# THE ENCYCLOPEDIA OF CLEVELAND HISTORY

# THE
# ENCYCLOPEDIA OF
# CLEVELAND
# HISTORY

EDITED BY

*David D. Van Tassel*

AND

*John J. Grabowski*

PUBLISHED IN ASSOCIATION WITH
CASE WESTERN RESERVE UNIVERSITY

INDIANA UNIVERSITY PRESS
*Bloomington & Indianapolis*

MANUFACTURED IN THE UNITED STATES OF AMERICA


**Library of Congress Cataloging-in-Publication Data**
The Encyclopedia of Cleveland history.

   "Published in association with Case Western
Reserve University."
   Includes index.
   1. Cleveland (Ohio)—History—Dictionaries.
2. Cuyahoga County (Ohio)—History—Dictionaries.
I. Van Tassel, David D. (David Dirck), 1928–
II. Grabowski, John J.   III. Case Western Reserve

*Third Printing*

# CONTENTS

# LIST OF MAPS

# LIST OF TABLES

# Preface

Cleveland is a city of paradoxes. It is a sprawling metropolis and a small town. It is a city that pioneered in social reforms of all kinds, and yet it is a bastion of conservatism. Founded and developed by a small group of Protestants from the New England and Middle Atlantic states, it is peopled by members of over 50 ethnic groups representing every part of the world and many of the world's religions. It is a blue-collar city that supports a unique cultural complex—University Circle—composed of nationally acclaimed institutions, and a park system—the "Emerald Necklace"—surpassed by none. A "city of cooperation," it became famous for confrontation politics. Cleveland's past is filled with soaring achievements, such as the building of the iron, steel, and oil industries, and a great transportation network of railroads and waterways. Its past is filled, too, with missed opportunities and reverses, such as the failure to become the center of the electrical, automotive, and aviation industries despite the prominence of these enterprises within the city during the early 1900s. Recently the decline and decay of heavy industry that has plagued the cities of the Northeast has made some of these missed opportunities doubly regretted as the traditional economic backbone of the city has disappeared. Nevertheless, and perhaps because of these paradoxes and changes, Cleveland's story is exciting and vibrant. It is filled with personalities who have made contributions as spectacular as electric street lighting, and as small as the modern golf ball. One writer rightly called Cleveland and its history "the best kept secret," but it deserves to be known, and that is the goal of the *Encyclopedia of Cleveland History*.

This work is the first history in encyclopedic format of a modern American city. It is, we hope, an up-to-date, accurate, and comprehensive account of every important aspect of the city's past. A number of histories have been written about Cleveland. One of the essays herein, "Histories of Cleveland," demonstrates the evolution and breadth of historical inquiry into the city's past. However, the last comprehensive history was written over 4 decades ago. In the intervening years, not only has the city greatly changed, but, more important, historians have broadened their definition of urban history to include much more than the great men or events in a city's past. Given this chronological gap and new areas of intellectual inquiry, it seemed appropriate that Cleveland's history be updated in an encyclopedic format where a multitude of professional views could be brought forth on all aspects of local development. Fortunately, rich new resources were available to support such inquiry, as the article "Libraries and Historical Societies" attests.

The task of fully exploring Cleveland's history has been enormous. It has taken nearly 6 years to plan and arrange for the writing of this volume. It contains over 2,500 articles, of which more than 2,300 are shorter factual accounts of individuals, events, and institutions that will serve as a ready reference source for facts relating to nearly every aspect of the city's past. We have included the good and the bad, so while one can find a sketch of Cleveland's notable Progressive mayor Tom L. Johnson, he can also find an entry relating to the city's fiscal default in 1978. Similarly, the many articles relating to businesses and industries not only detail their rise but in many cases also trace their decline in the post-World War II period. Taken as a whole, the business and industry entries provide a stunning exploration of the effect of internationalization on a local economy. Nearly 170 of the articles are longer reflective and interpretive examinations of major topics in local history prepared by local and national specialists. These interpretive essays, which constitute the scholarly backbone of the volume, explore topics such as agriculture, aviation, and business, and hitherto unexplored subjects such as fishing. The articles on immigration and migration and on philanthropy provide a much-needed synthesis of important local issues. The volume contains interpretive essays on every national war to have even remotely affected Cleveland; the pieces on the Korean and Vietnam wars are particularly noteworthy, as they analyze events that occurred after the compilation of the last comprehensive history of the city. Essays have been included that detail the history of all of the city's major ethnic groups. Most important, there is a mini-history entitled "Cleveland: A Historical Overview"; prepared by 3 historians, this entry represents the latest scholarship on the city's past.

In addition to exploring the obvious areas of local history, we have attempted to probe the hidden parts of the city's development in articles on streets, sanitation, and water supply. Similarly, sports, a topic ignored by many historians until recently, is given broad scope in this volume. In addition to an overarching essay on the subject, we have included special essays covering the history of particular major sports played in Cleveland, such as baseball, basketball, bowling, and football. In each case, we have tried to go beyond the "won/lost" column to explore the social and economic effects of such leisure-time endeavors. To assist the reader, we have also included a number of maps, charts, and lists that were devised especially for this volume. These follow the article that they best explain or illustrate, rather than being as-

signed to appendixes at the end. A second comprehensive index has been included to permit access to personal, institutional, and place names noted within the context of individual articles. The initial index lists the articles by subject, thereby permitting access to all articles relating to a particular category such as sports. We have aimed to make the text readable and comprehensible to high school students, laymen, and scholars alike.

In 1946, when the last great comprehensive history of the city was being completed, Cleveland was looking forward to its sesquicentennial, basking in its achievement and prosperity and enthusiastic about its plans for future growth. This encyclopedia was conceived during a period when the city seemed to languish in a slough of despondency, as its population declined and businesses moved elsewhere; but, during the course of this project, Cleveland began to stir, leadership reasserted itself, and there was a surge of enthusiasm for the future. The spark of this enthusiasm could be seen among the more than 250 people who worked on the project, as their growing knowledge of the city's past fueled their optimism about its future. We hope that, as the bicentennial of the city approaches, the *Encyclopedia of Cleveland History* will convey some of this enthusiasm and optimism to its readers, as well as inform them about the past of a city that has played a significant role in the growth of the United States.

David D. Van Tassel
July 1987, Cleveland

# Acknowledgments

When we embarked upon this project, we envisioned it as a cooperative effort to produce a new history of Cleveland. Perhaps naively, we foresaw that cooperation largely in terms of the contribution of articles and other content to this volume. We could never have foreseen the enormous fiscal, scholarly, and personal endeavors that have subsequently made this work possible. In the intervening 6 years, our definition of cooperation has been considerably broadened as hundreds of individuals and agencies have not only researched and written, but also funded, advised, creatively criticized, and otherwise assisted us in producing this encyclopedia; without their efforts, Cleveland would still lack a comprehensive history.

We cannot overstate the seminal role of the Cleveland Foundation in our work. It was at the suggestion of former foundation director Homer Wadsworth that David Van Tassel first began to explore the means of "updating" Cleveland's historical record. The Warner M. Bateman Fund, administered by the Cleveland Foundation, provided a substantial portion of the project's financial support. Mr. Bateman, a former director of the Cleveland Automobile Dealers Association, established the fund to encourage historical research and dissemination, believing that greater access to historical work would do much to promote the well-being of our country and its institutions. In addition to Mr. Wadsworth, Mr. Steven Minter, the foundation's current director, and assistant director, Dr. Susan LaJoie, maintained patience and faith throughout it all and subsequently helped support the creation of *Cleveland: A Tradition of Reform*, a work that grew from encyclopedia research. That this would be a long and expensive project soon became readily apparent, and over the ensuing years, the generosity of a number of families, foundations, and corporations added to the seed money provided by the foundation. This local funding was the key to unlocking additional support from the National Endowment for the Humanities. These donors, too numerous to mention here, are listed separately. The efforts of our advisory committee, brought together by James P. Conway and chaired by Ralph M. Besse and Robert M. Ginn, helped inform and convince potential contributors of the importance of the project. That these donors provided sustenance to the preparation of history is a measure of their foresight and understanding of Clio's role in both civic and personal fulfillment. The expertise and enthusiasm of committee members Robert D. Gries, Edward E. Worthington, and Betty Del Duca convinced many potential donors of the importance and worth of the project.

The content of this volume reflects the ideas and concerns of not only the editors but a large cross-section of the city's population as well. During the earliest years of the project, a national editorial advisory board, whose members are listed elsewhere in the front matter, provided valuable guidance and scholarly support for the concept of producing modern urban history in an encyclopedic format. At this time, Esther Rosenberg and, later, Cathy Miller, served as coordinators for the fledgling project. Over 200 individuals later provided suggestions for topics in more than 20 subject areas. Subsequently, over 200 people have written for the volume, as volunteers, contractual writers, or staff writers. Though a separate list provides the names of all of our authors, several deserve special mention. Among the volunteers, John Vacha and William Stark produced 115 and 88 articles respectively relating to journalistic and military history. William and Thea Becker performed yeoman service as contractual writers and together were responsible for 185 articles. Eric Johannesen not only helped define the architectural entries included in the volume but also produced several of the major essays in this subject and then went on to prepare, correct, and edit entries in a variety of fields. Nicholas Zentos undertook the difficult task of preparing the interpretive essays relating to a number of the city's nationality groups.

Early in the project, it became apparent that a substantial staff would be needed not only to coordinate and keep records but also to edit and check the accuracy of submissions, and research and write a large number of entries. In this regard, the work of Kenneth Rose and James Shelley deserves particular mention. Ken prepared nearly 400 articles, more than 14% of the volume. His enthusiasm and scholarship served as a model for his peers and make him, without doubt, one of the foremost experts in local history. Jim's work, particularly in the fields of art and medical history, helped the program through a busy and involved final year of writing. Central to all of this effort have been the efforts of Mary Stavish, who as project coordinator kept all of the records (and in doing so kept all of us on our toes concerning deadlines) as well as prepared an impressive series of articles relating to facets of the city's political history. That the entries in this volume meet certain standards of accuracy and content is due in large part to the work of a select group of people, including our editorial committee composed of Professors Carl W. Ubbelohde, Michael Altschul, and Michael Grossberg and our "veracity checkers," Thomas Pappas and Michael McCormick, who laboriously double- and triple-checked a large portion of the general entries for accuracy.

Underpinning all of this work are the excellent research resources with which the city of Cleveland is blessed; few cities are as fortunate. The collections at the Western Reserve Historical Society, Cleveland Public Library, and Cuyahoga County Archives proved central to this undertaking. All 3 institutions hosted encyclopedia workshops funded by the Ohio Humanities Council; additionally, the Historical Society waived its library entrance fee for encyclopedia researchers. The library of the Cleveland *Plain Dealer*, not normally open for outside researchers, was generously made avail-

able to the encyclopedia staff. It and the Cleveland Press Collection at Cleveland State University proved invaluable in tracing some of the area's more recent history. At each of these institutions, both executive and reference staff were constantly helpful and always supportive of the project. Also of particular assistance to our cartographer, Franklin Piccirillo, were the staffs of the Board of Elections, the Cleveland City Planning Commission, the Cuyahoga County Engineers Department, the Water Department of the City of Cleveland, the Regional Sewer District, and the Cuyahoga County Sewer District; their interest and Frank's diligence and skills have resulted in the new constant-scale maps to be found in this volume.

As the project came closer to publication, we were fortunate to have the advice and assistance of John Gallman of Indiana University Press and its thoroughly professional editorial, design, and production staff. Their patience in wading through and helping standardize over 2 file cabinets of manuscript was appreciated by all of us on the "Cleveland end" of this project.

Throughout the project, the editors have enjoyed the constant support of their colleagues and families as the enormity of its scope overwhelmed their offices, leisure time, and homes. The Department of History of Case Western Reserve University has endured the intrusions the project has created within the teaching and professional schedule of the editor-in-chief without complaint. The managing editor owes a debt to both Dr. Theodore A. Sande and Kermit J. Pike of the Western Reserve Historical Society for approving his participation in this project as well as maintaining a constant interest in his after-hours work as an encyclopedist. Helen Van Tassel and Diane Ewart Grabowski not only have endured the disruptions of home and family, but also have assisted their husbands editorially in the compilation of this volume. To them, and to the legions of of writers, supporters, and helpful critics, we can only extend a heartfelt thank you for assistance, patience, and understanding in our efforts to portray the history of a great and complex city in the best manner possible.

David D. Van Tassel
John J. Grabowski

# DONORS

*(listed in order of amount of gift and alphabetically within the same amount)*

FOUNDATIONS
The Cleveland Foundation
National Endowment for the Humanities
The Bolton Foundation
The William Bingham Foundation
The George Gund Foundation
The Ohio Humanities Council
Martha Holden Jennings Foundation
Kelvin and Eleanor Smith Foundation
The Treuhaft Foundation
The Forest City Enterprises Charitable Foundation
The Nathan L. Dauby Charity Fund
George M. and Pamela S. Humphrey Fund
Louise H. & David S. Ingalls Foundation
The H.M. O'Neill Charitable Trust
The George W. Codrington Charitable Foundation
Elizabeth Ring Mather and William Gwinn
    Mather Fund
Bicknell Fund
Firman Fund
The Lucille & Robert H. Gries Charity Fund
Kulas Foundation
The John P. Murphy Foundation
Britton Foundation
The Harry K. and Emma R. Fox Foundation
The Laub Foundation
The Hadden Foundation
The S. Livingston Mather Charitable Trust
The Wolpert Fund

COMPANIES
Cleveland Electric Illuminating Company
Leaseway of Ohio Incorporated
The Standard Oil Company
Chessie System Railroads
M.A. Hanna Company
TRW Incorporated
Ferro Corporation
Eaton Corporation
The Higbee Company
Jones, Day, Reavis & Pogue
Oglebay Norton Company
Ohio Bell Telephone Company
Premier Industrial Corporation

Squire, Sanders & Dempsey
White Consolidated Industries Inc.
The East Ohio Gas Company
May Company
Parker Hannifin Corporation
Sherwin-Williams Company
SIFCO Industries
Van Dorn Company
AmeriTrust Company
Huntington National Bank
The Lubrizol Corporation
Plain Dealer Publishing Company
Centran Corporation
Society National Bank
Baker Hostetler
Bearings, Inc.
Ernst & Whinney
Hauserman, Inc.
Reliance Electric Company
Cleveland Cliffs Incorporated
Arthur Andersen & Co.
Calfee, Halter & Griswold
Spieth, Bell, McCurdy & Newell
Price Waterhouse
The Standard Products Company
Stouffer Corporation

INDIVIDUALS AND ASSOCIATIONS
Mrs. C. Baldwin Sawyer
Mrs. Ralph S. Schmitt
S. Sterling McMillan
Early Settlers Association
Robert M. Ginn
Anonymous
David W. Swetland
Edward E. Worthington
James P. Conway
Ralph M. Besse
Betty Del Duca
Robert E. Glazer
Michael Altschul
Founders and Patriots
William S. Burton

# AUTHORS

*The following individuals have written articles for the Encyclopedia either as staff members, contractual agents, students, or volunteers.*

Abrams, Sylvia
Alewitz, Sam
Alexander, J. Heywood
Altschul, Michael
Anderson, Fleka J.
Baldanza, Lawrence
Banks, James
Barloon, Marvin
Barrett, Timothy
Barnum, George
Beal, Carol A.
Becker, Thea
Becker, William
Bellamy, Paul
Bergheger, Brian
Boieru, Olga
Borchert, James
Brachna, Gabor S.
Brinnon, Lillian
Brose, David
Brown, Jeffrey P.
Busch, Jane
Callahan, Nelson
Campbell, Thomas F.
Cauffield, Jane H.
Cetina, Judith G.
Chang, K. Laurence
Cheney, Nina
Chernen, June
Cimperman, John D.
Cline, Scott
Cohen, Paula
Colombi, Christopher A., Jr.
Connell, Timothy C.
Conti, Deborah
Copeland, Helen
Cross, James
Danielson, Elizabeth
Dardis, Kenneth
Dawson, Virginia P.
Day, Charles
Day, Jack G.
Deal, Mary
Decker, Timothy
Diaconoff, Peter
Dolezal, Brian J.
Duino, Russell
Durnbaugh, Linda
Edmonson, James

Erdey, Nancy
Farnham, Eleanor
Ferroni, Charles D.
Fertel, Eileen
Fischer, Scott
Freer, Frederick S.
Fugita, Stephen S.
Gaines, Ervin J.
Garfinkel, Stanley
Gerstner, Patsy
Gibans, Nina
Goetz, Heidi
Gorn, Cathy
Grabowski, Diane Ewart
Grabowski, John J.
Graham, Martin F.
Grant, H. Roger
Greppin, John
Grossberg, Michael
Hall, Maria
Hammack, David C.
Harris, Jill
Harrison, Dennis I.
Hategan, Vasile
Hauserman, Martin
Hehr, Russell
Herrick, Clay
Higgins, Bette Lou
Hoagland, Dorothy
Hruby, Frank
Hudson, Jean
Jackle, Robert C.
Janice, Christina
Jaquay, Robert
Johannesen, Eric
Johnston, Chris
Jones, Adrienne
Jones, Robert L.
Kabalan, Said S.
Kastner, Christine K.
Kelley, Karen
Kelling, Amy
Kipel, Vitaut
Klein, Richard
Klyver, Richard
Kollar, Mary Ellen
Kolson, Kenneth
Koozer, Sandra
Kosman, George

Kotrba, Karen
Krosel, Christine
Krumholz, Norman
Krzywicki, Marianne
Kuby, Donald J.
Kulchytsky, George P.
Kusmer, Kenneth
Landau, Earl
Lavelle, Kenneth
Laverty, Harriett
Lawler, Patrick
Leahy, John A.
Lee, Nancy A.
Leonard, Henry
Linke, Daniel
Loranth, Alice
Lupold, Harry
Lutz, Evelyn
Mack, Wayne
McCormick, Michael
McCracken, Martha G.
McNally, Edith
McTighe, Michael
Maciuszko, Jerzy
Mansfield, Herbert H.
Manthey, Ethel
Marsalek, Daniel E.
Masek, Linda
Maxwell, Marilyn J.
Mercer, Patricia
Metzger, Lynn
Miggins, Edward M.
Miller, Carol Poh
Miller, Craig S.
Miller, Genevieve
Miller, Ivan
Miller, Michael A.
Milner, Zelda
Morton, Marian J.
Musgrave, Tina
Nelson, Paul
Palermo, Anthony
Paley, Elizabeth
Papp, Susan
Pappas, Thomas
Pauly, Dorothy R.
Perry, Richard
Pershey, Edward Jay
Peters, Frances

Pfenninger, Allen
Pike, Kermit J.
Poole, Sarah
Porter, Roderick Boyd
Prpic, George J.
Psuik, Robert
Rarick, Holly M.
Reisman, Ellen
Reznick, Claudia
Rhoades, Camille
Richardson, James F.
Rodgers, Elizabeth G.
Rodis, Themistocles
Rose, Kenneth
Rose, Mark H.
Ross, David
Ross, Hugh
Ruksenas, Algis
Sabo, Gerald
Salgia, Tansukh
Sande, Theodore A.
Sanders, James W.
Sanko, Helene
Scharf, Lois
Schickler, Mildred J.
Schuld, Fred N.
Shelley, James
Sherrill, Charles

Shoup, Debbie
Sibley, Willis
Sidley, John David
Siney, Marion
Singer, Geoffrey A.
Sinnema, John R.
Solotko, Leslie Ann
Sords, Virginia A.
Sparrow, James
Spittler, Ernest
Stapleton, Darwin
Stark, Barbara
Stark, William
Stavish, Mary Ellen
Stavish, Mary B.
Steirer, Michael D.
Strasmyer, Robert
Susel, Rudolph M.
Swierenga, Robert P.
Szabo, Stephen
Szaniszlo, Elaine M.
Tanaka, Henry T.
Thrower, Glennis
Tipka, Donald
Toman, James A.
Topp, Walter
Traks, Andreas
Tussey, Jean Y.

Tuve, Jeanette
Ubbelohde, Carl
Vacha, John
Valencic, Joseph
Van Aken, William R.
Van Tassel, David D.
Vasilakes, Michael
Venkateswaran, Uma
Wallin, Harold E.
Weeks, Philip
Weiner, Ronald
Wells, Michael
Wertheim, Sally
Weymueller, Carl
Wheeler, Robert
Williams, John
Wilmer, Kathryn
Wing, Marie
Wollons, Roberta
Wood, James M.
Worthington, Edward W.
Wright, Richard
Wyatt-Brown, Bertram
Young, Dallas
Zentos, Nicholas J.
Zwolak, Loretta

# Readers' Guide

There are a number of aspects to this volume that the user should understand in order to obtain the greatest benefit from its content.

**Scope.** Although an Encyclopedia of Cleveland History, this work encompasses Cuyahoga County; the entries within relate to subjects, organizations and events, which in the opinion of the editors, have been central to the region's development. In each case, the subject of the entry, whether relating to a thematic area, individual, institution or event, must have had a substantive impact on the county in order to be considered for inclusion. Therefore, individuals who achieved fame outside of the area, after only a brief sojourn therein, are not included in the work. The work also limits biographical sketches to individuals who were deceased as of 1986. Researchers seeking data about individuals alive at that time are advised to consult the index which may lead them to information about a particular individual contained within the body of other entries. Similarly, institutional entries are limited to agencies, active or defunct, that are or were situated within Cuyahoga County; in several instances we have included sketches of businesses that had a long tenure or important effect on the county, but have now (1986) left the area. Institutional entries are, as far as possible, filed under their current (1986) corporate name. However, when the editors have determined that a former name would be more readily recognizable, we have made exceptions to this rule. Usually in such cases, we have, however, created an alphabetical entry under the popular name with a "See" instruction directing the reader to the proper title.

**Types of Entries.** There are two basic catagories of entries. The bulk of the work is composed of *general entries* which provide basic factual information about people, organizations and events. These entries are generally limited to 400 words each. As the general entries were written over a three year period, the most current information in any entry may date between 1983–1986, although the editorial staff has attempted to update early submissions throughout the project. In addition to the general entries there are 167 signed *interpretive essays* that explore major topical areas of local history. In these essays the authors have been asked to go beyond the simple provision of a factual explanation of a topic and to theorize about that topic and its importance to local history. Because these essays may represent such opinions, authorship is always indicated. The reader should also be aware that a major 40,000 word narrative history of the region precedes the alphabetical section of the volume. Those seeking a quick review of local history should consult this entry. Compiled in four chapters by three authors, this too is an interpretive essay and, as of 1986 incorporates the latest scholarly opinions about the region's development.

**Bibliographic Citations.** Many of the general entries and interpretive essays are followed by bibliographic citations. These do not necessarily indicate the authors' sources but are provided to direct the reader to additional information concerning the topic. Usually, the citations are for works or archival collections that relate specifically to the subject at hand. General histories of the city or of a particular subject, such as architecture or music are not generally cited. Readers wishing to pursue particular areas of inquiry in such works are directed to the essay entitled HISTORIES OF CLEVELAND for a selected listing of titles. Further information about general and specific works relating to Cleveland is contained in Matthew F. Browarek's *A Heritage of Books:*

*A Selected Bibliography of Books and Related Materials on Cleveland to be Found in The Cleveland Public Library*, (Cleveland: CPL, 1984). Most of the citations in this work have been given in short title form in order to save space. Several abbreviations have been routinely used: CPL (Cleveland Public Library), CWRU (Case Western Reserve University), CSU (Cleveland State University), and WRHS (Western Reserve Historical Society). The citation of any work in this volume does not constitute an editorial endorsement of its accuracy or scholarship.

**Indices & Cross Referencing.** Although history in an encyclopedic format has certain advantages in terms of breadth, it does tend to fragment the historical record. To overcome this problem we have provided three research tools. Within each article we have capitalized the names of individuals, organizations and events, as well as general topical terms when they duplicate or nearly duplicate the titles of other articles appearing elsewhere in the volume; this typographical device replaces the more standard "q.v." notation. At the end of various interpretive essays, "See also" references direct the reader to other, related interpretive essays provided the titles of those essays have not already appeared in the body of the article. Finally, two indices have been provided. The first provides selective subject access to the articles. A second lists names of individuals, organizations and places that appear within the body of the articles.

**Style.** The amount of information that had to .be compressed into this volume has made necessary several deviations from standard style. We have used the European form of date citation throughout the volume and abbreviated both terms and names whenever practical. Similarly, numbers are given in figures rather than being spelled out.

The editors would, of course, like to guarantee the accuracy of any information provided in this volume; to this end we can state that the data given is the most accurate available. However, six years of experience in compiling this work have taught us that truth is often an elusive commodity in local history. We therefore stand by the information as offered herein, but still remain open to correction. In a similar sense we realize that a single volume cannot encompass the history of an entire community. What is included between these covers reflects our decisions after entertaining much counsel and advice. We do realize that many other entries could have been added and that corrections of fact will inevitably need to be made; we hope to be able to do so in succeeding editions and supplements to this volume.

# Cleveland: A Historical Overview

## A COMMERCIAL HAMLET IS FOUNDED: 1796–1824

Cleveland was founded at the intersection of the CUY-AHOGA RIVER and Lake Erie, primarily because it was thought to be an ideal location for an agricultural center. The site was part of the WESTERN RESERVE, a portion of land extending from the Pennsylvania border 120 miles westward and 80 miles southward, comprising 2.5 million acres, which was sold to the CONNECTICUT LAND CO. by the state of Connecticut. While the land company and MOSES CLEAVELAND made a correct assessment of the location, they failed to realize that commercial development was a long way off. In the interim, many came to the site seeking a good place to live, raise their families, and harvest bountiful crops—they were often disappointed. Throughout the first 30 years, there was no harbor at Cleaveland (this spelling was gradually replaced—the modern spelling will be used hereafter), because the entrance to the river was blocked by sandbars that forced goods and passengers to be off-loaded onto smaller vessels in order to land. Moreover, the miasmic floodplain with its numerous swamps produced an environment filled with disease, which claimed the lives of many early settlers and convinced numerous others to move elsewhere. It was these elements, the commercial potential and the sickly atmosphere of the location, that determined much of the early history of the hamlet and the township that surrounded it.

*Formation: 1796–1800.* Through a series of protracted negotiations, the state of Connecticut had retained rights to western lands granted to it by a 17th-century charter. In order to settle this claim, the state was granted the "Western Reserve" tract in the Northwest Territory. Connecticut decided not to administer the land itself and sold it to a hastily gathered group of investors called the Connecticut Land Co. in Sept. 1795. The company wasted no time making arrangements to send a surveying party. One of its first jobs was to select the site for a capital of the Reserve. First, however, the Indians in the area had to agree that the land was owned by the company, because the grant from the U.S. did not remove Indian claims. Fortunately for the company, these claims were weakened by a series of battles that took place in western Ohio and ended in the defeat of the Indians at the Battle of Fallen Timbers in the fall of 1794. The treaty that followed reserved for

Indian use a rectangular tract beginning with the western bank of the Cuyahoga River and proceeding westward for about 60 miles and south for about 40 miles. The area east and south was open to white settlement. Finally, with only 60% of the Reserve available for survey, the Connecticut Land Co. sent its surveyors in the spring of 1796.

Moses Cleaveland and the 40-odd members of the party confirmed the company's title to the land in a meeting with the Indians near Buffalo and proceeded to the Reserve, arriving on 4 July. As the constitution of the company had directed, the principal town was laid out as quickly as possible. Cleaveland landed at the future site on 22 July but did not finally select it because he needed to get "more information of the extent of the ceded land and the traverses of the Lakes and Rivers." He did indicate his assessment: "I believe, as now informed, the Cuyahoga will be the place. It must command the greatest communication either by land or Water of any River on the purchase or in any ceded lands from the head of the Mohawk to the western extent or I am no prophet." Two weeks later, his investigation was complete; he was at the mouth of the river "to lay out [the] capital town," he told Zethan Butterfield on 20 Aug. When Cleaveland specified *communication* as the chief reason for his decision, he used the word in several ways. His immediate goal was to use the river to transport men, food, and the awkward instruments quickly to the interior in order to survey it. Fortunately, it was possible to go up the river 25 miles in a small boat. Had that been his only purpose, he could have established a temporary camp at the mouth, but he laid out the capital because he saw the commercial prospects of the river, which was navigable for lake sloops for 5 miles and for smaller vessels to the portage if the river was cleared of debris. That was a large "if," because little support for improvements to the river and harbor was forthcoming until the 1820s.

The town was planned to conform to New England and New York models of agricultural villages, because that was the heritage of the surveyors. While the surveyors did their best given their knowledge, other plans that would have incorporated the commercial potential of the area would have been preferable. In any case, the central feature of the plan was a 10-acre PUBLIC SQUARE, which was placed on the plateau near the ridge overlooking the riverbed. The square was divided by Ontario St., which ran north and south and was 90 feet wide. The east-west street,

Superior, was 40 feet wider than Ontario because it led to the river bank, where most of the river and lake traffic was expected to come into the town. Lots were laid out in an orderly fashion and made ready for sale by 1797, but virtually all of the "capital" was uninhabited for several years, and only gradually were the plots mapped by SETH PEASE and AMOS SPAFFORD cleared and settled. Consistently throughout the first decade, the company demonstrated that its primary goal was not settlement but quick sale for profit. Little encouragement was given, and no improvements were granted by the company to the capital site. In fact, other than a crude road cut through the woods from the Pennsylvania border to Cleveland, the company was interested only in land distribution. To that end, as soon as the final surveys were completed, tracts were chosen by lottery in Jan. 1798. At the same time, the company gave lots in Cleveland to several early residents because their presence encouraged other paying settlers. The lottery system itself made settlement haphazard, since investors picked land of varying qualities from separate boxes, which prevented them from owning contiguous tracts. Therefore, settlement of the entire Reserve was not orderly, and Cleveland, on the western edge of open land, was even more isolated. Some adventurous settlers did come to the area before 1800. They were more rugged frontier types interested in trade with Indians and supplying newcomers than they were farmers. The typical inhabitants during these first years did not stay long near the river: they either left the area altogether or moved to nearby townships away from the sickness that had begun to affect those who stayed near the village site. Undoubtedly, the most notable resident of these early years was LORENZO CARTER, who built a large log cabin where others could lodge and who quickly controlled most of the Indian trade. Others, such as JAMES KINGSBURY, NATHANIEL DOAN, and Ezekiel Hawley, came and liked the general area but moved out of the immediate Cleveland area. In Apr. 1800, Lorenzo Carter was the only resident of Cleveland.

***Survival Assured: 1800–1811.*** While the number of immigrants to the Reserve did not meet the expectations of the Connecticut Land Co., towns such as Warren had begun to grow significantly. In all of the Reserve, according to the federal census of 1800, there were 1,500 people. Ten years later, the number had grown to 17,000 in the Reserve, but to only 10 families in Cleveland. The reasons for this discrepancy are found in the pattern of migration from the East and in the problems with the site. Land in the Western Reserve was owned by residents of Connecticut, but most of them were content to remain landholders rather than become colonists in the new territory. Therefore, northeastern Ohio was not settled wholly by or even by a majority of settlers from Connecticut. Many residents were from other New England states, and 20% were from New York. Apparently, those in upper New England (Vermont and New Hampshire) as well as those from western Massachusetts were more likely to move in the early years of the century. These areas had been opened for settlement after the Revolutionary War, and many who went there did not find the prosperity they had hoped to achieve. Therefore, they were willing to move. Sometimes they moved to New York State first, and then on to the Reserve.

Fortunately, there were positive signs that Cleveland would be a political center, which helped bolster long-term prospects. First, the entire Western Reserve was declared part of the U.S. in 1800, which opened the way for formal political organization. The same year, Trumbull County was created to encompass the Reserve, with Warren as its county seat. Significantly, Cleveland was made one of the 8 townships in the county. Of course, it would have been

proper to name Cleveland the county seat, but because there was little population at the site, there was little need for a county seat in the area. It was also likely that new counties would be created quickly. Just 5 years later, Geauga County was formed from a portion of Trumbull, which included Cleveland. In 1807, the state legislature created Cuyahoga County, and after some debate, Cleveland was named the county seat in 1809 over the objections of its more populous neighbor, NEWBURGH. One additional form of recognition came when the federal government made Cleveland a port of entry in 1805 and appointed a collector to monitor trade from Canada as well as lake and river traffic. Each of these political changes added formal government responsibilities and officers to implement them. Throughout this early period, the primary political divisions were the township and county: no formal offices were created for the hamlet itself. The earliest positions insured that local elections were properly run and that the basic rules of government were observed. Because there were relatively few adult males in the entire township, many of them served in several offices simultaneously.

Several factors combined to inhibit long-term settlement in Cleveland. Early on, a conflict emerged between the rough group of settlers who lived "under the hill" near the river and those who thought the group was detrimental to the development of Cleveland. SAMUEL HUNTINGTON wrote to Moses Cleaveland on 10 Feb. 1802 that it was difficult to convince prospective settlers to stay, because Lorenzo Carter was "gather[ing] about him all the itinerant Vagabonds that he meets with out whom he gets all his labour done for their board and Wiskey: over whom he has an absolute control—organizing a phalanx of Desperadoes and setting all laws at defiance." Gideon Granger included these fears in a letter he wrote on 20 Oct. 1804 declaring his intention to settle in the Reserve. He said, "Cleveland has a Thousand Charms but I am detered from pitching on that place by the Sickness, the poorness of the Soil and the Inhabitants under the hill." Granger correctly identified the most important factor limiting the size of the hamlet—sickness. The most prevalent disease, described by contemporaries as fever and ague, was malaria, which affects its victims over a long period of time and debilitates them so they are more susceptible to other diseases. The Cuyahoga had changed its course to a new channel before the beginning of white settlement, and the abandoned channel had formed an extensive pool of stagnant water, which bred the mosquitos that carried the disease. Some residents observed that dry seasons reduced the problem, but none knew the cause or the cure.

In the wake of these realities, the population of the area grew slowly, which retarded institutional development and stunted economic progress. From 1802 to 1810, the entire township grew from 76 adult males (or about 200 people) to 300 people, and the hamlet itself managed only 57 residents by 1810. Political institutions were established quickly, but social and economic structures lagged behind. There were some cultural stirrings when a local lending library was formed in 1811 by 16 of the 18 families in Cleveland, and the Freemasons established a group, but formal schools would not appear until later, and no churches were organized, so the settlers relied on the occasional visits of missionary clergy such as JOSEPH BADGER. Residents were hampered in their attempts to prosper economically, because most were still in debt for their land and had not recovered from the expense involved in moving. In addition, they were forced to pay exorbitant prices for what they needed without having any way to earn money. The company turned a deaf ear to requests such as the one made by Huntington on 15 Nov. 1801 for funds to improve the harbor so that "our Salt, Iron, Potash, and Sugar Kettles and such Bulky articles" would cost less to buy and so that "we might supply the Ohio Country, if we had a harbour for Vessels, cheaper than they can be supplied from Pitt." Without this help, most residents planted crops in the marginal soil and bartered locally, for there was little hard money on the Reserve. They were aided by several local mills that ground flour and produced rough boards. Apart from these mills, the first signs of commercial life were the establishment of a merchant store in 1808 and the building of several lake vessels. One other positive sign was the opening of several communication links with other areas. In 1806, the company funded a road that connected Buffalo with the eastern boundary of its lands, where it joined the road to Cleveland. Impetus was provided for other roads when the western portion of the Reserve, which remained in Indian hands, opened for settlement as the result of a treaty in 1805. A road through this section from Cleveland to the Huron River opened 4 years later. In addition, Elijah Gun operated a ferry across the Cuyahoga to aid travelers and settlers. For all these reasons, the potential of the capital had grown, for it was now in the center of the Western Reserve.

*Hamlet as Village: 1812-1824.* During the 12 years that ended in 1824, Cleveland became a community with an adequate social and institutional base, a supportive political structure, and an economy poised to expand rapidly. Jessie Harris wrote home to Vermont in 1824 that Cleveland was a thriving town with 9 stores and 3 taverns. He added that there were 6 vessels owned in Cleveland constantly sailing the lakes and that all kinds of merchandise could be bought. He concluded that a canal from the Ohio River was scheduled to enter Lake Erie at the village site. Increased lake traffic and the likelihood of a canal terminus meant a total of 500 residents by 1825.

The population of all of Cleveland Twp. was only 605 in 1820, but even though it was not the most populous township in Cuyahoga County or the Reserve, it was the most significant commercial and manufacturing force in the area. A series of social and cultural institutions were founded in the years after the close of the WAR OF 1812, and political recognition of the hamlet as a village was successfully promoted in 1815. After years of accusations of irreligion, 4 churches were founded between 1815 and 1820. That same year, a Sunday school opened to keep idle boys off streets on the Sabbath, and within its first 3 months, 30 "scholars" attended weekly classes in reading, appearance, and behavior. Traditional schools were also founded during this time but were funded privately, since taxpayers were unwilling to take on the additional financial burden. A more socially motivated school designed for adults promised dancing lessons to students in 1820. Other cultural opportunities ranged from traveling exhibitions to a series of lectures on topics of the day. Displays of wax figures and a demonstration of gas were licensed by the village in the 1820s. Even before this time, several plays were performed, including weekly performances by a group called the Wags of Cleveland at the Shakespeare Gallery. By far the most impressive secular cultural institution was the Cleveland Forum, which held weekly meetings during the winter. Subjects for 1823 included "Is Love a Stronger Passion than Hatred?" "Are Agricultural Societies Beneficial?" "Ought the United States to Tax Unmarried Men over Thirty?" and "Is Slander Cause of More Mischief than Flattery?" One of the topics clearly met with approval, since in May 1823, the first meeting of the agricultural society was called. It was timed to coincide with the court of common pleas session in Cleveland, which would bring a large number of people to the village. Many informal social contacts were made at these sessions, where much business of all kinds took place. In sum, by 1824 these activities reflected a significant change from the frontier survival period. Furthermore, Cleveland had a newspaper beginning in 1818, which informed the growing local community and acted as an advocate of its growing importance.

As cultural activities increased, the social structure of the area became more differentiated. One observer noted that most Clevelanders did not dress fashionably. He found the typical dress of Cleveland women rather plain, and that men generally dressed in homespun cloth except on special days. However, some men and women did dress with good taste, many of whom were political and commercial leaders of the town. At the other end of the social spectrum, which admittedly was not as broad as that in eastern society, a number of poor appeared. The township warned several families to leave its jurisdiction to prevent their becoming dependent on the village and later paid for the removal of one family and for the funeral of another person. Other than court days, the 4th of July brought many members of the fledgling community together, perhaps because it celebrated both the founding of the nation and the date when Moses Cleaveland and his party entered the Reserve in 1796. In any case, there were elaborate celebrations for the time. Village leaders met to plan a celebration in 1819. All residents were invited to join the procession from Merwin's Hotel to the courthouse to hear the Declaration of Independence by REUBEN WOOD, Esq., and then to enjoy dinner at the Commercial Coffee House. Two years later, a list of celebrations in the *Herald* included 3 separate events for the area. Clearly, these events differed in tone from the early social problems between those under the hill and other residents.

Cultural opportunities and social differentiation complemented political changes, which gave the hamlet a measure of autonomy when it became a village in 1815. This new status required a village administrative structure, including a president, 3 trustees, a recorder, a treasurer, and a marshal. While the title of village was new, prominent political officeholders already knew who would be appropriate, and consequently the offices went to a small number of people. With the exception of the first year, there was only one treasurer before 1825, ASHBEL WALWORTH. Two men, DANIEL KELLEY and LEONARD CASE, served all but 2 of the 10 years as president of the village; Horace Perry was recorder for the 1810s, and Eleazar Waterman from 1821 to 1825. Horace Perry was recorder from 1815 to 1819, president in 1820, and a trustee from 1821 to 1825. During these same years, he also served the township as treasurer for 3 years, as justice of the peace for 7 years, as clerk for 3 years, and finally as trustee for 2 years. Clearly, Perry was one of the most important decision makers in Cleveland before 1825. Taken as a group, village officeholders were important economic leaders in both commerce and manufacturing.

Perry and his peers passed a series of rules governing the hamlet, which guaranteed a more orderly society and signaled the gradual end of the frontier period. In the first years, residents recorded earmarks that identified their animals, but by 1820 animals were a nuisance in the hamlet, and a set of ordinances regulated them. For instance, swine and cattle could not run in the streets, stray geese could be killed, and horse races were banned. Social controls prohibited discharging firearms or obstructing village officers. Economic regulations required all weights and measures to be sealed by the village inspector and all residents to use the village hay scales also run by the village inspector. The village fathers ruled that parents were liable for offenses their children committed. While these measures did not insure a peaceful, obedient society, they did suggest that most villagers preferred order to the disorder of the early years.

Village politics during this period were service-oriented, with few real rivalries. The most active races and the most significant political activity occurred on county, state, and national levels. Cleveland was the site of many political meetings to form slates of candidates for upcoming elections. Each township in the county sent 2 delegates to a county convention in 1818 to select a slate of candidates, for instance. Later the group published their preferred list in the Cleveland paper. On the national level, John Sloane ran against Peter Hitchcock for Congress from the area, but Sloane received few votes in the area because the people were not convinced by his recruiting sergeants. In spite of this lack of local support, Sloane won the election. On the state level, residents began to request aid through their representatives for harbor improvements and for communications with the south as early as the beginning of the 19th century. Proposals for funds to open a road to the south and to build a canal over the portage between the Tuscarawas and the Cuyahoga were presented, as were various plans to open the harbor. Generally, these requests failed. However, the most economically important one, the location of the canal terminus, succeeded after years of impatience. The idea was an old one, but the state legislature first seriously considered a canal proposal in 1817, the same year the Erie Canal in New York began construction. Two years later, legislation to incorporate a company to build a canal between Lake Erie and the Ohio River was before the state senate. After weeks of speculation on the great benefits this canal would bring to Cleveland, the *Herald* reported in Feb. 1819 that the bill was lost because the legislature had appointed several engineers to identify all practical routes. Fortunately for the Cleveland area, ALFRED KELLEY, a state legislator from Cleveland, served on the new commission. Over the next several years, each potential route from the lake to the river was surveyed. The politics were so intense that Kelley asked the *Herald* in 1822 not to publish news on the canal commission because it created regional jealousies, and he assured the public that no decision had been made. It would not be until Feb. 1825 that the final decision to locate the northern terminus where the Cuyahoga empties into Lake Erie was announced. While lake traffic would have continued to come to Cleveland, the location of the northern gateway in Cleveland was crucial to the quick rise in its fortunes. The positive impact that discussion of the canal had on the hamlet and its economic prospects was enormous and was undoubtedly the product as much of political influence as of sound engineering judgment.

Political help from the national level came slowly. As early as 1818, the hamlet petitioned Congress for funds to improve the harbor but failed. Consequently, all passengers and goods were landed on the shore in light boats. Six years later, Congress did allocate money for a lighthouse on Lake Erie, but at Grand River, not at Cleveland. Efforts to obtain funds to remove the sandbars and to build a public pier would wait until after 1824. Despite these setbacks, the economic history of Cleveland from 1812 to 1824 improved significantly after a shaky start. The War of 1812 helped Cleveland become a trade center, since supplies were stored in the hamlet and soldiers camped near the town, but the Panic of 1818 hurt economic opportunity, because it made barter pervasive and credit difficult to obtain. Finally, in the 1820s, lake traffic increased and the canal discussion intensified. Evidence of prosperity was nearly everywhere by the mid-1820s. The port of Cleveland was thriving by 1824, when exports exceeded $38,000 and imports $196,000, compared with 1809, when total exports were only $50.

Cleveland became the commercial center of Cuyahoga County during these years. The expansion took 2 paths: wholesale and retail trade and lake traffic. Trading posts were replaced by stores in growing numbers after the War of 1812, and merchants erected warehouses as early as 1815. The next year the COMMERCIAL BANK OF LAKE ERIE opened, partially to finance business and commercial operations. While no specific proof is available, there is little doubt that this bank gave the hamlet an advantage over its rivals, since it became the focal point of important economic decisions. Predictably, it failed in the aftermath of the national Panic of 1818. The shortage of hard currency was acute in the late 1810s, and the village issued corporation shinplasters or script to help residents pay taxes. Twenty businessmen, a considerable number given the small size of the hamlet, signed a notice informing the public that they would not accept the script. Retail outlets expanded during the early 1820s as furniture, books, shoes, and general merchandise of all sorts sold in the village. No doubt sales increased, because the first bridge linking the east and west banks of the Cuyahoga opened in 1822. By 1824 there were many local merchants selling eastern goods to local residents.

Significantly, the lake trade was also increasing in the late 1810s. At the peak of the shipping season in mid-July 1818, 21 boats entered or cleared the port for Buffalo and Detroit. Indicative of the lack of significant exports, they transported household goods, stoneware, dry goods, whiskey, livestock, pork, flour, butter, grindstones, and tallow. A ropewalk opened in the hamlet to supply rigging and other necessities to expanding shipping and boatbuilding enterprises. A new era in water travel arrived in Cleveland in 1818 as the first steamboat, *WALK-IN-THE-WATER*, arrived and was visited by a number of gentlemen and ladies from the village. The village entered the steamboat era with the launching of the 250-ton *Enterprise* in 1824. By the end of this initial stage of development, Cleveland was economically tied more to the lake than to the river, since most of its gross imports and exports came from the lake. Fortunately, it had all the necessary mercantile and financial institutions in place ready to meet any increased demand.

Robert Wheeler<br>
Cleveland State University

# COMMERCIAL VILLAGE TO COMMERCIAL CITY: 1825–1860

From 1825 to 1860, Cleveland, like other towns in the West, was swept through a series of changes at speeds far exceeding those experienced in the East as it quickly joined the nation in economic, cultural, social, and political terms. Cities such as Cleveland were better able to adapt to new ideas, because there was little to stand in the way—so much was to be lost by being left behind. Therefore, throughout the period, a nervous tension promoted change, while at the same time warning of the dramatic consequences of failure. Fortunately, Cleveland made few mistakes, partially because of its location and because it had sufficient reserves to make quick adjustments when needed. During the process, it quickly shed its frontier trappings to become the 19th-largest city in the U.S. by 1860. Also during the process, Cleveland participated in the passions of the antebellum era as a testing ground of what conservative easterners would become when transplanted to the Midwest.

Just a few of the changes can be quickly listed to demonstrate their pace and significance: in 1825, "the West" was very close to Cleveland; in 1860, it was far away both physically and culturally. In 1825, canal TECHNOLOGY was supreme; in 1860, canals were virtually unused. In 1825, Cleveland was an 8-month city that stopped functioning economically when the lake and canal were frozen; in 1860, the RAILROADS kept it open year-round. In 1825, Cleveland had a predominantly native population; in 1860, only a minority were born in the U.S. In 1825, some social distinctions were just beginning to appear; in 1860, social classes existed, there was some friction between them, and there were attempts to control less-desirable elements. In 1825, political officeholders served out of self-perceived duty; in 1860, party POLITICS controlled many elections, and local residents were caught up in a plethora of national issues. In 1825, most of those in the village knew each other; in 1860, anonymity had replaced familiarity as institutions replaced personal ties. In 1825, the city had yet to expand beyond the original bounds set by the 1796 survey; in 1860, it included both sides of the river and several annexed areas.

Some things did not change. Commerce continued to dominate the ECONOMY of the city. In addition, the geography of the riverbed and the high ground overlooking it on either side kept the commercial warehouses and transient housing "under the hill." Fortunately, this cloistering meant that the STREETS above were healthier and free of the intrusions that plagued most cities of the era. It is no happenstance that Cleveland's tree-lined avenues and increasingly elegant residences overlooked rather than emerged from the river banks. The physical well-being of the residents did improve significantly in the optimistic times of the late twenties and early thirties. Twenty years later, descriptions of the city heralded its location and spaciousness, and local HOTELS were filled not only with businessmen but also with those who were "summering" in Cleveland. Visitors judged the city as one of the most beautiful in the country.

*Canal Village to Provincial Center: 1825-1845.* The first 20 years of Cleveland's emergence began with the construction of the canal and ended with the return of good times afer a protracted depression, which began in 1837. In the process, a town developed that controlled its hinterland economically and was the focal point for culture and politics in northeastern Ohio. By far the most important single factor in the era was the transformation of the economy, for it drove all the other changes. Four events in 1825 determined the economic future of the village. First, in large part through the efforts of ALFRED KELLEY, the state of Ohio agreed to locate the northern terminus of the OHIO & ERIE CANAL at the mouth of the CUYAHOGA RIVER. Almost immediately, eastern funds began pouring into the village to take advantage of the predicted boom. Second, Clevelanders watched the progress of the Erie Canal closely and celebrated its completion in October with a dinner. More important, the *Herald* reported on 25 Nov. that a "procession of about 20 carts laden with the produce of the western country, brought from Lake Erie through the canal passed through several streets of New York city . . . carrying appropriate flags and banners. The produce was from Detroit, from Sandusky, from Cleveland, from Buffalo. . . ." For the near future, Cleveland did not need the Ohio Canal, because the village served as a gathering place where local farmers sent their produce destined for Buffalo, and ultimately for New York City. Moreover, the completion of the Erie Canal freed contractors and workers experienced in canal construction to come to Cleveland and begin work.

A third event that contributed to Cleveland's economic future was its selection as the site of the northern terminus of the canal. Engineers determined late in 1825 that a west side route would be less expensive if a wooden aqueduct was built to take the canal across the river 4 miles south of Cleveland. Public opinion, stated the *Herald* on 19 Nov., "cannot be mistaken, it is decidedly and unquestionably in favor of the eastern route." The final decision in favor of the east bank was made by the end of the year and sealed the relationship between the two sides of the river: retarding west side development and insuring the supremacy of the village of Cleveland. Fourth, efforts to obtain money from the federal GOVERNMENT for harbor improvements finally succeeded when $5,000 was appropriated, undoubtedly to accommodate the increased shipping requirements of the canal. With another, larger grant 2 years later, engineers successfully opened a new straight channel to the lake. The swift-flowing river eliminated the sandbars that had blocked the harbor from lakegoing vessels and removed the miasmic swamps from the mouth, which eliminated the pervasive sickness in the village.

The prosperity canal promoters had hoped for was confirmed by developments over the next 20 years. With improved TRANSPORTATION and reduced freight rates, demand for agricultural products increased along with farm productivity and prices, which, in turn, enticed more people to move to the hinterland and gave areas close to the canal a marked advantage over their rivals. In the process, the canal replaced the river route to New Orleans as a major conduit for goods headed to the East Coast from the Old Northwest Territory. Cleveland benefited particularly because it was the terminal point and a growing lake port. Consequently, it collected produce as it came north and sent manufactured goods south. Often overlooked is that Cleveland's hinterland did not include much of the WESTERN RESERVE, because it followed the canal route south to Akron, Columbus, and the Ohio River and passed through only 2 Reserve counties, Cuyahoga and Summit. The Cleveland-Akron portion of the canal was the first scheduled for completion, and construction contracts were issued quickly. As workers poured in, the cash they received for wages replaced the local barter economy and increased the number of bank notes in circulation, thereby facilitating the economic transactions. Within the year, hogs driven to Cleveland were slaughtered and sent east, and the latest goods from New York appeared in local stores. Cleveland had become "a mart of business for this section of the country," according to the charter of Western Reserve College in 1826, as forwarding and commission agents appeared to send property anywhere, sell it in any market, and advance funds for property deposited with them. Less than 2 years after construction had begun on 4 July 1827, the first canal boat arrived in Cleveland from Akron with the governor and other distinguished citizens on board and was greeted by a large number of spectators who lined the hills and banks. Five years later the canal was finally completed; however, Cleveland traded with the region from Columbus north, whereas goods south of the capital went to the Ohio River.

From 1827 to 1840, the Ohio Canal was the exclusive avenue to the lake and eastern connections by canal. The first year, flour, ashes, and butter and cheese came north, while salt, lumber, and over .5 million lbs. of merchandise went south from the village. As the canal pushed inland, the amount of merchandise grew to over 3 million lbs. in 1830, to 10 million in 1834, and to a high of 19 million by 1838. As wheat prices jumped from approximately $.30 per bushel before the canal to over $.60 in 1833, the amount of flour and wheat transshipped at Cleveland jumped 8 times by 1840, when over 2 million bushels of wheat and .5 million barrels of flour arrived via the canal. Significantly, the town's grain trade was almost totally dependent on this traffic, since, for example, in 1841, of the 461,000 barrels of flour shipped from Cleveland, 441,000 arrived by canal. By 1840, 44% of Ohio's wheat and flour came from the "wheat belt," a group of counties north and east of Columbus, making it the focus of the principal grain market of the Great Lakes. The other major agricultural products, corn and pork, rose at slightly less impressive levels.

Newspapers followed the rapid rise in local fortunes. The *Herald* commented in May 1830 that the amount of goods received by canal had already surpassed that of 1829 because of the abundant harvest and confidence in the canal. Seven years later, the *CLEVELAND HERALD & GAZETTE* observed that in 1832, much of the local economy had been limited to barter, and few farm products were exported, whereas now "the rich products of the interior [are] floating along" the docks. Enticed by canal products and aided by harbor improvements, more and more lake vessels arrived and cleared. From a begining of 350 arrivals and departures in 1831, the annual number rose to 1,000 by the late 1830s, and nearly 1,600 by 1844 exclusive of steamboats. Vessels increased in both number and size throughout the period. Nearly 50 of them made regular stops at Cleveland with passengers and some freights. It was not unusual for a visitor by the late 1830s to see the lake and harbor filled with sail- and steamboats waiting for their turn at the docks and regularly emptying large numbers of immigrants into the town. Without doubt, by the mid-1840s, Cleveland joined Detroit and Buffalo as the 3 dominant Great Lakes ports.

The dramatic increase in trade brought with it good news for the entire village and led to a period of speculative excitement. By 1830, Cleveland had 138 dwellings, 13 stores, and 15 warehouses as the banks along the river became the wholesale district. To complement the progress along the river, retail stores located along Superior indicated the beginnings of a central BUSINESS district. A residential neighborhood also emerged between Superior and the lake and Ontario and the river. Here early schools and the first church building, Trinity Church, were built. Architecturally, the village was a mix of log cabins, small frame houses, and several more contemporary buildings, with few traces of its primitive frontier beginnings. During the early 1830s, a series of real-estate schemes developed to exploit interest in tracts on both sides of the river. The floodplain on the west side was poorly drained land that had not been farmed. It was purchased by a group of Buffalo investors hoping northern Ohio would expand as Buffalo had done because of the Erie Canal. The marshlands were drained, and an elaborate hotel was built on the newly surveyed lands. Another scheme involved the development of the oxbow area of the river, which was named WILLEYVILLE and laid out in a pattern of radiating streets off a central circle. A bridge built by the investors connected it to the west side. In addition, a planned residential neighborhood, Clinton Square, located just beyond the city limits near the shore, had a central square and a goal of preserving the privacy of residents. All of these ventures temporarily raised land costs in the area, and a number of local investors did benefit. For instance, in Mar. 1835, a tavern located on the west bank changed hands at a profit of $3,000 in 1 day. Few investors received similar windfalls, however, since these ventures failed because of national economic developments. The real impact of these speculations was to raise land prices higher than they would be for 30 years.

While some did make money, it was only temporary in most cases, for surprisingly, not all the economic news during the thirties was positive. The Panic of 1837 and the depression that followed stopped much development in the village and stifled economic advance for 6 or 7 years. Previous cyclical economic downturns had had little impact before the canal brought national markets and national problems to northern Ohio. This time the impact was widespread. Banks failed, forcing local stores to produce their own currency called "shinplasters," which were not redeemable universally. These and other economic reversals doomed the dreams of many railroad companies that had been chartered by the state before 1836. Had it not been for the panic, railroad development would have been much quicker, and the era of the canal proportionately shorter. The hard times forced many new residents to leave town searching for work and housing. Also, many cultural institutions formed in the early 1830s disbanded, unable to collect dues from their membership. Only gradually did the country and Cleveland emerge from the depression by 1845.

Understandably, the panic not only ruined speculation, it also arrested a population spurt that had begun with canal construction in 1826. The village grew from 500 to over 5,000 in the 12 years after 1825, and the west bank of the river added another 1,000 persons. The greatest jump happened between 1833 and 1835, when more than 50% of the total arrived. Through 1836, immigrants poured into the village, and Cleveland and its smaller cross-river rival, OHIO CITY, were named cities in 1836 (even though by modern standards Cleveland was more accurately a town and Ohio City a village). The panic began to limit growth almost immediately. By 1840, 7,500 people lived at the mouth of the Cuyahoga, an increase of only 1,500 in 3 years—half that of the previous 3 years. Nevertheless, Cleveland's annual growth made it the fastest-growing city above 1,000 in the state. It was able to continue to grow gradually until in 1845, 12,000 lived on both banks. Cuyahoga, led by the growing towns, became the most populous county in the Reserve by 1840.

Many migrants settled in the area because of the opportunities offered by local commercial and manufacturing concerns, just as migrants had done before the canal era. The proportion of those involved in commerce grew so that in 1840, over 70% of them lived along the river at the lake. More and more workers were involved in small manufacturing establishments, which dotted the two towns. A relatively large number, over 100, worked on the west side at the CUYAHOGA STEAM FURNACE CO., the first and, for many years, the only heavy industry of importance in the Cuyahoga Valley. The firm, located on the west side partially because the east bank was crowded with warehouses, became the first of a majority of manufacturing companies established on the west side. Many workers employed by the Steam Furnace Co. arrived in the mid-thirties. Some were immigrants from Europe, but most were natives; foreign IMMIGRATION had just begun. The trend established in the late precanal period continued after 1825 as more and more settlers came from New York State, and relatively fewer from Connecticut and the rest of New England. The natives included more members from the middle and upper class who came with funds to invest in the future prosperity of Cleveland, much as the land speculators did. In 1830, the village was still overwhelmingly (96%) native. Apparently, the canal workers, who included a considerable number of IRISH, did not settle in Cleveland. European immigrants did come to the area in the 1830s. Newspapers record several self-help organizations serving Irish, GERMANS, and Scots during the decade. By 1840, it is likely that well over 25% of Cleveland household heads were foreign-born.

Throughout the 2 decades after 1825, BLACKS lived and worked in the village. Their numbers were never very large, and they were not isolated residentially. Cleveland newspapers frequently reported activities of local blacks and on occasion lauded their efforts. The community formed a church in 1830 and a school in 1832. In response to the formation of a young men's union in 1839, the *Herald* commented on 29 Mar., "The colored people of this city are not numerous, but of the better class of free blacks. They are industrious, peaceable, intelligent, and ambitious of improvement. A school is supported by them," as well as a lecture series and a library. An equally revealing statement was made by a black responding to a racist letter in the 5 Nov. 1845 *Herald*. He stated that there were 56 blacks from 20 families who had accumulated property of $55,000 since 1833 and were employed as canal boat owners and as stewards on boats. Without doubt, racism existed in Cleveland, but the city was a reasonably liberal environment for the times, and some blacks prospered here.

The growing population continued to become more and more differentiated as class and neighborhood distinctions grew and old conventions were outmoded. An upper social group existed in Cleveland during this time, and it was virtually all native. Several dress dances or cotillions occurred before 1845 and were attended by the town elite. Major celebrations, especially on Independence Day, were accompanied by speeches and a dinner where local leaders spoke. Signs of opulence appeared in some homes. In the 1830s, architectural design replaced the vernacular forms used previously. A Georgian-style home, the Crittenden house, built by a leading merchant, was completed in 1832 on PUBLIC SQUARE. Four years later, a more contemporary style, Greek Revival, began to take hold, and by the end of the thirties it had replaced Georgian. These new homes were brick and stone rather than wood and were much more imposing than earlier residences. While these are some indications of an elite in Cleveland, after 1845 a more conscious upper class emerged as members formed organizations to promote the city and their own particular view of its needs.

In contrast, the poor were increasingly apparent after the opening of the canal. WILLIAM CASE, a leading figure in the village, believed that by 1828, canal construction had "brought a great many irregular—drinking and rowdy persons" to the city and county. Six years later, in the aftermath of a Cholera Epidemic that attacked the town, the *Whig* on 9 Sept. 1834 said, "The class of persons among which the disease principally raged" was indicated by the fact that "of about one hundred victims . . . fifty-five were buried at the expense of the town." Many of the poor lived in the FLATS on either side of the river "under-the-hill." Here the thriving economy spawned numerous "groceries," which appeared on every wharf to dispense alcohol. A racecourse established in 1835 encouraged "a flood of imported depravity, strengthened by all the canaille that could be mustered from groceries and other dens of pollution," asserted the *Whig* of 14 Oct. 1835. Although he probably overstated the situation, Case said the city council had no power to force "suspicious persons" looking for public support to leave the city, so that at the beginning of the panic, "letters had been written to Ireland, England, Germany, that Cleveland took all the poor that came. In the spring of 1838, the poor came in swarms." Of course, many poor in Cleveland were not "black legs" or "out-laws," especially as the depression deepened. So obvious was the need that by the end of 1837, and for several years, a group of ladies coordinated efforts to feed and clothe the poor.

In between these two extremes were the working people of the town. Most laborers had problems of their own,

which included the scarcity of housing even to rent and exploitation by employers. As the population increased and canal connections brought eastern ideas and people to Cleveland, workers joined their counterparts and formed local unions. As early as 1834, journeymen printers united, and 2 years later a meeting of carpenters and joiners of both Cleveland and Ohio City demanded a 10-hour working day. The depression affected workers, and many left the town. Those who stayed probably had difficulty finding work. Just as the financial problems lifted in 1843, mechanics and laborers of both cities protested the return to barter and asserted that they would accept only cash for their services. Moreover, they promised to form a mechanics' and workingmen's society, and as one of their first acts, they held a parade where 350 workers protested their financial problems. Activity was not limited to these issues. In the early 1840s, a Mechanics' Lyceum formed, which promoted lectures on topics of interest to workingmen. All of these gatherings demonstrate an awareness among some workers that they had common interests that could best be served by united action.

Virtually all sectors of Cleveland society united in one form or another during the canal era. As population increased, ethnic and racial distinctions appeared, and social differentiation took place, residents were forced to establish institutions in order to express themselves in a city that lacked the homogeneity and harmony of traditional rural society. Moreover, Cleveland became a regional center during this period by forming branches of eastern institutions. In a sense, the canal brought both commodities and ideas. The first secular organizations were imported from the East just as canal construction began. Many had a distinctly religious cast and reflected the conservative New England background of their members. A branch of the American Colonization Society, a group devoted to sending blacks to Africa, was formed in 1826. It marked the first appearance of New England conservatism, which limited local response regarding slavery to the antislavery position rather than to more radical abolitionist views. Subsequently, in 1833, an antislavery society appeared to promote these views. Another popular movement, TEMPERANCE, reached Cleveland in 1830 and continued for many years. As with most voluntary organizations, members tended to be upperclass, and the targets of their attentions tended to be lowerclass. A series of groups were formed that were able to turn 4th of July celebrations in the thirties into celebrations of temperance. In 1834, for instance, children assembled from various Sunday schools, marched, and were treated to cakes, crackers, and cold water in an effort to rid the holiday of "rum and gunpowder." Throughout the period, hotels and steamboats converted to temperance principles. By 1843, Clevelanders joined a national movement to restrict the sale of liquor by the drink or to individuals who were drunk, but had little success.

National movements devoted to stimulating intellectual activity also prospered in Cleveland in the 1830s. Numerous public debates took place, especially in the winter months under the auspices of local branches of the lyceum movement, which continued a local tradition founded in the precanal era. As we have seen, mechanics and blacks founded their own versions of this popular format before 1840. Similar groups such as the Library Association, the Polemic Association, the Cleveland Reading Room, and various young men's unions provided refuge from the growing anonymity. They were supplemented by musical organizations such as the CLEVELAND MENDELSSOHN and MOZART societies. Service groups added to the institutional maze. The MASONS continued to be active despite an anti-Masonic movement that forced them out of sight during the late 1820s and much of the 1830s. Other groups, including the International Order of Odd Fellows, began to hold meetings as early as 1841. Another segment of the community formed private military units such as the CLEVELAND GRAYS and the Cleveland Guards. Composed of native-born, they served social and ceremonial functions in addition to their role in any military actions. Just at the end of the period, in 1843, local women who had been active in poor relief through their churches formed the MARTHA WASHINGTON & DORCAS SOCIETY to administer to all poor in Cleveland. They were attempting to supplement earlier mutual-aid groups formed to preserve ethnic, racial, religious, or fraternal bonds by Germans, Irish, Manx, blacks, firefighters, and BAPTISTS. These groups supported the temporary poor through a solitary gift to help them weather a difficult time. They made up the bulk of benevolence in the pre-1845 era, and while they continued after that time, other, more far-reaching relief was necessary.

Religious organizations formed quickly as population increased, and tended to be ethnically exclusive. From a beginning of 3 churches in 1830, the number rose to 12 Protestant congregations by 1845. The most prominent of these was the FIRST PRESBYTERIAN CHURCH, known as Old Stone Church, built in 1834 on Public Square. These congregations formed a series of social groups within their organizations, such as Sabbath schools, Bible classes, and female benevolent societies. Two Protestant churches were exclusively German and had about 600 communicants by 1845. By far the most significant change was the formation of the first Roman Catholic parish in 1835, which built ST. MARY'S ON THE FLATS in the oxbow area 3 years later. By 1845, there were also 2 Jewish congregations. In all, the directory estimated that there were over 8,000 members of religious organizations, many of whom made the church the center of their social activity.

While local children attended Sunday schools, Cleveland only gradually provided public EDUCATION for its citizens. Despite the rapid increase in population and in cultural and religious concerns, JOHN WILLEY, first mayor of Cleveland, told the city council in 1836: "Our character, our manners, our habits, and our means require an entire change, the introduction of a liberal and well adjusted system of education in our city" to replace private academies. The next year, a public school system began with a board of managers. After a shaky beginning, the system built 3 schoolhouses and was firmly established by 1845. HIGHER EDUCATION began near the end of the period, when the Cleveland Medical College opened in 1843. It immediately became successful and was viewed as one of the chief assets of the city. Other, similar institutions came only after 1845, when population and educational trends warranted expansion.

Just as the school system evolved over the 2 decades, politics and city government changed dramatically. Clevelanders not only joined national movements such as temperance and antislavery, they also participated in national politics. The stylistic change to mass appeal and party politics, which had not existed in earlier years, was exemplified by a convention of 15,000 WESTERN RESERVE and northern Ohio Whigs who met in Cleveland in Oct. 1844 to ratify Clay's presidential nomination. The evolution that led to this system began as early as 1827, when the first convention was held to determine local candidates. The political preferences of residents betrayed their New England heritage, since by and large they were for Clay and the American System of internal improvements beginning in the early twenties, and they consistently opposed Andrew Jackson to the point that no Jacksonian newspaper could survive in the city. In the mid-1830s they remained WHIG, and they supported Harrison's campaign in 1840 with great enthusiasm, as they did Clay's in 1844. Newspapers became more and more partisan during the era, and much of their news emphasized political issues. There were also significant changes in local political activity, where "caucusses" that nominated approved candidates were necessary "for the common good," according to the *Herald* on 9 Sept. 1835. Local party representatives established vigilance committees to police voting at each polling place and "to use all honorable means to secure the election of the candidates nominated." Not all means were honorable, however, as in 1843, 3 persons convicted of voting more than once at the spring election were each sentenced to 1 year in the penitentiary.

All this conscious political activity changed the nature of officeholding gradually during the canal era. It did not, however, change the ethnicity of officers, who remained native despite rising numbers of Germans and Irish in the community. Prior to 1836, village officers seemed to continue the tradition of public service by serving several years: JOHN W. ALLEN served 4 consecutive years as mayor; T. P. May was a trustee for 5; and David Worley served 5 years as treasurer. After Cleveland became a city, the mayor and city council, consisting of a president, 3 aldermen, and 3 councilmen from each of the 3 wards, formed the government. Over the next 9 years, there was no consistent pattern of officeholding. No officer served as mayor, alderman, or councilman more than 2 years, for instance. Perhaps a writer to the *Herald* on 25 Aug. 1837 correctly observed that Cleveland had "a central aristocracy composed of capitalists, [paper mill owners], and speculators" that shared offices among its members. A brief analysis of these men shows that virtually all were wealthy businessmen, and many were deeply involved in the land speculations of the mid-1830s. It is possible that they did not need to have long-term officers, since the increasing population brought many qualified men to the city. In any case, local leaders did begin to affiliate with political parties, according to Cleveland newspapers. In 1844, the *Herald* suggested that since local Democrats and Whigs had each nominated a candidate for mayor, and since both were old residents, well-qualified, and popular, the election of either would be good for the city. Later the same year, the newspaper put the local election into perspective when it stated that the Democrats had won the mayoralty by 32 out of 1,100 votes cast, but the spoils belonged to the Whigs, who held 9 of the 12 council seats. The paper continued that over the last 4 years, these mayoral elections had been so close that the Whigs had won by only 14 in 1841, and then the Democrats won by margins of 12, 45, and 32. Politics in the city were partisan, it seems, but the rival factions were drawn from the same ruling group before 1845.

These city leaders had a difficult task managing the transition from village to town over the 2 decades. From a village of few regulations and few responsibilities that relied on private institutions to provide needed services, Cleveland was forced to regulate more generally and to control more city services itself. Beginning in 1829, fire protection began when the village bought a fire engine and volunteers formed a fire department. By 1836, there were 4 firehouses manned by volunteers, and a fire warden examined houses to enforce ordinances designed to prevent fires. As crime increased, the village appointed a marshal in 1832 and 4 years later formed a city watch, including 8 companies of men. Also during this time, the city regulated MARKETS and attempted to centralize them. The condition of city streets was a continuing problem. Attempts to repair the dirt roads served little purpose, since they improved mobility but were not a permanent solution. All of these areas would force more permanent solutions on the city in the years after 1845, but before then only a piecemeal approach was used.

Just as efforts to provide city services did not keep pace with growing demands during the canal era, efforts to create a unified city on both sides of the river were stymied, as well. That part of BROOKLYN Twp. directly across the river grew quickly after 1830, and in the winter of 1835, a letter to the *Whig* stated: "I cannot see any good and sufficient reasons why Brooklyn should not be included in the proposed corporation [of Cleveland]. The interests of one place are closely connected and allied with the interests of the other." On 30 Dec., a Cleveland meeting rejected including the west side, because Clevelanders did not want the opposite bank to benefit from the larger population and tax base of the east side, and because residents feared the influence it would give Brooklyn, Buffalo, and New York speculators. The rejection erupted into a year-long confrontation rooted in the view that each city was fighting for the same business. The immediate issue was the repair or replacement of a floating bridge, but by June 1836, Cleveland removed the bridge because it obstructed navigation. A replacement, the COLUMBUS ST. BRIDGE, was built on the southern edge of Ohio City, diverting traffic to Cleveland rather than letting it pass through Ohio City's business district. After several incidents of vandalism to the new bridge, attributed to unhappy Ohio City residents, a skirmish took place on 31 Oct. 1836 when an attempt was made to saw through its timbers. The bridge's destruction was prevented by Cleveland citizens reinforced by the county sheriff, but according to an Ohio City paper describing the event, the mob began to destroy the structure only after they were fired upon. Subsequently, each village established a watch to protect BRIDGES and buildings. The controversy receded after a year but left scars so deep that any discussion of unification ceased for more than a decade.

These unsettled problems did not obscure Cleveland's progress from 1825 to 1845. A newspaper commented: "But a few short years have passed since our thriving town, (then a rude hamlet) stood upon the farther confines of the rising west. . . . Ours is no longer a western settlement, our children are surrounded by the comforts, the blessings, and the elegance of life." Within these 2 decades, a hamlet had become a commercial town justifying the foresight of its founders. It had become the capital of the Reserve. The town had expanded to over 12,000 people and was on the verge of becoming a legitimate city. It was also on the verge of several major changes that would make canals obsolete and would require more creative solutions to urban problems. During the next 15 years, ethnic consciousness increased, and the celebration of Yankee heritage grew markedly as Clevelanders coped with the final phase of the antebellum period.

*A National Urban Center Emerges: 1845-1860.* From 1845 to 1860, Cleveland became a city. Economically, railroads revolutionized transportation, laying the groundwork for the transition from commerce to manufacturing. Moreover, the city joined other Great Lakes ports in promoting regional economic development. Culturally, Cleveland shed its provincial perspective to become an integral if somewhat conservative part of national trends. Local politics, too, became embroiled in national issues. Significantly, Ohio City and Cleveland united following the trend of urban annexation. Finally, on the eve of the CIVIL WAR, some Clevelanders began to record the proud history of their progress. The economy continued to be the driving force of change during these years, as canal expansion and railroad construction led all other developments. After 1840,

feeder lines connecting the canal with Erie, Pa., the Mahoning Valley, Pittsburgh, and Marietta on the Ohio River ended the monopoly of the Ohio Canal's north-south trunk line as they provided alternate routes and commercial centers. These canals affected Cleveland in much the same way railroads would in the 1850s, for they strengthened its hold on certain commodities, such as grain, while they reduced traffic in other goods, such as foodstuffs. The Mahoning Canal was particularly important for Cleveland, since it opened a direct route to the interior of the Western Reserve and to the Mahoning Valley that funneled dairy products, wool, and coal to the city.

From 1845 to 1852, canals recovered from several poor years in the mid-1840s and reached their highest levels, at the same time that railroads finally attracted enough funds to begin construction. In 1851, the canal brought 2.5 million bushels of wheat, nearly 1 million bushels of corn, .66 million barrels of flour, and 3 million bushels of coal to Cleveland, breaking records for each commodity. The *Herald* of 20 Feb. 1849 praised the long-term impact of the canal, saying that it had "made Cleveland," because while it had cost $5 million to build, it had paid back 20 times that much. Also, without the canal, the paper estimated that the village population would have been 3,000 rather than 21,000, and its property worth only $3 million rather than $10 million. Few doubted the evaluation, and few predicted the reversal that followed. In the 9 years 1851–60, flour volume fell by ⅓, wheat by well over ½, and corn by ¾: the canal era had virtually ended.

While the end came quickly, prosperity in the 1840s masked the urgent need for railroad financing and meant that Cleveland was nearly left out of this next transportation revolution. Fortunately, such was not the case, for as the canal traffic reached its peak, the first rail connection was completed. Railroad promotion began in the 1830s and was revitalized in the mid-1840s. An editorial in late 1845 advocated support for a proposal to have the city of Cleveland purchase $2 million in stock of the Cleveland, Columbus & Cincinnati Railroad and added, "It has become a matter of surprise to our neighbors that Cleveland has been so stupid upon the project of this and other railroads." A letter to the editor of the *Herald* on 14 July 1846 argued that many businessmen and active young men left the city each year to settle in younger cities and towns along the lakes, such as Sandusky presumably, which had built several railroads because it had no canal connections to the interior. Advocates of trains constantly pointed out that Clevelanders were active only two-thirds of the year; for the other 4 months, "they burrow like animals." The iron horse, they argued, would initiate a year-round city. Finally, after several ill-organized attempts, the most promising line, the Cleveland, Columbus & Cincinnati (CC&C), was funded. Construction proceeded quickly, and by early 1851, plans for a celebration marking the arrival of the first train were quickly completed. By year's end, Cleveland was also connected with Painesville and Pittsburgh, and by 1853, with New York City, Chicago, and St. Louis. On the eve of the Civil War, it had become one of the major rail centers in the country.

The railroads revived commerce in Cleveland, which enhanced prosperity, but some observers saw problems unless the city's economic base broadened. Cleveland was a good place to live, said the *Leader*, 15 Mar. 1856, but there was "no living spirit of enterprise. . . . No thinking man with capital will stop in the city when we have only our commerce to sustain us. A manufacturing town gives a man of means full scope to his ambition . . . commerce alone cannot save Cleveland, as but few are benefited by it directly. Manufacturing creates a demand for merchandise, mechanical labor, all the necessaries of life, and gives tone to all legitimate business in and around it." Moreover, the city had all the right resources—mechanics, raw materials, places to erect factories, and cheap food prices compared to older towns. Despite these advantages, the paper continued, real-estate prices had declined for over 2 years, and some quick improvement was needed. Other arguments emphasized the ability to weather economic crises by diversifying and the benefit of wresting retail markets in the hinterland away from eastern manufacturers. Of course, manufacturing did exist in the area, and had ever since the founding of the Cuyahoga Steam Furnace Co. in the early 1830s. But as the 1853 city directory observed, investment in industry for a city of 33,000 people was much too small given "the capabilities of this location for sustaining manufactures." Most of the 150 establishments added between 1850 and 1860 were small and not related to the nascent iron and oil industries. Instead, they grew because the expanding population needed agricultural implements, woodenware, furniture, clothing, and sewing machines. While the number of inhabitants who worked in these factories continued to grow, they made up only 9% of the workforce on the eve of the Civil War. Iron manufacturing was still in its infancy as the first rolling mills began to produce in the 1850s, and therefore, the opening of the mineral resources of Lake Superior had only just begun to have an impact on the FOREST CITY by 1860.

Both commerce and manufacturing attracted people to the Cleveland area from 1845 to 1860. Fueled by canal expansion, the city's population jumped by 11,000, practically doubling in the first 5 years, and tripling the 7,000 residents of 1840. The excitement generated by the completion of the CC&C railroad generated another burst, which added 8,000 between 1850 and 1853. In all, the population increased by 30,000 to nearly 44,000 at the end of the 15 years, to lead all cities in the country of comparable size with a 10% annual growth rate. Other cities in northeast Ohio grew slowly from 1850 to 1860 in comparison; these increases, while not equivalent to that in Cleveland, were the beginning of a significant rural-urban movement as the proportion of urban residents in the Western Reserve rose. Clearly these changes suggest the continuing trend toward greater population concentrations. Another continuing trend was the rising proportion of foreign-born emigrating to Cleveland. At mid-century, the native-born made up only ⅓ of household heads in Cleveland, and only ⅖ of those in Ohio City. A decade later, both sides of the river were under 30% native, compared with 33% for German-born and 22% for the Irish-born residents. This native minority benefited from the influx of Europeans, who held occupations at the lower end of the economic ladder. Natives filled virtually all skilled positions, such as machinists and shipwrights, as well as more white-collar occupations, including merchants, physicians, and boatbuilders. Irish residents were at the bottom of the ladder. Half, who had no steady employment, were listed as day laborers, and the remainder had semiskilled jobs, such as shoemakers and sailors. Virtually no Irishmen held white-collar jobs. In contrast, 25% of the Germans were skilled craftsmen, and many semiskilled Germans worked in the more dependable building trades rather in the seasonal work along the wharves, as did the Irish.

Economic differences and preference concentrated the various ethnic divisions more and more in their own areas of the city. On the west side, for instance, the Irish began to dominate the lowlands near the river and the hillside leading onto the heights, where many natives lived in the fashionable FRANKLIN CIRCLE area. Germans made up less than ⅕ of the west side, except in a new residential area away from the lake south of Bridge St., where they constituted ⅔ of the households in 1860. These concentrations had their east side equivalents but should not be viewed as ghettos, since many residents were not forced into them by discrimination but chose to live close to countrymen. However, the increased presence of foreign-born undoubtedly raised ethnic consciousness in the city. A newspaper editorial on 18 Feb. 1851 offered a formula of assimilation that few followed when it advised foreigners to immediately become "Americanized" by "casting off" their European skins and encouraged natives to welcome them as brothers. Throughout the period, ethnic groups, especially Germans, created numerous organizations to preserve their languages and cultures in addition to the self-help groups formed in the 1830s. Germans added a German-language newspaper in 1846, a military group, the German Guards, in 1847, and a music society in 1848. In the 1850s, many Saengerbunden, German singing societies, were formed, and in 1859 the city hosted a North American SAENGERFEST, which included a group of 400 singers from Cleveland representing 24 separate local societies. Local churches expanded, as well, and by 1860, there were 6 German congregations. Some attempts to preserve culture were not successful, especially when they seemed to oppose AMERICANIZATION. The Ohio City Council denied a request to form a separate German school in 1853, for instance, but it did agree to print a city ordinance regulating dogs in both English and German.

Other ethnic groups did not form as many private organizations. Irish residents relied on churches and schools for their cultural activities, even though there were some organizations such as the HIBERNIAN GUARDS and the Irish Naturalization Society of Cleveland. By 1860, there were 4 churches and 7 parochial schools in the city. Throughout the period, there was little mention of the Irish in the newpapers. A great deal is made of the formation of the FATHER MATHEW TOTAL ABSTINENCE SOCIETY in 1851, which brought many Catholics into an essentially Protestant movement and promised an end to the heavy-drinking Irish stereotype that pervaded Cleveland newspapers. Immigrants from Scotland and the Isle of Man, who did not receive such negative characterizations, formed self-help organizations and were able to report in 1856 that only 1 countryman from each group had ever received city aid.

Blacks, too, increased in numbers and continued to associate in organizations for their social and economic improvement. They never made up more than 2% of the population, and they were not isolated residentially. Blacks worked at many levels of the occupational scale: ⅓ were unskilled; 45% were skilled; and 20% were semiskilled. Of course, serious questions of racism concerned all blacks. Three meetings held in Cleveland in 1847 considered a petition to Congress asking for enough land in a western area for blacks to form their own government and send representatives to Congress, but rejected it because slaveholders controlled the legislature. Several churches created new opportunities for religious and social activities, as did the Colored Young Men's Union Society, a debating club, and the Colored Association of Cleveland. The plight of blacks was explicitly highlighted by a newspaper, the ALIENED AMERICAN, published in 1853. The court system seemed to treat blacks with some fairness; a white in 1849 was found guilty of killing a black and was sentenced for the crime, while in 1854 a black man charged with raping a white girl was freed after it was learned she "did not sustain a good character."

The local upper class had formed a tight-knit society that entertained itself and attempted to control the destiny of the city. After 1845, when Cleveland became a boom town, one could have measured the social and cultural evolution of the upper class, because they began to copy eastern styles as quickly as they appeared in the East. By the late 1840s, Gothic houses had begun to replace earlier Greek Revival styles, and architectural provincialism had all but disappeared as eastern architects brought the latest fashion to Cleveland. A decade later, Italian villa designs such as the one built by AMASA STONE appeared along the posh section of EUCLID AVE. Stone's home featured rosewood and mahogany highlights and a heating system with a fireproof furnace that sent heated water to nearly every room. The house was the finest in the city.

The Protestant upper class did become more physically separated from the growing congestion of the central city, but at the same time it became more concerned with benevolence. What had been the purview of a few devoted wealthy women and ethnic self-help groups became an effort of prominent male leaders to instill the values of their heritage, especially self-discipline and Protestant morality, into the poor. Moreover, these leaders turned the attention of private and public organizations more toward the idle and begging class than to newly arrived immigrants or the ill. In so doing, they forged a movement that wished not only to help but also to control, as much out of fear as out of concern, and as further evidence of a growing class consciousness. There was legitimate reason for concern. The number of poor increased as the city population increased and as the cyclical downturns in the economy forced more newcomers out of work. Poor relief was a real problem, and when unemployment increased in 1856, the city provided outdoor relief. A survey of the beneficiaries concluded that 47% were Irish, 22% German, and only 12.5% "Americans." Throughout the 1850s, while the local economy weathered the panics reasonably well, each downturn reduced the number of workers dramatically, thereby increasing the number of needy.

The bulk of city residents fell between these two extremes. The working population continued to form groups to protect its interests during the late 1840s and 1850s. Cleveland's GARMENT INDUSTRY employed mostly women, and they protested wages and treatment in 1848 and formed a sewing society 20 years later. For a short time they ran their own shop. Throughout the 1850s, economic problems increased union activity. Most working-men settled in areas where they could afford housing. On the west side, housing costs dropped after the speculative boom of the thirties, and prices stayed low so that in contrast to Cleveland, separate houses were available to most people, and "nearly all had breathing room." Further opportunities meant that a large number of "men of small means" could buy lots on the west side, build houses there, and be nearer to work than those who had to live farther away from their work to afford housing costs on the east side. Less-affluent laborers and workers clustered around Lorain and south and west of Pearl. Consequently, financial considerations, along with ethnic loyalties and xenophobia, created residential segregation by the end of the antebellum period.

A great variety of private and public institutions were founded between 1845 and 1860 to accommodate the growing complexities of city life within a national cultural context. Some organizations, such as antislavery or temperance, expanded their activities and involved more than residents. In Cleveland, church leaders from congregational and Presbyterian churches dominated the abolition affiliates. While Cleveland was not a hotbed of ABOLITIONISM even in the 1850s, it was a stop for a few prominent abolitionist lecturers, including Frederick Douglass and Cassius Clay. One shortcoming of the city that kept it from more radical ideas and, in part, reflected its general propensities was the absence of an abolitionist press and the conservative editorial policies of the city's daily newspapers. More in keeping with its conservative New England heritage was local support for antislavery. Throughout the 1850s, some runaway slaves were helped, mostly through the efforts of local blacks, and occasionally by whites. Such actions were illegal, according to the Fugitive Slave Act of 1850, but many Clevelanders were proud of their defiance. The most dramatic indication of local sentiments was the excitement generated by the OBERLIN-WELLINGTON RESCUE and fugitive slave trial, when 37 rescuers were jailed. Throughout the proceedings, which took place in Cleveland, crowds gathered, and at one rally 10,000 attended. At the same time, soon-to-be-martyred John Brown, then a fugitive because of his actions in Kansas, stayed in the city. When he was hanged for his role at Harpers Ferry, flags flew at half-mast and bells tolled in Cleveland, partially because he represented courage and freedom in spite of his unacceptable methods.

In politics, local business leaders tried to replace Representative Joshua R. Giddings with a candidate of more moderate views on slavery but failed and were forced to rely on him. Throughout the 1840s, Clevelanders supported antislavery Whigs, but in the 1850s they joined the movement led by Giddings and others through the successive stages of antislavery parties from FREE-SOIL to the Whig-Free-Soil-Independent Democratic party known as the Republicans. So while local leaders and voters were reluctant followers of this limited national shift, they joined the organizations and were committed by the eve of the war. The temperance movement in Cleveland followed a similar path, as it too became involved in politics. The Washingtonians, a group prominent in the 1840s, expanded the temperance cause and paved the way for the SONS OF TEMPERANCE and the Independent Order of Good Templars. Both of these fraternal organizations offered fellowship and social events but were primarily devoted to protecting their numbers from drink and elevating their politics. Gradually in the 1850s, they became more active in politics. In 1853, they could not obtain a temperance position from either major gubernatorial candidate, so the Cleveland Temperance Alliance supported a Free Soil-Democrat. As we have seen, there were also Catholic temperance groups formed after the 1851 visit of Father Mathew, a protemperance priest. The numerous groups often participated in 4th of July parades to counteract the portrayal of intemperance among immigrants and offered direct aid to countrymen.

Private relief groups also sought to aid the poor in more systematic ways. The SOCIETY FOR THE RELIEF OF THE POOR, formed in 1850, and its successor the Relief Association, as well as the Sons of Malta, were upper-class, male-dominated groups that gave aid to those poor who were deserving because of their moral character and potential for improvement. Typical of the terms of relief were the stipulations of the City Mission of the Euclid St. Presbyterian Church, which stated that "no continued or permanent relief [would] be granted any family ... not ... connected with some Protestant [congregation]" and that they would be subject to periodic visitations to determine whether they were worthy of help. By the mid-1850s, leaders of these groups realized that they did not have the resources to deal with the problem and consequently began a campaign to have the government assume more responsibility. Uncared-for children created another problem, which church groups helped solve with the formation of the Protestant Orphan Asylum and similar Catholic institutions in the early 1850s. In addition, the Ragged School was founded to attract children too poor to attend public schools. Some of these institutions, especially the Ragged School, were partially or totally funded by the city after private efforts proved insufficient.

Not all voluntary groups sought to solve urban problems; some sought to improve the social and intellectual environment of their members. German MUSIC groups proliferated in the period, and in 1854 the Cleveland Academy of Music opened. From the foundation laid in the 1830s and partially destroyed by the depression of the 1840s, the CLEVELAND LIBRARY ASSOCIATION revived and by mid-century had a collection of more than 2,000 volumes. Moreover, business leaders who were involved in church groups and other benevolent societies also formed a Board of Trade here where they could discuss economic issues and meet peers. Fraternal associations such as the Masons and Odd Fellows met throughout the period. Social and athletic clubs such as the Ivanhoe Boat Club, the Cleveland Cricket Club, the Cleveland Chess Club, and local gymnasium groups all prospered during the period. In fact, SPORTS activities and public celebrations increased markedly in the 1850s. Horseracing revived and became an annual event, drawing as many as 3,000 people. Foot races and baseball also took place. By far the most popular celebration occurred annually on the 4th of July; it attracted 40,000 people in 1858. Residents also had opportunities to attend countless musical concerts and plays. In 1853, a theatrical rendition of *Uncle Tom's Cabin* played to 12,000 people in 15 performances.

Churches grew rapidly as they attracted new communicants. The number of Protestant congregations nearly tripled over the course of the 15 years, to 34, and they supported 38 Sunday schools. Just as the social order became more differentiated, so too did local churches. As we have seen, some church leaders were members of the local upper class who built new church buildings reflecting their own stature, and others took an active role in the political issues that permeated all levels of society. Churches after 1845 followed Gothic and Romanesque designs imported directly from the East. Political and moral beliefs were enmeshed in the antebellum period inevitably, and some local congregations felt the effects. In Mar. 1850, PRESBYTERIANS who favored abolition formed their own church. Catholic churches continued to expand, as well, so that in 1860 there were 4 separate churches. These congregations supported several orphan asylums and 4 parochial schools, including a seminary.

The realization that private institutions could no longer handle many urban social problems caused city government to take over some institutions founded by voluntary associations and to create others. The city poorhouse had served few poor in the late 1830s and 1840s, since private groups provided considerable aid, but as the problem increased, a Poorhouse & Hospital was built to house the sick, insane, and indigent and aged poor. The City Infirmary could minister only to meritorious cases who had been residents for at least 1 year. In 1857, the Ragged School, which had been founded by private groups, was taken over by the city. Its goal was to change "scholars from dangerous to industrious citizens." The city also saw the need for expanded educational opportunities for all residents. From 1846 to 1860, the number of school buildings rose from 13 to 17, and the number of students from 1,500 to 6,000. A Board of Education, formed in 1853, directed the system. In addition to the Ragged School, renamed the Industrial School in 1857, which trained poor youth, a high school opened in 1846 that trained those who wanted to learn the higher branches of education; and a night school opened in 1850 to aid those who needed to work but wished to learn, as well. In all, public education had virtually replaced private education on the eve of the Civil War, since only 3 secular schools remained in Cleveland in 1860, whereas a quarter-century before, nearly all pupils had attended private academies.

Other city services increased to meet the demands of the growing population. One obvious sign of the number of newcomers was an 1848 city ordinance placing street signs at various corners. Public utilities were also in demand. Water from wells supplied homes, but the business district needed a larger amount, which was provided when a large holding tank was constructed in 1849. It proved insufficient, so by 1856 a system was built that pumped lake water to the KENTUCKY ST. RESERVOIR on the west side and then distributed it. Gas lighting was introduced to downtown streets and buildings in 1850 and gradually spread south and east from Public Square, along the main streets going east and to the west side. Street surfaces continued to be a problem throughout the period, as surfaces constantly needed repair and as a primitive sewage system designed to drain main streets proved inadequate. Partially because of this problem as well as crowded housing, the city appointed a public health officer in 1856 and formed a board of health as a permanent structure, which replaced earlier boards created to deal with specific emergencies. Fire and police protection kept pace with other changes. Cleveland had 10 fire engines and a volunteer group of 500 firemen to cope with the growing number of fires. Police protection expanded as the small watch forces of the 1830s were replaced by a formal police department that employed 40 patrolmen by 1860. More local station houses appeared in immigrant communities and other areas where crime was more prevalent. The justice system also expanded to meet new demands, as a police court was formed in 1853. In addition, a federal district court was established in the city in 1855 as a result of the increasing financial position of the city.

All of these new services sought to make living and working better in a new city. The long, difficult period of contention between Cleveland and Ohio City ended when they united in 1854. The two had cooperated on bridge and harbor projects in the 1840s, which initiated attempts to unite them in the early 1850s. The reasons were obvious: the river would be under one authority; the harbor would receive federal money more easily; property values, especially of Ohio City lots close to the Flats, would increase; and administration would be streamlined. Nevertheless, while 88% of Ohio City voters wanted union, Clevelanders rallied behind an antiunion assault and rejected the proposal in 1851. Three years later, the issue returned with new benefits. New taxes, increased real-estate values for the east side business district, access to "fresh, pure water" from the west side's system, and the addition of the industrial capacity of "manufactories, iron works, machine shops, and warehouses" apparently convinced Clevelanders, who voted 4 to 1 in favor of union. Ohio City voters also approved annexation. The terms of the merger created 4 west side wards and guaranteed that a bridge joining the two banks would be built within 2 years, but also insured west side dependence by reserving revenues and assets of each before the union to that side exclusively. Cleveland benefited immediately because Ohio City brought a commitment to manufacturing and helped turn it away from commerce.

Local politics became more complex after the union, since more local offices were available as the number of wards reached 11 and the office of alderman was abolished. Just as religious and secular organizations became involved in national politics, so too did local elections. In the canal era, there was a constant turnover of officeholders as the pool of available men grew, but after 1848, officers often served more than 2 years, probably because of the rising effectiveness of local parties. Their new tactics included efforts to muster German and Irish voters, beginning in 1852. Three years later, the *DAILY TRUE DEMOCRAT* reported on 15 May a rather strong reversal of this approach, and one that was in concert with a national native American political movement, the Know-Nothing party. The paper reported that a crowd of "jackasses and hyenas and bawdy house bullies" had taken over the polls in the 1st and 2d wards, refusing to allow any anti-Know-Nothing foreigner to approach. All Germans were kept from voting and were beaten if they attempted to come too near. Whether these tactics continued is not known, but the Democratic party won virtually all the municipal offices in 1856. Clearly, local politics had become more organized and effective in the prewar years. Local connections to national parties were important as the rather conservative political views of many residents gradually joined the national trend to the left. Through the 1850s, Clevelanders supported Franklin Pierce over Winfield Scott in 1852, Fremont over Buchanan in 1856, and finally Lincoln in 1860. This shift toward the Republican coalition placed the area in the mainstream of American politics, just as it had gradually joined the economic and cultural mainstreams by the close of the antebellum period.

By 1860, Cleveland was one of the most beautiful cities in the country, with all the prospects associated with urban centers. It had matured quickly even by 19th-century standards. When the *Herald* compared the first city directory, published in 1837, to the one 20 years later, it saw major changes. Travel to Cincinnati had taken 80 hours by canal in 1837 but took only 10 in 1857. The number of names in the directory had increased from 1,300 to 11,000, while the number of factory workers had grown from 200 to 3,000. Other, more subtle differences included the rising separation of the city into a wholesale and commercial zone, a central business district, and numerous residential neighborhoods distinguished from one another by the quality of the houses and the spacing between them. This differentiation was not only economic but also social and cultural, as various institutions with more and more distinctly ethnic identities replaced the informal relationships of the precanal era. In effect, the social spectrum had widened, and organizations reflected this broadening. Cultural efforts to preserve traditional values by cultural associations became increasingly popular as many groups, especially natives, felt threatened by the majority foreign-born population. Conservative easterners had found ways to preserve their values by cultural associations and by joining national movements with a conservative bent. They also were able to form a ruling group that controlled the local economy and local politics. Urban problems and governmental solutions signaled the end to the era of voluntary associations providing most of the social services to the community. In the final analysis, in spite of all its problems, Cleveland in 1860 was a fully developed city with a brilliant economic future and a population capable of meeting the challenges it would present.

Robert Wheeler
Cleveland State University

# THE NEW INDUSTRIAL METROPOLIS: 1860–1929

**Introduction.** The 7 decades from 1860 through 1929 were the most exciting, eventful, and complex in Cleveland's history. From the beginning of the CIVIL WAR to the onset of the Great Depression, Cleveland rose from a small commercial city of 43,000 people to an industrial metropolis with a population nearing 1 million. During such a period of growth, the events, the people, and institutions loom bigger than life and were essential to the city's growth. The Civil War was a traumatic event for many Clevelanders who saw their sons and husbands and brothers off to fight for the Union cause, some never to come back. The whole city and surrounding population mourned the death of Abraham Lincoln, and everyone (an estimated 90,000 people) walked past the slain president's body, mounted on a catafalque in PUBLIC SQUARE. But the wartime boom had thrust the little commercial center on the road toward 60 years of industrial growth. Young JOHN D. ROCKEFELLER and Maurice B. Clark took the profits from government contracts to their produce-wholesaling business and invested in the new petroleum refining industry. SAMUEL B. MATHER, along with Otis & Co., went from iron-ore mining and smelting to the production of steel. In 1870 Messrs. Sherwin and Williams launched the paint-and-varnish industry in the city. Increasing numbers of immigrant groups, attracted by new jobs, families, and friends, populated Cleveland neighborhoods. Urban cultural institutions, such as the colleges and universities, the CLEVELAND MUSEUM OF ART, the WESTERN RESERVE HISTORICAL SOCIETY, and the CLEVELAND ORCHESTRA, were founded. Civic leaders such as TOM L. JOHNSON and NEWTON D. BAKER made the industrial metropolis a model for the 20th century city. WORLD WAR I, at the other end of the time period, further accelerated Cleveland's growth, attracting an internal migration adding to the already large foreign population and pushing the city into a period of suburban growth symbolized by the VAN SWERINGEN brothers' dual development of the suburb of SHAKER HEIGHTS and the downtown Terminal Tower complex.

These events and many more are important, and their story is fully told in other parts of this volume. But, in order to find meaning and to make sense of the bewildering array of particular achievements occurring during this 70-year period, one must step back and view it as a whole. In doing so, one begins to see the overarching continuities and the interrelations in trends. This section, therefore, will examine the growth of the city topically, over the whole period, treating the ECONOMY, demographic growth and change, geographic evolution, reform and the voluntary civic sector, and the political system. An understanding of the development of the economy is essential to understanding all other phases of the city's history. It explains the parallel demographic changes, which in turn influenced the evolution of the urban geography. Concurrently, the problems of poverty and SANITATION and demands for EDUCATION for the emerging metropolis spurred a variety of social and civic reforms, all of which explain and to some extent are explained by the political system and the development of the political structure of the new industrial metropolis.

*The Economy.* In the 7 decades 1860–1929, Cleveland's economy was a mirror of the American Industrial Revolution. Fueled initially in the 1860s by the Civil War, sustained in the latter decades of the century by the construction of a national TRANSPORTATION system, the growth of an internal market, and technological innovation, voracious growth continued into the first 3 decades of the 20th century on the crest of a wave of corporate consolidation, World War I, and a new industrial orientation toward consumer production. Highly sensitive to changes in the national economy, Cleveland made an economic transition from the commercial center of the Civil War era to the nation's 5th-largest industrial city by the close of the prosperity decade. AGRICULTURE was an important factor in this early growth. The opening of the Erie and Ohio canal systems made Cleveland the link in the transshipment of Ohio grains, most notably wheat, to Eastern Seaboard market centers. Much of the city's pre-Civil War growth and prosperity were the result of its advantageous geographic position.

Ohio's mid-century inclusion in the nation's growing RAILROAD network was accompanied by the realization by grain farmers tilling land bordering the canal that they could now ship directly to eastern markets and no longer needed to route their produce through Cleveland. The city's grain-oriented agricultural hinterland declined. However, the city's size soon influenced a second stage of regional agricultural development. Competition for land in the county between urban and rural uses had the effect of bidding up land prices and decreasing the size of farms. Those who owned small but high-priced farms now had to raise crops with high market prices. As early as the 1860s, Cuyahoga County farmers converted production to truck farming vegetables, fruits, livestock, and dairy products for the urban population. By the 1880s, when the county population was 197,000, agricultural production of the 5 surrounding counties was given over to truck farming and other high-intensity agricultural land uses, including greenhouse horticulture in Cuyahoga. In the 1920s, when the population of the city and its surrounding SUBURBS totaled over 1 million, 16 counties surrounding Cleveland produced agricultural goods for the consumption of Clevelanders and their agricultural processing industries. Cleveland's flour mills, breweries, and distillers became major consumers of regional agricultural output.

The commercial sector of Cleveland's economy comprised transportation, finance, and wholesale and retail trade. Until late in the 19th century, commerce was the city's leading sector, and transportation was the key to its rise. The state's railroad network was completed in the immediate post-Civil War period; by the 1880s, Cleveland could claim the densest network of railroad connections of any city between New York and Chicago. HIGHWAY construction in the 20th century paralleled the rail lines and reinforced Cleveland's position as a hinge between eastern markets and western sources of raw materials. Although the canal boom was spent by the 1870s, the city's Great Lakes water linkages remained important and expanded under the impetus of the iron and steel industry to include the iron ranges of the upper Great Lakes. In the 1870s and 1880s, oil pipelines added yet another transportation connection to the city. Pipelines linking Cleveland to the oil fields of Pennsylvania for a time made the city the nation's leading oil-refining center, and although this preeminence was short-lived, Cleveland did remain an important depot and refinery in the Standard Oil system. Gas from the West Virginia pipeline of the EAST OHIO GAS CO. completed the transportation network.

The locus of all modes of transportation was the mouth of the CUYAHOGA RIVER at Lake Erie. Very early in Cleveland's post-Civil War development, the inadequacies of the port became a primary source of local concern. The mouth of the river silted up with distressing regularity, while windstorms on Lake Erie battered the lakeshore, causing erosion and requiring constant repair of docks and unloading facilities. In the post-Civil War decades, unloading facilities were horse- and labor-intensive and were manifestly inadequate to meet the needs of a growing port. Cleveland's Board of Trade in the 1870s agonized over the loss of cargos to rival lake cities because Cleveland could

not unload ships expeditiously. Systematic dredging to widen the river was also necessary, and in the 1880s federal assistance was sought and won. These accomplishments allowed for greater ease of navigation and enabled city fathers to expand dry-dock and wharf facilities. A major accomplishment was a breakwater constructed east of the mouth of the river, which offered refuge for vessels and provided protection from the corrosive effects of wind and water. These pioneering efforts set the pattern for harbor improvements throughout the 19th and 20th centuries. Changes in nautical TECHNOLOGY resulted in larger ships, which required cargo-unloading apparatus suitable for state-of-the-art vessels. The resulting facility crises prompted the Cleveland Chamber of Commerce to create a standing committee on harbor improvements, which worked with the local congressional delegation to seek federal funds to assist with harbor maintenance and to fund capital improvements. That made it possible for local steel, mining, transport, and shipbuilding companies to construct their own docking and loading facilities within the river and lake harbor complex.

As a result of Cleveland's becoming a significant transportation hub, commerce intensified. The rise of Cleveland's banking industry was a sensitive barometer of its commercial climate. The history of money and banking in the U.S. between 1860 and 1929 was a saga of chaos and unpredictability, punctuated by wars, panics, depressions, sudden surges of business growth and attendant speculation, a deflationary federal monetary policy, and of course the Great Crash of 1929. The institutional history of Cleveland banks was determined by these larger national banking trends, but the BUSINESS history of Cleveland banking was shaped by the currents of local economic development. In the Jacksonian era, local banking institutions chartered as state banks in hopes of becoming the favored "pet banks" of the federal treasury; the Civil War reversed this trend. In his efforts to finance the Civil War and impose monetary restraints on the civilian economy, President Lincoln secured legislation (the Currency Act of 1863 and the National Bank Act of 1864) that had the effect of reorganizing the nation's banking industry by offering strong incentives for state banks to recharter as national banks. To discourage state banks, the legislation established new standards for the capitalization of banks, set standardized requirements for reserves, and placed a tax on state-bank-issued currency. Sixteen cities, including Cleveland, were designated by the new legislation as reserve cities in which local national banks were authorized to issue federal currency. In Cleveland, the new legislation prompted much activity as state banks rechartered as national banks in order to catch the anticipated windfall of new business.

Despite the chaotic conditions of the national banking system, the institutional history of Cleveland banking, dominated by the conservative descendants of the original New England settlers, appeared to be one of stable, steady growth. Local banks created during the war continued to flourish, and the 2 decades bracketing the change of centuries witnessed in most large cities the development of 2 new forms of banking institutions. The first of these were savings banks, frequently located in working-class and immigrant neighborhoods. They were to play a major role in financing neighborhood enterprises and promoting homeownership among property-conscious European immigrants. The other was of far greater monetary consequence. The state-chartered trust company was a late-19th-century bankers' attempt to break the logjam of antiquated banking legislation of the 1860s. National banks rechartered as state-regulated trust companies. Under the relaxed laws and indifferent supervision of the state, such local trust companies as Central National Bank, the Cleveland Trust Co., and the GUARDIAN SAVINGS & TRUST CO. were founded and rapidly expanded. They benefited from having greater investment decision-making authority over large amounts of cash, securities, and realty deposited in trust accounts with the bank. They exercised considerable influence over the direction the local economy would take, particularly in the early decades of the 20th century; and very early in their development, the Cleveland investment banking trusts established close financial ties with their larger counterparts in New York and Chicago. In 1913, the federal government created the Federal Reserve System, and Cleveland, because of a creative partnership between the business community, Newton D. Baker, and the Wilson administration, was made a regional FEDERAL RESERVE headquarters, recognition of the city's importance in the nation's banking system.

The business history of Cleveland's banks is more difficult to recount. Cleveland was a city that experienced rapid rates of growth in bank capitalization and deposits and rose in the first 15 years of the 20th century to the second tier in the nation's banking hierarchy, behind New York and Chicago but abreast of Boston, Philadelphia, Baltimore, and Pittsburgh. Paradoxically, the city's banking hinterland (the geographic area served by Cleveland banks) was substantially smaller than that of Cincinnati, Pittsburgh, Detroit, or St. Louis. Located midway between New York and Chicago, the nation's 2 strongest banking centers, Cleveland was also surrounded by the aforementioned strong regional banking centers. A second important reason for Cleveland's small banking hinterland can be found in the pattern of investment followed by local banks. Cleveland's economy in the late 19th century was rapidly making a transition from a commercial-sector-dominated economy to a manufacturing-sector-led economy. The city's banks were largely responsible for financing this transition. Cleveland banks were financing the growth of these manufacturing firms and were involved in the purchase of inventories, equipment, and the sale of finished goods. These activities required banking ties to New York and Chicago rather than a close investment relationship to other regional banks and businesses. In one area, however, Cleveland banks deviated from this practice. In the early 20th century, the city's banks shunned investments in the emerging automobile and aircraft industries, even though these local manufacturers were competitive with counterparts in other cities, with the result that Detroit and Los Angeles rather than Cleveland became the nation's production centers. In the speculation-fed 1920s, several Cleveland banks invested heavily in the rail and realty empire of the Van Sweringen brothers, and when that collapsed in 1929, several large city banks were devastated.

Wholesale and retail trade experienced a transitionary phase in the late 19th century. Many of Cleveland's leading bankers and industrialists, including MARCUS A. HANNA and John D. Rockefeller, began their business careers in countinghouses before the Civil War. In 1860, wholesaling, retailing, and light manufacturing activities were all housed in the same loft-type buildings between W. 6th St. and the FLATS. Competition for land for business uses drove up land prices at the same time wholesale and retail trade were becoming more specialized, more dependent on customer contact, and sensitive to changes in long-distance and commuter transportation. Considerable changes resulted in both businesses in the late 19th and early 20th centuries. Wholesaling, facing competition for space from heavy INDUSTRY and retailing and its own growing space requirements, abandoned the central area in favor of lower-cost land and larger buildings around the railroad beltline encircling the inner city. Separate wholesale districts emerged specializing

in food distribution, dry goods, and construction materials. In the 1860s, high-grade retailing broke away from general dry goods to serve the carriage trade along Superior Ave., but as the streetcar became the dominant mode of commuter transportation in the late 19th and early 20th centuries, there was a greater need for face-to-face contact with customers, and in consequence retailers competed for expensive land as close as possible to streetcar terminuses. Retailing became increasingly more specialized in the first decades of the 20th century, culminating in the department store.

Cleveland retailers and wholesalers served a local market primarily and did not, like those in Chicago, attract customers from great distances. That is reflected in employment statistics in wholesale and retail trade, which reveal an increase from 12% of the LABOR force in 1860 to 19% in 1900, only to decline to 12% in 1929. The rise and decline of employment in this sector of the local economy paralleled that of the nation, but the percentage of people employed in wholesale and retail trade never surpassed the national average. Transportation is credited with giving manufacturing in Cleveland its initial push. The canals made Cleveland a grain-processing center and provided stimulus for a BREWING INDUSTRY. The railroads, however, propelled the city into its industrial era, not only by giving it access to new markets and supplies of raw materials, but also because railroads were the major customers of the city's first industries. They stimulated a railroad rerolling industry, manufacturers of virgin rails, steam-engine factories, and the nation's largest railroad-repair industry.

Although transportation was also important in stimulating the growth of the iron- and steelmaking industries, geographic proximity to the requisite natural resources and local entrepreneurship also played a significant role. Cleveland was connected by water to the iron-ore regions of the upper Great Lakes and by rail to the coal fields of southern Ohio, West Virginia, and Pennsylvania. In the last quarter of the 19th century, Cleveland businessmen, who in the Civil War decade had been in wholesale trade, invested in mines in both regions and in transportation enterprises to transport the raw materials to Cleveland. With its superb location, it followed that Cleveland would also become a shipbuilding center. The iron and steel industry expanded considerably after the Civil War, and it in turn spawned foundries and castings shops, which made the city attractive to machine-tool entrepreneurs. By 1900, the iron and steel products industry was outstripping the original iron and steel industry in terms of value of product and number of hands employed. That set the stage for the development of the automobile and automobile-parts industries. The mining and iron- and steelmaking and -fabricating industries were greatly aided by the presence of the Case Institute of Technology, which graduated a steady stream of metallurgists, engineers, and chemists who not only served these industries but also in many cases founded their own businesses, such as LUBRIZOL.

Technology, transportation, and above all entrepreneurship joined in the rise of the oil industry. John D. Rockefeller exploited Cleveland's water, rail, and later pipeline linkages to bring Pennsylvania crude oil to his refineries. The presence of the STANDARD OIL CO. had a multiplier effect on the industrial and financial development of Cleveland. Nowhere was that more evident than in the city's large cooperage industry and in the growth of local CHEMICAL and paint industries. The mid-19th-century paper industry, in turn, was the seed for the PRINTING INDUSTRY. This development led the city to become an important manufacturer of printing presses, aided by the existence of the original iron and steel industry. The ELEC-TRICAL-apparatus industry emerged from a series of local inventions that themselves were the product not only of genius but also of an environment that educated and rewarded technicians. For example, CHARLES F. BRUSH, the inventor of the arc light, became a manufacturer of electrical apparatus. Twentieth-century Cleveland was not like Pittsburgh or Detroit, which specialized in the manufacture of a single product. Cleveland's economy evolved to the point where its manufacturing sector employed 223,000, or nearly half the city's labor force, all of which made Cleveland in these decades far more recession-proof than neighboring cities in the region.

Industrial growth between 1860 and 1929 included less-obvious but equally important changes in the business organizations manufacturing industrial products. These became apparent both in ownership and in the techniques of production and distribution. Cleveland's manufacturing concerns were founded by men who began their careers in the city's commercial sector and then invested their profits in mining, transportation, or manufacturing, or some combination of all three. In the 1870s, these enterprises were wholly owned by their principal founders or by a small group of limited partners. Ownership was frequently interlocking, which gave rise to a new elite locally based on industrial wealth. In the 1880s, the capital, managerial, technological, production, and distribution demands of these companies escalated to such a scale that the original principal founders were no longer able to meet them. The corporate device was then introduced, which pluralized ownership and allowed the company to raise sufficient capital to do business. Even in this phase of corporate evolution, Cleveland businessmen typically invested in one another's corporations. However, Cleveland's manufacturing sector was becoming integrated into the national economy, resulting also in removing corporate decision making from ownership.

By the 1880s, the capacity of these new enterprises outstripped reliable local supplies of raw materials and local marketing outlets. Efforts to market goods nationally ran into the limitations posed by relying on third-party commission merchants and wholesale jobbers in distant cities to sell products. The solution to these problems was to employ the capital raised through the corporate device to vertically integrate the firm backward to include transportation and sources of raw materials and forward to build a system for distributing and marketing the finished products. Backward integration was accomplished by purchase of firms in transportation and raw-materials extraction. Forward integration was accomplished by adding distribution and marketing arms to the parent firm. John D. Rockefeller was able to achieve both in the Standard Oil Co. by controlling his product from the wellhead to retail sales. Both required the expertise of professional managers. This action placed the daily decision making, and ultimately policy making, in the hands of professional managers, removing them from ownership. The professional managers, and the bankers financing these moves, preferred corporate policies that would insure long-term growth and stability over those that would maximize current profits.

As these and other new manufacturing firms came into existence in the late 19th and early 20th centuries, they produced complex lines of products requiring consumer credit for purchase and factory training in their installation, use, and maintenance. For example, one of Cleveland's rapidly growing industries was expensive and complex printing presses. To facilitate sales, manufacturers would install the machinery and train printing-press operators in its usage, creating still more production and distribution

demands on the parent firm and requiring still more integration of the organization. As further business expansion occurred in the 1893–1905 period and in the 1920s, business conditions dictated further vertical integration, which was accomplished in a wave of corporate mergers. Many Cleveland firms in iron- and steelmaking, iron and steel products, automobiles, automobile parts, and electrical apparatus found it attractive to merge into larger national corporations such as U.S. STEEL, REPUBLIC STEEL, GENERAL ELECTRIC, and WESTINGHOUSE. In these cases, corporate decision making was delegated to professional managers, who often were not resident in Cleveland. Strong local leadership in mining, transportation, shipbuilding, and communications enterprises initiated mergers, and Cleveland became the national headquarters of these locally conceived corporations. Other firms, particularly those in clothing, printing, and sewing-machine manufacture, had large enough local or regional markets for their products to withstand the pressures of vertical integration and hence retained their autonomous status and local ownership well into the 20th century. By the 1920s, decision making in Cleveland's manufacturing sector was divided among professional managers in distant cities, professional managers with their headquarters in Cleveland, and local owners of smaller manufacturing enterprises, which, by the 1920s, were not the city's dominant industries.

Rationalization of production had an important impact on labor. Because of heavy capital, technology, management, and energy costs, profit-boosting economies were frequently made at the expense of the workers. These cost-cutting measures included seasonal and inventory layoffs, low wages, and, as the production process modernized, replacement of skilled labor with less-skilled, low-paid workers. In Cleveland, skilled workers declined from 40% of the labor force in 1900 to 16% in 1930, while the percentage of semiskilled and unskilled increased from 25 to 45% during the same years. The number of salaried clerical workers increased threefold between 1900 and 1930. Salaried workers not only were better-paid than those in production, but their salaries increased at a faster rate than the wages of blue-collar workers. The changing nature of production and the inequities encountered in the workplace prompted an ever-mounting number of Cleveland workers to join unions. Unionization was accompanied by tough management resistance marked by intervals of labor violence.

In Cleveland, the local working class was split by ethnic and religious antagonisms, pitting the recently arrived Southern and Eastern European Catholics and JEWS against northern European Protestants. Northern Europeans, including IRISH Catholics, arrived in Cleveland after midcentury and were partially assimilated skilled workers by the time large numbers of unskilled Southern and Eastern European immigrants began arriving after 1890. They came to the city at a time when the production process was being modernized in the metalmaking industry, when management replaced higher-paid skilled workers with lower-paid unskilled workers. The unionized skilled workers refused to accept the unskilled as members, deepening antagonisms that were frequently exploited by management. The story was repeated in the metals-fabricating industries in the late 19th and early 20th centuries. Strikes and attendant violence characterized union activity in both industries. Unions still were unwilling to incorporate unskilled workers in an era when both industries were becoming increasingly dependent on semi- and unskilled labor. Thus, unions entered the 20th century in a weakened position, and in the antiradical, antiforeign, antiunion, open-shop atmosphere of the 1920s, the union movement in the metalmaking and metals-fabricating industries was further weakened. Craft unions in the transportation, food, clothing, and construction industries were far more successful, but even here, many union locals were ethnic satrapies that discriminated against less-favored ethnic groups. In the period following 1910, these practices were also directed against BLACKS.

Many working-class Clevelanders, denied opportunity in the formal economy, became participants in the city's informal economy. A dual economy evolved in Cleveland in which there existed a formal structure of income opportunities in enterprises that today would report their activities to the Internal Revenue Service alongside a second, informal, system, which included such activities as street peddling, barter, informal exchanges of services, illegitimate business enterprises, and petty and organized CRIME. Cleveland's declining rate of homeownership, increasing rates of cyclical and seasonal unemployment, the low wage structure, the rising crime rate, and the steadily mounting transfer of payments from public and private agencies serve as evidence that the informal economy existed but do not provide an accounting of its size. In the 20th century, American leaders had the choice of either reforming the formal economy so that it spread its rewards more equitably, or relying more heavily on the informal economy. That Cleveland's public transfer payments were at an all-time high, that the private welfare system was overhauled in the interest of greater efficiency in fundraising and delivery, and that local politicians and police systematically ignored the growing number of illegitimate business enterprises and activities, suggest that the latter was the course favored by decision makers national and local. It proved to be the path of least resistance.

***Demographic Growth and Change.*** Urbanization in the late 19th and early 20th centuries was usually an admixture of demography and industrialization, although there were important exceptions to the rule. London, Paris, and New York, the Victorian Era's largest cities, did not contain many large-scale manufacturing enterprises. Cleveland's urbanization, however, incorporated both demographic and industrial components. In 1860, Cleveland was a town of 43,417, but in the 7 decades that followed, the city added over 850,000 to its population and nearly 65 square miles to its geography. By the turn of the century, 1 in 10 Ohioans was a Clevelander. Cleveland in 1900 became the state's largest city, outstripping rival Cincinnati by a margin of 56,000. In 1930, Cleveland was the nation's 6th-largest city, with a population of 900,429. High population densities were a common feature of western urbanization. Paris, Berlin, and Liverpool by 1890 had broken the 100-persons-per-acre threshold. Only Brooklyn (44.6 ppa) among American cities approached Old World densities. The largest American cities ranged in density from 12 to 23 persons per acre. Cleveland's density in 1890 was 12 persons per acre, which increased to 22 by 1930. What alarmed Clevelanders about these statistics was the densities amassed in some urban neighborhoods. In Cleveland, the Central area, bordered by Woodland and Cedar avenues, had a 1910 density of 110 persons per acre. People living at these densities were frequently ill-housed, ill-clad, ill-nourished, and the victims of poverty, disease, and crime.

Despite what appeared to be dim prospects for some, immigrants and migrants flocked to cities such as Cleveland, accounting for a sizable proportion of their growth during the period 1860-1929. Population growth was the result of natural increase (a surplus of births over deaths) plus migration. Growth from migration occurs when in-migrants exceed out-migrants. Two streams of in-migration fed the city's growth. The first was composed of native-born migrants. They came to Cleveland from all the eastern states and in some measure from Ohio as well. Southern blacks were also part of the native-born migration stream to Cleveland. Except in the decade of the 1920s, when foreign IMMIGRATION from all sources flagged, black and white native-born in-migrants accounted for nearly 50% of the city's population increase.

The second stream of in-migrants swelling Cleveland's population was made up of the foreign-born. Virtually every European nationality group, plus a scattering of Orientals, was represented. They came in successive waves: first the Northern Europeans from the BRITISH Isles, then the GERMANS in large numbers, followed by the Irish and a small number of SCANDINAVIANS. Culturally and religiously disparate, they were, however, usually skilled and semiskilled workers. Between the mid-1870s and the outbreak of World War I, a second wave of immigration from Southern and Eastern Europe dwarfed the first wave: POLES, Russian Jews, HUNGARIANS, CZECHS, SLOVAKS, SLOVENIANS, CROATIANS, ITALIANS, and GREEKS. The new immigrants came from peasant societies and were overwhelmingly semi- and unskilled laborers who took their places in Cleveland's modernizing industries. In most decades, foreign-born migrants accounted for fully 25% percent of the city's growth. In the decade 1900-1910, immigrants were responsible for an estimated 40% of the city's population increase. In the 1920s, because of the restrictive provisions of the National Origins Act of 1924, foreign migration to the city slowed to a trickle. In 1920, perhaps the peak year of foreign migratory influence, the foreign element (the foreign-born plus native-born white with foreign parents) amounted to 75% of Cleveland's population.

Natural increase eventually became the major cause of Cleveland's population growth during the industrial era, but early in the era the indicators were not promising. In each of the 3 decades between 1890 and 1920, only 25% of the city's growth was the result of natural increase. In the decade 1920-1930, Cleveland's population growth was overwhelmingly the product of natural increase. Ironically, population growth through natural increase was achieved in the face of the declining birth rates achieved during these same years. Lowered birth and death rates are perhaps the most interesting feature of urban demography in the industrial era. Low birth rates are characteristic of urban lifestyles. That Cleveland's birth rates declined over time is an indicator of the city's growing urbanization. In 1870, the crude birth rate was 54 live births per thousand, a rate that dropped to 20 per thousand by 1930. The most impressive reductions occurred between 1870 and 1900. Although the great influx of immigrants in their childbearing years drove the birth rate up to the mid-twenties between 1910 and 1920, even these numbers did not rival the high birth rates of the mid-19th century. In order for Cleveland's population to grow through natural increase, an even more dramatic drop in the death rate was necessary. Most western cities in the latter decades of the 19th century and the first decade of the 20th realized the "urban demographic transition," where live births substantially outweigh deaths, and cities are able to add to their populations primarily through natural increase. Cleveland's vital statistics, albeit fragmentary, reflect this trend. The urban demographic transition occurred because life expectancy improved for people of all ages, but the most striking gains were made in the reduction of infant mortality. Cleveland experienced a 50% reduction in stillbirths alone between 1890 and 1930, a reflection of the positive trend in infant mortality.

The causes of lowered mortality were many: improved medical knowledge and health-care facilities, more nutritious diet, improved water-supply and drainage systems, the

PUBLIC-HEALTH movement, public regulation of food distribution and sales, and public imposition of sanitary and housing standards. A key element undergirding all of these efforts was the achievement of stable urban population densities. In 1910, population density stabilized at approximately 20 persons per acre, where it remained until 1930. Meanwhile, the vital index took its great leap forward to achieve values of between 167 and 192 births per 100 deaths. Densities in various neighborhoods, however, remained high throughout the first 3 decades of the 20th century, and so too did mortality rates in these neighborhoods.

*Geographic Evolution.* The first phase of the city's geographic evolution was the commercial city, a preindustrial settlement that took its shape from its initial advantages of site and situation. Cleveland in 1860 was a commercial city that had outgrown its original New England town plan with its historical focus at Public Square. Economically, the commercial city was oriented toward the mouth of the Cuyahoga River, where long-distance rail and water transportation fused. That, rather than Public Square, was the economic heart of Cleveland, the city's central business district (CBD). Production, distribution, sales, and services had yet to specialize, and all business functions might take place within a single loft-type building. Buildings of this nature were clustered on a narrow strip of land running from W. 6th St. down the steep hill to the Flats and the mouth of the river. North and south, this strip was bordered by the lake and Superior Ave. Land values in the CBD were substantially higher than anywhere else in the city; nearly 60% of Cleveland's business establishments were located in the central business district, and over 60% of the workforce found employment there. Virtually all businesses serving regional and national markets were located in the Flats end of the CBD, as were most of the nascent manufacturing enterprises. The transportation and construction companies of the city's commercial sector also favored central-business-district locations. Businesses in food wholesaling and retailing, finance, general dry goods, and services tended to locate in the W. 6th St. end of the CBD. Specialized retailers serving the carriage trade in the 1870s were opening shops on Superior east of Public Square toward Erie (E. 9th St.) and east along Euclid. Retailing also followed a less affluent clientele southeast along the banks of the river and due east following the shoreline of the lake. Still, most business activities in the commercial city were highly concentrated within the small central business district of the city.

Cleveland increased in size from 7 square miles in 1860 to 12 square miles in 1870, suggesting an increase in the city's radius from 2.5 to 3.5 miles. Population densities stabilized at 12 persons per acre, which remained the norm until the period of rapid industrial growth began in the 1880s. Population densities were symptomatic of the current state of commuter transportation technology. In a pedestrian city limited in size to the distance an individual could walk to work in an hour, the relatively high residential densities of the commercial city encouraged considerable social integration of housing within a small amount of space. Even though the commercial city was more integrated residentially than it would become in its industrial or metropolitan stages, patterns of residential separation did exist, which reveal that the choice residential land was found closest to and the least desirable land farthest from the central business district.

If the 6 Bureau of the Census occupational classifications of proprietors, professionals, clericals, skilled, semi-skilled, and unskilled are used as approximations of social class, it is possible to gain an understanding of the residential structure of the commercial city. Proprietors and professionals, approximating the upper and upper-middle classes, lived in wards closest to the central business district. In 1870, a higher-status EUCLID AVE. residential corridor was evolving. Professionals and proprietors traveled from this silk-stocking enclave to their CBD establishments by horse or carriage. Solidly middle-class clericals made their homes in the CBD wards, but an incipient pattern of residential dispersion showed clericals inhabiting a semicircle of lower-cost wards extending south and west of the CBD. Among the working classes, skilled workers were more highly integrated into the city's residential fabric than the two lower-status laboring groups. Skilled workers inhabited east and west side wards on the outskirts of the city, while semi- and unskilled workers lived in relatively segregated circumstances in a middle ring of wards forming a semicircle around the entire city, east and west sides.

Assimilation of migrant groups was a feature of 19th-century urbanization, and in the commercial city the melting-pot theory got its first test. The foreign-born inhabited wards south of the central business district on the east and west sides of the river bordering the Cuyahoga Valley. The immigrants from the United Kingdom, Ireland, and Germany were reasonably well assimilated into the residential structure of the city, but residual German and Irish colonies could be found on both east and west sides. In 1870, the most recently arrived immigrants were the Czechs. Virtually all Czechs were heavily segregated in 2 wards on the city's southeast side. Dense Czech concentrations in so few neighborhoods offered a glimpse of the residential segregation of the industrial future.

The industrial revolution gave its name to the second stage of urban geographic evolution. When the population of industrial Cleveland grew fourfold between 1870 and 1900, the limitations of its site had to be reckoned with. The city's topography embraced 5 features that did much to form the contours of the city during its industrial phase of growth: the Cuyahoga River, which presented challenges of navigation and docking through the 19th century; the Cuyahoga Valley, the east-west dividing line of both economic and social space; the shoreline of Lake Erie, which facilitated east-west radial expansion; the glacial ridges west of the mouth of the river, which impeded business expansion and residential settlement on the city's west side; and the level surface of glacial delta bordering the lake to the east, a permissive topographical feature that allowed rapid development east of the river. The land east of the river steadily rose in elevation, the earliest foothills of the Appalachian chain, affording attractive residential sites overlooking the industrial city below. It was within the limits of this topographical container that Cleveland evolved from a commercial town of 43,417 to an industrial city of 381,768 in the 40 years 1860-1900.

Industrial growth brought changes in the location of each type of business represented in the city's economy. Changes in the location of the manufacturing sector were perhaps the most far-reaching and of greatest social significance. Not only did the number of manufacturing firms and their volume increase during the period, but their spatial requirements were altered by the adoption of continuous-process production technology. The production requirements of these new enterprises and the limitations posed by the city's topography meant that only 4 distinct districts within the city could meet the spatial demands of the modern factory. The most important of these was the Flats, where 38% of all Cleveland manufacturing establishments were located in 1900. Beginning at the mouth of the river, where the lime and salt mines, the coal-storage area, and the oil-refining facilities congregated, the Flats industrial district followed along the banks of the crooked river. Giant metalmaking mills were built south to the southeastern industrial suburb of NEWBURGH, which formed a second industrial district, containing iron and steel mills, metals-manufacturing plants, clothing and bookbinding factories, and the bulk of the city's container industry. The Flats and Newburgh districts housed heavy industries dependent on both water and rail transportation. A third industrial district, developed by LEONARD CASE along the lakeshore east on St. Clair Ave. between E. 26th St. and E. 55th St., housed metals-fabricating and other factories dependent on rail rather than water transportation. Finally, land bordering the circumferential railroad belt surrounding the entire city, east and west, became Cleveland's fourth industrial district. But the inventory of industrial realty as early as 1909 was limited by the city's topography. Cleveland was hard-pressed to provide new factory sites for its expanding industrial base. The demand among competing businesses drove up the value of land in areas of the city where businesses congregated. Nowhere was that more apparent than in the CBD.

The increase in land values, the specialization of function within businesses, and the completion of the streetcar system combined to give the central business district its characteristic form in the industrial city. The most visible change was its location, which shifted from the W. 6th-Flats area to Public Square and the STREETS radiating from the Square. The major explanation for the eastward shift in location of the CBD was the completion of an electric streetcar system (see City of Cleveland Electric Street Railways map). That coincided with the decision of businesses to separate their production, distribution, and sales functions. Retailers became dependent on face-to-face contact with their customers. Public Square locations greatly improved the likelihood of meeting potential customers, who came twice a day to make trolley connections. Buildings appeared around the Square and on Euclid and Superior Ave. that housed retail specialty shops on the ground floor and offices on the upper floors. Department stores and almost all financial institutions and insurance and real-estate agents competed for adjacent office space in the central business district. The CBD became the center of white-collar employment. White-collar employers were willing to make the tradeoff of high-priced land for the advantages of face-to-face contact with customers and clients. Blue-collar employers in wholesaling, construction, and transportation, where possible, stayed in the Flats or moved to cheaper business sites on the fringe of the central business district, putting pressure on close-in residential neighborhoods for land.

The residential structure of the industrial city was determined by the ability to pay for housing and commuter transportation. More subtle forces of ethnic, racial, and class discrimination were also at work, as doubtless were the preferences of some groups to live together, most notably the elite groups and many of the immigrant groups. The least urbanized of the city's residents clustered in the wards nearest the central business district, east and west of the Flats industrial district, north and east of the lakeshore industrial district, north and south paralleling the railroad beltline industrial district, and on the west side adjacent to the Detroit-Lorain-W. 25th railroad beltline industrial district. The urbanized wards formed a wedge beginning at 13th St. and bordered by Superior and Cedar and extended to the easterly limits of settlement. A ring of urbanized wards formed the outer circle of west side settlement. The residential pattern of the industrial city was one in which the least affluent lived near places of employment in the industrial districts of the city, and the more affluent lived farthest from the economic core and commuted there by streetcar.

An interesting feature of Cleveland's industrial evolution was the residential separation of the native-born from the foreign-born. Cleveland, in effect, was 2 separate cities. With the exception of the western lakeshore wards, the heaviest concentrations of native-born Clevelanders were found on the east side. Although they were substantially represented in affluent, urbanized wards, not all native-born Clevelanders had attained that status. Native-born migrants clustered in wards around the central business district, the eastern lakeshore industrial district, and the eastern railroad beltline industrial district. They were most conspicuously absent from the Flats-area industrial district and the west side. The residential concentrations of the foreign-born were almost an exact reversal of those of the native-born. They were found in the urbanized outer ring of west side settlement and the west side industrial district, most prominently in the Flats-area industrial district, and some few spilled over into the east side railroad beltline industrial district.

Cleveland's ethnic duality was less apparent in the social geography of its classes, because class distinctions cut across ethnic lines. The residential concentrations of the upper-status proprietors and professionals roughly paralleled that of the more urbanized population. There was a concentration of this group on the near-west-side wards containing the west side retail district and its industrial site. The remainder of the proprietors and professionals were found on the east side in a wedge-shaped zone of settlement. This zone formed in the wards around the central business district and spread out the Euclid Ave. corridor to the edge of settlement of the proprietors and professionals, not unlike that observed in the same class in 1870. However, clericals were more likely to choose residences on the west side than on the east side. Of the lower-status groups, the unskilled workers provide the clearest examples of the residential structure of the industrial city. They were most heavily concentrated in wards containing the city's 5 industrial districts. The skilled and semiskilled workers followed a similar pattern, but they tended to live farther from their places of work. The skilled and semiskilled were least represented in the Flats and Newburgh industrial districts, which boasted the city's most modern, least skill-dependent factory operations. By World War I, Cleveland, a mature industrial city, with its segregated allotments of space to specific human activities, resembled a doughnut with a center containing the bulk of its business enterprises, and the most recently arrived, least urbanized, and least affluent of its citizens surrounded by a ring of relative comfort and affluence.

Cleveland's third phase of geographic evolution, the metropolitan region, was simply a geographic magnification of business and demographic spatial trends already underway. In the decade and a half between the war and the onset of the Depression, Cleveland's physical expansion would be brought to a halt at 71 square miles and 900,429 people by a surrounding ring of politically independent suburbs. The arrival of the metropolitan city was hastened after World War I when urban growth, spurred by fear of environmental and social contagion and smoothed by the extension of streetcar lines and the introduction of the automobile, culminated in the appearance of such suburban bedroom communities as EAST CLEVELAND, CLEVELAND HEIGHTS, Shaker Heights, and LAKEWOOD. The economic geography of the metropolis remained much the same as that of the industrial city. Dominant industries remained at their historical sites, although there was a growing tendency for retailers and service providers to decentralize with the spreading population. The metropolis was even more segregated by class, ethnicity, and race than its industrial predecessor, with affluent native-born Clevelanders monopolizing the suburban locations. The history of the metropolitan region can best be explained by the political geography of annexation and ZONING.

The annexation movement failed because of more intense racial, ethnic, and class antagonisms following World War I, new laws that facilitated incorporation and made annexation unworkable, and improved suburban services in suburban communities. Moreover, suburban municipalities discovered that restrictive zoning legislation could be used to keep undesirable businesses and people out of their communities. Cleveland added most of its foreign population between 1890 and 1914. They were usually impoverished Southern and Eastern European peoples who retained their native village subcultures in tightly segregated neighborhoods near the industrial districts. Concern was often voiced by the native-born about the foreign customs and radical politics of the immigrants. Black migration began in the World War I years and quickened in the 1920s, so that by 1929, the old Central neighborhood, southeast of the central business district, emerged as the city's first black ghetto. In the immediate postwar years, national attention was riveted on the communist ideology associated with the foreign-born and with the eugenic origins of migrating blacks, who were perceived as ignorant, frightening, and incapable of being incorporated into white society. To native-born Clevelanders, both types of people were resident in the corporate city in alarmingly large numbers. In the war decade and in the 1920s, the upper classes, together with a growing number of mobile middle-class professionals, moved to the suburbs, where they had the power to create economic and legal barriers between themselves and the objects of their fears.

Until 1914, Cleveland's annexations kept pace with population growth. After the Great War, annexation slowed to a trickle. In 1910 the suburban population was 44,000; it mounted to 130,000 in 1920; and in 1930 some 300,000 people were living in the suburban ring surrounding Cleveland, an increase of nearly 600% in 2 decades. Under Ohio law, annexations were accomplished by city ordinance coupled with the approval of the voters of the area designated for annexation. In the 19th century, voters proved compliant. Voters so willingly giving their approval were often residents of industrial districts where manufacturing and employment opportunities had spilled beyond the boundaries of the corporate city of Cleveland. They welcomed the prospect of sharing the cost of neighborhood services with Cleveland taxpayers. Twentieth-century suburbanites, however, were affluent and required no pooling of resources to meet the costs of services. Accordingly, they typically voted no on annexation, particularly after discovering that the state legislature could be persuaded to pass legislation facilitating municipal incorporation.

White-collar and working-class Clevelanders might have found the quality of services provided by the city of Cleveland acceptable, but the more affluent and educated classes grew ever more disenchanted as the 20th century advanced. In 1922, *Town Topics*, the newspaper that chronicled the leisure-time activities of socially prominent Clevelanders, assailed the specter of annexation, concluding that a suburb was "not going to increase its burden by adding to it the weight of paying to help mismanage Cleveland." All manner of Cleveland services, ranging from education to garbage pickup, were found wanting in a city whose political apparatus was increasingly controlled by the very people whose proximity suburbanites were fleeing. Zoning became a major weapon in a suburban arsenal dedicated to keeping undesirable elements out.

In 1916, the city of New York passed the nation's first zoning ordinance, and CLEVELAND CITY COUNCIL began in 1919 studying model zoning legislation that would not become a reality for another 9 years. In a heavily populated and congested city such as Cleveland, zoning ordinances were created to serve as guidelines for government-led environmental controls, but in practice zoning laws did little more than catalog existing land uses. Suburbs, however, were not laggard in their perception that zoning could give local government considerable sway over the future course of undeveloped land. Restrictive suburban zoning ordinances mushroomed thereafter, and all contained provisions either outlawing or severely restricting noxious businesses and incorporating provisions mandating lot size, setbacks, and even structural requirements for housing. These controls could be used to dictate the socioeconomic status of prospective residents. Ethnic and racial groups were specifically excluded under the common practice of issuing restrictive deed covenants. Cleveland's suburbs between 1910 and 1929 grew in accordance with these guidelines (see Population of Cuyahoga County maps).

Although restrictive covenants would not be struck down until the 1950s, restrictive suburban zoning ordinances were challenged in the court system in the 1920s. The village of EUCLID, an eastern lakeshore suburb of Cleveland, in 1922 passed a zoning ordinance that created several zones for various types of business and residential land use in the largely unbuilt village. The Euclid zoning ordinance was challenged by the Ambler Realty Co. on the grounds that zoning gave the municipal government police powers that abridged the company's right to use its property in accordance with rights assigned to corporate individuals under the 14th Amendment to the U.S. Constitution. In *VILLAGE OF EUCLID V. AMBLER REALTY*, the U.S. Supreme Court ruled against the company. This landmark decision gave the suburbs a legal stranglehold on corporate cities such as Cleveland. Thus, the political geography of annexation and zoning created the metropolitan region, in which the old industrial city would be forced to house the region's more undesirable industries and disadvantaged citizens and be in turn surrounded by a ring of environmentally pristine, affluent, and politically independent suburbs.

***Reform and the Voluntary Civic Sector.*** Cleveland's economic transformation added new groups to the city's traditional social class structure. Each developed its own values, institutions, and civic agendas. The agendas, wide-ranging and not infrequently in conflict, touched most areas of urban concern. Some of them were designed to improve the commonweal, others to advance the interests of a specific group or individual. A modern network of voluntary civic-sector organizations emerged late in the old century to collectively pursue both types of agendas. In consequence, GOVERNMENT was overhauled to deliver its services more effectively and equitably. Arts and educational institutions attempted to elevate the city culturally, set common standards of education, and teach American values. Other local organizations aroused themselves over the city's human and environmental needs, and all debated over what issues should be assigned to governmental institutions for resolution and which should be left to professionally managed and privately subscribed organizations in the voluntary civic sector. These organizations became advocates for a variety of conflicting political, social, and moral reform agendas, concerns originating in the social class structure of the industrial city.

The Cleveland Chamber of Commerce was by far the most powerful and most effective of the organizations in the voluntary civic sector. Founded in 1848 as the Board of Trade, it served for many years as the institutional voice of businessmen in the city's commercial sector. The rise of the manufacturing sector and the new class of entrepreneurs and managers made the old Board of Trade increasingly less representative of Cleveland's business concerns. By the 1880s, the organization was moribund. Under the guiding hand of Ryerson Ritchie, who became the new organization's first secretary, the Cleveland Chamber of Commerce emerged as a federation of business and professional "boards" representing manufacturers, wholesalers, retailers, realtors, and sundry professionals, but the real work of the chamber was done by a network of small issue-oriented committees whose portfolios included both business and civic concerns. Between 1890 and 1919, these chamber committees shaped a local agenda that would dominate policy making for the first third of the new century.

Local government was an early and ongoing concern of the chamber's Municipal Committee. Between 1890 and 1934, the committee supported such issues as structural reform in local government, HOME RULE, municipal finance, franchise regulation, at-large nonpartisan elections, annexation (for in 1916; against in 1923), REGIONAL GOVERNMENT, and the CITY MANAGER form of government for Cleveland. Other committees addressed the public-health issue in reports advocating municipal regulation of public markets and bath houses, improved sanitary and water-supply systems, water and air pollution, housing inspection, and school and visiting nurse services. The industrial rich and the middle-class professionals also used chamber committees to advance a variety of environmental reforms, such as neighborhood playgrounds, the PARKS that became the Cleveland and Metropolitan park systems, the Group Plan of public buildings, and city and later regional planning, and the Housing Committee over many years advocated such reforms as health and fire inspections, uniform building codes, zoning, and ultimately schemes to increase the inventory of new housing available to low-income Clevelanders. The chamber's committees on charities and corrections made recommendations that reformed the city's mosaic of charitable agencies and philanthropic institutions.

In each of these areas of concern—local government, public health, the urban environment, and charities—chamber committees followed a similar course of action. Initially the concern would be introduced to the full chamber, either by an influential Cleveland industrialist or by a lunchtime speaker of national distinction. The issue would then be assigned to a committee. Composed of industrialists and professionals, chamber committees studied problems exhaustively, even hiring professional staff and consulting with outside authorities. Local decision makers were drawn into the committee process as advisors. A final, comprehensive written report was submitted to the full chamber for discussion and approval. When approval was granted within the chamber, consensus was sought among local decision makers, and the public was informed in vigorous newspaper campaigns. Implementation of chamber-backed political reforms, for example, required an organizational coalition of voluntary civic and political groups. Reforms in public-health and environmental areas required that local government assume fiscal and management responsibility for implementation. In some cases, special-purpose districts, such as the Cleveland Metropolitan Park District, were created as implementation vehicles. Social welfare was regarded by the dominant groups within the chamber as a private rather than public policy matter, so implementation of social-welfare reforms was accomplished by purposely reducing

the role of municipal government and assigning fundraising, management, and delivery responsibilities to organizations in the voluntary civic sector.

In the 1890s, the chamber's Municipal Committee assigned to the Municipal Association (1895) responsibility for political reform. Guided by a board of trustees composed of young professionals, the association labored through these decades to achieve structural reform in local government and home rule, and to minimize the influence of the newcomers and the parties by advocating such "reforms" as at-large, nonpartisan elections and by screening candidates for local office. Municipal Association agendas could be realized only if the organization was willing to build consensus among elected officials and the two political parties. The coalition won the so-called federal charter, overhauling the structure of the municipal government, in 1892, home rule in 1912, and the city manager form of government passed in 1921.

The public-health movement saw the chamber at work in tandem with all varieties of middle- and upper-class reformer. All agreed that death rates could be reduced and health generally improved if a broad range of preventive measures were undertaken. The health problem was seen to have its roots in both human behavior and the local environment. This insured health movement support from both New England purity reformers, who maintained that social problems were rooted in human behavior, and the industrialists and professionals, who emphasized the environmental origins of social maladies. Responsibility for implementation was divided between public and private sectors. Public institutions, primarily the schools, instituted programs of public-health education, which were reinforced by voluntary civic-sector organizations such as the Public Health Nurses movement and the VISITING NURSES ASSOCIATION. Much of the effort was directed toward the working classes and their neighborhoods. Newcomers were encouraged to attend adult-hygiene classes in the schools and settlement houses and to avail themselves of public bath houses and the laundry facilities provided by the settlement houses. Municipal government, under pressure from the public-health movement, added to the inventory of public bathing facilities, modernized the system of water intake from Lake Erie, constructed a network of sanitary sewers throughout the city, and launched an inspection program of markets where food was sold. And industrialists were asked to voluntarily curb water and air pollution. If the branches of the public-health movement did not all bear equal fruit, there nevertheless was a quantifiable improvement in Cleveland's mortality statistics, beginning in the 1890s and realizing sustained gains after 1910.

Chamber committees early in the new century came to appreciate that the physical environment of the city had been despoiled by the city's industrial growth. Increasing population densities, traffic snarls, housing shortages, inadequate recreational space, and growth-induced urban sprawl not only were an aesthetic source of civic embarrassment but, as European social surveys had demonstrated, were held largely responsible for the pathologies observed in urban behavior. Moreover, from the viewpoint of businessmen, such conditions discouraged professional managers and the better sort of worker from accepting jobs in Cleveland.

The park movement was the earliest example of applying an environmental curative to a social ill. Neighborhood parks with supervised recreational programs were promoted by purity reformers as alternatives to the street life of vice and crime. The chamber's Parks Committee, dominated by business and professional environmentalists, initiated the remedy, and also planned on a grander scale when it proposed to encircle the city with a ring of planned parks to achieve "a continuous bower of verdant foliage" that would effect "a distinct and powerful influence along the line of good citizenship." In response, the city created a quasi-public Board of Park Commissioners empowered to design the system, acquire land, and raise private subscriptions for land acquisition. Even though the park board hired architect E. W. Bowditch of Boston to effect a park design, and several industrialists, including John D. Rockefeller, made generous donations of land, the Cleveland Park System made only halting gains until 1900, when the city absorbed the park board and assumed fiscal and operational responsibility for the fledgling system of parks. A decade later, it became apparent that the city's growth was going to leapfrog the now nearly built surrounding ring of Cleveland parks and spill over into the county. In 1911, the chamber, working with Cleveland parks director WILLIAM A. STINCHCOMB, began an intense lobbying effort in the state capital to win approval for a special-purpose regional park district with an independent board and separate taxing authority. In 1915, the Metropolitan Park District was empowered to design, build, and manage a ring of parks around the entire metropolitan region. With a park design crafted by Frederick Law Olmstead, the nationally famous designer of New York's Central Park, and an annual budget of $850,000 from park levies passed in 1917, 1918, 1920, and 1924, the Cleveland Metropolitan Park District (later called the CLEVELAND METROPARKS SYSTEM) began its task of building a park system for Greater Cleveland. The two park systems underscore the environmental-reform origins of both city and regional planning and demonstrate that a chamber-initiated environmental reform could be institutionalized with taxpayer support.

Public responsibility for CITY PLANNING was further stimulated by the chamber's advocacy of downtown development. In the last 2 decades of the 19th century, the shift of retail and commercial activities out of the historic Flats business district to Public Square occasioned a scramble for land along the streets radiating from the Square, which spilled into adjoining residential areas, impartially disrupting the residential settlements of rich and poor alike. The more immediate problem in the eyes of the chamber was that the eastward development of the central business district (CBD), though welcome, was taking place without the benefit of a central focal point that might impose some physical limits on the spread of the industrial city's CBD. Two young chamber activists, FREDERIC C. HOWE and MORRIS BLACK, aware that the city could acquire several new public buildings, including a federal court and customs house, county building, city hall, public library, railroad terminal, and possibly more, devised a scheme that would locate these civic buildings within a single comprehensive group plan to enhance the chaotic central business district. In 1895, the Beer & Skittles Club, of which Howe and Black were cheery members, persuaded the local chapter of the AMERICAN INSTITUTE OF ARCHITECTS to sponsor a design competition for local architects to create designs for harmoniously grouping the potential inventory of new buildings at a central location in downtown Cleveland. Surprised by the local enthusiasm for the project, the chamber responded by creating a Committee on Public Buildings (later called the Group Plan Committee). The object of the final plan—the Group Plan—was an orderly center for the industrial city's central business district, a community of classically designed public buildings setting an aesthetic standard for future development. Moreover, the municipality had been given authority to finance and build the project, an important precedent in the realization of institutionalized government city planning. The devel-

opment was to be monitored by a city planning commission created in 1913 and constituted largely of the industrialists and professionals who had supported the Group Plan.

A third chamber-inspired planning effort was the housing movement. The chamber created its Housing Committee in 1902. Initially, this committee saw the city's growing housing problem in environmental terms. It commissioned studies of working-class neighborhoods and concluded that the city's housing problem stemmed from low-quality housing stock, overcrowding, and poor sanitary conditions, an environment that was said to be at the heart of the mental, physical, and social maladies observed in Cleveland's slum districts. After consultation with housing experts in New York and Chicago, the Housing Committee recommended to the full chamber that these conditions would be remedied only if the municipality adopted a comprehensive housing code, incorporating construction standards for new buildings and guidelines for remodeling old housing. The code would also impose sanitary and room-occupancy standards and be enforced by the newly created municipal office of Housing Inspection. When council approval was finally given in 1914, the Housing Committee realized that the language and enforcement provisions of the building code were too vague to have the desired impact on slum housing. The committee then drafted a more exacting Tenement Code, which passed the city council in 1916 over the objections of newly emergent real-estate interests, who protested that public regulation of slum property was contrary to the principles of the free-market economy.

It was the free-market economy that brought home the realization that no amount of public regulation was going to solve Cleveland's housing problem. Initially, in 1913, the committee sought to build a block of model workmen's housing as a laboratory to demonstrate to the working classes how to maintain their houses and budget earnings into household accounts. But World War I brought huge increases in the number of workers migrating to the city, and postwar inflation and the continuing demand of a growing population for workers' housing forced a clearer perception of the city's housing problem on the Housing Committee: the free-market system was not producing enough housing stock for the workingman, and the filtering process of existing housing was also not bringing housing within his financial reach. The Housing Committee estimated in a 1920 report that 12,900 new families entered Cleveland each year, but only 4,200 new housing units were built annually. Homeownership among the working classes declined from 38% in 1918 to 19% in 1920 to 11% in the mid-1920s. The price of housing increased 12.7%, and lending institutions required a down payment of 80% of the purchase price, with the balance to be paid off within 2 years. In the 1920s, the committee promoted 2 privately funded limited-dividend companies to build and finance housing for the workingmen, a growing number of whom were black. This limited-dividend concept was held suspect by the prevailing free-enterprise value system and by the era's antagonism toward labor unions, foreigners, and blacks. In the end, the scheme failed. Only in the Depression decade was the housing problem addressed, and by then the solution came from the public sector.

Well before their era closed, the industrial elite put social reform on the agenda of the Cleveland Chamber of Commerce. Social awareness was forced by the city's late-19th-century industrialization. To cope with the growing problem of local poverty, which was particularly acute in recession years, a dual system of charities evolved. The first was funded and administered by the municipality's Department of Charities & Corrections and was chronically underfunded. The charity program included soup kitchens and a variety of work-relief activities, both of which were roundly resented by taxpayers and civic leaders. The second charity network was composed of a hodgepodge of private charity organizations and agencies loosely affiliated with local churches and funded by private subscription.

By the 1890s, this dual welfare system was drawing the fire of an unlikely coalition of concerned Clevelanders. The New England purity element was critical of the municipality's program because it was too costly and attempted no accounting of return for a charity dollar spent. The purity element was similarly critical of the private agencies, because their charity philosophy—known as the "Sweet Charity" approach—was too soft-hearted and failed to apply a rigorous remedial direction for recipients. There also was the frequently voiced suspicion that charity clients "worked the charity scam," that is, exploitation of the dual system's lack of administrative coordination by collecting benefits from both. The industrial and professional elite in the chamber were sympathetic to the concerns expressed by the purity element but felt that their common goals would not be reached until all charitable organizations were merged into a single umbrella organization with responsibility for fundraising and imposing management and accountability standards on each member organization. Once that was accomplished, both groups agreed, the municipality could get entirely out of the charity business. The third element involved in charity reform consisted of the professionals who were employed in the dual charity system. The professionals sought to rescue the private charity system from sectarian control and replace soft-hearted clergymen with college-trained social workers and other professionals who would combine efficiency in the delivery of services with a compassionate understanding of industrial reality. The WELFARE clients and their spokesmen, often ward politicians, sought not only the preservation of the dual system but also an increase in the amount of money available to both types of charitable agency with limited client surveillance. The middle- and upper-class coalition, however, proposed to police the system with an army of social workers, sundry clergy, YMCA secretaries, and visiting nurses. After these groups had struggled with the problem and each other throughout the latter decades of the 19th century, they witnessed early in the 20th century the triumph of the industrial elite's management philosophy. Used in large measure to implement the philosophy of the New England purity reformers, the operational details of modern management were put into effect by the newly intimidated social-welfare professionals. Repeated cycles of high unemployment induced by industrial recession and pressures from welfare clients and their representatives made it necessary for the city to remain involved in charity. The journey toward a systematic and orderly social-welfare system was not smooth.

After the Civil War era, charitable organizations were spawned in increasing numbers, and by the 1880s the city's dozens of such organizations were loosely affiliated with either the Protestant-dominated Associated Charities or the Irish Catholic-dominated BETHEL UNION. In 1884, the two organizations merged to form Bethel Associated Charities in an early attempt to coordinate fundraising and determine those charities deemed worthy of benefactor donations. In 1882, the New England element and the industrial elite both joined to support the Society for Organizing Charity, which in 1884 became the fundraising and budget arm of Bethel Associated Charities. Each member charity would be required to apply to Bethel for funds, which meant that each agency was subject to the budgetary and management restraints of the Society for Organizing Char-

ity. In operation, the system proved unworkable. A major obstacle to its success was a philosophy that "emphasized personal failure as the major cause of dependency" and that assumed that no one would work unless forced to do so. This initial effort to organize charity was dwarfed by the late-19th-century wave of immigration, industrial recession, and a new philosophy emphasizing the environmental origins of dependency.

In this environment, municipal assistance for the poor significantly increased, and charitable organizations outside the Bethel Associated Charities umbrella multiplied. The new radical environmental philosophy of the SALVATION ARMY, the institutional church, the YMCA, and the social-settlement house emerged as the Social Gospel, emphasizing that poverty took root in economic inequity. These local institutions promised to treat the causes rather than the symptoms of poverty and bring a halt to the practice of blaming the victim for his circumstances. At the same time, the attitudes of the New England purity element began to harden in the face of the onslaught of immigration. In rejecting the environmental origins of poverty among immigrants, they claimed that "to attempt to better the conditions of these homes as now grouped and huddled would be a waste of time and money." Many of the New England element thereafter broke ranks and gravitated toward TEMPERANCE as the remedy for the city's social ills.

At the dawn of the 20th century, Cleveland's charity problem was clearly out of hand, measured by rising public expenditures on charity and the proliferation of private charitable organizations, each motivated by conflicting philosophies and organizational objectives. Perhaps of most immediate concern was the competition among agencies for donations from the same small group of wealthy Clevelanders. In 1900, the chamber took charge of the problem when it created its Committee on Benevolent Associations, which in the next 20 years set in motion the process that would culminate in the creation of the Federation for Charity & Philanthropy (1913), the Welfare Federation (1917), and subsequently the Cleveland Community Fund (1919). The Welfare Federation (FEDERATION FOR COMMUNITY PLANNING) became the long-sought umbrella organization that would be used by the business and professional elite to distribute charity dollars and set policy for 88 approved charitable agencies. Western Reserve University was drawn in to establish the School of Applied Social Sciences to train the social workers who would serve in the agencies. The Cleveland Community Fund (now UNITED WAY SERVICES) was founded as the fundraising arm for the Welfare Federation. By means of a highly organized annual fundraising drive, it was able to transfer the cost of charity from the local rich to employees of the businesses they controlled by requiring each employee to pledge a percentage of his income to the Cleveland Community Fund. In its first year of operation, the Community Fund was able to raise in excess of $10 million. As part of this larger process, the CLEVELAND FOUNDATION was created in 1914 by FREDERICK GOFF, the president of Cleveland Trust Bank, to fund social surveys, study the shortcomings of local public institutions, and make recommendations for their improvement.

In the first 2 decades of the 20th century, volunteer PHILANTHROPY was dominated by the industrial and professional elite who were able to impose order and efficiency on Cleveland's charity network. The majority of the city's charitable agencies became dependent on the Cleveland Community Fund for raising money and the Welfare Federation for fiscal disbursement and policy and management guidelines. The elite's ability to control the flow of money into the system and set policy guidelines and management procedures made the work of the radical young professionals who served in the social-welfare agencies ineffectual and reduced the influence of the clients and their representatives.

Unlike the New England purity element, who blamed the individual for his condition, both the industrial elite and the more radical middle-class professionals were environmental reformers. But a distinction should be made between 2 varieties of environmental reform. The more radical middle-class reformers saw the economy as the core environmental issue, because the capitalist system distributed its benefits so unevenly. Dr. LOUIS B. TUCKERMAN, a radical clergyman, rejected an Associated Charities fund-raising appeal, claiming that "your society, with its board of trustees made up of steel magnates, coal operators, and employers is not really interested in charity. If it were it would stop the 12 hour day; it would increase wages and put an end to the cruel killing and maiming of men." This radical form of environmental reform was rejected in favor of an environmental approach that emphasized spatial solutions to social problems, seen in park-planning, Group Plan, zoning, and housing movements. The industrial elite was also cautious in the assignment of responsibility for implementation. Park planning was awarded to the public sector, but only in a carefully controlled special-purpose district. Implementation of the Group Plan and city planning generally was assigned to the City Planning Commission, whose membership included their representatives. Zoning, which proved a futile planning gesture, was awarded directly to the municipality. Housing was the least successful of the planning schemes, because it proffered solutions that implicitly undermined the free-market philosophy. Social-welfare reform was the most sensitive item on the industrial elite's agenda, but its resolution proved to be the most successful. Through employment of the newly created voluntary civic organizations, large amounts of money were raised, and modern bureaucratic methods of control were imposed throughout the welfare system. Thus, before the industrial elite moved to suburbia and began to play a more detached civic role as patrons of local cultural institutions, they were able to identify Cleveland's problems and impose their own methodology of order and businesslike efficiency on community decision making.

*The Political System.* A local historian wrote in 1896 that Cleveland's "commercial and private magnificence was equalled only by its municipal squalor." The problems of Cleveland's political system stemmed from 5 sources: the outmoded structure of the city's government; the quality of the city's political leadership; the manipulation of operating budgets and police powers to satisfy the demands of various interest groups, creating in the process a haphazard, inefficient system of service delivery; conflicts among elite-group reformers over means and ends of reform; and the conflicts attendant on the emergence of Cleveland as a metropolitan region, that is, a suburban periphery surrounding an inner-city core. These conditions were not unique to Cleveland and serve to explain the shortcomings of local political institutions throughout the nation.

In the middle third of the 19th century, Cleveland's municipal government was the ward of local businessmen. More businessmen than politicians, the part-time officeholders embraced the city booster philosophy of the day and used the municipality to promote civic growth with a mixture of boastful oratory and public spending on infrastructure improvements designed to attract new business to the city. Until the late 19th century, Cleveland was a low-tax, fiscally prudent municipality, unlike many American cities. In general, the 19th century was marked by speculation-induced financial panics, and cities emerged as irresponsible parties to the speculative fever in their flagrant issue of municipal bonds to fund local improvement schemes of dubious worth and inflated value. In the aftermath of each panic, state legislatures imposed more-restrictive city charters with respect to executive authority, policy initiatives, debt accumulation, and municipal independence of the state legislature. Cleveland's municipal charter, issued in 1852 and enduring until 1892, contained a full complement of restrictive provisions. The mayor was a figurehead who had little control over the city council, and only indirect control over his own administration. The executive, therefore, found it difficult to formulate policy, initiate legislation, or administer the public's day-to-day business. The charter forced the city to approach each problem on an ad hoc basis, often through the appointment of a special board to address a specific problem. In the latter decades of the century, the number of boards mushroomed, but none had a clear policy direction or sense of accountability to any level of public authority, the voters, the mayor, the council, or the bureaucracy. In the industrial era, this cumbersome, directionless system was manipulated at all levels. Power in the executive branch of government was exercised de facto by the bureaucracy, because by choice and design the mayor was a caretaker figure. Bureaucrats built their own satrapies and were virtually independent of the mayor, council, and public. In the final quarter of the century, there were repeated charges of bureaucratic mismanagement, favoritism, and embezzlement. City treasurers were especially vulnerable to charges of being unable to distinguish between legitimate and illegitimate means of remuneration. In 1886, city treasurer Thomas Axworthy absconded to Canada with $500,000 in public funds.

The legislative arm of municipal government was undermined through skillful manipulation of the ward system of councilmanic election. The key to this maneuver was to retain a high ratio of wards to the total population of the city; in 1900, Cleveland had 42 wards for a population of 381,768. With the franchise limited to male citizens over 21, these wards rarely generated over a thousand votes on election day. Such small numbers of votes were easily controlled by ward-level politicians. In key elections, fraud was transparently clear in these small geographies when bona fide registrants voted early and often, transients appeared at polling places sporting gift bottles of spirits, and the deceased rose, Lazarus-like, to claim their rights of franchise. These machinations elected a councilman who was powerful in his ward and who as a public servant faithfully represented the interests of those who elected him, including native- and foreign-born migrants, the elite, and businessmen seeking contracts and franchises from the municipality. Cleveland in these years was never dominated by a single boss, as New York, Chicago, Philadelphia, or Cincinnati was; instead, the city's ethnic, cultural, and class divisions produced a ward-level sachem, affiliated with either political party, who was, of course, powerful in his ward and by virtue of his electoral seniority able to win assignments to key city council committees where his power was in fact exercised. In addition, he often owned one or more companies doing business with the city. The councilman exercised a broker function, trading off the demands of various interest groups and on occasion advancing his own interests. By 1900, Cleveland City Council was highly representative of the city's ethnic and class composition.

Several ward-level political bosses achieved notoriety in the last quarter of the 19th century. In the 1870s, Silas Merchant emerged as a ward level-politician and dredging contractor dominant in the Republican party. In the 1880s and 1890s, William H. Gabriel, William Crawford, ROB-

ERT E. MCKISSON, and HARRY "CZAR" BERNSTEIN were powerful Republican figures with their political base in the wards and their financial support from those who did business with the city. With the backing of the ethnic vote loyal to Bernstein, McKisson became mayor in 1895. On the strength of his political influence in the city Republican party, McKisson attempted unsuccessfully to unseat Ohio Republican boss Marcus A. Hanna in a state senatorial primary. The old boss settled scores in 1899 when McKisson sought a second term as mayor. Hanna contributed $20,000 to McKisson's Democratic opponent, "Honest" JOHN FARLEY, a sum that one Farley supporter claimed was the margin of victory. Farley, a Democratic example of a Cleveland ward boss, was described by Frederic C. Howe as a "big raw boned, profane Irishman of substantial wealth, who made his money as a contractor" doing business with the city he served as a public official. This group was representative of the professional politicians who attempted to broker the interests of the low-tax, right-to-work, honesty-in-government New England element; the industrial and professional elite with their demands for efficiency in government and their antilabor and environmental-reform concerns; and the demands of the ethnic and native-born newcomers for favors, city contracts, jobs, and lax enforcement of laws restraining saloon operations, and other activities. The New England element, especially those wealthy members with holdings in Cleveland real property, were unyielding advocates of low taxes. These sentiments were shared by frugal, taxpaying immigrants. Here their influence was felt, for Cleveland remained throughout the entire period (1870–1900) one of the nation's low-tax cities. In this multicultural city, the New England element also expressed fears for the sanctity of property, law and order, right to work, and the enforcement of vice laws. Their right-to-work sentiments dovetailed with the antiunion sentiments of the industrial elite. The city's operating budget suggests that much of this agenda was met. Police and fire department expenditures steadily expanded during the period, and by 1900 the CLEVELAND FIRE DEPARTMENT was regarded as one of the nation's best. Local reformers and union officials frequently charged that CLEVELAND POLICE were used as scabs and strikebreakers. The operating budgets reveal that during years of labor strife, expenditures for police, courts, and the operation of correctional facilities increased as much as 33% and then declined in years of labor tranquility.

The businessmen and professionals who built the city's manufacturing sector required a local government that not only was antiunion but also would maintain existing infrastructure, and fund those environmental-reform measures that could not be legislated into special-purpose districts. In 1900, the public money spent on all the projects favored by the two elite groups amounted to 69% of all public monies raised from the tax duplicate in Cuyahoga County. Even so, this spending did not allay their concern for honesty and efficiency in local government and the need to overhaul the social-welfare system, the educational system, and the criminal-justice system. The newcomers, foreign-born and native-born alike, demanded representation, jobs, favors, contracts, and a laissez faire public attitude toward the informal economy, all to be accomplished within a low-tax environment. By the end of the century, virtually every ethnic group was represented on the city council—one of the benefits of having a great number of small wards. German and Irish mayors were also elected in the late 19th century. And with a payroll of $99,000 a month, the municipal government had jobs to dispense, and the names of ethnic newcomers appear with mounting frequency in the latter decades of the century.

As a growing city, Cleveland needed extensive bridge construction and repair, street paving, water supply, lighting, sewer construction, and, at the end of the century, garbage collection. It was in the provision of capital requirements for these improvements that the city was most frequently charged with corruption and favoritism. Between 1880 and 1900, municipal spending on these items increased by 300%, which in 1900 amounted to 42% of the municipality's $3.1 million budget. City council had committees devoted to each of these activities, and councilmen with greatest seniority and greatest ward-level power appeared most frequently on the committee rosters. They were charged with favoritism in hiring in these departments and in awarding contracts for construction work. Even though such charges were repeatedly made, these, like charges of electoral fraud, were seldom investigated. The professional politician was thus able to reward his ward-level constituents with jobs and contracts and distribute some of the benefits of civic largess to the newcomers. Through his influence within departments charged with law and code enforcement, the councilman was able to insure the continued operation of the informal side of the dual economy, although the two elite groups were highly incensed by the lax enforcement of saloon hours and by the flourishing trade in gambling and prostitution.

The municipality awarded franchises for the operation of public utilities and streetcar services. Tom L. Johnson, one of several streetcar-franchise operators, claimed that the franchise was the best of all business worlds: it gave the operator a long-term monopoly on the service rendered and the ability to set prices in defiance of normal market restrictions, and it allowed daily operation free from public scrutiny or meaningful consumer criticism. The difficulty was in winning the initial franchise award from the city council and keeping it when renewals came due. Both concerns kept actual and potential franchise operators active in municipal politics, especially at the councilmanic level. Although the great majority of Cleveland businessmen were not franchise holders, they were willing to ignore the corrupt relationship between the businessman franchise holders and the councilmen until Mayor Tom L. Johnson, in a complete about-face, sought to end the corrupt franchise alliances and replace them with public ownership of utilities and transportation. The influence of the ward-level political boss also spilled over into the system of public education, a large, growing institution with an expanding capital budget and an ample payroll reliably funded from the real property tax. The ward system, which had by the 20th century won the bosses' control of the municipal government, was also employed to elect ward politicians to the school board. Once they were in office, the familiar pattern of contract and patronage abuses came into view. These practices did, however, result in a roster of middle-level administrators and faculty who were remarkably representative of the diverse clientele the public school system served.

Less visible abuses appeared in Cleveland's system of criminal justice. These embraced the executive branch's law-enforcement responsibilities and extended into the judiciary. Sponsored by the Cleveland Foundation, a comprehensive study of the local system of criminal justice, prepared in 1921, concluded that the Cleveland Police Department was saddled with outmoded managerial techniques and professional incompetence. Although the department had added officers proportionate to the increase in the city's population since the 1880s, modern systems of staff and line management had not been adopted by the department, with the result that many police officers were spending time in station houses performing routine clerical duties instead of being in the street pursuing their line responsibilities as police officers. The department also did little to train officers and detectives in police work and modern principles of criminal detection. The 1922 survey inspired a furious round of changes in the system, as local newspapers for a time kept massive pressure on elected officials to institute reform. Accordingly, recordkeeping at all levels of the system improved, staff and line management was introduced, and recruiting and training programs were adopted.

Despite these criticisms, the Cleveland Police Department made 27,000 arrests each year, at which point the problem shifted to the prosecutor's office. Between 1863 and 1921, the number of indictments increased from 60 to 2,700, and crimes defined by statute increased from 249 to 1,053. These numbers reflect not only the increase in Cleveland's population but also the growing complexity of society. The number of employees in the municipal prosecutor's office, however, reflected only the increase in population. Staff and line responsibilities were not defined, nor was the office organized along functional lines corresponding to categories of criminal offense. In addition, the municipal prosecutor did not have authority to appoint those who served in his office. That was the function of the city's law director, who saw the prosecutor's office as part of the patronage network. The criminal court system gave clear evidence that merely expanding a system that had been adequate when Cleveland was a commercial town would not serve the needs of a modern industrial city. Although Cleveland was served by the municipal court and the county court of common pleas, neither court seemed able to define its own role in the system of justice, and both were plagued by whimsical systems of recordkeeping. The result was overcrowded dockets, court terms that ran continuously and concurrently, lengthy delays in trial dates, and inspired plea-bargaining arrangements. Sentences were glaringly inconsistent, causing some observers to suspect that sentencing bore a closer relationship to solvency of the offender than to statutory requirements. Yet, the juvenile court, created in the Johnson era, though burdened by the demands of a growing young population, won high marks from the criminal-justice survey.

Those unfortunates who traveled the full length of the Cleveland criminal-justice system ultimately found themselves jailed in one of the city or county lockups, where the woes of the system persisted. Segregation of inmates occurred only among the sexes; it was not extended to separate adult from juvenile offenders. The recordkeeping failures that plagued the entire criminal-justice system provided some embarrassing incidents of prisoners' being "lost," others' being freed before sentences had been served, and still others' being caged well beyond their terms. Faulty management, hiring, and training practices opened the penal system to patronage abuses, the hiring of sadists, a lack of educational and recreational opportunities for inmates, and even maintenance of minimal sanitary facilities. Inefficiency and incompetence also combined to flaw a well-conceived parole program. Many of Cleveland's civic activists agreed that the municipal system had failed but pursued conflicting reform agendas through the first 3 decades of the new century. The dramatic clashes of principle and personality, however, did generate some real change in the political system by the time the Great Depression cast its pall over the city.

Structural reform, embracing the home rule and city charter enthusiasms, was the most enduring reform issue. Between 1852 and 1931, Cleveland had 7 city charters, 6 of which were put into effect between 1891 and 1931. These repeated charter-reform episodes reflected the growth

pains of the city, as well as the fact that the reform coalition was built on a foundation of sand, which could shift with each political tide. When the home rule problem was resolved by state constitutional amendment in 1912, the reformers seemingly were free to shape their city's destiny; yet their efforts to shape a mayor-council government in 1913 and a city manager system in 1921 were to a large extent influenced by the city's growth in numbers, physical size, and institutional complexity. Thus, the municipality would never again suffer a caretaker administration of part-time businessmen-politicians. By 1916, the Board of Real Estate and good-government reformers were once again dissatisfied with the new city charter. The city manager system was the newest panacea for the weaknesses of municipal government. Although reform was in abeyance during the war, by 1921 the cumulative effect of several successive corrupt administrations gave the matter of charter reform renewed urgency. Support for the city manager system came from a coalition of reformers and businessmen. They persuaded the voters in 1921 to approve a city manager charter. The newly approved charter assigned policy making to a city council of 25 members elected at large from 4 districts essentially equal in population size. The intent was to eliminate the parochialism of the old ward system, although the east side-west side divisions of the city were perpetuated in the new ward scheme.

The suburbanization of Cleveland's upper and middle classes showed some local reformers that even if Cleveland could be given a satisfactory form of government, it would still be hampered by geographic restrictions imposed by its own political boundaries. As early as 1916, when only 100,000 lived in the suburbs, a small group of reformers resident in the suburbs called for a regional system of government embracing the entire county. The model was the Cleveland Metropolitan Park District. The regional-government scheme was advocated by the middle-class professionals of the Municipal League, who were unable to win the endorsement of the more powerful Chamber of Commerce, which still preferred annexation as the political solution to the problem of metropolitan sprawl. By 1924, when over 200,000 Clevelanders were living in the suburbs, the chamber changed its mind and established the Committee on Cooperative Metropolitan Government. No longer controlled by the industrialists, the chamber was now dominated by less powerful but nevertheless influential retailers, realtors, and publishers. The chamber, however, was unable to convince the state legislature to pass legislation permitting the formation of a regional government. Professional politicians both in the city and in the suburbs resisted metropolitan government because of the obvious threat it represented to the offices they held. Most significant, a unified political coalition of reformers could not be built around the issue of metropolitan government.

An important corollary of reform is that it costs money, and increased governmental responsibilities are usually accompanied by increases in revenue. During the entire 1860–1930 period, Cleveland was obligated to spend money on expanding infrastructure needs and on a steadily growing network of services in the 20th century, especially in the wake of the progressive redefinition of the role of government. In the Civil War decade, the city's budget was $.5 million; by 1930 the operating budget was $50 million. In the 19th century, per capita spending by the municipality remained constant at $8, while operating budgets increased nearly fourfold. The low tax burden was maintained through the simple device of physical growth, which added properties to the tax duplicate. During the progressive years of the century's first decade, per capita spending doubled, while the operating budget increased threefold. A local debate over taxation ensued, which pitted Progressive mayor Tom L. Johnson, who proposed to increase revenues with heavy property taxes on commercial and unimproved land, against those who proposed to keep the property tax low and raise additional revenue with a variety of new user taxes. Even though a 1910 property-tax reappraisal increased the value of the tax duplicate by 150%, the state legislature passed the Smith Act, which limited the municipality to taxing no more than 1% of appraised value, leaving the city with a budget shortfall of $3 million in 1910 alone. The Smith Act did allow an additional .5% through a voter referendum. In the next decade, the municipal budget increased 28%, but tax revenues remained level. The difference was made up in deficit financing. In 1920 alone, the city was forced to borrow nearly a quarter of its operating revenue, and debt service that year was 40% of the city's operating budget. In 1920 also, the state relaxed its strictures and allowed tax increases by local voter consent. A tax increase was won, but in 1925 it was neutralized by a lower property-tax valuation. The national economic crisis of the 1930s came to Cleveland early, and it made voters reluctant to approve new taxes. With the city now strangled by a surrounding ring of suburbs, it could not add to the tax duplicate substantially through new construction. The 1930 budget showed Cleveland sinking back into the same morass in which it had found itself in 1920, with 35% of its operating budget siphoned off to debt service. Many of Cleveland's higher-income people, who were now living in the suburbs, were also members of the civic organizations advocating higher taxes that residents of Cleveland would have to pay.

Through these years, the CLEVELAND PUBLIC SCHOOLS continued to be amply funded. Its problems were those of political control and pedagogical direction. Efforts were made to remove the school system from partisan politics throughout the industrial period. The municipality's Federal Plan charter of 1891 also reformed the school board by requiring nonpartisan, at-large elections, although subsequent charter reforms allowed 2 of the 7 board members to be elected from wards. Despite the reforms, suspicions of patronage abuse and fraudulently awarded contracts for construction, services, and textbooks were never far from the surface. Under pressure from the same civic coalition that had reformed the welfare system, the public school system's mission was broadened considerably between 1890 and 1930. When the performance of the schools inevitably failed to match the extravagant promises of the board and the professional educators, they were subjected to new rounds of bashing by reformers, newspapers, and the public. Educationally, the school system departed from the democratic ideal of the one-room New England schoolhouse to create commercial and vocational programs designed to serve the children of the city's growing body of newcomers. Critics claimed that these programs resulted in educational tracking. Tracking promoted social-class-based education, which predetermined the occupational futures of Cleveland's youth.

School superintendents, often the targets of local critics, were hired and fired frequently between 1890 and 1920, and their tenure seldom exceeded 4 years. Such shaky tenure was the result of school board politics, the tendency of board members to interject themselves into educational issues, and the superintendents' lack of management control over the entire system, including finances. Frank E. Spaulding (1916–1920), hired to implement the recommendations of the Cleveland Foundation's public-school survey, was the first superintendent with sufficiently sophisticated management skills to gain control over the entire system. Spaulding was able to integrate the fiscal and educational arms of the system into a single administrative unit. The superintendent's office became the center of management authority and systemwide planning and budgeting. Under Spaulding's leadership, the board became little more than a rubber stamp for policies initiated by the school system's professional managers. With the emergence of management control by professional educators, the history of the Cleveland public schools entered a new era.

In the 7 decades 1860–1930, Cleveland was transformed economically from a commercial village dependent on a regional economy to a city of nearly 1 million people integrated into an international industrial economy. Businesses changed from small countinghouses to large, bureaucratic organizations owned by anonymous stockholders, managed by professionals, and employing thousands of workers. Intensified social stratification occurred in the wake of population growth, a more complex economy, and modern business organizations. The city's institutional development was a reflection of its social stratification. Decisions were made collectively in the city's new institutions, and they were a reflection of the triumph of corporate values over the traditional values of individualism and community held by the descendants of the city's New England forebears and newcomers from rural Europe and America. Management techniques adapted from industrial engineering were applied indiscriminately to factory production and the delivery of social, governmental, and educational services. That was the birth of modern America, and it was conceived in industrial cities such as Cleveland.

Ronald Weiner
Cuyahoga Community College

# TOWARD THE POSTINDUSTRIAL CITY: 1930–1980

**An End to Prosperity: 1930–1939.** "It is something to make anyone glad he is a Clevelander." So was the *PLAIN DEALER* moved to comment on 19 Aug. 1927, the day after steelworkers unfurled a flag from the topmost peak of the Terminal Tower and doffed their hats with pride. The "city within a city" was nearing completion. Development of the CLEVELAND UNION TERMINAL group—consisting of the Terminal Tower, with the city's new railroad station below grade; the Builders Exchange, Medical Arts, and Midland buildings; and the HIGBEE department store (the Hotel Cleveland had been built in 1918)—was the biggest real-estate news in the city's history. It had a profound impact, eliminating a large area of squalor and making PUBLIC SQUARE, the traditional center of BUSINESS and civic life, once again the focus of downtown. It left Cleveland with the mark of a metropolis on it. In conceiving and building so comprehensive a project, brothers MANTIS J. AND ORIS P. VAN SWERINGEN created not only a profitable commercial center but also a new focus for Cleveland's pride and a distinctive visual symbol for the city—a landmark. Dedication of the new $150 million Cleveland Union Terminal was the outstanding civic event of 1930. On 28 June, some 2,500 of the city's leaders gathered for lunch in the station's main concourse. Surrounding them were more than 40 shops and restaurants operated by Harvey, Inc., said to be the world's largest unified merchandising service operated in conjunction with a railroad passenger station. Cleveland's new station handled 80 trains a day, as well as the rapid-transit line serving the Van Sweringens' new residential development of SHAKER HEIGHTS. *Railway Age* called it "a passenger terminal which ranks in magnitude and completeness with the best in the country."

Cleveland in 1930 had other reasons to celebrate. The 1920s had been a decade of great industrial, economic, and financial growth; of municipal progress and reform; of advancement in the arts, MEDICINE, EDUCATION, and CITY PLANNING and beautification. Large and important commercial buildings had been erected, including the FEDERAL RESERVE BANK, the OHIO BELL TELEPHONE, Hanna, and Union Trust buildings. New theaters and motion-picture palaces had opened at PLAYHOUSE SQUARE, and drew in their wake new shops and restaurants. Following on the heels of the turbulent FRED KOHLER administration, municipal affairs had been guided by the able city manager WILLIAM R. HOPKINS. The Muncipal Airport had been established, and construction of the new CLEVELAND MUNICIPAL STADIUM was about to begin. The Board of Education Building was nearing completion, and the city's Group Plan was progressing. Both the CLEVELAND PUBLIC LIBRARY and the PUBLIC AUDITORIUM had opened. The latter, promoted by the Convention Board of the Chamber of Commerce, attracted some of the country's largest gatherings--143,628 delegates would attend 237 conventions there in 1930—and materially aided the city's bid to become a convention capital. Beyond the city's borders, the development of LAKEWOOD, EAST CLEVELAND, CLEVELAND HEIGHTS, and Shaker Heights signaled the first flush of metropolitan expansion. For Cleveland, the year 1930 marked a watershed in the city's fortunes. The preceding decade had been a heady success for Cleveland, a period best symbolized, perhaps, by the ethereal images produced by the young photographer MARGARET BOURKE-WHITE of a brawny city ruled and shaped by powerful industries and equally powerful industrialists. In the space of a few months, however, tens of thousands of Clevelanders would be out of work, while more than a few of the city's barons—including the Van Sweringens—would face financial ruin. The depression years 1930–39 thus mark a distinct period in the city's life—an end to prosperity, from which, it might be argued, Cleveland has never fully recovered.

With a population of 900,429, Cleveland in 1930 was the nation's 6th-largest city, after New York, Chicago, Philadelphia, Detroit, and Los Angeles. With a combined city and county population of 1,201,455, it was the 3d-most-populated metropolitan area, after New York and Chicago. Startling changes had occurred since 1910. The population of Cuyahoga County outside of Cleveland had more than doubled, and now represented 25% of the total population of the county.

| | Cleveland | Cuyahoga County | City as % of County |
|---|---|---|---|
| 1910 | 560,663 | 637,425 | 88% |
| 1920 | 796,841 | 943,495 | 84% |
| 1930 | 900,429 | 1,201,455 | 75% |

The 4 largest adjacent cities—Lakewood, East Cleveland, Cleveland Heights, and Shaker Heights—in 1930 had a combined population of 178,904. These 4 cities, accounting for slightly more than 4% of the county's population in 1910, by 1930 accounted for as much as 15%.

For 30 years, statistician HOWARD WHIPPLE GREEN studied and reported on population trends in Greater Cleveland. His first major study, *Population Characteristics by Census Tracts, Cleveland, Ohio*, published by the Plain Dealer Publishing Co. in 1931, contained a wealth of information about the city's people and revealed trends that could not otherwise be discerned. The percentage of Cleveland's foreign-born white population had declined from 30.1% in 1920 to 25.5% in 1930. The greatest number of the city's foreign-born had come from Czechoslovakia (15.1%) and Poland (14.2%). Other countries with large numbers in Cleveland included Italy (10.3%), Germany (9.8%), Hungary (8.3%), Yugoslavia (8.0%), and Russia (6.6%). According to Green, each foreign-born, white, non-English-speaking group occupied a distinctly different section of the 5-city metropolitan area except the GERMANS, who had been integrated into the population "as evenly as the English, Welsh, Scotch, IRISH, or Canadians." Cleveland's black population had increased considerably, from 34,451, or 4.3% of the city's population, in 1920, to 71,899, or 8%, in 1930. Cleveland's BLACKS lived in a section bounded by E. 9th St. on the west, EUCLID AVE. on the north, E. 105th St. on the east, and, on the south, the tracks of the New York, Chicago & St. Louis Railroad just south of Woodland Ave. There was also a small concentration of blacks living in the southwest section of the city along Bellaire Rd. between W. 117th and W. 130th St., most of whom worked at the yards of the New York Central. Finally, some 1,200 blacks lived outside of Cleveland; these were largely house servants and chauffeurs living with their employers.

Cleveland's 394,898 gainful workers were employed largely in the manufacturing and mechanical industries (41%), trade (18%), domestic and personal service (10%), TRANSPORTATION and communication (11%), and building (7%). A total of 20% were in the service industries, including professional and semiprofessional service, public service, and domestic and personal service. Industries employing large numbers of Clevelanders in 1930 included (in round numbers) the building industry (28,000), blast furnaces and steel-rolling mills (19,000), other iron and steel industries (42,000), wholesale and retail trade (62,000), and steam RAILROADS (15,000). Prophetically, $1/7$ of Cleveland's gainful workers were not at work on the day in Apr. 1930 preceding the visit of the census enumerator. (One-third would be in this condition in Jan. 1931.)

By analyzing data for each census tract, Green statistically demonstrated for the first time in the city's history what he called the "great differences" among the economic areas within the 5-city region (Cleveland, Lakewood, East Cleveland, Cleveland Heights, and Shaker Heights)—differences in color, nativity, age, sex, literacy, employment, and the possession of radios and homes. Green identified 14 "economic areas" by ranking each census tract according to "equivalent monthly rental." The results showed that a disparity in wealth between the city and the SUBURBS was already well established. Only 21 of Cleveland's 201 census tracts ranked within the 7 highest economic areas (those paying $47 or more monthly rental), while all but 3 of the 51 census tracts outside of Cleveland ranked within the 7 highest economic areas. "In the high economic areas," Green wrote, "the picture is quite different than in the low economic areas. Homes are owned, families have radios, family heads are native white of native parentage, illiteracy is low, unemployment is uncommon, population is spread out over ample areas, the juvenile delinquency rate is low, likewise the infant mortality rate and the general death-rate are low."

As early as 1930, census figures showed that Cleveland was "decaying at the core," with increases of population occurring on the periphery of the metropolitan area and decreases occurring at the center. So Howard Whipple Green reported in the first Real Property Inventory of Greater Cleveland, published in 1933. The REAL PROPERTY INVENTORY OF METROPOLITAN CLEVELAND (RPI), of which Green served as director between 1932 and 1959, tracked movements of population into and out of census tracts in Greater Cleveland in the years between decennial census counts. Data of this kind, according to Green, were of great value for the "intelligent location and proper operation" of retail outlets, schools, branch banks, public transportation, and utilities. By charting trends, the RPI was designed to form the basis for "business judgments." In examining the periodic reports of the RPI over the city's long downward spiral, however, one cannot help but wonder whether RPI not only charted trends but initiated them as well. Census Tract M-7 (bounded by E. 55th and E. 71st streets and Central and Quincy avenues) is a case in point. This neighborhood centered at E. 55th and Woodland was home to large numbers of RUSSIANS, largely Orthodox JEWS, in 1920; 10 years later it was overwhelmingly black. "Few persons realized," Green wrote in the first edition of the RPI, "that census tract M-7 with 8.7% of its population Negro in 1920 would show 90.6% Negroes in 1930. An enormous increase in the number of Negroes in a particular section of the city with their influence on property values is always reflected sooner or later in mortgage finance."

By 1920, residential dispersion had already occurred among Cleveland's Irish and German populations. Between 1920 and 1930, once-strong enclaves of ITALIANS and Russians living on the near east side dispersed to other areas of the city and to the suburbs, while the black community became even more concentrated there, especially along Central and Scovill avenues. On the eve of the Depression, at least 90% of the city's blacks were concentrated in a ghetto bounded by Euclid and Woodland avenues and E. 14th and E. 105th streets. The first great migration of blacks to Cleveland had occurred during and after WORLD WAR I, when a need for workers in the North coincided with economic depression in the South. Between 1910 and 1920, the city's black population had increased 308%. IMMIGRATION from abroad, meanwhile, had fallen dramatically after 1914.

The new migration accelerated the process of residential segregation already underway, and the city faced the task of assimilating large numbers of uneducated blacks completely unaccustomed to urban life. The conditions of life of the typical black ghetto dweller were described by novelist CHARLES W. CHESNUTT: "The majority live in drab, middle or low class houses, none too well kept up . . . while the poor live in dilapidated, rack-rented shacks, sometimes a whole family in 1 or 2 rooms, as a rule paying higher rent than white tenants for the same space." Despite these conditions, by most measures of socioeconomic progress, the status of black migrants who came north after 1915 constituted an advance over their previous condition. In contrast to the 1960s, when northern blacks were experiencing "actual gains but psychological losses" (as one sociologist has put it), the blacks in the northern ghettos in the 1920s and 1930s recognized their improved status. Hence, Kenneth L. Kusmer has called this era the "Quiet Ghetto." Paradoxically, the consolidation of the ghetto after World War I produced a growing sense of black unity and a philosophy of self-help and race pride that would provide a basis for future struggle against racism in all its manifestations. Although the NATIONAL ASSOCIATION FOR THE ADVANCEMENT OF COLORED PEOPLE had been established in Cleveland in 1914, the organization did not gain strength until the 1920s, when it began to fight discrimination in theaters, restaurants, and other facilities. In 1931, the policy of segregating black patients at City Hospital came to an end, and the first black intern was admitted to the staff. Black political power, meanwhile, grew slowly but inexorably. THOMAS W. FLEMING, an accommodationist, was the sole black representative on city council until 1927. Within a few years, however, as the black population spread eastward, gradually engulfing formerly white wards, the ghetto was tranformed into an increasingly formidable political power.

In the months and years after the great stock market crash on Black Tuesday, 29 Oct. 1929, Cleveland coasted downhill at dizzying speed. The economic and cultural preeminence of the previous decade reversed to a fight for survival in the 1930s. There were an estimated 41,000 jobless in Cleveland in Apr. 1930, close to 100,000 by the following January. (In the Cleveland 5-city area, the numbers were 44,000 and 106,000 respectively.) Industrial conditions affected employment in Cleveland more seriously than in cities with small populations of gainful workers in the manufacturing and mechanical industries, including building. Detroit was the only other large American city with a higher percentage of workers so classified. Economic dislocation reached enormous proportions. The expenditure of $200 million for direct and work relief in Cuyahoga County in the 10-year period 1928-37 represented only 1/6 of the loss of $1.2 billion in normal wage and salary payments during the same period. According to one study, wages paid in industry in Cuyahoga County decreased from $251,942,813 in 1929 to $99,448,000 in 1933. To cope with rapidly shrinking tax revenues and the ever-growing need for massive amounts of direct relief (food, clothing, and shelter) to the unemployed, Mayor RAY T. MILLER turned to the enforcement of strict economy in GOVERNMENT. In 1931, $1 million was pared from municipal operating expenses and funneled to relief services, and a 1-mill county relief levy was adopted in 1932. But these measures fell far short of meeting the increasing cost of relief.

Within months of Pres. Franklin Delano Roosevelt's election, expanded federal assistance carried most of the relief burden. The Civil Works Administration (CWA), established in Nov. 1933, was followed by the Federal Emergency Relief Administration (FERA), which supplemented city, county, and state funds for direct relief and made work available to several thousand employable members of relief families. FERA's peak of activity in Cleveland occurred in July 1935, with 10,075 men and women on work relief. In 1935, care of the unemployable was given back to the Cuyahoga County Relief Administration, and the Work Progress Administration (later the WORK PROJECTS ADMINISTRATION) was established to provide work relief for 1 employable member of each relief family. Statistics demonstrate the intensity of the need in Cleveland. The monthly average of those receiving direct and (after 1933) work relief rose from 3,499 in 1928 to 52,995 in 1933 and 77,565 in 1936. Expenditures for relief (exclusive of administration) rose from $1,055,000 in 1928 to $14,506,000 in 1933 and $39,850,000 in 1936. The largest concentration of relief families and individuals, and the largest jobless ratios, were in those sections of the city Green had defined as "low economic areas" in 1930: the near west side and the east side south of Euclid Ave. Suburban areas were much less hard hit. In describing the geographic distribution of relief families, Green illustrated the disparity in concrete terms: "Families in the low economic tenths have little; many are on relief and the others are on the edge of dependence. Families living in the highest economic tenth have much; they pay high rents, own expensive homes, have telephones, automobiles, mechanical refrigerators, and most that the heart desires." By Mar. 1938, 54,849 residents of Cuyahoga County were receiving work relief under the CWA and WPA. These programs carried on much of the area's capital-improvements program, building STREETS, sewers, schools, and waterworks that would otherwise have been impossible. Aided by the WPA, the first portion of the lakefront highway (later called the Cleveland MEMORIAL SHOREWAY) was built between E. 9th St. and GORDON PARK. In 1938–39 the county, with WPA assistance, built the Main Ave. Bridge, which added another important high-level connection between the east and west sides of the city.

Cleveland's city and metropolitan parks especially benefited from the massive federal work projects. The CLEVELAND METROPARKS SYSTEM was substantially developed during this period, with the construction of roads, trails, picnic areas, shelterhouses, and other structures. The CLEVELAND PRESS on 22 July 1936 commented that the improvements financed with federal dollars were sweeping Cleveland's metropolitan parks into a completed system "a generation ahead of schedule." The once-beautiful city parks, meanwhile, had suffered from 3 decades of inadequate maintenance, and many of the homeless were using them for sleeping quarters. In the late 1930s, WPA forces working 2 shifts extensively rehabilitated the parks and built new playgrounds. In a radio address in 1936, PARKS Director Hugo E. Varga acknowledged that, without WPA help, "there would have been only a skeleton of the parks left as a bitter reminder of a pennywise and pound foolish policy. . . ." Another tangible legacy of work relief in Cleveland was the ART produced under the Public Works of Art Project and the other programs that followed it. Unemployed Cleveland artists produced graphics, murals, paintings, and sculpture of exceptional quality and enjoyed warm public support. Much of the New Deal art exemplified the "Cleveland Scene," stressing pride in Cleveland's heritage—its people, industries, ARCHITECTURE, and accomplishments.

A significant revolution of the 1930s was the change in historical assumptions about social responsibility. Government recognized for the first time an obligation to provide decent housing for the poor, although the construction of PUBLIC HOUSING, at least initially, was viewed in large measure as an emergency activity to put men to work. Under the leadership of ERNEST J. BOHN, who served as the first director of the Cleveland Metropolitan Housing Authority, Cleveland led the nation in establishing the first public-housing projects to be funded by the Public Works Administration. Construction began on 3 PWA projects in 1935: Cedar-Central Apts., located between E. 22nd and E. 30th streets and Cedar and Central avenues; Outhwaite Homes, between E. 40th and E. 46th streets and Scovill and Woodland avenues; and LAKEVIEW TERRACE, at W. 28th near the Main Ave. Bridge. The 3 projects, completed in 1937, provided apartments for 1,849 low-income families and resulted in the clearance of large slum areas. These were followed, in 1940, by Valley View Homes, at W. 7th St. and Starkweather Ave.; and Woodhill Homes, at Woodhill Rd. and Woodland Ave. (The latter utilized land formerly occupied by the popular amusement resort LUNA PARK.) All of the new housing projects were built in the modern functional style. One, Lakeview Terrace, received international recognition for its successful adaptation to a difficult site; its incorporation of the first community center in a public-housing project; and its use of the decorative arts, made possible by the Treasury Relief Art Project.

After Clevelanders voted to rescind the CITY MANAGER PLAN and return to an elected mayor and ward councilmen in 1931, successive city administrations struggled to provide relief to the destitute. As the numbers on relief swelled beyond the ability of local social-welfare organizations to cope, the burden of caring for the poor and unemployed fell on the city, dooming Ray T. Miller to be a 1-term mayor. Municipal government was in disarray under his successor, HARRY L. DAVIS. City finances were in sad condition, and the police department was corrupt and demoralized. In 1935, HAROLD H. BURTON was elected to the first of 3 terms. Burton, by 1938, brought order to the city, balancing the budget and cleaning up the police department. To accomplish the latter, he brought in a young federal agent who had helped break the hold of the Capone mob in Chicago to serve as safety director. ELIOT NESS was given free rein to conduct investigations wherever he suspected corruption.

Iron and steel, and iron and steel products, remained the city's mainstay. REPUBLIC STEEL acquired Cleveland's Corrigan, McKinney Steel Co. in 1935 and moved its headquarters from Youngstown to Cleveland. An improved economic outlook in 1936 encouraged Republic to undertake a major expansion of its Cleveland plant with the construction of a 98-inch continuous hot strip mill, then the widest in the world. The plant was continuously enlarged in the next 3 decades, and Republic until 1980 remained Cleveland's largest single employer. The first sign of the changes to come in the city's commercial life occurred in the late 1920s and early 1930s with construction of the first major stores and shopping areas to be built outside of the downtown area. These included new Sears department stores on the east and west sides of the city (1928), SHAKER SQUARE (1929), and branches of BAILEY's department store at Euclid-E. 105th and Detroit-Warren in Lakewood (1929–30). The Depression, then WORLD WAR II, postponed further decentralization of the city's retail industry. Cleveland's cultural growth was seemingly unimpeded by the economic hardship of these years. The decade saw the founding of the GARDEN CENTER OF GREATER CLEVELAND in 1930 and the opening of SEVERANCE HALL, the new home of the CLEVELAND ORCHESTRA, the following year. In 1936, DUNHAM TAVERN, Inc., was organized to preserve the famous inn, and on 30 July 1939, 35,000 people representing 47 countries attended the mass dedication of the chain of Cleveland Cultural Gardens, which covered 35 acres in ROCKEFELLER PARK, and paid tribute to the contributions of the city's diverse nationality groups. The decade also witnessed a protracted period of labor unrest. A sit-down strike of 7,000 workers at the FISHER BODY Co. plant on Coit Rd. was followed by strikes in auto plants in other cities. Other serious strikes in Cleveland during this period included those at Republic Steel and the Industrial Rayon Corp.

The Depression sharply curtailed construction, and, except for work-relief projects, few new buildings were erected in the 1930s. Two projects, however, would have a lasting impact on the city: Cleveland Municipal Stadium and the GREAT LAKES EXPOSITION. America in the 1920s was increasingly becoming a nation of spectators, and organized sports were becoming a popular and profitable activity. Other large cities, including Los Angeles, San Francisco, Chicago, and Baltimore, had built municipal stadiums, and Cleveland followed the trend. Promoted by City Manager William R. Hopkins, the new Municipal Stadium was seen as a fitting lakefront termination for the city's Group Plan. Voters approved a bond issue in 1928, and the Stadium made its debut in a program of song and speeches on 2 July 1931. The following year, on Sunday, 31 July 1932, the CLEVELAND INDIANS played their first game there. An astonishing 80,184 filled the ball park, and the next day's headline captured the moment: "From Noon to 3 They Pour into Big Horseshoe through All Routes; Railroads Bring Thousands; Akron Sends 1,200; Same Number from Pittsburgh Area; "NAP" LAJOIE and Other Stars of

Bygone Days Are Cheered; Depression Given Black Eye." Without a permanent lease, however, the Indians continued to play most of their games at LEAGUE PARK, in the HOUGH neighborhood, until 1947.

Another project helped revive the sagging spirits of Clevelanders. The Great Lakes Exposition was planned by business leaders to celebrate the industry and culture of the 8 Great Lakes states and the bordering provinces of Canada. The event also marked Cleveland's centennial as a city. The prospectus for the exposition summed up the important psychological benefits the event's promoters hoped for, stating, "Cleveland has for several years been so depressed by adverse circumstances that a forward-looking enterprise is needed to revive the sagging spirit of civic pride that formerly characterized the city." Financed by Cleveland business interests, the exposition ran from June through October over 2 years, 1936 and 1937. The lakefront exposition occupied the MALL from St. Clair Ave. north, and stretched from the Stadium to E. 20th St. Clevelanders witnessed the transformation of a former public dump into an attractively landscaped fairgrounds. The exposition offered exhibits of art, SCIENCE, industry, and horticulture, as well as popular entertainment. Extensive use of light as an architectural element showed off Cleveland's prominence as a center of lighting-industry research. The Great Lakes Exposition advertised Cleveland as a progressive, productive city and pointed the way toward economic recovery. Among its lasting benefits was the final realization of the Group Plan; the last building remaining in the area designated for the Mall was removed in 1935.

Dorothea D. Kahn, staff correspondent of the *Christian Science Monitor*, visited Cleveland in late summer 1938. She found a city appealing "in spite of its bigness," a city struggling with a serious relief problem but blessed with business and civic leaders "striving with rolled up sleeves to solve the city's problems, to improve business and so make more jobs, to provide better public and private housing, to increase educational opportunities, and to beautify the city." Kahn saw massive downtown buildings, but few skyscrapers; an abundance of tree-shaded homes, and new public-housing projects set down in slums; long viaducts that carried traffic high over the industrial valleys; and used-car lots with the legend, "We finance WPA workers." Public Square gave the big industrial city a New England "common" for a center. There, statues of the city's heroes brought the past tangibly into the present; much more than in other cities, Kahn wrote, "you find yourself reminded of the men who made the city." Nearby, a newly made lakefront stretched out beyond the factories and industries that had formerly claimed the shore, and the MALL stood as "a symbol of the city's long and patient efforts to bring its ambitious plan to realization." While the gathering clouds of war in Europe would soon mean the revival of Cleveland's economy, the resulting lure of jobs would also transform the character of its population, accelerating the move to the suburbs and prompting the first uneasy feelings that something was wrong.

**War and Renewal: 1940-1949.** The Depression had brought Cleveland to its knees. Industrialist CYRUS EATON would later say that Cleveland was hurt more by the Depression than any other city in the U.S. That assertion, George Condon wrote in 1967, "is plausible enough to people who remember the exuberant, dynamic Cleveland of pre-Depression days and who can compare it with the somber, convalescent city that walked with a dragging gait and a querulous expression until recent years. The Cleveland that the world knew from 1930 to 1955 was a hurt town and it showed in many ways. There was a disposition toward petty bickering among the civic leaders over petty

issues, while the large issue of Cleveland's future went untended and the sprawling downtown area turned gray and shabby." The period 1940-49 was marked by war and postwar renewal, by personal sacrifice and industrial expansion that would carry over into a peacetime economy. Long before war's end, Cleveland would begin planning for its future, charting new highways and other improvements and considering, for the first time, the problem of interracial relations. Economic well-being—even victory in the 1948 World Series—seemed to give credence to the claim, born in this decade, that Cleveland was "the best location in the nation." Cleveland in 1940 remained the nation's 6th-largest city, but for the first time its population count, 878,336, showed a small loss. Of this number, 20.4% were foreign-born white, while 10% were black. Outward migration to the suburbs had slowed during the Depression, and during World War II, shortages of men and materials continued to discourage new construction of homes in outlying areas. But at war's end, pent-up demand was met with large new housing projects in such suburbs as BROOKLYN, LYNDHURST, MAYFIELD HEIGHTS, MAPLE HEIGHTS, and SOUTH EUCLID, and Cleveland would see no abatement of the trend for the duration of its modern history.

As the decade opened, Cleveland faced publicly for the first time the phenomenon of decentralization. A report published in 1941 by the Cleveland Chamber of Commerce stated frankly: "It is evident that most people who live in Cleveland are anxious to move to the suburbs.... Experience has shown that if their economic status permits, the majority of Clevelanders prefer to live outside the central area." The reasons for this preference, according to the report, were several, ranging from smoke and dirt to congestion, vice and CRIME, deterioration, and, finally, the "proximity of races having a depreciatory effect on values." Although the population increased according to the 1950 census, the character of the city's inhabitants was changing. Native and foreign-born whites were leaving the city for the suburbs, and Appalachian whites and southern blacks were arriving in large numbers to seek work in Cleveland's expanding wartime industries. At the same time, migrant workers from Puerto Rico began arriving in Cleveland. Large numbers of Appalachians and Puerto Ricans settled on the near west side, and by 1970, some 20,000 Appalachians and 5,000 Puerto Ricans were living in that formerly Hungarian and Irish neighborhood. During the decade, Cleveland's black population grew from 85,000 to 148,000, and for the first time blacks began moving in substantial numbers into neighborhoods outside their traditional ghetto, including Hough, MT. PLEASANT, Miles Heights, and GLENVILLE. Glenville, annexed to Cleveland in 1905, was a predominantly Jewish neighborhood, many of whose residents had begun to move to Cleveland Heights when the first blacks moved there in the 1920s. Between 1940 and 1950, the black population in Glenville grew rapidly, from 1,069 to 20,517. In 1945, confronted by the problems of a changing neighborhood, residents formed the Glenville Community Council to address such areas of concern as interracial relations and the need for better recreational facilities, improved public safety, and stricter enforcement of the housing code. As early as 1945, Glenville's leaders recognized the presence of "potential powder kegs" in the crowded, changing neighborhood. Glenville was 67% black by 1960, and 95% black by the mid-1960s. The same pattern would occur again and again as white neighborhoods became black and segregation took hold of the city's east side.

While suburban residents continued to shop, visit, find entertainment, and earn their livings in Cleveland, they did not share its responsibilities, and they contributed nothing to the support of its services. As Cleveland advertising executive and historian WILLIAM GANSON ROSE put it in 1950, the thriving cities and villages that "nestled close to the sprawling, fan-shaped mother city" were "content in their municipal independence and the charm of their residential sections." Civic and business leaders, meanwhile, struggled to find solutions to the population decline revealed in the 1940 census. Rose, at a meeting of the Greater Cleveland Council of Smaller Business of America, Inc., presented a program to counteract the alarming trend. Among his suggestions were to revise zoning regulations; eliminate smoke nuisances and enforce SANITATION laws; foster the renovation of buildings worthy of future use and get rid of unsafe and unfit structures; promote development by private investors of better neighborhoods; and encourage development of the lakeshore as a practical and pleasant place to live. Rose's program was the first of literally hundreds that would be put forth over the next 4 decades as the city struggled to reverse its decline.

Cleveland industries in the 1940s expanded rapidly to meet demand for war materiel. Cleveland factories turned out planes, tanks, trucks, jeeps, artillery and small arms, bombs, binoculars, and telescopes. Production at the Thompson Aircraft Products Co., a Defense Plant Corp. subsidiary, began in 1941. At Municipal Airport, the Fisher Aircraft Assembly Plant No. 2 was erected in 1942 for the assembly of B-29s and, later, P-57 tanks. Nearby, the $20 million National Advisory Committee for Aeronautics (NACA) Aircraft Engine Research Laboratory (later NASA LEWIS RESEARCH CENTER) opened in 1943. Beginning with a national advertising slogan originated by the CLEVELAND ELECTRIC ILLUMINATING CO. in 1944 to help build postwar business, Cleveland claimed distinction as "the best location in the nation." The claim was based on the fact that within 500 miles of the city lived half the people of the U.S. and Canada; that Cleveland was the natural meeting place of iron ore, coal, copper, gypsum, stone, sand, and other vital raw materials; and that efficient water, rail, highway, and air transportation facilitated delivery and reduced costs. Cleveland further claimed—as a leader in the lighting industry and an important producer of machine tools, electrical goods, metal products, and paints and varnish—a diversified industrial base, a large supply of trained workers, and abundant low-cost power and water. Northern Ohio, embracing the Cleveland, Lorain, and Youngstown districts, remained the steel center of the nation. A survey of occupations made in 1946 showed that out of a total employment of 560,000 in Cuyahoga County, 4 industrial groups predominated: machinery (66,000 workers), iron and steel (50,000), transportation equipment (34,000), and electrical machinery (26,000). But a measure of the diversity of Cleveland industry can be seen in the fact that, in 1944, 4,000 workers were employed at the CLEVELAND UNION STOCKYARDS, while the city's 9 breweries employed more than 1,200. Industrial workers swelled the city's wartime population, and at war's end, an already severe housing shortage worsened with the return of servicemen eager to start new families. Throughout the city, single-family homes were subdivided into units housing several families, beginning a pattern of overuse and overcrowding, and laying the groundwork for future deterioration.

In 1943, at a luncheon at the Statler Hotel, Mayor Frank J. Lausche organized the Postwar Planning Council to begin the work of preparing Cleveland for the end of war-contract production and to coordinate planning at all levels of community life. The aim of the council, which was financed by donations from business, industry, and LABOR, was, in Mayor Lausche's words, "not only to build the bridge from war to peacetime production but also to lay plans for making Cleveland's industrial advantages so patent that we can keep all of the industries we have and attract new ones. . . ." Cleveland was in a race with all other industrial cities, Lausche warned, and the days of rapid growth were over. Under executive director S. Burns Weston, 5 panels were named to study transportation, public works, interracial relations, the needs of returning servicemen, and public finance. Two panels deserve special mention. The role of the public-works panel was to stimulate public agencies to rush the production of construction plans. Interestingly enough, the freeway system was seen as the one public-works project that would absorb the first impact of the suspension of war work, and one of the panel's tasks was to spur planning and land acquisition "mercilessly" (as one *Cleveland Press* reporter put it). A panel on interracial relations, chaired by Dr. Leonard Mayo, dean of the School of Applied Social Sciences at Western Reserve University, was charged with answering the question: Are the community and its facilities prepared to deal objectively with interracial relations? The panel defined areas where problems existed—such as housing, recreation, health, and employment practices—and recommended that the mayor follow a policy of preventive action rather than wait for problems to come to a head. As a result of the panel's work, the CLEVELAND COMMUNITY RELATIONS BOARD was established in 1945, with a mission "to promote amicable relations among the racial and cultural groups within the community."

During the late 1940s, Mayor THOMAS A. BURKE initiated the first major municipal projects since the erection of Cleveland Stadium in 1930–31. The popular Burke, who served as mayor for 9 years (1945–53), sponsored construction of the downtown airport and activated the dormant plan, first conceived by the Van Sweringens, for a system of rapid-transit lines serving Cleveland. In 1942, the city of Cleveland, with some reluctance, had acquired the near-bankrupt CLEVELAND RAILWAY CO., thereby becoming the owner and operator of a street railway system with 4,400 employees and an annual business of $15 million. The new Cleveland Transit System, under the supervision of the city's public utilities department, made the transition from streetcars to buses and completed construction of a new 19-mile rapid system in 1955. The line extended from Windermere Station near Euclid and Superior avenues on the east side to W. 140th and Lorain. An additional link to the airport, completed in 1968, gave Cleveland the first rapid-transit system in the country providing a direct rail connection between the downtown business district and the airport.

In Feb. 1944, a master freeway plan was completed by the Express Highway Subcommittee of the Regional Association of Cleveland. The plan followed on the heels of a freeway program and bond issue of $4.5 million endorsed by the voters 4 years earlier but delayed by war and the lack of a comprehensive plan. The plan called for a $240 million integrated freeway system as the solution to metropolitan Cleveland's traffic problems. While the plan bears striking similarity to the freeway system as built—it shows, for example, an inner belt, the WILLOW FREEWAY (I-77), an outer belt (I-271), and an outer belt south (I-480)—the differences are notable. The West Shoreway, following the lakefront as far as ROCKY RIVER, forms the major east-west roadway on the west side, not I-90, while the BEREA-Airport Freeway (I-71) as planned followed a substantially different route from that built. Finally, the proposed Medina, NEWBURGH, and Heights freeways were never built, though not until the 1970s were the later 2 projects put to rest. In addition to freeways, other major public-works projects were underway. By the mid-1940s, substantial progress had been made on improving the CUYAHOGA RIVER for navigation; plans called for widening, straightening, and deepening the river channel. The city's stock of public housing was enlarged with the extension of Outhwaite Homes and the construction of Carver Park, the latter consisting of 1,287 units at Unwin Rd. near Central Ave. and E. 43rd St.

Superficially at least, Cleveland was healthy during these years. Clevelanders had generally supported the war effort. The temporary War Service Center on Public Square, whose walls carried the names of the local men who had died in service to their country, represented the volunteer efforts of Clevelanders and was an active center for recruitment and the sale of War Bonds. ALEXANDER WINTON's pioneer automobile, built in 1896, and the Brush dynamo that gave the city light in 1893 at a plant on Lime St. were both donated for their scrap value, and victory gardens were planted throughout the city. The existence of racial tensions had been acknowledged and the first steps taken to ease them. The Cleveland Convention & Visitors Bureau reported that conventions brought 152,185 visitors to Cleveland during 1946. The same year, Bill Veeck purchased the Cleveland Indians and subsequently orchestrated the liveliest and most memorable period in Cleveland BASEBALL history. Throughout 1946, Clevelanders celebrated the city's 150th birthday with pageants, parades, and entertainment, drawing national attention. L. H. Robbins, in the *New York Times Magazine*, commented favorably on the city and its people: "Clevelanders display an exuberant enthusiasm for their town and their way of life such as you don't recall ever noting in any city east of the Alleghenies.... It really is remarkable, their town-boosting, their local pride and contentment...." Robbins reported on the city's industrial might (noting that the Terminal Tower is "blacked out, some days, in the smoke pall from the valley") and its fine public buildings ("Here is a civic center to shout about"), though he acknowledged that, beyond the downtown core, "the first miles aren't so good."

Indeed, there were signs of trouble ahead. Within the city, as Mayor Lausche noted in his speech launching the Postwar Planning Council, were slums with "living conditions unfit for human beings." The city had expanded carelessly, and the mansions that remained on Millionaires' Row (Euclid Ave.) rubbed shoulders with billboards and car-wash lots, tourist homes and factories. Metropolitan progress, many thought, was hampered by the disintegration of government into some 100 independent taxing units. Above all, the pace of decentralization was accelerating. Of $1.7 billion spent on postwar industrial expansion, $1 billion was spent in the suburbs. Of the resulting 170,000 new job opportunities, the suburbs got 100,000, the central city 70,000. And suburban home construction was outpacing home construction in the city 4 to 1. "Every metropolitan area is plagued by the paradox of suburbs siphoning off tax income," *Architectural Forum* would comment in 1955. "In Cleveland this parasitic situation reaches an extreme.... Suburban chauvinism in Cleveland is more than a political and financial problem. It is a social problem." The problem, in coming years, would only worsen.

***Exodus and Decline: 1950–1965.*** Cleveland, in the early 1950s, stood at a crossroads. Its central business district and its neighborhoods were deteriorating. Crime was worsening, and thousands of city residents were leaving for new homes in the suburbs. Over the next 15 years, civic and business leaders would struggle to define the problem, but answers would remain elusive. Urban renewal and the construction of freeways, meanwhile, would dramatically and

permanently change the face of the city. And while the ERIEVIEW plan would serve as a critical catalyst for future downtown renewal, the city's single-minded focus on the central business district would lead eventually to conflagration in Hough and yet another turning point in Cleveland's history.

Recognition that something was wrong unfolded gradually. In a speech to the ROTARY CLUB in Mar. 1953, Elmer L. Lindseth, president of the Illuminating Co., named some of the issues the city faced. These included downtown decay (no new office buildings had been built since the Terminal Group); slum areas and areas that threatened to become slums ("in some cases only for lack of enforcing our building codes"); inadequate transportation and parking; and a need for low-rent private housing and new schools, parks, and hospital beds. On 13 Oct. 1954, city leaders met at the MID-DAY CLUB to map strategies for making the downtown more attractive to shoppers; according to the next day's account of the meeting in the *Plain Dealer*, no one mentioned the huge new shopping centers that had been built on the periphery of "Greater" Cleveland. Several months later, in a front-page story, the newspaper asked: Is Cleveland's downtown district dying? Blight, it said, had settled on "whole chunks" of the downtown, including the old wholesale district northwest of the Public Square, and E. 9th St., the downtown's major north-south artery; retail sales in the central business district had failed to follow the upward curve of Greater Cleveland's growth in population and prosperity; and parking adjacent to Euclid Ave. was scarce. Yet, it reported, many businessmen believed the heart of Cleveland was strong compared with the downtowns of other large American cities, and that some postwar developments—for example, new access routes such as the East Shoreway, Chester Ave., and the Willow Freeway; express buses, which had replaced streetcars; and the CTS Rapid Transit and INNERBELT FREEWAY (both under construction)—had contributed to the health and prosperity of downtown Cleveland. *Plain Dealer* editor PHILIP PORTER has called this period in Cleveland's life the era of "coasting," of "abnormal goodwill." Industry appeared healthy, and the "Best Location" slogan was adopted enthusiastically by the newspapers and the Chamber of Commerce. Democrat Anthony J. Celebrezze, Cleveland's first and only 5-term mayor (1954–62), presided over much of the period. He maintained a minimum level of city services while keeping taxes low and, under urban renewal, oversaw sweeping changes downtown and in other areas of the city.

As a result of wartime in-migration, Cleveland's population in 1950 showed a small increase of 4.2%—up from 878,336 to 914,808. But Cuyahoga County population continued to increase at a much faster rate, so that slightly more than ⅓ (34%) of the county's population now lived outside of Cleveland. The foreign-born represented a decreasing proportion of the city's population in 1950 (15%, compared to 20% a decade earlier), blacks an increasing proportion (16%, compared to 10% in 1940). While the cities of Cleveland, Cleveland Heights, East Cleveland, and Lakewood all showed small increases in population, 8 cities had increased by more than 100%: Brooklyn (552%), Lyndhurst (240%), Mayfield Heights (193%), Maple Heights (181%), South Euclid (166%), Euclid (147%), PARMA (141%), and FAIRVIEW PARK (123%). Postwar prosperity, the construction of new HIGHWAYS, and the ready availability of low-cost, federally insured mortgages all accelerated the move to the suburbs. Racial transition in many of the city's east side neighborhoods was another major factor in the unprecedented white flight that took place during this period. Fortunes were made by blockbusting, a tactic the city's Community Relations Board was hard-pressed to stop. In poorer neighborhoods, large single-family houses were subdivided and, as rental income dwindled, often no longer maintained. Dramatic and rapid changes in the city's neighborhoods were accompanied by similarly dramatic and rapid growth in formerly rural areas outside the city's borders. Perhaps the most phenomenal change occurred in Parma, which grew from 28,000 in 1950 to 82,000 in 1960.

Retail stores followed the exodus. Prior to 1940, Shaker Square was the only shopping center in Cuyahoga County resembling the modern integrated centers of today. Developed by the Van Sweringens, it incorporated off-street parking, even though very limited by later standards. Suburban shopping centers mushroomed after World War II. Among these were Van Aken-Warrensville (Shaker Heights) in 1947; Eastgate (Mayfield Heights) and Westgate (Fairview Park) in 1954; SOUTHGATE (Maple Heights) in 1955; Parmatown (Parma) in 1956; and Golden Gate (Mayfield Heights) in 1958. Large suburban shopping centers evolved into climate-controlled regional malls, usually with 2 full-line department stores serving as anchors at either end. The first mall in the Cleveland area, SEVERANCE CENTER, opened in Cleveland Heights in 1963. While these suburban centers drained income from retail sales from the city center, Cleveland remained a powerful industrial center during these years. In 1950, 42% of Clevelanders who worked were engaged in manufacturing. The *Cleveland Press* (27 Jan. 1953) announced that 1952 had been one of the best business years of all time; 101 new manufacturing concerns were established, and existing industries spent more than $146 million for expansion and new equipment.

Cleveland looked forward to completion of the St. Lawrence Seaway, anticipating that it would restore the city to a position of prominence as a port of general commerce and create a new wave of industrial growth as manufacturers sought dockside locations to cash in on the lowest shipping and handling rates in history. An $8 million bond issue to improve port facilities was approved in 1955. From the perspective of 1959, when the Seaway opened, the Cleveland area's development potential looked promising: It was located in a favorable market; it enjoyed unlimited water resources, abundant electric power, a good labor reservoir, and an unexcelled combination of transportation facilities; and raw materials were near at hand. "New Era of Prosperity on the Way," read the headline in the special Cleveland supplement to the European edition of the *New York Herald Tribune* published in Mar. 1956.

Coincident with postwar industrial expansion was the implementation of 2 federal programs that would have a profound impact not only on Cleveland but also on virtually all large American cities: the Housing Act of 1949, which established the federal urban-renewal program, and the Federal Highway Act of 1956, which gave impetus to a nationwide network of freeways by providing federal funding of 90% of construction costs. The concept of urban renewal was simple: Using its power of eminent domain if necessary, the city purchased property in specific project areas that had been legislatively determined as blighted. The property was cleared and improved for redevelopment, then sold to private developers at a reduction (called a writedown) from its assembly cost. The federal government absorbed ⅔ of the net project cost. Until 1950, Cleveland—"with slums as vast and as wretched as are to be found anywhere in the country," according to the *Plain Dealer* (16 Apr. 1954)—had relied exclusively on the construction of public housing as a means of fighting blight. It had built 8 developments, with 5,179 units providing housing for

18,951 low-income persons. Urban renewal was seen as a solution to the problem of multiple ownerships in blighted areas and the high cost of assembling sites for new, large-scale redevelopment.

In Mar. 1955, residents living on E. 38th St. between Scovill and Woodland avenues were invited to witness demolition of the first house—at 2534 E. 38th St.—signaling the redevelopment of "Area B" (later called Longwood) and the start of urban renewal in Cleveland. By June 1958, 800 new dwelling units, new streets, and a playground had been built there, making it one of the first housing projects completed under urban renewal in the U.S. The next target, "Area C" (St. Vincent Center), was less successful. Launched in 1959, Cleveland's biggest urban-renewal project to date encompassed 114 acres between E. 19th and E. 33rd streets and Woodland and Central avenues. Deteriorated buildings housing some 1,800 families (95% nonwhite, 98% tenants) were demolished; new apartments housing up to 3,500 middle-income families were to be built in their place. No developers came forward, however, and in 1963 Redevelopment Director James M. Lister acknowledged that there was no longer a market for the kind of housing that had been envisioned.

The urban-renewal program in Cleveland, encompassing just over 6,000 acres, was the largest in the country. Seven inner-city areas, all on the east side, were targeted for urban renewal: Garden Valley, Longwood, East Woodland, University-Euclid, St. Vincent Center, Gladstone, and Erieview. Ultimately, residential projects (Garden Valley, Longwood, University-Euclid) were able to attract only developers of government-subsidized housing, and although Garden Valley was acclaimed as "one of the boldest and most imaginative redevelopment jobs conceived in any city," by 1963 occupancy had reached only about 50%, and the Garden Valley Housing Association defaulted on its mortgage. The East Woodland and Gladstone project areas, targeted for industrial reuse, actually experienced declines in assessed value from prerenewal levels, as did St. Vincent Center, which stood largely vacant until CUYAHOGA COMMUNITY COLLEGE was planned in the late 1960s. Only Erieview was successful in attracting substantial new private investment. A significant lesson from Cleveland's urban-renewal experience was the difficulty of creating effective demand for land in the inner city. Residents in these areas lacked adequate income to support new residential redevelopment without heavy subsidies, while industries often preferred to locate in suburban areas, near freeways and, usually, closer to their employees' homes. Further, the large-scale dispersal of the city's poorest residents naturally had major consequences for the adjoining neighborhoods that absorbed them. By 1958, council members were voicing their concerns about the effects of displaced slum dwellers in the Hough, Glenville, Mt. Pleasant, and upper Central areas. In addition to urban renewal, the construction of highways, facilitated by the Federal Highway Act of 1956, caused significant alterations in traditional land-use patterns. The network of freeways led first to the massive dispersal of population and demolition of housing, followed by the movement of commercial and industrial activities to the periphery of the city. By 1975, the interstate highway system had displaced an estimated 19,000 Clevelanders, resulting in significant losses not only of people but of income and property taxes as well.

Spurred by the availability of urban-renewal funds, planning thrived in Cleveland during these years. The City Planning Commission, under the direction of John T. Howard, had issued the General Plan of 1949 laying out general guidelines for the growth and development of the city. The downtown was expected to continue as the "natural" main business and shopping area, and the freeway plan of 1944 was made an integral part of the plan. Ten years later, the commission issued another plan, soon superseded by Erieview, called "Downtown Cleveland 1975." Envisioned was the virtual reorganization and redevelopment of the downtown, including the redesign of Public Square and Playhouse Square, and the construction of a subway under Euclid Ave. between E. 14th St. and the Terminal.

By the mid-1950s, many of the institutions at UNIVERSITY CIRCLE were embarked on large expansion programs. The University Circle Development Foundation (later UNIVERSITY CIRCLE, INC.) was created in 1957 to reinforce the commitment of cultural institutions to the Circle area and to implement a 20-year development plan. The plan proposed the creation of a "unified, beautiful, cultural center" and called for development of parking, new roadways, a shuttle-bus service, and a private police force. The ambitious plans also called for massive demolition—including a great deal of what Eric Johannesen would later call the "architectural museum" that constituted Magnolia Dr. and other streets in the historic WADE PARK area—much of which was later tempered by the economic constraints of the late 1960s–1970s. Many other plans, public and private, were frustrated and eventually abandoned because of a lack of money. Plans formulated between 1944 and 1967 for the city's near west side called for commercial revitalization by creating new parking lots, traffic arteries, and "open space." Planners ofen assumed that such low-income areas were "blighted" and, in some cases, recommended wholesale demolition. The City Planning Commission in 1944 and again in 1961 recommended major redevelopment of the near west side. Voters in 1963 rejected an $8 million urban-renewal bond issue that would have resulted in demolition of substantial portions of the neighborhood between W. 25th and W. 58th streets. Still another plan, in 1967, recommended the total clearance of what only a few years later would become the core of the OHIO CITY restoration effort.

The Erieview urban-renewal plan of 1960 was one of the most ambitious undertaken under the federal urban-redevelopment program. Prepared for the city by the internationally known firm of I. M. Pei & Associates, the plan called for clearance of the aging district northeast of downtown to provide sites for the construction of new office buildings, HOTELS, and housing. Erieview, it was hoped, would generate interest with the incentives provided by the urban-renewal program and encourage new private capital investment. Erieview embraced 163 acres located between E. 6th and E. 17th streets and between Chester Ave. and the lakefront. Almost 75% of the buildings in the project area were determined to be substandard; these and others that did not conform to the proposed plan were acquired and demolished. Parcels of land were assembled and gradually sold to private developers at substantial discounts. Erieview Tower, a 40-story office building at the heart of the project area, was erected first. The green glass curtain-wall building, incorporating a large plaza and reflecting pool, was completed in 1964 and served as a dramatic symbol of the entire redevelopment effort. Interestingly, it was built by a Columbus developer, John W. Galbreath; no Cleveland bank was prepared to take the gamble. A dozen other large buildings, private and public, followed over the next 2 decades. Among these were One Erieview Plaza (1965), the Federal Building (1967), the Bond Court Building (1971), the Public Utilities Building (1971), and Park Centre (1973). The latter consisted of two 20-story apartment buildings and a 2-story shopping mall. By 1972, over $220 million of construction had been committed to the Erieview project, and the following decade

would see the construction of many other large projects, including 2 new hotels, and the firm establishment of a new office and financial district with 9th St. as its spine.

Erieview was not without its critics. Philip Porter called it "the mistake that ruined downtown." Erieview, Porter contended, "was no slum," and its redevelopment accelerated the deterioration of Euclid Ave. as Cleveland's major shopping street by draining it of people. Others criticized Erieview for producing a boring consistency and for eliminating the color, variety, and continuity that give a city character. But Erieview attracted critical new private investment, and without it, the construction of new office space might have followed the flight to the suburbs. As one city planner put it in 1972, Erieview "could be viewed as the catalyst which pulled the downtown area out of an otherwise inevitable downward spiral." In future years, Erieview would accommodate the expansion of Cleveland's service economy and point the way toward development of the lakefront. Nevertheless, from the perspective of the 1960s, one criticism remains valid: Erieview during this period claimed all of the city's energy and attention, while other parts of the city were virtually neglected.

As Erieview made slow but sustained progress, yet another plan to "save" downtown Cleveland was unveiled in 1965. The 2-year, $150,000 study was made by the firm of Ernst & Ernst at the behest of the CLEVELAND DEVELOPMENT FOUNDATION. It offered recommendations to speed Cleveland's rebirth and called for, among other things, a dizzying program of new construction: 5,500 to 6,600 new residential units, 2,300 new hotel rooms, and 12,000 new parking spaces in multilevel garages by 1975; and 5,000 additional residential units, 900 additional hotel rooms, and 9,000 additional parking spaces by 1985. Noting that "Cleveland has serious problems with its image and business climate," Ernst & Ernst partner Kenneth C. Caldwell reported that in the 7 years since 1958, employment downtown had dropped from 125,000 to 116,000, and retail sales had declined by $52 million. The number of convention delegates was also down. On the eve of the HOUGH RIOTS, the city's focus remained firmly fixed on the downtown.

*The Loss of Confidence: 1966–1980.* Though the fountains on the Mall, a gift of the Leonard C. Hanna Fund, were turned on in Aug. 1964; though the new $17.5 million underground Convention Center was opened that month with the "Parade of Progress" showing off the best of the city's industry and technology, commerce, science, arts, and education; though Erieview was giving Cleveland a new physical image and Clevelanders a sense of pride and success some thought no longer possible—these signs of well-being were illusory. For as business and civic leaders focused on the rebirth of downtown Cleveland, the city's neighborhoods were in disarray. Nowhere was that more apparent than in Hough. Bounded by Superior and Euclid avenues and by E. 55th and E. 105th streets, Hough had changed from a middle- to a working-class neighborhood beginning in the 1940s. In 1950 its 2 square miles were home to 66,000 Clevelanders, 95% of whom were white. Many of the neighborhood's large houses had been subdivided into 3 or 4 units, and landlords routinely ignored housing-code violations. A neighborhood conservation drive launched in 1951 by the Hough Area Council targeted the problems of architectural eyesores, ill-run taverns, crime, and, later, blockbusting. During this decade, blacks displaced by urban renewal began moving to Hough, and by 1960 the neighborhood was 74% black. Four years later, the county WELFARE department opened its first neighborhood office in Hough, where 25% of welfare cases now lived. In a series of articles in Feb. 1965, the *Cleveland*

*Press* warned that Hough was "in crisis." Two months later, it reported insurance cancellations there because of widespread vandalism and arson. Meanwhile, progress in the University-Euclid urban-renewal project, launched in 1960, was dismal. University-Euclid was to have created a new model community and rehabilitated more than 1,400 existing homes in eastern Hough; instead, it was the nightmare of Cleveland's urban-renewal program. By 1965, almost $7 million had been spent, and there was virtually nothing to show for it.

Frustration was mounting. Mayor Ralph S. Locher-and other city leaders could not or would not see the trouble brewing despite sporadic outbreaks of violence during the early part of the summer of 1966. Roving gangs were harassing drivers and hurling rocks and bottles at businesses and passing vehicles on Superior Ave. A brief, uneasy lull was broken on Monday night, 18 July, by an outbreak of violence that would last for 4 days and result in the deaths of 4 blacks and millions of dollars of damage to property. Mayor Locher described the east side rioting as a "tragic day in the life of our city." The jeeps of the National Guard lining the major arteries shocked the white community out of its complacency. The mood of the city was one of fear and futility. The city whose vision had once made it a national leader now faced staggering losses on all sides. Over the next 15 years, Cleveland would struggle to regroup and survive.

In the space of a few years, it seemed, the fabric of the city, both physically and psychologically, was shredded. The much-vaunted CLEVELAND PUBLIC SCHOOL system was declining. Department stores—among them WM. TAYLOR & SON, the Bailey Co., and STERLING-LINDNER—were closing, as were the theaters at Playhouse Square. Cleveland was losing population and jobs. The heaviest job losses were in the manufacturing sector, once the city's mainstay. Formerly sound neighborhoods, now the province of the poor, deteriorated rapidly, and on streets where people had once lived and shopped, only rows of empty, gutted buildings remained. The city was hard-pressed to provide even a minimum level of service. Crime worsened, vacant lots became dumping grounds, and the empty hulks of heavy industry were bitter reminders of a prosperous past. Cleveland was an aging city where nothing seemed to go right, where even the river caught fire: Cleveland not only shared America's urban crisis, it epitomized it. The CLEVELAND LITTLE HOOVER COMMISSION, formed in Dec. 1965 to make an in-depth study of all city operations, submitted its reports in the aftermath of the Hough riots. It identified community relations as the city's "No. 1 problem." The commission was also extremely critical of the police department—which it called "defensive, isolated, parochial, and mistrustful of the public it serves"— and of the department's program of race relations, giving credence to long-standing complaints by blacks of unfair treatment. Though most of the problems had their roots long before Locher took office, he bore the blame. The newspapers turned on him—"Locher has had little or no rapport with that third of his city's population that is Negro," the *Plain Dealer* charged—and sought a replacement.

Many in Cleveland looked to State Representative Carl B. Stokes as insurance against further racial disorder, and as someone to give the city a chance to move forward again. In 1967, the eyes of the nation were on Cleveland as Carl Stokes narrowly defeated Republican Seth Taft to become the first black mayor of a major U.S. city. Only 7 months after Stokes took office, however, Cleveland police and black militants clashed in Glenville. A shootout on 23 July 1968 left 10 dead and dozens wounded. By daybreak, the Ohio National Guard was mobilized to arrest widespread sniping, looting, and arson. The GLENVILLE SHOOTOUT killed much of Stokes's support. Corporate Cleveland had supported a major Stokes initiative, the CLEVELAND: NOW! campaign, which collected money and channeled it into myriad improvement projects of Stokes's choosing. When Cleveland: NOW! money was later traced to Fred (Ahmed) Evans, the central figure in the Glenville shootout, donations plummeted. The predominantly white police force became Stokes's bitter foe, and racial division deepened throughout the city. Stokes and city council president James Stanton battled each other over virtually every issue. The newspapers got tough on Stokes. Later, in his autobiography *Promises of Power*, Stokes railed against their "simple-minded" interpretation that, "if only we could put our personalities and our vanities in the background and get along, the city could move ahead." In fact, Stokes wrote, he and Stanton were diametrically opposed on important issues—public housing, equal employment opportunity, gun control—on which there was no middle ground. Although Stokes managed to win reelection to a second term, he lost the support of many of his original backers and, tired of strife with city council, chose not to run for a third term.

Cleveland had been losing population since 1950, but the exodus accelerated dramatically after 1960, and by the early 1970s the rate of loss had climbed to some 20,000 persons a year. At the same time, the county outside of Cleveland continued to grow, though at a slower rate, until the 1980 census confirmed that it, too, was losing population.

| | Cleveland | Cuyahoga County |
|---|---|---|
| 1950 | 914,808 | 1,389,532 |
| 1960 | 876,050 | 1,647,895 |
| 1970 | 750,879 | 1,720,835 |
| 1980 | 573,822 | 1,498,400 |

As the city's population declined, the proportion of its black population rose dramatically, from 16% in 1950 to 38% in 1970 and 44% in 1980. The city was not only losing residents but also retaining a more dependent population. On the average, Cleveland residents were significantly poorer than the area's suburban population: in 1969, the average income for all city families ($9,717) was almost $6,000 below that for suburban families ($15,259), according to City Planning Commission statistics. Almost ⅓ of the city's families lived in substandard housing. By 1970, abandonment of entire neighborhoods—a phenomenon concentrated in all-black neighborhoods with high poverty, welfare, and crime rates—was well underway and spreading. Between 1966 and 1974, the city spent over $4 million on the demolition of abandoned buildings and still could not keep pace with abandonment, which was estimated at 3 units per day. A Brookings Institution study in 1975 ranked Cleveland 2d among 58 big cities having the worst social and economic problems. (Only Newark, N.J., ranked worse.)

Meanwhile, regional shifts confirmed that the city was becoming a less viable location for many kinds of economic activity. Although Cleveland's central business district was expanding as an office center, it lost dominance as a shopping center as its share of retail sales and employment declined. Vacant stores, however, were a citywide phenomenon: Real Property Inventory field counts showed that the number of occupied store units in Cleveland decreased from 15,768 in 1958 to 12,269 in 1972. The rest of the county, meanwhile, had gained store units: from 5,137 in 1958 to 6,735 in 1972. Many industries were abandoning obsolete, multistory buildings for modern one-story plants in the suburbs, usually on or near the freeway. The case of the

National Screw & Manufacturing Co. was typical. National Screw, a leader in the fastener industry, had occupied a large multistory plant at E. 75th and Stanton since 1889. In the 1940s it produced more than 50,000 different items; in 1936 the plant's amateur women's softball and bowling teams both won national championships. But in 1969, National Screw moved to a more efficient one-story plant in Mentor, taking with it more than a thousand jobs. The abandoned plant, empty and gutted, remained a startling sight for years, and a frequent target for arson. Between 1958 and 1977, Cleveland lost an estimated 130,000 jobs, while the suburbs of Cuyahoga County gained almost 210,000. By 1970, slightly more than half of all jobs in the Cleveland SMSA (Cuyahoga, Medina, Lake, and Geauga counties) were located in the suburbs. Many heavy industries, however, were leaving the region altogether, choosing to relocate to the Sun Belt or abroad, where wages and other costs were substantially lower. The bulk of the losses occurred in the durable-goods (metals) sector. Richard B. Tullis, president of the Harris-Intertype Corp., in 1972 told the *Plain Dealer* that Cleveland would have to face up to the inevitable trend of major industries being replaced by light manufacturing and service industries.

The early 1970s were sad, tumultuous years for Cleveland, years when the city seemed to be in the midst of its own Great Depression, years of physical and psychological erosion. The parks were, once again, virtual dumping grounds. The transit system was approaching financial disaster. The downtown, offering little to attract people, was largely dead at night, and the opening of the Coliseum in Richfield (Summit County) in 1974 further drained it of life while making it more difficult for Clevelanders to support the home teams. To outsiders, Cleveland was the butt of jokes on "Laugh-In," the "mistake-on-the-lake." Two projects that would later prove important to the city's well-being had their start in these years. By the late 1960s, modest efforts were underway to make the FLATS, site of the city's earliest industries, the center of Cleveland night life. The *Cleveland Press* recognized this trend in 1968 when it wrote: "There is a bit of the romantic down there . . ., with the rough and tumble seamen's bars, the cobblestone streets and the old buildings reeking [of] Cleveland's history." Settlers' Landing, a project of the Higbee Co., envisioned a complex of shops, restaurants, and entertainment facilities near the traditional landing site of city founder MOSES CLEAVELAND. Though that project failed, it succeeded in focusing attention on the waterfront, and by the mid-1970s an informal coalescing of bars, restaurants, and shops—many occupying former industrial buildings—had infused the area with new life. The historic-preservation movement began to make modest gains during this period. Particularly notable were the efforts of Ray K. Shepardson, who conceived the idea of saving the old movie and vaudeville palaces at Playhouse Square, for decades the center of the city's night life. The Playhouse Square Association was organized in 1970. With support from the Junior League and a cadre of other volunteers, the association created a cabaret theater in the lobby of the STATE THEATER. The production of *Jacques Brel* captured the public imagination and helped launch a concerted effort to preserve the theaters and restore them to their former glory. There were other, small signs of downtown renewal. Lunchtime concerts on the Mall, and at Huron Rd. Mall and Chester Commons (a new vest-pocket park of above-average design) drew thousands, while weekly "parties in the park," sponsored by the GREATER CLEVELAND GROWTH ASSOCIATION, helped keep young adults downtown after work and boost business at Cleveland restaurants and nightclubs.

Planning continued during these years, although it took a new tack. Between 1969 and 1979, under the direction of Norman Krumholz, the City Planning Commission worked to achieve what it called "equity objectives." Recognizing that Cleveland was not only losing population but also retaining a more dependent population, the commission staff deemphasized planners' traditional concerns with ZONING, land use, and urban design and instead focused on plans and issues aimed at ameliorating the worst problems of the city and its residents. The Planning Commission, for example, championed the needs of the transit-dependent (a 1969 survey showed that ⅓ of Cleveland's families had no automobile), securing reduced fares and service guarantees during the negotiations that led to the transfer of the Cleveland Transit System to the GREATER CLEVELAND REGIONAL TRANSIT AUTHORITY in 1975. Under 3 mayors who could not have been more different (Stokes, Perk, and Kucinich), Krumholz continued to urge that the city abandon its preoccupation with what urbanologist Jane Jacobs has called "cataclysmic change" and focus instead on strategies aimed at conservation and gradual improvement.

In the 1970s, Cleveland, like many other of the nation's ailing cities that found themselves competing for new development, offered public subsidies to stimulate the private real-estate market. It was hoped that property-tax abatement would lure investors, and thereby create jobs. Under Ralph Perk, the NATIONAL CITY BANK Building was built, and STOUFFER'S INN ON THE SQUARE developed, with the aid of tax abatement. A growing number of critics, however, claimed that the projects would have been built without tax abatement, and that such public largess served only to further erode the city's tax base. In 1975, the city of Cleveland, the Greater Cleveland Growth Association, and the CLEVELAND FOUNDATION together commissioned Lawrence Halprin & Associates of San Francisco to develop a plan to rejuvenate the downtown. Following a series of public workshops, Halprin unveiled his "Concept for Cleveland." It offered few ideas that went beyond the obvious and cliched responses to "urban blight." Among the recommendations was the creation of a pedestrian mall on Euclid Ave. Some of the plans—open trolleys, for example, and sidewalk cafes—failed to account for the Cleveland climate, while others—the depression of Superior Ave. underground and reconstruction of Public Square above it—failed to respect the city's historical sense of place. In a page-one editorial, the *Plain Dealer* praised the plan for its "color, pizzazz, magnetism, [and] lift. It could make Cleveland one of the most attractive cities of America. . . ." But the Halprin Plan, which cost over $300,000, came to nothing.

The final years in this, the most difficult period of the city's history, were marked by political turmoil, a court ruling whose consequences would persist long into the future, and, finally, a fiscal crisis. Though Republican mayor Ralph J. Perk had built a successful political career by articulating the grievances of his largely ethnic, working-class constituency, the mood of the city was changing. In the 1977 campaign, Councilman Dennis Kucinich successfully targeted 3 issues: saving Muny Light, ending tax abatement, and the need to concentrate the city's resources on its neighborhoods instead of the downtown. Shortly after taking office, however, the populist mayor who modeled himself after Mayor TOM L. JOHNSON came into conflict with virtually every group in the city. His and his young assistants' confrontational style alienated business and civic leaders, the news media, and, ultimately, even those neighborhood groups that had been his chief supporters. Though

Kucinich survived the bitter RECALL ELECTION OF 1978 by 236 votes, he was swept out of office a year later.

U.S. District Judge Frank J. Battisti, meanwhile, in 1976 ruled that the Cleveland and state boards of education were responsible for the racial segregation of Cleveland schools and must desegregate them. Over a period of 35 years, Judge Battisti found, school officials consistently chose to segregate pupils; the state knew about the situation and chose to do nothing about it. The historical problem of segregation in the schools was in part the consequence of segregation in the city's housing patterns. However, since at least the 1930s, school construction plans and decisions with respect to school boundaries and teacher assignments had elicited protests from the black community, many of whom believed that the Board of Education followed an unofficial policy of separating blacks and whites. A major school construction program undertaken by school superintendent Paul Briggs in the 1960s was perceived as a further attempt to strengthen de facto segregation. The desegregation remedy of crosstown busing helped accelerate a movement from the city of those who could afford a suburban home—blacks as well as whites—while resentment of busing helped defeat levy after levy. By 1980, the Cleveland school system was spending more than $12 million annually on transportation, and enrollment had declined by more than ⅓, from 123,00 in 1976 to 81,000.

On 15 Dec. 1978, Cleveland became the first major American city to DEFAULT since the Depression. The city could not repay $15.5 million in short-term notes that came due, and city officials were unable to agree with local banks on a program to avert default. The default was the product of the dramatic loss of jobs and population—with a consequent shrinkage of the tax base—and a unique political environment in which the mayor's actions were limited by an unwieldy 33-member city council and citizen demand for low tax rates. The roots of the city's fiscal problems reached back at least as far as 1965, when voters defeated a city income tax referendum, prompting creation of the Cleveland Little Hoover Commission to study city operations. In 1970, when Stokes found that revenues were inadequate to maintain the level of city services, he proposed an income tax increase from 1 to 1.8%, tying it, as an incentive, to a reduction in the school district property tax levy. Voters turned down the increase but approved the reduction, and at the end of Stokes's second term, the city had a $13 million budget deficit.

Stokes's successor, Ralph J. Perk, pledged not to seek any tax increases and kept his word. To cover revenue shortfalls, Perk borrowed heavily and tapped bond funds to cover operating deficits. In addition, federal categorical grant programs (including urban renewal) were replaced by community development revenue sharing beginning in 1974, which allowed cities to use the money returned by Washington for locally determined priorities; by 1977, federal aid supported over ⅓ of the city's budget. Finally, under Perk, the city of Cleveland sold a number of valuable city assets. The sale of its sewage-treatment facilities to a regional authority in 1972 brought in $32 million. Transfer of the Cleveland Transit System to a regional authority in 1975 brought in another $8.9 million. Perk also leased Cleveland Municipal Stadium to private interests and won city council approval of the sale of the Municipal Electric Light Plant, although the latter decision was eventually rescinded.

The sale of assets to cover general debt-service payments and operating costs failed to provide a long-term solution to the city's deteriorating financial condition. Expenditures were increasing rapidly, especially for debt service, while revenues continued to shrink. When Dennis

Kucinich was elected mayor in 1977, he faced a critical financial situation: $33 million in short-term debt was to come due by the end of 1978, $15.5 million of which was held by local banks. Kucinich, who had also promised no new taxes, continued to tap bond funds to cover operating expenses. However, he adamantly opposed the sale of city assets and halted the sale of Muny Light. Subsequent suspension of the city's bond rating by Standard & Poor's, and downgrading by Moody's, made it impossible to issue notes to the public to meet continuing obligations. In Dec. 1978, when local banks refused to roll over the city's short-term notes, default became a bleak reality. In Feb. 1980, under Mayor George V. Voinovich, voters approved a 50% income tax increase, an important first step toward the city's recovery of financial health. Of increasing concern, however, was the impact of the city's fiscal problems on capital investment in the city's physical plant. Streets, BRIDGES, and water and sewer systems were in poor condition, the result of a long history of neglect and a pattern of voter reluctance to raise taxes sufficiently to finance needed improvements.

It was, to be sure, a period of losses. The city had lost people, business, and industry. It had suffered unprecedented racial strife and the ignominy of default. But decisions to import "name" planners, to lure developers with land writedowns and tax abatement, to advertise the city nationally with such slogans as "The best things in life are here"—all had their roots in Cleveland's most important loss of this period: the loss of confidence. Cleveland in 1980 was far different from the city that had celebrated the opening of the Union Terminal with such pride a half-century ago. Once the nation's 6th-largest city, it was now 18th in size; once home to 75% of Cuyahoga County residents, it was now home to only 38%. By 1930, statistics showed, there already were 2 Clevelands. And the core of poverty and ring of affluence—begun with the introduction of the streetcar and reinforced by the automobile and the highway—were, in 1980, even more pronounced. Neighborhood erosion, epidemic after 1900, was still unabated. And although a multitude of grassroots conservation efforts were underway, the city remained home to a high proportion of low-income residents and to the county's poorest residents, while the economically well-off resided in suburbs that now reached into adjoining counties.

Although the city's historic ethnic groups and their descendants had largely departed for the suburbs, there were still distinct pockets of Italians, POLES, CZECHS, SLOVENIANS, CROATIANS, and HUNGARIANS. Foreign-language newspapers, though not so numerous as they had once been, were still published. New HISPANIC and Asian immigrants, meanwhile, had come to Cleveland, and their numbers were growing. While residential segregation persisted, blacks no longer were concentrated in crowded ghettos. Indeed, such areas as Hough and Central were now characterized by vast stretches of vacant land, with little prospect that anything would ever be built there. In the 1970s, for the first time, blacks in large numbers had found new homes in the suburbs. East Cleveland was now predominantly black, while Cleveland Heights, Shaker Heights, GARFIELD HEIGHTS, and EUCLID all had sizable black populations in 1980. Blacks had made substantial gains in all arenas, but especially in politics. The 21st Congressional District Caucus, organized in the late 1960s, continued to articulate the concerns of black voters. George L. Forbes had begun a long and powerful reign as city council president in 1973, and city council itself reflected a city now almost half black.

Like other cities in the nation's industrial crescent, Cleveland continued to struggle with wrenching economic change, with its transition from a blue-collar factory town to one where more than 70% were employed in service jobs. Of the city's 10 largest employers in 1980, only 3 (Republic Steel, JONES & LAUGHLIN STEEL, and ACME-CLEVELAND) represented the manufacturing sector. Cleveland was growing in importance as a center for education, applied research, and medicine—the CLEVELAND CLINIC FOUNDATION and UNIVERSITY HOSPITALS both ranked among the city's largest employers—and, though it had dropped in rank, it retained eminence as a corporate-headquarters city. In 1980, there were signs of interest in redeveloping such areas as the Flats, the WAREHOUSE DISTRICT, and the lakefront, projects that would prove important to Cleveland's economic well-being in the future. But some problems seemed as far from solution as ever. An aging capital plant, few high-income residents, and many high-cost residents were the recipe for ongoing fiscal trouble. Public housing, once the city's pride, was a shambles—often as deteriorated and as frightening as the slums it had replaced. Unemployment, especially among black youth, was high, as was the school dropout rate. Political volatility and fragmentation continued to characterize city hall, although voters in 1981 would reduce an unwieldy city council from 33 to 21 members and change the term of office for both council and the mayor from 2 to 4 years.

The legacy of highways, urban renewal, poverty, violence, and despair could all be seen in the Cleveland of 1980. Yet if the city had changed dramatically in the space of half a century, some things remained unchanged. Public Square, the original city center, was still the city's hub, and, despite repeated threats, the Group Plan was still intact. Clevelanders continued to shop at the WEST SIDE MARKET, at the Central Market, and on Coit Rd., where farmers from outlying areas still brought their produce. The Flats were still smoky from the remaining mills, and the crooked Cuyahoga was still crossed by a score of bridges. Blessed as it was with fine museums and theaters, a world-renowned orchestra, and numerous other institutions, Cleveland enjoyed its cultural maturity.

Cleveland's "steady march of progress" (to use the words of William Ganson Rose) had been interrupted—by depression, abandonment, economic decline, racial unrest, and fiscal crisis. But the city retained important advantages, not the least of which were hardworking and generous citizens proud of the city's past and hopeful for its future. For the fate of Cleveland, many realized, was not sealed by its past mix of industries and occupations, only influenced by it. The future depended in large part on the intelligence and wisdom with which those who remained would marshal their resources for the betterment of a gritty city determined not only to survive but also to rebuild.

Carol Poh Miller

*Epilogue: 1987.* There is ample evidence that rebuilding has begun. Despite the still-present dark cloud of racial tension lowering over the city, a new spirit of cooperation and optimism about the city's future appeared by the mid-1980s which was energized by such unique private organizations of business leaders as the New Cleveland Campaign and the Greater Cleveland Roundtable. Their activities were sparked by the growing evidence of success of many long-planned projects. The business community pulled together to support the MAYORAL ADMINISTRATION OF GEORGE VOINOVICH, contributing manpower to assist in putting the city's financial house in order. By the mid-1980's, the city was again considered a good risk by the nation's bond markets. The Playhouse Square complex of restored 1920s movie palaces was nearing completion, making it the 3d-largest theater complex in the country, and the result of a 10-year cooperation between citizens' groups, businesses, and the Cleveland Foundation. The Flats and the warehouse district had become a regional entertainment center, filled with restaurants and nightclubs teeming with people in the evening hours, contending with the problem of success—a shortage of parking. The Inner Harbor project was underway, as dredging began in the spring of 1987. The project was designed to bring the lake closer to downtown, with a marina, shopping malls, entertainment centers, and an aquarium. The International Exposition (IX) Center, a converted tank plant, was drawing huge crowds to record-breaking industrial expositions and consumer events, such as the Boat Show. A list of building and development could go on, but the best evidence of the new spirit of cooperation and optimism was the more-than-a-year-long effort on the part of people from all parts of the city to attract the ROCK 'N' ROLL Hall of Fame, beating out competition from cities such as Los Angeles, Chicago, and Philadelphia, to name only a few. Nevertheless, much has yet to be done, for most of the problems existing in 1980 still persist. The progress thus far, however, should portend a better future.

The Editors

# The
# Entries

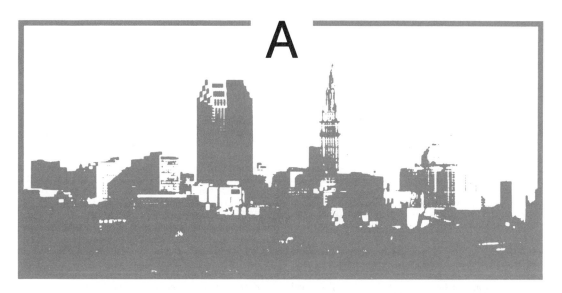

# A

The **AHS FOUNDATION** was founded in 1968 by Leland and Helen Schubert. Leland Schubert, a graduate and trustee of Ohio Wesleyan University, was an English teacher and head of the English Dept. of Madison College in Virginia before retiring to Cleveland in 1956. He was active in transcribing books into Braille and wrote a handbook that was first adopted at JOHN CARROLL UNIVERSITY. In 1985 he was on the board of the Society for the Blind, GILMOUR ACADEMY, and the Internatl. Scholarship Fund. Helen Schubert is active in OUR LADY OF FATIMA COMMUNITY CTR., an inner-city mission, and tutored in inner-city schools.

The AHS Foundation was established for the general purposes of urban education and programs for the handicapped. The family preferred to fund organizations for 3 or more years and emphasized alternative educational projects. The foundation will give only to nonprofit organizations; it does not fund individuals. In 1968, Leland Schubert gave Cleveland mayor Carl Stokes $1 million for the CLEVELAND NOW program. The foundation has made contributions to John Carroll University, United Independent Schools of E. Cleveland, and the FAIRMOUNT THEATRE FOR THE DEAF. Both the principal and the interest on the original bequest are used. In 1983, with holdings of $613,953, the operations of the foundation were turned over to the Schuberts' sons, who moved its headquarters to St. Paul, Minn.

**AM INTERNATIONAL, INC.** (the Addressograph-Multigraph Corp. until 1979), was formed in Cleveland on 5 May 1931 by the merger of 2 established office-machine manufacturers, the Addressograph Internatl. Corp. and the American Multigraph Co. of Cleveland. Addressograph, the older of the two, was organized in Illinois in 1893 and incorporated in 1896 by Joseph S. Duncan, inventor of an envelope-addressing device. In 1927 the company was sold to a group that included Joseph E. Rogers, senior vice-president of the Internatl. Business Machine Corp. As president and general manager, Rogers sought to expand Addressograph and merged it with American Multigraph in 1931. The American Multigraph Co. was organized by Harry C. Gammeter and Henry C. Osborn. In 1900 Gammeter, a sales engineer for the United Typewriter & Sales Co. of Louisville, Ky., invented a machine to duplicate letters; Osborn further developed the invention. They incorporated

on 12 Dec. 1902 and began production in a factory on E. 40th St. at Kelly Ave.

Addressograph-Multigraph consolidated its operations in 1932 in a new plant at 1200 Babbitt Rd. and grew steadily. Between 1952–66, under the leadership of J. Basil Ward, the company greatly expanded its operations. Its sales in 1953 totaled $68.4 million, and it had 5 subsidiaries. In 1955 the company began a vigorous program of expansion into foreign markets; by 1959 it had 11 subsidiaries and business transactions in 126 countries. In 1967 it had 27 subsidiaries and more than $400 million in sales. The company's rate of growth slowed in the late 1960s and 1970s. Sales of $572.9 million in 1976 brought a net income of $6.4 million. Roy L. Ash, cofounder and former president of Litton Industries, was elected chairman and chief executive officer of Addressograph-Multigraph in Sept. 1976. Before resigning in 1981, Ash made major cuts to improve efficiency; and, hoping to enter the field of high technology and establish a new corporate image, he moved corporate headquarters from Cleveland to Los Angeles in 1978 and changed the corporation's name in 1979.

AM Internatl. earned $5.8 million on sales of $909.6 million in 1980 but suffered severe losses in the next 2 years, losing $245 million in 1981 and $24.6 million in 1982. On 14 Apr. 1982, the firm filed for bankruptcy under Chap. 11 of the Bankruptcy Act. In Aug. 1982, workers at its Babbitt Rd. plant voted against a concession plan calling for them to give up $6 an hour, and AM Internatl. closed the plant in Oct. 1982. At the end of 1983, although bankrupt, the corporation ranked 427th among U.S. industrial corporations ranked by sales.

Brainard, George C., *A Page in the Colorful History of Our Modern Machine Age* (1950).

The **A. M. MCGREGOR HOME** was established in 1904 as a residence for white Protestants over 65 who had no other place to spend their last days. Mrs. Tootie McGregor Terry donated the house and land, on Terrace Rd. in E. CLEVELAND, in memory of her first husband, Ambrose McGregor. In 1904 the home was incorporated as a charitable organization by Seymour Adams, one of its early trustees. Mrs. McGregor Terry also donated an income of $5,000 per year to the home for a period of 5 years. The home opened in 1908, with Anna Huntley as its first matron. Dr. Marshall Terry, Mrs. McGregor Terry's second

3

husband, donated hospital equipment to the home and served as chairman of the board for many years.

The facility housed only 25 residents at first. Enlargements in 1916 and 1925 increased the capacity to 65, but the facility strove to remain as unlike an old-age home—as "homelike"—as possible. The early facilities were condemned by the E. Cleveland fire warden in 1940. The board raised the money to build a new structure on the site of the old one, which was finished in 1941. It contained a small hospital, as well as room for 72 residents. Further additions were made in 1961 and 1971, providing an overall capacity of 100. The additions also made possible the inclusion of more hospital facilities, a craft shop, a beauty shop, a snack bar, a gift shop, and an auditorium.

"History of the A. M. McGregor Home" (Compiled by Nina Kendrick for the A. M. McGregor Home and printed for the A. M. McGregor Home, 1984).

**ABOLITIONISM.** The contribution that Clevelanders made to the cause of black emancipation was related to 2 geographic factors: the location of the city in the puritan New England environment of the WESTERN RESERVE, and its position on Lake Erie opposite the shores of Canada, destination of so many hundreds of fugitives from the slave South. The village, town, and city that Cleveland became during the antebellum years did not wholly reflect the hard piety and humanitarian zeal for which the surrounding counties of Yankee settlers were long renowned. Instead, Cleveland was like most other fast-growing northern centers of trade: crass, money-conscious, pragmatic, and chauvinistic about Flag, Work, and Progress. Then and later, Clevelanders were generally skeptical of plans to rearrange society, but like most northerners they had little regard for slavery as a system. In time they came to despise the slaveholders for arrogance and undeserved pretensions to political power. Although Cleveland did not rally to the cause of root-and-branch abolitionism, its record of sympathy and help for the black man's plight in America matched, if not exceeded, that of any other metropolitan center in North America, with the exception, perhaps, of Boston and Toronto.

*Abolition.* At the outset, though, it should be understood that abolitionism was the most radical of several positions on slavery. The doctrine of "immediate emancipation," disseminated in the 1830s, was the product of eastern reformers. According to the theory of Boston's Wm. Lloyd Garrison and the American Anti-Slavery Society (1833), slavery was a personal and social sin requiring immediate repentance of slaveholders and all others who had failed to witness against the institution. Although the reform was theoretically akin to the temperance pledge and other conservative Evangelical goals, so extreme a position was bound to excite anger and fear because it threatened the very existence of the Union and foretold a shattering of racial customs and prejudices.

In Cleveland, a more popular organization was the American Colonization Society, founded in Washington in Jan. 1817 to repatriate blacks to Liberia. According to conservative supporters such as Elisha Whittlesey of nearby Tallmadge, Afro-Americans were too benighted and whites too antagonistic for both races to flourish in freedom in the same country. The county chapter of the organization had been founded in 1827 under the leadership of Jas. S. Clark, Samuel Cowles, and other town fathers. Although returning the entire southern labor force to Africa was hopelessly impractical, Cowles naively dreamed that American blacks would bring "the arts of civilized life" to the allegedly savage heathen there. The city elite soon heard from the rising Garrisonian reformers hoping to quench colonizationist enthusiasms and implant their own doctrines. In May 1833, Rev. Chas. Storrs, abolitionist president of Western Reserve College, Hudson, for instance, spoke at the Cuyahoga County courthouse on "the immediate emancipation of Slaves."

In Cleveland, indifference more than outright antagonism greeted the abolitionists, whose postal campaign of 1835 aroused, throughout the country, fierce mob action against the mailed propaganda and itinerant lecture agents. Protest was confined to a single meeting on 10 Sept. at the courthouse, where participants resolved that abolitionism threatened "the peace and permanence of the union" and assured southerners that they alone had "the right to free their slaves." Not until 1837 was the first chapter of the American Anti-Slavery Society established. S. L. Severance, W. T. Huntington, and JOHN. A. FOOTE, all Cleveland business and social leaders, took the chief posts, but the society left few traces. The circumspection contrasted with the high-mindedness and sermonizings of the students and professors at nearby Oberlin College, a chief center of abolitionist influence in the region, founded in 1834.

*Fugitive Slaves.* If abolition gained few converts, less radical approaches took root along the muddy banks of the Cuyahoga. Most important was the operation of the "Underground Railroad." The completion of the Ohio Canal in 1833 enhanced the strategic importance of the city in this regard, though the numbers assisted to freedom, especially by whites, were far lower than legend long claimed. For instance, the belfry of ST. JOHN'S EPISCOPAL CHURCH served as an occasional hiding place. Folklore, however, laid claim to a tunnel under the church that housed scores of slaves. Early–20th-century investigators exposed the fiction.

Not until the passage of the rigorously enforced Fugitive Slave Law in 1850 were Clevelanders aroused to concerted action. Antislavery meetings drew crowds, particularly when fugitives told their dramatic stories of punishment, escape, and freedom. A typical gathering was the one held at the Disciple Church in Solon on 17 and 18 June 1847. There Wm. Ferris, "a fugitive slave of Oberlin, addressed the afternoon meeting." Such incidents, as well as the denunciations of politicians such as Joshua Giddings at Cleveland rallies, encouraged otherwise law-abiding citizens to defy the hated Fugitive Slave Law. In 1855, for example, Jas. Adams of Big Kanawha, Va., fled with a cousin through Ohio, along a route used the previous year by 5 other fugitives from his neighborhood heading for Cleveland. A Cleveland antislavery clergyman, and then a white shoemaker whom the black travelers met on the outskirts of town, arranged their passage to Buffalo and from there to Canada. Such assistance kept the antislavery cause very much alive, but it rested largely on personal difficulties with which one could identify, not upon larger matters of polity and justice for the race as a whole.

Cleveland's most dramatic signal of white protest against southern high-handedness grew out of the famed OBERLIN-WELLINGTON RESCUE. Oberlinites of all colors and conditions mobbed a jail in nearby Wellington to rescue a fugitive long resident in their college community. Some 37, including Simeon Bushnell, a Cleveland store clerk who had helped to whisk the slave to Canadian freedom, were indicted by a federal grand jury in Cleveland and held in jail in the spring of 1859. Thousands attended a rally in the square, where Giddings, Benjamin Wade, and others denounced the Fugitive Slave Law, Democrats, and southerners. As Cleveland whites grew increasingly distressed about slavery and slave catchers, blacks also became more militant. For instance, in Nov. 1859, Deputy Marshal Wm.

4

L. Manson took into custody Henry Seaton, a Kentucky slave. Although the prisoner was returned to his master without incident, one Geo. Hartman, who had betrayed Seaton by luring him into a trap, had to seek refuge himself from an angry black crowd. He found safety in the city jail. John Brown, a native of Hudson in neighboring Geauga County, was the most famous beneficiary of Clevelanders' pride in protecting the hunted from their pursuers. At the time of the Oberlin rescuers' release and celebration assembly, Brown sojourned in Cleveland for 10 days, planning his assault on Harpers Ferry set for the fall of 1859. There was a price on his head for his Kansas guerrilla activities and the killings at Pottawatomie. Although he passed the federal marshal's office daily, no one turned him in.

By and large, such black activists as the Ohio canal boatman JOHN MALVIN and some white church people cooperated in aiding fugitives, but some local blacks, influenced in part by the record of race relations across the Canadian border, adopted the idea of emigration, one formerly held by the Western Reserve's colonization-minded elite—though for quite different reasons. On 24 Aug. 1854, the Negro Emigration Convention assembled in Cleveland to discuss plans for colonizing abroad. It could be said that the meeting was the birthplace of black nationalism—that is, a new consciousness of Afro-American culture. Although the *Cleveland Leader* accurately surmised that "the objects of the convention met with but little favor from our colored citizens" of the city, Cleveland black spokesmen agreed with the convention's protests against "insufferable Yankee intrusion," civil and social discrimination, and abuse—in Ohio as elsewhere in the nation.

*Political Antislavery.* Neither Cleveland nor Cuyahoga County played a decisive role in the development of third-party antislavery radicalism. Joshua R. Giddings, the dynamic though eccentric antislavery Whig congressman, represented Cleveland throughout the 1840s, but his base of strength in the district lay in the rural villages. In 1852, despite the Ohio legislators' gerrymandering to oust Giddings by removing Cuyahoga County from his district, Clevelanders helped to elect Edward Wade, another staunchly reform-minded Ashtabulan. Yet, the 2 Free-Soilers, Wade and his brother Benjamin, elevated to the Senate in 1851, and Giddings were careful to restrict their reform leanings to such popular matters as "Free soil" in the Mexican Cession territories and in "Bleeding" Kansas.

On the whole, the press was also relatively conservative on slavery issues. But in contrast to the wildly proslavery and Democratic *PLAIN DEALER*, the *CLEVELAND LEADER* usually took a reform position and helped to build a strong local Republican party. Wm. Day's *ALIENED AMERICAN* (est. 1852) served abolitionism in the black community, but the paper lasted only 2 years. Since there was no major college like Oberlin or Western Reserve at Hudson to give intellectual vitality to the antislavery impulse, and since political abolitionism was confined to conventional Republican efforts, abolitionism had no strong institutional base of support in the city.

*Church Abolition.* The only permanent bastion of rigorous immediatism was in a handful of churches. Though SAMUEL AIKEN of the FIRST PRESBYTERIAN (OLD STONE) CHURCH helped to launch the local antislavery society chapter, he was not dedicated enough to suit the abolitionist members of his church. Thereafter he became, however, increasingly hostile. Reform members of his church wheeled off in 1837 to form the Second Presbyterian Church; a larger antislavery group left in 1850 to establish the Free Presbyterian Church (later Plymouth Church of Shaker Hts.). It was said that in 1850 Aiken hid behind a pillar when authorities dragged a fugitive from sanctuary in the church.

Like Aiken's church, the First Methodist congregation also experienced antislavery defections in 1839 in protest against slavery and other matters of concern; soon afterward the dissidents formed the Wesleyan Methodist church. The larger church bodies—the Cleveland Presbytery and the Methodists' Erie, (later North Ohio) Conference, and the Cleveland Congregational Conference—made increasingly bold antislavery statements, especially after the Fugitive Slave Law was enacted. Yet there was no major abolitionist church leader in the city who commanded national attention.

The sole candidate to head local radicalism was JAS. A. THOME, a veteran church abolitionist and former Oberlin professor. His First Church (Congregational) in Ohio City was a lonely oasis of pure emancipationism. In 1862, Thome brought Theodore Weld out of retirement to address a throng on the meaning of the war effort. The occasion, though, was largely an exercise in nostalgia for the more innocent, less bloody era of youthful abolitionism 30 years before when the pair had traversed Ohio lecturing for black freedom. Tragically, guns and blockades were accomplishing more for racial justice than Garrisonian rhetoric ever did. In any event, the reform contribution of Cleveland—largely the work of its black residents—lay more in the succoring of fugitives from slavery than in any other aspect of the great humanitarian movement. Yet, one may safely guess that Cleveland's record of relative racial harmony owed something to the spirit of interracial cooperation in that cause. In 1865, the *Cleveland Leader* noted that "colored children attend our schools, colored people are permitted to attend lectures and public affairs," and had done so for years even before the war. Not many northern centers could boast of a similar attention to racial justice.

Indeed, any final assessment of Cleveland's antislavery position must acknowledge that its racial reform tradition more than matched that of most other northern cities. With their ethnic diversity, cities such as Boston, Cincinnati, New York, and Philadelphia and smaller places such as Utica and Rochester were sporadically torn by riots against blacks and abolitionists, a lawlessness that Clevelanders happily did not share. In any event, whatever the failings of Cleveland's civic leadership regarding formal abolition may have been, the commercial climate of the port and its locale in the heart of the Western Reserve made possible a relatively smooth transition from the era of slavery to the epoch of free-labor capitalism, to which Cleveland blacks and whites made their significant contribution.

Bertram Wyatt-Brown
University of Florida

McTighe, Michael J., "Embattled Establishment: Protestants and Power in Cleveland, 1836–60" (Ph.D. diss., University of Chicago, 1983).

Peskin, Allan, ed., *North into Freedom: The Autobiography of John Malvin, Free Negro, 1795–1880* (1966).

Reilley, Edward C., "The Early Slavery Controversy in the Western Reserve" (Ph.D. diss., Western Reserve University, 1940).

**ABRAHAM LINCOLN'S FUNERAL** included a wake for the late president held on Cleveland's Public Square on 28 Apr. 1865. Lincoln had been assassinated by John Wilkes Booth in Washington, D.C., on 14 Apr. Cleveland was one stop in a 1,700-mi. journey by train to Springfield, Ill., where Lincoln was buried alongside his 11-year-old son, Wm. Wallace (Willie), on 4 May. The funeral train arrived in Cleveland at UNION DEPOT from Buffalo, N.Y., at 6:50 a.m., pulled by the locomotive *L. Case*. The 9-car train was given another engine, the *Dispatch*, which pulled the train to the Euclid St. Station, arriving at 7:20 a.m. A 36-gun salute was presented. Accompanying Lincoln's remains to Springfield was a Military Guard of Honor of Veteran Reserve Corps troops, a Guard of Honor of Army and Navy commissioned officers, and an Escort of Honor of family and friends of the Lincoln family. Pallbearers lifted the coffin onto a hearse, and the procession left the station at 7:30 a.m. Col. JAS. BARNETT, 1st Ohio Volunteer Light Artillery, served as chief marshal. The procession included a local military escort commanded by Col. WM. H. HAYWARD, 150th Ohio Volunteer Infantry, consisting of the 29th Regiment, Ohio Natl. Guard; the 8th Ohio Independent Battery, Lt. Grenninger commanding; U.S. Army and Navy officers; Maj. General Hooker and staff; and governor of Ohio John Brough and staff. Six divisions, each with its own contingent of civic organizations, followed. The march route led up Euclid St. to Erie (E. 9th) St. A left turn led the procession to Public Square. Arrangements for public viewing of the body had been made by the Committee on the Location of the Remains, with the help of appropriate subcommittees. Lincoln's remains rested in a pagoda-style catafalque, which allowed 2 moving lines to view the body while walking over an inclined floor.

By 9:15, the procession had arrived at the Square. A portion of the 29th Ohio Natl. Guard was posted as guard, and the Veteran Reserve Corps troops stood as Military Guard of Honor around the remains. It rained throughout the day, sometimes quite heavily. Bp. CHAS. PETTIT MCILVAINE read from the *Book of Common Prayer of the Episcopal Church* as he conducted a short service for 9,000 people beginning at 10:00 a.m. Viewing began with the 29th Ohio Natl. Guard, Gen. Hooker and staff, and convalescents from the U.S. General Hospital on University Hts. By 6:00 p.m., 90,000 people had filed through the pagoda. The coffin was closed at 10 p.m. The 29th Ohio Natl. Guard, the "Civic Guard," and police headed the procession to Union Depot. They were followed by the hearse, the Military Guard of Honor, and the remainder of the civic organizations. The hearse, which had been removed from the Square at 10:30 p.m., was conducted to the depot via Superior St. and Vineyard. The Military Guard of Honor removed the coffin from the hearse and placed it on the funeral train. The train passed through BEREA at midnight, arriving in Columbus at 7:30 a.m. on 29 Apr.

**ABRAHAM LINCOLN'S VISIT TO CLEVELAND** took place 15–16 Feb. 1861 on the president-elect's way to Washington, D.C., at the written invitation of GEO. B. SENTER. Lincoln arrived from Columbus, Ohio, at the Euclid St. Station at 4 p.m. on 15 Feb. 1861. The station was guarded by 3 local military units: the Light Dragoons, the CLEVELAND LIGHT ARTILLERY, and the CLEVELAND GRAYS. Lincoln was greeted with cannon salutes, ringing bells, and blowing whistles. A great crowd, along with the local military escort, accompanied the president-elect and his son, Robt. Todd Lincoln, down Euclid to the west side of PUBLIC SQUARE to Ontario, St. Clair, Water, and Superior streets. Lincoln rode bareheaded, stovepipe hat in hand, in a drizzling rain, in an open carriage pulled by 4 white horses. The procession reached the WEDDELL HOUSE hotel at 5 p.m., where Lincoln was welcomed by IRVINE U. MASTERS, president of CLEVELAND CITY COUNCIL, and Judge SHERLOCK J. ANDREWS. Lincoln addressed the crowd fron the hotel balcony. He urged all citizens to support the Constitution and the Federal Union. He gave no indication of the impending crisis that threatened to embroil the nation in civil war. A reception was held later that evening from 7–9 p.m. The Lincoln party

occupied 20 suites of rooms at the Weddell House. The room in which Lincoln stayed was later maintained as a memorial. It was opened each year on his birthday, when a program was conducted by the Lincoln Society of Ohio. On 16 Feb. 1861, the Cleveland Grays escorted the Lincoln party to UNION DEPOT. The party left Cleveland for Buffalo at 9 a.m.

The **ACACIA COUNTRY CLUB,** located on the northeast corner of Cedar and Richmond roads in S. Euclid, opened on 31 May 1921, although only 9 holes of its golf course were completed, and it had no official clubhouse. Originally limited to Masons, it was later opened to non-Masons. The club covered 300 acres of land and offered some of the finest golfing in the area. Its course was designed by Donald Ross, a Boston golf expert. The first president and vice-president of Acacia were H. A. Tremaine and John R. Bentley respectively. There were approximately 400 members during the club's initial years.

Initially a golf club, Acacia steadily developed into a leading country club. On 4 July 1922, a $200,000 clubhouse was opened. In the summer of 1954, a $75,000 pool was added, complete with dressing rooms and a snack bar. Major additions to the clubhouse began in May 1963 and were finished by 1964. A new portico and stone front were added to the exterior. A new powder room was built by the main entranceway, and a large building to the west of the clubhouse was built to house a mixed grill, a men's card room and bar, and a new men's locker room. The interior decorators for the additions were Holzheimer's Interiors. The Acacia Country Club currently owns 176 acres and is managed by Geo. Hindley. There are 440 members. Leonard Wall was the president of the club in 1986.

The **ACADEMY OF MEDICINE OF CLEVELAND** was formed on 28 May 1902 through a merger of the Cuyahoga County and Cleveland medical societies. Incorporating the best features of its predecessors, the academy had business handled outside of meetings and set up sections on experimental medicine and chemical pathology to meet the specialized interests of members. From its founding, the Academy of Medicine was closely allied with the CLEVELAND MEDICAL LIBRARY ASSOC., which provided a temporary home for section meetings. Until the library group erected a new building in 1906 behind its headquarters at 2318 Prospect, the academy held its general meetings in the Chamber of Commerce Bldg.; the new facilities featured an auditorium that provided a forum for medical discussion for physicians and local medical school faculties. The academy later followed the Library Assoc. to its new building on the Case campus, donated by Mrs. Francis F. Prentiss, widow of Dr. DUDLEY P. ALLEN, prime mover of the association. The meetings attracted an initial membership of 459, which grew to over 600 by 1912. To improve organization, a full-time executive secretary was hired in 1919, which made the academy the first in the country to employ a professional administrator. This move boosted membership to over 700 within 2 years and was the turning point for the academy; by 1926, there were over 1,000 members. In 1924, the academy was incorporated.

Throughout its history, the academy has been involved in community health issues and has promoted modern techniques through the mass media. In the 1920s, it successfully moved tonsilectomies from school clinics to hospitals. The academy presented a radio program and later public-health lectures that were popular Depression recreation. Other media attempts to make the public more health-conscious included the 1953 TV series "Prescription for Living" (which featured a doctor and actors from the CLEVELAND PLAY

HOUSE who dramatized a medical situation) and the 1958 radio panel show "The Doctor Speaks" (which became Blue Cross/Blue Shield-sponsored "Healthlines"). After 1962, the academy, which had always managed its own publicity, turned to an advertising agency and other media professionals to create a logo and monitor its public image.

The academy has carried on the public-health tradition of its predecessor societies. In 1957 it set up one of the world's first poison information centers. It orchestrated the Salk and Sabin polio campaigns of the 1950s and 1960s and the rubella campaign of the 1970s. When rising concern for the poor and medically disadvantaged peaked with the creation of Medicare and Medicaid in the 1960s, the academy deliberated on the effects of such programs on the medical profession; ultimately, after public debates on Medicare and national health insurance, it accepted the new programs. Concerned members helped create the HOUGH-NORWOOD FAMILY HEALTH CTR. and have been active in regional planning. In 1976 the academy reorganized into 5 divisions that reflected contemporary concerns: legislative and political affairs, ethical standards, peer review, and negotiation with third-party carriers. The Academy of Medicine of Cleveland was located at 11001 Cedar in 1986.

The **ACADEMY OF MUSIC** was probably the most famous theater in the history of Cleveland and one of the most celebrated in the U.S. It was also among the nation's best drama schools. The theater was built in 1852 by Chas. Foster of Pittsburgh, who ran it for a short period and then leased it to JOHN A. ELLSLER. The academy occupied the 3d and 4th floors of a brick building on the east side of Bank (W. 6th) St. near St. Clair St. (Ave). The theater was 200' long, 80' wide, and 27' high. The stage was 80' by 60'. The theater had good acoustics and seated more than 2,000. Among its elegant and grand qualities were gas footlights and a high chandelier that hung from the center of the auditorium.

The first performance was *The School For Scandal*. In addition to the many great actors who trained at the academy, a large number of famous actors of the period held starring roles in its productions, including John Wilkes Booth, Charlotte Cushman, and Jas. O'Neill, the father of the playwright Eugene O'Neill. The Academy of Music was also known as the Natl. Hall (1853–54); Foster's Varieties (1854–55); the Cleveland Theater (1855–59); and the Theater Comique (1888). On 30 June 1889, the Academy of Music was partly destroyed by fire. It was quickly rebuilt. On 8 Sept. 1892, the theater was completely destroyed by fire. It was rebuilt as a dance hall. Its walls were later incorporated into the Academy Bldg., a commercial structure.

**ACKLEY, HORACE A.** (1815–24 Apr. 1859), a "pioneer surgeon of Northern Ohio" and the first local physician to use ether as an anesthetic in general surgery, was the founder of the Cleveland Medical College, now the medical school of CASE WESTERN RESERVE UNIVERSITY. Born in Genessee County, N.Y., in 1815, the son of a farmer, Ackley attended public schools. From 1833–34 he attended lectures at the College of Physicians & Surgeons of the Western District of the State of New York, where he was a student of JOHN DELAMATER and a classmate of JOHN LANG CASSELS. He also studied medicine under a preceptor in Rochester. Although he did not receive a medical degree, he was licensed to practice by the state of New York in 1834.

After practicing medicine in Rochester for several months, Ackley moved to Akron, Ohio, in 1835, where he served as demonstrator of anatomy at Willoughby Medical College until 1842. During this period he moved first to Toledo to practice, and then, in 1839, to Cleveland, where he opened an office in partnership with Dr. M. L. Hewitt. He began using ether as an anesthetic in his surgical practice in 1847, only 3 months after the first public demonstration of its use in Boston. The first known ether-assisted operation in the WESTERN RESERVE was an amputation performed by Dr. Ackley. By 1850 he decided to confine his practice to surgery. Ackley became so well known and respected that in 1855 Stephen A. Douglas traveled to Cleveland to have Ackley perform surgery on his throat. Ackley performed what was then considered a daring surgical technique, whereby he removed Douglas's uvula. Douglas recovered without complication and went on to his famous debates with Abraham Lincoln. In addition to his practice, Ackley held posts as the attending physician to Cleveland's City Hospital and surgeon to the UNITED STATES MARINE HOSPITAL, and he was a member of the city's board of health. He was also a member of the Ohio State Medical Society, which he presided over in 1852.

A dispute among the faculty of Willoughby Medical College in 1842 precipitated the departure of Ackley and Drs. Cassels, Delamater, and JARED POTTER KIRTLAND from the school. Together they founded the Cleveland Medical College, under the charter of Western Reserve University, then located in Hudson. Ackley was elected professor of surgery, anatomy, and physiology during the first session. Subsequently he confined his teaching to surgery. In addition to giving 30 lectures per week, he conducted clinics in surgery and medicine. He resigned his professorship in 1856 on account of family difficulties. In 1849 Ackley organized a relief effort of doctors to aid cholera-stricken Sandusky and was credited with single-handedly stopping the epidemic. He was also instrumental in founding the Northern Ohio Insane Asylum in NEWBURGH in 1851. Ackley was an avid hunter and fisherman. He financed the first experiments in the artificial propagation of fish, which were performed on his farm. He was a member and warden of Trinity Church. In 1837, he married Sophia Howell of Willoughby. They had 1 son.

The **ACME-CLEVELAND CORPORATION** was formed in 1968 by the merger of the Cleveland Twist Drill Co. and the Natl. Acme Co. By 1980 it was one of the largest machine-tool manufacturers in the U.S., with net sales of $405 million that year. Cleveland Twist Drill began in June 1876 when JACOB COX, invested in a Dunkirk, N.Y., machine shop, which he moved to Cleveland in Sept. 1876. In 1880 Cox bought his partner's share of the business and then sold 40% of the company to FRANCIS F. PRENTISS. The firm of Cox & Prentiss became the Cleveland Twist Drill Co. in 1883 and in June 1888 moved to its long-time location at Lakeside and E. 49th St. In 1896 the company began opening sales offices in other cities and offering various benefits to its employees. By 1905 it had stockrooms in New York and Chicago, had formed a Mutual Benefit Assoc. for sick and injured employees, had opened a reading room, and was offering evening classes. In 1915 it began a profit-sharing program. By 1955 the company had stockrooms in San Francisco, Detroit, Dallas, and Los Angeles and a plant in Scotland. Growth also came through acquisitions: by 1965 Cleveland Twist Drill had acquired the Bay State Tap & Die Co. of Massachusetts and had purchased the Eastern Machine Screw Co. of Connecticut; it had also established a Canadian subsidiary.

The Natl. Acme Co. began in Hartford, Conn., as the Acme Screw Machine Co., founded in 1895 by mechanics Edward C. Henn and Reinhold Hakewessell. In 1901 the company moved to Cleveland, merging with the Natl. Mfg. Co., a parts manufacturer using Acme machines, to form the Natl. Acme Mfg. Co., located at 7500 Stanton Ave. President of the new company was Wm. D. B. Alexander; Edward Henn was general superintendent, and his brother, Albert W. Henn, served as secretary. In 1915 Natl. Acme purchased a major competitor, the Windsor (Vt.) Machine Co. In 1916 the company was incorporated as the National Acme Co. and began building a new plant at E. 131st St. and Coit Rd. The company closed its Stanton Ave. plant in 1923, consolidated its Windsor operations into the Coit Rd. plant in 1933, and ceased to manufacture and sell screw machine products, concentrating instead on the production and sale of the machines themselves. In 1956 sales reached $36 million, and by 1961 the company was expanding into foreign markets.

Acme-Cleveland suffered through an industrywide depression shortly after its formation, losing $578,000 in 1971. It then sought to expand by acquiring other companies. Such expansion increased sales to more than $400 million in both 1980 and 1981, but Japanese competition, a recession, and the corporation's own inefficiencies led to a loss of $31.9 million in 1983, when sales plunged to $172 million, and a loss of $11.4 million in 1984. To reduce operating costs, Acme-Cleveland began to restructure its operations in 1982, cutting its workforce from 6,300 in 1980 to 2,600 by 1984 and moving operations out of its "antiquated and non-competitive Cleveland facilities." In Oct. 1984, Acme-Cleveland acquired the Communications Technology Corp., a telecommunications equipment company of Los Angeles, in order to diversify from its traditional machine-tool business.

Acme-Cleveland Corp., *Communique* (June 1976, Cleveland Twist Drill Co. Centennial Edition).

Chapin, Frederick H., *National Acme: An Informal History* (1949).

**ADAMS, SEYMOUR WEBSTER** (1 Aug. 1815–27 Sept. 1864), was pastor (1846–64) of Cleveland's FIRST BAPTIST CHURCH. He was born in Vernon, N.Y. His father, a farmer, was a deacon in the Baptist church, and his mother was a niece of Noah Webster. Adams decided on the ministry as a youth—perhaps because of his home environment. After graduation from Hamilton College, he attended the Hamilton Theological Seminary. Ordained in 1843, Adams served in 3 churches in New York before accepting First Baptist's second call to him. He first preached as its minister in Nov. 1846. He was pastor there until his death. Adams was a carefully prepared sermonizer who was known among his contemporaries as scholarly, shy, and retiring. During 1858–59, he wrote a memoir of Dr. Nathaniel Kendrick, founder of the Hamilton Theological Seminary.

Although not a socializer or conversationalist, Adams was thought of as a contributor to the moral development of Cleveland and Ohio. He was an active pastor who oversaw the growth of First Baptist and was equally influential in the new congregations that it spun off. His life served as an example of moral rectitude and high purpose to his fellow citizens. He was still mourned 50 years after his death. Adams married 3 times: first to Caroline E. Griggs, who died in 1847; then in 1849 to Mrs. Cordelia C. Peck, a widow, who died in 1852; and finally to Augusta Hoyt in 1855. In the summer of 1864, he joined other volunteers of the U.S. Christian Commission in nursing Union soldiers in Washington, D.C. That led to a fatal bout with typhoid.

Bishop, J. P., *Memoir of Rev. Seymour W. Adams, D.D.* (1866).

**ADDISON, HIRAM M.** (21 Nov. 1818–14 Jan. 1898), was an early Cleveland settler, an educator, and a reformer. He was born to a pioneer Western Reserve family in EUCLID. Addison was educated in local schools and began a career as a teacher in eastern Ohio and western Pennsylvania, achieving a considerable reputation as an educator. He married Anna McCaslin, one of his pupils, in Pennsylvania in 1844 and moved to Warrensville. They settled in Cleveland in 1856. After his marriage, Addison ventured into journalism, becoming a writer for the *Ohio Farmer* in the 1850s. He founded, edited, or was associated with several newspapers in the pre-Civil War years, all ill-fated, including the *American Advertiser*, *Temperance Banner*, *Harpoon* (a temperance paper), and *Cleveland Commercial*. Addison developed an active interest in various social causes, particularly ABOLITIONISM and the plight of poor urban children. In 1874 he put into operation his Fresh Air Camp, a farm in Warrensville Twp. where indigent children could escape the city in the hot summer months. Addison hoped to influence such children through exposure to nature and organized recreation to strive for higher goals than their backgrounds presumably allowed. This idea was copied in hundreds of locations during the following decades, and is still a part of urban social work today. In 1879, Addison founded the EARLY SETTLERS ASSOC. OF THE WESTERN RESERVE, which provided a meeting place for members of the area's early families, worked to preserve local history, and promoted pride in Cleveland. The association was active in planning Cleveland's centennial celebration, and Addison himself originated the idea for erecting a log cabin on PUBLIC SQUARE that became a focal point of the festivities. Because of Addison's enduring interest in local affairs and his paternal care for the city's poor, he was known as "Father" Addison.

**ADOMEIT, GEORGE GUSTAV** (15 Jan. 1879–22 Nov. 1967), was a prominent Cleveland businessman and artist and a founder of the CLEVELAND SOCIETY OF ARTISTS. Born in Memel, Germany, he moved to Cleveland with his parents and brother at the age of 4, settling in what later became part of E. CLEVELAND. He attended district school on Euclid Ave. In 1887 his parents bought a home in Woodland Hills adjoining a wooded field with a stream and fishing hole. It was here that Adomeit first developed an interest in drawing, and he received encouragement from a Mr. Aborn, who was then the drawing supervisor of the public schools. In 1894, while attending Bolton School, Adomeit won a competition for a 4-year scholarship at the Cleveland School of Art, then located on Wilson Ave. Because the award was not available until after graduation from high school, he was also permitted to attend Saturday class and a weekly sketching class. While at the Cleveland School of Art, Adomeit secured an apprenticeship in lithography, and after serving as an apprentice for 3 years, he accepted a position as head of the art department's photoengraving shop.

In 1902 Adomeit and W. H. Webster bought the Mason Engraving Co. and changed the name to the Caxton Engraving Co. They began with 5 employees and increased to 25 the following year. In 1905 they incorporated and added a printing department and changed the name to the Caxton Co., Printers & Engravers. In the early 1920s this firm was rated one of the 5 outstanding printing concerns in the country. In 1925 Adomeit was chosen as an honorary member of the Society of Calligraphers by W. A. Dwiggins; members of this society were chosen for their accomplishments in the graphic arts. In 1937 he was elected president of the Caxton Co. and continued there as president and art director until his retirement in 1956.

Throughout his life, Adomeit kept up his interest in art, painting at night, on weekends, and on vacations. He was a prominent member and founder of the Cleveland Society of Artists a member of Cleveland's ROWFANT CLUB, and a member of the American Institute of Graphic Arts. His paintings and drawings were exhibited at 40 consecutive MAY SHOWS, where he won 24 awards. His paintings were exhibited in several major art galleries, including the CLEVELAND MUSEUM OF ART, the Detroit Institute of Art, the Toledo Museum of Art, and the Whitney Museum of American Art. In 1932 his painting *Hills of Ohio* was one of 46 gathered from various regions of the U.S., featuring the native element in contemporary American painting.

**AEROSPACE INDUSTRY.** For a city fascinated with things mechanical, in 1903 Cleveland seemed unimpressed by the first flight of a heavier-than-air machine by two Ohioans from Dayton, Orville and Wilbur Wright. The event received little attention in local Cleveland papers. This period was the heyday of the railroad, the bicycle, and infatuation with the motorcar. While the railroad represented a firmly established transportation industry, the airplane joined the motorcar and the bicycle as the more dangerous amusements for the amateur.

The daredevils of the period prior to WORLD WAR I flew, and often perished, in variations on the "Wright Flyer," a biplane consisting of double wings supported by wire struts and rods, fabric-covered fuselage with open cockpit, and simple piston engine. The skies were the purview of barnstorming pilots such as the itinerant Paul Beck, who in 1912, in debt, no doubt, from his aerial adventures, delivered the first official airmail souvenir postcards to residents on farms within a radius of several miles of Cleveland. However, it was not until European recognition of the military importance of the airplane during World War I that Cleveland, like the rest of the country, realized its commercial potential. Thompson Prods., Inc., then known as the Steel Prods. Co., successfully transferred the complex valve technology of the automobile engine to the airplane. Thereafter, as other local companies made this transition, Cleveland became known as a major producer of aircraft engine parts.

In 1917, near the end of World War I, 10 prominent Clevelanders raised enough capital to attract a talented, though somewhat eccentric, airplane designer, Glenn L. Martin, to the city. The new company built the city's first aircraft factory on St. Clair Ave. Martin brought with him a striking array of talent: chief designer and engineer Donald W. Douglas, who founded the Douglas Aircraft Co. on the West Coast in 1920; Lawrence Bell, later of Bell Aircraft, the designer of the first supersonic plane; and Jas. H. "Dutch" Kindelberger, founder of North American Aviation, Inc. The Glenn L. Martin Co. produced a commercially successful plane, the Martin MB bomber, which, according to the historian John Rae, was "probably the best combat plane designed in the United States during the war; although it was not ready for wartime service, it became the Army's first-line bomber for a good many years."

Martin was a friend of Louis W. Greve, president of the CLEVELAND PNEUMATIC TOOL CO. Faced with a surplus of pneumatic tools produced for World War I, in 1918 the company developed a new product, the Cleco-Gruss shock absorber for cars and trucks. Application of the Cleco-Gruss air-oil principle (oil to cushion the shock and air to give spring) to airplanes was the next logical step. It seems no coincidence that in 1926 the first "aerol struts," or hydraulic landing gear, were designed for a Martin airplane. Louis Greve personally tested his aerols day after day, riding a board suspended under the body of a plane to take moving pictures of this innovation. Cleveland Pneu-

matic's "aerols" quickly became standard equipment on all airplanes and ensured the commercial success of the company until the end of WORLD WAR II, when the companies with whom Cleveland Pneumatic Tool had shared its aerol technology to assist in the war effort became competitors.

Martin played an active role in making the city cognizant of the need for a suitable airport. An active member of the Cleveland Chamber of Commerce and chair of the Subcommittee on the Airplane Industry, in 1918 he served on a special committee to study possible sites. The committee helped establish the first regular airmail service between Cleveland and Chicago, in 1919, but failed to get the city to act on its recommendation for a municipal airport. Not until 1921, when the threatened loss of a position on the coast-to-coast airmail route precipitated the decision, did the city approve the airport plan of City Manager WM. R. HOPKINS and issue $1.25 million in bonds to purchase 700 acres of land at Brookpark Rd. and Riverside Dr., the site of the present CLEVELAND-HOPKINS INTERNATL. AIRPORT. The city hired Major John Berry, a renowned airfield expert, to design the airport. Berry remained in Cleveland to become first the manager of the airport and then commissioner of airports.

Its strategic location on major airmail routes made the new airport one of the busiest in the U.S. by the late 1920s. The number of airplanes using it increased dramatically, from an average of 4,000 in 1925, when the airport was officially opened, to 17,600 in 1928. The federal Air Mail Service moved its division headquarters to Cleveland in 1925, and improvements to the airport were made at government expense. After the Kelly Act was passed in 1925, the Detroit-Cleveland air route, run by Henry Ford, became the nation's first commercial airmail venture. Regular air passenger service was established between Cleveland and neighboring cities, and by 1930 volume was high enough to warrant installation of the first radio traffic-control system. Just as Cleveland was a major transportation center in the days of the railroad because of its strategic location, it became a major connecting link on transcontinental air routes.

However, in 1929, just as the future potential of an aircraft industry in Cleveland seemed assured, Glenn L. Martin made the decision to move his company to Baltimore. The Martin all-metal monoplane, suitable for both commercial and military aviation, was at the forefront of American aircraft manufacturing. For example, after a visit on 29 Aug. 1928 to the Cleveland plant, Geo. W. Lewis, director of research for the Natl. Advisory Committee for Aeronautics (NACA), wrote to Martin: "I feel, after seeing the work you are doing in metal construction, that in this particular line of development you are far ahead of any other aircraft manufacturers." Whether the city could have prevented the Martin Co., now the Martin-Marietta Corp., from leaving Cleveland is a question that requires further research. The Great Lakes Aircraft Corp., a locally sponsored company that built Navy torpedo planes, took over the Martin plant, but not its tradition of innovation. By 1935 it was out of business.

Despite the Martin Co.'s departure, Louis W. Greve and Frederick C. Crawford continued to believe in Cleveland as a center for aviation. In 1929 they made a strong bid to hold the NATL. AIR RACES at the Cleveland Airport because of its excellent facilities and location, which offered "a level, well-graded, perfectly drained area one mile square with approaches as nearly perfect and free from hazard as ever greeted a man from the air." After the enormously popular first race in Cleveland, the city obtained a sanction to host future races, which were held through

1939 (with the exception of 1930, 1933, and 1936) and resumed after the war. The races were a proving ground for increasing the speeds of aircraft. Some of the improvements made by ingenious mechanics were later adopted by the aircraft engine industry, which at the time did little research of its own. Thus, the races made Cleveland known in the 1930s as the "Air Laboratory of the World." They attracted such nationally known fliers as Roscoe Turner, Jimmy Doolittle, and Amelia Earhart. Chas. Lindbergh shared the viewing stand with Frederick C. Crawford, president of Thompson Prods., which sponsored the Thompson Trophy Race, a popular free-for-all with a rigorous course and impressive trophy.

In contrast to the solid backing of the air races by the Cleveland industrial community, amateur enthusiasm for rocketry in Cleveland failed to attract investment capital on a scale large enough to influence industrial development. A young German, Ernst Loebell, brought knowledge and the dream of space travel to Cleveland. He founded the CLEVELAND ROCKET SOCIETY in 1933 with Edward L. Hanna, who provided substantial financial backing in its early years. However, the society, despite a well-equipped proving ground on the Hanna estate, never launched a successful rocket. The society's failure to interest either the military or private industry in rocket development, and the coming of World War II led to its demise.

While rocketry languished, the wartime economy stimulated Cleveland's air-related industries. In 1943 an aircraft industry publication, *Aerosphere*, listed no fewer than 189 firms in the area that contributed to the aviation parts industry, reportedly furnishing about 25% of the wartime needs of the nation's aircraft industries. Thompson Prods. expanded substantially during the war, as did Cleveland Pneumatic Tool, Cleveland Graphite Bronze, Chase Brass, and Jack & Heintz, Inc. In addition, a huge plant to manufacture Boeing "Super Fortresses" was built by the government adjacent to the Municipal Airport at a cost of $57 million and was operated by the Fisher Body Div. of General Motors. Because of the shortage of skilled labor, women were trained in aircraft riveting, welding, sheet-metal forming, and hydraulics to staff the bomber plant. That proved a short-term investment. In 1945, only 2 years after the plant began production, it stood empty, a victim of postwar recession.

World War II stimulated aviation-related industrial research in Cleveland. General Electric's branch at NELA PARK, for example, carried on secret research on radar and special electronic equipment for aircraft, and Cleveland Graphite Bronze did advanced research on aircraft bearings. The Pesco Prods. Co., which manufactured aircraft pumps, did important testing in its special altitude chamber at its Taft Ave. plant, while the ALUMINUM CO. OF AMERICA used x-ray equipment to determine the composition of metals. Case Institute of Technology was also actively involved in wartime research in the development of heat-resistant materials, the chemistry of fuels, and synthetic rubber.

However, by far the largest and most important investment in large-scale aeronautical research was made by the government. In 1940, NACA selected Cleveland over 62 other cities as the site for its Aircraft Engine Research Laboratory. Its location at the western end of Municipal Airport, on land where the stands for 20,000 spectators for the air races had been erected only 4 years earlier, again symbolized the important role that the airport played in the growth of Cleveland. Frederick C. Crawford, then president of the Chamber of Commerce, and Clifford Gildersleeve, the executive secretary, both actively participated in the effort to bring the engine laboratory to Cleveland.

While the American military thought that the war would be won with conventional aircraft piston engines, experimental work on a new aircraft power plant, the turbojet engine, began in England and Germany in the late 1930s. Great Britain, fearing defeat, arranged to share this new technology with the U.S. The completion of the Altitude Wind Tunnel in 1944, at the time the largest facility of its kind in the world, made the Cleveland laboratory the premier institution for the fundamental research on jet propulsion, which engine companies such as Pratt & Whitney and GE used in the development of new engine designs.

The 1950s were a time of consolidation and strengthening of existing Cleveland companies. Aircraft technology was too complicated and too costly for new companies to compete with the airframe industry, now concentrated on the West Coast, and the established engine companies in the East. The pioneering days of Glenn L. Martin and Louis Greve were over. However, established companies such as Thompson Prods. benefited from the research of the Cleveland NACA laboratory. Its early involvement in the transition from the piston to jet engines secured its position as a major producer of parts for jet engines. In 1957 the Russians launched Sputnik, the world's first satellite, and the U.S. hastened to recapture its lost prestige by the formation of the National Air & Space Admin. Cleveland's NACA Lewis Flight Propulsion Laboratory became part of NASA, and its research in air-breathing engines was curtailed. Rocket research, particularly development work on upper-stage launch vehicles, became the focus of the institution in the early 1960s.

Some Cleveland industries kept pace with the shift into space. Even before the formation of NASA, Thompson Prods. was involved in missile work through government contracts. In 1958 it merged with the Ramo-Wooldridge Corp. of California to form TRW. An extensive involvement in the space program began at this time, which has continued to the present, principally in advanced electronic systems. The company continues to manufacture turbojet components and has an extensive research and development program. With diversification into technology for rocket motors, Cleveland Pneumatic, now a subsidiary of the Pneumo Corp., joined the small list of Cleveland's aerospace industries, which also includes smaller companies such as Reutter-Stokes, Inc., which specializes in electronic instrumentation for satellites and jet planes, and the Thompson Aluminum Casting Co., Inc., which makes magnesium and aluminum castings for airplanes and spacecraft.

Why Cleveland has played a relatively minor role in the development of the national aerospace industry is a question that has not been fully analyzed. Certainly, the city's industrial leaders during World War I did anticipate the commercial importance of aircraft, and they attempted to establish an industry at a time when capital was available and the necessary technology simple. Despite the Depression and the loss of the Glenn L. Martin Co., the city did not lose its enthusiasm for aviation. Its sponsorship of the Natl. Air Races helped to sustain public interest at a time when the military and Congress did little to encourage its development. Moreover, the location of the NACA's laboratory in Cleveland in 1940 shows the foresight of Cleveland's leaders in recognizing that government-sponsored research would become increasingly important as aircraft technology became more scientific. But Cleveland's interminable gray skies meant that the city could not compete with the attraction of year-round flying weather on the West Coast. No Chamber of Commerce program could prevent the concentration of the airframe industry there. Since these same airframe companies became the nucleus for the missile and later space-related industries, it is not surprising that Cleveland industries, with the exception of TRW, failed to become major aerospace contractors. What is ironic is that the founders of 4 of the major aerospace industries once worked under the same roof on St. Clair Ave.

Virginia Dawson<br>
Lewis Research Center, NASA

NASA Lewis Research Ctr. Archives.

Holmfeld John, "The Site Selection for the NACA Engine Research Laboratory: A Meeting of Science and Politics" (Master's essay, Case Institute of Technology, 1967).

The **AFRO-AMERICAN CULTURAL & HISTORICAL SOCIETY MUSEUM,** 1765 Crawford Rd., is a nonprofit cultural and educational museum seeking to build an international African and Afro-American history museum in the area. The purpose of the organization is "to eliminate the distorted portrayal of the images of black people" and to educate young people about the positive contributions blacks have made to the cultures of the world. The museum is largely the result of the efforts of one man, Icabod Flewellen (6 July 1916- ). Born the son of a railroad brakeman in Williamson, W.Va., Flewellen developed an interest in black history at an early age as he listened to his father describe black inventors' contributions to the railroad. At age 13, Flewellen began collecting newspaper clippings and other material and artifacts pertaining to black history; his early collection was destroyed in the 1930s when someone set fire to his home in West Virginia. In 1953 Flewellen moved to Cleveland. His new collection of materials became the nucleus of the Afro-American Cultural & Historical Society Museum (est. 15 Apr. 1953, inc. Dec. 1960), located in Flewellen's home at 8716 Harkness Rd. from 1953 until Mar. 1968, when it was moved to a classroom at St. Marian's School, 2212 Petrarca Rd. In May 1973, the collection of more than 200,000 items was moved to 1839 E. 81st St., where it was housed until the CLEVELAND PUBLIC LIBRARY leased Flewellen its Treasure House building on Crawford Rd. in Feb. 1983. Flewellen was forced to work other jobs to support his historical project; he was a messenger for the Veteran's Admin. for 21 years, then worked as a maintenance man at Case Western Reserve University during the 1970s. As interest in black history increased, he began to receive grants for special projects, such as a $10,000 grant from the CLEVELAND FOUNDATION in 1970 to catalog his collection. The Ohio Humanities Council and the Natl. Endowment for the Humanities also provided support, and in 1983 the museum received a $50,000 community development block grant for lectures to schoolchildren and community groups. In 1980, Flewellen received a number of local awards to honor his educational and cultural service to the community.

The **AGORA** was the heart of Cleveland's rock music scene through much of the 1970s. It was a popular night spot where the city's youth came to listen and dance to the tunes of such rock 'n' roll bands as the Blind Mouses, the Gozongs, and the Three Stumps. Owned by Henry Lo-Conti, the Agora opened on 6 July 1967. Its clientele consisted largely of area college students, as the club's early policy limited admission to college students only. Originally located at 2175 Cornell Rd., the Agora had an informal setting that resembled the decor of a ski lodge. In addition to an 80-ft. bar, the club also housed a poolroom. But primarily it served as a showcase for local and national rock groups.

The Agora's national talent buyer, Ricci Iacoboni, was a major force in bringing such luminaries as the Police,

Hall & Oates, and Bruce Springsteen to the club's stage. Other staff members included Joyce Halasa, LoConti's assistant, vice-president Buddy Mayer, and publicist Suzy Peters. The Agora celebrated its 15th year with a newly remodeled club. By the mid-1970s, the club, which was located at 1730 E. 24th St., expanded its acts to include jazz artists. Though it continued to promote regular rock slots, it began reaching out to a more musically diverse audience. The Agora's popularity peaked between 1978–79. The club fell on hard times as the disco era emerged. Cleveland's dance crowd withdrew its support from the Agora, which still offered live music, and began to frequent the discos. However, the Agora still drew capacity crowds to concerts by nationally known groups. The club closed in Oct. 1984 as the result of a fire that caused an estimated $30,000 damage. As of 1985, the club was planning to reopen in August in the renovated WHK Auditorium at 5012 Euclid Ave.

**AGRICULTURE.** The first settlers in Cuyahoga County, both the squatters who occupied favorable sites in advance of the surveys and the conventional landseekers who came later, followed the usual pioneer routine. They made clearances, planted corn, buckwheat, and rye, fenced in garden patches, and kept some oxen, cows, and swine. When the soil had been "tamed" by other crops, they sowed wheat. They carried on their activities in spite of malaria, the ravaging of crops by multitudes of squirrels, and attacks on their livestock by wolves. Many were really professional land clearers who, after a few years, moved on to repeat the farm-making process elsewhere. The remainder, like the incomers who bought partially cleared holdings, became "regular farmers."

The first settlers in a community under clearance had the advantage of a "newcomers' market." Arriving immigrants often had few or no livestock and before long exhausted the food supplies they brought with them, so that they had to buy locally, with the necessaries they obtained selling for their price in an older settlement plus the estimated cost of transportation. In parts of Cuyahoga County, the newcomers' market lasted till ca. 1810. A replacement came when during the WAR OF 1812 Cleveland became an accumulating point for Army supplies. After the war, Cuyahoga County shared the general agricultural depression afflicting the western country. Wheat, regarded as a dependable cash crop in ordinary times, did not pay for the cost of production, and with the exception of potash, other farm products were unsalable.

The depression continued until after the opening of the Erie Canal in 1825, when there came to be a demand for wheat to go eastward. A few years later the construction work on the OHIO AND ERIE CANAL provided a local outlet for supplies of all kinds and for man-and-horse labor. When the canal opened, there was a ready demand in the adjacent territory for wheat and other farm products, and Cleveland changed from a village to a bustling urban center. At the same time, Cuyahoga County became a region of old cleared farms. Most of the occupants engaged in a mixed agriculture, relying on an income from the sale of wheat, wool, and cattle. Some, however, became specialists.

The most important specialization was in dairying. As elsewhere, butter was manufactured for sale to peddlers and storekeepers. On some farms, as a New England inheritance, cheese might be made. From the early 1830s, Cuyahoga County had some farm dairies producing 3 or 4 tons of cheese annually, with a market being found in the southern states. While the county was much less important in cheesemaking than the Western Reserve counties to the east, its output of butter and cheese in 1839 was together valued at $96,083. In 1859 the county's production of butter was put at 1,162,665 pounds and of cheese at 1,433,727 pounds. During the 1840s, many farmers within a short distance of the Cleveland city limits were delivering milk to urban residents. Some sold at a market or by peddling through the streets, others to milkmen with routes. Their competition came from urban dairies, not from farmers more distant. As was the Western Reserve practice, the dairy farmers bought their cows from drovers in the spring and sold them off in the fall, congratulating themselves on their good judgment when they found a few good milkers among the nondescripts.

A second type of specialization was in horticultural products. The commercial growing of orchard fruits was confined to farmers in the townships along Lake Erie and was almost entirely in cherries and peaches. By mid-century these were being shipped by boat and rail to both eastern and western markets. The value of the orchard output in the county in 1839 was placed at $18,179, and in 1859 at $67,437. During the 1840s, grapes were grown in Cleveland and the northernmost townships primarily as a garden crop. There was in 1850 only 1 vineyard in the county; it was in the Euclid area and comprised 3 acres. By 1855, however, there were about 200 acres of vineyards near EUCLID. There was only a small production of wine: most of the crop was sent by rail as table grapes to eastern and midwestern cities.

A third specialization was in market gardening. This industry, which involved the growing of a variety of vegetables plus strawberries and other small fruits, was limited to the thinly populated parts of Cleveland and to its environs. As native-born Americans had no relish for the incessant spading, hoeing, and weeding required, it was carried on almost exclusively by European immigrants and their families. The value of production in 1839 was given as $4,554 (which was probably an understatement), and in 1859 as $61,192.

In general, Cuyahoga County farmers prospered during the 3 decades preceding the CIVIL WAR. As a consequence, they were able to improve their buildings and buy new types of implements as they became available. A few were even carried away by the national silkworm mania of the 1830s, and many more by the rage for exotic fowls ("the hen fever") that swept the country in the early 1850s. Like other Ohio counties, Cuyahoga in the pre-Civil War era came to have agricultural societies. Its first was organized in 1823 and held a few fairs or "cattle shows," but it attracted little general support among farmers, and so it disappeared about 1830. A second society, organized in 1834, was short-lived. The third came into being in 1839, held fairs in 1839, 1840, and 1841, and then suspended operations in 1842. The fourth was established in 1846 under the new state law that provided for a subsidy from the county treasury on condition of complying with certain conditions. This society proved successful, mostly because, like others of its time, it found a drawing card at its fairs in horse trotting. This society is still (1985) in existence, but its fairs have long since ceased to be essentially agricultural and have become primarily community homecomings.

In the half-century or so after the Civil War, Cuyahoga County farming became more specialized, especially dairying. Increasing urban demand led to a considerable expansion in dairy buttermaking. Dairy cheesemaking was superseded by the factory system, introduced ca. 1863. In 1875 there were 16 of the new factories in operation, and in 1880 about 20. All of them made butter as a sideline. Those west of the CUYAHOGA RIVER were operated by proprietors ("cheese kings"), and those east of it by co-

operatives of the type found in Geauga and Portage counties. The most significant development, however, involved the supplying of milk to the Cleveland market. A change came in 1868, when the first milk train began operating into Cleveland, from Willoughby in Lake County. It was followed by others on all the lines leading into the city, and before the end of the century by still others on the INTERURBANS. The first milk trains were passenger trains that took on milk cans as an express item at a special rate, but later they might be local freights running on a schedule.

The advent of the milk trains had important consequences. The Cleveland milkshed was shortly extended to around 30 mi. from the city limits, into the counties adjoining Cuyahoga. As the railroads carried milk cans at a flat rate, the milk suppliers near the city were at a disadvantage compared to remoter farmers with cheaper land. New dairying country developed ribbon-fashion along the railroads. With dependable transportation available, some dairymen were encouraged to engage in "winter dairying" (i.e., year-around production), which in turn meant that an improved system of feeding the milking cows through the winter was necessary. The answer was the introduction of silage, and the first silo in Ohio was built at NEWBURGH in 1880. There were few others in Cuyahoga County till after the famous Silo Convention at Cleveland in 1889, when silo construction flourished. By the mid-1890s, Cuyahoga reputedly had more silos than any other Ohio county.

As soon as the milk-train system became established, dairymen ceased to sell directly to consumers but marketed through middlemen in the city. After a few years, some of these middlemen established depots near the stations for buying and shipping milk. In a subsequent variation, they set up "creameries"—skimming stations with machinery to separate cream from milk. When farmers began to have separators at home, the creameries bought cream from those that did not ship individually to the city. Most of these creameries were equipped to make butter but usually did so only when the cream market was glutted. As the milk depots and creameries operated throughout the year and paid better for their supplies than did the cheese factories, the factories began to shut down or sold their facilities to their rivals; by the mid-1890s none remained in the county.

The farmers involved in the market-milk industry found that the returns were regular and dependable, and so they gradually cut back on their sheep, swine, and wheat acreage. However, the economic security they gained was offset by an erosion of their independence. They had to comply with the increasingly strict regulations of the CLEVELAND BOARD OF HEALTH. To be competitive with other suppliers, they had to replace their ordinary cows with those of popular dairy breeds. When they shipped directly to dealers, they had to adjust their workday to the milk-train schedules, which were usually so arranged that the milk would arrive in the city by 8 a.m. Perhaps worst of all, they were disposing of a perishable product to buyers who had an interest in keeping prices low and who found ways of having the suppliers assume all the hazards of the market.

In response to the unsatisfactory dealer-farmer relationship, some suppliers in the Cleveland milkshed in 1901 organized the Northern Ohio Milk Producers' Assoc. to establish a fair price for milk. This entity had some success in public relations but little otherwise, for its members tended to make individual contracts with dealers whenever it was to their advantage to do so. Its first real success came in 1916, when the Cleveland milk dealers refused to raise prices to reflect the increasing costs of labor and feed. The association suddenly revived and provided leadership in a short strike that involved picketing, dumping of milk, and an embargo on milk shipping. Owing in large part to intervention by the Cleveland Chamber of Commerce, a settlement was reached that was a definite victory for the suppliers, with the association being recognized as a contracting agent. It shortly began to function as the Ohio Farmers' Cooperative Milk Co., one of several such organizations in Ohio.

After the Civil War, commercial orchard production declined; cherries, peaches, pears, and plums had all become uncertain crops because of insect and fungus problems and met effective competition when there was an occasional good year. Many of the orchardists therefore turned wholly or partially to viticulture, and by 1890 there were 5,000 acres of vineyards in the county. They stretched somewhat intermittently from the Lake County line westward to the market gardens on the outskirts of Cleveland, with a smaller development west of the city. At least during the 1870s, more table grapes were being shipped from COLLAMER (southwest of Euclid) than from any other railroad station in the country; its only near rival was Dover (now WESTLAKE). Grape production in the county reached its maximum in 1899 at 11,591 tons. In 1919 it was 3,753 tons.

Vegetable growing also expanded after the Civil War. Potatoes, which had always been important for farm consumption, developed outstanding commercial significance—partly because of market availability, but also because the crop would fit into whatever rotation was being used, would leave the soil in good tilth, and was tolerable in its labor aspect when farmers bought the available planters, sprayers, and diggers. In 1909 Cuyahoga was the leading potato-producing county in Ohio, with 1,141,469 bushels. Then the industry fell off rapidly. In 1919 production was only 35.4% of what it had been in 1909, and indeed was lower than in any other census year since 1859. The decline was attributable to the increasing prevalence of fungus diseases and to soil depletion. Continued lack of profitability in later years meant that in 1929 the crop was only 5.6% of the 1909 figure, and in 1949 only 2.4% thereof.

The market-garden specialty (now usually called truck farming) grew in the Cleveland area in proportion to the increasing population. Another phase developed near BEREA, where in the 1870s some operators began onion culture on muck land, relying for labor on the wives of the Czech and Polish workers in nearby quarries. The business was at best a gamble and after about a decade succumbed to competition from more efficient producers elsewhere. Of much more importance was the forcing industry, the growing of vegetables under glass for the out-of-season market. Many of the truck growers near Cleveland became at least partially involved in it. In 1900 they had about 21 acres in hotbeds or cold frames and 4 acres in greenhouses, the latter concentrated in the Brooklyn area.

Cuyahoga County agriculture in the years after WORLD WAR I was in some respects simply part of the national pattern, with a general increase in mechanization. Fundamentally, however, its course of development was determined by the continued expansion of metropolitan Cleveland. The table shows the decline in farmland acreage and the dwindling number of farms from 1900 on. The reversion to farmland in the 1930s was attributable to the fact that many failed real-estate promotions were sold or rented to farmers.

Concurrently there was a change in the concept of what was meant by a farm. Ca. 1920, with the exception of a few "showplaces" belonging to wealthy Clevelanders, the farms were still operated in conventional fashion by either owner or tenant. Farms of under 10 acres constituted about 10% of the total, but these were usually in intensively cultivated truck crops. With the advent of the automobile, country dwellers could work in the urban sector, and city wage earners could move miles beyond the suburbs. As a result, subdivisions appeared along the roads to the metropolis, with landlords selling off lots on their frontage. Though these parcels were classified as farms, in some cases they served as sites for antique stores, beauty parlors, dog kennels, and other small enterprises, and in many instances the occupants used them primarily as dormitories. Thus, in 1949 (the first year for which such figures are available) there were in the county 136 farms reporting no sales whatever of agricultural produce, and 563 "part-time farms" that reported sales of less than $400. Many were chicken-and-egg farms, a kind that practically disappeared during the next decade owing to the growth of "chicken factories" in the South. The areas cultivated on the low-output farms were so small that there were 404 farms in the county without a tractor, a horse, or a mule.

Changing times made for important developments in the market-milk industry. Beginning in 1917, owners of heavy trucks competed in milk hauling with the railroads and trolley lines, offering the advantages of charging $.04 a can less, picking up the cans from stands at the farmers' gates, and returning them later in the day. They established regular routes with fairly dependable schedules. As early as 1919, wherever there were hardtop roads, the system of taking cans to stations or milk depots was almost a thing of the past. By 1925 some of the trucking lines collecting for the Cleveland market reached as far as Ashtabula and Trumbull counties. During subsequent years, Cuyahoga County milk producers met competition in their home territory from distant milksheds owing to the introduction of insulated tank cars and "vacuum-bottle" trucks, and like other dairymen, they suffered from the perennial surplus-milk problem. Perhaps their worst problem was that the rising price of land made dairying uneconomical. The average value of Cuyahoga County farmland per acre (with buildings) was $359 in 1945, $747 in 1950, $1,064 in 1954, and $1,650 in 1959. For these reasons, market-milk production declined sharply after World War II. In 1944, 236 farms sold a total of 9,094,182 lbs. of milk; in 1949, 144 farms sold a total of 7,467,972 lbs.; in 1954, 47 farms sold a total of 4,508,254 lbs.; and in 1959, 10 farms sold a total of 124,190 lbs. In 1964 there were only 100 milk cows reported, on only 7 farms. The industry was gone, leaving useless equipment and empty silos as a memento.

The expansion of the metropolis steadily nibbled away at the fruit-growing areas. From the 1920s on, the only orchard product worth even a mention was apples, and by 1959 their average value per farm reporting was only about $75. In 1978 there were still orchards on 25 farms, but collectively they comprised only 136 rundown acres. Viticulture also was declining. The production of grapes in the county was 2,849 tons in 1939, and 213 tons in 1978. In the last year only 17 farms were still in the business, with a total of just 59 acres of vines.

While the market-milk industry and horticulturel were disappearing, the truck-farming business continued to expand. Shortly after the milk haulers invaded the country-

|  | Percentage of county acreage in farmland | Number of farms |
|---|---|---|
| 1900 | 80.2% | 4,571 |
| 1910 | 73.5% | 4,493 |
| 1920 | 58.6% | 3,375 |
| 1930 | 18.6% | 1,229 |
| 1940 | 28.0% | 2,500 |
| 1950 | 17.4% | 1,589 |
| 1959 | 6.8% | 576 |
| 1969 | 3.6% | 272 |
| 1982 | 3.0% | 193 |

side, some truck farmers acquired vehicles, enabling them to extend the sphere of market gardening 15 mi. or so into the rural areas. They often resorted to direct marketing, erecting roadside stands. Expenses in the industry were high on account of the cost of land, the dependence on hired labor, the need for fertilizers, pesticides, and (later) herbicides, and sometimes the installation of sprinkler systems. At the same time, the operators had increased yields as a consequence of better cultural practices and more mechanization and often benefited from appreciating land values. As roads improved, they were able to extend their marketing area to include urban centers other than Cleveland, and by selling through cooperative associations they got a larger share of the consumer's dollar. After WORLD WAR II, there was a steady decline in open-air vegetable growing as holding after holding was swallowed up by the advance of the metropolis. Truck-farming production, however, continued to increase because many of the open-air growers added to their facilities and entered the forcing business.

The greenhouse sector of truck farming, at least in its concentration in the Brooklyn community, was not displaced by urban development. Nevertheless, the rising price of land meant that new facilities tended to be in other areas, and especially around OLMSTED FALLS. In the mid-1920s Cuyahoga was supposed to have about 160 acres under glass—now meaning almost entirely in greenhouses—more than any other American county. The maximum area under glass appears to have been reached ca. 1959, when the census reported 236 acres. Some of the greenhouses specialized in flowers for the florist trade, but most were devoted entirely to lettuce, tomatoes, and cucumbers. Owing partially to consolidation, but chiefly to the investment required, most of the greenhouse operators by 1982 were corporations or partnerships. In that year there were 16 farms (greenhouse establishments) having sales of over $250,000 each, with an average of $542,813. The county then had 122.5 acres under glass and an output of "nursery and greenhouse products" valued at $11,673,000, or 89.5% of the stated agricultural sales ($13,039,000) of the county. The census did not distinguish between the two branches, but nurseries were a small element in the county; in 1969 their sales had been 8% of the greenhouse sales.

Until well into the 20th century, living conditions among Cuyahoga County farmers were similar to those in other parts of Ohio. Much of the old-time isolation had disappeared with the advent of organizations such as the Grange in the 1870s and Farmers' Institutes in the 1880s and the introduction of the telephone and free mail delivery. After World War I there was a great improvement in amenities throughout the rural area. In 1930 almost half the farm dwellings had water piped into them. Of the 1,589 farms enumerated in the 1950 census, 1,380 had telephones, 1,531 had electricity from power lines, and 1,490 were on hard-top roads. During the 1920s, nearly every farm had an automobile or a pickup truck or both, and practically all had radios, as they would later have televisions. There were a few one-room schools left in the early 1920s, but these were soon replaced by consolidated ones. There were new organizations, some being economic, such as those involved in cooperative marketing, and others being educational and social, such as the 4-H clubs. Many of these organizations became victims of advancing urbanization, and doubtless others will likewise disappear.

The steady encroachment of metropolitan Cleveland meant that in 1982 the agricultural census classified only 8,854 acres (13.8 sq. mi.) in the county as "land in farms." The open-country farmland did not have an even border on its urban side, so that portions might at any time be lost to a factory site or shopping mall or new subdivision.

Moreover, the open-country acreage was not consolidated but was fragmented by limited-access roads, parkways, airports, golf courses, parks, reservoirs, and wasteland. While the agriculture was concentrated in greenhouse operation and other truck farming, there were perhaps still a dozen farms engaged in general husbandry, selling soybeans, shelled corn, melons, sweet corn, and some livestock. Of the 8,854 acres of farmland, 2,364 were in woods. Of the remaining area—classified as "cropland"—336 acres were used only as pasture, and 959 acres were lying idle. That would suggest that the land was unprofitable for agricultural purposes or that it was being held for speculation, or both.

The 1982 census is misleading because it gives the number of farms in Cuyahoga County as 193. Of these, only 135 had any "harvested cropland." As had been the pattern since the 1920s, many of the operators were engaged in agriculture only part-time or even not at all. Out of the 193, 97 reported their chief occupation as something other than farming, 89 reported that they did no work on their farms, and 57 reported working off the farm for 200 days or more during the year. No doubt they commuted throughout the week to factory or other jobs in the Cleveland or Akron area. All in all, outside the truck-farming sector, Cuyahoga County agriculture in the 1980s had become a marginal operation. As in other old rural complexes surrounding a megalopolis, the prospects were for a gradual further decline.

Robert L. Jones

**AIKEN, SAMUEL CLARK** (21 Sept. 1791–1 Jan. 1879), was the first resident pastor of Cleveland's FIRST PRESBYTERIAN (OLD STONE) CHURCH and was one of the most prominent clergymen in the city in the mid-19th century. He was born in Windham, Vt. He entered Middlebury College in 1813 and after graduation studied for the ministry at the Andover Theological Seminary. He was married twice; his first wife, Delia Day, died in 1838, and he married Henrietta Day in 1839. Ordained and installed as a Presbyterian pastor in Utica, N.Y., in 1818, Aiken followed some of his flock to Cleveland in 1835 by accepting their call to the pastorate of First Presbyterian. Until 1861 he guided this prominent congregation, using a commanding presence and conservative outlook to deal with the philosophical, religious, and political vicissitudes of the day. He helped a frontier community develop into a city. A supporter of public improvements, Aiken spoke at the opening of the Erie Canal before Gov. DeWitt Clinton of New York and gave a well-publicized sermon from his own pulpit to Gov. Reuben Wood and other notables on the importance of railroad improvements in Ohio (1851).

The quicksands of Millerism, Mormonism, Universalism, and skepticism threatened the solidarity of many Cleveland churches. Similarly, the great debate over slavery caused congregational strife. It is to Aiken's credit that while his church debated these issues, it, with one exception, did not divide over them. Besides heading his church, Aiken found the time to play a prominent role in the civic and cultural affairs of Cleveland. He presided at the organizational meeting of the Cleveland YMCA (1854), and his addresses and sermons on topics such as theaters, public education, CRIME, and TEMPERANCE were important opinion pieces among the business and professional classes of the city. Aiken's denunciation of slavery before the 1857 Presbyterian General Assembly, meeting in Cleveland, helped the church on a national level to understand that accommodation on this issue was no longer possible. It symbolized the final position of no compromise reached by moderate opinion-makers.

14

*Annals of the First Presbyterian Church of Cleveland, 1820–1895* (1895).

The **AIR FOUNDATION** was a nonprofit organization that specialized in grants and scholarships for space- and aviation-related purposes in the 1940s, 1950s, and 1960s. The foundation was incorporated in 1945 by Frederick C. Crawford (of Thompson Prods.), Alvin C. Ernst (Ernst & Ernst), W. Trevor Holliday (Standard Oil), and Albert J. Weatherhead (the Weatherhead Co.). Its original purpose as stated in the bylaws was "to promote, encourage, finance, and conduct . . . scientific investigation and research relating to the science or art of aerial transportation and navigation, and the design of materials for, and processes which may be used for, the construction and manufacture of all types of aircraft and parts." Less specifically, it hoped to make Cleveland the aviation center of America. Crawford was the first and only president, and Benjamin T. Franklin was the general manager throughout the foundation's existence. Other officers who served lengthy tenures were J. D. Wright, vice-president; John L. Dampeer, secretary; and Sidney Congdon, treasurer. The founders raised $250,000 as seed money for the foundation's programs. Early programs included the Natl. Aircraft Show, held in Cleveland in 1946, and a Natl. Model Plane & Space Show, which it helped sponsor annually for over 20 years. The foundation also sponsored and underwrote Cleveland NATL. AIR RACES, Inc., which directed the affairs of the races from 1946–60, when they were discontinued. From 1964–66, the foundation cosponsored the CLEVELAND AIR SHOW. During the 1960s it withheld support from shows that featured air races in view of tragic mishaps in earlier races. By 1968 the Air Foundation had contributed $40,000 in scholarships to Case Institute of Technology and $150,000 into the U.S. Services Relief Societies Fund. Throughout its existence, the foundation worked periodically with the Cleveland Board of Education and U.S. Dept. of Defense to promote interest in aviation among America's youth. In 1964 it was awarded the Meritorious Service Award by the Air Force for its leadership in the Natl. Air Races and Natl. Aircraft Show. The Air Foundation was affiliated with the Cleveland Chamber of Commerce, and later with the GREATER CLEVELAND GROWTH ASSOC. The foundation was dissolved 8 June 1970, largely as a consequence of the Tax Reform Act of 1969. All assets, approximately $200,000, and records were donated to the WESTERN RESERVE HISTORICAL SOCIETY.

The **AIR-MAZE CORPORATION**, manufacturer of a variety of air and liquid filters, was organized in 1925 by Albert E. Schaaf, a business executive in bicycle and automobile manufacturing. First located at 321 the CAXTON BLDG., 800–820 Huron Rd., the company originally made air filters for automobiles, but it soon became a pioneer in the development of a variety of filters. By 1944 it had designed filters of more than 3,000 types and sizes, including for use in industry, by the military, and in air-conditioning systems for homes, restaurants, and office buildings. By 1939, Air-Maze had moved to larger quarters at 5200 Harvard Rd. in NEWBURGH HTS. It employed 550 people in July 1953 when it moved into a new $1.75 million plant at 25000 Miles Rd. in BEDFORD HTS. It was purchased in 1959 for $4 million by the Rockwell-Standard Corp. of Coraopolis, Pa., and operated as a subsidiary of the corporation until 1961, when it became a separate division. A name change in 1968 made Air-Maze a division of the North American Rockwell Corp. In 1975, Rockwell decided to sell Air-Maze and 12 other divisions in its Industrial Components Group. Along with 10 other divisions, Air-Maze was purchased by investors headed by Edward C. Mabbs and became part of the new Pittsburgh-based Incom Internatl., Inc. In Nov. 1984, Air-Maze was purchased by an investment group led by Robt. S. Jepson, Jr., of Chicago and renamed the Air-Maze Corp. The corporation, which employed 220 people in 1983, manufactures air filters, air-oil separators, and liquid filters for use in aviation and transportation. In addition to its Bedford Hts. plant, Air-Maze has a plant in Greeneville, Tenn., and another in Warrington, England, which it operates as part of a joint venture with Locker Air-Maze.

The **AITANEET BROTHERHOOD ASSOCIATION** is a Lebanese-American hometown society formed in 1927 by a group of natives from Aitaneet in Lebanon's Bekaa Valley. The association has aided needy Lebanese and Syrians in Cleveland and in the village of Aitaneet, helping to build schools and other facilities there. Founder and first president of the organization was JAMIL KAIM; also among the founding members were Jas. Abood, Ernest Sabath, Mufleh Nahra, Geo. Bird, and Tom Abood. The organization grew quickly; by 1935 it had 140 members and a junior group active in sports. By 1955 it was estimated that 700 immigrants from Aitaneet had made Cleveland their home.

**ALBANIANS.** *See* **BALKAN IMMIGRANTS**

The **ALCAN ALUMINUM CORPORATION,** the 4th-largest aluminum fabricator in the nation, was created on 6 Jan. 1965 by its parent company, Alcan Aluminum, Ltd. This Canadian firm, formed in 1928, had served the U.S. for years as a supplier of aluminum ingots. In the early 1960s, it sought to enter the U.S. fabrication market. In 1965, the firm purchased the plants of the Natl. Distillers & Chemical Corp. and the Cerro Corp. and organized its American subsidiary. Although none of its plants were situated in Cleveland, Alcan chose the city as its American headquarters (moving into Erieview Plaza in 1966) because of its strategic location in America's industrial market.

At the time of its formation, Alcan had already established itself as a a producer of aluminum sheet and plate, building products, cable, paste, and powder, with about 2,000 employees in 6 plants. Under Eric A. Trigg and Eric F. West, the company spent its early years consolidating its holdings and broadening its product line to make it more competitive with other aluminum fabricators. In 1969, it initiated an acquisition program, becoming a distributor of aluminum and other metal products and entering the foil business. By the early 1970s, Alcan was producing sheet metal for the canning industry. Within 10 years of its establishment, the company was among the top aluminum manufacturers in the country.

The late 1970s were a period of tremendous growth for Alcan, culminating in a record-breaking year in 1980. The firm continued to bolster its product lines through acquisitions and plant expansions, began to lay the groundwork for producing its own aluminum ingots in the U.S., and ventured into the recycling and automobile industries. The recession of the early 1980s brought an abrupt end to this growth, as Alcan lost $58 million in 1982. That led to some cost-cutting measures and studies of new product markets. By late 1983, the aluminum industry began to rebound, with Alcan maintaining a staff of 200 in Cleveland and 4,700 nationwide, with operations in 30 states.

The **ALCAZAR HOTEL,** at Surrey and Berkshire roads in CLEVELAND HTS., was built as a residential apartment hotel in 1923, one of the earliest suburban hotels in the Cleveland metropolitan area. It is designed in a Spanish-Moorish eclectic idiom, intentionally reminiscent of the complex in St. Augustine, Fla., that includes the hotels Ponce de Leon and Alcazar, built by Carrere & Hastings for HENRY FLAGLER, one of the original partners of Standard Oil, in the 1880s. The Spanish style is established by the overhanging red tile roofs, the arcade of long windows on the 4th floor of the facade, and the covered arcade in the patio. The hexagonal interior lounge is decorated with colored glazed tiles similar to those in the Alcazar in Seville. In the center of the patio garden is a circular fountain with a tall palm-tree finial and spouting frogs and turtles, copied from the one in the court of the Hotel Ponce de Leon. The architect was Harry T. Jeffry, and the sculptural work was by the firm of Fischer & Jirouch, the primary decorative artisans of Cleveland in the 1920s. The hotel catered to a residential and family clientele, and in the 1920s and 1930s dining and dancing, tea dances, and afternoon musicales were held. In the mid-1970s the hotel was acquired by Western Reserve Residences, a Christian Science organization, as a private retirement residence.

The **ALCO STANDARD CORPORATION** is a leading firm in the manufacturing, distribution, and resource fields. Although its headquarters are in Pennsylvania, Cleveland has played a significant role in the development of this company. Several Clevelanders helped to establish Alco Standard in 1965. It is the 7th-largest corporation in Cleveland, with approximately 20 facilities in the area employing 2,000 people. Its principal founder and first president, Clevelander Tinkham Veale II, conceived the company's philosophy of "corporate partnership"—acquiring numerous small, privately owned companies and allowing them to continue under their own management while providing them with financial support and advice.

Veale, with John T. Vaughn, first practiced this philosophy with the Cleveland-based Jackson Prods. Co., which they acquired in 1952 to manufacture and market technical products. In 1960, the firm began to diversify by acquiring small, privately owned companies, and a parent company, V&V Companies, Inc., organized in 1961. By 1964, V&V controlled 15 companies, including 2 Cleveland firms—the Gas Machinery Co. (founded 1902) and Gas Atmospheres, Inc. (1946), manufacturers of gas-producing equipment and industrial furnaces. Both Veale and V&V had purchased major interests in Philadelphia's Alco Chemical Corp., and in the fall of 1965, Veale directed the merger of V&V and Alco to produce the Alco Standard Corp., with interests in the chemical, electrical, and metallurgical fields.

Diversified from its inception, Alco Standard continued to broaden its holdings, but set strict standards for the firms it acquired. By 1971, it had acquired 80 companies, including several from the Cleveland area, manufacturing a variety of products—Pyronics, Inc. (1953), industrial combustion equipment; the Tempo Prods. Co. (1947), spray paint and parts for automobile, aviation, and marine industries; the Flodar Corp. (1945), hydraulic tube and pipe fittings; the Walker China Co. (1923), vitrified china for restaurants and institutions; Advanced Dynamics, Inc. (1957), thermocouples; the American Stamping Co. (1922), metal stampings and tools and dies for automobile and appliance industries; the Cleveland Range Co. (1933), the leading manufacturer of steam-cooking equipment; the Otto Konigslow Mfg. Co. (1876); the Kilroy Structural Steel Co. (1918), fabricators of steel for the aviation and construction in-

dustries; and Wheelock, Lovejoy & Co., Inc. (1846), distributor of steel.

Alco entered the leisure industry in 1967, the distribution business in 1968, the resource field in 1970, and the health-service industry in 1977. To manage its ever-growing number of companies, it periodically reorganized itself into various divisions. Two of these, the Specialty Prods. and the Metal Source groups, have their headquarters in Cleveland. After a disappointing year in 1972, Alco Standard halted its acquisitions and concentrated on internal growth. In 1976, the company resumed acquisition activity but maintained a policy of disposing of unprofitable firms, such as Advanced Dynamics, Walker China, Pyronics, and American Stamping. The diversity and acquisition/disposal policy of Alco brought it phenomenal growth into the early 1980s, despite the recession. By 1982, it had reached $2.8 billion in sales, with 17,000 employees in 368 facilities in 42 states and 10 foreign countries.

Alco Standard Corp., *The First Decade* (1976).

The **ALI-WEPNER FIGHT** on 24 Mar. 1975 was the first major boxing match in Cleveland since the SCHMELING-STRIBLING FIGHT of 1931. The contest unevenly matched the reigning heavyweight champion of the world, Mohammed Ali (formerly Cassius Clay), against Chuck Wepner, a liquor salesman from Bayonne, N.J. Because Wepner was not among the World Boxing Council's top 10 contenders (he ranked #13), the contest was not sanctioned as a title match, but it was promoted as seriously as if it were by the flamboyant local promoter Don King. The fight, to be held at the Richfield Coliseum, was to be preceded by a televised bout between Geo. Foreman and Oscar Bonavena; both spectacles would be seen at the Coliseum and 98 locations in Greater Cleveland via closed-circuit TV and broadcast throughout the world. Regardless of the outcome, Ali was guaranteed $1.5 million (plus $200,000 for training camp), and Wepner was guaranteed $100,000. Ticket prices were set at $10-$75, and 4,200 tickets were quickly sold. Don King tried to promote the fight in the black community, which was notoriously unsupportive of events at the Coliseum, since it was inaccessible to many inner-city people. When Ali arrived in Cleveland 10 days prior to the fight, he sported a roll of fat around the midriff, and was admittedly undertrained and overtired—but, he proclaimed, in good enough shape to beat Wepner. He trained, jogged through the Metroparks, and focused attention on his religion by underwriting a mosque that had formerly been a Federal's Dept. Store in the Lee-Harvard area. In the ring, Ali employed his game plan for 9 rounds until Wepner stepped on his toe, causing him to lose his balance and fall down. He had previously ignored Wepner's punches to the back of his head, but now Ali turned on his opponent for 6 more rounds scoring a technical knockout in round 15. The referee ended the fight when Wepner got up with 19 seconds of the countdown remaining but was obviously too weak to continue. Wepner, known as the Bayonne Bleeder for his tendency to bleed easily, was sent off to an Akron hospital, while Ali basked in victory. The fight, with its expected outcome, was fought before 14,000 fans.

The **ALIENED AMERICAN** not only was Cleveland's first black newspaper but apparently was also intended as a regional. It was founded at the urging of the Ohio and Natl. Conventions of Colored Freemen from 1849-53. Three editors finally produced the paper's inaugural issue on 9 Apr. 1853, at a time when they claimed there were only 2 other black papers in publication in the entire country. WM. H. DAY, a graduate of Oberlin College, was the paper's actual editor-in-residence. He obtained the aid of corresponding editors Rev. Jas. W. C. Pennington of New York and Samuel Ringgold Ward, a former slave then living in Toronto. After the appearance of the initial issue, the *Aliened American* seems to have suspended publication for several weeks in order to assemble its subscription list. Thereafter, it published weekly until 1855, when Day moved to a black settlement in Buxton, Ontario. It continued as a monthly, renamed the *People's Exposition* for another year. The void left by its passing was filled for a time by the appearance of another black paper, the *Herald of Freedom*, which was begun in Cincinnati by Peter H. Clark in 1853.

The **ALLEGHANY CORPORATION,** an investment holding company chartered in Maryland in 1929 and with its headquarters in Cleveland, was created in an attempt to secure ICC approval for a new railroad trunk line. Investing largely in railroad securities, Alleghany was originally financed through its holding of the Van Sweringen brothers' stock in 5 eastern railroads. Alleghany's collapse in 1935 resulted in congressional hearings that became the focal point of national railroad policy (see VAN SWERINGEN, M. J. & O. P.; CONRAIL; SHAKER HTS).

In 1915 the Van Sweringens sought the advice of their friend Alfred Smith, president of the New York Central Railroad, on securing public rail transportation between Cleveland and their suburban Shaker Hts. development. At that time the NYC was seeking to divest the Nickel Plate Railroad, which operated most of the right-of-way through Cleveland necessary for Shaker rail service. With the aid of Morgan & Co., owners of the NYC, the Van Sweringens in 1916 formed a holding company and secured the financing for the $8.5 million purchase of the Nickel Plate. With this purchase, the Van Sweringens began creating a complicated and convoluted railroad empire, which at its height had a value of $3 billion and operated more miles of main track than any other eastern line. During the following years, the Van Sweringens continued acquiring other railroads through newly created holding companies financed by Morgan and its satellite Guaranty Trust.

Alleghany was hard hit by the Depression, averting collapse only through loans from Morgan and Guaranty. By 1932 several Van Sweringen railroads were bankrupt, while Alleghany stock plummeted to several dollars a share, yet Alleghany remained solvent as the Reconstruction Finance Corp., and banks continued loaning it money for interest payments on its bonds. In 1935 the banks, deciding against further help, foreclosed in an attempt to salvage some of their holdings. At auction the Alleghany and the Van Sweringens' assets were purchased for almost $3 million by Midamerica, a holding company organized by Geo. Ball to salvage the Van Sweringen interests. With the death of the Van Sweringens in 1935 and 1936, Ball lost interest in Alleghany, selling it in 1937 to a group headed by Robt. Young, who moved its operations to New York City.

**ALLEN, DUDLEY PETER** (25 Mar. 1852–6 Jan. 1915), was the founder of the CLEVELAND MEDICAL LIBRARY ASSOC. and an eminent physician, surgeon, and professor. Born in Kinsman, Ohio, he was the son of Dudley Allen and the grandson of PETER ALLEN, both well-known and successful doctors. Following the death of his mother in 1862, Allen moved to Oberlin to attend the preparatory school of Oberlin College. He graduated with an A.B. from Oberlin in 1875 and went on to Harvard Medical School, where he received his M.D. in 1879. After graduation, Allen took a post as the house surgeon at Mas-

sachusetts General Hospital. A year later he resigned to continue his studies abroad. He settled in Cleveland in 1883.

Allen was primarily interested in surgical procedure and was one of the first Cleveland physicians to confine his practice to surgery. He was elected visiting surgeon of both Charity and Lakeside hospitals, where he became surgeon-in-chief. His contributions to medical literature include scholarly articles on surgery and medical ethics and a history of medicine in the WESTERN RESERVE. Allen began his teaching career as a lecturer in minor surgery at Western Reserve Medical College, a position he held from 1884–90. In 1893, he was elected to the Professorship of Principles & Practice of Surgery. He became professor emeritus of surgery in 1910 and senior professor of surgery in 1911. Allen was an active member of the Ohio State Medical Society, which he presided over in 1892, and the American Surgeons Assoc. He served as that organization's secretary in 1901 and a president from 1906–07. He was elected an honorary fellow of the Philadelphia Academy of Surgery in 1906 and of the American College of Surgeons in 1914.

A connoisseur of fine arts and a recognized expert in Chinese porcelain, Allen became one of the first trustees of the CLEVELAND MUSEUM OF ART. He was also a trustee and life member of the WESTERN RESERVE HISTORICAL SOCIETY. Oberlin honored him with an M.A. in 1883 and an LL.D. in 1908. He was elected a trustee of the college in 1898, a post he served until his death. One of Allen's most lasting legacies is the Cleveland Medical Library Assoc., founded in 1894. He was the driving force behind its development, served as president from 1903–06, and donated his entire library to it upon his retirement. The Allen Memorial Library building was made possible through the gift of his widow, Elisabeth Severance Prentiss, whom he married on 4 Aug. 1894. Allen was also active in nonprofessional organizations, including the UNION, ROWFANT, and UNIVERSITY clubs and the Second Presbyterian Church. In 1910, he resigned all of his positions and retired from practice. He and his wife toured around the world. Upon their return, Allen settled in New York City, although he maintained a residence in CLEVELAND HTS. He died of pneumonia.

Hudson, Dr., "Dudley P. Allen," Allen Memorial Library Archives, Cleveland.

**ALLEN, FLORENCE ELLINWOOD** (23 Mar. 1884–12 Sept. 1966), was a suffragette and jurist whose career marked a series of firsts for women serving in the legal field. Allen was born in Salt Lake City, Utah. Her parents came from collegiate backgrounds; her father was once a professor at Western Reserve University. She prepared for college at the Salt Lake Academy and the New Lyme Academy in Jefferson, Ohio, and attended WRU from 1900–04, majoring in music. From 1904–1906, Allen studied piano in Berlin while serving as assistant correspondent for the *Musical Courier* and music editor for the *German Times*. After a nerve injury ended her goal of a music career, she returned to Cleveland to become the *Plain Dealer*'s music critic and a teacher at LAUREL SCHOOL. Law then became her main interest; she received an M.A. in political science and constitutional law from WRU in 1908.

After being rejected by WRU's law school because of her sex, Allen attended law school at the University of Chicago (1909–10), and received her law degree from New York University (1911–13). In 1914, she was admitted to the Ohio bar and began practicing law. Allen was also an ardent suffragette. She successfully argued the E. Cleveland women's suffrage case before the Ohio Supreme Court in

1917; this case upheld the right of Ohio cities to grant women municipal suffrage.

Each of Allen's positions marked a first for women. She was appointed an assistant county prosecutor in 1919. In 1920, she was elected a common pleas court judge. Here she was the first woman to preside over a 1st-degree murder trial and to pronounce the death penalty. Her next first was election to the Ohio Supreme Court in 1922; she was reelected in 1928 by a wide margin. In 1934, Pres. Roosevelt appointed Allen a judge of the U.S. 6th Circuit Court of Appeals. One of her most noted cases was the 1937–38 TVA case; her opinion that the Tennessee Valley Authority was constitutional was upheld by the Supreme Court. Presidents Roosevelt and Eisenhower both considered her for a Supreme Court appointment. In 1958, Allen became chief judge of the 6th Circuit, the first woman chief judge of any federal court. She retired from active duty in 1959 but kept the title of chief judge and remained on call for special assignment.

Allen was a respected writer and worldwide speaker. Her books include *This Constitution of Ours* (1940), *The Treaty as an Instrument of Legislation* (1952), and her autobiography, *To Do Justly* (1965). Human rights, cultural relations, and international law were her favorite speaking topics. During the 1920s, she was active in the movement to outlaw warfare; throughout her career, she stressed the need for a substantive body of international law to prevent illegal warfare by nations. She never married.

Tuve, Jeanette, *First Lady of the Law* (1984).
Florence E. Allen Papers, WRHS.

**ALLEN, JOHN W.** (1802–5 Oct. 1887), was a pioneer, railroad developer, lawyer, and editor of the Whig publication *Cleaveland Advertiser*. He served 2 terms as mayor of Cleveland, 1841–43. Born in Litchfield, Conn., the son of a lawyer, Allen attended school in Chenango County and graduated from Harvard in 1825. He came to Cleveland in 1826 and studied law under Judge Samuel Cowles. In 1828 he married Anna Marie Perkins, who died a few months later. He married Harriet C. Mather in 1830; they had 3 children, James, William, and Louisa.

In 1831 Allen wrote the initial editorial for the *Cleaveland Advertiser* and thereafter served as an editor. In the following year he became director of the COMMERCIAL BANK OF LAKE ERIE, where he remained until 1842. He incorporated the CLEVELAND & NEWBURGH RAILROAD in 1834; he helped organize the Columbus & Cincinnati Railroad in 1835; and he was president of the CLEVELAND INSURANCE CO. and was among the 6 incorporators of the Ohio Railroad Co., which failed during the panic of 1837. He funded various other railroad ventures and in 1849 became the president of the Society for Savings. He assisted in the incorporation of the Trinity (Episcopalian) Parish of Cleveland in 1828. He was vestryman and warden of the parish.

Allen's public career began in 1828, when he petitioned Congress for aid to build a harbor in Cleveland. In 1832 he established the city's first board of health during the CHOLERA EPIDEMIC. From 1831–35 he was elected annually as president of the village of Cleveland's board of trustees. In 1833 he incorporated the CLEVELAND LYCEUM. He was elected to the Ohio Senate in 1835, and in 1836 he began 2 terms in Congress as a representative from Cuyahoga County; there he became good friends with H ary Clay. In 1841 Allen became Cleveland's fourth mayor. As mayor he led a delegation to the Chicago Convention of 1847 in opposition to Jas. K. Polk. He eventually became a Republican. In 1870 Allen was elected postmaster, a po-

sition he held for 2 terms. In 1879 he helped form the EARLY SETTLERS' ASSOC. of Cuyahoga County and served as its vice-president.

**ALLEN, PETER** (1 July 1787–1 Sept. 1864), was a prominent pioneer doctor in the WESTERN RESERVE. Born in Norwich, Conn., he obtained a preliminary education at the Norwich Academy and later taught there for 2 years. He received his medical education under Dr. Phineas Tracy in Norwich. In 1838 he received an honorary degree from Jefferson College. He married Charity Dudley on 13 May 1813. Their only child, Dudley Allen, succeeded his father in his practice. Allen began practice in the Kinsman, Ohio, area in 1808. In 1812 he was appointed surgeon in the Western Army under Gen. Simon Perkins and served in the campaign on the Maumee River. He served as censor at the Medical College in Willoughby and later in the Cleveland Medical College. In 1835 he was elected first president of the Ohio Medical Convention, an organization that later fostered the Ohio State Medical Society. He was elected president of the society in 1856.

Dr. Allen's practice at one time covered 12 townships in northeastern Ohio and western Pennsylvania. In addition to the general practice of medicine, he performed various surgical operations, which included ligation of the femoral artery for aneurysm; tracheotomy; amputations of the leg, thigh, arm, and shoulder joint; and operations for strangulated hernia and removal of tumors. These were performed without the use of an anesthetic. Before the establishment of medical schools, Allen usually had 3 or 4 students studying under him. His saddlebags and their contents are exhibited at the HOWARD DITTRICK MUSEUM OF HISTORICAL MEDICINE in Cleveland.

The **ALLEN THEATRE**, 1501 Euclid Ave., opened on 1 Apr. 1921. It joined the Ohio, State, and Hanna theaters, which had debuted only weeks before. The Allen was constructed in conjunction with the Bulkley Bldg., an 8-story office building on Euclid Ave., just east of E. 14th St. Designed by architect C. Howard Crane, the $1 million showplace was developed by 2 Canadian theater impresarios, Jules and Jay Allen of Toronto. An ornate lobby led to a pillared Italian Renaissance rotunda, its dome 33 ft. high. Travertine marble covered the floors, and Tennessee marble the walls. The balcony seating area was reached from another domed entrance hall, while yet a third dome graced the main arena. Altogether, the Allen could seat 3,003 patrons in opulent surroundings. *The Greatest Love* was the Allen's premiere feature. The silent movie was accompanied by music from a $40,000 pipe organ. Because the Allen brothers were not affiliated with a major motion-picture circuit, they experienced difficulty in securing first-run features. In 1932, RKO took over. In 1949, Warner Bros. joined in the theater's management, and finally, in 1953, Stanley-Warner Theatres assumed the lease of the theater. In 1961, $500,000 was spent to renovate the Allen. Seating was reduced to 2,800, the halls were refurbished, and new projection equipment was installed. The investment sought to strengthen the house's position at a time when downtown movie houses were losing audiences to newly built theaters in the suburbs. The investment, however, did not reverse the trend. Diminishing audiences led to Stanley-Warner's decision to close the theater. Its final day was 5 Mar. 1968. In 1970, the Playhouse Square Assoc. began an effort to restore theater life to the district. The Allen was the first theater to receive the group's attention. In 1971, the Budapest Symphony Orchestra played before a full house at the Allen, giving evidence that audiences could again be attracted to the downtown theaters. The

Allen hosted a total of 16 events before the association's attention shifted to the STATE THEATRE. In 1976, the Allen's lobby and rotunda were converted into a restaurant; its original architecture was carefully preserved. In July 1982, the CLEVELAND FOUNDATION purchased the Bulkley Bldg. and its component Allen Theatre. The foundation's intention was to guarantee the preservation of the theater until it could join the ranks of the newly restored neighboring PLAYHOUSE SQUARE edifices.

The **ALLIANCE OF POLES OF AMERICA**, with headquarters at 6968 Broadway, is a fraternal-insurance organization founded in Cleveland by 68 dissatisfied members of the Polish Natl. Alliance. By 1980 it had more than 20,000 members, and in 1983 it had assets of more than $7 million. The alliance was established in Sept. 1895 by members of Group 143 of the PNA. Led by Thos. Zolnowski, a grocer, these men were upset with the PNA's decision to admit as members Poles who were not Catholic. Resigning from the PNA, they met on 22 Sept. 1895 to create a new organization, and the following week they named their group the Alliance of Poles of Ohio. Zolnowski was elected chairman of the new organization, Teofil Golembiewski vice-chairman, Thos. Rutkowski secretary, and Joseph Deranek treasurer. Other disgruntled members of the PNA left it to join the new alliance, which held its first convention in St. Stanislaus's Parish Hall on 2 Jan. 1897. Its treasury then held $1,918. By its 1903 convention, the alliance had expanded its membership to other cities; the convention that year was held in Toledo. The treasury had also grown, to more than $20,000 in 1903. By 1906 membership had increased to 523, and the treasury to nearly $30,000.

By mid-1917 a sufficient number of Poles living outside of Ohio had joined the alliance to warrant a name change for the organization. In July the Alliance of Poles of Ohio became the Alliance of Poles of America. In 1925 the alliance began construction of its $180,000 headquarters at Broadway and Forman avenues; when the Alliance of Poles Hall was opened on 7 Feb. 1926, it contained an auditorium, offices, and meeting rooms. A library was soon added. The organization had 17,000 members at the time. Membership declined over the next decade, falling to 13,000 members in Ohio, Pennsylvania, and Michigan in 1935; 8,000 of these belonged to the 66 Cleveland branches of the alliance. Although membership fell, the alliance expanded its range of activities, beginning a newspaper, *Zwiazkowiec* (the Alliancer), and contributing to charitable and educational efforts to benefit Poles both in the homeland and in the U.S. Assets of the organization totaled more than $1 million in 1935, with $8 million worth of insurance in force.

The assets of the organization continued to grow, reaching $4 million in 1960. By 1973 the alliance had 15,000 members in 60 lodges in the Cleveland area and continued its work as both an insurance and a social organization. In addition to insurance, it offered mortgage loans, maintained a welfare fund for sick or disabled members, and awarded college scholarships. It also sponsored sports activities, a drama club, a scouting program, and showings of Polish films. By 1980, the number of lodges in the Cleveland area had declined to 29.

Alliance of Poles of America Records, WRHS.

The **ALLIANCE OF TRANSYLVANIAN SAXONS** is a national Saxon fraternal benefit society with its headquarters and origins in Cleveland. First organized as a sick-benefit society in 1895, the organization had grown to 9,000 members in 34 branches in 1981. The first Transylvanian Saxon Sick Benefit Society was organized by 27 men on 1 May 1895. Geo. Sift, a machinist, served as the first president. The Cleveland group took the lead in bringing together representatives of other Saxon groups in Erie, Pa., on 5 July 1902 to form the Central-Verband der Siebenburger Sachsen, which in 1965 changed its name to the English translation, the Alliance of Transylvanian Saxons. The first national convention of the national group, held in Cleveland on 31 Aug. 1902, established the branch system. The Cleveland group formed in 1895 became Branch 1, and 2 other Cleveland branches were recognized, branches 3 and 4. In 1907, Branch 1 purchased a site at 7001 Denison as the location for its meeting hall. The building was enlarged in 1910 to include a large dance hall, 2 bowling alleys, a dining room, and a music room; further remodeling occurred in 1925. Known as the WEST SIDE SACHSENHEIM and still in use in the 1980s, the hall became an important meeting hall and social center for the local Saxon community. In 1911, another local group, Branch 33 of the alliance, which had been formed in Sept. 1910 with Geo. Schneider as president, established its headquarters at 1300 E. 55th, known as the East Side Sachsenheim, which it used until ca. 1963. By 1935, Branch 1 had 550 members, and Branch 33, 300. Just as it took the lead in forming the national Transylvanian Saxon alliance, Branch 1 was active in forming other Saxon organizations in the Cleveland area. It established a youth branch in 1926, which lasted until 1967, and it helped form the Saxon Veterans Assoc. in 1946, a bowling league in 1954, an auxiliary committee in 1963 to bring in additional income for its Sachsenheim, and the German Music School in 1967. The cooperation among various Cleveland-area Saxon groups to raise funds and support the war effort during WORLD WAR II later led to the formation of the United Saxon Committee of Cleveland; it has served to promote Saxon customs and culture. In 1974, the national Alliance of Transylvanian Saxons bought a 2-story building at 5393 Pearl Rd. in PARMA as an investment and to serve as the group's national headquarters. By 1980, activities of the national organization, which had 4 branches in Cleveland, included a Saxon orphan fund and a fraternal insurance benefit fund with more than $8.8 million worth of insurance in force.

Souvenir Book, 75th Anniversary of Alliance of Transylvanian Saxons (1970).

**ALTA HOUSE**, serving Cleveland's LITTLE ITALY, is one of the city's oldest SETTLEMENT HOUSES. Alta House grew out of a day nursery established in 1895 to serve working Italian immigrant women in the Mayfield-Murray Hill Rd. district. The nursery soon came under the administration of the CLEVELAND DAY NURSERY ASSOC. Directed by Mrs. Louise (Marius E.) Rawson, the work at the nursery rapidly expanded. Along with local neighborhood leader JOSEPH CARABELLI, she approached JOHN D. ROCKEFELLER for funds to construct an expanded nursery building. Rockefeller agreed to finance the structure in 1898. By the time the building was dedicated on 20 Feb. 1900, the role of the operation had been expanded to that of a social settlement. Named after Rockefeller's daughter, Alta Rockefeller Prentice, Alta House provided clubs, classes, a nursery, and a center for various community activities. Rockefeller retained a strong interest in the settlement during its early years. In addition to providing the funds for annual operations, he continued to add to the physical plant. In 1910 he purchased an adjacent tract of land for use as a playground, and in 1913 he donated an additional building, which came to house a library, swimming pool, and gymnasium. In 1921, the Rockefeller family asked to be relieved of its responsibilities for maintaining the work, and in 1922, Alta House began to be funded by the Cleveland Community Fund (see UNITED WAY SERVICES).

Throughout its history, Alta House maintained an extraordinarily close relationship with the residents of its Italian-American neighborhood. Its board of trustees (est. 1900) always included neighborhood leaders, and its programs, in terms of clubs, classes, and recreation, often reflected the cultural background of its clients. Despite the destruction of the settlement's main building by fire in 1981, and the shifting population of its district, Alta House remains one of the area's most viable neighborhood centers in the 1980s, now operating both youth programs and senior citizens' services out of the former gymnasium building.

Alta Social Settlement Records, WRHS.
Reifsnider, Carl J., *Alta House* (1953).

The **ALTENHEIM** was founded in 1886 for the care of elderly people of German descent in the Cleveland area. It was established by the Westseite Deutschen Frauen Verein (the West Side German Women's Society), which itself had originally begun in 1876 for the purpose of sponsoring women who wished to enter the German Teachers Seminary in Milwaukee, Wis. In 1880, the society entered into a joint venture with a similar women's group on the east side to open a needlework school. This project was completed, and in 1886 the two groups could not agree on a second joint project, the west side ladies wishing to establish a home for the aged and the east-siders wishing to open a home for children. At this point the members of the West Side Society decided to pursue their project alone. The Altenheim was incorporated in 1887, and plans were begun to construct a facility. The home was specially designed to provide care for women and men of German descent over age 65. Land was purchased at 7719 Detroit Ave. in 1889, and the home was finished by 1890. This structure remained in use with only minor changes until 1980, when the Altenheim was moved to a home formally owned by Dr. Larsich at 15653 Pearl Rd.

The services offered by the Altenheim have remained constant throughout its existence. By 1923, there were no longer any restrictions upon the nationality or ancestry of the residents. The daily management of the home was guided by a matron, and the medical needs of the residents were the responsibility of a visiting physician. The Frauen Verein continued to set the policy of the home through the 1940s. The financial needs of the home were met by the society and through its endowment, membership fees, benefits, and gifts. During this time there was also an increase in social services offered to the residents, such as counseling and entertainment. In 1984, the Altenheim still provided a place for the elderly. It is equipped with hospital facilities and full nursing services. The staff provides counseling and programs for the residents.

Altenheim Records, WRHS.

**ALTERNATIVE SCHOOLS.** The alternative-schools movement emanated out of the 1960s milieu where parents began to demand choices in the schooling of their children. Specifically, alternative schools were institutions, often not state-accredited, serving the traditional school population but privately controlled and supported because the traditional systems were not meeting the needs. Cleveland has had several alternative schools. United Independent Schools of E. Cleveland (UISEC) began in 1968 with 2 preschool classes serving 50 children. Rev. and Mrs. J. David Brostrom started the Calvary Neighborhood School in the Calvary Lutheran Church, using the Montessori approach. Tuition and funds from the AHS FOUNDATION and Hudson Montessori Ctr. provided financial support. In 1969, these 2 classes, along with an additional class in the Chambers area, incorporated to form UISEC. Its goals were to develop independent learners and social awareness. By the fall of 1972, there were 7 classes, ages 3–10. The 141 students were predominantly black but integrated economically, socially, and racially from the suburbs and inner city. The Urban Community School, located on the near west side of Cleveland, educated multiracial and multicultural inner-city children growing up in a poor environment with substandard housing. It was founded in 1968 when St. Patrick's and St. Malachi's merged into an independent, nonprofit, interdenominational community school. In the public and parochial schools, these children faced learning and emotional problems, language barriers, and overcrowded classes. In contrast, UCS provided a creative, experimental education. The school used the near west side community as a learning resource. UCS was nongraded, but primary, intermediate, and junior-high levels were maintained. Many children were Puerto Rican and Appalachian. Children were admitted on a first-come basis, with tuition on a sliding scale. Initially UCS was operated by the P.M. Foundation, Inc., and supported mainly by a single benefactor. It was still in existence in 1986.

The Street Academy came about as a response to the high number of dropouts in Cleveland's lower-income neighborhoods. The URBAN LEAGUE OF CLEVELAND decided to replicate the street academy program that was operating in New York City. The program had 3 stages: street-academy level, which emphasized basic skills; transition level, which presented a more formalized style of learning; and precollege level, which focused on college preparation. In Mar. 1970, with funding from 3 major foundations and community organizations, the first street academy was opened in GLENVILLE. By November, 2 street academies, a transition academy, and the Circle Prep Academy were in operation. Then in 1972, the Street Academy consolidated into 1 site because of financial difficulty, at E. 83rd St. and Euclid Ave. Although the Street Academy lacked state accreditation, diplomas were granted through St. Joseph's High School. The program was structured to provide maximum individual experience to enable students to graduate in half the required time by eliminating study halls, by requiring only those courses necessary for graduation, and by offering a full summer program and counseling. The Street Academy was absorbed by the CLEVELAND PUBLIC SCHOOLS in 1975 and in 1978 was merged into the work-study program at the Woodland Job Ctr.

The Cleveland Urban Learning Community (CULC) was an alternative school approved through St. Ignatius High School. CULC was known as a "school without walls" because of its philosophy that learning should take place in the community. Fr. Thos. Shea, SJ, was its first director. The main objectives of CULC were to develop more self-direction, responsibility, and an increasing ability to make independent decisions. Students designed their own courses around real interests, needs, and state requirements and worked with a resource person. CULC was located on E. 4th St., central to the library, transportation, and other resources. Students were chosen on a lottery basis and did not pay tuition. The school closed in 1982 because of lack of funds and interest. In 1970, a group of Cleveland Hts. professional parents founded the Friends' School on Cornell Rd. because they believed the public schools were inflexible. The school developed to serve nonconforming students who were nonachievers. There was an individualized approach, with small classes of about 8 students. Later the school moved to Magnolia Dr. and became known as the School on Magnolia. In 1982 it became part of Child Guidance Services, and in 1984 it was renamed the Eleanor Gerson School in a new downtown location. In 1986 it served emotionally disturbed youth and worked with parents to develop student responsibility for learning. In addition to these schools, there were others that were less successful. The Sunrise Community School opened in 1971 with a focus on open classroom, individualized instruction, and an interdisciplinary approach. It served 25–40 children. The Learning Community school also opened in 1971, with a focus on open classroom and individualized instruction, serving about 35–40 students.

Alternative schools gained initial support from foundations and tuitions. Sustaining this financial support became a problem. Furthermore, interest in alternative schools waned as the country became more conservative, causing many to close, though some programs were adopted by public schools. As an offshoot of the alternative-schools movement, some public schools developed alternative programs, or schools within a school. Examples of these were the Concept I program at Beachwood High School, the Roaring 100s at Berea High, Education through Inquiry at Parma High, the New School at Heights High, and Catalyst at Shaker Hts. High. These programs provided alternative choices where students and teachers worked as communities and took more responsibility for learning, and where out-of-school experiences and interdisciplinary programming were encouraged. They also provided excellent models.

Sally H. Wertheim
John Carroll University

The **ALUMINUM COMPANY OF AMERICA** (Alcoa) was founded in 1888 as the Pittsburgh Reduction Co. and since 1900 has had a branch of its business in Cleveland, locating the headquarters of its forging division here in 1977. Alcoa established a sales office in Cleveland at 326 the Cuyahoga Bldg. in 1900; it moved to the Garfield Bldg. at 613 Euclid Ave. in 1907, the same year the company changed its name to the Aluminum Co. of America. In May 1909 it opened its first production facility in Cleveland, establishing a sand foundry at 6205 Carnegie Ave. to supply parts for automobile manufacturers in Cleveland and Detroit. In 1916 Alcoa began construction on a mold plant on farmland south of Harvard Ave. at E. 22nd St. Production at the plant began in July 1917. During WORLD WAR I, the plant's principal products were automotive and aircraft pistons for the Allies; after the war, the plant produced such items as automobile engine heads and pistons, diesel and marine engine parts, washing machine agitators, and vacuum cleaner parts.

Alcoa began expanding its Cleveland Works in 1938 in anticipation of increased military needs among America's European allies. During WORLD WAR II, the company invested $15 million to expand its Cleveland facility and became a principal supplier of forged aluminum for aircraft parts such as propeller blades. The Cleveland Works employed 10,300 people in 1943–44 and by 1945 had grown to include "the world's largest aluminum and magnesium forging plant," 2 aluminum foundries producing sand and permanent mold castings, an ingot plant, research and development facilities, and a magnesium sand foundry operated by an Alcoa subsidiary, the American Magnesium Corp. Modernization and expansion of the Cleveland Works continued from the 1950s into the 1980s, although employment dropped dramatically. In May 1955 Alcoa opened a $40 million plant that it built for and then leased from

the U.S. Air Force to make light alloy forgings for military aircraft; Alcoa bought the plant from the government in 1982. In June 1957 Alcoa installed an IBM computer to better manage production scheduling. By 1965, 3,000 people worked at Alcoa's Cleveland facilities, and the company expanded the works to include the forging of titanium. Between 1970–77, Alcoa invested $21.5 million to modernize and upgrade its Cleveland facility, including the construction of a wheel line facility in 1972. In July 1977 Alcoa consolidated its forging operations in Vernon, Calif., with its Cleveland operation to create the Alcoa Forging Div. with headquarters at 1600 Harvard Ave. The forging division employed 1,900 people in July 1980, when the company announced it was adding to its Cleveland Works a forging press to produce aluminum truck wheels.

The **AMALGAMATED CLOTHING AND TEXTILE WORKERS UNION** has been one of the most progressive and prosperous unions in Cleveland. It was originally organized nationally in 1914 as the independent Amalgamated Clothing Workers of America (ACWA). Soon the ACWA came to Cleveland to help organize and lift workers from the sweatshop conditions in the men's clothing industry. The ACWA was an early supporter of industrial unionism, and it scored some initial success in Cleveland. The 1920s were lean years for the union, as it was hindered by a recession in the industry. Under the guidance of BERYL PEPPERCORN, the ACWA began an organizing effort of the most formidable nonunion firm, JOSEPH & FEISS CO., in 1924. Ten years of persistent endeavor culminated in 1934 when Joseph & Feiss recognized the ACWA after 1,600 of its workers went on strike. This victory for the union encouraged a flurry of organizing activities in other Cleveland shops. By the mid-1930s, almost 95% of the men's clothing industry in Cleveland was unionized. Not only was the ACWA able to negotiate substantial improvements in wages and working conditions, but it also pioneered in the area of fringe benefits. During its organizing activities, the ACWA developed a close relationship with the manufacturers, and they eventually became one of its strongest supporters.

Although the ACWA joined the AFL in 1934, it split with the federation the following year and assisted in forming the CIO, including its local, central body, the CLEVELAND INDUSTRIAL UNION COUNCIL. As a well-organized and powerful union, the ACWA could now help other workers organize into industrial unions. The ACWA had always felt a close relationship with the textile workers, as they produced the yarn to make the clothes. Thus, the ACWA concentrated on unionizing this industry with the Textile Workers Organizing Committee. By 1939, the textile workers had formed their own union, the Textile Workers Union of America (TWUA). By this time, the ACWA had moved beyond the emphasis on economics. It developed superior cultural, recreational, and educational activities for its members. It became especially active in political affairs, helping to fund political campaigns at all levels and organizing the workers' voting power. The greatest pride of the ACWA was its Sidney Hillman Bldg., located at 2227 Payne Ave., opened in 1948. It was used not only by members but also by a variety of community groups.

Despite a recession in the industry in the 1950s, the ACWA held its own on wages and benefits and conducted a major union label campaign. In 1960, it launched a successful campaign into related clothing industries, such as firefighting and sporting clothes. To form an even stronger union, the TWUA merged with the ACWA in 1976 to form the ACTWU. By 1979, almost all of the industries in men's attire were represented in 1 union, as the shoemakers' union also joined the ACTWU.

Beryl Peppercorn Papers. WRHS.

The **AMASA STONE CHAPEL** on the Case Western Reserve University campus was erected by Mrs. John Hay and Mrs. Samuel Mather as a memorial to their father in 1911. It was designed by Henry Vaughan of Boston, first architect of the Natl. Cathedral in Washington, D.C. According to the architect, the chapel was designed in the late Decorated Gothic style and was closely based on English models. It is constructed of Indiana limestone. A keystone bearing the carved head of AMASA STONE, taken from the old UNION DEPOT on the lakefront that Stone built in 1866, was placed over the east entrance. The plan of the chapel consists of a nave and choir, with narrow side aisles divided by slender stone shafts. The nave accommodates 545 persons and is lighted by clerestory windows and larger east and west windows. The tower is 121 ft. high to the top of the corner pinnacles.

The **AMASA STONE HOUSE,** opened in 1877 as the Home for Aged Women, was established as an old-age home for "Protestant Gentlewomen" 60 and older. The purpose of the home was "to give old age the security it deserves, the care it needs, and the atmosphere of love and refinement it enjoys." The Home for Aged Women was built and endowed by AMASA STONE as a gift to the Women's Christian Assoc. Dedicated on 14 July 1877 and located at 194 Kennard (E. 46th) St. between Garden (Central) and Cedar streets, it served a total of 88 elderly women between 1877–96. According to the early regulations, residents paid a $250 admission fee and signed over their property to the home in exchange for lifelong care. In 1896 26 women lived there, and the home's expenses that year were $6,500.

The Women's Christian Assoc. operated the Home for Aged Women from 1877–1919. In 1919 an independent board of trustees took over the management of the home's endowment, a women's board was established to oversee daily operations of the home, and a junior board was created to organize special activities for the residents. On 11 May 1931, the 46 residents of the home moved to new facilities. Renamed the Amasa Stone House in honor of its benefactor, the new building was located at 975 East Blvd. on a 3-acre site donated by Wm. G. Pollock. Two-thirds of the cost of constructing the new building was donated by Amasa Stone's son-in-law SAMUEL MATHER. When it celebrated its 100th anniversary in 1977, the Amasa Stone House was home to 50 elderly women, and it employed 54 staff members to provide daily service and medical care to residents. Neither the religious requirement nor the provision requiring residents to sign property over to the home was still in effect.

Federation for Community Planning Records. WRHS.

**AMBLER HEIGHTS,** one of CLEVELAND HTS., Ohio's, oldest neighborhoods, is located in the southwest corner of the city. The boundaries include Cedar Glen Rd. (north), S. Overlook Rd. (east), East Blvd. and N. Park Blvd. (south), and Ambleside Rd. and East Boulevard (west). Streets in Ambler Hts. include Chestnut Hills, Denton, Devonshire, Elandon, and Harcourt roads and part of N. Park Blvd. The area is named after Dr. Nathan Hardy Ambler (1824–88). Ambler came to Cleveland in 1852 after 10 years as a dentist in Burlington, Vt., and the gold fields of California. He opened an office on Superior between Erie (E. 9th) and Bond (E. 6th) streets, later moving to the Northrup & Har-

rington Bldg. on Superior just west of Seneca (W. 3rd) St. As he practiced dentistry, Ambler also dealt in real estate, buying property on the outskirts of Cleveland, then reselling it as the city encroached upon his land. Using the gold dust in which he was paid in California for his services, Ambler increased his fortunes (he died a millionaire) to the extent that he quit his practice in 1868 to manage his money and real estate dealings. By 1872 he had purchased land past DOAN'S CORNERS on Fairmount St. (now Fairhill Blvd.). On that land he had built a mansion at the top of the hill now occupied by the grounds of the Baldwin Filtration Plant. Ambler called his mansion Rock Rest.

To aid in the management of his real-estate holdings, Ambler brought an adopted son, Daniel O. Caswell (1857–1906), from Lodi, Ohio. Caswell helped foster Blue Rock Springs Home, a mineral-water spa at the intersection of Cedar Rd. and DOAN BROOK. In addition, Caswell negotiated for sale some 350 acres of land, which included a parcel across from Rock Rest, to be known as Ambler Hts. Starting ca. 1900, Caswell with Wm. Eglin Ambler (1845–1925), no relation to Dr. Ambler of Curtiss-Ambler Realty, began a housing development in Ambler Hts., which consisted of large houses in a variety of styles, including Colonial Revival, Tudor, and Tudor Revival. Houses were built until ca. 1925 to designs by architects such as FRANK B. MEADE, CHAS. S. SCHNEIDER, and ABRAM GARFIELD. Homeowners in this neighborhood included Benjamin Bourne, president, Bourne-Fuller Co.; Chas. Cassingham, president, Cassingham Coal Co.; Samuel Halle of Halle Bros. Dept. Store; and Jerome Zerbe. This neighborhood was also called Ambler Park, and later Chestnut Hills.

**AMBULANCE SERVICES** began in Cleveland, as in most other U.S. cities, following the CIVIL WAR in the 1860s. City, Lakeside, Huron, and St. Alexis hospitals all operated ambulances in the late 19th century. Private ambulances began to appear in the 1880s and were preferred by the wealthy. For nonemergency conveyance, many funeral homes operated invalid carriages. Early ambulances were horse-drawn vehicles with box-shaped bodies; hard rubber tires and spring suspensions were added later. Equipment was rudimentary, usually consisting of a stretcher, blankets, and a bottle of brandy. In 1903, Lakeside Hospital introduced the first electric ambulance in Cleveland, which, although it had problems climbing steep hills, answered 750 calls its first year. As an early center of the auto industry, Cleveland benefited from gas-powered ambulances. The Peerless and White Motor companies by 1912 offered complete models. Styles varied from trucklike vans to luxury limousines. After WORLD WAR I, City was the only hospital to provide ambulance service. Of its 3 ambulances, 2 were usually broken down. At a time when municipal funding of hospital ambulances was becoming common in other cities, Cleveland's emergency services were left largely to the police and fire departments, and by 1920 to over 100 funeral homes. The funeral homes, in particular, were often criticized for not disinfecting their vehicles (usually with formaldehyde) after conveying a person with a contagious disease. In police emergency vehicles, basic equipment was little more than a tourniquet and rubber gloves.

Until the 1970s, despite occasional outcries from medical groups, very little was done to improve the training of ambulance attendants, largely because of the lack of state regulations. Vehicle improvements included the electric siren—replacing bells and gongs—and, in the 1940s, colored roof lights. After WORLD WAR II, 2-way radios were introduced. Many ambulances began to carry oxygen. Some even carried trained nurses, although they were not required to by city ordinance. In the 1960s, private firms began to compete with funeral homes for emergency service, mainly because of Medicare, which guaranteed 80% payment of the ambulance fee. Private firms took over in the 1970s when funeral homes, unable to afford compliance with new state regulations and federal wage laws, dropped completely out of the market. By the 1980s, most Cleveland suburbs were served by private companies, with several communities sometimes sharing a contract. Compared to other major cities, Cleveland was late in setting up its own ambulance service. In 1968, a study by the METROPOLITAN HEALTH PLANNING CORP. showed the need for such a service; one of the study's conclusions was that the police and fire departments were overburdened with medical-emergency calls. In 1974, the MHPC implemented a countywide 1-telephone-number service. Working with Mayor Ralph Perk, the following year MHPC helped set up the Emergency Medical Service System. Using federal and state funds, the EMSS began with 15 modern ambulances, 11 of which were stationed at Cleveland hospitals, and one at Hopkins Airport. As it was a division of the public safety department, all EMSS personnel were required to undergo extensive paramedic training at CUYAHOGA COMMUNITY COLLEGE.

The **AMERICAN AND CANADIAN SPORT, TRAVEL, AND OUTDOOR SHOW** is one of the oldest and largest of its kind. This annual event in Cleveland has been more commonly referred to as the Sportsman's Show. The first Sportsman's and Outdoors Show in Cleveland was held in 1927 in the PUBLIC AUDITORIUM. It was largely modeled after a similar outdoor show held annually in Boston. The Cleveland show ran for 1 week until 1930, when it was discontinued because of the Depression. It was resumed in 1937 and has taken place every year since then. The 1927 Sportsman's Show was the idea of 2 Clevelanders, Aaron W. Newman and Morris Ackerman. Ackerman was the outdoor writer for the *CLEVELAND PRESS*. Newman (later the president of Expositions, Inc.) ran the annual event until his death in 1963. The idea behind the first show was to provide manufacturers of outdoor and sports equipment with a promotional outlet for their products, and to encourage the public's growing interest in the recreational value of the outdoors.

The early shows, held in the Public Auditorium, featured exhibits and demonstrations relating to boating, hunting, fishing, and camping, as well as golf, baseball, and tennis gear. The auditorium was transformed into an outdoor setting with potted fir, spruce, and cedar, and in 1930 a meandering stream. The show reopened in 1937 as the American & Canadian Sportsman's Show. The show was sponsored by Expositions, Inc., under Newman, in conjunction with an advisory committee representing sportsmen's organizations and business organizations from across the U.S. and Canada. The show was one of the largest in the country, drawing an attendance of 105,000 from Ohio, western Pennsylvania, and southern Michigan. During the 1940s, one of its main attractions was a huge indoor tank used for demonstrations of log rolling, boating, and other water sports. In 1948, a 33,000-gallon exhibition tank collapsed, causing the week-long show to close for 2 days. Other features during this period included demonstrations by horseshoe-pitching champions and famous anglers, as well as a menagerie of live animals, including bears, from Canada. In the 1950s, the name was changed to the American & Canadian Sportsman's Vacation & Boat Show. In the 1960s, increasing emphasis was placed on the promotion of family vacations. Lucille Newman assumed management of the show after her husband's death in 1963. In

1968, Newman sold Expositions, Inc., to Dave Fassnacht and Betty Friedlander. The vacation theme was further expanded in the 1970s with more exhibits of recreational vehicles. Boating exhibits also grew in popularity. Travel booths had increased from 50 in 1958 to 263 in 1978, when over 200,000 were attending the show annually. Since the 1970s, the show has been officially known as the American & Canadian Sport, Travel, and Outdoor Show. In 1985 the Sportsman's Show was moved from the Cleveland Convention Ctr. and Public Hall Complex, where it had been held for many years, to the new I-X Ctr.

The **AMERICAN CHICLE COMPANY**, one of the world's leading chewing-gum manufacturers as a subsidiary of the Warner-Lambert Co., was established in New York by Cleveland chewing-gum manufacturer WM. J. WHITE, who merged his company with another Cleveland chewing-gum maker, the Beeman Chemical Co. Born at Rice Lake, Ontario, on 7 Oct. 1850, White worked as a confectioner from his Lorain Ave. home in the late 1870s, adding trinkets to bags of popcorn to increase sales. Ca. 1880 he found a way to make chicle more chewable and added flavor to it; in 1884 he established a plant at 57 S. Water (W. 9th) St. to manufacture chewing gum. In 1888 he built a new factory at 1675 Detroit Ave. to manufacture Yucatan gum, which he distributed to members of the U.S. Congress to launch his successful election campaign in 1892. Serving only 1 term in Congress, White returned to making Yucatan and Red Robin brand gums. By 1899, Wm. J. White & Son was the largest chewing-gum business in the world. In 1900, White, along with fellow Clevelanders Geo. H. Worthington and Dr. EDWIN E. BEEMAN, organized the $10 million American Chicle Co. in New York. White served as its president until forced out, probably in 1916, penniless. He attempted to make another fortune by establishing the Wm. J. White Chicle Co. in Niagara Falls, but that venture collapsed when he encountered legal difficulties with the American Chicle Co. Another attempt to rebuild his fortune ended with his death on 16 Feb. 1923.

American Chicle consolidated White's operations with those of another Cleveland company, Beeman Chemical, established by pepsin manufacturer Dr. Edwin E. Beeman in 1887. A physician who enjoyed research perhaps more than treating patients, Beeman found that pepsin, an extract from the stomach of hogs, provided relief from indigestion. He marketed pepsin in blue bottles graced with a picture of a pig on the label until an acquaintance suggested that he add pepsin to the current rage: chewing gum. With financial backing from Albert Johnson and Chris Grover, Beeman reorganized his business to manufacture pepsin-flavored chewing gum, and by 1893 Beeman Chemical's business had grown to $500,000. In 1900, Beeman sold his business to White. He died in Cleveland in Nov. 1906. American Chicle operated 2 plants in Cleveland: the Beeman plant at 78 Bank St. and the White factory on Detroit Ave.; after 1903, only the latter was in operation. In Mar. 1919, the company announced plans to build a $2 million plant in Long Island City, N.Y., and by 1921 it had ceased operations in Cleveland. In July 1962, American Chicle announced its merger with the Warner-Lambert Pharmaceutical Co. As a division of Warner-Lambert in 1976, its products included breath mints, convenience antacids, and cough drops, in addition to chewing gum.

The **AMERICAN GREETINGS CORPORATION**, founded in 1906 by Jacob Sapirstein, the son of a Polish rabbi and a recent immigrant, began as a one-man card-jobbing business. By the end of 1983 it was the 396th-largest U.S. corporation ranked by sales, with $722.4 million in sales and a net income of $41.7 million. In the 1930s the Sapirstein Greeting Card Co. included the founder and his 3 sons. After operating from the family residence at 852 E. 95th St., the company moved to larger quarters in 1932, and Sapirstein, dissatisfied with the cards then available, began to design and print his own. The company incorporated with $18,000 in capital in 1934 and opened a branch office in Detroit in 1936. By 1939 the company was operating as the American Greetings Publishers Co. and incorporated under that name on 29 Jan. 1944. Sales topped $1 million in 1940.

The company became the American Greetings Corp. in 1952 and offered stock to the public for the first time that year. By its 50th anniversary, in 1956, American Greetings operated 9 plants in Cleveland, turning out 1.8 million cards daily. Four years later Irving I. Stone succeeded Jacob Sapirstein, his father, as president. A series of new directions and innovations in the 1960s and 1970s boosted American Greetings' earnings considerably, enabling the company to launch in 1981 a serious challenge to Hallmark's supremacy in the greeting-card industry. In 1964 the company bought the House of Paper to better compete in the production and sale of ribbon, gift wrap, and other party goods. By 1966 it was the fastest-growing U.S. company in the industry; in 1968 sales surpassed $100 million.

Two innovations in the late 1960s also added to growth. In 1967 American Greetings introduced Holly Hobbie, the first of a series of characters that were licensed to appear on the products of other companies. In 1982 the company established a division to develop new licensing properties. In 1970 it introduced a new line of youth-oriented greeting cards, which were highly successful with all customers. As a result of these innovations, sales and income increased greatly. Total revenues in 1972 were $162.6 million; revenues for fiscal year 1984 were $840 million. Net income of $11.8 million in 1972 grew to nearly $60 million in 1984. In 1978 Morry Weiss, formerly in charge of marketing and sales, became president and chief operating officer. In Nov. 1983, American Greetings announced plans to phase out its last Cleveland-area plant, on W. 117th St. With 17 facilities employing 20,000 people nationwide, the corporation maintains its headquarters in the Cleveland suburb of Brooklyn.

The **AMERICAN HEART ASSOCIATION (AHA), NORTHEAST OHIO AFFILIATE, INC.**, is part of the not-for-profit, voluntary health organization funded by private contributions whose stated goal is to reduce early death and disability from heart disease, stroke, and related disorders. To achieve this goal, the AHA funds medical research, professional and public education, and community-service programs. Founded in 1924 by a group of eminent cardiologists, the AHA was originally a professional society. In 1948 it was reorganized as a national voluntary health agency involving lay people in the problem of combating cardiovascular disease. Operating out of its national center in Dallas, Tex., it had active organizations in all 50 states and Puerto Rico and branches in more than 3,000 communities in 1986. Greater Cleveland's affiliation with the AHA, then known as the Heart Society, a predecessor organization, began in 1948 when the annual February Heart Fund Drive was created. Five years later, in 1953, Heart Sunday, a 1-day door-to-door residential solicitation campaign, was initiated by the Northeast Ohio Affiliate, then called a chapter. This drive to solicit donations was the brainchild of Irving B. Hexter, president of the Industrial Publishing Co., who in 1953 was also board chairman of the Heart Society. Heart Sunday, now a nationwide observance, ranks as the largest single source of income na-

tionwide for the Heart Assoc. During the 1950s–1960s, the AHA funded primary research in Cleveland hospitals that resulted in the development of the heart-lung machine, the coronary bypass operation, and therapeutic treatments of heart disease.

During the late 1960s, the NE Ohio Chap. of the AHA proposed a plan to join with the Cancer Society and the Health Fund in a combined collection effort in a limited number of neighborhoods as a trial program to determine whether family contributions held up or fell below the amounts given to separate collections. Later, in the "Cleveland Plan," all 3 organizations joined in raising funds from business, industry, and employee deduction plans. In 1974, the NE Chap. became a direct affiliate of the national group. To qualify for direct affiliation, a local chapter must have raised $1 million for 3 consecutive years, serve an area with at least 2 million persons, and include 1 major research and teaching center. The local chapter is then represented on the national board of directors. Serving 8 Ohio counties since 1948, the Northeast Ohio Affiliate became the 4th metropolitan association in the nation, the others being in New York, Los Angeles, and Chicago. The Northeast Ohio Affiliate allocates more than 40% of its unrestricted divisible funds to research. In 1984–85 alone, investments in research in northeast Ohio totaled $871,000. Sixty researchers from local institutions received support from the affiliate in the form of grants-in-aid, fellowships, and summer stipends. In 1986, local headquarters were located at 1689 E. 115th St.

**AMERICAN INDIANS.** The tiny Indian community of early-20th-century Cleveland was largely a transient one. Census statistics show only 2 Indians resident in the city in 1900; 48 in 1910; and 34 in 1920. On the eve of WORLD WAR II, 47 American Indians resided in Cuyahoga County. Indians moved into and out of Cleveland, either individually or in family units, in response to prevailing economic conditions. Overwhelmingly they were members of the various tribes of the eastern U.S. The most common pattern found males moving to Cleveland to work for a few years in industrial factories. Once in the city, they often assimilated into urban life, in many cases completely eschewing identification as an Indian. This behavior was motivated less by a denial of their racial and cultural heritage than by an attempt to avoid discrimination and hostility from white inhabitants. Later, these Indians typically returned to their reservation or to the region where their families still resided, taking with them whatever savings they had accumulated. By the Depression of the 1930s, the Indian population in Cleveland was still small, with an informal group residing on the near east side. These people looked to a humanitarian male called CHIEF THUNDERWATER as their leader.

The city's Indian community increased notably following World War II. In 1950, 109 resided in the city, and an additional 57 elsewhere in the county. The goal of many Indians recently discharged from the armed forces was to seek work, and perhaps a new and better life, in the white world. They usually sought out a large city, where they felt it would be easier to find work than in a smaller community. Confidently, many sought employment in the expanding business community of postwar Cleveland. During the late 1940s and early 1950s, as the city's Indian population multiplied, many males joined together to form small Indian clubs. These clubs, whose locus was often small "Indian" taverns, provided members with camaraderie and fellowship with other Indians, including in their activities sports and social gatherings for the families of club members. The clubs also attempted to gather together Indians in an effort to help one another. The Indian population in Cleveland increased even more significantly in the late 1950s, a trend that continued until the 1970s. By 1960 the city population was 391, and the total county population 464. That was the direct result of the federal government's newly inaugurated program of "Termination and Relocation." Confronted with both a huge wartime public debt and an increasing role in international affairs, many federal officials believed that money spent maintaining the reservation system and policies could be better used in paying the national debt and in fighting the cold war. The government in Washington, in turn, opted for a new implementation of an old policy: a speeded-up assimilation of the Indian population into the dominant culture, to be brought about by the termination of the federal trust. By this new policy, Indians would move from their reservations and relocate, with the assistance of the federal government, in urban America. It was anticipated, incorrectly as it turned out, that reservations would be ultimately liquidated.

The Relocation Services Program, administered through the Bureau of Indian Affairs of the Interior Dept., designated Cleveland as one of the 8 cities in which to resettle reservation Indians. The bureau established an office in Cleveland in late 1952. It was responsible for administering the relocation program, which included finding housing and jobs for the newly arrived Indians. Training programs were also provided to help the new arrivals learn a skill and to adjust to urban life. Over 5,000 individuals were settled in Cleveland as a result of the federal government's relocation program. They came from a variety of tribes and, unlike the pre-World War II residents, were more likely to have come from the West. This period also saw a national questioning of educational standards for all Americans, in large part because of the Soviet success in putting *Sputnik* into orbit in Oct. 1957. The value of learning was reasserted with urgency. American Indian young people joined the trend toward more serious study. Their college registration rose by 200%. Many went on to graduate and professional schools. This trend carried with it 2 important consequences. It exposed Indian students to the rapidly growing civil-rights movement, which was particularly active on the nation's campuses. In turn, Indians perceived the relationship of civil-rights agitation for black Americans to the plight of their own people, both on and off the reservation. Activism bloomed among American Indians in the 1960s. Increasingly, Indian activists urged the federal government to become more concerned about the difficulties of Indian life. They pointed out bitterly that of all minority groups in the U.S., the American Indians were the poorest; 3 out of 5 lived below the federally established poverty line. They demanded that something be done, and done quickly, to address the blighted existence of their people.

Russell Means, a Dakota Sioux, emerged as a leader in Cleveland. A founding member of the American Indian Movement, an activist group drawing members from across the nation, Means also began a local organization in 1969 to unite the Indian community of Cleveland. At that time the city's Indian population was nearly 1,200. He hoped that the CLEVELAND AMERICAN INDIAN CTR. would be a place where the city's Indians could gather and be with others of their race, and where together they also could celebrate and preserve native traditions. The center first operated as a social organization, next developing a variety of cultural activities and social-service programs during the 1970s, such as youth job-training and placement programs. Rapidly it became a viable local agency, providing a publicly visible center for Indian activity in Cleveland. Many of the more active members of the Indian community in Greater Cleveland involved themselves with the center

and its work. By the late 1970s and early 1980s, the center's role was changing. The combination of greatly decreased federal funds for programs and increased cultural awareness among the Indian community in Cleveland convinced many to return to the reservation area, where they could live and work near their families. The center, obliged to reduce its own social-service programs, now sought to guide members in the more effective utilization of existing public services. Its activities increasingly focused upon job-training and -placement and cultural programs.

The average Indian individual who moved to Cleveland after 1950 had to struggle with the extreme determination to gain a satisfactory education, job security, and a comfortable life, both materially and emotionally. As a group, American Indians, nationally as well as in Cleveland, were plagued by a host of socioeconomic problems common also among other disadvantaged groups in society—problems such as poor education, inadequate housing, low pay, and alcoholism. Some merely foundered, caught precariously between a safer but economically desperate existence in the Indian world, and a new universe in the white world they could neither understand nor accept. For others, activism seemed the best method of addressing the pressing concerns of the Indian community. Yet another large group of relocated Indians did not see activism as the answer for themselves or for their families, nor did they judge it the best and most pragmatic solution to the myriad of problems facing them in urban America. Instead these people chose to identify less strongly as Indians. Often marrying non-Indians, they sought avenues by which to find a home in, and the acceptance of, mainstream America.

Philip Weeks and Lynn R. Metzger
University of Akron

The **AMERICAN INSTITUTE OF ARCHITECTS, CLEVELAND CHAPTER,** was established in the late 19th century. According to one source, it was organized on 7 Apr. 1887 from an earlier Cleveland Architectural Club. The existing chapter uses 1890 as its founding date. Throughout its existence, the chapter has been dedicated to architectural improvement in the city. In 1888 a joint committee of the institute and the Builders Exchange sponsored a bill in the Ohio legislature to create a department of building in Cleveland, and the city's earliest building permits date from this period. The introduction of the legislation that created the Group Plan Commission in 1902, a joint undertaking of the institute and the Chamber of Commerce, was an accomplishment of the utmost significance for the city. In 1921 the chapter organized the architectural course at the Cleveland School of Art, which subsequently became the Dept. of Architecture at CASE WESTERN RESERVE UNIVERSITY. In 1942 the chapter sponsored a series of lectures, "Planning Our Cities." For the 90th annual convention of the national institute, a committee of the chapter prepared *A Guide to Cleveland Architecture, 1796–1958*, published by Reinhold Publishing, and *Progressive Architecture* in 1958. In the 1970s and 1980s the chapter presented annual awards for the best restoration of historical buildings.

**AMERICAN MONARCH,** a manufacturer of screws, bolts, pins, and rivets, was formed by a merger of 2 Cleveland companies, Monarch Cap & Screw, founded by a Czechoslovakian immigrant, and American Rivet & Mfg. Monarch Cap & Screw was founded in 1922 as the Cleveland Brake Co. Frank J. Andel, a young toolmaker from Czechoslovakia, left another company he had founded, the Viaduct Tool & Machine Co. (later LEMPCO INDUSTRIES), to develop an auxiliary brake system for the Model T Ford.

By 1928, the firm, which began at 1950 E. 24th St. and moved in 1926 to 3444 E. 65th St., added king bolts and cap screws to its line. At this time, the company name was changed to reflect the product line. Throughout the years, Monarch Cap & Screw remained a small firm that provided stable employment for about 35 in the Newburgh Hts. area. Eventually moving to 5906 Park Ave., Monarch enjoyed war-related growth surges in the 1940s and 1950s. In 1956, it merged with the American Rivet & Mfg. Co. of 2140 Scranton, another small manufacturer with complementary lines of screws and fasteners. In an unusual move, American Rivet president Wm. L. Stein, a believer in employee ownership, encouraged workers to buy company stock; ultimately he owned less than 50%, while the workers owned 53%. This plan also enabled the new company, American Monarch, to liquidate a profit-sharing trust at Monarch. In 1985, the firm, still on Park Ave., reported sales of $1.5 million and employed 80.

The **AMERICAN MUTUAL LIFE ASSOCIATION** is a fraternal insurance society and the largest Slovenian-American organization in Ohio. Fraternal benefit societies provided Cleveland's SLOVENES with low-cost life, health, and accident insurance, as well as cultural and educational activities. Loans were also available. By 1910, over a dozen operated in the city. All were small, independent lodges, except for a handful affiliated with national organizations based in other states. One such group, the St. Barbara Society of Forest City, Pa., held a convention in Cleveland in 1910. Lodge No. 6 of Cleveland protested an increase in assessments and seceded shortly thereafter. On 11 Nov., the dissenting members met at Grdina's Hall on St. Clair Ave. to establish a fraternal society. The men wanted local control of finances and to keep investments within the community, plus impartiality to religious and political beliefs. They chose the name Slovenska Dobrodelna Zveza (Slovenian Mutual Benefit Assoc.) and voted John Gornik president. Auditing and jury committees were also elected. Membership was open to any Ohio resident of Slavic descent of good health and character age 16–45.

The group's first convention was held the following year. By 1913, SDZ numbered 1,100 members in 9 lodges. An office was opened in 1914 at 6120 St. Clair Ave., and the first real-estate loans were given. To attract young members, a juvenile department was created in 1919, and the first English-speaking lodge in 1920. A variety of life insurance plans were issued in the 1920s, starting at $500 coverage. The first bowling clubs and basketball leagues were organized in 1929, and sports olympiads attracted thousands of spectators. Individual lodges hosted picnics, dances, and holiday events. SDZ was active in the Natl. Fraternal Congress and local fundraising projects such as the construction of national halls and postwar reconstruction in the homeland. The official SDZ newspaper, *Our Voice* (Glas), debuted in English and Slovenian in 1939. SDZ had as many as 65 lodges and membership of over 20,000 in the 1960s. In 1962, a youth chorus was established in the NEWBURGH neighborhood, and the first college scholarships were given to qualified students. The group was renamed the American Mutual Life Assoc. in 1967. Ground was broken for a 110-acre recreation center in Leroy Twp., which opened in 1969. After nearly 50 years in the Slovenian Natl. Home building, AMLA offices were moved to S. Waterloo Rd. in 1981. In 1986, AMLA had $12.3 million in assets and $19.3 million of insurance in force. Past presidents have been Frank Cerne, Joseph Ponikvar, and John Susnik.

Klima, Margot A., *The Seventy-five Year Anniversary of the American Mutual Life Association, Diamond Jubilee, The American Mutual Life Association* (1985).

The **AMERICAN POSTAL WORKERS UNION, CLEVELAND CHAPTER,** was the largest major postal union active in the city in 1986. The group represented an amalgamation of earlier unions established to win rights for specific groups of postal employees. The APWU, with over 2,800 members in Cleveland, was created in 1971 after the Postal Reorganization Act of 1970, which established the U.S. Postal Service as an independent government agency. Postal unions, able to bargain over issues such as working conditions, promotional standards, grievance procedures, and safety since 1962, gained the right to engage in collective bargaining over wages, and all the rights won by their fellows in private industry except the right to strike. Nationally, the APWU is composed of 320,000 workers from the United Fed. of Postal Clerks, the Natl. Postal Union, the Natl. Assoc. of Post Office & General Service Maintenance Employees, the Natl. Fed. of Motor Vehicle Employees, and the Natl. Assoc. of Special Delivery Messengers. Each of these unions, active and separate since the turn of the century, shared a history of low wages and little ability to speak out about their jobs. Their attempts to influence representatives in Congress were squelched by "gag rules" that threatened dismissal if violated. In 1912, the Lloyd-La Follette Act permitted federal and postal workers to form unions, and subsequent legislation provided for workmen's compensation, retirement, and a nighttime differential. Wages, however, lagged behind those of private industry. Though federal jobs were secure during the Depression, postal workers were furloughed for a month and given a 15% pay cut. Despite wage gains in the 1940s and 1950s, the postal unions had limited power in the workplace. The unions had no bargaining clout, no effective grievance procedure, and no means of sidestepping repeated presidential vetoes on wage increases. Though John F. Kennedy's 1962 executive order authorized unions to bargain, wages and fringe benefits remained off limits. Continued frustration led to a walkout of postal workers that began in New York and spread to 200,000 workers throughout the country in Mar. 1970. The passage of the Postal Reorganization Act followed the wildcat strike.

In order to forge a stronger bargaining unit, the 5 unions formed the APWU; its corps of 89 elected national officials reflects its varied roots. Although some unionists hoped to merge letter carriers, mailhandlers, and other postal employees, the alliance that resulted joined those with the most similar job concerns. The Natl. Assoc. of Letter Carriers and other unions outside the APWU have occasionally negotiated jointly on contracts. The first 4 contracts (1971–78) emphasized wage issues, while working conditions have risen in importance since 1975. The Cleveland local shares the problems of stress and overwork common to other major urban centers, and was in the vanguard of job actions in 1970 and 1978. Prior to the passage of the Post Office Reorganization Act, the union was close to the Democratic party, and promotions within the system were often patronage appointments. Since 1970, seniority has been used exclusively, though post office management has tried to replace this valued union principle with the "best qualified" rule. Although the postal unions had chapters in Cleveland shortly after national formation, records are sketchy as to their founding dates and achievements. One union, the Natl. Fed. of Postal Clerks, was listed in the Cleveland city directory from 1915–17 and sporadically after 1925. The other components of the APWU were not listed until the 1970s.

The **AMERICAN RED CROSS, CLEVELAND CHAP-TER,** was organized by SAMUEL MATHER in 1905. Its initial purpose was to provide volunteer aid to the Army and Navy, to act as a channel of communication between families and members of the armed forces, and to carry on a system of disaster relief. The local chapter did not become directly linked to the national organization until 1910. Since its founding, the Cleveland Chap. has been served by many chairmen. Among those to receive special recognition were Judge Stanley L. Orr, chairman during the critical years 1941-45, and his successor, Albert M. Higley. In its first years, the Red Cross in Cleveland maintained an emergency committee and was active in welfare and training. Its services were substantially enlarged during WORLD WAR I, when the Cleveland Chap. was named headquarters of the Lake Div. (Ohio, Kentucky, and Indiana). A motor service and canteen were added, a program in Braille was developed, and the Jr. Red Cross (Cuyahoga County chapter) was founded.

As a member of the Community Chest, the Cleveland Chap.'s budget was severely reduced in the 1920s and 1930s. Services were shifted to help veterans, provide volunteers for hospital work, and offer lifesaving and first-aid training. In the aftermath of the Lorain tornado in 1924, the Red Cross provided disaster aid, feeding 3,000 families for the first 3 days. During the Depression, the Cleveland Chap. served as a distribution center for government supplies; over 50,000 families were fed and clothed. In 1938, the ANDREW SQUIRE mansion on EUCLID AVE. became the chapter's new headquarters. During WORLD WAR II, the local chapter again enlarged its services. The Nurses Aid Corps and Gray Ladies volunteer service were founded, providing valuable aid to local hospitals; the Dietitians Aide Corps was also started and served 7 Cleveland hospitals. During the war, Red Cross volunteers collected and produced knitted goods for war sufferers, operated canteens in Cleveland for servicemen, and recruited nurses. Cleveland was one of the cities chosen to set up a Red Cross blood-donor center for the purpose of securing blood to be processed into plasma for the Army and Navy. In 1951, the Red Cross Regional Blood Donor Ctr. opened, one of the largest regional centers in the country. Later known as the Northern Ohio Red Cross Blood Program, in 1980 it provided services to 87 hospitals in the region. In addition to collection and distribution services, the center includes a reference laboratory to assist hospitals in providing compatible blood for transfusions, and a laboratory that searches for and freezes rare units of blood. Into the 1980s, the Red Cross in Cleveland—receiving funds from the United Appeal—continued its disaster-relief services and expanded its Community Volunteer Services, Nursing & Health Services, and Youth Services (volunteer program). In 1985 it took over the TRAVELERS AID SOCIETY, which became a part of its Emergency Services.

The **AMERICAN SAVINGS BANK** was incorporated in 1887 at 220 Ontario St. opposite the Wheeling & Lake Erie Railroad Station. Begun as the German-American Savings Bank to meet the needs of produce merchants, it retained much of this trade while expanding into the commercial fields. It was noted for its large dividends to stockholders. The bank, which dropped *German* from its name during WORLD WAR I, withstood panics, 2 world wars, the Depression, and major inventory adjustments before becoming part of the Union Commerce Bank (Huntington) in 1955. It was located at 828 Huron Rd. at the time of its merger.

The **AMERICAN SHIP BUILDING COMPANY,** formed in 1899, was a major designer and builder of vessels for Great Lakes shipping. By 1960, uncertainty about the future of the shipping industry on the lakes led the company to diversify its operations, and by 1984 it had abandoned its Cleveland-area facilities. Incorporated in New Jersey on 16 Mar. 1899, American Ship Building consolidated 3 Cleveland firms—the Cleveland Ship Building Co., the Ship Owners' Dry Dock Co., and the Globe Iron Works—with 5 others in the Great Lakes region: the Chicago Ship Building Co., the Detroit Ship Building Co., the Milwaukee Dry Dock Co., the F. W. Wheeler Co. of Bay City, Mich., and the American Steel Barge Co. of Superior, Wis.; in 1901 the Buffalo Dry Dock Co. was added. Of the 3 Cleveland firms, the Globe Iron Works was the oldest; it began in 1869 when Robt. Wallace, Henry D. Coffinberry, John F. Pankhurst, and John B. Cowle bought an interest in Sanderson & Co., a small machine shop and foundry. Globe entered the shipbuilding industry when it purchased an interest in a dry dock under construction on the near west side along the CUYAHOGA RIVER by Stevens & Presley, operators of the Marine Railway. Soon Globe was building steel ships, and in 1880 it organized the Globe Ship Building Co., which launched the *Onoko* in Apr. 1882; the first compartmentalized iron-hulled freighter built for shipping on the lakes, the *Onoko* was a major step in the shipping industry's transition from wooden to iron hulls. In 1886 the Globe Iron Works reorganized as the Globe Iron Works Co. and absorbed the Globe Ship Building Co. Wallace and Coffinberry expanded their shipbuilding interests in 1886, when they organized the Cleveland Ship Building Co. The company began operations in the old CUYAHOGA STEAM FURNACE CO. plant on the Cuyahoga River; it built a plant in Lorain in 1897, and over the next 2 years it built there the largest dry docks on the lakes. Also in 1897, the Globe Iron Works Co. purchased the Ship Owners' Dry Dock Co. Organized in 1888 by veteran shipyard operator Wm. H. Redcliffe, the company had 2 docks in Cleveland when it was taken over by Globe.

The new American Ship Building Co. established its offices in Cleveland, at 120 Viaduct. Founding officers included Wm. L. Brown of Chicago, president; Robt. L. Ireland of the Ship Owners' Dry Dock Co., vice-president; Russell C. Wetmore, secretary-treasurer; and Jas. C. Wallace of the Cleveland Ship Building Co., general manager. In the early 1900s, the company grew with the steel industry's increased demand for new ore carriers. During WORLD WAR I, American Ship Building constructed 250 ships for the war effort; after the war, it returned to building passenger ships and large lake freighters, including the self-unloading freighter *Carl D. Bradley.* Under the direction of Wm. H. Gerhauser, president 1928-52, American Ship Building constructed a variety of vessels during WORLD WAR II, including minesweepers and Liberty Ships. By 1952 the company was the largest shipbuilder on the Great Lakes, but during the next 10 years American shipping on the lakes declined as a result of competition from both the railroads and Canadian shipping. With Edmund Q. Sylvester at the helm from 1957-62, the company began to diversify its operations: in 1959 it introduced a new sewage-treatment unit for use in ships and mines, and it bought Automobile Transport, Inc., a trucking firm that hauled cars; in 1966 it purchased the Cincinnati Sheet Metal & Roofing Co.

New president Wm. H. Jory continued diversification in 1963, but by 1967 a new group of younger investors thought they saw a brighter future for Great Lakes shipping. This group gained control of the board of directors, and one of its leaders, Geo. M. Steinbrenner III, became chief executive officer in Oct. 1967. The owner of the Kinsman Marine Co., Steinbrenner initiated a flurry of activity to build new ships, but by the 1980s he too had lost his optimism about the future of ore-boat construction on the Great Lakes. In 1972, the company bought the Tampa Ship & Dry Docks Co. in Florida; it expanded the facilities there in 1977 and moved its corporate headquarters from Cleveland to Tampa in 1979. Hit hard by the continuing decline in Great Lakes shipping and a strike that closed its shipyards in Lorain, Toledo, and Chicago in 1978–79, the company turned increasingly to defense contracts for its business and began to close its Great Lakes shipyards. It closed its Lorain shipyard in Dec. 1983.

The **AMERICAN SOCIALIST CONFERENCE** was held in Cleveland 28–30 Nov. 1958; 140 self-proclaimed socialists from 13 states and the District of Columbia convened at the Tudor Arms Hotel to study and discuss the need for socialism in America. The chairman of the conference was Eric J. Reinthaler of Willowick, Ohio. Although the Socialist and Socialist Labor parties declined to participate in or endorse the conference, several individuals claiming membership in these organizations and in the COMMUNIST PARTY were in attendance. Members of various labor unions and universities were also present. In fear of Communist or radical influences, the Cleveland antisubversive squad put the session under surveillance.

Claiming to be "Independent Socialists," the participants listened to speakers discuss the need for social and civil rights, world peace, and labor rights. The major discussions focused on civil rights and the need for independent political action on the part of labor. Clevelander Richard Tussey of the MECHANICS EDUCATIONAL SOCIETY OF AMERICA called for the formation of a labor party that would elect individuals pledged to the interests of workers. Although participants disagreed on several issues, all desired change in the electoral laws, which they felt discriminated against minority parties. The convention also advocated work toward correcting legislation that prevented the socialist program from being presented to voters on the presidential ticket in many states, including Ohio. Most also agreed that gaining the support of labor unions was essential in advancing socialism in America. The conference adjourned with the intention of establishing a committee that would maintain contact among the participants and arrange for local meetings to discuss issues of independent socialist action.

Proceedings of the National Conference of American Socialists, Cleveland, Ohio, 28–30 Nov. 1958, WRHS.

**AMERICAN STEEL & WIRE CO.** *See* **UNITED STATES STEEL CORP.**

The **AMERICAN WOMEN'S SUFFRAGE ASSOCIATION** held its first meeting in Cleveland 24–25 Nov. 1869. An enthusiastic audience, including delegates from 21 states, filled the large auditorium of CASE HALL. Susan B. Anthony, Rev. Antoinette Brown Blackwell, Lucy Stone, and Julia Ward Howe were among those attending. A constitution was written to provide for the national organization of state women's suffrage associations, to initiate new state associations, and to guide and coordinate their work in the women's suffrage movement. Henry Ward Beecher was elected president of the AWSA. The meeting was conducted with unusual efficiency and decorum, and the many speeches were warmly received and well reported.

**AMERICANIZATION.** The heavy influx of immigrants into cities such as Cleveland before and after the CIVIL WAR tested the belief that America could easily assimilate foreign newcomers. Hector Crevecoeur, an 18th-century

French writer, had popularized the image of America as a mix of races and nationalities blending into and forming a new culture. On the other hand, nativists who had organized the Know-Nothing party before the Civil War feared that the foreign customs and vices of non-Anglo-Saxon people would destroy America. Their solution was isolation from the rest of the world and deportation or restriction of aliens from our soil. Anglo-conformists shared a similar concern but believed that a less drastic solution could be found to make immigrants shed their foreign customs and assimilate into the mainstream of Protestant, middle-class America. The public schools were foremost among the institutions that were burdened with the task of fulfilling this mission.

One of the primary objectives of the CLEVELAND PUBLIC SCHOOLS since their beginning in 1836 had been the assimilation of foreign-born immigrants into American society. The leaders of the city's schools before the Civil War were transplanted New Englanders who believed that the public or common school was a panacea for the social and economic ills of American society. They claimed, like Horace Mann of Massachusetts, that the compulsory attendance of all children in the public schools would educate children not only in the "three Rs," but also in the cultural values of Anglo-Saxon America. In 1835, Calvin Stowe, one of the most influential leaders of Ohio's public-school movement, told teachers that it was essential for America's national strength that the foreigners who settled on our soil should cease to be Europeans and become Americans. But the public school found that immigrant children needed specialized programs to succeed in the classroom. In Mayflower School, built at the corner of 31st St. (Mayflower) and Orange in 1851, the majority of the students came from Czech families, and only 25% of the pupils could speak English by the 1870s. Teachers spent a portion of each day providing special lessons in the English language. In 1870, superintendent Andrew Rickoff and the school board instituted the teaching of German to successfully enroll the majority of the more than 2,000 children of German parentage who had previously attended private schools that taught subjects in German. Educational leaders in Cleveland before the turn of the century believed that Anglo-Saxon America would be strengthened by the addition of different nationalities as long as they conformed to the dominant culture. The goal of mixing all nationalities in the common schools was not endorsed by all immigrant groups in the 19th century. Cleveland's Irish Catholics followed the advice of Bp. RICHARD GILMOUR, who condemned the public schools as irreligious and told his congregants that they were Catholics first and citizens second. By 1884, 123 parochial schools had enrolled 26,000 pupils. Nationality churches served over 200,000 people by the turn of the century, and parochial schools of the Catholic diocese that taught foreign languages and customs flourished as Cleveland became the home of newcomers from Southern and Eastern Europe. Described as "the new immigrants," they increased from 43,281 to 115,870 people between 1900–10.

School reformers questioned the effectiveness of the policy of Anglo-conformity in the face of the growing cultural diversity of the student population. Some celebrated the philosophy of the "melting pot," or the mixing of nationalities together. Brownell School on Prospect Ave. had enrolled, for example, over 30 different nationalities by the turn of the century. Social settlements, such as HIRAM HOUSE in the Central-Woodland neighborhood of Russian Jews and ITALIANS, provided the city's first citizenship and vocational-education programs and became the social-service model for Cleveland's immigrants. In doing

28

so, the settlements carried forward citizenship programs that had been instituted early in the century by patriotic societies such as the Daughters of the American Revolution. In 1901, Harmon School provided "steamer classes," language instruction for foreign-born children. Evening schools taught adult immigrants civics and English to pass naturalization exams. Schools also expanded social-welfare programs to meet the needs of immigrant, working-class children. In 1907, a medical dispensary, the first of its kind, was opened in the Murray Hill district of Italian residents. Despite the public schools' efforts to reach immigrants, the CLEVELAND FOUNDATION's school survey of 1915 criticized the system for not providing enough steamer classes and other specialized programs for a student population in which over 50% came from homes in which a foreign language was spoken. It was estimated that over 60,000 un-naturalized immigrants lived in Cleveland and that ⅔ of the student population left school before the legally required age of 16 for girls and 15 for boys.

The entrance of America into WORLD WAR I increased the public's anxiety over the effectiveness of the public schools' Americanization program in securing the loyalty of foreign-born immigrants and their children. RAYMOND MOLEY, a political-science professor from Western Reserve University, was hired to direct its activities. On 6 Apr. 1917, Mayor HARRY L. DAVIS appointed the MAYOR'S ADVISORY WAR COMMITTEE, which created a "Committee of The Teaching of English to Foreigners." The mayor appointed businessman HAROLD T. CLARK as chairman and allowed the organization to be renamed the Cleveland Americanization Council. It coordinated 68 local organizations and worked with state and federal programs. The Board of Education trained language teachers, and the Citizens Bureau at city hall supplied instructors of naturalization. Both programs were offered at schools, factories, libraries, social settlements, churches, and community centers. Naturalization classes enrolled 2,067 students during the fall of 1919. The council launched a citywide publicity campaign, which included posters in different languages and advertisements in 22 nationality newspapers. The ideology of social efficiency was often used with employers to stress how the Americanization of foreign workers would increase their punctuality, orderliness, and productivity. Moley wrote *Lessons in Citizenship*, a civics handbook, to help immigrants pass naturalization exams. The War Advisory Committee asked ELEANOR LEDBETTER, a foreign-language librarian for the CLEVELAND PUBLIC LIBRARY, and other researchers to write a series of sympathetic studies of the city's nationality cultures and neighborhoods. The library also provided newspapers and books in over 20 different languages to reach the foreign-born. Despite the advocacy by Moley and Ledbetter of cultural pluralism as the basis for mutual exchange and respect between immigrant cultures and the public schools, the bitter controversies and feelings aroused during wartime America caused many Americans to lose faith in the assimilative capacities of the public schools.

Superintendent Frank Spaulding and the majority of the school board supported the removal and prosecution of a socialist board member who publicly opposed America's participation in World War I, under the Espionage Act of 1917. The board also terminated the teaching of German and required a loyalty oath from teachers as part of the wartime campaign for "100% Americanism." Events surrounding the MAY DAY RIOTS and Red Scare of 1919–20 aroused public anger against foreign immigrants who were supporters of radical or progressive causes. On 1 May 1919, the Socialist party's March in support of the Russian Revolution on Cleveland's PUBLIC SQUARE incited a riot and the arrest of 116 demonstrators. Local newspapers quickly pointed out that only 8 of those arrested had been born in the U.S. The city government immediately passed laws to restrict parades and the display of red flags. Newspapers and business, labor, and civic organizations called for the deportation of foreigners not wanting to become Americans. Others called for stronger Americanization programs.

Harold T. Clark asked for the passage of a law to compel young people to attend school until the age of 21 and for the adoption of methods used by the Army to teach soldiers English. Allen Burns, the former director of the Cleveland Foundation's survey program, conducted a series of studies to improve Americanization programs for the Carnegie Foundation. Cleveland's educators and social workers complained about the postwar financial cuts in citizenship training. The *PLAIN DEALER* alarmingly reported that the city's immigrant population contained over 85,000 unnaturalized males, and if their families were counted, the number of unnaturalized foreigners rose to approximately 212,000 out of a total residential population of 796,841. The postwar arrival of millions of Southern and Eastern Europeans created a sense of panic throughout America. Schools were judged incapable of assimilating what were seen as biologically inferior groups of immigrants. In 1924, Congress passed a quota law that drastically reduced the number of immigrants from Southern and Eastern Europe to 3% of their prewar level, and in effect banned Asians from coming to America.

Throughout the 1920s and 1930s, immigrant neighborhoods and organizations responded to the needs of the second generation. Often the American-born and -educated children clashed with the values and customs of their parents. Many no longer lived in the ethnic neighborhoods of their parents. Intermarriage between individuals of the same religious faith but different ethnic background created the triple melting pot among Catholics, Jews, and Protestants. Ethnic parishes and newspapers began to communicate in English as the second and third generations lost the urgency to speak their mother tongue. *LA VOCE DEL POPOLO ITALIANO*, an Italian nationality newspaper, advertised in English and urged its readers to naturalize. Some ethnic groups controlled their rate of assimilation by modifying and adapting their organizations. The Polish immigrant parish gradually changed, for example, to the hyphenated parish of the Polish-American community, and finally to the American parish of Polish ancestry. The nationality parish declined in membership in the central city and became a rarity in the suburbs because of restrictive immigration laws and demographic changes. Between 1930–40, Cleveland's foreign-born population decreased by 51,763, or 22.2%, and dropped to a total of 179,183. The proportion of foreign-born in the city's total population declined from 30.1% in 1920 to 14.5% in 1950. As the second and third generations became more successful economically and more Americanized, or less dependent on nationality organizations, they moved into what were once Protestant-dominated suburban areas after WORLD WAR II.

Different generations of immigrants continued to search for an identity that balanced both their ethnic heritage and the American environment. A conscious celebration of nationality cultures counteracted the host society's ethnocentrism. Folk festivals, sponsored by the CLEVELAND FOLK ARTS ASSOC., nationality holidays, fraternal organizations, the All Nations Festival, and the Cultural Gardens all celebrated immigrant contributions to the city. In 1948, the Mayfield Merchants' Assoc. in Cleveland's LITTLE ITALY sponsored a banquet to honor Miss Florence

Graham. Of Irish descent, she had faithfully served and fought discrimination against the city's Italian-American community since 1908 during her tenure as teacher and principal in the neighborhood's Murray Hill School. The YWCA's Internatl. Institute, organized in 1916, trained older immigrants to work with recent arrivals. The Citizens Bureau with the support of the Welfare Fed. supplied aid, advice, and naturalization classes. The bureau also cooperated with the citizenship and English classes for foreignborn pupils in the public schools. By 1929, 130,000 foreignspeaking students had attended these classes.

Eleanor Ledbetter expanded the foreign-language collection in the Cleveland Public Library and compiled a volume of Czech fairytales and a bibliography of Polish literature. HELEN HORVATH, who had immigrated from Hungary in 1897, began mothers' clubs and educational programs for foreign newcomers. The public schools asked her to join her efforts to their programs, and she was asked to discuss immigrant edcucation at many universities. John Dewey, the leading philosopher and proponent of progressive education, praised the work of Verdine Peck Hull, who had pioneered a course in interracial tolerance in the public schools in 1924. He declared that the program's emphasis on mutual understanding represented true Americanism. In 1973 the city created Senior Ethnic Find, a program to help elderly immigrants use available social services. The NATIONALITIES SERVICES CTR., created by a merger of the Internatl. Institute and the Citizens Bureau in 1954, and the LEAGUE FOR HUMAN RIGHTS, formed in 1934, helped immigrants displaced by the ravages of totalitarian regimes and World War II. The Cleveland Immigration & Naturalization Service helps residents sponsor the immigration of relatives, friends, and refugees from other countries and assists newcomers in becoming citizens.

With the decline in European immigration to America after World War I, Cleveland employers looked to the American South as a source of cheap labor. Over 100,000 Appalachians and 200,000 blacks migrated to the Greater Cleveland area in the ensuing years. The URBAN LEAGUE OF CLEVELAND helped blacks to find jobs and housing and, assisted by the NAACP, to fight discrimination. A plethora of black churches, KARAMU HOUSE, and fraternal organizations helped rural black newcomers adjust to their new urban environment. In the 1960s, the public schools began remedial and special education programs for minorities or those who were described as culturally disadvantaged learners. Cleveland's post-World War II population became even more diverse with the addition of Asians, Russian Jewish refugees, and Spanish-speaking people from Puerto Rico and Central or South America, Cuba, and Mexico. Displaced persons from Europe were the major foreign group in English classes, which enrolled over 2,000 students in the public schools in 1949. In 1965, Congress changed the immigration law. Ethnic origin was no longer a factor in admittance to the U.S. Preferential treatment was given to people with close relatives in the U.S. and those with occupational skills that America needed. People from the Far East and India were allowed to enter in large numbers. By the mid-1970s, almost ⅓ of America's immigrants came from Asia. Filipinos, Chinese, Koreans, Vietnamese, and Cambodians swelled the population of cities. In 1975, the greatest proportion of the 400,000 immigrants came from the West Indies and Mexico.

New and old organizations developed programs to meet the needs of Cleveland's changing immigrant population. The city's Vietnamese community established a refugee resettlement office to serve approximately 1,500 Vietnamese as well as Laotian and Cambodian immigrants. It offered social, employment, and translating services. The U.S. State Dept. asked the JEWISH FAMILY SERVICE ASSOC. to adapt their methods of resettlement to other groups. JFS helped over 600 Indo-Chinese settle locally. By the 1980s, Spanish-speaking groups had over 30,000 members in Cleveland. They were assisted by a variety of civic and fraternal organizations, the Spanish American Committee, an official liaison at city hall, and an employment-service bureau. Fifteen hundred Spanish-speaking students constituted the major group in the "English as a Second Language" program in the Cleveland public schools. Over 100 Vietnamese children were also enrolled in the bilingual course. The PACE ASSOC. (Program for Action by Citizens in Education), organized in 1963, developed a human-relations curriculum and trained teachers to increase multicultural understanding. The public schools also developed curriculum to promote an awareness of the history and contributions of minority groups.

Historically, the reaction of Clevelanders to immigrants and migrants has paralleled that of the country in general, and important differences between and among ethnic groups have shaped their responses to the culture of the host country. Birds of Passage, immigrants who came to America to earn as much money as quickly as possible before returning home, had little interest in becoming citizens or Americanized. Programs to assimilate immigrants depended heavily on the immigrants' reasons for coming to America, as well as the public's attitudes toward newcomers. When the economy of the city was expanding and in need of cheap labor, immigrants were seen as a vital part of the labor force and capable of becoming American. When the economy slumped in the 1890s and 1930s, or when the public became inflamed over patriotic unity, as occurred in the post-World War I and VIETNAM WAR eras, immigrants were viewed as threats to social harmony and incapable of assimilating. Native-born fears about new immigrants revealed their insecurities about American social and economic life. These conditions were directly connected to economic cycles of growth and decline.

By the 1970s, it became popular to note the rise of a "new ethnic consciousness," a movement strongly evidenced in Michael Novak's *The Rise of the Unmeltable Ethnics*. Novak believes that millions of ethnics who had tried to become Americanized according to the norms of the dominant culture were delighted to find that they no longer had to pay that price. Ethnic pride in cultural differences provided not only a stronger sense of community for immigrant groups, but also an antidote to an age in which modern systems of communication and commerce emphasized the greatest common denominators for a mass audience of supposedly like-minded individuals. This new attitude of cultural pluralism was quickly manifested in cities such as Cleveland. During the 1970s and 1980s, a series of programs were begun, including the Greater Cleveland Ethnographic Museum, Peoples & Cultures, the WESTERN RESERVE HISTORICAL SOCIETY's Cleveland Regional Ethnic Archives Program, the Public Library's Cleveland Heritage Program, CLEVELAND STATE UNIVERSITY's Multi-Cultural Education Ctr., and CUYAHOGA COMMUNITY COLLEGE's Community Studies Program and Oral History Ctr., that reflected this change in American attitudes. They served to continue the celebration of regional cultural vitality begun by people such as Eleanor Ledbetter and Helen Horvath, who created a sympathetic understanding of immigrant gifts as the basis for the Americanization of Cleveland.

Edward M. Miggins
Cuyahoga Community College

See also IMMIGRATION & MIGRATION and entries for specific ethnic groups.

**AMERICKE DELNICKE LISTY** (American Labor News), once the only Czech-language socialist weekly in the country, evolved in 1908 out of a mimeographed weekly founded by Karel Pintner. Located in Cleveland's Czech neighborhood on "Old Broadway," it was edited early in its career by JOSEPH MARTINEK, who later served as national secretary of the Czechoslovak Natl. Council of America, and subsequently by Vaclav H. Matousek. In 1928 it began printing 1 page in English, which later was edited by Frank Bardoun. As a Social Democratic publication, *Americke Delnicke Listy* espoused such political measures in the 1930s as social security, unemployment insurance, and old-age pensions. It advocated an independent Czechoslovakian republic in both world wars and prior to WORLD WAR II was the first American newspaper barred from Czechoslovakia by the Germans. In its own Czech-American community, it lent its support to such causes as the WORKERS GYMNASTIC UNION, workingmen's cooperative societies, Czech fraternal organizations, and freethinkers' schools. Although it survived to celebrate its 40th anniversary, *Americke Delnicke Listy* ceased publication in the early 1950s. Matousek, its last editor, then became an editor of the Czech daily *NOVY SVET*.

**AMERISKA DOMOVINA** (American Home), which became one of Cleveland's major ethnic dailies, could trace its lineage back to the origins of the city's SLOVENE press. It was preceded by *Narodna Beseda*, a semimonthly established on 11 Feb. 1899 and renamed *Nova Domovina* the following Nov. 1900. Although that venture went out of business on 25 Apr. 1908, Louis Pirc, one of the owners, replaced it on 5 June 1908 with a weekly named *Amerika*. That became *Clevelandska Amerika* when it went to twice weekly in Aug. 1908, and finally *Ameriska Domovina* in Feb. 1919. It was under that nameplate that it began daily publication on 3 Aug. 1929. In contrast to the freethinking daily *ENAKOPRAVNOST*, *Ameriska Domovina* has been strongly Catholic throughout its existence. Early issues gave recently arrived immigrants such practical advice as how to determine their house addresses. Politically, the paper favored the Democratic party nationally and opposed the spread of fascism abroad. By the 1930s, Pirc had acquired a partner, Jas. Debevec, who edited the paper and eventually became its owner. One of the few Slovenian newspapers to oppose the partisan party in Yugoslavia during WORLD WAR II, *Ameriska Domovina* maintained a staunch anti-Communist position afterward. Locally, it tended to follow the drift of young Slovenian-American politicians such as Geo. Voinovich toward the Republican party. Following Debevec's death in the early 1950s, control of the paper passed first to his wife, Mary, and then to his son, Jas. V. Debevec. Retrenchment began in the late 1960s, as *Ameriska Domovina* cut its issues back to 4, 3, and finally 2 times weekly. Addition of a weekly page in English helped stabilize the paper in the 1980s, when its Slovenian pages were edited by Rudolph M. Susel. Its home for over half a century was at 6117 St. Clair Ave.

**AMERITECH**—The **AMERICAN INFORMATION TECHNOLOGIES CORPORATION**—is the Chicago-based holding company founded in 1983 to receive from the divestiture of AT&T all shares of 5 telephone companies: Illinois Bell, Indiana Bell, Michigan Bell, Wisconsin Bell, and Ohio Bell. It also has subsidiaries for mobile communications service, directory advertising and publishing, customer sales and service, development, and lease financing for products and services. The Cleveland-based subsidiary of Ameritech, the Ohio Bell Telephone Co., began in Sept. 1879. Edward P. Wright, superintendent of the West-

ern Union Telegraph Co., organized the first telephone exchange in the city, located in the Board of Trade Bldg. on Water (W. 9th) St.; 76 people paid $72 per year to join the first exchange. Wright soon sold the exchange, valued at $3,700, for $16,300 and became vice-president of the new Cleveland Telephone Co. The company moved in 1880 to the top floor of the Kelly Bldg., 158 Superior Ave.; it moved again in 1888 to Seneca and Michigan Ave. (W. 3rd and Prospect), and yet again in 1898 to its new Main Bldg. at W. 3rd and Champlain.

When the Bell patents expired in 1894, independent telephone companies began to develop. The Home Telephone Co. was organized in Cleveland in 1895; it became the Cuyahoga Telephone Co. in 1898 and had installed 20,440 phones by 1906. In 1914 Cuyahoga Telephone Co. was absorbed by the Columbus-based independent, the Ohio State Telephone Co. In Oct. 1920, Cleveland Telephone changed its name to Ohio Bell and began to acquire other phone companies. It bought the Ohio properties of the Central Union Telephone Co. in Dec. 1920 and in 1921 merged with Ohio State Telephone, its only competitor in Cleveland. Eugene A. Reed served as the first president of the new company, which was worth $100 million. In July 1925 Ohio Bell began construction of its new $5 million, 22-story "Temple to Telephony" at 750 Huron Rd., which it officially occupied on 1 June 1927. In Dec. 1927, the Main and Cherry exchanges were switched to the new building's dial system facilities, enabling callers to bypass the operator and dial their numbers themselves.

Ohio Bell continued to expand and modernize its operations. In 1940, 154,700 residences and 33,800 businesses used Ohio Bell telephone service in Greater Cleveland; by 1951 Cleveland had 600,000 phones. In 1964 the company moved its headquarters to Erieview Plaza, and the next year it installed its one-millionth telephone in Greater Cleveland. By mid-April 1966, all Greater Cleveland phones had been given 7-digit numbers, replacing the exchange numbers used since 1897. Ohio Bell began using an electronic switching system in 1967, making available such services as call-waiting, call transfer, and 3-way calling. By 1982 the company was building a new $50 million, 16-story office building at E. 9th St. and Lakeside. Ohio Bell's sales totaled $1.4 billion in 1983.

**AMERITRUST** was established in 1894 as the Cleveland Trust Co., with $500,000 capital, and through mergers and a series of able leaders grew to become the largest bank in the Midwest. Within a decade of its founding, Cleveland Trust merged with the Western Reserve Trust Co. (1903) and kept their offices open as branches. Cleveland Trust, the first local bank to adopt the "branching" method of expansion popular in Canada and Europe, thus set the course for its own further expansion. By 1905, the bank outgrew a series of rented offices in the basement of the Garfield Bldg., and then in the Williamson Bldg., which served as its main office. It engaged the architectural firm of Geo. B. Post & Sons to build a domed Renaissance-style rotunda on property formerly owned by the First Methodist Church at E. 9th and Euclid. The granite building features 8 fluted Corinthian columns and a Karl Bitter pediment, *Allegorization of the Main Springs of Wealth*, arched above the main entrance.

By acquiring banks such as the Detroit St. Bank, the Garfield Savings Bank, and Lake Shore Banking & Trust, Cleveland Trust became the 6th-largest bank in the country by its 30th anniversary; 53 branches celebrated the event with a 1-ton cake. On the eve of the Depression, as it absorbed the Pearl St. Bank, Cleveland Trust had 58 branches, capital of $13.8 million, and a surplus of $23 million. Closed by the bank holiday in 1933, Cleveland Trust, being in a Federal Reserve city, was the first local bank to be examined and allowed to reopen, backed by the U.S. government. Pres. Harris Creech quelled any remaining panic among jittery depositors by extending bank hours to insure access to funds. Creech's firm handling of the crisis attracted an additional $8 million in deposits by year's end. With the hiring of GEO. GUND as a director in 1937 and as president in 1941, Cleveland Trust achieved even greater prominence in the financial community. By 1945, its billion-dollar assets nearly exceeded those of Cleveland's leading banks in 1929. Its wealth and influence were increased through interlocking directorates with major corporations; at one time Gund sat on 31 boards, while bank directors were often high-ranking corporate officials. The bank wielded additional power through its trust department, which managed and voted on corporate stock.

The investment and management policies of Cleveland Trust came under fire in the 1960s. First, the bank was challenged by CYRUS EATON for its policy of voting its own stock held by the trust department, and for its manipulation of other companies by voting their stock. Eaton, a major stockholder, won 2 early rounds in lower courts, but the bank's policy was upheld by the Ohio Supreme Court in Mar. 1970. Eaton sold his stock. The bank was then charged by the Justice Dept. with antitrust violations because of its control of stock in 4 competing machine-tool companies (WHITE CONSOLIDATED INDUSTRIES, WARNER & SWASEY CO., Pneumo-Dynamics, and ACME-CLEVELAND) and for its alleged role in the merger of Cleveland Twist Drill and Natl. Acme. The first case of its kind, the suit challenged a practice widespread in the banking industry of maintaining interlocking directorates and control over corporate stock. This suit was settled in 1975, when the Justice Dept. dismissed all but 1 issue; the bank agreed to refuse to hire as a director anyone who sat on the boards of 2 or more machine-tool companies.

Gund was succeeded as president and later chairman by Geo. Karch, who continued many of his predecessor's policies in the face of new challenges. Bounded in its ability to expand outside Cuyahoga County by a 1930s Ohio law, Cleveland Trust saturated the county market with branches. (Its 4 branches in Lake and Lorain counties existed under a grandfather provision in the law.) Anticipating a change in the law, the book acquired mortgage banking and realty companies out of state while delaying in-state expansion. By 1972, while Cleveland Trust searched for a successor to Karch, the bank's size and prominence were challenged by BancOhio of Columbus, a holding company. By its organization, BancOhio could skirt the law by acquiring banks throughout the state but set them up as corporations within counties. In mid-1972, when Cleveland Trust had 80 branches, BancOhio had 31 member banks and 143 offices in 30 counties. To compete, Cleveland Trust set up a holding company of its own, CleveTrust. With the coming of M. Brock Weir as president and CEO in Dec. 1972, the bank established affiliates throughout the state. In 1979, CleveTrust changed its name to the AmeriTrust Corp. to reflect its new horizons. An exchange of its state charter for a national one in 1983 permitted AmeriTrust to expand outside the state as well as outside the county, and to seek regional leadership.

As AmeriTrust increased its involvement outside the Greater Cleveland area, it had to fight off charges of abandoning its home town in favor of more lucrative investment opportunities elsewhere. In the 1960s, the bank pointed to its leadership in local home loans, its loan record to minority businesses and churches, the number of branches it maintained in the inner city, and its donation of outmoded buildings to community groups. AmeriTrust and its chairman were the targets of Dennis Kucinich's wrath in the 1970s when Cleveland was plunged into DEFAULT. Furthermore, the bank was charged with redlining by community action groups; this time, the bank was cleared of most charges but was found guilty of prescreening loan applications and of failing to meet the credit needs of low- and medium-income areas. In response, Weir promised a $5 million development corporation to create local jobs. Managed by chairman Jerry V. Jarrett, in 1986 the bank had assets of $7 billion and provided a full range of banking and trust services. Its local operation, the AmeriTrust Co. Natl. Assoc., operated many offices in Ohio and 1 in the Bahamas.

**AMUSEMENT PARKS.** The amusement park, a concept that originated in Europe, debuted in the U.S. at Coney Island, Brooklyn, N.Y. The island began as a summer resort for the wealthy of New York City; gradually the middle and working classes expropriated it and its expanding attractions for their use and entertainment. It became the prototype for amusement parks throughout the U.S. Two innovations at Coney Island deserve special mention. In 1884, La Marcus A. Thompson, an inventor originally from Ohio, built and operated the "Switchback," the nation's first roller coaster. The roller coaster went on to become the favorite attraction and most visible symbol of parks everywhere. Less noticeable but more important was the creation of a transportation network that fed the park. City rail lines carried visitors to the boat lines that served the island. Inexpensive transportation was critical in both the rise and the demise of the traditional urban park. By the early 1890s, Cleveland was ready to support such a recreational business. All of the factors that had made Coney Island a success were operative in Cleveland: a large, urban population, possessed of some disposable income, with access to trolley and interurban rail lines, living in cramped neighborhoods of numbing similarity. Once started, the parks sprang up quickly. The first for which documentation exists was Forest City Park. It was located between Beyerle Ave. and WASHINGTON PARK, with the Willson Ave. (E. 55th St.) trolley line running nearby. The park seems to have been an immediate success; 100,000 customers paid the $.15 admission fee in 1893. Attractions included a shooting gallery, a merry-go-round, shows and concerts in the theater, dancing, and BOWLING. However, as the years passed, the park began to suffer in comparison with newer competitors. Also, with no parking facilities, it could not host the newly developed automobile trade. Declining admissions and a major fire closed Forest City Park in the mid-1920s. Very few traces of it can be found today (1986).

Inspired in part by the success of Forest City, local investors formed a company to build a park on the eastern lakefront that, in time, became a Cleveland institution. EUCLID BEACH PARK, built on the site of the Cobb family farm between Collamer Ave. (E. 156th St.) and Ursuline Ave. NE, opened in 1895. A local trolley line ran to gate on Lake Shore Blvd., providing access to the park in its early years. The 1,700-ft. sand beach and 75 acres of wooded parkland drew bathers and picnickers. Entertainment attractions were varied and constantly expanded. Opening day at Euclid Beach became a harbinger of summer for generations of Clevelanders. Nevertheless, the park was not an immediate success. The original investor group gave way in 1901 to the Humphrey family. The Humphreys, previously known in Cleveland as candy and popcorn manufacturers, brought Euclid Beach into its glory years. Inventive and industrious, they made the park into a family entertainment center. In order to counteract the reputation of parks and carnival midways as hotbeds of iniquity and sensationalism, the Humphreys determined that nothing in Euclid Beach would "depress or demoralize" their customers. Further, they insured that nothing would physically injure their visitors by daily inspection of the rides. Finally, as an inducement to patrons, the Humphreys allowed free admission to the grounds and charged small fees for use of the attractions, among the more popular of which were La Marcus Thompson's 1896 reprise of the Coney Island Switchback, the baroque-styled carousel, the Thriller roller coaster, the Flying Turns, the Log Cabin, the Surprise House, the lakefront pier and fountain, the maple-floored dancing pavilion, and the skating rink, complete with a rococo-styled Gavioli organ. Over 100 rides and concessions made Euclid Beach the epitome of amusement parks. As the years passed, Euclid Beach Park changed. Trolleys were replaced by buses. Families in automobiles began to arrive more frequently. The park made provision to host these new guests. Even so, attendance began to decline after WORLD WAR II. Slowly at first, and then with startling rapidity in the 1960s, the once-loyal patrons turned to other diversions. The park closed forever on 28 Sept. 1969. Following a series of fires, only the entrance gate, designated a historic landmark, still stood in 1986 as a memorial to past glories. Still, in 1985 Ohio created Euclid Beach State Park on the easternmost 16 acres of the old amusement park. Some vestige of the land's original purpose remained.

In 1898, the first park on the west side of the city opened. PURITAS SPRINGS PARK, overlooking the Rocky River valley, stood astride a deep ravine from which flowed the artesian well that gave the park its name. Puritas Springs was also a "trolley park," served by the Cleveland & Southwestern interurban. Owner and manager John E. Gooding took his cue from Euclid Beach and offered free grounds admission. While the carousel, dance hall, and roller rink were popular, the truly outstanding attraction was the Cyclone roller coaster. Careening in and out of the ravine, the Cyclone was higher and faster than any other coaster in the Cleveland area. Puritas Springs drew west-siders for years. Still, its magnetism also began to fade after the war. In 1946, a fire destroyed the dance hall. In 1958, another fire forced the park to close. A residential neighborhood was developed on the Puritas Ave. site. In 1902, another east side park opened for what proved to be a brief run. WHITE CITY AMUSEMENT PARK was built on the lake at Lake Shore Blvd. and E. 140th St. It competed with, and imitated, Euclid Beach, a mile to the east. Served by the same streetcars, the 2 parks became a common destination for a day's outing. Unlike Euclid Beach, White City charged an admission fee. Attractions included the Shoot-the-Chutes water ride, the Scenic Railway roller coaster, the Flying Airships, Bostock's Animal Show, and the inevitable dance hall. However, catastrophe besieged the park. In May 1906, fire destroyed the grounds. The park was rebuilt, but a gale on 24 July 1907 destroyed it again, and White City did not reopen. The grounds are now (1986) the site of the Easterly Sewage Disposal Plant.

LUNA PARK opened in 1905 and proved to be Euclid Beach's most memorable competitor. Copied from the Coney Island park of the same name, Luna Park was a fantasy of "Oriental" architecture and electric lights. The 35-acre grounds were bounded by Woodland Ave., Woodhill, Mt. Carmel, and E. 110th St. The park was served by several local streetcar lines. The site is hilly, and patrons climbed a steep flight of stairs or later rode an early escalator to reach the gate. Luna Park also charged admission. The grounds were divided by a sharp rise, with the rides situated in the eastern half. Favorite rides included a carousel, a

ferris wheel, the Jack Rabbit and Pippin roller coasters, a Shoot-the-Chutes, a fun house, a roller rink, and a dance hall. Also, the park featured a concert garden, in which opera star Enrico Caruso once performed. The western half featured a picnic grove, swimming pool, motordome, and stadium for FOOTBALL and BASEBALL. Luna Park enjoyed brief but fervent popularity. It lost patronage in the late 1920s. By the late 1930s, only the skating rink remained open, but it was destroyed by fire. In 1940, the Woodhill Homes housing project was constructed on the site. The western suburbs got a park in 1906 with the opening of Lincoln Park, on Sloane Ave. in ROCKY RIVER. Built on grounds known formerly as Scenic Park, Lincoln Park was touted in the Cleveland newspapers as an investment opportunity. The Detroit and Clifton Ave. trolleys ran past, as did the Lake Shore Electric interurbans. Despite such major access lines and unique attractions such as the "only round dancing floor in Ohio," and an electrical race course over which "pitching wooden steeds operated by electricity" ran, Lincoln Park never became truly popular. One by one the attractions were disassembled, until only the grounds and the name were left. Gordon Gardens was the final venture in the Cleveland area, built in 1922. The smallest in size with only 8 acres, the park was located on the west side of E. 72nd St. between the lake and the New York Central tracks. The operators hoped to attract the automobile traffic on E. 72nd, but again, the small park could not compete with its larger, better-equipped competitors. The 1927 burning of the dance hall closed the park. In 1986, the grounds were occupied by the Shoreway and the CLEVELAND LAKEFRONT STATE PARK.

The golden age of urban amusement parks lasted only some 60 years. All across the U.S., the old parks closed in the 1960s and 1970s. There were several reasons for their passing. Perhaps primary was a change in taste for entertainment. Movies, and to a greater degree television, exposed the American public to fantasies far more compelling than those that the glitter and false fronts of the amusement parks could offer, and at a lower cost. Increased personal mobility, which had made the parks possible, continued to expand, carrying the public away with it. The parks had coped with the advent of the automobile by adding parking facilities, but they often reached the limits of their capacity. Also, family vacations more often became automobile trips to remote destinations. The local amusement park was simply too close. The nature of the direct competition changed, too. With the successful advent of Disneyland in 1955, "traditional" parks such as Cedar Pt. and Geauga Lake repackaged their offerings as complete vacation destinations, with accommodations and activities beyond the scope of the urban park. Racism in the postwar years also dealt a blow to the urban parks. Many whites ceased to attend parks once they had been successfully integrated, and as whites moved to suburban areas far removed from the parks, the loss of population further reduced the patronage of the parks and crippled their economic viability. Finally, the safety record of the old-style amusement parks was somewhat spotty. Wooden construction of high-speed rides and low profit margins often combined to produce neglect and unsafe conditions. The newer destination parks virtually insured that personal injury would not occur to their patrons. In the end, the traditional urban amusement parks proved to be both too tame and too dangerous for their audience.

Russell Allon Hehr

See also DANCE HALLS.

The **ANCIENT ORDER OF HIBERNIANS** is an Irish and Irish-American organization that traces its roots back to the organization of the Defenders in Ireland in 1565 to protect Roman Catholic priests and the church against English persecution. Branches were organized in the U.S beginning in 1836. A Cleveland branch reportedly was formed in the 1850s; by 1874, 3 branches of the benevolent society were active in Cleveland: one at ST. MALACHI'S CHURCH, one in NEWBURGH, and another that met at 99 Bank (W. 6th) St. Membership in the organization was open to Irish Roman Catholics of good moral character, and at a time when politics in Ireland led to friction between Irish nationalists and the Catholic church, members were not allowed to participate in secret societies condemned by the church. Local Irish historians suggest, however, that the moderate church-approved benevolent society became a means by which members of the ardent Irish nationalist Clan na Gael gained respectability and acceptance. A Cleveland branch of the latter group, the MacNevin Club (named in honor of Dr. Wm. J. MacNevin, a leader of the 1798 United Irish Movement), was formed in Cleveland in 1867 by Capt. P. J. Walsh. Local historians argue that despite its membership regulations, the local Ancient Order of Hibernians welcomed members of the Clan na Gael "with knowing nods, if not open arms." Cleveland hosted the national convention of the Ancient Order of Hibernians in May 1884, a meeting descibed as "a very stormy one throughout." The organization had grown to 15 divisions in Cleveland in 1896, when its headquarters were located at 219 Superior. The divisions held monthly meetings and came together quarterly for countywide meetings. They also took part in parades and other public events and sponsored their own social events. Between 1906–35, the order declined from 13 local branches to only 3, which met at Flynn Hall at Superior and E. 53rd, at 2702 Franklin Ave., and at Broadway and Harvard in Newburgh. In 1940, these 3 groups had a combined membership of 1,000.

**ANDORN, SIDNEY IGNATIUS** (25 Sept. 1906–25 Sept. 1981), made his mark in newspapers, radio, and television during a journalism career spanning over 50 years. Born in Newark, Ohio, he moved to Cleveland with his family in 1912. After graduating from Western Reserve University with a degree in English, he joined the staff of the *CLEVELAND PRESS* in 1929. Breaking in on the entertainment and sports beats, Andorn was soon assigned to write Cleveland's first gossip column for the *Press*. Modeled after Walter Winchell's pioneering "Your Broadway and Mine" in the *New York Evening Graphic*, Andorn's was called "The Minute Review" and subheaded "Read It While You Boil an Egg." In 1935, Andorn moved to the fledgling field of RADIO to do a gossip program for WGAR. Over the next 15 years, he also did news commentaries and a groundbreaking "Open Forum" program, in which listeners were invited to phone in questions on civic issues to be answered by experts visiting in the studio with Andorn. Other area firsts included the first broadcast from a moving train and the first from a mobile unit. In 1944, he won a commendation from the city council for his coverage of the EAST OHIO GAS CO. EXPLOSION AND FIRE.

Andorn broke into TELEVISION in 1950, when he became program director for WXEL (later WJW). He later recalled filling in gaps in live programming with shots of wallpaper patterns over a musical soundtrack. Later in his career he returned to Channel 8 as host of the "Cleveland Caucus" civic affairs program. Leaving television in 1954, Andorn wrote a column for the *CLEVELAND NEWS* until its demise in 1960, when he returned to WGAR for news commentaries and the "Open Forum." A City Club member, he served as president in 1966 and instituted its summer

outdoor debates in the Cleveland Public Library's Eastman Garden. He also taught broadcast journalism and mass communications at CUYAHOGA COMMUNITY COLLEGE. In the final years of his career, Andorn's news commentaries were heard over WCLV-FM, and his newspaper column resurfaced in the Sun suburban chain. He died on his 75th birthday, survived by his second wife, the former Miriam Cramer, and a daughter, Dr. Anne Andorn.

**ANDREW DALL & SON** was the firm of one of the most important building contractors in 19th-century Cleveland. Andrew Dall, Sr. (1821–1887), emigrated from Scotland in 1852. His son Andrew was born in 1850. The Dalls began primarily as stonecutters and masons, and by 1875 the family was well established as a contracting and building firm, having built the important Randall Wade and Backus houses on Euclid Ave., among others. It also built the EUCLID AVE. OPERA HOUSE (1875), St. Paul's Episcopal Church (1876), Adelbert College (1881), and the Wilshire Bldg. designed by John Edelman (1881). Other Euclid Ave. mansions erected by the Dalls were those of SYLVESTER EVERETT, Samuel Andrews (ANDREWS'S FOLLY), CHAS. BRUSH, and CHAS. BINGHAM (all demolished). Upon the death of Andrew, Sr., in 1887, Andrew Dall formed a partnership with Arthur McAllister. Among other buildings, McAllister & Dall erected the Samuel Mather home in Bratenahl, the Society for Savings by Burnham & Root, the SOLDIERS & SAILORS MONUMENT in PUBLIC SQUARE, the McClymonds house in Massillon, and the Erie County Savings Bank in Buffalo. After 1899 the firm continued as Andrew Dall & Son, building the CUYAHOGA COUNTY COURTHOUSE (1912) and the UNION CLUB (1905), as well as buildings in Dayton, Cincinnati, and Zanesville. The firm ceased to exist in 1913, and Andrew Dall died in 1923. The list of buildings constructed by the Dall firms indicates that they were among the most significant builders in late-19th-and early-20th-century Cleveland.

**ANDREWS, SAMUEL** (10 Feb. 1836–15 Apr. 1904), was a poor English immigrant who became a pioneer in the oil industry and cofounder of the STANDARD OIL CO. Born in Oaksey, England, Andrews received little formal education. A candlemaker by trade, he arrived in Cleveland in 1857. In 1859 he married Mary Cole. By 1859 he was an assistant to fellow Englishman Chas. A. Dean, an oil supplier who refined lard oil and manufactured coal oil from cannel coal. With Andrews's help, Dean's company became the first in Cleveland to refine kerosene from crude oil. Understanding the commercial possibilities of kerosene, Andrews decided to establish his own company to produce it and convinced another Englishman, Maurice B. Clark, and JOHN D. ROCKEFELLER to provide the financial support for his enterprise. Andrews, Clark & Co. was organized in 1863. With Andrews providing the practical knowledge for the company's operation and Rockefeller in charge of the financial aspects, the firm grew quickly, increasing production and taking on new partners. In 1870 Andrews's firm became the Standard Oil Co., with Andrews as works superintendent. Andrews often disagreed with Rockefeller over the direction of Standard Oil. Unhappy with its increasing number of mergers with companies outside Ohio, he sold his interests in the company to Rockefeller in the spring of 1874 for $1 million.

Andrews's fortune helped support several educational institutions in Cleveland. He helped build BROOKS MILITARY SCHOOL in 1875, and he served as a trustee of Adelbert College of Western Reserve University. He was also a member of the Erie St. Baptist Church. He also used his fortune to build one of the city's largest mansions, at the northeast corner of Euclid and Sterling (E. 30th) sts. Known as ANDREWS'S FOLLY, it was inefficient and costly to maintain and was razed in 1923.

**ANDREWS, SHERLOCK JAMES** (17 Nov. 1801–11 Feb. 1880), was one of the first lawyers in the Cleveland area; he was considered by many to be the father and head of the Cleveland bar. Andrews was born in Wallingford, Conn. His father, a doctor, taught him a preparatory course of study at the Episcopal Academy at Cheshire. After graduating with high honors from Union College in 1821, Andrews studied law at the New Haven Law School. During this period, he served as an assistant to Prof. Silliman in the chemistry department at Yale College. Andrews came to Cleveland in 1825 and formed a law partnership with Judge Samuel Cowles, which lasted until Cowles's retirement in 1832. Andrews then formed a partnership with JOHN A. FOOTE and JAS. M. HOYT (Andrews, Foote, & Hoyt). He quickly rose in prominence in his field and in the community. He was elected president of Cleveland's first city council in 1836 (resigning shortly thereafter) and also served as the prosecuting attorney for Cuyahoga County.

In 1840, Andrews was elected to the U.S. House of Representatives from the district that included Cleveland. Because of poor health, he retired after a single term. Returning to his law practice and still in poor health, he advised and pleaded only his firm's more important cases. The Ohio general assembly appointed Andrews to the Cuyahoga County Superior Court in 1848. The next year, he was a leading member of the Ohio Constitutional Convention, serving on the committees on judicial review and temperance. A new constitution abolished the superior courts, and again Andrews returned to his practice. After the convention, Andrews confined his practice mainly to the most important cases before the state and federal courts. During this period, he also had business interests; he served as president of the Merchants Bank and the Society for Savings. In 1873, another convention was called to revise the Ohio constitution; Andrews was elected as a delegate to the convention after receiving both the Republican and Democratic nominations. He also was unanimously elected to head the Cleveland district's delegation and served as chairman of the Committee on Revision of the Judiciary. After the convention, Andrews again returned to his practice and concentrated on important and complicated cases of equity. Before his death, he was elected vice-president of the EARLY SETTLERS ASSOC. OF THE WESTERN RESERVE. Andrews married Ursula Allen of Litchfield, Conn., in 1828. Her father, John Allen, was a member of Congress. The Andrewses had 4 daughters and 1 son.

**"ANDREWS'S FOLLY"** was the popular name for the home of SAMUEL ANDREWS, one of the original partners of the firm that became the STANDARD OIL CO. in 1870. Although he sold his shares in 1874 and thus did not reap the phenomemal riches that others did, Andrews determined to build the greatest house on the "Millionaires' Row" of Euclid Ave. Erected in 1882–85 and designed in a modified Victorian Gothic baronial style, the house had 80–100 rooms, an immense central hall, carved staircases and woodwork, stained glass, and 5 separate apartments for the financier's daughters. The architect was GEO. H. SMITH, one of the collaborators in the design of the ARCADE. Andrews's hope of entertaining Queen Victoria in the house never materialized. It was soon found that the plan of the house made it impossible for servants to function efficiently, and the house was closed. Thus it came to be known as "Andrews's Folly," standing vacant for 25 years until its demolition in 1923. The house was located on the northwest corner of Euclid and E. 30th St.

The **ANGLE** was an Irish ghetto that developed on Cleveland's near west side in the late 1860s. The Angle was generally defined as the parish of ST. MALACHI'S CHURCH, an area north of Detroit Ave., east of W. 28th St., and down Washington Ave. to WHISKEY ISLAND, which it included. This area had long been an Irish neighborhood, as it overlooked the ore docks where the early IRISH found employment. By the late 1860s, the Irish had become numerous enough for divisions to form within their own enclave, the poorer Irish remaining in the near west side area. A further artificial division was made when St. Malachi's was built in 1868, a parish that predominantly encompassed this poorer neighborhood. Despite their poverty, the "Angle Irish" were considered the most chauvinistic of Cleveland's Irish community. Closely knit, and resentful of outsiders, as an Irish parish ghetto, the Angle was a virtually "closed" community. Second and third generations of its sons and daughters married each other and endeavored to remain in the parish by building additions onto the rear of their parents' homes, or buying homes vacated by the deaths of older parishioners. The Angle raised countless numbers of future professional men, doctors, lawyers, priests, and politicians. Included among these were Tom Patton, a president of Republic Steel, and the boxing champion JOHNNY KILBANE. The Angle began to lose some of its cohesion with the death of parish leader Fr. Maloney in 1903. The encroachment of warehouses caused its eventual dispersion in the 1910s.

The **ANIMAL PROTECTIVE LEAGUE** is the chief organization in Cuyahoga County for the care of and prevention of cruelty to animals. The league was organized in 1912 by Miss Stella Hatch and Mrs. V. A. Dustin and was incorporated in 1913 as a private, charitable organization. It is a direct descendant of the Humane Society in Cleveland. The Humane Society, founded in 1873, had 2 branches: one for the prevention of cruelty to children, the other for the prevention of cruelty to animals. The latter branch became part of the Animal Protective League in 1927. The league's purpose since then has been to disseminate information about the care of animals and to prevent cruelty. The APL picks up and shelters homeless animals, which are then put up for adoption or put to sleep if not adopted. The league also accepts animals from people who wish to put their pets up for adoption. In its early days, the APL's attention was focused on small animals as well as draft animals used in city commerce. Later its attention was given mainly to small animals, primarily house pets. The league has always operated out of a building at 1729 Willey Ave. In 1934, the board of directors of the APL and the Cuyahoga County commissioners entered into a yearly contract. It allows the league to do all the animal-control work in Cuyahoga County: dogcatching and housing and destroying unwanted animals. Through this contract, in 1984 the county paid for 19 deputy dog wardens and humane agents. Outside of its dogcatching activities, the APL also attempts to disseminate information on how to care for animals. In order to accomplish its purpose, the league has various programs: educational programs coordinated with the public school system; investigations through legal channels of reports of cruelty, made with the full cooperation of the police and the courts; owner counseling on the care of pets; media advertising; outreach programs, which involve taking small pets to nursing homes; pet adoption services, with spaying and neutering facilities; and a regular newsletter to members of the league. The APL also offers veterinary services to those who cannot afford a private animal doctor. The funding for these activities comes from several sources. The county pays for services for which it has contracted. Other sources include endowments, membership fees, adoption fees, gifts, and bequests. The Animal Protective League has not changed its purpose during its history, but it has modernized its methods and placed more emphasis on education in recent decades.

**ANISFIELD, JOHN** (5 Mar. 1860–22 Apr. 1929), successful clothing manufacturer and real-estate executive, was a leader in the Fed. of Jewish Charities and active in several other civic and Jewish communal organizations. He was born in Cracow, Austria, near Vienna, and educated in the public schools of Europe. Before immigrating to America in 1876, he studied engineering. Upon his arrival in America, Anisfield settled in Cleveland, where he went to work for his uncle, Dr. Jas. Horowitz, who was a partner in the D. Black Cloak Co. Anisfield worked at D. Black for 6 years, attaining the position of manager. In 1882, he started his own cloakmaking factory. By the first decade of the 20th century, he was employing 700 workers at his factory at E. 22nd St. and Superior. In 1909, he was able to erect the Anisfield Bldg. at E. 9th St. and Huron. During his business career, Anisfield also served as president of the Garfield Realty, Anisfield Realty, and Broadway-Hamm companies.

Although he became active in Jewish communal activities organizations late in life, Anisfield held many high offices, including president of MT. SINAI HOSPITAL, the Jewish Orphan Home, and the HEBREW FREE LOAN ASSOC. At the time of his death, he was treasurer of the Fed. of Jewish Charities and was one of 2 Jews appointed to the Committee on Benevolent Associations of the Chamber of Commerce. Anisfield was married twice. In 1886 he married Daniela Guttenberg of Vienna, who died 10 years later. In 1904 he married Alice Strauss, the daughter of Adolph Strauss, an influential Jewish leader in New York. Anisfield had 1 daughter, Edith, by his first marriage.

The **ANNUNCIATION GREEK ORTHODOX CHURCH** was the first Greek Orthodox church established in Cleveland and formed the basis for all subsequent congregations. Greek immigrant men who came to Cleveland between 1894–1912 participated in the liturgy of the Greek Orthodox church sporadically, whenever itinerant priests conducted services in the coffeehouses, in communal apartments along Bolivar Rd., or in ST. THEODOSIUS RUSSIAN ORTHODOX CATHEDRAL. Organizing themselves as a formal society, the Pan-Hellenic Union, these men engaged the services of Fr. Geo. Scarpas, who commuted from Pittsburgh once a month. The first regular service was conducted on Christmas Eve 1910, in a hall above a movie house at Ontario and Bolivar. By 1912, the society had collected $12,000 and purchased a home on the corner of W. 14th St. and Fairfield Ave. Services were held there for over 2 years, after which they were transferred back downtown to Arch Hall on E. 4th and Ontario. With the arrival of more immigrants, including women, the congregation began to construct a church on the site of the house. The Greek Orthodox Church of the Annunciation, although not completed, became the sanctuary for the liturgy in 1919. In 1924, Fr. John Zografos became pastor. During his 4-year tenure, Fr. Zografos painted all 85 icons within the church. The first Greek school was established during his tenure. In 1930, Fr. Chrysogonos Lavriotis became pastor. He served the community until the mid-1950s. During the 1930s, when the church mortgage was saved from foreclosure by the intervention of Antony Hoty, to the postwar years, when the church was overcrowded with parishioners, he provided strong leadership and guided the Greek community in a period of rapid expansion.

With members moving to the suburbs, the demand for more churches grew. First SS. Constantine & Helen was built in CLEVELAND HTS. in 1956, and St. Demetrios in ROCKY RIVER in 1962. All three churches functioned as a single community, with the corporate name the American-Hellenic Community of Greater Cleveland, operating under a common state charter, until 1967, when each became autonomous. Numerous priests, from the early 1950s until 1967, circulated among the various churches. In 1967, Fr. John Protopapas assumed the pastoral duties at the Annunciation Church just a few weeks after all of the churches gained their autonomy. During his 20 years in that capacity, the church, its parochial school, and the Sunday schools have continued to grow, and Annunciation has continued to retain its central position among the area's Greek Orthodox churches.

**ANSHE CHESED** (Fairmount Temple) is the oldest existing Jewish congregation in Cleveland. It was established in 1841 and chartered on 28 Feb. 1842 after 30 members of the Israelitic Society of Cleveland, the city's first congregation, seceded in a dispute over religious ritual practices. Differences between the two groups were overcome in 1845, and a merger was effected under the name Israelitish Anshe Chesed Society of Cleveland, popularly known as Anshe Chesed. In 1846, Anshe Chesed erected the city's first synagogue, located on the south side of Eagle St. Four years later, Posen-born ISIDOR KALISCH was engaged as the congregation's first rabbi. However, soon after assuming the position, Kalisch and 20 members left Anshe Chesed to form Tifereth Israel. The congregation then hired Rabbi Bernard L. Fould, a native of Mulhausen, Bavaria, who remained in the pulpit until 1858. Established as a German Orthodox congregation, Anshe Chesed began introducing reforms during the 1860s. In 1861, chazan GUSTAVE M. COHEN, a religious liberal, became the congregation's spiritual leader; he instituted many of the reforms common throughout American Jewish congregations during the mid-19th century. Among these were introduction of a choir, an organ, and mixed seating.

Anshe Chesed continued on the road toward Reform after Cohen left in 1873. During the incumbency of Rabbi Michaelis Machol, a moderate Reform prayerbook was adopted, sermons were delivered in English, and the membership voted to worship with uncovered heads. In 1880, JAS. H. ROGERS was hired as organist. He served Anshe Chesed for 50 years while also working as the *Plain Dealer* music critic and organist for the First Unitarian Church. Anshe Chesed outgrew its Eagle St. Synagogue in the mid-1880s. In 1887, the congregation dedicated new quarters at 25th and Scovill and sold its old building to the Hungarian congregation, B'NAI JESHURUN. However, between 1887–1907, when Rabbi LOUIS WOLSEY was called to the pulpit, the congregation's membership witnessed little growth.

Wolsey, who initially espoused a conservative brand of Reform Judaism, became by the 1920s an adherent of Classical Reform and led Anshe Chesed in that direction. He expanded synagogue activities, supporting the creation of the Temple Sisterhood (1909), Alumni Assoc. (1911), and Men's Club (1924). Additionally, the congregation sponsored a Boy Scout troop, social and cultural events, and social-welfare services. Under Wolsey's leadership, the membership rose from 186 in 1907 to 1,200 by 1925. In 1912, Anshe Chesed dedicated the $250,000 Euclid Ave. Temple, located at 86th and Euclid Ave. In 1923, the Temple House, a facility that included a 1,400-seat auditorium, classrooms, and a library, was built as an addition to the Euclid Ave. Temple. After Wolsey's departure in 1925, Rabbi BARNETT BRICKNER was hired and served Anshe Chesed until his death in 1958. Brickner restored many of the traditional forms of religious service that had been victims of the move toward Classical Reform. One of his primary concerns was Jewish education. He created the position of director of education in 1927 to administer the 1,100-pupil Sunday school. Nathan Brilliant was hired and held the position until 1946, when he became director of the BUREAU OF JEWISH EDUCATION.

As Anshe Chesed's members moved farther eastward after WORLD WAR II, the congregation decided to relocate in the suburbs. A site was purchased in Beachwood on Fairmount Blvd., and following a lengthy court battle with the village over the construction of a synagogue, Anshe Chesed received permission to build. On 31 May 1957, the new synagogue, known as Fairmount Temple, was dedicated. Following Brickner's death, Rabbi Arthur J. Lelyveld was hired to serve the congregation. He had been national director of the B'nai B'rith Hillel Foundation from 1947–56. Lelyveld was an active civil-rights activist and a leader in the American Jewish Congress. He instituted the annual presentation of Ernest Bloch's Sacred Service at Anshe Chesed.

Anshe Chesed Congregation Records, WRHS.
Peskin, Allan, *This Tempting Freedom* (1973).
Rabbi Barnett R. Brickner Papers, WRHS.

**ANSHE EMETH** (Park Synagogue), the largest Conservative congregation in the U.S., was founded by Polish Jews in 1857. The congregation met for services in a series of rented halls until 1880, when it purchased the Erie St. Methodist Church near Woodland Ave. The congregation's membership remained small through its first 40 years; consequently, it could not afford a full-time rabbi. In 1902, Anshe Emeth merged with a smaller congregation, probably Baruch Ohel Chesed, with the result that in 1904 a new brick synagogue was erected at E. 37th and Scovill, and SAMUEL MARGOLIES was hired as rabbi. Under Margolies's leadership, Anshe Emeth became the most important and largest Orthodox congregation in the city. By 1916, when Margolies retired from the pulpit, Anshe Emeth had 300 members.

In 1916, Anshe Emeth merged with Congregation Beth Tefilah. The latter congregation was organized in 1912 in GLENVILLE and purchased a building at 105th and Hampton prior to the merger. In 1919, Samuel Benjamin, a graduate of the Jewish Theological Seminary, became rabbi and led the drive to build the Cleveland Jewish Ctr. The congregation moved into the new building in 1921 but did not dedicate it until construction was completed in Oct. 1922. In June 1922, SOLOMON GOLDMAN became the rabbi and led Anshe Emeth, now called the Cleveland Jewish Ctr., into the Conservative movement. Goldman served the congregation for only 6 years, but during that time it became the center of Jewish life in Glenville. The massive Jewish Ctr. building contained basketball and handball courts, a swimming pool, and a large auditorium. The congregation sponsored lectures, social functions, and entertainment, provided space for clubs, housed a branch of the CLEVELAND HEBREW SCHOOLS, and offered Americanization classes.

Anshe Emeth was the first "Jewish Center" west of the Alleghenies. By 1940, its membership reached 920 families, making it the largest congregation affiliated with the United Synagogue of America, the Conservative congregational

union. After Goldman left the congregation, Harry Dawidovitz became rabbi and served until 1935. He requested a leave of absence and subsequently resigned while on leave. The congregation then hired Cleveland-born Armond E. Cohen, who celebrated his 50th year as rabbi of the congregation in 1984. In 1947, the congregation sold the Cleveland Jewish Ctr. building on 105th and began holding services at a newly acquired location between Euclid Hts. Blvd. and Mayfield Rd. in CLEVELAND HTS. Construction soon began on a new synagogue designed by architect Eric Mendelsohn, and in 1951 the congregation dedicated the Park Synagogue complex.

**ANTISLAVERY SOCIETIES, BLACK,** were formed in the Cleveland area in the 1850s and were separate from the earlier, integrated societies (see CLEVELAND ANTISLAVERY SOCIETY and CUYAHOGA COUNTY ANTISLAVERY SOCIETY). A leader in forming these organizations was John Mercer Langston of Oberlin, who formed the Ohio Colored American League in 1850, reorganized it as the Ohio State Anti-Slavery Society in 1853, and revived that organization in 1858. By Jan. 1859, Cleveland-area BLACKS had formed the Cuyahoga Anti-Slavery Society as a branch of the Ohio State Society; it met at the AME Church on Bolivar St., with Rev. S. T. Jones presiding. On 7 Feb. 1859, the executive board of the Ohio State Anti-Slavery Society held its first quarterly meeting in Forest City Hall in Cleveland. Langston presided at the meeting, and Clevelanders Chas. H. Langston (secretary), JOHN MALVIN, and Joseph D. Harris were appointed general lecturers for the society. The Cuyahoga branch donated $5 to the state society, and a collection in Cleveland raised $13.30 for its work. By the fall of 1859, the state society had established its headquarters at the corner of Ontario and Michigan Sts. in Cleveland and was circulating 2 petitions throughout the state. One petition called upon the state legislature to repeal the state's BLACK LAWS and to eliminate racial distinctions from the state constitution. The other called for a law to "*fully protect* every inhabitant of this State in his inalienable right to *Liberty*, and which shall *effectually abolish* kidnapping and man stealing on the soil of Ohio." The Ohio State Anti-Slavery Society remained active until the outbreak of the CIVIL WAR, and black Clevelanders continued to play a prominent role in its work. At its annual meeting in Jan. 1860, John Langston continued to lead the organization, Malvin and Chas. Langston were reappointed lecturers, and Cleveland doctor ROBT. B. LEACH became a member of the executive board.

**ANTIOCH BAPTIST CHURCH,** organized as Antioch Missionary Baptist Church, was formally established in Jan. 1893 as the second Baptist church exclusively for black worshippers. It was begun by a small band of members of the SHILOH BAPTIST CHURCH who were unhappy with the leadership at that time. The group began meeting informally in Oct. 1892 in the home of Henry Myers at 10 Laurel (2327 E. 29th) St., with Rev. Wm. Ridley as the first acting pastor. In Mar. 1893, a student at Oberlin College, Rev. D. D. Minor, was engaged as the first official minister. The small congregation soon outgrew its small home meeting place and moved to the Odd Fellows Hall on Ontario St. at Prospect Ave. They purchased and remodeled a house on Central Ave. at Sked (E. 24th) St., which became their first church home. It was dedicated in July 1893. By 1905, the congregation had outgrown the small house and moved into a church building, built with the aid of matching funds donated by JOHN D. ROCKEFELLER. The congregation at E. 24th and Central Ave. became affiliated with the Northern Baptist Convention (later the American Baptist

Convention). They moved to their present (1985) location at the corner of E. 89th and Cedar Ave. in 1934, when the federal government chose to locate a public-housing project in the Central area, which would require razing the church at 24th and Central. Antioch Church is considered a leading institution among Cleveland's black population. Its consistent choice of educated, articulate ministers, including Rev. Horace C. Bailey (1903–23), WADE MCKINNEY (1928–62), and Emmanual Branch (1964–83), has kept the church visible and well-respected. It has also historically served as an institution that attempts to bring about inter-racial cooperation in the city, beginning with the ministry of Rev. Bailey. The church was often active in the political and social movement to gain equitable citizenship representation and rights for blacks. Antioch Church has one of the largest Protestant credit unions in Ohio, which serves its membership. The church also is cosponsor of a 12-story apartment building with UNIVERSITY CIRCLE, INC., and the CLEVELAND CLINIC FOUNDATION at E. 89th St. and Carnegie Ave.

The **ANVIL REVUE** is a satirical production presented annually by the CITY CLUB OF CLEVELAND in which club members and others poke fun at politics, institutions, and people in the news. Begun in 1913 as Stunt Nite at the City Club's first annual meeting, the production soon came under the direction of CARL FREIBOLIN, a bankruptcy court referee, and Joe Newman, *Cleveland Press* columnist and sporting-goods store owner. Freibolin, after being asked to participate in a poorly written skit, transformed the production into a fast-paced spoof of local politicians, party bosses, and public officials. The half-hour performances for club members soon expanded to a full evening's entertainment, with music, props, some professional actors, and a growing demand for admission. The show moved from club quarters in Weber's Restaurant on Superior Ave. to the Dutchess Theater, and then to the Prospect Theater; at one time an additional performance for women was scheduled. After 1924, Joe Newman wrote lyrics to accompany Freibolin's skits and became a partner in the annual production. Freibolin "retired" from his position as a writer and director in the late 1920s but resumed his "duties" in 1929. As the show expanded, so did the targets of its humor. Under the theme song "Its the Bull People Want," the Anvil Revue ribbed media people, lawyers, and other local figures. In the 1930s it took on national political figures and issues. The boldness of the satire attracted attention from out-of-town critics, who labeled Freibolin as Cleveland's Aristophanes. Though women were admitted first to a separate performance and then to the main event, the acting was a male prerogative until 1966. In 1939 a chameleonlike character, Ben Sapp, was introduced into the show. Sometimes a milquetoast, sometimes the toast of the town, Sapp was "Everyman," plodding through life and a foil to the policy-setting sophisticates lampooned in the skits. Newman retired from the show in 1958, and Freibolin in 1965. The show continued to run until 1976, when it was abandoned because of declining attendance. It returned in June 1979 in radio format and continued to be broadcast into the mid-1980s.

City Club of Cleveland Records. WRHS.

The **AQUARAMA,** the largest passenger ship to operate on the Great Lakes, started life as the *Marine Star* (1944). The 520-ft. ship was equipped with a single-screw, oil-fired, turbine-propelled engine. Gross tonnage was 12,773. It was the first auto ferry to use closed-circuit TV; the first to use stainless-steel sidings and rails; the first on the Great Lakes

to use escalators; and believed to be the first to use hy-draulically operated car entrance doors. In 1954, the *Marine Star*, a cargo and troop carrier, arrived in Muskegon, Mich., for conversion to a 9-deck cruise ship. The change to the *Aquarama* took 2 years and cost $5–8 million. With a passenger capacity of 2,500, the ship featured full picture windows, 5 bars, soda fountains, a restaurant, 2 dance floors, a movie theater, a television theater, a children's playroom, and all the latest equipment, including a gyro compass, a radio direction finder, radar, a fathometer, and ship-to-shore phones. Its cruising speed was 22 mph.

In 1956, Chicago and Cleveland were in competition for the Detroit run. Meanwhile, the *Aquarama* settled in Chicago as a floating amusement palace. Tied at the end of the Navy Pier, visitors were taken aboard by water taxi speedboats. Owner Mark McKee of Detroit preferred the Cleveland site, though dockage in Cleveland was not adequate. In an attempt to lease the W. 3rd St. Pier, the Michigan-Ohio Navigation Co., which operated the ship, made a bid to spend $152,800 to improve the pier space with ramp and parking space. This move, along with its other offerings, induced Cleveland officials to accept the proposal. The Aquarama wasoriginally scheduled to begin Cleveland operations in 1956, but the Cleveland pier was not yet ready. Scheduled runs began in 1957, taking passengers and their cars from Cleveland to Detroit in approximately 6 hours. Entertainment on ship was varied and included singers, name bands, dancers, marionette shows, games, and contests. Unable to turn a profit, the *Aquarama* made its last trip on 4 Sept. 1962. There was hope of using the ship for ferry service on Lake Michigan or as a floating convention center, but as of 1981, the *Aquarama* was still docked in Muskegon.

The **ARAB SOCIAL CLUB,** formed in the late 1970s, is described as "a local center for pro-Palestinian Arab-Americans." It serves as a social center and as a political center on Palestinian affairs, providing members access to Palestinian newspapers and magazines and video cassettes of speeches. Occasionally the club expresses its political views publicly, as it did in a telegram to Pres. Jimmy Carter in Mar. 1980 protesting Israel's establishment of a settlement in the Beit Hanina section of Jerusalem. The club also serves as a cultural center, sponsoring classes in Arabic and Palestinian history and culture for children on Saturdays. In 1986, the club moved from a converted storefront at 10313 Lorain to 7412 Lawn Ave. near Madison and W. 73rd.

**ARAB-AMERICANS.** Cleveland's Arab population, although among the smaller of the city's ethnic groups, has had a clear identity and historical development since Arabs began arriving here in the 19th century. There are today approximately 25,000 Americans of Arab descent residing in the Greater Cleveland area. The term *Arab* perhaps requires some clarification. As with most peoples, language is the defining factor; thus, an Arab-American is one whose ancestral tongue is Arabic. But unlike many nationality groups, whose members can trace their origins back to a single country or province, Arab immigrants could have come from a large region of western Asia and northern Africa (from Morocco to Egypt to Iraq) comprising 22 countries. Most Arab immigrants to Cleveland, however, like those to the rest of the U.S., came from Greater Syria. The Arab world, although predominantly Muslim, does have a significant Christian minority, and most of the earlier Arab immigrants to the U.S. were Christian. They had learned about the U.S. from the American Protestant missionaries who went to the Near East in the 19th century.

However, adherents of the various branches of Islam, including the Druze (actually a distinct sect of Islamic origin), also came here. It was ca. 1875 when Arab immigrants began to enter the U.S. in significant numbers. Most of these pioneers made a living peddling dry goods; many subsequently became storekeepers, importers, and manufacturers. (The first immigrants wrote home and, with some exaggeration, told of the freedom and the good life they had found in the U.S.) This initial wave of immigration lasted until the Quota Acts of 1920–24 drastically restricted the entry of many nationalities, including Arabs, into the country. Rather than being driven from the Old World by oppression and starvation, Arabs were drawn to America by the lure of economic opportunity; many planned to return to their homeland after making their fortunes (although many of these individuals changed their minds and remained in the New World). The political destabilization occurring in the Near East with the approach of World War I, and some dissatisfaction with the hegemony of the Turkish Ottoman Empire (which ruled the region at this time), provided additional but secondary incentives for going abroad. The first Arab immigrant to arrive in Cleveland, about 100 years ago, is said to have been a peddler who trekked his way from the East Coast. The city annual report first recorded Arab immigrants in Cleveland in 1895; it listed 12 individuals. That source indicates that during the period 1895–1907, 241 Arab immigrants came to Cleveland. The majority of the early immigrants were men, who generally worked as peddlers or as laborers in factories or in construction. Many, when they had saved enough money, went on to establish small businesses, particularly grocery stores, fruit stands, restaurants, dry-goods stores, and contracting firms. Increasingly, they sent for, or returned to the Near East to bring, wives, children, and other family members to the U.S., especially in the years around WORLD WAR I. The U.S. census of 1910 listed 497 individuals under the category "Turkey in Asia" (Asian subjects of the Ottoman Empire, most of whom were Arab); in 1920, the number was 1,320. Nearly all of these immigrants came from Syria, and especially from that part of it that is today the separate country of Lebanon. In Cleveland they initially settled in the Haymarket district on such streets as Bolivar Rd. and Eagle Ave., and across the CENTRAL VIADUCT in TREMONT. However, as they and their descendants prospered, they moved to various areas of Cleveland and its suburbs. The U.S. Census figures for individuals from Syria and Palestine were 1,180 in 1930 and 1,068 in 1940 (probably indicating movement out of Cleveland proper rather than a decrease in the area's Arab population). Partially because of this quick dispersal into the American mainstream, characteristic of Arab immigration to the U.S., and partially because of the relatively small number of people involved (compared to such groups as the ITALIANS, POLES, and HUNGARIANS), no real Arab neighborhood developed in Cleveland. The second large wave of Arab immigrants came to Cleveland after the founding of Israel in 1948, and consisted primarily of displaced Palestinian Arabs. The Israeli occupation of the West Bank of the Jordan River, the Golan Hts. of Syria, and the Sinai Peninsula of Egypt after the Six Day War of 1967 ensured that the immigration would continue. Intercommunal strife and, after 1975, civil war in Lebanon spurred a new Lebanese migration, as well. In addition, a number of students from Arab countries enrolled at Cleveland universities, becoming at least temporary members of the Arab community here. By 1960, Cleveland's Arab population had increased again, to 1,841, with most individuals coming from Lebanon, Egypt, occupied west bank of Palestine, and Syria. The figure for 1970 was 832 (reflecting the general decline in Cleveland's population during the period). Estimates for the total number of Arab-Americans (including individuals of American birth and mixed parentage) residing in the Greater Cleveland area during the 1970s and 1980s varied from 15,000 to 35,000. This more recent wave of Arab immigration differed from the earlier one in many particulars. First, the motivation for migration was often political rather than economic. At least some of the migrants planned to return to their homeland when conditions permitted. Second, these later immigrants were on the average better-educated; a number had university degrees. Thus, although some began their lives in Cleveland as laborers, many came with the requisite education and experience to enter academia and the professions here, or with sufficient funds to start small businesses. Third, the religious background of the new immigrants was more varied; specifically, more Muslims, as well as Coptic Christians from Egypt, were among them. The early immigrants had been overwhelmingly adherents of the Christian rites of Syria. Religious institutions provided a medium of self-identification for the Arab community in Cleveland, lacking as it did a specific neighborhood, or great numbers, and tending as it did toward assimilation. The several Syrian Christian groups all established their own churches early on. In 1906 the community founded its first church, ST. ELIAS MELKITE CHURCH (Byzantine Catholic), using a converted building at 2231 E. 9th St. St. Elias initially served all Arabic-speaking Christians in Cleveland. It is today (1986) located at 8023 Memphis Ave. in Brooklyn. The next church to be established was ST. MARON CHURCH (Maronite Catholic), presently (1986) located at 1245 Carnegie Ave. in Cleveland. The parish was created in 1915; its first home was a residence on E. 21st St. The other important Syrian rite, the Antiochian Orthodox, did not officially found its church, ST. GEORGE ORTHODOX CHURCH, until 1926, although the Arab Orthodox community had conducted services in several locations, including GRAYS ARMORY, for a number of years. In 1928 the congregation purchased and opened a church at 2587 W. 14th St. in Cleveland, the church's current (1986) address. The Druze community in Cleveland has no organized place of worship; however, its religious society, Al-Bakorat Ud-Durziet, was founded in 1916 to provide spiritual and material aid to all individuals in the Druze community. Its membership embraces all persons of the Druze faith in the Cleveland area. The ISLAMIC CTR. of Cleveland, at 9400 Detroit Ave., was founded in 1967 to serve the area's Muslims, many of whom were of Palestinian origin. The latest of the Arab community's religious groups to establish itself in the Cleveland area was the Coptic Christian church. The word *Copt* is derived from the Greek word for Egypt, and has come to mean the native Egyptian Christian church (it has a considerable number of followers in Ethiopia as well), which broke away from Rome in 451 C.E. and adheres to the Orthodox rite. With Egyptians having migrated to Cleveland in significant numbers only after the middle of the 20th century, it was not until 1971 that a Coptic church, St. Mark Coptic Orthodox, was officially established, and not until 1975 that its first full-time pastor (Fr. Mikhail E. Mikhail) was appointed. St. Mark, located at 5994 Ridge Rd. in Parma, serves the Coptic Christians not only of Cleveland but of Ohio and the surrounding region, as well.

Although religious institutions must be accorded the preeminent place in the Cleveland Arab community's organizational life, the group has also founded social, political, and other clubs, sometimes based on sectarian or geographic (referring to place of origin) identities, sometimes cutting across these differences. However, compared to some other ethnic groups of similar size in Cleveland, the Arab community has formed relatively few clubs and societies. Among the earliest of such organizations (dating from the 1930s or before) were the AITANEET BROTHERHOOD ASSOC., the Zahle Club, the Syrian Boys Club, the Syrian American Club, and the LEBANESE-SYRIAN JR. WOMEN'S LEAGUE. Clubs whose memberships had roots in a certain village or city, such as the Aitaneet Brotherhood, were founded by immigrants with strong ties to the homeland; thus the more recent American Ramallah Club, a Palestinian organization. Other social and cultural clubs included the ARAB SOCIAL CLUB, Arabian Nights, and the Union of Arab Women. Joining the Lebanese-Syrian Jr. Women's League on the list of service organizations were such groups as the Stars of Lebanon Christian Society and local chapters of the American Lebanese-Syrian Associated Charities and the United Holy Land Fund. The most noteworthy development of the post–1965 period was the growth of political and educational organizations in response to events in the Near East and their consequent coverage in the American news media and the policies of the U.S. government, both widely perceived as anti-Arab. In the late 1960s, the Middle East Relief Committee began by raising donations to aid Palestinian refugees, and subsequently, as the Cleveland Middle East Foundation, involved itself, apolitically, in welfare and educational activities both at home and overseas. The Cleveland Council on Arab-American Relations was founded as a political organization in the early 1970s. It changed its name to the Greater Cleveland Assoc. of Arab-Americans in 1973, and became closely associated with the Natl. Assoc. of Arab-Americans, established at about the same time to give Arab-Americans a national political voice.

Typically, Arab immigrants to the U.S. have tended to assimilate easily into the American mainstream; thus, no permanent Arab enclave developed in Cleveland, and relatively few Arab clubs and societies were formed. What ethnic self-awareness there was tended to be fragmented, focused on sectarian or geographic identity, a legacy of the Ottoman Turkish system of government in the homeland. The Arab-Israeli conflict, and its repercussions in the U.S., have perhaps done more than anything else to forge a heightened sense of common identity among Arab-Americans. Whether overseas rivalries within the Arab bloc and internal sectarian conflicts, especially in Lebanon, will be reflected here in new divisiveness within the Arab community, or whether the centripetal force of a common linguistic and cultural heritage will be strong enough to withstand such centrifugal tendencies, remains a question for the future, on the answer to which the size and composition of future Arab immigration to Cleveland will undoubtedly bear.

Said Kabalan

Macron, Mary Haddad, *Arab Americans and their Communities of Cleveland* (1979).

**ARBUTHNOT, MAY HILL** (27 Aug. 1884–2 Oct. 1969), was a nationally known educator and author whose particular interests were early childhood education and children's books. She was born May Hill in Mason City, Iowa, and received a B.A. degree from the University of Chicago in 1922 and an M.A. from Columbia University in 1924. Her first teaching experiences were at the State Teachers College in Superior, Wis., and the Ethical Culture School in New York City. In 1922 she came to Cleveland as principal of the Cleveland Kindergarten-Primary Training School, which later became a part of Western Reserve University. She was associate professor of education at WRU until her retirement in 1946. Arbuthnot was a distinguished author and lecturer. Her articles appeared in such journals as *Parents, National Education Association Journal*, and *Elementary English Review*. She was an associate editor for *Childhood Education*. She traveled giving lectures on education and children's books into her eighties. Two of her many books, *Children and Books* and *The Arbuthnot Anthology and Children's Literature*, remained standard texts in the children's literature field long after her death. Among her other books were *Time for Fairy Tales* (1952), *Time for True Tales* (1953), and *Children's Books Too Good to Miss* (1948). She coauthored a series of reading texts for the Scott-Foresman Co., and in 1969 the company established a lectureship at CASE WESTERN RESERVE UNIVERSITY in her honor. Arbuthnot was the recipient of an honorary Litt.D. degree from WRU in 1961 and the Constance Lindsey Skinner Award for Children's Literature in 1959. May Hill married Chas. Arbuthnot on 17 Dec. 1932. Dr. Arbuthnot was chairman of the economics department at WRU for 38 years.

The **ARCADE** is an internationally renowned structure bringing together the economic, technological, and aesthetic developments of the 1880s. It has no peer in the U.S. and has been compared with the Galleria Vittorio Emmanuele in Milan, Italy. Erected at a cost of $867,000, the Arcade opened on Memorial Day 1890. It was built by a company of which STEPHEN V. HARKNESS, one of the original partners of the STANDARD OIL CO., was president, and CHAS. F. BRUSH vice-president. Other heavy investors were JOHN D. ROCKEFELLER and Louis H. Severance. The architects were GEO. H. SMITH and JOHN EISENMANN, professor of civil engineering at the Case School of Applied Science.

The Arcade is a cross between a light court and a commercial passage or shopping street. The building is actually a complex of 3 structures, two 9-story office buildings facing Euclid and Superior aves., connected by the 5-story iron-and-glass enclosed arcade. The Euclid and Superior fronts are monumental facades of sandstone and brick in the Romanesque style. The great Richardsonian arched entrance on the Superior Ave. front is original, but the Euclid Ave. front was remodeled in 1939. The level of the Superior entrance is some 12′ lower than the Euclid one, so that in effect there are 2 main floors, connected by staircases at either end. Since Euclid and Superior are not parallel, a passage leads at a 23-degree angle from the Euclid entrance to a rotunda at the south end of the arcade. The arcade itself is a 300′-long covered light court ringed by 4 levels of balconies, which step back above the Euclid Ave. level. The effect of the vertical lines of the columns rising approximately 100′ to the glass roof creates the most breathtaking interior in the city. The visual appearance of the ceiling is a Gothic arch, because the lower sides of the roof trusses are curved, but the skylight itself is a gable roof that supports a light monitor along the ridge.

The Arcade reflects the time's rapid changes in building technology and contains a mixture of techniques and materials. First, the central entrance towers on both facades had load-bearing walls (before the alteration of the Euclid Ave. front, when steel beams had to be inserted). Second, the masonry facades above the ground story on either side of the towers are carried on I-beams that rest on brackets attached to steel columns. Thus, the facades utilize the skeletal principle that had been used in Chicago a few years earlier and that made the skyscraper possible. Third, the floors and roofs of the building are supported on a skeleton of iron columns and oak, wrought iron, and steel beams. The arcade roof trusses were of a new type, being hinged in 3 places, at the base and the apex. The roof monitor was also hinged at the top. The builder was the Detroit Bridge Co. The only major alteration of the interior has been the change in the stairs at the Superior entrance. At the same time, the original Art Nouveau light fixtures were removed and replaced with the present modernistic design.

**ARCHITECTURE.** Cleveland's innovations in certain areas of architectural planning have displayed a progressiveness and vision matched by few other cities. The 1903 Group Plan, which produced widespread national admiration at the time, is only one example. In the 1920s, the plan of the Union Terminal complex anticipated many of the features of Rockefeller Ctr. Greater Cleveland also developed the first comprehensive modern building code (1904), the first industrial research park (NELA PARK, 1911), and the most spectacular realization of the garden city suburb idea in SHAKER HTS. Moreover, Cleveland is not without its individual architectural landmarks that have no peer anywhere, the most notable being the ARCADE of 1890.

Architectural design in Cleveland during most of its history was typical of that in any growing midwestern commercial and industrial city. The building needs for various uses—domestic, commercial, religious, social, industrial, and so on—were common. The same is true of the styles used to clothe these uses; styles followed the general chronological development of those in the rest of the nation. The design of buildings was determined less by any discernible architectural philosophy than by the function or symbolism of the building, the wishes of the builder, the type of site or amount of money available, and the dictates of fashion. Because of the demand, the city attracted numerous fine architects, who generally produced buildings at a very high level of quality, though Cleveland is not known as the home of prophetic architects of national reputation.

At the time of Cleveland's beginnings in the early 19th century, there was no profession of architecture in the modern sense. The designer of buildings was sometimes a gentleman-scholar but more often a master builder in the late-18th-century tradition. The first master builder practicing in Cleveland who called himself "architect" was JONATHAN GOLDSMITH (1783–1847) of Painesville. Goldsmith built at least 10 houses on Euclid Ave. in the 1820s and 1830s. The most notable were the Federal-style Judge Samuel Cowles mansion (1834) and the Greek Revival Truman Handy mansion (1837). The modern profession of architecture began in the 1840s, and the individual private practice, performing most of the services of the modern architect, was established in Cleveland before the CIVIL WAR. Goldsmith's son-in-law CHAS. W. HEARD (1806–1876) was the most important architect from 1845 until his death. He worked in the Gothic Revival style as early as 1849. From 1849–59 he worked in partnership with SIMEON C. PORTER (1807–1871) from Hudson, Ohio. Heard and Porter designed predominantly in the Romanesque Revival style (Old Stone Church, 1855). They introduced the use of cast-iron columns in Cleveland in the mid-1850s. Heard designed the city hall, Cleveland's greatest Second Empire building, in 1875.

In the last quarter of the 19th century, Cleveland's most magnificent architectural ensemble was found on EUCLID AVE., lined with the fashionable mansions of wealthy executives in shipping, iron and steel, oil, electricity, and railroads. The fine residential street between E. 12th and E. 40th streets was known as "Millionaires' Row"; Clevelanders and many visitors called it "the most beautiful street in the world." Mansions remaining from the Greek Revival period, together with Gothic Revival and Tuscan villas from the 1850s and 1860s, stood side by side with great Romanesque Revival stone residences and eclectic houses in the Victorian Gothic, Renaissance, Queen Anne, and Neoclassic styles. The residences were designed both by Cleveland architects such as LEVI T. SCOFIELD, CHAS. F. SCHWEINFURTH, and GEO. H. SMITH and by out-of-town architects, including Peabody & Stearns, Richard M. Hunt, and Stanford White. Euclid Ave. remained fashionable until after the turn of the century, but virtually all of "Millionaires' Row" was destroyed in the years around WORLD WAR II.

At the same time, Cleveland participated in the revolution in commercial architecture that evolved simultaneously in Chicago, New York, and other large commercial cities, and which was characterized by 1) a concern for fireproof construction, 2) the provision of lighter and more open structure, and 3) the evolution of iron and steel skeletal construction. The foremost exponents of this development in Cleveland were FRANK E. CUDELL (1844–1916) and John N. Richardson (1837–1902), who produced a remarkable series of progressively lighter and more open structures between 1882–89—the Geo. Worthington Bldg., the Root & McBride-Bradley Bldg., and the PERRY-PAYNE BLDG., the first in Cleveland to utilize iron columns throughout all 8 stories, and containing an interior light court that attracted visitors from a considerable distance. The Chicago School of commercial building was actually represented by 3 buildings of Burnham & Root—the Society for Savings (1890), whose masonry load-bearing walls enclose an iron skeleton, and whose lobby is an unusually fine example of decorative art in the Wm. Morris tradition; the WESTERN RESERVE BUILDING (1891), a building of similar structure built on an unusual triangular site; and the CUYAHOGA BUILDING (1893), the first building in Cleveland with a complete steel frame. The Cuyahoga was demolished in 1982.

The development of skeletal structure and the interior light court reached a climax in Cleveland with the construction of the ARCADE. Opened in 1890, the Arcade is an architectural landmark that has remained without peer for nearly 100 years after its completion. Combining features of the light court and a commercial shopping street, the "bazaar" of stores and offices was built by a company whose officers included STEPHEN V. HARKNESS of Standard Oil and CHAS. F. BRUSH. The architects were JOHN EISENMANN and Geo. H. Smith. The 300′-long iron-and-glass arcade of 5 stories is surrounded by railed balconies and connects two 9-story office buildings designed in the Romanesque style. Because of the differences in grade, there are main floors on both the Euclid Ave. and Superior Ave. levels. The skeletal structure of the Arcade consists of iron columns and oak, wrought iron, and steel beams. The roof trusses were of a new type; since no local builder would bid on the construction, the work was done by the Detroit Bridge Co. The central well of the Arcade, with its dramatic open space and natural light, is the most impressive interior in the city, and its renown is international.

Other architects active in the last quarter of the century were ANDREW MITERMILER, planner of breweries, business blocks, and social halls; JOSEPH IRELAND, architect to AMASA STONE and DANIEL P. EELLS; Levi Scofield, designer of Cleveland's most important monument, the SOLDIERS & SAILORS MONUMENT (1894); and COBURN & BARNUM, whose major works were institutional and business buildings. By 1890, 36 architects were listed in the city directory, and in the same year the Cleveland chap. of the AMERICAN INSTITUTE OF ARCHITECTS was formed. In the 1890s many clients sought architects of national reputation to design important Cleveland buildings. Among the major architects represented were Burnham & Root, Richard M. Hunt, Henry Ives Cobb,

41

Shepley, Rutan & Coolidge, Geo. B. Post, Peabody & Stearns, and Geo. W. Keller. After the turn of the century, these included Stanford White and Cram, Goodhue & Ferguson.

When the profound change from Victorian revivalism to classicism took place in the 1890s, Cleveland architects responded with characteristic adaptability. Such architects as Geo. H. Smith, LEHMAN & SCHMITT, GEO. F. HAMMOND, and KNOX & ELLIOT began careers in the Richardsonian Romanesque and other revival styles and later were able to design tall office buildings and Beaux-Arts classical monuments with equal facility. One architect of this generation, Chas. F. Schweinfurth (1856–1919), was the first Cleveland architect to rank with those of national stature. Trained in New York, he came to Cleveland to design mansions, institutional buildings, and churches for the wealthy, especially in association with Mr. and Mrs. Samuel Mather. His early work was in the Richardsonian Romanesque style, and his masterpiece is generally agreed to be the Gothic TRINITY CATHEDRAL (1901–07).

The dominance of the classic revival was epitomized by the Group Plan of 1903, whose significance was immediately recognized across the country. The plan evolved as a result of the conception that newly planned federal, county, and city buildings could be placed in a monumental grouping. The Group Plan Commission consisted of Daniel H. Burnham, John M. Carrere, and Arnold W. Brunner. Uniformity of architectural character and building height was recommended, and the Beaux-Arts classical style was followed. The MALL, which is the center of the plan, was finally completed in 1936, and the major buildings include the Federal Courthouse (1910), CUYAHOGA COUNTY COURTHOUSE (1912), CLEVELAND CITY HALL (1916), PUBLIC AUDITORIUM (1922), Public Library (1925), and Board of Education Bldg. (1930). As an example of city planning inspired by the City Beautiful movement and specifically by the precedent of the Columbian Exposition of 1893, Cleveland's Group Plan brought the city a national reputation for progressive municipal vision.

A few Cleveland architects studied at the Beaux-Arts in Paris and brought its teachings with them, the most notable being J. MILTON DYER (1870–1957), architect of the city hall. By the first decade of the 20th century, the first generation of architects trained in an American architectural school was beginning to practice. In 1921 a group of architects established the Cleveland School of Architecture, with ABRAM GARFIELD as the first president. The school was affiliated with Western Reserve University in 1929. It later became a department of WRU (1952) and continued to operate until it was discontinued in 1972. Many architects were attracted to Cleveland by the opportunities to build in the growing and wealthy industrial city. The development of well-to-do suburban enclaves in LAKEWOOD, BRATENAHL, and the Heights between 1895–1939 fostered a climate in which excellent eclectic residential architects flourished. Among the finest were Meade & Hamilton, Abram Garfield, Philip Small, Chas. Schneider, FREDERIC W. STRIEBINGER, Clarence Mack, J. W. C. CORBUSIER, ANTONIO DI NARDO, and MUNROE COPPER.

The development of Shaker Hts. (1906–30) was probably the most spectacular embodiment of the suburban "garden city" idea in America. The subdivision was laid out so that curving roadways replaced the grid layout of city streets and were determined as much by the topography of the land as by the desire for informality. The apparently aimless meandering of the roads was actually calculated to provide access to the main arteries, as well as to create the best advantages for beautiful and livable home sites. Certain locations were reserved for the commercial areas, and certain lots were donated for schools and churches.

The homes of Shaker Hts. could be built for a wide range of prices, and there were neighborhoods of diverse character, from mansions to medium-sized residences to more humble homes. The architecture of the houses of the 1920s held few surprises; eclecticism was the accepted manner. The architects turned to styles that had developed satisfying and comfortable forms of domestic architecture. These might include American Colonial and English Manor (either Adam or Georgian), French, Italian, Elizabethan, Spanish, or Cotswold. But the similar plans and common scale, differentiated mainly in detail, resulted in familiar streets where the different styles stand side by side without jarring in the least.

The consistency of the domestic vision in the planned suburb was remarkable. Churches were designed to relate to the domestic architecture and were conceived in the same spirit. The two favorite styles were American Colonial and English Gothic. Schools, stores, libraries, hospitals, fire stations, and even the gasoline stations were designed in the Georgian and Tudor idioms. In 1927–29, the planned suburban shopping center at Shaker Square was built. The buildings were Georgian Colonial in style, and the plan of the square has been compared to a New England village green, but it owes a great deal to the concepts of mid-18th-century Neoclassic town planning in Europe; it has been suggested that the octagonal form of the square and its buildings was patterned after the Amalienborg Palace in Copenhagen. SHAKER SQUARE illustrates the continuing dependence on European models, combined with the expected references to American Georgian domestic building. It is also unusual in its integration of the rapid-transit line, which made the development of suburban Shaker Hts. possible.

The first 3 decades of the 20th century also saw a greatly increased demand for much larger and more formal private, institutional, and public buildings. Two architectural firms dominated the field—Hubbell & Benes, architects of the WEST SIDE MARKET, the CLEVELAND MUSEUM OF ART, various Wade Park plans, and the Ohio Bell Telephone Bldg., and Walker & Weeks, architects of the Federal Reserve Bank, Public Auditorium, the CLEVELAND PUBLIC LIBRARY, and SEVERANCE HALL. However, two of the largest such projects of the period, the Union Trust Bldg. and the Union Terminal Group and Terminal Tower, were entrusted to a Chicago firm—Graham, Anderson, Probst & White.

The Terminal Group (1922–31), an architectural complex that became the symbol of Cleveland, consists of 7 buildings occupying 17 acres. The group was notable for the development of commercial air rights over the station; all of the passenger facilities were below the street level. The arched portico on the PUBLIC SQUARE leads to the Terminal Bldg. lobby and to ramps going to the station concourse level. The Hotel Cleveland (1918) was incorporated into the group and balanced by Higbee's department store (1931). The Terminal Group may be compared with Rockefeller Ctr., which it predated by several years, in size, multipurpose use, and the incorporation of connecting underground concourses and an indoor parking garage. The 52-story Beaux-Arts-style tower, second-tallest in the world in 1928, is crowned by a classical spire, probably based on the New York Municipal Bldg. of 1913. Sometimes criticized as conservative in style, the Terminal Tower forms a focal point for the Public Square and the radiating avenues of Cleveland's street plan, and it expresses the enterprise of the Van Sweringen brothers, who built it. The Builders' Exchange (Guildhall), Medical Arts (Republic), and Midland buildings, also planned by Graham, Anderson, Probst & White, were designed in the modernistic style of 1929–30; their Art Deco lobbies were destroyed in 1981. The last building in the group, the U.S. Post Office, was completed in 1934.

The Depression era of the 1930s saw profound effects in architecture. Apart from the general decline in building and the consequent attrition in the number of practicing architects, the most important was the arrival of modernism under the influence of the European International style. That was most apparent in the design of federal public works. The first three public housing projects authorized and begun by the Public Works Admin. were built in Cleveland in 1935–37. They were the Cedar-Central apartments planned by Walter McCormack, Outhwaite homes by Maier, Walsh & Barrett, and LAKEVIEW TERRACE by Weinberg, Conrad & Teare. Lakeview Terrace is especially notable because of its adaptation to a difficult sloping site, and it appeared in international publications as a landmark in public housing. The simple design of the building units was clearly influenced by the European precedent of the International style. Other architects who adopted the new style with intelligence and vigor were J. Milton Dyer, Harold B. Burdick, Carl Bacon Rowley, J. Byers Hays, and Antonio di Nardo. The GREAT LAKES EXPOSITION in 1936 provided an opportunity for the display of the simple geometric forms of modernism, but the general acceptance of the style did not occur until after World War II.

The architecture of the postwar era is difficult to assess objectively from a recent perspective. New construction in Cleveland may have been more conservative in style and direction than at any other period in its history. Buildings continued to be built in traditional forms, as well as in the rectangular geometry of the assimilated International style. Many major projects were still awarded to nationally famous architects. Greater Cleveland saw structures designed by two of the old masters of modern architecture, Eric Mendelsohn and Walter Gropius. In the 1950s and 1960s, Cleveland firms such as Outcalt, Guenther & Associates filled the need for comprehensive planning on such projects as the Cleveland Hopkins Airport Terminal and master plans for CUYAHOGA COMMUNITY COLLEGE and CLEVELAND STATE UNIVERSITY. While the individual practice continued, a new type of complex design organization that could plan everything from a single structure to a megalopolitan transit system was typified by Dalton-Dalton-Little-Newport.

The Erieview urban-renewal plan of 1960 was one of the most ambitious undertaken under the Federal Urban Redevelopment program. The plan was prepared for the city by I. M. Pei & Associates. The clearance of nearly 100 acres between E. 6th and E. 14th streets, Chester Ave. and the lakefront provided sites for the building of new public, commercial, and apartment structures. The centerpiece of the plan was Erieview Tower (1964), designed by Harrison & Abramovitz. A new commercial and financial center developed that extended from Erieview to Euclid and E. 9th; from the late 1960s to the early 1980s, no fewer than 12 new office buildings were erected in and around the area between Euclid and Lakeside avenues, E. 9th and E. 12th streets. Virtually all of the new buildings represented variations on the formula of the late modern glass and metal skyscraper, with the exception of only 2 or 3 masonry-clad structures. The architects included Skidmore, Owings & Merrill, Chas. Luckman, Marcel Breuer, and local Cleveland design firms.

The most significant achievements in Cleveland architecture have been in large-scale planning—the Group Plan, the Terminal complex, Shaker Hts., PUBLIC HOUSING,

and urban renewal. Chronologically, architectural design has often lagged behind national developments, and its general standard has been typical of that in cities of the same size. Individual buildings of every period rival buildings anywhere in quality—the Arcade, the Terminal Tower, the Society Bank, and the Rockefeller Bldg., the motion picture palaces, and many churches. Several Cleveland architects, such as Chas. Schweinfurth and the firm of Walker & Weeks, achieved regional if not national reputations, and they will doubtless be more widely recognized when their work is fully documented. In conclusion, the architecture of Cleveland constitutes a representative index of the physical development and the taste of a large midwestern industrial and commercial city throughout its 19th-and 20th-century history.

Eric Johannesen<br>
Western Reserve Historical Society

Chapman, Edmund H., *Cleveland: Village to Metropolis* (1964).
Johannesen, Eric, *Cleveland Architecture, 1876-1976* (1979).
See also ARCHITECTURE, RESIDENTIAL; ARCHITECTURE, CIVIC; and ARCHITECTURE, SACRED.

**ARCHITECTURE, CIVIC.** In Cleveland, as elsewhere, the architecture of government is an indication of the civilization of the city. Almost without exception, the city's civic buildings have been in the classical modes that were the standard for government buildings throughout America's history. The majority of Cleveland's government buildings were erected during a period when the use of architectural style was understood to be symbolic. The most obvious precedents for civic buildings were the Greek style, because of the evolution of the democratic city-state in ancient Greece, and the Roman, because of the development of the body of civil law by the ancient Romans, as well as the various classical styles derived from them. These style references were consistent in federal, county, and city buildings alike, although Cleveland had no permanent state office building until the 1970s.

The first public building with any architectural character, and the most ambitious building of the period, was the second Cuyahoga County Courthouse, planned and constructed in 1826–28. It was a Federal-style building with facade of 6 Doric pilasters, a pediment, and an octagonal cupola and dome. It was planned just 2 years after the completion of the national Capitol's first dome and rotunda by Bulfinch. That precedent immediately established the domed classical building as the primary governmental symbol, imitated on most of the state capitols and many county courthouses. According to Edmund Chapman, the 1828 courthouse was "an attainment of considerable significance and reflects the national artistic revolution of these years." The building stood in the southwest quadrant of PUBLIC SQUARE until 1860, when a new courthouse was built and the city decided to clear the square of public buildings.

The culmination of the 19th-century phase of a national classical style came in a group of 3 buildings erected between 1858–75. The first U.S. Post Office, Custom House, and Courthouse was planned in 1856 and completed in 1858 on the east side of Public Square. It was designed by Ammi B. Young, official architect for the U.S. Dept. of the Treasury, as one of a large number of federal government buildings erected to serve the expanding western regions before the CIVIL WAR. The original central block of the 3-story building was Italian Renaissance rather than Greek or Roman in style, and in the 1880s large symmetrical wings were added in the same style. At the same time, the new courthouse was constructed in 1858–60 on the north side of Public Square. It was also a Renaissance building of simple proportions and relatively plain treatment, with arched windows and the use of quoins at the corners. When a fourth courthouse was needed, in 1875, it was built around the corner on W. 3rd St.; the somewhat more pretentious 4-story building was also Renaissance in style. Together, the federal building and the 2 county buildings summed up the civic aspirations of the city at mid-century. None of them is extant.

Though many 19th-century federal buildings, county courthouses, and city halls were built in the High Victorian mansard-roofed style, Cleveland would have bypassed that phase of civic architecture except for happenstance. The city of Cleveland built no permanent structure of its own until 1916. There was a competition for a city hall in 1869, and surviving drawings show a lavish domed and mansarded structure in the French Second Empire style; it was not built. After having occupied several commercial buildings, the city leased offices in the 5-story Case Block in 1875. Although it came to be known as City Hall, it was designed as a commercial block, not as a government building.

Throughout the 19th century, these early civic buildings were located wherever land was available in the general vicinity of Public Square. There was no thought of a unified ensemble until the concept of grouping the monumental public buildings occurred to several people in the 1890s. New federal, county, and city buildings were contemplated, and the logic of creating a grand ensemble was inescapable. A new U.S. Post Office, Custom House, and Courthouse was already projected on the same site as the 1858 building and extending east to E. 3rd St. This location became the south end of the MALL that resulted from the Group Plan. The Group Plan Commission was established in 1902, and its report the following year brought Cleveland into the forefront of national civic planning. The scale of its proposals caused *Harper's Weekly* to comment that Cleveland's commitment to the plan suggested "a new conception of municipality."

The inspiration of the "Great White City" at the Chicago Columbian Exposition of 1893, as well as the presence of Daniel Burnham on the commission, ensured that the Beaux-Arts Roman idiom would be the uniform style recommended. The Federal Bldg., erected in 1905–10 and designed by Arnold W. Brunner, member of the commission, is a 5-story granite structure with a rusticated basement, a colossal 3-story Corinthian colonnade, and a massive classical entablature. Since the Corinthian order was used on the Federal Bldg., the Ionic on the courthouse, and the Tuscan on city hall, it has been suggested that the classical orders were intended to symbolize the hierarchy of governments. Another important aspect of the Beaux-Arts ideal was the incorporation of decorative sculpture, paintings, and murals by the major artists of the day; in the case of the Federal Bldg. these included Daniel Chester French, Kenyon Cox, and Edwin H. Blashfield.

The CUYAHOGA COUNTY COURTHOUSE (1912) and the CITY HALL (1916) were planned as nearly symmetrical Beaux-Arts monuments to complete the north end of the Mall. Significantly, they were designed by architects of local rather than national reputation, the courthouse by Lehman & Schmitt and the city hall by J. Milton Dyer. The county building is more embellished, having pedimental sculptures of historic lawgivers and bronze statues of Jefferson and Hamilton. The interiors of both buildings are grand public spaces with high vaulted ceilings in the Roman style. More than any other places in the city, the courthouse and the city hall embody the classical symbolism of governmental architecture. Although not governmental buildings, the others in the vicinity of the Mall

carry out the idea of a uniform classicism. The PUBLIC AUDITORIUM, the Public Library and its annex (old Plain Dealer Bldg.), and the Board of Education Bldg. all reflect the uniform height and generally classical formula prescribed by the Group Plan Commission. The result is a civic ensemble in Cleveland that is unequaled among the cities of America.

The late 1920s brought the last generation of civic buildings to retain references to the ancient classical style, while exhibiting features that were transitional to the modernistic style characteristic of the 1930s. The Central Police Station, completed in 1926 to replace an old 3-story brick headquarters built in 1864, illustrates the transition perfectly. Wall piers are drastically simplified, and window spandrels contain geometric ornament that prefigures the Art Deco style, yet the 2 columns surmounted by eagles that flank the doorway are old authoritarian symbols. The Criminal Court Bldg. completed 4 years later on the same block is a completely modernistic building, all of whose geometric lines and ornament are in the Art Deco style. The simplified forms of the style were quite congenial to the classically trained architect; the idiom was symmetrical, it provided for the use of sculptured ornamentation, and building masses were treated in a way appropriate to the traditional use of masonry.

On the other hand, the innovative County Juvenile Court Bldg. (1932), housing the independent juvenile court and a detention home built around 3 sides of a quadrangle, is a 3-story brick building with a small tower and arched windows at the entrance. The reference here is to the eclectic domestic architecture of the period, a style that sought to express the security and comfort of home, and hence appropriate to a function dealing with juveniles. The last building of this period was the third U.S. Post Office, planned in the late 1920s and completed in 1934 as part of the Terminal Group. The customs, federal courts, and other federal agencies remained in the 1910 Federal Bldg. Like the Criminal Court Bldg., the post office is a thoroughly modernistic structure, exactly consonant with federal buildings of the Depression era's Public Works Admin. across the country. Bearing the stamp of the 1930s official style, its fluted vertical piers and long symmetrical sandstone facade mark the post office as the last of the classic government buildings in Cleveland.

In the decades between 1934 and the next group of civic buildings, a number of things took place in both government and architecture. The Great Depression and 2 wars provided the background for the greatest consolidation of centralized government in America's history. At the same time, all assumptions about the responsibility of government for social welfare were changed. In architecture, the period was marked by the complete dominance of the International style imported from Europe in the 1930s and 1940s. The expression of a building's function through its form, style, or ornament was relegated to the past, and commercial, institutional, and governmental buildings were frequently undifferentiated in appearance. These developments were reflected in the buildings erected by all branches of government between 1950–80. Cuyahoga County built a new administrative office building in 1956. It was located on the west side on the mall opposite the courthouse, as the north end of the Group Plan area once again became a focus for civic structures. The county administration building is a 4-story structure, bland and almost featureless, with the main entrance facing Ontario St. placed unsymmetrically at the north end of the facade. The symbolism of democracy and law was replaced by the expression of business efficiency.

In 1960, the Erieview urban-renewal plan designated the entire block east of the Mall and the Public Auditorium for a massive square federal office building adhering to the cornice line of the Group Plan buildings. As built in 1967, however, it became a 31-story office tower of utterly flat reflective surfaces of stainless steel and glass. It may be symptomatic that it was designed by 3 architectural firms in collaboration, and the Federal Bldg. enshrines the methodical and workaday aspects of bureaucracy even more eloquently than the county building. Also located in the Erieview area was the first new city office building in 30 years. At the north end of E. 12th St., the Public Utilities Bldg. was completed in 1971. The influence of Edward D. Stone, an exponent of the idea that an ornamental grace could counter the sterility of the glass box, was apparent. The symmetrical marble-clad structure, long and narrow with a cantilevered 5th floor, contains an interior atrium with a skylight. Because of the plan, the materials used, and the general effect of regularity, this building is the closest to the gestures of monumentality that still persisted in the federal buildings of the national capital through these years.

A different gesture toward monumentality was demonstrated in the Justice Ctr., completed in 1977 to house the county prosecutor, probation office, common pleas court, municipal courts, police headquarters, and corrections center. The combined county and city complex occupies a 26-story tower and an 8-story mass on the block opposite the earlier county administration building. Faced with pink granite and displaying ranks of windows set in deep horizontal reveals, the monolithic pile is articulated only by repetitious honeycomb units that are indistinguishable from those of a hotel, hospital, or laboratory. Abstract symbolism is not totally absent; just as the classical orders may have been used to express the hierarchy of federal, county, and municipal governments in 1910, the placement of the courts in a tower might be understood to symbolize their supremacy over the police function. The entrance sculpture by Isamu Noguchi was intended to suggest a gateway, but it remained incomprehensible to the general public.

The first State Office Bldg. in Cleveland was completed in 1979 and contains offices of the attorney general, taxation, the lottery commission, and workers' compensation, among others. The angular site west of the 1934 post office was an undeveloped parcel on the air rights over the rapid-transit tracks in the Terminal Group. The constraints of the site produced an irregular trapezoidal building of black-toned steel and glass with an acute angle facing the approach to Superior Ave. from the west. The form was conceived as a piece of monumental sculpture; but again, only a sign distinguishes it from a commercial office building.

Thus, Cleveland's most recent civic buildings were in the fully developed modern style that had dominated architecture since World War II. By the 1980s, the new architectural design called Postmodern was turning once again to representational forms that could express or symbolize the function of the building. As yet no general consensus has been reached as to what kind of forms might be appropriate for governmental buildings. Until such a consensus is realized, Cleveland's most characteristic civic buildings remain those of the classical period, and especially the Group Plan ensemble.

Eric Johannesen
Western Reserve Historical Society

See also ARCHITECTURE.

**ARCHITECTURE, RESIDENTIAL.** Throughout the city's history, the residential architecture of Cleveland has generally followed the typical trends of the rest of the nation. It cannot be said that Cleveland produced a distinctive architects' style like Chicago's Prairie style, or a characteristically regional style like that of the San Francisco Bay area. However, the character and quality of its residential architecture are comparable with the best examples of the same type anywhere. The most characteristic residential contributions have probably been in 3 areas: PUBLIC HOUSING, early-20th-century suburban homes, and the common detached neighborhood houses.

From the settlement of Cleveland in 1796 to the completion of the OHIO & ERIE CANAL in 1827, homes represented little that could be dignified by the name of architecture. The original settlers built log houses, and in 1810 there were only 3 frame houses. However, by 1830 the town began to acquire the appearance of a New England village, with numerous neat clapboarded houses based on Late Colonial vernacular practice. The only survival from this era is the DUNHAM TAVERN, which was far out on the Buffalo Rd. at that time. The growth of the village into a mercantile town at the terminus of the canal coincided with the spread of the Greek Revival style; moreover, Cleveland boasted a handful of first-rate master builders. During the 1830s and 1840s, many homes were erected that were the equal in every sense of those in Boston, New York, and Philadelphia, although of course none approached the scale of an antebellum southern plantation house. The characteristic feature of the Greek Revival, a full 2-story classic temple portico, appeared on many Euclid Ave. homes. Usually of 4 columns, the porticoes were either Doric (Erastus Gaylord house, 1836) or Ionic (Geo. Worthington house, 1852) in style, and usually the central colonnaded block was flanked by symmetrical wings.

Two other domestic revival styles appeared in Cleveland's homes before the CIVIL WAR, the Gothic and the Italianate. The former style could be rendered either as a Gothic cottage based on the pattern books of A. J. Downing (Thos. Bolton house, 1846), or as a pretentious stone mansion (Henry B. Payne house, 1849). The Italianate, Tuscan, or "bracketed" style achieved a far more widespread usage. It appeared in Cleveland as early as 1849 and was executed both as a Tuscan villa with a square tower (Jacob Perkins house, 1853) and as a squarish Italianate block with a cupola (Hurlbut house, 1855). The most extravagant and lushly ornamented house of this style was Amasa Stone's (1858). All of these houses have been razed. In the Civil War era, the introduction of a mansard roof on some of the late Italianate houses gave them a "French" look, but for some reason the Second Empire style never gained a strong foothold in Cleveland. Examples are the John D. Rockefeller (1866) and Anson Stager houses (1863). The latter, now the home of the UNIVERSITY CLUB, is the only Euclid Ave. mansion remaining from the first three-quarters of the century.

The street reached it heyday during the late Victorian period. The homes of the giant industrialists transformed Euclid Ave. from a picturesque Western Reserve street into "Millionaires' Row." Great houses, later called "monstrosities," rose in the High Victorian Gothic, Queen Anne, Richardsonian Romanesque, and various eclectic styles. The diversity of the mansions was unified by the generous setbacks, wide, spacious lawns, and tree-lined roadway, and this display of 19th-century architectural styles was equaled by few cities in America. However, the mansions of Euclid Ave. did not represent the entire picture of housing in a growing industrial city. The typical smaller homes of tradesmen, artisans, and factory laborers in the mid-19th century were in the common vernacular building style, which consisted of frame houses with a simple gable outline and a small stoop, or, less commonly, brick houses with stone lintels over doors and windows. These types were indistinguishable from the rural farmhouses being built in the Western Reserve countryside at the same time. There were very few row houses in the manner of eastern cities such as Philadelphia and Baltimore; this fact might be accounted for by the sense of unlimited space for expansion in the new West, and also by the greater distance from the European medieval tradition. In any case, the individual detached house was the rule and the row house the exception.

With the introduction of the railroads into the city and the development of heavy industry in the Flats, the disintegration of some of the more central neighborhoods had already begun by the last quarter of the century. To accommodate the rapidly growing working-class population at the beginning of the 20th century, the speculative developer flourished. Platted subdivisions, usually no more than a few streets in one direction and 3 or 4 blocks in the other, were the pattern. Duplicate or nearly identical houses were erected on speculation, on narrow lots laid out to afford the greatest possible return to the builder, and sold on a mortgage. Neighborhoods throughout the city were completed in this way on the west and east sides alike, and literally thousands of houses were constructed. By 1925 the city of Cleveland proper was practically built up to its final city limits.

Almost without exception, the developers' houses were wooden. The typical house was 2½ stories. Sometimes variety was added by an overhanging attic gable, a window, or classical porch columns. Around WORLD WAR I, this typical form became a 2-family house, with identical floorplans on each story, enabling the property owner to become an investor and a landlord. This type of income house became enormously popular and was endlessly duplicated throughout the city. Although many refer to these houses as "Cleveland doubles," there is no reason to suppose that the type was indigenous. At the same time, there was a sudden growth in the number of apartment buildings. Between 1900–10 alone, nearly 1,000 apartment buildings and terraces or row houses were built. They were seldom more than 4 stories tall, and usually were of brick and frame composite construction. Apartments were built in every style, from the simplest utilitarian block to ones with Queen Anne, Colonial, Tudor, or Spanish detail.

The first large movement to the suburbs began in the early 1890s. Suburban village developments were laid out at the same time on the Overlook at the northwest edge of CLEVELAND HTS., in AMBLER HTS. between Cedar Hill and DOAN BROOK, and in CLIFTON PARK on the western end of LAKEWOOD. Bratenahl's Lakeshore Blvd. and the former lands of the Shakers on the Heights also began to be developed. Although the spirit of 19th-century eclecticism was still firmly established, the house of the prosperous suburbanite began to develop a new and distinctive style between 1900–10. Its form tended toward a longer horizontal block with a low, hipped roof and a broad imposing front. In a reaction to Victorian ostentation, the interior plan was designed for more informal and practical modern living. The entrance hall was a circulation area that led on one side to a living room centered on a fireplace, and on the other to a dining room. Beyond the living room was a sun porch, and somewhere was a study, den, or library for privacy. The garage was detached and treated as the stable in the rear. The foremost exponent of this style was the partnership of FRANK B. MEADE and JAS. M. HAMILTON (Joseph O. Eaton house, 1917).

In the 1920s, the development of this progressive American type was cut short by the resurgent popularity of eclecticism. This fact has been attributed to a desire for a style expressing stability and security, and architects turned to historical styles from every period. The result is the suburban streets where Tudor, French, American Colonial, English, and Spanish homes stand adjacent to one another to form an attractive ensemble (Fairmount Blvd., Cleveland Hts.). It was the period of the full development of SHAKER HTS. (1915–30), and these assemblages of eclectic homes constitute a domestic architecture located in planned residential suburbs that have never been surpassed for livability and good taste.

However, the modern style that first gained currency in the 1930s never captured the public imagination as an alternative for domestic living. It remained an architects' style and an experimental method. During the Depression, a number of individual experimental houses were built showing either stylistic elements of the International style (flat roofs and corner windows) or new structural methods (steel framing, wallboard, and porcelain enamel shingles). The first complete statement of the modern house in Greater Cleveland was the home of architect Harold B. Burdick in Cleveland Hts. (1938). It displayed a square geometric shape, glass block and plate glass windows, a lack of historical ornament, and several "streamlined" features.

The extreme simplicity of the modern style, as well as some of its formal cliches, influenced postwar suburban architecture to some extent, but the "pure" modern style was bypassed by residential builders. Individual projects were built, especially architects' own homes, such as those of Ernst Payer, Clyde Patterson, and Don Hisaka, and in the 1950s, a unique private enclave of modern houses was completed in PEPPER PIKE. Located on a rural property that was not subject to the Van Sweringen Co.'s design restrictions, a dozen houses were designed by Robt. A. Little for a private cooperative community. The style of the homes largely reflected the functionalist style promulgated by Gropius at Harvard. Apart from such isolated instances, however, the modern style made little impact on Cleveland's private residential architecture.

The chief manifestation of modernism was in Cleveland's pioneer public housing. The first public-housing projects authorized and begun by the federal government were built in Cleveland in 1935–37. The Lakeview Terrace project was especially remarkable for its successful adaptation to the irregular hillside facing the lake. The development became internationally known and has been called a milestone in the history of American architecture. The design of the 44 residential units was clearly influenced by the work of European modernist architects, especially in features such as the windows arranged in horizontal bands, iron pipe railings, and the distinctive downturned hoods over the doorways. LAKEVIEW TERRACE also included the first community center in a public-housing project and was innovative in its use of the decorative arts. In the postwar period, the urban high-rise apartment became the standard for public-housing units. Regardless of the judgments that were made later on the failure of such densely populated blocks, Cleveland remained a leader in the provision of public housing under the leadership of ERNEST J. BOHN, director of the Cleveland Metropolitan Housing Authority from 1933–68. Bohn achieved a national reputation for his work in Cleveland, and the housing estates built under his direction included 9,537 units.

After WORLD WAR II, the new affluence of a growing middle class provided the means for thousands of families to seek a better home. The massive exodus to the suburbs in the 1950s made the suburban migrations of the teens seem like a mere trickle. The main directions of the movements were to the southwest and the southeast, and the most phenomenal growth took place in PARMA, Warrensville, and BROOK PARK. Unlike the older suburban homes, which were virtually without exception architect-designed, the 1950s suburban houses were builders' houses. Whether "Cape Cod," ranch-style, 2-story Colonial, or split-level, they consisted basically of a box or a set of boxes. Often the most distinguishing feature of these houses was the attached garage. This "packaged" housing provided homes for the urban emigrants in all the suburbs of Cleveland's metropolitan area.

However, by the 1970s and early 1980s, significant numbers began to reassess the benefits of living close to the city center. A movement to rehabilitate the near west side neighborhood revived the 19th-century name of OHIO CITY. A number of high-rise apartment buildings of 20 stories or more rose in the downtown (Park Centre, 1973), and there were tentative efforts to establish studio or loft living in the old WAREHOUSE DISTRICT. Whether the recovery of disintegrated residential areas such as HOUGH would be accomplished soon remained uncertain in the mid-1980s.

Eric Johannesen
Western Reserve Historical Society

See also ARCHITECTURE.

**ARCHITECTURE, SACRED.** Of the hundreds of sacred structures in Cleveland, there are several of national importance. ST. JOHN'S EPISCOPAL CHURCH (ded. 1838) is one of the earliest examples extant in the nation of the Gothic Revival style. National diversity is readily identifiable in the 13 onion domes atop ST. THEODOSIUS RUSSIAN ORTHODOX CATHEDRAL. Architecturally, Pilgrim Congregational Church (ded. 1894) expresses the late-19th-century American Protestant church's concern for social reform and functional efficiency. Unusual engineering is noted in the concrete dome of PARK SYNAGOGUE (ded. 1950) by internationally known architect Eric Mendelsohn. Not to be overlooked are some of the outstanding furnishings that heighten and lend a distinctive quality to local sacred buildings. Noteworthy is the imported wooden statuary by 19th-century German sculptor Josef Dressel installed during the early 1890s in the Church of St. Stephen (ded. 1876). The Von Beckrath tracker-action pipe organ installed in 1956–57 at Trinity Evangelical Lutheran Church (ded. 1873) is one of the first Baroque Revival organs built in this country. Fine examples of the stained glass of Louis C. Tiffany and noted Cleveland artist Toland Wright are to be found throughout Greater Cleveland (see CHURCH OF THE COVENANT, Presbyterian, ded. 1911).

Most early Cleveland churches were of a boxlike rectangular plan lacking columns, center aisles, chancels, or anything that might impede the sight or sound of the preacher or reader. Stylistically, most of these meeting-hall structures were commensurate with Cleveland's young population and were modest expressions of the reserved Federal and Greek Revival styles. The few churches that were constructed in this country in the Gothic form during the first half of the 19th century were by either Roman Catholic or the ritualistically attuned Protestant Episcopal congregations. Since the early settlers of Cleveland were primarily of English lineage, the first Gothic Revival edifices were limited to Episcopal builders; e.g., Trinity Church (ded. 1840) and Grace Church (ded. 1848). The first Roman Catholic church, Our Lady of the Lakes (ST. MARY'S ON THE FLATS, ded. 1840), displayed pointed windows, but the building itself was of the popular Greek Revival style. By mid-century, the country had tired of the classic austerity of the Greek Revival idiom and turned to romanticized picturesque forms of other, more exotic past styles. Despite the innate exotic characteristics of the pointed or ogee arch, the use of the Gothic form remained limited primarily to Roman Catholic and Episcopal structures. Another architectural form became fashionable that used all the popular "medieval" vocabulary, and was fenestrated with round arches. The Romanesque Revival, as it is sometimes called, presented a romantic but politically neutral edifice, and became popular for all denominations from the late 1840s to the early 1870s; e.g., Second Presbyterian Church (blt. 1850–52), Old Stone Church (ded. 1855), Plymouth Congregational/First Baptist Church (erected 1853), St. Mary's of the Assumption Roman Catholic Church (ded. 1865), ST. MALACHI CHURCH (ded. 1871), and the German Reform Church (cornerstone 1868). Since a specific Jewish sacred architectural form historically never evolved on its own, it was common for the design of a synagogue to reflect the fashion of its time and locale. During Oct. 1845, the *Herald* announced that the first local synagogue (ANSHE CHESED, whose cornerstone was laid that year) was "to be built in nearly the same style as the Baptist Church." When it was completed in 1846, it reflected the then-popular Romanesque Revival style.

When construction of sacred structures resumed after the CIVIL WAR, symbolism was slowly and sparingly reintroduced into American Protestant sacred buildings. The simplified symbolism that arose in the Protestant churches was usually confined to focal points such as the sanctuary, stained glass, and furnishings, and was as much decorative as it was symbolic. It was this reinterpretation of symbolism, including the lancet arch, that finally made the Gothic Revival an acceptable sacred style for all religious sects. The Gothic Revival idiom would remain popular for sacred buildings for the remainder of the 19th century, and throughout most of the 20th. A few 19th-century examples include Franklin Ave. Methodist Church (ded. 1870), FRANKLIN CIRCLE CHRISTIAN CHURCH (begun 1874, ded. 1883), and Zion Evangelical & Reformed Church (ded. 1885). The EPISCOPALIANS and the Roman Catholics continued to build several churches in the pointed style during this period. Running concurrently with the rise of Gothic form during the 1870s was the Richardsonian Romanesque, named after the American architect Henry Hobson Richardson of Boston. Architects throughout the country, including those in Cleveland, imitated Richardson's round arched, massive designs. The Richardsonian Romanesque form was openly adopted by most Protestant American churches, since it was promoted as an American form designed by an American architect. National interest in American-produced entities was also evident in the preference for the American-invented stained glass (by John La Farge and Louis C. Tiffany) used in the Protestant sects over the traditional, more translucent cathedral glass that remained a staple in ritually oriented churches.

The Richardsonian Romanesque style was ofen coupled with another American phenomenon formalized regionally, the "Akron Plan." Developed in 1868 by Louis Miller for the First Methodist Church of Akron, the Akron Plan served more fully the Protestant desire for a space where all could see and hear. It was designed as a Sunday school space contiguous with the sanctuary or auditorium. Centrally arranged, the Sunday school included a circumscribing balcony, with the floors of both levels pitched to give an uninterrupted view of the speaker. Sliding walls were placed so that portions of the gallery or space under the galleries could be closed off from the general auditorium. H. H. Richardson never built in Greater Cleveland, but there are many sacred structures that bear his influence. There are also some sterling examples of the Akron Plan, such as Bolton Presbyterian Church (ded. 1894), EUCLID AVE.

CHRISTIAN CHURCH (ded. 1908), and NORTH PRES-BYTERIAN CHURCH (ded. 1887). North is unusual in that the sanctuary and Sunday school are combined in the same space. America's pragmatic attitude is also noted in these Richardsonian/Akron Plan structures, in that many functions could be housed under 1 roof, including the auditorium, the Sunday school, social rooms for education and recreation, libraries, and swimming pools. A pertinent factor in these multifunctional buildings is that these services were opened to the entire public regardless of religious affiliation. The Reform Jews were part of this movement, as is evidenced in the Richardsonian Romanesque-inspired second synagogue for Tifereth Israel (occupied 1894). They also addressed social needs by opening several services of this functionally diverse building to the public. Of course, ritually oriented denominations were interested in social needs, but they were inclined, because of cultural differences, to remain ethnically exclusive. The efficient Akron Plan church was as foreign to them as the English language, and they continued to build their religious centers with separate buildings, each serving a different function according to their economic capacity.

Usually, only 1 or 2 styles dominated American architecture at any given time during the 19th century, but by the last quarter of that century and for the next 50 years, antiquarian eclecticism, as exemplified by the Ecole des Beaux-Arts and sanctioned by the Columbian Exhibition, ruled the day. America freely borrowed and mixed several styles from many antiquarian European and Classic Colonial American forms. People of English lineage tended to emulate English sacred monuments; e.g., AMASA STONE CHAPEL (ded. 1911) is strongly akin to St. Cuthbert, Somerset, England (ca. 1430). The so-called military tower of TRINITY CATHEDRAL (ded. 1907) bears a resemblance to the tower from the crossing of Wells Cathedral, England (13th century). Both Church of the Covenant (ded. 1911) and St. Peter Episcopal Church (ded. 1930) are said to be modeled after simple English and Scottish country churches. Interesting variations appeared, including First Methodist Church (1905), where the traditional Latin cross floor plan is truncated and capped by an overscaled, squat Gothic tower. That was apparently an attempt to present an exterior of a more academically Gothic building while retaining the open central interior plan typical of a late-19th-century Protestant church. Also, EPWORTH EUCLID METHODIST CHURCH (ded. 1928) is an unusual combination of English and French Gothic mixed with elements of the Art Deco period.

Prototypes such as the Roman Pantheon represent, among other things, an image of stability. Local sacred edifices were greatly influenced by this monument; e.g., First Church Christ Scientist (ded. 1931), Second Church Christ Scientist (ded. 1916, until the 1980s the 77th St. Playhouse), Fifth Church Christ Scientist (ded. 1926), and B'NAI JESHURUN (ded. 1905—SHILOH BAPTIST in 1986). At the turn of the century, there was a trend by older congregations to choose a prototype that reflected their religious or national origins. Several Roman Catholic churches were patterned after medieval and Renaissance monuments related to the history of their religion. The exterior of the Church of St. James (ded. 1935) was based on Cefalu Cathedral, and its interior on Monreale Cathedral (ca. 1166), both from Sicily. St. Agnes Church (ded. 1916 and demolished 1976) had a facade patterned after that of St. Gilles-du-Gard (ca. 1140), a Romanesque structure in the south of France. The facade of St. Colman Church (ded. 1918) is reminiscent of the Basilica of St. John Lateran, which is the cathedral see of the bishop of Rome. Past historical American forms also became popular. The

use of the American Colonial Georgian church form with its white-columned pedimented portico and slender spire or ogee-hooded cupola was often imitated. It grew to rival the Gothic style as the leading form for sacred structures throughout the 20th century; e.g., Plymouth Congregational Church (ded. 1923) and ARCHWOOD UNITED CHURCH OF CHRIST (ded. 1928).

The Jewish structures of this period were also eclectic. As indicated, this eclecticism allowed for an expression of one's own national or religious origins. Since many of the earliest-known synagogues were eastern in architectural form, 20th-century Jewish congregations often borrowed some of these ancient concepts. An early local example of this trend was seen in the eastern horseshoe arches designed throughout the facade of the Scovill Temple (ded. 1887, now demolished). More than any other form, the dome, supposedly eastern in origin, became a favorite theme dominating many early-20th-century synagogues; e.g., Euclid Ave. Temple (ded. 1912)—its dome parallels the contours of the Esicieserlierl Roruna Encumeni in Istanbul, as well as the Hagia Sophia, E. 82nd St. and Euclid Ave., the Temple on the Heights (ded. 1926), and the Temple (third structure of Tifereth Israel, ded. 1924). Although the dome was commonly used, it was never solely identified as a Jewish architectural form. During the same period, other non-eastern idioms were incorporated; e.g., ANSHE EMETH Synagogue (ded. 1904) is in the Gothic form, and OHEB ZEDEK Synagogue (ded. 1905) is Romanesque in form.

This eclectic environment was a timely setting for the development of a transplanted ethnic architectural expression. Several of the Central and Southern European groups who began arriving in large numbers during the 1880s were, by the 20th century, financially ready to build permanent churches. The exotic, nationally identifiable onion domes of the Russian, Rusin, Syrian, and Ukrainian churches did not seem as culturally foreign to the eclectic tastes of 20th-century America. Consequently, among all the many ethnic peoples who settled in Cleveland, this group of sacred structures is perhaps the closest example of authentic 1st-generation ethnic architecture: e.g., ST. THEODOSIUS RUSSIAN ORTHODOX CATHEDRAL (ded. 1911), St. Valdimar Ukrainian Orthodox Church (ded. 1924), and Holy Ghost Byzantine Catholic Church (ded. 1910).

During the 1930s and 1940s, the Depression and WORLD WAR II precluded the construction of many new sacred structures. It was not until the early 1950s that the plans to develop new suburban communities spurred the nation to build at a rapid pace. New houses of worship sprang up in response to the expansion of urban centers such as Cleveland. The conservative approach dominated sacred building through the mid-1960s. It was basically a continuation of some of the eclectic attitudes of 19th- and 20th-century America, which retained architectural religious motifs both universally and nationally symbolic. The American Colonial Georgian style became the most popular expression of the conservative movement; e.g., Parma South Presbyterian Church (ded. 1950), St. Martin Episcopal Church (ded. 1956), and Forest Hill Church, Presbyterian (ded. 1964). During the 1950s and early 1960s, many 2d- and 3d-generation descendants of Southern and Central European immigrants moved to the suburbs, but they maintained an unusually long allegiance to their first houses of worship in the inner city. As that changed and they began to build in the suburbs, many of the new Byzantine and Orthodox churches retained the traditional onion-dome form. In some cases, the chief difference between the churches built during the early 20th century by the 1st-generation immigrants and those built by their 3d-generation offspring is the use of contemporary building materials; e.g., St. Josaphat Ukrainian Catholic Church (ded. 1985) and St. Sava Eastern Orthodox Church (ded. 1982).

The opposite force or fashion is sometimes referred to as the modern movement. It began shortly after the turn of the century and was articulated by schools of design such as the Bauhaus. The austere designs of the modern movement were first seen in commercial and domestic structures, and did not find their way into sacred architecture until after World War II. In contrast to the conservative aproach, the modern sacred design presented an abstract facade where most visible religious associations were simplified or eliminated. The first truly modern and perhaps the most significant sacred structure built in Greater Cleveland is Park Synagogue (ded. 1950), built by renowned architect Eric Mendelsohn. Its lines are simple and details minimal, yet religious symbolism was not sacrificed. Here again the composition is dominated by a dome. Besides its eastern connotations, the dome universally symbolizes the protective heavens of God. At Park Synagogue, Mendelsohn has spiritually circumscribed the congregation within a symbol of heaven, a conceptual function of the dome, with earth seen through the glass in the seasons changing. Other designs favored reducing symbolism to simplified emblems affixed to streamlined basilica or box forms. These sacred structures suggest a greater kinship to the secular post-World War II modern buildings in their adherence to the modern postulate "Form follows function." Such a religious edifice became more a secular assembly hall, which is sometimes accompanied by a campanile or bell tower form; e.g., the Roman Catholic Church of the Gesu (ded. 1958), St. Rose of Lima Roman Catholic Church (ded. 1957), and the West Side Temple (ded. 1954). As utilitarian vernacular forms evolved to house the suburban middle class (the Cape Cod, bungalow, and ranch styles), a vernacular sacred form has also appeared. It is usually based on a rectangular or basilica plan enclosed by a gabled roof. The pitch of the roof ranges from nearly flat, like that of the ranch-style homes that surround it, to extremely steep, the A frame becoming a muted echo of the lancet arch of the Gothic style.

By the mid-1960s, with the occurrence of such events as the 2d Vatican Council in Rome and a movement toward ecumenical cooperation between some religious sects, a strong focus on building congregational participation developed. In order to bring the congregation closer to the ceremony and allow a greater appreciation of each other within the congregation, a circular or round seating configuration gained favor. This arrangement dictated that the exterior shell be based on a central plan, in contrast to the common rectangular plan. Of course, a central plan had been used by many Protestant and Jewish houses of worship since the 19th century. As a result, whether in a square or round format, the central plan dominates many designs for the newest sacred structures. Many of the more recent (1970s–1980s) sacred structures present a boldly abstract exterior design. When religious symbolism is retained, its presence is usually illusive. That lends a more secular appearance to the sacred structure comparable to current, equally dynamic, secular public and commercial buildings; e.g., Temple B'nai Jeshurun (Beachwood, ded. 1980) and St. Pascal Baylon Roman Catholic Church (ded. 1971). Even though Greater Cleveland did not produce any nationally recognized innovations in sacred architecture, its importance can be seen in the diversity of houses of worship built by more than 46 different nationalities in Cleveland.

Timothy Barrett
Western Reserve Historical Society

THE ARCHWOOD UNITED CHURCH OF CHRIST is an early "Plan of Union" church that survived in the 1980s in its west side neighborhood. The first settlers had established themselves in the large township of BROOKLYN in 1812, and itinerant Presbyterian and Congregationalist ministers held services from time to time in the area. The Plan of Union, under which these two denominations cooperated in a missionary effort to found churches in the WESTERN RESERVE, was responsible for establishing a church at Brooklyn in July 1819 called a Presbyterian church. Circuit preachers served the church until a permanent minister was hired in 1834. A town meeting house and members' homes were used for services until a building reportedly was built near the present (1986) corner of W. 25th St. and Willowdale Ave., and was in use by 1830. Following the usual pattern of Plan of Union churches, the Brooklyn congregation finally made a choice between the denominations and in 1831 was incorporated as the First Congregational Society of Brooklyn. In 1851 the frame building was moved to the corner of Liberty (W. 33rd) and Newburgh (Denison Ave.) streets. In 1879 a new brick building of Late Gothic style was built on the north side of Greenwood (Archwood) Ave. It was outgrown and in disrepair by the 1920s, and a new building in the Colonial Revival style was dedicated on the Archwood Ave. site in 1929.

National discussions concerning the merger of the Congregational and Evangelical & Reformed denominations began in the 1940s, and in 1957 the two formed the United Church of Christ. In 1967 the Archwood Church and Fourth Evangelical & Reformed were merged into the Archwood United Church of Christ. The Fourth Evangelical & Reformed Church was formed out of a German-speaking Sunday school begun in 1869 as a mission of the First Evangelical & Reformed Church at Penn Ave. (W. 32nd St.) and Carroll Ave. The Sunday school served German families in the area south of the area known as Walworth Run. In 1872 these families met in a home on Walton Ave. and chartered the Fourth Evangelical & Reformed Church. A lot was purchased on Louis (W. 32nd) St. south of Clark Ave., and a small frame church was dedicated in 1873. A Sunday school annex was added in 1884.

A second building was dedicated on Woodbridge Ave. in 1910. Until this time, all services were conducted in German; however, in the new church, evening services were said in English, and eventually English and German were used on alternating Sundays. Following the merger of the two congregations, the Evangelical & Reformed building was sold. The 1970s saw a decline in community involvement for the Archwood Church, but with renewed interest in neighborhood and community development, the church has become involved in many projects, including the Crossroads Development Corp. and Archwood Denison Concerned Citizens, the Brooklyn Centre Historical Society, and a hunger center. Church membership remained at approximately 250 in the 1980s.

ARENA. See CLEVELAND ARENA

ARMENIANS. Armenian immigration to Cleveland began in 1906 or 1907, when employees of the AMERICAN STEEL & WIRE CO. factory in Worcester, Mass., came to Cleveland to work in a newly opened branch of that firm. The company soon had 5 branches in the area, and Armenians who had earlier worked in its factory in Mass. were willing to come to the Midwest, lured by salaries that were often 1/3 higher. Most of the workers were young men without wives or family, and at first they numbered about 50. By 1913 there were more than 100, and some began to leave the mills to find employment as merchants, or in the small crafts, as barbers, shoemakers, or tailors, a trend that greatly increased in the 1920s. Many of the immigrants were from the Turkish city of Malatya, and they congregated after working hours in a coffeehouse at E. 71st and Broadway, near the rooming houses where many lived. By 1910, the 2 principal Armenian political parties had established headquarters in Cleveland. The Tashnags (Armenian Revolutionary Fed.) were eventually to locate at E. 55th and Broadway, while the Ramgavars (Armenian Constitutional Democratic party) came to E. 21st and Prospect. Migration slowed from WORLD WAR I until the early 1920s. It was then that the second wave of immigration occurred, though many had to come to America circuitously via Cuba, Mexico, or Canada because of the new immigration laws. A good number entered the U.S. illegally. Most found unskilled work at the mills, or often as workers in hotels. It was not until WORLD WAR II, when the Armenian population of Cleveland approached 1,500, that the community achieved economic security. Numerous societies aided them. Locally, the Educational Society of Malatya and the national Armenian General Benevolent Union were important. These organizations helped the young male workers to find jobs and housing and to learn the English language. They also assisted in the search for wives; many young Armenian women were brought directly to Cleveland from Cuba, to which they had come from the Middle East.

With prosperity, it became possible for the Armenian immigrants to consider building churches. The Tashnags purchased land for the Holy Cross Church & Community Ctr. on Wallings Rd. in N. Olmsted. The Ramgavars secured property for St. Gregory of Narek Church on Richmond Rd., Richmond Hts. Since there were no distinct areas in Cleveland where Armenians congregated, the sites of the churches were largely geographic compromises and did not reflect Armenian population centers. The Ramgavars were financially the most successful, buying their lot in the early 1960s, building a church shortly thereafter, and paying off the mortgage within 3 years. A few years later, they erected a community hall on the church ground. The Armenian church, the focus and protector of Armenian cultural life, continued that role in Cleveland. The parish halls of both the Tashnags and the Ramgavars supported the traditional Armenian culture. A Saturday school was established on the Richmond Rd. property in 1970, teaching Armenian language and history; this enterprise was supported by the Manoogian Foundation of Southfield, Mich. For more than 2 decades, beginning in the late 1950s, an Armenian radio program played on station WXEN, on Wednesdays from 8-9 p.m. During the 1970s, the time of political dislocation in Lebanon and Iran, countries with substantial Armenian minorities, few new families settled in Cleveland. The community has remained stable since 1960, with a population nearing 2,500.

John Greppin
Cleveland State University

**ARMSTRONG, WILLIAM W.** (18 Mar. 1833–21 Apr. 1905), was a local newspaper publisher and Democratic party political leader. He was born in New Lisbon, Ohio, and lived there until moving to Tiffin, Ohio, in 1854, where he bought and published a local newspaper. In 1857 he married Sarah Virginia Hedges. After serving as a registrar in the state treasurer's office in Columbus, Armstrong was elected secretary of state—the youngest man to hold that office in the history of Ohio (1862). He moved to Cleveland in 1865, bought the *PLAIN DEALER*, and edited it until 1883. In 1868 he testified at the impeachment trial of Pres. Andrew Johnson. Armstrong served as a delegate to the Democratic Natl. Conventions in 1868, 1880, and 1884. He also served on the Democratic Natl. Committee. In 1881 he declined the nomination to run for governor of Ohio. In 1891 the Democratic party adopted his rooster design as party symbol. Although often referred to as "Major" or "General," Armstrong never served in the military. The titles dated from his youth, when he was a member of a military organization for young boys. The fact that his father, Gen. John Armstrong, had been a military officer enhanced William's reputation of possessing a military background. Armstrong died in Tiffin, Ohio.

**ART.** The development of an art life in Cleveland primarily resulted from the efforts of 2 distinctly different groups within the community: the wealthy patrons of art and the artists themselves. The first group consisted of families who accumulated their wealth from industry and commerce; the artists derived mainly from the German community. Also important was the influence of the commercial arts on other aspects of Cleveland's art life. These contributing factors would change—to varying degrees—following WORLD WAR II. An established art life really did not begin in Cleveland until 1876. In earlier years the city managed to support a few itinerant portrait painters, woodcarvers, stonecutters, and sign painters. Traveling exhibitions were occasionally announced in the newspapers and were usually held in the courthouse or local churches. Typical of these was an exhibition in 1844 that featured reproductions of Italian and Flemish paintings. By 1857, the Cleveland directory listed 6 professional artists. They mainly subsisted on portrait commissions and fees for individual or class instruction. Painting was occasionally lucrative, as in the case of Julius Gollman, who received $400 for his group portrait of the Arkites. In 1876, 2 events combined to accelerate the growth of art in Cleveland. The Centennial Exhibition in Philadelphia, with its various displays of European and American art, is largely credited with encouraging the incipience of local art interest throughout America. The most popular painting at the exhibition was *THE SPIRIT OF '76* by a Cleveland painter, ARCHIBALD WILLARD. A celebrity, Willard returned to Cleveland and agreed to lead a group of young artists, who that year formed the Cleveland ART CLUB. Also known as the Old Bohemians, the artists obtained rent-free space on the top floor of the Case Block (the city hall annex), where they set up studios and offered classes. The Cleveland Art Club provided the city with its first nucleus of notable artists, most of them—such as FREDERICK GOTTWALD, Otto Bacher, and Max Bohm—the sons of German immigrants. Many received training abroad, primarily at the art schools in Munich and Dusseldorf.

In 1878, a group of women organized the first loan exhibition in Cleveland in order to raise money for social relief. The exhibition featured 167 oils, 67 watercolors, books and manuscripts, ceramics, bronze and statuary, gems, laces, and an Oriental collection. As in future loan exhibitions, artwork was borrowed from private collections in Cleveland, as well as from other cities, such as New York and Boston. Excursion trains came from such places as Erie, Dayton, and Toledo; attendance for the event exceeded 40,000. Many of the city's galleries and art stores mainly offered for sale reproductions of European paintings. Sales of original works by the old masters increased toward the end of the century. Although a few galleries set aside space for local artists, their works were seldom sold. Oscar Wilde's lecture in Cleveland in 1882 on the English Arts & Crafts Movement helped to encourage the founding later that year of the Western Reserve School of Design for Women (the future Cleveland School of Art). Such schools were proliferating throughout the country, mainly to prepare women—now joining the workforce—for careers as designers in local industries.

Art activity continued to increase in the 1890s with the founding of several new artists' and art organizations, and 2 more loan exhibitions, in 1894 and 1895. The catalog for the loan exhibition in 1894 reveals the steady growth of art in private homes in Cleveland since the first loan exhibition 14 years earlier. Names such as Olney, Brush, Holden, Huntington, Hanna, and Wade appear as contributors of oil paintings that included originals of da Vinci, Tintoretto, Rubens, and Van Dyke. The Cleveland Art Assoc. was the first organized effort among the city's wealthy industrialists to promote art in Cleveland. It was responsible for the loan exhibition in 1895. As the year before, half the proceeds were donated to the city's poor fund, and the other half for the purchase of artwork for a future museum. In terms of an overall art life, Cincinnati at this time was far ahead of Cleveland and all other western cities. Reasons included its location in the more developed Ohio River Valley, an established German population, and added patronage from wealthy Kentuckians. Moreover, Cleveland would not exceed Cincinnati in population until ca. 1900.

In the first decade of the 20th century, Cleveland experienced a lull in its art development. One reason was the defection of many of the city's finest artists to Europe in search of a more favorable art climate. Several of the Old Bohemians joined Hubert Herkomer in England, where Herkomer (later to become Sir Hubert) headed the Bushy-Hertz artists' colony near London. This emigration led in part to the dissolution of the Cleveland Art Club, the city's most vital artists' organization. Another factor for this period of inactivity was the delay in the establishment of an art museum. By 1891, 3 substantial funds had been bequeathed for this purpose, but problems arose from an inability to legally consolidate the separate trusts. Late in arriving (even Toledo had an art museum before Cleveland), the CLEVELAND MUSEUM OF ART was finally incorporated in 1913. No major exhibitions took place in the city during this period in view of the anticipated museum. Other exhibitions, usually well attended, were periodically held at Chas. Olney's private gallery and the Cleveland School of Art's new building (1906), which featured the city's first large exhibition room. From 1910–29, the city experienced its greatest period of art activity, reflected in the emergence of the Art Museum, the MAY SHOW, a resurgence in art and artists' organizations, and a number of exhibitions of current art from Europe. Cleveland's booming industrial growth naturally led to an increased desire for cultural distinction. In 1913, 10 cubist works from Paris were exhibited at the Taylor Dept. Store and caused quite a negative reaction in the community. The following year a Cleveland expatriate artist, ALEXANDER WARSHAWSKY, organized an exhibition of postimpressionist paintings that included the works of fellow Cleveland artists. This show also drew almost unanimous criticism, the *Plain Dealer* labeling it as the "Biggest Laugh in Town." Although the city wished to eliminate its provincial image, as late as the 1930s paintings of "undraped nudes" would still excite controversy in the newspapers.

The 1910s also saw the emergence of 2 dominant artists' organizations in the city. The CLEVELAND SOCIETY OF ARTISTS was founded in 1913 as a revival of the Cleveland Art Club. Its initial purpose was to continue the tradition of academic art. Its opposite was the KOKOON CLUB, founded in 1911. A cofounder, Carl Moellmen, had studied under Robt. Henri in New York. Henri despised academic rules and espoused an individualism and democracy in art more genuinely American. The Kokoon Club was based

on this conception. Cleveland at this time was becoming a thriving commercial-arts center. In lithography, the Morgan and Otis companies, and later Continental, were attracting artistic talent from around the country. The city also boasted well-known engraving and publishing houses such as the Caxton Co. In ceramics, the Cowan Pottery in ROCKY RIVER was gaining national recognition. For many years it recruited most of its craftsmen from the Cleveland School of Art. The artists' organizations drew the bulk of their membership from the commercial arts, providing artists with an uncensored outlet for their creative energies. The Kokoon Club was significant in that it provoked a struggle for the city to achieve a balance between progress and extremism. This struggle was based largely on a misconception among Americans that linked "new art" to political extremism and immoral behavior. Tension increased with city hall when the Kokoon Club's annual ball began to display some of the antisocial themes espoused by Dadaism, pervasive among America's avant-garde following WORLD WAR I. Fearing the loss of his job, Mayor FRED KOHLER banned the ball in 1923, claiming that the event fell within Lent. It was, however, resumed the next year and continued to attract enormous publicity (from outside the city, as well) as the yearly review of Cleveland's Latin Quarter.

This second generation of Cleveland artists still consisted largely of the sons and grandsons of German immigrants (of the 13 original members of the Kokoon Club, 9 were of German heritage). Many still received training in Germany, although the French postimpressionists—especially Cezanne—were also popularly emulated. Because many of the city's artists made a living as engravers, illustrators, and lithographers, fine draftsmanship often characterized their individual efforts—as in the paintings of WM. SOMMER. Overall, like most American artists until World War II, Cleveland artists generally sought a middle-of-the-road compromise between the old masters and moderns. The introduction of the May Show in 1919 helped considerably to bring attention to local artists. The Society of Artists, the Kokoon Club, and the WOMEN'S ART CLUB (organized in 1912) had each put on annual exhibitions, but these were generally received with little enthusiasm. The Cleveland Museum of Art and the new Cleveland Art Assoc. (revived in 1915) organized the first May Show to exhibit the works of local artists and craftsmen and to provide a market for their sale. Ultimate selection of the jurors was reserved for the museum's board of trustees. A similar show already existed in Chicago, but the Cleveland show was to become one of the country's largest and best-known. Traveling exhibits were sent around the country and did much to establish the reputation of Cleveland as an art center.

As the new center of art in Cleveland, the Art Museum implemented many programs and associated art organizations to promote art in the city. For the general public, various educational programs were offered. In 1918, in an *Art Museum Bulletin*, the museum stated an intention to build permanent collections in areas that would benefit the city's industries, such as printing, textiles, iron and steel, furniture, and woodcarving. That resulted in the founding of the PRINT CLUB OF CLEVELAND in 1919, and the Textile Art Club in 1934. In the 1920s, Cleveland surpassed Boston as the country's leading center in watercolor painting. The medium achieved popularity here because of the close-knit character of the artistic community; moreover, from 1924 it was the most important feature of the May Show. Many of these paintings won prizes at the prestigious Annual Internatl. Exhibition at the Carnegie Institute in Pittsburgh. Such attention helped to bring about the identification of a "Cleveland School" of artists. Despite growing recognition, the artists received a great unevenness of support in Cleveland itself. The May Show, ironically, was partly responsible. Removed from the show's prestige, the artists were more or less left stranded the remainder of the year. The various artists' organizations offered comparable works at yearly auctions, but these usually sold at disappointingly low prices. Dwelling in the shadow of the May Show, in later years such exhibitions indeed became popularly known as "reject shows." The wealthy in Cleveland were primarily dedicated to the collection of European art, and patronage of the Art Museum and May Show; unprotected, the artist fell prey to a swarm of middle-class bargain hunters. Artists in other cities usually fared no better; in Cleveland, the situation was only less consistent.

Like everything else, art in Cleveland suffered during the Depression. For the Cleveland Museum of Art, bequests were reduced, and purchases had to be curtailed. At the Cleveland School of Art, enrollment dropped 35% between 1930–33. Many artists and craftsmen dependent on the commercial arts for a living applied to the WPA's Federal Art Project. The Depression also contributed to the weakening of Cleveland's artists' organizations. The predecessor of the WPA/FAP was the Public Works of Art Project, established in 1933. Cleveland's quota of artists was fixed at 69, although twice that number applied. Those prominent in Cleveland art and museum circles—such as JOHN L. SEVERANCE and Mrs. Malcolm McBride—had influence on the selection committee. Under the PWAP, Cleveland artists produced 8 murals for the CLEVELAND PUBLIC LIBRARY, plaques for schools, historical maps, and other art objects. Later, in 1936, the FAP put 75 Cleveland artists to work in an old factory building to make signs, lantern slides, paintings, and sculptures. Ceramics were also produced and were very much in demand throughout the country, upholding Cleveland's national reputation in that area of art production. The Depression forced the artists' organizations to combine on exhibitions, auctions, and, in 1932, the first artists' curb market in Cleveland. Also that year, a gigantic exhibition of arts and crafts was held in the old Elysium Skating Rink; the profit of $6,500 was shared evenly among the organizations. By the late 1930s, there was a general demise among Cleveland's artists' organizations. The Depression and the increasing use of automation in the commercial arts, especially lithography, helped to check the flow of artists into Cleveland. European-trained artists, the majority of German heritage, were aging and giving way to a greater diversity of younger artists from the highly regarded Cleveland School of Art. As "new art" became more acceptable, the Kokoon Club and Cleveland Society of Artists blurred together. For these reasons and others that occurred after the war, Cleveland's artists' organizations would never again be as visibly active.

In the late 1930s and early 1940s, the art center of the world moved from Paris to New York. That also marked a turning point in the art life of Cleveland. After the war, a general shift took place in Cleveland from smaller commercial-art companies that mostly emphasized the graphic arts to a diversity of larger companies interested in industrial design. From the 1920s, the Cleveland School of Art had been placing a stronger emphasis on the practical uses of art and design in order better to serve the various industries in Cleveland. Following the war, this emphasis increased as manufacturing companies across America called for advertising artists and industrial designers to work in—among others—the automobile, home appliance, aluminumware, toy, ceramics, and greeting card industries. Theretofore, most of Cleveland's artists had been concentrated in several leading commercial art firms; now there was a general dispersion of artists, craftsmen, and designers among many industries. There was also the new and overpowering draw of New York for younger artists. These factors contributed to a further debilitation of the artists' organizations and led to a shift in focus from local to regional art, an emphasis that has continued to the present.

As the importance of the artists' organizations diminished, the void would be filled in the 1950s with a proliferation of neighborhood art centers and a multitude of art events sponsored by such diverse organizations as women's clubs, churches, cultural institutions, civic and ethnic groups, and department stores. In 1949, the CLEVELAND INSTITUTE OF ART Alumni Assoc. held its first annual art show and sale at SHAKER SQUARE. It was followed, in the 1950s, by a strong involvement from the Jewish community with the introduction of the JEWISH COMMUNITY CTR. show, and the annual benefit of the MT. SINAI MEDICAL CTR. Auxiliary. The annual exhibition at the PARK SYNAGOGUE, begun in 1960, helped to bring local attention to new movements in modern art such as abstract expressionism. Black artists in Cleveland were also making an important contribution. In 1940, 6 black artists under the auspices of the KARAMU HOUSE formed a new artists' organization. Known as the Karamu artists, within a few years they developed into the largest single group of black artists in the country. During the next decade, they exhibited at such notable institutions as the Cleveland Museum of Art and the Pennsylvania Academy of Fine Art. The Karamu House has also, since 1915, maintained a gallery with special interest in the works of talented black artists.

By the early 1960s, the diversity of local involvement had become considerable. In 1964, exhibitions included African art at the May Co., master prints at Higbee's, the Baycrafters' annual juried show, an exhibition of Cleveland artists at the Circle Gallery, the annual exhibition of work by teachers of art in Cleveland high schools, and a show by students of the Cooper School of Art—and that was only a fraction of the art events and sales that took place that year in Cleveland. Gallery openings and closings also proliferated at this time. The HOWARD WISE GALLERY of Present Day Painting, opened in 1957, attempted to bring works of contemporary European and American artists to Cleveland. The attempt faltered, and in 1961 the gallery moved to New York. In contrast to New York, where galleries are concentrated in specific parts of the city—such as Greenwich Village and Soho—galleries in Cleveland since the war have been dispersed throughout the greater metropolitan area. Decentralization has led to the closing of some galleries and has caused periodic movings of others in order to maintain a viable location. Recently, however, artists and galleries have been attracted to the Murray Hill area. In 1986, the second annual "Art Walk" was held, involving the participation of 20 private studios and 9 galleries in Murray Hill and nearby University Circle. In the 1970s, a number of outdoor art fairs were introduced in Cleveland. These include the Boston Mills Art Festival, the Lakewood and Cain Park festivals, and art displays as part of the Hessler and Coventry Village fairs. Many of these feature the art and handicrafts of local artists, while others have a more regional or national emphasis.

Among the artists working in Cleveland in 1986, 4 of the best-known are former instructors at the Cleveland Institute of Art (formerly the Cleveland School of Art). Viktor Schreckengost is a ceramicist, a painter, a sculptor, and a pioneer in industrial design. His works can be found in major museums, including the Cleveland Museum of Art and the Museum of Modern Art. Wm. M. McVey is one of the few sculptors in America today to earn a living from his skills; 80 of his works are on public display in northern

Ohio. His best-known work is the statue of Winston Churchill in front of the British Embassy in Washington, D.C. Kenneth Bates has long been considered the dean of American enameling. Internationally recognized, his enamel craftworks have appeared in every May Show since 1927, winning 32 prizes. Originally a ceramicist, Edris Eckardt in the 1950s switched to glass and bronze sculpture. Research led her to reformulate the ancient Egyptian gold glass technique: among glass artists, she is in the highest ranks internationally.

Since the 1950s, corporations have arrived on the local art scene in an area formerly dominated by the wealthy industrialists. Corporations have joined local foundations in making grants to art institutions in Cleveland; many corporate executives serve as board members for these institutions. Although its arrival was somewhat late in Cleveland, corporate art collecting has been a significant factor in the city's art life since 1975. Among Cleveland's financial institutions, some—such as AMERITRUST—have gone exclusively to New York for art objects; others, including BancOhio and Natl. City Bank, have provided patronage to local artists for reasons of public relations and cost.

In addition to its other exhibits, the Cleveland Museum of Art has customarily put together 1 major traveling exhibit yearly. One of its best-known shows nationally was a bicentennial exhibition, "THE EUROPEAN VISION OF AMERICA," which it cosponsored with the Natl. Gallery and the French government. The exhibit consisted of 340 paintings, decorative art objects, prints, artifacts, and books that depicted early America as seen by Europeans. Locally, the museum has installed extension exhibits in, among other places, the Beachwood Museum, the Beck Ctr. for the Cultural Arts, the Cleveland Public Library, and the Lakewood Civic Art Gallery. Also in 1976, Clevelanders were forced to confront modern sculpture in Isamu Noguchi's *The Portal*. The 15-ton, 36-ft.-high curving configuration of carbon steel piping is located at the W. 3rd St. entrance of the Justice Ctr. It was commissioned by the GEO. GUND FOUNDATION at a cost of $100,000. Quite visible, the sculpture was the subject of considerable controversy in the city. Sherman Lee, then director of the Cleveland Museum of Art, considered *The Portal* one of the most important monumental sculptures in the U.S. Public reaction—especially to its cost/value—was mostly opposite.

In recent years, Cleveland has seen the founding of several theme-based nonprofit art organizations. Contemporary art finally gained a foothold in the city with the establishment of the Cleveland Ctr. for Contemporary Art in 1968. A similarly oriented organization is the Spaces gallery, located in the warehouse district. Both organizations claim a commitment to Ohio artists. A revived interest in the "Cleveland School" artists led, in 1984, to the founding of the Cleveland Artists Foundation. The organization maintains the Northeast Ohio (NEO) Art Museum and, among its other activities, plans to revive the Kokoon Club Ball in 1986. NOVA (the New Organization for the Visual Arts) is dedicated to the advocation of the artist in the community, a responsibility previously held by the now-defunct Cleveland Area Arts Council. A subsidiary of NOVA, NovArt, was created to place works of regional artists in corporate homes. NOVA has implemented many new programs and exhibitions, including, in 1983, the Art in Special Places Program to expose art to people who do not frequent museums and galleries. The organization has coordinated, since 1980, the Cleveland Art Festival (now Cleveland Art Focus), which it hopes will become as big as the Three Rivers Festival in Pittsburgh.

Compared to cities with similar growth, an art life in Cleveland was late to arrive. But between 1910–29, Cleveland experienced a kind of renaissance in art that rivaled, and in some areas surpassed, that of other cities in America. The viability of the commercial arts in the city and the leadership of the Art Museum were strong contributing factors. With the possible exception of the May Show, Cleveland's art life has not been innovative but rather has accommodated, or expanded on, outside influences. Since World War II, Cleveland, like all other American cities, in terms of art has largely dwelt in the shadow of New York. The Cleveland Museum of Art, of course, has been a leader in such areas as Oriental art. Both the Art Museum and the Cleveland Institute of Art are proudly supported and remain among the finest of their kind in the country. But there is, perhaps, a tendency among Clevelanders to see these two institutions as the only centers for art in the city. That has led to Clevelanders' not fully taking advantage of the manifold offerings of the city's art life and, perhaps more seriously, has made it sometimes difficult for galleries, artists, and smaller art organizations to achieve a vital existence in the city.

James Shelley

Clark, Edna, *Ohio Art and Artists* (1932).
*Federal Art in Cleveland*, Cleveland Public Library (1974).
Smart, Jermayne, "Folk Art of the Western Reserve" (Ph.D. diss., WRU, 1939).
Wittke, Carl, *The Cleveland Museum of Art* (1966).
Wixom, Nancy Coe, *Cleveland Institute of Art* (1983).

The **ART CLUB** (also known as the Old Bohemians and the City Hall Colony) was founded by ARCHIBALD WILLARD in 1876. The group was initially composed of artists and friends, primarily of German extraction, who met at Willard's studio in the Union Natl. Bank Bldg. To discuss art and draw from live models. Later in 1876, after the group acquired rooms in City Hall in the Case Block, its aims were defined: to furnish instruction in drawing and painting of the same standard provided in foreign schools; to present exhibitions and lectures; and to assist art students. Prominent members of the group were Geo. Grossman, FREDERIC C. GOTTWALD, John Semon, Louis Loeb, Herman and JOHN HERKOMER, Daniel and Emil Wehrschmidt, Arthur Schneider, Chas. Henry Niehaus, and Max Bohm. Grossman later left Cleveland to found a New York City artists' colony. Gottwald painted figureheads and salon walls of lakeboats. Semon achieved national prominence as a landscapist. Loeb became an illustrator for *Harper's* magazine. The Herkomers became noted local woodcarvers. The Wehrschmidts eventually taught and painted in Bushey, near London. Schneider became court painter to the Sultan of Morocco. Niehaus became a prominent sculptor, and Max Bohm a successful mural painter in France. The club members fostered the Cleveland Art School, which operated out of the clubrooms until city officials required the space for additional offices in 1898. Soon after losing its clubrooms, the group dissolved. The Art Club should not be confused with 2 other groups, the Cleveland Arts Club or the later (1925) Cleveland Art Club.

The **ART LOAN EXHIBITIONS** were 2 special exhibitions held in 1893 and 1894 to benefit the unemployed of the city suffering from the national depression and to stimulate interest in art in Cleveland. The Loan Assoc. formed to organize the exhibition was headed by Prof. Chas. F. Olney, who with other members appealed to collectors all over the country for loans of paintings. The response was overwhelming; over 200 paintings were sent from across the U.S. Local Cleveland patrons, including Olney, CHAS. F. BRUSH, and William J. White, donated works from their collections. The first exhibition, housed in the Garfield Bldg., attracted huge crowds. Schoolchildren from throughout Cleveland attended and wrote compositions on works that they might not otherwise have had the chance to see. The exhibition raised a substantial amount of money and was so successful that an even larger show was planned for the following year. The second exhibition, also held in the Garfield Bldg., was made possible not only by the loan of artworks but also by significant financial donations by JOHN D. ROCKEFELLER, L. H. Severance, SAMUEL MATHER, and John F. Whitelaw. This second exhibition was larger than the first and included works by artists such as Claude Lorraine, Paolo Veronese, Albrecht Durer, Tintoretto, and Leonardo da Vinci. In addition, there were displays of textiles, fans, jewels, relics, curios, and statuary, as well as a public school exhibit. This event was also successful. At $.50 a ticket ($5 for a season ticket), a large amount of money was again raised to aid the poor of Cleveland. An extensive catalog of the paintings in the exhibition was published. After 1894, interest in the project waned, and no further art loan exhibitions were held although an Art Loan Exposition was undertaken to celebrate the 30th anniversary of the Cleveland School of Art in 1913.

**ARTER & HADDEN,** Cleveland's oldest legal partnership, has been engaged in the practice of law under this name since 1951, when a consolidation of 2 law firms created Arter, Hadden, Wykoff & Van Duzer. With offices in the Huntington Bldg., the firm employed 175 attorneys and did business in estate planning and corporate, communication, labor, hospital, and oil and gas law in 1986. Few law firms in the Cleveland area still practice under their original names. Arter & Hadden can directly trace its origins to the 1843 partnership of Willey & Cary. Opening an office in the Hancock Bldg., Geo. Willey started his law practice shortly after his admission to the Ohio bar in 1842. He was joined the following year by another recent admittant to the bar, John Cary. After 3 years in the Hancock Bldg., Willey & Cary moved to the Plain Dealer Bldg. at 53 Superior St. The firm remained there until 1851, when it moved to the WEDDELL HOUSE. In 1871, the firm changed its name to Willey, Cary & Terrell and moved its offices to 81 Public Square. When Cary left in 1877, the firm became known as Willey, Terrell & Sherman, followed by Willey, Sherman & Hoyt, and then, with Willey's departure, Sherman, Hoyt & Dustin. The firm had moved to the WESTERN RESERVE BLDG. by 1893 and with Sherman's leaving did business as HOYT, DUSTIN & KELLEY from 1898–1908. From 1908–18 it was known as Hoyt, Dustin, Kelley, McKeehan & Andrews. Between 1918–23, the firm practiced out of the Guardian Bldg. as Hoyt, Dustin, McKeehan & Andrews. In 1923 the firm added several new partners, including Chas. Arter, to become Austin, McKeehan, Merrick, Arter & Stewart. In 1930 it moved its offices to the Terminal Tower. With the departure of senior partner Alton Dustin, one of Cleveland's foremost trial lawyers and railroad attorneys, in the early 1930s, the firm became known as McKeehan, Merrick, Arter & Stewart and Geo. W. Cottrell. In 1951 the firm merged with John Hadden, Edwin Howe, John Beard, Jr., and Clyde Comstock, formerly of the law firm of Andrews, Hadden & Putnam.

Wykoff, L. C., *Scrapbook of a Century, 1843–1943* (1945).

**ARTHUR, ALFRED F.** (8 Oct. 1844–20 Nov. 1918), was a noted tenor, cornetist, conductor, educator, composer, and compiler. Born in Pittsburgh, Arthur received his early training in Ashland, Ohio, and at the Boston Music School. Following further education in Europe, he moved to Cleveland in 1871. He was active as a choral conductor, most notably with the CLEVELAND VOCAL SOCIETY, which he founded in 1873 and conducted through 29 seasons. Arthur was Cleveland's foremost choral conductor during the 19th century. The Cleveland Vocal Society gave a series of concerts yearly. Its programs show a wide variety of works performed, many with orchestra, and a fast-ripening taste for and laudable commitment to fine choral literature. It introduced major works such as Mendelssohn's *Saint Paul*, Handel's *Messiah*, and Verdi's *Requiem* to Cleveland audiences and mounted major May festivals during the 1880s and again in the mid-1890s. It won 1st prize in the world choral competition in Chicago in the World's Columbian Exposition in 1893. Commenting on the group's performance, *Brainard's Musical World* reported, "The Cleveland society is a mixed chorus, remarkable chiefly for its unity in singing and the clear quality of the tone produced." Arthur also conducted a short series of purely orchestral concerts at Brainard's Piano Rooms in 1872, which mark a real beginning for orchestral music in Cleveland. These programs included vocal solos, waltzes, and other light pieces by Strauss, along with overtures and parts or all of symphonies by Haydn, Beethoven, and Mendelssohn, a somewhat "popular" fare, the performance of which, however, elicited mixed reviews.

As an educator, Arthur founded the Cleveland School of Music (inc. 1875), to which he gave considerable attention. The school continued under the management of Arthur's son until his death in 1938. As a composer, Arthur wrote a number of songs and 3 operas, *The Water Carrier* (1875), *The Roundheads and Cavaliers* (1878), and *Adaline* (1879), none of them published. He authored several technical studies and compiled 2 hymnals, *The Evangelical Hymnal* and *The Spirit of Praise*, as well as a popular choral collection, *Brainard's Choir Anthems* (1879). Arthur was an important contributor to 19th-century music in Cleveland who was able to organize local forces, sometimes large in number, in landmark musical performances. He was also a positive force in the development of local musical taste and the training of local musicians, a number of whom went on to gain national prominence. Arthur was married to Kate Burnham. They had 3 children: a daughter, Ada, and 2 sons, Edwin and Alfred F.

**ARTHUR ANDERSEN AND COMPANY** is a major accounting firm providing a wide range of professional services in accounting, auditing, tax services, and management-information, systems, and manufacturing consulting through 176 offices in 49 countries. Established in Chicago in 1913 as Andersen, Delany & Co., it employed 17,600 in over 70 offices throughout 36 states and Washington, D.C., in 1986. Andersen opened its Cleveland office in 1946, transferring personnel from its Chicago and Detroit offices. During the 1940s, it became the first major accounting firm to formally recognize the special needs of the smaller business and to offer specifically designed services for entrepreneurs. It was also among the first firms to recognize the potential of computers and helped to develop the first major computer application for processing and recording business information. Another innovation that contributed to its growth in the area was encouraging its staff to develop expertise within specific industries. That enabled Andersen to serve efficiently the specialized needs of the widely diversified industries and businesses in the Cleveland area. By the opening of the Cincinnati office in 1957, Andersen was well established among Ohio's small and medium-size manufacturers. The 1960s saw its strongest growth in Cleveland. Its small-business emphasis paid off as many of its closely held clients became publicly owned corporations. In 1967, most of the public-utilities practice was transferred to the newly opened office in Columbus. By 1970, Andersen was the 2d-largest among the Big 8 firms in Cleveland. During the 1970s, the firm completed a transition to a practice based on manufacturing, retailing, and distribution firms, including 8 clients among the area's 44 largest companies. In 1986, Arthur Andersen & Co. was located at 1717 E. 9th St.

**ASBURY SEMINARY** was a Methodist institution in CHAGRIN FALLS that offered an advanced secondary education during the mid-1800s. Asbury was incorporated in 1839 by the Methodist Conference. The seminary was named after Rev. Francis Asbury, an early Methodist bishop in America. Rev. L. D. Williams, who had managed a small private school in Chagrin Falls, was the first principal. A building was erected in 1842. The seminary operated for 19 years until, in 1858, it was sold to the Chagrin Falls Board of Education for use as Union School.

**ASSOCIATED CHARITIES.** *See* **CENTER FOR HUMAN SERVICES**

**ASSOCIATED INDUSTRIES OF CLEVELAND** is an organization of employers dedicated to assisting business and industry in the field of labor relations. Associated Industries was founded as the American Plan Assoc. of Cleveland by 15 members of the UNION CLUB in 1920; it assumed its current name in 1930. Control of the group was vested in a 15-member board of governors. A general manager acted as chief administrator. WM. FREW LONG of Pittsburgh was hired as the first general manager in 1920 and served the association until his retirement in 1949. Initially dedicated to the principle of the open shop, the association solicited memberships from local industries, which paid dues proportionate to the number of employees on their payroll. In 1938, some 500 area industries were members. In 1982, over 600 companies were members. During its early history, the group fought unionization and legislation favoring organized labor. It mounted particularly strong opposition against the Wagner Labor Relations Act. During that decade, it also assisted the Ohio Rubber Co. of Akron during the United Rubber Workers strike (1934) and was very involved in the LITTLE STEEL STRIKE OF 1937. Its involvement in the latter strikes became the subject of a U.S. Senate investigation in which it was alleged that the association had hired strikebreakers, provided munitions, and conducted espionage in an attempt to break the strike. Associated Industries is currently located in the Leader Bldg. Its services include training programs, workshops, research, and communications activities directed toward assisting management in labor relations.

The **ASSOCIATION OF POLISH WOMEN IN THE U.S.A.** is a fraternal benefit society begun by local Polish women who preferred to have the dues they paid to the Polish Women's Alliance remain in the Cleveland area. Discussions leading to the formation of a separate organization were begun in 1911; the first general meeting was held on 12 Dec. 1912; and the first convention of the association met on 12 Feb. 1913. Officers elected at that convention were Teofila Twaragowski, president; Honorata Blazejczyk, vice-president; Elizabeth Sawicki, secretary; and Maria Kwarcianna, treasurer. The association had 146 charter members and was incorporated in 1917. By 1935 the Assoc. of Polish Women had grown to nearly 9,000 members in 49 Cleveland chapters and 1 in Erie, Pa. Its assets were more than $250,000, and it had paid out $75,000 in benefits. The association had also bought the site for its

headquarters (7526 Broadway) in 1927 and had established for its members a weekly newspaper, *Jednosc Polek*. In 1940 the association elected as president Frances Tesny, who guided it for the next 40 years. Under her leadership, the group built a new $250,000 meeting hall at 7526 Broadway in 1951. The society had 3,000 members when the hall was formally opened in Jan. 1952.

A major change in the association's policy was instituted on 9 Nov. 1952, when members voted to allow men to join. Since its formation, the Assoc. of Polish Women had been concerned with demonstrating that Polish women could be good citizens, involved in the life of the community just as their husbands were. The women thus not only established their own insurance fund and constructed a meeting hall but also undertook charitable projects to help people in Poland and others both within and outside of the Polish-American community. They also offered classes to teach the Polish language and heritage to young people and awarded scholarships to parochial schools, colleges, and universities. The association established a choir for adults and another for children, and it formed bowlers' clubs for both women and men. By 1973 the Assoc. of Polish Women had 42 lodges in Cleveland, with about 2,000 members. A decade later the assets of the organization were $855,282.

Assoc. of Polish Women in the U.S.A., "60 Years Diamond Jubilee Banquet" (Cleveland, 1971), Vertical File, WRHS.

The **ASTOR HOUSE** was for many years considered to be Cleveland's oldest structure. It was thought originally to have been used as a trading post prior to Cleveland's settlement in 1796. Although its authenticity was never established, the Astor House was generally believed to have been built in the 1780s by the Northwestern Fur Co., a venture associated with John Jacob Astor. Some accounts attribute its designation as the "Astor House" to Moses Cleaveland and his party of surveyors. It was thought to have been originally situated on the western side of the Cuyahoga River, near its mouth. Based on various accounts, it is possible that a few structures existed near this location prior to Cleaveland's arrival. One of these was purportedly a temporary shelter built by a shipwrecked British crew ca. 1786. Another was a small log trading house that a trader, Jas. Hillman, recalled passing in 1786 between TINKER'S CREEK and Lake Erie. Hillman later claimed that he built a small hut on the eastern side of the river a few years later. JAS. KINGSBURY, one of the first settlers, reportedly lived in one of these for a year before his own house was built.

In 1844, Robt. Sanderson purchased from JOEL SCRANTON what was considered to be the Astor House. As improvements to the mouth of the river threatened the house's destruction, Sanderson had it dismantled and moved to the west side, where he used it for several years as a carpentry shop and later as a residence. Sanderson based his belief in the house's authenticity on what he had learned of it through the previous owner, Joel Scranton. He also claimed that the chestnut timbers used in its construction had been hewn with a broadax. That suggested that the house was built before any sawmills existed in Cleveland. By the late 1800s, the Astor House was popularly believed to be the oldest house in Cleveland, and it was moved several times as the city grew. It finally ended up on the eastern edge of EDGEWATER PARK, where for many years it was under consideration as a museum. City officials ignored popular sentiment and ordered it destroyed on 12 Oct. 1922.

The **ASTRUP COMPANY,** manufacturer of awnings, awning hardware, and industrial fabric, was established in 1876 by Danish sailmaker Wm. J. O. Astrup, who had come to the U.S. and settled in Cleveland 10 years earlier. The company began as a manufacturer of sails for Great Lakes ships, but as sails became obsolete in the shipping industry, Astrup turned increasingly to the manufacture of other canvas products, especially awnings, which were growing in popularity with home and business owners. By 1880 Astrup was describing himself as an awningmaker, and by 1883 he had moved his operations to 1114 Pearl Rd. (2937 W. 25th St.), which remained the company's location in 1986. In addition to manufacturing awnings, Astrup began to make and sell awning hardware; in the 1890s he added tents to his line of products. From 1901-09, the company operated as the Astrup Mfg. Co.; it incorporated in 1909 as the Astrup Co. Wm. J. O. Astrup died in 1915, and his son Wm. E. Astrup became president; upon his death in 1916, the presidency fell to another of the founder's sons, Walter C. Astrup, who directed the company until his death in 1970.

When Walter Astrup took over the company in 1916, annual sales were $250,000. In 1924 the company built a modern factory at its W. 25th St. location, and in 1927 it opened a warehouse in New York to supply eastern awning manufacturers with awning hardware. By 1956 annual sales topped $10 million, and the Astrup Co. had become the country's largest manufacturer of awning hardware and distributor of awning fabric and canvas. By 1961 it employed 350 people and had sales offices in 5 other cities. After Walter Astrup's death in 1970, company leadership remained with the family, with 2 of his nephews, Kenneth W. Kirk and John D. Kirk, serving as officers. In 1983 the company employed 275 people, and sales of its awning hardware and industrial fabrics totaled $29 million annually. The company that began as a sail manufacturer attributed much of its later growth to the rise of the boating and recreation industry, for which it supplies canvas and other fabrics.

**ATKINS (NUSBAUM), LARRY (LAWRENCE)** (3 Mar. 1903-24 July 1981), was a nationally known Cleveland boxing matchmaker and fight promoter from the 1930s to the 1960s. During this period he was considered second only to Mike Jacobs of New York as a boxing match promoter. Atkins was born in Cleveland and attended East Tech and Glenville High School. A boyhood friend of Bob Hope and a bat boy for the CLEVELAND INDIANS, Atkins later studied at both Ohio Business College and John Marshall Law School. For a time in the early 1920s, he worked for the *CLEVELAND NEWS* and the *PLAIN DEALER* sports departments. Moving to Chicago, he helped Frank Churchill promote prizefights. During a 3-year period, which included the second Tunney fight in 1927, Atkins was Jack Dempsey's personal press agent. Returning to Cleveland in 1929, Atkins began promoting fights in the city. When CLEVELAND MUNICIPAL STADIUM opened, he became the public-relations director and assistant matchmaker for the facility. For a short period in 1934, Atkins was a radio sports announcer until he heard a tape of his voice. Moving to St. Louis in 1936, he was a professional fight promoter, master of ceremonies, and a comedian in a nightclub. Returning to Cleveland to stay in 1939, Atkins joined the new boxing promotion firm headed by Bob Brickman. During the next 25 years, he promoted boxing matches for firms including Natl. Sports Enterprises, Cleveland Sports Promotion, and Buckeye Sports Enterprise. For 19 years he was the matchmaker for the *News* Christmas Toyshop Fund boxing show. Realizing that tel-evised fights were damaging live boxing promotions, Atkins became a pioneer in lining up closed-circuit television for championship bouts. A member of Bill Veeck's "Jolly Set," Atkins had an amazing memory for first names. Married during the 1930s, Atkins was divorced by his wife, Molly. The couple had a daughter, Marcy.

The **AUSTIN COMPANY** was one of the most important innovators in the construction industry. The Austin Method of "undivided responsibility," the standardization of factory construction, the company's contribution to Depression modern design, and the development of the controlled-conditions plant are among its noteworthy achievements. The company was founded by Samuel Austin (1850-1936), who emigrated from England to the U.S. in 1872 and settled in Cleveland. In 1881 he began his own business, building and designing commercial, residential, and factory buildings, especially in the Broadway district. By 1900, the Austin Method was evolving, whereby the client contracted with one organization that handled all the activities of design, engineering, and construction. The method ensured speed, efficiency, and economy and brought engineering and architectural design together. The first major monument of this method was NELA PARK, begun in 1911.

In 1914 Samuel's son Wilbert J. Austin conceived of the standardization of factory design. Ten standard patterns for factory buildings were made available and found suitable for a large percentage of the demand. During WORLD WAR I, Austin built the Curtiss aircraft plant, covering 28 acres in Buffalo, and in the late 1920s the company built the first wide-span Hollywood sound stages for the film industry. In 1929 Austin erected the first all-welded steel frame building at 10465 Carnegie Ave. in Cleveland. In 1929-30 the company designed and built a giant automobile plant and an entire workers' city at Nizhni Novgorod in Russia as part of the Soviet attempt to industrialize rapidly under Stalin. With the onset of the Great Depression, Austin made important contributions to the modernistic design of the era, especially in 2 notable buildings, the Church & Dwight plant for Arm & Hammer Baking Soda in Syracuse, N.Y. (1939), and the NBC Radio City of the West in Hollywood, Calif. (1938). The company's prefabricated porcelain enamel service stations probably created its most visible impact across the country in the 1930s.

On the eve of WORLD WAR II, Austin built the first windowless, completely "controlled-conditions" factory for the Simonds Saw & Steel Co. (1938). During the war, it built 3 mammoth war plants in the Southwest, which had several innovative construction features in lighting and air conditioning. In the postwar period, the Austin Co. participated in the increasing suburbanization of industry, and in 1960 it became an international corporation with subsidiaries offering the same "undivided" services in a dozen countries around the world. The company's later work in the Cleveland area includes Kettering Hall at Oberlin (1961), CWRU Dormitories (1967), the CLEVELAND HEALTH EDUCATION MUSEUM (1971), and the Imax Theater at Cedar Pt. (1975).

Greif, Martin, *The New Industrial Landscape* (1978).

The **AUSTIN POWDER COMPANY** is the oldest manufacturing enterprise in Cleveland and remains one of the few U.S. manufacturers of black powder used in military ammunition. Begun in 1833 by the 5 Austin brothers to produce explosives used in blasting rock to build the OHIO & ERIE CANAL, the firm opened plants in Akron and Cleveland. Its Cleveland factory, bought from the Cleveland Powder Co. in 1867, at the 5 Mile Lock of the Ohio Canal (under what was in 1986 the Harvard-Denison Bridge), blew up in 1907. Austin also built at GLENWILLOW, a rural community it developed in 1888. The company built homes for its employees, a town hall, a school, and a general store in the village. In the 19th century, Austin products were used in eastern coal fields, while its real periods of growth occurred in wartime. In both world wars, the company was noted for its high-tonnage explosives. During WORLD WAR II, Austin also expanded its mine-tool business. Again in the Vietnam era, the company made the powder for over 250 types of ammunition. The government was the sole customer of the company's Glenwillow plant, where the workforce doubled to 200 to meet the demand. Because of the dangerous nature of the business, Austin powder manufacture was carried out in some 50 buildings at the Glenwillow site, and in other locations in 5 states. Headquarters were maintained in the ROCKEFELLER BLDG. in downtown Cleveland and then at 3735 Green Rd. in Beachwood. Though the company was safety-conscious, its history was marked by many explosions. As the isolation of Glenwillow ceased with the growth of neighboring Solon and Twinsburg, the company decided to close its Glenwillow plant. While the company could reduce the risk of widespread personal injury, it could not bar damage to windows and other property. After obtaining permission from the government, Austin moved its Ohio manufacturing operations to its plant in McArthur, Ohio, in 1972, where it had produced high explosives since 1930. Its move halved the annual budget of Glenwillow, a community dependent on 2 landfills, a sand and gravel company, a mobile home park, and an industrial park in addition to Austin. In 1986, Austin employed 65 people at its Beachwood headquarters.

**AUTOMOTIVE INDUSTRY.** The automotive industry includes the manufacture of automobiles, their parts, and accessories. Twentieth-century Cleveland is part of a nearly worldwide automotive culture dependent upon this industry. The city has played a major role in the rapid and revolutionary rise of the automotive industry since the 1890s, largely in the American Midwest. In fact, only Detroit has a better claim to being the heart of the automobile revolution. The automobile was developed in Germany and France in the 1880s and 1890s, with Americans making only minor contributions to the technology. The primary focus of European inventors was the gasoline-fueled internal-combustion engine, which was extremely powerful for its weight but required innovations in carburetion and ignition to make it reliable. Electric and steam engines also appeared promising but were heavier and had no advantages in power or speed. When Americans read newspaper accounts of the Paris-Bordeaux automobile race of 1895, in which 9 of 22 vehicles finished a 727-mi. course, they recognized that the automobile had come of age, and American inventors and manufacturers scrambled to enter the market.

In Cleveland, as elsewhere in the U.S., the horse-carriage and bicycle manufacturers were best equipped to become automobile makers. ALEXANDER WINTON was one of the first. Winton, a Scottish immigrant with metalworking skills, arrived in Cleveland in 1884 and a few years later founded the Winton Bicycle Co. The standard bicycle of the time incorporated many elements that were adaptable to automobile technology, such as chain-and-sprocket drive, wire-spoke wheels with rubber tires, tubular steel frames, and even accessories such as rear-view mirrors. Winton took these parts, learned the intricacies of internal-combustion engines, and built an automobile, which he exhib-

ited to Cleveland newspapermen in Oct. 1896. The next year he incorporated the WINTON MOTOR CARRIAGE CO. and completed an improved automobile with a 2-cyl., 2-hp engine. He showed it off by driving it to Elyria and back at an average speed of 12 mph. The next year Winton began producing a standard model in anticipation of a regular demand. Previously, American automakers (Duryea, for example) had manufactured automobiles to order. Thus, when Winton sold the first of his automobiles on 24 Mar. 1898, it marked the beginning of the American automobile industry as a whole, and the end of the period of experimentation and novelty.

Winton early demonstrated the genius for publicity by which the American automobile industry has become known. In 1897 he raced one of his cars and reached the then-incredible speed of 33.5 mph. In 1899 he drove from Cleveland to New York, accompanied by *Plain Dealer* reporter Chas. Shanks, whose exciting tales of that trip were read across the nation. When Winton reached New York, he was greeted by admiring crowds, and it was estimated that eventually a million people in that city saw his car. In 1903 a new 2-cyl., 20-hp Winton car was driven from San Francisco to New York in 64 days to establish distance and endurance records. The next year Winton brought representatives of the newspaper press in a special Pullman railroad car to see the Winton factory in Cleveland. Winton also continued to be a technological pioneer in the new industry. He was an early manufacturer of commercial vehicles, manufacturing 8 panel trucks in 1898 and adding a "business-wagon department" to his factory in 1900. Winton claimed to be the first American manufacturer to use the steering wheel as standard equipment (1900) rather than a tiller; to introduce the multiple-disc clutch; to make an 8-cyl. motor (1903); and to make available a self-starter as an option (using compressed air, in 1908). In the 1910s, Winton turned his ingenuity to diesel engines for ships and other purposes, however, and although the Winton was still known as a fine car, it lost its reputation for innovation. Numerous other Cleveland companies moved into the gasoline automobile business around the time Winton did. Companies such as Peerless and Stearns produced large, heavy, high-priced cars intended to appeal to wealthier buyers. There were few manufacturers in the U.S. who shared Henry Ford's vision that Americans of modest means could be induced to purchase a simple, unstyled, but durable automobile. It is therefore unsurprising that Cleveland's leading manufacturers of electric and steam automobiles also aimed at an upper-class market.

WALTER BAKER became involved in the vehicle business when he founded the American Ball Bearing Co. in Cleveland in 1895, selling some of his product to bicycle and carriage manufacturers. Three years later he organized the Baker Motor Vehicle Co., and in 1900 he exhibited his first electric car. It had 10 batteries, but only a ¾-hp motor. The batteries had to be recharged after 20 minutes of driving. Later Baker was able to install more powerful motors and longer-lasting batteries, but the Baker remained a relatively slow car with a limited cruising range. Since it was quiet and did not require shifting gears, it was regarded as an urban ladies' car. A 1909 Baker was part of the White House fleet in Washington, D.C., for several years. In 1915 Baker merged his company with Rauch & Lang, a distinguished Cleveland carriage manufacturer that had entered the electric vehicle business. But the gasoline automobile was the dominant force in the industry, and a few years later the new company stopped producing automobiles and focused on making electric vehicles for industrial purposes.

The leading steam automobile manufactured in Cleveland was the White. Since 1866, the White Sewing Machine

57

Co. had been a primary manufacturer in the city, making not only sewing machines but also roller skates, kerosene lamps, machine tools, phonographs, and bicycles. The company's founder, THOS. H. WHITE, had been trained in the firearms and sewing-machine industries of New England and had brought to Cleveland the knowledge of how to produce large quantities of standardized products with machine tools such as lathes and drill presses. His approach made it comparatively easy to adapt the machinery for making sewing machines to make many other metal items. While manufacturing automobile parts was an obvious step for a company such as White's in the 1890s, it was a considerably more expensive venture to manufacture automobiles. It took one of White's sons, ROLLIN H. WHITE, to initiate the automobile business. Rollin became involved with automobiles in the late 1890s by studying them at Cornell University, then joined Walter Baker in the early development of Baker's electric car, and visited Europe to study the automobile industry there. He returned a convert to steam vehicles, and in 1900 he patented a flash-steam boiler that allowed the operator to raise quickly enough steam to start a car. Steam boilers for railroad locomotives had required as much as several hours to get up steam for movement.

Rollin White publicly displayed 4 steam cars in 1900, and in the next year White Sewing Machine produced 193 cars for sale. White soon established a reputation for quality and dependability, and by 1906 reached an annual production of 1,500 cars, which the company claimed was twice that of any other automobile manufacturer in the world. That same year the automobile division split off from the parent company and established a new factory at E. 79th and St. Clair. On that site the company later made the shift from steam to gasoline engines (1909–11), and from largely automobiles to a total commitment to manufacturing trucks. White is regarded (with Stanley) as one of the 2 most important steam automakers in the U.S. and into the 1970s was one of the nation's major heavy-truck manufacturers.

Winton, Baker, and White were leaders in Cleveland's early rise to prominence in the American automotive industry. By 1909, the U.S. manufacturing census showed that automobile manufacture ranked as the 3d-largest industry in the city, with 32 factories employing over 7,000 workers and producing nearly $21 million worth of automobiles, an astonishing rise from 1899, when the census did not even list the industry as a category of industry. By 1909, Cleveland and Detroit were equal claimants to the title of "Motor City." Moreover, the industry did not stagnate in Cleveland, since other automobiles were introduced to the market after that time, such as the Chandler (1913), the Jordan (1916), and the Cleveland (1919). In all, over 80 different makes of automobiles were made in Cleveland up to 1931, when the last Peerless rolled out of the shop. But the several thousand of each Cleveland make that were manufactured paled in comparison to Henry Ford's Model T, first made in Detroit in 1908 but turned out in the hundreds of thousands per year after 1913. This rapid ascendancy of Detroit over Cleveland was symbolized by Ford's opening of a branch assembly here in 1914, making Model Ts from assembled parts brought by rail. Fords were manufactured here until 1932.

Why did Cleveland, arguably the early leader in the American automotive industry, lose out to Detroit? There is no single answer, but as historian John Rae has argued, the manufacturers and financiers of Detroit were more willing to take the risks involved in building the massive plants required to shift to assembly-line mass production of automobiles than were comparable businessmen in any other

manufacturing center of the nation. Still, Cleveland was an ideal location for the automotive industry: it had ready access to steel, glass, and rubber; it had many companies with the experience in using the machine tools necessary to make the equipment for assembly lines; it had large pools of both skilled and unskilled workers; and it was a major transportation center. For all of those reasons, as well as its early experience in automobile manufacturing, Cleveland became the 2d-largest center of the automotive industry in the U.S. Evidence for Cleveland's role in the second stage of automotive history came with the rise of parts manufacturing in the 1910s and 1920s. While companies producing cars were withering, others that made particular items were being founded in Cleveland. CLAUDE FOSTER, for example, invented successively the Gabriel horn and hydraulic shock absorber and manufactured them in Cleveland. Chas. E. Thompson began making valves for Winton's engines in 1904, establishing an automotive company that became Thompson Prods. in 1926, and later part of TRW. The Torbensen Gear & Axle Co. moved to Cleveland in 1915 and evolved into the EATON CORP., a major producer of gearing for commercial vehicles. Willard storage batteries were made in Cleveland from 1896 but were not specially made for the automotive market until 1908. A group of Case School of Applied Science graduates founded the LUBRIZOL CORP. in 1928 to manufacture a motor oil additive, and later marketed a variety of lubricants.

On a broader scale, by the 1920s, 70% of the steel made in Cleveland was destined for automotive manufacturing. Much of it was absorbed by frame and body manufacturers, who in the 1910s began to switch from the wooden carriage type of frame of early automobiles to the all-steel body standard by the later 1930s. The leading Cleveland factory was the Fisher Body plant on Coit Rd., opened in 1922 to make car bodies for General Motors. Innovations at this plant included the knockdown system of shipping, lacquer for body finish, safety devices on presses, and the building of bodies on a moving assembly line. Another industry much affected by the rise of the automobile was rubber manufacturing. Although the making of tires was concentrated in the Akron area, by 1920 there were nearly 40 rubber factories in the Cleveland area, and a number of Cleveland companies supplied equipment or chemicals to the rubber industry. Cleveland also emerged as a center for manufacture of vehicles other than passenger cars. White trucks became a leader in their field, and the Euclid Road Machinery Co. was incorporated in 1931 to make off-road trucks and construction vehicles. Cleveland's truck business became so important that the state of Ohio could claim in 1980 that it was the truck-manufacturing center of the U.S.

Cleveland's future in the automotive field was promoted by the creation of testing-and-research laboratories. Many of the city's nearly 50 industrial laboratories of 1930, for example, were involved partly or wholly in developing or assessing automotive parts and materials. Foundries and machine shops often had several people studying the production of engine blocks and cylinders, while Thompson Prods. had a staff of 13 engineers and scientists examining "heat-resisting steels for automotive valves; anti-corrosion materials; [and] automotive accessories." The Gabriel Co. and WILLARD STORAGE BATTERY CO. probably were typical of parts suppliers in that they kept staffs of 7 engaged in testing shock absorbers and 10 in battery research respectively. White Motor, on the other hand, had a staff of 15 exploring all problem areas and innovations in truck technology.

By the late 1930s, on the eve of WORLD WAR II, the automotive industry in Cleveland had assumed the role of the major American center of parts and accessory manufacturing. The U.S. census of manufacturing for 1937, a year of industrial depression, counted 23 makers of motor vehicle bodies and parts in the Cleveland region, employing 9,629 and producing over $86 million in products. Yet these statistics failed to account for many of the auto parts and accessories included in other census categories titled "machine shop products" or "electrical equipment" that were important sectors of Cleveland industry. Midway through the second stage of American automotive development, Cleveland was an exemplar of American commitment to the automobile. During World War II, Cleveland's automotive industry shifted to military production, producing few automobiles. The Euclid Road Machinery Co., however, expanded its production of trucks for both civilian and military purposes. Thompson Prods. became Cleveland's largest industrial employer, making both vehicle and aircraft parts. Many automotive workers found their skills much in demand by wartime plants, such as the Fisher Aircraft Assembly Plant, built near Cleveland's airport to assemble B–29s and P–75s. Immediately following the war, American automakers returned to automotive manfacturing to satisfy pent-up consumer demand, and the Cleveland automotive industry shared in the prosperity. The manufacturing census of 1947 listed 36 motor vehicle and parts companies in the Cleveland district, employing 22,452, more than 10% of the total industrial workforce.

Over the next 10 years, the 3 dominant American automakers made a series of major investments in the Cleveland area, further expanding its reliance on the automotive industry. The Chevrolet Div. of GM constructed in Parma the largest of the new plants. Opening in 1949, it was devoted largely to automatic transmissions. In 1963 it employed 7,740 workers. The FORD MOTOR CO. built 2 factories (opened in 1951 and 1955) and a foundry at Brook Park. By 1953, Brook Park was making most of Ford's 6-cyl. engines and all of the popular V–8 Mercury engines. That same year the *New York Times* reported that the shop for boring engine castings was "one of the best examples of automation" in the U.S. The *Times* noted that 250 men were doing "twice the work formerly produced by 2,500 men." When both engine plants and the foundry were in full operation, however, employment mushroomed: in 1978, when Brook Park produced its 30-millionth engine, about 16,000 worked there. Ford also built a car and truck assembly plant at Lorain, which opened in 1958, and has a stamping plant in Cleveland. Chrysler intended to enter the Cleveland area with the construction of a steel-stamping plant at Brooklyn, but eventually located it at Twinsburg.

With the construction of new plants and a boom in car buying in the 1950s and early 1960s, Cleveland's automobile industry reached its historical peak. The manufacturing census of 1963 recorded 59 motor vehicle assembly and equipment establishments in the district, with products worth over $559 million more than the raw materials taken in. Employment stood at 37,383, about 13% of Cleveland's total manufacturing force. Over the next 20 years, Cleveland's automotive industry entered its third phase of development. The industry had matured and stabilized, and rapid growth was no longer likely. Certain plants, such as Ford's at Brook Park, had intervals of expansion, but the general trend was downward. The American automotive industry as a whole suffered from overexpansion and the inability to respond effectively to consumers' growing interest in smaller, safer, and fuel-efficient automobiles. Automotive establishments in Cleveland shifted production patterns, reduced payrolls, and closed plants. GM ended production at the Coit Rd. Fisher Body plant in 1983, and

Euclid, Inc., the successor to the Euclid Road Machinery Co., closed its doors in 1985. That same year, workers at Brook Park were told that the company's V–8 engine work might be moved to Mexico. But there were hopeful signs. After some deliberation, GM decided in 1985 to invest $580 million in expanding and modernizing its Parma facility, with a company executive claiming that "modernization will assure the plant's operation for years to come."

The manufacturing census of 1982 found that the Cleveland area had 71 establishments making automotive parts, accessories, and stampings, but that they employed only 15,800. With the census taken during an economic recession, and encompassing only Cuyahoga, Lake, Geauga, and Medina counties, that figure was not fully reflective of the continued though diminished strength of the industry in northeastern Ohio. The Greater Cleveland Growth Assoc. found in Jan. 1986 that in a 7-county area (Cuyahoga, Lake, Geauga, Medina, Lorain, Portage, Summit), Ford, GM, and Chrysler employed 30,800 in all capacities. By the mid-1980s, the automotive industry had become a standard segment of the regional economy. The automobile was firmly embedded in American culture, with the average household owning 2 cars and daily usage increasing, but consumer demand for automobiles had not changed significantly for 15 years. The industry also faced a strong challenge from imported automobiles, which it was unable to turn back. It seemed unlikely that the automotive industry could be a major source of economic growth in the Cleveland area in the near future.

Darwin Stapleton
Rockefeller Archive Center

See also specific automotive companies.

**AVERILL, HOWARD EARL** (21 May 1902–17 Aug. 1983), was a player for the CLEVELAND INDIANS from 1929–39. An outstanding and popular centerfielder, the "Earl of Snohomish" was a consistent .300 hitter during the 1930s. Averill was born in Snohomish, Wash.; his father died when he was 18 months old. He completed 9 years of school and worked at various jobs, from construction camps to sawmills. He married Gladys Loette Hyatt on 15 May 1922, and they had 4 sons. One son, Earl Douglas Averill, played in the major leagues from 1956–63.

Averill played for semi-pro teams in central Washington before signing with the San Francisco Seals of the Pacific Coast League in 1926. After 3 successful seasons, his playing contract was sold to Cleveland in 1928. In his first time at bat in the major leagues, he hit a home run. On 17 Sept. 1930, Averill hit 4 home runs in a doubleheader, 3 coming in the first game. He played in the first All-Star game in 1933 and 4 later. His highest batting average was .378 in 1936, when he finished 2nd in the league. His lifetime home run total of 238 is the career record for an Indian. Averill was traded to Detroit in 1939 and completed his playing career in 1941 with Boston in the Natl. League, with a .318 lifetime batting average. After retiring from baseball, he operated a greenhouse and later owned a motel. In 1975 Averill was selected for the Baseball Hall of Fame at Cooperstown, N.Y.

**AVERY, ELROY MCKENDREE** (14 July 1844–1 Dec. 1935), author, historian, lecturer, scientist, and educator, was born in Erie, Monroe County, Mich., the eldest child of Casper H. and Dorothy Putnam Avery. Avery was educated at Union School (Monroe, Mich.) and at Monroe High School. At 17, he volunteered as a private in Co. A of the 4th Michigan Infantry, and in 1863 he joined Co. E, 11th Michigan Cavalry. He was mustered out as sergeant-major of his regiment. In addition to performing his military duties, he served as war correspondent for the *Detroit Daily Tribune*. Avery entered the University of Michigan in Sept. 1867 and became principal of Battle Creek (Mich.) High School at the beginning of his junior year. He later resigned his position, returned to the university, and assigned the principalship to Miss Catherine Hitchcock Tilden. Avery and Tilden were married at Battle Creek, 2 July 1870. She continued as principal of the high school, and he completed his college course, receiving the Ph.B. degree in June 1871. Soon after graduation, he was appointed superintendent of E. Cleveland (Ohio) schools. When the village of E. Cleveland was annexed to the city of Cleveland (1872), Avery became principal of East High School, with Mrs. Avery as first assistant. When East and CENTRAL HIGH SCHOOLs were consolidated (1878), he became principal of the Cleveland Normal School. For several years thereafter, Avery delivered a series of lectures about the new electric light and directed the formation of more than 40 Brush Electric Co. subsidiaries throughout the country (1879–85).

Avery wrote a series of high school textbooks on physical science, as well as several histories, including *Cleveland in a Nutshell* (1893), *History of the United States and Its People* (12 vols., 1912), and *History of Cleveland and Its Environs* (3 vols., 1918). From 1891–92, Avery served as a member of the city council (representing E. Cleveland), and from 1893–97 he served in the Ohio state senate. He founded the Children's Fresh Air Camp in 1890 and in 1895 was elected president, serving in that capacity for 13 successive terms. Afterward he was chosen honorary president. In 1905, Avery was one of 12 commissioners appointed by the Cleveland Board of Education to make a study of every department of the Cleveland public schools. Known as the "Avery Committee," it made a series of recommendations that were printed and distributed throughout the city and the country. Avery received many honors during his lifetime, including Master of Philosophy, University of Michigan (1874); Ph.D., Hillsdale College (1881); Doctor of Laws, Wilberforce University (1894); and Doctor of Civil Law, Hillsdale College (1911). He was a member of many professional organizations, including the American Assoc. for the Advancement of Science, the Ohio Archeological & Historical Society, and the American Economic Assoc. He was the founder and first president of the Western Reserve Chap. of the Sons of the American Revolution (chartered 5 May 1906) and a life member and trustee of the WESTERN RESERVE HISTORICAL SOCIETY. Catherine Avery died in Cleveland on 22 Dec. 1911. Avery married Miss Ella Wilson on 15 June 1916. They moved to Florida (1919) and settled in New Port Richey, where they took an active part in community affairs. Avery became the first mayor of New Port Richey (1924–25) and the first president of the First State Bank and was founder and president of the Avery Public Library of New Port Richey. He died in Florida and is buried in Knollwood Cemetery, Cleveland.

**AVIATION.** By 1930, Cleveland had emerged as one of America's aviation centers. A steady and at times rapid expansion continued, especially when after the 1950s the airplane replaced the passenger train as the most popular form of public intercity travel. Cleveland's initial contact with commercial aviation began during WORLD WAR I. Not passengers but mail generated the revenues; and the federal government, not the private sector, served as the driving force behind this development. It was not until the mid-1920s that modern air service materialized in the area. While some Clevelanders had flown in aircraft before that time, they likely had accompanied "barnstormers," who

since the prewar years had visited fairs and other outside events to perform their daring acts of aerial wizardry.

Just as Cleveland benefited from its position on the New York-to-Chicago railroad corridor, a similar geographic situation made the city fit ideally onto a coast-to-coast route for airmail delivery from New York City to San Francisco. It was, as Jay Morton, Cleveland commissioner of information and complaints, remarked in the mid-1920s, "a strategic point in the most direct coast-to-coast air route." During the latter part of 1918, federal officials, enthusiastically backed by the Cleveland Chamber of Commerce and other business groups, started construction of a transcontinental system of navigational beacons or "guide lights." The first phase involved work between New York and Chicago. Cleveland, because of its location and size, logically was selected as one of the principal stops. Quickly an airport, Woodland Hills Park, with its grassy landing strip and wooden airplane hangars, appeared near E. 93rd St. and Kinsman Rd. Then in mid-Dec. 1918, Cleveland's first regular airmail service began, when planes piloted by seasoned flyers from the U.S. Army flew the route between New York and Chicago. Problems with equipment and weather temporarily ended these flights; however, on 15 May 1919, the New York-Chicago route reopened. With considerable pride, the Cleveland *Plain Dealer* reported that "eight pilots, some of them 'aces' from the western front, have been employed." Planes on these runs carried 850 lbs. of mail (letters cost $.06 to send), and these flights experienced few major difficulties. On 8 Sept. 1920, the first transcontinental airmail trips in the nation, which took 3 days, started through Cleveland.

Cleveland's business community and government leaders realized that the east side airfield could not adequately serve the needs of increased mail volume. In 1922, for example, airmail service had begun between Cleveland and Cincinnati. So in 1925, a much larger facility, located on 1,040 acres on the city's southwest side, the future (after 1951) CLEVELAND HOPKINS INTERNATL. AIRPORT, started to take shape. This location, selected by a team of city officials and Army Air Service personnel, offered "a capacity in keeping with the future of air travel." While the project enjoyed the long-term benefits of good planning, the administration and passenger building did not open until 4 years later. The timing of this $1.125 million expenditure was ideal, for in 1925 Congress passed the Kelly Act, under which the federal government turned over operation of airmail routes to private parties through competitive bidding. This landmark legislation meant that civil aviation could realistically develop.

Aviation expansion affected Cleveland. Not only did private contract carriers fly mail to various cities, mostly in the Midwest, but airplane owners started to seek passengers. Ford Commercial Air lines inaugurated daily trips between Cleveland and Detroit on 1 July 1925, and soon Natl. Air Transport, a future component of United Airlines, launched what would become the first continuous service. (An earlier attempt had failed miserably; Aeropaire Airways in 1922 had been unable to sustain its "flying-boat" service between Cleveland's lakefront and Detroit's riverfront.) Traffic increased dramatically. In 1925, 4,000 planes cleared the field; in 1926, the total reached 11,000; and a year later, volume grew to 14,000. By Jan. 1929, Cleveland ranked 4th in the nation on the list of communities that had made airport improvements. Typical of the infant commercial carriers that emerged to serve Cleveland was STOUT AIRLINES. This Detroit-based company operated flights to Chicago and Cleveland. In 1929, travelers bound for either Detroit or Chicago left the Consolidated Air Travel ticket office at 712 Superior Ave. in a Stout company car for

Municipal (Hopkins) Airport. A maximum of 10 passengers boarded a Ford trimotored metal monoplane for either a 9:15 a.m. or 4:45 p.m. departure. The 100-minute flight to Detroit was expensive: $18 1 way and $35 round-trip. Stout Airlines, like sister carriers, repeatedly tried to assure potential patrons that air travel was safe. "The planes, pilots and mechanics are licensed by the Aeronautics branch of the Department of Commerce, and a rigid daily inspection of equipment insures maximum dependability at all times."

The Depression did not seriously retard commercial aviation in Cleveland. Well-to-do businessmen continued to prefer air to rail travel, except when poor weather conditions interfered. The decade witnessed a dramatic improvement in airline operational reliability. The Municipal Airport installed the world's first radio traffic system, thus making landings after 1930 much safer. General airport upgrading in the mid-1930s likewise made for better flying. Pilots favored the Cleveland field because of its relatively obstruction-free approaches. With the introduction of the Douglas DC-3 airplane in the late 1930s, the number of trips canceled by adverse conditions lessened significantly. The DC-3 made it possible for an airline to turn a profit on a flight without hauling mail. By WORLD WAR II, 3 airlines dominated the Cleveland scene: American, Pennsylvania Central, and United. Such earlier ones as Clifford Ball, Colonial Western, Embry-Riddle, Mercury, Pennsylvania Airlines & Transport, Thompson Aeronautical, and Universal either had folded or had merged. Once the war years ended, other carriers, some of which had developed into industry giants, successfully petitioned the Civil Aeronautics Board, the government regulatory agency created by the Civil Aeronautics Act of 1938, to enter the city. Eastern Airlines, the country's premier company, started service from Cleveland to Miami in 1945, although the route originated in Detroit and included intermediate stops in Charleston, W.Va.; Charlotte, N.C.; and Jacksonville, Fla. Soon thereafter, Trans-Canada (Air Canada), Transcontinental & Western (Trans World Airlines), and Northwest (Northwest Orient) paid daily calls at the ever-expanding facility in Cleveland.

Growth continued in the 1950s, 1960s, and 1970s. Ridership and mail increased, as did the number of flights, largely because of greater dependability, faster speeds, lower rates, and the decline in intercity railroad passenger service. Hopkins Internatl. Airport remained the aviation hub of the community, even though the administration of Mayor THOS. A. BURKE in 1944 decided to build a lakefront field (BURKE LAKEFRONT AIRPORT). The most significant technological advance during this period was likely the advent of the jet and the rapid disappearance of piston-driven craft. American Airlines, a Cleveland carrier since the early 1930s, made transportation history when it ordered 30 Boeing 707 jets in 1955. Not only did American subsequently dispatch these planes through Cleveland, but other trunk lines either followed suit with Boeing equipment or acquired comparable jets from Douglas—the DC-8s; from Convair—the 440s; or from other manufacturers. As in the early years, when the Ford Trimotor, Fokker Trimotor, Stinson A, and Lockheed Electra dominated commercial aviation, state-of-the-art aircraft continued to arrive in Cleveland. By the late 1970s, the day of the wide-body jets had dawned; 747s and DC-10s regularly landed at Hopkins. Only a few turbo-prop jets reminded travelers of the early jet age; these craft belonged almost exclusively to smaller feeder lines, such as the locally based WRIGHT AIRLINES.

With larger aircraft, the city of Cleveland embarked on various programs of modernization. Significant alterations occurred in the early 1950s as the result of $8 million worth of bonds that Cleveland voters approved in 1950 and 1952. Massive improvements began in 1973 and involved a $60 million terminal-expansion plan, including $9 million spent in the early 1980s on the rehabilitation of the west concourse. Hopkins Internatl. underwent the type of upgrading that has commonly occurred elsewhere, although unlike in Dallas and several other cities, the Cleveland airport was not relocated. Cleveland Hopkins is not the area's sole airport. To relieve congestion, especially traffic generated by private aircraft, Cleveland's downtown field, Burke Lakefront Airport, has continued to flourish since its opening in 1947, providing ready access to the central business district. Travelers who use their own or company planes or ride regularly scheduled commuter flights have found the Burke facility to be extremely convenient. The other major landing strip, CUYAHOGA COUNTY AIRPORT, also serves general aviation. But unlike Burke, this Richmond Hts. field has had a much longer history. It took shape in the spring of 1929 when Ohio Air Terminals, Inc., acquired a 272-acre parcel for a flying school and related activities. A powerful nearby property owner, however, brought legal action against the promoters because of airplane noise and danger. The courts agreed, and the airport closed on 1 Aug. 1930. A proaviation climate after World War II prompted small-plane enthusiasts to win voter approval for general county obligation bonds to pay for the field's rehabilitation. While some property owners again took legal steps to block the plan, they lost, and the Cuyahoga County Airport opened on 30 May 1950.

While physical improvements at Greater Cleveland's 3 airports were readily apparent, the traveler after 1978 also likely recognized that airlines themselves were changing, for the revolutionary process of deregulation swept the industry. This phenomenon took several forms. Trunk carriers often reduced the number of flights or ended service outright, especially to less-populated centers. Rates, too, frequently decreased to major cities, in part because new carriers could easily organize and enter what was rapidly becoming an intensely competitive field. United and American, for example, felt the sting of the recently created New York Air and Midway. Mergers also increased. Two regional giants, North Central and Southern, for instance, united on 1 July 1979 to form Republic. Wright Airlines, in operation since 1966, acquired the Clarksburg, W.Va.-based Aeromech Commuter Airlines in 1983. Similarly, a host of commuter companies developed. Clevelanders in the year of deregulation could fly Air Wisconsin, Best, Com-Air, Freedom, and Simmons or such limited scheduled carriers as American Internatl. and Jetstream Internatl. Indeed, these firms seemed as volatile as ones during the formative years of commercial aviation. The Sundorph Aeronautical Corp., which operated from both Burke Lakefront and Hopkins Internatl. To downtown Detroit, abandoned these flights in Mar. 1984 after about a year. Yet, like so many other commuter lines nationally, Sundorph continued to use its aircraft (in this case Navajo Chieftains) for charters and freight.

The story of Cleveland aviation involves more than the transporting of mail and people. From the mid-1930s to the present, the forwarding of express and freight has increased steadily. The first important event happened in Feb. 1936, when the Railway Express Agency's Air Div. started air-rail express service that linked Cleveland with cities on 20 American airlines and with most of Latin America through an interchange agreement with Pan American Airways. After World War II, air cargo service frequently became part of an individual carrier's Cleveland operation. American Airlines, for instance, inaugurated such service between Hopkins and 42 other cities on its far-flung system in Sept. 1946. And more recently, freight-only air forwarders have served the community, ranging from the giant Flying Tiger Line to the modest Midwest Air Charter.

Intimately linked to Cleveland aviation have been its world-famous NATL. AIR RACES, later recognized as the Natl. Air Show. The quality of the Cleveland airport together with the skilled organizational efforts of the Chamber of Commerce's Committee on Aviation and the support of local aircraft manufacturer Glenn L. Martin made possible the first contest and the satellite aeronautical exposition in 1929. The racing schedules were held intermittently throughout the 1930s, but they were suspended during the war years. They resumed, however, in 1946, only to end after 1949, when a racing plane crashed into a Berea house with the loss of 3 lives. In the 1950s, a new event, the Natl. Air Show, continued to make Cleveland "The Best Location for Sensation," with considerably reduced risks. The format consisted mostly of aircraft displays, both in the air and on the ground. Before the advent of the Natl. Air Show, the Thompson Trophy Race emerged as the event that captured the public's fancy. The brainchild of Thompson Prods. Co. (later TRW) executive Frederick C. Crawford, this contest received national network radio and later television coverage. While the alleged purpose of this event was to popularize aviation, its greatest legacy may well have been the fostering of considerable civic pride. As meaningful as the air races was Cleveland's role in aviation research and production. As early as 1918, inventor-entrepreneur Glenn L. Martin produced aircraft; his St. Clair Ave. factory built the first locally made plane during that summer. Although Martin moved his aviation plant to Baltimore in 1929, the Great Lakes Aircraft Corp. operated a portion of the former Martin facility until that company disbanded in the mid-1930s. Soon, though, this research/ production void was filled when the federal government's Natl. Advisory Committee for Aeronautics selected 200 acres of land adjacent to Municipal Airport for construction of its aircraft-engine research unit, the Flight Propulsion Laboratory, which became NASA LEWIS RESEARCH CTR. While Cleveland may no longer be the center of American aviation, it remains an important spot on that map.

H. Roger Grant
University of Akron

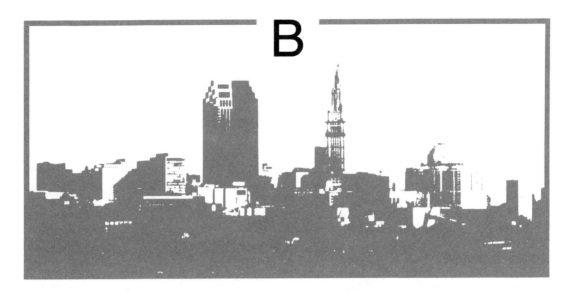

# B

The **B. F. GOODRICH COMPANY RESEARCH & DE-VELOPMENT CENTER,** 9921 Brecksville Rd., BRECKS-VILLE, was opened in 1948. In Oct. 1948 the *Clevelander* boasted that the new facility gave the Cleveland area "science's latest, most complete industrial workshop . . . in the Middle West," employing 225 scientists and technicians. The company encountered stiff opposition from some Brecksville residents when it announced in Aug. 1944 that it planned to locate a $1.5 million research center in the suburb. After much controversy, Brecksville residents on 7 Nov. 1944 passed a referendum that changed the zoning regulations and enabled the company to begin construction of the laboratory. The center's 6 original buildings, dedicated on 15 June 1948, were built on a 261-acre site that allowed further expansion, and between 1948-60 the company added another million dollars' worth of buildings. Employment at the center had grown to 398 in 1960 and to 525 in 1968. Among the projects carried out at the center under the direction of Dr. FRANK SCHOENFELD during this period of growth were tests of the durability of various materials using hurricane and rainmaking equipment; development of a chamber to simulate conditions in space in order to test space helmets and other equipment for space travel; and the development of new products and manufacturing processes in the rubber and plastic fields. The Brecksville Ctr. was expanded again as recently as 1977, and in the early 1980s the company was investing $60 million annually in research.

**BABCOCK, BRENTON D.** (2 Oct. 1830-10 Jan. 1906), was an entrepreneur and mayor of Cleveland, 1887-88. He was also the founder of Cleveland's Scottish Rite Masonry. Babcock was born in Adams, N.Y. He attended Adams Seminary and was a graduate of Watertown College, N.Y. In 1855, he accepted a clerkship from the Erie Railroad Co. in Buffalo. In 1865, he came to Cleveland as a bookkeeper for Cross, Payne & Co., a local coal dealership. Staying in the coal industry, Babcock became a partner in Chard & Babcock in 1869. In 1875 he became a traveling salesman for the firm of Tod, Morris, & Co. Three years later the company became Babcock, Morris, & Co. Babcock joined the Freemasons in 1859 and rose to a 33d-degree Mason. He gained additional honors and became a member of the Supreme Council for the Northern Masonic Jurisdiction of the USA. He also served as grand commander of the Knights Templar of Ohio, as well as the Oriental Commandery. He was a high priest of the chapter, and a member of the Royal Order of Scotland. He was the founder of the Scottish Rite. The Democratic party, looking for a potential mugwump politician, nominated Babcock as mayoral candidate to defeat Republican Wm. M. Bayne in 1886. As mayor, Babcock supported the reorganization of the city government on the Federal Plan, but otherwise he served only as a titular leader. On 6 Nov. 1867, Babcock married Elizabeth C. Smith (1837-1926) of Buffalo. They had no children. In 1900 the Babcocks donated several hundred volumes to the Adams Free Library, N.Y. The Babcock private library was donated to the Masonic Temple Assoc. of Cleveland.

**BABCOCK & WILCOX** was for many years the Barberton-based parent of the Bailey Controls Co. of Wickliffe, makers of instruments and controls. Bailey, a local employer of 1,500 and an industry leader, was among the first companies to utilize fiberoptics technology in its controls. Bailey Meter, as the company was first called, was organized in Boston in 1916 by Ervin G. Bailey with $50,000 capital. Within 3 years, Bailey saw a better market for his controls in the Midwest, and he relocated the company to Cleveland. The firm, with 100 employees, had its headquarters at E. 46th and Euclid. By 1921, the company established a Canadian subsidiary and opened additional branch offices in Cincinnati, Buffalo, and Pittsburgh. Bailey was purchased in 1924 by Babcock & Wilcox of Barberton, a major supplier of steam-generating equipment for the electric utilities industry. After the merger, the Barberton plant continued to make boilers, while Bailey produced meters and controls. In 1927, General Electric became ⅓ owner of the Bailey Meter division of the company, and the new entity took over GE's flow-meter business. Bailey, which moved to 1050 Ivanhoe Rd. in 1927, prospered and employed 1,000 at the onset of WORLD WAR II. The company became a major supplier of meters and controls on Navy ships. In 1953, Bailey became a wholly owned subsidiary of B&W. It opened an assembly plant, and later an administration building at 28901 Euclid. The Ivanhoe Rd. plant was operated until 1976, when facilities were consolidated. In 1978 the company was bought by Ray McDermott, after a stock bidding war with United Technologies to prevent an unfriendly takeover. Bailey Meter, now called Bailey Controls, was made a subsidiary of B&W by McDermott, a builder of oil rigs.

B&W, always heavily tied to the utility industry, was a major producer of controls and equipment for nuclear as well as fossil-fueled power plants. The company designed steam-supply systems, controls, and safety devices for nuclear plants at Three Mile Island, Harrisburg, Pa.; Indian Point, N.Y.; Nuclear One, Russellville, Alaska; and Davis-Besse, Port Clinton, Ohio. The Bailey division incorporated the latest electronic technology in the controls. In 1977, it made the first industrial use of fiberoptics, which made its products more immune to electrical impulses, a desirable feature in sensitive nuclear power plant controls. Equipment malfunctions at TMI, Davis-Besse, and other facilities put the company in the legal limelight in the 1970s and 1980s. Despite an expected boom in utility construction, B&W developed other markets—a wise move, as growth in utilities did not materialize. The company experienced increased sales in its chemical, petroleum, and industrial markets owing to widespread acceptance of electronic digital controls, which replaced mechanical ones. However, to compete in these markets, B&W had to streamline its organization; the result was layoffs of its labor force (which had tripled since 1946). When the company was founded, work rules were very strict, but since World War II the company has prided itself on its enlightened union relations. Workers at B&W were represented by the Natl. Brotherhood of Boilermen, but Bailey employees had no union. Management there kept workers informed of company events through videotapes and rewarded their suggestions. In 1972 the UAW organized the plant, winning a representation election. The Wickliffe plant was the site of a bitter strike in 1979.

**BABIN, VICTOR** (13 Dec. 1908–1 Mar. 1972), pianist, composer, and teacher, was the director of the CLEVELAND INSTITUTE OF MUSIC for 11 years. Born in Moscow, he studied in Riga before going to Berlin to study composition with Franz Schrecker and piano with Artur Schnabel at the Hochschule fur Musik. He came to the U.S. in 1937 and taught at the Aspen School of Music in Colorado, of which he was also director; the Berkshire Music Festival at Tanglewood, Mass.; and the Cleveland Institute of Music, of which he became director in 1961. As director, Babin brought distinguished musicians to the CIM faculty, broadened the course offerings, and established a cooperative relationship between CASE WESTERN RESERVE UNIVERSITY and the institute. He was made an adjunct professor at the university in 1969.

In 1933 Babin married another Schnabel student, Vitya Vronsky (b. 22 Aug. 1909 in the Crimea). They formed probably the best-known duo-piano team of their day. Their U.S. premiere was in New York in 1937, and they continued an active concert and recording career throughout their married life. A planned European tour was canceled by Babin's death in 1972. Vronsky remained on the piano faculty at the institute. Babin's compositions included concerti for 2 pianos and orchestra, chamber music, and songs. A song cycle, "Beloved Stranger," was set to texts by Witter Bynner. Babin was honored with the Cleveland Women's City Club Music Award and received an honorary Ph.D. from the University of New Mexico.

Grossman, F. Karl, *A History of Music in Cleveland* (1972).

The **BACH FESTIVAL** each year focuses worldwide attention on the Cleveland area through the interpretation and enjoyment of the works of Johann Sebastian Bach and his contemporaries. The festival was organized in 1933 at BALDWIN-WALLACE COLLEGE by professor Dr. Albert Riemenschneider to honor Bach. The first series of concerts was held 9 June 1933. Expanded to 2 days in 1934, the festival, held in early summer at the college conservatory, featured guest artists and outstanding students and faculty of the college. Riemenschneider and his wife, Selma, both taught at the school, piano and organ and piano and voice respectively. Besides the Riemenschneiders, Carl G. Schlyer (festival orchestra) and Cecil W. Munk (a cappella choir and brass choir) were active and influential during the early years of the festival. The festival consistently achieved a higher artistic standard and introduced seldom-heard works of Bach. Riemenschneider conducted the B Minor Mass (1935–36); the St. John Passion (1937, 1941); the Christmas Oratorio (1938); and the St. Matthew Passion, plus chamber music and motets.

With the dedication of the Kulas Memorial Arts Bldg. in 1940, the conservatory gained more room for festival functions as well as space for the 2,500 items Riemenschneider had collected that related to or were by the composer Bach. Riemenschneider retired in 1947, and Harold W. Baltz became conservatory director. Cecil W. Munk succeeded him in 1951. Geo. Poinar, head of the violin department at the conservatory, became festival director. In 1957, the Bach Festival celebrated its silver anniversary with the soprano Lois Marshall singing a solo cantata and Arthur Loesser, piano, and Joseph Knitzer, violin, playing sonatas 1, 2, and 4. In 1969, the festival broke with tradition by including "modern" music by Stravinsky and a modern dance by Joan Hartsborne choreographed to the second Brandenburg Concerto. Two years later, works by both Bach and his contempories were heard at the festival, including pieces by Buxtehude, Vivaldi, and Handel. Famed Bach scholar and conductor Helmuth Rilling was guest director in 1975. He reduced the size of the chorus to give more flexibility to the sound. Dwight Oltman became director in 1975. In 1985, a special festival was planned in celebration of the birthdays of Bach, Handel, and Scarlatti. It featured a display of rare Bach prints and manuscripts, with performances of music of all 3 composers, and ran for 4 days instead of 2.

**BACKUS, FRANKLIN THOMAS** (6 May 1813–14 May 1870), was a prominent Cleveland lawyer. Backus was born in Lee, Berkshire County, Mass. His father died when Backus was young, and the family moved to Lansing, N.Y., where Backus worked on the family farm. Completely self-taught, he was admitted as a junior-year student to Yale in 1834. In 1837 Backus came to Cleveland and opened a school for the classics. In 1839, after studying law with the firm of Bolton Kelley, he was admitted to the bar, and in 1840 he formed a law partnership with Jesse P. Bishop. In 1841, Backus was elected prosecuting attorney for Cuyahoga County; he was reelected in 1843. He was a member of the Ohio House of Representatives in 1846, and in 1848 he became a state senator. In 1854, Backus was on the commission that drafted the terms annexing OHIO CITY to Cleveland. In 1858, Backus, with 3 other prominent lawyers, RUFUS SPALDING, ALBERT G. RIDDLE, and Seneca O. Griswold, acted for the defense in the OBERLIN-WELLINGTON RESCUE case. During his lifetime, Backus, as a Republican, ran unsuccessfully for the Ohio Supreme Court and the U.S. House of Representatives. In 1868, he ran for Congress again, but as a Democrat, and lost. Despite the political losses, Backus was regarded as an excellent lawyer, having an extensive and profitable private law practice. The Cleveland bar said he had "sound judgement, vigorous intellect and unsurpassed integrity." In 1869, Backus helped establish the Cleveland Law Library; after his death, his law books were donated to it. He was also a founding member of the WESTERN RE-

SERVE HISTORICAL SOCIETY. In 1892, his wife, Lucy (Mygatt), donated $50,000 to Western Reserve University to found a law school to be named after her husband.

**BADGER, JOSEPH** (28 Feb. 1757–5 Apr. 1846), was the first missionary sent to the WESTERN RESERVE by the Connecticut Missionary Society and the founder of the first Congregational church in the Western Reserve (in Austinburg). He was one of the earliest clergymen in the area and, traditionally, preacher of the first sermon in Cleveland. Badger was born in Wilbraham, Mass. After service in the Continental Army, he started a career as a weaver but quit to prepare for Yale, where he secured his degree in 1785. Ordained a Congregational minister in 1786, Badger arrived in the Western Reserve in late 1800, after a 13-year career in a Massachusetts church, to serve both Congregationalists and Presbyterians under the Plan of Union. He spent 35 years as a missionary and resident minister, organizing churches and using his New England background and education to redress the emotionalism often associated with early-frontier religious meetings. Badger was interested in education; in 1801 he tried to secure a charter from the Territorial Assembly establishing a college, and in 1803 he sponsored the plans of the Erie Literary Society for an academy in Burton. It was Badger's work in the Western Reserve, first for the Connecticut Missionary Society and later for individual churches, that paved the way for the growth of organized religion in the area. For 26 years he was busy setting up churches and schools and giving counsel. His retirement in 1825 was interrupted by another 8-year tenure as pastor of a new congregation. His long service was the result of both invitations from the faithful and his sense that many pioneers needed reminding about the care of their souls. Under the auspices of the Plan of Union, Badger's work (1800–06) was the first Congregational effort to cooperate with Presbyterians in missionary activities on the frontier. His wilderness travels gave him a knowledge of the frontier, which brought him to the attention of Wm. Henry Harrison and led to his appointment as a brigade chaplain during the War of 1812. Badger's first wife, Lois Noble, died in 1818. He married Abigail Ely in 1819.

**BADGLEY, SIDNEY R.** (28 May 1850–29 Apr. 1917), was a prominent church architect in the U.S. and Canada who was active in Cleveland from 1887 until his death. Born at Ernestown, Ontario, Canada, he was educated at public schools and private academies in Canada and served as an apprentice in a Toronto architectural office. He came to the U.S. and Cleveland in 1887 and practiced under his own name and in a partnership with Wm. Nicklas. Several churches and a former orphanage designed by Badgley were still extant in 1984. They included the former Jones Home for Friendless Children (1903) at 3518 W. 25th St., the former Fourth Reformed Church (1909) at Woodbridge Ave. and W. 32nd St., the Lakewood United Methodist Church at 15700 Detroit Ave., and the former Pilgrim Congregational Church (1894) at W. 14th St. and Starkweather Ave. The Pilgrim Church is one of Badgley's finest structures and one of the first church buildings designed in the U.S. to function as both a religious and a community-service center. Badgley's pioneering design was exhibited at the Paris Exposition of 1900. Badgley was a vice-president of the Equity Savings & Loan Co. and a member of the Cleveland Chamber of Commerce. He was married twice. His first marriage, to Alma A. Clark in 1872, ended with her death 2 years later. He married Charlotte J. Billeland of St. Catherines, Ontario, on 21 Sept. 1876. Badgley is buried in St. Catherines.

**BAEHR, HERMAN C.** (16 Mar. 1866–4 Feb. 1942), was a businessman and politician who served as county recorder (1904–09) and mayor of Cleveland (1910–12). He was an officer of the CLEVELAND-SANDUSKY BREWING CO., vice-president of the Forest City Savings & Loan, and a director of Cleveland Trust bank. Baehr was born in Keokuk, Iowa, the son of Jacob and Magdalena Zipf Baehr. His parents had lived in Cleveland from 1850–62 before moving to Iowa and returned here shortly after the CIVIL WAR. He was educated in public schools, quitting school at age 14 to join his father's brewing company. He later attended Lehman's Scientific Academy at Worms-on-the-Rhine, and he graduated from the first scientific station of New York in 1887. After returning to Cleveland, Baehr was an official of the Baehr Brewing Co., which his father had founded, and became secretary and treasurer of the Cleveland-Sandusky Brewing Co. when it took over Baehr Brewing. He married Rose Schulte in 1898. Interested in Republican party politics, Baehr was elected county recorder, serving for 5 years, and defeated TOM L. JOHNSON for mayor in 1909. He declined to seek reelection in 1912 and returned to business, becoming first vice-president and director of the Forest City Savings & Trust Co. He became a director of the Cleveland Trust Bank (see AMERITRUST) when it took over Forest City Savings. He was also president of the Langenau Mfg. Co. He died in Los Angeles, Calif., at age 75.

The **BAGBY FUGITIVE SLAVE CASE**, heard in Cleveland's federal court in Jan. 1861, resulted in the return of one of the last fugitive slaves surrendered to the South before the CIVIL WAR. The defendant was Sara Lucy Bagby (ca. 1833–14 July 1906), who sought refuge as a domestic in Cleveland after running from her owner, Wm. S. Goshorn of Wheeling, Va. Tracing her to the city several months later, Goshorn had her arrested by U.S. marshals on 19 Jan. 1861. Before her scheduled federal hearing on 21 Jan., Bagby's counsel, RUFUS SPALDING, secured a habeas corpus hearing for his client. Probate Judge Daniel R. Tilden could find no reason to release her but ruled that neither could she be held in the local jail. Granting Spalding a 2-day recess to interview witnesses in Wheeling, U.S. Commissioner Bushnell White ordered a room fitted out for Bagby on federal property in the post office building. When the hearing resumed on 23 Jan., Spalding reported his failure to uncover any favorable evidence, and White restored Bagby to Goshorn.

It was widely believed at the time that the Bagby case was a test of the North's disposition to obey the Fugitive Slave Act. Both Tilden and White had cautioned that the city as well as the alleged fugitive was on trial. With 4 southern states already having announced their secession, even the radical Republican *CLEVELAND LEADER* counseled submission to the law for the sake of preserving the Union. The city was not entirely compliant, as several skirmishes were reported between deputies and bystanders during the passage of the prisoner from the local to the federal court. Precautions were taken on the train returning Bagby to Wheeling in order to foil a rumored rescue attempt. Although Cleveland was severly criticized by the abolition press for its submission, Bagby's reenslavement proved to be short-lived. She was released when Union forces occupied Wheeling and arrested Goshorn, who had subsequently supported Virginia's secession despite Cleveland's sacrifice. Bagby later moved to Pittsburgh and married a Union soldier, Geo. Johnson. She returned to live her last years in Cleveland, the scene of the trial that had briefly made her a symbol of the issues that had split the Union.

The **BAILEY COMPANY** was one of Cleveland's major department stores and a national pioneer in the establishment of branch operations. Its forerunner was a small dry-goods store opened by Lewis A. Bailey and Joseph W. Crothers at Ontario and Prospect avenues in 1881. By 1899, two well-known businessmen, Col. Louis Black and Chas. K. Sunshine, assumed the management of Bailey's store and incorporated it as the Bailey Co. By combining it with the neighboring Cleveland Dry Goods Co., they developed Bailey into a major department store, "the store for all the people," with a variety of home furnishings and clothing and 11 employees. The store was successful, and in 1903 Bailey erected a 10-story building at Ontario and Prospect; a 7-story addition was erected by 1910. In 1927, Bailey helped to organize a national holding company for several major-city department stores, the Natl. Dept. Stores Co. Bailey's president, Victor W. Sincere, became the first president of Natl. Dept. Stores, and Bailey was made a division of the firm. As Cleveland continued to grow, Bailey initiated a revolutionary precedent by establishing east and west side branches. An east side store was opened in 1929 at Euclid Ave. and E. 101st St., and the following year, a west side store was established at Detroit and Warren roads in LAKEWOOD.

In the late 1940s and 1950s, Bailey was involved in another expansion program. Its existing stores were remodeled, and 2 new suburban stores opened—in EUCLID in 1951 and MAYFIELD HTS. in 1960. In 1958, Natl. Dept. Stores sold Bailey to the Century Food Market Co. (later the CFM Co.) of Youngstown, Ohio. CFM began a $250,000 project to construct a new facade for the downtown store. In 1959, Bailey, with 1,400 employees, was noted in the labor movement when it became the first and only major Cleveland department store with a union contract covering sales clerks. Despite the downtown store's "facelift," Bailey encountered a decline in sales. In 1962, CFM closed Bailey's downtown and Euclid Ave. stores and placed emphasis on its suburban stores. The public outcry to this closing prompted Bailey to reopen a downtown store at 514 Prospect by the end of 1962. In 1965, Bailey sold its Lakewood store to Nevilles, Inc., which went bankrupt in 1968. CFM's interest in expanding into the booming discount store market was reflected in its action of Mar. 1966, when the 3 remaining Bailey stores were taken over by one of CFM's subsidiaries, Miracle Mart, Inc., of New York, and made into discount department stores, called Bailey Wonder Marts.

**BAILEY METER.** *See* **BABCOCK & WILCOX**

**BAKER, EDWARD MOSE** (18 Aug. 1875–17 Feb. 1957), broker and philanthropist, was one of the founders of the Fed. of Jewish Charities and a civic leader in Cleveland. He was born and educated in Erie, Pa., and matriculated at the University of Chicago, where he received his bachelor's degree in 1898. He conducted postgraduate studies in philosophy and sociology and studied for the rabbinate under the direction of his uncle and renowned Reform rabbi Emil Hirsch. Baker accepted a call to the pulpit of Temple Israel in Chicago in 1901. However, the death of his brother-in-law, Jacob Mayer, in Cleveland led him to settle in this city 6 months later. Upon his arrival, he took over Mayer's brokerage business. Before the year was over, he had been elected vice-president of the Cleveland Stock Exchange. He later served 15 years as its president.

A product of both the Progressive Era and the Reform Judaism that placed emphasis upon ethical monotheism and social reform, Baker believed that the test of wealth was the way it was used. He was among the founders of several charitable organizations and social-service agencies in Cleveland, including Associated Charities, the LEGAL AID SOCIETY, and the Community Fund. In 1903, he cofounded the Fed. of Jewish Charities and served as its first secretary. He was a member of the board of trustees for 50 years. Following the death of CHAS. EISENMAN in 1923, Baker served 4 years as president of the federation. He was active civically and politically in the city. In 1907–08 he was chairman of the Republican Executive Committee for Cuyahoga County. In 1912, he was a founder and 1st vice-president of the CITY CLUB OF CLEVELAND. He subsequently served as president. Baker's classical Reform training led him to argue that Judaism and Americanism were compatible and shared similar principles and could, in turn, place modern philanthropy easily in the framework of Judaism. In 1904, he wrote "Judaism and the American Spirit," in which he elaborated the similarity in ethical philosophy between the two. The article was published in *Arena* and later was issued as a pamphlet.

**BAKER, ELBERT H.** (25 July 1854–27 Sept. 1933), was the "fourth founder" of the *PLAIN DEALER*. He was born in Norwalk, Ohio. His family brought him to Cleveland in 1865, but in 1870 they moved to Kansas City. Baker returned to Cleveland in 1873. He went to work as an advertising salesman for the *CLEVELAND HERALD* in 1877 and moved to the *CLEVELAND LEADER* in 1882. In 1897, Baker followed Clevelander CHAS. E. KENNEDY to St. Louis to work for Joseph Pulitzer's *Post-Dispatch*. They returned the following year to take over the operation of the *Plain Dealer* under a lease signed with owner LIBERTY E. HOLDEN. While Kennedy assumed editorial control, Baker functioned as business manager. Among Baker's reforms were the compilation of reliable circulation figures and the adoption of uniform advertising rates. Since the *Plain Dealer*'s audited circulation was considerably lower than previous claims, Baker personally traveled to the East Coast to persuade the paper's national advertisers to maintain their accounts. He was also credited with eliminating partisan bias from news stories and expanding the *Plain Dealer*'s national and foreign news coverage, although in view of his position, Kennedy undoubtedly shared in the responsibility for those innovations.

With the withdrawal of Kennedy from the partnership in 1907, Baker assumed editorial as well as business direction of the *Plain Dealer* under the title of general manager. He represented a new breed of hired managers in American journalism, as the old editor-publishers relinquished personal direction of their enterprises. It was Baker, not Holden, who personified the *Plain Dealer*, and as such he became as influential a civic leader as his employer. He arranged the compromise that ended Cleveland's 10-year traction war under Mayor TOM L. JOHNSON, and later he twice orchestrated settlements between the city and the EAST OHIO GAS CO. In 1930, he became chairman of the board. He was a director of the Associated Press and the American Newspaper Publishers' Assoc., serving also as president of the latter group from 1912–14. Married in 1876 to Ida Smith, Baker had 2 daughters and 3 sons. In partnership with 2 of his sons, he became copublisher of 3 newpapers on the West Coast.

Kennedy, Charles E., *Fifty Years of Cleveland* (1925).
Shaw, Archer H., *The Plain Dealer* (1942).

**BAKER, NEWTON DIEHL** (3 Dec. 1871–25 Dec. 1937), was Democratic mayor of Cleveland (1912–16) and served as secretary of war in Pres. Woodrow Wilson's cabinet. Born in Martinsburg, W. Va., the son of Newton Diehl and Mary Ann Dukehart Baker, he attended local schools there and graduated from Episcopal High School near Alexandria, Va. He received a B.A. degree from Johns Hopkins University in 1892 and his law degree from Washington & Lee University in 1894. After brief service in Washington as secretary to Postmaster General Wm. Wilson, he returned to Martinsburg in 1897 to practice law. Baker came to Cleveland in 1899 to work in the law office of MARTIN FORAN. He was appointed assistant law director in Mayor Tom L. Johnson's administration in 1902 and became city solicitor in 1903. As solicitor, he handled many legal matters involved in Johnson's efforts to give Cleveland a municipally operated transit system, and he remained solicitor after Johnson's defeat in 1909. Baker managed the Democratic party's local campaign for state and congressional offices in 1910, and after Johnson's death he took over leadership of the county Democratic organization. In 1924 he turned over much of the party leadership to W. BURR GONGWER but remained chairman of the County Central Committee until 1936.

Active in promoting municipal HOME RULE, Baker helped write the amendment to the Ohio constitution giving municipalities the right to govern themselves. The amendment was passed by the state legislature in 1912, the same year Baker became mayor of Cleveland. As mayor he was influential in selecting the commission to write Cleveland's first home rule charter and campaigned for its successful passage in 1913. During his administration a new municipal light plant was built, and when it went into operation in 1914, it was the largest city-owned plant in the nation. Declining to run for a 3d term as mayor in 1916, he retired to practice law, founding the law firm of Baker, Hostetler & Sidlo (see BAKER & HOSTETLER).

Active in state and national Democratic politics as well, Baker was a leading supporter of Woodrow Wilson for president in 1912; however, he declined Wilson's offer to become secretary of the interior in 1913, preferring to remain in Cleveland as mayor. Two months after his retirement in 1916, he accepted an appointment as secretary of war in Wilson's cabinet. When the U.S. entered WORLD WAR I, Baker was responsible for drafting, organizing, outfitting, and provisioning an army of 2 million men to be sent overseas in the shortest possible time. When the war was over, his task included the demobilization of the troops and the negotiations to cancel numerous war contracts. Baker left Washington in the spring of 1921 after serving 5 years in Wilson's cabinet and returned to his law firm in Cleveland.

A successful lawyer, Baker was chief counsel for the Scripps-Howard newspapers, and the Van Sweringen interests were among his first clients. At the request of WM. R. HOPKINS, Baker represented the city of Cleveland in a suit contesting the right of the EAST OHIO GAS CO. To withdraw its service from the city without permission from the State Utilities Commission. Using the home rule provision that Baker had helped write into the state constitution, Cleveland had made a rate agreement with East Ohio Gas that permitted the company to withdraw when the contract expired. Baker, however, successfully argued that in the regulation of a public utility, state legislation takes precedence over the right of home rule municipalities to negotiate contracts.

An able speaker, Baker championed the cause of the League of Nations, which he felt would bring world peace. He also was active on many institutional, charitable, educational, and corporate boards and committees. He was given the Cleveland Chamber of Commerce Medal for public service in 1927, and in 1928 the U.S. government awarded him the Distinguished Service Medal. He was the author of *Why We Went to War*, published by Harper Bros. for the Council on Foreign Relations in 1936. Baker married Elizabeth Wells Leopold in June 1902, and they had 3 children: Elizabeth (Mrs. John Phillips McGean), Newton D. Baker III, and Margaret (Mrs. Fulton Wright). Baker died in Cleveland at the age of 66.

Newton D. Baker Papers, WRHS.
Cramer, Clarence H., *Newton D. Baker* (1961).

**BAKER, WALTER C.** (27 June 1868–26 Apr. 1955), was an engineer and an inventor instrumental in founding the American Ball Bearing Co. and in the development of the automobile industry. A manufacturer of electric cars, he developed several important automobile parts. Born in Hinsdale, N.H., Baker came to Cleveland with his parents in 1871. His father, Geo. W. Baker, was a founder and chief inventor for the White Sewing Machine Co. and also helped organize the Cleveland Machine Screw Co. Walter attended Cleveland public schools and graduated from Case School of Applied Science in 1891, when he joined Cleveland Machine Screw Co.

In 1895, Baker, John Grant, Rollin C. White, and F. Philip Dorn organized the American Ball Bearing Co. on Clarkwood Ave. near Central Ave. Originally formed to produce ball-bearing axles for horse-drawn vehicles, the company was supplying axles for the automobile industry by 1898. Baker served as the company's president from 1895–1918, when the firm and 13 others merged to form the Standard Parts Co. He served as a consulting engineer to the new company. In addition to adapting ball bearings to the automobile industry, Baker developed several other parts widely adopted by the industry. These include a steering knuckle for front wheels and a full-floating rear axle. Baker and Dorn built their own electrically powered automobile in 1897, and in 1898 they organized the Baker Motor Vehicle Co. Located at 116 Jessie (E. 69th) St., the company advertised its electric car as "the Most Elegant Automobile Made" and sold it for $850. The company is credited with introducing the left-handed steering system.

In 1905 the Baker Motor Vehicle Co. moved to a new plant on W. 83rd St. near the Lake Shore & Michigan Southern Railroad lines. Production had increased to 400 cars a year. The company introduced a truck model in 1907, and by 1913 more than 200 companies were using its trucks. In June 1915 the company merged with the Rauch & Lang Carriage Co. To form the Baker Rauch & Lang Co. The last Baker electric cars were produced in 1916. The company sold its electric passenger car business to the Stevens-Duryea Co. in 1920. Walter Baker served as vice-president of the electric car company until 1912, when he joined General Electric's Owen Magnetic Co. as the supervisor of its electric car construction. Baker was a member of several professional and social organizations, including the Cleveland Chamber of Commerce, the American Society of Mechanical Engineers, the Society of Automotive Engineers, the UNION CLUB, and the Lakewood Yacht Club. He married Fannie Elizabeth White in 1891.

**BAKER & HOSTETLER** was, in 1984, one of the most influential law firms in Cleveland. Known throughout the country, it employed at that time over 240 attorneys in 5 cities (124 in Cleveland, 55 in Washington, 34 in Columbus, 18 in Orlando, and 15 in Denver). The firm name had been changed 3 times over the years. The original name of Baker, Hostetler & Sidlo was changed in 1931 to Baker, Hostetler, Sidlo & Patterson. In 1938, the name was changed to Baker, Hostetler & Patterson, and in 1979 it was changed to Baker & Hostetler. The firm was founded by NEWTON D.

BAKER on 1 Jan. 1916—the day following the expiration of his second and final term as mayor of Cleveland. The founding partners were Baker, JOSEPH C. HOSTETLER (who had been Baker's assistant law director), and THOS. SIDLO (who had been Baker's public-service director). They had one associate, Paul Patterson. Baker, Hostetler & Sidlo's first office consisted of several rooms on the 5th floor of the new East Ohio Gas Bldg., located on E. 6th St. The firm moved in July 1916 to the 13th floor of another new building, the Union Natl. Bank Bldg., or, as it was more generally called, the 308 Euclid Bldg. By 1924, the firm needed more office space and moved to the 19th floor of the Union Trust Bldg. (HUNTINGTON BLDG). The firm remained there until Sept. 1980, when it moved to offices in the Natl. City Ctr. at E. 9th St. and Euclid.

Three months after founding the firm, Newton D. Baker was appointed secretary of war by Pres. Woodrow Wilson and went to Washington until Mar. 1921. Some of the firm's clients during its early years included the Internatl. Molders' Union of North America, the Natl. One Cent Letter Postage Assoc. (a lobbying organization for 1-cent postage), the Plain Dealer Publishing Co., the HOLLENDEN HOTEL, and the Midland Bank. After Newton D. Baker returned from his post in Washington, the firm grew rapidly. It acquired the business of E. W. Scripps and the Scripps newspapers, the Cleveland Trust Co., the Goodyear Tire & Rubber Co., and the business of the Van Sweringen brothers. Baker & Hostetler retained many of these companies as clients in 1984. Because Baker was so well known, the firm acquired a national reputation.

Some of the significant clients that Newton D. Baker represented included O. P. and M. J. VAN SWERINGEN before the Interstate Commerce Commission in matters involving the building of their railroad empire; and the General Electric Co., whom he represented in an antitrust suit in federal court. The entire office participated in the proxy fight in Youngstown involving the proposed merger of the Youngstown Sheet & Tube Co. with the Bethlehem Steel Co. The city of Cleveland was represented in a rate case against the EAST OHIO GAS CO. Baker was employed to represent utilities in many actions challenging New Deal legislation and power projects, including *Tennessee Electric Power Co.* v. *TVA (Tennessee Valley Authority), et al.*, seeking to have the TVA declared unconstitutional. Other clients of the firm included the American League of Professional Baseball Clubs, the Cleveland Baseball Co., and the CLEVELAND CLINIC FOUNDATION.

The **BAKER MATERIALS HANDLING COMPANY** was formed in 1915 by the merger of 2 Cleveland companies, the Rauch & Lang Carriage Co. and the Baker Motor Vehicle Co., which had been neighbors on W. 80th St. since 1898. Jacob Rauch, a German immigrant, originally opened the Wayside Smithy, a wagon-repair shop along the Cleveland-Cincinnati stagecoach route on Columbia Rd., in 1853. By 1860, he began building custom coaches at a new location on Pearl Rd. and selling them to an increasingly national market. Rauch added 2 partners, Chas. E. Lang and Chas. Rauch, his son, in 1881. The company, now called Rauch & Lang, expanded its line to include delivery vehicles. (The most famous Rauch delivery vehicle, however, had been built a decade earlier and was destined to become a Cleveland classic: an ice wagon embellished with a polar bear won a prize at the Philadelphia Centennial in 1876.) With the coming of the horseless carriage, Rauch & Lang turned to the manufacture of electric automobiles, building its first electric car in 1904 and beginning production of the pleasure car in 1905. Along with Fred R. White, WALTER C. BAKER began the Baker Motor Vehicle Co. in 1898, after building the experimental Electrobat for the 1892 Chicago Exhibition. He came to Cleveland, where he founded the America Bearings Co. To make small bearings and axles, an important development for the auto industry. Still fascinated with the concept of an electric vehicle, he formed a new company, the Baker Motor Vehicle Co., to build and market electric autos. By 1907, the company added electric load trucks to its line, and within 5 years, more than 200 companies were outfitted with Baker fleets, noted for their quality, streamlined appearance, and technological superiority. The introduction of the self-starter in 1912 and the rising popularity of the Model T doomed the electric car industry, but Baker's pioneering work in auto technology secured a place for his company in the infant gas-engined industry. Baker designed alloy steel transmissions and axles for the Model T and Packard lines. After he merged his firm with Rauch & Lang in 1915 (becoming Baker-Raulang), the new company developed the Owen-Magnetic, a gas-powered car with a magnetic ignition and a spiral bevel gas drive.

During WORLD WAR I, Baker was commissioned by the Army to make its first industrial trucks, which were used to unload supplies for the American Expeditionary Forces in Europe and to carry ammunition to the battle sites. This war contract shaped the future of Baker in 1920; the company sold off its electric car division to Stevens-Duryea and concentrated on the development of electric and gas-powered industrial lift trucks. In WORLD WAR II, Baker again supplied the military needs for ordnance and munitions trucks, as well as general-purpose loading trucks. Its innovations in the postwar years—namely, the Gas-O-Matic, the first transmissionless, clutchless, gas-powered electric motor-driven lift truck—made it an attractive acquisition for the century-old Otis Elevator Co. in 1953. Otis used Baker as the basis of its materials handling division; and it later acquired 2 local companies, the Moto-Truc Co. (1960) and the Euclid Crane & Hoist Co. (1970), and companies in California, Arkansas, and France. As part of Otis, Baker continued to make improvements in lift trucks and heavily experimented with electric vehicles, Baker's original product. In the 1970s, Baker electric trucks were tested by the post office for use by mail carriers, while other models were tested as people movers at CLEVELAND HOPKINS INTERNATIONAL AIRPORT and elsewhere throughout the country. In the midst of the oil crisis, Otis got more involved in the electrified urban transit field, and Cleveland's Baker plants at 8000 Baker Ave. and 12401 Taft Ave. (the old Moto-Truc plant) made many of the parts, as well as the electric motors. Otis became part of United Technologies in 1975 and in 1977 sold Baker to Linde-Akiengesellschaft, a German lift truck manufacturer, a firm with the international marketing strategy and technical expertise to complement Baker's quality and engineering excellence. The company now (1986) operates as the Baker Materials Handling Corp. and has its 2 local plants on Baker and Taft aves., which employ over 600 people locally.

**BALDWIN, CHARLES CANDEE** (2 Dec. 1834–2 Feb. 1895), was a corporate lawyer, a circuit judge, and a founder of the WESTERN RESERVE HISTORICAL SOCIETY. Baldwin was born in Middletown, Conn. His family moved to Elyria when he was 5 months old and returned to Connecticut in 1847. He attended a boarding school in Middletown and in 1855 graduated from Wesleyan University. In 1857, Baldwin received a degree from Harvard Law School. That same year he moved to Cleveland and was admitted to the Ohio bar. Baldwin began reading law in the office of Samuel B. and F. J. Prentiss. In 1863 he was made an equal partner. Over the years, he had successive partnerships with all 3 Prentiss brothers. He married their sister, Caroline, in 1862. As a lawyer, Baldwin achieved an expertise in corporate law.

His practice related largely to banks, corporations, and the management of trusts. More than once he represented large corporations in the U.S. Supreme Court. Despite ill health later in life, in 1884 Baldwin was elected to the first of 3 terms as a judge of the circuit court. He was one of 3 judges of the 6th district, consisting of Cuyahoga, Huron, Lorain, Medina, Summit, Sandusky, Lucas, and Ottawa counties. It was subdivided in 1887, and Baldwin eventually became presiding judge of the new 8th district—Cuyahoga, Summit, Lorain, and Medina counties. Almost all his time was spent hearing appeals. Very few of his decisions were overturned.

Baldwin was one of Cleveland's most civically active citizens. In 1882, he was chiefly responsible for the funds raised to secure a site in Cleveland for Western Reserve College of Hudson. He was also an active member of the Library Assoc., elected its vice-president in 1866. Among Baldwin's various other attainments, from 1875–78 he was president of the Cleveland Board of Underwriters, an original member of the American Bar Assoc., and a trustee for many cultural institutions in Cleveland. In 1867, with CHAS. WHITTLESEY, Baldwin organized what soon became the Western Reserve Historical Society. He served as its secretary for many years and in 1886 succeeded Whittlesey as president. Through his influence, he was able to gain support for the society from prominent citizens. He left his important cartographic collection to the WRHS. He was a member of several other historical societies and the author of many works on Ohio history and genealogy. He died while in office and was buried in LAKE VIEW CEMETERY.

**BALDWIN, NORMAN C.** (29 July 1802–12 June 1887), was a prominent businessman and politician in Cleveland and OHIO CITY during the mid-1800s. He achieved early success as a forwarding and commission merchant on the Ohio Canal, and later went into banking and real estate. Born in Goshen, Conn., Baldwin came to Hudson at the age of 15 and opened a general store. After 18 months, he entered into partnership with 2 brothers. His experience as a merchant led him, in 1839, to form a partnership with Noble H. Merwin in the produce commission business. A new firm was later formed—Giddings, Baldwin & Co.—which owned one of the first and largest steamship lines on the lake. The firm operated what became known as the Troy & Erie Line, a fleet of steamers and packets that moved goods from Portsmouth, on the Ohio River, via the Ohio Canal to Lake Erie, and then to New York and the Erie Canal. The company primarily transported wheat and passengers. Baldwin moved to Cleveland in 1830 and became actively involved in the development of land on the west side of the Cuyahoga in Ohio City. He was a member of the Buffalo Land Co., formed in 1833 to drain and improve land in Ohio City for houses and factories. In the first election held in Ohio City, in 1836, Baldwin was elected a councilman; from 1838–39 he served as Ohio City's third mayor. He lived there most of his later life. In 1834, Baldwin became the first president of the Bank of Cleveland; he ran its affairs until its closing in 1843. Earlier, in 1836, he had retired from mercantile life and entered a lucrative career in real-estate speculation. He and his brother Frederick at one time owned land in Cuyahoga, Summit, and Lucas counties. Baldwin later moved from Ohio City to Cleveland, into a large house on Euclid Ave.

**BALDWIN, SAMUEL S.** (ca. 1776–12 July 1822), was an early Cleveland and Cuyahoga County public official. Baldwin was born in Ridgefield, Conn., and moved to a farm in NEWBURGH in 1808. In addition to farming, he dabbled in real estate with LEONARD CASE. Baldwin's short public career revolved around politics. In 1809, he was elected justice of the peace in Cleveland. In 1810, he became the first surveyor and may have been sheriff of Cuyahoga County. (Several sources indicate Smith S. Baldwin was the first sheriff.) As surveyor he relaid, as a state road, the road between Cleveland and Aurora, and from Mantua to Warren. Sheriff Baldwin officiated at the murder trial and hanging of the Indian JOHN O'MIC. In 1812, he served in the state assembly. The next year, he was elected to the Board of County Commissioners and appointed by the board to act as clerk. Baldwin married Sarah Camp of Ridgefield, Conn., who died in 1818 at the age of 36. They had 6 daughters and 2 sons. In 1819, Baldwin married Rhoda Boughton of Grafton, Ohio.

The **BALDWIN BIRD RESEARCH LABORATORY** was a pioneering ornithological research facility established in 1914 by Samuel Prentiss Baldwin (26 Oct. 1868–31 Dec. 1938) at his estate in GATES MILLS. The son of CHAS. C. BALDWIN and his wife, Sophia Prentiss, Baldwin inherited his father's interests in archeology and geology and as a boy developed an interest in birds in the woods around Cleveland and SHAKER HTS. He studied biology and geology at Dartmouth, graduating in 1892; he earned a law degree from Western Reserve University in 1894, was admitted to the Ohio bar that year, and practiced law in Cleveland until ill health forced him to retire from active practice in 1902. He then entered business and became president of the Williamson Co. Baldwin spent much of his time pursuing his scientific interests in geology and ornithology; he went on several geological expeditions in the 1890s, but after 1900 he concentrated his efforts on ornithology. In 1914 he became interested in the method of banding birds for scientific study; he had been trapping English sparrows that were menacing the birds native to his Hillcrest estate in Gates Mills and decided to band them to see if these birds returned to his estate. At the time, the banding of birds in the U.S. was "largely sporadic and amateur work," but Baldwin's scientific approach is credited with revolutionizing the practice and launching "a great national scientific movement" that eventually was led by the U.S. Biological Survey. Between 1914–19, working at his Gates Mills estate and at his Innwood estate near Thomasville, Ga., Baldwin developed traps and methods of capturing and banding small birds. In the 1920s and 1930s, Baldwin, with the aid of several assistants, undertook more sophisticated studies of the lives and habits of individual birds, developing devices such as the potentiometer ("a recording electrical thermometer") and the wrenograph to permit round-the-clock study of individual birds. Specializing in the study of the house wren, Baldwin developed the latter device to keep a record of the birds' entrances into and exits from the nest to measure attentiveness to developing eggs. He also perfected a camera capable of making motion pictures of a bird embryo in the egg, thus enabling the researcher to view the successive stages of embryonic development. His potentiometer was important in one of his major works. "By an extensive study of body temperatures of the house wren," wrote one biographer, Baldwin proved that young birds develop from cold-blooded to warm-blooded animals, confirming the long-held theory that "a bird is a reptile which has grown feathers and wings." By 1936, Baldwin's research lab had produced more than 30 papers and scientific studies, including *Physiology of the*

*Temperature of Birds* (1932). Work at the lab ended with his death in 1938, but his widow, Lilian Converse Hanna, who he had married on 15 Feb. 1898, later donated much of their Gates Mills estate for a bird sanctuary and parks.

**BALDWIN RESERVOIR,** the covered reservoir of the Baldwin Filtration Plant and Fairmount Pumping Station, is believed to be the largest in the world. Completed in 1925 to store the treated water from the filtration plant before distribution to the service area, the underground clear-water reservoir is an engineering marvel. It is 500′ wide, 1,000′ long, and 35′ deep and has a capacity of 135 million gallons. It is roofed by a thin groin-vaulted concrete slab supported by 1,196 columns, which are 30 in. in diameter and spaced 18 ft. apart. Before the reservoir was filled, the underground space had the appearance of a vast and mysterious cathedral. The roof is covered with soil, making a parklike lawn adjacent to the filtration plant. The plant itself is a symmetrical Palladian structure 750′ long, which dominates the commanding site at the summit of Fairhill Rd.

**BALDWIN-WALLACE COLLEGE** is a liberal-arts college related to the United Methodist church. Located in BEREA, the college's campus extends from Eastland Rd. To the northeast corner of Front St. and Bagley Rd., the location of Baldwin University in 1871. In 1986, the total plant consisted of 41 buildings on 56 acres. The roots of the college date back to Mar. 1837, when the Berea Seminary was incorporated with John Baldwin as one of the trustees. It was part of a commune known as the Lyceum Community, which was devoted to working and teaching in agriculture and industry. Members had to relinquish all personal property to the lyceum and to "profess the Christian faith" and be of "unquestionable moral character." After the community failed in 1842, Baldwin offered in 1845 a "5 acre campus, 30 village lots and 50 acres of land having valuable inexhaustible stone quarries" to the North Ohio Conference of the Methodist Episcopal church to establish an institution of learning. The conference granted a charter to Baldwin Institute, a preparatory school. It opened on 9 Apr. 1846, admitting students of both sexes with no discrimination as to race, creed, or color. The institute included a normal school. Fifty-nine boys and 41 girls were enrolled.

In 1855, Baldwin Institute became Baldwin University. It expanded its offerings to include classical, scientific, and commercial courses and also gave emphasis to the study of music. Under the leadership of 2 German Methodist ministers, Wm. Nast and Jacob Rotweiler, a Dept. of German was created in 1857. In 1863, Jas. Wallace, a trustee, gave land for a separate school. The Dept. of German withdrew from the university and became the nucleus of the new German Wallace College, with Nast as its first president. An agreement was made not to duplicate course offerings, and the 2 schools shared academic studies. In 1900, the Nast Theological Seminary was added to German Wallace College. Through the leadership of Dr. Albert Riemenschneider of the Dept. of Music, a Conservatory of Music was added to the campus in 1912. The loss of the German Dept. and financial setbacks during the Civil War period placed Baldwin University in a precarious position. In 1874 the university incurred a debt of $10,000. Three years later its music department became a branch of the Cleveland School of Music. In 1888, the school was forced to sell its original campus to the Cleveland Stone Co. for $100,000. The funds were used to purchase a 20-acre campus at the northeast corner of Front St. and Bagley Rd. In 1911, Baldwin University was declared below standard, and

German Wallace College ended its association with the school. These events proved beneficial, for in 1912 the Methodist Episcopal Conference called for a union of the institutions. On 26 Aug. 1913, the schools merged to create Baldwin-Wallace College. German Wallace received ⅔ representation on the new board, and Dr. Arthur Breslich of German Wallace became president; Dr. G. A. Reeder of Baldwin University became vice-president. In 1986, the school had a full-time faculty of 133 and an undergraduate enrollment of 2,094. It offered the B.A., B.S., B.S. in Education, and Bachelor of Music Education in addition to master's degrees in business administration and education. It also participated in affiliate programs such as engineering, forestry, dental hygiene, criminal justice, and medical technology. The college's Conservatory of Music was particularly well known, as was the Riemenschneider Bach Institute and its annual BACH FESTIVAL. The institute sponsored the publication of the quarterly journal *Bach* and maintained the Bach Memorial Library, which held over 9,000 volumes, including over 800 rare manuscripts and first editions.

**BALKAN IMMIGRANTS.** Bulgarians, Albanians, and Montenegrins constitute the principal small Balkan groups in Cleveland. The major period of Balkan immigration to the U.S. occurred from 1880–1924, prompted by economic stress and political changes in the Balkan countries. Prior to the 19th century, the economic condition of the Balkan peasants had deteriorated as a result of industrialization, foreign competition, commercialization of agriculture, and population growth. Political unrest and demands for independence following retreat of the Ottoman Empire created an air of uncertainty and instability. Further disruption of village life because of a series of natural disasters prompted many Balkans to leave their farms and villages for the U.S.

Most of the immigrants were peasants, possessing few skills, no formal education, and very meager financial resources. They were attracted to large cities such as Cleveland that offered unskilled and manual labor opportunities in factories and iron and steel mills. Most of the desirable open land of rural America was already homesteaded, and the land available in the Southwest and Great Basin did not attract the peasants, who had neither the capital nor the technical skills needed to cultivate the arid earth. In the urban ghettos formed by the immigrants, they found social networks to replace those they had left behind. These ethnic communities provided the newcomers with the time and support necessary to adjust to their new environment. The Orthodox church became an expression of their ethnicity as well as religious loyalty, just as the church in their homeland had been their expression of nationalism and ethnicity since the Turkish invasion of the 15th and 16th centuries.

Although the Bulgarians, Albanians, and Montenegrins shared many of the same experiences, the ethnicity of each was unique, and hence the three groups must be considered separately.

*Bulgarians.* Bulgarian immigration to Cleveland may be divided into 2 periods: the turn-of-the-century immigration (1880–1924) and the post-World War II refugee immigration. The largest group of Bulgarian immigrants arrived in Cleveland during the first period. This group may be further divided based on whether the immigration occurred before or after the Balkan War of 1912. Bulgarians who arrived in Cleveland prior to 1912 represented every social and economic class—the wealthy and the destitute, the educated and the illiterate. Most were young men, some of whom had voluntarily fought for the Macedonians against the Turks in 1903. Others were inspired by Protestant missionaries and American schools in Bulgaria to seek further education in America. For the most part, these men had converted to Protestantism in Bulgaria and often were from wealthy families. Most of the immigrants of this period came with the intention of settling permanently in their new home.

The Bulgarians who arrived after 1912 were generally peasants who came to America for economic reasons. Many were men who planned to return to their homelands and families after making their fortunes. Eventually almost all of them changed their minds about leaving and instead brought their families to join them in America. The immigrants settled around Herman and Stone avenues. NW, Orange and Woodland avenues SE, E. 30th St. between Payne and Perkins avenues, and later W. 105th St. and Madison Ave. NW. Many of the men worked in nearby factories, although some started their own businesses, such as grocery stores and restaurants. It is impossible to determine the exact number of Bulgarian immigrants who came to America or who settled in Cleveland during the early period (1880–1924), because between 1899 and 1920, Bulgarians, Serbs, and Montenegrins were counted together by U.S. immigration authorities. The majority of the Bulgarian immigrants were from Thrace (Turkey), Greece, Serbia, and Bulgaria.

The most recent immigrants who arrived after WORLD WAR II were seeking to escape Communism. Since the Communists seized control of Bulgaria, only a small number have been able to leave that country for the U.S. The largest number of Bulgarian immigrants now come from Yugoslavia, the Macedonian Republic, and the autonomous region of Kosso-Metahija (Kosmet). The urban ghettos of the early Bulgarian immigrants no longer exist. These immigrants and their descendants now live in all parts of the city and number approximately 700. A weekly newspaper, the *Macedonian Tribune*, still enjoys a large circulation among people of Bulgarian descent. Two journals are also available. One, the *Rodolubie*, is from Bulgaria. The other, the *Bulgarian Exile Monitor*, is published in English and is written by a Clevelander, Mr. Geo. Petrov. It has subscribers throughout the U.S., in Australia, and in England.

Most of Cleveland's Bulgarians are EASTERN ORTHODOX, although some are Catholic, Jewish, and Protestant. The St. Dimitar Church Organization is the city's Eastern Orthodox church club. Efforts to establish an Eastern Orthodox church in the city have not been successful. ST. THEODOSIUS RUSSIAN ORTHODOX CATHEDRAL on Starkweather and St. Tikhon aves. was a church attended by Bulgarians in the early years. More recently, Bulgarians have attended Serbian or Greek Orthodox churches.

*Albanians.* Most of Cleveland's Albanians were originally from Koritza, the cultural and educational center of Albania. The immigrants came to Cleveland in 2 distinct waves: early-20th-century (1900–38) and post-World War II refugees. Most Cleveland Albanians settled in the city before 1938, when Albania was occupied by Italy. Before World War II, approximately 1,000 people of Albanian birth or descent lived in Cleveland. After World War II, some Albanians who were considered displaced persons came from refugee camps in Italy, Germany, and Austria. Other immigrants came from the Kosmet region of Yugoslavia. No Albanians have been allowed to leave their homeland since the Communists gained control of the country.

Almost all of the Albanian immigrants were illiterate peasants. Most were men, both single and married. Although many did not plan to be permanent U.S. residents, eventually most changed their minds and saved enough money to bring their families to join them in their new homes. The early immigrants first settled on the west side of Cleveland, on both sides of Detroit Ave. NW from W. 54th to W. 58th streets and in Linndale. Some settled on the east side around E. 30th and St. Clair. However, LINNDALE became the major Albanian community. Clevelanders of Albanian birth or descent are now scattered throughout the city and number approximately 500. Large Albanian communities are still found along W. 117th St. from Linndale to Lorain Ave., and along both sides of Detroit Ave. from W. 77th to W. 150th streets. Many of the early immigrants worked in the old roundhouse in Linndale and in factories within walking distance of their urban ghetto neighborhoods. Some established their own restaurants and little grocery stores.

The city's Albanians have several social clubs and 3 ethnic newspapers, the *Dielli, Liria,* and *Shqiptari i Lire.* Most of Cleveland's Albanians are of the Orthodox faith. In 1957 an Albanian Orthodox parish was founded in Cleveland by Rev. Campbell, a former Old Catholic. Services were conducted in a church hall on Jasper Ave. until 1965. Then the St. E. Premte Orthodox Church, an Albanian Orthodox church, was established at 10716 Jasper Rd. SW. At that time, the congregation numbered 60–90 families. Services are conducted in English.

*Montenegrins.* Montenegrins settled in Cleveland during 2 periods: around the turn of the century (1890–1914) and after World War II. The largest number arrived in Cleveland during the early period. It is difficult to determine the exact number of Montenegrins who immigrated to the U.S. during this period, because prior to WORLD WAR I, U.S. immigration authorities did not keep separate counts for Montenegrins, Serbians, and Bulgarians. Instead, these diverse groups were lumped together. Most of the Montenegrin immigrants were uneducated peasants who emigrated for a variety of economic, social, and political reasons. The economic condition of the peasants had deteriorated in their homeland. Their standard of living was the lowest in all of the Balkans. Wars and guerrilla fighting between the Montenegrins and their Moslem neighbors had ravaged the land. Blood feuds between clans were often bitter and long-standing. Frequently they generated more hostility toward fellow Montenegrins than toward their common enemy, the Turks. Political dissatisfaction with the autocracy prompted still more emigration.

Montenegrins and Serbs have been closely connected in both modern European history and Cleveland history. Prior to 1918, Montenegrins had had an independent country. They called themselves Crno Gorci. Their country was an ally of Serbia in the Serbian wars for liberation in 1912, 1913, and 1914. In 1915 both Serbia and Crno Gorci were occupied by the Central Powers. In 1918 Montenegro was absorbed by the Kingdom of the Serbs, Croats, and Slovenes, which in 1929 became Yugoslavia, or the country of the South Slavs. The spoken language of the Montenegrins is similar to Croatian, although culturally and religiously, Montenegrins are most like Serbians. Therefore, between the world wars, Montenegro was affiliated with Serbia. During this time, Cleveland's Montenegrins were absorbed by the city's Serbians. For example, since Montenegrins never had their own church in Cleveland, they attended the Serbian Orthodox Church and were assimilated into the Serbian culture. Montenegrins established settlements in the Serbian neighborhoods and worked in blue-collar positions similar to their neighbors'. Gradually it became impossible to distinguish between Serbians and Montenegrins in Cleveland. A memorial in the Yugoslav section of Cleveland's

Cultural Garden recognizes and celebrates this linking of Montenegrins with South Slavs and their ties with the Cleveland community. The memorial is a bust of Peter Petrovic Njigos, a 19th-century Montenegrin prince-bishop and poet. Following World War II, only a few thousand Montenegrins immigrated to the U.S. A small number settled in Cleveland. The Montenegrins constitute the smallest number of South Slav immigrants in the city. They are counted together with Serbs.

Nicholas J. Zentos
Lorain County Community College

Georgevich, Dragoslav, *Serbian Americans and Their Communities of Cleveland* (1977).
Works Projects Admin., *The Peoples of Cleveland* (1942).

**BALL, ERNEST R.** (21 July 1878–3 May 1927), was a composer of many popular songs from 1904–27. Born in Cleveland, he studied at the Cleveland Conservatory before moving to New York. There he became a vaudeville pianist, and he traveled throughout the U.S. playing vaudeville houses. He was described as the "American Tosti." Later, Litmark Music Publishing House hired him as a demonstrator and staff composer. Ball's first successful composition was "Will You Love Me in December as You Do in May?" He collaborated with Jas. J. Walker (later mayor of New York) on this song. Musical scores for Broadway shows were his next successful venture. He composed music for *Barry of Ballymore* (1910), *The Isle of Dreams* (1913), and *Heart of Paddy Whack* (1914) for Irish tenor Chauncey Olcott, with whom he collaborated. His other collaborators included Geo. Graff, Darl MacBoyle, J. Kiern Brennan, Arthur Penn, Annelu Burns, and David Reed.

Ball composed such songs as "Mother Machree," "When Irish Eyes Are Smiling," "A Little Bit of Heaven," "Dear Little Boy of Mine," and "Let the Rest of the World Go By." The ballad "Mother Machree" became associated with Irish tenors such as John McCormack. Ball's music, which has a sentimental aspect to it, appealed to cultured musicians as well as the general public. It has endured throughout the years. Ball became a charter member of ASCAP in 1914. He also had a successful career as a singer of his own ballads. He toured throughout the U.S. While on tour in Santa Ana, Calif., in 1927, he suffered a fatal heart attack and died. He was married twice, first to Jessie M. White, and later to Maude Lambert, a vaudeville entertainer.

**BALL, WEBB C. CO.** *See* **WEBB C. BALL CO.**

**BALTIMORE & OHIO RAILROAD.** *See* **CSX (CHESSIE SYSTEM)**

**BANCOHIO NATIONAL BANK** was a major banking presence in the Cleveland area for more than a decade after its acquisition of the local Capital Natl. Bank. Itself acquired by Natl. City Bank in 1984, it used the holding company concept as a means of overcoming geographic legal barriers in banking. Capital Natl. Bank, the major local component of BancOhio, was formed by Alex and Paul Wintner shortly after the onset of the Depression in 1929. With the establishment of New Deal programs, Capital became a pioneer in the FHA lending field. In 1933, only Natl. City, the oldest bank in Cleveland, and Capital, the newest, were operating without limitations on withdrawals. By 1946, the bank was sold to a new group of investors, who held control until a group headed by Joseph Cole bought it in 1963 as a subsidiary of Shelter Resources. Under the new management, the former state bank became a federal bank in 1964, and partly through its purchase of

St. Clair Savings, it doubled its assets within 2 years. In 1972, the bank was acquired by the Columbus-based BancOhio Natl. Bank, the largest holding company in Ohio, which sought a Cleveland base. That suited the needs of Shelter Resources, which wanted to expand its mobile-home interests and wished to divest its banking and mortgage interests under the terms of the bank holding company laws. With the acquisition, Capital Natl., Cleveland's 6th-largest bank, added its $121.3 million assets to the $2.327 billion of BancOhio. With changes in interstate banking laws, BancOhio was sought by Natl. City Bank in 1984. Although the assets of the two banks were comparable (NCB's $6.5 billion vs. BancOhio's $5.5 billion), BancOhio, a retail bank that had grown too fast, had little experience in corporate lending, and had made poor-quality loans that clouded its earnings picture. NCB, with strength in corporate lending, sought BancOhio's chain of 269 branches. As a result, in Oct. 1984, the two banks pooled their resources to become a dominant banking force throughout the state.

**BANDLOW, ROBERT** (1852–1912), was an organizer for the old Central Labor Union, predecessor to the CLEVELAND FED. OF LABOR, and for many years the business editor of the *CLEVELAND CITIZEN*. Of German ancestry, Bandlow migrated to Cleveland in 1854 and, after a public-school education, became a typesetter for the *Wachter am Erie* and an early participant in the labor movement. First organizing Local 16 of the German Typographical Workers in the 1870s, he quickly gained a reputation as a leader who could balance long- and short-term goals. When the CLU was formed in 1887, Bandlow worked days as a printer and nights and weekends as an organizer for this infant AFL affiliate. Within 2 years, he organized 26 unions linked to their respective internationals, and built CFL membership up to 500. His constant theme at union meetings, labor forums, and the FRANKLIN CLUB was the education of the worker, which he felt to be the best hope for instilling the discipline necessary to attain labor goals. By 1891, Bandlow, a Socialist, supported Henry C. Long and MAX S. HAYES in founding the *Citizen*, which Bandlow regarded as a solid educational tool. He mobilized CLU support in the form of guaranteed subscriptions. Within 2 years, he was the business editor. To the time of his death in 1912, Bandlow was instrumental in shaping the *Citizen* into a powerful organizing and educational tool for Cleveland labor.

**BANDS.** Paid professional instrumental groups of any size but restricted to woodwinds, brasses, and percussion, bands primarily played outdoor concerts and provided march music for parades. Until ca. 1840, Cleveland had virtually no organized bands that could qualify as professional. Among the easterners who settled the area, there were invariably amateur musicians to handle holiday celebrations, weddings, funerals, and dances. As the community grew, some of the bandsmen who had served in the army that established the prestatehood territory settled in the area. In this early era bands were, by modern standards, primitive—hardly more advanced than the fife-and-drum groups of Revolutionary War times. Indeed, the first account of band music in Cleveland notes that the only music available in Cleveland before 1840 was drums. And while the comment may be viewed critically, it obviously had its basis in fact. Jas. Burk was a drummer of renown in 1806, and Stafford's Corps of 6 drums performed in 1836, according to O. V. Schubert, author of a hand-written and hand-illustrated book, "A Brief Sketch of Cleveland's Noted Bands from 1840 to 1880." Schubert was the son of B. B.

(Ben) Schubert, who was born in Austria and was the cousin of the famous composer Franz Schubert.

By 1837 the CLEVELAND CITY BAND, which then had 18 members, had already been formed. In 1840, B. B. Schubert organized the City Grays Band, with 2 trumpets, 2 French horns, ophicleide, clarinet, flute, drums, cymbals, and slide trombone. Its first performance was held on PUBLIC SQUARE—the favorite place for band concerts at that time and the center of Cleveland's public activities. Schubert also organized the German Guards Band in 1845. One of the early important figures in Cleveland bands was JACKSON MILLER LELAND. First mention is made of him in 1844 in connection with the maiden voyage of the steamboat *Empire*. Leland's Band provided the entertainment for the passengers and in so doing showed the versatility of bands, for it was also for many years the leading marching band in Cleveland. To lead parades and processions, the colorful Leland bought a handsome bandwagon, which was later purchased by P. T. Barnum for use in circus parades. In 1848 the Jaeger Band was organized, and in 1850 Hecker's Band was noted as a favorite at public and private functions. While Cleveland usually prided itself on the quality and quantity of its bands, it was not averse to playing host to visiting groups. As early as 1851, "Dodsworth's Celebrated Cornet Band," consisting of 20 members, visited Cleveland for a concert in Melodeon Hall. The CLEVELAND GRAYS invited Dodsworth back several years later. In 1852 the Newark Band visited and got good local reviews.

During the CIVIL WAR, the various bands enlisted, but not necessarily in the Regular Army or for the duration. Heck's Band joined the 4th Michigan Regiment; a newspaper article covering its departure noted that it was the second band to leave for the war. While the account did not name the first, it is assumed that it was Jack Leland's band. Leland's Band returned from the war in June 1862 but left again in November of that year to join the 14th Ohio Regiment. By the next May, however, it was back in Cleveland giving park concerts. Leland evidently distinguished himself as a composer of band music. In Feb. 1863, the display window in Brainard's music store featured the "Seventh Regiment March" dedicated to Col. Leighton of the Ohio 7th and composed by Leland. Clark's Forest City Cornet Band was organized in 1863. Leland in 1867 organized a cornet band, and in 1869 Papworth reorganized his brass band. Leland and Papworth, in fact, were the two leading bandmasters during the mid-19th century. Gradually other men became prominent in the field: E. Hatfield, John Messer, Geo. Burt, Wm. Heydler, and Joseph Ballhouse all organized their own bands; but a glance at the few rosters available shows that frequently the players in the bands were interchangeable. As professionals, the various musicians played any jobs that came along, and it did not matter that several of them played in competing organizations. The chief differences in the bands were the leaders and the uniforms.

With the growth of the city in the latter half of the century, largely through the influx of immigrants from Central Europe, the number of bands expanded accordingly. In 1877, the Bohemian musician J. Mudra reorganized Carl Braetz's 10-year-old Great Western Band, which was to achieve and hold prominence through the early part of the 20th century under the direction of Frank HRUBY, another Bohemian, who took over in 1889. Under the latter's leadership, the band of 35–50 players played both locally and for national political conventions. On 4 July 1894, the Great Western Band played for the dedication of Public Square's SOLDIERS & SAILORS MONUMENT. GERMANS, one of the city's first major immigrant groups, always had in their midst some sort of "German Band" that could conveniently stretch itself from a small beer-hall outfit to one of marching and concert size. These, like the Czech and Italian bands that followed, were mostly amateur groups, though it was by no means rare for individual players to rise to professional status to join the established general-purpose bands. Visiting bands continued to be popular in the post-Civil War period. In 1867, the Western Band of Sandusky came to parade and concertize. In 1871, Marble's Band of Akron played at the corner of Superior and Bank streets; it went on excursion with the Knights Templar to Sandusky. In 1876, the Kaiser's own German Imperial Band, 35 pieces strong, came to town to play in HALTNORTH'S GARDENS. Four years earlier, both the Kaiser's band and the world-famous Garde Republicaine Band had made tours of the country, but despite the efforts of prominent Clevelanders to get one or both to town on off dates, lack of local financial support had doomed the effort. Also in 1876, Gilmore's Band from Cincinnati came up for a concert performance. The Cleveland Grays had an on-again, off-again romance with bands, both their own and guests. B. B. Schubert had organized the first Grays Band in 1840, but it apparently did not become a perennial organization. Newspaper accounts in the latter half of the century did from time to time mention Grays American Band, or sometimes just Grays Band, each time under a different leader. The inference is that the Grays simply went out and hired the band of the moment for their parades and other functions.

By 1900, Cleveland had grown considerably, and the number of city parks kept pace. Most of them had bandstands for band concerts: EDGEWATER, GORDON, LINCOLN, BROOKSIDE, and WADE were sites of summer concerts. The availability of such locales and a growing population provided the impetus for futher band development in the early years of the century. A major influence in local band growth during the early part of the century was the large influx of Italian immigrants. The ITALIANS brought with them the last great influx of European-trained bandleaders and musicians, many of them with extensive libraries of band music, principally arrangements of the operatic tunes and symphonic music that constituted the heart of the classical music played by bands in Italy. In Cleveland, Angelo Vitale, Frank Russo, August Caputo, and John Rinaldi were not only brilliant instrumental performers but band conductors, as well. Vitale, for example, spent his winters leading theater pit orchestras, and in the summers he conducted Vitale's Band in the various park concerts and parades.

After 1900, band music started to become associated more with national holidays and special celebratory events and less with regular concerts and parades. WORLD WAR I prompted a temporary reflowering of band music to go along with the general uplifting of the patriotic spirit. However, by that time, the armed services had bands of their own, and members were musicians who signed up for the duration. The same was also true in WORLD WAR II. Band music waned after World War I. However, Cleveland's 1936 GREAT LAKES EXPOSITION provided one last major outlet for organized band concerts. The exposition had its own series of band concerts under the direction of a half-dozen leaders, a special band shell having been erected for the purpose. That was the only prominent use of professional bands during the Depression. Not even World War II did more to revive, if only temporarily, Cleveland's professional bands. In 1946, the city of Cleveland sponsored a series of concerts on the Mall by a group called the Cleveland Band. The band was conducted by Leon Ruddick, head of music in the CLEVELAND PUBLIC

SCHOOLS. The Cleveland Band proved so popular that it was continued for several seasons, utilizing the services of guest conductors Angelo Vitale, Al Russo, and August Caputo, by then the elder statesmen of Cleveland bands. The period 1946–86 has shown 2 major developments in local band history. First, it belatedly recognized the validity of professional women musicians. The use of women in musical organizations had started in the late 19th century, but except for a very few in symphony orchestras, harpists usually, women were a rarity in musical life, particularly in professional bands, until after World War II. Second, the period has seen the twilight of professional concert bands, not only in Cleveland but also in the country as a whole. While bands did not disappear all at once, the pre-World War II bandleaders were forced to relinquish their positions because of both age and economic pressures.

The changes seriously affected professional bands. In the 1840s, according to O. V. Schubert, players were paid $3-$4 for a concert or a parade. They could command up to $1 for music lessons, $2 for a house party, and $2.50 for a dance. That provided a living wage. Schubert compared this level of income with that of schoolteachers at $20 a month, accountants at $8 a week, and laborers at $.75 a 7-day week. The relationship of bandsmen's pay to that of other professions was relatively constant throughout the 19th century, although because of the different natures and modes of work, comparisons must, of course, be considered imprecise. In 1986, professional bandsmen earned around $65 for a 2-hour rehearsal plus a 2-hour concert, not really a living wage when one considers that in 1986 a player could not count on as much work as in the 19th century. The size of the wage, however, had grown large enough to preclude the frequent use of professional band music on the part of municipalities or other organizations.

Such concerts as were given in the 1970s and 1980s were often billed as "Old Fashioned Band Concerts" and were a part of the general trend toward nostalgia at that time. The decline in band music in the post-World War II period can also be attributed to technological progress, changes in public taste, and economic shifts. The growth of a variety of forms of family entertainment, for instance, and the increasingly fast pace of contemporary living, in addition to the ever-changing tastes in music on the part of the general public, have cast professional bands into the background. The growth of high school and college bands encouraged their use in public parades and further obviated the need for professional bands. During the 19th century, band music had developed from drum-and-fife bands (5–15 players), to cornet and brass bands (15–20 players), to larger and fuller instrumentation capable of playing adaptations of the most orchestral pieces calling for up to 100 players. By World War II, however, high schools, colleges, and the armed forces were supporting organizations of this size. Local municipalities found it more and more difficult to find the money to pay for anything this large. Psychologically, the affordable 45- to 50-piece professional bands tended to seem rather puny compared with the others, and the glamor of the local professional bands inevitably wore off. What professional band music there has been since 1946 has been due largely to funds won from the phonograph-recording industry by the American Fed. of Musicians. These funds were established in the mid-20th century as a result of the federation's insistence on its members' being remunerated to some extent by the medium that helped wipe out a considerable portion of their work. In Cleveland during the 1980s, it is safe to say that whenever a professional band can be heard in concert or on parade, it is being paid for in large part by money earned by the music-recording industry. The only major reminders of the tremendous role of professional bands in providing local entertainment are the few remaining bandstands in the older small towns, such as Chagrin Falls, that surround the city. Though they still stand, they were, in the 1980s, rarely used relics.

Frank Hruby

See also MUSIC.

**BANG, EDWARD F. "ED"** (28 Apr. 1880–27 Apr. 1968), was sports editor of the *CLEVELAND NEWS* for 53 years of its 55-year existence. Born in Sandusky, Ohio, Bang broke into journalism with the *Sandusky Register*. After further experience in Youngstown, he was hired by the *News* and succeeded Grantland Rice as sports editor in 1907. Bang quickly became an influential figure on the local and national sports scene. A founder of the Baseball Writers' Assoc. of America, he also helped organize the Cleveland Baseball Fed., which sponsored one of the country's foremost sandlot baseball programs. In 1916, he played a persuasive role in the trade that brought outfielder TRIS SPEAKER from Boston to the CLEVELAND INDIANS. During most of his tenure, Bang turned out a daily column under the title "Between You and Me." He assembled a strong sports staff with writers such as Herman Goldstein, ED MCAULEY, and Regis McAuley. His pages promoted such events in Cleveland as professional basketball exhibitions and the 1931 SCHMELING-STRIBLING FIGHT in Municipal Stadium.

Reaching beyond the sports pages, Bang sponsored an annual News Toyshop Fund Boxing Show, which raised $500,000 over a 30-year period to provide Christmas presents for underprivileged youngsters. He was also a founder of the "Round Table," an informal gathering including I. S. (Nig) Rose and Judge SAMUEL H. SILBERT, which met daily at the Statler Grill. Bang retired shortly after the sale of the *News* to the CLEVELAND PRESS in 1960. He died at the Western Reserve Nursing Home in Kirtland and was survived by 2 sons and 2 daughters. His wife, the former Rose Schneider of Sandusky, died in 1950. From 1955–77, members of the Round Table sponsored an "Ed Bang Journalism Scholarship," which was awarded annually in his honor to 2 area high school graduates.

**BANK ONE CLEVELAND NA,** local affiliate of the Banc One Corp., the largest bank holding company in Ohio, was created from the former Euclid Natl. Bank. A relative newcomer to the Cleveland banking environment, Bank One popularized the bank holding company pattern of organization that challenged state laws limiting the geographic domain of banks. The local base of Bank One, Euclid Natl., began in 1953 as the Euclid Savings Assoc. In 1966, the small institution with $45 million in assets was converted to a national bank, under the name Euclid Natl. Bank. In 1975 it became a subsidiary of the Winters Natl. Corp., a small holding company anchored on the Winters Natl. Bank of Dayton, founded by the grandfather of comedian Jonathan Winters. ENB's growth was accelerated in 1976 when it absorbed the 10 Greater Cleveland offices of the Continental Bank, an older but foundering bank. Continental, founded as the Continental Industrial Bank by the Brotherhood of Railroad Trainmen at E. 9th and Superior in 1926, was bought out by businessmen in 1930. It specialized in loans to retail and small business establishments until financial problems resulting from some bad real-estate loans threatened its existence in the early 1970s. After a short-circuited merger attempt with Huntington Bancshares of Columbus in 1971, Continental joined Euclid

Natl. 5 years later. This merger gave ENB $232 million in assets and 17 offices. By 1983, it was the 5th-largest bank in the city owing to its aggressive attempt to win customers through free checking, Saturday banking, and personalized service.

As ENB was expanding within the county, many other banks throughout the state were reorganizing themselves as holding companies to permit even broader expansion. After changes in Ohio state banking law clarified the tax status of holding companies, institutions such as Bank One of Columbus established an umbrella corporation to encompass affiliated banks organized within counties. Established as the First Bank Corp. of Ohio, Inc., in 1967, the new holding company began its acquisition of banks around the state. After 1979, the Banc One Corp., as it was then known, courted Cleveland banks, which were cool to merger attempts. The corporation turned to encirclement tactics and bought up the Chardon Savings Bank, the Lake Natl. Bank of Painesville, and the Bank of Ashtabula to create Bank One Geauga County and Bank One of Northeast Ohio. It then merged with the Winters Natl. Corp. of Dayton, owner of ENB, to gain a Cleveland foothold. The merger made Banc One the largest holding company in Ohio, with $7 billion in assets. The resulting Bank One of Cleveland was itself merged with Bank One Geauga and Bank One of NE Ohio in Jan. 1984, to create a new Bank One of Cleveland with 53 offices in Cuyahoga, Geauga, Lake, and Ashtabula counties. Bank One's entry into Cleveland followed the takeover of the Union Commerce Bank by the Huntington Bankshares Corp.; to counter the Huntington media blitz that ignored the layoffs and management changes resulting from that takeover, Bank One advertising stressed that though the name was changed, the same reliable personnel would offer expanded service. As of the 1985 annual report, the Banc One Corp. owned the outstanding stock in 22 commercial banks operating in 328 locations in 46 counties, with the Columbus bank the largest affiliate.

Note: Variations in spelling of Bank One as Banc One are not typographical errors. The holding company that owns the local bank is Banc One, while the Cleveland bank is Bank One.

The **BANKS-BALDWIN LAW PUBLISHING COMPANY**, located in Cleveland since 1932, is the oldest law publishing house in the U.S. David Banks established the publishing firm of Gould & Banks in New York in 1804 with the encouragement of judges who saw a need for domestically published law books that would be less expensive than those then available from England. After Banks's death in 1871, his sons continued the business, then called Banks & Bros., but in 1880 2 of his sons divided the company; A. Bleecker Banks took over the Albany branch, which became Banks & Co., and his brother David maintained the New York firm as Banks Law Publishing.

In 1923, Wm. E. Baldwin became general manager of Banks Law Publishing. Baldwin earned a law degree in Kentucky in 1913, came to Cleveland as a law-book salesman in 1919, and established his own law publishing firm, the Baldwin Law Publishing Co., in 1920. His company's first publishing venture was to condense the 14 volumes of Ohio laws into 1 book, which was published in 1921 and eventually went through 7 editions; annual supplements recorded changes in the laws. Baldwin maintained his Cleveland firm while he managed the New York company. He became president of Banks in 1926 and merged that company with his own in 1932, moving the new Banks-Baldwin Law Publishing Co. to 3730 Euclid Ave., the former mansion of steel magnate Stewart H. Chisholm. In 1941 the company moved to a stately older home at 1904 Ansel Rd. In addition to publishing the statutes of Ohio and other states, Baldwin himself held copyrights to 500 books he had authored or edited. He remained president of the company until 1960, when he became chairman and Walter H. Drane took over as president. The company employed 30 people in 1966; by 1984 it had grown to 85 employees and had annual sales of more than $3 million.

**BAPTISTS.** The Baptists of Cleveland come from 2 distinct historical traditions, both ultimately derived from English Baptists, and before them from the Anabaptist groups of the Continent. Cleveland's white Baptists developed fairly directly from that tradition, as believers brought the religion from England to New England, and then to western settlements such as Cleveland. What had been a dissenting tradition in England and New England then developed into a religion of the well-established white middle and upper classes in Cleveland. A more circuitous path brought black Baptists and their religion to Cleveland (see BLACKS). The Baptist faith was brought from the South, where it was the product of a faith spread by white and black missionaries and shaped by slaves and, later, former slaves to meet the needs of a discriminated-against minority. As the dominant form of religion among black Clevelanders, the Baptist faith appealed to believers from the top to the bottom of the socioeconomic scale in the black community. Black Baptists maintained a religion more outwardly expressive and pietistic than white Baptists, but shared along with them the characteristic Baptist and evangelical insistence on an affirmation of the regenerating experience of Jesus Christ.

Baptists were a minor presence in the early years of the city. The original church of the denomination was FIRST BAPTIST CHURCH (1833), the 4th-oldest of the churches within the town. It was followed by Erie St. Baptist (1853; also known as Second Baptist Church) and First Baptist Church, Ohio City (1853; also known as Third Baptist Church). These were churches formed by settlers from New England. Black members coexisted uneasily in white Baptist churches in these years. JOHN MALVIN and his wife, Harriet, who were among the founders of the First and Second Baptist churches, successfully resisted efforts to prevent being segregated into a separate gallery. A mission sponsored by First Baptist led in 1849 to the founding of the first black Baptist church, SHILOH BAPTIST CHURCH. With these 4 churches, the Baptists were one of the smaller denominations of the early town. They were outnumbered by the churches of the Roman CATHOLICS (8), CONGREGATIONALISTS (4), EPISCOPALIANS (6), METHODISTS (7), and PRESBYTERIANS (6). The surge in Baptist church founding came after the CIVIL WAR. White Baptists from New England, the mid-Atlantic region, and the Appalachians and black migrants from the South gave the denomination the largest number of churches in the city. In 1929 there were 23 black and 87 white Baptist churches. The next-closest denomination was the Catholic, with 84 churches, while the chief rival for supremacy among the Protestant denominations, LUTHERANS, had 65. The early churches mounted extensive mission campaigns within the city and beyond its borders. More than a dozen churches could trace their origins to First Baptist alone, including Willson Ave. Baptist (1868; later, after a number of relocations and mergers, to become Church of the Master in CLEVELAND HTS.) and Superior Ave. Baptist (1870). Home and foreign missions occupied much of the attention of Cleveland's Baptists in these years. First Baptist and EUCLID AVE. BAPTIST CHURCH sponsored city missions in German, Italian, and Slovak areas. Euclid Ave. Baptist supported 4 missionaries in the South. Most churches also raised money to fund foreign missions. Euclid Ave. Baptist was the most prominent of the Baptist churches after the Civil War, counting among its members leading industrialists and citizens of the city, including JOHN D. ROCKEFELLER. Rockefeller had joined the church as a young man and at various times conducted Sunday school and served as a trustee.

White Baptist churches began moving to the suburbs in the early years of the 20th century, beginning a process that would leave only a handful within the city by the 1970s. First Baptist Church's pilgrimage was typical; it moved from W. 3rd (1836) to E. 9th (1855) to E. 46th (1886), and finally to Cleveland Hts. (1927). The city's black churches grew after the Civil War, particularly during the great migration in the early years of the 20th century. Shiloh Baptist was the largest of these, until, as a result of a schism in 1893, about half the members left to form ANTIOCH BAPTIST CHURCH. By the first decades of the 20th century, Antioch was the largest and most influential black church, with 1,200 members in 1923. Like comparable white churches, it was an institutional church, with recreational facilities and numerous clubs. Its charitable activities were extensive, claiming to have reached 2,000 homes in 1925. Some of the financial support for the churches came from white Baptist churches. John D. Rockefeller matched building-fund contributions for Shiloh Baptist and Antioch Baptist dollar for dollar. During the 1910s and 1920s, the larger black Baptist churches, including Shiloh, Triedstone, Friendship, and Liberty Hill, purchased the buildings of white churches and synagogues that were moving to the suburbs. The architectural evidence was still visible in 1986; the Star of David in the cornerstone of Triedstone Baptist Church, for example, was a reminder of the building's earlier occupants, the Jewish OHEB ZEDEK CONGREGATION. While the great migration of black settlers from the South during the first 2 decades of the 20th century swelled the larger Baptist churches, it also resulted in the creation of many smaller, often storefront, Baptist churches. These congregations reproduced the small scale and fervent piety of the small-town Baptist churches of the South. They attracted lower-income members of the black community, while the larger churches attracted the middle and upper classes.

The early-20th-century growth of white Baptist churches was not as spectacular as that of the black churches, but it was still enough to solidify the Baptists' status as the denomination with the greatest number of churches of any denomination in the area. In 1986 there were 337 churches listed under *Baptist* in the phone book. Catholics trailed with 157, and among the other Protestant groups, Lutherans were next with 98. Approximately ⅓ to ½ of the Baptist churches were black. The next-closest black denomination, the AME, had 14 churches listed. The largest of these Baptist churches was Shiloh Baptist, with 2,800 members, while the largest of the white churches was First Baptist, with about 700. Most of the suburban churches were medium-sized, with 150–500 members. Fifteen of the area's Baptist churches, all in the suburbs, were affiliated with the Southern Baptist Convention. Many of the largest black and white churches were affiliated with the CLEVELAND BAPTIST ASSOC. Of the 40 member churches, 25 were black. The association and its churches were active participants in the GREATER CLEVELAND INTERCHURCH COUNCIL and its social programs. It supported the West Side Ecumenical Ministries and the Inner-City Renewal Society (formerly the Inner-City Protestant Parish). The association was also active in larger centers and peace work. Many of the city's black Baptist ministers belonged to the Baptist Ministers' Conference. The group met weekly and brought together churches from the major national denominational bodies, the American, National, and Progressive Baptist conventions.

Although the city's black ministers were a potent political force, and Martin Luther King, Jr., Day celebrations became staples of black church life, services were little influenced by development in black and liberation theologies. Gospel songs and sermons that stressed the comfort and love of Jesus as a help for one's troubles, the Bible as a moral guide, and endurance as a survival strategy largely dominated the churches. The new message of pride and power was more often seen in church social groups, especially women's groups, and in special programs. Both white and black Baptist churches involved themselves in mission work and social activities in the 1960s and 1970s. The Cleveland Baptist Church, an unaffiliated church of 4,000 members, established outreach ministries in nursing homes, jails, and housing projects, and was active in conservative causes. Other white churches, such as First Baptist, occupied the other end of the political spectrum, joining in the support for improved housing, hunger centers, and missions abroad. Among black churches, Antioch Baptist was particularly active, joining 2 other groups to build the Randle Estates Townhouses, the first church-sponsored low-income housing in the area, and Antioch Towers, which provided housing for senior citizens. The city's black Baptist churches gained national prominence through nurses' programs and gospel music. In the 1930s, women from Mt. Sinai Baptist Church who had begun by assisting members who became ill at services broadened their duties to perform nursing services for the community. Their activity was instrumental in inaugurating the church nurses' movement. In 1945 they were accepted by the Ohio Baptist Convention. Part of the nationally organized Church & Community Health Advocacy Program in 1986, they received training from the Red Cross. A number of the city's choirs received national attention, among them the Prestonians, led by Earl Preston, Jr., minister of Morning Star Baptist Church. The Greater Cleveland Gospel Choir was named the Choir of the Year in 1980 by the Natl. Convention of Gospel Choirs & Choruses.

Michael J. McTighe
Gettysburg College

Beck, Joseph, "The Negro Store-Front Churches and Ministers in Cleveland" (Master's thesis, WRU, 1928).
Cleveland Baptist Assoc., *150 Years of Mission to Greater Cleveland, 1832–1982* (1982).

**BARBER, GERSHOM M.** (2 Oct. 1823–20 July 1903), was an educator, lawyer, and distinguished judge. He was also recognized for his service in the CIVIL WAR, for which he received a brevet commission as brigadier general of volunteers. Barber was born in Groton, N.Y., and came to Ohio at age 7 with his family. He worked on the family farm in Berlin Twp. until the age of 15, when he enrolled at Norwalk Seminary in order to prepare for college. After teaching in Kentucky for a few years, Barber matriculated at Western Reserve College in Hudson. After his sophomore year he was "honorably" dismissed and transferred to Michigan University, where he graduated in 1850. From 1850–56, Barber was a professor of mathematics and languages at Baldwin Institute; the last 2 years he served as principal, in which time he was credited with alleviating the college's debt. He resigned to study law under Samuel B. Prentiss in Cleveland, and was admitted to the bar in 1857. He then embarked on a career in law, within a few years interrupted by the war. A promoter of education, Barber later in life made notable gifts of money and books to such institutions as the Cleveland Law Library. As a Cleveland city councilman from 1872–73, he advocated state schooling, a cause he also worked for outside of politics. Barber entered the Civil War as a 2d lieutenant in Oct. 1862, assigned to the 5th Independent Co. of Ohio Sharpshooters. From Mar. 1863–Apr. 1865 he commanded a battalion of sharpshooters, attaining the rank of captain. He took part in all of the marches and battles of the Army of the Cumberland and was, at one point, attached to the headquarters of Gen. Rosecrans. Toward the war's end, he was promoted to lieutenant-colonel and was assigned to the 197th Ohio Volunteer Infantry. In June and July 1865, Barber served as president of the Military Examining Court under Gen. Hancock. Earlier, in April, he had personally been recommended by Gen. Thomas for a brevet commission of brigadier general. After the war, Barber developed a successful law practice in Cleveland with W. W. Andrews. In 1873, when the 2d Superior Court was created, Barber was one of 3 judges elected. This court was abolished in 1875, wherein Barber was elected to a 5-year term in the common pleas court; he was reelected in 1880. Barber married Huldah Lavinia Seeley in 1851.

**BARBER, JOSIAH** (1771–10 Dec. 1842), the first mayor of OHIO CITY, was a prime mover in west side residential, commercial, and industrial development. In 1809, when the last division of WESTERN RESERVE lands was made in Connecticut, Barber and his father-in-law Samuel Lord and brother-in-law RICHARD LORD received the portion along the western border of the CUYAHOGA RIVER to the lake. They arranged for a survey and sale of lands to settlers in the BROOKLYN section of Cleveland through the Lord & Barber Realty Co. In 1818, Barber constructed a log house at Pearl (W. 25th) and Franklin overlooking the river valley, which he later replaced with the first brick house in Cleveland. To entice settlers, Barber operated a store at Pearl and Lorain. In 1840, he and his partners dedicated a larger portion of land for an open-air market that was the forerunner of the WEST SIDE MARKET. In 1834, Barber was among the incorporators of the CUYAHOGA STEAM FURNACE CO., the first manufacturing concern in Cleveland. By the mid-1830s, Barber was increasingly active in the politics of Brooklyn Twp., which had been incorporated in 1818. Appointed a circuit judge in 1834, he stepped down to become the first elected mayor of Ohio City. Barber was an incorporator of Trinity Parish in downtown Cleveland and St. John's Parish at W. 26th and Church. As the vice-president of the CUYAHOGA COUNTY COLONIZATION SOCIETY, he favored gradual abolition of slavery and the colonization of blacks in Africa or South America.

**BARDONS & OLIVER, INC.,** is one of the chief machine-tool firms in Cleveland. Two former Warner & Swasey officials, Geo. Bardons and John Oliver, founded the firm in 1891 at 3 Walter (W. 9th) St. Originally it manufactured bicycle hubs and the machines to make them. Eventually it became a major manufacturer of turret lathes and parts, special machinery, and pipe and tube mill equipment. In 1895, Bardons & Oliver moved to the corner of Case Ave. and Hamilton. Eight years later, it relocated to its present (1984) site at 1133 W. 9th St. When Bardons died in 1924, John Oliver became the sole owner, and the Oliver family has remained active in the business ever since. In 1936, the firm was incorporated. In 1968, Bardons & Oliver made its only major acquisition, the Boom Boiler & Welding Co., one of the largest fabricators of custom-built industrial equipment in Cleveland. Wm. Birt Boom organized the company in 1915 on Merwin St. and incorporated it 2 years

later. The company divided its work between the manufacture of boilers, tanks, machine bases, and weldments and the repair of machines and metal equipment. Boom was a major repairer of boilers for lake vessel firms. By 1938, its business had grown to a point that it needed to expand from its 1-machine shop on Elm Ave. In 2 plants in the FLATS. By the 1960s, its boiler-repair business had become more seasonal, and it began to turn to space projects. With the addition of the $.5 million business of Boom, Bardons & Oliver's employment increased to 200. Since then, it has maintained annual sales of between $10 and $25 million.

**BARNETT, JAMES** (20 June 1821–13 Jan. 1911), was a distinguished businessman, politician, soldier, and philanthropist. He was noted for his influence in the organization of charitable societies, particularly the Associated Charities of Cleveland. Barnett was born in Cherry Valley, N.Y. His father, Melancthon Barnett, also figured prominently in the business and political interests of Cleveland. In 1825, the elder Barnett moved his family to Cleveland. Barnett attended CLEVELAND PUBLIC SCHOOLS and began his business career as a hardware clerk in the store of Potter & Clark. After 3 years he went to work as a clerk in the store of GEO. WORTHINGTON. He eventually came to serve as president of and was director on the board of the GEO. WORTHINGTON CO. He later was president and director of First Natl. Bank, Natl. Commercial Bank, Merchants Natl. Bank, GUARDIAN SAVINGS, the Big 4 Railroads, and the Cleveland Iron Mining Co. In 1839, Barnett became a member of the artillery section of the city's militia known as the CLEVELAND GRAYS. With the outbreak of the CIVIL WAR, he went to the front as colonel of the CLEVELAND LIGHT ARTILLERY by direct order of Gov. Wm. Dennison. He later opened a recruiting office on Superior St. to encourage enlistment. It was during the war that Barnett developed a keen appreciation for the plight of children left fatherless and homeless by the conflict. In 1862, on a return visit to Cleveland, he opened an office on Bank (W. 6th) St. To help enlisted men find homes for their children. During the war, Barnett distinguished himself by reorganizing the artillery section of the Cleveland Grays into the 1st Ohio Light Artillery. He participated in the key battles of Nashville and Shiloh and was honored with a promotion in rank to general and chief of artillery on Gen. Thos. Rosecrans's staff. He claimed the distinction of having held the highest rank of any soldier from Cuyahoga County who served in the Civil War.

Barnett's political interests materialized in 1856 when he helped organize the Republican party in Cleveland and served as a delegate from the 3d ward. His reputation for strong leadership made him a Union party candidate for waterworks commissioner of Cleveland. Under the Metropolitan Police Act of 1866, Barnett was appointed by Gov. Jacob D. Cox to serve as a police commissioner. At the urging of his party, he ran for city council and served for 2 years, 1873–74. Of his numerous affiliations, Barnett received the most satisfaction from working with Cleveland charities. His concern for children orphaned by war led to his becoming director of the board of managers for the Soldiers' & Sailors' Orphan Home in Xenia, Ohio. Alarmed at the lack of institutional care for war veterans, he was appointed to the board of managers for the Natl. Homes for Disabled Soldiers in 1881. Also that year, the Society for Organizing Charity was created in Cleveland. In 1886 the society merged with Bethel Mission to create the Bethel Associated Charities, the forerunner of the Associated Charities of Cleveland, of which Barnett was honorary president. He had expanded his sphere of influence from relief societies aiding those disabled by war to general relief programs for all persons in need. On 12 June 1845, Barnett married Maria H. Underhill, daughter of an Illinois physician. The Barnetts had 5 daughters. Upon his death, he was survived by his wife and 3 daughters.

Barnett, James, *Reminiscences of the Cleveland Light Artillery* (1906). Jas. Barnett Papers, WRHS.

**BARRICELLI, GIOVANNI ALFONSO** (23 Feb. 1873–16 Apr. 1934), was a cardiopulmonary specialist but is best known as one of the early leaders of the Italian community in Cleveland. Born in Benevenuto, Italy, he attended the University of Naples and completed courses in physics and chemistry. In 1889, at the age of 16, he arrived in the U.S. Barricelli remained in New York City for 8 years after passing his pharmacy examination. During that time, he owned and operated 3 drugstores. He studied medicine at St. Francis College of New York and completed his studies at the University of Illinois in Chicago, where he received his M.D. degree in Nov. 1902. In Cleveland, following postgraduate work in New York, Barricelli opened his cardiopulmonary practice at 419 Woodland SE in the area known as BIG ITALY.

Barricelli originated the Cleveland chapter of the Order of Sons of Italy and was its Grand Commander for a period of time. During WORLD WAR I, he served as a member of the U.S. Volunteer Medical Corps, as head of the Roman Legion in Cleveland, and as chairman of all the Liberty Loan campaigns among the Italians in Cleveland. He was made a Knight of the Crown of Italy for his services rendered to the Allies during the war. He married Orfea Malpezzi, known in Italy and in America as a scholar of philosophy and literature. She died in 1981. The Barricellis had 1 son, John Pierre.

**BARRY, FRANK T.** (9 Feb. 1881–31 Jan. 1956), was a minister, a social worker, and founder and director of Woodland Ctr. Neighborhood House for over 30 years. He was born in Lincoln, Nebr., and spent his boyhood in Topeka, Kans. He graduated from Lake Forest College, Lake Forest, Ill., in 1905; from McCormick Theological Seminary, Chicago, in 1908; and from Northwestern University in 1912. He served as Presbyterian minister in pastorates in Chicago, Evanston, Ill., and Minneapolis, Kans., before coming to Cleveland in 1918 as associate pastor and director of religious education at Woodland Ave. Presbyterian Church, at E. 46th St. and Woodland Ave. When Rev. Joel B. Hayden, the senior minister, resigned to serve FAIRMOUNT PRESBYTERIAN CHURCH in CLEVELAND HTS. in 1923, Rev. Barry became senior minister. During this time, he established and developed Woodland Ctr., a social-settlement house, as part of the church program. He continued to serve both as pastor of the church and as director of the center. In 1925, the congregation of Woodland Ave. united with the congregation of Kinsman-Union Congregational Church at E. 94th St. and Ramona Blvd. To form Woodland Hills Union Church. Rev. Barry was named minister. He continued to serve as director of Woodland Ctr., and under his leadership it expanded its social and recreational programs for people of all ages and of many ethnic backgrounds. At one time it was serving the needs of over 4,000 people in the neighborhood. In May 1938, Woodland Ave. Presbyterian Church was razed to make way for an extension of the Portland-Outhwaite Housing Project, and in Mar. 1941, Woodland Ctr. Neighborhood House, which had been located in an adjoining building, moved into new quarters at E. 71st St. and Kinsman Rd.; subsequently it was called Garden Valley Neighborhood House. Rev. Barry served as pastor of Woodland Hills from 1925–44, and he served Woodland Ctr. until 1948, when he retired and moved with his family to Florida. Rev. Barry married Sarah Prince McArthur in 1908. The couple had 4 children: Mary K. (Mrs. Raymond Gladieux); Dr. Frank McArthur Barry, a Cleveland physician; Martha Isabel (Mrs. Allen Mark); and Rev. David W. Barry. Mrs. Barry died in 1959.

**BASEBALL.** Professional baseball in Cleveland emerged in the late 1860s from the informal amateur baseball circuit that had developed in the area. In 1865, the FOREST CITY BASEBALL ASSOC. was organized to support an amateur team, the Forest Citys, which in 1869 turned partly professional and played its first professional game against the Cincinnati Red Stockings on 2 June. By Dec. 1870, it was apparent to observers that baseball was becoming a business, and stockholders in the club resolved to "organize the very best baseball team that could be secured." The Forest Citys joined the new Natl. Assoc. of Professional Baseball Players in Mar. 1871 and played in that league until forced to drop out in mid-1872 for financial reasons. In 1879, Wm. Hollinger and J. Ford Evans organized another team known as the Forest Citys, which played in the Natl. League through the 1884 season. In 1889, Cleveland fielded another team in the NL: the CLEVELAND SPIDERS, owned by Frank Robison and his brother Stanley, who together owned and operated the horse-drawn trolley system in Cleveland. Led by a local farm boy named Denton True "Cy" Young, the Spiders won the 1895 "pennant," then known as the Temple Cup, by winning 4 of 5 playoff games from Baltimore; they lost the cup to Baltimore in 4 straight games the following year. But these glory days had ended by 1899, when the Robisons shuttled the team's talented players to their NL team in St. Louis, and the Spiders finished the season 20–134. Cleveland fans stopped attending games, and many scheduled home games were switched to other cities. Cleveland was one of 4 teams eliminated by the NL at the end of the 1899 season.

When Ban Johnson laid the foundations for the new American League in 1900, he found 2 Cleveland businessmen ready to finance a franchise in the Forest City: Chas. W. Somers, who was in the coal business with his father, and John F. Kilfoyle, owner of a men's furnishings store (see CLEVELAND INDIANS). Somers had lots of ready cash, much of which went not only to finance the Cleveland team but to support other teams, as well. In 3 years, Somers bankrolled the new league, its teams, and its players to the tune of nearly $1 million. Somers and Kilfoyl brought professional baseball back to Cleveland, but the arrival in 1902 of second baseman NAPOLEON LAJOIE signaled the return of exciting baseball. Probably the greatest player of his time, Lajoie attracted the largest weekday baseball crowd in the city's history soon after his arrival, and in 1903 the team took the name "Naps" in his honor. The enthusiasm increased in 1908, when the Naps, then managed by Lajoie, finished 2d, beaten out by ½ game on the last day of the season. But the heady years under Lajoie ended in 1914, as the team performed badly (51–102) and fan interest waned. Lajoie faded at the end of the season and was released. But in no sense was baseball dead in Cleveland. The amateur competition that had spawned the pro game in the last half of the 1860s expanded and became more vigorous in the next 50 years. In 1910, the Cleveland Amateur Baseball Assoc. was formed to bring greater organization to amateur baseball in the area. As the performance of the local pros became less appealing to fans, they turned out to see amateur baseball in record numbers. Games at Brookside Park Stadium regularly drew 6,000–8,000 fans, and special games attracted audiences of 80,000–100,000 to the natural ampitheater.

In 1915–16, major changes set Cleveland's professional team on a new course. Somers was nearly $2 million in debt, and bankers advised him to sell the baseball team in order to save his other business interests. AL president Ban Johnson arranged the sale to several of his Chicago friends, led by Jas. C. Dunn, partner in a railroad construction firm, for $500,000. The team took on a new nickname, the Indians, and signed a player who would figure prominently in its future success: TRISTRAM (TRIS) SPEAKER. The 1920 season for the Cleveland Indians was a story of triumph born of tragedy. In August, star shortstop RAY CHAPMAN was hit in the head by a pitched ball and died the same day of a crushed skull. Although Cleveland fans reportedly were too deep in grief about Chapman's death to care what happened in the pennant race, by October they at last had what they had hoped for since 1901—a pennant and World Series winner. Playing the Brooklyn Dodgers in a best-of-9 World Series, the Indians lost 2 of the first 3 games in Brooklyn but returned home to LEAGUE PARK and won 4 straight to win the Series. Cleveland fans had many heroes from the 1920 World Series, as they witnessed Speaker's great fielding, STANLEY COVELESKI's 3 victories, and 2 "firsts" in World Series history: the first unassisted triple play, by Bill Wambsganss; and the first grand-slam home run, by Elmer Smith. In 1931, the city finished construction on the new CLEVELAND MUNICIPAL STADIUM, and in 1932 the Indians played 31 games there. The new stadium brought baseball fans downtown, where the new owners of the Tribe had numerous business interests. In 1927 the team had been purchased for $975,000 by a group of prominent Clevelanders: John Sherwin, Sr., Percy Morgan, NEWTON D. BAKER, JOSEPH C. HOSTETLER, and 2 sets of brothers: Chas. and ALVA BRADLEY, and O. P. and M. J. VAN SWERINGEN. Reporters hailed the return of ownership to Clevelanders, claiming that the team would now be operated as a "civic enterprise" as well as a business venture.

A new era for Indians baseball arrived in 1936 with the debut of a 17-year-old pitcher from Van Meter, Iowa. Bob Feller made his first major-league start on 23 Aug. 1936, striking out 15 St. Louis Browns, 1 short of the AL record; 3 weeks later he struck out 17 Philadelphia Athletics at League Park. In the first night game at the lakefront stadium, 27 June 1939, 53,305 fans watched Feller pitch a 1-hit shutout and strike out 13 Detroit Tigers. He opened the 1940 season by pitching the first opening-day no-hitter in major-league history. Behind Feller's pitching exploits, the Indians were exciting and competitive, finishing the 1940 season just 1 game out of first place. Clevelanders were interested in more than just professional baseball, however. The city has long claimed to be the "Sandlot Capital of the World." The Cleveland Baseball Fed. (formerly the Cleveland Amateur Baseball Assoc.), in cooperation with the city's Recreation Dept., has been the major force in promoting baseball as a summer pastime for men and boys. In 1938, the amateur sport received a boost when night sandlot baseball was introduced. Also in the late 1930s, I. S. "Nig" Rose, active for years in the Baseball Fed., took the lead in the formation of the Cleveland Municipal Softball Assoc., which adopted baseball rules and streamlined the game to make it more exciting for spectators and players. Amateur baseball and softball continue to be extremely popular summer pastimes, attracting thousands of players and spectators.

During the 1940s, Cleveland supported 2 professional teams: the Indians and the CLEVELAND BUCKEYES of the Negro American League. A series of teams in the Negro baseball leagues called Cleveland home for brief periods in the 1920s and 1930s, but the Buckeyes lasted the longest and were the most successful. But the Cleveland team attracting most of the attention in the late 1940s was the Indians, who were transformed into an exciting winner by a 32-year-old ex-Marine from Chicago named Bill Veeck, who put together a syndicate and bought the team in June 1946 for $1.5 million. A master showman and promoter, Veeck talked of "giving the Indians back to the fans" and attracted paying customers with strolling bands, fireworks displays, and orchids and nylons for the ladies. But he also put together a team of talented baseball players, one of whom was a 22-year-old rookie named Larry Doby. Doby had played for the Newark Eagles of the Negro League and in 1947 made his debut in the AL, becoming its first black player.

In 1948, euphoric Cleveland baseball fans witnessed their greatest triumph to date. At the lakefront Municipal Stadium, the Indians established new major-league records for the largest crowds at a single game, doubleheader, night game, and opening-day game, and for a season: 2,620,627 fans. Cleveland fans cheered many heroes during that wild and dramatic season. The Indians defeated the Boston Braves 4–3 in Boston to win the 6th and final game of the World Series; shortly after dawn the next morning, a crowd estimated at over 300,000 lined the entire 5-mi. length of EUCLID AVE. from UNIVERSITY CIRCLE to PUBLIC SQUARE to await the team's motorcade. The next year was Veeck's last in Cleveland; he experienced personal financial difficulties and sold the team for $2.2 million to a syndicate headed by Ellis Ryan and Hank Greenberg. The Indians continued to play outstanding baseball, but for the next 5 seasons they finished in 2d place behind the New York Yankees. The Indians returned to glory in 1954, amassing a record 111 victories for a pennant triumph over the Yankees behind perhaps the greatest pitching staff of all time. On 12 Sept., the Tribe took a doubleheader from the Yankees, shattering all Yankee hopes for a 6th straight pennant in front of the largest regular-season crowd in organized baseball history (84,587). But the 1954 season was tarnished somewhat with the disappointing loss of 4 straight World Series games to the New York Giants, and attendance in 1954 was nearly a million less than in 1948.

The Indians organization then embarked on several decades of instability. In Feb. 1956, local businessman Wm. R. Daley and Ignatius A. O'Shaughnessy bought the Tribe for $3.96 million. Despite the addition of new stars such as Herb Score and Rocky Colavito, performance and attendance lagged: in 1959, attendance dropped below 1 million for the first time since Veeck had come on the scene. In 1958, Cleveland baseball fans witnessed what would become a common pattern for the next 3 decades: shrinking crowds; threats to move the team to other cities; campaigns by business, civic, and political leaders to sell tickets and save the "civic enterprise" and maintain the city's image; and owners' claims that they kept the Indians in Cleveland, despite financial hardihps, out of "civic loyalty." The Indians enjoyed a revival in 1959, finishing in 2d place, 5 games out. But on 17 Apr. 1960, general manager Frank Lane traded the beloved Rocky Colavito to the Detroit Tigers after Colavito had hit 41 and 42 home runs in the 2 previous seasons. The Tribe changed hands again in Nov. 1962; a 19-man syndicate that included VERNON STOUFFER, Thos. J. Burke, F. J. O'Neill, and Gabe Paul paid $6 million for the team. By 1964, there was again talk of a possible move to another city, and the team's 5th-place finish was typical in the 1960s. To end the threats of a move, Vernon Stouffer bought control of the Indians in Aug. 1966; the team was then valued at $8 million. In 1968, city hall unveiled a proposal for a domed stadium, and backers predicted that the new sports palace might be ready in less than 3 years. Attendance at the stadium fell to 619,970 in 1969 as the team finished in last place. Stouffer turned down several offers to sell the club to out-of-town owners, but by 1972 a plan was in the works to have the Tribe play some "home" games in New Orleans. That plan was abandoned in Mar. 1972 when Stouffer sold the team for $9.7 million to a group of local investors headed by Nick Mileti. Mileti's ownership was an eventful one: it included a players' strike in 1972; an extremely unruly crowd and a forfeited game on Beer Night ($.10 a glass) on 4 June 1974; and major-league baseball's first black manager, Frank Robinson, who managed the Indians from 3 Oct. 1974 until he was fired on 19 June 1977. The Indians continued to play poorly during the 1970s, finishing above .500 only twice. In Feb. 1978, amid more rumors of an impending move, FRANCIS JOSEPH (STEVE) O'NEILL became the principal owner of the Indians.

In the 1980s, young Clevelanders had only the recollections of their elders to remind them of the grand tradition of Cleveland baseball, a tradition that had seen 14 future Hall of Famers earn their honors with Cleveland teams: pitchers DENTON TRUE (CY) YOUNG (with Cleveland 1890–98 and 1909–11, elected to the Hall of Fame in 1937), ADRIAN C. JOSS (1902–10, elected 1978), Stanley Coveleski (1916–24, elected 1969), Bob Feller (1936–56, elected 1962), Early Wynn (1949–57, elected 1971), Bob Lemon (1941–58, elected 1976), and the legendary black hurler LEROY (SATCHEL) PAIGE (1948–49, elected 1971); second baseman Napoleon Lajoie (1902–1914, elected 1937); shortstops Lou Boudreau (1938–50, elected 1970) and Joe Sewell (1920–30, elected 1977); and outfielders JESSE BURKETT (1891–98, elected 1946), Tris Speaker (1916–26, elected 1937), Elmer H. Flick (1902–1910, elected 1963), and HOWARD EARL AVERILL (1929–39, elected 1975). By 1985, talk of moving the team resurfaced and was countered by new proposals for a domed stadium; the team finished the year in last place (60–102), and its debt had grown to more than $11 million. In 1986, politicians and business leaders again jumped on the baseball bandwagon, and their campaign to sell tickets, aided immeasurably by a talented and exciting young team (84–78, 11.5 games behind), boosted attendance to nearly 1.5 million for the year. Adding to the excitement was the announcement in July that the O'Neill heirs had reached an agreement to sell the team for $35–40 million to Richard E. and David H. Jacobs, local developers who vowed to keep the Tribe in Cleveland. For Tribe fans, a hopeful and patient lot, the "civic institution" that was baseball in Cleveland was still alive and well.

Craig S. Miller

Lewis, Franklin, *The Cleveland Indians* (1949).

The **BASEBALL ALL-STAR GAMES** were held at CLEVELAND MUNICIPAL STADIUM 4 times, more than at any other stadium. The games were played on 8 July 1935, 13 July 1954, 9 July 1963, and 9 Aug. 1981. The 1935, 1954, and 1981 games set All-Star attendance records. The 1981 game was originally scheduled for 14 July but was postponed because of a mid-season players' strike. It was the first game played after the strike was settled. The 1935 game was the third All-Star Game. *Chicago Tribune* sports editor Arch Ward proposed such a game for the 1933 Chicago Century of Progress exposition. Its success and popularity led to its adoption as an annual event. The American League won the 1935 game, 4–1. A crowd of 69,381 watched New York Yankee pitcher Lefty Gomez and Cleveland pitcher

Mel Harder hold the Natl. League to just 4 hits. Gomez pitched the first 6 innings for the victory, and Harder pitched the final 3 to earn a save. Jimmie Foxx of the Philadelphia Athletics drove in 3 runs for the AL, including the game's only home run.

Cleveland's Al Rosen hit 2 home runs and drove in 5 runs to tie an All-Star Game record in the 1954 game, played before 68,751. The AL won the game 11–9, the highest-scoring All-Star Game in history. Washington's Dean Stone was the winning pitcher but did not retire a batter. Coming into the game with 2 on and 2 out in the 8th inning with the NL ahead 9–8, Stone caught the runner on third trying to steal home and threw him out at the plate. Cleveland's Larry Doby tied the score with a pinch-hit home run in the bottom of the 8th, and Chicago's Nellie Fox blooped a single later in the inning to drive in the go-ahead runs. Virgil Trucks pitched the 9th inning, blanking the NL and preserving the victory for Stone.

A disappointing crowd of 44,160 attended the 1963 game. San Francisco's Willie Mays led the NL to a 5–3 victory by driving in 2 runs, stealing 2 bases, scoring twice, and making a spectacular catch against the centerfield fence. The 1981 game was played before 72,086, the largest crowd to witness an All-Star Game. The NL won the game, its 10th consecutive victory, 5–4. All 5 NL runs came as the result of home runs—2 by Montreal's Gary Carter, and 1 each by Philadelphia's Mike Schmidt and Pittsburgh's Dave Parker.

**BASKETBALL.** Unlike other team games that evolved over a long period, basketball was invented to fill a specific need for an easy-to-learn, exciting, inexpensive team sport that could be played in a gym during the winter months. Created in 1891 by Jas. Naismith, physical-education instructor at the Internatl. YMCA Training School in Springfield, Mass., the game gained immediate popularity, spreading through the Ys all over the country. Basketball's growth and popularity in Cleveland paralleled its development in the rest of the Midwest. Basketball was introduced in 1894 at the Cleveland YMCA at E. 9th and Prospect, and by Jan. 1895 teams were organized and intramural games scheduled. In the early 1900s, basketball teams had been formed in local high schools, colleges, settlement houses, churches, shops, and businesses, as well. A Y-sponsored amateur basketball league was formally organized in 1906–07 with 8 teams, each of which had a representative on the league's executive committee, and the organization was made permanent the following year.

Each team was limited to 8 players, and all league participants had to be members in good standing of either the Athletic League of the YMCA or the Amateur Athletic Union, which had been founded in 1888 to supervise and promote amateur sports outside of high schools and colleges. Admission to the games was by free ticket or Y membership, a method introduced to control the size and rowdiness of the crowd. AAU basketball rules governed all games, and the two game officials were paid $.50 each per game. These organizational moves brought Cleveland in line with other YMCAs in the country. Citywide, however, only a few amateur teams played in leagues; most teams were informal aggregations with games arranged on a casual basis. Organized amateur basketball began to grow in 1915 with the formation of the Old Boys' Workers Group, made up of teams from YMCAs, SETTLEMENT HOUSES, and municipal (Muny) recreation centers.

Basketball spread throughout the nation's colleges in the late 1890s. The International Athletic Assoc. of the U.S., later the National Collegiate Athletic Assoc., assumed charge of the college rules in 1908. The first recorded basketball games played by Western Reserve University were in the 1897–98 season. In these early days, colleges scheduled games with whatever team was available, including high schools, Ys, and athletic clubs. Other local collegiate teams were fielded by German Wallace (1905) and Case Institute (1911). High school basketball developed about the same time in Cleveland. A team representing CENTRAL HIGH SCHOOL apparently played basketball at the YMCA in 1901, and the following year the team was part of a Y league. Regulation of Cleveland's high school athletic programs began in Dec. 1904 with the founding of the Senate league made up of Central, Collinwood, East, East Technical, Glenville, John Adams, Lincoln, South, West, and West Technical. Three years later, high school basketball came under the jurisdiction of the Ohio High School Athletic Assoc. Basketball and football were the most popular high school sports, and the proceeds from these games made the sports self-supporting.

Although Naismith had tried to devise a game that would eliminate the roughness of football, both players and fans contributed to the disorder that frequently accompanied basketball games. In Cleveland, the YMCA became disenchanted with the roughness of the game in 1900, when the annual formation of leagues was "not urged," and an editorial in the Y monthly magazine deplored the excessive enthusiasm for the game evident in many cities. In the close quarters of a gym, it was difficult for two officials to enforce the rules of the game, and they suffered abuse from both players and partisan fans. The Cleveland Y's ticket policy did help control the attendance at the games.

With the game's popularity came the realization that money could be made from the sport, and professional basketball teams were formed, touring the country playing all comers. The Buffalo Germans, considered the best professional team in the country at the time, were challenged by the Columbias of Cleveland in Feb. 1909. Unfortunately, the local team lost the game, 70–22. The early professional teams were disbanded with America's entry into World War I. Beginning in the 1920s, there was an upsurge of spectator interest in sporting events. Sports, which formerly had been player-centered almost exclusively, were being redesigned for consumer enjoyment. Professional basketball introduced an exciting, high-scoring, fast-paced, running style of play that eventually reached all levels of the game. The New York Celtics, an independent touring pro team, came to Cleveland's newly built public hall in the winter of 1922–23, playing to a capacity crowd and introducing the pivot play, which was in turn copied by the local amateur leagues. With its seating capacity of close to 12,000, the Public Hall was well suited to basketball events, which consisted of a main attraction, usually a game between popular professional or college teams, with preliminary games often featuring outstanding local amateur teams.

Cleveland developed a large and successful amateur basketball program, which served as a model for other cities to follow. The Muny leagues under the direct supervision of the city were formed in 1920, and in 1929 the Greater Cleveland Basketball Commission was formed to monitor the amateur basketball program. Whereas there had been a half-dozen teams in the early days, by 1935 there were approximately 1,000 teams for men, women, and teens. The backbone of amateur sports in Cleveland was the system whereby a firm or an individual would outfit a team with his or her name displayed on the back of the uniform, thereby gaining advertising and, in the event the team was successful, additional publicity. This practice did not compromise the teams' amateur standing with the AAU, which organized a branch here in 1931.

Collegiate basketball schedules became more standardized, with noncollegiate opponents gradually eliminated. Local rivalry was promoted with the formation of the "Big 4," an informal grouping of WRU, Case, John Carroll, and Baldwin-Wallace, established in the 1930s. With the growing number of high schools, the Cleveland Senate expanded in 1936, adding Jas. Ford Rhodes, John Hay, and John Marshall, and Benedictine, Cathedral Latin, Holy Name, and St. Ignatius, which previously had played in the Catholic league. An East Senate and West Senate were created, and the division winners played each other for the city basketball championship beginning in 1938.

The spectator orientation of basketball in the 1920s led to the formation of the American Basketball League in 1925, the first national professional basketball league in the country. The ABL standardized the rules of the game, which had varied from region to region; and, to prevent roster jumping, clubs were permitted to sign players to exclusive contracts. One of the leaders in establishing the league was MAX ROSENBLUM, owner of the Cleveland Rosenblums. His club won the first league championship, defeating the Brooklyn Arcadians 2 out of 3 games in the playoff. In the second year of the league's operation, the Celtics joined the ABL, dominating it so thoroughly the next 2 seasons that attendance declined and 3 teams folded. To equalize the competition, the ABL disbanded the Celtics, distributing the players to the remaining teams. The Cleveland Rosenblums acquired 3 former Celtics and won the next 2 championships. Attendance at the ABL games dwindled with the onset of the Depression, and the Cleveland team was forced to withdraw from the league in Dec. 1930. Losses mounted, and the ABL ceased to be a national circuit at the end of the 1930–31 season. The Cleveland Rosenblums continued to play touring pro teams during the 1930s, including the New York Renaissance, an all-black team featuring Clevelander Wm. T. (Wee Willie) Smith, who was inducted into the Natl. Basketball Hall of Fame in 1963.

Women's amateur basketball in Cleveland, played according to men's rules, began as early as 1918, and by the 1930s there were several women's amateur and industrial leagues. Locally the Newman-Stern girls' basketball team won the world championship in 1926, defeating the Edmonton, Alberta, Commercial Graduates. Two of their 4 games were played in Cleveland as preliminary contests to the Rosenblum-Arcadian matchup. Women's high school and collegiate basketball in Cleveland pursued a different course. Influenced by the Natl. Sec. on Women's Athletics of the American Physical Education Assoc., an anticompetitive athlete-centered program was adopted stressing intramural sports and a broad participation open to all girls. Basketball was generally played according to girls' rules, producing a slower, less strenuous game.

The coming of WORLD WAR II restricted amateur and collegiate as well as professional basketball, which was now represented by the Natl. Basketball League. As players and teams became scarce after 1941, the NBL was reduced to 3 teams, and in 1943 the Cleveland Chase Brass & Copper basketball team, an outstanding local amateur group, joined the league. In spite of the scoring of their best player, Mel Reibe, the Cleveland team was clearly outclassed. The next 2 seasons, the Cleveland entry was the Allmen Transfers; however, they left the league at the end of the 1945–46 season.

In the post-World War II era, basketball continued its popularity on the amateur, high school, and collegiate level, and a full-fledged professional basketball program developed. The competitive consumer-oriented game became more intense and remained so with the introduction of nationally televised games. The increased competitiveness of college basketball reached a crisis point with the basketball point-shaving scandal in 1951, when 33 players when accused of accepting money to keep the number of points between the winning and losing score within a range called for by gamblers. The NCAA, bowing to the reality of widespread recruiting violations, decided in 1952 to permit awards of full scholarships based solely on athletic ability, a key in the separation of sports from academic concerns. In contrast to this national development, athletics, including basketball, remained an integral part of the academic programs at Greater Cleveland colleges. In 1955, WRU, Case, and John Carroll helped form the President's Athletic Conference. Governed by the presidents of the member institutions, the PAC prohibited athletic scholarships, and student participants were required to report all sources of income to finance their college education. Case Western Reserve University withdrew from the PAC in 1983 to help found the North Coast Conference, which offered a conference program of both men's and women's varsity sports. Basketball, whether played in the PAC, the North Coast Conference, or the Ohio Conference, to which Baldwin-Wallace belonged, was noncommercial and athlete-centered. At CLEVELAND STATE UNIVERSITY (formerly Fenn College), basketball was the major sport, and CSU in recent years has developed the most extensive basketball program in the area. As a Div. I team in the NCAA, it plays basketball on a national major college level. CSU together with 7 other schools formed the Assoc. of Mid-Continent Universities in 1982.

High school basketball in the post-World War II era reflected the faster-paced, high-scoring game that had become popular. Players had greater physical abilities and were more skilled at playing the game. During this time, East Technical High School won the state championship 3 times, and CATHEDRAL LATIN SCHOOL won the state Class AA crown in 1977. In 1954 and 1956, the state high school basketball championships were held at the Cleveland Arena. With the coming of desegregation in 1979, the Cleveland Senate, now made up of Cleveland schools only, was realigned into North and South divisions.

Although the CLEVELAND REBELS and the CLEVELAND PIPERS played professional basketball briefly, the professional game was not a consistent part of the Cleveland scene until the CLEVELAND CAVALIERS were organized and admitted to the Natl. Basketball Assoc. in 1970. Their tenure in Cleveland has been the longest the area has had.

Varsity girls' basketball using boys' rules developed in the schools and colleges during the 1960s. Locally, women's teams representing John Carroll, Baldwin-Wallace, CWRU, Notre Dame, Ursuline, and Tri-C West were among those playing intercollegiate schedules in the early 1970s. Title IX passed by Congress in 1972 outlawed sexual discrimination by school districts or institutions. In order to comply with the law, Greater Cleveland school systems developed varsity girls' basketball programs.

In Cleveland as elsewhere, basketball's popularity was assured because it filled a need for an inexpensive, exciting, easy-to-learn winter sport. Its introduction and development through the Cleveland YMCA followed the national trends occurring at the time. During the post-World War II era, collegiate basketball here remained for the most part athlete-centered, in contrast to the commercialization characteristic of some collegiate basketball elsewhere. Locally the highly skilled, consumer-oriented, competitive basketball was played on the professional level.

Mary B. Stavish
Case Western Reserve University

Hiram House Papers, WRHS.
YMCA Papers, WRHS.
Case Western Reserve University Archives.

**BATH HOUSES** were opened in Cleveland at a time when the population density of city housing exceeded available bathing facilities. Humanitarians who promoted cleanliness and Americanism first made public showers available to neighborhood patrons of HIRAM HOUSE, a settlement opened in 1896. Amid rising concern for public health, City Councilman FREDERIC C. HOWE and others argued for the establishment of public baths throughout the city. He was appalled to find that in a district of 4,500 people, only 8 buildings had any type of bathing facilities. The few buildings with tubs often used them as coal bins or storage compartments because the residents had no money to buy coal to heat the water necessary to bathe.

By 1904, a 3-story public bath house was constructed at 1609 Orange Ave., a former Hiram House property. The bath house offered soap and towel plus a bath or shower for $.02. The Orange Ave. Bath House, run by the city, cost $28,000 to build and contained 49 bath compartments, 2 tubs for invalids, 26 showers, 2 open shower rooms, a gymnasium, and a laundry for the towels. Classes in wrestling, fencing, and boxing were held there, as were club meetings. The success of the Orange Ave. Bath House led to the opening of the Broadway Bath House in 1906 and the Clark Ave. Bath House in 1908, followed by 5 others modeled on Orange Ave. Ultimately, the price climbed to $.05 and then $.10 for laundering towels and staffing the houses. Some houses added swimming pools to attract more people. By 1929, only 2 of the baths were used exclusively for bathing; over 3,000 bars of soap and hundreds of towels lay in the property rooms. Revenues fell, even in the Depression. Headlines in 1941 proclaimed the bath trade "washed up" despite 3 million baths having been recorded the previous year, and all but the Broadway facility were razed or converted to other uses.

In 1954 the cost to operate the Broadway Bath House averaged $10 per bath, and the city decided to level the structure for a parking lot. Some neighborhood organizations protested that the baths still served the elderly, ill, and transient population. The city welfare director countered that the users could be sent to Turkish baths more economically, and the facility was closed as a result of the widespread availability of in-home bathtubs. Also considered as bath houses were the GORDON PARK and Edgewater Park Beach bath houses. These, however, were intended for changing before swimming. Ironically, they met a similar fate to that of the public bath houses, as swimmers began changing into their suits at home.

**BAUDER, LEVI F.** (28 Jan. 1840–1 Oct. 1913), was a Civil War soldier, a civic official, and permanent secretary of the Soldiers & Sailors Monument Commission. Bauder was born in Cleveland and graduated from CENTRAL HIGH SCHOOL in 1858. He studied at Oberlin College and taught school in Pickaway County until the CIVIL WAR broke out. He enlisted in the Sprague Cadets, which became Co. B, 7TH OHIO VOLUNTEER INFANTRY, on 20 July 1861. He was promoted to 1st sergeant from sergeant on 30 Sept. 1863. During the Chattanooga, Tenn., campaign of 1863, he served as a company commander, although he was never promoted to the rank of captain. He was mustered out with the 7th Ohio in Cleveland on 6 July 1864. After the war, Bauder married, practiced law, and served as Cuyahoga County auditor, 1877–83, and as justice of the peace, 1886–92. He maintained the records of the Soldiers & Sailors Monument Commission for 15 years. He resided at W. 20th St. at the time of his death. Bauder married Elizabeth Page in 1866. They had 5 children.

William P. Palmer Manuscript Collection, WRHS.

The city of **BAY VILLAGE** lies along the Lake Erie shore at the western edge of Cuyahoga County. Occupying 4.5 sq. mi., it borders the cities of ROCKY RIVER on the east, WESTLAKE on the south, and Avon Lake (Lorain County) on the west. It was incorporated as the village of Bay on 1 May 1903 and achieved city status in 1950. The name Bay Village was decided by ballot in a 1951 election. Bay Village was originally a portion of Dover Twp., formed in 1803, the same year that Cuyahoga County was created. The first permanent white settlers, the JOSEPH CAHOON family, arrived and settled on original lot No. 95 on 10 Oct. 1810. Cahoon built the first gristmill west of the CUYAHOGA RIVER in 1813. In the post-Civil War era, affluent Clevelanders began to look upon the shoreline of Lake Erie north of Dover Twp. as a suitable area to build summer homes and cottages. Dover Twp. flourished, but landowners felt cheated by township officials because of a lack of representative government. In 1901, residents gathered enough support to force an election, which resulted in the creation of Bay Village (also referred to as N. Dover). The area around Bay Village was never extensively used for farming. FISHING was an important industry until the late 19th century, as were vineyards and apple and peach orchards. In the early 20th century, the trend toward suburban homebuilding began encroaching upon the family farms. Bay became noted as a closely knit residential community that was highly interested in civic, social, and cultural advancement. Today, Bay Village has only 2 industries: a small machine-fabricating plant and a processing plant for food toppings. Commercial establishments are concentrated in 2 shopping centers. Population has grown from 450 in 1910, to 3,700 in 1940, to 17,846 in 1980. Recreational facilities include a municipal swimming pool, Clague Park, Huntington Park of the Metroparks System, and Cahoon Park, donated to the city in 1917 from the estate of Ida Marie Cahoon.

The **BAY VILLAGE HISTORICAL SOCIETY** was established in 1960 during the sesquicentennial celebration of Bay Village. A proposal had been made for the creation of a local historical society 50 years earlier by several area pioneers, including Reuben Hall and the Cahoon sisters. In 1973, the society was named manager of Rose Hill, the Cahoon family property located at 21715 Lake Rd., by the city of Bay Village. With funds provided by the city council, the society restored the property as a museum, in which furnishings and artifacts, primarily from the Cahoon family, were used to illustrate the community's history. A small research library was also housed at Rose Hill. In 1984, the society had nearly 200 members. Operated by volunteers, the organization operated the museum, sponsored the placement of landmark plaques on century homes, and hosted various historical programs. Revenues were derived from memberships and the proceeds of fundraising events such as an annual flea market.

**BAYERISCHER MAENNERCHOR**, sometimes referred to as the Bavarian Men's Choir, is one of several local German singing groups from the 19th century still in existence in 1986. The choir was formed on 20 Oct. 1893 with 70 charter members. During its history, it has performed widely, has held membership in several local and state singing societies, and has functioned as a social club for members as well as a singing group.

**BEACHWOOD** is a city located 10 mi. east of Cleveland and bounded by S. EUCLID and LYNDHURST on the north, SHAKER HTS. and UNIVERSITY HTS. on the west, WARRENSVILLE TWP. on the south, and PEPPER PIKE on the east. It occupies approximately 4.6 sq. mi. and was originally a part of Warrensville Twp. In 1915, a group of merchants, tradesmen, and farmers from the northeastern part of the township petitioned for permission to withdraw from the township. On 15 June 1915, the proposal passed, and on 26 June 1915, Beachwood Village was incorporated. In 1930, an unusual private cooperative subdivision was begun by Mrs. Dudley Blossom at Cedar and Richmond roads. Although much of Beachwoood's early history was characterized by boundary disputes, annexation disagreements, lack of funds, school reorganizations, and zoning problems, it grew substantially after WORLD WAR II. In 1960, Beachwood became a city, a residential community of homes, apartments, condominiums, schools, churches, synagogues, sports and recreational facilities, shopping centers, and many civic, cultural, and service organizations, as well as business associations. Accessibility to UNIVERSITY CIRCLE, to downtown Cleveland via rapid transit, and to interstate highways I–271, I–480, and I–90, as well as the Ohio Turnpike, contributed to Beachwood's development. Land was subsequently rezoned for limited business and industrial developments, including Corporate Park and Commerce Park Square, the first major office complex in the area. A third major development, Enterprise I in Science Park, was started in 1984. Much of this development was centered on Chagrin Blvd., particularly at its intersections with Green Rd. and Richmond Rd. Despite the growth of this office-industrial corridor, most of Beachwood remained residential. In 1980 its population was 9,983, much of which could be characterized as upper-middle- and upper-class. Its school system consisted of a high school, a middle school, and 3 elementary schools. The suburb was also home to the Cleveland College of Jewish Studies and several other private schools.

**BEARINGS, INC.**, with headquarters in Cleveland at 3600 Euclid Ave., was the country's largest distributor of ball bearings, bearing specialties, and power transmissions in 1986. It operated as a sales, distribution, and service organization, doing no manufacturing. Emphasizing the replacement market, the company in 1984 handled more than 147,000 types and sizes of ball, roller, linear, and thrust bearings through 13 distribution centers and 274 sales branches in 34 states. Bearings, Inc., was founded in 1923 when Joseph Bruening purchased the Cleveland branch of a Detroit-based bearings distributor. Named the Ohio Ball Bearing Co., it was originally located at 6715 Carnegie Ave. At first the company sold mostly automobile and truck replacement parts, but as industry shifted from belt-driven line shafts to individual motors to operate machinery, Bruening began concentrating on industrial customers. After just several years, the increase in business and the number of product lines being handled resulted in the need for larger quarters, and Ohio Bearings moved to 6537 Euclid Ave. In 1986, along with its corporate headquarters, Bearings, Inc., had its finance and control operations at 3950 Euclid and operated a branch office at 3634 Euclid Ave. Ohio Bearings' first branch operation outside of Cleveland was established in Youngstown in 1927, followed by branches in Akron, Cincinnati, and Columbus. Operations then branched out of Ohio with the founding of Indiana Bearings, Pennsylvania Bearings, and West Virginia Bearings. The 4 companies merged in 1952 to establish Bearings Specialists, Inc. The name Bearings, Inc., was acquired in 1953, when Bearings Specialists merged with a small Pennsylvania firm called Bearings, Inc. With the acquisition of Dixie Bearings, Inc., in 1957, Bearings, Inc., entered the southern market. In 1960 it acquired companies in Missouri, Illinois, Tennessee, and Arkansas, with some operations being placed under Dixie Bearings and others forming the subsidiary, Bruening Bearings, Inc. The West Coast division was created with the purchase of 3 companies in 1967 and expanded through another acquisition in 1972. Between 1980–84, Bearings, Inc., under the leadership of John Cunin, acquired additional companies, giving it entry into the New England market and expanding its market in the Southwest. It has also opened 24 new sales offices and has upgraded its employees' salaries and benefits in an effort to reach a sales goal of $1 billion a year by 1988.

**BEATTIE, H. W. & SONS CO.** *See* **H. W. BEATTIE & SONS CO.**

**BEAUMONT FOUNDATION.** *See* **LOUIS D. BEAUMONT FOUNDATION**

**BEAUMONT SCHOOL** traces its roots to the Ursuline Academy, which was founded in 1850. In 1850, Bp. AMADEUS RAPPE requested that URSULINE SISTERS from their community in Boulogne-sur-Mer, France, be sent to staff a school for girls in Cleveland. (Rappe had served as chaplain to their motherhouse in the 1830s before he came to America.) Four nuns, the first to arrive in the WESTERN RESERVE, began the academy, which was opened to 300 girls. It was incorporated to serve both elementary and secondary students in 1854. The school's first location was on the south side of EUCLID AVE., near Erie (E. 9th) St. As Cleveland expanded, a new location was needed. A new building was constructed at Scovill and Willson (E. 55th St.) avenues, with CHAS. F. SCHWEINFURTH as architect, and opened for the start of classes in Sept. 1893. The next major move occurred in 1941. Hard times had beset the Ursulines during the Depression, and it was necessary to sell the academy building and the motherhouse attached to it. The nuns were left without a building for the academy for the upcoming school year. In order to house the 160 nuns who had lived at the motherhouse, boarding students were eliminated from St. Joseph's Seminary and Villa Angela. The order then acquired the Painter estate at Lee and Fairmount in CLEVELAND HTS. The new location was given a new name, the Beaumont School for Girls, in honor of the first superior of the Ursulines in Cleveland. Enrollment in Sept. 1942, when the school reopened, was 100 students. As estate buildings such as an aviary and stables were converted to school use, enrollment grew markedly, to 400 by 1944. In the mid-1950s, a freshman building was added, and a few years later plans were set in motion to add 4 new buildings and triple enrollment to 1,200 students. Enrollment in 1986 was about 500. Beaumont in the 1980s remained much as it had over the previous 40 years. Its emphasis was on college preparation for young women in a Catholic setting. Almost all students continued on to college after graduation. The uniform and discipline code remained strict when compared to those of public schools and other private girls' schools that saw liberalized policies in the 1960s. No serious thought was ever given to coeducation, an issue faced by many single-sex schools in the 1960s and 1970s. Approximately 20% of the student body was non-Catholic.

**BECK, CLAUDE SCHAEFFER** (8 Nov. 1894–14 Oct. 1971), a surgeon active in Cleveland from the 1920s to the 1960s, achieved worldwide recognition for his pioneering contributions in the field of heart surgery and cardiopulmonary resuscitation. Beck was born in Shamokin, Pa. He received his A.B. degree from Franklin & Marshall College in Lancaster, Pa., in 1916, and his M.D. degree from Johns Hopkins University in 1921. He trained as a surgeon at Johns Hopkins, New Haven (Conn.), Peter Bent Brigham (Boston), and Lakeside hospitals; he worked under the tutelage of Dr. HARVEY CUSHING as a surgical research fellow at Harvard in 1923–24. Beck came to Cleveland, where he spent the rest of his professional career, in 1924. He joined the staff of UNIVERSITY HOSPITALS as resident and Crile Research Fellow in Surgery, and in 1928 he was appointed associate surgeon, a position he held until his retirement in 1965. His first faculty appointment at the Western Reserve University School of Medicine was as demonstrator of surgery (1924–25); he attained the rank of professor of neurosurgery in 1940. In 1952, the university created the first professorship of cardiovascular surgery in the U.S. for Beck, a position that he held until 1965.

Beck served as surgical consultant to the 5th Service Command of the U.S. Army from 1942–45, attaining the rank of colonel in the Medical Corps and receiving the Legion of Merit. He belonged to a number of medical and surgical organizations and was among the founding members of some, including the American Board of Surgery and the American Board of Thoracic Surgery. He also published many scientific papers, including monumental work on the effect of an uneven blood supply to the heart. However, Beck made his greatest contributions in the operating room, where his work laid the foundations for the surgical treatment of heart disease. As a young surgeon, he assisted Dr. ELLIOT CUTLER in the first mitral valve operations in the 1920s. He went on to perform the first operations for the surgical treatment of coronary artery disease in 1935; the first successful defibrillation of the human heart in 1947; the first successful reversal of an otherwise fatal heart attack in 1955; and the first successful removal of a heart tumor. Moreover, the work on defibrillation (restoring the regular rhythm of the heartbeat) involved the development of cardiopulmonary resuscitation techniques by Beck and his colleagues. They began offering a course in resuscitation for medical professionals in 1950, featuring experiment and practical exercise on living dogs. Sponsored by the Cleveland Area Heart Society, the course trained more than 3,000 doctors and nurses in less than 20 years. In 1963, a course in closed-chest cardiopulmonary resuscitation for lay persons was added. Beck married Ellen Manning in 1928; they had 3 daughters.

Claude S. Beck Papers, University Hospitals Archives.

**BECK, JOHANN HEINRICH** (12 Sept. 1856–26 May 1924), was a noted conductor, composer, teacher, and violinist. Born in Cleveland, Beck completed his musical education in Europe at the Leipzig Conservatory (1879–82), where he premiered his own String Quartet in C Minor at the Gewandhaus to much acclaim. Returning to Cleveland, he was active in music in the city for many years. His achievements were heralded in many reviews and articles across the nation. He was a solid craftsman who worked with integrity in his field. As a violinist, he was heard frequently in concert. He organized the Schubert String Quartet in 1877 and later the BECK STRING QUARTET, which gave frequent concerts during the 1880s. As a conductor, he directed the Detroit Symphony, 1895–96, and appeared with other important orchestras conducting his own works.

He led the short-lived CLEVELAND SYMPHONY ORCHESTRA, 1900–01. Later, together with EMIL RING, he led other orchestras under various names, preluding the formation of the CLEVELAND ORCHESTRA in 1918.

As a composer, Beck produced an unfinished opera, *Salammbo* (1887–    ), and over a dozen orchestral works, including *Skirnismael*, an unfinished cycle of 5 tone poems (ca. 1887–93), and 6 tone pictures for voice and orchestra (1876–89), also incomplete. The Cleveland Orchestra included his *Lara* overture in a concert on 18 Dec. 1919 at New Masonic Hall to critical acclaim. His chamber works include various piano pieces, songs, choral pieces, 3 string quartets (1877, incomplete), the Quartet in C Minor (1879–80), and the String Sextet in D Minor (1885–86), dedicated to his friend and teacher Henry Schradieck. Violin and cello pieces, an allegro for flute and piano, and various sketches complete his portfolio. Beck's bust now stands at the entry to the Fine Arts Div. of the CLEVELAND PUBLIC LIBRARY, which houses an extensive collection of his manuscripts. Only 1 of his works, the *Elegiac Song* (Op. 4, No. 1), has been published. Walter Logan, in the *Cleveland Weekly Review* of 17 June 1933, noted: "I know of no other Cleveland musician in the past half century that has left so pronounced a mark on the musical progress of Cleveland than has this distinguished violinist and composer." Beck married Mary Blanding Fellar of Tiffin, Ohio, in 1890. They had 1 son, Henry J., and a daughter, Hildegarde.

The **BECK STRING QUARTET** was formed in 1890 by noted Cleveland composer JOHANN BECK. It was one of the forerunners of the Chamber Music Society and contributed immensely to the cultural life of the community. The quartet was first known as the SCHUBERT STRING QUARTET. It had been organized in 1877 and followed an earlier quartet, the Cecilian (after the St. Cecilia Society). The Schubert String Quartet consisted of Johann Beck and Wm. Schramm, violins; J. H. Amme, viola; and Chas. Heydler, cello. Their 1884–85 season at Heard's Hall featured Beethoven, Brahms, and Mendelssohn. They also undertook a tour under the name of the Schubert String Quartette Concert Company, with Jeannie G. Cross plus pianist and musical director J. de Zielinski. On 16 Oct. 1890, the Beck String Quartet gave its first concert in Unity Church, with Beck and Julias Deiss, violins; Benjamin Beck, viola; and Max Droge, cello. They performed Beck's String Quartet in C Minor on 6 Nov. of that same year. Schubert's Piano Trio in B-Flat Major got its first Cleveland hearing in 1891 with Beck, Droge, and pianist JAS. H. ROGERS, and this concert rounded out the last season. They also performed with the German singing societies.

Alexander, J. Heywood, *It Must Be Heard* (1981).
Grossman, F. Karl, *A History of Music in Cleveland* (1972).

**BEDELL, GREGORY THURSTON** (27 Aug. 1817–11 Mar. 1892), was bishop coadjutor of the Protestant Episcopal Diocese of Ohio (1859–73) and third bishop of Ohio (1873–89). He is credited with advocating an Episcopal central cathedral, an idea contributing to the development of Cleveland's TRINITY CATHEDRAL (consecrated 1907). Bedell was born in Hudson, N.Y. He came from a family of Episcopal clergymen. He graduated from Bristol College in 1836 and from the Theological Seminary of Ohio in 1840. Ordained in 1841, Bedell came from New York City to take up his duties as bishop coadjutor. He was, however, no stranger to Ohio, having worked previously as Bp. Chas. McIlvaines's assistant for 14 years. In the early 1870s, Bedell was involved in an evangelical-versus-tractarian dispute

that decimated the administrative, faculty, and student ranks at Bexley Hall, the Episcopal seminary at Kenyon College. He eventually reconciled to high church practices and was able to accept vested choirs, hymn singing, surplices for the clergy, and a cross and flowers on the altar in the chancel. Ill health led to his retirement to New York City in 1889.

The Ohio Episcopal Church faced a crisis between 1881–87. The state's prosperity was not matched by church growth. Bedell took up traveling from parish to parish to counter the slump. He also worked on a plan for financial assistance to the diocese and developed the scheme of an annual parish sermon on the episcopacy and the need to endow it. Earlier (1874) Bedell presided over a statewide convention that divided Ohio into 2 dioceses, the northern 47 counties to be the Diocese of Ohio, the southern counties to be the Diocese of Southern Ohio. During the CIVIL WAR, Bedell, along with Bp. McIlvaine, preached loyalty to the Union and urged the Episcopal clergy to stay out of politics. He was married to Julia Strong. She died in New York City in 1897.

**BEDFORD** is a city located about 12 mi. southeast of downtown Cleveland, bounded by MAPLE HTS. on the northwest, the Bedford Reservation of the CLEVELAND METROPARKS SYSTEM on the southwest, OAKWOOD on the south, and BEDFORD HTS. on the east. It was originally part of Bedford Twp., and the present city comprises about 5.5 sq. mi. Bedford's early history is closely associated with TINKER'S CREEK, a tributary of the CUYAHOGA RIVER, whose rushing waterfall provided power for the settlers' mills and early industries. The first gristmill was erected in 1815; the same year, Benjamin Fitch arrived and began to make splint-bottom chairs, developing the industry that eventually became TAYLOR CHAIR. Bedford was named by Daniel Benedict after his home town in Conn. Bedford Twp. was organized in 1823, and the village of Bedford was incorporated in 1837 as the town of Bedford. The population in 1840 was 2,021. Hezekiah Dunham plotted the town center of the present city. Lots were set aside for a public square, a town hall, and a school. Dunham's own house remained opposite the square in the 1980s. The large Second Empire-style town hall was erected in 1874, and after the dissolution of the township in 1951, it became the home of the BEDFORD HISTORICAL SOCIETY. Bedford was the birthplace of ARCHIBALD M. WILLARD, painter of the *SPIRIT OF '76*, in 1836, and the home of Dr. THEODATUS A. GARLICK, eminent surgeon and scientist. The opening of the Ohio Canal in 1827 and the Cleveland & Pittsburgh Railroad in 1852 encouraged the industrial development of Bedford. In 1864, the 100-ft.-high stone arch railroad viaduct over Tinker's Creek was built, and in 1901 it was largely buried with fill when the railroad line was relocated. In 1881 the Connotton Valley Railroad was opened through Bedford, and in 1895 the Akron, Bedford & Cleveland interurban line was completed, operating until 1932.

Bedford is widely known for its chair-manufacturing industries. The Taylor Chair Co. was founded by Fitch's son-in-law Wm. O. Taylor in 1844 and was incorporated in 1885. The B. L. Marble Co., another maker of fine furniture, was incorporated in 1894. Other Bedford industries included HOLSEY GATES's Bedford Roller Mill (1876–1908), the McMyler-Interstate Co., pioneers in the design, development, and manufacturing of ore- and coal-handling equipment, Owen Tire & Rubber, the Bedford Distillery, and, in the post-World War II period, manufacturers of machine parts, china, and precision instruments. Bedford became a city in 1930. A charter was adopted, and a city manager plan of government became effective in 1932. The population of Bedford in 1940 was 7,390. The village of Maple Hts. had separated from the township in 1915; Bedford Hts., WALTON HILLS, and Oakwood withdrew in 1951, and the township ceased to exist. In the latter part of the 20th century, Bedford had 16 churches, including Catholic, Orthodox, and Protestant denominations. The Vincentian Sisters of Charity came to Bedford in 1928, and their Villa San Bernardo was erected in 1932.

Hubbell, Ned, *Life in Bedford* (1971).

**BEDFORD HEIGHTS** is a 7-sq.-mi. residential-industrial community located approximately 14 mi. southeast of Cleveland and bounded by BEDFORD and MAPLE HTS. on the west, SOLON on the east, OAKWOOD on the south, and WARRENSVILLE HTS. on the north. It was originally a part of Bedford Twp., named after Bedford, Conn. Its early history is synonymous with that of Bedford, a largely agricultural area with many dairy farms. In 1951, the village withdrew from the township and became the village of Bedford Hts. The village grew industrially, partly because of its proximity to the industrial area southeast of Cleveland and partly because of its location at the cross-roads of interstate highways I–271 and I–480 and the closeness of other highways, including I–71, I–70, I–90, and the Ohio Turnpike. In 1958, the voters approved a municipal charter creating a mayor-council form of government. On 4 Jan. 1961, Bedford Hts. became a city. In 1966, Mrs. Lucille J. (Donald) Reed was elected one of the first women mayors in Cuyahoga County, and a park and recreation area were named in her honor. The Bedford Reservation, one of the Cleveland Metropolitan Parks, is also located in Bedford Hts. The city is a community with a variety of homes, condominiums, apartments, schools (which are part of the Bedford School System), modern recreational facilities, industries, and warehouse facilities, as well as numerous churches, clubs, and civic organizations.

The **BEDFORD HISTORICAL SOCIETY** is an organization dedicated to the preservation of history of the original Bedford Twp. Its primary concerns are the management of the Bedford Historical Society Museum and the restoration and preservation of Bedford Commons. The society was organized in 1955. Its continuing focus is on the history of Bedford Twp., which originally included the present cities of BEDFORD, BEDFORD HTS., and MAPLE HTS. and the villages of OAKWOOD and WALTON HILLS. It opened in 1957 in a vacant classroom at Central Elementary School. In 1961 it was incorporated as a nonprofit organization to be governed by a 15-member board of directors. The museum was started in 1959 by Richard Squire and Wm. M. Jacka. As collectors of local historical relics, both men contributed to the museum's early collections. Squire has been the museum's director since its beginning. In 1963, for a token payment of $10, the society purchased the old Bedford Town Hall, built in 1874; $40,000 was spent on its restoration. The museum moved into the newly restored building, and over the next 2 decades it built up its collections. By 1982 these included a china and glass exhibit; the Willard Room, with a large woodcarving of Archibald Willard's *Spirit of '76*; Civil War material; the Jacka 1876 Centennial Medallic Collection; the Leonard Siegel Railway Collection; period room settings; and various paintings, prints, and lithographs. In addition to the museum, the society is dedicated to the upkeep of the historical Bedford Commons on the city's public square. It includes a gazebo, the Bedford Baptist Church, the old Wheeling & Lake Erie depot and tracks, and several war memorials. The society continues to be supported by membership dues, donations, book sales, and proceeds from the Strawberry Social held every June.

**BEECH BROOK, INC.,** is an institution devoted to the care of emotionally disturbed children and their families. It evolved from the Cleveland Protestant Orphan Asylum, established by the Dorcas Society of Cleveland, under the direction of REBECCA and BENJAMIN ROUSE, in 1852. The purpose of this institution was to care for children left orphaned by a recent cholera epidemic. The first chairman of the board was SHERLOCK J. ANDREWS, a prominent Cleveland lawyer. Under his direction, and with the help of Mrs. Stillman Witt, the asylum acquired enough money by 1855 to build a permanent residence at Wilson (E. 55th St.) and Woodland aves., where it remained for 23 years. In the 1870s, Mrs. Rouse convinced LEONARD CASE that the orphanage needed a new home. The new building, located at St. Clair Ave., was opened on 17 Nov. 1880. The purpose of the institution at that time was to find, feed, clothe, and educate homeless children who were "sound of mind and body" and, if possible, to find homes for them. The asylum also attempted to build a nursery, but it proved unsuccessful, and so care was restricted to older children of both sexes, and of all races and creeds.

By 1920, the asylum had again outgrown its facilities. A decision was made to build a new asylum, on the cottage plan, on land located on Lander Rd. in Pepper Pike that had been donated to the asylum by Jeptha Wade, Jr., in 1916. By 1926 the new buildings were completed, and the Cleveland Protestant Children's Asylum again moved. In 1958, the asylum stopped accepting orphans and began to admit emotionally disturbed children. It became a treatment center for these children and their families in 1960. In 1971, the name and charter of the asylum were formally changed to Beech Brook, Inc. Beech Brook, with both hospital and residential facilities, accepted only children between ages 5–12 who were referred to them by the Hanna Pavilion, the Mental Health Ctr., the Cleveland Clinic, and local schools. Its basic purpose was to help emotionally disturbed children reenter the regular school system and lead normal lives. Both medical and psychiatric treatments are used. Educational facilities are provided for children who cannot go through the regular public school system. Beech Brook coordinates with other area children's organizations by sending teachers and training people to work with emotionally disturbed children.

**BEEMAN, EDWIN E.** (Mar. 1839–6 Nov. 1906), was a physician who became known as "the Chewing Gum King" after he introduced the successful "Beeman's Pepsin Gum" in 1890. Beeman was born in LaGrange, Lorain County, Ohio, and grew up in Lorain and Erie counties. After an education in the public schools, he spent 2 years at Oberlin College and at age 18 began to read medicine under the supervision of his father, Dr. Julius Beeman. He graduated from Cincinnati Medical College in 1861. Beeman served 3 months in the CLEVELAND GRAYS in 1862, then joined his father in the drug business at 169 Ontario St. in Cleveland in 1863–64. He moved to Birmingham, Ohio, where he practiced medicine for 12 years, and then to Wakeman, Ohio, where he remained for 6 years. A specialist in digestive disorders, Beeman discovered through research that pepsin, an extract from the stomach of hogs, provided relief from indigestion. By 1883, Beeman had returned to Cleveland to manufacture pepsin, selling the white powder in a blue bottle with a picture of a pig on the label.

Beeman produced pepsin on a small scale until 1888, when he organized the Beeman Chemical Co. along with

Albert C. Johnson, Chris Grover, and Wm. Cain; from 1888–90, the company produced pepsin on a larger scale than before. In Jan. 1890, the company's bookkeeper, Nellie M. Horton, suggested that Beeman add pepsin to chewing gum. The following month, "Beeman's Pepsin Gum" appeared. The success of the product led to a reorganization of the company in 1891; Beeman's earlier partners sold their interests to Geo. H. Worthington, Jas. M. Worthington, and Jas. Nicholl. Nellie Horton also became a stockholder in the reorganized firm and served as assistant secretary and treasurer. The new Beeman Chemical Co., located at 40 Lake (Lakeside) Ave. from 1891–94 and then at 76 Bank (W. 6th) St. from 1895–99, produced both pepsin and chewing gum. In 1898, sales of chewing gum totaled $408,685; pepsin sales that year were $1,449; total profits then were $131,487. Meeting in New York City in June 1899, the directors of Beeman Chemical authorized the sale of the company to the American Chicle Co. Besides his business and medical interests, Beeman was active politically, serving 4 terms on CLEVELAND CITY COUNCIL. He was also a Royal Arch Mason. Beeman was married in 1862 to Mary Cobb.

**BEIDLER, JACOB A.** (2 Nov. 1852–13 Sept. 1912), was a prominent coal merchant who represented the 20th congressional district from 1901–06; he was a pioneer in the "back-to-the-farm" movement. Beidler was born near Valley Forge in Chester County, Pa. His father was a minister in the Mennonite Reformed church. Beidler worked on his father's farm until age 21, when he graduated from Lock's Seminary at Norristown, Pa. After graduation, he came to Cleveland and began a coal dealership. He married his wife, Hannah, in 1885 or 1886. They had 4 children: Mary, Mabel, Joseph, and Dudley. For over 40 years, Beidler was active in the coal business. He was president of the East Goshen Coal Co. and the Burton-Beidler-Phillips Coal Co.; at his death, he was president of the Rhodes & Beidler Coal Co. in Cleveland. Other business interests included his organizing the Belle Vernon-Mapes Dairy Co. and service as vice-president of the CLEVELAND, PAINESVILLE, & EASTERN RAILWAY. He also served for many years as a director of the Painesville *Telegraph-Republican*. Beidler began his political career on Cleveland's south side when he started a "marching campaign" in Jas. G. Blaine's presidential campaign of 1884; later he served on the CLEVELAND CITY COUNCIL, representing an east-end ward. He was a lifelong Republican.

A public feud between Beidler and JAS. R. GARFIELD began a political fight that resulted in Beidler's nomination and subsequent election to Congress representing Cuyahoga, Lake, and Medina counties in 1900. Beidler started *The Painesville Republican* newspaper when that city's existing paper endorsed Garfield. When the campaign began, Beidler had already moved from Cleveland to Belle Vernon, his Willoughby, Ohio, farm, where he raised Guernsey cattle. He was an advocate of the back-to-the-farm movement, which stressed the value of a rural, agrarian lifestyle. As a congressman, Beidler promoted rural interests. He was credited with obtaining 75 rural free delivery routes for his district and supporting the good-roads movement. Much of his time was spent helping military veterans obtain their pensions. Beidler was reelected in 1902 and 1904 but retired in 1907 because of a conflict with his business interests—he had spent more than his congressional salary. In 1907, he was appointed to the Ohio Board of Agriculture.

**BELGIANS.** Belgians form one of Cleveland's smallest immigrant groups. As of 1970, only 124 foreign-born Belgians resided in the city. Belgian immigration to Cleveland began in the 1870s. The 1880 census listed 75 Belgians in the city. The pre-World War I peak was reached in 1910, at 90. As a small country that never had a large transoceanic immigration in the late 19th century, Belgium's representation in Cleveland reflected relative levels in other American cities. Immigration did increase after the catastrophic effects of WORLD WAR I in the homeland. By 1930, Cleveland's Belgian population had risen to 130. Displacement caused by WORLD WAR II had a similar effect, and the city's Belgian population peaked at 298 in 1960. Many of the post-World War II immigrants were war brides or young professionals attracted by the city's technical and medical facilities. As a small community, and one that rapidly assimilated into American life, local Belgians founded no major or long-lasting organizations. However, the city has had an honorary Belgian consulate since 1923. Its presence reflects, to a degree, the trade relations between Belgium and Cleveland and, moreover, the city's sympathy with that country, which grew out of the disastrous events of World War I.

Ivan L. Miller

**BELL, ARCHIE** (17 Mar. 1877–26 Jan. 1943), covered drama and music for various Cleveland daily newspapers for more than 30 years. Born in Geneva, Ohio, he went to work shortly after graduation from Geneva High School as stenographer and secretary to publisher B. F. Bower of the *CLEVELAND WORLD*. Within a year, Bell became a reporter, Sunday editor, and finally managing editor for the *World*. Following an interview by Bell with a visiting actress, Bower persuaded him to become the *World's* drama critic at his managing editor's salary. When the *World* was merged into the *News* in 1905, Bell continued as a drama and literary editor of the *News*. He also took time off in the next few years to serve as a publicity director for the HIPPODROME THEATER and to manage tours for actress Olga Heghersole and soprano Ernestine Schumann-Heink.

In 1910, Bell joined the *PLAIN DEALER* as drama and music critic. He moved to the *Leader* about 1914. When that paper was sold in 1917, he moved with its Sunday edition to the *News*, where he remained for the rest of his career. He concentrated on theater but often covered music, as well. It was Bell who brought Fr. John Powers of St. Ann's Church together with ADELLA PRENTISS HUGHES of the MUSICAL ARTS ASSOC. for the benefit concert that marked the birth of the CLEVELAND ORCHESTRA in 1918. He also persuaded Morris Gest to bring *The Miracle* to Public Hall, which paved the way for the later visits of the Metropolitan Opera Co. in that location.

Beginning with a walking tour of Europe after his high school graduation, Bell became a prodigious world traveler, which led to a series of travel books, such as *The Spell of the Holy Land, The Spell of China,* and *The Spell of the Caribbean Islands.* He also wrote *The Clyde Fitch I Knew* (1910), and his popular fiction is exemplified by *The Clevelanders: An Expose of High Life in the Forest City* (1906), which is misleadingly but perhaps appropriately set mainly in Florida. Bell retired from the *News* in the mid-1930s because of a heart ailment. A bachelor, he lived quietly at his home on E. 85th St. until his death from pneumonia. His books and theatrical memorabilia had been donated to the Geneva Public Library.

**BELL, NOLAN D.** (1920–26 Feb. 1976), a veteran of the Karamu Theater stage, was recognized as one of the best nonprofessional actors/comedians in America. In order to support his wife, Viola, and their 7 children, he maintained

87

2 careers, working full-time as a worker for the Cleveland Sanitation Dept., while his love of the stage made him a veteran of more than 200 plays. Born in Gary, Ind., Bell moved with his family to Cleveland in the "Green Pastures" district of Cedar Ave. near the old Karamu Theater, then located on Central Ave. He appeared in his first production with the Karamu Children's Theater in 1926 at the age of 6. Under the direction of the drama center's cofounder, Rowena Jelliffe, Bell appeared as a child actor in numerous playhouse productions and radio plays. In 1935, after months of auditioning, Bell and a friend, Joseph Singleton, won roles on radio station WGAR portraying "Pin and Willie," building a reputation as the juvenile "Amos 'n' Andy" of the airwaves. Bell graduated from old CENTRAL HIGH SCHOOL with LANGSTON HUGHES, the internationally known black writer and playwright, who would later call Bell the finest actor and comedian of his day. After 2 years at the City College of Indiana and 1½ years at Indiana University, Bell entered the armed forces in 1940 as a warrant officer. His Army tour included 36 months in the Pacific Theater at Guadalcanal, the Fiji Islands, and the Philippines, where he studied for a year at the University of Manila. Discharged in 1946, Bell resumed his acting career at KARAMU HOUSE with lead roles in such plays as *Waiting for Godot* and *Golden Boy*. Often he appeared in the casts of 2 current productions while learning the lines for a third play. He was also an accomplished singer, performing several operatic roles at the Karamu. Bell also appeared at the MUSICARNIVAL in Cleveland and Florida, the DOBAMA THEATER, and the Chagrin Valley Little Theater. So widespread was his reputation that talent scouts from Hollywood and New York tried to lure him toward professional status, but Bell preferred freely sharing his talents within his own community. In 1968 he became the first black to join the regular staff at the CLEVELAND PLAY HOUSE. In 1968 Bell was honored for his talents with a listing in *Who's Who in America*, thus becoming the only Cleveland actor and the first garbage collector to be so listed. In 1972 he received national exposure when he starred in an episode of the television series *Maude*. He died peacefully in his sleep 4 years later.

The **BELL NEIGHBORHOOD CENTER**, a social-service center in the HOUGH area, was established in the late 1950s as a branch of the Goodrich Settlement House. Goodrich began its work in HOUGH as a result of construction of the INNERBELT FREEWAY through the old Goodrich neighborhood that it served; Goodrich officials looked for other areas in which to work and decided that the area with the greatest need was the eastern Hough area. Financed by a grant from the CLEVELAND FOUNDATION, Goodrich House staff began work in the area in Sept. 1958, designating the area bounded by E. 79th, Ansel Rd., Euclid, and Superior as its service area. In Feb. 1959, the Ohio Bell Telephone Co. donated its building at 1839 E. 81st St. as the headquarters for Goodrich's Hough branch; the project thus had both a location and a name, the Bell Neighborhood Ctr.

In its early years, the staff of the Bell Ctr. described its work as "social rehabilitation in the area," and early projects focused heavily on young people. In 1961, for example, Bell Ctr. received a $20,000 federal grant for a project that center director John W. Cox hoped would "raise the level of aspiration and motivation of youngsters" in fatherless families receiving welfare and "improve their work and play habits." Other projects in the early 1960s included voter-registration drives, cooperative cleanup campaigns with street clubs, a summer youth-employment agency, and interracial workshops. As the growing civil-rights movement made area residents more conscious of the problems in Hough, the Bell Neighborhood Ctr. began to receive greater financial and volunteer help; between 1963–65, volunteers from SHAKER HTS. and CLEVELAND HTS. established a nursery school and a library at the center. By late 1966, more than 50 people were associated with the staff of the Bell Neighborhood Ctr., and activities included a birth-control clinic, a Head Start program, a scholarship program to send high school students to college, a committee to improve relations between citizens and police, and programs to organize the community more effectively politically through civic education and the development of street clubs.

Throughout the 1960s, as both outsiders and Hough residents organized efforts to deal with the area's problems, the Bell Neighborhood Ctr. served as an important center of activity. It was a member of the E. 81st St. Corp., formed in May 1968 to provide housing for low- and moderate-income families; the center provided social services and a housing coordinator for the Hough Housing Corp., formed in 1966 by the Goodrich Settlement House and the CLEVELAND DEVELOPMENT FOUNDATION to rehabilitate housing in the area; and Citizens for Better Housing often met at the center. In June 1970, with assistance from the U.S. Dept. of Agriculture, the center began a year-round food program to provide needy children with breakfast and lunch. By 1973, the Bell Neighborhood Ctr. had moved to the new Hough Multi-Service Ctr., 8555 Hough.

Goodrich Bell Social Settlement Records, WRHS.

**BELLAMY, GEORGE ALBERT** (29 Sept. 1872–8 July 1960), was a pioneer and leader in social-settlement work in Cleveland. He is considered the founder of HIRAM HOUSE, the first social settlement in Cleveland. Bellamy was born in Cascade, Mich. His family's involvement in the Disciples (Christian) church provided him with a strong religious background. Desiring to enter the ministry, he studied at Hiram College from 1892–96. While at Hiram, he became interested in settlement work (see SETTLEMENT HOUSES) and joined a group of students in establishing a settlement house in Cleveland in 1896. Bellamy assumed control of the settlement, Hiram House, in 1897. In the ensuing decades he developed it into the largest and most financially secure settlement in the city.

A strong interest in urban, environmental reform characterized Bellamy's early career. He worked for housing-code regulation and served on the Cleveland Chamber of Commerce's Public Bath House Committee (1901) and its Committee on the Housing Problem (1903). He later directed his interests to recreational work, overseeing the creation of the city's first night-lighted playground at Hiram House in 1900. In 1912 he assisted Mayor NEWTON D. BAKER in the promotion of a recreational bond issue for Cleveland. In 1914 Baker named Bellamy unpaid supervisor of the city's playgrounds. Bellamy achieved a national reputation for his work in recreation. He served as a lecturer for the Natl. Playground Assoc., and during WORLD WAR I he directed the establishment of recreational facilities at military camps under the auspices of the War Dept.'s Commission on Training Camp Activities. Following the war, Bellamy accompanied former president Wm. H. Taft on a speaking tour in behalf of American entry into the League of Nations.

The postwar period brought about a dramatic change in Bellamy's social-work philosophy. In the 1920s he evolved a "Child Growth and Development Program," which was directed toward the molding of individual character traits. He committed a large portion of Hiram House's resources to this program and remained keenly interested in it after he retired from the settlement in 1946. Bellamy also became increasingly conservative in the post-World War I period. He was one of the few early settlement leaders to oppose Franklin Roosevelt's welfare programs. Bellamy was married twice. His first marriage, to Marie Laura Parker (a coworker at Hiram House), ended with her death in 1909. In 1912 he married Clara Horn.

Hiram House Records, WRHS.

Grabowski, John J., "A Social Settlement in a Neighborhood in Transition, Hiram House, 1896–1926" (Ph.D. diss., Case Western Reserve University, 1977).

**BELLAMY, PAUL** (26 Dec. 1884–12 Apr. 1956), was editor of the *PLAIN DEALER* from 1928–54. Son of utopian author Edward Bellamy (*Looking Backward, 2000–1888*), Bellamy was born in Chicopee Falls, Mass. After graduating from Harvard in 1906, he worked a year on the *Springfield* (Mass.) *Union* before coming to Cleveland as a reporter for the *Plain Dealer*. Two years later he was named the youngest city editor in the paper's history. Leaving the *Plain Dealer* briefly for work in a Chicago publishing firm and service in WORLD WAR I, Bellamy returned in 1919 and was made managing editor the following year. He took over the paper's editorial direction shortly after the death of editor ERIE C. HOPWOOD in 1928, although he didn't receive the title of editor until 5 years later. Bellamy remained editor of the *Plain Dealer* until Jan. 1954, when he was made editor emeritus.

As editor of the *Plain Dealer*, Bellamy kept a low profile in local affairs but was a national influence in his profession. While still managing editor, he had attracted notice in a speech before the American Society of Newspaper Editors, and he was elected president of that organization in 1933. Upon passage of the Natl. Recovery Act that same year, Bellamy was named by publishers to help draw up the NRA code for newspapers. A director of the Associated Press for 18 years, he used the occasion of the Don R. Mellett lecture at Ohio State University in 1943 to warn against excessive wartime censorship. Although he considered himself a Democrat and had known Pres. Franklin Roosevelt since his Harvard days, Bellamy became critical of the New Deal, and the traditionally Democratic *Plain Dealer* endorsed Wendell Willkie in 1940. Nonetheless, Roosevelt made Bellamy head of a wartime committee to formulate policies governing occupational draft deferments for federal employees.

A charter member of the CITY CLUB OF CLEVELAND, Bellamy served as its president in 1935–36. His first marriage, to Marguerite Scott Stark in 1908, ended in divorce in 1941 after producing 4 children. Bellamy subsequently married Mrs. Mary Mitchell Henry. Hindered by illness in his last years, he died in his Bratenahl home at age 72. His son, Peter Bellamy, has been a critic and columnist for the *CLEVELAND NEWS* and the *Plain Dealer*.

Paul Bellamy Papers, WRHS.

Porter, Phllip W., *Cleveland: Confused City on a Seesaw* (1976).

**BELLEFAIRE**, a residential home for children needing institutional care, is the oldest Jewish social-service agency in Cleveland. It was established in 1868 by the B'nai B'rith Grand Lodge District #2 as a regional institution, serving 17 states, to care for Jewish orphans. The B'nai B'rith had instituted a $1-per-year capitation tax in 1865 designed to fund a charitable or educational institution. Following the CIVIL WAR, the need for a Jewish orphanage was apparent, and the decision was made to locate in Cleveland. A large building, formerly Dr. Seeyle's water sanitorium at E. 51st St. and Woodland, was purchased for $31,000 and was dedicated on 14 July 1868 as the Jewish Orphan Asylum. It began operation 2 months later with over 80 residents. Under the direction of Rabbi Samuel Wolfenstein, formerly a rabbi at Congregation B'ani El in St. Louis, the asylum grew to include 400 orphans by the turn of the century. Wolfenstein served as its superintendent from 1878–1913.

The increasing number of orphans at the asylum and the deterioration of the facilities, coupled with the move of the Jewish population out of Woodland, led the board of trustees to search for a new location. In 1927 the asylum purchased land in UNIVERSITY HTS. on Fairmount Blvd. Following a court battle to override a discriminatory zoning ordinance, a new complex of buildings was constructed, and the orphanage occupied its new home in 1929. The home emphasized the care and education of orphans from its creation until 1940. That year, services were broadened to include therapeutic care for those children who could not receive it at home or in foster homes. Reflecting this change, the institutional name was changed in 1942 to Bellefaire. In 1941, Bellefaire merged its functions with the Welfare Assoc. for Jewish Children to create the JEWISH CHILDREN'S BUREAU. Bellefaire, which was still a regional organization, remained a residential-care facility, and the bureau, a local organization, provided casework, foster-home placement, group-home care, and daycare. By 1985, Bellefaire was a nonsectarian facility. It was no longer an orphanage but exclusively a residential home for children needing therapeutic care outside the nuclear family environment.

Bellefaire Records, WRHS.

Polster, Gary E. "A Member of the Herd: Growing Up in the Jewish Orphan Asylum 1868–1919" (Ph.D. diss., CWRU 1984).

**BEMIS, EDWARD W.** (7 Apr. 1860–25 Sept. 1930), a former college professor of history and economics, expert on public taxation, and ardent proponent of municipal ownership, was a political ally and appointee of TOM L. JOHNSON, serving as superintendent of the Cleveland Water Works from 1901–09. Born in Springfield, Mass., the son of Daniel W. and Mary W. Tinker Bemis, Edward Bemis received his education at Amherst College (A.B., 1880, and A.M., 1884) and at Johns Hopkins (Ph.D., 1885), where he studied history and economics. He reportedly taught the first university extension course in America, at Buffalo, N.Y., in 1885, then taught economics at Amherst (1885–86) and at various universities from 1886–88. From 1888–92, he served on the faculty at Vanderbilt University. He moved to the University of Chicago in 1892 but was forced to leave there in 1895, "because of views which were then considered radical by many." In 1896, he served as assistant statistician in the Illinois Bureau of Labor Statistics, and from 1897–99 he was professor of economics at Kansas State Agricultural College. During the 1880s and 1890s, Bemis was a prolific author of articles and reports about local government, tax policy, municipal ownership of utilities, working conditions, labor strikes, trade unions, socialism, and religion and social problems. He also published *Municipal Ownership of Gas Works in the United States* (1891) and *Municipal Monopolies* (1899). In 1892, he appeared in a Des Moines utility rate case, and in 1899 he was involved in the franchise valuation of Detroit Railways. His ideas, experience, and expertise made him an attractive ally for a Progressive mayor about to embark on a term in office, and Tom Johnson gave Bemis an opportunity to enact his suggested reforms.

Johnson placed Bemis in charge of the municipal water-works, a department described as "a nest of party hacks," and assigned him the task of removing the department from politics. Bemis replaced the spoils system with the merit system, unleashing protests from both the department and the local Democratic organization. With Johnson's firm support, Bemis ran the department in a scientific and businesslike manner, installing a record 70,000 meters and reducing rates. The elimination of graft and incompetent workers enabled completion of the water-intake tunnel. Bemis also continued his crusade for higher tax evaluations on properties owned by utilities and railroads in both Cleveland and other Ohio cities, testifying at many local and state meetings during his tenure at city hall. After 1909, Bemis moved to New York City, where he served as deputy commissioner of water supply, gas, and electricity in 1910, and later in other capacities. From 1913-23, he served on the advisory board of the Interstate Commerce Commission's valuation division. As a consultant in the 1910s and 1920s, Bemis investigated gas and telephone rates for Chicago, telephone rates in New York, and the valuation of utilities for Washington, D.C., and Dallas.

Biographical Notes on Edward W. Bemis, WRHS.

**BEN** was a fugitive slave who spent several months in Cleveland in 1806. He was the subject of an interesting episode in the city's early history that involved LORENZO CARTER and 2 slave owners from Kentucky. Ben's arrival in Cleveland was quite inauspicious. In the early spring of 1806, a small boat, or canoe, was driven ashore just east of ROCKY RIVER. The occupants were a man named Hunter, his family, and Ben. Hunter was from a settlement in Michigan and hoped to resettle in the WESTERN RESERVE. The boat was upset, and Ben was the only survivor; the others were drowned or within a few days died of exposure on the rocky shore of Lake Erie. After 3 or 4 days, French trappers enroute to Detroit rescued Ben from the shore and returned with him to Cleveland, where he was left under the care of Lorenzo Carter. He remained with Carter until October. At that time 2 men from Kentucky approached Carter, one of whom claimed to be Ben's owner. They demanded to see Ben. Carter purportedly stipulated that they could meet with Ben only if Ben himself consented to such a meeting. Ben eventually agreed to do so.

As a precaution, Carter arranged for Ben to stand on one side of the CUYAHOGA RIVER and the two men on the other. In this way communication passed between the two parties. The owner reportedly reminded Ben of his former good treatment under him and promised the same should Ben submit to his custody once again. Ben finally consented, and Carter relented—ostensibly expressing no dissatisfaction. The next day the two men, with Ben, departed Cleveland on horseback. Several miles away, in INDEPENDENCE, 2 men carrying rifles confronted the party and ordered Ben to flee into the woods, which he apparently did. These men, John Thompson and Jas. Geer, were considered to be employees of Carter's, or at least were frequenters of his tavern. In any case, Carter was largely credited with having a hand in the affair. Unable to find Ben after a brief search, the slave owners returned to Kentucky. For a while it was believed that Ben lived in a small hut, in either Independence or BRECKSVILLE. He eventually made his way to Canada, and nothing more is known of him thereafter.

**BENDER, GEORGE HARRISON** (29 Sept. 1896–18 June 1961), was a member of the Ohio Senate for 10 years, served as Republican congressman in the U.S. House of Representatives for 14 years, and was U.S. senator from Ohio for 2 years. Born in Cleveland, the son of Joseph and Anna Sir Bender, he attended Cleveland schools, graduating from West Commerce High School. After serving in WORLD WAR I, he returned to Cleveland, becoming advertising manager for the BAILEY CO. in 1920 and later general manager of the Bedell Co. He married Edna B. Eckhardt in June 1920, and they had 2 children, Barbara (Mrs. Ernest B. Stevenson) and Virginia (Mrs. Dorsey Joe Bartlett).

Attracted to politics, Bender was elected to the Ohio senate in 1920 and served there until 1930. Although he didn't drink, he was instrumental in defeating the Anti-Saloon League's bill to restore the authority of justices of the peace, who Bender felt were overzealous in their enforcement of Prohibition. He founded the G. H. Bender Insurance Co. while serving in the Ohio senate and during the 1930s was active in Republican party politics, publishing 2 magazines, the *Ohio Republican* and the *National Republican*. He authored a book, *The Challenge of 1940*, in which he promoted the candidacy of Wendell Willkie for president. He was chairman of the Republican Central Committee of Cuyahoga County from 1936–54; and from the time he was elected to Congress in 1938 until 1954, when he entered the Senate, Bender controlled Republican affairs in Cuyahoga County.

After 4 unsuccessful attempts, Bender was elected to the U.S. House of Representatives as a congressman-at-large in 1938 and remained there until 1948, when he was defeated by Stephen M. Young. He defeated Young in 1950 to return as congressman-at-large. After Ohio's congressional redistricting in 1951, he was again reelected to Congress, this time from the 23d district. An enthusiastic campaigner, he was perhaps best known for his bell-ringing support of Robt. Taft's unsuccessful bid to be the Republican presidential candidate in 1952. However, when Eisenhower won the nomination, Bender campaigned energetically for him in the presidential election. When Taft died in 1954, Bender won the election to fill out his Senate term, narrowly defeating THOS. A. BURKE. As senator, he worked to repeal the poll tax and advocated more federal action in areas such as school aid. In a bid to retain his Senate seat in 1956, he lost to Frank Lausche. In 1958, the ex-senator was hired by Jas. Hoffa to chair a 3-man commission to investigate racketeering in the Teamsters' Union. The Senate Rackets Committee and the court-appointed Teamster monitors denounced the Bender commission as a whitewash, and he resigned from the commission in Jan. 1960. At this point his political career ended, and he returned to his home in CHAGRIN FALLS, where he died at age 64.

**BENEDICT, GEORGE A.** (5 Aug. 1812–12 May 1876), was the editor of the CLEVELAND HERALD from 1857–76. Born in Watertown, N.Y., he moved to Cleveland in 1835, shortly after his admittance to the bar. He practiced law in Cleveland for the next several years, a period in which he also served briefly as city attorney, as well as president of the city council. In 1848 he was appointed to the position of clerk of the superior court, which he filled until the court's abolition under the Constitution of 1851. In 1853 Benedict purchased an interest in the *Cleveland Herald*, to which he had previously contributed articles. When JOSIAH A. HARRIS left the *Herald* in 1857, Benedict succeeded him as editor and formed a new partnership with the paper's other proprietor, A. W. Fairbanks, as Fairbanks, Benedict & Co.

Benedict kept the *Herald* on a steady course of conservative Republicanism through the Civil War and Reconstruction years. He was rewarded in 1865 by appointment as postmaster of Cleveland, a position he held for 4 years. His cautious stewardship was no match for the aggressive Republicanism of EDWIN COWLES, however. By the end of the war, the *Herald* had surrendered its competitive advantage to the upstart *Leader*. A vestryman of ST. PAUL'S EPISCOPAL CHURCH, Benedict was married with a son and 2 daughters. After the death of his son in 1871, his health began to deteriorate, and he died at age 63 after a long illness. His executor sold his interest in the *Herald* to his partner, Fairbanks.

**BENES, W. DOMINICK** (14 June 1857–15 May 1935), was a prominent architect whose most notable buildings were completed in Cleveland from 1895–30. With BENJAMIN S. HUBBELL, Benes was responsible for the design of some of Cleveland's most splendid classical revival buildings, including the CLEVELAND MUSEUM OF ART in 1916, as well as major early modern commercial structures, including the Ohio Bell Telephone Co. in 1927. Benes was born in Prague, Bohemia, and immigrated to the U.S. in 1866 with his parents, Joseph M. and Josephine Nowak Benes. He attended schools in Prague, public schools in Cleveland, and high school in Oberlin, Ohio. When he was 15, Benes left school and began a 3-year (1873–76) apprenticeship with another Bohemian-born architect, ANDREW MITERMILER.

In 1876 Benes began a 20-year association with the Cleveland architectural firm of COBURN & BARNUM, later Coburn, Barnum, Benes & Hubbell (1896). The latter was the architect for the WESTERN RESERVE HISTORICAL SOCIETY building at E. 107th St. and UNIVERSITY CIRCLE, completed in 1898 and since demolished. Benes and Hubbell subsequently established their own partnership, Hubbell & Benes (1897–1939), and completed their largest and most significant commissions as such. Other major Hubbell & Benes projects included the Citizens' Bldg. (1903); the Cleveland School of Art (1905), demolished; the Mather College Gymnasium (1908); the WEST SIDE MARKET (1912); the YMCA (1912); the Illuminating Bldg. (1915) on PUBLIC SQUARE; the Masonic Auditorium (1921); the current business wing (1922) of the CLEVELAND PUBLIC LIBRARY; the PHILLIS WHEATLEY ASSOC. (1927); and St. Luke's Hospital (1927). Benes was known by his contemporary colleagues as the "personal architect" to JEPTHA H. WADE. Wade's grandson commissioned Hubbell & Benes to design the Wade Memorial Chapel (1901) in Lake View Cemetery. Benes is credited alone for design of the Centennial Arch that was erected in Public Square during 1896.

Benes was a member of the Bohemian Turners' Society and the Cleveland Athletic, YMCA Business Men's, Century, Clifton, and Lakewood Yacht clubs. He served as a member of the West Cleveland Board of Education (1885–87), was a member of the Cleveland Chamber of Commerce, and was a member and past president of both the AMERICAN INSTITUTE OF ARCHITECTS CLEVELAND CHAP. and the CLEVELAND ARCHITECTURAL CLUB. Benes married Matilda F. Nowak on 9 Mar. 1881. Her parents were also early Bohemian immigrants. Her father, Frank Nowak, erected the first meeting house for various Bohemian societies. Matilda and Dominick Benes had 4 children: Grace, Clara, Matilda, and Jerome H.

Johannesen, Eric, *Cleveland Architecture, 1876–1976* (1979).

**BENESCH, ALFRED ABRAHAM** (7 Mar. 1879–21 May 1973), an attorney whose political and social views were shaped during the Progressive Era, was an active civic and Jewish community leader and senior partner in one of Cleveland's most prestigious law firms. He was born in Cleveland, the son of Bohemian immigrants, and attended public school here. After graduating from CENTRAL HIGH SCHOOL in 1896, Benesch matriculated at Harvard, where he eventually received his law degree in 1903. He married Helen Newman of Chicago in 1906. Benesch established a law practice in Cleveland in 1903 in partnership with Benjamin Star. Among his clients was the Peddlers' Self-Defense Assoc., established during the early 20th century to protect peddlers from street violence and robbery. Benesch was successful in obtaining better police protection and fair treatment in the courts for the predominantly Jewish peddlers.

Benesch's public career began in 1912, when he was elected to the city council. He served for 2 years. In 1914, Mayor NEWTON D. BAKER appointed him as public safety director. Benesch served as state director of commerce from 1935–39 and as area rent director for northeastern Ohio from 1942–45. Public education was one of his primary interests. He was a member of the Cleveland Board of Education from 1925–62, including 2 terms as its president, 1933–34. Benesch was an active member of B'NAI B'RITH. Representing that organization, he fought the quota system at Harvard University that restricted Jewish admissions to 10%. With considerable support from a past president of the university and a large number of the trustees, he was successful in removing the restriction.

Benesch was one of the founders of the BUREAU OF JEWISH EDUCATION in 1924 and was an active or honorary member of its board of trustees until his death. He also served on the boards of the JEWISH FAMILY SERVICE ASSOC., the JEWISH COMMUNITY FED., BELLEFAIRE, MT. SINAI Hospital, and the Natl. Jewish Hospital in Denver. He served the latter institution for over 50 years and was a vice-president during the 1950s and 1960s. In 1955, Benesch received the Eisenman Award from the Jewish Community Fed. for his civic and humanitarian activities.

Alfred A. Benesch Papers, WRHS.

**BENJAMIN, CHARLES H.** (29 Aug. 1856–3 Aug. 1937), was a mechanical engineer and an educator who taught at Case School of Applied Science from 1889–1907. He was responsible for establishing the school's mechanical engineering department. The son of Samuel E. and Ellen Fairfield Benjamin, Benjamin was born in Patten, Maine, where he attended Patten Academy and served as an apprentice in a machine shop prior to entering Maine State College (now the University of Maine) as a junior in 1877. He received his bachelor's degree in 1879, spent the next year at a machine shop in Lawrence, Mass., then returned to his alma mater to earn a master's degree in 1881. Benjamin began his teaching career at his alma mater in 1881, beginning as an instructor and advancing to professor of mechanical engineering before leaving in 1886 to become assistant manager at the McKay Bigelow Machine Co. in Boston. In 1889 he accepted the professorship of mechanical engineering at Case and became the head of the new department of mechanical engineering. He created the curriculum for the new department, supervised the planning for the department's new building (1892), and acquired the necessary equipment for the laboratory. Benjamin served as professor of mechanical engineering and department head from 1889–99, and again from 1903–07; between 1899–1903, professor of applied mechanics was added to his title. In 1907 he left Case to become dean of the School of

Engineering at Purdue University, a position he held until 1921, when he became director of the Engineering Experiment Station at Purdue. During his years at Case, Benjamin gave a number of public lectures and wrote 2 books, *Modern American Machine Tools* (1906) and *Machine Design* (1906); he later wrote *Steam Engine* (1909). He also served the city of Cleveland as supervising engineer in 1901 and as a smoke inspector. Benjamin married Cora L. Benson on 17 Aug. 1879.

CWRU Archives.

The **BENJAMIN ROSE INSTITUTE**, organized in Feb. 1909, was the first foundation established in the U.S. to deal primarily with the needs of the elderly. Designed to "grant assistance to older persons in trouble and in need, in such a way as to help them maintain their self-respect and place in the community," the institute has gained a national reputation for its innovative services to needy senior citizens in the Cleveland area. Upon his death in 1908, BENJAMIN ROSE left his estate and the proceeds from the Rose Bldg. for the establishment of an agency to help the elderly and crippled children. He named a 15-member board of trustees to direct the agency and stipulated that all future trustees be women, since he believed women to be more sympathetic than men. The institute began offering services in Apr. 1909 and worked thereafter to help the needy elderly remain at home rather than enter institutions. It began by granting monthly allowances to needy men past age 65 and women over 60. In 1910 it spent $7,998 to help 81 elderly Clevelanders; in 1920 the budget grew to $74,732 to help 276 people. From 1909–21 the institute helped 488 aged citizens. It also helped crippled children secure hospital treatment and rehabilitation services, spending $30,600 in 1920 to help 103 children.

MARGARET WAGNER served as director of the Benjamin Rose Institute from 1930 until her retirement in 1959. Under her innovative leadership, the institute broadened its services to the elderly, becoming a public advocate for their needs as well as providing much-needed services. It undertook a study of the growing number of nursing homes in the 1930s and helped to close unsanitary and poorly run ones; and it commissioned a survey of the needs of the chronically ill in the area in 1944. In 1937 it founded the first Golden Age Club, designed to break through the loneliness and isolation of many elderly citizens. The institute discontinued its services for crippled children in 1943, since other agencies had developed to meet this need. In 1941 the institute acquired Belford House, 11234 Bellflower Rd., a residential club for the elderly. It later acquired Juniper House, a nursing home at 11427 Bellflower Rd., and Braeburn House, formerly the Scottish Old Folks' Home.

The Scottish Old Folks' Home, located at 1835 N. Park Blvd., had been operated by the St. Andrews Scottish Benevolent Society, founded in Cleveland in 1846. In Apr. 1919 a committee of the society recommended establishing an old-age home for natives of Scotland, the descendants of natives, and descendants' spouses. By 1929 such a home had been established, with Mrs. Jessie L. Warnock as superintendent. The budget for the home rose from $4,592 in 1932 to $14,464 in 1948–49. When the home was taken over by the Benjamin Rose Institute in 1951 at the request of its trustees, it was renamed the Braeburn House. It continued under that name until the institute consolidated it along with Juniper House and Belford House into the new Margaret Wagner House, constructed at a cost of $2.2 million at 2373 Euclid Hts. Blvd. in CLEVELAND HTS. in 1961. For a number of years the institute was also a partner in a hospital designed to serve the medical needs

of the elderly. The Benjamin Rose Hospital, opened in 1953, was jointly operated by the institute and UNIVERSITY HOSPITALS. University Hospitals took over complete operation of the hospital in 1968, renaming it Abington House.

Additional bequests and donations over the years have increased the endowment of the institute. In 1982 it served 1,036 needy citizens with a budget of $2.9 million. With its headquarters in the Rose Bldg., the institute maintains 3 neighborhood offices to provide home visitation services to meet the health and social-service needs of the elderly.

St. Andrews Scottish Benevolent Society Records, WRHS.

**BENTLEYVILLE** is a 2.75-sq.-mi. residential village located approximately 20 mi. southeast of Cleveland. It is bounded on the north and east by CHAGRIN FALLS, on the north and west by MORELAND HILLS, and on the south by SOLON. Approximately 540 acres of the village are occupied by the S. Chagrin Reservation of the Metroparks System. Bentleyville was originally a part of CHAGRIN FALLS TWP. In 1831, a minister of the DISCIPLES OF CHRIST, Adamson Bentley, came to the area and bought land at the junction of the Aurora Branch and the CHAGRIN RIVER. He built a sawmill, a gristmill, and in 1836 a clothing store. He held Disciples meetings in a log schoolhouse. Other settlers built a triphammer shop, opened a tannery, and developed a stone quarry, chair and rake factories, and shops and stores. One of the important early settlers was Ralph Russell, founder of the N. UNION SHAKER COMMUNITY in 1822. In 1928, various proposals were suggested by the village of Chagrin Falls to annex all of Chagrin Falls Twp. Some residents, opposed to the annexation, wanted to separate and join Moreland Hills. However, another group of citizens circulated petitions for the formation of another village, voted to secede, and created Bentleyville, a separate incorporated village, in 1929. The population of Bentleyville has grown from 180 in 1950 to 301 in 1960, 338 in 1970, and 381 in 1980. There have been numerous proposals to annex the village to Chagrin Falls, Solon, or Moreland Hills, but its residents have chosen to remain independent.

**BENTON, ELBERT JAY** (23 Mar. 1871–28 Mar. 1946), was an author, educator, historian, and college administrator. He was born on a Dubuque, Iowa, farm, the son of Oliver Dustin and Sarah Proctor Benton. His family moved to a Kansas farm, where he spent his boyhood. He received his A.B. degree from Campbell College, Kansas City University. From 1895–97, he was principal of Holton (Kans.) High School, and from 1897–1900, he taught history at Lafayette (Ind.) High School. During this time, he was doing graduate work at the University of Chicago and at Johns Hopkins University, where he also served as a teaching assistant in history. Benton received his Ph.D from Johns Hopkins in 1903 and immediately afterward was appointed to the faculty of Adelbert College as instructor of history. In 1906, he became an assistant professor, and in 1909 he was named full professor. In 1925 he became the first dean of the newly organized Graduate School. He is credited with reorganizing and expanding the instructional program to include opportunities for related study in other university departments. In addition to his activities as dean, Benton continued to teach history. He retired in 1941 and was named dean emeritus. In 1942, upon the death of WALLACE H. CATHCART, director of the WESTERN RESERVE HISTORICAL SOCIETY, Benton, who had served the society as secretary and trustee since 1913, became its acting director, and subsequently its director. Benton wrote several books dealing with taxation in Kansas and the Spanish-American War. He wrote *Peace without Victory* (1918) and *A Short History of the Western Reserve Historical Society, 1867–1942*, both published by the society. He coauthored several histories with Western Reserve University professor Henry E. Bourne, including *Introductory American History* (1912), *History of the United States* (1913), *Story of America and Great Americans* (1923), and *A Unit History of the United States* (1932). He also wrote the 3-volume *Cultural History of Cleveland*. He was an editor of the *American Historical Review* and contributed articles to the *Dictionary of American Biography* and the *Dictionary of American History*. Benton married Emma Kaul in June 1895. She died in May 1925. In 1927 he married Irene J. Kaul (Mrs. Benton's sister), who died 22 Nov. 1977. In 1959, the Elbert Jay Benton Chair in History was established in his honor at Western Reserve University.

**BEREA** is a 4.88-sq.-mi. residential suburb located approximately 10 mi. southwest of downtown Cleveland, bounded on the north by BROOK PARK, on the east by MIDDLEBURG HTS., on the south by STRONGSVILLE, and on the west by OLMSTED FALLS. It was originally a part of Middleburg Twp. The first settler in Middleburg was Jared Hickox, who arrived in 1809. The history of the township really began with the arrival of John Baldwin and others in 1828 and their attempt to establish an experimental utopian Christian socialistic community. The founders of the Lyceum Village community and school purchased land, issued stock, and renounced personal property. The hamlet was known as Lyceum Village, but the post office was named Berea by Baldwin and Rev. Henry O. Sheldon in 1836. However, because of the small membership, the lyceum failed in 1844. In 1842, Baldwin founded the Baldwin Quarry Co., the beginning of the Berea sandstone industry. The Berea sandstone along the Rocky River had excellent qualities for grindstones and building stone. It eventually became known throughout the world, and during their heyday Berea quarries shipped 400 tons of stone daily throughout the U.S., Canada, Europe, and Australia. The quarries were consolidated in the Cleveland Stone Quarry Co. in 1886. Baldwin also established another educational institution, the Baldwin Institute, in 1845. He donated land to the Methodist Episcopal Church, which operated the institute. In 1855 its name was changed to Baldwin University. The school's German Dept. established the separate German Wallace College in 1863. In 1913, the two institutions were merged as BALDWIN-WALLACE COLLEGE.

Berea was incorporated as a village in 1850. The same year, the Cleveland, Columbus & Cincinnati Railroad was completed through the village, stimulating the local industry. The influence of Methodism also remained strong. In 1864, the first Methodist orphanage in the U.S. was established. It became the German Methodist Orphan Home in 1924, and the Methodist Children's Home of Berea in 1937. In 1894, the Cuyahoga County fairground, which had previously been located on Kinsman St. and in NEWBURGH and CHAGRIN FALLS, was permanently located on Eastland Rd. in Berea. Berea became a city in 1930. The location of CLEVELAND HOPKINS INTERNATL. AIRPORT in nearby Brook Park in 1925, the work of the NASA laboratory adjacent to the airport in the 1940s, and the completion of I-71 in the 1950s all contributed to the growth of the city. At the end of WORLD WAR II, its population was 6,025. The sandstone quarries finally closed in 1946. In 1960, Berea adopted a charter form of government. By 1980 its population was 19,567. The community

had more than 5,000 homes and apartments, more than 175 retail establishments, and more than 50 small manufacturers. Much of its postwar growth was attributable to the expansion of manufacturing in adjacent Brook Park. Berea was part of the Berea School District, which included Brook Park, Middleburg Hts., and RIVEREDGE TWP.

**BERNSTEIN, HARRY** (1856–1920), known as "Czar" Bernstein, was a neighborhood entrepreneur and political ward boss who could, according to contemporary accounts, deliver the votes he promised from his ward to a man. He was born in Poland, brought to Cleveland in 1868, and educated in the public schools. During his business career, Bernstein owned theaters, a restaurant, a saloon, a pool hall, and a hotel, established a neighborhood bank, and operated a junk business. He established the People's Theater and the less successful Perry Theater in the 1890s to present Yiddish entertainment in the heavily East European Jewish Woodland neighborhood. His Perry Bank was established specifically to serve the immigrant neighborhood. It later merged with the Cleveland Trust Co.

Bernstein's business activities provided a base for the political power he amassed. He was able to provide small favors for the needy immigrants in Cleveland's 16th (later 12th) ward. Bernstein became active in Republican politics ca. 1888 as an operative for the Hanna machine. He was one of Cleveland's most effective ward bosses, although his influence did not translate beyond the confines of the immigrant district. In the 1890s, Bernstein groomed a young protege, MAURICE MASCHKE, who within a decade became a leader of the county's Republican party. While Maschke's power grew, Bernstein's declined. In 1903, he was elected to the city council, the first and only time he held elective office. Although he supported Mayor TOM L. JOHNSON, Bernstein did not curry favor with the reformers. With the ascendancy of the Progressives and the beginning of a population shift in his ward, Bernstein lost much of his influence during the first decade of the 20th century.

**BETH HAKNESSETH ANSHE GRODNO** congregation, also known in its early years as the Synagogue of the Province of Grodno, was a typical example of the landsman-based congregation commonly established in East European Jewish immigrant communities. It was founded in 1904 by 11 Russian immigrants from Grodno, Lithuania, and was incorporated in August of that year by Morris Shapiro, Max Lifshitz, and Jacob Landy. Religious services were held initially in the home of Benjamin Zelling. After 3 months, a hall was rented at Perry (E. 22nd) and Orange, where the congregation met until it purchased a frame house on Osborn near Woodland in 1907. In 1912, the congregation followed the general move of Jews eastward and purchased a new building at E. 55th St. between Quincy and Central. Many of the congregation members during its early years were members of the Jewish Carpenters Union, Local 1750. The carpenters formed a conservative, tradition-minded Jewish union that experienced great success in winning wage concessions during the first 2 decades of the 20th century. Unlike the radical or largely secular trade unions, the carpenters, because of their religiosity, enjoyed the support of the Orthodox community. With the move of Jews out of Woodland, Anshe Grodno was forced to relocate. In 1924, a new synagogue was purchased at 105th and Columbia. For several years following the move to GLENVILLE, the congregation maintained a branch in Woodland for those members who were unable, primarily for economic reasons, to move from the neighborhood. During the 1930s, the congregation was served by Rabbi

Judah Levenberg, the head of the short-lived Jewish Orthodox Rabbinical Seminary. Levenberg acted as religious leader for a number of the smaller congregations of the city. In 1940, with a membership of 200 families, the congregation established a Hebrew school under the direction of Rabbi Milton Dalin. Like many small congregations, Anshe Grodno could not afford to relocate following WORLD WAR II when Jews were leaving Glenville for the suburbs. In 1947, it proposed to merge with the HEIGHTS JEWISH CTR. The proposal created considerable controversy within the congregation, and the objections were not overcome until Dec. 1950. The merger was consummated in Jan. 1951.

**BETH ISRAEL-THE WEST TEMPLE** was organized by 25 families in Apr. 1954 to provide a religious center for Reform Jews living on Cleveland's west side. In Oct. 1957, Beth Israel effected a merger with the West Side Jewish Ctr., formerly B'nai Israel, a Conservative congregation and at that time the only other congregation serving west side Jews. The congregation's first service, Rosh Hashanah, was held 27 Sept. 1954 at the First Universalist Church in N. OLMSTED. For the next 4 years, religious services were held at either the Universalist Church or the N. Olmsted Community Club House. After the merger with the West Side Jewish Ctr., construction of a synagogue was completed at 14308 Triskett Rd., and the structure was dedicated in May 1958. The congregation still occupies that site in 1986. During its first 7 years, Beth Israel was served by a succession of 6 student rabbis from Hebrew Union College in Cincinnati. The first, David Rose, returned to the congregation as rabbi in 1977 and serves in that capacity in 1986. Daniel Litt, another student, became its first full-time rabbi in 1961. Rabbi Sally Priesand, a graduate of Beth Israel's religious school, became the first woman ordained to the rabbinate in the U.S. As an outgrowth of a Social Action Committee, formed in 1961, several members of the congregation founded the CLEVELAND COUNCIL ON SOVIET ANTI-SEMITISM. Lou Rosenblum and Abe Silverstein, members of the congregation and of the CCSAS, became leaders in the national movement to assist Soviet Jewry.

Beth Israel draws its members from Cleveland's west side and the western suburbs. It expanded its facilities in 1965 with the construction of a new 8-room, 2-story wing. Also in 1965, the CLEVELAND FOUNDATION awarded the congregation library a $5,000 grant for book purchases to be expended over a 5-year period. By the end of the grant period, the library contained over 3,000 titles and provided service for the congregation and for high schools and colleges on the west side. Beth Israel since 1967 has also provided office space for CCSAS. The West Side Jewish Ctr., the first congregation on the west side, was organized as B'nai Israel by 10 families in 1910. It was formally incorporated in 1940, and for most of its existence religious services were conducted by lay leaders of the congregation. In 1953, the congregation applied to and was accepted by the United Synagogue of America, the national umbrella organization for Conservative Judaism. The merger with Beth Israel took the one-time Orthodox congregation into the Reform movement.

Beth Israel-West Temple Records, WRHS.

**BETHANY PRESBYTERIAN CHURCH**, 6415 W. Clinton Ave., originated from a mission Sunday school of the First Church (Old Stone) in Jan. 1888, when Chas. Fay, at the request of some Presbyterians on the west side of Cleveland and under the leadership and direction of Rev. Wilton

Merle Smith, associate pastor of Old Stone, organized a group of about 40 children who met in the Ohio Business University building at Pearl (W. 25th) St. near Franklin Ave. Membership grew to over 400. With the endorsement of the PRESBYTERIAN UNION, the request to the presbytery to establish a new church was granted, and on 2 July 1889, Bethany Church was organized with 61 charter members. On 1 Aug. 1889, Rev. Giles H. Dunning, who had served the Sunday school from the beginning, became the first pastor. In Feb. 1890, the church moved to quarters in the Wieber Block at the corner of W. 25th St. and Jay Ave. On 1 Apr. 1894, the congregation purchased a lot at the corner of W. 65th St. and Clinton Ave. With the financial assistance of the Presbyterian Union, construction was begun on a chapel on 29 Sept. 1894; it was dedicated on 2 June 1895. The membership grew, and through the years, Bethany has continued to offer programs that meet the needs of its changing neighborhood.

**BETHEL UNION** was organized on 31 Jan. 1867 as an auxiliary of the WESTERN SEAMEN'S FRIEND SOCIETY, an evangelical organization in Cleveland since 1830 devoted to working among the people and families in Cleveland's dock district. Loren Prentiss, Edward C. Pope, H. C. Tuttle, and Edwin R. Perkins were among the 20 organizers. Bethel Union was established to carry out evangelical work in the neighborhoods near the river and to maintain a home for friendless and poor people, and sailors between jobs. Bethel Union initially operated out of a church located on W. 9th St. It was sold in 1867, and the union moved into the "McCurdy Block" at the corner of Superior and W. 10th. The structure was purchased the next year, providing a 600-seat chapel, 30 sleeping rooms, a reading room, and 2 dining rooms. Lodging facilities were expanded during the following 2 years to include women. The union also provided a Sunday school, adult Bible classes, and missionaries to vessels in port. The Ladies' Bethel & Mission Aid Society, a women's auxiliary, provided physical as well as spiritual comfort to people in the neighborhood, distributing clothing and religious tracts. The trustees enlarged Bethel Union's work in 1873 to include all of Cleveland, and its name was changed to the Cleveland Bethel Relief Assoc. Ward committees were established to carry out the enlarged program of relief work, including soup kitchens and an employment agency. In 1884 it joined with the CHARITY ORGANIZATION SOCIETY to create the Bethel Associated Charities, and in 1900 its name was changed to the Cleveland Associated Charities, which became the Cleveland Associated Charities, Institute of Family Service, and in 1945 the Family Service Assoc. of Cleveland (see CENTER FOR HUMAN SERVICES).

**BETHLEHEM CONGREGATIONAL CHURCH** (1888–1954), located at the corner of Broadway and Fowler avenues, had its origins in the early Protestant missionary work among Czech immigrants in Cleveland in the early 1880s. One of the first Protestant churches for CZECHS in Cleveland was Olivet Chapel (Hill and Commercial streets), formed in 1882 with Dr. Henry A. Schauffler as pastor. It later merged with Plymouth Church (1888). In 1883, a Bohemian Mission Board of Cleveland was incorporated to coordinate the work of Cleveland Congregational churches with the Bohemian colony, and in 1884 Bethlehem Church was built at the corner of Broadway and Fowler. Named for the church in Prague in which John Huss, the Bohemian martyr, had preached, the new Bethlehem was dedicated in Jan. 1885 by Dr. Schauffler. In Mar. 1888, a wooden structure, Bethlehem Congregational Church, was organized with the aid of a council of Cleveland Congregational churches. The cornerstone for a new chapel was laid on the site of the original (1888) wooden structure on 2 Nov. 1919. The brick chapel served as a sanctuary and as a chapel for SCHAUFFLER COLLEGE OF RELIGIOUS & SOCIAL WORK. The merger of Schauffler College with Oberlin College, resulting in fewer students in attendance; gradual shifts in population; and steadily declining membership led to the dissolution of Bethlehem Congregational Church in 1954.

The **BICKNELL FUND** was incorporated in 1949 by Kate Hanna Bicknell (b. 1911) and Warren Bicknell, Jr. (1902–1975). Warren Bicknell, Jr., a director of the M. A. HANNA CO., was educated at UNIVERSITY SCHOOL, Taft School, and Williams College. He was also associated with the Cleveland Constr. Co. and the Society for Savings bank. Kate Hanna Bicknell is the granddaughter of Howard M. Hanna, Sr. The Bicknell Fund is designated primarily for local community grants and for higher and secondary educational institutions. No grants are given to individuals, or for loans. In 1985, assets of the fund were $2,207,686, with expenditures of $188,639 for 57 grants. Officers of the fund include Kate H. Bicknell, president and trustee; Warren Bicknell III, vice-president and trustee; and Donald J. Hofman, secretary and treasurer; with trustees Guthrie Bicknell, Kate B. Kirkham, Wendy H. Bicknell, Geo. D. Kirkham, and Lyman Treadway III.

The **BIEHLE FAMILY** were designers and painters who worked on frescoes and decorative painting for such clients as the Chamber of Commerce, churches, and several of Cleveland's foremost families. August Frederick Biehle (4 July 1856–10 Nov. 1918), the senior family member, was born in Freiberg, Baden. His father, a manufacturer of costume jewelry and trinkets, died when he was 4. Until he was 14 he attended school in his home town. He was apprenticed with a "master painter," went to a trade school, where he focused on drawing, and received other opportunities to educate himself. He traveled and worked in other European cities and completed a 3-year military service before deciding to emigrate to America in 1880. Biehle came directly to Cleveland and ultimately took a position with L. Cooks (later called Cooks Bros.), where he stayed for 16 years. During the last 8 of those years, he was under contract as chief designer and painter for the company. In 1897, he went into business for himself. He was contracted to do work for the firm of L. Rohrheimer and L. H. Hays (later Rorimer & Brooks). His works appeared in the Chamber of Commerce, the Casino, the Liberty E. Holden residence in Glenville, and many mansions and churches in the northeastern quarter of the country.

Biehle had 6 children. One son, August F., Jr. (13 Jan. 1885–7 Feb. 1979), was also a master decorator of mansions, a commercial artist and demonstrator for Sherwin Williams, a lithographer, an artist, and the winner of May Show awards and the Parma Fine Arts Award in 1961. He trained as an apprentice with his father at Rohrheimer's firm. Several of his commissions were for Euclid Ave. mansions, including that of Leonard Hanna. Later he worked with his father at the Biehle Bros. firm formed by 3 of the children of his father's brother Frederick A. Biehle, Sr. (1857–1916), a master decorator of mansions. The firm decorated in the Cleveland area ca. 1920–50 under the leadership of August W. Biehle (1882–1961), whose apprenticeship and college degree were received in interior design. Other members were his brothers Karl (1897?–1949) and Frederick A., Jr. (1881–1945), whose specialty was plasterwork and color mixing.

August F. Jr. had training as an art student, as well. In 1903, he went to Europe with Wm. Finkelstein and Dave Brubeck. He studied in Paris and in Munich (at the Kunst Gewerke). He developed a distinctive style of flat decorative patterns, absorbing the work of the Blue Rider, German Expressionist, and French Fauve painters—broad brush strokes and compositional elements. In 1912, he returned to Cleveland and worked for Sherwin Williams. Wallpaper had come into vogue, virtually eliminating decorator painting. Biehle then became a lithographer, and until his retirement in 1952, he produced mostly the lithography for billboard ads, theater marquees, and circus posters. He continued to paint landscapes, still lifes, and portraits. His paintings were so regularly noted in the MAY SHOW (25 years of inclusion) that he was allowed to exhibit without competition.

Always a student of painting, Biehle studied with HENRY KELLER in Summer School (an informal group) and with his friends PAUL TRAVIS and FRANK WILCOX. He worked for years at Otis Lithograph at Brandywine with WM. SOMMER and attended a session as late as 1956 with Max Weber. He also contributed covers for the *Bystander* and *Cygnet Monthly*, Cleveland art magazines, and programs and posters for the CLEVELAND PLAY HOUSE. Never content with one style of painting, Biehle painted abstractions as well as realistic landscapes and murals under WPA. He was responsible for 27 murals at the Alpine Village Restaurant and 12 at the Hofbrau House. He was also a member of the KOKOON CLUB. His son, Frederick August Biehle, an art educator and artist, carried on the family tradition in the 1980s.

The **BIG BROTHER/BIG SISTER MOVEMENT** began in the first decade of the 20th century as adults became increasingly concerned about the moral character of adolescents growing up in an urban environment. Big Brother and Big Sister organizations aim to help children in single-parent households by providing a friendly adult to serve as a positive role model in place of the absent parent. These organizations took shape in Cleveland during 2 periods of public concern about juvenile delinquency and have targeted increasingly younger children to receive their services by lowering age limits and initiating new programs.

Big Brother groups were first organized in Cincinnati in 1903 and in New York in 1904; Big Sisters were first established in New York in 1908. These organizations first appeared in Cleveland in 1919 with the formation of both the Jewish Big Brother and Jewish Big Sister associations. The Jewish Big Brother program was established by the Welfare Committee of the Euclid Ave. Temple Alumni Assoc., with Oscar H. Steiner as its first president. An all-volunteer program from 1920–25, the Jewish Big Brothers joined the Jewish Social Services Bureau in 1925, and professional caseworkers began to supervise the program. The Jewish Big Sister Assoc. was organized by the Council of Jewish Women. Mrs. Siegmund Herzog, president of the council, began the program as a result of her work at the council's Martha House, a home for working girls. Designed to serve girls with behavioral problems, the association joined the Jewish Social Services Bureau in 1926 and hired a full-time, paid supervisor. In 1932 the organization helped 88 Little Sisters. Both the Jewish Big Brothers and Big Sisters left the Jewish Social Services Bureau to join the JEWISH CHILDREN'S BUREAU in 1948.

Little information is available about the early Catholic Big Brother organization, but as early as 1922 the ST. VINCENT DEPAUL SOCIETY was offering Big Brother services at the juvenile court. Seeing the need for a similar service for girls, the society hired a social worker to train volunteer Big Sisters. In Mar. 1924, these volunteers were organized as the Catholic Big Sisters. Led by Catherine McNamee, this group of volunteers became an independent agency in 1931, establishing its own board of directors, joining both the Catholic Charities and the Welfare Fed., and taking over the Big Sister work of the St. Vincent dePaul Society. From Mar. 1930-Mar. 1931, the Catholic Big Sisters program helped 615 girls ages 14–21 and had 75 active Big Sisters; its 6-week summer camp, the Little Flower Lodge, served 68 girls in 1930. In 1938 the agency provided services to 714 girls, with 256 receiving long-term care.

During the 1920s and 1930s, Cleveland's Big Sister organizations in general seem to have been stronger than its Big Brother groups. Of the groups that formed the Big Brother & Big Sister Conference of Cleveland in Mar. 1927, 3 worked with girls (the Jewish and Catholic Big Sisters and the Big Sister Council, which later became part of the Women's Protective Assoc., which in turn became the Girls' Bureau) and 2 with boys (the Jewish and Catholic Big Brothers). The conference aimed to provide a clearinghouse for ideas and problems, to publicize the work of its member groups, and to develop and promote child-welfare legislation. In Apr. 1929 the conference joined the Welfare Fed.

The Big Brother/Big Sister movement appears to have declined in Cleveland during the 1940s. The Catholic Big Brothers group had to be organized anew at the decade's end, and in 1942 the Catholic Big Sisters withdrew from social-service work, deciding to concentrate their efforts on the development of the Christian Social Doctrine as a way of life, promoting it through a social hospice, institutes on Christian living, lectures, and study clubs. Although the organization reentered social work in 1947, only the Jewish Big Brothers worked continuously between the 1920s and the next important phase of the movement in the 1950s, when both the Catholic and Protestant Big Brothers were formed to combat male juvenile delinquency. A new Catholic Big Brother group was organized by Fr. Raymond J. Gallagher in the fall of 1949. It made its first Big Brother-Little Brother assignment in Feb. 1951. By 1960 the organization had 60 Catholic Big Brothers; the total grew to 150 in 1968. Between 1951-76, the Catholic Big Brothers helped 2,050 Little Brothers.

The sectarian nature of Cleveland's Big Brother organizations was not unique; religious distinctions led to multiple Big Brother groups in such cities as New York, Boston, Baltimore, Detroit, and Los Angeles. In Cleveland, a third group, the Protestant Big Brothers, was formed 1 Dec. 1956. Designed to serve Protestant and unchurched youths ages 8–18, the Protestant Big Brothers were founded by the Social Welfare Dept. of the Cleveland Area Church Fed. and were funded by a grant from the Cleveland Fed. Attorney Jay Standish led the group's formation; John Petten, a trained caseworker, was its first executive director. Fourteen volunteer Big Brothers were at work by Jan. 1957, and a second caseworker was hired in 1958; by 1960 there were 64 Protestant Big Brothers. Renamed the Big Brothers of Greater Cleveland by 1970, the organization claimed to be "the fastest growing" Big Brother group in the U.S., increasing its Big Brother-Little Brother assignments from 191 in May to 290 in Sept. 1970. Cleveland's 3 Big Brother groups worked closely during the 1950s and 1960s, promoting their work jointly during the annual Big Brother Week in January. This cooperation was formalized in 1967 with the formation of the Joint Big Brother Council of Greater Cleveland, designed to further increase cooperation and provide year-round publicity.

In 1977 the two national organizations, the Big Brothers of America and Big Sisters Internatl., merged to form Big Brothers/Big Sisters of America; accordingly, the two local groups changed their names and expanded their operations to meet new local demands for service. The Catholic Big Brothers began offering their services to girls and became the Catholic Big Brothers & Big Sisters, and the new Big Brothers/Big Sisters of Greater Cleveland received 3 foundation grants to begin a Big Sisters program for girls ages 5–17. The Jewish Big Brothers group continued to work only with boys, since it received few requests to expand its program to include girls. It worked closely with boys at Bellefaire, where a Big Sisters committee worked in the school and nursery. By Aug. 1980, 454 men and 111 women worked as volunteers for the Big Brothers/Big Sisters; in 1982 the organization matched 539 children with volunteer adults, and its budget of $240,000 was triple its 1970 budget. Both the number of volunteers and the amount of money in the budget declined sharply during the economic recession, however, and only 395 matches were possible in 1983.

Specialized programs similar to Big Brothers/Big Sisters also operated in Cleveland in the 1970s, such as Project Friendship, a United Way-funded program to help young girls referred to it by the juvenile court, and the Big Buddy/Little Buddy program in the Cleveland schools. Established in 1972 by veteran Big Brother Oscar Steiner and begun under the auspices of Big Brothers, the Big Buddy program matches fatherless inner-city youngsters ages 5–10 with more mature students, age 16 and older, who do well in school and are able to serve as respectable role models for their troubled Little Buddies. This "truancy prevention program" grew from 20 participants in 1972 to 500 in 1984 and is sponsored by the Child Conservation Council of Greater Cleveland, with assistance from the Student Activities Office of the CLEVELAND PUBLIC SCHOOLS.

**BIG ITALY** was Cleveland's first major Italian settlement and the center of the city's produce markets. In the late 1890s, Italians settled in the HAYMARKET along Woodland near the city center. By 1900 this formerly Jewish area was 93% Sicilian. Among the early settlers were Frank Catalano and G. V. Vittorio, who set up an Italian products-importing business and produce stand. Such ethnic entrepreneurs popularized oranges, bananas, figs, olive oil, anchovies, and garlic in Cleveland.

To serve the needs of the large Italian Catholic population, ST. ANTHONY'S CHURCH was established on E. 9th St. across from the ERIE ST. CEMETERY in 1887. St. Anthony's, the first Italian Catholic parish, relocated to 1245 Carnegie in 1904. As the Italian population of the neighborhood diminished, the parish merged with St. Bridget's at E. 22nd and Scovill. (St. Bridget's moved to Parma in 1956.) HIRAM HOUSE, the settlement house established on Orange Ave. in 1896, attempted to work with the Italian residents of the neighborhood. The immigrants, sensing an anti-Italian bias, shunned Hiram House at first but eventually joined some settlement activities in the 1910s after Hiram House hired an Italian worker. As the neighborhood of Big Italy deteriorated, residents moved to better housing in Collinwood, LITTLE ITALY, Kinsman, and Fulton Rd. Meanwhile, new immigrants to Cleveland bypassed the Woodland community for the newer settlements. The Italian population of Big Italy fell from a high of 4,429 in 1910 to 1,300 in 1940 and 180 by 1960.

Veronesi, Gene, *Italian Americans and Their Communities of Cleveland* (1977).

**BILL, ARTHUR HOLBROOK** (10 Nov. 1877–11 Mar. 1961), was an early innovator in techniques of hospital obstetrics and played a major role in establishing Cleveland's reputation for low maternal mortality. Bill was born in Cleveland to Herbert Weston and May McIlewain Bill. After attending CLEVELAND PUBLIC SCHOOLS, he received the B.A. degree from Adelbert College in 1897 and the M.A. degree from Western Reserve University in 1898. In 1901, he received the M.D. degree from WRU Medical School. Following graduation, he interned at Lakeside Hospital for 2 years; at Johns Hopkins Hospital in Baltimore in 1902; at Vassar Hospital in 1903; and at New York Lying-in Hospital in 1904, where he specialized in obstetrics. In 1905, he studied in Berlin, Vienna, and Paris. Bill returned to WRU in 1906, as an assistant in obstetrics. In 1907, he was promoted to demonstrator in obstetrics, and in 1908 he was made instructor. In 1909 he became associate professor and head of the department. In 1906, Bill became associated with Maternity Hospital. That year he began operating an out-patient clinic, using his home on E. 92nd St. Successful, the clinic increased its services, reaching a high of nearly 1,500 deliveries in a single year. In 1911, Bill became chief of staff; he moved Maternity to 3735 Cedar Ave. and helped to affiliate it with WRU. In the early 1920s, he started campaigning for a larger and better hospital. The campaign climaxed with the development of the University Hospitals complex adjacent to the university and the opening of the new Maternity Hospital on 30 Nov. 1925. Bill almost single-handedly structured the obstetrics training program at WRU so that by graduation, students had not simply witnessed confinements but had actually helped deliver as many as 40 babies and attended innumerable labors. By the time of his retirement from Reserve in 1948, Bill had helped train over 2,000 obstetricians-gynecologists and had played a major role in developing techniques to relieve childbirth pains. Bill was survived by his wife, Gladys Buttermore Bill.

The **BING FURNITURE COMPANY** was one of the largest furniture stores in Ohio. Louis S. Bing and Elias Nathan opened their first retail furniture store, with 10 employees, on Seneca (W. 3rd) St. on 25 Mar. 1891. By 1895, Bing was operating the store on his own. His brother Solomon joined him in the early 1900s. Business grew steadily, and in 1907 a new 4-story store opened on Prospect Ave. The new store fulfilled the company's slogan of selling "Everything for the Home." By 1935, it had furnished 100,000 homes in the area. Bing continued to expand its services in northern Ohio, and in 1945 it began to open branch stores in communities throughout the region. In the 1950s, the firm established its suburban Cleveland branches. By 1960, Bing had 14 stores, 4 of them in Cleveland. In 1961, the company was sold to interests controlled by the Schottenstein Bros. of Columbus, who operated several retail stores. Soon after the acquisition, Bing went out of business as its stock was liquidated. All of Bing's stores were closed in Sept. 1961 except for the one in EUCLID, which was bought by Louis Bing's grandson, George. He continued to operate that store as the Geo. L. Bing Furniture Co. until 1976.

**BINGHAM, CHARLES W.** (22 May 1846–3 Mar. 1929), was born in Cleveland, the son of William and Elizabeth Beardsley Bingham. He attended the CLEVELAND ACADEMY and, later, the New Haven Hopkins Grammar School before he entered Yale in 1864, from which he graduated with a B.A. in 1868. In college he mastered Latin, Greek, French, and German. After Yale, Bingham spent 3 years in Europe, primarily in France and Germany, studying geology, mining, and chemistry. He was caught in the activities of the Franco-Prussian War and was at one point

actually fired upon near the Pantheon. When he returned in 1870, he studied for and was granted the M.A. degree from Yale in 1871. He appears to have begun work in the Cleveland FLATS shortly afterward, although it is not known at what company (some sources suggest it was the Cleveland Iron Co., of which his father, WM. BINGHAM, was president). In 1879 he was a member of the firm of Wm. Bingham & Co. From 1881 until his death, he was president of the Standard Tool Co. During his life, he served on several banking boards and carried on business for members of his family, e.g., renting business properties and administering estates. As a result of this kind of business and family responsibility, the Perry-Payne Co. was established. On 8 June 1876, Bingham married Mary Perry Payne, the daughter of Henry B. and Mary Payne. There were 5 children: Oliver Perry, William II, Elizabeth Beardsley (Blossom), Frances Payne (Bolton), and Henry Payne. Bingham's philanthropic interests were widespread. From 1892 until his death, he was a trustee of the WESTERN RESERVE HISTORICAL SOCIETY; he served at various times as treasurer of the Case Library and president of the Case Library Assoc. He was one of the original trustees appointed under the will of John Huntington to conduct the Huntington Art & Polytechnic Trust; he was that trust's president and was a trustee of the Horace Kelley Art Foundation. He became the chairman of the joint building committee representing these 2 trusts in the construction of the CLEVELAND MUSEUM OF ART, of which he was an original incorporator. He remained a trustee from 1913–20. He was also a trustee of the Lake View Cemetery Assoc. Bingham was a member of the FIRST PRESBYTERIAN (OLD STONE) CHURCH from 1862, and from 1909 until his death was a trustee.

**BINGHAM, FLAVEL W.** (15 May 1803–1867), was a lawyer and politician who served 1 year as mayor of Cleveland. Born in New York, he came to Cleveland by 1837, where he set up a private law practice, Collins & Bingham. He was elected councilman and chosen city council president in 1845. In 1847 and 1848, he was elected as an alderman and again served as city council president. In 1849, he became mayor. Bingham was elected the city's first probate judge, serving from 1852–55. When his term expired, he returned to private law practice, forming the partnership Bingham & Hovey. During his life, he served as president of the Society for Savings bank and was well connected with local business interests. He left Cleveland for New Orleans in 1863, where he died. He and his wife, Emmeline, had 3 children, Frances, Charles, and Edward.

**BINGHAM, WILLIAM** (9 Mar. 1816–17 Apr. 1904), was born in Andover, Conn., the son of Capt. Cyrus and Abigail Foote Bingham. He was educated at the Andover village school and at the school in Monson, Mass. When he was 20, he traveled to the WESTERN RESERVE and settled in Cleveland. After 2 or 3 years of attempts to secure long-term employment, he received the assistance of his father in establishing a hardware business with GEO. WORTHINGTON. In 1841 he purchased the firm of Clark & Murfey and organized it under the name of Wm. Bingham & Co. On 2 Jan. 1843, Bingham married Elizabeth Beardsley, the daughter of David H. Beardsley, the first collector of tolls on the Ohio Canal at Cleveland. They had 3 children: Caroline Elizabeth, Chas. William, and Cassandra Hersh. Wm. Bingham & Co. prospered; it dealt not only in hardware materials but also in the metals trade. In 1846–47, Bingham served on CLEVELAND CITY COUNCIL, during which term he initiated the study that led to the establishment of a waterworks system for the city; he later supervised the construction of the first tunnel into the lake for drinking water. In 1862 he was appointed a member of the board of sinking fund trustees of the city. During the CIVIL WAR, he held several posts for the raising of volunteers, for the relief of disabled and wounded soldiers and their families, and for raising money for the Union. He appears to have been seriously considered for the nomination of the Republican party to be mayor of Cleveland in 1865 and 1867, but seems diligently to have avoided receiving the honor. In 1870 he served as delegate to the Southern Commercial Convention in Cincinnati, and in 1873 he was elected a senator, serving only 1 term. In 1876, Pres. Grant appointed him a member of the board of Indian commissioners, from which he resigned in 1877, apparently because he suffered a serious financial setback in Cleveland. He had endorsed a note for a colleague, who later defaulted, forcing Bingham to make good the payment. In 1884, Bingham was elected to the Military Order of the Loyal Legion of the U.S. His accomplishments in setting up early manufacturing and commercial ventures in Cleveland were many; they included not only the hardware and metal trades but also banking and railroads. He was also the first president of the UNION CLUB (1870). Among the companies with which he was associated were the Society for Savings and the Cincinnati, Wabash, & Michigan Railroad Co. He served as a trustee of the Case Library Assoc. and of the FIRST PRESBYTERIAN CHURCH.

**BINGHAM CO.** *See* **W. BINGHAM CO.**

**BINGHAM FOUNDATION.** *See* **WILLIAM BINGHAM FOUNDATION**

**BIRD, PHILIP SMEAD** (9 Nov. 1886–10 June 1948), was a clergyman, civic leader, and religious administrator. He was born in Newtonville, Mass., the son of Joseph Edward and Gertrude Hubbard Smead Bird. His early education was in Newtonville and Montclair, N.J. He graduated from Pomona College Preparatory School in Claremont, Calif., in 1905 and from Pomona College, where he received an A.B. degree, in 1909. He graduated from the University of California, where he received a Master of Literature degree, in 1910 and from Union Theological Seminary, New York, in 1913.

While attending Union, Bird was a student assistant at the Madison Ave. Presbyterian Church and was ordained there on 11 May 1913. He became an assistant pastor of the Claremont Congregational Church (1913–14) and associate pastor (1914–15). During these years he was also a lecturer on Biblical literature at Pomona College. On 15 May 1915 he became pastor of South Presbyterian Church, in Dobbs Ferry, N.Y., and while there he was also an instructor in Biblical literature at the Masters School (Dobbs Ferry). During the war he served as a religious director and camp speaker of the Natl. War Council of the YMCA at Camp Devens, Ayer, Mass. On 3 May 1920, he became pastor of the First Presbyterian Church of Utica, N.Y. While in Utica (1920–28), he was chairman of the committee on industrial relations of the Utica Chamber of Commerce and helped solve numerous labor disputes.

Dr. Bird was installed as pastor of the CHURCH OF THE COVENANT in Cleveland on 20 Feb. 1928. During his ministry, the 3 congregations that had merged in 1920 from 3 separate Presbyterian churches became united; membership increased (from 1,733 to 2,500); Christ Chapel was created as a separate but integral part of the main Gothic sanctuary; and the Williamson Chancel was restructured. Under Dr. Bird's leadership, the Covenant's influence on the Western Reserve University campus was ex-

tended by the establishment of the Student Christian Union and by making space and services of the church available to air cadets enrolled at WRU during WORLD WAR II. Bird was president of the Cleveland Church Fed. (1931–33). He was chairman of the Church Extension Committee of the Presbytery of Cleveland (1929–33) and moderator of the Presbytery (1942–43). In 1933 he helped organize the Cleveland Peace Committee, an interfaith group of widely representative citizens from many different organizations. When the committee was formally and officially established, on 9 Oct. 1936, Dr. Bird was elected chairman.

In addition to his pastoral work and his activities associated with the peace movement, Dr. Bird was a member of the board of the PHILLIS WHEATLEY ASSOC., a trustee of the YMCA, and a member of the board of trustees of Mather College, as well as the Executive Committee of the Board of Trustees, WRU. He was an honorary trustee of Schauffler College of Religious & Social Work. He was a member of the Neighborhood Assoc. of Cleveland and the Westminister Foundation of Ohio (1943); and a member of the New England Society of Cleveland and of the Western Reserve Society of Mayflower Descendants. He received an honorary D.D. degree from Hamilton College, Clinton, N.Y. (1924); an honorary D.D. degree from WRU (1928); and an LL.D. degree from the College of the Ozarks, Clarksville, Ark. (1933). Dr. Bird married Margaret Hubbell Kincaid of Utica, N.Y., on 11 July 1922; the couple had 1 daughter, Mrs. Joseph (Margaret Elizabeth) Kuder. Dr. Bird died in Cleveland and is buried in Lake View Cemetery.

Philip Smead Bird Papers, WRHS.

The **BIRD'S NEST** (or BIRDTOWN) is an area of LAKEWOOD settled in 1892 when the Natl. Carbon Co. (Union Carbide) laid out 8 narrow streets of 424 lots for factory housing. Populated by East European immigrants, the tiny community remains an ethnic enclave that still (1986) has a large Slovak population descended from the original settlers. Bordered by Madison on the north, W. 117th on the east, the rapid-transit tracks on the south, and Madison Park on the west, the Bird's Nest comprises streets named for birds: Thrush, Lark, Robin, Quail, and Plover. To accommodate the labor needs of Natl. Carbon, Glidden Bremley Storage, and other neighborhood businesses, foremen, often Slovak, hired friends and relatives. By 1910, SLOVAKS constituted 70% of the population. Immigrants, who walked to work, sought housing in cold-water flats 2 and 3 stories high. Double houses accommodated 6 to 8 families, and single-family lots often had a house at the front of the lot and one at the back that the owner would rent out to other immigrants. Much of the housing, built by the settlers and their friends, features architecture unique to Lakewood. The community was solidified by churches and shops, which in 1986 still remain a magnet for former residents who have moved out of Birdtown.

**BIRNS, ALEX "SHONDOR"** (21 Feb. 1905–29 Mar. 1975), was one of Cleveland's most notorious criminals. Between the days of Prohibition and his death in 1975, he was involved in rackets, PROSTITUTION, theft, assault, and murder. Birns came to America with his parents from Austria-Hungary in 1907. He grew up on Woodland Ave. between E. 45th and E. 59th streets, where he was known as the toughest kid on the block. He was an accomplished athlete and quick with his fists, and he had a volatile temper. Birns also had a strong need for prestige and respect. He enjoyed his later notoriety, treating the journalists who had labeled him "Public Enemy No. 1" very well. Birns's formal education ended in 1922, when he dropped out of high school after completing the 10th grade. In 1923 he enlisted in the Navy but was discharged after serving 6 months, because he was underage. He then sold newspapers for a short time and later began to sell bootleg whiskey. Birns's criminal record was extensive; charges ranged from vagrancy to murder. Most of the killing and maiming had more to do with his violent temper than with any rackets shootouts, however. In 1925 he was arrested for the first time, for car theft, and was sent to the Mansfield Reformatory, serving a little over a year. Over the years, Birns was arrested a number of times but served only a short time in jail. He had friends everywhere, including lawyers, judges, and policemen. He also expended considerable time and money buying off and silencing witnesses. Along with his interests in rackets and prostitution, Birns operated the Ten-Eleven Club and the Alhambra restaurant. At the Alhambra, he often treated off-duty policemen, lawyers, and journalists to free food. In 1942 he was arrested by U.S. immigration officials as an enemy alien. He never became a U.S. citizen; he was still a Hungarian citizen. For years, immigration officials tried to find a country to which they could deport Birns; however, none would accept him. In the spring of 1975, Birns was released from a short stay in jail. He made several announcements that he was going to retire from the rackets and go straight. However, he never got the chance. On Saturday, 29 Mar. 1975, he was killed by a bomb planted in his automobile, which was parked near a bar at W. 25th St. and Detroit. No one was arrested for his murder.

**BIRTHRIGHT, INC.** is a nonsectarian volunteer organization designed to offer pregnant women of all ages an alternative to abortion. It urges women with unwanted pregnancies to continue their pregnancies to term and offers them the medical and financial resources to do so. Modeled after and named for the Toronto, Ontario organization founded in 1968, Cleveland's Birthright, Inc. opened its first Cleveland office at W. 147th St. and Detroit Ave. in March 1971. By 1973, Birthright had opened an office on the east side and by 1978 had added an office in PARMA. The nonprofit service agency makes available a variety of resources for its clients. Those forced to leave home are provided shelter with a volunteer family. Birthright also offers counseling by clergy, lawyers, and other professionals; provides low-cost loans, maternity clothing, and items for the baby; and gives referral for placing newborns for adoption. Medical care is also available, as is help finding employment.

**BISHOP, ROBERT H., JR.** (1879–29 Sept. 1955), a Cleveland doctor, was a leader in the American public-health movement. He was internationally known for his efforts in forming public-health agencies to fight tuberculosis. Throughout his career, he also worked to raise the standards of medical education. Bishop was born on a ranch in Kansas, but at an early age, his family moved to Oxford, Ohio. A graduate of Miami University in 1904, he entered Western Reserve University Medical School and received his medical degree 4 years later. He interned at Lakeside Hospital under Dr. DUDLEY P. ALLEN. Bishop became the director of Lakeside Hospital in 1919 and was instrumental in consolidating that hospital with Maternity Hospital and Babies & Childrens Hospital into UNIVERSITY HOSPITALS. He became director at University in 1932. Throughout his medical career in Cleveland, he worked closely with the city's health department to implement public-health programs. During WORLD WAR I, he served as health commissioner in Cleveland, one of the youngest health commissioners in the country. Quite active in local

medical organizations, Bishop was a trustee for the Cleveland Welfare Fed., and his suggestions helped form the city's welfare department. He was also a board member of the Cleveland Hospital Council. In 1919, Bishop was defeated as the Democratic candidate for mayor. In 1947, he became head of the newly formed Joint Commission for the Advancement of Medical Education & Research. His later years were dedicated to stimulating interest in medical education at WRU. A member of many national medical and health organizations, Bishop was for 15 years director of the Natl. Social Hygiene Assoc. and a director of the Natl. Health Council, the American Hospital Assoc., and the American College of Hospital Administrators, of which he was also a president.

Early in his career, Bishop achieved national distinction for his innovative programs to fight tuberculosis. He was one of the founders of the Anti-Tuberculosis League and, in Cleveland, was responsible for the establishment of a bureau of tuberculosis in the city health department. As health commissioner, Bishop set up 8 TB control centers throughout Cuyahoga County and engineered special treatment programs in area hospitals. He also worked for a bond issue of several million dollars for a sanatorium at Sunny Acres, where he later served as chairman of the board. In 1918, Bishop organized and took to Italy the first overseas tuberculosis unit of the American Red Cross. In Italy, he initiated health-education programs and schools of nursing for the treatment of that disease. For his lifetime dedication to public health, Bishop was awarded the American Hygiene Assoc.'s Freeman Snow Medal for distinguished service to humanity. Bishop married Constance Mather in 1914.

———————

Mather Family Papers, WRHS.

**BLACK, MORRIS ALFRED** (31 May 1868–23 Apr. 1938), the son of Hungarian immigrants, rose through the garment industry to become one of Cleveland's influential leaders. He was involved with local voter education and city planning. Black was born in Toledo, Ohio, to Herman and Eva Judd Black, both of whom left Hungary because of political dissatisfaction and governmental conditions. In 1892 the Blacks moved to Cleveland, where Herman's uncle and aunt were the pioneer Hungarian family. Educated in Toledo and Cleveland public schools, Black graduated from Harvard University with the A.B. degree in 1890. That same year he began his career in the garment industry as a shipping clerk, and later he was a designer in the H. Black Co., manufacturers of women's outer garments. Founded in 1883 by Herman Black, the company was famous for its "Wooltex" coats and suits. He married Lenore E. Schwab on 21 Mar. 1898, and they had 1 son, Herman.

Black succeeded his father as president of the company from 1903–22. Under his guidance, H. Black was instrumental in making Cleveland one of the chief garment centers in America. Employing around 1,000 workers at its plant on Superior Ave. between E. 19th and E. 21st streets, the company reflected Black's philosophy that a factory not only should be efficient but should also be an attractive addition to the city and a pleasant workplace for the workers. In 1922 H. Black merged with the PRINTZ-BIEDERMAN CO. In 1923, Black became president of the Lindner Co., a garment manufacturer he had founded in 1913. He also served as president of the Blackmore Co. and the Cleveland Garment Mfrs.' Assoc. During his career, Black attempted to stabilize the garment industry by making agreements for impartial arbitration. Resigning as president of Lindner in 1936, he worked until his death as a business consultant.

In civic life, Black was best known for his service in the Civic League, the predecessor of the CITIZEN'S LEAGUE, and on the City Plan Commission. One of the league's founders in 1903, he served on its executive board until 1921. His interest in housing and city planning led him to become one of the organizers and the chairman of the City Plan Commission from 1915-25, and vice-president from 1915-20. From 1914-19, he served as president of the Cleveland Chamber of Commerce.

**BLACK BASEBALL TEAMS.** *See* **CLEVELAND BUCK-EYES**

**BLACK HAWK** (1767-1838) was an American Indian chief of the Sauk, and leader of the Black Hawk War against the U.S. in 1832. He came to Cleveland in 1833 to visit his mother's grave on the CUYAHOGA RIVER. Although some men from Cleveland served in the Black Hawk War, the village was unaffected by the war directly. Indirectly, 50 deaths resulted in Cleveland from an epidemic of cholera brought by a troop boat returning from the war. The boat had been denied docking in Detroit, but after consultation it was allowed to stop in Cleveland, where the epidemic soon spread. After the war, Black Hawk was taken into custody by the U.S. government and given a tour of eastern cities. Returning westward, he asked to stop in Cleveland for a day in order to visit his mother's grave. Black Hawk himself was possibly born in the area. In Cleveland, Black Hawk was given a canoe or boat, and he paddled up the river alone to a bluff overlooking the valley (possibly from the southeast corner of RIVERSIDE CEMETERY). He remained there for a short time, and upon returning, he reportedly had tears in his eyes.

The **BLACK LAWS** were a series of early-19th-century restrictions on Cleveland's black citizens imposed by the Ohio state constitution of 1802 and state law. Growing antislavery sentiment in the WESTERN RESERVE caused these laws to be repealed before the CIVIL WAR. Like many states carved out of the Northwest Territory, Ohio was influenced by southern attitudes toward race. Though slavery was not permitted in the state, the southern influence found its way into the state constitution in 1802. Blacks were not permitted to vote, to testify in court against whites, to hold office, or to serve in the state militia. Further legislation required blacks to file a $500 bond before settling in the state and to register their certificates of freedom in the county clerk's office before getting a job, and barred them from serving jury duty. Because of these laws, blacks were not permitted in the public school system until 1848, when a law was passed that permitted communities to establish segregated schools if they desired. While certificate and bond filing were loosely enforced, the balance of the laws were strictly followed in Cleveland, as well as the rest of Ohio. By the 1830s, as the Western Reserve became a hotbed of reform activity, attitudes toward blacks shifted from those held elsewhere in the state. Cleveland and other northeastern Ohio towns became stopping points on the Underground Railroad to Canada. While this activism was hardly universal acceptance of racial equality, by 1838 the CUYAHOGA COUNTY ANTI-SLAVERY SOCIETY pressured legislators to promote repeal of the black laws. Within 12 years that was accomplished through Free-Soil legislators from the Western Reserve. Cuyahoga County delegates prevented antiblack provisions in the 1851 constitution and in 1867 promoted Negro suffrage, which was defeated by the bulk of Ohio voters. Even with the black laws on the books, Cleveland was noted for its lenient racial policies. There was little segregation in public accommo-

dations, and even the school system was integrated within a decade of its founding. City blacks had greater access to skilled and semiskilled jobs and enjoyed a greater level of prosperity before the Civil War than their counterparts in other northern cities.

Meier, August, and Rudwick, Elliott, *From Plantation to Ghetto* (1976).

**BLACK MILITARY UNITS** were prohibited by state officials and state law until practical considerations prompted federal officials to authorize formation of such units during the CIVIL WAR. Not until 1878 was the state's militia law of 1803 revised to eliminate language that restricted militia service to whites. Cleveland blacks were eager to take up arms against the slaveholding Confederacy once war broke out in 1861. They repeatedly urged Ohio governors to form black military units, but their offers of service were refused. One local black, John H. Cisco, light enough in color to pass as a white man, enrolled as a white soldier in the 124TH OHIO VOLUNTEER INFANTRY; he was promoted to colonel in Aug. 1861. Cisco was an exception to the rule against black military service in Ohio prior to 1863. Since the state would not accept them, some blacks turned to the federal government: on 14 Aug. 1862, Newell Goodale issued a public call to form a regiment composed of local blacks and soon claimed to have 1,000 men. He sought direct admission for his troops into the federal armed service, but was refused by the secretary of war. In early 1863, local blacks found a way to serve in the war. Massachusetts had received permission to form black military units and recruited heavily among blacks in Ohio. In Feb. 1863, Joseph D. Green organized a military company, and in April he took about 30 men to Massachusetts to join its 54th and 55th regiments. Another group from Cleveland apparently left for Massachusetts later. In June 1863, Ohio received permission from the secretary of war to organize separate black military units. The first of these was the 127th OVI, which later became the 5th Regiment of the U.S. Colored Troop. Clevelanders Gustavus W. Fahrion, Eilery C. Ford, and Frank J. Ford served as captains in the unit, which saw action in N.C. and Va. In January the state organized a second black unit, the 27th USCT; it had 15 officers and 1,423 men when mustered into service.

After the war, the state returned to its discriminatory policy of an all-white militia. Black veterans in Cleveland were denied permission to form volunteer militia companies in 1866. But in 1870, blacks used their votes as a political bargaining chip to win Republican acceptance of black militia service. By 1875, Cleveland blacks had formed 2 militia units: the City Guards and the Barnett Guards. The City Guards were in existence by late 1874, when they held a Christmas festival to raise funds; in Aug. 1875 they celebrated the anniversary of the emancipation of the British West Indies, and in 1876 they joined other local militia units in the Washington's Birthday parade and at encampments that summer. The Barnett Guards also participated in the summer encampments that year. Such units were expensive to maintain, however, since the burden of buying arms, maintaining armories, and hosting socials rested with the militia men themselves. By 1877, Cleveland's 2 black militia units had become inactive. Changes in the militia law made the state and localities partners in sharing the costs of maintaining the militia, and in 1895 black Clevelanders organized another militia unit, L'Ouverture Rifles, named in honor of the Haitian patriot Toussaint L'Ouverture. With the the outbreak of the SPANISH-AMERICAN WAR, this unit of 67 men entered the Ohio Natl. Guard on 27 May 1898 as Co. D of the 9th Battalion. It did not see action during the war and was mustered out of federal service in Jan. 1899. It saw action on 21 July 1899, however, when, according to one historian, it "brutally restored order during a railway strike" in Cleveland. Pres. McKinley once praised officers of the company as being "the most conservative elements in American society." In 1900, popular Cleveland businessman John C. Fulton was elected commander of the 9th Battalion.

Discrimination in the military became apparent again during WORLD WAR I. Co. D was called into federal service in the summer of 1917 but was poorly supplied. Co. D later became Co. H of the 372d Regiment and was scheduled for overseas duty in 1918. But only days before the 9th's scheduled departure for Europe, a number of its ranking officers, including Clevelanders Maj. John C. Fulton and Capt. Wm. Green, were relieved of duty and discharged as physically unfit. Despite losing senior officers in a blatant move to eliminate high-ranking blacks from the service, the black troops performed well in Europe. The 372d was loaned to the French and saw considerable combat; the entire officer corps of Co. H was either killed or wounded in the Argonne in Sept. 1918. The 372d received the Croix de Guerre, France's highest military medal, and Co. H returned to a warm and ceremonious reception in Cleveland on 22 Feb. 1919. After the war, the Cleveland company returned to the Ohio Natl. Guard as Co. E of the 372d Infantry. It was called into federal service again in Mar. 1941; after training at Camp Dix, N.J., the unit served on the U.S. mainland until it was sent to the Pacific early in 1944. Transfers and its use as a training unit deprived the company of its Cleveland identity prior to its deactivation in Jan. 1946. In 1947, a branch of the Columbus-based 183d AAA (Automatic Weapons) Battalion was established in Cleveland. The 183d was redesignated the 137th AAA Battalion (Self-Propelled) in 1949 and was called into federal service on 15 Jan. 1952 for the Korean War, but saw no combat before reverting to a state unit in 1954. The Ohio Natl. Guard was integrated in 1954 by order of Gov. Frank Lausche.

Black, Lowell Dwight, *The Negro Volunteer Militia Units in the Ohio National Guard, 1870-1954* (1976).

**BLACKS.** Cleveland's black community is almost as old as the city itself. GEO. PEAKE, the first black settler, arrived in 1809, and by 1860 there were 799 blacks living in a growing community of over 43,000. As early as the 1850s, most of Cleveland's black population lived on the east side. But although blacks tended to live in a few neighborhoods, black and white families were usually interspersed within these areas; until the beginning of the 20th century, nothing resembling a black ghetto existed in the city. Throughout most of the 19th century, the social and economic status of Afro-Americans in the Forest City was superior to that in other communities in the north. By the late 1840s, the public schools were integrated, and segregation in theaters, restaurants, and hotels was infrequent; interracial violence seldom occurred. Black Clevelanders also suffered less occupational discrimination than blacks in other cities. Although many were forced to work as unskilled laborers or domestic servants, almost 1/3 were skilled workers, and a significant number were able to accumulate substantial wealth. Alfred Greenbrier became widely known for raising horses and cattle, and MADISON TILLEY employed 100 men in his excavating business. John Brown, a barber, became the city's wealthiest Negro through investment in real estate valued at $40,000 at the time of his death in 1869. Founded by New Englanders who favored reform, Cleveland was a center of abolitionism before the CIVIL WAR,

and the city's white leadership remained sympathetic to civil rights during the decade following the war. Black leaders were not complacent, however. Individuals such as John Brown and JOHN MALVIN often assisted escaped slaves, and by the end of the Civil War a number of black Clevelanders had served in the Union Army. Black leaders fought for integration rather than the development of separate black institutions in the 19th century. The city's first permanent black newspaper, the *CLEVELAND GAZETTE*, did not appear until 1883. Even the black church developed more slowly than elsewhere. ST. JOHN'S AME was founded in 1830, but it was not until 1864 that a second black church, MT. ZION CONGREGATIONAL, came into existence.

Between 1890-1915, the beginnings of mass migration from the South increased Cleveland's black population substantially; by the time of WORLD WAR I, about 10,000 blacks lived in the city. Most of these newcomers settled in the Central Ave. district between the CUYAHOGA RIVER and E. 40th St. At this time, the lower Central area also housed many poor Italian and Jewish immigrants. Nevertheless, the black population was becoming much more concentrated than it had been. In other ways, too, conditions were deteriorating for black Clevelanders. That was not true of the city's school system; black students were not segregated in separate schools or classrooms, as they often were in other cities. But exclusion of blacks from restaurants and theaters became commonplace, and by 1915 the city's YMCA and YWCA prohibited Negroes from membership. Hospitals excluded black doctors and began to segregate black patients in separate wards. The most serious discrimination occurred in the economic arena. Between 1870-1915, Cleveland became a major manufacturing center, but few blacks were able to take part in industrial jobs. Blacks were not hired to work in the steel mills and foundries that became the mainstay of the city's economy. The prejudice of employers was often matched by that of trade unions, which usually excluded blacks from membership. As a result, by 1910 only about 10% of black men in the city worked in skilled trades, while the number of blacks in service jobs doubled.

Increasing discrimination forced black Clevelanders back upon their own resources. The growth of black churches was the clearest example. Three new churches were founded between 1865-90, a dozen more during the next 25 years. The Baptist congregations grew most rapidly, and by 1915 ANTIOCH BAPTIST CHURCH had emerged as the largest black church in the city. Black fraternal orders also multiplied during this period, and in 1896 the Cleveland Home for Aged Colored People was established. With assistance from white philanthropists, the PHILLIS WHEATLEY ASSOC., a residential, job-training, and recreation center for black girls, was established in 1913 by JANE HUNTER, a black nurse. Blacks gained the right to vote in Ohio in 1870, and until the 1930s they usually voted Republican. The first black Clevelander to hold political office was JOHN PATTERSON GREEN, who was elected justice of the peace in 1873, served in the state legislature in the 1880s, and in 1891 became the first Negro in the North to win election to the state senate. After 1900, increasing racial prejudice made it difficult for blacks to win election to the state legislature, and a new group of black politicians began to build up a political base in the Central Ave. area. In 1915, THOS. W. FLEMING became the first black to win election to city council.

The period 1915-30 was one of both adversity and progress for black Clevelanders. Industrial demands and a decline in immigration from abroad during World War I created both a need and an opportunity for black labor in northern industries, and hundreds of thousands of black migrants came north after 1916. By 1930 there were 72,000 Afro-Americans in Cleveland. As a result of this migration, the Central Ave. ghetto consolidated and expanded eastward, as whites moved to outlying sections of the city. Increasing racial violence kept even middle-class Negroes within the Central-Woodland area. At the same time, discrimination in public accommodations increased. Restaurants overcharged blacks or refused them service; theaters excluded blacks or segregated them in the balcony; amusement parks were usually for whites only. Discrimination even began to affect the public schools. The growth of the ghetto created some segregated schools, but the new policy of allowing white students to transfer out of predominantly black schools increased segregation. In the 1920s and 1930s, school administrators often altered the curriculums of ghetto schools from liberal arts to an emphasis on manual training. Nevertheless, migrants continued to pour into the city in the 1920s, because for the first time they were able to obtain industrial jobs. Most of these jobs were in unskilled factory labor, but blacks were also able to move up into semiskilled and skilled positions. The rapid growth in the city's black population also created new opportunities for some black businessmen and professionals. Most black businesses, however, remained small: food stores, restaurants, and small retail stores predominated. Although the employment picture for blacks in the 1920s had improved, serious problems of discrimination still existed, especially in clerical work and the unionized skilled trades.

Black leadership underwent a fundamental shift in the post-World War I period. Prior to the war, Cleveland's most prominent blacks had been integrationists who not only fought discrimination by whites but also objected to blacks' creating their own secular institutions. After the war, a new elite, led by Thos. Fleming, Jane Hunter, and businessman Herbert Chauncey, gained ascendancy. This new elite did not favor agitation for civil rights; they accepted the necessity of separate black institutions and favored the development of a "group economy" based on the existence of the ghetto. By the mid-1920s, however, a younger group of black leaders was beginning to emerge. "New Negro" leaders such as lawyer HARRY E. DAVIS and physician CHAS. GARVIN tried to transcend the factionalism that had divided black leaders in the past. They believed in race pride and racial solidarity, but not at the expense of equal rights for the black citizens of the city. The postwar era also brought changes to the institutions of Cleveland's black community. The influx of migrants caused problems that the black churches were only partly able to deal with. The Negro Welfare Assoc., an affiliate of the Natl. Urban League founded in 1917, helped newcomers find jobs and suitable housing. The Phillis Wheatley Assoc. expanded its operations on behalf of homeless black girls, and a fundraising drive among white philanthropists made possible the construction of a 9-story building in 1928. The Cleveland branch of the NATL. ASSOC. FOR THE ADVANCEMENT OF COLORED PEOPLE (NAACP), led by "New Negroes," also expanded; by 1922 the branch had 1,600 members. The NAACP fought the rising tide of racism in the city by bringing suits against restaurants and theaters that excluded blacks, or intervened behind the scenes in an attempt to get white businessmen to end discriminatory practices. The FUTURE OUTLOOK LEAGUE, founded by John Holly, became the first black organization to successfully use the boycott to combat rising discriminatory practices.

The Depression temporarily reversed much of the progress that black Clevelanders had made during the previous 15 years. Although both races were devastated by the eco-

nomic collapse, blacks suffered much higher rates of unemployment at an earlier stage, and many black businesses went bankrupt. After 1933, the New Deal relief programs helped to reduce black unemployment substantially, but New Deal public-housing projects were segregated and contributed to overcrowding because they demolished more units than they built. Housing conditions in the Central area deteriorated during the 1930s, and blacks continued to suffer discrimination in many public accommodations. The period from the late 1920s to the mid-1940s was one of political change for black Clevelanders. Although migration from the South slowed to a trickle during the 1930s, the black population had already increased to the point where it was able to augment its political influence. In 1927, 3 blacks were elected to city council, and for the next 8 years they represented a balance of power on a council almost equally divided between Republicans and Democrats. As a result, they were able to obtain the election of Harry E. Davis to the city's Civil Service Commission and MARY BROWN MARTIN to the Board of Education, the first Negroes to hold such positions. They were also able to end discrimination and segregation at City Hospital. At the local level in the 1930s, black Clevelanders continued to vote Republican; they did not support a Democrat for mayor until 1943. In national politics, however, the New Deal relief policies convinced blacks to shift dramatically after 1932 from the Republican to the Democratic party. After WORLD WAR II, Pres. Harry Truman's strong civil-rights program solidified black support for the Democrats.

World War II was a turning point in other ways, also. The war revived industry and led to a new demand for black labor. This demand, and the more egalitarian labor-union practices of the newly formed Congress of Industrial Organizations, created new job opportunities for black Clevelanders and also led to a revival of mass migration from the South. The steady flow of newcomers increased Cleveland's black population from 85,000 in 1940 to 251,000 in 1960; by the early 1960s, blacks made up over 30% of the city's population. One effect of this population growth was increased political representation for blacks. In 1947, Harry E. Davis was elected to the state senate, and 2 years later Jean M. Capers became the first black woman to be elected to city council. By the mid-1960s, the number of blacks serving on council had increased to 10, and in 1968 Louis Stokes was elected to the U.S. House of Representatives. The postwar era also marked a period of progress in civil rights. In 1945 the CLEVELAND COMMUNITY RELATIONS BOARD was established; it soon developed a national reputation for promoting improvement in race relations. The following year, the city enacted a municipal civil-rights law that revoked the license of any business convicted of discriminating against blacks. The liberal atmosphere of the postwar period (partly a product of the democratic ideology of the war against fascism) also led to a gradual decline in discrimination against blacks in public accommodations during the late 1940s and 1950s. By the 1960s, segregated hospital wards and exclusion from downtown hotels and restaurants were a thing of the past.

Despite the improvements of the 1940–60 period, however, serious problems continued to plague the black community. The most important of these was housing. As the suburbanization of the city's white population accelerated, the black community expanded to the east and northeast of the Central-Woodland area, particularly into the Hough Ave. and Glenville sections. Expansion, however, did not lead to more integrated neighborhoods or provide better housing for blacks. "Blockbusting" techniques by realtors led to panic selling by whites in HOUGH in the 1950s;

once a neighborhood became all black, landlords would subdivide structures into small apartments and raise rents exorbitantly. The result, by 1960, was the transformation of Hough into a crowded ghetto of deteriorating housing stock. At the same time, segregation in public schools continued, abetted by school officials who routinely assigned black children to predominantly black schools. In 1964, violence between blacks and whites broke out when blacks protested the locations for the construction of 3 new schools. Frustration over inability to effect changes in housing and education, coupled with a rise in black unemployment that began in the late 1950s, finally ignited in a 4-day riot in the Hough ghetto (see HOUGH RIOTS) in 1966, which resulted in 47 people injured and millions of dollars in property damage. Two years later, a gun battle took place between black nationalists and police in GLENVILLE, and more rioting followed (see GLENVILLE SHOOT-OUT). The tension and hostility resulting from the riots did not entirely destroy the spirit of racial toleration in Cleveland, however, as evidenced by the election of Carl B. Stokes as mayor in 1967. Stokes, who would be reelected in 1969, became the first black to serve as mayor of a major American city. After he retired from politics in 1971, no black leader was able to replace him. Since then, however, blacks have continued to be the most influential group in city council.

As migration from the South came to an end, Cleveland's black population stabilized in the 1970s and 1980s. Although the ghetto continued to expand eastward (into E. CLEVELAND), fair-housing laws now made it possible for middle-class blacks to have greater choice of residency. Other eastern suburbs, SHAKER HTS. and CLEVELAND HTS., absorbed large numbers of black residents by the 1970s, but managed to maintain a balanced integrated population. In addition, some of the more blatant causes of the riots—such as the small number of black policemen—were partially resolved. But fundamental problems remained. Structural unemployment, exacerbated since 1970 as businesses moved to outlying suburbs or to the Sunbelt, adversely affected workers of both races, but the decline of manufacturing hurt blacks disproportionately. In the late 20th century, the most significant problems for black Clevelanders remained economic in nature.

Kenneth L. Kusmer
Temple University

Davis, Russell, *Black Americans in Cleveland* (1972).
Kusmer, Kenneth L., *A Ghetto Takes Shape* (1976).

**BLANCHARD, FERDINAND Q.** (23 July 1876-4 Mar. 1968), was a clergyman, poet, author, and civic leader. He was born in Jersey City Hts., N.J., the son of Edward Richmond and Anna Winifred Quincy Blanchard. His family moved to West Newton, Mass., where he received his early education; in 1894, he graduated from West Newton High School. He received his A.B. degree from Amherst College in 1898 and a B.D. degree from Yale Divinity School in 1901. On 29 May 1901 he was ordained as a Congregational minister, and on 19 June 1901 he married Ethel Hebard West. Dr. Blanchard served the Congregational Church in Southington, Conn., from 1901-04 and the First Congregational Church of East Orange, N.J., from 1904-15, when he accepted an invitation to become the minister of the EUCLID AVE. CONGREGATIONAL CHURCH at 9600 Euclid Ave., Cleveland. He was installed 25 Mar. 1915.

During WORLD WAR I, Blanchard was secretary of the YMCA at Camp Sherman, Chillicothe, Ohio. He received honorary D.D. degrees from Amherst College in 1918 and Oberlin College in Ohio in 1919. In addition to

his pastoral responsibilities, Dr. Blanchard was active in the religious, civic, and philanthropic life of the city, serving as president of the Cleveland Church Fed. (Greater Cleveland Council of Churches) from 1919-20; as secretary and board member of the AMERICAN RED CROSS, CLEVELAND CHAP.; as president and board member of the Associated Charities (Family Service Assoc.); and as a trustee of the URBAN LEAGUE OF CLEVELAND, KARAMU HOUSE, the Maternal Health Assoc. (PLANNED PARENTHOOD), and Schauffler College. He was active in the Society of Mayflower Descendants and in the organization that he founded (Jan. 1920), the Alathian Club, an ecumenical group of Cleveland clergy. He was a member of the executive committee of the Missionary Assoc. from 1908-36. For many years, he was a trustee (and later trustee emeritus) of Fisk University, Nashville, Tenn. In 1937, he was a delegate to the Oxford Conference on Life & Work held in Oxford, England.

On 14 June 1942, Blanchard was elected to the highest honor of his denomination—moderator of the General Council of the Congregational Christian Churches of the U.S. As moderator (1942-44), he provided leadership for over 6,000 Congregational churches with more than 1 million members. From 1944-50, Blanchard served as national chairman of the Congregational Commission of Interchurch Affairs. As one of the chief proponents for the union of the Congregational and the Evangelical & Reformed churches, he was instrumental in laying the foundation for the merger that was effected in Cleveland in June 1957 and resulted in the establishment of the United Church of Christ.

Blanchard wrote many articles for magazines, newspapers, and professional journals, as well as many poems and hymns. He also wrote several books, including *For the King's Sake* (1915), *How One Man Changed the World* (1928), and *Jesus and the World's Quests* (1930). He retired from the Euclid Ave. Congregational Church in 1951, became pastor emeritus, and continued to serve his church, his denomination, and his community. Mrs. Blanchard died 3 July 1966. The Blanchards had 2 children, a son, Edward R., a research chemist, and a daughter, Virginia (Mrs. Chas. S. Becker).

From *Village Green to City Center, 1843-1943* (Centennial of the Euclid Ave. Congregational Church, Cleveland, Ohio, 1943).

**BLEE, ROBERT E.** (31 Jan. 1839-26 Feb. 1898), was a railroad superintendent who served as mayor of Cleveland from 1893-95. He was born in Glenville, Ohio. His father, Hugh Blee, was one of the earliest settlers of Cuyahoga County. Blee attended district schools and the Shaw Academy at COLLAMER. He spent much of his childhood watching the trains on the nearby Lake Shore & Michigan Southern Railway. He was inspired by a Shaw graduation speaker to pursue a career in railroading; at age 15 he became a brakeman for the Cleveland, Columbus, & Cincinnati Railroad, the "Bee Line." During the CIVIL WAR, Blee supervised troop transportation for the Army between Cleveland's Camp Chase and Camp Dennison. After the war, he returned to the Bee Line, and by 1888 he had risen to the position of its general superintendent. Blee also had other business interests. He organized the Bee Line Insurance Co., serving as its president for 22 years. He was the president of the Ohio Natl. Bldg. & Loan Co. and a director for several other corporations. He never married.

During his life, Blee served in only 2 political positions. Elected as a Democrat, he was Cleveland's police commissioner from 1875-79; he is credited with ending the unpopular "star sessions" that typified police arrests until that time. As the result of a Republican split in 1893, Blee was elected mayor of Cleveland. During his term, he strongly advocated harbor improvements and the building of docks on the lakefront to maintain the city's position as a Great Lakes port. The police department also tried to register local prostitutes, but Blee was forced to stop them because of public outrage. Blee was defeated for reelection by ROBT. E. MCKISSON in 1895.

**BLISS, STOUGHTON** (18 Feb. 1823–19 Sept. 1896), was a Cleveland businessman and Army officer during the CIVIL WAR. Bliss was born in Cleveland. He worked as a post office clerk until going into the hat and fur business in 1846. Between 1850 and the outbreak of the Civil War, he was appointed colonel and served as assistant quartermaster of Ohio, a position that he held throughout the war. After the war he went into the stone business. At his death, he was affiliated with the Diamond Stone Quarry in BEREA, and was treasurer of the Grafton Stone Co. He was 1st vice-president of the Cleveland Light Artillery Assoc. Bliss married Mary Sweet in 1849. He never remarried after her death in 1851. There were no children. He is buried in Woodland Cemetery.

**BLIZZARDS** do not occur frequently in Cleveland, though heavy winter snowstorms are normal because of the proximity of Lake Erie and "lake effect" snows. Most snowstorms are not blizzards, with constant winds over 35 mph. The worst blizzards listed in the Natl. Weather Service records since 1871 occurred 9–11 Nov. 1913, 23–28 Nov. 1950, and 26–27 Jan. 1978. The 1913 blizzard began as 2 storms, one from the Canadian Northwest, which missed Cleveland, and another from Georgia, merged over New York and moved over the Great Lakes. Freezing rain fell early Sunday, 9 Nov. For over 7 hours that night, 60-mph winds blew out windows and spread fires; the barometer almost set a record, 28.78″. Downed electric wires electrocuted horses, halted trolleys, and severed communications with other cities. Plowing was futile; cleared areas were soon snow-covered. The Great Lakes shipping season had not ended; 32 ships were lost or severely damaged, as 277 sailors died. The storm subsided Tuesday, but food and coal supplies were low. Travel was paralyzed by 22.2″ of snow. Transit companies could not locate their cars. Obstacles blocked snow removal until Wednesday. Muddy city water required boiling. Food and fuel deliveries were resumed in the central city, but fresh goods could not be found past E. 55th or W. 25th streets; only canned foods were available. E. CLEVELAND and LAKEWOOD were isolated. Communication with the suburbs and the outside world was slowly reestablished. A thaw began on Thursday as temperatures reached 44 degrees; runoff water flooded some basements. Normal conditions returned by Friday. Transit lines reopened, and most utility wires were repaired; outages continued in fringe areas. The Weather Bureau called the storm the worst in its records.

On Thanksgiving 1950, an arctic air mass lowered temperatures to 7 degrees. The next day, 24 Nov., low pressure from Virginia moved into Ohio to cause a blizzard with high winds and heavy snow. The airport closed, and trolleys were immobile. The *Press* did not publish on Saturday, while a skeleton crew printed the *Plain Dealer*. Mayor THOS. BURKE called out the Natl. Guard and snow-removal equipment to clear the 22.1″ of snow brought by the 5-day storm. Sunday, Burke declared a state of emergency, banned unnecessary travel, and set up a city hall command post with service crews, transit authorities, and the Natl. Guard. Over 10,000 abandoned cars blocked snow removal; ice-packed track grooves closed 75% of CTS's streetcar lines. The storm weakened on Monday. Most area

schools closed; drifts still prevented clearing. The airport and downtown stores opened on Tuesday, but Burke asked downtown businesses to stagger hours to reduce transit burdens. Nonessential cars were banned downtown; parked cars blocked transit tracks. The storm ended, and all guardsmen were dismissed by Wednesday. Cleveland schools were to reopen that day but remained closed all week to keep children off transit lines. Some suburban systems reopened but then closed because of dangers from children walking in the streets. The emergency peaked on Thursday. Cleanup crews worked continuously; Burke ordered main arteries cleared curb to curb before side streets. Although the auto ban lasted until the last CTS line reopened on Saturday, parking problems remained, but police no longer monitored traffic. Normal conditions returned as the temperature hit 53 degrees. The storm had paralyzed the area for a week and cost over $1 million and 23 lives.

The worst blizzard in Cleveland history hit early Thursday, 26 Jan. 1978; low pressure from the Mississippi Valley met over southern Ohio with low pressure from the western Great Lakes. A cyclone formed as high winds rotated around low pressure; the eye reached Cleveland about 4–5 a.m., lowering the barometer to a record 28.26″. The temperature dropped 39 degrees in 6 hours; the wind chill exceeded −100 degrees F. Sustained winds blew 53 mph with 82-mph gusts as 8″ of snow fell. Hopkins Airport closed early with zero visibility. The Illuminating Co. sent 140 crews to repair 300 lines downed by wind and branches; 110,000 Greater Cleveland homes lost power, including 40% of Euclid. Fifty shelters opened. Mail delivery was halted for the first time since the 1950 blizzard. The blizzard, the third major storm of the winter of 1977–78, paralyzed much of the eastern U.S. Mayor Dennis Kucinich could not return from a Washington conference; finance director Joseph Tegreene set up a command post as acting mayor. The Natl. Guard, called up for the first time since 1950, was activated as Gov. Jas. Rhodes declared a statewide emergency. The storm hit before workers could depart for jobs, leaving fewer abandoned cars. RTA Rapids ran a few minutes late, but some buses were 90 minutes behind; RTA added 20 extra buses to meet demand. Many lines were rerouted because of closed roads. All area freeways were closed by the storm except for I–77; the entire Ohio Turnpike closed for the first time. Conditions improved the next day as winds averaged 20–30 mph; power was restored to all but 10,000 homes. Hopkins Airport reopened that afternoon. All major highways and the turnpike east of Elyria reopened. Guardsmen were reassigned to other areas of the state still hard-hit. Grocers anticipated shortages of milk and eggs if supplies did not arrive by the next week, but supplies began arriving over the weekend. The storm emphasized a major problem the city faced that winter, the second-snowiest ever: its snow-removal fleet was inadequate.

**BLOCH, ERNEST** (24 July 1880–15 July 1959), was an internationally known composer, conductor, teacher, and lecturer. He was recruited to found and direct the CLEVELAND INSTITUTE OF MUSIC in 1920. He stayed as its first administrator until 1925 (when he left to direct the San Francisco Conservatory of Music). Bloch was born in Geneva, Switzerland, to nonmusical parents. The son of a Jewish merchant, he showed musical talent early and determined that he would become a composer. By the age of 10, he was studying violin and composing pieces for the instrument. His teen years were marked by important study with violin and composition masters in Geneva and other European cities. His first main composition, the Symphony in C Sharp Minor, dates from his years in Munich (1901–03).

By 1904, Bloch returned to Geneva to enter his father's business. Between then and 1916, he juggled business responsibilities with composing and conducting. He delivered 115 lectures on aesthetics at the Geneva Conservatory. In 1916, in grave financial straits and with heavy family responsibilities, he accepted a job as conductor for dancer Maud Allen's American tour. The tour collapsed after 6 weeks, but performances of his works in New York and Boston created an immense impression, and his importance as a musical figure grew. Bloch devoted the years 1917–20 primarily to teaching in New York City (at David Mannes School and privately).

During the Cleveland years (1920–25), Bloch completed 21 works, among them the popular Concerto Grosso, which was composed for the students' orchestra at the Cleveland Institute of Music. His contributions included an institute chorus at the CLEVELAND MUSEUM OF ART, attention to pedagogy especially in composition and theory, and a concern that every student should have a direct and high-quality aesthetic experience. He taught several classes himself. After disagreements with Cleveland Institute of Music policy and policymakers, he moved to the directorship of the San Francisco Conservatory.

Bloch's Concerto for Violin and Orchestra had its premiere in Cleveland on 14 Dec. 1938 (Dmitri Mitropoulos conducting) by Joseph Szigetti. His students over the years included world-famous composer Roger Sessions and Cleveland composer HERBERT ELWELL. Bloch composed over 100 works for a variety of individual instruments and ensemble sizes. He won over a dozen prestigious awards, including the first Gold Medal in Music of the American Academy of Arts & Sciences (1947). His interests ranged far beyond music and included photography and metaphysics. He was married to Margaethe Schneider. They had 3 children.

**BLODGETT, WALTER** (1907–25 Oct. 1975), was an organist and teacher. He was also the curator of musical arts at the CLEVELAND MUSEUM OF ART from 1943–74. Blodgett was born in Grand Rapids, Mich. He came to Cleveland from Chicago in 1931, after holding a teaching post. He was a graduate of Oberlin College and the Julliard School of Music. He also studied at the College of St. Nicholas in England and studied organ design and construction in Germany. He was a career organist. His musical directions encompassed the EPWORTH EUCLID METHODIST CHURCH, St. James Episcopal, and the First Unitarian Church. Later, he was organist and director for 25 years at ST. PAUL'S EPISCOPAL CHURCH. On 1 Jan. 1943, Blodgett became the curator of musical arts at the Cleveland Museum of Art. He played nearly 1,200 organ recitals at the museum. He helped design its Gartner Auditorium, then tackled the "monster" (as he referred to it), rebuilding the P. J. McMyler Memorial Organ, located in the auditorium. In an interview with the *Plain Dealer* upon retiring after 33 years with the museum, Blodgett stated that his "most memorable evenings were spent conducting major choral works under museum sponsorship at St. Paul's Episcopal." His choir gave the Cleveland premiere of Beethoven's *Missa Solemnis*. The evening of his retirement, he played an all-Bach program and received a standing ovation. He is credited with generating considerable funds for the museum from endowments and also developing a network in Europe to bring new artists to Cleveland. He initiated the May Festival of Contemporary Music. Blodgett was music critic for the *Press* during WORLD WAR II. He contributed articles to various music magazines and was a faculty member at Western Reserve University from 1957–62. As soon as he retired as curator, he became, in 1974, the dean of faculty at the CLEVELAND MUSIC SCHOOL SETTLEMENT; he had been an advisory trustee for many years to the settlement. The same year, he won the Cleveland Arts Prize citation "for support and promotion for the creation and performance of new works, and encouraging and sustaining musical life in Cleveland." A resident of SHAKER HTS., Blodgett was unmarried.

**BLOSSOM, DUDLEY S.** (10 Mar. 1879–7 Oct. 1938), was a Cleveland businessman and philanthropist whose charitable contributions and activities eventually led him to civic office as city welfare director. Blossom, the son of Henry S. and Lela Stocking Blossom, received an A.B. degree from Yale. After returning to Cleveland, he began his associations with the Perry-Payne Corp., Payne-Bingham Co., Standard Tool Co., Cleveland Hobbing Machine Co., Blossom Lock Co., and Central Natl. Bank, in each of which he served as a director or officer. He served with the Red Cross in France during WORLD WAR I and in 1919 was appointed Cleveland city welfare director, a position he retained until 1921—then from 1924–32. As welfare director, Blossom was considered a progressive and an innovator, gaining national attention for city human-services projects, including City Hospital and Blossom Hill Home.

As a substantial contributor to the Community Fund, Blossom became fund chairman in 1934 and was appointed honorary chairman for life in 1938. He headed the campaign that raised the funds required to match JOHN L. SEVERANCE's $2.5 million donation to build SEVERANCE HALL. Blossom served as president of the MUSICAL ARTS ASSOC. and was a trustee of the Negro Welfare Fund, UNIVERSITY HOSPITALS, and Cleveland College. In the mid-1930s he was chairman of the GREAT LAKES EXPOSITION, and he also served 1 term as state representative. Blossom married Elizabeth Bingham, heiress to Oliver Hazard Payne's Standard Oil fortune, on 29 Sept. 1910. They had 2 children, Dudley S., Jr., and Mary.

**BLOSSOM, VOYAGE OF THE.** *See* **VOYAGE OF THE BLOSSOM**

The **BLOSSOM HILL SCHOOL FOR GIRLS** was a juvenile rehabilitation center that emphasized work away from home and continued secondary education as necessary steps in changing behavior and creating a more secure social setting. It was one of the first institutions of its type in the U.S. Initially named the Cleveland Girls' Farm, the institution began in 1914 and was located on a 37-acre tract on Kinsman Rd. In 1928 it moved to BRECKSVILLE and was renamed Blossom Hill in honor of DUDLEY S. BLOSSOM, one of its major benefactors. The Brecksville facility consisted of an administration building and 4 large brick homes that could house 75 girls. Although not all of the girls sent to Blossom Hill were delinquent, they were either wards of the court or referred by social-service agencies in Cleveland and Cuyahoga County. Girls ages 10–18 were eligible for the school; the average stay was 11 months. The rehabilitation program emphasized industrial and vocational training. The school attempted to create a stable social environment and prepare the girls for economic independence and responsible citizenship. Family members were encouraged to visit so as to retain strong family ties.

Since Blossom Hill became the girls' full-time home for an extended period, they received full school instruction. Teachers from the Cleveland Board of Education taught standard secondary as well as vocational courses. Recreation, medical care, and church programs were also provided. Since approximately 70% of the girls came from broken or unfit homes, they were eventually placed in private homes, where they usually worked as domestics. They were visited by the school's social worker weekly and remained under the institution's jurisdiction until age 21. In 1958 the school was taken over by Cuyahoga County. In 1974 the staff and girls moved to the site of the Hudson Boys Farm in Hudson, Ohio, which then became the Youth Development Ctr.

**BLUE CROSS AND BLUE SHIELD MUTUAL OF NORTHERN OHIO** resulted from the 1983 merger of BLUE CROSS OF NORTHEAST OHIO and MEDICAL MUTUAL OF CLEVELAND, INC., profferers of hospital insurance in northeast Ohio. The companies, which offered complementary benefits and shared headquarters, joined to cut operating costs, aid health care cost-containment efforts, and offer a comprehensive product line in a competitive marketplace. The merger was predicted to save $30 million in administrative costs within the first 3–5 years, and $9 million annually after that. Part of the savings was to accrue through staff reductions (mainly through attrition) of 400. Since its formation, BC/BS has attacked rising medical costs through the creation of a health-maintenance organization and the introduction of the CURE program. The HMO is a network of clinics that serve 10 northeastern Ohio counties, providing routine out-patient care for subscribers, who are then admitted to any of the 21 participating hospitals, if necessary. Meanwhile, the CURE program (Controlling Utilization Results Effectively), introduced in Oct. 1983, requires preadmission approval before a patient is checked into a hospital and prescribes the length of stay. Though the program has been criticized by physicians, who see their judgment called into question, and by patients, who resent being sent home too soon, CURE saved over $40 million in its first year of operation. Some savings, however, were shifted to out-patient care.

Another cost-containment measure developed by the new organization was the 1985 requirement that hospitals bid for Blue Cross business. Though 34 hospitals in Cuyahoga, Lake, and Lorain counties received invitations to bid, only those meeting certain standards for space utilization, efficiency, and economy were eligible for full Blue Cross/Blue Shield reimbursement. Hospitals that lost bids to become approved Blue Cross facilities claimed that political factors influenced the choices. Some, such as Lakewood Hospital, successfully challenged and overturned the Blue Cross decision in court. However, since BC/BS paid an average of 25% of area hospital bills, the company expected that the bidding process (and its CURE program) would eventually change hospital procedures and, in the long run, reduce unneeded hospital beds. In 1986, Blue Cross & Blue Shield Mutual of Northern Ohio served over 1 million subscribers in 11 counties. Although the company faced competition from self-insurance plans, private insurance companies, and Community Mutual, the Cinncinati-based Blue Cross affiliate, it remained the leader in hospital insurance in the area.

**BLUE CROSS OF NORTHEAST OHIO,** formed in 1957, united the CLEVELAND HOSPITAL SERVICE ASSOC. and the Akron Hospital Service Assoc. Like its Cleveland neighbor, the CHSA, founded in 1934, the AHSA was established in 1936 with the support of the business, social-service, and medical communities to offer prepaid hospitalization, and originally was funded by Akron Welfare Fed. loans. At the time of the merger, the Akron plan had 225,000 subscribers, while Cleveland had 1.5 million. The Blue Cross name originated in St. Paul, Minn., in 1933,

where the logo was created for the local hospitalization plan. Other plans copied the name and the distinctive blue emblem. By 1939, the American Hospital Assoc. adopted and took control of the name and the symbol; thereafter, only nonprofit hospital plans that met association standards could use the name. BCNO, based at 2066 E. 9th St., formerly the CHSA office, was heir to the dilemmas that challenged its predecessors: how to maintain reasonable rates in the face of spiraling hospital and medical costs. As medical science found new ways to prolong and improve the quality of life, Blue Cross responded by providing coverage for costly new procedures. With the aging of the U.S. population, further demands were put on the system to pay more claims. Costs were also increased by rising wages and supply costs. Moreover, the shortage of hospital beds that characterized the early days of the Blues was replaced by a surplus that was figured into hospital overhead.

When Blue Cross reached its 35th birthday in 1969, 600 people were on staff, compared to 5 at the start and 300 in 1965. The plan paid $1.4 billion in benefits during 35 years, with $100 million paid out in 1968 alone. With 1.8 million subscribers, the company's income was approximately $106.7 million annually. The Blue Cross policy, which at its inception offered 21 days of prepaid hospitalization for $.60 per month, now covered elongated stays, prescription drugs, and out-patient services, according to the terms of the policies, which were tailored to specific groups of subscribers. In an effort to control costs, BCNO installed a computerized recordkeeping system in 1970. The company instituted a cash incentive program to hospitals with above-average records on controlling costs, and required that hospitals submit expansion plans in advance to certain central health-planning agencies in order to receive certain benefits. The hiring of a financial expert as the new president of Blue Cross in 1976 further reflected the concern with cost containment. In the 1970s, BCNO provided benefit packages with increased out-patient coverage to minimize more costly hospital care. Coverage was also extended to single-parent maternity, alcoholism treatment, and mental health care at state institutions. Throughout Blue Cross history, physician care was covered by its sister organization, MEDICAL MUTUAL OF CLEVELAND, INC. This company was separately managed, but the coverages were intertwined and the products marketed together, which made them indistinguishable in the public mind. To better coordinate efforts to attack rising health costs, Medical Mutual and BCNO merged in Sept. 1983 to become BLUE CROSS & BLUE SHIELD MUTUAL OF NORTHERN OHIO.

Condon, George, *Fifty Years of Community Service* (1984).

**BLUE ROCK SPRING HOUSE** was a regionally renowned water cure located in Cedar Glen (Cedar Rd., south of UNIVERSITY CIRCLE). Between 1880–1908 it operated as a sanitarium or hotel, offering a variety of mineral-bath treatments and bottled spring water. For many years, area residents had drawn from the natural spring that produced a blue-green water containing large amounts of sulfur. It was believed to have therapeutic value, and its reputation increased. The owner of the land, Dr. Nathan H. Ambler, saw commercial possibilities, and in the late 1870s he fenced off the spring and began to bottle its water for sale to Cleveland restaurants and private residences. He invited Daniel O. Caswell, who had been helping him develop his real-estate interests, to take over the operation. The Blue Rock Spring Co. was incorporated in 1880, and facilities were constructed for a water cure. Water cure, or HYDROPATHY, was in vogue at the time and was administered for a variety of ailments. In the Blue Rock Spring House, baths were carved out of the rock on the ground floor of the building. Throughout the 1880s and 1890s, fashionable health treatments were offered under the direction of a professional medical staff. It was more of a resort in its early years, but the professional emphasis was later increased, and in 1901 the name was officially changed from Blue Rock Mineral Spring to Blue Rock Sanitarium Spring. Ambler, a dentist, made a fortune from the spring. Caswell, for many years president of the Blue Rock Spring Co., also benefited financially. His son, Daniel, Jr., was made Ambler's heir. The sanitarium closed in 1908, probably because of the waning popularity of hydropathy.

The **BLUESTONE QUARRIES** were situated in the small village of Bluestone near the intersection of Green and Bluestone roads in S. EUCLID. In its heyday, Bluestone was home to about 400 people and contained a general store and post office, 2 saloons, a temperance hall, a church, and boarding houses. The village sprang from a single industry: quarrying the rock from which the town took its name. In 1867 Duncan McFarland opened a quarry on the east bank of Euclid Creek in the southern section of Euclid Twp. In 1871 his sons, James and Thomas, opened one on the west bank. Two years later, Robert and John Maxwell opened a quarry and built a large mill on NINE MILE CREEK. The McFarland brothers sold their interest in 1875 to the Forest City Stone Co., which became one of the area's largest producers.

Euclid bluestone is a bluish-gray sandstone, dense and fine-grained, and harder, stronger, and less friable than the better-known Berea sandstone. The stone was used for sills and steps, foundations, and laundry tubs. Its greatest use, however, was for sidewalks. Bluestone reached the peak of its growth in the 1890s, when immigrant laborers from Sweden, Italy, Ireland, and Canada were working 5 quarries. In 1898 Bluestone's only church, the Swedish Evangelical Lutheran Church, was built overlooking Euclid Creek on property owned by the Maxwell-Rolf Stone Co. By 1910 concrete had begun to replace stone as a building material, and the quarries began to feel the effects of the competition. The post office, which had opened in 1884, closed that year, and by the end of the decade 1 company remained active. Bluestone became part of S. Euclid when that village was incorporated in 1917. All that remains of Bluestone today (1986) are Bluestone Rd. and the many bluestone walks on Cleveland's older streets.

**BLYTHIN, EDWARD** (10 Oct. 1884–14 Feb. 1958), served as Cleveland law director, mayor, and judge in the Court of Common Pleas for Cuyahoga County. Born in Newmarket, Wales, the son of Peter and Elizabeth Roberts Blythin, he attended elementary school in Newmarket and intermediate school in Rhyl, Wales, after which he spent 2 years as a bookkeeper for an English coal firm. Blythin came to Cleveland in 1906 and was immediately hired by the Walton Realty Co. To keep its books. He worked there for 10 years while studying law nights at Cleveland Law School. After receiving his LL.D. degree in 1916, he practiced law from 1916–41 and 1942–43, specializing in municipal law. He was appointed assistant law director of the city of Cleveland in 1935, became law director in 1940, and succeeded HAROLD H. BURTON as mayor of Cleveland when Burton became a U.S. senator in 1941. He served in that capacity for 11 months but lost to Frank Lausche in the election of 1941. During his brief tenure as mayor, Blythin was active in mobilizing available manpower for the national defense effort, and with Cleveland's unemployment rate at its lowest since 1929, Blythin urged companies and unions to remove all barriers to black employment.

From 1943–48, Blythin served as financial vice-president and secretary of Western Reserve University, and he was elected judge in the common pleas court in 1949. He presided at the trial of Dr. Samuel H. Sheppard for the murder of Sheppard's wife Marilyn in 1954 (see SHEPPARD, SAMUEL, MURDER CASE). Sheppard was convicted of 2d-degree murder and sentenced to life in prison. With the widespread publicity the case engendered, the defense maintained that Sheppard had not received a fair trial. Blythin defended both his conduct of the case and the propriety of holding the trial in Cleveland at that particular time. He remained judge in the common pleas court until his death at age 73. Blythin was a member of the Cleveland Transit Board from 1943–48 and was chairman of the board of the Shaker Savings Assoc. from 1944–58. He married Jane Rankin 5 Apr. 1913, and they had 5 children, Robert, Arthur, Glen (dec.), Jane (Mrs. Robt. Drake), and William.

Harold Burton and Edward Blythin Papers, WRHS.
"In Memory of Judge Edward Blythin" (Paper delivered to the Philosophical Club of Cleveland, 14 Jan. 1958, WRHS).

**B'NAI B'RITH**, originally a fraternal and social organization, is the oldest service organization in Cleveland. Solomon Lodge No. 16 of the Independent Order of B'nai B'rith was founded in Jan. 1853, 10 years after the first lodge of the order was established in New York City. The founders of the Cleveland lodge were SIMSON THORMAN, its first president; Abraham Wiener; BENJAMIN FRANKLIN PEIXOTTO, who would go on to become a national leader of the order; and Dr. Jas. Horwitz. A second lodge, Montefiore Lodge No. 54, was established in 1864. A year later it opened the first B'nai B'rith library in America. In 1863, Peixotto was elected Grand Saar (national president) of the Constitutional Grand Lodge. Three years later, he suggested that District Grand Lodge No. 2, the regional lodge with jurisdiction over Cleveland, create a Jewish orphan asylum for the Midwest. In 1868, the Jewish Orphan Home was dedicated in Cleveland.

The Cleveland B'nai B'rith lodge donated funds for various relief and charitable projects, including creating an aid committee to assist Russian immigrants (1881); establishing the Educational League (1897) to assure that qualified orphans could receive a college education; providing funds for pogrom victims (1901, 1905); sending aid to San Francisco earthquake victims (1906); "adopting" World War I orphans (1923); and raising funds for Ohio River Flood victims (1937). A third Cleveland lodge was established in 1896. Six years later, the three lodges merged and formed Cleveland Lodge No. 16. It was not until 1930 that another lodge was established in Cleveland. Over the course of the next 20 years, 11 additional lodges were created. In 1933, Heights Chapter 119, the first B'nai B'rith women's organization in Cleveland, was founded.

In 1942, the Cleveland Interlodge Council was formed to help coordinate activities. The B'nai B'rith Women's Council had begun operation in 1941. The Cleveland Hillel Foundation was created at Western Reserve University-Case Institute of Technology in 1945 to provide a Jewish cultural and educational center for the student body. Three years later, the Hillel House, erected at a cost of $40,000, was dedicated. Beyond its service function, B'nai B'rith played an important role in the social and economic mobility of Jews in Cleveland, especially during the late 19th and early 20th centuries. Like lodges in other cities, the Cleveland B'nai B'rith provided an arena in which Jews of varying cultural backgrounds could interact without being self-conscious.

**B'NAI JESHURUN,** Cleveland's third-oldest congregation, was established in 1866 by a handful of Hungarian Jews. Originally Orthodox in ritual, B'nai Jeshurun liberalized as its members acculturated, and by the early 20th century, it had joined the Conservative movement. B'nai Jeshurun's 16 members worshipped initially in the home of its first president, saloon owner Herman Sampliner, one of 3 brothers from Zemplin, Hungary. From 1870–87, services were held at either Halle's Hall on Superior or the German Theater on Michigan. When ANSHE CHESED congregation decided to vacate its Eagle St. synagogue, in 1886, B'Nai Jeshurun purchased the building for $15,000 and began conducting services there in 1887.

Sigmund Drechsler was hired as the congregation's first ordained rabbi in 1886. He replaced Morris Klein, who had been hired as teacher and chazan in 1875. Klein remained active at the congregation as Torah reader until his death in 1912. Drechsler, Hungarian-born and trained in the Orthodox rabbinical seminary in Berlin, oversaw B'Nai Jeshurun's move toward a liberal form of Orthodoxy. In 1904, a large group of newly arrived Hungarian immigrants who opposed the liberalism of the congregation attempted to put an end to the practice of mixed or family seating that had been instituted in 1873. When the proponents of family pews held firm, several members of the congregation seceded and formed OHEB ZEDEK congregation. B'nai Jeshurun purchased property at 55th and Scovill a year later, erected a new synagogue, and dedicated the building in Sept. 1906. Also in 1906, Drechsler left the pulpit and was replaced by Abraham E. Dobrin, the first rabbi trained at the Jewish Theological Seminary of the Conservative movement to serve a Cleveland congregation.

Dissension in the congregation led a succession of rabbis to serve for only short periods of time. Dobrin left in 1909 and was followed by Samuel Schwartz, who resigned after less than 3 years. Rabbi Jacob Klein served the congregation from 1912–18 and saw its membership increase from 450 to 725. Under Klein's leadership, the Hungarian background of the congregation was stressed less, and German gave way to English as the language of sermons. SOLOMON GOLDMAN was rabbi for less than 4 years. He solidified the Conservative nature of the congregation and witnessed a further increase in membership. However, he declined to remain in the pulpit because of internal dissension and left in 1922 to become rabbi at the Cleveland Jewish Ctr.

B'nai Jeshurun sold its Scovill Ave. synagogue in 1922, preparing to move into the Heights. In 1926, a new synagogue was dedicated in Cleveland Hts. on Mayfield Rd. The $1 million Moorish-Byzantine structure was designed by Chas. Greco, the New York architect who also designed the TEMPLE on Ansel Rd. B'nai Jeshurun, now popularly known as the Temple on the Heights, was the first congregation to relocate in the suburbs. Overseeing the construction of the new synagogue was Rabbi Abraham Nowak, a Conservative-trained Rabbi who was hired in 1923. He served the congregation for 10 years before being discharged in 1933. Nowak and a small group of the congregation's members then established the Community Temple.

Nowak was replaced by Clevelander RUDOLPH ROSENTHAL, who received his training at the Reform seminary. He served B'nai Jeshurun as rabbi and rabbi emeritus until his death in 1979. During Rosenthal's tenure, the congregation retired the mortgage on the synagogue (1941); constructed a new wing that included classrooms, offices, a study, and a chapel; became the first congregation in America to affiliate with the Zionist Organization of America; and increased its membership to 1,800 by 1966. As the Jewish population continued moving eastward, B'nai Jeshurun found itself isolated from its membership. A new synagogue was erected in Beachwood and was dedicated in 1980. The building complex was sold and now houses offices and a performing-arts center.

Rabbi Rudolph Rosenthal Papers, WRHS.

**BOARD OF TRADE.** *See* **GREATER CLEVELAND GROWTH ASSOC.**

**BOARDMAN, WILLIAM JARVIS** (15 Apr. 1832–2 Aug. 1915), was a lawyer active in Cleveland business, civic, and political affairs before moving to Washington, D.C., in the late 1880s. Born in Boardman, Ohio, Wm. J. Boardman received his early education there and in neighboring Poland. He spent 3 years at Kenyon College before transferring to Trinity College in Hartford, Conn. After graduating from Trinity in 1854, he entered Yale Law School, transferring to Harvard after a year. He graduated from Harvard Law School in 1856 and moved to Cleveland, where he worked briefly in the law offices of Samuel B. and Frederick J. Prentiss before being admitted to the bar and opening his own law office. Boardman was active in a number of local businesses. In 1859 he began a long tenure as a director of the Commerce Branch Bank of Cleveland and its successor in 1865, the Commercial Natl. Bank. In 1877 he became a director and general counsel of the Valley Railway Co. In the 1860s he served as president of the CLEVELAND LIBRARY ASSOC., later the Case Library; and in 1869 he became president of the Cleveland Law Library Assoc., later serving as a trustee of the law library. He was a trustee of both Kenyon College and Adelbert College of Western Reserve University. He was also active in the affairs of Trinity Church and in political organizations in the 5th ward. In Dec. 1859, Boardman married Florence Sheffield. In 1887, the Boardman family moved to the nation's capital, where they built a house the following year. Upon his death in 1915, Wm. J. Boardman was identified by newspaper headlines as the father of the leader of the Red Cross, Mabel Boardman.

**BOATING (RECREATIONAL).** Recreational boating, more specifically yachting, became an organized sport in Cleveland in 1878 when GEO. GARDNER founded the Cleveland Yachting Assoc., subsequently known as the CLEVELAND YACHT CLUB. Gardner, later elected mayor of Cleveland, is often referred to as the "Father of Yachting" in Cleveland. In the summer of 1884, Gardner and other members of the Cleveland Yacht Club, at the invitation of Henry Gerlach, sailed to Put-in-Bay aboard Gerlach's sloop, *Lulu*. There were other yacht clubs on Lake Erie, and it was Gardner's idea that Put-in-Bay would be a perfect site for a major regatta involving the other clubs on the lake. On 17 Jan. 1885, he called a meeting in Cleveland to form an association of clubs—and from this meeting the Inter-Lake Yachting Assoc. was born. The purpose of I-LYA was to foster camaraderie among Great Lakes yachtsmen and to adopt rules of measurement and handicaps to allow a variety of boats to compete in the regattas. The first official regatta was in Aug. 1894, at Put-in-Bay. It became the major regatta of I-LYA, and in the 1980s it (known as "Bay Week") extended throughout the first week of August.

Sailing yachts were not the only vessels used in the early days of racing competition. Naphtha-powered launches and steam-powered yachts competed in 1896. As more clubs, more types of boats, and 3 Great Lakes became involved, as well as some Canadian clubs, the creation of a continental governing body became necessary. Ernest W. Radder of the Cleveland Yacht Club chaired a committee that initially represented 109 yacht clubs and established the North American Racing Union, which evolved into the U.S. Yacht Racing Union. The complexity of current yachting rules springs from this early association. The Cleveland Yacht Club initiated a major race in 1901, named for its founder, Geo. Gardner. The Gardner Bowl was run on the 4th of July. In 1904, the first powerboat races were held on Lake Erie, and in 1908 the world record for speed on water was established at 28 mph. News of this event was relayed by carrier pigeons to eagerly awaiting enthusiasts in Cleveland, Sandusky, and Toledo. In 1914, another prominent Clevelander, ALEXANDER WINTON, had his name attached to the Winton Cup race. The longest race established by the CYC was the F. W. Roberts memorial trophy, a 180-mi. round trip between Rocky River and Port Stanley, Ontario. The most popular Cleveland-area regatta has been the Mentor Harbor Yacht Club's Falcon Cup, a 34-mi. race from Rocky River to Mentor. Established in 1938 by Richard Bostwick, it is run in cooperation with the Cleveland Yacht Club.

Two types of boaters emerged in the postwar era: powerboaters and sailors. With the development of the outboard motor and mass-production technology, powerboats became the foundation of the boating industry by a margin of 10:1. Those new to boating chose power over sail for a variety of reasons. The powerboat appeared to be an extension of the automobile, and the perception of simplicity of operation, as well as speed, versatility, and lower cost, combined to make the powerboat attractive to a wide variety of consumers. Sailing, on the other hand, had an elitist image and was perceived as complex, expensive, and restrictive. An important adjunct to recreational boating is sport fishing, which flourished in the post-WORLD WAR II period. Sport fishing was organized by the Lake Erie Sport Fishermen. Beginning in the early 1970s, the LESF stopped the commercial harvest of walleyed pike, and banned gill nets from Ohio waters. Sport fishing in the central basin of Lake Erie dramatically improved from its bleak days of the 1950s, when many proclaimed the lake "dead." Through the efforts of the Ohio Sea Grant program, operating as a cooperative extension service of the U.S. Dept. of Agriculture, based at Ohio State University, the first artificial reefs were constructed offshore from Lakewood and Edgewater parks (see FISHING).

With the introduction of mass-market boating, legal, political, and insurance-related issues began to surface. In 1946, the Greater Cleveland Boating Assoc. was established by Commodore W. Weir of the Forest City Yacht Club to "pressure city, state, and federal governments" to advance water recreation; 28 clubs affiliated with the GCBA, representing 50,000 club-affiliated boat owners. Safe operation of boats is the major goal of the association, and it also serves as an effective lobby. In this context, the GCBA was instrumental in repealing the state property tax on boats, and further achieved the inclusion of a .005% gasoline tax to be channeled to the state's Waterway & Safety Fund, for the construction and maintenance of boating facilities. Since the majority of boaters in the Cleveland area trailer their craft, launch ramps and parking lots have been a major concern of the organization. In 1952, 40,000 signatures were gathered and presented to Mayor Anthony Celebrezze seeking small boat-launching facilities for the Cleveland area. The mayor created the Dept. of Port Control, naming Wm. Rogers as the first director. The city established 5 ramp areas at Wildwood Park, GORDON PARK, E. 49th St., EDGEWATER PARK, and Donald Gray Garden. In 1986, only 2 public access areas remained, at E. 55th St.

and Gordon Park. In 1956, the Lake Erie Marine Trades Assoc. was established in Cleveland. The public role of this association has been the organization of various boat shows. However, its 116 members have also been involved in legal, political, promotional, and lobbying activities that affect the boating public.

As more consumers became involved in boating, the financial institutions sought registration and titling of boats. In 1960, through the combined efforts of the banking community and LEMTA, the state of Ohio responded by requiring the registration of all watercraft and the establishment of a waterway safety fund. In 1986 there were over 30,000 boats registered in Cuyahoga County. The appearance of private marinas and yacht clubs catered to a segment of the boating public that could afford such facilities. Historically, the yacht club has been associated with old-line monied elites. Social, economic, and vocational stratification were still factors in some of the clubs in the 1980s. The entrance requirements for the Cleveland Yacht Club are illustrative. A prospective member of the CYC must be proposed by a senior member, have been sponsored by another senior member, and have references from 3 other members. This selection process, plus the payment of a $4,000 initiation fee and monthly dues of $100, qualifies one for membership. Dock space requires additional fees. In 1986 there was a 3-year waiting period for dockage. Until 1986, none of the yacht clubs or their affiliate, the I-LYA, had had a woman or black man as a commodore; in that year Mrs. Davida Steinbrink was elected commodore of the Edgewater Yacht Club.

As the number of recreational boaters grew, safe operation became a major issue. The Coast Guard assumed the role of monitoring and responding to boaters in distress. The Boating Safety Div. of the 9th Coast Guard District in Cleveland maintained stations at Cleveland, Marblehead, Ashtabula, Fairport, and Lorain; over 1,200 people were assisted every year by just the Cleveland station. Boating safety regulations grew in response to changing conditions in the industry and attitudes of the public. In 1986 there were 40 rules governing the operation of boats. The USCG is assisted by the U.S. Coast Guard Auxiliary—a civilian volunteer, nonmilitary organization. The auxiliary conducts courtesy marine examinations and safe-boating courses and supports the Coast Guard in rescue and assistance missions. In the 1980s, Cleveland-area boaters were aided by a major renovation of the lakefront and the growth of recreational activity in the FLATS. The Cuyahoga River expanded services to recreational boaters. The ongoing efforts of Cleveland-area yacht clubs to improve facilities, the revitalization of Lake Erie, and the establishment of the CLEVELAND AIR SHOW and the BUDWEISER CLEVELAND 500 on the lakefront have served to make the "North Coast" into a major water recreational area with broad benefits for area boaters.

James Banks
Cuyahoga Community College

**BOBBIE BROOKS, INC.,** located at 3830 Kelly Ave., is a company with a national and international reputation for its leadership in the field of womenswear, particularly outerwear and swimwear. The company was established by Maurice Saltzman, a graduate of Cleveland Hts. High School and former resident of BELLEFAIRE. After a brief period of employment as a shipping clerk at Lampl Knitwear, Saltzman and a partner, Max Reiter, began their own enterprise, originally named Ritmore Sportswear, Inc., in a loft in the Bradley Bldg. on W. 6th St. Beginning with a $3,000 investment in 1939, they built the company into a multi-million-dollar operation within the next 15 years. In

1953, Saltzman bought out Reiter's share in the company for $1 million. By 1966, Saltzman's interest in the company had grown to $36 million, from which he contributed generously to many local charities. Originally, Bobbie Brooks focused on providing stylish clothes for teenage and junior-miss girls. Coordinated styling, colors, and fabrics made it possible for the junior girl to acquire her entire outerwear wardrobe at the company's 1-stop youth departments in retail stores. Bobbie Brooks also used computers to analyze and anticipate teenage fashion trends. Eventually, the company expanded its line to include "wardrobe conscious women 25–44 years of age." During the 1960s, the company continued to expand, adding production divisions in other cities. However, during the early 1980s, Bobbie Brooks suffered serious financial difficulties, which necessitated drastic reorganization. Though most of the company's production is now carried on in the South, it retains its headquarters in Cleveland.

**BOEHM, CHARLES** (1853–9 Apr. 1932), was an important missionary to the Hungarian immigrants in North America during the late 19th and early 20th centuries. Born in Selmecbanya, Hungary, he was the second of 6 children born to Felez and Julia Boehm. Orphaned at age 13, he was able to continue his education by means of academic scholarships. Boehm entered the minor seminary at Esztergom, where he displayed great academic brilliance. He was sent to the University of Vienna, where he completed his studies for the priesthood. John Cardinal Simor ordained him on 16 July 1876.

Boehm's first assignment was as associate pastor at Maria Nostra. From 1882–88 he served as administrator of the parish at Nagy-Modro before being sent back to Maria Nostra as its pastor. In 1892 he was the first Hungarian priest to be chosen by Kolos Cardinal Vaszary to work among the Hungarian Catholics in America. Boehm arrived in Cleveland in Dec. 1892 and established ST. ELIZABETH'S CHURCH. He started building a church and made provisions for a school. It was opened in 1893 under lay direction, but by 1895 the determined Fr. Boehm had gained the services of the URSULINE SISTERS. Boehm began the newspaper *Katolikus Magyarok Vasarnapja* (Catholic Hungarian Sunday) and also organized a number of spiritual and fraternal organizations.

Fr. Boehm was concerned about the spiritual welfare of other Hungarian communities. In 1907 he left the then-thriving parish of St. Elizabeth to devote himself to missionary work. Using Buffalo as headquarters, he traveled throughout the eastern U.S. and Canada, ministering to scattered Hungarian communities. In 1923 he returned to Cleveland to resume the pastorate of St. Elizabeth's. In recognition of his many services, Fr. Boehm was declared a domestic prelate by the Vatican and given the title of monsignor. Msgr. Boehm resigned his parish in 1927 because of advancing age. He did retire but took on a new apostolate. For 5 years he visited CLEVELAND STATE HOSPITAL and served as its unofficial chaplain. He died in St. Vincent Charity Hospital in 1932 after a brief illness. He is buried in Calvary Cemetery.

Papers of St. Elizabeth Parish, Archives, Diocese of Cleveland.

The **BOHEMIAN NATIONAL HALL** was built at 4939 Broadway in 1896–97 by Czech immigrants and reportedly was the first hall in the city owned by a nationality group. Planning for the building began in 1887, when Lodge Bratri v Kruhu called upon local freethinkers to erect a hall. The fundraising and planning were led by Vaclav Snajdr, editor of *DENNICE NOVOVEKU* (Morning Star), and the effort

involved not only Bohemian freethinkers but also most of the organizations in the Bohemian immigrant community. The building was designed by Cleveland architects ANDREW MITERMILER and John W. Hradek. The cornerstone was laid on 20 Dec. 1896, and the hall was dedicated 26 Sept. 1897. The building served as a meeting place for lodges, societies, and drama clubs, and in 1911 classrooms were added to teach Bohemian. Thos. G. Masaryk, founder and first president of Czechoslovakia, spoke in the hall in 1907 and again in 1918. By 1919, 73 societies met regularly at the hall.

The Bohemian Natl. Hall was managed by the Patronat, a board consisting of 2 delegates from each of the societies that owned stock in the building. The Patronat elected the 13 directors directly responsible for the hall's operation. Although the hall was a center for activities of the Czech immigrant community, it also was the site on 30 June 1967 of the Midnight Hour, "Cleveland's first psychedelic light show and dance," featuring the rock band Muther's Oats. In June 1975 the building was sold to SOKOL GREATER CLEVELAND, which began major restorations with funding from the CLEVELAND FOUNDATION and the Ohio Historical Society. The hall continued to host Sokol meetings, gymnastic events, lodge functions, and other Czech-oriented cultural events. In 1977 it was added to the Natl. Register of Historic Places.

Bohemian Natl. Hall Records, WRHS.

**BOHM, EDWARD H.** (7 Feb. 1838–7 May 1906), was a Civil War officer, newspaper publisher, and public official. Born in Alstedt, Saxe-Weimar, Germany, he moved to the U.S. in 1851. His family settled on a farm in NEWBURGH, Ohio. Bohm left the farm in 1856 to work on the Cleveland & Toledo Railroad until the CIVIL WAR broke out. He enlisted in Co. K, 7th Ohio Volunteer Infantry, on 18 Apr. 1861. Captured by Confederates on 20 Aug. 1861 on the Gauley River in western Virginia, he was imprisoned until 30 May 1862, when he was released at Washington, N.C. He was commissioned a 2d lieutenant in Co. D, 7th OVI, in Jan. 1863. Co. D saw heavy action at Chancellorsville, Va. (May 1863), where Bohm was wounded. He returned to Cleveland and was mustered out with the 7th on 6 July 1864.

In the postwar years, Bohm prosecuted soldiers' claims against the U.S. government. He was elected to the school board in 1870 and served as Cuyahoga County recorder from 1870–76. He founded the *Cleveland Anzeiger*, a German daily newspaper, but was forced to relinquish the paper after 4 years because of financial difficulties. He was president of the North American Saengerbund and the Saengerfest of 1874. A Republican, he served as presidential elector-at-large for Ohio in 1876 and was elected justice of the peace in 1885. He served as a member of the Soldiers & Sailors Monument Commission, 1896–1906.

**BOHN, ERNEST J.** (1901–15 Dec. 1975), was a nationally known pioneer and expert on PUBLIC HOUSING. Born of German parents in southern Hungary, he came to Cleveland with his father in 1911. He attended East Technical High School before graduating from Adelbert College in 1924 and Western Reserve Law School in 1926. He served briefly as an instructor of political science at Western Reserve College and People's University. In 1929 he was elected to the Ohio House as a Republican. Bohn left the legislature at the end of his term and ran for city council from the Hough district. He served as a councilman until 1940, becoming increasingly active in housing reform. In 1933 he authored the first state housing legislation to be passed by a state legislature. The Ohio law became a model for legislation in other states. As president and organizer of the Natl. Assoc. for Housing & Redevelopment Officials, Bohn worked to secure passage of the U.S. Housing Act of 1937.

Bohn is chiefly identified as director of the Cleveland Metropolitan Housing Authority (CUYAHOGA METROPOLITAN HOUSING AUTHORITY) from its founding in 1933 until 1968 and as chairman of the City Planning Commission from its founding in 1942 until 1966. His early work included slum clearance and redevelopment and focused attention on the idea that public housing was a federal concern. Following WORLD WAR II he became increasingly interested in housing for the elderly, recognizing a need for medical clinics, meal programs, and recreation facilities in his housing structures. The Golden Age Ctr. at E. 30th St. and Central Ave. was built under Bohn's direction and was the first such housing development in the U.S. for senior citizens. Deterioration of central-city housing in the mid-1960s led to charges that Bohn neglected to use his office to sufficiently meet the needs of poorer people in the city and had promoted racial discrimination in filling CMHA units.

Following his retirement, Bohn was a lecturer at Case Western Reserve University and was named to the board of directors of the Natl. Housing Conference and to the Ohio Commission on Aging. Bohn Tower and the Ernest J. Bohn Golden Age Ctr., an apartment building for the elderly, were named for him in recognition of his commitment and contributions to the city of Cleveland. Bohn never married.

Ernest J. Bohn Collection, Freiberger Library, CWRU.

**BOIARDI, HECTOR** (1897–21 June 1985), known to millions as Chef Boy-ar-dee of canned spaghetti products, was a local restaurateur who turned his zeal for the food of his native Italy into a multi-million-dollar business. The descendant of prominent chefs, Boiardi began cooking at age 10, left for New York about 1914 to work at the Ritz Carlton, and came to Cleveland 3 years later to be the chef at the new Hotel Winton (later the Hotel Carter), where he made his spaghetti dinners the talk of the Midwest. In 1924, he and his wife, Helen, opened their first restaurant, the Giardino d'Italia, at E. 9th St. and Woodland. To accommodate customers who wanted carryout spaghetti and sauce, the chef opened a second kitchen, above the restaurant. By 1928 the operation was so large that it required assembly-line production. It was moved to an empty factory, and products were packaged in a box designed by a Giardino d'Italia patron. The first 12 boxes were sold at Maxwell's grocery store on Woodland. As the product became popular and its fame expanded over a wider geographic area, the name was changed to a more pronounceable phonetic spelling (Chef Boy-ar-dee), and the chef's picture became the trademark.

The dinner for 4 contained a jar of the chef's secret-recipe spaghetti sauce, a packet of dry spaghetti, and a small container of Parmesan cheese, and was priced at $.60. When the amounts proved to be too much for the American appetite, the portions were reduced to 3 at $.35. Because the product was tasty and inexpensive, the Boiardi company prospered in the Depression and soon had a large plant at 5200 Harvard and 3 processing plants. By 1937, the company had an annual consumption of 9,000 tons of tomatoes, 7,000 steers, and several tons of other ingredients; to be close to the tomato fields, Boiardi sold the Harvard plant and moved to a 300,000-sq.-ft. factory in Milton, Pa., where the firm also had mushroom-growing facilities. Boiardi was approached by the government in WORLD WAR II

to develop tasty field rations for the armed services and converted part of his plant to handle military orders. By war's end, the sales of Chef Boy-ar-dee Quality Foods were $20 million annually, and the operation was sold to American Home Foods, the operating company of the American Home Prods. Corp., for $6 million. The chef was a consultant to the company until 1978.

Though Boiardi acquired national fame, he never abandoned the local restaurant scene. He opened Chef Boiardi's restaurant in 1931 with Albert Caminati at 823 Prospect. When the spaghetti business was sold in 1946, the name was changed to Chef Hector's, but the restaurant continued to offer the "good food at modest prices" that made it a favorite of downtown businessmen and families until it went out of business in 1967. Over the years, Boiardi acquired interests in other Cleveland restaurants, including Pierre's, Monaco's, and the Town & Country. Boiardi, whose spaghetti won international food contests and earned him Benito Mussolini's praise as the "world's greatest chef," was a talented businessman whose management skills extended beyond the food business. After a short-lived venture in 1946 to produce "barnyard ravioli," an animal food compressed into a brick made from restaurant scraps, he bought the Milton Steel Co. after a strike, and sold it for a large profit in 1951 (after the steel boom of the late 1940s ended). When Boiardi, whose picture still appeared on Chef Boy-ar-dee foods, died in 1985, his former company was selling $500 million a year of spaghetti and 100 other products. Boiardi, pioneer in convenience foods, had turned spaghetti from an "ethnic food" into a staple in the American diet.

**BOLLES, JAMES A.** (1810–19 Sept. 1894), was the rector of Trinity Church between 1855–59. His tenure was marked by controversy during a critical period in that church's history. Nationally, Bolles was known as the compiler of the a popularly used religious manual. Bolles was born in Norwich, Conn. He graduated from Trinity College in Hartford in 1830 and then entered the General Seminary in New York. He received his deacon's orders in 1833, and the following year he became a priest in the Episcopal church. Between 1834–55, Bolles was rector of St. James Church in Batavia, N.Y. In 1853, primarily through the influence of Samuel L. Mather, he was made rector of Trinity Church in Cleveland. Bolles distinguished himself as a scholar and churchman. Opposed to the evangelical movement, he advocated a written sermon and religious practices associated with the Catholic church. He strongly objected to the mass conversions of revival meetings and argued against the interdenominational movement, which he considered too superficial. Throughout his religious life, he worked hard to make the sacraments a more important part of the Episcopalian service. In the early 1850s, Bolles came into disagreement with the Episcopal bishop of Ohio over some of the aforementioned issues, and also over Bolles's iconoclastic emphasis on pastoral ministry rather than the preaching ministry. The two men entered into public debate, allowing their correspondence to be published. The ongoing debate drew national attention within the Episcopal church.

Within a few months of Bolles's accepting the rectorship of Trinity Church, the church burned down. Bolles was credited with providing the leadership needed to help it rebuild. During his ministry there, Bolles placed enormous emphasis on charity; he was responsible for implementing systematic giving and the founding of 2 mission churches. He was a strong advocate of the free church system, which included free (as opposed to rented) pews, and in 1859 he resigned as rector when the vestry refused to make Trinity a free parish. Other contributing factors to his resignation included divisiveness within the congregation over his advocation of daily services and other Catholic practices. In 1859, Bolles became rector of the Church of the Advent in Boston, but he returned to Cleveland in 1871 and for many years was a senior canon at Trinity Church. Bolles was widely known for his *Vade Mecum: A Manual for Pastoral Use*. Compiled with Scriptures and the Book of Common Prayer, the small volume achieved standard usage by a generation of pastors in their parochial work.

Pierce, Roderic Hall, *Trinity Cathedral* (1967).

**BOLT, RICHARD ARTHUR** ( 12 Mar. 1880–3 Aug. 1959), was a physician, and Director of the CLEVELAND CHILD HEALTH ASSOCIATION in the fields of maternal health, prenatal care and is noted for his work in child welfare. Bolt was born in St. Louis to Richard Orchard and Mary Virginia Belt Bolt. He graduated from St. Louis' Central High School 1898. After one year at Washington University, he transferred to the University of Michigan graduating with the A.B. degree in 1904, and the Ph.D. degree in 1906. During 1906–1907, he did post-graduate work in the Children's Hospital and Boston Lying-in Hospital. Bolt also did further post-graduate work at the University of California, 1916–1917, and Johns Hopkins University, 1925. Bolt came to Cleveland in 1907 as an intern at St. Vincent's Charity Hospital. He was then appointed pathologist and later visiting physician to the hospital's Gynecological Out-Patient Department. During 1909–1910, he was acting medical director of the Babies' Dispensary and Hospital. From 1911–1916, Bolt was medical director of the U.S. Indemnity College of the Tsing Hua College at Peking, China. In 1917, Bolt returned to Cleveland as chief of the city's bureau of child hygiene and as an instructor of pediatrics at Western Reserve University Medical School. In 1918–1919, he served as director of the child welfare division of the tuberculosis commission of the American Red Cross in Italy. In 1919–1920, he was director of the Alameda County (Cal.) Public Health Center. Between 1920–1925, he was a lecturer at Johns Hopkins. Bolt returned to Cleveland again in 1929 as Director of the Child Health Association and as an associate in hygiene and public health and pediatrics at Western Reserve. Despite the economically hard pressed years of the Depression and WORLD WAR II, Bolt pioneered many health related programs such as expectant mother classes and helped maintain others such as the babies' dispensaries' free milk program and the CLEVELAND PUBLIC SCHOOLS' dental program. As early as 1945, he advocated the use of flouride in the city's drinking water as a means of preventing tooth decay. Bolt retired in 1945 at the age of 65 to help organize the University of California's new public health school. Bolt married Rebecca Beatrice French on 21 July 1908. The Bolts had 4 children, Elizabeth, Richard, Marrion, and Robert.

**BOLTON, CHESTER CASTLE** (5 Sept. 1882–29 Oct. 1939), was an industrialist, Ohio senator, and U.S. congressman from Ohio's 22d district. He was born in Cleveland to Chas. C. and Julia Castle Bolton. His father was a prominent Cleveland businessman and philanthropist, and his mother was the daughter of former Cleveland mayor WM. B. CASTLE. He attended UNIVERSITY SCHOOL and received an A.B. degree from Harvard University in 1905. Returning to Cleveland, he joined the Bourne-Fuller Co., becoming the assistant treasurer. He resigned in 1917 to join the Army, and he attained the rank of lieutenant colonel in the Army Ordnance Dept.

After WORLD WAR I, Bolton was attracted to politics, beginning his career as a member of the municipal council of Lyndhurst village from 1918–21. As a Republican he was elected to the Ohio senate in 1922, serving from 1923–28. He was elected to Congress from the 22d district in 1928. As chairman of the Natl. Republican Congressional Campaign Committee, he was instrumental in bringing the REPUBLICAN NATL. CONVENTION OF 1936 to Cleveland. A critic of the New Deal, he lost his congressional seat in the 1936 election. He was again elected to Congress in 1938. Bolton married Frances Payne Bingham in 1907, and they had 3 sons, Chas. B., Kenyon C., and Oliver P., and a daughter, Elizabeth. Upon his death at age 57, his wife, FRANCES PAYNE BOLTON, was elected to serve out his term in Congress.

Chester C. Bolton Papers. WRHS.

**BOLTON, FRANCES PAYNE** (29 Mar. 1885–9 Mar. 1977), served as Republican congresswoman from Cleveland's 22d district for 29 years. She was also noted for her financial support of many projects, particularly in the fields of nursing, health, and education. She was born in Cleveland to Chas. W. and Mary Perry Payne Bingham. Her father was a prominent banker-industrialist. She was educated at Hathaway-Brown School and attended Miss Spence's School for Girls in New York City from 1902–04. On her return to Cleveland in 1904, she worked as a volunteer with the Visiting Nurse Assoc., accompanying the nurses on their rounds in the poor neighborhoods. This experience marked the beginning of a lifelong interest in the nursing profession.

During WORLD WAR I, Bolton was instrumental in persuading Secretary of War NEWTON D. BAKER to set up an Army School of Nursing rather than rely on untrained volunteers. She donated funds to establish a school of nursing at Western Reserve University, because she felt that nurses should have college educations as well as nursing training. Her substantial donation enabled WRU to raise the school of nursing from a department of the College of Women to the rank of a separate college in the university in 1923. In June 1935 it was renamed the Frances Payne Bolton School of Nursing in honor of her continued support and interest.

In 1907 she married CHESTER CASTLE BOLTON, and they had 4 children, Chas. B., Oliver P., Kenyon C., and Elizabeth. Her husband was Republican congressman from the 22d district when he died in 1939, and she served out his term. In the general election of 1940, she won the seat in her own right. During her long tenure in the U.S. House of Representatives, her major interests were nursing and foreign affairs. She sponsored the Bolton Bill creating the U.S. Cadet Nurse Corps in WORLD WAR II. As a long-time member of the House Foreign Affairs Committee, she was the first woman member of Congress to head an official mission abroad to the Middle East, in 1947. In July 1953, Pres. Eisenhower appointed her a congressional delegate to the U.N. She was defeated for reelection to Congress by Chas. Vanik in 1968 and returned to Cleveland. In addition to her interest in nursing, Bolton also founded the Payne Study & Experiment Fund in 1927 to finance projects that would benefit children. HAWKEN SCHOOL in LYNDHURST was built on land she and her husband had given to Jas. Hawken. She died at her home in Lyndhurst at age 91.

Loth, David, *A Long Way Forward* (1957).
Frances Payne Bolton Papers, WRHS.

**BOLTON, SARAH K.** (15 Sept. 1841–21 Feb. 1916), was a prolific writer of biographical studies, poetry, and a temperance novel. Born in Farmington, Conn., she came to Cleveland in 1866 after her marriage to Chas. E. Bolton, a Cleveland businessman and active worker in temperance activities. All of her books, regardless of type, reflect her contention that despite hardships, life can be worth living if one works hard and believes in God. Her own experiences as associate editor of the *Congregationalist* (1878–81), a Boston publication, and those of her husband as he labored for the cause of the workingman and the discouraged in heart, served as subject matter for her books. Her stories were published in 2 volumes: *A Country Idyll* and *Other Stories*. Although she was the most professional and prolific of local writers, her biographies received rightful acclaim, and her other books less.

**BOLTON, THOMAS** (29 Nov. 1809–1 Feb. 1871), was a prominent lawyer and common pleas judge. He served as a member of the CLEVELAND CITY COUNCIL and was its president from 1841–42. Born in Scipio, N.Y., he attended Temple Hill High School, where he developed an interest in law. He then attended Harvard University (1829–33), where he met his friend and future partner Moses Kelley. Bolton studied law in the office of John C. Spencer, Canandaigua, N.Y. In Sept. 1834 he settled in Cleveland, where he was admitted to the bar in 1835 in the office of Jas. L. Conger. In 1836 he invited Kelley to join him, and they formed the firm of Bolton & Kelley.

Bolton's public career began in 1835 when he was appointed to a committee to draft the charter for the City of Cleveland. He then served as clerk for the city's first elections. In 1839 he served as councilman, and in that year he served in the Office of the Judiciary, an appointment he again received for the term 1841–42. He also served on the city's Claims Committee and as alderman during the 1841–42 term. In 1841 he became the second president of the city council. In 1841 Bolton gained public attention and substantial criticism for defending 3 Negro slaves who were accused by their captors of having run away from their plantation. Despite several threats, Bolton proved that the captors who brought the slaves to a Cleveland jail had kidnapped them and claimed ownership.

Disillusioned with the Democratic party, Bolton joined the Free-Soilers' party in 1848. In 1856 he attended the Pittsburgh Convention as an organizer for the Republican party, and later that year he served as a delegate to the Republican Natl. Convention in Philadelphia. Also in 1856 he left legal practice to become judge of the court of common pleas, where he remained for 10 years until his retirement. Bolton was among the members of the first roster of the Cleveland City Guard, a private military company founded in 1837. He was also cofounder of ST. PAUL'S EPISCOPAL CHURCH, in Oct. 1846. He married Elizabeth L. Cone, whom he outlived. He then married Emeline Russel. He had 2 sons, Chas. C. and Jas. H.

The **BOLTON FOUNDATION** was founded in 1952 by Fanny Hanna Bolton (1907–1980). Bolton, the wife of Hanna Mining vice-president Julian Castle Bolton, was the daughter of Howard Melville Hanna, Jr. (1877–1945), president of the Hanna Mining Co. at the time of his death, and Jean Claire Hanna. Fanny Bolton was a trustee of UNIVERSITY HOSPITALS and was active in Cleveland civic life. The foundation was formed as a vehicle for charitable giving based on the philosophy of Fanny Bolton's grandfather, Howard Melville Hanna, Sr., who in 1904 advised his son to "be generous and liberal, but with true generosity and liberality, and thoughtfully . . . Thoughtless giving is more apt to be wicked and a curse, than a benefit." The Bolton Foundation supports Cleveland hospitals and health services primarily, with grants also going to secondary education. No grants are given to individuals. In 1985, the assets of the foundation were $4.4 million, of which $216,500 was expended for 30 grants. Officers of the foundation include Richard Stewart, president; Clair H. Bolton Jonklass, vice-president; Betsy Bolton Schafer, vice-president; and Paulette F. Kitko, secretary-treasurer.

The **BOND STORE** was the major example of Art Moderne commercial architecture in Cleveland. The Bond Clothing Co., which had occupied a store in the old Hickox Bldg. on the northwest corner of Euclid and E. 9th St. for many years since 1920, demolished the building in 1946 and erected its own store on the site. The design embodied the principles of commercial advertising display. It was conceived as a showpiece, apparently inspired by the World's Fair and film-musical architecture of the 1930s. The awkwardness of the acute angle at Euclid and E. 9th was solved by a cylindrical corner element topped by a floating roof canopy that was pierced with circular holes and illuminated by spotlights. In the 4-story interior, illuminated mirrored columns extended from the main floor through a 2d-floor ceiling well to the 3d floor, and a curving staircase ascended to the upper floors. The building materials were pink granite, terra cotta, steel, and aluminum. The architect was Herbert B. Beidler in association with Walker & Weeks. The store represented the climax of the 1930s brand of modernism in Cleveland. It was demolished in 1978.

**BONNE BELL, INC.,** was founded in 1927 by Jesse Grover Bell, a door-to-door cosmetics saleman from Salinas, Kans. When he decided to start his own cosmetics business, he was lured to Cleveland by the market promised by a bank advertisement that claimed that half of all Americans lived within 500 mi. of the city. He began the business, which he named after his daughter, with products he made on a hot plate in his basement, and he sold them on their merits, not fancy packaging. His door-to-door sales approach was so successful that after the Depression, he hired a crew of women who called on beauty shops to promote Bonne Bell facial products. By 1985 the company had grown to a $50 million enterprise that was still family-owned and -operated, with a unique style that penetrates Bonne Bell marketing, corporate concerns in employee relations, and even the corporate buildings.

The company has developed and chosen to perpetuate a wholesome image, and it focuses on markets in line with this image. Originally, the Bonne Bell line offered skin-care products primarily for the young. In 1936, Jesse Bell bought the formula for the company's major product, Ten-O-Six, a cleansing lotion developed by a local chemist that became a standard in the teenage beauty ritual. As Bonne Bell's original customers grew up and developed different skin needs, the company introduced products for women of all ages. The company spokesperson is its namesake, Bonne Bell Eckert, who in 1985 supplemented her duties as chairman of the board by answering volumes of mail from teenagers seeking skin-care advice.

Beginning in the 1950s, the company actively pursued the outdoor market and developed a line of sun blockers, heavy-duty moisturizers, and lip protectors for skiers, hikers, and joggers, marketing them under the slogan "Out there you need Bonne Bell." Under the leadership of Jess Bell, son of the founder, the company became an active sponsor of the outdoor life. Beginning with its sponsorship of the U.S. Ski Team in the 1960s, Bonne Bell backed many amateur and professional sports events for women, including tennis, skiing, bicycling, hiking, white-water canoeing, mountain climbing, and particularly running. Since Bell took up running in 1972 as an alternative to drinking, the company has sponsored 10K marathons in 15 cities and many charitable races. Approximately half of the company's ad budget is spent on promoting running and other outdoor activities.

The Bonne Bell "Be Fit. Look Good" philosophy is promoted at the company's headquarters. The main office and plant features a track, tennis courts, volleyball courts, exercise rooms, and other health-club facilities, which are open to production and office workers as well as executives. Employees are encouraged to use these facilities on their lunch hours. The company also encourages its employees to stay trim and in good health by offering bonuses for losing weight and stopping smoking. In addition, the company has offered employees short summer work weeks and extra vacation time at its expense. The personal style of the Bell family is even reflected in the corporate buildings. The main offices on Georgetown Row in LAKEWOOD have been remodeled to look like Williamsburg townhouses, while its Crocker Rd. manufacturing facility and warehouse in WESTLAKE were built in 1976 to resemble a Kentucky horse farm from the outside.

**BONNE BELL RUN** is an annual 10-kilometer race for women of all ages, sponsored by BONNE BELL, INC., of LAKEWOOD, Ohio. This run, one of the first in the nation open exclusively to women, is held on a Sunday in September or October every year. First organized in 1976, this race opened the door for women runners. Up to the time this race originated, there had been no races exclusively for women. Bonne Bell sponsored 10K races that year in 5 major cities—New York, Aspen, Boston, Cleveland, and Atlanta. At one time, Bonne Bell sponsored as many as 27 races for women annually. The race begins at the company's Manufacturing and Distributing Facility at 1006 Crocker Rd. in WESTLAKE, Ohio, proceeds through Westlake and BAY VILLAGE, and concludes at the company's Westlake facility. The 10th anniversary race in 1986, as well as the first race, originated at the company's corporate offices in Lakewood with the finish line at the Westlake facility. Although known as a race for women only, the first race and the 10th anniversary race were open to men and women. Women of all ages have participated in these races, as young as 8 years old and up to the ages of 65 and older. There are approximately 500 to 1,000 participants in the race each year.

**BOOTH MEMORIAL HOSPITAL** originated as a nameless "rescue home," established in 1892. Col. and Mrs. Henry Stillwell of the SALVATION ARMY, seeking to aid ostracized unwed mothers, had converted a house at 5905 Kinsman Rd. into hospital quarters. The home came under the supervision of the Army's women's social-service department in 1902 and expanded its building in 1904. It earned national recognition for its care of unwed mothers. In 1930 it moved into expanded facilities at 1881 Torbenson Dr. Delivery rooms and nurseries were added in 1953, and 5 years later 50 beds were added to offer more comprehensive prenatal and postnatal care.

An outreach program of the hospital was created in 1966, when Booth Memorial joined with the MARY B. TALBERT HOME to form the Booth-Talbert Clinic & Day Ctr. at 6010 Hough Ave. The program included hospitalization at Booth Memorial, an accredited school program, counseling, day nurseries, follow-up medical supervision, and Visiting Nurse Assoc. referral service. In 1977 Booth opened the Home-Life Birth Ctr. adjacent to the hospital. One of the first units of its kind in the U.S., the program allowed entire families to participate in the birth experience by moving into an apartmentlike home environment. Emphasis was on natural childbirth, and the average stay was to be 24 hours, with follow-up care provided in the patient's home.

**BOURKE-WHITE, MARGARET** (14 June 1904–27 Aug. 1971), was a prominent photojournalist who began her career in Cleveland. Born in New York, she graduated from Cornell University in 1927, where she had studied biology but took campus photos to earn money. After graduation and a failed first marriage, she came to Cleveland, where her widowed mother had moved. Here she explored the FLATS, which she called "a photographic paradise," and aspired to a freelance career as an architectural photographer. Bourke-White photographed stately homes for the local social publication *Town & Country Club News*; took several pictures for the *Clevelander*, a Chamber of Commerce publication; and produced several cover photos for *Trade Winds*, published by the Union Trust Co. She also photographed the newly completed Terminal Tower, where she opened her first studio. Her curiosity and interest in steelmaking led her to seek permission from Elroy Kulas to photograph in his mill, the Otis Steel Co. She experimented for 5 months in 1928, trying to overcome lighting problems in the mill while using artistic techniques to capture the drama of steelmaking. Kulas was so pleased with the results, he purchased 8 photos at $100 each and commissioned 8 more. He had them published in *The Story of Steel*, a booklet distributed to Otis Steel stockholders.

Bourke-White left Cleveland for New York in 1929 when Henry Luce, founder of *Time* magazine, saw the steel pictures and hired her for his new publication, *Fortune*. He later chose her as one of the 4 original staff photographers for *Life*. Her photo of the Ft. Peck Dam on the Columbia River, Mont., graced the first cover of *Life* on 23 Nov. 1936. Ultimately, Bourke-White produced 11 books of photo essays; became the first woman accredited as a war correspondent (1942); flew with the Air Force on a bombing mission (1943); traveled with Gen. Geo. Patton's 3d Army through Germany (1945); and traveled twice to India (where she photographed Gandhi a few hours before his assassination in 1948). She married novelist Erskine Caldwell in 1939 but was divorced in 1942. Although she had Parkinson's disease for 19 years, Bourke-White continued to work actively for *Life* until 1957 and published her autobiography (*Portrait of Myself*) in 1963. She died at the age of 67 in Stamford, Conn.

**BOURNE, HENRY E.** (13 Apr. 1862–19 June 1946), a history professor at Western Reserve University, was a leader in Cleveland's academic and civic life. He was one of the most active participants in the early growth of Flora Stone Mather College and, as an educator and scholar, was an early promoter of modern ways to teach history and a leading expert on the French Revolution. Bourne was born in East Hamburg, N.Y. He attended Yale University, where he received a B.A. in 1883 and a B.D. in 1887. The following year he was the assistant editor for the *Congregationalist* in Boston. He then taught history for 3 years at the Norwich (Conn.) Free Academy. Bourne became professor of history and registrar at Mather College in 1892, when the college was only 4 years old. As registrar (i.e., dean of the faculty), he was instrumental in raising the college's standing to one of the highest in the nation among colleges for women. As an educator, Bourne played an important role during the early decades of the 20th century in developing new teaching standards in history. Working with the American Historical Assoc., he helped establish standards for the preparation of history teachers at all levels, suggested material suitable for students in the various grades, and espoused the use of primary source material at the undergraduate level. Bourne's book *The Teaching of History and Civics in the Elementary Schools* (1902) served for many years as a standard guide for teachers. He also, in association with ELBERT J. BENTON, wrote textbooks on American history that presented a broader view than previous textbooks, showing the interplay of American and European history. Bourne served on the Mather faculty until 1930. Between 1930–36, he was a history consultant to the Library of Congress and managing editor for the *American Historical Review*. He returned to Cleveland in 1936. During his years in Cleveland, Bourne was founder and first secretary of the Municipal League (later the CITIZENS LEAGUE OF CLEVELAND) and served for 20 years as president of the Goodrich Settlement. Upon his retirement from Mather College, he presented the college library with a valuable collection of books on the French Revolution.

BOWLING. The leading participant sport in the nation, bowling's growth was tied to the development of the large urban areas where it was most popular. In its early days, it was essentially a workingman's sport played in taverns, where it was used to attract the drinking trade; however, as the sport grew, it distanced itself from its saloon-oriented beginnings and gained respectability. Participation grew dramatically during and after WORLD WAR II, when the combination of technological advances and prosperity encouraged the building of large, commodious establishments where whole families could enjoy the sport. Bowling's popularity leveled off in the 1970s and began to decline as other athletic interests claimed the public's attention.

For centuries, various forms of bowling with and without pins had developed in numerous countries. The American colonists, particularly the English and the Dutch, enjoyed bowling out of doors; however, the organized indoor sport as it evolved in this country was derived from the German game of ninepins, bowled on baked-clay alleys. The first indoor alleys were built in New York City in 1840, where the game was popular among German immigrants. As ninepins became closely associated with gambling, its play was forbidden by law in Connecticut and New York. To circumvent the law, a 10th pin was added to the game, and it was this indoor game of American tenpins that became popular in other areas of the country after the CIVIL WAR. The efforts to standardize the game's rules, equipment, and alley conditions were not successsful until the founding of the American Bowling Congress in 1895, and over a period of time, the ABC slowly gained authority over the game. It was in the growing midwestern cities such as Chicago, St. Louis, Detroit, Milwaukee, and Cleveland that the ABC's organizing efforts were concentrated, and it was there that the game flourished.

In Cleveland, the first bowling alley was established in 1872 at 97 Bank (now W. 6th) St., but the game did not enjoy substantial growth until the first decade of the 20th century. Between 1901–07, the number of bowling alleys more than doubled, and by 1905 the Cleveland Bowling Assoc., an affiliate of the ABC, had been organized to govern the sport. In 1907, the CBA identified 29 leagues made up of 240 teams, many of which were sponsored by local businesses. Independent teams and hundreds of occasional bowlers also utilized the alleys. Most of Cleveland's bowling facilities were operated in conjunction with saloons, where patrons could drink and gamble on the matches. Although the sport was popular with Germans here, and they owned a number of the major alleys, participation was citywide, encompassing most groups.

As women began to bowl, conditions in some alleys improved. By 1916, there was enough interest, particularly in the Midwest, to form the Women's Natl. Bowling Congress (later the Women's Internatl. Bowling Congress). Cleveland women were specifically encouraged to bowl at E. M. Helm's alleys on E. 13th St. in 1916, and 2 years later, the Cleveland Women's Bowling Assoc. was organized. Although it was still primarily a man's sport, by the mid-1930s about 7,000 women were bowling.

The game's popularity grew steadily throughout the 1920s and 1930s. In Cleveland by 1937 there were approximately 20,000–21,000 men and women bowling in 3,000 leagues, with another 12,000–13,000 occasional bowlers. The sport maintained its popularity during the Depression, but competition among proprietors was keen. The smaller alleys cut prices to attract more customers in the early thirties, and in an effort to establish uniform prices, a local committee of proprietors prepared an industry code under the Natl. Recovery Act. Approved by the Natl. Bowling Proprietors' Assoc., a standard price of $.20 a game was set, with pinboys to be paid $.04 for each game they worked. Their wages were raised in 1938 when billiard and bowling alley employees organized a union (Local 48A of the Bldg. Service Employees) and negotiated a contract with 46 of the 50 large bowling establishments. The contract, covering more than 500 pinsetters, pinboy supervisors, billiard-parlor rack boys, and janitorial help, called for a closed shop, with pinboys receiving $.06 for every league game they set and minimum wage increases of $2 per week for the other employees.

With the advent of World War II, the bowling boom began in earnest when a massive program was initiated to convince employers to sponsor teams in industrial leagues as a morale booster for war workers. The number of bowling centers in Cleveland increased from 59 in 1939 to 106 in 1945; and with many open from 8:00 a.m. to 3:00 a.m. 7 days a week, both league and open bowling provided needed recreation for men and women working all shifts. The game benefited from improved technology when American Machine & Foundry developed a rack into which 10 pins could be loaded by the pinboy and then reset. The rack provided a more consistent alignment of the pins, and games could be bowled more quickly. They were used in Cleveland by 1939 and became standard equipment in bowling centers during the war. As these centers installed modern lighting, comfortable furnishings, and air conditioning for year-round bowling and added lunch counters and soda fountains, they created a new environment in which the bar (now called a cocktail lounge) no longer was dominant but was an adjunct to the main business of bowling. The alleys welcomed teenagers, and during the war an interscholastic high school bowling league was formed. Whereas in 1940 there had been 12 million bowlers in America, by 1948 the figure had risen to about 20 million, making it the leading participant sport in the nation.

The spectacular growth continued after the war as further technological innovation and prosperity combined to expand the bowling population, which for the first time included black participation, in ABC-sanctioned leagues and tournaments. Previously barred from the ABC, BLACKS in Cleveland and other urban areas had formed their own leagues. Clevelander J. Elmer Reed organized the Cleveland Bowlers group in the 1930s (later known as the Cleveland Bowling Senate) and helped found the Natl. Negro Bowling Assoc., which governed black bowling. After World War II, industrial recreation groups were concerned about the ABC restriction, since black employment in manufacturing had increased significantly during the war, and industrial bowling leagues were still the backbone of the sport. Both the ABC and the WIBC were urged to change their policies, and in 1950, after being found guilty of racial discrimination in Illinois, the ABC opened up its leagues and tournaments to all; the WIBC immediately followed suit.

The technological innovation that truly revolutionized postwar bowling was the automatic pinspotter, which swept the alley clear of fallen pins, respotted the remaining pins, and returned the ball to the bowler, thus eliminating the need for pinboys. First demonstrated by AMF in 1946, it was made fully automatic by 1952 and installed in bowling centers all over the country. Bowling was now a big business; and although a large initial investment was required, lane owners could profitably operate 24 hours a day, 365 days a year, with little overhead. By 1971 there were approximately 51.8 million bowlers in the nation.

Cleveland shared in the national postwar bowling boom and the economic prosperity that fueled it. Automatic pinspotters had been installed in 10 bowling centers here by 1955, and larger and more luxurious alleys continued to be built, particularly in the suburbs, where many offered free bowling lessons, free coffee, and babysitting to attract homemakers to the alleys. Although construction costs were high (about $50,000 per lane for building, land, and equipment by 1970), the potential profit, availability of bank loans, and immediate cash flow when the lanes opened attracted groups of investors successful in business and professions unrelated to bowling. By the mid-1970s these alleys were filled with 100,000 men and women bowling in sanctioned leagues (governed by the ABC and WIBC), an increase of about 28% since 1954. Non-sanctioned-league participants, junior bowling programs, and recreational bowlers accounted for more than 200,000 additional bowlers. Much of this increase was due to women bowlers, whose participation doubled in 20 years. League competition became so popular, the dominance of factory worker teams was challenged by thousands of professional businessmen and women who took up the sport.

As a participant sport all age groups could enjoy, bowling was a social and economic success, and TELEVISION made it a popular spectator sport, as well, by presenting professional bowling tournaments as entertainment. The Professional Bowlers Assoc., founded in 1958, established a national tour by attracting corporate sponsorship of its televised tournaments. Cleveland has been a regular stop on the PBA national tour since 1974. Nationwide, bowling's growth leveled off in the mid-1970s, and by 1984 participation had declined by about 13%. There was increased competition for the recreational dollar from other athletic interests; and with the more unstructured lifestyle of the seventies, a weekly commitment to league bowling became a less attractive option. Women's participation in particular declined as more of them took jobs outside the home. In Cleveland these reasons, combined with the loss of jobs and population, resulted in a much sharper decline, averaging about 22% from 1974–84. In the 1980s, however, more senior citizens have taken up bowling here, and local proprietors have offered special promotions to lure open bowlers to the alleys. In 1985, these efforts brought a slight upturn in the number of open games bowled.

Over the years, Cleveland has produced outstanding bowlers, 7 of whom have been inducted into the ABC Hall of Fame: Walter Ward, Joe Bodis, Joe Kissoff, Steve Nagy, Harry Smith, Walter (Skang) Mercurio, and John Klares, along with Sam Levine, publisher of the *Cleveland Kegler*, and J. Elmer Reed, who were chosen for meritorious service to the sport. Local members of the WIBC Hall of Fame are bowlers Goldie Greenwald and Grayce Hatch and Josephine Mraz, a founder and long-time secretary of the Cleveland Women's Bowling Assoc. As an industrial urban area, Cleveland shared in the steady growth of bowling as a popular national sport from the turn of the century until the mid-1970s. Since that time, national interest in bowling has waned, but the decline in Cleveland has been more severe with the decrease in economic opportunity and loss of population.

Mary Stavish
Case Western Reserve University

American Bowling Congress, *History of Bowling* (ca. 1943).
Brunswick-Balk-Collender, *One Hundred Years of Recreation, 1845–1945* (ca. 1945).
Weiskopf, Herman, *The Perfect Game* (1978).

**BOXING & WRESTLING.** For most of the 19th century, the contact sports of boxing and wrestling were frowned on by the educated public and were seldom written about by Cleveland newspapers. As Cleveland grew in population, the demand for indoor recreation and spectator sports increased, and boxing and wrestling became more popular despite continued legal problems and newspaper criticism. Boxing refers to fighting with the fists, at first with bare knuckles and later with padded gloves, while wrestling involves grappling with the object of bringing one's opponent to the mat. Although there was a great deal of unorganized and impromptu fighting in early American history, little if any organized amateur and professional boxing and wrestling took place in Cleveland until the last few decades of the 19th century. One of the first mentions of boxing in Cleveland was in the *Leader* of 16 Oct. 1855, advertising classes by a Prof. Sheridan Mann in "the excellent ornamental and useful arts of sparring and fencing." Prizefighting was not written about until 21 Jan. 1863, when the *Leader* reported a fight in the Flats between Paste Horn of England and Jas. Hebard of Cleveland. Typical of Cleveland editorial comments was one in the *Leader* of 21 Mar. 1868: "It [prize fighting] is a crime against the peace of every civilized country." Later in that same year, the Ohio general assembly made it illegal "for a person to be in any way connected with a fight or to countenance it by his presence." For years boxing matches were held in Michigan, in Canada, or at times on boats in Lake Erie. By the 1890s, increased public interest in professional boxing in Cleveland was illustrated by vaudeville appearances by champion prizefighters, including John L. Sullivan, Jim Corbett, and Bob Fitzsimmons, and well-attended no-decision bouts in the newly constructed CLEVELAND ATHLETIC CLUB. Until 1898, private clubs supposedly for members only staged bouts. For a 3-year period boxing matches were permitted, including Cleveland's first championship match, a 20-round draw between Kid Lavigne and Jack Daly at the CENTRAL ARMORY on 17 Mar. 1898.

Upon taking office, Progressive mayor TOM L. JOHNSON banned professional boxing, but the city's interest in boxing did not wane. Clubs and gyms were organized and kept interest in local boxing high. Charley Marotta had a club on E. 79th St., Jack La Vack's gym was at Payne and E. 19th St., and Mike Ryan's gym was on Frankfort St. between what is now W. 6th and W. 9th streets. Fights moved out of Cleveland to Casey's Woods on Berea Rd. Phil Brock, a lightweight, was the first Cleveland boxer to win a championship. However, the emergence of JOHNNY KILBANE in 1907 was, in the words of boxing historian Dan Taylor, "the most important milestone in the history of boxing in Cleveland." Mayor HERMAN BAEHR tolerated fights, including one in Dec. 1911 at GRAYS ARMORY between Kilbane and Charley White. Returning in 1912 after winning the featherweight championship in California, Kilbane was greeted by a St. Patrick's Day crowd of over 100,000 Clevelanders. After a vicious fight between Kilbane and Monte Attell, Mayor NEWTON D. BAKER banned prizefighting in the city. In Jan. 1915, Mayor HARRY L. DAVIS reinstated professional boxing in Cleveland and appointed the city's first boxing commission, which included Billy Evans, baseball umpire, and Pat Pasini, athletic director of Case School. Bouts were to be no-decision matches limited to 10 rounds.

Amateur boxing's popularity grew during the years in which Mayor Newton D. Baker prohibited prizefighting in the city. The Cleveland Athletic Club imported teams to box local amateurs, and by 1914 4 Cleveland boxers were national champions at the AAU tournament in Boston. Scholastically, boxing was never popular in Cleveland, but for a time during the 1920s and 1930s, local colleges had boxing teams. Amateur boxing received a real boost in 1929 when the Golden Gloves program, started in Chicago by Arch Ward, held its first matches at the PUBLIC AUDITORIUM. In 1931 the Northeast Ohio AAU designated the Golden Gloves matches as the official tryouts for the national championships. At its peak, the Golden Gloves, sponsored by the *Plain Dealer* and the AAU, had over 800 young boxers entered. For years John Nagy, Cleveland recreation commissioner, served as president of the Golden Gloves Assoc., and the final bouts at the Arena regularly drew over 10,000 fans. By 1982 the AAU turned over the local program to the Amateur Boxing Fed. under the leadership of Wylie Farrier.

During the 1920s and 1930s, several important professional boxing matches were held in Cleveland. Local ring hero JOHNNY RISKO fought Max Schmeling, Gene Tunney, and Max Baer, future heavyweight champions. At the Cleveland Stadium on 3 July 1931, Max Schmeling knocked out Young Stribling in a match that had gate receipts of $349,000 (See SCHMELING-STRIBLING FIGHT). From 1926–36, Cleveland's boxing commission had a bad national reputation, with the fake Jones-Jeby fight in 1933 a vivid example. Mayor HAROLD H. BURTON appointed TRIS SPEAKER to the Boxing Commission in 1936, and for 6 years local professional boxing enjoyed its greatest growth. On 2 July 1947, welterweight boxer Jim Doyle died as a result of a title bout at the Arena against "Sugar Ray" Robinson. Doyle's death caused the Boxing Commission to rule that all boxers had to be licensed locally and that any boxer whose history showed a head injury would be banned. With the leadership of fight promoter LARRY ATKINS, live professional boxing was a major Cleveland spectator sport during the 1950s and 1960s, climaxed by the annual *News* Christmas Toyshop program. Eventually televised fights limited the attendance at local live professional boxing cards. The Mar. 1971 bout between Joe Frazier and Muhammed Ali brought out 16,000 fans for closed-circuit television viewing at 6 Cleveland locations and had a gate of $170,000. Flamboyant Cleveland-born fight promoter Don King attempted to revitalize boxing in northeast Ohio during the 1970s. The first black man to successfully promote boxing matches nationally, King brought the ALI-WEPNER FIGHT to the area in the mid-1970s. Although King promoted fights at the Public Hall as late as 1981, he was discouraged by the city's high cut of gate receipts. One of the last important live local fights in Cleveland was Gerrie Coetzee's knockout of Akron's Michael Dokes on 24 Sept. 1983. After many years of suggested changes in the governing of local boxing matches, the general assembly established in July 1981 the first boxing and wrestling commission in Ohio. The 3-person commission, appointed by the governor, writes regulations governing fights and issues licenses to boxers, trainers, and promoters. The Cleveland Boxing & Wrestling Commission no longer regulated professional fights but still was in charge of amateur boxing and professional wrestling matches.

Although wrestling had been the foremost sport of the Union Army during the CIVIL WAR, it was seldom reported in newspapers during the 19th century. Publicity about wrestling seemed limited to strong-man matches at circuses. It was not until the turn of the century that amateur wrestling became popular. Published records of early wrestling matches, considered "academic antics," were almost nonexistent. By the 1920s, Greater Cleveland scholastic wrestling tournaments were being held. In 1929, wrestling coaches Joe Begala of Kent State and Claude Sharer of Case School of Applied Science were the leaders in organizing the Northeast Ohio Assoc. of Wrestling Coaches & Officials. Beginning in 1939, the Ohio High School Athletic Assoc. held a state tournament, with Cleveland's John Hay High School winning 4 of the first 5 championships. From 1944–54, state invitational meets were held by the Greater Cleveland Wrestling Coaches & Officials Assoc. In 1955 the Ohio High School Athletic Assoc. reassumed the sponsorship of an annual state wrestling championship in Columbus. Greater Cleveland schools dominated the tournament from the beginning, with only 5 large schools from other areas of the state ever winning the team title.

Greater Cleveland scholastic wrestling took off after WORLD WAR II, because of many dedicated coaches and officials. Al Carroll was the secretary of the Greater Cleveland Wrestling Coaches & Officials Assoc. for over 40 years, while talented coaches, including Mike Milkovich of Maple Hts. and Howard Ferguson of Lakewood St. Edward's, coached dominating teams during the period. Milkovich's squads won 10 championships between 1956–74, and Ferguson's wrestlers won 10 straight state titles from 1978 on. Milkovich was especially important in involving the entire school and community in the wrestling program. Watching wrestlers was the thing to do on Saturday night in Maple Hts. Ferguson's young men continually defeated championship squads from other states. By the mid-1970s, the Natl. High School Fed. ranked Ohio highest in the number of boys, over 25,000, in scholastic wrestling. Holiday wrestling tournaments such as the pioneer one at BRECKSVILLE in 1960 have been consistent sellouts. The state tournament at Columbus now has 3 school divisions and attendance of over 30,000 fans for the 3 days. A Jr. Olympics program run by the AAU made it possible for young wrestlers to compete throughout the year. Local colleges and universities also had excellent wrestlers in the period following World War II. Joe Begala coached at Kent State for 42 years with 307 victories and 7 undefeated seasons, while CLEVELAND STATE UNIVERSITY, JOHN CARROLL UNIVERSITY, and CUYAHOGA COMMUNITY COLLEGE, Western Campus, consistently had nationally ranked wrestling squads.

Professional wrestling has been popular in Cleveland and has been helped by television in recent years. In GORDON COBBLEDICK's words, "rasslin' [is] not a sport but a superbly staged act." Peter Bellamy, *Plain Dealer* drama critic, described professional wrestling matches as "a harmless pleasure [providing] a fine howling and catharsis for people of childlike trust." In the 1980s local professional boxing matches were almost nonexistent. Under the leadership of the Amateur Boxing Fed., the Golden Gloves tournament and amateur boxing were having a renaissance. In the sports of scholastic and collegiate wrestling, the Greater Cleveland area was maintaining high quality programs, generating widespread public interest and support.

Fred Schuld
Independence High School

The **BOY SCOUTS OF AMERICA,** a national organization designed originally for middle-class urban adolescents ages 12–18, was modeled after the British scouting organization founded by Robt. S. S. Baden-Powell. Organized in the U.S. in 1910, the Boy Scouts promoted the development of skills and values in a standardized program that appealed to the cult of efficiency and to the moral concerns of the Progressive Era, enabling scouting to grow rapidly. Cleveland's first Boy Scout troop was organized in Sept. 1910 by Matthew D. Crackel, head of the West Side Boys' Club and the first local Scout commissioner. Six Scout troops were organized in Cleveland in 1910; in 1911 17 prominent Clevelanders formed the Cleveland Boy Scout Council to oversee these troops. Council organizers included NEWTON D. BAKER, Horatio Ford, and SAMUEL MATHER, its first president. The council was supervised by a volunteer or partially compensated Scout commissioner until 1918, when the commissioner was replaced by a paid Scout executive appointed by the national scouting office.

In 1914 the Cleveland council opened an 8-acre camp near GATES MILLS, held a summer camp near BRECKSVILLE, and began publishing the *Scout*, a weekly newspaper filled with stories of Scouts' good deeds, upcoming events, and editorial advice. The Scouts contributed to and benefited from the patriotic spirit during WORLD WAR I, selling Liberty Bonds, counting black walnut trees for potential use in making firearms, and growing to 2,000 members by 1917. In 1919 the Scouts went door to door collecting money for the Community Fund.

The national scouting office insisted upon a policy of English-only instruction, which alienated many immigrant parents in Cleveland. Scouting lagged in Cleveland in the 1920s but grew steadily under the leadership of Geo. E. Green, Scout executive from 1928–54. Green implemented national policies at the local level, establishing Cub Scouts for younger boys in 1933 and special-interest Explorer units for older youths in 1935 and lowering the age limits for all three classes of Scouts in 1949. He also expanded opportunities for Scouts through the development of campgrounds, such as the Beaumont Scout Reservation in Ashtabula County, opened in 1945. By 1963 the Greater Cleveland Council of the Boy Scouts owned 4 campgrounds. In 1962, after a series of temporary locations, the Cleveland Council built its own $475,000 office building at E. 22nd and Woodland Ave. The number of local Scouts reached 35,340 in 1965 but declined in the 1970s, prompting the development of new programs for disabled boys and inner-city youths. In 1981, 30,000 Greater Cleveland youngsters were in the Cub Scouts, Boy Scouts, or Explorers.

**BOYD, ALBERT DUNCAN "STARLIGHT"** (1871–8 Dec. 1921), was a colorful and influential Republican leader and businessman during the first 2 decades of the 20th century. His association with Republican county chairman MAURICE MASCHKE and his control of Ward 11 politics ranked him among the most powerful local blacks at that time. Boyd was born on a plantation in Oak Grove, Miss., and came to Cleveland while in his teens. He arrived without money, but soon secured employment as a handyman, clerk, and bookkeeper in a lodging house on Ontario St. By the age of 25, he had purchased his own tavern on Canal Rd., beginning a career as a tavernkeeper and real-estate speculator that netted him a small fortune. Boyd's tavern on Canal Rd., in the city's Ward 1, became a popular center of political activity. Following the drift of the black population to the lower Central-Scovill district, he built more elaborate quarters at E. 14th St. and Scovill Ave. His Starlight Cafe, remodeled in 1907 to include a barber shop, bath facilities, and a pool room, became unofficial headquarters for the Republican party in Ward 11. Boyd was able to gain the loyalty of a growing black population by providing aid to needy families in the ward. His control of ward voters was well respected despite charges of vice and corruption in his businesses. One of his ventures, the Z-Douglass Club, was frequently raided for gambling. He defended it as a place for recreation and card playing, asking, "Don't people play cards anywhere else in town?" Boyd's support for THOS. W. FLEMING, the city first black councilman, was the center of controversy during Fleming's campaigns for election, especially between 1917–21. Black political and religious leaders charged that under Boyd and Fleming's control, the ward had become the vice center of the city. The Republican party, however, continued to support Fleming with Boyd's active endorsement until his untimely death at age 50.

**BOYD, ELMER F.** (19 Mar. 1878–12 Feb. 1944), a native of Urbana, Ohio, came to Cleveland in 1898 and, after working for several years as a waiter and a clerk, entered one of the few professions open to blacks at the turn of the century: undertaking. He operated a funeral home in Cleveland from 1905 until his death. The son of Wm. F. Boyd and Anna Mariah Waters, Boyd learned his profession at Clark's College of Embalming in Cincinnati and Meyer's Embalming School in Springfield. He passed the state examination on 5 June 1905 and that fall opened an office at 2604 Central Ave. in Cleveland. In Apr. 1906 he took on a partner, Lewis J. Dean; their initial establishment was described as "a combination funeral parlor and haberdashery." In 1911 Dean left the business, and Boyd continued alone, moving his business to 2544 Central; by 1919 he had moved his operation to 2226 E. 43rd. By 1938, Boyd had bought the Slaughter Bros. Funeral Home, moved his operation to that location (2165 E. 89th St.), and changed the name of his establishment to E. F. Boyd & Son. The son, Wm. F. Boyd, continued the business after his father's death. Elmer F. Boyd was active in a number of local civic and fraternal organizations, as well as local, state, and national professional organizations. He was founder of the Cleveland Funeral Directors' Assoc. and was a member of the local Elk Lodge and the Mason Excelsior Lodge. He was also a member of the NAACP, the FUTURE OUTLOOK LEAGUE, the PHILLIS WHEATLEY ASSOC., and the Progressive Business Alliance, and was a trustee of ST. JOHN'S AME CHURCH. His obituary reports that he gave generously to charitable and religious institutions. In 1910, Boyd married Cora Stewart (1875–4 Jan. 1960) of Salem, Ohio. A schoolteacher for 15 years early in her career, Cora Boyd was active in the PTA in the Central area and was a member and officer in the local, state, and district branches of the Fed. of Colored Women's Clubs.

**BOYSTOWNS** were organized in 1939 as part of the city's new crime-prevention program. They were a means of combating juvenile delinquency by granting young boys a degree of self-government within their own recreation centers. It was believed the Boystowns would thus teach civic responsibility, as well as provide recreational activities. The idea for the Cleveland Boystowns came from the 1938 film *Boys Town,* starring Spencer Tracy and Mickey Rooney. City recreation commissioner J. Noble Richards proposed turning 6 police precinct stations vacated in the departmental reorganization into self-governing recreation centers supervised by the Recreation Div.; the Safety Dept. paid for heat, lights, water, and a watchman at each center, and the Welfare Dept. looked after the physical needs of the boys. Centers were established at Broadway and E. 55th, E. 79th and Woodland, E. 80th and Superior, E. 185th and Nottingham, W. 53rd and Clark, and W. 83rd and Detroit. Boys ages 8–18 in the vicinity of each center elected a mayor, 2 judges, and 7 councilmen to 1-year terms; the mayor appointed additional "town" officers. Each "town" also established a merit system, and violation of ordinances was punishable by demerits determined by a jury trial. For the primary elections on 1 Feb. 1939, 1,502 "citizens" registered to vote; turnout for the final election 2 weeks later dropped to 695 after elected councils levied taxes in the form of dues. Adult organizers of the clubs decided not to furnish the centers with any equipment "in order to establish an objective for Boystown officers," but by Feb. 1940 the project was "in danger of collapse through lack of funds and trained adult leadership." The result was an outpouring of volunteer service and supplies for the centers and the appointment of the first city employee assigned to Boystown full-time. The program was further strengthened in Mar. 1941 with the formation of the Cleveland Boystown Foundation to help finance and advise the Boystowns.

Boystowns declined during the war as city officials placed wartime services in the centers and crowded out the youngsters. In Apr. 1942, officials decided to mobilize the Boystowns' "citizens" into a junior civilian defense organization. Boystowns reappeared a year later, however, after "mounting juvenile delinquency emphasized the need to continue supervised recreation for children ages 10–16." Centers were opened at E. 55th and Perkins, E. 79th and Woodland, E. 80th and Superior, and W. 25th and Althen. The Boystowns were reorganized in 1947; the program was transferred from the Safety Dept. to the Joint Recreation Board, and emphasis shifted from explicit concerns about crime prevention and juvenile delinquency to education and recreation. Expansion of the program to include older boys and to offer a full program of sports helped boost the number of participants from 1,400 in 1947 to 2,000 in 1948. The KIWANIS CLUBs became involved heavily in Boystown activities in the 1940s and in 1963 were mentioned as cosponsor of the program with the Recreation Div. By late 1968 there were 3 Boystowns in operation and holding annual elections of mayors, but from the late 1940s the program had been far different from the self-governing and self-supporting clubs the adult founders had envisioned.

Writers Program of the Works Projects Admin., *Cleveland's Boystowns* (1940).

**BRADLEY, ALVA** (27 Nov. 1814–28 Nov. 1885), was a Great Lakes sailor, master, ship owner, and shipbuilder. As a partner in Bradley & Cobb, he contributed greatly to the development of Great Lakes shipping. Bradley was born in Ellington, Conn., to Leonard and Roxanne Thrall Bradley. In 1823, the family moved to Brownhelm, Ohio. At the age of 19, with all his possessions in a bundle, Bradley left home for the life of a sailor on the Great Lakes. He first served as a sailor on the schooner *Liberty*. During his sailing career, he served on numerous ships, including the *Young Leopold, Edward Bancroft,* and *Express.* The first ship on which he served as master was the small 15-ton vessel *Olive Branch*, which ran trade from the islands to the southern ports on Lake Erie. His next vessel as master was the 47-ton schooner *Commodore Lawrence,* owned by the Geauga Furnace Co. In 1853, Bradley, in partnership with Ahira Cobb, formed Bradley & Cobb, shipbuilders with yards in Vermilion. Bradley served as master on the *South America,* a 200-ton vessel built by his company. Among the many ships built by Bradley & Cobb was the 300-ton *Indiana,* one of the early propeller-driven ships on the Great Lakes.

In 1859, Bradley moved to Cleveland. In 1868, he centered all his interests in Cleveland, moving his Vermilion shipyards to the city. Building and launching at least 1 vessel each year, Bradley, in association with others, built a large fleet of 18 lake vessels between 1868–82. His business operations were so extensive and efficient that it became economical for him to carry his own insurance. He never experienced a wreck during his sailing career and suffered the loss of only 5 vessels as an owner. His wealth was estimated at $10 million, much of it invested in real estate. In 1880, Bradley helped found the Cleveland Vessel Owners Assoc. and became its first president. This group combined with its Buffalo counterpart to form the LAKE CARRIERS ASSOC. in 1892. On 6 Apr. 1880, Bradley became one of the original incorporators of the Case Institute of Technology. Bradley served as a trustee of the EUCLID AVE. CONGREGATIONAL CHURCH. He was honored by a set of memorial windows in the new church building in 1897. He was also active in the temperance movement in Cleveland. Bradley married Helen M. Burgess of Milan, Ohio, in 1851. They had 4 children: 3 daughters, Elizabeth, Eleanor, and Minetta, and a son, Morris, who succeeded his father in business.

**BRADLEY TRANSPORTATION** was a major local builder of lake vessels and at one time was the largest single vessel owner in the city. The firm was founded in 1868 by Ahira Cobb and Capt. ALVA BRADLEY, a Connecticut-born seaman who turned from sailing to shipbuilding in 1841. For a time Bradley lived in the home of Mrs. Edison, who named her son Thos. Alva after the captain. The business was centered in Vermilion until 1859, when Bradley came to Cleveland and Cobb sold out his interest. The shipyards were fully moved to Cleveland in 1868, and Bradley began building about 1 lake vessel a year. Bradley's son, Morris, came into the business in 1868 and urged its incorporation in 1882. The elder Bradley died in 1885, leaving his son with a fortune invested in real estate and iron and steel enterprises. Morris Bradley managed Bradley Transportation and made the company a prominent member of the Lake Carriers Assoc., an alliance of steamship companies. Increasingly, he turned his attention to real-estate development. When Morris died in 1926, the Bradley family was the largest holder of downtown real estate. As late as 1927, Bradley Transportation was apparently building vessels, its latest being the *Carl D. Bradley,* a 638-ft. freighter. However, the corporate listing no longer appeared in city directories after 1915.

**BRADSTREET'S DISASTER,** which occurred on 18 Oct. 1764, 1.7 mi. west of Rocky River, is one of the most notable events in the presettlement history of Cleveland. In late summer 1764, Col. John Bradstreet, a Nova Scotian in the English army and renowned as the hero of Ft. Frontenac, proceeded from Ft. Niagara as ordered by the Commander-in-Chief, Gen. Wm. Gage, with 2,300 British regulars, American provincials under Col. Israel Putnam, and Indians to Ft. Detroit. Stopovers on this westward trek included the Cuyahoga and Rocky rivers on 18 and 19 Aug. The expedition was initially part of a 3-pronged assault to put down Pontiac's Rebellion. After Indian acquiescence, the mission became one of reinforcement, exploration, retrieval of captives, challenge of hostile groups, and peacemaking.

Returning to Ft. Niagara, Bradstreet's party departed their extended Sandusky encampment, rowing their 46'-long bateaux to a swale near ROCKY RIVER (now the park, "Bradstreet's Landing"). Because of darkness, the rock-strewn but otherwise safe shelter of the river was too treacherous to navigate for the 60 boats and 9 canoes laden with 1,550 troops. An unexpected storm struck suddenly, with high waves causing the destruction of 25 boats and damaging others. Two days at the landing and 1 at Rocky River were required for repair before further travel could be undertaken. The path then again stopped at the Cuyahoga River (21-23 Oct.). The shortage of boats necessitated that a portion of the party proceed over land, carrying a minimum of provisions. Bad weather severely hampered the progress of the boats, while shortages of food and supplies, poor hunting, illness, and fire caused much hardship. Although rumors of marchers' perishing exist, only 1 fatality is confirmed in the struggle to return to Ft. Niagara. The last of the overland party arrived in the first week of November, shortly after the boats. With the crippling of the expedition and his accomplishments on the mission questioned, Bradstreet was open to the chastisement of his superiors, Gage and Sir Wm. Johnson, and his promotion to general was delayed.

**BRAINARD'S SONS.** *See* **S. BRAINARD'S SONS**

**BRATENAHL** is a residential community located on Lake Erie about 6 mi. east of downtown Cleveland. Approximately 4 mi. long and less than .5 mi. wide, it occupies 552 acres (.86 sq. mi.) and is surrounded by the city of Cleveland. It was originally part of the villages of GLENVILLE and COLLINWOOD. In 1902, when Glenville was anticipating annexation by Cleveland, a group of residents including LIBERTY E. HOLDEN, SAMUEL MATHER, and FREDERICK GOFF, mayor of Glenville, opposed annexation and decided to form an independent village. When Glenville was annexed in 1903, that portion north of the Lake Shore & Michigan Southern Railroad and extending from GORDON PARK to Coit Rd. seceded and was incorporated as the village of Bratenahl. In 1906, when the village of Collinwood was annexed, the area from Coit Rd. to E. 140th St. became part of Bratenahl.

In the mid-19th century, about 2 dozen families farmed the rural area. One of these early settlers was Chas. Bratenahl, who owned land on Lake Erie, and the path to his farms from St. Clair Ave. was called Bratenahl Rd. (E. 88th St.). On the lakeshore at Eddy Rd., Chas. Coit built a summer hotel known as Coit House. Later, this property was the site of the COUNTRY CLUB, which opened in 1889. The Country Club moved to PEPPER PIKE in 1930, and its 1908 building became the Lake Shore Country Club. It was razed in 1964 and replaced by the luxury apartment complex Bratenahl Place. In the late 19th century, some of Cleveland's wealthy families came to the lakeshore during the summer. Living first in elaborately furnished tents and later in summer cottages, many of them subsequently built large mansions on the lakefront in French, Tudor, Georgian, and Italian styles. These included such names as Corning, Hanna, Bolton, Mather, Goff, Ingalls, Haskell, Grasselli, Coit, and Cunningham. The area was characterized by the tree-lined Lake Shore Blvd., a succession of gardens accompanying the estates, curving drives, banks of trees and rolling lawns, and docks on the water's edge for family yachts. The population of Bratenahl was about 640 in 1910, increasing to 1,000 by 1920, 1,250 by 1933, and approximately 1,270 by 1960. In the 1980s, the population of 1,485 was diverse. Some families lived in modest homes along the side streets; others who were descendants of the original owners remained or returned to live in the lakefront mansions. Gwinn Estate, the Italianate villa of Wm. G. Mather, has been used as a conference center established by the family. Bratenahl is part of the Cleveland public school system, but many students attend parochial and private schools. The village, which in the 1980s had no commercial enterprises, had many community-oriented activities such as theater groups, town meetings, family nights, and a summer camp recreational program.

**BRAVERMAN, SIGMUND** (22 May 1894–27 Mar. 1960), was a prominent Jewish architect who designed more than 40 synagogues in the U.S. and Canada, and many diverse structures in Cleveland. Born in Austria-Hungary, Braverman came to the U.S. at age 10, received a B.S. from the Carnegie Institute of Technology in 1917, and served in the military during WORLD WAR I. In 1920 he came to Cleveland and opened an architectural practice. His work included apartments, theaters, shopping centers, schools, and hospitals, and from 1932–35 he was assistant, then acting, city architect for Cleveland. Among Braverman's best-known local designs are the Brantley Apts. (1937), the Cleveland Hebrew Schools Shaker-Kinsman Branch (1951), the BUREAU OF JEWISH EDUCATION (1952), Fairmount Temple, designed in association with Percival Goodman (1957), and Warrensville Ctr. Synagogue (1958). Active in Jewish community affairs, Braverman served as a director of the Bureau of Jewish Education, trustee of the Cleveland Jewish Welfare Fed., and vice-president and director of the JEWISH COMMUNITY CTR. and was a leader in Cleveland's Zionist movement. In 1924 he married Libbie Levin.

Sigmund Braverman Papers, WRHS.

**BRECKSVILLE,** located 14 mi. south of Cleveland on the southern border of Cuyahoga County, borders INDEPENDENCE on the north and BROADVIEW HTS. on the west. Breck Twp. was incorporated as the village of Brecksville in 1922 and achieved city status on 16 Dec. 1960. It operates under the mayor-council form of government. Brecksville occupies 19 sq. mi., and its population in 1980 was 10,132. In 1810, Seth Paine left Williamsburg, Mass., with his family and Melzer Clark for the WESTERN RESERVE. A land surveyor, Paine began work in the current Brecksville area in 1811 and also acted as land agent for the Breck family, owners of a substantial tract of land in the area. Paine selected 200 acres of flat land for himself and became known as the first white settler in Breck Twp., so named after the Breck heirs. Brecksville remained an agricultural community throughout the 19th century. In the 20th century, the construction of paved roads and the introduction of the automobile made Brecksville more accessible to Cleveland residents. In 1937–38, many farms in the village were uprooted to make room for the construction of Ohio Rt. 82. Post-WORLD WAR II migration from Cleveland to area suburbs, especially during the 1950s, contributed to Brecksville's growth. In 1960 its population reached 5,435, enabling it to incorporate as a city. By 1970, the population nearly doubled to 9,137. The Brecksville City School District operates 4 elementary, 1 junior and 1 senior high school, and a vocational school; 65% of Brecksville public-school graduates attend college. Other educational facilities include a branch campus of CUYAHOGA COMMUNITY COLLEGE, a parochial school, and the Advanced Bartending Institute. Among the city's largest employers are the Brecksville Veterans' Hospital, Ohio Bell, B. F. Goodrich, and the Brecksville Board of Education. Brecksville provides its residents with a variety of services. It is part of the CUYAHOGA COUNTY PUBLIC LIBRARY SYSTEM. Recreational facilities include the Brecksville Reservation of the Metropark System, 2 golf courses, baseball diamonds, tennis courts, riding stables, and a ski run.

Coates, W. R., *The Brecksville Centennial, 1811-1911* (1911).
Snow, Dorcas, *In and Out of Brecksville* (1982).
Wilcox, Frank, and Horrocks, Arthur, *A Reminiscent History of Brecksville* (1961).

**BREED, WALTER** (1867–9 Mar. 1939), was the rector of ST. PAUL'S EPISCOPAL CHURCH for over 30 years. He led the church's move from E. 40th and Euclid to Fairmount and Coventry in CLEVELAND HTS. and guided 2 generations of parishioners with his intellectual spirituality compressed into his hallmark 18-minute sermons. A descendant of the rector of Old North Church in Boston, Breed was born in Lynn, Mass. His New England heritage gave him an evangelical liberal point of view. He was ordained in May 1891 at Tarrytown, N.Y., after graduating from Wesleyan Union in Connecticut and Episcopal Theological Seminary in Cambridge, Mass. He received his D.D. at Harvard. In 1907, after serving in parishes in New England, he was assigned to St. Paul's, the most fashionable Episcopal church in Cleveland and the social center of Euclid Ave., located on the outskirts of downtown Cleveland when many wealthy families made their homes there. St. Paul's counted the Devereuxs, Mathers, Boltons, Seymours, and Scovills among its congregants. Breed won their loyalty with enlightened sermons grounded in the humanities and with his fresh and personal readings of familiar prayers. As downtown became less residential, Breed negotiated a merger with St. Martin's Episcopal Church and arranged the move to Cleveland Hts. At the suburban church, which he saw as warmer and friendlier, Breed developed a church school. Particularly interested in the religious education of children, he frequently taught classes, and he exhibited a gift for talking to children as young adults. Breed's philosophy for keeping perspective in his many duties was "Take long vacations and keep sermons short." Following his own advice, he visited England and Europe nearly every year. Breed died of pneumonia, leaving his wife, Ellen Broderick Breed, and 1 son.

**BRENTWOOD HOSPITAL**, located at 4110 Warrensville Ctr. Rd., is a small voluntary nonprofit general hospital in WARRENSVILLE HTS. It was established in 1957 by a group of osteopathic physicians and surgeons in response to the hospital bed shortage in the area. Brentwood was opened in 1957, and facilities were expanded in 1960, 1967, 1972, and 1975. It has approximately 181 beds and provides only the customary diagnostic and therapeutic services of a general hospital.

**BRETT, WILLIAM HOWARD** (1 July 1846–24 Aug. 1918), was librarian of the CLEVELAND PUBLIC LIBRARY and founder of the Western Reserve University Library School. Born in Braceville, Ohio, he attended public schools in Warren and became the school librarian at Warren High School at the age of 14. He enlisted and fought with the Ohio Infantry in the CIVIL WAR before entering the University of Michigan and later WRU, but he was forced by poverty to abandon his academic studies. Brett settled in Cleveland. He worked for a Cleveland bookdealer, the Cobb & Andrews Co., and expanded his acquaintanceship among bibliophiles, including JOHN G. WHITE, who was instrumental in appointing Brett librarian of the CPL in 1884. He soon distinguished himself for his contributions to cataloguing in the traditions set by Cutter and Dewey. By 1890 he was developing the concept of the open-shelf library, which led among other things to his being invited to London to deliver a paper on his ideas of free access to library collections.

Brett continued to grow and expand in almost every aspect of librarianship. Andrew Carnegie depended on his advice during the most fruitful years of the steel magnate's philanthropy. Brett was expert in building design. He published the first issue of his *Cumulative Index to the Selected List of Periodicals* in 1896, a publication that after several metamorphoses became the familiar *Reader's Guide to Periodical Literature*. In the same year he was elected president of the American Library Assoc. Brett campaigned vigorously for libraries for children and established an alcove for juvenile books in the CPL. Under his leadership, the first branch libraries were opened in Cleveland. Staff training came to occupy a large place in Brett's thinking; he realized the importance of specialized education to library work. His interest developed eventually into a plan for a library school at WRU, where in 1904 he was present at the birth of that school. He was its first dean even as he remained head of the public library. During the years before his death, Brett developed plans for the main library building on Superior Ave., which, although not opened until 1925, bore the imprint of his thought.

Eastman, Linda A., *Portrait of a Librarian* (1940).

**BREWING AND DISTILLING INDUSTRY.** Cleveland's distilling industry dates almost to the city's founding. In 1800 David and Gilman Bryant are said to have operated a secondhand distillery, brought from Virginia, on the banks of the CUYAHOGA RIVER at the foot of Superior St. Their output was "two quarts of raw spirits a day," according to historian Wm. Ganson Rose, which was used "in the household for medicinal purposes, as coin in commerce and trade, and as a pacifying influence over uneasy Indians." JOSIAH BARBER, who with his brother-in-law RICHARD LORD gave the village of Brooklyn (later the west side) its first economic boom, is said to have established that area's first industry, a distillery. By 1831, a distillery had been built on the narrow strip of land sheared off from the FLATS by the old river bed and the new channel of the Cuyahoga River, giving that district the name WHISKEY ISLAND. During the same period, Baptist clergyman Elijah F. Willey opened a brewery on Walworth Run, so that "the introduction among us of this wicked beverage cannot be laid at the door of the immigrant Teuton," John H. Sargent noted at a meeting of the EARLY SETTLERS' Assoc. in 1880.

There were 2 breweries in Cleveland when the first city directory was published in 1837-38. In 1845-46, 3 breweries employing 13 persons produced 177,000 gallons of beer and ale with an estimated value of $17,000. Thereafter, the directories trace the swift and sustained growth of the industry prior to Prohibition in 1920: in 1860, there were 11 breweries; in 1870, 17; in 1880, 23; in 1890, 19; in 1900, 23; and 1910, 26. The city's malt liquor output, valued at $1,249,502 in 1880, increased more than fourfold by 1910, to $5,124,478, and helped boost Ohio to third place, behind Wisconsin and Pennsylvania. The distilling industry, meanwhile, never attained the importance of brewing in Cleveland. In 1840, 2 distilleries produced 80,000 gallons of liquor, according to U.S. census figures. That number grew to 5 establishments producing products valued at $131,273 in 1860, but thereafter the industry declined as a factor in the city's economic life. The census gives no figures for the production of distilled liquor in Cleveland between 1870-1900. In 1910 the city's 4 distilleries produced products valued at only $14,341. Today PARAMOUNT DISTILLERS, in business since 1934, bottles its products—including blended and bourbon whiskey,

Scotch, gin, and vodka—in Cleveland but distills them elsewhere.

Throughout the 19th century, the brewing industry in Cleveland (as elsewhere) was characterized by small, family-owned breweries that had been founded by German or Bohemian immigrants. Deliveries of draft beer and ale were made by horse-drawn wagon to a small, local market, usually within a 30-mi. radius. Chas. Gehring, who opened his brewery in 1852, is credited with having produced Cleveland's first lager beer. By 1875, Gehring, Isaac Leisy (see LEISY BREWING CO.), Jacob Mall (see GUND BREWING CO.), and Leonard Schlather had all established breweries that would persist into the 20th century.

After 1860, several broad trends profoundly affected the brewing industry in Cleveland and nationwide. The Internal Revenue Act of 1862, instigated by the need for revenue to conduct the CIVIL WAR, introduced for the first time a tax on malt beverages and led to the formation of the U.S. Brewers' Assoc., America's oldest continuously incorporated trade association. (The Brewers' Assoc. would later form the industry's front-line defense against the threats posed by the growing temperance movement.) In the 1870s the development of pasteurization meant that beer could be bottled and sold to wider markets, while the spread of railroads also made it possible for brewers to look farther afield for customers and led to the emergence of the first national brewers. During the 1880s and 1890s, mechanical refrigeration was installed in the larger breweries, thereby completing the transformation of the brewmaster from a cook to a mechanic and engineer.

The period from 1880–1910 is often said to represent the palmy days of the industry. There were still a large number of breweries, the majority of which were small, family-owned enterprises, and production was constantly increasing. Cleveland in 1890 ranked 13th among U.S. cities in the production of malt liquor, after New York, St. Louis, Brooklyn, Milwaukee, Philadelphia, Chicago, Cincinnati, Newark, Boston, Baltimore, Buffalo, and Rochester. But though prosperous, the period also saw the beginnings of industry consolidation as larger brewers bought out competitors' plants and either continued to operate them or shut them down. Many smaller firms were helpless, beset as they were with the huge outlays required for new equipment, buildings, and personnel in order to compete.

In Cleveland this trend was most dramatically illustrated by the formation in 1899 of the Cleveland & Sandusky Brewing Co. through a merger of 11 northern Ohio breweries, 10 of them Cleveland firms. Cleveland & Sandusky quickly became embroiled in controversy; some independent brewers—among them GEORGE GUND of GUND BREWING and Otto Leisy of LEISY BREWING—were charging unfair competition. Leisy, in a letter to the *Plain Dealer* (19 Feb. 1899), charged that Cleveland & Sandusky purchased saloons, then coerced tenants "to sell their beer at their price or leave the premise." The Cleveland & Sandusky "trust" proceeded unhindered, closing unprofitable plants and adding others, although after repeal of Prohibition, brewers were prohibited from operating saloon tie-ins.

In terms of sheer numbers of breweries, the industry in Cleveland reached its zenith in 1910, when 26 breweries were operating in the city. In addition to Bohemian, Cleveland, Columbia, Gehring, Schlather, Star, and Fishel (all in the Cleveland & Sandusky fold), there were the Belz, Cleveland Home Brewing, DIEBOLT BREWERY, Excelsior, Forest City, Gund, Leisy, Pabst, PILSENER BREWING CO., Schlitz, STANDARD BREWING, and Stroh breweries. Leisy, Pilsener, and Standard, all located on the near west side, were the most formidable independents.

National Prohibition, which took effect on 16 Jan. 1920, dealt a serious blow to the industry. Brewers faced either the liquidation of their property without compensation or the manufacture of products other than alcoholic beer. For some Cleveland breweries, such as Gund, that meant the end of business. Others, including Pilsener and Standard, turned to the manufacture of low-alcohol (near) beer and dairy products, soft drinks, or fruit juices. Others, such as Leisy, simply closed down and waited. Prohibition ended on 7 Apr. 1933. By the following month, 4 of the city's breweries (Pilsener, Standard, Forest City, and Cleveland Home Brewing) were back in production, and others soon followed. All faced a significant amount of reinvestment, including new bottling machinery and whole fleets of motorized delivery trucks. From a merchandising standpoint, beer was a brand-new business after repeal. Consumer preference had shifted from draft to packaged beer, a trend favoring the larger "shipping" brewers, which took an increasingly larger share of the market at the expense of smaller brewers still selling draft beer to a local market. The larger brewers were better able to win and hold consumers through aggressive advertising campaigns, and to absorb the costs of new equipment.

Although the number of Cleveland brewers was decreasing, the output of the remaining firms continued to increase, so that in 1939 Cleveland's 9 breweries employed 1,265 persons (in 1910 the industry had employed 904), and malt liquor production was valued in excess of $10 million. Surviving were those companies that adopted bold new strategies to meet the competition head-on. The Standard Brewing Co., a strong contender that had long confined its market to a 50-mi. radius, embarked on a multi-million-dollar plant expansion after WORLD WAR II and broadened its market to include adjoining states. The Brewing Corp. of America, later known as the CARLING BREWING CO., used aggressive merchandising to make an unusually swift advance toward a leading position in the industry; Carling became one of the leaders in the multiple-plant idea, as well as Cleveland's largest brewer, ranking 15th in sales nationally in 1944.

Meanwhile, many smaller brewers were either absorbed or forced to close. The state excise tax, which averaged $.12 per case in the principal beer-producing states (New York, Michigan, Wisconsin, and Missouri) but was $.36 per case in Ohio, further aggravated the problems faced by smaller brewers. Leisy, Cleveland's oldest family-owned brewer, which as early as the 1870s had established markets well beyond the Cleveland area, pointed to the tax as an important factor in its decision to close in 1958. The city had 9 breweries in 1939, but by 1960 that number had dwindled to 5.

The phenomenon of brewery mortality, or shakeout, accelerated in the 1960s. Cleveland & Sandusky, Pilsener, and Standard all closed their doors, the latter two selling out to larger brewers (Duquesne and Schaefer respectively) attempting to expand their markets. The trend toward larger and larger brewing companies followed the pattern of industry in general, which increasingly turned to consolidation to meet such problems as financing and promotion. For the brewing industry, shakeout meant the end of malt liquor products having a distinctive taste and a regional identity: Gone were Black Forest beer (Cleveland Home Brewing), Gund's Clevelander beer, Erin Brew (Standard Brewing), Black Dallas malt liquor (Leisy), Old Timer's ale and Crystal Rock beer (Cleveland & Sandusky). By 1970 only 2 brewers remained in Cleveland, Carling and C. Schmidt & Sons. The following year Carling closed its Cleveland brewery, citing the plant's physical inefficiencies, and moved its headquarters to Waltham, Mass., near its modern brewery at Natick. Schmidt took over the vacant Carling plant and continued production there until 1984, when the city's last brewery closed. Schmidt blamed the closing on lack of sales.

Carol Poh Miller

**BREWSTER, WILLIAM H.** (b. 1814), was a Methodist minister who guided a Congregational church in Cleveland (1859–68) and was also a prominent local advocate of both abolition and temperance. Brewster was born in New Hampshire. His heritage, family background, and educational achievements are not known. Bucking the opposition of many of the city's clergy, Brewster left the haven of Euclid Ave.'s Wesleyan Methodist Episcopal Church to serve as first pastor of the University Hts. Congregational Church—an amalgam of Episcopal Methodists, EPISCO-PALIANS, PRESBYTERIANS, CONGREGATIONAL-ISTS, and Wesleyan Methodists. Its first services were held in Humiston's Cleveland Institute. Brewster wisely refrained from attempting to bestow an authoritative orthodoxy on this mixture of professions and instead relied upon common moral precepts and a recognition of Jesus as the Christ to keep the flock together. Abolition and temperance espousal were a primary concern of Brewster's. He made speeches in the service of both causes, championing the closing of saloons on Sunday in deference to the moral and religious rights of the community and accepting civil disobedience as appropriate action in opposing slavery. He also served as pastor of HUMISTON INSTITUTE. A popular lecturer, Brewster inaugurated a series of talks on the Bible (1859) and during the Civil War was not averse to selecting political topics for his speeches to Cleveland literary societies. He served as executive secretary of the Cuyahoga County Temperance Society (1862) and was appointed vice-president of the 1st General Conference of the Methodist Church (1867). He also served on the board of trustees of CLEVELAND UNIVERSITY. Brewster was one of the leaders of non-Episcopal and antislavery Methodists who split from the Episcopal branch of the church to organize (1842–43) the Wesleyan Connection of America. He also found himself compared to Henry Ward Beecher for the vehemence with which his sermons attacked slavery. Brewster's wife, Catherine, was born ca. 1821.

**BRICKNER, BARNETT ROBERT** (14 Sept. 1892–14 May 1958), communal leader, educator, Zionist, and orator, served as rabbi at ANSHE CHESED congregation for 33 years. The son of Yiddish-speaking East European immigrants, he was born in New York City on the Lower East Side and was educated in the city's public schools. He received his bachelor's (1913) and master's (1914) degrees from the Columbia University Teachers College. He was ordained in 1919 following graduation from the Reform movement's Hebrew Union College and received a Ph.D. in social science in 1920 from the University of Cincinnati.

Although only 33 years of age when he assumed the pulpit at Anshe Chesed, Brickner already had gained national stature as a community leader and educator. In 1910, he was among the founders of the Young Judea, a national Zionist youth organization. Between 1910–15, he was director of extension education at the Bureau of Jewish Education in New York City and with his mentor Samson Benderly was a cofounder of the Natl. Jewish Education Assoc. During WORLD WAR I, Brickner was the head of the Natl. Jewish Welfare Board's training school for Jewish welfare workers in military camps. And in 1919, he became the executive director of the United Jewish Social Agencies in Cincinnati. In 1920, Brickner decided to enter the pulpit and accepted a position at Holy Blossom Congregation in

Toronto. During 5 years in Toronto, he led his congregation from the Orthodox to the Reform movement, founded (1921) and was contribution editor for the *Canadian Jewish Review*, and served as president of the Toronto Federated Jewish Charities (1922–25).

Brickner succeeded LOUIS WOLSEY as rabbi of Anshe Chesed in 1925. During his tenure, he was responsible for increasing the membership from approximately 700 families to over 2,500, making it the largest Reform congregation in the country. He created the Young People's Congregation, the first of its kind, to encourage young couples to become involved in synagogue affairs. A proponent of Hebrew education, Brickner reinstituted Hebrew in the Anshe Chesed Sunday school curriculum. He was determined to improve interfaith relations and established an annual institute on Judaism at Anshe Chesed specifically for Christian religious schoolteachers and educators. For 25 years he delivered Easter Sunday sermons from the pulpit of the Boston Community Church. And from the late 1920s until WORLD WAR II, he had a weekly radio program on which he addressed common religious, cultural, social, and political concerns.

Brickner's reputation in the general Cleveland community was established in Feb. 1928 when he debated attorney Clarence Darrow at the Masonic Auditorium on the topic "Is Man a Machine?" Between 1928–36, he served as a labor arbitrator for disputes in the dry-cleaning, street railway, and baking industries. Within the Jewish community, Brickner succeeded Rabbi ABBA HILLEL SILVER as president of the BUREAU OF JEWISH EDUCATION (1932–40). He and Silver were influential in obtaining Jewish Welfare Fed. support for the bureau. In 1935, Brickner and Silver served as cochairs of the newly reorganized Jewish Welfare Fund, the fundraising arm of the federation. Brickner was also the president of the local Cleveland Zionist District, the local branch of the Zionist Organization of America.

On the national and international scene, Brickner attained several leadership positions. He was president of the Central Conference of American Rabbis, the rabbinical association of the Reform movement, from 1953–55, and also served as vice-president of the World Union for Progressive Judaism. As a leader in the conference, he was an early advocate of the ordination of women. During World War II, he chaired the Conference Committee on Chaplains and was administrative chairman of the Committee on Army & Navy Religious Activities of the Natl. Jewish Board. For his work in this endeavor and for his visits to camps during and after the war, Brickner was awarded the Medal of Merit in 1947 by Pres. Harry Truman.

Brickner served on the boards of the United Jewish Appeal, the Natl. Commission on Jewish Social Work, and the Religious Education Assoc. of America. He was a member of the executive committee of the Zionist Organization of America and the Actions Committee of the World Zionist Organization. He married Rebecca Ena Aaronson, a coworker at the Bureau of Jewish Education in New York, on 10 Aug. 1919. They had 2 children, Joy Marion and Arthur James Balfour.

Barnett R. Brickner Papers, WRHS.

The **BRICKNER-DARROW DEBATE** took place on Thursday evening, 9 Feb. 1928, before a standing-room-only crowd at Cleveland's Masonic Auditorium. The event captured the attention of the city, as an estimated Greater Cleveland audience of 500,000 listened to the 2-hour debate over radio station WHK. The CLEVELAND ADVERTISING CLUB, under the direction of president Wilbur Hyde, sponsored the debate, which pitted attorney Clarence Darrow against Rabbi BARNETT R. BRICKNER on the subject "Is Man a Machine?" Darrow, the most famous criminal lawyer in America and a celebrated agnostic, argued the affirmative. Rabbi Brickner, the spiritual leader of Cleveland's ANSHE CHESED congregation, argued the negative side of the question. Chief Justice of the Ohio Supreme Court Carrington T. Marshall was the moderator.

Each participant spoke 3 times on behalf of his argument. Darrow, who opened the debate, held that man's physiological composition and functions were exactly like those of a machine, including ingesting food for energy just as a steam engine needs coal. He continued, saying that all bodily organs operated in a mechanical manner. His argument also held that other animal forms as well as plant life are machines, using that premise to posit that although man is capable of thought and reason, so are animals. Brickner countered that it is the capability of thought and reason that differentiates man from a machine. Additionally, he argued that machines cannot write poetry or create works of art, nor can machines repair or reproduce themselves. Brickner also noted that a machine does not have a soul, a point Darrow challenged using his animal-as-machine premise to suggest that no one knows whether the lower orders have souls.

The *Cleveland Plain Dealer*, which used 2-1/2 pages to report the debate, chose 4 unofficial judges to select a winner. They included Maurice Bernon, former common pleas judge; Dr. Wm. Reed Veazey, professor of chemistry at Case School of Applied Science; Chas. W. Mears, advertising counselor; and John J. Sullivan, appellate judge. All four thought Brickner presented the stronger argument. Mayor JOHN D. MARSHALL called it a draw. A *Plain Dealer* survey of the audience prior to the debate indicated a 4:1 ratio favoring Brickner. Following the debate, another survey found the ratio was the same. The *Plain Dealer* reported that the debate brought together a man who was old and totally disillusioned (Darrow) and one who was young with unshattered idealism.

Rabbi Barnett R. Brickner Papers, WRHS.

**BRIDGE WAR.** *See* **COLUMBUS ST. BRIDGE**

**BRIDGES.** Cleveland, split firmly though unequally by the CUYAHOGA RIVER, is deeply dependent upon bridges. The city's east and west sides are joined today by both high fixed spans and lower-level opening bridges. Trains cannot climb steep grades, and their frequency of crossing is low enough to permit the use of opening spans of various sorts. Auto and truck traffic, however, is of such high density that delays occasioned by spans' opening for river traffic would be found intolerable. Autos and trucks are capable of climbing the relatively steep approaches to high-level bridges over the Cuyahoga River, and today the bridges carrying heavy traffic loads (the Innerbelt Bridge, the Lorain-Carnegie Bridge, the DETROIT-SUPERIOR BRIDGE, and the Main Ave. Bridge) all are high fixed spans. There are more than 330 bridges in the immediate Cleveland area, including both the Cuyahoga River bridges and those spanning other features of the area's mixed terrain and industrial complexes.

When Cleveland was first platted, just before 1800, the east and west sides were joined by ferries, which were supplanted soon by the first Center St. Bridge. The Center St. Bridge was based on a system of chained floating logs, a section of which would be pulled aside to permit the passage of vessels. A later version of this bridge was based on

pontoon boats, and ultimately on a succession of fixed structures. The first substantial bridge over the Cuyahoga appears to have been the first COLUMBUS ST. BRIDGE, erected ca. 1836, with a draw section permitting vessels to pass. The roofed bridge was 200 ft. long and 33 ft. wide, including sidewalks. In 1836, following the incorporation of both Cleveland and OHIO CITY, Cleveland ordered the destruction of its portion of the Center St. Bridge, which had the effect of directing commerce across the Columbus St. span, thereby bypassing Ohio City. Enraged Ohio City residents damaged the Columbus St. span, and hostilities commenced. The Cleveland marshal stopped the fray, yet west-siders ultimately gained their point, retaining a Center St. bridge along with the Columbus St. span. With Cleveland's annexation of Ohio City in 1854, traffic increases led to construction of the Main St. Bridge and the Seneca (W. 3rd) St. Bridge, and a rebuilding of the Center St. Bridge. In 1870, the Columbus bridge was replaced by an iron truss structure, which in turn was replaced by a 4th bridge in 1895. The Seneca span collapsed in 1857 and was replaced first by a timber draw span, and in 1888 by a Scherzer roller-lift bridge—the first of its kind in Cleveland. The Center St. Bridge had a similar sort of history, its wooden structure being replaced several times, finally with the unequal swinging span of iron built in 1900, which remained in service in 1986 as the sole swinging bridge in the city.

By 1986, 4 great vehicular bridges provided high-level spans over the Cuyahoga Valley. They were the Detroit-Superior Bridge (opened in 1918); the Lorain-Carnegie Bridge, renamed the HOPE MEMORIAL BRIDGE (1932); the Main Ave. Bridge (1939); and the Innerbelt Bridge (1959), which replaced the CENTRAL VIADUCT, demolished in 1941. Near the present Detroit-Superior Bridge may be seen the remains of one of Cleveland's great historical bridge achievements, the SUPERIOR VIADUCT, opened with great fanfare in Dec. 1878. Its great west side stone approaches were joined with a swinging metal span crossing the Cuyahoga toward PUBLIC SQUARE and downtown Cleveland. The viaduct served until the Detroit-Superior Bridge was opened in 1918. The Detroit-Superior Bridge resulted from continued traffic increases and complaints about delays in vehicular traffic from the frequent openings that river traffic required of the swinging span on the Superior Viaduct. Built as a 2-level structure, it permitted vehicular traffic on the top deck, with streetcars utilizing the lower deck until their demise in the 1950s. When inaugurated in 1918, it was the world's largest double-deck reinforced-concrete bridge structure.

Planned as early as 1916 but delayed by WORLD WAR I, the Lorain-Carnegie Bridge was opened in 1932. Though never used for traffic, the bridge possesses a lower deck, originally designed for rapid-transit trains and trucks. Four colossal pylons with figures symbolizing transportation progress make the bridge most distinctive. These pylons were preserved as the bridge underwent a thorough renovation process in the 1980s. In the mid-1980s, the bridge was renamed the Hope Memorial Bridge to honor the stonemason father of world-famed comedian Bob Hope. The new name, however, had not gained significant public appeal by 1986. Planned as early as 1930 to replace the low-level Main Ave. Bridge with its attendant traffic delays, the Main Ave. High-Level Bridge was opened in 1939 after a remarkably fast construction period largely financed with WPA funds. The bridge is 2,250 ft. long; with approaches, it is more than a mile in length. Eight truss-cantilever spans of varying lengths constitute the bridge itself, with added bridgework at the eastern end joining the bridge to the lakefront freeway. Having undergone significant emergency repairs in the 1980s, the Main Ave. Bridge was (in 1986) scheduled for early closure for a major rebuilding and renovation of the deck structure, sidewalks, and railings, estimated to cost in excess of $36 million.

The old Central Viaduct, opened in 1888, stood approximately at the location of the Innerbelt Bridge (1959). It was designed to bring southwest Cleveland traffic to downtown. The entire span consisted of 2 bridges of iron and steel placed on masonry piers. Originally the river was spanned with a swing section, which was replaced with an overhead truss in 1912 after an earlier tragic accident in which a streetcar fell to the river while the span was open. (see Central Viaduct Accident). Following additional accidents and structural problems, the bridge was condemned in 1941. Delayed by WORLD WAR II and by planning and financial concerns, the Central Viaduct was finally replaced by the Innerbelt Bridge (Ohio's widest) in 1959, with substantial funding resulting from the Federal Highway Act of 1956. The bridge is nearly a mile long, with the central portion consisting of a series of cantilever-deck trusses with a reinforced-concrete deck and asphaltic concrete driving surface. Because the bridge spans railroad tracks, industrial developments, and the Cuyahoga River, it involves a complex series of entrance and exit ramps along with the main structure. A substantial high-level rail bridge, the Cleveland Union Terminal Railway Bridge, just south of the Detroit-Superior Bridge, carries 2 rail tracks and 2 tracks used by commuter rapid trains of the Regional Transit Authority.

Nearly a dozen movable bridges remained across the Cuyahoga serving both vehicular traffic and railroads in 1986. Among the vehicular bridges, none of which are the same, are the old Center St. Swing Bridge, the Willow St. Lift Bridge (over the Old Cuyahoga Channel between the west side and WHISKEY ISLAND), the Columbus St. Lift Bridge, the Carter Rd. Bridge, and the W. 3rd St. Bridge. The remaining lift bridges serve various railroads; some were actively used, such as the ConRail Lift Bridge near the mouth of the Cuyahoga—the first bridge up the Cuyahoga from Cleveland Harbor—but many remained in lifted positions in the 1980s in response to industrial declines in the Cuyahoga Valley, and consequent declines in railroad traffic. The rail bridges included Scherzer roller-lift bridges, bascule structures, and jacknife bridges in addition to lift bridges such as the ConRail structure.

In addition to bridges spanning the Cuyahoga River, there are other bridges in Cleveland that are worthy of special note. CHAS. F. SCHWEINFURTH, noted for his design of the downtown TRINITY CATHEDRAL, the UNION CLUB, and the Mather mansion, designed 4 unusually fine bridges that span Martin Luther King, Jr. Dr. (formerly Liberty Blvd.) on Cleveland's east side. Structurally interesting in their combining of steel, concrete, and decorative stone, they include 3 vehicle bridges (Wade Park, Superior, and St. Clair avenues) and a railroad bridge (built for the Lake Shore & Michigan Southern Railway). Other noteworthy structures include the Forest Hills pedestrian bridge in nearby CLEVELAND HTS., the concrete-arch Monticello Bridge carrying Monticello Blvd. over Euclid Creek, and the 1910 Rocky River Bridge (demolished 1980). Other interesting bridges include the Hilliard Rd. Bridge over the Rocky River (1926) and the steel arched Lorain Rd. Bridge crossing the Metropolitan Park near the Rocky River.

Although a large number of engineers, designers, and architects, organizations, and consortia can be identified with recent bridge history in Cleveland, several individuals and organizations stand out prominently. One of these is Chas. Schweinfurth, whose designs were referred to earlier. Another prominent designer and builder associated mainly with midwestern railroad bridges was AMASA STONE, who, unfortunately, is often remembered for the tragic collapse of his innovative wrought-iron Howe truss bridge that spanned the Ashtabula River supporting the tracks of the Lake Shore & Michigan Southern Railroad, of which he was president. Cleveland firms that have had prominent roles in the history of Cleveland bridges are the firm of Wilbur J. Watson & Associates—known for the 1940 Columbus St. Bridge and later for pioneering concrete bridge structures—and Frank Osborn's OSBORN ENGINEERING CO., which began building local bridges at about the end of the 19th century. Another firm with historical prominence was the KING IRON BRIDGE & MFG. CO., which had important roles in the building of the Detroit-Superior Bridge, the old Central Viaduct, and the present (1986) Center St. Bridge. In the post-World War II period, the firm of Howard, Needles, Tammen, & Bergendoff was involved heavily with bridges in Cleveland, as attention shifted away from building bridges to rebuilding and rehabilitating existing structures.

Willis Sibley
Cleveland State University

Bluestone, Daniel M., ed., *Cleveland: An Inventory of Historic Engineering and Industrial Sites* (1978).
*Bridges of Cleveland and Cuyahoga County* (1918).
Watson, Sara Ruth, and Wolfs, John R., *Bridges of Metropolitan Cleveland* (1981).

**BRIGGS, JOSEPH W.** (1813–1872), while serving as the assistant postmaster in Cleveland during the CIVIL WAR, instituted free home mail delivery. He later was appointed by the federal government to supervise the establishment of such a system throughout the U.S. Briggs was born in Claremont, N.Y. In his youth, he was considered a mechanical genius, having made several inventions of merit in his career as a harnessmaker. During the early 1860s, Briggs was appointed clerk and assistant to the postmaster of Cleveland's first and only post office, on PUBLIC SQUARE. At this time, mail was handed out on request at windows and was not delivered to specific addresses unless by paid private carriers. Briggs claimed that he came up with the idea of free delivery during the winter of 1862–63; he observed that women, many of whom had come to receive letters from loved ones fighting in the war, were exposed to the cold while having to wait in slow-moving lines. Briggs's plan won the approval of the postmaster, EDWIN COWLES, who was also publisher of the *CLEVELAND LEADER*. Cowles believed that the circulation of his paper might also benefit from free delivery. The U.S. postmaster in Washington granted Briggs permission to implement the details of his system in Cleveland. Initially, the mail was sorted and taken to various grocery stores throughout the city, where it was distributed; later it was delivered to specific addresses. Briggs's system soon caught the attention of Congress, which on 3 Mar. 1863 passed a bill authorizing free mail delivery in cities throughout the country. Briggs was appointed as a special agent to implement the new system. He was later made national superintendent, and was chiefly responsible for organizing free mail delivery in 52 cities throughout the U.S., all of which he reportedly visited. Before he died, Briggs helped design the first mailman's uniform. A bronze plaque in the lobby of the Cleveland Federal Bldg. honors his achievements.

Joseph Wm. Briggs Papers, WRHS.

**BRITISH IMMIGRATION.** Immigrants from England, the Isle of Man, Scotland, and Wales were among the earliest to arrive in Cleveland. Because American society was, and

125

is, culturally and linguistically derived from that of Great Britain, they found in Cleveland a new home that was basically familiar and into which many readily assimilated, therefore leaving few traces, such as neighborhoods, churches, or clubs, through which historians can trace their progress.

*English* immigrants were the first British to arrive in the area, and over the years they largely remained, as characterized by Maldwyn A. Jones, "invisible immigrants." Indeed, Americans of English descent were the first to come to Cleveland and the WESTERN RESERVE, including MOSES CLEAVELAND and many in his surveying party. People of English birth or background thereafter compellingly determined the city's cultural, business, and industrial growth. Subsequent early immigrants became pioneer farmers, settling largely in the Newburgh area near Union Ave. Some, such as Jas. Wenham and Henry R. Hadlow and his son John, eventually became successful nurserymen. English immigration increased in the 1830s as the economic potential of the area grew. In 1830, over 1,200 Englishmen arrived in Cleveland; by 1848, 1,007 of the city's 13,696 inhabitants were English. Many opened small manufacturing establishments that subsequently grew into major commercial enterprises. They became stone contractors (John Spence), brick manufacturers (John Gynn), and paving contractors (Thos. Pharr). Some established shipyards that built Cleveland's wooden lake vessels (David T. Mitchell), while others were among the first to construct steel plate ships (John F. Pankhurst of Globe Iron Works). Some established extensive shipping interests (Col. Thos. Axworthy). They established the Cleveland Provision Co. (BENJAMIN ROSE) and jewelry businesses (Cowell & Hubbard).

Many initially settled in the area from E. 30th St. to E. 45th St. along Superior Ave., and also in parts of what later became E. CLEVELAND. Without barriers of custom or language, they consequently moved into all areas of the city. They did, however, establish various associations, including the St. George's Benevolent Society, a mutual-aid society for Britishers needing assistance (1858); the Sons and Daughters of St. George; and the Daughters of the British Empire. The ENGLISH SPEAKING UNION, which was established in the 20th century, did attract membership from the immigrant community, but more so from local anglophiles. Local admiration of English culture was substantial in the 19th and early 20th centuries, best exemplified by the architectural styles of many Protestant churches (see ARCHITECTURE, SACRED). The immigrants themselves were overwhelmingly Protestant of various denominations, but also included Catholics and Jews. Despite the popular perception that English immigration was confined to the pre-Civil War period, arrivals continued at a steady rate from the mid-19th century to the 1920s. It seems to have peaked in the period 1887–92. The city's English population rose from 4,530 in 1870 to 11,420 in 1910. Thereafter, the population in the city proper began to drop: to 11,126 in 1920, 6,542 in 1940, and 1,132 in 1970. However, English settlement in the Greater Cleveland area remained at a rather high level after WORLD WAR II. Many English joined the general movement to the suburbs; in 1980, 3,473 English lived in the Greater Cleveland area.

*Manx*, immigrants from the Isle of Man, located in the Irish Sea, form one of the city's unique ethnic groups. Cleveland, indeed, is the center of Manx immigration in the U.S. On 14 Mar. 1975, the Isle of Man issued 4 stamps to commemorate the settlement of Manx in the Western Reserve. Most Cleveland Manx came from the Kirk Andreas section of the Isle of Man located in the Irish Sea. Dr. Harrison, a physician in the British army, had visited the Reserve, and after returning to the Isle of Man told to

his brother, Rev. Harrison of the opportunity in Ohio. Manx farmers, many of whom faced adverse conditions in agriculture and fishing, and who resented class distinctions, welcomed this news. In 1822, the Corlett family came to America; they leased 50 acres of Newburgh land from the CONNECTICUT LAND CO., became farmers, and enthusiastically encouraged their fellow Manxmen to follow. In May 1826, 3 more Manx families (the Kelleys, Teares, and Kneens—13 people) arrived in Cleveland and settled in the Newburgh area near E. 93rd St. and Miles Ave. Each family purchased a farm, establishing a Manx settlement that drew further migrants. Another 70 Manx families settled in the Warrensville area on 25 May 1827. Primarily farmers, the settlers also engaged in weaving, tanning, sugar making, and chair or button making. Eventually the number of Manx and their descendants would grow to over 3,000. The Manx were bound by their own unique Gaelic language, which they used almost exclusively with each other and in their religious services. The first services in Manx were offered by Rev. Patrick Cannell, a Methodist preacher who came to NEWBURGH in 1826; he held services in his own log house, and later in the log schoolhouse on the Corlett farm. The original schoolhouse was replaced in 1842 by the "Manx St. School," located at Manx Ave. (Union) and Rice (E. 116th St.) which in turn was replaced in 1871, and in 1913 Mt. Pleasant school was built on the site. Like other ethnic communities, the Manx came to see a need for a mutual-aid society. Consequently, a group of 21 Manxmen established the Mona's Relief Society in 1851. It was designed to provide temporary relief for those who needed emergency assistance. On 7 Dec. 1899, a ladies' auxiliary was organized. In 1913, the group affiliated with the World Manx Society.

The community's major cultural organization, the Manx Choral Society, was organized in 1926 by John E. Christian. It performed at the 1st Internatl. Manx Convention, held in Cleveland in Aug. 1928, a gathering of Manx from all parts of the U.S., Canada, and the Isle of Man. The North American Manx Assoc. was organized at that convention; Christian was elected chairman. In 1923, the Cleveland Manx "sealed their link with the Isle of Man" when they presented a gold medal award at the Manx Musical Festival. This honor is awarded annually and is the strongest cultural bond between the homeland and Cleveland. Among noted Clevelanders of Manx descent are Dr. WM. T. CORLETT, internationally known skin specialist; lawyer W. Sheldon Kerruish; shipbuilder THOS. QUAYLE; and builders JOHN GILL & SONS, who handled construction of the Terminal Tower and other noted local buildings. Although immigration from the Isle of Man has nearly ceased, the closely knit Manx community, numbering an estimated 1,100 immigrants and descendants in 1970, continued to foster its culture and history into the 1980s.

*Scottish* immigrants first came to Cleveland ca. 1796; however, the largest Scottish immigrations occurred ca. 1830.

Many who came to Cleveland in the early 1830s came by way of Canada, Penna., Va., or the Carolinas. Most later arrivals came directly from Scotland. A number of the early immigrants were stonemasons, settling in the city. Most, however, were farmers and moved out to the farmland near Eddy Rd. The McIlrath, Eddy, and Shaw families were among those who were instrumental in the development of E. CLEVELAND. The second wave of migration settled around Denison and Fulton avenues on the west side, and E. 70th St. and Superior on the east side. It was not long before the Scots, like the English, moved out into all sections of Greater Cleveland. Those who came after 1830 adjusted quickly and achieved distinction in many fields, becoming industrial pioneers, particularly in the manufacture of iron. HENRY CHISHOLM was one of the founders of the Cleveland Rolling Mill in Newburgh, which grew out of the firm of Chisholm, Jones & Co. (1857) and ultimately became part of U.S. STEEL's American Steel & Wire Co. Later, his son William was instrumental in the Union Steel Screw Works and Chisholm Steel Shovel Works, being one of the first to manufacture steel screws made from steel produced by the Bessemer process. ALEXANDER WINTON was involved in the manufacture of bicycles and the Winton automobile. Alexander Campbell was a general contractor whose company paved many Cleveland streets. Wm. Knox, an architect, was responsible for the design of the ROCKEFELLER BLDG. and Trinity Congregational Church; Andrew Dall, Sr., and his son Andrew Dall, Jr., built some of Cleveland's finest structures.

The Scots were well represented in the leadership of the Presbyterian church. Rev. Andrew B. Meldrum, a Presbyterian clergyman originally from Fifeshire, Scotland, came to Cleveland in 1902 and became pastor of Old Stone Church; Dr. Alexander McGaffin, played a significant role in the establishment of Second Presbyterian Church, which later became part of the CHURCH OF THE COVENANT. Ironically, the second bishop of the Roman Catholic diocese was Bp. RICHARD GILMOUR, originally a Scotch Covenanter. The Scots moved quickly after their arrival to create cultural organizations. By May 1846, the Cleveland community had become large enough to establish the St. Andrews Benevolent Society, a branch of the St. Andrews Scottish Society of Edinburgh. Its purpose was to aid Scottish immigrants with counsel and financial assistance. Eventually the society established the Scottish Old Folks Home. In 1895, CLAN GRANT #17 (named in honor of Pres. U. S. Grant, who was of Scottish descent) was established as a fraternal organization. Other Scottish organizations included the Caledonia Literary Society, the Cleveland Kilty Band, the Caledonia Pipe Band, the Rob Roy Players Club (1929), and the Cleveland Scottish Choral Union (1928). In 1935 there were over 15 independent Scottish organizations. At one time, Cleveland was the headquarters of the Daughters of Scotland-Grand Lodge. Blue Bell No. 1, the first lodge of the Daughters of Scotland, was organized in 1900 to help needy Scotsmen. Emigration from Scotland decreased in the late 19th century; the poulation in Cleveland fell from 1,705 in 1880 to 1,474 in 1890. Then, during the early 20th century, it increased again. In 1900, the local population stood at 2,179; in 1910, at 2,880; in 1920, at 3,929; and in 1930, at 5,145. In 1930 an additional 1,376 Scottish immigrants lived in the city's 4 largest suburbs. Following World War II, the city population began to decline, to 4,866 in 1950; 3,895 in 1960; and 688 in 1970. In 1980, 1,896 Scottish immigrants lived in the Cleveland urbanized area. Despite this decline in the number of immigrants, local interest in Scottish culture seemed to have grown by the 1980s. The Ohio Scottish Games, held annually in nearby Oberlin, attracted thousands of participants and spectators, most of whom were several generations removed from their Scottish roots but were interested in their genealogy and ancestral culture nevertheless.

*Welsh* immigrants, as noted by Dr. CARL WITTKE, "can certainly claim a goodly share of credit for early development of Cleveland as one of the nation's most important iron and steel centers." One of the first Welsh immigrants, Jas. J. Chard, came from Wales in 1822 and in 1830 settled on a farm in EUCLID. He moved to Cleveland in 1832, opened a general leather business on Superior Ave. near Seneca (W. 3rd) St., and became one of the pioneer merchants of Cleveland. Welsh arrivals in Cleveland in the 1840s often settled in Newburgh. In 1848, 62 of

Cleveland's population of 13,696 had been born in Wales. They soon came in larger groups, particularly after DAVID I. AND JOHN JONES established an iron mill in Newburgh in 1856. The Joneses encouraged many of their fellow Welshmen, skilled in mining and ironworking, to come to Cleveland. The Welsh community grew rapidly around their mill, and by 1870 over 2,000 Welsh lived in Newburgh. Another Welshman, David James, built a competitive rolling mill called Crossing Mill, located where the Erie Railroad crossed the Pennsylvania Railroad. Subsequently it became the Empire Steel Co. Another Welsh settlement was established in Cleveland near the Otis Steel Mills along Lake Erie, near E. 40th St. and St. Clair. The group that settled there was smaller than that at Newburgh, and they became known as the "Lakeshore Welsh." Almost as soon as they settled in Cleveland, the deeply religious Welsh held cottage prayer meetings and services in their homes. A Sunday school was founded in 1850 with 13 pupils at the home of Robt. Edwards on Broadway, a Welsh Congregational Society was formed in 1858; 2 years later a chapel on Wales St. opened for worship. In July 1864, a church on Wales St. was completed and dedicated. As more Welsh came to work in the steel mills, their social and cultural activities, particularly singing societies, centered around the church, and the congregation gradually outgrew the building. In 1876 a larger church was constructed at 8000 Jones Rd., later known as the JONES RD. CONGREGATIONAL CHURCH in Newburgh. In 1890, Welsh Presbyterians organized a congregation at E. 55th St. and St. Clair Ave., which subsequently united with the Westminster Presbyterian Church at Addison Rd. and Wade Park Ave.

In the 1880s and 1890s, Polish immigrants settled in Newburgh gradually replacing the Welshmen at the mills. As Welsh ownership of the rolling mills became less dominant and Newburgh became part of Cleveland, the old Welsh community gradually disintegrated, and its families sifted into Cleveland's other neighborhoods. However, the Newburgh area continued to house Welsh families and their descendants into the 1960s. Indeed, during its later years, Newburgh and the Welsh community produced some of the city's most noted politicians, including HARRY L. DAVIS, DANIEL E. MORGAN, WM. R. HOPKINS, and EDWARD BLYTHIN. One of the activities that tended to unite the physically dispersed community was the Welsh love of 4-part singing. As soon as a few Welshmen settled in Newburgh, the traditional custom of singing in parts (especially after work in the mills) was revived. The Newburgh Welsh Chorus was organized in 1870 under the direction of Henry A. Jones, a leading choral director in the community. Ultimately it competed with the singing groups of Welsh communities of Youngstown and Pittsburgh at the traditional Welsh Eisteddfod, an institution from Wales dedicated to competitive singing and literary activities. Under Jones's leadership, the chorus won many 1st prizes in the Eisteddfod competitions. When Newburgh became part of Cleveland, the Welsh singers became the Mendelssohn Choir, and later they became members of the Forest City Glee Club under the direction of John R. Lodwick. The Welsh singers disbanded during WORLD WAR I and later joined the ORPHEUS MALE CHORUS under the leadership of a native Welshman, Dr. Chas. D. Dawe. Another Welsh singing group, the Cambrian Male Chorus, was directed by Wm. A. Hughes.

In 1900, the city's Welsh population peaked at 1,490. Seven years later the Cleveland Welsh Society was organized for the purpose of assisting impoverished Welsh and providing burial plots for indigent Welsh. On 6 Sept. 1911, a group of Welsh women organized an auxiliary to the

Welsh Society, and in 1912 the group's name was changed to the Welsh Women's Club of Cleveland. The Lakewood Women's Welsh Club was organized in 1923; the Women's Welsh Club of W. Cleveland in 1926; and the E. Cleveland Women's Welsh Club in 1927. The main purpose of these societies (with the assistance of the Welsh Women's Club of America) was to purchase and support the Welsh Home for the Aged. The first home, located on Mayfield Rd., was replaced later by the WELSH HOME on Center Ridge Rd. in ROCKY RIVER. Interestingly, these organizations were established in the face of a continuing decline in the city's Welsh population. By 1910 it had dropped to 1,298. Although it rose to 1,438 in 1930, the Depression proved disastrous, and the population dropped to 584 in 1940. By 1980, it was estimated that slightly more than 200 Welsh immigrants lived in the Greater Cleveland area.

Jean Hudson

The **BRITTON FUND** was incorporated in 1952 by Gertrude H. Britton (b. 1909), Brigham Britton (1907–1979), and M. J. Mitchell (b. 1906). Gertrude Hanna Britton is (1985) vice-president of the Britton Fund, and her son, Chas. S. Britton II, is president. Annually, approximately 50 grants are made in the range of $1,000-$20,000 each, the prominent exception being UNITED WAY SERVICES, which receives about 20% of the fund's annual giving. The fund generally supports charitable organizations in Ohio, particularly social agencies, higher and secondary education, hospitals and health services, and youth agencies. It does not give grants to individuals. In 1985 assets of the foundation were $4,371,373, with expenditures of $284,000 for 47 grants. Officers of the fund include Chas. S. Britton II, Gertrude H. Britton, Elizabeth C. Reed, and Donald C. Cook.

**BROADBENT, BIRDSALL HOLLY** (27 Sept. 1894–23 Dec. 1977) was a Cleveland dentist and orthodontist, internationally recognized for his invention of a head positioning device used in taking radiographs of the face and teeth. Broadbent was born in Lockport, New York, to James F. and Mabel Holly Broadbent. Broadbent graduated from the Western Reserve University Dental School with the D.D.S. degree in 1919 and entered private practice specializing in orthodontia. While doing research at WRU during the 1920s, Broadbent, along with Dr. T. Wingate Todd, developed the cephalometer, a machine designed to hold a patient's head stationary when x-rays were being taken of the mouth. The cephalometer provided dentists with a practical method of diagnosing abnormal growth and indicating the need for preventive or remedial therapies. For his work Broadbent received the Ohio Dental Association's 1952 John R. Callahan Memorial Award. In 1929, Broadbent became Director of the Bolton Fund of Western Reserve, the world's largest individually endowed fund for dental research. As research director for the fund's study of growth and development of the head and teeth, Broadbent helped to assemble the world's largest collection of serial cephalometric records. In 1933, the results of a three year study of facial growth and development done by Broadbent were desplayed at the Chicago World's Fair. In 1948, Broadbent was appointed clinical professor of dental facial anatomy at WRU. Here he created a new course studying the development of the face and how the teeth and jaws are formed in relationship to one another from infancy to adulthood. In 1960, Broadbent received an honorary degree from Dublin University. In 1965, he was named Western Reserve Dental Alumnus of the Year. In 1966, he was made an honorary fellow in dental surgery at the London Royal College of Surgeons. In 1967, he received an honorary Doctor of Science degree from WRU. As a youth Broadbent was among the first boys to join the Boy Scouts in America in 1910. When he began a 60 year association with Scouting in Cleveland, becoming the area's first fifty year veteran scout and the recipient of the Silver Beaver Award in 1952. Broadbent married Bernice Mathews on September 27, 1921. The Broadbents had four children, Ann Holden, Jane Paisley, Frances Philbrick and Dr. Birdsall Holly Broadbent, Jr.

**BROADVIEW HEIGHTS** is a 13-sq.-mi. residential suburb of wooded rolling hills located approximately 15 mi. south of Cleveland, bounded on the west by N. ROYALTON, on the north by PARMA, INDEPENDENCE, and SEVEN HILLS, on the east by BRECKSVILLE, and on the south by Medina County. Its name was derived from the hilly terrain.

Often referred to as the "highest of the heights," it has one of the highest elevations in Cuyahoga County, 1,275' above sea level. Broadview Hts. was originally part of both Royalton and Brecksville townships. After the villages of Brecksville and Royalton withdrew from their townships in 1915 and 1918 respectively, the residents on Broadview Rd., the original boundary line between the two townships, petitioned for the incorporation of a new village in 1926. The petition was granted by the Brecksville Twp. trustees, and the vote to incorporate was passed on 30 Nov. 1926. The village of Broadview Hts. had a population of 300 at that time. The population was 600 by 1928; in 1943 it had grown to 1,600, and in 1954 to 4,000. In 1960 the population was 5,400, and Broadview Hts. became a city. In 1971 the population was 11,400, in 1980 10,920, and in 1984 approximately 12,000. The city's commercial development is predominantly concentrated in 2 areas, a 75-acre industrial park located near the intersection of Rt. 82 and I–77, and an acre at the intersection of I–80 and Rt. 176. Residential developments have been interspersed among the rolling hills and wooded areas. Wallings School, built of stone ca. 1854 and located at the corner of Avery and Broadview roads, is one of the city's oldest structures. Broadview Hts. belongs to both the Brecksville and N. Royalton city school districts. A portion of the Brecksville Reservation of the Metroparks System winds through Broadview Hts.

The **BROADVIEW SAVINGS & LOAN COMPANY** began operation in 1919 with $250,000 and has grown to become one of the country's top 100 savings and loans, with assets of nearly $2 billion. Broadview opened for business on 19 July 1919, at the corner of Broadview and Pearl Rds. Its first officers included August E. Riester, president, Albert T. Case and Clayton C. Townes, vice-presidents, and W. Hoxie Hillary, secretary. Broadview moved its offices in 1924 to larger quarters at 3344 Broadview, and in 1948 to newly constructed offices at 4221 Pearl Rd., the first financial office in the area with drive-in teller windows. Under the direction of Edward J. Rupert, who began a 30-year tenure as president in 1942, Broadview became one of the largest savings and loans in the country. Assets of $21 million in 1948 made it the largest savings and loan in Cuyahoga County; the first to reach $50 million in assets, it was the 3d-largest savings and loan in Ohio and 36th in the nation in 1953. Its merger with County Savings & Loan in 1954 boosted Broadview's assets to $61 million. By 1956, Broadview was the largest savings and loan in Ohio, with assets of more than $97 million. Broadview continued to expand by merger and acquisition. Between 1954–64 it acquired or merged with Liberty Savings & Loan, Northern Ohio Savings & Loan, and Fairview Park Savings & Loan.

128

In 1973, Broadview Savings & Loan became the principal subsidiary of the newly established savings and loan holding company the Broadview Financial Corp. The savings and loan merged with St. Clair Savings in 1977, increasing its assets to $1 billion, and it acquired the savings deposits of the Washington Federal Savings Assoc. in Mar. 1980. Later that year it moved into new administrative offices at Rockside Rd. and I–77. By 1983, Broadview was the 2d-largest savings and loan in the state, with 44 branch offices and $1.9 billion in assets, placing the Broadview Financial Corp. 51st among U.S. diversified financial companies ranked by assets.

The **BROADWAY & NEWBURGH STREET RAILROAD COMPANY** began service on Christmas Day 1873, providing transportation for workers of the Newburgh steel mills. The line was chartered on 26 Aug. 1873. Double tracks were run down Broadway Ave. The line's western terminus was at Woodland Ave., where it met with other lines. The line continued east on Broadway to the Newburgh city limits. A horsecar line initially, the Broadway & Newburgh provided competition for the CLEVELAND & NEWBURGH DUMMY RAILROAD. By 1877, the Dummy line had gone into receivership. The Broadway & Newburgh had increased its system to 19 cars and 86 horses by 1879. The system also ran on Union Ave.

The 6-mi. line began equipping for electrification in 1890, converting to the Sprague overhead trolley system. Sixteen Brill electric motor cars with trailers were purchased for the newly electrified system. Part of the line's horse stable was converted into a powerhouse. The Broadway & Newburgh merged with the E. Cleveland and Brooklyn & South Side St. railways on 15 May 1893. The new line was called the CLEVELAND ELECTRIC RAILWAY, or "Big Consolidated." It was controlled by Henry Everrett, who later became one of the principals of the Everrett-Moore syndicate, a moving force in the development of interurban systems in the Midwest.

Christiansen, Harry, *Trolley Trails through Greater Cleveland and Northern Ohio* (1975).

**BROOK PARK** is an 11-sq.-mi. suburban community located 14 mi. southwest of Cleveland and bounded on the south by BEREA and MIDDLEBURG HTS., on the west by N. OLMSTED, on the east by PARMA, and on the north by Cleveland. It was originally a part of Middleburg Twp. In 1914, residents living in the northern part of the township, dissatisfied with schools, roads, and taxes, met secretly and voted to withdraw from the township and establish their own municipality. Wm. J. Sifleet, a leading proponent of secession, is often referred to as "the Father of Brook Park." Credited with naming the community for the brook that ran through the western portion of Middleburg, he was elected the first mayor. The first school and council hall were built at Five Points, considered a central location. In 1915–16, Brook Park was the scene of a short-lived gas well boom that started in LAKEWOOD and Rockport and then spread into Berea and Brook Park. The Brook Park council passed ordinances granting the Berea Pipe Line Co. and the EAST OHIO GAS CO. the right to lay, operate, and maintain pipelines for the purpose of supplying natural gas to villagers. The wells on the farms were productive for a short time. Brook Park's rural character changed dramatically when WM. R. HOPKINS, Cleveland city manager, selected its northwest section as the site of Hopkins Airport in 1925, and for a few years, the village had the distinction of being the location of the first and largest commercial airport in the world. Through the years, many legal disagreements, proposals, and counterproposals followed between Cleveland and Brook Park over annexation of the airport. These ended in 1947, when the city of Cleveland paid the village of Brook Park $85,000 to become the legal owner of more than 1,000 acres, including the airport.

On 3 Jan. 1941, ground was broken for the Natl. Advisory Committee for Aeronautics research laboratory, which became the Lewis Flight Propulsion Laboratory in 1948 and the NASA LEWIS RESEARCH CTR. in 1958, NASA's primary installation for the development of rocket propulsion. Brook Park's trend toward industrialization continued when the Fisher Aircraft Assembly Bomber Plant was constructed in 1943, and a whole new village came into being as the U.S. Housing Authority constructed many homes to accommodate the employees at the plant. Additional industries located in Brook Park after the war included Ferry Screw Prods., Inc., the Ford Motor Co.'s Engine Plants #1 and #2, the Firestone Tire & Rubber Co., the B. F. Goodrich Co., and the Goodyear Tire & Rubber Co. Brook Park became a city in 1961. A multipurpose recreation center, built in 1973, a variety of schools, churches, and many civic and social organizations serve the community. In 1980, the population was 26,195.

**BROOKLYN**, a portion of Cleveland bounded by BROOKSIDE PARK on the north, the CUYAHOGA RIVER on the east, Brookpark Rd. on the south, and Ridge Rd., W. 66th, and W. 61st on the west, was originally settled as the hamlet of Brighton, situated at what is now the intersection of Broadview and Pearl roads. The earliest pioneers in this area of Brooklyn Twp. south of Big Creek Valley settled in the fall of 1814. By the mid-1830s, the hamlet of Brighton, centered at Pearl and Broadview, extended perhaps ¼ mile, more or less, in each direction. Brighton was originally laid out on land belonging to a farmer named Warren Young. In Mar. 1838, the Ohio legislature passed an act incorporating Brighton Village. The new status was short-lived, however, for in Feb. 1839 the act was repealed, and Brighton returned to Brooklyn Twp. In 1889, the community boasted a population of 1,000 and again petitioned to incorporate, this time as S. Brooklyn Village. The request was granted on 10 June 1889. The S. Brooklyn community was an important market-gardening center for generations. The first experiment with market gardening was attempted by Alfred Tilton and J. L. Foote in 1860. They began by growing melons and common garden vegetables. A second milestone in S. Brooklyn gardening history was made by Gustave Ruetenik & Sons when they introduced greenhouse gardening in 1887. Public transportation came near to the community's borders in 1869 when the Brooklyn Street Railway Co. got an original 24-year grant to run down Pearl (W. 25th) St. from the center of Lorain south to the Cleveland city limits with a turntable at Bradwell Ave. One of the most interesting structures in S. Brooklyn was the Johnson house, which stood on the present site of the Cleveland Trust (now AmeriTrust) Bank Bldg. at the corner of Broadview and Pearl Rds. It replaced the old Brighton Hotel and was built by John L. Johnson with gold rush money. The Johnson house was the hub of commercial activity in the S. Brooklyn area for many years, being a well-known stopover for farmers coming to Cleveland to sell their produce. The Gates Elevator & Mills Co. Bldg. was constructed on the site of the current Pearl Rd. entrance to Brookside Park. A succession of bridges across the valley eased access to the north. S. Brooklyn led this section of the nation by using bituminous macadam to pave Pearl and State roads in 1903.

S. Brooklyn was annexed to the city of Cleveland in Dec. 1905. In 1915, 1916, and 1917, 3 more portions of Brooklyn Twp. (all adjacent to S. Brooklyn on the south and west) were annexed to Cleveland. In June 1927, when part of Brooklyn Hts. village joined the city, Cleveland acquired its present boundaries. With the passing years, the identity of the village of S. Brooklyn dimmed. By 1927, the annexations covered a much greater territory than the original village, and new residents were unacquainted with the old days. Gradually, especially after WORLD WAR II, all of Cleveland south of Big Creek came to be known as the Brooklyn section of the city. In 1976, the Old Brooklyn Community Development Corp. was formed. During the years 1975–76, the corporation enlisted the help of Kent State University students in the School of Architecture & Environmental Design to study the area and make recommendations for revitalization. In 1977, the board of trustees endorsed the Kent State study and retained the firm of Henshaw, Hartt, & Van Petten to develop a specific plan for community redevelopment and revitalization.

Wilmer, Kathryn Gasior, *Old Brooklyn/New Book I* (1979).
Wilmer, Kathryn Gasior, *Old Brooklyn/New Book II* (1984).

The **BROOKLYN ARTILLERY** was an artillery militia unit from the municipality of Brooklyn, south of Cleveland, or from Brooklyn Twp., on the west side of the CUYAHOGA RIVER. Little is known about the organization or personnel of the unit; however, it was in existence during the CIVIL WAR, 1861–65. Whether or not it was ever incorporated into the organization of any particular independent artillery battery or regiment during the war remains unknown. Vague references to the Brooklyn Artillery can be found in Cleveland newspapers published during the Civil War. The unit was also called the Brooklyn Light Artillery.

**BROOKLYN HEIGHTS** is a 1.73-sq.-mi. residential-industrial community located southeast of Cleveland and bounded on the west and north by Cleveland, on the east by the CUYAHOGA RIVER and INDEPENDENCE, on the south by Independence and SEVEN HILLS, and on the west by PARMA. It was one of the last municipalities formed from Brooklyn Twp. and Independence Twp. In 1902, a group of taxpayers in School District #4 discussed the possibility of withdrawing from Brooklyn Twp., primarily because they wanted to establish their own school district, and because of a dispute over taxes. In 1903, a petition for the incorporation of an independent village was presented to the trustees of the township. Following an election, the village of Brooklyn Hts. was incorporated in Feb. 1903. In 1920 the population was 605. Martin Ruetenik, the first mayor, and Hamilton Richardson were instrumental in creating the Cleveland Growers Marketing Co. of house and outdoor growers of fruits and vegetables, and helped the community to develop into one of the leading vegetable greenhouse areas in the U.S., with over 100 acres "under glass." In 1927, the area west of Brookpark Rd., representing about ⅔ of the area of the village and about half the population, was annexed to Cleveland. The remaining 413 people rebuilt their community. Geo. Thompson was the first mayor after annexation. The city gradually overcame financial difficulties, grew to 1,600 people in 1958, and in 1962 adopted the motto "the Greenhouse Center of America." In 1965, 53 acres of the total 1,178 were gardening and greenhouse enterprises. Since 1938, the schools of Brooklyn Hts. have been part of the Cuyahoga Hts. School District.

The greenhouses gradually gave way to industries. In 1984, the community of 1,653 people was characterized by over 100 industries, 500 residences, and about 5 greenhouses.

The **BROOKLYN MEMORIAL UNITED METHODIST CHURCH**, the first church organized in Brooklyn Twp., is also recognized as the oldest Methodist congregation in the Cleveland area. Methodist classes in the Brooklyn area began meeting as early as 1814 in members' homes. A Methodist society was recognized in 1818, with the name Brooklyn Methodist Episcopal Church. A log building was erected at the northeast corner of Denison and Pearl streets, and a frame addition was made in 1827. A new frame church was built on the same site in 1849 and was later moved to a lot on Greenwood (Archwood) Ave., west of Pearl (W. 25th St.). A brick Gothic building was dedicated on the Archwood site in 1882. A change in name was effected in 1896, making the church Brooklyn Memorial Methodist Episcopal Church.

With continued population growth in the area to the southwest of downtown, church membership increased, and by 1911 a new building was begun on the Archwood Ave. property. Dedicated in 1914, the building is of late Gothic Revival style, with twin square towers at the front and square projecting bays. A 6-sided dome with arched windows rises over the crossing of the bays. The interior is arranged as a preaching auditorium, with an Akron seating plan and a semicircular balcony. To the rear of the sanctuary is a Sunday school auditorium, separated by a sliding wall. Two levels of classrooms radiate off the auditorium from the main floor and a balcony. The church maintained an active Sunday school, women's society, and youth program. Membership has stood at approximately 200 into the early 1980s. The founding date of the church was used to fix the date of the celebration of the Centenary of Cleveland Methodism. A commemorative service was held in the church in Sept. 1918, with former Ohio governor Frank B. Willis speaking.

The **BROOKS MILITARY SCHOOL** was a college preparatory school for males that operated in Cleveland from 1874–91. Called at various times Brooks School, Brooks Academy, and Brooks Academy & Military Institute, the school was established by wealthy Clevelanders in honor of Rev. Frederick Brooks, rector of ST. PAUL'S EPISCOPAL CHURCH, who had dreamed of opening a prep school for young men. The school admitted "boys and young men from seven to twenty years of age" and was first located on Prospect at the southwest corner of Brownell (E. 14th) St. Its first headmaster was John S. White, a Harvard graduate.

In 1875 the school moved into a new building on Silbey near Hayward St. that had been built by a group of wealthy Clevelanders, including JOHN H. DEVEREUX, JEPTHA H. WADE, SAMUEL ANDREWS, and DANIEL P. EELLS. The new structure included a drill hall, an armory, a gymnasium, and a chemical laboratory. Military training at the school was conducted by an officer in the U.S. Army. President of the school after 1882 was Amos H. Thompson. The school was closed in 1891, and in 1908 the building was destroyed by fire. A separate school for young women was opened in 1876, the Brooks School for Young Ladies & Misses. Located first at Euclid and Willson (E. 55th) sts., the school moved several times between 1880–86, when it was purchased by Anne Hathaway Brown, moved to 768 Euclid Ave., and renamed HATHAWAY BROWN SCHOOL.

**BROOKSIDE PARK,** located in the southwestern part of the city at Fulton Rd. and Denison Ave., is one of Cleveland's oldest municipal parks. The parkland, purchased in 1894 by the Second Park Board, provided a natural setting for a playground in the wooded valley of Big Creek. The high bluff overlooking the lake and surrounding land was originally landscaped to provide for a variety of recreational facilities, including picnic grounds, a lake, tennis courts, and baseball diamonds. Additional landscaping was completed in the 1940s, but construction of I-71 destroyed a major portion of this park during the 1960s. The CLEVELAND METROPARKS ZOO, under the jurisdiction of the Cleveland Metroparks System, is located on the lower level of the park at the foot of Fulton Hill.

The **BROTHERHOOD OF LOCOMOTIVE ENGINEERS,** founded in 1863 as the Brotherhood of the Footboard, is the oldest of the railroad labor organizations. Having considered and rejected joining an organization that included all employees in mechanical departments, the original founders, engineers on the Michigan Central Railroad, decided instead that engineers could best be served by an organization limited to engineers and firemen. Meeting initially in a roundhouse in Marshall, Mich., the founders retired to more private surroundings at the home of one of the engineers. In 1867, the brotherhood established the Locomotive Engineers Mutual Life Insurance Assoc., which maintained a separate staff and constitution but required membership in the brotherhood as a precondition for insurance. The brotherood was conservative in nature, often eschewing strikes notwithstanding rank-and-file sentiments, choosing instead to aspire to be an "association of as intelligent men as one meets in money circles." A strike against the Chicago Burlington & Quincy Railroad in 1888 nearly destroyed the union. Bitterly contested, the brotherhood was forced to accept company conditions when the strike ended, which included the CB&Q giving preference in promotions to scab engineers hired during the strike.

In 1908, Cleveland was established as the permanent headquarters of the brotherhood, and in 1911 the Brotherhood of Locomotive Engineers Bldg. (Engineers Bldg.) was dedicated by Ohio governor Judson Harmon. It was the first building of its type built by a labor union in the U.S. During this period, under the leadership of Warren S. Stone, a strong supporter of the La Follette presidential candidacy, the brotherhood entered commercial ventures beyond its insurance services, including banking and real-estate investments totaling $150 million. In 1924, the Brotherhood of Locomotive Engineers Cooperative Natl. Bank Bldg. (Standard Bldg.) was completed and represented the zenith of its financial adventures. In Dec. 1931, the reorganized Cooperative Natl. Bank (Standard Trust Bank) was taken over by the State Banking Dept., and the bank's president was sentenced to the penitentiary for misapplication of funds. Between 1976–86, the brotherhood lost 8,000 members as deregulations and consolidations shook the railroad industry. As a result, the brotherhood commissioned its first study—to focus on economic trends, new technologies, and other issues affecting the industry and the union. One result was discussion of a possible merger with the UNITED TRANSPORTATION UNION—mostly "on train" workers—which has its national headquarters in LAKEWOOD. In 1986, the brotherhood had 4 divisions (locals) in Cleveland: No. 3 (CONRAIL), No. 31 (Baltimore & Ohio), No. 318 (ConRail), and No. 607 (Norfolk & Western). The brotherhood remains an independent labor organization unaffiliated with the AFL-CIO and other railroad brotherhoods. Its headquarters remain in the Engineers Bldg.

**BROWN, ANNA V.** (1914–12 Nov. 1985), earned a national reputation in the 1970s and 1980s for her work on behalf of the elderly. She developed Cleveland's office on aging in 1971 and continued to head it until her death. Brown was born in Vivian, W.Va., the only child of Dr. Joseph E. and Hattie Brown. Her father was a physician who also took a strong interest in politics and social conditions in their Appalachian region; he moved his family to Cleveland in 1941 and continued his medical practice. Brown was educated at the Northfield School for Girls in E. Northfield, Mass., then attended Oberlin College, receiving a bachelor's degree in sociology in 1938. She then earned a master's degree from New York University, majoring in race relations and politics. She began working as an auditor in the Cleveland office of the General Accounting Office, then as assistant executive secretary of the PHILLIS WHEATLEY ASSOC. In 1946 she became the secretary and manager of her father's office. In 1963 she mounted an unsuccessful bid for a seat on city council, running as a Republican and losing the election to Geo. Forbes.

Working with her father's patients, Brown came into close and daily contact with the problems of Cleveland's elderly and became an advocate on their behalf. In Feb. 1971, Mayor Carl Stokes appointed her the executive director of the Mayor's Commission on Aging, which became an official city department in July 1981 under Mayor Geo. Voinovich. Under her direction, the office on aging brought to Cleveland more than $2 million in federal funds in its first 2 years. Her office put together a comprehensive list of area services available to local elderly; worked as a proponent of Community Responsive Transit, winter assistance heating, and other programs; and developed a number of programs to meet various needs of the aged, such as Care-Ring, a phone service to check on those living alone. Brown's work took her onto the national political scene and earned her many honors. She was an Ohio delegate to the 1971 White House Conference on Aging and was a deputy chairman of the national advisory committee of the 1981 White House Conference on Aging. In 1984, she became the president of the Natl. Council on Aging, of which she had been a board member; she also served as president of the Urban Elderly Coalition and of the Ohio Chap. of the Caucus on the Black Aged, and was a consultant to the Congressional Black Caucus Brain Trust. Locally, she served on the boards of the ELIZA BRYANT HOME and the CLEVELAND CLINIC FOUNDATION. Brown was inducted into the Ohio Senior Citizens Hall of Fame, received several awards from local civic groups, and in 1985 received honorary degrees from Oberlin College and Miami University and was named Citizen of the Year by the Natl. Assoc. of Social Workers. Brown's husband, Elmer Brown, was a well-known artist who was responsible for the freedom mural in the City Club. He also worked for the AMERICAN GREETINGS CORP.

**BROWN, FAYETTE** (17 Dec. 1823–20 Jan. 1910), was a Cleveland businessman. During the CIVIL WAR, he served as a U.S. Army paymaster. Brown was born in N. Bloomfield, Ohio (Trumbull County). After his schooling, he worked for his brother at a wholesale dry-goods store in Pittsburgh, Pa. In 1845 he became a member of the firm, remaining at that position until moving to Cleveland, Ohio, in 1851. He formed a banking partnership with Geo. Mygatt under the name of Mygatt & Brown, taking over the business in 1857, when Mygatt retired. Brown closed his business at the outbreak of the Civil War. He served as paymaster, U.S. Army, 1861–62, before resigning his commission to return to private life. He returned to Cleveland to become general agent of the Jackson Iron Co. In the following years he became a powerful force in the iron industry. He served as president of the Union Steel Screw Co.; general manager of the Stewart Iron Co.; president of the Brown Hoisting & Conveying Machine Co.; and receiver of the Brown, Bonnell Co. of Youngstown, Ohio. Brown married Cornelia C. Curtiss of Allegheny City, Pa., on 15 July 1847. They raised 3 sons and 2 daughters. Because of Brown's military service, he was frequently referred to as "Major" or "Colonel."

Brown Family Papers, WRHS.

**BROWN, JERE A.** (1841–28 Mar. 1913), was an early black Republican politician and civil servant. A native of Pittsburgh, Pa., he attended Avery College in Allegheny, Pa. In 1858 he became an apprentice carpenter; in 1860 he moved to Canada with his parents. After 4 years he went to St. Louis, where he worked on the riverboats. In 1870 or 1871 Brown arrived in Cleveland and became active in politics as a means of improving his status. He first was appointed a bailiff for Judge Daniel R. Tilden, and in 1877 his Republican ties gained him an appointment as deputy sheriff, making Brown the first Afro-American to receive a political appointment in Cuyahoga County. He also served as clerk for the Board of Equalization & Assessment. In 1881 Brown became a letter carrier for the post office, thus gaining what was considered an elite occupation for blacks; he served in that capacity for 4 years but resigned because it kept him out of politics. In 1885 he was elected a state representative on the Republican ticket and served 2 terms in the state legislature (1886–87, 1888–89).

Brown's efforts on behalf of Ohio's black citizens during his legislative career displayed, in the words of one historian, "a tendency toward radicalism"; that tendency disappeared in his later career, however. As a legislator, Brown sponsored legislation to prevent life insurance companies from discriminating against blacks, helped secure funds for Wilberforce College, and is credited with playing a major role in the repeal of Ohio's BLACK LAWS. He supported the organization of the militant national civil-rights group the Afro-American League in 1890. Brown later became more interested in his own well-being and partisan politics than in civil rights for his race; he worked hard for Republican party candidates during the 1890s and fully expected to be rewarded with political appointments. His support for U.S. Sen. John Sherman was rewarded in 1890 by appointment as a customs inspector in Cleveland. Brown later gained appointment to the Ohio Dept. of Insurance, becoming the first black to serve there. In the last years of the decade, Brown served in the Dept. of Internal Revenue in Washington, D.C., before returning to Cleveland as an immigration inspector. Brown, who was married to Nina L., was also active in the Prince Hall Masons. He held several position in the order, including those of Grand Master of the Ohio Lodge and Grand Secretary of the Grand Lodge. He was also a member of the Republican State Executive Committee and a trustee of Wilberforce College, where he was buried.

**BROWNE, CHARLES FARRAR [ARTEMUS WARD, PSEUD.]** (26 Apr. 1834–6 Mar. 1867), was a nationally known journalist and humorist. Although he spent only 3 years in Cleveland, it was as a reporter for the *PLAIN DEALER* that he invented and developed his alter ego "Artemus Ward." Born at Waterford, Maine, Browne learned the printing trade and began writing in New England before setting out for Ohio in 1854. There he worked for the *Tiffin Seneca Advertiser* and the *Toledo Commercial*. JOSEPH W. GRAY recruited him as commercial editor and local writer for the *Plain Dealer* on 30 Oct. 1857.

Browne's first "Artemus Ward" letter appeared in the *Plain Dealer*'s local column for 30 Jan. 1858. Ostensibly written from Pittsburgh by an itinerant showman and waxworks proprietor, it requested information and publicity for a forthcoming Cleveland appearance and closed with the memorable tag line, "P.S pitsburg is a 1 horse town. A.W." Further communications in Ward's free-style spelling and grammar traced his peregrinations through neighboring cities and towns over the next 2 years, though, needless to say, the promised Cleveland date never materialized. Turning his humor to other subjects, such as the "three tigers of Cleveland journalism" (Joseph Gray, GEO. A. BENEDICT, and JOSIAH A. HARRIS), Browne also began sending copies of his material to *Vanity Fair* in New York. That led to friction with Gray, who wanted Browne's exclusive services but declined to raise his salary to what Browne thought they were worth. Announced in the *Plain Dealer* on 10 Nov. 1860, their parting was nevertheless cordial.

Browne went to New York, where he became editor of *Vanity Fair* and joined the lecture circuit in the guise of Artemus Ward. He published *Artemus Ward: His Book* in May 1862, from which Abraham Lincoln entertained members of his cabinet prior to the meeting at which he announced his issuance of the Preliminary Emancipation Proclamation. An offer by Browne to purchase the *Plain Dealer* after Gray's death was never realized, and he continued to follow the lecture trail to England, where he died of tuberculosis on the Isle of Jersey.

Shaw, Archer H., *The Plain Dealer: One Hundred Years in Cleveland* (1942).

**BROWNELL, ABNER** (1813–1857), was a member of the city council and mayor of Cleveland from 1852–55. Born in Massachusetts, he was educated in his local district and came to Cleveland in the 1840s while in the employ (1846–49) of the W. A. Otis Co. as a dealer in iron and glass. From 1849–53 he was a partner in the banking firm of Wick, Otis, & Brownell. His Massachusetts upbringing played a great role in shaping his personal and community life, and in 1853 he became president of the New England Society. In 1849 Brownell ran as a Democrat for city council, a post he held through 1852. In that year he then ran successfully for mayor with no opposition. He became the first Cleveland mayor to serve 2 terms in office (until 1855). While mayor, he supported city departments, new schools, new sewers, and loans for area roads. After leaving office, he became a commission merchant until his death in 1857. Brownell and his wife, Eliza, were married shortly before he settled in Cleveland. The couple had 4 children.

**BRUDNO, EZRA** (1877–12 Dec. 1954), attorney and author, was one of 2 notable Jewish writers in Cleveland during the first 2 decades of the 20th century. He was born in Lithuania and educated in a private European school. He was brought to America in 1891 by his parents and continued his studies at CENTRAL HIGH SCHOOL. After graduation, he attended Yale University and Western Reserve University, receiving a degree in law.

Brudno began his law practice in 1900 and continued to practice until his retirement in 1949. Soon after entering the legal profession, he turned his creative energies to writing. By 1910, he had 3 novels published: *The Fugitive*, *The Tether*, and *The Little Conscript*. In addition, his fiction and nonfiction were published in national magazines such as *Lippincott's* and locally in the *Jewish Review & Observer*. Although some of Brudno's fiction advocated shielding the young from the influence of America, he promoted the assimilation of Jews into western civilization in his nonfiction. He wrote that there was little, if anything, of value in Judaism and Jewish culture worth preserving. In 1920, he published a novel about the legal profession, *The Jugglers*, which met with little success. Fifteen years later, he wrote his only full-length piece of nonfiction, *Ghost of Yesterday: A Reappraisal of Moral Values and of Accepted Standards in This Changing World*.

**BRUSH, CHARLES FRANCIS** (17 Mar. 1849–15 June 1929), was one of America's most distinguished inventors. He was the youngest of 9 children born to Isaac Elbert and Delia Williams Phillips Brush at Walnut Hills Farm in EUCLID TWP. He attended public schools in Cleveland and received his mining engineering degree from the University of Michigan in 1869. He returned to Cleveland following graduation and spent the next 4 years working as a chemist. After being rejected by companies that had no use for his skills, he formed a partnership with Chas. E. Bingham, and they established a small business as iron dealers. In 1875, Brush married Mary Ellen Morris, and they raised 3 children, Edna, Helene, and Charles.

In 1876, Brush's experiments with electrical machines led to the patent of his "perfect" open coil-type dynamo, which became one of the predecessors of the modern generator. His development of the arc light in 1878 made him world-famous. These were 2 of the more than 50 patents issued to Brush during his career. In 1879 Brush demonstrated his arc light in Cleveland's PUBLIC SQUARE, and by 1882, "Brush Lights" were in use throughout the U.S., as well as in Canada, Mexico, Chile, England, and Japan. The Brush Electric Co., formed in Cleveland in 1880, was created out of the Telegraphic Supply Corp. In that same year, the Anglo-American Brush Electric Light Corp. was formed in London. Brush Electric was purchased by the Thomson Houston Electric Co. in 1889, which later merged with the Edison General Electric Co. in 1891 to form the General Electric Co. Brush then retired from the electric lighting field and spent the rest of his life vigorously pursuing some theoretical aspects of science. He became particularly interested in the fields of gravitation and heat, conducting experiments on the machines in the laboratory and basement of his Euclid Ave. home. The results of this work were presented in a series of articles published by the American Philosophical Society and the Royal Society.

Brush also continued to maintain a variety of business interests. He served variously as the founder and first president of the Linde Air Prods. Co., helped to form the Sandusky Portland Cement Co. (later Medusa), and served as president of the Cleveland Arcade Co., the Euclid Natl. Bank, and the Cleveland Chamber of Commerce. He was a director of the Cleveland School of Art and a corporator of Case School of Applied Science. He also served as a trustee of Western Reserve University and UNIVERSITY SCHOOL. In recognition of his outstanding work, Brush received many honorary degrees, including a Ph.D. from Western Reserve College in 1880, an M.S. from the University of Michigan (1899), an LL.D. from WRU (1900), and an LL.D. from Kenyon College (1903). His other honors included being made a chevalier of the Legion of Honor of France (1881) and receipt of the Rumford Medal from the American Academy of Arts & Sciences (1899), the Edison Medal from the American Institute of Electrical Engineers (1913), and the Franklin Medal from the Franklin Institute (1928).

Charles F. Brush Papers, Freiberger Library, CWRU.

The **BRUSH AND PALETTE CLUB** was one of the many small art groups founded in the late 19th century to support local artists and provide them an opportunity to discuss art with their colleagues and to display their work annually. As the name implies, the club was concerned specifically with painters. It was founded in 1893 by members of the city hall art colony, also known as the Old Bohemians or the ART CLUB. The first president of the club was ARCHIBALD M. WILLARD, and the first exhibition of its members' works was held in May 1894. The role of the Brush & Palette Club was to increase local awareness about painting and local painters and to encourage new talent.

Among the more prominent of the club's contributors were FREDERIC C. GOTTWALD, Orlando V. Schubert, Chas. Francis Deklyn, John Semon, and Adam Lehr. Gottwald traveled extensively in Europe, and his travels were reflected in his landscapes and street scenes. Semon was a reclusive landscape painter from BEDFORD, Ohio. Lehr was noted primarily for his still lifes and landscapes. As was the case with so many of the periphery art groups, there is no record of an official disbandment of the Brush & Palette Club. It may have merged with other groups, or its members may just have felt the club was no longer necessary. By 1912 it was no longer in existence.

The **BRUSH FOUNDATION** was established in 1928 by CHAS. F. BRUSH (1849–1929). Brush, inventor of the electric arc lamp, was born in Euclid, Ohio. He was president of the Cleveland Arcade Co. in 1887 and president of the Linde Air Prods. Co., now a division of the Union Carbide Corp. He was also a trustee of Western Reserve University, Adelbert College, UNIVERSITY SCHOOL, the Cleveland School of Art, and LAKE VIEW CEMETERY. Brush was married to Mary E. Morris in 1875, and they had 3 children, Chas. Francis II, Mrs. Edna Perkins, and Helene Brush.

The original intention of the Brush Foundation, a memorial to Brush's son, who died in 1927, was a bequest of $500,000 for the "furtherance of research in the field of eugenics and in the regulation of the increase of population." Brush feared that better health standards were contributing to a dangerous population explosion. He believed that some methods of birth control were essential to the future standard of living of the country. In 1985 the foundation continued to support projects for the control of population growth and the "betterment of the human race." Its current major interests are adolescent sexuality and the control of adolescent pregnancy, preserving women's freedom of choice to have abortions, and studying how laws and regulations may control population growth. No grants are given to individuals or for capital or endowment funds, scholarships and fellowships, or loans. In 1982, assets of the foundation were $2,020,188, with expenditures of $152,460 for 12 grants. Officers include Dr. David R. Weir, Meacham Hitchcock, Doris B. Dingle, Richard M. Donaldson, Dr. John J. Beeston, Chas. F. Brush, Sally F. Burton, Virginia P. Carter, Jane Perkins Moffett, Dr. Edward A. Mortimer, and Dr. Wm. C. Weir.

The **BRUSH-WELLMAN CORPORATION,** formerly the Brush Beryllium Co., is the world's largest processor of beryllium and beryllium compounds. Since its incorporation in 1931, the company has been a leader in finding new methods to increase the availability and commercial usefulness of beryllium, a lightweight metal noted for its high melting point, thermal conductivity, and rigidity at elevated temperatures. By 1985, Brush-Wellman supplied beryllium for instruments for missiles, aircraft, and satellites; fabricated components for guidance systems, missile skin panels, aircraft brake systems, and satellite structures; and produced beryllium copper and other alloys for the electronics industry. Founded by Chas. Baldwin Sawyer, a cofounder (with Chas. F. Brush, Jr.) of Brush Laboratories (see Gould), the company, initially located at 4301 Perkins Ave., was built on a process developed by Sawyer and former Brush Laboratories scientist Bengt Kjellgren to extract beryllium from beryl ore by thermal shock techniques. This process remained the basic one used to retrieve beryllium.

In its early years, Brush Beryllium contributed to the development of atomic energy for wartime and later peacetime uses. The company's sales of beryllium metal, alloys, oxides, and ceramics steadily increased to $4.5 million by 1955, but quadrupled by 1960 with the company's involvement in the space program. Brush Beryllium's product, the perfect Space Age metal, was used to form the heat shield for the reentry vehicle in the Project Mercury manned space flights. Though the aerospace program was curtailed, Brush Beryllium still prospered because of an increasing demand for the material in the aircraft and electronics industries. When beryl ore was found in the Topaz Mts. of Utah, Brush set up Beryllium Resources, which bought the rights to explore and later mine in the area, an operation that by 1961 yielded a plentiful supply of domestic ore. In 1971, Brush Beryllium acquired the S. K. Wellman Corp., a manufacturer of metallic friction material used in brakes and clutches for heavy-duty off-road equipment, and changed its name to the Brush-Wellman Corp. Brush-Wellman has its corporate offices at 1200 the Hanna Bldg. in Cleveland and since 1960 has maintained its Cleveland manufacturing facility at 17876 St. Clair Ave. in EUCLID. In contrast to its modest beginnings, the company also has plants and sales offices in 13 American cities and in Canada, Europe, and Japan. Its 1984 sales from all divisions were over $322 million.

**BUCKEYE-WOODLAND** is an east side Hungarian community established after 1880, which once held the largest concentration of HUNGARIANS in the U.S. Earlier Hungarian settlements at E. 79th and Holton eventually expanded to E. 72nd on the west, Woodland on the north, E. 140th on the east, and Kinsman on the south, with Buckeye Rd. being the prime location for homes and businesses. Population in the area grew from 1,500 in 1900, to 20,000 in 1920, to over 40,000 in 1940. Because there was no large existing Hungarian settlement in the 1880s, the Buckeye area became Cleveland's "Little Hungary." The new residents were able to set up old-country institutions, speak their native language, and do most of their business with former countrymen. They established 10 churches and synagogues, businesses, and a host of nationality organizations that reenacted native festivals and celebrations.

The Hungarian population of Buckeye was bolstered by the Hungarians displaced by WORLD WAR II and by the Hungarian Revolution of 1956, but these groups did not develop the intense loyalty to maintaining Little Hungary held by the old-timers, who were dying off. Younger Hungarian-Americans also abandoned the old neighborhood, leaving a Hungarian population of which over ⅓ was over 55 years old. BLACKS with different cultural traditions moved into the area and composed 43% of the population by 1972. Housing stock aged and deteriorated, and the percentage of renters skyrocketed. Banks refused to issue mortgages, and insurance companies canceled policies while denying new applications. Fear gripped the elderly residents and merchants, who often closed up shop in the face of muggings and robberies. Racial violence directed toward blacks as well as whites further threatened the neighborhood. During the late 1970s and 1980s, several neighborhood groups attempted to reverse blight, calm fears, and restore stability to the neighborhood. The Buckeye-Woodland Community Congress was established to fight redlining, foreclosures, dishonest real-estate tactics, and insurance cancellations, while the Buckeye Area Development Corp. was set up to attract federal, state, and local funds to refurbish homes and businesses in the area. Meanwhile, agencies such as the East End Neighborhood House and the Buckeye-Woodland Multi-Service Ctr. attempted to meet the needs of community residents, young and old, black and white. While the original ethnic flavor of the neighborhood could not be restored, decline was slowed through concerted efforts by new and old residents.

Papp, Susan M., *Hungarian-Americans and Their Communities in Cleveland* (1981).

**BUDDHISM.** The two major ethnic groups that have preserved Buddhist culture in Cleveland are the JAPANESE and the CHINESE. Each of these groups has its own temple. The largest Cleveland Buddhist temple is located at E. 214th St. and Euclid Ave. and is attended by approximately 90 families. Rev. Koshw Ogui has been the temple priest since 1980. Between 60–70% of the temple's members are second- and third-generation Japanese, 30% are American Caucasian who practice Zen Buddhism and use the temple twice a week to meditate, and the remainder are Chinese and Korean. In addition to this membership, 15–20 of Cleveland's approximately 500 Vietnamese Buddhists use the temple when a Vietnamese Buddhist priest visits. The Buddhist Church of America is the most liberal of Buddhist branches, and it represents the Jodo Shinshu sect.

The temple was organized in 1945 by Japanese-American evacuees from WORLD WAR II concentration camps. In the years following the war, Greater Cleveland's Japanese population swelled from only a few dozen (pre-World War II) to approximately 3,500. Services were originally held at a Unitarian church at 82nd St. and Euclid Ave., conducted first by Rev. Kono from Chicago on a temporary basis and later by Rev. Onoyama and Rev. Tsufura. In 1955, a building on E. 81st St. in the Hough area was purchased, and the temple was moved. At this time, 79th St. and Hough Ave. was the location of Cleveland's largest Japanese community. During the HOUGH RIOTS of July 1966, the temple was firebombed and repeatedly vandalized. The new priest, Rev. Taniguchi, lived there to safeguard it. Shortly thereafter, the congregation acquired the present location on Euclid Ave., and the temple and priest's residence were completed in 1968. The building that houses the temple is itself a simple, square, white-brick building. Inside, a gold-plated image of the Amida Buddha rests on the altar, and a large vat used for burning incense stands before it.

The Buddhist Temple of Cleveland has helped preserve ethnic ties and has sponsored social and community activities, as well as provides spiritual solace. For example, the temple's annual Bon Odori festival is an important community activity. The celebration honors one's ancestors. In April, the birthday of Buddha is celebrated, an event called Hanna Matsuri. Organizations such as the Japanese American Citizens' League cooperate with the temple to sponsor various activities.

The Chinese have a temple on the upper floor of a building owned by the ON LEONG TONG. It is located on Rockwell Ave. NE at E. 21st St. The temple was erected when the building was built in 1927. It is now open a few hours a week for worship and is used more often for community meetings. Only during the celebration of Chinese

New Year is the public allowed inside the temple to witness the traditional ceremony to welcome the New Year. The temple is a large room decorated to resemble a Chinese Joss House, with gold leaf, carvings, and silk wall hangings. The golden deity is Kwan Kung, a god of loyalty, and before him are three giant unburned joss sticks. Two friendly-looking pottery temple dogs flank the god on either side. In addition to the New Year's celebration, the Chinese of Cleveland celebrate a number of other festivals, such as the summertime Festival of the Ghost, when homage is paid to the dead, and the August moon festival, when the Chinese exchange moon cakes.

Nicholas J. Zentos
Lorain County Community College

Choi, Ching Yan, "Minority Status and Anomia: A Study of the Chinese in Metropolitan Cleveland" (Master's thesis, Western Reserve University, 1962).

Ishida, Eiko, "An Application of Gordan's Assimilation Theory: The Japanese-Americans in Cleveland, Ohio" (Master's Thesis, Kent State University, 1969).

Works Projects Admin., *The Peoples of Cleveland* (1942).

**THE BUDWEISER-CLEVELAND 500**, a Grand Prix auto race, has been held in the city on the July 4th weekend since 1982. Named for its primary corporate sponsor, the 500-km race was sited at BURKE LAKEFRONT AIRPORT. The concept of a local race in the style of the Indianapolis 500 was conceived by promoter Chas. K. Newcomb in 1981 and was approvided by CART (Championship Auto Racing Teams, Inc.). The race was expected to cost over $1 million to stage, with funding expected to come from the gate, a major sponsor, and grants from auto accessory companies. Its planned $200,000 prize money would make it one of the richest in America. The course, planned at the airport with the permission of the FAA, was designed to test both straight speed and turns. Two parallel runways (3 times wider than the Indy track) were linked to permit 125 2.48-mi. laps with 12 turns—8 to the right and 4 to the left. Cars were expected to reach speeds of 185 mph, although the record speed as of 1986 was the 135-mph run of Danny Sullivan in that year. Bleachers to seat 20,000 were to be constructed on the south side of the track to permit a full view of the course. Both the course and the seating were pronounced as excellent by the drivers and racing enthusiasts. The first race was held, as planned, on 4 July 1982, after 2 days of qualifying heats, and was won by Bobby Rahal. The quality of the course and the beauty of the lakeside site made the race popular with the drivers. Because the heat in the cars was magnified by the July temperatures, the race was shortened to 200 mi. in 1984, and the name was changed to the Cleveland Grand Prix. In 1985, the name was changed to the Budweiser-Cleveland 500. First-place winners have included Al Unser, Sr. (1983), Danny Sullivan (1984, 1986), and Al Unser, Jr. (1985).

**BUHRER, STEPHEN** (25 Dec. 1825-8 Dec. 1907), was Democratic mayor of Cleveland from 1867-71 and served 4 terms on the city council, 1855-57, 1863-67, and 1874-76. He was born on the Zoar farm in Tuscarawas County, Ohio, the son of Johann Casper and Anna Maria Miller Buhrer. When his father died in 1829, he and his older sister Catherine were bound to the Society of Separatists, who operated the communal farm at Zoar, until they came of age. As a child Buhrer worked on the farm, receiving his education in evening classes and at Sunday school, and when he was 12 years old, the society taught him the coopering trade. He left the farm when he was 17 and came to Cleveland, where he found work as a cooper. After a brief time as a traveling salesman in Indiana, Illinois, and Michigan, he returned to Cleveland in the late 1840s and opened his own coopering shop. He sold the shop in 1853, and by 1856 he had established a business on Merwin St. rectifying and distilling alcohol. His business expanded over the years to include the manufacture of gentian bitters and sewer gas traps and the bottling of mineral waters, and by the turn of the century, he was also a wholesale distributor of alcoholic beverages.

Attracted to politics, Buhrer served 3 terms on the city council and was elected mayor of Cleveland in 1867. As mayor, he urged the building of the Cleveland House of Correction & Workhouse, which was completed during his administration. Later he was appointed to the board of workhouse directors. After completing his second term as mayor in 1871, Buhrer returned to the city council for 1 more term. He remained in business until he died in Cleveland at age 81. Buhrer married Eva Maria Schneider in 1848, and they had 3 children, John, Mary Jane, and Lois Catherine (Mrs. Frank Q. Barstow). After the death of his wife in Mar. 1889, he married Marguerite Paterson.

The **BUILDERS EXCHANGE**, a nonprofit trade association, represents the allied interests of construction industry in northern Ohio. It was founded in 1888 and incorporated in 1892 for the "promotion of social enjoyment . . . , the advancement of all legitimate interests of the building trades of Cleveland, and to preserve affiliation with the National Association of Builders." Its incorporators were Ephraim H. Towson, its first president, Chas. C. Dewstoe, Geo. E. Heidenreich, Jacob A. Reaugh, Chas. A. Davidson, Arthur McAllister, Parker Shackleton, and Robt. McQuoid. The organization's first headquarters were located in the ARCADE. In 1899 the exchange moved its offices to the Chamber of Commerce building on PUBLIC SQUARE. Edward A. Roberts, the group's first permanent secretary, served in that position for 36 years. When the Builders Exchange moved its offices to the Rose Bldg. in 1916, it was the largest such organization in the country. Plans were made for an enlarged permanent exhibition of building materials to attract architects, engineers, and those about to build, and space was leased to builders so that they could maintain desks at the exchange. The exchange issued bulletins twice weekly to its members, containing news about contracts awarded and work projected.

In 1929 the exchange moved to the 18th floor of the Builders Exchange Bldg. (later the Guildhall Bldg.) in the Terminal Group. There, it mounted an elaborate "Home in the Sky" exhibit, which attracted wide attention for a number of years. In 1941 the exchange moved to its present location, 1737 Euclid Ave., where it opened a "Home Information Center" for homeowners and prospective homeowners and expanded its services to the public. The Builders Exchange had more than 600 member companies in 1961. It offered a permanent exhibit of building materials and equipment, product information for consumers, and a home counselor service. Contractors and suppliers used its plan room and files for information on new building projects, plans, and specifications. Chas. W. Jauch, who served as executive secretary for 34 years, retired in 1975. Today (1984) the Builders Exchange publishes *Building Construction News*, a monthly magazine, and *Construction Register* and *Construction Register Daily Update*, which report on projects throughout the state. It also promotes high standards of workmanship through its Craftsmanship Awards Program, introduced in 1956 and the first of its kind in the nation, and maintains an extensive product information library. Jas. A. Parks currently serves as executive secretary.

The **BUILDING CODE OF 1904** (Ordinances 46388-A and 44404-A), adopted by the city of Cleveland on 20 June, was the first modern comprehensive building code in the nation. Other cities had had building laws of various kinds; Cleveland's first was passed in 1888. JOHN EISENMANN, engineer of the ARCADE, studied many of these but finally rejected the idea of using any one as a model. Instead, he began with the fundamental premises of safety, public benefit, and the current state of building knowledge, and from these evolved the first "scientific" comprehensive code.

The code contained 5 major sections. The first created a department of building, specified the duties of inspectors in 6 areas according to structure, listed the regulations on permits and drawings, and provided for the process of appeal. The second section specified the rules applying to the erection of buildings and structures; these were written in minute detail but were arrangd with impeccable logic and good sense. The third section dealt with the relation of the building to its site, both the permanent situation and the occupation of public right-of-way during construction. The next section was entirely on fire protection, and the last was a separate section on elevators. Within 2 years, the commission found that it had evolved a model for a national building code; 29 cities had already used it as the basis for formulating their own codes, and there were also inquiries from foreign countries. The Cleveland Building Code of 1904 was a manifestation of the "radical democracy" of the city in the first decade of the century, in which rules applied equally to all, and a confirmation of the fact that Cleveland was leading the rest of the country in its idea of municipal responsibilities.

The **BUILDING OWNERS AND MANAGERS ASSOCIATION OF CLEVELAND** was formed in 1913 by 28 downtown building owners to look after their interests. Incorporated in 1914, the organization assumed the dual function of promoting high standards of property management among its members and of working with local government and the community on legislative, regulatory, and civic concerns. Throughout its history, BOMA has been an outspoken critic of school, municipal, and welfare operating levies that would affect property taxes, and has encouraged its own members to exercise fiscal restraint through efficient management and to charge reasonable rates to assure a satisfied, stable tenant population. In the 1980s the organization sponsored studies and energy audits of city buildings, conferences about the office-building industry, and educational programs that led to certification as a real property advisor. One of its most important activities has been as a legislative spokesman on industry issues in Columbus through its lobbying arm, Ohio BOMA, and in Washington as a part of BOMA Internatl.

BOMA works with other community groups to promote Cleveland as an office-building center. In the 1960s, BOMA led the public-relations effort to lure federal government agencies here, although they originally opposed the construction of the Federal Bldg. on E. 9th St. in view of the vacancy rates in downtown Cleveland. The organization also worked to improve the attractiveness of downtown to both owners and tenants by supporting issues such as vendor licensing, CEI reduction of steam-heat rates, and fair assessments on property owners for sewers and other capital improvements. From its offices at 1127 Euclid, BOMA provides information on the industry to its members through monthly newsletters and meetings, special reports and publications, and periodic seminars. Its membership is open to building owners and managers, major tenants, engineers, architects, real-estate professionals, appraisers, and those who supply and service the office-building industry.

**BULGARIANS.** *See* **BALKAN IMMIGRANTS**

**BULKLEY, ROBERT JOHNS** (8 Oct. 1880–21 July 1965), was a member of the U.S. House of Representatives from 1910–14 and served as U.S. senator from Ohio from 1930–39. A Democrat, he identified with the goals of progressivism and the New Deal. He was a prominent banker and businessman in Cleveland. Bulkley was born in Cleveland to Chas. Henry and Roberta Johns Bulkley. His father was a wealthy real-estate investor. He graduated from UNIVERSITY SCHOOL in 1898 and received an A.B. in 1902 and an M.A. in 1906, both from Harvard. After studying law with a Cleveland firm for a year, he was admitted to the Ohio bar in 1907.

Urged by Mayor TOM L. JOHNSON to run for Congress, Bulkley was elected from the 21st district in 1910. As a member of the Banking & Currency Committee, he helped frame the Federal Reserve Act of 1913, but he lost his bid for reelection in 1915. During WORLD WAR I he served in the legal departments of the General Munitions Board, the War Industries Board, and the U.S. Shipping Board Emergency Fleet Corp. After returning to Cleveland, he headed the Bulkley Bldg. Co. and helped found the Morris Plan Bank of Ohio, where he served as president and chairman of the board for over 30 years. He was one of the founders of the NORTHERN OHIO OPERA ASSOC. in 1927.

In 1930, Bulkley reentered politics as a candidate to fill the unexpired term of Sen. THEODORE BURTON. Advocating the repeal of Prohibition, he won election and was reelected to a full 6-year Senate term in 1932. He was a staunch supporter of the New Deal; his legislative accomplishments included the joint sponsorship of the Reconstruction Finance Corp., the Home Loan Bank Act, relief legislation, and the Federal Deposit Insurance Act. He also backed Roosevelt's controversial plan to enlarge the Supreme Court, which contributed to his defeat for reelection by Republican Robt. A. Taft in 1938. He returned to Cleveland to pursue his career as a businessman and lawyer, becoming senior partner in the firm of Bulkley & Butler. Bulkley married Katherine C. Pope in 1909, and they had 2 children, Robt. Johns and Katharine. Mrs. Bulkley died in 1932. In 1934 he married Helen Graham Robbins. He died at age 84.

Robert J. Bulkley Papers, WRHS.

**BUNDY, LEROY N.** (14 Apr. 1873–28 May 1943), was a Cleveland dentist and politician who served 4 terms as the black Republican councilman of Ward 17, located on the city's east side. Elected to city council in 1929, he devoted a lifetime toward working for the welfare of Cleveland's black community and was recognized as its outspoken defender. Born in Hamilton, Ohio, Bundy moved to Cleveland at an early age. He was educated at old CENTRAL HIGH SCHOOL and graduated from the Dental School of Western Reserve University in 1904. He practiced his profession in Cleveland with offices located on E. 55th St. until the 1920s, when his interests expanded and he chose to enter the political arena. In 1930, Bundy sponsored legislation to prevent the spread of tuberculosis in the E. 55th St. area and called upon city health authorities under his ordinance to clean up the junkyards in his ward. He also served as chairman of the council's Utilities Commission and wielded great influence in council later as a veteran member. In 1933, Bundy broadened his talents by studying law at the Law School of WRU; he won his law degree in 1936, which proved to be a pivotal year for blacks in Cleveland and across the nation. By 1936, the dominating influence Bundy exerted at council meetings led him to high places in the local Republican organization and won him recognition at the REPUBLICAN NATL. CONVENTION OF 1936. It was at this convention that he organized delegates from the southern states. Dr. Bundy's marriage produced no children; his wife, Vella, was his sole survivor upon his death.

**BUNTS, FRANK E.** (3 June 1861–28 Nov. 1928), was one of the 4 founders of the CLEVELAND CLINIC FOUNDATION and the first president of the ACADEMY OF MEDICINE in Cleveland. Bunts was born in Youngstown, Ohio, attended public school there, and graduated from the U.S. Naval Academy at Annapolis in 1881. He received his M.D. degree from the Western Reserve University School of Medicine in 1886 and served as house officer at Charity Hospital in Cleveland. Along with GEO. W. CRILE, SR., Bunts assisted Dr. Frank Weed in his practice on Cleveland's west side and did casualty work for the railroads and shipyards. He took additional medical training in Europe and served in the SPANISH-AMERICAN WAR before returning to practice medicine in Cleveland in 1896. He was named professor of principles of surgery and clinical surgery at WRU, and in 1902 he became the first president of the Academy of Medicine in Cleveland. In 1921, Bunts joined Geo. W. Crile, Sr., JOHN PHILLIPS, and WM. E. LOWER in establishing the Cleveland Clinic Foundation, patterned after the group-practice model of the Mayo brothers in Rochester, Minn. In addition to his important association with the Cleveland Clinic, Bunts continued to perform most of his surgical work at Charity Hospital (1885–1928) and served as its chief of staff (1913–28). His main surgical/medical interests were in gallbladder disease, breast tumors, and cancer. In addition to his medical interests, Bunts wrote a small volume of short stories entitled *The Soul of Henry Huntington.* In 1888 Bunts married Harriet Taylor; they had 2 children, Alexander Taylor Bunts and Clara Louise Bunts, who married Edward Dauost.

Bunts, Alexander T., and Crile, George W., Jr., eds., *To Act as a Unit* (1971).

Crile, George W., Jr., *George Crile* (1947).

The **BUREAU OF CHILD HYGIENE** was set up in 1912 by the Cleveland Health Dept. to reduce infant mortality. Because many illnesses of young children were caused by milk-borne pathogens, the bureau's main duty was to oversee milk production and distribution. As part of the Health Dept., the Bureau of Child Hygiene initially set up 12 stations—called Prophylactic Infant & Children's Dispensaries—throughout the city. The stations were staffed by medical personnel, including physicians, who advised mothers in infant care, referred sick infants to the Babies' Dispensary, and distributed specially processed milk. The bureau was established by the health commissioner, Clyde Ford. Dr. Chauncy Wyckoff, the first associate director of the Babies' Dispensary, was assigned as chief physician. Wyckoff was largely responsible for organizing the bureau and implementing its programs. After several years he was succeeded by Dr. R. J. Oschsner, who ran the bureau and its successors for over 20 years. To insure sanitary procedures in milk production, the bureau established the Bellamy-Ganderton dairy farm in Bedford. Wyckoff made biweekly inspections of the farm. Dairy workers, instructed in hand hygiene, were required to wear white overalls and collect the milk under clean conditions. After collection, the milk was immediately refrigerated in 10-gallon cans. All cows were tuberculin tested, and samples of milk were taken daily to the Cleveland city lab for bacterial count. Horse-drawn refrigerated wagons (and later motorized vehicles) delivered milk to the 12 stations and the Babies' Dispensary, where it sold for $.10 a quart; for mothers who could not pay, it was given without charge. Several volunteer organizations aided in its distribution and also helped to subsidize costs. As sanitation guards in milk production became more standardized in the 1920s, the bureau lost some of its importance. In the late 1920s it was replaced by the Chief Bureau of Child Welfare.

The **BUREAU OF JEWISH EDUCATION,** the central policy-making and resource agency for Jewish education in Cleveland, was established in 1924 following a recommendation laid out in a community survey completed the year before. The BJE was established to promote the efficient utilization of existing schools and facilities and to bring an estimated 12,000 Jewish children not receiving any formal Jewish education into contact with one of the community's schools. ABRAHAM H. FRIEDLAND, director of the CLEVELAND HEBREW SCHOOLS, was appointed executive director, and Rabbi ABBA HILLEL SILVER was selected as the first president. The bureau was not intially a beneficiary of the Fed. of Jewish Charities, because the latter received money from the Community Fund, which did not support religious education. Monetary support came from the 4 largest congregations and from 2 community-wide fundraisers prior to 1930. Under Friedland's leadership, the BJE was dominated by the Cleveland Hebrew Schools. Charges were made that he channeled funds to the Hebrew Schools to the detriment of other community schools. In the 1930s the bureau conducted a high school, a teacher-training program, a youth club, and children's programming for the Jewish holidays.

The bureau became a federation beneficiary in 1931 following the reorganization of the federation's fundraising arm. In 1936, the first major study of Jewish education in Cleveland extolled the excellence of the Hebrew Schools' education but noted that congregational schools would be the most important Jewish educational instrument in the future. With the death of Friedland in 1939, the controversy he engendered began to fade. Under the leadership of Azriel Eisenberg, and later Nathan Brilliant, and with increased federation funding, the bureau began to experience greater cohesion and community support. By the 1950s, the bureau comprised 15 member agencies, including 6 community schools, which received partial funding from the Jewish Welfare Fund, and 9 congregational schools (3 Reform, 3 Conservative, and 3 Orthodox), which were supported entirely by the congregations. Between the end of WORLD WAR II and the mid-1970s (with the exception of congregations), the only new Jewish institutions established in Cleveland were education-related. Support for Jewish education from the federation increased 14-fold during this period.

Bureau of Jewish Education Records, WRHS.

**BURKE, THOMAS A. (ALOYSIUS)** (30 Oct. 1898–5 Dec. 1971), was active in Cleveland politics for many years, serving as law director and mayor. He was born in Cleveland, the son of Thos. A. and Lillian McNeil Burke. He graduated from Loyola High School; he received his B.A. degree from Holy Cross College in 1920 and an LL.B. degree from Western Reserve University School of Law in 1923. Burke was assistant county prosecutor from 1930–36; and in 1937, the Ohio state attorney general appointed him special counsel to prosecute vote fraud. From 1937–41 he practiced law. Burke was appointed law director of Cleveland by Mayor Frank Lausche in 1941, and when Lausche left to become governor in 1945, he became mayor. As an independent Democrat, he was elected mayor in 1945 and served for 4 terms. During his administration, he presided over a large capital-improvement program, including a lakefront airport built on landfill, the first downtown airport in the country (see BURKE LAKEFRONT AIRPORT). He campaigned for a charter amendment passed in 1951 giving the mayor the power to appoint and dismiss the police chief and was instrumental in establishing a free municipal parking lot adjacent to the shoreway.

When U.S. Sen. Robt. Taft died in 1953, Gov. Lausche appointed Burke to fill Taft's Senate seat until the next Ohio general election, in 1954. In that election Burke narrowly lost his bid for the seat to Congressman GEO. H. BENDER. He retired from political life but continued to practice law as senior partner in the law firm Burke, Haber & Berwick. Burke married Josephine Lyon in 1923, and they had 2 daughters, Barbara (Mrs. Terrence J. Martin) and Jo Anne (Mrs. Stanley L. Orr). After Mrs. Burke's death in 1964, he married Evelyn Sedgwick. He died in 1971 at the age of 73.

Thomas Burke Papers, WRHS.

**BURKE LAKEFRONT AIRPORT** is a municipally operated inter-city facility located on Cleveland's lakefront, for the primary purpose of providing a downtown air terminal and relieving CLEVELAND HOPKINS INTERNATL. AIRPORT of the need to handle large numbers of smaller aircraft. A lakefront airport was first suggested by Wm. Rogers during the GREAT LAKES EXPOSITION of 1936. However, WORLD WAR II disrupted planning, and it was not until Aug. 1947 that operations began on a 3,600-ft. dirt runway served by a small operations headquarters. Only 202 flights were logged during the first month of operations; more than 9,000 were logged during Sept. 1984.

During the tenure of Mayor THOS. BURKE, major improvements were made in the facility, and it was subsequently named in his honor. In 1957 additional landfill in Lake Erie permitted the construction of a 5,200-ft. hard-surface runway. During the 1970s, the airport underwent considerable expansion. A new building, control tower, sales facilities, passenger accommodations, and a 6,200-ft. runway were added. The new runway enabled the airport to accommodate even large, multi-engine jet aircraft. Commercial operations out of the airport included Bolton's Helicopter Services beginning in 1984, Tag Airlines in 1956, WRIGHT AIRLINES in 1966, Midway Airlines in 1979–80, and Beaver Air Service in 1984. Beginning in 1981, the airport served as the racetrack for the BUDWEISER CLEVELAND 500, an Indianapolis-style road race. The NATL. AIR RACES, begun in Cleveland in 1929, were reestablished as the CLEVELAND AIR SHOW at the lakefront airport in 1964 and have been held annually each Labor Day weekend since then.

**BURKETT, JESSE CAIL "CRAB"** (12 Feb. 1870–27 May 1953), was a major-league baseball player for the CLEVELAND SPIDERS of the Natl. League between 1891–98. A left-handed outfielder, Burkett holds the record with Ty Cobb and Rogers Hornsby for hitting .400 or over during 3 seasons. Born in Wheeling, W.Va., Burkett began his professional career in 1888 as a pitcher with Scranton of the Central League. His ability to hit the baseball caused the New York Giants to transfer him to the outfield. By 1891 Burkett was playing for the Cleveland Spiders. His batting marks of .423 in 1895 and .410 in 1896 helped the Spiders play in the Temple Cup series, the 1890s equivalent of the World Series. The Spiders defeated Baltimore 4 games to 1 for the league championship in 1895. In 6 full seasons, Burkett never hit below a .345 average for Cleveland, leading the league 3 times in total base hits. At the beginning of the 1899 season, Frank De Hass Robinson, who owned 2 clubs in the NL, transferred the pick of the club, including Cy Young and Burkett, to St. Louis, where the outfielder hit .402 that season. After leading the NL in hitting during the 1901 season, Burkett jumped to the St. Louis team in the American League. Three seasons later, he was traded to the Boston Red Sox, where he finished his major-league career in 1905 with a .342 lifetime batting average. A fiery competitor, Burkett once pushed John McGraw of Baltimore off third base and sat on him while waiting for CY YOUNG to throw him the ball in order to tag McGraw out. Burkett was the owner and manager of Worcester in the New England League from 1906–13. Managing in the minor leagues as late as 1933, he also coached Holy Cross College from 1917–20 and Assumption College in 1928, 1931, and 1932. In 1946 he was selected for the Baseball Hall of Fame at Cooperstown, N.Y. Burkett's son, Howard, played minor-league ball for several years and tried out with the Chicago Cubs.

**BURNHAM, THOMAS** (18 June 1808–7 Apr. 1898), was one of the founders of the malleable iron business west of the Allegheny Mts. He first settled in OHIO CITY and from 1849–50 served as its mayor. Burnham was born in Moreau, N.Y. He was master of a freight boat on the Champlain Canal before settling in Brooklyn Twp., Ohio, in 1833. He took a job as a schoolteacher, and the following year he became one of the proprietors of the Burton House, a hotel at the corner of Pearl and Detroit Sts. Also in 1834, Burnham was employed by the Troy & Erie Line, a company doing a large business on the Ohio Canal, Lake Erie, and the Erie Canal. The company primarily shipped wheat. Burnham acquired an interest in the company and took control of a grain elevator on the CUYAHOGA RIVER, above the Superior St. viaduct. In 1851 he purchased the Erie elevator, one of the largest in Cleveland. He continued in the elevator business until 1871. Burnham was active in local government, in both Ohio City and Cleveland. Mayor of Ohio City when it was consolidated into Cleveland, Burnham was elected to CLEVELAND CITY COUNCIL. He later served as council president. A founder of the Cleveland Malleable Iron Co., Burnham served as its president for 5 years. He was also one of the founders of the Chicago Malleable Iron Co. In addition, he was the president of several smaller manufacturing interests in the Midwest.

**BURROWS** is the leading book, stationery, and office-supply firm in Ohio. It was founded by 2 brothers from New England, Chas. W. and Harris B. Burrows, who opened their first retail store on Euclid Ave. on 8 Nov. 1873. The Burrows Bros. Co.'s business in selling books and stationery started slowly, and within a year, it was almost bankrupt. Then Chas. Burrows introduced a circulating library in the store, which became quite popular and provided the firm with a profit by 1875. By the early 1880s, Burrows expanded, moving to larger quarters on Euclid Ave. and establishing publishing and jobbing services. In 1886 Burrows was incorporated, and 2 years later it acquired its major competitor, Cobb, Andrew, & Co., which was a descendant of one of the earliest bookstores in Cleveland, founded in 1837. In 1897, with around 200 employees, the company moved into the New England (Guardian) Bldg. on E. 6th St. and Euclid Ave.

By 1912, the Burrows brothers had left the firm and had sold the business to Jas. Robinson and John J. Wood. At this time, the company was exclusively a retail store, as Burrows had dropped its publishing and wholesale businesses. The store went into receivership during WORLD WAR I, but business revived when new interests bought it in 1919 and made Gordon B. Bingham general manager. In 1922, Bingham began to establish branch stores, and by World War II, there were 9 Burrows stores. In 1944, Burrows was sold interests headed by Howard Klein. Under Klein, the company moved its downtown store to 419 Euclid Ave. in 1948, expanded the number of suburban branches, and increased its line of products. In 1969, the HIGBEE CO. acquired Burrows but was forced to sell it in 1973 because of a federal antitrust suit against the merger. The new owners were headed by John J. Malloy, who guided Burrows from a 15-store chain with $7 million in sales in 1975 to 45 stores, 36 of them in Cleveland, with $18 million in sales in 1979. Burrows moved its flagship store to E. 6th St. and Euclid Ave. In 1982, Burrows was purchased by Bro-Dart Industries, Inc. (now known as BDI Investment, Inc.), of California, one of the nation's leading manufacturers and distributors of books and library supplies and equipment.

**BURTON, HAROLD HITZ** (22 June 1888–29 Oct. 1964), had a 30-year public-service career as mayor of Cleveland, U.S. senator, and associate justice of the U.S. Supreme Court. He was born in Jamaica Plains, Mass., the son of Dr. Alfred Edgar and Gertrude Hitz Burton. He graduated from Newton (Mass.) High School and attended Bowdoin College, graduating in 1909. He received his LL.B. from Harvard Law School in 1912. After graduation, he came to Cleveland and worked for 2 years. During WORLD WAR I he saw active service in Europe, receiving a citation from the U.S. government, the Purple Heart, and the Belgian Croix de Guerre.

After the war, Burton returned to Cleveland permanently and practiced law. He was elected to the Ohio state legislature in 1928 as an independent Republican. From 1930–31 he served as law director of Cleveland, becoming acting mayor for a brief period from Nov. 1931–Feb. 1932, and in 1935 he was elected mayor for the first of 3 terms. During his administration, the rackets that had flourished in Cleveland were broken up. The mayor actively promoted Cleveland as a convention center, and several major conventions were held here, including the REPUBLICAN CONVENTION OF 1936. Burton had great difficulty securing adequate relief funds from the state of Ohio for the destitute of Cleveland; however, in the end some $40 million was given to Cleveland for relief assistance. During his administration when there were strikes and labor unrest, the mayor encouraged negotiations between business and labor, but when violence threatened, he did what was necessary to preserve order.

In 1940, Burton was elected senator and served until 1945, when Pres. Truman appointed him to the Supreme Court. In 1951 he wrote the Court opinion outlawing racial segregation in railroad dining cars, and he participated in the *Brown v. Board of Education* decision outlawing school segregation. He retired from the Court in 1958, making his home in Washington, where he occasionally presided as judge in the U.S. District Court of Appeals and the Court of Claims. He married Selma Florence Smith on 15 June 1912 and had 4 children, Barbara (Mrs. H. Chas. Weidner), Deborah (Mrs. Wallace Adler), William, and Robert. He died in Washington, D.C., at age 76.

Harold H. Burton Papers, WRHS.

**BURTON, LEWIS** (3 July 1815–9 Oct. 1894), was a prominent Episcopal rector in the Cleveland area for 47 years, where he founded or managed a number of parishes. He was born just south of Erie, Pa. The inclinations of his early home life probably influenced his decision to follow his brother into the Episcopal priesthood. He graduated from Allegheny College in 1837, and he married Jane Wallace in 1841. Burton was known to his contemporaries as a handsome, dignified, genial, and able man. He used these qualities and a head for business to help his church meet the needs of its membership as it followed the southern and western expansion of Cleveland. Moved by the condition of a parishioner, Burton and his sister-in-law, Eliza Jennings, combined her gift of 7½ acres of land with community financial support to start the ELIZA JENNINGS HOME in 1888; it eventually became a well-endowed social-service agency for needy women.

Succeeding his brother as rector of Ohio City's St. John's parish in 1847, Burton led a successful rebuilding effort after fire destroyed the church in 1866. He started All Saints' and St. Mark's as missions of St. John's. He resigned from St. John's (1871) to take charge of both missions as they became full-fledged parishes. He led All Saints' until 1875 and was rector at St. Mark's until his retirement in 1887. He also developed a former Trinity mission into the Church of the Ascension (1875) and served as its first rector.

**BURTON, THEODORE ELIJAH** (20 Dec. 1851–28 Oct. 1929), was a recognized authority on river and harbor improvements and economic, monetary, and banking legislation. As a Republican, he served in the U.S. House of Representatives from 1889–91, 1895–1909, and 1921–28 and was U.S. senator from Ohio from 1909–15 and from 1928 until his death. Born in Jefferson, Ohio, the son of Rev. Wm. and Elizabeth Grant Burton, he attended Grand River Institute in Austinburg, Ohio. He and his brothers moved to Iowa in 1866, where he enrolled at Grinnell Academy & College. After 2 years of college, he returned to Ohio and received an A.B. degree from Oberlin College in 1872. He studied law with Lyman Trumbull in Chicago, was admitted to the Ohio bar in 1875, and came to Cleveland to practice law. He served on the city council from 1886–88 and was then elected to Congress from the 21st district. Defeated for reelection by Democrat TOM L. JOHNSON in 1890, he resumed law practice, specializing in estate administration. Burton was again elected to Congress in 1894, serving 7 terms.

At a time when Cleveland was improving the CUYAHOGA RIVER and its harbor, Congressman Burton became an active proponent of the development of the Great Lakes waterways, serving as a member and later chairman of the Rivers & Harbors Committee in the House of Representatives. A leading authority in the field, Burton was convinced that development could be accomplished efficiently and economically and was effective in curbing the overspending traditionally associated with rivers and harbors legislation.

Locally, Burton clashed with MARCUS A. HANNA in 1902, threatening to retire from Congress rather than allow the Hanna machine to conduct his reelection campaign. In a compromise, Burton chose the Republican campaign managers for his congressional district. In 1907 he returned to Cleveland to challenge Tom L. Johnson in the mayoral election. After his defeat, Burton returned to Congress, where Pres. Theodore Roosevelt appointed him chairman of his newly created Inland Waterways Commission in 1907 and its successor the Natl. Waterways Commission, where he served from 1908–12. From 1908–12 he also served on the Natl. Monetary Commission created by the Aldrich-Vreeland Emergency Currency Act to study worldwide banking systems.

Elected to the U.S. Senate by the Ohio legislature in 1909, Burton was in office until 1915, when he retired from the Senate and became president of Merchants' Natl. Bank in New York City (1917–19). He was again elected to the U.S. House of Representatives in 1921 and served on the World War Foreign Debt Commission organized to restructure the payment of wartime loans made to foreign countries. After WORLD WAR I, Burton was active in the world peace movement and was president of the American Peace Society for many years. At his behest, the society's 100th anniversary was celebrated by holding the 1st World Conference on Internatl. Justice in Cleveland on 7 May 1928. In order to pursue the cause of peace more effectively, Burton gave up his seat in the House in 1928 and was elected to the U.S. Senate. He died in Washington the following year at age 77, and his body was returned to Cleveland for burial in LAKE VIEW CEMETERY.

During his long career, Burton was the author of several books: *Financial Crises and Periods of Industrial and Commercial Depression* (1902); *Life of John Sherman* (1906); *Corporations and the State* (1911); *Modern Political Tendencies of the Times and the Effect of the War Thereon* (1919); and *The Constitution, Its Origin and Distinctive Features* (1923). On 16 Apr. 1928, the Cleveland Chamber of Commerce awarded him the Cleveland Public Service Medal in recognition of his promotion of civic, industrial, and business interests.

Theodore E. Burton Papers, WRHS.
Crissey, Forest, *Theodore E. Burton, American Statesman* (1956).

The **BUSINESS & PROFESSIONAL WOMEN'S CLUB OF GREATER CLEVELAND** was established in 1919 to provide a common meeting ground for women active in careers outside the home. Unlike study or social clubs organized mainly for entertainment and improvement, it offered women a comfortable place away from home to dine, relax, and discuss professional concerns with counterparts. The idea for the club originated during WORLD WAR I, when NEWTON D. BAKER, secretary of war, sent out a call for women to aid the war effort. Though the mobilization did not take place before armistice, the enthusiasm of working women led to the founding of the Business & Professional Women's Club of Greater Cleveland. The club was organized by politically active women, such as MARIE R. WING, FLORENCE E. ALLEN, FRANCES PAYNE BOLTON, Grace Doering McCord, and Margaret Mahoney, who invited Lena Phillips, a New York attorney and executive secretary of the newly formed Natl. Fed. of Business & Professional Women's Clubs, to address interested Cleveland women. By Nov. 1919, interest ran high enough that over 800 attended the first dinner meeting, presided over by Florence Allen at the Statler Hotel. Within a year, over 1,500 teachers, secretaries, stenographers, bookkeepers, nurses, cashiers, librarians, accountants, buyers, advertising women, artists, and public-relations specialists were numbered among the ranks. The women were bound by the necessity to support themselves in a man's world, while maintaining their femininity and female viewpoint.

Under the name the Businesswomen's Club of Cleveland, the organization was set up as a corporation managed by a 19-member board of directors and an executive secretary. The first president was Mary Rudd Cochran, a li-

brarian. The local club affiliated with the Natl. Fed. of Business & Professional Women's Clubs, and hosted a national convention in 1921. After meeting in the Statler for a few months, the club acquired the Billings mansion at 2728 Euclid, but it later returned to the Stillman Bldg. in the heart of downtown, near where many members worked. The new headquarters featured excellent kitchen facilities, a large auditorium, and a lounge for reading, eating, and conversation. Throughout its history, the organization fostered general and vocational education for women; in 1923, it endorsed a high school education as an appropriate foundation for women in business and established scholarships to enable young women to attain their diplomas. During the Depression, the Business & Professional Women's Club participated in the Natl. Fed.'s survey to determine the gravity of discrimination toward women in clerical and professional positions. In 1937, it joined the Natl. Fed. in endorsing the Equal Rights Amendment, the first major women's organization to do so. As the club continued to advance the cause of women in the domestic workplace, it also contributed to women's serving military needs throughout the world in WORLD WAR II. After the war, the organization resumed its work in support of women in the workplace. Despite its accomplishments and the importance of its work, membership declined over the decades. The Business & Professional Women's Club remained a viable organization into the 1980s.

Business & Professional Women's Club of Cleveland Records, WRHS.

**BUSINESS, RETAIL.** The segment of the economy that sells directly to the consumer diverse goods such as food items, clothing, furniture, appliances, medicines, cosmetics, building materials, and automobiles and supplies, has employed annually 13–16% of the Cleveland area's workers during the 20th century. Although the retail segment of the local economy has employed a fairly constant percentage of the area's workforce over time, the local retail business itself has gone through major changes. Foremost among these have been the locations of retail establishments and their size, structure, and methods of operation. The competition for the consumer's dollars from the 1830s to the 1980s led to new procedures in marketing and management, to larger stores offering low prices and greater selection, and to many concentrations of retail establishments spread throughout the suburbs in regional shopping malls and neighborhood shopping centers. There was little specialization among Cleveland merchants in the first half of the 19th century. The earliest merchants opened small trading shops and carried on trade with the Indians and the few settlers. Men such as Nathan Perry, Jr., JOEL SCRANTON, PETER M. WEDDELL, and Orlando Cutter were general merchants, serving as both importers and exporters and selling their goods both retail and wholesale. They purchased their supply of goods from eastern wholesalers and shipped grains and other western goods to eastern markets. In the 1810s and 1820s, merchants accepted in trade such items as pork, whiskey, corn, tallow, butter, "pot and pearl ashes, good clean rye, and a few barrels of good mercantile flour." Some offered "a liberal discount on Eastern cash." Newspaper advertising was extremely limited until the 1840s; advertisements served to announce new shipments, new stores, and the terms of trade and to call in debts prior to a merchant's departure from the city.

By the 1860s, local merchants had begun to specialize in retailing more exclusively and began to establish large dry-goods stores, such as that of Hower & Higbee, opened in 1860 (see HIGBEE CO.). The railroad gave merchants more reliable access to eastern markets, and cheaper newsprint made possible more and new forms of advertising that gave the retailer greater access to his customers. In the 1840s, advertisers departed from the usual "announcement" form by using catchy phrases and bold claims in ads. By 1851, store advertisements were using illustrations of goods, bold print, and more white space to attract the reader's eye. By 1860, advertisers were beginning to publish prices of their goods, to advertise clearance sales, and to make even bolder claims for their establishments. In June 1860, the eye-catching ad for Chas. H. Robison's Nonpareil Clothing Warehouse noted that the shop was located at the "Sign of the Live Yankee and the Big Red Coat," suggesting some of the visual aids retailers used to attract customers to their stores. Another way in which retailers sought to attract customers was with the location and distinctiveness of the stores themselves. From 1815 until the 1830s, Cleveland's retail businesses were centered on Superior St. west of PUBLIC SQUARE. Stores resembled the private dwellings they had taken over or shared with their proprietors. Between 1830-54, however, expansion of the warehouse district forced retailers to expand into the residential areas north from Superior along Ontario, Seneca (W. 3rd), Bank (W. 6th), and Water (W. 9th) streets. As the town and its businesses accumulated wealth and maturity, merchants built specialized blocks for businesses along Superior and its side streets; by 1854, Public Square had been surrounded by such 3- and 4-story commercial blocks. By 1850, distinct commercial centers also had formed on the west side at the intersections of Pearl (W. 25th) with Detroit and Lorain Rds.

The emerging business district was further congested in the 1860s and 1870s as industry displaced businesses in the FLATS and forced expansion of the warehouse and wholesale district farther into areas inhabited by retailers. Retailers east of the Cuyahoga moved their stores to the east and south; on the west side, businesses moved west and south to avoid the noise and dirt of industry along the river. By 1878, Euclid Ave. near Public Square was lined with stores on both sides. During the 1880s, the famous Millionaires' Row of mansions along Euclid Ave. sat between 2 expanding shopping districts, one growing east from Public Square and the other pushing west from the railroad crossing at Willson (E. 55th) and Euclid. Locations near transportation terminals and intersections became favorite ones for businesses. The convergence of streetcar lines at Public Square had made it a prime business location by the 1880s. Small retailers who followed the growing population into residential areas continued to locate near busy intersections and along heavily used streets.

The period 1860-1920 witnessed changes in business generally that laid the foundation for modern retailing and saw the development of a number of important local retail businesses. New technologies such as the railroad and the telegraph and improved administrative arrangements reduced the number of transactions involved in shipping, improved the flow of goods, enhanced the efficiency of operations, and thus lowered operating costs and prices. Along with large population increases, these developments made possible the rise of modern retailing by 1920. With the introduction of manufacturing at mid-century, Cleveland's population grew rapidly, from 43,417 in 1860 to 381,768 in 1900, and further to 796,841 in 1920. With this growth came an increase in the volume of retail sales and the number of retail establishments: the number of dry-goods stores increased from 20 to 200 between 1860-1900 and to 504 in 1920; the number of grocers jumped from 240 to 1,125 to 2,107. As some families began to acquire

a degree of wealth, they began to demand from retailers more than the necessities of life, giving rise to specialty stores such as the KINNEY & LEVAN CO. in home furnishings, COWELL & HUBBARD in jewelry, and specialty grocers CHANDLER & RUDD. Dry-goods establishments added new product lines to their inventories. The result was the beginnings of the department store, most of which developed from small dry-goods stores established in the last quarter of the 19th century. The department store did not come into full blossom locally until the leading retailers built new, palatial stores for themselves between 1900-15. Their impressive new buildings offered a wide variety of goods and catered to the expectations of their mostly female middle- and upper-class patrons. By 1915, the stores that would dominate Cleveland retailing until the 1960s—stores such as WM. TAYLOR SON & CO., the FRIES & SCHUELE CO., the BAILEY CO., the MAY CO., the HIGBEE CO., and HALLE BROS. CO.—were firmly entrenched as downtown landmarks to Cleveland's economic progress.

Emerging department stores took several measures to strengthen themselves financially and organizationally between 1880-1920. As Alfred Chandler has pointed out, the life of the typical 19th-century business usually was only as long as its proprietor; store and business names changed when owners took on new partners, died, retired, or sold their businesses to other owners who gave the stores their own names. But ca. 1880-1910, retailers and manufacturers began to incorporate and to adopt hierarchical and self-perpetuating forms of management, allowing the company to outlive its founders. At the same time, these merchants formed the RETAIL MERCHANTS BOARD to consider ways to promote business to their mutual benefit, to protect themselves against unscrupulous "itinerant merchants" and other unfair competition, and to guard against being cheated by both customers and employees. Like department stores elsewhere, the Cleveland stores also developed an elaborate plan of internal management to improve the efficiency of their operations. Each department was managed by its buyer, who purchased its goods and operated with a great deal of autonomy as long as the department performed well. On the lowest rung of the ladder of management were "cash boys," couriers between the various clerks in the departments, the wrapping desk, and the central cashier's desk. Cash boys could advance to wrapper and then further up the ladder. Technological innovation replaced cash boys with pneumatic tubes, which in turn were replaced by cash registers. While Cleveland's new department stores prided themselves on quality, integrity, and service, other merchants concentrated on lowering prices to attract customers. Some developed new policies that would systematically provide lower prices and thus enable their establishments to compete more effectively. One such effort was the chain store, which began to appear in Cleveland in the 1870s but did not become a major part of local retailing until the 1920s. National chains such as the Great Atlantic & Pacific Tea Co., Grand Union, the S. S. Kresge Co., F. W. Woolworth, and the United Cigar Stores Co. entered the local market gradually and added more and larger stores in the 1920s. In 1929, chain stores accounted for 35% of sales in Cleveland.

Grocery and drug chains were the first to make significant inroads into their respective local markets. The Marshall Drug Co., founded in 1884 by Wentworth G. Marshall, was an early important drug chain (see GRAY DRUGSTORES, INC.). It created a national controversy within the industry by introducing cut-rate prices in 1901. Other important local drug chains were the Standard Drug Co., formed in 1899 (see REVCO D.S., INC.), and Weinberger Drug Stores, which began in 1912 with a single store,

141

took shape as a chain in 1928, and provided the foundation for Gray Drug Stores, Inc. Development of these local chains and their later acquisitions by and mergers into larger regional and national organizations were part of an ongoing quest for more capital with which to expand further and to benefit from the economies of scale. Mergers, acquisitions, and cooperative buying and advertising agreements were frequent among local retailers after 1920.

The highly competitive local grocery business illustrates many of the general changes retailing has gone through in policies and operations. The number of grocery stores in the area grew steadily along with the population prior to 1930. As national chains entered the local market, local grocers fought back by opening their own branches and developed their own chains. By 1929, the leading chains in Cleveland were Kroger, with just over 200 stores, and the local Fisher Bros. and the national A&P, each of which operated about 300 stores locally. In all, Cleveland had 5,358 food stores that year, with 4,849 proprietors and 8,410 employees. The stores were small operations with an average of 1.57 employees per store (excluding proprietors), compared to the 28.8 employee-per-store average among general merchandisers that year. Food sales accounted for 22% of all retail business in 1929 and generally have remained between 22–26% of total retail sales since that time; in 1982, for example, food sales accounted for 23% of the county's retail sales and 26% of sales in the city. The food group historically has accounted for the largest percentage of retail sales in the area.

Although the percentage of retail food sales has remained stable, the consolidation of small neighborhood stores into much larger supermarkets sharply reduced the percentage of retail food stores and increased the average number of employees per store. The 5,358 food stores in the area in 1929 represented 43% of all retail stores; by 1954, the number of food stores had decreased to 3,114 (29% of all city retail establishments). The decline is illustrated by the decreased number of stores in the neighborhoods: on Broadway the number of stores dropped from 41 to 20, and the number of chains from 19 to 3; on Detroit grocery stores decreased from 86 to 24, the chains from 52 to 4. By 1982 the number of food stores had declined further to 1,235, and they were only 15% of the county's retail establishments. (In the city the food group's percentage of all retail establishments generally has been a few percentage points above the county's and was 19% in 1982.) At the same time, the average number of employees per store has increased from fewer than 2 per store in the 1920s and 1930s to 13.7 in the county in 1982 and 9.9 in the city. Several developments enabled the larger self-serve supermarkets to cut costs and lower prices. Increased use of the automobile and adoption of the cash-and-carry system helped eliminate deliveries; cash-and-carry also eliminated the costs of extending credit. Self-service and checkout counters in the front of the store eliminated the necessity of personal service for each customer. The larger stores, thus able to offer lower prices, also offered customers a much greater selection of items and brands than did the corner store. As it came to represent an effective retailing strategy, the supermarket was adopted by local grocers, who formed their own chains (see FISHER FOODS, INC., and FIRST NATL. SUPERMARKETS) and cooperative associations such as Foodtown (1948) and Stop-N-Shop (1961), both of which were creations of Julius "Julie" Kravitz, a leading grocery executive during the formative years of the local industry. The supermarket idea was elaborated into the "food warehouse" notion of the giant supermarket in the 1970s and 1980s.

As the supermarket developed in the 1940s and 1950s, its operational design proved attractive to other retailers, especially to the discount stores that became popular after WORLD WAR II and developed into major forces in retailing in the next several decades. Discount stores applied the large-volume, high-turnover, low-markup strategy of retailing first to appliances and hardware and later to clothing, furniture, and other department-store items. Discounters ignored and broke some accepted rules of business, first by taking less of a markup in order to undersell their competition, and then by breaking the Sunday closing laws and quickly eroding adherence to that custom. The local pioneer discounter was Louis Weisberg, who in 1947 established an operation known first as Big Bear and then Giant Tiger. Weisberg's operation had grown to 15 stores in 1968, when he sold it to Gaylords Internatl. Corp. of New York. Another early local discounter was Uncle Bill's, formed in 1955 by Sidney Axelrod. In 1961, Uncle Bill's became a complete discount department store by adding clothing and furniture to its offerings, and Axelrod sold his stores to the Cook Coffee Co. (see COOK UNITED, INC.). Although both Giant Tiger and Uncle Bill's suffered under the ownership of large, diversified corporations in the 1970s, the development of discount stores and the movement of people into the suburbs seriously hurt the department stores downtown. Between 1960–82, many of the prominent department stores were closed, and others were taken over by discount department-store chains.

Movement away from the central business district had been a gradual process. During the 1880s, 1890s, and early 1900s, smaller retail businesses serving the daily needs of customers for such items as groceries and meats moved into the residential districts. This process of residential movement continued and accelerated as the 20th century progressed. Business districts became more and more distinct as the automobile necessitated changes. Many neighborhood shopping centers were built in emerging SUBURBS such as LAKEWOOD and CLEVELAND HTS. At the turn of the century, these areas had few retail establishments and received regular visits from scissors grinders, oil salesmen, and peddlers of fish, meat, fruit, and tin. As these areas increased in population, however, retailers began to build shops along main thoroughfares and at important intersections. Eric Johannesen has described the neighborhood shopping center of the 1910s as typically being "a two-story block with ground floor stores and second floor apartments." In 1918, Cleveland Hts. had its first planned neighborhood shopping center at Cedar-Fairmount; by 1927, Cleveland Hts. had 220 retail establishments, E. CLEVELAND 423, and Lakewood 691. Together these close-in suburbs had 72% of the 1,848 retailers counted in a survey of 18 communities surrounding the Cleveland area.

The 1926 survey of retail businesses and 1935 sales figures suggest that suburban retailing first developed to attend to suburbanites' daily necessities, one of which was transportation. Of the 18 communities examined in 1926, all but 1 (SHAKER HTS.) had 1 or more establishments to service or repair automobiles, and exactly half had an automobile dealer; all but 1 had an ice-cream parlor, soft-drink stand, saloon, or cafe; 16 had grocers, 14 a butcher or meat shop, and 15 a hardware store. Other kinds of more specialized shops existed in fewer of the communities. In 1935, food stores in the suburbs accounted for 40.8% of all suburban retail sales, the automobile group for 17.26%, and filling stations for 10.56% Food and transportation thus accounted for 2/3 of all suburban retail sales in 1935. As the population of the suburbs grew in the 1950s and 1960s, a wider variety of retail businesses sprang up to serve customers in the convenience of their own neighborhoods. The suburban retail industry grew to resemble that of the city in its diversity. Between 1954–63, sales of the general merchandise group—department stores, variety stores, and the like—increased from 5.1% of all suburban retail sales to 17.9%, and groups such as apparel also increased their shares of the market. By 1982 the food group (21.8%) and the automobile group (16.96%) still dominated the suburban retail market, but with much lower percentages compared to 1935; the general merchandise group was the 3d-largest segment of suburban retail sales in 1982, with 15% of the market.

The suburban retail industry also came to resemble the city's retail industry in size and ultimately surpassed it in the mid-1960s. In 1929, Cleveland had 84% of the retail stores in the county and 87% of the county's retail business; by 1967 the city had 57% of the stores in the county but only 45% of the sales, and by 1982 only 35% of the stores and 28% of the business. While much of this decline is due to increased population in the suburbs and to the boom in suburban shopping mall construction, it also reflects the decline in the number of retail stores and in retail employment within the city. Between 1954–67, the number of retail establishments in Cleveland declined from 10,754 to 7,008; it dropped further to 3,727 stores with payrolls in 1982. During this same period, retail employment in the city declined from 63,225 in 1954 to 47,244 in 1967 and to 30,230 in 1982. In these same years, the county saw its number of stores shrink from 14,573 in 1954 to 12,403 in 1967 and to 10,612 with payrolls in 1982, yet employment increased from 82,130 in 1954 to 94,252 in 1967 and again to 104,183 in 1982. Retailers clearly followed the area's population as it moved farther away from downtown, but they followed with varying degrees of enthusiasm. Department stores were often reluctant to make the move, having heavy investments in their buildings, believing that downtown was still an important and accessible shopping district, and fearing that suburban branches would only compete with their downtown locations. Only at the end of the 1920s did department stores begin to move into important shopping districts that were still within the city limits. In 1928, Sears, Roebuck & Co., the large mail-order house that now recognized that the declining rural population meant it would have to change its marketing strategy to remain strong, built 2 large stores in Cleveland, 1 on each side of the city. In 1929, Bailey's became the first downtown department store to establish a branch in the outer part of the city, opening a store in the Euclid-E. 105th shopping center and following it in 1930 with a store in Lakewood. In 1948, Halle's became the first major local department store to move into the suburbs, opening a branch store in SHAKER SQUARE.

An early shopping center, Shaker Square was one of the first attempts to meet the special needs of automobile-oriented suburban shoppers. Easily accessible by public transportation, it also could accommodate patrons who came by automobile, something for which many early neighborhood shopping centers had not planned. By 1940, the Real Property Inventory counted 257 "shopping centers" in the Cleveland area; these often were no more than a "strip" of retail businesses along a major thoroughfare or a collection of stores at an intersection. Provisions for automobile parking at such centers were often inadequate. Merchants tried various schemes to remedy this defect, including parking lots in back of stores and off-street parking in front. Such ideas led in the 1950s to the development of the integrated shopping center: a group of storefronts built together, linked by a covered walkway, and served by 1 or more large parking lots. Such shopping centers as

SOUTHGATE sprang up throughout the suburbs in the 1950s. The design soon was modified by the introduction of "regional suburban shopping centers" containing 1 or more full-line department stores and a host of other stores; that concept in turn was altered by the enclosed, climate-controlled shopping mall, such as SEVERANCE CTR. Later area shopping centers were elaborations on this idea, with RANDALL PARK being the most elaborate locally and one of the world's largest malls.

Shopping centers went up at a surprising rate in the 1950s and 1960s and helped lure the major department stores out of downtown and into the suburbs. By Oct. 1956, according to the Real Property Inventory, Cuyahoga County had 26 modern or modernized shopping centers offering off-street parking; 10 had been built since 1951, and 23 more were built in the next 11 years. Erected on large plots of vacant land, many planned shopping centers attracted other construction and development in housing, offices, and businesses; developers such as the Glazer-Marotta Co. who specialized in shopping malls thus played an important role in the growth of suburbs. By 1966, 3 suburban communities had more than 400 retail establishments, and 14 others among the 37 surveyed had more than 100 stores. Between 1954–72, the number of retail stores in the suburbs increased by 3,079 (80.6%), creating 38,707 new jobs, a 204.7% increase. Large shopping malls, dominated by department stores and chain outlets for apparel and specialty items, are not, of course, the only word in retailing. Other forms of retailing exist; many area neighborhood shopping centers still are dominated by what Alfred Chandler has referred to as traditional business enterprises: single-unit operations owned by 1 or only a few people, dealing in a single product line, and governed by market and price mechanisms and thus highly vulnerable to changes in the market and the economy. But most marketing techniques are variations on old themes using new products (e.g., manufacturers' outlets retailing computers) or adaptations to fill gaps in the marketplace (e.g., the rise of convenience food stores in the 1960s and drugstores carrying food items in the 1970s). Still, there will always be room for the small entrepreneur such as Dan Gray who can see and seize the opportunity to capitalize on new fads and shifting tastes. In the 1970s, Gray turned $600 and the growing popularity of printed T-shirts into a lucrative operation known as Daffy Dan's. By 1980, his retail, wholesale, and custom printing operation had grown to more than 20 stores with more than 200 employees and sales of about $6 million.

Kenneth W. Rose
Case Western Reserve University

Klein, Richard, "Nineteenth Century Land Use Decisions in Cleveland, Ohio" (Ph.D. diss., University of Akron, 1983).
Retail Merchant Board Records, WRHS.
See also MARKETS AND MARKET HOUSES.

**BYELORUSSIANS.** Byelorussia (White Russia) is located in Eastern Europe. Part of it constitutes the Byelorussian Soviet Socialist Republic. Byelorussians have settled in Cleveland at least since the last decade of the 19th century. Numerous Eastern Orthodox churches, ST. THEODOSIUS RUSSIAN ORTHODOX CATHEDRAL among them, were built at the turn of the century, largely by Byelorussian rather than "Great Russian" immigrants. U.S. immigration authorities did not recognize Byelorussians as a separate ethnic group. As a result, during the last decade of the 19th century and the first 2 decades of the 20th, when the great wave of emigration from the Russian Empire was taking place, the immigrants to America were listed as Russians;

but for the most part, they were actually Byelorussians and Ukrainians. Byelorussian immigrants often referred to themselves as *tutejshy*, which in Byelorussian meant "local"; one estimate is that 2,000–3,000 Byelorussians in Cleveland derived from the *tutejshy*. The "locals" were for the most part those who came between 1894–1905. As many did not have a clear sense of who they were ethnically, they often joined Polish or Lithuanian Roman Catholic churches, while others gravitated to Eastern Orthodox parishes, invariably headed by a Russian priest. Byelorussian activities prior to WORLD WAR I were isolated and sporadic. An attempt was made to organize a fraternal insurance association, and bylaws for this organization were published. One group attempted to establish a Grodno-Vilna Brotherhood in 1913, but it also was short-lived. Byelorussian immigrants who came to Cleveland following World War I tended to be more visible. A number lived in the neighborhood of W. 14th St. and Professor Ave. During this period, some Byelorussians became associated with the Communist party, as it was the first political group to recognize Byelorussian ethnicity. During the mid-1920s, when the Byelorussian Socialist Hramada was being crushed in Poland, the Communists stepped up their activities among Byelorussian Americans. Because the Cleveland Byelorussian community sprang, for the most part, from the regions of Grodno and Vilna—areas where the Hramada was especially active—the appeal was strong and, not infrequently, effective.

Byelorussians who had established Byelorussian organizations in Chicago in the 1920s made organizational attempts in Cleveland as part of an active outreach program. Individual Byelorussians participated in the fraternal activities of other Slavic groups in Cleveland; close ties were maintained with both the UKRAINIANS and the CARPATHO-RUSSIAN groups. The Byelorussian community in Cleveland did not really begin to form its own organizations until the late 1940s. Shortly after the war, another wave of Byelorussian immigrants began to arrive. By 1950 the colony numbered over 100 persons, and by the mid-1950s there were over 1,000 new Byelorussian immigrants in Cleveland. In many respects, these immigrants differed from those who had arrived earlier—they were political immigrants and were conscious of their Byelorussian heritage; many had attended Byelorussian schools. The majority consisted of farmers from the western regions of Byelorussia: Pinsk, Brest, Bielastok, Grodno, Vilna, and Baranovichy; a few families were from Eastern Byelorussia: the Minsk, Gomel, Vitebsk, Mogilev, and Smolensk regions. The post-World War II community of Byelorussians in Cleveland numbered 2,500–3,000. The first Byelorussian-American organization in Cleveland (est. 1 Oct. 1950) was a chapter of the Byelorussian-American Assoc. of New York City. The Cleveland group was chartered on 15 Feb. 1951. It carried out cultural and social programs, assisted in finding jobs and helping Byelorussians in Europe, and was involved in political activities. Its goal was to promote an independent Byelorussian state. Other local organizations affiliated with the Byelorussian-American Assoc. are the Byelorussian-American Youth, the Byelorussian-American Veterans, the Women's Auxiliary, the Women's Ensemble, the "Vasilki," and a dance group.

The Byelorussians who came to Cleveland after WORLD WAR II were almost entirely EASTERN ORTHODOX. They could either join the existing Eastern Orthodox jurisdictions or organize their own church. A parish, the Mother of God of Zyrovicy, Byelorussian Autocephalic Orthodox Church, was established and chartered in 1951. The first services were held in a rented hall at W. 14th St. and Starkweather, since most parishioners lived in the TRE-MONT area. A new church building constructed at 3517 W. 25th St. was consecrated on Labor Day weekend 1960. It became the backbone of all social and cultural activities of the community. In the 1980s, the parish signed an agreement with the Riverside Cemetery Assoc. by which it set aside a separate section at the cemetery, and a Byelorussian monument was erected there. In the 1960s and 1970s, many Byelorussians moved beyond the city limits. Movement was largely to Strongsville, where the community acquired sizable property and began to establish a cultural and social center, "Polacak." The center, chartered as a nonprofit corporation, is planned to contain a research library, archives, and an ethnographic museum.

Vitaut Kipel
Byelorussian Institute of Arts & Sciences, Inc.

Kipel, Vitaut, *Byelorussian Americans and Their Communities in Cleveland* (1982).

**BYERS, EDGAR S.** (10 Apr. 1876–21 Feb. 1963), was an attorney and one of Cleveland's most outspoken, but respected, liberals from the Tom L. Johnson-Peter Witt era. A disciple of Henry George, the single taxer, he was a member of the CITY CLUB OF CLEVELAND and "dean" of its Soviet Table. Byers was born in Sharpsville, Pa., and came to Cleveland at age 10. He attended CENTRAL HIGH SCHOOL and graduated from Western Reserve University Law School. In 1901, he formed a law partnership with CARL D. FRIEBOLIN, which lasted until 1947. In 1915, Byers joined the City Club. Sometime during WORLD WAR I, Byers, JACK RAPER, Ed Doty, PETER WITT, and others formed the nucleus of the Soviet Table, an informal group that lunched together at the club. The origin of the group's name came from a humorous exaggeration of the liberal views held by most of its members. For decades, Byers served as an unofficial spokesman for the table by protesting against proposals he thought were contrary to the public interest. He also served as a director of the City Club from 1927–30. In 1924, Byers served as the Cuyahoga County manager for Sen. Robt. La Follette's Progressive party campaign for the presidency. Byers is credited with carrying Cuyahoga County for La Follette by over 10,000 votes; he started the campaign without an organization or any money and spent only $10,000. Byers, however, was unsuccessful when he headed Peter Witt's mayoralty primary campaign in 1932.

It has been estimated that Byers saved taxpayers several million dollars by his protests against the original plans for the Main Ave. Bridge, Municipal Stadium, and many other proposed civic projects. Byers and the Soviet Table were criticized by CITIZENS LEAGUE director MAYO FESLER after they led a successful campaign to eliminate the CITY MANAGER PLAN of government in Cleveland. Byers had objected to city manager WM. HOPKINS's use of authority and many of the city's land purchases during his tenure, including the site that later became CLEVELAND HOPKINS INTERNATL. AIRPORT. Other projects that Byers opposed included the construction of Union Terminal, the claim of several railways to public property on the lakefront, and the 1945 sale of the CLEVELAND RAILWAY CO. To the city. Although many of his efforts were unsuccessful, Byers felt that many of these projects were examples of private interests' benefiting from publicly owned resources. During his later years, the American Civil Liberties Union praised Byers for his legal work defending the civil liberties of his clients and opposing fast tax writeoffs for industrial facilities and the tax credit allowed on dividends from securities. Byers married Birja Wilkins in 1902; the Byerses had 3 daughters.

The **BYSTANDER** began publication as the *Country Club News*, probably ca. Jan. 1921. Strictly social in orientation, the monthly magazine seems to have been run largely by the efforts of female volunteers, among them GRACE GOULDER (IZANT). It became the *Town & Country Club News* in Dec. 1926, when it also acquired Chas. T. Henderson as editor. Shortly thereafter it was incorporated as the Town Publishing Co. by Warren C. Platt and moved to the Penton Bldg. on W. 3rd St. Conversion into a weekly on 21 Apr. 1928 put *Town & Country Club News* in a position to rival the cultural coverage of *Cleveland Town Topics*. Renamed the *Bystander* in Aug. 1928, it began running feature articles on subjects ranging from the Goodyear Blimp to PETER WITT. It absorbed its older rival on 14 Dec. 1929, when it appeared as the *Bystander Combined with Cleveland Town Topics*. Even the volume numbers of *Town Topics* were soon appropriated by the younger publication. Despite the benefits of the merger, the ensuing Depression eventually ate into the *Bystander*'s gains. "Cleveland's Pictorial News Magazine," as it billed itself in 1933, was less than half its pre-Depression size, and its price had been cut correspondingly from $.15 to $.10 cents. Although it started printing some material sympathetic to the New Deal, time had run out for the *Bystander*. Published on a biweekly schedule during the summer of 1933, it reverted to a monthly the following February and made its final appearance in Apr. 1934.

**BYZANTINE RITE CATHOLICS.** Most Americans know little about the Byzantine Rite church. The church came into existence as a result of efforts by the Roman Catholic church to convert Eastern Orthodox Christians in the old Austro-Hungarian Empire during the 16th and 17th centuries. Direct absorption into Roman Catholicism was unacceptable to many. Instead, a new institution representing a union of the two faiths resulted. Initially the name Uniate was used to designate the new institution; later Greek Catholic or Byzantine Rite Catholic church was preferred. The Byzantine Rite Catholic church retained various practices of the Eastern church while acknowledging the supreme leadership of the pope. For example, masses were performed in Old Slavonic rather than Latin; the Julian calendar (rather than the Gregorian) was observed; the Eastern form of the cross (3 crossbars, the lowest oblique) was retained; and clerical marriage was permitted. This latter practice caused an uproar among Latin Catholics in the U.S. with the arrival of Byzantine Catholic immigrants and their married clergy around the turn of the century. A decree in 1907 permitted only celibate priests to be admitted to America. As a result, thousands of Byzantine Rite Catholics defected to the Russian Orthodox church. The majority of Cleveland's early Russian Orthodox churches were built by these former Byzantine Rite Catholics in cooperation with the city's Carpatho-Russian Orthodox immigrants. Eventually, the celibacy decree was modified; as of 1924, married priests could enter the country, but married men could not be ordained in America. Clerical marriage continues among Europe's Byzantine Rite Catholics.

In 1916, 2 separate and distinct ecclesiastical administrations for Byzantine Rite Catholics in the U.S. were established by the Vatican. Reflecting this bifurcation, Cleveland has 2 dioceses, the Diocese of the Ruthenian (Rusin) Byzantine Catholic Church and the Ukrainian Byzantine Catholic Diocese of St. Josaphat, both of which were located in PARMA in 1986. The Ruthenian diocese (est. 1969) has included 11 Byzantine Rite churches in Greater Cleveland. Their membership is made up of Rusins and some HUNGARIANS, SLOVAKS, and CROATIANS. The Ukrainian diocese was established in 1984 and includes a majority of UKRAINIANS with some Lemkos. The ethnic groupings reflect historical divisions in their European homelands. Prior to WORLD WAR I, 2 separate groups existed among the Byzantine Rite Catholics in the Austro-Hungarian Empire: 60% were Rusins (Carpatho-Ruthenians whose region was annexed by Czechoslovakia between world wars I and II), and the remainder were Ukrainian (Galician-Ruthenians whose region was annexed by Poland between the world wars). The political allegiances of the two groups in Europe were different, and the immigrants to America brought with them these same loyalties. Although Rusin and Ukrainian immigrants at first cooperated in the new land, their regional and national differences soon made it impossible to maintain unity, and each group rallied around its own ecclesiastical administration. The oldest Rusin church in Cleveland in 1986 was St. John the Baptist Byzantine Rite Catholic Church. The parish was established in 1898, and a triple-domed church edifice was erected in 1913 at 2036 Scovill Ave. The structure was razed in 1961 to make way for the INNERBELT FREEWAY, and the church relocated to Parma. In 1969, St. John's was established as a cathedral. It is also the site of the Ruthenian Byzantine Catholic Diocese of Parma. For a time in the 1960s and early 1970s, a Byzantine Catholic high school was located on the church grounds. In the late 1960s, student enrollment peaked at 600. The school closed in 1975 and in 1986 housed diocesan offices and a Byzantine cultural-heritage institute. The largest Rusin parish in the 1950s was Holy Ghost Byzantine Catholic Church, with approximately 3,000 members. Its origin dates back to 1909, when west side parishioners of St. John's left the east side church and built Holy Ghost Church on W. 14th St. and Kenilworth Ave. The structure was topped with 3 of the "onion" domes characteristic of Byzantine churches. From 1918–62, Rev. Joseph P. Hanulya was assigned to Holy Ghost. During the 1930s, Rev. Hanulya started the Rusin Elite Society in his parish. He wrote the first history in English of Rusin literature in 1941 and later organized the Rusin Cultural Garden. Under his leadership, Holy Ghost School was built in 1958. Hanulya wrote the required grammar books, readers, Bible history books, and catechism, all in the Rusin language. In 1986, Holy Ghost was still located at its original address, but the school had been sold. In 1986, other churches under the jurisdiction of the Ruthenian Byzantine Catholic Diocese of Parma were St. Mary's Byzantine Catholic Church on State Rd. and Biddulph Ave., St. Gregory the Theologian on Quail Ave. in LAKEWOOD, St. Joseph's (originally at 9321 Orleans Ave.) in BRECKSVILLE, and 4 other suburban churches: St. Eugene, Holy Spirit, St. Mary Magdalene, and St. Stephen. Most parishes were made up of several different nationalities by the 1980s. The diocese publishes a newspaper, the *Horizon*.

Ukrainians from Galicia who arrived in Cleveland around the turn of the century initially joined St. John the Baptist Byzantine Rite Catholic parish. Nationality differences led the Ukrainians to secede from St. John and organize their own parish, SS. Peter & Paul Byzantine Catholic Church, in 1909. The building was located at the corner of W. 7th St. and College Ave., near the Ukrainian immigrant settlements. The church played an active role in community life. It sponsored drama productions and concerts, conducted Ukrainian language classes, and organized literacy drives directed at illiterate adults. Unprecedented growth of the parish following World War II occurred under the leadership of Rev. Dmytro Gresko. In 1947 he started an all-day parish school; a new convent was completed for the Sisters of St. Basil in 1953; and in 1956 both the interior and exterior of the church underwent major renovations. In addition, Rev. Gresko organized 3 new parishes: St. Mary's (originally on Kinsman Rd.) in SOLON, St. Josaphat's on State Rd. in Parma, and St. Andrew's on Hoertz Rd. in Parma. St. Josaphat's, completed in 1959, includes a convent for the Sisters of St. Basil the Great, the St. Josaphat Ukrainian Catholic Elementary School (K-Grade 8), and the Astrodome (a Ukrainian cultural center housing many Ukrainian organizations). The elementary school's curriculum includes study of the Ukrainian language, history, literature, and religion. A church surmounted by 5 golden-crossed domes was constructed by St. Josephat's parish in 1984. At that time, a Ukrainian diocese was established in Parma, and the church became a cathedral. The parish consisted of approximately 1,000 families in the 1980s.

Byzantine Rite Catholic churches identified with ROMANIANS, Croatians, and Hungarians were also to be found in Greater Cleveland. Two of the city's churches that are under the jurisdiction of the Romanian Byzantine Catholic Exarchate of Canton, Ohio, are ST. HELENA'S (founded in 1905 and located at its original address of 1367 W. 65th St.) and Most Holy Trinity Church (dedicated in 1916 at 2650 E. 93rd St., and relocated to 8549 Mayfield Rd. in Chesterland). The Croatian Byzantine Catholic parish of St. Nicholas, organized in 1901, bought a church building in 1913 at Superior and E. 36th St. St. Nicholas was the first Croatian Catholic church of Byzantine Rite in America. It was still at its original site in 1986. The congregation of St. John's Hungarian Byzantine Catholic Church was organized ca. 1892 and 16 years later built a church at Buckeye Rd. and Ambler Ave. In 1954, a new church was constructed on the Buckeye Rd. property, and the first Hungarian Byzantine Catholic elementary school in the U.S. was completed. In the 1980s, St. John's relocated to Solon. A Hungarian Byzantine Catholic church, St. Michael's, was established in 1925 on Cleveland's west side at 4505 Bridge Ave. It no longer existed in 1986.

In the U.S., Byzantine Rite Catholics have generally found themselves to be a small minority in comparison to Latin Rite Catholics. The fact that Byzantine Rite Catholics have their own hierarchy has helped to resolve some of the problems faced by Eastern Rite Catholics in America. However, at times the Byzantine Rite Catholic church has been unsuccessful in its attempts to maintain certain traditions regarded as alien and unacceptable to Latin Rite Catholics. As a result, some parishioners have rebelled and left the Byzantine Rite Catholic church for Orthodox churches or other religious bodies. However, Cleveland is one city that has retained a sufficiently large Byzantine Catholic population to support its own Byzantine Rite Catholic churches and elementary schools separate from those institutions belonging to Catholics of the Latin Rite. In 1986, it was estimated that 8,000 Ruthenians and 6,000 Ukrainians belonged to Greater Cleveland's Byzantine Rite Catholic churches.

Nicholas J. Zentos
Lorain County Community College

C

**CAMLS** (the Cleveland Area Metropolitan Library System) is a consortium of libraries that fosters increased access to the collections of area libraries and coordination of cooperative services among its members. It was established in 1975 under the provisions of a Library Services & Construction Act grant secured by CAMLS's predecessor, the Library Council of Greater Cleveland, an informal group organized in the early 1960s. Approximately 20 public, academic, and private libraries formed the original CAMLS, including BALDWIN-WALLACE COLLEGE, Case Western Reserve University Libraries, the Cleveland Hts./University Hts. Public Library, the CLEVELAND PUBLIC LIBRARY, the CUYAHOGA COUNTY LIBRARY SYSTEM, DYKE COLLEGE, and others.

CAMLS provides interlibrary loan services (members can borrow materials from one another with rapid service), a centralized service for photocopies of periodical articles, a listing of periodical holdings of member libraries, reciprocal agreements for borrowers in member libraries, continuing-education programs for librarians, a professional job-listing service, a radio program, and a clearinghouse for local library information. In 1986 42 libraries (academic, public, and corporate) were listed as members, covering a 5-county area. Several committees, including those for children's services, reference services, and technical services, assisted an executive director and project librarian. CAMLS continued to be funded by a federal LSCA Title III grant and from local membership fees.

The **CIO "PURGE" CONVENTION** took place in Cleveland 31 Oct.–4 Nov. 1949. Delegates to the national CIO convention voted to purge the organization of leftist and Fascist unions and union leaders. A change in leadership in 1947 put Philip Murray and several other right-wing leaders in power within the CIO. In May 1949, Murray issued an ultimatum to 12 leftist unions to follow CIO anti-Communist policy or face expulsion at the national convention in the fall. Those unions representing the left wing, led by the United Electrical Workers, the 3d-largest union in the CIO, demanded the right to remain in the CIO on their own terms and called for unity among CIO unions. The UEW also declared its intention to withhold its per capita tax to the CIO if Murray did not recognize its autonomy. But a meeting of the CIO's executive board on 24 Oct. 1949 further solidified Murray's intentions to oust leaders and unions following Communist or Fascist lines.

On 31 Oct., the opening day of the convention, Murray presented several amendments barring Communists and Fascists from serving on the executive board or as officers and giving the executive board the power to expel such officers and revoke the charters of leftist unions. An overwhelming majority of the 600 delegates approved the amendments. The following day the charters of the UEW and the Farm Equipment Workers' unions were revoked, and they were expelled from the CIO. Plans were made to expel the 10 remaining leftist unions. On 2 Nov. a new union, the Internatl. Union of Electrical Radio & Machine Workers, was formed. Members of the General Electric Corp. and the Westinghouse Corp. in Cleveland were expected to join. Plans were also made for CIO anti-Communist unions to absorb members of the expelled unions. Thus, leftist leaders who at one time had played important roles in the direction of the CIO were purged from its ranks as the fear of Communism began to spread across the country.

The **CSX CORPORATION** was by the mid-1980s one of 3 major railroad systems serving Greater Cleveland. It is the descendant of 2 of the oldest railroads in America, the Chesapeake & Ohio and the Baltimore & Ohio. The corporation is also composed of several railroads that were important in the early history of Cleveland. The CSX Corp. was formed by the merger of the Chessie System, Inc., and Seaboard Coastline Industries on 1 Nov. 1980. CSX is a natural-resources and transportation company. In addition to owning coal fields and gas and oil wells, the corporation operates railroads, barge lines, trucking companies, and pipelines. Corporate headquarters are located in Richmond, Va. In 1985, the chairman of the board and chief executive of CSX was Hays T. Watkins. One of the chief parts of the CSX Corp. was the Seaboard Coast Line Railroad, created in 1968 by the merger of the Seaboard Air Line and the Atlantic Coast Line railroads. In 1971, the Seaboard System gained control of the Louisville & Nashville and Monon systems, thereby giving it tracks reaching New Orleans, St. Louis, Cincinnati, and Chicago. The Seaboard System never had tracks or offices in Cleveland. The other major component of CSX is the Chessie System. It is the creation of the merger of the Chesapeake & Ohio and the Baltimore & Ohio railroads in 1962.

The Chesapeake & Ohio was created by an act of the Virginia legislature on 18 Feb. 1826. The charter provided a capital of $300,000 and empowered the new railroad to lay tracks through Louisa County, Va. In a few years, the tracks extended from Hanover Jct. to Louisa Courthouse, and the railroad became known as the Louisa Railroad. By 1868, the Louisa had become known as the Chesapeake & Ohio Railroad and had tracks running from Richmond, Va., to the Ohio River, a distance of nearly 405 mi. During the next century, the C & O continued to grow. New construction and mergers, most notably with the Pere Marquette and the Western Maryland railroads, allowed it to reach Buffalo, Chicago, Louisville, Milwaukee, and Newport News by 1960. After the merger with the Baltimore & Ohio, a merger with the Norfolk & Western Railway was considered. The idea was dropped shortly after the collapse of the Penn Central Railroad in 1970. A major source of the C & O's income was for many years hauling coal from the coal fields of Virginia and West Virginia to ports along the Potomac River and industries in the Midwest. Although the Chesapeake & Ohio never had tracks in Cleveland until its merger with the Baltimore & Ohio, it was linked to Cleveland by some of the men who controlled the railroad. During the 1920s, the C & O was owned by ORIS P. AND MANTIS J. VAN SWERINGEN. The Van Sweringens entered the railroad business by acquiring control of the New York, Chicago & St. Louis (Nickel Plate) Railroad in 1916. They soon acquired control of the C & O, Erie, Missouri Pacific, and Pere Marquette railroads. Their goal was to create a huge rail transportation system with Cleveland as the hub. The Terminal Tower was to be the building from which they would run the empire. The Van Sweringens lost their railroad empire in the Depression, but the Terminal Tower was built, and the C & O put its corporate offices in it. CYRUS EATON also controlled the C & O. Before he became chairman of the board in 1954, he had made his fortune in the steel and mining industries. Eaton served nearly 20 years as chairman. During his tenure, the corporate offices of the road remained in the Terminal. As many as 265 officers and employees worked there in the 1950s.

The Baltimore & Ohio Railroad, the other part of the Chessie System, was chartered in Maryland on 28 Feb. 1827. Operations began in 1830 on a 14-mi. section of track between Baltimore and Ellicott, Md. The B & O grew to become one of America's largest railroads. As with the C & O, mergers played an important part in this process. Among the many mergers orchestrated by the B & O were several concerning railroads that operated through Cleveland. One railroad was the Cleveland, Tuscarawas Valley & Wheeling Railroad, organized on 2 July 1870 as the Lake Shore & Tuscarawas Valley Railroad. The line was to extend from Elyria, Ohio, through Grafton to Dennison, Ohio. Coal was expected to make up most of the freight traffic. Access to markets for this coal was provided by connections with several larger railroads, including the Lake Shore & Michigan Southern and the Pittsburgh, Cincinnati & St. Louis railways. At Grafton, the Lake Shore & Tuscarawas Valley Railroad connected with the Cleveland, Columbus, Cincinnati & Indianapolis Railway.

The entire line of the Lake Shore & Tuscarawas Valley Railway formally opened on 18 Aug. 1873. The purchase of the Elyria & Black River Railway on 31 Oct. 1872 had added 8 more mi. of track to the system and caused the northern terminus to be at Black River Harbor (Lorain), Ohio. Uhrichsville, Ohio, had become the southern terminus. The entire length of the line was 101 mi. Clevelanders played an important role in the creation and operation of the Lake Shore & Tuscarawas Valley Railroad. In July 1871, WM. BINGHAM, Henry Chaflen, AMOS TOWNSEND, and 10 others were chosen by an executive com-

mittee of the railroad to solicit subscriptions of stock in Cleveland. The president in 1872 was Worthy S. Streator, while Wm. Grout and SYLVESTER T. EVERETT served as secretary and treasurer respectively. The central offices were in the Case Bldg. In Feb. 1872, Cleveland received its first Lake Shore & Tuscarawas Valley coal train. By 1873, there were 3 daily passenger trains leaving the city. Although the road did not have any tracks in Cleveland, its trains were able to reach Cleveland through an arrangement with the Lake Shore & Michigan Southern and the Cleveland, Columbus, Cincinnati & Indianapolis railways.

Debts from new construction and purchases of equipment combined with the Panic of 1873 to push the Lake Shore into receivership in 1874. Following sale under foreclosure, it was reorganized on 1 Feb. 1875 as the Cleveland, Tuscarawas Valley & Wheeling Railway. The new company prospered for a time. Net earnings for 1878 and 1879 were $165,482 and $162,319 respectively. Track had been constructed to reach W. Wheeling on the Ohio River. However, the railroad again went into receivership in Feb. 1882 and was sold under foreclosure on 5 Feb. 1883. It emerged from reorganization as the Cleveland, Lorain & Wheeling Railroad. The management and board of directors included numerous Clevelanders. SELAH CHAMBERLAIN and Worthy S. Streator, both of Cleveland, were president and vice-president respectively. AMASA STONE, Edwin Perkins, and Oscar Townsend were directors. The main offices were in the Merchants Bank Bldg. The Cleveland, Lorain & Wheeling fared better than its predecessors. Net earnings were $366,286 in 1884; $366,021 in 1888; and $346,517 in 1893. The railroad was also able to expand by completing the line to W. Wheeling in 1880 and consolidating with the Cleveland & Southwestern Railway in Nov. 1893. The Cleveland & Southwestern was a 30-mi. line from Cleveland to Medina. Consolidation with it gave the C, L & W a terminal in Cleveland, which was located on Literary St. on the Cuyahoga River. The C, L & W came under the operational control of the B & O Railroad in 1909. In 1915, the B & O purchased the entire system.

Another Cleveland-area railroad that eventually became part of CSX was the Valley Railway Co., which was organized in Aug. 1871. It was to run from Cleveland to Bowerstown in Monroe Twp., where it would connect with the Baltimore & Ohio. Work started in 1873, but a depression delayed the opening of the entire main line until 1 Jan. 1883. The road entered Cleveland by way of an abandoned canal bed on Merwin St. The freight station was located on Columbus St., while the passenger station was on Canal Rd. in the FLATS. Following the construction of a branch from NEWBURGH to Willow in 1894, the Valley Railway fell into receivership. It was unable to meet its debts, and the property was sold under foreclosure. Its successor was the Cleveland, Terminal & Valley Railway Co., which was chartered on 3 Oct. 1895. Soon after its creation, the B & O acquired a controlling interest through stock ownership. In 1915, all of the C, T & V's properties were bought by the B & O.

The Baltimore & Ohio Railroad had become one of America's largest railroad systems by 1915. Its tracks extended from New York City in the east to Chicago and St. Louis in the west. Baltimore, Cincinnati, Lexington, Pittsburgh, and Philadelphia were among the other major cities served. The entire system had 4,535 mi. of mainline track. The purchase of the Cleveland, Lorain & Wheeling and the Cleveland, Terminal & Valley properties was beneficial to the B & O for 2 reasons. By 1915, Cleveland was an important iron- and steel-producing center. With tracks running into Cleveland, the B & O had ready access to a large market for the coal in the Virginia tidewater areas, through which a portion of the B & O's tracks ran. Also, Cleveland's port provided access to other states bordering the Great Lakes. In the Cleveland area, the B & O had 2 main sets of tracks in 1915. The Cleveland, Lorain & Wheeling Railway tracks approached Cleveland on the extreme southwest, running through BROOKSIDE PARK and underneath Pearl Rd. The tracks then curved northward in the vicinity of the Harvard-Denison Bridge and proceeded into the Flats, where they ended in the area between W. 3rd and W. 4th streets. The total distance covered in the city limits was approximately 6.3 mi. The other set were those of the Cleveland, Terminal & Valley Railway; they entered the city limits in the south between Bradley Rd. and the CUYAHOGA RIVER and ran northward along the river and through the Flats before coming to an end on WHISKEY ISLAND. Within the city limits, the tracks of the old Cleveland, Terminal & Valley Railway covered a distance of 7 mi. Beginning in Independence Twp., there was a small branch (the Willow Branch) that entered the city limits around E. 73rd St. and ran for a mile along Mill Creek and Spring Brook to Broadway, where it ended.

The Baltimore & Ohio served numerous Cleveland businesses and industries during the early 1920s and 1930s. Among its largest customers were the CLEVELAND ELECTRIC ILLUMINATING CO., the Grasselli and Harshaw chemical companies, the Otis Steel Works, Sherwin-Williams Paints & Varnishes, Standard Oil, and the Theodore Kundtz Co. In 1915, its general offices were located in the ROCKEFELLER BLDG. The freight office was at 1997 W. 3rd St., while the freight depot was at 1681 Columbus Rd. Passengers could purchase tickets at an office at 341 Euclid Ave. and board passenger trains at the old Valley Railway Station on Canal Rd. The passenger service of the B & O in 1915 consisted of 8 daily trains. Four of these ran along the old Cleveland, Lorain & Wheeling tracks and stopped at Lester and Sterling. From there, passengers could catch a mainline passenger train to Chicago. The other 4 used the old Cleveland, Terminal & Valley tracks. These stopped at Akron and Youngstown before proceeding to Pittsburgh, Washington, and Baltimore. By the mid-20th century, the B & O continued to rank among the nation's major railroad systems. In 1950, the system was 6,188 mi. long and reached from New York and Jersey City in the east to Chicago and St. Louis in the west. In Cleveland, the B & O continued to use the same 2 sets of tracks during the 1950s that it had in 1915. B & O freight trains still served a mixture of chemical, petroleum, steel, and utility companies in Cleveland. Among the most important were the Harshaw Chemical Co., the Natl. Solvent Co., Cities Service Oil, Naphsol Refining, Jones & Laughlin Steel (formerly the Otis Steel Co.), and the Cleveland Electric Illuminating Co.

The road's freight and coal traffic offices had left their quarters on W. 3rd St. and had entered the Terminal Tower in Apr. 1934. In 1954, a new freight depot was built to replace the one on Columbus Ave. This facility had the ability to handle 44 boxcars and 70 trucks simultaneously. Also, by the 1950s, the Baltimore & Ohio was operating freight stations at 8222 Broadway and 4002 W. 25th St. The most dramatic changes however, occurred in the B & O's passenger facilities and services. Since mid-June 1934, the road had been using the Terminal Tower as its passenger station. The old Valley Railway passenger station on Canal Rd. had been changed into a freight office. The city ticket office had moved to 1110 Chester Ave. There were 2 types of B & O passenger trains serving Cleveland around 1950. The first picked up and delivered passengers directly at the Terminal Tower. The only train in this category was the Cleveland Night Express, which provided

overnight service between Baltimore and Cleveland. It had the dubious distinction of being the last B & O passenger train to leave the Terminal on 7 Dec. 1962. The second type of passenger train ran a route from Baltimore through Washington, Pittsburgh, and Toledo to Detroit. Passengers wishing to go to Cleveland had to get off at Pittsburgh. They were then transported to Youngstown via the Pittsburgh & Lake Erie Railway, and then to Cleveland by the Erie Railroad.

As of 1986, the Baltimore & Ohio Railroad was part of the CSX Corp. In Cleveland, CSX owned the 2 sets of tracks built by the Cleveland, Lorain & Wheeling and the Cleveland, Terminal & Valley railways. However, it used only the C, L & W tracks, which run from Cleveland to Lester and Sterling, Ohio. Two to 3 trains used these tracks daily. The C, T & V tracks, which run from Cleveland to Akron, were considered by CSX to be abandoned. While CSX owned title to them and paid taxes, it did not operate any trains over them. The only train that used them was the Cuyahoga Valley Steam Train, a weekend excursion train that takes passengers to Hale Farm and Akron. In the 1980s, one of the CSX Corp.'s major customers in the Cleveland area was the Cleveland Electric Illuminating Co. It operated unit trains that delivered coal to the CEI plant in Eastlake. CSX had an agreement with CONRAIL allowing the unit trains to travel over the Conrail tracks and reach the plant. Another chief customer was LTV Steel. CSX also transported oil and other petroleum products for Sohio. The CSX Corp. in 1986 used several of the old Chessie System facilities in Cleveland. The corporate offices of the old Chessie System, along with those of the coal traffic, merchandise sales, and public relations, are in the Terminal Tower. Because of a corporate reorganization, most of the employees in these offices were expected to be transferred to offices in Baltimore, Md., and Jacksonville, Fla., by 1 July 1986. The other facilities in Cleveland that CSX used included freight stations at 1001 Harvard Ave. and W. 130th and Brookpark Rd., a roundhouse on W. 3rd St., and a classification yard in the Flats. The old Valley Railway Station on Canal Rd. was used as the office of the terminal agent.

**CADWALLADER, STARR** (11 June 1869–2 June 1926), was a prominent social worker in Cleveland during the Progressive Era. Cadwallader was born in Howard, N.Y. He attended Hamilton College, graduating in 1893. He soon entered Union Theological Seminary. Following his graduation in 1897, he came to Cleveland and became the first head resident of the newly established Goodrich Social Settlement, serving until 1905. He worked there with NEWTON D. BAKER, FREDERIC C. HOWE, and other young men who later became prominent in local reform and political affairs. Cadwallader's interest in working with young people led him to assist efforts to establish a juvenile court in Cleveland, a goal that was realized in 1902. From 1902–04, Cadwallader served as director of schools under Mayor TOM L. JOHNSON. His adherence to a no-politics policy in appointing teachers and administrators caused many ward bosses to dislike him. From that position he moved on to become superintendent of the Cleveland Dept. of Health (1908–09) and was a member of the Ohio Board of Administration (of state institutions) under Gov. Jas. Cox.

During WORLD WAR I, Cadwallader served as head of the Cuyahoga County Draft Board, and in 1917 he became director of the Lake Div. of the American Red Cross, one of the largest and most active Red Cross groups. He was a member of the realty firm Stein, Cadwallader & Long, which was the agent for the Van Sweringen brothers in the sale of Shaker Hts. property from 1910–17. He married Harriet E. Gomph in Utica, N.Y., on 30 July 1896; she died in New York in 1935. They had 1 child, a son, Starr, Jr. Cadwallader died at his Shaker Hts. home at the age of 57.

**CADWELL, DARIUS** (13 Apr. 1821–26 Nov. 1905), was an attorney, state legislator, Union Army officer, and judge. Born in Andover, Ohio, in Ashtabula County, he attended county and select schools, completing 1 year at Allegheny College in 1841. After teaching in county schools for several years, he studied law under Benjamin Wade (later U.S. senator) in Jefferson, Ohio, and was admitted to the bar in 1844. He served as deputy clerk in Jefferson and in 1850 as a census agent in Ashtabula County. He served from 1856–58 as state representative and from 1858–60 as state senator, representing Lake, Geauga, and Ashtabula counties in Columbus. Turning down a captaincy in the Regular Army in 1862, Cadwell instead accepted the position of provost marshal of the 19th district, which had its headquarters in Youngstown, Ohio. In the fall of 1865, the 19th district was consolidated with the 14th, 16th, and 18th provost marshal districts, with headquarters in Cleveland. Caldwell maintained this position until the Cleveland provost marshal's office was closed in Dec. 1865 (see 18TH PROVOST MARSHALL DISTRICT OF OHIO). In 1873 he was elected to the Cuyahoga County Court of Common Pleas and served until 1884. Having opened a law office in Cleveland in the early 1870s, he practiced there after his second term expired.

Darius Cadwell Papers, WRHS.

**CAHOON, JOSEPH** (1762–1839), was an early settler of Cuyahoga County. He and his family were the first settlers of Dover Twp. (BAY VILLAGE). Cahoon was born in Rhode Island, where he was raised in a family of devout BAPTISTS. After several moves, he settled in Vergennes, Vt., where he lived until emigrating to the Western Reserve. A practical man, throughout his life he demonstrated a high degree of self-sufficiency. He was primarily a miller, with an additional talent for inventions. These included a cotton compress, a tie buckle machine, a grape hoe (drawn by 1 horse), and a shingle-making machine. In Vermont he had invented a nail-making machine but was unable to procure a patent because of "collusion and fraud" by a patent clerk.

With his family, Cahoon left Vergennes for the WESTERN RESERVE in 1810. To wish them well, a public meeting was held in the village square. Cahoon had visited Ohio in 1799 so as not to purchase land sight unseen. He chose land west of the Cuyahoga near the lakeshore, where the climate seemed more favorable for the fruit trees he wished to plant. The family took the land route to the Western Reserve and in autumn arrived in Cleveland, where they were briefly guests of JAS. KINGSBURY. On 10 Oct. 1810 they arrived in Dover Twp., and in 4 days they erected a log cabin on Lot #95 (north of Lake Rd., at the mouth of Cahoon Creek).

Within the first year, Cahoon planted seeds for apple and peach trees. On 10 Sept. 1813, the family erected the first gristmill in the Western Reserve west of the Cuyahoga. As they finished notching the beams together, they could hear the distant guns of Perry's fleet off Put-in-Bay. Cahoon later built a sawmill, which enabled him, with his son Joel, to build a frame house in 1818. When the fruit trees matured, Cahoon, always practical, took into account the excess fruit and built a distillery for the manufacturing of peach brandy. Cahoon was married to Lydia Kenyon. The Cahoon family remained in the original frame house, Rose

Hill, until 1917. At that time the house was deeded to the community and used as a library until 1960, when it became the Rose Hill Museum. It is maintained by the BAY VILLAGE HISTORICAL SOCIETY.

**CAIN PARK THEATER,** founded in 1934, is an outdoor theater in CLEVELAND HTS. Many college professors have called it one of the most significant theaters in America. It is situated in Cain Park, named after Frank C. Cain, mayor of Cleveland Hts. in the early 1930s. The park, part of the recreation system of Cleveland Hts., encompasses a wide ravine that extends along Superior Rd. from Taylor Rd. to Lee Rd. The theater was built by a group of Italian stonemasons working under the WPA. The amphitheater consists of 3 2-story brick buildings that occupy about 4 acres in the middle of the park. The auditorium seats 3,000 and has an 80-ft.-wide proscenium. The first production at Cain Park occurred in 1934.

Dina Rees Evans, executive director of the theater from 1934–50, offered plays, musicals, light opera, and band concerts utilizing local talent. Subsequently, a theatrical company was formed attracting students from college and university drama depts. By the 1940s, as many as 90,000 people attended during a season. After Evans's departure, the theater began to decline, expenses mounted, and bad weather often caused cancellations. By the 1970s the theater was often empty. In 1975, the Cain Park Theater Assoc. held a party in the park in an effort to revitalize interest in the park and raise funds for the theater. In the following city election, the voters in Cleveland Hts. overwhelmingly approved funding for the partial rehabilitation of the theater. In 1979, United Artists filmed the movie *Those Lips, Those Eyes* in the outdoor amphitheater, installing proper lighting and a new sound system for the theater. More productions were staged in the 1980s. The theater thrives today, a half-century after its founding.

Evans, Dina Rees, *Cain Park Theater* (1980).

**CALFEE, HALTER, AND GRISWOLD** specializes in corporate and securities law, commercial law and financing, municipal law and financing, civil litigation, taxation, labor relations, banking, real estate, health-care law, antitrust law, probate, and estate planning. The firm employed 107 full-time attorneys in 1986 and has always maintained offices in the Society Bldg. Calfee, Halter, one of Cleveland's oldest law firms, dates back to the formation of the partnership of Calfee & Fogg in 1908. Whereas many major law firms have grown through mergers, Calfee, Halter's growth has been internal. Over the years, the firm's name has changed to reflect the prominence of various key partners. Until the late 1960s, it was known as Calfee, Fogg, McChord & Halter. In 1968 it was doing business as Calfee, Halter, Calfee, Griswold & Sommer. The current (1986) name was adopted in 1974. The firm's founding partner, Robt. Calfee, graduated from Roanoke (Va.) College in 1893 and completed his law studies at Geo. Washington University in 1901. He received a Master of Law degree from National University in 1902 and began practicing in Washington, D.C., and Virginia before moving to Cleveland. Calfee and Fogg were joined in 1923 by a young Western Reserve Law School graduate, Edwin Halter, who served as the firm's managing partner from 1956–67. By 1950, the firm numbered no more than 10 attorneys. That year Bruce Griswold, WRU Law School graduate and former law clerk for U.S. Supreme Court Justice HAROLD H. BURTON, joined the firm; he was made a partner in 1951. The firm numbered 22 attorneys by 1962 and continued to grow rapidly over the next 20 years, reaching a total of 44 attorneys in 1972 and 88 in 1982. In 1985 it welcomed its 100th attorney. Major policy for the firm is determined by a 10-member executive committee elected annually by the partners. The average age of its 62 partners is the mid-40s. The firm maintains a strong tradition of participation in community affairs. All members, in addition to their professional responsibilities, are urged to participate in a broad range of educational, social, and charitable concerns.

**CALVARY PRESBYTERIAN CHURCH** began as a mission of FIRST PRESBYTERIAN CHURCH (OLD STONE). Calvary Mission was established in the east end by Old Stone's pastor HIRAM C. HAYDN before 1880. A Sunday school was begun in 1880, and an abandoned wood-frame chapel was purchased and moved from Ingleside Ave. (E. 75th St.) and Euclid Ave. to Euclid and E. Madison (E. 79th) St. A stone Gothic chapel was later built adjoining this chapel, which was then used for classrooms. In the first 12 years of its existence, the mission was served by rotating ministers from Old Stone. In 1892 the church was incorporated as Calvary Presbyterian Church, and the following year it called its first full-time pastor. There were 311 charter members recorded. A larger Romanesque stone church, designed by CHAS. F. SCHWEINFURTH and reminiscent of his renovation of Old Stone, was begun in 1888 and dedicated at E. 79th and Euclid in 1890. By the turn of the century, church membership had doubled, foreign missionaries were supported, and a gymnasium was built. The church served an increasingly working-class congregation as former well-to-do residents of the neighborhood moved to the suburbs.

In 1923 the Bolton Ave. Presbyterian Church was merged into Calvary Church. It had been located on Bolton Ave. (E. 89th St.) at Cedar Ave. By the 1950s the neighborhood had again changed, and an increasing number of black families attended the church. Eventually the ratio reached half black and half white. Ministers and officers of the church responded to the change by involving the congregation with civic and political issues and having the church support various community organizations and city and federal rehabilitative programs. Deterioration in the neighborhood spurred a campaign led by the church to improve the area and pressure the city for building-code enforcements and improved services. A relatively small number of pastors have served the church, including Rev. Thos. S. McWilliams, Rev. John Bruere, and Rev. Roger S. Shoup.

**THE CANAL BANK OF CLEVELAND** was one of several banks organized in Cleveland in 1845 after the state banking system was restructured by the passage of the Ohio Banking Act. E. F. Gaylord, S. H. Mann, and John L. Severance founded this independent bank, which primarily served canal shippers. It opened for business in 1846 in the Merchants' Exchange Bldg. on Superior St., with capital of $200,000. The firm was mismanaged from the start, and it quickly experienced financial problems. However, the adroit measures of Theodoric C. Severance, who became cashier in 1849, kept the bank in business for several years. As absolute manager of the business, Severance changed bank records to deceive state bank officials investigating its condition. Mismanagement of finances combined with the uncertain value of paper money and the rising threat of railroad competition to the canals finally brought about the bank's failure in Nov. 1854. That brought a "run" on the bank by its depositors. Several depositors refused to give in to the bank without a fight. Prominent Cleveland physician Dr. HORACE ACKLEY, a trustee of the new state lunatic asylum in NEWBURGH, demanded the institution's $9,000 deposit. When the bank refused, he turned

the matter over to the sheriff. The sheriff's deputies attempted to break open the bank's vault with sledgehammers until bank officials agreed to turn over its remaining assets to the asylum.

The **CANCER CENTER, INC., OF NORTHEAST OHIO** was a specialized cancer center as mandated by the Natl. Cancer Act of 1971 and 1974. The center was a consortium arrangement between the Case Western Reserve University School of Medicine and the CLEVELAND CLINIC FOUNDATION. In 1977 a third member, the Northeastern Ohio Universities College of Medicine, known as NEOUCM, was added to the consortium. The purposes of the center were to advance and aid the study of the causes, prevention, relief, and cure of cancer, to promote and provide techniques, treatment, and skills relating to cancer, and to engage in the conduct of research relating to cancer. It was to cooperate with other institutions of learning to advise and promote medical, surgical, and scientific education in the field of cancer. As a consortium, the center was independent and dedicated to catalyzing a communitywide effort directed at the cancer problem. It had no beds and provided no care except through member institutions. By a formalized agreement with the Health Services Admin. (HSA), the center provided reviews of requests for new cancer facilities and services in northeastern Ohio, thereby playing a role in city and regional health-planning efforts.

In 1974, the Cancer Ctr. received a planning grant from the federal government and was designated a "specialized cancer center" for northeast Ohio. It also received early and substantial financial support from local foundations, such as the CLEVELAND FOUNDATION, and the State Dept. of Health. The center's community-oriented programs included an at-home rehabilitation program; a cancer data registry system; the Cancer Information Service & Resource Clearing House, staffed by volunteers from the Jr. League; a newspaper column, "Cancer Answers," edited by Paul G. Dyment; educational programs for nurses; and visiting lectureships. The center served as a catalyst and planning agency for hospice activities in the Greater Cleveland area. After its dissolution in 1979, many of these successful programs were transferred to other health-care institutions in the Cleveland area. WM. C. TREUHAFT served as president of the board of trustees; other members of the board at various times were Frederick C. Robbins, Carl Wasmuth, Wm. S. Kiser, Robert Liebelt, Walter J. Pories, and Howard Metzenbaum. Executive directors of the center were Mortimer B. Lipsett (1975–76), Arthur Flynn (1976–78), and Abraham Brickner (1978–79). The center, located at 11000 Cedar Ave., was incorporated on 6 Mar. 1973, formally opened on 16 July 1975, and was legally dissolved on 21 June 1979.

Cancer Center, Inc., Records, CWRU Archives.

**CANFIELD, SHERMAN BOND** (25 Dec. 1810–5 Mar. 1871), was the first pastor of the Second Presbyterian Church of Cleveland, later to become CHURCH OF THE COVENANT. Canfield was born in Chardon, Ohio. He attended Western Reserve College, receiving his master's degree in 1838. Hamilton College conferred a Doctor of Divinity degree upon him in 1857. Canfield spent his career as a Presbyterian minister in Ohio and New York. His first pastorate (1839–41) was in OHIO CITY. He followed his service at Second Presbyterian with a long tenure (1854–70) as a pastor in Syracuse, N.Y. Although not physically prepossessing, he was a powerful speaker. The Second Presbyterian Church of Cleveland was organized around a

151

membership largely derived from the Old Stone Church. Canfield was the unanimous choice as pastor of this new congregation and guided it for the first decade. He was astute enough to realize that limited pew space caused bruised feelings and church divisions in many of Cleveland's rapidly growing houses of worship, so he insisted that the new structure for Second Presbyterian be roomy enough to accommodate an increase in membership; that resulted in one of the largest churches in the city. An ally of SAMUEL AIKEN in doctrinal matters, Canfield chaired an 1841 Cleveland Presbytery investigation into Chas. Finney's philosophy of Perfectionism (Oberlinism). On 4 July 1837, he performed the first marriage in CHAGRIN FALLS. Canfield married his first wife, Delia Slater, in 1836. In 1843 he married Sarah Winston White.

The **CANFIELD OIL COMPANY**, one of the early and most prominent independent oil refineries, was incorporated 23 Dec. 1886 by a former employee of the STANDARD OIL CO., Geo. R. Canfield (1 Dec. 1857–10 Nov. 1920), who presided over the company from its founding until his death. With capital of $25,000, Canfield established his oil company at the intersection of Willson Ave. (E. 55th St.) and the Erie Railroad tracks. Early in 1891, a fire destroyed most of this plant, but it was subsequently rebuilt. The refinery produced grease for lubrication and illuminating oils; another important early product was petrolatum, a substance sold by the pound and used by drug and cosmetic manufacturers as a base for cosmetics, ointments, and salves. Much of Canfield's growth resulted from mergers and the creation of companies by its stockholders, which were later absorbed into Canfield's operation. Canfield merged briefly in 1890–91 with the Cornplanter Refining Co. of Warren, Pa. In Dec. 1894, the Canfield stockholders incorporated the Clinton Oil Co., the first of several companies that consisted solely of company officers and an office staff; production and shipping were handled by Canfield. Other such office-only oil companies included Howard Oil & Grease and Crown Supply. Such organization was later deemed inefficient, and the companies were consolidated into the Clinton organization. In Dec. 1897, the Canfield stockholders founded the Penn Petrolatum Co. in Coraopolis, Pa., and in 1899 it was consolidated with Canfield; the American Petroleum Prods. Co. was founded in Findlay to manufacture grease in 1899, and in 1901 it also was absorbed by Canfield. In Sept. 1907, Canfield opened its second refinery in Cleveland at the intersection of E. 52nd St. and the Wheeling & Lake Erie Railroad tracks. The company opened its first gasoline service station on E. 18th St. between Prospect and Euclid in 1914; by 1921 it had 7 local stations. In 1922, Canfield opened a plant in Jersey City, N.J., to handle its foreign trade. The Depression reduced the company's earnings and forced a reduction in operations. Some service stations were closed, and attempts were made to lease other company-owned stations to independent operators on a commission basis. In 1945, Canfield Oil employed 260 people and became a subsidiary of Sohio. Operating under the Canfield name, the company employed fewer than 100 in 1957. In 1962, Canfield was merged with another Sohio subsidiary, the Fleet-Wing Corp., in order to eliminate duplicated effort and overlapping territory.

Jackson, John A., "The Canfield Oil Company, 1886–1945" (1945), WRHS.

*CANKARJEV GLASNIK* (Cankar's Herald) was a literary monthly published nationally in Slovenian, featuring fiction, essays, plays, and reviews. Literary gazettes had been part of Slovenian literary culture since the mid-19th century. Most SLOVENES settling in the U.S. were literate and sought to continue their language here with newspapers, almanacs, and other publications. A few literary magazines had been attempted in Cleveland and elsewhere, but were short-lived. *Cankarjev Glasnik* was published in Cleveland at a time when Slovenian-American cultural consciousness was at a peak. The nonprofit Cankarjeva Ustanova (Cankar Foundation) had been formed in 1936 to erect a memorial to Slovenian author Ivan Cankar in the Yugoslav Cultural Garden. Louis Kaferle was president, with Milan Medvesek as secretary. A literary monthly was proposed that would espouse progressive principles and appeal to the common man and intellectuals alike; 116 individuals and organizations joined the foundation to support the endeavor, and the first issue appeared in Aug. 1937, with one of Cankar's acquaintances, writer Etbin Kristan, as editor. In addition to subscriptions, funds were raised by events sponsored by the foundation and cultural groups in Cleveland, Detroit, and Pennsylvania. *Cankarjev Glasnik* showcased original fiction and plays by Slovenian-American writers such as Katka Zupancic, Anna Krasna, IVAN ZORMAN, and Louis Adamic. Some stories dealt with the immigrant experience using Cleveland as a backdrop. War commentaries documented events in Europe, Asia, and especially Slovenia. A 1942 article by Adamic provoked controversy for his support of Titoist forces in Yugoslavia. Poetry, political essays and satire, biographical and historical sketches, and literary and entertainment reviews shared space with Slovenian translations of short works by Mark Twain and Erskine Caldwell. It was believed to have been the only literary magazine in the Slovenian language in existence during part of WORLD WAR II. The magazine had never been on firm financial ground, and in spite of its quality, circulation was 1,100 at most. Ivan Jontez served as editor after Kristan's retirement. The magazine ceased publication with the Feb. 1943 issue.

The **CANTERBURY GOLF CLUB** was established in 1921 by John York, Lynn W. Ellis, and several other members of Cleveland's UNIVERSITY CLUB. It is located on S. Woodland Rd., a short distance east of Warrensville Ctr. Rd. Canterbury opened on 1 July 1922 as a men's-only club. In 1923, a women's golf committee forced it to open its course to women. The club is named after the Connecticut town of Canterbury, where the founder of Cleveland, MOSES CLEAVELAND, was born. Herbert Strong of New York designed the original course, which was enlarged and reconstructed in 1928 by J. H. Way, a Canterbury golf pro born in England. In 1928, the clubhouse, which was built in the "Old English" tradition, was also enlarged and remodeled. In 1938, a new outdoor swimming pool, designed by Wm. Pitkin, Jr., and Seward H. Mott, Inc., was built. C. Merrill Barber was the landscape architect for the new pool. Although Canterbury is currently considered a country club, its golf course is one of the finest in the country. The club has hosted some of the nation's most prestigious golf tournaments, such as the USGA Open (1940 and 1946) and PGA (1973) championships. The first president of Canterbury was Julian W. Tyler, and the first vice-president was Willard Fuller.

**CARABELLI, JOSEPH** (Apr. 1850–19 Apr. 1911), a skilled stonemason and influential businessman, was one of the first lay leaders in the LITTLE ITALY section of Cleveland. Unlike many other residents of Little Italy, Carabelli was a northern Italian Protestant. A native of Porto Ceresio, Como Province, he immigrated to America in 1870 at the age of 20, following an apprenticeship as a stonecutter. He spent 10 years in New York City as a sculptor, where he carved the statues for the city's Federal Bldg. Carabelli came to Cleveland in 1880 and quickly established the Lakeview Granite & Monumental Works, near LAKE VIEW CEMETERY. This enterprise soon attracted a large group of stonecutters from the province of Campobasso, who settled Mayfield Rd. near the cemetery.

Carabelli was responsible for the creation of a nursery and a kindergarten in 1895 for the children of working mothers in this neighborhood. With his financial assistance, and that of JOHN D. ROCKEFELLER, the nursery grew into ALTA HOUSE. Carabelli also played a major part in the creation of the first Cleveland Italian mutual benefit society, the Italian Fraternal Society, in 1888. This society served as the model for many other Italian benevolent groups, and by the mid-1890s it functioned as the arbiter. Carabelli went on to a successful business career and was elected to the Ohio House of Representatives in 1908 on a Republican ticket. He capped his career by pushing a bill through the legislature proclaiming Columbus Day an official holiday in 1910.

The **CARDINAL FEDERAL SAVINGS BANK** was formed on 1 Jan. 1974 by the merger of the Second Federal Savings & Loan Assoc. of Cleveland and Cleveland's oldest savings and loan, West Side Federal. At the end of 1981, Cardinal Federal was the 69th-largest savings and loan in the U.S. West Side Federal began operation in 1886 as the Cleveland West Seite Bauverein Co., changing its name to the West Side Savings & Loan Co. by 1911. Originally located at 2621 Lorain, the company had moved by 1916 to new offices at 2025 W. 25th St. In 1948, the company became a federally chartered institution, the West Side Federal Savings & Loan Assoc. of Greater Cleveland. It moved into a new main office building in Fairview Park in 1952. A merger with the Parma Savings Co. in 1967 gave West Side Federal more than $100 million in assets. Second Federal Savings & Loan, founded by Claire W. Grove, opened for business in the Arcade on 21 Apr. 1934. It moved to the Williamson Bldg. at 211 Euclid in Sept. 1934. After 10 years of operation, Second Federal's assets totaled $7.3 million. When it moved to its own building at 335 Euclid in July 1960, assets had increased to $85 million. The consolidation of these two institutions into Cardinal Federal in 1974 created a company with 19 offices and assets of nearly $.5 billion. Although it lost money in the recession of 1981–82 and was searching for a merger, Cardinal Federal had grown to 25 branch offices and $1.279 billion in assets by 1 July 1983. In Dec. 1983, Cardinal's board of directors voted to raise new capital by changing the company from a mutual savings association owned by depositors to a stock association owned by shareholders. The following month, Cardinal announced plans to change its name to the Cardinal Federal Savings Bank in order to reflect its wider range of services.

The **CARLING BREWING COMPANY**, originally incorporated as the Brewing Corp. of America, began operations in Cleveland in 1933. It was established by Jas. A. Bohannon, who had come to the city in 1929 as president of the PEERLESS MOTOR CAR CO. In 1931, after 2 years of the Depression, Bohannon informed stockholders that they could not sell luxury-class cars in the face of such poor economic conditions; he proposed that the 8-acre Peerless plant, at 9400 Quincy Ave., be converted to a brewery. Bohannon contracted with the Brewing Corp. of Canada for the American rights to Carling's Red Cap ale, which had been brewed in Canada since 1840. E. P. Taylor of Toronto became the first president of the Brewing Corp.

of America, bringing the technical and merchandising advice that went with the deal. The Peerless plant, which had been designed by J. MILTON DYER and built 1906–09, was converted to a brewery under the direction of J. C. Schultz, with Ernest McGeorge as resident engineer. The plant reopened in 1934.

After several false starts, including decisions to brew only ale and to package the product exclusively in nonreturnable bottles, the Brewing Corp. of America made an unusually swift advance toward the forefront of the industry. In 1944 it acquired Cleveland's Tip Top and Forest City breweries, increasing capacity by some 250,000 barrels to 1 million barrels annually. Aggressive merchandising lifted sales from 20th to 15th place. In 1944 Bohannon sold his stock holdings to Canadian Breweries, Ltd., giving that firm controlling interest. In 1954 the Brewing Corp. of America changed its name to the Carling Brewing Co. Beginning that year, Carling bought or built 6 additional plants to saturate all regions of the country with its Red Cap ale and Black Label beer. In 1971 Carling closed its Cleveland brewery, idling 385 workers, and moved its headquarters to Waltham, Mass., near its brewery at Natick. Carling president Henry E. Russell cited the brewery's "serious physical inefficiencies which result in excessive operating costs" as the reason for the move.

The **CARLON PRODUCTS CORPORATION** was founded by Chas. S. Britton and Geo. Quinn in 1929 as the Carter Prods. Corp., a metal specialties firm. By 1940, the firm turned to the production of plastic pipe and fittings, and over the decades it grew in the extrusion field to become known as the "U.S. Steel of Plastic Pipe." Carlon, the first company to make lightweight plastic pipe and conduit, introduced this product into a market dominated by copper and steel, believing that the lower cost, lighter weight, unlimited supply, and virtually impermeable nature of their product would win converts among electrical and plumbing contractors. Sales of Carlon pipe reached $9 million by 1960. The pipe was widely used for residential and industrial cold-water plumbing, golf-course irrigation, farm irrigation, urban gas, sewer, and water underground lines, missile parts, and ship plumbing. The company made 12 different kinds of pipe of varying dimensions, extruded from polyethelene, fiberglass, styrene, and other plastics from machines designed by Phillip Britton, one of the founder's sons. Carlon also developed special new techniques for well drilling and pipe laying. As the largest manufacturer of the products, the company set the standards for plastic pipe, offering engineers, code authorities, and builders a reliable guide for choosing the pipe. The company's growth took it from its original location on Front Ave. near the old UNION DEPOT to 10225 Meech Ave. in 1942, and eventually to Chamberlain Rd. in Aurora (Portage County) in 1960. In addition, the company had 6 other plants throughout the country. With the 1960 acquisition of the company by the Continental Oil Co. (Conoco), the corporate headquarters were moved in 1964 to Wilton, Conn., while a branch office was maintained at Commerce Park in Beachwood. When the Indian Head Corp., a conglomerate with holdings in textiles, information handling, and glass containers, bought Carlon in 1972 to enter the electrical and plastics field, corporate headquarters were returned to Cleveland, which was viewed as a leading industrial center and site of many plastics manufacturers. In 1984, the company occupied new headquarters on Science Park in BEACHWOOD.

In the 1960s, Carlon tried to penetrate the electrical market with its introduction of polyvinyl chloride conduit and fittings. It promoted its PVC products as chemically

153

resistant to corrosive fluids, self-extinguishing, noncombustible, nonrusting, and having low expansion-contraction and heat-conductivity values. Sales increased, but Carlon faced 2 major obstacles. First, the Natl. Fire Prevention Agency refused to approve the plastic pipe in the 1981 Natl. Electrical Code. Suspecting that this action resulted from vote packing by delegates representing a major competitor, the Allied Tube & Conduit Co., Carlon filed conspiracy and antitrust actions against both Allied and the NFPA. When in the 1984 NEC Code the NFPA approved the use of PVC tubing for residential construction, Carlon dropped the suit. Carlon also was at the center of a more serious health controversy over the electrical applications of PVC. According to some environmentalists, PVC releases toxic hydrogen chloride fumes when burned. The company maintained that the health threat was minor, especially for products made after 1977, when smoke and toxic-fume retardants were added, and that the claim is a last-ditch effort by the opposition to curb the growing use of plastic pipe at their expense. Despite recent NFPA approval, arguments over the safety of PVC conduit continued to rage in technical journals. Plastic conduit and fittings sales constituted some 60–70% of Carlon's business in 1985. Shortly after its purchase of Carlon, Indian Head itself was bought by Thyssen-Bornemisza N.V., a Dutch conglomerate owned by Baron Thyssen-Bornemisza, a descendant of a prominent West German steel mill owner and famous art collector. The celebrated ownership of Carlon has had little impact on the business, other than to make it (since 1980) a corporate sibling of Predicasts, another Cleveland company.

**CARPATHO-RUSSIANS.** Cleveland's Carpatho-Russians trace their heritage to the upper slopes and valleys of the Carpathian Mts. This region was part of the Austro-Hungarian Empire until 1918. It was annexed by Czechoslovakia between the world wars, and most of it was seized by the USSR after WORLD WAR II. The Carpatho-Russian people have always been a minority in a region ruled by foreign powers. This history of foreign domination was responsible, in part, for a weak sense of national identity among many immigrants. As a result, neither the immigrants themselves nor their institutions were consistent in their selection of terms they used to refer to themselves. Most of the immigrants accepted the designation Carpatho-Russian. However, a variety of terms were used to refer to some of the religious and regional subgroups. For example, early immigrants who belonged to the BYZANTINE RITE CATHOLIC church were called either Rusins or Ruthenians. Immigrants from Galicia (now southwest Poland) preferred to be called Lemkos—a name derived from Lemkovina, a territory in the Carpathian Mts. Religiously, the Lemkos were divided between the Russian Orthodox and the Byzantine Rite Catholic church. Other immigrants who belonged to the Russian Orthodox church, because of their deep sympathy toward the Russian nation, did not use any regional or ethnic designation other than the general Carpatho-Russian.

Carpatho-Russian immigrants arrived in Cleveland during 3 distinct periods, or waves: (1) around the turn of the century (1880–1914), (2) post-World War I (1920–38), and (3) post-World War II (displaced persons). The largest number of immigrants arrived in Cleveland during the first period, the time of a mass migration from Southern and Eastern Europe. The majority were men who came to America hoping to earn money and then return to families in the Old Country. Religious oppression by the Austro-Hungarian Empire also prompted some followers of the Eastern Orthodox faith to migrate to America. Between 125,000

and 150,000 Carpatho-Russians emigrated to the U.S. prior to WORLD WAR I. Virtually all emigration ceased during World War I. After 1920, women and children predominated among new immigrants, in contrast to the earlier period. Families joined husbands and fathers who, despite earlier resolve to return to their homeland, had decided to stay in Cleveland with its diverse employment opportunities. In 1924, the U.S. enacted a national quota system that severely restricted immigration from Eastern and Southern Europe. Between 1920–38, only 7,500 Carpatho-Russians left Europe for the U.S. In the 1930s, more than 30,000 Carpatho-Russians lived in Cleveland. Immigrants who arrived during the third wave of immigration were displaced persons, unable or unwilling to return to their European homeland for political reasons. These immigrants were of diverse backgrounds—some wealthy and educated, others poor and illiterate—but all sought permanent residence and citizenship. Since 1950, the Soviet Union and Eastern Bloc countries have effectively banned emigration. In 1983, approximately 25,000 Carpatho-Russians lived in Greater Cleveland.

One of the earliest Carpatho-Russian settlements in Cleveland dates back to the 1890s, when a group of immigrants moved in among the HUNGARIANS along Orange and Woodland avenues as far east as E. 30th St. As the groups prospered, the Hungarians moved eastward along Union and Buckeye avenues, and the Carpatho-Russians followed. The Carpatho-Russian settlements always centered around churches. Three early Carpatho-Russian churches on Cleveland's east side were the Cathedral of St. John the Baptist Byzantine Rite Church, St. Joseph's Byzantine Catholic Church, and St. Michael's Russian Orthodox Church. All 3 relocated to the suburbs. A second early Carpatho-Russian settlement was on the west side of the CUYAHOGA RIVER in TREMONT. The original Lemko settlement was also in this area, near W. 14th St. and around Starkweather and Professor avenues. ST. THEODOSIUS RUSSIAN ORTHODOX CATHEDRAL at St. Tikhon St. and Holy Ghost Catholic Church of the Byzantine Rite at W. 14th St. and Kenilworth Ave. served the community. These churches were still at their original locations in 1986. By 1906, Carpatho-Russians began to settle in LAKEWOOD. The area extended between Halstead and McGee avenues, south of Madison Ave., and was almost exclusively Carpatho-Russian. St. Gregory's Catholic Church of the Byzantine Rite and SS. Peter & Paul Orthodox Church (Carpatho-Russian) are 2 early churches that were still located in Lakewood in 1986. A large-scale move to the suburbs, especially PARMA, began after World War II. New parishes were formed. Some inner-city churches followed their members to the suburbs. Other times, new Byzantine Catholic and Orthodox churches were established. By the 1980s, most Byzantine Rite and Russian Orthodox congregations were made up of several different nationality groups.

The most important organizations in the immigrant community, after the churches, were the fraternal societies and brotherhoods. They sought to preserve the ethnic culture and traditions of Carpatho-Russians, as well as to provide for their members some degree of financial security. They accomplished the latter through such offerings as life-insurance policies and workmen's-compensation programs. Culturally, they sponsored youth clubs, sports organizations, social gatherings, and publications. Many early Carpatho-Russian clubs for members of the Orthodox faith bore the names of villages in the immigrants' homeland so as to attract former neighbors and create a sense of continuity in the new land. Most of these no longer existed in the 1980s. However, there still were other, national, clubs and groups for Orthodox Carpatho-Russians, such as the Russian Brotherhood Organization of the USA, the United Russian Brotherhood Organization of the USA, and the Federated Russian Orthodox Clubs of America. A newspaper for Orthodox Carpatho-Russians, *Rodina* (The Family), was published in Cleveland from 1927–40. It was written in a dialect of the Great Russian language. Several national journals and newspapers, such as the *American Orthodox Messenger*, the *Russian Orthodox Journal*, the *Orthodox Church in America*, and *Novoye Russkoyo Slovo* (New Russian Word), were still circulated among the Carpatho-Russians of Cleveland into the 1980s. Several fraternal, cultural, and athletic organizations were established in Cleveland by Rusins (Ruthenians). The Rusin Elite Society was founded in 1927 by Dr. Eugene Mankovich and Rev. Joseph P. Hanulya, pastor of the Holy Ghost Catholic Church of the Byzantine Rite, for the purpose of maintaining the Rusin culture and traditions among the youth. In 1935, the organization's name was changed to the Rusin Educational Society. Its monthly publication, the *Leader* (1929–30), was short-lived, but the organization sustained itself until the early 1960s.

In 1892, a Clevelander, Michael Lucak, Sr., helped to found the Greek Catholic Union, a national organization. It sought to promote unity among Greek Catholics who spoke Rusin, to provide insurance for members, and to encourage both academic and religious education. Its early newspaper was *Amerikansky Russky Vietnik* (American Russian Messenger). In the 1980s, the GCU was the largest Rusin fraternal organization. It served primarily as an insurance agency, although it provided scholarships for young people, organized golf and bowling tournaments, and participated in an annual Byzantine Catholic Day celebration (originally called Rusin Day). The GCU's publication, renamed the *Greek Catholic Union Messenger*, adopted an English-language format in 1953 and included but 1 page in the Rusin language. In 1939, an organization was founded to establish a Rusin Cultural Garden in Cleveland's ROCK-EFELLER PARK. As a result of its efforts, a bust of Aleksander Duchnovich, a 19th-century Rusin nationalist, was erected in 1952. It was the first and only public statue of a Rusin leader in the U.S.

Lemkos in Cleveland founded an organization in 1929 to preserve their ethnic traditions and cultural ties with their East European kinfolk. Two years later, representatives of various Lemko associations throughout the U.S. and Canada met in Cleveland to form a united organization of Lemkos. Headquarters for the national, the Lemko Assoc., were located in Cleveland from 1931–39, then moved to Yonkers, N.Y. The association's newspaper, *Lemko*, was published in Cleveland until 1939, when the paper followed the headquarters to Yonkers, where it merged with *Karpatska Rus*. During the 1950s, the local branch of the Lemko Assoc. moved to the Lemko Club at the corner of W. 11th St. and Literary Ave. in Tremont. Over the years, the local organization has published magazines, newspapers, schoolbooks, and a variety of other books in the native Lemko dialect. Efforts to attract young members have been generally unsuccessful. In the mid-1980s, the Lemko Club of Cleveland was sold, and the association planned to relocate in the suburbs. By the 1980s, most of the old Carpatho-Russian neighborhoods had been abandoned, and most of the descendants of the immigrants as well as new immigrants had relocated to suburban areas, the largest of which was Parma. By that time the Carpatho-Russian culture was being kept alive largely through the churches, which, for the most part, had also relocated.

Nicholas J. Zentos
Lorain County Community College

Pap, Michael S., *Ethnic Communities of Cleveland* (1973).
Works Projects Admin., *The Peoples of Cleveland* (1942).

**CARR LIGGETT, INC.**, founded in 1933, grew into a dominant force among Cleveland advertising agencies. It was one of the early ventures in Cleveland to offer advertising counsel to industrial and commercial clients. In 1920, Carr Liggett joined forces with another advertising man, Norman G. Krichbaum, to form the Krichbaum-Liggett Co. Krichbaum served as its president, with Liggett secretary-treasurer and lawyer Cedric G. Smith vice-president. Incorporated with $7,500 capital, the firm was located in the Engineers Bldg., 1365 Ontario. By 1928 Liggett was vice-president of the firm, and in 1933 he established his own firm, Carr Liggett, Inc., with offices in the Leader Bldg., 524 Superior. John A. Dougherty was vice-president of the new firm, and Thos. H. Liggett secretary. By 1937, Carr Liggett had moved to the NBC Bldg., 815 Superior. Liggett served as chief executive officer into the 1950s. On 1 July 1954, he sold his major interest in the firm to Jack Wilson and became senior counsel for the company. Wilson changed the company's philosophy from "copy-contact" to "a creative department agency." The agency added its own art department and, in 1958, its own media department. By 1966 it employed 46 people. In 1969, the company bought Merchandising Advertisers, Inc., of Mt. Pleasant, Ill., and the following year it acquired Rodgers & Co., a Cleveland Hts. industrial-advertising agency opened in 1959 by Robt. C. Rodgers. The latter acquisition increased Carr Liggett's staff to 69.

The firm was expanded further after new president Hal Shoup took control on 31 May 1978. Shoup added public relations, sales promotion, and special services such as HighTech and Creative Studio L to the firm's services. The agency also computerized operations to streamline all of its functions. Under executive vice-president Michael W. Carlton, the Liggett/36 Information System was successfully marketed to advertising agencies throughout the world. Carlton also formulated the agency's growing international operations, moving into global marketing for many clients. In 1980, Carr Liggett absorbed the Roberts Advertising Agency, expanding the employee-owned firm to 83 staff members. In 1984 the agency employed 90 people, and its capitalized billings were $35.3 million. In 1986, Carr Liggett agreed to merge with Lang, Fisher & Stashower Advertising, Inc., to form Liggett-Stashower, Inc. The new company, with 131 employees and estimated billings of $66.5 million a year, is one of the largest agencies in the Midwest. The chairman and chief executive officer of the new company is David L. Stashower.

**CARROLL, GENE** (13 Apr. 1897–5 Mar. 1972), was a prominent entertainer for 60 years. He had one of the longest-running television shows in Cleveland. Carroll was born in Chicago. His first acting experience, at the age of 5, was in the role of Cobweb in Shakespeare's *A Midsummer Night's Dream*, performed at Jane Addams's Hull House. He dropped out of high school and performed in amateur shows to compete for cash prizes. Next he appeared in small-time vaudeville but made very little money. He joined Jack Grady of Chicago in a song-and-dance act in 1924 and became successful. Grady became ill in 1929 and had to leave the act. Carroll then teamed up with Glenn Rowell of Cleveland. The partnership continued until 1943, when Rowell became a personnel manager in a Hartford, Conn., war plant. This act, known as Gene & Glenn, appeared in vaudeville and on the radio. In Cleveland they performed on station WTAM from 1930–35. In 1934, NBC began broadcasting a 15-minute version of the act. The radio show, called "Gene & Glenn," included the characters of Jake and Lena, which were created by Carroll. When Jake was to marry Lena in 1935, crowds gathered around the WTAM building in anticipation of a glimpse of the couple. Carroll and Rowell left Cleveland in 1935. They continued on NBC radio, performing out of Des Moines, Chicago, and Boston until 1943. After Rowell's departure, Carroll continued to perform alone. He appeared on the "Fibber McGee & Molly Show" on NBC for 1 season. He performed his Lena character on the show until 1947. He returned to Cleveland in Apr. 1948 to establish a talent school and begin a television variety show on WEWS. He continued these projects until his death. The television program was continued by his widow. Carroll was married 3 times. His first marriage, to Mary Carroll, ended in divorce in 1934. He married Sally Sage, a blues singer, in 1934. They were divorced in 1937. In 1940, he married Helen Olsen.

**CARTER, LORENZO** (1767–7 Feb. 1814), frontiersman, community leader, and tavernkeeper, was Cleveland's first permanent settler and the most versatile of its early citizens. Carter arrived in Cleveland on 2 May 1797 with his brother-in-law, Ezekiel Hawley (Holley, Holly), and their families after spending the winter in Canada. They had traveled to the area from Vermont. Lorenzo had been born in Rutland, Vt., and at age 22 on 28 Jan. 1789, he married Rebecca Fuller, also from Rutland. Until Apr. 1800, the Carters were the only white family in Cleveland. Other families settled briefly in the area but soon moved to Newburgh and Doan's Corners, to escape the swampy environment. The Carters stayed, however, and built a pretentious log cabin with a garret located on the east bank near the mouth of the CUYAHOGA RIVER. The cabin was used as an inn for travelers, and the garret as a jail. Cleveland's first wedding was performed in the Carter cabin, on 4 July 1797, when the Carters' house helper, Chloe Inches, married Wm. Clement of Ontario. The first social dance in Cleveland was also held in the front room of the Carter cabin, on 4 July 1801.

Carter, a Baptist, was described as a man of "action and energy." Among his many accomplishments were operating a ferry at the foot of Superior St.; constructing the first tavern in the city of Cleveland; and building the 30-ton schooner the *Zephyr*, the first vessel for lake trading (1808). He purchased 23-1/2 acres of land in 1802; 12 acres fronted on St. Clair, and the remainder was an irregular parcel of land on Superior St., Union Ln., and the river. It was here that Carter built the first frame house in Cleveland on the hill west of Water St. and north of Superior Ln. It was destroyed by fire before completion. The same year, he built a blockhouse on the same site, in which was located the Carter Tavern, consisting of a spacious living room, a kitchen, and 2 bedrooms on the first floor, with a large fireplace in the center. Several rooms and an attic were upstairs. Carter also built the first log warehouse in the city, in 1810.

Among the public offices or positions that Carter held were constable for Cleveland Twp. and major in the state militia. He was elected to the latter post in 1804 and subsequently was always referred to as "Major" Carter. The Carters had 9 children: 3 boys, Alonzo, Henry, and Lorenzo; and 6 girls, Laura, Rebecca, Polly, Rebecca (2d), Mercy, and Betsy. Their son Lorenzo and daughter Rebecca died in infancy. Henry drowned in the river at age 10. The Carters purchased a large farm on the west side of the Cuyahoga River in 1810. It later became the property of Alonzo Carter, upon his father's death. Alonzo farmed

the land until it was sold to the Buffalo Land Co. and cut up into city lots. Carter died at the age of 47. His wife, Rebecca, died on 19 Oct. 1827. Both are buried in the ERIE ST. CEMETERY.

**CASADESUS PIANO COMPETITION.** See **ROBERT CASADESUS PIANO COMPETITION**

**CASE, LEONARD, SR.** (29 July 1786–7 Dec. 1864), was an early settler in Cleveland and played a prominent role in developing businesses and promoting cultural and social institutions. The oldest of 8 children, he was born in Westmoreland County, Pa., near the Monongahela River. In Apr. 1800, his parents moved to a 200-acre frontier farm in Warren Twp. in Trumbull County, Ohio. In 1801, Case suffered exposure, which led to a crippling muscle paralysis. For the rest of his life, he had pain in his hips, knees, and ankles.

In 1806, Case was appointed clerk of the court of common pleas for Trumbull County. Later, he became the confidential clerk to Gen. Simon Perkins of the CONNECTICUT LAND CO. and became an authority on land titles in the WESTERN RESERVE. On the side, he studied law and eventually passed the bar, in 1814. Case moved to Cleveland in 1816 when the COMMERCIAL BANK OF LAKE ERIE was formed, and one of its founders hired him as the bank's cashier. The bank failed a few years later, but Case stayed in Cleveland, practicing law and becoming active in city politics. He married Elizabeth Gaylord in Stow, Portage County, in 1817. From 1821–25, he was president of the Cleveland village council. He was responsible for the ordinance regulating the planting of shade trees along streets, which led to Cleveland's nickname "FOREST CITY." From 1824–27, he served in the Ohio legislature, where he drafted tax laws that taxed land according to value rather than size. During this time he was a strong advocate of railroads and canals.

The next 30 years saw Case holding several jobs simultaneously. From 1827–55, he was an agent for the Connecticut Land Bank. In the Panic of 1837, he acquired large amounts of land from debtors who offered it as security for loans. In 1832, Case reorganized the Commercial Bank of Lake Erie and became its president. In 1847, he became vice-president of the Cleveland-Columbus-Cincinnati Railroad, which he had helped start with a $5,000 investment. In the late 1840s, he began turning his affairs over to his sons William and Leonard, Jr. During his life, Case generously gave money to many charitable organizations, including Cleveland's first school for the poor, the Cuyahoga County Historical Society, the Cleveland Medical College, and the city's first lyceum for the arts.

**CASE, LEONARD, JR.** (27 Jan. 1820–6 Jan. 1880), was a prominent philanthropist whose endowment of Case School of Applied Science capped a lifetime of contributions to science and learning. The son of LEONARD CASE, real-estate, banking, and railroad magnate, Leonard Case, Jr., was born in Cleveland and was educated in law at Yale. Sickly all his life, he neither married nor practiced his profession, but devoted himself to scholarly pursuits. Along with his brother WM. CASE, Leonard was a member of the Arkites, a group of prominent Clevelanders who met to read and converse about natural science in a small building (the Ark) filled with specimens of birds and animals he and his friends shot and mounted. Case and other Arkites were instrumental in the formation of the CLEVELAND LIBRARY ASSOC. Case was studious, eccentric, and wealthy, his only extravagance being a stable of expensive race horses, which he never rode because of his delicate health. Upon inheriting $15 million after his father's death in 1864, he regarded his added wealth as a trust to be used for the good of others and arranged for its disposal. In 1859, the Case brothers constructed Case Hall, a civic and cultural center, which provided space for the CLEVELAND ACADEMY OF NATURAL SCIENCES, the Cleveland Library Assoc., and the Ark club, as well as for theater productions and lectures. Case deeded the building to the Library Assoc. after 1876 (with the provision that there always be a meeting place for the Arkites); after 1880, it was known as the Case Library, a repository for valuable scientific and special book collections. In 1902, the library was removed to the CAXTON BLDG.; it eventually affiliated with Western Reserve University. Though Case had little taste for politics or business, he was responsible for creating the Case Block, a commercial building on Superior and Wood streets in 1875. The building provided retail and office space, and was used as city hall (at an annual rate of $36,000) until municipal affairs were relocated in a new building in 1916. The Case Block was razed to make way for the new Public Library building in 1921.

As the culmination of his generosity and love of knowledge, Case anonymously gave $1 million for the establishment of a technical school to teach pure science. In spite of his own classical education, he realized the need for people educated in mathematics, engineering, and chemistry in an industrializing society—an orientation that attracted support from the local business community and permitted the institution to become an important center for industrial research. To provide annual revenues, Case provided that upon his death, the rental income from his downtown properties be diverted to the new school. The Case School of Applied Science, as it came to be known, opened in 1881 on Rockwell Ave. and moved to UNIVERSITY CIRCLE in 1885. Among its first professors was John N. Stockwell, a prominent astronomer whose career Leonard Case, Jr., spurred by providing him with his own personal copy of La Place's *Mechanique Celeste*. The extent of Case's generosity was made known in 1880 when he died at age 60 of lung disease. His bequests to the Case School of Applied Technology shocked city officials, who expected Cleveland to be the heir to the Case Block and its revenues; the city, however, received 200 acres bounded by Willson (E. 55th), St. Clair, Minnesota (E. 25th St.), and Lake to be used for industrial plants and railroad rights-of-way. This area became the city's first comprehensive industrial district. Other beneficiaries of Case's philanthropy were the Old Stone Church, the Cleveland Orphan Asylum, the Industrial Aid Society, and the CLEVELAND FEMALE SEMINARY.

**CASE, WILLIAM** (10 Aug. 1818–19 Apr. 1862), the son of LEONARD CASE, SR., was a prominent businessman, politician, intellectual, and civic leader in Cleveland during the mid-19th century. Born in Cleveland, he received his education locally at Rev. Colley Foster's school and privately (1836–38) with FRANKLIN T. BACKUS. Backus urged him to attend Yale University, but Case chose to attend to business activities in Cleveland. However, he was also ambitious in other areas: in natural-history studies, architectural research, horticultural experiments, politics, and the founding of library and educational institutions. These interests all benefited Cleveland's public good.

Case's career was one of myriad memberships. In education, in particular, he helped form and served as first president (1846) of the CLEVELAND LIBRARY ASSOC. (later the Case Library); he was a founder of CLEVELAND UNIVERSITY (1850); and he chaired the national meeting in Cleveland of the American Assoc. of the Advancement of Education (1851). Case was president of the Cleveland, Painesville, & Ashtabula Railroad, using his business skills to secure the financing that allowed the line to complete its link in the Chicago-to-Buffalo route (1852). He later was president of the Lake Shore Railroad (1855–57). He was elected to the city council (1846) and served as an alderman (1847–49). He was the first Cleveland-born citizen to serve as mayor (1850–52), and during his 2 terms he organized the city workhouse, poorhouse, and house of refuge, as well as the city finances. His large real-estate holdings combined with his horticutural interests in a tree-planting campaign (1852), similar to his father's in the 1820s, that firmly established Cleveland's reputation as the "FOREST CITY." Case was the moving spirit of the Ark, a collection of individuals with a common interest in natural science who formed the nucleus of the organizers of the CLEVELAND MUSEUM OF NATURAL HISTORY. In 1859, he instituted the building of CASE HALL, modeling it on Boston's Faneuil Hall. Case epitomized the faith early-19th-century Americans had in growth and the future as they worked hard to boost their communities. He never married.

**CASE HALL** was a noted concert and lecture hall located in the Case Block on Superior, at PUBLIC SQUARE. Case Hall displaced private residences on Superior and necessitated the moving of the Ark, the meeting place for Cleveland's literary and scientific leaders. Built in 1867, the structure featured a mansard roof, a trend-setting design for future public buildings, and was constructed of red brick and stone at a cost of $200,000. With stores on the 1st floor and offices on the 2d, Case Hall had a 3d-floor auditorium that seated 2,000 on "patent opera chairs" and boasted a decor by the Italian artist Garibaldi. The first performance, by Signora Paradi and Signors Steffans and Bellini, commanded top ticket prices of $2 for reserved seats and $1.50 for general admission. Over the years, Case Hall was a stopping place on the lecture circuit of Horace Greeley, Henry Ward Beecher, and Mark Twain. German Clevelanders held a Peace Jubilee there at the end of the Franco-Prussian War, and English citizens celebrated the Golden Jubilee of the reign of Queen Victoria. The hall was the meeting place of the First Unitarian Society of Cleveland and of the first convention of the Natl. Assoc. of Woman Suffrage. In addition to cultural, social, and religious events, the building housed the CLEVELAND LIBRARY ASSOC. and by 1876 featured animal exhibits of the Kirtland Historical Society. Despite its fame as a cultural center and local landmark, Case Hall was converted totally to office space in 1894, its first tenant being the Citizens Savings & Loan. In 1902 it was leveled to make way for the main post office.

**CASE WESTERN RESERVE UNIVERSITY** (est. 1826) occupies 130 acres in UNIVERSITY CIRCLE and is the largest private university in Ohio. Nine schools make up the institution, which has affiliations with the CLEVELAND INSTITUTE OF MUSIC, the CLEVELAND INSTITUTE OF ART, and UNIVERSITY HOSPITALS. The 9 schools' enrollment in 1985 was as follows: the 2 undergraduate schools, Western Reserve College and Case Institute of Technology, 1,232 and 1,898 respectively; the Franklin Thomas Backus School of Law, 686; the Frances Payne Bolton School of Nursing, 268; the School of Medicine, 566; the Dental School, 363; the School of Applied Social Science, 251; the Weatherhead School of Management, 912; and the Graduate School, 1,880. The school offers over 110 undergraduate and graduate degrees, including 43 doctorates and 5 professional degrees. The faculty numbers over 1,400. CWRU evolved from a college founded by David Hudson in 1826 in Hudson, Ohio. As with many colleges founded during that time, there was more "faith and hope" than monetary support for the endeavor. For several years, the school struggled to keep its solvency and its faculty, who often went without pay. By 1860, 5 years after Henry Lawrence Hitchcock assumed the college's presidency, Western Reserve College was fiscally and academically sound. In addition to retiring the college's debt, Hitchcock encouraged the study of the sciences, bringing, among others, chemist EDWARD W. MORLEY to campus. The Cleveland Medical College, founded in 1843, was then a department of Western Reserve College. Located at E. 9th St. and St. Clair, it had a "distant and sometimes hostile" relationship with its parent institution. Until 1893, the medical faculty was virtually autonomous, appointing its own deans and making other major decisions. In 1893 the board of trustees and the university president assumed those responsibilities.

In 1880, LEONARD CASE, JR., and AMASA STONE made possible an important step in CWRU's development. The first bequeathed a portion of his estate to found the Case School of Applied Science. Stone donated over $500,000 to move Western Reserve College to Cleveland. He also gave 43 acres to both it and the fledgling Case School, so they could be located adjacent to one another, on land that the schools still occupied in the 1980s. In recognition of Stone's donation, Western Reserve University's men's undergraduate college was named Adelbert College, after Stone's son, Adelbert, who drowned while a student at Yale. It retained this name for the following 93 years. In 1888, the trustees of WRU decided to stop admitting women to Adelbert College and established the College for Women. Throughout its history, the school received substantial gifts from affluent Cleveland women. FLORA STONE MATHER, the college's second council president, was so generous that the school was renamed in her honor in 1932. Three of the 7 buildings on the women's campus were erected with donations from her or her family in her honor. From its inception, Mather College was closely linked with Adelbert College. Ten Adelbert faculty members donated their services to the new school for its first 3 years; afterward some professors held joint appointments. But in addition to the liberal arts, the school offered courses in home economics and education.

Thus, in 1890, the university consisted of 2 undergraduate colleges and a medical school. It was during the presidency (1890–1921) of CHAS. F. THWING that the school achieved a national reputation and became a true university. During his tenure, 6 schools were established: the Law, Dental, and Graduate schools, in 1892; the Library School, 1904 (closed in 1985); the Pharmacy School, 1908 (closed in 1949); and the School for the Applied Social Science, 1915. All had shaky financial beginnings yet gained solid academic reputations. The Law School opened with no endowment, dean, building, library, or experienced teachers. But it was one of the first schools to adopt the case method of study initiated at Harvard Law School, and the school's higher-than-required standards quickly put it among the country's best. An endowment and a name came from a bequest by the widow of FRANKLIN T. BACKUS. In 1986, the presidents of the National and American bar associations were both graduates of the school. The Dental School was a department of the Medical School until 1906, when, because of financial difficulties, the university sold it to Henry M. Brown, owner of the Cogswell Dental Supply Co. Though in name the Dental School was part of the university, Brown had complete control, which he used to unscrupulously pass out degrees. In 1916, the university repurchased the school from Brown and invested in equip-

ment and personnel, regaining the Dental Educational Council's top rating in 1922. In 1986, the school was housed in the Chas. Bingham Bolton Bldg., a $10 million structure erected in 1969 and located in the Health Sciences Ctr., between Abington and Cornell roads. The Graduate School of the university initially faced such a dearth of students that in 1921, 29 years after its founding, it was closed. In 1926, the school reopened with ELBERT JAY BENTON as dean, and it flourished. At the Case School, no formal graduate school was established until 1955. However, advanced studies were possible starting in 1930, and the first doctorate was conferred in 1939. Ironically, Case admitted women at the advanced level, but not as undergraduates. Except for several women who studied special programs during WORLD WAR II, the school would not be truly coeducational until 1960.

The Library School was founded by WM. HOWARD BRETT, head of the CLEVELAND PUBLIC LIBRARY and the school's first dean, who saw the need for professional training in Cleveland. Despite a $100,000 endowment from Andrew Carnegie, the school faced deficits annually. But it managed to survive with further contributions from Carnegie and the Cleveland Public Library. After World War II, JESSE HAUK SHERA, dean 1952–70, brought national recognition to the school, especially in the area of documentation and the doctoral program. In 1986, with enrollment significantly declining, the school was closed, despite some opposition from the university's faculty. The School of Applied Social Science was founded at a time when the concept of social work as a profession was questioned. Financial hardship and a continuing doubt about the school's validity plagued it during its early years. Twice the board of trustees considered closing it down. However, after World War II, a new dean, Leonard Mayo, raised endowment funds and erected a new building for the school. Its reputation grew and brought further donations, including almost $500,000 from the Ford Foundation in the early 1960s. The Dept. of Architecture evolved from a course organized by the AMERICAN INSTITUTE OF ARCHITECTS, CLEVELAND CHAP., in 1921 and taught at the Cleveland School of Art. It was incorporated as the Cleveland School of Architecture in 1924, with ABRAM GARFIELD, the architect son of Pres. JAS. A. GARFIELD, as president. CHAS. MORRIS, Philip Small, and CHAS. S. SCHNEIDER were other important Cleveland architects associated with the school. In 1929 the architecture school became a department of WRU. Its traditional curriculum was based upon that of the Beaux-Arts Institute of Design in New York until World War II, after which it came under the influences of international modernism. The department was closed in 1972.

In spite of the numerous new schools founded around the turn of the century and their deficits, the university flourished until 1930, when the Depression and a $6.5 million debt pushed it close to bankruptcy, forcing severe staff and salary cuts. The Case School survived this time relatively untroubled, as the businesslike leadership of the institution seldom borrowed money for expansion, preferring to do without necessities rather than go into debt. The Depression also ended the phenomenal growth of the university's downtown extension school, Cleveland College. In 1925, with financial help from NEWTON D. BAKER, the school had opened with 1,500 students at its downtown building at E. 20th and Euclid. It was dedicated to non-credit adult education, late-afternoon and evening credit courses for part-time students, and a business-administration program that would round out the other programs offered at Case and Reserve. By 1929, when the school moved to PUBLIC SQUARE, the student body had quadrupled to 6,000. But success came to a halt along with the nation's economy. From 1930 to the end of World War II, it was always close to bankruptcy. The GI Bill allowed a brief respite, propelling the school to new heights: 12,000 students in 1946–47 and a $1 million surplus. However, by 1953, the veterans were gone, and the school again faced financial hardship. The university decided to move it to University Circle, where the faculties of Adelbert, Mather, and Cleveland College merged into 1 body. Extension centers of Cleveland College were set up in Lakewood and Parma high schools to blunt criticisms that the school was not accessible to residents of the west side. Extension classes were held at Parma until 1959 and at Lakeland until 1962. In 1947, the Case School of Applied Science changed its name to Case Institute of Technology to better reflect the institution's rank and independence. The school expanded dramatically after World War II. Under T. Keith Glennan, president 1947–66, over $40 million was spent on new buildings, while the faculty increased by 60%. Long a commuter school, Case built dormitories to attract students from throughout the U.S. and the world. The graduate program increased from fewer than 75 students just after the war to 750 in 1967. In 1948, Case established a Div. of Humanities & Social Science, the first among engineering schools. Research grants and contracts increased and became the school's largest source of operating income.

Across Euclid Ave. at WRU, John S. Millis assumed the presidency in 1949, hoping to unify its loose confederation of schools. He initiated the founding of the University Circle Development Foundation, the predecessor of UNIVERSITY CIRCLE, INC. He also integrated resources at the CLEVELAND MUSEUM OF ART, Cleveland Institute of Art, Cleveland Institute of Music, Cleveland Hearing & Speech Ctr., and CLEVELAND MUSEUM OF NATURAL HISTORY into the curriculum at the university. He strengthened ties with long-time neighbor Case Institute and its president, Glennan. By 1960, the schools shared a health service, athletic facilities, and their geology and astronomy departments. Sharing departments was a significant move, because it required the 2 schools to coordinate their academic calendars. In 1964, Millis and Glennan agreed to a complete merger of their institutions and initiated the process that led to the formation of Case Western Reserve University in 1967. A byproduct of the federation of Case and Reserve was the new School of Management. Formed from the various business schools and departments within each institution, it remained nameless until the Weatherhead Foundation gave the school a $3 million grant in 1980, whereupon it became the Weatherhead School of Management. In 1972, the original 3 undergraduate schools of WRU, Adelbert, Mather, and Cleveland College, were combined into Western Reserve College. The school moved toward further consolidation in 1986, when university president David V. Ragone proposed the merger of the 2 undergraduate schools, Western Reserve College and Case Institute of Techology. In March 1987, the board of trustees approved the plan.

Cramer, C. H., *Case Western Reserve* (1976).
CWRU Archives.

**CASSELS, JOHN LANG** (15 Sept. 1808–11 June 1879), was one of the founders of the Cleveland Medical College, now the medical school of CASE WESTERN RESERVE UNIVERSITY. He was an expert geologist and naturalist, involved in the development of Cleveland's iron and steel industry. Born in Glasgow, Scotland, Cassels attended the University of Glasgow from 1824–26. He emigrated to the U.S. in 1827 and joined his brother in Utica, N.Y. He began

the study of medicine in 1830 under Dr. Moses Johnson and in 1831 enrolled at the College of Physicians & Surgeons of the Western District of the State of New York at Fairfield. Here he began his association with Dr. JOHN DELAMATER, professor of surgery. In 1833 Cassels became demonstrator of anatomy, and when he received his medical degree from Fairfield in 1834, he was promoted to professor of anatomy. He also taught chemistry, geology, mineralogy, and botany. In addition to his teaching duties, Cassels began a private practice in Chenango County, N.Y., in 1835.

Following Delamater to Ohio in the 1830s, Cassels became professor of midwifery and diseases of women and children, and professor of chemistry at Willoughby Medical College in Akron. He also served as dean and secretary of the faculty until 1843. He resigned these posts to establish, with Delamater, HORACE ACKLEY, and JARED POTTER KIRTLAND, the Cleveland Medical College. The college was founded under the charter of Western Reserve University, then located in Hudson. Cassels taught chemistry, pharmacy, materia medica, toxicology, and botany for 30 years. He also served as dean. In addition, he taught undergraduate chemistry and natural history in Hudson. In 1865 he procured the endowment for the Hurlbut Professor of Chemistry & Natural History.

As a natural scientist, Cassels had many interests outside the college. He maintained a private chemistry laboratory in the medical school, which he operated for 28 years. His work concentrated on toxicology, and he was often called as an expert witness at criminal trials. He studied food and water, making periodic checks of Lake Erie water for purity. Cassels was also a geologist, and in 1837 he was appointed the first assistant geologist of the New York State Geological Survey. He was employed by Cleveland industrialists to explore the Mississippi Valley for lead deposits, and in 1846, he claimed large deposits of iron ore on the southern shore of Lake Superior. This 1 sq. mi. of land, known as Cleveland Mountain, provided the city with the ore necessary to begin its iron and steel industries.

Cassels lectured publicly and contributed to many journals. He was made a corresponding member of the Imperial Royal Geological Institute of Vienna in 1861. He was a member of the Ohio State Medical Society and a curator and trustee for life of the CLEVELAND ACADEMY OF NATURAL SCIENCE. He never practiced medicine privately in Cleveland. Felled by a stroke in 1873, Cassels retired and was made professor emeritus of WRU. He was married in 1838 to Cornelia Olin of Vermont; they had 1 daughter.

**CASTLE, WILLIAM BAINBRIDGE** (30 Nov. 1814–28 Feb. 1872), was a businessman who served as mayor of OHIO CITY and Cleveland. He was born in Essex, Vt. In 1815, Castle's father, an architect, moved the family to Toronto, where he designed the Ontario Parliament Bldg. The family settled on a Cleveland farm in 1827 (one source indicates 1832). Later that year, Castle, his father, and Chas. Giddings opened the first lumberyard in Cleveland. Upon his father's death in either 1829 or 1832, Castle returned to Ontario and engaged in merchandising and manufacturing. In 1839, he moved to Ohio City; the next year he formed the hardware partnership of Castle & Field. Castle joined the CUYAHOGA STEAM FURNACE CO. as an accountant in 1843. He rose through the ranks and became manager of the firm upon the death of Elisha T. Sterling in 1859. During Castle's tenure, the company became an important ironmaking concern in Cleveland. Castle was associated with the company until his death.

For many years, Castle was a member of the Ohio City Common Council. He served as mayor of Ohio City in 1853–54; as mayor, he was a member of the special commission that wrote the 1854 agreement that merged Ohio City into Cleveland. Upon consolidation of the two cities, Castle resigned as mayor. In 1855, he was elected mayor of the consolidated city of Cleveland as a Whig. As mayor, Castle played a major role in the cutting of a shorter channel between Lake Erie and the Cuyahoga, which opened the river to larger ships; he also was a major participant in the building of a suitable harbor on the lakefront for the city. He supported reducing the city's debt and tax levels. He was a promoter and trustee of the city's waterworks, which went into operation in 1856. Castle was defeated for reelection in 1857. His last political activity came when he served as an at-large delegate to the 1868 Republican Natl. Convention. Castle had many other business interests. He was a member and director of the finance boards of the Peoples Gas & Light Co., the Citizens' Savings & Loan Co., and various railroads. Castle married twice. In 1836, he married Mary Derby; she died a year later. In 1840, he married Mary Newell; the Castles had 1 son and 3 daughters.

*William B. Castle (1872).*

**CASTO, FRANK M.** (30 May 1875–25 April 1965), was a noted dentist and educator at the Western Reserve University Dental School from 1904–37. Casto was born in Blanchester, Ohio, to Jas. Monroe and Margaret Watkins Casto. After attending Blanchester High School, he graduated from the Ohio State University Dental School with the D.D.S. degree in 1898, from the OSU Medical School with the M.D. degree in 1900, and from the OSU Pharmacy School with the Ph.D. degree in 1902. As a junior in dental school, Casto passed the Ohio state dental boards; he opened a private practice in 1897 in Plain City, Ohio. He began his teaching career in 1899 as an instructor at the OSU Dental School. In 1904 he was appointed professor of orthodontics at the WRU Dental School, where he organized its first orthodontic clinic. In 1917, when Casto was appointed dean of the Reserve Dental School, dental schools demanded only a high school education of their first-year students. During his tenure as dean, the program of instruction was raised to a 4-year curriculum. In 1922, WRU raised its entrance requirement to 1 year of college. By the time of Casto's retirement in 1937, WRU and all the country's leading dental schools demanded at least 2 years of preprofessional college training for admission. Casto also maintained a private practice in Cleveland and served as president of the local and state dental societies. He married Florence M. Andrus on 20 Feb. 1902 and had 3 children, William, Ruth, and Florence. Awarded emeritus status in 1937, Casto moved to California, where he practiced dentistry and medicine with his son.

The **CATARACT HOUSE**, a popular hotel, restaurant, and hostelry, was a landmark in the NEWBURGH area for many years. Located on the falls or cataract (hence the name) of MILL CREEK, the hotel was built in 1840 by Wm. Bergin. Attractive to patrons of nearby mills, the Cataract House was a favorite local eatery and meeting place, and a stopping place for visitors to NEWBURGH. When the wooden structure burned to the ground in 1852, the town gave Bergin the money to rebuild. The new building was more fire-resistant; the 3-story brick structure with an iron balcony over the doorway outlasted a succession of owners.

Beginning in 1852, the hotel was the site of balls and other festivities, which the new owner promoted in conjunction with an early version of the "getaway weekend" by encouraging guests to take the train to Newburgh for the affair and return home the next morning. The idea caught on; in the 1860s, the Cataract House ran a bus from the "dummy railroad" station to the hotel. Throughout its history, the hotel retained its name, except for a 10-year period from 1866–76, when it was known as Spencer House after its then-current owner. In 1905, the Pennsylvania Railroad bought the site of the Cataract House, as the company planned to level the falls and reroute Mill Creek for a new right-of-way. The hotel, however, continued to operate until ca. 1917, when the building was renovated for the South End Motor Co. The Cataract House premises were razed in 1931.

**CATHCART, WALLACE HUGH** (2 Apr. 1865–6 Sept. 1942), prominent bibliophile, is best known for his association with the WESTERN RESERVE HISTORICAL SOCIETY of Cleveland, first as its president (1907–13) and then as its director (1913–42). Totally devoted to the society and to the cultural life of Cleveland, he acquired many of his library's finest manuscript collections. His leadership made the WRHS one of the finest such institutions in the country. Born and raised in neighboring Elyria, Ohio, Cathcart first became fascinated with books as a bookstore clerk. As a student at Denison University, he served as librarian. Upon his graduation in 1890, he came to Cleveland to aid a book-dealing company, Taylor & Austin, during the holiday rush. He soon became secretary of the company and remained there for 7 years before joining the Burrows Bros. Co., a prosperous book dealer, where he quickly ascended from secretary to vice-president and general manager. As a prominent member of the book trade, Cathcart was one of the founders and later vice-president of the American Booksellers & Publishers Assoc.

Cathcart also was a civic and religious leader. He served as an officer in several of Cleveland's civic and mercantile organizations and as president of the Baptist City Mission Society for 7 years. His civic-mindedness and love of books attracted him to the WRHS. He acted as the organization's secretary for 3 years (1894–97). His continual commitment to the society was rewarded in 1907 when he was selected as president. Six years later he became the society's first full-time director when he resigned from Burrows Bros. As a book collector, Cathcart concentrated his energies in developing one of the best historical libraries in the nation. He spent the next 3 decades attempting to find and acquire early manuscripts and newspapers to enhance the research potential of the library. Many major, comprehensive collections were acquired. One of the most important was the Cathcart Shaker collection. It is considered the finest such collection in existence, with manuscripts and publications from 19 Shaker communities in 8 states, dating back to 1776. In addition to expanding the society's library, Cathcart gave attention to its other functions during his directorship. He expanded its educational and cultural programs and participated in the movement of both the museum and the library to new locations on East Blvd. in the late 1930s. His death in 1942 was seen as a great loss to Cleveland's cultural community. Cathcart and his wife, Elsie, raised 2 daughters, Genevieve and Evelyn.

*In Memory of Wallace Hugh Cathcart,* WRHS (1942).
Wallace Hugh Cathcart Papers, WRHS.

**CATHEDRAL LATIN SCHOOL** was a Catholic college preparatory school for boys that operated in UNIVERSITY

CIRCLE from 1916–79. It was founded by Bp. JOHN P. FARRELLY in 1916 on land at the corner of Euclid Ave. and East Blvd., with its administration building at 11105 Euclid (later Hitchcock Hall of CASE WESTERN RESERVE UNIVERSITY). The school name derived in part from Boston Latin School in Massachusetts; it was named "Cathedral" because it was located near where the Catholic diocese planned to build a cathedral on the present site of SEVERANCE HALL. The new school enrolled 130 students in 1916. Dr. Edward A. Mooney, who later became a priest and then cardinal-archbishop of Detroit, served as the school's first president (1916–22). The academic year was divided into 6 6-week periods, and for the first 6 years of the school's operation, diocesan priests taught academic subjects and religion, while scientific courses were taught by Brothers of the Society of Mary (Marianists) from Dayton, Ohio.

In the fall of 1918, the school moved into its new quarters at 2056 E. 107th St., and at the end of the academic year, 7 students graduated in its first class. In 1922 the Society of Mary took over complete operation of the school, which had 750 students. During the 1920s the school established a number of extracurricular activities, such as a newspaper (1923) and the band (1928), and began to develop a strong athletic program. In 1929–30 the first major expansion of facilities occurred, with construction of a gymnasium and additional classrooms.

By its 25th anniversary, in 1941, Cathedral Latin had 850 students and a faculty of 35. Enrollment peaked at 1,200 in the mid-1960s. In 1967 the school severed its 30-year membership in the East Senate athletic league, in which it had become a dominant force, because of financial losses in league play. Other programs in the late 1960s were designed to strengthen the school: it joined the University Circle Development Foundation in 1968, and in 1969 it launched a scholarship fundraising drive, bought land for new facilities, and reached agreements with neighboring CWRU that enabled its students to participate in CWRU computer, biology, and music programs.

By the late 1970s, declining enrollments and rising costs jeopardized the future of the school. Enrollment had fallen to 365 in 1979, and on 20 Feb., the Society of Mary announced that it would close the school at the end of the academic year. Parents and alumni formed the Committee for the Continuance of Cathedral Latin, chaired by Frank Vitale, and made plans to operate the school under a nonprofit corporation, but Bp. Jas. A. Hickey rejected their plan. The Cleveland Catholic Diocese sold the Cathedral Latin School property to the state of Ohio for about $500,000 in 1980; the land was to be used as the site of a new worker rehabilitation center.

The **CATHERINE HORSTMANN HOME,** 2155 Overlook Rd., was established to provide shelter and training for "young women who are dependent through no fault of their own." The Catherine Horstmann Society was founded in 1907 by Antoinette Callaghan and a small group of Catholic women. Callaghan was the wife of Hon. Thos. Callaghan, the first juvenile judge of Cleveland, who was distressed by the fact that as young women came to Cleveland from the farming communities to seek employment, they were often arrested for vagrancy; and as judge, he had to either remand them to jail or try to find them quarters at the Salvation Army Rescue Home. Those for whom facilities could not be found frequently ended up as victims of would-be employers. The society believed that through the establishment of a home, shelter and training could be provided for these young women, who could then take a rightful place in the community. The society approached

Bp. IGNATIUS F. HORSTMANN of the Cleveland Catholic Diocese, who approved their intentions with enthusiasm and a promise of support should it be needed. In gratitude for the bishop's unrestrictive acceptance of their plan, they named the society after his mother. The SISTERS OF THE GOOD SHEPHERD cooperated with the society, and in the first year, 40 girls were given shelter. The society had a paid worker at UNION DEPOT to meet incoming trains and to direct those who were indigent to temporary quarters. After several moves on the west side of Cleveland, the society was able to purchase a large home and grounds on the east side in 1950, where the home was still maintained in 1985. In 1969, the Welfare Fed. notified the society that it could no longer fund the Catherine Horstmann Home unless it merged with Family & Children's Services of Catholic Charities. Refusing to surrender its autonomy, the society withdrew from financial participation with the Welfare Fed. In Aug. 1969, the society closed its doors to the type of service it had been rendering since its inception, and after an eloquent presentation by Dr. Jane Kessler of CASE WESTERN RESERVE UNIVERSITY on the need for a home for retarded working women, the society, after meeting the requirements of the state of Ohio, found that in providing their unique approach to the retarded, they were again fulfilling their founder's purpose of caring for women "who are dependent through no fault of their own."

**CATHOLIC CEMETERIES.** *See* **ROMAN CATHOLIC CEMETERIES**

The **CATHOLIC CHARITIES CORPORATION** is the official fundraising agency for the Catholic Diocese of Cleveland. It was incorporated by the state of Ohio on 8 Apr. 1919 and today has a board of trustees comprising 213 laymen representing 90 parishes. The idea for the corporation came about during a meeting in 1918 between Fr. Chas. Hubert LeBlond, first diocesan director of Catholic charities, and Herman J. Trenkamp, a prominent Catholic businessman. They agreed that a group of Catholic laymen, organized for the purpose of raising funds, could relieve the problems of the diocese's growing annual deficit and its inability to expand its building program for shelter of needy people. The Catholic Charities Appeal, conducted annually, is the corporation's major fundraising activity. The first appeal raised $79,000. In 1957, the $1 million mark was reached; over $2 million was donated to the charity in 1980, and over $4.7 million in 1981. Funds from the appeal are distributed among social-service programs, programs for the aged, child and youth services, and such special programs as hunger centers, scholarships, and camps.

The *CATHOLIC UNIVERSE BULLETIN,* the official organ of the Roman Catholic Diocese of Cleveland, first appeared on 4 July 1874, as the *Catholic Universe.* Established by Bp. RICHARD GILMOUR, it began with a subscription list purchased from the *Celtic Index,* a failing clerical weekly from the Youngstown area. It was first edited by Rev. Thos. P. Thorpe, followed by layman MANLY TELLO, but Bp. Gilmour remained its guiding spirit. He subsidized it from his private means and those of his friends and even placed an early rival, the *Catholic Knight,* under interdict.

Upon Gilmour's death in 1891, the *Universe* came under the control of a private stock company owned by the diocese and individual laymen and priests. Editor Jas. Connelly resigned in the wake of criticism over his opposition to the SPANISH-AMERICAN WAR, whereupon Rev. Wm. F. McMahon, one of the shareholders, assumed the editorship in 1898. A new rival appeared in 1911, when the

*Catholic Bulletin* was begun as an education organ of the diocese's Catholic Young Men's Clubs. Within a few years, the *Bulletin* had broadened its appeal and outstripped the *Universe* in circulation. Under Bp. JOSEPH SCHREMBS, the two papers were merged into the *Catholic Universe Bulletin* on 28 May 1926. Ownership of the paper was vested in the Catholic Press Union, a nonprofit organization owned by the Diocese of Cleveland, which also began publishing diocesan papers for Toledo (*Chronicle*, 1934) and Youngstown (*Exponent*, 1944). A. G. Wey, business manager of the *Universe Bulletin* since the merger, also served as general manager of the Catholic Press Union until his retirement in 1967.

As the country and the Catholic church emerged from WORLD WAR II into the postwar baby boom, the *Universe Bulletin* reached its apogee. For 4 years, from 1951–54, it was judged the best Catholic paper in the country by the national Catholic Press Union, and at the end of 1963 its circulation peaked at 122,468. In the backlash against the Vatican II reforms and the civil-rights movement, circulation fell nearly 50,000 by 1972, although the *Universe Bulletin*'s strong stand for civil rights had brought it several interdenominational awards. Although circulation has held around 70,000, rising printing and postage costs caused the *Universe Bulletin* to convert to tabloid format in the 1970s and to switch from weekly to biweekly publication on 30 Apr. 1982. In editorial policy, it never endorses candidates, and it conforms to the bishop's stand on issues. Edgar V. Barmann became editor in 1974.

**CATHOLICS, ROMAN.** The history of Roman Catholicism in Cleveland has generally followed the patterns of the American Catholic experience in other industrial cities in the Midwest. The city's Catholic population grew dramatically in the 19th and early 20th centuries, especially as a result of European immigration. It then leveled off and declined as the city's industrial economy began to deteriorate after WORLD WAR II. Diocesan administrators successfully met the enormous financial challenges of providing churches, schools, and a wide variety of social-service institutions that these usually poor newcomers needed. They also met the challenge of enforcing discipline on an often fractious laity and clergy, though often only after numerous confrontations, many of which were the result of the insistent demands of ethnic groups for their own churches and schools regardless of the high cost of duplicate facilities. And Cleveland's bishops gradually established a modern administrative structure to control their increasingly complex organization. Vibrant inner-city parishes and schools, most organized along nationality and language lines rather than geography, were the heart of Cleveland Catholic life. But especially after World War II, their preeminence and, for some, their very existence were eroded as Catholics increasingly abandoned their ethnic heritage and trekked to the suburbs. And, indeed, the postwar years, marked by the currents unleashed by the 2d Vatican Council and the upheavals in American society generally in the 1960s, challenged much that was familiar to Cleveland's Catholics.

The first significant number of Catholics in Cleveland were German and especially Irish immigrants who came in the late 1820s and 1830s to work on the construction and maintenance of the OHIO & ERIE CANAL and in the commercial businesses that rapidly developed. Attended initially by itinerant missionaries, Catholics received the services of the city's first permanent priest in 1835 and the benefits of the city's first permanent Catholic church building, St. Mary's, located on the Flats, which was dedicated in 1840. There were soon a sufficient number of Catholics

that the Diocese of Cleveland (encompassing the northern third of Ohio until the creation of the separate dioceses of Toledo in 1910 and Youngstown in 1943) was erected in 1847. Its first bishop was LOUIS AMADEUS RAPPE (1847–70), who moved quickly to establish the institutional foundations of the new diocese. Within the city of Cleveland, 16 new parishes were erected, most of which soon possessed a parochial school. By 1872, approximately 4,700 students attended the parish schools, which were staffed by nuns whom Rappe had persuaded to come from Europe. Shortly after his arrival in Cleveland, the bishop founded ST. MARY'S SEMINARY for the training of priests, and, believing that Catholics should be cared for in their own facilities in order to safeguard their religion, he began the development of a growing network of Catholic institutions, including St. Vincent Charity Hospital. The success of Bp. Rappe's foundation work in Cleveland, however, was marred by a series of disruptions in the diocese. Believing that immigrants should be Americanized as quickly as possible, Rappe at first refused to erect ethnic parishes, a decision that angered the GERMANS, who complained to Rome so loudly that he was forced reluctantly to alter course and build separate churches for them. By the 1860s, he had stirred many IRISH to a frenzy by, among other steps, appointing French-speaking priests to their parishes. He had also disciplined a number of priests, who, feeling ill-treated, complained to an increasingly exasperated Rome, which forced Rappe to resign as bishop in 1870.

During the tenures of Bps. RICHARD GILMOUR (1872–91) and IGNATIUS F. HORSTMANN (1892–1908), the Catholic population of Cleveland continued to grow rapidly, primarily as a consequence of the flood of job-seeking immigrants, now increasingly from Southern and Eastern rather than Northern and Western Europe. The number of parishes, parochial schools, and social-welfare institutions grew correspondingly. Greater Cleveland's approximately 14 parishes in 1870 numbered 65 at the time of Bp. Horstmann's death in 1908, including more than 34 nationality ones, and even some of the territorial parishes were Irish in fact if not in name. Both Gilmour and Horstmann insisted on the obligation of parishes to build a schoolhouse, even before the construction of the church building, and on the obligation of parents to send their children to Catholic schools. Teaching sisters were encouraged to come to Cleveland, and, especially with the establishment of a diocesan school board in 1887, significant efforts were made to set and maintain standards so that parents would be assured that the quality of parish schools was at least equal to that of public institutions. There were 7,500 students enrolled in the city's parish schools in 1890; more than 20,000 were registered by 1909. These efforts to build a high-quality Catholic school system, however, did not occur without controversy. Indeed, Gilmour's insistence on parochial schools was in part stimulated by his belief that public schools were certainly Protestant and occasionally anti-Catholic. It was, in fact, Gilmour's awareness of nativist sentiment in the city that caused him as early as 1874 to found the *Catholic Universe*, both to publish news of special interest to Catholics and to defend their values against Cleveland's frequently anti-Catholic newspapers, especially Edwin Cowles's *CLEVELAND LEADER*. Nativism, indeed, had a strong following in Cleveland throughout the 19th century. Know-Nothingism flared in the 1850s, and anti-Catholic speakers always drew large audiences, but anti-Catholic sentiment was never as powerful or violent as in such cities as Philadelphia and Cincinnati.

If the growth of Cleveland Catholicism was occasionally marred by the attacks of nativists from without, its internal unity continued to be disrupted by divisions from within, as was the case in Chicago, Detroit, and Milwaukee, among other cities. Nationalities battled one another for control of church property, and they often made requests for separate institutions that the church administration could not satisfy. The danger of schism was thus ever present, and occasionally it was realized, as at St. Stanislaus parish in the early 1890s, where factionalism eventually resulted in 1894 in the formation of the schismatic IMMACULATE HEART OF MARY CHURCH. And factions of German and Irish priests, which had first appeared in Bp. Rappe's time, continued to disrupt the diocese. It was Bp. JOHN P. FARRELLY (1909-21) who brought Cleveland Catholicism into the modern era. A forceful administrator, he would simply not tolerate continued Irish/German bickering and interference in diocesan affairs. And although he was never able to eliminate it entirely, he significantly reduced its force. Especially significant, Farrelly sought to bring structure and administrative order to his diocese. Roman-trained and deferential to Roman authority, Farrelly personified a broad change in the style of episcopal leadership that occurred throughout the American church. Like his counterparts in Boston and Chicago, he would brook no opposition from either clergy or laity, and he sought to create in Cleveland the type of centralized control and bureaucratic management systems that increasingly characterized the operations of business and government as well as the Catholic church. Building on the work of his predecessors, he went a long way toward unifying and standardizing the parochial schools and teacher training on a diocesan scale. Numerous episcopal agencies and bureaus were established, including the CATHOLIC CHARITIES CORP. in 1919. The result was an administrative structure more adequate for the needs of an increasingly complex diocese.

Between 1909 and World War II, both Bps. Farrelly and JOSEPH SCHREMBS (1921-45) continued to broaden the facilities and programs that served Cleveland's Catholics. Except during the Depression, parochial school attendance grew, and resources on a large scale were devoted to establishing secondary schools and colleges for both men and women. The number of parishes in the city continued to increase, reaching about 90 in 1947. But more important than the expansion itself was its changing character. First, new parishes were increasingly territorial rather than national, because the restrictive immigration laws of the 1920s and then the Depression virtually halted the influx of newcomers at the same time that the earlier arrivals' American-born children, whose primary language was usually English, gradually came to dominate Cleveland Catholicism. And they frequently preferred to join territorial rather than nationality parishes. Second, new parishes were generally located on the edges of the city or in the suburbs as Catholics moved outward from older neighborhoods. Cleveland Catholics were not concerned, however, only with bricks and mortar. Like other Catholics, they participated increasingly in the activities of what was in fact a nationwide church and confronted the social and ideological issues that frequently agitated it. Bp. Schrembs was instrumental in the formation of the Natl. Catholic Welfare Conference, and in 1924 local units of the Natl. Conference of Catholic Men, as well as Catholic Women, were inaugurated. In 1935, the 7TH NATL. EUCHARISTIC CONGRESS was held in the city. Cleveland Catholics reacted to the impact of the Depression in a variety of ways, most supporting Franklin D. Roosevelt, others Dorothy Day and the Catholic Worker movement, and some the controversial Fr. Chas. E. Coughlin of Royal Oak, Mich. A group of Catholic Workers, with Bp. Schrembs's moral and fi-

nancial support, founded the Blessed Martin de Porres House of Hospitality in Cleveland in 1938 and Sacred Heart Hospice 1 year later. But Schrembs found himself in a dilemma in regard to his old friend Fr. Coughlin, whose supporters formed a branch of his Natl. Union for Social Justice in the city in 1936. As Coughlin increasingly engaged in invective and personal attacks, Schrembs began to distance himself, but he never entirely repudiated the Michigan priest.

The disruptive impact of suburbanization, already apparent to thoughtful Catholics by 1940, became starkly clear in Cleveland and other older American industrial cities soon after the end of World War II. The fact that the number of parishes (nearly 125) in Cleveland, as well as parochial school attendance, reached new highs in the early 1960s masked the fact that the growth of new suburban, almost exclusively territorial parishes went hand in hand with the decline of older, often nationality inner-city ones. The opportunities of suburbia were unfortunately counterbalanced by the decay of old neighborhoods and parishes. The construction of freeways and interstate highways disrupted once-stable communities at the same time that older parishioners gradually died or moved with their children to the more attractive suburbs. The exodus was heightened by urban renewal and by the movement of BLACKS into old, often ethnic neighborhoods, especially on the city's east side, which in 1966 was wracked by the HOUGH RIOTS, which only heightened white fear. The result was a series of parish and school closings, mergers, and reorganizations in the late 1950s and 1960s, carried out by Bp. EDWARD F. HOBAN (1945-66). Catholics in Cleveland, as elsewhere, were also affected by the forces released by the 2d Vatican Council (1962-65) and by the new ideologies exemplified by the counterculture movements of the 1960s and 1970s. In common with Americans of all faiths, beliefs and practices once accepted were now questioned. The number of seminarians studying for the priesthood declined steadily from the mid-1960s onward, as did the number of sisters serving the diocese and the number of students enrolled in the city's Catholic elementary and high schools. As a consequence, and also as a result of the growing crisis in Cleveland's industrial economy, which eliminated tens of thousands of jobs in the region, there were more parish and school closings and mergers. Lay teachers, who were outnumbered about 10 to 1 by sisters shortly after World War II, came to dominate the teaching force 3 to 1 by 1983.

But change did not always mean the crisis of closings and mergers or the task of building and staffing suburban churches and schools. Responding to the needs and opportunities of post-Vatican II Catholicism, Bp. CLARENCE G. ISSENMANN (1966-74) liberalized and broadened the governance of the diocese, a path followed by his successor, Bp. Jas. A. Hickey (1974-80), who also reorganized and streamlined the diocesan administrative apparatus. Attentive to the needs of Catholic newcomers in the city, as his predecessors had been, Bp. Hickey established SAN JUAN BAUTISTA CHURCH for Hispanics in 1975 and formed apostolates for Filipino- and Vietnamese-Americans 2 years later. Especially concerned about race relations in Cleveland, he issued strong pronouncements in 1976 and 1977, following court-ordered busing in the city, to prevent Catholic schools from becoming havens for those fleeing integration and to promote the hiring and enrollment of minorities in parochial schools. In 1978, he established the Bishop's Black Advisory Committee. And, recognizing the needs of the growing numbers of Catholic charismatics, Hickey organized the Charismatic Office in 1976. By the early 1980s, under the leadership of Bp. Anthony M. Pilla (1980- ), Cleveland Catholicism appeared to be responding successfully to the changes of the previous 30 years. The needs of a diverse urban and suburban Catholic population were being met; enrollments in Catholic elementary and high schools, though still declining, were no longer doing so precipitously; the number of seminarians had leveled off, and, indeed, had increased between 1982–84. Cleveland Catholics could therefore look forward to the future with considerable confidence.

Henry B. Leonard
Kent State University

Houck, George F., *A History of Catholicity in Northern Ohio and in the Diocese of Cleveland from 1749 to December 31, 1900* (1903).
Hynes, Michael J., *History of the Diocese of Cleveland* (1953).
Jurgens, W. A., *A History of the Diocese of Cleveland* (1980).
Work Projects Admin. Ohio Historical Records Survey Project, Parishes of the Catholic Church, Diocese of Cleveland, History and Records (1942).
See also PAROCHIAL SCHOOLS and specific Roman Catholic churches and religious orders.

The **CAXTON BUILDING** is one of the finest expressions of the tall steel-framed office building in Cleveland. It was erected in 1901–03. The president of the Caxton Bldg. Co. was AMBROSE SWASEY, founder of WARNER & SWASEY CO. and a promoter of the benefits of engineering to mankind. The Caxton Co. was a commercial printing and graphic-arts business, and the building has been devoted to occupants in the graphic-arts trades. It was named after Wm. Caxton, the first British printer in the 15th century. In 1905 it was occupied by the business of Alfred Cahen, which subsequently became the WORLD PUBLISHING CO. The architect was Frank S. Barnum, official Cleveland public school architect beginning in 1895, who specialized in functional, fireproof, utilitarian school construction. The main entrance of the 8-story building on Huron Rd. is a large, semicircular terra cotta archway with Romanesque details. The upper stories of the facade are treated, so the verticality of the construction is stressed. Some of the floors in the rear part of the building were designed and constructed to bear loads of 300 pounds per sq. ft., in order to accommodate printing presses.

**CELEBREZZE, ANTHONY.** *See* **MAYORAL ADMINISTRATION OF ANTHONY CELEBREZZE**

**CELEBREZZE, FRANK D.** (12 May 1899–21 Aug. 1953), had a long career of public service in Cleveland, where he was assistant county prosecutor, safety director, and municipal court judge. He was born in Cleveland to Rocco and Dorothy Marcoguiseppe Celebrezze (Cilibrizzi). When the family returned to Italy in 1908 to find employment, Frank attended Italian schools. After the family's return to Cleveland in 1912, his father worked as a track laborer, and Frank enrolled in Brownell School. Encouraged by one of his teachers to continue his schooling, he graduated from East Technical High School, enrolled in St. Ignatius College (now JOHN CARROLL UNIVERSITY) for a year, and attended Notre Dame University for 3 years, receiving an LL.B. degree in 1925. He was admitted to the bar in 1926 and went into private practice. He married Mary Delsander 24 Nov. 1927, and they had 6 children, Frank D., Jr., Gerald, Dorothy, Joanne, Monica, and James P.

Democratic party politics attracted Celebrezze, and he was appointed assistant county prosecutor in 1929. While in the prosecutor's office, he spearheaded a successful drive to break up racket operations in Cleveland, assisting Judge FRANK LAUSCHE in closing the large gambling clubs. He went to Italy to try Angelo Amato in connection with the Sly-Fanner murder case. Amato was sentenced to prison for 30 years. In 1942 Celebrezze was appointed safety director, replacing ELIOT NESS, and remained there until 1947, with a brief stint in the Army during WORLD WAR II. He was elected judge of the municipal court in 1947 and reelected in 1951. He died in 1953 at the age of 54.

Frank D. Celebrezze Papers, WRHS.

**CEMETERIES,** although meant for the dead, exist for the living, as artifacts of settlement, effected by circumstances, custom, and style. Cuyahoga County's cemeteries, after nearly 2 centuries, show variety. The more than 135 tallied recently include existing sites, cared for and abandoned; those relocated; and those only remembered. They are diverse—large and small; plain and fancy; public and private and sectarian; inclusive and exclusive; for animals as well as humans. Some cemetery myths obscure facts. The oldest tombstone, for example, seldom reliably dates a Cuyahoga County site, for as civilization encroached upon old graveyards, they were often moved to new, convenient locations that immediately aged beyond their years. Furthermore, cholera deaths were not the cause of cemeteries, nor were early sites embellished with prehistoric Indian mounds. By contrast, inexorably and unobtrusively, as Ohio cemetery laws have progressed from early indifference to current vigilance, they have increasingly affected this land use.

Several cemetery "styles"—burying grounds, rural cemeteries, memorial parks—having distinct looks connoting specific values, are represented in Greater Cleveland. First came burying grounds. Austere, small (seldom more than half an acre), and often lacking legal title, these plots befitted homogeneous hamlets or family or neighborhood groupings. Mid-19th-century urban gentry fancied the antithetical "rural cemetery," a designed landscape, often having written rules and a bucolic name, that prefigured the urban park in form, use, and governance. By the late 19th century, the mannered "rural" style evolved to the more aesthetically uniform and easily maintained "lawn plan" cemetery. The euphemistic memorial park, a 20th-century creation, is distinguished by features such as ground-level headstones easily maintained. Often, Greater Cleveland's memorial parks exhibited characteristics common to suburban real-estate practices, because real-estate agents were, for a while, drawn to the cemetery business.

The early burying grounds, 1786–1819, were casually established without legal title upon the death of a family member or neighbor, and were ignored by rudimentary governments. Such sites may be known only by written descriptions. Few family plots have remained intact. Some became the nucleus for public burial grounds; many more were removed to township or private cemeteries. In summer 1786, the first recorded nonaboriginal burial, place unknown, occurred among transient Moravian missionaries. In June 1797, when David Eldridge of the Connecticut Land Co.'s surveying party drowned in the Grand River, his body was returned to Cleveland for an impromptu burial on the north of in-lots 97 and 98, near the present northeast corner of the Ontario St.-Prospect Ave. intersection. Until 1826 that was Cleveland's first burial ground. Sites in Brooklyn, Newburgh, Warrensville, Dover, Rockport, Independence, and Middleburg townships are said to date from this time. Without the confirmation of public records, these claims rely as much on legend as on fact.

Public recordkeeping improved as governments, such as townships and school districts, were formed. Caretakers of informal but established public burying grounds might deed them to a government's care, as happened in Newburgh Twp. (1827). Or, township and village trustees might purchase land for burial grounds. These transactions' terms were very similar: land of an acre or less, restricted to cemetery use by covenant, was bought for a small sum, often $1. Cleveland's ERIE ST. CEMETERY, as well as at least 9 separate township cemeteries, was formed in these years. Some settlements established their own grounds: at DOAN'S CORNERS (1823) in Newburgh Twp.; at Brighton in Brooklyn Twp. (1836); and along York St. (ca. 1843) in Parma Twp. No opposition was raised to public purchase of a burying ground. Furthermore, since Ohio law did not, before 1850, mention municipal or township cemeteries, the township trustees must have seen their duty as providing "a public burying ground for said township and for no other purpose," as such deeds commonly read.

Ohio's first cemetery laws regulated religious associations' burying grounds. Unlike Greater Cincinnati, which had numerous sectarian graveyards, Greater Cleveland had only 2 identified ones before 1840: that of the Presbyterian-Congregationalist "Plan of Union" Church (ca. 1813) and that of the North Union Shakers (1827–88). All other burying grounds were public or private. During the 1830s and 1840s, however, European immigrants came to Cleveland. They were of Jewish, Roman Catholic, and Evangelical Lutheran beliefs, which stressed, when possible, apartness of their dead. The first of these sectarian cemeteries was the Jewish WILLETT ST. CEMETERY (1840); the second was the Roman Catholic St. Joseph Cemetery (1849). As adherents became more numerous, more Jewish and ROMAN CATHOLIC CEMETERIES were established. A third group, Protestant GERMANS, formed Evangelical and Lutheran congregations in rural Cuyahoga County. Eight surviving church graveyards attest to their distinct communities. Cemetery formation has continued into the 20th century. Five separate denominations have formed their own sites. When Jewish, Roman Catholic, and Evangelical Lutheran cemeteries have been formed, they have been confederated, rather than individual, congregational enterprises.

The success of the first rural or garden cemetery in the English-speaking world Mt. Auburn (1831) near Boston, Mass., inspired every town's urban gentry to develop their own. The garden cemetery appealed to a pastoral romanticism evident in the era's prose and poetry and to a gentlemanly interest in horticulture. The form's premeditated carriageways, paths, trees, shrubs, and flowers were civilized society's triumph over the unkempt burying ground's more "revolting" aspects. Although any cemetery could be ornamented, another attaction of the rural cemetery was the association of like-minded lot owners, a business aspect distinguishing this form from public grounds. Too, such a nonprofit incorporated association intimated—but did not assure—perpetual care of the site. The rural cemetery's much-publicized aesthetics and organization intrigued sophisticates everywhere.

The first rural cemeteries in Boston, New York, and Philadelphia had 2 effects on Ohio. From the mid-1830s, public cemetery trustees began to "ornament" their sites. Between 1838–48 the Ohio General Assembly considered, from municipalities large and small, over 25 separate rural cemetery association charters before it enacted a general law guiding their incorporation (1848). No separate charters came from Cuyahoga County. The first recorded incorporation was the Brooklyn Cemetery Assoc. (1849). Thereafter, county records show 9 associations in 20 years, including LAKE VIEW CEMETERY (1869) and RIVERSIDE CEMETERY (1875). More are known to have existed. By 1876, Greater Cleveland's fervor for forming nonprofit cemetery associations had abated. Still, the

movement's legacy was the cemetery association law and an abiding concern for the cemetery's beauty.

After the new Ohio constitution's promulgation (1851), state law first invested municipalities (1852) and townships (1853) with authority over burials and public cemeteries. As Ohio became more urban, many laws on public and private cemeteries were enacted. Cemeteries owned and operated by combinations of governments were permitted. In 1984, 3 public cemeteries in Cuyahoga County—Mayfield Union, Woodvale, and Chestnut Grove—are jointly administered. The county's role has been limited primarily to keeping records on, and providing graves for, veterans' burials. In the late 19th century, townships purchased new or additional cemeteries, when needed. Some townships assumed responsibility for the property of cemetery associations. The general assembly's manadate (1874) that townships care for neglected burial grounds brought some governments added burdens. Contributing to the dignity and utility of the main township cemetery was the vault for winter storage of the dead. Between 1870–95, 14 townships built vaults in Gothic or utilitarian styles. As municipalities engulfed townships, their cemeteries became city property, E. Cleveland Twp. (1859) excepted (though within Cleveland, this cemetery is overseen by CLEVELAND HTS. and E. CLEVELAND).

Cleveland operates 11 cemeteries. Five it developed: Erie St.; WOODLAND CEMETERY, possibly the city's first landscape architecture commission; Harvard Grove (1881); West Park (1900); and Highland Park (1904). Six were acquired through annexation: MONROE ST. CEMETERY; Brookmere; Brooklyn; Denison; Alger; and Scranton Rd. Jefferson Park, on W. Lorain Ave., is the site of the aborted Lorain Hts. Cemetery (1895). From village to city, maintaining a "burying ground" has been a municipal concern. Cleveland owned yet another cemetery, now eroded, on Lake Erie's shore in Lake County. In 1850 the city bought 1/4 acre as a mass grave for victims of the *Griffith* steamboat explosion.

From 1868–91, by Ohio law, Cleveland's cemeteries were governed by 3 elected trustees. When the "Federal Plan" abolished the arrangement, control first rested with the Dept. of Charities & Corrections. Currently, cemeteries are within the Dept. of Parks, Recreation, & Properties. One director, LOUISE DEWALD, was probably the first and only woman in the nation to oversee municipal cemeteries. In 1892 the private Cleveland Cremation Co. was founded. Unsuccessful, it was reconstituted successfully in 1900. In 1892 a municipal crematory was proposed; however, it was not built until 1924, in Highland Park. Cleveland was first to operate a municipal mausoleum and crematory.

The automobile, which with the motorized hearse had been banned from cemeteries, was admitted ca. 1910. Theretofore mourners had arrived by horse-drawn vehicles, on foot, or in a streetcar, often a specially fitted funeral car having a cemetery siding. The auto shrank a trip that had consumed a day into a few hours. The cemetery was never the same. Once-distant cemeteries, now surrounded by the city, seemed unfashionable. New cemeteries, memorial parks with acres of grassy lawns, ground-level markers, and selected plantings, beckoned the "modern way's" availability in faraway suburbs. Knollwood (1909), boasting Ohio's largest mausoleum, is a cemetery that bridged the changing fashions. Though having above-ground monuments, it began as a large land-holding corporation. When it became a nonprofit association, land was sold, some to Acacia Memorial Park (1927), Ohio's only Masonic cemetery, to comply with state laws.

Greater Cleveland real-estate agents speculating in suburban development often became memorial park entrepreneurs. Some memorial parks of the 1920s and 1930s, such as Parkside or Western Reserve, remained on paper. When others were developed, their managements sometimes illegally sheltered lot-sale profits under the nonprofit association's nontaxable status. The methods and extent of memorial park fraud were exposed in successfully prosecuted court cases and in Cuyahoga County grand jury investigations, commencing in Jan. 1936. Lot holders reported coercive salesmen; prosecutors impounded damning financial records. Seeking restored public confidence, the Ohio Assoc. of Cemetery Superintendents publicly decried these "promotional cemetery" organizations.

Entreprenurial memorial parks sold lots with racially restrictive covenants—"said land to be used solely for burial purposes for members of the Caucasian Race"—a technique derived from suburban real-estate practice. In the 1920s, before ZONING, many a homeowner's deed enumerated restrictions, some of which were designed implicitly, if not explicitly, to bar undesired non-Caucasians from suburbs such as SHAKER HTS. This undisguised restriction was new to Greater Cleveland, where cemeteries had not been overtly discriminatory, in contrast to other Ohio cities. Generally, BLACKS bought less-expensive cemetery lots, e.g., in Harvard Grove instead of Woodland, but they faced no outright prohibition until the memorial park era. In 1971 the Ohio Civil Rights Commission, supported by the Cuyahoga County Common Pleas Court, specifically voided Sunset Memorial Park's restrictive covenants. It was not the only Greater Cleveland memorial park that had enforced them.

Veterinarian Dr. W. C. Woodruff established the area's only pet cemetery, Woodhaven (1918), on Wilson Mills Rd. Over 5,000 domesticated animals were buried there. Residential encroachment, neglect, and new ownership have led to a new name, A Fond Memory (1983), and to the destruction of all older markers, save for the miniature mausoleum of Frenchie (1924–1929), magician Howard Thurston's performing monkey.

Mary H. Deal

Smith, Maxine Hartmann, ed., *Ohio Cemeteries* (1978).

The **CENTER FOR HEALTH AFFAIRS-GREATER CLEVELAND HOSPITAL ASSOCIATION** is an organization of Cleveland hospitals and health-care facilities formed to foster cooperation. It was the first such hospital organization in the country to maintain a staff and meet regularly. The Cleveland Hospital Council, as the body was first known, grew out of a series of conferences in 1914 between representatives of 15 hospitals to discuss common problems and more cost-effective ways of running hospitals. In 1916, the CHC was formally organized, with membership open to any public (not-for-profit) hospital. Among the 16 charter members were Lakeside, German (FAIRVIEW GENERAL), ST. ALEXIS, St. Clair, LUTHERAN, City (Metropolitan General), ST. LUKE'S, ST. VINCENT CHARITY, Maternity, St. Ann's, Babies' Dispensary & Hospital, HURON RD., MT. SINAI, and St. John's. A full-time secretary coordinated the work of the council, composed of 2 representatives from each member hospital. Offices were located in the Anisfield Bldg., the first of 6 locations. In its early days, the CHC encouraged its members to examine the role of the hospital in the community, and to adopt standardized procedures to increase public confidence. Members agreed that hospital rates must reflect actual costs of services rendered, and adopted a standardized reporting system that became a model for a national system by the American Hospital Assoc. The council also successfully lobbied for per diem reimbursement for indigent patients with the county. Through its first 3 decades, the council worked to develop uniform administrative policies, a hospital procedure manual, job descriptions for hospital personnel, and standard procedures for emergency care and autopsies.

To better assess the situation in Cleveland, the CHC conducted a Hospital & Health Survey in 1919. The survey found that only 6 hospitals had out-patient departments, ⅔ of the population lacked prenatal-care facilities, and Cleveland was short 1,500 hospital beds. The results were utilized to plan hospital expansion, promote better recording of vital statistics, and encourage the building of new water and sewage plants. The study was viewed throughout the country as a model document in the preventive medicine field, and was the first of many undertaken by the council. The Joint Hospital Committee was established in 1942 to recommend building when appropriate, and functioned until 1969. It was eventually replaced by the Regional Hospital Planning Board (initially the Metropolitan Health Planning Board). The group also set up a cooperative purchasing service in 1917, which was one of the first in the country. The council hired 2 people to handle buying, which replaced the haphazard buying practices of individual hospitals at a savings of thousands of dollars annually. Purchasing remained the largest single operation of the CHC's successor organization, the CTR. FOR HEALTH AFFAIRS.

By improving hospital admission procedures and then adding a collection service (1921) to its functions, the CHC encouraged members to inquire about a patient's ability to pay before service was rendered and then offered follow-up to insure that the monies were paid. During the Depression, the group developed a deferred-payment plan, the Hospital Finance Corp. of Cleveland, with lower-than-market interest rates. To address long-range needs for prepaid health care, the council sponsored John Mannix's hospitalization plan, which became the Cleveland Hospital Service Assoc. Ultimately, in 1975, the separate Cleveland Hospital Services, Inc., was created as the only shared debt-collection service in Ohio. The CHC also promoted employee education, disaster preparedness, and the development of new health-career programs. The group worked with the Board of Education and with area colleges to prepare students for jobs in hospital food service, housekeeping, recordkeeping, physician's assisting, and nursing. In 1969, the group expanded its functions and changed its name to the Greater Cleveland Hospital Assoc. After evaluation by the American Hospital Assoc., the GCHA opened membership to long- and short-term facilities such as nursing homes and convalescent centers. The restated purpose of the GCHA was to aid health-care facilities in effectively providing high-quality service to the public. With the restructuring, a larger role was given to the board of trustees and its executive council. Among the major concerns of the association were employee relations and benefits and government relations. In the face of increased union activity, association members were encouraged to develop responsive human-resources departments and attractive benefit plans. The group took over the administration of employee group life-insurance plans, and a restructured pension plan. The GCHA pension plan was, in 1986, the most comprehensive pension program offered by any hospital association in the U.S. and covered over 20,000 employees in 31 institutions.

The establishment of Medicare in 1966 placed increased pressure on the health-care system from state and national government. Hospitals were criticized for not providing enough care for indigents, and the medical delivery system was judged inadequate for their care. Legislators often supported health-care measures without full awareness of the needs of their constituents or of the institutions delivering the services. The GCHA confronted these problems by initiating dialogue between hospitals, community group representatives, and government officials, and by publishing a monthly newsletter to inform its members and legislators. In 1973, the GCHA applauded the development of the federally funded Cancer Data System to study the epidemiology of cancer in northeast Ohio; when funding ended in 1979, the association affiliated with the CDS to provide a central registry of cancer information for its members. As hospital operations changed in the 1980s to become more efficient and competitive, the GCHA broadened its name to the Ctr. for Health Affairs-Greater Cleveland Hospital Assoc. Its board was expanded to include representatives from business as well as health care. With cost containment a major goal, the association worked with its members to explore ways to deliver quality health care at a reasonable cost. In 1986, the Ctr. for Health Affairs was located at 1226 Huron Rd. in a historic building originally occupied by the WINTON MOTOR CARRIAGE CO.

The **CENTER FOR HUMAN SERVICES** is a professional, voluntary, nonprofit, multi-social-service agency that promotes the well-being of Greater Clevelanders through various programs designed with particular emphasis on the strengthening of individuals. The center offers family and youth counseling, homemaker services to assist in case of illness, and daycare centers for children of working or ill mothers. In 1969, the Welfare Fed. requested that 5 United Appeal-supported volunteer agencies—the Family Services Assoc., Youth Services, the Homemakers Service Assoc., the CLEVELAND DAY NURSERY ASSOC., and the TRAVELERS AID SOCIETY—study the possibility of merging. The subsequent merger in 1970 created 1 agency that was to centralize and streamline administrative responsibilities, provide a more efficient delivery system, allow greater flexibility in trying different methods of handling needs, and eliminate the need to shuffle people between agencies.

The Family Services Assoc. started in 1830 as the WESTERN SEAMEN'S FRIEND SOCIETY, a mission and lodge for destitute sailors. In 1867 the society was absorbed by the Cleveland Bethel Union's work of caring for sailors' families along the waterfront. Soup kitchens to feed the poor and a Ladies' Sewing Society to provide clothing for the poor followed. In 1881, the Charity Organization Society was created to oversee charitable activities in order to reduce pauperism and vagrancy, to prevent duplicate and indiscriminate relief efforts, and to care for all cases of distress. The name was changed to the Bethel Associated Charities in 1884 with the merger of the Bethel Relief Assoc. & the COS, with headquarters at Superior Ave. and Spring (W. 10th) St. In 1890, the name was changed to the Cleveland Associated Charities. As a Community Fund member agency, CAC struggled with direct relief efforts during the Depression until over 43,000 families were being cared for, and the government was forced to take over direct relief work. That left CAC free to deal with all other problems related to family adjustment, rehabilitation, and preservation. In 1945, the name was changed to the Family Services Assoc. One popular program during the 1940s was providing homemakers to manage homes and assume responsibility for handling children where the mother was absent. It was discontinued in 1947. That same year, FSA started a housekeeping service that enabled the elderly to

remain at home instead of having to enter nursing homes. After WORLD WAR II, many of FSA's efforts were directed toward counseling families and individuals in order to diagnose and work out family, marital, or individual problems. During the 1950s, a credit-counseling service was introduced to help families deep in debt. Since the 1950s, FSA has experienced a significant increase in problems among young children and the elderly.

Youth Services developed into a private casework counseling agency from an association dating back to 1916. Because of the deplorable conditions of Cleveland jails, the WOMEN'S PROTECTIVE ASSOC. was created to "protect and safeguard girls and women against social and moral dangers." Sterling House was established as a temporary home for girls in 1918, and in 1920 Prospect House was organized as a boarding house for women. The association became part of the Welfare Fed. The Big Sister Council became part of the system in 1922. As a direct result of the association's work, the Women's Police Bureau was created in 1925. In 1930, the Women's Protective Assoc. became the Girls Bureau, and in 1943 the Youth Bureau, expanding its services to care for all children 14–21 years of age.

The Day Nursery Assoc. and Kindergarten Assoc. were founded by the YWCA in 1882. In 1886, free kindergartens were open, and a decade later the program was taken over by the CLEVELAND PUBLIC SCHOOLS. In 1893, the association became independent of the YWCA. With headquarters at 2050 E. 96th St., DNA operated day nurseries at various locations throughout the years. Preference was given to children of mothers who were self-supporting and who had to work. At the time of the merger, DNA was operating 6 day nurseries, 25 daycare homes, and 2 centers, the Florence Harkness Camp and the Hanna-Perkins Therapeutic Nursery School for preschoolers with emotional problems. The Cleveland Homemakers Service Assoc. was established in 1967 as a Red Feather-supported private agency with an office in the Cuyahoga Savings Bldg. on E. 9th St. CHSA employed women to help in homes where the mother was ill or absent. Most of the trained homemakers were women in their fifties and sixties whose job was to tend children, cook, shop, and do light chores.

The Travelers Aid Society in Cleveland traces its roots back to the combined efforts of the Deaconesses of the Methodist Church, the Catholic Diocese, and the YWCA, which pooled their resources during the 1890s in order to provide aid to troubled travelers at the old Union Station. In 1919, the Cleveland Travelers Aid Society was formally organized and received financial support from the Community Fund. During its early days, TA operated around the clock at 5 railroad stations, the boat docks, the interurban station, and later the Terminal Tower. During the Depression, TA was hard-pressed to care for the increased numbers of transients. During World War II, TA operated a USO lounge in the Terminal Tower, providing countless services for traveling military personnel. Increased travel by automobile presented new problems for TA during the 1950s, while increased numbers of unemployed seeking new areas for jobs presented a different challenge during the 1960s. From 1970–85 it was affiliated with the Ctr. for Human Services.

Center for Human Services Records, WRHS.

The **CENTRAL ARMORY** was erected in 1893 at Lakeside Ave. and E. 6th St. (opposite the present city hall). It was built by the county to house units of the Natl. Guard but was also used for public events. For the 1896 centennial celebrations, it housed mass meetings, a concert and historical spectacle, gymnastic exhibitions by German, Czech, and Swiss groups, and a floral exposition. By 1909 it provided additional exhibition space for the INDUSTRIAL EXPOSITION, and it was connected by a bridge to the temporary exhibition hall north of Lakeside. In 1916 Chas. Evans Hughes addressed an audience in the armory during his presidential campaign. The Central Armory was designed by Cleveland architects LEHMAN & SCHMITT and was essentially a large covered hall. The 122' width was spanned by 6 arched plate girders. The balcony was suspended from the girders by iron rods. The exterior was constructed of stone in a castellated Gothic style derived from fortresslike medieval Italian municipal buildings. The Central Armory was demolished in 1965; the site is occupied by the Anthony J. Celebrezze federal office building.

**CENTRAL HIGH SCHOOL** was the first public high school in Cleveland. Established on 13 July 1846, it was the first such school west of the Alleghenies to provide free secondary education at public expense. Its founding was controversial because of the belief that education beyond the elementary level was the responsibility of the private school at private expense. Opponents of Central High alleged that operation of the school out of public funds was illegal under Ohio statutes. They argued that such funds should be used to expand or improve existing primary schools. These issues were resolved by state legislation in 1848 that made provisions for Central's funding. The major proponents of Central High were GEO. HOADLEY, Chas. Bradburn, and Geo. Willey. Its first principal was ANDREW FREESE, who later became superintendent in 1856. During this period, Central students included such eminent figures as JOHN L. SEVERANCE, JOHN D. ROCKEFELLER, MARCUS A. HANNA, SAMUEL MATHER, and, at a later date, LANGSTON HUGHES. The early curriculum of Central High included courses in English, mathematics, natural science, bookkeeping, rhetoric, and mental philosophy. In 1859, the length of the course was extended from 3 to 4 years, and German, Latin, and classics were offered in addition to English. The academic program was revised again in 1878 to include analytical geometry and mechanics. It was further expanded in 1891 to include a 2-year course in bookkeeping, commercial correspondence, law, and business forms and usages. In 1917, household economics, textiles, marketing, and home decoration were introduced. By 1928 the curriculum included courses in English, foreign languages, mathematics, social science, physical science, commercial education, technical education, art, home economics, and music. Central High was first housed in the Universalist Church on Prospect Ave. and changed locations 3 times in a span of 100 years. It moved to a new building on E. 40th St. in 1856, and in 1878 to a Gothic-style building on E. 55th St. The building, constructed at a cost of $74,000, was the pride of the community. In 1940 the school moved once again, to E. 40th St. By the time Central had its centennial celebration in 1946, it had graduated 10,000 pupils. In 1952 Central merged with EAST TECHNICAL HIGH, while its old site on E. 40th became Central Jr. High.

The **CENTRAL MARKET** is Cleveland's oldest market. It dates to Oct. 1856, when the city council approved a site for a market at the intersection of Ontario, Woodland, and Broadway. However, market men condemned the site as being too far uptown. The following year, the council forced acceptance of this site by moving the Michigan St. Market there and building a markethouse. Opposition to the Central Market continued until a new wooden markethouse was completed by the city on 14 Sept. 1867.

Although the Central Market was well patronized, with over 200 tenants, it soon became antiquated and lacked sanitary facilities. As early as 1890, it was declared inefficient; the city council considered a resolution to appropriate money to build a new markethouse, but no action was taken. The markethouse continued to deteriorate. In the 1920s, 1930s, and 1940s, several attempts were made by the city to raze, relocate, or repair the building, as the old markethouse was cited as a traffic, safety, and health hazard and impeded the development of the downtown area. In 1946, the voters passed a $1.35 million public market improvement bond to build a new markethouse. However, the administration of Mayor THOMAS BURKE did not expend the funds. On 17 Dec. 1949, the markethouse was destroyed by fire.

In 1950, the city council decided not to rebuild the market and used the bond money instead to renovate the WEST SIDE MARKET. Frustrated, the former tenants of the market, with the aid of former senator Frank E. Bubna, incorporated their own organization, the New Central Market, Inc., which leased the old Sheriff St. Market. For many years, the privately owned Sheriff St. Market, started in 1890 by the Sheriff St. Market & Storage Co., was the Central Market's major competition, located across the street at E. 4th and Bolivar. However, it was unable to compete successfully with the city-owned market, and by 1936, its large markethouse, built in 1891, was converted into a garage. The building was given a new life on 30 Mar. 1950, when 171 stands opened in it as the New Central Market. However, the market was continually plagued with financial problems. Many of its tenants left, and there were always rumors of its imminent closing. By 1981, it had fewer than 40 tenants, primarily serving the city's poor.

The **CENTRAL VIADUCT**, built between 1887–88, was a high-level bridge that linked the east and west sides of Cleveland. It stood where the Innerbelt Bridge (I-90) is now located. In Mar. 1879, Councilman Jas. M. Curtiss introduced a resolution asking that the city engineer undertake to determine the best site for a bridge linking downtown with neighborhoods southwest of Cleveland across the CUYAHOGA RIVER. The resolution met with some opposition and was not passed until 1883. Council authorized an expenditure of $1 million, and in Dec. 1885 the ordinance of construction was approved. Ground was finally broken in May 1887. The purpose of the bridge was to bring traffic from the southwestern parts of the city to the downtown area. The city engineer's office furnished the design and construction specifications; C. G. Force started the project and was succeeded by Walter W. Rice. W. M. Walters was in immediate charge of construction. Frank Osborn (founder of the OSBORN ENGINEERING CO.) was the engineer in charge of steelwork. The KING IRON BRIDGE & MFG. CO. was contracted to do most of the construction. The Central Viaduct was opened in Dec. 1888. It consisted of 2 bridges. The first structure, known as the Central Viaduct, was 2,839 ft. long and extended from Jennings Ave. (W. 14th) to Central Ave. (Carnegie). Known as a "stilt" type, the bridge consisted of a series of braced towers and deck spans of varying lengths. Originally it had a swing section over the river to allow taller ships to pass, which was removed in 1912 and replaced with an overhead truss. The roadway was approximately 100 ft. above the river. The second bridge, known as the Walworth Run section, is 1,088 ft. long and connects Abbey Ave. To Lorain Ave. at W. 25th. Its iron and steel spans are supported by iron towers on masonry foundations. A concrete mesh deck was added in 1930. The bridge, best seen from Scranton Rd., was still in use in 1986. The main bridge was completed at a cost of $675,000. It was opened on 2 Dec. 1888 with a parade and ceremony, followed by a banquet at the HOLLENDEN HOTEL attended by various local, state, and federal officials and other distinguished citizens. On the night of 16 Nov. 1895, a safety switch failed while the draw was open, causing a streetcar to plunge into the river; 17 people were killed. In Jan. 1939, the viaduct was razed after it was found to be unsafe.

The **CENTRAN CORPORATION** is one of the state's leading bank holding companies, with one of Cleveland's major banks, Central Natl., as its principal affiliate. Central Natl. Bank dates back to 1890, when JEREMIAH J. SULLIVAN, a national bank examiner, interested 10 prominent Clevelanders in organizing a bank. Central Natl. opened on 26 May 1890 with capital of $800,000 and 6 employees in the PERRY-PAYNE BLDG. on Superior Ave. The bank enjoyed immediate success because of the financial support it received from its board of directors, consisting of a number of prominent business leaders in the iron and steel and shipping industries. At the end of its first year, its resources had more than doubled, to $1.9 million; 10 years later, they had reached $4.5 million.

By 1905, Central had outgrown its original quarters and moved into the new Rockfeller Bldg. on W. 6th St. Despite its growth in commercial business, Central as a national bank was prohibited from offering certain services, such as savings accounts and trust services. In 1905, Jeremiah Sullivan organized the Superior Savings & Trust Co. To provide such services. When restrictions were lifted in 1921, the two banks merged as the Central Natl. Bank, Savings, & Trust Co., with an expanded capital of $4.5 million. In 1926, Central bought the bank building at 308 Euclid Ave.; it made it its headquarters the following year.

By the late 1920s, Central needed to increase its assets to maintain its business. It did so by acquiring one of the west side's largest banks, the United Banking & Trust Co., which was started in 1886 as the West Side Banking Co. at the corner of Lorain Ave. and Pearl St. With the merger, the firm's name was changed to the Central United Natl. Bank, Ohio's largest national bank. Jeremiah Sullivan's son, Corliss, guided Central through the Depression as it remained a sound financial firm and grew steadily. By the late 1930s, the bank had $130 million in deposits, $20 million in capital, 12 suburban branches, and 600 employees. In 1936, it shortened its name to Central Natl. Bank of Cleveland.

The postwar period witnessed even further growth for Central. By 1946, it was the 3d-largest bank in Ohio. In 1949, it moved its headquarters to the Midland Bldg. Central launched a branch-expansion program, acquired several smaller banks, and introduced many new banking services to the area. It was a pioneer and leader in international banking services. With 47 branch offices, Central reaffirmed its commitment to Cleveland in 1969 by building a 23-story main office building at the corner of E. 9th St. and Superior Ave. To ensure continued growth, the bank initiated the formation of a regional multi-bank holding company, the Centran Corp., in 1971. In the early 1980s, Centran experienced some financial problems, but by dissolving its financial companies, persuading Marine Midland Banks, Inc., to invest in it, and cutting its staff to 2,300, it began to revive. It was announced in Sept. 1984 that Centran would merge with the Society Corp., creating Ohio's 3d-largest holding company. The merger went into effect in Feb. 1986.

**CERMAK, ALBINA** (4 Apr. 1904–22 Dec. 1978), a lifelong Republican who held many political posts, was the first woman to run for mayor of Cleveland. The daughter of a Cleveland suffragette, Cermak dropped out of nursing school to aid her ailing mother and take over a position as bookkeeper-secretary-buyer in the family business, the Cermak Dry Goods Co. In 1933, after the business was sold, she became a bookkeeper for the city public utilities department; within 2 years, she was promoted to supervisor. Active as a Republican precinct committeewoman from 1925–53, Cermak served as vice-chairman and secretary of the Cuyahoga County Republican Central & Executive Committee and chairman of the Republican Women's Organization of Cuyahoga County from 1939–53. From 1946–53 she was a member of the Board of Elections, while holding many other positions in the organization: chairwoman, Republican State Central Committee; board member, Ohio Fed. of Republican Women's Clubs; secretary, State Central & Executive Committee; vice-president and secretary, Assoc. of Elected Officials; and board member and membership chairman, Natl. Fed. of Republican Women's Clubs. A delegate to the Republican Natl. Conventions in 1940, 1944, and 1952, she was on the resolutions committee in 1944 and 1952.

In 1953, Cermak resigned from many of her offices to become U.S. collector of customs. When the Republicans sought an opponent to run against Anthony Celebrezze in 1961, she stepped down to run against him, becoming the first woman to run for the mayoralty. She predicted that if elected, Celebrezze would abandon Cleveland for a cabinet post. As expected, she lost badly, while Celebrezze became secretary of HEW under JOHN F. Kennedy in 1962. Cermak was rewarded for her party loyalty with support for future office seeking and with choice and historic appointments. After unsuccessful campaigns for the state senate (1962) and clerk of Cleveland municipal courts (1963), she was the first woman appointed bailiff to the common pleas court in 1964. In 1965, State Auditor Roger Cloud selected her as an administrative specialist, while Gov. Jas. Rhodes named her vice-chairwoman of the Ohio Status of Women Committee in 1966. In 1971, she was a delegate-at-large to the White House Committee on Aging. In addition to Cermak's political affiliation, she was on the boards of the WOMEN'S CITY CLUB, the Council on Human Relations, the NATIONALITIES SERVICES CTR., the Grand Jury Assoc., the Catholic Board of Education, the DePaul Ctr. for Family & Children, and the Natl. Council of Catholic Women. Her club memberships in Republican activities alone exceeded 75. Single by choice to devote time to her many causes, she was considered among Cleveland's top career women and was a sought-after speaker. Frequently asked by women candidates for advice, she cautioned them against tugging at their skirts on the speaker's platform, and against trying to win votes through feminine wiles. Rather, she noted, their energies should be put into door-to-door campaigning and advocating what was best for Cleveland.

Albina Cermak Papers, WRHS.

**CHADSEY, MILDRED** (1883–3 Apr. 1940), was a prominent figure in local reform work. She came to Cleveland in 1912 after graduating from the University of Chicago. Chadsey was hired as the city's first housing commissioner, a post that included the duties of the chief city sanitary inspector. She went to work immediately, using her authority and a team of uniformed sanitary police to force landlords to repair plumbing, clean buildings, and provide fire protection. In the first year of her tenure, she caused over 200 tenements in the worst areas of Cleveland, primarily on the lower east side and in the FLATS, to be demolished or vacated. In 1913 Chadsey formed the Cleveland Bureau of Sanitation to oversee housing and sanitation, and she served as director of that bureau. A political move by the city council in 1915 threatened her job, but prominent citizens FREDERICK H. GOFF and SAMUEL MATHER vowed to give money to pay Chadsey's salary if the council would not. Some opposition to Chadsey was formed by city officials who owned tenements and resented her work.

Although Chadsey insisted she was not a reformer, she worked for progressive legislation and caused the city's dance hall ordinance of 1911 and housing code to be adopted. She was also active in the labor movement and served as executive secretary of the CONSUMERS LEAGUE OF OHIO. One of the founders of the WOMEN'S CITY CLUB in 1915, Chadsey left Cleveland during WORLD WAR I to manage Red Cross activities in Italy. From 1921–24 she was editor of the *Cleveland Year Book*, an annual report of events in Cleveland that outlined social progress and changes.

In 1919, Chadsey was hired by Western Reserve University to instruct students in social-work administration. She later became director of the group work services division of the School of Applied Social Sciences. She continued in this work until 1924, training young social workers to organize clubs and recreation at social settlements and community centers. Chadsey also helped found and directed the Adult Education Assoc. in 1925. She was vice-president of the CLEVELAND PLAY HOUSE and was very active in the CLEVELAND PUBLIC LIBRARY; a special book fund was established in her name at the library following her death. From 1937–38 she was president of the LEAGUE FOR HUMAN RIGHTS. Chadsey died in Cleveland at the age of 57.

**CHADWICK, CASSIE L.** (1857–10 Oct. 1907), was Cleveland's most famous female financial con artist. Her career as a swindler and her trial in Cleveland in 1905 drew the attention of the world. Chadwick was born Elizabeth Bigley in Eastwood, Ontario, Canada. During the course of her life, she assumed a number of names. At the age of 22, while still using her given name, she was arrested in Woodstock, Ontario, on a charge of forgery. She escaped conviction on the grounds of insanity. In 1882, Bigley married Dr. Wallace S. Springsteen of Cleveland, but after only 11 days of marriage, she was thrown out of his house when her background and true identity were revealed. She began a career as a fortuneteller, known as Lydia Scott, in 1886. In 1887 she assumed the name of Madame Lydia DeVere, also a clairvoyant. In 1889, she was sentenced to 9½ years in the state penitentiary for forgery in Toledo. Four years later, she was paroled by then-governor Wm. McKinley. She returned to Cleveland and between 1894–97 lived as Mrs. Hoover. In 1897, "Hoover" married Dr. Leroy Chadwick, who apparently knew nothing of her criminal activities until she was caught in 1905. Between 1897–1905, Cassie Chadwick obtained vast sums of money from Cleveland banks on forged notes. Claiming to be the illegitimate daughter of Andrew Carnegie, she borrowed substantial amounts from local banks, the loans secured by $5 million in securities and certificates forged with her name that she had deposited with the Wade Park Bank. She lived extravagantly, accumulating over $1 million in debts. She was exposed on 2 Nov. 1904, when H. B. Newton brought suit against her to recover $190,800. Until then, she had successfully duped several bankers out of hundreds of thousands of dollars. After fleeing to New York, where she was arrested, she stood trial in Cleveland in Mar. 1905. On 10 Mar. 1905, Chadwick was convicted on 7 counts of conspiracy against the government and conspiracy to wreck the Citizens Natl. Bank of Oberlin. She was sentenced to 14 years in prison and was fined $70,000. The key witness for the prosecution was Andrew Carnegie, who denied ever having met Chadwick. As the jury's verdict was read, Chadwick put on a dramatic show, denying her guilt. She arrived at the penitentiary on 12 Jan. 1906, where she died a year later.

**CHAGRIN FALLS VILLAGE** is located in Cuyahoga County in an area centered at the "High Falls" of the Chagrin River. Chagrin Falls has a land area of approximately 2.2 sq. mi., of which 57.5 acres are taken up by the river that flows through the town east to west. The river drew people who, for the most part, came from England and New England to develop its potential. The land around the "High Falls" was purchased by Seth Henderson of NEWBURGH and made ready as a base of operations. It was platted in 1837, and development of the river's potential began. Between then and 1870, 14 manufactories were established along its banks including an axe factory, a foundry, 2 flour mills, 4 woolen mills, 2 sawmills, 3 paper mills, and a woodenware factory. Of these 14, Geo. Fenkell's flour mill was still grinding grain for flour and processing feed for animals 93 years after it began.

Railway transportation, in the form of a narrow-gauge road, from Chagrin Falls to Solon (a distance of 4 mi.) was built in 1877 as a branch of the Painesville, Canton & Bridgeport Railroad. This and other short-lived roads failed. The Cleveland, Canton, & Southern Railroad, a standard-gauge road, failed in 1899, and its property was transferred to the Wheeling & Lake Erie Railroad. In 1949 the Nickel Plate Railroad assumed ownership until the Norfolk & Western (now the NORFOLK SOUTHERN CORP.) took it over 16 Oct. 1964. The Cleveland & Chagrin Falls Electric Railway Co. was granted a franchise to operate upon certain streets of the village in 1896. The first car over the route made the run from Cleveland on 8 May 1897, and in time it was extended to Hiram and Garretsville. By 1910, the entire line was in the hands of 2 receivers. It was reorganized as the Eastern Ohio Traction Co. but ceased to operate in Apr. 1925. When efforts to develop the power of the river were in progress, the community of people centered at the "High Falls" were in 2 counties and 3 townships, which complicated the business of government unnecessarily. It meant that 5 different governmental entities exercised control over parts of a community needing to be a unified town. An important step toward unification came 12 Mar. 1844, when the legislature passed an act "to incorporate the town of Chagrin Falls." An election was held 7 Sept. 1844, and Curtiss Bullard was elected mayor. In March of the following year (1845), the Twp. of Chagrin Falls was erected by the commissioners of Cuyahoga County on petition of "the inhabitants of parts of Solon and Orange Townships." These actions meant the town lay within one county and one township, and the people of the village finally were in control of their own affairs.

Chagrin Falls contained a variety of churches where social activities of the town were centered. The Congregational Church was established in 1836, the Free Will Baptist Church in 1841, the First Wesleyan Methodist Church in 1847, the Disciples of Christ in 1852, and the Bible Christian Church in 1869. The Congregational and Bible Christian churches united in 1884 to become the First Congregational Church, which joined with the Disciple Church in 1929 to become the Congregational-Disciple Church Federated. The Free Will Baptist Church disappeared with no fanfare ca. 1881. In 1875, the local newspaper, the *Exponent*, reported that the "Catholic people contemplate building a church in this place," but that was not accomplished until 1948. In 1916, the First Church of Christ, Scientist, was established in the village. The beliefs of the Spiritualists were accepted by some, as were those of the Seventh-Day Adventists (1892), but no actual organization of a church took place.

The people of the town had a third interest: education. They organized study groups and were their own teachers. The Congregational Church organized a class in spelling. Singing schools were conducted. A Dr. Harlow, M.D., was principal of the Chagrin Falls Commercial Institute. A small schoolhouse was erected on Main St. (date uncertain), probably near what is now No. 20. It was soon outgrown and abandoned. Rev. Lorenzo D. Williams conducted a "select school" on the 2d floor of Robt. Barrows's house on Pearl (now W. Washington) St., and it was well patronized from 1836–39. In Sept. 1843, the building erected for Asbury Seminary was ready for use as a school. There, the seminary provided teacher training, taught business education, and offered a college preparatory course. Rev. Mr. Williams was its principal until 1846. The first record of a board of education is dated 1849. The board conducted 3 schools, each located in a different part of the town, and pupils were permitted to attend the school of their choice. When Asbury Seminary ceased to exist, the board began negotiations (1850) to purchase the property. There is much discussion in the minutes of the board about paying for it and procuring a proper deed. These discussions notwithstanding, the property remains (1986) on the Cuyahoga County auditor's duplicate as the Asbury Seminary. In 1986, the site of the Asbury Seminary (torn down in 1893) contained Chagrin Falls middle school.

Changes in population of the town (from 2,505 in 1940 to 3,095 in 1950), the annexation of the school district of S. Russell (1927) to the school district of Chagrin Falls, and changes in curricular needs led the Chagrin Falls Exempted School District Board of Education to purchase, 29 Mar. 1955, the land occupied by the Cuyahoga County Agricultural Society for fair purposes from 1874–1924. The property was large enough to accommodate school facilities and a community recreational area. A swimming pool, built cooperatively by the WPA and the Cuyahoga County commissioners in 1937, was the starting point (1943) for the development of the Chagrin Valley Recreation Council. This group of volunteers maintained a recreational program for the residents of the Chagrin Valley. The Lewis Sands Elementary School was built in 1956 on the "fairgrounds" property. A complex of buildings (classroom, library, gymnasium) was ready for the high school in 1958, also on the "fairgrounds" property. These buildings, together with the Middle School, constitute the facilities of the Chagrin Falls Exempted Village Schools in 1986. The Gurney School, built in S. Russell in 1966 and added to in 1968 and 1972, was abandoned as a school in 1983 because of declining enrollment. Chagrin Falls, a town of 601 inhabitants in 1842, with 30 different businesses and 120 businessmen, had grown into a village of 4,286 inhabitants, in 1986, with 1,976 dwelling units and 335 businesses. It has evolved from a town made up of people determined to harness the power of the river for manufacturing to a residential community with 1 manufactory.

Elizabeth G. Rodgers

**THE CHAGRIN FALLS HISTORICAL SOCIETY** was established in 1946 to preserve documents and artifacts relating to the history of CHAGRIN FALLS. Until 1965 the organization's collections were stored in the village hall and in the homes of its members. In that year the society acquired the Shute Memorial Bldg. at 21 Walnut St. as a

museum through the bequest of Mrs. Laura Shute. In 1984 the society was staffed by a curator and librarian and had a membership of 137. Clothing, artifacts, and photographs were housed on the first floor of its museum and used to illustrate the early history of Chagrin Falls. The lower level of the museum housed a meeting room available for rental to outside organizations. Free monthly programs open to the public were offered between October and May, and special programs such as village house tours and period fashion shows were offered periodically.

**CHAGRIN FALLS TOWNSHIP** was created by action of the Board of Commissioners of Cuyahoga County at their Mar. 1845 session, on receipt of a petition from the inhabitants of the area. It is not one of the original townships of the WESTERN RESERVE. It was created a year after CHAGRIN FALLS VILLAGE was incorporated. According to established procedure, the government was put in place at a meeting of the qualified electors of Chagrin Falls Twp. at Griswold's Tavern on 7 Apr. 1845. Stoughton Bentley, Ralph Russell, and Boardman H. Bosworth were chosen trustees. Thos. Shaw was selected as treasurer, Alanson Knox as clerk, and Rev. John K. Halleck as assessor. The reasons inhabitants petitioned for erection of the township are not a matter of record. It is possible, however, that they wished to unify the area. Some of the inhabitants of the incorporated village of Chagrin Falls lived in Solon Twp., and others in Orange Twp. Noah Graves, an early inhabitant of the town, was a commissioner of Cuyahoga County at the time the request was made. It is not known whether Graves took a special interest in the procedure. Since Chagrin Falls Village lies wholly within the township of Chagrin Falls, property owners of the village are subject to the real property tax levied by the township. This tax is in addition to that levied by the village. That gives property owners beyond the boundaries of the village, but within the township, a tax advantage. Since the turn of the century, efforts to resolve this situation have not been successful. The township represents a layer of government with no legislative (or other) function to perform for the village.

The **CHAGRIN RIVER** has its headwaters above Bass Lake, near Chardon, in Geauga County. It rises at an elevation of 1,335' (above sea level), flows a distance of 47.9 mi., and empties into Lake Erie at Eastlake, in Lake County, at an elevation of 773'. From source to mouth, the river falls 762'. When measured directly, the distance from source to mouth is 14.5 mi. The river flows in a southwesterly direction from its source to a place approximately 1 mi. west of CHAGRIN FALLS. There it makes a *U* turn and flows on in a northerly direction to Lake Erie. The fall of the river, the place where it turns back, is at an elevation of 876'. The village of Chagrin Falls is centered at the waterfall, located just west of the Main St. Bridge. There the river falls about 20'. It falls about 74' within the corporate limits of the village, which gave the first settlers the idea that the energy of the river could be harnessed for manufacturing purposes. That was unsuccessfully tried in the 1840s. There were sawmills and gristmills along its length, notably the sawmill established by HOLSEY GATES and his two brothers at GATES MILLS, in 1826, and the gristmill that followed, and the sawmill put in place by Noah Graves and the gristmill built by Geo. Fenkell, in 1841, at Chagrin Falls.

The Chagrin River has 2 branches: the Aurora Branch and the East Branch. The Aurora Branch rises in Portage County and is formed by the confluence of 2 tributaries, approximately 1 mi. east of Aurora. The north-flowing tributary has its origin at Sunny Lake, and the west-flowing tributary in a swampy area north of Round Up Lake. The Aurora Branch flows 16.1 mi. and empties into the Chagrin River south of Miles Rd. in BENTLEYVILLE. The East Branch rises in Chester Twp., Geauga County, and flows in a southerly direction to a place near Wilson's Mills. There it turns back and flows northerly and then westerly to a place near Mitchell's Mills Rd. and on into the Chagrin River at Daniels Park, Willoughby. From source to mouth, the East Branch flows 19.4 mi. The Chagrin River has 4 other tributaries: Griswold Creek, Willey Creek, Silver Creek, and Beaver Creek. McFarland Creek is a tributary of the Aurora Branch. The Chagrin River was first called the Elk, and it appears as such on a map prepared by Lewis Evans in 1755. It was probably so named because of the great number of elk, buffalo, and other game in the area. It came to be called the Shaguin to memorialize SIEUR DE SAGUIN, a French trader, because the Indians had only a *sh* sound in their language. Seguin's name was further corrupted when SETH PEASE prepared a map of the WESTERN RESERVE in 1797. He anglicized the word and labeled the Shaguin the Chagrin.

The **CHAGRIN VALLEY COUNTRY CLUB,** 4700 SOM Ctr. Rd., MORELAND HILLS, is a private, invitational organization. On 5 Apr. 1921, the Chagrin Valley Country Club Co. opened a 9-hole golf course built on part of the Mapes farm located east of SOM Ctr. Rd. Under the leadership of Harry D. Sims and a group of citizens, the Chagrin Valley Country Club Co. and the Chagrin Valley Country Club Land Co. were reorganized, and the club was incorporated on 27 Jan. 1925. A land contract was drawn up with the Mapes family in July 1925 that covered the purchase of 23 acres on the west side of SOM Ctr. and 79 acres on the east side. By 1927, 9 holes had been constructed on the east side, and the "back 9" holes had been built on the west side. Subsequently, it was decided to sell the east side parcel and to expand the west side to 18 holes; later the east side became Moreland Hills Golf Course. Stanley Thompson, a noted golf-course architect from Toronto, designed the course, often described as "one of the most difficult in Northeast Ohio." In 1944, a new corporation, the Chagrin Valley Country Club Land Co., was formed and guided the further development of the club. Geo. Chalmers served the club as golf professional, golf instructor, and greens superintendent from 1921. Jas. Chapman, of Scotland, became golf pro in 1965 and continued in the position into the 1980s. A Colonial-style clubhouse, constructed in 1928 on the highest point of the 200-acre club, commands a 20-mi. view of the Chagrin Valley and is the site of many social events throughout the year.

The **CHAGRIN VALLEY HUNT CLUB,** located in GATES MILLS, Ohio, began in Sept. 1908 at a gathering at Tannenbaum Farm, the Waite Hill home of CHAS. A. OTIS, JR., Cleveland industrialist and sportsman. Otis and a group of like-minded Clevelanders (including Jacob B. Perkins, Arthur D. Baldwin, M. Clark Harvey, Allyn F. Harvey, John H. Hord, Frank C. Newcomer, Corliss E. Sullivan, and Samuel E. Strong) who enjoyed horseback riding and jumping decided to revive foxhunting in the Cleveland area. (An earlier organization, the Cleveland Hunt, had existed from 1897-99.) An agreement was drawn up, money was subscribed, and some English hounds were imported from Canada. The new group, called the Cuyahoga County Cross-Country Riding Assoc., elected Arthur D. Baldwin secretary. In the same year, membership grew from approximately 15 to 34; the name was changed to the Chagrin Valley Hunt Club, the pack was kenneled in the Red Barn near the Maple Leaf Inn, and Fred Harland was chosen

the first of many kennel huntsmen. The first meet was held 7 Nov. 1908, when Windsor T. White and Sullivan guided the group through the countryside south of Willoughby and in and around Gates Mills.

On 1 July 1909, the club purchased the Maple Leaf Inn in Gates Mills, including its buildings, equipment, and adjoining grounds, and on 10 July it became incorporated as the Chagrin Valley Hunt Club Co. Membership rules were again changed to accommodate first 100, then 150 members. The first official board of directors meeting, held 2 Nov. 1909, elected E. A. Merritt president; JEPTHA H. WADE, JR., and Corliss E. Sullivan vice-presidents; Frank C. Newcomer secretary; and Windsor T. White master of the foxhounds, a position he held until 1928. Through the years, club members—including many women—dressed in formal hunting attire have continued to follow the hounds through Gates Mills, HUNTING VALLEY, and nearby Amish farmlands. Membership has continued to expand (300) and includes many descendants of the founders.

**CHAMBER OF COMMERCE.** *See* **GREATER CLEVELAND GROWTH ASSOC.**

The **CHAMBER OF COMMERCE-CITY PLAN COMMITTEE** of Cleveland was an influential body, assuming "quasi-public commission" status with mayoral approval. In 1899 this special committee began modestly to investigate harmonizing the architectural styles of proposed public buildings. Within 4 years it spearheaded legislation for and implementation of the Group Plan. Purposely including architects and engineers in its ranks, the committee achieved authority when Mayor HERMAN BAEHR agreed to its review of "such public improvements as may come within its scope." Not only did the committee critique bath house and hospital designs, but in the teens and twenties it also promoted city and countywide schemes for rationalizing urban development, such as establishing planning commissions, accepting land-use zoning, and adopting in Cuyahoga County's communities a uniform platting ordinance. By 1938, with many of its programs implemented, the City Plan Committee's importance waned as its supporters retired and the chamber changed leadership.

Over 39 years, this committee had 6 prominent chairmen: Wm. G. Mather (1899-1911); Wm. H. Hunt (1911-15); MORRIS A. BLACK (1915-25); NEWTON D. BAKER (1925-27); Wm. C. Boyle (1927-32); and ABRAM GARFIELD (1932-38); 3 titles: Grouping Public Buildings (1899-1908); Municipal Art & Architecture (1908-17); and City Plan (1917-38); and numerous devoted members of experience and influence, including MOSES J. GRIES, FRANCIS F. PRENTISS, WM. A. STINCHCOMB, and BENJAMIN S. HUBBELL. Its prestige touched local, state, and national levels.

In 1915 Mayor Newton Baker appointed a separate City Plan Commission, several of whose members continued to serve on the committee. Thus began a long, intimate committee-commission association. In 1916 the 8th Natl. Conference on City Planning, sponsored by the committee, was held at the Chamber of Commerce. Over the years the committee advocated comprehensive street plans as well as widening, straightening, or extending specific streets. Subcommittees juried annual awards for apartment, commercial, and business buildings. Before bond issues came to ballot, their merits were assayed for voters. Area developments were promoted first through subcommittees that became separate corporations, e.g., the University Improvement Co. and Euclid Ave. Assoc. Legislation was drafted, and legal actions were taken at the committee's behest. The City Plan Committee considered itself an impartial forum as well as a source of experienced counsel.

**CHAMBERLAIN, SELAH** (4 May 1812–27 Dec. 1891), was one of the leading railroad developers in Ohio and the Midwest. One of Cleveland's most prominent businessmen, he was also successfully involved in the iron industry and banking. Chamberlain was born in Brattleboro, Vt. Raised on his father's farm, he acquired a basic education in the common schools. At the age of 21, he moved to Boston, where he obtained fundamental training in business as an apprentice in a grocery store. In 1835, Chamberlain formed his own company and was hired as a contractor to complete construction on an extension of the Erie & Pennsylvania Canal. His involvement in the transportation industry grew as he received larger contracts for work on the Wabash & Erie Canal. Later, in the 1840s, he supervised improvements on the St. Lawrence River in Canada. In 1847, he returned to Vermont and formed a new company to obtain contracts for building segments of the country's emerging railroad system. The company was largely responsible for the construction of the Rutland & Burlington Railroad to Boston, and the Lake Champlain Railroad. In 1849, Chamberlain moved to Cleveland to take advantage of railroad expansion in the Midwest. Chamberlain's other business involvements in Cleveland included, in the 1860s, the cofounding of the private banking house of Chamberlain, Gorham, & Perkins, which in 1880 was merged into Merchants Natl. Bank. Related to his railroad interests, in 1880 he was one of the founders of the Cleveland Iron Mining Co. (later to become CLEVELAND CLIFFS). Civically active in Cleveland, Chamberlain was a member of the Garfield Natl. Monument Assoc. To raise funds for the monument in 1882. Chamberlain's railroad interests in the Midwest were extensive. In 1849, he was given the entire contract for construction of the Cleveland & Pittsburgh Railroad. He was subsequently engaged, for several years, in railroad building in Iowa and Wisconsin and was a major stockholder in several railroad companies. In Ohio, he was one of the incorporators of the Cleveland, Lorain, & Wheeling Railroad Co. He was also instrumental in forming the Cleveland Transportation Co. and for many years was its president. Chamberlain married Arabella Cochran in 1844. The Chamberlains were one of the first families to own a mansion on "Prosperity Row" on Euclid Ave.

The **CHANDLER & RUDD COMPANY** is one of the most distinctive grocery stores in Cleveland, specializing in fine foods and delicacies. The firm started in 1864 as the Jones-Potter Co. Wm. Rudd was one of the first employees. Four years later, he and Geo. Chandler bought out the original owners and changed the name of the store, which was on the south side of PUBLIC SQUARE, to the Chandler & Rudd Co. With Cleveland's ethnic diversity and its growing wealth, Chandler & Rudd concentrated on imported delicacies but also carried a conventional line of groceries. Later, it added its own line of baked goods and candies. In 1888, the company incorporated and moved into a larger store on Euclid Ave., as well as an uptown branch at Euclid and E. 55th St. In 1894, Chandler left the business because of a dispute over the store's selling of liquor. Rudd and his brother, George, then managed the store.

Chandler & Rudd was the first grocery store in Cleveland to make extensive use of newspaper advertising. In 1910, it was one of the first grocery concerns in the nation to inaugurate a telephone ordering system. By 1930, the store had grown into a $2 million-per-year business. In the midst of the Depression, in 1932, the company undertook an expansion program, and by 1934, it had established 9 branch stores in shopping centers around the area. Although some of these branches were eventually abandoned, they marked the start of chain grocery stores in Cleveland. By 1940, the company had 4 stores and 175 employees. In the 1950s, the downtown store's business declined. In 1958, it moved into a smaller store on PLAYHOUSE SQUARE, dealing only in gifts and specialty foods. In 1960, the downtown store was closed. Chandler & Rudd moved its headquarters to its Shaker Hts. store at 20128 Chagrin Blvd., which had opened in 1952. Since 1960 the company has been run by the Marino family, which has maintained the remaining store in SHAKER HTS.

The **CHANDLER-CLEVELAND MOTORS CORPORATION** was established in 1926 by the consolidation of 2 successful Cleveland automobile companies, the Chandler Motor Car and Cleveland Automobile companies, both of which were founded by Frederick C. Chandler (12 July 1874–18 Feb. 1945). A native Clevelander, Chandler went to work for the Cleveland Bicycle Co. of Henry A. Lozier, staying with Lozier when he began to make boats and later automobiles. Chandler became general manager and later vice-president of the company. In Jan. 1913, Chandler and several other major Lozier executives resigned to establish their own company to produce a moderately priced 6-cylinder automobile. Chandler served as president of the new firm, Chas. F. Emise as vice-president, and Samuel Regar as treasurer. Establishing an office in the Swetland Bldg. on Euclid Ave. in 1913, the company purchased a 6-acre site on E. 131st St. north of St. Clair and began production in July 1913, producing in that year 550 cars that sold for $1,785 each. Production increased to 1950 automobiles in 1914 and 7,000 in 1915; the financial success of the company enabled it to expand its facilities in 1915, doubling its production capacity to 15,000 automobiles in 1916. During the war the company made 10-ton artillery tractors for the Army in addition to its own automobiles.

The great success of the Chandler Motor Car Co. encouraged Chandler to establish a second company to produce a lower-priced automobile. The Cleveland Automobile Co. was founded in Feb. 1919 and began production in July at a 17-acre site on Euclid Ave. near London Rd. Chandler and Regar served on the board of directors of the new company; John V. Whitbeck was president; Sidney Black, vice-president; and Joseph I. Krall, secretary. The company produced the Cleveland automobile, a 5-passenger touring car that sold for $1,385; 16,000 of them were made in 1920. Chandler Motor Car made 23,832 automobiles in 1920, the most of any car manufacturer in Cleveland and 13th in the nation. Sales, production, and profits declined for both companies in 1921; in 1926 the two firms were consolidated as the Chandler-Cleveland Motors Corp. The new firm stopped producing the Cleveland car in Mar. 1926, and in Dec. 1928 Chandler-Cleveland was sold to the Hupp Motor Car Corp. of Detroit, which stopped producing Chandler models in May 1929. After selling his automobile company, Frederick Chandler joined his son's Chandler Prods. Corp., which manufactured cap screws. He served as chairman of the board from 1929–42 after the death of his son, Frederick C. Chandler, Jr. The elder Chandler was married once, to Anna Nightingale in 1899.

**CHAPIN, HERMAN M.** (29 July 1823–24 May 1879), was a businessman who took a keen interest in Cleveland libraries and served 1 term as mayor of the city. Chapin was born in Walpole, N.H., and came to Cleveland in 1848 to become a partner in the wholesale grocery warehouse of Chas. Bradburn & Co. In 1852, he left to start his own business as a provision dealer and beef and pork packer. Shifting rail routes led Chapin to move his operation to Chicago in 1862, but he returned it to Cleveland a few years later when the routes shifted again. In 1865, he helped form the Hahnemann Life Insurance Co. and became its president. The firm later merged with the Republic Life Insurance Co. and moved to Chicago.

During the CIVIL WAR, Chapin helped raise money and equipment for the Union. While he was away assisting the war effort in the spring of 1865, he was elected mayor of Cleveland, even though he did not know he was nominated. During his term, the Metropolitan Police Act was passed. It transferred the police powers of the mayor, the police marshal, and the city council to a new board of police commissioners consisting of the mayor and 4 others appointed by the governor. In 1872, the act was changed to allow for the commissioners' election.

Chapin was involved in Cleveland libraries throughout his life. In 1854, he became president of the CLEVELAND LIBRARY ASSOC. and put the financially ailing organization on a sound fiscal base. He held the office again in 1858 and in 1870 became one of the directors for life of the reorganized association. He was also one of the members of the WESTERN RESERVE HISTORICAL SOCIETY at its founding in 1867. Chapin was a leader in the First Unitarian Church when it was founded in 1854. In the same year, he built the Chapin Block at the corner of Euclid and the Square. The third floor housed Concert Hall, an elegant public auditorium, later renamed Chapin Hall. Chapin married Matilda Fenno of Boston on 15 Oct. 1849. They had 6 children.

**CHAPMAN, RAYMOND JOHNSON "RAY"** (15 Jan. 1891-17 Aug. 1920), was a major-league baseball player for the CLEVELAND INDIANS between 1912-20. He was the last major-league player to die as a result of being hit by a pitched baseball. Chapman was born in Beaver Dam, Ky., but spent his childhood in Herrin, Ill. During 1910 and 1911 he played baseball with Springfield and Davenport in the Three III League. He joined the Toledo Mud Hens of the American Assoc., in 1911 and in August 1912 his contract was purchased by the Cleveland team in the American League. For the next 8 seasons, Chapman was the Indians' shortstop. More interested in his team's wins than his own accomplishments, Chapman led the league in sacrifice hits 3 years, setting a major-league record with 67 sacrifices in 1917. His team record of 55 stolen bases in 1917 was not broken until Miguel Dilone's mark of 61 in 1980. A competent fielder, Chapman was the league leader in putouts 2 seasons and in assists 1 year. In 1,303 baseball games with Cleveland, he had a batting average of .278. While playing for the pennant-contending Indians at the New York Polo Grounds on 16 Aug. 1920, Chapman was hit in the head by a pitched baseball from Carl Mays, an underhand pitcher for the Yankees. He died at a New York hospital 12 hours later. His funeral, held at ST. JOHN'S CATHEDRAL, was one of the largest in Cleveland's history. Chapman's grief-stricken teammates dedicated the rest of the season to him. Led by their playing manager, TRIS SPEAKER, the Indians won the league and world championships for the first time. Chapman was married on 29 Oct. 1919 to Kathleen Marie Daly, the daughter of Martin B. Daly, president of the EAST OHIO GAS CO.

The **CHARITY FOOTBALL GAME,** sponsored by the *PLAIN DEALER,* was begun in 1931 to raise money for the newspaper's Give-a-Christmas Fund and to determine an interscholastic football champion for the city. The game was played annually during the Thanksgiving holidays at the Cleveland Stadium through 1970; after 1970 the Senate Athletic Council moved the game to high school fields, and the *Plain Dealer* ceased its sponsorship. Cleveland's Charity Football Game was not unique during the Depression. The collegiate Big 10 conference, for example, arranged a charity schedule for its teams. The idea for the Cleveland high school game came from a remark by Owen D. Young, a member of Pres. Herbert Hoover's relief committee, who suggested that every city have a charity football game to help support its relief program. Officials from the Cleveland scholastic conferences agreed to suspend their rules prohibiting postseason play, making clear that this game was considered a special, emergency situation and was not to set a precedent.

John A. Crawford of the *Plain Dealer* managed the game for its first 15 years. Scholastic officials met each year to determine which two high school football teams in Cleveland were the best and should play in the championship game; beginning in 1937, when the Senate Conference was reorganized into East Side and West Side leagues, the champions in each league played for the title. From 1931-54 the game was held on the Friday or Saturday after Thanksgiving; from 1955-68 it was played on Thanksgiving Day. In an attempt to improve attendance, the game was moved to Saturday in 1969, and the event became a doubleheader, featuring the championship game of the Crown Conference in addition to the Senate game.

Through at least the mid-1950s, the game appears to have been a spectacle attracting citywide attention. The first game, in which CATHEDRAL LATIN SCHOOL defeated Central 18-0 before 19,304 spectators, raised $8,400 for charity and featured a high school marching-band competition in addition to the football game. Boy Scouts served as ushers for the 1932 game, the naval reserves fired a cannon during the flag-raising ceremonies, and competitions were held to select a poster and slogan to drum up support for the game. Tickets were later sold by high school alumni groups and students of all levels. By 1935, leading ticket sellers were eligible to win trips and other prizes. Attendance and proceeds varied according to the weather and the participating teams: in 1936, 19,000 spectators watched Collinwood and Cleveland Hts. play to a tie and raised $5,468 for charity; the following year the 47,315 people who saw John Adams defeat West Tech raised $15,655. The largest crowd for a Charity Game was 70,955 in 1946; they watched Cathedral Latin win over Holy Name for the 4th of its 5 straight Charity Game championships between 1943-47.

During the late 1960s, the Charity Game was marred by recurrent violence, what the *CLEVELAND PRESS* called "hoodlumism in broad daylight." Assaults, vandalism, and broken store windows in the downtown area after the 1969 event led councilman Gerald McFaul to urge that it be canceled. When the doubleheaders in 1969 and 1970 failed to improve attendance, the Senate Athletic Council moved the game out of the stadium, which the game's low attendance had made too costly to rent, to high school fields.

The **CHARITY ORGANIZATION SOCIETY,** organized in Jan. 1881, sought to coordinate charitable giving and organize it along scientific lines in order to prevent recipients from becoming "sadly pauperized in spirit" as a result of "injudicious and indiscriminate giving." The Cleveland society was one of 22 such organizations formed in the U.S. in the 5 years after the first appeared in Buffalo in 1877; the movement began in London in 1869. Officers in the Cleveland society included Howard M. Hanna, president; Walter S. Collins, secretary; W. S. Jones, treasurer; and Henry N. Reymond, general superintendent. The society's work was supported by $5 annual memberships and $100 life memberships.

Cleveland's Society for Organizing Charity shared the belief that there were 2 kinds of poor: "the honest poor, who prefer to work rather than to beg," and "the pauperized poor, who prefer to do anything rather than work." Society organizers believed that "the needy should be relieved, [but] the vagrant should not be supported in an idle life"; eliminating "injudicious giving" and making "*work* the basis of relief" would "restore" the idle, "clamoring" poor by forcing them to work for their own support. The society thus engaged in 2 kinds of work: "the repressive," by which it searched out "imposters," those for whom begging was a way of life, and "the provident, to educate the poor in ways of thrift and industry."

In Mar. 1881 the Cleveland Charity Organization Society opened a central office at 345 Superior St. Here it sought to register names of all people who received aid from the city and the various relief agencies. It urged Cleveland residents to send those who sought aid to the society's central office to apply for a certificate from the society. Applicants for certificates were investigated, and certificates were awarded "only to needy and worthy persons." The society aided 338 cases in 1881 and investigated 514 new family cases in 1882 and 538 in 1883.

As the society's work brought its investigators into regular contact with the city's poor, it became more aware of the social conditions that contributed to poverty and became more of an advocate for the poor. It called for day nurseries to enable more women to work, and it maintained a job registry where men could come in search of day work. In 1881, 405 men and boys sought work; the registry's 2,749 applicants in 1882 increased to 6,526 in 1883. More than 150 women sought work in 1881, and in Mar. 1882 the society opened a Matrons' & Servants' Employment Bureau, which was designed to allow the matrons to protect themselves against "incompetent or unworthy servants," but also to facilitate employment for deserving girls; 3,327 women registered at the bureau in 1882. In 1884, Cleveland's Charity Organization Society merged with Bethel Union to create Bethel Associated Charities, which later evolved into the Family Services Assoc. and subsequently the CENTER FOR HUMAN SERVICES.

**CHARLES DICKENS'S VISIT TO CLEVELAND** was part of a tour to the U.S. in 1842. Dickens, his wife, and a traveling friend, Mr. Putnam, arrived on Monday, 25 Apr. The author and his party had traveled on the steamboat *Constitution* after a rough voyage across Lake Erie from Sandusky. Dickens's journey could not be said to be particularly successful. While in Sandusky, he had read a newspaper article appearing in the *Cleveland Plain Dealer*. The article, according to Dickens, was an insulting piece of work, because it boasted of America's defeating England for a third time and of the singing of " 'Yankee Doodle' in Hyde Park and 'Hail Columbia' in the scarlet courts of Westminster." Unfortunately, Dickens's ire had not abated upon his stopover in Cleveland. Although he described the town in glowing terms, his reception, he felt, left much to be desired. Dickens and his friend, Mr. Putnam, walked around the town. Upon returning to the *Constitution* and his stateroom, the author and his wife were subjected to the curious stares of the local residents, who peered in the windows trying to get a look at the famous gentleman. Dickens was so upset by this unwanted attention that when the mayor, Dr. JOSHUA MILLS, came on board, the author refused to speak to him. Undaunted, the mayor moved to the end of the pier and passed the time whittling, hoping that Dickens would change his mind and make an ap-

pearance, but Dickens was adamant. The *Constitution* remained in port until 9 o'clock that morning, when it sailed, taking the author to his next stop, Erie, and then to Buffalo. Dickens did not return to Cleveland for another 25 years.

**CHEMICAL INDUSTRY.** For the first 60 years of its existence, Cleveland knew only the rather homespun chemical industries of a typical rural community, time-honored processes such as dyeing, tanning, soapmaking, and bleaching. Cleveland was essentially one of several small towns along Lake Erie. Completion of the OHIO & ERIE CANAL gave it an advantage in the 1830s. In the 1850s, a growing railroad network enhanced Cleveland's potential, giving it easy access to coal and oil from the east and south. Its lake harbor paved the way for its access to the ore fields of Michigan and Minnesota. Cleveland's chemical industry began to develop in the wake of the CIVIL WAR, in response to the emerging shipbuilding, oil, iron-and-steel, machine-tool, and automobile industries. In 1867, Eugene Ramiro Grasselli opened his first sulfuric acid plant in Cleveland adjacent to his major customer, the Rockefeller refinery on the banks of the CUYAHOGA RIVER. He soon moved the business he had founded in Cincinnati in 1839 to Cleveland, and found himself in competition with the Cleveland Chemical Works, whose interests he eventually acquired. He initiated a policy of expanding by establishing new plants, or acquiring facilities already in operation in those places where the oil industry was rapidly developing. After his death in 1882, his son, CAESAR A. GRASSELLI, continued to pursue the policies established by his father. By 1900, the GRASSELLI CHEMICAL CO. had built or acquired plants in Ohio, Pennsylvania, New York, New Jersey, Illinois, and Alabama. Their line of chemicals had expanded to include not only sulfuric acid, the staple used by the oil industry, but also hydrochloric, nitric, and acetic acids, a variety of salts, zinc pigments, phosphates, fertilizers, and even some coal-tar products. By 1903, it began to convert from the lead-chamber to the contact process for making sulfuric acid. At this time, the Frasch process was making domestic sulfur available at competitive prices. With other acid makers, Grasselli began to convert from imported pyrites to native sulfur as the basic raw material for making sulfuric acid.

During these years, 2 of Cleveland's important paint industries emerged to supply the growing construction, shipbuilding, machine-tool, and automobile industries. Henry A. Sherwin and Truman Dunham formed a partnership in 1866. Edward P. Williams joined the partnership in 1870, to form Sherwin, Williams & Co. By 1884, the name SHERWIN WILLIAMS CO. was adopted, and its paint products began to "cover the earth." The roots of the Glidden Co. were also being established, with the formation of the Glidden Varnish Co. in 1870. Both companies supplied coatings to the growing railroad car-building industry. In 1898, Wm. A. Harshaw effected a merger of 2 companies he had founded: the Cleveland Commercial Co. and the C. H. Price Co. of Elyria, to form the Harshaw, Fuller & Goodwin Co. to make oils, pigments, dry colors, and other chemical commodities. Many of these were consumed by the paint manufacturers. It retained this name until 1919, when it moved into new quarters on E. 97th St. and became the HARSHAW CHEMICAL CO.

The early decades of the 20th century, especially the decade following WORLD WAR I, saw the emergence of an American chemical industry of international significance. The war had removed important German chemical products from the market and, at the same time, involved the American industry in the production of munitions and other war material. Cleveland's chemical industries reflected this development. The Grasselli Chemical Co. diversified its products to include copper and barium sulfates, silicates, a variety of sodium- and sulfur-containing salts, insecticides, and fungicides. The Grasselli Powder Co. was formed by the merger of 3 powder companies in 1917. The Grasselli Dyestuff Corp. was incorporated in 1924, to take advantage of the growing need for dyestuff materials in the wake of World War I. Germany had been the principal international supplier until 1914. In 1928, Du Pont and Grasselli merged, and Grasselli became a division of Du Pont. At the time of the merger, Grasselli possessed 26 plants in the Midwest, Northeast, and South. The Grasselli Dyestuff Corp. came under the control of the American I. G. Chemical Corp., a branch of the principal German producer of dyestuffs, from 1928 until 1941, when it was reorganized and "Americanized" by the Foreign Funds Control Unit of the U.S. Treasury. The Harshaw, Fuller & Goodwin Co., on a more limited basis, diversified its product line to include glycerin refining (1914), anhydrous hydrogen fluoride and aluminum chloride, antimony products, calcium oxides and hydrated lime, and copper and uranium chemicals (1942–45). Because of its role in the production of uranium chemicals during WORLD WAR II, Harshaw received one of two 4-Star Army-Navy E awards given out in the nation.

Three major new companies appeared in Cleveland between the wars, the FERRO CORP., MCGEAN-ROHCO, INC., and the Glidden Co. The formation of Glidden is typical of the mergers that dominated the postwar years. Adrian D. Joyce acquired the assets of the Glidden Varnish Co. in 1917 and incorporated as the Glidden Co. By 1919, Glidden had purchased 11 other manufacturers of paint products in Illinois, Minnesota, Ohio, Pennsylvania, and even California (the Whittier-Coburn Co. of San Francisco). It achieved diversification and expansion by continued acquisitions: the Euston Lead Co., Scranton, Pa. (1924); American Zirconium Corp. (1933); Southern Pine Chemical Co. (1938); and E. R. Durkee Co. (1929), to name a few. By 1947, Glidden had 35 factories and 26 research and control laboratories, organized in 8 divisions: Paint & Varnish, Chemicals & Pigments, Metals Refining, Naval Stores, Vegetable Oils, Food Products, Soya Products, and Feed Mills. McGean-Rohco started out as 2 independent companies. John A. McGean founded the McGean Chemical Co. in May 1929, with himself as president and his son, Ralph L. McGean, as vice president. It became a leader in the manufacture of anodes and electroplating materials. Rohco was founded in 1947 by Richard O. Hull, a Cleveland chemist. It also specialized in electroplating chemicals and equipment for plating zinc, cadmium, copper, and chromium. The Ferro Corp. was founded in 1919 as the Ferro Enameling Co. Its main products were vitreous porcelain products, frits, glazes, and oxide colors for porcelain and ceramic products. The company changed its name to the Ferro Enameling Corp. in 1930, and finally to the Ferro Corp. in 1951.

The period following World War II can be characterized as one of internationalization and continued diversification through merger and acquisition, as is well illustrated by the development of McGean-Rohco. In 1965, the McGean Chemical Co. was bought out by Chemetron; in 1973, R. O. Hull & Co. was bought out by the LUBRIZOL CORP. Both were ultimately purchased by groups of private investors and reestablished as Rohco and the McGean Chemical Co. respectively. In 1974, McGean was purchased from Chemetron by a group of investors under Dickson Whitney, son-in-law of Ralph L. McGean; R. O. Hull was purchased from Lubrizol by a group of investors headed by its managers in 1979. Finally, in 1982, Rohco became

a part of McGean, and the name was changed to McGean-Rohco, Inc.

The gradual decline of Cleveland's oil and iron-and-steel industries in the years following World War II, especially in the 1960s and 1970s, had a major effect on the ancillary chemical industries. Under Dwight P. Joyce, Glidden continued to expand and diversify by acquisition. By 1966, it had reduced the number of its divisions to 4: Coatings & Resins, Foods, Chemicals, and International. It sold many of its interests in naval stores, soya products, and feedmills. In 1967, Glidden entered into a merger with the SCM Corp., eventually becoming GLIDDEN COATINGS & RESINS—SMC. Harshaw Chemical Co. also expanded, diversified, and internationalized during the years following World War II. Some of its important acquisitions were Rufert Chemical and Zinsser & Co. (1953), Kentucky Color & Chemical (1958), Fermo Labs (1962), and Hammer Electronics and Molechem, Inc. (1964). It also formed Harshaw Chemical, Ltd., in 1956 to manufacture and distribute its products in Europe and Great Britain, and in 1960 it acquired an 85% interest in Harshaw-van der Hoorn of the Netherlands. At the time of its acquisition by Kewanee Industries, Inc., in 1965, Harshaw employed over 1,900 people and had plants and labs in Ohio, Kentucky, New Jersey, Michigan, Illinois, Pennsylvania, and California. In 1977, Kewanee Industries was acquired by the Gulf Oil Co., which shortly became the Gulf Corp., and merged to form the Chevron Corp. in July 1985. Sherwin Williams also entered into this process of diversification and internationalization after World War II. Some of its important acquisitions included the Rubberset Co. (1956), the Maumee Chemical Co. and Sprayon Prods. (1966), the Levitt Bros. Co. (which ran the home improvement departments in K-Mart) (1967), the Osborn Mfg. Co. and Verffabrieken Ralson N.V. (1968), the Hadley Adhesives & Chemical Co. (1973), and some businesses of Dutch Boy, Inc., and the Ashland Chemical Co. and Eagle Picher Co. (1980). In 1983, it acquired GRAY DRUGSTORES, INC. During the late 1970s, Sherwin Williams disposed of certain businesses of its Chemicals Div., portions of its Coatings Chemicals and International segments, the Sherwin-Williams Container Corp., and about 100 company-operated stores, reducing its divisions to 3 basic ones: Paint Stores (1535), Drug Stores (423), and Coatings. In Dec. 1984, Sherwin-Williams employed over 19,000 throughout the world.

Ferro engaged in the merger and acquisition process following World War II, and even more so in the 1960s and 1970s. W. B. Lawson and the Ferro Drier & Chemical Co. were merged in 1946 to form the Ferro Chemical Corp. in BEDFORD. In the following years, at least 6 more domestic companies were acquired, and numerous foreign subsidiaries were set up. By 1966, Ferro possessed facilities in 11 states and foreign countries, including Japan, several South American countries, and South Africa, and employed 4,600, only half of these in the U.S. From 1966–86, Ferro averaged at least 1 new acquisition each year, as it expanded into 20 foreign countries and 12 states. In 1985, its employment stood at over 8,000. Its product lines included coatings, inorganic colorants, chemicals (esp. polymer additives), ceramics, and thermoplastics (esp. elastomeric).

Cleveland's chemical industries therefore followed many of the trends found in larger American industries. The major one was that toward greater diversification and expansion, and the formation of large, international conglomerates, such as SCM, Du Pont, and the Chevron Corp. This growth served 2 important purposes. It helped maintain profitability during transition periods, when a product or product line loses its importance, or when new products or product lines are being developed and tested, and it provided the broad economic base for an active and viable research-and-development program. The chemical industry in Cleveland has evolved from a locally operated one serving local manufacturing industries to an internationally diverse operation dependent upon an international market. Its viability in Cleveland in the 1980s was based not so much on proximity to natural resources or areas of product demand as upon the availability of a skilled research workforce and viable facilities to house that workforce.

Ernest G. Spittler
John Carroll University

The **CHESHIRE CHEESE CLUB OF CLEVELAND,** 1254 Euclid Ave., an invitational club of men, meets weekly to hear guest speakers, review books, and discuss "the topics of the day." The club began in 1917, when a group of businessmen who were meeting informally for luncheon at Chandler & Rudd (next to the MAY CO. on PUBLIC SQUARE) were invited by the manager, Harry D. Sims, to use a specially reserved table for their daily "book review" meetings. Thos. W. Larwood, Wm. A. Matthews, and Chas. L. Schwartz, founders, assisted by Sims and Harry D. Baker, patterned the club somewhat loosely on the original Cheshire Cheese Club of Fleet St. in London—made famous by Samuel Johnson and Jas. Boswell (1737). Through the years there has been a reciprocal relationship between the clubs in London and in Cleveland, resulting in an exchange of printed programs, occasional gifts, and personal visits of members to the club in London. The Cleveland club has met in a variety of locations, including the Public Square setting; the Nanking Restaurant (1930s); the Colonial Hotel (1940s); Stouffers (Playhouse Square–1950s); and the Hanna Bldg. until 1983, when the club moved to its present (1985) location at the Elegant Hog Restaurant. The club has "no constitution, no by-laws, no organized structure"; its main focus has been "good fellowship."

Herrick, Clay, *Brief History of the Cheshire Cheese Club* (ca. 1983).

**CHESNUTT, CHARLES WADDELL** (20 June 1858–15 Nov. 1932), was a black novelist, short-story writer, and lawyer. He was the first black writer to deal with the race question from the Negro's point of view. Chesnutt was born in Cleveland. After a brief stay in Oberlin, Ohio, his family moved to Fayetteville, N.C., where Chesnutt grew up during the years immediately following the CIVIL WAR. He attended the Howard School in Fayetteville, graduating at the age of 16. His formal education was augmented by extensive independent study and tutorial instruction in German, French, and Greek. He also taught himself stenography in order to make a living. After graduating from the Howard School, Chesnutt became a teacher in black schools in North Carolina. At the age of 19 he became assistant principal of the New Fayetteville Normal School, and later its principal. During this period he assiduously kept a journal, a source he later drew from for his short stories and novels. After brief employment in New York as a reporter, Chesnutt returned to Cleveland in 1883 and became a stenographer for Judge SAMUEL WILLIAMSON. He found time to study law and was admitted to the Ohio bar in 1887. For many years thereafter, he served as a court reporter in order to support his family and his writing.

As a writer, Chesnutt depicted blacks as human beings. That was a new departure in American literature, as theretofore blacks had been portrayed as stereotypes or subtypes. In his short stories and novels, he attempted to bridge the race gap and to raise the issue of civil rights and equal opportunity for blacks. In 1887, the *Atlantic Monthly* published its first of several Chesnutt stories, "The Gooph-

ered Grapevine." In 1899, selected stories of his were assembled into a single volume, *The Conjure Woman,* that was published by Houghton, Mifflin & Co. In April of that year it headed the bestseller list in Cleveland. Another volume of short stories followed, *The Wife of His Youth and Other Short Stories of the Color Line,* and then several novels. The most popular of these was *The House behind the Cedars* (1900), about intermarriage. That same year, in the May issue of the *Atlantic Monthly,* Wm. Dean Howells praised Chesnutt as being in the top rank of American short-story writers. Later in the decade, Chesnutt's popularity as a writer began to wane as white readers grew tired of his themes. He continued to write articles and lecture, and to be civically active in Cleveland, most notably as a member of the Chamber of Commerce. In 1878, Chesnutt married Susan Perry; they had 4 daughters.

Charles W. Chesnutt Papers, WRHS.

**CHESSIE SYSTEM.** *See* CSX (CHESSIE SYSTEM)

The **CHEVROLET PARMA PLANT OF GENERAL MOTORS CORPORATION** was built as part of GM's postwar expansion in the Cleveland area. Plans for the Parma facility at Brookpark and Stumph (later Chevrolet Blvd.) roads were announced in 1946. The plant opened in 1949 to build automatic transmissions for the Chevrolet division. By 1956, it employed 7,600 people in the manufacture of transmissions, propeller shafts, and pressed metal parts; employment rose to 7,740 in 1963. In 1979, employment at the plant was 7,500. Layoffs as a result of the recession in the automobile industry lowered the number of workers to 3,600 in Sept. 1984. In 1980 the plant made 3,900 transmissions a day for rear-drive cars and also produced hoods and other components for a new front-wheel-drive transmission, with the assembly of these parts handled elsewhere. In Nov. 1984 company officials decided to continue producing transmissions for light-duty trucks and vans at the plant at least through Aug. 1986.

**CHIEF THUNDERWATER** (10 Sept. 1865–10 June 1950), sometimes referred to by his Indian name, Oghema Niagara, was a native American Indian chief who worked to preserve the rights of his people and to improve their welfare. He also worked to preserve his native culture and undertook a variety of efforts to improve the image of AMERICAN INDIANS among white Americans. Niagara was born on the Tuscarora Indian reservation near Lewistown, N.Y. His mother, Au-Paw-Chee-Kaw-Paw-qua (Woman Whose Name Shall Never Die), a member of the Osaukee tribe, was the daughter of an important chief in the Black Hawk War, Chief Keokuk; his father, Jee-wan-gah, was a member of the Seneca tribe and was a hunter and trapper who also sold herbs. Niagara's parents had 2 other children, who were adopted by white parents. In alternate years he traveled with his parents between homes in Montreal and Iowa, often stopping to rest in Cleveland at the home of fellow Indian Peter (or Thomas) Bennett on Oregon St. (Rockwell Ave.) near Muirson (E. 12th).

Little information is available about Chief Thunderwater between 1875 and 1910. He apparently appeared in Wild West shows with Buffalo Bill Cody for about 9 years, and after 1883, he became an active combatant against "the excessive use of" liquor among Indians. It was apparently at this point that he began to work to improve the plight of native American Indians. In the early 1900s Niagara settled in Cleveland; by 1913 he was living at 6716 Baden Ct. in the E. 67th St.-Central Ave. area, and he was soon the president of the Preservative Cleaner Co., manufacturers of polish. He also sold his own Thunderwater's Mohawk Oil, for rheumatism and arthritis, and Jee-wan-ga tea. But the majority of his efforts went toward maintaining and improving the welfare, the rights, and the image of American Indians.

On 10 Mar. 1917, Oghema Niagara was among the incorporators in Ohio of the Supreme Council of the Tribes, an attempt to revive the renowned League of the Confederacy of Iroquois Nations in the Great Lakes region. The organization was formed to assist American Indians in sickness and distress, to promote their welfare, and "to propagate the doctrine of temperance and education among them and to legally protect and preserve their rights and interests generally." As chief of the Supreme Council, Niagara operated "the Council Sanctuary" in his home in Cleveland at his own expense, housing, feeding, clothing, and providing medical attention for what his neighbors said were hundreds of destitute, unemployed, and sick Indians and persons of all races. He also became involved in a variety of legal issues concerning both individual Indians and entire tribes.

Niagara's efforts to educate white Americans about the true nature of native American Indians and their culture took a variety of forms. He was an active member of the Early Settler's Assoc. in Cleveland and appeared at public ceremonies in full headdress, becoming known as Cleveland's "official Indian." He held an annual ceremony at the grave of JOC-O-SOT, placing maize on his grave in the ERIE ST. CEMETERY. Niagara remained active until ca. 1942, when illness forced him to give up many public appearances.

Chief Thunderwater Papers, WRHS.

**CHILD CARE.** Since the mid-19th century, Cleveland has provided care for children who are dependent, delinquent, neglected, or in need of daycare or medical services. Although child care has been both a private and a public responsibility, the public sector has played an increasingly significant role since the 1930s. The first public institution to care for children was the city infirmary, built in 1837, which housed all of Cleveland's dependent population, including the ill, elderly, disabled, and insane. In 1858, a separate house of correction or house of refuge was opened for vagrant or delinquent children under the age of 17, which operated in conjunction with the city workhouse from 1871 until its closing in 1891. From 1891–1901, delinquent children were kept in the Cuyahoga County Jail. From 1856–71, some public funding also supported dependent children given temporary shelter and training in the city industrial school. Most of the city's child-care institutions, however, were sponsored by private charities, most with strong ties to local churches, since in the absence of a viable public-relief system, churches played important social-welfare roles. Cleveland's predominantly Protestant population funded and administered several institutions for dependent and delinquent or predelinquent children from the mid-19th to the 20th century. These included the Protestant Orphan Asylum, founded in 1852 and supported by several Protestant denominations; the Jones Home, opened in `886; and the Cleveland Christian Home, affiliated with the Christian Church (Disciples of Christ).

The Cleveland Catholic Diocese also established orphanages to care for the dependent children of the city's growing Catholic population: St. Mary's Female Asylum (1851) and ST. JOSEPH'S ORPHANAGE (1863), administered by the Ladies of the Sacred Heart of Mary; and St. Vincent's for boys (1853) and St. Ann's Infant Asylum (1873) for foundlings and the children of the unwed mothers shel-

tered in St. Ann's Maternity Home, administered by the Sisters of Charity. In 1896, the Home of the Holy Family was incorporated to provide for Catholic orphans, although it was not under diocesan control. The Independent Order of B'NAI B'RITH founded the Jewish Orphan Asylum or Home in 1869 for the orphans of Jewish CIVIL WAR veterans. These orphanages provided long-term residential care for dependent or neglected children, but in the late 19th century there were also established several child-placing agencies that provided only temporary shelter until children could be returned to their parents and that also found foster or adoptive homes for children when return to the parental home was impossible. The CHILDREN'S AID SOCIETY was organized in 1858 as an outgrowth of the city industrial school. The Cleveland Humane Society, like others around the country, was at first a Society for the Prevention of Cruelty to Animals and began to serve children also in 1876, when it was charged by the city with the enforcement of a new state law that prohibited cruelty to children. The Humane Society also administered Lida Baldwin's Infants Rest for foundlings from 1884 until its closing in 1915.

Church-related institutions also provided preventive or protective services for children judged to be neglected, delinquent, or predelinquent. In 1869, the SISTERS OF THE GOOD SHEPHERD opened their convent for young women, and in 1892 the Women's Christian Temperance Union, Nonpartisan, opened its Training Home for Friendless Girls. The goal of these institutions was to reform and reclaim young women through religious training in a familial and domestic setting. Private funds and organizations also sponsored daycare facilities for the children of working mothers, beginning with the formation of the CLEVELAND DAY NURSERY & FREE KINDERGARTEN ASSOC. in 1882. By 1896, the association maintained 6 nurseries and 10 free kindergartens. In 1897, kindergarten education became a public responsibility of the city board of education. Four special medical facilities for children were established around the turn of the century. Rainbow Cottage opened in 1887 for convalescent children and became Rainbow Hospital for Crippled & Convalescent Children in 1913, and the Children's Fresh Air Camp, which later became HEALTH HILL HOSPITAL FOR CHILDREN, opened in 1889. Babies' Dispensary & Hospital began as a free milk dispensary in 1904, adding a clinic in 1907. The Episcopal Diocese of Ohio administered Holy Cross House for crippled and invalid children (est. 1903).

In the first 3 decades of this century, 2 significant trends in child care emerged: the growing role of the public sector, and the shift from institutional to noninstitutional care. The establishment of Cleveland's juvenile court in 1902 marked this new recognition of public responsibility. The court, established in reaction to the deplorable conditions of the children's facilities in the city jail, was empowered to make provisions for dependent and neglected children. Delinquent children might be placed on probation or in a public reformatory institution or detention home such as the Hudson Boys' Farm, opened in 1903, or BLOSSOM HILL SCHOOL FOR GIRLS, opened in 1914, or a private protective facility. The court was also responsible for collecting child-support money from negligent parents. In 1913, the state of Ohio also began to aid dependent children with a mothers' pension law, which provided funds for widowed or deserted mothers so that they could care for their children in their own homes. The growing preference for noninstitutional over institutional care gave the child-placing agencies new importance. In 1909, Cuyahoga County began to provide public funds for the Humane Society's child-placing services. In 1921 the Children's Bureau was established to standardize the placement of Protestant and Catholic children in foster and adoptive homes. Placement of Jewish children was handled by the Welfare Assoc. of Jewish Children, established in 1921 by the Jewish Welfare Fed. Several nonresidential protective services also developed during these years. The WOMEN'S PROTECTIVE ASSOC. was established in 1916 to safeguard young women and provide them with legal defense in court. It operated Sterling House as a place of detention and a temporary home for women from 1918–33. In 1930 the association became the Girls' Bureau, working closely with juvenile and municipal court probation officers. Friendly supervision of young people was also provided by the Big Brothers and Big Sisters. A Big Sisters Council was organized as part of the Girls' Bureau in 1922. A Jewish Big Sisters had been founded in 1919, Jewish Big Brothers in 1920, and Catholic Big Sisters in 1924.

Despite the trend away from institutional care, new facilities for predelinquent or neglected adolescents were established. The Catholic Diocese opened St. Anthony's Home for Boys in 1906 and the CATHERINE HORSTMANN HOME for girls of high school age, often referred by juvenile court, in 1907. The work of the Convent of the Good Shepherd was divided between the Sacred Heart Training School, which admitted girls referred by juvenile court, and the Angel Guardian School, which sheltered dependent girls. The Humane Society opened Leonard Hall for high school boys, which had formerly been Holy Cross House. The Cleveland Day Nursery & Free Kindergarten Assoc. founded the city's first nursery school in 1923. Since kindergarten education had become a public responsibility, nursery schools and daycare centers gradually replaced the association's free kindergartens. In 1931 the group changed its name to the Day Nursery Assoc. In 1922 the Sisters of the Holy Humility of Mary opened Rosemary Home for crippled children, later renamed the Johanna Grasselli Rehabilitation & Education Ctr. In addition, 2 new orphanages were founded: St. John's Orphanage for girls (1909), supported by the Episcopalian Diocese of Ohio, which moved from Cuyahoga County in 1929 and was staffed by the Sisters of the Transfiguration; and the Orthodox Jewish Orphan Home (1920). In the 1920s, the largest orphanages moved to the suburbs and expanded their facilities. In 1925, the Catholic Diocese combined the boys from St. Vincent's and from St. Louis Orphanage in Louisville, Ohio, into PARMADALE, in PARMA. The Protestant Orphan Asylum moved in 1926 to Orange Twp., changing its name to BEECH BROOK. The Jewish Orphan Home moved to UNIVERSITY HTS. in 1929, becoming BELLEFAIRE.

The onset of the Depression accelerated these trends toward public responsibility and away from institutional care. As the private funds that had traditionally supported the city's child-care institutions dwindled, the numbers of children who could be admitted into them dropped significantly: from a peak of 2,139 in 1928 to 1,346 in 1930. Public funding, particularly from the federal government, became more important, and public agencies, particularly at the county level, assumed responsibilities formerly taken by the private agencies. In 1930, for example, the Cuyahoga County Child Welfare Board took over the placement of more than 1,000 dependent childen then under the care of the Humane Society and the Welfare Assoc. for Jewish Children. The county also maintained a detention home, which gave temporary shelter until children could be placed elsewhere. In 1935, the federal Social Security Act provided federal funds, to be supplemented with local funds, for Aid to Families of Dependent Children. The precedent was the earlier mothers' pension laws. Since the 1930s, both the county and the federal governments have expanded these roles. The federal AFDC program has borne the chief re-

sponsibility for care of dependent children, usually within their own homes. From Dec. 1979-Dec. 1980, 90,300 persons in Cleveland received AFDC funds. The Cuyahoga County Dept. of Human Services handles child placement in foster and adoptive homes and in private child-care facilities and provides daycare as well as protective services for children within or outside of their homes. The county also maintains the Metzenbaum Children's Ctr., a temporary shelter and diagnostic center, a juvenile detention home, and the Youth Development Ctr. in Hudson, formed by the merger of Cleveland Boys School and Blossom Hill. The Ohio Dept. of Youth Services administers Cuyahoga Hills Boys School for juvenile offenders.

Since the 1940s, the private agencies have merged and diversified their services, most specializing in psychiatric or counseling services in residential or nonresidential settings. Since the need for institutional care for dependent children had been diminished by the AFDC program, as well as by other public-relief programs such as unemployment, old-age, and disability insurance, the orphanages and child-placing agencies have shifted their focus to children with emotional or behavioral problems who cannot be placed in foster homes or with their own families. The Children's Aid Society, the Cleveland Christian Home, and the Berea Children's Home, which opened in 1864 as the German Methodist Orphan Asylum, provide residential care for emotionally disturbed children. These services are also offered by Bellefaire, which merged in 1941 with the JEWISH CHILDREN'S BUREAU (formerly the Welfare Assoc. for Jewish Children) and in 1946 with the Orthodox Jewish Orphan Home; by Parmadale, which absorbed many of the smaller Catholic institutions; and by Beech Brook, which also has an adoption program for hard-to-place children. Residential protective facilities include Marycrest School, formerly the Sacred Heart Training School; the FLORENCE CRITTENTON HOME, which had served unwed mothers prior to 1971; Ohio Boys' Town;, and group homes run by the Augustine Society and the West Side Ecumenical Ministry. The Catherine Horstmann Home currently serves retarded young women. Family service agencies provide a wide range of programs. In 1945, the Humane Society and the Children's Bureau combined to form Children's Services, which in 1966 absorbed the Jones Home. Children's Services could then offer foster-home care, unmarried-parent counseling, a family daycare program, and, in the Jones Home, care for emotionally disturbed children. The Lutheran Children's Aid Society provides family counseling and foster-home placement. Catholic Social Services and the Jewish Children's Bureau also do child placement. Catholic Social Services and the JEWISH FAMILY SERVICE ASSOC. also do family and individual counseling, and Catholic Social Services and the Jewish Children's Bureau provide child placement and administer daycare facilities.

The increase in daycare facilities reflects the growing numbers of mothers in the paid workforce since WORLD WAR II. In 1949, only the Day Nursery Assoc., the JEWISH DAY NURSERY, and the WEST SIDE COMMUNITY HOUSE sponsored daycare centers. In 1962, 9 agencies administered centers, serving about 1,000 children. By 1982, in addition to facilities run by the CTR. FOR HUMAN SERVICES, the GREATER CLEVELAND NEIGHBORHOOD CTRS. ASSOC., the SALVATION ARMY, KARAMU HOUSE, Catholic Social Services, and the Jewish Children's Bureau, federal, state, and local funds supported a wide range of daycare facilities. The total capacity of these nonprofit centers was 6,140 children. The Ctr. for Human Services was the result of a merger in 1970 of the Day Nursery Assoc., the Family Service Assoc., and, later,

Travelers Aid and Youth Services, an outgrowth of the Girls' Bureau. The Babies' Dispensary had become part of UNIVERSITY HOSPITALS in 1925, and in 1971 it was joined by Rainbow Hospital to form Rainbow Babies & Childrens Hospital of University Hospitals. The expansion and diversification of these private institutions and agencies have been made possible in large part by public funds from the local, state, or federal governments. Although public funding has been provided mostly for the needs of dependent children, public agencies also buy from the private agencies the specialized professional services that these could more easily provide, such as daycare and psychiatric care and counseling. The availability of public monies, however, is dependent upon the general state of the economy, as well as the spending policies of elected officials.

Marian J. Morton
John Carroll University

Bing, Lucia Johnson, *Social Work in Greater Cleveland* (1938).
Federation for Community Planning Records, WRHS.
Polster, Gary, "A Member of the Herd: Growing Up in the Cleveland Jewish Orphan Asylum, 1868–1919" (Ph.D. diss. CWRU, 1984).

The **CHILD GUIDANCE CENTER OF GREATER CLEVELAND** is a private not-for-profit mental-health agency providing out-patient services to approximately 2,000 children and their families each year. Through its extensive outreach programs, the CGC provides the community such services as psychotherapy, psychological assessment, and consultation/education. With 6 branch offices, the CGC provided clinical services to children up to age 18 regardless of race, ethnicity, handicap, religion, or sex in 1986. A great need for child psychiatric services arose nationally during the 1920s. In 1924, with the help of the Welfare Fed. and the Natl. Committee for Mental Health, a demonstration Child Guidance Ctr. was established in Cleveland at the CHILDREN'S AID SOCIETY. Prompted by the clinic's success, the Welfare Fed. of Cleveland authorized a budget for a CGC Clinic. On 1 Jan. 1927, the CGC officially incorporated, appointed trustees, and named a director. The center's original constitution stated its objectives as the study and treatment of personality and behavioral problems of children. Using a "community network" approach, the CGC provided services to area children's camps and to the county juvenile court until a full-time psychiatrist was hired. The CGC also treated children with speech and reading difficulties until the establishment of the Cleveland Hearing & Speech Ctr. during the 1940s. In 1940, the trustees changed the name to the Cleveland Guidance Ctr. and broadened its objectives to include research and professional training. During the late 1940s and 1950s, the center developed training programs in psychology, psychiatry, and pediatrics with area colleges and received certification as a training center by the American Assoc. of Psychiatric Clinics for Children. Until 1961, half of the CGC's budget came from the state of Ohio. Fearing the loss of control over its own objectives and programs, the CGC voluntarily withdrew from the state's support program. With support from private funding, the center built a new clinic in 1963 at its present (1986) location at 2525 E. 22nd St. and adopted the name Child Guidance Ctr. With support received from the Cuyahoga County Mental Health & Retardation Board, the CGC expanded its services into a number of school systems, hospitals, daycare centers, women's shelters, and the CUYAHOGA COUNTY DOMESTIC RELATIONS COURT in the 1960s and 1970s.

The **CHILDREN'S AID SOCIETY** was Cleveland's first organization dedicated to the care and education of the city's poor children. Established in 1854, the society formally incorporated in 1865. It initially operated 3 industrial schools, whose students included homeless orphans, for whom the society also attempted to find homes. The society was under the direction of Robt. Waterton from 1857–76. When Rev. Wm. Sampson took over in 1876, the society had turned responsibility for the industrial schools over to the city of Cleveland and concentrated its efforts upon a school and farm on Detroit Rd. That had been donated by Mrs. Eliza Jennings 10 years earlier. This policy was determined by the trustees, who included SAMUEL MATHER, JOHN D. ROCKEFELLER, AMASA STONE (who donated funds for a new building on the farm), JEPTHA H. WADE, and Geo. Garretson Wade. The president of the society during this time was TRUMAN P. HANDY, who served from 1854–98. He helped form the policy that led the society in 1887 to offer an adoption service for children ages of 4–16. In 1898, DANIEL P. EELLS took over as president. He held the office for the next 19 years.

In 1921, a study by the Welfare Fed. of Cleveland recommended a change in the society's services. To this time the society had been a school, industrial home, and orphanage. Now, under the guidance of LEONARD C. HANNA, JR., C. G. Wade, J. A. Raymond, Dr. C. W. Stone, and Dr. ROBT. H. BISHOP, JR., the society turned its attention to becoming a mental-health center for retarded, neurotic, and psychopathic children. Under the direction of Dr. S. C. Lindsay, a child-guidance clinic was established and became so successful that it was separated from the society after only 2 years, in the mid-1920s. After going through various changes in the next 35 years, including a brief consolidation of the society with the Children's Bureau, the society followed the recommendations of a study made by Dr. Rudolf Ekstein, a prominent member of the Menninger Clinic, and converted to a full program of treatment. Under the guidance of Dr. Jas. F. Berwald, the society developed into a fully accredited, residential treatment center for emotionally disturbed children. The physical plant, 10427 Detroit Rd., was updated largely as a result of the efforts of Dr. S. Sterling McMillan. Since beginning this program, the society has maintained its goal of serving emotionally disturbed children and their families. It offers residential as well as daily treatment but accepts children on referral only. Children with physical disabilities are not usually accepted. The wards of the children are charged a fee, which is not to exceed the cost of the child's care. The work of the society is also supported by gifts and benefits, as well as the work of its 3 women's boards.

Children's Aid Society Records, WRHS.

**CHINESE.** Cleveland's Chinese population began to grow only after the 1860s. However, their numbers were small; in 1880, they were counted in the census with the Japanese, for a total of 23. The 1890 census showed 38 Chinese, and by 1900 their number exceeded 100. The settlers were all Cantonese—from China's southern province of Guangdong (Kwangtung), of which Canton, now Guangzhou, is the capital. The southerners among the Chinese were more ready to venture out of the country, and they had migrated to all the countries in Southeast Asia and to Australia and New Zealand. The Chinese who settled in Cleveland did not come directly from China but moved here eastward from the West Coast. Their first settlement was on the street west of Ontario St., now W. 3rd St., and then they occupied a row of brick buildings on Ontario St. between PUBLIC SQUARE and St. Clair Ave. Wong Kee, who moved here from Chicago, opened the first Chinese restaurant, at

1253 Ontario St., and later a second restaurant, the Golden Dragon, on the west side of Public Square. Most of the Chinese were proprietors of restaurants, waiters and cooks, or operators of laundries. Chinatown was a society of single men, as the 1882 Chinese Act barred them from bringing wives and children from China.

Even though they were a small colony, the Chinese established 2 merchant associations, the ON LEONG TONG and the Hip Sing Assoc. Affiliates of national associations, these were societies of merchants engaged in mutual aid, self-discipline, matching of funds and investment opportunities, and reconciliation of disputes. The two associations were competitive, and at times their rivalry took violent forms. The associations were called *tongs* in Chinese, so their fights and killings were referred to as "TONG WARS." In the late 1920s, as merchants needed the central sites around Public Square for major buildings, some of the Chinese moved east to areas around E. 55th St. at Cedar Ave. and Euclid Ave. Eventually, in the early 1930s, the Chinese colony settled around Rockwell Ave. and E. 21st St. By then the Chinese population had grown to 800. In 1930 the On Leong Tong, the larger of the 2 associations, moved into new headquarters at 2150 Rockwell Ave. Since 1930, the block on the south side of Rockwell Ave. between E. 21st St. and E. 24th St. has been the Chinatown of Cleveland. Among Chinatowns of American cities, Cleveland's is very small. By 1980, 2,000–2,500 Chinese were living there. In the 1980s, there were 3 Chinese restaurants and 2 Chinese grocery stores on this block. Next to one of the restaurants, the Shanghai, stands the On Leong Assoc. Bldg. On the 3d floor is the On Leong Temple, which is used for (Buddhist) worship a few hours a week, but more often serves as a meeting hall. The Sam Wah Yick Kee Co., the larger of the grocery stores, in its heyday delivered merchandise to 50 Chinese restaurants in Greater Cleveland and about 30 more downstate and around Pittsburgh.

From its beginning, the Chinese community maintained many Chinese values and traditions. They celebrated festivals on the Chinese calendar, most prominently the Chinese New Year in February. The Chinese were attached to their country of origin. Early in 1911, Dr. Sun Yat-sen stopped at Cleveland on one of his worldwide tours and spoke at Old Stone Church. Meetings were held at the Golden Dragon Restaurant on Public Square to rally support and to raise funds for his revolutionary movement to overthrow the rulers of the Qing (Ching) Dynasty. On 11 Feb. 1912, 4 months after the founding of the Republic of China, a celebration was held at Old Stone Church, and a telegram of congratulations was sent in the name of the Chinese residents of Ohio to Dr. Sun, President of the Chinese Republic. Twenty-six years later, the Chinese were again active in fundraising, to support the war effort and civilian relief in the Sino-Japanese War. They rallied behind the Chinese Consolidated Benevolent Assoc., the Cleveland Chinese Student Club, and later the Chinese Relief Assoc. About 500 Chinese residents pledged $3,000 a month. From 1937–43, $180,000 was donated for food, clothing, and medicine. In July 1938, the Cleveland Chinese Student Club published a quarterly, the *Voice of China*. Its editorials and articles strongly criticized the U.S. policy of selling scrap iron and oil to Japan; pointed out the weakness of the Neutrality Act; and urged the public to boycott Japanese silk. Three Caucasian Clevelanders served along with 4 Chinese on the editorial board. Sentiments toward the Chinese among segments of the Americans had been changing, and the Chinese Exclusion Act of 1882 was wiped off the books in 1943.

The Chinese population increased by about 100 between 1930–60. The 1960 census reported 905. After 1960 there was an influx of Chinese from Taiwan and Hong Kong. Some of the young Chinese who came to the U.S. in the late 1940s and early 1950s for university studies had chosen to stay permanently and were now establishing families in all parts of Cleveland and the suburbs. Beginning in the late 1970s, a small number of engineers and scientists from the People's Republic of China came to Cleveland for graduate study, and these increased to over 100 at CASE WESTERN RESERVE UNIVERSITY after 1980. By 1980, the Chinese population in Cleveland had risen to 6,000. The new residents had come from central and northern China and diluted the Cantonese concentration of the earlier settlers. Together with the offspring of the Chinatown residents, mostly college-educated, they advanced into the professions of engineering, medicine, and the sciences. The faculties of BALDWIN-WALLACE COLLEGE, Western Reserve University, Case Institute of Technology, and other colleges in Cleveland had increasing numbers of Chinese in their ranks. In the 1950s, the active mainstream of the Chinese population in Cleveland was the membership of the Chinese Students' Assoc. of Cleveland. As the students completed their studies and advanced in their professions, they changed their organization in the 1960s to the Chinese Student & Professional Assoc. of Cleveland, and in 1977, they adopted the name the Chinese Assoc. of Greater Cleveland.

One institution in Cleveland that worked with the Chinese from the time of their early settlement was the Christian church, specifically Old Stone Church. For 50 years, starting from 1892, the church conducted a Sunday school for the Chinese, teaching them English and the Gospel. The church viewed its work as a mission comparable to that carried out by the missionaries it sent to China. Instrumental in this work were 2 members of the church, Marian M. and Mary F. Trapp, sisters and public-school teachers who worked for 30 years among the Chinese residents living near the church. The sisters obtained a working knowledge of Chinese (Cantonese) and assisted the Chinese in business problems and other matters. In Dec. 1941, with the support of the Cleveland Church Fed., Old Stone Church, and the First Methodist Church, a Chinese Christian Ctr. was established in the EUCLID AVE. BAPTIST CHURCH. Language classes, worship services, and youth activities were transferred from Old Stone Church to the center. Dr. Wm. Fung came to Cleveland to serve as director, and his wife, Shao-ying Fung, assisted in teaching classes. In 1948, Dr. Fung was succeeded by Rev. In Pan Wan, a Baptist minister. The center's activities were continued until 1953, when Rev. Wan left. Language classes were conducted periodially at Euclid Ave. Baptist Church in the late 1950s, and Bible studies were held in homes.

In the early 1960s, the Protestants among the Chinese were meeting in homes for prayers and Bible study. In 1965, Kay Eng and Stanley Eng (not related) went to Rev. Lewis Raymond, pastor of Old Stone Church, and obtained the free use of the church's facilities. The Cleveland Chinese Christian Fellowship was formed, and Sunday worship services and classes began at Old Stone Church on 12 June 1966. In 1975, the Cleveland Chinese Christian Fellowship became the Cleveland Chinese Christian Church, and Rev. Peter Wong became its pastor. The average number of worshippers on Sunday rose to 110 by the end of the decade. In Jan. 1983, the church moved to its own building on Trebisky Rd. in RICHMOND HTS. By 1985, membership passed 265. The congregation has been led by 2 pastors, Rev. Kenneth Auyeung and Rev. Bill Jeung. Outside of the Chinese Christian Church, Chinese Protestants worship at various churches in Greater Cleveland. The number of Roman Catholics among the Chinese is estimated to be about 20–25% of that of Protestants.

Following the growth of the community in the 1960s, the movement to preserve ethnic cultural values became stronger. In 1966, Peter C. Wang, K. Laurence Chang, and Wen-hsiung Ko led in forming the Chinese Academy of Cleveland to provide Chinese children instruction in Chinese language and history in a formal school on Saturday mornings. After using the facilities of 2 other churches in Cleveland Hts., the academy settled at Noble Rd. Presbyterian Church in 1973. In 1980, Chinese residents on the west side, led by Emma (Mrs. C. H.) Wen and Alice (Mrs. H. C.) Kao, started the Academy of Chinese Culture. In 1981, classes were moved to Strongsville High School, meeting on Sunday afternoons. Other efforts were made to educate the general community about Chinese culture. Peter C. Wang, who founded the Chinese-American Cultural Assoc. in 1961, offered Chinese-language classes in public libraries in the early 1960s and edited *Pamir*, an English and Chinese monthly, between 1962–81. Through these, Clevelanders gained broader views of China and Chinese culture. Performing troupes from mainland China and Taiwan brought Chinese music and dances. In 1975, K. Laurence Chang wrote and produced 2 programs on "Values and Institutions of Chinese Culture," which were broadcast over WVIZ-TV in July. The growth of the local Chinese community during the post-1960 period was symbolized by the gift of a marble garden with a large bronze statue of Confucius to the city of Cleveland from the city of Taipei, Taiwan. The Chinese-style garden was dedicated as part of the Cleveland Cultural Gardens on a site in Wade Park on 21 Sept. 1985.

K. Laurence Chang
Case Western Reserve University

Fugita, Stephen, et al., *Asian Americans and their Communities of Cleveland* (1977).

**CHISHOLM, HENRY** (22 Apr. 1822–9 May 1881), was the primary stockholder and driving force behind the Cleveland Rolling Mill, the Cleveland steel company that eventually became part of U.S. STEEL. Born in Lochgelly, Fifeshire, Scotland, Chisholm was apprenticed at age 12 to a carpenter. After several years working in the trade, he emigrated to Montreal, Canada, where he established himself as a journeyman and contractor. In 1850, he came to Cleveland to execute a contract to build a breakwater for the Cleveland & Pittsburgh Railroad at the lake terminus of the road. He later secured contracts for the construction of piers and docks along the lakefront. Meanwhile, he developed a reputation as a technical genius and a superb handler of men that caught the attention of DAVID AND JOHN JONES, owners of the fledgling Jones & Co. Mill, an enterprise engaged in rolling iron rails. Chisholm invested heavily in the firm, which was first renamed Chisholm, Jones & Co., then Stone, Chisholm & Jones after Andros B. Stone was brought in as a partner. He reoriented the firm's operations toward the rerolling of worn-out rails. By 1858, the plant at NEWBURGH employed 75 and had 4 heating furnaces, a roughing mill, and a rail mill that produced 50 tons of rerolled rails daily. Chisholm personally managed the operation, including the precarious finances. To preserve scarce cash, he offered company-owned housing and company-store benefits to the workers, whom he knew by name and regarded as important to the company's success. Chisholm's vision dominated the concern. Seeing that steel would be the metal of the future, he sent his best ironmaster to Troy, N.Y., to learn the Bessemer process in use there. By 1866, the Cleveland Rolling Mill was committed to obtaining licensing and building a Bessemer furnace; in 1868, it was the 5th American plant to produce Bessemer steel, under the supervision of 2 experienced steel men from England. Soon the concern was producing steel rails for $225 a ton, as compared to $250 for French or English rails, with a workforce that was primarily IRISH, Scotch, Welsh, and English.

Chisholm, quick to realize the potential of steel, diversified mill operations to include the manufacture of wire, screws and nuts, and tools. In 1867, the mills purchased the Newburgh Wire Mill to utilize metal scraps. Chisholm brought experienced wire foremen from mills at Worchester, Mass., and under the direction of Wm. J. Hayes, soon built the new enterprise into the second-most-prominent wire mill in the country. Chisholm and other company principals organized the American Sheet & Boiler Plate Co. (1866), the Union Steel Screw Co. (1872), and the H. P. Horse Nail Co. (1877). Though the plate mill, nicknamed the Almighty Slow & Bad Pay Co., was a marginal operation, the other companies were innovators in the steel industry, because Chisholm was not afraid to experiment with new techniques or to hire innovative and knowledgeable personnel. According to some, Chisholm was in the same league as a steel man with his fellow townsman and friend Andrew Carnegie; had he lived longer, collaboration between the two would have been likely. Unfortunately, Chisholm died at age 59, leaving 5 children and his wife, the former Jean Allen. Upon his death, his workers contributed to a monument for him that stands in LAKE VIEW CEMETERY. His passing marked the end of paternalistic labor relations and of progressive management at the mill. Wm. Chisholm, who succeeded his father, provoked major strikes in 1882 and 1885 (see CLEVELAND ROLLING MILL STRIKES OF 1882 & 1885) and alienated Wm. Garrett, inventor of a new rodmaking process that the company needed to remain an industry leader. Aside from his Cleveland interests, Henry Chisholm held stock in the Union Steel Co. of Chicago, Indiana blast furnaces, and Lake Superior ore.

The **CHOLERA EPIDEMIC OF 1832** began in May when an emigrant ship landed at Quebec with cases of Asiatic cholera aboard. The disease, fatal in most cases, spread through the city with great virulence and moved quickly up the St. Lawrence River valley. Panic spread across the Great Lakes region as it became known that the course of the disease in that direction would be certain and rapid. A malaria epidemic in Cleveland in 1827 had left many residents generally discouraged and anxious to leave. Combined with the fears of Indian attacks ignited by the Black Hawk War in the West, the advent of a cholera epidemic occasioned further terror and discouragement. In June, Cleveland trustees met to devise plans to protect the villagers from the dangers of the expected epidemic. A board of health was appointed and empowered to inspect arriving vessels, examine all suspicious cases of diseases, remove all nuisances, and procure a suitable building for the treatment and isolation of all sufferers of cholera. The disease was introduced into the village with the arrival of the steamboat *Henry Clay* on 10 June. Engaged to transport soldiers to fight in the Black Hawk War, the boat was returning to Buffalo with a number of cholera cases. Having been prevented from docking in Detroit, the *Clay* was sorely in need of help. Its presence provoked great excitement in the village, and some proposed to burn it if it remained. The village trustees met immediately and determined that everything should be done to aid the sufferers but at the same time protect the citizens. The men from the *Clay* were removed to barracks on the west bank of the CUY-AHOGA RIVER, and physicians and supplies were furnished. The boat was fumigated and 3 days later departed for Buffalo. In the interim, several crewmen died, and the disease soon manifested itself in various locations in the village, among both those who had had no exposure to the boat or its crew and those who had ministered to them. The epidemic lasted a month, afflicting an unknown number and claiming 50 lives. In October an unexplained recurrence of the disease struck down 14 people, all of whom died within 3 days. Two years later another visitation of the disease took several lives, but it did not create any appreciable panic.

The **CHRISTCHILD SOCIETY,** Cleveland Chapter, is a Roman Catholic service organization founded in 1916, originally to provide layettes for needy children. The first Christchild Society was founded in 1886 in Washington, D.C., by Mary Merrick, out of concern that a poor child would have no Christmas presents. When she suggested that the boy write to the Christ child, he brought letters from his brothers, sisters, and friends as well as himself. Merrick asked her wealthy friends to give at least one gift to a needy child in honor of the Christ child. This generosity, informal at first, was organized into a club in 1886 and incorporated in 1906. The Cleveland chapter was established in 1916 by Mabel Higgins Mallingly, a professor at the School of Applied Social Sciences, who served as the group's president. Mirroring the national society, the Cleveland chapter of the Christchild Society had programs in 3 areas: health, character building, and relief. Most of the society's resources were directed toward providing Christmas gifts to the needy child, First Communion outfits for poor girls, and aid to servicemen. Using "Everything New for the New Baby" as their slogan, the group included everything down to the washcloth and soap in the packages for newborns. Each First Communion dress was different so as to make the day special for the recipient. After WORLD WAR I, funds remaining in the treasury of the Natl. Catholic Welfare Council were distributed throughout the country to establish postwar social-service programs. In Cleveland, the money was used to establish MERRICK HOUSE, a social settlement on W. 11th St. Christchild Society members turned their efforts toward the new organization. Also, the society organized a nutrition council that eventually became part of the school health program. The Christchild Society financed a library for Rosemary Home for Crippled Children and provided an ongoing supply of volunteers and hand-sewn items. The society currently (1986) raises money by selling handmade baby and children's clothing in its shops on the east and west sides.

**CHRISTIAN SCIENTISTS** were first organized in Cleveland by Gen. Erastus N. Bates in 1877. Bates secured 2 rooms in a downtown building and formed a ministry based on the teachings of Mary Baker Eddy, who had founded the Christian Science church 11 years earlier in Boston. Eddy's precepts were based on an interpretation of the Scriptures as upholding the idea that disease, sin, death, etc. are caused by mental error and have no real existence. The First Church of Christ, Scientist, received its charter from the state in 1891; it was largely modeled after the mother church, the First Church of Christ, Scientist, in Boston. Services were held at several locations before adequate quarters were found in the Pythian Temple. Services continued there until 1901, when the church moved into its own building at Cedar and Kennard streets. In keeping with the rule that Christian Science churches cannot be dedicated until free of all indebtedness, the new church

was not dedicated until 1904. In 1917, the congregation moved to a theater, where services were held for a year before the purchase of the Methodist Church building at Euclid Ave. and E. 93rd. In 1931, a new $1 million building was completed on Overlook Rd. In 1901, a group from First Church formed the Second Church of Christ, Scientist, and held its first service in a small white church at Euclid and E. 77th. The Third Church of Christ, Scientist, was formed in 1903. The First Church of Christ, Scientist, in LAKEWOOD had its beginnings in a business block at Detroit and Belle avenues in 1910, and completed its own building in 1922. The Fourth Church of Christ, Scientist, was founded in 1914, holding its first services in the Woodward Masonic Temple before moving into its own building in 1920. The Fifth Church held its first public services in a hall at W. 65th and Detroit Ave. in 1915, and later moved to Lake Ave. and W. 117th. With surplus from the Third and Fifth churches, the Sixth Church was formed in 1922. A group of members from the First Church (Cleveland) organized the First Church of Christ, Scientist, in CLEVELAND HTS. in 1924. Services were held in the Heights Masonic Temple until 1939, when the new church at Lee Rd. and Fairmount Blvd. was completed. This church is considered one of the most beautiful churches of early American design in the Cleveland area. The Seventh Church, in Cleveland, was organized in 1929. By 1933 there were more than 10,000 Christian Scientists in the Cleveland area.

Services in Christian Science churches are unique, in that there is no personal preaching. Two readers are elected to 3-year terms; the second reader reads passages from the Bible, while the first reads a spiritual interpretation of these passages from Eddy's book *Science and Health, with Key to the Scriptures*. In Cleveland, as elsewhere, testimonies are given at Wednesday-evening meetings. In addition, lectures are given from time to time by members of the Christian Science Board of Lectureship. In 1940, the 9 Cleveland-area churches formed the Christian Science War Relief Committee of Greater Cleveland. It was divided into 6 war-relief units, where volunteers made garments for civilian victims of WORLD WAR II in Europe. In 1952, the General Christian Science Reading Room was opened downtown; it has been jointly maintained by all the Christian Science churches in Cuyahoga County. In addition, all the churches support their own reading rooms, usually in the neighborhood of the church. These reading rooms are open to the public and offer, in addition to the Bible, the works of Mary Baker Eddy, the *Christian Science Monitor*, religious reference books, and organizational periodicals. In 1986, there were 14 Christian Science reading rooms in the Cleveland area. In the early 1980s, there were still 5 churches in Cleveland—the First, Third, Fifth, Seventh, and Eighth. Since 1940, several new churches have started in the suburbs of BEREA, CHAGRIN FALLS, BRECKSVILLE, EUCLID, LYNDHURST, PARMA HTS., and ROCKY RIVER. In addition, the churches jointly operated the Christian Science Visiting Nurse Service and the Christian Science Sanatorium-Overlook House, on Overlook Rd.

The **CHURCH OF THE COVENANT**, the Presbyterian Church, located at 11205 Euclid Ave. in UNIVERSITY CIRCLE, is a union of 3 different Presbyterian churches. The Euclid St. (United) Presbyterian Church, originally located at Euclid and E. 14th St., organized in 1853 and after 1880 known as the Euclid Ave. Church, merged in 1906 with Beckwith Memorial Presbyterian Church (organized in 1885), located at Fairmount (E. 107th) St. and Deering St. This union resulted in the formation of the Euclid Ave. Presbyterian Church, which in 1909 constructed the Gothic building known as the Church of the Covenant. In 1920, the Second Presbyterian Church (chartered in 1837), located at the corner of Prospect St. and E. 30th St., joined the Euclid Ave. Presbyterian Church, at which time the name the Church of the Covenant was adopted. Dr. Paul F. Sutphen of the Second Presbyterian Church and Dr. Alexander McGaffin of the Euclid Ave. Church served as associate pastors until 1928, when Dr. PHILIP SMEAD BIRD came from Utica, N.Y., to serve as the first minister of the 3 combined congregations. During his ministry, the Covenant became a united church supportive of Dr. Bird's participation in many civic and community activities. Following Dr. Bird's death (10 June 1948), Dr. Harry B. Taylor served as senior pastor from 1949–66.

In July 1967, Rev. Albert L. Jeandheur came from Rochester, N.Y., to be the senior pastor. He is assisted by an associate pastor, an assistant pastor, a director of music, and many volunteer organizations from the congregation, including the Board of Trustees, the Session, and the Deaconate. The Covenant's stated purpose, "To provide Christian outreach to persons of all ages," is carried out, in part, through the traditional Sunday morning worship service, the many church school programs, the Community Day Care Ctr., special programs designed for university students, a weekly radio ministry, and many overseas mission projects. In 1971 a community education building was added on to the original structure, and in 1980, the Church of the Covenant was listed in the Natl. Registry of Historic Landmarks. In 1983, the Covenant, as a participating member of the Presbytery of the Western Reserve, joined in the Natl. Plan of Union and adopted the name the Presbyterian Church (USA).

Bourne, Henry E., *The Church of the Covenant* (1945).
*The Covenant Speaks* (1954).

**CHURCH OF THE MASTER**, located at Monticello Blvd. and Quarry Rd. in CLEVELAND HTS., is the descendant of 6 Baptist churches. Its earliest progenitor was the Scovill Ave. Mission at Scovill and Hudson (E. 30th) St., organized as a Sunday school in 1858 by the Erie St. Baptist Church. A frame Gothic building was built the following year, and the church was operated as a mission by the Erie St. Church until Jan. 1868, when it was made independent and renamed Tabernacle Baptist Church. Farther east, at Garden St. (Central Ave.) and Baden (E. 67th) St., a chapel known as the Garden St. Mission was dedicated in Nov. 1873. Mr. and Mrs. JOHN D. ROCKEFELLER were active members of the mission, and Rockefeller served as superintendent for a time. In 1878 ground was broken for the Willson Ave. Baptist Church, at Willson Ave. (E. 55th St.) and Quincy. This congregation was the result of the merger of the Tabernacle and Garden St. congregations.

With continued growth to the east of the city, a Baptist congregation was started with 36 members at DOAN'S CORNERS in 1884, and a brick building was built on Euclid Ave. at Logan (E. 97th) St. The church was known as Logan Ave. Baptist. The building burned in Mar. 1890, and the congregation fell on difficult times. In 1892 the name of the church was changed to East End Baptist. Membership declined through the 1890s, but with the arrival of a new pastor in 1901, an upswing ensued, membership climbed to over 200, and by 1903 funds had been secured (in large part from John D. Rockefeller) and plans drawn by the firm of Hubbell & Benes for a large new building, which was dedicated in 1907. By 1914 the church claimed 562 members. The building was of Georgian Revival style, with a central tower and facade said to be modeled after Independence Hall. The sanctuary featured a large gallery and a raised baptistry at the rear of the speaker's platform and beneath a large choir gallery.

Fire gutted the building in 1916, and upon its rebuilding in 1917, a merger with the Willson Ave. Church was discussed. The merger was accomplished in 1921, and the congregation was named Church of the Master. By 1948 the church was faced with costly repairs to the building and a congregation that had largely left the immediate vicinity. A new site was chosen, on Monticello Blvd. at Quarry Rd. in Cleveland Hts. The first phase of the new building was dedicated in 1952. An education wing was added in the 1960s. Copper, Wade, & Associates designed the Colonial-style building.

**CHURCH OF THE SAVIOUR** in CLEVELAND HTS., with small beginnings similar to those of many Protestant congregations, grew to be a large and quintessentially suburban church, founded in the suburbs rather than transplanted from an inner-city neighborhood. A Methodist Episcopal church for the Heights was established on the Nottingham-Glenville Circuit in 1875. Meetings were held in schoolhouses and homes. In 1878 a frame building was built, largely with the labor of members, south of the intersection of Superior Rd. and Euclid Hts. Blvd. The area was known at the time as Fairmount, and the church was called Fairmount ME. A second building was constructed in 1904 at the corner of Superior and Hampshire roads. Membership had grown from 50 in 1878 to 113 in 1904, and the congregation was known as Cleveland Hts. ME. By 1924 membership had grown to 500, and a drive was started to erect a larger building. At this time the congregation adopted the name Church of the Saviour. A site was purchased on the east side of Lee Rd. between Bradford and E. Monmouth roads.

The cornerstone was laid in June 1927 for a building described as being in the 13th-century French Gothic style, but which features a number of English Gothic characteristics as well. An asymmetrically placed square tower was added to the south transept in 1953, and 2 wings containing classrooms, a chapel, and offices were added to the south and east in 1951 and 1953 respectively. The architect for the 1927 building was JOHN W. C. CORBUSIER, who designed more than 30 American churches. Upon his death, the project was completed by his associate, Wm. Foster. Two churches have been merged into Church of the Saviour: Moreland Blvd. Methodist in 1928 and Calvary United Methodist (formerly Calvary Evangelical United Brethren) in 1981.

The **CITIZENS LEAGUE**, successor to the Municipal Assoc. (1896) and the Civic League (1913), is a prominent civic organization promoting good government. It is known for its evaluations of candidates and issues and for the many reforms it has advocated. The nonpartisan Municipal Assoc. was organized by Harry Garfield when members of both political parties were outraged over questionable tactics of the parties in the 1895 mayoral and 1896 presidential elections in Cleveland. In 1897, the association tried to defeat Cleveland mayor ROBT. MCKISSON, who they thought was corrupt. A fact sheet of the candidates' qualifications was released, but McKisson was reelected. In 1899, a more determined association printed a 48-page report documenting McKisson's corruption; McKisson was decidedly defeated. In 1985, evaluations of candidates and voting issues were still the principal project of the Citizens League.

In 1910, MAYO FESLER was hired as the association's full-time secretary; previous work had been done by volunteers and part-time secretaries. Under Fesler, constructive aid to public officials was added to the investigative programs. Fesler convinced the executive board in 1913 that the name Civic League better represented the group's function. He resigned in 1917. To stimulate new membership, the league was reorganized as the Citizens League in 1923, and Fesler returned as director. The league's form basically remained the same, with minor changes; one was the replacement of the executive board with a board of 30 trustees.

Fesler stressed the need for research into the many problems of local government. In 1943, the Governmental Research Institute was created as the league's research arm and to monitor the activities and status of local government. The league prided itself on its reviews of governmental finances, including taxes. Fesler retired in 1945. Other notable directors have included Estal Sparlin (1953–73) and Blair Kost (1973–84). Over the years, the league lobbied for numerous reforms in state and local government, including municipal and county home rule, reapportionment of the general assembly, metropolitan government for Cuyahoga County, reductions in size of the CLEVELAND CITY COUNCIL, and an Ohio civil-service law. During the 1920s, the league was a major promoter of Cleveland's experiment with a city manager form of government.

Citizens League Records, WRHS. *Seventy-five Years of Doing Good* (1971).

The **CITY BLUE PRINTING COMPANY**, a photographic-reproduction and commercial printing firm, was begun in 1895 by John G. Sharp and John F. Schwanfelder; ownership has remained in the Sharp family into the 1980s. The company began in 1895 with 2 employees; the city directory for that year lists John F. Schwanfelder (1851?–1913) as a manufacturer and importer of blueprint papers, with his operation located at 451 Pearl Rd. By 1902 the business had moved to the roof of the Williamson Bldg. on Euclid Ave. at Public Square. It was incorporated in 1903 as the City Blue Printing Co., and remained in the Williamson Bldg. until moving to the Swetland Bldg. at 1010 Euclid in 1919. By 1909, John G. Sharp had become manager of the company; his son Trevelyan (1893?–1965) took over in 1920. The development of technology to reproduce and duplicate documents played an important role in the revolution in business management that took place in the late 19th and early 20th centuries, and the City Blue Printing Co. grew as that revolution took hold among Cleveland-area businesses. By 1922, the firm was advertising that it had 3 modern plants—one in the Swetland Bldg. and others at 1900 and 4300 Euclid Ave.—and offered commercial blueprinting, photographic reproductions, duplicate tracings, drawing materials, and a messenger service. It added a 4th branch in the Terminal Tower by 1930 and in 1947 employed 180 people. In 1960 the firm employed 140 people; it not only offered its own reproduction services but also was considered "the largest distributor of reproduction equipment and supplies to area industry." It also continued to supply drafting and engineering supplies. In 1968, City Blue moved its main plant from 1030 Euclid Ave. To 1937 Prospect Ave., where it occupied larger quarters that enabled it to centralize its operations and close its branch at 4300 Euclid. It continued to update its equipment to keep up with changing technology, yet in 1980 it claimed to be one of the few firms in the U.S. That continued to make "the original blue prints." In 1975 the City Blue Printing Co. received a national award for its policy of hiring disabled workers. Nearly half of its 109 employees that year were disabled, and the firm was named the employer of the year among small companies in the U.S.

The **CITY CLUB OF CLEVELAND**, often referred to as "Cleveland's Citadel of Free Speech," located in the Citizens Bldg., 850 Euclid Ave., provides a central meeting place for all dues-paying members (including women since 1971) of diverse beliefs and opinions to participate in free and open discussions about the social, political, and economic problems of the city, the state, the nation, and the world. The idea of a city club for Cleveland was formulated at an organizational luncheon at the Chamber of Commerce on 14 June 1912 by MAYO FESLER, Augustus R. Hatton, MORRIS A. BLACK, DANIEL E. MORGAN, Walter L. Flory, H. Melvin Roberts, and STARR CADWALLADER. A committee was formed to consider the project and on 30 July 1912 returned a favorable report for such an undertaking. The City Club was incorporated on 28 Oct. 1912. At its first meeting on 30 Oct., it was decided that the club would be an impartial, nonpartisan organization remaining neutral on all candidates and issues rather than an activist group making policy recommendations. The first board of directors' meeting, held 19 Nov. 1912, included Amasa S. Mather, Dr. ROBT. H. BISHOP, JR., Daniel E. Morgan, Walter L. Flory, Geo. A. Welch, Arthur D. Baldwin, Rabbi MOSES J. GRIES, Rev. Worth M. Tippy, EDWARD M. BAKER, Starr Cadwallader, ERIE C. HOPWOOD, and Augustus R. Hatton. The first officers included Daniel E. Morgan, president; Edward M. Baker, vice-president; Amasa Stone Mather, treasurer; and Mayo Fesler, secretary.

On 17 May 1913, the club leased the 3d floor of Weber's Restaurant at 244 Superior Ave. On 21 Sept. 1916, it moved to the 3d floor of the HOLLENDEN HOTEL, and on 12 Nov. 1929 it moved to its own clubhouse at 712 Vincent Ave.—adjoining Child's Restaurant. In July 1971, the club moved to the Cleveland Civic House in the Women's Federal Bldg., 320 Superior Ave., and in Dec. 1982, it moved to the Citizens Bldg.—its present (1986) location. The traditional City Club Forum, consisting of a formal (and often controversial) speech or a series of organized debates (often by political candidates), followed by a question-and-answer period involving audience participation, has been a trademark of the club for many years. The Forum Foundation Fund, endowing this activity, was established in 1940. The club's satirical musical, the ANVIL REVUE (originally called "Stunt Nite," 1914), written, acted, and staged by club members, was an annual feature of the City Club until 1976 and has since been revived as a radio broadcast. The Revue, for many years written by Judge CARL D. FRIEBOLIN and corroborator Joseph S. Newman, lampooned not only local citizens but state, national, and international events and personages, as well.

Campbell, Thomas F., *Freedom's Forum* (1963).
City Club of Cleveland Records, WRHS.

The **CITY MANAGER PLAN** was Cleveland's form of government from 1924–31. Cleveland was the largest city in the U.S. governed by such a system at the time. The plan was an effort to provide more efficient government by utilizing the managerial skills of a trained executive to run the city, and electing a smaller city council at large to remove the influence of the ward-based political machines. In Oct. 1919, the majority report of a committee established to study the plan recommended its adoption. Approved by the Cleveland voters in 1921, the City Manager Plan became effective in Jan. 1924. Under it, a city manager would be selected by city council to administer city affairs for as long as the council considered his service satisfactory. The manager enforced all city ordinances and was responsible for the conduct of all city departments. He had the right to appoint and remove all administrative officials except those covered by civil service. The city was divided into 4 districts, with each district electing 5–7 councilmen-at-large depending on its population. The election was nonpartisan, with a system of proportional representation. City council was reduced to 25 members serving 2-year terms, and it was hoped that under this system council would be more receptive to the needs of the city as a whole than had been the case under the ward-mayor form of government.

In Jan. 1924, council elected WM. R. HOPKINS as city manager and CLAYTON C. TOWNES as mayor. The mayor presided over city council meetings, had ceremonial duties, and was largely ignored by Hopkins. Townes served 2 years and was succeeded by JOHN D. MARSHALL, who remained until 1931. Although the plan was designed to remove political patronage, both Republican leader MAURICE MASCHKE and Democratic leader W. BURR GONGWER supported Hopkins's election and agreed to split the reduced patronage between them, with 60% going to the dominant Republicans and 40% to the Democrats. Hopkins exercised leadership in policy matters as well as administration, overshadowing city council's role in the governing process. HARRY L. DAVIS, hoping to return as mayor and take over leadership of the Republican party, led 3 unsuccessful attempts to abolish the City Manager Plan. In 1930, concerned with Hopkins's dominance, council voted to replace him with DANIEL MORGAN. Although Morgan had a better relationship with the council, a commission led by Saul Danaceau placed an amendment to abolish the City Manager Plan on the ballot in 1931. Generally, Republicans and reformers opposed the amendment, and Democrats supported it, in part because Morgan had hired many Republicans at city hall. The voters approved the change, Morgan resigned 4 days later, and the city returned to the ward-mayor form of government. The City Manager Plan had been abandoned because Hopkins's administration demonstrated that a city manager could acquire excessive power at the expense of city council. The voters disliked the complexity of proportional representation, and the rigors of the Depression left them dissatisfied with government in general. The plan failed to remove patronage from politics, as jobs and favors continued to be dispensed, although at a reduced level.

Bromage, Arthur, *Manager Plan Abandonments* (1959).
Campbell, Thomas F., *Daniel E. Morgan, 1877–1949* (1966).

The **CITY MISSION**, like 255 similar missions throughout the country, was started to provide aid in the form of food, lodging, and spiritual guidance to the homeless and needy. In 1910, a group of clergy and businessmen led by Fred Ramsey, the city welfare director, invited missionary Mel Trotter to Cleveland to set up a downtown mission. Trotter, a former drunk converted at the Pacific Mission in Chicago, raised $5,000 in 2 weeks and set up a mission in a former saloon at 1135 Superior. The City Mission, which promised "Hope to all who enter here," as well as a hot meal, was put under the supervision of Geo. Soerhide, a former Trotter assistant. Though affiliated with the Internatl. Union of Gospel Missions, the mission was interdenominational. The thrust of the nightly services was that belief in God can give men the power to change their lives. To the mission's founders, human kindness and divine love could help restore hope eroded by alcohol, industrial changes, unemployment, war, and domestic difficulty. Many of the mission's success stories became volunteers at the center. The message of local preachers such as Soerhide and later director Clifton Gregory was supplemented by those of major evangelists such as Bob Jones and Billy Sunday.

Supported by corporations and private donations, the mission primarily served meals and religion to "Skid Row" men but also put up the homeless at nearby hotels, gave clothes, meals, and food baskets to families, visited the sick and imprisoned, and taught classes at the county detention home. After 1950, it offered vacation Bible school to downtown children. In 1952, the mission opened dormitory facilities at 801 St. Clair NE, its home since 1926, to temporarily house 40 transients. The mission relocated to 408 St. Clair NW in 1964. Visitors to the mission did not have to embrace religion to enjoy its hospitality. However, the guests, who could stay 7 days a month (10 days in the winter), had to shower with soap, get their clothes fumigated, and refrain from smoking. Overnight guests were expected to earn their room and board by helping to maintain the building. In the 1980s, the City Mission served an evening meal of soup, coffee, and pastry to an average of 50 people. However, on holidays, hundreds came for a full-course dinner and a sandwich to take back on the streets. Although lodging at the mission was traditionally for men, in the 1970s the Angeline Christian Home was opened for women, first on W. 73rd St. and in 1986 at mission headquarters. As with the men's facilities, any needy women were welcomed, no questions asked.

*CITY OF EAST CLEVELAND, OHIO V. MOORE* resulted in a U.S. Supreme Court decision reversing an Ohio lower-court ruling and overturning an E. CLEVELAND zoning ordinance that prohibited members of an extended family, in this instance first cousins, from living together in the same residence. The Court treated as fundamental the right to live in an extended family as opposed to a nuclear family. It ruled that no city should be allowed to force its adults and children to live within certain narrowly defined family patterns.

Mrs. Inez Moore lived in her E. Cleveland home with her son, Dale, Sr., and her 2 grandchildren, Dale, Jr., and his first cousin, John Moore, Jr. Early in 1973, Mrs. Moore received from the city a notice of violation of the city's housing code ordinance. The notice stated that John, Jr., was an "illegal resident" and directed her to comply with the zoning ordinance, which limited the definition of a family member to one related to the nominal head of the household, provided that such person is not part of the extended family. Mrs. Moore refused to remove her grandson from her home. The city of E. Cleveland filed a criminal charge against her. Claiming that the ordinance was hostile and that it deprived her of the opportunity to live with her grandchildren, Mrs. Moore attempted to have the charge dismissed on the grounds that the ordinance was constitutionally invalid. Her motion was overruled. Found guilty, she was given 5 days in jail and a $25 fine. Her conviction was upheld in the appeals court. The Ohio Supreme Court declined to review the case, thus setting up the appeal to the U.S. Supreme Court.

In his opinion, Associate Justice Lewis Powell concluded that Mrs. Moore had been deprived of her liberty in violation of the due process clause of the 14th Amendment. The Court identified the fact that the zoning ordinance under dispute was clearly exclusionary in its attempt to restrict ethnic and racial minority groups from populating the community by decreasing the households by elimination of any nonimmediate family members. The Court's decision of 31 May 1977 noted that the predominance of nuclear families among the white middle and upper classes could not be used as a vehicle toward forcing ethnic and racial minority groups, among whom the extended family dominates, into decreasing the number in their households when the extended family is clearly necessary for economic survival among urban disadvantaged groups.

**CITY PLANNING.** Like most American cities, Cleveland began as a speculative venture in real estate. Conceived as the capital of New Connecticut, the city was laid out in 1796 by surveyors with the original Moses Cleaveland expedition. The plat, a faithful reproduction of a New England town with its characteristic commons, failed to treat either river or lakefront as a public amenity, a feature of the city's plan that was to be much lamented. After 1830, the Ohio Canal (which operated from the east bank of the river, much to the disadvantage of rival OHIO CITY on the west) provided a regular outlet for the region's goods, and harbor improvements promoted shipping. Roads entering the city from south and east gradually insinuated themselves into the orthogonal street plan, and several radiating diagonals, including Euclid, Prospect, and Kinsman streets, were cut through. Residences crept out along the east-west axes as the center of town increasingly was given over to retail trade. Property values also were inflated along the river and on the lakefront, where industrial development was centered.

Gradually, and sometimes reluctantly, city government responded to the demand for more public services. During the first half of the 19th century, the city assumed responsibility for planking and lighting the streets, installing sidewalks and culverts, and providing a water supply and gas works. Zoning was unknown except for a ban, in the interest of fire protection, on wooden structures in the business district. If there was a critical event in Cleveland's evolution from overgrown village to mature city, it occurred in 1851 when RAILROADS entered the city, occupying valuable waterfront properties and bringing factories and warehouses in their wake. The canal was soon overwhelmed by the competition from the railroads, but further harbor improvements were to prove critically important when ore boats from the Superior region sought the coal necessary for smelting and, later, for the open-hearth furnaces used in steel production. Good transportation also contributed to the city's becoming, late in the century, the hub of John D. Rockefeller's oil-refining empire. During the early industrial period, street extensions were still controlled by the original plat, but east of Willson Ave. (E. 55th St.) the pattern of growth no longer reflected the vision of the CONNECTICUT LAND CO. This period also saw the siting of educational and cultural institutions at UNIVERSITY CIRCLE, some 5 mi. from downtown. The city assumed responsibility for refuse collection and sewerage. Streets were improved and extended; bridges spanned the river (Ohio City was annexed in 1854). The poor, however, many of them immigrants, still lived in want of clean air and water and amenities as basic as parks. Until the turn of the 20th century, urban development proceeded irregularly; land use was subject to private whim rather than public control, and city planning had been confined to mundane engineering necessities.

The rise of progressivism brought a new and elevated conception of the possibilities of municipal life. Under Mayor TOM L. JOHNSON, the city gradually assumed responsibility for many services that had previously been left to the private sector; it also incurred a burdensome debt. Among many innovations that had to do directly or indirectly with city planning, none—not even the Municipal Light Plant—reflects as well the progressive spirit as the Group Plan calling for the organization of Cleveland's public buildings around a mall similar to that then under con-

struction in Washington, D.C. Unveiled by the leading architects of the day in 1903, Cleveland's civic center was conceived as the city's official gateway, a monumental corridor leading from a union railroad depot on the lakefront (never realized) to PUBLIC SQUARE. Few cities were as successful in putting their City Beautiful plans into effect, and Cleveland's Group Plan remains an eloquent expression of the Progressives' vision of a "city planned, built, and conducted as a community enterprise" (to quote FREDERIC C. HOWE). Because it antedated home rule, the Group Plan Commission was legally a creature of the state of Ohio. But when the state constitution was rewritten in 1912, Cleveland adopted its own charter, and with the passage of the requisite ordinance, Mayor NEWTON D. BAKER appointed Cleveland's City Plan Commission and charged it with overseeing the city's works of art, reviewing public works, public grounds, streets, and platting, and preparing a city plan. At about this time, the city's need for open space and recreation was met by the legislature's passage of an act authorizing creation of the Metropolitan Park Board. The father of Cleveland's Metroparks system, which was considered exemplary, was WM. A. STINCH-COMB, although many others, including Frederick Law Olmsted, Jr., made contributions. During the same period, General Electric's Lamp Div. developed NELA PARK in suburban Cleveland, an innovative wedding of the City Beautiful with the industrial park concept. On the eve of WORLD WAR I, the prospects for modern city planning in Cleveland must have seemed bright indeed.

But forces then at work were bent on demonstrating the continued efficacy of that older type of American city—the city as speculative real-estate venture. The ease of municipal incorporation made continued annexation difficult, and so Cleveland, much to the detriment of its tax base, was gradually hemmed in on all sides. Of Cleveland's suburbs, one—SHAKER HTS.—is particularly noteworthy. Building on the site of a utopian community that had disbanded in 1889, the Van Sweringen brothers developed the quintessential romantic suburb, where middle-class (i.e., property) values were protected through strict controls on land use, deeds, and architecture. Setting aside some of the most desirable tracts for schools and churches (and country clubs), they organized neighborhoods around elementary schools; commerce was confined to the periphery (most notably at SHAKER SQUARE); industry was excluded altogether, a departure from the Garden City concept with which the Van Sweringens are sometimes identified. As Shaker Village was too remote for streetcar service, the brothers undertook to build a light rail system, which obliged them to purchase the Nickel Plate Railroad (to acquire a few miles of right-of-way), to see to the passage of a referendum (substituting Public Square, where they owned property, for the lakefront as the site of a union station), and to construct the celebrated CLEVELAND UNION TERMINAL COMPLEX anchoring the western terminus of their Shaker Rapid.

The suburban movement seemed, for the sake of city as well as suburb, to render even more imperative the establishment of a planning profession rooted in the neutral principles of science. One of those principles was ZONING, and a case emanating from a Cleveland suburb served as the cornerstone of all zoning law in the U.S. In *VILLAGE OF EUCLID* V. *AMBLER REALTY COMPANY*, 272 U.S. 365 (1926), the Supreme Court upheld zoning as an appropriate exercise of the state police power. Cleveland's first zoning ordinance was adopted in 1929. During the 1930s, government addressed itself increasingly to urban problems, particularly housing. In the vanguard of the slum-clearance movement was Cleveland city councilman ER-

NEST J. BOHN. Bohn drafted the model for the public-housing statute adopted by the Ohio legislature in 1933; it was the first such act in the U.S. In the same year, Bohn became director of the Cleveland Metropolitan Housing Authority, where he oversaw construction of the nation's first public-housing estate, Cedar-Central Apts. Along with ABRAM GARFIELD, he spearheaded the creation in 1937 of the local chapter of the Regional Planning Assoc. of America, an organization founded by Lewis Mumford and others for the purpose of promoting the Garden City concept developed in England by Sir Ebenezer Howard.

The City Plan Commission, meanwhile, had proved somewhat disappointing. It met only twice monthly and was preoccupied with ordinary housekeeping duties; it had never produced a comprehensive city plan. A committee headed by Walter L. Flory recommended to Mayor Frank Lausche that vigorous planning be employed to combat the "slow insidious rot" spreading in every direction from the Central-area slum. Practically every one of the specific recommendations of the Flory Report was written into a proposed amendment to the city charter and approved by the voters in 1942. The charter amendment gave the commission, now called the City Planning Commission, a professional staff and greatly expanded scope, including "mandatory referral power." Bohn was named chairman and John T. Howard planning director, and by 1949 Cleveland finally had its first comprehensive plan. The 1949 General Plan represents the triumph of the City Efficient over the City Beautiful. More concerned with function than with form, it is preoccupied with infrastructure, and especially with traffic problems. In 1984, the General Plan still directed the work of the City Planning Commission and the professional staff. In the postwar period, federal policy was inconsistent: VA and FHA financing plans helped the middle class but encouraged urban sprawl. Other federal programs funded slum clearance and low-income housing, but they also aimed at downtown development. Cleveland pursued federal funds aggressively, the Longwood and Garden Valley public housing projects serving as national models. Bohn and Planning Director Jas. M. Lister expected the city's blight to be eradicated within a decade, but the truth is that here, as elsewhere, urban renewal probably destroyed more low-cost housing than it built.

Downtown redevelopment was a more glamorous enterprise, and in Cleveland it had powerful sponsors: Bohn; Lister, who was named head of the Dept. of Urban Renewal when it was created in 1957; Mayor Anthony J. Celebrezze; Upshur Evans of the CLEVELAND DEVELOPMENT FOUNDATION; and LOUIS SELTZER of the CLEVELAND PRESS. Shortly after Planning Director Eric Grubb unveiled a new downtown development plan, it was announced that the city would commence the most ambitious project yet undertaken with federal urban-renewal funds. Part residential and part commercial, the Erieview project carried a price tag of $250 million. The firm of I. M. Pei & Associates was retained to draw up the development plan, which was based on the premise that Cleveland was growing, needed more office space, and was ripe for regentrification. The 163-acre parcel was to be assembled, with the help of eminent domain, then turned over to private developers, who would erect a complex of steel-and-glass slabs on Pei's superblocks—all for the purpose of generating a "ripple effect" that would spread prosperity through the city. However inspiring the plan might have been, litigation, ghetto riots, and changing political and economic climates all conspired to litter Erieview with makeshift parking lots. Finally, in the 1980s, a construction boom generated the spectacular skyline that Erieview promised. Federal legislation also spawned the highway-

building boom of the late 1950s and 1960s, which changed the face of virtually every city in America. In Cleveland, as elsewhere, the interstate highway program spurred some economic development, but it was to prove an inadequate approach to urban transportation, tending to generate even more vehicular traffic, destroying neighborhoods, and facilitating the flight to suburbia that was eroding the city's tax base.

In the mid-1960s, disenchantment with the federal bulldozer helped fan the flames of ghetto riots in many cities, Cleveland included. Intellectually, it generated a backlash against physical planning and the profession's pretensions to neutrality. Critics charged that the development of the physical environment was virtually meaningless—if not cynically exploitative—when pursued with no consideration of justice and equality. Although this revisionism was influential in academic circles, it had little impact upon city planning departments—except in Cleveland, where the appointment of Norman Krumholz as planning director heralded a unique 10-year experiment in "advocacy planning." Shifting attention away from the General Plan and downtown and toward the neighborhoods and ordinary citizens, the City Planning Dept. proved effective in promoting the interests of those Clevelanders—approximately ⅓ of the city's population, by Krumholz's reckoning—dependent upon public transportation because they do not own automobiles. On many fronts, however, advocacy planning was routed by the city's implacable politics. During the mid-1980s, plans proceeded under Mayor Geo. V. Voinovich and Planning Director Hunter Morrison for development of the lakefront and the Euclid Ave. corridor. A slum-and-blight study permitted the demolition of the noted CUYAHOGA BLDG. and cleared the way for Sohio's $250 million headquarters on Public Square, while historic preservationists succeeded in saving the theaters at PLAYHOUSE SQUARE. The $200 million Tower City Ctr. project was imperiled by cutbacks in federal aid to the cities. Debate continued over the propriety and effectiveness of tax abatements and other inducements to investment, a debate with implications for those who saw the Mall as an ideal site for a new hotel. Plans for a domed stadium aimed both at retaining the city's professional baseball and football teams and at spawning further downtown development. The highest priority was placed on the lakefront, with optimists hoping that redevelopment will occur in time for the bicentennial celebration of the city's founding.

Kenneth Kolson
National Endowment for the Humanities

The **CIURLIONIS LITHUANIAN NATIONAL ART ENSEMBLE** is an internationally known group of entertainers. The group was formed in 1940 in Vilnius, Lithuania, by Alfonsas Mikulskis. It was organized to keep the nationalist spirit alive in the people despite Soviet and Nazi domination. The Ciurlionis, named after the noted Lithuanian composer Mikalojus K. Ciurlionis, featured Lithuanian dance, music, and song. The second invasion of Lithuania by the Soviets in 1944 created a wave of displaced persons. The ensemble escaped to Vienna, Austria, where they reestablished and began touring Austria and Germany. They eventually settled in Cleveland in 1949. Mikulskis, founder of the Ciurlionis Art Ensemble and its director until his death, studied at the Klaipeda and Kaunas conservatories and at the Stuttgart Academy of Music. He was a member of the Lithuanian State Opera and directed the Lithuanian Philharmonic Chorus and Symphony Orchestra. He was also a member of the Lithuanian underground during occupation. He was aided by his wife, Ona, who also studied music and directed the Lithuanian Kankles (a mandolinlike instrument) Natl. Ensemble. Mikulskis earned the title Myestro (maestro). After settling in Cleveland, the Ciurlionis gave its first concert in 1950 at SEVERANCE HALL. It appeared at the Lincoln Ctr. and Carnegie Hall and toured extensively throughout the U.S., Canada, and South America. Vladas Plechaitas joined the ensemble in 1959 as president to help the group's work. There were only about 40 members in 1949; in the 1980s the number had grown to nearly 70. The ensemble has also performed locally at Kulas Hall and at St. George's Parish Hall. They dress in traditional costumes while singing and dancing. The current (1985) conductor of the Ciurlionis is Rytas Babickas, who assumed the position in 1984.

Cadzow, John F., *Lithuanian Americans and Their Communities of Cleveland* (1976).

**CIVIL DEFENSE** programs, aimed at saving lives and preserving the operations of government and society in the event of nuclear attack, were carried out in a coordinated manner in Cuyahoga County from 1952–72. A product of the cold war and tensions between the U.S. and the USSR, civil-defense efforts locally received only minimal public support despite the efforts of local civil-defense officials and the press to make the preparations thought necessary to save lives and continue American civilization in case of attack. The outbreak of the KOREAN WAR combined with the development of atomic weapons by the USSR to spark fears of a possible attack by the Soviet Union. Cleveland was believed to be Russia's 4th "strategic target area" in the U.S. But in their haste to organize a defense against attack, city officials botched the effort. On 6 Dec. 1950, Mayor Burke appointed Ellsworth H. Augustus as Greater Cleveland civilian defense director; they envisioned a program modeled after the volunteer civilian-defense air-raid wardens of WORLD WAR II. But fewer than 10,000 of an expected 70,000 area residents registered as volunteers on 29 Mar. 1951. On 12 Apr. 1951, the state attorney general ruled that Augustus's appointment and creation of the Cuyahoga County Civilian Defense Council were "without legal authority from the State"; the council disbanded, Augustus resigned, and officials started over. By then, many people believed a more official and professional program was needed. In May 1951, CLEVELAND CITY COUNCIL established the post of civil defense director, a post soon assumed by John J. Pokorny. Under the Cuyahoga County Civil Defense Coordinating Agreement of 1952, various municipalities subscribed with the county commissioners to maintain an office to coordinate their efforts; Pokorny became county coordinator and organized drills and alerts during 1952. Clevelanders experienced their first "full-scale atomic age Civil Defense test" on 15 June 1954. By 1955, a complete air-raid warning system had been installed, an emergency radio-broadcasting system was in place, medical supplies were stockpiled, the ACADEMY OF MEDICINE had developed a medical-preparedness program, and a transportation program was mapped out. The transportation plan was part of the new civil-defense strategy of evacuating the city in case of imminent attack, a strategy made necessary by more powerful weapons and by radioactive fallout; it contrasted with the previous "duck-and-cover" strategy. The first "abandon-city drill" in July 1957 brought little public participation.

The late 1950s and early 1960s were a period of confusion and controversy. Local and federal officials disagreed over funding responsibility and over basic civil-defense strategy. By 1961, federal officials were urging people to build and stock fallout shelters in their own homes and chastised local officials for continuing to follow the "an-

tiquated mass evacuation concept." The Berlin and Cuban missile crises sparked new public interest in fallout shelters; in the early 1960s, 22 local firms specialized in the construction of home shelters. Stocking the area's 2,000 public shelters with food and other supplies began in 1963. During the remainder of the 1960s, interest in civil defense waned. In 1961, GARFIELD HTS. became the first jurisdiction to withdraw from the countywide agreement; in 1968, only 33 communities contributed to the county's civil-defense program. On 15 Apr. 1971, the county commissioners terminated the 1952 agreement, and the county civil-defense office officially closed on 30 Nov. 1972, with the $2 million in stockpiled supplies reverting to the communities, along with all other civil-defense responsibilities. The various communities gave these responsibilities varying degrees of priority but often did little, except for BROOK PARK, which maintained a strong program. The state continued to plan for evacuations of urban areas in case of nuclear attack. In 1977, the county established its Disaster Services Agency to plan for natural disasters, civil disturbances, or chemical or radiation emergencies. Civil defense returned to headlines locally in 1982. After the federal government revived mass evacuation plans, Cleveland City Council sided with anti-nuclear-weapons forces, who argued the impossibility of surviving an attack, and placed on the ballot a charter amendment prohibiting use of local tax money "for civil defense measures against nuclear or thermonuclear attack." Cleveland reportedly was the first city to hold a referendum on civil defense; the amendment passed by only 674 votes.

**CIVIL WAR.** Migrating Connecticut settlers, one historian holds, transplanted their religious, political, and social ideals to the WESTERN RESERVE. A principal feature of Connecticut New England, though, was the abhorrence of slavery, which inevitably led to an ideological confrontation with the slaveholding South. That, however, does not wholly delineate the feelings of Clevelanders toward the South on the eve of the Civil War. The way in which Clevelanders viewed the South depended largely on political-party affiliation. Not all Clevelanders, then, were in total abhorrence of slavery, nor were they convinced that a civil war would resolve deep-seated ideological differences between the North and the South. As the country moved toward the election of 1860, and closer toward war, Clevelanders found it difficult to objectively analyze the trend of national events as reported in Cleveland newspapers. The rhetoric and emotional appeal of partisan editorializing clouded issues. The Republican editors of the *CLEVELAND LEADER* and *HERALD*, for instance, maintained that John Brown had been driven to raid Harpers Ferry in Oct. 1859 by southern actions, which were wholly to blame—namely, if there had been no slavery, Brown would not have been forced to capture the arsenal. The Democratic *PLAIN DEALER* placed the blame on Brown as well as on abolitionist Republicans.

The victory of Abraham Lincoln in 9 of 11 wards for a plurality of 58% in Cleveland over the candidate of the northern faction of the Democratic party, Stephen A. Douglas, and 2 southern candidates was not necessarily an affirmation of the strength of abolitionism, or an indication of the desire to halt expansion of slavery into the western territories on the part of victorious Republicans in the city. Instead, recent research has suggested that the election of 1860 was a manifestation of a new trend in voting patterns that had emerged with the formation of the Republican party. Those who opposed the extension of slavery into the territories did so not because of any moral opposition to the perpetuation of chattel slavery, but because extension would close the West to white laboring settlers. Furthermore, Republicans gained prominence over the Democratic party in Cleveland by forming a coalition of antislavery Free-Soilers, native and foreign-born Protestants, and German freethinkers. Protestants tended to vote Republican, expressing a nativist hostility toward Roman Catholics of immigrant status on state and local issues, who in turn voted the Democratic ticket. Despite the new trend in voting patterns, the editors of local newspapers continued with the rhetoric of partisan politics as the secession crisis loomed closer. The *Leader*'s editor lightly dismissed the threat of the withdrawal of southern states from the Union as something that simply would not occur. The *Herald* proclaimed Lincoln's victory as one of right over wrong, of Unionists over secession-minded southern Democrats, and a repudiation of the commercial interests of northern Democrats. The *Plain Dealer*, bemoaning the triumph of Lincoln, the sectional president-elect of the North, warned that the South would surely secede. Civil war would certainly follow, but despite any Democratic opposition to the Lincoln administration, northern Democrats would be obligated to support Lincoln. When war finally broke out in Apr. 1861, that proved to be the case, as prowar Democrats and Republicans united to form the Union party in Cleveland to support Lincoln's war effort. The next 4 years would severely test this coalition and completely transform Cleveland.

The Civil War years brought economic prosperity to the city, prompting one historian to write, "Bloodshed and prosperity mixed well." Although the Panic of 1857 had increased unemployment in Cleveland by 25%, the majority of banks and businesses had survived into 1861. The city was completing the transition from a village, economically dependent on the north-south transshipment of goods on the Ohio Canal and the east-west transshipment on the lakes and RAILROADS, to a manufacturing center. C. Geo. Brownell stated in 1861 that like Pittsburgh's, Cleveland's future lay in manufacturing. The negative side effects of foul air and polluted river water of the Cuyahoga caused by oil-refinery and rolling-mill wastes in the FLATS would simply have to be tolerated, for the inconvenience would be greatly outweighed by industrial prosperity and high employment. The entire value of products produced in Cuyahoga County in 1860 totaled $6,973,737. Business leveled off between the beginning of hostilities in Apr. 1861, and September, when government contracts created an upswing. Compared to Columbus and Cincinnati, the number of Cleveland firms contracted to manufacture overt items of military hardware such as artillery, rifles, projectiles, ironclad naval ships, or explosives either were nonexistent or have remained one of Cleveland's best-kept secrets since 1861. It has come to light, however, that some ordnance was produced in limited amounts. Otis & Co. produced railroad iron for military use and gun-carriage axles. Four caissons and gun carriages were produced for the 9th Ohio Independent Battery by the Cleveland Agricultural Works. The firm of Peck, Kirby, & Masters built 2 steam-powered revenue cutters for the federal government. The Cleveland Powder Co. plant, which was leased and then bought by the Austin Powder Works Co. of Akron in 1860, was capable of manufacturing blasting and gun powder, although sources fail to indicate if any government contracting took place.

The young JOHN D. ROCKEFELLER, in partnership with Maurice B. Clark, found the war years particularly profitable. Their consignment firm, dealing in grain, meat, and produce, made a $4,000 profit in 1860. At the end of 1861, after selling Army messpork, salt, grain (breadstuffs), and other various commodities for government use, profits

rose to $17,000. In 1863, when Rockefeller entered the oil-refining business with Andrews, Clark, & Co., quite possibly a good percentage of kerosene and lubricants may have been sold to the government for use on the military railroads and in the Army and Navy. The tobacco trade with the South had ceased. Out of necessity, the first tobacco factory in Cleveland, T. Maxfield & Co., opened in 1862. The clothing business prospered also. Wool had for years been sent to the East for manufacture and then reshipped to Cleveland for sale. In 1862, the German Woolen Factory became the first company to manufacture wool cloth in Cleveland. The clothing firm of Davis, Peixotto & Co. filled at least 1 order for 2,000 uniforms for recruits and 500 officers' uniforms by Sept. 1861. The number of leather dealers increased from 9 to 16 by 1865. It is not inconceivable that boots, shoes, saddles, harnesses, carriage trunks, and other items may have been sold to the government for military use. A number of local merchants bought military equipment for sale to soldiers. Newspapers carried ads offering military headgear, tailored uniforms, Army manuals, rubber blankets, tent blankets, drums, flags, fifes, bugles, swords, sashes, belts, and shoulder straps for sale. H. Hattersly, gun dealer, sold revolvers and cavalry carbines. War claims agents offered a variety of services. Drugstores offered bottles of Porter's Cure of Pain, concocted to rid soldiers of stomach ailments. The Cleveland Worsted Co. advertised for 1,000 women to knit soldiers' socks, with payment of $.75 for each pound turned in.

The construction and establishment of Camp Cleveland and the U.S. GENERAL HOSPITAL, both on UNIVERSITY HTS. (TREMONT), provided employment for carpenters, washerwomen, cooks, and several physicians. The economy was stimulated by bids for cavalry horses and commissary supplies. Because certain ironworks had been manufacturing rifle barrels for the Springfield (Mass.) Armory, local leaders felt that the central location of steel, lumber, and coal in the area would make Cleveland an ideal location for the establishment of a national armory. Attempts to organize a citizens' committee with city council representatives to present the federal government its case succeeded, but for some unknown reason, council quashed the plan in Feb. 1862. Ordnance design remained in the hands of several inventors whose patents apparently never went into production. A Mr. Dickerson claimed to have designed a "centrifugal gun," which, similar to a Gatling gun, could fire 100–500 rounds per minute. Dickerson, finding no interested manufacturers in Cleveland, reportedly tried to sell the gun to enemy authorities in Richmond, Va. A Mr. Hugunin claimed to have developed an artillery projectile that could be fired up to a range of over 4 mi. in 25 seconds. W. H. Fargo experimented with a "faciliate" rifled cannon designed to fire all types of shot with greater ease than conventional cannon.

City leaders tried to establish a national military installation as a result of the threatened invasion from Canada by Confederate agents during the 1864 Johnson's Island Lake Erie Conspiracy. City council felt that Pres. Lincoln should forgo the Rush-Bagot Agreement of 1817 with Great Britain, which limited the number and armament of naval ships on the Great Lakes. Spokesmen GEO. B. SENTER and RICHARD C. PARSONS presented the case to the president and to the Congressional Committee on Naval Affairs, requesting that U.S. Navy ships be put on the Great Lakes to protect American shores and American commerce from foreign enemies. Furthermore, a U.S. Navy yard should be established at Cleveland to build, equip, and repair naval ships. Congressman RUFUS SPALDING had introduced a resolution to establish the yard, but it received no further consideration outside of the Committee on Naval Affairs.

As the war continued, industrial production increased. A number of banks provided ample capital, loans, and cash for expansion of businesses. City banks held $2.25 million in capital and $3.7 million in deposits by 1865. The number of incorporated iron companies had increased from 3 to 12. Iron-producing firms had begun to diversify their output from heavy castings and forgings to a variety of items such as hot- and cold-pressed nuts, washers, chain links, screws, bolts, and rivets. Demand for iron products had created a demand for more iron ore. During 1864-65, over half of the ore mined around Lake Superior had been shipped into Cleveland. That had spurred an increase in shipbuilding. In 1863, 22% of all ships built for use on the Great Lakes had been built in Cleveland. By 1865, the figure had increased to 44%. Shipbuilding had been aided by the local production of iron ship fittings, as well as steamboat engine shafts, engines, and screw propellers produced by firms such as the CUYAHOGA STEAM FURNACE CO. In addition, 4 lake steamer lines had located offices in Cleveland. Spurred on by the oil-refining industry, which had expanded to 30 refineries by 1865, railroad freight tonnage and receipts from passenger fares, mail expresses and rentals, and telegraph service increased dramatically. The number of railroad commission companies increased by 66%. Eight major railroads had located offices in the city. The Cleveland Board of Trade reported in 1865 that the total value of products produced totaled $39,000,000, compared to $6,973,937 for the entire county in 1860. Prosperity produced an inflation rate of 100% between 1860-64. Wages increased only 50%, but despite 2 major strikes, workers fared relatively well compared to those in less prosperous sections of the state. Prosperity in the 18TH PROVOST MARSHAL DISTRICT, in which Cuyahoga County was included, allowed working men to avoid military service by paying a commutation fee of $300 before 4 July 1864. After commutation was amended to include only conscientious objectors, a greater percentage could still avoid service by hiring substitutes at higher than the former $300 commutation fee. Working men of less prosperous districts simply could not afford to hire substitutes and had to submit to being drafted.

Throughout the war, Cleveland citizens supported the war policy of the Lincoln administration. This support found expression in 3 forms: election returns; positions of the editors of the *Leader*, the *Herald*, and, until 1862, the *Plain Dealer*; and the support that local government gave to military establishments and military-related activities, including the recruitment of volunteers. The Republican party had solid support in all counties of the Western Reserve except Huron by 1855. In 1859, Republican Geo. B. Senter was elected mayor with a majority of Republican councilmen. City elections were dominated by the "Union" party (Republican) ticket in the years 1863-65. The greatest threat to Ohio Republicans and to the Lincoln administration occurred during the gubernatorial election of 1863. Copperhead or Peace Democrat Clement L. Vallandigham of Dayton ran against Cleveland resident John Brough, a Democrat who ran on the statewide Union party ticket. Copperhead activity, although limited, found its major voice in the *Plain Dealer* editorial policy, which supported Vallandigham's candidacy and platform of a negotiated peace with the Confederacy. Anti-Copperhead sentiment led to the creation of the Cleveland Union League, or Loyal League, on 31 Mar. 1863, and later the formation of a national Union League in May 1863. League members took a secret oath of loyalty to the Lincoln administration's prosecution of the war to counterbalance the Copperhead-oriented Knights of the Golden Circle.

The Cuyahoga County Union Central Committee polled the county before the election. In Brooklyn Twp., 650 voters counted as potential Union party Brough supporters, and 225 as Vallandigham "traitors and doubtful" supporters. The poll excluded convalescent soldiers at the U.S. General Hospital on University Hts., but the officers there assured the Central Committee that the 200-300 patients were Brough men. Soldiers were particularly opposed to Vallandigham's peace position. Fifty to 75 men of the SECOND OHIO VOLUNTEER CAVALRY, many of them Clevelanders, destroyed the office and presses of the anti-Lincoln newspaper *Crisis* while wintering in Columbus, Ohio, in Mar. 1862. On another occasion, Clevelanders in another regiment threatened to ride Vallandigham out of their camp on a rail as he visited troops near Washington, D.C. Brough beat Vallandigham soundly in the Oct. election and carried a majority of 6,850 votes in Cuyahoga County. Of 1,141 soldiers' votes in the county, only 8 were cast for Vallandigham. Brough carried Cleveland by 2,400 votes. Support of the Lincoln administration continued through to the 1864 presidential race. Lincoln won against Democrat Geo. B. McClellan in Ohio by a majority of over 60,000. In Cuyahoga County, Lincoln's majority was 3,200, and in the city, 1,416. The Union party, which received support from Democrats who supported the Lincoln administration, found its voice in the *Herald*, a moderate newspaper, and in the *Leader*, which took a radical stance but by the war's end backed the Lincoln administration and not congressional control of Reconstruction. The *Plain Dealer*, edited by Democrat JOSEPH W. GRAY, supported Stephen Douglas's presidential candidacy in 1860 and, like Douglas, backed Lincoln during the secession crisis of 1861. Gray's death in 1862 led to the editorship of J. S. Stephenson, who turned the paper into an anti-Lincoln organ that supported Vallandigham for governor in 1863 and McClellan in 1864. Stephenson was replaced by WM. W. ARMSTRONG in Mar. 1865, who again made the *Plain Dealer* a responsible opposition publication of the Democratic party.

The issue of emancipation proved to be perhaps the most emotional issue of the war in Cleveland, next to the assassination of Lincoln. Of the proposed 1 Jan. 1863 Emancipation Proclamation, *Herald* editor JOSIAH A. HARRIS wrote that emancipation was necessary to defeat the South. *Leader* editor EDWIN COWLES held that the North was morally right in emancipating slaves and that Lincoln was to be commended "for the stalwart blow he struck for freedom and for the peace and future tranquility of the Union." Democrats, however, condemned emancipation. The war, they felt, was being fought to preserve the Union, not for purposes of abolition. Stephenson of the *Plain Dealer* wrote that Democrats wanted the country with "the Constitution as it is and the Union as it was." More caustically, he charged that emancipation would not be popularly accepted and that it would "make citizens of the entire black population—degrade your own race, and then when you have succeeded in ruining your country—hold mass meetings with negroes for Presidents—to rejoice and glory in your shame."

Emancipation was popularly accepted in Cuyahoga County and Cleveland, and support of the Lincoln administration's war effort continued. The support of the war effort by the citizens of Cleveland, except for a period in the winter of 1864, when volunteering waned, never faltered during the entire war. About 10,000 men from Cuyahoga County served in the military out of the 15,600 who were eligible for service. About 1,700 died during the war, and 2,000 left the military disabled or crippled. During the 3 drafts conducted, only in 1 instance did a crowd become

191

unruly enough to delay conscription (3 Oct. 1862). Drafting resumed as usual the next day, in contrast to the New York draft riots, which raged for 3 days in July 1863. Because of exemptions, payment of commutation, or the hiring of substitutes, few of the 10,000 who served from the county entered the service as drafted men. The city, the county, and individual wards earmarked or raised funds for payment as enlistment bonuses called bounties, in addition to bounties offered by the federal government. As wards and townships tried to clear their subdivisions from the draft with bounty offerings, they also collected food, clothing, and fuel for distribution to families of volunteers and drafted men. In 1864, ward committees formed mutual-protection associations, from which drafted members received money for the payment of the commutation fee or for hiring a substitute.

Civilian aid to the military was centered around establishment and maintenance of Camp Taylor (1861), Camp Cleveland (1862), the U.S. General Hospital (1862), the SOLDIERS AID SOCIETY OF NORTHERN OHIO (1861), and civic ceremonies and processions. Citizens provided food and blankets to recruits at both military camps until government stores and equipment could be brought in and distributed. Whenever regiments marched to UNION DEPOT for field service, citizens lined the route of march, bands played, and the "Secesh" cannon boomed salutes. The city earmarked funds to welcome troops home after service in the field. They were treated to a meal after detraining and a short welcoming ceremony on Public Square before marching to Camp Cleveland on University Hts. for payment and discharge from the Army. Citizens provided food to supplement Army rations for holiday dinner at the U.S. General Hospital. During the course of the war, over 3,020 wounded and diseased soldiers convalesced in the 300-bed hospital. Eighty-nine men died, a small number being buried in one of the government sections at WOODLAND CEMETERY. When the hospital was opened on 1 Jan. 1863, the government failed to provide transportation from Union Depot to University Hts. Citizens were asked, and responded, transporting dozens of wounded and sick soldiers in their private wagons and buggies. When convalescing soldiers requested donations of books, magazines, and newspapers, citizens responded with an adequate number of publications.

The chief agency for civilian aid was the Soldiers Aid Society, originally organized as the Cleveland Soldiers Aid Society in Apr. 1861. During the war, the populace contributed $982,481.25 in bedding and clothing, hospital furniture, medical supplies, foodstuffs and delicacies, and miscellaneous items to Ohio soldiers in the field through this agency, which acted as a branch of the U.S. Sanitary Commission. At the 1864 Sanitary Fair, held on Public Square, the society raised $100,191.06. A Soldiers' Home was opened near Union Depot in 1863 with an infirmary to house, feed, and care for furloughed and discharged soldiers plus men awaiting pensions. A less pleasant task for the citizenry was the honoring of war dead. On numerous occasions, the city's military units and fraternal organizations assembled for the funerals of Cleveland men who had perished in the field. By the end of hostilities, 2 monuments had been planned for Woodland Cemetery to honor the dead of the 7TH and the 23D OHIO VOLUNTEER INFANTRY regiments. With the war over, Clevelanders attended the most somber funeral of the period, as over 90,000 filed past the body of slain president Lincoln on the Square on 28 Apr. 1865. Five months later, Cleveland again responded to a war-related funeral—that of former governor John Brough, who died 29 Aug. and was buried in Woodland Cemetery.

The rapid increase in population during the war brought forth urban problems, which continued to concern city planners into the next century. The city's population grew from 43,417 in 1860 to over 67,500 by 1866. Some of these concerns were the need for efficient police and fire protection, adequate housing, public education, health services, transportation, and an improved network of roads and streets. One far-sighted individual, JOHN HUNTINGTON, a city councilman during the war, began working on practical solutions to some difficult problems. Through his efforts, and the belief that Cleveland would became an even greater industrial city in the postwar years, the following improvements became reality: the building of an adequate sewage drainage system (1862–63), the dredging of the CUYAHOGA RIVER, the replacement of fixed bridges across the Cuyahoga River with swinging spans, the introduction of steam-powered fire engines, and the installation of a police-fire alarm telegraph system. Other improvements included a reorganization of the waterworks, bringing the Mahoning Valley Railroad into the city on the bed of the Ohio Canal, the construction of the SUPERIOR VIADUCT (completed 1878), and the creation of Lake View Park. By 1870, Cleveland, with a population of 92,829, had entered the industrial age, owing to the prosperity experienced during the Civil War. The overall impact of the war on Cleveland has best been stated by historian Crisfield Johnson: "The effect of the war on Cleveland was very greatly to develop its manufactures. The iron business and the oil business in particular sprang forward into immense proportions, and it has been said, with but little exaggeration, that the war found Cleveland a commercial city and left it a manufacturing city. Not that it ceased to do a great deal of commercial business, but the predominant interests had become the manufacturing ones."

William C. Stark

Feuchter, Clyde E., "The Press in the Western Reserve during the Civil War, 1861–1866" (Ph.D. diss., WRU, 1941).

Flower, Phyllis Anne, "Cleveland, Ohio during the Civil War" (Master's thesis, Ohio State University, 1940).

**CIVIL WAR CAMPS IN CLEVELAND** (1861–1865) were situated in 2 general locations. Four camps (Taylor, Wood, Brown, and Tod) were located along what is now Woodland Ave. between E. 22nd and E. 55th streets. Two camps (Wade and Cleveland) were located west of the CUYAHOGA RIVER in the area now known as TREMONT. A seventh camp (Cuyahoga) was located on E. 55th St. Each was considered a camp of rendezvous and training where local regiments were organized and trained before being sent into service.

Camp Brown was used by the 37TH OHIO VOLUNTEER INFANTRY, a unit composed largely of German-Americans, from Aug.-Sept. 1861. The main camp was located on the corner of Park (E. 46th) St. and Euclid Ave. A separate parade ground was established at Kinsman St. (Woodland Ave.) and Case Ave. (E. 40th St.) on land owned by LEONARD CASE. Camp Cleveland was the largest and best-developed of the city's Civil War camps. It was organized in July 1862 on a 35½-acre site bounded by Hershal (W. 5th) St., University (W. 7th) St., Railway St. (Railway Ave.), and South St. (Marquandt Ave). Approximately 15,230 officers and men, or 4.9% of the troops raised in Ohio during the war, were trained there. The camp was also used to house federal units in transit from one assignment to another, as well as 2 groups of Confederate prisoners. At the war's end, over 11,000 troops were paid off and discharged at Camp Cleveland. The camp was closed in Aug. 1865.

Camp Cuyahoga was a militia drill and training camp located at Willson's Grove, along what is now E. 55th St. The camp was used from 2–9 Sept. 1863 as a place of muster and encampment for over 2,500 officers from the 7th Ohio Military District (composed of Cuyahoga, Lorain, Medina, Geauga, Ashland, Trumble, Summit, Mahoning, and Portage counties). Camp Taylor was Cleveland's first and most-used Civil War camp. It was located at the fairgrounds of the Cuyahoga County Agricultural Society at Sterling Ave. (E. 30th St.) and Kinsman (Woodland) Ave. The camp was used by 4 regiments—the 7th, 8th, 14th, and 21st Ohio Volunteer Infantry—between Apr.-Oct. 1861. From late Oct. To Dec. 1861, the camp was used by the 2D OHIO VOLUNTEER CAVALRY.

Camp Tod was used by the 45th Ohio Volunteer Infantry in Dec. 1861. It was located along Kinsman (Woodland) Ave. Its exact location has not, however, been determined. Camp Wade was used by the 2d Ohio Volunteer Cavalry from 26 Aug.–21 Oct. 1861. It was located on land later to be occupied by Camp Cleveland. Its boundaries were somewhat different from those of the later camp. Camp Wade was bounded by what is now W. 5th St., W. 7th St., Literary Rd., and Jefferson Ave. Camp Wood was located on 20 acres of land situated on the east side of Forest (E. 37th) St., ½ mile from Kinsman (Woodland) Ave. It was used by the 41ST OHIO VOLUNTEER INFANTRY from 17 Aug.–6 Nov. 1861.

**CIVIL WAR REGIMENTS** of volunteers were raised according to need through "calls" made by Pres. Abraham Lincoln and the War Dept. Quotas were given to each state. The governor of each state, in turn, oversaw the recruitment of troops in military districts set up throughout his state. A variety of regiments were raised in Cleveland, made up mostly of Clevelanders or men from Cuyahoga County. Other regiments, not totally recruited in Cleveland, also contained a number of Cleveland men. Together these were the 1st, 7th, 23d, 37th, 41st, 42d, 60th, 65th, 67th, 84th, 103d, 107th, 124th, 128th, 150th, and 177th Ohio Volunteer Infantry Regiments; the 29th Ohio Natl. Guard Regiment (Ohio Volunteer Militia); the 1st Ohio Volunteer Light Artillery; the 19th and 20th Ohio Independent Batteries; and the 2d, 10th, and 12th Ohio Volunteer Calvalry Regiments.

Harper, Robert S., *Ohio Handbook of the Civil War* (1961).
Reid, Whitelaw, *Ohio in the War: Her Statesmen, Her Generals, and Soldiers* (1868).

**CIVIL WAR ROUNDTABLES** were first formed throughout the country during the 1950s; in Cleveland, John W. Cullen and Kenneth S. Grant founded the Cleveland Civil War Roundtable in 1956. Members engage in researching, studying, and analyzing events and personalities associated with the American CIVIL WAR. In 1965 Wm. Mahoney, a member of the CCWRT and resident of OLMSTED FALLS, founded the Western Reserve Civil War Roundtable to serve the growing number of Civil War "buffs" in the southwestern suburbs of Cleveland. Each organization is governed by an elected body of officers and an executive committee. Both groups hold monthly dinner meetings with a featured speaker from Sept. Through May. Members as well as locally or nationally known Civil War scholars deliver presentations that usually center around battles and leaders of the war or other related topics. On occasion, topics at WRCWRT meetings have shifted to other facets of military history, such as the Revolutionary War, Gen. John "Blackjack" Pershing, and Gen. Custer at the Little Big Horn. In the 1980s, membership in the CCWRT was

100, and in the WRCWRT, 40. The previously all-male WRCWRT was opened to female membership in 1982 by a vote of the membership. Joint meetings were held in Sept. from 1973–78 at the renovated Grand Army of the Republic Hall in Peninsula, Ohio. In 1983 a joint meeting was held at the Armory of the CLEVELAND GRAYS, 1234 Bolivar Rd., Cleveland. Both organizations have given money to a number of Civil War preservation groups. The CCWRT sponsors an annual field trip to a Civil War battlefield, a book sale and quiz, and compiles a monthly newsletter, "The Charger," which contains book reviews and items of interest about the Civil War.

**CLAN GRANT NO. 17** of the Order of the Scottish Clans is a fraternal society organized on 13 Apr. 1885. It was named in honor of Pres. U. S. Grant, who was of Scottish descent. In its early years, the organization met in City Hall. Thos. S. Davies, the owner of a soap-manufacturing company, was chief in 1886; Peter Miller was secretary, and Chas. R. Stuart, the owner and operator of a bottling works, was treasurer. By the time of its 50th-anniversary celebration in 1935, Clan Grant No. 17 had 250 members and was the largest Scottish society in the area. A member of the United Scottish Societies, it regularly participated in annual Scottish events such as the celebration to honor the birthday of Scottish poet Robt. Burns.

**CLAPP, NETTIE MACKENZIE** (22 Aug. 1868–30 July 1935), was the first woman to be elected to the Ohio house of representatives from Cuyahoga County. She was born in Cincinnati and attended public and private schools there, as well as the Cincinnati School of Art. She came to Cleveland in 1911 and during WORLD WAR I helped organize the Cleveland Hts. auxiliary Red Cross. Her interest in politics grew out of her work for woman's suffrage, and she was elected to the Ohio house of representatives as a Republican in 1922, where she served for 3 terms. As chairman of the Committee on Benevolent & Penal Institutions, she supported a bill to establish the London prison farm. She was the only woman to serve on the executive committee of the Republican Natl. Convention held in Cleveland in 1924. Her bid for election to the Ohio senate in 1928 was unsuccessful. She married Harold T. Clapp, M.D., in 1912 and had 1 daughter, Dorothy Annette (Mrs. Daniel H. Petty). She died in Cleveland at age 66.

**CLARK, HAROLD TERRY** (4 Sept. 1882–31 May 1965), was a Cleveland lawyer and philanthropist. Clark was born in Derby, Conn., to Wm. Jared and Mary Josephine Terry Clark. He attended the public schools in Ansonis, Conn., and Hillhouse High School in New Haven. He graduated from Yale College with the A.B. degree in 1903 and from Harvard Law School with the LL.B. degree in 1906. Admitted to the Connecticut and Ohio bars, Clark settled in Cleveland in 1906. Starting work with SQUIRE, SANDERS & DEMPSEY that year, he became a member of the firm in 1913. In 1937, Clark withdrew from the firm to open his own law office, specializing in corporate and probate law. During WORLD WAR I he served as an assistant to the U.S. War Industries Board. After the war, he was attached to the American Commission to Negotiate Peace. Clark was the legal architect for the corporate structure of the Glidden Co. and Fisher Bros. Foods. He served as corporate counsel and a director for CLEVELAND QUARRIES and FISHER FOODS, as a director of the CLEVELAND ELECTRIC ILLUMINATING CO., as a trustee of Society Natl. Bank, and as the director of the Cleveland Chamber of Commerce. Clark's civic and philanthropic activities began in 1913, when he started a promotion to relocate the Holden Arboretum to Kirtland. In the following years, he guided the distribution of many millions of dollars to local cultural, educational, and charitable institutions. During the Depression and WORLD WAR II, Clark kept the CLEVELAND MUSEUM OF NATURAL HISTORY in operating funds almost single-handedly. He helped launch a drive to preserve Mentor Marsh as a nature sanctuary. He played a major role in the transformation of BROOKSIDE PARK into one of the country's finest zoos and was influential in the formation of the Metropolitan Park System. As vice-president and a trustee of the CLEVELAND SOCIETY FOR THE BLIND, Clark promoted sight-saving and Braille classes in the Cleveland schools and libraries. He authored numerous pamphlets on education for the blind and natural history. He was a founder of the Karamu Theater, a trustee of the CLEVELAND MUSEUM OF ART, and a promoter of U.S. participation in Davis Cup tennis. Clark married Mary Sanders in 1911. Mrs. Clark died in 1936, leaving 6 children, David, Mary, John, William, Annie, and Margaret. In 1940 Clark married Marie Odenkirk.

**CLARK, MERWIN** (5 Nov. 1843–30 Nov. 1864), was a volunteer soldier and commissioned Army officer in the CIVIL WAR. He was born in Cleveland and was raised by an uncle after both parents died. He attended local public schools. At the outbreak of the Civil War, he enlisted in the Sprague Zouave Cadets on 22 Apr. 1861. The Cadets became Co. B, 7th Ohio Volunteer Infantry, serving for a 3-month enlistment through 12 Oct. 1861. After campaigning in western Virginia, Clark reenlisted for 3 years on 19 June 1861. He survived the campaigns of 1862–63 in central Virginia and those in Georgia in 1864, to be mustered out with the 7th Regiment in Cleveland on 8 July 1864. He had been promoted to captain on 1 Sept. 1862.

In Cleveland, Clark enlisted in the Regular Army as a private. Gov. Brough of Ohio ordered his discharge from the Regular Army and appointed him lieutenant colonel of the 183d OVI on 12 Nov. 1864. Three weeks later, the 183d was assigned to the 2d Div., 3d Brigade of the 23d Army Corps (Army of the Ohio) commanded by Maj. Gen. John M. Schofield, near the center of the federal line at the Battle of Franklin, Tenn. on 30 Nov. 1864. During the battle, Clark was killed while rallying his regiment. He was only 21 years old and was referred to as "the boy officer." His body was buried in the field but was later removed to Cleveland for burial at WOODLAND CEMETERY. His bust stands in the SOLDIERS & SAILORS MONUMENT on PUBLIC SQUARE.

**CLARKE, JOHN HESSIN** (18 Sept. 1857–22 Mar. 1945), practiced law in Lisbon, Youngstown, and Cleveland. A Progressive and part-owner of a Youngstown newspaper, he rose through Democratic party ranks to the federal judiciary, and later to the U.S. Supreme Court. After his retirement, Clarke, who never married, became a tireless crusader for world peace. Born in Lisbon, Ohio, to John and Melissa Hessin Clarke, Clarke attended Western Reserve University, earning the A.B. degree in 1877 and the A.M. degree in 1880. He was admitted to the Ohio bar in 1878. He moved to Youngstown in 1880 after 2 years practicing in Lisbon. In 1882, he became part-owner of the *Youngstown Vindicator*. Through his editorials, Clarke was among the early supporters of the civil service reform movement. He also urged support for workmen's compensation in his editorials long before the idea gained statewide support.

In 1898, Clarke moved to Cleveland. Between 1899–1912, he served as general counsel for the Nickel Plate Railroad and later became the Cleveland attorney for the Pullman Co. Yet, he was not solely a corporate lawyer, for at the same time he fought for a $.02 railroad fare in Ohio. Active in Democratic party politics, Clarke was vice-president of the Ohio Anti-Imperialist League and worked for a short ballot in Ohio. In 1904, at the request of the party, he ran a hopeless campaign against Sen. MARCUS A. HANNA. Clarke's political ambitions were directed toward the judicial rather than the executive or legislative branches of government. A staunch supporter of Woodrow Wilson, he was appointed a U.S. district judge in the Northern district of Ohio in 1914. In 1916, Pres. Wilson appointed Clarke an associate judge of the U.S. Supreme Court. After retiring from the Court in 1922, Clarke became president of the League of Nations Non-Partisan Assoc. of the U.S. and a trustee for the World Peace Foundation. Believing that America would lead the way and that it was vital for the U.S. to join the League of Nations, he traveled throughout America speaking on behalf of world peace. In 1942, admitting the peace movement's failure, Clarke expressed his hopes that America would learn from its tragic mistake of failing to join the league.

**CLEANLAND, OHIO (RAPID RECOVERY)**, is an independent cleanup and beautification program for the city of Cleveland. Sponsored by corporations, groups, private citizens, foundations, and a grant from the Ohio Office of Litter Control, the nonprofit organization has been awarded the Natl. 1st Place Civic Organization Award twice by Keep America Beautiful, Inc. Cleanland, Ohio, originally named the Rapid Recovery Program, was formed in 1977 to beautify 32.6 mi. of land along the rapid-transit right-of-way. The program was initiated by a coalition of corporations and private citizens and was executed with volunteer labor. More than 107 beautification projects costing about $2 million were completed along the rapid-transit corridor by 1984.

In 1981, the program was expanded to include non-interstate transportation corridors, targeting a different one each year. The entire program's name then changed to Cleanland, while the rapid-transit corridor work became the Trackside Improvement Program. Work then expanded to include planting trees and gardens on Carnegie and Chester avenues, as well as gardens, called city side gardens, on vacant lots deemed too small or unlikely for development. In 1983, Cleanland, Ohio, received a Natl. Merit Award from Partners for Livable Places for its work along Chester Ave. and within the Hough area. Other programs included Litter Code Enforcement and litter cleanup programs organized in various communities; and an annual program of planting perennial flowers that would total an estimated 670,000 flowers by spring 1994. Board of trustee members in 1986 included J. Richard Kelso, president, EAST OHIO GAS CO.; Bruce Akers, vice-president, AMERITRUST; Wm. H. Bryant, GREATER CLEVELAND GROWTH ASSOC.; and Morton Mandel, PREMIER INDUSTRIAL CORP. Julius A. Zsako was executive director of the board, which totaled 64 members. A full-time staff with offices at 4614 Prospect managed day-to-day activities.

**CLEAVELAND, MOSES** (29 Jan. 1754–16 Nov. 1806), was a soldier, lawyer, frontiersman, and founder of the city of Cleveland. Cleaveland was born in Canterbury, Conn., the second child of Col. Aaron and Thankful Paine Cleaveland. The family was descended from early settlers to Canterbury, and his father had served in the French & Indian War. In 1777, Cleaveland became involved in the Revolutionary War, receiving a commission as a 2d lieutenant in the 2d Connecticut Continental Regiment. He was sent to Boston as part of the Lexington Alarm, and returned in

June to graduate from Yale. In 1778 he served with Gen. Washington at Valley Forge, and in 1779 he was appointed captain of a company of sappers and miners in the U.S. Army. He resigned his commission in 1781, after which he practiced law in Canterbury, represented his town in the Connecticut state legislature, and was a member of the state convention that helped to ratify the federal Constitution in 1788. On 2 Mar. 1794 he married Esther Champion, daughter of Henry Champion of Colchester, Conn. Four children were born to the couple. Two years later he was promoted to general, 5th Brigade, Connecticut State Militia. As one of the 36 founders of the CONNECTICUT LAND CO., Cleaveland was selected as one of its 7 directors and was sent out as the company's agent to survey and map the company's holdings. He had invested $32,600 in the venture.

After a strenuous journey through the uncharted wilderness, Cleaveland's surveying party eventually arrived at Canandaigua, N.Y., where Cleaveland spoke to the representatives of the Six Nations, including Capt. Brent of the Mohawk Indians. He convinced the Indians that their land had, in fact, already been ceded to the Americans through Gen. Anthony Wayne's Treaty of Greenville (following the Battle of Fallen Timbers). Although they had not signed the treaty, the Indians relinquished their claim to the land; Cleaveland gave them money, whiskey, and cattle in return for safe passage through the lands as far as the CUYAHOGA RIVER. The party traveled to the mouth of Conneaut Creek, where on 27 June Cleaveland negotiated with the MASSASAGOES tribe, who challenged his claim to their country. Cleaveland described his agreement with the Six Nations, promised not to disturb their people, and gave them trinkets, wampum, and whiskey, for which he received some clothing and a guarantee that the surveyors could explore the east bank of the Cuyahoga River in peace. Cleaveland and his surveyors arrived at the mouth of the Cuyahoga on 22 July 1796. They believed that the location, where river, lake, low banks, dense forests, and high bluffs provided both protection and shipping access, was the ideal location for the "capital city" of the Connecticut WESTERN RESERVE. Cleaveland paced out a 10-acre Public Square similar to those in New England; his surveyors plotted a town around it and subsequently named it Cleaveland in honor of their leader. In Oct. 1796, Cleaveland and most of his surveying party returned to Connecticut, where he continued his law practice. He remained involved in political and military affairs until his death, but never returned to the Western Reserve. A memorial near his grave in Canterbury, Conn., erected 16 Nov. 1906 by the Cleveland Chamber of Commerce, reads that Cleaveland was "a lawyer, a soldier, a legislator and a leader of men."

Moses Cleaveland Papers, WRHS.

The *CLEAVELAND GAZETTE & COMMERCIAL REGISTER* was Cleveland's first newspaper. It appeared on 31 July 1818, 22 years after the settlement's establishment. It was a 4-column, 4-page weekly, edited, published, and printed by Andrew Logan of Beaver, Pa., in a small shop at 220 Superior Ave. NW. Chief items of local interest in the inaugural issue were a list of ship arrivals and departures and an account of the sighting of a 32-ft. monster in Lake Erie. Because of an undependable paper supply, its issues often appeared at irregular intervals. On 6 Oct. 1818, its name was shortened to the *Cleaveland Register*. Its last issue was printed on 21 Mar. 1820.

**CLEMENT, KENNETH W.** (24 Feb. 1920–29 Nov. 1974), was a physician and civic leader whose activities ranged from medical practice and research to politics. He was considered the leading advisor in the election of Carl B. Stokes, the city's first black mayor. Clement was born in Vashti, Pittsylvania County, Va. His family moved to Cleveland when he was a child. He was educated in the public schools. After graduating from CENTRAL HIGH SCHOOL as class president and valedictorian in 1938, he received a 4-year scholarship to Oberlin College. He graduated in 1942, and with the aid of a scholarship he completed Howard Medical School in 1945. He interned at Harlem Hospital in New York City and completed his residency in general surgery at the Cleveland City Hospital. After serving in the U.S. Air Force, Clement returned to Cleveland to enter private practice. He served as assistant clinical professor of surgery at Western Reserve University and guest lecturer in intergroup relations in the School of Applied Social Work. His hospital affiliations included terms as chief of staff at FOREST CITY HOSPITAL, assistant surgeon at MARYMOUNT HOSPITAL, president-elect of the medical staff at ST. LUKE'S HOSPITAL, associate surgeon at Metropolitan General Hospital, and vice-chairman of the Cuyahoga County Hospital Board.

Among the numerous organizations in which Clement was involved at both the member and executive levels were the URBAN LEAGUE OF CLEVELAND, the NAACP, the American Civil Liberties Union, the Cancer Society, the ACADEMY OF MEDICINE, and the CLEVELAND FOUNDATION. He served as president of the CLEVELAND BAPTIST ASSOC., the first black layman to be elected to that post. He also served as a national director of the NAACP and Urban League and was a trustee of Kent State University, Howard University, and the OHIO COLLEGE OF PODIATRIC MEDICINE. As national president of the Natl. Medical Assoc., Clement was an ardent supporter of civil rights and Medicare legislation. Pres. Kennedy appointed him as the first black and first physician to the Natl. Social Security Advisory Council in 1963. Under Pres. Johnson, Clement served as a member of the Advisory Committee to the Disability Operation of Social Security and was a consultant on health resources to the Agency for Internatl. Development. Pres. Johnson also appointed him to the 3-member Presidential Appeals Board of the Natl. Selective Service System and to the first Hospital Insurance Benefits Advisory Council, which assisted in drafting the original Medicare regulations. Active in politics, Clement consulted with 3 presidents and a variety of national political leaders; his guidance and practical advice led Cleveland to become the first major American city to elect a black mayor. After serving as vice-chairman of the Cuyahoga County Democratic party, he waged an unsuccessful campaign for the U.S. Senate. Clement married Ruth Doss in 1942. They had 3 children.

**CLETRAC, INC.,** began in 1915 as the Cleveland Motor Plow Co., which grew out of the WHITE MOTOR CO. It was owned by the Oliver Corp. of Chicago from 1944–60 and was reacquired and closed by White in 1961. ROLLIN H. WHITE started the company as the Cleveland Motor Plow Co. in 1915 after a trip to the West interested him in finding a way to till land more efficiently and productively. The crawler-type tractor he developed—the first such vehicle for general farm use—was based on a principle that the company applied to heavy equipment used in highway construction, logging, and maintenance. In 1917, the company became the Cleveland Tractor Co. It was first located at Euclid and Lamb and later moved to 19300 Euclid.

In its first decade, Cleveland Tractor sold 40,000 tractors in the U.S. and 70 foreign countries and played a part in the agricultural revolution in the Soviet Union. While the firm was slowed by the Depression, the needs of the Civilian Conservation Corps and public works projects in the early 1930s kept the plant open and often operating at capacity. By 1937, the company enjoyed record tractor sales here and abroad and employed 1,500. Despite the diverse uses for its products, the firm remained committed to its farm market. On its 114-acre research farm in Summit County, Cleveland Tractor experimented with new equipment. By 1939, the company introduced 3 new lower-priced tractors for the small farmer. All featured a 4-cylinder engine and interchangeable parts; one model, "The General," was a radical departure from other Cleveland Tractor products, as it was a tricycle-type unit with rubber back tires that sold for $595, about the cost of a good 3-horse team.

Cleveland Tractor attracted military contracts after 1940. By the next year, the company offered the War Dept. a new high-speed model for artillery hauling and was awarded a contract. During the early years of the war, Cleveland Tractor produced over 350 military tractors per day and could have increased the output had materials been available. In 1944, the company was authorized to make a small number of its Model 35 tractors for civilian use. Though the company received a steady flow of orders, the low profit in defense work and the research costs for new products convinced officials that the firm would fare better as part of a larger unit. In 1944, Cleveland Tractor became part of the 96-year-old Oliver Corp. of Chicago.

As part of Oliver, Cleveland Tractor remained troubled. Oliver made a $3.5 million investment in the aging plant for tooling and engineeering for new products. Its defense contracts dwindled. Material shortages and work stoppages at other companies delayed the arrival of needed parts. Moreover, the farm market was cyclical and recession-prone. Because of cost problems, the company tried to restructure the wage scale for workers in 1950, who subsequently struck. The strike lasted 6 months, at the time the second-longest strike in Cleveland history. A federal mediator intervened, as the union charged that the company was unwilling to bargain in good faith. The strike ended when the company changed its position on the need for wage cuts as a result of the economic stimulation of the KOREAN WAR.

After a decade of failed merger attempts with larger companies, Oliver negotiated with the White Motor Corp., the former owner of the Cleveland operation, in 1959. Rather than buy the entire Oliver Corp., White took a 2-year option on the Cleveland plant that was contingent on its selling $12 million in tractors. Since White acquired exclusive rights to the Oliver name, Oliver stockholders changed the name of the facilities to Cletrac, Inc. By Nov. 1961, White exercised its option to buy its subsidiary. Because the Cleveland plant duplicated the product line of facilities at Charles City, Iowa, White decided to consolidate production and so bought local Cletrac inventories, engineering and designs, and machine tools but not the plant itself. It announced that the plant would be closed and the remaining equipment and office machinery auctioned off. The local plant idled 475 at its closing.

The **CLEVELAND ACADEMY** was created in 1821, when the trustees of the village of Cleveland raised over $200 for the construction of a new and larger school. The new 2-story brick schoolhouse, completed in 1822, was located on the north side of St. Clair Ave. On 26 June 1822, the academy was opened under the direction of Rev. Wm. McLean as headmaster. Other instructors included John Cogswell, who followed McLean, and HARVEY RICE, who served as instructor and principal until 1826. Curriculum at the academy consisted of reading, spelling, writing,

geography, Greek, Latin, and mathematics. Students, or "scholars," ranging in age from 8 to 21, were charged a tuition of $4 by the trustees for each term of 12 weeks. The academy was operated as a private primary school until 1830, when, because of competition with other private institutions in Cleveland, it was sold by the trustees. Following the incorporation of Cleveland in 1836, the Board of Managers repurchased the academy building and lot and rented space in the building to small classes and businesses. On 5 May 1847, Chas. Bradburn, school manager for Cleveland, recommended to the city council that the academy, now in disrepair, be demolished and the lot used for new schools. In the winter of 1849 the academy was demolished. In its place the city built a new school, the W. St. Clair St. School, which cost $6,000 and was finished in 1850.

Akers, William, *Cleveland Schools in the Nineteenth Century* (1901).
Freese, Andrew, *Early History of the Cleveland Public Schools* (1876).

The **CLEVELAND ACADEMY OF NATURAL SCIENCES** (also known as the Kirtland Society of Natural Sciences) was Cleveland's first scientific organization and the forerunner of the CLEVELAND MUSEUM OF NATURAL HISTORY. The origins of the academy go back to meetings at the "Ark" on PUBLIC SQUARE. It was formally organized on 24 Nov. 1845 by JARED P. KIRTLAND, JOHN LANG CASSELS, and SAMUEL ST. JOHN as trustees. Members of Cleveland's medical community were prominent as officers and members. Among the academy's early members were John Brainard, Erastus Cushing, HORACE ACKLEY, Jacob J. Delamater, THEODATUS GARLICK, WM. CASE, F. W. and W. Bingham, and CHAS. WHITTLESEY. The academy occupied a room, known as the Museum of the Cleveland Academy of Natural Sciences, in the Cleveland Medical College of Western Reserve at St. Clair and Erie (E. 9th) Sts. The museum had collections of specimens in mineralogy, geology, botany, zoology, natural history, and natural sciences. Lectures were held during the winter months. In 1876, the Kirtland Society of Natural Sciences opened a museum in CASE HALL. It contained the bird and mammal collection of Wm. Case, the bird collection of R. K. Winslow, the entomology collection of John Fitzpatrick, and fish specimens from the collections of Jared P. Kirtland and Elisha Sterling. After Kirtland's death, the geological, zoological, and botanical exhibits were moved to the Case School of Applied Science. The museum continued to function until 1920, when the Cleveland Museum of Natural History was established and the various collections were transferred to it.

Cleveland Academy of Natural Sciences Records, 1845–58, WRHS.

The **CLEVELAND ACADEMY OF OSTEOPATHIC MEDICINE** as a professional association encourages mutual understanding between public-health agencies and the practitioners of osteopathic medicine for the improvement of the public health. The academy is responsible for maintaining both the high standards of area osteopathic hospitals and institutions and ethical conduct in all phases of osteopathic medicine and surgery. It was located at 21821 Libby Rd. in BEDFORD HEIGHTS in 1986. The academy was created during the 1920s and operated as an unincorporated division of the Ohio Osteopathic Assoc. until 1966, when it was incorporated in Ohio as a not-for-profit institution. During the 1960s, the academy's headquarters were located downtown in the Bulkley Bldg. Its offices were moved to BRENTWOOD HOSPITAL in the early 1970s and to its present (1986) location during the late 1970s. The academy maintains professional affiliations with St. John and West Shore Hospital, RICHMOND HTS. GENERAL HOSPITAL, and Brentwood Hospital, the regional teaching site of the Ohio University College of Osteopathic Medicine. Aside from teaching, the academy also promotes the advancement of professional knowledge of surgery, obstetrics, and the diagnosis, prevention, and treatment of disease through the support and dissemination of original research and investigation. In 1986, the academy's membership was composed of 31 3d- and 4th-year students at the Ohio University College of Osteopathic Medicine, 26 interns, 31 residents, and 35 fellows at the CLEVELAND CLINIC FOUNDATION, and 170 regular members, many of whom hold professorships in American osteopathic medical schools.

The **CLEVELAND ADVERTISER**, from its first issue on 6 Jan. 1831, spelled *Cleveland* without the superfluous *a*, antedating the well-established *Herald* in that regard by more than a year. It was established as a Whig weekly by Henry Bolles and Madison Kelley, who ran it until 1833, when it was turned over to W. Woodward and converted into a Democratic organ. On 8 Jan. 1835, the *Advertiser* was purchased by Horace Canfield and Timothy P. Spencer, publishers of the *Ohio Review* at Cuyahoga Falls. Retaining the *Advertiser*'s Democratic orientation, Canfield and Spencer moved it above the post office on Superior Ave. In 1836 they followed the *Herald*'s lead by publishing a daily edition, although the weekly kept its identity as the *Cleveland Weekly Advertiser*. Canfield meanwhile dropped out of the partnership, but Spencer was joined by A. H. Curtis, who became active editor of both the weekly and the daily. After the demise of the daily in 1838, Spencer appeared as sole proprietor of the weekly *Advertiser* until 1841, when it was published by Calvin Hall. Still a Democratic paper, its last issue apparently was that of 17 Dec. 1841. It was then purchased by the brothers Admiral Nelson and JOSEPH WM. GRAY, who used its facilities to inaugurate a new Democratic weekly, the *PLAIN DEALER*, which first appeared on 7 Jan. 1842--11 years and a day after the debut of the *Advertiser*.

The **CLEVELAND ADVERTISING CLUB** is organized for the study of all matters related to advertising, to advance the public image of advertising and its image as a positive force in business, to promote Cleveland as an advertising center, and to advance the civic, cultural, and business interests of Greater Cleveland. Membership is open to all in good standing in the community who are interested in promoting the club's purposes. The initial meetings of the CAC took place in 1901 at the Forest City House and the Williamson Bldg. At the time, few businesses and manufacturers employed advertising in a systematic manner. Sharp trade practices and preposterous claims had brought the advertising industry into widespread disrepute, and admen were largely isolated practitioners suspicious of others in the field. From its inception, the club continually promoted credibility in advertising. It helped prepare state legislation promoting honesty in advertising in 1908. Formed in 1908, the CAC's Vigilance Committee was to encourage truth in advertising and good business ethics by monitoring careless and deceptive advertising. Renamed the Fair Practices Committee, it expanded its activities, eventually evolving into the Better Business Bureau. The club instituted the plan for "Truth and Believability in Advertising" in 1950, and in 1960 it put into operation the "Cleveland Plan for Maintaining Public Confidence in Advertising." Recognizing the need for skilled people, the Analad (analyzing ad-

vertising) Div. was formed in 1915 to offer courses in advertising. In 1919 the program was expanded, creating the School of Advertising. The annual classes produced thousands of graduates. In 1950 the school began offering courses in constructive public relations. In 1975 the CAC dedicated its Advertising Hall of Fame. The CAC not only supported but also originated civic projects of enduring value. The club launched the "Advertise Cleveland" movement in 1920 to help Cleveland know itself and the outside world know Cleveland. The "Come to Cleveland" Committee contributed to bringing about the GREAT LAKES EXPOSITION in 1936 and 1937. The Aviation Committee promoted Cleveland as an aeronautical center during the 1920s and successfully promoted a Cleveland-Hopkins Airport bond issue in 1950. The club has also successfully promoted Cleveland's FESTIVAL OF FREEDOM, the Downtown Festivals, and the Parade of Progress.

The **CLEVELAND ADVOCATE** was a black newspaper that flourished during the period of WORLD WAR I and the great migration of blacks from the South. It was established on 15 May 1914 by Ormond Adolphus Forte, a native of Barbados, British West Indies. According to Forte, who began working for the M. A. HANNA CO. after his arrival in Cleveland, the *Advocate* was launched with the financial backing of DANIEL RHODES HANNA, his employer and the owner of the *CLEVELAND LEADER* and the *CLEVELAND NEWS*. As the voice of moderate black leadership, the 8-page weekly was the logical successor of the *CLEVELAND JOURNAL* and the inevitable antagonist of the militant *CLEVELAND GAZETTE*. With America's entry into the war, the *Advocate*'s position began to harden. "This is the day of the radical Colored man," wrote Forte, who began to protest against segregated training camps for black soldiers and to question the state's support of Wilberforce University as conducive toward segregated education in Ohio. Ralph W. Tyler of Columbus, who joined the *Advocate* as contributing editor, went to France as war correspondent, where he exposed the efforts of some American officers to impose their own racist attitudes upon their French counterparts. Returning home, Tyler helped Forte to produce a 16-page "Soldiers' Edition" for the *Advocate* of 14 June 1919. During the 1920 presidential election, Forte withheld his endorsement almost until the last minute before giving Republican nominee Warren G. Harding an enthusiastic nod. Forte's efforts to keep the *Advocate* afloat failed by 1924. Subsequently, however, Forte published 2 more weeklies, the *CLEVELAND HERALD* and the *Cleveland Eagle*, along the same lines as the *Advocate*.

The **CLEVELAND AIR SHOW** is an indirect development (1964) of the NATL. AIR RACES, which were first held in Cleveland in 1929 as a competitive event. The first air show, in 1964 at BURKE LAKEFRONT AIRPORT, was underwritten by Geo. Steinbrenner. Approximately 10 years later, a corporation was formed to run the show, the Cleveland Natl. Air Show, Inc. The show continued along the same vein as earlier races, including such features as parachute teams, aerobatic teams, high-powered biplanes, and formula race heats. Some of the more famous acts included the Air Force Thunderbirds, the Red Devils, the Navy's Blue Angels, and the Army's Golden Knights parachute team. In 1976, a new dimension was added to the air show with an aviation industrial-educational exhibit in an Air Cleveland hangar. There were 60 exhibits by military and local firms and organizations. In 1981 a fatal accident involving the Air Force Thunderbirds took the life of Lt. Col. David L. Smith. The crash was caused by birds entering the engine through the air intakes on either side of the fuselage. Smith's was the 14th death in the Thunderbirds' 29 years of performing, and the second in 1981. The most prominent air show in the country, the Cleveland Air Show boasted military and civilian participants from around the world, with attendance estimates over 100,000 by 1978. The nonprofit corporation with 25 trustees hired C. K. Newcomb & Associates (a management company) to run the show, which was, by 1986, a continuing tradition for Cleveland's Labor Day weekend.

The **CLEVELAND AMERICAN INDIAN CENTER** was founded in Oct. 1969 by former Clevelander Russell Means to help resettled Indians adapt to urban life. The need for such a center grew out of federal policies that relocated Indians in urban areas. Since the mid-1950s, when the Eisenhower administration directed that native peoples should be removed from the reservations in order to blend them into the mainstream of American society, tribesmen had come to major urban cities in search of employment. Coming from a rural society where the pace of life, patterns of work, and cultural expectations were different, the migrants constituted the poorest of Cleveland's poor by the mid-1960s. With the passage of the Employment Assistance Program, which paid transportation, subsistence, and job training, the city became one of 8 relocation centers, though far from the western sites of most reservations. Cleveland offered good employment prospects, but high rates of alcoholism, child death, disease, and suicide indicated a low degree of social integration. While the Bureau of Indian Affairs was supposed to direct both the cultural and physical resettlement of Indians, budget cuts limited services, much to the dismay of Means, a Sioux Indian working as an accountant for the Council on Economic Opportunity. Spurred by the inefficiency and inadequacy of the bureau, Means sought a share of the federal dollars being channeled through his employer and other agencies to combat poverty. With the aid of CLEVELAND: NOW!, the Episcopal church, and the council, he opened a center in the basement of ST. JOHN'S EPISCOPAL CHURCH at 2600 Church Ave. The Cleveland American Indian Ctr., which aspired to administer programs controlled by the bureau, was a cultural center where native dancing and singing took place, and it also assumed some social-service functions for Indian migrants. The center has always been enmeshed in controversy. Shortly after its founding, the CEO threatened to cut off funds to the new organization; Means charged that the council's black administrators were hoarding federal dollars for the east side ghettos. When he mobilized the support of Puerto Ricans and poor west side whites to boycott the council (a move designed to cut off its federal funding), it dropped its opposition.

Internally, the center became a battleground for tribal rivalry, with the Navaho and Sioux and later the Choctaw and Sioux forces being the main opponents. Means proclaimed the need for unity to overcome the cultural emasculation of the Indian, symbolized by removal from the reservation as well as the past tyranny of the government, but his leadership was denounced as partisan. Forced out of office in 1972, Means went on to assume national prominence in the American Indian movement, while the dissidents installed Irma Yellow Eagle as director. More a social worker than an administrator, Yellow Eagle was in office when a major scandal erupted over a misappropriated federal grant intended to fund an alcoholism program. Within a year, the office passed to Jerome Warcloud (Gary Whitsel), formerly a Portage County high school teacher fired for supporting students demonstrating against the Kent State shootings. Like Means, Warcloud, 5/16 Cherokee, felt that Indians should get their fair share of federal largess,

and through effective grant writing, he multiplied the center's funds. He won CETA funds that permitted establishment of a training center at 4907 Lorain. Despite such successes, Warcloud came under attack for moving the center off its original course.

Another challenge to the power of both Warcloud and the Cleveland Indian Ctr. was presented by Robt. Hosick, leader of the rival North American Indian Cultural Ctr. Hosick, an Alaskan Indian, left the Cleveland center, where he was a part-time staff member, and set up a center in Akron. Casting aside Warcloud's census-supported claims that Cleveland was the major Indian population center in Ohio, Hosick effectively lobbied in Columbus to get control over 78 of Ohio's 88 counties, which gave Akron a larger funding base for federal job-training dollars. A feud developed between the 2 centers over whether Cleveland would get a mobile phone authorized by the state as Akron had. Hosick requested that the IRS and the FBI investigate the financial affairs of the Cleveland Indian Ctr., and then got the state director of special grants to cut off CETA funding during the probe; Hosick was temporarily put in charge of Cleveland funds. Though some questionable financial practices were uncovered that resulted in the Cleveland center's repaying some $18,000 in CETA funds, other charges were dropped when the Cleveland and Akron directors agreed that Cleveland should get 34.5% of federal funds, and Akron 65.5%. Despite the internal problems, the Cleveland American Indian Ctr. provides help to Indians adrift in an urban environment. It has been only peripherally involved in fights by Indians elsewhere to gain compensation for treaty violations, concentrating instead on jobs, counseling, alcoholism treatment, and the preservation of cultural identity. The center was located at 5500 Lorain Ave. in 1985.

The **CLEVELAND & BEREA STREET RAILWAY COMPANY** was the original line of track that eventually evolved into the CLEVELAND SOUTHWESTERN & COLUMBUS RAILWAY. The railway began in 1884 as a horsecar line in the college town of BEREA, Ohio, consisting of a 1½-mi. track from downtown Berea to the Lake Shore & Michigan Southern Railway depot. In 1890, the line was acquired by A. H. Pomeroy, a Berea businessman who was interested in the future possibilities of electric railways. He and his associate, W. D. Miller, who had operated horsecar lines in Sandusky, Ohio, and Mt. Clemens, Mich., had observed rapid development of street railways in Cleveland and other cities. Convinced that lines between communities would be a sound investment, they located additional investors, acquired the needed right-of-way, and laid rail on Rocky River Dr. from Berea to KAMM'S CORNERS (West Park), down Lorain Rd. to Cleveland's city limits at W. 98th St. There the passengers connected with the Woodland Ave. & West Side Street Railway. The 2 power companies serving Cleveland at that time said it was impossible to send power such a long distance through the wires to Berea. As a last resort, the railway used storage batteries for power. Service officially began on 2 Oct. 1893, with 1 car making 6 round trips a day. The batteries had to be charged after each round trip, which took about 2 hours. This line was eventually consolidated with other local street railways into the Cleveland & Southwestern Traction Co. After many years, through further consolidation with other railways, the lines became known as the Cleveland Southwestern & Columbus Railway Co.

Wilcox, Max E., *The Cleveland Southwestern & Columbus Railway Story* (ca. 1962).

The **CLEVELAND & BUFFALO TRANSIT COMPANY** was a popular steamship line and a trucking firm. It was established by Morris A. Bradley in 1885 and incorporated in 1892 with Bradley as president. Passenger and freight service was initiated between Cleveland and Buffalo on the *State of Ohio* and the *State of New York*, leaving Cleveland from the foot of St. Clair Ave. In 1896 the *City of Buffalo* was added, "the largest side-wheeler on the Great Lakes." The *City of Erie* replaced the *State of Ohio* in 1898, providing night service from Cleveland to Toledo. In 1914 Cedar Pt. and Put-in-Bay were added to the C&B route.

Passenger service became increasingly popular. In 1913 the *Seeandbee*, the largest and most costly sidewheel passenger steamer in the world, began regular trips between Cleveland and Buffalo, as well as special cruises. This 500-ft. all-steel ship could carry 1,500 passengers on 4 decks. An arrangement for lakefront development was negotiated in 1913. C&B and the Detroit & Cleveland line obtained a 50-yr. lease from the city for property at the foot of 9th St. for $55,000. There the two companies built the E. 9th St. Pier, a new lake terminal, which was dedicated in 1915. In exchange, the city built a bridge over the E. 9th St. railroad tracks, paved the E. 9th St. approach, and provided a street railway to the pier.

Expansion of passenger excursions in the 1920s led to the purchase of the *City of Detroit II* from the Detroit & Cleveland line. Rebuilt as the *Goodtime*, it provided excursions and "moonlight rides" on the Cleveland-Cedar Pt. and Put-in-Bay route. Fire destroyed the *State of Ohio* at the Cleveland dock in 1924, and automotive transportation began to erode the profitability of lake shipping. In 1930, C&B began tractor-trailer freight service during the winter months in an attempt to be competitive year-round. In 1938 another fire destroyed the *City of Buffalo*. That, along with resources already strained by the Depression and increasing competition from trucks and railroads, resulted in the collapse of the company. Liquidation began in 1939. The E. 9th St. Pier was transferred to the Lederer Terminal Warehouse Co. Both the *Goodtime* and the *City of Erie* were sold for salvage. The luxurious *Seeandbee* was eventually transformed in the 1940s into the USS *Wolverine*, an aircraft carrier training ship. The Cleveland & Buffalo Transit Co. did retain its trucks, however. Under the control of Cleveland capital, a successor appeared in 1943 and continued the trucking business. M. C. Portmann was the first president of the newly formed Cleveland & Buffalo Transit Co., Inc. By 1955, the firm grossed about $650,000 a year. That year it became a wholly owned subsidiary of Forest City Industries, Inc., of Cleveland.

The **CLEVELAND & NEWBURGH "DUMMY" RAILROAD COMPANY** was the first line to provide transit service in Cleveland powered by a source other than a horse, using steam engines in its "dummy" cars. The Cleveland & Newburgh Railroad Co., or Newburgh "Dummy" Line, began operation on 20 Oct. 1868. It began at Willson Ave. (E. 55th St.) and Kinsman Rd., meeting horsecar lines that extended to downtown Cleveland from that point. The line ran 3.33 mi., following Kinsman, crossing KINGSBURY RUN on a trestle, south on E. 65th St., east on Bessemer Ave., south on E. 75th St., then on to Broadway, which it followed to its eastern terminus at Harvard Ave. Fare was $.10. The line carried workers to the industrial Newburgh area, as well as provided transportation to the CATARACT HOUSE, a resort hotel near Broadway and Miles Ave. The hotel was near a natural waterfall, near Warner Rd. and Webb Terrace. The line's engines resembled streetcars from the outside, concealing a steam engine

in the car. A trailing car made up a train. Two trains operated initially.

The railroad was founded by industrialists JEPTHA H. WADE, AMASA STONE, STILLMAN WITT, and Hiram Garretson; initial funding was $68,000. In response to demands to end the required transfer at E. 55th to downtown, the line began running dummy trains to PUBLIC SQUARE in Nov. 1871. The chugging steam engines frightened horses, however, and the cars were banned from the downtown area. Later that month, an epidemic struck the Cleveland horse population, crippling the horse railway industry. The Newburgh line's steam trains were used by the E. Cleveland Railway Co., but the practice was discontinued once the epidemic passed. Accidents plagued the line throughout its history, damaging its financial health. That, along with a rival horsecar line that followed much of the same route (the BROADWAY & NEWBURGH ST. RAILWAY CO.), led to a decrease in revenues. The line went into receivership and ceased operation in 1877.

Christiansen, Harry, *Trolley Trails through Greater Cleveland and Northern Ohio* (1975).

The **CLEVELAND & NEWBURGH RAILWAY** was Cleveland's first attempt at passenger rail transit. It linked Newburgh Twp. from the area of DOAN'S CORNERS (E. 105th St. and Euclid Ave.) with PUBLIC SQUARE. The railway was incorporated on 3 Mar. 1834. It was started with capital of $50,000 subscribed by such prominent citizens as Aaron Barker (later Cleveland postmaster), David H. Beardsley (judge and Ohio Canal collector of Cleveland), Lyman Kendall, TRUMAN P. HANDY (banker), JOHN W. ALLEN (lawyer), Horace Perry (landowner and Cleveland village president, 1820), and Jas. S. Clark (businessman and real-estate investor).

The line was built by engineer and surveyor AHAZ MERCHANT. Rails and ties were of forest oak. Initially, the line carried stone and logs from Blue Stone Quarry atop Cedar Hill by gravity down the hill to Euclid Ave. From there, horses pulled flatcars to Public Square, where the freight was carted to the docks and building sites. The line had a franchise to extend to the docks, but it never did so. Passenger service was begun on 4 July 1835. Two cars with seats lengthwise and on the roof were added; round-trip fare from E. 101st St. to Public Square was $.25. The eastern station on the line was at the Billings Hotel, located at E. 101st and Euclid. It became known as the Railroad Hotel and also provided livery stables for the line's horses. The line followed Euclid Ave. to the southwest corner of Public Square, where it terminated behind the Cleveland House Hotel. Two round trips per day were made when passenger service was initiated; the number was increased to 6, but the line still lost money. Bankruptcy was declared in 1840. The line's officials asked for and received a subsidy from the Cuyahoga County commissioners—$49,866, but it continued to lose money. It was abandoned in 1842. Omnibus service replaced the railway, and its rails rotted in Euclid Ave. Seventeen years passed before another rail transit venture was begun in Cleveland.

Christiansen, Harry, *New Northern Ohio's Interurbans* (1983).
———, *Trolley Trails through Greater Cleveland and Northern Ohio* (1975).

**CLEVELAND ANNIVERSARY CELEBRATIONS** have been held regularly to commemorate the landing of MOSES CLEAVELAND on 22 July 1796. Observances have often been modest, consisting mainly of ceremonies on PUBLIC SQUARE sponsored by the EARLY SETTLERS

ASSOC. OF THE WESTERN RESERVE and featuring descendants of Moses Cleaveland; but on several occasions the observance has taken on a festive air. The two major anniversary celebrations have been the observances of the city's centennial in 1896 and sesquicentennial in 1946. The 100th birthday of the city was marked with a 3-month celebration from July–Sept. 1896. The Early Settlers Assoc. began planning for the event in 1893, but the official Centennial Commission was not appointed until May 1895. Original plans were quite ambitious, but, according to the commission's final report, "owing to the existing financial stringency and national political agitation, and to other causes, the celebration was not as extensive as at first proposed." The scaled-down celebration began with music from the chimes of TRINITY CATHEDRAL on Sunday, 19 July, and featured an Ohio Natl. Guard encampment, a log cabin built on Public Square, and a salute from the CLEVELAND LIGHT ARTILLERY at midnight to begin Founder's Day, 22 July. That day featured more public meetings and addresses, a parade of military and uniformed civic groups, the illumination of the Centennial Arch by Pres. Grover Cleveland (via telegraphic connection to Buzzard's Bay, Mass.), a procession of 24 floats, and a ball. Founder's Day was followed by New England Day (23 July), Wheelmen's Day (24 July, featuring a bicycle parade), Women's Day (28 July), Early Settlers' Day (29 July), and Western Reserve Day (30 July); August brought the Centennial Yacht Regatta, the Centennial Floral Exhibition, and the Knights of Pythias Encampment. Perry's Victory Day (11 Sept.) closed the official celebration, but on 18 Dec. the Women's Dept. of the Centennial Commission presented to the WESTERN RESERVE HISTORICAL SOCIETY a hermetically sealed aluminum container that held various documents, artifacts, and publications and that was to remain sealed until opened in 1996 by a lineal descendant of a member of the department's executive board.

The Cleveland Sesquicentennial Commission was established by Mayor THOS. A. BURKE in mid-Aug. 1945 to plan for the 150th anniversary of Cleveland's landing. The commission planned a series of events throughout the year, such as the Sesquicentennial Regatta, and used the sesquicentennial celebration to attract national events to the city, such as industrial shows and the broadcasts of national radio programs. Founder's Day was again the center of the special festivities; the historic landing was reenacted, and some 200,000 people gathered at the Mall for what the commission's report described as "a spirited Mardi Gras." Festive celebrations also marked the city's anniversaries during the 1920s and 1930s. Harper Garcia Smyth regularly penned scripts for elaborate historical pageants for these events. In 1921, as the week-long festivities marking the 125th anniversary neared an end, promoters were in debt by $25,000; they were saved by a rainstorm late in the week, which enabled them to collect $30,000 from a rain insurance policy. During the 1930s, civic leaders used the anniversary as an opportunity to promote the city and its business and industry. In 1931, the week of 18–25 July was proclaimed Made-in-Cleveland Week; in 1935, Founder's Day was part of Old Home Week; and in late 1934, the Come-to-Cleveland Committee of the CLEVELAND ADVERTISING CLUB announced a 35-point plan to attract 5 million visitors to the city in 1936 as Cleveland marked its 140th birthday and its 100th year as a chartered city.

Official Programme of the Centennial Celebration of the Founding of The City of Cleveland and the Settlement of the Western Reserve, WRHS.

Roberts, Edward A., comp., *Official Report of the Centennial Celebration* (1896).

*The Year of Celebration, 1946. A Report of the Cleveland Sesquicentennial* (1946).

The **CLEVELAND ANTI-SLAVERY SOCIETY,** organized in 1833, aimed "to procure the speedy abolition of" slavery, according to its constitution. Counting among its members prominent businessmen, professionals, blacks, and women, the society opposed both the schemes of colonization and the use of force to end slavery; instead, members placed their faith in reason and proposed to end the peculiar institution "by enlightening the public mind, in regards to the true character of Slavery." In the spring of 1833, Cleveland hosted 2 visitors who preached the evils of slavery and the urgent need for emancipation. In April, Chas. W. Denison of New York lectured on emancipation at the Episcopal church, and in early May the controversial abolitionist president of Hudson's Western Reserve College, Chas. B. Storrs, spoke at the courthouse. It appears that Storrs's speech prompted formation of the Cleveland society to give expression to rising antislavery sentiment, since the society's constitution stipulated that it was an "auxiliary to the 'Western Reserve Anti-Slavery Society,'" which had been chartered at Western Reserve College in Dec. 1832.

Experienced reformers provided the leadership for the Cleveland Anti-Slavery Society. These included the city's first resident physician, DAVID LONG, who served as the society's president; his son-in-law, merchant Solomon L. Severance, the society's secretary; law partners JOHN A. FOOTE and SHERLOCK J. ANDREWS; and Henry F. Brayton, active in New York City reform movements before returning to Cleveland in 1836 as a bookkeeper for the Bank of Cleveland. Long, Foote, and Harmon Kingsbury were also quite active in the society. Membership was easy to attain. "Any person" who signed the constitution became a voting member. Among the early signers were at least 2 blacks: JOHN MALVIN, an early black leader in the city who became a lecturer for the society, and Stephen Griffith, a mason. Although the issue of women's participation in the antislavery movement divided members of the American Anti-Slavery Society, women were apparently a sizable minority in the local society. Of the 131 signatures on the constitution, at least 30 are the those of women. The number of members in the Cleveland Anti-Slavery Society grew steadily. By Apr. 1836, the society had 70 members; the following year there were 200. The society's constitution called for annual July 4th meetings to choose leaders, but on 4 July 1837, Foote, Severance, and John M. Sterling—all members of the Cleveland society—led a meeting that created the CUYAHOGA COUNTY ANTI-SLAVERY SOCIETY. With Edward Wade of BROOKLYN as its president, Foote among its several vice-presidents, Brayton as its recording secretary, and Severance as its treasurer, the county society appears to have been the dominant local antislavery organization after 1837. But the national antislavery movement divided into warring factions in the early 1840s, and by 1842 the local organizations with national affiliation had disappeared.

The **CLEVELAND AQUARIUM** was located in GORDON PARK at 601 E. 72nd St. It was operated for the city of Cleveland by the CLEVELAND MUSEUM OF NATURAL HISTORY, which was responsible for stocking, staffing, maintenance, and making up the operating differences, while the city maintained ownership of the property and contributed toward annual operating expenses. The aquarium was open Tuesday through Sunday. It had 50 exhibit tanks, with the 5 largest systems each holding 12,000 gallons. Included in its freshwater and marine exhibits were sharks, piranhas, swordfish, sawfish, eels, squid, octopus, and coral. Among its highlights were the acquisition of a pair of lungfish in 1966 and their subsequent breeding; the acquisition of a school of red-bellied piranhas in 1970; and the arrival of river otters in 1971 and a sea lion in 1972. The original aquarium building was constructed as a bath house during the Depression and was abandoned after the park's bathing conditions deteriorated. Later it became a trailside museum featuring exhibits on the natural history of Lake Erie and the Doan Brook Valley. During the construction of the Lakeland Freeway, the museum became virtually isolated and was closed. The Cleveland Aquarium Society and the city reached an agreement in 1953 to convert the museum into an aquarium, with the city pledging participation in meeting annual operating costs and financial assistance with the completion of 10 500-gallon tanks. Local tropical-fish hobbyists volunteered, working at night, on weekends, and on holidays to make possible the aquarium's opening on 6 Sept. 1954.

The original structure was envisioned as a pilot plant, and under the Natural History Museum's direction, the aquarium often drew more visitors than the building could handle. A $300,000 gift from the Leonard C. Hanna Foundation financed the construction of a new octagonal wing in 1967 that tripled the aquarium's size and increased its tank capacity from 8,000 to 82,000 gallons. A gift from trustee Homer Everett enabled the aquarium to remodel its west wing in 1971. The aquarium underwent financial difficulties throughout the 1970s. In 1970 and 1971, the city proposed that the Cleveland Metropolitan Park Board assume the aquarium's operation. Despite annual deficits, it required a city council override of a mayoral veto in 1979 to increase the admission charges and keep aquarium operations with the museum. In June 1985, structural problems forced the closing of the aquarium to the public. On 1 Apr. 1986, operations were transferred to the Cleveland Metroparks, and the collection was transferred to new exhibits at the CLEVELAND METROPARKS ZOO.

The **CLEVELAND ARCHITECTURAL CLUB** was first formed in the early 1880s, but on 7 Apr. 1887, it was reorganized as the AMERICAN INSTITUTE OF ARCHITECTS CLEVELAND CHAPTER. In 1894 a second Cleveland Architectural Club was formed. The leading architects of the day were members, among them CHAS. F. SCHWEINFURTH, Frank A. Coburn, Frank Barnum, W. DOMINICK BENES, BENJAMIN HUBBELL, Geo. Steffens, and Herman Dercum. At that time, new city, county, and federal buildings were being planned, and one of the club's first and most important activities was to organize a competition for a "grouping of Cleveland public buildings." This action was a direct impetus for the historic Group Plan of 1903. The club then arranged important annual exhibitions of architectural drawings and photographs from firms around the country beginning in 1896, although there were no exhibitions in 1898–99. In 1899 the club was one of 4 to join an Assoc. of Technical Clubs organized by the Civil Engineers' Club. The association maintained offices and a library in the ARCADE. Later in the same year, the club became a member of the Architectural League of America, an association of architectural societies from 16 cities. In 1908 the members of the technical clubs formed the CLEVELAND ENGINEERING SOCIETY, whose members included all branches of the engineering, architectural, and scientific professions, and toward the end of WORLD WAR I the club went out of existence.

The **CLEVELAND AREA BOARD OF REALTORS**, known as the Cleveland Real Estate Board until July 1971,

began in the 1860s with small, informal meetings between local real-estate agents to promote better cooperation among themselves and to discuss community improvement. After the turn of the century, the board became a more aggressive professional organization concerned with standardizing the profession, improving its public image, promoting local residential and industrial development, and influencing legislation affecting the real-estate business. The Cleveland Real Estate Board was established informally in 1861, when agents began holding small meetings among themselves to discuss business standards, ideas for local development, and common problems.

An important leader in the transformation of the real-estate business from "a mere business transaction to a profession, requiring careful study of economics" was Daniel R. Taylor (28 Mar. 1838–19 Aug. 1924). Born in Twinsburg, the son of Col. Royal Taylor worked first as a schoolteacher and then as station agent for the Cleveland & Mahoning Railroad before coming to Cleveland in Nov. 1867 and embarking upon a career that earned him a reputation as "the pioneer real estate man in the city." Taylor worked as a general commission agent early in his real-estate career, opening and selling allotments; he later began to handle real-estate frontage for manufacturing purposes and served for many years as the purchasing agent for the Pennsylvania Railroad. He was also president of the Mfrs. Realty Co. and the Harbor View Co. Taylor was also among those most responsible for transforming EUCLID AVE. from a residential street to a business district. He and several partners bought the old St. Paul Church property on the southwest corner of Euclid and Sheriff (E. 4th) streets, razed the church, subdivided the land, and sold it for business development; they also obtained several homesteads on the north side of Euclid at E. 6th St. and similarly developed the property for business use. In a speech to the Real Estate Board in June 1911, Taylor recalled that "the greatest and most disastrous boom" in land prices had occurred in the late 1860s and early 1870s. Land prices "went soaring in and about the city, but when the panic came, what a fall there was. . . . From 1873–80 we were figuratively walking on hot plow shares. To keep taxes paid was indeed a burden. . . . In 1882 I bought land at $425 per acre that was held in 1872 at $3,000 per acre."

The Cleveland Real Estate Board was organized formally on 21 June 1892, to end what one member recalled as a period of "cut-throat competition and sign-smashing." "Our unscrupulous competitors would drive by at night and tear . . . down" recently posted for-sale signs, according to early board memeber A. S. Taylor. Board members acknowledged Daniel Taylor's leadership by choosing him as the organization's first president. Other officers included J. G. W. Cowles, vice-president; Chas. E. Ferrell, secretary; and Virgil C. Taylor, treasurer. Between 1892–1905, the board concentrated its efforts on internal, professional matters. Under the leadership of John Colahan, president of the board from 1898–1905, the board worked to standardize the real-estate business in Cleveland, to educate real-estate agents about their profession, and to develop codes of ethics to improve the public image of the profession. Such actions met one of the dual purposes of the board as spelled out in the preamble to its constitution: "To establish and maintain the calling of the real estate broker in a position of dignity and responsibility in the community, by insisting on principles of honesty and fair dealing in their business of buying and selling, renting, caring for, and loaning money on real estate."

By 1920, the board had become an elite organization with 7 classes of membership, and with a special title—"realtor"—which could be used only by its members and members of other affiliates of the Natl. Assoc. of Real Estate Boards, organized in 1908. Cleveland's was the 3d-largest board in the country in 1915. The board continued its efforts on behalf of the profession, lobbying in the state legislature for a state board to license real-estate agents (legislation passed in 1925; Ohio State Board of Real Estate Examiners est. in 1927 after the legislation was amended); protecting the profession in the 1930s against charges from the legal profession that realtors who filled out legal papers in real-estate transactions were practicing law illegally (resolved in Dec. 1940 when courts ruled in favor of Cleveland realtor V. C. Taylor & Son, who had been sued by the CUYAHOGA COUNTY BAR ASSOC.); and sponsoring a variety of services over the years designed to benefit its members, from real-estate classes to computerized multiple-listing services. It has also developed specialized affiliate groups such as local chapters of the Society of Industrial Realtors and the American Institute of Real Estate Appraisers.

In 1890, 24,453 Cuyahoga County residents owned their own homes, out of a population of 309,970. By 1900, population of the county had increased to 439,120, and homeownership had risen to 36,808; and by 1910, 54,206 county residents out of a population of 637,425 owned homes. As homeownership increased from 84,503 in 1920 to 125,296 in 1930, and the development of suburbs led realty firms to decentralize their offices and locate branch offices in outlying areas, individual round tables were established as regional divisions of the Real Estate Board, which coordinated their operations. The first such division was the Heights Round Table, organized in the fall of 1925, followed by the Lakewood-West Side Round Table in the fall of 1925; other regional divisions included the Southeast Round Table, the Brooklyn-Parma-Southwest Round Table, and the Northeast Round Table.

Another important goal of the board throughout its history has been "to advance the interests of Cleveland and its citizens by fostering public improvements, an equitable system of assessments and taxation, and the enforcement of laws for the protection, welfare and convenience of real estate owners and leaseholders, and generally to devise, advocate and support legislation calculated to improve the city of Cleveland. . . ." In 1911 or 1912, the board hired a permanent secretary to work in the interests of the real-estate business, and early in its history it established a valuation committee to appraise real-estate values. The board has also been active in proposing legislation in its interests and vigorously opposing legislation it believes would hurt property owners, building contractors, and the real-estate business. The board generally has opposed government intervention in the real-estate business through such programs as public housing, urban renewal, and, in the mid-1960s, fair-housing legislation. As early as 1950, the president of the board expressed a desire to develop the political power of homeowners, and in 1969 the board established a Home Owners Div. "to fight the growing octopus of big government."

The 1960s and early 1970s were difficult years for the board and for the local profession generally, as it came under public criticism for racial discrimination in its business practices and in its membership. In July 1961, the Cleveland Real Estate Board met for the first time with the Cleveland Assoc. of Real Estate Brokers, an organization of black real-estate agents who called themselves "realists" since the term *realtor* was protected for use by members of an organization they could not join, to plan ways to prevent the unethical practice of "block-busting." The Real Estate Board had no black members until Oct. 1963, when it voted to accept into its ranks J. Howard Battle; by 1972,

only 8 of its 568 members were black. The board also came under attack from federal and state officials for long-standing policies that it had established to protect and promote the profession. In 1970, the U.S. Dept. of Justice sued the board over its policy of establishing and publishing the rates that its members were allowed to charge for their services, and in 1975 the state's attorney general sued the board for attempting to monopolize training programs for real-estate agents.

The 1970s brought other changes, as well. The board became more active in general social issues, sponsoring a drug-abuse prevention program and the Light the Night anticrime program, and more actively promoting the fair-housing laws among both its members and the general public. The board had served for years as an information center about real-estate issues, and in the consumer-minded 1970s, it established a Housing Information Ctr. in 1973. In 1973 it also began Project Pride, a program to rehabilitate deteriorating properties to demonstrate to the public ways of maintaining and increasing property values. In 1976, the board voted to do away with its various classes of membership: rather than confer membership to only 600 real-estate broker members, it opened membership to all 6,000 salespeople in those firms. In 1977, after being located in various rented offices throughout its history, the Cleveland Area Board of Realtors purchased its own building at 2829 Euclid Ave. for $300,000.

The **CLEVELAND ARENA**, located at 3717 Euclid and commonly known as the Arena, was built in 1937 for $1.5 million by local sports promoter Albert C. Sutphin and a syndicate of stockholders. Sutphin acquired the property of the Brush estate in 1935, and on 16 May 1937, ground was broken for the 10,000-seat facility. Built primarily as the home of Sutphin's ice-hockey team, the CLEVELAND BARONS, the Arena was hailed as an "All-Sport Palace" and hosted many other kinds of entertainment. On opening night, 10 Nov. 1937, it was host to the Ice Follies of 1938; it hosted its first hockey match a week later, 17 Nov. By the 1940s, the Arena was hosting as many as 330 events a year; such events included shows by stars of radio, movies, and the stage; rodeos featuring the likes of Gene Autry and Roy Rogers; circuses; and a host of sporting events, from HOCKEY to wrestling to midget auto races to 6-day bicycle races. High school BASKETBALL tournaments, college and professional basketball games, and KNIGHTS OF COLUMBUS TRACK MEETS were also held there, and BOXING matches drew large crowds. The Arena was the scene of the tragic 24 June 1947 championship bout in which Jimmy Doyle died. It was also the site in Mar. 1952 of radio disc jockey Alan Freed's Moondog Coronation Ball. Sutphin owned and operated the Arena until Apr. 1949, when he sold it and the Barons to a group of Minneapolis sports promoters and businessmen. The Arena fell on hard times during the 1960s, hosting fewer than 100 events a year at its lowest point. Nick Mileti bought both the Arena and the Barons in 1968, but with the opening of the Coliseum in Richfield, the Arena ceased to host major sporting and entertainment events in 1974. Mileti's attempts to sell the Arena were unsuccessful, and the building was demolished in early 1977.

The **CLEVELAND ASSEMBLY OF 1855**, convened 17–20 Oct. at the Masonic Hall, was the first and last general synod of American Jewish religious and lay leaders. The meeting produced a statement of principles that synod organizers hoped would be the basis for uniting American Jewry. By 1855 there were approximately 110 congregations throughout America following various religious rituals, including Orthodox, traditional (Historical School), and moderate Reform, and radical Reform. Isaac Mayer Wise of Cincinnati, the leader of moderate Reform, and Isaac Leeser of Philadelphia, the leader of traditional Jewry, had been attempting to unify American Jews for a decade, albeit under their respective philosophies.

The Cleveland Assembly was the third attempt at organizing a synod and was successful largely because of the initial cooperation between Wise and Leeser under the slogan "Shalom Al Yisrael" (Peace be unto Israel). Among those attending the conference besides Wise and Leeser were Rabbis Leo Merzbacher of New York, Maximillian Lillienthal of Cincinnati, and Elkan Cohn of Albany and approximately a dozen other religious and lay leaders, primarily from the Midwest. Representing Cleveland were B. L. Fould, Joseph Levi, Asher Lehman of ANSHE CHESED CONGREGATION, and Rabbi ISIDOR KALISCH, F. I. Cohen, and Alexander Schwab of Congregation Tifereth Israel.

The statement issued by the synod resolved that the Bible is the revealed word of God; the Talmud is the traditional legal and logical exposition on Biblical law; the resolutions of the synod are legally valid; and illiberal assertions in the Talmud are not legally binding. Additionally, the conference established a committee to produce a new prayerbook that would reflect Jewish spiritual needs in the American environment, agreed to create Zion collegiate associations in all major American cities, and expressed opposition to all-day Hebrew schools in favor of public education supplemented by afternoon religious school. The latter three resolutions were introduced by Wise and his supporters but were opposed by Leeser, who had left Cleveland before the issues were discussed.

Despite the support of Wise and Leeser for the synod, the majority of religious leaders boycotted the meeting. The radical reformers, led by David Einhorn of Baltimore, rejected the resolutions because they did not believe that the Talmud was legally binding. Additionally, the radicals opposed Wise's moderate Reform and argued that he had capitulated to Leeser. The Orthodox and traditionalists welcomed the resolutions but stated their wariness of Wise, who they believed did not practice what he preached at the conference. In 1856, the committee appointed to produce a new prayerbook—Wise, Kalisch, and Dr. Rothenheim of Cincinnati—issued the *Minhag America* (American Ritual), which became the most popular ritual among moderate Reform congregations during the 1860s and 1870s. The new prayerbook eliminated many of the prayers found in the traditional ritual and was, therefore, opposed by Leeser and his followers. Rather than unifying American Jewry under the traditional umbrella as Leeser wished or under the native Judaism Wise hoped to create, the Cleveland Assembly illustrated that national religious unity was not possible for American Jewry.

Davis, Moshe, *The Emergence of Conservative Judaism* (1963).
Philipson, David, *Centenary Papers and Others* (1919).
Wise, Isaac Mayer, *Reminiscences* (1901).

The **CLEVELAND ASSOCIATION OF COLORED MEN** was organized in June 1908 as an effort of black business and professional men to work together to improve economic and social conditions for their race. The organization brought together the interests of community leaders in a variety of activities, which included sponsorship of a weekly lecture series, numerous social events, charitable projects, and, most important, weekly public meetings that provided a forum for discussion of issues of interest to blacks in Cleveland. As was typical during the pre-World War I period, the club concentrated their civic energies in "investigation" of situations where discriminatory practices were brought to their attention. Investigations were frequently followed up by meetings with officials where complaints of black citizens were aired. Committees of the organization sought to remedy race grievances through negotiation and conciliation. The association also stressed the philosophy of self-reliance, believing that demonstrations of upward mobility of individuals and group effort would result in eventual acceptance of blacks without regard to color. A favorite event sponsored by the group was an annual Emancipation Celebration picnic at LUNA PARK, a "whites only" facility that accommodated black patrons only on select occasions. The choice of this site was severely criticized by more militant black civil-rights activists. The day always included a speaker of national prominence, such as Judge Robt. Terrell, Washington, D.C.'s, first black judge. The Cleveland Assoc. of Colored Men was the successor of a smaller, more elite organization called the Cleveland Board of Trade (organized in 1905), an affiliate of Booker T. Washington's Natl. Negro Business League. The expanded organization attempted to broaden membership to include men of good standing who stood willing and ready "to advance the varied interests of the colored people of Cleveland." Officers in 1908 included THOS. W. FLEMING, president; Jacob Reed, vice-president; Robt. Cheeks, John Redd, Dr. E. A. Dale, Alexander Martin, Sr., and GARRETT MORGAN.

The **CLEVELAND ATHLETIC CLUB**, a private club catering to individuals interested in athletics, was established on 1 Feb. 1908. It was the second club in the city to bear the name. An earlier Cleveland Athletic Club had been established in 1885 and eventually faded out of existence in the 1890s. The first club established headquarters at 927 Euclid Ave. in 1886 and in 1891 moved to a new clubhouse and gymnasium located at 560 Euclid. It sponsored boxing matches, fielded a baseball team, and was active in the bicycling fad of the 1890s. In 1892 it had over 500 members. In 1895 the club was sponsoring a duplicate whist team, but little is known of its history after that time. The second Cleveland Athletic Club does not appear to be directly descended from the first. Incorporated by a group of prominent Clevelanders, including CHAS. OTIS, WALTER C. BAKER, and ELBERT H. BAKER, interested in a gentlemen's downtown sports club, it initially occupied space on the top floor of the New England Bank Bldg. at E. 6th St. and Euclid. Wm. Parmalee Murray, a banker and ore company executive, served as the first president. In 1910 the club built its own building at 1118 Euclid Ave., a 15-story structure in which it leased the top 8 floors for a period of 98 years. The club's offerings currently (1986) include swimming, bowling, billiards, and a card room. The Athletic Club building also has a dining room and 30 overnight guest rooms. Membership in the early 1980s was in excess of 2,000.

**CLEVELAND AUTOMBILE CLUB.** *See* **OHIO MOTORISTS ASSOCIATION**

The **CLEVELAND BALLET** was formed at an opportune moment in American dance by 2 respected and creative dancers, and grew in its first years from a fledgling troupe to a professional resident company with a national reputation for excellence. In 1972, Ian Horvath and Dennis Nahat, both formerly dancers with the American Ballet Theater of New York, bought a small ballet school operating in the basement of Cleveland's Masonic Auditorium. With their own financing and the support of a group known as the Ballet Guild of Cleveland, a small, non-professional company was formed, and the school became the School of Cleveland Ballet, moving to the Stouffer Bldg. on Euclid Ave. With seed money from the CLEVELAND FOUNDATION, a professional company of 16 dancers was recruited from around the country, and lecture-demonstrations and preview performances were given around the city in late 1975. Following a performance of a pastiche of American popular songs choreographed by Nahat and titled *US* at a benefit for the Garden Ctr. of Greater Cleveland, interest in the new company grew, and individual contributions and foundation funding expanded. The Cleveland Ballet gave its first public performances at the HANNA THEATER on 16 Nov. 1976.

The company grew in size and popularity rapidly. The founders had chosen a time when dance was enjoying unprecedented popularity in the public eye. Within the first few seasons, taped music was replaced by the OHIO CHAMBER ORCHESTRA, and in 1981, after several seasons of evenings composed of shorter works, the company presented its first evening-length story ballet, *The Nutcracker*, to sold-out houses. In 1983 a second evening-length work, *Coppelia*, was added to the repertory. The company is known for its eclectic style, performing these standards of the classical literature alongside many modern works. Much of the Cleveland Ballet's success can be attributed to its popular appeal and to the great ability of the founders and staff in raising the large sums of money required to operate a ballet company. The Cleveland Ballet has received major corporate and foundation support and sizable donations from individuals, and covers an unusually high percentage of its expenses by ticket sales. In 1984, Horvath resigned as co-artistic director, leaving Nahat solely responsible for the company, as well as for the direction of the School of Cleveland Ballet. The same year the company moved to a permanent home in the STATE THEATER in PLAYHOUSE SQUARE. The reputation of the Cleveland Ballet has been spread by means of small-scale tours, and reviews from around the country have been favorable. By 1985 the company had 38 dancers presenting a season lasting 32 weeks and including several new works (among them an evening-length *Romeo and Juliet*) and a long revival of *The Nutcracker*.

The **CLEVELAND BAPTIST ASSOCIATION** began as an early cooperative body for area Baptist churches that evolved into the official local organization of American Baptist churches. Although the Baptist religion shuns hierarchy, area Baptist churches realized a need for fellowship and for help in solving problems of doctrine, finance, and pastor selection that were beyond the scope of many small, newly founded parishes. As a result, in 1832, the Rocky River Baptist Assoc. was founded in a Methodist church with the help of the PRESBYTERIANS. Seven churches joined the first year, while 14, including the EUCLID AVE. BAPTIST CHURCH and the FIRST BAPTIST CHURCH of Cleveland, joined in the second and third years. The Lorain churches broke off to form their own society in 1839; by 1852, *Cleveland* was added to the name to reflect the geographic focus, while *Rocky River* was dropped from the name in 1859. Under the leadership of the CBA, area Baptist churches became the most prosperous in the state. The association carried on the work of establishing Sunday schools begun by BENJAMIN and REBECCA ROUSE, who were agents of the American Sabbath School Union of Philadelphia. Aside from its religious concerns, the association was a leader in many social causes over the years: antislavery, human rights, the Social Gospel movement, labor organization, equal opportunity, and world peace. For example, by 1849, a member church established a mission for BLACKS that became (by 1851) SHILOH BAPTIST CHURCH, the first black Baptist church in the local area and the mother of many area black churches. With the population shifts of the 1950s, followed by racial unrest in the 1960s, the CBA tried to adjust its programs to both meet the needs of those fleeing to the suburbs and promote racial harmony and social justice. It tried to involve blacks in American Baptist life, while many churches participated in the INTERCHURCH COUNCIL OF GREATER CLEVELAND, the Inner City Protestant Parish (the Innercity Renewal Society), and the West Side Ecumenical Society. Especially in the 1960s, the association was considered too conservative by many black activists. With its headquarters at E. 18th and Euclid, the CBA had 39 member churches (mostly black) in 1982 and was the official spokesman for the American Baptist Convention.

Cleveland Baptist Assoc., *150 Years of Mission to Greater Cleveland* (1982).

The **CLEVELAND BAR ASSOCIATION** was founded on 22 Mar. 1873 at an organizational meeting led by John W. Heisley and SAMUEL E. WILLIAMSON and attended by 51 other lawyers. SHERLOCK J. ANDREWS was elected president; John W. Heisley, Jas. Mason, and John C. Grannis, vice-presidents; Virgil P. Kline, recording secretary; Lyman R. Critchfield, corresponding secretary; and G. W. Barber, treasurer. The purpose of the association was "to maintain the honor and dignity of the Profession of the Law; to cultivate friendship and acquaintance among members of the Bar and to increase their usefulness in aiding the administration of justice and in promoting legal and judicial reform." Through the years, the CBA has sought to accomplish these objectives primarily through the activities of a series of committees. They have investigated misconduct of lawyers, judges, sheriffs, and police. Occasionally these investigations have led to resignations and/or disbarment. For example, the CBA supported the passage of a bill that made the solicitation of business by a lawyer an unethical procedure, legislation that has since, in part, been nullified.

In 1922, in an effort to keep partisan politics out of judicial races and to encourage the election of what it considered to be qualified candidates, the CBA began to poll its membership and to arrive at a list of endorsed or "preferred" candidates for the bench. This endorsement, known as the "bar slate," is publicized by local newspapers. The CBA has also held public forums and debates on a variety of issues related to the legal profession, including Prohibition, vote fraud, and divorce laws, and has made surveys leading to recommendations for adjustments in municipal court procedures, particularly in the instance of backlogged cases. The association has also come to the aid of people whose civil rights have been violated and endangered. One such instance came in 1955, when CBA lawyers volunteered to defend a number of Cleveland residents who had been indicted as subversives under the Smith Act. During WORLD WAR II, many CBA lawyers served on draft boards and advisory boards and were appeal agents. A War Aid Committee was formed to recruit lawyers to volunteer to give free legal advice to needy members of the armed forces and their families and dependents. The Cleveland Bar Assoc. was instrumental in the formation of the Ohio State Bar Assoc. (1880), and supported the organization of the CUYAHOGA COUNTY BAR ASSOC. (1927). By 1980, the Cleveland association's membership numbered in excess of 3,500.

Cleveland Bar Assoc. Records, WRHS.

Brady, Thomas J., *The First 100 Years* (1973).

The **CLEVELAND BARONS** were charter members of the American Hockey League in 1936 and played at the CLEVELAND ARENA until the team was moved to Jacksonville, Fla., in Jan. 1973. Called the "New York Yankees" of minor-league HOCKEY, the Barons won 9 regular-season titles and 8 Calder Cup playoff championships. The team that eventually evolved into the Cleveland Barons was begun in 1929 as the Cleveland Indians of the Internatl. League. Founded by retired Canadian goalie Harry Holmes, the team played its games at the ELYSIUM BLDG.; it drew well during the 1929–30 season as it played its way to the league championship. By 1933 the Indians were in serious financial trouble; in 1934 the team was purchased by former Central High goalie, boxing commissioner, and sports promoter Albert C. (Al) Sutphin of the Braden-Sutphin Ink Co. He immediately changed the team name from the Indians (1929–34) to the Cleveland Falcons (1934–37). In 1936 the team became a charter member of the new American Hockey League, formed by the merger of the Internatl. and Canadian-American minor leagues. In 1937 Sutphin built the 10,000-seat Arena on Euclid Ave. between E. 36th and E. 40th streets; he also held a public contest, which chose the Cleveland Barons as the new name of his team.

The years between 1936 and the late 1950s were golden years for the franchise, as the Barons were perennial winners. Crowds of over 10,000 were not unusual at a Saturday-night hockey game at the Arena. Cleveland was the largest metropolitan region in minor-league hockey. In 1949 Sutphin sold the Barons to a group of Detroit businessmen, who hired Jas. C. Hendy as general manager. During the spring of 1952, the Barons were set to be the 7th team in the Natl. Hockey League, but the deal fell through. In the late 1950s average attendance fell. Paul Bright bought the franchise after Hendy died, and he appointed Jackie Gordon general manager and Freddie Glover playing coach. Called the greatest Baron hockey player, Glover led the team to 1 more Calder Cup championship during the 1963–64 season. Nick Mileti bought the faltering franchise and the Arena for $2 million in 1968.

Mileti attempted to keep the Barons in Cleveland after he secured a World Hockey Assoc. franchise in 1972. They were competing with the new Cleveland Crusaders, and the Barons' attendance dropped to fewer than 1,000 fans per game. The Barons played their last game at the Arena on 8 Jan. 1973 before 412 fans and moved to Jacksonville, Fla. For a 2-year period between 1976–78, a franchise in the NHL christened the Barons played at the Coliseum. Brought to Cleveland from Oakland by Mel Swig and Geo. Gund III, the Barons were plagued by poor fan interest and low attendance. After finishing last in the Adams Div. for 2 seasons, the team was merged with the Minnesota North Stars, and professional hockey disappeared from the Cleveland metropolitan area.

The **CLEVELAND BICYCLE CLUB** was the 22d wheelmen's association to form in America. It was affiliated with the League of American Wheelmen. The Cleveland Bicycle Club published on a monthly basis the *Cleveland Mercury*, an official organ of the Ohio division of the LAW. The club was created by a group of 6 avid bicyclists on the evening of 30 Sept. 1879, at a meeting in St. Malachi's Hall, which at the time was used for a riding school. In the following month, membership increased to 14, and by 1882, active membership was up to 23. Headquarters for the club were at 147 Ontario St.

The CBC had 3 main purposes: 1) a mutual enjoyment by its members of the pursuit of bicycling as a pastime, to which end club meets, excursions, tours, races, etc. were arranged; 2) advancement of the privileges and protection of the rights of bicyclers—especially the members of the club; and 3) the promotion, in the public mind, of a favorable interest in bicycling. Membership in the CBC was confined to gentlemen amateurs over 19 years of age, members of the LAW, and owners of bicycles of a standard pattern. The eligibility of an applicant, as an amateur, was decided upon by the membership rules of the LAW. Application for membership was made to the secretary, proposed and seconded by 2 active club members, and accompanied by an initiation fee of $5, with quarterly dues of $2 in advance. Dues included the LAW initiation fee. Club meetings were held the first Wednesday in each month, with special meetings called by the president at any time, at the written request of 3 members of the club. The annual meeting was held on 30 Sept. Five members constituted a quorum at any meeting.

Founding members of the Cleveland Bicycle Club included T. B. Stevens, president; H. S. Stevens; Chas. Hopper, lieutenant; W. Leland; H. H. Higbee; and Alfred Ely, Jr., secretary/treasurer. The club probably went the way of most bicycle clubs, which dissolved in the early 1920s as a result of declining interest in bicycling and an increasing interest in the automobile. In fact, the LAW fell dormant for many years until there was a resurgence in recreational bicycling in the late 1950s and 1960s.

The **CLEVELAND BOARD OF HEALTH** was an appointed board of physicians and public officials who worked to improve public sanitation in Cleveland in order to prevent the spread of infectious diseases. Between 1832–1910 it was abolished and restored several times as an independent department of the city of Cleveland. The first board of health in Cleveland was founded in 1832 to combat an epidemic of Asiatic cholera. Appointed by the Cleveland village trustees, the board included Drs. EDWIN W. COWLES, JOSHUA MILLS, and Oran St. John, and 2 other men—S. Belden and Chas. Denison. It was empowered to inspect all vessels arriving from an infected port, to examine suspicious cases, and to provide a suitable building for isolation and treatment. A second cholera epidemic in 1849 brought into existence Cleveland's second board of health, consisting of A. Seymour, WM. CASE, and John Gill. The board reported daily to the community and helped pass an ordinance for city council prohibiting the sale of vegetables and fruits on the streets, especially in immigrant neighborhoods. On 7 Mar. 1850, the Ohio legislature authorized city council to establish a board of health with power to "abate nuisances" and implement necessary measures to control infectious diseases. In 1856, the council passed an ordinance creating a board of health. Dr. Frederick W. Marseilles was appointed health officer. The ordinance also provided that the mayor, city marshal, and director of the infirmary serve on the board.

In the 1870s, steps were taken to sample and analyze the milk supply, and soon after, a full-time milk inspector was appointed. The board also distributed circulars from house to house with information on diseases (cholera, diphtheria, etc.). In 1875, the board was merged into the Bureau of Police and became the Health Dept. In 1882 the board was restored and came more under the control of physicians, who appointed a health officer for each ward of the city. The board continued to work on improving the milk supply, attacked problems relating to sewage and garbage collection, and exposed "quacks" practicing medicine unlawfully. In 1886, the legislature authorized the board to appoint sanitary policemen, 1 for every 15,000 people. In 1893, revision in the Ohio sanitary laws helped increase the board's powers of inspection, extending to dairies, slaughterhouses, meat shops, food products, and a quarterly inspection of schoolhouses. The new laws were put into effect with city ordinances. The board was also given control of all registrations of births, deaths, and marriages and the granting of burial permits. Its power of quarantine was made absolute. Between 1892–1902, the duties of the board again came under the department of police. It was restored as an independent department in 1903. In 1905 there was a substantial increase in the number of district (ward) physicians and sanitary policemen. At this time the board included a food inspector, a meat inspector, a bacteriologist, a barber shop inspector, a plumbing and sewers inspector, 26 district physicians, and 37 sanitary policemen. In 1907 the Board of Health was once again abolished, its duties relegated to a bureau of the department of public service. In 1910 a new department was created, the Dept. of Public Health & Sanitation, which a few years later became the Div. of Health.

The **CLEVELAND BOYS' SCHOOL IN HUDSON**, also referred to as the Hudson Boys' School, was the city correctional school for delinquent boys. With its rural setting, it was one of the first schools of its kind in the country. Founded in 1903, for many years it was known as the Cleveland Boys' Farm. The idea for the facility was initiated by Wm. J. Akers, director of charities and corrections for the city of Cleveland. In 1902, action was finally taken by Akers's successor, Rev. HARRIS R. COOLEY, who was instrumental in getting the city to purchase 123 acres of land in Hudson for the establishment of a boys' farm. With the addition of 160 acres the following year, construction of a facility began. Cooley was an ardent promoter of a "back to the land" theory, believing that delinquent city boys would benefit through contact with nature. In later years, 2 other men, DUDLEY S. BLOSSOM and HARRY L. EASTMAN, became closely associated with the school. In 1938, the school received a substantial amount of money from the Blossom estate. Eastman was keenly interested in the school's development while serving as judge of the juvenile court. In the 1960s, a new physical education building was named in his honor.

The school's emphasis was on outdoor activities, including hunting, trapping, fishing, swimming, hiking, and farming. Up to 140 boys, ages 10–17, were housed in several cottages run by cottage "parents." Early buildings included 8 cottages, 4 barns, an engine house, a bakery, a laundry, a carpentry shop, and a gymnasium. It was considered an "open" facility; no fences were ever erected. The average length of stay was 7–9 months, which in later years increased to 2–3 years. Although the emphasis remained on outdoor activities, in later years, after it had been taken over by the Cleveland Board of Education, normal classroom instruction was introduced. By the 1950s, new programs were implemented to help the boys in meeting real-life situations and developing a sense of responsibility. These included various part-time job opportunities in the village of Hudson. An honor system was also developed whereby each boy could earn special privileges. In the late 1950s, the school was transferred from the city of Cleveland to Cuyahoga County, where it came under the control of the county commissioners. In 1961 the county, with $1.575 million from the sale of bonds, began a new building program. At this time, the emphasis on outdoor activities was further reduced, and new vocational programs were introduced, including classes in plumbing, printing, and painting. Overcrowding was reported during some years, and ad-

missions had to be refused. In 1968 the county procured $1.9 million through bond sales for additional expansion. In the mid-1970s, the BLOSSOM HILL SCHOOL FOR GIRLS was merged into the Cleveland Boys' School in Hudson. Since then it has been known as the Youth Development Ctr.

The **CLEVELAND BROWNS** are one of the most successful clubs in professional football history. Between 1946–83, they won 18 divisional titles, captured 8 league championships, and made the playoffs in 21 seasons. Eleven Browns are in the Pro Football Hall of Fame (see FOOTBALL). The Browns organization was founded on 20 Apr. 1945 by ARTHUR B. "MICKEY" MCBRIDE with the help of Robt. H. Gries, who had helped form the CLEVELAND RAMS in 1936 and whose family, including his son, Robt. D. Gries, continued to own an important minority share of the Browns into the 1980s. The team began playing in the All-American Football Conference in 1946. After the 1949 season, the Browns joined the Natl. Football League. McBride chose well-known high school and Ohio State coach Paul E. Brown to direct his new professional team; the club was even named after Brown. Brown, who served as head coach from 1946–62, was an innovative and influential coach whose many contributions to the game include its racial integration at the professional level: by signing Bill Willis and Marion Motley to contracts in 1946, the Browns joined the Los Angeles Rams in smashing the 13-year-old color barrier in professional football. During Brown's tenure as head coach, the team enjoyed its golden age. Led by such stars as Otto Graham, Dante Lavelli, Lou Groza, Marion Motley, and Bill Willis, the Browns won all 4 league championships in the AAFC (1946–49). In their first NFL season in 1950, the players proved to critics that they were a great team by defeating the defending NFL champion Philadelphia Eagles 35–10 in their first game and the Los Angeles Rams 30–28 in the NFL championship game, one of the greatest games in Browns history.

On 9 June 1953, McBride sold his interest in the Browns for $600,000; 50% went to a group of investors headed by local industrialist Dave R. Jones, and the remainder to Sol Silberman. It was the highest price paid for a football franchise up to that time. In 1955, the investors group bought out Silberman for $1.3 million. In 1954 and 1955, with Otto Graham still as quarterback, the Browns won back-to-back league championships. By the 1956 season, Graham and many other Browns stars had retired or been traded, and the team endured its first losing season, only to use its misfortune to its advantage in the draft, choosing Syracuse's Jim Brown in the first round. During his career (1957–65), Brown became one of football's greatest running backs, setting several NFL records. In 1961, former advertising executive Arthur B. "Art" Modell bought a majority share in the Browns for $3.925 million. In a controversial move, he fired Paul Brown in 1963. Under new head coach Blanton Collier, the Browns won the NFL crown in 1964 and from 1965–69 won 4 divisional titles but no league championship. The realignment of the league in 1970 following the merger of the NFL with the American Football League placed the Browns in the Central Div. of the new American Football Conference. Nick Skorich served as head coach from 1971–74 and led the team to the playoffs in 1971 and 1972. After Forrest Gregg served as head coach from 1975–77, Sam Rutigliano took over in 1978, leading the team to a divisional title in 1980 and an exciting loss in the playoffs; the Browns also lost in the playoffs in 1981. During Rutigliano's tenure, the Browns initiated the Inner Circle drug rehabilitation program to help players with drug problems. The team's poor performance at the beginning of the 1984 season prompted Modell to fire Rutigliano and to promote defensive coordinator Marty Schottenheimer to head coach. In 1986, under Schottenheimer and with Bernie Kosar as quarterback, the team won the Central Div. title.

The **CLEVELAND BUCKEYES** were the last of a number of Cleveland teams that played in the Negro baseball leagues. The Buckeyes played in the Negro American League from 1943–48 and returned for the first half of the 1950 season. In addition to being the last of Cleveland's black professional teams, the Buckeyes also lasted longer than any of the others and were the best, playing in 2 Negro World Series, winning in 1945.

Cleveland had a number of black professional baseball teams prior to the Buckeyes, but most of these ventures lasted a year or less, and the teams finished near the bottom in the standings. The Cleveland Tate Stars finished last in the Negro National League in 1922, as did the Cleveland Browns of 1924, the Cleveland Elites of 1926, and the Cleveland Hornets of 1927. In 1931 local attorney Alexander Martin and Thos. P. Wilson of Nashville brought the Nashville team (formerly the Kansas City franchise) to Cleveland as the Cleveland Cubs; featuring the legendary pitcher LEROY "SATCHEL" PAIGE, the Cubs played at Hardware Fld. at E. 79th and Kinsman before disbanding in July 1931. In 1932 the Cleveland Stars competed in the East-West League, and in 1933 the Cleveland Giants replaced the Columbus Blue Birds, who dropped out of the NNL in August. The Cleveland Red Sox won only 2 of their 24 games in the NNL in the first half of 1934 and played only 5 games in the second half of the season before dropping out of the league. Negro baseball returned to Cleveland in 1939 and 1940 with the Cleveland Bears, who played .500 ball in the NAL. The Cleveland Buckeyes were organized by Ernest Wright, a hotel and nightclub owner in Erie, Pa.; Wilbur Hayes, a local sports promoter, served as executive manager of the team. The team began play in Cleveland in 1943 with several former members of the 1942 Cincinnati Buckeyes, including outfielders Sam Jethroe and Willie Grace and pitcher Gene Bremmer. The Buckeyes had a number of star players during the 1940s, including Bremmer, who appeared in 2 all-star games; first baseman Archie Ware (4 all-star games); and catcher Quincy Trouppe (4 all-star appearances). Perhaps the best of the Buckeyes was Sam Jethroe, the centerfielder who appeared in 4 all-star games and was the league's most valuable player in 1945 (.393 batting average and 21 stolen bases). Jethroe was one of 3 black players given tryouts by the Boston Red Sox in Apr. 1945; another was Jackie Robinson. Jethroe played for the Boston Braves for 3 years (1950–52) and was named Natl. League Rookie of the Year at age 28.

The Buckeyes finished in the middle of the standings every season except for 1945 and 1947. In 1945 they finished in first place in both halves of the NAL season, compiling an overall record of 53–16. Managed by veteran catcher Quincy Trouppe and led by Sam Jethroe, the Buckeyes earned a spot in the Negro World Series against the defending champions, the Homestead Grays. Behind the pitching of Willie Jefferson and Gene Bremmer, the Clevelanders won the first series games at Cleveland Stadium and LEAGUE PARK, then completed the sweep by winning the next 2 games on the road, with Geo. Jefferson on the mound to shut out the Grays in Washington, D.C., and Big Frank Carswell throwing a shutout in Philadelphia. The Buckeyes again won the league pennant in 1947 and faced the New York Cubans in the Negro World Series. After beating the Cubans in the opening game in New York, the Buckeyes lost the next 3 games in Cleveland, Philadelphia,

and Chicago before dropping the final game at home in Cleveland. Despite success on the field, the Buckeyes lost money in 1947, and the team folded after a poor showing in 1948. It returned for the first half of the 1950 season, but after winning only 3 of its 36 games, the team again disbanded.

Peterson, Robert W., *Only the Ball was White* (1970).

The **CLEVELAND BULLDOGS** were a professional football team in Cleveland in 1924–25 and 1927. They were one of several attempts to establish the pro sport in the city in the 1920s and 1930s; although the attempt ultimately failed, it brought the first professional football championship to the city, in 1924. The major force behind the Bulldogs was Samuel H. Deutsch (2 Apr. 1892–4 Sept. 1958), a jeweler who eventually became president of his father's firm, Rudolph Deutsch & Co. On 28 July 1923, Deutsch obtained the Natl. Football League franchise for the Cleveland Indians; the team finished 5th in the 20-team league in 1923, with a record of 3 wins, 1 loss, and 3 ties.

On 3 Aug. 1924, Deutsch bought a professional championship football team for Cleveland: he paid $2,500 for the Canton Bulldogs, which had won the championship in 1922 and 1923. The Canton team had lost $13,000 on its way to a championship in 1923, and management had decided to suspend operations. Deutsch bought the Canton franchise and combined the best players from the 1923 Indians with the best of the championship Bulldogs to create the 1924 Cleveland Bulldogs. Coached by former Nebraska star and future Pro Football Hall of Famer Guy Chamberlin, the Bulldogs played their home games at Dunn Fld. (LEAGUE PARK) and finished 1st in the league with 7 wins, 1 loss, and 1 tie. A dispute arose over who was league champion, however; the Chicago Bears had defeated the Bulldogs on 7 Dec. and claimed the title, but the Bulldogs insisted that that game had been only an exhibition game, since it took place after the season was over. A league ruling declared Cleveland the champions.

The Cleveland NFL franchise was transferred to Herb Brandt of the Brandt food company on 1 Aug. 1925. The team fared poorly on the field and at the bank; rain kept it from playing on 7 Sundays, and by mid-November the organization was nearly bankrupt. It attempted to break even by canceling its remaining home games and playing only road games. The attempt apparently failed; on 11 July 1926, it suspended operations for the year. With 5 wins, 8 losses, and a tie, the team had finished 12th in 1925.

The Bulldogs returned in 1927, and again Deutsch tried to buy a championship for Cleveland. Along with fellow investors MAX ROSENBLUM, Herb Brandt, Harold Gould (assistant sales manager, Fairchild Milling Co.), and dentist Clinton C. Winfrey, Deutsch built the new Bulldogs around native Clevelander BENJAMIN (BENNY) FRIEDMAN, a star quarterback at Michigan. To complete the team, which was often referred to as "Benny Friedman's Cleveland Bulldogs," the owners bought a team with a reputation for passing, the "raw-boned, rangy lads" of the 1926 Kansas City Cowboys. Twelve of the 25 men on the Cowboys' roster played in Cleveland in 1927, but the attempt to buy another championship failed: the team finished 4th in the league, with 8 wins, 4 losses, and 1 tie. The new version of the Bulldogs apparently was no more prosperous than the earlier ones. Deutsch appears to have sold the team to Elliott Fisher of Detroit after the 1927 season; the 1928 Detroit Wolverines roster included 12 former Bulldogs, 7 of whom were Cowboys in 1926. When the Wolverines were sold to Tim Mara in 1929, 8 former Bulldogs became New York Giants, including 6 former Cowboys.

207

The **CLEVELAND CALL & POST** rose from somewhat obscure origins to the position of sole survivor in Cleveland's black newspaper field. It was created from the 1927 merger of 2 struggling weeklies, the *Call* and the *Post*, both of which dated from the beginning of the decade. The *Call* was founded ca. 1920 by a group that included local inventor GARRETT A. MORGAN and Edward E. Murrell, a printer from Kentucky. At about the same time, the *Post* was established as the organ of a fraternal group known as the Modern Crusaders of the World. Even after its self-described "marriage of misery," the *Call & Post* continued to flounder until the arrival in 1932 of WM. O. WALKER, a black businessman with publishing experience imported by the paper's stockholders from Baltimore. Over the following decade, Walker nursed the *Call & Post*'s size from 4 to 12 pages and its circulation from 300 to 10,000. He also acquired most of the paper and then gained capital for new equipment by forming a partnership, the P-W Publishing Co., with attorney LAWRENCE O. PAYNE in 1940.

Part of the *Call & Post*'s success may have stemmed from the sensational treatment of violence on its front page, a practice excused by some defenders on the basis of the paper's heavy dependence on over-the-counter sales. That was balanced by the paper's unrivaled coverage of the black community's religious and social news. Politically, the *Call & Post* combined frequent support of local black Democrats with generally Republican preferences on the national level, where it endorsed every Republican presidential candidate except Barry Goldwater in 1964. Following Payne's death in 1959, the *Call & Post* moved from its long-time address on E. 55th St. to its own building on E. 105th at Chester Ave. There the paper became one of the first in Ohio to convert to offset printing, as editions averaging 28–32 pages were prepared for a circulation that leveled off at about 25,000. Separate editions were also added for Columbus and Cincinnati. On 20 Jan. 1983, the weekly's traditional Saturday publication date was moved up to Thursday. Walker's death in 1981 ended a 49-year period of personal control. In accordance with previously made plans, his associates Harry Alexander and John H. Bustamante became copublishers, Alexander succeeding as president and Bustamante as editor. A recipient of several Russwurm Awards as an outstanding black weekly, the *Call & Post* numbers Chas. H. Loeb, Jas. L. Hicks, Wm. (Sheep) Jackson, and John Fuster among its former staffers.

The **CLEVELAND CAVALIERS** basketball team was organized by Nick Mileti and admitted to the Natl. Basketball Assoc. in 1970 along with the Buffalo Braves and the Portland Trail Blazers. With the league expansion, the Eastern and Western conferences were split into 2 divisions each, and the Cavs became part of the Central Div. of the Eastern Conference. The team opened their first season with a collection of players selected in the expansion and college drafts and finished in last place with a 15–67 won-lost record. They played their home games at the CLEVELAND ARENA until 1974, when they moved to the Coliseum built by Nick Mileti in Richfield, Ohio. With experience, the Cavs improved their record, winning their first division title and earning their first playoff spot in 1976. The defensive leadership of Nate Thurmond, who was inducted into the Natl. Basketball Hall of Fame in 1985, was instrumental in the team's success as the Cavs won the first round of the playoffs against the Washington Bullets but lost to the Boston Celtics in the semifinals. The Mileti era ended when he sold the team to Ted Stepien in 1980. Inexperienced in operating a professional basketball franchise, the Cavaliers' new owner was criticized during his 3-year reign for making questionable trades and numerous changes in the coaching staff; in the 1981–82 season, the Cavs finished 15–67. The team was soon in financial trouble, and Stepien found it necessary to sell players in order to continue operating the franchise. After losing approximately $15 million in 3 years, he sold the team in 1983 to Geo. and Gordon Gund. Although the Cavs made the playoffs in 1985, the new owners believed a management change would be beneficial and in 1986 hired a new general manager, Wayne Embry, and a new head coach, Lenny Wilkens.

**CLEVELAND CHAMBER OF COMMERCE.** *See* **GREATER CLEVELAND GROWTH ASSOC.**

The **CLEVELAND CHAMBER MUSIC SOCIETY** was organized to bring ensembles of the highest quality to Cleveland for chamber music performances. The society developed a school concert program and has from time to time commissioned new works. The Chamber Music Society was organized in 1949 by a small group of individuals. In 1951, it received a bequest from Grover Higgins "for one thing only, the nurturing of chamber music in some form—its creation, its interpretation, its publication and its nourishment." This stimulus and challenge led the society to maintain high standards and to expand its program. A full series of 7 concerts per season has been presented since 1952. From 1949–52, approximately 3 concerts a year were given. Favorite performing quartets and soloists have included the Guarneri String Quartet, the Beaux Arts Trio, the CLEVELAND QUARTET, the Bach Aria Group, Consentus Misucus, the Borodin Quartet, Jean-Pierre Rampal and Robt. Veyron-Lacrois, Wm. Parker, and many others of the same high quality. These concerts were held mostly in auditoriums in the University Circle area, but also in other locations such as Byron Jr. High School in SHAKER HTS. and Fairmount Temple in BEACHWOOD. In 1953, the society began its school concert program with the formation and participation of the Symphonia Quartet. Other ensembles also worked to communicate the appreciation of fine music to children of various ages and backgrounds. By 1968–69, the school program involved 82 concerts presented to 25,000 listeners. In 1969, the society affiliated with Young Audiences, Inc., a national organization that shared the same educational objectives. The society has commissioned works by ARTHUR SHEPHERD, Normand Lockwood, Sterling Cumberworth, Pat Pace, Walter Aschaffenburg, and Matthias Bamert.

The **CLEVELAND CHAMBER SYMPHONY** is a professional ensemble of 32 musicians based at CLEVELAND STATE UNIVERSITY. It was founded in 1980 by Albert Blaser, a CSU faculty member. Its purpose is "to bring to the community older and contemporary works, and to perform new pieces by area composers." Most of its players are freelance musicians recruited from theater pits, faculty recital halls, and commercial recording halls. The Chamber Symphony has no board of trustees and no formal CSU sponsorship. Edwin London, chairman of the CSU music department, is the ensemble's conductor. Blaser is associate conductor and orchestra manager, and also a clarinetist. Since 1980, the Cleveland Chamber Symphony has usually offered a series of 5 to 6 programs each year. Concerts are on Monday nights and are free and open to the public. Although the group brings old and new music together, it is mainly recognized for its commitment to 20th-century composers. It claims a commitment to spotlighting area soloists and composers.

The **CLEVELAND CHAPTER OF THE NATIONAL LAWYERS GUILD** is an organization of progressive lawyers, law students, and legal workers. It is one of 96 chapters (totaling 7,000 members) in the U.S. The NLG was founded in 1937 as a professional organization for lawyers who wished to break with the conservatism of other bar associations. The Cleveland chapter was formed that same year. Many of its early members were generally younger and wished an alternative to the Cleveland and Cuyahoga County bar associations, which they believed were dominated by corporate lawyers. The chapter's first meeting was held at Allendorf's Restaurant; Martin A. McCormack was elected president. Following the lead of the national organization, the Cleveland chapter opposed censorship of films and books and the appointment of certain judges; it supported Pres. Roosevelt's Supreme Court Plan. In the 1940s, the Cleveland and Ohio chapters joined forces under Cleveland lawyer Russell N. Chase to fight the state for disallowing the COMMUNIST PARTY and other minority parties on the state ballot. It continued its support of civil liberties and human rights into the 1950s by opposing special tests and loyalty oaths for public employees and teachers. Among its prominent members at this time was future U.S. senator Howard Metzenbaum. During the 1960s and 1970s, the Cleveland chapter began sponsorship of special events and programs, including a conference on prison issues in 1972 and, in 1976, classes in Cleveland neighborhoods on tenant rights, Social Security, welfare, and consumer rights. In 1980, the chapter boycotted Henry Kissinger's speech to the CLEVELAND BAR ASSOC., labeling him—in a letter to the bar association—an "infamous international outlaw." In 1986, the Cleveland chapter maintained an office at the John Marshall School of Law.

Russell N. Chase Papers, WRHS.

The **CLEVELAND CHILD HEALTH ASSOCIATION** was founded in the late 1920s to educate women on maternal and child health care. It was one of the most successful health and child-welfare programs in the U.S. The Child Health Assoc. was founded in 1929 as a result of the growing national movement to reduce maternal and infant mortality rates. Its purpose was to apply new social and scientific techniques for the health and safety of newborns, and children up to 15. Throughout its existence, the association's primary emphasis was on prenatal care. Dr. RICHARD A. BOLT was the director for 19 years and was strongly identified with the success of the CCHA's various programs. Bolt was an outspoken advocate for prenatal love and the child's need for sunlight, fresh air, and adequate play space. Ellen Nicely directed the prenatal program, which she organized under Dr. Bolt in 1932. The association was a member of the Welfare Fed. and was supported by the Community Fund. During the 1930s and 1940s, the CCHA sponsored health hygiene in schools, offered prenatal and mothercraft classes, and promoted the importance of nursery schools. It later expanded its program to include older children; in 1941, it focused on reducing the death rate due to accidents among children 2 to 15. The prenatal program consisted of classes at area hospitals, taught by trained nurses. The program achieved early success; in 1934, Cleveland had the lowest infant mortality rate among major American cities. Prenatal programs in other major cities were modeled after the Cleveland program. The Cleveland Child Health Assoc. disbanded shortly after Dr. Bolt retired in 1948.

**CLEVELAND CHURCH FEDERATION.** *See* INTER-CHURCH COUNCIL OF GREATER CLEVELAND

The **CLEVELAND CINEMA CLUB**, founded during the silent-film era, was dedicated to raising the moral and artistic standards of the motion-picture industry. It was the first local organization of its kind in the country. The Cleveland Cinema Club was organized in 1917, mainly through the efforts of Bertelle M. Lyttle. Stimulus to organize such a club came from the "better films" movement then current in America. Although an independent organization, the CCC adopted many of the standards of the Natl. Board of Review. The club's primary objective was "to study the art of the motion picture and its educational and moral effect and to promote a better understanding of its problems." Concerned with the moral quality of movies, the club sought to guide schools, clubs, settlement houses, and families by rating motion pictures for suitability. It occasionally tried to influence state and national legislation. The CCC also helped organize young people's motion-picture appreciation groups and cinema clubs, and interested itself in the latest developments in films by sending representatives to conventions of national organizations dealing with motion-pictures. The Cleveland club served as a model for motion-picture councils established in other U.S. cities. Among the club's many activities, in 1937 it started a children's program designed to create junior cinema clubs. It also presented, at the beginning of each school year, a list of films suitable for children to watch during school lunch hour. In 1938, it started an annual film festival—one of the first clubs in the country to introduce such an event. The club also published a bulletin 4 times a year, which listed ratings and recommendations of current films, and which it distributed throughout the U.S. The Cleveland Cinema Club lasted until 1968. In its later years, much of its effort went toward the establishment of a film library in the CLEVELAND PUBLIC LIBRARY's fine arts department.

Cleveland Cinema Club Records, WRHS.

The *CLEVELAND CITIZEN* began a career on 31 Jan. 1891 that eventually made it "America's oldest labor paper." It was founded on $30 capital by MAX S. HAYES and Henry C. Long, both members of the Cleveland Typographical Union No. 53. After 4 months, it was adopted by the Cleveland Central Labor Union, which financed its publication in exchange for free distribution to members of its constituent locals. Circulation of the *Citizen* climbed steadily from 1,000 to 10,000 during the first decade of the 20th century. Reflecting the stance of the CLU, the *Citizen* supported Eugene V. Debs and advocated independent political action by labor. It was largely to head off a move to have the *Citizen* adopted as the national organ of the American Federation of Labor that the conservative Samuel Gompers sponsored publication of the *Federationist*. Nevertheless, the *Citizen* remained an influential force on the national as well as the local labor scene.

Hayes regained full ownership of the *Citizen* in 1910, when internal schisms interrupted the sponsorship of the CLU. Henry Long having withdrawn in 1898, Hayes was solely in charge for the next 40 years, assisted first by ROBT. BANDLOW and later by David H. Jenkins as business managers. During the labor upheavals of the 1930s, Hayes was sympathetic to the goals of industrial unionism but reluctant to abet the splintering of the labor movement. While reporting objectively on the organizational efforts of the CIO, the *Citizen* intentionally soft-pedaled its differences with the AFL.

With circulation approaching 30,000 in 1940, Hayes suffered a stroke and relinquished control of the *Citizen* to his son-in-law, Albert I. (Bert) Davey, who had joined the staff on a part-time basis in 1932. Davey ran the *Citizen* for the next 37 years with the aid of Elizabeth Fanz, who became business manager in 1945 and Davey's second wife after the death of Maxine Hayes Davey in 1975. Reflecting the postwar merger of the AFL-CIO, the *Citizen* reported circulations of over 50,000 from the late 1940s through the early 1960s. When Davey terminated his editorship of the *Citizen* in 1977, the paper ended its existence as an independent organ. Ownership was assumed by the Cleveland Bldg. & Constr. Trades Council, which appointed Wm. G. Obbagy as editor under the supervision of a 9-member board. Although it still covered general labor-union activity in 1985, the *Citizen* devoted most of its resources to developments in the construction trades. Its circulation of approximately 25,000 went largely to members of the council's constituent unions.

The **CLEVELAND CITY COUNCIL** began with 3 trustees chosen to make laws for the township (1802) and later for the village (1814). Since that time, the council has ranged in size from 3 to 50 members (1885), and in the 1960s, with 33 members, it was second in size only to Chicago's 50-member council. Traditionally, a large council has been favored to represent the interests of Cleveland's many minority groups more effectively. When Cleveland was incorporated as a city in 1836, it had a council of 3 aldermen chosen at large and 3 representatives from each of 3 wards elected annually, as mandated by the Ohio state legislature. In addition to making laws, the council had administrative and executive powers, including regulation of the police and appointment of the city clerk. Councilmen were paid $1 for each meeting attended. The board of aldermen was abolished when Ohio passed a general act for the incorporation of all cities and villages in 1852. On the west side, OHIO CITY also became a city in 1836 with a council of 12 members, 4 from each of 3 wards. In 1853 its council was reorganized into 4 wards with 2 councilmen each. With Ohio City's annexation to Cleveland in 1854, the revised city council expanded to 11 wards, with 2 trustees elected from each ward. As the city grew, its expanding needs were dealt with on an ad hoc basis by creating boards to deal with city problems. With members on some of these boards and the power to appoint some officials, city council could, and did, on occasion, obstruct the administration of the city.

From 1886–91, a bicameral council was tried, with a board of 9 aldermen as the lower house and a 40-member council as the upper house. Council membership was halved in 1891, when the wards were combined into 10 districts, with 2 councilmen elected from each. Despite these changes, power and responsibility were so diffused that corruption was encouraged. In 1892, Cleveland was reorganized on the Federal Plan. The city council retained its legislative function, but all ordinances were submitted to the mayor for approval. Council could, however, pass a measure over his veto with a ⅔ majority. The new plan, modeled after the federal government, provided a clearer division between the executive and legislative branches. Mayor Tom L. Johnson's opponents, hoping to reduce his control of the council, challenged the Federal Plan in court, and in 1902 the Ohio Supreme Court ruled that Cleveland's charter under the plan was unconstitutional because it had been created by special legislation not applicable to the rest of the state. The ruling necessitated a new municipal code, which was approved by the Ohio legislature in 1903. The council was again reorganized with 1 councilman from each of 26 wards and 6 councilmen-at-large, remaining so until 1913.

When the HOME RULE amendment to the Ohio constitution passed in 1912, Cleveland gained control over its own municipal affairs. The commission elected to write a new city charter disagreed over the size of city council. Those advocating a small council elected at large maintained that it would be more efficient and less expensive and would eliminate the corruption associated with the political machines. Those favoring a large council elected by ward considered it more democratic, as it made councilmen answerable to the concerns of their wards. The charter approved in 1913 provided for nonpartisan election of a 26-member council (increased to 33 by 1923) on a ward basis.

Cleveland continued to experiment with its municipal government as corruption and machine politics persisted. Under the CITY MANAGER PLAN, adopted in 1921, the method of electing councilmen was changed. The city was divided into 4 districts, from each of which 5 to 7 councilmen, depending on population, were elected at large. They served a 2-year term and were paid $1,000 a year. Elections were nonpartisan, and a system of proportional representation was used. The council elected a manager to administer the city's business for as long as they considered his service satisfactory. In 1924, the first council elected under this plan chose WM. R. HOPKINS as city manager. In addition to administering the city's affairs, Hopkins, on his own initiative, also assumed the role of policy maker, thus diluting the city council's authority. In 1930 the council replaced him with DANIEL MORGAN. Although Morgan had a better relationship with the council, it was feared that the City Manager Plan might well lead to a municipal dictatorship, and in 1931, the city returned to the mayor-ward system. A nonpartisan primary was instituted, with a runoff between the 2 candidates receiving the highest number of votes in each of 33 wards. City councilmen served 2-year terms and were required to live in their wards. The checks and balances, including the mayor's veto and council's control of the purse, were retained. The council also had the right to investigate any official or department of the city to insure that it was properly administered.

In 1953, the city charter was amended so that the council candidate who received a majority of the votes cast in the primary election became the only formal nominee in the general election. That benefited the incumbents standing for reelection. In 1971 this 50% plus 1 rule was abolished. Another change in Nov. 1980 increased the councilmen's term of office to 4 years. It was felt that reducing the number of election campaigns would increase the council's efficiency. In response to Cleveland's declining population, the council was reduced from 33 to 21 members in July 1981. The reapportionment resulted in 8 wards on the west side and 13 wards on the east side, with an average population of 27,000 per ward.

Campbell, Thomas F., *Daniel E. Morgan, 1877–1949* (1966).
Durham, Frank, *Government in Greater Cleveland* (1963).
Greene, Kenneth R., *Influences on the Decision Making of the City Council* (1974).

**CLEVELAND CITY GOVERNMENT.** The government of the city of Cleveland took its present (1986) shape in 1914 with the establishment of the Home Rule Charter. This charter, which increased Cleveland's powers of self-government, was necessary because other government structures had proved incapable of handling modern, complex urban affairs. Prior to 1914, city services were provided by a combination of officers, boards, and commissions, many elected directly by the people or appointed by the council. The first act to incorporate the village of Cleveland was passed in the Ohio general assembly on 23 Dec. 1814. It directed that a president, a recorder, 3 trustees, a treas-

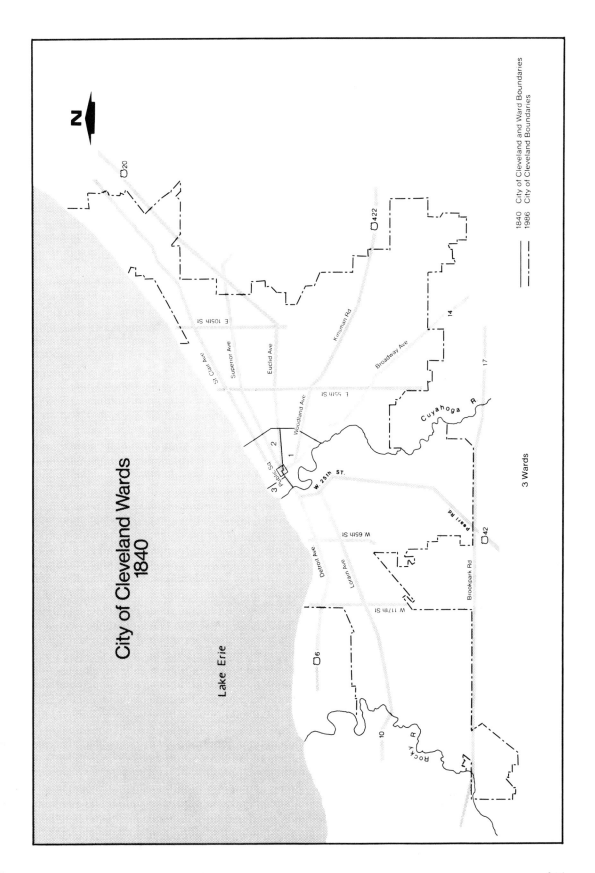

City of Cleveland Wards
1840

Lake Erie

N

1840   City of Cleveland and Ward Boundaries
1986   City of Cleveland Boundaries

211

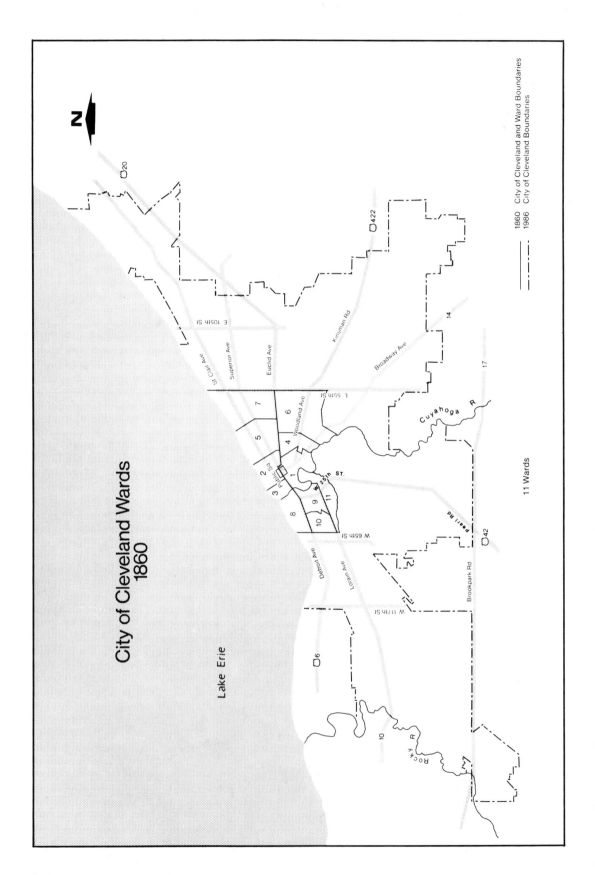

City of Cleveland Wards
1860

Lake Erie

N

1860    City of Cleveland and Ward Boundaries
1986    City of Cleveland Boundaries

11 Wards

212

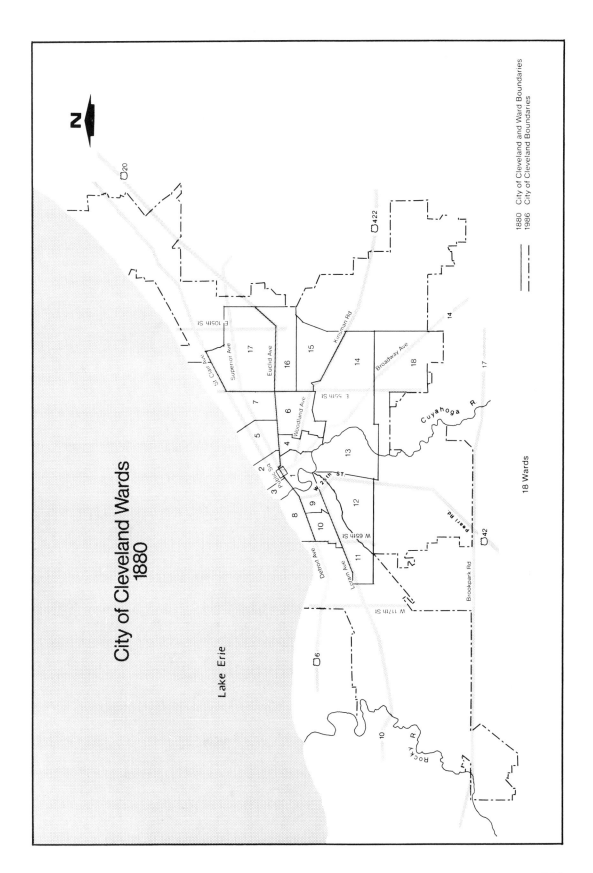

## City of Cleveland Wards
## 1880

Lake Erie

1880    City of Cleveland and Ward Boundaries
1986    City of Cleveland Boundaries

18 Wards

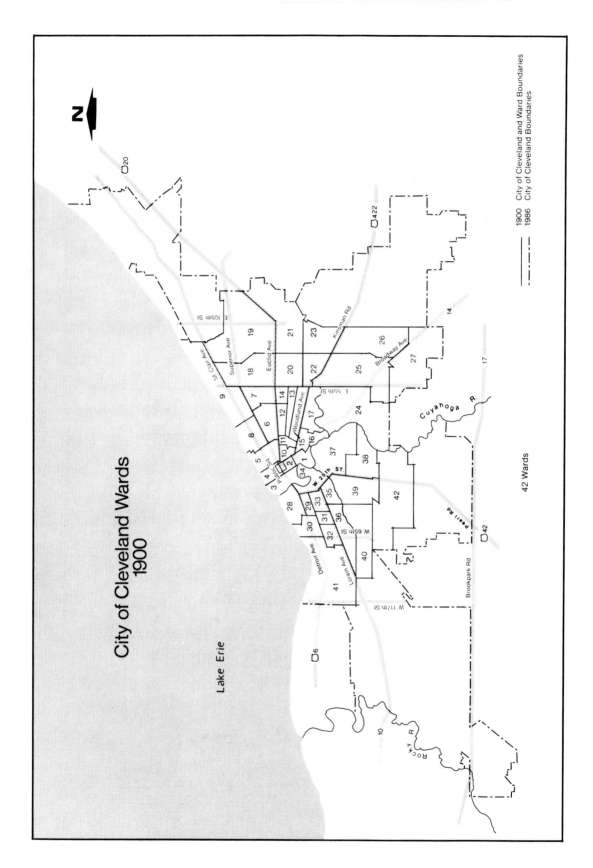

# City of Cleveland Wards
## 1900

Lake Erie

1900   City of Cleveland and Ward Boundaries
1986   City of Cleveland Boundaries

42 Wards

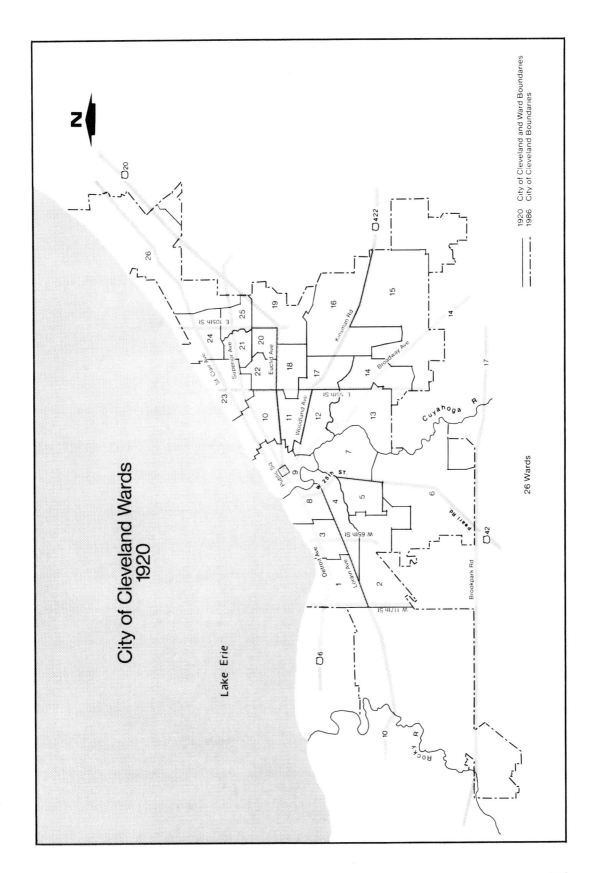

City of Cleveland Wards
1920

Lake Erie

N

26 Wards

1920   City of Cleveland and Ward Boundaries
1986   City of Cleveland Boundaries

215

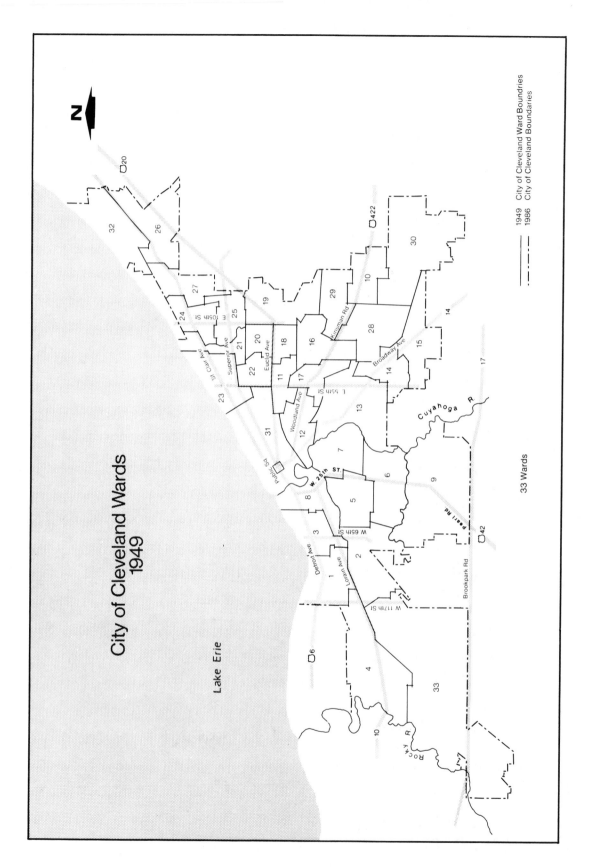

City of Cleveland Wards
1949

Lake Erie

N

Cuyahoga R.

ROCK R.

Pearl Rd

Brookpark Rd

Kinsman Rd

Broadway Ave

Woodland Ave

Euclid Ave

Superior Ave

St Clair Ave

Detroit Ave

Lorain Ave

W 25th ST.

W 65th St

W 117th St

E 65th St

E 105th St

Public Sq

1949    City of Cleveland Ward Boundries
1986    City of Cleveland Boundaries

33 Wards

216

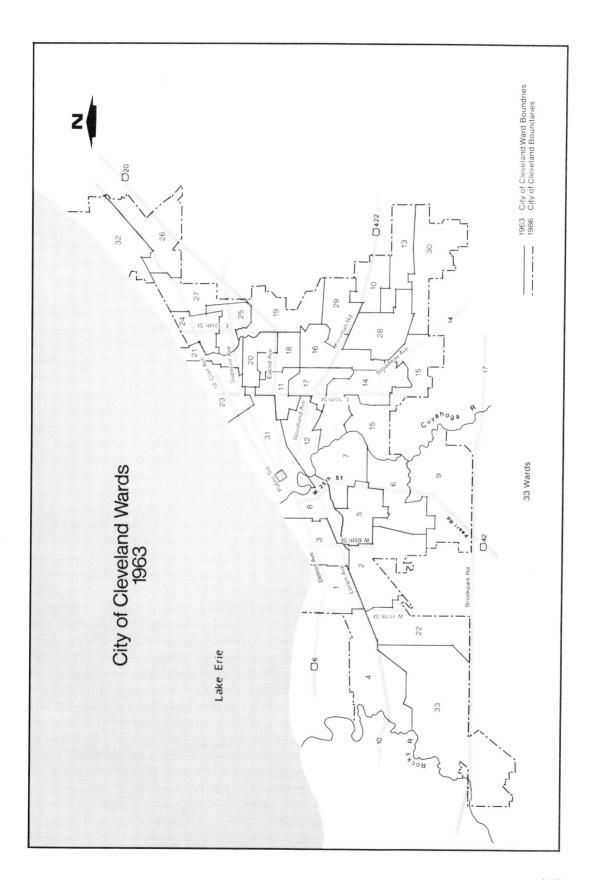

City of Cleveland Wards
1963

Lake Erie

33 Wards

1963   City of Cleveland Ward Boundries
1986   City of Cleveland Boundaries

N

20
32
26
27
24
25
19
21
23
E 105th St
Superior Ave
Euclid Ave
20
11
17
18
16
29
Kinsman Rd
28
10
422
13
30
14
Broadway Ave
15
31
12
Woodland Ave
17
14
E 55th St
15
Cuyahoga R
17
7
Public Sq
W 25th ST.
6
9
8
5
W 65th St
3
Detroit Ave
Lorain Ave
2
42
Pearl Rd
1
22
W 117th St
Brookpark Rd
6
4
10
Rocky R
33

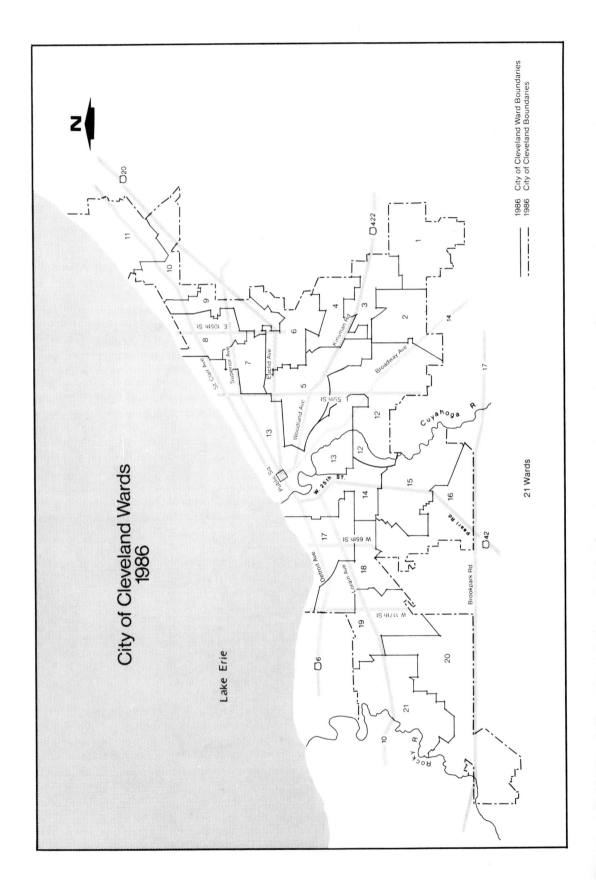

City of Cleveland Wards
1986

Lake Erie

N

□20

11

10

9

□422

1

E 105th St

8

6

4

3

2

14

St Clair Ave

Superior Ave

7

Kinsman Rd

Elgid Ave

5

Broadway Ave

Woodland Ave

E 55th St

12

17

13

Public Sq

13

12

Cuyahoga R

W 25th ST.

15

14

16

□42

Pearl Rd

17

W 65th St

Detroit Ave

18

2

Brookpark Rd

Loraine Ave

W 117th St

19

□6

20

10

21

ROCKY R

1986    City of Cleveland Ward Boundaries
1986    City of Cleveland Boundaries

21 Wards

218

urer, a village marshal, and 2 assessors be elected by the citizens of the village. By 1836, the population had increased sufficiently that the village charter was repealed and replaced with a new city charter incorporating Cleveland with a mayor-council form of government. City status was desirable for fiscal reasons; state law gave cities increased taxing and borrowing power. The council was preeminent at this time, with most administrative work resting in standing committees. As president of council, the mayor could vote in case of a tie. Without HOME RULE, Ohio cities depended upon the state legislature to alter their form of government; local matters took up a great deal of time in the general assembly. To reduce the number of municipal acts of incorporation, Ohio passed the General Municipal Corp. Act of 1852. Under this act, all municipalities were to conform to a standard governmental structure. Administrative boards were given authority over certain city services. The mayor was no longer president of the council and did not appoint standing committees. In addition, more appointed positions became elected offices. For example, in 1853, voters were called upon to choose not only the mayor and councilmen but also the police judge, police clerk, commissioner of waterworks, auditor, solicitor, treasurer, and city weigher, among others.

As the management of urban affairs became more complex, the number of boards and commissions multiplied. By 1891, voters recognized that government by boards and commissions was inefficient and adopted the so-called Federal Plan, a more centralized form of government. This plan called for the mayor to appoint directors of public safety and public service, concentrating responsibility for these departments under one elected official. However, the Ohio Supreme Court declared Cleveland's Federal Plan unconstitutional in 1902, making it necessary to adopt a new code. During the next 9 years, Cleveland enjoyed good government under Mayor TOM L. JOHNSON; although the mayor's and the city's desire for home rule remained strong. Cities needed to be able to respond to local needs, and there was confusion between executive and legislative

functions. Finally, in 1912, Ohio's 4th Constitutional Convention passed a home rule amendment allowing municipalities to enact their own charters. Accordingly, Clevelanders adopted a Home Rule Charter in July 1913. In 1923, the voters replaced the Home Rule Charter with the CITY MANAGER PLAN, favoring this system of government because they considered it nonpolitical. The 25-member council was elected by proportional representation, and a professional city manager was chosen. However, the city council continued to interfere with the manager's authority by pressing for jobs for political allies, and by 1931, the city returned to partisan elections for mayor and council.

In 1986, the government of the city of Cleveland was divided into 3 branches: the legislative branch, consisting of a 21-member council; the judicial branch, consisting of the municipal court and the clerk of courts; and the executive branch, consisting of the mayor, his adjunct offices, his advisors, and the administrative departments. The mayor is the chief executive of the city and is responsible for enforcing the city charter, city ordinances, and the laws of the state of Ohio. He has the right to introduce legislation and may take part in discussion in council, but he may not vote. The mayor supervises the administration of city services and appoints the directors of each department. The mayor and the directors constitute the Board of Control, which takes part in the awarding of contracts. Adjunct offices aid the mayor in his charter-mandated duties. The mayor is required to present a budget of estimated income and funds needed to run the city. The Office of Management & Budget was established in 1965 to aid in preparing the annual "Mayor's Estimate," as the budget is called. The other adjunct offices are the offices of Personnel, Consumer Affairs, and Equal Opportunity. The Office of Personnel works closely with the Civil Service Commission to perform personnel-management functions and assist the mayor with labor relations. The Office of Consumer Affairs was created in 1972 during the national consumers'-rights movement to protect consumers from fraudulent business practices by enforcing the city's Consumer Protection Code.

CLEVELAND MAYORS
(By Year)

| Year | Name | Year | Name |
|------|------|------|------|
| 1836–37 | John W. Willey | 1871–72 | Frederick W. Pelton |
| 1836 | Josiah Barber, Ohio City | 1873–74 | Chas. A. Otis |
| 1837, 1842 | Francis A. Burrows, Ohio City | 1875–76 | Nathan P. Payne |
| 1838–39 | Norman C. Baldwin, Ohio City | 1877–78, 1891–92 | William G. Rose |
| 1838–39, 1842 | Joshua Mills | 1879–82 | Rensselaer R. Herrick |
| 1840 | Nicholas Dockstader | 1883–84, 1899–1900 | John H. Farley |
| 1840–41 | Needham M. Standart, Ohio City | 1885–86, 1889–90 | George W. Gardner |
| 1841 | John W. Allen | 1887–88 | Brenton D. Babcock |
| 1843 | Nelson Hayward | 1893–94 | Robert Blee |
| 1843 | Richard Lord, Ohio City | 1895–98 | Robert E. McKisson |
| 1844–45, 1857–58 | Samuel Starkweather | 1901–09 | Tom L. Johnson |
| 1844–1846 | Daniel H. Lamb, Ohio City | 1910–11 | Herman C. Baehr |
| 1846 | George Hoadley | 1912–15 | Newton D. Baker |
| 1847 | Josiah A. Harris | 1916–19, 1934–35 | Harry L. Davis |
| 1847 | David Griffith, Ohio City | 1920–21 | William S. Fitzgerald |
| 1848 | Lorenzo A. Kelsey | 1922–23 | Fred Kohler |
| 1848 | John Beverlin, Ohio City | 1924–29 | William R. Hopkins, City Manager |
| 1849 | Flavel W. Bingham | 1930–31 | Daniel E. Morgan, City Manager |
| 1849–50 | Thomas Burnham, Ohio City | 1932–33 | Ray T. Miller |
| 1850–51 | William Case | 1936–40 | Harold H. Burton |
| 1851–52 | Benjamin Sheldon, Ohio City | 1941 | Edward Blythin |
| 1852–54 | Abner C. Brownell | 1942–45 | Frank J. Lausche |
| 1853–54 | William B. Castle, Ohio City | 1946–53 | Thomas A. Burke |
| 1855–56 | William B. Castle | 1954–61 | Anthony J. Celebrezze |
| 1859–60, 1864 | George B. Senter | 1962–67 | Ralph S. Locher |
| 1861–62 | Edward S. Flint | 1968–71 | Carl B. Stokes |
| 1863–64 | Irvine U. Masters | 1972–77 | Ralph J. Perk |
| 1865–66 | Herman M. Chapin | 1978–79 | Dennis J. Kucinich |
| 1867–70 | Stephen Buhrer | 1980– | George V. Voinovich |

The historical precedent for this office is the Weights & Measures Bureau, which was moved to Consumer Protection from the Dept. of Parks, Recreation & Public Properties. The director of the Office of Equal Opportunity establishes and monitors equal-employment and affirmative-action policies and programs required by federal, state, and municipal law. Within this office there are Minority Business Enterprise and Female Business Enterprise programs. The director of EEO is responsible for annual certification of MBE and FBE businesses. Thirteen administrative departments reporting directly to the mayor provide the city with the full range of municipal services. The Home Rule Charter provided for 6 departments and stated that council may create new departments by ordinance or charter amendments with the concurrence of the Board of Control. The original 6 departments were Law, Finance, Public Service, Public Safety, Public Utilities, and Public Welfare.

The Law Dept. was formed in 1903 by combining the formerly elective positions of city solicitor and police prosecutor. The law director is legal advisor, attorney, and counsel for the city, its officers, and its departments. He is acting mayor when necessary, and first to succeed the mayor in the event of the mayor's removal from office. The Law Dept. is responsible for defending the city in all suits as well as drafting or approving legislation, contracts, and bonds. The law director may be called upon to render an opinion on any question of law involving the powers or duties of the city council, directors of departments, or commissioners. There are 2 divisions in the Law Dept.: the Civil Div., headed by the chief counsel, and the Criminal Div., headed by the city prosecutor. The Finance Dept. is responsible for the city's fiscal affairs. The Div. of Accounts maintains the city's accounting records and certifies that funds are available and appropriated for expenditure before payment is made. The Treasury Div. serves as custodian of all monies, deposits, and investment securities. The Div. of Assessments & Licenses issues licenses and collects fees. The Purchases & Supplies Div. coordinates purchasing of all commodities, land, and services for city departments and assists the Board of Control with contract awards. Modern additions to the Dept. of Finance are the Central Collection Agency, established in 1966 to collect the municipal income tax; the Div. of Internal Audit, which performs audits of city departments and assists the city's external auditor; and the Printing & Reproduction Div., which was established in 1952 to assist in the printing of financial reports compiled by the departments.

The origin of the Dept. of Public Service can be found in an ordinance passed in 1836 permitting city council to appoint a commissioner of streets. Until that time, the village trustees were responsible for directing the work of grading the streets and devising the city plat. The General Municipal Corp. Act mandated a Board of Improvements consisting of the mayor, civil engineer, and 3 city commissioners, all elected offices. Later the street commissioner became a member of this board. In 1910, under the Paine Law, the mayor was given the authority to appoint a director of public service. The divisions of Streets and Engineering were combined under this department, as well as divisions for all public properties. Beginning in the late 1900s, the Engineering Div. was responsible for designing and constructing the city's sewer system and sewage-treatment plants. The first sewage-treatment plant, built in 1922, was placed under the Div. of Water so that revenues could pay for its operation. By this time, the sewer and water divisions had become part of the new Dept. of Public Utilities. Cleveland was providing sewer service to several suburbs when, in 1972, the newly formed Northeast Ohio Regional Sewer District took over control of the intercep-

tor sewers and treatment plants. In 1986, the primary functions of the Div. of Engineering were the preparation of all surveys, maps, and plats of the city and engineering plans, specifications, and cost estimates for all public improvements. This division is also responsible for city-owned bridges and the construction and maintenance of sidewalks, including ramped curbing for the handicapped. The Dept. of Public Service also includes divisions of Waste Collection, Architecture, and Motor Vehicle Maintenance.

The expenditures of the Dept. of Public Safety accounted for over half the total budget of Cleveland in 1986. With 3,355 full-time employees, this department is the city's largest. Its 5 operating divisions are Police, Fire, Emergency Medical Service, Traffic, and Dog Pound. Police and Fire were 2 separate departments until 1904, when the first Board of Public Safety was created to oversee the operations of both departments. This board was superseded by the Dept. of Public Safety in 1910. In 1837, a fire warden was appointed for each ward. The state legislature encouraged the organization of volunteer companies by granting members privileges and immunities such as exemption from military service. In 1862, the volunteer plan was discontinued in favor of a department headed by a chief engineer, who was appointed by the mayor. The first Fire Prevention Bureau was organized in 1896 with 2 fire wardens, whose duties were to inspect buildings for fire hazards and note violations of ordinances. In 1986, the Fire Div. operated 5 programs: Fire Prevention, Fire Suppression, Fire Communication, Fire Training Service, and Right-to-Know. The newest program, Right-to-Know, enforces the 1985 ordinance that requires employers to inform employees of hazardous substances in the workplace. The city council appointed the first night watch in 1850, after volunteer forces had proved inadequate. The watchmen had equal authority with the city marshal to preserve the peace of the city and make arrests. The Metropolitan Police Act was passed in the Ohio legislature in 1866, creating a BOARD OF POLICE COMMISSIONERS. The early Board of Police Commissioners passed levies to fund operations. The Emergency Medical Service provides prehospital emergency care, basic life support, and advanced life support on a 24-hour basis to the citizens of Cleveland. The EMS conducts its own communications, dispatch, and billing procedures.

Partly in response to the need for a reliable supply of water with which to fight fires, the first Board of Water Works Commissioners was elected in 1853. The voters then authorized the sale of bonds to finance construction of a waterworks. The first water flowed through the new city-owned system in 1856, when a 50″ intake was laid 300′ into Lake Erie. Electricity and gas were originally supplied by private companies supervised by a commissioner of franchises. Cleveland acquired electric light plants when it annexed the villages of S. BROOKLYN in 1905 and COLLINWOOD in 1910. After passage of the Home Rule Charter, which enabled the city to own and operate public utilities, a new light plant was opened in 1914, and the Dept. of Public Utilities was established. In 1986, the Div. of Water sold not only to Cleveland but also to 74 suburbs, and the Div. of Light & Power (also known as Cleveland Public Power) had become one of the largest municipally owned electric utilities in the U.S. Both divisions are self-supporting.

When it was established in 1913, the Dept. of Public Health & Welfare was one of the first in the U.S. to deal with recreation, charities, housing, employment, and corrections, as well as health and sanitation. At one time the department included in its operations the City Infirmary, City Farm, Workhouse, correctional institutions for both boys and girls, and Camp Cleveland. Eventually it was decided that most of the correctional and welfare institutions should be turned over to either the county or the state, in accordance with state law. In 1986, the focus of the Dept. of Public Health & Welfare was the enforcement of state and local health, environmental, and sanitation codes. That was accomplished by operating neighborhood health clinics, conducting inspections, and issuing licenses. The Air Pollution Control Div. was established in 1947 by ordinance and merged the activities of smoke abatement (which had belonged to the Div. of Building & Housing in the Safety Dept.) with the Bureau of Industrial Nuisances and the Bureau of Industrial Hygiene. Air Pollution Control is responsible for measuring the extent of pollutants and enforcing federal, state, and local regulations. The general fund of the city provides 30% of the funding for this division, while the federal and state governments provide the rest.

Cleveland was the benefactor of generous gifts of land for public parks and enjoyed the reputation of being the "FOREST CITY" because of its abundance of beautiful trees. In 1898, a Dept. of Forestry & Nurseries was established to safeguard this asset. By 1921, a 7th administrative department had been established, Parks & Public Property. In addition to parks and playgrounds, this department is responsible for public property such as CEMETERIES, markets, golf courses, and swimming pools. The maintenance and operation of the convention center are the responsibility of this department. In 1980, the name was changed to the Dept. of Parks, Recreation & Public Properties. A Div. of Airplane Landing was established in 1926 and was renamed the Div. of Cleveland Municipal Airport in 1942. The Office of Harbor Master was created in 1840 to regulate watercraft at city wharves; the harbor master reported to the Dept. of Public Service and its predecessor, the Board of Public Service. A 1952 charter amendment established the Dept. of Port Control, and the divisions of Airport and Harbor were transferred to it in 1954. The Dept. of Port Control administers activities at CLEVELAND HOPKINS and BURKE LAKEFRONT airports, and like the Dept. of Public Utilities, it is self-supporting. Port and harbor functions were transferred to the CLEVELAND-CUYAHOGA COUNTY PORT AUTHORITY at its inception in 1968.

Occasionally during times of fiscal or political crises, the mayor or council will call upon outside experts to study and recommend changes in the form and operations of city government. The most recent reorganization is the result of the Operations Improvement Task Force established by the mayor in 1979 to bring the city back to sound financial condition after its DEFAULT. The task force, composed of 89 loaned business executives, was funded by grants from foundations and corporations. The group published 650 recommendations for capital improvements as well as organizational changes, including a 4-year term for the mayor. Originally, the Dept. of Community Development was known as the Div. of Slum Clearance, operating as an executive branch of the mayor's office from 1954–59. The Div. of Buildings in the Dept. of Public Safety was created in 1904 to enforce the provisions of the first building code. In 1966, the first housing code was passed, and these 2 divisions were brought together with the newly created Div. of Housing to form the Dept. of Community Development. In 1980, the Operations Improvement Task Force recommended that the department add a Div. of Neighborhood Revitalization to handle planning for the Community Development Block Grant. The divisions of Building and Housing were combined to bring the code-enforcement functions together. The Dept. of Aging, which assists in administering all city programs relating to older persons, evolved from the Mayor's Commission on Aging established in 1971. Departmental status was conferred in 1981, as a result of the Operations Improvement Task Force. The Dept. of Human Resources & Economic Development was established in 1968 to implement programs for employment opportunities, manpower organization, and industrial development. After the Operations Improvement Task Force, Economic Development was given departmental status separate from the Dept. of Human Resources.

Besides the 3 branches of government, there are specialized boards and commissions that are appointed by the mayor and/or council to provide citizen involvement, assist in policy formation, or regulate activities of an administrative department. The Board of Building Standards & Building Appeals hears appeal cases of citizens who have grievances with the building code. The Board of Zoning Appeals performs a similar function with regards to the zoning code. The Board of Examiners of Plumbers certifies contractors to do work within the city. The City Planning Commission is composed of 7 members. One is a member of council, and 6 members are appointed by the mayor, with the approval of council. The charter mandates a planning director nominated by the commission and appointed by the mayor. The planning director is the ex-officio secretary of the commission. The City Planning Dept., the 13th administrative department, is the staff of the Planning Commission. The function of the Planning Commission is to make and adopt a general plan covering land use, transportation, recreation, and industrial, commercial, and residential development and improvements for the city. The commission also makes plans for specific improvements that it deems desirable for the city. One of the most important functions of the City Planning Commission is the recommendation to the mayor of a 5-year capital-improvement budget. The first City Plan Commission was established in 1915 after passage of the State Enabling Act, which permitted cities and villages to use their police powers in the planning and regulation of land.

The Landmarks Commission was established in 1971 to safeguard the heritage of the city by preserving sites and structures of cultural, social, economic, political, or architectural history. Coincidentally, there is the desire to stabilize and improve property values, thereby strengthening the local economy. The commissioner of architecture, the director of city planning, 7 mayoral appointments, and 2 city council appointments make up the Landmarks Commission. Friendly relations among the various racial and cultural groups in the city are the purpose behind the CLEVELAND COMMUNITY RELATIONS BOARD. This board, established by ordinance in 1945, consists of 14 mayoral appointments and 2 council appointments. The first Civil Service Commission took office in Jan. 1910, pursuant to the Ohio Municipal Civil Service Law. Three resident commissioners were appointed by the presidents of the Board of Education, city council, and the Sinking Fund Commission. The 1913 charter maintained the composition of the commission but vested appointing authority in the mayor. A 1967 charter amendment increased the number of commissioners to 5. The commission and staff are responsible for the testing and certification of individuals in the classified civil service, maintaining personnel records and files for city employees, and conducting hearings for disciplinary action against city employees. The ex-officio boards and commissions are those whose members are not appointed but serve by virtue of their positions in city government. This category includes the Sinking Fund Commission, the Board of Review for Income Tax, the Board of Review for Assessments, the Board of Sidewalk Appeals, and the Morals Claims Commission. The Sinking Fund Commission was established in 1862 to pay the indebtedness contracted in the construction of the city waterworks. This commission is responsible for accumulating funds from tax levies and income to discharge the outstanding debt of the city at maturity. It is composed of the mayor, the president of council, and the director of finance.

Some local government services that were formerly the responsibility of the city of Cleveland have been regionalized to achieve the benefits of a larger tax base. Regional authorities, established by state and local legislation, may be better able to apply for and receive state and federal subsidies. Urban transit was provided by the CLEVELAND RAILWAY CO., a private corporation, for 30 years before the city of Cleveland issued revenue bonds to buy the system in 1942. The Cleveland Transit System was operated as a city department under a Transit Board appointed by the mayor. The popularity of the automobile and the shift in population to the suburbs conspired to shrink revenues so that a subsidy would be necessary to keep the system in operation. In 1974, the Cleveland Transit System was transferred to the GREATER CLEVELAND REGIONAL TRANSIT AUTHORITY, which manages mass transit for the 5 counties including and surrounding the city. The authority is funded by sales taxes. The Cleveland Metropolitan Housing Authority was established during the Depression to replace slums with decent, affordable housing for low-income people. After WORLD WAR II, housing shortages increased not only in Cleveland but also in suburbs such as BEREA and EUCLID. The CUYAHOGA METROPOLITAN HOUSING AUTHORITY was established, with services extended throughout Cuyahoga County. Other regional authorities in the Cleveland area are the Northeast Ohio Regional Sewer District, the Cleveland-Cuyahoga County Port Authority, and the Metroparks. The mayor of Cleveland usually appoints at least 1 board member to regional authorities.

Mary Ellen Kollar
Public Administration Library

Snavely, Charles, "A History of the City Government of Cleveland, Ohio" (Ph.D. diss., 1902, WRHS).
See also GOVERNMENT, POLITICS

The **CLEVELAND CITY HALL**, dedicated in 1916, was the first such structure specifically built for and owned by the city. The earliest township government met in 1803 in a log cabin belonging to JAS. KINGSBURY. When the village was incorporated in 1815, a small frame building on Superior Ave. erected by Jas. Walworth was used as the village hall. In 1836 the city government was conducted in the Commercial Block on Superior near the west side of PUBLIC SQUARE. In 1856 it moved to rented quarters in the Jones Block, a brick building on the southwest corner of the square.

In 1869, a competition for a plan for a new city hall was held. Ten proposals were received. The 1st- and 3d-place schemes were designed by Heard & Blythe, and the 2d-place winner was Alexander Koehler, whose plans were discovered at the WESTERN RESERVE HISTORICAL SOCIETY in 1980. However, none of the competition plans was built. In 1875 the city leased the Case Block, a large commercial building built by LEONARD CASE at Superior and E. 3rd St. (the Public Library site). This Second Empire-style building was designed by CHAS. W. HEARD. In 1906 the city purchased the Case Block and continued to occupy it until the completion of the present building in 1916. In 1895 a city hall was approved by the voters, and a colossal Beaux-Arts building was planned for the 2 northern quadrants of Public Square, with an elliptical arch spanning Ontario St. Ground was actually broken on 4 June 1895, but within a week protests against building on the public land brought the project to a halt.

The present city hall was erected as part of the 1903 Group Plan ensemble of public buildings. Placed in symmetry with the county courthouse at the north end of the Mall, the city hall has an arcaded ground story, a 2-story Tuscan colonnade, and a central entrance bay characteristic of the Beaux-Arts style. The architect was J. MILTON DYER. Designed by 1907, the city hall was completed and dedicated on 4 July 1916. The building has a steel-framed and concrete structure with exterior walls of Vermont granite. The vaulted 2-story great hall is an impressive public space, and the commodious and workable arrangement of the interior has enabled the building to function well as a city hall for nearly 75 years.

The **CLEVELAND CLEARINGHOUSE ASSOCIATION**, a consortium of local banks, was one of the first organizations of its kind in the country. It was formed on 28 Dec. 1858 by the officers of 5 commercial and 4 private banks, with TRUMAN P. HANDY as president. Its first headquarters were in the City Bank of Cleveland at 21 Superior St. For its first 50 years, the association primarily served as a medium for the exchange of checks, drafted upon its members. In 1902, the clearinghouse adopted a new constitution, which increased its power to safeguard the city's financial interests. As part of the program of safeguards, the association hired a local bank examiner, Francis Coates, Jr., to augment the periodic examinations conducted by state and federal authorities. The examinations secured community safety by demonstrating and insuring the safety and solvency of each member bank.

The clearinghouse aided in getting the FEDERAL RESERVE BANK located in Cleveland in 1914 and supported the Liberty Loan drive during WORLD WAR I. After moving several times after 1858, the association relocated in the new Federal Reserve Bank Bldg. in 1923. Under the leadership of Harris Creech, it took a principal role in bringing relief to Cleveland banks in 1933. The strength of the association was demonstrated in that only 2 of its members failed during the Depression. For economic measures, the association suspended operations in 1942, and its functions were assumed by the Federal Reserve Bank of Cleveland. However, by 1945, the clearinghouse was operating again. Since WORLD WAR II, the association has been more loosely organized, with no central offices or staff. Its leadership is rotated among its 5 large member banks.

The **CLEVELAND CLIFFS IRON COMPANY** is the oldest iron-mining firm with its headquarters in Cleveland. The company's origin dates to 9 Nov. 1847, when 15 Cleveland men, who were interested in exploring the vast iron ore deposits on the Upper Peninsula of Michigan, formed the Cleveland Iron Mining Co. It was incorporated in Michigan in 1850 and reorganized in Ohio 3 years later. Samuel L. Mather was the leading force for the business in its first 50 years. After the opening of the Sault Canal in 1855 relieved a major transportation obstacle, Mather helped to make Cleveland Iron one of the chief iron companies on the Upper Peninsula. The company sent the first cargo of ore through the canal. It built railroads and docks in that area and, in 1869, started its own fleet of ore carriers, which were shipping 200,000 tons of ore annually by 1880. As surface mining was depleted in the 1880s, the firm pioneered in devising an underground mining system. The company's position was made even stronger in 1891, when it merged with one of its prime competitors, the Iron Cliffs Co., and became the Cleveland-Cliffs Iron Co.

Under Mather's son Wm. G. Mather, Cleveland-Cliffs began to diversify into ore-related industries. As it acquired 330,000 acres of timberland on the Upper Peninsula and built charcoal blast furnaces, the company moved into the forest-products and chemical industries. The firm was an innovator in the application of electricity to mining, which subsequently led to its involvement in the utility business, providing electricity not only to the mines but also to the Upper Peninsula communities. Desiring more control over its coal supply, the company entered this industry in the late 1910s by acquiring coal mines in Pennsylvania and West Virginia. Cleveland-Cliffs expanded its iron ore business by acquiring several smaller iron companies in the Marquette Range and eventually moving into the Mesabi Range during WORLD WAR I, giving it a total of 29 mines and 23 freighters. In 1929, the company, then the nation's largest independent producer of ore, became involved in CYRUS EATON's plan to form a consolidated Midwest Steel Co. As the Depression deepened and Eaton's project collapsed, the firm experienced serious financial problems. At this time, Mather turned the presidency over to Cleveland banker Edward B. Green, who brought the company out of its indebtedness and into a firm position to meet the demands of WORLD WAR II.

In the 1950s, Cleveland-Cliffs helped pioneer the development of taconite ore pellets. It expanded its iron ore operations to Australia and Canada in the 1960s. During the 1960s and 1970s, the firm continued to diversify into the uranium, shale oil, and petroleum fields. The recession of the 1980s forced a series of closings and reduced operations in the Lake Superior region and the decline of Cleveland-Cliffs' involvement in synthetic fuel programs. Despite the slumping steel industry, Cleveland-Cliffs still ranks as the largest iron ore producer that owns a majority of its domestic reserves, approximately 3 billion tons.

Cleveland-Cliffs Iron Co., *The Cleveland-Cliffs Iron Company* (1920).
Cleveland Iron Mining Co. Correspondence, WRHS.
Stuart, Harrison H., *The Cleveland-Cliffs Iron Company* (1974).

The **CLEVELAND CLINIC DISASTER** (also known as the CLINIC FIRE), which occurred on 15 May 1929, cost the lives of 123 people but stimulated the development and enforcement of safety regulations in hospitals in the U.S. The fire began as a result of the decomposition of stored nitro-cellulose x-ray film due to heat from an unguarded 100-watt incandescent light bulb, and released smoke and poisonous gases (primarily phosgene) throughout the main building of the CLEVELAND CLINIC FOUNDATION. Death or injury in almost all cases was due to the effects of inhalation of poisonous gases. Eighty visitors and patients and 43 employees of the clinic died in the disaster, while 92 were injured. Some of the deaths did not occur until several days after the fire. Dr. JOHN PHILLIPS, one of the founders of the Cleveland Clinic, died as a result of inhaling the gases. Several investigating commissions were established to look into the cause of the fire. Clinic officials were absolved from responsibility for the fire, but the tragedy was one of the largest in the U.S. up to that time.

As a result of the fire, the City's Manager's Commission investigating the disaster recommended that Cleveland's police and fire departments be supplied with gas masks and that a municipal ambulance service be established to provide suitable transportation for emergency cases needing hospital care. On the national level, the clinic disaster resulted in the development of new standards for storage and labeling of hazardous materials, especially x-ray film. The

storage of nitro-cellulose film was abandoned. Poisonous gas was recognized as a hazard, and fire insurance companies began to revise and strictly enforce safety regulations.

The **CLEVELAND CLINIC FOUNDATION** is an independent nonprofit institution dedicated to providing quality specialized patient care within a setting of education and research. In 1979, Congress recognized the foundation as a center of medical excellence—a Natl. Health Resource. The Cleveland Clinic was founded by 4 Cleveland physicians—Drs. GEO. W. CRILE, SR., FRANK E. BUNTS, WM. E. LOWER, and JOHN PHILLIPS. During WORLD WAR I, Drs. Crile, Bunts, and Lower established the first U.S. military hospital (see LAKESIDE UNIT) near the battlefields of France and were impressed by the practicality of having teams of medical specialists working together. When they returned to Cleveland in 1919, they formed a group practice with Dr. Phillips with the intention of ultimately opening a clinic. The Cleveland Clinic Foundation was incorporated on 21 Feb. 1921, and a clinic building was opened on Euclid Ave. near E. 93rd. The initial aim of the founders was outlined as "better care of the sick; investigation of their problems; and more teaching of those who serve." About 25% of the income was to be put into research, education, and expansion. A new 184-bed hospital was opened in 1924. On 15 May 1929, a fire in a basement storeroom ignited x-ray films, spewing a toxic yellow cloud of fumes throughout the clinic building and killing 123. The foundation slowly recovered from the fire and the stock market crash, but it was not until after WORLD WAR II that substantial growth occurred, particularly in the areas of research and education. The formation of the research and education divisions further stressed the clinic's emphasis on specialty care. Since its founding, emphasis within the Div. of Research has been on diseases of the kidneys, circulation, and the heart. Among the numerous developments, the clinic was one of the first institutions to recognize neurosurgery as a medical specialty; developed the first feasible artificial kidney, which cleanses toxic waste from the blood of patients whose kidneys no longer function; established the world's first training program for enterostomal therapists; pioneered work in kidney transplants and kidney revascularization; made important discoveries related to high blood pressure; and developed coronary bypass surgery.

Since the 1950s, innovations such as the coronary bypass operation and other procedures related to cardiology and cardiovascular surgery have accounted for much of the foundation's expansion. By 1980, 25% of the hospital, including a 351-bed cardiovascular wing, was set aside for heart patients. Treating and evaluating about 6,000 patients a year, the foundation's department became the largest of its kind in the world. The foundation has also been a pioneer in medical education. Its Div. of Education was incorporated in 1935 and was one of the first institutions to promote continuing medical education. By the 1980s, it was recognized as the largest postgraduate medical facility in the U.S. not connected with a medical school or university. In addition to the education and research divisions, the foundation has maintained 2 other major additions—a large specialty clinic and a 1,008-bed hospital. The clinic, founded in 1921, and the hospital, founded in 1924, were the 2 original divisions of the foundation. In the mid-1970s, the clinic launched a long-range planning process to study its clinical, research, and education needs; it began acquiring land in 1974, purchasing nearby lots as they became available. By 1986 the process was essentially completed, and the clinic owned virtually all the land (about 100 acres) between E. 88th and E. 105th from Chester to Cedar Ave. As of 1986, it intends to remain within those boundaries, and future purchases would be in-fill. In 1985, $185 million in improvements and additions were dedicated, chief among them the new 12-story Pelli Clinic building for out-patient services. Plans were also announced for a new $50 million research center. The clinic was, by this time, the largest nongovernment employer in Cleveland; in 1985 it employed 8,000 people. It has also become one of the largest privately funded, not-for-profit medical centers in the world. Its international reputation for specialized medical care has attracted patients from all over the world.

The **CLEVELAND COALITION OF LABOR UNION WOMEN** is a chapter of a national organization of women and men unionists who are united by their special concerns for women workers and are working within the framework of their own unions to achieve their goals. CLUW is not a union. The national organization was founded in Chicago in Mar. 1974 by 3,200 women representing 58 unions. In the 1980s, CLUW has thousands of members and has many chapters nationally. The Ohio CLUW has 4 local chapters, located in the Warren-Trimble-Youngstown area, Columbus, Toledo, and Cleveland. In 1983, the president of Cleveland CLUW was Sue Wilson. The Cleveland chapter did not have an office. Instead, most of the work was done out of the homes of the officers. The monthly meeting was held at an affiliated union hall. The Cleveland coalition attempts to sponsor 2 conferences a year. Past topics have included organizing the unorganized, occupational hazards, and sexual harassment. Cleveland CLUW is financed through fundraisers and membership dues. The organization has also helped to raise money for various strikes. It is considered to be one of the national organization's most active chapters.

The **CLEVELAND COMMISSION ON HIGHER EDU-CATION** was the driving force in establishing community colleges in Ohio and CUYAHOGA COMMUNITY COLLEGE in Cleveland, and was responsible for many communitywide higher-education activities involving the cooperative efforts of its member institutions—colleges and universities in Cuyahoga County. The commission was first organized in 1952, with a $75,000 grant from the CLEVELAND FOUNDATION. It consisted of a committee of 7 community leaders who were to survey higher education in Cleveland, using accredited liberal-arts colleges and universities in Cuyahoga County as a base for the study. When the study was completed, the group was unsuccessfully restructured as the Joint Committee for Cleveland Higher Education (1954–56). It was reorganized as the Cleveland Commission on Higher Education in early 1956.

The commission was organized to provide a forum to explore all avenues of potential cooperation between local colleges, and to try to solve common problems for its members cooperatively. It also functioned as a catalyst and facilitator to encourage long-range and development planning and to promote higher education in the community. The pattern of operations involved a continuous study, survey, and reporting process to determine educational needs and areas of duplication and/or gaps in educational offerings. Evaluating the purpose of the commission and the services provided to its members was also an ongoing process. The commission is a voluntary organization whose influence and prestige derive from the stature of its members. It is supported by member institutions and by corporate contributions and foundation grants.

Since 1956, the commission has been composed of the presidents of the member institutions and a corresponding number, plus 1, of public members, who are appointed for 3-year terms. Initial institutional members included Case Institute of Technology, Western Reserve University, Fenn College, BALDWIN-WALLACE COLLEGE, and JOHN CARROLL UNIVERSITY. The group was later joined by Cuyahoga Community College, NOTRE DAME COLLEGE, URSULINE COLLEGE, DYKE COLLEGE, and the CLEVELAND INSTITUTE OF ART; Fenn became CLEVELAND STATE UNIVERSITY, and Case and WRU federated. The survey committee was chaired by W. R. Burwell, chairman of the Brush Development Corp., and included civic leader Frank E. Joseph, a driving force in the activities of the commission. From 1956–69, former CLEVELAND ELECTRIC ILLUMINATING Co. chairman Ralph Besse led the group during an era of considerable accomplishment. Subsequent chairmen included Federal Reserve Bank president W. Braddock Hickman; former school board member and attorney Hugh Calkins; Nolan Ellison, president of Cuyahoga Community College; Notre Dame president Sr. Mary Marthe SND; and Robt. M. Ginn, chairman of the Illuminating Co. Public members have traditionally been corporate leaders with a strong commitment to civic activities. The day-to-day functioning of the commission has been administered by a salaried director and secretary. At various times, associates or consultants have been hired to administer special programs.

The changes in purpose of the commission have reflected the changing needs and demands facing area colleges and universities. The goals of the Besse years (1956–69) were to help members prepare for anticipated massive enrollments through planning, support, and development activities, and to take the leadership in establishing a community college. Under Hugh Calkins (1971–76), the commission took on a more active posture in response to the changing social climate. Programs to prepare inner-city teachers to counsel and prepare minority students to attend college and to explore approaches in nontraditional education marked this period. Since the mid-1970s, with colleges and universities experiencing dropping enrollments, reduced funding, and a loss of prestige, the commission has reduced its budget and office staff and limited its activities to serve as an information exchange, a monitor of educational needs in the community, and a facilitator of cooperative interests to its members.

Cleveland Commission on Higher Education Records, WRHS.

The **CLEVELAND COMMUNITY RELATIONS BOARD** was one of hundreds of boards established in cities across the country to promote racial harmony after WORLD WAR II, but the Cleveland board was the first to be established as a part of the city government. Created by city council in Mar. 1945, the board is designed "to promote amicable relations among the racial and cultural groups within the community" and "to take appropriate steps to deal with conditions which strain relationships." With a paid director and staff and unpaid members appointed by the mayor with council's approval, the board had a good record in its first 5 years. By 1950 it had helped end blatant discrimination in hotels and restaurants, banned discrimination in PUBLIC HOUSING and by numerous other social agencies, and established a policy that prohibited segregation in PARKS, playgrounds, and pools. In 1950 it convinced the American Bowling Congress to eliminate discrimination within its ranks. After city council passed the fair employment practices ordinance in 1950, the Community Relations Board was reorganized and placed in charge of administering the new law. Frank W. Baldau remained as director of the board, with Roosevelt S. Dickey as assistant director, but board membership was increased from 12 to 17. In its first 3 years of administering the new law, the board settled 171 cases without resorting to public hearings or prosecution. The board's 3-member staff was expanded to 12 in 1959 to deal with increasing tensions brought about by the influx of large numbers of migrant whites and blacks from the South. But the creation in 1959 of the Ohio Civil Rights Commission, which lured away the director of the Cleveland board, Frank Baldau, as its executive director, led many people to believe that the Cleveland board was no longer needed. Such confusion, exacerbated by staff changes, city council's rejection of a fair-housing ordinance proposed by the board in 1960, and the belief on the part of many officials that board investigations stirred up rather than soothed racial tensions, made it difficult for the board to be effective during the early 1960s.

The board was strengthened in 1963 by new appointments, especially that of Ellsworth H. Harpole, who served as director from 1963–66. As the civil-rights movement became more active in Cleveland after 1963, the board more strongly advocated the concerns of the city's black community. It worked with civil-rights groups, business and industry, and labor unions to improve employment for blacks and the acceptance of black applicants into union apprenticeship programs. In 1965, city council made easier the board's administration of the fair employment practices legislation by giving it the power to initiate investigations rather than wait for a formal complaint. During the 1960s, the board worked to improve relations between the police and Cleveland citizens, especially in the black community. From 1963–74 it also sponsored an annual home visitation program that allowed black and white Greater Clevelanders to visit in one another's homes (and later churches) to discuss race relations. In the latter half of the 1970s, the board worked to ease fears about court-ordered busing to desegregate Cleveland schools. It also continued to monitor racial tensions and discrimination in the city. By its 35th anniversary in the spring of 1980, the Community Relations Board had a staff of 23 and a budget of $400,000.

The **CLEVELAND COMPOSERS' GUILD** is one of the oldest continuously operating composers' groups in the U.S. It evolved from the activities of the Manuscript Sec. of the FORTNIGHTLY MUSICAL CLUB. The club had been recognizing the importance of the work of Cleveland composers as early as 1912, when compositions by JAS. H. ROGERS, WILSON G. SMITH, JOHANN BECK, and CHAS. V. RYCHLIK were performed. Later other composers such as ARTHUR SHEPHERD, HERBERT EL-WELL, F. KARL GROSSMAN, Patty Stair, Harriet Ware, and others were included on club programs. This interest led to the creation of the Manuscript Sec. in 1928 by Mrs. Carl Radde, a former president of the club. The Manuscript Sec. became the Composers' Guild in 1957, with Jane Corner Young as chairman.

The guild, made up of men and women who have had their works performed before an audience, schedules programs of works by its members and has made recordings of some of the best work. Among those whose works appear on recordings are Marcel Dick, Donald Erb, Rudolf Bubalo, Jane Corner Young, Klaus G. Roy, Howard Whittaker, Raymond Wilding-White, and Bain Murray. The composers represented in the guild have won laurels individually for the guild and for Cleveland in Europe and South America, and widely within the U.S. The recordings through the years have been made with Composers' Recordings, Inc., sponsored by the KULAS FOUNDATION, Century Advent, and Crystal of Los Angeles, Calif. Publication projects with Galaxy, Ludwig Music Co. have been undertaken, as well as special concerts in New York City, Pittsburgh, Cincinnati, and elsewhere. Among the noted artists who have performed in guild projects are Robt. Shaw, Marie Kraft, ARTHUR LOESSER, David Burge, and Seth McCoy. In 1985, guild membership included composers from Oberlin, Akron, Kent, Youngstown, and Baldwin-Wallace, as well as the Greater Cleveland area. Dennis Eberhard was president in 1985; he was preceded by Walter Watson, Rudolf Bubalo, Bain Murray, and Donald Erb. The guild has been supported for many years by the Bascom Little Fund in its many projects.

**CLEVELAND CONGRESS OF MOTHERS.** *See* CLEVELAND COUNCIL OF PARENT-TEACHER ASSOCIATIONS

The **CLEVELAND CONVENTION** (31 May 1864) brought together a group of anti-Lincoln Republicans in order to form a new political party and nominate a candidate for president and vice-president to run in the 1864 presidential election. The convention met in Cleveland at Chapin Hall on 31 May with about 200–300 delegates representing 10 states. United in their opposition to Lincoln's conduct of the war, they named their new party Radical Democracy and adopted a platform that included the abolition of slavery by constitutional amendment, a 1-term presidency, and direct election of the president by the people. John C. Fremont was nominated by acclamation as the party's presidential candidate, with Gen. John Cochrane of New York as vice-presidential candidate. Although Fremont accepted the nomination by letter in June, he withdrew his name in Sept. to prevent a split in the Republican party for the 1864 election.

McKinney, Effie, *The Cleveland Convention* (1928).

The **CLEVELAND COUNCIL OF PARENT-TEACHER ASSOCIATIONS** was organized in Apr. 1902 in the Old Stone Church. Known from 1902–27 as the Cleveland Congress of Mothers, the local organization was affiliated with the Ohio Congress of Mothers, which had been formed in 1901 at the national convention in Columbus of the Natl. Congress of Mothers. Formation of the Cleveland congress was prompted by the organization of the state group. Mrs. Martin Striebinger, a charter member of the Ohio congress and its first recording secretary, was instrumental in forming the Cleveland congress; she was elected its first president, serving from 1902–04, and was president of the Ohio congress from 1903–06. Others active in the early years of the CCM included Mrs. C. E. James, Mrs. Jas. Logan, and Mrs. Walter Lister. Like the national and state organizations, the CCM was a federation of the various mothers' clubs associated with kindergartens and schools in the area. Its membership grew quickly, from 95 individual members in 1905 to 3,000 in 53 affiliated mothers' clubs in 1923. Its purpose was to promote cooperation between parents and teachers in the education of children and "to raise the standard of home life; to develop wiser, better trained parenthood; and to promote laws for the protection and care of children." The CCM worked to combat juvenile delinquency, on behalf of teachers' pensions, and for the education of the deaf and mute; other projects included financial assistance to St. Luke's Hospital's maternity dispensary (1911–12) and a successful campaign against long hat pins.

By 1927, when the Cleveland Congress of Mothers became the Cleveland Council of Parent-Teacher Associations, it had 101 affiliates and about 10,000 members. It grew to 124 units and 28,000 members in 1946 and to 167 units in 1977. But during the 1970s, membership in PTAs declined nationwide by 37%, and by 56% in Ohio; by 1980, membership in Cleveland Council affiliates was 6,000. The decline was blamed on the increased number of working mothers and on the need to travel cross-town for PTA meetings as a result of busing. Membership and activities in the suburbs remained strong, while the PTA in Ohio's big cities was described as fighting "for its life." Leaders in Cleveland vowed to refocus priorities and to improve both membership and the organization's role in school issues. Locally, parents were criticized for being apathetic, unorganized, and ineffective in helping the Cleveland schools deal with the serious problems of the 1970s, but at the state level, the PTA continued to discuss, take stands, and lobby on such social and educational issues as the problems of "latchkey" children, child sexual abuse, standards for teachers, academic standards for athletes, and asbestos in schools.

Natl. Congress of Parents & Teachers, Ohio Branch, *50 Years: Ohio Golden Jubilee Year, 1901-1951* (1951).

The **CLEVELAND COUNCIL ON SOVIET ANTI-SEMITISM**, a grassroots organization whose goal is to educate the public on the plight of Soviet Jews, was the first group of its kind established anywhere in the world. It was formed in 1963 by Jews living on Cleveland's west side, including Louis Rosenblum, Herbert Caron, and Abe Silverstein. Although the council was not affiliated with BETH ISRAEL-THE WEST TEMPLE, many of the initial members of the former were also members of the latter, and the CCSA periodically gave reports to the congregation's Social Action Committee.

Between 1964-69, the council developed educational tools and devised protest strategies that became staples of the Soviet Jewry movement. It organized letter-writing campaigns, requested appeals to Soviet leaders from prominent individuals, produced and distributed handbooks designed to assist other communities in the organization of their own councils, produced motion pictures and slide shows depicting the plight of Soviet Jews, published the first newsletter, *Spotlight*, to address the issue, and devised confrontational patterns of protest. One of the most successful activities created by the council was the People-to-People program established in the late 1960s. This activity demanded little of its participants but, at the same time, involved and educated a large number of people. Included in the People-to-People activity were greeting-card campaigns, letters-to-Soviet-Jews campaigns, and adopt-a-family and adopt-a-prisoner campaigns.

By 1969, there were 5 other councils nationwide, most established with the assistance of the Cleveland group. In 1970, these councils and the Cleveland council formed the Union of Councils for Soviet Jewry in order better to share information and resources. Louis Rosenblum served as the first union chair, and the national headquarters were in Cleveland. Until 1972, the union was an all-volunteer organization. That year, an office with a staff of 1 was established in Washington, D.C., to provide congressional liaison and to channel information to the news media regarding Soviet Jewry. The union included 18 councils by 1973, and 10 years later included 32 councils representing 50,000 members. Although the Cleveland council was still active in 1985, by the late 1970s the JEWISH COMMUNITY FED. had taken over the major organizing effort locally for Soviet Jewry.

Cleveland Council on Soviet Anti-Semitism Records, WRHS.

The **CLEVELAND COUNCIL ON WORLD AFFAIRS** is a nonpartisan, nonprofit organization with a membership of 1,060 that seeks to educate the public in foreign affairs. Council services include lectures and panel discussions with world-affairs experts, discussion groups, international tours, special programs for secondary-school students and teachers, and hosting foreign students and visitors. Funding is obtained through membership, contributions, and tourist and investment income. The council's origin dates from 11 Nov. 1919, when, on the 1st anniversary of Armistice Day, a discussion group sponsored by the newly formed LEAGUE OF WOMEN VOTERS was formed at the CITY CLUB. Its purpose was to provide leaders and speakers in the cause of international cooperation. A council composed of women's clubs involved in peace programs was instrumental in founding the Council for the Prevention of War in 1921. Changing its name in 1923 to the Council for the Promotion of Peace, the group merged in 1929 with business and professional leaders to form the Internatl. Affairs Committee. In 1933 the committee became the Foreign Affairs Council, and in 1943 it incorporated as the Cleveland Council on World Affairs. In 1947, the council in conjunction with *TIME MAGAZINE* cosponsored an Institute on World Affairs, which served as a precursor of the Marshall Plan and the 1949 Atlantic Alliance. Under Brooks Emeny, director and president 1935-47, the council achieved national recognition. It was Emeny's philosophy that the ideal of democracy is an informed public opinion. As council director and an assistant professor of international politics at Cleveland College, Emeny created an adult education program on world affairs, holding meetings 4 or 5 times a year. The council's impact on the community results from the work of its numerous groups. The Cleveland Committee on Foreign Relations is an invitational group of prominent business and professional leaders. The Women's Forum sponsors a series of morning and luncheon programs. The council hosts the annual Model United Nations program for high school students and teachers. Composed of volunteers who serve as host families and escorts, the Internatl. Visitors Committee provides services to foreign visitors and students temporarily residing in Greater Cleveland.

Emeny, Brooks, *A History of the Founding of the Cleveland Council on World Affairs, 1935-1948* (1975).

The **CLEVELAND CULTURAL GARDEN FEDERATION** is the body that oversees the operations of the Cultural Gardens, a series of landscaped gardens with statuary that honor the various nationality and racial groups in Cleveland. Situated along East Blvd. and Martin Luther King, Jr. Blvd., the gardens are unique in the nation. The CCGF was founded in 1925 by Cleveland newspaperman LEO WEIDENTHAL as the Civic Progress League. Weidenthal first envisioned the concept of the gardens when he witnessed the dedication of the Shakespeare Garden in ROCKEFELLER PARK in 1916; he felt that a similar site should be prepared for each of the city's nationality communities. In 1926 the name of the organization was changed to the Cultural Garden League. Weidenthal, Chas. J. Wolfram (president of the federation for 25 years), and Jennie Zwick were prominent during the early years of the organization. In 1926 a Hebrew garden was established. The city cooperated with this concept by passing an ordinance on 9 May 1927 that set aside areas of Rockefeller Park adjacent to the Hebrew and Shakespeare gardens for the development of future ethnic gardens. The next gardens were the Italian, German, Lithuanian, Slovak, and Ukrainian in 1930, followed by the Polish, Hungarian, Czech, and Yugoslav gardens in 1934. In 1938 the American, Rusin, Irish, Greek, and Syrian gardens were established. In the years since the 1930s, Romanian, Estonian, Afro-American, Chinese, Finnish, and Indian gardens have been created. As of 1986, the gardens included 24 different sites.

Much of the work on the earlier gardens was accomplished with labor from the WPA. The planning and fundraising for each of the gardens were undertaken, however, within the various ethnic communities, while the Cleveland Cultural Garden Fed. (this name was adopted in 1952) has overseen overall planning and coordinated various joint programs. These have included the 2d UNESCO Conference in Cleveland in 1949 and the annual celebration of One World Day, which began in 1945. During the 1960s and 1970s, many of the gardens suffered severe vandalism. In response, many of the ethnic groups removed statuary for safekeeping. In 1985–86, a major restructuring of the Martin Luther King, Jr. Blvd. area was undertaken, and plans were discussed for the rehabilitation of the garden areas. The federation, which included 40 members from the nationalities affiliated with the gardens, continued to work for their rehabilitation. In 1986, the governing body of the CCGF consisted of a president, vice-presidents, an executive secretary, a treasurer, a recording secretary, and an executive board.

Cleveland Cultural Garden Fed. Records, WRHS.
Lederer, Clara, *Their Paths Are Peace* (1954).

The **CLEVELAND-CUYAHOGA COUNTY PORT AUTHORITY** is the joint city- county board formed in 1968 to operate the port of Cleveland. The authority is governed by 9 directors, 6 appointed by the city of Cleveland and 3 by the county. A staff of 10 handles day-to-day operations. The authority is financed by 5-year .13 mill levies and revenues from ships using port facilities. Port authority proposals began circulating in the 1920s. In 1924, the *PLAIN DEALER* promoted a nonpartisan harbor commission to manage and improve the port. In 1931, City Manager DANIEL MORGAN formed a Cleveland Port Advisory Board to study improvements, but nothing major resulted. The port authority idea was revived in the 1950s as Clevelanders anticipated increased trade from the St. Lawrence Seaway. In 1955, the general assembly authorized the creation of city, county, or joint city/county port authorities to operate ports with voter-approved tax levies up to .55 mills. Also in 1955, the city hired New York port consultant Jas. C. Bulkley to study the port. The *Bulkley Report* proposed new facilities and an independent port authority free from political pressure; the mayor, however, rejected an authority. Between 1955 and the opening of the Seaway in 1959, the city took little action to prepare for increased trade. The idea resurfaced in 1962 when councilman Anthony Pecyk proposed to remove the port from city control to a port authority; Mayor Anthony Celebrezze rejected the idea, but Pecyk and council president Jas. Stanton continued to promote it. They felt that a port authority would help create jobs and equalize the tax burden throughout the county. In 1964, the Cuyahoga County commissioners proposed a joint city-county port authority; the city would receive a majority, since it developed the existing facilities. The commissioners noted that Cleveland had lost business to the Toledo-Lucas County Port Authority and other ports; they felt that, although Cleveland's port business had recently increased, the port had not benefited from the Seaway as had other ports and that Cleveland was unable to develop and promote its facilities. The city could not match the huge advertising budgets of other ports; the port of New York even operated a Cleveland office.

County and city officials met during 1964 and early 1965 to discuss an authority; Mayor Ralph S. Locher opposed the idea. In 1965, Stanton introduced a charter amendment to create a port authority; a 1965 study by Ernst & Ernst, an accounting firm, called for port expansion and a city/county port authority. Locher denounced authorities as governmental units, not directly accountable to voters, that would take city assets. County commissioners tried to revive the proposal in Apr. 1966 after Jas. C. Bulkley's firm advocated an authority in another study. A port authority was an issue of the 1967 mayoral campaign. Supporting an authority, Democrat Carl Stokes defeated Republican Seth Taft, who shared Locher's opinion that too much power would be placed in too few hands. Stokes made an authority a major priority and received support from Gov. Jas. A. Rhodes. On 4 Jan. 1968, the city and county agreed to create a joint port authority with a majority of city-appointed directors; they also agreed that the authority would eventually buy the port facilities. Directors were appointed on 22 and 23 Jan.; the Cleveland-Cuyahoga County Port Authority first met on 30 Jan. Lacking a development plan, the directors submitted only a .13 mill operating levy on the May 1968 ballot instead of the .55 mills allowed by the 1955 Ohio port authority law; city voters had to approve a charter amendment for lease negotiations to begin. On 8 May, city voters approved the charter amendment, while county voters approved the port authority levy. Voters renewed the 5-year levy in 1972, 1977, and 1982. Although the first lease-purchase agreement between the city and the port authority was signed 21 Mar. 1969, the authority still, in 1986, leased several docks from the city. In 1975, the city released the authority from a lease provision, forcing it to seek an additional levy to purchase the city facilities; the authority, however, purchased 55 acres of land, including 18 acres from Penn Central, in 1973 and the old Postal Annex in 1978. In 1979, the federal government licensed the authority to operate a foreign free trade zone; in 1985, the authority created a subzone at the I-X Trade Ctr. in BROOK PARK.

Most of the major long-term development projects proposed in the 1970s were never developed, although the authority built 2 warehouses, expanded a third, and installed minor improvements. Republic Steel proposed a 1,000' ore dock, which was rejected by Mayor Dennis Kucinich in 1979. Although a smaller dock was built, Republic Steel built a state-of-the-art dock in Lorain. When the Ohio House considered a bill in 1979 giving authorities increased taxing authority and the power of eminant domain, Kucinich threatened to end the authority. Scandals rocked the authority in the 1980s. The firm that had agreed to renovate the postal annex and operate the free trade zone defaulted on its contract; in 1986, demolition of the aging building began. Two former directors were convicted, John Felice for extortion and Arnold Pinkney for a conflict of interest in a sale of liability insurance to the authority, and others were under investigation. The Cleveland-Cuyahoga County Port Authority did not dramatically increase Seaway traffic into Cleveland. Budget cutbacks were necessary in 1985. The port's success hinged on the economies of other ports; in 1984, Cleveland benefited from the overflow business of crowded eastern ports. Local firms still found it cheaper to ship goods by rail to the port of Baltimore. Most of the cargo entering the port during the 1980s was foreign steel, although there was also a small trickle of iron ore.

The *CLEVELAND DAILY ARGUS*, an evening daily, made its first appearance on 3 Mar. 1885, 2 weeks before the death of the *CLEVELAND HERALD*. Priced at $.01, it was an attempt to test the market for a working-class paper with Republican leanings. As such, it advocated high tariffs and sound currency, while offering free want ads to the unemployed and calling for municipal supervision of the retail weighing of coal. Early in its career, the "Reporter Printing Co." was briefly listed as publisher of the *Daily Argus*. C. M. Fairbanks was later identified as editor, and the paper appeared to have been printed in the Frankfort St. plant of Abel W. Fairbanks, publisher of the *Herald* prior to 1877. Declaring itself the victim of a labor boycott, the *Argus* evidently suspended publication on 27 Feb. 1886, a few days short of its first anniversary.

The **CLEVELAND DAILY GAZETTE** was an expanded version of the biweekly edition of L. L. Rice's *CLEVELAND WHIG*. The paper made its first appearance in May 1836. It replaced the biweekly *Whig*, although Rice, largely using material from the *Daily Gazette*, continued publication of the weekly *Whig* from the same office. Together with the *Advertiser*, which was converted about the same time, and the *Herald*, which had converted a year earlier, it briefly provided Cleveland with 3 daily newspapers. Evidently that was too much for the traffic to bear, for Rice admitted after 6 months that he was still operating at a loss, even though 3 of the *Gazette*'s 4 pages consisted of advertisements. Having taken in CHAS. WHITTLESEY and A. H. Lewis as editorial associates, Rice sold both the *Daily Gazette* and the *Whig* to the pair on 17 Dec. 1836. Whittlesey and Lewis formally took charge on 3 Jan. 1837, at which time they changed the name of the weekly edition from *Whig* to *Gazette*. On 21 Mar. Whittlesey announced the merger of the *Gazette* with the *Cleveland Herald*, which he had purchased in partnership with JOSIAH A. HARRIS. Its name survived as part of the *Herald & Gazette* until 1843, when the combined publication reverted to the name of the older *Herald*.

The **CLEVELAND DAILY REVIEW** briefly provided the city with its first Sunday newspaper. After 2 months of publication in a prototype 2-page format, it reappeared permanently on 29 Aug. 1857 as a 6-day penny daily of 4 5-column pages. Published by Edward A. Munson & Co., the paper gave Geo. Spear and Henry Newcomb Johnson equal billing with Munson as coeditors. It professed to be neutral in politics and within 2 weeks claimed a larger circulation than any 2 of the other Cleveland dailies. The first issue of the *Sunday Morning Review* appeared on 18 June 1858. Although identical in format to the *Daily Review* and offered free to patrons of the latter, there were no editors listed on its masthead, nor was any mention made in the *Daily Review* of this Sunday connection. Advertising patronage in the Sunday edition was extremely sparse, and after 11 weeks it metamorphosed into the *Saturday Evening Review* on 11 July. Though still dated for Sunday in its first issue, subsequent issues were dated on Saturdays until its expiration near the end of the year. Spears and Johnson apparently severed their connection with the *Daily Review* shortly after the commencement of the Sunday experiment. Early in 1859, Munson sold out to Thomas L. Wilcox, and Johnson rejoined the staff as editor. In 1860 the *Daily Review* was owned by Walter H. Shupe, and Max H. Allardt published it in 1861, by which time it had expanded to a full 7-column format and raised its price to the prevailing \$.03. It suspended publication in May of that year.

The **CLEVELAND DAY NURSERY AND FREE KINDERGARTEN ASSOCIATION** promoted and supported middle-class family-centered values through child-development programs that were eventually incorporated into the public school system. Incorporated in 1894, the association had its roots in the Young Ladies' Seminary and

the Young Ladies' Temperance League, 2 organizations founded by LINDA THAYER GUILFORD in 1874. Seminary pupils, who included FLORA STONE MATHER, Jane Foote Tracy, and Julia Bolton Castle, were inculcated with a belief in the value of education, a sense of moral responsibility for the poor, and a missionary spirit to spread their values through concrete programs. The first expression of the Guilford philosophy was the Young Women's Temperance League. Ladies who joined the league signed pledges promising to personally abstain from liquor and to discourage its use among family and friends. The league expanded its mission to include services for working girls that ranged from reading and sitting rooms, where they could come for enlightening Christian education, to temporary lodging and job searches. The emphasis soon changed from temperance to promoting the general welfare of women and children. By 1877, a short-lived charity kindergarten was set up at Olivet Chapel, but it was abandoned in favor of a day nursery program, which began in 1880.

As the league's work resembled that of the Women's Christian Assoc., the two organizations merged in 1882. Former league members organized the Young Ladies' Branch of the WCA for special work among children. The branch opened several nurseries—the Bethel, Perry St. (later called the St. Clair St. and then the Perkins), and West Side—and a kindergarten at the Perkins site. As a supplementary activity, the ladies established the Flower Mission to distribute flowers among the elderly, sick, hospitalized, and poor. For \$.05 a day, the nurseries offered food, clothing, medical care, and a safe place for children while their mothers worked. The benefactresses disapproved of women's working outside the home but welcomed the chance to counteract what they considered to be the lax home training of the children. Often, the middle-class values and the occasionally patronizing attitudes of the wealthy Protestant ladies alienated the working-class, illiterate, and often Roman Catholic mothers, who sometimes shifted their children from nursery to nursery, stopped sending them altogether, or stopped paying the daily nickel. Yet, the mothers accepted the concept of the day nursery and responded to the good intentions of the ladies.

The branch then began to found kindergartens, as aids to character formation of all children, not just the children of working mothers. The kindergarten movement forged ahead under the direction of Louise Barron Rawson, president of the branch from 1885-1911. A close friend and fellow teacher of Linda Guilford, Rawson united social reformers behind the kindergarten cause and gave the organization the goal of directing all charity kindergartens in the city. Within 6 months of her election, the branch opened a kindergarten at the Perkins Nursery, followed by 13 others by 1898. Settlement houses also ran their own programs, but kindergarten work became the branch's most important work. In 1893, the branch split off from the WCA to concentrate all its resources on its work with children. Within a year, the resulting body, the Cleveland Day Nursery & Free Kindergarten Assoc., was incorporated as a nonprofit organization. Its membership, funding, and mission remained unchanged. By the turn of the century, the association moved into a golden era, marked by increased funding and rising attendance in its programs. It also operated vacation schools, supervised playgrounds at several public schools, and sponsored Saturday morning sewing classes, mothers' meetings, and summer outings. When the group opened the Cleveland Kindergarten Training School in 1894, its control over the local kindergarten system was increased as the school trained professional teachers for the growing system of public kindergartens as well as for the charity schools. The Cleveland Board of Education incorporated kindergarten programs into the curriculum in 1897, and the association gradually dissolved its kindergartens; by the 1930s, there were enough public facilities to serve poor neighborhoods, and the remaining association kindergartens were closed. As the first generation of association members died off, professionals were hired to manage and staff the organization, which operated nurseries and other programs until 1969, when it was absorbed by the Family Service Assoc., which subsequently became part of the CTR. FOR HUMAN SERVICES.

Cleveland Day Nursery Assoc. Records, WRHS.

The **CLEVELAND DENTAL SOCIETY** was established in 1886 by 13 Cleveland-area dentists. In its centennial year, membership stood at approximately 1,100. The organization's goal is to provide continuing education for professionals and community education on dental care. Each spring, the group sponsors the North Coast Annual Spring Meeting, a 2-day event with exhibitors, continuing-education programs, and speakers. During its existence, the CDS has developed constructive programs that have made significant progress in dental education and provided generous clinical aid to the needy. In 1897, the group appointed a committee for dental education in public schools. They prepared literature related to dental care for distribution to children. A free dental clinic for the poor was established at City Hospital on Scranton Rd. in 1906. The dentists on the committee donated several hours a week to working in this clinic. However, the program did not live up to expectations; no children came, and the clinic attracted only hospital personnel and people living in the immediate area. In 1910, the dentists examined children in 4 public schools, and found that 97% of them needed dental attention. As a result, 4 free clinics were established throughout Cleveland. The CDS expanded its examination program to include all public school children, and in 1928 included children in all PAROCHIAL SCHOOLS. This program was later abandoned because of lack of funding. A major accomplishment of the organization was convincing legislators to approve fluoridation of the Cleveland water supply in 1957. The CDS auxiliary produced the "Big Tooth" display at the CLEVELAND HEALTH EDUCATION MUSEUM. Meetings are held 6–8 times per year. Officers for 1986–87 were Dr. Louis J. Juliano, president, and Dr. Ronald L. Occhionero, president-elect.

The **CLEVELAND DEVELOPMENT FOUNDATION** was established by local business leaders to assist urban-renewal and slum-clearance efforts. It provided financial and planning assistance for a number of projects in the 1950s and 1960s. Planning for the foundation began in the spring of 1954. Inspired by the work of the Allegheny Conference on Community Development in Pittsburgh, John C. Virden of the Federal Reserve Bank, Elmer Lindseth of CEI, and Thos. F. Patton of Republic Steel proposed that Cleveland's business leaders organize a $2 million foundation to help finance and plan projects to eliminate "slum conditions" and otherwise promote "urban redevelopment." The Cleveland Development Foundation was incorporated on 23 June 1954; Virden served as its first president, and Upshur Evans of Standard Oil became its executive director, a position he held until resigning in 1968. At the last minute, a representative of the city administration was added to the foundation's board of trustees, increasing its membership to 21. The CDF raised its $2 million revolving fund through membership subscriptions and the sale of 10-year, 4% development notes. It provided seed money for a number of urban-renewal and redevelopment projects over the

next 15 years, most of which were in housing; its first major project was the Garden Valley housing project on reclaimed land at E. 79th St. and KINGSBURY RUN, to house people from urban-renewal districts so that redevelopment of those districts could proceed. Other housing projects in which the foundation participated were the Longwood housing project at E. 40th St., the East Woodland Community Apts., Kerruish Park (construction of 200 single-family homes at Lee and McCracken roads), and the renovation of homes and apartments in the Hough-E. 90th St. area.

By 1958, the foundation attracted national attention. Housing remained an important component of its work, but in the 1960s it moved into other areas, especially the development of downtown Cleveland. In Jan. 1960, the CDF unveiled a $500 million citywide redevelopment program that called for construction of commercial, office, and apartment buildings in the Erieview Project downtown, redevelopment in the University Circle-Hough area, and rehabilitation of buildings on the west side. The foundation subsequently supported redevelopment in the St. Vincent, Gladstone, and University-Euclid areas, provided initial funding for the Ohio City Community Development Assoc., and funded preparation of a development plan for CLEVELAND STATE UNIVERSITY. By 1963, however, the foundation's main project, Garden Valley, was in trouble. The nonprofit Garden Valley Housing Assoc. was formed in May 1963 to manage, operate, and refinance the project, which was in default on its mortgage. In 1972 the foundation transferred operation and management of both Garden Valley and Longwood Homes, which was also in default, to other nonprofit housing agencies. In 1968, the foundation was reorganized and essentially merged into the new GREATER CLEVELAND GROWTH ASSOC. Its new 8-member executive committee included 6 members of the Growth Assoc.'s executive committee, and the foundation's president, Geo. Grabner, also headed the Growth Assoc.

Cleveland Development Foundation Records, WRHS.

The **CLEVELAND DIESEL ENGINE DIVISION OF GENERAL MOTORS CORPORATION**, a leading research facility in the development of diesel engines and a major supplier of diesel engines for Navy submarines during WORLD WAR II, began operation in Nov. 1912 as the Winton Gas Engine & Mfg. Co. at 2116 W. 106th St. Cleveland automobile manufacturer ALEXANDER WINTON founded the company after he was unable to find a satisfactory gasoline engine to power his yacht. He decided to design and manufacture his own marine gasoline engine but soon became interested in the diesel engine then being developed in Europe. In 1913 the company built its first diesel engine. Winton Gas Engine & Mfg. became the Winton Engine Works in 1916. It manufactured diesel engines for a variety of marine craft, including freighters, tugboats, private yachts, and government vessels; it later produced engines for locomotives. In 1928 Geo. W. Codrington replaced Winton as president of the company, which became the Winton Engine Corp. in 1930, when it was purchased by GM. It continued as the Winton Engine Corp. until its name officially became the Cleveland Diesel Engine Div. of General Motors Corp. in 1937.

In 1938 Cleveland Diesel employed 750 people, and by 1939 98% of its business was work performed for the government. In 1930 Carl D. Salisbury and his engineering department had begun to reduce the weight of the diesel engine and to give it more speed and flexibility; these were important innovations during wartime. Called "Cleveland's foremost defense industry" in 1941, Cleveland Diesel expanded its plant, employed 5,000 people, and produced diesel engines for an estimated 70% of the Navy's submarines during World War II. Employment dropped to 1,000 in 1947, but plant expansion continued in the 1950s; in 1953 Cleveland Diesel occupied the plant on W. 106th St. and another plant at 8200 Clinton Rd. But in Sept. 1961 the 500 Cleveland Diesel employees received word that GM was closing the Cleveland plant and combining its operations with facilities in LaGrange, Ill. The development of atomic-powered submarines had diminished the Navy's demand for diesel engines.

The **CLEVELAND DISCIPLES UNION** was formed in 1887 to promote the cause of the Disciples of Christ church in Cleveland. Spurred on by the Baptists, who had been organized for half a century, the Disciples met at the FRANKLIN CIRCLE CHRISTIAN CHURCH in Aug. 1887. With 1,100 initial members, the union grew to 30,000 within 5 years. The organization, listed in the Cleveland telephone book as late as 1968 at 2056 E. 4th St., did missionary work and helped organize and support new congregations.

The **CLEVELAND ELECTRIC ILLUMINATING COMPANY** (CEI) served an area of only ¼ sq. mi. when it began operations in 1892; by 1980 it had grown to serve a 1,700-sq.-mi. area with more than 700,000 customers and had a net income of more than $100 million a year. The Illuminating Co. was organized on 29 Sept. 1892 as the Cleveland General Electric Co.; it adopted its present name on 21 July 1894. Cleveland General Electric resulted from the merger of the Brush Electric Light & Power Co. and the Cleveland Electric Light Co. The former was founded by inventor and electric light pioneer CHAS. F. BRUSH along with Richard C. Parsons, Wm. H. Barris, and Eugene H. Cowles. Incorporated on 16 Mar. 1881, with offices at 71 Ontario St., the firm used Brush arc lamps to light PUBLIC SQUARE, several main streets, and a number of stores.

The Cleveland Electric Light Co. was established on 21 June 1884; its early officers included Stiles C. Smith, president, and Frank J. Stafford, secretary and manager. Cleveland Electric Light bought a power-generating station on Johnson St. between Bank (W. 6th) and Water (W. 9th) streets and used the power to supply its Edison incandescent lights in several downtown stores. The new Cleveland General Electric Co. replaced the Brush arc lamps with the superior Edison incandescent system and by 1894 had invested more than $1.2 million to light Cleveland. In 1895 the company built a generating plant on Canal Rd., considered "the most modern in the world." It attracted interested engineers from all over the world.

By 1900 CEI had 1,400 customers. With offices in the CUYAHOGA BLDG., the firm began to expand service by decentralizing its power-distribution centers. By 1910 it had 31,000 customers in a service area that included BRATENAHL, E. CLEVELAND, EUCLID, CLEVELAND HTS., LAKEWOOD, and almost all of Cleveland. In 1911 it opened its Lake Shore steam generating plant at E. 70th St., and in Mar. 1913 the company moved into the new 15-story Illuminating Bldg. at 75 Public Square, which served as the firm's headquarters until the company moved into another new Illuminating Bldg. at 55 Public Square in Feb. 1958. Further expansion in Cuyahoga County gave CEI 167,000 customers in 1920. Under Robt. Lindsay's direction from 1921-33, CEI continued its expansion. Ten substations were built between 1921-26; between 1925-29 the company entered Lake, Geauga, and Ashtabula counties and part of Lorain County, opening generating plants in Avon Lake in 1926 and Ashtabula in 1930. In the early

1940s, CEI began promoting Cleveland as "the best location in the nation" in hopes of attracting new industries to the area and increasing its business. In 1946 it purchased the Cleveland Light & Power Co., organized in 1893. CEI customers numbered 370,000 in 1946.

The Illuminating Co. continued to expand and construct new plants through the 1970s. It opened the Eastlake steam generating plant in 1953, gas turbine generating plants in Eastlake and Avon Lake in 1973, and a steam plant in Mansfield in 1976. In Sept. 1967 CEI became a charter member of the Central Area Power Coordination Group (CAPCO), which included Toledo Edison, Ohio Edison, the Duquesne Light Co., and the Pennsylvania Power Co. CAPCO was designed to create a power pool to provide greater reliability of service and lower costs. CAPCO members also pooled financial resources to build generating facilities. The Seneca Hydroelectric Plant, of which CEI owned 80%, began service in 1970; in 1974 CEI began construction of the Perry Nuclear Power Plant near North Perry; and in 1977 service began from the Davis-Besse Nuclear Power Station, of which CEI owns 51%.

The 1970s were a difficult decade for the company. Municipal governments often challenged proposed rate increases and were joined by consumer groups that regularly fought such proposals before the Public Utilities Commission. Suburban and rural residents protested planned routes for power lines; environmental and antinuclear groups warned the public about the dangers of pollution and nuclear power; and from the early 1970s, CEI was engaged in a running battle with the city of Cleveland over arrangements to provide emergency power to the city's municipal light plant and the city's failure to promptly pay for that power. The Muny Light issue culminated in an antitrust suit against CEI filed by the city in 1975, charging the company with monopolistic practices designed to force Muny Light out of business. The city eventually lost the suit. CEI continued to grow and remained profitable. On operating revenues of $328 million in 1973, the company had a net income of $73 million; in 1983 revenues of $1.2 billion produced a net income of $258 million, and CEI employed 5,339.

The **CLEVELAND ELECTRIC RAILWAY COMPANY**, known as Big Con(solidated), was created by a merger of the E. Cleveland, Broadway & Newburgh, Brooklyn, and South Side railway companies on 15 May 1893. On 29 May, the Cleveland City Cable Co. and the Woodland Ave. & West Side Street Railway Co. merged to form the Cleveland City Railway Co., or Little Con(solidated), leaving Cleveland with only 2 street railway companies. The company operated the Abbey, Broadway, Cedar, Central, Clark, Euclid, Fairhill, Mayfield, Scovill, Scranton, Union, Wade Park, W. 14th St., W. 25th St., and partial E. 55th St. lines. In 1897 it owned 127 mi. of track, 344 motor cars, and 145 trailers. By 1901 there were 135 mi. of track, 426 motor cars, and 83 trailers. Cleveland's first severe transit strike began 10 June 1899 against the Cleveland Electric Railway as workers struck for improved pay and working conditions and union recognition. Violence and lawlessness marked the extended strike as the company imported strikebreakers. On 1 July 1903, the company acquired and merged operations with the Cleveland City Railway Co. The merger eliminated the need for riders to pay separate fares to different companies and gave the company a virtual streetcar monopoly. Known as Con-Con, it owned 901 motor cars and 236 mi. of track. From the 1901 municipal elections until 1909, CER officials, who favored a 5-cent fare, were embroiled in a legal battle with Mayor TOM L. JOHNSON over the issue of municipal ownership and a 3-cent fare. The period was marked by numerous legal proceedings, the organizing of "low-fare" rail companies who were given franchises as quickly as old grants expired, and middle-of-the-night maneuverings. During this period, the CER experimented with zone fares, penny transfers with a 3-cent fare, and 7 tickets for a quarter as ways of strengthening its position with the public. In 1907 the company gave in to Johnson, agreeing to lease its operations to the Municipal Traction Co. The 3-cent fare was a reality, but operating economies and a violent transit strike resulted in a 1908 referendum election defeat for the municipal system, forcing it into receivership. In 1910, voters approved the compromise "Tayler Grant" as authored by Judge ROBT. W. TAYLER. The agreement provided "service at cost" and a 3-cent fare. It also returned railway operations to the company, now reorganized as the Cleveland Railway Co. under city supervision.

The **CLEVELAND ENGINEERING SOCIETY** was founded in 1880 as the Civil Engineers' Club to counter a rival society that promoted the supposed mathematical and physical properties of the Great Pyramids. Putting their stake in the metric system, the 8 local civil engineers that formed the core of the club met in the surveyor's office in the old courthouse. Both the membership and the goals of the organization broadened to include representation from all branches of engineers who met to discuss challenges within the profession. The society soon became known as a local "Sorbonne of Technology," which served as a forum and a means of continuing education for its members and a technical education center for the community at large. It offered "afterwork training" for engineers and technical personnel, and opened its classrooms and other facilities to professional groups for meetings, review courses, and seminars. It also had a student loan fund to aid students who sought technical education.

Before the Depression, the society had over 1,500 members. During hard times, however, the number of dues-paying members fell off. Though the society could not provide work for its out-of-work members, it encouraged engineers to meet with industrialists at its offices to find ways to help their companies out of the Depression. In the early 1970s, when engineers, especially those trained in aerospace, again faced mass layoffs, the society tried to reorient the jobless to new specialties. Throughout its history, the society has issued useful publications of its members; journals, transactions, and bulletins provide for an exchange of information among different subspecialties, plus keep members informed of local happenings. Aside from its own publications, the society has collected books on technical subjects; in 1959, the organization donated over 14,000 technical titles to the CLEVELAND PUBLIC LIBRARY to make the material more accessible to the public.

In its first 100 years, the society had many homes in the downtown area that were quickly outgrown. In 1958, it used the contributions of over 250 companies and 3,000 individuals to erect a permanent home at 3100 Chester on a uniquely appropriate site: that of the old John Huntington estate and Polytechnical Institute that provided free technical education to the public. The facility featured classrooms, office space, a banquet hall and catering service, and an auditorium to serve the varied needs of the society. By 1980, more than 60 trade and professional associations regularly used the building for conferences, luncheons, or special presentations. In addition, many of the rooms of the center were used for CETA job retraining. Though it had over 2,000 members, the society yielded to mounting economic pressures and in 1983 was forced to reduce its staff and sell its building. In 1985, the Cleveland Engineering Society continued its educational and professional activities at the same site.

The **CLEVELAND FEDERATION OF LABOR,** the old craft wing of the Cleveland AFL-CIO, was the first successful coalition of tradesmen in the city. Chartered by the American Fed. of Labor in 1887, the organization was called the Central Labor Union until 1902, when it became the United Trades & Labor Council. In 1910, the council adopted the name it would retain until the merger with the CLEVELAND INDUSTRIAL UNION COUNCIL, the Cleveland Fed. of Labor. Before the formation of the Central Labor Union, trade unionists had loosely allied in the 1870s as the Industrial Council, which later became the KNIGHTS OF LABOR TRADES & LABOR ASSEMBLY 47. By 1886, there were 50 locals that composed Local 47, which loosely subscribed to the reform unionism promoted by the Knights. Shortly after the AFL was formed in 1881, organizers were sent to Cleveland to win local support for the new union movement. As a result of clashes between the rival organizations, many Cleveland trade unionists seceded from the Knights and began to meet informally to discuss organization of a central labor body. In Sept. 1887, the Typographical Union #54, Cigar Makers #7, Iron Molders #218, Typographical #6 (German), Amalgamated Carpenters, Brewery Workers #17, and Bakery Workers #19 applied for a federation charter, which was granted the next month. By 1890, the CLU formed 26 locals through the efforts of organizer ROBT. BANDLOW; within 10 years, the number grew to 71. The organizational effort was aided by the *CLEVELAND CITIZEN,* a labor paper founded by MAX S. HAYES and Henry C. Long of the Typographical Union in 1891, which became a useful forum for presenting local issues to the working man.

In 1902, the CLU merged with the Building Trades Council to become the United Trades & Labor Council. Until the rise of the TEAMSTERS UNION after 1912, the building trades dominated the labor body and brought it more into line with the conservatism of the national federation. By 1914, the only alternative to the approach of the AFL was the IWW. The Cleveland branch, however moderate, faced an uphill battle in gaining acceptance from the Cleveland business community. Under such colorful early leaders as Chas. "Big Boy" Smith and Larry McLaughlin, the CFL fought for the right to organize and for the open shop (especially among city workers) in a largely antiunion atmosphere through to the 1920s, and enjoyed some success with a low level of violence. As the country moved into a deepening depression in the 1930s, organized labor lost members who could no longer pay dues. As WPA rolls increased, the CFL feared the establishment of a dual organization, which would lure members with nominal dues and weaken the "legitimate" labor movement. When masses of less skilled, previously unorganized workers sought to negotiate better wages, hours, and working conditions as a result of the passage of Sec. 7A of the NIRA, the federation fought hard to establish loyalty and discipline. After 2 years of wildcat strikes, the most solid of the newly established unions were clearly the drivers in various industries (laundry, beverages, bakery, newspapers, etc.), the UNITED AUTO WORKERS, the clothing workers, and gasoline-station operators. Meanwhile, older, more established unions such as the Teamsters and Building Trades experienced major growth.

Beginning in 1935, the craft orientation of the federation was challenged by a group led by United Mine Workers president John L. Lewis, who favored the organization of workers in mass industries—steel, rubber, autos—along vertical industrial lines rather than laterally by trade. Locally, an uneasy peace between representatives of the two factions was threatened by membership raids on federation unions. When several industrial unions left the national federation and formed a separate organization, the Congress of Industrial Organizations, Clevelanders formed the Cleveland Industrial Union Council. In the face of competition from the council, the CFL was split by internal leadership squabbles. The Building Trades numerically dominated the organization, while the Teamsters under EDWARD MURPHY were a counterbalancing force. When key unions in the Building Trades Council seceded from that body in 1936, antagonism spilled over into the federation, and construction in the city was threatened as the warring unions controlled completion of various projects. Murphy exercised his considerable organizing skills to work out a truce, and built support for the ouster of Building Tradesman Albert Dalton as executive secretary in 1938 and the election of Thos. "Mr. Labor" Lenahan to that post. Murphy then engineered a truce that minimized jurisdictional fights.

Throughout the 1940s, the CFL supported the war effort through a 14-point program that discouraged strikes and promoted conservation. While chiding labor for absenteeism, the federation spoke out against employers who exploited workers in sweatshop conditions. The federation effort to maintain a united front with the council in war planning was undercut by the council's initial condemnation of the war, and by continuing raids of AFL unions by CIO organizers. By 1948 it became obvious to Ed Murphy and other CFL leaders that labor must have a more vigorous presence in the community than that provided by the then-current regime. Murphy led a group to topple Lenahan and elect Wm. Finegan as executive secretary. Finegan led the organization until it merged with the council in 1958 and became the Cleveland AFL-CIO.

The **CLEVELAND FEDERATION OF MUSICIANS**, Local No. 4, is one of the city's oldest labor unions. Local 4 had its origins as the Musicians' Mutual Protective Assoc. when it was founded on 4 Dec. 1877. In 1895 the association joined the American Fed. of Musicians and became known as the American Fed. of Musicians, Local No. 4. In 1910 a division between black and white musicians occurred; it resulted in the formation of the black musicians' own local—the American Fed. of Musicians, Local No. 550. However, the two groups were later reunited in 1962 as the Cleveland Fed. of Musicians, Local No. 4. The primary goal of Local No. 4 was to establish and enforce a minimum-wage standard that its members should charge for their services. The purpose was to enforce "good faith and fair dealings" among its members. Women received membership privileges in the local in 1901, as the protection of female musicians became a part of its purpose.

Local No. 4 actively supported the formation of local and national unions. It also supported other area trade unions by forbidding its members to work in restaurants and hotels that were nonunion, and it helped lobby for an 8-hour working day. The local also played a role in establishing the Cleveland and American Federations of Labor and the United Trade & Labor Council in Cleveland. The *CLEVELAND CITIZEN*, the oldest labor newspaper in Ohio, was established with Local No. 4's assistance. The *Cleveland Musician*, established and printed under the guidance of the Cleveland Fed. of Musicians Local No. 4, is the local's official organ. Local No. 4 has traditionally maintained a strict discipline over its members. Those members who were found to be in violation of the union's constitution or bylaws were fined and penalized. Harsh warnings appear frequently in issues of the *Cleveland Mu-*

*sician*, reminding its members to carry their union cards and to maintain the minimum-wage standard.

Cleveland Fed. of Musicians Local No. 4 Records, WRHS.

The **CLEVELAND FEMALE ORPHAN ASYLUM**, incorporated on 3 Apr. 1837, was apparently a short-lived attempt to help orphaned young girls in the area. It was established by a group of about 13 women from Trinity Church, including Laura Willey, Martha Kendall, and Sophia K. Ford, but its method of operation and how long the asylum existed are unclear. The Cleveland Female Orphan Asylum is mentioned in only the 1837 city directory; later directories list no other institutions specifically for orphans until the establishment of the Orphans' Asylum on St. Clair St. in 1852. Roderic H. Peirce's history of TRINITY CATHEDRAL mentions the Cleveland Female Orphan Asylum as the predecessor to the Trinity Church Home for the Sick & Friendless, which was established in Mar. 1856, but gives no further details. The benevolent women of Trinity Church apparently established several other charitable endeavors in the interim.

The **CLEVELAND FEMALE SEMINARY**, a boarding and day school for girls, was a forerunner of colleges for women. Founded by Rev. Eli N. Sawtell, the seminary opened on 3 May 1854 (an earlier enterprise by the same name had been established in Apr. 1837). Rev. Sawtell and several leading citizens of Cleveland, including LEONARD CASE, JR., JAS. M. HOYT, John M. Woolsey, and Oliver Perry, had formed a joint stock company the preceding year to underwrite the venture. Prof. SAMUEL ST. JOHN was chosen as the first principal. Located in a new $50,000 building on Kinsman Ave. between Wallingford Ct. (E. 45th Pl.) and Sawtell (E. 51st) St., the school initially enrolled 120 students, who paid an annual tuition of $300. The seminary had 2 major departments, Preparatory (which admitted girls under 12 years of age) and Academic (for those over 12). Emphasis was placed on teaching both languages and science so students could acquire a wholesome mental discipline. The Preparatory Dept. offered courses in English, reading, science, history, arithmetic, drawing, penmanship, and Latin. The Academic courses, which were taken over a 4-year period, included algebra, physiology, chemistry, astronomy, zoology, botany, trigonometry, mental philosophy, natural philosophy, analytical geometry, political economy, mythology, and science of government. Optional courses in French, German, and Greek were offered. In 1865, a Telegraph Dept. was established to provide instruction in the principles of telegraphy for students in natural philosophy and chemistry. The seminary suffered financial setbacks in its early years and accumulated an increasing floating debt. In 1863, Prof. Solomon N. Sanford purchased the school, at which time it became a private enterprise. It was reincorporated in 1871 as the Cleveland Seminary for Girls, and at this time acquired the rights and privileges of a college, including the authority to grant degrees. In 1868, the seminary opened a branch on Euclid Ave. for day students. That branch closed in 1874. The school closed in 1883 as a result of continuing financial problems.

The **CLEVELAND FIRE DEPARTMENT** evolved from the village's first firefighting organization, the Live Oaks No. 1 volunteer fire association, which formed in 1829. The first hand-operated fire engine in the village had been purchased in 1829. Prior to that, the only firefighting equipment available had been cisterns and buckets. The city's first regularly organized firefighting company followed in

1834, when the volunteer company Eagle No. 1 was established. Capt. John McCurdy was Eagle's first foreman. Further development was rapid, and by 1835 there were 4 volunteer fire companies, including 2 engine companies, a hook-and-ladder company, and a hose company. The first chief of the volunteer department was Samuel Cook.

By 1853 the department had grown to include 8 engine companies and a hook-and-ladder company. Growth of the department was not uneventful. Many volunteer companies were organized and disbanded in this time. In addition, several serious fires caused considerable damage in the growing city in the late 1850s. The CIVIL WAR contributed to the disruption of the volunteer department. Fully two-thirds of Cleveland's volunteer firemen served in the armed forces. With these factors in mind, the city council in 1863 authorized a paid steam fire department of 53 men. Jas. A. Craw was chief engineer. At that time the city owned 4 steam pumping engines and a hook and ladder. In 1864 a fifth steam engine was purchased, and a fire alarm telegraph system was installed. The city's system of water mains was also under construction. In 1865 there were 167 fire hydrants and 75 reservoirs throughout the city.

The next several decades saw the department grow steadily in an effort to keep pace with the growing city. By 1873 it had 147 members. It was a time of technological advancement, also. In 1875 the city purchased its first piston pump fire engine. The first use of suspended harness and the purchase of the department's first aerial ladder occurred in 1877. In 1880 newly appointed chief Jas. Dickinson reorganized the 17 existing companies into 3 battalions. The first sliding poles were used in 1881, and in 1882 the city purchased 5 new engines and an extension ladder that could extend 85 ft. Despite these strides, the department was barely able to keep up with the growth of the city. In 1884 2 disastrous fires caused widespread destruction in the FLATS. Much new equipment was purchased as a result of these fires, including the department's first fireboat, the *Joseph L. Weatherly*. By 1893 the department had 287 members in 18 engine companies, 7 hook-and-ladder companies, and a hose company. This period was one of remarkable growth for the department. New men and equipment were added at a steady rate. By 1909 the department had grown to over 500 men.

In 1901 GEO. A. WALLACE was named chief. He had joined the department in 1869 and would serve as chief until 1931, a career of over 61 years. At the time of his retirement, he was considered America's best-known firefighter. Growth of the fire department continued into the 1930s, when it reached a strength of over 1,400 members. In 1930 the 13-battalion department responded to over 8,800 alarms. While the size of the department remained relatively stable for the next several decades, the number of alarms rose steadily. In 1963 the 1,250-member department answered over 14,000 alarms. In 1975, with 1,190 members, the department responded to over 35,000 alarms. In 1963 7 firefighters were killed in the line of duty, including 4 in the downtown explosion of a leaking propane gas truck on 13 Aug. It was both the worst single disaster and the largest number of firemen killed in a single year in the department's history. On 4 Aug. 1966 4 firefighters were killed and 8 injured in an explosion at Metallurgical, Inc. In 1963 Wm. E. Barry was appointed chief. He served until 1981.

The **CLEVELAND FOLK ARTS ASSOCIATION**, an organization dedicated to the preservation and public display of traditional songs, dances, and crafts within Cleveland's various ethnic and racial groups, was formed in 1950 by the 24 nationality groups that organized the first annual Cleveland Folk Arts Festival on 28 Jan. 1950 at the Music Hall. The purpose of the association was "to gather and disseminate information through the media of arts and literature what each nationality, racial and cultural group had contributed and is contributing to the United States of America." The first officers of the association were Theodore Andrica, president; municipal judge Louis Petrash, vice-president; Margaret Fergusson, secretary; and Frances Tesny, treasurer. Andrica, for many years the nationalities editor for the *CLEVELAND PRESS*, still served as president when the association and the *Press* cosponsored the 30th annual Cleveland Folk Arts Festival at Lakewood Civic Auditorium on 2 Nov. 1980. In each of those 30 years, more than 500 performers, dressed in traditional costumes, presented songs and dances from their native lands; through 1980, more than 128 local groups had participated in the festival.

In addition to the folk arts festival, the association undertook other projects to call attention to the traditional arts. In Mar. 1952 it began publishing the *Folk Arts News*, a newsletter publicizing the festival and other events in the various local ethnic communities. More important, in 1960 it used the proceeds from festival ticket sales to establish the Folk Arts Corner in the Foreign Language Div. at the CLEVELAND PUBLIC LIBRARY. The association purchased several display cases, in which were exhibited traditional costumes and craftwork donated by association members or other groups.

Andrica, Theodore, *Thirtieth Anniversary Folk Festival* (1980).
Theodore Andrica Papers, 1928–1956. WRHS.

The **CLEVELAND FORCE SOCCER TEAM** proved to be the city's most consistently successful professional sports organization in the late 1970s and early 1980s. Riding on increased interest in the sport of soccer in the U.S., the Force debuted with the Major Indoor Soccer League in 1978. Playing a modified version of the outdoor game, the Force held their home games at the Richfield Coliseum in rural Summit County. The season began in October and ran for 24 games through April. The first season produced a losing record on both the field (5–19) and the balance sheet. The club could not fill the coliseum's 17,217 seats or sell even 1 season ticket. Like many other new sport franchises, the Force had trouble establishing recognition and attracting attention. Original franchisee Eric Henderson held out for the first year but was forced to sell the team during the off-season. The purchasers were the Wolstein family. Bart Wolstein became the president and his son, Scott, the executive vice-president. The Wolsteins set about to make the team a contender in the MISL and, hence, profitable. While the league established its credibility and expanded its schedule, from 32 games in the 1979–80 season to 48 in 1982–83, the Wolsteins acquired the best players available. The nucleus of a contender was formed with the signing of forward Keith Furphy in 1981 and forward Craig Allen, midfielder Kai Haaskivi, and goalie Chris Vaccaro in 1982. One casualty, however, was original coach Eddie McCreadie. He moved to the team's front office and was replaced by Timo Liekoski. Liekoski and the new players changed the Force's fortunes. In the 4 seasons under Liekoski (1982–83 to 1985–86), the Force compiled a regular-season record of 114–78 and reached the MISL championship playoffs every year. The last 2 years the team was eliminated from the playoffs only in the semifinals. The Force currently (1986) holds one of the best records in the league. The improved quality of play and active marketing of the team began to pay off in terms of increased fan interest and attendance. Ticket sales climbed to nearly 400,000 in 1985–86, including 2,500 season tickets. The team's consistent winning record, contrasted with those of the other professional sports franchises in the area, generated a great deal of excitement among sports enthusiasts, especially during the 1984–85 and 1985–86 playoffs. Clevelanders, anxious to have a winning sports club, found a team they could cheer.

The **CLEVELAND FOUNDATION**, the pioneer community trust in America, was the creation of FREDERICK H. GOFF. Goff, a distinguished lawyer and president of the Cleveland Trust Co. (see AMERITRUST), was concerned about the obsolescence of wills and trust funds that made no provision for changing circumstances. Impressed with the philosophy of Sir Arthur Hobhouse (London, 1880), who advocated that property be managed by the "living hand" through public tribunal rather than by the dead hand, Goff created and structured his community trust to alleviate these problems. Accordingly, the Cleveland Foundation was established on 2 Jan. 1914 under the trusteeship of the Cleveland Trust Co. Throughout its history, the foundation has been guided by 4 main principles: (1) Its funds are the union of numerous gifts of various sizes left at different times by a variety of donors. (2) These funds are placed in the custody of local financial institutions, which are trustees of the Cleveland Foundation. These institutions invest the funds for the foundation. (3) The income from the funds is disbursed by a distribution committee of 5 having a membership that changes by rotation of appointments; 2 are appointed by the trustee institutions and 3 by public officials. (4) Any contributor may designate his or her preferred charity, and his or her wishes will be observed unless changing conditions make such purposes unnecessary, undesirable, impractical, or impossible. Several changes have occurred in the foundation's operations during its history. Multiple trusteeships were inaugurated in 1931, in which additional banks became trustees, therefore giving wider service to potential donors. This program was again expanded in 1955. In 1943 the foundation established a combined fund, under which memorials and small gifts could be made to the foundation, with these gifts retaining their identity though they were commingled for investment purposes. In 1967 the Cleveland Foundation and the Greater Cleveland Associated Foundation combined their staffs in an effort to increase the effectiveness of foundation philanthropy in Greater Cleveland. The two foundations, however, continue to exist as legally separate entities, and their differing purposes are observed.

Pledges to the foundation during its first year totaled $40,000. However, expendable funds were not generated until 1919. Funds from Goff's personal wealth and monies from the Cleveland Trust Co. were used to underwrite the foundation's activities during this early period. These consisted principally of a series of surveys, the most important of which were the Cleveland School Survey of 1916 and the criminal justice survey of 1921–23 (see CRIME). The recommendations put forth by these surveys had a significant effect within the respective areas. By 1923, the assets of the fund were $367,452, and $7,637 was distributed. In 1979, the total market value of the fund was $202,390,308, and over $14,000,000 was distributed. This growth was attributable not only to wise investment and the continuing generosity of donors, but also to support from several other large funds, including the Ford Foundation and the Hanna Fund. Thirteen trusts of over $1 million each, plus a large combined fund trust including many small and medium-sized gifts, enhance the foundation. Funds from the foundation have been used to support innumerable organizations and activities as diverse as the GREAT LAKES EX-POSITION and the CLEVELAND COMMISSION ON HIGHER EDUCATION. Cultural activities such as the CLEVELAND ORCHESTRA, the CLEVELAND BALLET, and the CLEVELAND OPERA have also benefited. Almost every educational organization in the Greater Cleveland area has had programs funded through the foundation. Currently, monies from the Cleveland Foundation are distributed on a statewide basis, with the largest portion (35%) being allocated to health-oriented programs and institutions.

Cleveland Foundation Records, WRHS.
Howard, Nathaniel R., *Trust for All Time* (1963).
Miggins, Edward M., "Businessmen, Pedagogues, and Progressive Reform: The Cleveland Foundation's 1915 School Survey" (Ph.D. diss., CWRU, 1975).

The **CLEVELAND FREE SCHOOL**, or Colored Free School, was organized by a committee of black citizens who were concerned about the lack of educational opportunities for Cleveland's black children between 1832 and the early 1850s. The school, open intermittently during the period in several locations, also helped to educate adults whose education had been banned in southern states. In 1832, JOHN MALVIN, a black citizen who had arrived in Cleveland only a year earlier, called together a group of black men, including John Brown, a prosperous barber, David Smith, and Alexander Bowman. The group met to find some way to rally support for a school for blacks in Cleveland, since a state law passed in 1829 specifically prohibited their attendance in tax-supported schools. The small group succeeded in instituting a subscription system of monthly payments from black citizens of the city. John H. Hudson, a white mill owner, granted the group the use of one of his mill rooms for school purposes. Later the school was held in Millers Block on Superior just west of W. 3rd St. Guaranteeing a salary of $20 per month, the school secured a "half-breed" Indian to teach. He was replaced by a young white woman, Clarissa Wright, who was forced to resign because of illness, and later a young black man, Matthew M. Clark.

Three-month sessions, over a period of 3 or 4 years, were managed by the small group of subscribers. However, the need for a more comprehensive approach to the matter of education for blacks in Ohio became apparent to the small Cleveland group. In 1835, Malvin convened a state convention in Columbus, which led to the formation of a formal organization, the School Fund Society, which succeeded in sponsoring schools in Cleveland, Columbus, Cincinnati, and Springfield. The state group also persistently attacked exclusive state laws. In 1848, a law was passed providing for the use of tax monies collected from colored taxpayers in towns where there were 20 or more black schoolchildren to be used to maintain black community-directed separate schools. In districts where there were fewer than 20 black schoolchildren, the schools would be integrated. The original Cleveland city charter of 1835 stated that schools were to be "accessible to all white children." However, after first refusing to subsidize an all-black school in 1843, the city council assigned limited funds to the struggling private black organization. The city schools were completely integrated by 1850 and remained so until well into the 20th century.

The **CLEVELAND GATHERER** was a weekly newspaper of 6 columns introduced in Dec. 1841 by a partnership identified as Bagley & Fisher. Also known as the *Gatherer & Weekly News Scroll*, it professed temperance and "independent politics." It was edited by Edward Burke Fisher and managed to survive for at least a year, by which time Fisher was also the sole apparent proprietor.

The **CLEVELAND GATLING GUN BATTERY** was an independent military organization formed by prominent Clevelanders who were concerned about the maintenance of law and order in the city in the face of increasing labor disorders in the late 1870s. Although placed on alert several times, the unit was never called into action. A citizens' committee to plan for the battery began after the labor disorders in 1877. Using funds contributed to it, the committee purchased 2 Gatling guns and then issued a call for volunteers to man the guns. At a June 1878 meeting in the mayor's office, the Cleveland Gatling Gun Battery was established with 25 charter members. Among its initial members were Maj. W. F. Goodspeed, elected captain; 1st sergeant Thos. Goodwillie; 2d sergeant Leonard C. Hanna (later captain, 1882–93); 3d sergeant John R. Ranney; and quartermaster J. Ford Evans. On 6 Mar. 1880 the Ohio legislature enacted a bill to authorize Cleveland citizens to establish a Gatling gun battery, placed it under control of the mayor in emergencies and made it subject to the regulations governing Ohio Natl. Guard units. The unit was incorporated on 17 May 1880. An armory was constructed at E. Prospect and Sibley (3433 Carnegie). In 1885 the battery had 2 guns (valued with caissons at $2,500), 80 sabers, and 1 revolver. It billed the city $242 for the services of its members on guard during the iron workers' strike at Newburgh, 8–13 and 17–21 July 1885, and in 1896 it again billed the city, requesting $260 for "services rendered" 3–11 July. The majority of the unit's activities appear to have been social events; its annual target practice, for example, was held at such resorts as St. Clair Springs, Mich., and Chautauqua Lake, N.Y., and included dances and other social occasions. In April the battery's members voted to establish the 2d Div. of the 2d Battalion of the Ohio Naval Reserves, and members so desiring enlisted in that unit. In June 1897, the battery charter was amended to make its new purpose one of maintaining the battery's property and promoting among members "reciprocal feelings of mutual benefit and social intercourse" and "the spirit of military excellence." The Gatling Gun Battery was briefly reestablished as an independent military unit in 1900, but in Feb. 1905 the members voted to dispose of the battery's property. In Apr. 1924 the armory site was sold to Troop A for $33,000.

Cleveland Military Units Records, WRHS.

The *CLEVELAND GAZETTE* gave local blacks their own newspaper for the first time since before the CIVIL WAR. Although founded on 25 Aug. 1883 by a partnership of 4 men, within 3 years it had come under the sole control of its original managing editor, HARRY C. SMITH. By the time of Smith's death, it had become the longest-publishing black weekly in the U.S., earning its nickname "The Old Reliable" by never missing a Saturday publication date in 58 years. With Smith as editor and publisher, the *Gazette* exemplified personal journalism long after that commodity had disappeared from the daily press. Smith's causes became the *Gazette*'s causes, as he mobilized its 4 pages—"big enough when a newspaper is editorial all over," said the *Chicago Defender*—against segregated schools, minstrel shows, and the last of Ohio's "BLACK LAWS." Regarding the debate over vocational training versus college education, the *Gazette* recommended the latter whenever possible. In the spirit of an older age, Smith often engaged in printed debates with fellow editors, notably Wendell P.

Dabney of the *Cincinnati Union*. Circulation of the *Gazette* remained fairly constant at 5,000 for its first 20 years. Around WORLD WAR I, it was reported at 18,000, where it remained, perhaps somewhat inflated, until the end. It inhabited a succession of addresses in its lifetime, including Euclid and Superior avenues, W. 3rd St., and Smith's final headquarters at 2322 E. 30th St. Two constants were its 4-page format and its Republican allegiance, which not even the New Deal could sway. Following Smith's death on 10 Dec. 1941, the *Gazette* was continued for a time by his associate, Talbert White. Although gaps appear in the file, it surfaced in 1944 as a 12-page paper under the ownership of the Cleveland Publishing Co., with Dr. Geo. W. Brown as managing editor. Diminished to tabloid size, its final issue apparently appeared on 20 May 1945.

The **CLEVELAND GRAND ORCHESTRA** was a forerunner of the CLEVELAND ORCHESTRA. CONRAD MIZER, a local impresario, decided after the demise of the CLEVELAND SYMPHONY ORCHESTRA in 1902 to try a series of winter concerts. With the financial support of some prominent citizens, Mizer (as business manager and chairman of the executive committee) formed a new symphony, known alternately as the Cleveland Symphony Orchestra, the Cleveland Grand Orchestra, and the Cleveland Orchestra. The first program was held at GRAYS ARMORY on 4 Jan. 1903. The concert played to standing room only. American pianist Wm. Sherwood played Liszt's E-Flat Major Piano Concerto. Also on the program was Borodin's *Steppes of Central Asia*, Weber's overture to *Euryanthe*, a selection from *Carmen*, and the Wedding March from *A Midsummer Night's Dream*. JOHANN BECK and EMIL RING both conducted. A Sunday concert series was started in the summer and was held in HALTNORTH'S GARDENS. It proved successful. The price for a concert was $.10, $.15, or $.25. Mizer died suddenly in 1904; during that one season, the group was known as the Cleveland Orchestra. Also associated with the orchestra at that time was ADELLA PRENTISS HUGHES, who functioned as concert manager. Many soloists appeared, including Sol Marcosson, Wm. Becker, Grace Probert, and Francis Sadlier. Besides playing the standard literature, the orchestra played the works of local composers and songwriters, including JAS. H. ROGERS, Chas. Sommer, CHAS. V. RYCHLIK, Isabelle Beaton, Carl Groenwald, Fanny Snow Knowlton, and Albert Gehring. The Cleveland Grand Orchestra was the name adopted through 1909, when the group played citizens' pop concerts. The series then became the People's Symphony Orchestra, still conducted by Ring and Beck. The final program was given in Mar. 1912. The dissolution occurred, according to Adella Prentiss Hughes, because "the pops had begun to be monotonous."

**CLEVELAND GRAPHITE BRONZE.** *See* **CLEVITE**

The **CLEVELAND GRAPHITE BRONZE SEIZURE**, which occurred 6 Sept.–11 Nov. 1944, put the Cleveland Graphite Bronze Co. plants (see CLEVITE, GOULD) into the hands of the Army after a strike crippled war production there. It was the first war plant seizure in Ohio and only the fourth in the 5th Regional Jurisdiction of the War Labor Board (WLB). Cleveland Graphite Bronze, manufacturer of automotive and aircraft bearings, employed 2,500 at the onset of WORLD WAR II, with workers represented by the MECHANICS EDUCATIONAL SOCIETY OF AMERICA, an independent union known for its assertiveness in gaining recognition and rights for its workers. The company tried to anticipate union concerns by offering benefits, and prided itself on its familial labor relations, harmonious until 1940. Bickering over wages led to a series of strikes in 1940–41 that were brought before the Natl. Defense Mediation Board, but a major change in the climate at Graphite occurred after the company, to meet demands for its products, expanded its plant, hired 5,000 people, including women and furloughed soldiers, and ran 3 shifts per day. Vacations were canceled, and days off were limited to 1 in 7. Employees who took time off were subject to dismissal. Tensions ran high in the fatigued, poorly integrated workforce. MESA accused the company of exaggerating its percentage of war work to exploit employees. As a result, strikes became more frequent.

On 31 Aug. 1944, employee Elmer Torok was fired for allegedly breaking a 75-cent lock to gain entry to his locker. Although after subsequent investigations it is still unclear whether he lost his key or whether the lock was changed without notice, 5,000 struck. A statement issued by the company claimed that Torok's destruction of property was the last straw in a series of incidents involving him. The union countered that Torok's dismissal was their last straw, too, as at least 18 people had been fired over 2 years for petty causes. Torok offered to pay for the lock and key, but the company claimed he had tried to provoke a disciplinary action that would result in a work release (which he had been trying to get); MESA disputed this charge and asserted that the penalty was too harsh. The company refused to reinstate him and further charged that the union violated the law by striking rather than referring the matter to the WLB. The 5th Regional WLB, concerned about the effect on war production, referred the matter to the national WLB for action. Pres. Roosevelt issued an executive order that put the War Dept. in charge of Cleveland Graphite Bronze operations. As of 6 Sept., the company reopened, under a flag symbolizing federal authority and under the control of the Army, with Lt. Col. Geo. D. Lynn in charge. This action took the strike out of the hands of the WLB and made settlement a matter between the company, the Army, and the union, with the help of the Natl. Conciliation Service. MESA president Matthew Smith claimed victory for the strikers, as the MESA dispute with the company management was settled by the Army takeover. The trouble that erupted at Graphite was part of a broader battle being waged by MESA to fend off CIO raids on membership and to gain proper representation on the local and national WLB. Although CIO intrusion did not surface as an issue in the strike, the composition of the WLB was a rallying cry for MESA, which protested the empowerment of Mayor Frank Lausche to name arbiters. After the Army took control, the CIO did begin serious organizing efforts, which were not eliminated until an election was held in 1947 that gave MESA a decisive victory. After 2 months, when the Army felt that labor and management could again cooperate, the plant was released from military control. The Torok case was still in arbitration, but the seizure effectively neutralized it as an issue; when the U.S. Conciliation Service eventually decided for the company, the union took no further action.

The **CLEVELAND GRAYS** were an independent military organization when they were formed as the Cleveland City Guard on Washington's birthday, 22 Feb. 1837. The Grays eventually fought as a unit in the CIVIL WAR, the SPANISH-AMERICAN WAR, the Mexican Border Dispute in 1916–17, and WORLD WAR I. They have also served at ceremonial functions and have annually held a parade on or near George Washington's birthday. Organized with 74 active members and 44 associate members, the Grays reportedly were the first uniformed troops west of the Allegheny Mts. The unit changed its name from the Cleveland City Guard on 7 June 1838, when the members adopted a gray, Colonial-style uniform; they later adopted bearskin shakos as their headdress. Under the command of Capt. Timothy Ingram from 1837–53, the unit held a number of military exercises, such as its first encampment, 3–7 July 1839, on the outskirts of the city at Superior and E. 9th streets. Such exercises were as much social events as military practices; they often included parades and a visiting military unit from another city, as well as drilling. The Grays also organized other units in their early years, such as a gun squad in 1839 that in 1845 became the CLEVELAND LIGHT ARTILLERY, and a band in 1840 that reportedly was the first in the city. Taking the motto "Always Ready," the Grays were the first Clevelanders to fight in the Civil War. Mustered into service on 16 Apr. 1861, and serving as the 1st Co., 1st Regiment, Ohio Volunteer Infantry, they first saw action at Bull Run and served throughout most of the war. As an independent unit, the Grays had difficulty getting into the Spanish-American War; the federal government favored the use of Natl. Guard units, and it took a special act of the Ohio legislature to create a battalion of engineers to muster the Grays into the Ohio Natl. Guard as the 3d Battalion, 10th OVI. After serving for 9 months, the Grays were reorganized as an independent unit after the war; the unit thus had to join the Natl. Guard again in 1916 to fight in the Mexican border dispute and remained in the Natl. Guard to take part in World War I as the 148th Infantry, 37th Div. The unit again became independent after the war. During WORLD WAR II and subsequent conflicts, the Grays served in the armed forces not as a unit but as individuals.

In addition to their military service, the Cleveland Grays have often served at public ceremonies, and have participated in many celebrations and parades locally and in other cities. From their earliest days, the Grays have also been a social organization, holding their first reception and military ball on 23 Jan. 1839. Their various armories over the years have served as social centers. The present GRAYS ARMORY, built in 1893 at 1234 Bolivar Rd., has hosted a variety of events, from the Metropolitan Opera (1902) to the first local automobile show (1903). The Grays became less of a military organization after World War II, turning over the shooting range in the basement of their armory to the CLEVELAND POLICE DEPT. and dropping the military-service requirement for membership. In 1972, the Grays and the Western Reserve Theater Organ Society began to cosponsor regular concerts on the armory's refurbished Wurlitzer organ, and in 1974 efforts were launched to establish the Cleveland Grays Military Museum. In 1980, the Cleveland Grays Armory was placed on the Natl. Register of Historic Places, and in 1985 the 250 members of the ceremonial unit began a campaign to raise $2.5 million for repairs and restoration of the building.

The **CLEVELAND GREENHOUSE VEGETABLE GROWERS' COOPERATIVE ASSOCIATION** is an organization designed to help the Cleveland-area greenhouse vegetable industry by funding scientific research, providing marketing information to growers, and promoting locally grown products to consumers. The association was formed in 1926 as the Cleveland Hothouse Vegetable Growers' Cooperative Assoc.; the name of the group was changed in 1949. The 19 growers who founded the organization had a total of 25 acres of land under glass in 1926; by 1937 there were 225 acres of greenhouses in the Cleveland area. The organization had about 100 members in 1956 and was active in national and local legislation, research, and the distribution of seeds, the purchase and supply of greenhouse materials, and the promotion of greenhouse-grown products. By the mid-1950s the association boasted that the Cleveland area, with 350 acres of greenhouses, had "the third largest concentration of greenhouses" in the U.S. and the third-largest in the world. Of the Cleveland greenhouse crop, 80% was tomatoes, 10% was lettuce, and the other 10% was split evenly between watercress and cucumbers.

The local industry had grown to more than 400 acres and a $10 million annual income by 1961. Between 1957–67, the association spent $70,000 on research; in 1951 the group spearheaded a drive within the Ohio. Vegetable Growers' Assoc. that donated an $18,000 greenhouse to the Ohio Agricultural Experiment Station at Wooster. But in the late 1960s and 1970s, the local industry declined. The energy crisis and the increasing cost of natural gas and oil made greenhouses more expensive to maintain, and the number of acres under glass fell from 250 in 1973 to 75 in 1982 and 60 in 1984. In 1983 the association began to explore new marketing strategies to improve sales, and in Jan. 1985 it launched an advertising campaign for Western Reserve Gourmet Cucumbers, followed later by a similar campaign for tomatoes.

The **CLEVELAND HADASSAH** (est. 1913) was the third national chapter of the Women's Zionist Organization formed in the U.S. On 25 June 1913, a small group of women met in the home of Dr. Isidore and Kate Biskind to hear the founder of Hadassah, Henrietta Szold, call for the organization of a Cleveland chapter. A week later, 21 charter members established the Shoshana Chap. By the end of the year, the Cleveland group had enrolled 400 members, and by 1919 membership was over 1,000. Prior to the formation of the Cleveland chapter, Rachel Landy, a local nurse, was sent to Palestine along with Rose Kaplan of New York by the New York and Baltimore chapters to conduct district nursing visits. Landy and Kaplan established the first Hadassah House nursing center in the Mea Shearim section of Jerusalem. Out of their efforts grew the Hadassah Medical Organization, which became and remains the focus for Hadassah fundraising. Elsa Rogat served as Cleveland Hadassah's first president. During her 2-year tenure, Hadassah established Hebrew classes for members and instituted the annual dinner dance and raffle for fundraising. Kate Biskind served as president from 1915–19 and broadened the fundraising activities as Hadassah participated in the Zionist Organization of America's Palestine Restoration Fund drives. Biskind resigned in 1919 to move to Palestine, where her husband became the first director of the Hadassah Medical Unit.

Although American Zionism suffered a serious schism at the ZOA CONVENTION OF 1921, Cleveland Hadassah (as well as the Natl. Hadassah) continued to grow. In 1923, the Jr. Hadassah was established for young women. It enrolled 80 members during its first year. During the mid-1920s, the Cleveland Hadassah received an award from the Natl. Hadassah for the largest proportional increase in membership among all the chapters. Cleveland Hadassah, as part of the national effort, raised funds and provided material aid for the war-stricken populace of Jerusalem during and after World War I; established a program for adoption of Palestinian Jewish orphans; and sold war bonds during World War II. In 1935, Cleveland hosted the national Hadassah convention, at which the Youth Aliyah program to assist German Jewish children to immigrate to Palestine was established. Besides offering Hebrew classes for members, Hadassah provided Zionist study groups, discussion groups on cultural and political topics, and various social activities. In the area of fundraising, the Cleveland chapter innovated nationally the donor luncheon, which became a major source of funds. In civic affairs, Hadassah

has been active in making health kits for the Head Start program and has offered tutorial services at Glenville High School. In 1963, Cleveland Hadassah had over 6,000 members, a figure that has decreased only slightly since that time.

Hadassah Records, WRHS.

The **CLEVELAND HALL OF FAME** consists of deceased individuals from the Greater Cleveland area who received national or international acclaim. It was unveiled at Cleveland's PUBLIC SQUARE on 22 July 1971 as the highlight of the city's 175th birthday. The idea for the Hall of Fame was conceived by Ruth Ketteringham, a trustee of the EARLY SETTLERS ASSOC. OF THE WESTERN RESERVE. Under the auspices of the association, Ketteringham was appointed chairman of the project. A selection committee was assembled, consisting of local experts in various fields and officers of the Early Settlers Assoc. Persons selected to the Hall of Fame must be listed in *The Dictionary of American Biography* and must have died at least 25 years before selection. At the unveiling in 1971, there were 29 names. They were NEWTON D. BAKER, CHAS. F. BRUSH, LEONARD CASE, JR., CHAS. W. CHESNUTT, MOSES CLEAVELAND, Dr. HARVEY K. CUSHING, JAS. A. GARFIELD, CAESAR A. GRASSELLI, MARCUS A. HANNA, JOHN M. HAY, MYRON T. HERRICK, TOM L. JOHNSON, ALFRED KELLEY, JARED POTTER KIRTLAND, SAMUEL L. MATHER, Dr. ALBERT A. MICHELSON, Prof. EDWARD W. MORLEY, Oliver Hazard Perry, JAS. FORD RHODES, JOHN D. ROCKEFELLER, EDWARD W. SCRIPPS, AMBROSE SWASEY, CHAS. F. THWING, MANTIS J. VAN SWERINGEN, ORIS P. VAN SWERINGEN, JEPTHA WADE, ARTEMUS WARD, and ARCHIBALD M. WILLARD. After the unveiling in July, black-and-white portraits of the honorees were displayed by the MAY CO. A similar exhibition, featuring 29 oil paintings, ran at the WESTERN RESERVE HISTORICAL SOCIETY between August and September. In 1972, the black-and-white portraits went on permanent display in the new Utilities Bldg. at Lakeside and 12th. In 1981, the permanent exhibit was moved to the back wall of the city hall rotunda, and 7 new names were added: GEO. W. CRILE, Thos. Alva Edison, Chas. Martin Hall, Adm. Ernest J. King, Wm. McKinley, RUFUS P. RANNEY, and ALEXANDER WINTON. The committee plans to add new names every 5 years.

The **CLEVELAND HARMONIC SOCIETY** was one of the earliest musical organizations in Cleveland. The society was organized in 1835 by 7 amateur instrumental performers. Its emphasis soon shifted to choral music; it was one of 2 such societies that existed in Cleveland in the mid-1830s. In 1837, the society gave a number of concerts under the leadership of G. W. Pratt. A spring concert in 1839 presented 26 pieces, including works by Handel and Haydn. The Harmonic Society was one of the few choral groups in Cleveland in the mid-19th century of non-German origin; it was categorized as an English choral society. It was also one of the few choral societies in Cleveland to survive the CIVIL WAR. In 1870 it participated in a concert by the Theodore Thomas Orchestra, in which it supplied the choral section for Beethoven's *Choral Fantasy*. The following year the society performed *Martha* with the Germania Orchestra. The performance was repeated later that year at a benefit for sufferers of the Chicago fire. Other performances from this time included Mendelssohn's *Elijah* and a grand opera. The Cleveland Harmonic Society (not to be confused with the Cleveland Harmonic Club) faded in the

1870s with the emergence of the CLEVELAND VOCAL SOCIETY.

The **CLEVELAND HEALTH EDUCATION MUSEUM** is a nonprofit institution devoted to educating the public in matters of health. It was the first permanent health museum in the country. The museum was incorporated on 28 Dec. 1936. It officially opened on 13 Nov. 1940 through the efforts of the ACADEMY OF MEDICINE in Cleveland in cooperation with area medical, dental, public-health, civic, and cultural organizations. Its original purpose was to portray the advances made in medical and health science, and to promote personal and community hygiene.

The original incorporators of the Health Museum were Dr. Lester Taylor, Dr. Hubert C. King, Dr. Jas. A. Doull, Howard W. Green, and H. Van Y. Caldwell. It was, and continues to be, governed by a board of trustees, of which Dr. Lester M. Stecher was chairman until 1972. Dr. Bruno Gebhard, an eminent authority on hygiene, was the museum's first director. Lowell F. Bernard succeeded him in 1970. The Health Museum's early emphasis was on 3-dimensional health exhibits, classes in health education, group tours, and special film showings. Its main focus, however, was on its exhibits. Many of these were inherited from the American Museum of Health in New York, which had exhibited at the 1939 World's Fair. Others came from individual donors, which included Robt. Latou Dickinson's 100-piece collection of birth models, added in 1945. These exhibits have always been of 2 kinds: permanent ones on human biology, and temporary ones dealing with current medical and health problems.

Since its founding, the museum has engaged in a program of steady expansion. Its original home was at 8811 Euclid Ave., a gift of Elisabeth S. Prentiss, who also established $420,000 in trust funds for the museum and a national award for public service in the health-education field. In 1945 the museum acquired the 43-room Treadway mansion at 8911 Euclid Ave.; it was completely remodeled in the early 1970s through a $2.5 million expansion program that included the addition of 2 new wings. In 1969 the Health Museum divided into 2 main functions: a museum and an educational center. At this time it began to place heavier emphasis on its educational aspects. The old museum was remodeled to include 13 self-contained classrooms, each with its own exhibits, supplementary audiovisual equipment, and materials relating to specific subject matter, such as "The Five Senses," "Nutrition," "Human Reproduction," and "Drug Addiction." By 1978 over 50,000 schoolchildren a year were receiving 2 hours of instruction from 15 health educators. Other programs, aimed at adults and families, included workshops on aging, and health and safety in sports. This focus on education continued into the 1980s.

The **CLEVELAND HEALTH SCIENCES LIBRARY** was created in Feb. 1965 by the action of Western Reserve University and the CLEVELAND MEDICAL LIBRARY ASSOC. By an agreement signed at that time, the university's libraries of medicine, dentistry, and nursing were joined with the library of the association in an administrative entity controlled by a joint trustee committee and a joint executive council, and advised on operations by a joint advisory council. Both founding organizations retain their individual independence as legally constituted organizations. The libraries involved had existed in close physical proximity for many years, and there was considerable duplication of collections. In addition, the university health-sciences libraries had some strengths that were complemented by those of the Library Assoc., and vice versa. The

creation of the administrative entity discouraged duplication of resources. Through the combining and streamlining of their operations, both libraries were improved.

The Cleveland Health Sciences Library began formal operations on 1 July 1966 under the direction of Robt. G. Cheshier. In 1971 the libraries of the university departments of biology and nutrition were added. In 1972, all of the university libraries involved were physically combined in the Health Ctr. Library, located in Sears Tower, 2119 Abington Rd., adjacent to the health-sciences schools of the university. The Cleveland Medical Library Assoc. collection remained in the Allen Memorial Medical Library at 11000 Euclid Ave., where it has been since 1926. While the collection at the Health Ctr. Library is primarily for students and faculty, that at the Allen Library is oriented toward the needs of the practicing health-sciences professional. The Allen collection also has a large historical component, including rare books, an archives, and the HOWARD DITTRICK MUSEUM OF HISTORICAL MEDICINE. In 1986, the Health Sciences Library served the needs of a health-sciences faculty of approximately 1,100, a student body of about 1,200, and at least 2,000 practitioners in the local area. It is a designated resource library for northeast Ohio under the Regional Medical Library Program of the Natl. Library of Medicine, and a major lender of materials to other libraries. It also provides direct staff assistance to many area hospital libraries.

The **CLEVELAND HEBREW SCHOOLS** are a community afternoon supplemental school for instruction in Hebrew. The nondenominational school is principally involved in teaching Hebrew to children who do not attend Jewish day schools and whose parents want more Hebrew than can be gained from the Sunday school curriculum of the congregations. The school traces its origins to the creation of the Sir Moses Montefiore Hebrew School in 1885. This Talmud Torah, located at Broadway and Cross Sts., served 50 children from primarily poor families. The school offered the rudiments of Hebrew and religious studies. In 1890, the school was reorganized and later moved to E. 35th St. In 1904–05, its income was only $3,800, derived from tuition, contributions, seat rental in its synagogue, and the sale of Manischewitz matzoh at Passover. The Hebrew Schools held the local distribution rights for Passover matzoh for several years.

The Talmud Torah received a boost in the first decade of the century when Jules Flock and Aaron Garber, who previously operated a competing school, joined the staff. Their innovative approach to Hebrew instruction changed the method from rote learning to an organic approach in which Hebrew became the language of use for all school activities. The Bible and Hebrew were taught in Hebrew and English. Yiddish, the first language of most of the pupils, was no longer employed. Another innovation was the introduction of modern Hebrew literature. Classes were held after public school, and depending on the age of the child, they ran well into the evening. During the summer, classes were all day.

Rabbi SAMUEL MARGOLIES of ANSHE EMETH CONGREGATION was the most outspoken proponent of the Talmud Torah during the 1910s. Under his direction, the student population increased, and the school became a center for Jewish cultural activity. Margolies was a Zionist leader in Cleveland, and under his direction the Hebrew Schools assumed a decidedly nationalist profile. Following Margolies's death in 1917, a campaign that he had started to raise funds for a large Talmud Torah building was continued. Its end product was the Cleveland Jewish Ctr. in GLENVILLE, which housed a branch of the Hebrew

Schools. In 1920, there was a branch in Glenville, which with the main school on E. 55th St. served nearly 900 students.

In 1921, ABRAHAM FRIEDLAND became superintendent of the school and led it through growth and decline and much controversy. By 1923, the student population had increased to 2,300, owing in great measure to Friedland's charismatic leadership. However, at the same time, Friedland was embroiled in a struggle with those who opposed his Zionist views and the nationalist tone of the school's curriculum. While Friedland was recognized nationally as a great educator, he was not as good an administrator. By 1926, the school faced a growing debt in excess of $60,000, and student enrollment was dropping. In 1929, the student body was 1,500; 7 years later it was only 716. A 1936 report on Jewish education noted that most Jews had moved from the old Woodland neighborhood and that of those remaining, 40% were on relief. That robbed the school of much of its tuition income base. In addition, the congregations that had relocated in Glenville, Kinsman, and the Heights were taking over much of the responsibility of Jewish Hebrew education. In 1948, there were 7 branches of the Cleveland Hebrew Schools. However, in the coming years, the proliferation of Jewish day schools and the continued offering by the congregations of afternoon Jewish Hebrew classes eventually led to the consolidation of the Cleveland Hebrew Schools' classes into locations at 25400 Fairmount Blvd. and (branch) 1690 Lander Rd.

Cleveland Hebrew School Records, WRHS.
Bureau of Jewish Education Records, WRHS.

**CLEVELAND HEIGHTS** is an incorporated city adjacent to Cleveland and 6 mi. east of downtown. It comprises 8 sq. mi. and is bounded on the north by E. CLEVELAND, on the east by S. EUCLID and UNIVERSITY HTS., and on the south by SHAKER HTS. Geologically, the heights to the east of Cleveland are the western edge of the Appalachian Plateau. The area occupied by Cleveland Hts. was originally farmland in E. Cleveland and S. Euclid townships. The oldest surviving house, built ca. 1820, stands on Superior Rd., and several early-19th-century farmhouses remain on Fairmount Blvd. and elsewhere in the city. In 1895, real-estate developers Patrick Calhoun and John Harkness Brown created the Euclid Hts. subdivision, conceived as a "garden suburb," north of Cedar Rd. and west of Coventry Rd. Other developments followed, including the Euclid Golf development at the western end of Fairmount Rd., Mayfield Hts. east of Coventry, and AMBLER HTS. between Cedar and N. Park Blvd. From the 1890s until well into the 20th century, the city was a "streetcar suburb," with lines running on Mayfield to Lee Rd., and up Cedar Hill and Fairmount to Taylor Rd.

The hamlet of Cleveland Hts. was created in 1901, and the village of Cleveland Hts. was incorporated in 1903 with a population of 1,500. The longest-serving mayor was Frank C. Cain, 1914–45. Cleveland Hts. became a city in 1921 and the same year established the first zoning ordinance in Ohio. In 1922, the council-city manager plan of government was adopted. A handsome Georgian Revival city hall was built in 1924; it was demolished in 1986 when a new city hall was built at SEVERANCE CTR. At the time of incorporation, a volunteer fire department was established. The public school system began in 1901 in the old E. Cleveland district school (1882) on Superior at Euclid Hts. Blvd. The high school started in 1904 with 2 classes. The first public library opened in 1911 in Coventry School. The public school system and the public library were later con-

solidated with those of University Hts. There are 10 elementary schools, 3 junior high and 1 senior high school, and 4 public library branches. There are also 2 parochial schools, a Baptist school, Lutheran East High School, the HEBREW ACADEMY, BEAUMONT SCHOOL, a school for learning-disabled children, and 2 MONTESSORI SCHOOLS. Between 1910–40, the population grew from 3,000 to 55,000. Street patterns and neighborhoods developed around the old established rural roads. Although there was no central downtown, the major shopping areas developed at Cedar and Lee, Fairmount and Cedar, and Mayfield and Coventry in the 1910s and 1920s. The Cedar-Taylor area became the center of a strong Jewish community in the 1920s. Cleveland Hts. has 135 acres of public parks and began to develop its extensive park system early, passing a bond issue in 1916 for the purchase of parkland. FOREST HILL PARK, covering 60 acres and formerly the summer home of JOHN D. ROCKEFELLER, was donated by John D., Jr., in 1938 and is jointly administered by the cities of Cleveland Hts. and E. Cleveland. Cain Park was developed in the ravine along Superior Rd. between Lee and Taylor roads. There are recreational areas and picnic grounds, and Cain Park is most widely known for its outdoor theater complex (see CAIN PARK THEATER), built by the WPA and opened for its first season of theater, music, and community programs in 1938. There are 2 municipal swimming pools and an ice-skating pavilion in the city.

The headquarters of the AUSTIN CO. and MEDUSA CORP. are located in the city. Severance Ctr., one of the earliest and largest enclosed regional shopping centers, was built in 1963 on the site of the JOHN L. SEVERANCE estate after much controversy. However, there is no industry in the city, and 76% of the land is used for residential purposes. A large proportion of the residents are professional, including university faculty, museum curators, CLEVELAND ORCHESTRA members, and doctors and lawyers. In 1970, the population was 60,767; there were roughly equal numbers of Catholics, Protestants, and Jews. In 1960, black residents made up less than 1% of the population, but in the 1960s and 1970s a sizable immigration of black families occurred. The Real Estate Advisory Committee to the State was formed, and the Heights Community Congress, representing 200 groups, was organized to facilitate racial integration. There was a dispersed pattern of homebuying, and Cleveland Hts. developed a high percentage of racially integrated neighborhoods. In 1980, the population fell to 56,907, including 41,192 whites, 14,061 BLACKS, 59 native Americans, 674 Asians, 469 Hispanics, and 452 others. In 1970, 73% of those 25 or older were high school graduates; by 1980, the percentage had increased to 83.4%. There are approximately 13,000 single-family residences, nearly 2,000 duplex and multifamily dwellings, and more than 200 commercial structures, including a number of professional buildings. Many religious and professional groups were established in the city. A Carmelite monastery, the JEWISH COMMUNITY CTR., and YMCA and YWCA branches are located in the city. There are also the MONTEFIORE HOME FOR THE AGED, the MARGARET WAGNER HOUSE of the BENAJMIN ROSE INSTITUTE, and more than 25 nursery and daycare centers. There are 2 Roman Catholic churches, a Greek Orthodox church, several synagogues, including Eric Mendelsohn's nationally known PARK SYNAGOGUE, and Protestant churches of many denominations.

The **CLEVELAND HERALD** was the second attempt by Ormond A. Forte to found a black newspaper. Like Forte's

*Cleveland Advocate* (1914–24), it attempted to reconcile the self-help tradition of the older black leadership with the more aggressive tactics of a newer generation. Begun in 1925 as a campaign paper, the *Herald* outlasted the campaign by 2 years before the withdrawal of backing forced its suspension. Forte returned to publishing ca. 1935 with the *Cleveland Eagle*, which he established and continued to 1938. Shortly thereafter he revived the *Herald* and managed to keep this reincarnation alive for over a decade. Originally a 16-page tabloid, by 1946 the *Herald* was an extremely well-printed, full-sized weekly of 8 pages. Essentially it was also a 1-man operation, although Forte occasionally acknowledged the assistance of an associate editor or business manager. In politics he kept the *Herald* fairly solidly Republican. Reverting to tabloid size in 1949, the *Herald* raised its price from 5 to 10 cents a few months later. Incorporation as Ohio Daily Enterprise may have brought Forte fresh capital, for on 4 July 1950, the *Herald* celebrated the acquisition of its own printing press with a 46-page "Negro Achievement" Edition featuring thumbnail sketches of over 100 prominent black Clevelanders. By 1951, the *Herald* had cut back to 8 pages. However, by 1954, Forte evidently ended his last newspaper.

The ***CLEVELAND HERALD AND GAZETTE*** was first published on 19 Oct. 1819. It was the city's second newspaper and, after the death of the *Register* in 1820, its only newspaper for the next 7 years. It was founded by Eber D. Howe, who personally delivered the weekly to subscribers in a 2-day circuit on horseback to Painesville and back and often accepted payment in kind. After Howe's withdrawal in 1821, with circulation painfully built up to 300, the paper was published by its printer, A. Willes & Co. Willes ran the paper for several years, after which it was briefly operated by Jewett Paine and John R. St. John. Benjamin Andrews assumed control on 17 Apr. 1832. He dropped the *a* from the word *Cleaveland* in the paper's title and, in 1835, made the *Herald* Cleveland's first daily newspaper. In 1837, JOSIAH A. HARRIS and CHAS. WHITTLESEY purchased the *Herald* and combined it with the *CLEVELAND DAILY GAZETTE* as the *Herald & Gazette*. Whittlesey left the partnership in 1838, leaving Harris as sole editor of the *Herald*, which resumed its former name in 1843. Under Harris, the *Herald* established itself as the city's chief Whig organ, prospering in spite of its opposition to the MEXICAN AMERICAN WAR. It installed the city's first steam-power press in 1845 and moved into its own 4-story building on Bank (W. 6th) St. at the beginning of 1851. It was receiving news by telegraph by 1847 and, in conjunction with the *PLAIN DEALER*, arranged to receive the reports of the Associated Press from New York in 1854.

With the retirement of Harris in 1857, the *Herald* passed into the hands of GEO. A. BENEDICT and A. W. Fairbanks, Harris's partner since 1850. After the death of the Whigs, it switched its allegiance to the Republicans, but its support lagged behind that given to the newly formed *CLEVELAND LEADER*. While the *Leader* became an early proponent of emancipation in the CIVIL WAR, the *Herald* tried to hold the line as long as possible for the Crittenden resolution, which declared the war's sole purpose to be the preservation of the Union. By the time of Benedict's death in 1876, the *Leader* had passed the *Herald* as the city's leading newspaper. Fairbanks sold the paper in 1877 to RICHARD C. PARSONS and WM. P. FOGG, who organized the Herald Publishing Co. by the end of that year. Among the investors was MARCUS A. HANNA, who eventually assumed personal management of the paper after the withdrawal of Parsons in 1880. In a final attempt to keep up with the *Leader*, the *Herald* began a Sunday edition in 1877 and appointed Robt. S. Pierce as Cleveland's first sports editor. Hanna eventually wrote off the *Herald* as a bad investment and sold it in 1885 to the *Leader* and the *Plain Dealer*, which sealed its fate. Its name and subscription list went to the *Leader*, while the *Plain Dealer* moved into the *Herald* plant and immediately began issuing a morning edition with much of the *Herald*'s staff. Editorial writer John H. A. Bone wrote the *Herald*'s obituary, considered a local journalistic classic, in its final edition of 15 Mar. 1885.

Shaw, Archer H., *The Plain Dealer* (1942).

The **CLEVELAND HOME BREWING COMPANY** was organized in 1907 by Ernst W. Mueller (1851–1931). Mueller, a native of Bavaria, emigrated to Cleveland in 1856 and followed his father, Peter Mueller, in the malting business. In 1887 he purchased the Schmidt & Hoffman brewery at Hough and Ansel aves. and started the Cleveland Brewing Co. This company merged in 1897 with the Cleveland & Sandusky Brewing Co., of which Mueller became 2d vice-president and then, in 1901, president. In 1907 Mueller left Cleveland & Sandusky and purchased the Beltz Brewing Co. plant at 2501 E. 61st St. (at Outhwaite Ave.), which he enlarged and reequipped. Beltz family members remained associated with the new Cleveland Home Brewing Co., Joseph Beltz serving as vice-president and John J. Beltz as superintendent. Otto W. Beltz succeeded Ernst Mueller as president upon Mueller's death in 1931.

Cleveland Home Brewing stayed in business during Prohibition, manufacturing ice, malt liquid, and a beverage called "Yako." Ernst Mueller's son, Omar E., served as president from the mid-1930s until his death in 1947. Sales, meanwhile, gradually declined, from 111,000 barrels in 1945 to 35,000 barrels in 1951, the brewery's last year of operation. During its last years, ALESSANDRO L. DE-MAIORIBUS, Republican leader and one-time city councilman, served as president, general manager, and brewmaster. In 1952 the business was liquidated and its property sold at auction. Trade names of Cleveland Home Brewing Co. products included Black Forest and Sonny's beers.

The **CLEVELAND HOMEOPATHIC HOSPITAL**, founded by Dr. S. R. Beckwith in May 1856, was one of the first hospitals formed in Cleveland. Beckwith took over a 2-story house on Lake St. and modified it to accommodate 20 patients, mainly sick and injured employees of the Lake Shore and the Cleveland, Columbus, & Cincinnati railroads. In 1869, homeopathic physicians withdrew from the Willson St. Hospital and opened Cleveland Protestant Hospital. In 1873, that hospital moved into the Humiston Institute building on Huron Rd. The hospital consolidated with Beckwith's hospital, and the following year was incorporated as the Cleveland Homeopathic Hospital (sometimes referred to as the Cleveland Homeopathic Hospital Society). The incorporators were Drs. Beckwith, H. F. Biggar, and John C. Sanders. Dr. H. H. Baxter was also prominently identified with the project. A new hospital was constructed on the Huron Rd. site in 1879, and a larger building replaced that one in 1895. The Cleveland Homeopathic Hospital closed in 1917 because of competition from ST. VINCENT CHARITY HOSPITAL, and became HURON RD. HOSPITAL.

The **CLEVELAND-HOPKINS INTERNATIONAL AIRPORT** is located 8 mi. southwest of PUBLIC SQUARE at Brookpark Rd. and Riverside Dr., adjacent to the eastern ridge of the Rocky River Valley. It is among the world's largest, finest, and busiest commercial airport terminals. A municipal airport for the city had been envisioned shortly after WORLD WAR I, but it took the threat of Cleveland's being bypassed as a U.S. Air Mail stop to spur city leaders into making an airfield a reality. Cleveland would be a stop on the coast-to-coast flight only if the federal government could be satisfied that the city would make the necessary investment in an airfield. In 1925, City Manager WM. R. HOPKINS presented city council the recommendations of an advisory committee along with options on 1,040 acres of land at the Brookpark and Riverside intersection. Council approved, and bonds were issued. Clearing and grading took place at record speed so that the U.S. Air Mail could inaugurate night flights on 1 July 1925. The local news media criticized the airfield's distant location as folly. However, not only did the passengers make the long trek, but so did the general public, who curiously viewed the activity at the field. The NATL. AIR RACES were first held in Cleveland in 1929 as part of the ceremonies dedicating Cleveland's Municipal Airport. The field's superior facilities and enthusiastic audiences made the show and the Thompson Trophy Race an annual event (except during WORLD WAR II) until 1949, when it was discontinued.

Constructed in 1927, the first terminal building was the location of the world's first airport control tower. Throughout the years, the city has expanded and modernized the facilities at Hopkins to meet the increasing passenger demands. The original terminal building was replaced with a modern building in 1956. Since then, additional concourses and gates have been added, including the South Concourse, opened in Apr. 1968, and the North Concourse, opened in Aug. 1978. The baggage-handling facilities have been expanded; a parking garage was added to the expanded parking 'ot; and moving sidewalks and escalators were installed. On 15 Nov. 1968, rapid-transit service to the airport began, and with this expansion of service, Cleveland became the first American city to have such a link between its downtown and airport. The problems of jet noise and the need for more and longer runways have brought the city into conflict with the airport's neighbors. With the Rocky River Valley and the NASA LEWIS RESEARCH CTR. blocking expansion to the west and southwest, the airport has had to expand in other directions, into developed neighborhoods. In 1984, both Cleveland and FAIRVIEW PARK began an attempt to annex RIVEREDGE TWP. and relocated its residents to provide for immediate expansion. The airport, originally known as Cleveland Municipal, was renamed Cleveland-Hopkins Internatl. Airport on 26 July 1951, to commemorate the 82d birthday of Wm. Hopkins, who founded the airport.

The **CLEVELAND HOSPITAL ASSOCIATION** was a failed attempt to gain hospital privileges for black doctors and freer access to hospital care for Negro patients. The idea, unsuccessful in 1915, was reintroduced with more urgency in 1921 after Cleveland's black population was increased by WORLD WAR I southern migrations. Before 1900, the black graduates of Cleveland medical schools had difficulty making a living, as the black population was less than 3,000, and most black doctors were unwelcome as staff members at Cleveland hospitals. By 1910, there were 5 Negro doctors to serve a black population of 8,500. White patients seldom patronized black doctors. As blacks came from the South during and after the war, the inability of black doctors to treat patients in hospitals threatened the health of the community, since black doctors and nurses were unable to practice modern skills in the institutions where black patients were confined. To aid both professionals and patients, Dr. E. A. Dale proposed in 1915 a hospital for people of all races where black medical professionals could practice; because of opposition by black doctors and by the Cleveland Assoc. of Colored Men, the new hospital did not materialize. In 1921, Dr. Joe Thomas took a different approach. Arguing that a new Cleveland hospital was needed to alleviate overcrowding, he established the Cleveland Hospital Assoc., which in turn proposed the $250,000 Lincoln Memorial Hospital. The facility would offer nurse training for all women and an arena for physicians to practice their skills. The idea was rejected by the Cleveland Hospital Council of the Welfare Fed. and by the community at large. Undaunted, Thomas began to build a facility at his home on E. 40th St., but it was never completed. The Cleveland Hospital Assoc. faded along with the hopes for Lincoln Memorial Hospital.

A similar body, the Mercy Hospital Assoc., got no further in its campaign to establish a black hospital because of fear by the black community that the establishment of such a hospital would lead to segregation in hospitals that were previously open to blacks. The agitation led to the formation of a committee to study the problem of black hospital privileges at City Hospital, which was supported by taxpayers of all races. Though the report did not favor any policy changes in hiring practices because of the likely prejudice of white patients toward black doctors, a black physician and 2 black nurses were employed by City Hospital. By 1930, when DANIEL P. MORGAN came into office as city manager, the official attitude toward the hospital changed, and city council passed a resolution that gave all citizens of Cleveland equal opportunity to secure training as nurses and interns at City Hospital.

Davis, Russell H., *Black Americans in Cleveland* (1972).

The **CLEVELAND HOSPITAL SERVICE ASSOCIATION,** organizational forerunner of BLUE CROSS & BLUE SHIELD MUTUAL OF NORTHERN OHIO, administered the first prepaid hospitalization plan in the U.S. directed to the general public, which was endorsed by the American Hospital Assoc., the Cleveland Hospital Council, and the medical profession. The CHSA was incorporated in 1934, a time when widespread economic distress exacerbated a crisis in health-care delivery. By the 1920s, hospitals had gained general acceptance as the preferred treatment site for serious illness, but rising costs for building, equipping, and operating made many persons reluctant to seek hospital care. These concerns led to the formation of the Committee on the Costs of Medical Care, a national group that made a unified attempt to analyze the economics of health care. By 1932, the committee concluded that the public needed more health care but that hospitals were underutilized. Further, it suggested that the health-care system could be put in balance by creating a pooled fund through insurance or taxes (or both) to be used for payment of individual health care. In Cleveland, as well as many other cities, this concept was already under study. John Mannix, a 20-year-old accounting clerk at Mt. Sinai, began studying hospital costs in response to the outrage of patients provoked at receiving bills twice the expected size. (Hospital room rates averaged $6 a day, but extra services hiked the bill to $15.) Such charges provided 33% of hospital income. Mannix devised a plan to absorb the cost of extra services. When, at age 24, he became administrator of Elyria Hospital, he experimented with an all-inclusive rate for maternity coverage and tonsillectomies. Meanwhile, his study of hospital usage in Lorain County showed that the average person spent only $.50 per month on hospital care. When further study of the Greater Cleveland area supported his data, he devised an insurance plan.

Mannix tried unsuccessfully to interest insurance companies in selling health-care policies. Following the release of the preliminary report of the Committee on the Costs of Medical Care, he approached the Cleveland Hospital Council with his ideas for hospital finance and prepaid group hospitalization. The council adopted the concept of inclusive rates, which Mannix had further tried as an administrator at UNIVERSITY HOSPITALS, and after the committee issued its final report, it set up a local body chaired by Mannix. By Dec. 1933, Mannix called a meeting of hospital administrators and trustees, ACADEMY OF MEDICINE representatives, the Welfare Fed., and other groups who agreed to test the plan through a not-for-profit corporation to be called the Cleveland Hospital Service Assoc. Backed with a $7,500 loan from the Welfare Fed., the organization set up headquarters in Rm. 237 of the 1900 Bldg. on Euclid Ave. under the direction of John McNamara. (Mannix declined the offer to head the program at that time.) With a staff of 4, McNamara enrolled 13,000 the first year. The plan was so successful that by Sept. 1935, the association paid off its loan to the Welfare Fed. ahead of schedule and established a small reserve fund after paying claims.

The first plan cost $.60 a month for 21 days of ward coverage, or $.75 for a semiprivate room. "Hospitalization" was defined to include hospital bed and board, general nursing care, routine hospital lab service, use of the x-ray department, use of the operating room, administration of anesthesia by a hospital employee (not a physician), ordinary drugs, and surgical dressings incident to illness or injury. The policy did not apply to maternity care, mental illness, tuberculosis, contagious diseases, or workmen's-compensation cases. Subscribers could be sent to any of the 13 member hospitals by their physicians. The plan did not cover doctor costs, though its sister plan, MEDICAL MUTUAL, did so after 1945. CHSA tried to enroll groups at area companies with 10 or more employees. The first enrollees were Fairview Park Hospital, followed by Cleveland Trust. White Sewing Machine, Royal Typewriter, the STANDARD OIL CO., the U.S. Postal Service, the WARNER & SWASEY CO., and the YWCA-YMCA quickly followed. The companies collected the premium and forwarded the money to the CHSA. Contracting companies had to guarantee that 60% of the employees would subscribe; Cleveland companies averaged 75% enrollment. As the plan, known after 1939 as Blue Cross, gained widespread acceptance, it was broadened to include maternity and family coverage, nongroup coverage, and longer stays. Management of the Blue Cross organization ultimately came into the hands of John Mannix, who developed plans in Detroit and Chicago after leaving his administrative post at University Hospitals. Mannix, who had enhanced enrollment figures nationally by successfully wooing the auto companies as subscribers, came back to Cleveland at the onset of an escalating financial crisis.

After WORLD WAR II, a new wave of inflation destroyed rate stability as overhead costs for hospitals raised daily charges and Blue Cross payouts. Moreover, the plan was blamed for a scarcity of hospital beds. A special fund was established to double the number of beds in the area; such building increased the potential for claims from hospital stays and, ultimately, resulted in excess capacity. By 1953, the CHSA was paying out $356,000 a year more than it was collecting, and announced rate increases as high as 59%. Despite public outrage, additional double-digit increases followed in subsequent years: in 1956, a public hearing aired Blue Cross's problems and verified that the

company's requests were justified. Its administrative costs averaged less than 5% (a national record). To pool risks over a larger area as well as improve service and benefits, the CHSA merged with the Akron Hospital Service Assoc. to become Blue Cross of Northeast Ohio in July 1957. At that time, CHSA had 1.5 million subscribers, while the combined membership in BCNO was 1.7 million for 10,000 enrolled groups.

Condon, George, *Fifty Years of Community Service* (1984).

The **CLEVELAND INDIANS** baseball team is a charter member of the American League, founded in 1901. It is one of 4 teams (along with Boston, Chicago, and Detroit) to have remained in the same city since the league's inception. Originally named the Blues, then the Broncos, from 1903–11 the team was known as the Naps, in honor of player-manager NAPOLEON LAJOIE. From 1912–14 the team was officially named the Molly McGuires but popularly was still called the Naps. In 1915 Lajoie was traded, and, partially based on newspaper polls of fans, the team became permanently known as the Indians, a nickname that had been popularized in the 1890s when the Amerindian LOUIS "CHIEF" SOCKALEXIS played for the old Natl. League CLEVELAND SPIDERS.

The original owners of the franchise were 2 Cleveland businessmen, John Kilfoyle (president, 1901–08) and Chas. Somers (1908–15). Under their aegis, the team, which played in LEAGUE PARK at 65th St. and Lexington Ave., essentially a trolley-car stadium, began to develop a farm system and to prove competitive on the field. However, the team was a serious pennant contender only in 1908, when it finished ½ game behind Detroit. In 1915–16 a series of major changes affected the club: the trade of Lajoie, the adoption of the "Indians" nickname, and the sale of the team to a Chicago-based group headed by Jas. Dunn. On the field, the team's fortunes immediately improved with the acquisition of player-manager TRISTAM "TRIS" SPEAKER. In 1920, the Indians won their first pennant and went on to defeat the Brooklyn Dodgers in the World Series. In the 1920s and 1930s, the team usually finished in the first division, but only in 1921 and 1926 did it seriously challenge for the pennant, finishing a close 2d both times.

In 1927 a Cleveland syndicate, including the Van Sweringen brothers, NEWTON D. BAKER, and Alva Bradley (who served as president until 1946), purchased the team and began construction of a new playing field—CLEVELAND MUNICIPAL STADIUM, on the lakefront, more than twice the capacity of League Park and, unlike it, essentially designed for access by automobile. Municipal Stadium opened in July 1931, although some games continued to be played at League Park, with decreasing frequency, until 1946. In Bradley's era, the team was at its strongest in the late 1930s; in 1940 it was the preseason favorite to win the pennant, but personal hostilities between manager Oscar Vitt and his leading players, dubbed the "Cry Babies," contributed to another 2d-place finish.

In 1946 another Chicago businessman, Bill Veeck, purchased the Indians. While his tenure was brief—he sold the team to a Cleveland syndicate headed by Ellis Ryan and Hank Greenberg after the 1949 season—it is still remembered as the team's golden age. Veeck brought an uninhibited enthusiasm and imagination to promotional matters, dramatically increasing attendance. Of equal or greater importance to the fans, the team rapidly improved its play on the field, creating a momentum that outlasted the Veeck era by a decade. Under player-manager Lou Boudreau, and then under Al Lopez, the Indians became a consistently powerful team, regularly challenging the New York Yankees for the pennant. Its main strength lay in its dominant pitching, featuring Bob Feller, Bob Lemon, and Early Wynn, among others. The 1948 season was undoubtedly the most exciting and memorable in the team's history and in popular perceptions of that history. Led by Boudreau, the Indians beat the Boston Red Sox 8–3 in a 1-game pennant playoff, and went on to defeat the Boston Braves in the World Series. The team also won the 1954 pennant under Lopez, setting a record for most regular-season victories (111), but lost the World Series to the New York Giants in a demoralizing 4-game sweep.

From 1960s, the Indians had difficulties in maintaining consistency and competitive respectability. Declining attendance, frequent managerial changes, and a slow disintegration of the farm-team and scouting systems all contributed to, and were prompted by, instability in team ownership. Ryan sold out to Myron Wilson in 1953, and he in turn to Wm. Daley. In 1961–62 Gabe Paul became president and general manager. While he retained the latter position (apart from a few years' stint with the Yankees in the early 1970s) until his forced retirement in 1985, team ownership and the presidency were assumed by VERNON STOUFFER in 1966 and a decade later by Nick Mileti, both of whom lost money amid rumors that the team might even be moved to another city. At the start of the 1980s, the club was purchased by the O'Neill family, and the threat of relocation elsewhere faded; but by the mid-1980s the O'Neills, too, were seeking new ownership for the team. On the playing field the Indians were a .500 team at best: only once, in 1968, did they finish as high as 3d place. League expansion and realignment put the Indians into baseball's most competitive division, and the team was not successful in attracting free-agent star players. In the mid-1970s the double experiment of hiring still another player-manager, and baseball's first black manager, Frank Robinson, failed to reverse the downward trend. In the mid-1980s the prospects for a rejuvenated operational stability under new president Peter Bavasi, for renewed fiscal solvency under new ownership, and perhaps for new playing quarters in a domed stadium, seemed to be the Indians' brightest hopes in quite some time for a revival of the team's competitive respectability that its fans had long and earnestly awaited. The highly successful 1986 season seemed to bear out these hopes.

Lewis, Franklin, *The Cleveland Indians* (1949).

The **CLEVELAND INDUSTRIAL UNION COUNCIL** was the Cleveland affiliate of the Congress of Industrial Organizations. At odds with the CLEVELAND FED. OF LABOR for most of its history, the CIUC merged with the CFL in 1958 and became the Cleveland AFL-CIO. The drive to organize workers along industrywide lines intensified after the NIRA gave workers the right to organize in 1933. The federation, bound by traditions of organization by craft, fearful of worker militancy, and conciliatory to government and employers, not only failed to aggressively reach out to the less skilled but also expelled those within its ranks who tried to do so. Despite this difference in ideology, the real issues between the federation and the CIO were power and tactics. Cleveland labor leaders shared CFL attitudes about the CIO. When local auto workers staged sitdown strikes at the FISHER BODY General Motors plant in Dec. 1936, members initially voted their support for the strikes. Old-line craft-union members—metal polishers, electricians, plumbers, machinists, bricklayers—were angry, however, that police had closed the plant to them and demanded that it be reopened; by Jan. 1937, the

Cleveland Fed. reversed its earlier vote and condemned the "outlaw work stoppage" spearheaded by the CIO. In response, CIO leaders and friends met at Public Music Hall to show support and raise money for the strikers; some $1,350 per week was pledged, much of it from the COMMUNIST PARTY. When the strike at Fisher Body proved successful, the CFL refused to send congratulations to the strikers, and federation metal-trades locals immediately began an organizing drive at the plant. In Mar. 1937, the CFL followed national directives and expelled 5 unions: the UAW, Amalgamated Clothing Workers, Textile Workers, Steel Workers (Amalgamated Assoc. of Iron, Steel & Tin Workers), and INTERNATL. LADIES GARMENT WORKERS UNION. Led by BERYL PEPPERCORN of the Amalgamated Clothing Workers, leaders from these unions met to form the United Labor Congress, later the Cleveland Industrial Council, and by 1938 the Cleveland Industrial Union Council.

When national settlement of the GM strike was reached in mid-Mar. 1937, Fisher Body workers marched through the streets, setting off a CIO organizing drive that would push CIO ranks from 10,000 in 1937 to over 100,000 in 1947. Attempts by CFL leaders to keep peace were punctuated by a series of raids on rival unions and by new organizing drives in plants already affiliated with the opposite union. By 1939, Cleveland workers had tied their hopes for harmony between their parent unions on Franklin D. Roosevelt's attempts to reconcile the AFL and CIO. Though "one big union" did not result from the talks, efforts of local leaders and a change in national CIO leadership in 1940 reduced strains. Both bodies sat on the city War Planning Board, but jurisdictional squabbling and federation antipathy toward the alleged Communist influence in the council prevented cooperation until the Communists were purged from the ranks in 1949.

In the wake of WORLD WAR II, the CIUC attempted to improve its status in the eyes of the antiunion, anti-Communist public, and more specifically hoped to prevent passage of the Taft-Hartley bill. Long an advocate of political action, it mobilized grassroots opposition to the bill—a tactic finally emulated by the CFL, which then set up ward- and precinct-level coalitions of its own. The council and the railroad brotherhoods waged a united campaign to minimize strikes, a major spur to Taft-Hartley, but the Cleveland Fed., lacking national approval, did not join in. With the passage of Taft-Hartley came the requirement that union officials sign anti-Communist affidavits. Though the CIO (like the AFL) opposed the bill on principle, the CIO had denounced the Communist party in 1946 and was anxious to expel the radical element from its ranks. Many council members feared that their unions would lose NLRB certification, and sought affiliation with the CFL. Federation officials requested that national president Wm. Green send an organizer to the Cleveland Fed. to handle the avalanche of requests. The CIUC proposed that each organization halt raids on the other's membership, but the federation claimed that it was only responding to workers' needs. To stop the membership drain, the council ousted Chas. McLennon, the community service director, Fay Stephenson, Cleveland-based president of the CIO Women's Auxiliary, and other leaders with ties to the Communist party. Several months later, the national CIO convention held in Cleveland expelled the United Electrical Workers and 10 other unions for radicalism (see CIO PURGE CONVENTION, 1949). Despite continuing jurisdictional fights, this severing of leftist ties removed a major barrier to CFL-CIUC cooperation. The first official joint act was to mount an unsuccessful campaign against the election of Sen. Robt. Taft. In 1958, 3 years after a national merger, the council combined with the CFL to become the Cleveland AFL-CIO. At the time of the merger, the council claimed 200,000 members and had its headquarters at 1000 Walnut Ave.

The **CLEVELAND INSTITUTE OF ART** was founded as a professional school for artists at a time when Cleveland witnessed an increased cultural awareness and an increasing market for artists in the working world. The institute began as the Western Reserve School of Design for Women and was founded in the fall of 1882 in the home of Sarah M. Kimball, 1265 Euclid Ave. Within weeks classes had grown and were moved to quarters in the Case Block. In 1883 the school had 8 students, and as enrollment climbed in subsequent years, men as well as women were admitted. From its inception, the school sought to train students for careers; it represents the convergence of the interest in decorative art and crafts in the late 19th century and the need for trained designers in industry.

In 1892, after an unsuccessful attempt to merge the school into Western Reserve University (in which much of the "practical" instruction was dropped in favor of a more "academic" discipline), the school reverted to being an independent institution under the name Cleveland School of Art. At this time the school came under the direction of Georgie Leighton Norton, who led it over the next 30 years. Under her direction a new building was constructed in 1904 on Juniper and Magnolia Dr., in UNIVERSITY CIRCLE. The building was designed by Hubbell & Benes and was built on property donated by JEPTHA H. WADE. By 1913 an endowment had been established, securing the future of the institution.

While the Depression and WORLD WAR II significantly reduced enrollment, various programs were added to keep the school viable. It played a part in the WPA Federal Art Project in the Cleveland area, and during the war such studies as mapmaking and medical drawing were incorporated alongside the usual courses in drawing, painting, and sculpture. By the early 1950s, enrollment climbed as industry again sought trained designers and craftspersons. In 1955–56 a new building in the International style was built on the corner of East Blvd. and Bellflower Rd. The building provided classrooms, a library, galleries, studios, and an auditorium. As its standards had risen through the years, the school was renamed the Cleveland Institute of Art in 1948. The bachelor of fine arts degree was first offered in 1947, and by 1969 the program was a 5-year-long curriculum (the 5th year had been optional to that point) providing an academic as well as professional education. In the mid-1970s, enrollment was halted at 525. In 1981 the former Ford assembly plant on Euclid Ave. east of Mayfield Rd. was purchased and converted into studio space, classrooms, and space for other services. Additionally, the school operates an extramural program in southern France. Students specializing in painting, graphic design, sculpture, textiles, jewelry making, and other forms receive the B.F.A. degree.

The **CLEVELAND INSTITUTE OF MUSIC** is a nationally recognized conservatory, which has produced many outstanding musicians and claimed many others as members of its faculty. It was founded in 1920 by a group of supporters led by Mrs. Franklyn B. Sanders and Mrs. Joseph T. Smith. Classes were first held in the Statler Hotel and then moved to the Hall residence at E. 31st St. and Euclid Ave. ERNEST BLOCH, a Swiss composer and teacher, was appointed director, and Mrs. Sanders was executive director. The Institute moved from the Hall residence to the Chisholm home at E. 28th and Euclid in 1923, then to the Samuel Mather home at E. 26th and Euclid in 1932, and

the Cox home at 34th and Euclid in 1941, where a 400-seat auditorium was added. In 1961 a new International-style building was constructed at East Blvd. and Hazel Dr. in UNIVERSITY CIRCLE, with a concert hall, greatly expanded classrooms, studio and practice space, and a library and offices.

Beginning with Ernest Bloch, the institute has engaged a distinguished faculty. Bloch's successors as artistic director have been musicians with great reputations: BERYL RUBINSTEIN (1932–52), Ward Davenny (1954–61), VICTOR BABIN (1961–72), Grant Johannesen (1974–85), and David Cerone (1985– ). Among the faculty have been Roger Sessions (composition), Nathan Freyer (violin), Quincy Porter (composition), Louis Persinger (violin), Joseph Knitzer (violin), Raphael Drurian (violin), ARTHUR LOESSER (piano), Marcel Salzinger (violin), Nevada van der Veer (voice), Marie Simmelink Kraft (voice), Eleanor Steber (voice), Boris Goldovsky (opera), Marcel Dick (composition), and HERBERT ELWELL (composition), among others. The institute operates 2 divisions: the collegiate conservatory, offering bachelor's, master's, and Ph.D. degrees (since 1952 in cooperation with Western Reserve University and its successor CASE WESTERN RESERVE UNIVERSITY), and the preparatory department for younger students. Branches of the preparatory department have operated at various times in FAIRVIEW PARK, PARMA, ORANGE, SHAKER HTS., and CHAGRIN FALLS.

Early in the development of the institute, Ernest Bloch began the teaching of Dalcroze Eurythmics, a method of musical and movement instruction. Dalcroze methodology and technique are taught to conservatory students, and children in the preparatory department receive Eurythmic instruction. Opera has been an important department, as well, and the piano, voice, and composition departments have been particularly recognized. Highly trained and successful players in most instruments are products of the institute. A long and close relationship with the CLEVELAND ORCHESTRA has provided many orchestra members for the faculty of CIM. A cooperative program in music education was begun with CWRU in 1968 to train music educators. By 1985 the Cleveland Institute of Music's enrollment had grown from the initial 5 students in 1920 to a student body of 230 collegiate and 2,000 preparatory and adult education students and 130 faculty members.

The **CLEVELAND INSURANCE COMPANY** was a banking and insurance company that was organized in 1830 and forced out of business as a result of the great Chicago Fire of 1871. Standard histories of Cleveland report that the company received a perpetual charter in 1830 to operate as both an insurance and banking business, but that it functioned solely as an insurance business until reorganized to operate solely as as an insurance business in 1861. City directories indicate that the leading figures in the business during this time were Edmund Clark (1799–30 Dec. 1861) and Seth W. Crittenden. The directories also indicate that in 1861 Crittenden and Clark were operating their banking business as S. W. Crittenden & Co.; the Cleveland Insurance Co. does not appear in the city directories in the 1860s until 1868. Active as officers in the insurance company between 1868–71 were HENRY B. PAYNE, S. D. McMillan, S. S. Coe, Ralph P. Myers, and Richard R. Lyon.

The **CLEVELAND INTERNATIONAL PROGRAM** is a private, voluntary organization that seeks to build international understanding by an annual international program of cultural and professional exchanges in the fields of social work, community planning, special education, and other human services. The program was founded in 1956 by

HENRY OLLENDORFF as a vehicle to secure "person to person diplomacy" throughout the world, utilizing professionals to witness the skills and knowledge of the visited country and to transfer those experiences upon their return. Since 1956, the Cleveland Internatl. Program has spread throughout the U.S. and has 12 affiliates, operating under the Cleveland-based Council of Internatl. Programs. The secretary general in 1985 was Dr. Tom Hatcher, and the executive director was Dorothy Faller, both of Cleveland.

The **CLEVELAND JETPORT** (LAKE ERIE INTERNATIONAL JETPORT) was a project proposed during the 1960s and 1970s to build a new international airport off Cleveland's shoreline. Mayor Ralph Locher introduced the first proposal for a jetport in June 1966. In 1969, Dr. Abe Silverstein, director of NASA'S LEWIS RESEARCH CTR., unveiled a more comprehensive plan that proposed the construction of such an airport 1 mi. north of Cleveland's downtown at the cost of $1.185 billion. The premise of both proposals was that by the 1990s, CLEVELAND HOPKINS INTERNATL. AIRPORT would be insufficient to serve the region's commercial air transportation needs. Thus, in 1971 the county commissioners formed the Lake Erie Regional Transportation Authority (LERTA) with the authority to apply for federal funds for an in-depth feasibility study. LERTA was formed largely through the urging of Jas. C. Davis, chairman of the GREATER CLEVELAND GROWTH ASSOC. LERTA's board of trustees consisted of 10 members, 4 of whom were appointed by the county commissioners, and 6 by the city. Dr. Cameron M. Smith was the executive director. In 1972, LERTA began a $4.3 million feasibility study to be completed in 5 years. The initial $1.2 million came from the Growth Assoc.; the Federal Aviation Admin. later provided most of the additional money. A private firm completed the study in 1977, proposing the building of an airport inside a stone-and-sand dike 5 mi. off Cleveland's shoreline. The 13-mi. dike would surround a 6-sided land mass reclaimed from the lake, 40 ft. below the lake's surface. The new jetport would be accessible by an RTA train and a highway connecting it to the innerbelt. Other sites for a regional jetport, Ravenna and the Grafton-Beldon area in Medina and Lorain counties, were also considered but were rejected.

The study received severe opposition from Mayor Dennis Kucinich, who, along with other key city officials, disavowed himself from LERTA in 1977. Other opponents included the League of Women Voters. Detractors cited the cost-benefit ratio, airport renovation at Cleveland Hopkins, weather conditions on the lake, and the failure to explore alternate forms of transportation. Proponents refuted these claims and argued the practical need for a new airport, the additional jobs it would create, and its favorable effects on Cleveland's image and business climate. LERTA received a critical blow in 1977 when an FAA study rejected the need for a new airport in Cleveland, at least until the year 2000. This decision was related to the Dept. of Transportation's shifting of funds for improvements at existing airports rather than to the building of new ones. In 1978, the FAA discontinued its support of the project, and LERTA was forced to dismiss its remaining employees and restrict its functions to yearly board meetings.

The *CLEVELAND JEWISH NEWS* became heir to the tradition of the city's English-language Jewish press in 1964, when it was born of the merger of the *Jewish Review & Observer* with the *Jewish Independent*. It could be traced back to the founding of Cleveland's first Jewish newspaper, the *Hebrew Observer*, by Hiram Straus and Sam Oppenheimer on 5 July 1889. Oppenheimer then teamed with

Jack Machol in 1893 to start the *Jewish Review*, which was purchased 3 years later by Dan S. Wertheimer. Both weeklies were merged by Wertheimer in 1899 into the *Jewish Review & Observer*, which remained in the control of the family for the next 65 years. Originally edited by Miss Jessie Cohen, the paper was located in the Ajax Bldg. on St. Clair and later moved into the Crown Bldg. on Lakeside Ave. Along with their newspaper, the Wertheimers maintained a successful printing business. Established on 9 Mar. 1906, the *Jewish Independent* became another family enterprise when Maurice Weidenthal of the *PLAIN DEALER* became editor several weeks later. Circulation had approached 20,000 by 1917, when Weidenthal died and was succeeded by his brother, Leo. A renowned literary and theatrical scholar, LEO WEIDENTHAL guided the *Independent* for nearly 50 years. His nephew, David L. Sperling, was long-time manager of the weekly, which moved in 1934 from Bolivar Rd. to the Film Bldg. at Payne and E. 21st St. Weidenthal's impending retirement in 1964 served as the catalyst for a reorganization of Cleveland's Jewish press by a civic group incorporated as the Cleveland Jewish Publication Co. Headed by Lloyd S. Schwenger, the board drew upon a credit of $155,000 to purchase both the *Independent* and the *Jewish Review & Observer*, which published their last editions on 23 Oct. 1964. Under the editorship of Arthur Weyne, the *Cleveland Jewish News* made its bow as a 32-page tabloid on 30 Oct. 1964. Within 10 years, the *Cleveland Jewish News* had paid off its loan and moved from the Film Bldg. to new quarters at 13910 Cedar Rd. Circulation was maintained at 15,000–20,000, while average size increased from 16 to 36 pages. Weyne was succeeded as editor by Jerry D. Barach and Cynthia Dettelbach; all of them were assisted by Bernice Green as associate editor.

The **CLEVELAND JOB CORPS** was one of over 100 job-training programs created by the Economic Opportunity Act of 1964. It produced the first program graduates in the country. The Job Corps recruited high school dropouts ages 16–21 and sent them to a residential center where they could obtain a GED, if necessary, and work skills. Because the program was national in scope, applicants were often sent to urban or rural settings far from home. In Cleveland, the program was sponsored by the Alpha Kappa Alpha Sorority, a predominantly black women's service organization that received a contract from the Dept. of Labor to operate the local center. The group maintained a house at 1588 Ansel Rd. for nearly 400 girls until 1971, when the center relocated into the old Tudor Arms Hotel at E. 107th and Carnegie, which had been used by CASE WESTERN RESERVE UNIVERSITY as student housing during the 1960s. While only women lived at the facility, men were accepted into the program after 1976. Program offerings varied throughout the country, but in Cleveland the corpsmen were trained in business and clerical fields, health occupations, food services, and other service occupations. Through the cooperation of the Brotherhood of Railway & Airline Clerks, the center offered a union training program that guaranteed job placement as train attendants and Amtrak office workers.

The Cleveland Job Corps, founded as part of the War on Poverty, has withstood budget cuts and proposed reorganizations since the Nixon era. Critics questioned the cost of maintaining such residences, but studies on Job Corps effectiveness emphasized the social benefits. Research in 1969 showed that Job Corps graduates earned about $1,200 more after completing the program and that black enrollees had increased perceptions of their abilities to advance if given equal opportunity. The Nixon administration, however, closed 57 centers (many in rural areas) and hoped to shift the remaining centers to state and local control, where they could be financed through federal revenue-sharing funds. Cleveland Corps director Dr. Zelma George argued that any change in the program would endanger its effectiveness. She felt that most enrollees needed to be temporarily removed from home environments that often bred despair and hopelessness and had to be given social skills and good work habits along with vocational training. She won her point, although because of a change in policy, applicants were sent somewhat nearer to home than previously to minimize culture shock and high dropout rates. In 1980, the program was economically stable. In 2 decades, the Cleveland Job Corps trained over 12,000 people, mostly black women from out of state. Three directors have led the program, including Dr. George (1966–74).

The CLEVELAND JOURNAL came into existence on 21 Mar. 1903, with the intention of providing an organ for black business interests. Among the businessmen who founded it were Welcome T. Blue, president of the Journal Publishing Co., and Nahum Daniel Brascher, who edited it during most of its existence. As suggested by the early slogan "Labor Conquers All Things," the Journal was a vigorous supporter of the self-help racial philosophy of black educator Booker T. Washington. Politically, like most black leadership at the time, it was Republican. Evidently prosperous for a time, the weekly Journal expanded to 8 pages early in its second year. On 25 Feb. 1905, it published a 16-page "Woman's Edition" written and edited by members of the City Fed. of Colored Women's Clubs. Each year it celebrated its anniversary by sponsoring a public reception in one of Cleveland's black churches. Located originally in the American Trust Bldg. on PUBLIC SQUARE, it later moved to the black business district on Central Ave. While shunning the militant posture of the rival Cleveland Gazette, the Journal was not complacent on racial issues. Notable was a 4-part series, "Discrimination in Cleveland." In 1909, the paper's vice-president, THOS. W. FLEMING, became the first black elected to Cleveland City Council, while Brascher was made a city storekeeper. Political success did not insure economic survival, however, as the Journal ceased publication in 1912.

The CLEVELAND LAKEFRONT STATE PARK, with administrative headquarters at GORDON PARK, 740 E. 72nd St., was established in 1978 by the Ohio Dept. of Natural Resources (Div. of Parks) at the request of the city of Cleveland and functions under a lease agreement (1977) between the department and the city. The agreement provides that the state, which allocated $5 million for capital improvements for Cleveland lakefront parks, be responsible for the maintenance, development, and improvement of 450 acres of park areas along the Lake Erie shoreline, including EDGEWATER PARK, located at the west end of the shoreway; the E. 55th St. Marina; Gordon Park at the foot of Martin Luther King Blvd.; Wildwood Park at the foot of Neff Rd.; and EUCLID BEACH PARK. By 1984, a 100-year master plan detailing systematic development of the park was partially implemented by many additions and improvements, including facilities for fishing, boating, swimming, and picnicking and day-use facilities at all designated park areas. Robt. M. Bacon, park manager 1978–80, was succeeded by Dave Stites.

The CLEVELAND LAW COLLEGE was created through the efforts of RUFUS P. RANNEY. It was granted a charter and authorized to grant degrees on 5 Jan. 1882. Judge E.

J. Blandin of the common pleas court was elected dean, and classes began in the fall of 1885. All of the faculty were either on the bench or full-time lawyers. Classes were held in the old courthouse on PUBLIC SQUARE, and students were allowed to use the county law library in that building. The school suspended operations after 1 academic year. There is no record of why it failed in spite of substantial support by the bar. The best assumption is that the faculty, as senior members of the bar during a period of major expansion of industry and commerce in Cleveland, increased their legal work, which impaired their ability to operate a school. They also failed to recognize the need for full-time instructors, which would require a substantial initial capital investment. The failure of the school in 1885 was a major impetus for the establishment of the Law School at Western Reserve University in 1891. Judge SAMUEL E. WILLIAMSON of the common pleas court, who had taught the course in property at the college, became chairman of a committee of prominent lawyers that sought to permanently establish the school or to take steps to establish another law school in Cleveland. In May 1891, Williamson was chairman of a committee of 11 Cleveland lawyers and judges that voted unanimously to ask WRU to establish a full-time university law school, with a permanent endowment and a full-time faculty.

The CLEVELAND LEADER, one of the city's major newspapers, grew out of the merger of the True Democrat into Joseph Medill's DAILY FOREST CITY as the Forest City Democrat in 1853. EDWIN COWLES, who joined the new venture as Medill's partner, changed the name to the Cleveland Leader on 16 Mar. 1854 and shortly thereafter bought out his partners to become the paper's principal owner and, after 1859, editor, as well. Cowles made the Leader an uncompromising organ for the newly formed Republican party, in whose birth he had assisted. With the party's victory in 1860, the Leader emerged as the local organ for the dominant radical wing, while the Herald espoused the interests of the more moderate Whiggish branch. In Cleveland's BAGBY FUGITIVE SLAVE CASE of 1861, however, the Leader reluctantly joined the Herald in counseling submission to the law as proof that southern rights could be respected under the Union. Immediately after Bull Run, the Leader returned to the faith with a call for immediate emancipation. It fought staunchly against the 1862 Negro exclusion campaign in Ohio and supported the Union candidates for governor and Lincoln's reelection campaign in 1864.

Emerging from the war as Cleveland's leading daily, the Leader was organized as a joint stock company with $300,000 capitalization on 3 July 1865. Its evening edition, begun in 1861 as the Evening Leader, was renamed the Evening News in 1868. By 1875, its circulation of 13,000 was double that of the Herald and 5 times that of the PLAIN DEALER. Cowles kept the paper technologically up to date, importing Cleveland's first perfecting press in 1877 after seeing one at the Philadelphia Exposition and pioneering the use of electrotype plates in Ohio. Together with the Plain Dealer in 1885, the Leader bought out its old rival, the Herald, thus securing the Evening Herald's AP franchise for its own afternoon edition, which then became the News & Herald. Its editorial page and policy remained a duplicate of the Leader's. Editorially, the Leader was an extension of its editor's strong personality. Alone among Cleveland papers, it urged the construction of the SUPERIOR VIADUCT in the 1870s. It scooped its rivals on the coverage of such stories as the Lake Shore & Michigan Southern Railroad disaster in Ashtabula County in 1876. Yet, as former staff member CHAS. E. KENNEDY observed, the *Leader* ultimately suffered from its editor's two grand passions: unflinching loyalty to the Republican party and uncompromising opposition to the Catholic church.

After Cowles's death in 1890, the *Leader* lost direction. With most of the profits going into dividends for the Cowles heirs, the *Leader* quickly lost its edge in the morning field to the aggressive *Plain Dealer.* In 1905, it was purchased by CHAS. A. OTIS, owner of the *CLEVELAND NEWS.* Otis sold a half-interest in both the *News* and *Leader* to Medill McCormick, the grandson of Joseph Medill and son-in-law of MARCUS A. HANNA. Assuming personal control of the *Leader,* McCormick moved it from its long-time location on Lower Superior near W. 6th St. to the corner of E. 6th and Superior Ave. For the mayoral campaign of 1907, he imported cartoonist Homer Davenport from the *New York Evening Mail* to contend against his father-in-law's nemesis, Mayor TOM L. JOHNSON. In 1909 he leased the *Leader* to a triumvirate headed by Chas. E. Kennedy. Although Kennedy and his partners streamlined the *Leader* and returned the Sunday edition to profitability, the paper was sold in 1910 to McCormack's brother-in-law DANIEL R. HANNA, who also purchased the *News* as the *Sunday News-Leader.* Prominent among the *Leader's* editorial staff were editor Jas. B. Morrow, city editors Jas. H. Kennedy and Sam Anson, and reporter Bob Larkin.

The **CLEVELAND LIBERALIST** was the personal organ of Dr. Samuel Underhill, a semiretired physician of advanced rationalist philosophy. Introduced on 10 Sept. 1836, the 8-page, 3-column weekly was nearly as much magazine as newspaper in format, preferring leaders devoted to scientific expositions over political manifestoes. During most of its first year, its favorite target was Harmon Kingsbury's *Cleveland Messenger,* whose campaigns to sanctify the Sabbath were denounced by Underhill as "humbug and quackery." Underhill apparently financed the *Liberalist* largely from his own resources, aided by the services of his son, James S. Underhill, as printer and publisher. While he could accept phrenology as a serious science, he was far ahead of his time in his crusade against the false claims of patent medicines.

After more than a 100 issues, Underhill announced the suspension of the *Liberalist* for lack of financial support on 27 Oct. 1838. Within a few weeks, however, he and a partner named Thompson revived it as a semiweekly called the *Bald Eagle.* In an attempt to capitalize on Anglo-American tensions following the *Caroline* affair, the *Bald Eagle* struck a patriotic stance and promised "the earliest Canada News." Although it printed a prospectus for daily publication, the paper evidently expired early in 1839.

The **CLEVELAND LIBRARY ASSOCIATION** was a leading intellectual organization in Cleveland during the latter half of the 19th century. It later became the Case Library. The CLA was chartered in 1848 by the YOUNG MEN'S LITERARY ASSOC. It was incorporated with 200 shares of stock at $.10 cents each, the yearly profit to be used for the acquisition of books. Its original purpose was to maintain a library, a reading room, a museum, and an annual series of lectures. WM. CASE, president of the Young Men's Literary Assoc., and CHAS. WHITTLESEY were largely responsible for its founding. An annually elected board of trustees controlled the association until 1870, when 5 directors were appointed for life. The first 5 directors were SAMUEL WILLIAMSON, JAS. BARNETT, HERMAN M. CHAPIN, WM. BINGHAM, and Benjamin A. Standard. Dr. John W. Perrin was for many years head librarian.

The CLA initially occupied a small room on Superior with 500 volumes and was open to the public on a subscription basis. By 1858, its library had increased to 3,000 volumes, and membership to 500 subscribers. At that time it was the largest library in Cleveland. In addition to its library, a winter lecture series was offered. Ralph Waldo Emerson was the featured lecturer in 1853, 1859, and 1867. In 1867, the CLA began a decade of rapid expansion. That year it moved to the 2d floor of CASE HALL (E. 3rd and Superior), and with a grand inauguration concert it was opened to the general public. In 1870, LEONARD CASE gave an endowment of $25,000 and a perpetual lease of its rooms on the 2d floor. In addition to maintaining a circulating library, the CLA also collected special books and manuscripts, material relating to local history, and relics of natural history. In 1867, the WESTERN RESERVE HISTORICAL SOCIETY was founded as a department of the association. Another department, the Kirtland Society of Natural Sciences, was founded in 1870; it would later evolve into the CLEVELAND MUSEUM OF NATURAL HISTORY. Both departments eventually achieved autonomy. In 1876, Leonard Case deeded Case Hall to the Library Assoc. Thereafter, it was known as the Case Library. The name was later changed to the Leonard Case Reference Library, and it was consolidated into Western Reserve University in 1941.

The **CLEVELAND LIGHT ARTILLERY** was organized 6 July 1839 by 9 members of the CLEVELAND GRAYS gun squad. Like the Grays, the CLA drew its membership from young men representing the area's best families. As Ohio militia law did not recognize artillery as a military service, the original artillerymen received no state support. They purchased their own uniforms and procured their own 6-lb. cannon, for which they built the carriage and caisson, and made their own ammunition. Nevertheless, artillery membership increased, and in 1845, the gun squad detached itself from the Grays and elected drill sergeant David Wood as captain. Following an encampment at Wooster in 1846, the CLA traveled west, attending conventions and ceremonial functions, inspiring other cities to establish their own artillery services. Increased popularity resulted in increased membership, and by 1851 the CLA had enough influence to induce state authorities to furnish needed guns and harnesses. In 1852, the Light Artillery was called to its first duty: suppressing a riot that had broken out at a medical school on the corner of Ontario and Prospect avenues. After 48 hours, the rioters were subdued, and the CLA's popularity surged. In 1859 the state legislature revised militia law, permitting artillery to muster. Subsequently, 6 companies were formed, 4 in Cleveland and 1 each in Brooklyn and Geneva. Organized together, the 6 companies were commissioned as Battery A, the 1st Regiment of Light Artillery, Ohio Volunteer Militia, by Gov. Chase in Aug. 1860. Led by Col. JAS. BARNETT, the regiment made its first public appearance in Sept. 1860. When the CIVIL WAR broke out in Apr. 1861, the CLA did a 3-month tour of duty in the mountains of (West) Virginia, the first of many engagements during the war. The first Cleveland unit to experience battle, the Light Artillery also suffered the first casualty from the area, Geo. Tillotson. After the Civil War, the CLA made many public appearances during holidays and special events. It later served as the cornerstone of the formation of Battery B, 135th Field Artillery, Ohio Natl. Guard. (See FIRST OHIO VOLUNTEER LIGHT ARTILLERY.)

Davidson, Henry M., *History of Battery A, First Regiment of Ohio Volunteer Light Artillery* (1865).

The **CLEVELAND LITTLE HOOVER COMMISSION** was appointed in Dec. 1965 by Mayor Ralph Locher and council president Jas. Stanton to make an in-depth study of all city of Cleveland operations. The commission was inspired by the Hoover Commission, created by Pres. Truman (and again by Eisenhower) to investigate inefficiencies and recommend streamlining of the federal government. Former president Herbert Hoover was chairman of both federal commissions. The Cleveland Little Hoover Commission was composed of 24 business and community leaders and drew funds from private sources. The project was designed to set guidelines for future policy decisions concerning city income tax, city-county transfer of functions, and expansion or reduction of city operations. The need for such a study was partly due to the defeat of a city income tax in 1965. Carter Kessel, vice-president of the Midland-Ross Corp., was chairman, and Donald Witzke the executive director. The total study was divided into a number of projects assigned to contributed and professional analysts, who generally devoted full time to the study. The 52 analysts, assigned to various city departments, were charged "to analyze the above operations, determine their adequacy and make specific recommendations for improvements and/or financial savings." That resulted in 19 reports, on personnel, purchasing, motor-vehicle maintenance, urban renewal, inspection, police, fire, finance, port control, utilities, water pollution-technical, engineering, construction, recreation and parks, waste collection, law and judicial, city planning, health, and wrap-up. Of the commission's 600 recommendations, over 70% were acted on in some way. Those carried out in full included the establishment of a water pollution control lab and a sanitary landfill for refuse disposal, and insistence on a 40-hour work week for building inspectors. Among those rejected was the use of 1-man police cars in low-crime areas. The last reports were published and distributed early in 1967. The Little Hoover Commission was briefly retained to help implement recommendations, and then was disbanded.

**CLEVELAND LUTHERAN SCHOOLS** began at the elementary level in the 1850s when individual parishes established schools to teach the doctrines of the faith and to maintain the heritage of the German immigrant members of the parishes. Instruction until the turn of the century was in German. ZION EVANGELICAL LUTHERAN CHURCH, under the direction of its pastor, Rev. Henry C. Schwan, established the first school in 1851. It remained open until 1974. Other early schools included those established by Trinity Lutheran Church (1853); IMMANUEL EVANGELICAL LUTHERAN CHURCH (1874); ST. JOHN'S EVANGELICAL LUTHERAN CHURCH (1878); St. Paul Lutheran (1880); and Christ Lutheran (1889). In Nov. 1946, 11 Lutheran congregations formed the Cleveland Lutheran High School Assoc. to establish a Lutheran high school in the city. When the appropriate funds had been raised, Cleveland Lutheran High School was opened at the Lutheran Veterans Ctr. at 2612 Prospect Ave. on 7 Sept. 1948. It was the first under the auspices of the Protestant church in the state and the 9th in the nation. Seventy-five students composed the first 9th-grade class. Erwin F. Sagehorn of St. Louis, Mo., served as first principal. Eventually, 3 structures (former homes) at the Prospect site were remodeled to house the growing school. It was formally dedicated on 22 May 1949. In 1957, the school was razed to make way for the INNERBELT FREEWAY. A state payment of $1 million was used to construct 2 new, identical high schools: Lutheran High School West, at 3850 Linden Ave., Rocky River, and Lutheran High School East,

at Yellowstone and Mayfield Rds., Cleveland Hts. Until the west side school opened in Oct. 1958, classes were held at SS. Peter & Paul Church in Lakewood. East side classes were held at PARK SYNAGOGUE until the east side structure was opened in Sept. 1959. Walter Harting was named principal of Lutheran West, and Henry L. Felton of Lutheran East. In the 1980s, both schools were supported by tuition, and while many students came from church-related families, the student bodies of both were religiously and racially diverse.

The **CLEVELAND LYCEUM** was an early cultural organization for young men, providing a local forum for the exchange of literature and ideas. The lyceum was incorporated by SHERLOCK J. ANDREWS, JOHN W. ALLEN, IRAD KELLEY, John Barr, LEONARD CASE, Edward Baldwin, Richard Hussey, Jas. Conger, and Thos. Kelley. It was founded as part of a national movement that originated in Connecticut in 1826. The purpose of the lyceum movement was to encourage adult education and self-improvement through lectures, debates, museums, libraries, and educational associations. The Cleveland Lyceum offered a reading room, for members only, and public debates and lectures. In 1836, members debated the question "Would it be a good policy for our Government to admit Texas into the Union?" Another topic for debate that year was "Ought the Right of Suffrage be extended to Females?" In 1838, the question of whether or not corporal punishment was necessary in the training of children was addressed. A lecture series, using outside and local talent, was also an important event on the lyceum's yearly agenda. By 1837, the lyceum had a membership of 110. In 1838, an attempt was made to unite with the Cleveland Library Co., the Cleveland Reading Room Assoc., and the YOUNG MEN'S LITERARY ASSOC. The attempt failed, but despite economic hard times for the city's library undertakings, the lyceum managed to linger until ca. 1843. When it closed, its library was divided among members, many of whom later joined other, similar organizations.

Benton, Elbert J., *Cultural Story of an American City* (1944).

The **CLEVELAND MAENNERCHOR,** also known as the Heights Maennerchor, was one of the first German singing societies founded in Cleveland. It was formed in 1873, a full 25 years after the first society, the FROHSINN SINGING SOCIETY. The purpose was not necessarily to compete with other singing guilds but rather to add to the amount of Germanic song in the area. Originally under the leadership of Reinhold Henninges, the Maennerchor performed at various functions, including the 1874, 1893, and 1927 SAENGERFESTS in Cleveland, as well as various "German Days." In 1904, the group became part of the UNITED GERMAN SINGERS of Cleveland, with a total membership of 415 persons. However, it still maintained and sang under the old name. After the 1927 Saengerfest, German Day celebrations continued to be popular; in 1933 the Maenerchor performed before 20,000 people attending a German Day festival at EDGEWATER PARK. Membership in the group was stable and long-term; 31 of its 1935 members (with Fritz Wesiphal, president) had been with it for 25 years. The Maennerchor held meetings every Wednesday night at the home of the society on W. 10th St. and Starkweather Ave. Its headquarters moved in 1950 to 4311 W. 35th St. The Maennerchor gave concerts and was well received at the 81st German Day celebration in 1971. It dissolved in 1974.

Cleveland Maennerchor Records, WRHS.

*CLEVELAND MAGAZINE* made its debut in Apr. 1972, as part of a nationwide city magazine movement. It was the brainchild of Oliver Emerson, president of the Emerson Press, and Lute Harmon, a marketing researcher for the Cleveland Electric Illuminating Co. Harmon became publisher, while Emerson sought local backing and served as chairman of Cleveland Magazine, Inc. "The whole idea was to do stories nobody else was doing," said Michael Roberts, who joined the staff early in 1973 and soon succeeded John Mearns as editor. For the first 2 years, it was edited and printed at the Emerson Press on Chester Ave. After circulation passed 20,000, however, editorial offices were moved to the Keith Bldg., while production was taken over by the Penton Press.

Among the special areas that *Cleveland Magazine* staked out for itself were media, politics, organized crime, and courts. A critical cover story on the Kucinich administration, which broke on the day of the firing of police chief Richard Hongisto (Apr. 1978), became the magazine's all-time bestseller. An expose of Cleveland's federal district court in May 1982 led to an investigation by a federal grand jury. On the lighter side, the magazine also set or followed local trends with its lifestyle coverage, notably in its restaurant reviews and listings. In 1978, Cleveland Magazine, Inc., changed its name to City Magazines, Inc., when it founded *Monthly Detroit*; *Tampa Magazine* was begun in 1980, followed by the purchase of *Milwaukee Magazine* in 1981. By 1983, however, it had sold off these properties in order to concentrate on the parent *Cleveland Magazine*. Robt. F. Pincus became *Cleveland Magazine*'s publisher in 1982. Key editorial positions have been filled by Gary W. Diedrichs and Edward P. Whelan, while *Cleveland* contributors have included Don Robertson, Geo. Condon, and Dick Feagler. Circulation in 1984 was 50,000.

The **CLEVELAND MANX SOCIETY,** organized as Mona's Relief Society in 1851, and Mona's Mutual Benefit Society, organized in 1855, were the 2 oldest organizations established to provide assistance to immigrants from the Isle of Man and their descendants. The name Mona, adopted by both these organizations, was once the name of the Isle of Man. Mona's Relief Society was organized by 21 Manx settlers in 1851, 25 years after the first Manxmen arrived in Cleveland. Formed for "the mutual improvement of its members, and the charitable relief of" Manxmen in need, and for their "better establishment and good government," the relief society was supplemented 4 years later by the establishment of Mona's Mutual Benefit Society, a fraternal insurance society that charged its members monthly dues and provided sick and death benefits. In 1935, the Mutual Benefit Society had 200 members. Between 1876–86, Mona's Relief Society had 268 applicants for relief and paid out $1,745. In addition to the sick, the society helped those Manx people who had no relatives or friends able to care for them in death. It bought a burial lot in WOODLAND CEMETERY and buried 60 people there until 1911, when it bought a larger lot at Highland Park Cemetery. Mona's Relief Society became a major social and cultural institution in the Manx community, in addition to providing help to the sick and needy. In Dec. 1853 it began holding annual Manx festivals, and in Aug. 1880 it initiated an annual picnic; both events were held to raise funds for the society's relief work, as well as to celebrate the Manx heritage. By 1886 the society had 65 members; it began a debating club for young people in the late 19th century. In 1899, an endowment fund was created, and the Ladies' Auxiliary

was established; through its quilting and sewing meetings, it provided a more regular income for the society's relief work. The society continued both its relief work and its social and cultural activities into the 1920s and 1930s, supporting what its historian called the First Great Manx Homecoming—a visit to the homeland—in 1927. By the mid-1970s, Mona's Relief Society was known as the Cleveland Manx Society, and its membership directory contained 133 listings.

Cleveland Manx Society, Membership Directory (Nov. 1974).

**CLEVELAND MEDAL OF HONOR WINNERS.** Twelve Greater Cleveland servicemen have won the Medal of Honor. The recipients were:

| Name | Unit | War |
| --- | --- | --- |
| Barton, Thomas C. | U.S Navy | Civil War |
| Frey, Franz | 37th Ohio Vol. Inf. | Civil War |
| Rock, Frederick | 37th Ohio Vol. Inf. | Civil War |
| Dowling, James | 8th U.S. Cavalry | Indian Wars |
| Richmond, Samuel | 8th U.S. Cavalry | Indian Wars |
| Stupka, Loddie | U.S. Navy | Peacetime |
| Baesel, Albert D. | 37th Division | World War I* |
| Foster, William A. | U.S. Marine Corps Res. | World War II* |
| KIDD, ISAAC C. | U.S. Navy | World War II* |
| Petrarca, Frank J. | 37th Inf. Div. | World War II* |
| Towle, John R. | 82d Airborne Div. | World War II* |
| Herda, Frank A. | 101st Airborne Div. | Vietnam |

* awarded posthumously

**CLEVELAND MEDICAL COLLEGE.** *See* **CASE WESTERN RESERVE UNIVERSITY**

The **CLEVELAND MEDICAL LIBRARY ASSOCIATION** was created on 27 Nov. 1894, when a committee representing 3 Cleveland medical societies met for the purpose of adopting a constitution and bylaws for a medical library. Members of the CUYAHOGA COUNTY MEDICAL SOCIETY, the SOCIETY OF MEDICAL SCIENCES, and the CLEVELAND MEDICAL SOCIETY thus established the Cleveland Medical Library Assoc. as an independent organization whose purpose was to provide and maintain a medical library for the practicing physicians of the area. Space for the library was made available at the Case Library in downtown Cleveland. In 1898, the association purchased the Henry Childs residence on Prospect for its rapidly growing library. In 1906, a fireproof wing was added to the structure, but continued growth necessitated further development, and in 1919, additional land was purchased at the Prospect Ave. location for a new building. Hearing of the proposed building, Mrs. Francis Fleury (Elisabeth Severance) Prentiss, widow of DUDLEY P. ALLEN, M.D., suggested that the library building be erected on land adjoining the proposed site for UNIVERSITY HOSPITALS. Dr. Allen had been an active member of the CMLA and had left a large endowment for library operations at the time of his death in 1925. Mrs. Prentiss offered additional funds for the building's construction on its present site at 11000 Euclid Ave., and on 13 Nov. 1926, the Dudley P. Allen Memorial Medical Library was opened.

The CMLA is supported by endowment and membership fees. Its collection is primarily clinical in nature; that is, it serves the direct library needs of practitioners in the health-sciences fields. Membership provides a number of specialized library services, but the library is fully accessible to the public. Since 1966, the CMLA has been a partner in the CLEVELAND HEALTH SCIENCES LIBRARY, an administrative entity that includes the Allen Library, and the Health Ctr. Library of Case Western Reserve University.

The united library operations center provides health-sciences faculty, students, and practitioners with a resource of nearly 350,000 books and 2,500 journal titles. The Allen Library was designed by the Cleveland architectural firm of FRANK R. WALKER and HARRY E. WEEKS, and is considered to be one of their very fine Neoclassic buildings. It is constructed of Indiana limestone with a pink Geor !'3 :PLE BASE. In 1983, the Allen Library was placed on the Natl. Register of Historic Places. From 1931–44, the association occasionally published the *Bulletin of the Cleveland Medical Library*, and between 1944–54 an occasional *News-Letter* appeared. In 1954, a new series of the *Bulletin* began; with the exception of the period 1973–75, it has appeared regularly since that time.

The **CLEVELAND MEDICAL READING CLUB**, an organization of black physicians, was, in 1986, the oldest continually meeting medical club in the city. It was founded in Nov. 1925 by black physicians, who were excluded because of race from other medical organizations. At the time of its conception, there were only 4 hospitals in the country where black physicians could get internship training; none were in Cleveland. Therefore, local black doctors formed the club to keep abreast of programs and advances in the medical field. To do so, members prepared papers for discussion with the group. Founding members were Drs. L. O. Baumgartner, E. J. Gunn, L. T. Rodgers, CHAS. GARVIN, Leon Evans, Armand Evans, Geo. Ferguson, J. A. Owens, O. A. Taylor, and J. H. McMorris. The club has no elective structure; one member is usually asked to assign topics and notify members of meetings. Members rotate in hosting the dinner meeting. As of 1986, membership was limited to 20 elected physicians. The club continued to meet monthly, except for July and August.

The **CLEVELAND MEDICAL SOCIETY** was organized in 1893 to advance medical science, promote the interests of the medical profession in Cleveland, and foster fraternal feeling among physicians. It was organized by physicians as a protest against the orientation and policies of the CUYAHOGA COUNTY MEDICAL SOCIETY. Dominated by older doctors, the county society held secretive afternoon meetings and made little attempt to attract new members. Younger physicians desired regular and vigorous discussion with their colleagues on current medical issues; a permanent home; and access to a full spectrum of medical literature. The resultant Cleveland Medical Society, organized 3 Feb. 1893 and incorporated in 1894, had 125 initial members, and by the end of the first year, 200 members from northeast Ohio. The society did not shy from controversy, and its quarterly meetings with out-of-town speakers—a national innovation—attracted 300–400. Its tolerance toward homeopathic practitioners earned rebuke from the American Medical Assoc. More important, the legislative committee headed by the social reformer-physician LOUIS B. TUCKERMAN lobbied for public-health issues in Columbus. When Dr. Albert Ohlamacher, a professor of pathology and bacteriology at the College of Wooster, reported his pioneer work on antitoxins, Tuckerman got society backing for the use of such antitoxins for free vaccines to combat diphtheria and tetanus. The society also supported the Cuyahoga County Medical Society and the Society for Medical Sciences in forming the CLEVELAND MEDICAL LIBRARY ASSOC. in 1894. Under pressure from the AMA, the Cleveland Medical Society joined forces with the Cuyahoga County Medical Society to form the Cleveland ACADEMY OF MEDICINE.

The **CLEVELAND MEETING OF THE RELIGIOUS SOCIETY OF FRIENDS (QUAKERS)**, while not the original Quakers organization in Cleveland (an evangelical or "pastoral" Quaker meeting was formed in 1871, known as First Friends Church), carries on the tradition of "unprogrammed" worship and social and community involvement that has distinguished the sect throughout its history. The Cleveland Meeting began in homes in the early 1920s and by 1925 met in Eldred Hall, and later Adelbert Hall of Western Reserve University. In 1940 the meeting moved to the CLEVELAND MUSIC SCHOOL SETTLEMENT, and finally, in 1956, it purchased a house at 10916 Magnolia Dr., designed by ABRAM GARFIELD and built for Edward M. Williams in 1915. At first there was little formal organization within the meeting, and little connection to other Quaker groups. In 1937 the Cleveland Monthly Meeting was formed as a new and united meeting under the American Friends' Fellowship Council, created in the same year by the American Friends' Service Committee, a national group claiming to represent most or all Quaker groups in the U.S. The Monthly Meeting is the business session of Quaker polity, directing the operation of the organization, admitting new members, managing properties, and carrying out other administrative duties.

The Cleveland Meeting differs from the earlier Quaker organization in the city in its adherence to the "unprogrammed" meeting, that is, worship without creed, liturgy, or clerical leadership, wherein members gather and participate as they are moved. The Cleveland Meeting has grown from its original 10–20 members to approximately 100. It has sponsored activities ranging from reading and sewing groups to a course in seeking alternatives to violent behavior, support of a local hunger center, and the Friends' Round Table, a discussion group. Additionally, a part of the Meeting House is given over to several social-action organizations and is known as Peace House. Such activities are in keeping with the Quaker ideal of serving "that of God in every man." In 1965, disagreement regarding the degree of meeting response to the American involvement in Southeast Asia, among other factors, resulted in the formation of a second meeting, known as Community Meeting. The two operated separately until 1975, when the differences were resolved and a merger was accomplished.

**CLEVELAND MEMORIAL SHOREWAY.** *See* **MEMORIAL SHOREWAY**

The **CLEVELAND MENDELSSOHN SOCIETY** was an early local musical society that performed sacred music. It was organized in Dec. 1850 and became a vital influence in the community. The first officers of the society were TRUMAN P. HANDY, president; Elijah Bingham, vice-president; J. H. Stanley, secretary; and John L. Severance, treasurer. Jarvis F. Hanks was the director of music. The group's membership was confined to the families of early local settlers. It was organized for the performance of oratorios and other sacred music. There were about 100 vocal performers in the group, and an orchestra of 25 musicians. The Mendelssohn Society performed works such as Haydn's oratorio *The Creation*. The concerts were held in the Melodeon Hall. New officers were elected for the society on 4 Nov. 1852 for the following year. Handy was again elected president; John L. Severance, vice-president; Oliver P. Hanks, secretary; and Theodoric C. Severance, treasurer. J. P. Holbrook was the conductor. Membership at this time was 112. That was the last listing of the society in the *Annals of Cleveland*, and one can assume that it ceased to exist.

The **CLEVELAND MESSENGER** was a religious weekly founded to promote the principles of Sabbatarianism. Published by the music firm of Breck & Tuttle, it first appeared in May 1836 and lasted about a year. It was edited by Harmon Kingsbury, who was joined and then superseded by Rev. Stephen J. Bradstreet in 1837. In accordance with its avowed object, the front page was regularly taken up by a lengthy article under the standing head of "The Sabbath." Advertising was sporadic, and secular news appeared primarily as filler.

The **CLEVELAND METROPARKS SYSTEM**, an extensive network of parklands in Cuyahoga and Medina counties, consists of 11 reservations: Huntington, Bradley Woods, Rocky River, Big Creek, Mill Stream Run, Hinckley, Brecksville, Bedford, S. Chagrin, N. Chagrin, and Euclid Creek. In 1976 the district assumed responsibility for operation of the Cleveland Zoo, now called the CLEVELAND METROPARKS ZOO. Together with a chain of parkways, these Metroparks virtually surround the city on the east, south, and west, giving rise to the nickname the "Emerald Necklace." The Park District was the brainchild of WM. A. STINCHCOMB (1878–1959). As early as 1905, as Cleveland city park engineer, Stinchcomb urged that Greater Cleveland take advantage of the exceptional character of the county's natural areas by creating a park and boulevard system that eventually would encircle the entire metropolitan area. The proposal arose out of Stinchcomb's belief that the shorter workweek introduced a new problem, that of the proper use of leisure time, and that contact with nature was essential to the well-being of urban dwellers. Stinchcomb's efforts secured passage of state legislation permitting the establishment of park districts and the creation of the Cleveland Metropolitan Park District as a separate subdivision of the state of Ohio. The district was created on 23 July 1917, and the first park property was acquired 2 years later. Stinchcomb was appointed director of the district in 1921 and served in that position until 1957. In its early years, the district concentrated its efforts on acquiring land before advancing values and private development placed it beyond reach. Later, during the Depression, funds were used to provide maximum employment, and at the same time to develop and improve the parks for greater public use. Federal work projects contributed in a substantial way to the further development of the parks. CCC and WPA workers laid water mains and built roads, trails, and shelterhouses still in use today.

The district's activities are directed by a Board of Park Commissioners consisting of 3 citizens, each serving 3-year terms without pay, appointed by the administrative judge of the Probate Court of Cuyahoga County. The district is financed by a tax levy on all real estate in the district and by miscellaneous receipts from district operations, such as golf-course greens fees. The district has acquired more than 18,500 acres of parkland since its inception. Major acquisitions and developments have been in Cuyahoga County, although the district owns land in Summit, Lorain, and Lake counties, in addition to the Hinckley Reservation in Medina County. The policy of the Board of Park Commissioners has been to maintain the parklands in a natural state, limiting development to that consistent with conservation. Interpretive trails, bridle and hiking trails, park drives, picnic areas and shelterhouses, trailside interpretive centers, wildlife management areas, and swimming beaches are among the major developments in the district. In addition, the Park District maintains 6 golf courses and 3 riding stables. Lou E. Tsipis has served as executive director-secretary since 1980.

The **CLEVELAND METROPARKS ZOO** is located in BROOKSIDE PARK on the southwest side of Cleveland. Occupying 166 acres, the zoo is home to 2,500 animals of over 500 different species, and by the 1980s had an annual attendance of 850,000 visitors. Known as the Cleveland Zoological Park until 1975, it had been operated by the city of Cleveland, the CLEVELAND MUSEUM OF NATURAL HISTORY, and the Cleveland Zoological Society. In 1986, the zoo was operated by a board of directors as part of the CLEVELAND METROPARKS SYSTEM and received its operating budget through the passage of tax levies. On 15 Sept. 1882, JEPTHA H. WADE I donated land to the city of Cleveland on the east side for WADE PARK, in which was placed a herd of American deer. During the next few years, other animals were added, and in 1889 a small building was erected in the park. Because of increased residential development and the opening of the CLEVELAND MUSEUM OF ART in Wade Park in 1916, the zoological collections were gradually moved to Brookside Park near W. 25th St. Growth of the collection led many civic groups to realize that its continued successful operation required expert scientific guidance. In Oct. 1940, the city entrusted management of the zoo's day-to-day operations to the Cleveland Museum of Natural History, with Fletcher Reynolds as the zoo's first director. Zoo operations under city management resulted in significant growth. In Oct. 1944, CLEVELAND CITY COUNCIL approved the acquisition of the portion of Brookside Park east of Fulton Rd., increasing the zoo's size to 110 acres. In both 1946 and 1952, Cleveland voters approved $1 million bond issues for the construction of the Bird Bldg. and the Pachyderm Bldg., which opened in 1950 and 1955 respectively. The Cleveland Zoological Society was formed in Apr. 1957 and was entrusted with the operation of the zoo under contract with the city. Under the direction of Dr. Leonard Goss, 1958–79, the zoo continued to expand. The new $3.7 million Cat & Ape Bldg., one of the zoo's major attractions, opened in 1978. In 1986 the zoo took over CLEVELAND AQUARIUM operations, moving the exhibits to Brookside Park. Plans for future expansion included a new Rain Forest exhibit and the revitalization of the Children's Zoo.

**CLEVELAND METROPOLITAN HOUSING AUTHORITY.** *See* **CUYAHOGA METROPOLITAN HOUSING AUTHORITY**

The **CLEVELAND MODERN DANCE ASSOCIATION** was established in 1956 to promote modern dance in Greater Cleveland. A nationally recognized organization, the CMDA has, from the outset, focused its classes and programs on progressive concepts in dance and defined its purpose in public involvement and performance presentation. By donating its reference collection of books to the Cleveland Hts. Public Library, the league made accessible the region's first substantial collection of dance materials. Since 1956, CMDA has annually coordinated modern-dance concerts and related activities for schoolchildren; in 1973 it introduced the Dance Component of the Natl. Endowment for the Arts' Artists-in-the-School project, which, with the assistance of the Ohio and Cleveland Area arts councils, provided schools with performers for considerable lengths of time. The association's annual public workshops have provided courses in techniques of modern dance, jazz movement, and dance composition and have been conducted by guest artists distinguished as principal dancers, internationally renowned choreographers, and accomplished teachers. Nationally recognized dance-therapy workshops for mental-health and medical professionals have been offered 4 or 5 times yearly since 1979. Also in 1979, CMDA established an unprecedented annual subscription series, which, in conjunction with the Playhouse Square Foundation, presented 1 to 5 separate productions, including bookings of nationally recognized troupes. The society has been affiliated with all Cleveland-based modern dance ensembles and has encouraged the formation of 40 major dance companies, more than 100 workshops, and the enrollment of 7,000 students in master classes. Institutions that have cooperated with CMDA have included CLEVELAND STATE UNIVERSITY, CASE WESTERN RESERVE UNIVERSITY, the Beck Ctr., the CLEVELAND MUSIC SCHOOL SETTLEMENT, JOHN CARROLL UNIVERSITY, CUYAHOGA COMMUNITY COLLEGE, and Shaker Hts. High School.

The **CLEVELAND MOZART SOCIETY** was one of the first musical organizations in Cleveland. The society, a choral group, was established in 1837 by TRUMAN P. HANDY. Its goal was the promotion of musical science and the cultivation of refined taste in its members and the community. It did so by promoting concerts in Cleveland and encouraging the development of singing talent among Cleveland's adults. In 1838, the society began to broaden its scope when it established an instrumental group. It also opened a singing school and provided musical education for children. In its later years the society experienced financial problems and began to charge for its once-free concerts. Although no specific date is given for the society's demise, it did not survive the CIVIL WAR.

The **CLEVELAND MUNICIPAL STADIUM**, constructed on reclaimed land on the city's lakefront, was completed in 1931; at that time it boasted the largest individual seating capacity (78,189) of any outdoor arena in the world. The first discussion of a municipal stadium occurred in the early 1900s, when Floyd Rowe, city supervisor of health and physical education, mentioned the possibility of providing a site for high school athletic contests. City Manager WM. R. HOPKINS raised the issue again in 1923, and in 1928, Cleveland voters approved a $2.5 million bond issue to support construction. The facility was not conceived as a great financial benefit to the city, but it was felt that an attractive facility would bring major events to the community, and that would offset the minor revenues realized by the city from club rentals and concession percentages. Construction proceeded despite projected cost overruns and the financial difficulties of the Depression. Designed by OSBORN ENGINEERING and the architectural firm of Walker & Weeks, the stadium was completed on 1 July 1931. The first event held in the new arena was a championship boxing match between Max Schmeling and Young Stribling on 3 July 1931 (see SCHMELING-STRIBLING FIGHT). The CLEVELAND INDIANS played their first game in the park on 31 July 1932; however, that team continued to split its home season between the stadium and LEAGUE PARK until 1947, when it finally moved its entire home season to the stadium. During that year, professional football also came to the stadium. By the 1960s, football, as played by the CLEVELAND BROWNS, became the major attraction, in terms of overall attendance, at the facility.

During its history, the stadium has been used for a variety of sporting and nonsporting events, including rock concerts in the 1970s and 1980s, opera, circuses, the FESTIVAL OF FREEDOM, and the 7TH NATIONAL EUCHARISTIC CONGRESS of 1935; this last event holds the all-time attendance record for the facility, 125,000. By the 1960s, the stadium began to show its age, and the financially

troubled city was hard-pressed to maintain it. In 1966 the city issued $3,375,000 in bonds to provide for improvements, including a new Cleveland Browns office, new ticket facilities, new paint, and new box seats and escalators. However, with the construction of new stadiums throughout the country, Cleveland's facility was still considered outmoded. Given further municipal fiscal problems, Cleveland Browns owner Art Modell offered to manage the facility and provide $10 million for repairs and modifications. In 1974 Modell was given a 25-year lease on the facility. His Stadium Corp. then proceeded to put $8 million worth of improvements into the structure, including 108 loges built under the edge of the upper deck. Nevertheless, a strong movement surfaced in the 1980s for the construction of an entirely new domed stadium for Cleveland. By 1986, a planning body for the new stadium had been formed, and after controversy concerning the siting of the new facility (lakefront vs. central downtown), the domed-stadium group began acquiring property in the vicinity of the CENTRAL MARKET.

Toman, James A., *Cleveland Municipal Stadium* (1981).

The **CLEVELAND MUSEUM OF ART** is acknowledged as one of the finest art museums in the U.S., and its collections, facilities, and programs have an international reputation. The museum, which opened to the public on 6 June 1916, had been planned for a number of years. Its creation was made possible by Hinman B. Hurlbut, JOHN HUNTINGTON, and real-estate heir Horace Kelley, all of whom had bequeathed money specifically for an art museum, as well as by JEPTHA H. WADE I, whose WADE PARK property had been donated in part for the site of such a facility. The Neoclassic building of white Georgian marble that formed the original museum was designed by the Cleveland firm of Hubbell & Benes and was constructed at a cost of $1.25 million. It was situated north of the Wade lagoon, which subsequently formed the focus of the Fine Arts Garden.

Frederic Allen Whiting served as the CMA's first director (1913–30). During his tenure, a number of local families, including the Allens, Holdens, Huntingtons, Hurlbuts, Nortons, Warners, Severances, and Wades, contributed works of art to the growing facility. In 1919 the first Annual Exhibition of Cleveland Artists & Craftsmen was held; this exhibition soon became known as the MAY SHOW. WM. M. MILLIKEN, initially curator of decorative arts at the museum, served as its second director, from 1930–58. During his tenure, the CMA continued to grow and prosper, particularly during the 1940s and 1950s, when a series of large bequests, including the Rogers Bequest and the Severance Fund, allowed it to purchase works and build its collections on a regular basis.

In 1958, 3 important events occurred. On 4 Mar. the museum's first addition was completed. Designed by J. Byers Hays and Paul C. Ruth, it doubled the size of the museum and included the enclosure of its outdoor garden court. During that year the CMA also received the sizable Leonard Hanna, Jr., bequest, which provided it with the funds necessary to function in the mainstream of national and international art collecting. Finally, in 1958, Sherman Emery Lee became the museum's third director. Lee was primarily responsible for the development of the museum's Oriental collection, which ranks as one of the finest in the country. During his directorship, another wing, designed by Marcel Breuer and Hamilton Smith, was opened in 1971. It contained special exhibition galleries, classrooms, lecture halls, and the headquarters for the education department. In 1983, Evan Hopkins Turner became the fourth director of the

CMA. During his tenure, another addition to the museum was opened. Designed by Cleveland architect Peter van Dijk, it contained the museum's extensive library, as well as 9 new galleries. In addition to its collections of fine arts, the CMA has 2 150-seat lecture halls and a 765-seat auditorium, which are used for frequent film and musical presentations. Presidents of the museum since its inception have been WM. B. SANDERS, JEPTHA H. WADE II, JOHN L. SEVERANCE, Wm. G. Mather, HAROLD T. CLARK, and Mrs. EMERY MAY NORWEB.

Cleveland Museum of Art Archives, Cleveland Museum of Art.
Wittke, Carl. *The First Fifty Years (A History of the Cleveland Museum of Art From 1916–1966)* (1966).

The **CLEVELAND MUSEUM OF NATURAL HISTORY** was incorporated in 1920. However, its roots can be traced back to 1835, when a group of young men began meeting in a small building, owned by the Case family near PUBLIC SQUARE, called the "Ark." The "Arkites" held a mutual interest in natural history and filled the Ark with animal specimens. Under the guidance of the eminent naturalist and physician Dr. JARED POTTER KIRTLAND, this group formed the CLEVELAND ACADEMY OF NATURAL SCIENCES and then renamed it the Kirtland Society of Natural Sciences in honor of its leader. This organization disappeared by the end of the century. The idea of establishing a natural-history museum in Cleveland was rekindled in the 20th century by HAROLD T. CLARK. He successfully gained the interest and support of 26 civic leaders, who founded the Cleveland Museum of Natural History in early Dec. 1920. Seven years later, the museum became the legal successor of the Kirtland Society and inherited much of its collection. The museum had a humble start, with a small collection and no programs. Its first headquarters were a business office in the Lennox Bldg. at E. 9th St. and Euclid Ave. The staff immediately began to purchase collections, as well as to organize collecting expeditions in Ohio and eventually throughout the world. By 1922, they were able to display these acquisitions in the museum's new home, the former Leonard Hanna mansion on Euclid Ave. The next 30 years witnessed rapid growth in the museum, with an ever-increasing collection and more exhibits and services for the public. By the 1950s, when the institution was outgrowing its old home, which was also threatened by highway construction, plans were begun for a new museum. From 1958–61, 5 building units opened at University Circle, including 3 large display galleries, a living-animal section, a planetarium, and an observatory. With a continuing development in programs, collections, and exhibits, a large addition was dedicated in 1972 with more space for the research library, temporary exhibits, and an auditorium. In the early 1980s, a 4th major exhibit area was opened.

Early in the museum's history, the trustees and staff realized that they needed to provide public services beyond the confines of the museum. Thus, starting in the 1930s, the museum played an important role in establishing Holden Aboretum in Kirtland, Ohio, and the Trailside Museums in Cleveland's Metropolitan Park System. For several years, it was also responsible for operating the Cleveland Zoo. The museum was a leading force behind the construction of the Cleveland Aquarium. In 1985 it transferred management of the aquarium to the CLEVELAND METROPARKS. Four natural areas in surrounding counties are also maintained by the museum as sanctuaries. One of the most prominent areas for this institution has been its educational programs. Over the years, the museum has taught millions to appreciate the natural environment—"to

inspire a love of nature." Its founders wasted little time in initiating such a program—6 weeks after incorporation, it established an education department, one of the first in any American museum. In the past 6 decades, the museum has developed and refined various special-education programs for preschoolers to college students and adults. For the general public, it has also offered a lecture program, which has brought many famous scientists and naturalists to Cleveland.

Sixty years of gathering specimens, primarily by expeditions and donations, has provided the museum with unique, comprehensive collections. What enhances the value of these collections is the sequential manner in which they are displayed in the museum—beginning with the formation of the universe and ending with an analysis of man's relationship to his environment. Only a small number of the over 1 million specimens can be displayed. The remainder are utilized for research purposes. Students and prominent scientists from around the world come to study these collections. Dr. Donald C. Johanson, who was curator of physical anthropology at the museum, utilized the well-known Hamman-Todd scientific collection of human and primate skeletal remains to analyze and compare with his discoveries in Ethiopia. The organization's publication program disseminates further information on its collections through various books and papers, its nationwide magazine, the *Explorer*, and its newsletter, "Tracks." Although the Cleveland Museum of Natural History has never relied on tax-based support, the strong support of Clevelanders in membership and contributions and the dedication of the staff and trustees have continually maintained the quality of this major cultural institution in educating man to respect nature.

Papers on Origin and History of, Library of the Cleveland Museum of Natural History.
Hendrickson, Walter B., *The Arkites and Other Pioneer Natural History Organizations of Cleveland* (1962).

The **CLEVELAND MUSIC SCHOOL SETTLEMENT**, opened in Oct. 1911 with 50 pupils, was designed to provide inexpensive or free musical training and to give students a place to find help with personal problems. By 1984 it was the largest school of its kind in the U.S. and had become an important cultural institution locally, serving 3,000 students in a variety of programs with an annual budget of $1 million. Inspired by a New York music school settlement, Almeda Adams, a music teacher blind since birth, founded the Cleveland school with the help of ADELLA PRENTISS HUGHES. Initial funding for the school was a $1,000 donation from the FORTNIGHTLY MUSIC CLUB, a society founded in 1894 to promote music in Cleveland. The school was funded by private donations until 1919, when it became a charter member of the Welfare Fed.

From 1911–18, the Cleveland Music School Settlement was located in the Goodrich Settlement House. Growth forced several moves until 1938, when it moved to 11125 Magnolia Dr., the 42-room former home of Edmund S. Burke, governor of the Federal Reserve Bank. In 1955 the school bought the adjoining property, and by 1973 it had 6 buildings at its main school. In 1947, the school's $40,000 budget supported 40 faculty members, who taught theory, piano, voice, and string instruments to 475 pupils. In 1948, Howard Whittaker was appointed director of the school; he served in that capacity until retiring in 1984. Under his direction, the Cleveland Music School Settlement greatly expanded its activities and became a promotional force for the arts in the community, helping to found the Lake Erie

Opera Theater in 1964 and the Cleveland Summer Arts Festival in 1967.

With a grant from the CLEVELAND FOUNDATION, the Music School Settlement began in 1953 a program to extend its music instruction services to social-service agencies such as neighborhood centers, orphanages, hospitals, and institutions and homes for the retarded, disabled, and aged. Directed by Richard Kauffman, the extension program was a pioneering effort in the use of music therapy. By 1973 it served 35 agencies and had led the school to establish a music therapy institute to teach others to use music therapy. The Music School Settlement has also expanded its services geographically: in Sept. 1958 it opened a branch in the WEST SIDE COMMUNITY HOUSE; by 1969 it had a south side branch on Harvard Rd.; it merged with the Koch School of Music in ROCKY RIVER in 1970; and, petitioned by 1,200 local residents in 1980, it opened a branch at 5415 Broadway, former home of the Hruby Conservatory of Music, which closed in 1968.

Cleveland Music School Settlement Records, WRHS.

The **CLEVELAND MUSICAL SOCIETY** was one of the earliest organizations in the city devoted to music. Its founding in 1832 coincided with the arrival of the first piano in Cleveland. The first president of the society was A. S. Sanford. Members met every Monday and Tuesday at 7 p.m. In its early years, the society essentially served as a club for those who shared a common interest in music. Later it began to sponsor occasional musical events that were opened to the public. With the emergence of several new singing societies in the late 1830s and early 1840s, the society became less publicly active. Occasional concerts usually featured choral music. The Cleveland Musical Society probably disbanded during the CIVIL WAR. It sponsored 2 concerts in 1861: Mendelssohn's *Capriccio Brillante*, and the "Tower Scene" from Verdi's *Il Trovatore*.

The **CLEVELAND NETS** (1974–77) were the local franchise in the innovative World Team Tennis league. Native Clevelander Joe Zingale, a former disc jockey turned radio station owner, bought the Nets franchise for $50,000 and, after 4 years of poor performances both on the court and at the box office, moved the team to New Orleans before the start of the 1978 season. World Team Tennis was a short-lived (1973–78) experiment that infuriated many tennis devotees by encouraging booing and cheering in support of the home team. Founded by tennis star Billie Jean King, her husband, Larry, and sports entrepreneur Dennis Murphy, the team tennis effort began in May 1974, fielding 16 teams to play a schedule of 44 contests each. Teams offered large salaries to lure players away from the traditional tennis tournament game. The Nets began the 1974 campaign with player-coach Clark Graebner, Peaches Bartkowicz, South African Ray Moore, and the brother-sister duo of Cliff Richey and Nancy Gunter, but Zingale eventually signed some of the game's biggest stars to play for the Nets, including Marty Riessen (player-coach 1975–77 and 1975 Rookie of the Year), Martina Navratilova (1976), and Bjorn Borg (1977).

In their 4 years of operation in Cleveland, the Nets never had a winning season, but they managed to make the playoffs twice. Playing home matches at Public Hall in 1974, they won 21 of their 44 matches (.477) to finish in 4th place in the Central Sec. of the Eastern Div.; that record was good enough to make the playoffs, but there the Nets lost to the Philadelphia Freedoms in 2 straight matches. For 1975 the Nets hired a new coach and moved to the Richfield Coliseum; the new location helped improve total attendance from 48,887 in 1974 to 55,924 in 1975, but the team finished in last place in its division with only 16 wins (.364). Total attendance increased to more than 73,108 in 1976, when the team won 20 of 44 matches (.455), but a season-ending slump in which they lost 4 of their last 5 contests kept the Nets out of the playoffs. The Nets averaged 3,323 fans per match in 1976, which was higher than the league average. For 1977, Zingale did what other owners had begun to do to boost attendance—he scheduled half of the Nets' "home" matches for cities other than Cleveland: in Pittsburgh, St. Louis, Nashville, Miami, Baton Rouge, and the New Orleans Superdome. Zingale also counted on the signing of top male player Bjorn Borg and "the world famous transsexual" Dr. Renee Richards to help the Nets at the box office. The Nets again fared poorly on the court, however, winning only 16 games (.364), but nevertheless qualified for the playoffs, thanks only to what one sportswriter called "the ineptness of the traveling Soviet team," which won only 12 matches. The Nets lost to the Boston Lobsters in the playoffs, 3 matches to 2. The team averaged about 3,000 spectators per match in 1977 and made a profit of $165,000; of that, $125,000 was the result of a trade. On 14 Feb. 1978, Zingale officially moved the Nets to New Orleans, where the team had drawn well during its 1977 "home" game.

The *CLEVELAND NEWS* was one of the city's major daily newspapers during the 20th century. Although the *News* began publication in 1905, its lineage can be traced back to 1868, when the *CLEVELAND LEADER* began issuing its evening edition under the banner of the *Evening News*. When the *Cleveland Herald* ceased publication in 1885, the *Leader*, which had acquired rights to the name, amended the evening edition's title to the *News & Herald*. Cleveland banker CHAS. A. OTIS created the "modern" *News* in 1905, to further his political campaign against Mayor TOM L. JOHNSON. Having bought the *CLEVELAND WORLD* in 1904, he then acquired the *News & Herald* through his purchase of the morning *Leader*. Adding the *Evening Plain Dealer* to his acquisitions, Otis merged the 3 afternoon papers into a single daily, which premiered as the *World-News* on 3 July 1905 and became simply the *Cleveland News* on 13 Sept. Through the *News & Herald*, it possessed the valuable AP franchise in Cleveland.

In 1912, Otis sold the *News* to his brother-in-law, DANIEL R. HANNA, SR., who had acquired the *Leader* 2 years earlier. Hanna enlisted the *News* in support of Theodore Roosevelt's Bull Moose campaign and a year later consolidated its operation with that of the *Leader* in his newly erected Leader Bldg. at E. 6th St. and Superior. When the *Leader* was sold to the *PLAIN DEALER* in 1917, the *News* inherited the *Sunday Leader*, which appeared first as the *Sunday News-Leader* and then as the *Sunday News*. After WORLD WAR I, in an effort to catch up with the front-running *CLEVELAND PRESS*, Hanna imported ARTHUR B. "MICKEY" MCBRIDE from Chicago to serve as the *News's* circulation manager. Under sports editor ED BANG, the paper also began the annual *Cleveland News* Toyshop in 1926, raising money through boxing matches to provide for the needy at Christmas. That was the same year that the *News* moved into its modern publishing plant at E. 18th St. and Superior.

Still failing to overtake the *Press*, the *News* was pushed to the edge of extinction by circulation and advertising declines during the Depression. In 1932, the heirs of Dan R. Hanna, Sr., transferred control of the paper to the FOREST CITY PUBLISHING CO., which also acquired the stock of the *Plain Dealer*. With 5 members on the board to 2 for the *News*, the *Plain Dealer* was the senior partner

254

of the enterprise, a fact underscored by the subsequent suspension of the *Sunday News* on 3 Jan. 1933. As the junior partner, the daily *News* managed to survive for nearly 30 more years, providing the *Plain Dealer* with a certain nuisance value against the *Press*. It remained staunchly Republican in orientation, although it began to support some Democrats on the local level.

Postwar *News* circulation peaked at 148,752 in 1952, but shortly began to decline after a price hike from 5 to 7 cents. In 1959 its circulation stood at 130,368, against 320,271 for the *Press*. On 23 Jan. 1960, Forest City Publishing Co. announced the sale of the *News* to the *Press*, and the last edition appeared that Saturday afternoon. The *Plain Dealer* moved into the *News* plant, which provides its current address. For several months the phrase "and News" was entered below the nameplate of the *Cleveland Press* in constantly diminishing type, until it disappeared completely. Prominent *News* staffers included editor NATHANIEL R. HOWARD, city editor Albert E. M. Bergener, drama critic ARCHIE BELL, columnists John B. Mullaney and Howard Preston, radio-television critic Maurice Van Metre, and sports writer ED MCAULEY.

Shaw, Archer H., *The Plain Dealer: One Hundred Years in Cleveland* (1942).

The **CLEVELAND NEWSPAPER GUILD, LOCAL 1,** merited its designation by antedating the formation of the American Newspaper Guild (ANG) by several months. During the Depression summer of 1933, a group of *Cleveland Press* reporters began meeting under the leadership of Robert L. Bordner and Garland Ashcraft to discuss salary cuts and other adverse job conditions. Encouraged by the Heywood Broun column in the *New York World Telegram* urging unionization for newspapermen, they joined with writers from the *CLEVELAND NEWS* to organize the Cleveland Editorial Employees Assoc. on 20 Aug. 1933. Over the next few months, the Clevelanders spread the union message among journalists in other cities and urged Broun to assume leadership of the movement. After changing their name to the Cleveland Newspaper Guild on 17 Oct., they attended the first ANG national convention in Washington, D.C., on 15 Dec. 1933. Broun was elected its first president, and the Cleveland chapter was recognized for its pivotal role with the nation's first local chapter. Early in 1934, Local 1 appointed Wm. M. Davy, a former mineworker from Tuscarawas County, as its first executive secretary. By the end of the year, Davy had negotiated the ANG's first contested contract when he won an agreement from the *Cleveland News*. A contract signed 2 years later with the *CLEVELAND PRESS* set the precedent of collective bargaining for the entire Scripps-Howard newspaper chain. By 1944, guild jurisdiction had been extended to editorial rooms of the *PLAIN DEALER* and the *CATHOLIC UNIVERSE BULLETIN.* Beginning in 1946, Local 1 was also involved in several newspaper strikes. Although it failed to secure a union shop in the devastating strike of 1962–63, it subsequently secured a guild shop in all active units, requiring employees to join the guild and pay dues within 30 days of employment. Davy, who retired at the end of 1963, was followed as executive secretary by Jack F. Weir and, after 1978, J. Stephen Hatch. Membership inevitably declined from a high of over 700 to around 450 following the death of the *Cleveland Press* in 1982. Losses from the *Press* and *News* units were partially made up by the accession to Local 1 of units from the *Canton Repository* in 1968 and the *Massillon Evening Independent* in 1970. Local 1 served as host for national conventions of the ANG in 1935, 1968, and 1983.

The **CLEVELAND NEWSPAPER STRIKE OF 1962,** the city's third, turned out to be the most consequential in the history of local journalism. It was triggered by a walkout of drivers (Teamsters Local 473) at the *PLAIN DEALER* on the night of 29 Nov. 1962, but the underlying cause was the effort of the CLEVELAND NEWSPAPER GUILD (Local 1) to secure a closed shop in the *Cleveland Press* business department. As only little more than half the employees in that department belonged to the union, the guild wanted a contract provision requiring membership or at least compulsory dues payment from all who worked there. Although the *Plain Dealer*'s business department was completely unorganized by anyone, that paper was pulled into the strike by union membership of employees in other departments. In all, 2,400 members of 11 different unions joined the work stoppage. Although the TEAMSTERS UNION broke the picket lines after a week, they rejoined the strike 10 days later. An estimated $2.6 million in wages was lost by the strikers, while the two newspapers estimated their losses at $19 million, much of it in canceled Christmas advertising. As the 129-day strike dragged on, various expedients were adopted in efforts to circumvent the news blackout, rendered even more complete by a simultaneous 114-day newspaper strike in New York. Department store owners temporarily revived the CLEVELAND SHOPPING NEWS, while the weekly *Heights Sun-Press* began appearing twice a week. The chief stopgap was provided by the Newspaper Guild itself, which published a strike paper, the *CLEVELAND RECORD*, from 21 Jan. 1963 to the end of the strike. With the ratification of new contracts by the Printers' and Machinists' unions on 4 Apr., the way was clear for the reappearance of the *Plain Dealer* and the *Press* on 8 Apr. Although the guild failed to obtain its union shop, the ultimate loser in the strike was the *CLEVELAND PRESS.* Debating one of his employees on TELEVISION during the strike, *Press* editor LOUIS B. SELTZER had struck many observers as unnecessarily overbearing in his manner. Upon resumption of publication, the *Press* suffered a circulation drop of 40,000 readers, to only 12,000 for the *Plain Dealer.* The *Press* never really recovered that loss, as it surrendered its circulation edge to the *Plain Dealer* within 5 years. Other newspaper strikes occurred locally in 1946, 1956, 1972, and 1974.

**CLEVELAND: NOW!,** a joint public and private program for wide urban renewal and revitalization in Cleveland, was created by Mayor Carl B. Stokes in response to the 4 Apr. 1968 assassination of Dr. Martin Luther King, Jr. Stokes announced the program on 1 May 1968 in a television documentary jointly produced and televised by WKYC-TV, WEWS-TV, and WJW-TV, in which the mayor toured the city's problem areas and talked with residents. The program was originally to have raised $1.5 billion over 10 years. The first 2-year phase called for $177 million for projects in the areas of employment, youth activities and employment, community centers, health-clinic facilities, housing units, and economic renewal projects. Funding came from business donations, countrywide public solicitations, city and state funds, and $143 million in federal funds. The program called for countywide public sponsorship; Geo. Steinbrenner III, head of the Group '66 organization of business leaders, committed the organization to heading a public collection for $1.25 million, which included schoolchildren, workers, and shoppers. Also included in funding was a .5% city income tax increase.

Funding goals were quickly met for the first few months; however, public outrage to the program arose after the GLENVILLE SHOOT-OUT of 23 July 1968, and donations declined. NOW funds had indirectly gone to purchase arms used in the shootout. Fred "Ahmed" Evans had bought guns with his paychecks from starting an African cultural shop in HOUGH. The funds had originated with NOW but passed through several agencies before the Hough Area Community Agency paid Evans; he dispensed arms to about 20 members of the Black Nationalist Organization of New Libya. Evans and his accomplices were sentenced to life terms.

NOW actively operated until 1970 and met many of its initial goals. On 26 Feb. 1970, Stokes announced that NOW would fund 4 new community centers, its last major commitment. A month later, on 24 Mar., Stokes announced that a second fund drive would begin in several weeks; however, the drive never materialized. In 1970, 8 Cleveland policemen and a tow-truck driver wounded in Glenville sued Stokes and the NOW trustees for $8.8 million, charging that Evans had purchased the arms and ammunition that wounded the plaintiffs with NOW funds and that Stokes had personally authorized that Evans and other militants be paid to keep the peace and not commit crimes in the summer of 1968. The suits were not heard in common pleas court until Apr. 1977 and were dismissed a month later. Evans's funds had originated with Cleveland: NOW! to set up the cultural shop, but no witnesses confirmed the payoff theory. An appeal was rejected in 1978. Cleveland: NOW! was not formally dissolved until Oct. 1980. The remaining $220,000 was donated to the CLEVELAND FOUNDATION to use for youth employment and low-income housing.

Stokes, Carl B., *Promises of Power* (1973).

The **CLEVELAND OPERA** was organized in 1976 by David and Carola Bamberger and John Heavenrich as the New Cleveland Opera Co. Cleveland Opera was formed to be the city's resident producing opera company. It sought to develop new audiences by being accessible intellectually (performing primarily in English) and financially (prices were well below those for the Metropolitan Opera's Cleveland tour). Besides its internationally known general manager/ artistic director David Bamberger, the opera board has included many prominent Cleveland-area citizens, including Nicholas Peay and Dr. David Klein. Its singers have included veterans of the Met and the New York City and San Francisco operas. The company has featured outstanding younger American singers, many of whom have later risen to national and international prominence. The opera has been led by some of the finest conductors, including Franz Allers; Sixten Ehrling; Anton Guadagno; Scott Bergeson; and Clevelanders Robt. Page, Geo. Posell, and Stuart Raleigh. Famed comic Victor Borge made his operatic conducting debut with *The Magic Flute* at the Cleveland Opera. Beginning at Byron Auditorium in SHAKER HTS., the company moved to the HANNA THEATER by the 1980/ 81 season. In 1984 it took up residence at the Playhouse Square Ctr.'s STATE THEATER. Its productions have covered the full range of world music theater, from *Aida* and *Faust* to *Naughty Marietta* and *Kiss Me, Kate*. Its "Cleveland Verdi Festival" (1982/83) was the first season by any American company dedicated to the works of a single composer. Jan Bach's *The Student from Salamanca*, winner of the New York City Opera's first national 1-act opera competition, was presented 43 days after its premiere at Lincoln Ctr. Cleveland Opera won an Emmy for Best Production of Cultural Significance (1978) for its televised staging of Britten's *The Little Sweep*. The opera's tour department has performed throughout the state 150–200 times annually for community groups, schools, and social-service institutions. Its tour to golden age centers is the only series in the state designed to serve the needs of institutionalized senior citizens. Cleveland Opera has received funding from a variety of foundations (the CLEVELAND FOUNDATION, the GEO. GUND FOUNDATION, the Natl. Endowment for the Arts), individuals, and corporations (TRW, EATON, Sohio).

The **CLEVELAND OPERA COMPANY** grew out of the Studio Club in 1920. In 1917, the Studio Club, under the direction of Francis Sadlier, gave light operas in local theaters. In 1920, they offered a week's run of Victor Herbert's *Serenade* at the COLONIAL THEATER on Superior Ave. NE near Rockwell. They then reorganized the company as the Cleveland Opera Co., for the purpose of producing grand and light operas. The company started with light works and gradually moved into opera on a larger scale. Its first season (1921) consisted of *Mikado, Serenade*, and *Fortuneteller* at the Colonial Theater. By 1923, it had moved up to *Il Trovatore*, in which Metropolitan Opera star Lila Robeson sang. The Cleveland Opera Co. was engaged for the premiere of a new "all-American" opera, *Alglala*, by Akronite Francesco de Leone (composer) and Cecil Fanning (librettist). This premiere took place at the Akron Armory on 23 May 1924. Mabel Garrison and Edward Johnson of the Met were in the cast. The orchestra was made up of 40 musicians from the Cleveland Orchestra conducted by F. KARL GROSSMAN. *Alglala* was then performed in Nov. 1924 at Masonic Hall in Cleveland. Another premiere produced by the Cleveland Opera was based on Marion Campbell's play *Love's Wishing Well*. The first performance of this opera set in Ireland was at the Masonic Auditorium on 7 Mar. 1927, sponsored by the combined Eastern Star Chapters of Greater Cleveland. In 1928, Grossman left for Europe, and Francesco de Leone became musical director of the company, which continued to perform light opera for several seasons. Around this time, the company came to be called the Cleveland Opera Assoc., and then the Opera Guild. The Cleveland Opera Co. "merged" with a group formed in 1932 by Rudolf Schueler called Friends of the Opera. They were funded by the Federal Musical Project, and all members of the troupe were paid. For several years during the 1930s, this group performed in school auditoriums, Public Hall, CAIN PARK THEATER, and churches. They presented standard operas such as *Carmen, Cavalleria Rusticana*, and *The Marriage of Figaro* in English. The Cleveland Opera Co. continued until 1937, "when there was no further need apparently for its continuance," although more likely it disbanded because of the end of the Federal Music Project, which was discontinued at this time.

The **CLEVELAND ORCHESTRA** is one of the premier orchestras of the world. It was established in 1918 through the efforts of ADELLA PRENTISS HUGHES and the MUSICAL ARTS ASSOC. Hughes had been active since the turn of the century in bringing major orchestras and musicians to perform in Cleveland, and in the process became keenly aware of the need to provide the city with its own orchestra. A benefit concert performed for St. Ann's Parish in CLEVELAND HTS. on 11 Dec. 1918 marked the beginning of the orchestra. The musical personnel recruited for the concert, including NIKOLAI SOKOLOFF as conductor, went on to form the core of a permanent Cleveland Orchestra under the management of Hughes and the direction of the Musical Arts Assoc. During the 1920s, the orchestra built a firm base of local support, and through travels in Ohio and to the East Coast, it began to achieve broader notice. Concerts were given in the Masonic Auditorium, and later in the Music Hall. A substantial gift from Mr. and Mrs. JOHN L. SEVERANCE enabled the Musical Arts Assoc. To build a permanent home, SEVERANCE HALL, for the orchestra at Euclid Ave. and East Blvd. in UNIVERSITY CIRCLE. The orchestra first played there in 1931.

The orchestra has had 6 musical directors/conductors: Nikolai Sokoloff, 1918–33; ARTUR RODZINSKI, 1933–43; Erich Leinsdorf, 1943–46; GEO. SZELL, 1946–70; Lorin Maazel, 1971–82; and Christoph Von Dohnanyi, 1984–. Each of these men contributed to the growth of the orchestra in a variety of ways. However, it was under the direction of Szell that the orchestra undertook an extensive series of foreign tours that greatly enhanced its international reputation. Maazel continued the tours while expanding the orchestra's commercial recording work.

Since the orchestra's inception, one of the major facets of its work has been educational, accomplished principally through series of concerts held for local schoolchildren. These concerts are in addition to the orchestra's normal Thursday, Friday, and Saturday evening performances during the fall-through-spring season. In 1968, the orchestra began a new phase of its history with its inaugural performance at the Blossom Music Ctr. Located in Northampton Twp. in Summit County, the Music Ctr. serves as the orchestra's summer home, attracting large audiences from the Cleveland-Akron area to its spacious lawn and pavilion seating. Throughout its history, the Cleveland Orchestra has existed largely on privately donated monies raised by the Musical Arts Assoc. from individuals throughout the community. During the 1960s and 1970s, it also benefited from monies made available through various federal programs for the arts.

Grossman, F. Karl, *A History of Music in Cleveland* (1972).
Marsh, Robert, *The Cleveland Orchestra* (1972).
Musical Arts Assoc. Archives, Severance Hall.

The **CLEVELAND, PAINESVILLE & ASHTABULA (CP & A)** interurban extended the CLEVELAND, PAINESVILLE & EASTERN (CP & E) interurban line 27 mi. farther east to Ashtabula. It formed a link with other interurbans at its Ashtabula terminus that allowed passengers to travel on to Erie, Pa., and Buffalo, N.Y. The line was incorporated in Apr. 1901 by the Everrett-Moore syndicate, owner of the already existing CP & E. The CP & A was established as a subsidiary, primarily for bookkeeping reasons. Stops along the route from Ashtabula included Madison, Perry, Unionville, and Geneva. The majority of planned right-of-way was through open country, to allow for speed, but the line traveled on the city streets of Geneva and Madison. Just as the line opened, in Oct. 1903, the Everrett-Moore syndicate lost control of the line, because of financial problems. J. W. Holcomb and E. J. Latimer became the new owners of the CP & A. Internal problems gripped the new line. Directors could not decide upon a location for the CP & A's main offices and car shops. Finally, in 1906, the Everrett-Moore syndicate reacquired the line and operated it as a part of the CP & E, as originally planned. The rolling stock kept its CP & A designation, however, and different books were kept for the CP & A until its demise in 1926.

The interurban lines linking the CP & A with points eastward at Ashtabula were never on strong financial ground, and traffic to and from the east, both passenger and freight, was never substantial. One of the linking lines, the Cleveland & Erie, went into receivership in 1920; the second, the Pennsylvania & Ohio, closed down its Ashtabula-Conneaut link in Feb. 1924, effectively dead-ending the CP & A in Ashtabula. Automobiles and bus lines began eating away at the CP & A's remaining passenger business, while trucks did the same to its freight traffic. The line was burdened with financial losses in 1923 and 1924; it went into receivership on 23 Feb. 1926. Service stopped within 24 hours. The parent line, the CP & E, lasted just 3 months longer, making its final run on 20 May 1926.

Christiansen, Harry, *New Northern Ohio's Interurbans* (1983).

The **CLEVELAND, PAINESVILLE & EASTERN** was the primary interurban line carrying passengers east from Cleveland to Painesville. A subsidiary line, the CLEVELAND, PAINESVILLE & ASHTABULA, extended the line farther east to Ashtabula. The CP&E was chartered 25 Apr. 1895, as part of the Everrett-Moore syndicate. Henry A. Everrett and Edward W. Moore were well-known figures in midwestern public utilities and had holdings in traction companies in both the U.S. and Canada. Their syndicate, which included officers of the CLEVELAND ELECTRIC RAILWAY CO., was involved in the building and operation of interurban systems. The syndicate controlled all northern Ohio interurbans except the Southwestern. The CP&E began service between Cleveland and Painesville on 4 July 1896. The initial Cleveland terminus was at Ivanhoe Rd. and Euclid Ave.; the line was extended to PUBLIC SQUARE in 1897. The original, or "main," line included stations in Euclid, Wickliffe, Willoughby, Mentor, and Painesville. A northern, or "shore," line was added in 1898, with stops at COLLINWOOD and Willoughbeach Park. Willoughbeach Park was a trolley park, owned and operated by the CP&E. It stood across from what is now (1985) Shoregate Shopping Ctr., on Lake Shore Blvd. The line promoted day trips to the park, which featured a dance hall, picnic groves, swimming, and a few rides.

The CP&E acquired the Painesville, Fairport & Richmond Street Railway in 1898, a 6-mi. spur that added an extension from Painesville to Fairport. In 1900, the CP&E established the Cleveland, Painesville & Ashtabula, set up as a subsidiary for bookkeeping purposes. The CP&A extended the road 27 mi. east of Painesville to Ashtabula, where it linked with 2 other interurban lines. These lines provided rail links with Erie and, farther east, Buffalo. The CP&A opened in Oct. 1903, but the Everrett-Moore syndicate lost control of it owing to financial difficulties. Everrett & Moore reacquired the CP&A in 1906. Both Everrett and Moore maintained summer estates along the line, near Mentor. The 27-room Moore mansion, Mooreland, was purchased by Lakeland Community College in 1982. The CP&E was handicapped by connection with weak lines at its eastern terminus, Ashtabula. As the connecting lines failed, anticipated passenger traffic between Cleveland and Buffalo never materialized. Freight service dwindled as truck service became established in the 1920s. Buses and private autos began to take away passenger fares, as well. Successive losses in both 1923 and 1924 caused the line's demise, although it never went bankrupt. The CP&A was closed first, in Feb. 1926. Willoughbeach Park did not reopen for the 1926 season. The only moneymaking operation of the line, an electric plant that provided power to several thousand customers between Mentor and Geneva, was sold to the CLEVELAND ELECTRIC ILLUMINATING CO. The final CP&E run was on 20 May 1926.

Christiansen, Harry, *New Northern Ohio's Interurbans* (1983).
Christiansen, Harry, *Trolley Trails through Greater Cleveland* (1975).

The **CLEVELAND PANTHERS** were a semiprofessional football team in the 1920s; that was also the name of the Cleveland team in the short-lived 1926 American Football

League and was the original name selected for the organization that eventually became the CLEVELAND BROWNS. Little information is available about the semiprofessional Panthers until the team turned professional in 1926. That year the Panthers joined the AFL, the first professional league organized to compete directly with the young National Football League. The Cleveland franchise in the league was obtained by Chas. X. Zimmerman, president of the Amiesite Asphalt Co. of Ohio; he was also vice-president of the 9-team league. Geo. T. Jones was secretary of the organization; Frank Garden, vice-president; and Herman Zapf, treasurer. They signed players that Clevelanders would recognize, such as former Cleveland Bulldogs players Doc Elliott and Dick Wolf and Ohio State stars Al Michaels and Cookie Cunningham. Clad in gold-and-black uniforms, the team played its home games at the new Luna Park stadium.

The season began impressively: 22,000 spectators watched the Panthers defeat Red Grange's New York All-Americans 10–0 at LUNA PARK on 26 Sept. One observer called the crowd "the largest ever to watch a football game in Cleveland," and added that the Panthers themselves "looked like a real collegiate eleven." Although the Panthers won 2 of their next 3 games, only 1,000 people attended the 31 Oct. game at Luna Park. The following week, as the Panthers were in Philadelphia preparing for a game, the Stearns Advertising Co. sued the team for $1,000, and the organization was placed in receivership by the court. The team was disfranchised by the league and disbanded, stranding the players in Philadelphia. Herb Brandt, owner of the NFL franchise for Cleveland, quickly signed most of the Panthers' players and revived the CLEVELAND BULLDOGS for at least 1 game in what was left of the season. The Panthers returned in 1927 but were apparently an independent semiprofessional team managed by Jones, whose next major appearance on the Cleveland sports scene was in the summer of 1945. After a newspaper contest chose the Panthers as the name for the Cleveland franchise in the All-America Football Conference, Jones reminded owner ARTHUR B. (MICKEY) MCBRIDE of the earlier Panther teams and apparently demanded several thousand dollars for the use of the name. McBride refused to pay, reopened the contest, and selected the Browns as the name for his team.

The **CLEVELAND PHILHARMONIC ORCHESTRA** became a source of fine music for Clevelanders in the late 1930s. It also served as a means by which young area musicians gained valuable concert experience. The orchestra was founded in 1938 by 3 Cleveland musicians: bass clarinetist Alfred Zetzer, oboist Robt. Zupnick, and cellist Irving Klein. They approached Dr. F. KARL GROSSMAN, a professor at Western Reserve University, with a proposal to conduct an orchestra in which they could acquire concert experience that would better prepare them for professional careers. Grossman, impressed with the musicians' performance after hearing just one rehearsal, decided to accept their offer, and became the orchestra's first conductor and director. He remained conductor and director throughout the Cleveland Philharmonic Orchestra's first 25 seasons. Other directors included Robt. Marcellus, Jose Serebrier, Zolton Rosznyai, Geo. Cleve, and Wm. Slocum. The orchestra's musicians performed on a voluntary basis. The only salaried members were the director and concertmaster. The group's financial support came from private and corporate donations. The chief corporate contributors were the Sohio Co. and Natl. City Bank. In the early 1980s, the orchestra became active in presenting concerts for specific ethnic groups in the Cleveland area. Past concerts have

included celebrations of Czechoslovakian Independence Day, the rededication of BOHEMIAN NATL. HALL, and Martin Luther King Day. In 1973 the orchestra began sponsoring a Young Persons' Concert competition, selecting a young musician by audition to perform a concerto at the Young Persons' Concert. The orchestra established a tradition of providing special outreach programs to the community. It sponsored a joint program with the Lake Erie Girl Scout Council, providing concerts as a part of the music badge program. It was also active in working with the city's senior citizens by sponsoring lectures related to their concerts through the Elders Program of CUYAHOGA COMMUNITY COLLEGE and the CLEVELAND PUBLIC LIBRARY. In the 1980s, the Philharmonic Orchestra's primary purpose continued to be as a source of opportunity for aspiring musicans.

The **CLEVELAND PHOTOGRAPHIC SOCIETY** was established on 25 Jan. 1887 as the Cleveland Camera Club. It was founded to advocate the leisure aspect of photography. By 18 June 1913, a controversial reorganization of the club for financial solvency resulted in the Cleveland Photographic Society, incorporated 9 Oct. 1920. In 1921, the society instituted the School of Photography, within which John Steinke conducted most classes until a faculty was assembled in 1928. Enrollees studied commercial practices, portraiture, composition, technique, pictorialism, photochemicals, and bromoil processing. The society's traveling shows premiered in 1922, when prints mounted on 8'x4' flats were exhibited at select locations throughout the city. Twice, works of members hung at the Smithsonian Institute in Washington, D.C.; during May and June 1926, 26 persons exhibited 88 photographs, and in 1927, 46 respondents to the administration's invitation displayed 127 pictures. Additionally, during the early 1930s, prints were posted on the excursion train to the popular Pittsburgh Salon. "Through the Darkroom Door," conceived in 1923, is the CPS's newsletter and accounting of events, photographic suggestions, techniques, and competition results. The publication has won numerous Photographic Society of America bulletin contests. Some accomplished members of the society have been Will Higbee, founder of the HIGBEE CO.; Henry Mayer, a newspaper photoengraver whose primary studies were industry and nature and who chaired the school, taught industrial class, held office as vice-president, and donated annual trophies to encourage nature shootings; Arnold Weinberger, a photographer who assumed duties at nearly all levels of operation; John Moddejonge, an associate of the Photographic Society of America and judge of international and domestic competitions, whose participation was oriented toward print production and color slide instruction; and Wm. Meyer, cofounder of the Northeastern Ohio Camera Club Council. In the 1980s, the Cleveland Photographic Society retained its initial objectives in offering darkroom and clubroom facilities, seminars, showings, photo essays, outings, slide and print competitions, awards, and participation in the Northeastern Ohio Camera Club Council and the Photographic Society of America.

The **CLEVELAND PIPERS** professional basketball team was acquired by Geo. Steinbrenner in 1961 as part of a new American Basketball League organized by Abe Saperstein, owner of the Harlem Globetrotters. Before joining the ABL, the Pipers had played in the Industrial Basketball League in 1959–60 and 1960–61, winning the league championship and the national Amateur Athletic Union crown in 1960–61. Cleveland was part of the ABL's Eastern division, which included Pittsburgh, Washington, and Chicago; the Western division was made up of San Francisco, Kansas City, Los Angeles, and Hawaii. The team, coached by John McLendon, the first black coach in professional basketball, included Ben Worley, John Barnhill, Rossi Johnson, Dick Barnett, and Larry Siegfried. They defeated the Hawaii Chiefs in their first home game, played 21 Nov. 1961 at the Public Hall before an announced crowd of 3,318. In spite of efforts to attract fans by scheduling preliminary games featuring the Harlem Globetrotters and a basketball team consisting of Cleveland Browns football players, interest in the team declined. In early Feb., Bill Sharman took over as coach, but attendance was poor, even though the Pipers won the league championship. The playoff between Cleveland and Kansas City was marred by a dispute between Steinbrenner and Saperstein over the location of the final game. Although Steinbrenner signed Jerry Lucas of Ohio State University to a generous contract for the 1962-63 season, the Pipers were financially unable to field a team. The league collapsed at the end of 1962, and Lucas joined the Cincinnati Royals of the National Basketball League.

*CLEVELAND PLAIN DEALER. See* **PLAIN DEALER**

The **CLEVELAND PLAY HOUSE** is the nation's oldest continuously running resident theater company. The idea for the Cleveland Play House developed from a discussion group held weekly at the home of Chas. S. Brooks. In 1916, members of the group formed the Play House Co. for the purpose of establishing an art theater based on the bohemian spirit of art theaters in Paris and Moscow. Brooks was the company's first president, and Raymond O'Neil its first art director. Frederick McConnell became director in 1921, a post he held until his retirement in 1958. His successors have been K. Elmo Lowe, 1958-69, and Richard Oberlin, 1971-85. The director has been primarily responsible for the annual budget and the season's productions. The Play House is governed by 24 trustees elected to 3-year terms; throughout the years they have played a considerable role in fundraising efforts. In 1917, the Play House acquired the former Cedar Ave. Church on E. 73rd St. and converted it into a 200-seat theater. In 1926 the Drurys donated land between Carnegie and Euclid near E. 86th St., and a new Play House was built. The new complex consisted of the 522-seat Drury Theater and the 160-seat Brooks Theater. Later, in 1949, an open stage was acquired when a church at the corner of Euclid and E. 77th St. was converted into a 560-seat theater. In its early years as an art theater, the Play House staged many performances of European modernist playwrights. During the 1920s, this emphasis on avant-garde theater began to soften as the Play House moved into more mainstream theater production, although the smaller Brooks Theater continued to feature experimental works. During this period, an average of 20 plays were produced each year, and the company became increasingly professionalized.

In the 1930s, the Play House incurred its first deficit. It managed to keep most of its programs alive, including a children's theater with an enrollment of over 500, an affiliation with Western Reserve University's theater department, and a School for Theater that offered tuition-free training in return for work connected with the theater. The Play House emerged from its deficit in the 1940s and continued to present 10-month seasons that ran from September-June. Its professional staff at this time included 13 actors and 9 technical workers. By the mid-1950s, the staff had doubled; it continued to grow, reaching 100 in 1971. During this period, the Play House continued to receive most of its support from subscribers, donations, and grants.

New developments included, in 1958, its becoming an equity company in which only members of Actors' Equity could join the permanent company, and, in 1960, the opening of the Play House Club. The Play House remained fairly conservative in its theater offerings throughout the 1960s and 1970s, for which it occasionally was criticized. During the 1970s it again began to operate at a deficit and cut productions 15-20 per year to an average of 13. In Nov. 1983, the Play House closed its theaters and opened a new $14 million complex on an adjoining site. The complex, designed by Phillip Johnson, is one of the largest in America, housing all 3 theaters under one roof, including the 644-seat Kenyon C. Bolton Theater.

Oldenburg, Chloe Warner, *Leaps of Faith: History of the Cleveland Play House, 1915-85* (1985).

The **CLEVELAND PNEUMATIC TOOL CO.**, a division of IC Industries since 1984, is the world's largest manufacturer of aircraft landing gears. Founded in 1894 as the Union Electric Co. by Claus Greve, the company manufactured electric generators for 4 years before turning to the manufacture of pneumatic tools. The Cleveland Pneumatic Tool Co., as it was then called, made drills, valves, and couplings. In 1908, it produced the rock hammer drill used to dig the Panama Canal. With the onset of WORLD WAR I, the company moved to a new factory at 3734 E. 78th St. Its wartime production consisted mainly of riveters for Navy shipbuilding. To compensate for a small tool market after the war, the company introduced the Gruss Air Spring, a shock absorber used on luxury cars. By 1926 it had adapted this pneumatic technique to aircraft, and built the first aircraft landing gear, which became standard throughout the industry. Cleveland Pneumatic's growing expertise made it the major landing-gear supplier for military and commercial aircraft. During WORLD WAR II, in the interest of national defense, It trained other companies to produce its product, thus laying the groundwork for postwar competition. Over the years, Cleveland Pneumatic has outfitted such planes as the 747, 707, DC-8, DC-9, B-17, and B-52. As a major military subcontractor, its corporate fortunes have followed defense spending; when the SST was authorized by Congress, the company soared, but when the plane was canceled, Cleveland Pneumatic laid off 1,200 employees. A second plant opened in 1968, when employment peaked because of 747 production; it was closed in 1972. Aside from landing gear, Cleveland Pneumatic's product line includes hydraulic, pneumatic, mechanical, and electromechanical equipment for aeronautical and industrial uses.

For a time, Cleveland Pneumatic was unique, because it was owned by its employees. In 1953, 2 employee trusts, the 77th St. Trust for salaried employees and the Cleveland Pneumatic Tool Co. Profit Sharing Trust for hourly people, were established and financed by company contributions. Disagreement over management of the trusts led to several bitter strikes in the 1950s and to stockholder discontent. Textron, which had managed the trusts through its 60 Trust of Boston arm, wanted to merge with Cleveland Pneumatic; instead, the Pneumo Dynamic Co. was created by joining 4 divisions of Cleveland Pneumatic and a subsidiary corporation, and stock ownership was opened to the public. Company headquarters were moved to Boston. In 1984, the company was acquired by IC Industries, owner of the Pepsi Cola Bottling Co. and the Illinois Central Gulf Railroad. The purchase provisions included a "shark repellent" feature to ward off unwelcomed merger partners by guaranteeing IC Industries the option to purchase Cleveland Pneumatic and its unissued stock. In 1986 the company maintained its plant at 3781 E. 77th St. Though its hourly employees have been courted by the Internatl. Assoc. of Machinists and the United Mine Workers, the bargaining agent for the company remained an independent union, the Aerol Aircraft Employees Assoc.

The **CLEVELAND POLICE DEPARTMENT** was formed in 1866 under the auspices of the Metropolitan Police Act enacted by the Ohio general assembly. Prior to the act, police services were provided by an elected city marshal assisted by a small number of constables and volunteer night watchmen. The "Metropolitan System" was based upon the success of the Metropolitan Police of London, and was then in effect in several large American cities. It was adopted in Cleveland largely through the efforts of Jacob W. Schmitt, the incumbent city marshal who later became chief of police. The act created a board of police commissioners with authority to appoint a superintendent of police and a number of patrol officers, not to exceed 1 officer for each 1,000 citizens. As first formed, the department consisted of a superintendent, 6 officers, and 29 patrol officers. They were divided into a day platoon and a night platoon and were responsible for providing protection to a city of 67,000 people.

Samuel Furnal was appointed acting superintendent. Within a few months he was replaced by John N. Frazee, who served as superintendent until 1867. Turnover was rapid, and the next 4 years saw 3 men occupy the office of superintendent. In 1871 the department was reorganized, and Jacob W. Schmitt was appointed chief of police. In 1872 the department was again reorganized through an act of the Ohio general assembly. Chief Schmitt was retained, serving until 1893. The major impact of this reorganization was the appointment of several additional patrol officers. The department was shaken in 1876 when a group of recently dismissed patrol officers appealed to the Ohio general assembly. As a result of their challenge, the entire department was dismissed and legislation passed disestablishing the current board of police commissioners. Following the creation of a new board, nearly all members of the department were reappointed.

After these turbulent beginnings, the police department settled into a period of relative calm. Attention was given to the improvement of service. The final decades of the century saw the institution of patrol wagons and the call-box system in the city. In 1894 the department established its mounted unit. These were years of growth for both the city and the department. By 1898, with the city's population exceeding 350,000. The department had grown to a force of 355 members assigned to 12 different precincts. While most officers manned footposts, there were also a detective bureau and a citizens' dress squad, whose members participated in various anticrime details and special investigations.

In 1903 the department assumed its modern form when the state legislature abolished the Metropolitan Police Act. Control of the department was shifted to the municipal government. The plan adopted provided for a department of public safety headed by a director appointed by the mayor. The director had charge of both the police and fire departments and appointed their respective chiefs. The chiefs appointed the members of their departments from a list of eligible candidates prepared by the Civil Service Commission. This system has remained in use through the present.

From 1900–20 the department's energies were directed at the management of rapid growth. The population of the city climbed from 381,000 in 1901, to 568,000 in 1911, to 831,000 in 1921, and the police department grew from 388 members in 1901 to 534 in 1911 and 1,384 in 1921. Efforts were also made to modernize operations. In 1903 the first

mobile patrols were instituted as officers began to patrol on bicycles. Upon the introduction of automobiles, the last horse-drawn vehicle was withdrawn from service in 1916. Most officers still walked footposts, however. Motorcars were reserved for wagons, ambulances, detectives, and other special uses.

As the period of expansion passed, the police department in the 1920s and 1930s experimented with new technologies and procedures. As a result, it became widely recognized as one of the most progressive and efficient departments in the U.S. In 1925 the department established its women's bureau. In 1927 it installed its first teletype machine, and in 1929 its first radio transmitter. Cleveland was the first city to have its own station and to be assigned a wavelength by the FCC. In 1929 several police cars were equipped with radio receivers. Cleveland was the second American city to experiment with this new technology. In 1931 the Scientific Unit, forerunner of the present Scientific Identification Unit, was established. Geo. J. Matowitz was appointed chief in 1931. He served until 1950, becoming one of the most respected chiefs in the department's history.

Following the appointment of ELIOT NESS as safety director in 1938, the police department was again reorganized. Ness abolished the existing system of precincts and instituted a system of districts, each commanded by a captain. The 5 districts were subdivided into 32 zones, which were patrolled by radio-equipped zone cars 24 hours a day. Cleveland was the first city to replace completely its system of foot patrols with radio-dispatched motor patrols. In addition to the zone cars, the city was also patrolled by units of the Accident Prevention Bureau, the Emergency Ambulance Service, the Motorcycle Div., and the Detective Bureau. Other innovations pioneered by the department included the Uniplex car-to-car communications system, the electronic-visual system used to recall officers to their cars, and the system of automatically triggered cameras used in banks and stores to photograph robbery attempts.

The end of WORLD WAR II saw the department grow from a strength of 1,316 in 1944 to 1,843 in 1950. In 1945 a 6th police district was added. While the population of the city remained stable throughout the 1950s, the police department continued to expand, reaching a total of 1,947 members in 1960. Frank W. Story replaced Chief Matowitz in 1950 and served until 1962. The 1960s saw relations between the police department and the city's growing black community deteriorate significantly. Rioting occurred in the Hough area in July 1966. On 23 July 1968, police and black militants engaged in a 4-hour gun battle in Glenville that killed 3 police officers and 4 civilians; 12 police and 3 civilians were wounded (see GLENVILLE SHOOT-OUT). It was the bloodiest day in the history of the police department.

In the 1970s the department suffered from the city's deteriorating financial condition. Aging equipment was not replaced, and the department decreased in size through attrition and layoffs. From a peak of 2,464 members in 1970, the department declined to a total of 1,857 in 1980. In the 13 years prior to 1979, the department had 12 different chiefs. Coupled with rising crime rates and increasing demands for service, these factors contributed to a perception of the department as disorganized and demoralized. The 1980s saw efforts on the part of the city administration to improve the police department. Much new equipment was purchased, and an increased emphasis was placed on community relations. Financial problems persisted, however, and a layoff of 269 patrol officers in 1984 reduced the department's strength to a total of 1,551 members.

The **CLEVELAND PRESS** was the flagship of the communications chain founded by EDWARD W. SCRIPPS. Five years after helping his brother James start the *Detroit News*, Scripps came to Cleveland, where he started the *Penny Press* in a 4-room office on Frankfort St. on 2 Nov. 1878. A small, 4-page afternoon daily, it reflected Scripps's predilection for news condensation and announced its independence of party politics. Scripps sought to capture the working-class reader with the *Penny Press*, and to this end he refused to print "puff" pieces for advertisers or supress unfavorable news items concerning the city's more prominent citizens. Although Scripps relinquished personal direction of the *Penny Press* within 3 years, the paper continued to prosper. Its name was shortened to the *Press* in 1884, and it finally became the *Cleveland Press* in 1889. Under the editorship of Robt. Findley Paine, its circulation surpassed 100,000 during the SPANISH-AMERICAN WAR.

By its 25th anniversary, in 1903, the *Press* was Cleveland's leading daily newspaper. It exposed the Cassie Chadwick bank-swindling case and promoted the renaming and numbering of Cleveland's streets in 1905. In 1913 the *Press* moved into a new plant at E. 9th and Rockwell (the present BancOhio Bldg. site), published its first 20-page edition, and introduced a women's feature into its columns. During WORLD WAR I it was the first newspaper in the country to report the results of the draft lottery, printing the names of over 17,000 Greater Clevelanders in the order of their liability. As it entered the 1920s, the *Press* neared 200,000 in circulation and maintained its political independence by proposing the city manager form of government for Cleveland and supporting Progressive candidate Robt. La Follette for president in 1924.

LOUIS B. SELTZER became the 12th editor of the *Press* in 1928, and under his 38-year stewardship the *Press* became one of the country's most influential newspapers. Seltzer readjusted the *Press*'s original working-class bias into a less controversial neighborhood orientation, stressing personal contacts and promoting the slogan "The Newspaper That Serves Its Readers." This public-service ideal reached its zenith during WORLD WAR II, when the *Press* published special clip-out sections for servicemen, sent them pictures of their newborn infants via "Heir Mail", kept an honor roll for their names in its lobby, and finally raised money for the WAR MEMORIAL FOUNTAIN on the Mall to honor those who were killed.

In the postwar period the *Press* continued its public-service campaigns, from a crusade to legalize the artificial coloration of oleomargarine to sponsorship of a $50,000 "mercy flight" of medicine and clothing for Hungarian refugees in 1956. It was also an unrivaled force in Ohio politics, as demonstrated by its successful promotion of Frank J. Lausche and Anthony J. Celebrezze as mayors of Cleveland, and the former as governor of Ohio for an unprecedented 5 terms. In 1954, the *Press* played an aggressive, controversial role in the prosecution of Dr. Sam Sheppard for the 4 July murder of his wife, Marilyn, in their Bay Village home (see SHEPPARD MURDER CASE). Seltzer-written front-page editorials under such heads as "Somebody Is Getting Away with Murder" and "Quit Stalling—Bring Him In" were a major factor in the U.S. Supreme Court's decision to order a new trial 10 years later on the grounds that press coverage had unduly influenced the original verdict.

Despite this single major setback, the *Press* maintained its preeminence in the city and state through Seltzer's retirement in 1966. It moved into its modern printing plant at Lakeside and E. 9th in 1959 and 1 year later purchased the *CLEVELAND NEWS* from the FOREST CITY PUBLISHING CO., merging it into the *Press* and thereby becoming the city's only surviving afternoon daily. In 1964, the *Press* was named one of America's 10 best newspapers in a list compiled by *Time* magazine. Under Seltzer's successor, Thos. L. Boardman, however, the *Press* began a decline that was shared in general with other large afternoon dailies throughout the country. Evening television news programs, the flight to the SUBURBS, and the switch from public to private transportation by commuters were cited as the chief factors in the decline, which saw the *Press* surrender its circulation lead to the morning *PLAIN DEALER* in 1968. Prompted by a national shortage of newsprint in 1978, the *Press* converted its Saturday edition into a tabloid format. Circulation, which had nudged 400,000 under Seltzer, was down to around 300,000.

Shortly after Boardman's retirement in favor of Herb Kamm at the end of 1979, rumors began circulating to the effect that the *Press* would shortly suspend publication unless it could be sold. That was confirmed by the parent Scripps-Howard organization, and Cleveland businessman Joseph E. Cole was identified as a prospective purchaser. Before negotiating for the paper, however, Cole exacted concessions from 9 *Press* unions, which included a 1-year wage freeze and over 100 layoffs. Sale of the *Press* to Cole was announced on 31 Oct. 1980, at a rumored price of $20 million. In an effort to restore the paper's competitive position, Cole introduced a Sunday edition of the *Press* on 2 Aug. 1981, and a morning edition on 22 Mar. 1982. A retrenchment followed shortly thereafter, however, in which the *Sunday Press* was pulled back to a Saturday publication schedule, and the Saturday tabloid edition was eliminated. Citing the depressed economy and consequent losses in advertising, Cole announced the paper's closing on 17 June 1982, and the final edition of the *Press* appeared that afternoon. Notable *Press* staff members also included editors Earl Martin and Victor Morgan, city editor LOUIS CLIFFORD, columnists MAURICE PERKINS, JACK RAPER, DAVID DIETZ, MILTON WIDDER, and Dick Feagler, sports editor FRANKLIN (WHITEY) LEWIS, music critic Frank Hruby, photographer Fred Bottomer, and cartoonist Bill Roberts.

Cleveland Press Collection, CSU.

The **CLEVELAND PROVISION COMPANY**, founded in 1854 as Rose & Prentiss by BENJAMIN ROSE, financier and philanthropist, and Chauncey Prentiss, and incorporated as the Cleveland Provision Co. in 1876, was the leading meat packer in Cleveland for over a century. Established at a time when farmers began turning over the slaughter of their livestock to city packinghouses, Cleveland Provision was exclusively a pork-packing facility until 1887, when it expanded to include beef and lamb. The company was first located on Ontario St., but moved to 2527 Canal Rd. in the Flats to be near the Ohio Canal, a shipping point and a source of cut ice. Before the widespread use of mechanical refrigeration in the 1890s, animals were slaughtered in the winter and preserved with ice slabs cut from the canal. Cleveland Provision then moved to the heart of the stockyard district at 3378 W. 65th St. At this time, the company discontinued its own killing and was able to select a better grade of meat for processing at a better price. Under the direction of John Nash, Cleveland Provision developed the Wiltshire and Rose Premium brands of smoked meats. It was among the first to package bacon in see-through boxes, and was the largest of two dozen local packinghouses. Although the firm remained in business under the name the Cleveland Provision Co. until the 1950s, it was successively bought out by 2 other Cleveland firms. In 1937, Lake Erie Provision (est. 1865), operated by the

Newcomb family, bought the brand names, formula, supplies, and goods of the financially troubled Cleveland Provision Co. Ohio Provision, established in 1895 by the McCrea family and located at 2254 W. 61st St., bought out the resulting company in 1954 and moved to 6101 Walworth Ave. As a consequence of changes in the meatpacking industry, food marketing, and the American diet (see CLEVELAND UNION STOCKYARDS CO.), the company, processor of Sandy Mac brand meats, closed in 1962. At the time of its closure, it was the largest pork packer in Cleveland, and the largest remaining meat packer, as Swift & Co. and 3 local packinghouses had recently suspended operations. The building, acquired by the Schaeffer Brewing Co, was destroyed in a 1963 fire.

The **CLEVELAND PSYCHIATRIC INSTITUTE** is a short-term psychiatric-care hospital for the observation, care, and treatment of the mentally ill, especially those patients with mild conditions in the early stages and possibly of short duration. Located at 1708 Aiken Ave., in 1986 CPI was the only state short-term psychiatric-care hospital serving Cuyahoga and its 4 neighboring counties. It employed a staff of 16 full-time and 3 part-time doctors and a support staff of 500. With a 226-bed capacity, the hospital maintained 211 beds for acute-care patients, who stayed for periods of up to 20 days. The other 15 beds were reserved for patients who stayed up to 90 days under the courts' forensic evaluation program. In addition to administering short-term care, CPI provides psychiatric training for resident physicians from Metro General Hospital and Case Western Reserve University Medical School, and nursing training for students from Lorain Community College. It also provides social-work training for students from CWRU's School of Applied Social Sciences, psychiatric training for students from CWRU and Kent State and Cleveland State universities, and psychiatric and counseling training for clergy students at Ashland College. CPI was originally established in 1945 as the Cleveland State Receiving Hospital when the Ohio legislature approved the creation of a statewide system of receiving hospitals, including one in Cuyahoga County. After successful negotiations, state officials entered into an agreement with Cleveland City Hospital (Metro General) to assume control of the acute-care facility at Hoover Pavilion on 1 Nov. 1946. The name CPI has been in use since the early 1960s. Poor state management practices and bureaucratic red tape demoralized the hospital's staff and delayed improvements. Crowded conditions were exacerbated by the admission of alcoholics and by "patients" using the hospital as a refuge from the law. Doctors resigned because of low pay and regulations banning private patients. Western Reserve University temporarily withdrew its affiliation in 1949, criticizing the state's handling of hospital conditions. Program and physical-plant improvements have been slowly made since the 1950s. An out-patient clinic was opened in 1952 to provide follow-up care for discharged patients. Originally built in 1922, a therapy wing was added to Hoover Pavilion in 1957. In 1981, CPI combined its operations with the Fairhill Receiving Hospital.

The **CLEVELAND PUBLIC LIBRARY**, one of the nation's major urban library systems, evolved from the Public School Library. Since 1869 it has provided free public access to books and information. Classed as a school-district library under Ohio law, Cleveland's library has a 7-member board of trustees appointed by the Cleveland Board of Education for 7-year, rotating terms in 1984. The CPL initiated service on 17 Feb. 1869, in modest rented quarters located in the Harrington Block, at Superior and Public Square. Luther M. Oviatt was the first librarian. The early philosophic foundations of the library were set largely by 3 people: WM. H. BRETT, LINDA A. EASTMAN, and JOHN G. WHITE. Beginning with Brett, the library sought to bring books within the reach of the entire community. Services to children and youth and extension work through branches and schools were initiated in the 1890s. Service to the blind began in 1903 with a collection of books in Braille. The specialized requirements of Cleveland's business and labor communities were addressed first by Eastman, who founded the Business Information Bureau in 1928. Through Brett's persuasion, Andrew Carnegie financed construction of 15 neighborhood branch libraries, through gifts that totaled $590,000.

The library moved its downtown collections several times before passage of bond issues in 1912 and 1921 provided for the construction of the present building at 325 Superior Ave. Designed by architects Walker & Weeks to conform with other civic buildings in Daniel Burnham's Group Plan for the Mall, the main library was opened to the public on 6 May 1925. The adjacent Plain Dealer Bldg. was acquired in 1959 to serve as the library's Business & Science Bldg. The Eastman Reading Garden, maintained by the library since 1937, lies between the 2 buildings. Over a period of several decades, between the Great Depression of the 1930s and the social activism of the Great Society in the 1960s, the prestige and civic utility of the library declined severely. The most visible deterioration occurred in branches, where dated collections and shabby facilities discouraged public use.

In 1976, the most extensive reorganization and renovation plan in the history of the CPL was initiated by its 11th director, ERVIN J. GAINES. The modern-day renaissance of the library addressed every aspect of the organization, from buildings to collections, staffing, and all technical services. A $20 million building program for branches, unparalleled in American public libraries, brought 18 new or remodeled branches to Cleveland's citizens. Attractive, modern library buildings and fresh, new book stocks spurred renewed public use of Cleveland's neighborhood libraries. Circulation of books, which had plunged during the years of neglect, increased steadily. The Cleveland Public Library's on-line bibliographic data base made information about the entire collection available instantly in the main library and the 31 neighborhood branches. A growing network of other libraries in a 6-county area was linked through access to Cleveland's on-line data base, illustrating the library's continuing commitment to extending access to books and information.

Cramer, C. H. *Open Shelves and Open Minds: A History of the Cleveland Public Library* (1972).

**CLEVELAND PUBLIC SCHOOLS.** Cleveland's public schools are rooted in the campaign to provide a tax-supported, compulsory system of education that began with Horace Mann in Massachusetts and Henry Barnard in Connecticut during the late 1820s. They and other reformers in the antebellum era fought to create a legal and financial basis for public education and to include secondary schooling in the system. Between the CIVIL WAR and WORLD WAR I, America's public schools expanded their role by attempting to compensate for the deficiencies of their students. They instituted specialized programs for vocational-technical students, immigrant and needy children, the adult learner, and the handicapped. Between this period and WORLD WAR II, public education developed extracurricular activities, psychological testing and tracking of students, and expanded adult and vocational education. After the war, America's inner-city school systems were burdened with both a declining tax base and a growing student population as southern blacks migrated to the North. They also had to deal with the effects of poverty and racial discrimination. The federal government played a larger role in financing and controlling public education, especially in school systems under a court desegregaton order. Through these periods, the schools have always expected to build good character, promote mobility and social harmony, and educate the general public. This mission became the philosophical foundation of public education, but every generation struggled and debated how best to achieve it amid socioeconomic change and political conflicts. In 1836, the state legislature of Ohio incorporated Cleveland as a city and allowed it to organize a tax-supported, public school system. The city council appointed a board of school managers, which took over a school located at the Protestant Bethel Union Chapel on Superior Hill. The BETHEL UNION provided free education for mainly poor children who attended its Sunday school and lived in the FLATS. It was nicknamed the "Ragged School" because of the poor condition of the children's clothes. Most parents employed tutors at their own expense or sent their children to private schools such as the CLEVELAND ACADEMY, a secondary school established in 1821. The public saw no need for schooling beyond the basics of "the 3 Rs" in a rural economy. The home, the church, and the workplace were considered more important than formal schooling.

To accommodate 800 students, the city built separate schools for boys and girls in each of the city's wards and purchased the Cleveland Academy in 1837. Samuel Lewis, the first state superintendent of schools, authored a law that provided a tax levy for the state common school fund in 1838. In 1840, Cleveland City Council built 2 45-ft.-square buildings on Rockwell and Prospect avenues. It also appointed Chas. Bradburn, a retailer and wholesaler, and Geo. Willey, a lawyer and brother of the mayor, to the Board of Managers. Both led the campaign for the expansion and improvement of the public schools for over a decade. By 1842, there were 15 public schools with an enrollment of 1,200 students. Public education had a difficult time overcoming the image of still being a charity organization, since many students were housed in rented, overcrowded, and inadequate buildings. Faced with cuts from state funds, the managers reduced the wages of teachers, shortened the school year, and even sold a school bell in 1842. Progress and reform occurred despite these circumstances. The board prescribed a uniform system of textbooks, and teachers divided their schools into as many classes as possible. They were required to take competency tests and demonstrate evidence of good moral character for employment. Regardless of their social or economic backgrounds, all students were to receive a common education as they sat together in the antebellum schoolhouse. In 1844, Bradburn led the crusade to establish the first public high school against those who decried any higher taxes and the failure of the elementary schools to enroll the over 2,000 children of school age not in attendance. One critic also questioned whether a citywide high school would qualify as "a common school," since the council had the right only to lobby for district schools in the city's wards. School reformers throughout America liked to describe the high school as "the people's college," for it was expected to provide a secondary education for those who could not afford private academies. Requirements and entrance exams also gave educators greater control over the grammar schools. Bradburn and his supporters proudly opened CENTRAL HIGH SCHOOL on 13 July 1845—the first public high school west of the Alleghenies.

In 1847, the state authorized the election of a board of education to control all schools in a single district. In 1853, Ohio established school levies to eliminate student fees and authorized local school boards to organize primary and secondary schools. The newly appointed board chose ANDREW FREESE, the first principal of Central High School, as the superintendent. In 1859 the state allowed each of the city's 11 wards to elect members to the school board for a term of 1 year. Freese attempted to grade and classify the schools by dividing the elementary system into 3 divisions and introducing a course of study for each grade. "Object lessons" that used games or physical artifacts and gymnastics were introduced during the period of the Civil War. The 3-story Brownell St. School enrolled 1,386 pupils during its first year of operation in 1865. The school's size was indicative of the city's growing population, as factories expanded rapidly and employed thousands of native- and foreign-born workers during the industrial era. In 1866, superintendent ANSON SMYTHE, a graduate of Western Reserve College and former state superintendent, stated that the public schools, with a population of 9,270 students, could compensate for a lack of moral culture and religious instruction.

Andrew Rickoff, the former head of Cincinnati's public schools, was chosen superintendent in the post-Civil War era. No predecessor or successor had a greater impact on the development of public education. He classified students into 12 grades and 3 divisions—primary, grammar, and high school. That was a major step away from the one room of mixed grades in the common school and the basis for placing students in a graded curriculum according to their age and ability. In 1848, John Philbrick had pioneered the Quincy School in Boston that became the model for the rest of America. Each teacher had a separate classroom for the one grade she taught, and each student his own desk. Proficiency tests ranked and placed students in a standardized curriculum. Teachers and students were expected to work more efficiently under this modern division of labor. Rickoff expected teachers to fit their students into a new course of study that was prescribed for each term. Semiannual promotion of students was introduced, and the separation of boys and girls was eliminated. In 1872, German became part of a bilingual program to attract the city's German children who were attending private schools. The superintendent and the board had far greater control of the public schools after the state reduced the city council's authority except for the approval of new school locations and buildings. Rickoff made the principals of grammar schools that were closed assistant superintendents and established the office of supervising principal. Women were chosen for the latter position because they were not involved in partisan politics. In 1874, a normal school for training teachers was founded. During Rickoff's 15-year tenure as superintendent, the schools expanded from 9,643 to 26,990 students and from 123 to 473 teachers. High praise was given to the school buildings—which included a new and imposing Gothic building for Central High School—and the educational exhibits of the Cleveland public schools at the Centennial Exhibition of 1876. Despite national acclaim, local newspapers attacked the unsanitary and overcrowded conditions in the schools and the political manipulations of the school board. Burke Hinsdale, the president of Hiram College and friend of Pres. JAS. A. GARFIELD, criticized the mechanical nature of the educational environment. A newly elected school board appointed him as the next superintendent. He visited and encouraged teachers to return to a thorough grounding of each student in the essentials of a good education.

Like his predecessor, Hinsdale and his Republican friends on the school board were defeated by a new political coalition, which selected a former teacher and administrator to direct the public schools. In 1884, an after-school program called the Manual Training School opened in a rented barn on E. 40th St. It included classes in carpentry, woodturning, and mechanical drawing, machine shop, and a course in cooking. In 1887 the state paid the students' tuition. The school board opened the West Manual Training School in the upper floor of the West High School and added a 2-year business course to the secondary curriculum. The evening schools increasingly focused on helping immigrants learn English and civics to pass naturalization exams as a heavy influx of foreign-born people from Southern and Western Europe arrived in the city. In 1889, the school board hired its first truant officer to enforce the new compulsory-attendance law requiring children of school age to attend 20 weeks a year.

In 1891, a coalition of reformers from Cleveland secured the passage of the Federal Plan, which allowed the public to elect a school board of 7 members as a legislative branch and a school director as an executive branch. The latter appointed Andrew Draper, a former lawyer, as superintendent. Draper attempted to improve the teaching staff and opened a manual training room in Central High School and a school for deaf children. Lewis Jones, his successor, opened the first kindergartens in 1896 and began a medical inspection program. In 1904, the state abolished the Federal Plan and allowed 5 members to be elected at large and 2 by wards for the school board. After the board heard the recommendations of an education commission that investigated the schools in 1905, it appointed Wm. H. Elson as the new superintendent. He pioneered vocational education by opening a technical high school in 1908. Courses in general education were related to the demands of the business world. Each teacher was also assigned a group of students to counsel in a homeroom. Male students could take courses in cabinetmaking, pottery, drawing, woodturning, pattern making, foundry work, and machine shop. Female enrollees could study home economics and applied or commercial art. In response to the business community, which wanted better preparation of graduates for office or retail work, a commercial high school was established in 1909. During that year, the board also permitted an industrial school to open at the Brownell Bldg. for the non-academically talented boy or girl who dropped out of school after the 7th or 8th grade. This school devoted a half-day to academic work and the remainder to courses in industrial work, home economics, and physical education. This program became the basis for the junior high program.

As part of the progressive movement in education at the turn of the century, America's public schools expanded their role in society. They provided programs and services to compensate for the deficiencies of students, which were often attributed to their poverty, family background, or blighted neighborhoods. In 1903, Cleveland's public schools opened playgrounds and summer vacation schools. The board expanded the physical education program and instituted a school gardening program. In 1908, the first medical dispensary in the history of public education opened at Murray Hill School in Cleveland's LITTLE ITALY. In 1910 the Cleveland Dental Society began inspecting children's teeth in the public schools. Elson instituted luncheon rooms in the high schools, classes for the blind, social centers, and a normal school at UNIVERSITY CIRCLE. Despite his innovative reforms—the epitome of educational progressivism—Elson and his supporters were defeated at the polls amid charges about fraudulent school contracts awarded after the COLLINWOOD SCHOOL FIRE killed 173 students in 1908 and complaints about overcrowding of the schools, which enrolled 64,409 students in 1912.

In 1915, the CLEVELAND FOUNDATION conducted a comprehensive survey of the public schools. Its reports criticized the system's inefficiency and lack of programs to deal with the needs of the city's children. Two-thirds of the student population left school before the legally required age. In 1917, a new school board chose Frank E. Spalding from Minneapolis to implement the survey. He centralized the decision making in the schools and expanded the junior highs established during his predecessor's tenure as the key to retaining more children in the middle grades. Guidance counselors, testing, and grouping of students by ability were also introduced to reduce the failure rate. The public schools increased their efforts to Americanize immigrants and their children, dropping the teaching of German, and required a loyalty oath of teachers as part of the patriotic campaigning of the World War I era. By 1918, the school population—sorted into a variety of specialized programs and ability groups—numbered 106,862 students. There were 4,715 students—almost half of the secondary enrollment—in the commercial-technical high schools. The Smith Hughes Act of 1917 had provided federal funds for the expansion of vocational education.

Robt. J. Jones, the deputy superintendent who organized 15 junior high schools during Elson's administration, became superintendent in 1918. He served 15 years and supported the growth of music education and services for crippled and mentally deficient students. The schools expanded and initiated extracurricular activities, such as glee clubs, school newspapers, student council, and sports programs to develop "the good character" of pupils. Influenced by a conference on the student failure rate, the schools developed a "Progress Plan" in 1928. Nine elementary curriculum centers organized an ungraded program for the least capable students with the lowest IQs and attempted to individualize the curriculum by adapting it to the students' abilities and needs. Responding to the decline in the neighborhood around Central High School and to the arrival of black students who had been denied access to a decent education in the South, a clinic was established to study and remedy the educational and social problems of the neighborhood's youth. In 1922, the school board approved the creation of the Major Work Program of special classes for gifted children. A reduction in fees led to the enrollment of over 10,000 students in adult education by Sept. 1927. Aided by the Bing Act (1921), which required attendance until the age of 18 and graduation from high school, daily enrollment expanded to 144,000 students. Between 1920-30, the school system spent over $18 million to construct 32 buildings.

Greater emphasis was given to vocational and special education classes in the 1920s. In 1920, a program for students interested in the trades permitted them to work as apprentices 4 hours per week. In 1924, a new vocational program, the Girls Opportunity School, was opened at Miles Standish School. It helped female students, who were often forced to leave school early because of or became discouraged with their inability to perform the traditional academic work. The program included courses in cooking, hygiene, home nursing, English, and math. It later became Jane Addams School, which enrolled 1,500 students by 1930. In 1927, Eagle School was converted into a trade school for male students—the basis for Max Hayes Vocational School, which began in 1957. In 1924, Thos. A. Edison School—the successor to a program for "incorrigible children"—enrolled male students with disciplinary problems. It offered courses in millwork, mechanical drawing, metalwork, and handwork. In 1926 Outhwaite School for Boys, and in 1929 Longwood School for Girls began offering special education for students who were below average for their grades. Students were expected to transfer back to the regular classroom after they were brought up to their grade level.

After World War I, the black student population grew from 9,066 in 1923 to 13,430 in 1929. The total enrollment of the schools increased by 11,216 students, while the number of black pupils grew 4,364 during this 6-year period. The *Call & Post*, a black newspaper, complained on 7 Jan. 1937 that too many black students were enrolled at Longwood and Outhwaite schools. The paper claimed that they had become a permanent dumping ground for not only the average but also the mentally deficient and slow-learning students. Their educational program provided only half as many subjects as traditional high schools and lowered the morale of their students. The black community also complained about the deterioration and poor quality of the programs at Central High School by the 1930s. In 1936, blacks threatened to oppose future school levies unless improvements were made. Physical repairs were made in the special-education schools, and in 1939 a cornerstone was laid for a new Central High School. Three years earlier, HAZEL MOUNTAIN WALKER had become the first black principal in the school system.

The Depression decreased the city's tax duplicate and forced the school system to curtail expenses through reductions in programs and staff. The schools managed to feed over 44,000 needy children daily. The medical inspection and health programs increased their efforts. The federal government also paid the wages of people who could teach in the adult education program. With the advent of World War II, the schools expanded their vocational-technical program. Over 50,000 people were trained for jobs in war industries. Superintendent Mark Schinnerer contended that that was a permanent priority, as only a minority of students were going to college.

The Cleveland public schools emphasized "life adjustment" classes in the 1950s to reduce the dropout rate of students who failed to finish high school and to help young adults find their appropriate vocation. The need to provide facilities for the growing population of pupils became the dominant issue in this decade, as well as in the 1960s. Enrollment increased from 99,686 in 1950 to 148,793 students in 1963. In 1960, Cleveland ranked as one of the lowest (38) in professional staff per 1,000 pupils in comparison to other large cities in the nation. In 1966, BEACHWOOD, a wealthy suburb of Cleveland, had 63 staff members per 1,000 students. In that same year, Cleveland ranked lowest with a per pupil expenditure of $480 in Cuyahoga County, and 90 of its 174 schools were over 50 years old. Faced with a dwindling tax base because of depopulation and industrial decline, the school system struggled to educate a growing student population. It also increasingly enrolled low-income and minority students as white middle-class families and jobs fled to the suburbs after World War II. Hope appeared, however, when private foundations and the federal government attempted to come to the aid of central city school systems such as Cleveland during this era.

In 1960, the city's schools could not adequately house the enrollment of 134,765 students; 14,000 were put on half-days because of the shortage of teachers and classrooms, mainly in the city's east side black neighborhoods. In 1960, the Ford Foundation funded a project at Addison Jr. High School in HOUGH to reduce the dropout and juvenile-delinquency rates among black adolescents. As part of its Great Cities Grey Areas Program, the federal government also supported the Hough Community Project, which included home visitation, work study, and remedial programs. In addition, it provided in 1963 more funds for vocational education. Max Hayes was open from 8 a.m. To 10:30 p.m. and enrolled 796 high school students, 1,250 apprentices, and 1,493 adult education students. To relieve overcrowding, superintendent Wm. B. Levenson, a 30-year veteran of the school system, proposed to rent space from the Catholic Diocese. Lee Howley, vice-president of the CLEVELAND ELECTRIC ILLUMINATING CO. and chairman of a citizens' committee on school finances, campaigned for a bond issue to build more facilities. In 1962, 70% of the voting public approved a bond program and a levy to improve the schools, but the building plans met resistance from civil-rights groups led by Clarence H. Holmes, the president of the UNITED FREEDOM MOVEMENT. Pickets, demonstrations, public meetings, and a school boycott were organized to protest the continuing segregation of black students. Civil-rights leaders argued that it was better to bus black students to unused classrooms than to build new schools that perpetuated segregation. Violence erupted in the Murray Hill School District, and Rev. Bruce Klunder, a young Presbyterian minister, was accidentally killed by a bulldozer in 1964 while participating in a protest against the construction of a new school. The head of the school board promised to bus blacks to integrate the system. The superintendent resigned, and ALFRED BENESCH, a veteran of the school board, contended that the present board should resign for interfering with the superintendent.

In 1963, the Program for Action by Citizens in Education (the PACE ASSOC.), organized with the support of the Cleveland Associated Foundation, advocated a variety of school reforms in its report: early reading assistance, libraries in elementary schools, a human-relations curriculum, black teacher recruitment, a tutor corps, interdistrict vocational training and summer schools, and the establishment of an agency to promote its recommendations. The latter became a foundation-supported organization, which developed a wide variety of programs that improved public education in Cuyahoga County before its demise in 1974. ALTERNATIVE SCHOOLS such as the Cleveland Urban Learning Community of St. Ignatius High School, the United Independent Schools of E. Cleveland, and the Urban League's Street Academy provided nontraditional options in the 1970s and demonstrated the need for reform. In 1964, Paul Briggs, the head of the Parma schools, took command of the superintendency. The board also ended the "dual system" of administration that had existed since 1904 by making the Business Dept. report to him. Briggs announced that the Cleveland public schools would also have "a new look" through federal assistance that would expand preschool education and a new center for adult education. The enrollment of adults in literacy classes almost doubled. Antipoverty programs and the Elementary & Secondary Education Act of 1965 funded many new programs in the district. Assisted by PACE, the system opened 105 elementary libraries in 1966. Briggs launched an ambitious building program in 1968 that included a downtown Supplementary Education Ctr. for students from all sections of the city and an extensive school-building program. The public supported his efforts by passing another bond issue to build enough schools for the enrollment of over 150,000 students.

After a survey demonstrated that ⅔ of high school dropouts were unemployed, the federal government helped establish a Student Neighborhood Youth Corps, which provided after-school jobs to encourage the retention of students. In 1965, the government's Manpower & Training

Ctr. was established in a public school. The State Employment Office referred trainees, who received a stipend to attend the program, which included basic or remedial courses and vocational education in the areas of trade and industry or clerical and professional services. Programs in cooperative and distributive education in the high school provided students with the opportunity for on-the-job work experience. A vocational Occupational Program was instituted at Thos. Edison to reduce the number of dropouts without marketable skills. In addition, the school cooperated with the Bureau of Vocational Rehabilitation to provide work-study programs for boys who qualified. An Occupational Work Experience Program, which included a work laboratory with wood- and metalworking equipment to prepare the student for employment, was begun for below-average students in high school. Under contract with the U.S. Dept. of Labor, the Woodland Job Training Ctr. enrolled over 1,000 trainees in what was described as a factory school in 1968. The school trained the ranks of hard-core, unemployed city residents.

Briggs recruited black teachers and administrators for the school system. He appointed Jas. B. Tanner, a black educator, as his assistant superintendent and helped organize a Master of Arts in Teaching at JOHN CARROLL UNIVERSITY. He declared that the federal government's Aid to Dependent Children program would provide in the first 6 months of 1968 over $1 million to finance 11 new programs for 29,289 disadvantaged learners in 81 schools. But in 1973, the NAACP filed a suit claiming that quality education was not legal or possible in a segregated environment. On 6 Feb. 1978, Federal Judge Frank Battisti issued a remedial order as a result of his finding the previous year that the Cleveland school system and the state board of education were guilty of de facto and de jure segregation of black students in Cleveland. Briggs and the school board, headed by Arnold Pinkney, a black businessman, had defended the existence of neighborhood schools and claimed that segregation was the result of residential housing patterns they were not obligated to correct. The desegregation case demonstrated that the board's actions, which included busing, constructing schools, and reassigning students for the purposes of segregation, had racially isolated and violated the 14th Amendment rights of the city's black children. Briggs predicted that the court order would increase both white flight from the city and the dual system of public education that had left schools in central cities with predominantly disadvantaged minority children. His problems were increased when the public rejected by an almost 2-to-1 margin a request for a school levy to remedy the school system's deficits. He resigned his position in the midst of conflicts and troubles engulfing the public schools. In Sept. 1978, the school system had to obtain a $20 million loan from Ohio's Emergency School Assistance Fund. The state also found Cleveland's public schools below minimum standards and made compliance and the appointment of a financial administrator the basis of a second loan in 1981.

The federal court established a Dept. of School Desegregation Relations to develop and implement a remedy with 2 main objectives: eliminating the effects of prior desegregation and providing an integrated educational environment. The Office of School Monitoring & Community Relations was also established to foster the public's understanding of desegregation and to report on its progress. Chas. Leftwich, the court-appointed deputy superintendent, had the school department report directly to him. After Leftwich resigned, the court approved the board's appointment of Margaret Fleming, the former director of the Dept. of Research, as his replacement in Nov. 1978. She worked diligently to help the schools comply with the court order. The Monitoring Commission reported to the court, however, that the school system had resegregated black students who had been transported from the Addison Jr. High district and should be held in contempt of court for obstructing the court's desegregation plan. The court removed Fleming from her position after lengthy hearings and appointed Donald Waldrip to head the Dept. of Desegregation in 1980.

Superintendent Peter Carlin, the successor of Briggs and a veteran teacher and administrator of the school system, described his efforts as "Working Together for Excellence." He and the school board had to immediately address the needs of teachers. Cleveland's United Fed. of Teachers, which had been organized in 1933, successfully obtained better wages and benefits for the instructional staff after striking in 1978 and 1979. Carlin reported that the schools made progress toward integration by daily transporting over 30,000 students in 550 vehicles. The schools now served over 12 million free or reduced meals. The superintendent cited other positive signs: a computerized scheduling program, School Community Councils and a Parent Awareness Project, human-relations training of staff and teachers, improvement in reading scores in the elementary grades, compliance with the state's minimum standards except for facilities, repayment of both loans from the state, and a Code of Rights, Responsibilities & Discipline for students. But conflicts among school-board members, school closings and program reductions, layoffs, the continuing poor performance of students, and decline in enrollment diminished the public's confidence. In 1982, Carlin left the system and sued it for its failure to evaluate him before his nonreappointment. Two years later, Waldrip departed under a dark cloud for both his inability to obtain funding for the expansion of magnet schools and his purchase of a million reading programs from a firm he had represented.

The cost per pupil, which went up more than 100% between 1971-80, ranked the expenditures of the Cleveland public schools in the top 10% of districts in Ohio. The percentage of the system's budget spent on educational programs and teachers declined, but the expense of maintenance, administration, and nonteaching personnel increased as enrollment dropped. In 1983, an accounting firm's study of the schools estimated that the board was expecting to spend $1.3 million for custodial employee overtime. A coalition to reform the school-board budget had continually criticized the board's spending priorities.

The debate about the role and performance of the public schools revolves around the larger question of how America can live up to its commitment to human rights and equality. The court's desegregation order reaffirmed the importance of the schools as part of the nation's democratic heritage. But their poor performance eroded the belief that schools can cure the problems of American society. Cleveland's public schools freed themselves of political control and the image of being a charity organization before the Civil War but were, by the 1980s, reverting to these conditions. The continued crisis of public education in Cleveland had prompted proposals for its takeover by either the state or the mayor. After Carlin's departure, superintendent Frederick Holliday committed suicide, and his successor was forced to resign. Alfred Tutela, who came from Boston as a member of the court's desegregation team in 1978, was appointed superintendent in 1986. He announced that the school system needed over $50 million to repair its facilities, including many buildings from the Briggs era. In a period of diminishing federal support and local taxes—as graphically illustrated by the multi-million-dollar revenue loss from the bankruptcy of LTV Steel—the prospects for such massive rehabilitation looked remote in 1986. Diminishing resources jeopardized the school system's ability to survive its escalating problems.

Over 70% of Cleveland's schoolchildren received some form of public assistance as single-headed impoverished families became the norm for many inner-city children by the mid-1980s. Integration became more difficult as the percentage of black enrollment increased from 58% in 1976 to 66% in 1981. Almost 50% of the system's students failed to graduate from high school in an era when employers increasingly required secondary and postsecondary degrees. For those who remained, the longer they stayed in school, the poorer became their performance on reading-comprehension tests. Attendance in the junior and senior divisions was the second-worst in the state. Only 37% of the city's adults had a secondary education by 1986. Nancy Oakley, the director of Project Learn, a volunteer tutorial program, estimated that 47,000 illiterate persons lived in Cleveland. Poverty and the culturally different learner had been inextricably bound with illiteracy and student failure throughout the history of public education. The consequences of the shortcomings of the schools were a direct result of confused priorities resulting in public reluctance to bear the responsibility for providing a system of universal education that included those who have the greatest needs but the least resources. The condition of public education reveals society's values and priorities. What improved schools in the past was the belief that they were more important than any other institution outside the family and could meet the needs of different learners; this belief/priority seemed sadly lacking in the 1980s.

Edward M. Miggins
Cuyahoga Community College

See also EDUCATION.

The **CLEVELAND QUARRIES COMPANY** is a major extractor of sandstone deposits at Amherst and formerly BEREA. The history and prospects of the company are closely linked with those of the city of Berea and BALDWIN-WALLACE COLLEGE. The first corporate ancestor of the Cleveland Quarries Co. was founded in 1833 by John Baldwin, organizer of Baldwin University. While traversing his farm on a moonlit night, pondering the sagging fortunes of his seminary, Baldwin came across a piece of stone that had marvelous knife-sharpening abilities. He saw that the sandstone, soon called "Berea grit," was the key to the future of his academic enterprises; he set up a lathe to cut grindstones and leased out his land to others (including Jas. Wallace, another college pioneer) who mined the product. Soon there were a number of small quarry companies operating along the Rocky River, under such names as the Baldwin Quarry Co., Diamond Quarry Co., Ensign Quarry Co., Berea Stone Co., Murphy Stone Co., and Cuyahoga Stone Co. The grindstones produced in the area became popular among farmers for sharpening tools. They were also used in Cuba to sharpen machetes for chopping sugar cane. Meanwhile, sandstone became a desirable building material, and the quarries at Berea and Amherst, where the sandstone was also found, supplied commercial needs. In 1886, the Cleveland Stone Co. was formed from several small companies operating in both locations. Though labor in the quarries was always hazardous, working conditions deteriorated under Cleveland Stone Co. management, and in 1896, Berea was the scene of a bloody strike. Later (1929), Cleveland Stone merged with Ohio Quarries and Ohio Cut Stone to become the Cleveland Quarries Co.

The quarries at Berea and Amherst supplied stone for buildings throughout the U.S. In the decades after the CIVIL WAR, 20 gangs operated saws around the clock to produce 12,000 carloads of stone per year. In 1880 the company got its biggest order to date—stone to build the massive old SUPERIOR VIADUCT. Other local users included the Old Stone Church, the FAIRMOUNT PRESBYTERIAN CHURCH, the Lorain-Carnegie Bridge, the Board of Education Bldg., and John Hay High School. After local quarries became part of Cleveland Stone, the corporate owners affronted Berea townsmen by buying the land from underneath the financially strapped Baldwin-Wallace College; though the city was fearful of losing the college, it was rebuilt there with stone donated by the corporation. Eventually, the Berea quarries were exhausted; the cavernous pits that remained provided local swimming holes and later, the basis of Berea Quarries Park in the Rocky River Reservation. When the last Berea stone was quarried in 1939, the company moved its mining operations to Amherst, where it estimated that another 100 years' supply of stone remained. The deposits at Amherst, which cover over 1,000 acres, are among the largest and deepest in the world. Aside from building materials, the sandstone from Amherst is used as refractory and soaking-pit linings in steel mills and as a liner for Bessamer converters. In addition, crushed stone, previously discarded as waste before the development of crushing equipment in the 1950s, is in demand as highway building aggregate, and as hearth-bottom material in foundries. The Cleveland Quarries Co. is currently owned by the Standard Slag Co. of Youngstown, Ohio, which also owns Cleveland Builders' Supply.

The **CLEVELAND QUARTET**, originally made up of Donald Weilerstein and Peter Salaff, violins, Martha Strongin Katz, viola, and Paul Katz, cello, was the first in-residence string quartet at the CLEVELAND INSTITUTE OF MUSIC. In 1986 they were artists-in-residence at the Eastman School of Music in Rochester, N.Y. When CIM director VICTOR BABIN secured funding for an in-residence string quartet, he appointed institute instructor Weilerstein as its first violin and charged him with finding candidates for the group. Weilerstein formed the group in 1969 at a time when all 4 members were residents at the music school in Marlboro, Vt. Known as the New Cleveland Quartet, the group made their debut that summer at Marlboro and were invited to become the resident quartet at CIM. After 2 years of residency at CIM, a disagreement in 1971 with the institute over teaching loads resulted in the group's moving to the University of New York at Buffalo. Here they dropped the *New* from their name, becoming the Cleveland Quartet. In 1976 the quartet was appointed the resident quartet at the Eastman School of Music. In 1980, Atar Arad replaced Martha Katz. The quartet's repertory, in addition to the standard classical repertory, includes works by Brahms, Mendelssohn, Debussy, Bartok, Ives, and Slominsky. The group has been described as 4 virtuoso musicians who, while complementing each other, have not allowed their individual personalities to be submerged.

The **CLEVELAND RAILWAY COMPANY** held the city's public-transit franchise from 1910–42. The streetcar lines operated by the company annually carried hundreds of millions of passengers on a fleet that numbered as many as 1,702 streetcars and buses. The street railway industry in Cleveland began in 1860 and quickly expanded. At the time, the practice was for the city to award private companies exclusive franchises to operate their horse-drawn cars along specified streets. The number of these companies grew steadily until the horsecar began to give way to the electric streetcar in the late 1880s. The capitalization of the electric lines prompted a period of amalgamation. By 1893 only 2 companies remained, the CLEVELAND ELECTRIC RAILWAY CO. and the Cleveland City Railway Co. (the former dubbed the "Big Con" and the latter the "Little Con"). These companies merged in 1903, forming the Cleveland Electric Railway Co., popularly referred to as "ConCon."

In 1906, however, mayor TOM L. JOHNSON organized a municipal traction company to compete with the privately held giant, his line offering a $.03 fare. That started what became known as the "traction wars" and led to both the Cleveland Electric Railway Co. and the Municipal Traction Co. entering receivership in 1908. Federal Judge ROBT. W. TAYLER, overseeing the receivership, then produced a new franchise agreement between the city and the old Cleveland Electric Railway Co.—renamed the Cleveland Railway Co.—in which the company would provide transit services at cost (which included a return to stockholders), while the city would have regulatory control vested in a traction commissioner. The voters approved the Tayler Grant in Feb. 1910, and on 3 Mar. The Cleveland Railway Co. era began.

Under the leadership of its first president, John J. Stanley, the company saw ridership jump from 228 million in 1910 to 450 million in 1920. Then competition from the auto, and later the effects of the Great Depression, diminished ridership. Control of the company was wrested from the stockholders by the Van Sweringen brothers in 1930, and their interests controlled its management until 1937. By that time many changes had occurred. The first buses appeared in 1925, and the first trackless trolleys in 1936. The company found it ever more difficult to maintain the system, and the expenses demanded by the fixed nature of the streetcar lines prompted rubber-tired substitution. The Tayler Grant expired in 1935, and though it was extended, the city, under the prodding of traction commissioner Edward J. Schweid, began pressing for municipal ownership as the key to needed improvements. Four years of negotiations led to an agreement. The city issued revenue bonds in the amount of $17.5 million to purchase the shares of the company, and on 28 Apr. 1942, the municipally owned Cleveland Transit System took over the city's transit operations.

The **CLEVELAND RAILWAY FIGHT** of 1879 pitted TOM L. JOHNSON against MARCUS A. HANNA, Elias Simms, and the 6 other owners of established street railway lines in the city. Johnson, a wealthy young entrepreneur new to Cleveland, hoped to establish a street railway business here. The controversy began when he bid against the streetcar company of Simms & Hanna for a railway grant. Although Johnson had offered the lowest bid, the Cleveland city council granted Simms the line by invoking an obscure technicality in the city charter that allowed grants to be given to companies for extension of their existing lines. Johnson altered his attack and bought the Pearl St. line on Cleveland's west side, thereby qualifying for grants under the extension provision and giving him an opportunity to underbid Simms for future grants. Johnson continued to expand his line by buying up grants from the other companies and eventually winning new grants from the council.

At this time, street railway passengers in Cleveland needed to take several different systems to reach one destination and paid a new fare at every line change. Johnson wanted to offer a single-fare ride from the west side to downtown Cleveland. This idea forced him once again into confrontation with the powerful Simms & Hanna Co. Access to downtown from the west side was achieved via the

SUPERIOR VIADUCT. Connecting the viaduct track with downtown were 4 tracks on Superior St. That could be used by all car companies. In order for Johnson to attain his 1-fare plan, he needed to connect his line with the viaduct and the free tracks beyond it. The Simms-Hanna Co. owned a half-mile track running from Johnson's line to the viaduct. They would not agree to Johnson's proposal for a transfer program between the lines, insisting instead on charging Johnson's customers again for the short half-mile trip. To avoid this charge, Johnson circumvented the Simms-Hanna track by offering free omnibus service for his passengers. The new program was successful.

One year after Johnson instituted his bus idea, the Simms-Hanna franchise, including the pivotal half-mile of track, came up for renewal, and the city council, aware of the public's support of Johnson's plan, and cognizant of the upcoming city elections, refused to grant the renewal except on the condition that Johnson's cars be permitted to operate on the half-mile line. Simms & Hanna were forced to surrender, and Johnson had won a major victory. After this success, Johnson's next goal was to create a system that offered a crosstown ride. He bought the Jennings Ave. line running through the Flats, giving him control of the west and central sections of Cleveland. He hoped to add an east side line to complete his system, but Hanna, realizing this idea would precipitate a struggle for ridership, moved to consolidate his interests by buying out Simms and other stockholders in his railway company and thereby became directly involved in a struggle to stop Johnson's plan.

The fight between the two men concerning the right-of-way grants for Johnson's eastern branch developed into a struggle for control of the city council. Two council members who had originally been strong Simms-Hanna supporters switched to Johnson's side. Simms had revengefully influenced them to support Johnson—thus enabling him to win the council votes required to complete his crosstown system. Subsequently Johnson worked to increase his ridership by reducing the fare he charged on his lines. His crosstown plan was successful. (The other companies were forced to offer the same benefits to their customers in order to compete with Johnson.) These two years of confrontation not only reformed Cleveland's street railway system but, perhaps more important, also thrust the vigorous and ambitious Tom L. Johnson into an open rivalry with a strong political opponent, the powerful Republican leader Mark Hanna, which would continue for years to come.

The **CLEVELAND RAMS** were the first prolonged and well-financed attempt to establish a professional football team in Cleveland. Initially organized in 1936 as a member of the short-lived American Football League, the Rams joined the National Football League in 1937 and played in Cleveland for 8 seasons before moving to Los Angeles in Jan. 1946. Damon "Buzz" Wetzel, star fullback at Ohio State University from 1932–34, organized the Rams in 1936 as part of the new 6-team AFL. Financed by a group of local businessmen headed by attorney Homer H. Marshman, the team was a success on the gridiron, finishing 2d in the league, but it struggled financially. After the Boston team canceled the championship game because its unpaid players refused to participate, Wetzel and Marshman arranged for the Rams to leave the poorly managed AFL and join the NFL on 12 Feb. 1937.

Marshman and the other Rams stockholders paid $10,000 for a franchise in the NFL, then put up $55,000 to capitalize the new club. The new league proved to be much tougher, however, and the Rams fared poorly on the field. Between 1937–42, the Rams' best finish was 3d place in the Western division, with 5 wins and 6 losses in 1942. In June 1941 Marshman and his partners sold the Rams to Daniel F. Reeves and Frederick Levy, Jr., for about $100,000. The two new absentee owners' original plan to move the team to Boston collapsed, and the Rams remained in Cleveland, although the club suspended operations in 1943 while both Reeves and Levy served in the military. Reeves later purchased Levy's share of the team.

After another poor season in 1944, the Rams had an excellent year in 1945. Under new head coach Adam Walsh and behind rookie quarterback BOB WATERFIELD, they won 9 games and lost only 1, finished 1st in the Western division, and earned a narrow victory over the Washington Redskins in the NFL championship game. Despite the successful 1945 season, the club continually finished its seasons in debt. As the CLEVELAND BROWNS prepared to bring a well-publicized second professional football team to the city in 1946, Reeves decided to escape this added competition in an already difficult market by moving the Rams to the potentially more lucrative market of Los Angeles. Dan Reeves (30 June 1912–15 Apr. 1971) thus opened the West Coast to major sports and became an innovative team owner. His contributions to the game earned him a spot in the Pro Football Hall of Fame in 1967.

The **CLEVELAND RAPE CRISIS CENTER**, founded in 1974, has played a leading role in advocating women's safety, counseling victims of sexual abuse, and educating the public about issues regarding sexuality and women's safety. More than 150 rape crisis centers were founded in the U.S. in the 5 years after the first was organized in Washington, D.C., in the summer of 1972. The Cleveland Rape Crisis Ctr. was founded in Feb. 1974 by Lynn Hammond, a women's counselor at the FREE MEDICAL CLINIC, and Carol Zander, head of the rape task force of the Cleveland Natl. Organization of Women. They were soon joined by *Call & Post* reporter Jeanne Van Atta and Lorraine Schalamon. They began the center as a late-night telephone hotline for rape victims. From an office in the Free Clinic, the all-volunteer staff provided extensive counseling and support for rape victims and members of their families. In Apr. 1976, $50,000 in grants from the Cleveland and Gund foundations enabled the center to expand its activities. It moved to new offices in the YWCA building at 3201 Euclid, hired a small full-time staff, and kept the hotline open all day. After a number of rapes occurred in downtown office buildings in 1977, the Rape Crisis Ctr. joined with the Safety Task Force of CLEVELAND WOMEN WORKING to launch a campaign to encourage building managers to improve security. The center also began to offer inexpensive self-defense classes for women.

The center received 800 calls from rape victims in 1980, and in December it implemented a program designed to improve the rate of indictment of accused rapists. Representatives from the Rape Crisis Ctr. began to make presentations to new members of the grand jury during their 2-week training period. The presentations discussed the motives for rape and described the psychological trauma suffered by the victims. With this educational program in place, the rate of indictment for sex offenders in Cuyahoga County increased from 5% in 1978 to 90% in 1981. Although founded to help female victims of rape, the Rape Crisis Ctr. has expanded its activities to encompass other issues, as well. Male counselors help male victims of homosexual rape and the male family members of female rape victims. Of the 1,370 rape victims counseled by the center in 1980, 40 were men. In 1975 the center led the campaign urging a federal ban on use of the "morning after" contraceptive DES because of the possibility it caused vaginal

cancer. By 1983 the Rape Crisis Ctr. had hired a youth coordinator to provide counseling for sexually abused children.

---

*The Voice of the Nightingale* (1984).

The **CLEVELAND REBELS** basketball team was organized in 1946 by Al Sutphin, owner of the CLEVELAND ARENA. It was part of the newly organized Basketball Assoc. of America, whose aim was to bring professional basketball to the major cities of the country. Cleveland was in the Western division, which included teams from St. Louis, Chicago, Detroit, and Pittsburgh. The Eastern division was made up of Providence, Philadelphia, New York, Washington, Toronto, and Boston. Sutphin was president of the club, and Roy Clifford was business manager. The coach at the beginning of the season was ex-Celtic Henry "Dutch" Dehnert, and the team he had assembled included Mel Riebe, Frankie Baumholtz, Clarence Hermsen, Leo Mogus, Ken Sailors, Irving Rothenberg, and Bobby Faught. The first game was played at the Arena 3 Nov. 1946, and 7,594 fans saw the Rebels beat the Toronto Huskies 71–60. By the spring of 1947, Roy Clifford was the coach, and fan interest had declined. The Rebels finished in 3d place, with a record of 30–30. Cleveland was one of 4 teams that disbanded after the first season.

The *CLEVELAND RECORD* was published by members of the CLEVELAND NEWSPAPER GUILD to alleviate the news blackout that accompanied their strike of the *CLEVELAND PRESS* and *PLAIN DEALER* on 29 Nov. 1962. Published 5 times a week (daily except Thursday and Sunday), it first appeared on 21 Jan. 1963, edited by John Blair of the *Plain Dealer* with the assistance of managing editor Matt Fenn of the *Press*. Editorial and business offices were in the Euclid Arcade, while the paper was printed by the Collinwood Publishing Co. Issues averaged 8–12 pages, with daily runs of 100,000. Among the local events covered in the *Record* were a record-breaking cold spell and the engagement of Dr. Sam Sheppard to Mrs. Ariane Tebbenjohanns. With the settlement of the strike, it printed its 55th and final edition on 6 Apr. 1963.

The *CLEVELAND RECORDER* was launched as a morning daily on 9 Sept. 1895. Cleveland's last example of personal journalism, it remained the organ of its founder, veteran newspaperman Geo. A. Robertson, from its beginning to practically the end. It enthusiastically backed Wm. Jennings Bryan in 1896, and TOM L. JOHNSON later admitted having invested $80,000 in hopes of making the *Recorder* a more reliable Democratic organ than the *PLAIN DEALER*. Evidence of Johnson's contributions may have been provided by the *Recorder*'s expansion from 4 to 8 pages on 1 Dec. 1896. A year later, at about the time Johnson claimed to have withdrawn his support because of losses in the panic, the *Recorder* was thrown into receivership. At that point it was neither sold to the *Plain Dealer* nor converted into a court calendar, as stated in standard sources. Although cut back to 4 pages, it entered the evening field and continued as a general newspaper for at least another dozen years.

If anything, Robertson made the *Recorder* more outspokenly Democratic than ever. It supported Bryan again in 1900 but was originally hostile toward Tom Johnson's mayoral bid the following year. Questioning his sincerity on the $.03 fare issue, the *Recorder* sarcastically referred to Johnson as "Five Cent Tom." It announced its conversion prior to the primary, however, and thereafter gave Johnson its support. Politics was the *Recorder*'s principal fare, and its "Town Gossip" column, undoubtedly written by Robertson, was a prime daily source of political rumors and news. Other than that, there were standard wire reports and occasional columns on the theater and boxing. Early in the 1900s, the *Recorder* went through a yellow phase, colored with such heads as "PLACED HIS CHILD ON A RED HOT STOVE." Circulation, once over 42,000, later was generally reported at around 30,000. By 1908, Robertson had acquired the *Daily Legal News*, which he began to publish as the morning edition of the *Recorder*. When he died on 20 Feb. of that year, however, the primary impulse behind the *Recorder* was gone. By 1913 the *Daily Legal News*, established in 1888, had swallowed the *Recorder*, which survived in 1985 in the nameplate of the former.

The *CLEVELAND REPORTER* was established midway through a 4-week newspaper strike in Nov. 1956, as a substitute for Cleveland's 3 closed dailies. The tabloid made its first appearance on 5 Nov. 1956, 3 days after publication ceased on a combined edition of the *Plain Dealer, News*, and *Press*. It was published by striking newsmen and printers under the designation of the Valley News Co., using the facilities of the United Publishing Co. at 6875 Broadway. Although crediting no editor, the masthead listed Mike Lapine as business manager and Ken Rankin as advertising manager. Selling at the then-current price of $.07, the *Reporter* circulated about 100,000 copies a day and covered such events as the Hungarian Rebellion, the Suez Crisis, and the 1956 elections. It ceased publication upon a preliminary strike settlement on 16 Nov., although complications kept the regular dailies closed through 28 Nov. 1956.

The *CLEVELAND REPUBLICAN* was a campaign paper issued to promote the election of John Tyler as president. Published and edited by Emanuel Fisher, it first appeared on 2 May 1844, and at irregular intervals thereafter, at least through 18 July. Besides Tyler, it advocated first D. R. Porter of Pennsylvania, then Wm. Shannon of Ohio for vice-president, and David Tod for governor. Tyler withdrew from the race in favor of the Democratic nominee, Jas. K. Polk, on 20 Aug.

The **CLEVELAND ROCKET SOCIETY**, formed ca. 1933, was an organization of area residents interested in the possibilities of liquid-propelled rocket flight and engaged in experimental work in that field. It was active for less than 5 years. The group was founded and led by Ernst Loebell, an engineer born and trained in Germany and acquainted with German rocketbuilder Karl Poggensee. After graduation from engineering school in 1927, Loebell went to work at the German branch of the Otis Elevator Co.; he was eventually transferred to the U.S. and then to Cleveland, where he later joined the WHITE MOTOR CORP. In Cleveland, Loebell discussed his interest in rocketry with fellow members of the CLEVELAND ENGINEERING SOCIETY, and with the encouragement and aid of Chas. St. Clair, he formed the Cleveland Rocket Society, establishing its office in the Hanna Bldg. The society grew to about 100 members at its peak, including Western Reserve University German professor Hugo K. Polt, attorney John V. Crist, civil engineer Fred W. Donley, and machine-shop operator Harold C. Haar, as well as interested high school students.

Loebell and the society were not space-oriented but were interested in "more practical and attainable" uses of rocket technology: its use in transcontinental, supersonic mail delivery and in passenger service. Loebell, St. Clair,

and another early member, Edward L. Hanna, planned a program of experiments that they hoped would produce a 1,000-mph rocket that could carry mail, precious cargos such as medicine, and weather-recording and other scientific instruments. Supported by an annual $5 membership fee and donations of material and labor, the society carried out a series of 5 experiments in 1933–34. Working first on the basic problem of developing a practical propulsion system, the society ended its experiments in the face of what its historian called "the chief technical problem which plagued all the rocketeers of the 1930s: to find an adequate means of cooling." Although Loebell designed "a regeneratively-cooled, heat absorbent aluminum motor," construction of an acceptable motor took a year, and it was not tested by the society. By then the Depression had drawn members' attention away from society activities. Loebell left Cleveland temporarily after losing his job, and the society's publication, *Space*, begun in Dec. 1933, ceased publication after the 5th issue in Sept. 1934. The society was continued by some members but conducted no more experiments, built no more motors, and may not have held any more meetings. The work of the society was well-publicized in the local press and the national popular scientific press, and in 1937 it enjoyed a final moment of fame when the French Ministry of Commerce & Industry invited it to send an exhibit to the 1937 Paris Internatl. Exhibition. The society's exhibit, a scale model of the long-distance, radio-equipped mail rocket Loebell hoped to build and one of the regeneratively cooled motors, received good reviews in French and British journals.

The **CLEVELAND ROLLING MILL STRIKES** occurred during the summer of 1882 and 1885 and involved skilled workers who were largely of British origin, as well as Polish and Czech unskilled laborers who were working in the company's facilities near present-day Jones Rd. and Broadway. In May 1882, skilled workers who had joined the Amalgamated Assoc. of Iron & Steel Workers issued demands to the company, including a wage set by the union and a closed shop for skilled workers. These were rejected by the company's president, Wm. Chisholm, and the workers walked out. The company responded by hiring unskilled Polish and Czech workers from outside of Cleveland. On 5 June the company reopened. The union's decision to use nonviolent tactics to keep the POLES and CZECHS out of work failed. Serious violence errupted on 13 June as Czech workers and police were stoned by strikers. The public, which had previously sympathized with the strikers, now turned to the side of the company and strikebreakers. By the end of July, the strike had virtually collapsed as a result of the city's support of the company, the attitude of the public, and the union's inability to gain support of the large numbers of new unskilled workers.

In the summer of 1885 a more massive and violent strike occurred, this time led by the Poles and Czechs who had been recruited 3 years before. In July, a recession caused Chisholm to cut wages for the third time that year. The wire mill workers walked out and, violently invading the other mills, forced the entire company to shut down. Most of the English-speaking, skilled workers also walked out; however, they did not approve of the violent tactics of the unskilled, who were later viewed as radicals by the public and the press. On 6 July, 1,500 workers marched to Chisholm's downtown office and demanded a restoration of June wages. They were refused. The next day, 1,000 Poles and Czechs forced the H. P. Nail Co. and the Union Steel Screw Co. (Chisholm owned stock in both) to close, and severely beat the latter company's president. The Rolling Mill Co. tried to reopen on 13 July but to no avail, as a mob attacked policemen on duty, causing yet another riot. A strikers' association was begun by the English-speaking workers and the Poles and Czechs, but with little success. In September, many skilled workers began returning to work. On 25 Sept., Poles and Czechs decided to attack the mills the next day. However, Mayor GEO. GARDNER ordered Chisholm to restore the June wage. The strike ended, but Chisholm refused to rehire many Poles and Czechs. Those responsible for the strike and its eventual success found themselves without jobs.

The **CLEVELAND ROLLING MILLS.** *See* **UNITED STATES STEEL CORP.**

**THE CLEVELAND-SANDUSKY BREWING CORPORATION** was known for many years as the Cleveland & Sandusky Brewing Co.; it was formed in 1898 through a merger of 11 northern Ohio breweries. These were, in Cleveland, the Baehr, Barrett, Bohemian, Cleveland, Columbia, Gehring, Phoenix (later Baehr-Phoenix), Star, and Union breweries; and, in Sandusky, Kuebeler-Stang (actually 2 breweries, Kuebeler and Stang, which had consolidated 2 years earlier). The Baehr, Barrett, and Union breweries were closed shortly after the merger, while 3 others were added to the chain: Schlather (1902) and Fishel (1907) in Cleveland, and the Lorain brewery (1905) in Lorain, Ohio.

The oldest of the Cleveland & Sandusky breweries, Gehring and Schlather, had been established in the 1850s by Chas. E. Gehring and Leonard Schlather respectively. In Sandusky, brothers Jacob and August Kuebeler had established their brewery in 1867, while Granz Stang in 1880 assumed control of a brewery begun ca. 1852 by Philip Dauch. The first officers of the Cleveland & Sandusky Brewing Co. were F. W. Gehring, president; Jacob Kuebeler (Sandusky), 1st vice-president; Ernst Mueller, 2d vice-president; and Wm. H. Chapman, secretary and treasurer. HERMAN C. BAEHR, who would later deny TOM L. JOHNSON a fifth term as mayor of Cleveland, served for several years as secretary and treasurer. The company's general offices were in the American Trust Bldg. on PUBLIC SQUARE.

Simon Fishel, a former manager of the Bohemian Brewing Co. who had founded the Fishel Brewing Company in 1904, became president of Cleveland & Sandusky when that company absorbed Fishel in 1907. He served in that position until his death in 1917; sons Theodore and, later, Oscar succeeded him. Over the years, most of the chain's smaller breweries were closed, so that by 1919, of the company's Cleveland plants, only Gehring, Fishel, and Schlather remained. During Prohibition, the company manufactured carbonated beverages and near-beer at the Schlather bottling plant at 2600 Carroll Ave. After repeal, the only Cleveland brewery to reopen was Fishel, located at 2764 E. 55th St.; it resumed production of Gold Bond beer in July 1933 and produced Gold Bond and Crystal Rock beer and Old Timer's ale into the 1960s. In Sandusky, the Stang plant reopened but was closed again in 1935 following a 2-month strike by brewery workers. Oscar J. Fishel headed the company during this turbulent decade but resigned in 1940 after a proposal to sell the brewery's assets to the Brewing Corp. of America (see CARLING BREWING CO.) was defeated by stockholders. The company was reorganized, and Frank P. Van De Westelaken was elected president.

In 1956, Marvin Bilsky left his family bakery business to join the brewery as vice-president and general manager; 3 months later he became president. The brewery had suffered 3 successive years of losses. But Bilsky's aggressive advertising and merchandising—in 1958 Cleveland-Sandusky became the first brewery in the nation to toast its malt (a process claimed to enhance taste), and in 1959 it introduced the throwaway bottle—were not enough to reverse the company's fortunes. The Cleveland-Sandusky Brewing Corp., as it was last known, closed in the mid-1960s.

The **CLEVELAND SHOPPING NEWS** thrived between the two world wars on the concept of a newspaper consisting wholly of ads and delivered gratis. Though claiming to be the first of its breed, the paper had remote antecedents on the local scene in 2 pre-Civil War publications, the *Commercial Gazette* and the *Commercial Advertiser* (ca. 1856–61). Both were devoted mainly to advertisements and distributed at nominal or no cost. From its initial issue of 15 Oct. 1921, however, the *Cleveland Shopping News* pioneered a formula eventually copied in 60 other cities, from St. Petersburg to Seattle. It was owned and operated principally by the large downtown department stores, which invited Edward L. Greene of the Cleveland Better Business Bureau to draw up a code of advertising standards to govern the publication. President of the Cleveland Shopping News Co. for much of its history was Chas. H. Strong of WM. TAYLOR SON & CO., while Sam B. Anson, former city editor of the *CLEVELAND LEADER*, served as publisher. After 1926, printing of the *Shopping News* was handled in its own plant at 5309 Hamilton Ave. Originally a weekly, the paper at its height was delivered twice a week by 1,200 carriers to 345,000 households. Excessive operating costs were blamed for the suspension of regular publication with the issue of 1 July 1954, although the name was revived thereafter for direct-mail advertising campaigns.

The **CLEVELAND SKATING CLUB**, 2500 Kemper Rd., SHAKER HTS., was founded in 1936 by a group of families who wanted their own private indoor skating rink. It was one of the first figure-skating clubs in the U.S. To own its own club building. Additional impetus came when the Toronto Skating Club visited Cleveland in 1935 and requested that a skating club be used for its performances rather than the Elysium rink located at E. 107th and Euclid Ave. The club acquired the property, clubhouse, and other facilities of the Cleveland Tennis & Racquet Club at Fairhill and Kemper Rds. It subsequently acquired icemaking equipment that had been used in downtown Cleveland during the 1936 GREAT LAKES EXPOSITION. Indoor skating and indoor tennis began the winter of 1936–37, and in 1938 single membership included both activities. The building for the rink was built alongside the old tennis clubhouse, with the space between the buildings enclosed to provide a viewing and dining area overlooking the rink. This glass-enclosed gallery just off the upper lounge has been a special attraction of the Cleveland Skating Club. The club offers a full schedule of classes and lessons to its members, providing them with a variety of opportunities for training and experience. Several Olympic gold medalists and world champions began their skating careers at the CSC, including Carol Heiss, Hayes Alan Jenkins, David Jenkins, and Wm. Fauver. The club also hosts an annual ice show that benefits the Memorial Fund of the U.S. Figure Skating Assoc., which provides scholarships to young skaters. Through the years, the CSC's facilities have continued to expand. In 1970, the adjacent armory and grounds of the Natl. Guard (see TROOP A) were acquired, thus enabling members and guests to participate in an expanded variety of programs and activities, including year-round skating, ballroom dancing on ice, hockey, squirt, and curling, as well as year-round tennis, paddle tennis, and swimming.

The **CLEVELAND SOCIETY FOR THE BLIND** provides special services that enable blind people of the community to cope with problems of sightlessness. A pioneer in developing such services, it has served as a model for similar agencies in other cities. The society grew out of an experiment at Goodrich House begun in 1898 that, among other concerns, urged instruction of blind children in CLEVELAND PUBLIC SCHOOLS. Interest generated from the experiment led to the formation of a small reading group for the blind in 1906, which in turn led to the formal establishment later that year of the Cleveland Society for the Blind by representatives of the CLEVELAND PUBLIC LIBRARY, the VISITING NURSES ASSOC., Associated Charities, and Cleveland settlement houses. Prominent early participants included LINDA EASTMAN, who founded the reading group, and Mrs. E. B. Palmer, who was executive secretary during the society's first 25 years. Robt. B. Irwin, later director of the American Foundation for the Blind, was an early innovator for the society who helped develop and supervise public school Braille classes.

The primary goal of the society was to find ways for blind people to work independently. In 1907, a broom shop was instituted. By 1910 the society was one of the leaders in promoting selective placement of the blind in private industry. It had also been instrumental in getting the state involved when, in 1908, it sponsored 2 bills that led to the establishment of the Ohio Commission for the Blind. Other services at this time included a social-services committee to assist society in meeting the needs of blind people, especially those destitute or homebound, and public school classes for blind children, sponsored by the Board of Education. In 1927, the society moved into the CAESAR A. GRASSELLI house on E. 55th. Through the 1930s it continued efforts to secure work for the blind and obtain for them instruction in Braille, typewriting, and shop work. By the 1950s, its volunteer services had been expanded to invite involvement from various civic groups, such as the Council of Jewish Women. Volunteers established special committees such as the Sterling Committee, which provided reading services and recreation programs on the east side. The society was one of the first agencies in the country to develop a contract department that worked with industry in doing subcontract work. It was also the first to establish a community glaucoma society program (1953). Other employment services that were developed included a centrally managed vending-stand program, a retail sales program (discontinued in 1966), and a marketing program for products made by the blind. In 1966, the society moved to the Sight Ctr. on Chester Ave. at E. 105th St. Receiving much of its support from the United Appeal, it continued to offer services in employment, sales, recreation, social work, and rehabilitation, as well as a program of public education.

The **CLEVELAND SOCIETY OF ARTISTS** was founded in Mar. 1913 by GEO. ADOMEIT and Chas. Shackelton to provide a means of communication between artists, art lovers, and practitioners in the applied arts and crafts. The group carried on the traditions of 2 earlier Cleveland art groups, the Cleveland Art Club, founded in 1876 by ARCHIBALD M. WILLARD, and the Cleveland Arts Club, founded in 1889. The society had several locations during its 70-year existence. It first gathered at members' houses, then in the HOLLENDEN HOTEL, the GAGE GALLERIES, and Wm. Edmondson's Studio, and in 1920 in its own clubrooms on Prospect Ave. In this same year a building fund was started, which led to the purchase of a site at 2022 E. 88th St. in 1938. John Kelly, an authority on early American architecture, designed a 2-story brick gallery that was constructed at this address.

One of the primary yearly activities of the society was an auction held for the purpose of establishing a Cleveland School of Art scholarship. In addition, in 1930 the society started a collection of works by Cleveland artists, selecting as the first piece Frederick C. Gottwald's *The Dreamer*, which had won the Penton medal at the 1919 MAY SHOW of the CLEVELAND MUSEUM OF ART. In 1945 Lawrence E. Blazey was elected president of the society. Under his leadership, the group was particularly successful in attempts to encourage local area talent. The society continued to function, successfully encouraging and fostering a love of art in the community, until it was disbanded in Sept. 1983.

The **CLEVELAND SOROSIS SOCIETY** was a 19th-century club that focused on women's growing sense of power to change themselves, their condition, and the society around them. The Cleveland group, organized in 1891, grew out of the Western Reserve Club of Cleveland and was patterned after clubs established in New York and California. Its name, a contraction of *sorority sisters*, was consciously chosen from botany, where *sorosis* means a collective fruit formed by a union of many flowers. Like a pineapple, fig, or mulberry, Sorosis gathered many literary, philanthropic, scientific, artistic, and social pursuits into one umbrella organization. Committees, which functioned like separate clubs and had their own officers, goals, and policies, took turns making presentations about their programs to the general group. Members of the various committees tended to be professionals, socially prominent, and intellectual. Far from being radical, the women were nonetheless influenced by mounting campaigns for suffrage and women's rights to channel their energies into useful activities. For example, one group incorporated into Sorosis was the Women's Employment Society, which was operated like a business to hire women to sew garments for sale; in 1885, the society sold 500 pairs of jeans and 300 gray flannel shirts destined for Indian reservations to the Dept. of the Interior. With similar enterprise, the Health Protective Assoc. campaigned for clean streets, better sanitation, and separate play areas for children. The separate groups shared the view that women's basic abilities would be enhanced by a knowledge of science. Knowledge of modern sanitation, public health, and childrearing could turn a woman's lot into a respected profession wherein she became a domestic engineer who efficiently promoted a clean home and nutritious meals. Health could be improved by a conscious program of physical culture. While Sorosis shied away from accepting suffrage clubs into its fold, members of the individual groups reevaluated their roles as women and ultimately were more prepared to accept suffrage and a larger role in society. In 1902, the Cleveland Sorosis became part of the FED. OF WOMEN'S CLUBS OF GREATER CLEVELAND, but it remained active well into the 1950s. After 1917 the club met in its home at 2040 E. 100th St.

Cleveland Sorosis Club Records, WRHS.

The **CLEVELAND, SOUTHWESTERN & COLUMBUS RAILWAY** was the 2d-largest interurban in the state. Only the Ohio Electric Railway, which ran in western Ohio, was larger. The CS&C connected Cleveland with Columbus to the south and Norwalk to the west. The line originated in 1876 as a horsecar line known as the CLEVELAND & BEREA STREET RAILWAY. It was newly chartered in

1891, when electric rail traction was coming of age. An electric-powered railway, running from Cleveland to BEREA, was opened in 1895. It was owned by the Pomeroy family. Later in 1895, the Pomeroys formed a partnership with the Cleveland banking firm of M. J. Mandelbaum & Co., providing cash to extend the line to Elyria. The Pomeroy-Mandelbaum syndicate, as the partnership was known, continued purchasing and operating other short rail lines; in 1903, the lines were merged into the Cleveland & Southwestern Traction Co., providing service as far west as Norwalk and as far south as Wooster. Southern routes to Bucyrus and farther on to Columbus were then acquired, and on 4 Mar. 1907, the Cleveland, Southwestern & Columbus Railway was chartered. The line covered 225 rail miles. Known as the Green Line for its dark-green cars, the CS&C operated several amusement parks along its routes, as was the practice of the interurban companies, to draw riders. PURITAS SPRINGS PARK in Cleveland opened in 1900 and continued to operate long after the road's demise, finally closing in the late 1950s. The CS&C stopped at Chippewa Lake near Medina, although it did not own the park. It also operated parks in Mansfield (Casino Park) and between Galion and Bucyrus (Seccaium Park).

The CS&C went into receivership in 1922 but returned a profit in 1923 after abandoning its Norwalk-Oberlin run. It was the last profit recorded by the line. Continued losses led to the abandonment of 2 more sections of the line in 1926 and the replacment of rail service with buses. In 1927, the CS&C's cars were painted orange to be easier for auto and truck traffic to distinguish in the hope of preventing grade-crossing accidents. After that, the line became known as the Southwestern. A unique move for survival came in 1928 when the Southwestern made transportation history by offering the first coordinated rail-air service package. Passengers could purchase a through ticket to Detroit. The CS&C dropped off riders at the Cleveland Airport, from which STOUT AIR SERVICES flew on to Detroit. Revenues continued to plunge, and in 1929, the line went into receivership. A federal judge ordered the line abandoned in Jan. 1931. The Southwestern made its final trip on 28 Feb. 1931. Some of its bus operations were taken over by the N. Olmsted Municipal Bus Co., whose buses were painted in the old Southwestern dark-green-and-orange color scheme.

Christiansen, Harry, *New Northern Ohio's Interurbans* (1983).

The **CLEVELAND SPIDERS** were a professional baseball team in the American Assoc. in 1887–88 before moving to the Natl. League for the 1889 season. Owned by streetcar tycoon Frank DeHaas Robison and managed in the 1890s by Oliver "Pat" Tebeau, the Spiders became one of the best teams in professional baseball before Robison dismantled its talent and the club was laughed out of town in 1899. In 1886 Robison received a franchise for a Cleveland team to play in the AA in 1887. With Geo. W. Howe as secretary and Davis Hawley as treasurer, Robison put together a team known first as the Forest Citys and after 1889 as the Spiders. Robison built a ballpark on his streetcar line at Payne Ave. and E. 39th St. The team fared poorly in its 2 years in the AA, finishing the 1887 season in 7th (last) place and improving only to 6th place in 1888. At the end of the 1888 season, however, the team was chosen to replace Detroit in the NL.

Another change in 1889 was the team name. Because of the "skinny and spindly" appearance of many of the players, the team acquired the nickname Spiders. The Spiders fared little better in the NL in 1889, finishing in 6th place. Some players, such as Pat Tebeau, jumped to the

Cleveland team in a rival league in 1890 but returned to the Spiders in 1891. Also in 1891 the Spiders moved to a new ballpark (still on a Robison streetcar line) at Lexington and E. 66th, and for the last half of the season, Tebeau took over as manager and transformed the team; in 1892 the Spiders became a contender. Tebeau, "an advocate of rowdy baseball," often harassed opposing players and umpires, and once said that "a milk and water, goody-goody player can't ever wear a Cleveland uniform." Cleveland challenged Baltimore for the title of "rowdiest" team in baseball.

In 1892 the Spiders, led by the pitching of DENTON TRUE "CY" YOUNG, George "Nig" Cuppy, and John Clarkson, and with Chas. "Chief" Zimmer behind the plate, finished in 2d place, behind the Boston Beaneaters. Cleveland was one of only 2 teams that made money in 1892. The Spiders slipped to 3d place in 1893 and to 6th in 1894 before regaining their form in 1895 and 1896, finishing 2d to the Baltimore Orioles both seasons and playing the Orioles in the postseason series for baseball's Temple Cup. In the 1895 series, worthy of baseball's 2 rowdiest teams, the Spiders emerged victorious, winning the first 3 games at home (aided, Baltimore sportswriters claimed, by a barrage of potatoes and other missiles from spectators aimed at Oriole players), losing the next contest in Baltimore amid what baseball historian David Voigt called "a bombardment of eggs and rocks," and finally clinching the series with a win in Baltimore, after which "an angry crowd threatened [the Spiders'] safety." In 1896 the Orioles avenged the defeat by winning the Temple Cup series in 4 straight games.

The Spiders were never contenders after 1896, finishing 5th in both 1897 and 1898. Poor attendance at their home games angered Robison, and after the 1898 season, he punished local fans for their disloyalty by transferring talented players from the Spiders to the St. Louis team he had purchased in July 1898. His move served only to further alienate the Cleveland fans. Only 500 spectators saw the Spiders' opening-day doubleheader in 1899, and later attendance was so poor that Robison announced that the team would play no more home games after 1 July. A crowd of 1,500 at a doubleheader after that apparently forced him to modify that policy, but the team did transfer many home games to other cities, leading sportswriters to call them "the Wanderers." For their extremely poor performance on the field, the Spiders were regularly called "the Misfits," and bookies gave 4-1 odds that the club would not win 2 games in a row, something the team did only once on its way to compiling a record of 20–134 (.129). Cleveland was one of 4 teams dropped from the league in 1900.

The **CLEVELAND STATE HOSPITAL** was a state-supported psychiatric facility for long-term care. Originally known as the Northern Ohio Lunatic Asylum, it was the second of 6 public asylums established in Ohio during the 1850s. In later years it was commonly known as Newburgh State Hospital. NOLA was authorized by an act of the Ohio legislature in 1852. The main building, containing 100 beds, was completed in 1855 on land in NEWBURGH donated by the Garfield family. Previously, many of those considered insane had been kept in jails or almshouses. The purpose of the asylum was to provide the mentally ill a quiet place outside the city with a moral environment where healthy living habits could be learned. NOLA was run by a 5-member board of trustees appointed by the governor. Dr. HORACE ACKLEY was the first chairman and superintendent. A professor of surgery in the Medical Dept. of Western Reserve College, Ackley was an important figure

273

in the building of the hospital and its early development. In its first 100 years, the hospital had an enormously high turnover of superintendents—21 within that span. The hospital's last superintendent, Dr. Wm. Grover, served for 18 years.

In its early years, the hospital had a homelike atmosphere; patients and staff usually dined together. It was largely an "open" facility, and most patients were free to make use of the grounds. Management of disturbed patients included seclusion, cuffs, straps, strait-jackets, and cribs. Treatment, however, was largely based on providing a healthful environment. After a fire in 1872, a more substantial structure was built, with a capacity for 650 patients. But as early as 1874 there were reports of overcrowding, a problem that would plague the hospital over the next 100 years. By 1900, over 10,000 patients, most of them long-term, had been cared for. At this time the hospital began to treat mainly poorer patients, as an increase in the number of private hospitals attracted the wealthy. An increasing number of patients were also being admitted by the courts, further adding to overcrowded conditions. By 1920, the census had risen to 2,000. Although CSH managed to keep pace with progress in medicine, conditions—because of overcrowding and irregular state support—continued to decline in the 1920s and 1930s. In 1946, investigations by the *CLEVELAND PRESS* and the newly formed Cleveland Mental Health Assoc. revealed a history of brutality and criminal neglect, and squalid conditions in many of the wards. Although overcrowding persisted, conditions began to improve with the development of social services, psychology, group work, occupational therapy, volunteer services, and the establishment of out-patient clinics. Severe budget cutbacks in 1961 eliminated 29 activity programs. In 1962, for 2,700 patients there were 12 ward doctors and 10 RNs to supervise 250 attendants. During the 1960s, the patient population dropped from 3,000 to 1,800, closer to the intended capacity of 1,500. The state began to phase out CSH in 1972; in 1975 it became the Cleveland Development Ctr., a care facility for the mentally retarded. The old main building was demolished in 1977.

**CLEVELAND STATE UNIVERSITY** (est. 1965) occupies a campus of approximately 60 acres, between E. 18th St. and the Innerbelt Freeway, with most of its major buildings located between Euclid and Chester avenues. Its establishment and location were intended to stimulate urban revitalization. The university consists of 5 undergraduate colleges: Fenn College of Engineering, the James J. Nance College of Business Admin., Arts & Sciences, Education, and Urban Affairs together with a College of Graduate Studies and the Cleveland-Marshall College of Law. CSU offers over 90 undergraduate and graduate degree programs, including 4 doctorates and 2 professional degrees in law. Enrollment in 1984 was approximately 14,000 undergraduate and 5,000 graduate students, including almost 1,000 in the law college. The faculty numbered nearly 570.

Fenn College, CSU's private college predecessor, was the outgrowth of the Cleveland YMCA's evening educational program, started in the 1880s. A newly created day-school program was combined with the evening school in 1906 under the name the Association Institute. Four different day schools were established in 1909: the School of Commerce & Finance, the Technical School, the Preparatory School, and the Special School (dropped in 1913). The Preparatory School received accreditation from the state in 1915, and from the North Central Assoc. of Colleges & Secondary Schools in 1920. The first female students were admitted in 1918. In 1921 the YMCA's edu-

cational branch was renamed the Cleveland School of Technology.

The first college credit classes in engineering and business were offered in 1923. Classes were held in the Central YMCA Bldg. on Prospect Ave. and E. 22nd St., and in 3 former residences located on Prospect east of the YMCA Bldg.: the Johnson Bldg., the Edwards Bldg., and the Medical Bldg. The first building erected for the college was the Fenn Bldg., in 1928. Two significant events marked 1927: the first graduating college class, and the beginnings of plans for a junior college program that became Nash Jr. College in 1931. The educational program was again reorganized in 1929, uniting both the day and evening programs and changing the school's name to Fenn College in honor of SERENO PECK FENN, Cleveland YMCA president and benefactor of its educational program. The Preparatory School and Nash Jr. College ceased operations in 1934. A liberal arts division was added to the original engineering and business schools in 1932.

Fenn College offered a quality low-cost educational program designed to attract those for whom a college education might be financially unattainable. In line with this policy, Fenn became the second college in Ohio to adopt the cooperative education program. By alternating classroom work with actual employment, the program enabled many Fenn students to finance their educations, as well as to gain practical work experience. The purchase of the Natl. Town & Country Club Bldg. at Euclid Ave. and E. 24th St. in 1937 gave Fenn needed classroom and office space. Renamed Fenn Tower in 1939, it also provided the college with a prestigious Euclid Ave. address. Fenn's reputation was further enhanced in 1940, when it received accreditation from the North Central Assoc.

Dr. Cecil V. Thomas, serving simultaneously as Fenn's first president (1930–47) and the YMCA's executive director, was responsible for the college's early development. Under the administration of Dr. Edward Hodnett (1948–51), Fenn College constructed Foster Hall, financed by a donation from Cleveland entrepreneur CLAUDE H. FOSTER, and separated from the YMCA in 1951. Dr. G. Brooks Earnest served as president (1952–65) until the state's takeover. In 1953, Fenn expanded again by purchasing the Ohio Motors Bldg. on E. 24th St. Renovated for classroom use, the building was dedicated in 1959 as Stilwell Hall, in honor of Chas. J. Stilwell, chairman of the board of trustees.

Increasing operating costs, competition from a new community college, and rumors of a possible state takeover placed Fenn in financial straits by 1963. That year the college released "A Plan for Unified Higher Education in Cleveland-Northeastern Ohio." The plan called upon the state to develop a state university in Cleveland using Fenn College and its personnel as the nucleus. On 18 Dec. 1964, Gov. Jas. A. Rhodes signed legislation creating Cleveland State University, Ohio's 7th state university, and announced the appointment of 9 trustees, with Jas. J. Nance as chairman. Negotiating committees from Fenn and CSU reached an agreement in Mar. 1965, whereby the state would take control of Fenn College, its facilities, and personnel on 1 Sept. 1965. Dr. Harry K. Newburn, appointed by the CSU trustees as an educational consultant, served as acting president until the appointment in Feb. 1966 of Dr. Harold L. Enarson as CSU's first president. Dr. Newburn returned in 1972 as interim president, serving until Dr. Walter B. Waetjen assumed the presidency.

Dr. Enarson's tenure (1966–72) marked a period of tremendous growth. Enrollment increased 3-fold, from 5,000 to 15,000. The faculty increased from 90 to 450 members. The academic program added a college of education (1966), the first graduate-degree programs (1967), and doctoral-degree programs (1969). The campus expanded from 9 acres and 3 buildings to over 27 acres with 4 new classroom and office buildings. Dr. Waetjen's tenure (1973– ) has marked a period of maturation for CSU. Its programs have grown, and significant research and public-service programs, such as the Legal Clinic, the Speech & Hearing Clinic, and the Ctr. for Neighborhood Development, have been developed.

Cleveland-Marshall Law School, an important facet of the university, grew out of the merger of the Cleveland and John Marshall law schools. The former dates from 1897, when judges Willis Vickery, Arthur Rowley, Chas. Bentley, FREDERIC C. HOWE, and Clifford Neff organized the Baldwin University Law School. At the same time, F. J. Wing founded the Cleveland Law School. The 2 schools merged in 1899 and incorporated under the name the Cleveland Law School as the law department of Baldwin University (later BALDWIN-WALLACE COLLEGE), an association that lasted through 1926. It was Ohio's first evening law school and the first to admit women. The school began instruction in the America Trust Bldg. in downtown Cleveland but soon moved into the Engineers' Bldg. Willis Vickery took the lead in the school's early development, serving as a faculty member, business manager, and dean. He was succeeded as dean by his son, Melville Vickery, who served from 1932–37. Judge Lee Skeel was selected to fill the decanal vacancy and in 1945 became president of the school. Wilson G. Stapleton, faculty member and trustee, was then appointed dean, serving until 1967.

Established by Cleveland attorneys ALFRED A. BENESCH, Frank T. Cullitan, and David C. Meck, Sr., the John Marshall Law School began classes on 20 Sept. 1916, in the New Guardian Bldg. on Euclid Ave. The successful results of its first year's instruction resulted in affiliation with Ohio Northern University in May 1917. In 1920, Ohio Northern organized the John Marshall Preparatory School to meet the needs of Marshall students who needed additional academic work before entrance to law school. After 6 years, the relationship cordially ended, and Marshall received authorization to confer degrees under its own name.

Serving as dean, Judge David C. Meck, Sr., was instrumental in the early growth of the school. Secretary-treasurer Dean B. Meck served from Marshall's founding until 1935. He was succeeded by David C. Meck, Jr., who was designated dean in 1939. In 1919, Marshall moved to the old courthouse on PUBLIC SQUARE. Two years later it moved to 242–248 Superior Ave. In 1938, Marshall moved again, to the Hippodrome Bldg., 720 Euclid Ave.

On 24 June 1946, the two downtown evening law schools consolidated as the Cleveland-Marshall Law School. That same year operations moved to 1240 the Ontario Bldg., a site occupied until the building was razed to make way for the Justice Ctr. Between 1963–67, the school had a nominal relationship with Baldwin-Wallace College. After regaining independent status, Cleveland-Marshall initiated its first full-time legal educational program, graduating its first full-time class in 1970. Cleveland-Marshall received state institutional status in 1969, becoming the Cleveland-Marshall College of Law, the 6th of the colleges constituting CSU. The largest law college in Ohio, it has 60% of its students in the day program and 40% in the evening program.

University Archives, CSU.

The **CLEVELAND STRING QUARTET** was a chamber music group attached to the CLEVELAND ORCHESTRA in the 1920s and 1930s. It was composed of principal play-ers from the orchestra's string section. The quartet was formed in 1919, a year after the birth of the Cleveland Orchestra. It was organized largely through the efforts of the orchestra's first conductor, NIKOLAI SOKOLOFF. Its original and continued purpose was to provide Cleveland with a first-rate chamber music ensemble. Sokoloff relinquished leadership of the quartet to concertmaster Louis Edlin in 1922. Its personnel changed several times during the 1920s, eventually solidifying in the 1930s with Josepf Fuchs, 1st violin; RUDOLPH RINGWALL, 2d violin; Carlton Cooley, viola; and Victor de Gomez (the only original member), cello. ADELLA PRENTISS HUGHES managed the quartet from 1919–33; Carl J. Vosburgh succeeded her in 1934. The CLEVELAND MUSICAL ARTS ASSOC. sponsored the quartet throughout its existence. The Cleveland String Quartet had its most successful years under Josepf Fuchs, who joined the group in 1926. Over the next 7 years it presented concerts in London, New York, Washington, and 27 other American cities, including an engagement by the Elizabeth Sprague Coolidge Foundation for 8 concerts at various educational centers. The quartet also played at private recitals in Cleveland and elsewhere in Ohio, including an annual concert at the Cleveland Country Club. With the opening of the Severance Chamber Music Hall in 1931, the quartet began a more regular schedule of concerts and recitals. It presented a chamber music series at Severance every autumn, usually consisting of 6 evenings a season. A spring series was added later and in 1936 featured a Johannes Brahms Chamber Music Festival. Other local activities included the launching, in 1934, of a commercial series over WHK radio. In 1939, the quartet was reorganized, with Fuchs as the only continuing member. Attendance at its concerts began to drop, and in 1941, soon after the departure of Fuchs, the quartet disbanded.

Cleveland Musical Arts Assoc. Archives.

The **CLEVELAND SUNDAY SUN** was introduced on 10 Oct. 1880 by W. Scott Robison, one of the original founders of the Sunday Voice. Like its contemporary competitors, it contained 8 pages and sold for $.05. Editorial offices were at 134 St. Clair Ave. Besides the emphasis placed on graphics, the Sun began a women's feature and opened a column to amateur poets. A memorial edition published upon the death of Pres. JAS. A. GARFIELD in 1881 accommodated a total of 17 engravings, and the Sun claimed that the demand had necessitated the printing of 20,000 additional copies. Capitalizing on interest in a new invention, a political gossip column headed "The Sun's Telephone" employed the device of reporting its items in the vernacular of transcribed telephone conversations. Robison's name was removed from the masthead in 1882, possibly because he seems to have also become a police magistrate at the time. Although the Sun claimed Ohio's largest Sunday circulation, it was sold on 10 Nov. 1885 to C. C. Ruthrauff, who merged it into the Sun & Voice by the following Sunday, 15 Nov. 1885.

The **CLEVELAND SUNDAY TIMES** served as the name for 3 different publications in the 1870s. First came the Cleveland Sunday Times of 17 Sept. 1871, the first Sunday newspaper issued in Cleveland since the short-lived Sunday Morning Review of 1858. Published by Mr. Saltiel and Mr. Luse at 268 Superior, it professed independence in politics, since the two main parties were "both corrupt to the core." It hoped to sell for $2.50 per year but evidently succumbed after half a dozen issues to the even newer Sunday Morning Voice. A second Cleveland Sunday Times appeared around 18 July 1875. Its 20th number, dated 28 Nov. 1875, contained 8 pages and only the name "Times Printing Co." as a clue to its ownership. Known simply as the *Sunday Morning Times*, the third paper of this appellation was much longer-lived than its namesakes. Probably begun on 7 May 1876, its issue of 6 Aug. 1876 (no. 14) contained 8 6-column pages selling for $.05. Through most of its career it was owned and edited by J. P. O'Brien, who marshaled its columns in support of the Democratic party. Its address was less consistent, moving from Seneca to Long St. and finally to 63 Public Square. O'Brien also launched a penny daily edition of dubious longevity, the *Evening Times*, on 24 Apr. 1879. Appearing in 1881 as the *New Sunday Morning Times*, the weekly by that time was listed under the management of J. D. Shannon, followed shortly by H. Adnett, apparently not long before its expiration.

The **CLEVELAND SURVEY OF CRIMINAL JUSTICE** of 1921 was the first thorough study of the criminal-justice system of a major American city. It analyzed the work of the police, prosecutors, coroner's office, criminal courts, and correctional system; probed legal education; weighed the role of psychiatry in criminal justice; and assessed the adequacy of crime reporting in the local press. Funded by the CLEVELAND FOUNDATION and promoted by its director RAYMOND MOLEY, the survey was codirected by Roscoe Pound and Felix Frankfurter of Harvard Law School. They assembled a team of nationally known experts and drew as well on such local talent as Western Reserve University sociologist Chas. E. Gehlke, who conducted the statistical research. Recommendations proposed by these experts included the reorganization of the police department with a view to the improvement of the training and discipline of officers; the creation of effective court administrative procedures and recordkeeping; the abolition of the grand jury as a means of indictment; the establishment of court dockets organized to reflect the gravity and complexity of cases; the improvement of the method of appointing judges; the replacement of the coroner's office with a medical examiner; the employment of psychiatric procedures in the prevention of crime and the treatment of offenders; the upgrading of legal education; the curbing of newspaper sensationalism and interference with justice through self-restraint; and, finally, the establishment of a citizens' organization to educate the public and press for these reforms. The last recommendation led to the establishment of the Cleveland Assoc. for Criminal Justice. A coalition of business, professional, and civic groups, the organization achieved only limited success in reforming the justice system, but it served as a useful civic watchdog in matters of crime and justice for 3 decades. The survey was more successful in setting the pattern for future studies, serving as a model for surveys in at least 7 states and for Pres. Hoover's Commission on Law Observance & Enforcement (popularly known as the Wickersham Commission), the first national assessment of criminal justice. Seen in a larger cultural perspective, the Cleveland survey epitomized the outlook of the Progressive Era. It was characterized by reliance on professional experts who, through objective fact-finding, would provide the basis for nonpartisan civic reform and efficient public administration.

The **CLEVELAND TANK PLANT** was built at 6300 Riverside Dr. in BROOK PARK in 1942 as the Cleveland Bomber Plant, its name reflecting its major wartime product. The plant, which ultimately made tanks under a variety of contractors, was closed for manufacturing in 1972 but remains a focal point for Cleveland's hope of attracting new industry. During WORLD WAR II, the Bomber Plant, owned by the Dept. of Defense, was operated by General Motors as the Fisher Body Aircraft Plant No. 2, and made the B-29 bomber. One of its other products, the P-75, was scrapped after several fatal test runs.

In its heyday, the Bomber Plant employed 15,000 workers at the relatively high rate of $.95 an hour ($.25 above the wage paid at other big plants), with a 55-hour work week. The labor force, largely composed of inexperienced workers, was inefficient at first, but the facility was overstaffed to maximize the cost of the contract. In the absence of quotas, the workers caught on to the work and were encouraged to turn out quality parts. To aid production, employees named aisles and work areas after battlefields such as Iwo Jima and Guadalcanal. Many of the workers lived in housing projects built on Triskett and Berea roads and rode to work in a CTS bus dubbed the "Bomber Bus." When the war ended, the workforce was abruptly disbanded, and the plant closed, triggering a 5-year debate as to its fate. The city of Cleveland considered leasing the facility for future airport expansion at a bargain rate of $1 a year, but decided against it for fear it could not afford the maintenance costs. GM and Ford rejected the plant as a potential location for their expanded operations. After a brief tenure as an exhibition hall and sales center, and talk of converting the facility to apartment housing for returning servicemen, the plant was leased to Natl. Terminals for soybean storage.

By 1950, as the KOREAN WAR heated up, the production contract for the Army tank was awarded to GM's Cadillac Div., which selected the Bomber Plant as the manufacturing site. The Cadillac Tank Plant, as it was renamed, promised immediate employment to 6,000. After 2 years of production, the Army rejected all tanks made at Cadillac because of a problem with the gun mechanism. GM offered its engineering expertise and designed a new gun sight; the Walker Bulldog was put into service in Korea by May 1953 and was produced successfully until 1955. With the nation at peace in the late 1950s, the fate of the plant was again uncertain; after closing in 1959, it reopened in 1960, when Cadillac was awarded contracts to build the self-propelled T-195 and T-196 howitzers and M-114 armed personnel carriers. In 1964, Chrysler outbid GM on the M-114 and M-109, though Cadillac remained in charge of engineering, research, and administration. GM regained most of the contracts in 1965. In that same year, GM shifted management of the tank plant (now usually called the Cleveland Tank Plant or the Cleveland Ordnance Plant) to its Allison Div. To complete its contracts, GM again had to recruit a workforce; to attract employees in the "seller's market" of the 1960s, the company promised that in case of cutbacks, it would absorb workers into other GM divisions. Also, Allison absorbed the hardcore unemployed, who were bused in from the West Park Rapid Station.

Among the products of the Cleveland Tank Plant operation was the controversial M-551 16-ton Sheridan tank, billed as the most versatile and mobile tank ever built. Congress decided to discontinue the program when the GM contract was completed in 1972. The Defense Dept., which in the past had wanted to retain ownership of the plant, announced its intention to sell it. The two most likely buyers were the city of Cleveland and GM. In hopes of increasing its tax base by enticing GM or another industrial buyer to its city limits, Brook Park entered the bidding and offered $16 million, compared to Cleveland's $5 million. Cleveland dropped out of the bidding, but Mayor Ralph Perk threatened to seize the property under eminent domain for airport expansion after Brook Park purchased it. Brook Park was unable to raise the funds, so the ownership remained with the Defense Dept. GM lost interest in the property because of unreasonable demands made by the

General Services Admin., which was handling the sale. Meanwhile, Brook Park unsuccessfully wooed several major companies.

In 1977, the Park Corp. of Charleston, W. Va., bought the facility to create an international trade mart. Then-governor Jas. Rhodes tried to link this development with his plans for a World Trade Ctr. Rhodes's plans did not materialize, but Park renovated the office space and part of the plant after fighting for tax abatement from Brook Park, in hopes of finding major tenants. As of 1986, the main part of the plant operates under the name Capital Goods Trade Fair, but is known more generally as the I-X Center, site of boat and other large industrial shows.

The **CLEVELAND TEACHERS' UNION** was chartered in Cleveland in 1934 as the American Fed. of Teachers Local 279; its name was changed in 1940. The union was organized to counter the problems of layoffs, transfers, class size, long hours, and low wages, which had worsened during the Depression. Between 1932–33, teachers' salaries were cut by 40%. Teachers were sometimes paid in scrip, and sometimes not at all. Union membership at that time was not viewed favorably by the school board, yet 150 teachers joined. Their first task was to make 1,000 calls on delinquent taxpayers, making the union directly responsible for bringing $350,000 to the county treasury, which went to the school system. The union also began to campaign to restore the salary cuts of the Depression years. Steady progress was made, but it was not until 1941 that Cleveland teachers received 100% of their former salaries. During the next several decades, the union fought to enable married women to teach, for salary gains and benefits such as hospitalization and maternity and paternity leave, and for due process for nontenured teachers.

The union also pursued educational issues and civil and democratic rights and provided scholarships for Cleveland students. In 1964 it won the first election to select an official bargaining agent in the school district, and the following year it was reaffirmed as the sole bargaining agent. In an effort to increase wages, the union struck in 1978 and again in 1979. The first strike, 7 Sept.–16 Oct. 1978, resulted in an 8% increase. The following year the strike continued for 11 weeks, 18 Oct. 1979–11 Jan. 1980, and led to a 26% salary increase, as well as other benefits. In 1983 the Cleveland Teachers' Union ratified a "Bridge Agreement," which enabled schools to remain open and a levy to pass, and brought membership a 9.5% raise and other benefits.

The **CLEVELAND THEATER** was known as the city's melodrama theater. It was built by Chas. H. Bulkley and was located at the northeast corner of St. Clair Ave. along the W. 2nd St. alley. The theater opened on 19 Oct. 1885 under the management of Frank M. Drew. The first performance was by the Chas. L. Andrews Co. in *Michael Strogoff*. Drew quit at the close of the first season. In Sept. 1886, H. R. Jacobs, the "King of Diamonds," purchased the theater and changed the name to H. R. Jacobs Theater. His first season opened that month with *The Lights o' London*. On 7 Dec. 1891, the interior of the theater was damaged by fire. Jacobs reopened it on 21 Mar. 1892 with *Ship Ahoy* by the Miller Opera Co. Jacobs changed managers frequently. Finally, after many problems, he gave up the theater in the mid-1890s. The Brady & Stair syndicate then secured possession of the theater and restored the original name. The new Cleveland Theater became a variety show house. In Mar. 1910, the theater opened as a cheap vaudeville and moving-picture house. A few years later it returned to low-grade stock. The theater was closed and put to commercial uses in late 1910. It was later remodeled

for use by the Union Paper & Twine Co., which burned down on 11 Mar. 1912.

The **CLEVELAND TIGERS**, often referred to as the Cleveland Indians, were the first Cleveland franchise in what became the National Football League. Owned by local sports promoter Jimmie O'Donnell, the team began in 1919 as an experiment in the so-called Ohio League; in 1920, when owners of professional teams decided to form a better-organized league, O'Donnell obtained the Cleveland franchise. O'Donnell, also the owner of a semipro baseball team called the Tigers, was aided in his football venture by Stanley B. "Stan" Cofall, a football star at East Technical and later East High schools, then at Notre Dame (1914–16), and professionally with the Massillon Tigers. Cofall helped organize the Cleveland team in 1919 and, along with O'Donnell, attended the 17 Sept. 1920 meeting at Ralph Hay's Hupmobile Agency in Canton that founded the American Professional Football Assoc., which became the NFL the following year. In 1920 he was player-coach of Cleveland for the first half of the season; he was also elected vice-president of the new league.

In the first year of operation, the Cleveland Tigers compiled a record of 1–4–2. The Tigers had an excellent defense, but no offense; they scored only 2 touchdowns all year and lost 3 games by 7-0 scores. In 1921 the Tigers returned with 2 future Hall of Famers, Joe Guyon and player-coach Jim Thorpe. The team won its first 2 games, but in the second game the legendary Thorpe injured his ribs and was lost for most of the remainder of the season; he tried to play, against doctor's orders, but was unable to continue. The Tigers narrowly lost the next 4 games. When Thorpe returned to action in a postseason game against the Giants in December, the Tigers were again victorious. Early in 1922, O'Donnell received permission from the league to suspend operations for a year, but when he was unable to post the $1,000 annual guarantee the league required, his franchise was canceled. The franchise was later purchased by Samuel Deutsch (see CLEVELAND BULLDOGS), who operated the team as the Cleveland Indians in 1923, finishing in 5th place with a 3–1–3 record.

The *CLEVELAND TIMES* (1845) first appeared on a local masthead as the name of a Democratic weekly started on 10 Sept. 1845. Published by Horace Steele and Peter Baxter, it was edited by the former and appeared on Wednesdays. Within a few weeks it claimed 400 subscribers in Cleveland, as well as 100 in Painesville, which appeared to have been Steele's former base of operations. Much of its energy was devoted to infighting with the rival Democratic daily, the *PLAIN DEALER*, which the *Times* accused of being controlled by "the Bank Clique." Steele had withdrawn from the partnership by Apr. 1846, leaving Baxter in control until he was joined by R. Haddock in Aug. Haddock assumed full control by December, meanwhile keeping up the running battle with JOSEPH W. GRAY of the *Plain Dealer*. Haddock also began publishing a daily edition, probably late in 1847, under the nameplate of the *Daily Cleveland Times*. After relocating from the Phoenix to the Franklin Bldg. the following year, he took on John G. Miller, Jr., as associate editor. In Feb. 1849, however, the *Times* was merged into the *Plain Dealer*.

The *CLEVELAND TIMES* (1922) represented the last serious attempt to establish another daily newspaper in Cleveland. It survived for 5 years in the mid-1920s. The paper began as the *Cleveland Commercial* on 2 Mar. 1922; it was renamed the *Cleveland Times & Commercial* by the following year and eventually became simply the *Times*.

Published by the Cleveland Commercial Publishing Co. and edited by O. K. Shimansky, the *Times* reputedly had the backing of the local utilities and the Van Sweringen brothers. It hoped to challenge the *Plain Dealer*'s morning monopoly by producing a "businessman's paper" of conservative mien, exemplified by the slogan "Clean—Alert—Reliable." Lacking the *Plain Dealer*'s AP franchise, it used the UP night wire and relied heavily upon the *New York World* for syndicated material.

In its efforts to become competitive, the *Times* lowered its price from $.03 to $.02 and began publishing a tabloid Sunday edition. Circulation rose slowly, from 20,000 in 1923 to 32,000 in 1926. Fresh capital was secured from MANTIS J. AND ORIS P. VAN SWERINGEN, and Samuel Scovil, former president of the CLEVELAND ELECTRIC ILLUMINATING CO., emerged as president of the Commercial Publishing Co. The *Times* moved from its offices at 307 Superior into a new 2-story plant constructed for it at 2160 Payne Ave. Earl E. Martin, former editor of the CLEVELAND PRESS, was hired to edit the *Times* in 1926. Martin set out to broaden the paper's general appeal by building up a solid local staff, but his efforts proved too late. Regretting the lack of "a comparatively little more advertising support," Scovil announced the suspension of the *Times* on 3 Mar. 1927. Its circulation lists and good will were purchased by the *PLAIN DEALER* for $100,000. Among its staff members, Gordon Cobbledick, Spencer Irwin, and Eleanor Clarage moved to the *Plain Dealer*, while Robt. M. Seltzer was hired by the *Press*.

**CLEVELAND TOWN TOPICS** was the "Bible" of Cleveland's social and cultural sets for over 40 years. Billed as "A Weekly Review of Society, Art and Literature," it was founded on 17 Dec. 1887 by Felix Rosenberg, who served as editor, and T. J. Rose, who became business manager. Its magazine format organized coverage into regular departments in lieu of feature articles. A lively lead column of gossip and commentary appeared under the heading "Talk of the Town," later renamed "The Lounger." Following the departures of Rose and then Rosenberg, *Town Topics* went through a period of instability around the turn of the century. Norman C. McLoud and C. H. Wright appeared as short-lived editors, the former also as proprietor, and the publication's address moved from the Arcade and Vincent St. to the Garfield Bldg., before finally settling in the CAXTON BLDG. There it came under the proprietorship of Chas. S. Britton, owner of the Britton Printing Co., who published it for the next quarter-century. Another mainstay came with the arrival in 1903 of Helen DeKay Townsend as society editor, a position she filled for the remainder of the magazine's history.

Although not overly political, *Town Topics* served its elite readership with a moderate dose of Republicanism. It was generally antilabor in tone and a consistent opponent of Mayor TOM L. JOHNSON. It was an early automobile enthusiast, giving the horseless carriage regular coverage as early as 1901, when it was largely regarded as a rich man's plaything. During the next few years, automobile ads pumped its annual Automobile Show issues to over 50 pages. Britton's inability to find a permanent editor evidently made *Town Topics* an increasing liability for him in the 1920s. Circulation of the "intimate newspaper," in Myron T. Herrick's words, was never more than a few thousand. On 7 Dec. 1929, Britton announced its merger into the *BYSTANDER*, a newer rival that thereafter would be printed in his plant. Apparently the marriage did not succeed, because a year later former staffers announced the "return of a conservative family journal" under the name *Cleveland Town Tidings*. Appearing on 28 Mar. 1931, the

weekly later formed an affiliation with the FED. OF WOMEN'S CLUBS OF GREATER CLEVELAND in an effort to acquire a circulation base. Even that could not compensate for the reverses of the Depression. After a 6-week suspension in the summer of 1932, *Town Tidings* returned in a newspaper format on 17 Sept., fought the lost cause of Herbert Hoover's reelection, and apparently expired after 19 Nov. 1932.

**CLEVELAND TRANSIT SYSTEM.** *See* **GREATER CLEVELAND REGIONAL TRANSIT AUTHORITY**

**CLEVELAND TRUST COMPANY.** *See* **AMERITRUST**

**CLEVELAND TWIST DRILL.** *See* **ACME-CLEVELAND**

The **CLEVELAND UNION LEADER** arose amid the turbulent labor disputes of the 1930s to provide a voice for the ideal of industrial organization. It was launched on Labor Day, 3 Sept. 1937, not long after the birth of the Congress of Industrial Organizations, which endorsed and supported the weekly newspaper through its local affiliate, the CLEVELAND INDUSTRIAL UNION COUNCIL. Disclaiming any intention of competing with the AFL-oriented *CLEVELAND CITIZEN*, the *Union Leader* concentrated on the allegedly antilabor bias of Cleveland's daily press, particularly the *PLAIN DEALER*. Originally edited by Ted Cox, the *Cleveland Union Leader* eventually fell under the direction of business manager John F. Cummins, who became publisher. From its original 4 full-sized pages, it was later converted into an 8-page tabloid with extra pages for Labor Day and election issues. It was aggressively anti-Communist in the period following WORLD WAR II, attacking Progressive candidate Henry Wallace and backing the CIO-endorsed Harry Truman in 1948. Emulating the reconciliation of the AFL and CIO in 1955, the *Union Leader* was merged into the *Cleveland Citizen* on 1 May 1959.

The **CLEVELAND UNION STOCKYARDS COMPANY**, a marketplace for livestock growers, was organized as the Cleveland Union Stockyards in 1881 and incorporated as the Cleveland Union Stockyards Co. in 1892. In 1893, it acquired the Farmers & Drovers' Stockyards Co. Originally located on Scranton Rd., it moved to 3200 W. 65th after a landslide destroyed the first site. Dubbed the "Hotel de la Hoof," where the guests walked in and were carted out as steaks, hams, and sausages, it provided the hostelry and feedstation for cows, pigs, and sheep until the animals were sold to meat packers. Its phenomenal growth up through the 1940s, when Cleveland was among the largest meat-processing centers in the U.S., and its fight for survival in the 1950s reflected the changing trends in meat packing, marketing, and the American diet.

The stockyards, over 60 acres of pens, troughs, brick walkways, and bidding areas, were the 7th-largest in the country in the 1920s. Livestock was shipped to terminal yards such as the Union Stockyards and sold by commission merchants to local and out-of-state buyers. The stockyards featured a hotel and bar for farmers who accompanied their livestock to market; when commission merchants increasingly assumed the responsibility for shipping, the facilities were converted for chickens. In 1923, Cleveland handled 1.3 million hogs, 125,000 cattle, 145,000 calves, and 308,000 sheep and lambs raised in Ohio and the Midwest. Though 90% of all stock sold was dressed and consumed locally, buyers from New York, Newark, Boston, and Baltimore supplied their local markets here because the Cleveland Union Stockyards attracted excellent-quality stock at reasonable prices and were near reliable rail-shipping connections. Often these buyers took the entire lot of lambs and hogs at higher prices than local buyers were willing to pay. Though Cleveland Union Stockyards activity was only a fraction of that which took place in Chicago, Cleveland could ship U.S.-inspected meat to the East Coast in 48 hours.

In the years following WORLD WAR II, livestock raising moved westward; the stockyard industry declined in importance as livestock transactions were localized and trucking replaced the railroad as the prime method of transporting stock. Since trucking gave the farmer more freedom to choose his market, he began to transport his stock to local stations, where his overhead (shipping, storage, feeding, commission) was less. By 1960, 90% of livestock previously moved by train was trucked to the point of sale. Representatives from packinghouses and chain stores began patronizing the local centers or went directly to the farmers, rather than to the stockyards.

Accompanying this moved toward decentralized buying and slaughter was a move to centralize meat processing; most operations were concentrated in Omaha. Local plants of nationwide concerns such as Swift closed in cities such as Cleveland; old Cleveland firms folded or merged (see CLEVELAND PROVISION CO.). Meanwhile, Americans began to eat less pork, which affected both the stockyard population and the meat-processing industry. The Cleveland Union Stockyards, like most other stockyards, had a heavy capital investment in its property and was too immobile to keep pace with the trends. As the focus of the local industry moved west to Berea, the stockyard business declined. In 1968, the stockyards, then only 35 acres, closed down—only 3 years before the Chicago stockyards faced the same fate.

The **CLEVELAND UNION TERMINAL** and Terminal Tower, Cleveland's most familiar landmark, was the largest construction project of the 1920s in the city. The railroad terminal, originally intended for the north end of the MALL, was located on PUBLIC SQUARE following a public referendum in 1919. It was planned by the MANTIS J. AND ORIS P. VAN SWERINGEN in response to traffic difficulties with the lakefront railroad depot in WORLD WAR I. Excavation of the site began in 1924, and the plans for the 52-story office tower were first shown in Feb. 1925. The entire depot and office complex was designed by Chicago architects Graham Anderson, Probst & White. Construction on the steelwork began in 1926, and the 708-ft. Terminal Tower was completed in 1927, the tallest building in the world outside New York City until 1967. The unprecedented engineering for the project included foundations 250 ft. deep for the tower, the demolition of more than 1,000 buildings, and the construction of many bridges and viaducts for the railroad approaches.

The first train entered the depot on 23 Oct. 1929, and regular passenger service began in June 1930. The formal opening of the terminal group, including the Guildhall, Republic, and Midland buildings across Prospect Ave., took place on 29 June 1930. The office buildings were constructed on airrights over the depot. The complex also includes the Hotel Cleveland, which was built in 1918 (STOUFFERS INN ON THE SQUARE), Higbee's Dept. Store (1931), and the U.S. Post Office, completed in 1934. All of these buildings are connected by public underground passages. The area occupied by the depot and the air-rights buildings covers 17 acres. A distinctive feature of the terminal was the amount of commercial space on the concourse level, with Harvey restaurants and retail stores forming "the world's largest unified merchandising service" in connection with a union passenger station. The terminal was used by the New York Central, Nickel Plate, Big 4, Erie, and Baltimore & Ohio railroads, but the Pennsylvania Railroad continued to use the lakefront depot. The height of train service through the terminal was during WORLD WAR II, 1941–45. The station was also the main terminal for the SHAKER RAPID TRANSIT and in 1955 for the crosstown rapid line, and for the first rapid transit in the country connecting a downtown business district with a major airport in 1968. The last passenger service left the terminal in 1977, and the through railroad tracks were removed. The Lausche State Office Bldg. was erected on the northwest corner of the terminal air-rights area in 1979. The post office removed its operations and closed the 1934 building in 1982. The Terminal Tower Bldg. and station were acquired by Forest City Enterprises for development as a retail center in 1982 and were renamed Tower City Ctr.

Toman, James A., *The Terminal Tower Complex* (1980).

**CLEVELAND UNIVERSITY** became the city's first institution of higher learning in a brief career lasting from 1851–53. It was chartered by the Ohio general assembly on 5 Mar. 1851, its trustees included WM. CASE, TRUMAN P. HANDY, AHAZ MERCHANT, SAMUEL STARKWEATHER, and Richard Hilliard. For president, they tapped the recently resigned head of Oberlin Institute, Asa Mahan, who brought most of the new university's first students from Oberlin with him. Classes began on 2 Apr. 1851, in temporary quarters in the Mechanics' Block on Ontario St. The school's future, however, was closely bound to a proposed campus planned for an area on the west side, hopefully named University Hts. Most of the trustees appeared to be speculating in property in the neighborhood, later known as TREMONT. They set aside a 275-acre parcel for the university, part for the campus and part to raise an endowment fund. Streets in the area were endowed with such academic names as College, Literary, Professor, and Jefferson, and a 3-story building was raised among them for the future home of Cleveland University.

Philosophically, Mahan charted the university along a progressive, non-sectarian course. Citing the examples of Brown and Rochester University, he advocated a practical as opposed to a classical course of study. Among its 13 chairs of instruction was one devoted to "Practical & Scientific Agriculture & Horticulture." Included in the ultimate plans of Mahan and the trustees was a visionary complex encompassing not only a national university of European scope but an orphan asylum, old-age retreat, and female seminary, as well. After a full year of operation in its new home, culminating with the awarding of 8 degrees in June 1852, Cleveland University declined rapidly the following fall. Mahan resigned as president on 13 Dec., possibly because of a clash of personalities with some of the trustees. One of the school's chief sponsors, Mrs. Thirsa Pelton, died shortly thereafter, on 19 Feb. 1853. Although the board of trustees was reorganized that year, the university apparently was liquidated by the end of the academic year. Mahan served briefly as president of the Homeopathic College of Cleveland before rounding out his career as president of Adrian College in Michigan. From 1859–68, the Cleveland University building was occupied by Humiston's Cleveland Institute, a college preparatory school operated by Ransom F. Humiston.

Holtz, Maude E., "Cleveland University: A Forgotten Chapter in Cleveland's History" (Masters thesis, Western Reserve University, 1934).

279

The **CLEVELAND VOCAL SOCIETY**, 1874–1902, under the leadership of ALFRED ARTHUR fashioned a record of substantial musical achievement. Building upon a basic repertoire of 19th-century part songs, the society moved into the arena of major festival events. Its most noteworthy contributions were the many introductory performances in Cleveland of major chorale works with orchestra, which emphasized the importance of involvement with this genre of literature. The development of chorale-music performances in Cleveland is directly related to Arthur's arrival in Cleveland in 1871. In 1873, he interested a group of men in organizing a chorale-performing group that was to become the Cleveland Vocal Society. The "First Complimentary Rehearsal" of the new society was presented on 10 Feb. 1874 at Brainard's Opera House. The group consisted of 49 singers performing 10 selections, from the popular "You Stole My Love" to Mozart's "Ave Verum Corpus," with accompaniment provided on piano and cabinet organ. On 5 May 1874, the society presented a May Festival at CASE HALL.

Traditionally the CVS presented 3 concerts a year, in December, February, and April or May. By 1875 it was performing works with orchestral accompaniment, the Vocal Society Orchestra. By 1880 there were about 70 singers, divided equally between men and women, and an orchestra of 30 players. In May 1880, the society arranged a May Festival at the Tabernacle on Ontario St., the first of regular biennial festivals that lasted until 1886, when financial deficits and the amount of work involved brought the series to a close. The idea was revived in 1895 and 1897 when the Boston Festival Chorus joined the society for May Festival concerts in the Music Hall. In Apr. 1889, CVS announced plans to intensify its concentration on major works, maintain a complete orchestra throughout the entire season, and establish an auxiliary chorus to train and provide additional voices. In 1890 the chorus numbered 119, with 57 in the orchestra. At the world choral competition held at the 1893 World's Columbian Exposition, the society enhanced its reputation by winning 1st prize. The CVS concentrated on major chorale works during the 1880s and 1890s, including Handel's *Messiah* and the requiems of Mozart, Verdi, and Berlioz. Its practice of presenting works with large chorale and orchestral forces was similar to the practices of other such contemporary groups. The society continued until 1902, amassing an impressive list of credits, including works by Mendelssohn, Bruch, Palestrina, and Gounod.

Alexander, J. Heywood, *It Must Be Heard* (1981).

The **CLEVELAND WATER CURE ESTABLISHMENT** was a combination sanitarium and resort for the treatment of various ailments and diseases through HYDROPATHY. Founded in 1848 by Dr. Thos. T. Seelye, it was one of many such establishments that came into vogue in the U.S., particularly in Ohio and New York, during the 1840s and 1850s. Seelye built his sanitarium, a 3-story brick building, near a soft-water spring in a wooded glen between Wallingford Ct. and Sawtell Ave. (E. 51st St.). In a rural setting, the sanitarium was known for its beautiful landscaping that included curving walks and drives. Water cure, or hydropathy, was a therapy that originated in Germany. It was used to treat almost every known physical malady, from the common cold to various chronic diseases. It was believed that immersion in cold water of certain parts of the body would draw blood from the diseased parts and cause the affliction to eventually dissipate. The various types of treatment included a douche bath, shower bath, hose bath, cataract bath, rubbing wet sheet, plunge bath, and sitzbad.

The sitzbad, or sitting bath, required the patient to sit waist-deep in ice water, with a blanket thrown over the shoulders and tub, for 15–30 minutes. This specific treatment was commonly used for head and chest colds and headaches. The Cleveland Water Cure specialized in "treatment of diseases peculiar to females," including those related to childbirth. In 1851, the charge for "board, medical advice, and all ordinary attendance of nurses" was $8 per week, payable weekly. In addition to hydropathy, diet and exercise were also emphasized. Despite the disapproval of many Cleveland physicians, who were opposed to the therapeutic claims of hydropathy, the Cleveland Water Cure enjoyed a regional reputation for nearly 2 decades. In 1868 it was sold to a national Jewish organization for $25,000 and became the Jewish Orphan Asylum (see BELLEFAIRE).

The **CLEVELAND WHIG**, after the appearance of a specimen issue on 20 Aug., began regular weekly publication under the editorship of Lewis L. Rice on 10 Sept. 1834. Politically, it advanced the cause of the party for which it was named and was sympathetic toward the rising antislavery movement. Francis B. Penniman of Utica, N.Y., joined Rice in a partnership, which lasted from Jan. 1835 to Apr. 1836. Shortly before the *Cleveland Herald* became a daily, Rice converted the *Whig* into a semiweekly on 3 Mar. 1835. It was published on Tuesdays and Fridays, but the weekly Wednesday edition, now consisting mostly of reprinted material from the semiweekly, was maintained for circulation in outlying areas. When Rice began the CLEVELAND *DAILY GAZETTE* in May 1836, the semiweekly was absorbed by the new venture, and the weekly *Whig* survived to the end of the year, mainly on reprints from the *Gazette*.

The **CLEVELAND WOMAN'S CLUB** provided Cleveland women with a place to hold meetings, entertain guests, and attend lectures and musical entertainments for more than 30 years. The club was organized in 1908 with the goal of acquiring property for this purpose. Set up as the not-for-profit Womens's Club House Assoc. in 1908, the organization changed its charter to become a for-profit body in 1910 so as to realize its objectives. In 1912, the club's directors authorized a lease on temporary quarters in the new Cleveland Athletic Club Bldg. at 1146 Euclid. The club's purpose was largely social; it served as a site for club meetings. However, music, literature, and art were promoted among the members, as was an acquaintance with civic affairs; club facilities were made available for concerts and other cultural activities and for roundtable discussions. In 1914, the club made its long-anticipated move into a permanent home, the James Jared Tracy mansion at 3535 Euclid Ave. Within 7 years, the club raised the funds to purchase the property, but the ownership was short-lived, and in 1926, the club sold it to the Masonic Order. The Cleveland Woman's Club continued to rent the home until 1942, when Fenn College leased the premises for use as a training center for Air Force recruits, and later for a girls' dormitory. The mansion was razed to make way for a parking lot for the Masonic Auditorium in 1951. The club, perhaps a victim of changing roles that cast women as wartime wage earners, with less leisure to pursue clubwork, disappeared from the telephone directory in 1942.

**CLEVELAND WOMEN WORKING** is an advocacy organization dedicated to securing equal pay and rights for women in the workplace. Currently one of 10 chapters of a national organization, Cleveland Women Working was established in 1975, primarily through the efforts of Helen Williams. The organization attempts to combine documented research with action in order to achieve its objectives. It also counsels and educates women about job problems and legal rights and attempts to increase public awareness of the problems women face in the workplace. Since its establishment, Cleveland Women Working has initiated a federal investigation of employment practices in major Cleveland banks, has held hearings before government officials to document discriminatory practices, has published class-action charges on behalf of women against specific employers, and has campaigned to increase security measures in downtown Cleveland office buildings. The primary theme underlying these and other activities has been "Raises, rights, and respect." Membership in the organization, which has its headquarters at 1224 Huron Rd., is open on a dues-paying basis, with dues keyed to a member's income.

The **CLEVELAND WOMEN'S ORCHESTRA** was formed in 1935 to give women with a desire for a musical outlet the opportunity to participate in an orchestral experience. Hyman Schandler, the founder and a member of the Cleveland Orchestra, noted the dearth of women participating in symphony orchestras. The Cleveland group is among the oldest continuous groups in the country, if not the oldest ongoing women's orchestra. Hyman Schandler has (as of 1985) been the sole principal conductor of the group. With the encouragement of his wife, Rebecca White Schandler, a musician in her own right, he has kept the enterprise alive almost single-handedly. A core of 75 women, ranging in age from 16 to 60, representing housewives, nurses, students, teachers, secretaries, etc., have practiced and performed a minimum of 10 benefit concerts annually throughout the Cleveland area in locations such as nursing homes, hospitals, senior citizens' homes, and social-service agencies. The orchestra presents an annual spring concert at SEVERANCE HALL.

The orchestra has featured many distinguished soloists, including Natalie Hindiras, Eunice Podis, Philip Setzer, Joseph Knitzer, Lynn Harrell, ARTHUR LOESSER, and Jan Peerce. The orchestra has premiered many compositions, including the Concerto for Piano in C Minor by Taktakishvili and the first Cleveland performance of Benjamin Britten's *Young Person's Guide to the Orchestra*. The orchestra's advisory board has been chaired over the years by many distinguished persons, including Helen Hunt Clark and Martha Joseph. Aside from his positions as a violinist with the CLEVELAND ORCHESTRA and as conductor of the Cleveland Women's Orchestra, Hyman Schandler was a violin teacher at the CLEVELAND MUSIC SCHOOL SETTLEMENT for over 65 years and a consultant to various musical organizations. Mrs. Schandler died 18 Apr. 1985, less than 1 month before the 50th-year anniversary concert.

The **CLEVELAND WORKHOUSE** at Cooley Farms was recognized throughout the U.S. as one of the finest and most progressive penal institutions of its kind. It became a model for similar institutions around the world. It moved to Cooley Farms in 1912. The city's first workhouse was established in 1855 and was located on Scranton Rd. with the city infirmary. In 1871 it moved to a new building on Woodland Ave. at E. 79th St., where it remained until 1912. Dr. HARRIS R. COOLEY, pastor of the Cedar Ave. Church of Christ, was the person after whom the farms were named, because of his role in their creation. Appointed city welfare director under mayor TOM L. JOHNSON, he recognized the need for new facilities to house the city's penal, philanthropic, and sanitary institutions. He was convinced that the residents of these institutions could best be helped by exposure to a wholesome environment that would aid their

rehabilitation or recuperation. At his urging, the city purchased 25 neighboring farms in rural WARRENSVILLE TWP. Purchases began in 1904 and by 1912 totaled over 2,000 acres, costing the city more than $350,000. It was originally intended to add another 3,000 acres to the holdings, but those plans were never fulfilled. The Warrensville site was selected because the city had already begun to acquire land there for use as a cemetery in 1902.

The farms were originally divided into 4 institutions. Colony Farms was the city infirmary or poorhouse. In addition to dormitories, it included a number of small cottages for elderly couples and a halfway house. Overlook Farm was the tuberculosis sanatorium. Highland Park Farm was the municipal cemetery, and the Correction Farm was the workhouse and the house of corrections. Each was distinct from the others, and each held about 500 acres of land. The Correction Farm was located 1 and ½ miles from the remainder of Cooley Farms. Much of the construction was completed by prisoners. Inmates lived in dormitories, with separate buildings for men and women. All inmates were expected to work, as the primary purpose of the farm was to provide productive work for the prisoners. Work was divided into 4 main activities: farm, dairy, garden, and orchard. The farm was nearly self-sufficient. In addition to growing vegetables and feed, the prisoners cleared and maintained the grounds and operated a dairy, a piggery, a greenhouse, a blacksmith shop, and a sawmill. A cannery produced 40,000 gallon cans of fruits and vegetables each year. Farm products were used by the various welfare institutions, which saved the city considerable money. There was even a quarry on the property where prisoners produced stone for use in concrete and road grading.

Medical, religious, educational, and vocational guidance services and a liberal parole program were provided. The CLEVELAND PUBLIC LIBRARY operated a branch, and the Cleveland public schools provided a program of grade-school education. Some problems existed at the workhouse from the very beginning, however. By 1925 the larger number of Prohibition and speeding convictions rendered the facility inadequate and overcrowded. To alleviate the problem, a new women's building was constructed in 1927, the old building being converted for use by men. The average daily population exceeded 750. By the 1960s, conditions at the workhouse had deteriorated significantly. The city's worsening financial condition and the aging of the facilities created serious problems. Rapid turnover of staff was symptomatic of the upheavals occurring. In 1971, 75 inmates attempted to storm the main gate, and 100 police were required to maintain order. By 1975 all forms of inmate labor had been abandoned. By the mid-1980s some corrective steps had been taken. Although no large-scale farming was attempted, inmates did maintain a large garden, the products of which were sent to food banks and other charities. In 1984 a susbstance-abuse program was in place, as were 2 separate work-release programs. In 1985 plans were announced for a new facility to be built at the site.

Cleveland Workhouse and House of Correction Records, WRHS.

The *CLEVELAND WORLD* was the city's closest approximation to the "yellow journalism" of the 1890s. An outgrowth of the *Sunday World*, it first appeared as an afternoon daily in the summer of 1889. Throughout its 16-year existence, it was published on Ontario St. near St. Clair and sold for $.01. Shortly after its birth as a daily, the *World* became the property of B. F. Bower of Detroit and Cleveland newspaperman Geo. A. Robertson. With a UP franchise, it was regarded as a serious threat to the afternoon

281

supremacy of the *Press*. In Apr. 1895, however, Bower and Robertson sold the *World* to Robt. P. Porter, former director of the U.S. Census. Under Porter, the *World* became outspokenly Republican, espousing Wm. McKinley in its news as well as editorial columns during the 1896 presidential canvass. Though McKinley won the election, the *World* went into receivership and again came under the control of Bower in Nov. 1896. While retaining its Republican sympathies, the *World* was steered by Bower from politics toward sensational coverage of crime and disaster stories.

During the growing crisis in Spanish-American relations in 1898, the *World* closely followed public opinion as it turned against Spain. It was reconciled to war within 2 days after the sinking of the *Maine*, though it was not sharply critical of McKinley's delays. As the crisis deepened, the *World*'s headlines increased in size and column width until they finally towered over 2 in. and stretched across the entire front page. Occasionally they indulged in trick styles, such as "WAR DECLARED AGAINST SPAIN," qualified in smaller type by "Unless She Immediately Withdraws Her Army and Navy from Cuba." Claimed circulation jumped from 21,695 in February to 33,892 in May. In the early 1900s, the *World* added halftones and Sunday color supplements to its repertoire. Advertising lineage dropped, however, and in 1904 Bower took the desperate step of reducing the price of the *Sunday World* from $.05-$.02. Later that year he sold the *World* to Cleveland industrialist CHAS. A. OTIS. On 12 June 1905, Otis purchased the *Cleveland News & Herald* and consolidated it with the *World* as the *World-News*. He added the *Evening Plain Dealer* to the combination on 16 July, simultaneously killing the *Sunday World* as a quid pro quo. On 13 Sept. the name *World-News* was dropped in favor of the *CLEVELAND NEWS*.

The **CLEVELAND WORLD TRADE ASSOCIATION** (est. 1946) is the Internatl. Div. of the GREATER CLEVELAND GROWTH ASSOC. The association's basic purpose is to perpetuate and expand international trade in the Greater Cleveland area, and to promote and implement foreign investments in the northeast Ohio area. It was formed when the Cleveland Export-Import Assoc. merged with the Cleveland Inter-American Council and became the Cleveland World Trade Organization. The association's office, located at 690 the Union Commerce Bldg., collects and disseminates up-to-date trade information through its Internatl. Trade Library and its *World Trade Bulletin*, which summarize important trade legislation, new international trade agreements and procedures, and import and export opportunities. In addition, the CWTA also provides services for certification of commercial documents, assists in market research, and helps with investment studies and recommendations. It conducts many activities of a trade-education nature, including workshops and seminars having to do with trade expansion, international banking and financing, legal aspects of licensing, and joint ventures. Monthly luncheon meetings, an important feature of the association, offer members an opportunity to hear authoritative speakers discuss current topics of international interest. One of the CWTA's most significant activities is the organization and cosponsorship of an annual conference devoted to a better understanding of world trade and expansion. A tradition for more than 30 years, these conferences have offered a variety of programs concerning world markets, national and international trade legislation, and trade relations, with speakers from leading national and foreign corporations and international legal firms presenting papers dealing with international affairs. The association has organized support for legislation that affects free world trade—working to promote legislation important to Cleveland's international business community, and it has encouraged foreign corporations to locate in Greater Cleveland, establishing a network of contacts in "investment-producing" countries throughout the world.

The **CLEVELAND WORSTED MILL COMPANY**, established in 1902 at 6114 Broadway by Oliver M. Stafford and Geo. H. Hodgson, grew out of the small Turner Worsted Mill founded by Joseph Turner in 1878. One of the largest worsted mills in the country by 1920, Cleveland Worsted was an important local employer in the Fleet-Broadway area for more than 70 years. As the owners were unable to meet their labor needs in the Cleveland area, they bought additional plants in the East. In its prime, Cleveland Worsted Mills controlled 11 plants in N.Y., N.J., Pa., R.I., and Ohio, each of which performed a specialized function and retained its own name. The Cleveland plant was the most complete and handled every operation, from the scouring and sorting of wool to the boiling of the cloth; dyeing and finishing were handled at a company plant in Ravenna, using chemical-free water from Lakes Hodgson and Stafford in Portage County (these lakes were purchased by the company and named after the owners). The local plant had 185,000 worsted spindles and 1,800 broad looms, as compared to the 460,000 worsted spindles, 290,000 woolen spindles, and 9,800 looms owned by the American Woolen Co., a major New England firm.

The company hired CZECHS and POLES from the neighborhood and LITHUANIANS from St. Clair, because they viewed these groups as the hardest workers, and shunned ITALIANS and IRISH. Management positions were held by New Englanders brought from eastern mills rather than ethnics until the mid-1920s, when the company sold stock to workers and then tried to win their support by offering promotions and company picnics to prevent a takeover by American Woolen. Before the Depression, skilled workers such as weavers were paid $12 a week and a $1 bonus for each perfect yard they produced. When the Depression hit, wages fell to an average $7 a week. After the NRA established a minimum wage, Cleveland Worsted guaranteed workers the required $.30 an hour by drawing on future weeks' earnings if piecework rates for a single week did not equal the minimum. Irate employees, penalized by equipment failures beyond their control, appealed the practice to the Natl. Labor Relations Board and were compensated with back pay. The wage cuts motivated workers to organize, at first informally, and then as part of the United Textile Workers. Aided by organizers blackballed from mills in the East, workers waged 2 bitter strikes in the 1930s. The company took advantage of the hard times to break the strikes but did institute less-prohibitive work rules and more internal promotions of neighborhood workers. There were no further successful attempts to organize until the mid-1940s.

Throughout its history, the company produced luxury fabrics as well as its staples—serge and gabardine. During WORLD WAR II, the company refused to accept government orders and stockpiled woolens for civilian use. The government retaliated by padlocking the warehouses of woolens until the company agreed to run 4 looms of uniform serge for every 1 loom of civilian fabrics. Technological improvements in textiles increased both the number of looms a worker tended and his/her productivity. In 1920, workers tended 1 loom that might produce a 64-yd. bolt of cloth in 4 days. By 1935 innovations such as the automatic magazine that transferred bobbins permitted workers to manage 4, then 6, then 12 looms. When Cleveland Worsted Mills adapted the Warner & Swasey power loom in the 1950s, each worker was responsible for 24 looms that each wove a bolt in 6–8 hours. Despite advances in technology, worsted plants such as Cleveland Worsted faced competition from textile plants in the South and from synthetic fibers. After a bitter strike over union recognition in 1955–56, Louis O. Poss, the then-current owner, liquidated the plant on Broadway, as well as other Ohio locations, rather than acknowledge the union victory. The plant was briefly reopened in 1956 to complete work in progress, but key strike organizers were not called back. When the plant finally closed, many middle-aged workers were left without pensions, as the company had successfully opposed the establishment of a pension plan over the years.

The **CLEVELAND WRITERS' CLUB** was founded in 1886 as the Cleveland Woman's Press Club by 10 writers who felt the need for cooperation and association. It was the first of its kind in Ohio. Two prominent presswomen, Harriet Ellen Grannis Arey and GERTRUDE VAN RENSSELAER WICKHAM, helped to found the Cleveland club. Arey served as its first president. Several of the other early presidents were Catherine H. T. (Mrs. Elroy McKendree) Avery, Sarah E. Bierce, LINDA T. GUILFORD, Lizzie Hyer Neff, and Adele E. Thompson. When a similar club was founded in Cincinnati in 1888, the two organizations united to form the Ohio Women's Press Assoc. The Cincinnati branch subsequently withdrew, and in 1912 the name was changed again to the Cleveland Woman's Press Club. The club became affiliated with the Cleveland Fed. of Women's Clubs in 1916 and with the Ohio Fed. of Women's Clubs in 1919. In May 1922 a new constitution was adopted, and the organization became the Cleveland Writers' Club. The CWC was made up of professional women writers in the Greater Cleveland area. Its purpose was to bring members together to encourage writing and publication, offer criticism and advice, exchange experiences, and study literary models. To achieve these goals, the club, in addition to regular business meetings, presented lectures and public readings intended to educate and inform, and to entertain. It also sponsored an annual writing contest, offering prizes for the best entry in each of several categories, and a monthly newsletter entitled "Write Face" to keep members informed of club news and activities. The work of the CWC included short stories, poems, and children's literature, which was published in popular magazines. Scripts and stories for radio, including the club's own 15-minute program, were also written, as were some novels and nonfiction works. The club remained active into the 1970s.

Cleveland Writers' Club Records, WRHS.

The **CLEVELAND YACHT CLUB**, originally organized in 1878 as the Cleveland Yachting Assoc., and part of the Inter-Lake Yachting Assoc., was founded by GEO. W. GARDNER, a pioneer in yacht racing who also served as mayor of Cleveland. The original headquarters of the club were in the old Case Block at Superior and E. 3rd streets. A dock building was erected near the mouth of the CUYAHOGA RIVER. T. H. Smead was elected the first commodore in 1878, followed by Gardner, who held the position from 1879–94, when Luther Allen, banker and industrialist, took over for a 1-year term. Geo. H. Worthington succeeded Allen. In 1879, the Cleveland Yachting Assoc.'s fleet consisted of 15 yachts, including Gardner's steam yacht, *Rosaline*. On 3 Oct. 1888, the club was incorporated as the Cleveland Yacht Club. At that time, the U.S. secretary of the treasury granted the club lease of the lakefront at the rear of the U.S. MARINE HOSPITAL, just east of "Suicide" Pier at the foot of Erie (E. 9th) St. The cornerstone for a new clubhouse was laid in 1891, and the building was dedicated on 15 Sept. 1895. Worthington became commodore in 1895 and held that office until 1914. The CYC directed the Cleveland centennial regatta in 1896, the largest ever held on fresh water up to that time. In Apr. 1913, the Lakewood Yacht Club, which had selected the island in the Rocky River lagoon as its clubhouse site (1901), merged with the Cleveland Yacht Club. The new constitution and bylaws stated that the Cleveland Yacht Club was "formed for the purpose of encouraging, fostering, and otherwise engaging in sailing, boating, rowing, canoeing, and manly exercise, improving Naval Architecture, [and] promoting sociability among its members. . . ." On 29 Nov. 1914, the club moved its E. 9th St. clubhouse to the Rocky River location known as Indian Island. Capt. Nelson Simonson, club member and president of the American Constr. Co., directed the move by barge of the downtown clubhouse. A veranda facing Lake Erie was added, and the old Lakewood Yacht Club building was attached and used as a dining room. The downtown location became known as the E. 9th St. Station.

By 1918, the club, with over 1,000 members, had become one of the nation's finest. JOSIAH KIRBY, president of the Cleveland Discount Co., was then commodore. Kirby's business failures probably led to the bankruptcy of the club, since its affairs and those of his company were closely linked. The CYC went into foreclosure because it did not maintain rent payments on its property as stipulated in the 3-year lease entered into in 1926. Lakewood Municipal Court granted the Midland Bank permission to oust the club from its headquarters. Midland and the Cleveland Securities Corp. sued the yacht club jointly, testifying that the club owed them $4,500. All appeals failed. A new Cleveland Yacht Club was subsequently formed; it was planned as a yachting club and not a social club, as it had been prior to the bankruptcy action. The club survived the Depression without any employees. The commodore served as club manager. Dues at the time were $19 plus $1 excise tax. The club slowly became solvent and by 1949 was able to buy Rocky River Island. It became profitable again in 1933, under the leadership of Commodore Milton N. Gallup, whose term was completed with the club's debts paid and a cash balance in the bank. During Gallup's term, the Rocky River Yacht Harbor Co. took a lease on the island until 1943, when the Rocky River Island Co. took over. The CYC was given a lease on its Snug Harbor building on the island, which was remodeled into a clubhouse. In 1963, a new clubhouse was built.

**CLEVELAND ZOO.** *See* **CLEVELAND METROPARKS ZOO**

The *CLEVELANDER* has survived 3 major format changes as the organ of the Cleveland Chamber of Commerce and its successor, the GREATER CLEVELAND GROWTH ASSOC. Premiering as a monthly publication in May 1926, it contained 36 pages edited by Munson Havens and Lawrence L. Jewell and printed by the Stratford Press. Strongly civic in profile, its guest writers during the first year included WM. R. HOPKINS, NEWTON D. BAKER, TRIS SPEAKER, MYRON T. HERRICK, DUDLEY S. BLOSSOM, LINDA EASTMAN, and Bp. JOSEPH SCHREMBS. By WORLD WAR II, the *Clevelander* was being coedited by Carl E. Stahley and Iris Shimp. From a Depression low of 16 pages, including covers, wartime prosperity had once again fattened its size to a 1945 "Roster Issue" of 128 pages. Though becoming perceptibly more business-oriented, the magazine still featured articles by such civic figures as ARTUR RODZINSKI, WM. M. MILLIKEN, ELIOT NESS, Frank J. Lausche, and WM. GANSON ROSE.

After the metamorphosis of the Chamber of Commerce into the Greater Cleveland Growth Assoc., an attempt was made to transform the *Clevelander* into a hardcover quarterly in Apr. 1970. Printed at the Penton Press, the redesigned magazine resembled the contemporary *American Heritage* in size and outward appearance. Civic boosterism again dominated its content, though articles were written mostly by professionals rather than guests. Circulation of the quarterly was nearly 15,000. Only 8 issues of the new quarterly had appeared before the *Clevelander* abandoned its hardcover format. It printed a 9th number in soft covers in Apr. 1972, the same month that saw the birth of *CLEVELAND MAGAZINE*. One impetus for the new magazine, published independently of the Growth Assoc., was the imminent demise of the older *Clevelander*, from which *Cleveland* recruited some of its early staff. With its civic functions assumed by the new *Cleveland Magazine*, the *Clevelander* was converted into a monthly newsletter by the Growth Assoc. on 1 May 1972. Assuming the nature of a house organ, its issues ranged from 8–20 pages in length.

The **CLEVITE CORPORATION** was founded in 1919 as Cleveland Graphite Bronze to make bearings and bushings for the automotive industry. It was bought by Gould-Natl. Battery in 1969 to form GOULD, INC. Two of the founders of Cleveland Graphite Bronze, Jas. J. McIntyre and Carl Johnson, had previously owned Dann Prods., a small company founded ca. 1912 that pioneered the self-lubricating bearing. When the company went bankrupt after WORLD WAR I, stockholders asked Ben Hopkins to organize, finance, and manage a new company to sell the bearings used to support engine crankshafts and piston rods. Under a name derived from the graphite baked into the interior of the oilless bearing, Hopkins, McIntyre, Johnson, and Jas. Myers began CGB operations at 2906 Chester with 20 employees and a commitment to maintaining quality, research, and exemplary employee relations. The demand for bearings followed the rise of the auto industry throughout the 1920s and 1930s; by 1937, the company, then located at 8880 E. 72nd St., made 183 million parts annually and employed 2,300. This growth was due largely to the introduction of the Thinwall bearing in 1930, which doubled the company's business. As WORLD WAR II approached, CGB anticipated the need for aircraft bearings, and after 2 years of research it developed a silver-plated bearing that could be mass-produced and could withstand heavy wear. During the war, Graphite plated 2 tons of silver per day onto aircraft bearings, and by VJ day it had used more silver than the U.S. Mint had in the same period.

The aircraft business tripled the CGB workforce to 7,000 by 1945 and necessitated the building of a large new plant at 17000 St. Clair (the former site of Great Lakes Aircraft) and a $3 million addition in 1941. From 1939 on, the plants ran 24 hours per day, 7 days a week, and workers got a maximum of 1 day off per week and no vacations. The expanded workforce included women and soldiers stationed in Cleveland and, according to the company, "incendiary, self-seeking labor leaders." As a result of the strains produced by overwork and the unassimilated workforce, CGB was the scene of strikes over wages, company terminations of workers over petty infractions of rules, and failure to bargain throughout the war. The strikes, called by the MECHANICS EDUCATIONAL SOCIETY OF AMERICA, the then-unaffiliated union that represented the workers, were part of a nationwide confrontation between MESA and the CIO, which was trying to organize the war industries. In 1944, one strike culminated in seizure of the plant by the Army (see CLEVELAND GRAPHITE BRONZE SEIZURE). After the war, CGB retained a foothold in aviation; it regained its growing replacement business but saw the importance of broadening its base. As a result, in 1949, it bought out 2 Cleveland companies as its first subsidiaries: the Harris Prods. Co., makers of the Silentbloc metal and rubber bearing, and Monmouth Prods., a replacement-bearing maker.

In 1952, CGB purchased the Brush Development Corp. for $7 million, a historic move that gave it diversity and entry into the expanding electronics field. Brush, founded in 1930 by heirs of arc light inventor CHAS. F. BRUSH, manufactured recording and sound-reproduction equipment and was the world's largest producer of artificially grown crystals for use in phonograph pickups, microphones, hearing-aid components, and underwater signaling devices. To reflect the new product lines, Cleveland Graphite Bronze changed its corporate name to Clevite, but the bearing division retained its former name. The company bolstered its electronics sector with purchases of transistor and semiconductor firms. By 1959, over 1/3 of the company's sales were in electronics, and that segment was split into 4 units: Clevite Transistor Prods.; Brush Instruments; Clevite Electronic Components; and Clevite Ordnance. Clevite's electronics expertise won it major defense contracts to produce torpedoes, sub tracking systems and simulators, guided missiles, and oceanographic equipment, and in 1967, the company opened a new ordnance plant at 18901 Euclid to double its size, production, and workforce.

Because of its dominance in both bearings and electronics, Clevite was the object of merger bids in 1968 by some 20 companies, with the most serious contenders being Weatherhead, the U.S. Smelting, Refining, & Mining Co. of New York, TRW, and Gould-Natl. Battery of St. Paul, Minn. After a year-long battle, Clevite merged with Gould, a battery firm 1/4 its size, under the name Gould, Inc. However, the Clevite name was retained for the bushing and bearing division, and Clevite's president, Wm. Laffer, became chairman of Gould. The new company sought to be an "integrated technology" company that concentrated on batteries, electronics, and defense. As a result, the Clevite division that made bearings was sold in 1981 to get cash for further electronics expansion to the Reading Co., the bankrupt but reorganized railroad. Reading also bought the Imperial Brass Co., a supplier of tube fittings to the auto industry, and called its new purchases Imperial Clevite. Within a year, the new owners began talking about laying off half the workforce of 600 or of closing the plant entirely unless workers accepted a 13% pay cut and other concessions. Claiming inescapable "structural changes in the U.S. auto industry," Reading charged that the company was overproducing Thinwall bearings. MESA, still the Clevite union, twice turned down the concessions, despite contrary recommendations by their international. In 1985, Reading carried out its threats and closed the Imperial Clevite engine plant on St. Clair and a distribution center in VALLEY VIEW. In 1985, only the technical center at 540 E. 105th St. remained open, with a drastically reduced labor force.

**CLIFFORD, LOUIS L.** (24 June 1906–25 May 1968), held the key position of city editor during the post-World War II hegemony of the *CLEVELAND PRESS*. Born in Wabash, Ill., he moved to Cleveland and graduated from CATHEDRAL LATIN HIGH SCHOOL in 1924. He immediately began work as a police and criminal-courts reporter for the *CLEVELAND NEWS*, under the tutelage of its legendary city editor, A. E. M. Bergener. Joining the *Press* in 1928, Clifford earned a reputation as a human-interest writer. After service as assistant city editor, he was named city editor in 1943. Clifford's 25-year tenure at the city desk coincided almost perfectly with the *Press*'s domination of Cleveland politics and journalism. He trained and directed the strong local staff, which both executed the political campaigns of Editor LOUIS B. SELTZER and pursued the "big" stories of crime and corruption that interested Clifford. Seltzer extolled Clifford as the best city editor he had worked with, a judgment concurred in by both friendly and rival local journalists. Unlike Seltzer, Clifford preferred to maintain a relatively low profile outside of his job. He also eschewed the flamboyant theatrics of traditional city editors such as Bergener in favor of a lower-key, but no less authoritative, approach. He made 2 appearances at Columbia University, where he addressed professional gatherings on staff training and municipal affairs. A resident of Euclid, Clifford was married to the former Patricia Sloan and was the father of 3 children, John E., Thos. S., and Mrs. Donna O'Donnel. He served on the Euclid Charter Commission and the Euclid-Glenville Hospital board. He died of a heart attack in the *Press* parking lot as he was preparing to leave for a week's vacation.

**CLIFFORD, WILLIAM H.** (8 Apr. 1862–10 Jan. 1929), was a black public servant and Republican politician who served 2 terms in the Ohio legislature in the 1890s. As a legislator, he played an important role in the election of MARCUS A. HANNA to the U.S. Senate, accepting money from the influential black powerbroker GEO. A. MEYERS to cast the deciding vote in Hanna's favor in Jan. 1898. A native Clevelander, Clifford spent 7 years in the employ of the Woodruff Palace Car Co. before embarking on a career in public service and politics. In 1888 he took a job in the county clerk's office; in Sept. 1888 he was appointed cost clerk, the 3d-highest-paid job in the office, and became the highest-paid black man in local, county, or state government up to that time. He held various offices in the Republican party, including vice-president of the Ohio Republican League in 1889 and membership on the State Republican Executive Committee in 1891. He served as assistant sergeant-at-arms at the 1896 and 1900 Republican national conventions. Clifford was elected to the state legislature twice. He served in the 71st (1894–95) and 73d (1898–99) sessions of the Ohio House of Representatives. In 1902 he graduated from the Cleveland Law School, and ca. 1908 he was appointed to a position in the auditor's office in the War Dept. in Washington, D.C. He held that position until his death.

Clifford's wife, Carrie Williams Clifford (d. 10 Nov. 1934), was prominent in the social and civic life of Cleveland and later Washington. A native of Chillicothe, she grew up in Columbus, where she was educated as a teacher. She taught school in Parkersburg W.Va., until her marriage brought her to Cleveland. She was influential in the formation of the Ohio State Fed. of Colored Women, of which she was the first president; she organized branches of the group in various cities and founded and edited its official publication, the *Queen's Garden*. She was active in the theater and in literary societies, wrote and published poetry and magazine articles, and was a public speaker of some renown, giving public readings in Cleveland and elsewhere. She was also an outspoken advocate of the rights of Afro-Americans. The *New York Times* called her "the most fiery of [the] speakers who addressed the National Negro Business League's Convention" in New York City in 1905, and her obituary described her as "the first woman in the country who became interested in the Niagara Movement and espoused its cause in unmistakable terms." She helped or-

ganize the Washington, D.C., chapter of the NAACP and served it in various capacities.

The **CLIFTON CLUB**, 17884 Lake Rd., LAKEWOOD, Ohio, a private social and recreational club, was originally organized by and for residents of suburban CLIFTON PARK who desired a clubhouse for their gatherings along the lakefront. They leased (and subsequently purchased in 1916) property from the Clifton Park Land & Improvement Co., were incorporated 28 May 1902, and financed the construction of a 3-story clubhouse of wood and stucco at 17884 Lake Rd. on the brow of the hill overlooking the mouth of the Rocky River. The formal opening was held on 22 Aug. 1903. Capt. Russell E. Burdick was the first president. Subsequently, families from Lakewood, ROCKY RIVER, and BAY VILLAGE joined the club. On 11 Jan. 1942, the Clifton Club was completely destroyed by fire; however, the membership agreed to keep the organization intact. Wartime building restrictions delayed reconstruction, but in 1948 ground was broken for a new building, and on 3 June 1950, the club was reopened. Through the years, the club has continued to fulfill its purpose by "providing a setting for entertainment, recreation and enjoyment" for its members and guests, including wedding receptions, dances, parties, and family gatherings.

*The Clifton Club, 1903–1978* (75th Anniversary Booklet).

**CLIFTON PARK**, a residential neighborhood in LAKEWOOD, is located on the high eastern bluffs at the mouth of the Rocky River. The name dates from 1866, when a group of Cleveland businessmen—among them Elias Sims, Daniel P. Rhodes, Ezra Nicholson, and JOSIAH BARBER—formed the Clifton Park Assoc. to promote the area as a summer resort. Transportation was needed for the venture to succeed, and by 1868 members of the association had built the Rocky River Railroad. The line originated at Bridge St. at the city limits and extended to what is today Sloane Ave. in Lakewood. There passengers disembarked to enjoy boating, bathing, large picnic groves, and beer gardens. In 1894 the Clifton Park Assoc. commissioned Ernest W. Bowditch, a landscape architect with offices in Boston and New York, to prepare plans for an exclusive residential district. Wm. J. Starkweather built the first house, in 1897 (now demolished). In 1899 the association sold its interest to the Clifton Park Land Improvement Co., which began to promote the area in earnest. A map published ca. 1899 touted Clifton Park as "the finest suburban residence property accessible to Cleveland . . . with the exceptional advantages of pure air, forest grounds, private parks, bathing, beaches, boating and fishing privileges with every lot."

All the most important lakefront residences were built between 1900–15, many in the Neoclassic, Georgian, and Renaissance Revival styles popular during that period. Clifton Park became home to some of Cleveland's leading citizens, including WALTER C. BAKER, founder of the Baker Motor Vehicle Co.; Francis H. Glidden, founder of the Glidden Varnish Co.; and W. DOMINICK BENES, partner of the architectural firm of Hubbell & Benes. In 1912 the Clifton Park Land Improvement Co. was dissolved, and a trusteeship of 5 Clifton Park residents was formed to hold in trust for lot owners the common property of the park, including Clifton Beach. In the early 1960s, after extensive litigation, Clifton Blvd. was extended through Clifton Park to connect with a new bridge over the Rocky River. The project required the demolition or relocation of a number of houses and cut the neighborhood in two. The northern section of Clifton Park, where the oldest and most imposing houses are located, is listed in the Natl. Register of Historic Places. It remains a neighborhood of stately, well-maintained homes characterized by winding drives and the heavy screen of trees.

**CLINGMAN, ANDREW R.** (1844-14 May 1864), was a soldier depicted by LEVI T. SCOFIELD in the infantry sculpture group *The Color Guard* on the SOLDIERS & SAILORS MONUMENT. Clingman (sometimes spelled Klingman) was enlisted in Co. E, 103d Ohio Volunteer Infantry, on 8 Aug. 1862 by Capt. Levi T. Scofield in Cleveland. He was described as being 5'7½" tall, of dark complexion with hazel eyes and brown hair. His place of birth was listed as "Atlantic Ocean," and his occupation as sailmaker. He was one of the color guard killed during an assault at the battle at Resaca, Ga., on 14 May 1864. Capt. Scofield, 23d Army Corps engineers, observed the assault and claimed to have seen Clingman carried off the field in a blanket. After the war, Scofield depicted Clingman in the *Color Guard* group as the soldier on the right flank, lying on his back, suffering from a mortal wound. He was one of 2 103d soldiers depicted by name. (See also MARTIN STREIBLER.)

Board of Monument Commissioners, *Brief Historical Sketch of the Cuyahoga County Soldiers and Sailors Monument* (1965).
Members of the One Hundred and Third Ohio Volunteer Infantry, *Personal Reminiscences and Experiences—Campaign Life in the Union Army, 1862-1865* (1900).

The **COALITION OF BLACK TRADE UNIONISTS** was founded in 1972 after AFL-CIO president Geo. Meany refused to endorse a presidential candidate. By 1976, the group, organized by Wm. Lacy, president of AFCSME, had 9,000 members nationally, with 150 in Cleveland. In that election year, the coalition held its 5th annual convention in Cleveland at the Convention Ctr., where it endorsed Jimmy Carter for president and urged BLACKS to register and vote for a candidate with their interests in mind. An overriding concern of the coalition was the lack of blacks in union leadership positions. Of 35 members of the AFL-CIO executive council, only 3 were black—A. Phillip Randolph of the Brotherhood of Sleeping Car Porters, and representatives of 2 smaller unions. Locally, the few black leaders included Bruce Foster of the Amalgamated Transit Union, Paul Wells of Local 1099 of the Municipal Firemen's & Laborers' Union, and John Vingard of Local 10 of the Hotel, Motel, & Restaurant Supply & Bartenders' Union. Resolutions that came out of the convention included endorsements for the Humphrey-Hawkins Bill for full employment, busing to achieve school integration, tax reform, national health care, federal aid to cities with high unemployment, and protests against apartheid in South Africa.

**COBBLEDICK, GORDON** (31 Dec. 1898-2 Oct. 1969), covered the local and national sports scenes in the *PLAIN DEALER* for most of his 40-year career. Born in Cleveland, he attended EAST TECH HIGH SCHOOL and studied mining engineering at Case School of Applied Science. Joining the *Plain Dealer* in 1923, he first covered the police beat and city hall. He left the *Plain Dealer* to work for the *CLEVELAND TIMES* in 1926 but returned shortly before the suspension of the rival morning daily. Soon after his return, Cobbledick succeeded Henry P. Edwards as the *Plain Dealer's* baseball writer. His coverage of the Cleveland Indians throughout the 1930s culminated in his exposure of the famous "players' rebellion" in 1940 against manager Oscar Vitt. As a war correspondent during WORLD

WAR II, Cobbledick saw service in the Pacific Theater. V-E Day found him on Okinawa, where his dispatch contrasting the news from Europe with the costly campaign still continuing against Japan was widely reprinted and eventually canonized in Richard Morris and Louis Snyder's *A Treasury of Great Reporting.*

Although Cobbledick was rewarded with a general column upon his return to the *Plain Dealer*, he was called back to athletics in 1946 upon the death of sports editor Sam D. Otis. From the 1948 Indians to the 1964 Browns, "Cobby" edited the sports section during the golden age of Cleveland sports. His "Plain Dealing" column was one of the paper's most popular features, despite (or because of) such whimsical conceits as his insistence that GOLF was not a "sport" but merely a "game." Retiring from the *Plain Dealer* in 1964, Cobbledick conducted a sports program on WEWS-TV for a time and authored a 1966 biography of Indians slugger Rocky Colavito, entitled *Don't Knock the Rock.* His wife was the former Doris V. Mathews of Cleveland, and they had 2 sons, William and Raymond. He died shortly after moving to Tuscon, Ariz., in 1969.

**COBURN & BARNUM** was an architectural firm active in Cleveland from 1878–97. Forrest A. Coburn (1848-l Dec. 1897) and Frank Seymour Barnum (1851–17 Dec. 1927) formed a partnership after both had worked as draftsmen for established Cleveland architects, Coburn with Walter Blythe and Barnum with JOSEPH IRELAND. Coburn executed a famous and often-published lithograph, "Bird's-Eye View of the Flats," showing the new Superior Viaduct, in 1878. During their 20-year association, Coburn & Barnum planned some of Cleveland's most distinguished buildings, including churches and commercial, institutional, and resident buildings. The Furniture Block and the Blackstone Bldg. were 2 of their most important commercial buildings, built in 1881–82. The Blackstone in particular was a superior example of fire-resistant mill construction with a remarkable 4-story interior light court. One of the firm's draftsmen who worked on the building was John H. Edelman, who subsequently moved to Chicago and is credited with being the mentor of Louis Sullivan.

Coburn & Barnum's churches included the Woodland Ave. Presbyterian, First Congregational on Franklin Ave., Brooklyn Congregational, and EUCLID AVE. CONGREGATIONAL churches. Their residential commissions included additions to the home of JEPTHA H. WADE II; residences for Wm. J. Morgan, president of Morgan Lithography, and Geo. Howe (later the VIXSEBOXSE GALLERY) on Euclid Ave.; the spectacular Washington H. Lawrence mansion (Bay View Hospital) in 1898; and the imposing memorial library added to Pres. Garfield's home in Mentor by his wife in 1885. The firm's institutional and cultural buildings included the Medical School (1885-87) and Guilford College (1892) for Western Reserve University, the Electricity Bldg. for Case School in 1896, the OLNEY ART GALLERY on W. 14th St. (1893), and the Western Reserve Historical Society building at E. 107th St. in UNIVERSITY CIRCLE in 1898.

During the entire life of the firm, one of Coburn & Barnum's assistants was W. DOMINICK BENES. Later they were also joined by BENJAMIN S. HUBBELL, and the firm was named Coburn, Barnum, Benes & Hubbell for 1 year, after which Hubbell & Benes left in 1897 to establish their own partnership. Upon the departure of Hubbell and Benes, and Coburn's untimely death in 1897 at the age of 49, Barnum formed F. S. Barnum & Co., in association with Albert Skeel, Harry S. Nelson, Herbert Briggs, and Wilbur M. Hall. In 1895 Barnum was appointed consulting architect to the Cleveland Board of Education. Between that date and his retirement in 1915, the office planned and constructed more than 75 school buildings, many of which were notable for pioneering fireproof construction, especially in response to the disastrous COLLINWOOD SCHOOL FIRE of 1908. Barnum's schools were modern in plan and structure compared with those of the 19th century, and they served several generations well.

In 1901 Barnum designed the CAXTON BLDG., completed in 1903, for AMBROSE SWASEY. It was an 8-story steel-framed building for the commercial printing and graphic-arts trades and an excellent example of the Chicago commercial style. In 1904 Barnum designed the Park Bldg. on PUBLIC SQUARE for the Swetland family; it was said to be one of the first office buildings in Cleveland to utilize floor slabs of reinforced concrete. After Barnum retired in 1915, the firm continued under the name of Briggs & Nelson. Barnum moved to Coconut Grove, Fla., and died in Miami. He was buried in LAKE VIEW CEMETERY on 29 May 1928.

**CODRINGTON CHARITABLE FOUNDATION.** *See* **GEORGE W. CODRINGTON CHARITABLE FOUNDATION**

**COHEN, GUSTAVE M.** (26 Mar. 1820–13 Dec. 1902), chazan, teacher, and spiritual leader at ANSHE CHESED CONGREGATION from 1861–73, was probably the first musically trained cantor in America. Born in Walsdorf, Meinengen, Germany, Cohen was educated in music, pedagogy, Hebrew, and German at Heidelberghausen in Meinengen. He immigrated to America in 1844, settling in New York City, where he became chazan at Temple Emanu-El. He organized the first Jewish choir at Emanu-El and introduced organ music to the religious service. He also taught in the Hebrew day school sponsored by the congregation. In 1856, he accepted a position at Congregation Anshe Maariv in Chicago, but he moved to Cincinnati within a year. He remained there for 4-1/2 years. In 1861, Cohen was hired by Anshe Chesed Congregation in Cleveland. Although he promised not to introduce any reforms at the still-Orthodox congregation, he opened the 1863 Rosh Hashanah service with a German song and made liberal use of an organ and choir during the service. He later introduced the confirmation service at the congregation.

Late in 1865, 30 members of Anshe Chesed petitioned Congregation Tifereth Israel for membership on the condition that Cohen be hired as cantor. The latter congregation refused. In February of the following year, Cohen left Cleveland for Milwaukee, where he remained for 4 months. Upon his return to Cleveland, 34 members of Anshe Chesed, including founders Isaac Hoffman and Moses Alsbacher, again petitioned Tifereth Israel for membership under the same conditions. The congregation agreed, and Cohen was offered the position. Anshe Chesed offered Cohen a raise from his previous salary of $1,200 per year to $2,000, but he accepted the Tifereth Israel offer. In 1867, Tifereth Israel decided to hire an ordained rabbi to act as teacher, preacher, and leader of the congregation. Cohen was released, and he returned to Anshe Chesed, where he continued as the congregation's spiritual leader until 1873, when Rabbi Michael Machol was hired.

Cohen was an accomplished musician, composing several musical pieces during his lifetime. In 1864 he published a collection of works entitled *The Harp of Judah*. Other published collections include *Orpheus, or Musical Recreations* (undated), *Musical Relaxations* (undated), and *The Sacred Harp of Judah, or Musical Recreations* (1878). Cohen was active in several Jewish communal organizations. In 1862, he founded the Zion Musical Society, probably the first Jewish musical society in America. The society performed several concerts at Melodeon Hall. In 1863, he was involved in the reorganization of the Hebrew Benevolent Society, which was orignally established in 1855. And in the late 1860s he was a moving force in the creation of the Hebrew Young Ladies' Literary & Social Society. After leaving the employ of Anshe Chesed, Cohen held several jobs, including grocer, bailiff, music teacher, and insurance agent. He lived the last decade of his life at the MONTEFIORE HOME.

**COLE, ALLEN E.** (1 Sept. 1883–6 Feb. 1970), was a professional photographer in Cleveland's black community. His years of photographing the working- and middle-class community produced a collection of some 27,000 negatives at the time of his death; the negatives were acquired in 1980 by the WESTERN RESERVE HISTORICAL SOCIETY, which reproduced a selection of Cole's photographs in a book that takes its title from the motto of his business, *Somebody, Somewhere, Wants Your Photograph* (1980). A native of Kearneysville, W.Va., Cole was one of 13 children born to blacksmith Allen Cole and his wife, Sarah. After graduating from Storer College in nearby Harper's Ferry, young Cole went to Atlantic City, where he worked as a waiter, and then to Cincinnati, where he was a railroad porter and later a cook on a dining car until he was injured in a train accident. He then formed a real-estate partnership, but when business proved to be slower than expected, Cole moved to Cleveland, working as a waiter at the CLEVELAND ATHLETIC CLUB and eventually becoming head waiter, a position he held for over 10 years.

At the Athletic Club, Cole met Joseph Opet, manager of Frank Moore Studios, who introduced him to photography. He assisted in Opet's studios in his spare time over the next 6 years, and finally decided to leave the Athletic Club to make his living as a photographer. In 1922, he opened his own studio at his home on E. 103rd St., later moving to 9909 Cedar. When individual orders declined in the Great Depression, Cole equipped his studio for commercial work and did commission work for 8 white studios. As his health declined over the years, he was confined to studio work and photographing small outside groups. Cole contributed photographs to the *CLEVELAND CALL & POST*, and his work earned prizes and praise at state and local exhibitions. In addition to serving as the photographer of the black community, Cole was an active participant in its civic and fraternal affairs. He was a founder and treasurer of the Progressive Business League, an officer of the Dunbar Life Insurance Co., a member of ST. JAMES AME CHURCH, and active in the Elks and the MASONS. He was a member of the Internatl. Photographic Assoc. and for years was the only black member of the Cleveland Society of Professional Photographers. His wife, Frances T. Cole (1 Jan. 1889–29 Apr. 1979), served as his assistant and business manager.

*Somebody, Somewhere, Wants Your Photograph* (1980)
Allen E. Cole Papers, WRHS.

The **COLE NATIONAL CORPORATION** is a specialty retailer with 5 chains offering keys, prescription eyewear, engraved gifts, toys, and pastries. With headquarters at 29001 Cedar Rd. in LYNDHURST, it had over 1,700 retail outlets operating in 47 states and over 10,500 employees in 1986. Joseph Cole entered the key business in 1936 with the Natl. Key Co. in Cleveland. In 1944, he left to start the key division at Curtis Industries. Starting with a small key shop in the parking lot of the Sears Roebuck store on Carnegie

Ave., Cole turned the key division into the second-largest next to National. In 1950, he purchased both the Natl. Key Co. and the keymaking accounts of Curtis, making his company the largest of its kind in the country. Cole became known as the "key king." Manufacturing neither keys nor keymaking equipment, Natl. Key relied upon over 100 suppliers to provide its growing network of outlets with a product line of over 3,000 different types of keys and accessories. In 1958, Natl. Key went public, selling out its stock subscription in 1 day. Becoming Cole Natl. in 1960, the company began expanding into different product areas. It acquired Fairfield Publishing, a greeting-card firm, and Shore Mfg., producers of business incentives and specialties. The acquisition of Masco Optical served as the foundation for Cole Natl.'s optical division and its operation of the optical departments in Sears and Montgomery Ward stores. In 1961, Cole Natl. acquired both Automatic Concessions, manufacturers of amusement devices, and Sterling Industries, a Cleveland manufacturer of aluminum, steel, and plastic products, and became the exclusive producer of gifts for Welcome Wagon. In 1965, the key division introduced colored aluminum automobile keys. Cole Natl. merged in 1966 with Susan Crane, producers of giftwrap, and acquired the Gene Upton Co., manufacturers of self-adhesive metal letters and numbers. In 1967, Cole opened its Things Remembered gift-store chain. It acquired Manco, Inc., a manufacturer of watchbands, in 1968 and Griffon Cutlery in 1969. In 1977, Cole Natl. moved its headquarters from Grant Ave. in CUYAHOGA HTS. to Lyndhurst. In 1978, it spun off its Canadian retail operations and its distribution business, creating Cole Consumer Prods. In 1980, Cole opened its first French Oven stores and acquired the toy supermarket Child's World, Inc.

## COLKET, MEREDITH BRIGHT JR.
(18 Aug. 1912–19 May 1985), was an archivist, a historical agency administrator, and one of the foremost genealogists in America. Colket was born in Strafford, Chester County, Pa. He studied history at Haverford College, where he earned B.A. (1935) and M.A. (1940) degrees and was elected to Phi Beta Kappa. In 1974, he was awarded an honorary Litt.D. degree from BALDWIN-WALLACE COLLEGE. Colket joined the staff of the fledgling Natl. Archives in Washington, D.C., in 1937. He was a staff specialist until 1950, when he was appointed genealogy and local-history specialist. There he was particularly active in the preservation of records of historical and genealogical research value. He compiled A Guide to the Genealogical Records in the National Archives (1964), the first comprehensive finding aid to the vast resources of that institution. In 1957, Colket left the archives to assume the directorship of the WESTERN RESERVE HISTORICAL SOCIETY, which, under his leadership, grew to become the largest privately funded historical society in the country. Upon his retirement in 1980, he was made director emeritus.

Colket believed that citizens could achieve greater understanding of what it meant to be Americans through studying their own family's history. He stimulated interest in the history of local communities and encouraged recognition of the achievements of earlier generations. Colket's first publication, on the ancestry of Anne Hutchinson and Katherine Marbury Scott (1936), was followed by genealogical accounts of several other American families, including the Fairbrothers (1939), Pelhams (1940–43), Jenkses (1956), Pelots (1980), and Chisholms (1984). His Creating a Worthwhile Family Genealogy (1968) continues to serve as a model for those who set about to publish a family history. One of Colket's special interests, the English origins of America, led to the publication of his classic study Foun-

ders of Early American Families, Emigrants from Europe, 1607–1657 (1975, rev. ed. 1985). During Colket's tenure, the WRHS experienced the most dramatic growth in its history, expanding its main physical plant on East Blvd. and acquiring outlying properties, including the Jonathan Hale farm in Bath, Ohio; under his directorship, the library became one of the foremost local-history and genealogy research centers in America. He was a founding member (1940) of the Assoc. for State & Local History and founder and first director (1950–60) of the Natl. Institute for Genealogical Research. In Cleveland, he served as vice-president of the NATIONALITIES SERVICES CTR. and chairman (1978–82) of the Cleveland Hts. Landmarks Commission. Colket married Julia Beatrice Pelot in 1945.

## COLLAMER
was the section of the present city of E. CLEVELAND that stretched from Lakeview on the west and Ivanhoe on the east. Bisected by Euclid Ave., Collamer was intersected by such roads as Noble, Taylor, and Lee to the south, and Doan, Shaw, and Collamer to the north. The original settlement of Collamer was established in 1812 when a tannery and gristmill were started by David Crocker near Collamer St. and Euclid Ave., where NINE MILE CREEK crossed. Named for Judge Jacob Collamer, postmaster general under Pres. Zachary Taylor, the little colony was occasionally referred to as Nine Mile Creek or Euclid Village before 1850. Some of the earliest churches in the Western Reserve were established in Collamer, including the Plan of Union Church (later the First Presbyterian Church of E. Cleveland). Because of the large number of ministers who came to reside there, the area was referred to as Saints' Row. The land of Collamer was noted for its fertility, especially for grapes, peaches, and cherries. From 1870–79, Collamer was the largest shipping point in the U.S., followed by Dover, Ohio. It was also noted as the territory of the Lakeview & Collamer Railroad, which ran north of Superior, turned east, and ran north of Euclid, where it again turned east to Chardon. Part of this route was used for streetcars and later the rapid transit, which ran from E. Cleveland to PUBLIC SQUARE. Collamer was included in the township of E. Cleveland (est. 1847) and the village (later the city) of E. Cleveland (est. 1895.)

Price, Ellen Loughry, A History of East Cleveland (1970).

The **COLLEGE CLUB OF CLEVELAND**, 2348 Overlook Rd., CLEVELAND HTS., a social, civic, educational, and philanthropic organization of (and for) women who have graduated from an accredited college and who have been approved for membership, was originated in 1897 by Louise Pope and Carolyn Shipman for the purpose of "promoting social, philanthropic and literary interests." An invitational meeting held on 20 Nov. 1897 at Clark Hall on the Mather Campus of Western Reserve University proved successful and led to a second decision-making meeting, on 4 Dec. 1897. Later, an official organizational meeting held on 15 Jan. 1898 at the Hotel Stillman on Euclid Ave. elected Pope (later Mrs. Homer H. Johnson) president and Shipman secretary. The original group consisted of 88 charter members, representing 17 colleges.

At first, meetings were held every 2 weeks in the homes of members or in college buildings. In 1900 a suite of rooms in the Wedge Bldg. on Euclid Ave. near Erie (E. 9th) St. became the club headquarters. Various alumnae groups furnished the rooms and acted as hostesses for the daily teas held for members and guests. Later the club moved to the Bangor Bldg., and then to the CAXTON BLDG. In 1908, Channing Hall in the Unitarian Church became the club's meeting place. The club was incorporated on 15 Jan. 1908 as the College Club Co. On 15 Jan. 1913, the club purchased the stable, with adjoining coachman's quarters, attached to the Chas. Wm. Wason property at 1958 E. 93rd St. Members remodeled, redecorated, and added extensively to this building, which was their home for 38 years. During WORLD WAR I, members volunteered in many war-relief organizations. A scholarship was established in 1922. Participation in organizations for war relief characterized volunteer activities again during WORLD WAR II.

In Jan. 1948, the club reorganized and became the College Club of Cleveland, a nonprofit organization, and in Mar. 1951 it purchased its present clubhouse, the Wm. D. B. Alexander home, from the estate of D. Edward Angler. The mansion was remodeled and redecorated, and the new headquarters were opened in Oct. 1951. The club sponsors varied programs, including classes, lectures, and meetings, as well as social activities such as luncheons, dinners, benefits, and traditional parties. On 9 Oct. 1978, "the Alexander House" was designated a Cleveland Hts. landmark.

The **COLLINWOOD** neighborhood of Cleveland is located about 7 mi. northeast of PUBLIC SQUARE, near Lake Erie. Originally part of E. Cleveland Twp., Collinwood was a village separate from Cleveland until 1910. It was initially called COLLAMER after Judge Jacob Collamer, appointed postmaster for the district in 1850. By 1860, an omnibus line operated between Cleveland and Collamer via St. Clair Ave., and in the 1870s Collamer was the largest shipping point for grapes in the U.S. The main axis of the village was Collamer (E. 152nd) St. The first church in the community, the First Congregational Church of Collinwood, was organized in 1876. The Collinwood Christian Church was organized 2 years later. By 1890, Collinwood was a major switching point of the Lake Shore & Michigan Southern (later New York Central) Railroad and the location of its vast freightyards. In 1903 and again in 1929, the COLLINWOOD YARDS were expanded; they eventually included over 120 mi. of track and extensive repair shops. Cutting a wide swath through the northern section of the community on either side of E. 152nd St., they were the basis for the area's early growth. Disaster struck the Collinwood community on 4 Mar. 1908, when the COLLINWOOD SCHOOL FIRE claimed the lives of 172 schoolchildren and 2 teachers. The fire resulted in the safer construction of school buildings and more rigid fire inspection of public buildings throughout the nation.

Collinwood was annexed to Cleveland on 21 Jan. 1910. The neighborhood became home to large Irish, Italian, and Slovenian populations, and during WORLD WAR I a small colony of blacks settled in the Thames-Darwin section near the railyards to work the New York Central. FIVE POINTS—the intersection of E. 152nd St. and St. Clair and Ivanhoe avenues—was the commercial hub of the neighborhood. During WORLD WAR II, Collinwood encompassed one of the heaviest industrial areas in the world, and Five Points business property became more valuable than any other location outside the downtown area with the exception of Euclid-E. 105th (see DOAN'S CORNERS). Within its boundaries, in addition to the New York Central yards, were FISHER BODY, Thompson Prods. (See TRW), GENERAL ELECTRIC, LINCOLN ELECTRIC, Eaton Axle (See EATON CORP.), Bailey Meter (See BABCOCK & WILCOX), Hamilton Steel, Lindsay Wire, and a dozen other firms. Householders for the first time took in roomers, many of whom were migrants from the Virginias, Kentucky, and Tennessee. During the 1950s, Collinwood experienced the beginning of social problems that would persist over the next several decades. High delinquency and

crime rates, including problems with street gangs, were followed by racial turbulence in the 1960s and 1970s as BLACKS moved into the formerly solid white neighborhood. Collinwood High School became the focus of many of these clashes. The Collinwood Community Services Ctr. was established in 1967 to provide youth programs in the neighborhood. In 1970, the Collinwood Better Business Assoc. was formed to revitalize the Five Points shopping district, but it ultimately failed to fight the cycle that was leaving lines of empty storefronts across the city. Collinwood in 1985 was an uneasy amalgam of racial and ethnic groups, all of which have suffered from the departure of some of the neighborhood's largest industries, including Fisher Body and Eaton. CONRAIL, successor to the bankrupt Penn-Central Railroad, closed the Collinwood Yards in 1981.

The **COLLINWOOD RAILROAD YARDS** & Diesel Terminal, centered on present-day E. 152nd St. just south of the Lakeland Freeway, are important switching and repair facilities for the Cleveland division of the CONRAIL System. The Collinwood Yard is one of 2 modern classification yards serving the Cleveland area, especially east and south side industries. The associated diesel terminal employs nearly 300 persons in the refueling and repair of locomotives. Trailvan piggyback service is provided at Collinwood, along with a Flexi-Flo terminal permitting rail car/tank truck liquid and dry bulk commodity transfer. The Collinwood Yards also provide a vital interchange link to the NORFOLK SOUTHERN CORP.

Historically, the property now encompassing the Collinwood Yards & Diesel Terminal has been strategically important for rail development. The yards trace their lineage to the establishment of the Cleveland, Painesville & Ashtabula Railroad in 1848. From the early 1850s this small trunk system was a link in the larger Buffalo-to-Chicago route, which eventually was merged to form the Lake Shore & Southern Michigan. A 100'-wide right-of-way supporting double trackage was established in 1852, with 4 tracks laid by 1900. Repair shops and a railyard were established in 1873 near COLLINWOOD to handle the rapidly growing system's large freight car and locomotive inventory.

The village of Collinwood, which surrounded the growing rail facilities to the north and south, was incorporated into the city of Cleveland on 21 Jan. 1910. The railyards have had an important impact on 2 different neighborhoods in the Collinwood area. The territory just south has been extensively settled by individuals of Italian heritage, some of whom migrated eastward from LITTLE ITALY. The neighborhood north of the tracks to the lakeshore and referred to as Waterloo Beach or N. Collinwood has been widely settled by persons of Slovenian birth. Employment in S. Collinwood is blue-collar-oriented; Waterloo Beach contains no more individuals of white-collar employment. Thus, the Collinwood Yards not only are important transportation facilities but serve as neighborhood boundaries, as well, with the newly constructed E. 152nd St. Bridge providing a passage point and vista of a thriving transport network.

Staufer, Alvin F., *New York Central's Early Power, 1831–1916* (1967).

The **COLLINWOOD SCHOOL FIRE** occurred on 4 Mar. 1908, killing 172 children and 2 teachers at Lakeview Elementary School in the village of COLLINWOOD. The fire, caused by an overheated steam pipe in contact with wooden joists under the front stairs, began shortly after 9 a.m. Nearly all of the 366 students enrolled were in attendance, but only 194 escaped; the others were trapped inside the rear first-floor exit. By the time volunteer firemen arrived, nothing could be done to save the trapped students. The parents of the students fought to drag bodies from the heap, and later searched through a makeshift morgue in hopes of identifying their children. Nineteen bodies could not be identified and were buried in a common grave in LAKE VIEW CEMETERY, along with 150 identified students.

The intitial report blamed the children's failure to escape on the rear doors of the school. It was claimed that the doors opened inward; children were unable to open them because bodies were jammed against the doors because of the panic of other children pushing from behind. The coroner's inquest, which included reports from witnesses and the architects who designed the building, and an examination of the building proved the initial report to be erroneous. The report concluded that the children's failure to escape resulted from their own panic, which caused them to become jammed and congested on the rear steps. The inner vestibule doors were narrower than the outer doors; the children therefore wedged tightly between the vestibule doors, while others pressed them from behind. The outer doors did open outward. Laws requiring school doors to open outward were already in effect at the time of the blaze. But the horror of the Collinwood fire caused numerous school inspections across the country, which resulted in stricter laws.

Neil, Henry, *Complete Story of the Collinwood Disaster and How Such Horrors Can Be Prevented* (1908).

**COLONIAL DAMES OF AMERICA.** *See* **PATRIOTIC SOCIETIES**

**COLONIAL DAMES OF THE XVII CENTURY.** *See* **PATRIOTIC SOCIETIES**

The **COLONIAL THEATER** opened on 16 Mar. 1903. It was located at Superior Ave. near E. 9th St. Built by the McMillans of Detroit, Mich., it was a distinguished house for almost 30 years. Shortly after it opened, it was leased by Drew & Campbell of the Star Theater and for several years was used for vaudeville productions. The name of the theater was changed to the Shubert-Colonial Theater on 9 Sept. 1918. Theatrical attractions were presented during the regular seasons, while in the summer, stock companies used its facilities. The theater was demolished in 1932.

The **COLONY THEATER**, located on SHAKER SQUARE, is one of Cleveland's major movie houses and one of the Square's most notable architectural features. Completed in Dec. 1937, the Colony was designed for Warner Bros. by John Eberson, a Chicago and New York theater designer. Though the exterior of the building harmonized with the Georgian theme of the Square's other structures, the interior was completely modern, making use of bakelite, Italian marble, and the clean, flowing lines of the late Art Deco period. The auditorium seated 1,500 on the main level and in a balcony. Seats were originally equipped with the Acousticon system, which consisted of an earphone to be used by viewers with hearing problems. The lower-level lounge featured a mural, painted by internationally known muralist Arthur Crisp, depicting the adventures of Aladdin. The theater prospered throughout the 1940s and 1950s. However, like many movie houses it eventually lost much patronage to TELEVISION, and on 11 Feb. 1979 it closed. At that time it was operated by Natl. Theater, Inc. Beginning in July 1980, the theater was reopened by the Friends of Shaker Square for occasional shows. In June 1981, it reopened on a full-time basis under the management of Morris Zryl for movies and live performances, specializing in the exhibition of 70mm films and classic movies.

The **COLUMBIA THEATER**, 2071 E. 9th St., opened on 26 Oct. 1913 as the Miles Theater under the direction of president and general manager Chas. H. Miles. It was billed as "America's most beautiful vaudeville palace." It was decorated in the Louis XIV style in a color scheme of old rose, ivory, cream, and gold, with DuBarry damask on the walls and mahogany seats upholstered in rich green velour, which matched the carpeting. The backs of the seats contained slot machines that would dispense candy for $.05. Rose velour curtains with deep-gold galloons draped the boxes. The stuccoed walls contained 2 French murals on the spaces over the proscenium boxes. The proscenium itself was decorated with acanthus leaf and satyr-head designs. The auditorium contained 12 proscenium boxes, 26 mezzanine boxes, and 2 aero boxes. The 2,000-seat theater cost nearly $500,000. Beginning at noon was a 5-hour program of vaudeville and movies, with such popular figures as "Gentleman Jim" Corbett, Joe Pinner, and Joe Yule (Mickey Rooney's father) with Bert Lahr. Tickets cost $.10, $.20, and $.30.

In 1920 the Miles Theater became a burlesque house and changed its name to the Columbia. It changed again in 1931, when the movies were introduced and it became the Great Lakes Theater. Between 1935–37, the theater suffered an identity crisis. For a while in 1935 it was called the Miles again and featured vaudeville and first-run movies under the management of Ed Flannigan, Geo. Young, and Warren Irons. Then it was a movie theater under the name of the Carter. In 1936 it became the Federal Theater—part of the Federal Theater Project of the WPA. The first production was the Broadway play *Triple A Plowed Under*, a 22-scene dramatization of the farm problem. Operating as the Miles again, it was called by a 1937 article in the *Plain Dealer* a "flophouse with a soundtrack." Sometime in 1937 it became the Carter again—owned by the Community Theater Circuit, which operated 15 houses in Cleveland. In 1954 the plaster ceiling fell, injuring 10 patrons. The theater was torn down in Dec. 1959.

The **COLUMBUS STREET BRIDGE** was the first permanent bridge over the CUYAHOGA RIVER. Constructed in 1836, it led to further commercial development of Cleveland at the expense of OHIO CITY, which led to the "Bridge War" between the cities in 1837. The Columbus St. Bridge was built by a group of real-estate speculators, led by Jas. S. Clark, who were developing Cleveland Ctr., a commercial district at Ox Bow Bend in the FLATS. It provided a direct route to Cleveland Ctr. from the Medina & Wooster turnpike (Pearl Rd.), a main artery from the south. The covered bridge was given to the city of Cleveland by Clark on 18 Apr. 1836. It cost $15,000 and was 200′ long, 33′ wide, and 24′ high, with a draw at the center allowing ships up to 49′ wide to pass. Travelers and farmers delivering crops could now bypass Ohio City entirely by crossing into Cleveland over the new structure instead of using the old floating bridge owned jointly by Ohio City and Cleveland. Seeing their trade diverted to Cleveland, Ohio City residents boycotted the new bridge, and in retaliation, CLEVELAND CITY COUNCIL had their half of the floating bridge removed, further irritating Ohio City residents. This action in the spring of 1836 began the so-called Bridge War.

The west-siders, rallying to the cry of "Two Bridges or None," declared the Columbus St. Bridge a nuisance and proceeded to cut away the southern draw of the bridge. In late Oct. 1836, they tried to blow up the western end of the bridge with a powder charge, but the explosion did little damage. A group of 1,000 Ohio City volunteers then turned to shovels, digging deep ditches in front of both ends of the bridge, making it impossible for horses and wagons to reach the structure. Unsatisfied with that, some Ohio City residents armed with guns, crowbars, axes, and other weapons set off to finish the destruction, only to be met by Cleveland mayor JOHN W. WILLEY and a group of armed Cleveland militiamen. A riot ensued on the bridge, and 3 men were seriously wounded before the county sheriff arrived to end the violence and make several arrests. A court injunction prevented any further interference with the bridge, and as a result, during November, an armed guard from Cleveland was kept there while the courts resolved the issue by ruling that there should be more than one bridge crossing. Thus ended what one commentator called "one of the most exciting events" in early Cleveland history. The Columbus St. Bridge stayed (an iron bridge replaced it in 1870), but builder Clark's real-estate venture collapsed, and the properties were sold by the sheriff in 1837. Although Ohio City grew, the bridge ended any hopes of its rivaling Cleveland.

The **COMMERCIAL BANK OF LAKE ERIE** was the first bank in Cleveland and, though short-lived, played an active role in the early economic life of the town. Incorporated by 8 Clevelanders who chartered it for 25 years with $45,000 in capital, the bank opened for business on 6 Aug. 1816 in a parlor of a house at the corner of Superior and Bank (W. 6th) streets. ALFRED KELLEY was president. For 2 years, the firm carried on an active business in mercantile credits and real-estate loans. However, it fell victim to the Panic of 1819. In 1820 it was unable to redeem $10,000 worth of its paper money with specie funds to the Second Bank of the U.S. The debt to the federal government was placed on the bank's books. Although the bank could not conduct any business, the directors continued to meet periodically to maintain the charter.

In 1832, the bank was reorganized when an eastern investment group, headed by the Dwight family through its representative Geo. Bancroft, negotiated with the bank's stockholders to buy a majority of the firm and pay off its federal debt. The bank reopened on 2 Apr. 1832, with LEONARD CASE as president, whose residence served as the bank's office. Bancroft sent New Yorker TRUMAN P. HANDY to Cleveland to help manage the bank as a cashier. The Dwight family placed considerable assets in the bank to provide it with a firm base for operation. The enterprise was successful at first. Reorganization coincided with the tremendous growth of the canal trade in Cleveland in the 1830s. The bank extended credit to Cleveland's merchants for importation of eastern merchandise and bought bills of exchange to finance eastern shipments of Ohio farm surpluses. It also secured major deposits of public funds from the state and federal governments.

During the Panic of 1837, the bank was unable to collect its heavy loans to Cleveland merchants. It suspended payment of specie for over a year. Although it survived the panic, the Commercial Bank never recovered. When its charter expired in 1842, the state legislature refused to recharter it. The bank then applied for receivership with Truman Handy and 2 other men appointed to complete the firm's affairs. By 1845, they had distributed its remaining assets, including prime parcels of downtown real estate.

Commercial Bank of Lake Erie Records, WRHS.

The **COMMERCIAL INTELLIGENCER** was a Whig daily introduced by Benjamin Andrews, formerly publisher of

the *Cleveland Herald*. Cleveland's 4th daily, it appeared in Jan. 1838, after the merger of the *Daily Gazette* into the *Herald* and shortly before the reversion of the *Advertiser* to weekly status. Committed to the presidential candidacy of Henry Clay, the *Commercial Intelligencer* was designated the city's "official paper" under the administration of Mayor JOSHUA MILLS. True to its title, it was also heavy with advertising and business news. Habitually referred to as "the disorganizer" by the *Herald & Gazette*, the *Commercial Intelligencer* was condemned by that paper as the creation of "leading loco focos" (Democrats) seeking the disruption of the Whig party. Although indignantly denying the charge, the *Commercial Intelligencer* unsuccessfully backed the candidacy of an independent Whig candidate for the lower house of the state legislature. After more than a year of existence, it finally suspended publication on 11 June 1839. Andrews was named postmaster of Cleveland in 1842.

The **COMMISSION ON CATHOLIC COMMUNITY ACTION** is the social-justice arm of the Diocese of Cleveland. It was begun by Bp. CLARENCE G. ISSENMAN in June 1969 to provide a creative response to the problems of racism, discrimination, and poverty that faced the church and society at large. Aux. Bp. Wm. M. Cosgrove and Geo. A. Moore, a journalist and founder of the Catholic Interracial Council, served as the commission's first cochairmen. Richard M. Kelley became the first executive director. The commission's members assessed and promoted policies, and its staff carried them out. It strove to involve both parishes and individuals in its activities and cooperated with public and private agencies to achieve its goals. This work included the evaluation of various diocesan offices and recommendations of ways to make them more responsive to the needs of the poor and minorities. In 1971 Harry Fagan, a commission staff member, launched Action for a Change, a course that applied Gospel principles to social problems. Individuals were trained at the parish level and could involve themselves in issues such as housing, self-help, and hunger programs. In 1972 Fr. Daniel Reidy became executive director of the commission. During his tenure, the commission provided assistance to local grassroots organizations, such as the Buckeye-Woodland Community Congress, the St. Clair-Superior Coalition, the Heights Community Congress, Active Clevelanders Together, and the Senior Citizens' Coalition. It also organized a hunger center network, helped publicize the hunger problem, and launched a coordinated effort to deal with problems in the criminal-justice system. Fr. Reidy was succeeded by Harry Fagan in 1975. The director of the commission in 1985 was David Hoehnen.

Archives, Diocese of Cleveland.

The **COMMUNIST PARTY** in Cleveland was a small, disciplined group of men and women involved in both political and labor activities who believed it was necessary to overthrow American capitalism by revolutionary means in order to establish proletarian rule. The party has not played a significant role in Cleveland's history. The local Communist party was founded by Ohio and Cuyahoga County socialists belonging to the left-wing section of the natl. Socialist party. At a section meeting in New York on 21 June 1919, the Cuyahoga County group unsuccessfully promoted a party referendum to reverse the Natl. Executive Committee's nullification of election results believed to be favorable to the left wing. Led by CHAS. E. RUTHENBERG, the left-wing section declared themselves the true national executive committee of the Socialist party at a meeting held in Cleveland on 26 July 1919. One of 4 splinter groups, they left the Socialist party to help form the Communist Labor Party, which joined with the Communist Party of America in May 1920.

In Cuyahoga County, the Workers Party of America, the Communists' political arm, nominated congressional candidates in the 1924 election but received few votes. The county gave national party leader Wm. Z. Foster 2,437 votes when he ran for president in 1932. There were periodic attempts to unite with the Socialists and the SOCIALIST LABOR PARTY in order to increase their political strength, but the groups were unable to reconcile their differences. In the 1930s, the Communist party turned its attention to organizing the automobile workers at the White Motor Co. and the GM Fisher Body Plant on Coit Rd. In order to promote more aggressive union activity, party member Wyndham Mortimer, who worked at White Motor, formed the Cleveland District Automobile Council (CDAC), made up of 9 locals. Mortimer and others represented only a small part of the organizing effort, but their discipline and unity made them influential. Both Mortimer and John Williamson, Ohio party secretary, advised the local leaders during the sit-down strike at Cleveland's Fisher Body Plant begun 28 Dec. 1936. The strike, which became companywide, ended early in Feb. 1937 with the recognition of the UNITED AUTO WORKERS as the bargaining agent at GM. After WORLD WAR II, possible Communist influence in the United Electrical Workers' Union (see FA-WICK-AIRFLEX STRIKE) was removed when the union was expelled from the CIO in 1949 (see CIO "PURGE" CONVENTION). In the early 1950s Andrew Onda was secretary of the Cuyahoga County Communist Party, and Benjamin Gray was listed as head of the security division. Since that time little party activity has been evident.

Keeran, Roger, *The Communist Party and the Auto Workers' Unions* (1980).

Benjamin Gray Papers, WRHS.

**COMMUNITY CHEST.** See **UNITED WAY SERVICES**

**COMMUNITY FUND.** See **UNITED WAY SERVICES**

**COMMUNITY HOSPITAL OF BEDFORD** (also known as BEDFORD MUNICIPAL HOSPITAL), located at 44 Blaine St., BEDFORD, Ohio, is a city-owned nonprofit short-term general hospital. It was originally established in 1908 in the home of Mr. and Mrs. W. H. Lascher on North St. This effort ended within 2 years. In 1925 another small hospital was opened, in the Martin Silver house at the corner of Broadway and Grace St., but it later was moved to the Senter house nearby. The hospital was supported by the local Parent Teachers' Assoc., various city service clubs, and a hospital guild. In Mar. 1926 a bond issue was proposed and passed authorizing the city council to procure land and build and equip a municipal hospital. Bedford Municipal Hospital opened in 1928 with 24 beds; it expanded its facilities in 1943, 1949, and 1951. In the early 1950s there were various offers from private physicians' and citizens' groups, the Kaiser system, and other private institutions to purchase the hospital from the city. In the 1960s there were major fundraising campaigns to expand the hospital, but expansion was eventually financed through passage of a bond issue in 1966. From 1968-73 the hospital was embroiled in a controversy over a city charter amendment that gave the city council of Bedford the right to appoint the hospital administrator. After the resignation in 1968 of Eleanor Cline, who had served as administrator of Bedford hospital for 32 years, there was a rapid succession of administrators for the next 5 years. Despite these problems, Bedford Hospital was expanded with the opening of a new building in 1970 and remains a city-owned general hospital.

"Hospitals" Collection, Archives, Howard Dittrick Museum of Historical Medicine. *The Northeast Ohio Health Services Area and Its Hospital Needs* (1976).

The **CONDUCTORS' STRIKE OF 1918-19** involved the Cleveland Railway Co.'s female streetcar conductors and Local 268 of the Amalgamated Assoc. of Street, Electric Railway & Motor Coach Employees of America. The strike was sparked by the railway company's employment of female conductors to relieve wartime labor shortages and possibly undermine the Amalgamated Assoc. In May 1918, in fear of economic and social threats, the union announced its opposition to the employment of women as conductors or motormen and its intention not to grant women union membership. It also called for an investigation of the labor shortage by the Dept. of Labor. The Labor Dept., claiming that the company had created a labor shortage, issued a mandate for the dismissal of the women by 1 Nov. 1918. In an effort to counter the union and Labor Dept.'s actions, the women formed the Assoc. of Women Street Railway Employees and enlisted the help of FLORENCE ALLEN, Cleveland lawyer and suffragist, the Women's Trade Union League, and several other reformers, suffragists, and feminists. The women were successful in inducing Labor Dept. secretary Wm. B. Wilson to defer the dismissal until 1 Dec. and refer the case to the Natl. War Labor Board. Local 268 did not wait for the board to hold a hearing and threatened a walkout if the company did not dismiss the women. The board issued a restraining order against the dismissal until it could reach a decision; on 3 Dec. 1918 the union announced a strike.

The mayor of Cleveland immediately went to Washington to urge the board to reach a decision. It ruled that the women be dismissed by 3 Jan. 1919 and claimed that since the armistice had been signed, the labor shortage was over. The "conductorettes" filed for a new hearing, which the board agreed to hold in March. But although the March hearing caused the board to reverse its earlier decision and order the reinstatement of 64 female conductors, the union claimed that the board's jurisdiction had ended with the war, and the company refused to recognize the ruling. The female conductors lost the case and their jobs.

The **CONFERENCE FOR PROGRESSIVE POLITICAL ACTION,** held at Cleveland's Public Hall 4-5 July 1924, endorsed Sen. Robt. M. La Follette of Wisconsin as a candidate for the U.S. presidency. The 800 delegates to the conference consisted largely of farmers and trade unionists who felt that the Republican and Democratic parties had failed in their obligations to the American people. Also attending were several delegates from the Socialist party. In a telegram in which La Follette was recognized as "the outstanding leader of the progressive forces in the United States," the national committee of the Progressive Political Alliance asked him to become a candidate. On 4 July 1924, the first day of the conference, La Follette sent word through his son that he intended to run as an independent presidential candidate, but not on a third-party ticket, for fear of alienating independents in Congress who had been elected on party tickets. His independent platform advocated public ownership of RAILROADS; abolition of injunctions in labor disputes; a constitutional amendment to prohibit child labor; and a government marketing corporation. The conference delegates enthusiastically supported La Follette's announcement of candidacy and his platform; however, formal endorsement of his candidacy was postponed until 5 July, when a vote by acclamation won La Follette the support of representatives of the Socialist party, the Farmer-Labor party, and the NAACP.

**CONGREGATIONALISTS.** Congregationalist churches, now part of the United Church of Christ (UCC), were among the city's first and most influential religious institutions. They were active in the first years of the town's growth and later conducted much of the mission work that was designed to "Americanize" and evangelize the immigrants who arrived at the end of the 19th century. In recent years, they have maintained their traditionally autonomous churches, liberal theology, ecumenical orientation, and vigorous social activity. In the town's early years, Congregationalists vied with PRESBYTERIANS to establish churches. Under an agreement known as the Plan of Union, Presbyterians and Congregationalists had agreed to unite to evangelize the West. Most of the churches under the plan, after brief attempts to combine Presbyterian and Congregational organizational forms, chose one or the other. Many of the oldest and most influential of the city's Congregational churches began as Presbyterian churches. ARCHWOOD UNITED CHURCH OF CHRIST, the first of the present city's Congregational churches, was organized in 1819 with a Presbyterian Confession of Faith, and maintained links to a nearby synod. It was not until 1867 that it associated with the Cleveland Congregational Conference. First Congregational Church (Cleveland) was organized as First Presbyterian Church of Brooklyn in 1834. It was discontinued in 1954. It left the Presbyterians in 1848 to become an independent Congregational church, and 10 years later joined the Cleveland Congregational Conference. EUCLID AVE. CONGREGATIONAL CHURCH started as First Presbyterian Church in 1807, but became Congregational in 1854.

Plymouth Congregational Church resulted from the dissension and instability introduced by the conflicting Presbyterian and Congregational forces in FIRST PRESBYTERIAN CHURCH (OLD STONE.) The church was nurtured by Congregationalists but adopted a mixed form of government. It was not until 1835, under Rev. SAMUEL AIKEN, that the church settled into the Presbyterian camp. A number of religions and new churches can be traced at least partly to dissatisfaction with the form of organization. The most significant defection, Free Presbyterian Church 1850, came as the result of opposition to the church's moderate stand on antislavery and its practice of charging for pews, in addition to misgivings about its structure. Two years later, to mark its new denominational leanings, Free Presbyterian took the name Plymouth Congregational Church at the suggestion of New York's Rev. Henry Ward Beecher. Plymouth Congregational itself disbanded in 1913 but, with the aid of the Congregational Union, was reconstituted in 1916 as one of the 5 churches provided for by the VAN SWERINGEN brothers in their planned community, SHAKER HTS. One Congregational church that began as such in 1855 had its own mixed denominational heritage. When it was organized in 1859, Heights (now Pilgrim) Congregational Church combined members, confessions, and organizational forms of Congregational, Methodist, Wesleyan Methodist, and Presbyterian churches.

In general, Congregationalism suffered in Cleveland under the Plan of Union. The Congregational form of government, with autonomous churches, was considered by many inappropriate for a region where support and supervision from the denomination were needed to nurture churches through their early years. In addition, Presbyterians were closer, in nearby Pennsylvania. As a result, Plan of Union churches in the city tended to be Presbyterian. Those outside the town were more likely to be Congregational; most likely because the churches of the smaller settlements were not seen as requiring major outside support. The characterization of the historian of the Plan of Union, Wm. S. Kennedy, that the milk from Congregational cows was being turned into Presbyterian butter, is an apt one. By 1865 there were 4 Congregational churches in the city, including 2 that had just left the Presbyterians, as compared to 6 Presbyterian churches. The city as a whole had 50 churches. Although individual Congregational churches were self-governing, the need to establish some connections with other churches led in 1853 to the formation of the Cleveland Congregational Conference. The conference exercised no supervisory functions, but rather served to provide a forum for discussion and a base for joint efforts. The conference provided the organizational framework for much of the mission and benevolent work of the denomination.

In the years 1880–1910, Congregationalists mounted the most extensive city mission work of all the area's denominations. They established missions spread throughout the city designed to reach nearly 2 dozen different ethnic and language groups. To further their work, Congregationalists founded the Bible Readers' School in 1886. It later took the name SCHAUFFLER COLLEGE OF RELIGIOUS & SOCIAL WORK, after its leader, Henry Albert Schauffler. The school trained young women to proselytize among their own ethnic group. The women were sent out to both "Americanize" and evangelize their compatriots. Many of the individual Congregational churches were involved in their own mission work. Plymouth Congregational's Olivet Chapel worked in the Czech community. Pilgrim Congregational broadened its activities to reach out to the new residents of its neighborhood. By 1895, Pilgrim had become the city's first institutional church, so-called because it concerned itself not just with worship but also with a variety of educational and recreational functions. It conducted classes in English, trained immigrants for jobs, and sponsored clubs for all ages and interests. The church building itself was constructed with outreach in mind. It was built according to the Akron Plan as an auditorium rather than a cross. Sliding doors and walls created adaptable meeting space for its multiple activities. In addition to churches that grew from missions, Congregationalists established churches outside downtown and in the suburbs. From 9 churches in 1880, Congregationalism had increased to 21 by 1896. Only Boston and Chicago claimed more.

Congregational churches also lent their efforts to a variety of social and moral reforms. First Congregational Church (earlier known as First Presbyterian Church, Ohio City) was one of the most socially active. Its long-time minister, JAS. A. THOME, joined the antislavery effort wholeheartedly. He had been one of the "Lane rebels," students who left Lane Seminary in Cincinnati over the antislavery issue. Like others, he attended Oberlin, where he also taught. Congregational churches were active in TEMPERANCE activity and in work aiding the poor and orphans. Congregational churches continued their moral reform efforts in the years after the Civil War. They were particularly active in the Women's Crusade of 1873 against the liquor traffic. In 1886, Pilgrim Congregational Church established the JONES HOME for Friendless Children. Benevolent work sponsored by women's organizations of the churches has been a regular feature of Congregational church activity; Christian Endeavor societies were popular around the turn of the century as a channel for social and missionary work for younger members.

With their distaste for limiting creeds and strict organizational forms, the city's Congregationalists have been active in ecumenical efforts. At various times early in the 20th century, for example, Pilgrim Congregational Church held services that included the pastor and chorus of ST. THEODOSIUS RUSSIAN ORTHODOX CATHEDRAL, the members of Methodist and German Evangelical churches, and the rabbi of Tifereth Israel. Formal ecumenical agreements have shaped 20th-century Congregationalism. Some diversity was introduced in 1931 with the merger of Congregational churches with Christian (or Christian Congregational) churches. Among other changes, that brought more black members to the Congregational church. The ecumenical process went a step further in 1957, when the Congregational churches nationwide merged with the Evangelical & Reformed church to form the United Church of Christ. The Uniting Synod was held in Cleveland's Music Hall. The merger brought some additional new elements to the Congregational churches, including the German and Methodist influences of the Evangelical & Reformed denomination. In 1986 the UCC numbered 48 churches, compared to 43 for the Presbyterians, of the metropolitan area's more than 1,300 churches. Although predominantly a white denomination until the 1970s, Congregationalists had 1 black church, MT. ZION CONGREGATIONAL CHURCH (1864), known for serving an upper-class leadership elite in the black community. Other black UCC churches were the result of the moving of blacks into formerly all-white areas. Thus, a number of churches with connections to Congregationalism, such as East View UCC and Shaker Community Church (a former Evangelical & Reformed church), are now black. In recent years, the UCC churches have been among the most active in the Greater Cleveland Interchurch Council and the Inner-City Renewal Society. Recent efforts to promote civil rights, peace, and economic justice mark a continuation of the generally liberal, socially involved activity that has characterized Congregationalists in the city.

Michael J. McTighe
Gettysburg College

Cristy, Rev. A. B., *Cleveland Congregationalists, 1895* (1896).

The **CONNECTICUT LAND COMPANY** (1795–1809) was authorized by the state of Connecticut to purchase and resell a majority of the WESTERN RESERVE, the area of northeast Ohio that Connecticut had reserved for her citizens in 1786, in exchange for ceding all western land claims to the U.S. government. The Western Reserve comprised all land south of Lake Erie to 41' latitude and within 120 mi. of Pennsylvania's western border. The Connecticut Land Co. received title to all Reserve land except for the Firelands, 500,000 acres on the extreme west that were reserved for Connecticut victims whose lands were burned by the British in the American Revolution, and a previously sold salt tract in the Mahoning Valley. On 14 Oct. 1795, a citizens' committee formed by Connecticut's general assembly reported that the company, a syndicate of 35 purchasing groups representing 58 individuals, had agreed to purchase all remaining Reserve lands for $1.2 million on 2 Sept. 1795. The sale was on credit; each purchasing group issued personal securities, some of which were later converted into mortgages on the purchased land. The proceeds of the sale formed the Connecticut School Fund. The company adopted articles of association on 5 Sept. 1795. Each purchasing group received a number of shares equal to the amount of money invested. Company proprietors were joined in a deed of trust to 3 trustees, John Caldwell, Jonathan Brace, and John Morgan; the trustees' deeds are the original title source to most property in the Reserve. Under the Articles of Association, 7 directors were appointed to settle Indian claims to Reserve lands, survey the land into townships, sell the land, and establish settlements, and were given extensive authority to run the company. The first directors included MOSES CLEAVELAND, who was also the company's general agent, Samuel Mather, Jr., Samuel Johnson, Roger Newberry, Henry Champion, and Ephraim Kirby. Augustus Porter was appointed chief engineer. Moses Cleaveland led the first company survey party to the Reserve in 1796 and negotiated a treaty with the Iroquois whereby the tribe gave up claim to all land east of the CUYAHOGA RIVER. Cleaveland also founded the settlement of Cleveland on this trip. The surveys of the Reserve took the company several years to complete, but Cleaveland returned to Connecticut later that year and never returned to Ohio.

Settlers were slow to purchase Reserve lands. The company had not made provisions for education within the Reserve, and other land was more conveniently available in western New York. Other states also claimed the territory; the title to the land and the right to govern it were disputed. In 1800, a congressional committee led by John Marshall reported, "As the purchasers of the land commonly called the Connecticut Reserve hold their title under the state of Connecticut, they cannot submit to the government established by the United States in the Northwest Territory and the jurisdiction of Connecticut could not be extended over them without much inconvenience." Settlers ignored the authority of the governor of the Northwest Territory, while Connecticut refused company pleas that the state exercise the authority, and territorial rights ceded in 1786. On 28 Apr. 1800, Pres. Adams signed the "Quieting Act," in which the U.S. gave Connecticut claim to the Reserve so that the company's land titles would be quieted and guaranteed. The bill assumed that Connecticut would then grant the U.S. jurisdiction over the Reserve; that was accomplished on 10 July 1800, when the Western Reserve became Trumbull County, a part of the Northwest Territory. The company divided its lands in drafts in 1796, 1802, 1807, and 1809. In each draft, some townships were subdivided and sold to benefit the entire company, while others were divided among company proprietors themselves. The three trustees were responsible for making the property deeds. During the early years, slow land sales forced the company to offer settlers moderate rates, free bonus land for running grist- and sawmills, and other incentives. Because of company mismanagement, not many of the original proprietors made profits. Many proprietors had not moved to the Reserve; the company never opened a sales office in Cleveland or anywhere else in the Reserve. The 1809 annual report on the Connecticut School Fund showed that a large amount of interest on the company's debt was unpaid and that the collateral of the original debt was not safe; the debtors also were scattered in different states. The company was dissolved with the last draft on 5 Jan. 1809, when all remaining land was divided among the proprietors.

Connecticut Land Co. and Accompanying Papers, WRHS.

**CONRAIL** (the Consolidated Rail Corporation) was by the mid-1980s the major railroad system serving Greater Cleveland. A combination of railroads that had been prominent throughout Cleveland's history, it saved from abandonment approximately 900 of a total of 1,528 mi. of railroad right-of-way in Ohio. In Cleveland, ConRail combined the operations of the Penn-Central and Erie-Lackawanna railroads with tracks between Cleveland and Chicago, Buffalo, Cincinnati via Columbus, and Pittsburgh via Youngstown.

ConRail was established by Congress in 1975 to reorganize and consolidate 5 of 7 bankrupt northeastern railroads. Designed as a 10-year federal government experiment, ConRail was technically a private, for-profit corporation operating under a board of directors dominated by government appointees until it had repaid most of its debts, after which time ownership was to be returned to private interests. The Penn Central was the most substantial of the railroads serving Cleveland. The New York Central and the Pennsylvania were the nation's 2 largest trunklines, extending from the Atlantic to the western gateways. On both lines, Cleveland proved to be a strategically located terminal along the "lifeline of national welfare." The merger of the 2 financially troubled railroads in 1968 to form the Penn Central Transportation Co. created the world's largest privately owned transportation company. The merger, however, was marred by the fact that both railroads had poor records of equipment and labor utilization, histories of shipper complaints, and increasing signs of poor management that could not be cured by the merger. The Penn Central's fall into bankruptcy in 1970 demonstrated that nothing short of complete regulation or nationalization could save the railroads from their own mistakes and was one factor directly responsible for the creation of ConRail. When the Penn Central collapsed, the Cuyahoga County auditor figured the debt owed to Cleveland and surrounding suburbs in excess of $32 million, most of which was payable to various school systems. Following a federal court decision allowing Penn Central to pay a percentage of the debt owed, Penn Central officials offered to pay 50% of its back property taxes. Penn Central owned 2 yards in Cleveland, the COLLINWOOD YARDS and one at E. 82nd and Kinsman Rd. Disapproval by Cleveland city officials prompted Penn Central to increase the offer to 60%, or approximately $18 million.

New York Central operations in Cleveland date back to 1836, when financial backing was secured for the construction of a rail line from Cleveland to Cincinnati via Columbus and Wilmington. The line was chartered on 14 Mar. as the Cleveland, Columbus & Cincinnati Railroad. The financial panic of 1837 shelved all plans for construction, and not until 1845 were commercial interests sufficiently revived to consider the railroad as a financially feasible means of freight and passenger service. In 1845, the original charter was amended to include building the line as far as Columbus, a more central location for easier connections with other rail lines. A $200,000 line of credit from the city and an additional $65,000 from private sources enabled actual construction to begin in 1847. Ground was broken at a point in the meadows just north of Walworth Run known as "Cleveland's FLATS." The railroad was built from St. Clair to Superior and parallel to River St. In 1849, the first train in Cleveland pulled wooden flatcars into the city along River (W. 11th) St. at the speed of 6 mph. In Nov. 1849, city council passed the first ordinance regulating train speeds down to the safe rate of 4–5 mph.

Beginning in 1862, the CCC bought a number of rail lines, which by 1882 gave the system a through line between Cleveland, Columbus, Cincinnati, Indianapolis, and St. Louis. In 1889 the Cleveland, Columbus, Cincinnati & Indianapolis, known as the "Bee Line," merged with the Indianapolis & St. Louis and the Cincinnati, Indianapolis, St. Louis & Chicago, the original "Big 4" railroad, to create the Cleveland, Cincinnati, Chicago & St. Louis Railroad. The "Big 4," which had its headquarters in Cincinnati, lost its identity in July 1929 when the ICC authorized the NYC, owner of stock in the "Big 4," to acquire control under a 99-year lease as part of the NYC's unification plan. Cleveland operations benefited from the acquisition. In 1929, a

new $100,000 passenger depot and switchyards were constructed at Grand Ave. near LINNDALE along with improvements at the Collinwood Yards. In 1931, the "Big 4" moved their accounting offices from Cincinnati, centralizing their base operations in Cleveland and New York. An additional track was then added to parallel the 2 tracks already running from BEREA to the Union Terminal. At its height, the "Big 4" operated 2,629 mi. of track.

The Lake Shore & Michigan Southern Railroad was the NYC's western territory connection. Incorporated in 1869, this strategic trunkline was a union of disjointed roads into 1 line that depended upon through traffic for business. The Lake Shore Line was a great factor in Cleveland's growth. The New York Central Bldg., a 5-story structure originally constructed in 1883 for the Lake Shore Line, was one of the largest and most imposing buildings in downtown Cleveland before the city began to expand east of PUBLIC SQUARE. The Cleveland-to-Toledo development of the Lake Shore Line began in 1846 when the state chartered the Junction Railroad Co. to build from a point on the Cleveland, Columbus & Cincinnati. In 1850, the Toledo, Norwalk & Cleveland Railroad was incorporated to build a narrow gauge line from Toledo eastward to Grafton, passing through Norwalk and connecting with the CCC line at Wellington. In 1852, the Port Clinton Railroad Co. was chartered to extend to Toledo. The merger of these 3 lines in 1853 produced the Cleveland & Toledo Railroad Co. and completed the development of the Lake Shore Line from Buffalo to Erie and from Cleveland to Chicago.

The Cleveland, Painesville & Ashtabula Railroad, chartered in 1848, brought to the Lake Shore Line the Cleveland-Erie connection. The CP&A was built on a road eastward from Cleveland through Painesville and Ashtabula to the state line. This line was the first step in forging a connecting link in a Buffalo-Chicago through route. Construction began in 1850, and although the city of Cleveland had pledged a $100,000 credit line, financing still proved to be difficult. The line was built using T-rail. Passenger coaches were an unprecedented 56 ft. in length, with 8 wheels and brakes. Freight cars were 25 ft. in length, supplied with brakes. Traffic on the line was handled by 6 30-ton wood-burning engines with 6 foot drivers, 2 of which were built in OHIO CITY by the CUYAHOGA STEAM FURNACE CO. In 1852, a CP&A train traveled the entire length from Cleveland to the state line. In 1854, the CP&A endeavored to complete its connection across northwest Pennsylvania through Erie with the NYC. Granted authority by the Pennsylvania legislature, provided it subscribe to $500,000 shares of stock in the Sunbury & Erie Co., the CP&A established a through link between New York and Cincinnati via Buffalo and Cleveland. In 1867, the CP&A leased the Cleveland & Toledo Co. The CP&A then proceeded to merge with the Lake Shore Line in 1868. In 1869, the Lake Shore Line united with the Michigan Southern & Northern Indiana Railroad to form the Lake Shore & Michigan Southern. Absorption of the Buffalo & Erie later that year brought 1,013 mi. of track into 1 massive system. In 1873, the LS&MS merged with the NYC.

Both the NYC and the Pennsylvania owned substantial real-estate interests in Cleveland. In 1914, a tentative agreement was reached whereby the city of Cleveland conveyed its rights in the "Bath St." tract located between W. 9th St. and the CUYAHOGA RIVER to the railroads in exchange for an equivalent amount of acreage of submerged and filled land east of E. 9th St. The railroads were also to purchase from the city a site for a depot at a cost of $1 million. Although the provisions were never fully executed, both railroads claimed street rights along the lakefront for many years. The NYC was heavily involved in the development of the Van Sweringens' Terminal Tower complex. Heavily involved in the development of SHAKER HTS., the Van Sweringens bought control of the Nickel Plate Railroad from the NYC in order to get the right-of-way for a rapid-transit line to downtown Cleveland. Taking advantage of the Nickel Plate's high-level crossing of the Cuyahoga Valley, the Van Sweringens built their Union Terminal complex on 4 acres of land purchased on Public Square. Before completion of the terminal, the NYC used the old UNION DEPOT on the lakefront at W. 9th St. In 1921, the NYC joined its subsidiary, the "Big 4," and the Nickel Plate to form the Cleveland Union Terminal Co., one of 3 companies that owned the terminal complex. It turned out to be an expensive venture for the NYC, as bonds from this venture were still outstanding even after the last passenger train had departed from the terminal in 1971.

Operations of the Pennsylvania Railroad in Cleveland date back to 1836, when the Cleveland & Pittsburgh was chartered in response to local interest to build a rail line from Cleveland to Pittsburgh. Originally known as the Cleveland, Warren & Pittsburgh, the first charter was set aside until 1845, when interest in building a rail line from Cleveland to the Pennsylvania state line was revived. Lack of funding delayed construction in Cleveland and forced the city council at a public hearing in 1847 to ask for construction support. In 1848, an election provided financial support in the form of a $100,000 stock subscription. Toward the end of 1850, the line had extended to New Philadelphia. By 1852 the Pittsburgh connections had been laid, with the first trains covering the 98.5 mi. to Pittsburgh and Wheeling. In 1853, the Pennsylvania legislature incorporated the C&P line in order to connect it with the Ohio company.

In 1851, the C&P was granted the charter of the Cleveland, Mt. Vernon & Delaware, formerly the Cleveland, Akron & Columbus Railway Co., in order to construct a line from Hudson, Cuyahoga Falls, and Akron to connect with a road located between Massillon and Wooster. In 1852 the company's Akron branch was organized, and a road was built from Hudson south to Millersburg. In 1853 the line became known as the Cleveland, Zanesville & Cincinnati. Falling upon hard times, the line entered receivership from 1861–64 and in 1865 was transferred to the Pittsburgh, Ft. Wayne & Chicago, a line that came under the control of the Pennsylvania in 1869. The Pittsburgh, Mt. Vernon, Columbus & London Railroad purchased the CZ&C from the Pennsylvania in 1869. The new line created that year, the Cleveland, Mt. Vernon & Delaware Railroad Co., completed its line from Hudson to Columbus on the C&P line. In 1881, the line went into default and was sold at a foreclosure sale to the Cleveland, Akron & Columbus Railroad Co. In 1882 the courts set aside the sale and appointed a receiver, who sold the road to the Cleveland, Akron & Columbus Railway Co., and by 1899 the Pennsylvania had purchased a majority of its capital stock. In 1856, a C&P train became the first train to burn coal as a fuel as it departed Cleveland. It traveled 101 mi. in 11 hours, 25 minutes, using 9,798 lbs. of coal. Operators, convinced of the advantages, soon abandoned wood as a fuel. In 1871, the C&P was leased for 99 years to the Pennsylvania Railroad. It provided a valuable western connection for both the Pennsylvania and Cleveland. At its height in 1908, the line operated 256 mi. and carried over 1.8 million passengers from the Euclid and E. 55th St. station. The *Steeler*, the first post-World War II passenger train to operate out of Cleveland, reduced travel time to Pittsburgh by over 30 minutes.

Like its rival the NYC, the Pennsylvania grew through mergers and absorptions into one of the largest rail systems in the country. By the 1920s, it was one of 7 trunk lines that gave Cleveland a reputation of having one of the best transportation systems in the country. At its height, the Pennsylvania Railroad operated over 66 trains a day through Cleveland. It owned a substantial amount of property in the Cleveland area, including the Union Depot on the lakefront and 11 acres from E. 9th St. to E. 14th St. along Lakeside Ave., and passenger stations located at Euclid and East 55th St., Davenport Ave., Harvard Ave., Woodland Ave., and Wason St. A 1955 management reorganization changed company operations from a 3-region and 18-division system to one of 9 regions, with Cleveland becoming headquarters for the Lake Region. In 1959, the Pennsylvania eliminated Cleveland service on several commuter routes. The Dan Hanna Special, named for the man who persuaded Pennsylvania officials to run a train for him from his home in Ravenna, abandoned shuttle runs from Alliance. The *Clevelander*, running from New York, was the last Pennsylvania passenger train running in and out of Cleveland able to carry those passengers. In 1964 the Pennsylvania cut the Cleveland-to-Pittsburgh run, ending service at Youngstown. In 1965 the PUCO allowed the Pennsylvania to end passenger service to Youngstown, Bedford, Macedonia, Hudson, and Ravenna, after which the Pennsylvania closed its main station at Euclid and E. 55th St.

The other major component of the ConRail network in Cleveland is made up of the Erie-Lackawanna. The Erie Railroad was chartered in 1832–33, and began operations in 1841. Originally called the New York & Erie Railroad Co., the line was formed in an effort to build a line connecting the Hudson River to Lake Erie. The history of the Erie is one of its regularly being the target of 19th-century "robber barons" and numerous falls into receivership. Chartered in 1848, the Cleveland & Mahoning Valley Railroad encountered early financial problems that postponed construction until 1853. By 1857, the C&MV reached from Cleveland to Youngstown via Warren, opening the Mahoning Valley coal fields to Cleveland and other lake ports and dealing a blow to canal commerce. The C&MV was leased by the Atlantic & Great Western Railroad in 1863 and was purchased by the Erie in 1938. When the Erie fell into receivership in 1862, the old NY&E disappeared under foreclosure, and the Erie Railway Co. took its place. In 1865, Erie built a passenger station in Cleveland on Scranton Rd. In 1881, a passenger station in the Flats was opened at what became the east end of the DETROIT-SUPERIOR BRIDGE on land owned by the "Big 4" railroad. The station, whose second floor had been sheared off to make way for a viaduct to bring trains directly into the tower complex, remained open until 1949, when Erie moved into the Terminal Tower.

Completion of the broad-gauge Atlantic & Great Western Railroad into Cleveland in 1863 provided a new route to the east and increased the movement of oil from the northern Pennsylvania fields. With the realization that Chicago was needed as a western terminal, the Erie in 1874 sought unsuccessfully to acquire by lease the unprofitable but valuable A&GW. Soon after, the A&GW entered receivership and was reorganized as the New York, Pennsylvania & Ohio Railroad, its headquarters being moved from Erie to Cleveland. In 1883, the Erie leased the NYP&O, acquiring its capital stock in 1896. In 1941, the entire property was conveyed to the Erie. In 1927, the Van Sweringen brothers began buying into the Erie through the Chesapeake & Ohio Railroad, and by 1929 they owned 55% of the controlling stock. They installed their own man as president and moved the corporate headquarters to Cleveland.

Encountering financial difficulties and unable to negotiate a substantial loan, the Van Sweringens saw their financial empire collapse and were forced to turn to the U.S. district courts for protection. The resultant reorganization broke up the railroad empire into its component roads. In 1948, the Erie dedicated a new Lee-Heights suburban passenger station near Lee and Miles roads. In 1949, using tracks rented from the NYC, the Erie moved into the Terminal Tower and began laying new track between E. 27th St. and the E. 55th St. yards. Another of its financial declines led the Erie into becoming a subsidiary of Dereco, a company that also owned all the stock of the Delaware & Hudson through its parent company, the Norfolk & Western Railway system. Dereco formally adopted the Erie by merging it in 1960 with the Delaware, Lackawanna & Western Railroad, creating the Erie-Lackawanna, and Cleveland replacing New York as the principal place of business.

The E-L operated the last commuter train in Cleveland. By 1972, intercity trains had stopped using the Terminal Tower. In June the E-L went bankrupt, with part of its operations absorbed by ConRail, which allowed commuter trains to continue operating with a federal subsidy. However, in 1976, when the Youngstown-to-Cleveland run failed to show a profit and both the state of Ohio and ConRail declined to subsidize it further, the E-L discontinued the service. The E-L had provided strong competition for the newly mergered Penn Central Railroads. It was no small effort on the E-L's part that it survived almost intact through the 1960s. When the Penn Central principals discussed merger, the N&W stood as its strongest competitor. The E-L, however, did not figure in either system's future merger plan. It was only by court order that the bankrupt E-L properties were included both as a part of ConRail and as part of N&W's merger plans for a northeast empire.

The **CONSUMERS LEAGUE OF OHIO**, a prominent reform organization with its headquarters in Cleveland, has played a major role as a means for women, who had been excluded from political activity, to influence society, especially in the areas of workers' welfare and feminist reform. The league, affiliated with the Natl. Consumers League, was founded in 1900 in Cleveland by a small group of prominent women who were members of a literary society, the Book & Thimble Club. The league's initial purpose was to further the welfare of workers who produced or sold consumer goods. It distributed "white lists," which named stores or companies whose workers were adults, were paid fair wages, and worked in good working conditions, thereby encouraging patronage of these businesses while advocating a boycott of those that did not meet these standards. The league's two most prominent members were MYRTA JONES, who served as president from 1908-23, and ELIZABETH MAGEE, who was the its executive secretary from 1925-65.

In later years, the league grew stronger and expanded its goals and activities. In 1909 it began to endorse and campaign for labor legislation that mandated better working conditions and wages. What began as a local movement later became statewide, as the league, along with the Ohio State Fed. of Labor, began lobbying for state labor legislation. In 1917 the Consumers' League of Ohio served as the Committee on Women & Children in Industry for the state and the U.S. Council of Natl. Defense; the league's president, Myrta Jones, chaired the committee. Under the direction of Jones, the league was able to push through a program of state legislation that regulated working conditions for women.

During the 1920s, the league met with little success in securing legislative reforms despite extensive campaigning

for issues such as a minimum-wage law for women, stricter control of child-labor, and a federal child-labor amendment. Nevertheless, the league continued to grow in terms of membership and support. It added men to its ranks in 1921. In 1925 the league's new executive secretary, Elizabeth Magee, began developing a close relationship with the labor movement and labor leaders in state and federal government. In 1928 she began a study of unemployment compensation, developing and securing the implementation of a statewide program that served as a model for many other states. The Ohio Plan stressed larger benefits and more secure funding as part of unemployment insurance. In 1933 it was instrumental in the passage of a minimum-wage law for women and the Ohio ratification of the federal child-labor amendment. In 1937 it conducted a successful campaign for a shorter work week for women.

As more women entered the workforce during WORLD WAR II, the league saw that laws were enforced to prevent child labor, regulate working hours, and provide daycare centers for the children of working mothers. After the war, the league worked to improve the status of Ohio's migrant workers and worked with the NAACP to secure an Ohio law for fair employment practices. The league has continued its support of social-welfare issues. It has sponsored women in workers' education programs in women's colleges, fought against sexual discrimination, and sought to establish daycare centers and maternity leave.

Consumers' League of Ohio Records, WRHS.

Harrison, Dennis I., "The Consumers' League of Ohio Women and Reform, 1909-1937" (Ph.D. diss., CWRU, 1978).

The **CONTEMPORARY ART CENTER OF CLEVELAND** is located at 11427 Bellflower Rd. in UNIVERSITY CIRCLE. It was originally established in 1968 as the New Gallery of Contemporary Art, and was located on Euclid Ave. It functioned originally as a private art gallery and became a nonprofit institution in Oct. 1974. The purposes of the gallery are 1) to bring to Cleveland the works of new and innovative contemporary artists who are recognized nationally and internationally but are not being shown in other Cleveland galleries; 2) to introduce recent trends and innovations in contemporary art to the community; 3) to give support and recognition to both emerging and established Ohio artists; 4) to educate adults and area schoolchildren regarding contemporary art; and 5) to sponsor or participate in regional arts events and to cooperate with other art organizations. The decision to change the name of the gallery from the New Gallery of Contemporary Art to the Contemporary Art Ctr. of Cleveland was made in 1984 so that the name would better reflect the programs and activities of the organization. The gallery presents approximately 10 exhibitions annually and has hosted over 280 exhibitions since its inception. It also presents a fall lecture series and art education programs and publishes exhibition catalogs. In the past the gallery has shown the works of such internationally famous artists as Christo, Robt. Rauschenberg, and David Hockney. It has also presented the works of several Ohio artists, among them Patrick Kelly, Paul Oberst, Gene Kangas, and Heide Fasnacht.

**CONTINENTAL, A DIVISION OF DOLLAR SAVINGS BANK**, began operation as a savings association in 1892, serving the German population; 90 years later it had more than $1 billion in assets and was the 98th-largest savings and loan in the U.S. Continental was first organized as the South Side German Bldg. & Loan Assoc. on 18 Jan. 1892. The first elected officers were Phil Voelke, president; Christ Behlke, vice-president; John Zervis, secretary; and Chas.

Kuenzer, treasurer. The association met weekly in temporary quarters at the corner of Clark Ave. and W. 25th St. until 1910, when it built its own offices at 3115 W. 25th St. In 1920, with assets totaling $1.5 million, the building and loan association dropped its German identification and became the South Side Savings & Loan Assoc. When it received its federal charter on 20 Apr. 1938, it became South Side Federal Savings & Loan. By 1955, South Side Federal's assets were more than $50 million; when it purchased Heights Savings & Loan in 1956, it increased its assets to $75 million, and it saw them surpass $100 million in 1958. South Side Federal became Cleveland Federal Savings & Loan in 1961 and moved into new offices at 614 Euclid Ave. in Sept. 1962. Five years later its assets were more than $200 million; by 1974, they were $430 million. In Dec. 1979, Cleveland Federal merged with Citizens Savings & Loan of Painesville. Cleveland Federal became the Continental Federal Savings & Loan Assoc. on 1 Mar. 1980, at the beginning of a difficult period for the company. Between 1980 and the end of 1983, Continental Federal lost $61 million. With assets of $1.05 billion at the end of 1983, it had a negative net worth of $16.1 million. In 1984 Continental merged with the Dollar Savings Bank of Pittsburgh.

The **CONVENTION AND VISITORS BUREAU OF GREATER CLEVELAND, INC.**, an independent organization responsible for the marketing and promotion of Greater Cleveland, grew out of the Cleveland Chamber of Commerce. The bureau was organized in Feb. 1934 from the Convention Board of the Cleveland Chamber of Commerce, which had been formed in the early 1920s. Its first president was F. J. Andre. A. J. Kennedy managed the bureau until July 1935, when Mark Egan became executive secretary and manager. Dale Finley was president in 1985. The bureau's principal job has been to promote Cleveland through national and regional programs directed at attracting visitors and conventions to the Greater Cleveland area. Its membership consists of small businesses and major corporations, and its board of directors includes many prominent citizens of the city. During the 1920s, the Convention Board was instrumental in the development of Cleveland's Convention Ctr. When the PUBLIC AUDITORIUM was built in 1922, it was one of the first and largest meeting/exhibit facilities in the U.S. By 1928, with the addition of the Music Hall, the building complex became one of the 3 largest facilities in the country outside of New York and Chicago. The Cleveland Convention Ctr. grew again in 1963 with the addition of the underground exhibit facililty. In 1984, 208 conventions were hosted in the area, with 103,755 delegates spending an average of $370 each per 3-day stay. The bureau also booked 100 meetings for future years, estimated to generate $22,940,000 worth of income for the area. In 1985, the bureau was conducting a "Cleveland's Got It" community awareness campaign to enlighten Clevelanders about area assets.

**COOK UNITED, INC.**, has been involved in various retail and wholesale fields and was, at one time, one of the country's leading home-service-route, supermarket, and discount department store chains. Max Freeman and Hyman C. Broder started the firm on St. Clair Ave. as the Cook Coffee Co. in 1921 and incorporated it 4 years later. For its first 30 years, Cook grew by operating retail truck routes that sold coffee, tea, and other grocery and household items in 15 states. By the early 1950s, it began to expand. It first issued public stock in 1950, and the following year, the company entered the supermarket field by acquiring the local 10-store Pick-n-Pay Supermarket chain (see FIRST NATL. SUPERMARKETS, INC.). Its retail food business was strengthened in 1959 when Pick-n-Pay purchased the 24-store Foodtown chain. Cook then moved its headquarters from its Chester Ave. plant to Foodtown's offices at 16501 Rockside Rd., MAPLE HTS.

In 1961, Cook moved into another retail business when it acquired 5 Uncle Bill's Discount Dept. Stores, which had been founded in Brooklyn by a pioneer in that field, Sidney Axelrod, in 1956. Over the next several years, Cook acquired 3 other discount department store chains in the Midwest and East and added retail drugstores in 1967. It also acquired several food-manufacturing firms to supply its supermarkets and provide institutional food service. It entered the wholesale hardware business by acquiring several Midwest firms in the late 1960s and early 1970s. To reflect this diversified $360 million firm, with over 70 supermarkets, 90 discount department stores, and 40 home-service routes, its name was changed to Cook United, Inc., in 1969.

However, the random growth and indiscriminate expansion that typified the discount industry during the boom years of the 1960s brought trouble to Cook in the 1970s. The company's far-flung, diversified operations and weak market position became unmanageable. The first to be affected was its food industries. Unable to rejuvenate the ailing Pick-n-Pay chain, Cook sold it in 1972. The following year, the firm divested itself of its original home-service-route business. By 1974, Cook was close to bankruptcy, with a $22 million operating loss. A bitter proxy fight left Martin M. Lewis in charge. He quickly closed numerous stores and decreased inventory. By 1976, Cook was completely out of the retail food and drug business. The smaller firm, with 7,000 employees, showed a profit. Despite consolidation of its operations, Cook continued to be besieged by financial problems. After acquiring the 47-store Rink's Discount Dept. Store chain from GRAY DRUGSTORES, INC., in 1981, Cook decided to concentrate its resources on its discount department store business. By 1984, the firm had divested itself of all wholesale operations, and a $26 million operating loss in 1983 resulted in retail closings. Later in the year Cook went into Chapter 11 of the federal bankruptcy code, giving it a chance to reorganize without pressures from its creditors.

**COOLEY, HARRIS REID** (18 Oct. 1857–24 Oct. 1936), was a minister and leader of reform movements in Cleveland during the Progressive Era. Cooley was born in Royalton, Ohio, to Rev. LATHROP COOLEY of the DISCIPLES OF CHRIST CHURCH and Laura Reid Cooley. He attended Hiram College, where he received his ministerial training, graduating with a B.A. in 1877. Three years later he received his M.A. from Oberlin College. Following postgraduate work at Oberlin, he served 1-year pastorates in Disciples churches in Brunswick and Aurora, Ohio. In 1882, Cooley became pastor of the Cedar Ave. Christian Church in Cleveland, a position that he retained for 21 years. He drew a large congregation to his church, among whom was TOM L. JOHNSON. Johnson and Cooley became close friends, their relationship bonded by Cooley's support of Johnson when the latter was ill with typhoid fever, and their shared ideals in the areas of politics and reform. Cooley was almost alone among the city's Protestant clergy in his support of Johnson's radical democracy. When Johnson was elected mayor in 1901, one of his first acts was to appoint Cooley director of charities and correction. Cooley retained this position for 10 years, continuing as director into the administration of NEWTON D. BAKER. Cooley's major action as director was the creation of a farm colony on 2,000 acres purchased in WARRENSVILLE TWP. to house the CLEVELAND WORKHOUSE, the county poorhouse, and a tuberculosis sanatorium. Acquired in 1902 at a cost of $350,000, the "Cooley Farms" came to be considered an outstanding example of progressive penology and health care. In 1903, Cooley supervised the opening of the City Farm School in Hudson, Ohio. Popularly known as the CLEVELAND BOYS' SCHOOL, this farm provided a rehabilitative setting where orphaned or incorrigible boys under 14 could be guided by a professional staff. The only city clergyman to enter actively into politics during the Progressive Era, Cooley also served on the City Plan Commission beginning in 1915. He held this position until dismissed by Mayor HARRY L. DAVIS in 1934. He was also active in the construction of City Hospital and the Girl's Home. In 1900, Cooley married Cora Clark, a Hiram College professor and suffragette. He died in Cleveland at the age of 79.

**COOLEY, LATHROP** (25 Oct. 1821–2 Jan. 1910), was a Disciples of Christ minister in the city of Cleveland and northeast Ohio, where he served many churches. Cooley was born in Genese County, N.Y., to a farm family that moved to Portage and then to Lorain County, Ohio. His rural primary education was followed by attendance at the Brooklyn Academy. He finished his studies in Bethany, W.Va. Although he taught school at the beginning of his career, Cooley was also attracted to the ministry and began preaching in 1843 at N. Eaton in Lorain County. Except for a year in Chicago, he was an active minister for 60 years in the WESTERN RESERVE. He was both a missionary and a resident pastor in Cleveland, Akron, Painesville, and N. Royalton. Cooley was interested in business. He made sound real-estate investments, was a director of the Citizens Savings & Trust Co., and was involved in other Cleveland businesses. His interest in education led to a 30-year tenure as a benefactor and trustee of Hiram College. Becoming a prominent and influential citizen, Cooley used his eloquence and forceful personality to support ventures he considered important for Cleveland's public good. He preached in the workhouse, the city jail, and the Aged Women's Home. In 1880, he was appointed superintendent and chaplain of the Cleveland Bethel Union, a reorganized seamen's mission that eventually sheltered women, offered an outdoor work-relief program, and conducted missionary services. In 1877, Cooley founded the Disciples Mission, which in 1883 became the Cedar Ave. Church of Christ, the church attended by TOM L. JOHNSON. His business investments led to a last will and testament containing a legacy for the establishment of what became HURON RD. HOSPITAL. Cooley was responsible for financing a chain of Disciples of Christ missions around the world. He was twice married; his first wife, Laura Reid, died in 1893. In 1895 he married Letta E. Searles.

**COPPER, MUNROE W., JR.** (1897–12 Nov. 1985), was a prolific designer of traditional ARCHITECTURE in Cleveland from 1921–85. He was born in Philadelphia to Munroe and Priscilla Van Tin Copper. He earned scholarships to the Philadelphia School of Industrial Art and the Philadelphia School of Art. He attended the University of Pennsylvania and graduated in 1920 after serving in the Navy during WORLD WAR I. In 1921 Copper came to Cleveland and was employed by the firm of Walker & Weeks. He worked on the design of the Federal Reserve Bank. He began his own office in partnership with Donald Dunn in 1924. Later he worked with his son, Munroe W. Copper III.

Copper became known for his adaptation of Pennsylvania Colonial domestic architecture, incorporating shallow gabled or hipped roofs and fieldstone walls. He also worked in the Georgian, English, and French styles and designed more than 2,000 homes, of which over 100 were in SHAKER HTS. He planned homes for such Ohio families as Bolton, Harvey Firestone, and Hoover. He also designed 59 churches, as well as office buildings, restaurants, hospitals, and condominiums. His principal later works included St. Peter's Episcopal Church, Ashtabula (1964); First Presbyterian Church, Mansfield (1965); Lake Ridge Academy, N. Ridgeville (1968); and the Bonne Bell offices and laboratory, LAKEWOOD (1969). Copper built his own home in GATES MILLS in 1931. He was elected to the village council of Gates Mills and was appointed chairman of the zoning and planning board in 1946. He was an enthusiastic horseman, woodcarver, restorer of antiques, and watercolorist. Copper married Marguerite Letts in 1921. Their children were Mrs. Marguerite Wright, Mrs. Lois MacAllister, Munroe III, and Craig.

**CORBUSIER, JOHN WILLIAM CRESWELL** (31 Oct. 1878–8 June 1928), was a national authority on church architecture who helped design the CHURCH OF THE COVENANT in UNIVERSITY CIRCLE and the CHURCH OF THE SAVIOUR in CLEVELAND HTS. Born in Rochester, N.Y., Corbusier was educated there and in Paris at L'Ecole des Beaux Arts. He moved to Cleveland in 1905 and practiced architecture under his own name, as well as in a partnership called Corbusier, Lenski & Foster. At the time of his death, Corbusier was the architect for at least 30 churches throughout the U.S. Two examples of his work were extant in Cleveland in 1984. They are the Church of the Saviour (1928) at 2537 Lee Rd. in Cleveland Hts., and the Church of the Covenant (1911) at 11205 Euclid Ave., a design in which he was associated with the national architectural firm of Cram, Goodhue & Ferguson. Corbusier, Lenski & Foster were the architects for the home of Salmon P. Halle, a prominent Cleveland department store owner, who built a grand French provincial villa on Park Rd. in SHAKER HTS. A resident of Hudson from 1913–28, Corbusier was an elder at the First Congregational Church of Hudson, a former director of the choir at the Church of the Covenant, and a member of the Chamber of Commerce and the Cleveland Athletic, Kiwanis, and Hudson clubs. He married Katherine Lyman (1881–1932) in 1905. Both are buried in Hudson, Ohio.

**CORLETT, WILLIAM THOMAS** (15 Apr. 1854–11 June 1948), was a Cleveland physician and dermatologist who introduced new methods for the treatment of skin and venereal diseases in a number of Cleveland-area hospitals. His notable contributions included original research on the effect of climate, particularly cold, on skin diseases. Corlett was born to William and Ann Avery Corlett on the family farm in Orange, Ohio. He attended the public schools in Orange, graduated from Chagrin Falls Academy in 1870, and attended Oberlin College from 1870–73. Enrolling in the Wooster University Medical College (College of Wooster), he graduated with the M.D. degree in 1877. Appointed demonstrator of anatomy at Wooster, Corlett resigned the position 2 years later, in 1879, in order to study abroad. He entered the London Hospital as surgical dresser in the medical department. Upon completion of his studies in London, he entered the Hospital St. Louis and Hotel Dieu in Paris. While in Europe, he specialized in diseases of the skin, and upon his return to London he qualified as a fellow in the Royal College of Physicians. Returning to Cleveland, Corlett established a general medical practice but soon began devoting his energies to his chosen specialty. In 1882, he was appointed lecturer on skin and genito-urinary diseases in the medical department at Wooster. He received appointment as professor in 1884, the first such in northeastern Ohio, but resigned to take a lecturership in the same branch at Western Reserve University Medical School. He was appointed professor of dermatology in 1887. Returning to Europe in 1889, Corlett visited medical centers in Vienna, Berlin, London, and Paris. In 1890, his title at WRU was changed to professor of dermatology and syphilology, a chair he held until 1914, when he was appointed senior professor. In 1924, he was appointed professor emeritus. In 1893, Corlett was appointed to the Charity Hospital medical staff; he was on the consulting staff of both ST. ALEXIS and City (Metropolitan General) hospitals from the time of their organization and was dermatologist at Lakeside Hospital. He was responsible for bringing the first x-ray machine to the area from Vienna. As a member of the Board of Health in 1893, Corlett fought for better lighting and ventilation in public schools, as well as instituting Health Board visits to the schools. Corlett married Amanda Marie Leisy at Rheinpflatz, Germany, on 28 June 1895.

**CORRIGAN, LAURA MAE** (1888–22 Jan. 1948), received widespread attention as an international socialite. She was the wife of Jas. W. Corrigan, a Cleveland steel magnate. Little is known of Corrigan's early life. She was born in Wisconsin, the daughter of a gardener. She married physician Duncan R. MacMartin in Chicago, later divorcing him. In 1917 she married Corrigan, the son of one of the founders of the Corrigan-McKinney Steel Co. The marriage received a good deal of publicity in Cleveland; as a wedding present, Corrigan gave his wife a $15,000 Rolls Royce. Possibly because of her earlier divorce, Laura Corrigan was never really accepted into Cleveland social circles. As a result, she and her husband—who previously had had something of a playboy image—spent much of their time in Europe. They soon became part of the international social set, moving to and from London and Paris. Corrigan's lavish parties received considerable attention in the society columns of newspapers in both Europe and the U.S. Among her frequent guests was the Prince of Wales, later King Edward VIII. She also became friends with the young Duchess of York, now Queen Elizabeth II. In 1925, Jas. Corrigan returned to Cleveland, where, in a well-publicized takeover, he regained control of Corrigan-McKinney Steel. He reestablished residency in Cleveland, while Laura, except for visits, remained in Europe. James died in 1928, leaving his wife an enormous fortune. The money remained in Cleveland banks; in 1938, 3 armored trucks and 20 armed guards were used to move her $21 million a few blocks from the Union Trust Co. to Natl. City Bank.

After her husband's death, Corrigan resided almost permanently in Europe. In Paris when WORLD WAR II broke out, she was forced to escape to England via Portugal. During the war she was widely recognized for her work on behalf of French soldiers and refugees; to aid the latter, she organized a group of French women known as La Bien Venue. Corrigan also extended aid to U.S. citizens who were unable to leave Europe for financial reasons. In Buckinghamshire, England, she ran the Wings Club, a popular place for Allied officers. Before the war, Corrigan received a yearly income of $800,000. During the war, the U.S. State Dept. allowed her only $500/month. In order to finance her wartime activities, she sold almost all of her jewelry, tapestries, and furniture. After the war, she received from the French government the Croix de Guerre, Legion of Honor, and Croix de Combattant, and from the British government the King's Medal. Corrigan had no children by either marriage.

**CORY UNITED METHODIST CHURCH,** one of the oldest black churches in Cleveland, grew from a small congregation of 15 members in 1875 to an important institutional church by the 1960s. Cory United Methodist Church was founded on 25 Mar. 1875 by Rev. Henry Steen (or Stein) of Cadiz, Ohio, at a meeting of 15 people in the home of Jas. Hankins at 38 Hackman (E. 36th) St. First known as Cory Chapel, the church was named in honor of Rev. J. B. Cory, a white Methodist missionary in the city. Services were held in several locations before the church moved into a rented building at Forest and Garden (E. 37th and Central) streets; the building was dedicated on 6 Nov. 1887, and in Oct. 1890 the congregation bought the property. The church had 109 members by 1892. The church was located at E. 37th and Central until Sept. 1911, when the congregation, under the leadership of Rev. Geo. Sissle, acquired a building at E. 35th and Scovill Ave. A fire in Feb. 1921 necessitated moving the services elsewhere until repairs were completed; by 1926, the rebuilt church had become too small for the growing congregation, and a campaign was begun to raise funds for a larger church. The Depression postponed the purchase of larger quarters until Sept. 1946, when, under the leadership of Rev. Dr. Oliver B. Quick, the congregation paid $125,000 for the Jewish Ctr. at 1117 E. 105th St. After spending another $35,000 on improvements and repairs, Cory United Methodist Church moved into its new quarters on 2 Mar. 1947. During Rev. Quick's tenure at Cory, church membership increased from a few hundred in the late 1930s to more than 3,000 members in 1952.

From its earliest years, the congregation at Cory had been interested in more than religious issues—the Ladies Church Aid & Literary Society sponsored lively debates on social issues in the 1880s—and with the purchase of the facilities of the Jewish Ctr., the church acquired the means by which it could become an important community and recreation center as well as a religious institution. By early 1949 it was operating a library, a gymnasium, a swimming pool, and a music school, and it had 3 choirs and a concert hall. In 1961, the city Div. of Recreation leased the church's recreational facilities for the Cory Recreation Ctr., which offered craft, dance, and music classes, and meeting and game rooms in addition to the pool and gymnasium. Also in 1961, the church began to sponsor boys' football teams as a way to "eliminate the temptation to get into trouble." The church offered its facilities for other purposes, as well, serving as a community meeting place and as a site for a Hunger Task Force Food Ctr. in the 1970s. Church membership was estimated at 1,400 in June 1975.

The **COSMOPOLITAN DEMOCRATIC LEAGUE OF CUYAHOGA COUNTY** is a political organization of elected officials that represents the interests of Greater Cleveland's ethnic groups within the Democratic party. The league was formed on 2 Nov. 1932 by Felix T. Matia, who was the director of public parks. Its first officers included Matia as president; Municipal Judge Geo. S. Tenesy, 1st vice-president; Associate County Prosecutor FRANK D. CELEBREZZE, 2d vice-president; Councilman Emil J. Crown, secretary; and State Representative John DeRighter, treasurer. Monthly meetings at the Hotel Statler brought together representatives of the area's Polish, Czech, Slovak, Hungarian, Italian, Slovene, Serbian, Ukrainian, Russian, Croatian, Rusin, Romanian, Greek, and German communities to discuss political issues and to endorse candidates at election time. Over the years the league's endorsements have gone to candidates active in the affairs of the ethnic community, and in primary elections the league often has differed with the CUYAHOGA COUNTY DEMOCRATIC PARTY in its endorsements.

The **COTILLION SOCIETY OF CLEVELAND**, a private social nonprofit organization, originated at a preliminary planning meeting at the home of Mr. and Mrs. Chas. W. Steadman in Jan. 1964. A second meeting held at the UNION CLUB established the society and selected a steering committee to plan bylaws, a scholarship fund, and membership policies. Twenty-eight charter members of the society held their first membership meeting on 9 Feb. 1964 at the MAYFIELD COUNTRY CLUB and elected a board of governors. The first officers included Chas. W. Steadman, chairman; Wm. Feather, Jr., 1st vice-chairman; Henry J. Nave, 2d vice-chairman; Keith S. Benson, secretary; and Robt. Berger, Jr., treasurer. The society filed incorporation papers 11 Feb. as a nonprofit organization. The first annual meeting of the Cotillion was held 11 Oct. 1964 at the Mayfield Country Club, when 83 new families became members and the charter was established stating the society's purposes: (1) "To establish, promote and operate a charitable foundation devoted to furthering the education of young people who otherwise would be unable to attend the college of their choice and (2) to provide wholesome supervised social activities for the young people whose parents are members in the Society." The first Cotillion Ball sponsored by the society was held on 3 Sept. 1964 at the COUNTRY CLUB as 25 girls, freshmen and sophomores in college, made their debut. Through the years, the tradition has continued; the dance subsequently was limited to debutantes who would be college freshmen in the fall. Each year a group from the Women's Committee reviews and ultimately selects the scholarship recipients—the funds coming from members' dues and sustaining fees. Over the past 20 years, the Cotillion Society of Cleveland has awarded scholarships worth over $275,000. In Nov. 1979, the Cotillion Society hosted the first Collegiate Dance to honor the sons of members in the organization. This dance and the Cotillion Ball have become traditional social events in Cleveland.

The **COUNCIL FOR ECONOMIC OPPORTUNITIES IN GREATER CLEVELAND**, 1350 W. 3rd St., was established in 1964 to develop, administer, and coordinate the local front in Pres. Lyndon Johnson's War on Poverty. Under the leadership of Ralph W. Findley until his retirement in 1979, the federally financed Cleveland CEO established a number of programs to provide various services to the area's needy. Created by national politicians to employ controversial measures to deal with difficult social problems, local councils such as the Cleveland CEO were embroiled in controversy from the beginning. Such councils were mandated by the 1964 Economic Opportunity Act and reported directly to the federal Office of Economic Opportunity, thus bypassing established state and local agencies. The act's call for the "maximum feasible participation" of the poor in the operation of antipoverty programs created early political difficulties for the CEO in Cleveland. Mayor Ralph Locher appointed the members of the CEO's board of trustees, and his first appointments aroused much criticism from representatives of the poor and civil-rights leaders, who succeeded in delaying federal funding for the local program until membership of the board was expanded and modified to satisfy federal administrators that the concerns of the poor would be heard. The community-action programs of the CEO also proved disturbing to some city councilmen, who complained that CEO employees were creating political problems for them by fostering demands for services among the poor.

The Cleveland CEO concentrated on providing increased opportunity and services for the area's poor. Its first $12 million federal grant went to support a Job Corps center for women, a job-training program for welfare recipients, a part-time jobs program for youths, and a community-action program. In Apr. 1966, the CEO dedicated Neighborhood Opportunity Ctrs. in Central, Kinsman, HOUGH, and GLENVILLE, and on the west side; these housed offices for legal-aid services, food-stamp registration, information services, maternal and infant care programs, the Cleveland Small Business Development Corp., and the Ohio State Employment Service. Prominent CEO programs included health services, such as the HOUGH-NORWOOD FAMILY HEALTH CARE CTR., job training for youths, and children's services, such as daycare centers, the preschool Head Start program, and nutrition programs. The CEO also funded Project HOPE (Housing Our People Economically, Inc.), programs for senior citizens, consumer education, the Foster Grandparents Program, and energy assistance and weatherization programs. The antipoverty program came under repeated political attacks at the national level as conservatives attempted to slash its funding or eliminate it altogether. In 1982 the Cleveland CEO's budget was cut from $12 million to $9 million, and funding of such local councils was altered, coming no longer directly from the federal government but in the form of earmarked funds channeled through state and local governments.

The **COUNCIL FOR HIGH BLOOD PRESSURE**, operating as a council of the AMERICAN HEART ASSOC. to encourage research into the causes of high blood pressure, was originally founded in Cleveland in 1945 as the Natl. Foundation for High Blood Pressure. The founders were Irvine Page, Geo. E. Merrifield, Frank E. Joseph, and Alva Bradley. The foundation was formed to stimulate interest in high-blood-pressure research, because there had been so little attention paid to it in the past. In 1947, the name was changed to the American Foundation for High Blood Pressure. Two years later it merged with the American Heart Assoc. to become its council on high-blood-pressure research. Since the merger, the council has been managed by the Heart Assoc.'s national office in Dallas. The council encourages research in hypertension, primarily through the awarding each year of the Stouffer Prize and an annual fall conference held in Cleveland. The Stouffer Prize was started in 1966 by the Vernon Stouffer Foundation for exceptional breakthroughs in research in blood pressure and hardening of the arteries. The prize is $50,000 and is conferred at the annual meeting; it is considered one of the most prestigious awards for research in the field of heart disease. The fall conference has annually attracted scientists from around the world; in 1973, 300 scientists from the U.S. and 16 other countries were in attendance at the 2-day symposium to discuss research. The council has also supported research locally, making Cleveland a leading center for high-blood-pressure research.

The **COUNTRY CLUB**, 2825 Lander Rd., PEPPER PIKE, one of Cleveland's most prestigious country clubs, provides a variety of recreational facilities, including golf, swimming, and tennis, for its members, their families, and guests. The club's origin dates from 1889, when a small, informal group of horseback riders, known as the Bit & Bridle Club, frequently rode from their mansions on Euclid Ave. out to open country along Lake Erie. They purchased a site near the intersection of Eddy Rd. and Lake Shore Blvd. in Glenville Twp. (now BRATENAHL) and originally planned to build a cabin-shelter clubhouse, but so many acquaintances wanted to join that the log cabin idea was abandoned and the Country Club was formed as "a club in the country for picnics and parties," with a membership limited to 100. The first officers included SAMUEL MATHER, president; JEPTHA H. WADE II, vice-president; Chas. C. Bolton, treasurer; and Jas. Parmalee, secretary. The chartered club dedicated the newly built clubhouse (1889) to "fun in the open air."

During the club's early years, Mather visited the St. Andrews Golf Club (Yonkers, N.Y.) and became enthusiastic about the game; on 23 Mar. 1895 he held an organizational meeting to form a Cleveland golf club. The club was organized, and the following officers were elected: Samuel Mather, president; Horace E. Andrews, vice-president; and Robt. H. Clark, secretary-treasurer. Subsequently a short 9-hole course was laid out near the lake adjacent to the Country Club. The Cleveland Golf Club formally opened on 13 July 1895 as a subsidiary of the Country Club but in 1898 was incorporated as a separate organization. The Clay home on Coit Rd. was rented as a clubhouse, and Joe Mitchell from Scotland was employed as the first professional. In 1902, the Cleveland Golf Club and the Country Club consolidated; the golfers gave up their Coit Rd. home, and golf became an integral part of the Country Club's activities. Fire had destroyed the Country Club's first clubhouse (1889-99) and a second in 1906. Subsequently, ABRAM GARFIELD, architect and club member, designed the club's third structure at 11405 Lake Shore Blvd. Opened in 1908, it was the scene of many of the club's social events through the years. The golf course was also extended to 18 holes.

In 1928, the club accepted an offer from O. P. AND M. J. VAN SWERINGEN to relocate on 200 acres of their Pepper Pike property. Financial arrangements were agreed upon; Depression reverses surmounted, and in 1929 ground was broken for the new clubhouse on Lander Rd. It was formally opened on 10 Aug. 1930. The first game was played on 16 Aug. 1930. In 1935, the Natl. Amateur Tournament was held at the Country Club, and Lawson Little made golfing history by completing his "little slam," winning both the British and American titles in 2 successive seasons. The Country Club completed purchase of the property in 1939-40. In the ensuing years, many additions have been made to meet the recreational needs of club members.

Arthur, Alan, *The Country Club . . . Its First 75 Years, 1889-1964* (1964).

The **COURT OF NISI PRIUS**, an invitational social club limited to a special membership of lawyers and judges that meets every week for companionship, began during the winter of 1899, when a group of young lawyers that had been gathering informally for fellowship was officially organized by 2 Cleveland lawyers, Homer H. McKeehan and John W. Hart. The first official meeting, held on 19 May 1900 in the Turkish Room of the Bismarck Hotel on Huron St., elected McKeehan as "judge," while Hart was designated "clerk of court." Other charter members included FREDERIC C. HOWE, Jas. J. Hogan, David M. Glascock, Benjamin A. Gage, John E. Morley, NEWTON D. BAKER, Frank S. Masten, John MacGregor, Jr., Thos. H. Hogsett, Wm. J. Starkweather, John A. Thompson, John H. Clarke, and Wm. C. Boyle.

The club's activities, including their Saturday meetings, are characterized by a spirit of mock solemnity in which the club is a "court," meetings are "sessions," and written notices are "writs," "pleas," "warrants," "judgments," "summonses," and "subpoenas"; the "judge" is "Mr. Justice," and members are "sergeants." For many years the club met at the HOLLENDEN HOTEL; they later transferred their headquarters to the Terminal Tower but subsequently returned to the Hollenden. On Election Day in November, the court "elects" a new "judge," and a new "clerk of courts" is appointed. The entertainment at the court's annual dinner, traditionally held in March, features satirical skits and comic sketches. These stunts, often based on song parodies and well-known operettas, are written and produced by club members and are designed to satirize and ridicule their colleagues, public officials, invited guests, and current events of universal interest. On 30 Jan. 1915, the first "Grand Order of the Double Cross" awards were presented to JEREMIAH J. SULLIVAN, David C. Westenhaver, Newton D. Baker, ROBT. J. BULKLEY, and JAS. R. GARFIELD. Although this honor is annually awarded to prominent citizens in jest, it contains an oblique reference to their contributions to the city of Cleveland. The court's humorous buffoonery has contributed to its goal of friendship and conviviality through the years.

**COVELESKI, STANLEY ANTHONY "STAN"** (13 July 1889-20 Mar. 1984), was a major-league baseball pitcher for the CLEVELAND INDIANS between 1916-24. His 3 victories in the 1920 World Series helped the team win its first world championship. Born in Shamokin, Pa., Coveleski was working in the coal mines at 12 years of age. He was one of 5 brothers who played baseball; his older brother Harry was a pitcher for Philadelphia and Detroit. In 1908, Coveleski signed to pitch for Lancaster, but he did not make the major leagues as a regular pitcher until 1916. Coveleski's best pitch was a spitball, which he could make break down or up. From 1917-21 he won 20 or more games a season, with 24 victories in the 1920 championship season his best mark. His 3 wins in the World Series were each 5-hit complete games. Traded to Washington in 1925, Coveleski won 20 games for the Senators and pitched in another World Series. He ended his major-league career in 1928 after pitching for the Yankees. Coveleski won 215 and lost 141 games during his 14-year career and posted a low 2.88 earned run average per 9 innings pitched. He was elected to the Baseball Hall of Fame at Cooperstown, N.Y., in 1969. He married Frances Chivetts in Jan. 1922.

The **COVENTRY VILLAGE BUSINESS DISTRICT** is situated on Coventry Rd. between Mayfield Rd. and Euclid Hts. Blvd. in CLEVELAND HTS. Coventry Rd. was originally built as a part of Patrick Calhoun's 1890s suburb of Euclid Hts. The Coventry business district was established and grew to serve the rapidly increasing populations of Euclid Hts. and the adjacent Mayfield Hts. (M. M. Brown) developments. The inauguration of streetcar service up Cedar Glen Hill and Euclid (Hts.) Blvd. to Hts. Circle (Edgehill) in 1897 and a later 1907 extension down Coventry and out Mayfield to Lee improved accessibility, thus furthering residential growth. After suffering a number of financial reversals, Calhoun went bankrupt in 1914. Many of the undeveloped Euclid Hts. lots were broken up and auctioned off in smaller parcels. Many apartment residences were built shortly thereafter, causing a dramatic population increase and an accompanying demand for goods and services. Before the Coventry business district was developed, the nearest commercial center of any size was at DOAN'S CORNERS. Most of the buildings on Coventry were constructed between 1913-33, with the greatest growth occurring between 1921-25, when 18 commercial buildings were erected.

Euclid Hts. originally was a mostly upper-income community for Protestants of Anglo-Saxon heritage. By the early 1920s, however, a large and thriving Jewish community blossomed in the newly constructed apartment districts. Most Jewish migration to Coventry was from the Mt. Pleasant-Kinsman area of Cleveland. Until the late 1960s, Coventry had a large and thriving Jewish business and residential presence. A major change in Coventry's merchant composition began in the autumn of 1967, as businesses catering to the new "counterculture" were opened. Over the next 10 years, the Jewish influence in Coventry greatly declined and gave way to a new generation of stores that served a younger and more affluent market. The Coventry Village of the early 1980s evolved into a marketplace that not only served the needs of the local populace but also featured shops and boutiques serving a wide range of Cleveland-area consumer tastes.

**COWLES, EDWIN W.** (19 Sept. 1825–4 Mar. 1890), was a prominent newspaper editor. Descended from New England stock, Cowles was born in Austinburg, Ohio. In 1839 his father brought him to Cleveland, where he was apprenticed to learn the printing trade. In 1844 Cowles formed a job-printing partnership with Timothy Smead, and Cowles handled the printing of both the *OHIO AMERICAN* and the *True Democrat*. When the latter was merged into the *Forest City Democrat* in 1853, Cowles acquired interest in the paper and became the dominant force behind its conversion into the *CLEVELAND LEADER* the following year.

At the same time, Cowles played a leading role in the formation of the Republican party in Cleveland. With his new partner, Joseph Medill, he hosted a meeting in the *Leader*'s office, which resulted in the issuance of a call for the first Republican Natl. Convention, held in Pittsburgh in 1855. Cowles then secured sole control of the *Leader*. By the time he assumed the position of editor as well as publisher, in 1859, he had made it the leading radical Republican voice in northern Ohio. As a result of the Republican victory in 1860, Cowles was rewarded with the traditional plum of the Cleveland postmastership. Under his administration, the Cleveland post office pioneered in the free-delivery system of mail in urban areas. Throughout the war he continued to attack slavery and defend the Union cause in the *Leader*. However, under the administration of Pres. Andrew Johnson, he was replaced as postmaster by GEO. A. BENEDICT, editor of the more moderate *Herald*.

Cowles continued to play an influential role in Republican politics after the war, attending the national conventions of 1876 and 1884 as a delegate and lending his support to Grant, Garfield, and Jas. Blaine. He was as outspoken a nativist as he was a Republican, heading the Cleveland chapter of the anti-Catholic Order of the American Union and carrying on a running editorial war with MANLY TELLO, editor of the *Catholic Universe*. Cowles was credited with securing the insertion of a plank in the 1876 Republican platform advocating a constitutional amendment against any appropriation of public funds for parochial education.

Called "the Horace Greely of the west" by one Cleveland historian, Cowles was the city's last surviving representative of the era of personal journalism. As eulogized by the rival *Plain Dealer*, "in newspaper fighting he considered the sledge hammer a more effective weapon than the rapier and he went at a policy, a party, or a rival paper with smashing blows instead of with keen thrusts." Even late in his career, he carried a pistol and practiced target shooting on a brick wall in his office. Cowles married Elizabeth C. Hutchinson in 1849 and fathered 3 sons and 2 daughters. When two of his sons invented a new melting process for aluminum, Cowles loosened his reins on the *Leader* and devoted his declining energies to the promotion

of a company formed to exploit their discovery. He died in his home at 769 Case Ave. (E. 40th).

**COX, JACOB D., JR.** (1 Nov. 1881–16 Feb. 1953), as president of the Cleveland Twist Drill Co., was widely known in the metals-processing industry as a pioneer in profit sharing and employee stock participation planning. Cox was born in Cleveland. He came from a well-known family; his grandfather was a major general in the Union Army and governor of Ohio, and his father was prominent in tool manufacturing as founder, in 1876, of Cleveland Twist Drill. Cox grew up in the family mansion on Euclid Ave. He attended Williams College, where he graduated as a Phi Beta Kappa. After college, Cox spent several years working in the western logging industry, his work often interrupted by poor health. In 1911 he became assistant to his father, and in 1919 he succeeded him as president of Cleveland Twist Drill. He held that position until his death in 1953. Cox had a deep interest in relations between management and labor; while he was president of the company, there was never a work stoppage due to a labor dispute. Cox introduced many employee benefits that are standard today, including 2 weeks of vacation (after 2 years' service); a share in the company's profits at Christmas; profit sharing and participation in the company's investment; old-age pension on retirement at age 65; a sickness and accident fund; payment for suggestions that led to better efficiency and increased production; group life insurance; discussion groups in the factory; and promotion from the ranks. Cox formulated his profit-sharing plan in 1915. He later wrote a book, *The Economic Basis of Fair Wages*. Cox's innovative policies, which also included hiring handicapped persons whenever possible, served as models for similar programs in companies throughout the country. He was married to the former Phyllis Graves.

**CRAIG, LILLIAN** (12 June 1937–14 Nov. 1979), was a leader in the local welfare-rights movement and a founding member of the Natl. Welfare Rights Organization in 1967. A native Clevelander, Craig was the oldest of 3 daughters born to an abusive, alcoholic father. Her mother died when Lillian was 12; 2 years later the children were separated because of their father's drinking problem. After problems with her foster parents, Craig was sent to Marycrest School for Girls; upon graduation she was offered a scholarship to St. John's College. She was unable to accept the scholarship because it made no allowances for living expenses, and relatives refused to allow her to live with them. Craig described herself as "very bitter" by age 18.

As a divorced mother with 3 children, Craig found it too difficult to hold a job and adequately care for her children. She applied for and began receiving welfare payments; the stigma attached to welfare further estranged her from her relatives. In the early 1960s, Craig found a crucial source of support at St. Paul's Community Church, a member of the Inner City Protestant Parish. Rev. Paul Younger had founded there a group of welfare mothers who helped one another cope with their problems. Younger's group, Clevelanders United for Adequate Welfare, became a politically active organization in the mid-1960s, working for larger welfare payments, free school lunches for children of welfare recipients, and better overall treatment from the welfare bureaucracy. Craig and CUFAW were aided by the radical community organizers of the STUDENTS FOR A DEMOCRATIC SOCIETY's Economic Research & Action Project. Along with SDS members Carol McEldowney and Kathy Boudin, Craig helped to write *The Welfare Rights Manual*, a welfare manual written "in 'people terms'."

As a spokesperson for CUFAW, Craig became a well-known and controversial leader of the local welfare-rights movement, taking part in sit-ins, marches, and public confrontations. She made national headlines in 1966 when she grabbed a microphone away from Sargent Shriver, head of the Office of Economic Opportunities, and confronted him about the administration's welfare policies. Craig's reputation as a controversial leader made it difficult for her to find employment in the late 1960s as her friends in SDS and the Inner City Protestant Parish left Cleveland. She worked at the McCafferty Health Ctr. on the near west side from 1971–76, and in June 1976 she became the director of the Near West Side Multi-Service Ctr. She also volunteered at the Crisis Ctr. on Bridge Ave. and served on a child-abuse task force.

Grevatt, Marge, *Just a Woman* (1981).

**CRAMER, CLARENCE HENLEY** (23 June 1905–15 Mar. 1982), was the author of 9 books, dean of Adelbert College, and professor of history at Western Reserve University. He was born in Eureka, Kans., the son of Rev. and Mrs. D. H. Cramer. After living in several states, his family settled in Mt. Gilead, Ohio where he graduated from Mt. Gilead High School in 1923. He attended Ohio State University, receiving his B.A. and M.A. degrees in 1927 and 1928 respectively and his Ph.D. in history in 1931. From 1931–42 he was associate professor of history at Southern Illinois University at Carbondale. During and after WORLD WAR II, he served in various governmental posts including: director of personnel for the Natl. War Labor Board, 1943–44; chief personnel officer for the United Nations Relief & Rehabilitation Admin. in Germany, 1945–46; and director of personnel for the Internatl. Refugee Organization in Geneva, 1947–48.

Cramer came to Cleveland in 1949, when he was named associate professor of history and business at WRU. After serving as acting dean of the School of Business from 1952–54, he became dean of Adelbert College, serving from 1954–69, after which he returned to teaching. "Red" Cramer was always accessible to the students, and he was known for his wise counsel and ability to uncover financial resources to help those that showed promise. During his academic career he specialized in economic and diplomatic history, and he wrote biographies of Robt. G. Ingersoll and NEWTON D. BAKER, *American Enterprise—Free and Not So Free* (1972), and *Open Shelves and Open Minds: A History of the Cleveland Public Library* (1972). After his retirement in 1973, he published *Case Western Reserve University: A History of the University, 1826-1976* in 1976, and *Case Institute of Technology: A Centennial History, 1880-1980* in 1980. He also wrote histories of the law school, the school of library science, and the school of dentistry at CWRU. He married Elizabeth Garman of Denver, Colo., in Dec. 1949. He died in Cleveland at age 76.

**CRANE, HART** (21 July 1899–27 Apr. 1932), was a modern, lyrical romantic poet whose position is firmly established in American letters. He is considered a pioneer of the spirit in the tradition of Ralph Waldo Emerson and Walt Whitman, but in the context of the machine and jazz age of the 1920s. He was an influence on poet Dylan Thomas; contemporary poet Robt. Lowell called him "the greatest voice of his generation." Born in Garrettsville, Ohio, Crane and his mother, Grace Hart Crane, moved to Cleveland in 1909 after she separated from C. A. Crane, millionaire candy manufacturer. Crane said his parents' stormy marriage and the "bloody battleground of their sex lives" laid the groundwork for his lifelong instability.

Crane began to write verse when he was 13, influenced by the Elizabethan poets, Whitman, Emerson, the French Symbolists, Plato, Blake, Poe, and others. He published his first poem at age 16 (1915) in *Bruno's Weekly*, while attending East High School. He attempted a college education but was mainly self-taught. While writing and studying, he held jobs with advertising companies in Cleveland and served a brief stint as a *PLAIN DEALER* reporter. Moving to New York after frequent trips there, his finances always shaky, Crane made his reputation with poems such as "Praise from an Urn" (1922), "For the Marriage of Faustus and Helen" (1923), and "Voyages I-VI" (1926), publishing in the small-press literary magazines *Dial, Seven Arts, Poetry*, and others. His first collection, *White Buildings* (1926), was well received and established him as a major voice. A wild and passionate life, including alcoholism and homosexual debaucheries (as they were then referred to), established him as a legendary figure. His contemporaries and friends included Edna St. Vincent Millay; friend and mentor Waldo Frank, who was a well-known critic and novelist; critic Allen Tate; and Sherwood Anderson. As they were of him, Crane was a champion and promoter of many writers and artists.

In his poetry, Crane sought to master the immediate continuity of experience in a world he saw as increasingly chaotic and to reconcile the spirit with the machine age. He traveled through California in 1927–28 and Europe in 1928–29. In 1930 he published *The Bridge*, his most famous collection, which used the Brooklyn Bridge as a metaphor for American life and destiny. It won him greater critical acclaim and a Guggenheim Fellowship in 1931. The lyrical genius and brilliance of Crane's talent were such that it could weather the extreme instability of his life, which deteriorated with his increasing alcoholism. In 1931, Crane sailed to Mexico, where he lived in an artists' colony outside of Mexico City and worked on an epic poem about Montezuma's conquest of Mexico, which he never finished. In 1932, Crane's personal problems, including depression brought on by his father's death, alcoholism, and the feeling that he had lost his poetic powers, caught up with him, and while sailing back to America on the *Orizaba* to settle his father's estate, he jumped ship and drowned. His body was never recovered. His collected poems were published posthumously in 1933.

**CRANE, ORRIN J.** (1828–27 Nov. 1863), was a volunteer Civil War Army officer killed in battle at Ringgold, Ga. Crane was born in Troy, N.Y. At the outbreak of the CIVIL WAR, he was employed as a carpenter for a local Cleveland shipbuilder. He enlisted in the Cleveland Light Guard Zouaves on 17 Apr. 1861 as a private and was elected 1st lieutenant on 19 Apr., when the company became Co. A, 7th Ohio Volunteer Infantry. He was appointed captain on 14 May 1861 and mustered out 13 June 1863, to accept the captaincy of Co. A when the 7th Ohio reenlisted for 3 years. He learned the rudiments of military science from Col. WM. R. CREIGHTON and excelled in supervising the building of bridges, barracks, and corduroy roads. He participated in the major campaigns of the Army of the Potomac in Virginia during 1862–63. At the Battle of Antietam (17 Sept. 1862), he commanded the 1st Brigade of the 2d Div. of the 12th Army corps for a time.

Crane was promoted to lieutenant colonel on 6 Oct. 1862, and was in command of the 7th Ohio on 27 Nov. 1863. On that date, the 1st Brigade, commanded by Wm. R. Creighton, was ordered to assault Taylor's Ridge, a 500-ft. summit near Ringgold, Ga. The 7th Ohio, on the left end of the assaulting line, was forced to move through a ravine and was mauled by enfilading Confederate fire. The brigade failed to occupy the summit, suffering heavy casualties. Crane was killed near the top. Col. Creighton tried to have Crane's body brought down from the ridge but failed and was mortally wounded—shot through the heart. The 7th Ohio held a position about halfway down the ridge with the other regiments of the 1st Brigade until the Confederates were finally routed. Both Crane's and Creighton's remains were transported back to Cleveland, where they lay in state at City Hall the night of 7-8 Dec. 1863. After a memorial service at the Old Stone Church, where Crane was a member, both were deposited in the ERIE ST. CEMETERY in the Bradburn family vault. Thousands of citizens lined the street for the procession, as local military units participated. In July 1864, both bodies were buried in WOODLAND CEMETERY, side by side.

**CREIGHTON, WILLIAM R.** (June 1837–27 Nov. 1863), was a volunteer Civil War officer killed at Ringgold, Ga., in 1863. Creighton was born in June 1837 in Pittsburgh, Pa. At the beginning of the CIVIL WAR, he worked as a printer at the *Cleveland Herald*. He had previously served as 1st lieutenant of the Cleveland Light Guard Zouaves. Creighton recruited a company of infantry on 17 Apr. 1861 and took them into Camp Taylor in Cleveland, where they were mustered as Co. A, 7TH OHIO VOLUNTEER INFANTRY. Elected lieutenant colonel of the regiment in May 1861 at Camp Dennison, Ohio, he became known as an expert drillmaster. He was promoted to colonel on 23 Mar. 1862, after meritorious service at the Battle of Winchester, Va. On 9 Aug. 1862, he was severely wounded in the shoulder at the battle of Clear Mountain, Va., and did not rejoin the 7th until Sept. 1862.

By the fall of 1863, the 7th Regiment had been assigned to the Army of the Cumberland, XII Corps, 2d Div., in the Western Theater. On 27 Nov., Creighton was in command of the 1st Brigade. At 8 a.m., his 1st Brigade was ordered to assault the 500-ft.-high summit of Taylor's Ridge near Ringgold, Ga. Under a galling fire, the brigade struggled toward the top but failed to occupy their objective. Creighton, in rallying his former regiment, the 7th Ohio, then commanded by Lt. Col. ORRIN J. CRANE, was shot through the heart and carried down the ridge, dying 6 hours later. There were 2 versions published concerning his mortal wounding. One account claims that Creighton rallied the 7th Regiment to reach the body of Crane, who had been killed close to the summit. The attempt failed, and Creighton was actually killed during the retreat. A second account claims that he was mortally wounded just after fixing a tourniquet on the leg of a wounded friend.

Creighton's and Crane's remains were transported back to Cleveland. Both bodies were kept at City Hall the night of 7-8 Dec. 1863 and were taken to Old Stone Church for a memorial service on 8 Dec. The bodies were transported to the ERIE ST. CEMETERY and temporarily deposited in the Bradburn family vault. Thousands of citizens lined the streets for the procession, in which several local military units participated. At a later date, both Creighton and Crane were buried side by side in WOODLAND CEMETERY. Ft. Wood at Chattanooga, Tenn., was renamed Ft. Creighton in the colonel's honor. Creighton was survived by his widow, the former Eleanor L. Quirk, whom he had married on 2 May 1861. A bust of Creighton is displayed in the SOLDIERS & SAILORS MONUMENT.

Wm. R. Creighton Papers, 1862-64. In Regimental Papers of the Civil War, WRHS.

**CRILE, GEORGE WASHINGTON, SR.** (11 Nov. 1864–7 Jan. 1943), was a surgeon, a medical researcher, and one of the founders of the CLEVELAND CLINIC FOUNDATION. Crile, born in Chili, Ohio, was the 5th of 8 children of Michael and Margaret Deeds Crile. He was educated in the Crawford Twp. public schools and received his A.B. degree from Ohio Northern University in 1885. After receiving his medical degree in 1887 from Wooster Medical College (Cleveland), he received additional surgical training in the leading medical centers in Vienna, London, and Paris. Along with FRANK E. BUNTS, he worked as a physician and surgeon for Dr. Frank Weed and served on the staffs of several Cleveland hospitals (Lakeside, Charity, St. Alexis). He performed the first successful human blood transfusion at ST. ALEXIS HOSPITAL in 1906. During the SPANISH-AMERICAN WAR, Crile served as 1st lieutenant, U.S. Army Medical Corps. While serving in Puerto Rico, he became interested in military surgery, field sanitation, and tropical diseases. During WORLD WAR I, he served as surgical director of the American Ambulance Hospital in Neuilly, France (1915), and later organized U.S. Army Base Hospital No. 4 (LAKESIDE UNIT) for service in France (1917–18). During his service in France, he did research in war neurasthenia, shell concussion, effects of poison gas, wound infection, and shock. As the result of his military service, Crile received many military honors, including the Legion of Honor of France (1922). Along with Drs. WM. E. LOWER, Frank E. Bunts, and JOHN PHILLIPS, Crile founded the Cleveland Clinic, which was a medical group practice modeled after the group practice of the Mayo brothers in Rochester, Minn. He served as the president of the foundation (1921–40) and trustee (1921–36). In addition to his research in surgical shock, he perfected the operation for goiter and thyroid disease. Crile also had an interest in the study of intelligence, power, and personality in man and animals and developed the theory that the human organism is an electrochemical mechanism. Crile authored numerous medical articles and books on surgical shock, thyroid disease, and blood transfusion, as well as other aspects of surgery. Among his many awards for medical achievement was the Cartwright Prize (1897 and 1903) of Columbia University and the Third Laureate Lannelongue Foundation of the Societe Internationale de Chirurgie de Paris (1925). He was a member of numerous American and international medical and surgical societies, including the American Heart Assoc. and Natl. Academy of Sciences, and a fellow of the Royal Academy of Medicine of England, Ireland, and Rome. He was a founding member of the American College of Surgeons and served as its second president (1916–17). He held academic appointments at the University of Wooster (1890–1900) and Western Reserve School of Medicine (1900–43). He was married to Grace McBride of Cleveland and had 4 children (George, Jr., Robert, Margaret, and Elizabeth).

Geo. W. Crile, Sr., Papers, WRHS.

**CRILE HOSPITAL** was built by the U.S. Army as a hospital for the treatment of soldiers and military veterans. Located on York Rd. in PARMA, Ohio, it opened in June 1943 and was named in honor of Col. GEO. W. CRILE, SR., of the U.S. Army, who served as clinical director of the U.S. Army Base Hospital #4 (LAKESIDE UNIT) in Rouen during WORLD WAR I. The hospital had 108 beds scattered through 83 buildings located on 152 acres. Plans to convert it into a neuro-psychiatric hospital for veterans were opposed by the city of Parma, and the hospital was closed in 1964 when the Wade Park (Veteran's) Hospital was opened. The site was donated to CUYAHOGA COMMUNITY COLLEGE in 1965 to be used for educational purposes.

CRIME. Although crimes were committed in Cleveland almost immediately after the arrival of the first settlers, it is hard to find criminal acts documented in any of the social or intellectual histories of the life of the city or the WESTERN RESERVE. This historical quiet persisted, even though as Cleveland grew and became more complex, crime statistics grew and the social and individual circumstances leading to illegal misbehavior became more involved. With the exception of the sensational murder, historians of the Western Reserve have been reluctant to chronicle the area's crime life, even though abundant documentary evidence exists attesting to this particular aspect of the area's history. Cleveland's first instance of crime traditionally occurred when the early settler LORENZO CARTER punched a fellow frontiersman. Since the town's early regulations were known familiarly as Carter's Law, it should come as no surprise that no punishment is recorded as having been levied against Carter. A desire to cash in on frontier land speculation and to leave the stifling atmosphere of New England towns meant that Cleveland's early settlers could be a crude and coarse lot, not always attuned to legal niceties. However, by 1802, the settlers found it necessary to elect JAS. KINGSBURY as the first justice of the peace for the township of Cleveland. This beginning of a court system received further development in 1810 when Cuyahoga County established a court of common pleas and issued a grand jury indictment against David Miller for keeping a tavern without a license.

Alcohol consumption was linked with sensational crime as early as 1802, when the murder of a Chippewa medicine man by a member of the Seneca tribe was blamed partially on excessive drinking. By 1836, Cleveland's citizens were complaining that too many liquor licenses caused too much drinking, which in turn was responsible for an epidemic of lawlessness. Alcohol and its use and abuse even early on became entwined in the public mind as a reason for crime. Even when not stimulated by drink, the clash of the Indian and white cultures stirred up emotions enough to provide early Clevelanders with sensational criminal cases. The lack of ethnic sympathy between different aspects of city society thus also showed up early. In 1807, a Seneca Indian was murdered in a revenge killing that included his being mistaken for another Indian accused of killing a Hudson man; and Cleveland's first public execution in 1812 was a bizarre affair involving an Indian defendant, O'MIC, the first person tried for murder and executed in Cuyahoga County. By 1812, crime in Cleveland had grown to the point that a jail became necessary, and construction began on the first public courthouse and jail, erected on the northwest corner of PUBLIC SQUARE. Robbers, murderers, thieves, and counterfeiters all shared the county's hospitality in this building, but they were sometimes able to elude the law officers charged with escorting them from one place to another.

The numbers of law officers continued to grow. In 1836, a City Watch of volunteers began policing Cleveland from sundown to sunrise, and an early instance of detective work occurred in 1851 when a justice of the peace, David L. Wightman, traced footsteps on the embankment of a railroad derailment and discovered who was responsible for the engine leaving the tracks and killing the engineer. This kind of police efficiency was appreciated by citizens concerned that Cleveland was protected from crime by only a handful of acting constables and watchmen. By 1853, the establishment of the city's first municipal court, the police court, became a fact. This court replaced the mayor sitting as a police judge. The police court was joined by a city police force on 1 May 1866, when Jacob W. Schmitt persuaded the Ohio legislature to pass the Metropolitan Police Act. The new police system replaced the night watchmen

and consisted of 36 officers. By 1872, the city was divided into 7 police districts as fewer than 60 officers attempted to contain crime in a rapidly growing city. Michael Kick was the first officer killed while on duty, when confronting a gang of burglars in 1875.

As the city changed, the CLEVELAND POLICE DEPARTMENT had to accommodate these changes in order to fight crime and stay current with social conditions. A bicycle squad was added in 1903, the wharf detail in 1904, and the motorcycle detail in 1910, and policewomen joined the force in 1924. The Bureau of Ballistics was founded in 1929; in 1934, more than 500 officers attended the first of a series of 21 continuing-education lectures on the law. The first women detectives appeared in 1965, and the department added a community-relations unit and a sex-crime unit in 1967. All east side police patrol cars were integrated in 1968, and the police applicant examination was offered in English and Spanish in 1970. By the late 19th century, Cleveland's image was that of a hard-drinking city of working-class citizens. However, this working class, by adding population to the city, also crowded into neighborhoods where poverty, lack of public health, and despair combined to produce those conditions that fostered crime. By 1905, Cleveland police officers were arresting 27,926 persons annually, the culmination of a steady climb from 9,369 arrests in 1882. Drunkenness, PROSTITUTION, and automobile offenses accounted for most of the 1905 arrests. However, there were also 18 people arrested for murder, and 47 bodies were found in the city. In 1911, the Cleveland Baptist Brotherhood identified liquor, lack of adequate policemen, and social vices such as dance halls and moving pictures as the reason for high crime in the city. Eleven years later, the Cleveland Foundation's study of the city's criminal justice system (*Criminal Justice in Cleveland*) concluded that the alarming crime rate reflected an unstable population and a breakdown in the administration of criminal law caused by a proliferation of laws not representative of community standards or desires. By 1920, many Clevelanders felt insecure about their lives and property. A crime involving the chief judge of the municipal court, WM. H. MCGANNON, brought this feeling to a head, and the city's establishment, particularly the CLEVELAND BAR ASSOC., decided to utilize the CLEVELAND FOUNDATION to study the city's criminal-justice system (see CLEVELAND SURVEY OF CRIMINAL JUSTICE). The study's conclusions mapped out an ambitious plan of social engineering in order to begin the containment of crime. Over 20 years later, facets of this plan were still debated.

The introduction of PROHIBITION in 1919 ushered in a Cleveland era of the rackets. Mob violence, gang slayings, hijackings, and bootlegging carried out by groups such as the MAYFIELD RD. MOB characterized the city's most prominent criminal activities, and Cleveland became nationally known as the producer of underworld alumni destined to assume important mob positions in other big cities. The advent of the mob also meant the beginning of organized gambling, and on 9 Jan. 1924, local police agencies opened their war on this activity by seizing slot machines. Even when Prohibition ended, the gambling rackets remained, as the city's wealthier citizens frequented city and county casinos, and the less-well-off took advantage of the numbers games and the slot machines found in the neighborhood bars and tobacco stores. These avenues of recreation were controlled by the Mafia, and when the police pressure in Cleveland became too intense, gambling moved into suburban and country areas. Cleveland's gambling clubs (the Pettibone Club, Jungle Inn, Mounds Club, and Colony Club) achieved local and national notoriety until closed down by primarily state effort.

The post-WORLD WAR II era saw a new emphasis on crime and its relationship with social conditions. Juvenile delinquency and the domestic life that spawned it became a concern to Cleveland's police department. Broken homes and the easy availability of liquor were identified as the chief culprits. This analysis also brought home the importance of realizing that the causes of crime lay in a complicated connection of domestic, economic, and social elements. Clevelanders mirrored the citizens of other large urban centers as they wrestled with the racial factors in their crime statistics. The apportioning of blame for black on black crime touched off a multiyear debate in the late 1950s and the 1960s and 1970s about who or what was responsible for an increase in crime. Newspaper reports about suburban workers or visitors in Cleveland who fell victim to robbery, rape, or murder, coupled with a citizenry confused and frightened by what seemed to be constantly mounting criminal and racial tension, engaged public officials, police officers, and voters in a search for scapegoats and solutions. Increased police foot or cruiser patrols, better street lighting, and a sophisticated police communications center vied with calls for better educational and employment opportunities and decent housing availability as Clevelanders grappled with the causes of the supposed pandemic of crime. In actuality, these late-20th-century debates about crime in Cleveland were only the larger and more complicated versions of discourses on crime debated by Clevelanders in the early 19th century as they struggled to implement Carter's Law. The growth of crime had simply mirrored the development of the city and would continue to do so in the future.

Michael V. Wells
Cleveland State University

**CROATIANS.** Greater Cleveland contains 10,000 Croatians, the 4th-largest concentration of Croatians in the U.S. after those in Pittsburgh, Chicago, and New York. During the two world wars, and in the period 1950–70, Cleveland was one of the main centers of Croatian and South Slavic political, fraternal, and cultural activities. A South Slavic people, the Croatian immigrants to Cleveland were a part of centuries-long migrations from Croatia. The exodus reached its peak ca. 1910 and then was repeated some 50 years later. All waves of Croatian immigration to Cleveland and America were caused by the political and economic situations of a homeland under the oppressive regimes of Austria-Hungary and both royal and Communist Yugoslavia. Before 1919, most Cleveland Croatians were natives of southern and northwestern Croatia; afterward they arrived from all Croatian lands: Croatia-Slavonia, Bosnia-Hercegovina, Dalmatia, and Istria. Most were of peasant stock. The periods of their arrival may be divided as follows: 1860s–1918; 1919–41; and 1945–1980s. The first Croatians came to Cleveland during the late 1860s from neighboring states. They were attracted by jobs in industry and construction, and induced by the SLOVENIANS who were their neighbors in the old country. There was a large influx of them by 1890. They joined the Slovenians along St. Clair (from E. 9th to E. 79th streets), north of Superior, and along the lake near the factories, and also inhabited parts of W. 26th St., Scovill, and Woodland. Before the early 1900s, many were single males who lived in boarding houses. The area on E. 40th St. and St. Clair became the heart of the Croatian settlement. By 1910, many Croatians lived in GLENVILLE, NOTTINGHAM, COLLINWOOD, EUCLID, Randall, and WEST PARK. They worked for American Steel & Wire, the Van Dorn Iron Works, Otis Steel, the Patterson Sargent Paint Co., Cleveland Twist Drill, and other shops and factories, and for the New York

Central, Pennsylvania, and other railroad companies. The majority were unskilled workers and laborers. The period 1890–1919 was the era when the foundations were laid for religious, fraternal, educational, social, cultural, and political activities.

To pay for burials and aid the injured and sick, the Croatians founded mutual-benefit and fraternal societies. The most important was the Natl. Croatian Society of Pittsburgh (1894), which had many members in Cleveland. The first lodges of the NCS were established here in 1895 and 1897. These, and those established later, usually bore names of saints. Lodge 235, founded in 1906 in Collinwood, was named "Croatian Liberty." Over the years it became an important center for social and patriotic activities. The 3d Natl. Convention of the NCS was held in Cleveland in 1896, while its 12th Convention met here in 1915. Some 70% of all Croatians belong to the Catholic church (most of them Roman Catholic, and about 100,000 Byzantine Rite). About 20% adhere to Islam; most of the rest are Eastern Orthodox or Protestant, and a few are Jewish. Among the early settlers here, a great majority were Catholics of both rites. The first Croatian church was St. Nicholas (Byzantine Rite), founded by Rev. Mile Golubic and some 50 families from Zumberak. From E. 41st and St. Clair, it moved in 1913 to E. 36th and Superior under the leadership of Rev. Milan Hranilovic. The Roman Catholic St. Paul parish was founded in Nov. 1902 by Rev. Milan Sutlic. The newly built church on E. 40th was opened on Easter Sunday 1904. Niko Grskovic, who succeeded Rev. Sutlic, built a primary school in 1910. He left the parish of some 6,000 people in 1917 to devote full time to the Yugoslav Committee in Washington, D.C. He was a nationally known Croatian activist, journalist, publisher, and editor of newspapers, and a leading fraternalist.

By the 1920s, there were approximately 12,000 Croatians in Cleveland. The period 1920–40 was the peak of Croatian community activity. The first convention of the newly formed Croatian Fraternal Union (CFU) met at the Slovenian Auditorium 3–22 May 1926. Several English-speaking CFU lodges were established in the 1920s. One of the first lodges of the new Croatian Catholic Union (organized in Gary, Ind., in Oct. 1921) was Lodge No. 10 at St. Paul parish. The CCU national convention met here in Apr. 1921. After the establishment of Yugoslavia in 1918, the masses of Croatian immigrants in America, including thousands of those in Cleveland, opposed the new government in Belgrade. Many immigrants arriving here during the 1920s were followers of Stephen Radich and his Croatian Peasant party. A branch was established in Collinwood in Nov. 1923. After Radich's assassination in 1928 and the introduction of royal dictatorship in Yugoslavia in 1929, the Cleveland Croatians joined nationwide activities against it. The CPP and other organizations held protest meetings, issued memoranda, and published newspapers condemning conditions in Croatia. Also organized were huge annual Croatian Days, starting in 1933, that attracted thousands and were widely publicized in the American press. A new Croatian Home was built on Waterloo Rd. (Collinwood) and became the center of many community activities into the 1980s. (An older Croatian Home on St. Clair became inadequate.) Established Croatian immigrants were able after May 1945 to help their war-ravaged homeland and assist thousands of refugees, including numerous close relatives, who were now fleeing Communist Yugoslavia. The Displaced Persons Act of 1948 made it possible for thousands of Croatians to immigrate to Cleveland. The Society for Croatian Migration brought over and assisted over 5,000 immigrants with the assistance of the Natl. Catholic Welfare Conference. Many newcomers settled in the St. Clair area and gradually rejuvenated the old settlement. Some 40% of these newcomers were below the age of 39; many were highly educated, skilled, and professional people.

The post-World War II immigration, coming in several waves, was more political than economic. The young generation that grew up under Communism brought with them an intense nationalism, fierce opposition to the regime at home, and imported ideas of violence. Among the problems that arose was the rift between the "old" and "new" immigrants. The main political organization is the Croatian Natl. Congress, advocating complete independence for Croatia. The 1940 census counted 12,540 Croatians in Cleveland. Following the influx of the immediate postwar period, immigration continued at a substantial pace; between 1967–71, some 8,000 additional Croatians arrived in Greater Cleveland. In 1985, over 25,000 Croatians and people of partial Croatian extraction were living in the area. During the 1950s–70s, many new organizations were founded: the United American Croatians, the "Lisinski" Singing Society, the American-Croatian Academic Club (Society), the Croatian Foundation, several folklore groups, soccer clubs, and a variety of political, cultural, and fraternal societies. The churches also expanded during this period. St. Nicholas parish dedicated a newly built church at the site of the old one in Apr. 1975. This parish had some 250 families, while the St. Paul congregation had some 5,000 parishioners. In 1972, in a unified effort, the Croatians acquired the Croatian Ctr., with over 100 acres of land on Mulberry Rd. in Chesterland. On 29 Sept. 1984, the large, newly built Croatian Natl. Home was dedicated in Eastlake on Lakeshore Blvd. Costing over $2.5 million, it was, in the 1980s, the centerpiece of Cleveland's Croatian community.

George J. Prpic
John Carroll University

**CROGHAN, GEORGE** (d. 31 Aug. 1782), was a notable frontiersman, trader, and Indian agent. He served as a captain under Gen. Braddock, and later as Sir Wm. Johnson's deputy superintendent of Indian affairs. Before the French & Indian War (1754–63), Croghan established trading posts throughout the upper Ohio country in the present states of Ohio, Indiana, and Illinois. When not representing his own interests, he served those of the British, often facilitating negotiations with the Indians that opposed them to the French. Croghan is significant in Cleveland's history as the first identifiable white man to maintain a trading post at the mouth of the CUYAHOGA RIVER. He visited there periodically between 1745–48.

**CROSSER, ROBERT** (7 June 1874–3 June 1957), represented the Cleveland area in Congress for 38 years between 1912–54. Influenced by Mayor TOM L. JOHNSON and the writings of Henry George, Crosser believed in equal rights for all and was dedicated to the elimination of poverty. He was born in Holytown, Lanarkshire, Scotland, to James and Barbara C. Crosser. His parents emigrated to America in 1881, settling in Salineville, Ohio, where Crosser attended public schools. He graduated from Kenyon College with the A.B. degree in 1897. He attended Columbia University Law School and Cincinnati Law School, earning the LL.B. degree in 1901, when he was admitted to the Ohio bar.

Crosser practiced law in Cleveland from 1901–23. He soon became involved in politics, working for Mayor Tom L. Johnson. In 1910 he was elected to the Ohio house of representatives. In 1912 he was chosen as a delegate to Ohio's 4th constitutional convention, where he chaired the committee and authored the section relating to initiatives and referendums. Crosser won election as congressman-at-large in 1912 and as representative of Ohio's 21st congressional district in 1914 and 1916. He was defeated for the congressional seat in 1918 and 1920, largely because of his opposition to the military draft. In 1922 Crosser was reelected to Congress. He held the seat until 1954, when he was defeated by Chas. Vanik in the Democratic party primary.

Although a member of the Democratic party, Crosser considered himself an independent. He won the nickname of "Fighting Bob" for his soapbox street-corner campaign and upset victory in the 1912 congressional election. Reluctant to accept outside advice, Crosser chose to follow the dictates of his conscience. In Congress, his independent stance resulted in his being passed over for the powerful leadership positions. On the local level it often cost him the support of the Democratic party in the primaries.

Considered an authority on transportation in Congress, Crosser served as chairman of the Interstate & Foreign Commerce Committee (1948–52) and the first congressional Flood Control Committee. A strong supporter of postal and railroad workers, he enjoyed strong support at election time from both groups. In Congress, Crosser authored legislation giving railroad workers security benefits that were the most liberal of its day. Crosser married Isabelle D. Hogg on 18 Apr. 1906. The Crossers had 4 children, Justine, Barbara, Robert, and James. Crosser suffered from arthritis and from 1934 was confined to a wheelchair.

**CROWELL, BENEDICT** (21 Oct. 1869–8 Sept. 1952), was a banker, a brigadier general in the U.S. Army, and a chemical engineer. During WORLD WAR I he served as assistant secretary of war under NEWTON D. BAKER. Crowell was born in a small house on Euclid Ave. After graduation from Rockwell School and St. Paul's, he attended Case Institute of Technology. He transferred to Yale, where he majored in chemistry, earning a Ph.B. in 1891. In 1918 he was awarded an M.A. from Yale. After graduation, Crowell worked for the Otis Steel Co. in Cleveland as a chemical engineer. There he developed a process for determining phosphorus content in steel that took only 20 minutes instead of the 3 hours required by the old method. He then worked as a mining engineer in Brazil, Mexico, and Alaska before starting the Crowell & Little Constr. Co. After service during World War I, he returned to the construction business. In 1938 he was named president of the Central Natl. Bank, where he remained until shortly before his death in 1952. He was also appointed to the board of directors of the Nickel Plate Railroad in 1941.

Crowell's public service started when Newton D. Baker appointed him to the Civil Service Commission. In 1916 he served on the Kernan Board, which was charged with determining the feasibility of manufacturing all armaments in government arsenals. When war was declared, Crowell received officer training and was ordered to Washington to supervise artillery castings as a major of ordnance. He then headed the Washington office of the Panama Canal Zone. In 1917, Secretary of War Baker appointed him assistant secretary of war, and a year later he gave him the additional job of director of munitions. During Baker's trips to Europe, Crowell served as acting secretary of war. After the war, Pres. Wilson twice sent him to France on special missions. He went first to Europe, to study aviation developments, and later to France, where he disposed of $4 million worth of military equipment. In 1922, a Washington grand jury indicted Crowell and 6 of his aides from the Emergency Constr. Committee of the Council of Defense, charging them with altering the contract bidding system to enrich construction firms in which they had some interest. The charges were dropped in 1925 for lack of evidence. Between the wars, Crowell served in a number of capacities. He was a member of the Bituminous Coal Authority for the Central States, state director of the Natl. Emergency Council during the Depression, director for the regional boards of the Natl. Recovery and Social Security administrations, and chairman of the Ohio Repeal Council against Prohibition. In 1931, Pres. Hoover promoted Crowell to brigadier general. Later, during WORLD WAR II, he was appointed special consultant to the secretary of war. Crowell was founder and first president of the Army Ordnance Assoc., an organization advocating national defense preparedness, and president of the Natl. Rifle Assoc. He was also the author of several books. Crowell married Julia Cobb in Dec. 1904; they had 2 children, Florence and Benedict. Crowell is buried in Arlington Natl. Cemetery.

Benedict Crowell Papers, WRHS.

**CUDELL** is a neighborhood located around the Cudell Recreation Ctr. in the West Blvd. district of the west side. It is named after FRANK (FRANZ) E. CUDELL, who gave the center to the city. The area includes approximately 6 city blocks between W. 98th and W. 100th streets and Detroit and Cudell avenues. This area is about half of a tract originally owned by Franklin Reuben Elliott, who built the nucleus of the Cudell house in 1845. In 1860 Elliott sold this portion of the tract to JACOB MUELLER (1822–1905), a German immigrant, lawyer, and founder and editor of the German-language newspaper *WACHTER UND ANZEIGER*. In 1872–74 Mueller was lieutenant governor of Ohio. In the 1870s and 1880s, his large estate comprised a deer park, orchards, and extensive produce and flower gardens. In the late 1880s Mueller transferred the property to Cudell, who had married Mueller's daughter Emma.

Frank Cudell (1844–1916), a German immigrant from Aachen, was an important Cleveland architect of churches and commercial blocks in partnership with John N. Richardson. He was a promoter of the Group Plan, a liberal thinker, a pamphleteer, and an inventor. Cudell remodeled the Mueller house, built 2 apartment terraces (the Cudell Dwellings) on W. 99th St., and deeded a portion of the property along West Blvd. to the city as a public park. He proposed a clock tower to be the centerpiece of a public garden in the parkway. When Cudell died in 1916, he bequeathed the house to the city, and his widow built the Cudell Tower as a memorial in 1917. After Emma Cudell's death in 1937, the house was opened by the Dept. of Parks & Recreation as the Cudell Arts & Crafts Ctr. in 1939. It was also the home of the west side branch of the GARDEN CTR. OF GREATER CLEVELAND. The center served as a meeting place for all kinds of recreational, educational, and cultural groups, and it was considered to be one of the first municipally operated arts and crafts centers in the country. In 1964 a large new brick recreation center and gymnasium was built by the city on the property. In 1977 the right-of-way of West Blvd. was relocated, and the Cudell House, 10013 Detroit Ave., was moved a short distance to the east.

**CUDELL, FRANK (FRANZ) E.** (1844–25 Oct. 1916), was a partner in the firm of Cudell & Richardson, the most important and innovative architects in Cleveland during the 1880s. Cudell was born at Herzogenrath, near Aachen (Aix-la-Chapelle), Germany. His parents were Dr. Karl and Louise Krauthausen Cudell. Cudell emigrated in 1866 and was employed briefly in the office of Leopold Eidlitz in New York. His younger brother Adolph became the senior part-

ner of the Chicago architectural firm of Cudell & Blumenthal. Franz Cudell came to Cleveland in 1867 and formed a partnership with John N. Richardson (1837–1902) in 1870. The most important early work of Cudell & Richardson was a series of churches in the Victorian Gothic style, for which Cudell's familiarity with German Gothic architecture undoubtedly provided precedents. Among the most European of the churches erected in Cleveland in the 1870s, especially significant were St. Joseph Catholic Church (1871–99), St. Stephen Catholic Church (1873–81), and FRANKLIN CIRCLE CHRISTIAN CHURCH (1874–75). Cudell & Richardson also designed institutional buildings such as the Jewish Orphan Asylum (1888) and residences for the well-to-do, of which 2 were known to be standing in the 1980s, the Jacob Goldsmith house (1880) and the TIEDEMANN HOUSE (1881).

Cudell's firm also designed many commercial buildings, especially a set of notable structures in the 1880s embodying an increased striving for lighter structure, more open walls, and the use of the new materials of cast and wrought iron. The development of these structures was contemporary with those of the Chicago School and can be seen in the Geo. Worthington Bldg. (1882), the Root & McBride-Bradley Bldg. (1884–85), and the PERRY-PAYNE BLDG. (1889). The latter was the first in Cleveland to use iron columns throughout all 8 stories (not a steel frame) and was celebrated for its interior light court. The firm of Cudell & Richardson dissolved following the completion of the Perry-Payne Bldg., and Cudell retired in 1903. He took an active interest in the development of the Group Plan. He wrote letters and broadsides pointing out flaws in the plan of the Group Plan Commission of Burnham, Carrere, and Brunner. These included *The Grouping of Cleveland's Public Buildings* (1903, *The Proposed Revised Plan of 1903 to Fit Present Conditions* (1916), and *The Columns upon Which to Support Our Republic* (1905), in which it was clear that Cudell felt that his own ideas had been ignored. Cudell was a liberal thinker, a pamphleteer, and an inventor. He bequeathed the property for the Cudell Ctr. to the city (see CUDELL). Cudell was married twice. His first wife, Marie (Heffenmuller), died in 1887. He married Emma Mueller, daughter of former lieutenant governor JACOB MUELLER, in 1889.

**CULTURAL GARDENS.** *See* **CLEVELAND CULTURAL GARDEN FEDERATION**

The **CUNNINGHAM SANITARIUM** was located at 18485 Lakeshore Blvd. at 185th St. The sanitarium was a 5-story-high spherical steel structure designed to maintain a pressurized atmosphere to aid in the treatment of various diseases, especially diabetes. Although oxygen therapy had been in use for over 8 years, Cleveland's sphere was the first to carry out such therapy on a large scale; it allegedly remained the only one of its kind in the world. This treatment, developed by Orval J. Cunningham of the University of Kansas, was founded on the belief that the higher air pressure introduced oxygen in abundance into the body system and aided in the therapy of various diseases. The Cunningham Sanitarium was built in 1928 by H. H. Timkin, owner of the Timkin Roller Bearing Co. of Canton, Ohio, after a friend of his underwent successful treatment by Dr. Cunningham. The site was chosen because of its location on the lake and the quiet and beauty of the surroundings. The structure, a 900-ton ball 64′ high with 38 rooms and 350 portholes, was built by the Melbourne Constr. Co. at a cost of $1 million. The ball was attached to a 3-story sanitarium hotel by a series of steel tanks resembling gas storage tanks. Patients taking the air cure could eat, sleep, read, and play games in the pressurized tanks.

The Cunningham Sanitarium was opened in 1928 and managed by Dr. Cunningham himself until 1934, when it was sold to Jas. H. Rand II, son of the cofounder of Remington Rand. Rand reorganized the hospital in 1935 and renamed it the Ohio Institute of Oxygen Therapy and used the air-pressure facilities for various research projects under his direction. In 1936 the hospital was again reorganized, as a general hospital known as Boulevard Hospital. Financial problems forced its closing in 1937. The site remained unused until purchased by the Diocese of Cleveland as a potential site for Catholic youth organization activities. The Cunningham Sanitarium was razed in 1942, and the scrap steel, valued at $25,000, went to help the war effort. St. Joseph High School was built on its site.

**CUSHING, ERASTUS** (15 July 1802–4 Apr. 1893), was one of Cleveland's most respected practicing physicians. The son of David, Jr., and Freelove Brown Cushing, he was born in Cheshire, Mass., in 1802. His father died in 1814, when Erastus was 12. In 1820 Erastus went to study medicine under Dr. Wm. Tyler of Lanesboro, Mass. Between 1822–23, he attended the New York College of Physicians & Surgeons in New York City; he was certified to practice in 1823. He continued his education at the Berkshire Medical Institute of Williams College in Pittsfield, Mass., where he was a student of JOHN DELAMATER. He received his medical degree from Berkshire in 1824. Cushing practiced medicine in Lanesboro, where in 1826 he married Mary Ann Platt. He also practiced briefly in Troy, N.Y. Interested in furthering his education, he attended lectures at the Medical Dept. of the University of Pennsylvania in Philadelphia between 1834–35. For health reasons he decided to leave New England and settle in Cleveland in Oct. 1835. He opened a practice on PUBLIC SQUARE as a family physician. Eventually he went into partnership with his son, Henry Kirk, who also became a physician. In 1837 Cushing served on the committee that organized the Willoughby Medical College in Akron, Ohio. He induced his former professor, Dr. John Delamater, to teach at Willoughby. Delamater subsequently left Willoughby to aid in the formation of the Cleveland Medical College, founded under the charter of Western Reserve University. Dr. Cushing was also involved in this endeavor, being appointed by the board of trustees of WRU to a committee charged with presenting to the board suitable candidates for the M.D. degree. Known as a kind and distinguished gentleman, easily recognizable by the long black cape he wore, Cushing continued in his lucrative private practice. He worked steadily until age 62, when he went into semiretirement. He retired fully at the age of 70. Cushing had 4 children and was the scion of a family of physicians. His son, HENRY KIRK CUSHING, grandsons Harvey and Edward F. Cushing, and great-grandsons E. H. and Kirke W. Cushing all received medical degrees.

**CUSHING, HARVEY W.** (8 Apr. 1869–7 Oct. 1939), the son of Henry Cushing, was America's first neurosurgeon and one of the most prominent physicians born in Cleveland. During the early decades of the 20th century, he developed techniques for operating on the brain and central nervous system that revolutionized neurosurgery. Born in Cleveland, Cushing was a graduate of CENTRAL HIGH SCHOOL. He received his medical degree from Harvard in 1895. He began his career as a general surgeon and only gradually became interested in the developing field of surgery of the brain and spinal cord. After a year of study in England and Germany, he became an associate professor of surgery of the central nervous system at Johns Hopkins University, where he came into contact with Sir Wm. Osler, a Canadian physician renowned for his earlier work on malaria, cerebral palsy, and diseases of the spleen, heart, and blood. He later wrote a biography of Osler, which won him a Pulitzer Prize in 1926. From 1912–32, Cushing was professor of surgery at Harvard Medical School, and from 1932–37 he was the Sterling Professor of Neurology at Yale. Cushing introduced a method of operating on the brain with a local anesthesia. Through preoperative studies, the use of tourniquets and silver clips to control bleeding, and new checks on blood pressure and oxygen levels, he reduced mortality from brain surgery to 10% at a time when most doctors were losing 33 to 50%. Cushing was also the first to use electrocautery in brain surgery. He was able to classify brain tumors and was the first to link them with gastric ulcers. An internationally known expert on the pituitary gland, in 1931 he discovered a new disease, Cushing's disease, in which there is overstimulation of the basophil cells of the pituitary. In 1969 a plaque was unveiled at the southeast corner of PUBLIC SQUARE honoring Cushing as America's first neurosurgeon. He was married to Katherine Crowell of Cleveland. They are buried together in LAKE VIEW CEMETERY.

**CUSHING, HENRY K.** (29 July 1827–12 Feb. 1910), was a prominent Cleveland physician during the late 19th century. He was one of the most active participants in Cleveland medical societies and during his career was a leader in local efforts to raise the professional and educational standards of the medical profession. Cushing was born in Lanesboro, Mass., the son of a physician, Dr. ERASTUS CUSHING. The family moved to Cleveland when Cushing was 8. He graduated from Union College in 1848 and then studied medicine under his father while also attending lectures at Cleveland Medical College. He received his medical degree in 1851 from the University of Pennsylvania in Philadelphia and soon after returned to Cleveland. In 1856, Cushing became a member of the faculty of the Western Reserve Medical Dept. He stayed on the faculty until 1883, primarily teaching obstetrics and gynecology. During the Civil War he served as surgeon-major in the 7TH OHIO VOLUNTEER INFANTRY. After the war he became a trustee of Western Reserve University, which conferred upon him an honorary degree in 1884. Through his involvement in medical societies, Cushing helped promote a more scientific approach to the study and practice of medicine. He was one of the organizers of the (early) Cleveland Academy of Medicine in 1867. He later served as president of the CUYAHOGA COUNTY MEDICAL ASSOC., during which time he organized an effort to purchase medical journals for the Case Library. In 1887, Cushing was made first president of the Cleveland Society of Medical Sciences, which intended to elevate the medical profession and raise money for a medical library. He later served on the joint committee of 3 Cleveland medical societies, which led to the founding of the CLEVELAND MEDICAL LIBRARY ASSOC. in 1894. In 1906 the Dept. of Experimental Medicine was formed at the Medical School of WRU and named in honor of Cushing. He married Betsey M. Williams in 1852; she died in 1903, leaving him with 6 children. Two sons, Edward and Harvey, followed their father's profession.

**CUTLER, ELLIOT CARR** (30 July 1888–16 Aug. 1947), was internationally known for his work in heart and brain surgery. Cutler was born in Bangor, Maine, to Geo. Chalmer and Mary Franklin Wilson Cutler. He received the A.B. degree from Harvard University in 1909 and the M.D. degree in 1913, graduating first in his class. After graduation, he was appointed surgical house officer at Peter Bent Brigham Hospital in Boston. In 1915, he became resident surgeon at Massachusetts General Hospital in Boston and alumni assistant at the Harvard Medical School. In 1916, he took an assistantship working in immunology and bacteriology at the Rockefeller Institute in New York City. During WORLD WAR I, Cutler was commissioned as a captain and given charge of Base Hospital No. 6. Later promoted to major, he was awarded the Distinguished Service Medal by the U.S. Congress for his work in the evacuation hospital in Boulogne, France. He returned to Harvard and Peter Bent Brigham Hospital in 1919, beginning his private practice in 1921. In 1924 Cutler was appointed professor of surgery at Western Reserve University Medical School and director of surgery at Lakeside Hospital, serving until 1932, when he was appointed to the Moseley Professorship of Surgery at Harvard and the directorship of surgery at Peter Bent Brigham Hospital. While in Cleveland, Cutler, collaborating with CLAUDE BECK, developed a surgical treatment, cardiovalvulotomy, for the heart condition mitral stenosis, a thickening and narrowing of the valve between the left auricle and left ventricle which hampers blood circulation. Used only 6 years, this procedure was responsible for opening the field of direct surgical approach to not only chronic valvular disease but also other congenital and acquired mechanical abnormalities of the heart. Cutler married Caroline Pollard Parker on 24 May 1919. The Cutlers had 4 children, Elliot, Thomas, David, and Marjorie Parker.

The **CUYAHOGA BUILDING** was one of 3 tall office buildings (the others being the Society for Savings Bldg. and the WESTERN RESERVE BLDG.) in Cleveland designed by Burnham & Root or Daniel H. Burnham & Co. of Chicago. Erected on PUBLIC SQUARE in 1892–93, the 8-story building was the last of the three, a fine example of the Chicago-style office building, and the first building in Cleveland with a complete structural steel frame. It was built by MYRON T. HERRICK and Jas. Parmalee and housed the offices of Herrick, secretary of the Society for Savings, advisor to Wm. McKinley, and later governor of Ohio and ambassador to France. TOM L. JOHNSON had his office in the building, and the CLEVELAND ELECTRIC ILLUMINATING CO. was a major tenant. The corner drugstore was occupied in turn by Meyer & Gleim, E. R. Selzer, and Schroeder's Drugs. When the Cuyahoga was demolished for the site of the Sohio building in 1982, the arched terra cotta entrance facing Superior Ave. was dismantled and reassembled as part of the Western Reserve Historical Society library building.

**CUYAHOGA COMMUNITY COLLEGE** was opened in Sept. 1963, 2 years after the Ohio legislature passed enabling legislation to create a statewide system of community colleges. Tri-C was designed to meet the need for low-cost, convenient, skill-oriented career and academic training among minorities, women, older students, and displaced workers in an era marked by a growing awareness of society's responsibility to offer equal opportunities to all its citizens. Following state action, the Cuyahoga County commissioners established the Cuyahoga Community College District in Oct. 1961 and appointed the first board of trustees the following January. Chairman Robt. Lewis raised $400,000 from the CLEVELAND FOUNDATION and business and private sources and submitted a plan to the state, and by Dec. 1962 the college was chartered under the leadership of its first president, Dr. Chas. Chapman. Facilities were first located in the old Brownell School Bldg. at Brownell Ct. and E. 14th St. A dedicated new faculty

worked to bring education to 3,039 students who enrolled in fall 1963. Aided by a levy passed in late 1963, the college expanded to other buildings and began planning a permanent home. Since the college aimed to bring affordable education to all county residents, the downtown construction was complemented by expansion westward to PARMA at the old CRILE HOSPITAL and eastward, where classes were held in area schools. The Metropolitan Campus opened in 1966, while the permanent Western Campus was built in 1975. The country club-like Eastern Campus was opened at Harvard and Richmond roads in 1981. Planning for the 3 campuses was centralized at the district office at 900 Carnegie Ave.

In line with the varied goals and levels of preparation of CCC students, the college offers freshman- and sophomore-level academic coursework that can be transferred to a 4-year college; remedial work to compensate for deficiencies in reading, grammar, and math; and career programs in allied health fields, engineering, business, and public service. Graduates receive an Associate of Applied Sciences degree, and those taking work in fields such as dental hygiene, registered nursing, medical assisting, and occupational therapy assisting are prepared for state certification and licensing. In addition to the degree programs, CCC offers off-campus general courses, noncredit courses for professional improvement and hobbies, and TV courses that can be taken for credit. While the 3 campuses offer most courses, each has its program specialties: Metro, nursing, dental hygiene, hospitality management; Western, aviation technology, physician assisting, transportation; Eastern, commercial art, ophthalmic dispensing technology. Campus facilities are also open to the community, and all campuses offer cultural events, with Metro the scene of many jazz, dance, dramatic, and classical music programs. After an enrollment boom in the 1960s and 1970s, Tri-C, like most Ohio colleges in the 1980s, suffered an enrollment decline. Such fluctuations in student population have led the college to realign its mission in terms of current needs. Following the recession of 1980, with its many layoffs in heavy industry, CCC entered the retraining field for the unemployed and the skills-obsolescent. In 1984, the college broke ground for a state-funded Unified Technologies Ctr. adjacent to the Metropolitan Campus that was to provide modern training facilities for business, industry, government, and labor. In 1986, Cuyahoga Community College had a full-time equivalent enrollment of about 20,000 students per quarter. Full-time faculty, represented by the American Assoc. of University Professors, numbered about 400, with part-timers hired each quarter as needed. The college was part of a statewide system that included 3 state community colleges, 5 county community colleges, 16 technical institutes, and 24 university branches.

The **CUYAHOGA COUNTY AIRPORT** is the main airport in Cuyahoga County of service to privately and corporately owned aircraft. It is also a regional center of aviation-related industries. With the increase in private aviation during the 1940s, the Board of County Commissioners appropriated funds through the issuance of general obligation bonds to develop a county airport. That ultimately led, in Dec. 1946, to the purchase of the former Herrick Airport on Richmond Rd. The Cuyahoga County Airport was officially dedicated on 30 May 1950 for the intended use of light, single-engine planes. Early proponents of the County Airport included the Cleveland Chamber of Commerce, the Cleveland Aviation Club, and the Board of Commissioners. Among the latter, Joseph F. Gorman was a particularly strong advocate. The airport continues to be a department of the county commissioners. Robt. D. Shea was airport director until 1969, when he was appointed director of aviation for county affairs.

During the airport's early years, the county confronted severe opposition from neighboring residents in Richmond Hts. and Highland Hts., who sought relocation of the airport elsewhere. The common pleas court ruled against a taxpayer's suit in 1947, a decision that was later upheld in the court of appeals. Periodically since then, legal battles have been waged to prevent various airport operations and improvements. These have been largely unsuccessful. Despite local opposition, the airport underwent enormous expansion in the 1950s and 1960s, including several extensions to the runway and the building of additional hangars to house the increasing number of planes using the airport. Through steady acquisition of land, by 1970 the airport had doubled its original size, to 585 acres. Most of the money for expansion came from county land sales and matching federal funds. In the 1960s, primary use of the County Airport began to shift in favor of corporately owned aircraft. In 1967, businesses were responsible for 60% of the airport traffic. By the end of the decade, its 3 main tenants were the Ohio Aviation Co., the Mercury Aviation Co., and TRW. Among the corporations that built hangars were TRW (1969), the EATON CORP. (1973), and Diamond Shamrock (1975). Although the Cuyahoga County Airport continued to serve private pilots throughout the 1970s, it also attracted more businesses. This trend carried into the 1980s with the completion, in 1984, of a $2.5 million office building and a proposed industrial park.

The **CUYAHOGA COUNTY ANTI-SLAVERY SOCIETY** was organized on 4 July 1837 at a meeting in the Old Stone Church. "The object of this society," according to its constitution, was "the entire abolition of slavery throughout the United States and the elevation of our colored brethren to their proper rank as men." Several of the professional and business men who took the lead in forming the new society were also prominent in the CLEVELAND ANTI-SLAVERY SOCIETY, formed in 1833. JOHN A. FOOTE presided over the organizational meeting of the county group and became a vice-president; John M. Sterling helped draw up the constitution and was president in 1841; Henry F. Brayton served as recording secretary; and Solomon L. Severance was treasurer. Each of these men was also a leader of the Cleveland society. Other officers in the county society were Edward Wade of BROOKLYN, president; and serving as vice-presidents, Samuel Freeman of PARMA, Asa Cody of EUCLID, J. L. Tomlinson of ROCKPORT, and Samuel Williamson of Willoughby. L. L. Rice served as the corresponding secretary. Similarities in leadership and in the constitutions of the two groups suggest that the Cuyahoga County Anti-Slavery Society may have been formed as the successor to the Cleveland society as antislavery sentiment spread throughout the county. The constitution of the Cleveland group called for annual 4 July meetings to elect officers; that the county group was organized on 4 July 1837, and the absence of newspaper references to the Cleveland society after this date, indicate that the county group was formed to replace the city society. In the early 1840s, the national antislavery movement split into warring factions, and after 1841 there are no references in local newspapers to either a Cuyahoga County or a Cleveland Anti-Slavery Society until Jan. 1859, when the *Leader* refers to single meetings of both organizations. On 10 Jan. 1859, an apparently new county society met at the African Methodist Episcopal Church on Bolivar St. to hear an antislavery speech.

The **CUYAHOGA COUNTY ARCHIVES** are the repository for the historical records of Cuyahoga County. The office encompasses the Office of Archives, Records Management, and Printing & Reproduction Services. The County Archives were created in June 1975 as a department of the Board of Cuyahoga County Commissioners. Their original purpose was manifold: to insure the useful administrative, fiscal, and legal life of all county records; and to save for present and future study, research, and use those records of significant historical importance. As part of their conception, they were also to assist in neighborhood preservation and restoration. The budget and essential operation of the County Archives are determined by the county commissioners. The commissioners responsible for their establishment were Hugh A. Corrigan, Seth Taft, and Frank R. Pokorny. Roderick B. Porter was director between 1975–85. After his resignation, he was succeeded in the management of the archives by Judith G. Cetina, curator of county manuscripts.

Prior to 1975, the county's efforts at records retention and disposal were sporadic. Records, some dating from 1810, were stored in several county buildings under various conditions. Some valuable records were inadvertently destroyed, and the overall use of space was inefficient. With the aid of guidelines published by the Ohio Historical Society, the County Archives were established to meet these needs. Their first endeavors were to microfilm documents of permanent historical value (court of common pleas transcripts and auditor records) and to remove poorly stored records from the Gross Bldg. on W. 9th St. They then became concerned with record scheduling, acquisition, and preservation and the arrangement and description of their more important holdings.

In Jan. 1974 the County Archives moved into the newly restored Rhodes House (1874) on Franklin Blvd. in OHIO CITY. The move increased visibility and allowed the public greater accessibility to county records. Among their holdings are death records (1863–1908), naturalization records (1818–1971), and county tax records (up to 1973), as well as mortgage records and land deeds. The archives also assumed a role as liaison between the county and cultural institutions that received money from the county, such as the Playhouse Square Foundation. In 1985 severe budget cutbacks constricted the operation of the archives. It was reduced to a minimal staff, and only work required by law was continued.

The **CUYAHOGA COUNTY BAR ASSOCIATION** has long been a supporter of civil rights and liberties of the individual. The association was organized in 1927 by 64 former members of the CLEVELAND BAR ASSOC. Originally the Cleveland Law Assoc., its initial purpose was "to form a progressive lawyers' association aimed at protecting the rights of the public in any instance whether in the courts, the legislature, or in city government matters." Its first trustees were Judge Frederick P. Walther, Judge Thos. E. Greene, Judge Bradley Hull, and J. P. Mooney, and HARRY F. PAYER was elected the first president in 1927. Both officers and trustees were elected by the members and held office for 1 year. In 1939, the association became involved in opposing the bar integration issue, where membership, dues, and licensing are mandatory before practicing law. In 1948, it endorsed the Gwynne Bill, which allowed lawyers to practice without further testing before administrative agencies, and limited the same standards of advertising and soliciting to both groups. In the same year it supported fair employment practices and set up a committee to study chronic alcoholism. In 1949, it recommended that judges in divorce cases send attorneys cards notifying them of overdue decrees and setting up a new date when due, and requiring decrees to be filed as soon as the case was heard. In addition, it organized and demanded a judge's removal from pretrial procedures for improper case handling while being paid at public expense. During that same year, the Cleveland Bar Assoc. offered to assist in bringing to trial the editor of a local newspaper who had allowed a reporter to criticize the divorce court. It also opposed the Bartunek-Seibert Bill, believing it violated due process of law. In 1951, after investigating charges of illegal adoption practices involving attorneys, it found no wrongdoing. In 1961, it became the first association favoring abolishing capital punishment. In 1985, the association had over 2,000 members.

Cuyahoga County Bar Assoc. Records, WRHS.

The **CUYAHOGA COUNTY CENTENNIAL** was observed with a week-long celebration, 10–15 Oct. 1910. The festivities included a carnival, an air show, a boat regatta, an Indian village, concerts, and fireworks. The celebration officially opened at noon on Monday, 10 Oct., with a 100-gun salute from the naval vessel the U.S.S. *Dorothea* in Cleveland harbor, and the flag-raising ceremony of pioneer settlers. Daily features of the centennial celebration included afternoon and evening band concerts on PUBLIC SQUARE, a carnival and sideshows on the Mall, and an Indian village of 3 teepees and 14 Chippewas brought in from an Indian reservation in Michigan and erected on the Square. Monday's major event was the dedication of the new Harvard-Denison Bridge by the Cuyahoga County commissioners. On Tuesday, 300,000 spectators viewed a parade of floral decorated automobiles traveling from WADE PARK along Euclid Ave. downtown past the judging stand on Public Square and proceeding across the SUPERIOR VIADUCT and along Detroit Ave. to the western end of LAKEWOOD, where dedication ceremonies were held by the county commissioners for the new Rocky River Bridge. Wednesday activities, held under the auspices of Cleveland's Italian-American societies, celebrated the anniversary of Christopher Columbus's discovery of the Americas and featured a downtown fireworks display on the lakefront. Thursday was designated as "Cleveland Day." Open houses were held at all Cleveland firehouses, a peacepipe ceremony was held between the Chippewas and Cleveland city officials, and the centennial anniversary fireworks display was held on the lakefront. Special seating arrangements for 10,000 were set up along the embankment overlooking the lakefront airfield as aviators Glenn Curtiss, Augustus Post, Bud Mars, Chas. Willard, J. D. McCurdy, and N. C. Adosides performed on Thursday for the first of a 2-day aerial show. Using 2 8-cyl., 69-hp aircraft and 1 4-cyl., 25-hp aircraft, the aviators competed in a series of 12 different speed, skill, and endurance competitions. Saturday's closing festivities included a powerboat regatta and races at EDGEWATER PARK, the play *Hiawatha*, as performed by the Chippewa Indians, and the biggest parade in Cleveland's history, featuring Cleveland's military and fraternal orders and 26 marching bands.

The **CUYAHOGA COUNTY COLONIZATION SOCIETY** was formed at a meeting at the Academy on 8 Jan. 1827. The society favored bringing an end to slavery by colonization: the government would buy slaves from their masters and transport the newly freed blacks to Africa. Supporters of colonization, which gained a national following in the 1820s and early 1830s, believed the plan offered inducements to slaveholders that would hasten the end of the peculiar institution. Prominent citizens of the area were among the leaders of the Cuyahoga County Colonization Society. Its president was businessman and at-torney Samuel Cowles. The colonization plan drew much criticism from supporters of the immediate abolition of slavery. As antislavery sentiment and abolitionist fervor grew in the 1830s, the local colonization society faded from existence. The last meeting of the Cuyahoga County Colonization Society mentioned in the *Annals of Cleveland* is the annual meeting in Jan. 1830.

The **CUYAHOGA COUNTY COURTHOUSE** is the fifth structure erected for that purpose. The first was a 2-story log building constructed in 1813. It contained jail cells, a living room for the sheriff, and a 2d-floor courtroom. It was replaced in 1830 after the completion of the second courthouse. For a brief description of the second, third, and fourth courthouses, see ARCHITECTURE-CIVIC. The fifth courthouse was erected on Lakeside Ave. at Ontario St. as part of the Group Plan scheme proposed in 1903. The building was begun in 1906 and completed in 1911, at a cost of $4 million. The architects of the modern steel-and-concrete, granite-faced structure were LEHMAN & SCHMITT, with CHAS. MORRIS as chief designer. The courthouse is one of the finest examples of the Beaux-Arts style in the city and is ornamented with sculptures representing historic lawgivers. At the entrance stand bronze statues of Jefferson and Hamilton. Above the cornice are marble statues of Stephen Langton and Simon de Montfort by Herbert Adams, Edward I and John Hampton by Daniel Chester French, and John Sommers and Lord Mansfield by Karl Bitter. On the north side of the building are statues of Moses and Gregory IX by Herman Matzen, and of Justinian, Alfred, John Marshall, and RUFUS RANNEY. The interior is noteworthy for the grand 3-story central court with vaulted ceilings, marble Ionic columns, and a balustraded mezzanine. The interior decorative scheme was under the direction of CHAS. SCHWEINFURTH. An elegant curving marble staircase rises past a large stained-glass window representing Law & Justice. In the 2d-floor corridor are murals of *The Signing of the Magna Carta* by Frank Brangwyn and *The Constitutional Convention of 1787* by Violet Oakley. The contractors for the courthouse were ANDREW DALL & SON, the largest masonry and building contractors in the city at the turn of the century, who were also responsible for the SOLDIERS & SAILORS MONUMENT, the Society for Savings Bldg., and many of the great Euclid Ave. mansions. With its magnificent classical architecture and the best of decorative and symbolic art, the Cuyahoga County Courthouse is one of the most significant governmental structures in the city.

The **CUYAHOGA COUNTY DEMOCRATIC PARTY** gradually organized when the national Democratic party began to take shape. Known at first as the Democratic-Republican party, by the early 1830s it had shortened its name to the Democratic party. It favored an agrarian society, expansion of suffrage, and the preeminence of local and state governments over the national government. Cuyahoga County was the basic unit of local party organization. The first recorded county meeting was held 18 Sept. 1818 at the Commercial Coffee House to nominate candidates for the state legislature. Thereafter, delegates from the townships in the county assembled in convention several weeks before the October elections to select nominees for county and state offices and the federal Congress. If in agreement, they would print 1 slate of candidates; if not, rival slates of candidates emerged. As national issues such as the Natl. Bank, internal improvements, and slavery arose, parties became more formal, and the county conventions appointed committees to oversee party concerns between elections.

In the village of Cleveland, the early party was a spontaneous grouping of men around a leader. The residents knew the potential candidates for local office personally, and nominations were made at an informal meeting of citizens. The newspaper published their selections, as well as any additional nominees suggested by other residents. Elections were usually held in the courthouse or schoolhouse until the city was incorporated in 1836, when a voting place was designated for each ward. In the 1830s and 1840s, the Democratic party and the Whigs divided the governing of the city between them. As time went on, political campaigns became social occasions, with speeches, posters, marching, singing, parades, and flags. Local newspapers were politically active. The PLAIN DEALER, founded in 1842, served as the voice of the Democratic party. Party meetings were held a few days before the April elections to choose candidates for city offices, and as with the county, they were announced in the newspapers. Local Democrat and Ohio senator REUBEN WOOD was elected governor of Ohio in 1850. With the annexation of OHIO CITY in 1853, the number of wards increased from 4 to 11, and ward meetings and committees were organized.

As antislavery sentiment grew and the CIVIL WAR came, the Republican party became dominant, and the Democratic party declined in influence. With the postwar growth of Cleveland, politics became a year-round endeavor, and Democratic Clubs were formed to maintain party activities between elections. Recognized Democratic leaders in the latter half of the 19th century included JOHN FARLEY, CHAS. P. SALEN, Wm. Crawford, and HARRY "CZAR" BERNSTEIN. The party regained strength, sending MARTIN FORAN and then TOM L. JOHNSON to Congress in the late 1880s and early 1890s, and between 1891–1901 divided mayoralty honors equally with the Republicans. In 1895, the local party split over the tariff issue and the free coinage of silver. Solid gold democrats led by *Plain Dealer* publisher LIBERTY E. HOLDEN and John Farley opposed the silverites led by Chas. Salen. This split allowed the Republicans to win the mayoral election that year.

The Democrats regained city hall from 1899–1910 by electing John Farley mayor in 1899 and Tom Johnson in 1901. The support of former populists PETER WITT and Tom Fitzsimmons, who were able to attract both the labor and the German vote, made the party dominant in the 1901 election. Johnson controlled city council as well as the city and county party committees, and built an organization loyal to him. In 1904, the Ohio legislature, which controlled municipal affairs, changed municipal elections from April to November to coincide with the presidential, state, congressional, judicial, and county elections. It was expected that there would be less independent voting for local offices. To curb the influence of political parties in the electoral process, the legislature also replaced party-nominating conventions with direct primaries, making them mandatory for county, township, municipal, and school board offices in 1908, and for congressional seats and delegates to the national party conventions in 1910. The party therefore had to devote more of its time and resources to election campaigning. Nonpartisan primaries were introduced in Cleveland's home rule charter in 1913. NEWTON D. BAKER succeeded Johnson as head of the local Democratic party organization in 1910 and served as mayor of Cleveland from 1912–16. He relinquished active leadership of the party to his chief lieutenant, W. BURR GONGWER, in 1924, but remained chairman of the County Central Committee until 1936.

The Democrats were a minority party during the years of the CITY MANAGER PLAN. However, with the demise of the plan in 1931, Democrat RAY T. MILLER was elected mayor. The party split into factions in the 1930s as Miller and MARTIN L. SWEENEY fought for control, and Miller later sought to replace Gongwer as party chairman. Although he was elected chairman in 1938, lawsuits and countersuits followed until 1940, when the state central committee finally declared Miller county chairman. Miller then made Cleveland a Democratic stronghold by securing the political allegiance of both the black community and the nationality groups.

In the late 1940s and 1950s, the Democratic party consolidated its city organization. However, as more Democrats moved to the suburbs in the early 1960s, they began to organize their latent suburban strength. Party unity was challenged when a group of black Democrats broke away from the regulars in 1970 to organize the 21st District Caucus. The caucus's name and membership boundaries came from the congressional district of Louis Stokes, who was elected chairman. It was felt that the caucus would have more political influence by providing unified backing for the candidates of their choice. In 1972, in an effort to reestablish party unity, the regular Democratic party named 3 cochairmen, Geo. Forbes, Anthony Garofoli, and Hugh Corrigan. Corrigan resigned in 1976, leaving Forbes and Garofoli to run the party. They reverted to a single chairman in 1978 with the election of Timothy Hagan. When Hagan was elected county commissioner in 1984, John M. Coyne succeeded him as chairman.

The Cuyahoga County Democratic party in 1984 consisted of ward or precinct committeemen elected in the primaries by the registered Democrats in each ward or precinct in the county. The committeemen made up the County Central Committee, who in turn elected the county chairman and 400 of the 750-member Executive Committee. The remaining 350 members of the committee were selected by the county chairman. All committeemen, as well as the county chairman, were elected in even-numbered years and served 2-year terms. The Executive Committee was the decision-making body of the party and formally met twice a year to endorse Democratic candidates for the primary elections.

Powell, Thomas Edward, *The Democratic Party in the State of Ohio* (1913).

The **CUYAHOGA COUNTY DEPARTMENT OF HUMAN SERVICES** (Welfare Dept.) is the division of county government responsible for financially assisting and supervising the disabled and disadvantaged residents of the county. Its establishment formally acknowledged the county as the agent in charge of human services, rather than private, city, or state agencies. Formed 1 Jan. 1948 by a resolution of Cuyahoga County commissioners Curry, Pekarek, and Gorman, the Welfare Dept. was charged with administration of sections of the Ohio code that dealt with public welfare. These include aid to dependent children and the needy blind, poor relief and burials, emergency aid in war- or peacetime, and cooperation with state and federal authorities in these activities. John J. Schaffer was appointed by the county commissioners as the first director of the department, and he and his staff were responsible to the commissioners. The Welfare Dept. was an outgrowth of several agencies that had been in place prior to 1948. Before 1933, welfare had been the province of the Associated Charities and the Jewish Social Service Bureau, both private agencies under the jurisdiction of the Community Fund. From 1933–48, public welfare was variously handled by the county (the Cuyahoga County Relief Admin.); the city of Cleveland (the Wayfarers' Lodge, furnished rooms, boarding houses, and nursing homes); and the U.S. government (the Federal Emergency Relief Admin.).

As a result of national legislation and changes in the Ohio code, the Cuyahoga County Welfare Dept. greatly increased its sphere of responsibility during the 1960s and 1970s. By 1983, the department was the largest of the county's governmental divisions, with 2,500 employees providing services to 250,000 county residents each month. Functions were later divided into social services, income maintenance, and shared services. Social services include nonfinancial supportive assistance to help people achieve self-sufficiency, to protect children and adults, and to preserve families, through programs such as shelters for abused children and adults, adoption and foster care, daycare, family planning, homemaker services, and alcohol and drug rehabilitation. Income maintenance includes administration of Supplemental Security Income, Aid to Dependent Children, Title XX funds, and general relief funds, as well as determination of eligibility. Specific activities include the work-supplement program, food stamps, home-delivered meals, and medical assistance. Shared services are internally focused systems, planning and training, management information, and administration and finance. In 1983, the Cuyahoga County Welfare Dept.'s cost of operation represented 38% of the county's general fund. On 20 July 1984, the Dept. of Welfare was renamed the Dept. of Human Services.

The **CUYAHOGA COUNTY DOMESTIC RELATIONS COURT** is a subdivision of the court of common pleas. It has full equitable power and jurisdiction over all domestic-relations matters, including authority to terminate marriages, divide property, and determine child custody and support payments. Located in the old courthouse on Lakeside Ave., the Domestic Relations Court consisted of 5 judges, 5 trial referees, and 7 Central Motion Docket (CMD) referees in 1986. Cases are heard only by the judges or their trial referees, while the CMDs entertain all pre- and postdecree motions. Alarmed at the rising number of divorce suits, common pleas court judges in 1920 voted to establish the Domestic Relations Bureau. Located on the 2d floor of the new courthouse on St. Clair Ave., the bureau's goal was to prevent divorce, thereby saving Cleveland from gaining a reputation as a "divorce center." Since many applicants were found to be from out of state, the bureau was designated to investigate residence qualifications of those seeking divorce and, when possible, to reconcile the litigants. The bureau merely forwarded domestic-relations cases to the common pleas judges, who heard divorce cases as "fillers" between regular civil cases. In 1929, the bureau was replaced by a new Domestic Relations Court. Under this new arrangement, all domestic matters were assigned to one courtroom and heard by the common pleas judges on a rotating basis. By 1944, Cuyahoga County remained the only large Ohio county without a permanent domestic-relations court with judges specifically elected for the position. In 1959, the Ohio legislature voted to create a Domestic Relations Branch of the Cuyahoga County Court of Common Pleas and to create 2 new judicial positions to hear exclusively domestic-relations matters. The Div. of Domestic Relations presently (1986) comprises 4 departments. The Family Conciliation Service, created in 1979, is staffed by a psychologist, a psychiatrist, and 4 social workers who attempt to help litigants mediate their differences. The Legal Dept., composed of 4 attorneys, provides legal research and assistance for the judges and referees. The Dept. of Investigations is called into cases at the court's discretion. The Bureau of Child Support enforces court-established child- and spousal-support orders.

The **CUYAHOGA COUNTY FAIR** began in 1893 and has run every summer except for 1932 (because of the Depression), 1942, and 1943 (because of WORLD WAR II). The first agricultural fair held in the county was in 1829. During the 1850s, the Cuyahoga Agricultural Society supported the county fair in CHAGRIN FALLS, which remained in existence until 1914. At that time, the county commissioners decided to leave Chagrin Falls and consolidate the event in BEREA. Before that time, fairs were held in several scattered areas throughout the county, including Dover (originating there in 1861), Warren, and Cleveland. Basically, there were 2 main fairs—the one in Chagrin Falls, for the east side of the county, and one in various locations surrounding Berea, for the west side. By 1871, the Berea Agricultural Society had been formed. At this time the fair was held in late September/early October. This group began to decline and in 1884 asked the state legislature for a permit to sell the land and buildings of the society. The West Cuyahoga County Fair Society was established in 1893. They located their fairgrounds on the current (1986) site in Berea and MIDDLEBURG HTS., where the fair has remained ever since. By 1899, the Berea fair had made the one in Dover unprofitable, and it ceased to operate. Originally, the fair was held only during the daylight. In 1914, a "night fair" was tried, and the evening crowds outnumbered the daytime patrons. Schools closed for the day, and practically all business was suspended for the fair during the first 2 decades of the 1900s. In 1924, 40 acres were added to the grounds; and in 1929, the main entrance was decorated with an ornamental steel arch designed by Fred J. Hartman. Additional ground improvements were undertaken during the Depression by the WPA. Another 18 acres were added to the grounds in Feb. 1950. On 10 Sept. 1931, the West Cuyahoga County Agricultural Society changed its name to the Cuyahoga County Agricultural Society. Over the years, the agricultural nature of the fair declined, and it took on more of a carnival atmosphere. However, into the 1980s, the participation of the 4-H clubs has helped to maintain the agricultural aspect.

**CUYAHOGA COUNTY GOVERNMENT.** On 16 July 1810, the General Assembly of Ohio approved an act calling for the organization of the county of Cuyahoga. This statute did not, however, include a unique plan for the political structure of the new county, because the state constitution had established that the general assembly would provide, by general law, for the government of all Ohio counties according to the same organization. However, as Cuyahoga County grew in the ensuing 170 years, particularly in the period following WORLD WAR I, this standard structure was greatly modified to meet the needs of an increasingly urban area. At the center of county government in Ohio is a board of commissioners, a panel of 3 persons first provided for by statute in 1804. The commissioners serve as the county's executive and legislative branches of government and conduct business in concert with 8 independently elected administrative officials. These officers, the auditor, clerk of courts, coroner, engineer, prosecuting attorney, recorder, treasurer, and sheriff, elected for terms of 4 years, derive their power and receive their duties from the state. The court of common pleas, the "backbone" of the state's judicial system, assumes the primary responsibility, with the assistance of the prosecuting attorney, clerk of courts, sheriff, and coroner, for the administration of justice in the county.

Although each elected official has separate and distinct responsibilities within this framework, largely carried out by administrative, professional, and clerical staffs, the historical development of each of Cuyahoga County's offices has been similar in many ways. All of the county's elected officers have identifiable predecessors that served under English law or under the laws of the Northwest Territory. All of the offices, with the exception of the coroner and sheriff, were originally occupied by individuals appointed to the position, by either the state legislature or the courts, and only gradually did state law require that officeholders be elected by the people for terms that would vary in their duration during the 19th and 20th centuries. The offices of the sheriff and coroner were specifically provided for in the Ohio Constitution of 1802 and made elective, originally for terms of 2 years. This structure remained fundamentally the same throughout most of the 19th century, as did the basic duties and responsibilities originally assigned to the offices. The activities of these major departments gradually increased and broadened, however, as the business of governing became more complex. The first real modifications in the basic structure of county government did not occur until the late 19th century, and by 1913, several new offices and agencies had been added. In the years that followed, the growth of government was steady and marked as the county, particularly through the action of the Board of Cuyahoga County Commissioners, as empowered by the state, continued to respond to the needs of a growing urban population and the problems posed by an increasingly complex industrial society, through the creation of new agencies and institutions in the fields of health, human services, justice affairs, PUBLIC SAFETY, and TRANSPORTATION.

By 1913, the structure of county government, largely static throughout most of the 19th century, had expanded to include several new agencies and divisions. The organization of the court system, for example, was modified to include courts of appeal (1912) and insolvency (1896), as well as a juvenile court. The CUYAHOGA COUNTY JUVENILE COURT, created by state legislation passed in 1902, represented the second such entity in the U.S. The provisions of the Ohio measure made it applicable to Cuyahoga County only, and the legislation was promoted and supported by local-interest groups who advocated the creation of a separate court, and thus distinction in treatment, for the juvenile offender. The juvenile court was linked to a detention home for minors made possible by state legislation passed in 1908 granting the commissioners authority, with the advice and recommendation of a duly authorized judge, to establish such an institution for delinquent, dependent, or neglected youth. The juvenile court also presided over the Mothers' Pension program, created by state law in 1913, which allowed a stipend to women with children under the age of 16 who lacked traditional means of support.

The responsibilities of the probate court, originally established under the provisions of the Ohio Constitution of 1851, had also expanded to include, by 1913, the power to appoint 4 county residents to constitute a board of park commissioners known in Cuyahoga County as the County Park Commission. In 1913 the probate judge also received the power to appoint the county board of visitors, a body authorized by an act of the Ohio general assembly in 1882 with responsibility to keep apprised of the conditions and management of all charitable and correctional facilities supported in whole, or in part, by county or municipal taxation. By 1913, the court of common pleas also had its authority expanded to include jurisdiction over a jury commission (1894) and the SOLDIERS & SAILORS RELIEF COMMISSION. The Board of County Commissioners also had new departments to supervise, including divisions of blind relief and soldiers' and sailors' burial, as well as a purchasing agent. Through the activities of 2 of these new

agencies, the commissioners became involved in the business of providing assistance to the needy. In 1884, for example, the general assembly empowered the commissioners to appoint 3 persons in each township of their county with the duty of providing for the burial of any honorably discharged soldier, sailor, or marine who died without the means to pay his funeral expenses. In 1913, the commissioners also assumed the duties of administering state aid to visually handicapped citizens through the operation of the blind-relief division.

The years after 1913 saw a continued expansion of county responsibilities. By 1936, a number of new agencies, boards, and divisions had been integrated into the county system. The business of the court of common pleas attained an increasing level of professionalization during the 1920s with the establishment of a criminal-record department, to more systematically compile individual crime records; a probation department; and a psychiatric clinic, to furnish the trial judge with a report on the mental condition of a prisoner to assist him in determining whether hospitalization was preferable to punishment. The addition of a domestic-relations bureau to the court of common pleas reflected a continuing trend toward specialization in legal matters. Although the bureau was organized in 1920, it was not until 1929 that the litigation pertaining to divorce and domestic-relations matters was actually segregated and given to 1 judge for disposition (see CUYAHOGA COUNTY DOMESTIC RELATIONS COURT).

By 1936, there were 13 divisions under the direct authority of the county commissioners. Two of these departments were created to alleviate the hardships brought to county residents by the Depression. The Cuyahoga County Relief Admin. served as the agency for the disposition of public-relief funds in the county; while under the provisions of state legislation passed in 1933, the commissioners were authorized to administer funds for housing relief in the county. A third agency, the recreation division, was formed directly by the commissioners to see that funds were distributed to the best advantage on work-relief projects related to recreation, including playground, MUSIC, and theatrical projects. This action did not represent a temporary commitment made necessary by the conditions of the era. When the activities of the CCRA were terminated, the county commissioners continued their responsibility in the area of public welfare by accepting control of the "Central Bureau" from the city of Cleveland in 1937. By this action, the new County Relief Bureau assumed the duty of providing for the transient, paupers, and the disabled, with an administrative staff to coordinate and organize its actions. The Relief Bureau remained part of the county structure until 1947, when the commissioners, by authority granted to them by state law, created the County Welfare Dept. In the tradition of the CCRA and the County Relief Bureau, the new department assumed the responsibility for the welfare services provided by the board. In 1952 the child welfare board, established in 1929 to care for neglected and dependent children, was transferred to the County Welfare Dept., and in 1953 its name was changed to the Div. of Child Welfare.

The county commissioners also became involved in the care of the elderly and chronically ill by establishing a county nursing home in 1938. This responsibility increased during the 1940s and 1950s as the county assumed duties formerly handled by the city of Cleveland. In 1942 the Sunny Acres tuberculosis sanitarium was deeded from the city to the county, and in 1953, Highland View Hospital for the chronically ill was opened as a county facility. The postwar years witnessed the creation of additional agencies. In 1946 the commissioners took the first step toward the development of additional airport facilities, recognizing that with the development of airline travel as a major mode of private and commercial transportation, it was necessary for Cuyahoga County, as an important urban area, to supply adequate landing fields and air terminals. The CUYAH-OGA COUNTY AIRPORT on Richmond Rd. was officially opened and dedicated in 1950.

During the cold-war years, the county became actively involved in CIVIL DEFENSE. In 1952, the commissioners empowered their board president to enter into agreements with the various municipalities for the purpose of coordinating civil-defense activities. Additional postwar cooperation between the county and its surrounding municipalities was also made necessary by the high rate of urban development. In 1947, the county commissioners approved an agreement for cooperation with area municipalities in the creation and maintenance of a Regional Planning Commission to work toward rational planning for local growth. Another legacy of the postwar period was the county's involvement in coordinating housing for returning veterans. In 1946, under authority granted by the Ohio general assembly, the commissioners provided for the establishment of the Cuyahoga County Veterans Emergency Housing Project and appointed an administrator to take charge of the "acquisition, planning, construction, operation and maintenance" of such a project. The creation of these new offices and agencies imposed upon the board an increasing number of administrative duties. To assist them in carrying out their responsibilities, the commissioners were the first in the state to establish the position of the county administrative officer. The commissioners assigned to the county administrator a variety of tasks that included the daily supervision of the county's offices, departments, and services and the responsibility of assisting the board in administering and enforcing its policies and resolutions.

Following 1952, county structure continued to change as some obsolete departments were abolished and new ones were created to meet changing circumstances. In 1958, the county's veterans' housing program was terminated, as it no longer rendered a vital service. In 1975, the commissioners approved the establishment of an archival agency to give life to the county's largely moribund records commission; to control the growing mountain of paperwork by offering records-management services to the various county offices and agencies; and to make available the county's documentary heritage to the public. Earlier the commissioners had attempted to better organize their system of information gathering by establishing a data-processing board in 1967. This board, consisting of the auditor, treasurer, and 1 of the commissioners, approves the acquisition of automatic data-processing equipment and is authorized to establish a centralized data-processing system for all county offices. In the area of justice services, the commissioners created a public defender's commission in Nov. 1976 with the goal of its becoming the "principal source of representation . . . of those persons eligible for publicly provided counsel in criminal, juvenile, and probate proceedings." By Mar. 1978, a public defender was hired, assisted initially by a staff of 16 attorneys.

Additional changes during the post-World War II period occurred when older agencies were reorganized but retained their basic functions. The Welfare Dept., established in 1947, was by 1986 known as the CUYAHOGA COUNTY DEPT. OF HUMAN SERVICES. The services offered by the department had so increased that they were reorganized within 3 major divisions: social services, income maintenance, and shared services. Each division, in turn, administered a plethora of special projects and programs. The social-services division administered adoption and foster care, an alcoholic and drug rehabilitation unit, and homemaker services, among other programs. The Metzenbaum Children's Ctr., also under the jurisdiction of social services, was opened in 1966, replacing the Winifred Fryer County Children's Receiving Home. It functioned as an emergency shelter for abused and neglected children who were wards of the county. The civil-defense activities of the 1950s, marked by the establishment of fallout shelters and the regular testing of air-raid sirens, were outdated by the 1980s, but the county's charge to preserve public safety during times of emergency continued, particularly under the Disaster Services Agency, established in 1977, which has the responsibility to prepare plans and coordinate emergency activities in the face of disaster, whether natural or manmade.

By the 1980s, services to the chronically ill had been expanded and reorganized. In 1979, the county merged the Highland View chronic hospital with Metropolitan General Hospital, and in June of that year the Highland View chronic and rehabilitation hospital on the campus of Metro General was formally dedicated. The county's work with the elderly expanded greatly in this period to meet the needs of the growing segment of older people in the general population. In 1976, the county was designated as Area Agency on Aging for Cuyahoga, Geauga, Lake, Lorain, and Medina counties. As such, it directs federal funds and matching local grants to city aging offices and private nonprofit agencies to be used for such services as nutrition programs and the purchase or renovation of senior centers for the elderly. In 1968, another planning agency, the NORTHEAST OHIO AREAWIDE COORDINATING AGENCY, was established, as the county board joined the commissioners from 5 neighboring counties to form an agency with responsibility for solving the joint problems of a multicounty region. By the 1980s, NOACA was involved in issues such as land use, housing, transportation, waste treatment, and water quality. The years after WORLD WAR II also witnessed the development of several substantially autonomous local government agencies that, although not directly controlled by the electorate, developed out of needs for special services in the areas of health, transportation, education, and library facilities. Most of these boards and commissions are associated with the county's structure, as the commissioners either appoint a certain number of persons to serve as their members of the board or actually serve as ex-officio members of the agencies. These included (in 1986) the Mental Retardation Board (1967), the Community Mental Health & Retardation Board (1968), the Cuyahoga Community College District Board (1962), the CLEVELAND CUYAHOGA COUNTY PORT AUTHORITY (1968), and the GREATER CLEVELAND REGIONAL TRANSIT AUTHORITY (1975).

The growing complexity of Cuyahoga County's governmental structure and the proliferation of the services it provides were a natural product of the overall growth of the area during the 20th century and reflected the need to provide uniform, coordinated services to meet the common needs that may formerly have been met by individual municipalities. This evolution of responsibility has been used by advocates of a regional governmental structure to illustrate the necessity of such a structure. However, by the 1980s, all formal efforts to achieve regional government had been defeated, and the growth of county services to meet common area needs seemed destined to continue.

Judith G. Cetina
Cuyahoga County Archives

See also GOVERNMENT, POLITICS.

The **CUYAHOGA COUNTY HOSPITAL SYSTEM,** recognized as the nation's first public hospital system, consisted of Metro General/Highland View Hospital, Sunny Acres Skilled Nursing Facility, the Kenneth W. Clement Ctr. for Family Health Care, and the Chronic Illness Ctr. in 1986. The system also provided ambulatory medical and community health services through several facilities. The system was officially organized in 1958, when the county electorate approved the transfer of the City Hospital of Cleveland to the county hospital board's authority. The purpose was to provide multiple patient services and health programs largely financed by the county. As a public hospital, over the years it has mainly served indigent patients. The system is governed by a 10-member county hospital board composed of electors of the county. Board members serve 6-year, overlapping terms, with appointment by the Board of County Commissioners. Funds for rebuilding the system's physical plant came largely from capital-improvement levies in 1963, 1966, and 1971. Voters also approved operating levies to help finance multiple patient services and health programs. By the 1980s, it had become the largest system of its kind in the state of Ohio (1,000 beds), offering tertiary, secondary, and primary care, with extensive ancillary facilities and a number of highly specialized services. In addition, it has a teaching program in affiliation with CASE WESTERN RESERVE UNIVERSITY. In the early 1980s, the focus of the system's planning shifted from capital improvements to operational matters. At this time, the system was—in addition to its major facilities—maintaining several community health programs, including Project GOH (Golden Age Outreach for Health), a program to improve neighborhood care of the elderly in the Fairfax area; the Maternity & Infant Care Project, offering no-charge maternity care and family-planning services to women living within designated social-planning areas in Cleveland; the Women, Infants, & Children Program, a specialized supplemental food program; and a tuberculosis control program. Throughout much of its existence, the system has served more patients in the Medicare, Medicaid, county indigent, and other governmental programs than any other hospital in the area.

The oldest and largest component of the CCHS is Cleveland Metro General Hospital. Until the 1950s it operated as the City Hospital of Cleveland, which was founded in 1837. Its initial purpose was to serve as a municipal institution for healing the sick; the need for such a facility originated from a CHOLERA EPIDEMIC in 1832. Management was under the control of the Board of Health, the mayor, and 3 members of council. Located on E. 14th, within a few years it disintegrated into an almshouse for the infirm, poor, and insane. Interest in reorganizing the City Hospital culminated in the construction of a new hospital on Scranton Rd. in 1889. Within a few years, the hospital had a medical staff of 28 doctors and a training school for nurses. In 1903 a tuberculosis sanatorium was set up, the first of its kind in the U.S. Although the hospital cared for a large number of sick patients, mainly indigent or tubercular, it also continued to operate as an asylum for the insane until 1909, when emphasis was shifted to its function as a general hospital.

The hospital saw its greatest development in the 1920s, when a number of new buildings were constructed under the leadership of city welfare director DUDLEY S. BLOSSOM. The new complex, at the Scranton Rd. site, consisting of 16 buildings covering 28 acres, was, by 1932, the 6th-largest general hospital in the nation, and considered one of the best municipal hospitals. In 1930, 55% of its costs were paid by the city, and 45% by the county. By the early 1930s, despite a good medical staff, the hospital was being consistently criticized for inefficiencies due to poor political planning. To reduce political interference in its operation, a Citizen's Advisory Committee was appointed in 1934. However, the hospital continued to suffer from operational problems through the 1940s. Studies done in the 1950s showed a lack of facilities, equipment, and funds, as well as poor administration, so in 1958 the electorate of Cuyahoga County voted that the hospital be turned over to the authority of the Cuyahoga County commissioners. It was renamed Cleveland Metro General Hospital. Throughout the 1960s and 1970s, Metro General continued, as a public hospital, to admit all patients in need of care, regardless of financial ability. Between 1962–72, the hospital was virtually rebuilt as $40 million was spent on expansion, including, in 1973, the opening of a 12-story, twin-tower structure with 558 beds. Over the next 10 years, the hospital increased its out-patient clinics as a result of cutbacks for indigent care in other hospitals, and also developed specialized acute-care services that began to bring in a broader range of patients. The hospital's burn center has become its best-known specialized service. In 1979, 27% of Cleveland Metro General's patients were suburbanites, 9% were from outside the county, and 64% were from Cleveland.

Highland View Hospital specialized in treatment and rehabilitation of the chronically crippled, victims of strokes, and those afflicted with neuromuscular diseases. It is one of the leading facilities of its type in the country. It opened in WARRENSVILLE TWP. in 1953. The project was initiated by a hospital building commission appointed by the county. Its purpose has always been to provide treatment for the chronically ill. Initially designated as Cuyahoga County Hospital, the name Highland View was used in order to make it seem more like a private hospital. Since it opened, the hospital has been affiliated with CWRU's medical school. Although Highland View opened with 445 beds, throughout most of the 1950s many beds were vacant because of a staff shortage. The lack of nearby affordable housing was cited as the major reason. As a public hospital, Highland View mainly treated indigent patients, although later—because of its specialized services—it began to draw a broader range. The number of self-pay patients increased in the 1960s as a result of Medicare legislation and an increase in private hospital insurance payments. The average stay was 67 days; no patients were accepted for permanent placement. All patients suffered from long-term chronic illnesses other than tubercular, mental, or alcoholic cases. In 1971, the county electorate approved plans to consolidate the county's medical facilities. As a result, plans were made to relocate Highland View's services to the Metro General Hospital site on Scranton Rd. In addition to financial reasons, it was thought that the move would improve Highland View's occupancy rate. Because of strong opposition, the move did not occur until 1980. Despite consolidation, Highland View continued to operate as a general hospital for care and rehabilitation of chronically ill patients. Most of the patients admitted in the early 1980s suffered from chronic illnesses such as arthritis, stroke, spinal-cord injury, and cardiac and neuromuscular diseases, as well as cases of temporary injury such as head trauma or back strain.

Sunny Acres is a 320-bed skilled-nursing facility in Warrensville Twp. As part of the Cuyahoga County Hospital System, it functions as a long-term-care unit. The idea for Sunny Acres was conceived by HARRIS R. COOLEY, director of charities for the city of Cleveland, who saw the need for a facility devoted to the care of tubercular patients. During its first few years, it operated as a 60-bed tuberculosis hospital in a house on Richmond Rd. A new facility with 238 beds—known as the Warrensville Sanatorium—was completed near the original site in 1913. In 1931, the sanatorium was expanded to accommodate 430 patients, and the staff increased to 210. The city transferred ownership to Cuyahoga County in 1942, and the name was changed to Sunny Acres Tuberculosis Hospital. Ten years later, a new building, financed through a $4.9 million bond issue, was opened, increasing capacity to 500 beds. By the late 1950s, the TB-patient census had declined dramatically, and in 1961 the Board of County Commissioners approved a 10-year program to transform the hospital into one specializing in the care of the chronically ill. An extended-care unit opened in 1966, and many of the older buildings were demolished. Treatment of Sunny Acres' former TB patients was transferred to Metro General Hospital or to out-patient services at the county's tuberculosis clinic. The merger of Sunny Acres into the CCHS was finalized in 1972. Since the merger, most patients have come through referrals from Metro General/Highland View Hospital. As a 320-bed skilled-nursing facility, it treats mostly victims of stroke, multiple sclerosis, muscular dystrophy, mental disorders, cancer, and spinal-cord injuries. In 1981, the 500-person staff included 8 full-time physicians, 74 nurses, nurses' assistants, occupational and physical therapists, speech audiologists, lab technicians, pharmacists, and social-service employees. Sunny Acres has all the equipment and services of an acute-care hospital, with the exception of emergency and operating rooms.

The Clement Ctr. offers specialized medical diagnoses and treatment to families living in 5 of Cleveland's poorer areas. It also helps coordinate efforts of other area health providers and resources to implement programs needed in the community. The center was named for Dr. KENNETH W. CLEMENT, well-known black surgeon and humanitarian. Clement was a trustee of the CCHS for 6 years, and vice-chairman of the board at the time of his death in 1974. The Clement Ctr. opened on E. 79th in Mar. 1976. Although it is open to all county residents, its primary purpose was to serve 5 social-planning areas: Central, Central East, Central West, Kinsman, and Woodland Hills. These areas, with a population of 85,000, had been designated by the METROPOLITAN HEALTH PLANNING CORP. and the U.S. Dept. of Health & Human Resources as medically underserved. The clinic's programs are directed toward the psychosocial as well as the medical aspects of health care, with special emphasis on disease prevention and health maintenance. From the beginning, its services have been linked to Metro General Hospital. In addition to county funds, the center, until 1981, received support from the CLEVELAND CLINIC FOUNDATION. The foundation also assisted in recruiting staff. In 1980, only 10% of the center's patients were able to pay entire bills; 10% were covered by Medicare, and the remainder by county taxpayers. For some services, such as the Child Development Program, there was no charge. Medical care at the center was designed to be provided by 3 family-based teams, 1 mental-health team, 1 dental team, and 1 social-service team, as well as an optometrist.

The Chronic Illness Ctr. provides assistance to elderly and chronically ill residents of Cuyahoga County. The center developed from a chronic-illness information, screening, and placement center founded in 1954. It was sponsored by the Welfare Fed. until 1961, when it became part of the County Hospital System. It was conceived as a public-service agency to serve the growing number of people in the county over 65. A program was developed by Dr. Joseph B. Stoklen, Cuyahoga County chronic-illness coordinator. Located on E. 55th, the center receives funding from the county health board. Its clients are usually older persons with chronic medical conditions complicated by severe emotional stress and social problems; few can manage the affairs of day-to-day living without assistance. In 1980, the staff included 14 social workers, 5 geriatric outreach workers, 3 RNs, and medical, legal, and psychiatric consultants.

The **CUYAHOGA COUNTY JUVENILE COURT** was the second of its kind in the U.S. It initiated new concepts in the juvenile-justice movement and was instrumental in setting national standards for more enlightened treatment of juvenile offenders. Created by a legislative act on 8 Apr. 1902, the Insolvency & Juvenile Court, as it was first named, owed its existence to the foresight and interest of city solicitor NEWTON D. BAKER and Glen K. Shurtleff, who was for many years general secretary of the YMCA. In 1901, they had studied the unfavorable conditions of children in the jails of the county and began a movement through the Social Service Club and the Bar Assoc. for the establishment of a court for children. Thos. E. Callahan, who was elected judge of the county's insolvency court in 1901, also became interested in the juvenile-court concept. Based on the Illinois Act of 1899, which created a juvenile court in Cook County, Ill., and guided through the Ohio legislature by Sen. John F. Herrick, a 1902 law established the Cuyahoga County Juvenile Court, combining it with the insolvency court. Judge Callahan presided over both. Upon his death in 1904, he was succeeded by Judge Thos. H. Bushnell until Nov. 1905, when Judge Geo. S. Addams was elected. From 1926–60, the court was run by Judge HARRY L. EASTMAN. Operating under the philosophy of treatment and rehabilitation rather than punishment, the early court found employment for "neglected" juveniles under 16, appointed guardians, opened a boarding home, and established the CLEVELAND BOYS SCHOOL at Hudson (1903) and a special detention home (1906). At first it had no authority to deal with adults contributing to the delinquency of minors, but in 1904, the court was given the power to impose fines on adults. An amendment in 1908 raised the jurisdictional age to 17 years. It provided that a boy over 16 who had committed a felony could be sent to the Ohio State Reformatory, and contributing adults could be punished by a fine and jail sentence. In 1913, jurisdictional age was raised to 18. The crucial terms *delinquent, dependent,* and *proper parental care* were defined, and all children were assured a physical and mental examination. The Mothers' Pension Law was enacted at this time.

During Eastman's tenure, many improvements were made in the physical, mental, and emotional evaluation and treatment of juvenile offenders. Sept. 1926 saw the appointment of Dr. Eleanor R. Wembridge, psychologist and astute social worker, as girls' referee. She was to become nationally known for her published work. Miss Lottie Bialosky was another experienced professional who supervised the probation staff at this time. In the 1920s, juvenile court cases were at times subordinated to insolvency cases, as the court tried nearly all the cases of the appropriation of property for the Union Terminal and the Food Terminal. The volume of work was so great that in 1931, the insolvency court was abolished, and the juvenile court became a separate entity. In 1932, a new juvenile court complex was occupied, located on E. 22nd St. between Cedar and Central. The homelike Tudor buildings represented an effort to provide a less threatening atmosphere for the activity of the court. Changes in the court's purpose during the 1960s and 1970s involved the trend toward lessening its jurisdiction over noncriminal misbehavior or status offenses. Children under 18 are now afforded most of the due-process rights held by adults. In the 1970s and 1980s, branches handling probation and intake were established in many of Cleveland's neighborhoods. In early 1982, a 15-member Youth Services Advisory Board was formed to assist in planning and recommendation of services and programs for young people.

Cuyahoga County Juvenile Court Citizens' Committee, *Golden Jubilee* (1952).

The **CUYAHOGA COUNTY MEDICAL SOCIETY** was organized in 1859 to carry out the functions of the defunct 19th District Medical Society: to assure the competence of medical professionals in Greater Cleveland. The society emphasized continuing medical education, and quarterly meetings featured a paper by one of 25 members. During the CIVIL WAR, the society was inactive, as most physicians were involved in war work. The need for a medical association resurfaced after the war, and rival organizations competed for area physicians. In June 1867, the (first) Cleveland Academy of Medicine was formed by many whose names appear on the rolls of the county society; in 1868, younger physicians enamored with the pathology research of Rudolf Virchow formed the short-lived Pathological Assoc., which merged with the Cleveland Academy of Medicine to become the Cleveland Medical Assoc. By 1874 this latter group joined the Cuyahoga County Medical Society.

The resulting Cuyahoga County Medical Society, 100 members strong, continued to meet the social and educational needs of members through quarterly afternoon meetings. Part of the group's income was used to buy books and journals through an arrangement made with the Case Library; in return for $1 per year per member, the library cared for and controlled lending of society books. Within a decade, some members sought an organization that met more frequently, in the evening, and offered more of a forum for scientific discussion. The county society lost some members to the fledgling SOCIETY OF MEDICAL SCIENCES OF CLEVELAND in 1887. To respond to member desires, the older body moved its meeting to 3:30 p.m. and increased dues to expand the book and journal fund.

Another challenge came when the Cleveland Medical Society organized in 1893. Younger physicians bypassed the more static county society to join the new, more progressive body. In an effort to attract a broader spectrum of physicians, the county society adopted an amendment to provide sections to study special areas of medicine. The first of these was the medico-legal section, active until 1898, which fostered the study of forensic medicine and was open to all reputable physicians and lawyers. The Cuyahoga County Medical Society joined its rivals in 1894 to form the CLEVELAND MEDICAL LIBRARY ASSOC. The result was to render useless the Society of Medical Sciences (disbanded 1896) and pave the way for the union of the Cuyahoga County Medical Society and the Cleveland Medical Society in the ACADEMY OF MEDICINE in 1902.

The **CUYAHOGA COUNTY MILITARY COMMITTEE** was formed by order of Gov. Wm. Dennison, Ohio's first Civil War governor, in 1861. Each of Ohio's 88 counties had such a military committee, with members appointed by the governor to oversee recruitment of volunteers for service in the Union Army and Navy. The members of the Cuyahoga County Military Committee at the end of 1863 were WM. B. CASTLE (chairman), WM. BINGHAM, F. Nicola, EDWARD HESSENMUELLER, Col. GEO. B. SENTER, STILLMAN WITT, M. Barlow (secretary), Wm. Edwards, Wm. F. Cary. It was also the responsibility of the committee to stimulate recruitment to fill quotas set by the governor, lest conscription need be implemented. Gov. Tod,

Dennison's successor, retained the County Military Committee system when he took office in 1862, and on 8 July 1862, by proclamation, he established 11 military recruiting districts in Ohio. Cuyahoga County was included in the 11th military district, which also included the counties of Summit, Columbiana, Medina, Stark, Portage, Mahoning, Trumbull, Lorain, Geauga, Lake, and Ashland. Enlistments were encouraged by offering bounty or enlistment bonuses at the city ward or township level at "war meetings." The meetings were sponsored not necessarily by the Cuyahoga County Military Committee but by local ward or township officials and patriotic citizens. Another function of the committee was to provide relief money for Cuyahoga County families whose men had enlisted. Most of the relief money came from voluntary contributions by concerned citizens. The Cuyahoga County Military Committee served without pay.

Cuyahoga County Military Committee Records, WRHS.

The **CUYAHOGA COUNTY NURSING HOME**, located at 3305 Franklin Blvd., was first opened in 1938 as an experimental shelter for relief patients who were permanently and totally disabled. BELL GREVE, director of the County Relief Bureau, was aware that during the Depression, many ill and disabled persons were living under adverse circumstances in attics, cellars, and low-quality nursing homes. She persuaded the county commissioners to provide a home for the county's chronically ill, aged, and infirm. In 1938 the commissioners authorized the alteration of a county building on Franklin Blvd. for use as a nursing home. The nursing home staff, headed by Edith L. Marsh, superintendent, and Dr. Joseph I. Goodnow, medical director, adopted a policy of self-help and rehabilitation for its patients and stressed wholesome food, adequate vitamins, massage, and exercise as part of its medical treatment. Physical, occupational, and recreational therapy were also essential components of the home's pilot program for the chronically ill. Today the County Nursing Home provides intermediate care to individuals who are ambulatory and do not require constant attention. It also operates a living and training center for mentally retarded adults.

The **CUYAHOGA COUNTY PUBLIC LIBRARY SYSTEM** is composed of 4 regional libraries and 22 branch libraries, serving 48 suburban communities with a total population of more than 617,000. In addition to traditional library services, it offers a variety of free services, including a comprehensive consumer and community-services information and referral service. The County Library System had a collection of more than 2 million circulating items in 1986. In 1985, its patrons borrowed more than 5.6 million items. The system also has access to nearly 6 million items through the Cleveland Area Metropolitan Library System (CAMLS), which was created in 1975 to promote library cooperation and resource sharing among the area's different libraries. Through 1985, Ohio public libraries received funding through taxes collected on intangible personal property, such as stocks and bonds. Beginning in Jan. 1986, public libraries in the state were funded through the state income tax. Like all libraries in Ohio, the system has a 7-member board of trustees with members serving rotating 7-year terms. Three members are appointed by the court of common pleas, and 4 by the county commissioners. The system's administrative building is at 4510 Memphis Ave. The County Library System was established by referendum in the Nov. 1922 general election. The original petition called for the inclusion of all of Cuyahoga County not then served by an existing public library. In 1922, only

8 communities had tax-supported library service: BAY VILLAGE, BRECKSVILLE, Cleveland, CLEVELAND HTS., Dover (WESTLAKE), E. CLEVELAND, Idlewood (UNIVERSITY HTS.), and LAKEWOOD. Only a few other communities had libraries supported by private funds. The County Library System opened its doors on 1 Apr. 1924 on the 3d floor of the Kinney & Levan Bldg., and Margaret Thayer was appointed County Library head. During the first year, 8 branches and 15 stations were organized, extending service to rural districts where people were scattered and unable to reach a library. In 1925, the Brecksville board voted to merge with the County Library System. Other privately supported libraries, such as those in N. OLMSTED and CHAGRIN FALLS, turned over their collections to the county as branches were opened in their communities. The N. Olmsted collection included books that had originally been brought by covered wagon from New England and had been part of the WESTERN RESERVE's first circulating library collection.

The **CUYAHOGA COUNTY REGIONAL PLANNING COMMISSION (RPC)** was established in 1947 to offer advisory services to member communities and operate as a regional planning agency. Early efforts at regional planning were made by the Cleveland Metropolitan Planning Commission, formed in 1921; the Cuyahoga County Planning Commission, appointed in 1924; and the Regional Assoc. of Cleveland, a nonprofit citizens' organization that was instrumental in producing a master plan for the integrated freeway system that was built in the 1950s with the aid of state and federal funds. After WORLD WAR II, a survey made by the president of the Cuyahoga County Planning Commission showed there was need for an areawide agency to address regional problems. As a result, the Cuyahoga County Regional Planning Commission was established by the county commissioners and 19 county municipalities in Sept. 1947. The commission, made up of the 3 commissioners, the county engineer, the county administrator, 5 citizen members appointed by the commissioners, 2 members from the Cleveland Plannning Commission, and 1 member from each city and village wishing to participate, had 2 planning divisions, 1 for the entire region and 1 to help local communities in the county.

On the regional level, the RPC began preparing a regional building code that would coordinate with the revised Cleveland code, and made studies of sewer and water, highway, and transportation services. It gathered information on problems of ZONING, location of business centers, and recreational facilities for local communities. As an advisory group, the commission was often the only official body where problems, conflicts, and inequities could be discussed and solutions offered. Two important land-use reports issued in the 1950s were financed in part through an urban-planning grant under the provisions of the Federal Housing Act of 1954, and a major report titled "People and Their Homes" was published in 1964. The RPC also provided consultant services to local urban-renewal agencies and participated in the Cleveland–7 County Transportation-Land Use Study—a joint effort in planning by the governments and technical agencies in northeastern Ohio. Local planning on a long-range basis was stimulated by the Federal Urban Planning Financial Assistance program, which became available in Ohio in 1959. Communities asked the RPC to prepare series of planning activities with the aim of establishing continuous comprehensive planning in local subdivisions. In 1971, the RPC had a staff of 24; however, available money for planning projects decreased during the 1970s, and by 1983 the staff was reduced to 14. The commission was funded mainly by the Cuyahoga County government and membership dues from the county's municipalities.

Durham, Frank, *Government in Greater Cleveland* (1963).

The **CUYAHOGA COUNTY REPUBLICAN PARTY** began in Ohio with a statewide convention held in Columbus 22 Mar. 1854 to oppose the passage of the Kansas-Nebraska Act. The act, by allowing the two territories to decide for themselves whether or not to permit slavery, in effect repealed the Missouri Compromise, which had prohibited slavery in those western lands. The convention agreed to meet again. By the time of that meeting, 13 July 1854, the Kansas-Nebraska Act had been passed by Congress, and the nucleus of a new political party emerged, calling for its repeal and no further extension of slavery. At first it was known variously as the Anti-Nebraska, People's, Fusion, and Anti-Slavery party; however, the name Republican gradually came into widespread use. In Cuyahoga County, the People's party, formed in Sept. 1854, pledged its support of the July anti-Nebraska convention and campaigned for the reelection of anti-Nebraska candidate EDWARD WADE to Congress. Wade received more than twice the number of votes given to his opponent. Elsewhere in the state, party congressional candidates were successful in all but 6 counties. The Cuyahoga County party, made up of conservative Whigs, Free-Soilers, Union Democrats, and Know-Nothings, was using the name Republican by 1855, but in the municipal elections of 1855 and 1856, it ran candidates as the People's party. The first presidential candidate of the national Republican party (organized in Feb. 1856) was John C. Fremont, who won a majority in both Cleveland and Cuyahoga County in the fall elections. The Democrats, however, won the municipal election that year.

As antislavery sentiment grew, so did the fortunes of the Republican party both locally and nationally, and it became dominant in Cleveland during and after the CIVIL WAR. More interested in local than national affairs, the local party by and large did not support the radical Republican program after the war. With the postwar growth of Cleveland, political activity became more professionalized, but local businessmen still actively participated in the practical work of the party. Prominent party leaders during the latter part of the 19th century included Silas Merchant in the 1870s and Wm. H. Gabriel from 1885–90. Locally, candidates for political office were chosen by the party about a week before the April election at conventions made up of delegates elected at ward meetings throughout the city. Names of the candidates were then printed in the local newspapers. The Republicans received the best press from the *CLEVELAND LEADER*, their major supporter. The first effective countywide voter registration went into effect in May 1885. City council divided the city wards into precincts and appointed 2 registrars for each precinct, 1 for each political party. The registrars were stationed at the voting places on specified days to record the names of voters who presented themselves. The Tippecanoe Club, originally founded by the Whigs to campaign for Wm. Henry Harrison in 1840, was revived by the Republicans when his grandson Benjamin Harrison ran for president in 1888. Clubrooms were established in Cleveland, and the organization remained in operation after the election. In 1896, the local club chartered a train to Canton, Ohio, in order to be the first delegation to offer congratulations to president-elect Wm. McKinley, whose successful campaign had been managed by Cleveland industrialist MARCUS HANNA.

In municipal elections, political lines were not always sharply drawn, and party affiliation did not necessarily follow economic or social lines. The Republicans wooed the labor and immigrant vote by emphasizing their support for protective tariffs as a way of maintaining local employment. The Republican organization in Cleveland had its greatest successes in local campaigns compromised by factional fights, revolts against regular nominations, and unexpected independence on the part of the voters. In the 1890s, there was a struggle for power within the local party between Hanna and Mayor ROBT. MCKISSON, who had built a political machine of Republican shop clubs and ward organizations loyal to him. In 1898 their fight for control moved to the state, where McKisson came within 4 votes of defeating Hanna in his bid to become U.S. senator from Ohio. After Hanna's death in 1904, Sen. THEODORE BURTON, and later MAURICE MASCHKE, took over party leadership. As chairman of the Central Committee of the Cuyahoga County Republican party, Maschke successfully appealed to the nationality and minority groups. The party regained the mayoral seat and control of city council in 1916. When the CITY MANAGER PLAN went into effect in 1924, Maschke and Democratic leader Gongwer agreed to the selection of WM. HOPKINS as city manager and learned to live with the reduced patronage during the operation of the plan. With the return of partisan politics in 1931 and the retirement of Maschke, a conflict between the ward leaders and Republican Mayor HAROLD H. BURTON developed in 1936 and 1937 over the distribution of patronage. GEO. BENDER gained control of the county organization in 1938 and was county chairman until 1955, when ALESSANDRO "SONNY" DEMAIORIBUS succeeded him.

The Republicans had been the dominant party in the 1920s and 1930s. By 1947, however, the the party's decline was evident. In the post-World War II era, increasing numbers of Republicans moved to the suburbs, and a substantial number of those migrating into Cleveland were Democrats. Unable to produce vote-getting candidates, the Republicans suffered defeat in both county and city elective offices. Their Cleveland City Council representation declined from 13 out of 33 councilmen in 1953 to 2 by 1965. When DeMaioribus died in 1968, Robt. Hughes and Saul Stillman became cochairmen. Stillman resigned in 1975 to accept an appointment to the common pleas bench, and Hughes continued as chairman of both the Central and Executive committees. In 1984, Claudia Guzzo assumed the chairmanship of the Central Committee. She is believed to be the first woman ever to chair a major committee of either party in Cuyahoga County. By the late 1960s, the Republicans were again successful, electing candidates to county offices and 2 Cleveland mayors, Ralph Perk (1972-77) and Geo. Voinovich (1980- ). In 1984, the Cuyahoga County Republican party consisted of ward or precinct committeemen elected in primary elections by the registered Republicans in each ward or precinct in the county. The committeemen who made up the County Central Committee elected the county chairman and the Executive Committee. All committeemen and the county chairman were elected in even-numbered years and served 2-year terms. The Executive Committee was the decision-making body of the party, formally meeting twice a year to endorse Republican candidates for the primary elections.

Sego, Michael A., ed., *Politics in the Making* (1967).
Smith, Joseph Patterson, *History of the Republican Party in Ohio* (1898).
Stumbo, Frank, *Ohio GOP* (1980).

The **CUYAHOGA COUNTY SABBATH SOCIETY** was a mid-19th-century organization dedicated to preserving the Sabbath as a sacred day of rest. Little information is available about the society; the *Annals of Cleveland* mention only 1 of its meetings, but the resolutions adopted at that 10 Mar. 1844 gathering at a Baptist church suggest that the large audience present had strong concerns about the sacred nature of Sunday was being eroded by the secular acts of men and governments. With lawyer and prominent reformer JOHN A. FOOTE serving as chairman and exchange broker TRUMAN P. HANDY as secretary, the meeting opened with a prayer and then proceeded to adopt a series of resolutions urging local citizens to avoid performing secular work on Sundays. The gathering resolved that since God had "appointed and sanctified the Sabbath, its strict observance . . . must always be in accordance with the highest interest of all His creatures"; that the laws of God take precedence over those of human governments; that maintaining the Sabbath is a matter not only of "true piety" but also of "patriotism and philanthropy"; and that "all secular employments on the Sabbath, excepting those works of mercy by individuals, chartered companies, or governments, call down the wrath of Heaven, impoverish the land, and inflict cruelty and injustice on all the people, but especially on the laboring poor." The society apparently took little other action in its efforts to preserve the Sabbath, since this meeting adjourned after it agreed to publish these resolutions in the newspapers.

**CUYAHOGA COUNTY SOLDIERS & SAILORS MONUMENT.** *See* **SOLDIERS & SAILORS MONUMENT**

The **CUYAHOGA COUNTY SOLDIERS' RELIEF COMMISSION** is a county agency, organized under the provisions of a state law first passed in 1886 and since revised, charged with providing relief for indigent military veterans. It was known until ca. 1945 as the Soldiers' & Sailors' Relief Commission; its responsibilities have diminished over the years as federally sponsored welfare programs have expanded. The county apparently began providing relief for soldiers and sailors in the late 1860s; when the state mandated that each county establish a commission to aid "honorably discharged, indigent Union soldiers, sailors and marines" and their families, the county program was reorganized under the new law. By 1896, the 3-man commission (at least 2 of whom were to be Union veterans) appointed by the judge of the common pleas court regularly was providing aid for 500 persons at an annual cost of about $40,000. By the 1920s, its caseload was about the same, even though its clients included veterans of 2 more wars, but the tax-supported budget had increased to $100,000. By the 1930s, it was customary that one commissioner be a Civil War veteran, another be a veteran of the SPANISH-AMERICAN WAR, and the third be a member of the American Legion; the commissioners were exempt from civil-service requirements.

The commission's caseload expanded greatly during the Depression. The commission spent $83,000 in 1928; the caseload grew to 3,500 veterans and the cost to $600,000 in 1933. By 1935, the commission helped 1,800 families a month and sponsored work-relief projects. By the mid-1940s, the caseload had declined, the budget was $127,000, and the agency was spending more and more time finding jobs for applicants. The commission was reorganized and expanded ca. 1945 in anticipation of increased demands for relief after WORLD WAR II. The 1986 law stipulates that "wherever possible," the 5-member commission include a veteran of WORLD WAR I, a member of the American Legion, a member of the Veterans of Foreign

Wars, a member of the Disabled American Veterans, and a veteran of World War II who is a member of American Veterans of World War II. Since 1945, the expansion of federal and state welfare programs has diminished the commission's responsibilities somewhat, and on several occasions it has been accused of mismanagement. County judges accused it of poor management in 1951; it was criticized for high operating costs in 1958; and in 1960, an attempt to merge it into the county welfare department failed. In the early 1970s, the commission was the subject of an investigation by the county auditor, the county prosecutor, and the county welfare department; in 1973, 2 former commissioners pleaded guilty to using their offices to commit larceny by trick. Partly as a result of these scandals, and partly because the welfare department sought part of the commission's budget in order to qualify for additional federal matching funds, the county welfare department took over distribution of relief funds to veterans' families, leaving the commission with distribution of funds to single persons and childless couples.

The **CUYAHOGA COUNTY UNIT OF THE AMERICAN CANCER SOCIETY** is an organization dedicated to raising money for cancer research, both locally and nationally, and educating the public on cancer, as well as providing services to those suffering from cancer. The Cuyahoga County Unit developed from the Cleveland advisory board of the American Society for the Control of Cancer, Inc. It became a chapter of the newly formed American Cancer Society in the mid-1940s. Its initial purpose was to educate people to recognize early symptoms of cancer. Early active members included Joseph S. Silber, who served several terms as president in the 1950s; Sidney Conger, treasurer for the unit's first 10 years; Mrs. Paul Lawrence, who directed the cancer dressing program; and Mrs. Don Cadot, chairman of the education committee. The unit is run by officers elected to 1-year terms and a board of trustees; although it is locally run, its activities are planned in conjunction with the American Cancer Society. Most money raised by the Cuyahoga unit goes to the parent organization, which, working with local officers, then allocates funds for cancer research and programs in the Cleveland area.

By 1948, the Cuyahoga unit had established 8 cancer-detection clinics throughout Cleveland. The clinics, in area hospitals, examined patients free of charge who were brought in by doctors and were suspected of having cancer. By 1951, the Cuyahoga unit was assisted by 1,900 volunteers and 184 civic and social organizations. Volunteers assisted in delivering dressings to cancer patients and transporting them to treatment centers, and in the house-to-house solicitation of funds. In the 1950s, several more diagnostic and treatment clinics were established, as were 3 cytology laboratories—at UNIVERSITY, ST. LUKE'S, and City hospitals. An average of $500,000 was raised annually for the American Cancer Society. In 1953, the unit moved into larger offices in the ARCADE. In the 1960s, suburban chapters were established. Some of the unit's allocations went toward the purchase of sickroom equipment and drugs for indigent patients, as well as nursing care. The unit provided area doctors with free Pap test supplies, and grants for continuing research and rehabilitation programs at local hospitals and clinics, including a grant to the Cleveland Hearing & Speech Ctr. to retrain patients who had lost their larynxes to cancer. To aid its fundraising, the unit joined forces with United Torch in the early 1970s. New programs were launched, including an antismoking program that has become one of its most important public programs. Because Cleveland is a center for medical care and research, the Cuyahoga unit has generally received more funds from the American Cancer Society than it has contributed.

**CUYAHOGA HEIGHTS** is an industrialized suburb of 4.5 sq. mi. located approximately 6 mi. southeast of Cleveland and bounded on the west by Cleveland, on the east by GARFIELD HTS., on the north by NEWBURGH HTS., and on the south by INDEPENDENCE and BROOKLYN HTS. It was originally part of Newburgh Twp. and later Newburgh Hts. In 1917, Newburgh Hts. experienced a building boom, farms were subdivided into residential lots, and citizens faced rising taxes. A group of farmers led by Jesse W. Hammersley met to discuss secession in a partition that would leave the residential area in Newburgh Hts. and the industrial and farm property in what became Cuyahoga Hts. Following an election in 1918, the village of Cuyahoga Hts. was established. Many industries, including the Ferro Corp., American Steel & Wire, REPUBLIC STEEL, Ohio Crankshaft, the Benjamin Moore Paint Co., the Harris-Seybold-Potter Co., the ALUMINUM CO. OF AMERICA, U.S. STEEL, and E. F. Hauserman were attracted to Cuyahoga Hts. because of its strategic location on the CUYAHOGA RIVER, its proximity to the New York Central Railroad, and the abundance of natural resources, including lumber, sand, and natural gas. In 1920, the village adopted a charter that encouraged industrial and commercial development. During WORLD WAR II, industrial expansion continued, and in 1967 approximately 64 industries and 18 trucking and shipping firms were located in Cuyahoga Hts. At that time its population was approximately 800, many of whom traced their lineage to the Italian and Polish immigrants who had settled in the area in the 1920s. In 1984, the strategic location of Cuyahoga Hts. within the heart of Cleveland and near the I-77-I-480 interchange, as well as community and municipal support, continued to attract and maintain over 100 businesses and industries, including STANDARD OIL of Ohio, E. F. Hauserman, and the RELIANCE ELECTRIC CO. They occupy over 2,000 acres, and the daily population expands from 761 to more than 18,000 as workers commute from nearby communities. Cuyahoga Hts. maintains a school system and recreational facilities for its citizens.

*The Village of Cuyahoga Heights in the Bicentennial Year 1976–1977 (n.d.).*

The **CUYAHOGA METROPOLITAN HOUSING AUTHORITY**, the first community housing authority in the nation, was established as the Cleveland Metropolitan Housing Authority in 1933, largely through the efforts of ERNEST J. BOHN, who served as its director until 1968. Also instrumental in the formation of CMHA was a survey by Msgr. ROBT. B. NAVIN, "An Analysis of a Slum Area in Cleveland." CMHA was created as an advisory and coordinating agency for the improvement of housing conditions of low-income families, and for the elimination of slum areas. The passage of the U.S. Housing Act in 1937 enabled CMHA to plan, construct, and manage federally subsidized housing facilities. CMHA was granted authority to borrow money, issue bonds and notes, and appropriate property at fair market prices. Cedar Apts. at Cedar and E. 30th and Outhwaite Homes at E. 55th and Outhwaite Ave. were completed in 1937, and the money for their construction was the first allocation made in the U.S. for low-rent housing through the Public Works Admin.

CMHA focused on providing housing for war workers and their families during WORLD WAR II. The operation of housing units for returning veterans was the chief concern following 1945. High-rise PUBLIC HOUSING for the elderly, such as the Golden Age Ctrs., were established in the mid-1950s and were praised as models for geriatric housing. The idea of high-rise housing expanded to include family units. High crime statistics, charges of racial discrimination, and the Federal Housing Act of 1968 initiated changes in CMHA's approach to subsidized housing in the late 1960s. Tenant organizations requested more social-service programs, such as daycare, "Meals-on-Wheels," and Head Start. The Housing Act recognized the inadequacy of concentrating large developments of low-income housing in small areas and made provision for the rehabilitation of single-family units as scattersite housing. In 1971, wishing to emphasize a willingness to create housing wherever low-income and elderly people live, the Cleveland Metropolitan Housing Authority changed its name to the Cuyahoga Metropolitan Housing Authority. Subsequent to the passage of the Federal Housing Act of 1974, CMHA has administered the "Section Eight Program," which allows selected families to choose their own housing scattered throughout the county. CMHA is an independent public agency regulated by the Ohio Housing Board and governed by a board composed of 5 unpaid members who serve 5-year terms.

Ernest J. Bohn Collection, Freiberger Library, CWRU.

The **CUYAHOGA RIVER** divides the east and west sides of the city of Cleveland. It originates in springs in the highlands of Geauga County, in the adjoining townships of Hambden and Montville. The 2 sources, which form the East and West branches of the river, are 35 mi. east of Cleveland and, paradoxically, farther north than the river's mouth. The river flows southwest to Cuyahoga Falls, on the northern edge of Akron, where it drops into a large, deep valley and turns sharply north. Thus, it forms the letter U as it courses through Geauga, Portage, Summit, and Cuyahoga counties. It is 80 mi. long. Upon reaching Cleveland, about 6 mi. from its mouth, it becomes a sharply twisting stream before emptying into Lake Erie. Its mouth forms part of Cleveland's harbor, and the river is navigable about 5 mi. upstream.

It is believed that the Mohawk Indians meant "crooked river" when they called it "Cayagaga," although the Senecas called it "Cuyohaga," or "place of the jawbone." In 1796, when the future city of Cleveland was surveyed by the CONNECTICUT LAND CO., the Cuyahoga River formed the western boundary of U.S. territory not still in Indian hands. The OHIO & ERIE CANAL, completed to Portsmouth on the Ohio River in 1832, paralleled the Cuyahoga between Akron and Cleveland. The business district of the early city fronted on the river, and the canal terminated at Superior St., where steamers, schooners, and canal boats exchanged imported goods for the products of local industry. The Cuyahoga's irregular course allowed ample space for docks, warehouses, and storage yards. In the 1850s and 1860s, shipyards lining the old ship channel on the west side turned out hundreds of vessels of all classifications, while docks receiving iron ore grew in size and value of receipts. Industry had claimed virtually all of Cleveland's riverfront by 1881, when the discharge from factories and oil refineries made it, according to Mayor RENSSELAER R. HERRICK, "an open sewer through the center of the city." With federal assistance, the river mouth was widened beginning in 1898, and beginning in 1936 the river was widened, sharp bends were cut back, and the channel was deepened so that by 1941, 600-ft. freighters could navigate safely.

On 22 June 1969, a burning oil slick floating on the river caused extensive damage to 2 railroad trestles at the foot of Campbell Rd. Hill. The incident received national attention, and several weeks later *Time* magazine (1 Aug. 1969) branded the Cuyahoga as one of the most polluted rivers in the U.S. Water quality was improved over the next decade with the construction of sewer interceptors and wastewater-treatment plants and remedial measures taken by industry in response to lawsuits brought by the U.S. attorney, the Sierra Club, and others. The challenge of communication between the east and west sides of the city has necessitated the construction of dozens of BRIDGES over the years, many of them engineering feats. In 1941, 26 bridges spanned the Cuyahoga and the old ship channel, causing one writer to assert that "Cleveland, once so aptly called the Forest City, now . . . should be known as the City of Bridges."

The **CUYAHOGA RIVER FIRE** took place at approximately 12 p.m. on Sunday, 22 June 1969. The fire was brought under control at approximately 12:20 p.m., but not before it had done $50,000 worth of damage to 2 key railroad trestles at the foot of Campbell Rd. Hill SE in Cleveland. An oil slick on the river caught fire and floated under the wooden bridges, setting fire to both. Witnesses reported that the flames from the bridges reached as high as 5 stories. What caused the oil slick to ignite was never determined. A fireboat battled the blaze on the water while units from 3 fire battalions brought the flames on the trestles under control. The bridge, belonging to the Norfolk & Western Railway Co., sustained $45,000 worth of damage, forcing the company to close both of its tracks to traffic. The other, 1-track trestle, belonging to the NEWBURGH & SOUTH SHORE RAILROAD CO., remained open; however, it incurred damages estimated at $5,000. Responsibility for the oil slick was placed on the waterfront industries, which used the river as a dumping ground for oil wastes instead of reclaiming the waste products. The railroad trestles were not all that sustained damage in the fire. Cleveland's reputation was severely damaged by the occurrence. The city became the brunt of numerous jokes from comedians and the media across the country, characterized as the only city with a river that had burned. Ironically, another oil slick burned on the Cuyahoga River in 1952 causing an estimated $1.5 million damage without attracting national attention.

The **CUYAHOGA STEAM FURNACE COMPANY** was the first iron manufacturer in the Cleveland area. Chas. Hoyt started the company in the Cuyahoga Valley in 1827 at Center and Detroit Sts. in Brooklyn Twp. It was the first shop to utilize steam power in the region. Hoyt's cast- and wrought-iron business prospered, and on 3 Mar. 1834, it became Cleveland's first incorporated manufacturing plant, with JOSIAH BARBER, RICHARD LORD, Chas. Hoyt, and Luke Risely as stockholders. Soon afterward, a fire swept the shop, and 2 years later, a larger plant was erected, producing over 500 tons of castings annually and employing up to 100 workers. Cuyahoga Steam Furnace grew by adapting to the region's changing needs for metal forms. Originally, it produced mill gearings, but after the Panic of 1837, it entered new lines of work. In 1840, it began to make stationary steam engines. In 1842, as RAILROADS entered the WESTERN RESERVE, the plant started to manufacture railroad equipment. With the increase in lake traffic, Cuyahoga moved into the marine engine field by the following year. It also produced plows, axes, and cannons during the 1840s.

By 1849, the firm had no debts and had become the state's largest producer of steam engines. It then ventured into locomotive construction, building the first locomotive west of the Alleghenies in 1849. With a growing locomotive business, the company erected a substantial plant near the old shop in 1853. By 1857, the plant had produced 100 locomotives, with $60,000 in annual sales. However, the Panic of 1857 hurt the firm, and it decided to close its locomotive works and return to safer, more profitable lines of work at its Detroit St. plant. During the CIVIL WAR it was a large supplier of railroad iron to the Union forces. Cuyahoga maintained its business for the next 20 years, until it was purchased by the Cleveland Shipbuilding Co., the forerunner of the AMERICAN SHIP BUILDING CO., in 1887.

Cuyahoga Steam Furnace Co. Records, WRHS.

The **CUYAHOGA VALLEY LINE** is a steam railroad that provides historical and nostalgic weekend rail excursions from Cleveland (Independence) to Akron during the summer months. The train runs through the Cuyahoga River Valley and includes a stop at historic Hale Farm & Village. The Cuyahoga Valley Line was incorporated in 1972 by a group of private citizens interested in preserving the memory of the days of steam railroading. Actual operation began in the summer of 1975. It became a successful tourist attraction, operating June through October. The group, known as the Cuyahoga Valley Preservation & Scenic Railway Assoc., is a nonprofit organization that operates the line primarily from the fares. State and Cuyahoga County grants have aided the association, as have private donations. The association works closely with the Midwest Railway Historical Foundation, a local chapter (currently based in Copley, Ohio) of the Natl. Railway Historical Foundation, a nonprofit foundation of private citizens interested in finding, restoring, and maintaining old railway rolling stock and equipment. The Cuyahoga Valley Line rents its equipment from the foundation. Foundation volunteers operate the train during its summer run. The primary attraction of the line is its 1918 "Mikado"-style steam locomotive. The train is composed of antique cars. First-class seating is available in a restored 1930s Pullman car, the *Mt. Baxter*. Much of the train's journey passes through the Cuyahoga Valley Natl. Recreation Area, at many points along the Ohio Canal. U.S. park rangers accompany the train, describing the scenic and historic area to passengers. The train runs on tracks leased from the Baltimore & Ohio (Chessie System).

The **CUYAHOGA VALLEY NATIONAL RECREATION AREA** was created by an act of Congress sponsored by Rep. John F. Seiberling and signed by Pres. Gerald Ford on 27 Dec. 1974. It designated 32,000 acres along 22 mi. of the CUYAHOGA RIVER in southern Cuyahoga and northern Summit counties as the third urban park in the Natl. Park system; the Golden Gate Natl. Recreation Area in San Francisco and the Gateway Natl. Recreation Area in New York City were established in 1972. The northern boundary of the park is at Rockside Rd. in VALLEY VIEW. CVNRA was established to preserve the "scenic, recreational, natural, and historic" values of undeveloped land between Cleveland and Akron, land threatened by commercial development and rapid population growth. The national recreation area was established officially on 26 June 1975 and included such already developed recreational facilities as the Virginia Kendall Park, Blossom Music Ctr., and Hale Farm & Village. Congress had authorized $34.5 million for land acquisition over a 5-year period, and under the direction of Superintendent Wm. C. Birdsell, the Natl. Park Service and the Army Corps of Engineers embarked on a controversial land-buying spree that angered many people residing in the park area and politicians. By 1980, only 60% of the land had been acquired at a cost of more than $42 million, and the Park Service had bought 306 of the 750 homes in the park area. A series of articles in the *CLEVELAND PRESS* in Apr. 1980 criticized the Park Service for its acquisition policies, its limited use of scenic easements, and poor management of the area.

By the fall of 1980, CVNRA was offering visitors' biking and nature tours, programs for children, concerts, and craft programs. After Birdsell's death on 18 Aug. 1980, Lewis S. Albert became the superintendent of CVNRA; under his direction and that of the Reagan administration in Washington, policies at CVNRA were changed. CVNRA stopped purchasing land not needed for park purposes and sought other ways to preserve it. By Nov. 1984, the Natl. Park Service had bought 14,444 acres of land for CVNRA for $78 million and had plans to buy 3,000 additional acres. It had also spent $2 million to restore 50 historic structures and was working on restoration of such landmarks as the Jaite paper mill and the nearby company town. CVNRA continued to expand its offering of cultural and recreational activities and hosted the Natl. Folk Festival from 1983–85. By the time it celebrated its 10th anniversary in Sept. 1985, the Cuyahoga Valley Recreation Area had an annual operating budget of $3 million and 84 employees (down from 125 in 1980). By 1984, 7 million visitors a year enjoyed its natural beauty and recreational facilities.

The **CZECH CATHOLIC UNION** is a national fraternal benefit society with its national headquarters located in Cleveland at 5349 Dolloff Rd. Organized in 1879 in Cleveland's St. Wenceslaus parish by Rev. Anthony Hynek, the union developed from that parish's St. Anne's Society, organized in 1867, and was known originally as the Bohemian Roman Catholic Central Union of Women. The union's first 2 branches were St. Anne's in Cleveland and St. Ludmilla's in New York. Both lodges had religious, charitable, and cultural purposes. In the early years, members of the benefit society agreed to pay $.25 each upon the death of a member. In 1881 the society had 629 members, and its death benefit was increased from $100 to $150. As both membership and competition from other benefit societies increased, the society continued to increase its death benefit; it had been increased to $275 in 1889, but in 1895 competition pushed the benefit to $500, and soon thereafter to $1,000.

During the 1920s–1930s, the union strengthened its organizational structure and financial management. In 1928 it formally organized its juvenile division, which absorbed the loosely affiliated members of the Pannenske Spolky. Improvements in financial management came about largely at the insistence of the state of Ohio, which in 1934 ordered the union to become 100% solvent. Soon thereafter the union merged with the Czech Catholic Cleveland Union of Men and the Czech Catholic Cleveland Union of Women; by 1939 the Bohemian Roman Catholic Central Union of Women had become known as the Czech Catholic Union. Marie L. Kral, the society's long-time president, guided the union through this period of reorganization; her fellow officer Anna M. Veverka served as secretary for many years and led the union as president after 1968. For many years the organization was located in the Atlas Bldg. at 5644 Broadway. By 1960 it had moved to its own building on Dolloff Rd. Its paper, *Posel* (Messenger), kept members apprised of the society's news. By 1973 the Czech Catholic Union had 12,000 members across the country, with 4,000 members in 8 lodges in the Cleveland area. It continues to support religious institutions and cultural, charitable, and educational efforts. By 1984 it had 36 lodges nationally, assets of more than $4.7 million, and more than $6.2 million of life insurance in force in 4,470 policies.

**CZECHS.** Cleveland's Czech community forms one of the city's oldest and largest ethnic groups. Approximately 37,000 people of Czech birth or background reside in the metropolitan area in the 1980s. The term *Czech* refers collectively to Bohemians, Moravians, and Silesians. Czechs immigrated to America and settled in Cleveland in 3 distinct periods, or waves. The first major migration began when political persecution by the Austrian government forced many well-educated Czechs to flee their homeland. Some had participated in an unsuccessful revolt against the Austrian government in 1848. Peasants and skilled craftsmen from the villages also immigrated to America between 1848–70. Unlike some immigrant groups of this period, the Czech immigrants consisted primarily of family units whose intention was to settle permanently. Many of the early immigrants hoped to homestead in Nebraska, Iowa, and Wisconsin. Immigrants who stopped to rest along the way at cities such as Cleveland often found a haven where they settled and welcomed fellow immigrants. In 1850, there were 3 Czech families in Cleveland; by 1860, 15; in 1870, 696 Czech families, or 3,252 individuals, resided in the city.

The largest wave of Czech migration occurred between 1870 and WORLD WAR I. It was prompted primarily by economic conditions in the homeland; employment opportunities were meager, incomes low, and taxes intolerable. The Austrian government's demand that young Czech men serve 3 years in the army contributed another reason for migration. The Czech immigrants as a group had an extraordinarily low illiteracy rate, as they had enjoyed one of the best education systems in the Austro-Hungarian Empire. The illiteracy rate of 1.5% among post-1880 immigrants was lower than that of most states in the Union at that time. In 1890 there were 10,000 Czechs in Cleveland. The years 1900–14 witnessed the greatest influx of Czech immigrants to the Cleveland area. Czech migration to the U.S. declined significantly between the world wars for political reasons in both the U.S. and the Czechs' own homeland. The U.S. Natl. Origins Act in 1924 restricted immigration into the country. In Europe, a democratic Czechoslovakian nation was established following World War I. That removed a major motive for earlier migrations. The third, or post-World War II, wave of migration consisted of Czech refugees, exiles, and expatriates whose flight was prompted by 3 major events: the conclusion of WORLD WAR II, the Communist takeover of Czechoslovakia in 1948, and the ill-fated Dubcek revolt in 1968. Approximately 30,000 Czechoslovakians arrived in the U.S. between 1948–62. In 1970, roughly 47,000 Czechs lived in metropolitan Cleveland. By 1983 the number had fallen to 37,000 because of immigration restrictions of the Communist government in Czechoslovakia, and a general decline in Cleveland's total population.

Early Czech immigrants of the 1850s settled on Hill, Cross, and Commercial streets, now part of the FLATS. Czechs did not settle in old neighborhoods but preferred to build their own settlements on the outskirts of the city, away from downtown congestion, where they could cultivate small vegetable and flower gardens. During the 1870s and 1880s, Czechs built 2 settlements. One was on the west bank of the CUYAHOGA RIVER south of OHIO CITY. The other was on the east bank of the river near Croton St. As industry began to intrude into the enclaves, the residents moved farther west, toward W. 41st St. between Denison and Clark avenues, and farther east and southeast toward Quincy Ave. and E. 80th St., Buckeye Rd. and nearby streets, lower Fleet Ave. near E. 55th St., and Broadway around E. 55th St. The Broadway area from E. 37th St. to Union Ave. was known as "Little Bohemia." From the late 1870s to the end of World War I, this district was the largest and most prosperous Czech settlement in Cleveland. The influx of immigrants prior to World War I, coupled with encroachment by large industrial plants into the Broadway section, led to a new Czech settlement around E. 131st St. After World War I, the move to the SUBURBS began. MAPLE HTS. soon became one of the most important Czech communities in the county. Other suburbs such as GARFIELD HTS., NEWBURGH HTS., UNIVERSITY HTS., CUYAHOGA HTS., SHAKER HTS., CLEVELAND HTS., BEDFORD, WARRENSVILLE, CHAGRIN FALLS, INDEPENDENCE, PARMA, and LAKEWOOD gained significant Czech populations. However, in Cleveland in 1986, the Broadway-Fleet and Clark-Fulton areas still retained a small Czech population. Many of the early immigrants were tailors, shoemakers, masons, stonecutters, blacksmiths, and carpenters. The unskilled immigrants often worked on farms or for John D. Rockefeller's refineries making barrels. The Broadway section of the city offered easy access to the factories. By the turn of the century, Czechs were engaged in every kind of business. The first Czech industrialist in Cleveland was Frank J. Vlchek, founder of the VLCHEK TOOL CO., which manufactured tool kits for cars.

Czechs were bound together by a common language and by shared customs. Religiously, however, the community was fractured into 2 antagonistic groups: Catholics and freethinkers. Nearly all Czech immigrants had identified themselves as Catholic at the time they entered the U.S., but by the end of the 1880s, more than half of Czech-Americans had left the church. Most of the disaffected rejected any religious affiliation and were known as "freethinkers." Their views were anticlerical. The majority of freethinkers were agnostic, with beliefs similar to those of Thos. Jefferson, Benjamin Franklin, and Thos. Paine. A minority were atheist, and others were simply indifferent toward organized religion. Some Czech-Americans who rejected Catholicism were either converted or joined Protestant churches, primarily Methodist, Baptist, or Congregational. The philosophies of the two groups were irreconcilable. Rivalry forced every Czech-American to make a choice. Each settlement in Cleveland contained at least 1 church, established by the religious, and a hall, founded by freethinkers, both of which provided many services to the community; they were cultural, civic, and social centers, and housed ethnic schools. Not until the 1930s did freethinkers and Catholics freely associate with each other. In recent decades, the number of positive freethinkers has declined, as the younger generation has not been attracted to the movement, and is instead indifferent toward religion.

Of the city's Czech-Americans who are members of an organized religion, the majority are Catholic, some are Protestant, and some are Jewish. The first Czech Catholic church in Cleveland was ST. WENCESLAS CHURCH, named after the first Czech saint. It was founded in 1867 at the corner of Arch and Burwell streets. The second Czech parish was St. Prokop (1874), on the west side of the city. In 1892, the St. Wenceslas congregation built a new church at the corner of Broadway and E. 37th St. In 1923, with the move to the suburbs, another St. Wenceslas church was built in Maple Hts. Eventually both St. Wenceslas churches within the city proper were razed. In 1986 there were 5 Catholic churches and 1 Protestant church, SCRANTON RD. BAPTIST, which retained a moderate complement of Czechs in their congregations. The Catholic churches included St. Wenceslas, Our Lady of Lourdes, St. John Nepomucene, and Holy Family Roman Catholic

Church. In 1986, Cleveland still had 3 Czech halls: the Sokol Greater Cleveland Hall (BOHEMIAN NATL. HALL) and Ceska Sin Sokol Hall, which were established by freethinkers, and the Czech Karlin Hall, which was established by Catholics. Fraternal organizations also reflected the break in the community. Each Czech fraternal has identified itself with either Catholicism or free thought. The organizations thereby institutionalized the schism so that Catholic and non-Catholic fraternals remain distinct to this day. The first Czech society organized in Cleveland was the Slovanska Lipa, organized in the 1860s. Among the active Catholic bodies in the 1980s were the CZECH CATHOLIC UNION, the Czechoslovak Society of America, and the Catholic Order of the Foresters, while the WESTERN FRATERNAL LIFE ASSOC. grew out of the freethinking community. In addition to providing social, educational, cultural, and recreational activities, an important contribution of the organizations was the provision of financial resources through savings and loan societies and insurance groups. Czechs also founded a number of savings and loans to meet similar needs; these included the First Federal Saving & Loan Assoc. of Cleveland and the People's Savings & Loan Assoc.

Gymnastic training, with strong nationalist overtones, has been a vital part of Czech-American life. Many of the athletic groups have been branches of the Sokol organization. The first Sokol unit in Cleveland, Sokol Czech, was organized in 1879. Sokols also provided dramatic and musical training, offered lectures, helped establish libraries, and fostered a sense of Czech brotherhood. One Cleveland Sokol unit, the WORKERS GYMNASTIC UNION, sponsors gymnastic exhibitions and social events at Taborville, a Czech cooperative community southeast of CHAGRIN FALLS. Two other major Czech gymnastic units in the 1980s were SOKOL GREATER CLEVELAND and Sokols of Ceska Sin. The Sokols were responsive to the aspirations of Czechs for a free nation-state. Before the U.S. entered World War I, several members of Cleveland's Sokols participated in the Czechoslovak Legions that fought with the Allies in Europe. A total of 360 Czech and Slovak volunteers from the Cleveland area eventually joined the Czechoslovak Legionnaires. In 1915, in Cleveland, Czechs and Slovaks met to plan a strategy to liberate and unify Czech and Slovak regions in an independent republic. During World War I, Czech-American publications and ethnic leaders lobbied to influence American public opinion. Msgr. OLDRICH ZLAMAL, pastor of Our Lady of Lourdes Church, encouraged Cleveland Czechs to become politically active and to petition for the independence of Czechoslovakia. The democratic Czechoslovakian nation state created at the conclusion of World War I was a source of personal gratification for Czechs in this country until its Nazi occupation in 1938 and its fall to Communism in 1948.

Drama, musical, and dance groups have helped preserve the Czechs' ethnic heritage since the 1860s. In 1867 a musical organization, the LUMIR-HLAHOL-TYL SINGING SOCIETY, was established in Cleveland. Groups such as the VOJAN SINGING & DRAMATIC SOCIETY and the Vcelka Czech Dramatic Society were founded afterward. Music was an area of the arts in which many Czechs excelled; 10 of the 57 members of the first CLEVELAND ORCHESTRA were Czech. CHAS. V. RYCHLIK, a member of that first orchestra, was a successful composer and respected music teacher until his death in 1962. Families such as the HRUBYs and the Machans were active as performers and composers.

Czech newspapers in Cleveland presented the views of 3 different segments of Czech society: freethinkers, social-

ists, and religious. Toward the latter part of the 19th century, Cleveland was one of the major cities in the nation with a large population of Czech progressives or freethinkers. Thus, the city offered an attractive market for a chain of newspapers that represented the freethinkers. *Pokrok* (Progress), established in 1871, was the first progressive Czech newspaper in the city. It was followed by a progressive weekly, *DENNICE NOVEVEKU* (Star of the New Era), and a daily *Svet* (The World) under the same management. Cleveland was also a major center of Czech socialism. In 1909 the weekly *AMERICKE DELNICKE LISTY* (American Workman's News) began publication. Its editor, JOSEPH MARTINEK, was active in the struggle for old-age pensions in Ohio. The *Americke Delnicke Listy* continued to be published until 1953. Catholics preferred the *American*, a Czech newspaper founded by FRANK J. SVOBODA. In 1939, *Svet* bought out the *American* and became the *SVET-AMERICAN*. From then until the summer of 1950, when it ceased publication, the *Svet-American* was the only Czech daily newspaper published in Cleveland. In the fall of 1950, a new Czech daily, *NOVY SVET* (New World), began publication. Although published out of New Jersey in the 1980s, *Novy Svet* still contained articles about Cleveland Czechs contributed by its local editor.

The movement of Czechs toward the suburbs, which began shortly after World War I, has weakened the old neighborhoods and many of the institutions located in them and has made it difficult to maintain ethnicity. The Communist takeover of Czechoslovakia in 1948 further alienated Czech-Americans from their Old World roots. In the 1980s, however, Czech-American culture in Cleveland was still evident in gymnastic meets and congresses, in folklore demonstrations and fetes, in religious festivals, in commemorations of events significant to Czechs in Bohemia and Moravia as well as in America, and in the instruction in Czech history, language, and culture available at education centers. Much of this activity seemed attributable, however, to the general resurgence of interest in ethnicity in the 1980s. Without a strong new immigration, however, it remains to be seen how such activities can endure with the general dispersal of the Czech population.

Nicholas J. Zentos
Lorain County Community College

Ledbetter, Eleanor, *The Czechs of Cleveland* (1919).
Works Projects Admin., *The Peoples of Cleveland* (1942).

**CZOLGOSZ, LEON F.** (1873–29 Oct. 1901), the assassin of Pres. Wm. McKinley, was a resident of Cleveland for a number of years. He was born in Detroit, one of 8 children of Polish immigrants. The family moved several times before settling in Cleveland in 1891, where the father operated a saloon at Tod and 3rd streets (E. 65th and Gertrude Ave.). Later the family pooled its money and bought a farm in Warrensville Twp. Czolgosz had only 5½ years of schooling, yet he was regarded as the family intellectual because he could read and write English. He found work in the Newburgh Wire Mill in Cleveland in 1891. He participated in a strike at the mill in 1893, which failed; consequently, he grew bitter toward RELIGION and capitalism, regarding them as tools of the wealthy. He quit the mill in 1898 because of supposed ill health and did not work again, spending most of his time on the family farm, where he became increasingly restless and moody. Czolgosz became attracted to the anarchist movement in the late 1890s. He attempted to become a member of the Liberty Club, a Cleveland anarchist group, but its leaders did not trust him. While they did not turn him away, they gave him a wide berth. He apparently got the idea of shooting

McKinley after reading of an anarchist's assassination of King Humbert I of Italy in 1900. Later he claimed that a speech delivered by noted anarchist Emma Goldman at Cleveland's FRANKLIN CLUB in May 1901 incited him to commit the assassination.

It had been advertised that McKinley would visit the Pan-American Exposition in Buffalo in Sept. 1901. Czolgosz left Cleveland in mid-1901 and on 31 Aug. rented a room while awaiting McKinley's arrival. On 6 Sept., he was among a crowd of people in the exposition's Temple of Music, waiting to shake hands with the president. Czolgosz had concealed a revolver under a handkerchief wrapped about his right hand. When it came his turn to shake McKinley's hand, he fired twice, hitting the president in the breastbone and abdomen. He was captured immediately. McKinley died of the abdominal wound 8 days later. Czolgosz was tried by the Supreme Court of the State of New York and found guilty of murder in 2 days. He was electrocuted at the Auburn (N.Y.) State Prison on 29 Oct. 1901, and his body was placed in an unmarked grave on the prison grounds. Czolgosz's act, the third presidential assassination, brought the wrath of the press and public upon anarchist groups. It also resulted in full-time presidential protection by the Secret Service.

---

Johns, A. Wesley, *The Man Who Shot McKinley* (1970).

# D

The ***DAILY CLEVELANDER*** provided Cleveland with its first penny newspaper on 1 Oct. 1855. It was edited by W. J. May, formerly of the *Cleveland Herald*, who provided its 4 5-column pages with some lively writing. Avoiding politics at first, the *Clevelander* instead displayed a passion for the THEATER; theatrical events were regularly listed under the masthead. Its most serious political fight, in fact, was a successful campaign against a nearly prohibitive theater tax passed by the city council. As the national election campaign progressed in 1856, the *Clevelander* professed boredom with all candidates as late as July. By September, however, it hoisted the colors of Millard Fillmore to its masthead, while claiming no sympathy for the nativist principles of his American party supporters. Shortly after the election and its own first anniversary, the *Daily Clevelander* suspended publication on 18 Nov. 1856.

The ***DAILY FOREST CITY*** was founded on 26 Apr. 1852 by Joseph Meharry Medill, who had moved to Cleveland after brief publishing experiences in Coshocton and Newark, Ohio. A penny paper of 4 pages, it supported Whig politics and soon claimed a circulation of 5,000. By its second year, Medill had been joined as partner and coeditor by his brother, Jas. C. Medill. On 15 Oct. 1853, the *Daily Forest City* and *DAILY TRUE DEMOCRAT* were consolidated into the *Daily Forest City Democrat*. As explained by the new paper, "The publication ... of two Journals of an anti-slavery and progressive character, in the same place, was a waste of moral strength and of pecuniary resources." The Medills were joined in the new partnership by John C. Vaughn of the *True Democrat* and job printer EDWIN W. COWLES. Cowles soon became the dominant figure in the new enterprise, as the paper was renamed the *CLEVELAND LEADER* at his insistence. By the spring of 1855, Medill sold out to Cowles and moved to Chicago, where he eventually became publisher of the *Chicago Tribune*. His grandson, Medill McCormick, long afterward briefly returned to Cleveland as publisher of the *Leader*.

The ***DAILY MORNING MERCURY*** was one of the half-dozen publications that made their debuts in the local media explosion of 1841. Specializing in police reports, it was started in early September by Edward Burke Fisher and Calvin Hall. By November it had been combined by Fisher with Gage Mortimer Shipper's *DAILY MORNING NEWS* as the *Daily Mercury & News*. According to the *Cleveland*

*Herald*, Shipper had withdrawn from the enterprise by 1 Mar. 1842, when the paper was reported to be under the enterprise of Fisher and the proprietorship of "Messrs. Cottrell & Bagley." Since Bagley and Fisher had also been identified as publishers of the weekly *CLEVELAND GATHERER*, a connection between that publication and the contemporaneous *Mercury & News* is likely.

The ***DAILY MORNING NEWS*** may have been a regeneration of the *EAGLE-EYED NEWS-CATCHER*, since publisher Gage Mortimer Shipper had been associated with David L. Wood in the publication of that newspaper. Further evidence is provided by a reference in the *Cleveland Herald* of 2 Aug. 1841, which states that the *Morning News* had been recently enlarged into a sheet of "respectable size." By 23 Nov. 1841, however, the *Herald* reported that the *Morning News* had been merged with the *Daily Mercury* into the *Daily Mercury & News*.

The ***DAILY NATIONAL DEMOCRAT***, established by proadministration Democrats in reproof of the pro-Douglas position of the *PLAIN DEALER*, first appeared on 3 Jan. 1859. Benjamin Harrington, who also replaced *Plain Dealer* publisher JOSEPH W. GRAY as Cleveland postmaster, was reportedly the new paper's backer, in partnership with U.S. Marshal Matt Johnson. By May, however, E. A. Munson of the *CLEVELAND DAILY REVIEW* appeared on the masthead as publisher, "For the Proprietors." The *National Democrat* was edited by Chas. B. Flood, aided by Alphonse Minor Griswold as associate editor. In the presidential campaign of 1860, the *National Democrat* found itself in the untenable position of supporting the southern Democratic ticket of Breckinridge and Lane in the capital of the WESTERN RESERVE. Griswold had left the staff, turning up before the end of the year as Chas. F. Browne's replacement on the *Plain Dealer*. After the suspension of the *National Democrat* on 12 Feb. 1861, Flood served as the *Plain Dealer*'s Columbus correspondent.

The ***DAILY TRUE DEMOCRAT*** began as the *True Democrat*, a weekly published in N. OLMSTED, Ohio, in 1846. From its first daily issue of 12 Jan. 1847, however, the *Daily True Democrat* carried a Cleveland dateline. It was founded as an organ of the antislavery Whigs by Edward Stowe Hamlin, a former Congressman from Elyria, Ohio, with E.

L. Stevens as coeditor. Published in the Merchants' Exchange Bldg., the *Daily True Democrat* served as a forum for Congressman Joshua R. Giddings and supported Martin Van Buren, the candidate of the Free-Soil Democrats, for president in 1848. Hamlin left midway in the campaign to start a Free-Soil paper in Columbus, leaving the *Daily True Democrat* in the hands of T. G. Turner. With the aid of JAS. A. BRIGGS as editor, Turner continued the *Daily True Democrat* for nearly a year before turning it over to Thos. Brown in June 1849. Although Brown maintained the paper's Free-Soil principles, he also succeeded in making it less a political and more a general sheet in the next 4 years between national elections. John Champion Vaughan, a reformed southern slaveholder, was appointed editor. Increased space was devoted to nonpolitical news events, such as the city's first gas streetlights and the completion of the Cleveland-Columbus railroad, and a regular "local" column made its appearance. Under the administration of Mayor WM. CASE, the *Daily True Democrat* was designated "Official Paper of the City."

A new partner, Bostonian Geo. Bradburn, joined Brown and Vaughan to form an editorial triumvirate in Sept. 1851. It was not a harmonious arrangement, as Bradburn later charged Vaughan with censorship of his copy, failure adequately to requite his labors, and even physical abuse. New investors headed by H. C. Gray of Painesville took over the paper in May 1853, and on 17 Oct. 1853, it was merged with Joseph Medill's *DAILY FOREST CITY* to form the *Daily Forest City Democrat*. Gray, Medill, and EDWIN COWLES, who had printed the *Daily True Democrat*, were listed as publishers of the combined paper. Gray withdrew in favor of the latter two the following February, and the paper was rechristened the *Cleveland Morning Leader* on 16 Mar. 1854.

**DAISY HILL** was the country estate and farm of O. P. AND M. J. VAN SWERINGEN, developers of SHAKER HTS. and the CLEVELAND UNION TERMINAL complex. Situated in the suburb of HUNTING VALLEY east of Cleveland, it was developed by the two bachelor brothers between 1920-27 at an estimated cost of $2 million. Located on acres of rolling land at the edge of the Chagrin Valley, the estate included the main house, stables, nursery and greenhouse, a manmade lake, and 22 garages. The stone walls, bridges, and round towers in the Norman style were built by local stonemason Geo. Brown. The low, rambling main house contained 54 rooms and was designed in a mixture of styles. It has a 2-story Colonial portico, high-ceilinged informal parlors, and a large indoor swimming pool. A Dickens collection contained many first or limited editions, and the mansion was furnished with expensive antiques, American paintings, and Dresden and Spode china. The Van Sweringens occasionally entertained there but often held business meetings at Daisy Hill. The architect was Philip Small, who also planned SHAKER SQUARE for the Van Sweringens. Following the deaths of the two brothers in 1935 and 1936, their personal property was sold at auction in 1938, and the mansion was purchased in 1946 by Gordon Stouffer.

Haberman, Ian, *The Van Sweringens of Cleveland* (1979).

**DANCE HALLS.** During much of the 20th century, social dancing was one of the major recreational activities in industrial cities such as Cleveland. During the peak years between the 1920s and the 1950s, there were over 150 dance halls accessible to Greater Clevelanders, not including several hundred more dance floors in HOTELS, nightclubs, and private halls. These included facilities extending to Conneaut Lake Park, Pa., in the east; Meyers Lake Park, Canton, in the south; and Cedar Pt. Park, Sandusky, in the west. Although cities such as New York, Chicago, and Los Angeles had larger facilities, Cleveland became well known to musicians and bandleaders as a place to develop with a chance to move into a position of national prominence. One of the earliest social dances in Cleveland was held at Ballow's Hall in 1854. Dances at that time included the two-step, the waltz, and later the cakewalk and other syncopated steps. Ca. 1910, popular sheet music started to appear with parts for dance-band instrumentation, and by that time dancing in public parks became viewed as an adjunct to other activities such as swimming and sports; several dance pavilions were built at parks in the early 1900s. At EDGEWATER PARK, a dance pavilion overlooked a bath house on the beach below. GORDON PARK had a dance area in conjunction with a large bath house extending over the lake near E. 72nd St., and a park building at Brookside, off Fulton and Denison Ave., included a dance area on the 2d floor. Another city pavilion was located at Woodland Hills Park, at Kinsman and Woodland avenues. Both the Woodland Hills and Edgewater pavilions closed in 1914. Private amusement parks, which also formed at this time, offered dancing, in addition to a variety of other activities suited to families and group outings. PARKS with dance floors included Silver Lake Park in Cuyahoga Falls, built in 1876; LUNA PARK, where the dance pavilion was of generous size with the dance floor at ground level; EUCLID BEACH, which had one of the finest dance floors in the region and which for a time offered outdoor dancing; and PURITAS SPRINGS PARK, which had a plain ballroom and also featured an outdoor dance area.

The society dance craze, influenced by the popularity of Irene and Vernon Castle, led during the WORLD WAR I period to a changing social pattern. Before this time, dance halls were not always considered places where members of polite society might properly go. Therefore, dances were generally private functions. Some of the more affluent and prominent citizens built their homes with a ballroom and party facility, generally on the 3d floor, with access by special stairs or elevator. On the lower end of the social scale, saloons offered some dancing. Saloon dance floors disappeared after the 18th Amendment, the Volstead Act, took effect in 1920. They were replaced during Prohibition by supper clubs with a more sophisticated atmosphere that reflected the influence of society dancing. Most hotels countrywide included ballrooms or party rooms to provide for dancing as well as other group activities. When supper clubs flourished, local hotels created their own special clubs, with the potential clientele already staying as guests of the hotel. Radio broadcasts originated from hotel supper clubs on a regular basis during the 1930s and 1940s, with some broadcasts carried on a national network, publicizing both the orchestra and the hotel. Numerous private clubs and fraternal organizations provided a room in their building suitable for dances as well as other group functions related to the organization.

With the increased popularity of dancing in the 1910s and 1920s, many localities enacted laws to regulate conduct in the dance halls, which were viewed by some citizens as potential havens for moral laxness between the sexes. By 1930, 28 states and 60 large cities had adopted laws or ordinances to regulate public dancing; Cleveland developed Ordinance 690, defining regulations for dance places and dancers. *Public Dance Hall* meant any academy, room, place, restaurant, or nightclub where dancing was held, or any room, place, hall, or academy in which classes in dancing were held or instruction in dancing was held or given for a fee. The ordinance included restrictions on intoxi-

Aragon (Olympic Winter Garden; Shadyside), 3179 W. 25th St., 1915– .
Argonne, 18810 Bridge Approach, 1930– .
Arnolds, 945 E. 152nd St.
Banater Hall, 11934 Lorain Ave.
Baumeils Hall, E. 34th & Woodland Ave.
Bedford Glens, Glen Rd. off Willis, Bedford, 1905–44.
Berea Ballroom, Eastland Rd. at Berea Fairgrounds.
Big Barn, Lorain Ave. at Lorain County line.
Boles, E. 93rd & Broadway.
Botts, W. 25th & Franklin Blvd.
Bowl, The, 3739 E. 93rd St.
Blue Moon (Shadyside), State Rd. near Pearl Rd.
Bradlee's, 1715 Euclid Ave., 2d floor.
Brighton Park (Flappers Paradise), off Denison near Brookside Park.
Brookside Park Pavilion, at Brookside Park off Pearl Rd.
Brunswick, 1480 Pearl Rd.
Burns (Trostler's), 2064 E. 55th.
Cain Park, Pavilion and Amphitheater, 14591 Superior Rd., active-summer.
Capital, W. 65th & Lorain Ave.
Carnegie Hall, 1220 Huron Rd.
Central Armory, E. 6th & Lakeside, 1903–19.
Circle Ballroom (Zimmermans; Bradlees; Crystal Roller Gardens; Circle "O"), 10300 Euclid Ave., 2d floor.
Cleveland Heights Pavilion, Mayfield & Superior roads, semiactive.
Cleveland Public Hall Ballroom, E. 6th & Lakeside Ave., semiactive.
Continental Ballroom (Fosters; Glicks), 13929 Euclid Ave., 2d floor.
Danceland, with summer roof garden (Skateland), 9810 Euclid Ave.
Dreamland Ballroom, E. 13th near Chester Ave.
Eagle House, Miles & Broadway avenues, 1840–1900.
Edgewater Pavilion, Edgewater Park, Edgewater Dr., 1800s–1914.
Euclid Beach Pavilion, Euclid Beach Park, E. 160th & Lake Shore Blvd.
Flynn Hall, E. 53rd & Superior Ave.
Freemans, W. 25th & Lorain Ave.
Gilberts (Green Parrot), 14623 Detroit Ave., Lakewood.
Gordon Park Pavilion, Gordon Park, near E. 72nd & Lake Shore Blvd.
Grays Armory, 1234 Bolivar Rd.,1893– .
Grdinas Hall, E. 59th & St Clair Ave.
Green Gables, 13107 Broadway Ave.
Guild Hall, Builders Exchange Bldg.
Hansons, 1900 W. 25th St.

Harmony Hall, 2515 Franklin Ave.
Hillside, E. 72nd & Broadway.
Hollywood Gardens, 1214 E. 79th St.
Homestead Ballroom, 11806 Detroit Ave., 2d floor.
Hopkins, Grace, 8329 Euclid Ave., 2d floor.
Jiendo Dance Hall, 4105 Clark Ave.
Klings Hall, 3241 W. 50th St.
Lorraine, 11938 Lorain Ave.
Luna Park Pavilion, Luna Park, 10911 Woodland Ave.
Madison Park Dancing Academy, 13222 Madison Ave., Lakewood.
Mahalls (Mahall's Bowling Lanes), 13300 Madison Ave., Lakewood.
Marigold, E. 185th St. at Lake Erie.
Marcane (Ritz; Greystone), 3705 Euclid Ave.
Martha Lee Club, E. 17th & Euclid Ave.
Merrils, W. 25th & Caroline Ave.
Metropolitan Gardens, off 160 Adams Ct., Berea, Ohio.
Metropolitan Hall, 10609 Superior Ave.
O'Laughlin's, 6415 Detroit Ave.
Old Brewery, behind Mt. Sinai Hospital.
Old Taylor Bowl, E. 36th & Harvard Ave.
Osters (Oster & O'Laughlins), 2052 E. 105th St. (party center).
Pennsylvania Hall, E. 55th St. & Euclid Ave.
Puritas Springs Ballroom, Puritas Springs Park, west end of Puritas Rd.
Rauscharts, near E. 55th & Euclid Ave.
Remenys, E. 55th & Woodland Ave., 2d floor.
Sachsenheim Hall, 7001 Denison Ave., semiactive.
Shaw-Hayden Dance Hall, 1381 Hayden Ave.
Sojacks, 1699 W. 25th St., 3d floor (E. 79th & St. Clair Ave.).
Sommers Hall, 2945 W. 25th.
Springvale Ballroom, 5871 Canterbury Rd., N. Olmsted, Ohio, active.
Starlight, Cedar & Lee roads.
Starlight Ballroom, 27070 Detroit Rd., active-party center.
Steamer City of Erie (1900s).
Steamer Goodtime, E. 9th St. Pier, 1924–40.
Steamer St. Ignace, E. 9th St. Pier, ?–1924.
Trianon (Crystal Slipper; Trianon Bowling Lanes), 9802 Euclid Ave., 1927– .
Twilight Ballroom, 6021 St. Clair Ave. NE, 1940s.
Vega Hall, 3025 Vega Ave.
Virginia Hall, 10529 Superior Ave.
Walters Grove Dance Pavilion, 5486 State Rd., 2d floor.
White City Pavilion, E. 140th St. & Lake Shore Blvd., 1800s–1906.
Windermere Ballroom, 14250 Euclid Ave., 1940s.
Woodland Hills Pavilion, Woodland Hills Park, Kinsman & Woodland avenues.

cating liquor and gambling and required decorum of behavior and dress. Smoking was restricted to designated rooms. Dance-hall inspectors were first hired by the city in 1929 to check places covered by the ordinance. By 1930, there were nearly 150 dance-hall inspectors covering the city. Dance halls also had an employee assigned to check decorum and dress. Dancing too close or cheek to cheek was discouraged. After a marathon dance contest held at the Old Taylor Bowl, at E. 36th St. and Harvard, the city ordinance was amended to prohibit such activities. Dance-hall activity in Cleveland reached a peak during the Big Band era of the 1930s and 1940s. Many of the major ensembles of that era, including those of Glenn Miller and Artie Shaw, played at locations in the Greater Cleveland area. However, interest in ballroom dancing declined through the 1950s as musical tastes changed and other forms of entertainment, such as TELEVISION, became available. Ballroom and club owners experienced a rise in operating expenses and increased fees for bands. That, along with diminishing attendance, especially in some urban areas where social unrest brought a few roving gangs to disrupt dances, forced many operations to close or cut back their

schedules. Owners changed their halls from dancing to party centers, roller rinks, bowling lanes, or a variety of commercial enterprises.

Although some dance halls existed during the 1800s, most of Greater Cleveland's most prominent, nonpark facilities were built between 1900–30. The Aragon, 3179 W. 25th St., remained one of the few ballrooms operating in the 1980s. It was originally built in 1919 as the Olympic Winter Garden, catering to dances, roller skating, banquets, weddings, and prizefights; ownership changed in 1930, and the name became Shadyside Gardens. Several years later, after remodeling, the ballroom was renamed the Aragon, after one of Chicago's finest ballrooms. From the 1930s to the 1950s, most of the traveling name bands made a stop at the Aragon, generally on Sunday. Radio broadcasts were a weekly feature continuing into the 1960s. Dances were scheduled for Wednesday, Friday, Saturday, and Sunday. Wednesdays were designated as Polka Night until the demand subsided. The Crystal Slipper, 9810 Euclid Ave., opened in 1927 as the largest and finest of the city ballrooms. Within several years the name was changed to the Trianon, after another famous ballroom in Chicago. Dances

331

were held nightly, and popular name bands were featured for a night or short-term engagement. During the early 1940s, the Trianon, under new ownership, became the Trianon Bowling Lanes, which operated through the 1950s, when the property was acquired by the CLEVELAND CLINIC FOUNDATION. Danceland, 9001 Euclid Ave., operated as a dance hall through the 1920s and 1930s, when, under new ownership, it was converted to a roller rink and renamed Skateland. Danceland had featured a summer roof garden. By the 1960s, new owners converted and remodeled the building for commercial use as a food store and other shops.

The Ritz Ballroom, 3705 Euclid Ave., was active through the 1930s, with the name changing to the Greystone and later to the Marcane, which continued into the 1950s, when the structure was given over to commercial use. Later the entire block, including the Cleveland Arena, was demolished, leaving an area used as a parking lot in the 1980s. Bedford Glens, located off Glen Rd. in BEDFORD, began as a park in the early 1900s; soon after, a barnlike structure was built, and it became a year-round dance and bowling resort. Bedford Glens became popular and was remodeled, becoming well-known from Cleveland to Akron; it had the advantage of an interurban stop nearby. Ed Day was the proprietor and orchestra leader, directing a group known as Ed Day and His Ten Knights. Although the ballroom was successful, a fire closed it in 1944. Springvale Ballroom, 5871 Canterbury Rd., N. OLMSTED, was still operating in the 1980s. It was built in 1923 by the Biddulph family and managed by it throughout its history. This ballroom was remodeled on at least 2 occasions, and in the 1980s dances were held on Wednesday and Saturday evenings, with private parties at other times. Only a few dance halls continued to operate in the 1980s, and these averaged fewer than 2 nights of dances per week. Hotels, clubs, and fraternal organizations continued to hold special dances: one hotel, Swingos, regularly scheduled Sunday brunches with dancing, capitalizing on a revival of interest in Big Band music during the 1980s. However, despite predictions of a revival of ballroom dancing and music, such activities continued only at a minor level in the 1980s when compared to their peak period of popularity during the 1930s and 1940s.

Robert Strasmyer

See also MUSIC, POLKAS, JAZZ.

**DANDRIDGE, DOROTHY** (9 Nov. 1923–8 Sept. 1965), was a Cleveland-born black nightclub entertainer turned movie actress who had starring roles in such film classics as *Porgy and Bess* and *Carmen Jones*, which earned her a Best Actress Oscar nomination in 1954. She enjoyed a successful career that made her world-famous. The daughter of a minister, Rev. April Dandridge, Dorothy was influenced most by her mother, Ruby, who was a screen and radio actress best known for her roles with the late Hattie McDaniel on the old "Beulah" television show. Dorothy entered show business at the age of 5 as part of a singing trio that included her mother and a sister, Vivian. Dandridge also performed acrobatic ballet at various Cleveland churches and schools. She and her sisters became known as the Wonder Children. The family moved to Los Angeles when Dorothy was 9 years old. After being tutored by an aunt in theater dressing rooms, Dorothy and her sisters were enrolled in regular schools upon reaching California. Encouraged by her mother's success in Hollywood, Dorothy dropped out of high school and formed a trio with her sister Vivian and friend Etta Jones, and they sang with Jimmy Lunceford, a top bandleader from the "Big Band"

era. The trio won small parts in movies, and in 1940 they opened at the famous Cotton Club in New York City, where Dandridge met dancer Harold Nicholas, one-half of the famed Nicholas Bros. dance act. The couple married in 1941, had a daughter, Harolyn, in 1944, and divorced in 1951.

Following her divorce, Dandridge enrolled in a Hollywood drama school. A turning point in her career came when she sang with the Desi Arnaz band at the Hollywood Mocambo, and after a string of successes as a singer on the supper-show circuit, she was chosen to star opposite Harry Belafonte in *Carmen Jones*, a black Broadway musical based on Bizet's opera. She appeared in the title role when the play was performed at the Palace in Cleveland in 1954. In 1959, she costarred with Sidney Poitier in *Porgy and Bess*. On 30 June 1959, Dandridge married Jack Dennison, a white nightclub owner on Las Vegas's famed Strip. The second marriage for both produced no children and ended in divorce in 1962. In 1963, Dandridge filed for bankruptcy, claiming debts in excess of $100,000. In 1965, at the age of 41, she collapsed in her West Hollywood apartment, the victim of a rare complication resulting from a fractured foot.

**DAUBY, NATHAN L.** (31 May 1873–17 May 1964), began his career as a clerk in a shoe store and eventually joined and built the MAY CO. into the city's largest department store. He was a prominent local philanthropist. Dauby was born in Cleveland, the son of David Dauby. He began his business career at age 15; he became manager of the Star Shoe Co. at 384 Ontario 2 years later and soon gained a reputation as a skilled merchant. In 1892, Dauby went into business for himself. Along with Emil Strauss, he opened the Dauby & Strauss boot and shoe store at the corner of Ontario and Huron. It was the city's first one-price shoe store, and its success surprised the merchants who had predicted that the process of customer and merchant's negotiating the price of an item would not die out. Dauby bought Strauss out in 1898. Dauby's success as a shoe merchant led the May Co. to lease him its shoe department ca. 1902. In 1904 he became manager of the entire May Co. store in Cleveland. He served as both general manager and merchandise manager until 1933. He continued to serve as general manager until 1945. He shortened his hours and relinquished total control in that year, but remained involved with the company for an additional 16 years. In 1961, at the age of 88, he left and took offices in the Natl. City Bank Bldg., from which he directed his philanthropic activities.

During his tenure as general manager, Dauby became known as an innovative retailer and built the May Co.'s Cleveland store into the largest department store in Ohio. In 1912 he convinced May Co. officials to build a 6-story, $2.5 million building on PUBLIC SQUARE, which was completed in 1914. Dauby introduced into the store a number of features designed for the comfort and convenience of customers, such as the first escalator (1914) and a parking garage for patrons (1925); as early as 1904 the store had a children's playground. Dauby was also one of the first to entice customers into his store by offering Eagle Trading Stamps, and later double stamps. Dauby became a director of the national May Co. operation in 1910 and by 1918 was a vice-president. From 1945 until his death, Dauby devoted considerable energies to philanthropic work, especially to the direction of the LOUIS D. BEAUMONT FOUNDATION. Dauby had been a long-time contributor to various charitable efforts in the Cleveland area, giving to the BOY SCOUTS, the YMCA, the YWCA, and various churches. He became a trustee of MT. SINAI HOSPITAL in 1913 and was a leader in the Community Fund campaigns. In 1952 he donated his mansion at 11212 Euclid Ave. to the Cleveland Hearing & Speech Ctr. Upon his death, he left an estate of $10 million, of which $1.5 million went to a variety of local institutions. A respected community leader, Dauby shunned public tributes, but in 1946 the Chamber of Commerce awarded him its Medal for Public Service. Dauby and his wife, Bessie, had a son, David, and a daughter, Mrs. Lucile D. Gries. Mrs. Dauby died in 1939.

The **DAUBY CHARITY FUND** was founded in 1944 by NATHAN L. DAUBY. Dauby, a native of Cleveland, went into the shoe business in 1892 at the age of 19. In 1899 he leased the shoe department of May's Dept. Store, and he went on to become a manager and chief executive officer of the May Co. from 1912 to his retirement in 1945. Dauby remained as an advisor to the company until 1961, and at the same time devoted himself to running the LOUIS D. BEAUMONT FOUNDATION, one of the largest private foundations in Cleveland's history. (Commodore Beaumont was a cofounder of the MAY CO. At its peak, the foundation had assets of $30 million, the principal of which was disbursed by 1977.) Dauby was married to Bessie Dauby (d. 1939), with whom he had a son, David, and a daughter, Lucile D. Gries. The purposes of the fund are general, primarily local in Cuyahoga County. In 1952, Dauby donated his mansion at 11212 Euclid Ave. to the Cleveland Hearing & Speech Ctr. Upon his death, grants from his estate went to Western Reserve University, the Cleveland Hearing & Speech Ctr., and the Natl. Jewish Hospital of Denver. No grants are given to individuals, for endowment funds, or for loans. In 1983, the assets of the fund were $2,228,394, of which $125,462 waas disbursed for 26 grants. Under the terms of Dauby's will, the full fund must be paid out within 20 years of his daughter's death (Mrs. Lucile D. Gries, 1902–1968). Officers of the fund in 1985 included Richard Brezic, Ellen G. Cole, and Robt. D. Gries.

## DAUGHTERS OF THE AMERICAN REVOLUTION.
*See* **PATRIOTIC SOCIETIES**

**DAVIS, HARRY E.** (26 Dec. 1882–4 Feb. 1955), lawyer and politician, was active for more than 50 years in Cleveland Republican party politics and black community affairs, including the NAACP, black Masonry, and KARAMU HOUSE. Davis was born in Cleveland and educated in the CLEVELAND PUBLIC SCHOOLS. He attended Hiram College, 1904–05, and graduated from the Western Reserve University Law School with the LL.B. degree in 1908. Admitted to the state bar that same year, he went into private practice. Davis's involvement in local black community affairs and the Republican party was lifelong. He was a member of the Lincoln League of Colored Voters of Cuyahoga County and was involved with the annual Republican Lincoln-Douglass dinners. In 1909, using the 1896 Ohio civil-rights law, Davis brought racial-discrimination charges against a Burrows Store ticket seller who had refused to sell to him. Even though the ticket seller was found guilty, a common pleas court jury denied Davis civil damages.

In 1920, Davis was elected to the first of 4 consecutive terms in the Ohio general assembly, the first black elected since 1910. As chair of the assembly's Codes Committee, he introduced a resolution calling for a general referendum to remove from the Ohio constitution a provision that limited the elective franchise to "white male citizens." The resolution was approved by the electorate in 1923. In 1928, Davis became the first black elected by city council to the Cleveland Civil Service Commission. He served his last 2 years on the commission, 1932–34, as its president. Elected to the Ohio senate in 1947, Davis was only the second black and the first since 1893 to serve there. In the senate, he introduced a bill creating a municipal police court in E. CLEVELAND and had the distinction of being the first black legislator to preside over the senate. With his reelection to the senate in 1953, he became the only successful black candidate for the Ohio legislature during the 1950s. Davis was married in 1917 to Louise Wormley, who died in 1948. Davis served as a trustee of Karamu House and the EUCLID AVE. CHRISTIAN CHURCH. Active in Masonry since 1910, he was a 33d-degree mason and had authored a manuscript on BLACKS in Masonry. His work on the history of blacks in Cleveland was carried on and completed by his brother, RUSSELL H. DAVIS. His memory was honored in 1962 by the Cleveland Board of Education with the naming of Harry E. Davis Jr. High School.

Russell H. Davis Papers, WRHS.

**DAVIS, HARRY LYMAN** (25 Jan. 1878–21 May 1950), was elected to 4 terms as mayor of Cleveland (1916–20, 1933–35) and served as governor of Ohio from 1921–23. Davis was born in NEWBURGH, the son of Evan and Barbara C. Davis. He left school at the age of 13 and took a job in the steel mills, completing his education studying at home and at night school. At 21, he became a solicitor for the Cleveland Telephone Co., and 3 years later he founded the Davis Rate Adjustment Co. to sell telephone securities to the general public. He later turned to the insurance and liability field, establishing the Harry L. Davis Co. He married Lucy V. Fegan in 1905, and they had a son, Harry L., Jr.

Davis's first venture into politics was his election as city treasurer on the Republican ticket in 1909. He lost his bid for reelection in 1911. He successfully campaigned for mayor in 1915. In that election, the preferential election process used (see HOME RULE) gave his opponent, PETER WITT, more first-place votes; however, Davis won with a plurality of over 2,800 on a combination of first, second, and other choice votes. The affable mayor was perhaps best known for establishing the MAYOR'S ADVISORY WAR COMMITTEE, which worked with the Army and the draft boards during WORLD WAR I and organized receptions and banquets for the returning troops after the armistice. Davis was reelected mayor for 2 more terms but resigned in May 1920 to campaign successfully for governor of Ohio. During his term as governor, he restructured the executive branch to include a cabinet of 7 directors to help administer state affairs. He did not stand for reelection in 1922 but did campaign for the governorship in 1924, losing to incumbent Vic Donahey. Returning to Cleveland, Davis, a believer in the ward-mayor form of city government, opposed the CITY MANAGER PLAN. His amendment to abolish the plan was rejected by the voters in 1927 and 1928. In 1929, together with Saul Danaceau and Edward Downer, tried again with the Three-D amendment; however, it, too, was unsuccessful. In 1931, Davis took little part in the successful campaign, led by Saul Danaceau, to abolish the City Manager Plan. With the return of the ward-mayor form of government, Davis was again elected mayor and served from 1933–35. He died in Cleveland at age 72.

**DAVIS, RUSSELL H.** (29 Oct. 1897–14 Nov. 1976), was a teacher, a school administrator, a civic activist, and the historian of Cleveland's black community. The son of a black mail carrier and a French woman, Davis was born in Cleveland and attended Bolton School and CENTRAL HIGH SCHOOL, graduating from the latter in 1916. He then entered Adelbert College of Western Reserve University, receiving his bachelor's degree in 1920, and Case School of Applied Science, earning a degree in chemical engineering in 1922. He received a master's degree in education from WRU in 1933. Davis worked as a chemical engineer for the GRASSELLI CHEMICAL CO. before embarking on a career in education. In Jan. 1928, he became a math and science teacher at Kennard Jr. High School, thus becoming the first black male to serve in the Cleveland school system's secondary schools. In 1932 he was transferred to Central High School; in 1940, when a new Central High was built, Davis remained at the old E. 55th St. facility as principal of Central Jr. High School. In 1951 he was transferred to Rawlings Jr. High, where he remained until Jan. 1962, when he became the principal of the new Harry E. Davis Jr. High School, named for his brother. He retired from the Cleveland school system in 1965. In addition to his work as a teacher and school administrator, Davis was a member of the Ohio School Survey Committee (1953–54) and served 2 years on the state Board of Education (1968–69). He later served as a member of the Bratenahl school board.

Davis also was active in civic affairs. In 1943 he spearheaded the Welfare Fed.'s Central Area Social Study, which resulted in the creation of the Central Area Community Council, of which he was an executive committee member. He also helped organize the Glenville Area Community Council and was its first president. He was an incorporator and executive committee member of the Neighborhood Settlement Assoc. and a trustee of the Family Service Assoc., KARAMU HOUSE, the Garden Valley Neighborhood House, and the Maternal Health Assoc. He was an officer in the local chapter of the Ohio Retired Teachers Assoc. and Seniors of Ohio, and a member of the Citizens Advisory Board of Cleveland City Hospital. Davis also chronicled the history of Cleveland's black community in newspaper columns and books. He wrote *Memorable Negroes in Cleveland's Past* and completed a project begun by his brother, Harry E. Davis, publishing the encyclopedic *Black Americans in Cleveland* in 1972. Davis's wife, Claire, was a teacher for 35 years before her retirement in 1960.

Russell H. Davis Papers, WRHS.

**DAVIS CUP MATCHES** have been played in the Cleveland area 10 times in the history of the international tennis competition. Cleveland hosted preliminary rounds of the competition for 3 years before hosting its first championship Challenge Round in 1964. In all, the Cleveland area has hosted 6 preliminary Davis Cup rounds (1960, 1961, 1962, 1966, 1968, 1979) and 4 championship matches (1964, 1969, 1970, 1973). Until 1960, Davis Cup matches in the U.S. were the property of 3 East Coast cities—New York, Boston, and Philadelphia—and the successful campaign to bring Davis Cup tennis to Cleveland was quite a coup in the tennis world. The campaign was led by local attorney and former high school and collegiate tennis star Robt. S. Malaga. It brought the first Davis Cup event to the CLEVELAND SKATING CLUB on 16–18 Sept. 1960; the U.S. team defeated Venezuela in that American Zone final, 5–0. The Cleveland Skating Club hosted the next 2 American Zone matches as well, and the U.S. team was victorious in both, defeating Mexico 3–2 in 1961 and Canada 4–1 in 1962.

In early 1964, Cleveland mounted a strong civic campaign to win the privilege of hosting the Davis Cup finals later that year. Cleveland beat New York and Los Angeles after Malaga guaranteed promoters $100,000 and a new facility in which to stage the event; the money was the clincher. The 1964 Davis Cup final was played at the new

7,500-seat tennis stadium at Roxboro Jr. High School in CLEVELAND HTS., where the Australian team captured the cup on 28 Sept., defeating the U.S. 3–2. The first Davis Cup final played in the Midwest was the most financially successful final up to that time; other firsts that year included the first black on the U.S. team (Arthur Ashe). Two more preliminary rounds were played in Cleveland before the championship returned in 1969. In the 1966 American Zone match, the U.S. blanked Mexico 5–0, and in the 1968 Interzone match, the U.S. defeated Spain 4–1. From 19–21 Sept. 1969, the Romanian team challenged the Americans for the cup at the HAROLD T. CLARK COURTS in Cleveland Hts. but were shut out by the U.S., 5–0. The U.S. successfully defended the cup in late Aug. 1970 at the Cleveland Hts. site, shutting out the West German team 5–0. When the Davis Cup final returned to Cleveland on 30 Nov. 1973, the location of the match was moved downtown to Public Hall, where the Americans lost the cup to Australia, 5–0. The Cleveland Skating Club hosted the last Davis Cup event held in Cleveland, the American Zone final, on 16–18 Mar. 1979, won by the U.S. over Colombia, 5–0.

The **DAVY MCKEE CORPORATION**, a multinational engineering corporation with a net worth of $50 million in 1978, began on 1 Nov. 1905, when metallurgical engineer Arthur G. McKee set up an iron and steel consulting firm in the ROCKEFELLER BLDG. at Superior and W. 6th St. In 1906, the former district engineer for the American Steel & Wire Co. formed a partnership with 2 other engineers, Robt. E. Baker and Donald D. Herr; they incorporated in 1915 as Arthur G. McKee & Co. McKee served as president until 1946. The company offered complete engineering and construction services for iron and steel projects. It did business with nearly two-thirds of the American and Canadian iron and steel producers in its first 10 years. By 1919, it required larger facilities and moved to 2422 Euclid Ave. McKee increased its operations significantly in 1926 when it merged with the Oklahoma-based Widdell Engineering Co., an oil-refinery engineering firm. Henry E. Widdell directed the company's oil department and later succeeded McKee as company president, serving in that capacity until 1964. In 1941, the company relocated to 2300 Chester Ave., and from its new location it played an important role in the design and construction of World War II defense plants, building 7 new blast furnaces in the U.S. and all of the new Canadian furnaces installed during the war. In the 1950s and 1960s, McKee expanded its foreign operations, setting up subsidiaries in Canada, Australia, Europe, and South America.

The company expanded in a new direction in 1961 with the acquisition of the Western Knapp Engineering Co., a San Francisco-based firm that designed and constructed plants to process nonferrous metals and minerals. But McKee's greatest growth came in the 1970s. After losing $2 million in 1971, the company earned more than $8 million in 1976, 1977, and 1978. Net worth increased from $18 million in 1971 to $50 million in 1978. Acquisitions helped the company's growth; in 1977, McKee acquired the Dresser Engineering Co., a Tulsa, Okla., firm that designed and constructed plants to produce natural gas, and the Toledo-based Campbell, DeBoe & Associates, designers of power-generating facilities for municipalities and industries. Arthur G. McKee & Co. merged with the Davy Corp. of London, England, in Nov. 1978 and in June 1979 became the Davy McKee Corp., a subsidiary of the U.S. holding company Davy, Inc. In 1981, Davy McKee employed 1,400 people in the Cleveland area. Hit hard by the 1981–82 recession, the company employed fewer than 400

Greater Clevelanders in Apr. 1983, when it announced plans to relocate its petroleum-processing and chemicals-engineering operations from facilities in Independence to Houston, Tex.

**DAY, WILLIAM HOWARD** (16 Oct. 1825–3 Dec. 1900), was an abolitionist, editor, printer, publisher, lecturer, civic leader, and clergyman who devoted his life to improving the conditions of his fellow blacks, both in Cleveland and elsewhere. He was born in New York City, the son of John and Eliza Dixon Day. He was educated at a private school, and later attended high school in Northampton, Mass., where he learned printing in the offices of the *Northampton Gazette*. He entered Oberlin College in 1843 and graduated in 1847, the only black in a class of 40 students. In 1859 he received an M.A. from Oberlin, and in 1887 he received a D.D. degree from Livingstone College, Salisbury, N.C. Following graduation from Oberlin, Day lived in Cleveland and worked toward the repeal of the oppressive BLACK LAWS of Ohio. In 1848 he sponsored and chaired the NATL. CONVENTION OF COLORED FREEDMEN, which was held in Cleveland. Following this meeting, he helped organize the Negro Suffrage Society. From 1851–53 Day was compositor and editor of the Cleveland *DAILY TRUE DEMOCRAT*, which later merged with the *CLEVELAND LEADER*. In 1853–54 he established, edited, and published the weekly *ALIENED AMERICAN*, the first black newspaper in Cleveland. He later became editor of its successor, the *People's Exposition* (1855). Day, who taught Latin, Greek, math, and rhetoric, was also appointed librarian of the CLEVELAND LIBRARY ASSOC. in 1854.

During 1856–59, Day worked with many of the fugitive slaves who had fled to Canada, teaching particularly in the Elgin settlement of Buxton, Ontario. He was elected president of the Natl. Board of Commissioners of Colored People of Canada & the U.S. in 1858—just prior to his visit to Great Britain, where he spent several years addressing British, Irish, and Scottish audiences. While there he raised over $35,000 for schools and churches for blacks in Canada. Returning to America after the CIVIL WAR, he worked with the Freedman's Aid Assoc. In 1866 he was ordained a minister in the African Methodist Episcopal Zion church. He later became general secretary of the General Conference. He continued to gain fame as a lecturer and was the featured speaker at the Emancipation Meeting held at the Cooper Union in New York City. In 1867 he became inspector general of schools for refugees and freedmen in Maryland and Delaware, and in 1869 he worked for black voter registration in Wilmington, Del. In 1872 Day moved to Harrisburg, Pa., where he was made a clerk in the Corporation Dept. of the state auditor general's office. He was elected to the Board of Education (representing his 8th ward) in 1878 and was repeatedly reelected; he served as president from 1891–93.

On 25 Nov. 1852, Day married Lucy Ann Stanton, the first black woman to graduate (1850) from the Ladies' Literary Course of Oberlin College. During their marriage, Lucy Stanton Day worked along with her husband in abolitionist and temperance organizations. In 1854, she published a short story on slavery in the *Aliened American*, making her one of the nation's earliest black women writers to be published. Lucy was committed to finding a way to aid newly freed slaves in the South. After the American Missionary Assoc. rejected her application to teach because she was, by then, separated from her husband, she finally was able to go south in 1866 when the Cleveland Freedmen's Assoc. sent her to Georgia to work as a teacher. She later moved to Florence, Miss., as a teacher under the Reconstruction Act. Lucy Stanton and William Howard Day

were divorced in 1872. He married Georgia F. Bell of Washington, D.C., in June 1873. Lucy Day became Mrs. Levi N. Sessions in June 1878 and moved to Chattanooga, Tenn., where she was active as an officer in the Women's Relief Corp., the Order of the Eastern Star, and the Women's Christian Temperance Union. She died in Los Angeles in 1910. Day died in Harrisburg. Following his death, an elementary school, a federal housing project, a cemetery, and a memorial society were named in his honor.

Davis, Russell H., *Memorable Negroes in Cleveland's Past* (1969).
Lawson, Ellen N., *The Three Sarahs: Documents of Antebellum Black College Women* (1984).

**DAY, WILLIAM L.** (13 Aug. 1876–15 July 1936), was a lawyer who served as a U.S. district attorney and federal judge for the Northern District of Ohio. Day was born in Canton to Wm. R. and Mary Schaefer Day. He came from a family of lawyers and judges. His father was an associate justice of the U.S. Supreme Court; his grandfather, Luther Day, and his great-grandfather, Rufus Spalding, were both justices on the Ohio Supreme Court. He also had 3 uncles and 3 brothers who were lawyers. Day received his early education in the Canton public schools and attended Williston Academy in E. Hampton, Mass. Like his father and brothers, he received his legal education at the University of Michigan, graduating with the LL.B. degree in 1900. Day was admitted to the Ohio bar in June 1900 and began the practice of law in the firm of Lynch, Day & Day in Canton. In 1908 Day moved to Cleveland, having been appointed the U.S. district attorney for northern Ohio by Pres. Theodore Roosevelt. He served in that office until 1911, when he was appointed U.S. district court judge. Day resigned the bench in 1914, citing the low salary, which did not allow him adequately to support his family. Day joined the firm of SQUIRE, SANDERS & DEMPSEY, remaining until 1919, when he left to join the firm of Day, Day & Wilkin. From 1925 until his death, Day practiced with his brother Luther in the firm of Day & Day. In 1919, Day & Wilkin were appointed special assistants to the Ohio attorney general to investigate CRIME in Cleveland. Conducting thousands of interviews with people involved in gambling, vice, and other criminal activities, Day & Wilkin were instrumental in uncovering bail-bond scandals and secured an indictment for the murder of a Cleveland police patrolman. Day married Elizabeth E. McKay on 10 Sept. 1902. The Days had 2 children, Wm. R. and Jean C. Day was a member of the American, Ohio, and Cleveland bar associations.

**DEACONESS HOSPITAL OF CLEVELAND,** located at 4229 Pearl Rd., was established in 1914 by the Evangelical Deaconess Society as a training institution for deaconesses (religious sisters) who would provide nursing and administrative services for hospitals in the U.S. affiliated with the Evangelical church. In 1919 the society purchased the Johnson property on Pearl Rd. and decided to open a small church-affiliated community hospital. Deaconess Hospital opened in 1923 with 22 beds. In 1925, Rev. Armin A. Kitterer was hired as the hospital's administrator; he served in that capacity for 50 years. The original medical staff at Deaconess tried to bring new qualified physicians into the "Old Brooklyn" area of the west side to practice medicine. The hospital's tuberculosis ward and facilities provided the main income during hard financial times. Additions and renovations to the main hospital occurred incrementally and throughout its history (1927, 1948, 1953, 1957, 1961–62, 1972–73, and 1977). John H. Budd, M.D., president of the American Medical Assoc., was active on the hospital medical staff.

"Hospitals" Collection, Archives, Howard Dittrick Museum of Historical Medicine.
Kitterer, Armin A., "Historical Summary 1914–1967 of Deaconess Hospital" (Unpub. manuscript, Deaconess Hospital of Cleveland).

The **DEBS FEDERAL COURT TRIAL** (*The United States v. Eugene V. Debs*) in Cleveland resulted from an antiwar speech that the Socialist leader gave in Canton, Ohio, on 16 June 1918. Debs was charged with the violation of the Espionage Act. The trial took place in Judge Paul Westenhaver's courts from 9–12 Sept. 1918 and captured national interest. Debs's position as the leader of American socialism, as well as his crusade for freedom of speech, created national public interest in the case. U.S. District Attorney Edward S. Wertz was in charge of the case for the government. He was assisted by Francis B. Kavanagh, who prepared the case for the government, and Joseph C. Bretenstein. Debs was represented by Seymour Stedman, W. A. Cunnea, Joseph Sharts, and Morris Wolf. The chief witnesses were Clyde R. Miller, Edward Sterling, and CHAS. RUTHENBERG.

The trial centered about the content of Debs's Canton speech. Two versions were read before the jury. In the speech, Debs denounced war, expressed solidarity with the Bolesheviks, sympathized with Socialist leaders in prison, and praised the INDUSTRIAL WORKERS OF THE WORLD. The principles espoused in the speech included freedom of speech and the goals of international socialism and social justice. The antiwar sentiments around which the prosecution built its case were focused in one sentence: "The master class has always declared the wars, the subject class has always fought it." Debs also endorsed the Socialist Proclamation of St. Louis, which explicitly stated the party's opposition to war. During the trial, no witnesses were called for the defendant. Rather, Debs defended his actions by a speech to the jury. He did not deny, repudiate, or retract any of his statements, indicating that his speech had been a clear and courageous exposition of his principles. The jury found him guilty on 3 counts: attempting to incite insubordination, disloyalty, mutiny, and refusal of duty in the military and naval forces of the U.S.; obstructing and attempting to obstruct the recruiting and enlistment service; and uttering language to incite, provoke, and encourage resistance to the U.S. Judge Westenhaver sentenced Debs to 10 years' imprisonment pending an appeal to the Supreme Court. The court upheld Debs's conviction. However, he was pardoned by Pres. Warren Harding in 1921.

**DECKER, EDGAR** (18 Feb. 1832–1 Dec. 1905), was one of Cleveland's earliest and most prominent photographers. He was primarily known for his portraits, some of which earned him national honors. Decker spent his boyhood on a farm in New York State. He attended district schools and later was largely self-taught. At the age of 13, he became a clerk in a store, where he worked for 7 years. During the next 4 years he managed his own store, where he developed an interest in photography. He moved to Cleveland in 1857 and worked in various studios for 2 years before opening his own on Superior St. in 1859. He maintained a studio in Cleveland for over 40 years. In 1883 he moved it to a more fashionable location on EUCLID AVE. Decker produced an enormous volume of work that included portraits of old pioneers, lawyers, businessmen, physicians, society women, and families. In 1862 he photographed Cleveland regiments encamped outside the city prior to their involvement in the CIVIL WAR. Decker won many prizes for his portraits of famous statesmen, soldiers, diplomats, and actors and actresses. Among these were 4 presidents—Garfield, Grant, Hayes, and McKinley—as well as Gen. Sheridan. His original photographic portraits were tipped in the book *Cleveland, Past and Present; Its Representative Men* (1869). Active in photographic societies, in 1887 Decker was elected president of the Natl. Photographic Assoc. His work was continued by his protege GEO. EDMONDSON, who also became a well-known Cleveland photographer. Edmondson acquired Decker's studio at the turn of the century. Decker also served on city council from 1878–82. He was married to the former Julia English.

**DEFAULT** (15 Dec. 1978–16 Nov. 1980) occurred when Cleveland was unable to repay $14 million in loans owed to 6 local banks. The city remained in default for almost 2 years before an agreement to refinance the loans was negotiated. Its inability to meet its financial obligations meant that Cleveland was unable to borrow money in the nation's financial markets. The city's financial problems became acute during the administration of Mayor Ralph Perk, 1971–77. When general expenditures increased approximately 30% and revenues were unable to cover the shortfall, the city increased its short-term borrowing by almost $130 million, and the subsequent debt service charges the city was obligated to pay increased from $10.1 million to $16.6 million. In addition, the Perk administration tapped bond funds set aside for capital expenditure to cover operating deficits and obtained additional funds from the sale of the sewage system and the transit system to a regional authority. Dennis Kucinich, elected mayor in 1977, continued to use money from capital funds to meet operating expenses. In July 1978, the banks refused to roll over $7.8 million in short-term notes. At that time, however, Cleveland was able to buy up the notes. When the city was subsequently unable to explain what had happened to $56 million in capital-improvement bonds, the national bond-rating organizations Standard & Poor and Moody's downgraded its rating, thereby alerting investors to the increased risk in buying its bonds and notes.

In Dec. 1978, $15.5 million in short-term notes came due, of which $14 million were held by 6 local banks, Cleveland Trust, Natl. City, Central Natl., Society Natl., Euclid Natl., and Capital Natl. The Kucinich administration put together a plan to guarantee payment of the notes, which included issuing long-term bonds to replace the short-term notes; guaranteeing the bank loans coming due with the 1979 tax receipts; seeking a 50% income tax increase; and accepting an outside fiscal watchdog. The plan was rejected by the banks, who insisted on payment of the $14 million owed them. When the city was unable to come up with the money, Cleveland became the first major city since the Depression to default on its financial obligations. The default meant that investors in the national bond markets would no longer be willing to buy city bonds to finance improvements. It was also necessary for the city to submit to state financial supervision in return for loans to continue operations. Geo. Voinovich replaced Kucinich as mayor in Nov. 1979 and formed an Operations Improvement Task Force made up of 90 loaned business executives to examine city government and recommend ways to improve its operation. The mayor put together a 3-year fiscal plan to enable the city to escape from default. In Nov. 1980, the city and 8 area banks closed a $36.2 million refinancing deal to pay off the defaulted loans.

Marschall, Dan, ed., *The Battle of Cleveland: Public Interest Challenges Corporate Power* (1979).

DELAMATER, JOHN (18 Apr. 1787–28 Mar. 1867), was an influential teacher of medicine and was instrumental in the founding of 3 medical colleges, including the Cleveland Medical College, the forerunner of Case Western Reserve University's medical school. He was also one of the country's leading authorities on surgery and obstetrics and gynecology. The son of Jacob, a prosperous farmer, and Elizabeth Dorr Delamater, John was born in Chatham, N.Y. A childhood injury left him unfit for farming, prompting his parents to prepare him for the ministry. Delamater wanted to go into law, but his father objected. He compromised by studying medicine, apprenticed to his uncle, Dr. Russell Dorr, betwen 1804–07. In 1807 Delamater was licensed to practice by the Medical Society of Oswego County, N.Y. Between 1807–22 he remained in private practice. Delamater began his teaching career in 1823, when he was appointed one of 6 original professors of the Berkshire Medical Institute, the medical department of Williams College, which was founded in that year in Pittsfield, Mass. He received an honorary M.D. from Williams College in 1824. At Berkshire he taught courses in materia medica and pharmacy. In 1827 he began teaching surgery at the College of Physicians & Surgeons of the Western District of the State of New York, at Fairfield. There he taught surgery, pharmacy, and obstetrics for 10 years. Between 1823–43, Delamater held professorships at Geneva College, the Medical School of Maine (Bowdoin), the Medical School of New Hampshire (Dartmouth), the University of Vermont, the Medical College of Ohio, and Willoughby College in Akron, of which he was one of the founders in 1837. The only subjects Delamater did not teach during his career were anatomy and chemistry. In addition, he conducted a private medical school in Palmyra, N.Y., for several months each year.

In 1840, Delamater moved from New York to Willoughby, Ohio. A faculty schism at Willoughby College in 1842 prompted him to move to Cleveland, where he founded, along with Drs. Ackley, Cassels, and Kirtland, the Cleveland Medical College. Delamater was appointed dean and professor of midwifery, diseases of women and children, and general pathology. He held these posts for 17 years. After moving to Cleveland, he stopped his peripatetic teaching, although he did give a private course of medical lectures after the close of the regular session at Western Reserve. Delamater was a member of many professional organizations, including the Massachusetts, New York State, and Ohio State medical societies. In 1819 he was one of the organizers of the Berkshire District Medical Society, serving twice as vice-president. Devoutly religious, Delamater was a deacon of the Congregational church and an elder of the Presbyterian church. He was politically outspoken, especially against slavery. A temperance advocate, he lectured on the subject both in class and out. When he retired from teaching in 1860, Western Reserve honored him by electing him the first professor emeritus of the university. He was also awarded an honorary LL.D. He continued in private practice and filled temporary teaching vacancies nearly until his death. Known for his charity and negligence in collecting fees, he retired in near-poverty. His colleagues collected funds to furnish him with a home in Cleveland. Married in 1811, Delamater had 8 children.

DE LERY, JOSEPH GASPARD CHAUSSEGROS (21 July 1721–11 Dec. 1797), a French lieutenant, described in his private journal the earliest recorded account of the complete transit of the south shore of Lake Erie. In it he noted the first recorded encampment at the CUYAHOGA RIVER, on 2 Aug. 1754, and drew a sketch of the river, which he called "Riviere a Seguin or Blanch, also Goyahague." The transit of the south shore occurred in the summer of 1754. In the latter part of Apr. 1754, de Lery was ordered by the Marquis Dequesne to journey to Detroit to reinforce the garrison and to serve there as second in command under Sieur Pierre Joseph de Celoron de Blainville. He departed Presque Isle on 30 July 1754 with a force of 285 men in 27 canoes and arrived at Ft. Detroit on 6 Aug. His journal includes detailed directions, distances, descriptions of the shoreline, and drawings of numerous rivers and creeks. While earlier descriptions of the south shore of Lake Erie exist, they are limited to either end of the lake and exclude the Cuyahoga River.

DEMAIORIBUS, ALESSANDRO LOUIS "SONNY" (25 Apr. 1898–5 May 1968), was a member of CLEVELAND CITY COUNCIL for 20 years and was a long-time leader in Cuyahoga County Republican affairs, serving as party chairman 1955–68. One of 9 children, DeMaioribus was born in Cleveland, the son of Dominic and Lucia DeMaioribus. The family lived behind the grocery store operated by his father at 1930 Coltman Rd. Nicknamed "Sonny" as a child, he attended Murray Hill School and East High School. He went to work for the CLEVELAND HOME BREWING CO. in 1925 as a bookkeeper, becoming general manager by 1934 and eventually president of the firm until it was liquidated in 1952. Attracted to politics, DeMaioribus was first elected to city council in 1927. At that time, the Republican party was in the majority, and he gained political influence serving as council president from 1934–42. Resigning from the council in 1947, he worked at the Cuyahoga County Republican headquarters until 1955, when he became party chairman, succeeding GEO. BENDER. During this time, the Democratic party was in the ascendancy, and the Republicans suffered electoral defeats consistently. By cooperating with the Democrats, however, DeMaioribus was able to obtain some of the available patronage for his party. DeMaioribus was preparing to retire as county chairman when he died suddenly at age 70.

DEMOCRATIC PARTY. See CUYAHOGA COUNTY DEMOCRATIC PARTY

DEMORE, MATTHEW (Apr. 1903–18 Mar. 1976), was a prominent local labor leader active in the Internatl. Assoc. of Machinists for 4 decades. Born of Italian immigrants, DeMore was raised in LITTLE ITALY and attended East High until age 16, when he quit school to work as a machinist's apprentice for the Michigan Central Railroad in Detroit. He returned to Cleveland in 1920 to work for the maintenance department at the Vacuum Cleaner Div. of General Electric, a position he held until 1926, when he became active in the fledgling IAM. Within 3 years, he headed a reform slate of officers on a platform pledged to streamline the operations of District 54, which included the Cleveland area. Under his leadership, the district was practically free of strikes, and membership jumped from 4,500 to 6,000. He led the district as president from 1938–61. While DeMore was an active participant in strikes, he advocated the strike weapon only as a last resort. He was regarded in the community as a fair-minded and honest leader, which led to his appointment to the War Labor Board, the War Manpower Committee, Mayor Lausche's War Production Committee in WORLD WAR II, the War Stabilization Board during the KOREAN WAR, the Advisory Committee on Workmen's Compensation, and the Community Relations Board. In 1946, he also unsuccessfully challenged incumbent representative FRANCES P. BOLTON for Congress. Also, he served as the vice-president for the Ohio AFL-CIO and the Cleveland AFL-CIO, and was a director for the State Council for Machinists. In 1961, DeMore was elected an international vice-president of the IAM, and he moved to New York to manage its northeast region. Within 3 years, he was a regional vice-president at the IAM Washington office. He was elected general secretary-treasurer in 1965. When his 4-year term expired in 1969, DeMore stepped down from union office and devoted his time to the Natl. Council of Senior Citizens, a lobbying group, and other activities for senior citizens. He and his wife, Mary, had 5 children.

**DEMPSEY, JAMES HOWARD** (29 Mar. 1859–2 May 1920), was a prominent lawyer and one of the founding partners of SQUIRE, SANDERS & DEMPSEY. Born in Shelby, Ohio, he was the son of John and Martha C. Davis Dempsey. He received his early education from the public schools in Shelby, and from Gilmor Hall Grammar School in Gambier, Ohio. He then went to Kenyon College. Upon graduation in 1882, he went on to study law at Columbia University. The summer following his first year at Columbia, Dempsey gained employment at the Cleveland firm of Estep, Dickey & Squire. Persuaded to stay, he continued his studies under Judge Estep, the senior partner. Upon passing the bar in 1884, Dempsey became a partner. He stayed with the firm until 1890, when he left with ANDREW SQUIRE to establish, along with Judge WM. SANDERS, the firm of Squire, Sanders & Dempsey. Devoted to improving education, Dempsey was on the board of trustees of UNIVERSITY SCHOOL in Cleveland and his alma mater, Kenyon College, which bestowed on him the LL.B. degree in 1912. He was also on the board of trustees of LAKE VIEW CEMETERY. Dempsey was president of the Factory Site Co. and director of many Cleveland companies, including the Union Commerce Natl. Bank, Grasselli Chemical Co., and Bourne-Fuller Co. He was a member of the Union, University, and Tavern clubs and the Cleveland, Ohio, and American bar associations. Dempsey was married twice. His first wife, Emma Norris Bourne, whom he married on 24 Sept. 1885, died on 14 Mar. 1893. They had 2 sons, John Bourne Dempsey and Ernest Cook Dempsey. He then married Ada Hunt on 30 Oct. 1915. They had 2 children, Jas. H., Jr., and Isabel.

*DENNICE NOVOVEKU* was both the direct and spiritual successor of *Pokrok*, a Czech rationalist weekly that was moved to Cleveland from Chicago in 1871. Brought here by its editor, G. B. Zdrubek, *Pokrok* (Progress) was located on Croton St. Zdrubek's anticlerical zeal shortly made him the object of a libel suit brought by Fr. Wm. Repis of ST. WENCESLAS CHURCH. Although he had imported Vaclav Snajdr and humorist John V. Capek for assistance, Zdrubek abandoned *Pokrok* ca. 1875 and returned to Chicago to found the daily *Svornost*. Snajdr remained in Cleveland to establish *Dennice Novoveku* (New Era Journal) in 1877. An admirer of the American agnostic Robt. Ingersoll, he edited his weekly for the local Czech intelligentsia and arrayed it against the Catholic clergy, whose alleged perfidies were regularly exposed in a "Confessions" column. For a time his paper served as the official organ of the Czech Slavic Benevolent Society and the Union of Czech Women. One of his contributors was Dr. Ales Hrdlicka, later editor of the *American Journal of Physical Anthropology*. Like *Pokrok*, *Dennice Novoveku* generally supported the Democratic party. Circulation peaked at over 3,000 in the 1890s, but high costs and delinquent accounts made the paper a marginal operation. In 1911, Snajdr apparently merged it into the newly formed Czech daily *Svet* and retired from active journalism.

**DENTISTRY.** In the first half of the 19th century, dentistry in Cleveland was just emerging as a profession in its own right. Its professional development was hampered by preoccupation with technical proficiency and a corresponding lack of concern for the need to understand dental pathology that would advance dentists' ability to diagnose and treat patients' disorders. A further barrier to professionalization was the absence of accepted criteria or qualifications required to practice dentistry in Cleveland or Ohio until 1868. As a result, dentistry in early Cleveland was dominated by itinerant tooth-drawers and uneducated practitioners who had been trained in the traditional way, by a form of apprenticeship. A notable exception to this pattern was BENJAMIN STRICKLAND, the first resident dentist in Cleveland. Strickland, who settled here in 1835, was unusual in that he had apparently earned the M.D. degree (although from which school or college we do not know) and received an honorary D.D.S. degree in 1843 from the Baltimore College of Dental Surgery, the first school of dentistry in the U.S. But Strickland's academic background was indeed exceptional for the time; before 1860, more than ⅔ of all dental practitioners held no degree, either dental or medical. There was a shared feeling among the leading dentists of Cleveland, however, that the standards of the dental profession needed to be raised. The first evidence came in 1857, when 36 dentists met in Cleveland and formed the Dental Convention of Northern Ohio (later known as the Northern Ohio Dental Assoc.). This group held meetings twice yearly to hear papers addressing topics of common interest, and their first resolution in 1857 endorsed an increase in the standards of dental education. In 1862, a further demonstration of Cleveland dentists' commitment to advancing their professional status came when the city played host to the 3d annual meeting of the American Dental Assoc. (formed in 1859). This organization had as its second president Dr. Wm. H. Atkinson of Cleveland, one of the leading dentists in the city. Cleveland dentists, led by Dr. W. P. Horton, were subsequently active in the formation of the Ohio State Dental Assoc. (1867), which secured legislation creating a board of dental examiners for Ohio in 1868.

Despite these early efforts by Cleveland dentists to enhance their professional standing, concerns over education and credentials remained subordinate to their involvement in the technical advances in their field and with ways to gain greater financial security. That delayed dentistry's break with its tradelike heritage. Part of the problem lay in dentists' near-obsession with mechanical improvements and new materials that they could patent and from which they could derive profits from licensing agreements. While this technical bent brought American dentistry to the forefront of world acclaim, it did not bring about a general increase of disinterested professional conduct among dentists. For example, when Wm. T. G. Morton, a Boston dentist, introduced ether for dental and surgical anesthesia during the period 1844–46, he patented it under the name "Letheon" and offered it for use by his colleagues only after payment of licensing fees. Cleveland dentists, led by Drs. M. L. Wright and Benjamin Strickland, began using Morton's "Letheon" as early as Jan. 1847, only 3 months after its first public demonstration in Boston. To these men the whole licensing and patent system was a normal, accepted part of dentistry. Another example of the influence of the patent system and its potential abuse can be found in the introduction of Vulcanite, a hard rubber used for artificial denture bases. The process of making hard rubber was introduced in 1851 by Nelson Goodyear, brother of rubber-industry pioneer Chas. Goodyear. Goodyear did not patent the process or product at that time, however, and dentists were free to use the material for making dentures. In Cleveland, Wm. H. Atkinson was using Vulcanite as early as the period 1859-60, but he was compelled to abandon the practice (or at least pay a fee) in 1864, when Dr. John A. Cummings patented the process and sold his rights to the Goodyear Dental Vulcanite Co. From 1864-81, Goodyear required licensing and prosecuted those who did not comply. Consequently, business interest hampered the flow of new techniques in dentistry.

In the early part of the 1900s, some dentists in Cleveland began to set aside their concern for immediate financial reward, which had limited the free exchange of innovation in dentistry. The best example of this new openness is found in the introduction of x-ray in Cleveland. Roentgen's discovery of x-ray in 1895 promised to revolutionize diagnostic procedures in both medicine and dentistry, and its rapid presentation in the scientific press mitigated efforts to constrict its use by either secrecy or licensing encumbrances. Nevertheless, managing the early x-ray equipment was not simple, and opportunities to derive personal profit by not sharing new knowledge and expertise did exist. In Cleveland's dental community that did not happen, thanks chiefly to Dr. Weston A. Price. Price, a founding member of the American Roentgen Ray Society, demonstrated the practical application of x-ray before the CLEVELAND DENTAL SOCIETY, the Northern Ohio Dental Assoc., and the Ohio State Dental Society during the period 1897-99. He also designed and patented lead-lined gloves for protection against x-ray burns, but placed his innovation in the public domain instead of commanding fees from those who made use of it.

By 1920, the cumulative technical achievements of American dentists ushered in the modern era of "painless" dentistry. The basic equipment making painless dentistry possible was introduced between 1900-20. In these decades, Cleveland dentists adopted the dental unit or equipment stand (combining high-speed electric drill, electric light, fountain spittoon, and built-in power supply), the hydraulic lift chair, and the x-ray machine. An important addition to dental anesthetics in this period was Novocain, a local anesthetic discovered by Alfred Einhorn in 1905. Dental practice, as embodied in its technology, would not change substantially between 1920 and the 1960s, when dental chairs, turbine drills, and other equipment assumed their present (1986) form, and new synthetic materials found greater use in dentistry. Associated with technical change was the emergence of dental specialties in Cleveland. Nationally, societies and academies for these specialties came into being between 1900-30, and included orthodontia (1901), periodontia (1914), oral surgery (1918), and pedodontia (1927). In dental directories ca. 1900, a few Cleveland dentists began to announce that they had restricted practice to a variety of these fledgling specialties. In 1914, for example, Drs. Chas. and Wm. Teter claimed that they had a "practice limited to minor oral operations, extracting teeth and administering nitrous oxide and oxygen for surgical purposes." By the early 1920s, around 10 dentists chose to limit their practices to a single distinct specialty, usually either oral surgery or periodontia. The number of dental specialists increased gradually in succeeding decades to around 45 in the period 1945-60, when statistics from the American Dental Assoc. show that Cleveland supported 12 oral surgeons, 24 orthodontists, and fewer than 5 each in the fields of periodontia, pedodontia, prosthodontia, and endodontia. The incidence of specialization increased substantially in the 1960s and then leveled off in the 1970s, reaching an average figure of 1 specialist for every 20 general practitioners. The role of these specialists remains, in general, ancillary and supportive to the nonspecialist dentist, in contrast to medicine, where several specialties (particularly internal medicine and gynecology) have assumed the position of primary care providers, a role filled formerly by the general practitioner or family doctor.

As important as specialization, and perhaps even more so, was a new emphasis upon preventive dentistry in Cleveland at the turn of the century. Preventive dentistry, based upon periodic examination, cleaning, and treatment of teeth, was intended to prevent minor dental problems from becoming serious ones. Convincing the general public that such preventive measures would indeed be effective was not easy, however. People needed dramatic proof and continued reminders. In Cleveland, the "Marion School Experiment" provided the necessary proof. Subsequent efforts by the Cleveland Dental Society and the Mouth Hygiene Assoc. kept preventive dentistry in the public eye, reminding people that a regular checkup at the dentist was preferable to the suffering that followed neglect of one's teeth.

The advent of preventive dentistry was, in Cleveland, a direct outgrowth of efforts by the Cleveland Dental Society (formed 1886) to offer "free dental service for needy children." The society, under the leadership of Henry Lovejoy Ambler and Wm. George Ebersole, formed a Committee on Dental Instruction in 1897 to promote dental hygiene in the public schools. To plan an effective program that would help all children in the city, members of the society met with HARRIS R. COOLEY, director of charities for Cleveland, in 1906. With Cooley's support, the Cleveland Board of Education established dental clinics, which in 1909 were staffed by the Cleveland Dental Society and furnished by loans from dental-equipment manufacturers. As part of this program, Dr. Wm. G. Ebersole conducted the "Marion School Experiment" in 1910. Ebersole selected for study and observation a group of 40 children in grades 4 through 7 at Marion School. For a period of 6 months, these children underwent dental examinations and received training in proper methods of chewing their food and brushing their teeth daily. Necessary dental care, from fillings to oral surgery, was provided without charge. The results of the "Marion School Experiment" confirmed Cleveland dentists' claims that proper mouth hygiene contributed substantially to better overall health and academic performance among school-age children. Buoyed by Ebersole's findings, the Cleveland Dental Society inaugurated the Mouth Hygiene Assoc., which came under the sponsorship of the Cleveland Fed. for Charity & Philanthropy in 1916. Thereafter, the dental-hygiene movement gradually outgrew its relief orientation and increasingly came to emphasize the virtues of preventive dentistry, as extolled in window displays, health fairs, and parades. Such efforts ultimately culminated in the creation of Children's Health Day in 1941 by the Cleveland Dental Society and dental-hygiene exhibits organized in cooperation with the CLEVELAND HEALTH EDUCATION MUSEUM.

In Cleveland, the key to achieving a professional standing for dentistry was education, particularly at a dental school associated with a university. In a general sense, education at a university dental college was favored, since it would give prospective dentists a firmer grounding in the health sciences, which in turn would enable them to master new knowledge in the fields of oral and dental pathology and physiology. Moreover, in the absence of a large institutional base, such as the hospital constitutes for medical doctors and surgeons, the university-affiliated dental college constituted the chief place where students could acquire clinical experience under close supervision, and also where professors and students could carry out research programs or concentrate upon developing the dental specialist's skills and knowledge. Perhaps most important, education at a state-certified school of dentistry could become the essential qualification for professional status among dentists.

Dental education in Cleveland actually began in the Medical Dept. of Western Reserve University, where Lewis Buffet lectured on oral and dental pathology and oral surgery from 1874–81. This professorship fell victim to a merger of the medical faculties of WRU and the University of Wooster, and there was no university-level instruction in dental subjects until 1892, when WRU established a dental school. At first the dental and medical schools of WRU were intimately associated, sharing entrance requirements and classes and occupying the same building erected for the medical school in 1884. Liberal endowments received by the medical school from businessman John L. Woods led to a general upgrading of the curriculum and entrance requirements that elevated the medical school to a position of nationally recognized excellence; the school of dentistry could not keep pace, owing to its own meager resources. In consequence, the two schools went their separate ways in 1896, much to the detriment of dental education in Cleveland. The fledgling school of dentistry found new quarters in the Bangor Bldg. on Prospect Ave., but the school's fortunes deteriorated over the subsequent decade. The financial situation was so bleak by 1906 that WRU welcomed an offer to purchase the school made by dental-supply entrepreneur Henry Milton Brown. Brown bought the school and ran it as a profit-making proprietary institution, while retaining the name and degree-granting privileges of WRU. For its part, Western Reserve was relieved to be free of the rising debts the school incurred but later came to regret the arrangement made with Brown. The quality of education plummeted while Brown ran the school; the failure rate of graduates taking the state licensing exams ran as high as 35% at one point. To correct this situation, WRU bought back the school, which by 1917 occupied a new site in UNIVERSITY CIRCLE.

Following the troubled proprietary decade (1906–17), WRU found in FRANK MONROE CASTO a capable and energetic dean for the school of dentistry. Casto had impeccable academic credentials, including a specialization in orthodontia, and possessed a solid sense of how to create an outstanding institution of dental education. During his 2 decades as dean (1917–37), Casto raised entrance standards, increased the number of full-time faculty from 2 to 8, developed a respected library, and transformed the school's clinic from profit-making venture to a true center of learning for students, where dental care was available to anyone regardless of their ability to pay. Casto's tenure also initiated the tradition of research projects that won national recognition in the field of dentistry. Among these was a landmark study of the development of the jaws and teeth of children conducted by THOS. WINGATE TODD, M.D., and BIRDSALL HOLLY BROADBENT, D.D.S. The success of Casto and his successors in bringing WRU into the front ranks of American dental schools is confirmed by the dominant role the School of Dentistry has played in training dentists who practice here; in its first 80 years of existence, WRU has graduated ⅓ of all dentists in Ohio and ⅔ of dentists in northeast Ohio.

In the postwar period, 2 issues have attracted attention to dentistry and the dental profession in Cleveland. The first, which properly lies in the domain of PUBLIC HEALTH, is the question of fluoridation of drinking water. The second is a matter of dental economics, namely, the emergence of retail-store dentistry. In 1950, the Cleveland Dental Society inaugurated a campaign to gain public support and acceptance of fluoridated water, which promised to reduce dental caries by 60%. CLEVELAND CITY COUNCIL authorized fluoridation in 1951, but it was not

until 1956 that it was achieved, owing to delays incurred by the controversy and legal action enveloping the fluoridation program. Subsequent studies of Cleveland school-children demonstrated that between 1956–63, the incidence of tooth decay dropped by 66%. Cleveland's example stimulated statewide action, as mandated by the Ohio legislature in 1969. A resolution passed by city council in 1976 officially recognized the leadership role played by the Cleveland Dental Society in achieving these results.

Perhaps the most profound of recent changes in dentistry fall in the domain of economics, particularly as manifested in the problems that confront beginning dentists establishing themselves in practice and in the choices made by patients in selecting a dentist and determining how they will pay for dental services. While medical and hospital expenses are increasingly met by third-party payers, dentistry has not fared so well. As of 1980, dental services constituted only 2% of total federal expenditures for health care, and less than 25% of dental expenses were covered by prepaid insurance plans. One consequence has been the advent of retail-store and franchise dentistry, which in the Cleveland area far exceeds the national average. The increase of retail-store dentistry must be explained by a mix of factors, part involving fledgling dentists' ability to establish an independent practice, and part stemming from patients' choice of ways to pay for dental care. In 1986, graduates of a dental school, particularly of a private institution such as the School of Dentistry of CASE WESTERN RESERVE UNIVERSITY, can expect to face a financial burden of around $25,000, which compels them to seek immediate remunerative employment. Added to this indebtedness is the prospect of high initial capital investment in equipment and instruments for private practice, ranging anywhere from $25,000 to $100,000. A solution for many is franchise dentistry in a large retail-store facility. Consumers, for their part, seem to prefer the convenience of credit-card payment and proximity to other commercial establishments. The result is a marked increase in retail-store dentistry in Greater Cleveland, and this trend is likely to be on the rise elsewhere throughout the U.S. in the future.

James Edmonson
Howard Dittrick Museum of Historical Medicine

**DEPAOLO, LOUIS** (1894–5 Dec. 1977), was a businessman and political and civic leader who earned the title "mayor of LITTLE ITALY" for the variety of services he provided for residents of Cleveland's Italian immigrant community. Born in Italy, DePaolo attended elementary school and 2 years of technical school there before leaving Campobasso for Cleveland in 1910. He joined 4 uncles in Cleveland, where he continued his education with 2 years of private night school. Trained as a tailor by one of his uncles, DePaolo worked as a tailor, then as a bank clerk, before going into business for himself as the owner of a bookstore, then a confectionery, and then a paint store, and finally as an insurance and real-estate agent. Italian immigrants found much more than books or paint in DePaolo's stores and offices. He spoke 18 Italian dialects and was often called upon as a translator, serving in that capacity for the Dept. of Justice for many years. He provided help with visas, coached those preparing for the citizenship examinations, offered advice about income taxes, sold Alitalia airline tickets, and, beginning in the 1950s, led an annual tour of Italy. From 1941 until ca. 1975, DePaolo produced, directed, and hosted the "Italian Radio Hour"; he also published the Italian weekly newspaper *L'ARALDO* (The Herald) from 1952–59. In addition to providing such services for the Italian community, DePaolo was active in political and civic affairs. He was a trustee of ALTA HOUSE, was a member of the Community Relations Board, and served as president of the Mayfield Merchants Assoc., the Mayfield-Murray Hill District Council, and the Democratic Italian League. He also chaired the Italian American Div. of the Natl. Democratic Committee of Ohio, and he ran for state representative in 1952. DePaolo did not limit his charitable efforts to the local Italian community. After WORLD WAR II, he received the Star of Solidarity from the Italian government for his work in helping to rebuild his native country. He was survived by his wife, Theresa.

**DE SAUZE, EMILE BIALS** (7 Dec. 1878–11 July 1964), was an innovative foreign-language educator. As director of foreign languages for the CLEVELAND PUBLIC SCHOOLS from 1918–49, he developed and implemented a conversational method that brought world renown to Cleveland. De Sauze was born in Tours, France, and received his first degree from the University of Poitiers in 1900. He came to the U.S. in 1905 and received an American Ph.D. degree from St. Joseph College in Philadelphia. Before coming to Cleveland in 1918, he was head of Romance languages at Temple University (1905–16) and head of the French department at the University of Pennsylvania (1916–18). He became an American citizen in 1917.

The de Sauze method, which came to be known as the "Cleveland Plan," emphasized listening and speaking skills as well as reading and writing. The target language was used exclusively in the classroom, so that the pupil heard and practiced only that language. At that time, this approach was a distinct departure from the traditional grammar-translation method commonly in use. Under de Sauze's direction, his textbook *Cours pratique de Francais* (lst ed. 1919) was used as the beginning text in the Cleveland schools; later it was supplemented by advanced-level readers he either authored or edited, from 1924–39, such as *Contes gais, Jean Valjean, Lisons donc, Un peu de tout,* and *Commincons a lire.* The 1946 revised version of *Nouveau Cours pratique* is still used in many schools. Because so many of his original ideas are standard teaching practice today, de Sauze may be remembered only as the pioneer of foreign-language teaching for children. During the 1920s, as part of the Major Work program, a specialized program for gifted elementary school children, French was added to the curriculum as an extra challenge. Classwork, entirely oral and in French, was based on a systematic plan of active participation. The de Sauze plan for French is still used: adapted to other foreign languages, it has been widely imitated. Contributing to the success of his methods was the fact that de Sauze was able to train his teachers himself. He founded and for many years directed the School of French of Western Reserve University, as well as the Demonstration School of Foreign Languages, where, during the summer, educators from all over the world came to observe his methodology in practice. He was the author of numerous articles and a leading member of all American professional language associations. He also founded the MAISON FRANCAISE, a continuing cultural organization for the Cleveland Francophone community. De Sauze died in Cleveland at age 85. His wife, Melanie Philips, whom he married in 1903, preceded him in death, in 1946, as did their daughter, Marcelle (Mrs. Oliver J. Deex), who died in 1961.

The **DETROIT-ROCKY RIVER BRIDGE** (1910–80) was the 4th bridge built at that location connecting Detroit Rd. between LAKEWOOD and ROCKY RIVER. It was designed by civil engineer Alfred Felgate, with Wilbur Watson serving as consulting engineer. Construction, which cost $225,000, began in Sept. 1908, and the bridge was dedicated on 12 Oct. 1910. The bridge was an early example of the 2-ribbed, open-spandrel type. Upon completion, it briefly held the record as the largest masonry arch in America, at 280'. The main span had 2 arch ribs 18' wide and 16' apart. The 5 end spans were 44' each. The bridge's overall length was 708', and its width was 60'. The central span alone weighed 16,000 tons. The vertical pressure at the crown was 6,220 tons. Remarkable for its time, the concrete on the span was not reinforced with steel. The concrete mixture contained an aggregate of sand and stones, some the size of fairly large boulders. The facing mixture used on all exposed surfaces was composed of carefully selected aggregate. The bridge's concrete columns and deck were of reinforced concrete. During construction, steel-arch centering, designed by Watson, was used for the first time instead of timbers for the concrete forms. Many area residents at first thought the bridge too big and impractical. But by the mid-1920s, rush-hour traffic jams on the 4-lane span were commonplace. Into the 1970s, various public officials and groups proposed constructing another bridge to connect the northern ends of Rocky River and Lakewood. In the 1960s, deterioration of the Rocky River Bridge became a serious problem. Concrete chunks fell off into the valley below, and holes appeared in the deck. It was closed several times for emergency repairs. Traffic was limited to 2 lanes, a 4-ton weight limit, and a 10-mph speed limit. In 1978, construction began on a new bridge just south of the old. A modern haunched, plated girders bridge with concrete piers, it was designed by Adache-Ciuni-Lynn Associates and built by the Natl. Engineering & Contracting Co. The new bridge opened in Oct. 1980 at a cost of $4 million. The old bridge was demolished by dynamite on 13 Feb. 1981. The west piers remained intact, with plans to use them as the foundation for a new office building.

Watson, Sara, and Wolf, John, *Bridges of Cleveland* (1981).

**DETROIT-SHOREWAY** is a community on Cleveland's west side, centered around W. 65th St. and Detroit, bounded by OHIO CITY (W. 45th) on the east, W. 85th on the west, EDGEWATER PARK on the north, and Lorain on the south. The heart of the area was known as Gordon Square until the building of the Shoreway in the late 1930s and early 1940s. The Gordon Square Arcade at W. 65th and Detroit remains the commercial center of the neighborhood. The area was originally purchased by the CONNECTICUT LAND CO. from Indian tribes; after the land was surveyed, it became part of Brooklyn Twp. in 1818. The neighborhood economy prospered when the Ohio Canal was built, although rivalry with the Cleveland east side resulted in isolation of the area. When Ohio City and Cleveland were merged, the Detroit-Shoreway neighborhood itself was annexed to Cleveland. With the construction of the Lake Shore & Michigan Southern Railroad along Lake Erie in 1852, industries such as Walker Mfg. (later Westinghouse), Baker-Raulang, and Union Carbide moved into the neighborhood. Streetcar development after 1863 encouraged commercial development along Detroit.

Though the community began as a Yankee enclave, immigrants carved out sections for themselves and built churches and other institutions that provided cohesiveness to the neighborhood. Among the earliest settlers were the IRISH, who settled between W. 45th and W. 65th, later moving west to the W. 70s and then to W. 117th St. St. Colman's Church at W. 65th (organized 1880), the old Irish-American Club, and numerous pubs remained ethnic strongholds for many years. GERMANS inhabited the south part of the neighborhood around W. 76th after 1830, when

341

many came to work on the Ohio Canal. The early settlers were joined by additional countrymen between 1900–15. Social life centered around Snyder's Beer Garden and nationality clubs. In the early 20th century, ITALIANS and ROMANIANS dominated the area. Though a few Italians managed orchards between W. 58th and W. 69th from Lorain north to the Lake Erie coast from the mid-19th century, substantial numbers of Italians did not settle there until 1900. The center of the Italian community life became Our Lady of Mt. Carmel West, built in 1926 after Italian Catholics relentlessly petitioned the diocese for a parish of their own.

Romanians located between W. 52nd and W. 61st streets north of Detroit, previously an Irish area. They established ST. HELENA'S CHURCH on W. 65th, as well as the Union and League of Romanian Societies of America. Ethnic entrepreneurs opened the only Romanian banking institution, the Romanian Savings & Loan (which later merged with the Pioneer Savings & Loan), at 5501 Detroit. By the late 1950s, many neighborhood people had moved to Warren Rd., and the St. Helena building was sold to a Russian Orthodox congregation. After WORLD WAR II, many ethnics, such as the Romanians, moved to the suburbs, opening the area to new occupants. The availability of low-cost housing in the neighborhood attracted impoverished immigrants and migrants, often Puerto Ricans, Mexicans, Appalachians, and AMERICAN INDIANS. These groups failed to build the type of institutions that preserved neighborhood stability in a postindustrial society. To build cohesiveness, the Detroit-Shoreway Assoc. was formed in 1973. The group, umbrella to many block clubs, protested the deteriorating quality of the Detroit commercial strip, overrun by adult bookstores, strip joints, and bars. In 1981, the association became an administrator for Small Business Assoc. loans for area businesses. Among the projects backed by the Detroit-Shoreway Neighborhood Assoc. is the restoration of the Gordon Square Arcade. Formerly a dance hall, the building, with its 124,000 sq. ft., is among the largest multiuse buildings in any Cleveland neighborhood. The arcade houses a bank, a restaurant, variety stores, medical, legal, and dental clinics, a theater, and other retail and service businesses.

The **DETROIT-SUPERIOR BRIDGE**, which was opened to traffic on Thanksgiving Day 1917; was the city's first high-level bridge over the CUYAHOGA RIVER. Connecting Detroit and Superior avenues, it was engineered to relieve the significant traffic congestion that had clogged the old SUPERIOR VIADUCT, located just north of the new span. Built at a cost of $5.284 million, the bridge took 5 years to complete. It rises 96' above the Cuyahoga River. Its outer ends consist of a series of 12 concrete arches; its center span is an overhead arch of steel, 591' in length. Altogether the bridge is 3,112' long and, including approaches, stretches 5,630'. The bridge carries 2 decks. The upper deck was designed for vehicular and pedestrian traffic, while the lower deck was to carry streetcars. The subway, as the lower deck was called, had entry ramps at W. 6th St. and Superior Ave., on W. 25th St., and on Detroit Ave. Four sets of tracks ran along the lower level, with passenger stations located at each end of the subway. By 1930, traffic over the bridge had reached a volume of 70,400 automobiles a day, a total that led to the bridge's being called the "nation's busiest." With the subsequent opening of the Lorain-Carnegie Bridge in 1932 and the Main Ave. Bridge in 1939, that traffic toll was subsequently reduced.

With the ending of streetcar operations in 1954, the subway level stood empty, but the upper deck had once again become clogged with traffic as buses and trackless trolleys, which replaced the streetcars, were forced to share the upper deck with automobile traffic. Studies showed that these larger vehicles could not clear the lower level's tight curves. Subsequent suggestions that the lower level be paved for automobile traffic were similarly blocked on the grounds that clearances were too restrictive to allow safe passage. The ramps leading to the lower level were covered over in Nov. 1955. The opening of the Innerbelt Bridge in 1959 relieved some congestion, but the Detroit-Superior Bridge remained a rush-hour bottleneck, its 4 traffic lanes not sufficient for the demand. In 1967, work was begun on renovating the structure. The renovation, completed in May 1969 at a cost of $6 million, included adding 2 additional traffic lanes by narrowing existing sidewalks from 15 to 5 ft. and cantilevering the new lanes outside the central arch.

**DEVEREUX, HENRY KELSEY "HARRY K."** (10 Oct. 1859–1 May 1932), was the son of Gen. JOHN H. DEVEREUX and Antoinette Kelsey. Though young Harry ably followed in the business footsteps of his father, his greatest contributions were to the gentlemanly sport of harness racing. He was called the "greatest driver of them all"; his prowess in trotting was compared at the time to that of Babe Ruth in baseball. As a youth, Devereux attended Brooks Military Academy, where he was chosen at age 16 as the model for the drummer boy in ARCHIBALD WILLARD's painting *THE SPIRIT OF '76*. After graduating from Yale in 1883, he was employed by the Cleveland, Columbus, Cincinnati & Indianapolis Railroad, first as a civil engineer and then as a real-estate agent. Later, he was the manager of the Chicago-Cleveland Roofing Co. From an early age, when he hitched the family dog to a sled, Devereux was fascinated with harness racing and with horses. Never a bettor, he invested his pocket money in an increasingly better grade of horses, often past their prime but with a bit of spark left, and drove them in amateur races at the old GLENVILLE RACE TRACK. He became an accomplished driver, and over the course of his life he won over 3,000 cups and ribbons, accumulated 14 driving and riding records, and outpaced even professional drivers in skills on the rack. One of his first racing successes was with John A. McKerron, who ran unparalleled heats of 2:10 and 2:11 in th 1900 Boston Cup Race, followed by victories in 1901 and 1902 as well. A man of aristocratic bearing, Devereux felt that his own cool confidence was transmitted to his horses.

Devereux devoted considerable amounts of time and capital to the advancement of harness racing as a sport for the moneyed classes, who were fond of viewing matinee races from posh boxes at Glenville, and of participating in this genteel sport. In 1895, he organized the Gentlemen's Driving Club of Cleveland, which sponsored harness races; the club drew sportsmen from all over northeastern Ohio and soon became the leading such club in the U.S. Friendly competition between Cleveland's club and those of other cities (New York, Boston, Syracuse, Lexington, Memphis, Columbus, Toledo) was promoted through the League of American Driving Clubs, which he organized in 1901. Though he was not the originator of such racing leagues, he professionalized the sport and focused attention on Cleveland as a first-rate trotter town. The races his organizations promoted also showcased his considerable driving skills. When a leading proponent of the Glenville Race Track died, the mayor of the village of Glenville declared betting illegal, a move that assured the closing of the track (1909) and spurred race supporters such as Devereux to establish an alternative: in 1908, sportsmen organized the village of N. RANDALL, where the major industry was horseracing. While some were involved for profits, Devereux saw it as a semiphilanthropic endeavor that would endow future men of bearing with racing skills. Through the Forest City Livestock & Fair Co., he financed the building of RANDALL PARK Race Track and was its first president. Over the years, Devereux lamented the declining popularity of light harness racing, due largely, he felt, to the rising popularity of the auto. The club died out in 1910, though Randall Park itself was open until it was razed for the building of RANDALL PARK MALL in the early 1970s. Nonetheless, until the end of his life, Devereux trained horses at his winter home in Thomasville, Ga., and drove them at his beloved Randall Park in the summer. When he died, he left his horses and all his racing paraphernalia to a pair of faithful stablemen. Devereux was married to Mildred French and had 2 children, Julian French and Aileen (Mrs. Lanier Winslow).

Devereux Family Papers, WRHS.
Gentlemen's Driving Club of Cleveland Records, WRHS.

**DEVEREUX, JOHN H.** (5 Apr. 1832–17 Mar. 1886), a civil engineer and businessman, became one of the leading railroad managers in the Midwest. During the CIVIL WAR, he earned distinction as controller and chief of Union military railroads in Virginia. Devereux was born in Boston, the son of a merchant sea captain. He attended the Portsmouth Academy in New Hampshire and at the age of 16 emigrated to Cleveland, where he obtained employment as a construction engineer on the Cleveland, Columbus & Cincinnati Railroad. With the completion of that line, he found similar employment on the Cleveland, Painesville & Ashtabula Railroad. In 1852 he moved to Tennessee, where for the next 8 years he was division and resident engineer of the Tennesee & Alabama Railroad. From 1860–61 he was a civil engineer in Nashville. When the Civil War began, Devereux elected to join the Union Army. In 1862, as a colonel, he was placed in charge of all Union rail lines in Virginia. At this time the military railroads in Virginia were in a state of disarray because of repeated damage inflicted by Confederate units and conflicts between the various Army and government departments using the lines. Devereux was largely credited with greatly improving efficiency by organizing inspection and repair units, obtaining much-needed equipment, enforcing rules concerning use of the railroads, and smoothing differences between the different departments. Under his supervision, the trains were used to move large bodies of troops, artillery, and the sick and wounded. Devereux resigned as a general in the spring of 1864.

After the war, Devereux returned to Cleveland, where he was made general superintendent of the Cleveland & Pittsburgh Railroad; he was later made vice-president. In 1868 he became vice-president of the Lake Shore Railroad, and then president. When that railroad was consolidated into the Lake Shore & Michigan Southern, he became general manager of the entire line. Under Devereux, the Lakeshore & Michigan Southern was very successful and earned a reputation for safety. In 1873 he was made president of the Cleveland, Columbus, Cincinnati & Indianapolis Railroad, a line he had earlier helped build, and at the same time served as president of the Atlantic & Great Western Railroad Co. Under Devereux's leadership, the former became one of the model railroad lines in the country. Devereux was also president of several smaller companies, and politically was twice defeated for Congress. The Devereux residence, built in 1873, was part of "Millionaires' Row" on EUCLID AVE. near E. 22nd St. In 1851, Devereux married Antoinette Kelsey in Cleveland; the couple had 4 children.

Devereux Family Papers, WRHS.

**DEWALD, LOUISE** (3 Nov. 1877–12 Oct. 1954), for many years the highest-ranking woman in Cleveland's city government as commissioner of cemeteries (1925–42) and possibly the only woman cemetery commissioner in the U.S., had a significant, turbulent career. Rising through cemetery department ranks and serving 12 mayors for more than 40 years, she resigned under pressure in Feb. 1942. A Cleveland native and public school graduate, Dewald began with the department in 1900 at Woodland, which her brother supervised. In 1911 a high civil-service exam score placed Dewald on a classified list, from which she was picked for departmental secretary in 1912. In Mar. 1917, after another successful examination, she was appointed supervisor of cemeteries. Under the 1924 city charter authorizing a city manager form of government, Dewald became commissioner of cemeteries. Popular with employees and the press, she strove to enhance the department's self-sufficiency by promoting the nation's first municipally owned mausoleum and crematory at Highland Park in 1928.

When mayoral government was restored in 1932, RAY T. MILLER became the first Democrat in city hall since NEWTON D. BAKER. With the Depression deepening, Miller, desiring to distribute patronage, fired officeholders, including Dewald. Immediately after her dismissal in Mar. 1932, she petitioned the Ohio Supreme Court for reinstatement, *State ex rel. Dewald* v. *Matia, Dir. of Parks and Public Property*, which the justices unanimously granted in June 1932. "Woman Upsets Democratic Machine in Court Test," announced the *CLEVELAND PRESS* in this vindication of municipal civil service. Dewald resumed her post after Harry L. Davis's reelection in Nov. 1933. In June 1934, contending that women work twice as hard as men, she drew from the city council's finance committee bipartisan criticism for exploiting women when her practice of employing them for cemetery work at hourly rates below men's, $.37½ per hour versus $.60 per hour, was revealed. Described as a model career woman, Dewald was active in the Business & Professional Women, the WOMEN'S CITY CLUB, the YWCA, and Altrusa. She was fond of BASEBALL, GOLF, and swimming. However, in late 1941 and early 1942, this political survivor was accused of embezzling over $19,000, allegedly for racetrack and club gambling. After restoring the funds by May 1942, she was placed on 5 years' probation for technical embezzlement.

The **DIABETES ASSOCIATION OF GREATER CLEVELAND** is a nonprofit UNITED WAY SERVICES agency that provides services and support for individuals with diabetes and their spouses and family members; promotes diabetes research; and assists professionals in diabetes treatment. The Diabetes Assoc. was founded from 2 organizations. The Cleveland Diabetes Society, with Dr. Joseph Goodman as president, was established in 1946 for professional members. The Diabetes League of Greater Cleveland, with Mrs. Earl Hoover as president, was founded in 1948 for laypersons. In 1954, the organizations merged, with Dr. Goodman as president and Mrs. Hoover as vice-president. A major objective of the association has been to promote research by financially supporting local efforts. DAGC encourages nationally recognized physicians specializing in diabetes care to conduct research in Cleveland. Since 1956, DAGC has awarded $1.6 million for research activities. The Diabetes Assoc. has undertaken mass screening projects in the Cleveland area. In 1957, over 400,000 Clinistix were distributed to Cleveland-area residents for self-testing. In 1962, finger blood testing was done using mobile units throughout the community. Although these projects were no longer done citywide in 1986, DAGC offered a detection test as a community service. The association has sponsored many educational programs, with speakers available for community groups and local health fairs. Nutritional information sheets and cookbooks are made available at a nominal cost. For the health professional, the Diabetes Assoc. sponsors symposiums and seminars and publishes professional bulletins on current issues, including advances in treatment of diabetes and developments in research. Instant Glucose, a cherry-flavored gel for treatment of an insulin reaction, which was developed for the Diabetes Assoc., is available for sale by the association. DAGC financially supports a summer camp, Camp Ho Mita Koda, in Newberry, Ohio (25 mi. east of Cleveland), for children ages 7–15 with diabetes, open for 3 summer sessions. Membership in 1986 was 625, of which 150 were professionals. The executive director was Harriet L. Schwartz, and the president for 1986–88 was Chas. J. Berkey, senior vice-president, Private Banking Div., AMERITRUST CO. DAGC is located at 2022 Lee Rd. in CLEVELAND HTS.

The **DIAMOND SHAMROCK CORPORATION** was incorporated in Delaware in 1983 as the successor to various corporations, the oldest of which was founded in 1910. DS is an integrated oil and gas company whose operations consist of exploration, production, refining, marketing, sale of crude oil and natural gas, and the development of geothermal reserves. The Diamond Alkali Corp., a forerunner of Diamond Shamrock, was incorporated in Delaware in 1929 as the successor to a company with the same name incorporated in West Virginia in 1910. DA manufactured and marketed a large number of basic inorganic and organic chemical products, such as soda ash, caustic ash, laundry soda, soda crystal, bichromates, polyvinyl chloride, chlorine, alkalis, and coke. Raymond Evans, one of the founders, chose Painesville in 1911 as the site of DA's main chemical plant, because of its strategic location. Painesville had salt deposits and an abundant Lake Erie water supply and was easily accessible by both lake freighters carrying Michigan limestone and railroads hauling West Virginia coal.

A pioneer in the development of alkali-based products, the company found that new products often produced side effects that resulted in the development of still other products. By the mid-1960s, DA's product line had grown to over 1,400 products. It was a major employer in the area, and the economy of many surrounding communities was directly tied to the fortunes of the company. Labor disputes were matters of immediate community concern, as better than half the workforce in some communities was employed at DA. Another complication was that DA was the area's supplier for cooking and heating gas. When work stoppages occurred, many local residents found their gas supplies cut off. DA moved its corporate headquarters to the Union Commerce Bldg. in Cleveland in 1948. In 1967, the merger with the Shamrock Oil & Gas Corp. created the Diamond Shamrock Corp. The major focus of the new company moved to oil and away from industrial chemicals, and in 1979 corporate headquarters were moved to Dallas. In 1982, DS consolidated its chemical businesses, establishing their headquarters in Cleveland. The closing of the Painesville chemical plant in 1976 left many medical, environmental, and community problems, the effects of which continued to be felt in the 1980s.

**DICKENS, CHARLES VISIT TO CLEVELAND.** *See* **CHARLES DICKENS'S VISIT TO CLEVELAND**

The **DIEBOLT BREWING COMPANY** was a small, family-run brewery located on Pittsburgh Ave. at the corner of Jackson (E. 27th) St. Its history is obscure. It began in 1888 as Diebolt & Uehlin, a partnership of Anthony J. Diebolt and August Uehlin. A year later, Edward A. Ruble succeeded Uehlin. But from 1892 until it closed in 1928, the firm was known as the Diebolt Brewing Co. Anthony Diebolt was secretary and treasurer. When the brewery closed to make way for the Union Terminal development, all three company officers entered the real-estate business, forming the Diebolt Co., with offices in the Keith Bldg. The 3-story red-brick stable that once housed the brewery's beerwagon horses was still standing in 1980, when it was photographed for the Historic American Engineering Record of the Natl. Park Service and then torn down for construction of a new main post office.

**DIETZ, DAVID** (6 Oct. 1897–9 Dec. 1984), covered science and medicine for the *CLEVELAND PRESS* and all Scripps-Howard newspapers for over 50 years. Born in Cleveland, he graduated from CENTRAL HIGH SCHOOL in 1915 and began writing for the *Press* while attending Western Reserve University. After brief stints covering movies and radio, he was designated science editor for the entire Scripps-Howard chain in 1921. Pursuing his new beat, Dietz was one of only 4 reporters to cover the 1922 meeting of the American Assoc. for the Advancement of Science in Boston. Written at his *Press* desk, his daily science column began appearing in Scripps-Howard papers the following year. In 1934 he was one of a dozen charter members and first president of the Natl. Assoc. of Science Writers. Their coverage of the scientific meetings held in conjunction with the Harvard tercentenary brought Dietz and 4 other science correspondents the 1937 Pulitzer Prize in reporting.

During WORLD WAR II, Dietz served as consultant to the surgeon general of the Army and on a committee of the Office of Scientific Research & Development. His book *Atomic Energy in the Coming Era* appeared in 1945, and shortly after the war he covered the atom bomb tests at Bikini Atoll and contributed the article on the atomic bomb that appeared in the 1946 edition of the *Encyclopedia Britannica*. Respected for his ability to render scientific jargon into readable prose, Dietz also served in the 1940s as science correspondent for the NBC radio network. Dietz lectured at WRU, Columbia, Harvard, and Yale, and his numerous honors included membership in the Royal Astronomical Society and the Societe Astronomique de France. Besides honorary degrees from WRU and Bowling Green State universities, he also collected the Lasker Medical Journalism Award, the B. F. Goodrich Award for Distinguished Public Service, and the Jas. T. Grady Medal of the American Chemical Society. Among his 9 books, written at both the adult and young-reader levels, are *The Story of Science* (1931), *Medical Magic* (1937), and *Stars and the Universe* (1969). His *All about Satellites and Space Ships* (1958) sold over 250,000 copies. Dietz was married to Dorothy Cohen and was the father of 2 daughters and a son. After an estimated production of 9 million column words, he retired to his home in SHAKER HTS. in 1977.

**DINARDO, ANTONIO** (1887–29 June 1948), was an architect active in Cleveland from 1921–48. DiNardo was born in Italy, where his father was a builder of bridges. After coming to America, he attended the University of Pennsylvania and the Beaux-Arts Institute of Design in Philadelphia. In 1910 he received a scholarship that enabled him to study in Europe. Upon his return, he worked in the office of Paul Cret, and later in the New York office of

Arnold Brunner, who planned the Federal Bldg. in Cleveland and was a member of the Group Plan Commission. While in Brunner's office, diNardo designed a building for the north end of the Mall, which was apparently the earliest conception of the tower design that became the Terminal Tower. He also made studies with Brunner for the Capitol Park in Harrisburg, Pa.

DiNardo served in the Army in WORLD WAR I, after which he taught at the Carnegie Institute of Technology in Pittsburgh for 1½ years. He came to Cleveland in 1921. He became a designer in the office of Hubbell & Benes; among other buildings, he designed their Pearl St. Bank. His own work included St. Augustine Academy in LAKEWOOD, St. Margaret of Hungary Church, portions of the McGregor Home for the Aged, St. Cecilia Church in Detroit, and St. Augustine Church in Barberton. In 1928 he made the original plans for the Fairhill Rd. "village," but as built they were executed by Harold Fullerton. He planned a number of private residences, of which the one for Robt. Black in Mansfield is among the most notable. In 1936, diNardo designed one of the modern experimental structures for the GREAT LAKES EXPOSITION, the Transportation Bldg. In 1945–46 he made designs for a proposed new criminal court building in Cleveland, but it was not built. DiNardo was also an accomplished artist in both oil and watercolor painting, and he exhibited frequently in the Cleveland MAY SHOW. Following his graduate trip to Europe, he published a volume of lithographs in 1924 entitled *French Farmhouses, Churches, and Small Chateaux*. He was a member of the Cleveland Chap. of the American Institute of Architects. In WORLD WAR II he served as a major in the Air Force at Wright Field in Dayton. After his death in 1948, his wife, Alida, preserved many of his architectural drawings.

*DIRVA* (The Field) appeared on 26 Aug. 1916 and became Cleveland's major Lithuanian-language newspaper. Organized by A. B. Bartusevicius, it succeeded a short-lived predecessor named *Santaika* (Peace). Vincas K. Jokubynas was *Dirva*'s original editor, but Kazys S. Karpius took over by 1918 for what became a 30-year tenure. Equally at home in the editorial and printing departments, Karpius acquired a controlling interest in the paper in 1925. Through the WORLD WAR II era, he attempted to maintain an even-handed policy of antifascism, as well as anticommunism. Several editors followed Karpius from 1948 until 1964, when Vytautas Gedgaudas commenced an editorship of more than 20 years' duration. Reorganized under the direction of Viltis, Inc., *Dirva* became the organ of the Lithuanian Natl. Alliance of America. In response to increased postwar immigration, its publication schedule expanded to thrice weekly during the 1960s but eventually returned to its original weekly frequency. Located on St. Clair Ave., the 16-page tabloid maintained a circulation of more than 2,000 of the 4,000 it had claimed between the world wars.

**DISCIPLES OF CHRIST.** Although small in the number of their churches and of only minor public influence, the Disciples of Christ can claim an acquaintance with national prominence not shared by other Cleveland denominations. For a brief stretch in 1857, JAS. A. GARFIELD, the 20th president of the U.S., served as one of the rotating ministers of FRANKLIN CIRCLE CHRISTIAN CHURCH. Another of the Disciples churches, Crawford Rd. Christian Church, added to the denomination's political luster by being able to claim as one of its members Cleveland's best-known mayor, the Progressive reformer TOM. L. JOHNSON. The Disciples of Christ (or Christian) denomination was organized in 1832 as the result of the merger of a number of restorationist groups. Based on the ideas of a former Scottish Presbyterian, Alexander Campbell, and the preaching of Walter Scott and Barton Stone, these groups wanted to restore 1st-century Christianity by paring away centuries of what they considered to be non-Scriptural accretions. They created a direct, practical faith with a simple and informal worship, which included only those activities positively mandated by the Bible. Added to that was a rationalism at odds with the emotional, revivalistic style of many of the religions of 19th-century America. The movement's strength was more to the east, in and around the Mahoning Valley of Ohio and in the border states, than in cities such as Cleveland, but Disciples churches gained a following in the years before the CIVIL WAR. The first Disciples church in the area was organized in Collamer in 1830 (it eventually became EUCLID AVE. CHRISTIAN CHURCH). Its first minister, Sidney Rigdon, was in the midst of a spiritual pilgrimage that took him from the Baptists to the Disciples and then, in 1830, to the Mormon settlement in Kirtland, Ohio. In 1843, the church moved to DOAN'S CORNERS, 4 mi. east of the city center. It was not until 1864 that the church employed a permanent minister. Franklin Circle Christian Church (1842) was the first Disciples church within the city limits. Alexander Campbell himself had spread the faith in the city by participating in debates in the mid-1830s defending Christianity against nonbelievers and his form of Christianity against other Christians. The debates were held in the courthouse and in FIRST PRESBYTERIAN CHURCH over a number of days.

With far fewer churches than other Christian denominations, the Disciples made less of an impact on moral and social reform and missions than groups such as CONGREGATIONALISTS or PRESBYTERIANS. Still, their activity was substantial. With the success of the Baptists' union in mind, churches joined together in the Disciples' Union in 1885. The union coordinated mission and social work, as well as provided a mechanism for Disciples churches to keep in touch with one another. Like other Protestant denominations, the Disciples engaged in extensive efforts to reach the city's immigrants. Euclid Ave. Christian Church even joined with 2 churches from other denominations, Epworth Memorial, a Methodist church, and Pilgrim Congregational, in evangelical efforts. The churches sent out 2-person teams without regard to church affiliation, to go door to door to spread their message. Franklin Circle Christian Church conducted a Bible school for Chinese immigrants. Disciples churches were active in the Federated Churches of Cleveland, Protestantism's umbrella organization for supervising and coordinating mission work. Benevolent efforts of the Disciples churches included employing a city missionary to work in a hospital, sponsoring the Cleveland Christian Home for Children (founded in 1901), and joining in the activities of the YWCA and the Red Cross. The Disciples also joined in the activities of the Christian Endeavor Society, a Protestant interdenominational organization that was a popular vehicle for mission and social work for youth. Rev. Joseph Zachary Taylor of Euclid Ave. Christian Church served as national superintendent in the 1890s.

In the mid-20th century, some of the Disciples churches joined in the suburbanization and diversification that faced all Protestant churches. Heights Christian Church was organized in 1929 in SHAKER HTS. with a nucleus of almost 200 members drawn from Euclid Ave. Christian Church. The congregation's integrated membership numbered 300 in 1986. The Euclid Ave. Christian Church itself moved to CLEVELAND HTS. In recent years, it continued the outreach that has marked the history of the Disciples in Cleveland by housing a hunger center and aiding close to 50

Cambodian families resettle and get jobs. Other Disciples churches stayed as their neighborhoods changed. Franklin Circle Church of Christ received black, Indian, Filipino, and other newcomers attracted to the near west side, often to work at the LUTHERAN MEDICAL CTR. Once a month the church conducted services in a senior citizens' high-rise only a few blocks away. In 1986, Disciples churches were almost evenly divided between city and suburban churches. The number of Disciples churches has remained small throughout the years from the organization of the first church in 1830 to the 1980s. In 1865, there was only 1 Disciples church out of the 50 in the city. In 1986, 22 of the approximately 1,300 churches in the metropolitan area were Disciples churches. Disciples churches remained small, usually 200–500 members, and they still maintained the vision of restoring a religion closer to 1st-century Christianity amid the social, ethnic, and racial diversity of the 20th century.

Michael J. McTighe
Gettysburg College

The **DISPLACED HOMEMAKER PROGRAM** was one of a number of social programs begun in the 1970s as the women's movement called attention to the needs of various women. Established in 1978 with a $200,000 grant from the state of Ohio, the Displaced Homemaker Program is designed to help women who have lost the financial support of their spouses through divorce, separation, disability, or death. The program is located on the 3 campuses of CUYAHOGA COMMUNITY COLLEGE and consists of a 10-week course aimed at helping these women become self-sufficient and financially independent. The classes function as support groups and offer instruction in such areas as assertiveness training, legal issues, budgeting, career opportunities, and self-marketing techniques for job hunting.

**DIVORCE EQUITY, INC.,** is a nonprofit organization that promotes fairness in divorce through research, advocacy, and educational programs. Based in Cleveland, the organization has chapters in Akron, Cincinnati, Toledo, and Columbus. Divorce Equity was founded in 1971 as Cleveland Women's Counseling, an all-volunteer advocacy group concerned with abortion and women's health issues. Its telephone referral service advised women where to seek abortion services and alternatives to abortion. In 1973, Cleveland Women's Counseling expanded its referral service to include employment services, education, consciousness-raising and self-help groups, psychological counseling, and daycare. Expanded services required larger offices, and the organization moved to larger quarters at 2420 Taylor Rd. in Dec. 1975.

Between 1973–78, Cleveland Women's Counseling served more than 10,000 women, 35% of whom received help with problems related to divorce. Because of this demand for divorce services, the group transferred its telephone referral service to WOMENSPACE and reorganized its operation to devote greater attention to the economic needs of divorced women. To more accurately reflect its purpose and because of its expansion to other cities, Cleveland Women's Counseling changed its name to Divorce Equity, Inc., in 1982. By 1983 it had relocated its headquarters to the Civic at 3130 Mayfield Rd. Since 1976, the organization has made available to divorcing couples a "Dissolution of Marriage Kit," a package of materials enabling a couple to divorce without the services of lawyers. It has also sponsored seminars for those considering divorce and has published manuals on divorce and child custody. Initially concerned with the impact of divorce on women, Divorce Equity by 1984 had broadened its focus

to explore the effects of divorce on all parties involved. Its operations are funded by individual contributions and foundation grants.

The **DNIPRO CHORUS** was formed in 1955 by post-World War II refugees to continue their native Ukrainian traditions of choral singing. Named for the most powerful river in the Ukraine, the group was organized by Eugene Sadowsky, the choir director at St. Mary Ukrainian Catholic Church. The group had 50 male members in 1959 and that year presented its program of religious music, ballads, operettas, and Cossack songs to audiences in Detroit and Pittsburgh, as well as in Cleveland. By 1964, the chorus had grown to 100 members; during the 1960s it appeared on television and at the World's Fair in Montreal in 1967. Ca. 1962, the Dnipro Chorus began to sponsor an annual debutante ball; the 20th ball was held in 1982. In 1973, one local ethnic historian praised the Dnipro Chorus as "one of the best vocal groups in the free world."

**DOAN, NATHANIEL** (1 June 1762–29 Nov. 1815), was a member of the second expedition of the Connecticut Land Co. surveyors in 1796. He served as a blacksmith and was in charge of the cows, oxen, and horses the surveyors brought with them. Doan was born in Middle Haddam, Conn., where he had married Sarah Adams (1771–4 Mar. 1853). Along with JAS. KINGSBURY, JOB STILES, and others, he received city lots from the CONNECTICUT LAND CO. In 1798 he returned to Connecticut and brought his wife and 6 children back on a trip that took 92 days. Doan was required to set up a blacksmith shop on his property on Superior St., opposite Bank (W. 6th) St. The shop was Cleveland's first light industry. Doan shod pack horses for the company and also made tools. Within months, the Doans were forced out of the area by the scourge of fever, ague, and mosquitos, and in 1799, Doan bought 100 acres of land in Euclid Twp. (later E. Cleveland, now part of Cleveland) for $1 an acre. He built a hotel and tavern, a famous landmark for almost 50 years, on the northwest corner of what is now Euclid Ave. and E. 107th, which he occupied until his death. A store was also added. A saleratus factory was needed by the community, and Doan built a plant and began production. A blacksmith shop completed the group of buildings. Doan served as justice of the peace, postmaster, and clergyman. When the first military company was organized in Cleveland in 1804, he was elected as first lieutenant, and as captain in the following year. He was town clerk for many years, and in 1809 he became one of the associate judges of Cuyahoga County.

Post, Charles Asa, *Doan's Corners and the City Four Miles West* (1930).

**DOAN BROOK** is a 7-mi. stream emptying into Lake Erie that separates Cleveland and GLENVILLE, runs through WADE PARK, crosses EUCLID AVE., and ultimately feeds from the SHAKER LAKES. The brook powered a mill and tannery, a sawmill, and a gristmill for the Shaker community established in 1823. Because of its beauty, the city of Cleveland regarded Doan Brook and its surrounding valleys as the core of park development. After acquiring the Shaker properties in 1892, the Shaker Hts. Land Co. donated about 280 acres to the city of Cleveland to form the basis of a park system (Shaker Hts. Park). In 1896, JOHN D. ROCKEFELLER donated the 276 acres of Doan Brook Valley land that became ROCKEFELLER PARK. The connecting link between the two parks had been partially donated by Martha Ambler and partially bought by the city in 1894.

**DOAN'S CORNERS** "definitely and accurately were the corners of Euclid Avenue and what are now 105th and 107th Streets." So wrote Cleveland historian Chas. Asa Post, a product of the neighborhood, in 1930. Doan's Corners takes its name from NATHANIEL DOAN, an early settler in Cleveland who left his home and blacksmith shop on lower Superior St. in 1799, migrated 4 mi. east, and built a log hotel and tavern on the northwest corner of Euclid Ave. and Fairmount (E. 107th) St. It became a regular stop for travelers between Buffalo and Cleveland. Doan also built a store on the southwest corner and later operated both a blacksmith shop and saleratus (baking soda) factory. By the 1870s, Doan's initial settlement was a flourishing crossroads town of stores, churches, small industries, a hotel, and a post office. The area became part of E. Cleveland Twp. in 1866 and 6 years later was annexed to Cleveland.

The area's annexation marked the passing of the "old-time Corners" and the beginning of changes wrought by a growing city. Case School (1881) and Adelbert College (1882) were established nearby, and Doan's Corners assumed the air of a college town. Euclid Ave. between Willson Ave. (E. 55th St.) and the Corners was filled in with fine residences. By the early 20th century, the expanding city had largely engulfed Doan's Corners. In 1930, on the site where Doan had erected his log tavern, now stood a hotel and business block, surrounded by other hotels, theaters, banks, commercial buildings, and apartment houses. In the 1920s, vaudeville, and later motion pictures, brought thousands to the Park, Keith's E. 105th, the Circle, the University, and the Alhambra theaters, all located in what had become Cleveland's "second downtown." Through the 1950s, Doan's Corners—as it was still called—was a weekend haven for a generation of Clevelanders, many of whom still recall youthful visits there for shopping and entertainment. By 1970, Doan's Corners was overcome by the epidemic urban blight that claimed the surrounding neighborhoods of the east side. Half the buildings had been torn down, and what remained, one newspaper reporter observed, was "a honky tonk shambles that looks as if it's been bombed, or ought to be." Virtually no remnant of Doan's Corners remains today (1986). The area has been cleared for expansion of the CLEVELAND CLINIC FOUNDATION. In 1984 the state of Ohio broke ground for the W. O. Walker Industrial Rehabilitation Ctr., for the treatment of injured workers, on the south side of Euclid Ave. between E. 105th and E. 107th streets.

The **DOBAMA THEATER** was founded in 1960 by Marilyn and Don Bianchi. Named for its founders (Dobama is an anagram of the first syllables of the Bianchis' names), it was conceived as a performing-arts environment where the Bianchis could produce their own shows and avoid the usual community-theater politics. The first 2 productions were staged in May 1960 and Sept. 1961 at the Chagrin Valley Little Theater on a short-term rental basis. Between 1 May 1962 and June 1963, Dobama offered 8 productions in its own theater in the Quad Hall hotel at E. 75th and Euclid Ave. Eight years later, Dobama opened in a renovated bowling alley on Coventry Rd. in CLEVELAND HTS. with the Cleveland premiere of Lorraine Hansberry's *The Sign in Sidney Brustein's Window*.

Over the years, Dobama has offered a variety of productions, 90% of which have been world, American, or Cleveland premieres; the remainder have been revivals of American classics. These productions have reinforced the basic premises upon which the Bianchis founded Dobama, including the obligation of the nonprofessional theater to bring responsible production to superior play scripts that otherwise might not be seen in a community and to func-

tion so that individual vanities are subordinated to a mutual pride in accomplishment. In 1977, the creativity and force behind Dobama, Marilyn Bianchi, passed away. Her legacy, a week of free theater at the season's end and the Marilyn Bianchi Kids' Play Writing Festival, a competition open to all children in the country, remains. Everyone entering a play receives some reward; and the best plays are produced at Dobama during the renamed "Marilyn's Free Theater."

**DOCKSTADTER, NICHOLAS** (4 Jan. 1802–9 Nov. 1871), was a pioneer, merchant, and banker. He was mayor of Cleveland from 1840–41. Dockstadter was born in Albany, N.Y., where he was educated locally. In 1826 he came to Cleveland with 2 of his brothers, Richard and Butler. Once in Cleveland, Dockstadter embarked on an independent dealership in hats, caps, and furs, which he received in trade with local Indians. He soon became the leading fur trader in the region. In 1834 he became treasurer of the Cleveland & Newburgh Railroad. In 1835, Dockstadter was chosen to be treasurer of the village of Cleveland. In the following year, he was elected alderman of the newly incorporated city. In 1838 he was elected alderman again. During the years 1837–38, Dockstadter was chosen as a delegate to the county and state Whig conventions. His popularity brought him a victory in the 1840 election for mayor. He served only 1 term, after which he returned to private business. Dockstadter was married to Harriett Judd (1805–1837). The couple had 5 children.

**DOCTORS' HOSPITAL**, originally located in CLEVELAND HTS., was the forerunner of HILLCREST HOSPITAL. In an attempt to relieve the hospital-bed shortage in Cleveland in 1935, 157 physicians of the ACADEMY OF MEDICINE of Cleveland began a fundraising drive to build a hospital in Cleveland Hts. Abandoning the idea of building a new structure, the Edgehill Apt. building located at the junction of Cedar and Euclid Hts. Blvd. (12337–49 Cedar Rd.) was purchased by the Cleveland Memorial Medical Foundation and converted into a general medical and surgical hospital. Doctors' Hospital opened on 6 Aug. 1946. By 1955, the apartment building had been converted into an accredited modern 200-bed hospital. Doctors' was governed by a lay board of trustees; Dr. Arthur Culler, pastor of Heights Christian Church, served as president of the board of trustees and was succeeded by Chas. E. Silvers. Russell H. Stimson served as director of the hospital. Trustees of the organization of Doctors' Hospital included Drs. R. Richard Renner, F. D. Butchart, and Wm. A. Sommerfield and Mr. Wilbur F. McCann. From its earliest days, Doctors' had a special interest in fostering cancer research. It received research support from the Rand Corp. In 1968, the hospital was purchased by the city of Cleveland Hts. for use of the land as a parking lot and fire station. In 1968, the staff and services of Doctors' Hospital moved to Mayfield Hts. (6760 Mayfield Rd.) and became known as Hillcrest Hospital. The apartment building that served as Doctors' Hospital was razed. As a result of its absorption by Hillcrest Hospital, it is now part of STRATEGIC HEALTH SYSTEMS.

**DOLLAR SAVINGS BANK.** *See* **CONTINENTAL DIVISION OF DOLLAR SAVINGS BANK**

The **DOMESTIC WORKERS OF AMERICA** were organized in Cleveland in 1965 as a nonprofit association to study and respond to the personal, economic, and social needs of domestic workers. The first successful attempt to organize noncommercial domestic workers in the country, the DWA operated as an employment referral service for area day workers. In 1986, its headquarters were at 2388 Unwin Ave. It had approximately 60 members, down from a peak of over 500 in the early 1970s, when operations were financed by members' dues. In the 1960s, most domestic workers were struggling at the bottom of the economic ladder. Many were older women who had less than a high school education and who worked for less than $1 an hour. As domestics they were denied many of the benefits enjoyed by most American workers: social security, unemployment compensation, workers' compensation, minimum wage, sick time, and vacation and holiday pay. In 1965, Geraldine Roberts was fired as a domestic from a home in SHAKER HTS. after speaking out against unfair treatment. Having seen television news stories of strikes by schoolteachers and police, she decided that domestics should organize in order to change their unfair working conditions. About 20 day workers attended the first DWA organizational meeting at ST. JAMES AME CHURCH on Cedar Ave. in Sept. 1965. With the assistance of the LEGAL AID SOCIETY, CORE, and Burt Griffin, the group applied for an association charter and approved a constitution and bylaws. With a grant from the Council of Economic Opportunity to help finance its early operations, the DWA opened its headquarters at the Bruce Klunder Freedom House, 5120 Woodland Ave. In the late 1960s, the DWA moved its headquarters to a rented house at 8510 Cedar Ave. and opened a west side office at 3500 Lorain Ave. During the 1970s, it moved its headquarters to the Central Opportunity Ctr., 2018 E. 55th St., and later to offices at WOMENSPACE, 1228 Euclid Ave. In addition to its referral service, the DWA helped improve working conditions for domestic workers by successfully lobbying for legislation to include domestics under state workers' compensation and helping to establish a standard minimum wage for domestics. The DWA also has sponsored a speakers' bureau and workshops designed to help employees and employers better understand their responsibilities and the workers' needs. In addition, it has provided scholarships to enable domestic workers to improve their occupations.

**DONAHEY, JAMES HARRISON "HAL"** (8 Apr. 1875–1 June 1949), was chief editorial cartoonist of the PLAIN DEALER for half a century. Born in West Chester, Tuscarawas County, Ohio, he was the brother of Ohio governor and U.S. senator Vic Donahey. Moving with his family to New Philadelphia, he gained his first newspaper experience there with the *Ohio Democrat*. He then came to Cleveland, where he studied at the Cleveland School of Art and in 1896 became an illustrator for the *CLEVELAND WORLD*. Hired by editorial manager CHAS. E. KENNEDY, Donahey began drawing for the *Plain Dealer* on 1 Jan. 1900. During the mayoral campaign of 1907, observers declared Donahey the winner in an artists' duel with Homer Davenport, whom the *Leader* had borrowed from New York to do battle against Mayor TOM L. JOHNSON. On 23 Apr. 1910, Donahey published probably his most famous cartoon, in observance of the death of Mark Twain. It depicted 2 somber boys rafting a flower-draped bier "Down the River."

His increasing national reputation brought Donahey an invitation to work for the *New York Journal* in 1911, but after a week's trial he returned to Cleveland, where he felt his subtle style was better suited. Combining work with his love of travel, Donahey provided the *Plain Dealer* with pictorial accounts of such diverse locales as Egypt and Alaska. His travels in the Southwest and Mexico led to a scholarly interest in Mayan and Anasazi culture. Donahey also took an active part in community affairs; he was a member of the ROWFANT CLUB and received the Cleve-

land Community Fund's Distinguished Service Award in 1938. He often sketched on public occasions, from illustrated lectures to Liberty Bond rallies during WORLD WAR I. Some of his originals were prominently displayed in the GREAT LAKES EXPOSITION of 1936. After the death of his first wife, Beatrice, in 1939, Donahey married Mrs. Josephine Rhodes, a widow. He had one stepdaughter, Mrs. K. M. Haber, but no children of his own. After the 1920s, he lived on a farm in Aurora, where he pursued such hobbies as grafting fruit trees and refinishing antique furniture. He died shortly after suffering a stroke and was buried in New Philadelphia.

James H. Donahey Collection, WRHS.

The **DORCAS HOME**, founded in 1884 as a refuge for sick and destitute women, had become by 1917 a rest home for elderly women. It was operated by the Dorcas Society, a charitable organization formed by a small group of women who met regularly to sew for the poor. Adopting the name of a Biblical figure described as "full of good works and alms," 14 women, led by veteran philanthropists Mrs. Josiah A. Harris and Mrs. Hiram H. Little, formally established the Dorcas Society in 1867 to provide nursing care in the homes of the city's sick and poor women. In 1884, 3 Dorcas Society members—Mrs. Chas. E. Wheeler, Mrs. Maria C. Worthington, and Mrs. Chas. L. Rhodes—rented a small cottage on Hamilton St. to care for "two feeble women each with a child to care for in her weakness." Soon they asked the Dorcas Society to help with their project. The society joined in the operation of the home on 20 Dec. 1884, and in the spring of 1885 the Dorcas Invalids Home was incorporated. The home was moved to St. Clair St., then to 1255 Garden St. in Aug. 1885, and again in Apr. 1886, to 1643 Euclid, where it was regularly filled to capacity with 22 residents, prompting another move, on 15 Oct. 1892, to its final location on E. Madison Ave. (1380 Addison Rd.), which was remodeled and enlarged in 1907 and again in 1929.

By 1892 the annual budget of the home was $3,700, and the rules of admission made clear that this money went to support only the deserving poor. By the Dorcas Society's 50th anniversary in 1917, the home had cared for 314 women, and the budget had grown to more than $13,000. Forty-six elderly women lived in the home in 1928, when the fundraising campaign to remodel the facility stressed its "homelike character." By 1938, 52 women lived there. Throughout the 1940s and 1950s, the Dorcas Home offered the 52 annual members of its "family" a private room, food, laundry service, nursing and medical care, weekly church services, occasional movies, and activities in conjunction with other social agencies. Annual activities included summer picnics, a Christmas party, and a recital tea. The home's budget had grown to $110,070 in 1963, and its directors had begun to look for a new, safer neighborhood for the facility. Unable to make suitable arrangements to move the home, the directors placed the 28 remaining residents in other facilities and closed the Dorcas Home in 1967. The Dorcas property was given to the ELIZA BRYANT HOME in 1968.

**DORR, DAVID**, was the author of the first book known to be published by a black in Cleveland. His travelogue, *The Colored Man around the World*, was published in 1858. Dorr traveled to Europe, North Africa, and Asia as a slave. He escaped after his arrival back in the U.S. when the freedom he had been promised by his master was denied. The diary of his experiences during this journey formed the content of the book. Little more is known of Dorr except that he served as a soldier in the 7TH OHIO VOL-UNTEER INFANTRY during the CIVIL WAR.

**DOVER.** *See* **WESTLAKE**

**DOVER VINEYARDS, INC.,** was established coopera-tively in 1932 by a group of local winegrowers. All wine was made from the growers' grapes. In 1958 the winery was sold to the current owner, Zolton Wolovits. In 1986, the vineyards were gone. All wines were produced and bottled at the winery, but the grapes were purchased from other Ohio vineyards. Twenty-three varieties of wine were sold in a retail shop on the premises at 24945 Detroit Rd. and distributed throughout Ohio. Dover stores 100,000 gallons and produces 50,000 cases a year.

**DOW, HERBERT H.** (26 Feb. 1866–15 Oct. 1930), was a chemistry student at Case School of Applied Science when he developed an interest in the subjects that led him to develop the Dow Chemical Co. Born in Belleville, Ontario, the son of Joseph H. and Sarah Bunnell Dow, he came to Cleveland with his parents when his father became master mechanic at the Chisholm Steam Shovel Works. Dow en-tered Case School in 1884 and graduated in 1888 with a B.S. degree. His senior thesis dealt in part with brines in Ohio. At the urging of his instructors, Dow presented a paper that summer at the meeting of the American Assoc. for the Advancement of Science, held in Cleveland. Ad-ditional research for the paper included a trip to collect brine samples in Ohio, Michigan, West Virginia, and Penn-sylvania; the collecting trip furthered Dow's interest in the value of brines and provided information about brine de-posits that proved useful later.

In 1888–89, Dow served as professor of chemistry at the Huron St. Hospital College. During that time he de-veloped a process for manufacturing bromine from brine; he received a patent for the process on 12 Apr. 1892. In 1889 he organized a company to work with brines in the fields near Canton. That venture failed, however, and in 1890 he started a new venture in Midland, Mich., where, as in Canton, the brines contained a heavy concentration of bromine. The Dow Process Co. was organized to pro-duce bromine and its derivatives. Dow organized the Mid-land Chemical Co. in 1892 and in 1895 began to manu-facture chlorine and its derivatives. He formed the Dow Chemical Co. in 1897 to manufacture chlorine and caustic soda; in 1900, Dow Chemical absorbed the older Midland Chemical Co. as part of an expansion of its product line. In establishing both the Midland and Dow chemical com-panies, Dow had the financial and technical assistance of his Case classmate ALBERT W. SMITH. Dow served as president and general manager of Dow Chemical and was responsible for developing many new chemical processes, for which more than 100 patents were granted. For his contributions to chemistry, he received honorary degrees from the Case School of Applied Science (where he also served as a trustee) in 1924 and the University of Michigan in 1929 and received the Perkin Medal from the Society of the Chemical Industry in 1930. He was a member of a number of professional societies, including the American Assoc. for the Advancement of Science, and served on both the Board of Public Works and the Board of Education in Midland, Mich. On 16 Nov. 1892, Herbert Dow married Grace A. Ball of Midland, Mich.

**DOWELL, DORSEY MAXFIELD** (28 Apr. 1903–3 Apr. 1964), was the rector (1942–64) of Christ Episcopal Church in SHAKER HTS., Ohio. He was also affiliated with the Church of the Epiphany, St. Mark's Church, the Church

of the Redeemer, and St. Thomas Church. Dowell was born in Clarksburg, W.Va., the son of an Episcopal clergyman. He received a degree from Kenyon College and then at-tended Bexley Hall, where he graduated in 1928. Ordained a priest in 1929, Dowell, except for a stint in Piqua, Ohio, spent his entire life in the Cleveland area. Reflecting his times, he was concerned about racial and religious harmony within the church and the community. He married Eliza-beth Hubbard in 1928. An untimely, sudden death cut his career short. As a counselor for Alcoholics Anonymous, Dowell saw the AA unit at Christ Episcopal develop 12 sister units. He served on the board of the American Cancer Society. He was also known as a builder of churches. He organized the Church of the Epiphany in EUCLID (1928–29), led St. Mark's and the Church of the Redeemer's uni-fication to form a new St. Mark's, and served as rector of St. Thomas in BEREA (1938–42). He guided Christ Epis-copal through a disastrous fire and the flooding of its re-placement as the church's congregation grew from 125 to 1,100 families. At the time of his death, he was president of the standing committee of the diocese.

Clergy Records, Episcopal Diocese of Ohio Archives.

The **DRAVO WELLMAN COMPANY** is a pioneer man-ufacturer of steel plant equipment and has gained an in-ternational reputation for engineering some of the largest material-handling projects ever built. The firm started in 1896 as the Wellman-Seaver Engineering Co., founded by the inventor of the first open-hearth furnace in the U.S., Samuel T. Wellman, his brother, Chas. H. Wellman, and John W. Seaver, to engineer and design steel mills and industrial plant equipment. In 1897, the company built the first mechanical gas producer, and by the early 1900s, it was installing all types of plant equipment around the U.S., as well as in foreign countries. In 1901, it constructed a plant at Central Ave. and E. 71st St. The following year, Thos. R. Morgan joined the firm, and it was incorporated as the Wellman-Seaver-Morgan Co. in 1903. That enabled it to acquire the Webster, Camp, & Lane Co. of Akron, manufacturer of mining machinery and iron- and coal-han-dling equipment. This acquisition allowed the firm to begin to engineer and build integrated mills for handling, trans-porting, and manufacturing raw material into finished prod-ucts. As Wellman-Seaver-Morgan contracted business from all over the world, it concentrated on expanding its ma-terial-handling equipment. One of the company's execu-tives invented the Hulett unloader, which revolutionized the Great Lakes ore industry. In 1931, excavating buckets were added to its production line when the firm acquired the G. H. Williams Co. of Erie, Pa. A year earlier, the corporate name had been changed to the Wellman Engi-neering Co.

During both world wars, Wellman manufactured gun carriages, and afterward it exported cranes to Europe. In 1954, the Cleveland-based McDowell, Inc., an interna-tional construction and engineering firm, acquired Wellman to fulfill McDowell's goal of erecting turnkey plants for basic industries. In 1963, there was an official merger of these 2 companies, producing the McDowell-Wellman En-gineering Co., with its headquarters in the Vulcan Bldg. at 113 St. Clair Ave. A year later, it acquired the Lewis Weld-ing & Engineering Co. of SOLON, founded in 1938 as a diversified designer and manufacturer of special product machines and equipment. Throughout the 1960s and 1970s, McDowell-Wellman built coal docks and port loading fa-cilities. The Massachusetts firm Helix Technology Corp. purchased McDowell-Wellman in 1978 and sold its bulk material-handling unit and research center to Pittsburgh's

Dravo Corp. in 1980. Dravo reorganized the Cleveland units as the Dravo Wellman Co., which gave the corporation diversity in designing and building coal- and energy-related plants and equipment. Employing 160 people, Dravo Wellman became the world leader in the design of unit-train unloading systems. Its research center is being utilized for making coke pellets and refining shale oil.

Wellman Engineering Co., *A Pictorial Record of Engineering Achievements . . .* (1944).
Wellman-Seaver-Morgan Co., *The Wellman-Seaver-Morgan Co.* (n.d.)

The **DREHER PIANO COMPANY** originated in 1853 when Baptiste Dreher (Sept. 1830–9 Apr. 1890) came to Cleveland and began to make melodeons. Dreher's grandfather, Meinard Dreher, was an organ builder in Illreichen near Ulm, Germany, and was an acquaintance of Johann Sebastian Bach. By 1859, Baptiste Dreher had formed a partnership with Wm. J. Kinnard and had established a shop on Superior St. By 1870 he was in business on his own, advertising himself as the general agent for Decker Bros. pianos. Ten years later he was selling organs as well as pianos. His sons Henry (8 Aug. 1864–19 Mar. 1929) and Oscar (1860–23 Feb. 1921) had joined the company by 1887, and the name was changed to the B. Dreher & Sons Co.; after their father's death, the sons changed the name to the B. Dreher's Sons Co., with Frederick W. Bruch as president, Henry Dreher as vice-president, and Oscar Dreher as secretary and treasurer. From ca. 1891–1912, they had a shop on Superior and another in the ARCADE; by 1912 Henry Dreher had become president of the company, which had moved to 1028 Euclid. In 1922 it moved to the corner of 1226 Huron Rd.; by then it sold phonographs, records, and music rolls in addition to instruments. By 1923 the company had become the Dreher Piano Co. Poor health forced Henry Dreher to sell the company in July 1928 to Chicago-based Lyon & Healy, which expanded its offerings and moved the store to 1007 Huron in the 1930s before closing the operation in 1953.

**DUMOULIN, FRANK** (9 July 1870–9 July 1947), was an Episcopal priest, the third dean and rector of TRINITY CATHEDRAL (1907–14), and bishop coadjutor of the Protestant Episcopal Church of Ohio (1914–24). He was born in Montreal, Canada. His father was a Canadian bishop of the Church of England. DuMoulin received his B.A. and M.A. degrees from Trinity College, University of Toronto, in 1894. Ordained a deacon in the Church of England in 1894 and priest in 1895, DuMoulin had a number of pastorates and rectorships in Toronto, Chicago (where he was naturalized in 1904), and Cleveland before taking up his posts at Trinity. Plagued with ill health almost from the start of his bishopric, DuMoulin resigned his Ohio position and spent 1924–25 in Egypt and Asia Minor while trying to get fit enough to resume his clerical duties. Although his health was still shaky, starting in 1925 DuMoulin resumed his career with a series of rectorships in Philadelphia, North Carolina, and New York before retiring in 1943. He was an excellent orator, interested in uniting his church with social and welfare needs.

DuMoulin was interested in Cleveland's civic and charitable affairs. He helped organize the Fed. for Charity & Philanthropy and in 1913 was appointed by Mayor NEWTON D. BAKER as a delegate to a conference called to discuss the needs and rights of cities under the new Ohio constitution. He also worked with the CITY MISSION. As dean and bishop, DuMoulin was responsible for a number of developments while in Ohio. While dean, he chaired

the social betterment committee of the Pastors' Union and was first president of the Federated Churches of Cleveland. He continued the cathedralization of Trinity, began a vacation Bible school, and established a playground for underprivileged children. As bishop coadjutor, he laid to rest the little-understood and -used diocese convocation and substituted for it a division of the diocese into 7 geographic areas. DuMoulin chaired the Federal Council of Churches of Christ in America committee on motion pictures, which in 1936 submitted a report condemning movies that were morally offensive or harmful to the minds of young people. DuMoulin married twice. His first wife, Ethel King, died in 1928. He married Cora Stiles in 1929.

The **DUNHAM TAVERN**, one of Cleveland's oldest buildings and a representative Colonial farmhouse of pioneer days, is still standing in its original location. The tavern, now known as the Dunham Tavern Museum, located at 6709 Euclid Ave. and believed to be the first building constructed on Euclid east of E. 55th St., was originally the home of Rufus and Jane Pratt Dunham, a young couple who came to Cleveland in 1819 (sometimes given as 1823) from Mansfield, Mass. The Dunhams, who had purchased property that extended from Euclid Ave. to what is now Hough Ave., struggled with subsistence farming and lived at first in a log cabin built on the rear of the property. A new structure completed in 1824 was located near the old Buffalo-Cleveland-Detroit Rd., and it became a popular stagecoach stop and hostelry. Through a series of changes and additions, including a taproom, the house became known as Dunham Tavern—a popular social and political center. In 1853 the Dunhams sold the tavern and accompanying buildings, and in the intervening years it was reportedly used as a tavern, but gradually it was reconverted into a private home used by a succession of Cleveland families, including Dr. and Mrs. Jas. A. Stephens. The Stephenses, who had lived in the house since 1886, bought it in 1896, and Mrs. Stephens (Oriana B.) remained there until 1930—several years after Dr. Stephens's death.

During the 1930s, when Euclid Ave. was changing dramatically from a residential community to a business area, the survival of the Dunham Tavern was threatened. Several eminent Cleveland artists and architects began to use it for studios and offices. Prominent among these was A. DONALD GRAY, a Cleveland landscape architect who was particularly devoted to the tavern and who was instrumental in its preservation. In 1936 he encouraged a group of similarly concerned citizens, including Mrs. Benjamin P. Bole and Ihna Thayer Frary, to establish the Dunham Tavern Corp., with Mrs. Bole as president. Funds came from many other individuals and groups, notably the Society of Collectors, Inc., which assumed responsibility for the tavern in 1941 and has subsequently continued to restore significant features and to furnish it with appropriate antiques. The building is listed in the Natl. Register of Historic Places and was designated a Cleveland landmark in 1973. In 1982, Dunham Tavern, Inc., and the Society of Collectors, Inc., merged into one corporate entity, the Corp. of Dunham Tavern Museum. In 1985 the tavern had a membership of 145, and expenses of operating the structure as a museum were defrayed through an annual antiques show, a small endowment, membership dues, and an annual sustaining-fund drive.

**DUNMORE, WALTER T.** (15 July 1877–23 Jan. 1945), was one of the most noted law professors in early-20th-century America. A legal scholar and specialist in several branches of the law, he was involved in a number of unusual and lengthy legal battles. His civic passion was the

Cleveland LEGAL AID SOCIETY. Dunmore was born in Cleveland. His parents moved to Norwalk when he was a small boy, where he attended the public schools. He graduated from Oberlin College with the A.B. degree in 1900. From 1900–02, he clerked in the Norwalk probate court. The experience led to his enrollment in the Western Reserve University Law School, where he earned the LL.B. degree in 1904. He then returned to Oberlin and completed the A.M. degree in 1905. Admitted to the Ohio bar in 1904, Dunmore was appointed an instructor of real property law at WRU Law School in 1905. Later, he also taught evidence, wills, and conflicts of law. In 1911, he was appointed dean of WRU's law school, serving at that post until his death.

Dunmore was a vocal critic of the American legal-education system. He felt that there were too many lawyers graduating from law schools whose chief aim was profit. Instead of training students to think like lawyers, he believed the schools attempted to "pour" legal training into their students and then hope for the best. Dunmore had a national reputation in his specialty, real property law. In 1938, he was appointed special master by Common Pleas Judge Walter McMahon in a lawsuit brought by landowners along the shores of Lake Erie to recover damages from the city for the building of the MEMORIAL SHOREWAY. Dunmore served on the executive committee of the Cleveland Legal Aid Society. He devoted much time and greatly aided the society's effort to help the underprivileged to be aware of and secure in their legal rights and protection. Dunmore wrote extensively on legal matters. His book *Ship Subsidies* was awarded the Hart, Shaffner & Marx Economic Prize. He assisted ARCHIBALD THROCHMORTON with the preparation of the *Ohio General Code* (1921). Dunmore loved to travel, making trips to South America, Asia, the Middle East, Europe, and the Pacific Islands. Dunmore's first wife, Mabel Curtis, died in 1931. They had 2 daughters, Marjorie Curtis Oliver and Helen Elizabeth Ayers. In 1939, Dunmore married Kathleen Townsend Firestone.

**DUNN, DANIEL A. "DANNY"** (17 Sept. 1884–17 Jan. 1968), was a noted Cleveland boxing trainer, promoter, and manager during the 1920s and 1930s. His most famous boxer was JOHNNY RISKO, who fought and defeated several heavyweight contenders during his career. Dunn was born in New York City. As a newsboy there, he learned to fight early in order to protect his business on the city's west side. A 5'2", 120-lb. contender, he fought as an amateur and professional in and around New York City. For his first match in Harlem, he received $2. In 1910, Dunn came to Cleveland and continued his professional boxing career. He taught boxing and operated health clubs at the CLEVELAND ATHLETIC CLUB and in the Sloan Bldg. In 1923 he opened a gym in an old building at 2861 Detroit Ave. One day Johnny Risko came in to learn boxing, and Dunn became his trainer and manager. Although Risko's first fight paid him only $2, before his career was finished, Risko and Dunn had earned over $250,000. Several times Risko was only a bout away from a championship fight. Dunn invested in real estate and advised Risko to establish a $100,000 trust fund. When Dunn suggested Risko retire from boxing, the fighter dropped him as his manager in 1935. Dunn never found another Risko, and he closed his gymnasium. By 1942 he was working as a laborer in the Cleveland Service Dept. for $.72½ an hour. He was married to Gerda Marie Bergland. The couple had no children.

**DUNN FIELD.** *See* **LEAGUE PARK**

**DUTCH.** Persons of Dutch birth or ancestry have lived in Cleveland from its pioneer days. Initially, the city served the Dutch primarily as a Great Lakes gateway to the Midwest. By 1850 there were only 161 Dutch-born in Cuyahoga County, but from 1850–70 the Dutch community doubled in each decade, reaching 603 Dutch-born in 1870, plus several thousand more with Dutch parentage or ancestry. The high point was reached in 1910 at 1,076 Dutch-born, plus an estimated 5,000 of Dutch parentage or ancestry. The 1980 census reported 4,211 persons of single Dutch ancestry in the Cleveland Standard Metropolitan Area. Adding those with multiple Dutch ancestry and those no longer aware of their Dutch ancestry brings the total today in Greater Cleveland to an estimated 20,000. The comparatively small Dutch population in Cleveland reflects the fact that the overall Dutch immigration was minimal. In 1980 the Dutch ranked only 17th among non-native-speaking groups in the U.S. Their homeland, the Netherlands never experienced a mass emigration that emptied ⅓ to ½ of the countryside, as happened in Ireland. Instead of being driven out by famine, most Dutch immigrants chose to leave the fatherland for economic reasons; cultural, political, and religious motives were secondary. Family, faith, and work were the watchwords of the Dutch immigrants, not liberty, fraternity, and equality.

Dutch immigration to North America had 3 major phases: the commercial expansion of the Dutch West India Co. in Colonial New York (1614–64); the free migration in the years 1815–1915; and the planned and largely refugee migration after WORLD WAR II. The Dutch community in Cleveland was greatly influenced by these migrations. The earliest Dutch in Cleveland were descendants of the Colonial "Old Dutch," such as the business leader Wm. H. Van Tine, Sr. (b. 1820), and the noted Brecksville agriculturalist Burr Van Noate (b. 1826), who followed the frontier into the WESTERN RESERVE. The Old Dutch were thoroughly Americanized before coming to Cleveland, and the "Young Dutch" came directly from the Netherlands. Finally, after World War II, several hundred more Dutch arrived, including refugees from newly independent Indonesia (formerly the Dutch East Indies). The postwar immigrants revived the lagging awareness of Dutch culture and language among the Young Dutch. Even the Dutch Indonesians, while bringing an Asian cultural blend that set them apart, were Dutch-speaking and very loyal to their Dutch tradition.

The first Young Dutch of the 19th century in Cleveland merely passed through the city on the way west, such as Klass Janszoon Beukma, who in 1835 followed the Ohio Canal from Cleveland en route to Lafayette, Ind. The first permanent contingent of Dutch in Cleveland was a group of 16 persons, all Roman Catholics—a minority group in the Netherlands—from the municipality of Aalten (Gelderland Province), located near the German border in an area known as the Achterhoek. They were led by Harmanus Bernardus Wamelink, a dyer of textiles, with his family of 9; along with Joannes Gerhardus Jansen, a ropemaker, with a family of 6; and a 24-year-old bachelor musician, Bernard Breugelman. The group settled near the southern city limits bordering Woodland Ave. The next major group of Hollanders, all Protestants of Reformed (Calvinist) background, arrived in the spring of 1847, after wintering in Rochester. They hailed mainly from Zeeland Province, particularly from the islands of Schouwen and Duiveland. Other Calvinist Zeelanders arrived later in 1847, and more followed in the next decade, particularly in 1854. Even more Gelderlanders from the Achterhoek, both Catholics and Calvinists, settled in Cleveland, with the largest group arriving in 1870–71. By then, about half the Dutch in Cleveland were from the Achterhoek, and a third were from Schouwen and Duiveland. The connection of Cleveland Dutch to only 2 small regions of the Netherlands conforms to the general pattern of chain migration that resulted in transplanted communities from specific European villages.

The Cleveland Dutch also settled in a segregated pattern according to the place of origin and religion, as was typical of Dutch communities elsewhere and reflected the cultural diversity and provincial localism in the Dutch homeland. The Zeelanders and some from Overijssel Province lived in 3 neighborhoods on the east side: along Central Ave. between E. 33rd (Blair) and E. 39th (Osborne) streets, where the True Holland Reformed Church (later East Side Christian Reformed Church) was built in 1872 on E. 35th St. (Calvert); along Lexington Ave. and E. 55th St. (Willson), where the First Holland Reformed Church was built in 1864 and remained until the congregation disbanded in 1929 after many members had moved from the area; and at E. 75th Street (Carr) and Woodland Ave. in a settlement dubbed "Dutch Alley." The Gelderlanders, both Reformed and Catholics, mainly chose the west side, settling in 3 areas: alongside the City Infirmary between W. 14th (Jennings) St. and W. 25th (Pearl) St.; farther south along the hillside of Holmden Ave. that was known popularly as "Dutch Hill"; and along Lorain Ave., from W. 54th (Courtland) to W. 65th (Gordon) streets in an area known as "Wooden Shoe Alley." The Catholics were centered around St. Stephen's Church (opened in 1870), while the Calvinists were a few blocks farther south, between W. 58th (Waverly) and W. 65th streets south of Lorain, where the True Holland Reformed Church (later West Side Christian Reformed Church) was built in 1872 on W. 58th St. In 1881, Calvary (Second) Reformed Church began meeting in a small chapel at W. 73rd St. and Lawn Ave., and in 1910 they moved to their present location in the 1900 block of W. 65th St. After World War II, as members moved to the suburbs, Calvary mothered 5 new Reformed churches in the western suburbs (in order: Riverside, Brooklyn, Parkview, Parma Park, and Brunswick). In 1950, West Side also moved to its present (1986) location on Triskett Rd. Both the east and west side settlements boasted the usual panoply of Dutch shops, stores, and offices to serve their fellow ethnics. Today there are 6 Reformed churches in Greater Cleveland, totaling 1,300 members, of whom fewer than 10% are of Dutch ancestry. The junior denomination, the Christian Reformed church, which had long been more Dutch and more resistant to Americanization, today has 3 churches (on Triskett Rd., in WARRENSVILLE HTS., and in MAPLE HTS.) with a total of 650 members, of whom more than half are yet of Dutch birth of ancestry.

Occupationally, the censuses of the 19th century reveal that ½ of the Cleveland-area Dutch were skilled craftsmen (primarily carpenters, coopers, and tailors), ⅓ were factory workers and unskilled laborers, and the remainder were retail merchants, clerks, and professionals (clerics, teachers, doctors, and nurses). In the 20th century, as the city industrialized and newer immigrants filled the lower ranks of the labor force, the Dutch moved increasingly into white-collar positions and professional careers, and became self-employed craftsmen and small businessmen.

By WORLD WAR I, the Dutch in Cleveland were rapidly assimilating. At its founding in 1890, the Second Dutch Reformed church instituted the first English-language worship service among the 4 Dutch Calvinist congregations then in the city. In 1914 the church changed its name to Calvary Reformed Church, thus eliminating the overt ethnic identity, and the congregational minutes were first recorded in English. In 1918 the English service at Calvary

was shifted from the secondary evening service to the primary morning service, because few members by then could command the mother tongue as well as the English language. By 1930, even the 2 more conservative Christian Reformed churches in Cleveland had gradually shifted to English in the morning service, and by 1940 the last Dutch language service was held in Cleveland. In contrast to the Calvinists, the Dutch Catholics had lost their mother tongue by the second generation because of the multinational nature of the Roman Catholic church. St. Stephen's was mainly a German parish, and there was no Dutch-language priest for confession and instruction. Since the 1930s, social clubs have sought to preserve a sense of cultural identity among the disparate Dutch in Greater Cleveland. The Hollandia Club headed by John Dykeman was active until the early 1950s, when it was supplanted by the Netherlands American Society of Ohio, led primarily by Harry and Virginia Kerkheide, which presently has a membership of 70 with a core group of 20. This society has successfully integrated Dutch Indonesians with the Dutch from the mother country, including both Catholics and the unchurched. But the Calvinist Dutch remain aloof, preferring instead the fellowship and social life of their churches. By the 1980s, the Dutch in Greater Cleveland have dispersed to the city fringes and the suburbs, where considerable numbers of Calvinists still cluster within easy driving distance of their churches. These, together with the Netherlands American Society, preserve what little remains of Dutch group life and culture.

Robert P. Swierenga
Kent State University

**DYER, J. MILTON** (22 Apr. 1870–29 May 1957), was a prominent architect who designed Cleveland's CITY HALL (1916) on Lakeside Ave. Born in Middletown, Pa., Dyer moved with his family to Cleveland in 1881. He attended the Outhwaite School, graduated from CENTRAL HIGH SCHOOL, attended a local training school for machinists, and studied at the Cleveland Institute of Technology and L'ecole des Beaux Arts in Paris (1900). After returning to Cleveland from Europe, Dyer had an active practice in the first 2 decades of the 1900s. Some of his major commissions were the Brooklyn Savings & Loan Assoc. (1904) at W. 25th St. and Archwood Ave.; the TAVERN CLUB (1905) at E. 36th and Prospect Ave.; the First Methodist Church (1905) at Euclid Ave. and E. 30th St.; the PEERLESS MOTOR CAR CO. (1906), now C. Schmidt's & Sons brewery at E. 93rd St. and Quincy Ave.; the CLEVELAND ATHLETIC CLUB (1911); and City Hall (1916). After a period of inactivity, Dyer designed the U.S. Coast Guard station (1940) on WHISKEY ISLAND at the mouth of the CUYAHOGA RIVER. Early residences designed by Dyer include one for Edmund Burke (1910) on Magnolia Dr. in UNIVERSITY CIRCLE (now used by the CLEVELAND MUSIC SCHOOL SETTLEMENT) and the Lyman Treadway house (1911) at E. 89th St. and Euclid Ave. (now part of the CLEVELAND HEALTH EDUCATION MUSEUM). Dyer was a member of the University, Union, Euclid, Tavern, and Hermit clubs, as well as the Cleveland Chamber of Commerce.

**DYKE COLLEGE** is a private, independent, nonprofit college that awards associate and baccalaureate degrees, mainly in occupational programs in business and commerce technologies. It was the first school of its kind in the country and is the oldest college formed in Cleveland. The present Dyke College was formed as the result of a merger between Spencerian Business College and Dyke School of Commerce in 1942. The former was originally founded by E.

G. Folsom as FOLSOM'S MERCANTILE COLLEGE in 1848. In 1852 it became a part of the Bryant & Stratton chain of business schools, and after a few more changes in name it became, in 1876, Spencerian Business College. A former graduate, Frank L. Dyke, established Dyke School of Commerce in 1894. Folsom's Mercantile College was initially founded to provide continuing education in Cleveland beyond secondary education "for those with aspiring careers in the work world." Courses consisted primarily of penmanship, bookkeeping, drawing, and chirhythography. The singular purpose was to prepare men for clerical functions in business offices. The focus shifted as clerical duties did. In the 1870s, when it had become Spencerian Business College under Platt R. Spencer, it was one of the first schools in the country to emphasize typewriting, and later shorthand.

The main difference between the two schools, until their merger, was that Dyke emphasized short-term instruction, while Spencerian grew increasingly more collegiate. After 1904, under Ernest E. Merville, Spencerian began to offer B.A. degrees in business administration, commercial science, accounting and auditing, and law. Through the years, both schools were variously located in the downtown area. On 17 Sept. 1942, the two schools merged under Jay R. Gates and became Dyke & Spencerian College. Enrollment, down from the Depression years, increased after WORLD WAR II to 750 day students and 400 night students. Classes were held in the Standard Bldg. until 1958, when the college moved to E. 6th St. *Spencerian* was dropped from the name, and it became Dyke College. During the 1960s and continuing through the 1970s, several factors contributed to hurting Dyke's image as a college. These included its downtown location, competition with CUYAHOGA COMMUNITY COLLEGE and CLEVELAND STATE UNIVERSITY, and the misconception that it was only a clerical school. In response, the school augmented its liberal-arts offerings and, in 1972, became a member of the Ohio College Assoc. Throughout the 1970s and into the 1980s, special educational programs were developed to appeal to jobless blue-collar workers, Hispanics, and inner-city children, including, in 1984, the establishment of a $100,000 scholarship fund for local high school graduates. In 1984, Dyke College moved to a new location on Prospect Ave. Jay R. Gates was president of the college from 1942–71. He was succeeded by John C. Corfias.

**DYKSTRA, CLARENCE ADDISON** (25 Feb. 1883–6 May 1950), was an educator and political scientist who promoted the city manager form of government in Cleveland and later was city manager of Cincinnati. Dykstra was born in Cleveland but grew up and attended public school in Chicago; as a youth he was inspired by the reform ideas of TOM L. JOHNSON. Dykstra received a B.A. from the University of Iowa in 1903; he then became a history fellow and an assistant in political science at the University of Chicago. He held several teaching positions in Florida, an instructorship in history and government at Ohio State (1908–09), and the political science chair at the University of Kansas (1909–18), where he became nationally known as a leader in state and municipal administration. Dykstra resigned his chair in 1918 to return to Cleveland as executive secretary of the Civic League. Encouraged by A. R. Hatton, chair of Western Reserve University's political science department, he started the movement for instituting a city manager form of government in Cleveland. Dykstra served on the 1919 committee to improve Cleveland's city charter; he also drafted an unsuccessful amendment that would have allowed county home rule in Ohio and the consolidation of city and county governments. He unsuccessfully fought the Van Sweringen proposal to put CLEVELAND UNION TERMINAL on PUBLIC SQUARE. The Civic League did not rehire Dykstra as executive secretary in 1920; many attributed this decision to the Van Sweringens' opposition.

In Chicago and then Los Angeles, Dykstra held similar positions to his Civic League position. In Los Angeles, he helped establish the Metropolitan Water District and start construction on a major water aqueduct to serve the area; he also taught part-time at newly formed UCLA. In 1930 he became the second city manager of Cincinnati. Dykstra returned to academia as president of the University of Wisconsin, where he served until 1945. During this period, he also served on several national boards: as president of the Natl. Municipal League (1937–40), the first director of the Selective Service Board (1940), and chairman of the Natl. Defense Mediation Board (1941–45). In 1945 he returned to UCLA as provost; he served there until his death 5 years later. On 31 July 1903, Dykstra married Ada Hartley, who died in 1926; the couple had 1 daughter, Elizabeth. Dykstra married Lillian K. Rickaby, a former dean of women at the Riverside School in California, on 25 Dec. 1927; Dykstra adopted his stepson, Franz Lee Dykstra. Dykstra is noted for several publications, including *The Commission-Manager Plan of City Government*, 1915; *Democracy and Education*, 1938; and *Democracy and the Manpower Crisis*, 1944.

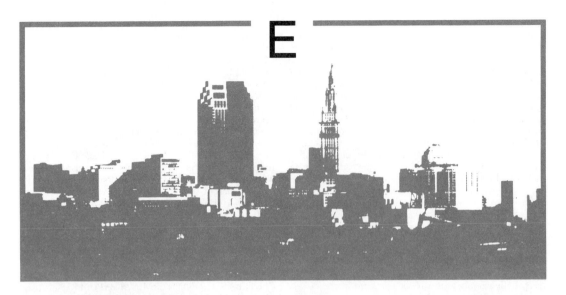

E

The *EAGLE-EYED NEWS-CATCHER* began its short career on 29 Apr. 1841. Published by Gage Mortimer Shipper and David L. Wood, it was seemingly inspired by Benjamin Day's successful *New York Sun* (1833) in every respect but price, going for $.03 instead of Day's revolutionary penny. Like the *Sun*, it printed in a 3-column format on an extremely small page, approximately 9″ x 12″. It also aspired to be a nonpartisan tribune of the people, whom it characterized as "we 'poor folks' . . . ground between two millstones." References in other papers raise the possibility that the *News-Catcher* may have been converted by Shipper into the *DAILY MORNING NEWS* within a few months of its inception.

The **EARLY SETTLERS ASSOCIATION OF THE WESTERN RESERVE** is a voluntary organization of citizens who have lived in the WESTERN RESERVE for over 25 years, who are dedicated to preserving the ideals, principles, and motivations of the pioneers of the Western Reserve, and who sponsor and participate in a variety of historical celebrations. In the summer of 1879, HIRAM M. ADDISON, philanthropist, educator, and newspaperman, wrote numerous articles urging the establishment of an organization that would honor the city's founding and perpetuate the memory of Cleveland's pioneers. He issued a written call for a public meeting concerning such an organization. On 19 Nov. 1879 in the probate courtroom of Judge Daniel R. Tilden, "a goodly number" (20–30) convened to appoint Hon. Jas. W. Allen chairman and Addison secretary, establish the Early Settlers Assoc. of Cuyahoga County (later changed to the Western Reserve), and write a constitution. At a meeting held on 12 Jan. 1880, the following officers were elected: president, HARVEY RICE (1880–91); vice-presidents, Allen and Jesse T. Bishop; secretary, Thos. Jones, Jr.; and treasurer, Geo. C. Dodge. A new constitution was written in which the following purposes were stated: "to record the deeds of pioneers, to collect all facts, incidents, relics, and personal reminiscences respecting the early history and settlement of the county and other parts of the Western Reserve regarded of permanent value." In May 1880, the first "annual convention" was held in the Euclid Ave. Presbyterian Church; subsequently annual meetings were held on 22 July, but after 1902 they were held every 10 Sept., commemorating Commodore Perry's victory on Lake Erie. Records of the proceedings of these meetings (including addresses made

and speeches given, as well as invaluable data about early Cleveland) have been published by the ESA in the *Annals,* published annually from 1880–1933, 7 times from 1934–61, and every 5 years since 1961.

The association commissioned and funded the statue of Gen. MOSES CLEAVELAND that was placed on the PUBLIC SQUARE, was instrumental in erecting the Harvey Rice monument in 1889, and was responsible for the erection of the bronze replica of the Commodore Perry monument dedicated 14 June 1929. It also funded the statue of Geo. Washington located at the Federal Bldg. Plaza, E. 6th St. and Lakeside Ave.; it was dedicated on 14 June 1973. The ESA has been responsible for the restoration and preservation of the ERIE ST. CEMETERY (July 1950), for the establishment of Ft. Huntington Park, just west of the CUYAHOGA COUNTY COURTHOUSE (1938), and for the erection of the boundary markers designating the 4 corners of the Western Reserve. In addition to participating in the annual celebration at the Public Square on 22 July, the Early Settlers Assoc. has taken an active part in the 100th, 125th, 150th, and 175th observances of the city's anniversary. During the sesquicentennial, the ESA participated in numerous activities, including assisting in the naming of the MOSES CLEAVELAND TREES (they also marked the trees in 1971 and 1976). During the 1971 (supersesquicentennial) celebration, the association established and selected the CLEVELAND HALL OF FAME. The Early Settlers Assoc. has continued to sponsor and to participate in many other activities in accordance with their bylaws of 1947: "to inspire great interest in the history of Cleveland and the Western Reserve, to preserve traditions; to honor all important historical events with appropriate observances and to mark historical places with enduring signs; to further the best interest of Cleveland and the Western Reserve by cooperating with other organizations." It published numerous maps and brochures and in 1963 cooperated with the WESTERN RESERVE HISTORICAL SOCIETY in the publication of *A Pictorial History of the Western Reserve* by Margaret Manor Butler.

Annals of the Early Settlers Assoc. of Cuyahoga County.

**EAST CLEVELAND** is a residential city located about 7 mi. from downtown Cleveland and occupying 3 sq. mi. It is adjacent to Cleveland on the north and west and bounded by CLEVELAND HTS. on the east and south. It was originally part of E. Cleveland (organized 1805) and Euclid townships. The oldest remaining early-19th-century house is that of Thos. Phillips on Eddy Rd., where it was moved from a corner on EUCLID AVE. The name E. Cleveland has been carried by at least 5 political entities in Cuyahoga County—township, hamlet, and villages reduced by repeated annexations by the city of Cleveland. The present city was incorporated as E. Cleveland Village in 1895. There followed a period of growth, during which gas and water lines were installed, Euclid Ave. was paved, and streetcar service from Cleveland began. The population reached 10,000 in 1910, and E. Cleveland became a city in 1911, with a mayor-council form of government. A charter was drafted in 1915, and in 1918 the city adopted a city manager plan. The charter adopted in 1916 provided for women's suffrage in municipal elections, giving E. Cleveland the only enfranchised women east of Chicago. During the teens and twenties, the majority of the city's housing was built, including large Euclid Ave. residences, many apartments and large terraces, and single-family subdivisions. They were served by commercial centers at the major Euclid Ave. intersections at Superior, Taylor, and Lee roads. In 1920 the population was over 27,000. One of the early manufacturers was the Natl. Bindery Co. (1905). Beginning in 1911, the Natl. Electric Lamp Assoc., later the lamp division of General Electric, began the construction of NELA PARK on Noble Rd., often called the first suburban industrial research park in the nation. Other light industries were established along the Norfolk & Western and New York Central railroads during WORLD WAR II.

In 1929-30, John D. Rockefeller, Jr., began a residential development on part of the Forest Hill estate that had belonged to his father. Only 80 of the planned 600 homes were built before the project was abandoned because of the Depression. In 1938, FOREST HILL PARK, comprising 60 acres, was donated by Rockefeller to the cities of E. Cleveland and Cleveland Hts. The Rockefeller family made many contributions to E. Cleveland, including land for the public library, the hospital, and the junior high school. The E. Cleveland Public Library was made possible by a donation from Andrew Carnegie and was completed in 1916. The McGregor Home for the Aged on Terrace and Lee roads was built in 1908 and enlarged in 1941. In 1931 the HURON RD. HOSPITAL, which had moved from its downtown Cleveland location, was erected on Terrace Rd. In 1920 the Warner & Swasey Astronomical Observatory for Case School was built on Taylor Rd. It contained a 9" telescope, and in 1939 a 24" telescope was donated by the WARNER & SWASEY CO. The school system includes 6 elementary schools, 1 junior high, and Shaw High School. The city has many churches of all denominations, many lining Euclid Ave., from St. Paul Episcopal Church to the Hare Krishna Temple. First United Presbyterian Church, the oldest church in Cuyahoga County and one of the first in the Western Reserve, was formed in 1807 as the First Church of Christ in Euclid. In the second half of the 20th century, many Euclid Ave. homes were replaced with small businesses and fast-food outlets. When the Cleveland rapid-transit system was opened in 1955, the eastern terminus was located at Windermere, from where it was possible to ride directly to CLEVELAND-HOPKINS INTERNATL. AIRPORT. In 1969, the population was 37,991. During the 1960s, E. Cleveland experienced a major population shift as black residents constituted an increasingly larger proportion of the population. By 1984, E. Cleveland was one of the largest predominantly black communities in the county, with a population of 36,957.

The **EAST CLEVELAND CONGREGATIONAL CHURCH** (United Church of Christ), located at Euclid Ave. and 1813 Page Ave., was established on 18 Nov. 1931 as a result of the merger of East Congregational Church (1900) and the Mayflower Church Congregational (1920); each had been formed as the result of several separate mergers. East Congregational, originally located at the corner of Euclid and Prospect (Shaw Ave.), was organized in 1900 from the merger of the Congregational Union of Cleveland, the Congregational City Missionary Society (1892), and the "Free Congregational Church of Euclid" (organized 4 July 1852 by a small group of people who had originally been members of the First Presbyterian Church of Euclid [1807], but who had withdrawn because they wanted to take a more active stand against slavery). The Congregational City Missionary Society acquired the site at Euclid and Page in 1894, but did not worship there until 6 years later when the new stone chapel was completed on 21 Oct. 1900. In the meantime, the church, formally organized in Apr. 1900, met in the little frame schoolhouse on the site of Shaw High School until the new stone chapel at the corner of Page and Euclid was completed on 21 Oct. 1900. Mr. H. Clark Ford contributed to the purchase of the property. The first pastor of East Congregational was Rev. Wm. H. Pound (1900); he was succeeded by Rev. Herman F. Swartz (1901-06), who expedited the move to the new building.

The Mayflower Church Congregational, Euclid Ave. at Lockwood, was formed in Dec. 1920 from the merger of the Park Congregational (1890) and Calvary Congregational churches (1909). Park Congregational originated as an interdenominational Sunday school (July 1886), subsequently became the Union Chapel, and in Jan. 1888 became a mission or "North Branch" of the Euclid Ave. Congregational Church. Rev. I. W. Metcalf was the first pastor. It was organized as an independent church on 2 Oct. 1890 as Park Congregational Church, moving to the corner of Cullison and Crawford (Ashbury St.) in 1892. Calvary Congregational (1909-20), also a mission church under the auspices of the Euclid Ave. Congregational Church, was originally organized as Lake View Chapel (1890); it then became an independent church named Lakeview Congregational Church of Cleveland. Rev. Albert B. Christy was the first pastor (1894). Under the pastorate of Rev. Louis J. Luethi, the church moved to Euclid and Lockwood and in 1909 became Calvary Congregational Church. In 1920 it merged with the Park Congregational Church to form the Mayflower Church Congregational.

In 1931, Rev. Howard Lee Torbet, who had served as pastor of the Mayflower Church Congregational (1913-20), became the first pastor of the East Cleveland Congregational Church. He served from 1931-37. During Rev. Earle C. Hochwald's pastorate (1948-58), a dial-a-prayer service was initiated, and in 1955 a new educational wing, Pilgrim Hall, was dedicated to accommodate the expanding membership. Rev. Dewey F. Fagerburg, who became minister in 1962, sought to involve the church in many political-action programs and civil-rights projects. His ministry came during a time of transition for both the church and the neighborhood and was characterized by dissension and controversy.

In 1970, Rev. Fagerburg and some of his parishioners dissolved the existing church organization, changed the form of worship, and established "the People's Church," designed to meet the needs of "blacks and oppressed peoples." An opposition group, the Mayflower Group, sought to preserve the traditional forms of work and worship. Subsequently the Western Reserve Assoc. of the United Church of Christ and the Ohio Conference withdrew financial support from the church. Rev. Fagerburg resigned (1977), and the building was sold to a group of families who had organized the Messiah Congregational Church and who have continued to worship in private homes. In 1986 they were in the process of selling the building to the Second New Hope Institutional Church of God in Christ, which had used the building since 1980.

The **EAST CLEVELAND RAILWAY COMPANY** was established on 6 Aug. 1860, when company president Harry Stevens broke ground at Euclid and Willson (E. 55th St.) avenues. By 3 Sept., 3.339 mi. of single track had been laid from Willson through Prospect to Bank (W. 6th) St., and horsecars began carrying passengers for a 5-cent fare on the iron-strapped wooden rails. Later that year, the company's franchise was extended on Euclid from Willson to Case (E. 40th St.), then to Prospect, and also from Case to Sterling (E. 30th St.) and Prospect. In 1868, the company received extensions for lines running on Brownell and Prospect to Garden, and on Garden to Willson. Rights were later extended to the Cleveland & Pittsburgh Railroad tracks and to the city limits on Quincy. The company's unsuccessful attempt to use electricity was a first in the country. ECRY had placed trolley wires in a trench in the street along its Garden St. line, but improper drainage permitted the trench to fill with rainwater, shorting out the lines.

On 30 Sept. 1875, ECRY held a trial operation of a "fireless" locomotive on the Euclid line between Willson and Doan. The steam-powered experiment proved successful, but city council, influenced by powerful horsecar operators, passed legislation banning steam from the city streets. In 1879, the company was awarded a 25-year franchise renewal. In Feb. 1882, an extension franchise was granted from Prospect to Haywood, to Cedar, east to Fairmount. In Apr. 1883, ECRY received an extension on Euclid from Fairmount to DOAN BROOK, and the same extension on Cedar in 1884. On 24 June 1884, the East Cleveland Railway Co. operated the first electric railway for public use in America for 1 mi. along its Garden St. line. In 1886, city council extended the company's franchise on Water (W. 9th), Bank (W. 6th), and Lake streets and east on Euclid Ave. to the city limits. In 1888, ECRY received the right to lay a double track along Cedar to Willson, on to Hough, east to Dunham and to Wade Park, and eastward to the city limits. On 30 June 1889, it extended overhead trolley-line service on the Euclid line to downtown Cleveland. By the late 1880s, the large number of competing railway lines awarded franchises had made operating conditions impractical and inefficient. On 15 May 1893, city council authorized the consolidation of the E. Cleveland, Broadway & Newburgh, Brooklyn, and South Side traction companies into the CLEVELAND ELECTRIC RAILWAY CO.

The **EAST END NEIGHBORHOOD HOUSE** was established in 1907 by Hedwig and Anna Kosbab, daughters of Josip Kosbab, a Hungarian immigrant. The settlement serves the Buckeye-Woodland-Woodhill community and is located at 2749 Woodhill Rd. Initially, the Kosbabs offered classes in sewing and cooking for their neighbors, but as demands grew as immigrants poured into the neighborhood principally from Hungary, but also from Italy and other parts of Southern Europe, they formalized their work by incorporating in 1911. Their first board of trustees included SAMUEL MATHER, ROLLIN WHITE, and ORIS P. VAN SWERINGEN. By the time of Hedwig's death in 1922, the settlement had served nearly 70,000 people in cooking and sewing classes, boys'and girls' clubs, mothers' clubs, and language classes, and through activities such as dances, sum-

mer recreation, and crafts programs. Lester Liles, an experienced settlement worker and graduate of Ohio State University, and his wife succeeded Hedwig. He introduced programs such as gardening and camping during his tenure. In 1930 he resigned and was replaced by Lillian Amiraux. Amiraux's brief tenure of 4 years saw an expansion of the settlement's recreation program. Geneva Mathiasen, a housewife and volunteer, assumed direction of the settlement in 1934. She guided it through various World War II activities, such as scrap drives and blood donations, and was instrumental in the settlement's controversial program of relocating Japanese-American families within its neighborhood in 1944.

Mathiasen's successor, DOROTHY SMITH, a Vassar graduate, worked to mend rifts between the community and settlement that had been caused by issues such as Japanese resettlement. Smith worked closely with board member MARIE WING to insure representation of the community on the settlement's board; such representation had not existed to this time. Robt. Bond, head worker of Goodrich House, assumed control of East End after a brief period following Dorothy Smith's resignation in 1955. Bond, retaining his directorship of Goodrich, jointly operated both settlements as the United Neighborhood Ctrs. He launched a number of new programs to address the needs of the aging, changing neighborhood. These included "Meals on Wheels," an effort to bring hot, nutritional meals to senior citizens in the area, and a crafts program designed to better tenant/landlord relationships. Bond resigned in 1963 to become the director of the GREATER CLEVELAND NEIGHBORHOOD CTRS. ASSOC. In the years following Bond's resignation, the settlement has had to cope with a rapidly changing neighborhood. Originally Hungarian, the East End neighborhood became largely black during the 1960s and 1970s. The settlement was faced with problems not only in reconciling differences within the neighborhood but also in changing its own board and administrative staff to reflect its new clientele. During this period, the settlement continued to change its program, in part to meet the needs of the area, but also to take advantage of newly available federal funds. To this end its programs for the 1960s and 1970s not only reflected increased attention to the needs of senior citizens but also included expanded daycare programs and mental-health programs. Much of the club and class work that initially had characterized settlement work was dropped. By 1975, federal funding accounted for 65% of the settlement's $540,000 budget.

East End Settlement House Records, WRHS.

The **EAST OHIO GAS COMPANY** has supplied natural gas to the Cleveland area since receiving a controversial franchise from the city in 1902. Founded in 1898 to market an often wasted by-product of the Standard Oil Co.'s drilling operations, East Ohio had gas sales of $1.1 billion in 1986. STANDARD OIL CO. established the East Ohio Gas Co. to pipe natural gas from its wells in West Virginia to Akron for use in lighting and heating homes and businesses there and in communities along the pipeline route. Incorporated on 8 Sept. 1898, with Elizur Strong as president and headquarters in Lima, East Ohio obtained its first franchise in Dennison, soon adding New Philadelphia, Dover, Canton, Massillon, and Akron; by 1900 it had 3,874 customers. In 1902 the company sought a franchise to extend its services to Cleveland. The 2 companies providing artificial gas to Cleveland opposed the East Ohio franchise. The Cleveland Gas Light & Coke Co., incorporated on 6 Feb. 1846 to light city streets and distribute gas to homes and businesses, had been dormant until MOSES C. YOUN-

GLOVE and Benajah Barker gained control of its operations in 1848. Barker built the gas works in 1849 and served as company president for 5 years. In 1851, the company served 233 customers and lighted 82 public lamps, all on the eastern side of the Cuyahoga; not until 1856 did it apply for a franchise to light the west side. The People's Gas Light Co., organized in Dec. 1866 by John H. Sargent, Sanford L. Lewis, and John Bousfield, took over gas service on the west side in May 1868 when it purchased the Cleveland Gas Light & Coke Co.'s properties there.

Although rates were regulated by the city council, customers complained regularly about artificial-gas prices and service. A recurring complaint was that the companies lighted city streets according to the almanac: critics charged that if the almanac said a night would be bright, then the street lamps went unlit, regardless of actual conditions. In addition to this complaint about company service, consumers found natural gas attractive because it was less expensive and more efficient than artificial gas. The availability of natural gas from East Ohio would mean difficult times for artificial-gas suppliers and coal dealers, and they fought the new company's proposed entry into the market, allegedly offering councilmen thousands of dollars in exchange for votes against granting East Ohio's franchise. Mayor TOM L. JOHNSON favored granting the franchise, amid charges that Standard Oil had offered him a million dollars for his support. During council's debate on the franchise, one councilman dramatically displayed the money offered him by opponents of the franchise, and council then approved East Ohio's request on 23 June 1902.

The company grew quickly after it entered the Cleveland market. Martin B. Daly, general manager of the firm's Cleveland operations and later East Ohio president (1906–26), established an office at 437 the ARCADE. Natural gas was first supplied to the city in 1903; by 1905 the company had 280 business and 30,000 residential customers. On 24 Feb. 1910, the company was reorganized to include the Cleveland Gas Light & Coke Co., with its 46,225 services, and the People's Gas Light Co., with 19,000 services. The new East Ohio Gas Co., located at 1447 E. 6th St. in Cleveland, had capital of $20 million. In 1916 the company moved into a new office building at 1405 E. 6th St.; it moved into another new building at 1717 E. 9th St. in Apr. 1959. Growth continued as the company extended its service into other northeastern Ohio communities. By 1938, it served 67 communities with 500,000 customers; it served 167 communities in 1958 with 750,000 customers. In Apr. 1955, East Ohio acquired the Lake County Gas Co., and in Apr. 1959 it purchased Painesville's municipally owned gas-distribution system. By 1970 it served 258 communities and employed more than 3,400 people. In 1943, East Ohio began to expand its supply of natural gas by supplementing gas from Appalachian fields with gas from Texas; in 1958 it began buying Mexican gas. On 20 Oct. 1944, an explosion and fire destroyed the company's storage facilities and offices on E. 62nd St. between St. Clair and the lakefront, killing 133 people (see EAST OHIO GAS COMPANY EXPLOSION AND FIRE). East Ohio remained a subsidiary of Standard Oil until the Public Utilities Holding Co. Act and rulings by the Securities & Exchange Commission forced the oil company to divest itself of East Ohio and other public utilities in 1943. The Consolidated Natural Gas Co. was formed then to receive these companies. East Ohio is the largest gas distrubutor among Consolidated's subsidiaries. Of total revenues of $1.1 billion in 1986, East Ohio's net income was $3.7 million.

East Ohio Gas Co., *Fifty Years of Service, 1898–1948* (ca. 1948).

The **EAST OHIO GAS COMPANY EXPLOSION AND FIRE** took place on 20 Oct. 1944 when a tank holding millions of gallons of liquid natural gas exploded. The most disastrous fire in Cleveland's history engulfed more than 1 sq. mi. of Cleveland's east side bounded by St. Clair Ave. NE, E. 55th St., E. 67th St., and the MEMORIAL SHOREWAY. At approximately 2:30 p.m., white vapor began leaking out of Tank No. 4 of the EAST OHIO GAS CO., located at the end of E. 61st St. It quickly spread toward E. 61st St. and was ignited by a spark. The earth trembled as No. 4 exploded, sending fragments of metal thousands of feet away. Houses on both sides of E. 61st St. and E. 62nd St. burst into flames. The fire ran for 20 blocks, engulfing rows of houses while missing others.

At 3 p.m., the tank next to No. 4 exploded. The ball of flame was seen as far away as John Adams High School, 7 mi. away. Houses and factories a half-mile away were scorched by the heat. The liquid gas ran down the street and into sewers, where it turned into vapor and seeped into basements. Houses exploded, and manhole covers were blown hundreds of feet into the air. Birds, burned to death by heat waves estimated at 3,000 degrees Fahrenheit, fell from the sky. Some employees of East Ohio Gas tried to escape by hiding in metal lockers; only their bones and jewelry survived. In an effort to escape, people ran across the Shoreway toward Lake Erie. Others ran down E. 55th St. The immediate area surrounding the burning district was evacuated, and refugees were sheltered in Willson Jr. High School on E. 55th St., where the Red Cross tried to care for approximately 680 homeless victims. By late afternoon the following day, much of the fire had burned itself out, and most of the firemen were sent home. Electricity was restored in some areas. Property damage was estimated at $6 million. The fire destroyed 79 homes, 2 factories, 217 cars, 7 trailers, and 1 tractor. The death toll reached 130 victims, 50 of whom were gas company employees; 52 bodies were not identified. The fire hampered the Cleveland war effort. The fire and subsequent analysis of its cause led to new and safer methods for the cryogenic storage of natural gas.

**EAST SIDE IRISH AMERICAN CLUB.** *See* **IRISH AMERICAN CLUB EAST SIDE**

**EAST TECHNICAL HIGH SCHOOL,** a comprehensive coeducational high school, was the first public trade school in the Greater Cleveland area. In 1905, Francis E. Haserot, president of the Cleveland Board of Education, reported on the inadequacy of industrial education in Cleveland high schools. In Feb. 1905, under the leadership of Superintendent Wm. H. Elson, appointed a 12-man commission to examine the existing courses of study; the commission recommended the establishment of a "Manual Training School." On 5 Mar. 1906, the board unanimously adopted a resolution authorizing the issuance of bonds for the purpose of building a manual training high school (almost immediately changed to Technical High School). The new enterprise, a pioneer in technical education, was one of 5 technical high schools in the country and the first trade school in this area. The location, 2470 E. 55th St., was selected on 13 Aug. 1906; ground was broken and construction began on 30 Aug. 1907, and on 5 Oct. 1908, the Technical High School, a brown-and-yellow brick building with Gothic facade, was opened. Classes began on 12 Oct. with an enrollment of 700 pupils. East Tech, as it was called after 1910, was originally coeducational. It became an all-male school in 1929 when female pupils were transferred to John Hay High School, and it became coeducational again in 1952 when CENTRAL HIGH SCHOOL and East Tech were merged. Jas. F. Barker of Muskegon, Mich., the school's first principal (1908–16), often referred to as "the

Father of East Tech," was instrumental in establishing a new type of secondary training, which combined a general education with technical training in a specialized field. He extended the school day as well as the school year; he selected the scarab as the school's official emblem and brown and gold as the school's colors (representing the colors of the building). An *armillary* sphere, an astronomical model made of iron and steel circular tubings representing the great circle of the heavens containing signs of the zodiac (symbolizing the "whole life"), was installed on top of the roof, becoming a distinctive feature of the building. In 1972 it was transferred to the inner courtyard of the new building.

East Tech's enrollment increased as young Clevelanders, predominantly students of immigrant families, enrolled in the program. Graduates were often able to secure employment immediately upon graduation and/or were equipped to enter college, including technical universities. Later the school became one of the city's predominantly black secondary schools. The school became a leader in interscholastic athletics, winning city championships in football (1915–23); innumerable Senate, city, sectional, state, district, and regional championships in basketball (1950s); and over 13 state championships in track, particularly during the days of future Olympic stars JESSE OWENS, Dave Albritton, and Harrison Dillard. In Jan. 1970, ground was broken at 2439 E. 55th St. for construction of a new building almost diagonally across the street from the original structure. Many East Tech alumni participated in the dedication of the new "space-age" building on 11–12 Oct. 1972. (The original building was demolished in the early 1970s.)

Garrett, Zulieme, *The Story of East Technical High School* (1936).

**EASTER, LUSCIOUS "LUKE"** (4 Aug. 1915–29 Mar. 1979), was a major-league baseball player for the CLEVELAND INDIANS between 1949–54. A 6'4", 240-lb. first baseman, he was noted for his long home runs at the Cleveland Stadium. Easter was born in St. Louis, Mo. He was a renowned softball player until signed by the Cincinnati Crescents of the Negro American League in 1946. During 1947–48, he was a member of the Homestead Grays. Bill Veeck, owner of the Cleveland Indians, purchased his contract in 1949 and sent him to San Diego to play. After 80 games in the Pacific Coast League, Easter had a .363 average and 25 home runs. Recalled to play for the Indians in Aug. 1949, he began a 6-year major-league career. Plagued by numerous injuries, Easter had chronic knee problems that limited his career to 491 games with Cleveland. Although Easter hit only 93 major-league home runs, his long drives made him a fan favorite. JACK GRANEY, the Cleveland radio announcer, called Easter's home runs "bazooka blasts." On 23 June 1950, Easter hit a baseball into the upper deck that was measured at 477' from home plate and is considered the longest home run hit at CLEVELAND MUNICIPAL STADIUM. After leaving the major leagues, Easter played in the Internatl. League until 1966. He returned to Cleveland and began working as a polisher at TRW in EUCLID. The Indians hired him as a batting coach in 1969. By 1979, Easter had become a shop steward at TRW. On 29 Mar. 1979, he was killed by bank robbers while cashing his fellow workers' paychecks. Easter was married to Virgil Lowe and had 3 sons and a daughter.

**EASTERN ORTHODOX CHURCHES.** There are many parallels in the beliefs of the Eastern Orthodox church and the Roman Catholic church, but are there are also fundamental differences between them. Some of the beliefs and traditions unique to Eastern Orthodoxy help to explain both the role of the church in the life of Cleveland's Orthodox immigrants and the impact of American society on the churches. Eastern Orthodox Christians contend that all bishops have equal authority. They reject Roman Catholicism's claim of universal supremacy of the bishop of Rome, i.e., the pope. During the Middle Ages, Eastern Orthodoxy evolved into several independent exarchates and patriarchies. For historical reasons, the patriarch of Constantinople was recognized as honorary leader of Eastern Orthodoxy. However, each of the patriarchies was autocephalous, that is, a separate entity with its own leader or patriarch. Supreme authority resided in the Ecumenical Council. Each patriarchy was identified by region or nationality, such as Greek Orthodox or Russian Orthodox. Such designations were really a convenient, but inaccurate, way of saying, for example, "the Eastern Orthodox churches of the Greek Rite." Thus, the Orthodox churches in the homelands of immigrants were closely tied to the people's regional, national, and cultural heritage. In some areas, the church had become the people's sole expression of nationality.

Many Eastern Orthodox immigrants from Eastern Europe, the Balkans, and the Near East settled in Cleveland between 1880–1924. They brought with them strong allegiances to the mother churches in their homelands. Formation of a parish was one of the first tasks undertaken after settling in the city. These ethnic churches maintained ties to the mother churches and helped to preserve ethnic traditions. Liturgies continued to be performed in the languages of the first-generation immigrants, and priests were generally born and educated in the Old World. The tradition of autonomy of Eastern Orthodox churches was observed among the various ethnic Orthodox churches in Cleveland. Ethnic-language liturgies discouraged multiethnic congregations. Gradually, changes occurred both within the churches themselves and in their ties to the mother churches in Europe and the Middle East. The causes were varied. Communist takeovers of certain countries in Eastern Europe, the Balkans, and the Soviet Union strained relations between the mother churches and their branches in America. Questions of allegiance and politics created internal conflicts and divided parishioners. In one case, such a dispute found no resolution short of schism within the church and a lengthy legal battle. Second- and third-generation descendants, no longer fluent in the language of their ancestors, found it difficult to understand ethnic-language liturgies. Many churches requested bilingual priests, and some churches adopted English as the liturgical language. At the same time, assimilation of ethnic descendants into mainstream American culture and a weakening sense of identity with European nationalities produced a sense of religious community among some members of the Orthodox faith. One expression of this feeling was the creation of the Orthodox Church of America and subsequent membership of several Cleveland churches.

Another challenge faced by early Eastern Orthodox churches in Cleveland involved the movement of parishioners to the SUBURBS. By the 1950s, older Orthodox churches were often to be found in inner-city neighborhoods containing few members of the original ethnic community. In some cases, these churches were able to attract ethnic members throughout Greater Cleveland and to continue to serve as the cultural, social, and spiritual center for their ethnic congregations. Other churches followed their parishioners and relocated to areas deemed more convenient by suburbanites. New parishes were also formed in the suburbs as the Orthodox population increased through recent immigration from some Orthodox countries and movement of city dwellers to the suburbs. By the 1960s, more than 100,000 Clevelanders were members of the city's several Orthodox Christian churches. In the 1980s, the community of Eastern Orthodox churches in the U.S. did not have one central headquarters. Many of the churches were organized along national lines and were still connected with their respective mother churches in Europe and the Middle East. In 1986, Eastern Orthodox churches in Greater Cleveland included the Russian, Greek, Carpatho-Russian, Ukrainian, Byelorussian, Romanian, Serbian, Armenian, Syrian, Albanian, and American Orthodox. A Greek Orthodox monastery was also located in the city.

Although all of the Eastern Orthodox churches in Cleveland shared many of the same experiences because of the process of immigration and the pressures of American society, each church also enjoyed a unique ethnicity. Thus, responses of the various churches to the pressures from within and without were varied. Some of these responses are evident in brief chronicles of various Eastern Orthodox parishes in Cleveland. The homelands of the CARPATHO-RUSSIANS, UKRAINIANS, and BYELO-RUSSIANS are now (1986) under the control of the Soviet Union. However, in this country, each group has its own ethnic Orthodox church. The majority of Cleveland's early Russian Eastern Orthodox churches were established by Carpatho-Russian immigrants from the nothern Carpathian region of Eastern Europe. Most Clevelanders considering themselves as "RUSSIANS" trace their heritage to this area, which was part of the Austro-Hungarian Empire prior to WORLD WAR I. The city's Ukrainian Orthodox churches, which are not consolidated with the Russian Orthodox churches, were founded by Ukrainian immigrants primarily from the Carpathian Mountain regions and the Western Ukraine. Most of Cleveland's Byelorussians came here as White Russian refugees from Germany, Belgium, and England after WORLD WAR II.

The first Orthodox parish in Cleveland was St. Theodosius, founded in 1896. In the course of 15 years, this Russian Orthodox church grew from a simple frame structure on Literary Rd. at W. 6th St. to the ST. THEODOSIUS RUSSIAN ORTHODOX CATHEDRAL, which was still one of the foremost Russian Orthodox churches in America in the 1980s. In 1904, the first Ukrainian Orthodox services in Cleveland were conducted in a small hall on W. 14th St. The St. Vladimir Ukrainian Orthodox Church was completed in 1933 at 2280 W. 11th St. As parishioners moved to the suburbs, the church followed. From 1957–66, worship was held in the old Parma city hall. In 1966, a new St. Vladimir Church at 5913 State Rd. in PARMA was completed. The traditional onion-shaped domes were constructed in 1974. Several other Russian and Ukrainian Orthodox churches were located in Greater Cleveland in 1986. These included St. Michael Russian Orthodox Church, Holy Resurrection Russian Orthodox Church, St. Sergius Russian Orthodox Church, SS. Peter & Paul Orthodox Church, Holy Trinity Ukrainian Autocephalos Orthodox Church, St. Andrew Eastern Orthodox Church, and St. Nicholas Ukrainian Orthodox Church.

Cleveland's only Byelorussian parish was formed in 1950 and conducted worship in a W. 25th St. residence until a new Byelorussian Autocephalic Orthodox church, Our Lady of Zyrovicy, was constructed on W. 25th and Scranton Rd. SW. Fifteen Greek immigrants started the Greek Orthodox Church of Annunciation in 1912 in the Arch Hall at the corner of Ontario and Bolivar. One year later, the church moved to a hall at W. 14th St. and Fairfield. The building was razed in 1917 and replaced in 1919 by the present (1986) ANNUNCIATION GREEK ORTHODOX CHURCH. The newer parishes of SS. Constantine & He-

len, St. Demetrios Greek Orthodox, and St. Paul Greek Orthodox were established as people moved to the suburbs. In 1904, Romanian immigrants organized St. Mary's parish, which was reportedly the first Romanian Orthodox parish in America. In 1960, the church was relocated from its Detroit Ave. site to 3256 Warren Rd. NW. In addition to ST. MARY'S ROMANIAN ORTHODOX CHURCH, there is a smaller Romanian Orthodox parish in Greater Cleveland named Bunavestire Church.

Serbian immigrants founded a Serbian school-church congregation and named it St. Sava in 1909. The parish soon outgrew the small house in which services had been held, and the St. Sava Serbian Orthodox Church was relocated to E. 36th St. and Paine Ave. in 1918. After World War II, as membership in the church increased and more Orthodox Serbs settled in the suburbs of Cleveland, church members decided to build a new church at 6303 Broadview Rd. in Parma. However, before this church could be consecrated, 2 factions emerged within the congregation, each fighting for control of the church. The main issue was whether the church should remain under the control of the patriarchate in Yugoslavia, a country governed by a Communist regime, or whether it should sever ties with the mother church and be autonomous. Twelve years of litigation ended 23 March 1975, when the church property was divided between the groups (see ST. SAVA CONTROVERSY).

ARMENIANS settled in Cleveland between 1908 and the end of World War I. Services were initially held in space made available by several local Protestant churches, especially Episcopal churches. In 1963, the St. Gregory of Narek Armenian Apostolic Church was built on Richmond Rd. in RICHMOND HTS. It was the first Armenian church in Ohio. In 1928, ST. GEORGE'S ORTHODOX CHURCH-Antiochian was founded by Syrian immigrants. The church occupied a former Methodist church building at Starkweather and W. 14th St. in the heart of the largest Syrian community in Cleveland, remaining in this location into the 1980s. Albanian immigrants first arrived in Cleveland in the 1910s. In 1957, Rev. Campbell, an Old Catholic, founded an Albanian parish. A church hall on Jasper Ave. served the needs of the parish until the St. E. Premte Orthodox Church, an Albanian Orthodox church, was established in 1965 at 10716 Jasper Rd. SW.

The continuing process of Americanization is evident in several of Cleveland's Eastern Orthodox churches. The first parish in the U.S. to call itself the American Orthodox church was the city's Christ the Saviour American Orthodox Church. The church was founded in 1964 in Parma by Rev. Stephen Jula, associate pastor of St. Theodosius Russian Orthodox Cathedral. In 1976, the 250-member church relocated to N. ROYALTON. The church is part of the Carpatho-Russian Orthodox Diocese in America. English is used throughout the church services; the liturgy is the same as that used by all Eastern Orthodox churches. The first Orthodox church in Greater Cleveland to conduct all its services in English was Holy Trinity. This parish was organized in 1963 and conducted services at Parma Memorial Hall. In 1965, when ground was broken for a new church, the congregation had grown to 400 people. Similar to Holy Trinity was St. Innocent Orthodox Church in WESTLAKE. The parish was organized in 1983 and has been conducting services since 1984 in a chapel rented from a Protestant church on Hilliard Blvd. There were approximately 60–70 individuals in the congregation in 1986.

Nicholas J. Zentos
Lorain County Community College

359

See also specific Orthodox immigrant groups.

**EASTMAN, HARRY LLOYD** (9 Apr. 1882–7 July 1963), was judge of the Cuyahoga County Insolvency & Juvenile Court from 1926–60. He was responsible for innovations that made that court the model system for the entire country during the 1940s. He was a leading advocate of the juvenile-court philosophy, which combined traditional legal processes with techniques of medical and social sciences, the goal being to provide protection and care, as well as correction. Eastman was born in Butler, Pa., but was educated in the Findlay, Ohio, public school system. He became a photoengraver and invented a "perfect ratio rule" measuring device for photoengravers. After working at the *PLAIN DEALER* and the *CLEVELAND LEADER* for a few years, he did odd jobs in photoengraving to work his way through the Western Reserve School of Law. In 1913, he received his LL.B. degree and was admitted to the Ohio bar. He served as assistant U.S. attorney for the Northern District of Ohio from 1919–21 and practiced law with several Cleveland firms until 1926. He married Marcella J. Dalgleish on 30 Sept. 1922.

In May 1926, Gov. Alvin V. Donahey appointed Eastman judge of the Cuyahoga County Insolvency & Juvenile Court to fill an unexpired term. The following year, he was elected to that office; successively reelected, he held the position for 34 years. Eastman was a member of the CITIZENS LEAGUE OF CLEVELAND, the Welfare Fed., the CLEVELAND ATHLETIC CLUB, the GREATER CLEVELAND SAFETY COUNCIL, the LEGAL AID SOCIETY, the Masonic Lodges, the Natl. Council of Juvenile Court Judges (founder and president, 1937–42), and the Natl. Probation & Parole Assoc., 1934–42. During Eastman's terms of office, the County Detention Home and juvenile court buildings were built (completed in 1932). The juvenile court became an independent branch of the county court system in 1934. Administrative changes were made and services added, making it one of the most progressive in the nation. Eastman improved personnel standards by raising the requirements for civil service, by cooperation with schools of social work, and by instituting the professional casework training of probation officers. He established the first juvenile-court psychiatric clinic and founded a department of child support. Recognized as an authority, Eastman was invited to participate in the 1940 White House Conference on Children in a Democracy. In 1950, he was the only representative of the CUYAHOGA COUNTY JUVENILE COURT on the important Fact Finding Committee of the Mid-Century White House Conference of Children & Youth. Judge Eastman retired from the bench in May 1960.

Harry Lloyd Eastman Papers, WRHS.

**EASTMAN, LINDA ANNE** (17 July 1867–5 Apr. 1963), was the fourth librarian of the CLEVELAND PUBLIC LIBRARY, succeeding her friend and mentor WM. HOWARD BRETT. She was the first woman in the world to head a library of its size when she assumed the position. Eastman was born in Oberlin, Ohio, to a family whose New England ancestors included Miles Standish. When she was 7, her parents, Wm. Harvey and Sarah Redrup Eastman, moved the family to Cleveland, where Eastman attended public school, graduating with honors from West High. Completing a course at Cleveland Normal School, Eastman entered into teaching but soon found herself attracted to library work. She became an assistant at the CPL in 1892 and was promoted to vice-librarian under Brett in

1895. Eastman was named librarian in 1918, a position she held until her retirement 20 years later. Her first years were dominated by the construction and occupancy of the $4.5 million main library building, opened in 1925. Later in her tenure, she developed several specialized operations, including a travel section, a business information bureau, and services to the blind and handicapped. Eastman's achievements within her profession were highly regarded and recognized nationally. She was president of both the Ohio Library Assoc. and the American Library Assoc. and held a professorship at the Library School of Western Reserve University. She retired as librarian in 1938, when she was 71. She died at the age of 95.

Archives, Cleveland Public Library, Cleveland, Ohio.

**EASTON'S SONS, INC.** *See* **THOMAS W. EASTON'S SONS, INC.**

**EATON, CYRUS S.** (27 Dec, 1883–9 May 1979), was a controversial capitalist and financier who was outspoken in his criticisms of other businessmen, his support of labor after the 1930s, and his promotion of better U.S.-Soviet relations. Eaton was born in Pugwash, Nova Scotia, the son of a successful merchant and farmer. After graduating from Amherst Academy in Amherst, Nova Scotia, he briefly attended Woodstock College before transferring to McMaster University, where he majored in philosophy to prepare himself for theological school and the Baptist ministry. His career plans began to change in the summer of 1901. On a trip to Cleveland to vist his uncle, Rev. Dr. Chas. Aubrey Eaton, then minister at the EUCLID AVE. BAPTIST CHURCH, Cyrus Eaton met and later went to work for JOHN D. ROCKEFELLER. Shortly after he graduated from McMaster in 1905, he returned to Cleveland to work for the EAST OHIO GAS CO.

With direct assistance from Rockefeller, Eaton went into business for himself in 1907. Representing a New York banking syndicate in which Rockefeller had an interest, Eaton went to Manitoba, Canada, to secure natural-gas franchises. He succeeded in obtaining the franchises, but the firm he represented collapsed during a financial panic. Still holding the franchises, Eaton received financing from a Canadian bank to organize the Canada Gas & Electric Corp. and proceeded to develop gas and electric companies throughout Canada and the American Midwest. In 1912 he consolidated these holdings into the Continental Gas & Electric Corp. Eaton's wealth was estimated to be $2 million by the time he became a naturalized American citizen and settled in Cleveland in 1913. Eaton diversified his interests in the 1920s. In 1916 he became a partner in Otis & Co., an investment banking firm. In 1926 he organized his own investment trust, Continental Shares, Inc., and began investing in rubber and steel. In Dec. 1929, he consolidated his steel holdings into the Republic Steel Corp., the 3d-largest steel firm in the U.S. Eaton's wealth in 1929 was estimated to be $100 million, most of which he lost in the Great Depression.

In Apr. 1931, Eaton resigned as chairman of Continental Shares, but he remained as majority owner of Otis & Co. and rebuilt his fortune in the 1940s and 1950s, serving as a director of the Chesapeake & Ohio Railroad after 1943 and becoming its chairman of the board in 1954. He also became chairman of the board of the West Kentucky Coal Co. in 1953. In the mid-1950s, Eaton turned his attention to broader issues. Transforming his boyhood home in Pugwash into a "Thinker's Lodge," he invited a number of scholars to spend a week at his retreat in Aug. 1955. A Soviet scholar was invited to the second Pugwash Conference in 1956, and in 1957 the first Pugwash Conference of Nuclear Scientists brought together scientists from around the world to discuss international issues. During the cold war, Eaton cultivated friendships with Soviet leaders and urged the U.S. and the Soviet Union to develop better relations. He received the Lenin Peace Prize in 1960 for his efforts to promote international peace and understanding.

Eaton was active in Cleveland affairs, as well. In 1942 he negotiated the municipal purchase of the CLEVELAND RAILWAY CO. and arranged financing for the new Cleveland Transit System. From 1930–39 he served as a trustee of the Cleveland Metropolitan Park District; he donated 58 acres of land to the parks in 1955. He was most active in educational endeavors: he was a founder and trustee of the CLEVELAND MUSEUM OF NATURAL HISTORY; he helped transform the YMCA night school into Fenn College; and he was a trustee and benefactor of Case School of Applied Science. He was also a trustee of Denison University, the University of Chicago, and the Harry S. Truman Library. He was a fellow of the American Academy of Arts & Sciences and a member of the American Council of Learned Societies and 3 other scholarly societies. Eaton was married twice. His first marriage, in Dec. 1907 to Margaret House, ended in divorce in Aug. 1934; after her death in 1956, he married Anne Kinder Jones in Dec. 1957.

Cyrus S. Eaton Papers, WRHS.

The **EATON CORPORATION** was founded as the Torbensen Gear & Axle Co. in 1911 by Joseph Oriel Eaton and Viggo Torbensen to manufacture truck axles. In a year when truck production in the U.S. was less than 11,000, Torbensen produced only 7 axles. The company moved from New Jersey to Cleveland in 1915, was incorporated in 1916 as the Torbensen Axle Co., and in 1918 became a subsidiary of its largest customer, the Republic Motor Truck Co. Eaton left Republic in 1919 to form the Eaton Axle Co., which quickly became a leader in the axle field. From its new plant in E. CLEVELAND (until 1983 the Axle Div. of the present-day Eaton Corp.), Eaton bought control of Torbensen Axle and diversified to include auto components with its acquisition of 2 spring manufacturers (including the Perfection Spring Co. of Cleveland) and a heater manufacturer in 1928. Additional purchases gave the company expertise in the manufacture of valves, pumps, and precision engine parts, as well as plants in several states. One of the largest automotive-parts manufacturers in the U.S., Eaton Axle survived the Depression because of its diverse product line.

After Eaton died in 1949, the Eaton Mfg. Co. continued its expansion and intensified its research efforts; it profited from the popularity of power steering and air conditioning, which it introduced in 1955. In 1958, the company acquired a major axle and transmission manufacturer, the Fuller Mfg. Co. of Kalamazoo, Mich., that entrenched its position in the truck components field. Its worldwide acquisitions solidified its reputation in vehicle components, as well in a new area—electronics. Its merger in 1966 with Yale & Towne, Inc., a major producer of locks and material-handling products with facilities around the world, moved Eaton into new markets and changed its corporate name to Eaton, Yale & Towne, Inc. Among its local acquisitions in this period were Cleveland Worm & Gear (1959), which made worm gears and worm drive speed reducers, and the Tinnerman Prods. Co. (1969), which made fasteners. During the 1970s, the company (known as the Eaton Corp. as of 1971) was adversely affected by falling vehicle sales. Under the leadership of E. Mandell de Windt, it carefully planned its future acquisitions with an eye to recession-

resistant diversity and balance. Its biggest step in this direction was the acquisition of electronics and electric control producer Cutler-Hammer, Inc., of Milwaukee (1978).

As Eaton merged with high-tech firms, the company sold off some of its vehicle divisions and closed unprofitable plants. In 1980, Eaton sold the local Industrial Drives Div. (formerly Cleveland Worm & Gear), which employed 340 and generated $27 million in sales, to the Vesper Corp. of Pennsylvania. Meanwhile, Eaton shortened the workweek at the Axle plant to 4 days and laid off workers. By 1983, the company announced that both the Axle plant at 739 E. 140th St. and the old Tinnerman plant at 8700 Brookpark would close unless the workers agreed to concessions. When the workers refused, the company announced the closing of both plants at the expense of 1,100 jobs. At this time the axle plant was operating at only 25% capacity in response to the falling demand for heavy-duty axles (212,000 in 1979 as compared to 82,000 in 1982) and falling heavy-duty truck sales (340,000 in 1973 as compared to 115,000 in 1982). The result of its high-tech thrust was a realignment of its source of sales revenues; in 1984, the company had record sales of over $3.5 billion, with 51.2% coming from its electric and electronic products and 48.7% from vehicle components. Defense work was among the fastest-growing sectors. In 1982, the company reaffirmed its commitment to remain in Cleveland by moving its headquarters from 100 Erieview to 1111 Superior.

**ECONOMY.** Metropolitan Cleveland grew on the expanding 19th-century technologies of waterborne shipping, railroad, and telegraph. Oriented to the geographic disposition of soils and minerals, of lakes, and of eastern mountains, these lines of transport and communication converged upon the strategic location at the mouth of the CUYAHOGA RIVER to beget a metropolis. The era of spectacular growth terminated with the onset of the Depression. But the Depression was not the culprit. Even with the outbreak of WORLD WAR II, Cleveland's growth resumed only at a retarded pace, and the city's course in the postwar years trailed the national expansion. The technologies of transport and communication that had previously fixed the location and powered the urban growth had lost much of their magnetism, yielding to the dispersive influences of the motor vehicle, the airplane, the computer, and electronic communication. Thus, Cleveland matured with the maturity of its technological base. The forces that engendered the city's growth were impersonal. The destiny of Cleveland, as of any city, was cast in the mold of its functions. With respect to Cleveland (and most older American cities), 3 such functions can be named: an entrepot function; the logistical function; and the function of specialization. An entrepot is a site at which nature has placed a barrier to the otherwise uninterrupted flow of freight. At this point, all goods must be shifted from one conveyance to another. This circumstance marked the mouth of the Cuyahoga River as the terminus of the OHIO & ERIE CANAL upon its completion in 1832 and marked the site where the metropolis would flower. From the entrepot, the logistical function emerged. An entrepot is an economical point for processing raw materials, commonly a number of such materials in combination, and for distributing products to dispersed markets. The site thus becomes strategic to the logistics of manufacturing and distribution activities that cluster about the locus of interchange. Manhattan's garment industry and Cleveland's metalworking shops are illustrative.

The specialization function is related (but not confined) to the logistics. Numerous enterprises specialize by process—foundries, forges, bookbinders, and the like. Thus,

361

an entrepreneur with a new product to put on the market can farm out much of the production to such processors and confine his own shop to design and assembly. An extreme specialization is patronized by only a minute portion of the total population. To assemble a clientele adequate for its sustenance, therefore, the specialization must be practiced where the total population is great. Only in a large city can one find antitrust lawyers, marine lawyers, patent lawyers, domestic-relations lawyers, and labor lawyers, as well as landscape architects and stores selling only artificial limbs. Many of the people in the city neither patronize nor participate in any of these urban functions. The city is home to 2 intermingled populations; one consists of those engaged primarily in the employments that explain the city's existence and can be considered the functional population. Its members provide services mainly for export beyond the city's boundaries. The other consists of those drawn to the city to serve primarily local needs and can be designated as the collateral population. It includes such persons as retailers, most doctors, and schoolteachers, for example. The city is there because of the functional population; the collateral population is there because of the city.

To trace the record of Cleveland's economy, we must concentrate attention on the functional activities. Cleveland emerged from its frontier cocoon as an entrepot in the 1830s. The Ohio Canal had been completed to Akron in 1827 and to Portsmouth on the Ohio River in 1832. Prior to the railroad era, the only way to move large quantities of goods at low cost was by water. On land in the 1830s, the charge per ton for 100 mi. of wagon haulage on the best turnpikes ranged generally from $10 to $15. On the Ohio Canal it averaged only $1. The Erie Canal had been completed from the Hudson River to Buffalo in 1825, giving the shores of Lake Erie initial waterway access to populous eastern and overseas markets. With its opening, freight rates between Lake Erie and New York had dropped to 10% of their former level. The Ohio Canal, which, with its branches, eventually constituted a system of some 500 mi., extended this access from Cleveland southward into central and eastern Ohio. The canal thus opened Cleveland's hinterland and established Cleveland as the growing region's principal outlet to the world. Previously, much of northern Ohio had been a sparsely settled wilderness. Low-cost shipment on the canal greatly augmented the potential incomes to be earned from newly cultivated farms and newly opened mines. Wheat, which formerly had a farm value in northern Ohio of $.20-.30 a bushel, now yielded the farmer $.50-.75. On this advantage, settlement accelerated, and Cleveland's hinterland became populous. Cleveland thus began to thrive because of freight transshipment. All freight arriving at the mouth of the Cuyahoga, whether by canal or lake, had to be unloaded, stored, and either processed or transferred to another vessel. Waterfront storage required warehouses. In 1838, for example, the *CLEVELAND HERALD* announced that, in spite of the depression, 9 large warehouses were erected. In 1837, 2 ropewalks were operating in Cleveland. Ship-repair yards expanded into shipbuilding.

In 1827, as the canal reached Akron, Cleveland's first manufacturing establishment appeared: the CUYAHOGA STEAM FURNACE CO. The canal system, supplemented by lake and road haulage, channeled into the town the coal, iron, tallow, and other materials for foundries, fabricators of steam engines, soap and candle factories, millstone shops, sash and door works, and stoneware potteries. The directory of Cleveland and OHIO CITY for the years 1837–38 lists 17 such establishments in the city. On this foundation, Cleveland's downtown center of commerce

and finance emerged. Warehouses and other storage and transfer centers were convenient points of sale, inviting merchandising and brokerage. Insurance offices opened to protect against the hazards of flood and fire. Newly opened banks met the demand for funds by cash-hungry inland farmers and other shippers, as well as the needs of local fabricators.

When all communication was by foot messenger or face-to-face, the offices of the commercial and financial firms had to cluster within walking distance of the waterfront. The Cleveland city directory of 1852–53 listed 6 insurance companies, 43 insurance agents, 6 commercial banks, 6 private banking houses, 2 exchange brokers, and the Society for Savings. Thus, Cleveland's downtown business district came into being—sited near the mouth of the Cuyahoga River by the technology of the horse-drawn canal barge—where, with the umbilical cord to the canal long severed, it remained in the 1980s. In the 1850s, the railroad initiated the town's subsequent surge to metropolitan dimensions. The railroad, in association with the telegraph, constituted a quantum leap in the conquest of distance. In 1850, before railroad connections, 10 days elapsed in good weather in the movement of people, freight, and news from New York to Cleveland—in the winter as much as a month. In 1865, the people and cargo made the railway trip in a day and a night, and news via the telegraph was instantaneous.

The RAILROADS accelerated the growth of existing cities. The lines were built to the urban waterfront for interchange with established waterborne commerce. Railroads offered substantially lower rates between larger centers. In 1851, railroad rates averaged in the neighborhood of 1.8 cents per ton-mile; in 1881 they were down to about 1.2 cents, and in 1891 to about 0.9 cent. For one thing, the urban concentrations provided the large tonnages essential to the economy of longer and more heavily laden trains. Long intercity movements, uninterrupted by switching at intermediate points, also reduced railway costs. Besides, railway competition was more keen, and rates therefore lower, between larger cities, where the shipper normally had a choice of several alternative routings. Rail transportation thus reinforced the previously water-based supremacy of urban logistics. In 1850, 5.1% of the American people lived in cities of more than 100,000 inhabitants; in 1880, 12.4%, and in 1910, 22.1%. Railroad development was a catalyst of this urbanization. Cleveland's first railroad was completed to Cincinnati in 1851. In 1863, the first through train arrived in Cleveland from New York. By 1870, some 6 railroad lines converged upon the Cleveland waterfront from virtually all landward points of the compass, and population had soared to 92,829, more than fivefold that of 1850. Centered on its new railroad and its lake connections, Cleveland embarked upon an 80-year career of spectacular growth. The transportation network poured into Cleveland a growing volume of basic raw materials and fuels. Cleveland enterprise opened the Lake Superior ranges to the nation's fledgling steel industry and transshipped the lake-borne ores by rail to Ohio Valley furnaces. The new railroads brought crude oil from Pennsylvania to the largest oil-refining center in the world and carried its products via the low-cost Mohawk Valley route, consigned to coastal and foreign markets. Railborne Ohio Basin coal funneled into Cleveland to multiplying foundries and coke ovens—much transshipped also to upper-lake consumers.

The low-cost abundance of metals, fuels, and components attracted a complex of related ventures. Fabricators of such products as sewing machines, machine tools, locomotives, bolts and nuts, and innumerable other metallic devices either initiated operations or moved existing works to Cleveland, coming from such origins as Massachusetts, Chicago, and the Ohio Valley. A CHEMICAL INDUSTRY grew up on the combination of local industrial demand and the availability of lakeborne and railborne minerals. The ever-growing numbers of immigrant families whose men found jobs in these industries expanded the supply of underemployed wives and children, a capable labor force for the GARMENT INDUSTRY. For all of these industries, the railroads reached out to nationwide markets on a scale previously unknown and thereby gave the spur to large-scale manufacturing and mass production. Canal traffic languished under the impact of water-competitive railroad rates. It has been estimated that, as of 1881, the average cost of a 500-mi. shipment by rail was about $6 per ton; as of 1891, only $4.50; and, on routings competitive with canals and rivers, much less. Everything landborne went by rail, and the network placed Cleveland within 500 mi. of low-cost access to most of the nation's markets. Admittedly, by the standards of the late-20th century, rail shipment was slow. But by the standards of the 19th, it was swift beyond precedent.

Industrial expansion generated related professional and administrative employment. Cleveland became an important center of industrial and architectural engineering. Industrial publishing flourished. Most of Cleveland's industry was home-grown, and home office administration thus grew in pace with the industrial works. Administrative control was enhanced, not only by proximity to local operations but, as well, by the convergence in Cleveland of rail connections for executive travel, mail service, and superior telegraphic communication. The era was one of revolutionary invention, not only affecting the telegraph, railroad, and steamship but including, as well, such innovations as the Bessemer converter, the open-hearth furnace, the by-product coke oven, the catalytic cracker, the sewing machine, the grain binder, the AC electric motor, the electric streetcar, the diesel engine, the gasoline automobile, the incandescent lamp, the telephone, and the wireless telegraph—devices to recast industry, conquer distance, and redraw the pattern of American life. Cleveland invention was in the vanguard, creating, for example, the open-hearth charging machine, the Hulett unloader, the oil expeller, the automatic screw-cutting machine, and the famous arc light system of CHAS. F. BRUSH.

The value of the city's manufactures in 1929 was nearly 120 times what it had been in 1860 (stated in dollars of constant purchasing power), and the population of Cuyahoga County in the same period had leaped 25-fold, from a mere 48,000 to over 1.2 million. In the 1920s, Cleveland observed its emergence into greatness by a program of massive civic construction, marked by harmony of design and lofty purpose—an extensive system of gracious parks, completion of the Group Plan centered on the lakeside MALL, and the monumental CLEVELAND UNION TERMINAL Group linked by a new rapid-transit line to SHAKER HTS., to name the most notable of these works. But now the lifelines of transport and commerce were beginning to fray. The motor vehicle on paved highways and telecommunications were weaving a new logistical and administrative fabric disruptive to urban concentration. In 1929, the railroads carried 96% of the nation's overland freight tonnage; and in 1983, only 43%. The motor vehicle severed the chains that had bound the factories to the urban railroad terminals. Rail freight moves only in trains. Trains must be assembled mainly in the big urban switching yards from points where the interconnecting main lines fan out across the map. In the pretrucking era, for access to dispersed markets, most factories had to locate near these centers.

But for the truck, no train assembly is required, and direct highway connections are ubiquitous.

The production of finished products commonly requires a daily intake of components, parts, and supplies from process specialists, such as foundries and electroplating shops. Rail shipment of small lots is slow, and delivery times are unpredictable. Thus, before trucking, shops with related operations clustered near each other for local transfer by horse-drawn wagon or pushcart. By contrast, trucking provided overnight or second-day delivery over hundreds of miles, permitting specialization without proximity. Plants sited off the rail lines were subjected to the cumbersome and costly process of transfer by plodding dray wagon to and from the nearest railroad. Before automobiles, workers either walked to work or took the electric streetcar. It was no accident that the grimy working-class neighborhoods were built in the shadow of the smokestacks. Workers in automobiles could commute many miles in any direction. Thus, the motor vehicle transferred to the countryside much of the former urban functions of logistics and specialization. Industry became more footloose, drifting toward regions, such as the South, where low labor cost, favorable tax rates, comfortable climate, and cultural and recreational ambience displaced urban logistics as a controlling locational influence. Air conditioning relieved something of the discomfort of southern summers, and the lack of winter's snow and ice on southern HIGHWAYS enhanced the service of trucking.

Meanwhile, a revolution in communications abetted the centrifugal pull. The cellular phone, microwave tower, satellite relay, and fiberoptics, all integrated with the computer, virtually eliminated the city's entrepot function. No longer need the commercial and financial offices locate within walking distance of the waterfront. Administration, likewise, was liberated from proximity to operations. Linked by computerized controls to a home office far away, chain stores, chain factories, and chain hotels proliferated in formerly rural regions, leaving the rail- and water-based urban centers behind. The process of displacement was slow and largely unperceived. Half-concealed by the distortions of Depression and war, the underlying diastrophic process of the nation's logistical restructuring crept relentlessly forward. During the 50 years 1880–1930, the population of Cuyahoga County had increased by over 1 million. During the following 50 years to 1980, it increased by fewer than 300,000. Had the pre-1930 rate of growth continued, Cuyahoga County in 1980 would have been home to over 7 million people. During the decade preceding 1980, the county actually lost population, as highway transport and telecommunications continued to exact their toll.

Cleveland's maturity need not foreshadow decline. While the city's entrepot and logistical base have been eroded by the revolution in transport and communications, the equally vital function of fostering specialization has not been as seriously affected. In Cleveland, specialization flourishes conspicuously in health care and in other professional and industrial activities, as well as in the arts and various cultural endeavors. The specialization function may be inadequate to restore rapid growth, but it can sustain and enrich the life of the existing city. Also, higher income levels, widely distributed, are associated with advancement and democratization of the arts. While the volume of manufacturing and population of Cuyahoga County fell from 1970 to 1980, the money income per capita rose 11.9% (after correction for inflation). The continuing distinction of the CLEVELAND ORCHESTRA, the emergence of the CLEVELAND BALLET, the multiplication of theaters, and the sustained vitality of the visual arts and of the CLEVE-

LAND MUSEUM OF ART are integral to this development. Some have lamented Cleveland's loss of the AUTOMOTIVE INDUSTRY early in the 20th century. But few have cited Detroit for superior quality of life. Amsterdam and Florence do not rank among the world's most rapidly growing cities, but they are surely among the greatest. The greatness of a city is measured not by quantity but by quality. And by this criterion, Cleveland reaches toward her ultimate fulfillment.

Marvin J. Barloon
Case Western Reserve University

See also BUSINESS, LAKE TRANSPORT, TRANSPORTATION.

**EDGEWATER PARK,** located along Lake Erie at the west end of the Shoreway (at W. 58th St.), was purchased in 1894 by the city's Second Park Board from Jacob B. Perkins, Cleveland industrialist. The land, consisting of 2 parcels, became Perkins Beach and Edgewater Park. Many recreational facilities were subsequently provided, including beach maintenance, bath houses, a pavilion, baseball diamonds, and numerous picnic and playground areas. The eastern half of Edgewater Park at the lower level contained additional athletic fields, the Edgewater Yacht Club, and the Edgewater Lagoon. Clevelanders used this park for many years, until much of it was destroyed by construction of the Shoreway freeway and it fell into disrepair in the 1960s. In 1978, Edgewater Park became part of the CLEVELAND LAKEFRONT STATE PARK, and since that time many of the park's recreational facilities have been restored, including offshore fishing platforms, a 900' bathing beach (one of the largest in Cleveland), a renovated pavilion, picnic areas, a boat-launching ramp, the Edgewater Yacht Club, and the Edgewater Marina.

**EDMONDSON, GEORGE MOUNTAIN** (23 Aug. 1866– 8 Nov. 1948), was a leading portrait photographer. He was born in Norwalk, Ohio, and educated in the public school system. His father, born in England, was a well-known photographer, and George began the study and practice of the art at the age of 16. He worked for his father for a short time, then moved to Cleveland in 1887 at the request of JAS. F. RYDER. He became assistant to the veteran photographer in his Superior St. studio. Edmondson used his knowledge of enlarging on the new bromide paper for Ryder, and in turn, the studio won several prizes. After a year and a half, he joined the studio of Decker & Wilbur (see EDGAR DECKER). In 1891, the firm dissolved partnership when Wilbur retired. Edmondson remained and 6 years later was taken into partnership. In 1903, he succeeded to the business and moved to larger facilities at 510 Euclid Ave. Edmondson concentrated on portrait photography. He was the recipient of numerous medals and awards for his endeavors. He made an effort to keep his studio up to date in equipment and technique. He was in the forefront of color photography in the early 1900s. Edmondson belonged to many clubs. In 1902, he was chosen president of the Photography Assoc. of America. He was also elected president of the Photographers Assoc. of Ohio. He was secretary and treasurer in 1910 of the Professional Photographers Society of Ohio and a member of this society in New York. He belonged to the Chamber of Commerce, the Lakewood Yacht Club, the CLEVELAND ATHLETIC CLUB, and the Unitarian church. He was married to Wilhelmina Neason Edmondson and had 2 children, Geo. Mountain, Jr., and Ivy Jane.

**EDUCATION.** The early history of education in Cleveland paralleled developments in Ohio and America, since education was a state initiative and local efforts reflected those of the state. The immigration of the 1830s and 1840s aroused feelings of nationalism and patriotism. The Catholic population grew rapidly and provided for a separate system of education during the 19th century. Many reform movements sprang up, focusing on such causes as ABOLITIONISM, women's rights, temperance, prison reform, and education. Education provided the unifying, homogenizing element needed in the society to deal with this diversity. Reformers such as Horace Mann in Massachusetts, Henry Barnard in Connecticut, and Samuel Lewis in Ohio led a simultaneous movement to establish a common school— not a school only for the common man, but a school for all, publicly supported and controlled, to train people for citizenship and economic power and to provide suitable moral training. The first state education act was passed in 1821 (though there are records of schools as early as 1803); it provided for control and support of common schools in the state. The language of the law was permissive, not mandatory. In 1825, a second law became more specific, providing for taxation for the use of schools, a Board of County Examiners, and the employment of only certificated persons as teachers. In 1837, the state passed a law establishing the position of state superintendent, to which Samuel Lewis was appointed. In 1853, a stronger law provided an augmented school fund, established a state education office, and strengthened local control. School enrollments began to increase, from a total of 456,191 in 1854 to 817,490 in 1895. The length of the school year also increased.

The first school reported in Cleveland was opened in 1817 and charged tuition. The CLEVELAND ACADEMY, built upon subscription, followed in 1821. When Cleveland was chartered in 1836, the first school supported by public money was opened. Two sections of the law related to schools allowed taxation for their support and gave the council the authority to fix the school year and to appoint a board of managers to administer the schools. These schools were to serve only white children at the elementary level. The first school for Negroes was opened in 1832 by JOHN MALVIN and was supported by subscription. The Board of Education built its first 2 schoolhouses in 1839–40. The first high school, CENTRAL HIGH SCHOOL, was opened in 1845, with ANDREW FREESE as principal. Superintendence of the schools began in 1841, and some of the notables included Freese, HARVEY RICE, Luther M. Oviatt, Rev. Anson Smythe, and Andrew J. Rickoff. The Board of Education was appointed by the council at first, but by 1859 it was elected, becoming fully autonomous in 1865 to levy and expend its own funds. Following the act of 1853, there were attempts to unify schools. A system of grades and classification of pupils was instituted, including a graded course of study, the adoption of methods of promotion, and the use of suitable graded textbooks. Students were often tested monthly, and records of their progress were kept. Even then many educators questioned this practice and whether it allowed for the individuality of the child. In 1877 the school board established a school for disruptive students. At this same time, the state passed a law compelling parents to send children ages 8–14 to school a minimum of 12 weeks a year.

At the turn of the 20th century, as the city grew and became more industrialized, the bureaucratic ethic and the cult of efficiency prevailed and influenced school practice. The schools used a pediocentric approach to students. An interest in education as a science was precipitated by the work of G. Stanley Hall, Edward L. Thorndike, and Sigmund Freud on a national level. The fledgling science of psychology provided an understanding of child growth and development. John Dewey and his colleagues at Columbia

University wrote of the needs of the individual students and the importance of experience as it relates to education. It was within this context of ferment that the education system in Cleveland grew. A program in manual training for high school students began in response to many of these events, and also to a growing pressure from the business community for more practical programs. This program later moved to Central High School and the Manual Training School in 1893. In 1887 a course in cooking was added, a first in the country. By 1909 the first technical and commercial high schools had been established. The school system met the needs of many of the immigrants by providing a place where they could learn English and civics. The board hired its first truant officer to enforce the compulsory attendance law of 1889. After passage of a state law mandating the education of disabled persons, the board opened the Cleveland Day School for the deaf, and it provided for the gifted by establishing the major work classes in 1922.

Further response to outside forces moved education beyond the traditional classroom. The schools offered children's concerts in cooperation with the CLEVELAND ORCHESTRA in 1921 and used RADIO (WBOE) as a means of instruction in 1931. By 1947, all grades in public, parochial, and private schools used this service. As a result of the strong influence of the field of child psychology, Lewis H. Jones, superintendent, established 6 kindergartens from 1896–97. Prior to this time, the YWCA had founded the DAY NURSERY & FREE KINDERGARTEN ASSOC. in 1882, with a free kindergarten in 1886. By 1903, the schools started vacation schools and playgrounds to keep the children off the streets and involved in physical activity. They also opened a gardening program for both normal and problem children and added medical services to the system in 1908. By 1918, the schools enrolled over 100,000 students in their many specialized schools and programs to provide an education best suited to each individual child. Citizenship training was studied by the Cleveland Chamber of Commerce in 1935. It recommended that public education be involved in training citizens who were informed about economic conditions. As a result, teachers toured industrial plants and attended lectures to see the application of business to their own classrooms.

Although the public school reforms of the Progressive Era, geared to the needs of the industrial commercial life of the times, were apparently beneficial to the society and the children, these efforts often were developed to limit the emerging political threat of the immigrants and the poor. These efforts continued, even though there were those such as Prof. Wm. Bagley of the University of Illinois who early warned of the social stratification created by separate vocational schools, and others who cautioned against the undue expansion of the public schools into areas that should be served by other institutions in the society. Investigations of the schools were also part of the efficiency cult. Commissions were formed to study student dropouts or new facilities. In 1905, SAMUEL ORTH, head of the school board, appointed an education study commission. Its report recommended a differentiation in the functions of the high schools and the establishment of separate commercial high schools. A much more significant study followed between 1915–16. The Ayres School Survey sponsored by the CLEVELAND FOUNDATION criticized the school system as inefficient and unprogressive and recommended a more centralized administration. In response, new superintendent Frank E. Spaulding developed new junior high and vocational programs and instituted a department of mental testing and a double-shift plan to relieve overcrowding and differentiation among students. Many felt an educational revival had occurred, though others would argue

that these new systems served better only those they had always served well.

Following WORLD WAR II, the launching of *Sputnik* affected the curriculum of the schools, emphasizing a turn to the study of languages and the hard sciences. Neoprogressivism then followed, where schools were asked to stop demanding the right answers from students, to stop being repressive, and to move to a reemphasis on the child as reflected in the informal classroom movement. This period was also one of growth, with many buildings being added to school districts, notably those in Cleveland led by Superintendent Paul Briggs, who was appointed in 1964. Focus was also placed upon the inequitable features of American education and the racial caste system the school had maintained. Opportunity for education was to be made available to all youngsters, without regard to race, creed, national origin, sex, or family background. The nation had been alerted, and it was necessary to act once again through the schools, even if that action took the form of court cases. Such was the situation in the Cleveland schools. The Cleveland School Desegregation Case (*Reed* v. *Rhodes*) was filed in the U.S. District Court on 12 Dec. 1973. The trial began before Chief Judge Frank J. Battisti on 24 Nov. 1975 and concluded on 19 Mar. 1976. An opinion was issued where state and local defendants were held liable for policies that intentionally created and/or maintained a segregated system. In Dec. 1976, the court issued guidelines for desegregation planning, to begin by 8 Sept. 1977. The state and local boards appealed the case to the 6th Circuit Court of Appeals. Judge Battisti felt that the Cleveland school officials were resisting the court order, and several desegregation plans were mandated, rejected, and resubmitted. By Dec. 1977, the court ordered the establishment of a Dept. of Desegregation Implementation responsible only to the court; it was terminated in 1982. In May 1978, the court established an office of school monitoring and community relations to monitor the schools, an unprecedented action. In June 1978, a final desegregation plan necessitated the closing of 36 schools and the transportation of students. By 23 Aug. 1979, the 6th Circuit Court affirmed the district court's decision of the board's liability and the remedy, which included educational remedies such as special reading programs. Desegregation began and was often met with resistance, but busing was implemented peacefully, and it appeared that the educational results were positive.

Paralleling the events in public education were strong private, parochial, and alternative school initiatives. These movements evolved out of political movements and the goals of parents who wanted more control over the governance of schooling for their children. Early-19th-century reformers saw the common school as a vehicle to mix nationality, socioeconomic, and immigrant groups. Their vision often did not coincide with the wishes of their constituency. Cleveland's Catholic population followed the prescriptions of the bishops, who began as early as 1825 to question public education, which they deemed to be Protestant-oriented. By 1884, the 3d Plenary Council of Baltimore required schools for Catholic children to be built next to each church. The first Catholic school in Cleveland was opened in 1848, and by 1884 there were 123 PAROCHIAL SCHOOLS with 26,000 children enrolled. By 1909, several significant schools were added by Bp. JOHN P. FARRELLY, including CATHEDRAL LATIN SCHOOL. Catholic education was organized under the Diocese of Cleveland, and the first superintendent of schools was Rev. Wm. A. Kane, appointed in 1913, with the first school board appointed by Bp. JOSEPH SCHREMBS in 1922. Other religious groups followed. The first Lutheran school was established in 1848, and by 1943 there were 16 others. Other nationality and religious groups also ran schools, often meeting after the public school day had finished or as Sunday schools.

PRIVATE SCHOOLS were an important part of Cleveland's educational history, evolving from the academic movement of the 20th century. A Mission School for poor children became the Ragged School in 1853 and then the City Industrial School, from which the CHILDREN'S AID SOCIETY developed in 1858. One of the early private independent schools, UNIVERSITY SCHOOL, was started by Newton M. Anderson in 1890, as a result of a perceived overcrowding in public schools and a desire for needed new trends in education. LAUREL SCHOOL had its beginnings as Wade Park School for Girls in 1896, and HATHAWAY BROWN was founded in 1886, its forerunner being MISS MITTLEBERGER'S SCHOOL. HAWKEN SCHOOL was founded in 1915. Reflecting the 1960s political milieu, parents started the alternative-schools movement. These ALTERNATIVE SCHOOLS ranged from the Urban Community School, founded in 1968, which was neoprogressivist in philosophy, serving a multicultural population, to the Cleveland Urban Learning Community (CULC), a school without walls whose classes occurred in the community and that appealed to nontraditional students. In addition, many public schools developed alternative programs on the model of a school within a school. These were programs that emphasized individualized approaches geared in nontraditional delivery formats. The alternative-schools movement was supported mainly through foundation funds. These provided for initial costs, but the schools could not be sustained on this basis. They began to experience financial difficulties, forcing several to close as a result. However, some continued by garnering ongoing support or by affiliating with established institutions.

The Western Reserve area can also claim credit for efforts in TEACHER EDUCATION with the organization of the Ohio State Teachers Assoc., and in 1869 the NORTHEAST OHIO TEACHERS ASSOC. The CLEVELAND TEACHERS UNION, an affiliate of the American Fed. of Teachers, was founded in 1933. Some of the early academies, such as Wadsworth, were institutions similar to high schools and prepared students for higher education and/or teaching. This area became known as a source of teachers for the state. In 1839 the Western Reserve Teachers Seminary was opened at Kirtland, founded only 2 years after the first normal school in the U.S. Superintendent Andrew Rickoff inaugurated a week-long teacher-training institute in 1869 and a normal school in 1876 at Eagle Elementary School. He also proposed a merit pay system. Subsequently, the Cleveland School of Education, Western Reserve University, and the Board of Education offered courses for teacher in-service training. In 1928 the university established a School of Education, which was a merger of the Cleveland Kindergarten-Primary Training School, a private school founded in 1894, and the Senior Teachers College. Secondary teachers were prepared at WRU. Later, in 1945, the university established a division of education, responsible for providing the professional education courses required for state certification, and a graduate program, which was discontinued in the 1970s.

The first CLEVELAND UNIVERSITY in 1852 had a brief rise and a rapid decline in 1856. Cleveland had already established its first medical school in 1845 when 6 doctors seceded from Willoughby Medical College and reorganized in Cleveland as the medical school of Hudson's Western Reserve College. Other institutions that were established were the Western Reserve College of Homeopathic Medicine in 1850, lasting for several decades, and a School of

Commerce, also in the 1850s. In 1880, Case School of Applied Science was founded to offer an engineering curriculum, the first west of the Alleghenies. Western Reserve College, originally founded in Hudson, Ohio, moved to Cleveland. AMASA STONE provided for endowment and buildings for the move, stipulating that the college be renamed for his son, Adelbert, and located close to Case School. In 1888 the trustees created a separate women's college, which eventually was named Flora Stone Mather College. It was the first coordinate college in the country. At the end of the 19th century, WRU added a graduate school, a law school, nursing and dental schools, a school of library science, and a school of applied social sciences. CASE WESTERN RESERVE UNIVERSITY resulted as a merger of the two institutions in 1967. BALDWIN-WALLACE COLLEGE in BEREA was founded by Methodists in the mid-1850s. These private colleges were primarily Protestant-oriented. The growing number of Catholic immigrants at the end of the 19th century sought another environment. St. Ignatius College was established by the Jesuits on the near west side of Cleveland in 1886. It was later renamed JOHN CARROLL UNIVERSITY and moved to UNIVERSITY HTS. in the 1920s. The first chartered women's college in Ohio was founded by Ursuline sisters in 1871. The Sisters of Notre Dame established an academy in downtown Cleveland in the 1870s, and later NOTRE DAME COLLEGE. The YMCA sponsored evening college-level classes for working students. By 1923, they added day classes and a cooperative plan whereby students held jobs related to their business courses and engineers pursued courses at Fenn College. In the 1920s, Cleveland College of WRU was established in downtown Cleveland to serve the needs of the employed population. DYKE COLLEGE resulted in 1942 from a merger of one of the nation's oldest private commercial schools, Spencerian, with Dyke School of Commerce, dating from 1893.

Colleges did not grow in any major way until the sudden increase in the number of young people of college age in the 1960s. Formerly the emphasis had been on the private colleges, but after World War II, there was a steady increase in the percentage of students attending public institutions. The CLEVELAND COMMISSION ON HIGHER EDUCATION, a coalition of college presidents and business interests, completed a study in the 1950s that recommended that some type of public higher education be offered in Cleveland. In 1958 the Ohio Commission on Education beyond the High School was established, and it made recommendations for the founding of 2-year colleges or technical institutes financed by the state, local funds, and student fees. That led finally to the founding of CUYAHOGA COMMUNITY COLLEGE in 1963, and later to its 3 campuses. In 1964, CLEVELAND STATE UNIVERSITY was established to provide a public university education in the downtown Cleveland area. It included the old Fenn College, a law school, and science and health structures, among others. Higher education experienced significant growth, but as it moves into the last 2 decades of the century, it will increasingly deal with the effects of a declining traditional student population, unless it decides to attract nontraditional student groups such as older students.

Sally H. Wertheim
John Carroll University

The **EDUCATIONAL RESEARCH COUNCIL OF AMERICA,** located in the ROCKEFELLER BLDG., was originally known as the Educational Research Council of Greater Cleveland. An independent, not-for-profit, nongovernmental research and development center, it was founded in 1957–58 by Dr. Geo. H. Baird, Cleveland educator, administrator, and businessman, who believed that elementary and secondary school EDUCATION in America needed to be improved, primarily through curriculum reform. He initially gained the support of Van H. Leichliter, Cleveland industrialist, and subsequently obtained the necessary financial support from foundations, Cleveland businessmen, and grants from private industry. The council incorporated in July 1958 with Dr. Baird as executive director.

The council began functioning in Mar. 1959, after 9 school systems (public, private, and parochial) in the Greater Cleveland area joined. Initially, their membership fee entitled them to curriculum material devised by the council and the opportunity to participate in conferences, workshops, and in-service training programs. Original curriculum materials, both student books and accompanying teacher guides, were prepared collaboratively by the professional council staff, teams of classroom teachers, school administrators, and educational consultants who were specialists in their respective fields. The first of these, a series of books on mathematics, achieved nationwide attention for its innovative approaches and was used in many school systems throughout the country. In 1962, Science Research Associates, Inc., of Chicago published these materials.

In Mar. 1962, the council published an interdisciplinary, sequential, concept-oriented social-science program. Materials were tested in the classrooms, revised, and retested before final publication. It was estimated that students from more than 27 participating school districts across the country used this material; subsequently the Allyn & Bacon Co. published the program. In addition to these programs, materials for a reading program, a career awareness program, and a physical education program were developed. In Sept. 1967, the Educational Research Council of Greater Cleveland became the Educational Research Council of America. The council continued to receive funds from participating school systems, from numerous foundations, and from Cleveland industry for its services'; however, as more and more school districts developed their own research programs, they withdrew from the council, and it gradually curtailed many of its activities. Dr. Baird retired from the organization in 1983.

**EELLS, DAN PARMELEE** (16 Apr. 1825–23 Aug. 1903), was a banker and financier active in a number of business ventures and philanthropic organizations in Cleveland. Eells was born in Westmoreland, N.Y., the son of a Presbyterian minister. The family moved to Ohio in 1831, settling in Amherst in 1837. Eells attended high school in Elyria in 1839–40 and in Oberlin in 1841; he entered Oberlin College in 1843 but transferred to Hamilton College in Clinton, N.Y., in 1844. He left college to support himself in 1846, teaching district school in Amherst in 1846–47, then working as a bookkeeper in the Cleveland commission house of Barney, Warring & Co. until 1849. He continued his studies by correspondence, however, and graduated from Hamilton in 1848. In Mar. 1849, Eells became a bookkeeper in the Commercial Branch of the State Bank of Ohio in Cleveland. He advanced, becoming a teller in 1853 and a cashier in 1858. When the bank was reorganized as the Commercial Natl. Bank of Cleveland in 1865, Eells was vice-president of the new institution; he was elected its president on 7 Dec. 1868 and served in that capacity until retiring in July 1897. As a bank officer, Eells played a role in financing a number of companies. He served as a director of 32 firms in various cities and held an executive position in 15 of these. He held interests in oil refineries, iron and

steel companies, cement manufacturers, coke and gas works, and 6 railroads.

Eells was also active in educational, charitable, and religious organizations in Cleveland and elsewhere. He was a member of the Cleveland Board of Education from 1865–68 and served as a trustee of Lane Theological Seminary, Lake Erie College, Oberlin College, and his alma mater, Hamilton College. He was president and trustee of the Cleveland YMCA; president of the Cleveland Bible Society; treasurer of both the Protestant Orphans' Asylum and the Home for Aged Women; and both treasurer and vice-president of the CHILDREN'S AID SOCIETY and the BETHEL UNION. In 1882, Eells bought land at the corner of Lexington and Willson (E. 55th St.) avenues and built the Willson Ave. Presbyterian Church, which was renamed the Eells Memorial Presbyterian Church in 1903. In Sept. 1849, Eells married Mary M. Howard, who died in 1859. He was married again, in Jan. 1861, to Mary Witt. Eells's son, Howard Parmelee Eells (16 June 1855–11 Feb. 1919), had a son whom he named Dan Parmelee Eells (24 Sept. 1884–14 Oct. 1959). The younger Dan Eells spent most of his career in Milwaukee, where he went in 1907 to work for the Bucyrus Steam Shovel & Dredge Co., which had been formed by his father and grandfather in Cleveland in 1880 as the Bucyrus Foundry & Mfg. Co. It was renamed and moved to Milwaukee in 1892.

Howard P. Eells, Jr., Family Papers, WRHS.

The **EIGHTEENTH PROVOST MARSHAL DISTRICT OF OHIO** (1863–65), with headquarters in Cleveland, was created by the Enrollment Act of 3 Mar. 1863, passed by the U.S. Congress, to furnish additional federal troops for service in the CIVIL WAR. The 18th District supplanted the 11TH MILITARY DISTRICT as the coordinating body for troop recruitment in the Cleveland area. Its administration extended to Cuyahoga, Lake, and Summit counties. The district was administered through an enrollment board consisting of the district provost marshal, a licensed physician, and a commissioner, all of whom were federally appointed. The board was empowered to enroll men eligible for military service, conscript and draft troops, determine draft exemptions, muster drafted men into service, locate and apprehend draft evaders, and arrest deserters and spies. During 1864, the district administered 3 federal drafts (Feb.-Mar., July, and Dec.). Only 4,250 men were drafted throughout the state in this period, and because of exemptions only 54 men actually saw service. The 18th District was considered one of the most poorly administered of the 19 established in Ohio. Frederick Nash, who administered the district from 1863-Feb. 1865, was brought to trial several times on charges that he extorted money from draftees and accepted bribes in return for exemptions. Nash, a captain in federal service, was eventually acquitted of the charges and honorably discharged from the service.

Murdock, Eugene C., *Ohio's Bounty System in the Civil War* (1963).

The **EIGHTH OHIO VOLUNTEER INFANTRY REGIMENT** was organized 29 Apr.–2 May 1861 at Camp Taylor, located at the corner of Hudson and Kinsman streets. The 9 companies of the 8th were made up of men from northern Ohio. Co. B represented the Hibernian Guards, a military society of Cleveland. The regiment was mustered into service for 3 months on 2 May. It transferred on 3 May to Camp Dennison, located 15 mi. from Cincinnati. When Lincoln called for regiments of 3 years' duration, the 9 companies answered the call on 22 June. In July, the regiment was transferred to the West Virginia theater of operations, where it engaged in a number of skirmishes. It participated in the Shenandoah Valley Campaign against the forces of Gen. "Stonewall" Jackson from Mar.-June 1862, when it was sent to the Peninsula region of Virginia. The regiment was involved in the Maryland Campaign from 6–22 Sept. It gained distinction at the Battle of Antietam of 17 Sept. From that point on, the 8th Ohio was recognized as one of the most disciplined and dependable regiments of the Army of the Potomac.

The 8th played an honorable role in the Battle of Fredericksburg on 13 Dec. 1862 and the Chancellorsville Campaign from 27 Apr.-6 May 1863. Its greatest glory, however, was achieved during the Battle of Gettysburg. On 2 July, the regiment was ordered forward beyond the Emmitsburg Rd. to drive Confederate skirmishers from a position where they had been annoying the Union line. It remained entrenched at this point, unrelieved and undergoing constant enemy fire, throughout 2–3 July. It was still in this advanced position during what has commonly been called Pickett's Charge. The regiment was attacked by superior numbers and not only was able to successfully repel the enemy but also nearly captured all the surviving members of 3 Confederate regiments. Following the Battle of Gettysburg, the 8th was placed on detached duty to New York City in order to restore order following the draft riots of July. It returned to the Army of the Potomac in September and was engaged in a number of skirmishes until spring 1864.

The regiment participated in the Wilderness Campaign from 3 May–15 June 1864, where it again gained distinction for its gallant service. It remained entrenched before Petersburg, Va., until 25 June, when its term of service expired. The 8th returned to Cleveland on 3 July and was met at the train station by Mayor GEO. B. SENTER, a delegation from the Military Committee of Cleveland, and the Temperance Brass Band. After the reception, the regiment marched to Wheeler & Russell's Dining Hall for breakfast. A program followed, ending in a procession down Water and Superior streets to Camp Cleveland, located in TREMONT. The regiment was officially mustered out of service on 13 July 1864. A total of 205 members of the 8th Ohio died during its term of service, including 8 officers and 124 enlisted men killed or mortally wounded in battle and 1 officer and 72 enlisted men from disease. Monuments to the 8th Ohio stand prominently at the battlefield sites of Antietam and Gettysburg.

Galwey, Thomas Francis, *The Valiant Hours* (1961).
Sawyer, Franklin, *A Military History of the Eighth Regiment* (1881).

The **EIGHTY-FOURTH OHIO VOLUNTEER INFANTRY REGIMENT** (1862) contained 2 companies from Cleveland during its 3-month period of service in the CIVIL WAR. The 84th was organized at Camp Chase in Columbus, Ohio, in May and June 1862. Companies D and E were recruited by the CLEVELAND GRAYS. The regiment was ordered to Cumberland, Md., on 11 June 1862, where it became part of the Railroad District Dept. of the Mountains until July 1862. Its operations and actions there included provost duty, after which it was assigned to the 8th Army Corps, Middle Dept., until September. The regiment was then sent to Columbus and mustered out at Camp Chase on 14 Oct. Losses were listed as 14 men killed by disease.

Henry L. Burnham Diary, WRHS.

**EINSTEIN, RUTH** (1883–20 June 1977), was a Jewish community leader for over half a century and was the principal moving force behind the creation of Council Gardens. She was born in Cleveland, the daughter of Abraham Wiener and granddaughter of Abraham Aub, a founder and long-time president of the Jewish Orphan Home (see BELLEFAIRE). She was a graduate of the College for Women of Western Reserve University. Einstein joined the board of trustees of the NATL. COUNCIL OF JEWISH WOMEN, CLEVELAND SEC., in 1920 and remained a trustee until her death. In 1920, she was among the founders of the Jewish Big Sisters Assoc., an affiliate of NCJW. In 1922, she suggested the idea of training volunteers, which subsequently became a major part of the NCJW program. During the Depression, she helped establish educational and vocational classes for the unemployed through NCJW and conceived the idea for Council Thrift Shops, which became a major fundraising vehicle for the organization. In 1954, Einstein developed the idea for a low-rent, nonsectarian apartment complex for the well elderly. Through her fundraising and lobbying efforts, the Council Gardens project was begun in 1960. The units, located at Mayfield and Taylor roads, were opened in 1963. Einstein was chair of the Council Gardens board of directors from 1960–64. Besides her work for NCJW, Einstein was a board member of Bellefaire, the JEWISH COMMUNITY FED., the JEWISH FAMILY SERVICE ASSOC., and the MONTEFIORE HOME. In 1964, she was given the Chas. Eisenman Service Award for community service by the JCF. In 1965, she received a special citation for service from the United Appeal, and in 1972 she was given the Hannah Solomon Award by the national office of the NCJW for service to the organization. Einstein was married in 1903 to Jac L. Einstein, who died in 1919. They had 2 children, Paul Eden and Edith.

**EISENMAN, CHARLES** (1865–9 March 1923), clothing manufacturer and philanthropist, was an organizer and first president of the Fed. of Jewish Charities in Cleveland. Born in New York City, he moved to Cleveland as a young man and was cofounder of the K & E Co. (later the Kaynee Co.), manufacturers of shirts and blouses. Eisenman was a product of the Progressive Era and brought to his business endeavors the belief in the oneness of business and social action. He believed that good working conditions and fair treatment of employees encouraged productivity, and he opposed the organizing of trade unions as an infringement on the rights of the employer to provide for the welfare of the workers. Following the accumulation of considerable wealth, Eisenman retired in 1906 to devote his energies to PHILANTHROPY.

In 1903, Eisenman was one of 9 men who met to form the Fed. of Jewish Charities for the purpose of organizing the local Jewish charitable organizations in order better to facilitate fundraising and curtail duplication of services. He was elected president, a position he held until his death. Unlike many of the other organizers of the FJC, Eisenman did not represent the interests of an existing charitable agency. His view of charitable activity was broad but practically based. He opposed including organizations in the FJC that could not demonstrate an ability to raise funds from their constituents. He proposed including only "matured" immigrant organizations as federation affiliates. Eisenman was one of the principal supporters of the establishment of a Jewish hospital in Cleveland. He favored the attempt to establish a kosher kitchen at MT. SINAI HOSPITAL, although he recognized that the attempt would be a failure. Eisenman was active in the American Jewish Committee and the American Jewish Relief Committee, an organization created to assist European Jews who suffered disabilities during WORLD WAR I. He was an organizer and active member of the Cleveland Community Fund Council until his death. During World War I, he was chairman of the Council of the Natl. Defense Committee on Purchases & Supplies and was awarded the District Service Medal for his work. Eisenman was survived by his wife, the former Bertha Hays, who died in Nov. 1941.

**EISENMANN, JOHN** (1851–6 Jan. 1924), architect of the ARCADE and author of Cleveland's first comprehensive building code, was born in Detroit. He received his early education in Monroe, Mich., and graduated from the University of Michigan in 1871. He headed the U.S. geodetic survey of the Great Lakes and the St. Lawrence and Mississippi rivers until he contracted jaundice and was forced to take a 2-year leave of absence. During this period he studied architecture at the polytechnics of Munich and Stuttgart, graduating from the latter institution. He returned to his former post with the geodetic survey and in 1882 came to Cleveland to take a position as professor of civil engineering at the Case School of Applied Science. When Case was moved from Rockwell Ave. downtown to UNIVERSITY CIRCLE, Eisenmann drew the plans for the first building (1885). In 1880–90 he designed, with GEO. H. SMITH, the Arcade. In 1904, at the request of Mayor TOM L. JOHNSON, Eisenmann wrote the first comprehensive building code for the city of Cleveland, on which many other cities later modeled their own codes (see BUILDING CODE 1904).

Eisenmann was a member of the AMERICAN INSTITUTE OF ARCHITECTS CLEVELAND CHAP. and of the Civil Engineering Club of Cleveland. As a member of the Wade Park Commission, he participated in the early planning of the Wade Park area. He is also credited with designing the Ohio state flag. Among the pioneers of structural-steel construction, Eisenmann also invented and patented "Mannel," a hollow building tile. Upon his death in 1924, his widow, Anna M., revealed that Eisenmann had mortgaged their Crawford Rd. home to raise funds with which to draw up plans for the Perry Memorial at Put-in-Bay when the project was first proposed. Another plan had been chosen, and, bitterly disappointed, Eisenmann began to fail in health. Before he died, he requested that his ashes be scattered from the top of the Perry monument.

**ELECTRICAL AND ELECTRONICS INDUSTRIES.** The first significant application of controlled electricity in Cleveland was telegraphy, which made its appearance in the city in 1847 on the premises of the Lake Erie Telegraph Co. Fire-alarm boxes were the second useful manifestation of the "new" power in the city, and by 1865 there were 24 of them. The telephone came in 1877. Besides these communications uses, the other main areas of electric-industrial progress in the latter part of the 19th century were lighting, traction, and industrial motors, and in these areas, as well, Cleveland's technical-entrepreneurial talent was quick to perceive opportunities and act on them.

In the lighting field, CHAS. F. BRUSH was the most prominent innovator and entrepreneur of the period. His major renown was based on the practical development and commercial exploitation of the arc light. Although the latter was invented in England in 1808, it was Brush who brought it into practical application by developing an improved dynamo to provide a steady current, and by making design changes in the arc fixture itself that improved the quality of the light and extended the working life of the carbon electrodes. He also redesigned the lamp's circuit in such a way as to make arc lighting from central stations possible. Brush began to sell arc lighting systems of limited size in the late 1870s for use in such locations as stores,

factories, and hotels. However, the extensive future potential of this equipment was first realized with Brush's demonstration of its street-lighting possibilities on 29 Apr. 1879, in Cleveland's PUBLIC SQUARE. The brilliance of the light produced at this well-attended event by his 12 lamps caused a sensation and foretold the decline of the gas-lighting era. Brush was soon selling central power stations to cities such as San Francisco, New York, Baltimore, Boston, and Philadelphia. The Cleveland Telegraph Supply Co., where he had done the developmental work, was bought out by Brush in 1880 and renamed the Brush Electric Co. The battle between electric lighting and gas was a vigorous one. In 1883, CLEVELAND CITY COUNCIL, viewing comparative costs, voted to go back to gas light. (It reversed itself, however, 17 days later.) Advances were made in gas-lighting technology, and the struggle between the two systems lasted a total of some 30 years before electricity won out. At the same time that Brush was bringing out his arc light, Thos. Edison was designing a practical incandescent lamp at his Menlo Park, N.J., laboratory. This development later came to have great significance for Cleveland, because the companies that came together in 1906 to form the Natl. Electric Lamp Assoc. centered much of their light-bulb production in this area. When the NELA was taken over fully by the GENERAL ELECTRIC CO. in 1912, becoming the Natl. Quality Lamp Div. of that corporation, it moved to a unique setting in the eastern Cleveland SUBURBS. NELA PARK, as it was named, was a new phenomenon—the industrial park. It took the leading role in GE's incandescent lighting development program from 1915 until 1935, when fluorescent lighting research became prominent.

The equipment for the first electric streetcar line in the Cleveland area was worked out and tested in the shops of the Brush Electric Co., and it was a Brush generator in the car barn that powered the line from its start-up, in 1884. The line, which operated as the E. CLEVELAND RAILWAY CO., had technical problems with its underground power supply cable and closed down the following year. Work continued, however, and a successor line reached Public Square from its home station in E. CLEVELAND in 1889. It was followed by the electrification of other local car lines in the area.

Led by the expansion of applications in communications, lighting, and traction, the Cleveland-area electrical industry grew rapidly during the 1800s. The Brush Electric Co. added the manufacture of arc light carbons to its activities and also began marketing an incandescent lighting system, the rights for which it had purchased from a British firm. As the use of electricity expanded, the need grew for added power-generation and -distribution facilities. In 1892, the Brush Electric & Power Co. merged with the Cleveland Electric Light Co., and a large powerhouse was constructed on Canal St. These developments led to the formation, during the same year, of the CLEVELAND ELECTRIC ILLUMINATING CO. By 1900, Cleveland ranked first in the production of electric automobiles. At the end of the century's first decade, it also claimed first place in the production of carbons, lamps, and electrical hoisting apparatus. Its status as the site of a major exposition of the electrical industry in 1914 further promoted Cleveland's claim to primacy.

The 1895 discovery of "x-rays" by the German scientist Wilhelm Roentgen touched off considerable activity in Cleveland. A professor of physics at the Case School of Applied Science, DAYTON C. MILLER, was interested in exploiting the potential medical applications of the newly discovered form of electromagnetic radiation. He worked diligently to improve the x-raying process, which at first was slow and expensive. The x-ray industry in Cleveland had another pioneer at the turn of the century in Henry P. Engeln. Engeln, in collaboration with Dr. Geo. Iddings, established the Engeln Electric Co. which, by the time of its merger into the American X-Ray Corp. in 1929, had 200 employees. This merger was unsuccessful, and the new company was acquired by the Westinghouse Electric & Mfg. Co. in 1930. During its independent life, the Engeln Co. did highly innovative work in the development and marketing of x-ray equipment. Soon after the acquisition of the company by Westinghouse, its plant at E. 30th St. and Superior was purchased by Picker X-Ray (see PICKER INTERNATL.), which became a leading firm in that field.

An important industrial application of electrical technology that flourished in Cleveland was arc welding. Here, the entrepreneurial skill of John C. Lincoln, founder of the LINCOLN ELECTRIC CO., was noteworthy. Lincoln, who had gained experience working in Chas. F. Brush's shops, started a small business in 1896 producing electric motors. As the firm grew, it became specialized in arc-welding equipment, and by 1938 it was an international company claiming to be the largest manufacturer of that line in the world. The electrical motor concerns became the province of a separate entity, the Lincoln Motor Co., which was incorporated in 1906 and changed its name to the RELIANCE ELECTRIC CO. in 1909.

From 1901–06, the federation of companies in the lighting business known as the Natl. Electric Lamp Co. was in an unusual sort of "friendly competition" with General Electric—i.e., the latter actually held a majority ownership position in the NELC, acting as "silent partner" in this ostensibly competing group. This unusual arrangement persisted until 1911, when a federal court ruling required GE to take over the NELA (the word *Company* in the federation's title had been changed to *Association* in 1906), formally and fully. Nela Park, opened the next year, thus became a GE venture—although it required some initial argumentation by National's leaders to convince GE that the project made business sense.

In addition to lighting, traction, and industrial applications, the electrical home-appliance field was richly represented in Cleveland production enterprises by the time of WORLD WAR I. Heating-related appliances included coffee percolators, hot plates, frying pans, corn poppers, baby-bottle warmers, kitchen ranges, hair dryers, and radiant heaters. In addition, there was heavy production of vacuum cleaners, washing machines, fans, vibrators, and sewing machines. By 1919, Cleveland led the nation in the production of electric batteries and vacuum cleaners (7 different makes of vacuum cleaners were being produced in the city in 1931). As of the mid-1920s, Cleveland ranked 3d in the production of radios, after New York and Chicago. Theodore A. Willard, whose WILLARD STORAGE BATTERY CO. was Cleveland's largest battery producer, founded the city's first high-powered radio station, WTAM. By 1938, the Willard Co.'s 15-acre plant, built in 1914, was turning out 15,000 batteries per day.

In the 1920s, John A. Victoreen, an inventive Cleveland radio amateur, started a radio parts business. Soon, however, his attention turned to radiation measurement, and he developed the Condenser R-Meter, an instrument for measuring accurately the intensity and total dosage of x-ray delivery, which gained international fame. The Victoreen Instrument Co. was founded in 1928, in CLEVELAND HTS. Radiation measurement remained a central concern; the company provided 95% of the instrumentation for the Bikini atomic bomb tests, soon after WORLD WAR II, earning itself claim to the title of "first nuclear company."

With the coming of World War II, Cleveland electrical firms reorganized their production around the needs of the military. One example was the manufacture of miniature radio tubes at Nela Park for use in proximity fuses for antiaircraft artillery shells. Lighting and visibility research of varied kinds, devoted to military problems, also occupied much of the time of the GE laboratories there. War production helped bring about the establishment of the new Electronics Dept. at GE, with formal inauguration in 1947. The postwar period, as well, was one of rapid growth for the industry. In the Cleveland metropolitan area, electrical machinery manufacturing, for example, grew in value-added terms by 21% in the 1947–54 period. *Fortune* magazine's list of the 500 largest industrial corporations for 1958 included 2 electrically related Cleveland-area firms, Reliance Electric and the Addressograph-Multigraph Corp.

The demand for power was growing rapidly even before the onset of war pressed it more urgently. Between 1939–44, the Cleveland Electric Illuminating Co.'s output increased by 30%. In the last year of that period, 76% of the power the company produced went to industry, with an estimated 90% of that being war industry. By 1946, CEI could count 370,000 customers, in contrast to the 1,400 it had had at the turn of the century. Its service covered 132 communities, with a total population of 1.5 million. Relatively low power rates attracted new industries to the area. Growth continued, and in 1954 the company was serving 465,000 customers in 137 communities, from Avon Lake on the west to Conneaut in the east. CEI's rates have on occasion become a political issue in Cleveland, the sensitivity of the question being increased by the fact that the city early established, and has maintained, a municipally owned power company. That has caused disputes over comparative rates, and has also brought up for recurring debate the question of whether the city should sell its electrical utility and thus get out of the competitive power business (see MUNICIPAL OWNERSHIP).

Leading the list of Cleveland companies active in the electronics field during the immediate postwar period were the Hickok Electrical Instruments Co., Victoreen Instrument Co., and Brush Development Co. In 1946, Victoreen was the city's major producer of electronic tubes, employed 75 people, and achieved a total output worth $4.5 million. Cleveland Electronics, Inc., was representative of other firms in the area engaged in the production of electronic goods. By 1946, it was turning out 50,000–60,000 radio loudspeakers per month and preparing to manufacture similar components for the new television industry. The Hickok Co. manufactured precision radio and radar test equipment, and was active in exporting. Brush Development, which was founded in 1930 to exploit some of the products developed by Brush Laboratories, was producing voice-recording equipment. It had entered that field in 1938, and during the war was the main supplier of wire recording equipment to the armed forces. For industry, Brush made oscillographs and hypersonic analyzers, piezoelectric crystals, and other products. Natl. Spectrographic Laboratories, Inc., another Cleveland firm, made electrical excitation units for spectrographic analysis. Phasing devices and tuning-fork frequency controls were produced by Acme Telectronix, while the Bird Electronic Corp. manufactured testing equipment, filters, and high-frequency antennas. The total value of the city's electronic products for the year 1946 was more than $10 million.

Cleveland, while not industrially top-ranked among centers of the rapidly developing microelectronics field, has establishments that have made a considerable mark in it nonetheless. On the research and development side, the well-established solid-state microelectronics laboratory at

CASE WESTERN RESERVE UNIVERSITY pursues studies in the area of integrated circuits, electronic materials, and new processing technologies. The university's programs contribute importantly to the area's electronic industry by providing graduate engineers and computer specialists. The NASA LEWIS RESEARCH CTR. is heavily involved in applied microelectronics in connection with its responsibilities in space communications. Among larger Cleveland-area manufacturing firms having a substantial stake in the electronics field is TRW, Inc. This company plays an active part in the aerospace and defense industries, developing both spacecraft and the payloads for them, communications and guidance systems, and ground station equipment. Bailey Controls, the electronics arm of the BABCOCK & WILCOX CO., has its world headquarters in Wickliffe, just east of Cleveland. While its industrial-controls products also include pneumatic, hydraulic, and mechanical components, the heart of the technology is electronics. The firm provides analog and digital circuit design, producing control systems of varying complexity. With a long history of supplying equipment for utilities, Bailey Controls has provided instrumentation for the nuclear power-generating industry since the latter's inception.

Allen-Bradley, now a subsidiary of Rockwell Internatl., is a long-established area firm producing programmable controllers and similar capital goods, incorporating electronics, for manufacturing industries. Keithley Instruments, Inc., based in SOLON, had its beginnings in a high-impedance amplifier, called the "Phantom Repeater," invented by Joseph Keithley in 1946. For the next 5 years, this and other Keithley-developed instruments were manufactured for him by another firm under contractual arrangements; then, in 1951, Keithley moved his operation to larger quarters and began manufacturing on his own. Sensitive measuring instruments remained the core of the company's output, which came to include voltmeters, ammeters, digital multimeters, and complex testing systems incorporating both computer hardware and software. The company's product-development path in itself traces some of the most important steps in the technological advance of electronics since the 1940s—vacuum tubes to discrete transistors to integrated circuits, and finally, to complex computer-linked systems that can handle the tasks of measurement and computation virtually simultaneously.

Peter Diaconoff

See also INDUSTRY, TELEGRAPHY & TELEPHONES.

The **ELEVENTH MILITARY DISTRICT OF OHIO,** with headquarters in Cleveland, was one of 11 recruiting districts established throughout the state by proclamation of Gov. David Tod on 8 July 1862. The districts were established to coordinate the recruitment of soldiers for service in the CIVIL WAR. A total of 22 regiments, totaling over 30,000 men, were to be created in the state. Each district was limited to the recruitment of men from within its boundaries. The 11th District included Cuyahoga, Lorain, Medina, Mahoning, Trumbull, Geauga, Lake, and Ashtabula counties. Of the 4 regiments raised in the district, 2, the 103D OHIO VOLUNTEER INFANTRY and the 124TH VOLUNTEER INFANTRY, consisted largely of Cleveland-area men and were trained at Camp Cleveland (see CIVIL WAR CAMPS).

Harper, Robert S., *Ohio Handbook of the Civil War* (1961).

The **ELISABETH SEVERANCE PRENTISS FOUNDATION** was founded in 1939 by Elisabeth Severance Allen Prentiss (1865–1944), Luther L. Miller, and Kate W. Miller.

Elisabeth Prentiss was the daughter of Louis H. and Fannie Benedict Severance. Her father, a pioneer in the oil industry, was an associate of JOHN D. ROCKEFELLER in the original STANDARD OIL CO. of Ohio. Elisabeth Severance married twice, first to one of Cleveland's most distinguished surgeons, DUDLEY PETER ALLEN, for whom the Allen Memorial Library was named. After Dr. Allen's death, she married (1917) FRANCIS FLEURY PRENTISS, Cleveland industrialist and philanthropist. Mrs. Prentiss was awarded the Cleveland Medal for Public Service in 1928 and an honorary Doctor of Humanities degree from Western Reserve University in 1942 for her gifts to ART, MUSIC, and health care in Cleveland. She was a trustee of and donor to the CLEVELAND MUSEUM OF ART, a trustee of the MUSICAL ARTS ASSOC., and a patron of hospitals and medical associations, both at Oberlin College and in Cleveland.

The purpose of the Prentiss Foundation is specifically medical, "for the promotion of medical and surgical research, to assist in the acquisition, advancement and dissemination of knowledge of medicine and surgery, and of means of maintaining health; to improve methods of hospital management and administration; to support programs to make hospital and medical care available to all." Grants are limited to the Greater Cleveland area, especially to ST. LUKE'S HOSPITAL. No grants are given to individuals, national fundraising organizations, or foundations, for scholarships or fellowships, or for matching gifts or loans. In 1983, the assets of the foundation were $30,350,195, with expenditures of $2,003,653 for 15 grants. Officers of the foundation include Theodore W. Jones, Quentin Alexander, Harry J. Bolwell, Wm. J. DeLancey, and Wm. A. Mattie.

The **ELIZA BRYANT CENTER,** opened in 1897 as the Cleveland Home for Aged Colored People, was the first nonreligious institution sponsored by blacks in Cleveland. Eliza Bryant, born into slavery in North Carolina but a free resident of Cleveland after 1858, began efforts to establish a home for elderly black women in the city in 1893, aided by Sarah Green and Letitia Fleming. On 1 Sept. 1896, the Home for Aged Colored People was incorporated; on 11 Aug. 1897, the first residents were admitted into the $2,000 home at 284 Giddings (E. 71st) St., near Lexington Ave. The home had no gas, no furnace, and no bath, and in 1901 the trustees purchased better facilities at 186 Osborne (2520 E. 39th) St., which the home occupied in May 1902. It was moved again in Mar. 1914; the new house, at 4807 Cedar, purchased for $9,000, remained its location for 53 years. By 1957, the Home for Aged Colored People was accepting both men and women but was rarely filled to its capacity of 16 residents. With assistance from the Welfare Fed., it was reorganized and renamed the Eliza Bryant Home for the Aged in Apr. 1960. On 5 Sept. 1967, the home moved into the former DORCAS HOME at 1380 Addison Rd., which the Bryant Home leased. The new facility enabled the home to more than double its capacity; its 43 residents included both blacks and whites. In 1968, the Dorcas Society donated its property to the Bryant Home, and the heavily endowed A. M. MCGREGOR HOME gave the Bryant Home $1.5 million to continue its operations. Renamed the Eliza Bryant Ctr., the home announced an ambitious expansion program in Apr. 1984. With a $1.1 million gift from the defunct FOREST CITY HOSPITAL and other donations and grants, the center planned to develop a geriatric village to accommodate 100 elderly residents at Wade Park and Addison roads.

Federation for Community Planning Records, WRHS.
Eliza Bryant Home Records, WRHS.

The **ELIZA JENNINGS HOME** is one of the oldest facilities for the care of the elderly in Cleveland. At one time it also served as a home for patients with incurable diseases. The Eliza Jennings Home for Incurables was opened in Oct. 1888, with its facilities and operation underwritten by Mrs. ELIZA JENNINGS. Jennings heard the plight of an elderly woman in her church who had become poor and had no place to live, and decided to establish a home for such indigent gentlewomen. Constructed on land donated by Jennings on Detroit Rd. (now 10603 Detroit Rd.), the home was operated by the Women's Christian Assoc. Soon after its opening, the trustees decided to house only the elderly. The requisites for admittance were certificates of at least 5 years' residence in Cleveland and testimonials of satisfactory character. Women who had mental troubles or infectious diseases were not admitted. The YOUNG WOMEN'S CHRISTIAN ASSOC., successor to the Women's Christian Assoc., operated the home until 1922. Women have always managed the home, from its organization to the board of trustees of the present day, and women have been its prime movers. In 1922, the home was formally separated from the association and incorporated as a private, nonprofit organization under the chairmanship of Mrs. Chas. Orr. With the aid of C. Perry Burgess, the home raised enough money to build a new facility (completed in 1925) on the site of the old one on Detroit Rd., next to the CHILDREN'S AID SOCIETY (also on land given by Mrs. Jennings). Since then, Eliza Jennings has been enlarged by the addition of the Tomlinson Pavilion in 1955 and the Laub Nursing Pavilion, donated by Elsie Laub and Chas. Morris, in 1966. In the 1980s, the home served the elderly of both sexes, housing 60 residents, and had a nonresident member plan, which enabled nonresidents to utilize its programs and medical facilities. At the same time, plans were being made to build a retirement community as well. A section of the home was also equipped for full-time nursing care. Support for these activities came through endowments, gifts, and membership fees.

The **ELIZABETH RING AND WILLIAM GWINN MATHER FUND** was founded in 1954 by Elizabeth Ring Mather (1891–1957), from her husband's estate. Wm. Gwinn Mather (1857–1951) was born in Cleveland, the son of Samuel Livingston Mather and Elizabeth Lucy Gwinn, and descendant of the Colonial New England Mathers. He graduated from Trinity College in 1877 and received his master's degree from Trinity in 1885. He was president of the CLEVELAND CLIFFS IRON CO. from 1890–1933, after which he was chairman of the board until 1947, and honorary chairman until 1951. He was director of the Republic Steel Corp., Kelley Island Lime & Transport Co., Medusa Portland Cement Co., and American Trust Co. (Union Bank of America). Mather was also first president of the Cleveland Stock Exchange and president of the CLEVELAND MUSEUM OF ART from 1933–49. He was a member of the American Antiquarian Society, the Bibliographic Society of London, the Bibliographic Society of the American Historical Society, and the WESTERN RESERVE HISTORICAL SOCIETY. He married Elizabeth Ring Ireland in 1929, who had 1 son, Jas. D. Ireland. The fund was established for specific civic purposes in the Cleveland area, including the arts, hospitals and health agencies, secondary and higher education, conservation, and social welfare. No grants are awarded to individuals or for scholarships, fellowships, matching gifts, or loans. Applications for grants are not encouraged. In 1982, assets of the fund were $3,847,094, with expenditures of $1,146,444 for 76 grants. Officers and trustees of the fund in 1984 included Jas. D. Ireland, president, Theodore R. Colborn, Cornelia

I. Hallenan, Cornelia W. Ireland, Jas. D. Ireland III, Lucy S. Ireland, and R. Henry Norweb, Jr.

**ELLSLER, EFFIE** (4 Apr. 1854–8 Oct. 1942), was a Cleveland-born actress of the gaslight theaters of the 1880s, and of the early motion pictures at the turn of the century. Fondly titled "Cleveland's Sweetheart," Ellsler achieved stardom in 1870 and through the early 1900s was renowned as one of the finest American actresses of her day. As a member of the famous Ellsler theatrical family of Cleveland, she learned to perfect the art of emotional distress and extravagant gesture that was so popular during the pre-Ibsen period of stage and screen. Ellsler was named for her mother, Euphemia Emma Ellsler, who, with her husband, JOHN A. ELLSLER, performed on stage as "Uncle John A. and Effie E." Formerly of Philadelphia, Ellsler's parents played with a theater company in the early 1850s at the Cleveland Varieties, Cleveland's first permanent playhouse. Approximately 1 year after Effie's birth, her father made his debut as local manager of that theater, which he named for Cleveland. In addition to his credits as a character actor, Effie's father was a producer, and later manager of the old ACADEMY OF MUSIC, located on Bank (W. 6th) St.

Little Effie made her first stage appearance at an early age, portraying Little Eva in Harriet Beecher Stowe's *Uncle Tom's Cabin*, and later playing Cricket in *The Cricket on the Hearth*. Through childhood, Effie was trained in the dramatic arts by her father, and later, she was taught by the sisters of the Ursuline Academy in Cleveland. At the age of 18, she was called away from the convent school to take the role of Virginia in a production called *Virginius*. One of the happiest occasions in her life in Cleveland came on 6 Sept. 1875, when her father opened the new $200,000 Forest City Opera House, which had been built largely through his efforts in promoting construction of a playhouse for a quarter-century. The opening play was Bronson Howard's *Saratoga*, in which he had a part and young Effie was leading lady. On 1 Dec. 1880, Effie's performance as Hazel in Steele MacKaye's melodrama *Hazel Kirke* gave the opera house its most brilliant first night of the winter season. She is best remembered for this tear-inducing role, which opened in Madison Square Theater on 4 Feb. 1880 and made a record run on Broadway in the early 1880s that was not surpassed until 1906. Her portrayal of Hazel was said to have influenced an entire generation of mothers who chose that name for their new babies. Ellsler's last appearance in Cleveland occurred on 29 May 1919 at the Shubert-Colonial Theater in a play called *Old Lady 31*. She was married to Frank Weston, a gifted actor who appeared with her in *Hazel Kirke* and many other plays. They had no children.

**ELLSLER, JOHN ADAM** (22 Sept. 1821–21 Aug. 1903), was a leading figure in Cleveland's theatrical history. As an actor, producer, manager, and theater builder, he helped bring to Cleveland what has been described as "the Golden Era of the American Stage." Ellsler was born in Philadelphia. His family moved to Baltimore, where he worked as a young man in a printing shop that published the programs and posters for the most fashionable theater in the city. Responsible for delivering the posters, he stayed on for the performances and developed a great love for the theater, eventually deciding to make it his life's work. He returned to Philadelphia, where he acquired a job as the assistant treasurer of Peale's Museum. He also worked as a property man and acted in minor roles. In 1846 he became a member of the Arch St. Theater and gained important acting experience. From there he moved to the Chatham St. Theater in New York, where he met and married the actress Euphemia Emma Myers. They remained at the Chatham until Dec. 1849, at which time they began to travel throughout the South and Northeast, with Ellsler acting as producer and manager.

The Ellslers first came to Cleveland in the mid-1850s for a 3-month contract at the Cleveland Theater. Ellsler subsequently assumed the management of the ACADEMY OF MUSIC. Though the city's population did not seem substantial enough to support a full-time theatrical company, Ellsler proceeded to establish one. He set up a schedule that began in Cleveland, moved to Columbus during sessions of the legislature, moved back to Cleveland until the 4th of July, and ended with road trips to nearby cities such as Akron and Canton. Not only did Ellsler bring a permanent theatrical company to Cleveland, but he also succeeded in attracting some of the most prominent figures from the THEATER, opera, and burlesque to the academy's stage from 1855–73. He also assisted many new actors, including his daughter Effie, in getting started. As a result of his kind and helpful demeanor, he was nicknamed "Uncle John" by those who worked with him. Encouraged by the success of the academy, Ellsler arranged in 1873 for the construction of the EUCLID AVE. OPERA HOUSE. He invested his life savings in the project, but cost overruns and the financial panic of 1873 forced him to sell the house to MARCUS HANNA in 1879. Ellsler remained in Cleveland for several more years as manager of the Park Theater. In 1886 he gave up all activity in Cleveland and moved his family to New York, where he continued his acting career, often taking bit parts as an "old man." He died in New York.

**ELWELL, HERBERT** (10 May 1898–17 Apr. 1974), wrote with the authority of a composer in his own right as the *Plain Dealer*'s music critic. A native of Minneapolis, he came to Cleveland by way of Europe. After 2 years' study in New York with ERNEST BLOCH, Elwell went to Paris in 1921, where he joined a famed coterie including Aaron Copland and Virgil Thomson, all studying under Nadia Boulanger. In 1923 he received a fellowship from the American Academy in Rome, where he conducted the premiere of his ballet suite *The Happy Hypocrite*. Elwell came to Cleveland in 1928 to head the Cleveland Institute of Music's composition and advanced theory department, a position formerly held by his mentor, Bloch. During his 17 years there, he also served as assistant director. Other teaching positions included classes at the Oberlin Conservatory of Music, summer sessions at the Eastman School of Music in Rochester, and direction of the composition department of the CLEVELAND MUSIC SCHOOL SETTLEMENT. From 1930–36, he was also program annotator for the CLEVELAND ORCHESTRA.

As music critic for the *PLAIN DEALER* from 1932–64, Elwell cut a magisterial figure in local music circles. Even the most popular artists were held by him to exacting standards, as when he observed of Geo. Gershwin that "as a pianist he is a good composer." He was not beyond breaking into the middle of an avant-garde concert with a "Bravo!" for an unexpectedly harmonic chord. His Sunday pieces were leisurely discourses that fulfilled the educational function of criticism. Nothing else Elwell wrote as a composer quite equaled the success of *The Happy Hypocrite*, which was programmed by GEO. SZELL on the Cleveland Orchestra's 1965 European tour. His *Lincoln Requiem Aeternam* for chorus and orchestra received the Paderewski Prize and a nationwide radio presentation in 1947. Also notable were a Concert Suite for violin and orchestra, a score of songs, and several pieces arranged by his friend Robt. E. Nelson for concert band. Among other

prizes, Elwell was recipient of the music prize in the Women's City Club's first creative fine arts awards in 1961. He was a resident of CLEVELAND HTS. with his wife, Maria.

**ELWELL, JOHN JOHNSON** (22 June 1820–16 Mar. 1900), was a physician, attorney, author, educator, and Union Army officer. Elwell was born in Warren, Ohio. He began a career in medicine after graduating from Cleveland Medical College in 1846. Following a 9-year period of practice in Orwell, Ohio, he served in the Ohio legislature (1853–55). Admitted to the Ohio bar in 1855, he practiced law in Cleveland. During the 5 years prior to the outbreak of the Civil War, he edited and published the *Western Law Monthly* and taught at the Ohio & Union Law College and at Cleveland Medical College. A text on medical jurisprudence that he authored remained in popular usage through 4 editions.

After the outbreak of the CIVIL WAR, Elwell was appointed a quartermaster on 3 Aug. 1861. He equipped the 2D OHIO VOLUNTEER CAVALRY then being raised in Cleveland. He also equipped the 3d Ohio Volunteer Cavalry, raised in Huron County in Sept. 1861, and the Sherman Brigade. Elwell served as volunteer aide-de-camp to Gen. Henry W. Benham at the Battle of Secessionville (also known as James Island), S.C., on 16 June 1862. At the assault of Ft. Wagner, 18 July 1862, he rallied troops in line of battle, although Union forces commanded by Gen. Quincy Gillmore failed to gain their objective. On 8 Nov. 1862, Elwell was promoted to lieutenant colonel; he served as chief quartermaster of the Dept. of the South until 1 Feb. 1864. He also served as chief quartermaster for Gen. David Hunter. Because of attacks of yellow fever, Elwell was removed from service in the field to Elmira, N.Y. As quartermaster there, he purchased over 17,000 horses and had them delivered to the cavalry bureau in Washington, D.C. He was also quartermaster of Elmira Prison, which held thousands of Confederate prisoners, and of the rendezvous at Elmira for drafted men. Elwell was breveted 4 times for gallantry in battle and received the Gillmore Medal for his meritorious conduct in South Carolina. His brevet generalship dated from Mar. 1865. After the war, he returned to Cleveland and resumed his career in medicine and law. He became editor of John Bouvier's *Law Directory* and served on the Soldiers & Sailors Monument Commission, 1888–1900. At death, his residence was listed as 2190 Detroit Ave. He is buried in WOODLAND CEMETERY.

The **ELWELL PARKER ELECTRIC COMPANY**, organized in 1893 to build motors, developed the industrial truck in 1906 and pioneered its use and development to transport and handle industrial materials. The Elwell-Parker Electric Co. of America was incorporated in West Virginia on 6 July 1893, with capital provided by Alexander E. Brown, Henry D. Coffinberry, and Stewart H. Chisholm. The principal incorporator was Brown, inventor of hoisting and conveying machinery used to load and unload bulk cargoes in Great Lakes shipping. Searching for a source of electric motors for his machines, Brown obtained the rights to manufacture in the U.S. motors designed by Englishman Thos. Parker and his partner P. Bedford Elwell. The American company began slowly during the depression of 1893. Located in the St. Clair St. plant of the Brown Hoisting & Conveying Machinery Co., Elwell-Parker had 23 employees by 1896. By 1897 the company had moved to its own plant on Hamilton Ave. at the corner of Belden; in 1907 it moved to its present (1984) site on St. Clair between E. 40th and E. 45th streets. In May 1899, the firm made its first motors for battery-driven vehicles, selling them to WALTER C. BAKER. By 1901, it supplied motors to 7 automobile companies, and in 1903 it developed the motor and chassis for street trucks. In 1909, the Anderson Carriage Co. of Detroit purchased a majority interest in Elwell-Parker to ensure itself a supply of motors for its vehicles. But by then Elwell-Parker had charted a new direction for its growth.

Morris S. Towson (4 June 1865–17 Mar. 1942), an innovative engineer who joined the firm in 1896, designed an electric truck in 1906 to help the Pennsylvania Railroad more quickly move luggage at its Jersey City terminal. In 1910, Elwell-Parker began to extend the use of these trucks to general industry; its "electric porters" in train terminals were known as "electric stevedores" when used on the docks by steamship companies. By 1913, Elwell-Parker was exporting its trucks to British railway companies. A major innovation in 1914 expanded the use of these industrial trucks: they were given a platform that enabled them to raise and carry cargo; these low-lift trucks were produced beginning in 1915. In the 1920s, these trucks became increasingly specialized: a series of trucks to lift and transport automobile body dies were introduced between 1928–30; trucks were also designed for use in the steel industry and in newsprint paper mills. The development of the high-lift fork truck in 1927 and of the pallet a short time later made possible new and more efficient storage methods. The company was reorganized in 1920 with Towson as president, a position he held until his death. The new firm manufactured only industrial trucks. By 1943, 30 companies were using its equipment. In 1956, the company had sales of $6.5 million and employed about 300 people. Annual sales approached $20 million during the mid-1970s, but in the early 1980s the depression in the automobile and basic metals industries sharply reduced the company's sales and employment; sales fell to $8.1 million in 1983, and employment plunged from 360 to 130. In 1984 the company began to recover, enjoying sales of $12.5 million.

Love, John W., *Lengthened Shadows* (1943).

The **ELYSIUM**, once a grand landmark at the corner of E. 107th St. and Euclid, was an indoor skating palace. Conceived and built by Dudley Humphrey, the "popcorn king," and his brothers of EUCLID BEACH PARK, it was once the largest indoor skating rink in the world. A lifelong skating enthusiast, Dudley Humphrey sold popcorn and sharpened skates at an outdoor rink owned by his father, Harvey Humphrey, at WADE PARK; disregarding skeptics who doubted the success of an indoor facility, he broke ground in 1907 and invested, by some reports, $150,000 in the rink. The Elysium, so named after a contest was held, was beset with technical problems. Over 12 mi. of water pipes were laid over bare earth to permit the rink to open on time; when the 100' x 300' ice surface would not properly freeze, tons of cracked ice were brought in to fill in the holes. When the facility opened in Nov. 1907, crowds flocked there to skate and to watch the giant glass-encased ice machines. From October to May, when Euclid Beach was closed for the season, the Elysium offered afternoon and evening skating sessions to the music of popular bands, as well as skating lessons. Schools, colleges, and professional hockey teams used the rink and built a popular following for ice HOCKEY.

The Elysium was home to the Cleveland Falcons, later the CLEVELAND BARONS. In addition, it was the site of international and local figure-skating contests. Its operations were interrupted during WORLD WAR I when the building was used as a barracks for the Student Army Training Corps for Case Institute. When the Elysium reopened as a skating rink, it prospered until the Depression, when employees received half cash, half scrip in their pay

envelopes. As both ice hockey and figure skating became more popular in the 1930s, the Elysium suffered because of lack of audience capacity. The Barons moved to the CLEVELAND ARENA, and the CLEVELAND SKATING CLUB, a group of figure skaters, purchased the facilities of the disbanding Cleveland Tennis & Racquet Club on Fairhill Rd. Revenues fell to a trickle from their previous high of $90,000. With the onset of WORLD WAR II, the fate of the Elysium became clear; wartime shortages and impending takeover of the building by the military caused the rink to close in 1941. By 1942, the land reverted to its original owner, the Case School of Applied Science, and the famed ice-making machinery was removed. The building, however, stood for another decade, used as a bowling alley and used-car showroom. Talk of building an office building or a park on the site never materialized. After the city of Cleveland acquired the property in 1951, the building, by then dilapidated and an eyesore, was razed and the land used to widen Chester Ave.

The **EMBASSY THEATER,** 709 Euclid Ave., one of downtown Cleveland's last movie theaters, was built by Waldemar Otis as the Columbia Theater and opened 12 Sept. 1887, premiering Hanlon's *Fantasma.* It boasted a tunnel leading to the Oaks Cafe on Vincent St. and marble stairs leading to a mahogany bar on Euclid Ave. The Columbia was built in the continental style, with boxes on either side of the auditorium. The main floor and balcony formed a horseshoe. On 17 Feb. 1889, it became the Star Theater, managed by W. Scott Robinson and Jas. S. Cockett until 29 Aug., when Frank M. Drew took over. Vaudeville, melodrama, and comic opera were offered until the 1890s, when burlesque was introduced. The Star was a "refined" burlesque house; women viewed the show from a side balcony, separated from the male audience by a heavy curtain. Some of the stars who played there included the Al G. Fields Minstrels, Ted Healy, Weber & Fields, and Rose—Wild Girl from the Yucatan. It was renamed the Cameo Theater in 1926 when it opened as a motion-picture house. Loews took over the theater in 1931, and the building was remodeled. The new color scheme was flame, green, and gold, and the seating capacity was 1,500. A new Wurlitzer organ was purchased.

In 1938, the Cameo was razed (except for the east and west walls); the Embassy Theater went up on the site and opened on 16 Oct. The tunnel was removed, and the theater was furnished with air conditioning, gleaming chromium, velvet hangings, and indirect lighting. The Embassy had a larger lobby than the Cameo, an inner rotunda, and an auditorium "streamlined with curves running toward the screen." Seating capacity was 1,200. During the 1970s, it became a showplace for action-type karate films. The Embassy was owned by Community Circuit Theaters. Then the oldest theater building in downtown Cleveland, the Embassy was closed on 1 Dec. 1977 and razed to make way for the Natl. City Bank building.

The **EMERALD CIVIC SOCIETY** was established in 1968 to enhance the social and cultural life of the Irish-American community in Cleveland. The organization was founded by a group of Cleveland men who had been impressed by the exhilarating atmosphere surrounding the St. Patrick's Day parade in New York City and who decided to add a touch of class and excitement to Cleveland's annual parade by bringing in a well-known marching band; society members also began marching in the parade themselves, dressed in top hats, tails, and gloves, and wearing carnations. Led by Joseph Patrick Rochford, the nonprofit society was chartered in Apr. 1968. In order to raise money to bring a prominent marching unit such as the Notre Dame University band to each St. Patrick's Day Parade, the society began to sponsor annual fundraising events, such as the Emerald Ball and Irish Nights in the FLATS. By 1970, these events were also funding a scholarship program for students entering Catholic high schools; 3 $400 scholarships were awarded that year. By 1972, the scholarship program had grown to $6,000 in aid, and the society had grown to 200 members.

**EMMANUEL CHURCH (EPISCOPAL)** dates from 1871, when ST. PAUL'S EPISCOPAL at Euclid and Case (E. 40th) St. opened Emmanuel Chapel at Prospect and Hayward (E. 36th) streets. Still under the supervision of St. Paul's, a new Emmanuel Chapel was built in 1874 on Euclid Ave. east of Glen Park Place (E. 86th St.), and it, in 1876, was admitted to the Episcopal Diocese of Ohio as Emmanuel Church. In 1880, the frame Gothic building was moved slightly west and enlarged. In 1889, conflict between the rector and members of the parish resulted in the rector and a large number of parishioners' leaving the Episcopal church altogether. They formed the Church of the Epiphany, Reformed Episcopal, and built a church on the other side of Euclid Ave. A period of growth for Emmanuel Church followed the split; a Sunday school was started in 1890, and a chapel, which later became St. Alban's Parish, was started in 1892.

In 1900, the firm of Cram, Goodhue, & Ferguson was commissioned to design a new building for the Euclid Ave. site. A late Gothic Revival structure of stone was drawn by Ralph Adams Cram. The building was planned so it could be built in stages, as funds became available. The first section, 6 bays of the nave and a temporary chancel, was built in 1902. The remaining 2 bays and the interior were completed in 1904. A new brick-and-stone parish house replaced the older wooden one in 1924; the tower of the original plan remained uncompleted. With the sale of adjoining property, the building debt was liquidated and the church consecrated in 1926. The parish was, like many east end churches, in the center of great social and economic change in the surrounding neighborhood during the 1950s–1970s. In order to remain viable, a variety of programs, keeping pace with the change, were started. A tutorial program providing individual assistance to schoolchildren, a legal aid project, and a larger hunger center (serving as many as 1,900 families per month) characterized these services to the community in the 1980s.

The **EMPIRE SAVINGS & LOAN** was a black-owned and -operated financial institution formed to meet the needs of BLACKS migrating from the South. Empire was founded in 1911 by Herbert Chauncey, a railroad mail clerk who attended night school to become a lawyer. Upon opening his practice, he gathered capital from his friends to open a savings and loan company. With $100,000 in hand, he opened an office at 2316 E. 55th St. The business prospered, and Chauncey turned his own attentions to real-estate and insurance ventures, putting Empire management into the hands of Howard Murrell. By 1928, the company opened a short-lived branch on Cedar. In the Depression, Empire was faced with the same problems as most banking institutions: savers withdrew funds to live on, and borrowers could not make their payments. When the company could not meet expenses, taxes, and interest, the state took over its operations and liquidated the remaining assets. When final liquidation payment was made in 1958, over 60% of the funds had been returned to depositors. The company disappeared from the telephone directory in 1954; its final address was at 1277 E. 105th.

*ENAKOPRAVNOST* (Equality) offered Cleveland's Slovenian residents their first daily newspaper when it began publication in Apr. 1918. A primary impetus behind its appearance was the movement that resulted in the establishment of an independent Yugoslav state in the final months of WORLD WAR I. Liberal in its political orientation, *Enakopravnost* avoided any religious affiliation but became the official organ of the Slovene Progressive Benefit Society in 1924. Edited for most of its first 2 decades by VATRO J. GRILL, it was published by Frank Oglar, president of the American Jugoslav Printing & Publishing Co. on St. Clair Ave. In the 1930s it printed 1 page per week in English. It became staunchly antifascist with the approach of WORLD WAR II, when it was edited by Anton Sabec. *Enakopravnost* emerged from World War II as a defender of the Communist Tito regime in Yugoslavia. That, plus its support of Henry Wallace in the 1948 presidential election, won it the unfavorable notice of the House Committee on Un-American Activities. It was also plagued by a steady turnover of editors, which included Ivan Bostjancic and a return stint by Grill. Leaving the local field to its rival daily, *AMERISKA DOMOVINA*, *Enakopravnost* ceased publication on 3 Apr. 1957.

**ENGLISH.** *See* **BRITISH IMMIGRATION**

The **ENGLISH-SPEAKING UNION, CLEVELAND BRANCH** was founded on 15 Mar. 1923. The Cleveland branch is part of the parent organization, the English-Speaking Union of the U.S., which is closely affiliated with but completely separate from the group in Great Britain. It is a nonprofit, nongovernmental organization whose sole purpose is "to draw together in the bond of comradeship the English-speaking peoples of the world [and] to strengthen the friendly relationship between peoples of the United States of America and of the British Commonwealth by disseminating knowledge of each to the other, and by inspiring reverence for their common traditions." The first president of the Cleveland branch was John A. Penton, founder of the Penton Publishing Co. In 1925 the E-SU established headquarters in the Union Trust Bldg. under the guidance of its officers DAVID S. INGALLS, CHAS. F. THWING, Edith Charlesworth, and ANDREW SQUIRE. In 1929, new headquarters were established in the Citizen's Bldg. under the presidency of ABRAM GARFIELD. He remained president through WORLD WAR II. During the war, the E-SU Committee for British War Relief united local Scottish, Welsh, Manx, and English organizations to support the war effort. This committee contributed money and warm clothing, placed exiled British children in Cleveland homes, and cooperated with the American Friends of France to raise money for French refugee relief. This work was carried on at the Dunham Tavern Museum. After World War II, the E-SU disbanded. The organization was reactivated 6 Dec. 1960. The officers elected were Dr. Harlan Hamilton, Chilton Thomson, Molly Strachen, and Clay Hollister. Projects undertaken by the union included scholarships for British children to study in the U.S. and fellowships for college students and librarians offered on an exchange basis. Another project, Books across the Sea, provided American books to Commonwealth countries. The organization helped sponsor the Winston Churchill Memorial Fund and the visits of Prince Charles of Great Britain in 1964 and 1977.

English-Speaking Union, Cleveland Branch Records, WRHS.

**EPISCOPALIANS.** As the WESTERN RESERVE opened up as part of the new frontier, the Episcopal church found that its reliance on this hierarchy meant difficulties in keeping up with a restless population marching continually westward. A frontier was no place for a bishop, and without a bishop, the early-19th-century Episcopal missionaries working in central and northeastern Ohio (Joseph Doddridge, Roger Searle, and Jas. Kilbourne) did so almost without official church sanction. A bishop meant a diocese, and it was not until 1817 that the Episcopal church's General Convention officially formed the Ohio Diocese. By that time Congregational and Presbyterian pastors and their flocks were proving that religion was not absent in the Western Reserve. The Episcopalians were eager to catch up; by 1818 they had organized the Ohio Diocese and elected Philander Chase, a relative newcomer to Ohio and the church, as their first bishop (1818–31). Chase acquired a national reputation as "the frontier bishop." While he was no stranger to Cleveland, his missionary travels all over Ohio and his ultimate settlement in Gambier set the stage for the double focus between Cleveland and central Ohio that existed in the diocese for nearly 80 years. Chase founded and consecrated many churches, including a number in the Cleveland area, of which Trinity (1829) was later to assume primacy in the diocese. Bp. CHAS. PETTIT MCILVAINE (1832–73) built on Chase's efforts. By the end of Chase's episcopacy, Cleveland had a population of 4,000 and a full Episcopal parish on the southeast corner of St. Clair and W. 3rd St. McIlvaine's tenure included additions to this city parish; he attended the founding of ST. JOHN'S (1836) and consecrated Trinity (1854) and ST. PAUL'S (1859). Episcopal church growth was not, however, unimpeded; the western stretches of the area were not always hospitable to parish growth. Here again there was a lack of both ministers and buildings, and Presbyterian churches and sometimes school buildings were pressed into Episcopalian service.

Episcopalian emotionalism crept into the church in Cleveland, as it did everywhere in the U.S., because of the resurgence of the high church-low church debate, instigated by the English publication of "Tracts for the Times" (1833). These tracts quickly crossed the Atlantic, and Cleveland Episcopalians engaged in the ancient debate about the place of clerical vestments, medieval ceremonies, the keeping of holy days, and making the sign of the cross in their religious services. The Protestant Episcopal Church of America and its Ohio Diocese were generally low-church (or evangelical) in their principles. But as this low-versus-high dispute continued during the middle years of the 19th century, Cleveland's Trinity and Grace churches became identified as high-church and St. John's and St. Paul's as low-church. As the diocese became more urbanized, high-church tendencies began to edge into Episcopal services in Cleveland. By 1880, Bp. GREGORY BEDELL (1873–89) had to admonish the rectors of Trinity, Grace, and St. Mary's about wearing white and colored stoles. Earlier, Bp. McIlvaine had explained why processional singing by surpliced choirs was not consistent with church policy. Although the CIVIL WAR interrupted these doctrinal discussions, Cleveland was to witness sporadic breakouts of this debate well into the 20th century.

The Civil War was another source of Episcopalian concern. McIlvaine was a staunch Union supporter and made sure that his ideas were known to both clergy and laity, and they became the inspiration for Bp. Bedell's pastoral letter approved by the Episcopal House of Bishops in 1862. The letter supported the Northern cause, and up to its time was the only Episcopal position that pledged the support of the church to the state in a political matter. Unlike other national churches, the Protestant Episcopal church in America did not split over the issue of slavery. Cleveland Episcopal churches before the Civil War did not use their forums to examine the peculiar institution, and during the war they focused on the Union cause and not the moral question of slavery. Even the 1861 diocesan convention meeting in Cleveland 2 months after Ft. Sumter concerned itself with politics, not morality. But both Episcopal clergy and laity could let political discussions carry them away, and by 1863 both McIlvaine and Bedell had to warn the clergy about discussing politics in the pulpit. After the Civil War, the Ohio Diocese's dominion gained the attention of the 4 Episcopal parishes in Cleveland, and so politics remained an important component of parish affairs. By 1867, the Convocation of Cleveland was asking that it be allowed to form a separate diocese. That touched off a full diocesan debate, leading to an 1873 decision to examine a division of the diocese. This division materialized in 1875, when the 41 southern counties in Ohio became the Diocese of Southern Ohio, while the 47 northern counties remained as the Diocese of Ohio, with its headquarters in Cleveland. Bp. Bedell's relocation from Gambier to Cleveland and a Huron St. address recognized this fact and refocused the attention of the Ohio Diocese on the city. The theretofore peripatetic bishops now resided in the city, and it was not long before an idea for a cathedral surfaced.

The division of the state into 2 dioceses did not, however, guarantee prosperity. The booming post-Civil War years helped Cleveland's economy, but they were not as kind to the diocese. Spending for missions lagged, parishes were faulted for lack of leadership and coordinated missionary efforts, and church membership fell. Partially, these troubles stemmed from the church's inability to come to grips with the new wave of immigrants. From the arrival in Cleveland of many immigrants from Germany in the 1860s to the flood tide of East Europeans later in the century, Episcopal church leaders pondered how to attract these newcomers. While other Protestant denominations were successful in recruiting members from the immigrants, the Episcopal church in Cleveland followed the national Episcopal example in demonstrating little success in this effort. The only real achievement was the foundation of Christ German Protestant Episcopal Church on Orange St. (1870). More success was had in facing the social needs brought on by the rapid post-Civil War industrialization. Along with the Congregational churches, the Episcopal church nationally was credited with many leaders of the Social Gospel. That was also true in Cleveland: Chas. D. Williams, dean of TRINITY CATHEDRAL, served as first president of HIRAM HOUSE (1896); Lewis Burton, rector in a number of Cleveland parishes, helped initiate the founding of the ELIZA JENNINGS HOME (1888); and FRANK DUMOULIN, while a dean at Trinity, spurred the efforts leading to the formation of the Federated Churches of Greater Cleveland (1911).

Individual parishes were also involved in efforts to alleviate problems. In 1874 and 1875, Trinity founded a children's charity, the Scovill Ave. Home for Helpless Children, and in 1916 it opened Trinity House on E. 22nd St. The EAST END NEIGHBORHOOD HOUSE on Croton Ave. sprang from the efforts of Emmanuel Church (1908). During the 1930s, Trinity helped sponsor an effort to provide musical and film entertainment along with refreshments to those suffering from the economic downturn of the Depression. The missionary activities of the city's parishes were more coordinated than the piecemeal social-work efforts. Population shifts between 1890–1918 meant movement to the SUBURBS. For example, Christ German relocated to SHAKER HTS. To insure membership as people drifted out of the central city area, a Cleveland Church Club was formed in 1898. This drift from the city was ironically taking place at the same time that the idea for the construction of an Episcopal cathedral in Cleveland was reaching a formulation stage. During the 1890s, church construction nationally was affected by prosperity, allowing many denominations to vie with each other in the construction of edifices reflecting Gothic or Romanesque influences. So it was in Cleveland.

Bp. WM. LEONARD (1889–1930), Wm. G. Mather, and Cleveland architect CHAS. F. SCHWEINFURTH were instrumental in planning and completing the cathedralization of Trinity parish and the building of a suitable church as the headquarters for the diocese's ecclesiastical government. A $1 million donation from SAMUEL MATHER insured the construction of a perpendicular Gothic 15th-century English cathedral at Euclid and E. 22nd St. The cornerstone was laid in 1903, and the building was consecrated in 1907. Cleveland's arrival as a regional center for business and cultural achievements was now suitably recognized in an appropriate religious monument. The cathedral, along with mission development and the need to expand parish facilities to keep up with a growing population moving into the suburbs, meant a new attention to the constant quest for money. Early national Episcopal fundraising efforts can be dated to 1780, and from the beginning the Ohio Diocese petitioned the church hierarchy for money. Mostly, though, the diocese had to rely on its own resources, and that often meant rough times. In the early days, bishops and rectors often went unpaid; even as late as the Depression, Bp. WARREN RODGERS (1930–38) had to severely cut his salary in order to make ends meet. All the bishops after Bedell copied his efforts in planning a series of fundraising campaigns. These efforts meant that the diocese had to communicate effectively with all church members. The founding of *Church Life* was an effort to meet this need. Its first issue was 2 July 1887, and in different forms it has continued publication under the same name. The pages of *Church Life* and other publications reflect the church's opinion on political concerns. As early as 1876, the diocese's 59th convention agreed that women should be allowed to vote in the election of church officers (although not agreeing to make them eligible for actual office). By the 1970s, this opinion had developed into a not-so-unanimous agreement to the ordination of women priests, and 2 women priests were accepted by the Ohio Diocese. The 1960s and 1970s also showed an Episcopal willingness to embrace other liberal or reformist ideas. Bp. John Burt (1968–84) spoke out against the VIETNAM WAR, and other Cleveland clergy worked for racial and ecumenical progress and harmony. From a denomination struggling for survival in adverse frontier conditions, the Episcopal church has become a staunch pillar of a metropolitan religious community.

Michael V. Wells
Cleveland State University

See also RELIGION.

The "EPIZOOTIC," or "CANADIAN HORSE EPIDEMIC," struck Cleveland in Oct. 1872, severely affecting the city's transportation for almost a month. Also referred to as the "epizootic catarrh," it was thought to be a type of influenza originating in Canada, affecting only horses. The virus spread along the U.S. East Coast during early Oct. 1872 and rapidly moved westward. False reports of the virus circulated through Cleveland for 2 weeks before the first case was officially acknowledged by veterinarians on 28 Oct. Within a week, transportation in Cleveland was brought to a virtual standstill. The public stables were hardest hit, while private stables suffered less. The Fire Dept. was forced to use stricken horses at reduced speed, and several streetcar stables closed down completely. Many of Cleveland's metal industries had to reduce workers' hours. In some cases, oxen were used in place of horses. Cleveland suffered less than most eastern cities. By the time the epidemic reached Cleveland, it was known that dry feed and not putting the horses back to work too early would prevent fatalities, although some did occur. Veterinarians also urgently warned against "bleeding" as a cure. By the end of November, most of the city's horses had fully recovered.

The **EPWORTH-EUCLID UNITED METHODIST CHURCH** is descended from Cleveland's earliest Methodist societies, having been formed from 2 historic congregations: Euclid Ave. Methodist Episcopal and Epworth Memorial Church. The congregation now occupies a landmark of the UNIVERSITY CIRCLE area, one of Cleveland's most recognizable buildings. The Euclid Ave. Methodist Episcopal Church traced its history to Methodist classes established permanently at DOAN'S CORNERS in 1831. A church building was constructed in 1837 on Doan St. (E. 105th), and the church was known as Doan St. ME. A second building was built in 1870 and razed in 1885. In 1887 a new building went up on Euclid Ave. at Oakdale (E. 93rd), and the church became known as Euclid Ave. ME. Epworth Memorial Methodist Episcopal looked to the Erie St. ME Church, formed in 1850 and located on Erie St. (E. 9th) between Eagle St. and Ohio (Central Ave.), as its original predecessor. In 1875 the Erie St. Church purchased a building on the corner of Prospect and Huntington (E. 18th) and became known as the Prospect St. or Christ ME Church. In 1882 a merger took place with a mission church at Prospect and Willson St. (E. 55th), known as Cottage Chapel, which had been started by Rev. DILLON PROSSER in 1875. The merger produced Central ME, renamed Epworth Memorial when a new building was built in 1891–93. Yet another church, Scovill Ave. ME, was merged into Epworth Memorial in 1895. It was in Central ME on 14 May 1889 that a coalition of young people's groups known as the EPWORTH LEAGUE was formed. The league spread worldwide, and by the turn of the century it claimed 19,500 chapters and over a million members. The league promoted missions, temperance, and social activities. It later became the Methodist Youth Fellowship.

In 1919–20, the Euclid Ave. and Epworth Memorial congregations merged to construct a large building on a site between E. 107th St. and Chester Ave. Bertram Grosvenor Goodhue was commissioned to design the church shortly before his death in 1924. Plans were completed by Goodhue's firm in association with the Cleveland firm of Walker & Weeks. Construction began in 1926 and was completed in 1928. The building is a modern adaptation of Gothic themes. The form and grouping of elements on the slope above the Wade Park Lagoon are said to be reminiscent of Mont Saint-Michel; however, the details of the structure are highly stylized rather than rigidly Gothic. The plan is cruciform with a high central fleche and tapering octagonal roof rising over the crossing. The exterior mass is ornamented with sculptured figures by New York sculptor Leo Freidlander. On the interior, the roof is supported by 4 great arches. A large rose window to the east, arched transept windows, and 4 small lancets in the tower are the only openings. The attached educational wing is low and rectangular. The entire structure is faced with Plymouth granite. In 1961, Wade Park Methodist Church, organized in 1892 on the corner of Wade Park and Marcy avenues, was merged into Epworth-Euclid Church.

The **EPWORTH LEAGUE,** a Methodist organization that set the pattern for most church youth organizations, was founded in a Cleveland Methodist church and within 10 years claimed over a million members internationally. Prior to 1889, as many as 5 organized young people's groups existed in the Methodist Episcopal church, among them the Methodist Alliance, claiming 20,000 members in 1883; the Oxford League, organized at the Methodist Centennial Conference, a large chapter of which existed at Cleveland's Central Methodist Church; the Young People's Christian League; and others. In 1889 the groups began discussions of a merger into a single body, and on 14 and 15 May of that year, 27 persons gathered at Central Methodist and formed the Epworth League. The constitution of the Oxford League was modified and adopted along with the well-known motto of the Young People's Christian League, "Look Up, Lift Up." The league spread nation- and world-wide, claiming a peak of 1.75 million members in 19,500 chapters by 1899. It carried out a portion of the social-service work of the denomination. It worked in 6 "departments": Spiritual Life, Social Work, Literary Work, Correspondence, Mercy and Help, and Finance. Locally, chapters organized "Fresh Air Work" (day camps for city children), literary events, lecture series, and fellowship gatherings. Central Methodist Church was renamed Epworth Memorial Church in 1891, in honor of the worldwide movement that had begun there, and 6 panels of stained glass were contributed to the church by league chapters across the country to commemorate its founding. Epworth Memorial later became a part of EPWORTH EUCLID METHODIST CHURCH. With the merger of Methodist denominations in the 1930s, the Epworth League became known as the Methodist Youth Fellowship; it survives to the present (1985) as the United Methodist Youth Fellowship.

**ERIE RAILROAD.** *See* **CONRAIL**

**ERIE STREET CEMETERY,** preserving 9th St.'s original name, has been a municipal cemetery of controversy since 1826. Cleveland village trustees, desperate to replace the informal community burial ground south of PUBLIC SQUARE with a permanent site, purchased from LEONARD CASE, SR., for $1 the "whole of lots 144, 143, and the northpart of 142," which were in deep woods. So remote and spacious was the land that the council permitted a gunpowder magazine (1836) and a poorhouse-hospital on the unused portion. Disgruntled heirs of the original lot owners, claiming infringement of a covenant restricting use to burials, fruitlessly sued Cleveland in federal court (1836–42). In 1839, Cleveland's council passed a cemetery-management ordinance specifying a site survey and subdivision into salable lots; rules for lot holders; a fee schedule; and the appointment of a sexton, whose job included preventing "horses, hogs, or dogs from roaming within the limits of the burial ground." Since there were no other church or private cemeteries nearby, this city cemetery buried all faiths until strict enforcement of the "lots only sold" rule led the Israelitic Society to establish WILLETT ST. CEMETERY (1840). The first of the ROMAN CATHOLIC CEMETERIES, St. Joseph, was organized in 1849.

By 1850, the city cemetery, on the busy town's edge, was, despite ornamentation, old-fashioned. After WOODLAND CEMETERY opened in 1853, the old city cemetery retained favor with Cleveland's pioneer generation, such as the Cases, who were at first buried there. But no improvement—including plantings, fencings, and a formal gateway—could disguise Erie St.'s infirmities. By 1900, it was a departmental debit. For Progressives, beginning with Mayor

TOM L. JOHNSON, the cemetery mocked an efficient city. His administration, which developed Highland Park Cemetery (1904), reinterred bodies there, not without opposition, and reclaimed land from Erie St. for city streets. The struggle begat the Pioneers' Memorial Assoc. (1915). It was most influential as the battle climaxed in the 1920s over the approach to the proposed Lorain-Carnegie Ave. bridge—through or around Erie St. Cemetery? "Around," City Manager WM. HOPKINS decreed in 1925. With that, serious attempts to remove the cemetery ended. Complaints of neglect inspired WPA action, including erecting a fence fashioned from the demolished Superior Ave. viaduct's sandstone. In 1940, this refurbished cemetery of historic graves, including that of Algonquian Chief JOC-O-SOT, was rededicated, a grassy haven in Cleveland's midst.

**ERIEVIEW** was an urban plan adopted by the city of Cleveland in 1960. It was designed to eliminate much of the existing blight and decay in the aging district northeast of the downtown, and to take advantage of federal urban-renewal funds. The project area extended roughly from E. 6th to E. 17th Sts. and from Chester Ave. to the lakefront. The area west of 14th St. was intended for public and commercial uses, and the area to the east for residential use. Erieview was the most ambitious program undertaken to that date under the Federal Urban Redevelopment Program. Land was acquired by the city, structures were cleared, and assembled parcels of land were sold to private developers. Guidelines were established with regard to land use, building height and setback, population density, site coverage, and parking. The plan was prepared by internationally known architect I. M. Pei & Associates. The general concept provided for groups of low buildings accented by vertical towers. A 40-story tower at E. 12th St. and St. Clair was the hub of the plan, and a plaza with a reflecting pool stretched west to E. 9th St. E. 12th St. was made into a divided boulevard, with a hotel and a city office building at the north end. At E. 12th St. and Chester, an open space or plaza called Chester Commons was created for pedestrians, shoppers, and leisure activities. Thus, the plan provided for public and commercial office space, hotels, and entertainment.

The buildings erected during the first phase included Erieview Tower (1964), the Federal Bldg. (1967), One Erieview Plaza (1965), the Bond Court office building (1971), the Public Utilities Bldg. (1971), and Park Ctr. (1973), a combination 20-story apartment building and shopping mall. The buildings were designed in the modern idioms inspired by the International style by both local and national architects. New buildings continued to be built in the project area into the 1980s, including the Ohio Bell Bldg., Ctr. One, Eaton Ctr., and Northpoint. While many of the features of the original plan were not carried out, and the project was seriously criticized in the mid-1970s on various grounds, it served the purpose of stimulating a large amount of new commercial office construction northeast of the downtown.

**ERNST & WHINNEY** is an international accounting firm with more than 350 offices in over 75 countries, including 115 offices in the U.S. Originally founded in Cleveland as Ernst & Ernst, Ernst & Whinney Internatl. was formed in 1979. One of the country's "Big 8" accounting firms, it has its national headquarters in Cleveland in the Natl. City Ctr. In 1903, Alwyn C. and Theodore Ernst opened an accounting office in the Schofield Bldg. (E. 9th St. Tower). Known as Ernst & Ernst, the 2-man operation struggled for existence at a time when accounting was considered little more than routine bookkeeping. By 1906, Theodore had left the firm in order to enter the commercial laundry business. Carrying on the business alone, A. C. remained the managing partner until his death in 1948. Novel for its time, A. C.'s concept of accounting as a creative discipline was the foundation of Ernst & Ernst's success. He believed that accountants should be thoroughly knowledgeable about their clients' operations, and use that knowledge to help their clients by drawing attention to weaknesses and offering constructive suggestions. Implementing his philosophy, Ernst created the Special Services Dept. in 1908, the predecessor of current management-consulting services. Tax services were first offered after the introduction of the federal income tax in 1913.

Beginning in 1908, Ernst & Ernst experienced rapid growth. The first offices outside Cleveland were opened in Chicago and New York in 1909, followed by several other cities in quick succession. In 1919, 6 new offices were opened, to bring the total to 19. During the 1920s, the firm became national in scope, opening 26 more offices and moving its Cleveland office to the Union Trust (Huntington) Bldg. Having clients with foreign operations, Ernst considered for some time establishing international operations. In 1923, Ernst entered into a working agreement with Sir Arthur Whinney and Sir Chas. Palmour, partners of the British accounting firm Whinney, Murray & Co. The arrangement proved to be mutually satisfactory, and over the years it evolved into Whinney, Murray, Ernst & Ernst, the international operations of Ernst & Ernst. The death of Ernst led to the formation of a management committee, which selected Hassell Tippett as the new managing partner. Under his leadership, the Ernst & Ernst Internatl. Div. was created, and 66 new offices in the U.S. and Canada were opened. With its international headquarters in New York City, Ernst & Whinney was, in 1986, one of the fastest-growing major accounting firms in the world, employing 3,000 people in the U.S. and 5,000 in other countries.

**ERNSTHAUSEN FOUNDATION.** *See* **JOHN F. & DORIS E. ERNSTHAUSEN CHARITABLE FOUNDATION**

**ESTONIANS.** Estonia, situated on the northeastern shores of the Baltic Sea, became a republic in 1918 after winning independence from Russia. In June 1940, it was invaded and occupied by the Soviets and subsequently was annexed to the USSR. WORLD WAR II brought alternate Soviet and German occupations, ending in 1944 with the reimposition of Soviet rule. It is difficult to trace Estonian immigrants to America in the late 19th and early 20th centuries, because prior to 1918 they carried Russian passports and were entered on immigration records as Russians. It is believed that the first Estonian settler in Cleveland was Geo. Tammik, who arrived in 1903. Until 1945, only about 35 more people were recorded here as Estonian immigrants. After World War II, a substantially greater number of Estonians came to the U.S., mostly political refugees. During the years 1945–61, about 11,200 Estonian refugees were admitted to the U.S.; about 200 of them found homes in the Greater Cleveland area.

Although Estonians are one of the smallest ethnic groups in the Cleveland area, their national consciousness has remained very high. Cultural, social, and political activities of the community are centered in their organizations. The oldest Cleveland Estonian association, Arendaja, was founded over 60 years ago (1925) by the first Estonian settlers in the area. In 1986 it still served as a social and cultural club promoting good fellowship, understanding, and mutual help among its members. Ohio Eesti Vaba-

dusvoitlejate Uhing the Estonian Freedom Federation, Inc., Ohio Chap.) was founded in 1953. Its major aim has been the continuation of the struggle for Estonian independence. Its activities also include observations of historical holidays of Estonia and preservation of traditions and customs of the homeland. Estonians are overwhelmingly Lutheran. Their church, Eelk Cleveland, Ohio Kogudus (the Estonian Evangelical Lutheran Church of Cleveland, Ohio), is at 3245 W. 98th St. In 1986, services were conducted by clergy from Toronto, Canada. Most of the 1st-generation immigrants are members of this church. Estonians are one of 21 nationalities belonging to the CLEVELAND CULTURAL GARDEN FED. The Estonian Garden was officially dedicated in 1966. It is dominated by a tall concrete monument, which is surrounded by white birches and other native plants that depict a typical Estonian landscape.

Andreas Traks

**EUCLID** is a city located on the lakeshore to the east of Cleveland, bounded on the east by Lake County and on the south by RICHMOND HTS. It was incorporated as a village in 1903 out of a large portion of EUCLID TWP. and soon grew into one of Cuyahoga County's major industrial cities. Over 140 firms, including Euclid, Inc., Chase Brass & Copper, the LINCOLN ELECTRIC CO., Fisher Body, and the RELIANCE ELECTRIC CO., are currently located in the city. Euclid was named for the Greek mathematician by a member of the CONNECTICUT LAND CO.'s surveying party. Its population at the time of incorporation was 1,640. In 1914, a portion of the village's western edge was annexed to Cleveland, reducing its size to its current 10 sq. mi. In 1930, Euclid became a city when its population reached 12,751. In 1980, its population stood at 64,000, making it the 13th-largest city in Ohio. The local school system, which became independent of the county in 1922, has an enrollment of 6,400 students in 8 elementary, 3 junior high, and 1 high school. There are 26 churches representing 16 denominations in the city. Seven Catholic and 1 Lutheran grade school are operated by various churches. A variety of ethnic groups are represented in the local population, with individuals of Slovenian extraction predominating. In 1980, 9% of the population was black. The city is governed by a mayor-council system. All city offices, as well as the police station, library, school board, and recreational facilities, are located in Memorial Park on E. 222nd St. Briardale Greens, a public golf course, is located nearby. The Nottingham Filtration Plant was constructed in Euclid in 1951.

Voorhees, Leonard B., *Euclid, Ohio, 1797–1847* (rev. ed., 1977).

**EUCLID AVENUE** follows the historic Lake Shore Trail of the Indians. It was laid out by Cleveland village trustees in 1815 and was surveyed the following year. It takes its name from the small settlement of surveyors to the east in EUCLID, Ohio, but as late as 1825 it was known as the Buffalo Rd. because it served as the major route to that city. In the 1820s, Euclid was a narrow road through the woods, unpaved and unlighted. It was recognized by the state legislature as a highway in 1832, and 2 years later it was covered with planks to the city limits. The street soon became the first choice of residence for many Clevelanders, and by mid-century it was well on its way to becoming "the most beautiful street in the world." Between Erie (E. 9th) St. and Willson Ave. (E. 55th St.), Cleveland's foremost men of wealth began to build mansions set in deep, spacious lawns. JOHN D. ROCKEFELLER purchased a home there in 1868, where he lived until moving to New York

City in 1884. The street gained the official status of an avenue in 1870, and no avenue in the world, it was claimed, presented such a "continuous succession of charming residences and such uniformly beautiful grounds." In the 1870s, fine residences began to fill the open spaces east of Willson Ave., and the 1880s saw many of the avenue's largest houses built. Cleveland architect CHAS. F. SCHWEINFURTH, the premier residential architect of Euclid Ave., designed no fewer than 15 mansions there over the years, many in the Romanesque idiom. That style seemed to be an architectural equivalent for the ambitions and achievements of Cleveland's most prominent industrialists and financiers of the period. It was still fashionable in the early 1900s to build a mansion on Euclid Ave.—those of Leonard C. Hanna (1904) and SAMUEL MATHER (1910) were among the last to be built—but Cleveland's commercial center pushed inexorably eastward, and Euclid Ave. became an increasingly important traffic artery. The commercial and industrial crossroads at Euclid and E. 55th St. grew, too, further hastening the abandonment of the avenue as a residential street. By 1937, of the 40 great houses that had formed "Millionaires' Row," 7 remained standing. In 1986, the T. Sterling Beckwith House (ca. 1863), home of the UNIVERSITY CLUB, was the only 19th-century mansion still surviving.

Wilson, Ella G., *Famous Old Euclid Ave.* (1932).

The **EUCLID AVENUE BAPTIST CHURCH,** located at E. 18th St. and Euclid Ave., referred to as "Mr. Rockefeller's church," had its origins in the spring of 1846 when a group of teachers from the FIRST BAPTIST CHURCH and several other churches organized the Cleveland Union Sabbath School. They met in the building at Eagle St. and Erie (E. 9th) St. Miss Frances Twitt, one of the teachers, is credited with being the founder. In 1848 the Sunday school, which had moved to the corner of Kinsman and Erie St., had so expanded that property at Erie St. and Ohio St. (Central Ave.) was purchased, and a new building was erected in 1850. When the congregation of the Second Presbyterian Church moved to Superior St., the Baptists purchased their church on Rockwell St., and in Mar. 1851 they moved it to the Erie St. property. Rev. J. Hyatt-Smith became pastor in Apr. 1851; religious services began on 20 July 1851. In August, a group of 44 members of First Baptist received permission to separate from the church in order to help form the new congregation, and on 19 Aug. 1851, the Erie St. Baptist Church was organized.

During the pastorate of S. B. Page (1861–66),the church assumed control of the Scovill Ave. Baptist Mission at Sterling (E. 30th) and Scovill Ave. The name was changed to Second Baptist Church of Cleveland in 1868. With a substantial increase in membership, it was decided to relocate; the building was sold to the German Evangelical Protestant Church; and property at the southwest corner of Euclid Ave. and Huntington (E. 18th) St. was purchased; and on 14 June 1871 the cornerstone was laid. With a new location, the name was changed to Euclid Ave. Baptist Church. JOHN D. ROCKEFELLER, who had joined the church when he was a teenager, had taught Sunday school, and had served as superintendent at the Scovill Mission, was named superintendent of the new church Sunday school in 1872 and served until 1905. He served as a trustee (1883) and was one of the church's most generous benefactors. Over the years the church was active in missionary work, organizing the Judson Missionary Society, the Garden St. Mission, the St. Clair Mission, and the Baptist Home for Old People.

When membership rose to over 2,000, it was decided that a larger building was needed; the church property was sold to John D. Rockefeller, Jr., and property on the northeast corner of Euclid and E. 18th St. was purchased. A new sanctuary was built in which the first services were held 23 May 1926. In June 1926, John D. Rockefeller, Sr., contributed $200,000 and $100,000 conditional on matching gifts from other parishioners. John D. Rockefeller, Jr., also contributed $50,000 toward completion of the new auditorium. The building, designed by Walker & Weeks, was constructed of glazed terra cotta brick. It had a 234-ft. frontage on the west side of E. 18th; an auditorium seating over 2,300 people; and a 2-story Sunday school unit. During the week of 3–8 Apr. 1927, Dr. John Snape led formal dedicatory services for the $1.25 million building. Although the church prospered for several years, it was threatened with foreclosure on the mortgage in Feb. 1934. In Oct. 1936 Dr. D. R. Sharpe, executive secretary of the Baptist Assoc. of Cleveland, appealed to the Rockefellers for assistance. They contributed $250,000 for purchase of the land and the building but stipulated that the titles be transferred to the Baptist Assoc., and that they not be asked again for any contributions. During the pastorate of Dr. Bernard C. Clausen in the 1940s, the neighborhood changed; there was dissension within the congregation over his preaching and his stand on political issues; and there was a steady decline in membership. Dr. Clausen resigned in 1950. In Jan. 1956, the 300-member congregation decided to discontinue the church, and on 1 July 1956, Rev. Richard Waka conducted the final service in the chapel. For the next several years, the church building served as headquarters for the Cleveland Area Church Fed., the CLEVELAND BAPTIST ASSOC., and the Inner City Protestant Parish. On 8 July 1957, the delegates to the Cleveland Baptist Assoc. voted to dispose of the 30-year-old structure and empowered the trustees to sell or lease the building. The building was not sold but was demolished in the fall of 1961, and the property eventually became a parking lot.

*Historical Sketches: Seventy-five Years of the Euclid Avenue Baptist Church, Cleveland, Ohio 1851–1926* (1927).

The **EUCLID AVENUE CHRISTIAN CHURCH,** begun in 1843, became one of the largest Disciples of Christ congregations in the city. Members of the Disciples Church in Euclid, which itself originated in the FRANKLIN CIRCLE CHURCH OF CHRIST, desired a church near their own Doan Brook neighborhood. As a result, on 4 July 1843, a group assembled in a maple grove near where the brook crosses Euclid Ave. Thirty conversions resulted from this assembly, as well as the plans for a new church. Within a month, the congregation requested formal dismissal from the mother church. The church met in homes until 1848, when a church was constructed on Euclid between Doan (E. 105th) and Republic. At the turn of the century, the church moved to a magnificent green stone building at E. 100th and Euclid in a residential section. Peak membership was reached in 1929, when 130 of its 2,088 members left to form the Heights Christian Church in Shaker Hts. As the neighborhood changed, membership declined to fewer than 900, who came largely from E. CLEVELAND and CLEVELAND HTS. to attend services. To better serve its parishioners, the Euclid Ave. Christian Church followed the pattern set by several other denominations and moved east to 3663 Mayfield Rd. in Cleveland Hts. The old church building was sold to the East Mt. Zion Baptist Church, the first black church to hold services on Euclid Ave.

The **EUCLID AVENUE CONGREGATIONAL CHURCH** was organized as the First Presbyterian Church of E. Cleveland in Nov. 1843, the outgrowth of a Sunday school started in 1828 at DOAN'S CORNERS by Sally Cozad Mather Hale and associated with the "Plan of Union," a cooperative church-founding effort between Presbyterians and Congregationalists dating to 1801. The congregation met in homes and barns until a plain 2-story brick building was built in 1845 at the corner of Euclid Ave. and Doan (E. 105th) St. The church was incorporated in 1847 with a membership of 62. In Feb. 1852, the members of the church severed their connection with the presbytery, and for a decade the congregation was known as the Independent Presbyterian Church. This break, the end of the pioneer Plan of Union, was sparked by dissent over the Presbyterian General Assembly's stand on abolition. The congregation was largely in favor of abolition and adopted the Congregational style of church government. In 1862 the church became known as First Congregational Church of E. Cleveland, and in 1867 a larger brick building was built on the corner of Euclid and Logan (E. 96th) St. It had a capacity of 600 persons and cost $25,000. The congregation numbered 109. In 1872 the name was again changed, to Euclid Ave. Congregational Church. The present (1986) building was dedicated on the Euclid and Logan site in 1887. It is a Romanesque building of stone, with a large Sunday school building at the rear. Four churches were started as missions of Euclid Ave. Congregational in the late 19th century, including Park Congregational, at Crawford and Hough avenues, and Lakeview Congregational, all ca. 1890. Hough Ave. Congregational was merged into Euclid Ave. Congregational in 1934. As the population of the surrounding neighborhood changed in the late 1940s and 1950s, the church considered following the lead of other neighboring congregations and relocating in the suburbs, but a decision was made to remain in the inner-city neighborhood. The church then embarked on an ambitious community outreach program, including daycare and the Hough House Service Ctr.

One Hundred Twenty-fifth Anniversary of Euclid Avenue Congregational Church, Cleveland, Ohio, 1843-1968 (1968).
Euclid Ave. Congregational Church Records, WRHS.

The **EUCLID AVENUE OPERA HOUSE** was known as one of the finest theaters in the U.S. Located at the corner of Euclid Ave. and Sheriff St., it was built in 1875. The theater cost $200,000 and was described on its opening night (6 Sept. 1875) as elaborate, luxurious, and very beautiful. It was completely carpeted, with a painted dome and intricate plasterwork. The interior, 70' deep x 65' wide, included a 54' x 76' stage and proscenium that measured 34' high x 37' wide. D. Graham, a specialist in theater architecture, designed the structure. The opera house seated 1,638. When refitted from gas to electricity in 1885, it was among the first theaters in the U.S. to make this move. JOHN A. ELLSLER, formerly of the ACADEMY OF MUSIC, formed a stock company that established the Euclid Ave. Opera House. Soon after its founding, Ellsler lost his fortune, and the opera house was sold at a sheriff's sale to MARCUS A. HANNA. On 24 Oct. 1892, the theater was destroyed by fire, but it was rebuilt on a grander scale than before. It reopened on 11 Sept. 1893. It thrived throughout the early 20th century. It was demolished in 1922. The HANNA THEATER, located at Euclid Ave. and E. 14th St., became its successor.

**EUCLID BEACH PARK,** one of the nation's best-known amusement centers, was located on the southern shore of Lake Erie at E. 156th St. and Nottingham Rd., about 8 mi. from PUBLIC SQUARE. The park, incorporated on 23 Oct.

1894 by a group of Cleveland investors, was originally managed by Wm. R. Ryan, Sr., a local businessman and politician. Ryan patterned the park after New York's Coney Island, offering a beer garden, freak shows, and gambling operations. Ryan severed his connection with the park in 1897 and opened a competing park, WHITE CITY, nearby. Lee Holtzman became the new director of Euclid Beach, but the enterprise failed and was offered for sale in 1901.

Dudley S. Humphrey II and 6 members of his family took over management of the park in 1901 after obtaining a 5-year lease. They had previously operated popcorn-vending machines and a concession at the facility, but they left in 1899 because they were dissatisfied with behavior at Euclid Beach. The Humphreys completely changed the character of the park in keeping with their own personal philosophy, which was embodied in the slogan "Nothing to depress or demoralize." They added many entertainment features to the facility, expanded beach and bathing facilities, and instituted a policy of "one fare, free gate and no beer." That allowed patrons to reach the park with only 1 street railway fare, and to enter free (paying only for whatever rides or facilities were used). This policy was maintained until the park closed. The Humphreys' policies attracted many families, as well as company and community groups, to the facility. The park was the scene of political gatherings, such as the local Democratic party "steer roast," and in 1910 the site of an important exhibition flight by aviator Glen Curtis. Euclid Beach remained extremely popular into the 1960s, when changing lifestyles, lake pollution, rising operational costs, and racial incidents caused its attendance and receipts to decline. The park closed on 28 Sept. 1969. The carved archway entrance, declared a historic Cleveland landmark in 1973, is the only restored feature that remains at the site.

Bush, Lee O.; Chukayne, Edward C.; Hehr, Russell A.; and Hershey, Richard F., Euclid Beach Park, A Second Look (1979).
Euclid Beach Park Is Closed for the Season (1977).

The **EUCLID BEACH PARK RIOT** was a disturbance on 23 Aug. 1946, one of a series of protests that summer against racial discrimination at the amusement park. EUCLID BEACH PARK had a long history of discrimination against black patrons. Discrimination suits against the park can be traced back to 1899; by ca. 1915, Euclid Beach and LUNA PARK had established policies of admitting blacks to their facilities only on certain days. Euclid Beach employed a special police force to expel any rowdy, intemperate, or otherwise unwelcome guests, including blacks; historians of the park note that management took steps to guarantee that patrons would find little there to offend them. The 1946 protests against racial discrimination at the park began on 21 July, when 20 people from American Youth for Democracy, the United Negroes and Allied Veterans of America, and the Natl. Negro Congress formed an interracial group to visit the park. A park policeman reportedly told the group that park policy permitted "no sitting, no talking, no mixing of any kind . . . between the races" and evicted the group. In a subsequent interview with the Call & Post, park manager Harris C. Shannon explained that the ban on black participation in "close contact" activities such as dancing, swimming, and skating was not discrimination but "business necessity": the park could afford to pay damages as a result of the few discrimination cases filed against it, but it could not afford to lose the business of its white patrons. Subsequent protests by black organizations aimed to dramatize discrimination and to make it unprofitable for park management, who claimed such protests were Communist-inspired.

Veterans' groups and civil-rights organizations mounted pickets at the park on several occasions, and violent disturbances inside park gates in August and September further angered the black community. On 23 Aug., 12 black and white members of the Committee of Racial Equality (CORE) visited the park but were escorted out by park police. City Transit employee Albert T. Luster, a black who had gone to the park to join the CORE group but never met it, was later attacked and beaten by a park policeman. Luster's beating prompted more protests and picketing; several lawsuits were filed against the park as a result of the evening's events. The summer's protests culminated on 21 Sept. in the most serious disturbance. A 6-member interracial group from CORE visited the park; as they were being evicted from the dance pavilion by park police, 2 off-duty black Cleveland policemen, Lynn Coleman and Henry MacKey, intervened on behalf of the group. After explaining to park police that evicting the CORE group was a violation of their civil rights, a scuffle broke out between park police and the two city policemen, and Coleman was shot in the leg with his own revolver. The event sparked a series of investigations and prompted city council legislation providing for licensing of amusement parks and revocation of a license for racial discrimination. At the mayor's request, the park closed for the season a week earlier than planned. When the park reopened in 1947, the dance pavilion was operated by a private dance club.

**EUCLID GENERAL HOSPITAL** (also known as Parkwood Hospital, Glenville Hospital, and Euclid-Glenville Hospital) is a voluntary, nonprofit community hospital located at 101 E. 185th St. and Lakeshore Blvd. in EUCLID, Ohio. Lack of hospital facilities in the Collinwood area spurred the formation of a hospital in the Glenville area in 1907 by the Parkwood Hospital Assoc. The hospital, located in an apartmentlike building at 701 Parkwood Ave., was known as Glenville Hospital and sometimes as Parkwood Hospital. Dr. Hudson Fowler, Sr., company surgeon for the New York Central Railroad, and Dr. JACOB E. TUCKERMAN were among the founders of the hospital and directed its early efforts. A training school for nurses was an integral part of the hospital from its beginning. Glenville was incorporated as a nonprofit hospital in 1927 and retained an all-physician board of trustees until 1944. The original hospital was replaced by a more modern facility in 1933. In 1950 the Euclid-Glenville Hospital Assoc. was formed, and plans were developed to build a new hospital at a site in Euclid. In 1952, Euclid-Glenville Hospital was built on the 185th St. and Lake Erie site. Euclid General underwent corporate restructuring in 1983 and became part of Lakeshore Health Systems and then STRATEGIC HEALTH SYSTEMS.

"Hospitals" Collection, Archives, Howard Dittrick Museum of Historical Medicine.

**EUCLID, INC.,** is one of the world's leading firms in the manufacture of off-highway, earthmoving, and hauling equipment. It started in 1926 as the off-highway business of the Euclid Crane & Hoist Co., a firm founded by Geo. Armington in 1909 in EUCLID. In 1931, Armington's son, Arthur, took over a small shop adjoining Euclid Crane & Hoist at 1368 Chardon Rd. and began his own business by incorporating the off-highway division as a separate firm, the Euclid Road Machinery Co. It began with 300 employees, producing as many as 20 15-ton trucks per month for the construction and mining industries. Euclid tripled its production during WORLD WAR II. After the war, the company continued to prosper. In 1946, it built a new plant

at E. 222nd St. and St. Clair Ave. It bought another plant nearby 3 years later and greatly expanded both by the early 1950s. The firm also gained an international reputation for its quality equipment and extended its overseas business by establishing a British subsidiary in 1950. By 1953, Euclid was a $33 million business with 1,600 employees, turning out 170 trucks per month—over half of the nation's off-highway dump trucks.

In 1953, General Motors acquired Euclid for $20 million to gain entry into the off-highway business. As a division of GM, Euclid continued to develop larger types of equipment and to expand by building a new plant in Hudson in 1959. However, GM was charged in an antitrust suit by the U.S. government and ordered to dispose of the Euclid Div. GM acquiesced in 1968 and sold Euclid to the WHITE MOTOR CO. It was then reorganized as Euclid, Inc. Under White, Euclid remained profitable but felt the financial difficulties of its parent company in the 1970s. In 1977, Daimler-Benz of West Germany purchased Euclid. Daimler-Benz provided Euclid with a source of funds and new markets, particularly overseas, as Euclid established plants in several foreign countries. Overseas sales accounted for almost 80% of its $200 million business. Euclid suffered through the recession of the early 1980s as the number of employees dropped to 800. As the construction-equipment industry remained sluggish, Daimler-Benz decided to sell Euclid, Inc., to a construction equipment firm, the Clark Michigan Co.—a subsidiary of the Clark Equipment Co.—in 1984. Clark subsequently announced the closing of the Cleveland plant.

**EUCLID NATIONAL BANK.** See **BANK ONE OF CLEVELAND**

**EUCLID TOWNSHIP** originated from actions taken by Gen. MOSES CLEAVELAND several months after the surveying of the Western Reserve was begun in July 1796. Forty-one of Cleaveland's surveyors camped at Conneaut Creek demanded considerations in excess of their original contracts because of the nearly intolerable working conditions they faced. Cleaveland settled by drawing up a new contract with the surveyors on 30 Sept. for their joint purchase of a township of 25 sq. mi. at $1 per acre. Each man was granted lakefront property, as well as a farm back in the rocky hills and plateaus. The surveyors were obligated to clear land, erect houses, sow wheat and grass, and settle a specified number of families during the next 3 years. The new owners named the area Euclid Twp. in honor of the Greek mathematician who was considered the "patron saint" of surveyors.

The area was first settled in 1797 but was not officially incorporated as a township until 1809. The western boundary of the area began at approximately E. 140th St.; the southern limit was near what is now Cedar Rd. The eastern limit was near present-day Winchester Rd., while the lake formed the northern edge of the township. Portions of the township were later incorporated into Cleveland, E. CLEVELAND, EUCLID, CLEVELAND HTS., S. EUCLID, LYNDHURST, and RICHMOND HTS. In 1828, the township trustees divided the area into 9 school districts. Two additional districts were added in 1900. Farming, fishing, and their allied trades were the main occupations of the township's residents during the 19th century. Quarries, sawmills, and shipbuilding made up other portions of the economy. In 1900 the population was 3,573. On 15 Aug. 1899, the northwest portion of Euclid Twp. voted to incorporate separately as Nottingham Village (now part of Cleveland). On 14 Feb. 1903, Euclid Village (now Euclid) incorporated. In 1917, Euclidville (now Lyndhurst), S. Euclid, and Claribel (now Richmond Hts.) incorporated as an independent village, causing Euclid Twp. to cease to exist as a political entity.

The **EUROPEAN VISION OF AMERICA** was the title given to an art exhibition sponsored jointly by the CLEVELAND MUSEUM OF ART, the Natl. Gallery of Art, Washington, D.C., and the Reunion des Musees Nationaux France in celebration of the U.S. bicentennial in 1976. The exhibition traced the way European nations had viewed the Americas from the time of Columbus's landing up until the 19th century. In 1973, Wai Kam Ho, curator of Chinese art at the Cleveland Museum of Art, proposed an exhibition that would explore the European view of America. English art historian Hugh Honour was invited to be guest curator and to write the catalog for the exhibition, which featured over 350 objects spanning 400 years. The exhibition included sculptures, paintings, drawings, prints, books, furniture, tapestries, maps, porcelains, and silverwork from 12 countries and over 50 museums and private collections. The oldest item was an illustrated edition of Columbus's report to King Ferdinand and Queen Isabella, published in 1493.

The exhibition opened in Dec. 1975 for a 10-week showing at the Natl. Gallery in Washington, D.C., prior to traveling to Cleveland for the 13-week period encompassing the 4th of July bicentennial celebrations. A final showing was held at the Grand Palais in Paris. While in Cleveland, the exhibition was the subject of a 1-hour television special, hosted by actor Peter Ustinov, shown nationwide on Public Broadcasting stations. When the exhibition closed in Cleveland on 8 Aug. 1976, an estimated 108,000 people from 30 states and 20 foreign countries had viewed the works of art, an average of 7,700 visitors a week. A grant from the Central Natl. Bank of Cleveland made it possible for those visitors to see the exhibition free of charge. *Time* magazine described the exhibition as the "most entertaining [bicentennial] exhibition in America."

**EVERETT, SYLVESTER T.** (27 Nov. 1838–13 Jan. 1922), was one of Cleveland's best-known financiers and business leaders. He financed and promoted the construction of some of the country's first electric railways. Everett was born in Liberty Twp. He worked on the family farm and attended a district school until the age of 12, when he joined an older brother in Cleveland. Everett attended public schools for a year and then obtained a job as a general utility boy in a dry-goods house. At the age of 13, he became a messenger boy for the banking house of Brockway, Wason, Everett (an older brother) & Co. Within a few years he became a cashier, leaving that position in 1858 to work briefly in a bank in Philadelphia. He then became superintendent of a petroleum company with oil-producing farms in the Oil Creek district of Pennsylvania. Everett returned to Cleveland in 1868 to assume management of Everett, Weddell & Co. (previously Brockway, Wason, Everett & Co.). In 1876, he joined the Second Natl. Bank, serving as its president, and then organized the Union Natl. Bank, which, under his management, became one of the city's leading financial institutions.

Everett was identified with many large interests in the mining and transportation industries. He was also active in city government, serving 7 terms as city treasurer between 1869–83. In that office he was credited with many reforms, including an enormous increase in public investment in municipal bonds. A staunch Republican, he was a delegate to several Republican conventions and was a close friend and supporter of both JAS. A. GARFIELD and Wm. McKinley. Pres. Garfield appointed Everett as the U.S. government director of the Union Pacific Railroad; McKinley offered him the ambassadorship to Austria-Hungary. Everett was personally acquainted with, or at least had met, every Republican president from Lincoln to Harding. Everett was also widely known as a pioneer in the promotion of electric railway construction. He promoted, financed, and built 2 of the first street railways (electric) in the U.S.—in Akron and in Erie, Pa—as well as several other lines. Everett was a leading art collector in Cleveland, owning some of Europe's finest art treasures. He was also a founder and charter member of the UNION CLUB. At his home at E. 40th and Euclid Ave., Everett entertained many famous Americans, including his friends Andrew Carnegie and J. P. Morgan. Everett married his first wife, Mary, of Philadelphia in 1860. After her death, he married Alice Wade, the granddaughter of JEPTHA WADE I, in 1879.

**EXCELSIOR** was a Jewish club established "for the purpose of establishing intimate friendly relations among ourselves, and to enjoy the advantages of an Association calculated to produce enlightened social and literary pleasure." Twenty-two men met on 20 Oct. 1872 in Halle Hall on Superior at the call of Solomon Austrian to form a social club. By the end of the year, 30 men had purchased a share of stock apiece at $50 per share. The club was established, in part, as a reaction to Jewish exclusion from the social clubs of Cleveland, such as the UNION CLUB and the Century Club. It included in its membership only upwardly mobile Jews with German cultural backgrounds and was typical of the Jewish social clubs of the emerging upper-middle class founded throughout the U.S. in the 1870s and 1880s.

During its existence, the Excelsior Club met at 5 locations. In its first year, meetings were held at Weisgerber's Hall on Prospect and Brownell. In 1873, the club entered into a 3-year lease for use of the Corlett Bldg. on Erie (E. 9th) St. In 1876, it moved into the specially designed 2d and 3d floors of the newly constructed Halle Bldg. at Erie and Woodland. In 1887, a large building designed by Cudell & Richardson was dedicated at 38th and Woodland. It was built on property formerly owned by Dr. Jas. Horwitz, a charter member of the club. In 1908, Excelsior moved into a new home on Euclid Ave. in the Wade Park district. This latter building is today (1985) Thwing Hall of CASE WESTERN RESERVE UNIVERSITY. The club sponsored a variety of social events for its members, including balls, musicals, and plays, as well as provided dining facilities, card and billiard rooms, reading rooms, a library, a bowling alley, and other recreational and social facilities. In 1931, the Excelsior leadership recognized that the OAKWOOD CLUB, founded in 1905, included many of the Excelsior members and provided similar and expanded activities. A merger of the two clubs was effected in Jan. 1931.

Oakwood Club Records, WRHS.

**EXECUTIONS** of convicted criminals sentenced to die were carried out at the local level in Ohio prior to 1885, when the state legislature moved all executions to the state penitentiary. Between 1812–85, 9 convicted murderers were executed by hanging in Cuyahoga County; the last execution occurred in 1879. The first execution in Cleveland was the only public hanging in the city. JOHN O'MIC (given variously as Omic, O'Mick, Poccon, and Beaver), an Indian convicted of the murder of trapper Daniel Buell, was hanged on 24 June 1812 (sometimes given as 26 June). In 1844 the state legislature prohibited public executions, and the next 8 men executed in Cuyahoga County were hanged inside the jail.

English immigrant Jas. Parks was hanged on 1 June 1855 for the 1853 murder of Wm. Beatson in Cuyahoga Falls. Dr. John W. Hughes, a local physician convicted of murdering his mistress, Tamzen Parsons, in the streets of BEDFORD, was hanged on 9 Feb. 1866, on the same gallows used to hang Parks. The cases of Parks and Hughes attracted much public interest and aroused much sympathy on their behalf; those who followed their footsteps to the gallows were less colorful, and their plights failed to attract similar feelings of sympathy. Alexander McConnell, an Irish immigrant who lived with his wife and 6 children in Canada, was executed on 10 Aug. 1866 for the 24 Mar. murder of Rosa Colvin. Lewis (or Louis) R. Davis was executed on 9 Feb. 1869 for firing the murder weapon during the 12 Sept. 1868 robbery of prosperous farmer and dairyman David P. Skinner of INDEPENDENCE. John Cooper was hanged on 25 Apr. 1872 for killing and robbing a friend who had refused to loan him money for train fare. Stephen Hood, convicted of the 17 July 1873 murder of his adopted 14-year-old son, was executed on 29 Apr. 1874. On 22 June 1876, Wm. Adin was hanged for the 4 Dec. 1875 murders of his wife, his stepdaughter, and the latter's friend. The last execution in Cleveland occurred on 13 Feb. 1879, when Chas. R. McGill was hanged for the 2 Dec. 1877 murder of his mistress, Mary Kelley.

As the history of executions in northeastern Ohio unfolded, the execution process became a grim ritual: the same gallows and rope traveled throughout the region for use in hanging condemned men. The efficiency of the execution itself was a constant concern, and the *Plain Dealer* praised Sheriff John M. Wilcox in 1879 for showing "how a man ought to be hanged." Despite the law against public executions, large crowds were present at several hangings inside the jail; the crowds were admitted by special passes distributed by the sheriff. Larger crowds gathered outside the jail and sometimes did not disperse until allowed to view the body. Newspapers gave detailed accounts of the lives and crimes of the condemned men, drawing moral lessons from their fates, and gave detailed descriptions of each execution, recording how long the heart continued to beat after the hanging and even in one instance describing the removal of the brain for an autopsy.

**EXPLORATIONS.** The map *Amerique Septentrionale*, published by Nicholas Sanson in 1650, not only was the first to adequately show Lake Erie but also charted the southern shore with an accuracy unmatched for more than a century. Earlier French maps, from 1612-42, not only were vague and inaccurate but also were admittedly based on reports from Indians living farther north or east. Although some French Recollet or Jesuit missionary must actually have visited the region of Cleveland prior to 1648, when and from whom Sanson obtained his information remains unknown. Iroquois warfare prevented European travel into the lower Great Lakes from 1649-54, but it appears that Pierre Esprit Radisson visited northern Ohio as an Onondaga captive in the winter of 1652. For the next 20 years, the numerous French explorers, including the 1669 expeditions of Joliet, Galinee, and Casson and the 1673/74 voyage of Joliet, followed the northern shore of Lake Erie. La Salle's 1679 voyage of the *Griffin* went eastward along Lake Erie's south shore en route to its ultimate disappearance in western Lake Michigan. Hennepin's account of this voyage suggested that northern Ohio was unoccupied, and the Cleveland region was not closely inspected. While N. Perrot noted that unlicensed English Indian traders were captured near Michilimacinac in 1684 and 1686, their identities and their routes to Lake Huron are unrecorded. The French, English, and Dutch maps published between 1650-1723 suggest little direct information from northeastern Ohio, despite Cadillac's establishment of Ft. Ponchartrain at Detroit in 1701 and the persistence of French missions in western New York State until 1713, and later at Niagara. Indeed, both the Bellin maps and Charlevoix's accounts of his 1721 journey from Niagara to Detroit indicate that the southern interior was still unknown. The next vague French descriptions of the lower Cuyahoga and environs are probably attributable to CHAUSSEGROS DE LERY, engineer at Ft. Niagara who traveled down the Ohio in 1729, or Jacques Sabrevois, who in 1734 crossed from Detroit back to Presque Isle (Erie, Pa.). There are few new accurate data for northern Ohio in Fr. J. P. Bonnecamp's maps of the 1749 Bienville Expedition down the Ohio, although by that date the French had a post at the Wyandot village of "Sandoski" (1739), and the English had posts at Pickawillany on the Upper Miami.

The first European residence of the Cleveland area was the 1742-43 trading post established by Francois Saguin (see SIEUR DE SAGUIN), probably some 5-8 mi. up the Cuyahoga. That the official inspection report by Robt. Navarre of Detroit provided so little significant geographic information suggests that during the past decades the region had become well known. Although no individuals are noted, Navarre clearly indicates that both French and English traders were traversing northeast Ohio to deal with Detroit and Oswego. It seems likely that Conrad Weiser had visited the area between 1744 and 1748. Christopher Gist's journals describe it very clearly, and GEO. CROGHAN's 1748 letters to Richard Peters clearly indicate his familiarity with the region. Croghan's journal suggests that he had established an English post at the mouth of the Gichawaga (Cuyahoga) sometime prior to 1750. DeLery again crossed along the southern shore in 1754, briefly describing and charting the Cuyahoga River mouth.

The geographic details on the 1755 John Mitchell Map for the British Board of Trade are attributable to the explorations of these Pennsylvania explorers. Although much of Mitchell's inland geography is excellent, he showed a straight east-west Erie shoreline. The area from Sandusky Bay to Cleveland is described as *Canahoque*: The seat of War. The Mart of Trade, & Chief Hunting Grounds of the six N.Y. Iroquois on the Lakes & the Ohio.

The Gwahago (Cuyahoga) River is shown flowing about 50 mi. straight north from a large lake, with an Iroquois town, Gwahogo, on the east bank just above TINKER'S CREEK, although Mitchell shows 30 mi. from the site to the lake along the trail that ran from the forks of the Ohio River to Sandusky Bay. The slightly later Lewis Evans maps (after 1755) give a better picture of the Cleveland area, including descriptions of topography and mineral outcrops. Evans showed a French house and a Mingo town on the west bank of the CUYAHOGA RIVER opposite a village of (Ot)Tawas on the trail from Pennsylvania that now crosses the river to run 90 mi. west to Sandusky. But these towns and posts appear to have disappeared by the winter of 1757/58, according to the captivity narrative of Jas. Smith.

In the fall of 1760, Maj. Robt. Rogers (see ROGERS EXPEDITION) sailed from Presque Isle along the south shore. Other than describing the (old) mouth of the Cuyahoga as 25 yds. wide, Rogers provided no new information beyond his later and questionable claim that Pontiac attended his meeting with a party of Ottawa Indians at the mouth of either Conneaut Creek, the Grand River, or the Cuyahoga River. Early the following year, Sir Wm. Johnson, British agent for Northern Indians, was summoned from Oswego to Detroit, spending at least 1 night at the Cuyahoga.

Both of the British expeditions sent to deal with the warring western Indians in 1764 were accompanied by geographers. Thos. Hutchins, who accompanied Henri Bouquet from Ft. Pitt to the forks of the Muskingum, produced a detailed map in 1765 showing the true course of the Cuyahoga, with a Cuyahoga (Indian) town just below modern Akron, and an Ottawa town farther downstream on the east bank. The ill-fated Bradstreet voyage (see BRADSTREET'S DISASTER) along the lakeshore was documented by Lt. JOHN MONTRESOR, who going west described the Cuyahoga (which he terms *asseequesix*, or *au saquein*) as being "the river where the Upper Nations hunt, and also paddle six leagues (13.2 to 16.6 miles) up this river, land on the east side, and from thence march loaded to Fort Duquesne, now Fort Pitt, in six days. . . . The river is navigable for birch canoes 60 miles up. . . ." On his return from Detroit, Montressor discovered that for a barge the Cuyahoga was navigable upstream only for 5 mi., to a place called *le petit rapide*.

The increasingly bitter Indian reaction to the English colonists' westward incursion farther south again rendered northeast Ohio dangerous after 1764. It appears likely that some Indian agents operating out of Montreal, such as Matthew Elliot, were able to maintain temporary posts at the Cuyahoga mouth. And the Moravian missionary John Heckewelder, who had first visited Ohio with Christian Post in the late 1760s, was able to pass through the region accompanied by David Zeisberger in 1772. Yet during the American Revolution itself, virtually all of northeast Ohio was uninhabited. Heckewelder returned from Canada with his surviving Delaware converts in the spring of 1786, to establish the temporary village of PILGERRUHE on the east bank of the Cuyahoga just below Tinker's Creek. At that time, or within a few months, John Askin of Detroit had at least 2 British trading posts on the Cuyahoga. About 7 mi. above the lake was a house operated by Elliot, Wm. Caldwell, and Alexander McKee, and another post was operated by Duncan and/or Neil near the lake. During the next decade, the exploration of the region was beyond the military limits of the newly formed United States of America. Following Jay's Treaty and the Treaty of Greenville, those Loyalist posts and the associated Moravian sites were abandoned. Heckewelder left his now-famous 1796 map for the first CONNECTICUT LAND CO. survey party under the direction of MOSES CLEAVELAND. The period of exploration had ended, and that of resettling had begun.

David Brose
Cleveland Museum of Natural History

**EXPOSITIONS.** *See* **FAIRS AND EXPOSITIONS**

# F

The **F. B. STEARNS COMPANY,** founded by Frank B. Stearns (6 Nov. 1878–5 July 1955), produced automobiles in Cleveland from 1898 until Dec. 1929. Inspired by a display of self-propelled vehicles at the Chicago World's Fair in 1893, Stearns produced his own 1-cylinder automobile in 1896. In 1898, he and 2 partners—Ralph R. and Raymond M. Owen—established F. B. Stearns & Co. Working in a shop behind the Stearns family home at Euclid and Republic (E. 101st) St., the company made about 50 2-cylinder, 4-passenger automobiles between 1898–1900. The Owenses left the firm in 1900, and by 1901 Stearns had rented a shop at the corner of Euclid and Lakeview Ave. (E. 110th St.). He reorganized and incorporated the firm in 1902 as the F. B. Stearns Co. and served as president, general manager, and treasurer; his father, Frank M. Stearns, was vice-president and secretary.

Stearns began introducing new automobile models in 1903; the 80 cars it produced that year were all painted bright red. By 1906, production had increased to 300 cars a year. The company took pride in its workmanship, spending about 2,000 hours on each car. It was also proud of its cars' performances in races, endurance runs, and hill climbs. Refusing to build special racers, Stearns entered its stripped-down stock cars in these events, winning several times. By 1910, production had increased to 1,000 cars a year, and in 1911 Stearns introduced its first truck. Also in 1911, the company introduced its first automobile with a special Knight engine; the company had received the first U.S. license to build the British Knight sleeve-valve engines. From 1912–29, the company's cars were known as Stearn-Knights.

Stearns had branches and dealers in 125 cities in 1912 and produced 875 cars that year; by 1917 it was producing 4,000 cars yearly. During the war, the company produced Rolls Royce airplane engines as well as its own automobiles. Automobile production fell to 1,256 in 1919 but rose to 3,850 in 1920. In Dec. 1925, John N. Willys, head of the Willys-Overland Co. of Toledo, bought the controlling interest in F. B. Stearns. Stearns was almost bankrupt at the time of Willys's purchase and never completely recovered; production was stopped on 12 Dec. 1929, and the company dissolved on 30 Dec. Frank B. Stearns had retired from the firm at the end of 1917. He later worked to improve the diesel engine, obtaining 16 patents for his work and selling his engine to the Navy in 1935. He later took up organic farming. He married Mabelle Wilson in 1902.

Wager, Richard, *Golden Wheels* (1975).

**FACTORY HOSPITALS** were medical facilities that began to appear in the 1880s specializing in the treatment of emergency cases from Cleveland's industrial areas. Only a few such hospitals were actually attached to a specific factory. These were always larger companies engaged in the manufacture of metal products, usually with a high accident rate and without any emergency medical services nearby. The American Steel & Wire Co. for many years maintained such a facility in NEWBURGH. It was used only for casualty surgery and treatment of minor ailments. In 1884, St. Alexis Hospital was created to serve primarily the Cuyahoga Valley industrial area. A Dispensary & Accident Dept. was officially formed in 1887. For many years ST. ALEXIS HOSPITAL was mainly a surgical hospital, with a continuous major load of accident and industrial cases. With a similar purpose, St. Clair Hospital was chartered in 1891 to serve the industrial area between E. 26th and E. 45th, an area that by 1913 included 100 factories employing 50,000 men. Most of its patients were surgical or emergency cases, men injured on railroads or in factories. St. Clair had 30 beds in 1896, and 43 in 1920. It was supported by annual contributions, most of which came from corporations and manufacturers in the vicinity. In the 1910s, many of the larger factories began to incorporate infirmaries with either a full- or part-time medical staff. The reasons were partly humanitarian, but also cost-efficient, as adequate health care reduced the number of days lost per year per worker due to accidents or sickness. By 1920, 50% of industrial workers in Cleveland were receiving some sort of medical treatment in industrial plants. At that time in the city, there were 7 full-time and over 20 part-time physicians devoted exclusively to industrial medicine, many of whom were shared by more than 1 company. Industrial nursing also began to develop at this time and eventually led to the founding of an Industrial Nurses' Club in Cleveland.

Cleveland Hospital Council, *Cleveland Hospital and Health Survey, 1919–1920* (1920).

**FAIR HOUSING PROGRAMS** developed in the 1960s and 1970s as a result of the civil-rights movement to promote open, nondiscriminatory housing and the integration of the Cleveland area's residential neighborhoods. As the area's black population increased in the decades prior to 1960, BLACKS were restricted to increasingly segregated neighborhoods such as HOUGH, GLENVILLE, MT. PLEASANT, and Central. In the 1950s, black homebuyers began to escape these overcrowded neighborhoods for homes in the suburbs. They encountered what one historian called a "complex network of discrimination and prejudice" that included the use of restrictive covenants, problems securing mortgages, and the hostility of whites, which occasionally resulted in violence. In some neighborhoods, however, such as Ludlow and Lomond in SHAKER HTS., some white residents worked to calm the fears of others and to promote integration (see LUDLOW COMMUNITY ASSOC. and LOMOND ASSOC.). With the development of the civil-rights movement in the 1960s, a number of community-based "human rights" groups were formed to promote open housing. Many of these joined together in Feb. 1964 to form the Fair Housing Council, a federation of neighborhood groups, which, with funding from the Businessmen's Interracial Committee on Community Affairs, hired a housing coordinator in late 1965. It also helped people file complaints with the Ohio Civil Rights Commission. While the numerous community-based organizations did much to promote a liberal consensus on fair housing, the most important and active fair-housing organizations were Fair Housing, Inc., PATH, Operation Equality, and the Cuyahoga Plan. Fair Housing, Inc., incorporated in Apr. 1962 by Joseph E. Finley, KENNETH W. CLEMENT, and Gilbert J. Seldin, described its purposes as "opening up all of Cleveland's suburbs, east and west, to Negro buyers" in order "to ease the pressure on certain areas." It financed its operations through the sale of stock at $10 a share and hired a real-estate broker, Stuart E. Wallace, to locate homes in white neighborhoods for blacks and to find homes in integrated communities for interested white buyers. The agency sold 350 homes, 199 to black families, before the stockholders decided in Sept. 1971 that their goals had been accomplished and voted to dissolve Fair Housing, Inc. It was succeeded by Stuart E. Wallace & Co. Realtors.

The PATH (Plan of Action for Tomorrow's Housing) Assoc. developed from the PATH Committee, appointed in Sept. 1966 by the Greater Cleveland Associated Foundation to investigate "the nature and extent of housing problems" in the area and to establish housing goals. In Mar. 1967, the 30-member committee, headed by attorney Jas. Huston, issued The PATH Report, which described "a housing crisis in Greater Cleveland," argued that "the housing problems of the City of Cleveland and those of the suburbs are interrelated," outlined steps to improve the housing situation, and promoted neighborhood integration. To implement the proposals, board members formed the PATH Assoc. on 16 Mar. 1967 and hired Irving Kriegsfeld as executive director. Like the PACE ASSOC. in education, PATH became an important political force on behalf of better and open housing, working with city government and the private sector to improve housing in the area, especially the inner city. It established the Contractor's Assistance Corp. to help small contractors in housing construction and rehabilitation, supported the Lee-Seville public-housing project, worked with realtors and with the insurance industry, lobbied federal and state legislators, and, in the 1970s, unsuccessfully sued 5 local suburbs for racial discrimination. By mid-1974, PATH was unable to secure funding from foundations and closed its office.

Operation Equality, a national program sponsored by the Urban League, began in Cleveland in Nov. 1966 and worked closely with the Fair Housing Council. Financed by a 3-year, $1.5-million Ford Foundation grant, it maintained a list of open-occupancy housing and established a housing office to help black buyers and renters find homes. It provided prospective black buyers with information about the various suburban communities and in May 1968 began taking them on bus tours of suburban homes. In Dec. 1967, Operation Equality launched a campaign to lobby the 57 communities in the area to pass open-housing resolutions. As federal legislation and Supreme Court rulings increasingly made fair housing the law of the land, Operation Equality shifted its focus in 1969 from trying to get homes listed on the open market to convincing real-estate brokers to work with black buyers, and to working with blacks to file discrimination suits and complaints in the courts and with federal and state agencies. Grants from the Ford and Cleveland foundations supported the work of Operation Equality during the early 1970s as it worked to obtain open-housing agreements from large apartment-management firms, promoted economic integration through the use of scattersite public housing in the suburbs, and served as a consultant for federal and local agencies.

Since the mid-1970s, Cleveland's fair-housing watchdog has been the Cuyahoga Plan of Ohio, Inc., incorporated on 13 Mar. 1974. This "private, non-profit corporation" began operation on 18 Nov. 1974 with $134,000 in grants from the CLEVELAND and GEO. GUND FOUNDATIONS. Its aims are to "end discriminatory housing practices; desegregate neighborhoods throughout the county; [and] strengthen and maintain already integrated neighborhoods." Like earlier fair-housing groups, it established a housing information service and negotiated with the real-estate industry and with lending institutions to eliminate discriminatory practices. It also works closely with government agencies, and in the mid-1980s put together a pilot program to use state funds for low-interest loans for first-time homebuyers moving into segregated neighborhoods. In the early 1980s, the Cuyahoga Plan released a series of reports on housing in the area, which found continued improvements in the racial diversity in the eastern suburbs, but not in the western suburbs. These reports suggested that, despite all of the gradual progress and all the effort expended on behalf of fair housing, Cleveland remained "the second most segregated area in the nation."

**FAIRFAX, FLORENCE BUNDY** (1907–6 Mar. 1970), was a long-time black employee of the city's Recreation Dept. who became assistant commissioner of recreation in 1966. The Fairfax Recreation Ctr., built at 2335 E. 82nd St. in 1959, was named in her honor. A native Clevelander, Fairfax was a graduate of Cleveland Hts. High School and the College for Women of Western Reserve University. In 1928 she became physical-education director in the city's Div. of Recreation, and following graduation from college in 1929, she became physical-education director of the Central Recreation Ctr. In 1934 she was appointed playground supervisor in the Central District. She became superintendent of the Bureau of Recreation Ctrs. in 1944. On 16 Aug. 1953, Fairfax suffered severe injuries in an automobile accident, which took the life of her husband, Lawrence E. Fairfax. After 7 months she was back at work, and in May 1954 she was appointed superintendent of the new Bureau of Special Activities, which was designed to help "the unattached youngster or independent street club or gang . . . find better ways and better places to play" and to help solve the problem of juvenile delinquency by guiding problem youth to appropriate social agencies. She hoped the bureau would be able "to help children to form good social patterns of behavior through recreation." In recognition of her years of devotion to the recreational needs of Cleveland's inner-city youth, the Fairfax Recreation Ctr. was dedicated in her honor in 1959. In 1966, Mayor Ralph

Locher appointed her assistant commissioner of recreation, a position she held until her death.

The **FAIRHILL MENTAL HEALTH CENTER** was a state psychiatric facility in Cleveland dedicated to short-term care. Fairhill Psychiatric Hospital opened in 1959 as one of 5 state psychiatric facilities in Cleveland. It occupied the former U.S. MARINE HOSPITAL on Fairhill Rd. Its initial purpose was as an intensive, short-term hospital. Many of its patients were transferred to long-term hospitals. Although Fairhill was originally given a capacity of 200 beds, by 1960 only 70 were in use because of staffing problems. With the enactment of the Community Mental Health Ctrs. Act by Congress in 1963, the name was changed to Fairhill Mental Health Ctr. Its emphasis remained on short-term care, although its overall purpose was slightly revised, "to provide comprehensive psychiatric services to all residents of a given geographical area, regardless of socio-economic status." Fairhill's area primarily consisted of Cleveland's east side and eastern suburbs. As a state psychiatric hospital, Fairhill attempted to minimize many of the negative aspects attributed to state hospitals. Its interior design was cheerful and bright. Many innovative therapeutic programs were developed to encourage patient involvement. Such programs included a daily meeting of patients in the various wards, the creation of a patient disciplinary and rules committee, and, to counter withdrawal, current-events sessions, mental-health films, and other group activities. A "neighboring" program was also introduced to link up patients with volunteers in the community. In 1966, Fairhill became an "open hospital" (no locked doors), one of 3 such hospitals in the country.

From the mid-1960s, Fairhill began to suffer from budgetary restrictions and constantly changing state directives. One result was overcrowding: in 1966, admissions were limited to only 50%, because of delays in transferring patients to long-term hospitals. In 1974 the state urged a shift in mental-health services to community health organizations. That coincided with the dismissal of the hospital's superintendent, Dr. Aladar E. Mako. His replacement was Robt. McMillen. In 1975, a budget crisis resulted in the transfer of 38 employees to institutions for the mentally retarded. Two years later, in 1977, the hospital's out-patient clinic was closed. Despite a $3 million renovation in 1980, Fairhill continued to be burdened with a tremendous clinical load. Overcrowded conditions persisted, and the hospital was criticized for early discharges. By 1983 it was in danger of being decertified for Medicare and Medicaid because it did not meet federal standards. As the Cleveland Psychiatric Institute was in a similar situation, the Ohio Dept. of Mental Hygiene & Correction decided to consolidate the two hospitals rather than make improvements on each separately. Despite community opposition, Fairhill Mental Health Ctr. closed in Dec. 1983.

**FAIRMOUNT PRESBYTERIAN CHURCH** at Fairmount Blvd. and Coventry Rd. in CLEVELAND HTS. grew out of Presbyterian Sunday school classes organized by Dr. Paul F. Sutphen of Second Presbyterian Church and his assistant, Rev. Edward C. Young. Classes were held in the homes of neighborhood families in 1912-13, then in a real-estate office at the corner of Fairmount Blvd. and Wellington Rd., and subsequently (1915-16) in a frame chapel built (1915) by the Presbyterian Union on land purchased at the corner of Fairmount and Coventry Rd. A petition for the organization of a church was presented 11 Oct. 1916 to the Presbytery of Cleveland by Thos. E. Borton and others; the request was granted, and Fairmount Presbyterian Church of Cleveland Hts. was granted a charter in Oct. 1916. The

first service was conducted on 5 Nov. 1916 and Rev. Percy Elwood Erickson of Newark, N.J., Fairmount's first permanent minister, conducted his first service on 3 June 1917. Unfortunately, 3 months later, the chapel, struck by lightning, was destroyed by fire, but the structure was replaced almost immediately by another frame building constructed on an adjacent site. On 7 Dec. 1917, the congregation voted to incorporate as a nonprofit organization, the Fairmount Presbyterian Church. A parish house, including a religious-education unit, was built in the 1920s. The indebtedness of the parish house was paid off in 1937, and a campaign for funds for the building of a new sanctuary was launched. A traditional English-village, parish-type church was completed. Constructed of Ohio sandstone, it featured a stone tower surmounted by a stone spire, a series of 37 stained-glass windows created by Dutch artist Joep Nicolas, and a pipe organ built by WALTER HOLTKAMP. The first service was held on 29 Mar. 1942; the formal dedication was 18 Apr. 1942. During the tenure of Rev. Dr. John Magill (1967–72), a housing development, Fairmount Village, located at E. 90th St. and Hough Ave., was completed, and a yoked fellowship with Greater Avery AME Church at 7503 Wade Park was inaugurated. Rev. Henry W. Andersen, Fairmount's 6th minister, founded the Cleveland Covenant Concept in Dec. 1979, which subsequently led to the establishment of the GREATER CLEVELAND ROUNDTABLE—a multiracial urban forum that addressed the areas of public education, employment, housing and community well-being, and racism.

**FAIRMOUNT TEMPLE.** *See* **ANSHE CHESED**

The **FAIRMOUNT THEATRE FOR THE DEAF** was America's first professional resident theater for the deaf. Conceived in 1975 as part of the Fairmount Ctr. of the Creative Performing Arts, it significantly developed deaf theater as an artform. Though part of the center, it was founded by Brian Kilpatrick, a deaf actor, and Chas. St. Clair. Their intentions were to stage plays and make them available to the hearing-impaired by translating them into American Sign Language. They also wished to provide the hearing part of the audience with the added dramatic effects of sign language. Performances were carried out by speaking actors with a signing counterpart or by actors who signed as well as spoke their parts. Beginning in 1975, the theater presented *My Eyes Are My Ears with These Hands*, an original musical, which was videotaped and aired on local television. It won a local Emmy Award for Outstanding Service Program. *Alice in Deafinity*, a musical based on *Alice in Wonderland*, also played that season and later toured to New York at Lincoln Ctr.'s Summer Theater Festival. First-time deaf-theater presentations were done with plays such as Tennessee Williams's *Glass Menagerie*, Moliere's *The Doctor in Spite of Himself*, and Beckett's *Waiting for Godot*. In 1983, the Fairmount Theatre for the Deaf was awarded "The Most Popular Show" for its presentation *Smircus—A Mime Circus* at the 8th Internatl. Pantomime Festival of the Deaf in Brno, Czechoslovakia, where it represented the U.S. against 12 other competing countries. Debbie Anne Rennie, one of the theater's 5 actors, won an award for overall best actor. In Aug. 1984, the theater was chosen by the U.S. government (as part of a cultural-exchange program) to perform at the Jerash Festival in Amman, Jordan.

**FAIRS AND EXPOSITIONS.** Fairs and expositions have always provided an outlet for the public expression of the fundamental temper and economy of a community. As a midwestern county seat, Cleveland participated early in the enthusiasm for agricultural fairs, which were so much a part of 19th-century rural life. In addition, historical and commemorative celebrations served as occasions for this public expression of the community spirit. The transformation of the city into a manufacturing and commercial power inspired industrial expositions that were tributes to the dynamics of the 20th century. These events demonstrated the latest developments in technology and style, and although not as large as the more famous "world's fairs," several of them were landmarks in Cleveland's history.

County agricultural societies and fairs sprang up from New England to the Mississippi in the 1820s, based on the model of the Berkshire County Fair, Mass., in 1810. The Cuyahoga County Agricultural Society was established in 1823, the same year as the Geauga County Agricultural Society and fair, which claimed 160 years later to be the oldest continuously operating county fair in the U.S. The first CUYAHOGA COUNTY FAIR did not take place until 1829. It was held in PUBLIC SQUARE and the courthouse (see ARCHITECTURE, CIVIC). Livestock was exhibited in the Square, and the household and domestic arts were displayed in the FIRST PRESBYTERIAN (OLD STONE) CHURCH. An oddity of the 1820s was a craze for silkworm culture and the planting of mulberry trees, and various silken products were shown. However, the operation of the Cuyahoga County agricultural fair was not continuous. Revived in the late 1840s and 1850s, fairs were held on fairgrounds on Kinsman St., and in NEWBURGH and CHAGRIN FALLS. In 1894 the fair became established in BEREA at the Eastland Rd. site, where it continued to flourish for the next 90 years.

In 1870, the State Board of Agriculture selected Springfield as the location of the Ohio State Fair, and a group of Cleveland businessmen, including AMASA STONE and JEPTHA H. WADE I, decided that Cleveland would have its own fair. A private company, the Northern Ohio Fair Assoc., was incorporated in Feb. 1870. The purpose of the association was to promote agriculture, horticulture, and the mechanical arts and, because of the gentlemen's interests, to develop trotting races. Ninety acres of land were purchased on St. Clair Ave. in GLENVILLE, and exhibition buildings were erected, including an amphitheater seating 12,000. The first fair was held 4–7 Oct. 1870. The attendance was 85,000, more than the state fair attracted. There were cash premiums for exhibits of livestock, agriculture, mechanical arts, and domestic and household arts. In 1874, the premium list amounted to $30,000. The Northern Ohio Fair was discontinued after 1881, and the buildings were sold.

Beginning in the mid-19th century, a special impetus for public events was provided by the collective experience of a nation at war. The NORTHERN OHIO SANITARY FAIR in 1864 was a fundraising effort to help the CIVIL WAR, and the $78,000 it raised went to the Soldiers Aid Society and the U.S. Sanitary Commission. A large cross-shaped building was erected in Public Square, which had been enclosed by fences shutting off Superior Ave. and Ontario St. in 1852. The wings of the building contained an assembly hall seating 3,000, a floral hall, a dining hall, and the exhibition hall. Exhibits included livestock, implements, and art objects, and many of them were auctioned for the fund. The fair was held in February and March, and the building was lighted with gas and heated with stoves. In the 20th century, the Allied War Exposition came to Cleveland in 1918 to promote the sale of war-saving stamps for WORLD WAR I. Three miles of trenches represented a battlefield on the lakefront between E. 9th and W. 9th Sts. A mock battle was enacted, and weapons, machinery, and other war equipment were displayed. Iron-

ically, the exposition opened on 16 Nov., 5 days after the signing of the armistice. During the World War II years (1939–45), an annual FESTIVAL OF FREEDOM was presented, called "the nation's largest" 4th of July celebration. Pageants, mock battles, fireworks, and demonstrations by patriotic and military organizations drew capacity crowds to the CLEVELAND MUNICIPAL STADIUM every year.

Twice in the course of its history, Cleveland has mounted a major centennial exposition. The 100th anniversary of Moses Cleaveland's landing in 1796 was the occasion of a great celebration from 19 July–10 Sept. 1896. Among the features of the celebration were a replica of a pioneer log cabin erected in Public Square, a historical float parade, an evening reception and ball in GRAYS ARMORY, a bicycle parade from WADE PARK to Public Square, and a series of historical conferences on education, religion, and philanthropy. A large temporary triumphal arch was erected over Superior Ave. directly north of the recently completed SOLDIERS & SAILORS MONUMENT. The Centennial Arch was 79' high, 106' wide, and 20' thick. Constructed of a wooden frame covered with lath and plaster, it was ornamented with 6 plaster-cast groups and a sculptured frieze. At night it was illuminated with 900 electric lamps. The new CENTRAL ARMORY, erected in 1893, was the scene of mass meetings, concerts and a historical musical spectacle, gymnastic exhibitions by German, Czech, and Swiss groups, and a floral exhibition. The last day brought a celebration of Commodore Perry's victory at the Battle of Lake Erie, with a great industrial and military parade and an evening banquet, ending with a fireworks display over the lake.

The most memorable exhibition in Cleveland's history was the GREAT LAKES EXPOSITION of 1936 and 1937, planned to commemorate the centennial of Cleveland's incorporation as a city, as well as to celebrate the industrial trade empire of the 8 states bordering on the Great Lakes. The exposition benefited from the experimental work on quick and inexpensive construction at Chicago's Century of Progress in 1933–34. The style of the exposition's buildings was "simple, straight-forward, colorful and severe," and the architects hoped that they would "establish a trend in modern design just as did the buildings of the Columbian Exposition and the Century of Progress."

The fair was held on the Mall, in the PUBLIC AUDITORIUM and underground exhibition hall, and on the lakefront area created on filled land and reached by a bridge over the railroad tracks. Five major structures were erected, plus many notable smaller buildings and industrial exhibits. The five were the Horticulture Bldg., the Hall of Progress, the Automotive Bldg., an amphitheater for a transportation pageant, and the Marine Theater, rebuilt in 1937 for Billy Rose's Aquacade. A permanent 3½-acre horticultural garden was designed by A. DONALD GRAY and built on the lake side of the new municipal stadium. The festival atmosphere was enhanced through color and light. Ever since 1896, Cleveland's expositions have made artificial illumination an important feature, and the use of light as an architectural element was one of the major contributions of the Great Lakes Exposition. As a demonstration of 20th-century scientific systems and functional design, the lighting and architecture of the exposition made a contribution that has been unjustly overshadowed by the more renowned world's fairs. In 1941, Clevelanders were able to compare their exposition with parts of the New York World's Fair of 1939–40, as the exhibits of 22 nations were brought to the auditorium for the Cleveland Internatl. Exposition.

As an industrial exposition, the 1936 exposition was the climax of a series of expositions that began early in the century, when influential citizens realized that Cleveland was one of the most important industrial and commercial centers in America. In 1908, the Chamber of Commerce began planning a Cleveland INDUSTRIAL EXPOSITION of the products of local manufacturers. The exposition committee "wanted Clevelanders to understand the message of stack, and hammer, and wheel, and to realize the extent and variety and quality of Cleveland-made products." FRANCIS F. PRENTISS was chairman of the committee, and CHAS. F. BRUSH was president of the Chamber of Commerce.

No existing public hall could accommodate the 280 exhibitors, and a temporary building was constructed on the present city hall site at the foot of E. 6th St. The exposition building covered 57,036 sq. ft. It was described as being larger than the arena floor of New York's Madison Square Garden and larger than any existing exposition structure in the U.S. The Central Armory provided additional exhibition space, and the two buildings were connected by a bridge over Lakeside Ave. The exposition was held in June 1909 and was attended by 215,000 persons, breaking all records for such expositions. The combined area of the buildings was 4 times that of any previous exposition. The temporary building was an innovative structure with outer walls of wood covered with plaster and roofed with a tent. Three 70-ft. masts with radiating steel struts like an umbrella supported a network of cables that held the fireproof canvas roof. There was an exotic ornamental gateway at the 6th St. entrance, with plaster ornament representing wheels, gears, and hammers. The street approaches were elaborately decorated, and the exposition lighting was supplied by 20,000 electric lamps.

In 1914, the Cleveland Electrical Exposition was held to demonstrate the efficiency of electricity in illuminating, power, and household use. The exhibit was inaugurated on 20 May by Thos. A. Edison in the Wigmore Coliseum (Dodge–13th Bldg.). The displays confirmed Cleveland's leadership in the industry, owing in part to the work of Chas. F. Brush and the presence of the Natl. Electric Lamp Assoc. and Westinghouse in Cleveland. In 1915, the Cleveland Automobile Show was held in the coliseum, demonstrating Cleveland's preeminence in the automotive manufacturing field before it was superseded by Detroit in the 1920s. Of the 29 makes displayed, nearly all were defunct just 20 years later. The most important exhibition of the twenties was the Cleveland Industrial Exposition of 1927. It took place from 6–28 Aug. in the Public Auditorium, the plaza that had been cleared so far for the Mall, and a temporary west wing on the west side of the plaza. The latter was a large rectangular steel-framed exhibition shed approximately equal in size to the auditorium. The exposition attracted 650,000 visitors during 23 days. A band shell occupied one end of the plaza, and the centerpiece was the 225-ft. "Tower of Jewels," a classical tower with a fountain at the base and surmounted by a steel mast, illuminated with constantly changing colored floodlights.

Until 1922, Cleveland's fairs, expositions, and celebrations were held in Public Square, the Central Armory, temporary structures, and various other locations. With the completion of the Public Auditorium in 1922, and 10 years later the Lakeside underground exhibition hall, Cleveland was provided with a permanent public convention and exhibition center for the first time. The first exhibit in the auditorium was the American Bldg. Exposition, which featured an installation of 6 full-sized houses and 3 miniature homes. The Annual Automobile Show became a regular attraction; in Jan. 1924, 58 manufacturers displayed 240 models. Another regular exhibitor was the Natl. Machine Tool Builders Assoc., which began annual exhibitions in 1927. For several years the Public Auditorium and con-

vention hall was the largest such facility in the country, and in the 1930s and 1940s Cleveland was a national convention center. In the postwar period, the parade of industrial exhibitions continued, but any attempt to list the innumerable shows would be impossible. One of the most popular perennial exhibitions was the GREATER CLEVELAND HOME & FLOWER SHOW, first held in 1942. In 1964, the convention center was greatly enlarged by the construction of additional display areas and underground parking beneath the Mall and its new Hanna Fountains. In part because of these facilities, by the last quarter of the century the constant schedule of industrial and trade shows seems to have replaced the major exposition as the means of promoting Cleveland marketing across a wide region.

Eric Johannesen
Western Reserve Historical Society

**FAIRVIEW GENERAL HOSPITAL,** located at 18101 Lorain Ave., was founded in July 1892 by a group of local ministers and laymen of the Reformed church as a training school for religious sisters to provide care and religious instruction to the community. It was originally established as the Society for Christian Care of the Sick & Needy (also known as the Bethesda Deaconess House). In 1894 the "German Hospital," as it was then known, was located in a small house on Scranton Rd. and served the west side German community. From 1896–1955, it was located at 3305 Franklin Circle. In 1913 the German Hospital had a sanatorium for some of the city's tuberculosis patients. It changed its name from the German Hospital during WORLD WAR I, taking the name Fairview Park Hospital because of its location near a park named Fairview. In 1955, Fairview Park Hospital moved to its present location on Lorain Ave., and in 1960 it again changed its name, to Fairview General Hospital, to reflect its provision of all basic hospital services. It renovated and expanded its facilities in 1970 and again in 1974. Since its inception, the hospital has been involved in nursing and medical education. Its School of Nursing was formally established in 1909 and later moved to Codrington Hall in 1956. In July 1986, Fairview General Hospital affiliated with Lutheran Medical Ctr. in a joint venture called Health Cleveland, Inc. Health Cleveland, Inc., is a holding company for Fairview General Hospital and LUTHERAN MEDICAL CTR. and their subsidiaries and foundations.

**FAIRVIEW PARK,** located approximately 8 mi. from downtown Cleveland, is bounded on the west by N. OLMSTED, on the north by ROCKY RIVER, and on the east and south by the Rocky River Reservation of the Metroparks System. It occupies approximately 4.5 sq. mi. and was originally part of Rockport Twp., organized in 1812. In 1910, the area south of Center Ridge Rd. separated from Rocky River to form the village of Fairview. Its official incorporation took place in Sept. 1910. There were approximately 35 families and 300 people living in Fairview at that time. In 1948, the name was changed to Fairview Park, and in 1951 the village became a city. The first city charter was adopted in Nov. 1958. At the turn of the century, transportation to ROCKPORT was provided by the interurban Cleveland Southwestern Railway Co., which also served 3 amusement parks, Puritas Springs, Chippewa Lake, and Seccaium Park. As automobiles became more common, many new streets were platted and paved in a street program between 1927–30. With the demise of the interurban in 1931, the N. Olmsted municipal bus line began to serve Fairview. Fairview's main street, called at different times Sugar Ridge, Coe Ridge, and State St., finally took the name Lorain Rd., designated State Rt. 10 in 1934. Utility services in Fairview began with electricity in 1913, gas in 1916, the first streetlights in 1921, and water service from Cleveland in 1923. The first school was located on Lorain Rd. in 1840. In 1914, 47 children attended local schools. Enrollment peaked at 3,640 in 1969–70, and in 1984 it had dropped to 1,769. In 1984 there were 2 elementary schools, 1 junior high, 1 high school, and 2 parochial schools. Library services were first provided by the Cuyahoga County Library in 1925, and the Fairview Park Regional Library opened in a new building in 1957. In 1985 there were 6 churches in Fairview Park. The oldest was the Lutheran Church of Our Savior (1919). Much of the city's growth took place after WORLD WAR II as part of the general movement to the SUBURBS. During this period, the Fairview Shopping Ctr. opened in 1947 on Lorain Rd., and the Westgate Shopping Ctr. was constructed in 1954. By 1960 the population had increased to 14,624, and it reached its height in 1970 at 21,681. The total population in 1980 was 19,311. Over 79% were born in Ohio, and 7.4% were foreign-born. The predominant ethnic groups were German and IRISH.

**FAMILY PLANNING.** Cleveland's first family-planning program began in 1928 in a small, privately funded "maternal health clinic" that provided services only to married women. By 1984, responding to changing social and economic pressures, major hospitals, city health clinics, the Cuyahoga County Dept. of Human Services, and Planned Parenthood served thousands of Cleveland women. Family-planning services aid families to achieve their desired size; they are usually identified with the control of fertility but may also involve the control of infertility. Impeded in the late 19th century by the prohibitions against contraceptives by Roman Catholic doctrine and other moral systems that maintain that reproduction is the primary purpose of sexual intercourse, family planning since the 1960s has become a widely used health and welfare service, often funded by public monies.

The steady decline of the American birthrate throughout the 19th century suggests the widening use of a variety of birth-control methods to achieve the smaller family size made desirable by urbanization and modernization. These methods included sexual abstinence, the use of contraceptives, and abortion. Both to halt this decline and to reinforce the restrictive sexual mores of the late 19th century, Congress in 1873 passed the Comstock Law, which, by describing birth-control information as pornography, barred it from the federal mails. States and cities followed the federal lead, passing similar laws against the distribution of birth-control information and devices. Simultaneously, although abortion until the time of "quickening," when the fetus showed signs of life, had been legal in most states, many states in the post-Civil War period passed stringent laws that prohibited abortion unless it was necessary to save the mother's life.

The restrictions on birth control were challenged in the first 2 decades of the 20th century, when family limitation became an increasingly attractive option for the middle class. The most famous of the challengers was Margaret Sanger, whose experience as a public-health nurse in the slums of New York City persuaded her that women must be permitted to limit their pregnancies through the use of contraceptives. Sanger's first efforts to distribute birth-control information and devices were halted by local police, but in 1918 a New York court of appeals decided that contraceptives could be distributed by doctors "for the cure or prevention of disease." In this context, Clevelanders formed the city's first family-planning organization. Initiated by women volunteers in a prenatal clinic who, like

Sanger, saw women's lives ruined by unwanted pregnancies, this "maternal health clinic" at first attempted to establish birth-control clinics in the city's hospitals. Thwarted by city ordinances, however, the group opened an independent clinic in 1928, changing its own name to the Maternal Health Assoc. The association was privately funded. Significant financial support came from the Brush Foundation, whose founder, CHAS. F. BRUSH, was concerned with eugenics and world overpopulation.

In order to keep within the law, the clinic was staffed by 2 doctors, both women, and also had a medical advisory board of prominent physicians. The clinic offered services at first only to married women with serious health problems, but then to women needing contraceptives for other than health reasons. The association's report for 1928–30 stated that the clinic staff had seen 510 patients, of whom 379 were white and 131 were black, with an average age of 30.1 years. In the 1930s, the clinic established a marriage-counseling service and became a center for the training of doctors and nurses in family planning. In 1936, a second clinic was opened on Cleveland's west side. Studies of clinic patients during these years also became the basis for the infertility clinic established in 1946. These expanded services reflected the economic pressures of the Depression, which made family limitation more desirable at both the private and public levels. In 1930, the advertisement and shipping of contraceptives for permissible use, such as the prevention of venereal disease, became legal, and the sales of birth-control devices rapidly soared. In 1936, a federal circuit court upheld the right of physicians to provide contraceptive information and services for the purpose of preserving health. In 1942, the U.S. Public Health Service ruled that states might use federal health-service funds for family-planning programs. However, the retention by many states of anticontraceptive legislation impeded the wider use of public funds and the establishment of public birth-control clinics that would make available contraceptive information to those who could not afford to obtain it through private physicians.

In the post-World War II years, renewed impetus for family-planning programs came from growing concern about a rapidly increasing world population and its threat to available natural resources. By the mid-1960s, this concern was compounded by a heightened awareness of poverty in the U.S., and the interrelationships between poverty, uncontrolled fertility, and the unavailability of medical services. Shifts in attitudes about family planning were also evident in its endorsement by the 1960 White House Conference on Children & Youth. Beginning in 1965, federal legislation provided funds for local family-planning programs, requiring that these services be made available to anyone, but with special emphasis on welfare recipients and the medically indigent. At the same time, as the feminist movement began to demand fuller reproductive rights for women, some states liberalized their abortion laws. In 1973, the Supreme Court in *Roe v. Wade* followed suit, permitting abortion with the advice of a physician in the first trimester of pregnancy but allowing the states to regulate abortion in the second and third trimesters. Although this decision originally allowed public payments for abortions of Medicaid recipients, the 1978 Hyde amendment prohibited this use of federal funds.

These changes were reflected in the expanded services of the Maternal Health Assoc., which in 1966 became Planned Parenthood, affiliated with the national Planned Parenthood. In 1960, the association's clinic served 1,611 patients; in 1964, 2,967. In 1965 the association provided staff and volunteers for the city's first public family-planning clinic at Metropolitan General Hospital, and in 1968

391

the group sponsored the Community Family Planning Project, which was funded by the Cleveland Foundation and industry. Federal support for Cleveland family-planning services began in 1971 with the establishment of the Metropolitan Health Planning Corp., which distributed federal funds and coordinated family-planning programs in Cuyahoga and 3 adjacent counties. Since 1976, the FED. FOR COMMUNITY PLANNING, which had endorsed family planning itself in 1966, has taken over this responsibility. Public recipients of federal funds have included the Metropolitan General Hospital clinics and its Maternal & Infant Care Project and the health centers run by the city of Cleveland Dept. of Public Health & Welfare. Private recipients of federal funds for their clinics for the medically indigent include Planned Parenthood and MT. SINAI, BOOTH MEMORIAL, and UNIVERSITY HOSPITALS.

Family-planning services include counseling about birth-control methods, the distribution of contraceptives, medical examinations, and referral to appropriate medical and social services, as well as infertility examinations and out-patient sterilization. Clients for these services must be low-income persons who do not have access to private family-planning services, and although there are no age limitations, the client must be able to give an informed consent. In 1984, an estimated 34,000 women in the 4-county area received such services. Planned Parenthood's clinics served 10,828 clients in 1983. Planned Parenthood also specializes in sexuality counseling, trains counselors through the public schools and churches, and with the Fed. for Community Planning sponsors a Teenage Pregnancy Prevention Panel. THE CUYAHOGA COUNTY DEPT. OF HUMAN SERVICES also has a family-planning program for welfare recipients, which provides information about contraception and referral to medical facilities. Family-planning information is also available through the county's Services for Young Families program, which is designed for teenage unwed mothers. The 1973 Supreme Court decision was confirmed by the passage in that same year of a Cleveland city ordinance that permitted abortion in licensed facilities. These included several free-standing abortion clinics, as well as hospitals.

Marian J. Morton
John Carroll University

Bremner, Robt., ed., *Children and Youth in America* (1974).
Isaacs, Stephen L., *Population Law and Policy* (1981).
Kennedy, David M., *Birth Control in America* (1970).
Mohr, James C., *Abortion in America* (1978).
Reed, James, *From Private Vice to Public Virtue* (1978).

**FAMILY SERVICES ASSOCIATION.** *See* **CENTER FOR HUMAN SERVICES**

**FARLEY, JOHN HARRINGTON** (5 Feb. 1846–10 Feb. 1922), was a member of city council, 1871–77, and was elected mayor, serving 1883–85 and 1899–1901. Farley was born in Cleveland, the son of Patrick and Ann Schwartz Farley. He received a public-school education. Interested in politics, he was elected to city council in 1871 as a Democrat and served 3 terms. Known as "Honest John" Farley, he was elected mayor in 1883. After 1 term in office, he was appointed collector of internal revenue by Pres. Grover Cleveland and was made director of public works in Cleveland under Mayor ROBT. BLEE in 1893. With the support of the Municipal Assoc. (now the CITIZENS LEAGUE), he defeated incumbent Republican mayor ROBT. MCKISSON in Apr. 1899. During his term in office, Farley had to request the state militia to support the Cleveland police in maintaining order during the streetcar strike

in 1899. In business, Farley was a contractor and served as president of the Mutual Bldg. & Investment Co. He participated in the founding of the Central Natl. Bank and also was an officer of the GUARDIAN SAVINGS & TRUST CO. Farley married Margaret Kenney on 23 Nov. 1884. He died suddenly of a stroke at age 76.

**FARRELLY, JOHN PATRICK** (15 Mar. 1856–12 Feb. 1921), was the fourth bishop of Cleveland. He was born in Memphis, Tenn., the only child of John Patrick Farrelly and his wife, Martha Moore Clay. Mrs. Farrelly and her son converted to Catholicism when the future bishop was a child. Farrelly was educated at Georgetown University, the Jesuit College at Nemur in Belgium, and North American College in Rome. He was ordained to the priesthood on 22 May 1880 in the Lateran Basilica in Rome. He spent 2 years of study in Palestine after ordination. He was noted as a Scripture scholar, a linguist, and an archeologist. In 1882 he returned to Nashville, where he was assigned to the Cathedral. In 1883 he became chancellor of the diocese. In 1887, Farrelly was named secretary to Bp. Dennis J. O'Connell, rector of North American College. Prior to the founding of the Apostolic Delegation, the North American College staff served as the intermediary between Rome and the American bishops. Farrelly traveled widely in this regard. In 1894 he was named spiritual director of the college. He was named the new bishop of Cleveland on 16 Mar. 1909 and was consecrated in the chapel of North American College on 1 May 1909.

Farrelly was concerned over the inefficient bazaars used for fundraising by various charitable organizations. He established the Board of Charities (the forerunner of Catholic Charities) in 1910 under the direction of Fr. C. Hubert LeBlond. Farrelly built new buildings for the health-care facilities in the diocese, established a ministry to the deaf and hearing-impaired, and opened Merrick House and Catholic Young Women's Hall. He established the office of superintendent of schools in his efforts to standardize parochial education. Several secondary schools, including CATHEDRAL LATIN, were opened. Farrelly had planned to build a new seminary, but his plans were cut short by his untimely death. He had been visiting Knoxville, Tenn., when he contracted a fatal case of pneumonia and died.

The **FATHER MATHEW TOTAL ABSTINENCE SOCIETY** was the name taken by several Catholic temperance and fraternal-benefit societies in the mid- and late 19th century. Catholic temperance work was begun in Cleveland in the 1840s by Rev. Peter McLaughlin, who organized the Catholic Total Abstinence Society at ST. MARY'S ON THE FLATS in 1840. The Irish organization took part in parades and other public celebrations in the 1840s. The local total abstinence movement among Catholics received strong support from Bp. AMADEUS RAPPE upon his arrival in Cleveland. Organization of the Catholic Total Abstinence Society may have been inspired in part by the work then being done in Ireland by Fr. Theobald Mathew. Although Fr. Mathew received only "half-hearted cooperation" in his work from most of the American Catholic hierarchy, Bp. Rappe was a strong supporter of his efforts and was among those who invited Fr. Mathew to the U.S. During his long U.S. tour (1849–51), Fr. Mathew visited Cleveland and revitalized the local movement against drink. In 1851, he addressed large audiences on 3 and 10 Aug. About 3,000 people listened to his first address in the unfinished Cathedral, and many, including the bishop and the clergy, took the pledge; the next week the mayor and city council were reportedly among those who took the pledge of the "T-totalers." During Fr. Mathew's 2-week visit to

Cleveland, 5,000–6,000 people took the pledge, according to newspaper estimates.

Fr. Mathew's visit prompted the organization of the Fr. Mathew Total Abstinence Society, which claimed 180 members in 1852. The object of the society was "the promotion of the cause of Temperance" and the relief of members who became ill. The society was reorganized on 3 May 1857, with Bp. Rappe as president; over the next several years, the 3d-floor auditorium of the Cathedral school became known as Fr. Mathew Hall. The society claimed as many as 1,200 members in the early and mid-1860s, and continued to meet into the late 1880s. Cleveland hosted the national conventions of the Catholic Total Abstinence Union in 1872 and 1889. By 1870, Cleveland had a second Fr. Mathew Total Abstinence Society: the Fr. Mathew Total Abstinence & Benevolent Society of NEWBURGH. Presided over at first by Rev. J. Conlan of ST. PATRICK'S CHURCH, the organization by 1877 was meeting at St. Columba's Academy on Broadway. It continued to meet until ca. 1896. These societies were only 2 of many Catholic temperance groups active in Cleveland during this period. But by 1912 these Catholic groups had disappeared.

**FAWICK, THOMAS L.** (14 Apr. 1889–8 Jan. 1978), was an internationally known industrialist, inventor, and art collector. He patented over 250 inventions, ranging from automotive parts to wood treatment used in the making of violins. Fawick was born in Sioux Falls, S.D., of Norwegian parents. He quit school at the age of 15 to become a plumber. He soon became interested in cars, and at the age of 20 he built reportedly the first 4-door touring car in America. In 1912, he moved to Waterloo, Iowa, where, while working for the Galloway Tractor Co., he designed the first single-unit drive casting for a tractor, which vastly increased vehicle maneuverability. Throughout his life, Fawick discouraged the use of books, claiming that book learning was an impediment to human ingenuity. In 1917, Fawick was one of 3 incorporators of the Twin Disc Clutch Co. in Racine, Wis. A natural mechanical genius, by the 1930s, he had over 100 patents on automotive and industrial clutches, making Twin Disc Clutch the nation's leading manufacturer in the latter category. He also invented what was said to have been the first internally geared overdrive for automobiles. In 1936, Fawick sold his interests in the Twin Disc Clutch Co. and organized the Fawick Clutch Co. He moved the company to Cleveland in 1942. For the airflex clutch, used in industry and in naval landing craft during WORLD WAR II, Fawick in 1949 received the Franklin Institute's coveted John Price Wetherill Medal for outstanding achievement in the field of engineering. During the 1950s and 1960s, the Fawick Corp., with Fawick as chairman and president, expanded to Europe, Japan, and Canada. Fawick also continued to invent in other fields. He patented a combination rubber-and-cork handgrip for golf clubs in 1965 and established a company in Akron to manufacture it. He also designed and improved sound systems for Public Hall and the Stadium.

A self-taught violinist, Fawick composed and had published numerous pieces for the violin. He was also the owner of 2 Stradivarius violins, one of which was valued at over $100,000. During the 1950s, Fawick became interested in the making of violins and other string instruments. He developed a secret treatment that accelerated the aging of wood and kept the instrument even-tempered during temperature fluctuations. The Fawick violin gained international acceptance and was praised by many of the world's leading violinists. Fawick claimed that the tone was almost identical to that of a Stradivarius. In 1968, the Fawick Corp. was merged with the EATON CORP. Fawick, at age 79,

retired to devote 7 days a week to the Fawick Museum at W. 57th and Detroit Ave. A private museum, it contained the artworks Fawick had collected over the years, including ivories, bronzes, marbles, paintings, furniture, porcelain, and rugs. The collection was auctioned off in 1979, the year following Fawick's death. Of the $1.2 million in proceeds, ⅔ went to the CLEVELAND MUSEUM OF ART, and the remainder to BALDWIN-WALLACE COLLEGE.

Depke, John E., *The Tom Fawick Story* (1972).

The **FAWICK-AIRFLEX STRIKE,** which officially lasted 8 Mar.–6 June 1949, was called by Local 735 of the United Electrical Workers (UEW), an allegedly left-wing CIO union. At issue was the union's failure to sign non-Communist affidavits as required by the Taft-Hartley Act. The strike was a classic example of AFL-CIO rivalry. When the Fawick-Airflex Corp. refused to bargain with Local 735 because it failed to obey the law, workers voted 99–16 to strike the plant. Business agent Marie Reed called the company charges of Communist domination and Taft-Hartley violations a smokescreen that hid the real issues of wages and working conditions. The company had threatened to fire 7 union members, refused to make a wage offer, and wanted to institute a new job-evaluation program and weaken the seniority system. The strike that followed, however, focused attention on possible Communist links in a Communist-sensitive era. Fawick immediately challenged union picketing, and in the first of many bitter court battles during the strike, the union was restricted to 7 pickets. When Fawick vice-president Richard Huxtable was put on the stand, he introduced charges of Communist domination and asserted that the company would never bargain with the UEW but would bargain with the AFL-UAW, which had filed to hold an election at Fawick. Though the UEW offered to end the strike if all strikers were rehired without discrimination, the company consented to an election and agreed to bargain with the winner, and if it withdrew its picketing injunction, Fawick reasserted that it would not bargain with the UEW. Sanctioned by the NLRB, the UAW held an election on 22 Mar. As the UEW was ineligible, since its leaders had not signed the affidavits, the choices were AFL-UAW or no union. The AFL lost 75–50, which gave the UEW a moral victory, but the company still barred the UEW. Undaunted by defeat, the AFL initiated a back-to-work movement that infuriated UEW leaders, who filed unfair-labor charges against Fawick for acting in collusion with the AFL to interfere with a duly elected bargaining agent. As the AFL took a more active role, violence was introduced to the picket line, as strikers pelted AFL-driven cars with stones and nuts and bolts.

Strikers who were arrested for picketing violations were treated harshly by a series of judges who underscored the leftist ties of strike leaders. Judge Jas. C. Connell, who presided over most of the trials, called the picketing a "treasonous act" in a strike that was a "communist conspiracy" and exacted high bonds ($2.4 million in one case), stiff fines, and jail terms for violators. Marie Reed, Morris Stamm, and other UEW leaders tried to get him removed 3 times for bias after censure by the court of appeals, but Connell was cleared of the charges by Chief Justice CARL WEYGANDT and the Ohio Supreme Court. By May 1949, striker Joseph Kuess had been convicted of contempt 13 times and was assessed $6,500 in fines and 130 days in jail. Other leaders were similarly treated: Marie Reed, $3,000 and 60 days; Morris Stamm, $4,000 and 80 days; and Paul Shepard, $4,000 and 80 days. The UAW back-to-work drive undercut support for the UEW. With the assurance of company support, the AFL-UAW applied for a charter and petitioned to hold an election, which it won. On 6 June the AFL-UAW signed a 2-year contract, which effectively ended the strike and evicted the UEW from Fawick. At a cost of $1,000 a day, the UEW continued the action with dwindling support for another month. Despite its links to the CIO, the strikers at Fawick received little support from the CLEVELAND INDUSTRIAL UNION COUNCIL. This body, which had repelled its own leftist elements, aided some individual strikers and decried AFL interference, but condemned Local 735 for disobeying the court order against picketing and violence. The strike received some support from other UEW locals, such as 707 at GE, which had as its business agent Fred Haug (husband of Marie Reed). After losing appeals, most of the convicted strike leaders served reduced prison terms. The UEW Internatl. paid the $38,000 in fines, while the UEW was expelled from the CIO in Nov. 1949 for alleged Communist ties.

Morris and Eleanor Stamm Papers, WRHS.

**FEATHER, WILLIAM CO.** *See* **WILLIAM FEATHER COMPANY**

The **FEDERAL RESERVE BANK OF CLEVELAND** has been one of 12 banks in the Federal Reserve System. A well-organized campaign by a group of Cleveland businessmen, financiers, and politicians, including Mayor NEWTON D. BAKER, JEREMIAH J. SULLIVAN, Warren S. Hayden, ELBERT H. BAKER, and FREDERICK H. GOFF, led to the decision to locate the headquarters of the 4th Federal Reserve District in Cleveland in 1914. The district included all of Ohio, western Pennsylvania, eastern Kentucky, and northern West Virginia. The bank opened on 16 Nov. 1914 in the Williamson Bldg., with 23 employees and Elvadore R. Fancher as governor.

The Federal Reserve Bank primarily serves as a banker's bank and a fiscal agent of the federal government. It collects checks, supplies as well as destroys currency, wraps coins, transfers funds by wire, provides facilities for the safekeeping of securities, makes loans, and regulates member banks within its region. Its largest client is the federal government, which keeps a share of its working balance on deposit here. It issues, redeems, and services U.S. government obligations, such as savings bonds, maintains records of treasury tax and loan accounts, processes deposits of federal taxes, and acts as an agent for the government in defense contract financing. One of its primary functions is to gather information concerning the state of banking in the district and to make credit policies for the nation as a whole. The bank's research department issues analyses of current economic conditions of the district in periodic reports to all media.

The Federal Reserve Bank grew quickly in Cleveland. In 1918, 2 branches were established in Pittsburgh and Cincinnati. By 1923, the bank had 882 members and 600 employees. On 27 Aug. 1923, the $8 million Federal Reserve Bank Bldg. was opened at the corner of Superior Ave. and E. 6th St. Designed by the architectural firm of Walker & Weeks, it is considered one of the nation's finest banking homes, with the world's largest vault. The bank's governors (later referred to as presidents) have played an important role in Cleveland. Fancher (1914–35) took a leading role in attempting to bring relief to area banks in 1933. Willis J. Winn (1971–82) served as a catalyst in bringing community leaders together to discuss the problems facing Cleveland. In 1982, Karen Horn became president—the first woman president of a Federal Reserve Bank—overseeing about 400 member banks and 1,500 employees.

**FEDERATED CHURCHES OF GREATER CLEVELAND.** *See* **INTER CHURCH COUNCIL OF GREATER CLEVELAND**

The **FEDERATION FOR COMMUNITY PLANNING** is a nonprofit, citizen-led organization whose primary work, research and planning, is closely linked to other functions: policy development, legislative advocacy, public information, and agency coordination. Its staff works with a network of volunteer committees and a membership of 220 health, social-service, and civic organizations. The FCP's antecedents lie in the early-20th-century movement to systematize philanthropic work. The organization was established by the Cleveland Chamber of Commerce in 1913, upon recommendation of its Committee on Benevolent Associations, and initially was called the Fed. for Charity & Philanthropy. The new body implemented a plan relatively untried in the nation in which donors to charities made their contributions to the federation, which in turn allocated them to private social-service and health agencies. This federated approach sought to eliminate numerous individual agency campaigns then in existence. In 1913, the first year of operation, the FCP's drive raised $126,735, which was disbursed among 55 approved private agencies.

In Dec. 1916, the FCP merged with the Welfare Council of Cleveland and assumed a new name, the Welfare Fed. of Cleveland. The council, composed of agency executives, had served as an advisory body to the city's Dept. of Welfare. This merger created a multifunction organization unique for its time. In 1919, the federation helped organize the Community Chest to handle solicitation of funds. The FCP maintained its allocation role through 1971, when it transferred this function to UNITED WAY SERVICES. At this juncture it adopted its current (1986) name, the Fed. for Community Planning. Immediately upon its establishment, the federation began to develop a group of interrelated functions—planning, research, advocacy, agency coordination, and public information. The FCP's first project was a study of "cripples," their problems and job opportunities (1913), followed by work on the issue of illegitimate children and unwed mothers (1914). During the Depression, a project in TREMONT and Central brought improvements in social conditions in these neighborhoods. Children-oriented programs focused on wartime daycare and delinquency prevention (1943), establishing the county Receiving Home for Children in 1948 (the Metzenbaum Ctr. in 1986), the development of daycare programs (1960), and child-abuse prevention (1966). The FCP was instrumental in the founding of Blue Cross (1934), the postwar expansion of the area's hospital system, and the Health Goals Project (1966) that led to improvements in dental care, neighborhood health care, and the county health-care system. Other areas of activity included services to youth, older persons, and the handicapped; occupational planning; nursing homes; and social-work education.

The FCP gave continuing attention to the government's role in funding and providing assistance to the poor, children in distressed circumstances, and other vulnerable populations. An early federation action was to support a 1913 city ordinance outlawing substandard day nurseries. By the 1940s, the FCP had begun a major effort to enlarge federal, state, and county responsibilities in light of the broader tax bases these units of government had available. In 1965, a 20-year effort to reorganize public welfare in Ohio culminated in the enactment of state legislation that consolidated public assistance and a variety of social services within the county welfare department and provided state funds based on need, not happenstance. In the same decade, the federation secured legislation that created mental-health boards and mental-retardation boards in each county responsible for planning and funding services. The principle of purchase of social services by government agencies from voluntary agencies was pioneered by the FCP in the 1950s when it arranged for the Cuyahoga Board of County Commissioners to purchase care for emotionally disturbed children. With the appearance of federal purchase of service funds in the 1960s, this principle became an integral part of the social-service scene. Activity in public information began in 1913 with the formation of the Committee on Preventative Propaganda to work for reduced infant mortality, and the publication of the *Social Year Book*, the first in a continuing series of informational reports. In 1944, the FCP held its first Health & Human Services Institute, an annual 1-day convening of human-service professionals and volunteers. In 1950, the federation initiated an informational and referral service to provide a single place for people to seek help.

Federation for Community Planning Records, WRHS.

**FEDERATION FOR JEWISH CHARITIES.** *See* **JEWISH COMMUNITY FEDERATION**

The **FEDERATION OF CATHOLIC COMMUNITY SERVICES** is an "umbrella" agency, a voluntary association of social-service agencies operating within the structure of the Cleveland Catholic Diocese. The FCCS is the administrative, financing, planning, and research section of the Cleveland Catholic Charities (CCC), while the CATHOLIC CHARITIES CORP. is responsible for fundraising and management of diocesan properties. In 1970, a diocesan-wide task force was formed to evaluate social services in the Catholic community. Two years later, the results came in the form of a list of recommendations made to the then-bishop of Cleveland, CLARENCE G. ISSENMANN. Included among the suggestions was the need for a coordinated social-service structure suited to the resources of the diocese, one that while respecting the autonomy of each service agency would strengthen the delivery of services and improve communication and coordination of activities among organizations. In 1972, 30 agencies and institutions, such as PARMADALE Children's Village of St. Vincent De Paul and the Catholic Youth Organization, joined together to form a centralized programming, planning, and administrative body that would provide services such as auditing, bookkeeping, and collecting (due bills) and give technical assistance in the areas of grantsmanship, managerial and program consultation, periodic reviews, and budget management and reviews. In 1984, there were members in FCCS receiving such services as coordinated approaches to programs on aging and youth; legislative and legal advice; telephone referral; and a parish social ministry program designed to aid individual parishes. At the time of its founding, the FCCS consisted of a chairman of the board; the bishop; a board of trustees; an executive committee; a council of executives, consisting of directors of individual agencies; an executive director; and a program staff. The first executive director was Frank Catliota, who served until 1983.

Federation of Catholic Community Services Records, Catholic Diocesan Archives.

The **FEDERATION OF GERMAN-AMERICAN SOCIETIES OF GREATER CLEVELAND** and similar organizations to coordinate the activities of the numerous German-American groups in the area have been formed in Cleveland 3 separate times over the last 100 years. The first

such organization was formed in the 1880s but dissolved during WORLD WAR I. In late Mar. 1932, more than 50 groups joined together to reorganize the federation as the Cleveland Stadtverband, or the United German Societies. Led by OTTO L. FRICKE, Carl Raid, Geo. Gaul, Julius Boenisch, Wm. H. Engelman, and others, the Depression-era Stadtverband aimed initially to provide relief support for unemployed German-Americans; it also sponsored the annual German Day celebrations at the GERMAN CENTRAL FARM and sponsored speakers and films about issues and events of interest to the German-American community. In the years prior to WORLD WAR II, pro-Nazi elements within the community attempted to gain control of the Stadtverband, but its leaders were able to thwart their efforts. Nevertheless, the internal struggles weakened the organization, and growing anti-German sentiment contributed to its demise ca. 1940. In the 1950s, the Fed. of German-American Societies of Greater Cleveland was formed to coordinate the efforts of German-American groups; it continued the German Day celebrations and undertook various projects for the benefit of the German-American community and to promote and commemorate the German experience in America.

Cleveland Stadtverband Records, WRHS.

The **FEDERATION OF ITALIAN-AMERICAN SOCIETIES OF GREATER CLEVELAND** is a service organization formed in 1963 to coordinate the work of local Italian societies and to work on behalf of the Italian community. Since 1968 it has sponsored the annual Italian Day celebration and other events to raise funds for charities and scholarships. In 1985 the federation had 45 member organizations with 160,000 total members.

The **FEDERATION OF ORGANIZED TRADES AND LABOR UNIONS OF THE UNITED STATES AND CANADA'S SECOND ANNUAL CONVENTION** was held in Cleveland 21–24 Nov. 1882. It was the first such meeting held in the city. The federation, which was formed in Pittsburgh in 1881, was the precursor of the American Fed. of Labor. Of the 19 delegates, 3 were from Cleveland: Geo. A. Collins, president of the Cleveland Trades Assembly; Donald McIntosh of the Carpenters; and W. J. Cannon of Cigarmakers Local 17. The other 16 delegates represented 10 unions and 8 national or international unions, and came from 15 cities in 9 states. Samuel Gompers of New York (who would become president of the AFL in later years) was one of the more vocal delegates. The Cleveland convention passed various resolutions concerned with child labor, prison labor, education, and apprenticeships. Two other resolutions were of particular note. A lengthy discussion was conducted over Internatl. Typographical Union representative F. K. Foster's paper "Protection vs. Wages." The result put the congress on record against a high or protective tariff, which overturned its decision of a year before, which had been in favor of a protective tariff. The congress also adopted a motion demanding that the national 8-hour law be enforced. The secretary of the congress was instructed to notify Pres. Arthur and ask him to enforce the statute. Several resolutions were also passed that condemned actions taken by various companies against workers and unions. In an effort to further unite the labor movement, the congress voted to allow the Knights of Labor, the Women's Natl. Labor Union, and all "bona fide" labor unions of men and women to be represented in the federation.

The **FEDERATION OF WOMEN'S CLUBS OF GREATER CLEVELAND** is a voluntary nonprofit, non-political, nonsectarian association of leaders of Cleveland's women's clubs, supported by membership dues and contributions. The club assists its members in a variety of ways and cooperates in many civic, educational, and philanthropic activities. In the winter of 1901, Mrs. Sarah (Chas. Edwin) Porter, as president of the U. & I. Literary Society, initiated the idea of the federation and invited 18 club presidents to a guest day, 27 Mar. 1902, at the home of Mrs. Summer G. Ryder, 65 Ingleside Ave., for a preliminary discussion. Subsequently, representatives from 37 clubs met in April, when a constitution and bylaws committee was appointed. It was adopted by 18 clubs representing 700 women at a meeting on 6 May 1902. The name the City Fed. of Women's Clubs was selected, and the following officers were elected: Mrs. Porter, president; Mrs. Mattie C. Smith, secretary; and Mrs. Lottie L. Saunders, treasurer. The first meeting, held on 4 Nov. (sometimes given as 7 Nov.) 1902 at the Pythian Temple, was attended by 100 women. Its purposes included achieving closer communication with member clubs and serving the community through civic improvement, education, industrial, and philanthropic committees.

In 1904, the name was changed to the Cleveland Fed. of Women's Clubs; the group met in the EAST CLEVELAND CONGREGATIONAL CHURCH (Euclid Ave. and Page Ave.), later in the Women's Club of the CLEVELAND ATHLETIC CLUB, and subsequently in the EUCLID AVE. CHRISTIAN CHURCH. In 1918, the federation moved to its own headquarters in the Hotel Statler, where it remained until 1939. It joined the Ohio Fed. in 1911 and the General Fed. in 1915. By 1923, the Cleveland Fed. had grown to a membership of 40,000 members affiliated in 180 clubs. Six departments reflected their activities: American Citizenship, Applied Education, Civic Legislation, Fine Arts, Welfare, and a Jr. Council. The federation was incorporated not-for-profit in 1929, when the present name was adopted. Through the years, the federation has continued to coordinate the educational, civic, and welfare activities of women's clubs in the Cleveland area as they work on special projects determined by the Ohio Fed. and/or the General Fed. In addition, the federation has served on countless city committees and has sponsored and/or cosponsored many civic enterprises, including city beautification, health and nutrition, crime prevention, service to schoolchildren, scholarships and loans to high school and college students, and volunteer work during both world wars (including its own Civilian Service Corps). In 1982, the federation comprised 25 clubs representing 3,000 women; it continued to be represented on many major civic committees and continued to work through its departments: Conservation, Education, Fine Arts, Home Life, Internatl. Affairs, and Public Affairs.

Fleming, Abigail B., *History of the Cleveland Federation of Women's Clubs* (1902–29).
Federation of Women's Clubs of Greater Cleveland Records, WRHS.

The **FEMALE PROTECTIVE UNION** was a labor union organized in Cleveland in late 1850. The union, which had features of a mutual-aid society, was formed by sewing women to combat long hours, low wages, and merchants who refused to accept payment on orders at face value. At first, benevolent Clevelanders concerned with the plight of the sewing women offered them conventional charitable aid, such as was given to the poor and sick. The union refused to accept the dependent status associated with such aid. Rather than charity, the FPU desired a loan that would allow them to market their own goods through the establishment of a cooperative store. On 1 May 1851, the Female Cooperative Union Store opened for business. However, it and its union were short-lived. After some activity during Nov.-Dec. 1851, both the union and its store dissolved.

The **FENCE WAR OF PUBLIC SQUARE** arose between Cleveland residents, who wanted the entire PUBLIC SQUARE fenced in as a central park, and the local commercial interests, who felt that the closing of Superior and Ontario streets at the Square hindered the area's commercial development. By 1839, the city had fenced in each individual quadrant of Public Square. Erected to improve the Square and prevent depredation by cattle and swine, the fence was, over the years, the subject of considerable city council legislation. Ordinances were enacted to keep boys and loafers from occupying it and annoying traffic and to prevent the Square from being used as a ball ground. By 1852, with the open country boundaries being pushed farther out, attention turned to the need for city parks. Residents near the Square wanted it fenced in and the street entrances closed to form a central park. A petition was introduced to city council on 22 July asking that the streets be vacated, but the law department declared the petition illegal. Between 1852–57, public discussion in city council and the newspapers continued as to whether or not the Square should be fenced in entirely. In Jan. 1857, council voted to vacate all intersecting streets at Public Square, and on 24 Mar., the Square was entirely enclosed by a fence erected at night in order to circumvent any court injunctions that might have been issued. The Square became a popular recreation area, as traffic was obliged to circle it.

Opposition to the enclosed Public Square continued, especially among the local commercial interests on Superior east of the Square, who felt the fence hindered business activity. Aided by the city's having allowed the fence to fall into disrepair, the completion of the Post Office & Custom House, and a street railway company's wanting the right-of-way through the closed streets, opponents of the enclosed Square presented city council a petition against the further blockading of Superior in 1867. City council appointed a special committee to study the question. When the committee failed to agree, council adopted the committee's minority recommendation that the courts should adjudicate all legal issues. Municipal Court Judge Samuel B. Prentiss ruled that Superior Ave. had been dedicated as a continuous street and that the closing was unconstitutional. On 24 Aug., Superior was reopened. The following week, petitions were presented asking for the opening of Ontario St., and the obstructions were removed, thus ending Cleveland's "great central park."

**FENN, SERENO PECK** (25 Apr. 1844–3 Jan. 1927), was one of the 3 principal founders of the SHERWIN-WILLIAMS CO., serving as treasurer and vice-president. His major community interests were the YOUNG MEN'S CHRISTIAN ASSOC. and the FIRST PRESBYTERIAN (OLD STONE) CHURCH. Fenn was born in Tallmadge, Ohio, to Sereno and Elizabeth Carrothers Fenn. He grew up on his parents' farm, graduating from the district school. He arrived in Cleveland in 1862 to attend the HUMISTON INSTITUTE. In 1864, he enlisted in the Ohio 164th Infantry, serving in Co. B for 4 months. After his discharge he worked as a clerk in the Cleveland office of the U.S. Pension Office. In 1865, Fenn began working as a clerk in the Cleveland, Columbus & Indianapolis Railroad freight office. Rather than violate his religious convictions by working on Sundays, he quit the railroad in 1870.

In 1869, Fenn had attended an international YMCA convention. During the trip, he became acquainted with Henry A. Sherwin, a fellow delegate. The friendship led to Sherwin's hiring Fenn in Apr. 1870 as cashier-bookkeeper in the newly organized partnership of Sherwin-Williams & Co. In 1880, Fenn was taken in as a partner and made treasurer. In 1884 the partnership was incorporated, with Fenn as one of the incorporators and a significant stockholder. He continued as treasurer until 1921, when he became vice-president. His death ended a 57-year career devoted to the business. Fenn served as a director of the Cleveland YMCA from 1868–1920. As its president for 25 years, he provided strong leadership. His special interest was in the association's educational programs. Fenn contributed considerable support for the YMCA's national and international programs, as well as the Cleveland educational program. In 1930, the Cleveland YMCA School of Technology was renamed Fenn College in his honor. Fenn was an active member of the Old Stone Church from 1865 to his death, serving as elder, trustee, and superintendent of the Sunday school. He married twice. His first marriage, to Mary Augusta DeWitt in May 1870, ended with her death in 1917. His second marriage, to Helen Barry Wright in July 1918, ended with her death in June 1923. Fenn had no children of his own. His stepdaughter, Elizabeth Huntington DeWitt, married JOHN L. SEVERANCE.

**FENN COLLEGE.** *See* **CLEVELAND STATE UNIVERSITY**

**FENSTER, LEO** (1904–22 Sept. 1984), was a UAW activist who survived attempts to remove him from office because of his Communist sympathies. Until the end of his life, he was a spokesman for radical causes. Born in New York, Fenster moved to Cleveland as a child, graduated from Glenville High School, and attended Western Reserve University for a year. His interest in the labor movement resulted from an early job as a furrier's assistant. Later, as a clerk at the Coit Rd. Fisher Body Plant, he helped organize Local 45 of the CIO-Auto Workers' Union (later the Cleveland District Council-UAW), and over the years he held many offices, including that of recording secretary. He was viewed as the guiding force of the local. Fenster's leftist influence was particularly felt in the pages of the *Eye Opener*, the local's paper. Critical of both UAW and government policies, the journal was accused of following the Communist party line, especially after Fenster declared himself a Communist in 1942. The *Eye Opener* denounced both Roosevelt and Truman as warmongers, supported Henry Wallace as a third-party candidate for president in 1948, and condemned the Marshall Plan. Fenster criticized UAW support of the cost-of-living clause negotiated with GM, as wages could decline as well as increase with inflation; instead he advocated a salaried 40-hour week for autoworkers. He clashed with Walter Reuther, a former Socialist who led an antileftist slate of candidates on the national level in 1947, and in a debate accused him of supporting the auto companies in their quest for speedup. Opposed to the UAW support of signing the Taft-Hartley anti-Communist affidavits, he rallied support among his coworkers in Local 45 to defy national directives.

Fenster's politics came increasingly under attack in the late 1940s as "right-wing" forces in the union tried to oust "left-wing" forces, in a move parallel to actions in the national CIO and UAW and the local CUIC and UAW bodies. Opposition forces charged that funds had been diverted to political causes and that the *Eye Opener* was too costly. Fenster countered that the house organ cost less than half per copy of what the official UAW paper cost.

For 2 years, Fenster's slate of candidates won Local 45 elections; by Oct. 1950, Fenster was replaced as *Eye Opener* editor for his refusal to run a guest column in support of the KOREAN WAR. The international tried unsuccessfully to get him removed from any position of power in the local; he ultimately resigned. Like many early Communist supporters, Fenster grew disenchanted with Kremlin abuses of power but remained a leftist critic of social policy. He was an advocate of troop withdrawal from Vietnam by 1968, and in 1970 was a member of a citizens' committee that met with peace negotiators. After a stroke in 1968, Fenster retired and spent his time writing and lecturing about the history of the labor movement. In 1971, he edited the autobiography of Wyndham Mortimer. Fenster died after another stroke. He left his wife, Bertha, and 4 children.

The **FERRO CORPORATION** is a worldwide producer of specialty materials using organic and inorganic chemistry. It operates principal manufacturing facilities either directly or through wholly owned subsidiaries or partially owned affiliates in 32 countries on 6 continents. Most of Ferro's products—coatings, ceramics, chemicals, thermoplastics, and colors—are formulated and designed to the specific needs of its customers' manufacturing processes. Its major markets are construction, home appliances, household furnishings, industrial products, transportation, and government purchases. Founded in Cleveland as the Ferro Enameling Co. by Robt. Weaver, the company was incorporated under Ohio laws in 1919. In 1930 the name was changed to the Ferro Enamel Corp. The present name was adopted in 1951. Ferro is among the top 500 corporations in the country; its corporate offices are located in Cleveland, in Erieview Plaza, as is its Coating Div. on E. 56th St. Its Color Div. and Bedford Chemical Div. are located in BEDFORD, and its Corporate Research & Technical Ctr. is located in INDEPENDENCE. Ferro's most important product is frit, the basic ingredient for porcelain enamel and ceramic glaze. Research done during the 1930s at the Cleveland Coatings Div., then the Frit Div., resulted in the development of an industrial process that successfully thinned the inorganic frit so that only 32 grams were needed to cover each square foot, compared with 246 grams by older methods. In 1986, Ferro was the world's largest producer of frit. The Coatings Div. produces porcelain enamel frit for steel and aluminum, ceramic frit and glaze coatings for floor and wall tile and dinnerware, resin-based organic powder coatings and inorganic porcelain enamel powder coatings for metal applications, and specialty glasses. The Color Div., started in 1939, manufactures inorganic pigments, porcelain enamels, and ceramic colors for the plastics and coatings industries. The Bedford Chemical Div. traces its roots back to the company's acquisition of the Chase Drier & Chemical Co. in 1940. It produces a broad line of additives for plastic and rubber polymers, including heat and light stabilizers, catalysts, plasticizers, antimicrobials, antioxidants, and flame retardants for industrial, pharmaceutical, and cosmetic applications.

**FESLER, MAYO** (19 Nov. 1871–6 May 1945), was a leading reformer for good government in the Cleveland area; for over 20 years, his name was synonymous with the CITIZENS LEAGUE, which he directed. Fesler was born in Morgantown, Ind. He grew up with an interest in politics and civic affairs. After high school, he attended DePaul University and the University of Chicago, where he received his degree in 1897. For the next 5 years, he taught high school in Indiana, and he was a substitute professor of political science at Indiana University for 1 year. Fesler's first civic position came in 1903, when he was appointed secretary of the St. Louis Civic League. In 1910, the Cleveland Municipal Assoc. hired him as its secretary. Fesler, NEWTON D. BAKER, and A. R. Hatton led a statewide campaign for municipal home rule; Fesler served as secretary of the Ohio Municipal League, which was formed to promote the cause. This effort resulted in the adoption of HOME RULE in the 1912 state constitution; Fesler helped the charter commission draft the first city charter for Cleveland. In 1913, he changed the name of the association to the Civic League. He was also involved in movements that led to the implementation of the merit system of appointment and promotion of city employees and to the general assembly's passage of a civil service act in 1914; both acts were intended to end any incentive for patronage hiring in public offices. Fesler helped organize the CITY CLUB OF CLEVELAND in 1912 and served as its first secretary.

Fesler left Cleveland in 1917 to become secretary of the Brooklyn (N.Y.) Chamber of Commerce; in 1922, he went to Chicago to be the secretary of its city club. The Civic League was reorganized as the Citizens League in 1923. Fesler returned to Cleveland to serve as the league's first director; he held this position until he retired 2 months before his death. Fesler is credited with starting the movement that led to the recodification of Ohio's election code in 1929; to prevent fraud, permanent voter registration became mandatory. Nationally, he served as vice-president of the Natl. Municipal League and as a member of the council of the Natl. Civil Service Reform League. Fesler often lobbied before CLEVELAND CITY COUNCIL and the Ohio general assembly. He was praised by many civic leaders as a reformer but was disliked by many officials for his continual criticism of government operations and for the league's public opposition to candidates felt to be unqualified. Fesler married Gertrude Fails in 1903; they had 1 daughter, Jean Louise.

The **FESTIVAL OF FREEDOM** has been Cleveland's official 4th of July celebration since 1938. Begun as part of the national convention of the Grottos of the U.S. and Canada, the festival has continued as an event of its own. The first festival was part of the Grottos' Mardi Gras on 29 June 1938, entitled "Festival of Beauty and Fire." The program attracted 250,000. This success prompted a proposal that a similar event be staged in 1939 as the city's official 4th of July celebration. The 1939 festival, organized by the Come-to-Cleveland Committee of the CLEVELAND ADVERTISING CLUB headed by Geo. Buehler, was called "Festival of Freedom and Fireworks." It commemorated Independence Day and honored local organizations. A cloudburst forced the cancellation of the program, which was rescheduled for Saturday, 8 July 1939, when 33,643 people attended the show at the stadium. That was the only time an admission was charged. The program received national attention in 1940, when NBC presented live radio coverage to the nation. The 1940 program was the first year funded by private contributions. Because of its success, the festival group decided to make the program an annual event. They incorporated as a nonprofit organization. During the 1940s, the festivals included bands, orchestras, ethnic music and dancers, military demonstrations, parades, and the fireworks display. By 1948, the festival had become so popular that the limited seating capacity at the Stadium forced the trustees to move it to BURKE LAKEFRONT AIRPORT. In 1954, the show moved to EDGEWATER PARK, where it was still located in 1986. In 1986 the festival remained totally underwritten by Cleveland businesses, organizations, and individuals. The program was administered by the Cleveland Independence Day Assoc., a volunteer group from the city's business community. Attendance was estimated at 200,000 annually.

**FETZER, HERMAN** (24 June 1899–17 Jan. 1935), was better known as "Jake Falstaff" to readers of the *Akron Times* and the *CLEVELAND PRESS*. He was born in Maple Valley, Ohio, near Akron. After graduating from Akron's West High School, he went to work as suburban reporter for the *Akron Times*, where in 1920 he began his column "Pippins and Cheese," taking its title as well as his pen name from Shakespeare's *Merry Wives of Windsor*. Except for a short sabbatical, during which he served as managing editor of the *St. Petersburg* (Fla.) *Times* and head of the *Cleveland Plain Dealer*'s Akron bureau, Fetzer remained with the *Times* until its merger by Scripps-Howard into the *Akron Times-Press*. He worked briefly for the *Akron Beacon Journal* and published 3 books, 2 of them based on his Teutonic folk hero, Reini Kugel.

Fetzer's reputation spread as he published articles, poems, and stories in the *New Yorker*, the *Nation, Collier's*, and *Liberty*. In the summers of 1929 and 1930, he was invited by the vacationing Franklin Pierce Adams to write Adams's "Conning Tower" column in the *New York World*. Lured to Cleveland early in 1930 by the *Cleveland Press*, Fetzer not only contributed "Pippins and Cheese" but also did rewrites, editorials, and features until his early death from pneumonia. Largely through the efforts of his widow, the former Hazel Stevenson of Akron, several volumes of his work were published posthumously. Upon the appearance of *The Bulls of Spring: Selected Poems* in 1937, Ted Robinson in the *PLAIN DEALER* hailed Fetzer as "the finest lyric poet Ohio has ever produced." This book was followed by 3 volumes of Ohio farm stories culled from a "Rural Vacation" series he had done for the *Press*. A representative Fetzer anthology appeared under the title *Pippins and Cheese* in 1960.

The **1525 FOUNDATION** was incorporated in 1971 by KENT HALE SMITH (1894–1980). Smith was president of the LUBRIZOL CORP. from 1928–51 and chairman of the board until 1958. His father was ALBERT W. SMITH, once head of the Case Institute of Technology chemistry and chemical engineering departments and cofounder of the Dow Chemical Corp. Smith received his B.S. degree from Dartmouth College in 1915 in physics, and a second B.S. in 1917 from Case Institute of Technology. He was awarded an honorary Ph.D. in 1954 from Case. Smith worked for Dow Chemical from 1917–19, and then formed the Ce-Fair Development Co., which built the ALCAZAR HOTEL and the Fairmount-Cedar Bldg. In 1928, Kent joined his brothers Kelvin and Vincent to form the Cleveland Graphite Oil Prods. Co., the parent company of Lubrizol. Smith was acting president of Case Institute of Technology from 1958–61 and gained national notice in 1972 with his contribution of $244,000 to Richard Nixon's presidential campaign fund. Over the years, he received numerous awards for community service and for his support of higher education. Activities of the foundation are for general local charitable giving, with special support for CASE WESTERN RESERVE UNIVERSITY, environmental protection, UNIVERSITY CIRCLE, and social service. In 1984, assets of the foundation were $29,457,887, with expenditures of $1,039,851 for 22 grants. Officers of the foundation included Hubert H. Schneider, Thelma G. Smith, and Phillip A. Ranney.

The **FIFTEENTH OHIO NATIONAL GUARD REGIMENT**, formed in June 1879 and disbanded in 1881, was composed of local and regional militia companies. The regiment was the dominant military organization in Cleveland during this period. Its principal officers were Col. Allan T. Brinsmade, Lt. Col. Geo. A. McKay, and Maj. Henry Richardson. The regiment was a federation of 5 Cleveland companies—the Emmett Guards (Co. A), the Veteran Guards (Co. C), the Forest City Guards (Co. D), the Townsend Light Guards (Co. E), and the Washington Guards (Co. I)—and 5 units from other towns: the Brooklyn Blues (Co. B), the Buckeye Guards (Co. F) from Geneva, the Ely Guards (Co. G) from Elyria, the Chagrin Falls Guards (Co. H), and the Berea Light Guards (Co. K).

Of the 5 Cleveland units, the oldest and best-known was the Emmett Guards, formed in 1873 by Irish-American Civil War veterans. Led by Capt. MARTIN A. FORAN, the Emmett Guards were one of the most active local military units in the mid-1870s, participating in numerous public ceremonies and parades and holding a variety of social events and fundraisers. Members met weekly at 99 Bank (W. 6th) St. in 1874 and became embroiled in a controversy with the CLEVELAND GRAYS about use of the Frankfort St. armory, a dispute that reached the chambers of the city council. The Washington Guards, led by Capt. Vincent Shafer, may have been older than the Emmetts: a German unit known as the Washington Guards was formed in 1850 and was active until at least 1857 (drilling on Lorain near Abbey), but city directories and newspapers indicate that it did not last into the 1860s. The Veteran Guards, with an armory at Erie (E. 9th) and Sumner in 1878; the Townsend Light Guards, armory at Scovill and Kennard (E. 46th) in 1878; and the new Washington Guards, armory on Garden (Central) near Greenwood (E. 28th) in 1878, all first appeared in the city directory in 1877 or 1878, although each may have existed prior to formation of the regiment in 1877.

In 1881, local newspaper criticism of the regiment's inefficiency prompted the adjutant general to order an inspection of its companies. The inspection apparently led him to agree with the newspapers, for the regiment was disbanded, and 4 of the 5 Cleveland companies were dissolved. Other units, such as those from CHAGRIN FALLS and BEREA, later became part of the new 5th Regiment of the Ohio Natl. Guard. The only Cleveland troop deemed worthy of survival when the 15th Regiment was disbanded was the Forest City Guards. Begun in Nov. 1876 by Geo. A. Fiske (its first captain), the troop attracted 10 charter members to its first regular meeting on 2 Jan. 1877. In early 1878, it occupied its first armory at St. Clair and Muirson (E. 12th). When the 15th Regiment was dissolved, the Forest City Guards became Co. A of the 5th Regiment of the Ohio Natl. Guard on 10 July 1881. During its first 25 years, the troop was called to readiness during the railroad strike in July 1877 and during rioting in Cincinnati in Mar. 1884 and in Cleveland that June, and helped fight a large fire in a local lumberyard in the fall of 1884. It also was sent to Fairport in Dec. 1887 for service during a strike by the ore handlers. Other than such brief periods of service, only parades, encampments, and social events varied "the monotonous existence" of the troop prior to 1891.

**FIGGIE INTERNATIONAL, INC.,** is a diversified operating company put together by native Clevelander Harry E. Figgie, Jr. In Dec. 1963, Figgie bought the family-oriented "Automatic" Sprinkler Corp. of America; through acquisitions he increased its annual sales of $22 million to $742 million in 1984, making Figgie the 367th-largest corporation in the U.S. "Automatic" Sprinkler began in 1910 as the result of the merger of 4 small companies. Incorporated in Delaware in 1919, the firm was bought in 1926 by John A. Coakley, whose family maintained ownership until 1963. Main offices of the company were located in New York City and then Cleveland before being moved to Youngstown—the site of the firm's plant—in 1936. It had sales offices in Cleveland by 1924. In the early 1960s, the firm made little money; it was put up for sale in 1962. Figgie bought it for $5.8 million on 31 Dec. 1963. In May 1965 he established his office in the CEI Bldg. in Cleveland, and in Aug. 1970 he moved the company headquarters from Youngstown to a new building at 4420 Sherwin Rd., Willoughby. In 1965, Figgie began to diversify the company. He targeted 4 markets around which to build: fire protection; fluid controls and hydraulic equipment; industrial labor-saving equipment; and electronic instrumentation and components. Between 1965–69, "Automatic" Sprinkler acquired more than 50 divisions to serve these markets and increased its sales from $25 million in 1964 to $379 million in 1969; net income rose from $1.2 million to $8.6 million in the same period. To reflect this diversity, the company adopted a new name on 29 Oct. 1969, becoming A-T-O, Inc.

In 1970, the company began to concentrate on internal growth and to transform its internal service centers in data processing, corporate insurance, and real estate into autonomous profit centers serving both the company and outside businesses. By 1981, net sales had increased to $769.9 million, and net income to $25.7 million. During the early 1980s, the corporation undertook several major changes. On 1 June 1981, it changed its name to Figgie Internatl., Inc., and in 1982 it moved its administrative headquarters to Richmond, Va., with plans eventually to move its executive offices there, as well. On 18 July 1983, Figgie Internatl. Holdings, Inc., was incorporated in Delaware and became the parent company of Figgie Internatl. As a result of the losses the company suffered in the recession in 1982–83, Figgie began to sell, close, or consolidate some of its weaker divisions in 1984; among those it began to close in early 1985 was American LaFrance, founded in 1832, which had been "the largest custom-builder of fire apparatus" in 1981.

**FINE ARTS MAGAZINE** was one of the few subscription periodicals devoted entirely to the arts and their promotion. It evolved from a weekly FM radio programming guide called *Fine Music*, which had its home base in Chicago. The first issue of *Fine Arts* was in Jan. 1961. Alla V. Wakefield, editor; Linda Kraus and James B. Gidney, associate editors; Clement A. Miller, recordings editor; and Wm. Ward, art director, produced the magazine. The advisory committee included Walter Blodgett, curator of musical arts at the CLEVELAND MUSEUM OF ART; Edward G. Evans, chairman of Western Reserve University's music department; L. A. Graham of the Akron Symphony Orchestra; ARTHUR LOESSER, author and pianist; and Clement A. Miller, dean at the CLEVELAND INSTITUTE OF MUSIC. *Fine Arts* listed concerts (classical and jazz), theater dates, museum and gallery openings, lectures, noteworthy films and television showings, and AM and FM radio programs. In addition, it printed concert reviews and featured photos and paintings on the cover. In June 1962, the publication nearly failed because of lack of money. It was rescued by its loyal following and some accountants who suggested the magazine move to a for-profit status instead of nonprofit. The staff subsequently expanded with new business, circulation, and promotion managers. Wakefield, now editor and publisher, also hired feature writers such as Nina Gibans (art) and Reuben Silver (drama). Rost Warden became managing editor. During the mid-1960s, the magazine started writing about the turmoil of the times with articles about unrest on the campus and general policies. The last issue of *Fine Arts* was published on 2 Feb. 1973. It featured an article on the defunct *Life* magazine.

**FINKLE, HERMAN** (Apr. 1891-Oct. 1952), referred to as the "Little Napoleon of Ward 12," served as a city councilman for a record-breaking 35 consecutive years. He had one of the more colorful and contrasting political careers in Cleveland. Early in his career, Finkle was considered a ruthless, corrupt sergeant of the Republican machine; but by the time of his death, he was recognized as one of the most knowledgeable and able members of city council. Born in Detroit, Mich., Finkle moved at age 11 into the Woodland Ave.-E. 55th St. district of Cleveland. He received his education in the public schools and graduated from the Cleveland Law School in 1913. Through his law practice, Finkle was able to place himself in the Republican organization by becoming a law partner and brother-in-law to "Czar" ALEX BERNSTEIN. He soon became the protege of Republican boss MAURICE MASCHKE. In 1917, Finkle decided to run for council in his 12th ward; with the support of the Republcan machine, he easily won. The Republican organization then aided him in getting reelected 18 times. Upon his reelection in 1921, Finkle became Republican floor leader, a position he held until the Democrats took over city hall in 1932. During these years Finkle was associated with various land, patronage, and financial scandals, and several attempts were made by the CITIZENS LEAGUE to oust him from council. Finkle always came out of these confrontations unscathed.

It may have been coincidence, but Finkle's behavior and viewpoints seemed to change soon after the death of his only daughter in the mid-1930s. His interests began to extend beyond the boundaries of his ward as he became involved with citywide problems such as street lighting, the establishment of health centers, mass transportation, airport development, and minority-rights issues. As minority leader of the council, he was able successfully to pass legislation in these areas. Finkle's great expertise was in city finances, as he served many years as chairman of the powerful finance committee. Mayors, Republicans as well as Democrats, relied on Finkle's advice on Cleveland's financial matters. By the 1940s, many, including the Citizens League, lauded Finkle as a respectable political leader and authority in municipal government. He was urged to run for mayor several times, but each time he declined, as he preferred to maintain his council seat. Finkle was still a member of council at the time of his death.

Herman Finkle Vertical File, WRHS.

**FINNS.** Immigrants from Finland settled in Cleveland as early as 1885. By 1900, 79 foreign-born Finns lived in Cleveland, and 86 in Cuyahoga County. Between 1901-10, 304 more Finns came to the city, and during the following decade, an additional 288. By the 1930s, approximately 3,000 people of Finnish descent lived in Cleveland. Most Finns came to America for economic reasons. Wages in their homeland were meager, working and living conditions were substandard, and land was difficult to acquire. Compulsory military service in the Russian Army also prompted many to emigrate. Most came from rural areas, especially from the province of Vaasa in western Finland, where they had received some schooling but no advanced education. Large Finnish communities were established in Fairport Harbor, Ashtabula, Conneaut, and Cleveland, where manual labor on the iron-ore docks was needed. Soon Finns were to be found in Cleveland's shipyards, on lake vessels as sailors and fishermen, and in automobile-manufacturing

plants. Among the immigrants were some skilled workers from the cities. A number of Cleveland's tailors and carpenters around the turn of the century were Finns. The city also attracted Finnish women by its opportunities for domestic work. In 1916 it was estimated that Finnish women outnumbered men 3:2. The first Finnish settlement in Cleveland was around Clinton Ave., from W. 25th to W. 38th St. In the 1930s, approximately 1,500 people of Finnish descent lived in this neighborhood. Linndale contained the city's 2d-largest Finnish settlement. Suburbs with Finnish families were LAKEWOOD, CLEVELAND HTS., SHAKER HTS., and EUCLID.

The majority of Cleveland's Finns are Lutheran. Early Finnish immigrants established 2 churches, Gethsemane Evangelical Lutheran Church and Bethany Natl. Evangelical Lutheran Church. The older, Gethsemane, was organized in 1903 and soon affiliated with the Suomi Synod (Finnish American Evangelical Lutheran Church). After holding services at various rented halls, the church moved in 1914 to 1433 W. 57th St. Membership grew from 85 in 1904 to 200 in the 1950s. Visiting pastors were provided by larger churches of the synod. Bethany Natl. Evangelical, founded in 1919, was located at 1449 W. 48th St. on the corner of Franklin Blvd. It was a member of the Missouri Synod. Among the cultural organizations that attempted to preserve Finnish culture and language was the Talko Club, a drama society. It was founded in 1948. Its activities included plays, musicals, folk music and folk dancing, arts and crafts, carnivals, dinners, and dances. Membership peaked at 50 members. The final play was presented in 1957, and by the mid-1960s, club activities had virtually ceased. Choral music was another important cultural activity in the Finnish community. One ensemble, the SAVEL FINNISH CHOIR of Cleveland, was organized in 1936. It was active until 1962. Cleveland's first Finnish temperance unit, the Young People's Temperance Society, was reportedly organized in 1898. After 1910, the society was located in a hall at 3509 Detroit Ave. In addition to housing the Temperance Society, its libraries, and reading rooms, it also hosted meetings, concerts, and parties sponsored by Finnish societies, such as the Finnish-American Relief Committee, the Finnish Musical Arts Assoc., the Talko Club, the Finnish Camp of Royal Neighbors (Insurance Co.), the Finnish Stagers' Club, the Finnish Socialist Club, and the Finnish Nationalist Club. Finnish immigrant co-operatives were formed in the early settlements. One of the best-known was the Finnish Co-operative Boarding House at W. 32nd St. and Clinton Ave. NW. It was begun in 1912. Members of the co-operative, generally unmarried male Finnish immigrants, were entitled to use the house's kitchen, dining room, sleeping room, and Finnish steambath (sauna). Residents of the Finnish community also purchased shares in the co-operative and frequently used the sauna facilities.

Politically, the great majority of the Finns were conservative. Most were Republican, although a fairly large number joined the Democratic party during Franklin D. Roosevelt's presidency. The first socialist club in Cleveland, and the second in the state of Ohio, was founded by Finns in 1904. Its impact on local politics was minimal because of language barriers and the tendency of Finns to keep to themselves. However, the socialist group significantly increased the political clout of Finns in general by waging an effective campaign that urged every Finn in the city to become a U.S. citizen. In 1920 the group purchased a hall at 3147 W. 25th St., but 4 years later a split in the ranks of the club's members caused it to lose the hall. Thereafter, the Socialist Club declined. Several publications served the Finnish immigrants in Cleveland. In 1928 a weekly Finnish newspaper, the *Kausan Lehti*, began publication. Although its circulation numbered 2,000 copies, a shortage of funds forced a move of the paper to Ashtabula Harbor in 1931. Handwritten journals or newspapers were prepared by many organizations, including the Temperance Society and the Socialists of Cleveland.

Finnish settlements in Cleveland never grew to be permanent ghettos. In size, they remained relatively small. Second- and third-generation descendants were often unwilling to accept Old Country values, with strict codes of behavior and religious orthodoxy. They displayed an indifference toward, and sometimes outright rejection of, immigrant heritage and sought to move away from the original ethnic enclaves. This dispersion of Finnish-Americans accelerated their assimilation into American culture. As identification with the ethnic group waned, mixed marriages with other religious and ethnic groups further diluted Finnish traditions. Americanization of the Finnish church was also inevitable. As congregations came to contain more American-born members, services frequently were conducted in English. The new generation of American-born clergymen believed that an ethnically isolated "Finnish" church would not have the personnel or the funds needed to survive. Therefore, they encouraged Americanization of the church. In 1986, Cleveland had no Finnish Lutheran church. The bath houses and co-operative boarding houses had also long since disappeared. Despite the once-vigorous efforts of the early immmigrants to preserve their ethnic heritage, "Little Finland" had ceased to exist in Cleveland by the 1980s.

Nicholas J. Zentos
Lorain County Community College

Kolehmainen, John I., "A History of the Finns in the Western Reserve" (Ph.D. diss., WRU 1937).

The **FIRMAN FUND** was incorporated in 1951 by Pamela Humphrey Hanna Firman (b. 1913). Pamela (Mrs. Royal) Firman is the daughter of U.S. Treasurer GEO. M. HUMPHREY. In 1958 she was appointed to the distribution committee of the CLEVELAND FOUNDATION by then-mayor Anthony J. Celebrezze. She has served as the chair of the University Hospitals' women's committee, on the University Circle planning commission, and as president of the board of Rainbow Babies & Childrens Hospital. The fund is broadly for support of hospitals, higher and secondary education, cultural programs, youth agencies, and community funds. It has been most visible in its support for UNIVERSITY HOSPITALS. No grants are given to individuals, for research, or for loans. In 1985, assets of the fund were $4,415,124, with expenditures of $257,215 for 86 grants. Trustees of the fund included Pamela H. Firman; Carol L. Colangelo, secretary; M. G. Mikolaj, treasurer; Cynthia F. Webster; and Royal Firman III.

The **FIRST BANK NATIONAL ASSOCIATION** was established in June 1974 by Cleveland lawyer John H. Bustamante and 4 partners. The first bank in Cleveland owned by "minority groups," as the newspapers often describe it, First Bank was founded as a result of Bustamante's legal work on the incorporation of local black-owned companies and his realization of the difficulty such firms had in getting financing. Bustamante set out to establish a financial institution able and willing to support such businesses. Originally known as the First Bank & Trust and with $2.5 million in capital, First Bank opened for business in June 1974 at 232 Superior Ave. Its first transaction was a deposit by the General Motors Corp. By the end of 1974, the bank had assets of $11.2 million but had lost $49,023; in 1975 its assets grew to $15.2 million, and it had a net income

of $90,336. In Jan. 1976, the shareholders approved the change in the name to First Bank Natl. Assoc., and federal officials approved the bank's plans to become a national bank. In June 1976, First Bank acquired Community Natl. Bank; the acquisition doubled First Bank's assets to $32 million and gave it branches at 4567 Northfield and 26777 Lorain; it added a branch in UNIVERSITY CIRCLE in 1978, and in Oct. 1981 it announced plans to move its main office from the CUYAHOGA BLDG. to the Terminal Tower. In May 1982, the First Bank Natl. Assoc., the 4th-largest black-owned bank in the U.S. with 110 employees and assets of $68.7 million, was named bank of the year by *Black Enterprise* magazine. By the end of 1982, First Bank's assets had grown to $73.9 million, and in Mar. 1983 stockholders approved the reorganization of First Bank as a subsidiary of the First Intercity Banc Corp., "the first black one-bank holding company in the country." The holding company was formed to insulate the bank from takeovers, to increase its capacity to raise capital, and to enable it to expand services.

The **FIRST BAPTIST CHURCH OF GREATER CLEVELAND,** located at 3630 Fairmount Blvd. and Eaton Rd., CLEVELAND HTS., is the result of a union of the First Baptist Church of Cleveland and the Cleveland Hts. Baptist Church. In 1816, Moses White, one of the first Baptists to settle in the village of Cleveland, and BENJAMIN and REBECCA ROUSE were among the first group of Baptists who met in the upper rooms of the "Old Academy" at St. Clair and W. 6th St. Rev. Richmond Taggart, a Baptist minister who had stopped in Cleveland on his way west, preached to them on 19 Nov. 1832, and on that day the "First Baptist Society of Cleveland, Ohio" was organized. Subsequently, on 16 Feb. 1833, 17 BAPTISTS formally established the First Baptist Church of Cleveland. The membership grew rapidly, and in 1834 they built a 55 × 80-ft. brick sanctuary with a 150-ft. spire at the corner of Seneca (W. 3rd) St. and Champlain St. In Apr. 1836, Rev. Levi Tucker became the first permanent pastor, serving until 1842. The church grew in members and strength and the congregation purchased the Plymouth Bldg. at the northwest corner of Euclid Ave. and Erie (E. 9th) St. in 1855.

Through the years, First Baptist—through gifts of money and members—organized many other churches and mission Sunday schools throughout the city, including the Idaka Chapel, built in 1874 at the corner of Prospect Ave. and Kennard (E. 46th) St. by STILLMAN WITT and his daughter, Mrs. Dan P. Eells, as a memorial to Witt's granddaughter, Idaka Eells. In 1887 it was joined by the congregation of First Baptist, and they built their own Romanesque-style church adjacent to the Idaka Chapel and dedicated it on 9 Sept. 1889. It remained at this location for over 40 years. Many members of First Baptist continued to move eastward, and in Dec. 1919, a group of 25 people formally organized the Baptist Church on the Heights. They worshipped in Coventry Elementary School in Cleveland Hts., and within 2 years they had over 300 members.

Rev. Theodore R. Adams helped plan the merger of the Heights Church and First Baptist to establish the First Baptist Church of Greater Cleveland in 1927. The downtown building was sold, and an 8-acre tract of land bounded by Fairmount Blvd., Eaton Rd., and Shelburne Rd. was purchased. On 12 June 1928, the cornerstone was laid, and on 14 Oct. 1928, Dr. Harold Cooke Phillips, who had been serving both congregations, was formally installed as pastor. The Gothic church, built of light-colored Indiana limestone, including the 130-ft. Swasey Tower and several memorial stained-glass windows, was dedicated during the week of 2–9 June 1929. Membership grew to over 3,000 parishioners as the music program was expanded and the programs of outreach to both the community and the foreign-mission field were extended.

The **FIRST CATHOLIC SLOVAK LADIES ASSOCIATION,** a national fraternal benefit society with national headquarters located at 24950 Chagrin Blvd., was established by 9 women in Cleveland's ST. LADISLAUS CHURCH in Jan. 1892. By 1984, the association had 742 lodges nationwide, assets of more than $86 million, and nearly $251 million of insurance in force. Known until July 1967 as the First Catholic Slovak Ladies Union, the association was founded in 1892 by Anna Hurban (1855–1928), a Slovak immigrant who came to the U.S. in 1880. Hurban founded the society with the assistance of Rev. STEPHAN FURDEK. The first group of 9 women had assets of $77, but the organization grew quickly; by the time it held its first convention, in Pittsburgh in 1893, it had grown to 226 members in 16 lodges. The union was incorporated in Ohio on 18 Oct. 1899; by then it had 84 branches in 5 states, with membership of 1,859 and assets of $1,949.81.

The organization expanded its activities during the next 3 decades. To insure its own perpetuation, in 1905 it formed a youth division for members' daughters ages 16–18; in 1914 it began to publish its own newspaper, *Zenska Jednota*. By 1922, the union's assets had grown to $1.3 million, and the organization began to contribute regularly to Slovak educational and religious institutions. It donated $5,000 to the Matica Skolska fund to build Slovak schools in Cleveland and other cities. Between 1922–35, the union contributed more than $100,000 to Slovak schools and religious institutions. It also spent more than $100,000 in 1929 to build its first headquarters, located at 3756 Lee Rd. in SHAKER HTS.; the new building was dedicated on 5 July 1930. Membership in the union continued to grow. By 1935, the national organization had total membership of more than 62,500 (37,500 in 459 senior chapters with $34.5 million of insurance in force, and 25,000 junior members in 390 chapters with $5 million of insurance in force). Cleveland itself had 25 senior lodges with 3,769 members and 13 junior chapters with 1,870 members. By its 75th anniversary, in 1967, the First Catholic Slovak Ladies Assoc. had 103,792 members nationwide in 900 branches, and its assets totaled more than $40 million. In Apr. 1967, the association began building a new national headquarters on Chagrin Blvd. near the VILLA SANCTA ANNA HOME FOR THE AGED, which the association had built in 1960. The new headquarters were dedicated on 20 Oct. 1968. With increasing assets and more than 700 lodges nationally, the association continued to provide financial support for Slovak and Catholic agencies and institutions in the 1980s.

The **FIRST CATHOLIC SLOVAK UNION OF THE USA AND CANADA** is a fraternal benefit society founded in Cleveland in 1890 by 11 men from 4 states. By 1933, the union had more than 100,000 members and assets of more than $9 million; by 1983, its assets had grown to more than $49 million. The union was established by Rev. STEPHAN FURDEK during a period of debate within the American Slovak community about how best to achieve unity among the various local Slovak lodges and societies. The union, or jednota, was formed by men who believed that the Natl. Slovak Society was too secular an organization and perhaps even anticlerical. Believing that Slovak unions should be ⌐rganized along religious lines, Furdek and members of the St. Joseph Society, a group organized by Furdek on 5 May 1889, called for a mass meeting of SLOVAKS on 4 Sept. 1890, at which time the First Catholic Slovak Union was

organized. Taking as its motto "For God and Nation!" the union aimed to help members deepen their religious faith and required them to become U.S. citizens within 6 years of their arrival. It also established an insurance fund to support members and their widows and orphans, began publishing *Jednota*, a weekly newspaper, and served as a cultural organization to protect the Slovak language and heritage.

The organization grew steadily. By 1918, it had branches in 29 states and Canada and 50,000 members. It had more than $1.5 million in capital and had paid out $5 million in benefits. By 1933, the union had more than 100,000 members, and its assets were in excess of $9 million. It dedicated a new national headquarters at 3289 E. 55th St. in Aug. 1933. The union's activities had grown by the mid-1930s to include operation of an orphanage for 150 children in Middletown, Pa., and contributions toward the support of Benedictine High School in Cleveland and 2 girls' schools in Pennsylvania. Membership remained around 100,000 into the late 1970s. Between 1978–82, the number of lodges declined from 471 to 453, and insurance certificates in force from 104,053 to 98,220; during the same period, the union's assets increased from $42 million to $47.8 million, and its insurance in force from $125.8 million to $141.2 million. Other activities of the union in 1982 included the operation of its own printing plant and publishing house, a relief fund, support for other Catholic and Slovak organizations, a $14,000 annual college scholarship program, and sponsorship of national bowling and golf tournaments.

Ledbetter, Eleanor E., *The Slovaks of Cleveland* (1918).
Megles, Susi; Stolarik, Mark; and Tybor, Martina, *Slovak Americans and Their Communities of Cleveland* (1978).

The **FIRST HUNGARIAN LUTHERAN CHURCH,** located at Buckeye Rd. and East Blvd., was chartered on 23 Apr. 1906 to fulfill the spiritual and social needs of Hungarian Lutherans resident in Cleveland. The congregation initially met in a church building they had purchased on Rawlings Ave. in 1907. Within 6 years, they had established the first Hungarian orphanage in America (also located on Rawlings Ave.) and the Martin Luther Sick & Death Benefit Society. By 1923, they supported a Lutheran seminary located in Budapest, Hungary. In 1941, the congregation moved to a new Transylvanian Gothic-style church at East Blvd. and Buckeye. Kossuth Hall, which housed educational work, was built at this location in 1954, at which time the congregation numbered more than 1,000 members. In 1949–50, the church sponsored the immigration of approximately 200 displaced persons, and in 1956 it sponsored the immigration of more than 100 "freedom fighters" from the Hungarian Revolution. The congregation was also active in preserving Hungarian culture, sponsoring at first an annual Grape Harvest Festival, and by 1967 an annual "Hungarian Heritage Days" event. The congregation's pastors have included Steven Ruzsa (1907–23), Ladislaus Ruzsa (1923–34), Andor Leffler, Ph.D. (1934–54), and Gabor Brachna, D.D. (1955–80).

The **FIRST HUNGARIAN REFORMED CHURCH OF CLEVELAND, OHIO,** was organized by Rev. Gustav Juranyi and 60 charter members on 3 May 1891. In 1894, a wooden church was built on Madison Ave. (E. 79th St.). Five years later, a stone church was built at the same location by Rev. Alexander Csutoros. In 1925, the congregation purchased 1 acre of land on the corner of Buckeye and East Blvd. in order to relocate. In 1932, Bethelen Hall Education Ctr. was built on this site under the pastorate of Dr. Joseph Herceg with the leadership of Emery Kiraly.

Under the pastorate and leadership of Rev. Dr. Stephen Szabo, a magnificent Romanesque Cathedral-style church was built adjoining Bethelen Hall (with an impressive 155-ft.-high tower). The new church was dedicated on 4 Sept. 1949 with 4,000 people present, including Ohio governor Frank Lausche. The church building with numerous facilities became an important meeting place for conventions and conferences of many local and national organizations of American HUNGARIANS. In 1957, the mortgage was retired. In that year more than 250 refugees of the 1956 Hungarian Freedom Fight were settled here by the congregation. In 1977, the church was designated as an architectural & historical Cleveland landmark. Rev. Dr. Stephen Szabo retired in 1983 after 36 years of service.

**FIRST NATIONAL SUPERMARKETS, INC.**, is one of the leading food chains in the country and the largest supermarket chain in the Cleveland area with its Pick-N-Pay stores. The origin of Pick-N-Pay can be traced to 1928, when Edward Silverberg incorporated a firm called Farmview Creamery, Inc., which opened a small dairy store in CLEVELAND HTS. In the 1930s, Silverberg expanded his company into a chain called Farmview Creamery Stores. In 1938, he introduced the supermarket to Cleveland when he opened a store on E. 185th St. called Pick-N-Pay, which carried dairy products as well as grocery items. After the opening of a second Pick-N-Pay, Silverberg changed the corporate name of all his stores to Pick-N-Pay Supermarkets in 1940. Pick-N-Pay continued to grow, and in 1951, when it had 10 supermarkets, it was acquired by the Cook Coffee Co. of Cleveland (now COOK UNITED, INC.), which operated retail truck routes, selling grocery and household items.

Under Cook, Pick-N-Pay continued to prosper in the 1950s. In 1959, Cook made a substantial addition to Pick-N-Pay by acquiring the 25-store Foodtown, Inc., a supermarket chain from ACF-Wrigley Stores of Detroit, which had acquired Foodtown in 1956. Julius and Milton Kravitz of Cleveland opened the first Foodtown store on E. 88th St. and Superior Ave. in 1941. Six years later, Julius Kravitz guided the formation of a chain of independently owned Foodtown supermarkets. Foodtown strengthened its distribution network in 1952 when it acquired the pioneer manufacturer and wholesaler of food products in Cleveland, the Wm. Edwards Co. Marcus A. Treat started the firm as a partnership on River St. in 1853, and it was incorporated in 1906. After its acquisition by Cook, Pick-N-Pay increased its stores to 38, acquired the right to distribute "Edwards Brand" products, and moved into Foodtown's headquarters in MAPLE HTS.

In the early 1960s, Pick-N-Pay continued to expand by building its own food-manufacturing plants. But by the mid-1960s, it began to experience financial and operating difficulties. Cook was unable to reverse this downward trend and in 1972 sold Pick-N-Pay's 57 stores to a group of investors headed by Julius Kravitz. Pick-N-Pay enjoyed immediate success as the new management upgraded its facilities and opened larger stores. That increased sales to $300 million and employment to 5,000 by 1975. Pick-N-Pay became the leading supermarket chain in Cleveland. Competition remained keen, though, with the other major grocery chains, Fazios (see FISHER FOODS, INC.) and Stop-N-Shop. A price war between these firms in 1977 led to an indictment against all of them for price fixing in 1982. In 1978, Pick-N-Pay moved beyond northern Ohio by acquiring the First Natl. Stores of Boston, a major New England food chain, to form First Natl. Supermarkets, Inc., with headquarters in Maple Hts. By closing many of the declining New England stores and introducing new product techniques, First Natl. Supermarket was able to remain profitable into the 1980s, with 155 stores in 7 states and $1.3 billion in sales by 1983.

The **FIRST OHIO VOLUNTEER LIGHT ARTILLERY** carried 886 Cleveland-area men into the CIVIL WAR. It began with a 3-month service tour, Apr.-July 1861, which produced the area's first casualties. Later the company underwent reorganization, continuing in the war effort for 3 years, principally in the Kentucky, Tennessee, and Georgia theaters. The 1st Ohio was created in 1860 by the union of 6 artillery companies from Cleveland, Brooklyn, and Geneva, including the former gun squad of the CLEVELAND GRAYS. The resulting union produced a battle-ready regiment commanded by Col. JAS. BARNETT. The outbreak of the Civil War in 1861 prompted Barnett to offer the artillery's services to the Ohio adjutant general. On 20 Apr., Adj. Gen. Carrington wired Barnett to report with his men within 48 hours. On 22 Apr., Barnett and 160 men with 6 guns and caissons started for Columbus by rail, but were diverted to Marietta in order to protect the north-south frontier. On 23 Apr., the 1st arrived on the Ohio border to find itself standing alone against Confederate troops threatening to invade Ohio. The 1st Ohio served its first 3-month tour in (West) Virginia. Along with other Ohio and Indiana regiments, it moved into (West) Virginia on 28 May in an effort to prevent an invasion of Ohio. On 4 June, at Phillippi, the Cleveland artillerymen exchanged fire for the first time with Confederate forces. On 7 July, at Laurel Hill, Geo. Tillotson became the first soldier from Cleveland killed for the Union cause. At the Battle of Carrick's Ford on 14 July, the 1st Ohio made its first capture of enemy men and materials. Barnett later presented the captured Confederate cannon (which in 1986 stood on PUBLIC SQUARE) as a gift to the city. On 30 July 1861, the 1st Ohio returned to Cleveland for a heroes' welcome. Pres. Lincoln's call for troops to aid the Union cause resulted in the reorganization of the 1st Ohio for 3 years' service. Col. Barnett was promoted to general and was appointed chief of artillery on the staff of Gen. Rosecrans, while the regiment was enlarged to 12 batteries and dispersed to different theaters for the war's duration.

A *Military History of Battery D, First Ohio Veterans' Volunteers Light Artillery* (1908).

The **FIRST PRESBYTERIAN CHURCH (OLD STONE)** grew from a Plan of Union Sunday school established in 1820, which was incorporated as the First Presbyterian Society in 1827. The church building, which became known as "Old Stone," was the second within the Cleveland limits and was built on the corner of Ontario St. and PUBLIC SQUARE between 1831-33. This first Georgian Revival-style building was razed and the cornerstone laid for a Romanesque Revival church in 1853, designed by the firm of Heard & Porter. Shortly after its completion in 1857, the building was severely damaged by fire, and although the exterior walls survived, the interior was entirely rebuilt in 1858. A spire was added to the east tower in 1868 but was removed following a second fire, in 1884, which necessitated another rebuilding of the interior, this time in the later Romanesque Revival style by CHAS. F. SCHWEINFURTH.

Since early in its existence, Old Stone Church has dealt with the dilemma of a migrating congregation, since residential areas began their move eastward, away from Public Square, as early as the 1850s. The church's decision throughout its history has been to remain in the original Public Square location. The church has supported a variety

403

of inner-city ministries, including Goodrich House, a settlement house founded in 1897, and the Home for the Friendless, which was opened in the church parlors during the CIVIL WAR to care for Southern refugees (and which later became part of Cleveland City Hospital). A high degree of community leadership was provided by such pastors as Robt. B. Whyte, Wm. H. Goodrich, HIRAM C. HAYDN, and Lewis Raymond. Dr. Haydn was pastor for nearly 3 decades, beginning in 1872. Under his leadership, the Cleveland Presbyterian Union was formed and worked for the extension of church work in the city. Old Stone Church has been the mother church for many Cleveland-area Presbyterian churches, including First Presbyterian of Brooklyn (1835), Bethel (1835), Second Presbyterian (1837), NORTH (1870), CALVARY (1892), Windermere, Glenville (1893), Trinity, and Lakewood (1912). In 1984 the Old Stone Church stood amid modern buildings clustered around Public Square, the oldest structure in the center of the city. With a large, active congregation, it was one of the few of Cleveland's early churches remaining in its original location for its entire history.

Ludlow, Arthur C., *Old Stone Church* (1920).

The **FIRST UNITED METHODIST CHURCH OF CLEVELAND** was, true to its name, the first Methodist congregation organized in the Cleveland area. The First Methodist Episcopal Society was formed by 9 hearers on the Cleveland circuit in 1827. The circuit included part or all of Cuyahoga, Lake, Geauga, and Summit counties. At the time of the Cleveland society's organization, Revs. John Crawford and Cornelius Jones were the itinerant preachers for the circuit. Cleveland was made a permanent station in 1830, and in 1841, after years of meetings in rented rooms and homes, a building was dedicated, after 5 years of work, at the corner of St. Clair and Wood (E. 3rd) streets. The first resident minister was D. C. Wright, in 1860. Plans had been made for a new church at Euclid and Erie (E. 9th) streets in 1865, but they were struck down because of the cost. A smaller chapel was built on the site, serving until 1874, when a larger Gothic building was built. By 1901, the formerly residential neighborhood on Euclid had become commercial, and the church sold its property to the Cleveland Trust Co. It relocated to Euclid and Sterling (E. 30th) St., where it constructed a new edifice designed by J. MILTON DYER, and opened in 1905. The design bears a strong resemblance to its contemporary TRINITY CATHEDRAL but is primarily an adaptation of the Perpendicular Gothic style. The church has remained at the E. 30th St. location despite the movement to the suburbs, and in the 1980s, the congregation was made up of a mixture of inner-city and suburban members.

The **FIRST UNITED PRESBYTERIAN CHURCH OF EAST CLEVELAND**, located at 16200 Euclid Ave., is a pioneer among congregations of the early outlying areas and holds the distinction of having occupied the same plot of land for its entire history, an uncommon record among city churches. The church was organized out of a Plan of Union Sunday school, which built a white frame meeting house to replace a log structure on a rise above Euclid St. in EUCLID TWP. in 1816. The Plan of Union was a cooperative effort between Presbyterians and Congregationalists to found churches and Sunday schools in the new communities of the WESTERN RESERVE. The resulting congregations eventually allied themselves with whichever denomination matched the background of the members or the sentiments of the time. Rev. Thos. Barr was minister until 1820, ministers from Cleveland preached until 1825,

and in 1825 Rev. Stephen Peet was ordained. In 1828, the First Presbyterian Society of Euclid was officially organized, and it continued to occupy the 1816 building. In typical fashion, a cemetery adjoined the church overlooking the valley of NINE MILE CREEK.

In 1895, the congregation dedicated a new building on the same site. The building is of dark stone in the Romanesque Revival style. In 1896, the name of the church was changed to match the newer name of the community: First Presbyterian Church of E. Cleveland. (It should be noted that the church has no direct relationship to the earlier congregation of the same name that met at DOAN'S CORNERS and later became EUCLID AVE. CONGREGATIONAL CHURCH.) The church has been served by noted clergymen, including Wm. H. Beecher (brother of the famous preacher Henry Ward Beecher), Dormer L. Hickok, and Henry S. Brown. With the assistance of Rev. Brown, the "Old First" Noble Hts. Bible Chapel was organized in 1921, and subsequently became Noble Rd. Presbyterian Church. The church remains in its original location, with an addition constructed in 1962.

Price, Ellen Loughry, *A History of East Cleveland, Ohio* (1970).

The **FISHER BODY DIVISION OF GENERAL MOTORS CORPORATION** has operated 2 plants in the Cleveland area: the Cleveland plant at E. 140th St. and Coit Rd., and the Euclid plant at 20001 Euclid Ave. The older of the 2 plants was the Coit Rd. facility, opened in June 1921 by the Fisher Body Co., which had been formed in Detroit in 1908 by the 6 Fisher brothers from Norwalk, Ohio. Managed by Edward F. Fisher, the 6-story Coit Rd. plant was originally intended to build automobile bodies for the Cleveland Automobile Co. and the Chandler Motor Car Co.(see CHANDLER-CLEVELAND MOTORS), but its first completed order was for Chevrolet. The plant was enlarged soon after it opened, and in 1922 it turned out 150 bodies a day; by 1924, the plant employed 7,000 workers and produced 600 bodies daily. Fisher Body became a division of GM in 1926, and the following year the plant stopped producing bodies for other companies.

On 28 Dec. 1936, 300 workers at the Cleveland Fisher Body plant initiated a sit-down strike that quickly spread to the Flint, Mich., plant and nearly paralyzed the company. The Cleveland plant was occupied for 3 days, but the strike continued until GM recognized the United Auto Workers as the bargaining agent for its employees in Feb. 1937. During WORLD WAR II, the Coit Rd. plant produced tank and gun parts and engine nacelles for B–29 airplanes. Wartime employment at the plant was 14,000 and included women; by 1946, employment had declined to 4,000 workers, who produced 5,000 bodies daily. Postwar employment at the plant peaked at 5,600 in 1949 and declined to 3,490 in 1964 and 3,200 in 1971, when the plant produced large stamping dies and upholstery and trim sets rather than bodies. Employment stood at 1,530 with 1,240 workers on indefinite layoff in Feb. 1982, when GM announced plans to close the plant. Production ended in Aug. 1983, and the facility was sold in 1984 to the Park Corp.

Fisher Body's Euclid plant was built in 1943 by the Cleveland Pneumatic Aerol Co. to produce parts for aircraft landing gears during the war; Fisher Body bought the plant in 1947. The plant produced bodies for Chevrolet and Pontiac station wagons and panel trucks from 1948–60; between 1960–65 it produced bodies for Chevrolet convertibles, and in 1966 it began assembling Buick Riviera and Oldsmobile Toronado bodies. In 1970, body production was moved from the Euclid plant to more modern plants in Michigan, and the Euclid plant began turning out interior trim and upholstery. From its peak of 2,958 in 1955, employment at the plant declined to 1,860 in 1964. It declined to 1,143 with 300 other workers on layoff in Feb. 1982, when GM announced plans to close the plant. Worker concessions during contract negotiations enabled the company to keep the plant open, however.

Wager, Richard, *Golden Wheels* (1975).

**FISHER FOODS, INC.,** has been one of the major food retailers in Cleveland. It began as the Fisher Bros. Co. in Feb. 1907 when 3 New York grocers, Manning F. and Chas. Fisher and Joseph Salmon, opened a grocery store with 4 employees at W. 47th St. and Lorain Ave. The company was incorporated in 1908. With 48 stores around the city by 1916, Fisher Bros. built a new warehouse and bakery at 2323 Lakeside Ave. That same year, the firm introduced the cash-and-carry system, which lowered prices and increased the company's business. In 1928, the chain had $18 million in sales from its 323 stores across northern Ohio. In that year it began to install meat departments in its stores. The firm continued to expand during the Depression, building fewer but larger stores. In 1937, Fisher Bros. opened its first self-service "master market." The 1950s were a period of continued expansion and modernization as Fisher Bros. moved out to the SUBURBS. In 1961, the name was changed to Fisher Foods, Inc., to reflect changes in its operation. Until the 1960s, Fisher was the largest retail food distributor in Cleveland, but its sales then began to fall, as did its share of the market. In 1965, Fisher Foods was acquired by a group of investors, consisting of Carl and John Fazio, whose father had started the Fazio grocery stores in 1927; Sam Costa, owner of the largest supermarket in the area; and Julius (Julie) Kravitz, founder of the Stop-N-Shop Supermarket Assoc. in 1961.

Within a year, the new owners had turned the company around under the Fazio store name. In 1968, the company moved its headquarters to BEDFORD HTS. In the late 1960s and early 1970s, when it pursued an aggressive acquisition program, purchasing grocery stores in the Midwest and California as well as related food industries, Fisher Foods became the second-fastest-growing supermarket chain in the country. By the mid-1970s, this diversification led to a deterioration of its supermarket business in Cleveland and caused internal dissension, leading Kravitz and Costa to leave the company. The Fazios instigated a "price war" in 1977 to regain some of Fisher's Cleveland market from Pick-N-Pay (see FIRST NATL. SUPERMARKETS, INC.) and Stop-N-Shop. A consequence was that all 3 firms were charged with price fixing in 1982 and forced to make restitution to area customers. In the 1980s, Fisher Foods began to restrengthen itself by consolidating its holdings. By 1983, Fisher had 48 stores and a new wholesale business, with over $500 million in sales and 4,300 employees. In 1984, the American Financial Corp. of Cincinnati took control of the firm from the Fazio family.

**FISHING INDUSTRY.** Although Cleveland is situated on a lake that historically ranked among the world's great fisheries, Clevelanders never looked to Lake Erie as a food source in any major sense. After 1796 the fishery was a marginal commerce, overshadowed by the port's role as a transportation hub and industrial depot. Four major factors, geography, technology, consumer taste, and chronological coincidence, steered commercial fishermen to other ports on Lake Erie, particularly Sandusky, Ohio, and Erie, Pa. By 1850, the port of Cleveland looked to the Great Lakes for resources that proved of far greater economic importance than inexpensive protein. The topography of the Ohio shore and lake bottom made the establishment of a fishing fleet in Cleveland impractical. High and rockbound from just east of the CUYAHOGA RIVER west to Cedar Pt., the shoreline presents as great a navigational hazard as any stretch of water on the Great Lakes. Only the few river mouths provide safe refuge from the sudden storms. On 19 Apr. 1808, Capt. Joseph Plumb of NEWBURGH, acting on reports of large schools of "yellow Catfish" gathered at the mouth of the Black River, fitted out a sailing scow for a seining expedition. Among others accompanying Plumb was AMOS SPAFFORD's son Adolphus. A sudden squall wrecked the boat at Dover Pt. (BAY VILLAGE), drowning all aboard except Capt. Plumb. Plumb was saved in a daring rescue, but the event exposed the difficulties of offshore fishing from Cleveland. Geography placed the richest fishing grounds at the far ends of the lake. The shallow, warm western basin has always been home to most of the lake's fish. The deep eastern basin, on which Cleveland is sited, holds comparatively few. Because of its depth, it is not as easily fished as the west. Further, the species available off Cleveland were not as profitable to fishermen as the highly desirable fish of the west. Thus, a Cleveland-based boat faced the choice of sailing west past the dangerous shore, or east an uneconomical distance, to the fishing grounds. Geography gave Cleveland's competitors another advantage. Both Sandusky and Erie grew beside the only natural harbors on Lake Erie. Sandusky and Presque Isle bays provided both refuge and terrain favorable for early fishing equipment.

The earliest extensive commercial fishing in Ohio began during the 1830s in Sandusky Bay. Its calm, shallow water and abundance of fish permitted simple, inexpensive onshore seining. A seine was a large bag-shaped net carried out on the water by rowboat, dropped overboard, and then dragged ashore. The rocky shore of Cleveland was not appropriate for this operation. Thus, while a Cleveland shoreline farmer might supplement his income with an occasional haul from the lake, a whole fish-processing industry was encouraged by the geography of the richest fishing ground. When the Ohio Canal was awarded to Cleveland instead of Sandusky, the western city needed another economic base. It responded by expanding exploitation of its greatest resource and developed an export trade in fish. Shortly after the canal's opening, Cleveland was handling large quantities of fish caught elsewhere for transshipment to Ohio hinterland markets. Other technological changes confirmed the industrial differences of the cities. During the 1850s, commercial fishermen moved out into the main fetch of the lake, significantly increasing their catch. About this time, a sufficent inventory of used vessels came within their financial reach. Simultaneously, however, another important commodity for Cleveland's industrial history arrived on the crowded wharves of the Cuyahoga. In 1852 the first shipment of iron ore from the Marquette Range was off-loaded. This new traffic further congested the busy river, pushing out less profitable vessels. Still, despite the gathering industrial boom, a real commerce in fish did exist in the Flats. The wholesale grocers who had transshipped import fish on the canal had evolved into commission merchants who brokered all varieties of commodities. These merchants purchased boatloads of fish from as far away as Lake Superior. They would then pack the fish on ice for local sale, or in salt for transport inland. The latter proved more profitable. W. L. Standart was the most notable merchant in this trade. Cited as the most prominent commercial fisherman in Cleveland, Standart operated 2 boats from the city. However, he was also a grocer, commission merchant, and saloon keeper. Clearly, Standart was not the professional lakeman seen in other ports.

Consumer taste also retarded the development of a fishing fleet in Cleveland. Both Native Americans and Europeans pursued the coldwater species of fish, especially whitefish and lake trout. This demand remained constant until the decline of those populations in the 1930s and 1940s. While found throughout the Great Lakes, neither was particularly numerous in comparatively warm Lake Erie. With the fishing fleets of the upper lakes supplying the premium species and those of Sandusky and Erie providing other needs, Clevelanders chose to invest in fleets of freighters to serve the transportation and steel industries. By the 1860s, the economic role of the port of Cleveland had been established. The city would be a consumer, not a producer, of raw resources such as foodstuffs. However, some fishing boats sailed from the Cuyahoga, and processing plants continued to clean and preserve the catch. This marginal commerce would last for many years. In fact, the industry did enjoy some growth in the late 19th century. In 1883, for example, the demand of a booming urban population kept 4 major processing houses and several independent operators profitable. Two of the large firms specialized in ocean fish and shellfish, which had sold in Cleveland since the opening of the Erie Canal in 1825. The other 2 handled imported lake fish. The independents generally sold their catch directly to grocers or through the municipal market. John W. Averill, Jr., was typical of the owner-operators of this period. His fleet consisted of 4 steam tugs and 1 sailboat, somewhat smaller than the comparable Sandusky firms. Even so, Averill especially advertised his whitefish and lake trout, indicating that he also imported fish.

In 1899, Chicago-based A. Booth & Co., then the largest fishing company on the lakes, opened a fishing station and processing plant in the Flats. Booth (est. 1848) was the first to apply sophisticated management and financial procedures to a rough-and-tumble industry. The company soon had stations on all major fishing grounds and plants in most lake cities. True to form, Booth quickly grew to be the largest commercial fishing company in Cleveland. However, the long decline of the fishery began at about this time. The first evidence was the collapse of the lake sturgeon population. Relentless fishing and environmental changes caused by pollution and soil erosion decimated this once-valuable species. The period 1880–1915 regularly saw catches of 40 million lbs. of all varieties in Ohio waters. After that, species after species was subjected to the same pressures that had driven the sturgeon to near-extinction. The waters off Cleveland were particularly affected. Contrary to popular belief, the arrival of the sea lamprey did not cause the decline of the fish populations of Lake Erie. The lamprey does not breed in the warm streams feeding into the lake. By the 1920s, the average yearly catch had fallen to 16 million lbs. The collapse of the cisco, or lake herring, accounted for most of this loss. This failure was extremely damaging to the industry, as the cisco had accounted for the bulk of sales. Some of the older firms, such as Averill, went out of business at this time. However, while the industry as a whole grew smaller during the 1920s and 1930s, the companies that have survived were founded then. Fulton Fish, Euclid Fish, and State Fish all began as fleet owners and processors. Social changes added to the competitive pressures. The industry was unionized during the 1930s, which drove up wages and costs. World War II drafted every available sailor into the armed forces, leaving only 1 boat operating out of Cleveland. Postwar consumer taste turned increasingly to beef. By 1950, only 7 boats sailed from the port. Cleveland was not the only city so affected. Throughout the Great Lakes, the industry was withering.

The nature of the lakes' ecosystem was changing because of human action. Commercially valuable fish were vanishing, to be replaced by "rough" fish such as carp and smelt, which flourished despite the habitat degradation. All these environmental factors, so pronounced in overutilized Lake Erie, culminated in a single great ecological catastrophe; the mayfly hatch of 1954 failed. The loss of this food source was disastrous for fish populations. The number of sauger, blue pike, walleye, and perch plummeted. More, the mayflies served as an environmental indicator. Polluted and oxygen-depleted, Lake Erie increasingly could not sustain life. This general collapse finished several companies. In 1955, Booth closed its Cleveland station. Star Fisheries, the predecessor to the State Fish Co., occupied their property in the FLATS. Lean years followed. In the absence of pollution controls, the lake was increasingly fouled. Unheralded, the boats departed Cleveland for more promising waters. In 1970, when Gov. Jas. Rhodes was forced to suspend fishing because of mercury contamination, only 1 boat, Fred Wittal's *Shark*, was left on the river. By 1973, even it was gone. Nevertheless, the abandonment of Cleveland as a fishing harbor did not mean an end to the fish-processing industry. The surviving companies continued to import and distribute fish from the ocean and upper lakes. Prospects brightened in the 1970s. Pollution control stemmed the habitat degradation. Fish stocks first stabilized, then grew. Demand for fish, spurred by a cholesterol-conscious society, increased. However, the fishing industry did not revive. The lucrative tourist industry lobbied for restrictions on the lakemen. Recreational fishermen, arguing that overfishing was responsible for the depletion of the stocks, met increasing success in Columbus. Strict netting regulations were applied. The Ohio Dept. of Natural Resources instituted a phased ban on gill nets in 1983. In 1985, the ban became complete. Fisherman sold their equipment and quit the industry. By the late 1980s, the majority of lake fish consumed by Clevelanders were caught across the lake in Canada.

Michael McCormick
Western Reserve Historical Society

---

See also BOATING.

**FITCH, JABEZ W.** (1823–1884), was a native Clevelander who served as commandant of Camp Taylor in Cleveland during the CIVIL WAR. Fitch was an attorney by profession. In 1852 he served as Cleveland fire chief; he was appointed U.S. marshal in 1855 when the seat of the Northern District of the U.S. Federal Court was established in Cleveland. In the spring and summer of 1861, he served as commandant of Camp Taylor, a camp of rendezvous and preliminary instruction. He later enlisted as a private in the 19th Ohio Volunteer Infantry and served as quartermaster. After the Civil War, Fitch returned to Cleveland and sold real estate. In 1873 he was elected president of the Cleveland Society for the Prevention of Cruelty to Animals, which later became known as the Cleveland Humane Society. In 1874 he became president of a statewide humane society. The following year, he was elected lieutenant governor of Ohio under Gov. Bishop.

*Annals of the Early Settlers Association of Cuyahoga County* (1886).

**FITCH, ZALMON** (1785–28 Apr. 1860), was a leader in the financial circles of Cleveland and Warren, Ohio. Fitch was born in Norwalk, Conn. Little is known about his education or early life. In 1810, he established a general store in Canfield, Ohio, the second one in the Reserve. He moved to Warren in 1813 and soon became a leading businessman. When the Western Reserve Bank was established in 1816, he became a cashier and held the position until he became president 23 years later. He also served as the land agent for several of the original stockholders of the CONNECTICUT LAND CO. In 1838, the receivers of the then-closed Bank of Cleveland appointed him trustee to settle its affairs after it collapsed in the Panic of 1837. Fitch served on the board of trustees of the newly formed Western Reserve College in Hudson, Ohio, in 1826. He served as a trustee of the Warren Municipal Court in 1836, 1842, 1847–48, and 1854–55, even after his move to Cleveland in 1838. He was a member of the board of agency of the Cleveland Medical College in 1843. Fitch was a member of the Warren Board of Education in 1849. He was one of the founding members of the Euclid St. Presbyterian Church in 1853. He served on the board of directors of the Cleveland & Pittsburgh Railroad in 1859. Fitch married Betsey Mygatt of Canfield, Ohio, in 1808. They had 3 children. She died in 1838. Fitch later married Rebecca H. Salter of New Haven, Conn., who died in 1879 at the age of 89.

Zalmon Fitch Papers, WRHS.

**FITZGERALD, WILLIAM SINTON** (6 Oct. 1880–3 Oct. 1937), was a member of city council for 4 years and was appointed mayor by HARRY L. DAVIS in 1921. Fitzgerald was born in Washington, D.C., the son of David and Esther Sinton Fitzgerald. He was educated in Washington's public schools and received a Master of Laws degree from Geo. Washington University in 1903. He came to Cleveland in 1904, was admitted to the Ohio bar that same year, and practiced law. In 1911 he was elected to city council from the 11th ward as a Republican and served 2 terms. Fitzgerald was appointed law director by Mayor Harry L. Davis, and when Davis resigned in 1920 to campaign for governor, Fitzgerald became mayor. He was defeated in his mayoral bid by FRED KOHLER in 1921 and afterward resumed his law practice. He died in N. ROYALTON at age 56. He had married Margaret Chilton Tucker on 14 Jan. 1920, and they had a son, Wm. Sinton, Jr. They were divorced in 1922, and he married Carolina Granger on 23 Mar. 1933.

**FIVE POINTS** is the area of COLLINWOOD where St. Clair Ave., E. 152nd St., and Ivanhoe Rd. come together to form a star. The name is more loosely given to all of Collinwood, that area of Cleveland bounded by E. 152nd on the west, St. Clair on the north, the Conrail tracks on the south, and E. 171st St. on the east. Other areas of Collinwood, as defined by a 1975 Kent State University study, are Four Points (near the Conrail bridge), mid-E. 152nd St., the industrial district, and the residential district. The Five Points intersection is home to Collinwood High School and the commercial hub of Collinwood. Settled ca. 1910, the area was the destination of many ITALIANS who had previously resided in BIG ITALY. As more migrants came to Collinwood to work in the industry concentrated there, the neighborhood expanded to its present boundaries.

At one time, Five Points was considered the most valuable industrial land in the city. Among the businesses located in the 20-block rectangle were Apex Electric, General Electric, Bailey Meter, Murray-Ohio, Fisher Body, Bryant Heater, Cleveland Graphite Bronze, Eaton Axle, Weatherhead, WILLARD STORAGE BATTERY, LINCOLN ELECTRIC, RELIANCE ELECTRIC, Clark Controller, Steel & Tube, Hamilton Steel, Natl. Acme, LINDSAY WIRE WEAVING, and Marquette Tube. Workers, neighborhood people, and students made the stores and restaurants at the

Five Points intersection prosperous well into the 1950s. By the 1960s, the changing racial balance of the neighborhood led to the flight of white residents and the alarm of merchants, who let their property deteriorate as they agonized over whether to remain in the neighborhood. A revitalized merchants' group, the Collinwood Better Business Assoc., fought for better city services and better cooperation among its members to reverse the pattern of fright and flight. In 1975, Collinwood got $100 million of Title I money to refurbish Five Points and other sections of Collinwood.

**FLAGLER, HENRY M.** (2 Jan. 1830–20 May 1913), was a businessman who was a founder and strategist in the development of the STANDARD OIL CO. He later played a major role in the development of Florida's east coast. Born in Hopewell, N.Y., the son of an itinerant Presbyterian minister, Isaac Flagler, and his third wife, Elizabeth Harkness, Flagler attended school through the 8th grade. At 14 he left home to live with his Harkness relatives in Republic, Ohio. His relation to the Harknesses gave him important business opportunities. In 1852 he joined with Dan and Lamon Harkness to buy out F. C. Chapman's interest in Chapman & Harkness and formed Harkness & Co., establishing a distillery, which made $50,000 for Flagler by 1863, when he sold his interest. During the CIVIL WAR he worked as a business agent dealing in salt, pork, and other provisions. After losing $100,000 in the salt industry in Michigan in the mid-1860s, Flagler moved to Cleveland in the summer of 1866 to try to manufacture a horseshoe he had patented and to rebuild his fortune. He worked briefly selling barrels to oil refiners, then became a commission merchant with Maurice B. Clark and T. S. Sanford. By 1867 he had made enough money to buy the firm and establish H. M. Flagler & Co. with his brother-in-law Barney York and Henry T. Collins.

Flagler's connections to the Harknesses paid off again in 1867. STEPHEN HARKNESS invested $100,000 in JOHN D. ROCKEFELLER's growing oil business and placed Flagler in charge of his investment; the firm became Rockefeller, Andrews, & Flagler. Described as "a grim, shrewd, rather ruthless man of business" by one biographer, Flagler developed the idea of absorbing smaller refineries in the Cleveland area, negotiated many of the purchases, and negotiated with the railroads for the reduced shipping rates that the company enjoyed. He also developed the plan to replace the partnership with a joint stock company and drew up the articles of incorporation for Standard Oil in 1870. He served as secretary and treasurer of the corporation and in 1879 proposed creation of a trust to hold and administer all Standard Oil properties; when the plan was revised in 1882, Flagler was one of the 9 trustees. Flagler served as vice-president of Standard Oil until 1908 and as a director until 1911, but he ceased to play an active role in its affairs after ca. 1881. By the 1880s he had moved to New York. During his years in Cleveland, Flagler was a member of the Board of Trade and the Mfg. Assoc. and actively supported the Republican party. During the 1880s he began investing heavily in Florida, building luxurious hotels along the eastern coast, building the Florida East Coast Railway, promoting agriculture in the region, and developing Palm Beach and Miami. Flagler was married 3 times. On 9 Nov. 1853, he married Mary Harkness; she died on 18 May 1881. On 6 June 1883, he married Mary's nurse, Ida Alice Shourds; she was later committed to an insane asylum. Flagler obtained an expensive divorce in 1901 and on 24 Aug. 1901 married Mary Lily Kenan.

Chandler, David Leon, *Henry Flagler* (1986).

The **FLATS** are located along the CUYAHOGA RIVER within the city of Cleveland where the river pursues a sinuous course through a valley about ½ mi. wide. This bottom land, the floodplain of the river, separates the high plateaus on which the city stands and is known as the "Flats." The lowlands near the mouth of the river were the site chosen by Cleveland's earliest settlers for their cabins. Its swampy character, however, caused so much illness that many soon migrated to higher ground. The unhealthful Flats ultimately were abandoned to commerce and industry, while the plateaus were chosen for farms and residences. The opening of the OHIO & ERIE CANAL between Cleveland and Akron in 1827, and as far as the Ohio River in 1832, spurred a tremendous increase in lake shipping. The Flats offered abundant room for docks and warehouses and, later, convenient manufacturing sites. Beginning in the 1850s, the RAILROADS found the broad expanse of the Flats advantageous in the storage and handling of freight. In the second half of the 19th century, the Flats were crowded with iron furnaces, rolling mills, foundries, lumberyards, shipyards, flour mills, oil refineries, paint and chemical factories, and other industries.

While the Flats facilitated commerce and manufacturing, they hindered communication between the east and west sides of the city. In 1878, after a decade of often bitter debate, the 2 sections were finally united with the completion of the SUPERIOR VIADUCT. Travelers no longer had to negotiate the precipitous valley walls to reach river crossings in the Flats. Other "high-level" BRIDGES followed. In the 20th century, as industries grew less dependent on water and rail transportation, the Flats gradually lost their concentration of industry. Some industries moved to modern plants in the SUBURBS, while others relocated to other parts of the country; some, rendered obsolete, simply closed. Although the Flats today are still the site of industry, including the huge works of the Republic Steel Corp., they harbor many more abandoned relics that bear silent witness to the city's industrial growth and development. In the 1970s and 1980s, the Flats enjoyed a new vitality as nightclubs and restaurants sprouted along Old River Rd. and other streets. In 1978, the nonprofit Flats Oxbow Assoc. was organized to promote the economic well-being of the area. In recent years, however, a number of ambitious projects—such as the Higbee Co.'s Settlers' Landing development and a proposal to renovate a remnant of the Superior Viaduct as a public park—were begun and then abandoned. Today the Flats are an amalgamation of commerce, industry, nightlife, and (with the construction of a series of condominiums in 1983–84) residences.

**FLEMING, THOMAS W.** (13 May 1874-Dec. 1948) and **LETHIA COUSINS** (7 Nov. 1876-25 Sept. 1963), were among the most influential BLACKS in the city's political and civic life during the first half of the 20th century. The first black to be elected to CLEVELAND CITY COUNCIL, Thos. Fleming was an active Republican until his departure from politics in 1929. Lethia Fleming, also a Republican activist, was a leader in numerous civic and women's organizations. Thos. W. Fleming was born in Mercer County, Pa. He arrived in Cleveland in 1893 to follow his trade as a barber. He soon became active in Republican politics as a protege of HARRY SMITH, black newspaper editor and state legislator. During his first year in the city, he led a group of young black Republicans to challenge the established black Republicans when they failed to endorse a black as a candidate for city council, and began to attend council meetings in order to learn what he called "the art of government." He attended the Cleveland Law School in the evening, and in 1906 he passed the teachers' examination (the equivalent of a high school diploma) and the bar examination. Appointed a member of the Repub-

lican State Executive Committee in that year, he made his first, unsuccessful, bid to gain a council seat in 1907. The 1909 Republican sweep of the city elections brought Fleming to council, where he served for 2 years as councilman-at-large. He was elected councilman from Ward 11 in 1916, serving until his indictment on a much-disputed charge of unlawful soliciting and corruption in office. He served 3 years in the Ohio Penitentiary. During his tenure on council, Fleming took pride in his part in facilitating the appointment of blacks to city jobs, which had previously been denied to members of the race. He also introduced ordinances to build a public bath house, gymnasium, and swimming pool in the Central area and to prevent the organization of a Ku Klux Klan chapter in Cleveland. Fleming was active in black business and social organizations. He was a cofounder of the *CLEVELAND JOURNAL* in 1903 with Nahum Brascher, Welcome T. Blue, and Leroy Crawford. Together with ALBERT D. "STARLIGHT" BOYD he formed the Starlight Realty & Investment Co. in 1919 to buy and rent properties in the Central area. They erected a business block at Central Ave. and E. 40th St.

Fleming's first marriage, to Mary Ingels Thompson, ended in divorce in 1910. Lethia Cousins was a schoolteacher when she married Fleming in 1912. Born in Tazewell, Va., she attended high school in Ironton, Ohio, and received her teacher's training in Morristown College in Tennessee. Before her marriage, she had taught for 20 years in West Virginia, where she also was an active worker for women's suffrage. Upon her marriage and subsequent move to Cleveland, she immediately became affiliated with the movement in the city. She was among the founders of the Negro Welfare Assoc., which later affiliated with the Natl. Urban League. Lethia Fleming was a zealous activist and organizer for the Republican party. Beginning in 1920, she directed the national campaigns of 4 presidential candidates among Negro women. She also organized, chartered, and incorporated the Natl. Assoc. of Republican Women in the U.S., with headquarters in Washington. Lethia Fleming served for 20 years as a worker with the County Child Welfare Board. She became interested in the Bahai movement in 1912 and, in later life put politics aside to follow its tenets.

Thomas and Lethia Fleming Papers, WRHS.

**FLINT, EDWARD SHERRILL** (3 Jan. 1819–29 Jan. 1902), was a railroad executive and banker and mayor of Cleveland, 1861–63. Flint was born in Warren, Ohio, but the early deaths of both parents left him to be raised and educated by his grandparents in Vermont. He initially worked as a bookkeeper. By 1851 he relocated himself and his family to Cleveland to start a real-estate firm. Finding his interest to be railroads, Flint became superintendent of the Cleveland, Columbus, Cincinnati, & Indianapolis Railroad, 1859–78. In 1860, Flint became a member of the Cleveland School Board. The following year he was elected mayor. The outbreak of the CIVIL WAR made Flint decide to become a Republican. He later became a War Democrat. During his term in office, he supported the cause of the North in the Civil War and took measures for the city to aid the families of local soldiers. Flint was defeated in his second mayoral election by IRVINE MASTERS. He retired from public life, remaining in the railroad business until his retirement in 1879. At that time he remained only as a trustee of the Society for Savings. Flint was married to Caroline E. Lemen of Cleveland. The couple had 5 children.

**FLORA AND FAUNA.** The early settler who cleared a bit of the forest for his cabin and garden patch began a series of changes in the plant and animal life in the area that has become Greater Cleveland. In the forest that surrounded his cabin, he could hunt deer, bear, wild turkey, and smaller animals necessary for daily living. Indians before him may even have encountered elk and wood buffalo. The rapid rise in population and industrialization had nearly wiped out the native vegetation and forest-living animals by the mid-1800s. From then on, the native plants and animals were replaced by human importation, either on purpose or by accident. Plants and animals so introduced thrived and sometimes crowded out the native species. Written accounts of the nature of the forests encountered are sketchy at best, but there are enough living remnants and accounts to reconstruct their nature and content. From the practice of early surveyors to use living trees as markers for lot corners, we can get a picture of the forest community of that location. There are records of some 20 species of trees so marked. Our best clue to what the original forests were like is the sizable areas that are being preserved by the Cleveland Metropolitan Park District throughout the Cleveland area. Many of these areas were timbered, some were farmed, but many have recovered naturally or by planting trees that would quickly provide forest cover, such as white and red pine, which are American, and Scotch and Austrian pine, which are European. In the main, however, there are forest ecosystems in most of the reservations that look much as they did in the days of MOSES CLEAVE-LAND.

In the reservations of the eastern highlands, there are good examples of the climax forest of the eastern U.S., dominated by American beech and sugar maple trees. A detailed study of this forest ecosystem was made in the N. Chagrin Reservation from 1930–40 by Arthur B. Williams, ecologist for the CLEVELAND MUSEUM OF NATURAL HISTORY and park naturalist for the Metropolitan Park District. In this study, he found that 51% of the trees that measured 3.5 in. in diameter were American beech, 26.5% were sugar maple. The remaining 22.5% were made up of 16 species, with red maple, tulip, red oak, white ash, basswood, and cucumber the most prominent. The nature of the soil resulting from the decay of leaves, trunks, and branches over the years is in the middle range of the pH scale, not too acid or too alkaline. The area is not too wet or too dry. This combination provides an excellent display of spring wildflowers, beginning early with spring beauties, hepaticas, and bloodroot and continuing through mass displays of red and white trilliums, yellow adder's-tongue, Dutchman's-breeches, squirrel corn, and foamflowers, to mention a few of the 61 species of wildflowers and low shrubby plants listed in the report. Fourteen species of ferns were identified and reported. The 4-year study revealed 29 species of birds nesting in the 65-acre study plot. Heading the list in numbers was the red-eyed vireo, followed by wood thrush and 5 warblers—American redstart, ovenbird, Louisiana water thrush, and black-throated green. Williams listed wild turkey as a former but no longer present resident. Of the 25 species of mammals listed, the short-tailed shrew and white-footed mouse were the most numerous. Red, gray, and flying squirrels and chipmunks were next. Of the larger mammals were woodchucks, opossums, raccoons, skunks, and red and gray foxes. Williams listed Virginia deer, bobcat, and black bear as formerly present. The Virginia deer is the only one of this group to return; abandoned farms in eastern counties and changing agricultural practices allowed shrubs and young trees to grow that provided ideal food for deer and encouraged their migration from Pennsylvania and West Virginia.

The broad floodplains of the Chagrin, Cuyahoga, and Rocky rivers provide an entirely different forest ecosystem from that of the eastern uplands. Here will survive only trees and plants that can withstand the frequent flooding, with subsequent deposit of sediment over their roots. The dominant trees of the floodplains are cottonwood, American sycamore, Ohio buckeye, black walnut, butternut, American and slippery elm, ash-leaved maple (also called box elder), and black rock maple. Two wildflower displays are provided by the conditions of the floodplain. In addition to the woodland flowers of the hillsides, which are basically the same as those of the eastern uplands, the floor of the floodplain has white as well as yellow adder's-tongue, giant Solomon's seal, cow parsnip, Virginia bluebell, and Canada lily, to mention a few in spring. In the late summer and early fall, rather than a relatively bare floor, the floodplain is covered with tall plants dominated by the yellows of several species of wild sunflowers, green-headed cone flower, Indian cup plant, and yellow and orange touch-me-not. The birds that are unique to the floodplain are those that are adapted to the river and river edge. Great blue, green-backed, black-crowned, yellow-crowned night herons, American bittern, and kingfisher find food in the river. Spotted sandpipers nest on the gravel edges and islands; wood ducks nest in the forest trees; song sparrows and yellow and yellowthroat warblers nest in the shrubs along the river's edge. Similarly, the mammals oriented to rivers such as raccoon, muskrat, and mink are present. With the abundance of nuts, squirrels find plenty of food. Deer populations are increasing and are being studied by wildlife specialists.

Rocky River Valley is also unique, in that a number of species of plants are found here that are not found in the floodplains of the Cuyahoga or the Chagrin. Sessile trillium, isopyrum related to rue and wood anemone, white adder's-tongue, and giant Solomon's seal are common in western Ohio and neighboring Indiana but are not found farther east than the Rocky River Valley. Oak-hickory forests grow best on the tops of ridges of the deeply dissected terrain of the southern portion of Cuyahoga County and the flat lands of the western suburbs. Red, black, and scarlet oaks and shagbark, pignut, and bitternut hickories thrive on drier soils and provide a more acid soil as the leaves, branches, and trunks decay. Only plants that can tolerate these conditions can survive. Wildflowers such as partridge berry, wintergreen, spotted wintergreen, coral root orchid, and rattlesnake plantain all prefer this type of forest. Low bush blueberries and several species of mosses prefer these drier and more acid soils. Birds and mammals are similar to those of the beech-maple forest to the east. The exception is the fox squirrel, which prefers the more open forest and forest edges provided by the oak-hickory community. These are present more often to the west, where the forest extends into the grassland of the prairie. As forest conditions have changed, fox squirrels have moved eastward and now are nearly equal in numbers to the original gray squirrels.

Trees and plants that are more at home farther north are found on east- and north-facing slopes of the CHAGRIN and CUYAHOGA RIVERs, as well as in deep ravines having an east/west orientation. Formerly in this area, white pine was harvested for lumber by early settlers. Now hemlock, black and yellow birch, American yew, native juniper, and mountain maple are found in this type of habitat. Here the rare lady's-slipper orchid and trailing arbutus find a favorable habitat. Northern birds such as black-throated green warblers nest, and in a few localities the nests of dark-eyed junco have been found. The Hudson Bay jumping mouse is the only northern mammal to be found here.

Early reports indicate that there were a number of wet areas and swamps between EUCLID AVE. and Lake Erie. These have all been reclaimed, thus eliminating habitats favorable to this type of ecosystem. This vast array of forest ecosystems that exists due to variety of terrain provides the greatest diversity of plants and animals in the state. Cleveland is indeed a place where the influence of east, west, north, and south intermix. But what of the urban community? Here human activities have provided habitat for plants and animals that can tolerate congestion and adverse atmosphere conditions. By the early 1900s, a portion of Euclid Ave. became "Millionaires' Row," and landscape architects planted the estates of the wealthy industrialists with such novelties as southern magnolias and the newly discovered ginkgo imported from China. Other residential streets were planted with fast-growing trees such as silver maple, pin oak, Norway maple, and London plane tree—a hybrid cross between the native sycamore and the Oriental sycamore. This tree is now (1986) the most common street tree in the city. Horse chestnuts from Europe, both the white and pink varieties, have replaced the Ohio buckeye, and the native American elms were replaced with either European or Oriental elms. The little leaf linden from Europe was found to be so adaptable to city conditions that it can be planted in tubs along downtown streets. Flowering cherry trees brighten suburban boulevards. In the early 1940s, the city's Div. of Shade Trees developed several trees, such as the globe and columnar maples, that grow to proportions more suitable to crowded street conditions in the early 1940s. The native honey locust, a tree with an array of multiple thorns, was developed into a variety that was not only thornless but also without unsightly seed pods in the late 1920s.

A number of plants can be found along arteries of transportation. Sunflowers from Kansas and nodding thistles from Midwest prairies are familiar plants along highway innerbelts and in the FLATS of the Cuyahoga River. These and other exotic species have grown from spillage of shipments of grain on highway and railroad rights-of-way. Sand reed grass, beach grass, sand cherry, and the rare pitcher thistle, plants native to the great dunes of Lake Michigan, are growing on an unused pile of sand near the mouth of the Cuyahoga River, brought by a freighter from the Michigan shore of Lake Michigan. Highway beautification was given increased emphasis by Lady Bird (Mrs. Lyndon B.) Johnson. Since that time, various agencies have brought a number of unusual plants to brighten highways and to hold soil on steep embankments. The popular use of crown vetch is an example of this kind of introduction. Mammals in the surrounding natural areas have remained fairly constant. In the early 1940s, there was evidence that the Virginia deer had returned to the area. They have since become a nuisance in some suburban areas. Beaver began to return to northeastern Ohio as early as the 1940s. Their return to streams is causing flooding in some instances and doing considerable damage to trees in others. In the more densely populated areas, raccoons, opossums, skunks, and chipmunks are making themselves at home. Transportation arteries have contributed unwanted rats and mice from the beginning of urbanization.

The shoreline of Lake Erie is a natural pathway for spring and fall migrating birds. Thousands of blue jays stream along the shoreline during a week in early May, probably to make a crossing at Erie or Buffalo. In the fall, there is a similar flight of bank swallows moving west. Many species can be seen in downtown Cleveland and in parks along the lake awaiting favorable weather conditions to cross the lake or resting after an overwater flight in the late summer and fall. In general, the bird population has remained reasonably constant during the time that systematic records have been kept. Some new species have been added for one reason or another. The cardinal was considered a rare bird in the early 1900s; now it is a common year-round resident. In fact, it has become so abundant and is so attractive that it was adopted as the state bird in 1959. After an importation in 1850 and 1852 and a direct importation to Cleveland in 1869, the English sparrow, or house sparrow as it is now called, has become a door-yard pest. In 1890, 80 European starlings were released in Central Park in New York City. A count of starlings roosting on buildings on PUBLIC SQUARE during the winters of 1930–31 and 1932–33 was estimated to be as high as 19,900. A few pairs of house finches were released in New York in 1940. Their spread from that introduction has been incredible. The first house finch was reported by Benjamin P. Bole, Jr., in the Holden Arboretum on 5 Jan. 1964. Now it has become a regular nester around homes and gardens, even nesting in hanging flower baskets on balconies of high-rise apartments. Perhaps because of more persistent and well-informed observers, many new gulls have been reported wintering along our lakefront. Great and lesser black-backed gulls from the Arctic, Franklin's gull from the Midwest, the California gull from the Far West, and the little gull from Europe have all been reported in the last few years. This great diversity of plants and animals continues to keep Greater Cleveland the "FOREST CITY."

Harold E. Wallin
Cleveland State University

The **FLORENCE CRITTENTON HOME** of Cleveland originally provided for the needs of unwed mothers and their children, and also operated an adoption service for the infants. Chartered by the Ohio legislature in 1911, the Florence Crittenton Home for Unwed Mothers was organized as a branch of the Natl. Florence Crittenton Mission. Its purpose was to provide a temporary home and medical care for unwed mothers and their children. In order to remove the social stigma of unwed motherhood, the mission guaranteed anonymity to its residents.

The home first opened at 523 Eddy Rd. It accepted girls from all stations of life, and charged only the amount it cost to provide residential and medical services. Some exceptions were made on the basis of need. Mothers were required to stay in the home until the baby was 6 months old. A matron took charge of the daily activities of the home, and medical care was provided by a part-time nursing staff and a visiting physician. The first matron was Mrs. Margaret Rutter. During the 1930s and 1940s, Miss Zona Scott was the matron. Under her leadership the mission moved to a newer, larger building at 8615 Euclid Ave. Scott also made possible increased adoption services and larger, more modern medical facilities for the home. By this time, the requisite 6-month postnatal stay had been eliminated.

In the late 1950s and early 1960s, Florence Crittenton experienced financial difficulties. The number of applications had dropped, and costs had risen, until it was able to serve only those who could pay. In an attempt to lower costs, the medical facilities were eliminated, and babies were delivered at the CLEVELAND CLINIC and, later, BOOTH MEMORIAL HOSPITAL. Finally, in 1971, a study of the usefulness of the home was completed by the Welfare Fed. It concluded that the number of unwed mothers who wished to preserve their anonymity had dropped, and that rising fees had made the home inaccessible to all but those of middle income or greater. The federation threatened to withdraw funding unless the home reacted in some way to the study. In response, the Florence Crittenton Mission changed its focus, becoming an "attention" home. Renamed Florence Crittenton Services of Greater Cleveland, Inc., its main concern was the care of adolescent women who either had suffered neglect at home or were in minor trouble with the law. In the late 1970s, Florence Crittenton Services relocated to 3737 Lander Rd.; its operations are supported by contributions rather than fees.

Florence Crittenton Home Records, WRHS.

**FOGG, WILLIAM PERRY** (27 July 1826–1909), was an adventurer and writer. Fogg was born in Exeter, N.H., and moved to Cleveland as a child. A conferred but transplanted "Yankee," he was an early member and president of the New England Society, which promised to promote a kindred spirit among the offspring of New England pioneers. Initially a chinaware merchant, Fogg became active in city affairs and was appointed to the Board of Commissioners in 1866. Cleveland Mayor HERMAN M. CHAPIN, Fogg, and the other commissioners drafted the Metropolitan Police Act of 1866. In 1868, Fogg began his round-the-world travels. He was one of the first Americans to travel through the interior of Japan. The *CLEVELAND LEADER* published his letters; they were later published as the book *Round the World Letters*. This edition also included letters from China. His second book, *Arabistan, or The Land of the Arabian Nights* (1872), was first published in England and is an account of his journey through Egypt, Arabia, and Persia to Baghdad. His final book is simply the revised American edition of *Land of the Arabian Nights*. When he returned to America, Fogg and Richard C. Parsons acquired the business of the Herald Publishing Co. in 1877. The venture was doomed, and it failed, leaving the lawyer Parsons to go back to his practice and Fogg to go abroad again. Fogg later came back to the U.S. and lived in Roselle, N.J., from 1901–08. He then lived in Morris Plains for the last year of his life. He had married Mary Ann Gould on 20 May 1852.

**FOLK ARTS FESTIVALS.** *See* **CLEVELAND FOLK ARTS ASSOCIATION**

**FOLSOM'S MERCANTILE COLLEGE** was the first college founded in Cleveland. R. C. Bacon opened the college on W. 3rd St. in 1848. A few months later, E. G. Folsom, who had taught penmanship in common school in Cleveland, became sole owner. Folsom was instrumental in obtaining support for the college from prominent business and professional leaders in Cleveland. A visiting committee of 12 men made the initial investment in the college. Its original purpose was to provide young men with rudimentary training in business skills in order to fill positions in Cleveland's rapidly growing business community. In 1850 it became known as E. G. Folsom's Commercial College. At this time penmanship, speed, and legibility were important qualifications for success in business, so Folsom's offered 4 courses—in penmanship, bookkeeping, drawing, and chirhythmology. Night classes were offered for those who worked during the day. Schooling lasted only 2–3 months. In 1854, the college moved into the 4th floor of the new Rouse Block, and the name was changed to Folsom's Mercantile College. JOHN D. ROCKEFELLER graduated from Folsom's in 1855. Soon after, the school became known as Bryant, Lusk & Stratton Business College. The college served as a model for the chain of Bryant & Stratton business schools established throughout the country. After successive changes in ownership, it became Spencerian Business College in the 1870s. Spencerian later merged with another school to form DYKE COLLEGE.

**FOOTBALL.** The first organized football game in Cleveland was reportedly played in 1887, when a Central High School team defeated a group of freshmen from Case School of Applied Science. Newspapers provided general coverage of eastern college football, but locally the game remained a little-known sport until 1890, when interest in football grew quickly. Graduates of eastern colleges living, working, and teaching in Cleveland passed along their knowledge of football rules and strategies to local men and boys. Their knowledge, experience, and ability made possible several important local games in 1890, which further promoted and popularized football. These games included the first high school game in the city's history (25 Oct., University School 20, Central 0); a series of games between UNIVERSITY SCHOOL, Central, Case, and Adelbert College; and a charity game that attracted 1,500–3,000 spectators to Natl. League Park to watch the Crescent football club of New York defeat a team from Cleveland. So excited was the crowd that it spilled onto the field several times during play, a common problem before seats were provided. By 1895, a number of schools and athletic clubs in the area had 1 or more football teams, and by 1900 local newspapers were giving extensive coverage to the daily practices of high school and college teams. But problems were emerging. During the early years, the sport was informal, disorganized, and rough. Players formed football clubs with little regard for eligibility rules or game schedules; arranging games through the newspapers was common practice at various levels into the 1900s. Eligibility rules for high school and college games were vague and impossible to enforce short of refusing to play, which happened only rarely. Another problem was "ringers" who played for money: some accepted money to play for 1 or more college teams during the course of a season, and high school and college athletes sometimes were paid to play for athletic clubs.

High school administrators soon moved to gain control over the sport at their institutions in order to prevent abuses and to protect their schools' reputations. In Nov. 1904, the Athletic Senate, made up of school administrators, adopted new eligibility rules and academic standards to govern athletics in the elementary and high schools. In 1936 the high school Senate was expanded to include PAROCHIAL SCHOOLS and additional public schools, and was reorganized into East and West divisions to improve competitiveness in order to help the schools maintain self-supporting athletic programs. Organizations such as the Senate and the Ohio High School Athletic Assoc., formed in 1907, brought order to the sport but did little to support the individual school's football program; as late as 1940, the financial management of local high school football programs rested with the faculty manager, coach, or principal in each school, and only 4 of the 17 Senate teams had their own playing fields. Athletic associations composed of students and interested alumni and faculty controlled the sport at Western Reserve College until 1919, and at Case until 1947. Under the strong guidance of athletic association president FRANK VAN HORN, Case reigned as the state's football powerhouse between 1902–11. In the early 1900s, critics raised serious objections to various aspects of the sport. In Nov. 1910, local ministers "bitterly denounced" the violent nature of football, called for the game's abolition, and lodged a protest against the scheduling of the annual Thanksgiving morning game between Case and Western Reserve, which had begun in 1891. Safety became a major issue between 1900–10, leading football boosters to adopt several new rules designed to make less important plays that emphasized strength and force, such as the flying wedge. By 1912, a more modern version of the game had developed, with legalized passing, 4 downs to make 10 yards and retain possession of the ball, and touchdowns worth 6 points. Locally, the chaotic situation of the 1890s had become more ordered: no longer did high schools, colleges, and athletic clubs play one another, but there were separate leagues for each. As early as 1903, an amateur football league had been organized with divisions in various weight classes and teams composed of former high school and college players.

As the 1920s approached, football in Cleveland shifted from a player-controlled sport to one increasingly controlled by others and geared more toward the spectator. By 1915, for example, the team names in the amateur league had changed from the likes of the Madison Athletic Club, the Kickoffs, and the Archwood Bible Club to names such as Bartlett Drugs, Favorite Knits, Langgreths Tailors, and Blepp Knits as businesses and industries sponsored amateur teams. Men gradually discovered that football could be used to advertise a business, to enhance the reputation of educational institutions, to build strong characters in young players, to demonstrate the worthy Americanness of an ethnic or racial group, to turn a profit in professional football, and to rally pride around the performance of a team, whether at the ethnic, neighborhood, or city level. Fans developed their own meanings for the game and its stars. Star quarterback BENJAMIN (BENNY) FRIEDMAN, for example, became more than a star athlete to many Cleveland Jews. As he combated prejudice in his rise to stardom in high school, in college, and in the pros, he became a symbol of Jewish pride and ability, a shining example to show other Americans that Jews could excel in manly sports and other areas of American life. Other ethnic and racial groups had their own symbols and sources of pride on the gridiron, both individuals—such as Ted Green, the black star at Case in 1902 and 1903 and then at Reserve while in law school in 1905, and Bill Willis and Marion Motley, who helped smash the color barrier in pro football with the Browns in 1946—and entire teams, such as the Mohawks, an all-Italian team that claimed the city championship from 1914–18, and the Slovak Catholic Benedictine High School team, which was formed 2 years after the school was organized in 1927. The players might play simply for the enjoyment of the game, but fans and others invested the gridiron struggles with their own meanings.

High school and college administrators also discovered uses for football. In elementary and high schools, sports were used as tools to enhance the moral development of children; football became a way to teach boys self-discipline and character and a way to save potential juvenile delinquents. Moral rhetoric over football in the high schools gave way to the values of the marketplace in local colleges such as John Carroll and Western Reserve, where a strong football program was seen as good for business, attracting publicity, new students, and financial contributions to the schools. Local college football was extremely popular between 1920–45. The Big 4 of Case, Western Reserve, JOHN CARROLL UNIVERSITY, and BALDWIN-WALLACE COLLEGE had been organized in the 1930s, and those schools, along with big-time college programs such as Ohio State and Notre Dame, dominated the attention of the fans. But by 1950, local college football was in serious trouble. The increasing commercialization of big-time college football made it much more difficult for the small, private schools in the Cleveland area to compete for talent and finance their programs. The NCAA decision in 1952 to allow colleges to award full scholarships solely on the basis of athletic ability further increased the pressures on local schools, where football attendance was on the decline and the athletic programs were losing money. In Dec. 1954, the presidents of small colleges in the region formed the Presidents' Athletic Conference, which banned athletic scholarships and sought to create an atmosphere conducive to competitive athletics on a regional basis without great expense. Although the conference went through several reorganizations, local college football has remained less spectator-oriented since 1955.

Marketplace values and football also came together in the development of professional football in Cleveland. The pro game flourished in surrounding northeastern Ohio towns after 1903, but no pro team developed in Cleveland until 1916, when the Cleveland Indians were organized by Gene Watson "Peggy" Parratt and sports promoter Herman Schleman. Parratt had been a baseball and football star at Case, but in 1905 he accepted money to play for the Shelby Athletic Club on Sundays as Jimmy Murphy. After his identity was revealed and he admitted to breaking the amateur code, Parratt was barred from Case athletics. He maintained his connections with area football and in 1916 introduced professional football in Cleveland in a more legitimate manner. Despite an impressive home opener at LEAGUE PARK, defeating the Carlisle Indians in the first pro football game played in Cleveland by a Cleveland team, 8 Oct. 1916, and a successful season on the field (8–3–1), the team did not enjoy the financial success its organizers had hoped.

Two decades of failed attempts passed before pro football caught on in Cleveland. In 1919 the CLEVELAND TIGERS (sometimes Indians) played in the last year of the so-called Ohio League. On 17 Sept. 1920, the owners of professional football teams met in the showroom of Ralph Hay's Hupmobile Agency in Canton to discuss formation of a stronger league, the American Professional Football Assoc., which became the NFL. Representing the Cleveland franchise were Stanley B. "Stan" Cofall (d. 21 Sept. 1961), former Cleveland high school star, standout at Notre Dame (1914–16), organizer of the 1919 Indians, and vice-president of the new league, and Jas. M. "Jimmie" O'Donnell (1871–1 Oct. 1946), who had owned the 1919 team. But the pro game had difficulty establishing itself against the college game in Cleveland: O'Donnell could not sustain his franchise beyond 1922 and sold it in 1923 to Samuel H. Deutsch, who literally bought the city its first professional football championship in 1924 when he purchased the champion Canton franchise and moved it to Cleveland (see CLEVELAND BULLDOGS). But Deutsch also encountered difficulties and transferred his franchise in 1925 to Herb Brandt; after a financially disastrous season, Brandt suspended operations before the 1926 season. The void was filled that year by the CLEVELAND PANTHERS of Red Grange's short-lived American Football League. Deutsch revived the Cleveland Bulldogs in 1927 behind the many talents of Benny Friedman, but he sold the team when the venture failed. The league placed a temporary franchise (the Indians) in the city as an experiment in 1931, but the team fared poorly on the field (2–8) and at the box office and was not continued.

Despite the lack of a popular pro team, the sport was integrated into the social life of the community during the 1920s, 1930s, and 1940s because of the uses people found for the sport. During the Depression, civic leaders inaugurated the *Plain Dealer* CHARITY FOOTBALL GAME as a means of raising funds for charity. In the late 1930s and 1940s, civic boosters used football to promote the city, using the 80,000-seat Stadium and its potential for large gate receipts to lure to the city major college games such as Navy vs. Notre Dame and Ohio State vs. Illinois, pleasing local football fans, making money for the city and local businesses, and putting the city in the national spotlight, if only briefly. Two new amateur leagues—the Catholic Youth Organization, founded in late 1937, and the Muny Football Assoc., led by Fr. Joseph Andel as president from 1946–

60—also helped integrate football into the fabric of the city's social life by providing leisure activities for young boys and men. The increasing popularity of professional football in the post-World War II years further made the sport part of the city's social fabric and a symbol of the middle-class good life. Professional football finally established a foothold in the city when attorney Homer Marshman formed the CLEVELAND RAMS in the short-lived American Football League in 1936 and then the NFL after 1937. Marshman and his partners sold the club to Dan Reeves in 1941. Shortly after the Rams won the city's second pro championship in 1945, Reeves moved the club to the sunnier financial climate of Los Angeles.

Appetites whetted by the 1945 championship were satiated the next season and in seasons to come by the CLEVELAND BROWNS, organized by ARTHUR B. "MICKEY" MCBRIDE and led by head coach Paul E. Brown (b. 7 Sept. 1908), whose systematic approach to the game helped influence the styles of numerous coaches at all levels of the sport in the postwar years. An innovative and highly successful coach at the high school, college, and professional levels, Brown emphasized character, intelligence, and speed and developed many of the coaching procedures that revolutionized and rationalized the game. As coach of a new team entering a new pro league just after the war had disrupted college football, Brown was able to nearly handpick his new team from the best players he had seen during his coaching career. Inducted into the Pro Football Hall of Fame in 1967, Brown was joined in that shrine by 6 of his initial pro recruits: quarterback Otto Graham, inducted in 1965; fullback Marion Motley, 1968; offensive tackle and placekicker Lou Groza, 1974; pass receiver Dante Lavelli, 1975; defensive middle guard Bill Willis, 1977 (College Hall of Fame, 1971); and center Frank Gatski, 1985. Brown brought 3 other future Hall of Famers to the Browns: record-setting running back Jim Brown, inducted in 1973; defensive end LEN FORD, 1976; and offensive tackle Mike McCormack, 1984. Former Cleveland Ram BOB WATERFIELD was elected to the Hall of Fame in 1965, and wide receiver Paul Warfield was enshrined in 1983. Paul Brown's tenure as Browns coach ended in 1963, when he was fired by owner Arthur B. "Art" Modell (b. 23 June 1925), a young advertising executive and former television producer from New York. An energetic man on the make in the spirit of Jimmie O'Donnell, Sam Deutsch, and Mickey McBride, Modell was much more successful than they in parlaying his franchise into power and status in the community. He bought the team in 1961 and soon became a leading force among NFL owners, serving as league president 1967-70 and piloting the league through its merger with the American Football League and subsequent reorganization. By the mid-1970s, Modell was receiving honors as a civic leader in his adopted town and was considering a foray into politics.

After 1960, Cleveland football was affected by economic considerations and general social changes. At the high school level, recurrent violence at the Charity Football Game in the 1960s contributed to a decline in attendance and a change in the site of the game. Beginning in 1968, the parochial schools withdrew from the Senate for economic reasons, and after the school desegregation order, the Senate was reorganized in the fall of 1979 from East and West divisions, suggestive of the racial divisions within the city, into North and South divisions. In 1981, civic and business leaders expressed concern about the future of interscholastic sports in the financially troubled public schools. That pro football is a business and also shares in the general ills of society became painfully apparent to fans as a result of players' strikes, a 1982 court battle between Modell and

Browns minority stockholder Robt. D. Gries, revelations in 1982 and 1983 that several Browns players had drug problems, and the tragic cocaine-induced death of defensive back Don Rogers in 1986. Such events went far toward debunking the myth of the necessarily virtuous athlete, yet in high schools and elsewhere, coaches still shared longtime Benedictine coach Augie Bossu's goal of turning out "good Christian young men." To these men, football remained what it had long been: one way to instill in boys and young men character and the important values in life. Although the spectator and his dollars attracted the attention of football promoters at all levels at one time or another, many coaches and administrators maintained an interest in the character, welfare, and moral development of players, and players in high schools and such leagues as the Northern Ohio Touch Football League continued to play for pure enjoyment and dreams of gridiron glory. The tension and ambivalence between moral principle and character, on the one hand, and the supreme goal of "winning," on the other, were part of football from its earliest days, both locally and nationally. That tension, after all, is one element that makes the sport uniquely American.

Kenneth W. Rose

Case Western Reserve University

Brown, Paul, with Clary, Jack, *PB: The Paul Brown Story* (1979).
Rader, Benjamin G., *American Sports* (1983).

FOOTE, JOHN A. (22 Nov. 1803–16 July 1891), was a leading reformer and politician during Cleveland's early history. Foote was born in New Haven, Conn. His father, Samuel A. Foote, was governor of Connecticut and a member of both the U.S. House of Representatives and the U.S. Senate. John was also the elder brother of Adm. Andrew H. Foote, of naval fame during the CIVIL WAR. Educated at Yale College, Foote went on to study law at Litchfield after his graduation in 1823. He practiced law for 7 years and served 2 Whig terms in the Connecticut legislature before coming to Cleveland in 1833. Foote's illustrious career in Cleveland began when he formed a law partnership with SHERLOCK J. ANDREWS, which continued until 1848, when Andrews was elected to the bench. Foote, a member of the WHIG PARTY, served 1 term in the Ohio legislature, 1837-39. In 1839 he was elected president of Cleveland's city council, a position that he held under Mayor JOSHUA MILLS until 1840. Several years later, in 1844, Foote ran as the Whig candidate for mayor but was defeated. His political career reached a pinnacle when he was elected to the Ohio state senate in 1853. Foote became a convert to the Republican principle after that party was formed in 1854.

As an adept man of business, Foote worked zealously to secure public favor for the early railroad ventures of Cleveland. He served as director of the Cleveland, Columbus & Cincinnati and the Cleveland & Pittsburgh railroads. He also was a trustee of the Society for Savings. One of the most important and useful features of his life was his connection with work in juvenile education and reform in Cleveland and Ohio. In addition, he was a proponent of the temperance and antislavery movements. As a member of city council in 1839, Foote served on a committee that made the first purchases of land for school purposes. In 1856, Gov. Chase selected Foote as one of 3 commissioners for the reform of schools in the state of Ohio. His colleagues on the reform commission were Chas. Reemilen and Jas. D. Ladd. The commission adopted, from its studies on school reform in Europe, the "family" system. The Ohio reform farm was the result of the commission's study and became a model for other reformatory establishments. In the Cleveland area, Foote, along with HARVEY RICE, started the Industrial School of Cleveland and the CHILDREN'S AID SOCIETY.

Foote had a strong interest in TEMPERANCE and played an important role with his proposals in city council, calling for ordinances against the proliferation of liquor. In 1839 he proposed that a committee on licenses be created to regulate the expansion of "dram shops." Although much debated, Foote's ordinance was passed on 6 May 1840 with some revisions. The ordinance was entitled "An ordinance to regulate taverns, and prohibit the sale of ardent spirits or other intoxicating liquors by less quantity than one quart." It was provided, further, "that no licensed tavern keeper should give or sell ardent spirits to any child, apprentice, or servant, without the consent of parent, guardian, or employer, or to any intoxicated person." Foote was subsequently elected president of the Cleveland Temperance Society. He was actively opposed to slavery and served as treasurer of the CLEVELAND ANTI-SLAVERY SOCIETY in 1833, and he became vice-president of the CUYAHOGA COUNTY ANTI-SLAVERY SOCIETY in 1837. Foote was a member of the FIRST PRESBYTERIAN CHURCH of Cleveland. He was married twice: first to Francis A. Hitchcock, of Cheshire, Conn., who died in 1855, leaving 8 children, and next, in 1858, to Mary S. Cutter of Cleveland.

The **FOOTPATH DANCE COMPANY,** a nonprofit troupe based in SHAKER HTS., was the first modern dance company from Greater Cleveland to perform both nationally and internationally. Footpath was formed in 1976 by artistic director Alice Rubenstein. Initially, the company consisted only of women. Original members included Charlotte Barker, Paulette Sears, Tamar Kotoske, Jackque Lunn Bell, Tara Deaodhar, and Rubenstein, who choreographed and directed. Besides performing at area colleges and arts festivals, Footpath immediately formed a touring company, which performed in Ohio, surrounding states, and Canada. The company also offered children's and adults' classes in modern dance. In 1977, Footpath received a grant from the Ohio Arts Council, which allowed them to increase the frequency of their appearances. From the first, Rubenstein selected dances for the repertoire with the intent of balancing nonnarrative pieces with works of dramatic content. Footpath accepted its first male dancer, Mark Schmucher, in 1981. At this time the company began a series of lunchtime performances at the Engineers Auditorium, in order to build local recognition. This series was continued in 1982 with the support of the CLEVELAND FOUNDATION. The company continues to grow, and performs regularly in Cleveland. In Aug. 1986, Footpath was one of 4 American companies invited to participate in the prestigious competition in Paris, France (Dance A. Paris). That marked the first time that American modern dance companies were selected for international competition. Footpath had its offices and studio at 16704 Chagrin Blvd. in 1986.

**FORAN, MARTIN A.** (11 Nov. 1844–28 June 1921), served in the U.S. Congress from the 20th and 21st districts from 1883–89. He was a member of the Ohio Constitutional Convention and county prosecutor and judge of the court of common pleas. Foran was born in Choconut Twp., Susquehanna County, Pa., the son of Jas. and Catherine O'Donnell Foran. He grew up on his father's farm, was educated in public school, and learned the coopering trade. He attended St. Joseph's College in Susquehanna County for 2 years. During the Civil War, he served in the 4th Pennsylvania Cavalry. In 1868 he came to Cleveland and

practiced his trade, serving as president of the Coopers International Union, and from 1870–74 he was editor of the *Coopers' Journal.* During this time he studied law; he served as a member of the Ohio Constitutional Convention in 1873, and after being admitted to the Ohio bar in 1874, he practiced law in Cleveland.

Active in local Democratic party politics, Foran was elected prosecuting attorney for Cuyahoga County, serving 1875–77. He supported the local chapter of the KNIGHTS OF LABOR and was considered a moderate reformer who tried to bridge the gap between capital and labor. With strong support from labor, he was elected to Congress in 1882 and served 3 terms. During this time he wrote a novel, *The Other Side: A Social Study Based on Fact,* which described the life of the working man. Declining to run for a 4th term in 1888, Foran returned to Cleveland and practiced law. He continued to be active in politics and brought the talents of NEWTON D. BAKER to the attention of Mayor TOM L. JOHNSON. He was elected judge of the court of common pleas in 1910, where he served until his death in Cleveland at age 76. On 29 Dec. 1868, Foran married Kate Kavanaugh, and they had 2 children, Gertrude M. (Mrs. Franklin A. Handrick) and Margaret O. (Mrs. Jas. Connolly). After the death of his wife in 1893, he married Emma Kenny the same year.

**FORD, HORATIO** (23 June 1881–28 Nov. 1952), was a Cleveland-area banker and lawyer. His civic involvements included the BOY SCOUTS OF AMERICA and forest conservation. Ford was born to Horatio Clark and Ida May Thorp Ford. His family had first come to Cleveland in 1840 and had been involved in the Underground Railroad. Educated in the CLEVELAND PUBLIC SCHOOLS, Ford graduated from CENTRAL HIGH in 1900. He earned the A.B. from Yale University in 1904 and the LL.B. degree from Western Reserve University Law School and was admitted to the Ohio bar in 1907. In 1906, Ford started as a cashier in the Gordon Park branch of the Garfield Savings Bank. By the time of Garfield's merger with Cleveland Trust Bank in 1922, Ford had served as bookkeeper, secretary, attorney, and a director of the bank. After the merger, he continued as a cotrustee for certain trusts, an attorney, a director, and an assistant vice-president for Cleveland Trust. A member of the law firm of Snyder, Henry Thomsen, Ford & Seagrave from 1913–26, Ford retired from banking in 1940 to return to the practice of law, joining the firm of Ford & Reece, later Ford, Reece, Baskins & Howland.

In 1910, Ford helped organize the Boy Scouts in the Cleveland area, serving on the area executive committee from 1910–20. Possessing a deep feeling for and understanding of nature and the outdoors, Ford was able to qualify 1,500 acres of family-owned Whitfield Woods property in Middlefield, Ohio, as one of the first tree farms in Ohio. From 1950 until his death, he served as president of the Ohio Forestry Assoc. Ford served as an officer or director of the Federal Improvement Co., the New Amsterdam Co., the One Euclid Ave. Co., the Mayfair Realty Co., the Cleveland & Eastern Traction Co., the Cleveland & Chagrin Traction Co., the Realty Bond & Mortgage Co., and the Cleveland YMCA. Ford married Ella Almira White on 7 May 1908. The Fords had 6 children, Horatio, Andrew, Thomas, Jonathon, Baldwin, and Almira.

**FORD, LEONARD "LENNY"** (18 Feb. 1926–14 Mar. 1972), was a star defensive end for the CLEVELAND BROWNS professional football team from 1950–57. He was inducted into the Pro Football Hall of Fame in 1976. Born and raised in Washington, D.C., Ford attended Armstrong High School, where he was captain of the football, baseball, and basketball teams in his senior year. He began college at Morgan State, then transferred to the University of Michigan. He was an All-American in football at Michigan in 1946 and 1947 and played in the 1948 Rose Bowl game. Ford began his professional football career playing both offensive and defensive end for the Los Angeles Dons of the ill-fated All-America Football Conference in 1948 and 1949, catching 67 passes on offense. The Browns acquired Ford after the 1949 season in the draft held to allocate players from failed AAFC teams. Coach Paul Brown used Ford strictly on defense, and although he missed most of the 1950 season with a fractured jaw, Ford returned to the lineup during the 1950 championship game to tackle Los Angeles Rams ball carriers for losses on 3 successive plays. Standing 6'5" tall and weighing 260 lbs., Ford played a more important role in Cleveland's defense beginning in 1951. An excellent pass rusher, he was named to the all-NFL all-star team each year from 1951–55. On 19 May 1958, however, the Browns, seeking to use younger players in the lineup, traded the 32-year-old Ford to the Green Bay Packers. He played 1 season for the Packers, then retired. During his 11-year professional career, he recovered 20 fumbles. After his retirement, Ford and his wife Geraldine lived in Detroit, where he served as assistant director of recreation at the time of his death.

The **FORD MOTOR COMPANY** began operating in Cleveland in 1906, establishing a sales and service office at 1900 Euclid Ave. In 1911, Ford moved its Cleveland operation to E. 72nd St. and St. Clair Ave. (at a railroad siding there); workers assembled Model Ts from sections received from Detroit. In 1913, Ford constructed a branch assembly plant at 11610 Euclid Ave. The 4-story brick building was designed by Albert Kahn, an architect who designed factories for several automobile companies. Production at the facility began on 29 June 1914. The plant was turned over to the government in 1917 for the storage of war materials. Production of automobiles resumed in 1919, and in 1921 the factory was enlarged by the addition of a 5-story wing; in 1923 the stationary assembly line was replaced by Henry Ford's innovative moving assembly line. Production at the plant peaked at 225 Model T cars daily in 1925; employment was 1,600 that year. From 1927–31, the Euclid Ave. plant turned out Model A cars; in May 1932 it began to produce Model Bs, but the effects of the Great Depression prompted Ford to halt production at the plant later that year.

The Euclid Ave. facility was converted to general offices and a distribution center for Ford in 1933; it was turned over to the government again during WORLD WAR II and later was sold. Beginning in 1975, the former plant was remodeled to house art studios, and in 1976 the building was placed on the U.S. Dept. of Interior's Natl. Register of Historic Places. Following World War II, Ford began an expansion program that located several production plants in northeastern Ohio, making the Cleveland area second only to the company headquarters in Dearborn, Mich., as a base of operations. The Canton Forge Plant began operation in 1948; construction of a stamping plant in WALTON HILLS was announced in 1953; and the Lorain assembly plant began production in May 1958. Ford's engine plants at 17601 Brookpark Rd. were also constructed in the 1950s. Engine Plant No. 1, considered to be "the most modern, automated engine plant in the world," began production in Sept. 1951; in 1952, a casting plant was constructed on the same site to make engine blocks for the plant. The popularity of the larger Ford V–8 engines prompted the company to build a second engine plant at the site in 1955. In 1978, these engine plants produced their 30-millionth engine and were making engines for more than half of Ford's domestic cars. But the recession in the automobile industry reduced employment at the engine complex from 16,000 in 1978 to 11,000 in 1980. More jobs were lost in 1982 when Engine Plant No. 2 stopped producing the large 8-cyl. engines and began producing engine parts. Employment at Engine Plant No. 1 fell from 4,000 in 1980 to 2,750 in 1982.

**"FOREST CITY,"** Cleveland's long-time nickname, has murky origins. An obituary of Timothy Smead, editor of the short-lived *OHIO CITY ARGUS*, claims that "while in an editorial capacity Mr. Smead gave to Cleveland the name of Forest City" (*Plain Dealer*, 4 Jan. 1890). Credit for inspiring the name, however, is generally given to WM. CASE, secretary of the Cleveland Horticultural Society in the 1840s and mayor 1850–51, who encouraged the planting of shade and fruit trees. The Forest City Race Track, opened in 1850, is the earliest-known business use of the name. It was followed in 1851 by the Forest City Agricultural Warehouse, Bank, Bath House, Cricket Club, and Lyceum. A hotel using the name, the Forest City House, was incorporated in Mar. 1851. A city Dept. of Forestry & Nurseries was established in 1897; Cleveland's fame as the Forest City was waning, and the city launched a new effort to save trees. In the late 1930s, with Works Progress (later Work Projects) Admin. aid, the city's Bureau of Horticulture planted more than 13,000 trees in city parks. A count in 1940 found 221,198 trees in the city in addition to 100,000 others in the parks. "Forest City" was still the name of some 35 large and small firms in Greater Cleveland in 1985.

The **FOREST CITY BASEBALL CLUB,** or the Forest Citys, was the name of several early amateur and professional baseball teams in Cleveland. The first Forest City team was an amateur team sponsored by the Forest City Baseball Club, organized in 1865. The team played other squads around the city and in the northern Ohio area, such as the Penfields of Oberlin. In 1868 the club had 150 members and enjoyed a good reputation locally until 24 June, when it suffered a humiliating 85–11 defeat at the hands of the Athletics of Philadelphia. It finished the season with 12 wins and 11 losses. The loss to Philadelphia may well have been the catalyst for the organization of a professional Forest City team the following year. In Jan. 1869, the *Leader* reported that the 300 members of the Forest City club were determined "to bring out a 'crack nine' next season," and by May the club had hired several players. Among them were outfielder and first baseman Arthur Allison, pitcher Albert G. "Uncle Al" Pratt, and Jas. L. "Deacon" White, each of whom would remain with the team until its demise in 1872. With a team that was half amateur—several players wished to remain "pure" and refused payment for their services—and half professional, the Forest Citys played the first pro baseball game in Cleveland on 2 June 1869, losing 25–6 to the original pro team, the Cincinnati Red Stockings, in front of 2,000 spectators at Case Commons at Putnam Ave. (E. 38th St.) between Scovill and Central avenues. The Forest Citys continued as a pro team in 1870.

On 17 Mar. 1871, the Forest Citys became a charter member of the Natl. Assoc. of Professional Baseball Players, a loosely knit league that lasted through 1875. Playing their home games on a new field at Willson (E. 55th St.) and Garden (Central Ave.), the team fared poorly. It finished the 1871 season in 7th place in the 9-team league, with a record of 10–19 (.345). A new manager proved no more inspirational in 1872; the team won only 6 of 21 games and reportedly dropped out of the league in midseason because of financial problems. For the next several years, Cleveland had no professional baseball team, but from 1879–84 it fielded a Natl. League team that was known as the Forest Citys. Organized by businessman Wm. Hollinger and J. Ford Evans, a veteran of the earlier pro effort, the team played its home games on a field at Kennard (E. 46th St.) and Cedar. It had a new manager in each of its 6 years of operation and recorded 3 winning seasons: 1880 (47–37, 3d place), 1882 (42–40, 5th place), and 1883 (55–42, 4th place). It made baseball history on 12 June 1880, when it was the victim of the first perfect game in organized baseball, pitched by John Lee Richmond of the Worcester, Mass., team. The Forest Citys' star pitcher during these years was iron-armed Jim McCormick, who appeared in 62 games in 1879 with a 20–40 record, and in 74 games in 1880 with a 45–28 record, to lead the league in most wins and most innings pitched (658). The Forest Citys finished the 1884 season with a dismal 35–77 record to place 7th in the 8-team league. The club lost several star players to a rival league, and in early 1885 it resigned from the NL. Cleveland's next pro team in 1887 was called the Forest Citys before it became known as the Spiders, and amateur teams revived the Forest Citys name in later years.

**FOREST CITY ENTERPRISES, INC.,** is involved in 3 related areas—real estate, commercial building and development, and the retailing of building supplies. It was founded in 1922 when a Jewish Polish immigrant, Chas. Ratner, opened a lumberyard at E. 93rd St. and Harvard Ave., called the Forest City Materials Co. The company was incorporated in 1924, and by the following year, Ratner's 2 brothers, Leonard and Max, joined him in the business. By 1928, Chas. Ratner had sold the business to his brothers, with Max as president of the firm. The Ratners' primary business was selling lumber and building materials to professional builders in the area. As Forest City thrived, the Ratners began to move into other related businesses, such as building garages, cottages, and unfinished furniture. During the Depression, the Ratners were able to buy land at bargain prices. In 1941, Forest City became one of the nation's first firms to manufacture prefabricated homes. The company then became involved in the postwar building boom, helping to develop many of Cleveland's suburbs. It was a pioneer in the "do-it-yourself" home-improvement market when it opened its first retail store in 1955. Two years later, the company built a large lumberyard and building-materials center on Brookpark Rd. in Brooklyn, which became its headquarters in 1965. By the late 1950s, Forest City was Ohio's largest building-materials firm.

In 1960, the Ratner family consolidated its interests in the lumber and building-materials field and the management of commercial properties into a new firm, Forest City Enterprises, Inc. The company then placed more emphasis on retail as it opened more stores in the Midwest. By 1983, it had 20 home-center stores, 7 of them in the Cleveland area. Its wholesale business continued to grow, especially after it acquired one of the country's largest lumber distributors in Oregon in 1969. Forest City also maintained its building-materials business, until the recession caused its liquidation in 1983. The area of greatest growth for Forest City after its reorganization in 1960 was in real estate and development. In the 1960s and 1970s, it gained interests in building, owning, and operating numerous malls, shopping centers, office and industrial buildings, hotels, and apartment complexes across the nation. In 1968, Forest City acquired the construction firm of Thos. J. Dillon & Co., Inc., in Akron. In the early 1970s, Dillon developed modular units, which allowed for a fast and efficient building system for mass-produced housing. Soon, Forest City

became Cleveland's largest apartment and home builder. Its real-estate business was strengthened when Forest City formed a separate company in 1969, Forest City Rental Properties, Inc. In the late 1970s, the firm sold many of its smaller projects to devote its capital to larger, urban developments. Two important ones in Cleveland are the Tower City project, which it began in 1980, and the Halle Bldg. (see HALLE BROS. CO.), which it purchased in 1982.

**FOREST CITY HOSPITAL** was a 103-bed general hospital that served the Glenville area. It was commonly referred to as Cleveland's first interracial hospital. In 1939, the Forest City Hospital Assoc. was formed by a group of black doctors in order to raise support for a hospital free of color restrictions. One of its ultimate aims was to offer black doctors the opportunity to participate in the total operations of a hospital. In 1954, the association received support from the Cleveland Hospital Fund, and ground was broken for a new hospital on the site of old Glenville Hospital. Most of the old hospital was razed and a new building constructed, and in 1957 Forest City Hospital opened its doors. Among the founders were Dr. U. G. Mason, Dr. M. H. Lambright, Walter M. Weil, and Dr. S. O. Friedlander. Wm. G. Laffer, president of the CLEVITE CORP., was a leading fundraiser. The hospital was governed by a 30-member board of trustees and a 35-member medical advisory board. Forest City opened as a modern general hospital providing departments of medicine, surgery, obstetrics and gynecology, general practice, x-ray, laboratory, outpatient, and emergency facilities. By the late 1950s, the Glenville neighborhood it served had become predominantly black. Of the 53 doctors on active staff, 50% were white; most of the employees, however, were black. Because of the changing neighborhood and the predominantly black staff, Forest City was generally perceived as a "colored hospital." Through its first 10 years, the hospital had an average bed occupancy of 70%. But despite the finest of acute and ambulatory health services, its reputation suffered. Criticism of the hospital's physical layout led to a campaign in 1967 to double the beds and institute various renovations. But by the early 1970s, admissions began to decline, and the plan was dropped. In the 1970s, Forest City placed greater emphasis on its out-patient facilities, which included high-quality emergency care, 2 or 3 mobile units, dental, podiatry, and eye services, and specialized supportive services. As admissions continued to decline and black doctors found their place in other Cleveland hospitals, the hospital's role in the community it served diminished, and in 1978 it closed.

The **FOREST CITY PUBLISHING COMPANY** was a holding company formed on 29 Sept. 1932 to facilitate the *PLAIN DEALER*'s purchase of the *CLEVELAND NEWS*. The new company acquired the stock of the Plain Dealer Publishing Co., publisher of the *Plain Dealer*, and of the Cleveland News Co., publisher of the *Cleveland News*. Benjamin P. Bole, president of Plain Dealer Publishing, became president of the new company, and the initial 7-member board of directors included 5 men associated with the *Plain Dealer*. Forest City Publishing soon expanded its interests beyond newspaper publishing. In 1934, it bought Cleveland's pioneer radio station, WHK, and it later bought controlling interest in radio stations in Akron, Columbus, Cincinnati, and Youngstown. In 1937, it augmented its newspaper business with the incorporation of the Art Gravure Corp. of Ohio. Located in a new building at 1845 Superior Ave., the firm printed the *Plain Dealer* as well as other newspapers and magazines such as *Ohio Farmer* and *Michigan Farmer*. In the 1950s, Forest City Publishing began to dismantle its regional media empire, which it had never operated as a coordinated unit. Between 1952–54, it sold its radio stations outside of Cleveland, and in Jan. 1958 it sold WHK to Metromedia, Inc. In Jan. 1960 it sold the *News* to the *CLEVELAND PRESS*, which promptly ceased publication of its new acquisition. Forest City Publishing continued as publisher of the *Plain Dealer* until it sold that paper to Samuel Newhouse in Mar. 1967, at which time the company, in the words of Philip Porter, "degenerated into a dummy corporation" with little role in decision making.

**FOREST HILL,** now a residential neighborhood in E. CLEVELAND and CLEVELAND HTS., originally was the summer home of the John D. Rockefeller family. In 1873, Rockefeller purchased a large tract of land bordering Euclid Ave. in E. Cleveland. He sold it to the Euclid Ave. Forest Hill Assoc. in 1875 and bought shares in the company, which set out to establish a "water-cure and place of public resort." Rockefeller, with others, earlier had organized the Lake View & Collamer Railroad, whose eastern terminus was near the resort underway at Forest Hill. Both ventures failed. The large, rambling building intended to house the sanitarium was half-finished when work stopped. Rockefeller completed the house and operated it for 1 summer (1878) as a club for paying guests. Thereafter, he maintained Forest Hill exclusively as a summer home for his family. Rockefeller gradually added to the grounds until he had acquired some 700 acres that stretched beyond E. Cleveland into Cleveland Hts. He laid out 18 mi. of roadways, carved out trails, built a lake and a half-mile track for his trotters, and later added a 9-hole golf course. John D. Rockefeller, Jr.'s, generous support of conservation projects is said to have stemmed from his boyhood days at Forest Hill, where, under the tutelage of his father, he developed his lifelong love of nature.

In 1884, Rockefeller established his legal residence in New York City, but he returned with his family to Cleveland every spring to live at Forest Hill until late fall. After his wife Laura's death in 1915, Rockefeller returned to Forest Hill for only brief and infrequent stays, and he last visited the "Homestead," as it was known, in July 1917. On 17 Dec. 1917, the house was destroyed by a fire of unknown cause, and Rockefeller never returned to Cleveland again. Under John D. Rockefeller, Jr.'s, custody, the Forest Hill estate was broken up. Portions provided sites for a new HURON RD. HOSPITAL and for Kirk Jr. High School, both in E. Cleveland. Forest Hill Blvd. was cut through the estate, and New York architect Andrew J. Thomas was hired to prepare plans for the Forest Hill subdivision. He designed the 81 French Norman-style houses that were built, beginning in 1925, out of a projected 600 homes. A little less than a third of the original estate was set aside as a public park, which John, Jr., donated in memory of his father to the cities of E. Cleveland and Cleveland Hts. FOREST HILL PARK, opened in 1942, today occupies what was once the heart of the original Forest Hill estate.

Goulder, Grace, *John D. Rockefeller: The Cleveland Years.*

**FOREST HILL CHURCH, PRESBYTERIAN,** located at the intersection of 3031 Monticello Blvd. and Lee Rd., CLEVELAND HTS., and originally known as Cleveland Hts. Presbyterian Church, began as a mission branch of Beckwith Memorial Church, located at Fairmount (E. 107th) St. and Deering Ave. In Nov. 1903, a small group of people from Beckwith Memorial began holding Sunday-morning classes, and Rev. Albert J. Alexander, minister of Beckwith,

began conducting their Sunday-evening services in a private home on Radnor Rd., Cleveland Hts. On 5 Feb. 1905, this group established the Mayfield Hts. Branch of Beckwith Memorial and moved to the 1st floor of the Superior St. School House at the corner of Euclid Hts. Blvd. and Superior Rd. Membership increased, and a larger sanctuary was needed; a building campaign was started, and on 14 June 1908 a cornerstone was laid for the Cleveland Hts. Presbyterian Church at the corner of Mayfield and Preyer Ave. Dedicated on 24 June 1909, it was still considered a branch of Beckwith Memorial until 1 Mar. 1910, when it separated from Beckwith, which subsequently became a part of the CHURCH OF THE COVENANT (Presbyterian). Rev. J. J. Weber, the first minister, served from 1909–10 but resigned because of illness. He was succeeded by Rev. Edward S. Claflin, who served from 1910–16, when the church received its charter. Rev. W. F. Dickens-Lewis served from 1917–34. During his ministry, a new education wing was built to meet the needs of the expanding Sunday school enrollment. Rev. Clem E. Biniger, who served the church from 1935–43, instituted many new fellowship groups and mission programs. He was succeeded by Rev. C. M. Stewart (1943–45). On 5 Apr. 1946, Rev. Yoder P. Leith began a 24-year pastorate. Membership continued to grow, and a larger building was needed; therefore, in Oct. 1946, property at the intersection of Lee Rd. and Monticello Blvd. was purchased from the estate of JOHN D. ROCKEFELLER, and a building fund for a new church was started in 1948. Ground was broken on 7 May 1950, the cornerstone was laid 17 Sept. 1950, and on 21 May 1951, the newly named Forest Hill Church, Presbyterian, a brick Georgian Colonial church, was dedicated. A new education wing was added in 1956, and in 1964 another addition, Fellowship Hall, was dedicated. Rev. Dr. Ned W. Edwards, who had served as assistant minister from 1963–70, became the senior minister in Sept. 1970, following Rev. Leith's retirement.

**FOREST HILL PARK,** located east of Lee Rd. and south of Euclid Ave. on Cleveland's east side, was originally part of the estate of JOHN D. ROCKEFELLER. In 1873, Rockefeller bought land south of Euclid Ave.—the midpoint of frontage being the Forest Hill Block. More land was acquired later. The high sloping land topped by a plateau was developed as a private country estate including trees, shrubs, lawns, gravel roads, bridle trails, several lakes, and tracks for fast horses. BRIDGES built from stone from the quarry on the property were constructed over the north and south branches of Dugway Creek. The property was used by the family as a summer estate until Mrs. Rockefeller's death (1915). Between 1900–36, Rockefeller donated property in order to widen the bordering streets, Terrace Rd. and Forest Hill Blvd. In 1939 John D. Rockefeller, Jr., transferred the property to CLEVELAND HTS. (⅓) and E. CLEVELAND (⅔), with the stipulation that the land be used and developed for recreational purposes. Subsequently, the park was improved, with a swimming pool, basketball courts, fields for football and baseball diamonds, tennis courts, and picnic areas. In the ensuing years, recurrent vandalism has caused deteriorating conditions in certain sections of the park.

**FORT HUNTINGTON,** located on a site west of the county courthouse at Ontario and Lakeside, was a fortress and supply depot of the Army of the Northwest during the WAR OF 1812, built at the direction of Pres. Jas. Madison to protect the settlement. The fort was named after Samuel Huntington (1765–1817), governor of Ohio 1808–10. A camp was established at the site in 1812 by local militia under the command of Gen. Simon Perkins. It was called Camp Harrison, in honor of Wm. Henry Harrison, commander of the Army of the Northwest. In early spring 1813, a Maj. Jessup, Regular Army, took charge of the troops. Under his command, Capt. Stanton Sholes, a hero of the Revolutionary War, commissioned by Pres. Madison to the 2d Div. of the U.S. Artillery, arrived in Cleveland. It was under his command that the fort, stockade, and hospital were built. Ft. Huntington was visited by Adm. Oliver H. Perry before the Battle of Lake Erie, and he returned there to celebrate victory. Wm. Henry Harrison, destined to become the 9th president of the U.S., visited the fort after taking command of the Army of the Northwest. He inspected the troops in midsummer 1813. The site was rededicated as a park in 1977. In 1982, a sculpture, executed by Wm. McVey, was added to the park to commemorate the 1936 victory of Clevelander JESSE OWENS in the Olympics.

The **FORTNIGHTLY MUSICAL CLUB** is one of the oldest continuous music clubs in Ohio and among the oldest in the country. Fortnightly was organized in Jan. 1894 by Mrs. Curtis Webster. It was federated with the National Fed. of Music Clubs in 1898 and became a charter member of the Ohio Fed. of Music Clubs on its organization in 1919. It continues (1986) to be important in the federation. During its first 25 years especially, Fortnightly served as a concert agency for Cleveland, bringing many of the orchestras and artists who performed here. The Cleveland group and ADELLA PRENTISS HUGHES, a charter member who took charge of Fortnightly's public concerts after the third season, became known for their well-managed concert seasons. Because of early success, Mrs. Hughes and Fortnightly went into partnership for the presentations then called Symphony Orchestra Concerts, and the profits were shared equally between them. It could be said that the interest developed in symphonic music through these concerts made it possible to organize the CLEVELAND ORCHESTRA. Mrs. Hughes became the Cleveland Orchestra's first general manager, and Fortnightly backed the new enterprise with a $1,000 gift in 1917, the first organization to do so. It became the first founder-supporter also of the CLEVELAND MUSIC SCHOOL SETTLEMENT. The Fortnightly Club also backed the organization of the CLEVELAND INSTITUTE OF MUSIC. Mrs. Franklyn B. Sanders, chairman of the Fortnightly Program Committee for 18 years at the turn of the century, was active in the founding of the institute.

As Cleveland developed into a music center, the need for the concert-agency function diminished. Fortnightly turned its attention to awarding performing opportunities for its members and other musicians in the Cleveland area. Concerts were presented the first Tuesday morning and third Tuesday afternoon of each month in 1985. The club's activities have expanded over the years. For instance, the CLEVELAND COMPOSERS' GUILD had its beginnings in the late 1920s as a "Manuscript Section" of Fortnightly. The club's Jr. Division helps school-aged musicians find outlets for their talents. Fortnightly has organized pianists and instrumentalists into workshops and music-appreciation groups. The membership as a whole provides an audience, as needed, for active performers. The working committees that organize scholarship auditioning and social events are made up of associate members of the club.

Fortnightly Musical Club Records, WRHS.

The **41ST OHIO VOLUNTEER INFANTRY REGIMENT**, 1861-65, rendezvoused and was organized for 3 years' service in the CIVIL WAR between 26 Aug. 1861-29 Oct. 1861, at Camp Wood in Cleveland. There the 41st was mustered into federal service on 31 Oct. 1861. Approximately 407 Cleveland men served in its ranks. After duty at Camp Dennison near Cincinnati, the 41st was assigned to the 15th Brigade, Army of the Ohio, from Dec. 1861-Jan. 1862, and then to the 4th Div. until Feb. 1862, serving at Camp Wycliffe, Ky. The 41st was assigned to the 19th Brigade, 4th Div., Army of the Ohio, from Feb.-Sept. 1862, and to the 2d Corps from Sept.-Nov. 1862, during which time it saw action at Shiloh, Tenn., and Corinth, Miss.

From Nov. 1862-Jan. 1863, the 41st was assigned to the 2d Brigade, 2d Div., Left Wing, 14th Army Corps, Army of the Cumberland. It participated in the Battle of Stone's River. From Jan.-Oct. 1863, the regiment was assigned to the 2d Brigade, 2d Div., 21st Army Corps, Army of the Cumberland, under which it fought in the Tullahoma, Tenn., Campaign, the Battle of Chickamauga, Ga., and the siege of Chattanooga, Tenn. Between Oct. 1863-Aug. 1865, the 41st was assigned to the 2d Brigade, 3d Div., 4th Army Corps, Army of the Cumberland, and was active in Tennessee, Alabama, and Georgia. Between Aug.-Nov. 1865, the regiment was assigned to the Dept. of Texas and was on duty at San Antonio until mustered out on 27 Nov. 1865 and discharged and paid off at Camp Chase in Columbus, Ohio. The 41st had achieved veteran status in Jan. 1864 and had taken its veteran furlough, passing through Camp Cleveland, Ohio, in Feb.-March. Losses were reported as 8 officers and 168 enlisted men dead from hostile causes and 1 officer and 153 enlisted men dead from disease, for a total of 330. Regimental commanders included Wm. B. Hazen and Aquila Wiley.

Kimberly, Robert L., and Holloway, Aphraim S., *The Forty-first Ohio Veteran Volunteer Infantry . . .* (1897).

**FOSTER, CLAUD HANSCOMB** (23 Dec. 1872-21 June 1965), was a pioneer automotive inventor, industrialist, and philanthropist. He was born on the family homestead in Brooklyn, a suburb of Cleveland, the second son of George and Julia Wells Foster. As a youth he demonstrated a flair for mathematics, music, and tinkering with mechanical devices. In 1891, he opened a machine shop in the Britton Bldg. on Erie (E. 9th) St. To support his fledgling business, he played the trombone for 11 years in the Euclid Ave. Opera House orchestra. In 1896, the Britton Bldg. burned, destroying Foster's business and all his worldly possessions. Starting anew, Foster became an automobile dealer, selling the Cleveland-built General automobile, located in the Electric Bldg. on Prospect St. In 1900, he also acquired the Peerless and Ajax automobile agencies. Finding inspiration watching a clarinetist adjusting his reeds, Foster developed the Gabriel Horn, a multitone automobile horn powered by exhaust gases. Starting with $1,500 in 1904, he founded the Gabriel Co. in a small shop on Superior Ave. The horn proved so successful that the company was unable to meet the demand. In 1907, Foster moved Gabriel to 1411 E. 40th St. Foster next became concerned with developing a practical automobile shock absorber. His design was inspired by watching a deckhand "snubbing" a lake steamer into its dock position by wrapping a spring line around 2 steel posts. In 1914, he patented his "Snubber" shock absorber, capitalizing its production at $1 million.

From 1920-25, the Gabriel Co. earned annual profits of more than $1 million, selling 75% of all shock absorbers marketed in the world. Foster was among the first employers to develop an employee profit-sharing incentive program. Between 1917-25, he paid his employees more than $600,000 in addition to their salaries. He sold the Gabriel Co. in 1925 to Otis & Co. for $4 million, taking only half the company's evaluated price. Foster made provisions for his business associates in the company to purchase its stock at a fair price. He remained as the company's chairman until 24 Feb. 1928. Known as the "Doctor of Car Riding," Foster was often consulted by automobile manufacturers when new car models developed riding difficulties. In 1939, as chairman of Pressure Castings, Inc., Foster established a "40–40–20" profit-sharing plan, 40% each to stockholders and employees and 20% to a reserve sinking fund. Throughout his career, Foster made numerous large anonymous gifts to hospitals and charitable institutions. The peak of his philanthropic activities came on 22 July 1952. At a dinner party, he announced to the heads of 16 educational and charitable institutions that he was dividing the bulk of his wealth, almost $4 million, among them. Married to Emma Schultz, Foster had 2 sons, Earl and Daniel. Foster is buried in RIVERSIDE CEMETERY.

Thomasson, Wayman H., *Claud Foster: A Biography* (1949).

**FOURTH GENERAL HOSPITAL** (Lakeside Unit, World War II), staffed primarily by Cleveland-area physicians and nurses, was the first U.S. Armed Forces general hospital unit to go overseas in WORLD WAR II. Although the 4th General had existed on paper since 1933 as a successor to Base Hospital No. 4 (LAKESIDE UNIT), actual preparations for mobilization of the unit began in 1940. The U.S. surgeon general sent a letter to the dean of the Western Reserve University School of Medicine asking for the formation of a medical unit staffed by faculty members and professional personnel from associated hospitals. On 24 Dec. 1941, 17 days after Pearl Harbor, the surgeon general's office offered the 4th General the opportunity to set up the first U.S. Armed Forces general hospital overseas. The historical association with the WORLD WAR I unit and the fact that a number of its professional personnel were on the staff of UNIVERSITY HOSPITALS justified the unit's informal designation as the Lakeside Unit; however, physicians and nurses from the medical school and several Cleveland hospitals, as well as private-duty nurses, joined the unit. On 9 Jan. 1942, the unit's 54 medical officers were ordered to active duty at Ft. Jackson, S.C., where the Cleveland unit combined with the old 56th General Hospital to form the new U.S. Army 4th General Hospital, before going on to New York City. The unit's 72 Cleveland-area nurses, plus 48 nurses transferred from military hospitals, were also ordered to New York; the convoy departed on 23 Jan., its destination unknown to the physicians, nurses, and 500 enlisted men of the unit. They disembarked in Melbourne, Australia, on 27 Feb. and set up operations in the newly built Royal Melbourne Hospital with a capacity of 1,000 beds (eventually expanded to 2,900). As the Pacific Theater's first American hospital, the 4th General cared for American and Allied troops from various locations in Australia and the campaign fronts in New Guinea and the Solomon Islands. At this point, medical cases, especially malaria, outnumbered surgical cases.

The unit was stationed in Melbourne for 2 years, where it admitted more than 35,000 patients. Also during this time, the 4th General participated in pioneering the Army's "portable hospital" concept. Two 25-bed hospitals, each carrying light equipment and designed to be staffed by 4 officers and 25 men, went out in Sept. 1942 to receive casualties on the front line of battle during the early phases of the Buna (New Guinea) campaign. The 1st Portable Surgical Hospital subsequently took part in the landing at Aitape in June 1944; the 2d later staffed the hospital ship

*Tasman*. In the spring of 1944, the 4th General Hospital, following the northward sweep of battle, moved to the military installation at Finschhaven, New Guinea. When the unit arrived on 14 Apr., a rudimentary 500-bed hospital was nearly completed; the first patients arrived on 23 Apr. Within several months, the hospital had expanded to 2,000 beds, having built tent wards and absorbed the 63d and 126th station hospitals. In New Guinea, the unit tended more surgical cases than it had in Melbourne, as well as medical and psychiatric cases. As more territory was recaptured in the Philippines during 1945, the base at Finschhaven closed down; the hospital closed on 23 July 1945, and the 4th General was sent north to Manila in anticipation of the invasion of Japan. With Japan's surrender, the unit never actually admitted patients in Manila, and its personnel were transferred to other units or sent back to the U.S. The 4th General Hospital operated wards and treated patients for 3 years and 3½ months between 12 Jan. 1942 and VJ day; it admitted 46,200 patients.

**FOX FOUNDATION.** *See* **HARRY K. & EMMA ROSENFELD FOX CHARITABLE FOUNDATION**

The **FRANCISCAN COMMUNITY AND APOSTOLATE** in Cleveland once encompassed a seminary and college, as well as monastic orders for men and women, a secular order for the laity, and parishes and schools. In 1879, Cleveland was established as the core of the Province of the Sacred Heart, which extended west to Platte City, Nebr., and north and south from Superior, Wis., to Memphis, Tenn. The Franciscans were invited to Cleveland in 1869 by Cleveland's first bishop, Rt. Rev. AMADEUS RAPPE. Several fathers came from Saxony to erect a residence that was later (1877) raised to the status of a convent. The Franciscans took over a small German parish called St. Bernard's that began in 1855 in 2 rented rooms on E. 25th St. The parish, the third in Cleveland, had a school at E. 25th and Orange, but because of the distance between the church and the school, worshippers converted one of the classrooms into a chapel. In 1863, a frame church was constructed at E. 23rd and Woodland and dedicated to St. Joseph. A school was built the following year. Within 2 years of the coming of the Franciscans, a magnificent Gothic structure was constructed to replace the older structure, which then became the parish hall. The church, often called "the cathedral of the East Side," was a showplace for the woodcarving skills of the Saxon friars. Statues were sent from the Saxon monasteries, while the pulpit, high altars, and sacred picture frames were carved by local friars. The priests opened a college on the site in 1876 that enrolled about 70 students in the first years, but a shortage of teachers forced them to abandon the venture and transfer the students to Teutopolis, Ill., the home of Quincy College. In 1906, the fathers answered the call to pastor to another ethnic group, the Poles, and were put in charge of ST. STANISLAUS CHURCH at E. 65th and Forman. In addition, the priests took on the chaplaincies of several area colleges and hospitals and became confessors to some 23 religious orders.

In the Franciscan tradition, the priests and brothers, the First Order of St. Francis, were accompanied by a Second and Third Order, for women and the laity respectively. A cloistered convent of the Poor Clares was established for nuns, while the Third Order called the laity to a life of moderation and piety. The laity who belonged to the Tertiate, as the Third Order was called, were exhorted at monthly meetings to pray daily, visit the sick, and avoid occasions of sin. Their ranks were increased locally by many diocesan clergy attracted by the special Franciscan call to charity and sacrifice. Since 1929, the Third Order has had a junior branch for men and women 14–35 that also sponsors activities ranging from sports to music and drama. In 1986, the Tertiate, which was then called the Secular Order of St. Francis, had 6 chapters throughout Greater Cleveland. Beginning in 1907, young Franciscan priests received part of their seminary training at the Seminary of Our Lady of the Angels on Rocky River Dr. Young priests came to the seminary for 3 years to study philosophy after completing the novitiate and 2 years of college in Illinois, and before completing the prerequisite 4 years of sacred theology before ordination. In 1960, as a result of a decision to make Cleveland the center for philosophy studies for all Franciscan seminarians, a new seminary was built. However, a shift in plans before the opening consolidated philosophy and novitiate studies in Illinois, and all seminary activity ceased in Cleveland. The new facility was used as a center for pastoral theology for newly ordained priests, and briefly, in the 1970s, was a school for those studying to become Franciscan brothers. In addition to St. Stanislaus and St. Joseph (scheduled to close in 1986), the Franciscans pastored 3 other parishes: Our Lady of Angels at 3644 Rocky River Dr. (on the site of the seminary), St. Jude's at 4771 Richmond Rd., and St. Anthony of Padua at 6800 State Rd.

The **FRANCO-PRUSSIAN WAR PEACE JUBILEE** was held on Monday, 10 Apr. 1871, to celebrate the German victory that ended the Franco-Prussian War (1870–71). Cleveland's German societies began planning the celebration in Mar. 1871, electing Rev. Dr. Jacob Mayer of the Tifereth Israel Congregation as president of the committee in charge of organizing the event. A temporary triumphal arch, 85' tall, was erected on Superior St. just east of the PERRY MONUMENT. The first event of the jubilee was a concert of all the German singing societies and the Orchestra of Germany Band in CASE HALL on 8 Apr. The Jubilee Day began with a 101-gun salute at daybreak on the lakefront. By mid-morning the "elaborate preparations" were ready; an "immense throng" of visitors was arriving from the surrounding area via the railroads, which were offering reduced fares; and the city streets and businesses were decorated with "thousands of banners" and flags. The highlight of the day was the long parade, which, according to the *Leader's* correspondent, took 58 minutes to pass and included 490 horsemen, 1,700 marchers on foot, and 39 carriages, including decorated firewagons and butchers' and brewers' wagons. After winding through the city streets for nearly 3 hours, the procession returned to the square for addresses by Rev. Mayer and August Thieme of the *Waechter am Erie.* The celebration, which cost the German societies about $3,000, ended in the Central Rink with a ball, which lasted until 4 a.m.

**FRANKLIN CIRCLE,** on the near west side, is unique as the only example of radial planning in Cleveland. Franklin Place, as it was originally known, was surveyed in 1836 and dedicated to public use by early landowners JOSIAH BARBER and RICHARD LORD. It had a radius of 140' and until 1857 was used as an open-air farmers' market. That year CLEVELAND CITY COUNCIL appropriated the circle to park use and erected a white wooden fence, leaving a street 30' wide around the perimeter. A wooden pavilion and a lily fountain were placed in the center. In 1872, Cleveland's newly created Board of Park Commissioners had the lily fountain removed to the northwest quadrant of PUBLIC SQUARE and set out to "resurrect and beautify" the circle. Franklin St. was laid through the center of the park, the circle was graded, and trees and

shrubbery were planted. A stone pavilion took the place of the old wooden one, and a large rockwork sculpture was added to the now greatly diminished grounds. The area was nicknamed "Modoc Park" and gained a reputation as a political forum; the young congressman Wm. McKinley spoke there, among others. The FRANKLIN CIRCLE CHURCH OF CHRIST was erected on the south side of the circle and dedicated in 1883. Prominent citizens built fine homes in the vicinity, among them Daniel P. Rhodes, JAS. F. RHODES, MARCUS A. HANNA, and John H. Sargent. Ohio historian Henry Howe, visiting Cleveland in 1890, called Franklin Circle "a delightful summer evening resort."

In 1907–08, TOM L. JOHNSON's Forest City Railway Co. extended its line through the circle. Two large yellow-brick apartment houses, the Beckwith (now demolished) and the Heyse, were built facing the circle, and the only remnant of the once finely landscaped park was the trees. Franklin Circle's importance as a social center dwindled. With the proliferation of the automobile, the circle eventually was given over entirely to asphalt paving, so that its original, imaginative design was all but obliterated, and the circle no longer served its intended function as a public park. In 1969, the city of Cleveland sold a small portion of the Circle to Lutheran Hospital for construction of a hospital addition. In 1984, plans were underway to alter the circle to a 4-way intersection, remove the asphalt paving to expose the brick street below, and plant trees.

The **FRANKLIN CIRCLE CHRISTIAN CHURCH (DISCIPLES OF CHRIST),** one of the earliest west side Protestant congregations, has served not only in its role as a neighborhood institution but also as the parent of other west side congregations. The Franklin Circle Christian Church was organized in OHIO CITY in Feb. 1842, the outgrowth of a meeting called by Disciples preacher John Henry. Initially, services were held in a building on Vermont Ave., near W. 28th St. For a time, between 1843–46, services were held in various rented rooms across the river in Cleveland. The congregation returned to Ohio City in 1846 and in 1848 erected a large frame church building, known locally as "God's Barn." Many of the church's early members were lake captains and their families, and at one time 7 ship's captains were listed on the membership rolls. Among those who served the church as pastor was JAS. A. GARFIELD, in 1857, then recently graduated from Hiram College. A building, designed by the firm of Cudell & Richardson, was begun on a neighboring lot to the south of the "barn" in 1874, and was completed in 1883. A Sunday school wing was added in 1916. As members left the immediate neighborhood, the church remained in its original location, supported by a largely "commuter" congregation. The work of the church has been dedicated to the inner-city neighborhood surrounding it, and has included a Chinese Sunday school, a preschool, senior-citizen and low-income meal programs, and summer youth programs. Franklin Circle was the parent church of 5 west side Disciple congregations: Lakewood, West Boulevard, Highland, Parma, and Westlake.

The **FRANKLIN CLUB** was a forum devoted initially to discussing economics and monitoring the policies of government officials. Originally known as the Union Labor Club, it was founded sometime between 1893 and 1895 as a consequence of the Panic of 1893. The name was changed to the Franklin Club when member Dr. JACOB TUCKERMAN noted that the term *Union* implied that the organization was national in scope. In 1895 the club met every Sunday at Forester's Hall, 125 Champlain St. In later years it met at 7 Ontario St. Club members came from all walks of life and included doctors, a fish dealer, and a mail carrier. There were no membership dues, but voluntary contributions were used to maintain the club's library.

Club members believed that "error is harmless if truth is free to combat it," and therefore adopted a policy permitting the discussion of any topic of public interest. Topics addressed at the club included free love, ethics, economics, prohibition, PROSTITUTION, the role of women, and anarchy. Members of the club also took an active part in local political activity by writing to local officials and governmental agencies. They thus expressed their displeasure with the School Council of Cleveland for not complying with fire-escape regulations and with the CLEVELAND CITY COUNCIL for permitting the United Salt Co. to lay pipes in the public streets. On 23 Dec. 1900, the club reorganized and became the Progressive Liberty Assoc. It was under the association's auspices that Emma Goldman addressed the organization on 5 May 1901 on the topic of anarchy. It was this lecture that supposedly incited LEON CZOLGOSZ to assassinate Pres. Wm. McKinley later in the year. Following the assassination, the club's records were confiscated by the police, and the organization declined in importance.

Franklin Club Records, WRHS.

**FRARY, IHNA THAYER** (13 Apr. 1873–18 Mar. 1965), was an author, lecturer, and teacher of ARCHITECTURE and architectural history. He was born in Cleveland and grew up in the Doan's Corners area. He studied at the Cleveland School of Art and in 1894 became an interior designer for the Brooks Household Art Co. (later Rorimer Brooks), where he remained until 1914. He became an independent designer after leaving the company. During his association with Rorimer Brooks, Frary designed furniture, including that for 2 Statler hotels. For a time he worked for the F. B. STEARNS CO. designing auto interiors, and in 1918 he went to work for the American YMCA as educational director for the southwest region, based in San Antonio, Tex. In 1920, Frary returned to Cleveland to become membership and publicity secretary for the CLEVELAND MUSEUM OF ART, a position he occupied until his retirement in 1946. He was a member of the faculty of the Cleveland School of Art and was a lecturer at the Cleveland School of Architecture of Western Reserve University and at the JOHN HUNTINGTON POLYTECHNIC INSTITUTE. He served as a trustee for the Museum of Art and the WESTERN RESERVE HISTORICAL SOCIETY. His interest and study in architectural history brought forth his books *Thomas Jefferson, Architect and Builder* (1931), *Early Homes of Ohio* (1936), *Early American Doorways* (1938), *They Built the Capitol* (1940), and *Ohio in Homespun and Calico* (1942). Frary married Mabel Guild on 2 June 1904, and they had 2 sons, Spencer G. and Allen T.

Ihna Thayer Frary papers, WRHS.

**FRASCH, HERMAN** (25 Dec. 1851–1 May 1914), was a chemical engineer and inventor whose work proved valuable to the STANDARD OIL CO. Frasch was born in Wurttemberg, Germany, and was an apprentice to a druggist before coming to the U.S. in 1868. He settled first in Philadelphia, where he worked in a laboratory at the College of Pharmacy. He went into business for himself in 1873, opening a shop to apply chemical science to the problems of industry. In 1876 he developed a new process for refining paraffin wax from petroleum; he patented the process and sold the patent to the Cleveland Petroleum Co., a subsidiary of Standard Oil. Impressed by Frasch's achievement, officials of Standard Oil offered the German immigrant a position in the company's research department in Cleveland, and Frasch moved there in 1877. Although most of his work was with petroleum, he made innovations in several areas: he developed a new oil lamp; developed a new process to produce white lead; and introduced new methods to manufacture salt and carbonate soda. He also worked with electricity.

In 1885, Frasch decided to go into the oil business for himself and purchased some oil fields near Ontario, Canada, establishing the Empire Oil Co. He had been able to buy the fields at a low price because the crude from them was high in sulfur and of poor quality. His experiments to rid the crude of sulfur led to a new process to desulfurize crude petroleum, and between 1887–94 Frasch received 21 U.S. patents for refining petroleum. He sold both his Ontario operations and the patents for the desulfurization process to Standard Oil. The new process enabled Standard Oil to produce high-quality refined oil from poor-quality crude supplies. In 1891, Frasch developed and patented a process for mining sulfur using water heated to more than 300 degrees. The following year he organized the Union Sulfur Co. Frasch moved to Paris after he retired from business. His innovations were honored in 1912, when he received the Perkins Gold Medal in chemistry. Frasch was married twice. He married his first wife, Romalda Berks, while he was living in Philadelphia. She died in 1889. In 1892 he married Elizabeth Blee of Cleveland.

Sutton, William Ralph, "Herman Frasch" (Ph.D. diss., Louisiana State University, 1984).

**FRAZEE, JOHN N.** (3 Sept. 1829–21 Jan. 1917), was a volunteer Civil War officer and law-enforcement official. Frazee (sometimes misspelled "Frazer") was born in Wyantskill, N.Y. He came to Cleveland in 1850 and took a job as a west side patrolman with the Cleveland police. Following a reorganization of the department, he was appointed chief of police in 1852—the first chief in the department's history. Frazee served as a corporal in the CLEVELAND GRAYS before the outbreak of the CIVIL WAR. He left the police department to enlist in Co. E, 1st Ohio Volunteer Infantry, on 16 Apr. 1861. He was promoted to sergeant on 21 Apr. 1861, 1st sergeant on 1 June 1861, and 2d lieutenant on 2 July 1861. He was mustered out with Co. E (consisting mostly of Cleveland Grays) on 1 Aug. 1861. Frazee then served 4 months as a captain in the 84th OVI. In Aug. 1863, he was appointed lieutenant colonel of the 29th Ohio Volunteer Militia. In May 1864, he was appointed to the same rank in the 150th OVI and saw service around the defenses of Washington, D.C., that summer, being mustered out with that regiment in Cleveland on 23 Aug. 1864. After the war, Frazee served as captain of the Cleveland Grays. In 1888 he established a successful laundry business, from which he retired in 1915. His funeral was held at GRAYS ARMORY on 23 Jan. 1917. At the time of his death, he resided at 1720 E. 81st St. He is buried in WOODLAND CEMETERY.

The **FRED A. LENNON FOUNDATION** was established in 1965 by Fred A. Lennon. Lennon was born in 1906 in Providence, R.I., and was brought to Cleveland as a child. He began his career with IBM in 1927, then organized the Crawford Fitting Co. in 1948. In 1965, he became president of the Midwestern Natl. Life Insurance Co. During his career, he has been director of the United Screw & Bolt Co. and the Union Commerce Bank. In 1965, Lennon acted as interim president of Bede Aviation, and in 1984 he was awarded the Distinguished Contributions Award from the Society of Mfg. Engineers. Lennon is married to Alice Lennon, and they have 2 children, Mrs. Thos. Ryan and John Lennon. The primary emphasis of the fund is to support higher education and the Roman Catholic church. Grants are also made to hospitals, cultural programs, public policy, and community funds. In 1985, assets of the foundation were $5,211,000, with expenditures of $679,250 for 115 grants. Officers of the foundation included Lennon and John F. Fant, Jr.

The **FREE MEDICAL CLINIC OF GREATER CLEVELAND** was established in 1970 to provide free, nonpunitive, nonjudgmental medical care to young people with drug problems. One of the few free clinics from that period to survive, it steadily expanded its services to meet changing community needs and became one of the most respected and important medical and social-service agencies in the city. The Free Clinic evolved from Jeanne Sonville's Together Telephone Hotline, a counseling service for young people with drug problems, which began operation in Feb. 1970. Statistics from the hotline showed the need for a facility to deal with the medical needs of people reluctant to take their drug problems to traditional doctors and hospitals. With a $100,000 grant from the GUND, Weatherhead, and CLEVELAND FOUNDATIONS, Sonville and 25 volunteers opened the Free Clinic in June 1970 at 2039 Cornell Rd., offering therapy for drug addiction and full medical, dental, and psychiatric care.

Dependent upon grants, donations, and the service of volunteers, the clinic struggled through its first 3 years. Nevertheless, it expanded its services and overcame the initial suspicions of some community members who saw it as part of the emerging counterculture. It began offering birth-control information and counseling for pregnant women in 1971, helping runaway children in 1972, and providing pediatric care for poor children in 1973. In 1974, the Free Clinic received the Anisfield-Wolf Award for the most outstanding community service. Under the direction of David Roth from 1974–80, the clinic enjoyed a period of growth and stability. The Friends of the Free Clinic provided a secure source of financial support, and the expansion of services continued, with the addition of a legal clinic (1975), a program to treat hypertension (1977), and the Safe Space Station to provide temporary shelter for runaways (1977). The clinic moved into larger quarters at 12201 Euclid Ave. in 1974 and launched a major renovation of the building in July 1980. When Roth resigned as director in 1980, the clinic's annual budget of $900,000 supported 19 programs and served 50,000 people. The recession of the early 1980s brought both a money shortage and an increased demand for the clinic's services. Unemployed men and women whose medical insurance had run out found the clinic indispensable. In Dec. 1982, the clinic received the largest gift in its history—$100,000 from the TRW Foundation—enabling it to serve 3,000 additional patients a year.

The **FREE SOIL PARTY** of Cuyahoga County was organized in the summer of 1848 as part of a national third-party movement which supported free grants of public land to settlers and opposed the extension of slavery to the western territories. In order to further limit slavery, the party advocated the separation of the federal government from any aspect of the institution—a proposal first enunciated by Salmon P. Chase of Cincinnati.

In Ohio, the Free-Soilers were concentrated in the WESTERN RESERVE, where the party drew its support from antislavery elements in both the Whig and Democratic parties and the Liberty party, which had been politically active in the mid-1840s. At the Ohio Free Territory Convention held in Columbus on 21 June 1848, Edward Stowe Hamlin, editor of the Cleveland *DAILY TRUE DEMOCRAT*, took the lead in securing a resolution approving the free-soil doctrine. The Cuyahoga County group was organized by THOS. BOLTON and Huron Beebe, who along with EDWARD WADE attended the national organizing convention of the Free-Soil party held in Buffalo on 9–10 Aug. 1848. Ex-president Martin Van Buren was nominated as the party's presidential candidate, and on 12 Aug. in Cleveland, a ratification meeting was held on PUBLIC SQUARE affirming Van Buren's nomination. In the 1848 election, Van Buren won the county by the slim margin of 226 votes but came in 3d nationally behind Zachary Taylor and Lewis Cass.

The local party continued its activities in 1849 and 1850 but began to lose strength. On 13 June 1849, Free-Soil Democrats held a mass meeting at Public Square to celebrate the 62d anniversary of the Northwest Ordinance, which had prohibited slavery in the northwest territories. Using the ordinance as a precedent, they continued to demand that the federal government prohibit slavery in the western territories. At the state Free-Soil convention in Cleveland on 22 Aug. 1850, Rev. Edward Smith was nominated for governor; however, he failed to win a majority in either the county or the state. Free-Soil candidates continued to be nominated for office until 1854, when the party became part of the Anti-Nebraska movement.

The **FREEDMEN'S FESTIVAL** was an annual early-fall celebration held by Cleveland blacks beginning in 1863. Frederick Douglass, the first speaker for the celebration, paid tribute to the valiant deeds of blacks in arms in the CIVIL WAR and prayed for the souls of the dead. At each celebration, great emphasis was placed on the role blacks had played in the fight to save the Union. At the 1868 celebration, for example, a list of Cleveland's black soldiers was read as their company colors were raised. The festival was a new acknowledgment of the struggle to end slavery in the U.S. Prior to 1863, blacks throughout the North, including Cleveland, had celebrated the end of slavery in Haiti at an event called the West Indian Emancipation Celebration. These annual festivities served as fundraisers for the Cleveland Freedmen's Aid Society and the Freedmen's Education Society.

**FREESE, ANDREW J.** (1 Nov. 1816–2 Sept. 1904), was a pioneer schoolmaster and educator, and the first superintendent of Cleveland schools. He was born in Levant, Penobscot, Maine, the son of Gordon and Hanna Allen Freese. Young Freese, determined to become a teacher, attended college irregularly for about 3 years and taught school in order to finance his college education. He traveled extensively throughout New England and consulted with Horace Mann to further his knowledge of existing school systems. He taught in Bangor, Maine, became greatly respected, and subsequently became secretary of the Penobscot Assoc. of Maine. Freese came to Cleveland in 1840, taught at the Prospect St. School, and later became division principal. With the support of the Board of Managers, he was instrumental in effecting changes in state laws that eventually led to a graded school system, better textbooks, and the establishment of a public high school. GEO. HOADLEY, mayor of Cleveland 1846–48, recommended in his inaugural address that a public high school be established; accordingly, the first free public high school in Cleveland, as well as in Ohio, was opened on 13 July 1846 for 34 boys in the basement of a Universalist church on Prospect St., with Freese as principal. Among his students were Laura Spelman (Mrs. John D. Rockefeller), JOHN D. ROCKE-FELLER, and MARCUS A. HANNA. The school subsequently became CENTRAL HIGH SCHOOL. In 1847, Western Reserve University conferred an honorary M.A. degree upon Freese.

In June 1853, the Board of Education (formerly the Board of Managers) created the office of superintendent of instruction and appointed Freese to the position. For the next 3 years, Freese continued as principal of Central High School, while also fulfilling his responsibilities as superintendent. In 1861 he resigned because of ill health. He taught at the Eagle School for several years and in 1868 became principal of Central High School; he resigned in 1869 because of illness. Following his retirement from teaching, he originated a series of outline maps, assisted the editor of the *Ohio Journal of Education*, and authored a series of books about education. At the request of the Cleveland Centennial Commission, he wrote the *Early History of Cleveland Public Schools*, published in 1896. On 17 June 1847, Freese married Elizabeth Merrill, a descendant of Rev. Moses and Nancy Lee Merrill of Haverhill, N.H.

**FREIBERGER, ISADORE FRED** (12 Dec. 1879–27 Apr. 1969), was a Cleveland banker who was active in many social, educational, and civic activities throughout the city. Freiberger was born in New York City to Esther and Samuel Freiberger; they moved to Cleveland when he was 3, settling in the St. Clair-Hamilton Ave. area. Freiberger's working career started at age 7, when he started selling newspapers. He attended CENTRAL HIGH SCHOOL and then, working at odd jobs, paid his way through Adelbert College, graduating in 1901. He then worked as a clerk at the Cleveland Trust Co. but attended BALDWIN-WALLACE COLLEGE at night, earning an LL.B. in 1904. Freiberger was promoted steadily at Cleveland Trust, eventually becoming chairman of the board in 1941. He was also a director for the FOREST CITY PUBLISHING CO., which published the *PLAIN DEALER* and the *CLEVELAND NEWS*, and became its president in 1943. He was a director of 9 other local businesses, including the Youhiogeny & Ohio Coal Co. However, it was Freiberger's many outside affiliations that brought him notice. He was president of the Cleveland Chamber of Commerce in 1927 and vice-president of the Great Lakes Exposition in 1936. During his life, he was a member of over 50 religious, civic, business, and charitable organizations. He was a trustee of MT. SINAI HOSPITAL, the Playhouse Foundation, Western Reserve University, Cleveland-Marshall Law School, and the JEWISH COMMUNITY FED. He was a member of the American Bar Assoc. and the CITY CLUB, and sat on the executive and finance committees of the board of trustees of WRU. He won numerous honors in his life, including the Cleveland Chamber of Commerce Medal for Public Service, the American Heart Assoc.'s Award of Merit for Distinguished Service (1957), and an honorary doctorate of humanities given by WRU in 1947. He helped the university with a $20 million development program, and in 1956 the school named its new library in his honor. In 1968, he was awarded Adelbert College's Distinguished Alumnus Award. He was married to Fannie Fertel, and they had 2 children, Lloyd Stanton Freiberger and Ruth Gilbert.

**FRENCH.** The story of the French in Cleveland is one of individuals and not of a national group. The few French who did come, however, exerted a cultural influence out of proportion to the ethnic group's size. The French were among the first white men to explore what is now Greater Cleveland. Later, traders came to the area. A French trading post was reported to be at the CUYAHOGA RIVER at TINKER'S CREEK in 1775. After the explorers and the traders came French Roman Catholic priests and nuns. Most prominent among these were URSULINE SISTERS, who arrived in Cleveland in 1850 from Boulogne-sur-Mer, France, to fill the need for educators. Within the Cleveland Diocese, they staffed 25 elementary schools. In Cleveland, 2 high schools—BEAUMONT SCHOOL and Villa Angela—and URSULINE COLLEGE in PEPPER PIKE carry out the curriculums structured after the French system of education. The Ursulines were followed by the Ladies of the Sacred Heart of Mary, of the sisterhood in France, who established a temporary asylum for orphan girls in 1851. In 1870, the Catholic Parish of the Annunciation was organized for the French on Hurd St. By 1880, 506 French lived in the city. French people who came to Cleveland during the last century never settled in a neighborhood centered around a church as many other immigrant groups did. Independent and individualistic, they scattered to all parts of the city, never really assimilating into the host culture.

However, the French presence was very much felt, since French culture was generally admired by educated Americans. Therefore, concerts of French music or the appearance of noted French actress Sarah Bernhardt served not only the small local French community but cultured members of the general population, as well. Although French people by nature avoid "clubs," attempts to create some were made in the 1910s. By that time, 494 French were listed as resident in Cleveland. The oldest club, no longer in existence in the 1980s, was the French Table (La Table Francaise), composed mostly of men who wanted to perfect their knowledge of French and meet fellow Frenchmen. Then in 1916, the Circle of French Lectures (Cercle des Conferences Francaises), mostly for women, was established. It was still in existence in the 1980s. The organizations attracted both resident immigrants and native Americans who were desirous of participating in French cultural activities. In 1918, the French House (La MAISON FRANCAISE) was founded by a teacher, Dr. EMILE DE SAUZE who was noted for his pedagogical method for teaching the French language. The headquarters of this club are in Paris, France; it is the French Alliance—L'Alliance Francaise. Membership in this organization is also open to all: especially to French teachers and their students. Other small clubs were established in later years. By 1930, the number of French living in Cleveland had risen to 846, with over 1,000 resident in the Greater Cleveland area. The growth was caused, in part, by an influx of war brides. The French War Bride Club—La Gauloise—organized in 1935, and the Ohio chapter of the Natl. French War Brides Club served this new segment of the population and continued to do so for a new generation of war brides after WORLD WAR II; this new influx helped raise the city's French population from 517 in 1940 to 836 in 1950. Two other groups were founded in the postwar period, Les Bavards for west side French-speaking Clevelanders, and the Friendship Club (L'Amicale) for the east-siders. L'Amicale started in 1970 in Chesterland, Ohio. The club gathers professional men and women who are doctors, lawyers, businesswomen, university professors, poets, and writers.

From the 1960s through the 1970s, the area's French population never exceeded 1,000. In 1980, only 604 persons of French birth were estimated to be living in Cuyahoga County. However, the traditional high stature of French culture and art continue to exert strong influence in the city. For instance, in 1986, the CLEVELAND INSTITUTE OF MUSIC celebrated 55 years of teaching one of the oldest instruments of music, the harp, by Carlos Salzedo (born in Arcachon, France) and his foremost student, Alice Chalifoux. The CLEVELAND ORCHESTRA has hosted many French performers and composers. The establishment of the Darius Milhaud Society in Cleveland in 1984 had national significance, as its chief purpose is to encourage the performance of a wide repertoire of Milhaud's music all over the U.S. It is, of course, impossible to determine the exact role exerted by the small numbers of French immigrants upon the city's continuing and growing interest in French culture. Undoubtedly, given the professional status of many of the immigrants, particularly after World War II, they did play a role in furthering such an interest. What can be concluded from an analysis of French immigration to Cleveland is that this small immigrant group has, directly or indirectly, exerted proportinately more of a cultural influence on the city than any other group.

Helene N. Sanko
John Carroll University

**FRENCH, WINSOR** (24 Dec. 1904–6 Mar. 1973), chronicled the doings of the "beautiful people" of Cleveland and the world as a society columnist for the *CLEVELAND PRESS*. Born in Saratoga Springs, N.Y., he became the stepson of Joseph O. Eaton, founder of the EATON CORP., after the death of his own father. He moved to Cleveland along with his family and Eaton Mfg. in 1915. After sporadic educational experiences, which included 2 months at Kenyon College, French worked briefly for the *CLEVELAND NEWS* and for *TIME MAGAZINE* during its Cleveland period. He was married in 1933 to Margaret Hall Frueauff in a lavish New York wedding followed by a European honeymoon. Returning to Cleveland, French joined the *Press*, and the couple entertained in their CLEVELAND HTS. home for a year, until Mrs. French obtained a divorce. She became noted as an actress under the name Margaret Perry.

Familiar with New York's Algonquin group, French wrote some drama citicism for the *Press* but found his true calling as a society reporter. Listed among his friends were Lucius Beebe, Marlene Dietrich, Clark Gable, Libby Holman, John O'Hara, and Cole Porter. He left the *Press* to live in New York in 1941 but returned at the conclusion of WORLD WAR II. Sent to Europe to report on the condition of the average European in 1946, he cabled back a series of interviews with such representatives of the downtrodden as Noel Coward, Beatrice Lillie, and Somerset Maugham. Never remarried, French was able to live in the style of the people he wrote about partly through the casual gift of some IBM stock from his Cleveland friend Leonard Hanna. He was probably the only working journalist in Cleveland history to own a Rolls Royce. Failing in health and confined to a wheelchair late in his career, French turned serious and used his column to campaign for the rights of the handicapped. Because of these efforts, Mayor Ralph Locher ordered City Hall and other city-owned buildings to be made accessible to handicapped persons, and French received a presidential citation in 1966. He retired from the *Press* in 1968. He was buried with his parents in Williamstown, Mass.

**FRICKE, OTTO L.** (1886–4 June 1951), was a German-American lawyer in Cleveland active in the affairs of organizations serving the German community in the 1930s and 1940s. His continued support for the people in his native land made him a controversial figure during this period. Born in Germany, Fricke received his basic education there. He came to the U.S. in 1909 and worked at various jobs before graduating from Cleveland Law School. He worked as a clerk, a bookkeeper, and an auditor in the 1910s; by 1920 he had become the treasurer for the Theo Gutscher Co., a sausage manufacturer. By 1923 he had entered the real-estate business, and by 1926 he had established a law practice with Joseph C. Calhoun, Jr., and Henry W. MacLeod. Fricke was active in a variety of local and several national German-American organizations. He served as president of the German-American Congress, which met in Cleveland in 1934, and as the national secretary of the German-American Natl. Alliance of Philadelphia. Locally, he was a member and for 10 years the president of the German Central Organization; a founder and the first president of the Cleveland Stadtverband; and a member of the German-American Businessmen's Club, the Heights Maennerchor, the Socialer Turnverein, and the Concordia Masonic Lodge.

Fricke's strong identification with his German heritage led to an ongoing interest in the affairs of his native land, which made him a controversial figure in the eyes of the anti-Nazi and anti-German forces in the 1930s and 1940s. Speaking at a German Day celebration in June 1940, Fricke made what one listener described as "a bitter attack on newspapers, politicians, and all those 'who foment hatred against Americans of German descent,'" asserting that "'Americans of German stock are Americans first, last and all the time.'" His critics had a difficult time believing that assertion in light of some of Fricke's other activities. He served as counsel to the German consulate in Cleveland before it closed in June 1941; was the chairman of the Cleveland chapter of American Aid for German War Prisoners, established in the fall of 1940; and was the lawyer who represented Karl Zanzinger, the only Clevelander arrested in the 1941 national roundup of suspected German agents accused of recruiting skilled craftsmen to work in factories in Nazi Germany. Fricke became the center of further controversy in the fall of 1945 when the *WAECHTER UND ANZEIGER* published a letter from him urging German-Americans to protest postwar policies of the Allies, which he believed were detrimental to the German people and to Germany's future. Fricke's wife, the former Serena Cooks, died on 16 May 1973.

**FRIEBOLIN, CARL DAVID** (19 Jan. 1878–2 Sept. 1967), was a lawyer, a teacher, a federal bankruptcy referee for 50 years, and a well-known wit and satirist who wrote the City Club's *ANVIL REVUE* for many years. He was born in Owatonna, Minn., the son of Rev. Wm. and Kate Dennerline Friebolin. The family moved to Cleveland in 1885, where he attended old CENTRAL HIGH SCHOOL. He received his law degree from Western Reserve University in 1899 and practiced law in Cleveland. With the encouragement and support of Mayor TOM L. JOHNSON, he was elected to the Ohio House of Representatives in 1911 and to the Ohio senate in 1913. Before his term in the senate was completed, he was appointed to the common pleas bench but lost when he ran for election to the post. In 1916 he was appointed federal bankruptcy referee and continued in that position until his death. He became a nationally known expert on bankruptcy law, contributing to the drafting of the 1938 Natl. Bankruptcy Act. He also drafted the rules of uniform procedure adopted by the Natl. Assoc. of Referees. From 1934–59 he taught bankruptcy law at WRU. In Cleveland, Friebolin is perhaps best known as the author of the *Anvil Revue*, a satiric look at the Cleveland scene put on each year by the CITY CLUB. For the revue, he created the character Ben Sapp, the confused ordinary citizen who "got over the fence last." Friebolin died in Cleveland at the age of 89. After his death, the Carl Friebolin Memorial Scholarship was established at the Case Western Reserve Law School. He married Florence Brookes on 30 June 1906, and they had a son, Brookes, born in 1910.

**FRIEDLAND, ABRAHAM HAYYIM** (1891–3 Aug. 1939), educator, author, poet, and Hebraist, was the first director of the BUREAU OF JEWISH EDUCATION in Cleveland. Born in Gorodok, a village near Vilna, Lithuania, Friedland received a traditional yeshiva education as a young boy and was touted as a prodigy because he had memorized 7 tractates of the Talmud by the age of 12. His family came to New York when he was 14 years old, and he continued his studies at the Isaac Elchanan Yeshiva while also studying for his public high school exams. Following graduation from Columbia University, Friedland helped, in 1911, to establish the Natl. Hebrew School for Girls in New York. It was the first school of its kind in the U.S. He remained at the school until 1920, when he accepted the position of superintendent of the CLEVELAND HEBREW SCHOOLS. In 1924, when the Bureau of Jewish Education was established to provide coordination and foster cooperation among all the institutions offering Jewish education, Friedland became its first director. As director, Friedland established teacher-training programs, youth clubs, children's theater programs, a program for advanced Hebrew studies, and the Institute for Jewish Studies. An ardent Zionist, Friedland was often the focus of criticism for those who felt he was teaching secular Jewish nationalism. Despite some controversy and constant financial problems, Friedland built a network of 8 Hebrew schools and 5 religious schools, and an adult institute by the time of his death in 1939. In 1926, he declined an invitation to become the director of the Jewish educational system in Palestine.

Friedland was active in local and national Jewish communal affairs. He served as president of the Cleveland Zionist District, the Ohio Region of the Zionist Organization of America, the Histadrut Ivrith, and the Natl. Council of Jewish Education. A particular interest of Friedland's was the creation of learning aids to teach Hebrew to children. His works written for the young include *Torah-Li*, for teaching Bible passages; *Shiron*, jingles that teach Hebrew; *Gilenu*, written with Emmanuel Gamoran, the director of education for the Union of American Hebrew Congregations; and *Sippurim Yofim*, a series of simple stories in Hebrew. The latter work was published in 3 volumes by the Bureau of Jewish Education in 1962 and has been used widely in the U.S., Canada, England, India, Australia, and South Africa. Among Friedland's other works are *Hashvil*, written with Rabbi SOLOMON GOLDMAN; *Sonettot*; and a posthumous compilation of his poetry, *Shirim*. He also translated Hebrew literature into English and the English poets, especially Shelley, into Hebrew. He married his wife, Yonina, a native of Palestine, in 1916. They had 1 daughter, Aviva.

Bureau of Jewish Education Records, WRHS.
Abraham H. Friedland Papers, American Jewish Archives, Cincinnati, Ohio.

**FRIEDMAN, BENJAMIN "BENNY"** (18 Mar. 1905–23 Nov. 1982), a native Clevelander, became a star quarterback in college and professional football in the 1920s and 1930s. He was elected to the College Football Hall of Fame in 1952, and many feel he deserved a spot in the Pro Football Hall of Fame. The son of Russian Jewish immigrants, Benny Friedman first became a football star at Glenville High School, leading the team to an undefeated season and the city championship in 1922. He entered the University

of Michigan in 1923 and played football there in 1924, 1925, and 1926; he was a consensus All-American in the latter 2 years. Following his collegiate career, Friedman returned to Cleveland to play professional football in 1927 for the CLEVELAND BULLDOGS of the National Football League. At a time when most players made about $150 per game, Friedman received an $18,000 salary for the season and $750 for each of the 5 postseason games. In addition to quarterbacking the team, he traveled with the team publicity man, Ed Bang, to promote upcoming games. He played for the Detroit Wolverines in 1928, and in 1929 New York Giants owner Tim Mara bought the entire Detroit team to obtain the rights to Friedman, who became the Giants' first big star, from 1929–31. He then played for the Brooklyn Dodgers (1932–34) before retiring as a player. During his professional career, he threw 71 touchdown passes and scored a total of 179 points.

Friedman was a multitalented player. His specialty was accurate passing, but he was also a threat running with the ball and did the place-kicking. He was a 60-minute man, playing defense as well as offense. An inventive and colorful player, he was one of the biggest attractions in football during his era, and his play and promotional efforts helped keep the pro sport alive in New York in the early years of the Depression. Friedman became a coach after his playing career ended, serving as the head football coach at City College of New York (1934–41) and as the head football coach and athletic director at Brandeis University (1949–63). For many years he operated a summer camp in Oxford, Maine; in 1964 he began a 1-week quarterback camp there. In 1980, Benny Friedman was inducted into the Glenville High School Hall of Fame. In 1982, suffering from cancer and a circulatory ailment and having lost a leg to amputation, he took his own life.

The **FRIENDLY INN SOCIAL SETTLEMENT**, founded in 1874 to offer slum residents a wholesome gathering place free from the evils of liquor, soon evolved into one of the city's first SETTLEMENT HOUSES. Using the Holly Tree Inns of Boston as a model, members of the Women's Christian Temperance Union (WCTU) established 3 Friendly Inns in Cleveland in 1874: the St. Clair St. Friendly Inn, 634 St. Clair, managed by Mrs. Mary B. Stacy; the River St. Friendly Inn, 34 River (W. 11th) St., operated by Jas. Richards; and the Central Place Friendly Inn, 71 Central Place, which became the main branch of the Friendly Inns. Opened as a reading room operated by Edwin T. Abbott, by 1876 the Central Place Friendly Inn offered room and board, as well. By 1880 there were 5 Friendly Inn reading rooms throughout Cleveland.

In 1888, the Friendly Inn managers consolidated the expanding social-service functions of the "inns" in a new building at the corner of Broadway and Ohio streets (522 Central Ave.). The new Central Friendly Inn served recent immigrants of various nationalities, providing playgrounds and kindergartens for children, clubs to teach mothers and daughters basic housekeeping and child care, bathing facilities for men, and vocational training for boys. By 1907 a dispensary had been added, and each nationality served by the settlement had its own department headed by someone who spoke the native language; these departments offered advice and guidance on personal matters and classes in American customs, speech, and law. Each department also aimed "to renew the memory of the homeland." Disagreements within the WCTU in the 1880s led to the formation of a separate Non-Partisan Women's Christian Temperance Union, which managed the Friendly Inn until 1926, when the Women's Philanthropic Union was created to govern the settlement and to promote other philanthropic endeavors.

In 1924, changes in the surrounding neighborhood prompted the relocation of the Friendly Inn to 3754 Woodland Ave., former home of the Council Educational Alliance and the original home of the EXCELSIOR Club for Jewish businessmen. The settlement continued to serve many ethnic immigrant groups, but by then more than a third of those using its services were black Americans recently arrived in the city. By 1925, the Friendly Inn was operating a summer camp, which enabled 326 children to escape the congested city for 2 weeks that summer. In 1957, the resident camp was supplemented by day camps. More than 140,000 people used the settlement's services in 1925; attendance grew to 222,858 in 1935. The Friendly Inn was forced to relocate again in 1954, when its Woodland neighborhood was included in an urban redevelopment program. The settlement moved to the community center building of the Carver Park Estates, 2382 Unwin Rd. By 1957 the settlement was sponsoring various boys' clubs and athletic teams in an attempt to reduce juvenile delinquency in the area. By 1962 it had added a golden-age club for senior citizens. As poverty, public housing conditions, and educational opportunities for minorities became issues of public concern in the mid-1960s, the Friendly Inn addressed these issues with a Head Start program, vocational rehabilitation programs, and housekeeping classes for public housing residents. The Friendly Inn continues to provide meeting places for community groups and to offer programs oriented toward health and family services, the needs of children and the aged, and the vocational and recreational needs of teenagers and adults.

Friendly Inn Social Settlement Records, WRHS.

The **FRIES & SCHUELE COMPANY** was one of Cleveland's pioneer dry-goods stores, as well as the west side's oldest department store. Chas. Fries and Geo. Klein opened their small store, Fries, Klein & Co., on 13 Apr. 1868 at Pearl (W. 25th) St. and Carrol Ave. It was a full-service department store, specializing in custom-made carpets, curtains, and draperies. Chas. Hoover soon joined the venture, which became Fries, Klein, & Hoover. By 1879, both Klein and Hoover had died, and a store clerk, Christian Schuele, became a partner in the Fries & Schuele Co. In 1885, the growing store had moved 1 block south to a building at 1948 W. 25th St. across the street from the WEST SIDE MARKET. Fries & Schuele continued to prosper. Coinciding with its incorporation in 1909, the company erected a 5-story building adjoining its former location. The attraction of the new West Side Market House, opened in 1912, greatly benefited the nearby store. Its carpet and drapery installation business remained quite profitable, as Fries & Schuele became one of the nation's largest carpet-selling firms. To handle its growing business, the store was expanded and renovated several times. By 1968, the company had 150 employees. In the mid-1920s, the Fries family sold its interest in the store, but the descendants of Christian Schuele continued to run the business until it closed on 13 Jan. 1979. The store could no longer compete with discount stores, and many of its customers had moved to the SUBURBS.

**FROHRING FOUNDATION.** See **WILLIAM O. & GERTRUDE L. FROHRING FOUNDATION, INC.**

The **FROHSINN SINGING SOCIETY** was the first German music club in Cleveland. Its work brought national attention to the city. The Frohsinn was begun in 1848 by German immigrants led by a man named Heber. The society's rehearsals, informal at best, were held from time to time in Seifert's Casino. Gottlieb Votteler assumed direction of the group in 1849 after several of its founders, including Heber, left for the California gold fields. The Frohsinn attended the first exchange festival (Saengerfest) in Cincinnati in June of that year, where the society received high praise. Heber returned in late 1849 to resume his position as director. With former members of the Frohsinn and others, Heber organized an informal group, which constituted the mixed chorus section in the Freimaennen Band in 1850. This act forced the dissolution of the Frohsinn Singing Society in 1850.

Alexander, Heywood J., *It Must Be Heard* (1981).

The **FRONT ROW THEATER,** built at an approximate cost of $3 million, was completed in 1974 and opened on 5 July of that year. It is located in HIGHLAND HTS. on Wilson Mills Rd. near I-271. The Front Row has featured some of the major figures in show business. Among its most popular attractions have been celebrities such as Sammy Davis, Jr., Wayne Newton, Liberace, and Steve Lawrence and Eydie Gorme. Richard Jencen, who lived in SHAKER HTS., designed the Front Row. It was the first all-weather theater to be built in Greater Cleveland since the CLEVELAND PLAY HOUSE in 1927. It seats 3,200 people and is approximately 300' x 270'. Since it is a theater in the round, the last row is 59' from the stage, which is 29' in diameter with its orchestra pit. A circular curtain conceals the stage lighting. The entire stage slowly revolves during each performance in order to provide a clear view for all the spectators. Also, the circular domed auditorium has no pillars to block spectators' views. The theater has 3 concession stands, including an elegant champagne bar. The original 5 owners of the Front Row were president Nate Dolin and his wife, Mollie, of Bratenahl; Dominic Visconsi of CHAGRIN FALLS; general manager Lawrence Dolin of BEACHWOOD; and Len Luxemborg. The house manager is Wm. Swann.

**FURDEK, STEPHAN** (2 Sept. 1855–18 Jan. 1915), was a Cleveland priest who worked with Czech and Slovak immigrants in the 19th century. He also organized the national fraternal insurance society the FIRST CATHOLIC SLOVAK UNION. Furdek was born in Frztena, Hungary. He studied at Nitra before enrolling in the Prague Seminary to study for the priesthood. Bp. RICHARD GILMOUR had written the Prague Seminary asking them to locate a priest who was fluent in Czech and Slovak who could come to Cleveland to work with the immigrants. Furdek, who was nearing the end of his studies, was chosen for the assignment. He arrived in Mar. 1882 and studied at ST. MARY SEMINARY. Bp. Gilmour ordained him on 2 July 1882 and assigned him to ST. WENCESLAS CHURCH at E. 37th St. and Broadway. Fr. Furdek worked there until May 1883, when he was asked to organize a parish for the CZECHS residing in the vicinity of E. 55th and Broadway.

The new parish was placed under the patronage of Our Lady of Lourdes. Fr. Furdek had ministered to many of his new parishioners when he served at St. Wenceslaus. He quickly built a small church and school. He was briefly assigned to St. Procop's, but the parish of Our Lady of Lourdes demanded his return. He came back to spend the rest of his priestly ministry there. In 1888 he organized ST. LADISLAUS CHURCH, the first parish to serve both SLOVAKS and HUNGARIANS in Cleveland. In 1891 Furdek founded the national fraternal insurance organization the First Catholic Slovak Union, whose membership had grown to 45,000 in 1915. He became the founder and publisher of *Jednota*, its journal. Furdek wrote numerous books and pamphlets on religious and educational themes in Slovak and Bohemian. He published a reader for Slovak students. He served as a diocesan consultor and advisor to the bishop.

Archives, Diocese of Cleveland.

The **FUTURE OUTLOOK LEAGUE** was formed in the midst of the Depression, in Feb. 1935, with the intention of obtaining jobs for Afro-American residents of the Central area. The idea for the league grew out of dissatisfaction with the achievements of existing Negro organizations concerning employment. John O. Holly, a political officeholder in the area, was instrumental in the FOL's founding and served as its first president. The league was governed by an executive board and executive officers. Initially the FOL appealed to semiskilled, unskilled, and newly located Negro residents in search of jobs. It strove to persuade white-owned businesses in Negro neighborhoods to hire Negro employees and further advocate Negro ownership of businesses in these neighborhoods. Unlike most Negro organizations at this time, the league promoted the use of pickets and economic boycotts in order to achieve its goals. Jobs were won in this fashion for several hundred residents in the Central area. From 1937–41, the FOL published a newspaper, *Voice of the League*, and broadened its base of support in the community as businessmen, ministers, and professionals joined in membership or advocacy. However, its activities declined during WORLD WAR II, because jobs were created in defense and war-related industries. The league rebounded with several boycott and picket campaigns in the years just after the war. Since 1950, however, it has been less active in Cleveland.

Zinz, Kenneth M., "The Future Outlook League of Cleveland: A Negro Protest Organization" (Master's thesis, Kent State University, 1973).

The **GABRIEL COMPANY,** established in 1904 to manufacture automobile horns, became a major supplier of shock absorbers for the original-equipment and automotive aftermarkets. Founded by CLAUD H. FOSTER, a cornetist in a theater orchestra, the Gabriel Mfg. Co. marketed a horn he had created and named for the Angel Gabriel. The Gabriel Horn was popular on luxury cars throughout the world, including Germany, where Kaiser Wilhelm forbade anyone from buying one to compete with his. Within 5 years, Foster invented a shock absorber that dominated the market until the 1920s and made him a multimillionaire; in 1923, he paid $838,000 in Ohio taxes, the largest amount collected to that date from an individual.

In 1925, the Gabriel Snubber Co. was reorganized with eastern and Canadian capital and continued to prosper. Foster sold his interest for $5 million, a fraction of its worth, and divided the profits among his employees. After Foster's departure, the company, which officially changed its name to the Gabriel Co., went into a slump when many of its customers went out of business. A new "air-type" shock absorber that was lighter, less expensive, and more efficient was developed by the company and was adopted by Ford, and it revitalized corporate fortunes. Variations on the product were used in WORLD WAR II in jeeps, armored cars, and glider planes. The company also secured government contracts to manufacture ordnance, shells, and fan assemblies—all of which propelled its 1940 sales of $346,000 to over $5 million in 1944. Gabriel outgrew its facilities at 1407 E. 40th St. and leased a government plant at E. 140th and Darley.

Under the leadership of John Briggs, a Chicago investment banker, Gabriel resumed its national ad campaign in the 1940s and began to diversify. The company bought out Internatl. Metal Hose, makers of hoses and tubing, in 1942, followed by Ward Prods. (radios, antennas, cable, 1942) and Workshop Associates (radios, microwave antennas, 1951). These companies increased Gabriel's foothold in the original-equipment and replacement auto-parts markets and expanded its customer base. In addition, Gabriel acquired from a British company the exclusive manufacturing rights for a revolutionary oil-filled shock absorber used in RAF warplanes, and after several years of modifications, he introduced the device to the American automotive industry.

By the mid-1950s, Gabriel expanded its corporate family with the purchase of the Burd Piston Ring Co. (1951); EA Laboratories (heaters, 1951); divisions of Houdaille Industries, Inc. (hydraulic shock absorbers, 1956); the Gladden Co. (guided-missile and aircraft parts, 1957); and the Bohannon Mfg. Co. (aerospace technology, 1958). Gabriel opened a rocket power division in Mesa, Ariz., and an electronics plant in Millis, Mass. While the Cleveland shock absorber division was the largest, the others acquired lucrative government contracts. Gabriel's rocket power plant developed solid rocket propellant and other aerospace innovations.

In 1962, Pres. Briggs suddenly resigned; he reportedly was behind a stock buyout by the Maremont Co. of Chicago. When Maremont ownership reached 50%, Gabriel directors resigned. With the acquisition of Gabriel, Maremont, already a major supplier of exhaust systems, brake components, clutches, and cam shafts, acquired 70% of the shock absorber business. Though Maremont claimed it would maintain the Cleveland facilities and 1,000 employees, protracted labor troubles caused the company to reassess its position. The Internatl. Assoc. of Machinists (IAM), which represented Gabriel employees, was challenged by the TEAMSTERS UNION in 1962; a series of contested elections (which resulted in a Teamster victory) disrupted company operations for about 4 years. In 1966, Maremont claimed that declining orders at the Cleveland plant necessitated a shutdown, and equipment was shipped to the company's Tennessee and Canadian plants; the IAM claimed a "sweetheart deal" between Maremont and the Teamsters. The old Gabriel facilities were closed in 1966, putting over 450 people out of work.

**GAERTNER, CARL FREDERICK** (1898–4 Nov. 1952), was a nationally known landscape artist whose frequent and best medium was watercolor. The son of H. Frederick Gaertner, manager of the BURROWS BROS. CO., he was born in Cleveland and graduated from EAST TECHNICAL HIGH SCHOOL. He intended to be an engineer. He began attending Western Reserve College in 1918 and finished at the CLEVELAND INSTITUTE OF ART. In 1918, while still a student, he began instructing at South High School in Willoughby. In 1925, Gaertner started teaching at the Cleveland Institute of Art and Western Reserve College, as well as at JOHN CARROLL UNIVERSITY. Gaertner exhibited in 27 Cleveland May Shows. His paintings hang in galleries all over the country, including the CLEVELAND MUSEUM OF ART, the Metropolitan Museum, the Chicago Art Institute, and the Whitney Gallery. He was also responsible for the fresco in the Cleveland Greyhound bus station. Gaertner is best known for his Ohio landscapes, with their dark, dramatic skies. He traveled frequently to such places as Cape Cod, Hudson River Bay, the Allegheny Mts., and the Monongahela Valley to find variety in landscapes, but he always returned to the Chagrin Valley and his farm in Willoughby. Gaertner won the Natl. Academy of Design Award in 1953 for an oil painting entitled *Barge Men*. His portrait hangs there in tribute to him. He was a member of the Masons, a past president of the CLEVELAND SOCIETY OF ARTISTS, and a member of the Audubon Club and the American Watercolor Society. The Carl Gaertner Memorial Prize in painting is offered at the Institute of Art. A retrospective of his work was held at the Cleveland Museum of Art in June 1953. Gaertner was married in 1938 to Adelle Potter and had 2 sons.

The **GAGE GALLERY OF FINE ARTS** was a privately owned art gallery established by Geo. E. Gage in 1910. Gage, born in Hudson, N.Y., was the son of a collector of fine china. During the early years of the century, he worked in a variety of fields and once owned a small art store in Hudson, where he became acquainted with members of the famous Hudson River School. While on a trip to New York, he met Maj. Chas. J. Strong of WM. TAYLOR SON & CO. in an art store. As a result of their conversation, Strong suggested that Gage move to Cleveland and set up an art department in Wm. Taylor Son & Co., a suggestion that Gage followed. In 1910, Gage opened his own gallery at 2258 Euclid Ave. There he sold and exhibited fine paintings, drawings, etchings, bronzes, and porcelains. Many of the artworks sold through his store to leading citizens were later donated to the CLEVELAND MUSEUM OF ART. Among these were Anne Hyatt's bronze groups of horses entitled *Up-Hill and Down-Hill*, given to the museum by Ralph King, and George Bellows's *Blue Boy* and Gari Melcher's *Christ with Halo*, which were a bequest of Mrs. Henry A. Everett. The WOMEN'S ART CLUB OF CLEVELAND was organized in Belle Kaufmann's studio at the Gage Gallery in 1912, and the CLEVELAND SOCIETY OF ARTISTS often held meetings there before they moved into their own clubrooms. In 1935, the gallery moved to 13100 Shaker Square following a robbery at the Euclid Gallery in which over $10,000 worth of bronzes and paintings were stolen. Gage died on 7 May 1940 at the age of 79, and the galleries closed the following year.

**GAHN, HARRY C.** (26 Apr. 1880–2 Nov. 1962), was a lawyer, city council member, congressman, and public official. Gahn was born in Elmore, Ohio, to Dr. Louis and Esther Knight Gahn. Educated in Elmore public schools, he graduated from Elmore High School in 1897 and taught in a nearby country school. He graduated from the University of Michigan with the LL.B. degree and was admitted to the Ohio bar in 1904. Specializing in trial practice, he worked in private practice with Wm. Patterson, 1904–06, and with the law firm of THEODORE BURTON, 1906–08. In 1909, Gahn became legal counsel for the LEGAL AID SOCIETY, serving until 1912, while working in the law office of Harry Howell.

Elected from the 14th ward to the CLEVELAND CITY COUNCIL, 1911–21, Gahn served as council president between 1918–19. As a member of the Cleveland River & Harbor Commission, 1911–21, he made a special study of Cleveland harbor development, port administration, and the merchant marine. He advocated the public ownership of harbor facilities in order to make them the best on the Great Lakes so that when the St. Lawrence River was made navigable to ocean vessels, Cleveland would become an important world seaport. In 1921, Gahn was elected to the U.S. Congress from Ohio's 21st district. Defeated for re-election in 1923, he returned to the general practice of law, with special attention to the handling of estates and personal-injury cases. He became counsel for the Methodist Children's Home in Berea in 1913 and was president of the Cleveland Chevrolet Dealers' Assoc., 1924–37. In 1936, he was appointed solicitor for the city of INDEPENDENCE; he retired after 20 years in 1956. Gahn married Grace Gerrard in June 1917. They were divorced in 1929. He had 2 daughters, Marjorie and May.

Harry C. Gahn Scrapbook, WRHS.

**GAINES, ERVIN J.** (8 Dec. 1916–21 June 1986), modernized and improved operations at the CLEVELAND PUBLIC LIBRARY during his tenure as the system's director from Nov. 1974 until his retirement at the end of 1985. The son of Ervin J. and Helen Hennessey Gaines, Ervin was born and educated in New York City. He attended the public schools and graduated from Columbia University in 1942, then joined the Navy's submarine service and saw action in the Pacific. He returned to Columbia as an English instructor (1946–53) and earned a master's degree in English (1947) and a doctorate in comparative literature (1952). From 1953–56, Gaines worked for the CIA-sponsored anti-Soviet radio station Radio Liberation, based in Munich. He then entered personnel management, working for the Teleregister Corp. (1956–57) and as a freelance consultant (1957–58), during which time he worked with the Boston Public Library on personnel problems. That led to an interest in libraries and to a position as assistant director of the Boston Public Library (1958–64). In 1964, he became director of the Minneapolis Public Library, a position he held until being hired by the Cleveland system.

In Cleveland, Gaines found a system in which circulation was declining rapidly, the large staff was underpaid, the board was divided by issues of race and patronage, the system's operations and procedures were outmoded, and libraries were deteriorating physically. Public displeasure with the system had resulted in a narrow defeat for a levy in Nov. 1974. Gaines moved quickly, eliminating little-used programs and books to cut costs, increasing salaries by 20% in 1975, closing and consolidating branch libraries, and implementing use of the Library of Congress book-numbering system. To help finance such changes, he directed a successful campaign in 1975 for a tax levy, which brought the library $4.3 million over 5 years. By 1979, the system's decline had been halted. Through closings and consolidation, the number of branch libraries was reduced from 39 in 1974 to 31 in 1984, including 8 new buildings and 10 remodeled ones; through attrition, the number of library employees was reduced from 649 to 451. After declining to a low of 2.6 million items in 1978, circulation increased to 4.1 million items in 1984. Gaines's modernization program included replacing the traditional card catalog with a computerized system. Other programs he launched were the valuable index of local papers (1976– ) and the Cleveland Heritage Project. Praised for having "dragged the library into the modern age," Gaines, with his blunt manner, and his changes often received severe criticism from retired and older staff members and patrons. But the public in general approved: the last tax levy of Gaines's administration (Nov. 1985) was approved by a 20,000-vote majority. As executive director of the Urban Libraries Council, Gaines was a proponent of federal aid to libraries. He was also a member of the Internatl. Assoc. of Metropolitan City Libraries and hosted one of its meetings in Cleveland, in Aug.

1985. He was also a member of the American Library Assoc. Gaines married Martha Zirbel on 11 Feb. 1938.

**GANNETT, ALICE** (1876–23 May 1962), prominent settlement-house worker and reformer, was born in Bath, Maine. Her father, Henry Gannett, was a chief geographer of the Geologic Survey and one of the founders of the Natl. Geographic Society. Gannett attended schools in Washington, D.C., and earned a degree from Bryn Mawr College. She taught school for 3 years before traveling to New York City in 1906, where she took a room in a tenement among poor social conditions. There she became devoted to the settlement-house idea and the promotion of social welfare. She served briefly at Welcome Hall in Buffalo, N.Y., before her return to New York City, where she headed Lenox Hill House for 6 years. She also served as associate director of the Henry St. Settlement in that city for many years. Gannett came to Cleveland in 1917 as a settlement leader. Here she headed Goodrich House (see GOODRICH-GANNETT NEIGH. CENT.) at 1420 E. 31st St. for 30 years. During her tenure, the settlement established a tradition of free thought and speech, commitment to neighborhood, and improved working conditions. Gannett was president of the Cleveland Fed. of Settlements for 5 years, was president of the Natl. Fed. of Settlements for 2 years, and headed the CONSUMERS LEAGUE OF OHIO for 8 years. She also served as a trustee of the Welfare Fed. of Cleveland. In the 1950s she founded the Neighborhood Group, a senior citizens' organization for civic improvement. Gannett died in Harrisburg, Pa., and is buried in Washington, D.C.

The **GARDEN CENTER OF GREATER CLEVELAND** is the country's oldest civic garden center. It was establshed on 4 Dec. 1930 and was originally located in a boathouse at Wade Park Lagoon. The center was founded by Mrs. Thos. Howell, Mrs. Wm. Mather, Mrs. Chas. Otis, Mrs. John Sherwin, Mrs. Walter C. White, and Mrs. Windsor T. White. The founders stated their purpose as follows: "The Garden Center of Greater Cleveland is formed for the purpose of providing a place or places where knowledge and appreciation of gardening and horticulture are promoted." Its establishment can be dated to a 24 Jan. 1930 meeting of the Garden Club of Greater Cleveland, where Mrs. Walter C. White explained that the club library (which had been donated by Mrs. Andrew Squire) had grown so much that it needed a permanent home. The CLEVELAND MUSEUM OF ART had been providing storage, but the museum was in need of the space. Mrs. White suggested storing the books in the boathouse at the edge of the lagoon. This idea was approved by art museum director Frederick Whiting. To raise money for the center, the Garden Club held a French Street Fair in front of the Art Museum on 12–14 June 1930, raising $17,000. Margaret Asborn, graduate of Lowthorpe School of Landscape Architecture, was the center's first director. The new center issued a newsletter, and by the end of its first year had had 47 lectures/demonstrations and 20,000 visitors. Reorganized in 1933, the center became the Garden Ctr. of Greater Cleveland, ending its sponsorship by the Garden Club. That was also the first year of the White Elephant Sale fundraiser, which has since become an important charity event, often billed as the world's largest rummage sale. The Garden Ctr. incorporated as a nonprofit organization in 1937, and in 1939 it enlarged its center with 2 wings. A west side branch was opened at Cudell House, 10013 Detroit Ave., on 6 Apr. 1940. It moved to the Beck Ctr. for more space in 1977. Because of parking problems and danger of flooding, the center decided to relocate. Ground was broken on 9 Oct. 1964 at the center's present (1986) site at 11030 East Blvd. The Garden Ctr. and its programs have continued to grow. By 1980 the budget was $450,000, and membership was more than 4,000, plus 50 corporate members.

**GARDNER, GEORGE W.** (7 Feb. 1834–18 Dec. 1911), was a prominent businessman and politician who served in city council for 8 years and for 2 terms as mayor of Cleveland. Gardner was born in Pittsfield, Mass., the son of James and Griselda Porter Gardner. The family came to Cleveland in 1837, where he attended public schools. Leaving school at 14, he sailed the Great Lakes for 5 years. Returning to Cleveland, he was employed in the private banking house of Wick, Otis, & Brownell from 1853–57, after which he became a junior partner in Otis, Brownell & Co., grain dealers. Gardner continued as a grain merchant when he joined M. B. Clarke and JOHN D. ROCKEFELLER to found Clarke, Gardner & Co. in 1859. Two years later, together with Peter Thatcher, Geo. H. Burt, and A. C. McNairy, he built the Union Elevator in 1861, the largest grain elevator in the area at the time. Later the firm became Gardner & Clark and added the manufacture of flour to their elevator business with the purchase of Natl. Flour Mills in 1878. Gardner was one of the incorporators of the Cleveland Board of Trade, which later became the Chamber of Commerce, and served as its president in 1868. He also was president of the Buckeye Stove Co., the Buttman Furnace Co., and the Walker Mfg. Co. as well as a director of the Merchants Natl. Bank. Gardner was one of the organizers of the CLEVELAND YACHT CLUB. Gardner was active in Republican politics, serving as a city councilman 1863–64 and 1876–81 and as president of council 1879–81. He was mayor in 1885–86 and 1889–91. He died in Dayton, Ohio, at age 78 but is buried at WOODLAND CEMETERY in Cleveland. He married Rosaline (or Rosilda) Oviatt in 1857, and they had 7 children.

**GARFIELD, ABRAM** (21 Nov. 1872–16 Oct. 1958), son of former U.S. president JAS. A. GARFIELD, was a prominent residential architect, founded one of Cleveland's most active architectural firms, and was a leader in both local and national city planning and redevelopment efforts. Garfield was born in Washington, D.C., and moved to Cleveland after his father's death in 1881. He attended public and private elementary schools in Cleveland and St. Paul's School in Concord, N.H. He received a B.A. degree from Williams College in 1893 and a B.S. from the MIT in 1896. He traveled in Europe for a year and returned to Cleveland to begin his architectural practice in 1897. The following year he formed a partnership with FRANK MEADE, and as Meade & Garfield the architects completed several major commissions for prominent Cleveland families that established them as 2 of the city's premier residential designers.

From 1905–22, Garfield practiced as Abram Garfield, Architect. As the firm expanded, he added partners. Garfield's firm operated as Garfield, Stanley-Brown, Harris & Robinson (1926–34); Garfield, Harris, Robinson & Schafer (1936–56); and Garfield, Harris, Schafer, Flynn & Williams (1957–59). After his death, the firm continued as Schafer, Flynn, & Associates (1962–66); Schafer, Flynn, Van Dijk & Associates (1966–68); Schafer, Flynn, Van Dijk & Dalton, Grimm, Johnson (1968–70); Flynn, Dalton, Van Dijk & Partners (1970–73); and Dalton, Van Dijk, Johnson & Partners from 1973 on. Garfield was personally responsible for the design of Mrs. John Hay's residence (1910), now part of the WESTERN RESERVE HISTORICAL SOCIETY in UNIVERSITY CIRCLE; large homes in SHAKER HTS. and BRATENAHL; the original Babies & Childrens and Maternity Hospital (1923) in the University Hospitals group; Bratenahl School (1901); and the Woodhill and Seville homes for the Cleveland Metropolitan Housing Authority. He was a founder and first president of the Cleveland School of Architecture (1924–29). When the school became part of Western Reserve University, he served as vice-president and vice-chairman of the board (1929–41). Garfield was made a trustee of WRU in 1941, was elected an honorary lifetime member in 1943, and received an honorary Doctor of Humanities degree from the university in 1945.

An advocate of CITY PLANNING, Garfield served on the Group Plan Commission and was a member of the Cleveland Planning Commission (1928–42) and its chairman (1930–42). He helped found the Regional Assoc. of Cleveland with ERNEST BOHN and served as its president until 1957. Garfield was appointed by Pres. Theodore Roosevelt to the Natl. Council of Fine Arts (1909), by Pres. Coolidge to the Natl. Commission on Fine Arts (1925), and by Pres. Hoover to the Committee on Blighted Areas & Slums (1932). He served this last group as chairman. Garfield was a member, director, and officer of the American Institute of Architects, the ENGLISH SPEAKING UNION, the Century Assoc. of New York, the Natl. Academy of Design, and the Union and Tavern clubs in Cleveland. On 14 Oct. 1897, Garfield married Sarah Grainger Williams, the daughter of Edward Porter Williams, a founder of the SHERWIN-WILLIAMS CO. She died in Feb. 1945. He married Helen Grannis Matthews on 12 Apr. 1947.

**GARFIELD, JAMES ABRAM** (19 Nov. 1831–19 Sept. 1881), the 20th president of the U.S., was born on a farm in Orange Twp., Cuyahoga County, Ohio. Garfield was the youngest of 4 children. Fatherless at the age of 4, he faced poverty as a youth, working as a farmer, carpenter, and canal boatman. He studied at Geauga Seminary in Chester, Ohio, and at the Western Reserve Eclectic Institute (now Hiram College) from 1851–54. He graduated from Williams College in Massachusetts in 1856. He returned to Hiram to teach classics at the college and later, 1857–61, served as its president. At the same time, he served as a lay minister in the DISCIPLES OF CHRIST church. In 1858 he married Lucretia Rudolph, and in 1859 he was admitted to the bar and elected to the Ohio senate. At the outbreak of the CIVIL WAR, Garfield volunteered in the Union Army. He was commisioned as a lieutenant colonel in 1861 in the 42d Ohio Regiment. His command defeated the superior forces of Gen. Humphrey Marshall at Middle Creek, Ky., in 1862, after which he was promoted to brigadier general. He later took part in the Battle of Shiloh and won distinction at the Battle of Chickamauga (19 Sept. 1863), receiving the rank of major general. Garfield resigned his commission in Dec. 1863 after being elected to the U.S. House of Representatives. He served in the House for 17 years, with membership on the Military Affairs, Ways & Means, Appropriations, and Banking & Currency committees.

In Jan. 1880, Garfield was elected to the U.S. Senate. Before his term began, he attended the Republican Convention in Chicago (June 1880) as campaign manager for John Sherman of Ohio. Garfield, however, became the Republican candidate for president, nominated on the 36th ballot as a compromise candidate between former president Ulysses S. Grant and Sen. Jas. G. Blaine. Chester Alan Arthur of New York was selected as his running mate. Garfield and Arthur opposed the Democratic candidates Winfield Scott Hancock and Wm. H. English. The Republican platform advocated civil-service reform, a protective tariff, veterans' legislation, and restriction of Chinese immigra-

tion. Headquarters for the campaign were in Cleveland, but Garfield spent most of the time receiving various delegations of voters at his home, "Lawnfield," in Mentor, Ohio. Garfield and Arthur won the election by less than a 10,000-vote plurality, but they garnered 214 of the 369 electoral votes that were cast. Pres. Garfield, confronted with problems of patronage, spent most of his brief time in office trying to ameliorate the two conflicting factions within his party. Indebted to Blaine and his group for election support, Garfield appointed him secretary of state, angering Roscoe Conkling and his group, who unsuccessfully attempted to block Senate approval; the Senate confirmed the appointment, and Conkling resigned from the Senate. On 2 July 1881, while on his way to a Williams College reunion, Pres. Garfield was shot at the Washington, D.C., railroad station by Chas. Julius Guiteau, a disappointed office seeker. Garfield suffered through agonizing attempts by various physicians to save his life before he finally died on 19 Sept. 1881 at Elberon, N.J. He was buried, in accordance with his wishes, at LAKE VIEW CEMETERY in Cleveland, and the GARFIELD MONUMENT was erected to his memory in May 1890. Two of Garfield's sons, Harry A. and JAS. RUDOLPH, went on to distinguished careers of their own.

Peskin, Alan, *Garfield* (1978).

**GARFIELD, JAMES RUDOLPH** (17 Oct. 1865–24 Mar. 1950), was a lawyer and activist in civic and charitable affairs in Cleveland. Involved in Republican party politics, he served at numerous appointed federal posts, including on the Civil Service Commission and as secretary of the interior. Garfield was the third child of Pres. Jas. A. and Lucretia Rudolph Garfield. He attended public schools in Washington, D.C., and St. Paul's School in Concord, N.H. He received the B.A. degree from Williams College in 1885 and the LL.D. degree from Columbia University. Admitted to the Ohio bar in 1888, Garfield started practice in Cleveland with his older brother, Harry. His attachment to his law practice continued for more than 60 years; he became the senior partner in the firm of Garfield, Baldwin, Jameson, Hope & Ulrich.

From 1896–1900, Garfield served in the Ohio senate, where he authored an election-reforms bill. In 1902, Pres. Roosevelt appointed him to the Federal Civil Service Commission, established as a result of the assassination of Garfield's father. In 1903, Garfield was appointed to the U.S. Commission of Corporations in the Dept. of Commerce & Labor. Roosevelt appointed Garfield as secretary of the interior in 1907, and he quickly became part of Roosevelt's "lawn tennis" cabinet. Considered by many to be the best interior secretary to that time, Garfield sought to modernize the department. He spearheaded Roosevelt's efforts to conserve public resources. He was also active in Indian affairs, traveling to Montana and Wyoming to handle matters affecting the Indian nations. He was later closely associated with the Progressive party.

With his return to his Cleveland law practice in 1909, Garfield was called upon from time to time for public service. During WORLD WAR I he served on the Cleveland War Council. Pres. Coolidge appointed him to the emergency board for the investigation of railroad labor disputes in the Southwest. In 1929, Pres. Hoover appointed him as chairman of the Federal Commission of the Conservation of the Public Domain. Garfield also played a prominent role in Cleveland civic and charitable affairs. He was one of the founders and trustees of the Community Fund. He was the first legal counsel for the CLEVELAND FOUNDATION, vice-president of the Cleveland Welfare Fed.

from 1917–20, and trustee of the Speech & Hearing Clinic, the Humane Society, the LAKE VIEW CEMETERY, Lake Erie College, and the WESTERN RESERVE HISTORICAL SOCIETY. Garfield married Helen Newell in 1890. The Garfields had 3 sons, John, R. H., and Abram.

**GARFIELD HEIGHTS** is a suburb southeast of Cleveland occupying about 6.75 sq. mi. It is bounded on the north by Cleveland, on the east by MAPLE HTS., on the south by VALLEY VIEW, and on the west by CUYAHOGA HTS. Originally part of the village of NEWBURGH, it split off in 1907 as the village of S. Newburgh. When the village became a city in 1930, it took its name from GARFIELD PARK. The former Newburgh Park had been renamed in 1897 in memory of Pres. JAS. A. GARFIELD, whose father was one of the early settlers of the area. In the 19th century, the heights above the Cuyahoga Valley were more desirable to settlers than the swamps of the river. Early settlers were farmers who supplemented their income by producing "black salt," a mixture of lye and potash from burned timber that was more profitable to ship to eastern markets than grain. Farms dominated the landscape until real-estate developers began to develop the area as a residential community in the 1920s. The population jumped from 2,550 in 1920 to nearly 16,000 by 1930. Whereas early residents were German, the residential immigration after 1920 consisted of working-class POLES, other Slavs, and ITALIANS. The population in 1980 was 35,000. Garfield Hts., like many commuter SUBURBS, had a small industrial base, which led to budgetary difficulties. Overbuilding in the 1920s led to an 80% delinquency rate in the Depression. For many years, the major industries were the Round Chain Co. and General Chemical. Exhausted quarries in the area were utilized as a landfill by Garfield Hts. and other suburbs. Despite the tax revenues such operations brought in, they created a public nuisance because of the pollution problems associated with them. In 1978, the city sought legal remedies to close the landfills. Currently, the largest component of the tax base is the Garfield Mall, built in 1971. In 1985 the community maintained police and fire departments and a school system consisting of 2 elementary, 1 junior high, and 1 high school. MARYMOUNT HOSPITAL and Convent were located in Garfield Hts. beginning in 1925.

The **GARFIELD MONUMENT,** located on a sloping hill near Mayfield Rd. in LAKE VIEW CEMETERY, was built as a tomb and memorial to Pres. JAS. A. GARFIELD. Construction of the monument began in 1885 with funds raised by the Garfield Natl. Monument Assoc. headed by JEPTHA H. WADE, HENRY B. PAYNE, and JOSEPH PERKINS. Construction was completed in 1890, and the monument was dedicated on 30 May of that year, with a procession of notables including Pres. Benjamin Harrison, former president Rutherford B. Hayes, Vice-Pres. Levi P. Morton, and members of the Garfield family. The monument is constructed of native Ohio sandstone upon a design by Geo. Keller, architect of Hartford, Conn., who had won the commission in a national competition. Keller was assisted by John S. Chapple of London, who supervised the work on the mosaics and stained-glass windows. A combination of Romanesque, Gothic, and Byzantine architecture, the structure has been called the first true mausoleum in America, combining both tomb and memorial functions. The monument, pinnacled by a 3-tiered circular tower 50′ in diameter and 180′ in height flanked by 2 small octagonal towers, stands upon a broad stone terrace. The exterior of the base is decorated with 5 life-size bas relief panels depicting Garfield in different phases of his life and

career. Inside the monument in the memorial room, a white Carrara marble life-size statue of Garfield stands in front of a marble replica of the chair he used in the White House. The memorial hall is surrounded by polished red granite columns supporting a beehive dome decorated with gold leaf and mosaics. Stone mosaic panes depicting various mourning processions decorate the sides of the chamber below the dome. The caskets of Garfield and his wife, Lucretia, and urns containing the ashes of his daughter and son-in-law lie in a crypt directly beneath the memorial hall.

**GARFIELD PARK,** located at Broadway and Garfield Pkwy. in GARFIELD HTS., was acquired by the city of Cleveland in 1895 as part of the city's centennial celebration (1896). It consisted of a series of high promontories and creek valleys providing a natural setting for the development of many recreational facilities, including baseball diamonds, tennis courts, football fields, and a swimming pool on the upper level and boating and fishing on the lakes on the lower level. A German howitzer captured in the Argonne Forest (1918) was moved to Garfield Park in 1931 and dedicated on 29 May 1932 by an American Legion post. In 1942 the howitzer was melted down as scrap for war purposes. The park continued to be one of Cleveland's most widely used recreation spots until it deteriorated through vandalism, littering, and dumping during the 1950s and 1960s. Since it is owned by the city of Cleveland but is located in Garfield Hts., there have been many disputes over its jurisdiction. By 1986 it had been taken over by the CLEVELAND METROPARKS SYSTEM and was being rehabilitated.

The **GARFIELD-PERRY STAMP CLUB,** one of the first stamp clubs in the U.S., was formed by area collectors on 17 Mar. 1890. Its organization was initiated by Geo. J. Bailey, a stamp collector and agent for the Harkness estate. He invited area collectors to a meeting to form a local branch of the American Philatelic Assoc.; they were chartered as Branch No. 7. Bailey was elected the club's first president, along with W. H. Schneider as vice-president, W. Wallace MacLaren as secretary, and C. A. Brobst as treasurer. The club was named to honor JAS. A. GARFIELD and Oliver Hazard Perry, because the portraits of these men that appeared on the $.05 and $.90 stamps had originated in Cleveland: Garfield's was from a photograph by JAS. F. RYDER, and Perry's was copied from his monument. The club's membership grew slowly but steadily during its early years. It had 16 charter members by mid-Jan. 1894, and 54 resident and 16 nonresident members by 1917. The club gave up its charter in the American Philatelic Assoc. ca. 1900 and became an independent club; in 1914, it took the 2-year charter of Cleveland Branch No. 30 of the American Philatelic Society. In addition to regular meetings, the club held annual dinners and exhibitions, where trophies were awarded for best displays in various categories. Its exhibitions, as well as the large stamp collections assembled by many of its members, helped the club achieve a national and international reputation for its philatelic work. By 1950, its nonresident members included the postmaster general of Sweden, and total membership was about 280. In 1957, the club hosted the first spring meeting of the American Philatelic Society, which returned in 1965 for another spring meeting. In honor of the Garfield-Perry Stamp Club, the U.S. Bureau of Engraving & Printing issued a souvenir card on the occasion of the club's Mar. 1986 show. *Plain Dealer* stamp columnist Stephen G. Ersati found the souvenir card to be "one of the greatest ironies," since it "salutes the progress of women by featuring the 1902 Martha Washington stamp, the first U.S.

stamp featuring an American woman," but the club continued to bar women from membership, arguing that "few women collect stamps and . . . those who do don't collect them very seriously."

**GARLICK, THEODATUS A.** (30 Mar. 1805–9 Dec. 1884), was a surgeon, a sculptor, Cleveland's first photographer, and the first American to breed fish artificially. Garlick was born in Middlebury, Vt., a nephew of Ephraim Kirby, a CONNECTICUT LAND CO. director. In 1818, he joined his brother Abel, a Cleveland stonecutter, and helped produce the village's first shipped goods, burr millstones. He supported himself as a blacksmith and tombstone carver in Cleveland, Newbury, and Brookfield (Trumbull Co.), where he also studied medicine with local physicians. He was admitted to Baltimore's Washington Medical College in 1832 and graduated from the University of Maryland 2 years later. He practiced surgery in Youngstown until 1852, when he was offered a partnership with Dr. HORACE A. ACKLEY at the Cleveland Medical College. Garlick developed new procedures in plastic and facial surgery and operative midwifery. He invented splints and instruments for amputation, trepanning, and obstetrics. His skill in surgery, combined with his background in sculpture, made him an adept portraitist. He achieved notice for wax medallion reliefs of his professors and was invited to Washington, D.C., where Pres. Jackson and Henry Clay posed for him. His painted plaster models of anatomy and pathological specimens for the Cleveland Medical College were admired for their precision, and several medical schools commissioned models from him. Locally, he sculpted portrait busts of his friend Dr. JARED KIRTLAND and others.

Garlick's insatiable curiosity led him to widely varied avocations. In 1820, he and his brother excavated an Indian mound on the southeast corner of Euclid and Erie streets, possibly Cleveland's first archeological dig. Following Daguerre's methods, he built a camera and, in Dec. 1839, made the first photograph in the WESTERN RESERVE, a landscape, using a silvered brass plate. He accomplished some of the first photographic portraits without sunlight and produced the first daguerreotype in Cleveland 9 Sept. 1841. Garlick was an avid fisherman and coauthored essays on angling. Accounts of artificial fish breeding by French scientists interested him in the idea of controlling reproduction in food fish. He experimented at Dr. Ackley's farm outside of Cleveland and, in 1853, successfully fertilized trout eggs in vitro. Ackley helped him build a series of ponds and flumes—the country's first fish hatchery. Garlick presented his findings in lectures, exhibits, and a series of articles for the *Ohio Farmer*, published in 1857 as *A Treatise on the Artificial Propagation of Certain Kinds of Fish*. The book detailed fertilization, hatching, stocking, hatchery construction, and fly fishing, and included discussions of trout, bass, perch, pickerel, sunfish, and eels. The U.S. Fish Commission acknowledged his pioneering efforts in 1880. At age 75, Garlick took up Greek, and within 2 years he was able to translate the Bible. He died in Bedford in 1884. He was married 3 times; his first 2 wives were daughters of a Brookfield mentor. Several of his children pursued medical careers. He served on the Board of Censors of the Cleveland Medical College and was a founder of the CLEVELAND ACADEMY OF NATURAL SCIENCES.

"Theodatus A. Garlick," *Nineteenth Annual Meeting of the Western Reserve and Northern Ohio History Society* (May 1869).

**GARMENT INDUSTRY.** As early as 1860, the manufacture of ready-to-wear clothing became one of Cleveland's leading industries. The garment industry probably reached its peak during the 1920s, when Cleveland ranked close to New York as one of the country's leading centers for garment production. During the Depression and continuing after WORLD WAR II, the garment industry in Cleveland declined. Scores of plants moved out of the area, were sold, or closed their doors. Local factors certainly played their part, but the rise of the ready-to-wear industry in Cleveland, as well as its decline, paralleled the growth and decline of the industry nationwide. Thus, the story of the garment industry in Cleveland is a local or regional variant of a much broader phenomenon. In the early 19th century, clothing was still handmade, produced for the family by women in the household or custom-made for the more well-to-do by tailors and seamstresses. The first production of ready-to-wear garments was stimulated by the needs of sailors, slaves, and miners. Although still hand-produced, this early ready-to-wear industry laid the foundations for the vast expansion and mechanization of the industry that occurred after mid-century. The ready-to-wear industry grew enormously from the 1860s to the 1880s, and for a variety of reasons. Increasing mechanization was one factor. In addition, systems for sizing men's and boys' clothing were highly developed, based on millions of measurements obtained by the U.S. Army during the CIVIL WAR. Eventually, accurate sizing for women's clothing was also developed. The Depression of 1873 contributed to the growth and growing acceptance of men's ready-to-wear, because men found in off-the-rack garments a satisfactory and less costly alternative to custom-made clothing. The production of ready-made men's trousers or "pants," separate from suits, was also stimulated during the depression of the 1870s. Separate trousers allowed men to supplement their outfit without having to purchase a complete suit. In general, however, the great expansion of the ready-to-wear industry coincided with and was partly the result of the tremendous urbanization and the great wave of immigrants that the U.S. experienced in the last decades of the 19th century and the early decades of the 20th. That was the period in which industrial cities such as Cleveland also experienced rapid growth, and it was during this period that Cleveland's ready-to-wear clothing industry was launched and blossomed.

Stimulated by the needs of the military during the Civil War, the garment industry in Cleveland continued to grow in the postwar years. In general, the first clothing manufacturers started out as retailers. The early entrepreneurs of the clothing industry in Cleveland were often JEWS of German or Austro-Hungarian extraction. Their previous experience in retailing prepared them for the transition to manufacturing and wholesaling and for the great opportunities of the ready-to-wear industry. One example was Kaufman Koch, a clothing retailer whose firm eventually evolved into the JOSEPH & FEISS CO., a leading manufacturer of men's clothing. The company still exists in the late 1980s, although it is no longer locally owned. The entry-level manufacturer needed relatively little capital to launch a garment factory. H. Black & Co., which would become a major Cleveland manufacturer of women's suits and cloaks, started out as a notions house. The Black family, Jews of Hungarian origin, decided to produce ready-to-wear clothing based on European patterns in their own home. Later, fabric was contracted out to home sewers and then returned to the factory for final assembly. The system of contracting out to home sewers was widely practiced at this stage of the garment industry's development. By the close of the 19th century, home work had been generally superseded by factory production. Garment manufacturing started in the FLATS on Water St. By the early

433

20th century, it was concentrated in what is now called the WAREHOUSE DISTRICT, an area bounded by W. 6th and W. 9th streets and Lakeside and Superior avenues. One company that established itself in the growing garment district between W. 6th and W. 9th was the L. N. Gross Co. Founded in 1900, it specialized in the production of women's shirtwaists. In the 1890s, many women wore suits. The separate shirtwaist provided a relatively inexpensive way to modify and vary their wardrobe. By 1900, women were wearing the shirtwaist and skirt popularized by Chas. Dana Gibson and the "Gibson Girl." L. N. Gross pioneered in the specialization and division of labor in the manufacturing process. Instead of having one person produce an entire garment, each garment worker specialized in one procedure, and then the entire garment was assembled. L. N. Gross continues to operate in the 1980s, although in 1984 ownership passed from the Gross family to other Cleveland investors.

The garment industry was concentrated in the Warehouse District, but it spread to other areas of the city as well, on both the east and west sides. For example, the landmark building of the CLEVELAND WORSTED MILLS dominates the skyline on Broadway near E. 55th St. First organized in the 1870s and controlled after 1893 by KAUFMAN HAYS, a leading Cleveland businessman of German-Jewish extraction and by other Cleveland businessmen, the Worsted Mills produced fabric for Cleveland manufacturers as well as for garment manufacturers in other parts of the country. The company owned and operated a total of 11 mills in Ohio and on the East Coast. During the first 3 decades of the 20th century, the garment industry spread from downtown to the east side along Superior Ave. between E. 22nd and E. 26th. One of the outstanding structures in that area was the Wooltex Co. plant, a portion of which subsequently housed the Tower Press. The RICHMAN BROS. CO. built a large plant on E. 55th St. near St. Clair. The company was founded in Portsmouth, Ohio, and in the late 1890s moved to the thriving industrial metropolis of Cleveland. Richman Bros. specialized in the production of men's suits and coats, an activity in which Cleveland was a close runner-up to New York. In order to reduce the risk of large cancellations by wholesalers, Richman distributed its product directly to the customer in its own retail outlets. The plants of other garment manufacturers dotted the east side well into the 1960s, including BOBBIE BROOKS on Perkins Ave. and the Dalton Co. at E 66th and Euclid. The PRINTZ-BIEDERMAN CO. had been founded in 1893 by Moritz Printz, for many years the chief designer for H. Black & Co. Printz-Biederman specialized in the production of women's suits and coats, a branch of the garment industry in which Cleveland ranked second to New York. Located first on St. Clair opposite the main fire station, moving later to a larger St. Clair location between W. 3rd and W. 6th streets, in 1934 the company built a larger modern factory on E. 61st between Euclid and Chester. The large knitwear firm of Bamberg-Reinthal built a plant on Kinsman at E. 61st. Joseph & Feiss was located on the west side on W. 53rd, Federal Knitting had a plant on W. 28th and Detroit, and the Phoenix Dye Works was still located on W. 150th St. in 1986.

For approximately 50 years after the 1890s, about 7% of Cleveland's workforce toiled in the garment factories. The ethnic origins of those who worked in the industry were as varied as the immigrants who flowed to the U.S. in the early decades of the 20th century. Jewish workers played a prominent role in this period, but other immigrant groups such as CZECHS, POLES, GERMANS, and ITALIANS were also employed in large numbers. Many of the garment factories were located in ethnic neighborhoods,

from which they drew their workforce. Examples include Joseph & Feiss, LION KNITTING MILLS, Cleveland Worsted Mills, and the Richman Bros. Co. These companies, though not with the original owners, were still operating in the late 1980s. Small workshops also proliferated in the ethnic neighborhoods, and many garment workers labored in sweatshop conditions. Unlike in New York, however, where the majority of shops employed 5 or fewer workers, by 1910, 80% of Cleveland's approximately 10,000 apparel workers were employed in large and well-equipped factories. Although working conditions were somewhat better in Cleveland than in New York, Cleveland garment workers generally received low wages and worked long hours with few, if any, benefits. Like garment workers in New York and elsewhere, they sought to improve their wages and working conditions by organizing. In 1900, a number of small craft and trade unions joined together in New York City to form the INTERNATL. LADIES GARMENT WORKERS UNION. This union spearheaded organizing activities throughout the industry. In Cleveland, 1911 was a critical year in labor history. Garment workers staged a massive strike. On 6 June the employees of H. Black & Co. walked out, and up to 6,000 of Cleveland garment workers followed them. The ILGWU sent officials from New York to encourage the strikers. In spite of considerable support for the strikers in the community at large, the owners resisted. Attempts to negotiate a settlement failed, and by October those who could returned to work. The strike had been lost (see GARMENT WORKERS STRIKE OF 1911).

During WORLD WAR I, the garment industry produced a variety of apparel to keep the soldiers and sailors in uniform and to keep them warm. Wartime inflation and prosperity prompted the ILGWU to organize another massive work stoppage in Cleveland involving approximately 5,000 workers. To avoid a long strike that might jeopardize the production of military uniforms, Secretary of War and former Cleveland mayor NEWTON D. BAKER intervened, prevailing on both sides to accept a board of referees. The board then gave the workers a substantial increase in wages. This event marked a watershed in relations between management and labor in Cleveland's garment industry. Because of the threat of unionization, and because of the influence of "Taylorism" or "Scientific Management," large Cleveland garment factories began to provide a variety of amenities for their workers. This process had begun before 1920 but reached a peak during that decade. Of special importance in this movement was Joseph & Feiss. Paul Feiss, in particular, was a convinced exponent of scientific management. Time and motion studies were implemented in order to make production more efficient and cost-effective; working conditions were improved in order to reduce employee turnover and to provide the best possible environment for maximum productivity. Thus, factories such as Joseph & Feiss or the Cleveland Worsted Mills began to provide clean and well-run cafeterias, clinics, libraries, and nurseries for children. Employees of both sexes were urged to participate in sports, theatricals, and other activities. The factory was also a place where immigrants became Americanized. They learned English and a variety of homemaking skills. One consequence of paternalism was a brake on the growth of unionism.

The Depression and the New Deal had a major impact on the garment industry. Many manufacturers did not survive the Depression. Those who did were faced with a powerful new labor movement bent on organizing the unorganized workers of many industries, including the garment industry. Bolstered by the provisions of the NRA and the Natl. Labor Relations Act, both the ILGWU and the

Amalgamated Clothing Workers, which represented workers in the men's garment factories, actively and successfully waged organizing campaigns. Some owners acquiesced. Others resisted, and that led to protracted, damaging strikes. Some owners used the occasion to simply close their doors. The process of decline in Cleveland's garment industry began during the Depression. During World War II, the industry was once again geared for war production. Factories produced uniforms, knit scarves, and parachutes. Lion Knitting Mills were famous for their production of the knitted Navy watch cap. Following the war, a number of garment manufacturers were unable to adjust to new market conditions and to new price levels. But while some companies fell by the way, new and vigorous garment factories grew, especially in the 1950s. Among them was Bobbie Brooks, founded by Morry Saltzman, and the Dalton Co., founded by Arthur Dery. In fact, the Cleveland garment industry was still so large and influential in the 1950s that Cleveland manufacturers were able to convince the Phoenix Dye Works of Chicago to relocate in Cleveland, where the company had so many customers. Throughout the years, other businesses ancillary to garment manufacturing also flourished in Cleveland.

The once-vigorous Cleveland garment industry has dwindled considerably since World War II, and especially since the 1960s and 1970s. Signs of trouble for the industry appeared even before World War II. By the 1970s, the decline accelerated. In some instances, management has transferred manufacturing operations elsewhere while retaining offices in Cleveland. In some cases an entire operation has moved from the Cleveland area, usually to the South. Many companies sold off all or part of their businesses or simply closed. In several parts of Cleveland, there exist substantial factory buildings that once housed portions of the garment industry. A few have been partially or completely recycled for other uses, while others stand empty and deserted. The reasons for this rather dramatic shift are complex and varied, some deriving from local conditions and some from conditions that are national or even global in nature and that have affected the industry as a whole throughout the U.S.

The garment industry is traditionally a low-paying industry, and rising labor costs aggravated the industry's problems. Some Cleveland manufacturers have suggested that unionization of garment workers significantly damaged the industry's ability to compete. It is true that most of the large Cleveland manufacturers were unionized, as much of the industry nationwide. In that sense, unionization itself did not necessarily mean that one company had an unfair advantage over another. On the other hand, the garment unions in Cleveland generally sought and received wage settlements above the national minimum. Labor costs were frequently lower in areas outside Cleveland, and even in New York manufacturers managed to cut labor costs. Labor costs were considerably less in the South, and Cleveland manufacturers as well as garment and textile workers throughout the U.S. faced and still (1986) face growing competition from lower-paid workers in other parts of the world. For example, knitwear and other textile products produced in South Korea, Taiwan, Hong Kong, or Singapore could be sold in the U.S. at considerably less than the same products manufactured in the U.S. Another factor that may have played a role in discouraging some Cleveland manufacturers was the changing workforce. In the early years of the century, and until the 1950s and 1960s, many women workers had a limited number of employment opportunities. That was particularly true for the European immigrant women who dominated the workforce of the garment industry. By the 1950s, 1960s, and 1970s, there

was a new generation of women working who had many more employment opportunities at wages much higher than could be earned in the garment industry. It was thus more difficult to find a suitable workforce at wages the garment industry could afford to pay. Some authorities in the industry contend that, in fact, while labor costs in Cleveland were relatively high in comparison with some regions, there were additional factors that also contributed to the industry's decline. For example, some family-owned concerns were sold or simply dissolved when family shareholders could no longer agree on management decisions. In other cases, the heirs preferred some profession or occupation other than the garment industry.

The apparel industry is extremely competitive. It is also subject to changes in technology and to the rapidly changing conditions of the marketplace. Cleveland firms often did not or could not respond with sufficient alacrity or astuteness to such changing conditions. Cleveland was perhaps too divorced from the center of the market in New York. It lacked a regional market of importance, and thus many manufacturers lost touch with what consumers wanted. When the price structure changed after World War II, some companies foundered, unable to sell the same garments to the same customers at about twice the prewar price. Sometimes manufacturers had to aim at new markets and constantly modify or develop new products to meet new market conditions or to develop new markets. Some companies were unable to respond to a shifting and rapidly changing marketplace. Until the 1950s, all the major fabric houses had representatives in Cleveland. In 1986 there were none. New York has come to dominate the industry as both a marketplace and a manufacturing center. Substantial Cleveland manufacturers must have a presence in New York and must constantly study and test the marketplace trends in New York City. There are other important regional markets such as Dallas and Los Angeles, thus moving the focus of the industry away from Cleveland. Perhaps that is part of a larger underlying transformation of the American economy resulting in the loss of preeminence of the older industrial centers of the Great Lakes region and Middle West. On the other hand, Cleveland garment manufacturers who take advantage of new technologies, who learn to cut costs, and who learn to respond effectively to the marketplace may still survive and even flourish.

Stanley Garfinkel
Kent State University

See also LABOR.

The **GARMENT WORKERS' STRIKE** OF 1911 began on 7 June when 4,000 workers took to the streets to picket for improved working conditions in their factories. The strike was planned and executed by the INTERNATL. LADIES GARMENT WORKERS UNION. Though Cleveland ranked 4th among American cities in garment production, the union felt that it would be the best city in which to organize, as it still rivaled New York in its importance as a supplier to the national market. The workers' demands, presented to the individual employing companies on 3 June, included a 50-hour week with Saturday afternoons and Sundays off, no charges for the use of machines and materials, and a closed shop on subcontracting. The employers categorically rejected all of the demands and refused arbitration.

The 4-month strike was marked by violence. Strikers surrounded and stoned the Printz-Biederman factory and, at one time, tried to drag an accused strikebreaker out of her home. The local newspapers, which had initially supported the strikers, slowly turned against them as the violence continued. While the real causes of the violence cannot be accurately determined, there is evidence that the manufacturers encouraged such action in order to turn sentiment against the strikers. One member of the picket committee later admitted that he had been paid $10 a day and all expenses by the Cloak Mfrs.' Assoc. to instigate violence. In addition to the violence, other factors worked against the strikers. The employers were able to continue to fill their orders by contracting to other shops in smaller communities in Ohio. They were also able to buy and sell in the New York market. Unable to meet the financial requirements of the strikers, the international finally called off the action in Oct. 1911, without gaining any concessions. The strike cost the unions more than $300,000. For several years after, the union was unable to organize worker support against the Garment Mfrs.' Assoc. in Cleveland.

**GARVIN, CHARLES H.** (27 Oct. 1890–17 July 1968), was a distinguished physician, civic leader, and businessman in Cleveland. His interest in black social and economic programs was particularly notable. Garvin was born in Jacksonville, Fla., where he received his early education. He attended Atlanta University and graduated from Howard University and its medical school in 1915. He lived and practiced medicine in Cleveland from 1916 until his death. During WORLD WAR I, he became the first black physician commissioned in the U.S. Army, serving in France as a commanding officer in the 92d Div. Garvin's interest in medicine extended beyond his practice to research and writing numerous articles for medical journals. His avocation, tracing the history of Africans and Afro-Americans in the field of medicine, led him to amass an important collection of books on the black experience. He also completed a manuscript (unpublished as of 1986) and wrote several articles on the subject. His account of the history of blacks in medicine in Cleveland was published in 1939 in the *Women's Voice,* a national women's magazine. An article published in the *Journal of Negro Education* recounted the experience of blacks in the special services of the U.S. Army during World War I. Garvin was active in the local black business community. He was a founder of the Dunbar Life Insurance Co. and helped organize the QUINCY SAVINGS & LOAN CO., where he served as a director and chairman of the board. He was also a pioneer in integrated housing during a period of intense racial separation in the city. Despite threats of violence and 2 bombings, he remained determined to live in the home he had built on Wade Park Ave., at that time an exclusive allotment. His experience became a symbol for blacks in the city and the nation. As a civic leader, Garvin served as a trustee of KARAMU HOUSE, the URBAN LEAGUE OF CLEVELAND, and the Cleveland branch of the NAACP. He was appointed by the Cleveland Board of Education to be a trustee of the CLEVELAND PUBLIC LIBRARY in 1938, serving as board president in 1940 and 1941. He also served as national president of the Alpha Phi Alpha fraternity.

Chas. Garvin Papers, WRHS.

**GASSAWAY, HAROLD T.** (5 Aug. 1893–13 Apr. 1952), was a black Cleveland lawyer and city politician who represented Ward 18 as the Republican leader. He served as an alternate delegate to the Republican Natl. Convention from 1940. His political platform demanded good government efficiently administered. Gassaway was a prominent figure in Cleveland's developing black community, involving himself in numerous church, fraternal, and civic organizations. Born in Anderson, S.C., Gassaway adopted

Cleveland as his home in the early 1920s. He was educated in the public schools of Anderson until his education was interrupted by WORLD WAR I, when he served as a sergeant in the 349th Field Artillery, serving 9 months in France and 4 weeks on the western front. Following his discharge, Gassaway continued his education at Clark University, from which he graduated, and then at Howard University in Washington, D.C., where he received his law degree in 1922. Admitted to the Ohio bar in 1923, Gassaway opened his first office in Cleveland, practicing in all the courts.

A growing black population during the early 1920s localized black political strength in wards 11 and 12, located west of E. 55th and south of Euclid to KINGSBURY RUN. By the late 1920s, the area east of E. 55th between Euclid and Woodland avenues was settled by BLACKS in sufficient numbers to enable black leaders to take control of the Republican party organization in this area, which included wards 17, 18, and 19. Against this background, Gassaway decided to enter the political arena. In 1928, a struggle for control of Ward 18 developed between CLAYBORNE GEORGE and Gassaway, who had been elected president of the Ward 18 Republican Club over opposition from George. Together with L. L. Yancy, then ward leader, Gassaway assumed control of Ward 18 and backed John Hubbard for council. From 1939 until his retirement from politics in 1951 because of declining health, Gassaway served as councilman from Ward 18, succeeding in every election year. When not in the political limelight, Gassaway busied himself as senior partner of the firm of Gassaway, Collum, Tyler & Kellogg, located in the Prospect & 4th Bldg. He was a member of the Cleveland, Cuyahoga, and American bar associations. In addition, he served as president of his own business, the Gassaway Broom Mfg. Co. Gassaway married former schoolteacher Ethel Sutton of Pomeroy, Ohio, in 1926. He was survived by her and their 2 daughters, Margaret and Carol, all of whom resided at 2317 E. 85th St. in Cleveland.

**GATES, HOLSEY or HALSEY** (1797–2 Nov. 1865), was, with his brothers, an early settler in Mayfield Twp. The village of GATES MILLS was named after him. Gates came to the WESTERN RESERVE from Delhi, N.Y., in 1826. He brought with him gearing for a sawmill; additional machinery and lumber were hauled from Cleveland, and in 6 weeks construction of the mill was completed. The next year he added a gristmill, and with these 2 essential industries Gates Mills became a center for settlement. In later years Gates rebuilt the gristmill; he also dismantled the sawmill and rented it out as a rake factory. Other buildings that he built included the Gates Mills Inn (now part of the CHAGRIN VALLEY HUNT CLUB) and the Gates Mills Methodist Episcopal Church (now St. Christopher's-by-the-River). Gates contributed $800 of the $1,300 needed to build the church. The wooden-pegged floorboards were cut in his mill. In 1834, Gates was appointed the first postmaster in Gates Mills. For 1 year he carried the mail between the village and Cleveland. He also surveyed the first road connecting those places. Gates married Lucy Ann Bralley; the union produced 9 children.

**GATES MILLS** is a village located in the Chagrin Valley and bounded by MAYFIELD HTS. on the west, Geauga County on the east, and HUNTING VALLEY on the south. Originally part of Mayfield Twp., it occupies 8.8 sq. mi. Gates Mills was founded in 1826 by HOLSEY GATES, who bought 130 acres of Chagrin River land from the CONNECTICUT LAND CO. in order to have a good water supply for a sawmill. The excellent location and abundant water supply led to the construction of several more mills, which gave the area its name. AGRICULTURE flourished, and potash, cheese, and rake factories were established. By 1850, Gates Mills was a thriving community exporting manufactured products. The area had mail service, a school, a tavern, and an organized social and religious life. During the post-CIVIL WAR period, the water-powered mills languished, and the vitality of the village declined. In the 1890s, Cleveland professional men such as S. Prentiss Baldwin, FRANK GINN, and FRANK WALKER established the village as their country retreat. These men backed the Maple Leaf Land Co., which promoted the village, and the Cleveland & Eastern interurban railway, which connected the village with Cleveland in 1899. The Gates Mills Improvement Society, formed in 1905, was primarily made up of landowners, who shaped the exclusive, well-to-do New England character that Gates Mills maintained into the 1980s. The CHAGRIN VALLEY HUNT CLUB was formed in 1909 and occupied the old Holsey Gates house. The village of Gates Mills was incorporated in 1920, and Frank Walker was the first mayor. In 1930, a village hall was built to house the police, fire, and streets departments. The village is governed by a mayor-council form of government. Little has changed the residential character of Gates Mills. Following the close of the mills, no new industry came into the area. Two churches, 2 PRIVATE SCHOOLS, 2 tennis courts, 1 library, and the N. Chagrin Reservation of the CLEVELAND METROPARKS SYSTEM serve the community of 2,236 residents.

**GAY COMMUNITY.** To the extent that a community can be defined by its organizations and institutions, Cleveland's gay community can be said to date from ca. 1970, when a chapter of the Gay Activists Alliance was formed at CASE WESTERN RESERVE UNIVERSITY. In one sense, the history of the community dates to whenever homosexuals first recognized one another and formed social ties. Groups of homosexuals were always aware of themselves as a separate underground society, and although that society became more visible in bars and other places that catered to this group in the years after WORLD WAR II, information on this society through the first three quarters of the 20th century is sketchy, largely anecdotal, and not relevant to the discussions of organized communities.

Cleveland's gay community, then, a group with a collective perception of itself as set apart from the rest of society by common interests and concerns reflected in its organizations, movement, and institutions, can date its earliest history to an event in New York City and the subsequent coalescence of social climate and perceived need in the late 1960s, which played a large role in creating what is identified as the gay community both in Cleveland and throughout the country. On 27 June 1969, a group of homosexuals defended themselves against a police raid on the Stonewall Inn in Greenwich Village, New York City. This "Stonewall Uprising" marked the first large public event demanding equal rights and protection for homosexuals. The movements for civil rights for BLACKS, women, and others, and the tone of liberal thought in the late 1960s and early 1970s, took this isolated event and set in motion a wave of activism that resulted in the movement for "gay rights," which saw the formation of groups, services, and institutions specifically geared to homosexuals as a community of interests. While the Cleveland chapter of the Gay Activists Alliance, that national organization that grew directly out of the Stonewall Uprising, did not last, another group was organized at CLEVELAND STATE UNIVERSITY, also ca. 1970, which became the Gay Educational & Awareness Resources Foundation. The GEAR Foundation originated not as a political group but as an edu-

cational and coordinating organization that developed into an umbrella agency for a variety of services, smaller organizations, and activities. A telephone hotline for counseling, referral, and information, support groups, a community center, counseling, and a publication, *High Gear*, have been among its many activities. Organizations for youth, lesbians, and other interest groups have operated under its aegis.

The activism of the early gay-rights movement took many forms. Most visible were the organizations in large cities, principally New York and San Francisco, that worked for social and political change, largely as a response to specific issues such as police harassment and job or housing discrimination. Much of the emphasis of the GEAR Foundation was on advocacy and service within the gay community, since harassment and discrimination were not overt or widespread in the Cleveland area, and since cooperation within the gay community was a prerequisite for effective work beyond. Without the kinds of provocation that stirred activism in other cities, and because the necessary cooperation was more a goal than an achievement, Cleveland has been judged a difficult city in which to be an activist. The GEAR Foundation's most visible work in the community has been its Community Ctr., providing meeting space for the various groups under the GEAR umbrella and space for services such as the hotline and counseling. The center was located for a time in a building at W. 14th St., and subsequently moved to Fulton Rd. near Lorain Ave. By 1986, after many years of budget constraints and strained resources, the foundation and its staff began to concentrate on a smaller number of services, thus encouraging less fragmentation. The public face of the foundation was renamed the Lesbian/Gay Community Service Ctr. and embraced a telephone hotline, an Ohio Dept. of Health AIDS hotline, a counseling center, rap groups, a youth group, and a speakers' bureau.

A much later organization in the Cleveland community responded swiftly to issues facing virtually all gay communities since the advent of the Acquired Immune Deficiency Syndrome (AIDS) epidemic, which affected a large number of gay men beginning in the early 1980s (principally in the gay population centers on the coasts) and which appeared in Cleveland at a slow but rising rate soon after. In 1982, a group of individuals concerned with the rising number of AIDS cases nationally and locally formed the Health Issues Task Force. The group, modeled on similar groups elsewhere, seeks to educate the entire community on AIDS issues and prevention, and strives to assist persons with AIDS in obtaining services and assistance. Active in the group are medical and social-service professionals and interested laypersons, gay and straight, reflecting the widespread concern in the community at large over the potential effects of the disease on the entire society. Through the efforts of the task force, a variety of educational events have been held, and in cooperation with UNIVERSITY HOSPITALS and the CLEVELAND CLINIC, a survey and clinical study were undertaken in the Cleveland area.

In any emergent community, publications play an important role in building any sense of cohesiveness. The newsletter *High Gear* was started by the GEAR Foundation in 1975 and was the first attempt to produce a newspaper exclusively for the gay community. Printed in tabloid form and circulated free at various points around the city, *High Gear* carried local and national news, various features and editorials, and advertising. Although beset at various times by financial and organizational difficulties, it survived until 1982. After its demise, the GEAR Foundation became involved in another publication, primarily an advertising medium with little editorial content, distributed at bars, and which was soon abandoned. In 1984, a new attempt at a gay newspaper began, known as the *Gay People's Chronicle*. It was an independent organization governed by a publication board, and published a mixture of editorial, feature, and national and local news in a monthly tabloid. Like its predecessor, it had a largely free distribution and a small list of subscribers.

A large variety of smaller and more specialized organizations have existed in the Cleveland gay community. Among the earliest were religious groups, both within mainline denominations and independent of them. The gay religious organizations sought to foster the support and acceptance normally sought from churches. In the early 1970s, a religious group called the Community of Celebration flourished for a time; it was succeeded by a chapter of the national organization for gay Catholics, Dignity. A local congregation of the Metropolitan Community church, a national denomination with a primarily gay membership, existed for a time (ca. 1973). The most lasting of the religious groups have been Dignity and the Episcopal organization Integrity, both of which continued to be active into the 1980s. A Jewish group known as Chevrei Tikvah began in 1983 and held many social functions as well as religious services. A new Protestant congregation was started in 1986 known as Emmanuel Community Christian Church. A club addressing political issues, orginally called the Eleanor Roosevelt Gay Democratic Club (and later changing *Democratic* to *Political*), was formed in 1980. It studied political issues, took stands on issues of importance to the gay community, endorsed candidates for office in local and state campaigns, and advocated civil-rights legislation on the local and state levels. As the movement has grown and provided increased visibility for the gay community, a number of organizations have come into existence with a specifically gay identity. At various times, volleyball and bowling leagues, social clubs, an archives and oral history project, a gay academic union, and an organization addressing gay and lesbian issues, known as the Gay & Lesbian Institute, existed. CWRU's Lesbian & Gay Student Union began sponsorship of an annual conference on gay and lesbian issues, which attracted nationally known speakers and significant audiences, and later was constituted as its own organization. Support groups for gay fathers, gay mothers, and parents of gays, as well as student groups at various Greater Cleveland colleges and universities, have assisted both gay and concerned straight people.

Included in any look at a homosexual community, but separate because of a variety of influences, is the lesbian community. Lesbian groups in Cleveland, as elsewhere, had close alliances to the women's-rights movement of the late 1960s and 1970s, and given the difference in concerns between feminist and gay reformers, it is probably only in the mid-1980s that dividing lines within the community became less pronounced. Collectives such as Oven Productions, which produced cultural events for women, coffeehouses, and the feminist publication collective *What She Wants* are representative of the alliance with the feminist movement and the activity of the lesbian community. Other groups are purely social and supportive. A lesbian group, LIGHT (Lesbians in GEAR Hanging Together), existed for a time as part of the GEAR Foundation, followed by the North Coast Lesbian Alliance in the early 1980s, ultimately leaving GEAR and operating independently, with involvement in the Women's Building Project in CLEVELAND HTS. Another independent group, Wonderful West Side Women, began in the early 1980s.

According to the accepted estimate that 10% of the population is homosexual, Greater Cleveland's gay community should have numbered approximately 150,000 persons in the 1980s. Included in this approximation are men and women of all races and classes living and working in virtually every part of the city, and involved in all aspects of the life of the city from the auto assembly lines to government, from cultural institutions to BUSINESS to SPORTS. Of this number, a large number are "in the closet," that is, not living openly gay lifestyles. Among both men and women, the population can be divided among those who are active in the organizations, those whose involvement in the community is through the bars and other social situations, and those who do not participate in the community at all, because of either lack of interest or fear of discovery. The last category embraces both individuals who are not out at all and those who confine their gay identity to private situations. Even allowing for a large closeted population and the overlap between these arbitrary distinctions, the gulf between the total population and those active in the organizations is significant. In general, the climate toward homosexuals has improved throughout the U.S., probably as a result of the increased visibility and education brought about by the gay-rights movement. There is certainly a larger openly gay population in most cities than ever before. Cleveland represents that improved climate, certainly not to the extent of the very general acceptance in cities the size of New York or San Francisco, or in similar forms, but rather in being a benign, generally open city with little or no police harassment, little visible housing or job discrimination, and generally high levels of respect and tolerance.

The gay community is somewhat visible and not without its impact on the life of the city. While no single ward or area has become a truly central gay area, at various times a number of areas of the city have housed large concentrations of gay population: Cleveland Hts., the area around SHAKER SQUARE, OHIO CITY, and the area around W. 117th St. and Clifton Blvd. in LAKEWOOD. In the early 1970s, many of the social activities became concentrated in a group of establishments on W. 6th and W. 9th streets north of Superior Ave. Formerly, a number of clubs had been located in the DOAN'S CORNERS area, and later several bars were scattered on the eastern fringes of downtown. Although not a highly organized or activist city for gay people, Cleveland continued into the 1980s to have an established, visible, and largely accepted gay community with significant involvement in the larger community and effective institutions of its own. Its contributions as a community do not have a long history, but certainly the work of organizations has been significant and has opened the door to further development of a cohesive community.

George D. Barnum
Case Western Reserve University Libraries

The **GENERAL ELECTRIC COMPANY,** a major manufacturer of electrical appliances and a leader in the development of electrical lighting, has maintained important manufacturing and research-and-development facilities in Cleveland since 1901. GE was established on 1 June 1892 by the consolidation of the Edison General Co. of Schenectady, N.Y., and the Thomson-Houston Electric Co. of Lynn, Mass. The latter firm had acquired Cleveland's Brush Electric Co., which was established in 1880 by lighting pioneer CHAS. F. BRUSH along with patent attorney Mortimer D. Leggett and Geo. W. Stockley, the firm's vice-president, treasurer, and business manager. As part of the new General Electric Co., the Brush Electric facilities at Mason (Hough) and Belden (E. 45th) streets became the home of a venture secretly entered into by GE: the Natl. Electric Lamp Assoc. (NELA).

Established on 3 May 1901 as the Natl. Electric Lamp Co. and renamed in 1906, NELA resulted from an agreement between small electric companies to pool their resources for research and development, share the results of these engineering efforts, and thus more effectively compete against industry giants GE and Westinghouse. Lacking the capital to establish such an operation, the originators of the plan—Franklin S. Terry of the Sunbeam Incandescent Lamp Co. of Chicago and Burton G. Tremaine of the Fostoria Incandescent Lamp Co. of Fostoria, Ohio—convinced GE president Chas. A. Coffin to finance their proposed business and leave control of its operations to the independent companies. Coffin agreed to do so if the agreement was kept secret and if the operation worked out of the former Brush plant. GE secretly owned 75% of NELA stock, and NELA moved into the Brush plant at E. 45th in 1902. GE's relationship with NELA remained a secret until an antitrust suit filed against GE by the federal government in 1911 forced the disclosure of the arrangement. GE then absorbed NELA as its Natl. Quality Lamp Works Div.

By 1911, the NELA facilities at E. 45th St. were no longer adequate, and Tremaine and Terry proposed building new, more spacious facilities in the countryside east of the city. On 18 Apr. 1913, GE moved its facilities from E. 45th St. into 7 new buildings in the nation's first industrial park, located on 37 acres of land in E. CLEVELAND. Called "the University of Light" because of its emphasis on research and development and its campuslike design, NELA PARK grew to include 24 major buildings located on 90 acres of land in 1963; the 300 people employed there in 1913 increased to more than 2,000 by 1963 and 2,800 in 1975. By 1931, GE had made Nela Park the headquarters of its Incandescent Lamp Dept. Between 1913–63, a constant ⅔ of the work performed at Nela Park involved research and development. The products developed there included high- and low-beam headlights for automobiles (1924), camera flashbulbs (1930), and the fluorescent lamp (1938). Since 1926, Nela Park engineers have also designed and constructed elaborate lighting displays at Christmas time. GE has also been responsible for lighting and decorating the national Christmas tree in Washington, D.C., since 1963.

GE has maintained various production facilities in Cleveland over the years, many involved in lampmaking. Among them in 1954 were the Pitney Glass Works, which began producing lightbulbs in 1919, making 65,000 a day; the Chemical Prods. Works, making fluorescent powders and chemicals; the Cleveland Weld Works; and a vacuum cleaner plant. The latter two operations were closed in 1972, as was a refractory metals laboratory that had opened in 1955. GE employed a total of 7,000 workers in Cleveland in 1954. In 1983 the company announced plans to close the Cuyahoga Lamp Plant at Nela Park and to reduce operations at other local plants as part of a consolidation of its manufacturing operations to eliminate the firm's excess capacity. The move left a total of 5,500 employees in Cleveland-area GE facilities.

**GENUTH, DAVID L.** (12 Apr. 1901–23 Feb. 1974), rabbi and Jewish community leader, was one of Cleveland's most influential Orthodox rabbis for 4 decades. Born in Marmoresh Sziget, Hungary, Genuth received a traditional yeshiva education before coming to the U.S. in 1924. He continued his studies at Yeshiva University in New York and Yale University Divinity School in New Haven, Conn. Genuth was ordained in 1926 and subsequently accepted a pulpit in South Norwalk, Conn. In 1931 he moved to Cleveland, where in 1933 he was called by a group of Marmoresher landsmen to serve as rabbi at the newly es-

tablished KINSMAN JEWISH CTR. He combined a modern view of Orthodoxy with an ability to cope with the radical labor element at the KJC to forge the center into one of the city's most important Orthodox congregations. In 1948, Genuth left the KJC and with 8 families established Temple Beth El, the first congregation in SHAKER HTS. Beth El was a family-centered congregation; its popularity grew until in 1966 it could boast 500 families. An ardent Zionist, Genuth was a member of the Cleveland Zionist Society and an active supporter of the Jewish Natl. Fund and Bonds for Israel. Other communal involvements included being one of the organizers of the Jewish Community Council and serving as a representative to its delegate assembly. Additionally, he was chaplain for Jewish patients at Highland View Hospital, gave monthly lectures at the MONTEFIORE HOME, and provided bar mitzvah lessons for the deaf and mentally retarded. Genuth married Anne Einhorn, the daughter of Rabbi Henry Einhorn of New Haven, prior to moving to Cleveland. They had 3 children, Saul, Phyllis, and Esther.

**GEOLOGY & NATURAL RESOURCES.** The city of Cleveland, Ohio, sits at the junction of 2 major land types. From the Portage Escarpment lying to the southeast and east of the city, the glaciated Allegheny Plateau rises in gradually higher ridges to the Appalachian Crest in Virginia, Kentucky, and Pennsylvania. To the west the Central Lowlands roll across the prairies of Illinois to the trans-Mississippi plains. Abutting the Portage Escarpment and overlapping the Central Lowlands plains, a series of ancient lake beds and beach ridges lie across the northern 2 to 6 mi. of the region. These extend up the Cuyahoga Valley nearly as far south as Akron. Within northeast Ohio, all mineral and stone sources are sedimentary. The closest nonsedimentary minerals are the upper surfaces of the igneous and metamorphic basement rock buried at depths approaching 6,000'. These may have recrystallized as much as 2 billion years ago, during the Precambrian eons. During the Ordovician period from ca. 600–500 million years ago, the area from Indiana through New York formed a vast but narrowing tropical sea off the coast of an ancient continent. The first deposits were lime from shells, then silty clays washed from the land to the southeast. As the basin grew shallower, sands and then fragments of the corals and limey reefs that grew in the warm waters were deposited. Continental uplift and the development of volcanic island arcs resulted in the formation of shallow and brackish marine bays during the following Silurian period (500–400 million years ago). These formed the earliest sedimentary rocks in the area, called the Albion or Newburgh sandstones and silty limestones. Within those basins, rapid evaporation crystallized and deposited more lime, then thick layers of salts and thin lenses of gypsum and dolomite, the Middle Salina formation of interbedded siltstone, rock salt, dolomite, and gypsum; and the lower Niagara (reef) dolomite.

During the Devonian and Mississippian periods, from 400–300 million years ago, continued erosion from the continent to the north and northeast began filling the shallow seas with red, gray, and black clays and with limey silts. Finally, vast channels and deltas cut through and spread across the exposed mudflats and then filled with sand. Today these sediments have been compressed into the bedded Mississippian deposits of siltstones and shales belonging to the Cuyahoga Formation; the deltaic sandstones of the Berea Formation; and, still lower, the silty shales of the Cuyahoga Formation. These are underlain by the lithographic Cleveland shales, which yield the world-famous fish fauna. In the areas east of Cleveland, or where major tributaries

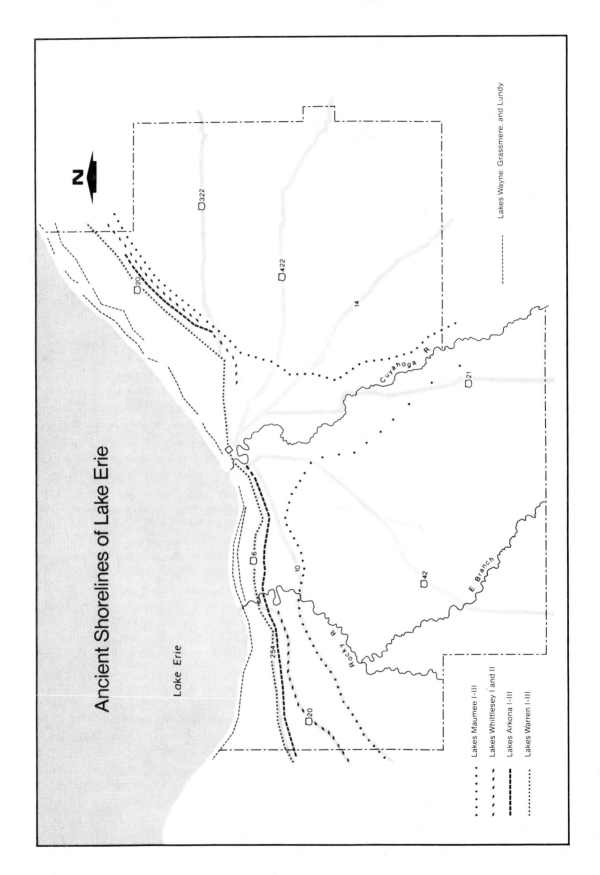

# Ancient Shorelines of Lake Erie

Lake Erie

Lakes Wayne, Grassmere, and Lundy

Lakes Maumee I-III
Lakes Whittlesey I and II
Lakes Arkona I-III
Lakes Warren I-III

Cuyahoga R

ROCKY R

E Branch

322
422
14
20
21
42
6
10
254
20

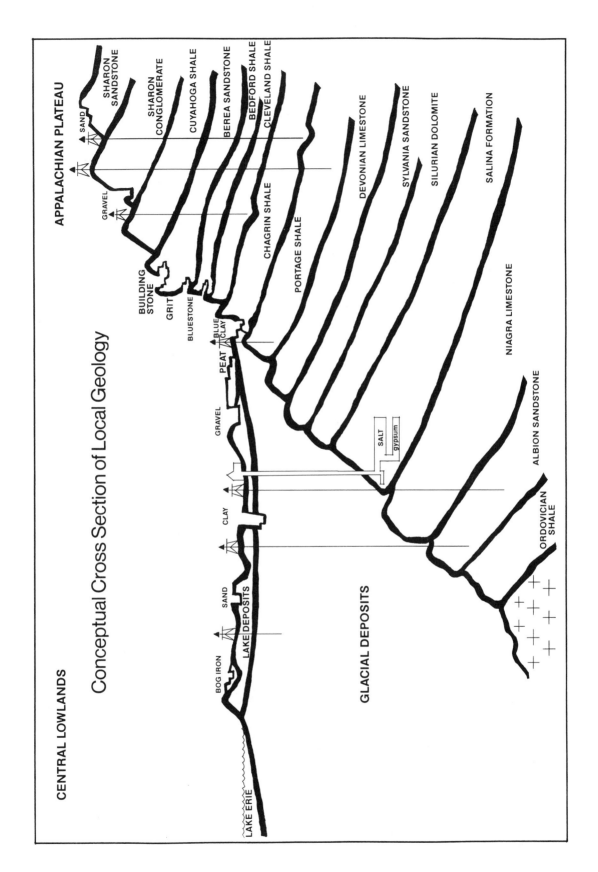

Conceptual Cross Section of Local Geology

441

cut down to meet the Cuyahoga, the exposed bases of these bedrock deposits are the Devonian shales of the Chagrin Formation. Below the Chagrin shale lies the Devonian series of Huron/Portage shales, Bass Island limestone, and, at the base, the Sylvania silica sandstone. Throughout the Pennsylvanian period from 300–200 million years ago, fluctuating and gradually deepening seas in turn covered these deposits with an alternating series of thin organic iron and limey silts; thin stringers of bituminous coal; and finally a thick series of coarse sands and gravels. Today these sediments have been compressed into the Sharon sandstone and conglomerate of the Pottsville series.

Ca. 180 million years ago, the slow collision of the African and North American continental plates crumpled these earlier deposits, tilting them up to the west, and finally lifting the entire Apalachian Plateau above sea level. Erosion replaced sedimentation in the region of northern Ohio until the last onset of continental glaciation during the Pleistocene epoch, beginning ca. 1.3 million years ago. During that epoch, glacial ice expanded southward from the Laurentian Highlands to override northern Ohio. Alternating advances and retreats stripped the soils and ground down the rock outcrops of the Allegheny Plateau, filling the highland valleys and central lowlands with deposits of sands and gravels, clays and boulders. Little evidence of the earliest glacial events, prior to 250,000 years ago, or the soils developed in interglacial times is preserved in northern Ohio. In general, the glacial advances followed the topography of the underlying bedrock but smoothed it out. During several periods of late glacial history, drainage to the north was blocked by melting ice, resulting in ice-dammed lakes that drained to the south across this region. Some remnants of sands and gravels washed from Illinoian glaciers, ca. 200,000 years ago, remain in the area. However, most of those deposits were removed by the later Wisconsinan ice advances, which began ca. 125,000 years ago. During that Wisconsinan glacial period, thick deposits of sand and silt mixed with boulders, gravels, and pockets of clay washed from the melting ice were left on the eroded surface of the Central Lowland province, west of the escarpment of the Allegheny Plateau. These deposits are called "drift" or till. Ice from what is called the Erie Lobe made 5 different readvances into the northeastern Ohio region during the Wisconsinan event. These advances were separated into 2 different lobes of ice by resistant outcrops of sedimentary rock. The margins of those lobes of glacial ice, which joined south of Canton, influenced the location of the early headwaters of the CUYAHOGA RIVER. The Killbuck ice advanced from the northwest, while the Grand River ice advanced southward through the Grand River lowland. The sequence of meltwater deposits comprises Mogodore till; Kent till; Lavery till; Hiram till; and Ashtabula till. Most of Cuyahoga County is covered by clays, sands, and gravels deposited as Hiram till more than 14,500 years ago.

The major event shaping the modern local drainage systems began when the ice melted northward from the Akron region, leaving a boundary ridge of drift called the Wabash End Moraine ca. 16,000 years ago. This moraine stood for 10,000 years as a drainage divide between the southward-flowing upper Cuyahoga River and Lake Erie. An ancient Lake Cuyahoga was ponded between the Wabash Moraine and the retreating Hiram-age ice. During a subsequent readvance of the Hiram ice ca. 14,800 years ago, the Defiance Moraine was deposited just north of Peninsula. When this ice began to retreat again ca. 14,300 years ago, another short-lived lake, called Lake Independence, was formed. The major fill of the Cuyahoga Valley between Cleveland and Akron consists of the deposits from

these two lakes. Lake Cuyahoga sediments extended to a height of 970′ above mean sea level, and Lake Independence deposits occur below 800′. Even after the northward retreat of the ice into Canada, minor climatic fluctuations resulted in changing water levels of the Great Lakes. These changes were related to shifts in the edges of the Canadian ice sheets, as well as to the downcutting of some lake outlets and the rising of others owing to the slow rebound of the earth's crust, freed of the weight of miles of ice. The changes in the lake levels resulted alternately in erosion or deposition in the river valleys.

From ca. 14,000–12,500 years ago, the basin of Lake Erie was occupied by a gradually falling series of large lakes, all at higher elevations than the modern Lake Erie. Erosion and deposition along the southern shore of these lakes formed wave-cut terraces and beach ridges that generally parallel the modern lakeshore. Lakes Maumee I-III were at elevations that, between 14,500–14,100 years ago, fell from 780 to 764′ above sea level (represented today by Lorain Rd. west of the Cuyahoga and Johnny Cake Ridge Rd. at the eastern edge of the county). Ca. 13,800 years ago, Lakes Whittlesey I and II were formed at elevations between 740 and 730′ above sea level (Center Ridge Rd.). Lakes Arkona I-III were formed between 13,600–13,300 years ago at elevations from 711 to 690′ above sea level (modern wave-cut Terrace Rd. in E. CLEVELAND and the Franklin-Hilliard Rd. beach ridge west of the Cuyahoga). A further drop to elevations of 686 and 670′ above sea level formed Lakes Warren I-III between 13,000–12,900 years ago (modern Detroit and Euclid avenues, as well as modern Mentor Rd.). Between 12,900–12,600 years ago, the opening of the Niagara Falls outlet resulted in a rapidly lowering series of lakes (Wayne, Grassmere, and Lundy), which are not marked by strong or continuous beaches much east of Cleveland. (Today's Clifton and Lake roads, St. Clair Ave., and Lake Shore and Lakeland boulevards generally follow these ancient beach ridges.) By 12,200 years ago, the inflow of water from the upper Great Lakes had been diverted northeast, and the level of early Lake Erie had fallen 40 meters below the modern level of 571′ above sea level (to about 440′ above sea level). There was a slow rise to a near-modern level of 565′ between ca. 4,500–2,500 b.c. It was during this period that erosion to the lowered lake levels downcut the old southern divide, enabling the upper Cuyahoga to join the flow northward into Lake Erie, the last major geological event to affect this area. Beyond shaping the topography, these geological events have been responsible for the materials of economic significance to Cleveland's future development.

Throughout the Cleveland area, many of the glacial sediments and some of the rock layers carry water. The till plains and the western outlier of the Glaciated Appalachian Plateau also contain major subsurface water resources within the ancient buried river valleys filled by more recent glacial deposits. The Cuyahoga, Rocky, and Chagrin rivers and their major tributaries in places cut through postglacial soils into the underlying bedrock. Throughout the region, these soils had developed differentially over the past 12,000 years. Their specific forms are dependent upon the local "bedrock," the slope and drainage, and the climate and vegetation. On the uplands of the Allegheny Plateau, most soils are of glacial origin, derived from sand and gravel till mixed with fragments of the shale or sandstone bedrock. These poorly drained upland soils are rather unproductive heavy clay loam. Occasional patches of more well-drained sandy soils exist as small terraces along some large streams. In areas near the glacial moraines, or on the lakeshore behind the beach ridges themselves, soils range from sandy clay loam to coarse sandy gravels. Along the slopes of the escarpment rimming the city of Cleveland, erosion prevents soil development, and the surface consists of poorly consolidated shales and sandstones. Upon the Central Lowland till plains, as well as within most of the Cuyahoga River Valley and many of its larger tributaries that flow across the old lake beds, soils consist of a mixture of sands, gravels, clays, and silts. Dry sandy soils characterize most of the rest of this zone. Prior to drainage, the clayey subsoils were considered unproductive. The occasional floodplain terraces that occur along the Cuyahoga and lower Chagrin and Rocky rivers represent long, narrow soil zones of deep, well-drained, sandy silt loams. These are the major fertile soils in the region and have always been considered prime agricultural land. Equally productive, although of limited extent in the region of Cleveland, were the ancient beach ridges and the fragile and quickly depleted organically rich peat-filled lakes. The latter occurred scattered from the old Collamer Bog, near the present COLLINWOOD RAILROAD YARDS, to Lake Abrahams, near the Internatl. Airport.

Naturally, the mineral resources of the more recent, exposed sediments were the earliest to be exploited. Extensive deposits of sands, gravels, and clays occur so widely across most of the region that there has never been commercial centralization. Iron-rich deposits of yellowish or bluish glacial clays occurred in pockets from 3–75' thick throughout the till plains. In the early 19th century, these were extracted from open pits and locally fired for earthenware. The ancient beach ridges provided an easily obtainable source of well-sorted quartzite sands, which were exploited as aggregate and were used as early as 1802 for glassmaking. The old Cuyahoga River delta deposits on the Central Lowlands and, on the plateau, numerous kames (glacial steam deposits) yielded gravels used first as road metals, and subsequently for concrete.

Two rather ephemeral surface deposits were also significant in Cleveland's early history. On several portions of the Central Lowland till plains, as well as at a few locations along the lakeshore to the east of Painesville, old postglacial "kettle" lakes had filled with organic peat. First avoided, then exploited as truck gardens for the growing urban population of the early 20th century, these deposits were being cut and dried to be sold as fertilizer for landscaping by the 1930s. While "Lake Abrahams" was the largest, other peat bogs existed in N. OLMSTED, in E. Cleveland, at Dover and Middle Ridge, at Columbia Ctr., just south of the Berea railroad station, and southeast of Northfield. Far more significant for Cleveland's long-term economy were the deposits of bog iron scattered across northeastern Ohio. First encountered as aberrant compass readings during the original land survey of Bath Twp. in Summit County, larger deposits, economically exploitable by open-pit mining, were found behind the old Lake Arkona beach ridges from Cleveland east to Conneaut. Open-hearth furnaces at Painesville and Ashtabula were processing some of the surprisingly high-grade ore as early as 1833, but most of the production finishing and a good amount of initial reduction between 1837–59 were centered in the Cuyahoga flats. Indeed, although there are no economic deposits of coal closer to Cleveland than those that outcrop along the Copley-Ravenna line to the south, even these thin stringers of Mississippian/Pennsylvanian age were providing Cleveland's ironworks with 250,000 tons annually. The Union demand for iron during the CIVIL WAR virtually exhausted these local ore deposits. Nevertheless, while many of the early furnaces in Lake and Ashtabula counties became archeological sites, those in Cleveland became a focus of the Great Lakes iron industry. But with improvements in internal bulk transportation, by the 1860s more uniform

sources of sand and gravel were obtained by crushing the pure and well-sorted Sharon sandstone and conglomerate, where these outcropped in areas to the east of Cleveland. Most production of finer ceramicware had moved to Akron, where quality glacial clays were available, while the successors of the antebellum glass industry of the WESTERN RESERVE relocated adjacent to the Sylvania sandstone outcrops at Toledo.

As early as 1870, shallow open-pit extraction at Dover and Wickliffe was recovering the Dekalb or Erie blue clays weathered from the Chagrin shale. These were used for paving brick and firebrick. Outcrops of the Chagrin shales were also being mined in NEWBURGH, MILL CREEK, INDEPENDENCE, and COLLINWOOD for the production of drain tile, paving brick, and common brick. Clays for face brick, fire brick, and hollow tile were extracted from the Bedford shale, and the lower (Euclid) shales of the Cuyahoga formation at BEREA and BROOKLYN, Independence, and Newburgh. Indeed, most of the brick used in the construction of Cleveland's streets and structures is still obtained from these local deposits. Perhaps the most enduring natural resource of the region has been Berea sandstone. In use for building walls and foundations as early as 1799, it is still one of the region's major bulk exports. Occurring in beds of variable size, stratigraphic complexity, and compactness, the Berea deposit has an average thickness of 30–130', although in deep channel fill, as at the major quarries at Berea, it may exceed 225' in thickness. The lower levels, if not cross-bedded, are usually very well cemented and coarse. That is the famous Berea "grit," which since 1840 has been cut and turned into grindstones. The upper levels are finer, moderately well cemented, and rather flat-bedded. They have provided most of the curbing, building and bridge block, flagging, and trim for northeast Ohio, found in public and private buildings throughout the Midwest. Under the Berea sandstone lie the Bedford shales whose lowest (Euclid) levels in eastern Cuyahoga County are a 20'-thick lens of hard blue-gray shale called "Bluestone." The stone splits easily into even, thin layers, each from 3–6" thick. As early as 1834, a quarry at the top of Woodland Hill (modern SHAKER HTS.) provided Cleveland with flagging and cap and sill stone. "Bluestone" quarries were opened at Newburgh in 1847. The large S. EUCLID quarry operated from before 1880 through the Great Depression.

One result of the 1859 Pennsylvania petroleum boom was a brief flurry of wildcat exploration in northeastern Ohio. In the early 1860s, wells drilled into the Devonian shales were started at Brighton, at the KINGSBURY (RUN) quarry in the Cuyahoga Valley, and in the Rocky River Valley near Berea. Wells were also drilled in Mayfield, Warrensville, and Euclid townships, where small oil seeps in the Bluestone had been reported. While some of these wells yielded as much as 25 barrels per day, all were exhausted within several weeks. An equally deep well drilled by the Newburgh Brick & Clay Co. in 1911 yielded 100 barrels per day for the first week, and then 35–40 barrels per day until it was exhausted in 3 months. While the oil was high-grade (17% gasoline, 35% kerosene) with little sulfur, the sources were both localized and extremely small. The first significant by-product of the oil "boom" (which never materialized) was the 1883 discovery of natural gas at a well drilled in ROCKPORT Twp. Some of the early natural gas exploited occurred in pockets at 1,800' on the base of the Cleveland shales, but far larger fields were tapped in 1886 by the Cleveland Rolling Mill at Newburgh in the lower Portage shales at a depth of 2,660'. The largest gas fields (in the Albion sandstones) were encountered between 1905–07 by the EAST OHIO GAS CO. and Logan Gas & Fuel wells near Kamms and Berea. By 1911, wells at Warner and Canal roads had encountered smaller fields of oil and gas in thin sandstones within the Niagara limestones, and in 1912 a well started jointly by the Natl. Carbon Co. and the WINTON MOTOR CARRIAGE CO. hit gas in the Berea sandstone, setting off a 1913–14 boom in LAKEWOOD and a 1914–15 boom in WEST PARK. By the 1930s, the last major natural gas pockets in the Central Lowlands province were being tapped in the Denison-Harvard district. Gas exploration and new production on the Allegheny Plateau continues today.

"Rock Gas" was not the only natural methane available. Small decomposed organic deposits, buried in the glacial till overlying the Central Lowlands, also yielded "drift gas" at depths between 125–450′. THOS. WHITE was the first to provide his home at 8218 Euclid Ave. with privately owned well gas for heat, light, and cooking, from 1890–92. There are a number of similar individual wells still operating. The deep exploitation for natural gas had unforeseen results. In 1886 the Cleveland Rolling Mill gas well No. 2 encountered salt brine in the Salina formation 1,990–2,154′ below the surface. By 1889 the Newburgh Salt Co. had 3 brine wells at Madison (Addison) and the New York Central Railroad crossing, and from 1905–30 the Cleveland Salt Co. operated 3 brine wells at Ashland and Central Ave. SE. By 1944, the Union (Morton) Salt Co. had opened a deep-shaft mine near Lake Shore Blvd. and E. 65th St., which went down into several levels of this same Salina formation. Since 1957, large salt mines at WHISKEY ISLAND have been operated by the INTERNATL. SALT CO. The upper levels of massive rock salt deposits exceed 350′ in thickness and are mined by galaries extended below the lake basin for as much as 6 mi., while lower levels yielded limited amounts of anhydrite gypsum used for cement.

David S. Brose
Cleveland Museum of Natural History

See also INDUSTRY.

**GEORGE, CLAYBORNE** (26 Mar. 1888–24 Dec. 1970), was an important city councilman and a long-time member of the Civil Service Commission. He and his well-known wife, Zelma Watson George (8 Dec. 1903- ), were prominent leaders in the political, cultural, and social affairs of the local black community. George was born in Surry, Va., the son of Bolling T. and Cornelia George. His father was a peanut farmer who taught himself to read and write; Clayborne received limited education in a 1-room country school but at age 17 entered 6th grade at the academy at Howard University. After graduating from the academy in 1911, he received his bachelor's degree from Howard in 1915 and graduated from the law school there in 1917. George then entered the 1st Negro Officers Training Camp in Ft. Des Moines, Iowa; commissioned a 1st lieutenant, he spent 8 months in France in WORLD WAR I. Discharged in Mar. 1919, George enrolled in Boston University the next fall, and in 1920 he received a master's degree in law. George was admitted to the Ohio bar in 1920 and began to practice law in Cleveland. He quickly became active in the political affairs of the city's black community. He was named to the executive committee of the local NAACP in 1922 and served as the organization's president from 1924–26; George was one of the leaders responsible for the growth of the local NAACP in the 1920s. He ran unsuccessfully for city council in 1925, then established the East End Political Club as a political base and became a strong advocate of independent politics for the black community. George was successful in campaigns for city council

in 1927, 1929, and 1931. George, LAWRENCE O. PAYNE, and LEROY N. BUNDY constituted the effective "black triumvirate" on city council during this period, taking advantage of political disputes and power struggles and using the power of the collective black vote to make political gains for the black community. George became a Republican ward leader in 1930 and in 1931 was named chairman of city council's safety committee. In Aug. 1933, he resigned from council to run for municipal court judge; he lost that race, but in 1934 Mayor HARRY L. DAVIS appointed him to the Civil Service Commission. George was reappointed to the commission 5 times, serving as a member until his retirement in Dec. 1969. In Jan. 1970 he retired from law practice. He had been a founder of the John M. Harlan Law Club and a member of the CUYAHOGA COUNTY BAR ASSOC. He also served as the first chairman of the Negro College Fund in Cleveland and was a 3-term president of the Central Areas Community Council.

George's marriage to Zelma Watson on 2 Sept. 1944 was the second marriage for both. Zelma Watson's first marriage ended in divorce; George's first wife, Enola, died in 1941. Zelma Watson was a native of Hearn, Tex., the oldest child of Samuel E. J. and Lena Thomas Watson. She graduated from the University of Chicago in 1924, and after her father's death in 1925, she worked to help her 5 brothers and sisters earn their college degrees. After 2 years as a caseworker for Associated Charities, she was a probation officer for the Chicago Juvenile Court (1925–32), then became the dean of women at Tennessee State University. Her first marriage took her to Los Angeles, where she was founder and executive director of the Avalon Community Ctr. (1937–42). She was a Rockefeller Foundation research fellow in New York before marriage took her to Cleveland in 1944. In Cleveland, Zelma Watson George became involved in a variety of activities. Her knowledge of Negro music and culture won her appointment to the women's advisory board of KARAMU HOUSE in 1944. In 1949 she sang the title role in *The Medium* at the Karamu Theater; she took that role to Broadway in 1950 and later appeared in other productions in Cleveland. During the 1950s, she was active in the YWCA and several organizations promoting intercultural and interracial relations; she received her doctorate in intercultural relations from New York University in 1954. In 1959 she served as a goodwill ambassador and lecturer for the U.S. State Dept., and in June 1960 she was appointed an alternate member of the U.S. delegation to the UN General Assembly. She served as director of the CLEVELAND JOB CORPS from 1966–74.

*Here's Zelma* (1971).
*Obsequies in Memory of Clayborne George, March 26, 1888-December 24, 1970* (1970).

The **GEORGE M. AND PAMELA S. HUMPHREY FUND** was established in 1951 by Geo. M. (1890–1970) and Pamela S. (1890–1979) Humphrey. GEO. M. HUMPHREY, noted businessman, was distinguished for his service as the 55th secretary of the treasury under Pres. Dwight D. Eisenhower from 1953–57. Humphrey married Pamela Stark in 1913, and they had 4 children: Gilbert W. Humphrey; Caroline Butler; Geo. M., Jr., who died in infancy; and Pamela Firman. Pamela Humphrey was active in the Garden Club of Cleveland and the Rainbow Hospital for Crippled Children, forerunner of Rainbow Babies & Childrens Hospital. The fund broadly supports hospitals, higher and secondary education, and community funds, as well as cultural programs and health agencies. Giving is primarily in Ohio, and the fund does not give grants to individuals. In 1985, assets of the fund were $5,086,353, with expenditures of 426,450 for 56 grants. Officers include Carol H. Butler, president; John G. Butler, vice-president; and Herbert N. Putnam, Jr., treasurer; with Pamela Rutter.

The **GEORGE GUND FOUNDATION** was founded in 1951 by GEO. GUND (1888–1966). Gund was born in La Crosse, Wisc, and settled in Cleveland with his family in 1897. He graduated from University School in 1905 and was a member of the first graduating class of the Harvard Business School in 1909. He took his first job with Seattle Natl. Bank but returned to Cleveland when his father died. In Cleveland he created the Kaffee Hag Corporation, which produced decaffeinated coffee and sold the caffein to Coca-Cola. In 1929 he sold the business to the Kellogg Corporation for $10 million paid largely in Kellogg stock. With the proceeds from the sale, Gund invested in securities during the depression, including large shares of Ohio's largest bank, the Cleveland Trust Company (AMERITRUST). He became the director of Cleveland Trust in 1937, and president in 1941. Gund succeeded I. F. FREIBERGER as chairman of the board in 1962. Over the course of his career, he was director of some 30 corporations. He married Jessica Roesler (1904–54) in 1936, and they had 6 children.

Gund's personal estate was valued at $600 million, the largest in Cleveland's history. On his death, the Gund Foundation received an additional $40 million for the purposes of education and the fine arts, bringing the Foundation assets to a total of $83.5 million, second only to the CLEVELAND FOUNDATION. The Gund Foundation supports new concepts and methods of teaching and educational opportunities to the disadvantaged. The board in 1985 also funded projects leading to community organizing, social change, and innovative projects. Generally no grants are given to individuals, buildings, endowments, equipment, or research. In 1983 the assets were $113,856,000 with expenditures of $6,158,000 for 366 grants. Members of the board in 1985 included: Frederick Cox, president and treasurer; Geoffrey Gund, vice president; William G. Caples, secretary; Kathleen Barber; Geo. Gund III; Graham Gund; and Laura A. Gund.

The **GEORGE R. KLEIN NEWS COMPANY**, located at 1771 E. 30th St., is a wholesale distributor of a wide range of magazines, paperback books, and out-of-town newspapers. The company sells about 25 million pieces of reading material each year and regards itself as the 3d-largest provider of reading material in the area, behind the *PLAIN DEALER* and the library system. The company was founded on W. 3rd St. in 1927 by Geo. R. Klein, and control of the business has remained in the family; brothers G. Robt. and Wm. C. Klein guided the company before their retirements in 1978, passing the presidency to Geo. R. Klein, Jr. The company's early business was in newspapers and magazines, and as paperback books began to appear in the 1930s, publishers turned to pulp magazine distributors such as the Klein Co. as natural distributors. The company's business grew steadily; by the mid-1950s, growth had prompted it to change locations several times. In 1957 it bought its property on E. 30th St. In the early 1950s, the company became known for its early use of data processing. G. Robt. Klein had served in the Navy during the war and gained knowledge of the developing computer technology through his experience with the Navy payroll computer in Cleveland. He made the company the first in Cleveland to use the first generation of IBM computers. The company also used innovative measures to promote reading and to interest students and teachers in its inexpensive paperback books. During the 1950s and 1960s, it made do-

nations of books to school libraries; many of these donations were made by the Klein Foundation, established by the firm to use part of each year's profits for a project of benefit to the community. The company also put together a bookmobile to travel to schools to acquaint students with low-priced books, and sponsored book festivals at area schools to offer paperbacks for sale; it even experimented with book-vending machines in inner-city schools. By 1966, the company, which distributed all mass-market paperbacks in the area, also was the distributor of 51 out-of-town newspapers and 1,200 magazines to 850 dealers; by 1977 it sold to 1,978 dealers in northeast Ohio and had distribution facilities in Warren, Ashtabula, and Sandusky, in addition to Cleveland.

The **GEORGE W. CODRINGTON CHARITABLE FOUNDATION** was founded in 1955 by Geo. W. Codrington (1886–1961). Codrington was a ferryboat operator before coming to Cleveland in 1917 at the request of ALEXANDER WINTON, pioneer in auto manufacturing and president of Winton Diesel. When Winton retired in 1928, Codrington took over the company. Winton Diesel was acquired by the General Motors Corp. in 1930, and the company became the CLEVELAND DIESEL ENGINE DIV. OF GM in 1938. During WORLD WAR II, Cleveland Diesel grew by 800%, manufacturing engines for Coast Guard and naval submarines, cruisers, gunboats, and other war-related equipment. Codrington retired in 1950 as a vice-president of GM. Foundation grants are limited to Cuyahoga County in the areas of HIGHER EDUCATION, hospitals, youth and health agencies, MUSIC, and museums. Fairview Park Hospital, the School of Nursing, and CASE WESTERN RESERVE UNIVERSITY have been primary recipients of Codrington grants. No grants are given to individuals. The foundation assets in 1983 were $5.9 million, producing an income of $357,800 for disbursement. Officers of the foundation were Raymond Sawyer, secretary; Earl P. Schneider, chairman of the board; W. Paul Cooper, vice-chairman; John J. Dwyer; Wm. E. McDonald; and Homer D. Webb, Jr.

The **GEORGE WORTHINGTON COMPANY** is Cleveland's oldest business existing under its original name and one of the nation's leading hardware wholesalers and industrial distributors. The firm began in 1829 when 16-year-old Geo. Worthington rode into Cleveland from New York on horseback. He stopped to watch work on the OHIO & ERIE CANAL and noted the lack of proper tools. Seeing a sales opportunity, Worthington rode back to New York, borrowed $500 from his brother, purchased picks, shovels, wheelbarrows, and other implements, and shipped them to Cleveland. The supply sold quickly, and Worthington doubled his money. He bought more stock, with which he opened his first store at Superior and W. 10th streets. Worthington's hardware store was an instant success. In 1835, it acquired its foremost competitor, McCurdy & Conklin, and moved into its store at Superior and Water (W. 6th) streets. Business volume enabled Worthington to hire clerks to run the store while he traveled northern Ohio on horseback, securing more business and delivering wares by oxcart. He also helped to form the Cleveland Iron Co., which produced bar iron that was sold by his hardware store.

The advent of the railroad and the CIVIL WAR stimulated the growth of the company. By 1868, it was necessary for Worthington to build a new store and warehouse at 802 W. St. Clair Ave. near Water (W. 9th) St. The store burned in 1874, but a larger store was soon erected on the same site. The company continued to expand its headquarters until it had 13 structures on St. Clair Ave. Wor-

445

thington also widened its line of products. By 1870, with 2,000 items being sold, the firm began issuing yearly catalogs as sales reached $1.5 million. The company was incorporated in 1887. During WORLD WAR I, the firm's sales territory spread through 10 northeastern and midwestern states. In 1920, Worthington discontinued its retail business and devoted its resources to the wholesale trade. With the introduction of discount department stores after WORLD WAR II, the neighborhood hardware stores that Worthington serviced began to fail. In response in 1960, the company helped to form the Sentry Hardware Corp., a national affiliation of hardware wholesalers. In 1979, Worthington under Sentry had annual sales of $60 million, with 450 employees and 35,000 items in its catalog. In 1984, Worthington moved from its downtown headquarters to a more modern plant in Mentor. By 1985, the employee-owned company was supplying 1,500 independent hardware retailers. In Sept. 1986, the company filed for protection under Chapter 11 of the U.S. bankruptcy law.

George Worthington Co., *Eighty-seven Years of Progress* (1916).
George Worthington Co. Records, 1849–70, WRHS.

**GERMAN AMERICAN RESETTLEMENT SERVICES, INC.,** incorporated in Apr. 1952, was formed "to aid and assist needy displaced persons of German ethnic origin" whose lives were disrupted by political changes in postwar Europe. The group was organized and headed by Rev. John Foisel, its first president, Robt. A. Baerwalde, vice-president, and M. A. Schneider, secretary. Both Rev. Foisel and Schneider were officers in the Lutheran Relief for Transylvanian Saxons, Inc. The latter organization, formed in Nov. 1945, had several branches throughout Ohio and Pennsylvania by 1952. It took the lead in calling a meeting for 29 Feb. 1952 at the East Side Sachsenheim to form "a local committee of all German American Societies" in Cleveland for the purpose of aiding refugees of German ethnicity. At its initial meeting, the new group called itself the Federated German American Relief for Expellees Organizing Committee, but at its March meeting it became German American Resettlement Services, Inc. Membership was open to any church, lodge, club, singing society, or dramatic group in the Greater Cleveland area that had "a membership of predominantly German origin." The major activities of the organization involved providing financial and material donations to refugee camps in Europe and helping new immigrants in the Cleveland area. German American Resettlement Services, Inc., continued to operate into the early 1960s.

The **GERMAN CENTRAL FARM** occupies more than 30 acres of land at 7863 York Rd. in PARMA. Used for meetings, picnics, and sports and cultural events, the site was established by the German Central Organization (GCO), which bought the farm in 1926 for $24,000 and created there a soccer field, tennis courts, a rifle range, a swimming pool, a meeting hall, and other accommodations. By the mid-1930s, the farm was a popular meeting and recreational place for members of Cleveland's German-American community. The GCO was a social organization made up mostly of immigrants who arrived in the U.S. after WORLD WAR I. It was established in Oct. 1924 by a committee of 15 men headed by Felix Schmit, an editor of the *WAECHTER UND ANZEIGER*. It was incorporated on 5 Feb. 1925; its first president was OTTO L. FRICKE, a lawyer. The organization was designed to help its members with matters of American citizenship, to provide them with a social center, and to provide material help to its needy members. To achieve the latter purpose, the organization established a

free employment bureau; it also dispensed food and other aid to the poor. Between 1924–35, it distributed $10,000 to needy GERMANS.

By 1935, the GCO had 1,000 members; in January of that year the Frauenbund Der Deutschen Zentrale, the ladies' unit of the organization, was formed, and within months it had 200 members. In 1933, other units of the organization included sports groups, a dance orchestra, a drama club, mandolin and symphony orchestras, and a concert string quartet. By 1939, the GCO had 5,000 members. The late 1930s and the war years were difficult ones for the organization, however. The rise of Nazism in Germany made many Clevelanders suspicious of local Germans, and of the GCO in particular. In 1937, Dr. Herbert S. Reichle, head of City Hospital's pathology department, was president; he was later accused of being a Nazi sympathizer. In Jan. 1942, the suspicions of some Clevelanders toward the area's German population turned violent, and the German Central Farm was the target of vandalism more than once. By the time the 30-acre site celebrated its 50th anniversary in 1976, however, it was again a popular recreational area for German-Americans. It also hosted the celebrations and events of other ethnic organizations, as well as the annual picnics of local businesses.

The **GERMAN CONCERT ORCHESTRA,** also known as the Germania, was an ensemble used for all musical purposes in the German community and was the longest-lasting orchestra in early Cleveland. The Germania's first appearance was in Feb. 1868 at CASE HALL with a chorus in performance of Rossini's *Stabat Mater* under the direction of John Underner. The orchestra was probably an offshoot of or related to an earlier ensemble, the ST. CECILIA SOCIETY, which played (as the Germania did) overtures, waltzes, polkas, and support music for the various German clubs. Made up of German musicians, the group had no regular conductor. FERDINAND PUEHRINGER worked with it to raise the standard of playing and is credited with developing a concert subscription series. That, in turn, made the orchestra more viable.

The Germania's primary function remained broad; it was available for any engagement. In 1870 it performed works by Haydn, Handel, and Weber. In 1871, it supported the German Harmonie Singing Societies in a production of *Martha* at the ACADEMY OF MUSIC. Philip Groterath conducted the group at Case Hall in Oct. 1873, when it supported many local singing societies, including the Cleveland Gesangverein, Harmonie, Orpheus, Harmonia, and Turnverein. Adam Nuss of the Cleveland Gesangverein conducted the orchestra and his own chorus, as well as appeared as a guest violinist and pianist. Though not the principal orchestra at the 1874 Saengerfest, the Germania still supported local singing societies at the festival. The PHILHARMONIC ORCHESTRA, formed in 1881, eventually supplanted the Germania as a professional group. The Germania, however, did continue to support local vocal societies for several years.

*GERMANIA* was Cleveland's first German newspaper, which gained it the distinction of also being the city's first printed foreign-language paper. Although it was preceded by Maximilian Heinrich Allart's *Monatliche Journal* of July 1844, the earlier effort must be disqualified for its handwritten format. Founded by EDWARD HESSENMUELLER, *Germania* came off the press at 24 Water St. in 1846. Like its owner, the weekly paper was Democratic in politics. By 1852, *Germania* had acquired a competitor in the *Waechter am Erie*, established that year. It also switched its allegiance to the WHIG PARTY at about that time, leaving the Democratic field to the newer paper. While some sources place *Germania*'s expiration in 1853, it was evidently involved in a libel suit as late as 1855, when Ernest Scheuffler was mentioned as editor. A Cleveland *Germania* cited by historian CARL WITTKE as active on the side of Republicanism after the CIVIL WAR, however, was an entirely different publication.

**GERMANIA HALL,** located at 532 Erie (2416 E. 9th) St., was built by the Germania Turnverein in 1888 to house their gymnastic facilities and serve as a meeting place. Germania Turnverein was organized on 7 Sept. 1876 by east side residents who were former members of the Cleveland Turnverein. Their new $65,000 hall on Erie St. was built under the leadership of Wilhelm Kauffmann with assistance from Paul Schneider, Adolf Mayer, Dr. Carl Zapp, Louis Uhl, and others. The hall included a bowling alley, a long bar, a gym, a restaurant, and a 3d-floor ballroom. The hall was used by the Germania Turnverein for 20 years. In 1908 the group merged with Turnverein Vorwaerts and moved into the latter organization's hall (See VORWAERTS TURNER HALL). Germania Hall then became known as Acme Hall. As such it was used by the Cleveland Cheese Club of stagehands as the site of their parties. During WORLD WAR I, it was used by radicals as a site for meetings, one of which featured an antiwar speech by Eugene V. Debs. By 1920, the hall had gained such a reputation as a radical meeting place that Rev. Frank Baker, director of its new occupant, GOODWILL INDUSTRIES, claimed that the first thing he did was to raise the American flag over the hall. The former Germania Hall, described in the 1930s as "an old castle-like building" at E. 9th and Carnegie, served as the local headquarters of Goodwill Industries until it was scheduled for demolition to make way for the INNERBELT FREEWAY in the mid-1950s.

**GERMANS.** Germans formed one of Cleveland's largest and most influential nationality groups in the 19th and 20th centuries. Although not as large as the German communities in other northern cities, the local community had an important influence on the city's economic, educational, and cultural life. The first significant period of commercial growth in Cleveland, brought about chiefly by the opening of the Ohio Canal in 1832, coincided with the arrival of German immigrants in substantial numbers. Cleveland and other lake cities lagged a few years behind Cincinnati and St. Louis in the influx of Germans, for both of these cities gained German immigrants via the riverways and the National Road. Prior to the opening of the OHIO & ERIE CANAL, Cleveland's Germans were chiefly those of German descent from Pennsylvania, New York, and Maryland whose forebears had generally come to America before the Revolutionary War; many of Cleveland's early civic leaders, such as LEONARD CASE, claimed German heritage of this kind. Germans arriving in Cleveland during the 1830s first settled along Lorain St. in Brooklyn, and along Superior and Garden (Central Ave.) streets on the east side. As the city expanded during the 19th century, succeeding generations moved east, west, and south, eventually fusing with other elements of the total population.

Many German newcomers to America in the 1830s were motivated to leave their German homelands by a combination of factors that included political oppression, religious persecution, and economic depression—especially crop failure in the Rhineland. Between 1840–46, when Cleveland's population grew from 6,000 to 10,000, German immigrants constituted ⅓ of this new growth. As a new wave of political refugees began arriving in 1848–49 via the RAILROADS, the German-born population reached 2,590,

about 60 less than the total of all other foreign-born residents. The Germans arriving after the unsuccessful Revolution of 1848 were freedom lovers and were generally well educated. Opposed to slavery, they later showed strong support for the Northern cause during the CIVIL WAR. After a lull during the Civil War, emigration to America resumed substantially until 1873. Some of this exodus included people unfriendly to Prussia and unhappy with the formation of the German Empire in 1871. The 1873 financial panic in the U.S. and a concurrent industrial boom in the new Germany were probable causes of a temporary waning in emigration to America in the late 1870s. Except for some influx into Cleveland of German-speaking groups from Austria-Hungary, German immigration declined after 1882. However, Germans remained the largest group arriving in the city on an annual basis until the mid-1890s. By 1900, over 40,000 Germans resided in the city, and over 45,000 in the county. Later immigration was on a smaller scale but continual, and often consisted of German-speaking peoples from outside of the German state, particularly from Austria-Hungary and including groups of Gottscheer, "Metzies" from Unter-Metzenseifen and Saxons from Siebenburgen, Transylvania, in Romania. Except for those escaping economic depression in the mid-1920s and Nazism in the 1930s, relatively few settlers have come to Cleveland from Germany in the 20th century. German-speaking immigrants have been in the main those fleeing Communism in German-speaking communities outside Germany proper, the so-called Volksdeutsche. Many of these are members of the large Cleveland Danube-Swabian organization. German immigration in Cleveland began to slacken at a time when the immigration of most other nationality groups in the city was just beginning. As a result, Germans assimilated earlier, and their influence was most directly felt during the 19th century; most of the old German neighborhoods had already disappeared by the time of WORLD WAR I.

Among skilled craftsmen ca. 1850, Germans outnumbered all others, even though they composed a lesser proportion of the total population. They worked as jewelers, tailors, makers of musical instruments (e.g., pianos, such as those built by the DREHER PIANO CO.), cabinetmakers, and "machinists" (i.e., mechanics). The Germans' introduction of beer as a beverage perhaps aided in tempering the drinking habits of Cleveland natives, in that the consumption of hard liquors was diminished. Initially, the German BREWING INDUSTRY in Cleveland consisted of small breweries, each intended to serve only the brewer's own tavern. The breweries later expanded to become wholesale suppliers—notably LEISY BREWING CO., GUND BREWING CO., Schlather, and PILSENER BREWING CO. After the Civil War, Cleveland Germans—like other American Germans—distinguished themselves in the manufacturing of pianos, furniture, coffins, clothing, stoves, metal products, and carriages, and later in the tool-and-die industry and building trades. THEODOR KUNDTZ was a particularly important cabinet manufacturer. Germans were also prominent in the wholesale and large-scale food business, the grocery business, and baked goods, as well as in smaller restaurant and bakery enterprises such as the LAUB BAKING CO. In AGRICULTURE, Germans introduced advanced soil-conservation methods to the Cleveland area. Rather than seeking land previously uncultivated, they often took over farms deserted because of soil depletion and rejuvenated the soil through methods unknown in America. Louis Harms, a viticulturist, experimented with various kinds of grapes until he found the type best suited to the climate and soil of EUCLID. Cleveland Germans also made significant contributions in the field of science and technology. The first seismograph for measuring the intensity of earthquakes was made by Fr. FREDERICK L. ODENBACH of St. Ignatius University, now JOHN CARROLL UNIVERSITY. Other German-Americans connected with Cleveland universities and colleges, such as ALBERT A. MICHELSON, achieved significant breakthroughs in science, or developed new instruments and methods useful in science or industry.

Unlike most other nationality groups that came to Cleveland, the Germans came from a variety of religious backgrounds. The total number of churches with services in German reached 120 or more in Greater Cleveland. The first was founded in 1835 and split early into Evangelical and Lutheran congregations. The latter one (ZION EVANGELICAL LUTHERAN CHURCH) introduced the Christmas tree and other German Christmas customs to Cleveland. After 1840, other German religious groups followed in quick order, including Lutheran, Evangelical, Jewish, Evangelical Assoc., Catholic, United Brethren, Methodist, Baptist, Episcopal, Seventh-Day Adventist, and Reformed congregations. Only a few new German churches were founded after 1900. Some churches continued to hold services in German until WORLD WAR II. The German churches in Cleveland were also responsible for founding many benevolent societies and hospitals. In 1864, the Central German Conference of the Methodist Episcopal church established an orphan home in BEREA. As of 1987, it still served children of all faiths as the Berea Children's Home. German churches also founded 3 hospitals, still flourishing on the west side in the 1980s. A committee of Reformed church ministers opened a health-care facility on Scranton Rd. in 1898. Later it moved to Franklin Blvd., where it was known as German Hospital until World War I, when its name was changed to Fairview Park Hospital (FAIRVIEW GENERAL HOSPITAL on Lorain Ave.). The LUTHERAN MEDICAL CTR. on Franklin Blvd. grew from modest beginnings in 1896. The third hospital, DEACONESS HOSPITAL OF CLEVELAND, was founded in 1920 by the Evangelical Synod of North America. The ALTENHEIM, a skilled-nursing facility in STRONGSVILLE, was located on Detroit Ave. from 1892–1980. It was organized by the West Seite Deutscher Frauenverein, which was originally interested in supporting the training of teachers of German.

It was primarily through their schools, social clubs, and cultural organizations that the Germans attempted to preserve their language and culture. Cleveland's German churches and private organizations, notably the Freimaennerverein, sponsored German schools from the mid-19th century to 1870, when the German language was introduced into the curriculum of the public elementary schools. Lutheran and Catholic churches continued to offer German in their schools until early in the 20th century. The removal of German from the public elementary schools was not caused solely by the anti-German feeling at the time of World War I; rather, it was to be expected, inasmuch as German immigration had slackened over a complete generation, while the arrival of other ethnic groups had increased. The elimination of German in the high schools, however, was brought about largely by the lack of interest among pupils imbued with patriotism. Beyond the primary and secondary levels, several institutions of higher learning were organized by Germans. The first of these was German Wallace College, founded in Berea in 1863 as an outgrowth of the German Dept. of Baldwin University. German was the language of instruction for most of the courses at German Wallace College; in 1913 it merged with Baldwin University to become BALDWIN-WALLACE COLLEGE. Other colleges with German beginnings were NOTRE DAME COLLEGE, founded by a group of Sisters of Notre Dame from Germany, and Calvin College (1881–99), an institution founded by the Reformed church. John Carroll University was originally founded by German Jesuits as St. Ignatius College at W. 39th and Carroll St.

The Germans made perhaps their most significant impact in Cleveland on the city's cultural life, especially in the field of ART. The Cleveland Art Club, also known as the Old Bohemians, was founded in 1876 and provided the city with its first nucleus of notable artists, most of them—such as FREDERICK C. GOTTWALD, Otto Bacher, and Max Bohm—the sons of German immigrants. Many received training abroad, primarily at the art schools in Munich and Dusseldorf. A succeeding generation of German-descended artists would dominate the city's art life until World War II. When the KOKOON ARTS CLUB was founded in 1911, 11 of its 13 charter members were of German descent. Many from this next generation of artists also received their instruction abroad, and helped make Cleveland during the 1920s a leading center of art activity. Germans also distinguished themselves in ARCHITECTURE; prominent architects in Cleveland of German extraction included FRANK E. CUDELL, CHAS. F. SCHWEINFURTH, and JOHN EISENMANN.

Germans were also quite influential in raising the standards of MUSIC in the city. In the newspapers of the 1830s and 1840s, German music teachers advertised their availability for lessons. Balthasar Schubert, nephew of composer Franz Schubert, was the first director of the Cleveland Grays Band in 1840. German orchestras, BANDS, and singing societies proliferated throughout the second half of the 19th century. In 1855, 1859, 1874, 1893, 1927, and 1986, Cleveland was host to the North American Saengerbund's SAENGERFESTS. In 1858, the Cleveland Gesangverein began a long tradition of locally produced opera with a performance of Flotow's *Alessandro Stradella*. German organizations and directors such as FERDINAND PUEHRINGER continued to offer Cleveland-produced opera well into the 20th century. The German community also produced some notable composers and conductors, such as JOHANN BECK. In the mid-1980s, there were still half a dozen German music groups in Cleveland that had 19th-century roots. Since the days of heavy German immigrations, Cleveland has not been without a German newspaper. The first one, GERMANIA, did not survive long after its 1847 beginning. Five years later, in 1852, the *Waechter am Erie* began serving the German community and continued to due so in the 1980s as the *WAECHTER UND ANZEIGER*, having merged with the *Anzeiger* in 1893.

Despite some disturbances, Cleveland Germans did not suffer excessively from anti-German hysteria during World War I. Although it has been asserted that many German street names were eliminated, the loss of German names may actually have come during the change of north-south street names to numbered streets in 1906. In 1980, there were 9,435 residents of Cleveland claiming German birth; for 2,201, German was the language spoken at home. However, these Germans and the descendants of earlier German immigrant groups constituted the largest white ethnic group in the county at that time. It is possible that Cleveland's Germans lag behind Cincinnati's in their attempts to preserve their ethnic past, and also behind Columbus's, where the 19th-century German Village has been restored. Cleveland Germans, with the city of Cleveland, have, however, paid homage to the great cultural heroes of Germany in the German Cultural Garden on Martin Luther King Blvd. In 1983, the FED. OF GERMAN AMERICAN SOCIETIES was instrumental in having a downtown street named for Daniel Pastorius, organizer of the first German emigration to America in 1683. German culture and customs in Cleveland have perhaps been most visibly preserved in *Gemuetlichkeit*, expressed through love of music, dancing, and conviviality. This "old world" spirit has been centered in a number of German beer gardens, restaurants, festivals, and performing groups, and at such places—and events—as the GERMAN CENTRAL FARM, the Sachsenheim, Lenau Park, and the Oktoberfest. In the 1970s, the SCHUHPLATTLER AND TRACHTENVEREIN BAVARIA has won 1st place in 6 of 10 biennial North American competitions. That the German clubs have the future of their ethnic culture in mind is evidenced by the emphasis on the appeal to youth; several societies continue, in the 1980s, to have vigorous music and dance programs for young people. They include the Danube-Swabians, relative newcomers, who erected a large multipurpose German Cultural Ctr. on Columbia Rd.

John R. Sinnema
Baldwin-Wallace College

See also LUTHERANS.

**GERSTENBERGER, HENRY JOHN** (9 Jan. 1881–24 June 1954), a widely recognized Cleveland pediatrician, helped to establish the Babies & Childrens Hospital and to develop SMA (Synthetic Milk Adapted), an artificial milk formula. His many contributions influenced the development of pediatric medicine both locally and worldwide. Gerstenberger was born in Cleveland to John H. and Clara E. Schake Gerstenberger. Attending Western Reserve University Medical School, he graduated with the M.D. degree in 1903. Encouraged to study pediatric medicine abroad, Gerstenberger, in 1903, first went to Berlin, Germany, and then on to pediatric centers in Vienna, Austria. His studies were interrupted when he contracted tuberculosis.

Gerstenberger returned to Cleveland in 1906 as head of the pediatrics department at City Hospital (Metropolitan General Hospital); director of the Tuberculosis Contact Clinic, the first of its kind in the Western Hemisphere; and professor of pediatrics at Western Reserve University Medical School. Recognizing the need for inner-city infant and child care, he was instrumental in creating the Bureau of Child Hygiene as part of Cleveland's Dept. of Health. When the Babies' Dispensary & Hospital formally opened in 1911, Gerstenberger was its first medical director. Located on Euclid Ave. near E. 30th St., the dispensary was open 6 days a week, with physicians donating their service to the indigent. Partly financed by income from the production of the SMA formula, the Babies & Childrens Hospital relocated on University Hospitals' new campus in 1925. As professor of pediatrics, Gerstenberger found that a combined treatment of cod liver oil and ultraviolet light eased the symptoms of spasmophilia, a convulsion caused by a reaction to slight amounts of sunshine in springtime by children who suffer from rickets. Gerstenberger married Else B. Schweitzer on 28 Mar. 1913. The Gerstenbergers had 4 daughters, Paula Ruth, Else Louise, Gretel, and Katherine.

The **GILBERT W. AND LOUISE IRELAND HUMPHREY FOUNDATION** (formerly the Louise Foundation) was incorporated in 1951 by Gilbert W. (1916–1979) and Louise Ireland (b. 1918) Humphrey. Gilbert W. Humphrey was president of the Hanna Mining Co. from 1960–61 and chairman of the board from 1961–79. His father, GEO. M. HUMPHREY, was secretary of the treasury under Pres. Dwight D. Eisenhower and president of the Hanna Mining Co. from 1929–52. G. W. Humphrey graduated from Yale in 1939 and from Yale Law School in 1942.

After WORLD WAR II, he practiced law in Cleveland with the firm of Jones Day Cockley & Reavis, before joining M. A. Hanna in 1948. He was an active board member of numerous businesses and agencies, including UNIVERSITY HOSPITALS and Case Institute of Technology. Louise Ireland Humphrey, daughter of R. Livingston Ireland, was president of the NORTHERN OHIO OPERA ASSOC. They had 3 children, Geo. M. Humphrey II, vice-president of Hanna Mining; G. Watts Humphrey, Jr., president of Mid-West Steel; and Margaret Humphrey Bindhardt. The purposes of the foundation are to emphasize educational institutions, music, cultural programs, community funds, hospitals, and social agencies. No grants are given to individuals. Giving is primarily local. In 1985, assets of the foundation were $1,252,000, with expenditures of $165,800 for 35 grants. Officers include Mrs. Louise Ireland Humphrey, Margaret H. Bindhardt, M. G. Mikolaj, Irene E. Manni, and Geo. M. Humphrey II.

**GILL, JOHN & SONS CO.** *See* **JOHN GILL & SONS COMPANY**

**GILLESPIE, CHESTER K.** (4 Apr. 1897–22 Mar. 1985), known as "Mr. Civil Rights" in Cleveland, was a black lawyer and Republican politician who served 3 terms in the state legislature between 1933–43. Gillespie was part of the militant segment of Cleveland's black community who agitated for immediate integration in the 1930s and 1940s. The son of Warren and Lulu Trail Gillespie, he was born in Home City, Ohio, a small town near Cincinnati. He moved to Cleveland about 1909. After attending Ohio State University, Gillespie earned a law degree from the Baldwin-Wallace College Law School in 1920. He soon became active in Cleveland politics. He served as assistant law director for the city in 1921 and ran unsuccessfully for the state legislature in the 1920s. But he soon became the leading civil-rights attorney in Cleveland; in the words of one historian, Gillespie brought "more antidiscrimination suits against Cleveland theater, restaurant, and amusement park owners than any other attorney in the city."

Many of Gillespie's antidiscrimination suits were unsuccessful, however, and the difficulties he encountered as a civil-rights lawyer influenced his actions as a state legislator. Gillespie served 3 terms in the Ohio general assembly (1933–34, 1939–40, 1943–44), and during his tenure there he sponsored legislation that extended the Ohio civil-rights law to prohibit discrimination in retail establishments. He also included in the state liquor law a provision that made racial discrimination grounds for revoking a liquor license. As a legislator, he also provided much assistance to Central State University in Wilberforce, Ohio. Gillespie's civil-rights activities included a stint as president of the local NAACP chapter in 1936–37, and along with fellow attorney CLAYBORNE GEORGE, he led the fight for downtown office space for black lawyers and other professionals in the 1930s and 1940s.

Gillespie was active in Republican politics at the state and national levels. He was a member of the Republican State Central Committee, a delegate to the 1948 and 1968 national conventions, and an alternate delegate to the 1964 national convention. His Republican ties undoubtedly helped him gain appointment to the State Board of Education in the spring of 1963; in the fall he won election to complete the unexpired term to which he had been appointed. In Oct. 1965 he was appointed interim chief justice of Cleveland Municipal Court; he served in that capacity only 2 months. Gillespie retired from both law and politics in 1971 and moved to Los Angeles. Gillespie also was active in the Masons, the Elks, and the Moose, and he was a member of the American Legion and Kappa Alpha Psi. On 27 Sept. 1924, he married Dorothy Thomas. As members of the CLEVELAND COUNCIL ON WORLD AFFAIRS, they traveled widely together.

Chester K. Gillespie Scrapbooks, WRHS.

**GILMOUR, RICHARD** (24 Sept. 1824–13 Apr. 1891), was the second bishop of Cleveland. Gilmour was born in Dumbarton, Scotland. His family emigrated first to Nova Scotia and then to Pennsylvania when he was a child. In Cumbola, Pa., Gilmour, of Scotch-Presbyterian background, became acquainted with Catholicism and decided in 1842 to convert and begin studies for the priesthood. He studied privately and at seminaries in Pittsburgh and Loretto, Pa., before completing his studies at Mt. St. Mary Seminary in Emmitsburg, Md. He was ordained to the priesthood on 30 Aug. 1852 in Cincinnati by Archbp. John B. Purcell. Gilmour was named pastor of St. Mary in Portsmouth, Ohio, with the responsibility for Catholics in the nearby areas of Ohio, Kentucky, and Virginia. In 1857 he was assigned to St. Patrick Church in Cincinnati, where he started a model school. Gilmour adapted and translated a popular Bible history, which won papal commendation. He also authored a series of readers, which were widely used in Catholic schools. From 1868–69 he served as a seminary professor before being transferred to the pastorate of St. Joseph Church in Dayton. On 28 Feb. 1872, Gilmour was named the new bishop of Cleveland. His episcopal consecration took place at Cincinnati on 14 Apr. 1872.

The number of Catholics had increased, and they had begun to move into the mainstream of Cleveland society. However, a significant amount of nativism and know-nothingism existed. Gilmour became an ardent defender of the rights of Catholics. To counter such prejudice, he founded and subsidized the newspaper *Catholic Universe* in 1874. Gilmour also defended the PAROCHIAL SCHOOLS when in 1877 the Cuyahoga County auditor declared them to be taxable and demanded that the buildings be sold at auction. A bitter though successful 6-year court battle ensued. Gilmour endorsed the creation of church schools, because he argued that public schools were sectarian in nature. He also established a school board to maintain uniformity and high standards. Under the bishop's direction, services to the poor and sick were expanded. St. Ann's Asylum & Maternity Home, ST. ALEXIS HOSPITAL, and ST. JOHN HOSPITAL were all founded with his support. Gilmour held an important role in the national church. He served as an expert on church property and its legal aspects for the bishops who met at the Provincial Council of Cincinnati in 1882. He provided expertise at the III Plenary Council of Baltimore in 1884 and was on the committee that journeyed to Rome to present the findings of that council. Gilmour's health had begun to deteriorate, and he traveled to Florida to recuperate in Mar. 1891. His death occurred at St. Augustine in April.

**GILMOUR ACADEMY,** located at SOM Ctr. and Cedar roads in GATES MILLS, was founded in 1946 by the Brothers of the Holy Cross. The inspiration for its founding came from Bp. EDWARD HOBAN, who had been educated by the brothers. Although Bp. Hoban advocated such a school, Gilmour's founding resulted from a serendipitous occurrence. While traveling to Cleveland on his yearly tour to encourage vocations to the order, Br. Theophane learned that the Drury Estate in Gates Mills was vacant and was being considered as the site of a paint factory. The estate had been vacant for about 20 years, having been abandoned by Francis E. Drury and his wife after they had lived for there for only a year. At this point, Br. Theophane had no knowledge of Bp. Hoban's desire for a school in Cleveland. Upon returning to Indiana, he was asked to attend a meeting to consider such a request from Bp. Hoban. Br. Theophane suggested that if a new school was indeed planned, he knew the perfect site, the Drury estate. Within a few months, the brothers had purchased the estate, and Br. Theophane was appointed headmaster. Gilmour Academy was designed as both a boarding school and a day school to educate the boys of affluent Catholics in the Cleveland area. It emphasized small class size and close teacher-student relationships. In 1946, 35 students were enrolled. In its relatively short history, Gilmour has experienced a number of changes, all a reflection of its growth. That is shown clearly in the enrollment figures. By 1966, enrollment was 230, and 20 years later it stood at 400 for grades 9–12. The school expanded to include a middle school (grades 7–8) in 1970, and a Montessori preschool was added in 1985. Currently (1986), plans are to add 1 grade per year so that Gilmour will offer education from preschool to grade 12. Perhaps the most significant development was the merger with GLEN OAK SCHOOL in 1982. Glen Oak had been founded as an all-girls' school in 1969 on a campus adjoining Gilmour. From the beginning, the schools had shared faculty, classes, and programs. The union was a logical one. In 1986, Gilmour remained both a day and a boarding school (for high school students). Approximately 45 boys and 30 girls were boarders. Most of the remaining students come from Cleveland's eastern suburbs. Although the student body was still predominantly Catholic, there were a number of Protestant, Jewish, and Moslem students. The total enrollment in 1986 was 500.

**GINN, FRANK HADLEY** (25 Feb. 1868–6 Feb. 1938), was one of Cleveland's leading corporation lawyers and one of the city's most active patrons of MUSIC and ART. He was born in Fremont, Ohio, to Francis Marion and Millicent Ophelia Pope Ginn. He attended public schools in Fremont and Clyde and spent 1 year at Kenyon Military Academy. He graduated from Kenyon College with a Ph.B. in 1890. After coming to Cleveland in 1890, Ginn studied law under Judge Edwin Blandin and was admitted to the Ohio bar in 1892. In 1899, he became a member of the firm of Blandin, Rice & Ginn, later Blandin, Hogsett & Ginn. The firm joined with Kline, Tolles & Morley in 1913 to form TOLLES, HOGSETT, GINN & MORLEY. Appearing in court only infrequently, Ginn did most of his work in his office. Through a wide holding of stocks and connections built up in his practice, he became a potent figure in Ohio industry. An active participant in the management of numerous corporations, Ginn was reported to be an officer or on the board of more companies than anyone else in Ohio. Although credited with considerable influence, Ginn made few public appearances and had little open involvement in politics. However, he was intimately involved with many of the powerful figures in Cleveland's financial life. For years he was closely associated with the interests of the Van Sweringen brothers, actively counseling them through the legal manuevers involved in the building of their railroad empire.

As a patron of music and art, Ginn was one of Cleveland's most active and colorful citizens. But most of his activities did not receive public recognition, as he studiously avoided publicity. Ginn was one of the founders and officers of the MUSICAL ARTS ASSOC. He was one of the prime movers in the founding of the CLEVELAND ORCHESTRA and the CLEVELAND STRING QUARTET, as well as a financial supporter. He served as chairman of the building committee for SEVERANCE HALL and was on the Cleveland Committee of the NORTHERN OHIO OPERA ASSOC. Ginn served on the Cleveland Art Museum's advisory Board of Council. In his private life, he gathered a large collection of paintings, especially of modern French painters, and tapestries. Ginn married Cornelia Root on 25 June 1899. The Ginns had 2 sons, Francis and Alexander, and 2 daughters, Mrs. W. Powell Jones and Barbara Root Ginn.

**GIRDLER, TOM MERCER** (19 May 1877–4 Feb. 1965), was one of Cleveland's leading steel industrialists and one of the nation's most outspoken critics of organized labor and the New Deal. He was the first president and chairman of the board of the REPUBLIC STEEL CORP. Girdler was born on a farm in Silver Creek Twp., Clark County, Ind. He attended Manual Training High School in Louisville, Ky., and graduated from Lehigh University in 1901 with a degree in mechanical engineering. Even before graduation, Girdler went to England for the Buffalo Forge Co. (1901–02). He then worked for the Oliver Iron & Steel Co. of Pittsburgh (1902–05), the Colorado Fuel Co. (1905–07), the Atlantic Steel Co. of Atlanta (1908–14), and the Jones & Laughlin Steel Co. (1914–29). In 1929, Girdler accepted an offer from CYRUS S. EATON and Wm. G. Mather to assist in negotiations leading to the formation of the Republic Steel Corp. in Cleveland. He then became the company's first president and board chairman. Under his direction, Republic became a major producer of light alloys, with profits exceeding $87 million between 1936–43. At first Girdler supported Pres. Roosevelt's Natl. Industrial Recovery Act. In order to comply with the act's requirement that employers bargain collectively with their employees, Republic established a representation plan for its employees. When enactment of the Wagner Act outlawed plans such as that instituted by Republic and promoted negotiations with regular unions such as the CIO, Girdler lost all affinity for the New Deal. He refused to bargain with the CIO, which he termed an "irresponsible, racketeering, violent, communistic body." Though Girdler conceded the need for collective bargaining in modern industry, he refused to do so when directed to by what he considered "govenment edict." Girdler and Republic's refusal to bargain with the CIO and allow union elections in his plant in 1937 resulted in the LITTLE STEEL STRIKE in May of that year. In 1942, under order of the War Labor Board, such elections were held, and the CIO organized Republic. Girdler resigned from the presidency of Republic in 1937 but continued as chairman of the board. He later became chairman of the board and chief executive officer of Vultee and Consolidated and engineered their merger in 1943. Girdler retired from Republic in 1956. He continued his hobbies of breeding and racing horses and traveling while in retirement. He died at his estate in Easton, Md.

Girdler, Tom M., *Boot Straps* (1944).

The **GIRL SCOUTS,** founded nationally by Juliette Gordon Low in 1912 and modeled after Robt. S. S. Baden-Powell's British Boy Scouts, were designed "to help girls realize the ideals of womanhood as preparation for their responsibilities in the home and as active citizens in the community and the world." As in the Boy Scouts, adult Girl Scout leaders sought to teach their charges to master useful skills, perform civic duties, and hold upstanding values. The first Girl Scout troop in Cleveland was the Pansy Troop, organized in 1914 and led by Rhoda Piggott. Its activities included hikes, cookouts, camping at Euclid Beach, marching in parades, and visits to shut-ins, orphanages, and patients in the City Hospital. By 1916, 20 troops had been organized in the area, and in 1921 Mrs. Julia Crowell, Mrs. Newton D. Baker, and 22 other women established the Cleveland Girl Scout Council to provide direction for scouting in the area.

In the early 1930s, Cleveland Girl Scouts, like those in other cities, began selling cookies to support their activities; sales of the cookies grew annually, and in 1981 gross receipts from the sales in the Cleveland area reached $1.5 million. In 1937 the Girl Scouts in Cuyahoga County numbered 3,626, with 1,400 in Cleveland. That year the Cleveland council bought a 243-acre site in W. Richfield to serve as a permanent campground. By 1976, the council owned 5 campsites. In 1950, after a series of temporary offices, the Cleveland council moved into the Community Service Bldg. at 1001 Huron Rd. The local council continued to grow, serving 19,000 members in 1957 with an annual budget of $196,905. The Cleveland council was expanded in 1962 to include Geauga County; in 1963 it merged with the Lake County council to create the new Lake Erie Girl Scout Council. The new council had 36,834 Scouts and 9,809 adult leaders by Jan. 1964.

The local Scouts undertook several innovative programs in the 1960s and 1970s to both increase membership and expand their activities to meet the needs of minorities and other overlooked social groups. In 1964, the Lake Erie Council received a $7,500 grant from Community Action for Youth to establish a demonstration project in the Hough neighborhood and strengthen its minority recruitment program. In 1968, the success of Cadette Troop 435's service project at the Parma Hts. Southwest Senior Ctr. led to the development of the Senior Citizen Scouting Program. Scout membership fell from 45,000 in 1971 to 41,000 in 1976, the year the Lake Erie Council established its Plus Four clubs for boys and girls in elementary schools in COLLINWOOD and Euclid Park. By 1982, men were active as coleaders in local troops, expanding the range of activities available to the Scouts.

**GITTELSOHN, BENJAMIN** (1853–1 Jan. 1932), rabbi and scholar, was born in Lithuania. He was descended from a long line of rabbis, but because his widowed mother was impoverished, he was forced to wander from town to town for charitable donations that enabled him to receive a traditional yeshiva education. He became rabbi of the town of Avanta in 1878 and in 1883 left to become rabbi of Trashkun. He remained very poor, because the Jewish community was unable to pay an adequate salary. In 1890, Gittelsohn was asked to settle in Cleveland by the growing community of Lithuanian Jews in the city. He became rabbi at Beth Hamidrosh Hagodol, serving that congregation until 1901. He assumed the pulpit of Oer Chodosh Anshe Sfard the following year and remained its rabbi until his death. Gittelsohn was a quiet, learned man who eschewed an active communal role among Cleveland's Orthodox Jews. However, the force of his religious knowledge led him to become the spiritual authority for other small congregations during his rabbinate. Among these were (at various times) Ohave Emuna Anshe Russia, Shaari Torah, and Agudath Achim. Gittelsohn provided the community with responsa and discourses on Jewish law and custom. He was Cleveland's first rabbinic scholar. He published 2 scholarly works. The first, *Ha-Poteah ve-ha-Hotem* (New York, 1898), was a collection of Talmudic discourses, many of which were given before Cleveland congregations. The second, *Seder Haggada shel Pesah 'im Be'ur Nagid ve-Nafik* (Jerusalem, 1904), was a detailed commentary on the Passover Haggadah. Additionally, he wrote a commentary on the prayerbook that was never published.

GLASBENA MATICA is one of America's most highly regarded Slovenian choruses, having presented operas and classical works at the SLOVENIAN NATL. HOME on St. Clair Ave. By 1930, cultural life in Cleveland's Slovenian community was at a peak. The ZARJA SINGING SOCIETY successfully introduced operas in the late 1920s and was considered the leading exponent of Slovenian music outside of Europe. Differences over finances and the Chicago-based parent organization split the society into 2 choruses, Samostojna (Independent) Zarja and Socialisticna (Socialist) Zarja, in 1930. Both continued to operate from the St. Clair auditorium and even shared the same director, John Ivanusch, for a while. Samostojna Zarja was made up of many of the original group's strongest talents and continued to present full-length operas and an ambitious repertoire in concert. The new chorus debuted with a Slovenian folk opera and reprised the work for the Theater of Nations festival at PUBLIC AUDITORIUM. Throughout the 1930s, concerts alternated with staged works such as *Il Trovatore*, Ivanusch's *Turjaska Rozamunda*, Smetana's *Hubicka* in Czech, and a Croatian opera. A 1932 performance of Flotow's *Martha*, with a cast of 80, was acclaimed by the *Cleveland Press* as one of the best musical productions of the year. Featured singers in this period included Carolyn Budan, Mary Ivanusch, Josephine Milavec, Antoinette Simcic, Louis Belle, Frank Plut, and Frank Bradach. Ivanusch resigned in 1940, and the group changed its name to Glasbena Matica (the Music Society). Anton Schubel of the Metropolitan Opera Chorus directed for 2 years, followed by local poet and composer IVAN ZORMAN, who led the chorus in concerts and occasional operas. Schubel returned in 1949 and resumed regular productions of standard operas in Slovenian with orchestral accompaniment, such as *Carmen, La Traviata, Mignon,* and *The Tales of Hoffman,* and a new generation of singers performed, including June Price, Ann Safred, and Edward Kenik. After Schubel's death in 1965, Valentina Fillinger directed the chorus in semiannual concerts, a recording, and a tour of Slovenia in 1966. She retired in 1974 and was succeeded by Vladimir Maleckar. A second tour took place in 1978. The chorus numbered 35 members in 1986.

Frank, Molly, *Glasbena Matica 50th* (1980).

GLASER, OTTO (2 Sept. 1895–11 Dec. 1964), was a pioneer in radiology, radium therapy, and nuclear medicine. He developed the first instrument to measure dosage precisely, thereby laying the foundation for the development of therapeutic radiology. Glaser received his Ph.D in physics from the University of Frieberg (Germany) in 1919 and served instructorships at the Radiological Institute of Frieberg (1919–21) and the University of Frieberg Medical School (1921–22). In 1922 he married Emily von Eherenberg and emigrated to the U.S.; he became a U.S. citizen in 1929. Dr. Glaser served at Howard Kelly Hospital in Baltimore, 1922–23; in the Dept. of Biophysical Research, Cleveland Clinic, 1923–24; and as assistant professor of biophysics at the New York Postgraduate Medical School, Columbia, 1925–27. In 1927 he returned to Cleveland and was appointed head of the Dept. of Biophysics at the CLEVELAND CLINIC FOUNDATION (1926–61). He served as emeritus consultant at the Cleveland Clinic Foundation from 1961–64.

In collaboration with Dr. U. V. Portmann and Valentine B. Seitz at the Cleveland Clinic, Glaser developed the condenser dosimeter for measurement of x-rays and radiation from radioactive substances. Following WORLD WAR II, he was principally interested in radioactive isotopes and their application to the diagnosis and treatment of disease.

He was one of the first scientists to measure radioactive fallout and helped standardize measurement of radioactivity. In addition to his work in radiobiology, Dr. Glaser, along with Dr. Irvine Page, did work in hemorrhagic shock and arterial transfusions, was one of the first to work in the field of aviation medicine, and with Dr. GEO. W. CRILE, SR., simulated "bends" in animals to test physiologic results and treatments. Glaser was also the world's foremost authority on the life and accomplishments of Wilhelm Conrad Roentgen, the discoverer of x-rays, publishing a life of Roentgen in 1931 in German and in English in 1933 and 1934. He published over 100 scientific articles; his major scientific work was *Medical Physics* (1944, 1950, 1960), and he collaborated on the *Physical Foundations of Radiology* (1944, 1952, 1961). He was a diplomate of the American Board of Radiology and a member of mumerous radiological societies in Cleveland, the U.S., and abroad. Among Glaser's honors were the Gold Medical Achievement Award of the Radiological Society of North America (1936), the Olympia Decoration (1938), the Janeway Medal of the American Radium Society (1950), the John S. Coulter Plaque of the American C̶̶̶̶̶̶̶̶̶ ̶̶̶̶̶̶̶Physical Medicine (1952), and the Commander̶ ̶ ̶ ̶ ̶ ̶ many, 1960). Otto and E̶r̶ Hannelore Glaser, who tea̶

Otto Glaser Papers, Archives, ̶

GLEASON, WILLIAM J. (2̶ a volunteer Civil War sol̶ Soldiers & Sailors Monum̶ born in County Clare, Irela̶ moved to Vermont when h̶ thereafter to Cleveland. H̶ CIVIL WAR broke out, a̶ "devil" for the *PLAIN D̶* with troops gathering at ̶ spent 3 months drumming a̶t̶ ̶t̶h̶e̶ ̶c̶a̶m̶p̶.̶ ̶ he lied about his age and enlisted in the 60TH OHIO VOLUNTEER INFANTRY. He served 1 week before his parents obtained a writ of habeas corpus and brought him home. His parents opted to allow him to join the 29th Regiment, Ohio Natl. Guard, Co. E, as a drummer boy. He continued to work at the *Plain Dealer* but ran away to enlist in the 150th OVI at 17 years of age. He served with the 150th in the defenses of Washington, D.C., in the summer of 1864. After the war, Gleason worked as a compositor in the printing trade and in the insurance business. He served on the board of elections and as secretary of the Cleveland Public Library board, controller of the city of Cleveland, president of the Irish Natl. League, and nationally as a staff member of the commander of the Grand Army of the Republic. He served on the Soldiers & Sailors Monument Commission, 1894–1905. He is buried in Calvary Cemetery.

Gleason, William J., *History of the Cuyahoga County Soldiers and Sailors Monument* (1894).

GLEN OAK SCHOOL was founded in 1969 as an all-girls' school by the Religious of the Sacred Heart (Madams of the Sacred Heart). Before the founding of Glen Oak, the order had no schools in the Cleveland area, but a number of area women who had been educated by the Madams encouraged them to establish a school in Cleveland. In the mid-1960s, the order reached an agreement whereby they acquired some land and a building adjacent to GILMOUR ACADEMY in GATES MILLS. The school was not designed to be a traditional Catholic girls' school. Although religious instruction was important, an ecumenical approach was taken. For example, the religious-studies program was guided by not only a Catholic priest but also a Protestant minister and a Jewish rabbi. Neither was the school's pedagogy traditional. Team-teaching, the open classroom, interdisciplinary studies, and nongraded evaluations were foundations of the school. In addition, education was to be coordinated with Gilmour; facilities and faculty were shared. The Madams of the Sacred Heart remained at Glen Oak for 3 years. In 1972, an Episcopalian minister, Rev. Lloyd Gesner, was appointed headmaster. He directed the school until 1977, when the URSULINE SISTERS, long associated with education in the Cleveland area, were asked by the board of trustees to take over the school. Sister Claudia Klyn was appointed director. In the early 1980s, plans were adopted for the merger of Glen Oak and Gilmour, and a merger was finalized in time for the 1982–83 school year.

The **GLENVILLE** neighborhood is located on Cleveland's east side in the area of St. Clair Ave. and E. 105th St. Incorporated as a village on 4 Oct. 1870, it was formally annexed to the city of Cleveland on 19 June 1905. Once known as a resort for the wealthy and the "garden spot" of Cuyahoga County, Glenville is an example of an ever-changing urban America. Glenville was born out of an early Irish settlement on the lakeshore between E. CLEVELAND and COLLINWOOD in 1873. Shady, thick glens through which little streams tumbled gave the area its picturesque name. Early New England farmers were the first to settle in the area, followed by immigrants from Scotland, Ireland, and England. Gradually, Glenville grew into a secluded rural village. Almost surrounding the flourishing village center at St. Clair and Doan (E. 105th) St. were truck farms operated by German-Americans, who hauled their produce to the city. In time the St. Clair horsecar line was extended in the form of a horse-drawn truck. Glenville residents could also reach Cleveland by boarding the Ashtabula accommodation train at the Coit Rd. Station.

During the "Gay Nineties," when EUCLID AVE. was celebrated as the most beautiful street in the country, Glenville's lakeshore location made it a fashionable summer residence for Cleveland's affluent families. Occupying nearly all of Cleveland's northeast portion from Superior Ave. north to Lake Erie, the village attracted the finest in society and sport. Glenville attracted national attention at the turn of the century as a horseracing center with the Northern Ohio Fairgrounds, built in 1870 at St. Clair and E. 88th St. With the GLENVILLE RACE TRACK, it became the racing center of the country. The village also attracted national attention on 14 July 1895 with the opening of the Cleveland Golf Club, with SAMUEL MATHER as its first president. Industrial expansion in Cleveland contributed to the first great increases in the city's black population, beginning in 1910. Forced to settle in small pockets throughout the city, blacks by 1930 constituted 8% of Glenville's population. Much of the population at that time was of Jewish background. Forced to live in increasingly segregated areas, blacks by 1950 constituted 90% of the population in Glenville, with the area coming under the control of black political leadership with the election of black city council members in the 1960s. On 23 July 1968, riots erupted, causing widespread neighborhood arsons, and looting (see GLENVILLE SHOOT-OUT). In 1985, Glenville remained a depressed area representative of the problems facing urban America.

The **GLENVILLE HEALTH ASSOCIATION** is a private urban health center that provides services to the poor in the GLENVILLE area. It receives no tax monies and is supported in part by private foundations. The GHA was organized in 1970 as an outgrowth of the Forest City Hospital Assoc. The need for such an organization was prompted by an ACADEMY OF MEDICINE report listing only 21 physicians' offices and 100 hospital beds (at FOREST CITY HOSPITAL) to serve Glenville's 80,000 people. The GHA's first objective was to develop an ambulatory care program in Glenville. The long-range goal was to erect a center that offered comprehensive health care 24 hours a day, 7 days a week. The GHA is directed by a board of 40 trustees. The original board was headed by Leonard Howard. Through its trustees, the GHA is affiliated with Forest City Hospital, MT. SINAI, UNIVERSITY HOSPITALS, and CASE WESTERN RESERVE UNIVERSITY. In 1973, the GHA received $500,000 in grants from private foundations—including $400,000 from the Robt. Wood Johnson Foundation of Brunswick, N.J.—to run a walk-in clinic for 2 years. With additional grant money, a new medical facility was built at 10640 St. Clair Ave., staffed by 6 doctors and 2 dentists. As opposed to other urban health centers, the GHA attempted to emulate the personal style of practice typical of private doctors and dentists. The clinic, however, was often underused during the 1970s, as many Glenville residents believed that quality health care could be obtained only outside the community. Because of that and the increase in medical costs, the GHA was forced to reduce its staff in the late 1970s. By 1984, however, it became almost self-supporting, generating 89% of its $1.6 million annual budget from patient revenues and contracts. Since 1974, the GHA has operated in conjunction with Forest City Hospital and as a teaching facility for CWRU. In 1975 it received the $5,000 Anisfield-Wolf Memorial Award from the CLEVELAND FOUNDATION for outstanding community service.

The **GLENVILLE RACE TRACK** was once the site of horse, auto, bicycle, and foot races. Located on St. Clair between E. 88th and E. 101st streets, it was considered a first-class course for both cars and horses in an era when both sports were pastimes of the wealthy. The Glenville track was built in 1870 by the Cleveland Driving Park Co. as part of the Northern Ohio Fair, whose major grounds were located across the street from the track. The Northern Ohio Fair Assoc., a stock company formed by leading citizens, promoted AGRICULTURE, horticulture, the mechanical arts, and trotting races. The track was part of an 87-acre development that attracted the city's wealthy sportsmen in the summer. The fairground was abandoned in 1881, but the driving-company venture remained successful for another 3 decades. Included among the original stockholders were Frank Rockefeller, SYLVESTER EVERETT, Warren H. Corning, and Howard M. Hanna. Harness races were the principal attraction at the track, where many world speed records were set. The track solidified Cleveland's prominence in the racing world. In 1872, Cleveland joined with Buffalo, Utica, and Rochester to become the Quadrilateral Circuit; within a year the group became part of the Grand Circuit, the major league of harness racing. A famous race at the track in July 1876 pitted the famed Goldsmith Maid against Smuggler and was immortalized in verse by Oliver Wendell Holmes. On 30 July 1885, Wm. H. Vanderbilt's Maud S. set the world record for trotting (2:08 ¾) at the track. Horseracing at Glenville was later promoted by the Gentlemen's Driving Club, organized in May 1895 by HARRY K. DEVEREUX, Col. Billy Edwards, and DANIEL RHODES HANNA. The club introduced matinee races, often run before 10,000 people. Amateurs such as Devereux, the most prominent of the local drivers, amassed records and awards; at the high point of his career, the Boston Challenge Cup Race of 1902, he drove the horse John McKerron to victory in 2 heats, with times of 2:07 ½ and 2:08, and went on to win a pacing cup with Ananias.

The sporting life of the track overflowed into the nearby Roadside Club, where race spectators and participants wined and dined after the matinee. According to local tradition, the winners treated the losers to extravagant champagne dinners. Even after harness racing lost its appeal, the Roadside Club prospered as a gambling club until 1935 (from 1926 until its closing, it was known as the 9100 to correspond to its St. Clair Ave. address). The track was also used for auto racing; its dirt surface was one of the few mile courses in the country where speed trials and match races, featuring popular drivers such as Barney Oldfield, were held. The track's popularity corresponded with the growth of Cleveland's AUTOMOTIVE INDUSTRY. Many cars were tested at the track, including locally built Baker Electrics and Wintons. Despite the popularity of racing at Glenville, the track was abandoned in 1908 when GLENVILLE mayor FREDERICK GOFF declared betting illegal. Through the efforts of Devereux and other racing devotees, the center of local racing was subsequently shifted to the village of N. RANDALL, which was incorporated specifically to accommodate the sport. The matinee harness races were held at the new N. Randall track known as the Golden Oval, while auto racing moved to Summit County. The popularity of trotting races, the main attraction at Glenville, waned within a decade of its closing. The new N. Randall track was less accessible to the general public, which began to prefer running to trotting races. As the wealthy deans of Cleveland racing reached retirement age, the newly rich businessmen did not take up the sport. The Gentlemen's Driving Club passed out of existence prior to WORLD WAR I.

The **GLENVILLE SHOOTOUT** was a violent episode that began the evening of 23 July 1968 in the eastern section of GLENVILLE. It was a spontaneous action against police by an armed, purposeful black militant group, resulting in casualties on both sides. After the initial shootout, the violence resulted in destruction of property throughout the Glenville area. On the evening of 23 July, there were 2 police surveillance teams in the Superior-Lakeview area watching Fred "Ahmed" Evans and his militant group, who were suspected of buying illegal weapons, as well as a police tow truck making a routine pickup of an abandoned car. Although it is not clear who shot first, there was an exchange of gunfire between Evans's group and the police. Before the night was over, 7 people were dead: 3 policemen, 3 suspects, and 1 civilian; and 15 were wounded. The shootings attracted a large crowd, mostly black, young, and hostile, and it became clear that the police were neither trained nor equipped to handle the situation. Mayor Carl Stokes requested and received the assistance of the Natl. Guard.

On the afternoon of 24 July, the mayor decided that in order to prevent further casualties, only black policemen and black community leaders would be allowed in the Glenville area. Their job was to patrol the area that night to ease the tensions in the neighborhood. The rest of the police and the guard were stationed on the perimeter of the cordoned-off area. Stokes believed that putting BLACKS in control of their own community would prevent further bloodshed, and that proved to be the case. However, there was continued looting and arson in the 6-sq.-mi. area. On 25 July, the Natl. Guard and the police reentered Glenville, and a curfew was established. The arson and looting gradually diminished, and by 28 July order had been restored.

Sixty-three businesses were damaged, with a total loss set at $2.6 million. Evans surrendered to the police the morning of 24 July. The following spring he was tried for murder, found guilty, and sentenced to life in prison, where he died in 1978. At his trial it was confirmed that Evans had received funds from CLEVELAND: NOW!, a program for urban rehabilitation. As a result, contributions to the program dried up. The presence of a black mayor in Cleveland had not provided insurance against racial confrontation, and racial tensions in the city were exacerbated by the shootout. The episode showed that for many Cleveland blacks, the expectation of a better life had not been fulfilled, and the potential for violence was still present.

Masotti, Louis H., and Corsi, Jerome R., *Shoot-out in Cleveland* (1969).

**GLENWILLOW** is a village occupying 2.2 sq. mi. in the southeastern corner of Cuyahoga County. It is bounded by SOLON on the north and east, OAKWOOD on the west, and Twinsburg in Summit County on the south. Originally part of Solon Twp., Glenwillow was created as a company town in the 1890s, when the AUSTIN POWDER CO. purchased 1,200 acres of isolated territory to produce mining tools and blasting powder for mines and quarries. The unsettled rural area was chosen because of the hazardous nature of the work. Austin built 30 rental homes for employees and reserved 400 acres of farmland to raise cattle and produce hay. Glenwillow prospered and was able to attract nearly a dozen other industrial concerns, including Miller Industries. Its growth was further enhanced by the prosperity of the neighboring communities of Solon, BEDFORD, and Oakwood. The relationship between the village and the Austin Co. ended in 1972, when the company closed and moved; it had at one time occupied one-half the area of Glenwillow. That helped develop the village into a tightly knit community, and the absence of crime, debt, and any relief burden led to Glenwillow's being characterized as a modern-day utopia. During the 1970s, annexation attempts by Solon and MAPLE HTS. threatened the village's existence. Once the only Cuyahoga County community without a city income tax, Glenwillow was forced to adopt a 1% tax to raise revenues for basic operations. No longer a "company town," Glenwillow still retained several trucking and construction firms and the Glenwillow Mobile Home Park. Glenwillow is part of the Solon School System and contracts with Solon for fire protection. It has no city water or sewer system, and only a part-time police force. Village residents rely on shopping areas in nearby communities. Recreational facilities are limited and include 1 golf course. The population in 1980 was 528.

The **GLIDDEN COATINGS & RESINS DIVISION (IMPERIAL CHEMICAL INDUSTRIES)**, in 1986 a part of Britain's largest industrial company, is the descendant of a small paint-and-varnish firm begun over 100 years ago. Before its mergers with ICI and earlier with SCM, Glidden revolutionized the coatings world with its chemical research that had applications to food technology as well as paint. The company was founded as the Glidden Varnish Co. by Francis Harrington Glidden and was operated from a 1-story building on Woodland. In 1875, Glidden and partner Levi C. Brackett bought out the Forest City Paint & Varnish Co. (founded 1875) and renamed the company Glidden & Brackett. With the coming of a new partner, the company again modified its name, to the Glidden & Joy Varnish Co. Glidden manufactured varnish and a lacquer known as Jap a lac. In 1917, when it was purchased by Adrian Joyce (and became the Glidden Co.), the firm averaged annual sales of $2 million. Within 2 years, Joyce acquired 11 paint manufacturers and distributors that expanded the company's expertise in pigments, dry colors, chemicals, and metals. Realizing the linkage between the oils used in paint and those used in food, the company began acquiring vegetable oil-processing plants and food processors and distributors in the 1920s. By 1934, Glidden owned the E. R. Durkee Co. of New York, maker of condiments, spices, and sauces, and 6 other companies that produced over half of its sales volume. The diversification enabled Glidden to utilize both the edible and inedible components of oils. In 1932, Joyce went to Germany to study the use of soybeans. He returned convinced that soybean oil's chemical composition and purity would make it an excellent paint oil, because of its color retention, nonyellowing properties, and wearability. Also, the bean had excellent food value and was a source of lecithin, a phosphorus-rich compound previously extracted (at high cost) from egg yolks. As a result of Joyce's convictions, Glidden began construction of a $1 million soya protein plant. Along with Henry Ford, Adrian Joyce is credited with promoting the growth of soybeans as a cash crop in America, and by 1939, his company was one of the largest soybean processors in North America. It also ranked as the largest manufacturer of cadmium pigments, the 2d-largest paint and varnish maker, and one of the largest margarine manufacturers in the world.

With its headquarters in Cleveland, Glidden manufactured much of its paint and varnish line here, while it organized its newly acquired plants under autonomous regional directors. Research and development for the paint-and-resins division was centered in Cleveland, while food research for its Durkee Famous Foods line was in Chicago. The paint factory was located at 11000 Madison Ave., while the research center was on Elmwood Ave. in LAKEWOOD until it moved to STRONGSVILLE in 1966. Through research and merger, the Glidden paint division introduced such innovations as interior latex (1948), porcelain paint (1953), exterior latex (1957), strip coating (1959), electroplating (1961), and insulating paint (1978). Accompanying these developments was research in synthetic resins and polyesters and turpentine fractionating and production. In addition to its technical prowess, Glidden was noted for its successful marketing of its commercial, industrial, and consumer product lines. In 1939, the company opened a color center, which featured miniature rooms to aid customers in selecting products from their local Glidden retail store. Glidden routinely modernized its product lines and monitored their profitability.

Glidden's visibility in all markets made it a likely takeover target by the mid-1960s. To ward off an unfriendly merger by the Greatamerica Co. of Dallas, Glidden considered merging with General Analine and Fil, before merging with SCM (Smith Corona Merchant), manufacturer of typewriters, copy machines, data-processing equipment, and household appliances. Within a decade, the Glidden-Durkee division of the company accounted for 2/3 of the company's sales. In 1976, the division was split into 4 operating divisions: Glidden Coatings & Resins, Durkee Fine Foods, Inorganic Chemicals, and Organic Chemicals. Though the headquarters for coatings and foods remained in the city, the paint plant was phased out in 1976. The company asserted that the Cleveland factory was the most expensive plant to run of all Glidden facilities, despite partial rebuilding after a major fire in 1957. The closing affected 180 salaried and hourly people. In 1986, SCM was itself acquired by Hansen Trust PLC. The company retained SCM's chemical, paper-products, and consumer-goods lines,

including Durkee Foods, but sold the Glidden Coatings & Resins Div. to Imperial Chemical Industries in Aug. 1986. IPC, a leading international chemical manufacturer, sought Glidden to reinforce its position as a paint company. Glidden had an important position in the can, industrial, appliance, and powder coatings market, and its acquisition made ICI the 3d-largest producer in the $9 million U.S. coatings-and-resin industry. Glidden's renowned research effort was viewed as a complement to that of ICI. At the time of the sale, Glidden employed 1,200 in the Greater Cleveland area and had annual sales of $650 million and net assets of $200 million.

The **GLOBE THEATER** was one of the first theaters in the city of Cleveland. Built by J. W. Watson in 1840, it was located on the 2d floor of a business building on the north side of Superior Ave., approximately midway between Bank (W. 6th) St. and Seneca (W. 3rd) St. The theater was 60′ wide by 100′ long and approximately 25′ high. It had a shallow stage 40′ wide and 15′ deep. The Globe had good acoustics and seated nearly 1,000. Although quite handsome, it was redecorated frequently because of changes in ownership and name. Over the years the facility was known as Watson's Hall (1840–45); Melodeon Hall (1845–60); Brainard's Hall (1860–72); Brainard's Opera House (1872–75); and the Globe Theater (from 1875 until its demolition in 1880). There were many interesting attractions held at the theater. Ralph Waldo Emerson lectured on 10 Jan. 1847 on the "Man of the World." The Great Royal Japanese Troupe from the Imperial Theater of Yeddo appeared on 28 Feb. 1873. Louis Kossuth, an orator and eminent Hungarian patriot, spoke on 2 Feb. 1852. The last performance, *Uncle Tom's Cabin*, was held on 29 Jan. 1880.

**GOFF, FREDERICK H.** (15 Dec. 1858–14 Mar. 1923), was a lawyer, banker, and civic leader who developed the ideas for both the living trust and the community trust, using the latter idea to establish the CLEVELAND FOUNDATION in 1914. Goff was born in Blackbury, Ill., the son of Frederick C. and Catherine Brown Goff. His family later moved to Cleveland, where his father became a prominent coal dealer. Goff attended CLEVELAND PUBLIC SCHOOLS and graduated from CENTRAL HIGH SCHOOL. In 1881 he graduated from the University of Michigan with a Ph.B. degree. He returned to Cleveland and worked as a librarian in the Cleveland Law Library, taking advantage of the opportunity to read and study law. In either 1883 or 1884 he was admitted to the Ohio bar.

Over the next quarter-century, Goff was a partner in a succession of law firms: Carr & Goff, 1884–90; Estep, Dickey, Carr & Goff, 1890–96; and Kline, Tolles & Goff, 1896–1908. He worked primarily in corporate law, and he became a specialist in reorganization and financial problems. By the early 1900s, his annual income was estimated to be $100,000. On 8 June 1908, Goff left the legal profession to become the president of the Cleveland Trust Co., which grew tremendously during his tenure. He established new rules of operation that improved the bank's image and its financial position; these rules included no loans to directors, a continuous daily audit, and new safeguards for assets. Under Goff's leadership from 1908–23, Cleveland Trust increased the number of its offices from 15 to 52, its depositors from 70,000 to 397,000, and its resources from $30 million to $176 million. Goff also oversaw the bank's merger in 1922 with the Lake Shore Banking & Trust Co. and the Garfield Savings & Trust Co.

As both lawyer and banker, Goff helped a number of wealthy Clevelanders plan their estates, and from this experience grew his 2 contributions in the development of trusts: the living trust and the community trust. The living trust enabled wealthy men and women to convey their property to a trustee prior to their deaths and to specify how it should be managed. The idea for the community trust was influenced by Sir Arthur Hobhouse's *The Dead Hand* (1880), which argued that too often trusts and funds established for limited purposes later become outmoded. The community trust enabled the wealthy to place their property in a central community fund administered by trustees who would possess sufficient latitude to manage the funds for the continual improvement of a changing community. Goff was instrumental in establishing the Cleveland Foundation in 1914 and in publicizing the idea in other communities. By the time of his death, more than 50 such community trusts had been established in the U.S.

Goff's community service took other forms, as well. Elected mayor of GLENVILLE in 1903, he ended gambling at the local racetrack and endorsed a proposal for Cleveland to annex Glenville. In 1907 he represented the CLEVELAND ELECTRIC RAILWAY CO. during negotiations with Mayor TOM L. JOHNSON over the street railway controversy. During WORLD WAR I, he served on the executive committee of the MAYOR'S ADVISORY WAR COMMITTEE and was appointed by Pres. Woodrow Wilson as vice-chairman of the War Finance Corp.'s capital issues committee. He also served as a trustee of the Community Fund, of HIRAM HOUSE, and of Western Reserve University and was treasurer of the Chamber of Commerce, president of the Cleveland Law Assoc. (1908), and a founder and director of the Assoc. for Criminal Justice. He also served as a director or officer in a number of local railroad, manufacturing, and service companies. He married Frances Southworth on 16 Oct. 1894.

**GOLDBLATT, HARRY** (14 Mar. 1891–6 Jan. 1977), was an eminent research scientist and physician. He was internationally recognized for his pioneering research in the causes of high blood pressure. Goldblatt was born in Iowa, but grew up in Canada. He received a B.A. from McGill University, where he developed an interest in biology. In 1916 he graduated from McGill's medical school at the top of his class. After briefly serving as a resident in surgery at the Royal Victoria Hospital in Montreal, he claimed U.S. citizenship and from 1917–18 served in the Medical Reserve Corps of the U.S. Army. After a 2-year interval in which he served as resident pathologist of Lakeside Hospital in Cleveland, Goldblatt continued his education in Europe, including a fellowship at the Lister Institute of Preventative Medicine, where he won honors for his research. While at Lakeside, Goldblatt developed a research interest in the field of experimental pathology. From 1924–27 he was an assistant professor of pathology at Western Reserve University; he was associate professor from 1927–35. Between 1935–46 he was professor of experimental pathology, at the same time serving as associate director of WRU's Institute of Pathology. After a 7-year absence—during which time he served as director of medical research at Cedars of Lebanon Hospital in Los Angeles—Goldblatt returned to Cleveland to become Mt. Sinai's director of laboratories. From 1961 he was director of the Louis D. Beaumont Research Laboratories.

Early in his career, Goldblatt developed an intense interest in discovering the cause of essential hypertension. That led to a famous experiment in the early 1930s, which is believed to have stimulated more research than any single experiment in medical history. Almost by accident, Goldblatt discovered that by clamping off part of the main arteries to the kidneys, high blood pressure was caused. That

established the theory that alterations in blood flow to the kidneys played an important role in blood-pressure elevation. The experiment opened an entirely new field in research of the disease. Throughout his life, Goldblatt continued to research the causes of high blood pressure. He was specifically dedicated to finding unequivocal proof that renin, an agent found in normal kidneys, was the origin of essential hypertension. In 1965, with the assistance of Dr. Erwin Haas, he was able to isolate enough renin to provide 4,000 ampoules to the World Health Organization, which voted to make Goldblatt's renin—called Goldblatt units—the international standard of measurement of human renin. Later, with Drs. Haas and Sharad Deodhar, Goldblatt achieved a breakthrough in basic knowlege by producing antirenin with acetylated homologous renin. Goldblatt was the recipient of many honors, most significantly the Scientific Achievement Award of the American Medical Assoc. in 1976, and appointment to the Natl. Academy of Sciences in 1973. Because of the scientific implications of his work internationally, the American Heart Assoc. established the Dr. Harry Goldblatt Fellowship.

**GOLDMAN, SOLOMON** (18 Aug. 1893–1953), religious leader, educator, author, and national Zionist figure, served Cleveland's congregations B'NAI JESHURUN and ANSHE EMETH for 10 tumultuous years. He led Anshe Emeth, then known as the Cleveland Jewish Ctr., from liberal Orthodoxy into the Conservative movement. Born in Kozin, Poland, Goldman was brought to the U.S. as a child. He received a traditional Jewish education at the Orthodox Yitzchak Elchanan Yeshiva in New York until 1912, when he entered the Jewish Theological Seminary, the Conservative rabbinical college. He was ordained in 1918. Goldman's first pulpit was Cleveland's Congregation B'nai Jeshurun, a post he accepted in 1918. Although the congregation's membership increased during his tenure and moved completely within the Conservative movement, internal conflict and resistance to his attempts at making it a Jewish center led Goldman to resign in 1923. He then accepted the pulpit at Anshe Emeth, which less then a year earlier had dedicated the massive Cleveland Jewish Ctr. on E. 105th St. in the Glenville neighborhood. Goldman's leadership made the Jewish Ctr. the spiritual, cultural, and social focus for the Jews of GLENVILLE. During his years there, it became the largest institution of its kind in the U.S.

Despite this success, Goldman faced open hostility from the Orthodox within the congregation. They challenged him on the issue of mixed seating for men and women, which they opposed. The dissidents, in an attempt to reinstitute separate seating, took their case to the Union of Orthodox Rabbis, which called Goldman to appear before a rabbinical court. Goldman refused on the grounds that he and his congregation were Conservative, and the Orthodox rabbis had no jurisdiction in the matter. The dissidents then filed 38 complaints in the Court of Common Pleas of Cuyahoga County against Goldman and 31 trustees. The court, after hearing arguments, refused to intervene, thus allowing mixed seating to remain. Several of the men who opposed Goldman left the congregation and joined OHEB ZEDEK.

Goldman was an advocate of Hebrew education. He collaborated with A. H. FRIEDLAND in the development of educational materials and was active in support of the CLEVELAND HEBREW SCHOOLS, a branch of which met at the Cleveland Jewish Ctr., and the BUREAU OF JEWISH EDUCATION. While in Cleveland, Goldman began to develop a national reputation in the Zionist movement. In 1925, he opposed American Jewish Committee leader Louis Marshall and refused to serve on a national committee to raise funds for the distressed East European Jews. He argued that the money should be used to transport Jews to Palestine rather than to aid them where they were. Goldman left Cleveland in 1929 to become the rabbi of Congregation Anshe Emet in Chicago. He served in that position until his death in 1953. After leaving Cleveland, he continued to be a major force in the Zionist movement and served as president of the Zionist Organization of America (1938-39). Goldman was a Biblical scholar and published several works, including *A Rabbi Takes Stock* (1931), *The Jew and the Universe* (1936), *Crisis and Decision* (1938), *Undefeated* (1940), *The Book of Books* (1948), *In the Beginning* (1949), and *From Slavery to Freedom* (1958). In 1933 he wrote a pageant, *Romance of a People*, that was performed at the Chicago World's Fair.

**GOLDNER, JACOB H.** (8 Aug. 1871–30 Dec. 1949), was pastor of EUCLID AVE. CHRISTIAN CHURCH, E. 100th and Euclid Ave., for 45 years and pastor emeritus from 1945-49, one of the longest continuous pastorates of any minister of the DISCIPLES OF CHRIST. He was born in Beaver, Pa., the son of George and Caroline Vogt Goldner. Left motherless at the age of 6, he lived with his grandparents, and later with a farmer, who encouraged him in his efforts to secure an education, which subsequently included graduation from Rayen High School (Youngstown) in 1893 and from Hiram College in 1896. While attending Hiram, he served as student minister at the Austintown Church. His first full pastorate, the Chagrin Falls Church (1896-98), was followed by graduate studies at the Divinity School, University of Chicago. Before completing his degree, he accepted an invitation (Jan. 1900) to become pastor at the Euclid Ave. Christian Church. The then-existing structure, which accommodated 400 people, soon grew too small for the increasing membership. Accordingly, work on a new church at the same location began in Sept. 1905. It was dedicated on 12 April 1908. The church, which became known as the greenstone church because of the serpentine green stone of volcanic origin from West Chester, Pa., was in the Romanesque style, with its notable stained-glass windows and a Siena marble baptistry. It seated over 1,100. Soon after Dr. Goldner began his service to the church, he embarked on an experimental adventure in personal evangelism, calling on people within the community—at that time a residential, noncommercial area of the city. The plan worked, and hundreds were received into membership; evangelism was taken up by churches, replacing the revival meetings.

Dr. Goldner was a member of the committee that organized the Cleveland Fed. of Churches (later the Cleveland Church Fed.) and served as its president (1921-22). He was president of the Ohio Christian Missionary Society (1920), served as a commissioner of the Assoc. for the Promotion of Christian Unity, and in 1924 was elected president of the Internatl. Convention of the Disciples of Christ. An alumni trustee of Hiram College, Dr. Goldner also did graduate work at Harvard University (1897) and at Western Reserve University (1903). He traveled extensively in Europe and the Middle East. Dr. Goldner resigned on 1 Oct. 1945 and was immediately named pastor emeritus. From 1945 until his death in 1949, he was ad interim pastor of 7 churches. He died several days before the celebration of the 50th anniversary of his ministry in Cleveland (Jan. 1950). His wife, Harriet Marks Goldner, whom he had married 10 Aug. 1904, had been killed 13 Oct. 1920 by a hit-and-run driver. The couple had 2 sons, Dr. Jacob H. Goldner, Jr., a physician in California, and Rev. Gerould R. Goldner, pastor of Lakewood Christian Church.

**GOLDSMITH, JONATHAN** (1783-1847), was a master builder active in Lake County and Cleveland between 1819-43. Goldsmith was born in Milford, Conn., and after a brief apprenticeship as a shoemaker, he apprenticed himself to a carpenter-joiner at the age of 17. He worked in Hebron, Conn., and Berkshire County, Mass., before moving to Ohio in 1811. Goldsmith's known buildings include 30 homes and commercial buildings in Painesville, another handful around Lake County, and 10 houses in Cleveland. The Cleveland residences were all built between 1830-37 on Euclid Ave., when it was a prime residential street. None of them is extant. They were built for such prominent citizens as SHERLOCK J. ANDREWS, PETER WEDDELL, Samuel Cowles, and TRUMAN P. HANDY. All were executed in the current late Federal and early Greek Revival styles. Some were true mansions, especially the Handy home and the Judge Thos. Kelly house, both of which boasted a colossal Ionic portico. Goldsmith's apprentice and assistant on the Cleveland jobs was his son-in-law CHAS. W. HEARD, who continued to practice architecture in Cleveland until 1876. Goldsmith is better-documented than most early 19th-century master builders, because many of his drawings have survived in the WESTERN RESERVE HISTORICAL SOCIETY, as well as account books, contracts, and letters. His drawings were included in the Metropolitan Museum's exhibition "The Greek Revival in the United States" in 1943, and he is mentioned in Talbot Hamlin's *Greek Revival Architecture in America.*

**GOLF.** Golf is a sport that originated in Scotland in the 15th century. It is played on a large, open tract of land. The object of the game is to hit a small, hard ball across a distance with clubs, and ultimately to sink the ball into a hole, utilizing the least possible number of strokes. In 1986, golf was a very popular sport in Cleveland, and was played throughout most of the year. SAMUEL MATHER is credited with introducing the game to Cleveland. Traveling in the East on business in 1895, Mather was invited to play the St. Andrew's course at Mount Hope, N.Y., then recognized as the best and most prestigious golf club in the U.S. He became quite enthusiastic about the game. On his return to Ohio, he set about organizing a golf club, whose membership would comprise the social and business elite of Cleveland. Mather's efforts resulted in the creation of the Cleveland Golf Club, located in GLENVILLE. He served the club as its first president, and R. H. S. Clarke as secretary. The grounds opened 13 July 1895 with a glittering social occasion, and a demonstration of the game by T. Sterling Beckwith, Jr., and J. D. Maclennin, two of the city's wealthy sportsmen. The game rapidly took hold among the circles that Mather had intended. In 1897, Wm. H. Boardman, another wealthy sportsman, led the first Cleveland golf team to Buffalo, where they defeated the best that the city could offer. That same year, the original COUNTRY CLUB established a golf course at its grounds on Lake Erie in BRATENAHL. From the first, golf was perceived as a sport that both men and women could play with dignity. In 1899, Clevelanders contributed a technological innovation that revolutionized the game. Previously, golf had been played with a ball made from gutta percha, a substance that resembled rubber. However, these balls were hard and lacked resilience. It occurred to COBURN HASKELL, a member of the Country Club, that a true rubber ball might improve distance. Working with Joseph Mitchell, the professional golfer at the club, and Bertram Work of the B. F. Goodrich Corp., Haskell developed the wound-rubber-core golf ball. Scores dipped markedly, and

457

the ball became the official standard until the 1960s and the development of the solid-core ball.

Golf began a period of rapid growth with the turn of the century. Exhibitions were staged to popularize the game. On 28 July 1900, Harry Vardon, then the greatest contemporary American golfer, played 36 holes at the Cleveland Golf Club. More courses were established. The Euclid Club, the second to be devoted primarily to golf, was opened 4 July 1900. Wm. B. Chisholm, president of the Cleveland Rolling Mills, served as the club's president. Chisholm induced his friend JOHN D. ROCKEFELLER (an avid golfer who had built a course on the grounds of his Forest Hill estate) to provide part of the land for the club. The Western Open, a national amateur tournament, was played there in 1902. By 1915, 7 golf clubs were located in Cuyahoga County. The 2 original clubs, the Cleveland Golf Club and the Euclid Club, had merged respectively with the Country Club and the MAYFIELD COUNTRY CLUB.

Golf had clearly become established in Cleveland. However, it remained a sport of the wealthy. The middle class generally could command neither the large spaces required for courses nor the time required for the leisurely pace of the sport. However, the prosperity created by Cleveland's rapid growth as an industrial center was fueling a revolution of rising expectations. The middle class became more numerous and influential. While private clubs continued to open, most notably the CANTERBURY GOLF CLUB in 1921 and ACACIA COUNTRY CLUB in 1923, demand for public courses began to mount. WM. A. STINCHCOMB, of the Metropolitan Park system, recognizing the need, opened Metropolitan No. 1 in the Rocky River Reservation in 1925. The Depression had comparatively little effect on a sport that attracted the financially secure. By 1930, 8 courses admitted the general public. Two of these were publicly owned, one by the Metro Parks, the other by the city of Cleveland. By 1941 the county had 16 private, 15 semiprivate, and 2 public courses. WORLD WAR II retarded the growth of the sport, so that in 1951 the same number of courses were available. However, the postwar boom would reinvigorate the factors that had driven the first round of growth.

The utility of the golf course as a business venue continued to draw the commercially minded middle class. The introduction of televised matches, and of large cash prizes on the professional circuit, drew national attention to the game. Perhaps most important, professional players emerged whose golf skills were great but whose personalities meshed well with their upwardly mobile audience. Arnold Palmer was the most notable example of this group. Palmer first achieved recognition for his play as an amateur at the Pine Ridge Country Club, while stationed by the Coast Guard in Cleveland in 1952–53. He turned professional in 1955 and went on to become the most popular, and one of the most successful, golfers of the 1950s, 1960s, and 1970s. Further, he parlayed his winnings and endorsement fees into a small business empire through shrewd management. Palmer personified the aspirations of the increasingly wealthy middle class. The professional tournaments grew more lucrative and visible. Prior to 1946, Cleveland had hosted 4 Western Opens, 2 U.S. Opens, 1 Women's Western Open, 1 Women's Natl. Championship, 1 Cleveland Open, and several Ohio State Championships. However, the professional purses had been small, never exceeding $10,000. After the war, corporate sponsorship and television fees became available. The Carling Open, held at Manakiki Country Club in 1953 and 1954, offered $15,000 in combined prizes. The Cleveland Open, established in 1963, boasted a purse of $100,000. The prizes grew steadily, but the event was discontinued in 1975. The Ladies Professional Golf Assoc.

has staged several tournaments here since 1976, including the Babe Zaharias Invitational Classic that year, and the World Championship of Women's Golf, 1981–84. In 1986, 44 golf courses existed in metropolitan Cleveland and Cuyahoga County, including 26 that were listed as open to the public. Nine organizations, representing and organizing all levels of play, served the golfing public.

Edward E. Worthington

**GOMBOS, ZOLTAN** (21 Jan. 1905–26 Nov. 1984), was a key figure not only in the Cleveland ethnic community, where he published the Hungarian daily *SZABADSAG*, but in the larger civic arena, as well. He became a soccer star as a student in his native Hungary. When he emigrated to the U.S. in 1925, he briefly stopped in Indianapolis prior to settling in Cleveland later that year as a student at Western Reserve University. There he studied business, played soccer, and earned expenses as a sports columnist for a Hungarian paper before graduating in 1929. With business careers severely limited by the Depression, Gombos became one of Cleveland's first foreign-film exhibitors in various rented theaters. He even opened a Gypsy theme restaurant at the 1936 GREAT LAKES EXPOSITION. Since 1932 he had covered sports and amusements for *Szabadsag*, where he won promotion to city and then managing editor. He also won the hand of his first wife, Magda, whose father was one of the paper's officials. Gombos began his 45-year tenure as editor and publisher of *Szabadsag* in 1939. As president of the Liberty Publishing Co., he also acquired a New York Hungarian daily, the *Amerikai Magyar Nepszava* (American Hungarian People's Voice). He moved the New York paper's printing operation to Cleveland, where he also acquired several English neighborhood papers, including the *Buckeye Press*. In the 1950s he also published a national Hungarian weekly, *A Jo Pasztor* (The Good Shepherd). As one of the country's most prominent Hungarian-Americans, Gombos was appointed to the delegation that returned St. Stephen's Crown from the U.S. to Hungary in 1978. He received the American Hungarian Foundation's Geo. Washington Award in 1978. He served on the Cleveland zoning board for 11 years and was chairman of the Ohio Racing Commission from 1953–58. As an original member of the Playhouse Square Foundation, he often sponsored appearances in the downtown theaters of such attractions as the Budapest Symphony. By the time Gombos sold his publishing interests in Sept. 1984, both *Szabadsag* and the New York paper had become weeklies. He was survived by his second wife, Lenke Schaar, formerly a Hungarian actress and singer, and a stepdaughter, Suzanne Webster.

Zoltan Gombos Papers, WRHS.

**GONGWER, W. BURR** (1873–28 Sept. 1948), was considered the last of the "old time" political bosses as he ruled over the Democratic party in Cuyahoga County for 35 years. With his control over patronage, he was personally responsible for the careers of many prominent public officials in Cleveland. A warm, intense politician, Gongwer emphasized strict party loyalty. This principle led to much party turbulence during his reign. Born on a farm near Mansfield, Ohio, Gongwer grew up as a Republican. After beginning as a journalist in Mansfield, he came to Cleveland in 1899 as political reporter for the *PLAIN DEALER*. In 1900, he was assigned to interview the Democrat TOM JOHNSON, who was running for mayor. They soon became friends, and when Johnson was elected mayor the following year, he made Gongwer his secretary. Although still a Republican at the time, Gongwer was so inspired by

Johnson's leadership that he eventually turned Democrat. As Johnson's secretary for 8 years, Gongwer began to gain power in the party as he was entrusted with more and more of the party details, including the distribution of patronage.

Gongwer's political fortunes grew when he became deputy clerk of the Board of Elections in 1910 and chief clerk 2 years later. From 1915–21, he served as collector of customs. With Johnson's death, the leadership of the Democratic party passed to NEWTON D. BAKER, while Gongwer became his chief lieutenant. Baker gradually relinquished some of his party duties to Gongwer, until Gongwer was practically party boss by 1915. However, it was not until 1924 that Gongwer was officially made executive committee chairman of the party. In the 1920s, though, the Democratic party was in a weakened condition, and Gongwer did not have much to govern. He was able to keep the party alive by implementing the "60–40 deal," which allowed the Democrats to keep a portion of the jobs in a Republican-controlled, CITY MANAGER PLAN. In the early 1930s, Gongwer helped to produce Democratic victories locally and statewide, and by 1932, he ruled one of the strongest and most formidable political organizations in the history of the city. However, the party was debilitated at this time by a 5-year internal debate between Gongwer and Congressman MARTIN SWEENEY and U.S. Sen. ROBT. BULKLEY. Gongwer maintained his power during this turbulent time, but he eventually lost his position to RAY MILLER in 1940. At that time he retired from politics and spent his remaining years in an insurance business that he had established in the 1920s.

W. Burr Gongwer Papers, WRHS.

## GOODRICH, B. F. RESEARCH & DEVELOPMENT CENTER. *See* B. F. GOODRICH RESEARCH & DEVELOPMENT CENTER

The **GOODRICH-GANNETT NEIGHBORHOOD CENTER,** originally the Goodrich Social Settlement, was organized in 1897. It was founded by FLORA STONE MATHER in conjunction with Old Stone Church. Mather donated the original building, paid the settlement's expenses during its early years, and established its first endowment fund. As the settlement expanded, it began to receive much of its financial support from the Community Chest. The first grant from that agency was made in 1920, and the sums rose appreciably over the next few years. Working to promote a sense of neighborhood pride and responsibility, the settlement organized street associations and clubs for all ages, and offered classes and workshops for arts and crafts, cooking, sewing, gymnastics, and other activities. Pride in one's self and a sense of community were seen as important goals for those involved at Goodrich, and many who were later prominent Clevelanders socialized there as youth. The first settlement director was STARR CADWALLADER, who served until 1902. Cadwallader began with a 4-year plan, which included a drive for cleaner streets. Other prominent directors and residents who helped Goodrich to foster many outstanding "firsts" in phases of urban life include FREDERIC C. HOWE, NEWTON D. BAKER, and ALICE P. GANNETT. Gannett served as director of Goodrich House from 1917–47. During its early years, the organizations that grew from Goodrich House projects included the CONSUMERS LEAGUE OF OHIO, the LEGAL AID SOCIETY, the CLEVELAND MUSIC SCHOOL SETTLEMENT, the Society for the Blind, the Home Gardening Assoc., and the Sunbeam School for Crippled Children.

As the downtown area rapidly became a commercial district, the settlement moved its headquarters eastward. From its original location on Bond (E. 6th) St. at St. Clair, it moved in 1914 to E. 31st St., where a gym and auditorium were added to the settlement house. In 1952 the E. 55th St. Ctr. was opened to serve residents between E. 40th and E. 65th. That same year, the Downtown Neighborhood Ctr. began to operate near the area where the Goodrich House had begun, serving grade-school and teenage children living between E. 9th and E. 26th. In 1969, the settlement again moved its headquarters east, to the E. 55th St. Ctr. During the settlement's history, a wide variety of ethnic groups have benefited from its programs. The original German and Irish residents were replaced by East European immigrants, who in turn were replaced by Appalachian whites and southern blacks. Over the years, the settlement has provided a full range of services for these people, including adult education, day nursery facilities, and camp programs.

Goodrich Social Settlement Records, WRHS.

**GOODWILL INDUSTRIES** of Greater Cleveland, organized in 1918 and incorporated in 1919, specializes in providing job training and employment for disabled men and women by soliciting donations of used clothing, toys, furniture, and appliances to be repaired by its handicapped employees and resold. Cleveland Goodwill was one of 27 groups organized during Goodwill Industries' national expansion campaign in 1918–19, funded by the Methodist Centenary Fund. The local group was founded by Rev. Frank M. Baker with an initial budget of $5,000. A Methodist minister, Baker served as Goodwill's local director until his death in 1950. By 1920, Goodwill Industries had established its main headquarters at 2416 E. 9th St., where it remained until construction of the INNERBELT FREEWAY forced it to move to 930 E. 70th St. in 1954. Although most of its financial support came from the resale of repaired goods, Goodwill began receiving aid from the Community Fund in 1922. That was also the year in which the national organization adopted as its own the motto used by the Cleveland branch, "Not Charity, But a Chance." Providing work for the handicapped and aged was its first priority, but Goodwill sponsored social activities, as well, including a Boy Scout troop and other clubs for children. Clubs for its adult employees offered debates and baseball for men and health talks and housekeeping demonstrations for women. In addition, Goodwill Industries held morning religious services in its chapel.

After WORLD WAR II, the national organization decided to concentrate efforts on providing vocational services for the handicapped and began to receive federal and state funds for its rehabilitation services. In 1963, Cleveland Goodwill described itself as a "non-sectarian workshop." In 1972 it centralized its operations in a new facility at 2295 E. 55th St. Since the 1950s, Cleveland Goodwill had subcontracted to perform a variety of services for private industry. Employee dissatisfaction with that practice led Goodwill to begin making its own wooden toys in 1978 as a way to teach its trainees marketable skills in woodworking. By 1981, Goodwill Industries of Greater Cleveland had an annual budget of $2.5 million and provided training for 950 disabled people a year. Like other social-service organizations, it faced economic problems during the recession of 1981–82 as donations declined and both operating costs and demand for services increased.

Kimbrell, Horace Warren, *This Is Goodwill Industries* (1962).

**GORDON, WILLIAM J.** (30 Sept. 1818–23 Nov. 1892), was a businessman who operated a major wholesale grocery and was a pioneer in opening the iron-ore regions around Lake Superior. He is best remembered for his gift of GORDON PARK to Cleveland. Gordon was born in Monmouth County, N.J. Orphaned at 13, he learned the wholesale grocery business as a young man in New York City. Arriving in Cleveland in 1839, he started W. J. Gordon & Co. and quickly gained the public's confidence. Within a few short years, his was the largest and most important grocery establishment in Ohio. In 1856, Gordon became partners with Geo. Fellows for the purpose of conducting business in New York City. To accommodate their vast Cleveland business, they erected a new building on the corner of Superior and Merwin sts., which provided 2.5 acres of floor space, the largest in the west at that time. Later Solomon D. McMillan and Martin R. Cook were added as partners.

In 1853, the first load of iron ore was shipped to Cleveland from the Lake Superior region by Samuel Kimball and Gordon. Gordon had been convinced that the iron ore from that region could serve the manufacturing interests of Cleveland, and after visiting the area, he helped establish the Cleveland Iron Mining Co., serving as its president from 1856–66. With John H. Gorham, he also founded the first woodenware-manufacturing firm in Cleveland. In 1865, Gordon began purchasing several large tracts of land east of Cleveland and laying out an extensive park. The result was a 122-acre park that had few equals in the country. At Gordon's death, it was deeded to the city of Cleveland, provided that it should forever be maintained and at all times be kept open to the public under the exclusive name of Gordon Park. In 1872, Gordon began improving large tracts of unused land on both sides of the CUYAHOGA RIVER. He purchased the tracts, laid out streets, and erected houses built with economy and taste. These he sold at moderate prices and on easy payment terms, enabling many Clevelanders to afford comfortable homes. Gordon married Charlotte Gertrude Champlin on 25 May 1843. The Gordons had 4 children, only 2 of whom, Georgina and Charles, survived to adulthood.

The **GORDON BENNETT INTERNATIONAL BALLOON RACES** were hosted in Cleveland on 1 Sept. 1930 as part of the NATL. AIR RACES. Clifford Gildersleeve, Ohio governor of the Natl. Aeronautic Assoc., was instrumental in bringing the races to Cleveland. Jas. Gordon Bennett, publisher and sportsman, spurred competition balloon flying by offering a trophy and money to the winner of a long-distance competition (1906). The rules stipulated that the winning nation would hold the trophy and host the race the next year. A nation winning the race 3 times in succession would permanently keep the trophy. In 1924, Belgium gained permanent possession of the first trophy. For the 1925 races, the Belgium Aero Club donated a second trophy for the continuation of the races. The U.S. gained possession of this second cup in 1928. For the 1929 races in St. Louis, a new trophy was donated by the Detroit Board of Commerce. The U.S. gained possession of this third cup during the 1932 races. Poland had possession of the cup in 1939, when the races were discontinued because of WORLD WAR II. The races were not held again until 1983 (Paris). They have been held every year since. The Cleveland race started from the Cleveland Airport for unknown destinations. The entrants included balloons from France, Belgium, Germany, and America. The U.S. had 3 entries: *Goodyear VIII*, piloted by Ward T. Van Orman; *City of Cleveland*, piloted by R. J. Blair; and *City of Detroit*, piloted by Edward J. Hill. The race official was Capt. H. E. Honeywell, a previous Gordon Bennett winner who had made 573 flights in 30 years. Each balloonist carried several dozen large red paper envelopes labeled "Balloon Message." Pilots would send their altitude, time, and direction to earth in these envelopes weighted with lead and carrying colored streamers. Finders were asked to send the envelopes directly to Cleveland. The balloonists were scheduled to leave Cleveland at 4:30 p.m. on 1 Sept. By 3 Sept., all balloons except the *Goodyear* were down, making Akronite Ward T. Van Orman the winner.

**GORDON PARK** consists of 2 sections: one part located along the lakefront (E. 72nd St. and East Shoreway at the tip of Martin Luther King, Jr. Dr.), and the inland part south of MEMORIAL SHOREWAY. The original land, part of the Doan Brook Valley, stretched along the lake from E. 71st St. to E. 38th St. and contained a beach, many natural caves, and upper and lower drives. It was the private estate of WM. J. GORDON, who landscaped his Doan Brook property with graveled paths, rustic bridges, groves of trees, and shrubs. Opening his private park to visitors every week, he stipulated that it would become a public park at the time of his death. After his death in 1892, the city of Cleveland received the title (Oct. 1893), and Gordon Park became a city playground with many recreational facilities, including fishing, boating, bathing, and picnicking. Eventually it was joined to ROCKEFELLER PARK and WADE PARK by a series of bridges, and the whole area became a popular spot for many years.

Subsequently, misuse, vandalism, and the construction of the Lakeland Freeway (1952), which divided the park, almost totally destroyed it. Deterioration continued, and in 1978 the Ohio Dept. of Natural Resources, through a lease agreement with the city of Cleveland, established the CLEVELAND LAKEFRONT STATE PARK, which assumed responsibility for restoration of Cleveland's lakefront—including the lakefront part of Gordon Park. Within 7 years (1977–84), provisions had been made for fishing, boating, and swimming through the establishment of the Gordon Fishing Pier, the Inner City Yacht Club, and the Gordon Launch Ramp Area. The park also incorporates the CLEVELAND AQUARIUM, administrative offices of the Cleveland Lakefront State Park, and the Navy Finance Ctr. Plans are underway by the city of Cleveland for major restoration of the inland section of Gordon Park.

**GOTTWALD, FREDERICK CARL** (15 Aug. 1860–23 June 1941), was a painter, a long-time instructor at the Cleveland School of Art (later the CLEVELAND INSTITUTE OF ART), and one of the foremost members of the Cleveland artistic community for over 40 years. He is sometimes referred to as the dean of Cleveland painters. Born in Austria, Gottwald immigrated to Cleveland before his first birthday. He attended public schools here and had his first artistic training in 1874 with ARCHIBALD M. WILLARD. In 1876 he joined with Willard in founding the ART CLUB. Gottwald earned money to study art in New York City and abroad by painting landscapes in the cabins and salons of lakeboats and by gilding figureheads for boats. He later studied at the Cooper Institute in New York City, the Art Students' League in Munich, and the Julien Academy in Paris. He returned to Cleveland in the late 1880s, where he accepted a post on the staff on the newly formed School of Art, an institution he would be associated with for the next 41 years. He also taught at Western Reserve School of Design, the JOHN HUNTINGTON POLYTECHNIC INSTITUTE, and Oberlin College. In 1899, Gottwald married Myria Scott. He and his wife enjoyed traveling, particularly in Europe. Many of his landscapes are based on scenes from his travels in Italy, England, and Germany. In 1921 he spent his sabbatical year in Italy, and later, after his retirement in 1926, he moved there. He returned to

Cleveland for a short time in 1930 before retiring to California in 1932, where he spent the remaining years of his life. In 1919, Gottwald received the Penton Medal at the Cleveland Museum of Art MAY SHOW for his work entitled *The Thinker.*

**GOULD, INC.**, established in 1918 and incorporated in Delaware in 1928, began doing business in Cleveland in 1945 as Gould Storage Battery, and later as the Gould-Natl. Batteries Co. (1950) at 4500 Euclid. The company became a major force in the local economy after its 1969 purchase of CLEVITE. Before that merger, Gould Natl. Battery's holdings were primarily in automotive and industrial products. Gould beat out 3 serious contenders (WEATHERHEAD, TRW, and U.S. Smelting, Refining, & Mining) and 17 others to gain entry into Clevite's lucrative high-tech and ordnance markets. The company name was changed to Gould, Inc., and under the direction of Wm. Laffer, former president of Clevite, the new corporation aspired to build an integrated-technology company that would concentrate on underwater technology, precision measurement and controls, pollution control, business-machine components, data display, recording instruments, and computers.

The cornerstone of the new Gould was the Clevite Ordnance Div., renamed Ocean Systems. Based on work pioneered at the Brush Development Co., a 1952 acquisition, Clevite had become a major supplier for the U.S. Navy in the 1950s and 1960s. Before the merger, this division moved from 540 E. 105th St. to a new facility at 18901 Euclid to double its size, productive capacity, and labor force. Considered the leading civilian authority on torpedo design, the firm developed the Polaris submarine, a major underwater tracking system, and the Mark 6 torpedo. After the firm became Gould, contracts continued to flow in; in 1971, Gould triumphed over Westinghouse to win a $1.5 million military contract for the computerized Mark 8 torpedo. To achieve its corporate goals, Gould acquired many new subsidiaries in the 1970s that increased its expertise in electronics and computer technology, and in the 1980s began divesting itself of its electrical and industrial interests. As early as 1972, Gould complained that the Clevite engine-parts plant at 17000 St. Clair was outdated and was laid out in such a way that it would be difficult to sell; by 1981, the division and its building were sold to the Reading Co. for $500 million. In 1982, Gould announced its intention to sell off most of its electrical-products business, except for batteries, which it reorganized into a separate subsidiary, GNB Batteries.

In 1985, Gould, Inc., had met its goal of becoming an integrated developer and marketer of electric systems. The company had sales of $1.4 billion in 1984 and employed 21,000 worldwide. Despite several diverse holdings (i.e., the Penske Corp., which leases Hertz trucks and promotes auto racing, and Gould Florida, a land-development company), most of the company's sales result from electronics, electrical systems, products, and components, and defense systems. Though it sold the historic bearings division, Gould employed over 2,500 at its Ocean Systems, Foil, Recording Systems, & Controls Div. in 1985. With its headquarters in Rolling Meadows, Ill., Gould has tried to be a good municipal citizen through such ventures as the "Make It in Cleveland" program in 1980 to seek local suppliers for its torpedo production.

**GOULDER, GRACE [IZANT]** (27 Mar. 1893–17 Nov. 1984), was a writer on Ohio history and lore, known widely for her long-running column in the *Plain Dealer Magazine* and for her several books. Born in Cleveland, she was ed-

ucated at Vassar College, graduating in 1914. At that time she was employed by the *PLAIN DEALER* as society editor. With the outbreak of WORLD WAR I, she went to work for the national board of the YMCA in New York and Europe. After her marriage in 1919, she ceased working full-time until an article by her on the Ohio state capitol was bought by the *Plain Dealer* and became the first of her "Ohio Scenes and Citizens" columns, which ran weekly in the *Sunday Magazine* until 1969. Each article featured an interesting person, historical sidelight, or unusual place from around Ohio. Goulder's first book, *This Is Ohio*, was a collection of brief anecdotal histories of each of Ohio's 88 counties. It was published first in 1953 and was revised in 1965. The "Ohio Scenes and Citizens" pieces were collected into a book of the same title in 1964. A third book, *John D. Rockefeller, The Cleveland Years* (1972), documented the earlier life and Cleveland connections of the oil tycoon. A history of Hudson, Ohio, where Goulder lived from 1923 onward, was in preparation at the time of her death. Goulder was the recipient of the Martha Kinney Cooper Ohioana Award, the Cleveland Women's City Club Creative Fine Arts Prize, and awards and citations from the New England Society, the American Assoc. for State & Local History, the WESTERN RESERVE HISTORICAL SOCIETY (of which she was a trustee), and the Harding Memorial Assoc. Goulder married Robt. Izant (a vice-president of Central Natl. Bank) in 1919. She was survived by 2 children, Robt. J. and Mary.

**GOVERNMENT.** The tract of land that was to become Cleveland had at one time or another been claimed by Spain, France, and Great Britain. When American independence had been secured, the new federal government tried to resolve the disputes that arose among the several states, all the while contending with Indians who had a claim of their own, and who were made the more restive by British troops slow to give up their western posts. The key event was passage of the Ordinance of 1787, for that made administration of the sparsely settled territories possible. Although the first real effort to enforce white man's law in the area was initiated in the 1790s under the auspices of the CONNECTICUT LAND CO., the truth is that during the early years of Cleveland's history, law and justice seem to have been meted out—with very little evidence of resistance—by the redoubtable LORENZO CARTER. The formal origins of municipal government are traceable to the creation of Washington and Wayne counties, which were divided at the CUYAHOGA RIVER and administered out of Marietta and Detroit respectively. After some further reorganization, Trumbull County was organized in 1800; the court of quarter sessions convened soon afterward in Warren, designated the county seat. Officers of Cleveland Twp. were chosen in an 1802 election, and a rudimentary civil government was in place when Ohio was admitted to the union in 1803. The next year saw a $10 tax imposed on residents by the town meeting, the political institution most often identified with New England. Cleveland became the seat of Cuyahoga County when it was created in 1807, and the court of common pleas met in 1810. Late in 1814, Cleveland received a village charter, and the next year ALFRED KELLEY was elected first president. Still, the village was a precarious frontier outpost.

During the next few years, ordinances set penalties for (among other things) discharging firearms and allowing livestock to run at large. LEONARD CASE served as president from 1821–25, the latter date also marking the choice of Cleveland as northern terminus of the Ohio Canal and local adoption of a property tax. In succeeding years, the delinquent tax rolls were, according to one account, "rather robust." The public's view of local government is indicated by a revealing story told by WM. GANSON ROSE: responding to the trustees' decision in 1828 to set aside a little money for public improvements, citizens demanded to know "what on earth the trustees could find to spend two hundred dollars on." In 1832, a CHOLERA EPIDEMIC spawned a short-lived board of health. In 1836, Cleveland attained the status of a city and adopted a government more closely resembling that of the present day. Voters elected city councilmen (3 from each of 3 wards), aldermen (1 per ward), and a mayor with little real executive authority. The mayor's salary was set at $500 per annum. Council authorized a school levy, and the first public school recognizable as such opened the next year. City offices were established in the Commercial Block on Superior St. In 1837 the city raised $16,077.53 and spent $13,297.14, an example of fiscal responsibility that was not always to be followed.

Municipal government gradually widened its scope. The Superior Court of Cleveland was created in 1847. In 1849, the city was authorized to establish a poorhouse and hospital for the poor. As late as mid-century, public service—road work, particularly—was sometimes rendered in kind. By 1852, the city was served by the railroad, and the legislature passed an act that resulted in Cleveland's designation as a second-class city. Council was now composed of 2 members elected from each of 4 wards; their compensation was $1 per session. Executive powers were exercised not so much by the mayor as by various officials and bodies, including a board of city commissioners, marshal, treasurer, city solicitor, market superintendent, civil engineer, auditor, and police court, including judge, clerk, and prosecutor. In 1853, voters elected the first Board of Water Works Commissioners, and council established a Board of Education, which in turn appointed a superintendent. When Cleveland merged with OHIO CITY in 1854, 4 additional wards were created, bringing the total for the united city to 11. During the late 1850s, a modern sanitary system was gradually put in place. A paid fire dept. was created in 1863, and the first police superintendent was appointed in 1866. The Board of Education established the CLEVELAND PUBLIC LIBRARY in 1867, and a Board of Park Commissioners was put in place 2 years later, although that did not end complaints about a lack of adequate open space and park facilities. During the last half of the 19th century, annexation kept pace with the city's growth, which tended to be in the direction of Brooklyn, Newburgh, and E. Cleveland townships.

Municipal government was modernized again with the passage of state legislation in 1878. Under the new scheme, voters elected the mayor, city council, treasurer, police judge, and prosecutor. Council appointed an auditor, city clerk, and civil engineer. The administrative boards that distinguished this form of government were variously chosen: voters were to elect the police commissioners and cemetery trustees; council appointed the board of health and, if it chose to do so, a board of improvements, and inspectors of various kinds; the mayor appointed (with council's consent) park commissioners and a superintendent of markets, and he named the directors of the house of refuge and correction. Rose is not alone in arguing that although that was generally a more efficient form of government, the fact that nearly all board members were unpaid resulted in "indifferent service" or worse. It was during this period that patronage, or the "spoils system" identified with Jacksonian democracy, came into disrepute, in part because of the assassination of Pres. Garfield by a lunatic invariably described as a "disappointed office seeker." The response at the federal level was the Pendleton Act, and local government followed suit. Thus, in 1886 Cleveland adopted legislation requiring that positions in the police department be filled by competitive examination. In the same year, a board of elections was created, and in 1891 the state substituted the Australian (secret) ballot for the old system whereby "tickets" were printed and distributed by the parties. Old-line politicians were placated by the adoption of the party-column ballot, which encourages straight-ticket voting.

Even late in the 19th century, cities did not presume to perform many services directly. Although they were gradually assuming responsibility for libraries, parks, and poor relief, utilities, such as street lighting and street railways, still tended to be franchise operations. Cleveland seems to have operated no industries of its own save the waterworks. But the pressures brought on by growth and the special needs of immigrant groups resulted in the expansion of municipal services during this period, and that inevitably meant more expensive government. Since the increase in municipal expenditures occurred during a period of deflation, cities not only were spending more money, they were spending more precious money. As a result, they often had to borrow. Apparently Cleveland was not atypical in having to spend, ca. 1880, about ⅓ of its income on debt service.

Increasing dissatisfaction with city government led to the adoption in 1891 of a form of government modeled directly after that at the national level. Under the Federal Plan, power that had been distributed among various boards, commissions, and officials now was to be shared by a legislature and executive responsible to the electorate. The mayor, who received an annual salary of $6,000, and 6 department heads (appointed by the mayor with approval of council) made up the Board of Control. Council consisted of 20 members, 2 from each of the 10 districts representing the 40 wards, and each received $5 for attending a regular weekly meeting. The city treasurer, police judge, prosecuting attorney, and police-court clerk were elected by the people. Adoption of the Federal Plan did not spell an end to the franchise system, nor did it eliminate corruption. And the separation of powers made it difficult for real leadership to be exercised. The extent to which things got done in those days often depended upon the efficacy of informal agencies—bosses and machines—that tended to be the engines driving the formal municipal government. These institutions, while efficient in their own way, bred corruption.

Party machines also reflected the contentiousness of a population split along class, religious, and ethnic lines, the 1890 census showing that of the 261,353 people living in the city, 164,258 were native-born, and only about 25% of these were of native parentage. While certain of Cleveland's leading citizens seemed quite adept at the rough and tumble of electoral politics (MARCUS A. HANNA, for instance), white Anglo-Saxon Protestants generally were put off by a political system that was not instinctively deferential, and which was often ungentlemanly. It was in this spirit that Harry Garfield, son of the late president, and other leading Clevelanders organized the Municipal Assoc. of the City of Cleveland, rechristened the Civic League, and later the CITIZENS LEAGUE OF GREATER CLEVELAND. Derived from the same spirit of progressive middle-class reform is the unique and venerable City Club Forum, which is dedicated to the proposition that the marketplace of ideas is best kept free and open to all.

That progressivism was a multifaceted phenomenon can be seen in the career of TOM L. JOHNSON, who was elected mayor in 1901. During his administration, Cleveland's Progressives operated a municipal garbage plant; they

462

took over street cleaning; they built BATH HOUSES and a tuberculosis hospital. The penal system was reformed and a juvenile court established. This municipal expansiveness cost money, of course, and the city's indebtedness, $14,503,000 in 1900, rose to $27,688,000 by 1906. The structure of local government also changed several times during this period. Progressives here and elsewhere were convinced that the sorry state of municipal affairs was due largely to the "political" interference of state legislatures, and the home rule movement sought to cut the cities loose from legislative control. The redrafting of the state constitution in 1912 was a great triumph for reformers, and Cleveland's HOME RULE charter, a progressive document, went into effect in 1914. In general, Progressives stood for nonpartisan elections and the principle of at-large (rather than ward) representation and tended to support the strengthening of executive powers. The CITY MANAGER PLAN was perhaps the archetypal Progressive contribution to municipal government in the U.S. The idea was to put city government on a sound business footing by having a competent, neutral manager not subject to favoritism and cronyism. Cleveland was the first (and only) major American city to adopt, and then to abandon, the council-manager form of government. Certainly, reformers must have been bitterly disappointed when the nonpartisan election of councilmen by proportional representation from large districts proved to have no noticeable impact on corruption. In 1931, voters dumped the manager and proportional representation, bringing back the old mayor-council form and the ward principle.

In the years after WORLD WAR I, it was becoming increasingly evident that Cleveland was suffering from an erosion of its tax base. By that time, the more affluent SUBURBS were no longer anxious to be annexed to Cleveland, as city services were no longer demonstratively better than theirs. Suburban communities were gradually becoming independent of the central city as more people moved to the outlying areas. Aware that city and suburb shared some concerns, reformers began to press for the adoption of a dual form of metropolitan government, in which the county would assume some areawide functions but existing municipal powers would be preserved. The county had been considered the administrative arm of the state since 1810, when the first Cuyahoga County officers were inaugurated. With the organization of the last Ohio county in 1851, a new state constitution was passed giving the general assembly the authority to provide for the election of such county officers as it deemed necessary. Cuyahoga County government had only those powers given to it by the state (see CUYAHOGA COUNTY GOVERNMENT), and any reorganization leading to metropolitan government would require an amendment to the Ohio state constitution allowing the county to write its own home rule charter. After several unsuccessful attempts, that was accomplished by initiative petition in 1933; Ohio was the fourth state in the country to do so.

Two years after the amendment had passed, a Cuyahoga County home rule charter to reorganize the existing government was approved by the voters. The Ohio Supreme Court, however, ruled in 1936 that the reorganization transferred municipal functions to the county and, therefore, needed the more comprehensive majorities called for in the Ohio constitution (see REGIONAL GOVERNMENT MOVEMENT). During this time, Cleveland politics focused on the multiple ethnic groups who were acquiring visible political power. It is significant, too, that while cities were taking on certain new responsibilities in response to the Depression—specifically, slum clearance and public housing—the federal government, by providing social-welfare benefits, undermined the power of the party machines; the bosses and precinct captains had once been the only source of such services. As the machine's role in local politics began its long decline, the newspapers to some extent took over the task of promoting those politicians who had a knack for making headlines, a circumstance that might have given further impetus to ethnic (and later racial) politics. This point may be best illustrated by the career of Frank J. Lausche, mayor 1941–44, and later governor and U.S. senator. Thanks to the papers and the loyal support of Eastern and Southern European nationality groups, Lausche was a force in Ohio politics for the better part of 3 decades, despite a stormy relationship with Democratic political bosses in the city. The same formula was employed by Anthony J. Celebrezze, who was elected mayor in 1953. It did not matter that Democratic boss RAY T. MILLER opposed Celebrezze, because he had the support of influential *Press* editor LOUIS B. SELTZER. Together, they championed the cause of urban renewal, and the city increasingly looked to Washington for needed funds.

There was some tinkering with the city charter during this period. A partisan mayoral primary was introduced, as was the so-called knock-out rule stipulating that council candidates would run unopposed if they garnered more than 50% of the vote in the primary election, which remained officially nonpartisan. In the Progressive tradition, middle-class reformers continued to work for metropolitan government; however, these efforts proved fruitless. To the voters, the virtues of efficient and economic areawide public services were more than offset by the fear that metropolitan government would lead to the transfer of municipal functions to the county, and that they would lose both access to and control of any government covering a larger geographic area. These fears were shared by both suburbanites anxious to guard the prerogatives of their municipalities and city residents who viewed metropolitan government as a scheme to dilute their power.

Even without metropolitan government, the increasing complexity of state government had widened the scope of county responsibility, primarily in the health and welfare field. Other specific needs, the regional sewer district and transit authorities, for example, were administered by special agencies staffed by professional managers who operated for the most part in anonymity and were not subject to direct control by the electorate. As an ad hoc solution to the need for larger jurisdictional units without creating a full metropolitan government, these agencies enjoyed phenomenal growth both locally and nationally after WORLD WAR II. In the city of Cleveland, the focus shifted from areawide concerns to a resurgence of interest in neighborhood governmental units (little city halls) in the 1960s and early 1970s. With the turbulence of the sixties, there were doubts about the ability of city administrations to deal with problems that were surfacing. Both the development of these small quasi-governmental units and the special agencies as an alternative to metropolitan government represented a critique on the ability of existing local governments to meet the changing needs of their populations.

New problems surfaced that severely taxed the ability of city administrations to govern Cleveland. Although the opening of the St. Lawrence Seaway in 1959 symbolized the optimism generated in the community by post-World War II prosperity, the area's economic base began to erode as the number of manufacturing jobs began to decline. However, the heavy in-migration to the city of people seeking employment continued, and a serious shortage of affordable housing and overcrowded schools developed. These problems were critical in the black community, which by 1963 had grown to about 32% of Cleveland's population, and the inability of Mayor Ralph Locher's administration to deal effectively with them exacerbated black-white hostilities superimposed upon a city already riven by nationality politics. Governing Cleveland became more arduous as violence in the city's black ghettos, begun in earnest in 1965, continued into the administration of Carl B. Stokes, elected in 1967. There was no respite from municipal problems during the Perk administration, as the city's shrinking tax base and voter opposition to a city income tax increase compounded Cleveland's financial problems, which by this time were already quite severe, and federal revenue-sharing funds had to be used to meet the city's payroll.

The financial shortfall continued under Democratic Mayor Dennis J. Kucinich, elected in 1977—an urban populist leading a crusade against privilege, particularly that of the city's business and banking establishment. The ill will generated by his zeal led to an unsuccessful recall attempt by his opponents in 1978 and the withdrawal of the business and financial community's support from his administration. Later that year, local banks refused to roll over the city's notes, and Cleveland, unable to pay them off, was forced to default on its financial obligations. The shock of DEFAULT persuaded the voters to raise the income tax and enabled Republican Geo. Voinovich, elected mayor in 1979, to reorganize the city's administration and restore its financial credibility. Cleveland's immediate problems appeared to be contained, and in a more cooperative atmosphere, long-discussed changes in the city charter were made with a 4-year mayoral and councilmanic term of office, approved in 1980, and a reduction of city council from 33 to 21 members, established in 1981. A truce between white Republican Mayor Voinovich and Geo. Forbes, the black Democratic council president, made the city's politics less abrasive than in previous years.

Kenneth Kolson
National Endowment for the Humanities

Mary B. Stavish
Case Western Reserve University

Durham, Frank, *Government in Greater Cleveland* (1963).
Sacks, Seymour, *Financing Government in a Metropolitan Area: The Cleveland Experience* (1961).
Sego, Michael A., ed., *Politics in the Making: Greater Cleveland* (1967).
Snavely, Charles, *A History of the City Government of Cleveland, Ohio* (1902).
See also POLITICS, CLEVELAND CITY GOVERNMENT, CUYAHOGA COUNTY GOVERNMENT, specific mayors, and, for recent mayors, MAYORAL ADMINISTRATION OF.

**GRACE CONGREGATIONAL CHURCH,** located for many years at Gordon Ave. (W. 65th St.) and Colgate St., originated in 1867 as a Methodist-Congregational Union Sabbath school in a brick schoolhouse near the corner of Ridge Rd. and Denison Ave. organized by the First Congregational & Methodist Church. In 1870, the First Congregational Church accepted complete responsibility for the school, and in 1874 it was moved to Union Chapel (built by First Church) at 73rd St. and Brimsmade Ave. In 1875, Rev. Elisha A. Hoffman was put in charge of the Union Sabbath School, and in 1878 it moved from Union Chapel to Harbor St. Congregational Chapel, a mission chapel that had also been established by First Church. When the New York Central & St. Louis Railway Co. wanted the Harbor St. Congregational Chapel property for its right-of-way, the First Congregational Church sold the property and gave the proceeds to Union Sabbath School. Nineteen members of this Sabbath school had voted on 7 Dec. 1881 to form Grace Congregational Church, with Rev. Hoffman as their pastor. On 9 July 1882, they dedicated their new "gothic edifice with stained glass windows" located on Train St. near Clark St. The congregation grew, but because of the changing neighborhood, the property was transferred to the Cleveland Bohemian Mission Board in 1884, and it ultimately became Cyril Church, used by Rev. Henry A. Schauffler for his work with the Czech community. Grace Congregational Church built its new sanctuary at Gordon and Colgate Ave.; it was dedicated on 28 June 1885, and the old Union Chapel on Ridge Ave. was moved to the property as an addition to the new church. Rev. Hoffman resigned his pastorate 1 Apr. 1886 and was succeeded by Rev. John H. Hull. The church was instrumental in starting several missions, including one on Lorain Ave. that later became West Park Church. In 1953, the original First Congregational Church merged with Grace Church, and in 1979 Grace Church voted to merge with Faith Community Church (organized in 1958 in N. ROYALTON). The merger was consummated on 20 Jan. 1980 when both congregations unanimously decided to name their merged church the First Congregational Church. Rev. Garred W. Johnstone served as the first pastor of the church, located at 10383 Albion Rd., N. Royalton.

The **GRACE HOSPITAL ASSOCIATION** (Grace Hospital) is located at 2307 W. 14th and Fairfield Ave. It was the first small hospital in Ohio to be accredited by the American College of Surgeons. Grace Hospital was founded in 1910 by a small group of homeopathic physicians who believed there was a need for a medical/surgical hospital on Cleveland's near south side, because the area contained no voluntary hospital. It was located on the old Brainard property (W. 25th St. and Scranton). In 1913 it moved to its present site and acquired and remodeled 2 houses. Grace became a nonprofit hospital in 1920, and in 1935, Col. Joseph H. Alexander, former president of the CLEVELAND RAILWAY CO., became head of the board of trustees. A new brick hospital was built and dedicated in 1938. The hospital was again remodeled and modernized in the 1950s with the addition of 2 wings. In 1953, Grace Hospital was renamed the Grace Hospital Assoc.

The **GRAND ARMY OF THE REPUBLIC** was a national association of Union Civil War veterans founded in Springfield, Ill., in 1866. Ohio was one of 10 states and the District of Columbia that sent representatives to the GAR's first national convention in Indianapolis, Ind., in Nov. 1866. The first meeting of the Dept. of Ohio, GAR, was held in Jan. 1867 in Columbus. By late 1868, some 303 local "posts" had been established throughout the state, including a number in Cleveland. With its membership centered in the local posts, the organization worked on both the state and national levels for issues such as pensions and the establishment of soldiers' homes. A number of Clevelanders, including Wm. C. Bunts, JAS. BARNETT, and Theodore Vogues, held positions in the state organization of the GAR. By 1908 there were a total of 8 GAR posts in Cleveland, with a membership of 886. Five additional posts were located elsewhere in Cuyahoga County, with 129 additional members. Two national GAR encampments (conventions) were held in Cleveland. Over 30,000 veterans attended the 35th Encampment, 12–13 Sept. 1901. This event saw the "greatest" military parade in the history of the city. Considerably fewer veterans attended the 81st Encampment in the city in Aug. 1947. This event had been organized by John H. Grate, a 102-year-old veteran from Atwater, Ohio. The last Cuyahoga County GAR member, Peter J. Diemer, had died several years before this event, on 23 Feb. 1943.

Following the demise of many of the local posts, their record books were transferred to the WESTERN RESERVE HISTORICAL SOCIETY and to various smaller societies and libraries in Cuyahoga County.

Grand Army of the Republic, Dept. of Ohio, Records, WRHS.

**GRANEY, JOHN GLADSTONE "JACK"** (10 June 1886–19 Apr. 1978), was a major-league baseball player for the Cleveland team from 1910–22. He was the popular radio announcer of the Indians games between 1932–53. Graney was born in St. Thomas, Ontario, Canada. He played rugby and HOCKEY as a boy, but he was an excellent left-handed baseball pitcher. He intended to enroll at the University of Toronto, but after a tryout in Buffalo, Geo. Stallings signed him to a contract and shipped him to Erie. Graney finished the season at Wilkes-Barre with 24–4 record; his contract was purchased in 1908 by the Cleveland Naps. In spring training, he hit manager NAPOLEON LAJOIE in the head with a pitch and was sold to Portland. After hitting 6 more batters in the head during the season, he was switched to the outfield. By 1910 he was back with Cleveland. Only a journeyman ball player, Graney had a lifetime batting average of .250 in 1,402 games. He played on the 1920 World Championship team, alternating in left field with Charley Jamieson. Graney was well liked by Cleveland youngsters. When he walked into LEAGUE PARK, boys would start yelling his nickname, "Mick Mick," and grab hold of him. Anyone touching Graney could enter the park free.

In 1921, Graney became a partner in the Kane-Graney Motor Co., a Ford agency, in Brooklyn. Selling out in 1929, Graney began his radio-announcing career in 1932 without an audition. His salty voice and enthusiastic manner made him the most popular baseball announcer in Cleveland sports history. Every game was opened by Graney's saying, "Here's the windup . . . here's the pitch." Asked the reason for his radio-announcing success, Graney explained, "I tried to follow the ball, stay with the play and leave fancy words to others." Over the years, he teamed with several announcers, including Pinky Hunter, Van Patrick, and Jimmy Dudley. Graney even made commercials such as "Never give a bug a break. Give 'em Bugaboo" exciting and memorable. Graney tried television sportscasting at WEWS in 1954 but then retired to Bowling Green, Mo. He and his wife, Pauline, were married on 14 June 1916. They had a daughter, Margaret, and a son, Jack, Jr., who was killed in an airplane crash during WORLD WAR II.

**GRASSELLI, CAESAR AUGUSTIN** (1850–1927), president and later chairman of the board of the GRASSELLI CHEMICAL CO., was one of this country's leading manufacturing chemists. He was also an important figure in the industrial, civic, and social life of Cleveland for more than 50 years. Grasselli—universally known to his friends and associates as "C. A."—was born in Cincinnati, the 5th of 8 children of Fredericka Eisenbarth and Eugene Ramiro Grasselli (1810–1882). His father, an important pioneer chemist, gave him a solid grounding in chemical-plant construction and operation, and he attended Mt. St. Mary's College in Emmitsburg, Md. Grasselli would later write: "I cannot remember the time when I was not interested in chemistry and did not expect to follow my father in this business." He was 17 when Eugene Grasselli moved his chemical business to Cleveland in 1867. In 1873 he was made a partner.

As a young man, Grasselli assisted materially in the development of high-explosives manufacture. In 1885 he introduced American saltcake, or sodium sulfate, to the glass industry, which formerly had been dependent upon British supply. After his father's death, Grasselli became president of the Grasselli Chemical Co., a position he held from 1885–1916, when he became chairman of the board and his son, Thos. S., succeeded him as president. During that period, company assets grew from $600,000 to $30 million. Sulfuric acid remained a major product. Convinced that it ought to be produced close to its market, Grasselli acquired or built additional plants. In 1889, Grasselli absorbed the Marsh & Harwood Co. and bought the Standard Acid Works in New Jersey. He later erected furnaces for the manufacture of zinc and plants for zinc smelting in West Virginia and Indiana. In all, the Grasselli empire encompassed some 14 plants scattered over the eastern part of the U.S. when it merged with Du Pont in 1928.

Grasselli's interests were not confined to chemicals. In 1886 he became the first president of the Woodland Ave. Savings & Trust Co., and in 1893 he was named president of the Broadway Savings & Trust Co.; in 1920, when these two institutions merged with 27 others to form the Union Trust Co., Grasselli remained as a director. He also played a prominent role in Cleveland civic life. He was a founder of the CLEVELAND MUSEUM OF ART and the CLEVELAND INSTITUTE OF MUSIC, and he helped organize the Cleveland Chamber of Commerce in 1893. He gave the old family home at 2275 E. 55th St. to the CLEVELAND SOCIETY FOR THE BLIND, and in 1922 he gave the Rose-Mary Home for Crippled Children, 19359 Euclid Ave., to the Catholic Diocese of Cleveland, in memory of his wife, Johanna Ireland Grasselli.

Grasselli Family Papers, WRHS.

The **GRASSELLI CHEMICAL COMPANY** traced its origin to Cincinnati, where Eugene Ramiro Grasselli (1810–1882) established a chemical works for the manufacture of sulfuric acid in 1839. Born in Strasbourg and educated at the universities of Strasbourg and Heidelberg, Grasselli was descended from an Italian family that, since medieval times, had been druggists and chemists. He emigrated to America in 1837 with the ambition of supplying chemicals to new and growing markets. In 1866, Grasselli erected a plant on Independence Rd. near Broadway in Cleveland, and he moved his headquarters there the following year. He began large-scale manufacturing of sulfuric acid to meet the demands of oil refiners in the city's Kingsbury Run section. Situated next to the Standard Oil Co. refinery, Grasselli shared in and aided the tremendous growth of that company. In 1873 he admitted his son, CAESAR AUGUSTIN GRASSELLI (1850–1927), as partner in the works and continued business under the name E. Grasselli & Son.

Eugene Grasselli died in 1882. In 1885 the partnership was dissolved, and the Grasselli Chemical Co. was formed, with Caesar A. Grasselli, president; Eugene Grasselli (his brother), vice-president; David K. Bailey, secretary; and Kenneth B. Bailey, treasurer. By acquisition and consolidation, the company grew in size and prosperity, establishing plants in New Jersey, Illinois, Indiana, West Virginia, Kentucky, Alabama, New York, Pennsylvania, and Ohio. As other chemical-dependent industries grew, Grasselli manufactured more diverse chemical products, including acid phosphate, acetic acid, silicate of soda, fertilizers, and zinc. During WORLD WAR I the company entered the explosives field, and after the war it produced dynamite and black powder for blasting. In 1928, the Grasselli Chemical Co. consolidated with the E. I. Du Pont de Nemours Co. of Wilmington, Del. Thos. S. Grasselli, who had succeeded his father as president in 1916, became vice-president and a director of Du Pont. In 1936 the Grasselli Chemical Co. was dissolved, and the Grasselli Chemical Dept.

took over this phase of the Du Pont business. Du Pont's Chemicals & Pigments Dept. operated at the original Grasselli site in 1984, producing sulfuric acid, zinc chloride, galvanizing fluxes, sodium bisulfate, and silicates.

Grasselli Family Papers, WRHS.

**GRAUL, JACOB** (5 Nov. 1868–14 Feb. 1938), served on the Cleveland police force, 1897–1930, and as chief of police, 1922–30. His term as chief was colorless in view of his personal service, yet he faced more political battles within the department and between department members and the administration than any other chief. Not popular within the department, he was considered the strictest disciplinarian ever to serve it. Graul was born in Cleveland and attended CLEVELAND PUBLIC SCHOOLS. As a young man he learned the plumbing trade, and although adept at his craft, he grew bored and changed careers, gaining appointment to the CLEVELAND POLICE DEPT. Graul joined the force with the idea of becoming chief and worked methodically to achieve that ambition. Lacking the brawn, deep voice, and other attributes characteristic of other members of the police force, he made his reputation as a plainclothesman at the old Central Station and later the detective bureau.

Graul's career was uneventful. Through hard work, he rose through the ranks: first to sergeant, in 1903; lieutenant in 1909; captain in 1912; and deputy inspector in 1918. He was scrupulously obedient to every order given him, a quality he expected and demanded later from all those who served under him. He was one of the few policemen to remain loyal to FRED KOHLER when Kohler was ousted as police chief in 1913. When Kohler was elected mayor in 1922, he installed Graul as chief. Although Graul maintained a reputation for honesty, fine character, and personal integrity, he was often hampered by politics in the operation of the department, as Kohler punished those who opposed him, rewarded his supporters, and prevented raids on slot machines and gambling spots. Graul remained chief during the years of city manager rule, but he was overshadowed by Safety Director Edwin Barry, who ran the police department from city hall. Graul incurred the wrath of the "Drys" when he publicly declared that in terms of enforcement, Prohibition was unworkable. He was eased out of office by City Manager DANIEL MORGAN in 1930 with the promise of a big pension, only to see it later reduced by two-thirds. Graul was married to the former Alma Lentz; the Grauls had 3 children, Alfred, Walter, and Mrs. Eldon Lewis. Graul died of a cerebral hemorrhage while serving as foreman of the grand jury and was buried in Highland Park Cemetery.

**GRAY, A. DONALD** (24 Feb. 1891–30 May 1939), was a landscape architect and designer active in Cleveland from 1920–39. Gray was born in Tyrone, Pa. He graduated from Bucknell University in Pennsylvania and attended Harvard University, after which he worked briefly with Frederick Law Olmsted, Jr., in the Olmsted Bros. firm in Brookline, Mass., the premier landscape architects in America at the time. Gray came to Cleveland in 1920. He established a practice in landscape architecture and designed many private gardens and estates in Cleveland, the Heights, and outlying SUBURBS. In 1925 he made a trip to England to study the gardens of the great houses there. He designed the landscaping for the noted private development of Fairhill Rd. houses in 1931, and made his own home there for several years. Among his important public works were the landscape design for the Cedar-Center apartments, the first federal public-housing project in the nation, plans for FOR-

EST HILL PARK, and some of the designs for the chain of Cleveland Cultural Gardens in ROCKEFELLER PARK. Dedicated to "making a beautiful city of Cleveland," Gray worked closely on the development of the Cleveland Garden Ctr. in collaboration with Mrs. Wm. G. Mather and Mrs. Chas. A. Otis.

In 1936, Gray was influential in the preservation of DUNHAM TAVERN, Cleveland's oldest remaining house (1842). He contributed to its restoration, proposed the idea of making it a museum of early Americana, and for a time maintained his office there. In the mid-thirties he contributed a regular gardening column to the CLEVELAND PRESS. One of Gray's most permanent contributions was the Horticultural Gardens for the GREAT LAKES EXPOSITION of 1936–37, which remained after the exposition on the site north of the CLEVELAND MUNICIPAL STADIUM. The gardens were named for Gray as a memorial after his death, and continued to be maintained by the city in the 1980s. Gray married Florence Ball, daughter of Webb C. Ball, on 11 Jan. 1928. They had 1 daughter, Virginia.

A. Donald Gray Papers, WRHS.

**GRAY, JOSEPH WILLIAM** (5 Aug. 1813–26 May 1862), was the founder of the PLAIN DEALER. Gray was born in Bridgeport, Vt. He was raised and educated through the academy level in upstate New York; he and his brother, Admiral Nelson Gray, emigrated to Cleveland in 1836. After several terms of teaching in local schools, including the St. Clair Academy, Gray read law under HENRY B. PAYNE and HIRAM V. WILLSON and was admitted to the bar. In partnership with his brother, Gray purchased the CLEVELAND ADVERTISER, a faltering Democratic weekly, in Dec. 1841. It was resurrected by the two brothers on 7 Jan. 1842, as the Cleveland Plain Dealer. A. N. Gray served the paper as business manager until shortly after the weekly was converted to a daily in 1845, when he left the Plain Dealer solely in his brother Joseph's charge.

Gray became personally as well as editorially involved in Democratic politics. Appointed postmaster of Cleveland by Pres. Franklin Pierce in 1853, he was dismissed from that position by Pres. Jas. Buchanan in 1858 for his editorial support of Illinois senator Stephen A. Douglas in opposition to the Lecompton Constitution. Receiving the Democratic nomination for Congress in 1858, Gray lost the election in the normally Republican district to Edward Wade. Gray went to both the Charleston and Baltimore Democratic conventions in 1860 as a delegate pledged to Douglas. He maintained his support of Douglas even through defeat, endorsing the senator's pledge of loyalty to the Union after the secession of the South in 1861. For 20 years, Gray managed to keep his Democratic paper alive in the heart of a Whig, and later Republican, stronghold. His politics evidently placed no hindrance on his social life, in which his fondness for dancing was well known locally. He married Mary K. Foster in 1845 and fathered a daughter and 2 sons. A household accident with a son's toy cap pistol cost him the sight of one eye in 1858, and his health soon after deteriorated. He died after a short illness at home and was buried in the ERIE ST. CEMETERY.

**GRAY DRUG STORES, INC.,** is one of the nation's leading drugstore chains and a pioneer in merchandising techniques. Its founder, Adolph Weinberger, a Hungarian immigrant, opened his first drugstore at E. 30th St. and Scovill Ave. in 1912. Weinberger moved his store several times before he introduced cut-rate prices at a Prospect Ave. location. This technique sparked his business, and by 1928 he had 7 drugstores, which he formed into Weinberger Drug Stores, Inc. Despite the Depression, Weinberger pursued a rapid expansion program, and by the mid-1930s, with the acquisition of a Columbus firm and aggressive discount pricing, the chain had grown to 29 stores. In 1936, it established headquarters at 2400 Superior Ave. By 1945, the company had expanded to a point where it was operating under 6 different names. That year, it consolidated all of its stores under one name, Gray Drug Stores, Inc., the shortest and most easily remembered name. Gray continued to grow after WORLD WAR II by being one of the first companies to build stores, mainly in Ohio, and through a $40 million expansion program. It diversified into another major retail field, discount department stores, by leasing drug departments in such stores and by acquiring the Rink's Dept. Store chain of Cincinnati in 1964. Two years later, Gray moved into larger headquarters at 666 Euclid Ave.

By the late 1960s, Gray experienced a decline in business. After a proposed merger with COOK UNITED, INC., was blocked in 1969, Weinberger's son Jerome resolved to rebuild the company, initiating a vigorous expansion program with emphasis on newer and larger drugstores, especially in Florida, with a greater variety of goods and health services. In 1981, Gray decided to concentrate on its discount drugstore business. It sold its 47 Rink's stores to Cook United and then acquired the 181-store Drug Fair chain, with headquarters in the Washington, D.C., area. That gave Gray over 360 stores in the Midwest and East. To prevent a takeover by a Texas firm, Gray merged into the SHERWIN-WILLIAMS CO., the Cleveland-based paint and chemical firm, in Sept. 1981. Gray continued to thrive under Sherwin-Williams as it acquired the 26 Cleveland-area Cunningham Drug Stores in 1982. Cunningham's predecessor in Cleveland was the pioneer Marshall Drug Co., which began as a partnership between Wentworth G. Marshall and Arthur F. May in a Public Square drugstore in 1884. Marshall also strove to introduce the cut-rate policy into the drugstore industry in the early 1900s. Detroit-based Cunningham acquired Marshall in 1941 and closed the last Marshall store in 1978.

**GRAYS ARMORY,** built by Cleveland's long-standing private military company the CLEVELAND GRAYS, has served not only as a meeting lodge and assembly hall for that group but also as a stage for a wide variety of performances. The armory was designed by Cleveland architect Fenimore C. Bates and was built on Bolivar St. at Prospect Ave. The cornerstone was laid on Decoration Day, 1893. The appearance of the structure is, appropriately enough for an organization that provided trained men for military service and to serve as honor guards at local, state, and national functions, that of a military fortress. A great 5-story tower with rows of progressively smaller windows and a turreted cap, and the rusticated stone foundation at the street level surmounted by massive brick walls suggest a sturdy bastion. The rounded arch of the entrance and the stone and brick details suggest the Neo-Romanesque style of H. H. Richardson. The interior contains offices and meeting rooms at the front and a large drill hall with a clerestoried roof supported by exposed iron trusswork at the rear.

The Grays Armory was one of 2 such structures begun in Cleveland in 1893, the other being the CENTRAL ARMORY built by the county for Natl. Guard units at E. 6th St. and Lakeside. The armory's drill hall not only was used for training and assemblies of the Grays but also was rented out for various social and cultural events. Programs for the 1896 Cleveland Centennial were held there. Performers such as opera star Emma Calve appeared, along with popular revues and touring companies. In 1918 it was the scene of the first concert of the newly formed CLEVELAND ORCHESTRA. In later years, as more elaborate theaters and halls were opened, fewer performances were held at the armory. However, in the 1970s the Western Reserve Theatre Organ Society installed and refurbished a large Wurlitzer theater pipe organ in the drill hall, and concerts were given regularly. The Cleveland Grays have continued to operate from their armory on Bolivar Rd. into the 1980s.

**GRDINA, ANTON** (27 Apr. 1874–1 Dec. 1957), called "perhaps the best known Slovenian leader in this country" at the time of his death, was a prominent businessman and a civic and cultural leader in the Slovenian community. The son of a poor farmer, Grdina grew up in Ljubljana, Yugoslavia, where he received an elementary school education. On 24 Aug. 1897 he arrived in Cleveland, his trip financed by a brother already living there. In the next 5 years he worked on canals and roads, in a hat factory, and as a street cleaner; by 1904 he had saved enough money to buy a hardware store on St. Clair Ave. By 1906 Grdina was also selling furniture, and in 1910 he became an undertaker. He had interests in 2 companies by 1920, the Grdina Furniture Co. at 6019 St. Clair, and Grdina & Co., a hardware store at 6127 St. Clair. In 1928 he incorporated Anton Grdina & Sons, home furnishers and funeral directors; he served as president of the company until his death. Grdina helped organize 2 banking institutions to serve the Slovenian community. In Dec. 1916 he helped found the Slovenian Bldg. & Loan Assoc., which became the St. Clair Savings Assoc. in 1937; and in the winter of 1919–20 he was among the organizers of the North American Bldg. & Savings Co., later the NORTH AMERICAN BANK. Grdina served as president of the latter institution from 1939 until his death.

Prominent in the community as a businessman and banker, Grdina took the lead in rebuilding that part of the St. Clair neighborhood destroyed by the EAST OHIO GAS CO. EXPLOSION & FIRE on 20 Oct. 1944. He organized the nonprofit St. Clair-Norwood Rehabilitation Corp. to finance reconstruction in the area. Grdina himself gave $5,000 to the effort and led the campaign that raised an additional $17,900 from 26 local merchants. The corporation bought the sites of the destroyed houses and built and sold 16 new homes. Grdina was also an important cultural leader in the Slovenian community. He served as treasurer of the CLEVELAND CULTURAL GARDENS FED. from its founding in 1926 until 1957; was president of the Yugoslav Cultural Garden; organized the Grand Carnolian Slovenian Catholic Union; was a founder of the Natl. Slovene Catholic Union; and held memberships in 16 Slovenian lodges. He also maintained close ties to people in the homeland, making available to those in the U.S. films, newspapers, and magazines from the native land and soliciting funds in the U.S. for specific needs in Yugoslavia. For his efforts, Grdina was the first Slovenian in the U.S. to receive the Third Order of the Yugoslav Crown, awarded to him by King Peter in 1938. In 1954 he was made a knight in the Order of St. Gregory by papal decree. Grdina was married in 1899 to Antoija Bizelj.

**The GREAT LAKES DREDGE AND DOCK COMPANY** was established when larger ships on the Great Lakes created a need for deeper channels and sturdier docks. The company was founded in 1890 by Wm. A. Lydon. Since then it has grown, and its operations have expanded to Central and South America, as well as the Middle East, Africa, and the Caribbean Islands. In addition to dredging and dock construction, the company has also fabricated and laid subsequeous pipelines, installed piers for bridges, built up breakwaters, and added sand to eroding beaches. Initially, a facility for manufacturing premolded reinforced concrete piles and poles was built on WHISKEY ISLAND. These were used in harbor and dock improvements, piers, heavy foundations, and electric power-transmission lines. In 1914-15 the company participated in the construction of piers and abutments for the Detroit-Superior and Clark Ave. bridges.

In the 50-year period 1920-70, Great Lakes Dredge & Dock worked on the McArthur Lock at Sault Ste. Marie and built the southwest pier at this location to protect the Power Canal from out-of-control freighters. On the lower lakes, its dredges worked on the Livingston, Fighting Island, and Amherstburg channels. Dredging the Cuyahoga River was an annual task. Among other projects managed by the Cleveland office during these years were installing a 5-mi. pipeline for Rochester, N.Y., and a water intake for Buffalo, revamping the breakwater at the Avon Lake Power Plant, and doing marine work at the CLEVELAND ELECTRIC ILLUMINATING CO. Great Lakes Dredge & Dock also participated in construction of the St. Lawrence Seaway. In 1977, the Great Lakes Dredge & Dock Co. established the North American Trailing Co. as a wholly owned subsidiary. This latter company took delivery of the first hopper dredge to operate on the Great Lakes. The unique design of this vessel permits it to split longitudinally from stem to stern to discharge its cargo. In 1979, Great Lakes Internatl. became the holding company of Great Lakes Dredge & Dock and its subsidiaries. The most recent management change took place in early Nov. 1985, when Great Lakes Internatl. was taken over by real-estate magnate Sam Zell.

The **GREAT LAKES EXPOSITION** of 1936 and 1937 provided Clevelanders with relief from the dreariness of the Depression years and helped them celebrate the centennial of the incorporation of their home town as a city. The exposition was the idea of Frank J. Ryan and Lincoln G. Dickey, who had served as the city's first public hall commissioner. They conceived of using the downtown lakefront as an exhibition area that would emphasize the strengths of the Great Lakes region. They then sold community leaders on the merits of the plan, and DUDLEY S. BLOSSOM became chairman of á civic committee that contributed $1.5 million to transform the idea into reality. The exposition was built on land extending along the lakefront from W. 3rd St. to about E. 20th St. It also used the Mall area, Public Hall, and Municipal Stadium. Altogether the fairgrounds covered 135 acres. Work on transforming the site began in Apr. 1936, and in just 80 days the complex had been completed. The exposition opened to the public on 27 June 1936 for a 100-day run.

A variety of attractions drew throngs to the lakefront. The Mall was transformed into a grand entranceway with brilliantly lighted pylons and a promenade leading toward the water. There was a "Streets of the World" district that featured 200 cafes and bazaars reminiscent of the countries they represented. There was a midway with rides and sideshows. There were many historical and industrial exhibits, such as a Court of the Presidents, a Hall of Progress, and an Automotive Bldg. An art gallery, a Marine Theater, and horticultural gardens were other popular attractions. Opening day lured 61,206 visitors to the lakefront, and on Labor Day 125,192 people set the exposition's attendance record. When the season ended, nearly 4 million visitors from across the nation had attended. Sponsors decided to carry the show over for a second season. The 1937 season opened on 29 May with a new attraction which became

its most popular feature: an Aquacade that featured water ballet shows and starred Eleanor Holm and Johnny Weismuller. By the time the second season came to an end on 15 Sept., another 3 million visitors had been logged. Nearly $70 million had been spent by exposition visitors over the 2 years. By Apr. 1938, the entire exposition site east and south of the stadium had been cleared. The only vestiges of the festival remaining in 1985 were the Donald Gray Gardens and the columned promenade directly north of the stadium, once part of the exhibit's Horticultural Gardens.

The **GREAT LAKES HISTORICAL SOCIETY** is devoted to the presentation and study of history on the Great Lakes. Its principal attraction is the Great Lakes Historical Society Museum, the largest and oldest marine museum on the Great Lakes. The Great Lakes Historical Society was organized on 27 Apr. 1944 in a meeting that took place at the CLEVELAND PUBLIC LIBRARY. The founders were Frederick Wakefield, A. A. Mastics, Milton N. Gallup, and Wm. Stage. Its initial purpose was "to promote interest in the collection and preservation of written material and objects dealing with the history, geology, and folklore of the Great Lakes." Since its founding, the society has been governed by a board of trustees. The original officers were Alva Bradley, president; Clarence S. Metcalf, vice-president; and Louis C. Sabin, Donna L. Root, Leo P. Johnson, and A. A. Mastics. Capt. H. Chesley Inches was museum director from 1958-70. Alexander Cook succeeded him as the museum's curator.

The society originally housed its collections at the Cleveland Public Library. In 1953 it moved to its present (1986) home in Vermilion, where it established a museum in Frederick Wakefield's old mansion. For a time it was known as the Wakefield Nautical Museum. In 1968 a $250,000 addition was built; it later was dedicated to Capt. Inches. The museum's collections include ship models (the largest such collection of any marine museum on the Great Lakes), marine relics and artifacts, paintings, photographs, and special displays dealing with Great Lakes history. Among the displays are a large collection of ships' engines, an exhibit of tools used in the construction of wooden ships, and a simulated ship's bridge. The society also maintains the U.S.S. *Cod* submarine on Cleveland's lakefront, publishes a quarterly journal on Great Lakes History, *Inland Seas,* and houses the Clarence S. Metcalf Library. Since 1955 it has also given attention to the history of the Vermilion area. Since the 1970s, the museum has been considered for relocation to Cleveland as part of the lakefront development schemes that have arisen there.

The **GREAT LAKES THEATER FESTIVAL** opened as the Great Lakes Shakespeare Festival on 11 July 1962 with a 30-member acting company performing 6 plays during the summer. It began at the Lakewood Civic Auditorium with the financial backing of the Parma Fine Arts Council and the JEWISH COMMUNITY CTR. The festival draws audiences from all over Ohio, including Akron, Toledo, and Ashtabula. Its original producer/director was Arthur Lithgow, formerly a member of Princeton University's faculty and the general director of the McCarter Theater at Princeton. Lithgow was replaced in 1966 by Lawrence Carra, who resigned in 1976 and was replaced by Vincent Dowling. Dowling resigned in July 1984. From the beginning, the Great Lakes Shakespeare Festival had difficulty funding its season. In its first year, only 18,000 people attended its series of 6 plays, which led to a $25,000 loss. By 1964, the deficit rose to a total of $32,000. Fortunately, the CLEVELAND FOUNDATION made a $20,000 2-year grant to the festival, which was then used to subsidize the low-priced student matinees. In July 1982, the festival moved to the refurbished Loew's Ohio Theater. In 1982, Dowling won the lucrative production rights to the 8-hour drama *The Life and Adventures of Nicholas Nickleby.* Although the show did well in 1982, it had a low attendance record when it played again in 1984, and at that time the festival faced the largest deficit in its 22-year history. The festival opened a second theater on 9 July 1983, called the Inn Theater. It seated 99 people and was located in the Parthenon Lounge across EUCLID AVE. from the OHIO THEATER. In 1985 the festival changed its name to the Great Lakes Theater Festival, and Gerald Freedman was appointed its new artistic director.

The **GREATER CLEVELAND GROWTH ASSOCIATION,** founded in 1848 as the Board of Trade and reorganized in 1893 as the Cleveland Chamber of Commerce, has been a leader in promoting BUSINESS, INDUSTRY, and the image of the Greater Cleveland area and has played a major role in bringing a greater degree of rationality and order to the local urban environment in the early decades of the 20th century. The Board of Trade was organized on 7 July 1848 by 36 local merchants led by insurance agent Joseph L. Weatherly. The board's activities were designed to help its members operate their businesses more efficiently. It met 6 days a week and issued market and shipping reports on such items as coal and agricultural products; its efforts were especially helpful to merchants dealing in grains and provisions. By the time it issued its first annual report in 1866, the board had 230 members. It was incorporated in Apr. 1866.

In 1892, the Board of Trade began to promote industry in the city, forming a committee to encourage new industries and businesses to locate in Cleveland. From the work of this committee grew plans to reorganize the board and expand its activities beyond commerce to include general civic affairs. On 6 Feb. 1893, the Board of Trade became the Cleveland Chamber of Commerce, and its committee began work on such issues as EDUCATION, legislation, TRANSPORTATION, municipal affairs, and entertainment. The chamber helped raise funds for the relief of the poor during the economic depression of the 1890s, built an armory on Bank (W. 6th) St., persuaded the federal government to locate a hydrographic office in the city, and planned the Cleveland presentation at the World's Fair in Chicago.

By 1899, membership in the chamber had grown to 1,100, and on 2 May the chamber dedicated its own office building on the northeast corner of PUBLIC SQUARE, adjacent to the Society for Savings building. Its expanded program of civic involvement continued over the next 3 decades as it attempted to bring a sense of geographic and social order to the rapidly growing city. Among its activities were development of the Group Plan for the Mall (1900); establishment of the juvenile court (1902) and the municipal court (1910); development of a sanitary code for the city, which included meat and milk inspections (1904) and the city's first comprehensive traffic ordinance (1911); successful promotion of a new street-numbering plan (1905); sponsorship of 2 industrial expositions (1909 and 1927); organization of the University Improvement Co. to develop UNIVERSITY CIRCLE (1919); and organization of the Fed. for Charity & Philanthropy in 1913, the predecessor to the Community Fund and UNITED WAY. During the 1920s and 1930s, the chamber was active at both the state and national levels, opposing wage and hour legislation and lobbying against state income tax bills.

Dependent as it was upon support from business, the chamber suffered the loss of both members and income during the Depression; membership dropped from 5,200 in 1929 to 2,100 in 1933. Bewildered by the depth of the Depression, the chamber was unable to provide much help to local businesses, although it did bring the NATL. AIR RACES to Cleveland beginning in 1929, and it sponsored the GREAT LAKES EXPOSITION in 1936 and 1937. Beginning in 1936, the chamber was reorganized under the leadership of Alwyn C. Ernst. Ernst initiated a new phase of chamber activities by introducing corporate membership, soliciting suggestions from businessmen for chamber projects, and hiring specialists from other cities to lead the chamber's civic-improvement projects, such as river and harbor improvements and trade expansion.

The chamber continued its growth and its active involvement in civic affairs. By 1948 it had 5,000 members, and in Dec. 1967 it merged with the Greater Cleveland Growth Board and adopted its present (1985) title. The Growth Board had been organized in Jan. 1962 to maintain jobs in the city by working to solve problems that caused employers to leave. By 1979, membership in the Growth Assoc. had grown to 6,400, with 96 employees and a $7 million budget, which included $5 million in federal funds for job training and minority business assistance. After the social turmoil in Cleveland in the 1960s, the new Growth Assoc. planned to address social issues in addition to traditional business concerns. By 1980, however, it recognized that its efforts in such social spheres as housing, justice, welfare, education, and recreation were not proving effective; the Growth Assoc. then reduced the number of its departments from 11 to 4 in order to concentrate its efforts on economic development. Its new programs were the Cleveland Area Development Corp., the Council of Smaller Enterprises, the Metropolitan Cleveland Jobs Council, and the Community Resources Ctr.

Baker, Samuel B., "The Cleveland Chamber of Commerce in the Great Depression" (Ph.D. diss., Case Western Reserve University, 1984).
Greater Cleveland Growth Assoc. Records, WRHS.

The **GREATER CLEVELAND HOME AND FLOWER SHOW,** a popular annual event, was first held in Public Hall in 1941. Before that, home shows and flower shows were held separately in Cleveland. The first home and building show was run in 1916 by Ralph P. Stoddard, a Cleveland newspaper man, and the Complete Cleveland Bldg. Show Co. Other shows followed in 1922 and 1923. The 1922 show was the first event to take place in Public Hall. The first flower show was staged in 1919 and was held in the Wigmore Coliseum located on E. 13th St. It was Stoddard who originally conceived the idea of combining the two shows. The combined Home & Flower Show in 1941 started small. It occupied only a portion of North Hall, the Arcade, and the upper and lower Lakeside Halls in Public Hall (also known as PUBLIC AUDITORIUM). It was an instant success; attendance was 100,625. The show was staged as a nonprofit, civic enterprise, with the chief interests being home construction, home furnishing, landscaping, flower gardening, and flowers. The main idea was to make people want to build or improve their homes. The Home & Flower Show was held at about the same time every year, the last part of February, and ran through the first part of March. It soon became the most popular annual event held in Public Hall. People from all parts of the state came to see the latest in home equipment and home appliances, to learn about the newest types of building materials, and to get new ideas from the full-scale homes that were exhibited. Eventually the show became such a large-scale production that staff had to be hired to work year-round on the project. The original staff included Ralph P. Stoddard, the show's first managing director; Louise Madison, assistant to the manager; and Joseph M. Schultz, secretary and treasurer. Other directors included Chas. Hutaff and Edward J. Baugh.

**GREATER CLEVELAND HOSPITAL ASSOCIATION.** *See* **CENTER FOR HEALTH-GREATER CLEVELAND HOSPITAL ASSOC.**

The **GREATER CLEVELAND NEIGHBORHOOD CENTERS ASSOCIATION** was organized in 1963 as the administrative body for neighborhood centers throughout the city. The GCNCA centralized the planning and budgeting and coordinated the activities of some 20 neighborhood agencies. Built on the Neighborhood Settlement Assoc., organized in 1948 by HIRAM HOUSE, FRIENDLY INN, and UNIVERSITY SETTLEMENT, the group drew in unaffiliated SETTLEMENT HOUSES to meet the needs of the 1960s. The consolidation of many centers that shared goals but differed in programs was considered very innovative in 1963, and in successive years, the association has been a local arena for many trends in social welfare. At the time the Neighborhood Settlement Assoc. was established, settlement houses were redefining their role as one of enriching the lives of their new neighborhood clients through recreation and other services increasingly administered by professional social workers. The new clients of the houses tended to be migrants from the South, Puerto Rico, and Appalachia. Under the auspices of the association, the old settlement houses, whose name had come to connote a slum, became neighborhood centers and, ultimately, multiservice centers. Funded by the United Appeal, the Welfare Fed., and the CLEVELAND FOUNDATION, the association became a clearinghouse for federal funds destined for programs for job training, housing, neighborhood redevelopment, daycare, drug abuse, social services, food stamps, youth activities, and the like. The association experimented with creative programs such as daycare for the elderly, 24-hour daycare for children of shift workers, and drop-in centers for teens. While some programs were funded for only a short time, long-term innovations included the LEGAL AID SOCIETY, Meals on Wheels, and the Sunbeam School. Founding members of the Greater Cleveland Neighborhood Crtrs. Assoc. included ALTA HOUSE, the Chagrin Falls Park Community Ctr., the Collinwood Community Services Ctr., the EAST END NEIGHBORHOOD HOUSE, Friendly Inn, the Garden Valley Neighborhood House, the Glenville Neighborhood Community Ctrs., Goodrich House, the Harvard Community Services Ctr., Hiram House Camp (successor to Hiram House), the League Park Ctr., the Lexington Square Community Ctr., MERRICK HOUSE, the Mt. Pleasant Community Ctrs., the PHILLIS WHEATLEY ASSOC., the RAINEY INSTITUTE, University Settlement, and WEST SIDE COMMUNITY HOUSE. Associate members included the CLEVELAND MUSIC SCHOOL SETTLEMENT. Additional centers have raised the number of members to 23.

Greater Cleveland Neighborhood Centers Assoc. Records, WRHS.

The **GREATER CLEVELAND NURSES ASSOCIATION,** District #4 of the Ohio Nurses Assoc., has been active under various names in Cleveland since 1900. Throughout its existence, its general purpose has been to promote the nursing profession in Cleveland. The GCNA was founded on 28 May 1900 by a group of nurses who hoped "to improve the standard of the profession of trained NURSING in Cleveland and elsewhere and to improve the conditions affecting the members in the practice of their profession, to raise a fund for the purpose of furnishing nurses to deserving persons unable themselves to pay in full for the services of nurses, to stimulate an interest in nursing affairs and to conduct a central registry." The group soon became known as the Graduate Nurses' Assoc. Of initial importance was the central registry, which provided both hospitals and private patients with trained nurses, and continued to do so until its closing in 1974. Fifty-five nurses were on the registry after the first year. The association was incorporated in 1909. During this early period, it received financial aid from the Isabel Hampton Robb Memorial Committee. Isabel Robb was a leader in the nursing profession and a member of the Graduate Nurses' Assoc. until her death in 1910.

In June 1918, the association merged with the newly formed (Nov. 1917) District #4 of the Ohio State Graduate Nurses' Assoc., which included the Cleveland area. Another group, the Visiting Nurse Club, also joined District #4 at this time. In 1921, the district filed new articles of incorporation, with greater emphasis on education and increased efficiency in nursing care. During the 1930s, the association was concerned with advancing its profession by calling for the establishment of a nursing division in the State Dept. of Health. It also worked for proper salary and position recognition of public-health nurses, and for an 8-hour day for private nurses working in hospitals. During the early 1940s, the association became involved in the defense movement, working with agencies such as the American Red Cross and the Ohio Council of Defense. After WORLD WAR II, and into the 1970s, the association established committees to meet the interests of nurses working in specialized areas of the profession. These included industrial nursing and public health committees, a Psychiatric-Mental Health Practice Div. (est. 1971), and nurse practitioner and cardiovascular nursing conference groups. In the 1970s and 1980s, the association increased its public-health awareness programs, including—in the early 1970s—sponsorship of symposiums on drug abuse and referral services for those suffering from drug addiction. It also became more active in advocating the rights of nurses in the workplace. As an example, in 1969, the association passed a resolution supporting nurses at ST. VINCENT CHARITY HOSPITAL who were attempting to secure a contract through collective bargaining. The association has also supported legal action against employers who discriminate against nurses as women.

Greater Cleveland Nurses Assoc. Records, WRHS.

The **GREATER CLEVELAND POISON CONTROL CENTER** has provided a 24-hour emergency telephone "hotline" service for both health-care professionals and the public, and poison-prevention materials, exhibits, and education programs for community groups. It is the oldest such countywide facility in the country. The GCPCC was organized in 1957 by the ACADEMY OF MEDICINE as a public-service agency to help reduce childhood accidents due to poisoning. From the start, the program consisted of 2 components: a telephone emergency service and an educational (preventive) program. Throughout its existence, the GCPCC has been primarily funded by the Board of Commissioners of Cuyahoga County; it has also received grants from private foundations and federal funds. Between 1957-81, it was sponsored by the Academy of Medicine, with additional help from the FED. FOR COMMUNITY

PLANNING and UNITED WAY. Since 1981, it has been located on the CASE WESTERN RESERVE UNIVERSITY campus, cosponsored by the Dept. of Pediatrics of the School of Medicine and Rainbow Babies & Childrens Hospital. While at the Academy of Medicine, the GCPCC specialized mainly in the chemical hazards of household products and treatment if swallowed. Since moving to CWRU, the program has expanded to include drug information services and an industrial toxicology program providing services to local industry. The number of emergency calls received increased from 12,000 in 1981 to 20,000 in 1985.

The **GREATER CLEVELAND REGIONAL TRANSIT AUTHORITY** was established in Dec. 1974. It was charged with creating a countywide system of public transportation, to be built primarily upon the foundation of the existing Cleveland Transit System. CTS had come into existence in Nov. 1941 with the municipal purchase of the CLEVELAND RAILWAY CO., which had held the city's transit franchise since 1910. It officially took over operations on 28 Apr. 1942. CTS assumed control of public transit at a time of climbing ridership due to wartime conditions. It was faced with improving services and modernizing an operation that had been short of cash for several years. In 1946 the all-time high in ridership occurred, with 493 million passengers. Following the war, ridership began to decline, and CTS began to modernize its operations. By Jan. 1954, streetcars were eliminated from the city's streets in favor of buses and trackless trolleys. Construction of a $29.5 million rapid-transit line began in Feb. 1952. On 15 Mar. 1955, east side service was inaugurated between Windermere and CLEVELAND UNION TERMINAL, and on 14 Aug. 1955, the west side portion was opened from the terminal to W. 117th St. Two extensions to the west side line were subsequently undertaken. In 1958 the tracks were extended to West Park, and in 1968 they were extended to CLEVELAND HOPKINS INTERNATL. AIRPORT. The airport extension made Cleveland the first city in the U.S. to have a rail link connecting its downtown with its airport.

Problems with the system began to surface in 1967. That was the last year in which CTS operated out of farebox revenues. Ridership had declined to 162 million, attributable to people's preferring their automobiles and to CTS's failure to establish new lines in suburban areas where residential and commercial growth had taken place. As revenue continued to decline, CTS raised fares and cut service, a process that led to further declines. In 1973 the city loaned CTS $7.3 million to help meet its debt. That loan allowed the system to continue operating into 1975, and it also gave impetus to the birth of the GCRTA. The first board members of the newly created authority were appointed in Jan. 1975. Richard Stoddart became president of the 10-member board, and Leonard Ronis was named the system's first general manager. The first item of business was to work out arrangements for consolidating all the separate transit systems in the county under the RTA umbrella. Besides CTS, the authority agreed to absorb the SHAKER HTS. RAPID TRANSIT, and it established contracts with the bus lines that served GARFIELD HTS., BRECKSVILLE, EUCLID, N. OLMSTED, and MAPLE HTS. All these arrangements, however, were contingent upon voter approval of a 1% increase in the county sales tax. Voters, lured by the promise of lower fares and improved service, approved the tax levy on 22 July 1975.

RTA began transit operations on 5 Oct. 1975, offering a $.25 local fare and $.35 express ride. Ridership, which had plummeted to 78 million in 1974, rose rapidly. By 1980

passenger totals had climbed 76%. In that year, however, financial troubles began to be felt by RTA. A reduction in federal subsidies and a decline in anticipated revenues from sales taxes due to an economic recession forced RTA to raise fares. Additional increases were made in 1981, and again in 1982. This latter increase brought the fares to $.85 for a local ride and $1 for an express trip. Increased fares led to passengers' once again turning to their cars, and ridership declined by 30% by the end of 1983. In its first 10 years of operations, RTA accomplished many of its goals. It established central coordination of the county's transit services, significantly expanded routes, created special services for the aged and handicapped, rebuilt its rapid-transit lines, updated its fleets of railcars and buses, and built new vehicle-maintenance facilities.

The **GREATER CLEVELAND ROUNDTABLE** is an organization of Cleveland leaders bound together by a commitment to solve community problems. Organized in 1981, the organization was originally composed of some 60 representatives of business, labor, churches, suburbs, neighborhood organizations, social agencies, and the black community. To achieve a cross-section of Cleveland leadership, members are appointed by a board of trustees. Funding comes from corporations and foundation grants. The aim of the roundtable is to provide a forum for discussion of issues crucial to the Greater Cleveland area. It would then increase the public's awareness of alternative courses of action. Discussion has centered around 5 major areas: public education, economic development, housing and neighborhood development, and race relations. Among the causes the roundtable has supported are the 1984 CLEVELAND PUBLIC SCHOOL levy (the first successful one in 12 years), the need for a domed stadium, and the management crisis at the CUYAHOGA METROPOLITAN HOUSING ASSOC. Until 1986, the roundtable was chaired by Sarah Short Austin, a former executive of the Natl. Urban Coalition. Facing increasing opposition from other BLACKS who questioned her leadership, Austin was replaced by Ralph S. Tyler of TRW as acting chairman.

The **GREATER CLEVELAND SAFETY COUNCIL** has been a nationally recognized leader in the field of safety education and training. Organized in 1919, it was the third local safety council to be established following the creation of the Natl. Safety Council in 1913. The national council was formed as a response to the high number of serious industrial accidents and the lack of comprehensive workers' compensation laws. It was conceived as a permanent group dedicated to encouraging safety in INDUSTRY. The Cleveland council's purpose was the prevention of accidents through education and training. An independent organization financed entirely by membership and contributions, it emphasized the partnership of safety education, law enforcement, and the development of effective safety devices as a means of accident prevention. It presented programs, distributed literature, gave classes, and provided safety information in Cleveland and surrounding communities. The council worked closely with a variety of organizations, including the Cleveland police and fire departments, the Ohio Bureau of Motor Vehicles, the Ohio Dept. of Highway Safety, and many local school districts.

The council's first budget was $15,000. By the 1980s, with corporate and individual memberships totaling more than 1,200, its annual budget exceeded $125,000. The first president of the council was Stephen W. Tener. Col. Joseph H. Alexander, president of the council in 1926, was instrumental in elevating it to the forefront of the national safety effort. In 1939, 1943, and 1947, Cleveland was ranked first in large cities in traffic safety. In 1956 the Cleveland Safety Council developed a successful industrial safety program, Patterns for Progress, that was later adopted statewide. In the late 1950s the council changed its name to the Greater Cleveland Safety Council, recognizing the important role played outside of the city of Cleveland. Through the 1980s, the council continued efforts to achieve its goals of accident prevention through safety education and training. Bolstered by the work of over 300 volunteers, it maintained its position of leadership in the safety field. In 1981 the Greater Cleveland Safety Council won the State of Ohio Grand Award for Excellence & Dedication in the Promotion of Safety, the highest award given to a council in the state of Ohio.

The **GREATER CLEVELAND SPORTS HALL OF FAME** was organized in Aug. 1976 to recognize the contributions Greater Cleveland men and women have made to this area through their sports achievements. The Hall of Fame originated as a project of the Greater Cleveland Bicentennial Sports Committee at the suggestion of Sam Levine. A committee was created in 1975, and a year later a nonprofit foundation was set up to raise money and organize the Hall of Fame. The first induction of members took place in Sept. 1977; however, it wasn't until July 1978 that the Hall of Fame was officially opened in the Grand Lobby of the Cleveland PUBLIC AUDITORIUM. Inductees included both amateur and professional athletes in BASEBALL, BASKETBALL, BOWLING, boxing, fencing, FOOTBALL, GOLF, gymnastics, HOCKEY, swimming and diving, TENNIS, track and field, and wrestling, and there was a general category for meritorious service in all sports. In 1980 a new division was added for all sports not originally recognized by the hall. Eligibility for membership was restricted to outstanding sports figures who were born and raised in Cleveland, brought recognition to the area through their sports accomplishments here, and remained as residents. All candidates must either have competed in their sports for 12 years or more or have been retired for 3 years or more, whichever came first.

The **GREATER CLEVELAND VETERANS COUNCIL,** formed in 1946, celebrated its 35th anniversary on 29 Jan. 1983. Member organizations are the VETERANS OF FOREIGN WARS, American Legion, Disabled American Veterans, American Veterans of World War I, and American Veterans of World War II. Each organization sends representatives to monthly meetings, held at the Disabled American Veterans Hall at 1423 E. 39th St. near Superior Ave. The purpose of the GCVC is to unite veterans of Cuyahoga County in their concern for and discussion of legislation, nationally, statewide, and locally, that affects veterans' benefits. In addition, the council participates in memorial observances and parades on Veterans' Day, Memorial Day, and Pearl Harbor Day. Pearl Harbor Survivors Assoc. representatives attend meetings but are not members of the Veterans Council. The first president of the council was E. J. Sklenicka of Cleveland. All member organizations are chartered by the U.S. Congress. At one time, GCVC members were part of the Joint Veterans Commission, but they opted to form their own organization.

The **GREATER CLEVELAND VOLUNTEER HEALTH PLAN** is a volunteer group that in 1982 replaced the METROPOLITAN HEALTH PLANNING CORP. as Greater Cleveland's health-care planner. The group was formed by business executives in 1982 and was privately funded. Donald C. Flagg, a Stouffer Corp. vice-president, was the main organizer. Like its predecessor, the MHPC, the Volunteer

Health Plan's main purpose was to "slow the increase in health costs without sacrificing the quality, availability, and accessibility of health care in the Cleveland area." More specifically, the group hoped to prevent unreasonable expansion of a health-care system already over capacity; encourage price competition among health-care providers; and arouse consumer awareness and action. The GCVHP is a 2-tier organization with an 18-member board of trustees and a 30-member board of governors. The trustees meet 3 or 4 times a year, and the board of governors, all volunteers, carry out their directives. Harry J. Bolwell was elected chairman of the board of trustees. Stephen F. Sears was the executive director in 1986. In 1984, the state designated the GCVHP as the Greater Cleveland health planner to act as an advisory group to the Ohio Dept. of Health. The GCVHP is also empowered to lobby on proposed health-care legislation. It handles almost $500,000 in federal funds annually.

**GREEKS.** Greeks formed one of Cleveland's smaller but most cohesive nationality groups in the 20th century. In Cleveland, as in other American cities, Greeks have demonstrated a penchant for individual small-business enterprise and the preservation of their culture through their central institution, the Greek Orthodox church. The first Greek to settle in Cleveland reportedly was Panagiotis Koutalianos, a fabled "strong man," who came to the city sometime before 1880. Out of 370,007 Greeks who emigrated to the U.S. between 1890–1920, 5,000 settled in Cleveland. Difficult economic conditions in Greece during this period were primarily responsible for this migration. Because most of the early Greek immigrants initially intended to return to Greece after working in America, about 95% of them were male, probably the largest percentage of male immigrants from any country at this time. Finding that the promised economic opportunities were exaggerated, most, however, remained in Cleveland and eventually arranged to have their families join them, or, if unmarried, returned to Greece in order to find a wife to bring to the U.S. Without women, most of the men formed nonfamily groups averaging 4–8 individuals. Renting or leasing apartments and sometimes entire houses, these men lived under varied conditions. The sections of the city in which they first settled are where most later raised their families. The largest concentration of Greeks formed around Bradley Ct. off of Bolivar Rd. between Erie (E. 9th) and Ontario, which soon became known as "Greek Town." A second area on the near east side was farther to the southeast along Woodland Ave., E. 79th, and Hough Ave. TREMONT, bounded by W. 14th, Fairfield Ave., W. 11th, and Clark Ave., was the only Greek settlement on the west side; it was formed largely by immigrants who moved across the river valley from Greek Town. Although most of these men, in time, married women who either came or were brought from Greece, there were more marriages with non-Greek women than were acknowledged at the time. By the 1920s, when immigration from Greece was legally restricted to 100 persons annually, the Greek population of Cleveland had stabilized at 5,000–6,000.

Because of their lack of skills, their ignorance of the English language, and the discrimination generally directed against southeastern Europeans, Greeks were initially forced to accept menial work. Despite their predominant agrarian background, Greeks in Cleveland took such jobs as railroad construction, bootblacking, dishwashing, waiting tables, cooking, hat cleaning, and street vending. Within an average of 5 to 10 years, however, many were able to become managers or owners of coffee shops, grocery stores, barbershops, restaurants, candy stores, bakeries, florist shops, and cleaning, pressing, and laundry services. Involvement in small business enterprises largely established the pattern for Greek economic involvement in Cleveland through the early half of the 20th century. The largest concentration of Greek enterprises, patronized by both Greeks and other East Mediterranean immigrants, was on Bolivar Rd. Larger enterprises, such as Perides Bros. Cigarette Mfrs. and the Peppas & Alex Co., manufacturers, wholesalers, and exporters, also developed. In 1922, the latter firm had capital stock in excess of $1 million and offices in both Cleveland and Chicago. In 1922, there were at least 137 Greek-owned enterprises in Cleveland, including 5 coffeehouses, 6 grocery stores, 25 confectioneries, 27 shoeshine parlors, and 60 restaurants. There was also a print shop, and later, in the 1930s, a newspaper, the Mentor, that served the Greek community.

The Greek Orthodox church became the cultural and social center of Cleveland's Greek community. During the early years, religious services were held in private homes. By 1910, space was rented for that purpose in Arch Hall on Ontario St. In 1912, a house and lot were purchased on the corner of W. 14th and Fairfield Ave., the site of the first, and until 1937 the only, Greek Orthodox church in Cleveland, ANNUNCIATION GREEK ORTHODOX CHURCH. A second church, St. Spyridon, appeared in 1937 on E. 65th and Addison Ave. on the near east side. This church, whose pastor was Rev. Wm. Lambert, followed the Julian calendar. St. Spyridon was absorbed by the Annunciation parish in 1950 along with its other properties, including the St. Elias Cemetery in BEDFORD HTS., which was later divested. Most burials, however, both before as well as since, were conducted at the St. Theodosius Russian Orthodox Cemetery at Biddulph and Ridge roads in BROOKLYN.

Greek culture was also preserved and taught in the schools. Besides the Annunciation Church School, 3 other schools were established simultaneously, which resulted in 2 schools on each side of the CUYAHOGA RIVER. The other west side school (in addition to the Annunciation's school) was the Greek American Progressive Assoc. School on the 2d floor of the Kranidis Bldg. on the corner of W. 11th and Fairfield Ave. The east side Greeks sent their children to either the Woodland School, which occupied the back of a grocery store, or the Lexington School, which was held at various premises off of E. 55th. In the 1920s and 1930s, classes were held 5 afternoons a week for 3 hours immediately after public school. Not only were the children expected to learn the Greek language, history, literature, and religious catechism, but on major holidays they performed in plays, presented songs, participated in dances, and recited lengthy poems and dialogues—all in Greek. Priests and secular teachers ran the schools.

Outside the church, a favorite meeting place for men—in addition to the many coffeehouses—was the regional or provincial social clubs. By the 1930s they had developed into self-help or beneficial associations. Most of them persisted into the 1980s, such as the Achaean, Arcadian, Chian, Cretan, Karpathian, Lacademonian, Laconian, Macedonian, Messinian, Microasiatic, Mykonian, Pan-Icarian, Rhodian, and Samian societies. Two other organizations appeared in the 1920s that were national in both scope and purpose. The first of these was the American Hellenic Educational & Progressive Assoc. It was founded in Atlanta in 1922, partly in response to discriminatory practices against Greeks; assimilation was one of its major goals. The Greek American Progressive Assoc. was founded in 1923 in Pittsburgh and, in contrast to the AHEPA, made ethnicity its major purpose. Both organizations had charter chapters in Cleveland by 1925; AHEPA had 3 chapters here as of 1984.

After WORLD WAR II, the Hellenic University Club, with professional and educational aims, appeared in Cleveland. Restricted to college graduates of Greek birth or descent, it had fewer members than the other 2 organizations but made an impact through its communitywide programs, which included lectures, seminars, and panel discussions on current educational, social, medical, legal, and political topics, as well as dramatic and musical presentations.

Most of these organizations provided activities for youth, including sports, dances, and other forms of recreation. Later, they also began to offer scholarships and internships for Greek students to attend undergraduate and graduate schools. AHEPA and GAPA have been notable in their efforts to encourage high school graduates to pursue their studies in higher institutions of learning. The Hellenic University Club has tended to concentrate its efforts in offering scholarships to Greek youth already in college or graduate schools. Noneducational activities included a boys' marching band sponsored by the local GAPA chapter, which from the late 1920s and into the 1930s was in demand to appear in many cities, including Detroit, Pittsburgh, Toledo, Canton, and Youngstown. Each year, along with the Annunciation Choir, the GAPA Jrs. Band accompanied Christ's bier on Good Friday as it was carried by mourners to neighboring St. George's Orthodox Antiochian Church on W. 14th, and then to St. Vladimir's Ukrainian Orthodox Church on W. 11th. In the late 1930s, the Sons & Daughters of Hellas, for teenagers, was formed. Following World War II, with the return of the veterans—many of whom were former members of SDH—another club was formed for young adults, the Hellenic Orthodox Youth League. With one of its major aims to present the youth's view of community affairs, HOYL became increasingly involved in parish and community activities. Both SDH and HOYL, with the support of parish councils, published during the 1940s and 1950s a community newspaper, the Hellenic Herald. The paper ceased publication soon after the appearance of the archdiocesan-sponsored national youth group the Greek Orthodox Youth of America, which replaced both SDH and HOYL. Two other youth societies have formed since then: the Jr. Orthodox Youth for 8-to-12-year-olds, and the Greek Orthodox Young Adult League.

World War II was significant for most Greek-Americans as a major turning point in their acceptance by other Americans. Although it defended itself successfully against the Italian invasion, Greece proved unable to duplicate that effort against the German forces, which quickly crushed it. But by its well-known effort of resistance, Greece became overnight a much admired and appreciated member of the Allied Forces. In America, the Greek War Relief Assoc. was formed, composed of Greek Orthodox church parishes, societies, and individuals who pledged money and supplies, and their services to assist the Greek people under German occupation. AHEPA and GAPA probably exerted the greatest efforts at the local level; Cleveland Greeks frequently oversubscribed the quotas assigned to them.

Following the war, the Greek population of Cleveland, mostly by natural increase, doubled, reaching approximately 10,000. Since 1965, with passage of the nonquota immigration law, population in the Greater Cleveland area has been estimated at 10,000–20,000. In 1980, there were 2,603 people of Greek birth living in Cleveland proper. Because of increased population, the elimination of St. Spyridon in 1950, and increased movement of parishioners into the eastern suburbs, a new church was built on the east side as a complement to the Annunciation Church. Rev. John Gerainios promoted the building of SS. Constantine & Helen Greek Orthodox Church in 1956 on Mayfield Rd. in CLEVELAND HTS. Later, 2 other churches were built in the western suburbs: St. Demetrios Greek Orthodox Parish was organized in 1962 under Rev. Peter Metallinos, and the St. Paul Greek Orthodox Parish in 1967. In 1955, the Annunciation parish had reorganized itself into a corporation, the American Hellenic Community of Greater Cleveland. St. Paul's was the first parish to develop outside the corporation. The charter of the American Hellenic Community was later amended to permit each parish to be "autonomous and autocephalic, as provided by the First Ecumenical Council of Nicaea in 325 A.D." Membership in each of these 4 separate parishes, as of 1980, varied between 300 and 600. Each maintained a Greek school, with classes meeting either 2 afternoons a week or on Saturday mornings, the number of students at each averaging 100–200. The Annunciation School is one of the few in the U.S. whose graduates' credits are accepted without examination by the public schools of Greece. Each of the 4 parishes holds a "Greek Festival" at different times of each year.

On the whole, the 2d, 3d, and even 4th Greek-American generations seem to be following the pattern of the *Protporoi* (pioneers) in their continuing involvement in small and middle business enterprises. While many have remained in the retail business in which their forebears made their mark, increasingly younger Greeks have shown an interest in such fields as real estate, insurance, small manufacturing, and stockbroking. There are also more who are beginning to emerge in the legal, academic, medical, and service professions. Economically conservative, Cleveland Greeks, with few exceptions, did not generally involve themselves politically until after World War II. While most voted as Democrats prior to the war, afterward the Republican party seemed more attractive to many.

Themistocles Rodis
Baldwin-Wallace College

**GREEN, HOWARD WHIPPLE** (25 Apr. 1893–8 July 1959), a statistician, studied and reported population trends in Greater Cleveland for 30 years. Born in Woonsocket, R.I., he received his B.A. degree from Clark University and attended Harvard University before receiving his B.S. degree from MIT. Green worked briefly for the H. Koppers Co. in Lorain before going to work as a bacteriologist for the War Dept. in the Panama Canal Zone. He worked with the Rockefeller Fund on malaria control in Arkansas, Louisiana, and Puerto Rico before coming to Cleveland in 1923 as director of the Bureau of Statistics & Research of the Cuyahoga County Public Health Assoc., forerunner of the Cleveland Health Council. Beginning in 1925, he served as secretary of that council for 34 years. Among his early projects was a 2-year survey of atmospheric pollution in Cleveland.

Green supervised the 1930 federal census in Cleveland. The following year he prepared, for the Plain Dealer Publishing Co., *Population Characteristics by Census Tracts, Cleveland, Ohio*. This volume broke down census figures into smaller units, revealing trends that could not otherwise be discerned and allowing more efficient approaches to community health and welfare problems. In 1932 Green organized the nonprofit REAL PROPERTY INVENTORY OF METROPOLITAN CLEVELAND (RPI) and served as its director until his death in 1959. RPI furnished data on family units, housing, utilities, retail stores, and industry and became the model for similar organizations throughout the country. Green's work on the inventory led *Properties* magazine to say, "Cleveland, Ohio, knows more about itself than any other city in the United States." Beginning in 1933, Green circulated "A Sheet-a-Week" among several hundred Cleveland subscribers; the fact sheet was founded

on his belief that business could profit from the information contained in government reports if it was abbreviated and simplified. In later years Green was senior partner of Howard Whipple Green, Ober & Associates, a consulting firm. He was a long-time resident of CLEVELAND HTS. "Howard Whipple Green was Cleveland's personal Univac, and then some," the *Cleveland Press* editorialized upon his death.

**GREEN, JOHN PATTERSON** (2 Apr. 1845–1 Sept. 1940), the "Father of Labor Day," was a lawyer who became an important black Republican politician and civil servant. He was the first black elected to political office in Cleveland and later became the only northern black elected to a state senate in the 19th century. Green was born in Newberne, N.C., the son of John R. and Temperance Green, free blacks of mixed ancestry. His father died when John was young, and in June 1857 Temperance Green moved her family to Cleveland. John attended Mayflower School, but he left in 1859 because of family financial difficulties and took odd jobs to bring in money. Studying on the side, he published *Essays on Miscellaneous Subjects by a Self-Educated Colored Youth* in 1866. After a lecture tour to promote the book, he attended Cleveland's CENTRAL HIGH SCHOOL (1866–69); in 1870 he graduated from Union Law School and moved to South Carolina, where he was admitted to the bar in Sept. 1870. He began his political career in South Carolina in 1872 as a delegate to the state and national Republican conventions. Green returned to Cleveland in late 1872 and received the Republican nomination for justice of the peace. His victory in the election made him the first black elected to office in Cleveland; he held the post for 9 years (1873–82). In 1877 he lost a controversial election for the Ohio House of Representatives, but he won a seat in that body in 1881. He was defeated for renomination but was again elected to the Ohio legislature in 1890. There he introduced the bill that established Labor Day as a state holiday; the U.S. Congress made it a national holiday in 1894.

In 1892 Green was elected to the Ohio senate, representing a district that was largely white. He was that body's first black member and served 1 term there. During the 1890s he became closely acquainted with leading Ohio Republicans MARCUS A. HANNA and GEO. A. MYERS, and his campaigning for the national Republican ticket earned him appointment in 1897 to the newly created position of U.S. postage stamp agent (1897–1905). He served briefly as the acting superintendent of finance in the Post Office Dept. before leaving government service in 1906 and resuming his law practice in Cleveland. His participation in national politics after 1906 was limited to occasional speeches. A writer as well as a politician, Green published several books and articles. In addition to the 1866 essays, he published *Recollections of the Carolinas* (1881) and his autobiography, *Fact Stranger Than Fiction* (1920). During the 1890s he wrote articles for the Afro-American News Syndicate. He continued to practice law until his death at age 95. Green took what one historian has called an "amicable position" on racial matters; he was friends with influential people in both Washington and Cleveland. He was the first black member of the Logos Club, an exclusive discussion group; he was also a member of the Social Circle and a founding member of St. Andrew's Episcopal Church. Green was married twice, first on 23 Dec. 1869 to Annie Walker, who died on 15 Jan. 1912. On 6 Sept. 1912, he married a widow, Mrs. Lottie Mitchell Richardson.

Green, John P., *Fact Stranger Than Fiction* (1920).
John P. Green Papers, WRHS.

**GREEN, SAMUEL CLAYTON** (1872–25 Apr. 1915), was an early-20th-century black businessman who established a number of business ventures between 1902 and the onset of illness in 1913. Little biographical information is available about Green other than his business ventures, but one historian has called him "the most successful legitimate businessman" among a new generation of elite black entrepreneurs in Cleveland at the turn of the century. City directories suggest that he began his business career with the apparently short-lived S. C. Green Hardwood Lumber Co. at 405 Prospect in 1901; his career began to prosper the next year, when he patented a sofa bed and, with 16 stockholders, organized the New Leonard Sofa Bed Co. to manufacture and sell his product. The New Leonard Co., sometimes referred to as the Leonard Sofa Bed Co., appears to have grown out of Lyman B. Leonard's sofa bed company; the exact relationship is unclear. The venture was owned by blacks and employed only blacks. From that initial success, Green moved into real estate and construction in 1903, incorporating the Mohawk Realty Co. along with Welcome T. Blue. Mohawk built homes on Cedar and Blaine avenues and erected the Clayton Bldg., with stores, offices, apartments, and meeting rooms, at 2828 Central. He also invested in a laundry (the Eureka Co.) and a restaurant at 2840 Central, and in 1906 he established the Clayton Grocery Store (2826 Central) and People's Drug Store (3315 Central). In 1907 he purchased a church building at E. 37th and Cedar and remodeled it into a skating rink and dance hall, and in 1911 he purchased a motion-picture and vaudeville theater at 3136 Central, forming the S. C. Green Amusement Co. to operate it as the Alpha Theater. He added the Dunbar Theater in Columbus to his holdings in 1913. Green's various business ventures were designed initially to turn segregation and discrimination to his advantage, but the drug and grocery stores lasted less than 5 years because of insufficient support from the black customers Green intended to serve. Insufficient black patronage for another of his all-black ventures, the Central roller rink, led him to institute "white only" nights twice a week to lure the dollars of whites into his coffers. One result was a 1909 lawsuit by Walter L. Brown charging discrimination after he had been refused entry on a "white night"; Brown won the suit.

**GREEN ROAD SYNAGOGUE,** one of Cleveland's largest Orthodox congregations, traces its origins to a handful of immigrants from Marmaresher Sziget, Hungary, who established the Marmaresher B'nai Jacob Society in the Woodland neighborhood in 1910. The members of this self-help society rented a room at E. 26th St. and Woodland Ave. in that same year and held religious services. In 1911, they purchased a building at E. 25th St. near Woodland. The congregation moved to a rented building at E. 30th St. and Scovill in 1920. In May 1922, the congregation incorporated as the First Marmaresher B'nai Jacob Congregation. Although it was not a large congregation, it purchased a brick building in GLENVILLE in 1922 from the Cleveland Jewish Ctr. in order to serve those members who had moved out of the Woodland neighborhood. The following year, the congregation hired its first rabbi, Meyer Leifer, a graduate of the Huszt Seminary in Hungary.

The Woodland branch of the congregation moved to E. 61st St. and Woodland Ave. in 1922 and remained there until 1932, when the property was sold and the membership joined the Glenville branch. Reflecting the broadening of activities sponsored by synagogues during this era, the congregation changed its name to Anshe Marmaresher Congregation in 1937 and was popularly known as the Marmaresher Jewish Ctr. Following the move of Jews out of Glenville after WORLD WAR II, Anshe Marmaresher relocated in the Heights. As the Orthodox community settled between Taylor Rd. and Green Rd. in the 1960s, another move became imminent. With a loan from the HEIGHTS JEWISH CTR., Anshe Marmaresher purchased property on Green Rd. and in 1972 dedicated a new synagogue. Recognizing that it was no longer a landsman congregation and following the lead of other congregations that adopted names based on their street location, the congregation became known as the Green Rd. Synagogue.

Green Road Synagogue Records, WRHS.

**GREENE, DANIEL J. "DANNY"** (Nov. 1929–6 Oct. 1977), was known as the Cleveland king of racketeering. He was heavily involved in loan sharking and gambling. He also had a legitimate business in land speculation. Greene, the son of a newspaper printer, grew up in Collinwood. He dropped out of high school and quickly earned a reputation as an alley fighter. In 1957 he became a stevedore on Cleveland's waterfront. Shortly thereafter he was elected president of Local 1317 of the longshoremen's union. In 1964, Greene was indicted for taking kickbacks in return for casual labor assignments. He was convicted of embezzling $11,000. However, the conviction was reversed on an appeal because of prejudicial cross-examination by the government. In 1970 Greene pleaded guilty to violating union laws and was fined $10,000; as a result, he lost his union position. He then turned his attention to organizing trash haulers.

Tales of a feud between Greene and Michael Frato, a hauler who had pulled out of Greene's guild, began to circulate. Arthur Sneperger, a Greene associate, was killed when a bomb he was carrying toward Frato's car exploded. Police suspected that Greene detonated the bomb because he believed someone was leaking information to Frato. On 26 Nov. 1971, while Greene was jogging near White City Beach, a car pulled alongside, and from within, Frato aimed a gun at Greene. Greene pulled out his own gun and fired, killing Frato. He was acquitted on the grounds of self-defense. Greene also took control of running rackets and numbers in the absence of racketsman ALEX (SHONDOR) BIRNS, who was in jail for bribing a Parma policeman. After Birns's release, Greene continued in the rackets game. Greene escaped unharmed in June 1975 when a bomb destroyed his home and office on Waterloo Rd. He had survived a previous bombing and 2 shooting attempts before he was killed on 6 Oct. 1977. As Greene returned to his car from a visit to his dentist, the car next to his exploded, killing Greene. His death may have been the result of a vendetta or clash with other organized-crime groups.

**GREVE, BELL** (4 Jan. 1894–9 Jan. 1957), a pioneer in the development and provision of relief and rehabilitation services to the poor, sick, and disabled, gained an international reputation for her work with local, state, and international social-service agencies. Greve was a native Clevelander, daughter of railroad worker Louis Greve. She graduated from Glenville High School and entered Hiram College with plans to become a missionary, but after working at HIRAM HOUSE in Cleveland one summer, she became interested in social work. She transferred to Flora Stone Mather College at Western Reserve University, where she received her degree. She later earned a law degree from Cleveland Law School.

Greve began her social work career in 1918, as a charity visitor in Cleveland's red-light district for the city's Charities Bureau. In 1921 she began her career in international relief and rehabilitation, spending 3 years in Europe as the head of a Red Cross child-health center in Hodonin, Czechoslovakia, and as the director of an orphanage of 3,000 children in Alexandropol, Armenia. Upon returning to the U.S., Greve joined the administration of Ohio governor Vic Donahey as superintendent of the division of charities in the Dept. of Public Welfare. After 5 years in this position, she became director of the Community Chest in Charleston, W.Va., a position she held for 5 years. In Apr. 1933, Greve became director of the Assoc. for the Crippled & Disabled, which became the Cleveland Rehabilitation Ctr. in 1943. She directed this agency until 1953. Under her leadership, it gained a reputation as one of the nation's foremost rehabilitation institutions. Greve initiated the agency's Curative Playroom for disabled preschool children in 1934, and in 1935 she opened a work treatment shop to provide light work for disabled adults and to help them gain employment in private industry. Construction of a new building for the agency in 1938 made it one of the few in the country to offer a variety of specialized rehabilitation services under one roof.

From 1937–44, Greve also served as the director of the Cuyahoga County Relief Bureau. In this capacity she supervised the transformation of the infirmary from city to county control. She also established the first county nursing home to care for the aged and ill. In 1953 Mayor Anthony J. Celebrezze appointed Greve as director of the city's Dept. of Health & Welfare, a position she held until her death. The first woman cabinet member in the city in 20 years, Greve won approval for a $2.4 million bond issue to improve the city's correctional facilities: CLEVELAND BOYS' SCHOOL, the BLOSSOM HILL SCHOOL FOR GIRLS, and the workhouse. In addition to her local social work and government service, Greve remained active in international relief and rehabilitation agencies. She helped organize the 1936 World Congress for Workers for the Crippled in Budapest, and in 1941 she was elected secretary-general of the Internatl. Society for the Welfare of Cripples, a position she held for 10 years. During the 1940s she helped Mexico and the West Indies develop rehabilitation programs for their disabled residents, and she made several trips to Greece to help implement rehabilitation services for victims of the war. Bell Greve (sometimes given as Belle) was a member of the Collinwood Christian Church for more than 50 years. She never married.

**GRIES, MOSES J.** (25 Jan. 1868–30 Oct. 1918), a proponent of Classical Reform Judaism, served as spiritual leader of the TEMPLE for 25 years (1892–1917). Gries, whose family was of Austro-Hungarian background, was born in Newark, N.J. He attended the University of Cincinnati and Hebrew Union College, graduating and receiving ordination in 1889. Gries's first rabbinical position was in Chattanooga, Tenn., where he served until 1892, when he accepted the pulpit at the Temple. He succeeded Rabbi Aaron Hahn and was the first native-born HUC-educated rabbi to serve in Cleveland. During his first 8 years at the Temple, Gries effected radical changes in the congregation. All vestiges of German were discarded, the *Union Prayer Book* was adopted, Sabbath morning services were moved from Saturday to Sunday, English was substituted for Hebrew in Torah readings and most prayers, and Hebrew was removed from the the religious school curriculum. Gries's religious philosophy was that Reform Judaism should be Americanized. In keeping with most Protestant denominations at the turn of the century, Gries created an array of congregational groups and services, including the Temple Women's Assoc., the Temple Library, the Temple Alumni Assoc., the Educational League, the Temple Orchestra, and the Temple Society.

Gries was a political and social progressive, imbued with the philosophy of the social gospel. He had close ties to the liberal Protestant clergy of the city and was active in ecumenical affairs. He believed it was incumbent upon the wealthy to use their money for the common good in charitable and benevolent activities, as well as for civic improvement. In 1897, he advocated the building of a city hall, city library, art museum, and public auditorium. He was one of the small group that founded the CITIZENS LEAGUE OF CLEVELAND. Gries took an active part in the communal affairs of Cleveland Jewry. He was instrumental in founding the Council Educational Alliance, a settlement house established by NATL. COUNCIL OF JEWISH WOMEN, CLEVELAND SEC., in 1899. In 1897, Gries called for a general federation of charities to consolidate and coordinate charitable efforts in the community. When the Fed. for Jewish Charities was established in 1903, he became one of its most active members.

Gries led local protests against pogroms in Eastern Europe and urged social welfare work among the newly arrived Jewish immigrants. At the same time, he remained far removed from the largely Orthodox, Yiddish-speaking immigrants. In 1907 he denounced Zionism, which was gaining considerable strength in Cleveland among the East European immigrants. He believed political Zionism raised unwanted questions concerning Jewish identity and loyalty. He argued that Zionism raised the issue of dual loyalty, which threatened the security of the Jewish community in America. For health reasons, Gries resigned from the Temple in 1917. He died a year later. He was survived by his wife, Frances (Fannie) Hays Gries, the daughter of businessman KAUFMAN HAYS. Through his marriage to Frances Hays in 1898, he also became the brother-in-law of MARTIN MARKS, who served 23 years as president of the Temple, all but 3 of those years during Gries's tenure.

Rabbi Moses Gries Family Papers, WRHS.
Rabbi Moses J. Gries Papers, American Jewish Archives, Cincinnati, Ohio.

**GRIES CHARITABLE FUND.** See **LUCILE & ROBERT GRIES CHARITABLE FUND**

**GRILL, VATRO J.** (1899–21 Mar. 1976), was the head of a Slovenian publishing company and an important leader in the Slovenian community of Cleveland. Active in politics, he became assistant police prosecutor, assistant prosecutor in the city Dept. of Law, and assistant attorney general in Columbus. Born in Slovenia, Grill attended the first 3 grades of the gymnasium at Ljubljana before coming to the U.S. with his parents in 1914. He finished his high school courses at Cleveland Preparatory School in 1915. In 1919, at age 20, Grill was named editor of the Slovenian daily newspaper *ENAKOPRAVNOST* (Equality); he soon began to study law at Cleveland Law School, and in 1925 he passed the bar examination.

By 1929, Vatro Grill was considered "one of the most versatile Slovenian leaders in the country." In addition to being an editor and a practicing attorney, he was a teacher in the Slovenian school, director of dramatics of the Ivan Cankar Slovenian Dramatic Society, a singer in the ZARJA SINGING SOCIETY, and a member of the board of directors of the SLOVENIAN NATL. HOME, and in 1928 he had been elected national president of the Chicago-based Slovenian Progressive Society. He later edited the society's official organ, *Napredek* (Progress). Grill was quite active politically, serving frequently as a speaker at meetings and mounting an unsuccessful campaign in 1940 for the state legislature. In Feb. 1942 he was named assistant police prosecutor by Law Director Thos. A. Burke, Jr.; he resigned as editor of *Enakopravnost* but maintained his post as president of the American Jugoslav Publishing Co., a post he held until 1959. By 1954 Grill had become assistant prosecutor in the city's law department, but by 1956 he had returned to publishing and editing, serving as the editor of the *New Era Semi Monthly* in 1958 and 1959. Grill also served as a referee for the Industrial Compensation Board and as assistant attorney general in Columbus before his retirement. He moved to Yugoslavia in ca. 1971 and lived there for 4 years before returning to the U.S. to live in Santa Clara, Calif., where he died. His wife, Anna, survived him.

Klancar, Anthony J., comp., *Who's Who among the Yugoslavs* (1940).

**GRISWOLD, INC.,** with its headquarters in the Illuminating Bldg. on PUBLIC SQUARE and known for 70 years as the Griswold-Eshleman Co. before changing its name in 1983, is one of Cleveland's most prominent advertising agencies. Chas. Eshleman and Ray H. Griswold founded the agency in 1912 with $200 in capital. Known initially as the Advertising Dept. Co., the firm had no home office but maintained desks in the offices of its clients. By 1913, the agency was known as Griswold-Eshleman. By 1927, the company had 15 employees; that year Chas. J. Farran joined the firm as a copywriter and began steadily to advance, ascending to the presidency in 1957 and to chairman of the board in 1969. During his tenure as president (1957-69), Farran transformed the company into an international agency, adding offices in Amsterdam, Brussels, Paris, Milan, and Dusseldorf, as well as in New York City, Chicago, and Pittsburgh. He built the company's business from about $9 million in billings in 1957 to more than $42 million in 1972. In the 1950s and 1960s, Griswold added to its list of clients such companies as GENERAL ELECTRIC, SHERWIN-WILLIAMS, and Penton Publishing. By 1970, Griswold was the largest advertising agency in Ohio and the 38th-largest in the U.S. By 1985, Griswold, Inc., had sold or closed many of its offices in other cities. It employed 100 people in offices in Cleveland and Columbus and had billings of $38 million that year. In Sept. 1985, Griswold announced that it had agreed to merge with and become a wholly owned subsidiary of the Detroit-based advertising agency Roy Ross, Inc.

**GROSSMAN, F. KARL** (1886-16 May 1969), was a prominent figure in Cleveland's musical life, distinguishing himself as a conductor and teacher. He was perhaps best known as the long-time director of the CLEVELAND PHILHARMONIC ORCHESTRA. Born in Cleveland, Grossman began formal training on the violin at age 11. He later studied piano theory and composition in this country, and then in Paris and Berlin. During his life, Grossman was involved in almost every aspect of the city's musical life. His compositions were performed by some of the various ensembles in the city, including, when he was a young man, the FORTNIGHTLY MUSICAL CLUB. In 1914 he began a long association with music programs in area churches, that year establishing a professional quartet at the Lakewood Christian Church. He later served as conductor for the Lakewood Methodist Church Choir. In 1920 he became conductor and musical director of the Cleveland Opera Co., and in 1924 he became the 5th conductor of the Hermit Club Orchestra. Grossman later conducted the Madame Butterfly Co., and orchestras at the CLEVELAND MUSIC SCHOOL SETTLEMENT and Western Reserve University. He also, as a violinist, was a concertmaster for the Cleveland Municipal Symphony. As an educator, Grossman

in 1929 joined the faculty of Cleveland College (on PUBLIC SQUARE) as an instructor in chamber music and music history. He was later made head of the music department. His academic career continued at WRU, where he served on the faculty from 1942-57, for many years as head of the music department. He received an honorary degree in music from BALDWIN-WALLACE COLLEGE. In 1938, the Cleveland Philharmonic Orchestra was founded to provide opportunity for instrumental students in Cleveland to acquire professional experience. Grossman directed its debut concert and remained as its conductor until the 1960s. Grossman is also the author of the book *A History of Music in Cleveland* (1972).

**GROSSMAN, MARY B.** (10 June 1879-Jan. 1977), one of the early women lawyers in Cleveland, was active in the fight for women's suffrage and in the early 1920s became the first woman municipal judge in the U.S. Grossman was born in Cleveland, the daughter of Hungarian Jews Louis and Fannie Engle Grossman. She attended public schools and studied at the Euclid Ave. Business College. From 1896-1912 she worked as a stenographer and a bookkeeper in the law office of her cousin, Louis J. Grossman; she became interested in law and enrolled in the law school at BALDWIN-WALLACE COLLEGE, receiving her law degree and passing the Ohio bar examination in 1912. She was only the third woman lawyer in Cleveland and in 1918 was one of the first 2 women admitted to membership in the American Bar Assoc. Grossman maintained a private practice in Cleveland from 1912-23. During that time she was active in the struggle for women's suffrage and served as chairwoman of the League of Woman's Suffrage. Once women won the right to vote, Grossman decided to run for municipal judge; she lost her bid for the bench in 1921, but in 1923 her campaign proved successful, and she became the first woman municipal judge in the U.S. She continued to win election to the Municipal Court of Cleveland until she retired at age 80 at the end of 1959; she also served on the traffic court (1925-59) and organized the morals court in 1926, serving there until her retirement. As a judge, Grossman earned a reputation as, according to her obituary, "a severe, rigidly honest jurist, sometimes irreverently referred to as Hardboiled Mary." When she took a day off to observe a Jewish holiday in 1927, 39 bail jumpers wanted on outstanding warrants reportedly took advantage of her absence and turned themselves in so they would not have to face her brand of justice. Grossman was also quite active in community affairs and professional organizations. She was a charter member of the WOMEN'S CITY CLUB and the LEAGUE OF WOMEN VOTERS. She was a trustee and a member of the board of the Diabetes League of Greater Cleveland, and served as chairman of the board of ALTA HOUSE. She never married.

Mary Grossman Papers, WRHS.

**GROUP PLAN.** *See* **MALL**

The **GUARDIAN ANGELS** were an organization of volunteers who patrolled areas of the city in an attempt to deter CRIME. They were the focus of much interest and debate when they were formed. The Guardian Angels were established by Curtis Sliwa in New York City in 1979 as a citizens' group organized in response to the high levels of crime in the New York subway system. Wearing distinctive clothing, including red berets, they patrolled streets and subway platforms in an attempt to deter street crimes. The Angels were unarmed but did have training in self-defense. They patrolled in groups of 8 to compensate for their lack of weapons. Although open to anyone, the Guardian Angels were composed almost exclusively of young men from the inner city. Although not sanctioned by the New York City authorities, the Guardian Angels were popular with the general public and received much attention in the media. As a result, local chapters were formed in several large cities. In 1981, U.S. Congressman Ronald M. Mottl, representing Cleveland's suburban 23d district, invited Sliwa to open a chapter in Cleveland. Despite the reluctance of city officials to endorse his organization, Sliwa agreed. The formation of the Cleveland chapter was announced in June 1981. Eric Brewer was its first director. By Mar. 1982 there were 55 members of the Guardian Angels in Cleveland. All had undergone 10 weeks of training. The Angels patrolled the area around PUBLIC SQUARE. In their first 9 months they made 2 citizen's arrests and assisted in the apprehension of 13 other persons. They were generally well received by the public. In Feb. 1983, the Guardian Angels were given permission to patrol RTA buses and trains.

The **GUARDIAN SAVINGS AND TRUST COMPANY** was one of Cleveland's principal banks in the early 20th century. It began in 1894 after several prominent Clevelanders, including MARCUS A. HANNA and Gen. JAS. BARNETT, helped to modify state laws to make it easier to organize a trust company in Cleveland. Guardian Trust was incorporated on 28 June 1894 with capital of $500,000, which was doubled by the end of the year. The bank was opened on 10 Dec. 1894 in the Wade Bldg. on lower Superior Ave. with 4 employees. In 1898, Henry P. McIntosh became president. In 1902, an "uptown" office was opened in the Arcade. Four years later, with assets of $14 million, Guardian needed larger quarters and erected a 12-story building at 322 Euclid Ave. Its original office in the Wade Bldg. was consolidated with its newer quarters in 1912. In 1914, the company purchased the largest office building in Cleveland, the New England Bldg. (erected 1895) at 619 Euclid Ave. After Guardian remodeled and expanded it and renamed it the Guardian Bldg., it was considered one of the nation's finest bank buildings.

Under J. Arthur House, Guardian continued to expand. From 1919–21, the firm purchased several smaller, local banks. Its major acquisition was one of Cleveland's earliest banks, the Natl. Commercial Bank, which dated back to 1845 (sometimes given as 1846), when it was established in the Atwater Block on Superior Ave. as the Commercial Branch Bank—one of the 2 state branch banks in Cleveland. It was reorganized as the Commercial Natl. Bank in 1865 and as the Natl. Bank in 1905. In the 1920s, Guardian also began to establish neighborhood branch offices, which totaled 19 by 1931. By the late 1920s, Guardian was a web of 26 companies, including a large number of investment and real-estate firms. The bank had 725 employees, with over $140 million in deposits and $16 million in capital. However, during this period of growth, several of the bank's top offices made unwise and often illegal business policies, especially in regard to its investment and real-estate dealings. Guardian was near insolvency in 1932 but "window-dressed" its banking statements. After the bank holidays of Mar. 1933, Guardian was ordered into liquidation. A state banking committee investigated the bank and uncovered many of the illegal dealings, which resulted in the conviction and imprisonment of Pres. House and another officer for the mismanagement of the institution. It took years to unravel the legal entanglements and complete the liquidation. A $1 million lawsuit against the bank directors was settled in 1947. After the final dividend was paid to depositors and creditors in 1950, the bank's affairs were closed on 19 Feb. 1952, and its records were destroyed in 1958.

The **GUENTHER ART GALLERIES COMPANY** was established in 1868 by Felix Guenther in the Old Forest City House Hotel on PUBLIC SQUARE. Over the years, the Guenther Galleries made a series of moves up Euclid Ave. to the Stone Bldg., the King Bldg., the Siegel Store Bldg., the site of the Cowell & Hubbard Block, the site of the Keith Bldg., and eventually 1725-27 Euclid Ave. In 1934 the galleries made their final move, to the 2d floor of the Kinney & Levan Bldg. in PLAYHOUSE SQUARE. The Guenther Galleries supplied objets d'art to many of the wealthy families of Cleveland at the turn of the century and boasted works by such names as Greuze, Parmiginano, Corot, and Daubignay. In 1931, the Guenther Galleries merged with the Leamon Galleries to become Guenther Art Galleries. In 1933 it was the largest exclusive picture store between New York City and Chicago and remained one of the outstanding art galleries of the Midwest until May 1963, when the MAY CO. bought its entire stock and sold it at an exhibition and sale on 22 May 1963.

**GUILFORD, LINDA (LUCINDA) THAYER** (22 Nov. 1823-1 Mar. 1911), was a pioneer educator, author, and administrator of some of Cleveland's earliest PRIVATE SCHOOLS. She was born in Lanesboro, Mass. Her mother died when Linda was still a young girl; her father, a shoemaker, was often ill. The eldest of 5 children, Linda, at 16 years of age, worked in a paper mill at Dalton, Mass. In 1845, several friends made it possible for her to attend Mt. Holyoke Seminary, South Hadley, Mass., from which she graduated in 1847. On 14 Oct. 1848, Guilford arrived in Cleveland, and on 16 Oct., she assumed her duties as principal of the Young Ladies Seminary, a new private school located on the corner of Ontario and Prospect St. The enterprise, promoted by Rev. Darius Morris, opened with an enrollment of 12 pupils, grew to 20 students, and closed at the end of the academic year because of lack of funds. In 1851, Guilford became principal of the first Female Academy in a building at Huron and Prospect streets (the Osborn Bldg. site). It was often referred to as "the Point," and over 200 girls received academic instruction—including Latin, the classics, and Bible study—during its 3 years of existence (1851–54).

In May 1854, Guilford became vice-principal of a second school, the CLEVELAND FEMALE SEMINARY, a boarding and day school directed by Dr. SAMUEL ST. JOHN (LL.D.). It was the largest private school in Cleveland at that time, with an enrollment of 120 pupils; it was located on Kinsman Rd. between Sawtell and Wallingford Ct. and was often referred to as "Miss Guilford's School." She closed her association with it in 1860. In Nov. 1861, after a trip abroad, she opened her own private day school for boys and girls—once again at "the Point" (1861–66). In the spring of 1865, several families who wished to send their children to a private school organized and incorporated the second Cleveland Academy (23 June 1865). Under the leadership of STILLMAN WITT, president; JOSEPH PERKINS, secretary; Amasa Stone, Jr.; TRUMAN P. HANDY; and many others, they bought land on the south side of Huron St. and erected a 2-story brick building. The school, also known as "the Brick Academy," opened 29 Jan. 1866 with 90 students. Guilford, the principal, remained for 14 years until it closed on 17 June 1881 because of declining enrollment.

Following her teaching years, Guilford was active in the Young Women's Temperance League; she became president of the WCTU and often wrote and lectured on its behalf. She volunteered at the FRIENDLY INN SOCIAL SETTLEMENT, was active in Mt. Holyoke alumnae activities, and was named to the Advisory Committee of the College for Women of Western Reserve University. In 1885 she published *The Use of Life*. In 1892, Guilford published *The Story of a Cleveland School from 1848–1881*, a memoir about her teaching experiences and a tribute to her former students. One of these, FLORA STONE MATHER, presented a new dormitory for girls to the College for Women (24 Oct. 1892) and named it Guilford Cottage in honor of her former teacher. It was to be the scene of many reunions for Guilford, as her former students often returned to visit her. She was elected to the Ohio Women's Press Club (1888), and in 1896, at Cleveland's centennial celebration, she read a paper entitled "Some Early Teachers in Cleveland." Guilford died in Cleveland. Her funeral service, conducted by Dr. Paul Sutphen, pastor of Second Presbyterian Church, where she had been a member since 1852, was attended by many of her former students, from many of Cleveland's "first families." She was buried in WOODLAND CEMETERY.

**GUND, GEORGE** (13 Apr. 1888–15 Nov. 1966), was the long-time head of the Cleveland Trust Bank (AMERITRUST) and a local philanthropist. Born in La Crosse, Wis., Gund was the son of a Cleveland brewery owner and real-estate man. He was educated at UNIVERSITY SCHOOL before completing an A.B. at Harvard, where he was the editor of the *Daily Crimson*. A student in the first graduating class of the Harvard Business School, he learned about investment interest from J. P. Morgan and was further grounded in banking, insurance, and commerce. Gund started his banking career at Seattle Natl. Bank, where he developed a life-long love of the West. Away from the bank, he panned gold in Alaska, captained a regional polo championship team, skipped kayaks on the Bering Sea, and ranched and cowpoked in Nevada. When his father died, he returned to Cleveland to manage the family business, but his interests were diverted to a venture of his own. He acquired the Kaffee Hag Corp., which made decaffeinated coffee. After refining the process of extracting caffeine (which he sold to Coca-Cola), he sold the company to Kellogg for $10 million in cash and stock. He then turned his attention to real estate and banking.

During the Depression, Gund solidified his growing personal fortune by buying good-quality stocks at bargain prices. One of his favorite investments was in insurance companies; throughout his life, he sat on the boards of several companies. By 1937, he was hired by Cleveland Trust, first as a director, and then, in 1941, as president. When he took office, the bank was 17th in the country, with $800 million in deposits. As banking throughout the country became more sophisticated, Gund expanded the bank's financial power base in Cuyahoga County through loans and investments and by increasing the number of branches. To strengthen the bank's ties to the business community, he served on more than 30 corporate boards and encouraged the appointment of directors with similar ties. In addition to his role at the bank as president until 1962 and chairman of the board from 1962–66, Gund served as an officer, trustee, or director of 14 civic, philanthropic, and educational institutions. Among his favorite charities were the CLEVELAND MUSEUM OF ART, the CLEVELAND FOUNDATION, the SALVATION ARMY, TRINITY CATHEDRAL, and Harvard University. In honor of his leadership in the financial community and his generosity to the school, 2 professorships (in commercial banking and in economics and business administration) were established in his honor in 1964 and 1966. Gund merged his love of art and the West in his large collection of western art, notably the work of Frederic Remington. Many pieces, especially the bronzes, were displayed in the windows of the Cleveland Trust rotunda and later became part of a traveling exhibit. Aside from his art expenditures and his collection of toy banks, Gund was noted for his frugal lifestyle; he drove a mid-priced car and wore a patched overcoat long past its prime. A bachelor until age 48, Gund married Jessica Roesler, granddaughter of Henry B. Laidlaw, founder of the Laidlaw banking house of New York, in 1936. Within a decade, she bore him 6 children: George III, Agnes, Gordon, Graham, Geoffrey, and Louise. Mrs. Gund, very prominent in civic affairs, died in 1954 at age 50. Gund died of acute leukemia. Having provided for his children before his death, he left most of his $600 million estate to his GEO. GUND FOUNDATION.

The **GUND BREWING COMPANY** was a small independent brewery located at 1476 Davenport St. on the city's near east side. It was known as the Jacob Mall Brewing Co. and had an annual capacity of 8,000 barrels when Geo. F. Gund (1855–1916) purchased it in 1897. Gund was born and educated in La Crosse, Wis. From 1895–97 he served as president of the Seattle Brewing & Malting Co. in Seattle, Wash.; he then moved to Cleveland, and on 1 Apr. 1897, he purchased Jacob Mall Brewing. Gund served as president and treasurer, Gustav A. Kaercher as vice-president, and Jacob Fickel as treasurer. On 1 Jan. 1900, the firm name was changed to the Gund Brewing Co. That year the company produced 12,000 barrels, still a small output compared to those of other Cleveland breweries of the period. Geo. Gund was active in the industry, serving as a trustee of the U.S. Brewers' Assoc. and as secretary of the Cleveland Brewers' Board of Trade. In 1899 he testified before State Attorney General Frank S. Monnett against the combination created by the CLEVELAND-SANDUSKY BREWING CO., which Monnett had previously declared to be an illegal trust. Citing "fierce" competition between the combination and independent brewers, Gund testified that the combination loaned money without interest to saloon keepers who would take its product, and leased buildings and then turned out the customers of independent breweries in order to establish saloons that would sell its product. Prior to Prohibition, Gund Brewing brewed 2 beers, Gund's "Finest" and Gund's "Clevelander," which it promoted with the slogan "A Wonderful City—A Wonderful Beer." During Prohibition, the Gund interests turned toward previously established real-estate and coffee businesses. The Gund Realty Co. (inc. 1922) and the Kaffee Hag Corp. (inc. 1914) were headed respectively by Anna M. Gund, Gund's widow, and his son GEO. GUND; both were based at the brewery address. After Prohibition, the brewery was operated for a short time by the Sunrise Brewing Company (1933–39), then by the Tip Top Brewing Co. It closed in 1944.

**GUND FOUNDATION.** *See* **GEORGE GUND FOUNDATION**

# H

The **HBSU,** the oldest Jewish benevolent society in Cleveland, was organized on 16 Apr. 1881 as the Hungarian Benevolent & Social Union and received its state charter 2 years later. It was established to aid its members in case of illness or death, to assist nonmembers in "unfortunate circumstances," and to cultivate friendly and social relations among its members. The HBSU was formed by 24 Hungarian Jews, who gathered for their first meeting in the shoe store of Ben Schlesinger, the society's first president. Membership was over 100 by 1885, increasing to 763 in 1916. During the early 1980s, membership was approximately 500. In 1919, the Hungarian Benevolent & Social Union officially changed its name to the HBSU, indicating that membership was no longer based on Jewish national origin. In the late 1960s, the organization adopted the name Heights Benevolent & Social Union for publicity uses. The HBSU never had its own meeting hall. Over the years it has held meetings in many locations, including the Gesangverein Hall, Knights of Pythias Temple Hall, B'nai B'rith Bldg., Gates of Hope Synagogue, WARRENSVILLE CTR. SYNAGOGUE, and B'NAI JESHURUN synagogue, among others.

The HBSU has provided typical benevolent and aid society forms of assistance, including partial payment of hospital bills, death benefits for members and their families, and visits to sick members. It has also expended a large portion of its annual expense budget as charitable donations, both locally and in the national and international arena. Recipients have included persecuted Romanian Jews, World War I sufferers, and the Red Cross Society for Italian sufferers. Additionally, the HBSU has donated money to or subscribed to membership in Cleveland Jewish organizations, such as the HEBREW FREE LOAN ASSOC., The Fed. of Jewish Charities, the Infant Orphans Mothers Society, and the Jewish Orthodox Home for the Aged. The primary funtion of the HBSU in recent years has been as a social outlet for its members. The organization sponsors picnics, dinners, balls, lectures, and other special programs. Its *Bulletin* was first published in 1908 and has been in continuous publication since. In 1953, a women's auxiliary was created. During the early 1980s, the HBSU officially incorporated as a fraternal organization. Two lodges were established, one in Florida, composed of Clevelanders who moved to the South, and one in Cleveland. The Cleveland lodge also serves as the Grand Lodge of the HBSU.

HBSU Records, WRHS.

The **HCS FOUNDATION** was established in 1959 by Harold C. Schott (1907–1977). Schott, with his brother Walter, came to Cleveland from Cincinnati in 1940 as Willys-Overland auto distributors for the Midwest. They bought the Columbia Axle Co. and continued acquiring businesses until, at the height of their careers, they owned some 31 companies. The partnership dissolved in 1952 when Harold and another brother, Joseph, bought BEARINGS, INC. Gifts from the foundation are limited to Ohio and go primarily to the Roman Catholic church. Grants also support higher and secondary education and hospitals. In 1984, assets of the foundation were $4,613,643, with expenditures of $172,895 for 7 grants. Trustees included Francie S. Hiltz, L. Thos. Hiltz, B. J. Mulcahy, Wm. Dunne Saal, and Milton B. Schott, Jr.

**H. W. BEATTIE AND SONS, INC.,** is one of Cleveland's foremost diamond merchants. Hugh W. Beattie, a Canadian jeweler and watchmaker, came to Cleveland in 1884 and started his own business by renting a window in the Chas. Stein store at the corner of Ontario and Prospect. He worked in the store as a watchmaker while carrying on his jewelry business there. Soon Beattie had enough money to rent his own store at Scovill and Kennard (E. 46th) streets. In 1890, he moved downtown when he purchased the partnership of Baxter & Craig and relocated his store in the newly opened ARCADE. In the 1890s, his brother, Geo. Beattie, joined the partnership. As it began to concentrate more on selling precious stones, Beattie started to mount displays of such jewels in his store window and soon gained world fame for these artistic displays. By 1907, the business dealt exclusively in jewels.

In 1917, Geo. Beattie began his own jewelry firm in the Arcade. Two years later, H. W. Beattie took his 3 sons into the partnership, which was incorporated in 1926. In 1920, Beattie opened a second store, designed by the decorating firm of Rorimer Brooks, in the Bulkley Bldg. on PLAYHOUSE SQUARE. Twelve years later, it relocated the store and all its furnishings to 1117 Euclid Ave. Over the years, Beattie continued to furnish exclusive service and quality diamonds to his customers. In 1959, after Geo. Beattie's death, Beattie & Sons bought out his store in the Arcade, and in 1976, Beattie closed the Arcade store. The

480

firm also started to issue an annual catalog in the 1970s with a national mailing list of 11,000. Beattie has remained a family-owned business, with several family members among its 18 employees.

**HAAS, VINCENT P.** (23 Oct. 1912–2 Apr. 1977), was a Cleveland diocesan priest who devoted much of his ministry to working with the poor, racial minorities, and alcoholics. Fr. Haas was born in Cleveland. He was educated at CATHEDRAL LATIN and JOHN CARROLL UNIVERSITY before entering ST. MARY SEMINARY in Cleveland to study for the priesthood. He was ordained on 2 Apr. 1938. He served at parishes in Akron and S. EUCLID before being named pastor in 1946. His assignment was to organize the parish of St. Peter Claver for black Catholics. Fr. Haas spent the next dozen years successfully integrating his black parishioners into neighboring churches. He also served as a chaplain at St. Thomas Hospital, where he gave support and direction to the founders of Alcoholics Anonymous, Dr. Bob Bill and Sister Ignatia. In 1961, Fr. Haas became the spiritual director of the St. Augustine Guild, the forerunner of the Catholic Interracial Council. From 1962–66 he served as pastor of the Conversion of St. Paul Shrine. In 1963 he led a group of Clevelanders to Washington, D.C., for the Freedom March. During the HOUGH RIOTS of 1966, Fr. Haas organized a group of priests who went into the neighborhoods and urged the people to be calm and to return to their homes. He also served as an unofficial advisor to the Ohio bishops on racial problems and possible solutions. In 1966 he was transferred to the pastorate of St. Colman's in Cleveland. Here he encouraged and directed an outreach ministry to the poor and senior citizens. He died in Cleveland.

Archives, Diocese of Cleveland.

**HADDEN, ALEXANDER** (2 July 1850–22 Apr. 1926), was born in Wheeling, (W.)Va., the son of Alexander Hadden (of Ballygawley, Ireland) and Mary Eliza Welch of Wheeling. At the age of 5 he moved with his family to a farm in Parkersburg, Ohio; in 1857 the family moved to EUCLID. Hadden attended the district school and the high school (Shaw Academy, later Shaw High School). He graduated from Oberlin College in 1873. That same year he began to study law at the office of Spalding & Dickman, where he stayed until he was admitted to the bar in Oct. 1875. He practiced law until Feb. 1882, when he was appointed by Carlos M. Stone (Cuyahoga County prosecuting attorney) to be an assistant prosecuting attorney. Hadden married Frances Hawthorne on 17 July 1883; she was originally from Coshocton, Ohio. He was elected prosecuting attorney of Cuyahoga County in 1884 and held the office for 3 terms until 1893. In 1896 he ran for the common pleas bench but was not elected. Gov. MYRON T. HERRICK appointed Hadden the third judge of the Probate Court of Cuyahoga County in 1905. Previously he had continued to practice law in association with Sheldon, Sterling, Horace, & Leonard Parks, and later with CARL D. FRIEBOLIN and Jas. H. Griswold. In 1902 he formed a partnership with Frank N. Wilcox—Wilcox, Collister, Hadden, & Parks. This firm's principal business was representing a syndicate that promoted the development of interurban electric lines throughout the WESTERN RESERVE and northern Ohio. At the time of his appointment to the probate bench to succeed the deceased Henry C. White, the office was on a fee basis, and the compensation was, while not exorbitant, rather more than the salary of a common pleas judge. Hadden held the office continuously (he first stood for election in 1906) from 1905 until his death. Hadden taught the science and theory of criminal law at the Wm. T. Backus School of Law at Western Reserve University from 1894 until his death. He was widely regarded for the clarity of his written judicial opinions and achieved some considerable fame through the writing and subsequent publication of an essay for the PHILOSOPHICAL CLUB OF CLEVELAND in 1918: *Why Are There No Common Law Crimes in Ohio?* During his tenure on the probate bench, Hadden had a particular concern for the insane, who were the responsibility of the court, and argued forcibly for the advancement of modes of treatment and the expansion of available facilities for their treatment. Hadden had 2 children, Alice (1884) and JOHN A. (1886).

**HADDEN, JOHN A.** (11 July 1886–1 Jan. 1979), was born in Cleveland, the son of ALEXANDER HADDEN. He attended CLEVELAND PUBLIC SCHOOLS before going to Harvard, from which he graduated with the B.A. degree in 1908 and the Bachelor of Laws in 1910. After returning to Cleveland that year, where he began to practice law in a small firm, he joined TROOP A. In 1912–13, Hadden was an assistant federal district attorney for the northern district of Ohio. In 1916 he went with Troop A to do service on the Mexican border. From there he went to Europe as part of the American Expeditionary Forces and commanded Battery F of the 135th Field Artillery of the 37th Div. in France. During this time, he served as judge advocate of 2 general courts, 1 in Alabama and 1 in France. When he returned to Cleveland, he took up the practice of law as an assistant prosecuting attorney for Cuyahoga County.

Early in 1922, Hadden married Marianne Elisabeth Millikin. He went into private practice in the firm of Griswold, Green, & Palmer. In 1925 he was elected a Republican member of the Ohio House of Representatives and served until 1931. During that time, he introduced a joint resolution calling for the submission of a constitutional amendment to the Ohio electors that would provide for the classification and taxation of personal property; this resolution was approved, and the amendment was then adopted in a general election. The result was the elimination of an older taxation of all property, including intangibles, according to uniform rule. Hadden's practice consisted largely of probate and corporation reorganization. He was appointed a trustee in the bankruptcy of the Erie Railroad Co., whose reorganization he successfully carried out in company with Robt. Woodruff and Chas. Denny. In the early 1930s he was a founding partner of the firm of Andrews, Hadden, & Burton, which later merged with McKeehan, Merrick, Arter, & Stewart and with Geo. Wm. Cottrell to become Arter, Hadden, Wykoff, & Stewart; it is now (1986) ARTER & HADDEN. In 1942, Hadden was appointed deputy regional director of the war production board for Cleveland, in which office he served for a year. He was later involved in the development of SEVERANCE CTR. in CLEVELAND HTS. in the early 1960s with Severance A. Millikin, his brother-in-law. Hadden was active in local Republican politics and was chairman of the CUYAHOGA COUNTY REPUBLICAN PARTY finance committee. He was a trustee and member of the executive committee of UNIVERSITY HOSPITALS, a trustee of the ELISABETH SEVERANCE PRENTISS FOUNDATION, and a director of the Youngstown Steel Door Co., the Union Commerce Bank, the Enos Coal Mining Co., and Enoco Collieries, Inc. He had 3 children: John A., Jr., Alexander H., and Elisabeth S.

The **HADDEN FOUNDATION** was established in 1957 by JOHN ALEXANDER HADDEN (1886–1979). Hadden, state representative and lawyer, was the son of ALEX-

481

ANDER HADDEN (1850–1926), probate judge in Cuyahoga County from 1905 until his death, and professor of criminal law at Western Reserve Law School. John Hadden was a partner of ARTER & HADDEN, founded in 1843 as Willey & Cary, the oldest and one of the largest law firms in Ohio. He graduated from East High in 1904, Harvard College in 1908, and Harvard Law School in 1910. He was an assistant federal district attorney from 1912–13 and a member of the Ohio general assembly from 1925–31. Hadden was married to Marianne Elisabeth Millikin and had 2 sons, John Alexander, Jr., and Alexander H., and a daughter, Elisabeth H. Alexander. Recent recipients of Hadden Foundation grants have been UNIVERSITY HOSPITALs and the medical and law schools of CWRU, as well as the UNITED WAY, LAUREL SCHOOL, HAWKEN SCHOOL, the WESTERN RESERVE HISTORICAL SOCIETY, and the BENJAMIN ROSE INSTITUTE. In 1985, foundation assets were $949,784, with expenditures of $36,200. Officers of the foundation included Alexander H. Hadden, president; John Hadden; and Quentin Alexander.

HAGAN, JOHN RAPHAEL (26 Feb. 1890–2 Sept. 1946), was an auxiliary bishop of Cleveland who was first president of Sisters' (later St. John) College. Consecrated a bishop only 4 months before his untimely death, he advanced the quality of Catholic elementary education throughout the country. The son of a railroad man, Hagan was brought to Cleveland from his native Pittsburgh at age 2. After graduation from CATHEDRAL LATIN SCHOOL, he entered the priesthood and began studies at North American College in Rome. In 1914, he was ordained with special permission, as he was a year short of the required 25 years of age. Through study at the University of Bonn (Germany) and the Catholic University of America, he acquired a D.S.T., a D.S.Ed., and a Ph.D. After 9 years as a parish priest at St. Augustine (1914–16), ST. PATRICK'S (1916–21), and St. Mary's, Bedford (1921–23), where he was pastor, Fr. Hagan was then named superintendent of schools by Bp. JOSEPH SCHREMBS. Soon after assuming the position he would hold for 23 years, he was recognized as a great educator with a keen sense of the essentials of teacher training.

As in many dioceses, education of elementary teachers was conducted in normal schools run by religious communities with unequal resources. As a result, there was little uniformity among the graduates. Hagan negotiated with the communities for 5 years to persuade them to entrust the training to a diocese-run school, Sisters' College, which was opened in 1928. Within 4 years of its establishment, the institution, in response to changing state directives, switched from a 3-year normal school to a 4-year program leading to a bachelor's degree. With the assistance of Msgr. ROBT. NAVIN, Hagan built Sisters' College into an innovative training center that provided consistency but not overstandardization of the teachers who staffed diocesan schools. In addition to his work at the college, Hagan helped found the Experimental School at Catholic University, aided the NEA, and founded the Catholic PTA movement. He taught at Cathedral Latin, Sisters' College, the seminary, and Catholic University, and authored texts. An advocate of federal aid to parochial education, he was a popular speaker in education circles. In 1946, Hagan was named auxiliary bishop of Cleveland by Pope Pius XII. Though he had no jurisdiction in the diocese unless delegated by Archbp. ROBT. HOBAN, he was appointed titular head of the dormant diocese of Limata, in the ancient Roman province of Numidia, North Africa. This move was in keeping with a policy of never vacating a see; Numidia, in a desert area overrun by Mohammedans, was vacated in the 8th century. His more substantial duties included continuing his work with the diocesan schools, though he resigned the presidency of ST. JOHN COLLEGE and the school superintendency. His consecration took place in May 1946 at St. Agnes Church, his home parish, as ST. JOHN CATHEDRAL was undergoing remodeling. In Aug. 1946, Hagan was taken ill; he died following abdominal surgery. He was 56.

HAHN, EDGAR A. (24 Nov. 1882–16 July 1970), was a lawyer whose contributions to Cleveland extended beyond the legal community to embrace cultural, civic, philanthropic, and educational endeavors. Hahn was born in Cleveland to Aaron and Therese Kolb Hahn. He attended the CLEVELAND PUBLIC SCHOOLS, graduating from CENTRAL HIGH SCHOOL. He earned the LL.B. degree from Western Reserve University in 1903 and did postgraduate work at Columbia University. Upon admittance to the Ohio bar in 1904, he started practicing law with his father. In 1912, the new state constitution enabled Ohio cities to adopt their own charters. At the September elections, Cleveland voters determined to assume the powers of self-government and elected Hahn to the commission responsible for forming a home-rule charter for the city. Hahn joined the law firm of Mooney, Hahn, Loeser & Keough as senior partner in 1920. The firm eventually became Hahn, Loeser, Freedheim, Dean & Wellman. As a lawyer, Hahn possessed an instinctive appreciation of the relationship between banking and society, and in 1933, he played a major role in untangling the confusion produced in Cleveland by the national bank holiday.

Hahn was one of the founders and original trustees of the NORTHERN OHIO OPERA ASSOC. in 1927. He donated generous amounts of time and effort to making Cleveland one of the foremost stops on the Metropolitan Opera's annual spring tour. In 1963, Northern Ohio Opera honored Hahn by making him its first honorary life trustee. As vice-chairman of the MUSICAL ARTS ASSOC., Hahn helped to initiate the tradition of summer concerts by the CLEVELAND ORCHESTRA in 1938. In 1959, he was appointed a trustee of the CLEVELAND MUSEUM OF ART, and he was chiefly responsible for the museum's acquisition of a number of fine 18th-century paintings. Hahn also served as treasurer and trustee of the LOUIS D. BEAUMONT FOUNDATION and as a director of Natl. City Bank. In Apr. 1964, Hahn was presented the Cleveland Medal for Public Service by the Cleveland Chamber of Commerce for his many noteworthy achievements of immeasurable value to the community. In 1967, he was selected Sr. Citizen of the Year. Hahn married Irene Moss on 13 Jan. 1910. The Hahns had 2 daughters, Katherine Hahn Bercovici and Mrs. Stanley Goodman.

The HALLE BROTHERS COMPANY was one of Cleveland's leading and most stylish department stores. It opened its doors with 20 employees on 7 Feb. 1891, when brothers Salmon P. and Samuel H. Halle bought T. S. Paddock & Co.'s hat and furrier shop, which had operated since 1846 at 221 Superior St. near W. 3rd St. In 1893, the Halles moved the business to the Nottingham Bldg. at Euclid Ave. and Sheriff (E. 4th) St. and expanded into ready-to-wear clothing. By 1896, it had become one of Cleveland's foremost fur shops. With its incorporation in 1902, the store expanded in space and goods. By 1907 it reached $1 million in sales. In 1910, Halle Bros. moved up Euclid Ave. to E. 12th St., where it occupied an imposing new 10-story building. Four years later, the store doubled its size and became a full-fledged department store carrying exclusive merchandise. Halle Bros. continued to grow in the 1920s. In 1927, the company opened its new $5 million, 6-story Huron-Prospect Bldg. It was a pioneer in establishing branch stores in the region, opening 5 in 1929 and 1930. Samuel Halle held the company together during the Depression. After WORLD WAR II, the business began to grow again as Halle Bros. started to develop suburban branches in 1948, completed a $10 million modernization and expansion program in 1949, and increased its workforce to over 3,000. However, by the mid-1950s, the company had slipped behind the MAY and HIGBEE companies in annual sales. Its downtown store was losing money as the company attempted to consolidate its space there, while its suburban stores subsidized the large downtown facility.

In 1970, Chicago's Marshall Field, Inc., purchased Halle Bros.' 9 stores. This merger was hailed as a "new era" for Halle Bros., as Marshall Field's greater resources were expected to increase the company's financial leverage and expansion plans in the competitive marketplace. The euphoria ended as Marshall Field ignored Halle Bros., and its operations became more troubled. The Halle family tradition, which had provided the business with its quality reputation, disappeared when Chisholm Halle was forced to resign as president in 1974, and Marshall Field began to introduce medium-priced goods. In the late 1970s, Halle Bros. was losing $1 million annually. Marshall Field considered either consolidating its expensive selling space at PLAYHOUSE SQUARE or moving to a new location nearer PUBLIC SQUARE. Finally, in Nov. 1981, Marshall Field sold the then–15 Halle stores to Associated Investors Corp., headed by Jerome Schottenstein. Schottenstein pledged to keep the Halle Bros. stores open, but within 2 months, he decided to close the entire chain. The downtown and most of the suburban stores closed in Mar. 1982. However, Schottenstein was persuaded to try to operate Halle Bros. as a smaller business with 6 stores, including the one at Westgate Mall. But by the fall of 1982, these stores were either sold or closed.

Crooks, Edwin W., "The History of the Halle Bros. Co." (Ph.D. diss., Indiana University School of Business, 1959), WRHS.

**HALLORAN, WILLIAM L.** (23 July 1915–7 Dec. 1941), was a rising young journalist and reserve naval officer who was the first Cleveland casualty of WORLD WAR II. Halloran was born and raised on Cleveland's west side and attended St. Ignatius Elementary School. After graduation from Cathedral Latin in 1933, he worked as editor of the *Shopping News Junior* while attending JOHN CARROLL UNIVERSITY. He transferred to OSU in 1936 where he was on the staff of the *Ohio State Lantern*, graduating with a B.S. in journalism in 1938. He immediately landed a job as a United Press Internatl. reporter with the *Columbus Citizen*, where he covered a variety of beats.

In early 1940, UPI transferred Halloran back home to Cleveland, where he worked as the UPI representative in the *Cleveland Press* building. With a deteriorating world situation (the war in Europe had begun in 1939), he left the *Press* to volunteer for active duty in the U.S. Naval Reserve, in 1940. His reasons for volunteering were expressed in a well-known letter to his former employer in Columbus, which was printed, in part, in the 14 Dec. 1941 issue of the *Citizen*. After attending the U.S. Naval Reserve Midshipmen's School at Northwestern University, Halloran received an ensign's commission in June 1941. He last visited Cleveland on 25 June 1941 and reported for duty aboard the *Arizona* 5 days later. Ens. Halloran perished aboard the *Arizona* on 7 Dec. 1941, when it was sunk during the surprise attack on Pearl Harbor that thrust the U.S. into World War II.

Halloran became a symbol of Cleveland's and America's tragic loss at Pearl Harbor, as hundreds attended a memorial service at St. Ignatius Church on 17 Dec. 1941. The Ensign William I. Halloran Club, dedicated to furthering Navy interests, was formed on 21 Dec. 1941. Mr. and Mrs. Halloran attended the launching of the U.S.S. *Halloran* in 1944 at the Mare Island Naval Yard in California, with Mrs. Halloran christening the vessel. In 1945, a city park in Cleveland located at W. 117th St. and Linnett Ave. was named in the ensign's honor. Halloran was posthumously awarded the the Purple Heart; American Defense Fleet Medal, 1939–41; Asiatic Pacific Campaign Medal, 1941–45; and World War II Freedom Medal, 1941–45.

**HALTNORTH'S GARDENS**, located at the corner of Woodland and Willson (E. 55th St.) avenues (1001 Woodland), was a popular German beer garden. Haltnorth's Gardens was a picturesque setting in which Clevelanders could enjoy a picnic or an evening of beer and opera. Situated on a wooded lot, the establishment literally was a garden: tables were scattered among fruit trees, the trunks of which were whitewashed up to the branches and encircled at the bottom by whitewashed cobblestones. A rustic bridge crossed a pond on the grounds. Patrons entered through the Willson Ave. gate of "a high whitewashed wooden fence" that enclosed the garden. From June through September, a stock company managed by Chas. L. LaMarche presented light opera in the covered theater, which seated 600–800 people. The CLEVELAND PHILHARMONIC ORCHESTRA presented concerts in the gardens. Although the Haltnorth's Gardens of the 1880s and 1890s was a pleasant, relaxed gathering place, that of the 1860s and 1870s appears to have been altogether different, judging from accounts in the *Leader*. These beer gardens were apparently established by Frederick Haltnorth (1825–1882), a native of Desson, Germany, who came to the U.S. in 1849. After arriving in Cleveland in 1851, Haltnorth established the William Tell House, a hotel at the corner of Front and Meadow Sts. In 1864 he entered the brewing business; about the same time he opened a saloon on PUBLIC SQUARE.

Haltnorth's Gardens is first mentioned in the *Leader* in 1863; a proponent of temperance, the *Leader* complained that the beer garden, then located on Kinsman St., was a gathering place for thieves, pickpockets, prostitutes, and "shoulder-hitters," was the site of many fights, and was the greatest "nuisance" the city had ever faced. Attempts were made to prevent the streetcars from running to the gardens on Sunday in order to hold business and sin there to a minimum, since "scenes are enacted there every Sabbath that should excite a blaze of indignation in the breast of every respectable citizen." By 1867, however, the gardens had become a meeting place for a variety of organizations holding special meetings and celebrations, and there were concerts by German singing societies and other musical groups. By 1872, Haltnorth's Gardens had moved from Kinsman to the corner of Woodland and Willson and was under the proprietorship of Geo. Mueller. It had several proprietors over the years, and by 1905 it had become the Coliseum Theater, featuring comedies by the Ralph C. Herz Co. and later Yiddish drama under the direction of I. R. Copperman.

**HAMANN, CARL AUGUST** (26 Jan. 1865–12 Jan. 1930), was dean of Western Reserve University Medical School, 1912–19, and visiting surgeon at Charity and City hospitals, 1896–1930. He was an outstanding surgeon, and his abilities as a diagnostician were almost legendary. He was called "the King" by his colleagues and students in tribute to his professional abilities. Hamann was born in Davenport, Iowa, to Claus H. and Marie Koenig Hamann, German immigrants. He graduated from Davenport High School in 1885 and taught school the next 2 years. He entered the University of Pennsylvania Medical School in 1887, graduating with the M.D. degree in 1890. During 1890–91, Hamann was a resident physician at the Lankenau Hospital in Philadelphia. He returned to the University of Pennsylvania as an assistant demonstrator of anatomy from 1891–93.

Arriving in Cleveland in 1893, Hamann established his private practice in addition to his appointment as professor of anatomy at WRU Medical School. In 1912, he was appointed dean and professor of applied anatomy and clinical surgery. A stern and painstaking instructor, Hamann was beloved by his students. As dean, he headed the medical school during a period of rapid growth and is credited with helping to build one of the world's finest medical centers in Cleveland. As founder of the Hamann Museum of Comparative Anthropology at the medical school, he devoted much time and effort to the task of preparing, recording, and mounting materials he gathered for his anatomical teaching museum. Hamann was modest and soft-spoken and gave of his skills and talents freely. As he gained recognition and success, he maintained a large number of patients from all walks of life. Sympathetic and compassionate, Hamann came to be regarded by many of his patients almost as a parent. He was reputed to have done more charity practice than any other physician in the city. Hamann performed over 10,000 operations, and even in his later years he would perform up to 20 a day. For many years he shared the administrative burden for the department of surgery at Charity Hospital with Dr. FRANK BUNTS. With Bunts's death in 1928, Hamann shouldered the entire burden until he was struck down with heart disease shortly before his own death. Hamann married Ella F. Ampt on 31 Oct. 1900. The Hamanns had 2 children, Carl A. and Elizabeth Marie.

**HAMILTON, JAMES MONTGOMERY** (27 June 1876–12 Jan. 1941), was a prominent architect active in Cleveland from 1905 until the 1930s. In partnership with FRANK B. MEADE, he was responsible for the design of several hundred homes in historical revival styles for notable Cleveland residents. Hamilton was born in Ft. Wayne, Ind., and educated in public schools there, graduating from high school in 1894. He attended MIT in Boston and moved to Cleveland in 1901. Hamilton traveled in Europe for 2 years (1903–04) to study architecture, then returned to Cleveland, where he worked for the firm of Meade & Garfield. In 1911, he formed a partnership with Meade—Meade & Hamilton, which lasted until 1941. During this time, the two architects designed great many residences for industrialists living in the northeastern U.S. Among Meade & Hamilton's projects in the Greater Cleveland area were the Euclid Ave. homes of Francis E. Drury, H. G. Otis, NATHAN L. DAUBY, Kenyon V. Painter, and Henry White, and the WADE PARK homes of Eugene R. Grasselli, A. A. Augustus, Justin Sholes, and EMIL JOSEPH. In the emerging SUBURBS of Euclid and AMBLER HTS. (now CLEVELAND HTS.), the firm designed homes for MYRON T. HERRICK, John Sherwin, and John G. W. Cowles. In SHAKER HTS., homes were designed for CAESAR A. GRASSELLI, A. H. Diebold, C. K. Chisholm, ROLLIN H. WHITE, and Ira H. Baker. In addition to the residential buildings, Meade & Hamilton designed 6 clubhouses, including the SHAKER HTS. COUNTRY CLUB, the MAYFIELD COUNTRY CLUB, and the HERMIT CLUB.

Johannesen, Eric, *Cleveland Architecture, 1876–1976* (1979).

**HAMILTON, MARGARET** (1902–15 May 1985), was a stage-and-screen actress born in Cleveland and best remembered for her role as the "Wicked Witch of the West" in the film classic *The Wizard of Oz*. Hamilton was raised at 2058 E. 96th St. Her father was an attorney. She attended Bolton School, and then HATHAWAY BROWN, graduating in 1921. Her family wanted her to become a teacher, so she went to Boston for training at Wheelock Kindergarten Training School. It was there that she received her first acting experience in a production of *Little Women*. She returned to Cleveland and taught at Hough Elementary School, then operated her own nursery for the Cleveland Hts. Presbyterian Church. She went to New York in 1922, where she taught day school. There she saw Gertrude Lawrence in the play *Okay* and again became enamored with the theater. She quit teaching, returned to Cleveland, and worked at the CLEVELAND PLAY HOUSE from 1927–30. During this time, she met and married landscape architect Paul Meserue. After the Play House, Hamilton did summer work in Massachusetts. Arthur Beckworth "discovered" Hamilton in a play entitled *The Hallems*. The Broadway version was called *Another Language*. It was the surprise hit of 1932 and was made into a film with Hamilton and Helen Hayes. That launched Hamilton's Hollywood career. Because of her distinctive profile, however, her roles were never very diverse; she usually played aunts and spinsters. Her role as the wicked witch came in 1939. The role further helped typecast Hamilton, but she still remembered it fondly many years later. She continued making films and doing plays, appearing in more than 75 of each before her death. She also did guest roles on television shows and made television commercials, most notably for Maxwell House coffee. In her later years, Hamilton returned several times to the Play House to appear in productions such as *The Importance of Being Earnest* and *Night Must Fall*. She also continued to teach Sunday school and worked as a volunteer in various causes. Hamilton divorced her husband in 1938; they had 1 son.

**HAMMOND, GEORGE FRANCIS** (26 Nov. 1855–26 Apr. 1938), was an important classical architect active in Cleveland from 1886–1926. Hammond was born in Roxbury, Mass., the son of George and Cornelia Johnson Hammond. He attended Roxbury Latin School, Roxbury High School, and the Massachusetts Normal Art School. He also studied with Wm. R. Ware, founder of the first American curriculum based on the Beaux-Arts system of architectural training, at MIT. In 1876, Hammond worked as a draftsman in the office of Wm. G. Preston in Boston. He began independent work in 1878 and set up his own office in 1884.

In 1886 Hammond moved to Cleveland, having designed the first HOLLENDEN HOTEL on Superior Ave. in 1885, one of the first large fireproof hotels in Cleveland (see HOTELS). Among his works in Ohio were the Electric Bldg., 702 Prospect, 1900; the First Church of Christ, Scientist (Lane Metropolitan CME Church), 1904; the master campus plan and 5 original buildings of the Ohio State Normal College (Kent State University), 1911–15; McKinley High School, Canton; and the U.S. Post Office in Zanesville. He designed hospitals, schools, factories, and power buildings in Chicago, Kansas City, New Orleans, Toronto, and Montreal. Hammond's own home at 1863 Caldwell Rd. in CLEVELAND HTS. is a fine Colonial Revival residence, and he designed a number of suburban homes, especially in the Clifton Park area of LAKEWOOD. He published *A Treatise on Hospital and Asylum Con-*

*struction* in 1891 and was elected a fellow of the American Institute of Architects. He retired in 1926 and died in Falls Village, Conn. Hammond married Annie Borland Barstow in 1883. Following her death in 1886, he married Annie E. Butcher of Toronto on 2 June 1897.

**HAMPSON, JAMES B.** (1841–28 May 1864), was a volunteer Civil War officer killed in action during the Atlanta Campaign in Georgia. Hampson was a printer by trade, who was listed as 4th corporal of the CLEVELAND GRAYS in June 1860. He enlisted in Co. E, 1st Ohio Volunteer Infantry, for 3 months' service, 23 Apr. 1861. Hampson was promoted to 2d lieutenant on 17 June 1861 and to 1st lieutenant on 2 July 1861. He was mustered out with his company on 1 Aug. 1861. Hampson enlisted in the 124TH OVI as a major, dating from 1 Jan. 1863. While on staff duty with Gen. Wood, commander of the 3d Div., 4th Army Corps, Army of the Cumberland, at the Battle of Pickett's Mills, Ga., he was mortally wounded. He had stated many times that he would be killed in the line of duty. Hampson is buried in Marietta Natl. Cemetery. His bust is displayed in a medallion in the SOLDIERS & SAILORS MONUMENT on Cleveland's PUBLIC SQUARE. Hampson Post, No. 23, GRAND ARMY OF THE REPUBLIC, which met at 184 Superior, was named in his honor.

Lewis, George W., *The Campaigns of the One Hundred and Twenty-fourth Regiment* (1894).

**HANDY, TRUMAN P.** (17 Jan. 1807–25 Mar. 1898), was an early banker and financier active in establishing educational, philanthropic, and musical institutions in the city. Born in Paris in Oneida County, N.Y., Handy received a common-school education and entered the banking profession at age 18, becoming a clerk in the Bank of Geneva, N.Y. In 1830 he moved to Buffalo, where he helped organize the Bank of Buffalo and served as a teller. He moved to Cleveland in Mar. 1832 at the request of historian Geo. Bancroft, who, along with several associates, had acquired control of the defunct COMMERCIAL BANK OF LAKE ERIE, which they planned to reopen. Handy was the cashier of the Commercial Bank when it reopened in Apr. 1832; he remained with that institution for the next 10 years. When the state legislature refused to renew the bank's charter, Handy was one of the commissioners appointed to settle its affairs. In 1843 he opened his own banking office, T. P. Handy & Co., which existed until 1845, when the State Bank of Ohio was organized. Handy was a director, a cashier, the largest stockholder, and chief executive officer of the Commercial Branch Bank when it opened in Nov. 1845. In Jan. 1862 he became president of the troubled Merchants Branch Bank, and within a year he had made that institution profitable. He became president of the Merchants Natl. Bank in Feb. 1865 and continued as president of its successor, the Mercantile Natl. Bank, from 1885 until his retirement in 1892.

As a banker and financier, Handy was involved in the organization of a number of railroad and manufacturing enterprises. He was an incorporator of the CLEVELAND & NEWBURGH RAILROAD CO., treasurer and director of the Cleveland, Columbus & Cincinnati Railroad Co., a stockholder and director of the Cleveland Iron Mining Co., and a stockholder in the Cleveland Rolling Mill Co. He was also president and executive committee member of the CLEVELAND CLEARINGHOUSE ASSOC., formed in 1858 to facilitate exchanges between banks. Handy was also active in civic and educational affairs. A member of the first school board, he helped establish public schools in the city; he also helped organize CLEVELAND UNIVERSITY in 1850, was an incorporator of the Case School of Applied Science and Western Reserve University, and was a trustee of Lane Theological Seminary. He also served as superintendent of the Sabbath School, as treasurer of the Cleveland Sanitary Commission, and as president of the Homeopathic Hospital, and he was a founder and president of the Cleveland Industrial School. He was a founding member of the Second Presbyterian Church in 1844. Handy also took part in several musical societies. He was the first president of the CLEVELAND MOZART SOCIETY and a member (and president in 1853) of the CLEVELAND MENDELSSOHN SOCIETY. Handy was married in Mar. 1832 to Harriet N. Hall of Geneva, N.Y.; their arrival in Cleveland by stage was their bridal trip. His wife died in July 1880.

*Annals of the Early Settlers Assoc.* (1898).

**HANNA, DANIEL RHODES** (26 Dec. 1866–3 Nov. 1921), was owner and publisher of the *CLEVELAND NEWS* and the *Sunday News-Leader*, and a partner in the M. A. HANNA CO. Hanna was the son of MARCUS A. HANNA and a prominent member of the Rhodes-Hanna coal and iron clan. He was a partner in the M. A. Hanna Co. from 1891–1915 and was considered a leader in the development of iron ore in the northwestern Great Lakes region and in the bituminous coal and blast furnace industries. In 1910, Hanna purchased the *CLEVELAND LEADER* from Joseph M. McCormick, publisher of the *Chicago Tribune*, and in 1912 he acquired the *Cleveland News* from CHAS. A. OTIS, JR. He published the *News* and *Leader* until 1917, when the *Leader* was sold to the *PLAIN DEALER*. The Sunday edition of the *Leader* continued to be published with the *News* as the *Sunday News-Leader*. Hanna built the Leader-News Bldg. on Superior at E. 6th St. in 1912 and the Hanna Bldg. and Theater as a memorial to his father in 1921. Both buildings were planned by Chas. A. Platt, the eminent New York residential architect.

Hanna was a member of the COUNTRY CLUB, the TAVERN CLUB, and the UNIVERSITY CLUB. A lover of horses, he belonged to the Gentlemen's Driving Club and the Four-in-Hand & Tandem Club, among others. Hanna lived at various times on Franklin Ave., Lake Ave. (LAKEWOOD), Euclid Ave., and Bratenahl Rd., and had homes in Ravenna, Ohio, Lenox, Mass., and Ossining, N.Y. He remodeled the home in Ravenna, a Rhodes-Hanna house constructed in 1817, in the early 1900s, incorporating portions of 2 rooms that were purported to have come from Buckingham Palace when it was renovated by Edward VII. Hanna was married to Daisy Gordon and later to May Harrington and had 8 children, Mark A., Carl H., Dan R., Jr., Elizabeth, Natalie, Ruth, Charlotte, and Mary. He died at his home in Ossining, N.Y., and was buried in LAKE VIEW CEMETERY, Cleveland.

**HANNA, DANIEL RHODES, JR.** (28 May 1894–13 Sept. 1962), was a leading publisher and journalist. He was born in Cleveland to DANIEL RHODES HANNA, SR., and May Harrington Hanna. He had 2 older brothers, Marcus Alonzo Hanna II and Carl Harrington Hanna. Hanna attended the CLEVELAND PUBLIC SCHOOLS, Taft School in Watertown, Conn., and Phillips Andover Academy, Andover, Mass. At the age of 19, he joined his father at the *CLEVELAND NEWS*, which the elder Hanna owned. When his father died in 1921, Hanna took over the paper. In 1925 he became president and general manager of the Cleveland Co., which owned and operated the daily and Sunday *Cleveland News*. In 1932 the FOREST CITY PUB-

LISHING CO. acquired the stock of the *Cleveland News* and the *PLAIN DEALER*. By 1946, Hanna was vice-president and director of the Forest City Publishing Co., but he had little influence on the *News*'s direction. In 1951 he became vice-president and chairman of the Hanna Bldg. Corp. and the Hanna Theater Corp., replacing his brother Carl. Hanna remained associated with the Hanna Bldg. until his death, even though it and the theater had been purchased by the T. W. Grogan Co. in 1958. Hanna was a member of the Kirtland, Mayfield, Pepper Pike, Tavern, Hermit, and Mid-Day clubs and was a principal founder of the Chagrin Valley Kennel Club. He married Ruth Randall in 1917. They had 4 children. The marriage ended in divorce. Hanna married Lucia Otis Newell on 25 July 1936.

**HANNA, LEONARD C., JR.** (5 Nov. 1889–5 Oct. 1957), was one of the major philanthropic figures in Cleveland history. During his lifetime he contributed over $90 million to cultural and charitable institutions in and around Cleveland. He was also a director of the M. A. HANNA & CO., a coal- and iron ore-shipping concern started by his father, Leonard Colton Hanna, and his uncles, Howard and MARCUS HANNA. Hanna was born in Cleveland. He attended University School, the Hill School in Pottstown, Pa., and Yale University. After graduation from Yale, he worked in the iron and steel industry to gain experience. He then served as a 1st lieutenant with the aviation section of the Army Signal Corps in WORLD WAR I. After the war he returned to Cleveland and was admitted to the partnership of M. A. Hanna & Co. (which later became Hanna Mining) in 1917.

Hanna was an avid art collector, theatergoer, and patron of the arts, as well as a fan of boxing and BASEBALL. In 1914 he joined the Cleveland Museum of Art's advisory committee, and beginning in 1920 he served as a trustee and member of the Accessions Committee. In 1941 he incorporated the Leonard C. Hanna Jr. Fund, and as president and one of its trustees, he was responsible for dispensing millions of dollars to institutions in Ohio, including KARAMU HOUSE, the CLEVELAND PLAY HOUSE, UNIVERSITY HOSPITALS, and Western Reserve University. From 1942–44 he served with the American Red Cross in England, establishing and directing recreational centers for American airmen stationed in England. Hanna was a member of the UNION CLUB and the ROWFANT CLUB and at one time was president of the TAVERN CLUB. At his death at age 67, he left a bequest of over $33 million to the CLEVELAND MUSEUM OF ART, which helped make it one of the country's truly great museums.

**HANNA, M. A. CO.** *See* **M. A. HANNA COMPANY**

**HANNA, MARCUS ALONZO** (24 Sept. 1837–15 Feb. 1904), was a leading businessman who founded the M. A. HANNA CO., and a national leader of the Republican party who managed Wm. McKinley's successful presidential campaigns in 1896 and 1900. He also served as U.S. senator from Ohio from 1898 until his death. Hanna was born in New Lisbon, Ohio, the son of Leonard and Samantha Converse Hanna. He attended school there until his family came to Cleveland in 1852. In Cleveland he attended CENTRAL HIGH SCHOOL, and later he spent a few months at Western Reserve College in Hudson, 1857–58. He entered his father's business, Hanna, Garretson & Co., wholesale grocers, and after his marriage to Charlotte Rhodes, he joined his father-in-law's firm, Rhodes & Co., iron and coal merchants. When Daniel P. Rhodes died, Hanna gradually assumed control of the company, and in 1885 it became the M. A. Hanna Co. Hanna's other busi-

ness interests included ownership of the West Side Railway, which later became the WOODLAND AVE. & WEST SIDE RAILWAY. In the late 1880s Hanna began electrifying his street railways and consolidated the company with the Cleveland City Cable Co. to form the Cleveland City Railway Co. Competition for streetcar franchises put him in opposition to TOM L. JOHNSON. He had a lively interest in drama and the THEATER and bought the EUCLID AVE. OPERA HOUSE in the late 1870s.

During his successful career as a businessman, Hanna was attracted to politics, an interest that apparently began when he was elected to the Cleveland Board of Education ca. 1869. As a Republican, he was active in the ward level, helping to get out the vote and insure an honest count. He organized a Businessman's Republican Campaign Club and proved to be an effective collector of funds for the party, as well as a generous donor himself. As his political influence grew, Hanna utilized his skills as a political campaigner, managing Jas. B. Foraker's successful campaign for governor of Ohio in 1885. Although his efforts to make John Sherman the Republican presidential nominee in 1888 failed, he was instrumental in securing Sherman's reelection to the Senate in 1892 over Gov. Foraker. Hanna withdrew from active participation in the business of M. A. Hanna in 1894 in order to devote his time to nominating Ohio governor Wm. McKinley for president. Setting up headquarters in the PERRY-PAYNE BLDG. in the spring of 1895, he organized committees to promote McKinley's nomination in key states, bearing almost the entire cost of this enterprise. McKinley was nominated for president at the Republican Natl. Convention in St. Louis, and as chairman of the Natl. Committee, Hanna organized McKinley's successful presidential campaign in 1896 and again in 1900. In 1897 Hanna was appointed by Ohio governor Asa Bushnell to replace U.S. senator John Sherman when Sherman became secretary of state. In a close election, the Ohio legislature elected Hanna to the Senate in Jan. 1898, and he was reelected to another 6-year term in 1904.

As a senator, Hanna participated in shaping legislation to subsidize U.S. shipping and favored building a canal across Panama. In 1901 he was chosen chairman of the Executive Committee of the Civic Fed., the purpose of which was to informally mediate disputes between labor and management. Hanna was a powerful Republican political leader and retained that leadership on the national and state levels after McKinley's death in 1901; however, he did not succeed in keeping the control of Cleveland politics in Republican hands. Locally, Democratic mayor Tom L. Johnson was the dominant force at that time. Hanna married Charlotte Augusta Rhodes in Sept. 1864, and they had 2 children, Daniel Rhodes and Ruth Hanna McCormick Simms. Hanna died in Washington at age 66. His funeral was held in Cleveland on 19 Feb. 1904, with burial at LAKE VIEW CEMETERY. Four years later a memorial of Sen. Hanna was unveiled at UNIVERSITY CIRCLE.

Beer, Thomas, *Hanna* (1929).
Croly, Herbert, *Marcus Alonzo Hanna: His Life and Work* (1912).
McCook, Henry Christopher, *The Senator: A Threnody* (1905).

The **HANNA THEATER** has served as a pioneer in the world of legitimate THEATER in Cleveland for over 60 years, providing Clevelanders with a source of quality theatrical entertainment rivaling Broadway. Located in the Hanna Bldg., the theater opened on 29 Mar. 1921. It was built by DAN R. HANNA, who dedicated it to the memory of his father, Sen. MARCUS A. HANNA, a theater lover and former owner of the EUCLID AVE. OPERA HOUSE. Sen. Hanna believed that the stage was "one of the great pulpits of the world, a public forum for the discussion and presentation of the great questions of life, while it afforded one of the best forms of amusement for the people—a relaxation from the workaday world." The first production at the Hanna Theater was a presentation of *The Prince and the Pauper*. In the ensuing years, it hosted a number of major touring Broadway shows. It is the only "road theater" in the country that has been in operation for 50 or more consecutive years; most were forced to close during the Depression. Milton Krantz was the general manager of the Hanna for 42 years, known as "Mr. First-Nighter" for his tradition of walking up the aisles from the first row to the last, shaking hands with people he knew. Krantz accepted the challenge of running the Depression-weary Hanna in 1941. At that time, it was staging shows that stayed open for 3-day runs. Soon, under Krantz's philosophy that a theater should be run like a business, the Hanna hosted longer runs. Krantz retired in 1983, having attended over 1,000 opening nights. Wm. Roudebush served as president and producing director of the Hanna in 1984. The Hanna Theater, Building, and Annex were constructed of Indiana limestone, designed by Chas. A. E. Platt, built by JOHN GILL & SONS, and decorated by Faustino Sampietro. The exterior and interior were based on purely classic traditional architectural design. It has a seating capacity of 1,535, and was operated by Uptown Productions of Cleveland in 1984.

**HARCOURT BRACE JOVANOVICH** is a leading publisher of textbooks and periodicals and has operations in testing services, broadcasting, theme parks, and insurance. Begun in 1918, it has been a force in American education and important internationally to belles-lettres and scholarly research. The firm, by the 1980s a Fortune 500 corporation, undertook a major reorganization and relocation early in the decade. That, in part, involved the transfer to Cleveland, from New York City and Chicago, of HBJ Publications, which produces business periodicals; the Psychological Corp. (which moved again to San Antonio in 1986), producing materials and services; and Beckley-Cardy (which moved to Duluth, Minn.), managing school and office supplies sales and distribution. In 1982, Cleveland was established as a third corporate headquarters, along with San Diego, Calif., and Orlando, Fla. The headquarters building in Cleveland (7500 Old Oak Blvd., MIDDLEBURG HTS.) was designed by Tufts & Wenzel, Architects, Inc., and has won several awards for energy efficiency and its effective and daring design. Sea World Enterprises, one of HBJ's business segments, operates 3 marine theme parks, which provide instructional entertainment and sell food and merchandise. A Sea World Park is located near Cleveland in Aurora, Ohio. A fourth Sea World Park was scheduled to open in San Antonio, Tex., in Apr. 1987.

**HARD, DUDLEY JACKSON** (4 Aug. 1873–9 Oct. 1950), was for many years a leader in military affairs whose first experience was in the SPANISH-AMERICAN WAR. Born in Wooster, Ohio, to Curtis V. and Adeline Jackson Hard, Hard graduated from the College of Wooster in 1893 and shortly thereafter moved to Cleveland. In 1894 he joined the newly organized Cleveland Light & Power Co., with offices at the northwest corner of St. Clair and Ontario streets. At that time, electric light and power were being produced on a small scale by a steam engine belonging to the Williams Publishing Co., for use by its immediate neighbors. In 1893, Cleveland Light & Power took over the Williams business; when Hard joined the firm, he became its treasurer, and by 1946 he was president when the com-

pany's interests were purchased by the CLEVELAND ELECTRIC ILLUMINATING CO.

In 1898, Hard decided to leave his private business interests to follow in the footsteps of both his father and grandfather, who had been career servicemen. In that year he enlisted as a private in Ohio's 8th Volunteer Infantry, serving in the Spanish-American War campaign in Santiago. From 1906–10, Hard served in Troop A of the Ohio Cavalry, as a 1st lieutenant. By 1916, he had attained the rank of major, commanding a battalion from Ohio in the Mexican border campaign. During WORLD WAR I, Hard was a colonel commanding the 135th Field Artillery. In 1923 he was promoted to colonel, chief of staff, of Ohio's 37th Div., and by 1928 he was brigadier general of the 54th Ohio Cavalry Brigade, which commanded troops from Ohio, Kentucky, Louisiana, and Georgia. Hard's string of military accomplishments earned him a reputation as one of the most decorated military men from Ohio.

In 1936, following nearly 20 years of continuous military service, Hard was again promoted, this time to major general, commanding the 37th Div. of the Ohio Natl. Guard. Retiring from military service in that same year, he served as the first county commander in Cleveland of the American Legion. Ohio's first county council of the American Legion was formed in Cuyahoga County at the HOLLENDEN HOTEL on 2 July 1919, with Hard as acting chairman. The Cleveland Medal for Public Service was awarded to Hard on 21 Apr. 1836 for distinguished military service, resulting in many essential improvements in the organization and discipline of the Natl. Guard of Ohio. Living after retirement as a private citizen, Hard pursued civic activities with the same enthusiasm he had exhibited during his military years, becoming involved with the Cleveland Welfare Fed., the Cleveland and Ohio chambers of commerce, and the Cuyahoga County Boy Scouts. He was survived by his wife, Mildred J. Hopkins, whom he married in St. Louis, Mo., on 18 Nov. 1903, and their 2 children, Dudley J., Jr., and Mrs. Jane Russell.

Dudley Hard Papers, WRHS.

**HARKNESS, STEPHEN V.** (18 Nov. 1818–6 Mar. 1888), was a leading Cleveland financier who provided crucial financial support for the STANDARD OIL CO., of which he was cofounder. Born in Fayette, N.Y., Harkness lost both of his parents at an early age. Raised by relatives, he was apprenticed to a harnessmaker after his formal education ended at age 15. When his apprenticeship was over at age 21, he moved to Bellevue, Ohio, to practice his trade. Moving often in the 1850s, Harkness soon left harnessmaking for other ventures. In 1855 he established a distillery in Monroeville, Ohio, and by 1860 he was a leading businessman in the Monroeville-Bellevue area. He organized a bank in Monroeville in 1860, and in 1864 he formed a partnership with Wm. Halsey Doan to supply crude oil to refineries.

His fortune made, Harkness sold his various enterprises in the Monroeville-Bellevue area in 1866 and moved to Cleveland. Although he retired from daily involvement in business management, he continued to invest in business enterprises, the most successful of which was Standard Oil. Harkness invested between $60,000 and $90,000 in the firm's forerunner, Rockefeller, Andrews & Flagler, and in 1870 he became a charter member of the Standard Oil Co. He was a director of the firm until his death. From 1869–72, Harkness owned ⅓ of the Union Elevator firm with GEO. W. GARDNER and Geo. H. Burt. In 1876 he built the Harkness Block at the corner of Euclid and Willson (E. 55th) sts. He served as a director of the Euclid Ave.

487

Natl. Bank and the Ohio River Railway Co. and as president of both the Iron Belt Mining Co. and the Cleveland Arcade Co. He was a member of the WESTERN RESERVE HISTORICAL SOCIETY and contributed to the Central Friendly Inn, to various churches, and to the effort to bring Western Reserve University to Cleveland. Harkness was married twice—to Laura Osborn in 1842 and to Anna M. Richardson in 1853.

The **HARMONIA CHOPIN SINGING SOCIETY,** established in 1902 by young Polish immigrants interested in preserving their heritage, was by 1972 "the oldest active male chorus in Ohio." It was formed on 2 Aug. 1902 as the Harmonia Choir by B. W. Ruszkowski, Stanislaw Rakwitz, John Kaczmarski, Boleslaw Szbarbach, Joseph Sznajder, and John Mendrzycki. The group soon took over the Kosciuszko House, a small hall over a tavern at E. 65th St. opposite Baxter Rd. In 1912 it merged with the Fryderyk Chopin Choir, formed in 1907; by 1919 the new Harmonia Chopin Choir had 100 voices, was holding weekly practice meetings, and had branches for both boys and girls. By 1923 the group had moved to its present location at 3736 E. 71st St. The group took on a broad scope of activities, serving the Polish community but also performing outside it to introduce the larger population of Cleveland to Polish culture. It sang for many religious, fraternal, and civic gatherings, as well as at important Polish affairs, including fundraising events to benefit fellow Poles. The group has received a number of awards and trophies for its singing.

The **HAROLD T. CLARK TENNIS COURTS** are located on S. Marginal Rd. opposite BURKE LAKEFRONT AIRPORT. They were named in honor of Cleveland philanthropist and lawyer HAROLD TERRY CLARK, an avid promoter of American participation in Davis Cup competition. Since their opening in July 1978, the courts have hosted numerous amateur and professional competitions, including the Western Open, the U.S. Natl. Amateur Hardcourt Tennis Championship, the Championship of the Americas, the Natl. Public Parks Tennis Tournament, and the Urban League Annual Tennis Tournament. Early in 1964, an ad hoc committee was created to promote Cleveland as the site of the 1964 DAVIS CUP MATCHES. Their bid was accepted, and a committee, headed by Robt. Malaga, was formed to raise funds for the construction of a new stadium for the matches. The site selected was at Ambler Park, near Roxboro Jr. High School. Although located in CLEVELAND HTS., Ambler Park was owned by the city of Cleveland. The committee obtained a building permit from the Cleveland Public Properties Dept. on condition that when the matches were concluded, the bleachers would be dismantled and the playing court left as a permanent improvement to the park. The stadium, however, was not dismantled in 1964, and during the succeeding years the park permit was renewed. Between 1966–72, the stadium was the biennial host site for the women's Wrightman Cup tennis matches. In 1973 it was again the host site for the Davis Cup matches. In 1970 an unsuccessful campaign was launched to raise financing for a proposed new Harold T. Clark Tennis Stadium in PEPPER PIKE. To be located at the Cleveland Racquet Club, it was to be the host site for both the Davis Cup and Wrightman Cup matches. By 1972, plans had been altered for the construction of a $150,000 stadium at an unspecified site. In 1972 the Clark Stadium spectator stands were sold to an Indianapolis group, who dismantled the stands after the 1973 Davis Cup matches. During the administration of Mayor Ralph Perk, a final location for the new Clark Stadium was approved on city land on S. Marginal Rd. Financed at a cost of $230,000 of city funds and $150,000 raised by Greater Cleveland tennis groups, the stadium features seating for 5,000 and an earthen mound on the north side, 6 to 8′ above the level of the East Shoreway, that screens out noise and traffic.

**HARRIS, ALFRED WILSON** (18 Aug. 1884–19 Mar. 1932), was an architect active in Cleveland from 1917–32. Harris was born in Tremont, Ill. He attended the University of Illinois, where he studied architecture, and then lived in Peoria for several years. He served in the Air Force during WORLD WAR I, was in charge of aviation training camps abroad, and attained the rank of major. Harris began practicing as an architect in Cleveland in 1917. He was considered one of the most competent designers of English-style houses, of which several were built in SHAKER HTS. He is best known for the grand design for Moreland Courts, a $30 million apartment and commercial development announced by JOSIAH KIRBY in 1922. The concept included the MORELAND COURTS APARTMENTS linking the western edge of Shaker Hts. with a shopping center at Moreland Circle (now SHAKER SQUARE). In addition to the 1,500-ft.-long apartment building on Shaker Blvd., it included terrace homes on Van Aken Blvd., business buildings, stores, and a theater on the circle, and a market house, central heating plant, and parking garage southwest of the circle. Harris spent 14 months on the preliminary planning. His plans for the commercial buildings showed a variety of form and detail comparable to that executed in the apartments, creating the feeling of a medieval street.

When Kirby's development failed in 1923, less than a year after it was announced, the VAN SWERINGEN brothers employed Harris to prepare a scheme to develop Shaker Blvd. west to E. 93rd St. However, the Harris plan was never carried out, and Philip L. Small and Carl B. Rowley were engaged by the Van Sweringens to complete Moreland Courts and to plan Shaker Square. Although Harris's scheme was not completely realized, the effect of his intentions can be seen in the irregular block of smaller apartments south of Shaker Square and bounded by Drexmore, S. Moreland, Hampton, and S. Woodland. Nearly all of them were designed by Harris, although they were built by different developers. They constitute a picturesque combination of round towers, bay windows, steep slate roofs, half-timbered gables, brick, stone, wood, and stucco. Maj. Harris's artistic bent was also expressed in painting and sculpture. Aviation remained a lifelong pursuit, and he was one of the charter members of the Cleveland Aviation Club, founded in 1919. He married Mary E. Harris, and they had 2 sons, Alfred, Jr., and Thomas.

**HARRIS, JOSIAH A.** (15 Jan. 1808–21 Aug. 1876), prominent publisher and editor, was eulogized as "the Nestor of Cleveland journalism." He moved with his family in 1818 to N. Amherst in Lorain County, where he attended and taught briefly in the local schools. Settling in Elyria, Harris married another Massachusetts native, Esther M. Race, and was elected sheriff for 2 terms. He also revived Elyria's first newspaper, the *Lorain Gazette,* as the *Ohio Atlas & Elyria Advertiser,* which appeared as a weekly in 1832. After selling the paper, Harris worked briefly in Columbus and did some traveling in the South before coming to Cleveland in 1837. In partnership with Judge CHAS. WHITTLESEY, he purchased the *CLEVELAND HERALD & GAZETTE,* although Whittlesey gave up his share after 1 year. Harris proceeded to establish the *Herald* as the city's most solid newspaper, paying off its debts and providing it with its own printing office.

Harris won local support by scrupulously printing notices of marriages, deaths, and meetings, and furnishing free copies of the paper to all clergymen. The public was invited into the *Herald*'s office to read the exchange papers laid out on the "Old Round Table." A confirmed advocate of TEMPERANCE since youth, Harris also abstained from tobacco, coffee, and tea. He refused to print ads for the more notorious quack medicines in the *Herald*, or notices for the return of runaway slaves. Harris also kept the *Herald* solidly behind the WHIG PARTY. During the 1840 presidential canvass, he published a Harrison campaign paper called the *Axe*, and in 1844 and 1852 he served as a delegate to the Whig Natl. Convention. He was elected mayor of Cleveland for 1 term in 1847. Joined by partners A. W. Fairbanks in 1849 and GEO. A. BENEDICT in 1853, Harris began loosening his ties with the *Herald*. Benedict took over as editor in 1857, when Harris moved over to Edwin Cowles's *Leader*, which he edited from Feb. 1857-Nov. 1860. Although Harris briefly returned thereafter to the *Herald*, he quit journalism permanently after the CIVIL WAR. His retirement was spent on a small farm in ROCKY RIVER, where he raised grapes, which frequently took prizes at regional and state fairs. After suffering a series of strokes over a period of 2 years, Harris died at the Franklin Ave. home of his daughter, Mrs. F. X. Byerly, on 21 Aug. 1876. He was also survived by 2 sons, Byron C. and Brougham F. Harris.

The **HARRIS CALORIFIC COMPANY** is the oldest leading producer of gas welding and cutting apparatus in the U.S. A pioneer in the field, it manufactured the nation's first flame-cutting torch. Its founder, John Harris, accidentally discovered the oxyacetylene (oxygen flame) method of cutting and welding tools in 1899. In 1904, he exhibited his cutting torch at the St. Louis World's Fair, and the following year, he started the company in a small shop on the west side with a few workers. Harris continued to refine its gas torches and began to produce related accessories, such as gas pressure regulators. The U.S. Welding Co. of Minnesota purchased Harris in 1926, and U.S. Welding's founder, Lorne Campbell, Jr., became its president, serving until the 1950s. After WORLD WAR II, Harris found important new markets in research laboratories and aircraft and missile applications. For years, the company had been content to remain a small but quality manufacturer with its business primarily in the Northeast. Under Clarence Taylor, Harris flourished in the late 1950s and early 1960s at its new plant on Cass Ave. Taylor launched a program to widen the company's distribution organization in the West, pushed development work on new equipment, and intensified the advertising program. The firm also broadened its foreign business. For several years, Harris had maintained distributorships in South America and South Africa. Taylor established subsidiaries and distributorships in Mexico, Italy, Australia, the United Kingdom, India, and New Zealand. By 1960, 20% of its sales were from abroad. Between 1957-63, Harris's annual sales quadrupled to over $4 million, and employment increased to 150 people. By 1963, the company was able to begin a major diversification program into the area of anesthesia equipment for medical purposes. Harris Calorific continued to grow throughout the 1960s, with about 230 employees by 1970. In 1973, the Emerson Electric Co. of St. Louis, manufacturer of a a wide range of electrical and electronic products, acquired Harris as a subsidiary. The purchase was the beginning of Emerson's international diversification program. Emerson experienced great growth in the late 1970s, and Harris benefited from it, expanding its domestic and European facilities and markets, and building an assembly plant in Geor-

gia. By 1983, the firm was also considering moving its Cleveland manufacturing operations to Georgia, leaving only the sales office in this city.

The **HARRIS CORPORATION,** founded in Cleveland in 1895 as the Harris Automatic Press Co., is a worldwide leader in the information-processing industry. It was an early leader in printing-press technology, and its growth by acquisition of complementary enterprises pulled it toward electronic communications and away from its Cleveland base. In 1926, Harris Automatic Press merged with the Seybold Machine Co. and the Premier Potter Premium Press Co. of Derby, Conn., and incorporated in Delaware as the Harris-Seybold-Potter Co. It became Harris-Seybold in 1946 and the Harris Intertype Corp. in 1957, after its merger with the Intertype Corp. The company adopted its present title, the Harris Corp., in 1974.

In its first 50 years, Harris was a growing manufacturer of commercial printing presses and a pioneer in printing, especially offset lithography. In 1951, it introduced the 5-color sheet-fed press, an evolutionary successor to its 1-color press (1906) and more recent 4-color press (1931). Its "flying printing press," developed for the Army in 1951, a relatively light (8,000 lbs.), portable unit for on-site development of multicolor maps, aerial charts, and reconnaissance photos, showed the potential of compact, professional-quality printing equipment. From 1947 on, the directions of the corporation were shaped by Geo. S. Dively, who articulated, in a series of 5-year plans, the strategy of Harris management and corporate acquisition. Harris not only would seek expansion in the growing graphic-arts market, which tends to double every 12-15 years, but also would seek diversification through the purchase of heavy or light industry subdivisions that might benefit from its management skill. Though Harris acquisitions strengthened the corporate foothold in printing and the expanding copy-machine field, purchases of such firms as Autronics Research (1956) and Gates Radio (1957) further involved the company in the electronics field and in defense work.

The 1967 merger of Harris with Radiation, Inc., a manufacturer of electronic communications products, increased Harris's involvement in nonprofit communications and gave it the electronic control technology to refine its own typesetting equipment. By 1970, electronics provided 50% of the company's $380 million sales, and Harris opened a new plant in Melbourne, Fla., to triple its capacity for manufacturing integrated circuits. The increasing concentration of Harris employees in Florida (and other Sunbelt locations) encouraged the company to move its headquarters to Melbourne in 1978. In 1982, Harris set its Printing Equipment Sector afloat. The Harris Graphics Corp. incorporated in Dec. 1982. The new company, which designs, manufactures, and markets printing equipment, is also based in Melbourne, Fla. The firm's Cleveland plant at 4510 E. 71st St. makes parts for a line of sheet-fed presses that was discontinued in 1975. Since the plant was operating at less than $\frac{1}{3}$ capacity, its closure was imminent in 1985. The Harris Corp., meanwhile, has continued its immersion in electronic communications with the purchase of Lanier Business Systems in 1983 and the installed rental base of Exxon Office Systems in 1985.

**HARRISON, MARVIN CLINTON** (13 July 1890-29 Aug. 1954), was a Cleveland attorney who offered his counsel to numerous labor-management and intraunion disputes in Cleveland. He was also active in politics and reform legislation. Harrison spent his childhood in Scribner, Nebr. After graduating from Harvard Law School in 1915, he worked for a Boston law firm. At that time Harrison considered himself a socialist and was in favor of many progressive issues, including women's suffrage. However, his socialist views changed during WORLD WAR I. In Sept. 1916, Harrison moved to Cleveland, where he worked briefly for Payer, Winch & Rogers, a firm that specialized in accident litigation. He soon left this firm and went into partnership with Geo. Seith as a corporate attorney for the General Insurance Co. During the war, Harrison served a brief term in the Naval Reserve, 1917–18. After the war he returned to Cleveland and resumed his private practice.

Harrison's partnership with Homer Marshman began in 1934 and ended in 1947, when he joined another firm, Harrison, Thomas, Spangenberg & Hull. The firm dealt primarily with accident litigation; however, Harrison involved himself in numerous cases involving labor unions and industrial accidents. He became involved in the LITTLE STEEL STRIKE OF 1937 when he helped win settlements for strike victims who had been harmed by the Republic Steel Corp.'s attacks on strikers. Harrison and Marshman spent 4 years gathering evidence as they sought to prove that Republic Steel had tried to break the strike through violent confrontations in hope of creating antiunion sentiments that would lead to a back-to-work movement. The case came to trial in 1941; and on the basis of the trial, Republic Steel settled claims against it from the Cleveland, Chicago, and Massillon areas. Harrison was also involved in labor-management disputes at Thompson Prods. and Hercules Motors of Cleveland, and in intraunion disputes in the Brotherhood of Railroad Trainmen and the United Furniture Workers Local #450. In 1944 he helped win settlements for victims of the EAST OHIO GAS EXPLOSION. He was also involved in cases arising out of the Fair Labor Standards Act and its amendment, the Portal-to-Portal Act of 1947.

During the 1930s, Harrison became active in politics and reform legislation. In 1931 he drafted an unemployment-compensation bill for the Ohio legislature. He was an Ohio state senator from 1933–34 and played a large role in the ratification of the Natl. Child Labor Amendment and the passage of the Ohio minimum-wage law. During the Depression, Harrison supported the New Deal and participated in a Senate investigation of defaulted banks in Cleveland. In 1936 he chaired Roosevelt's Cuyahoga County campaign. He ran unsuccessfully for the U.S. Senate in 1944 and 1946 in the Democratic primaries. His career was characterized by an interest in civil rights. He was a member of the NAACP, the Natl. Consumers League, and the Natl. Committee of the American Civil Liberties Union and was president of the CONSUMERS LEAGUE OF OHIO between 1934–54.

Consumers League of Ohio Records, WRHS.
Marvin Clinton Harrison Papers, WRHS.

The **HARRY K. AND EMMA ROSENFELD FOX CHARITABLE FOUNDATION** was founded in 1959 by Emma Fox (d. 1961). Harry and Emma Fox were owners of the Grabler Mfg. Co. The original funds for the foundation came from the proceeds of Emma Fox's family inheritance. Grants are given primarily in northeast Ohio for the general purposes of supporting hospitals, education, cultural programs, youth agencies, and human services. Major recipients of Fox grants have been Hiram College and, at Western Reserve University, the Medical School, the History Dept., the Nursing School, and the School for the Applied Social Sciences. Grants have also gone to smaller projects and fledgling organizations aimed at social problems and arts support, rather than larger institutions. No grants are given to individuals or for endowment funds, matching

gifts, or loans. In 1983, assets of the foundation were $3.25 million, of which $201,000 was disbursed in 62 grants. In the 1980s, the foundation preferred to fund more projects at smaller amounts than fewer large organizations. Officers of the foundation included Harold E. Friedman, Mrs. Marjorie S. Schwied, and George Rosenfeld.

The **HARSHAW CHEMICAL COMPANY,** established in 1892 to deal in chemicals, oils, and dry colors, had become by 1982 a diversified industrial chemical producer employing nearly 1,700 people in northern Ohio. Harshaw Chemical was founded by Wm. A. Harshaw as the Cleveland Commercial Co., located at first in a rented office on S. Water St. (Columbus Rd.). He gradually took on RALPH L. FULLER and Wallace B. Goodwin as partners. In the mid-1890s, the company bought interests in several manufacturing firms, and in 1897 it formed the C. H. Price Co. to take over one of these, a small linseed-oil mill in Elyria. In 1898, Cleveland Commercial and C. H. Price were merged to form the Harshaw, Fuller & Goodwin Co., with glycerine-refining and electroplating operations in Elyria and headquarters in Cleveland. Wm. A. Harshaw served as president of the company until retiring in 1936; his son, Wm. J. Harshaw, served as president from 1936–56. During the early 1900s, the company concentrated on expanding its manufacturing operations. In 1905 it bought land in Cleveland's industrial valley for a new plant (its Harvard-Denison plant, 1000 Harvard Rd.), and in 1913 it built a glycerine refinery in Philadelphia. Business grew during the 1910s as WORLD WAR I increased the demand for the firm's products; in the 1920s, the firm improved and enlarged existing facilities and expanded its manufacturing operations into New Jersey.

After outgrowing several locations in Cleveland, the company bought the old Hathaway Brown School building at 1945 E. 97th St. in 1929 and moved its headquarters there in the spring of 1930. It also shortened its name to the Harshaw Chemical Co. in 1929. Sales fell more than a third in the early 1930s. During this time, however, the company's new research department developed several processes and substances important to the company's later success. The process it developed for the bright plating of nickel required no buffing and was a boon to the auto industry. By 1945, Harshaw's annual sales had increased to $23.9 million, income was $313,265, and the firm employed 1,461 people. WORLD WAR II had increased the demand for Harshaw products, and the company, unknowingly at the time, contributed to the development of the atomic bomb by producing uranium chemicals for government scientists. Production of these chemicals at the Harvard-Denison plant left behind low levels of radiation that were still detectable in the mid-1970s. The company continued to grow after the war; it expanded by acquiring other companies and by forming subsidiaries in France (1954) and Germany (1962). Sales were $60.8 million in 1955, with income of $2.5 million and 1,683 employees. During the 1960s, it contributed to the space program and to the military technology used in the VIETNAM WAR.

In 1966, Harshaw merged with the Kewanee Oil Co. of Bryn Mawr, Pa., in order to avoid a stock takeover by the Sun Chemical Corp. of New York. Although Harshaw continued to grow, the late 1960s and early 1970s were a difficult period; environmentalists charged that the firm was polluting the CUYAHOGA RIVER, and the company was hit by long strikes by its employees. After a decline in 1975, sales rose to $184 million in 1976, and earnings to $10 million. In 1977, the Gulf Oil Corp. acquired Harshaw's parent company, Kewanee Industries, Inc.; Gulf was primarily interested in Kewanee's oil reserves, and by 1982 it wanted to sell Harshaw. In 1983, Gulf and the Kaiser Aluminum & Chemical Corp. began a joint venture by combining their chemical units into the Harshaw/Filtrol Partnership, which brought operations of Harshaw together with those of Kaiser's California-based Filtrol Corp. to produce specialty chemicals under Filtrol management. In June 1984, Harshaw announced that it had sold its building on E. 97th St. and was moving its headquarters to the Corporate Circle Complex on Chagrin Blvd. in PEPPER PIKE.

Harshaw Chemical Co., *Tested by Time* (1956).

**HART, ALBERT GAILORD** (17 Aug. 1821–10 Oct. 1907), was a local Cleveland physician and Civil War Army surgeon. Hart was born in Hartford, Ohio (Trumbull County). He attended school in Hudson, Ohio, beginning in 1834, and graduated from Western Reserve College on 16 Aug. 1840 with a bachelor's degree. Between 1841–43, Hart studied medicine in Mercer County, Pa., and attended lectures at the University of Pennsylvania. In 1844, he received his master's degree from Western Reserve College, and on 6 June he married Mary Crosley Hornell in White Lake, Mich. From 1844–52, he practiced medicine in Middlesex, Pa. Hart received his medical degree from Jefferson Medical College in Philadelphia, Pa., in 1852. Between 1852–60, he established a medical practice in Clarksville (Mercer County), Pa. In 1860 he moved to Hartford, Ohio, and he invested in the oil business, 1860–61, in Mecca, Ohio. When the CIVIL WAR broke out, Hart was appointed assistant surgeon, 41ST OHIO VOLUNTEER INFANTRY, on 5 Sept. 1861. He spent 2 periods of time at home on sick leave (28 Mar.–27 Apr. 1862; 30 Mar.–19 Apr. 1863). On 19 Jan. 1864, Hart returned to Ohio, accompanying Col. AQUILA WILEY of the 41st Regiment to Cleveland. The 41st spent most of Feb. 1864 on veteran furlough in northern Ohio. Hart apparently returned to the field with his regiment, then resigned on 5 or 9 Nov. 1864.

Hart had moved his family to Brooklyn Twp. in 1864. He settled in University Hts. on Scranton Ave. near Starkweather. That apparently allowed him to live with his family while serving on the medical staff at the U.S. GENERAL HOSPITAL in University Hts., which later became known as Lincoln Hts. and the south end. He became a member of the Medical Society of Cleveland in 1870 (later known as the Cleveland Academy of Medicine), served on the Cleveland Board of Education, 1871–73, and was a member of the CLEVELAND BOARD OF HEALTH in 1880. Hart was a member of the Grand Army of the Republic Post 546 in 1889, and a member of the Military Order of the Loyal Legion of the U.S., dating from 1892. The elder of his 2 sons, Hastings Cornell Hart (b. 1851), became a well-known penologist, and a younger son, Albert Bushnell Hart (1854–1943), became a leading historian. He also had 2 daughters, Helen Marcia (1846–1886) and Mary Jeanette (1856–1875). Hart is buried in WOODLAND CEMETERY.

Albert Gailord Hart Papers, WRHS.

**HARTMAN, CHARLES A.** (1827–2 May 1863), was an Army surgeon in the CIVIL WAR. Hartman served as Cuyahoga County coroner prior to his entrance into the Army as surgeon of the 107TH OHIO VOLUNTEER INFANTRY on 26 Aug. 1862. The 107th was organized and given preliminary training at Camp Cleveland, Aug.-Sept. 1862. A physician in civilian life, Hartman was listed as killed at the Battle of Chancellorsville, Va., on 2 May 1863. He was listed as being buried at Fredericksburg but is not in the register of burials at Fredericksburg Natl. Cemetery. Hart-

man is remembered in Cleveland by a large medallion of his bust in the SOLDIERS & SAILORS MONUMENT.

**HARTZ, AUGUSTUS "GUS" FREDERIC** (8 Sept. 1843–22 May 1929), was one of the best-known theatrical figures in Cleveland's history. Born in Liverpool, England, Hartz was apprenticed to a stage magician at the age of 8 and studied with a tutor in the evenings. Arriving in the U.S. in 1863, he pursued a stage career until 1880, when he settled in Cleveland. He was manager of the Park Theater, which opened in Cleveland on 22 Oct. 1883 with a comedy, *The School for Scandal*. This playhouse was part of the 3-story Wick Block, erected in 1883 on PUBLIC SQUARE by the Wick family as the home of the private banking house of Henry Wick & Co. In 1884, the Park Theater was destroyed by fire; it was not reopened until 6 Sept. 1886. But during the period of restoration, Hartz decided to join the EUCLID AVE. OPERA HOUSE. He was both lessee and manager of the opera house from 1 June 1884 until 1 June 1920, when the lease expired. The Euclid Ave. Opera House also succumbed to flames, on 24 Oct. 1892, and when it reopened on 11 Sept. 1893 with a production of *Beau Brummel*, Hartz was still present as manager, giving Cleveland audiences the best stars and performances for many years. Under the management skill of Hartz, the Euclid Ave. Opera House reigned as Cleveland's favorite playhouse for many years, until it was displaced by the HANNA THEATER, the new "legitimate" favorite. In addition to his extensive theater skills and interests, Hartz displayed talents in the business field as president of the Majestic Oil Co. and the Trenton Rock Oil & Gas Co. Hartz married in Rhode Island on 24 Feb. 1894 and was survived by his wife and 2 children.

The **HARVARD CLUB** (1930–41), an illegal gambling casino located at various addresses (at least 6, including 3111, 3201, 4200, and 4209) on Harvard Ave., near E. 42nd St., NEWBURGH HTS., was one of the largest gambling operations between New York and Chicago, accommodating 500–1,000 gamblers a night, who came from all over the country to play the crap games, the slot machines, roulette, and all-night poker. Originally run by Wm. Fergus, who was forced to flee, and later owned by Frank Joiner, who was killed gangland style, it was eventually owned and operated (3111 Harvard Ave.) in 1933 by Jas. "Shimmy" Patton, Arthur Hebebrand, and Daniel T. Gallagher. A celebrated raid, initiated by County Prosecutor Jas. T. Cullitan and led by Safety Director ELIOT NESS, with a group of volunteer off-duty policemen, closed the club on the night of 10 Jan. 1936. It reopened at 4209 Harvard Ave. on 15 Feb. 1936 with expanded gambling operations, including a fleet of limousines for free customer pickup from downtown Cleveland. The club continued despite repeated scandals, many threatened lawsuits, police raids, grand jury investigations, ownership changes, and a succession of different locations until 1941, when Common Pleas Judge Frank J. Lausche ordered it closed. It defied the order. Finally Judge Lausche constituted Detective Capt. Michael Blackwell, an officer of the court, to close the club, and in Apr. 1941 it was closed by Blackwell and his squad of Cleveland police.

**HASKELL, COBURN** (1868–14 Dec. 1922), a prominent Cleveland businessman and sportsman, was widely known as the inventor of the modern golf ball. Haskell came to Cleveland from Boston in 1892 as the result of a friendship between his father and MARCUS A. HANNA. In Cleveland, Haskell became closely associated with the Hanna family; he worked for the M. A. HANNA CO. and married Gertrude Hanna, the daughter of Howard Melville Hanna.

An avid golfer, Haskell patented a ball with a rubber-wound core on 11 Apr. 1899. In 1901, he retired from M. A. Hanna to organize the Haskell Golf Ball Co. The "Haskell golf ball" replaced the universally used gutta-percha ball and revolutionized the manufacture of golf balls. Because of its greater distance, the Haskell ball reduced scores and helped considerably to increase the popularity of golf. Haskell Golf Ball was dissolved in 1917, selling its patents to other companies, including the A. G. Spalding Co. In addition to his interest in sports, Haskell was also known as a lover of music, art, and books. He owned many first editions of the early illustrators, and he belonged to the ROWFANT CLUB, the Groiler Club of New York, and the Bibliophile Society of Boston.

The **HASKELL FUND** was established in 1955 by Melville H. Haskell (1901-1984), Coburn HASKELL, and Melville H. Haskell, Jr. Melville H. Haskell was the oldest son of the late Coburn and Mary Gertrude Hanna Haskell. Presently, the fund is administered by the Haskells' oldest son, Coburn Haskell. Annually, 30 to 35 grants are made in the range of $1,000-$6,000 each, the prominent exception being the University of Arizona, which represents about 13% of the fund's giving. Most grants are for community, medical, and educational purposes. The fund does not give grants to individuals. In 1985, assets of the Haskell Fund were $1,618,276, with expenditures of $110,700 to 38 charities. Officers included Coburn Haskell, Schuyler A. Haskell, Betty J. Tuite, and Donald C. Cook.

**HATHAWAY BROWN** was, in 1986, the oldest surviving private girls' school in the Cleveland area. The school was founded in 1876 as an adjunct to the BROOKS MILITARY SCHOOL, the foremost private school for boys at the time. Its original name was the Brooks School for Ladies. The early years were tenuous. The school was proprietary in nature and had several owners, including Miss Anne Hathaway Brown. Brown's stay was relatively short, as she sold the school after 4 years (in 1890) and moved to New Jersey. She had left her mark, however, securing for the school not only its permanent name but also a reputation for excellence in the education of young women. Brown was succeeded as both owner and principal by Miss Mary E. Spencer, who remained in control for 12 years (1890-1902). The school continued to prosper under the direction of other capable and dedicated headmistresses, especially Miss Mary Elizabeth Raymond (1912-38) and Miss Ann Cutter Coburn (1938-68).

The school's early mission was twofold: to prepare upper-class women for a career in society and to equip them with well-trained minds. These two goals were seen not as mutually exclusive but as interdependent. The early curriculum included Latin, grammar, Greek, English, Bible study, elocution, and calisthenics. The course of study was revised often and at various times included mathematics, music, cooking, woodcarving, and science. Grades kindergarten through 12 were offered. The school was housed in several different places in its early years. The most prominent of its early buildings was erected in 1905 on Logan (E. 97th) St. through a substantial gift by FLORA STONE MATHER. In 1927 the school moved to its present (1986) location at 19600 N. Park Blvd. in SHAKER HTS. The move was made at the behest of the VAN SWERINGEN brothers, who hoped that Hathaway Brown and other private schools would help attract the upper class to their new community. Throughout its history, Hathaway Brown has educated the daughters of some of Cleveland's most well-known families. In the 1980s, the school emphasizes college preparation and academic foundations rather than the

"agreeable manners and fine conversational powers" that were thought to be so important to one of the school's early headmistresses. It has developed a national reputation for its academic program. In 1963, *Harper's* magazine called it "one of the best schools in the country." In 1985 it was awarded a prestigious national award called "Excellence in English."

Needham, Ruth Crofut, and Hudson, Ruth Strong, *The First Hundred Years: Hathaway Brown School* (1977).

**HAUSER, ELIZABETH** (b. 15 Mar. 1873), an able leader in an era when few women had developed such skills, spearheaded countywide efforts to gain statewide and national suffrage. This movement led to the founding of the LEAGUE OF WOMEN VOTERS. A native of Girard, Ohio, Hauser brought to Cleveland over a decade of experience as a writer for the *Warren Tribune Chronicle* and other papers. Her editorial and publishing skills won her a job as secretary to TOM L. JOHNSON, and as the editor of his autobiography, *My Story*. Hauser arrived in Cleveland in 1910 to organize Cuyahoga County women to win suffrage through constitutional change at the upcoming Constitutional Convention. As director of the Cuyahoga County Women's Suffrage Assoc., she rented an office in the Old ARCADE and issued an open invitation to all Cleveland women to attend a meeting at the old Hollenden Hotel. With the aid of Zara DuPont, MYRTA JONES, and others, Hauser arranged a picnic at Cedar Pt. that drew small crowds of women who were interested in but reluctant to openly embrace the suffrage cause. Hauser found women willing to buy discreet badges, but many shied from waving "Votes for Women" flags. To increase the acceptability of supporting the suffrage cause, Hauser and her colleagues wooed socially prominent women to attend lectures and luncheons, and to allow their names to be used in conjunction with suffrage activities. The feminists built a growing core of workers to canvass neighborhoods for signatures to be presented to the 1912 Constitutional Convention; the 15,000 signatures collected won over a majority of Cuyahoga County delegates. Hauser and Mrs. Myron Vorce accompanied Harriet Taylor Upton, president of the Ohio Women's Suffrage Assoc., to the state capital, where the convention voted 76-34 in favor of submitting Amendment 23 for women's suffrage to a special election on 3 Sept. 1912.

In the 6 months before the election, the group sought broader support for the cause. Adding such innovative techniques as soapbox oratory, motor trips through the neighborhoods, and stops at factory gates to the more familiar rallies and parades, the suffragettes proclaimed their cause to all who would listen. When the Cuyahoga County Women's Assoc. became the Cuyahoga County Women's Suffrage party, the suffragists acquired a new organizational framework of wards and precincts, similar to that of the regular political parties. Hauser and organizers such as DuPont built a strong grassroots base of support that brought out the vote in the 1912 election. Though Amendment 23 lost because of sabotage by the whiskey lobby, the machinery was in place for further campaigns. In the years before 1919-20, when women's suffrage became law in Ohio and in the land, Elizabeth Hauser battled antisuffragists, financial difficulties, and uninformed attitudes by orchestrating a whirlwind of lectures, debates, bake sales, rallies, whistlestops, suffrage suppers, and pageants. With the passage of suffrage amendments, the work of Hauser's Women's Suffrage party was complete. To continue the important work of political education for women, the League of Women Voters was organized in Apr. 1920 and led by former suffrage leaders. BELLE SHERWIN was elected the first president, while Hauser became a national officer (director of the 4th Region, which included Ohio). Hauser went on to become the first chair of the Committee for Internatl. Cooperation to prevent war and a vice-president in charge of a department for efficiency in government. Hauser remained active in the league throughout her life and was among the leaders who reminisced about early struggles at the 25th anniversary of the league in 1945.

Abbott, Virgina Clark, *The History of Woman Suffrage and the League of Women Voters in Cuyahoga County, 1911-1945* (1949).

**HAUSERMAN, INC.,** a leader of the office-interiors industry, is the world's first and largest producer of movable interior walls. The company's founder, Earl F. Hauserman, was the secretary of the Hunt, Quiesser, Bliss Co., a dealer in building supplies, when on 24 Mar. 1913 he bought out a portion of that company and organized the E. F. Hauserman Co. to produce steel sashes. Hauserman's policy of erecting complete sashes provided for an initial boom in sales. During WORLD WAR I, the firm began to develop steel partitions, and by 1927 it became the exclusive manufacturer of movable steel partitions. That same year, a fire almost leveled its 9-year-old plant on Grant Ave. in CUYAHOGA HTS. Although Hauserman suspended much of its production of steel partitions during WORLD WAR II, its past experience led to the development of "Master Walls," prefabricated steel houses, and aircraft parts built for the government. Earl F. Hauserman's sons, Fred M. and Wm. F., guided the company into a postwar period of great expansion. Fred Hauserman returned to the production of movable steel walls and increased the number of customers by organizing a network of direct sales offices. By 1956, Hauserman was conducting $45 million worth of business per year. The company built a new Cleveland plant in 1958 in Cuyahoga Hts., acquired a steel ceiling firm the following year, and by the early 1960s began to introduce its products in Canada and Europe through subsidiaries. In 1969, the company entered new, growing markets when it acquired the Educator Mfg. Co. and the Gotham Education Equipment Co., manufacturers of furniture and wall systems for schools and offices. Hauserman then became involved in office-system design programs, producing all types of wood and metal office furniture. To keep pace with this growth, the company was reorganized as Hauserman, Inc., in 1972, with the E. F. Hauserman Co. becoming the U.S. subsidiary. In 1978, Wm. Hauserman strengthened the company's position by acquiring Sunar, a Canadian manufacturer of office furniture and interior designs. This move increased sales, which by 1982 reached a record level of $135.7 million. In 1983, Hauserman, Inc., merged its 2 North American subsidiaries into Sunar Hauserman, Inc., an even stronger interior-furnishing firm with 8 plants and over 60 sales offices.

**HAWKEN SCHOOL** was the last of Cleveland's prominent independent schools (the others were UNIVERSITY SCHOOL, LAUREL, and HATHAWAY BROWN) to be founded. It was founded in 1915 by Jas. Hawken. He was able to convince the Boltons, Prescotts, Hannas, Perkinses, and other prominent Clevelanders that schools were paying too much attention to academic training and not enough to good citizenship, physical well-being, character development, and spiritual growth. It was in this context that Hawken School opened on Ansel Rd. in Cleveland as an all-boys' elementary school with 19 students and 3 teachers. The school strongly reflected Hawken's ideas about education. He believed that it was more important "for a boy of 14 to have a vigorous and active body, mind, and conscience than pass a college entrance exam or make his class in a fashionable preparatory school." Values such as initiative, truthfulness, courage, and sincerity were emphasized. This kind of training would produce "vigorous, sturdy, well-balanced leaders of vision and ability." Boys were given a value of life based on the concept of man as a spiritual being. The school's emphasis was Christian, but nondenominational. Hawken's distinguishing pedagogical method was small class size (8–10 students), which would allow for the "intimate teaching of the individual boy." Not only grades were given, but also written reports assessing the boys in terms of their own individuality.

Over the years, Hawken has reaffirmed its commitment to its early goals while at the same time undergoing a series of changes. By the 1920s, class size, though still relatively small, increased to 10–15 students. As the school grew, new quarters were needed, and in 1922 Hawken moved to a site on Clubside Rd. in S. EUCLID donated by Mr. and Mrs. CHESTER BOLTON. At that time, the school experimented with a high school, but the expansion was not permanent and was discontinued in 1932. Hawken clarified its mission to providing rigorous preparation for other Cleveland secondary schools, as well as eastern boarding schools. In 1960, land in Chesterland was donated to the school by the Walter C. White family, and an upper school was permanently added in the fall of 1961. In the 1970s, Hawken became Cleveland's first and only coeducational independent school. In 1974, the upper school accepted girls at all grades. The lower school (grades kindergarten–8) adopted a grade-by-grade transition so that in 1981, coeducation was complete. Hawken in the 1980s was a strong coeducational school emphasizing college preparation for its students while still endeavoring to recognize and develop individual talents and creative abilities.

**HAY, JOHN MILTON** (8 Oct. 1838–1 July 1905), was a diplomat, statesman, U.S. secretary of state, historian, author, and poet. Hay was born in Salem, Ind., the son of Dr. Chas. and Helen Leonard Hay. He was educated in Warsaw, Ill.; at the Academy of Pittsfield, Pike County, Ill.; and at the state college at Springfield, Ill., and graduated from Brown University, Providence, R.I., in 1858. After graduation, he studied law with his uncle, Milton Hay, whose offices adjoined those of Abraham Lincoln. Hay was admitted to the bar in 1861 and, after Lincoln's election, accompanied him to Washington, where he served as the president's private secretary. He was subsequently given the rank of colonel and assigned to the White House officially as a military aide. He served with Lincoln until the president's assassination. Secretary of State Wm. H. Seward launched Hay on his diplomatic career, appointing him secretary to the legations in Paris (1865–67), Vienna (1867–68), and Madrid (1869–70). Hay returned to the U.S. in 1870, where he served as an editorial writer for the *New York Tribune*. In 1874, he married Clara Louise Stone, daughter of AMASA STONE. Hay moved to Cleveland in 1875, remaining in the city until 1886. While in Cleveland he worked for his father-in-law and served on various civic and cultural boards, including the board of trustees of Western Reserve University (see CASE WESTERN RESERVE UNIVERSITY). Hay was a local celebrity, noted for his fine manners and an ability to deliver witty speeches. He, however, became bored with Cleveland society, expressing his views in *The Bread Winners*, a volume that he authored anonymously. After leaving Cleveland, Hay and his family moved to Washington, where he continued his literary and political career. In 1890 he and his lifelong friend John Nicolay authored the notable 10-volume work

493

*Abraham Lincoln: A History.* In 1896 Hay campaigned for Wm. McKinley, and in 1897 he was rewarded with the appointment of ambassador to Great Britain. Appointed secretary of state in 1898, Hay participated in events attendant upon the Spanish-American War, enunciated the "Open Door" policy concerning relations with China, and, during the term of Theodore Roosevelt, was instrumental in treaty negotiations that paved the way for the construction of the Panama Canal. Hay died in Newbury, N.H., but was buried in Cleveland at LAKE VIEW CEMETERY.

Dennett, Tyler, *John Hay* (1933).
John Hay Papers, Illinois Historical Society, Springfield, Ill.

**HAYDN, HIRAM COLLINS** (11 Dec. 1831–31 July 1913), was a distinguished Cleveland clergyman, long-time pastor of FIRST PRESBYTERIAN CHURCH (OLD STONE), and a president of Western Reserve University. Born in Pompey, N.Y., of farming parents, Haydn was educated at a local academy, graduated from Amherst College in 1856, and received a D.D. from Union Theological Seminary in 1859. He served pastorates in Connecticut before coming to Ohio in 1866 as pastor of the First Congregational Church of Painesville. Haydn was called to be associate pastor of Old Stone Church in 1871 and soon after succeeded Rev. Wm. Henry Goodrich as senior pastor. He remained in that position until 1880, when he became secretary of the Congregational Mission Board in New York. He returned to Cleveland in 1884 to resume his pastorate at Old Stone and to serve for 2 years as president of WRU. As president he was instrumental in founding the College for Women, with the assistance and support of FLORA STONE MATHER, an influential member of the Old Stone congregation and benefactor of the university. Mrs. Mather gave the university the building that carried Haydn's name. As pastor of Old Stone, Haydn was an active and highly visible leader in the community. He was involved in the founding of Goodrich House (see GOODRICH-GANNETT NEIGH. CTR.), a settlement house sponsored by the church; the PRESBYTERIAN UNION, of which he served as president from 1907 until his death; and many Cleveland-area Presbyterian churches initially sponsored by Old Stone. His second Old Stone pastorate lasted until 1902, when he became pastor emeritus. Haydn was married twice, to Elizabeth Coit in 1851 and, following her death, to Sarah Merriman in 1864.

**HAYES, MAX S. (MAXIMILIAN SEBASTIAN)** (25 May 1866–11 Oct. 1945), was a Cleveland printer who became a lifelong social activist and spokesman for LABOR. He gained national repute as editor of the *CLEVELAND CITIZEN* and as a leader for 3 decades of the socialist opposition to the Samuel Gompers administration within the American Fed. of Labor. Hayes was born on a farm in Huron County and educated in the common schools of Havana and Fremont, Ohio, until the age of 13, when he started working in the printing trade. He completed his apprenticeship in Cleveland and was initiated as a journeyman in TYPOGRAPHICAL WORKERS UNION NO. 53 in 1884. He served the local as organizer, president, and delegate to the Central Labor Union, to conventions of the Internatl. Typographical Union, and to state printers' and AFL bodies. He was an organizer for the ITU for 15 years, helped found many printers' local unions in Ohio, and was repeatedly elected to represent the ITU at national conventions of the AFL.

On 31 Jan. 1891, Hayes helped launch the *Cleveland Citizen* to serve the local labor movement. For almost 50 years, he combined editing the paper with his energetic

labor and political activities. He was the People's party (Populist) candidate for CLEVELAND CITY COUNCIL in the spring and for state senate in the fall of 1893. By 1896, he was a leading activist in the local Socialist Labor party and secretary of the Central Labor Union. Two years later he was elected CLU delegate to the national convention of the AFL for the first time. That was the beginning of his long battle with Sam Gompers over implementation of demands for union democracy, organization of the unorganized, solidarity, and, especially, independent political action by labor. He received ⅓ of the vote for president when he ran against Gompers at the 1912 convention.

In 1900, Hayes was nominated for vice-president of the U.S. by a Socialist Labor party convention but withdrew in the interest of a merger with the Social Democrats headed by Eugene V. Debs to form the Socialist Party of America. He campaigned as a Socialist candidate for Congress in 1900, for Ohio secretary of state in 1902, and, for the last time, as Farmer-Labor party candidate for vice-president in 1920. Hayes was a fraternal delegate of the AFL at the 1903 British Trade Union Congress in Leicester, England. He participated in congress sessions by day and addressed Labour party, trade union, and socialist meetings at night. As labor's advocate in local and state reform movements, Hayes helped found the CONSUMERS LEAGUE OF OHIO in 1900 and the Anti-Tuberculosis League in 1904, participated in drafting the Ohio Workmen's Compensation Law of 1911, and was appointed to the Cleveland Metropolitan Housing Authority in 1933 and to the Ohio State Adjustment Board of the Natl. Recovery Admin. in 1934.

Despite his differences with national AFL policies, Hayes argued that the correct course for socialists and militants was to fight from within rather than divide their forces in dual organizations. For that reason he opposed the Socialist Trades & Labor Alliance of the SOCIALIST LABOR PARTY in the 1890s, the INDUSTRIAL WORKERS OF THE WORLD in 1905, and the CIO split in the 1930s. Hayes was married to Dora Schneider on 11 Dec. 1900. They had 1 child, Maxine Elizabeth, who married A. I. Davey, Jr., in 1931. Davey became editor of the *Citizen* when Max was incapacitated by a stroke in Oct. 1939. Max, Dora, and Maxine are buried in LAKE VIEW CEMETERY. In recognition of Hayes's role as a builder of the local union movement, Max Hayes Vocational High School was named after him in 1957 on the recommendation of the Cleveland Fed. of Labor.

Max S. Hayes Papers, Ohio Historical Society.

The **HAYMARKET** was an area of downtown Cleveland that lay to the south and west of PUBLIC SQUARE near the east end of the HOPE MEMORIAL (Lorain-Carnegie) BRIDGE; it began as a marketplace, evolved into a residential, business, and commercial district, and degenerated into the city's first slum. Covering about 4 acres, the Haymarket district was bounded on the north by Race Ave. SE, on the south by Harrison St. and the CENTRAL VIADUCT, on the east by Ontario St., and on the west by the CUYAHOGA RIVER. It developed after 1839, when a small wooden building was constructed as the first municipal marketplace at the corner of Michigan and Ontario. Before sunrise on Tuesday, Thursday, and Saturday, farmers would drive their wagons to stables on Central Ave. and Race Ct. and sell produce and hay while their horses sampled the hay. By 1856, city council voted to build a new market at Pittsburgh (Broadway) and Bolivar, but the area remained a feed station for horses. Early in its history, the Haymarket was surrounded by fine homes, but owing to the influx of thirsty and tired farmers, canal men, and lake seamen, it was also dotted with saloons--30 on Commercial St. alone—and lodging houses. After the CIVIL WAR, cheap housing made the Haymarket attractive to impoverished immigrants. Though ITALIANS and Slavs predominated in 1870, later contemporary observers counted 40 nationalities and 14 languages. For some, the Haymarket was a stopping place; for others, enmeshed in the cycle of poverty, its deteriorating housing provided permanent residence. The area and nearby Whiskey Hill became an overcrowded refuge for the unemployed, derelicts, transients, and criminals who preyed on the other hapless residents. Nearby factories and passing trains polluted the area with dirty smoke.

At a time when 2 quarts of beer cost $.05 and neighborhood people sat on the curb drinking it from pails, the Haymarket became a focal point for temperance activities by the newly formed Women's Christian Temperance Union and the YOUNG WOMEN'S CHRISTIAN ASSOC., both of which tried to divert immigrants from the lure of drink. In 1874, the YWCA attempted to preserve a wholesome atmosphere in the neighborhood by opening the Central Friendly Inn at Central Place. The inn had a reading room and meeting hall for men and boys, and later a restaurant, kindergarten, playground, children's library, and commercial laundry. When the inn moved to Central and Broadway in 1888, it included low-rate boarding rooms for drunks, chapel services, and nightly temperance meetings. In a similar vein, the WCTU opened storefront canteens, and the SALVATION ARMY opened a barracks. To meet the medical needs of Haymarket residents, especially women and girls, Dr. MYRA MERRICK organized the Children's Free Medical & Surgical Dispensary in 1878 on Webster St. The hospital, a precursor of WOMAN'S GENERAL HOSPITAL, offered women doctors a place to practice their skills as well as aided the needy. The Haymarket was regarded as such a tough area after 1880 that the police patrolled the "Hill"—the crest of Commercial St. SE—in threes or fours. Early crime kings "Blinkey" Morgan and "Johnny" Coughlin terrorized the downtown area from headquarters in the Haymarket and created a crime lore that was thinly disguised in the fiction of Alfred Henry Lewis. Much of the area was razed for the building of the CLEVELAND UNION TERMINAL in the 1920s, and its residents nearest to Public Square were displaced. The remains of the Haymarket were wiped out by innerbelt construction in the 1950s.

**HAYR, JAMES** (1 July 1838–1 Aug. 1927), was a volunteer Civil War soldier and early custodian of the SOLDIERS & SAILORS MONUMENT. Hayr was born in Hamilton, Ontario, Canada. He and his family moved to Niagara Falls, N.Y., in 1851. He worked as a painter in Rochester, New York City, and Cleveland. Hayr enlisted in the Zouave Light Guards, which became Co. B, 23D OHIO VOLUNTEER INFANTRY, in 1861. He was promoted to corporal on 4 July 1864 and to sergeant in Sept. 1864. He was severely wounded at the battle of Cedar Creek, Va., in Oct. 1864. He was mustered out of service on 1 Aug. 1865 at Cumberland, Md. Returning to Cleveland after the war, he became active in veterans' affairs. He served as commander of the Hampson Post (Grand Army of the Republic) and as an officer on the Cuyahoga County Soldiers & Sailors Monument Commission, beginning in 1884, and served as custodian of the Soldiers & Sailors Monument for a number of years. He is buried in WOODLAND CEMETERY.

**HAYS, J. BYERS** (11 Feb. 1891–26 Aug. 1968), was an important local architect active in Cleveland from 1920–63, who designed both traditional and modern experimen-

tal structures. Hays was born in Sewickley, Pa., and graduated in architecture from the Carnegie Institute of Technology in 1914. In 1916 he joined the office of Raymond Hood in New York as Hood's first and only draftsman. Hays came to Cleveland in 1920 to join the firm of Walker & Weeks. He soon became a principal designer in the firm; among the works he designed for it were the Federal Reserve Bank (1923), the great Indiana War Memorial in Indianapolis (1927), the exterior of the CLEVELAND MUNICIPAL STADIUM (1926), and St. Paul Episcopal Church of Cleveland Hts. (1927–51). In 1930, Hays set up his own office in partnership with Russell Simpson. In 1935, Hays & Simpson planned an experimental modular house for GE that was erected at NELA PARK. It was an attempt to provide a prototype for a small house specifically designed for family living and prompted by the economic strictures of the Depression. In 1936, Hays & Simpson designed the Hall of Progress, with a new and unique system of rigid wooden trusses, for the GREAT LAKES EXPOSITION. Hays was also a member of the architectural committee for the exposition. The partnership of Hays & Simpson lasted until 1950.

During WORLD WAR II, Hays was briefly associated with the renowned civil engineer WILBUR J. WATSON in the design of war housing projects. After the war, he founded the firm of Conrad, Hays, Simpson & Ruth, which continued as Hays & Ruth from the mid-1950s until Hays's retirement in 1963. Hays drew the master plan for the Cleveland Zoo in 1948 and designed the bird and pachyderm buildings. Hays & Ruth planned the first major addition to the CLEVELAND MUSEUM OF ART in 1958, which provided an interior court facing the original structure of 1916, but which was completely obscured from the exterior by Marcel Breuer's 1971 addition. Hays & Ruth also planned the Lakewood High School auditorium (1960) and the Riverview public-housing development (1963). Hays served on the Fine Arts Advisory Committee of the Cleveland Planning Commission and the Cleveland Hts. Planning Commission. He was a consultant to the Rocky River planning and zoning boards, president of the AMERICAN INSTITUTE OF ARCHITECTS CLEVELAND CHAP., and a fellow of the AIA. He also served on the architectural advisory committee of UNIVERSITY CIRCLE and was a trustee of Western Reserve University. Hays was married to Charlotte M. Hays and had 2 children, Mrs. Raymond Schoenfeld and Alden F.

**HAYS, KAUFMAN** (9 Mar. 1835–12 Apr. 1916), merchant, banker, and civic leader, was born in Stormdorf, Hesse-Darmstadt, Germany. He immigrated to the U.S. in Sept. 1852 and settled immediately in Cleveland, where his sister Rosa had been living since 1850. As a young man, Hays worked in several local retail stores owned by Jewish merchants. In 1860, he joined SIMSON THORMAN as a junior partner in the latter's hides-and-wool business. Hays left the business in 1864 to establish a retail clothing store with his brother Joseph. Hays Bros. remained in operation until 1885, when it was sold to Klein & Lehman. Hays was among the organizers of the Teutonia Insurance Co. in 1867. Against his advice, the company directors decided to heavily insure businesses in Chicago, and the company was subsequently wiped out financially by the great fire of 1871. In 1868, Hays purchased stock in the Citizens Savings & Loan Co., and in 1875 he became a member of the board of directors. He also held stock in the City Natl. Bank. In 1886, he established the Euclid Ave. Natl. Bank with MYRON T. HERRICK, CHAS. F. BRUSH, and SOLON L. SEVERANCE. Hays was elected vice-president of the bank in 1893 and held that position until 1905, when the bank merged with Park Natl. Bank to form the Euclid-Park Natl. Bank, which in turn became the First Natl. Bank of Cleveland and ultimately part of the Union Trust Co., of which Hays was a vice-president at his death.

When the Turner Mfg. Co., a textile company, failed in 1893, Hays became secretary of the reorganized company. He and Geo. H. Hodgson were asked by the directors to manage the firm. They encountered great success and built it into the CLEVELAND WORSTED MILLS, which by the turn of the century was the city's largest textile mill. Hays was elected to CLEVELAND CITY COUNCIL in 1886 and became chairman of the city's finance committee. Two years later, he was elected vice-president of council. Following the embezzlement of city funds by the city treasurer in 1888, Hays was appointed acting treasurer. He is generally credited with saving the city's credit and returning the city to sound financial ground. Hays was among the founders of the Hebrew Benevolent Society in the late 1850s. He was a member of Tifereth Israel (The TEMPLE) and served as the congregation's president from 1867–71. He married Lizzie Thorman on 8 May 1861. They had 4 daughters, Frances (Mrs. MOSES GRIES), Belle (Mrs. MARTIN MARKS), Rolinda, and Nettie.

Kaufman Hays Papers, WRHS.

**HAYWARD, NELSON** (1810–14 Apr. 1857), was mayor of Cleveland, 1843–44. Hayward was born in Braintree, Mass., where he was locally educated. He came to Cleveland in 1825 with his 2 brothers, Joseph and John, and joined in various small enterprises with them. In 1840, he became the assistant chief of the Old Volunteer Fire Dept. Hayward's political philosophy was that of a Jacksonian Democrat. It was this new trend of thought that won him the mayoralty in 1843, after he had served as alderman in 1841 and 1842. He was never reelected to public office, however, as the political trend of the city became partisan Whig and Republican. Hayward was vice-president of the city's Temperance Society in 1842. The following year he became a member of the Cleveland Lodge of the Odd Fellows. He never married.

**HAYWARD, WILLIAM HENRY** (6 Dec. 1822–1 Mar. 1904), was a Cleveland printer, organizer of the CLEVELAND GRAYS, and Civil War Army officer. Hayward was born in Lebanon, Conn., and moved to Cleveland with his family in 1825 via the Erie Canal and lake schooner. At age 15, he began work with Sanford & Lott in the printing business. He helped organize the Cleveland Grays in 1837, became 1st sergeant in 1852, and served as president, 1858–59. When the CIVIL WAR broke out, he was commissioned lieutenant colonel of the 1ST OHIO VOLUNTEER LIGHT ARTILLERY. He served until resigning because of illness on 1 Apr. 1863. He returned to Cleveland, where in Aug. 1863 he was elected colonel of the 29th Ohio Volunteer Militia, referred to as the City Regiment, Volunteer Militia. On 5 May 1864, Hayward was commissioned colonel of the 150th Ohio Volunteer Infantry. He led the 150th, made up largely of Clevelanders, during its period of service in the defenses of Washington, D.C., until it was mustered out in Cleveland on 23 Aug. 1864. In the postwar years he was an active member of the GRAND ARMY OF THE REPUBLIC and the Cleveland Light Artillery Assoc. In 1846 he married Jane E. Willis. He died at the home of his daughter at 729 Prospect St. He is buried in WOODLAND CEMETERY.

Cleveland Light Artillery Assoc. Records, WRHS.
Tibbits, George W., A Brief Sketch of the Cleveland Grays (1903).

**HEALTH HILL HOSPITAL FOR CHILDREN** (also known as Health Hill Hospital for Convalescent Children), located at 2801 Martin Luther King, Jr. Dr. (East Blvd.), was incorporated in 1895 as the Children's Fresh Air Camp & Hospital. The Fresh Air Camp was the result of Hiram Addison's desire to provide a healthy environment for ill children and their mothers. The hospital was built on land donated by Jacob Perkins in Woodland Hills. The Children's Fresh Air Camp & Hospital originally provided convalescent care and dietary treatment for children, but under the leadership of Isabel H. Smith, who served as executive director 1944–67, the 52-bed hospital developed a broad range of rehabilitation services and programs for chronically ill children. The hospital was renamed Health Hill Hospital for Children in 1967. Health Hill opened a pediatric ventilator-dependent unit in 1986. The only pediatric specialty hospital of its kind in Ohio, it is affiliated with Case Western Reserve University School of Medicine.

Brown, Kent L., ed., Medicine in Cleveland and Cuyahoga County, 1810–1976 (1977).

**HEARD, CHARLES WALLACE** (1806–29 Aug. 1876), was a major architect of the Midwest during the Victorian era. He was born in Onondaga, N.Y., and moved to Painesville, Ohio, 3 years later. In 1822 he was apprenticed to JONATHAN GOLDSMITH, a master of Greek Revival architecture, whose daughter he married in 1830. He became Goldsmith's partner and remained so until Goldsmith's death in 1847, working primarily in Cleveland beginning in 1833. Of the several Late Colonial and Classic-style homes that they built near PUBLIC SQUARE and on Euclid St., the Chas. M. Giddings house on Rockwell and Ontario streets is generally attributed primarily to Heard. Heard made the usual progression from carpenter to master builder to architect, and after Goldsmith's death, he took Warham J. Warner as his partner. Together they built the first Gothic residence in Cleveland—the Henry B. Payne house on Euclid and Perry streets (razed in 1940). Perhaps Heard's most important building in the early Gothic Revival style was St. Paul's Episcopal Church, at Euclid and Sheriff (E. 4th) streets (1851, demolished in 1874), for which SIMEON PORTER was the master builder. Heard & Porter became the leading Cleveland building company in the decade preceding the Civil War. Before they dissolved their partnership in 1859, they built the Second Presbyterian Church (1852, destroyed by fire in 1876), the Old Stone Church (1855), the Eagle St. School (1855), CENTRAL HIGH SCHOOL (1856), Payne & Perry's Block (1855), and the I. S. Converse Block (1859), the homes of Chas. Hickox and Hinman B. Hurlbut (1855), the Lake Erie Female Seminary (Painesville, Ohio, 1859), and the Cleveland Orphan Asylum (1859).

In 1863, Heard & Warner were cited as the builders of CASE HALL, a huge "French style" business block and lecture and music hall—which became the cultural center of Cleveland—on the present site of the CLEVELAND PUBLIC LIBRARY. By 1864, Heard was in partnership with his son-in-law, Walter Blythe, with whom he designed the First United Presbyterian Church of Erie St. (E. 9th) near Huron and Prospect (1867). Heard & Blythe also built the Case Block (1875) at Superior and Wood streets, a building of grand scale that housed city hall, a hotel, commercial space, offices, and studios. The Case Block was considered the climax of Heard's eclectic tradition, but his productive days were not over: his last large public building was the EUCLID AVE. OPERA HOUSE (1875) on Sheriff (E. 4th) St. near Euclid, entered through Heard's own business block, which he had finished the year before. Other buildings in Cleveland for which Heard was responsible include the Geo. Merwin house (ROWFANT CLUB, 3028 Prospect), most of the public school buildings of the 1860s, including the Sterling School (1867, E. 30th at Carnegie, demolished 1982), the St. Clair School, the Rockwell School, and the Arlington Block on Euclid St. (1875).

Heard & Sons, as his firm was eventually called, was selected to build the Ohio state building at the Philadelphia Centennial Exhibition in 1876. Of all of the state buildings offered to the city of Philadelphia after this temporary exposition, only Heard's 2-story gabled structure was retained; and it, unlike most of Heard's work, was still standing for the Bicentennial. Heard was an architect with a mastery of current styles, which he was able to portray with restraint because of his classical training with Jonathan Goldsmith. He was also able to incorporate innovations such as folding partitions, cast-iron columns, and plumbing and heating trends already widely used in eastern cities. He was active in community affairs, including Democratic politics, the fire department, and the CLEVELAND ACADEMY OF NATURAL SCIENCE.

Johannesen, Eric, *Cleveland Architecture, 1876-1976* (1979).

The **HEBREW ACADEMY** is an Orthodox day school that provides a full religious and secular education from prekindergarten to high school. The academy was established in 1943 through the efforts of Rabbi Elijah M. Bloch and Rabbi Chaim M. Katz of the TELSHE YESHIVA. Their goal was to provide a Torah-oriented education for Cleveland's Jewish youth. Classes began in Sept. 1943 with 24 students of elementary-school age meeting in the basement of the Cleveland Jewish Ctr. A year later, the Hebrew Academy moved into a house on East Blvd. recently vacated and provided by the Telshe Yeshiva. However, increased enrollment and the need for greater space caused the school to return to the Cleveland Jewish Ctr., where it occupied 10 rooms. By 1946, the academy's enrollment was 170, and construction began on a new building on Taylor Rd. A 1-story structure was dedicated in Jan. 1949. A year earlier, the Hebrew Academy had become an affiliate of the JEWISH COMMUNITY FED. by joining the BUREAU OF JEWISH EDUCATION following 4 years of negotiation. From its original enrollment of 24 students, the academy grew to 600 in 1965 and to 800 in 1983. This increase created the periodic need for expansion of the physical facilities. In 1953, a second story was added to the school. New classroom and multipurpose wings were added to the original building in 1964, 1966, and 1981.

The Hebrew Academy expanded its age-group offering beginning in 1951, when a Jr. High School department was added. The Yavne High School for Girls was established in 1957 and held classes at Taylor Rd. Synagogue until 1966, when it moved to the academy's complex. A boys' high school, Mesivta, was created in 1965. Three years later, Irving Stone, president of the academy's board of directors, donated 6½ acres of land with existing buildings for the high school, which is now known as the Jacob Sapirstein Mesivta High School in honor of Stone's father, the founder of AMERICAN GREETINGS CORP. The high schools are accredited by the Ohio State Board of Regents and received college preparatory charters in 1967. In 1979, a foreign-student division was created to provide religious and secular classes for Iranian and Russian children. Classes meet at Taylor Rd. Synagogue, with enrollment near 100. Rabbi N. W. Dessler has served as principal since 1944.

Bureau of Jewish Education Records, WRHS.

The **HEBREW FREE LOAN ASSOCIATION** was established in 1903 to provide interest-free loans to needy Jewish immigrants. Following the Biblical injunction demanding that Jews not charge interest from the needy, Cleveland merchants Chas. Ettinger and Maurice Black each donated $200 to create the loan fund to assist newly arrived East European Jews. The association was formally incorporated on 9 Sept. 1904 as the Gmilus Chassodim Society. Loans provided by the association in its early years generally were for $25-50 and were given to cover medical expenses, to purchase food and clothing, or to provide temporary room and board, and in some cases included assistance funds for establishing small businesses. Early records of the association indicate that the repayment rate on the loans ran between 97-99%.

In 1909, the association provided approximately 700 loans averaging nearly $30 each. Since its founding, the function and purpose of the association had changed. From an immigrant aid society, it evolved into a general relief agency during the Depression. Following WORLD WAR II, it provided small capital loans to returning veterans. In the 1980s, its loans covered emergency assistance, medical expenses, lump-sum tuition, and home improvement. The association was an early beneficiary of the Fed. of Jewish Charities. It is a nonsectarian, nonprofit, self-supporting organization that operates on dues from its 700 members and income from investments. It has a loan fund in excess of $100,000 and is managed by volunteers and a paid executive secretary. In 1982, the association became a charter member of the Assoc. of Hebrew Free Loans, a national organization established by similar groups. In 1984, the association received the Isaiah Award for Human Relations from the Cleveland Chap. of the American Jewish Committee.

Hebrew Free Loan Assoc. Records, WRHS.

The **HEIGHTS AREA PROJECT** was established by the JEWISH COMMUNITY FED. in 1969 in an attempt to stabilize the Heights and halt or slow the move of Jews and Jewish institutions into the far eastern suburbs. This action, supporting stabilization and commitment to neighborhood, marked a change from the post-World War II era, when the JCF assisted organizations in the flight from GLENVILLE and Kinsman. By the late 1960s, Jewish institutions were concentrated in a small area, along and adjacent to S. Taylor Rd., to a greater degree than at any time in the community's history. Among these were PARK SYNAGOGUE, Taylor Rd. Synagogue, the JEWISH COMMUNITY CTR., the JEWISH FAMILY SERVICE ASSOC., the MONTEFIORE HOME, the BUREAU OF JEWISH EDUCATION, and a host of smaller synagogues and institutions. The estimated cost of relocation in 1969 was $100 million.

With the desegregation of the Heights in the 1960s, the JCF feared the same kind of Jewish panic selling and eastward flight that had characterized the changes in E. Cleveland. To insure against that possibility, the JCF extracted promises from the heads of the principal organizations that they would not move from their present location. At the same time, the Cleveland Hts. Project was established to provide mortgage assistance for Jewish homebuyers in the Heights, to create a public-relations program to "market" the Heights as a livable and vibrant neighborhood, to foster creation of street clubs for sociability and security, and to lobby for improved city services. The project also cooperated with non-Jewish Heights-area organizations in the formation of the Cleveland Hts. Congress in an effort to maintain and insure an orderly neighborhood integration. The CHP and JCF sponsored committees to deal with security and policing and to guard against blockbusting and

497

discriminatory real-estate practices. In addition, the JCF used its power in 1973 to block the Bureau of Jewish Education's plan to move from S. Taylor Rd. to a facility in BEACHWOOD. As the Jewish population increased in S. EUCLID and UNIVERSITY HTS., the CHP expanded the geographic limits of its mortgage program and changed its name to the Heights Area Project. In the mid-1980s, the project provided low-interest mortgage assistance in the form of down-payment loans or monthly mortgage-assistance payments.

The **HEIGHTS JEWISH CENTER** was the first congregation established in Cleveland's eastern suburbs. Established on 1 July 1923 as the Heights Orthodox Congregation to serve the handful of Orthodox Jews who had moved into CLEVELAND HTS., it initially met in the home of Jacob Makoff on Euclid Hts. Blvd. Four years later, the congregation purchased and remodeled a brick building at 14274 Superior. Jacob Berkowitz served as the first president. In 1936, Seymour Zambrowsky was hired as the congregation's first ordained rabbi. Zambrowsky received his ordination at the short-lived Orthodox Rabbinical Seminary of America, which was located in Cleveland between 1929-38 and run by Rabbi Judah Levenberg. In 1937, under the leadership of Zambrowsky and with the support of its younger members, the congregation changed its name to the Heights Jewish Ctr., a move designed to appeal to young Jewish families in the Heights. By 1940, membership had grown from the initial 30 families to over 250, with approximately 80% of the members under the age of 40.

Rabbi ISRAEL PORATH, Cleveland's leading Orthodox rabbi, assumed the pulpit in 1946 after 20 years at OHEB ZEDEK CONGREGATION and Nevéh Zedek. A year later, the congregation merged with Beth Hamidrash Hogodol, a congregation that sought to move out of GLENVILLE during the general post-World War II movement of Jewish institutions into the suburbs. The latter congregation was established in 1865 by Lithuanian Jews. In 1941, it merged with Ohave Emuna Anshe Russia, a once-Orthodox congregation that had been founded in 1882. In 1948, Beth Hamidrash Hagodol Ohave Emuna-The Heights Jewish Ctr., known popularly by the final 4 words of its name, began construction of a new synagogue on Cedar Rd. near Green Rd. in University Hts. In 1951, the congregation merged with Anshe Grodno following 4 years of controversial merger discussions. Porath remained as rabbi of the congregation until his retirement in 1972, when he was succeeded by Rabbi Daniel Schur.

Heights Jewish Ctr. Records, WRHS.

**HEINEN'S, INC.**, is one of the chief grocery-store chains in the Cleveland area. The company was established in 1929, when Joseph H. Heinen, a German immigrant who had worked at various food and meat markets since childhood, opened his own neighborhood butcher shop in the Kinsman-Lee district of SHAKER HTS. Heinen built his business on a variety of quality meats. By 1933, it had prospered to a point that he moved across the street to a larger store and opened it as a complete food-service center. The firm's reputation for high quality, service, and cleanliness increased as it continued to specialize in meats. In 1939, Heinen's began a prudent expansion program by opening other supermarkets in middle- and upper-income neighborhoods. Ten years later, it opened its first self-serve supermarket on SHAKER SQUARE. By 1962, Heinen's had 5 stores and a new $1.5 million warehouse and headquarters at 20601 Aurora Rd., WARRENSVILLE HTS. In the 1960s, it began to establish stores on Cleveland's west side.

The company has always remained a family-owned operation, and Joseph Heinen and his son, John J., have been honored as Retailers of the Year. The company has been involved in civic affairs, including its annual benefit program for the American Cancer Society, which began in 1978. By 1981, it was the 5th-largest grocery chain in Cleveland, with 11 stores, 1,000 employees, and $90 million in annual sales, which represented about 8% of the area food market.

**HEISE, GEORGE W.** (b. 27 June 1888), was a chemist and researcher for Natl. Carbon Research Laboratories. The son of German immigrants Paul E. and Dora Tyre Heise, George was educated in the public schools in his native Milwaukee and then attended the University of Wisconsin, where he received a B.S. degree in 1909 and an M.S. degree in 1912. He served as a chemistry instructor at Grinell College (1909–10) and taught chemistry and physics at DePaul University (1910–11) before returning to the University of Wisconsin as an assistant and later a fellow in chemistry (1912–13). From 1913–17, Heise served as a physical chemist in the Bureau of Science in Manila, the Philippine Islands, performing chemical and bacteriological tests on the water. In 1917 he became a captain in the U.S. Army Reserve Corps and was assigned to the Utilities Div. at Camp Grant, Ill., to work on water softening, sanitation, and other technical problems. He was transferred to the Chemical Warfare Service in 1918 before returning to civilian life in 1919. During WORLD WAR II, he worked again with the Chemical Warfare Service and with the Natl. Defense Research Council. In 1919, Heise went to work for Natl. Carbon Research Laboratories as a research chemist and engineer. He worked first in Fremont, was transferred to Long Island in 1921, and came to Cleveland in 1925. In Cleveland, Heise led a group in electrochemical research and made contributions to the development of commercial dry batteries. He was responsible for more than 75 patents and wrote many technical papers. He was a fellow of the American Assoc. for the Advancement of Science and a member of the American Chemical Society, the Electrochemical Society (president, 1947–48), and other professional and industrial organizations. On 6 Aug. 1915, Heise married Margaret Armstrong.

**HEISMAN, JOHN W.** (23 Oct. 1869–3 Oct. 1936), the highly successful and innovative college football coach for whom the Heisman Trophy is named, was born in Cleveland and began his coaching career in northern Ohio. Heisman's parents immigrated to Cleveland from Germany; they christened their son Johann Wilhelm. A cooper, the elder Heisman moved his family to the oil fields around Titusville, Pa., where he opened a barrel shop. After attending Titusville High School, young Heisman entered Brown University, where he played FOOTBALL in 1888, and then transferred to Pennsylvania, where he was on the football team in 1890 and 1891. He received a law degree from Pennsylvania in 1892.

Heisman began his coaching career as a player and coach at Oberlin College in 1892, leading his team to a perfect season of 7-0, and twice shutting out Ohio State University (40-0 and 50-0). In 1893 he coached all sports at Buchtel College (later the University of Akron); again as a player and coach, he led his team against OSU, defeating the Buckeyes in overtime at the state fair in Columbus. At Buchtel, Heisman encountered faculty opposition toward his extremely competitive approach to football. In 1894 he returned to coach at Oberlin, winning 4 football games, losing 3, and tying 1. Heisman's coaching career then took him southward. He coached at Alabama Polytechnic Institute (later Auburn) (1895–99), Clemson (1900–03), Georgia Institute of Technology (1904–19), Pennsylvania (1920–22), Washington & Jefferson (1923), and Rice Institute in Houston, Tex. (1924–27).

Heisman's innovations changed the game of football. He was an early proponent of legalizing the forward pass; used guards to lead the interference on sweeps; and introduced the direct snap from center. In 1898 his teams began to use audible signals to begin each offensive play. He also introduced a special shift that was the forerunner of the T and I formations. After his retirement from coaching, Heisman became an organizer and first president of the New York Touchdown Club and director of athletics at the Downtown Athletic Club of New York. In 1935, the latter club began awarding an annual trophy to the nation's best college football player; following Heisman's death, the trophy was named in his honor. Heisman married twice. His marriage to Evelyn McCollum Cox in 1903 ended in divorce in 1918; in 1924 he wed Edith Maora Cole, who died in 1964.

**HENNIG, EDWARD A.** (1880–28 Aug. 1960), was a leading amateur athlete both locally and nationally prior to 1950. He was the first athlete from Cleveland to participate in the Olympics, winning 1 gold medal and finishing in a tie for another in the 1904 games. Hennig was an active gymnast from age 8, when a doctor recommended that he take up gymnastic exercise to build himself up. Twice a week he walked 4 mi. from his home to a gymnasium downtown for his workouts. He was a member of the Cleveland East Side Turners for 73 years and a member of the Central YMCA for nearly 60 years. Hennig was one of 496 athletes from 10 countries to participate in the 1904 Olympic Games in St. Louis. He captured top honors in 2 gymnastic events, winning the gold medal in Indian club swinging (since discontinued) and finishing in a tie for 1st place in the horizontal bars with another American, Anton Heida. Hennig also competed in national Amateur Athletic Union competitions; he won first place for both Indian club swinging and the horizontal bars in the 1911 competition, and in AAU contests between 1933–50 he won 10 1st-place medals and 3 2d-place awards. Throughout his athletic career, Hennig won 14 national AAU championships and 3 national Turner titles. He was voted the outstanding amateur athlete in northeastern Ohio in 1942, when he was 62, and placed 3d that year in the voting for the AAU's Sullivan Trophy, presented to the outstanding amateur athlete of the year. He was later inducted into the GREATER CLEVELAND SPORTS HALL OF FAME. An engineer by trade, Hennig was employed by the McMeyer Interstate Corp., builders of hoist machines, and later became chief engineer for the R. A. Kaltenbach Corp., engineering consultants. Hennig's wife, the former Alma Warnke, died in 1949.

**HENRIETTA, SISTER, CSA** (1902–17 Oct. 1983), operated the Our Lady of Fatima Mission in HOUGH for Cleveland's poor. Blending compassion with self-reliance, she provided food and clothing to the down-and-out while teaching them skills. Born Marie Gross in Cleveland, she entered the Sisters of Charity of St. Augustine after graduating from Mercy School of Nursing in Canton as an R.N. She served as the night nursing supervisor at Canton's Mercy Hospital from 1928–31 and as the supervisor of surgery from 1931–49. She was appointed the assistant administrator until 1951, when she became the hospital administrator. When the hospital acquired the former Timken estate in 1963, she perfected her fundraising skills to build the new Timken Mercy Medical Ctr. Though the old Mercy facilities were phased out in 1970, during her tenure Sr.

Henrietta managed the dual operation. For her work in establishing the first hospital civil defense program, she was cited by Pres. Eisenhower. A member of the Ohio Hospital Assoc., she was instrumental in organizing Stark County's first school of practical nursing. She also promoted the establishment of the first cardiac catheterization program in a community hospital. In 1963, Sr. Henrietta returned to her native Cleveland, where she was assigned to St. Vincent Charity Hospital as nursing administrator. When Fr. Albert Koklowsky asked for a nun to help in his work at OUR LADY OF FATIMA MISSION in Hough, Sr. Henrietta, with the support of her order, answered the call. The priest felt that a nun sitting on the porch would help the image of the mission; as Sr. Henrietta frequently commented, she never had much time for sitting at Our Lady of Fatima. During the HOUGH RIOTS of 1966, she commuted from St. Vincent, but eventually she moved to the area so as to immerse herself totally in her work. Sr. Henrietta approached her position with the mind of a caring, tough hospital administrator. She was intolerant of squalor. To combat the rats, litter, and filth of the area, she mobilized volunteers from the neighborhood and the suburbs to clean up the streets and homes.

Although Sr. Henrietta's mission provided emergency food, clothes, furniture, and holiday baskets, she saw herself and her work as teaching rather than giving. She made certain that people took charge of their own lives. To make sure that the lessons were well learned, she made spot checks on homes and presented Spic and Span Home Awards to those who passed the inspections. Within months, the area served by the mission—bounded by Superior, Chester, E. 55th, and E. 79th streets—appeared noticeably cleaner than the surrounding areas, and the turnover rate of occupancy decreased in line with one of Sr. Henrietta's mottos: Don't move, improve! As residents became more sophisticated in basic skills, she encouraged the formation of the Caridad and the Family Cooperators groups to plan and carry out local improvement projects. The Famicos Foundation was set up to buy and refurbish homes and sell them to families who otherwise could not obtain credit. To finance her work, Sr. Henrietta relied on donations of money, materials, jobs, and labor, which she skillfully obtained from individuals and corporations. Her self-help approach won her support, respect, and many personal awards, including the Catholic Interracial Council Award for Social Justice (1976), the Distinguished Community Service Award from the Natl. Urban Coalition (1979), and the Mura Award from the American Jewish Committee (1983). Though her order adopted a modern short habit in the 1970s, Sr. Henrietta preferred the older white garb to reinforce the values she preached.

**HERBERT, THOMAS JOHN** (28 Oct. 1894–26 Oct. 1974), served as the 56th governor of Ohio. He also served on the Ohio State Supreme Court and as state attorney general. Herbert was born at E. 65th St. and Utica Ave. in Cleveland to John T. and Jane A. Jones Herbert. He attended Dunham School and East High School. Working various jobs, including ushering at LEAGUE PARK, he earned his way through Western Reserve University, receiving the A.B. degree in 1915. Herbert had to drop out of law school after 1 year because of lack of money. With America's entry into WORLD WAR I, he became a 1st lieutenant in the U.S. Air Service. In Europe he ferried aircraft from England to France. Later, while serving with the 56th Royal Air Corps Squadron, Herbert shot down 1 German plane and was himself shot down, suffering a wounded leg. He received both the U.S. and British Distinguished Service Cross and the Purple Heart.

Returning to WRU's law school, Herbert graduated with the LL.B. degree, was admitted to the Ohio bar, and was appointed assistant law director in Cleveland in 1920. He served as an assistant county prosecutor from 1923–24 and entered private practice until 1928, when he was appointed an assistant state attorney general. In 1932 he was defeated for a congressional seat. In 1933 he became a special counsel to the state attorney general in the liquidation of the Union Trust Co. In 1938, Herbert was elected Ohio attorney general for the first of 3 terms. In 1944, he was defeated for the Republican governor's nomination. Herbert defeated Frank Lausche for governor in 1946, but he lost to Lausche in a 1948 rematch. He returned to private practice until 1952, when he lost the Republican primary for governor. In 1953, Pres. Dwight Eisenhower appointed Herbert chairman of the Subversive Activities Control Board in Washington, D.C. In 1956, Herbert won election to the Ohio Supreme Court, but a severe stroke prevented his seeking reelection. Herbert married Jeanette Judson (d. Dec. 1945) on 30 Apr. 1919. He married Mildred Helen Stevenson in 1948. Herbert had 3 children, Metta Jane Stevers, Daniel, and John.

**HERKOMER, JOHN** (1821–1913), was a woodcarver, born in Waal, Bavaria. He practiced his craft in Cleveland from 1851–83. He is best known for the staircases and interior decorations he carved for the homes of prominent Cleveland families. Herkomer was the youngest of 4 brothers. He left Bavaria in the late 1840s and traveled to New York City. In 1851 he was joined by his brother Lorenz. They set up a woodcarving and portrait shop, first in New York City, and later in Rochester, before finally settling in Cleveland, where they opened a shop on Prospect St. In 1857, Lorenz and his family moved to England. Soon after their departure, John married and moved his woodcarving establishment to new quarters on Erie (E. 9th) St. Herkomer left for England in 1883, after over 30 years in Cleveland. He was employed to design and carve interior decorations for the home of his nephew, Sir Hubert Herkomer, a famous painter, in Bushey, England. He died there. Clevelanders who had residences decorated by Herkomer include Col. JOHN HAY, SAMUEL ANDREWS, and Amasa Stone, Jr. The stairway of the original Hay house on Euclid Ave. was removed and incorporated into the Hay house on East Blvd. (later the WESTERN RESERVE HISTORICAL SOCIETY). Herkomer was also responsible for the lions' heads on the West Side Branch of the YMCA. Most of the homes he decorated have since been torn down to make way for business and industry. Herkomer was one of the members of the original ART CLUB with ARCHIBALD WILLARD.

Baldry, A. L., *Hubert von Herkomer R.A.: A Study and a Biography* (1901).
Herkomer, Sir Hubert von, *The Herkomers* (1911).

The **HERMIT CLUB** is a meeting place for businessmen and professionals with talent in and appreciation of the performing arts. Its abbey, or headquarters, is located on Dodge Ct. Membership is limited to 400, and it has a ladies' auxiliary composed of widows of members. Organized by Cleveland architect FRANK BELL MEADE, it was patterned after the Lambs Club in New York. The Hermits' first abbey, designed by Meade, was built on Hickox Pl. (3rd St.) in the heart of the downtown theatrical district of that day. Beginning in 1904, annual theatrical productions of musical comedies were staged by the Hermits as an outlet for their creative talents and as a means of paying off the abbey's indebtedness. These productions continued until they were interrupted by WORLD WAR I, then resumed biennially until they were interrupted by the Depression. Two public presentations were staged following that period, but they were the last in a long battle with the exigencies of the commercial theater. It was estimated that the Hermits' productions drew a total audience of over 100,000. Since then the Hermits' shows have been staged only for the pleasure of their members and friends. Out of these shows have evolved many of the Hermits' specialized performing groups, such as the Hermit Symphony Orchestra, the Hermit Jazz Group (known earlier as the Hermit Blues), the Hermit Chorus, the Hermit Drama Group, and the Hermitcrafters. The Hermit Club is best symbolized by its present (1986) abbey. The move to the new abbey in 1928 reflected the shift of the focal point of theater in Cleveland from lower Euclid Ave. to PLAYHOUSE SQUARE. Also designed by Meade, the abbey incorporated many of the interior decorations of the Hermits' original home. Located at the stage entrance of the OHIO THEATRE, it exudes an Old World atmosphere that stands in stark contrast to the neighboring buildings. The English Tudor exterior blends plaster walls with hand-hewn timbers. On the front of the structure and along its sides is an elaborately carved frieze. The interior features Gothic architecture and includes dining rooms, card rooms, reading rooms, and a lounge.

Thomas, William H., *The Pit, the Footlights, and the Wings: The Dramatic Record of the Hermit Club, 1904–1954* (1954).

**HERRICK, JOHN FRENCH** (23 Feb. 1836–5 July 1909), was a volunteer Army officer in the CIVIL WAR and a Cleveland attorney. Herrick was born in Wellington, Lorain County, Ohio. He attended Wellington Academy and Oberlin College (1856–62). He raised Co. D, 87th Ohio Volunteer Infantry, in Lorain County for 3 months' service and was appointed captain on 11 June 1862. Unfortunately, the 87th was captured at Harper's Ferry, W.Va., by the forces of Confederate Gen. Thos. J. "Stonewall" Jackson on 15 Sept. 1862, 2 days before the Battle of Antietam was fought. Paroled, and out of the war, he returned to Cleveland and studied law at the Union and Ohio State law colleges, graduating in 1863.

In 1863, after receiving word that the proper exchange of prisoners had been made with the Confederate States government, Herrick was again eligible for military service. He raised a company of recruits for the 12TH OHIO VOLUNTEER CAVALRY, placed on detached duty on Johnson's Island during the Nov. 1863 invasion scare at the island's Confederate prison. In the field, Herrick was promoted to lieutenant colonel, dating from 15 July 1865, and commanded the regiment during the last year of the war. Returning to Cleveland at the war's end, he practiced law with his brother, Gamaliel E. Herrick, in partnership until 1892. He was for a time senior partner of the legal firm of Herrick, Athey & Bliss but withdrew to practice law alone. He was elected senator to the Ohio state legislature in 1901 and was noted for a bill that established juvenile courts in Ohio. Herrick spent his last years representing the E. Cleveland Street Railroad Co. and the Cowell Platform & Coupler Co. He was a member of the Brough Post, No. 359, Grand Army of the Republic, and of the Military Order of the Loyal Legion of the U.S., and he was a Mason. He preceded his wife in death, with whom he had raised a family of 7 children. He is buried in LAKE VIEW CEMETERY.

Mason, F. H., *The Twelfth Ohio Cavalry* (1871).
Grand Army of the Republic, Dept. of Ohio, Brough Post No. 359. Collinwood, Ohio, Records, WRHS.

**HERRICK, MARIA M.,** was a 19th-century reformer and literary personage, active in the Female Moral Reform Society and publisher of Cleveland's earliest magazine. After coming to OHIO CITY from New York in 1836, Herrick became active in the Maternal Assoc. of Ohio City. From 1837-40 she edited and wrote for a monthly journal, the *MOTHERS & YOUNG LADIES' GUIDE.* Among the subjects discussed in the magazine were "Family Government," "Duties of Mothers," "Fashion," "Self Consecration," and "The Orphan's Tale." Though the magazine lasted for only a few issues, the concerns of Maria Herrick were carried on in the Female Moral Reform Society. This society was organized in Sept. 1842 to promote family values and return runaway children to their homes. Formed by Herrick along with REBECCA ROUSE and others, the society decried "sin abroad in the land" that infiltrated homes and weakened the family. Because discipline and purity were not promoted there, children got into trouble outside the home and took to petty crime and PROSTITUTION. Between 1842-43, the society investigated cases of women and children who had been lured into wickedness, and cared for them in members' homes until they could be returned to their families. The last recorded minutes of the society were dated Jan. 1844, when its work was taken over by the MARTHA WASHINGTON & DORCAS SOCIETY. Maria Herrick, disabled at an early age by a fall from a carriage, remained active in social-reform causes well into her nineties.

Ingham, Mary B., *Women of Cleveland* (1893).

**HERRICK, MYRON TIMOTHY** (9 Oct. 1854-31 Mar. 1929), served the city of Cleveland, the state of Ohio, and the nation as a lawyer, businessman, politician, and diplomat. Born in Huntington, Lorain County, Ohio, Herrick attended the district school at Huntington and the Union School in Wellington. He worked at numerous jobs to obtain enough money to go to Oberlin Academy and then Ohio Wesleyan College. Herrick did not complete his college degree but instead came to Cleveland to study law in 1875. He was admitted to the bar 3 years later and practiced law for the next 8 years before turning his interests to the banking business. In 1886, he organized the Euclid Ave. Natl. Bank and also began his long association with the Society for Savings, where he served in various executive positions until 1921. He became involved in many other business enterprises in Cleveland, such as the building of the ARCADE, and others throughout the country. It was also in the late 1880s that Herrick first became interested in politics. He served on CLEVELAND CITY COUNCIL from 1885-90. As a staunch Republican, he aided MARCUS HANNA in grooming Wm. McKinley for the presidency in 1896. He continued to move up in the Republican ranks, and by 1903, he was the Republican nominee for governor of Ohio. Herrick was elected by a large majority over the prominent Democrat TOM JOHNSON. He was a conservative, though controversial, governor and thus was defeated in his reelection attempt in 1905.

With the Republicans controlling the White House, Herrick had been asked several times since 1897 to accept a cabinet position or diplomatic post; each time he refused. Finally, in 1912, he accepted the ambassadorship to France from Pres. Taft. Although he was to be replaced in his post in 1914, he remained in Paris after the outbreak of WORLD WAR I. Herrick was commended for his assistance in evacuating stranded Americans out of Europe and providing relief to the war victims. He then returned to Cleveland to lead various civic committees organized for the war effort. In 1921, Pres. Harding reappointed Herrick ambassador to

France. Postwar relations with the U.S. were worsening until Herrick skillfully helped in handling Chas. Lindbergh's historic landing in Paris in 1927. He was the first to greet Lindbergh after his transatlantic flight. Two years later, while still serving as ambassador, Herrick died in Paris. Herrick had married Carolyn M. Parmely in 1880, and they had 1 son, Parmely.

Mott, Col. T. Bently, *Myron T. Herrick Friend of France* (1929). Myron T. Herrick Papers, WRHS.

**HERRICK, RENSSELAER RUSSELL** (29 Jan. 1826-30 Jan. 1899), was an entrepreneur, city council member, and mayor of Cleveland for 2 terms, 1879-82. Herrick was born in Utica, N.Y., the son of a successful merchant. His father died when he was 2, leaving Herrick to educate himself during his childhood with only limited formal instruction. He was one of 4 children raised by MARIA MARCIA SMITH HERRICK, a successful magazine editor. In 1836, Herrick came to Cleveland as an apprentice to a printer. He also learned carpentry during his apprenticeship. For several years he worked in carpentry, and finally he became president of the Dover Bay Grape & Wine Co. Herrick began his public life in 1855, when he became a member of CLEVELAND CITY COUNCIL, a post he held for 5 terms. He served on the City Board of Improvements in 1873-76 and 1877. As a Republican, he successfully ran for mayor in 1879 and served until 1882. As mayor, Herrick lowered the indebtedness of the city and also the levy rates. He also instituted the annual census by the police department. After his term in office, Herrick returned to private life and became the vice-president of the Society for Savings. In 1891, however, he returned to public life as the director of the city's Public Works, a position he held for 1 year. In 1846 Herrick married Adelaide Cushman. He later married a widow, Mrs. Laura White Hunt. Neither marriage produced any children.

**HESSENMUELLER, EDWARD** (1811-27 Jan. 1884), was a lawyer who became a prominent Cleveland German-American leader. A strong and active Democrat, he was elected to 5 terms as a justice of the peace and to 2 terms as a judge in the police court. Hessenmueller was born in Wolfenbuettel, Braunschweig, Germany, and was educated at the University of Halle. With his young wife, Minna, he arrived in Cuyahoga County in 1836. He was admitted to the bar in 1839 and the following year moved to Cleveland. Within 3 years he became a leader in the local German-American community, taking a leading role in organizing that community's celebration of American independence in 1843. Later that year he was elected to the first of 5 3-year terms as a justice of the peace; he became a police court judge in 1860.

Hessenmueller served the Cleveland community in a variety of ways. From 1846-53 he published the *GERMANIA,* the first German newspaper published in the area. In 1850 he was a member of a committee established to investigate the causes and prevention of steamboat accidents, and in 1853 he was appointed U.S. commissioner and pension agent for Cleveland. In Oct. 1861, he was part of a small committee appointed by city council to visit troops from Cuyahoga County serving in western Virginia; he helped the soldiers arrange to send money home to relatives and returned with letters to family members. He also served on the disbursing committee to distribute relief funds raised to help the families of volunteers serving in the war, and he was president of the German Central military committee, which raised funds for the support of the German 107th regiment. He was also a director of the City

Infirmary. In addition to his legal and civic services, Hessenmueller had a number of business interests. He was elected a trustee of the Society for Savings in 1850 and was secretary of the Teutonia Insurance Co. He was also active in fraternal and cultural organizations, including the Odd Fellows and the Cleveland Gesangverein, serving as president of the latter.

The **HIBERNIAN GUARDS** were an independent military company made up of Irish-American volunteers. The unit made its first public appearance during the July 4th parade in 1847, marching under the direction of Capt. P. A. McBarron, and was extremely active in the 1850s under Capt. Wm. Kinney, establishing an armory on Oregon St. (Rockwell Ave.) and holding annual parades, dinners, and balls to celebrate such events as Washington's birthday, St. Patrick's Day, and July 4th. By 1861, the Hibernian Guards numbered 49 men and muskets. Still under Kinney's leadership in June 1861, the Guards were mustered into service for 3-year stints as Co. B in the 8th Regiment of the Ohio Volunteer Army. The company saw action in such battles as Antietam and Gettysburg before its original members were mustered out of service on 13 July 1864. As a unit, the Hibernian Guards lost their identity as a result of becoming part of a larger unit during the CIVIL WAR. In Sept. 1874, the Guards were formed anew by Capt. E. B. Campbell. The new unit held a ball that Thanksgiving, marched in the 1875 Washington's Birthday Parade, and established an armory at 161 Detroit, but apparently did not last until 1876, perhaps losing the competition for members to a new unit of Irish-American Civil War veterans, the Emmett Guards (see 15TH REGIMENT, OHIO NATL. GUARD).

The **HIGBEE COMPANY,** a major area retailer operating department stores throughout northeastern Ohio, began as a dry-goods and ready-to-wear clothing store operated by John G. Hower and Edwin C. Higbee. By 1985, the company was part of the holdings of an international investment corporation, Industrial Equity (Pacific), Ltd., of Australia, and its annual sales were approaching $250 million. Located at 237 Superior St., 1 door east of Seneca (W. 3rd) St., the Hower & Higbee store first opened its doors on 10 Sept. 1860 to capitalize on the crowds at the dedication of Perry's Monument. In 1870 the store moved to larger quarters across the street (238-40 Superior); by 1886 it employed 25 cash boys and had added a telephone and 3 delivery wagons. Hower died on 10 June 1897, and in 1902 the firm was reorganized as the Higbee Co.; Higbee served as president from 1897 until his death on 17 Jan. 1906, when his son, Wm. T., became president. The addition of an annex in 1904 connected the store to PUBLIC SQUARE, but in 1910 Higbee's moved to a new store at Euclid and E. 13th St. Among the separate departments in the new store were furs, shoes, linens, silks, toiletries, women's outer garments, and "a section devoted to the exploitation of waists." In 1913, Higbee sold the controlling interest in the company to a group of investors that included Asa Shiverick, who was elected president and served in that capacity until his death in 1937. On 29 May 1913, the firm was incorporated in Delaware with $1.1 million in capital. By 1929, annual sales had reached $11.8 million; that year the company became part of the Van Sweringen empire, and in Sept. 1931 it moved back to Public Square as part of the Terminal Tower group of buildings. During the Depression, Higbee's annual sales were about $10 million, half of what management expected in the expensive ($19.5 million) new quarters. In 1935 the company filed for bankruptcy; it was reorganized in 1937 and acquired by a group

of investors that included Chas. Bradley (president, 1937-44) and John P. Murphy. In 1946, sales climbed to $37.5 million, and in 1949 the company bought the Public Square store from the Metropolitan Insurance Co. for $18 million.

Sales continued to increase in the 1940s and 1950s, despite management's refusal to establish branches in suburban shopping centers. Higbee's decided instead to renovate and add attractions to its downtown store, such as a music center, an expanded hospitality center on the 10th floor, and an annual import fair in 1956. In 1958, the store began to improve its selection of merchandise and expand its organization. Annual sales were more than $52 million by the time of the company's centennial celebration. In the 1960s, Higbee's reversed its policy and entered suburban shopping centers, moving into an existing store at Westgate in 1961, then building its own store at SEVERANCE CTR. in 1963. By 1970, Higbee's had 6 suburban stores and annual sales of more than $100 million. It expanded its operation in other ways, as well, establishing the Red Cross Shoe Div. in the mid-1960s (sold in 1983), acquiring the G. M. McKelvey Co. department store in Youngstown in 1969, and establishing real-estate and development subsidiaries. Under the leadership of Herbert E. Strawbridge, Higbee's acquired land along the riverfront at the foot of Superior Hill in 1971, designated the area as Settlers' Landing, and in the next several years renovated and sold several historic buildings, prompting other investment and redevelopment in the area. In 1983, the Higbee Co. had annual sales of $245.3 million and a net income of $6.3 million. In 1981, 2 foreign investment groups began buying Higbee stock, and in Sept. 1984 negotiations between the Higbee board of directors and the 2 investment groups resulted in the 11 Higbee stores' merging with one of the investors, Industrial Equity.

*Fifty Years of Service Celebrated by the Higbee Company in Its New Store* (1910).

**HIGHER EDUCATION.** The origins of the institutions of higher education in Cleveland can be traced in many respects to the needs and belief systems of their early founders. These emerging institutions were often a reflection of the larger society within which they were founded. Developments in American higher education were closely related to the major events in the nation's social and political history, worldwide intellectual and technical revolution, rising egalitarianism, and population growth. The pre-Civil War years were emphatically the age of the college and witnessed the proliferation of colleges on both the national and local levels, some of which remain in existence in Ohio over a century later. Most of these colleges were originally religiously affiliated and privately sponsored. The period after 1865 was dominated by the rise of the university based on the German system, which stressed publication, research, and graduate study. Early Cleveland colleges were founded by prominent community and church leaders in order to provide for a trained ministry who could transmit the values of the society. Western Reserve College, for example, largely a Presbyterian endeavor, chose Hudson as its first site in 1826, although it had considered Cleveland and later moved there in 1882. In 1850, several Baptist ministers were involved in the founding of CLEVELAND UNIVERSITY across the CUYAHOGA RIVER from downtown. It had a brief life until 1856, when it was closed. The 1850s saw the opening of Western College of Homeopathic Medicine, which lasted for several decades. Dyke School of Commerce, a proprietary school, was established in the early 1850s to serve the growing needs of the mercantile community. Practical courses for office workers, such as bookkeeping, were taught. Later it merged and became Duke & Spencerian College in 1942, and then developed into DYKE COLLEGE, a non-profit educational institution granting 2- and 4-year business degrees.

As Cleveland grew and became industrialized, its educational needs expanded. In 1880, Case School of Applied Science was founded, and 2 years later Western Reserve College moved from Hudson to Cleveland. Case offered an engineering curriculum, the first west of the Alleghenies. It was characterized by linear growth in applied science and engineering from its founding until 1947. From 1947–67, it experienced a transition to Case Institute of Technology and became nationally recognized. Thereafter, it struggled to retain its identity, and by 1973 it enjoyed a renaissance and reassertion of its position as a technical institute as part of CASE WESTERN RESERVE UNIVERSITY, which had resulted from a federation with Western Reserve University in 1967.

Western Reserve College, with the assistance of a donation of $500,000 from AMASA STONE for buildings and endowment, moved from Hudson, Ohio, to Cleveland in 1882, after having deliberated the action for some time. It had experienced great financial difficulty, often unable to pay its president, and lost many students and faculty during the CIVIL WAR. Stone controlled the board of trustees and stipulated that the college be named for his son, Adelbert. He also mandated that the college and Case School be located in close proximity on a site about 5 mi. east of downtown Cleveland. Many wanted Adelbert to admit only men, even though Western Reserve College had admitted women. So in 1888, a separate women's college was established across the street. It was later known as Flora Stone Mather College and was the first coordinated college in the country. By the end of the 19th century, WRU added a graduate school, law school, nursing school, dental school, school of library science, and school of applied social science, reflecting the German model of higher education with its graduate programs. In 1846, METHODISTS founded Baldwin Institute in Berea. In 1864, German Methodists separated the German department from Baldwin and established German Wallace College. BALDWIN-WALLACE COLLEGE resulted from a merger of these two institutions, still affiliated with the Methodist church, in 1913. Following WORLD WAR II, Baldwin-Wallace broadened its traditional liberal-arts curriculum to include business and evening programs.

Most of the private colleges continued their Protestant church affiliation and orientation toward middle-class and upper-middle-class values. Though WRU discontinued its formal affiliation with any denomination after the move to Cleveland, most of its presidents were Protestant clergymen. These types of orientations did not seem to meet the needs of an emerging economically successful Catholic population. The Catholic community began to establish its own colleges. St. Ignatius College was founded by the Society of Jesus in 1886. In 1923 it was renamed JOHN CARROLL UNIVERSITY after the first archbishop of the Catholic church in the U.S. In 1935, it moved from its original location on Cleveland's west side to its current location in UNIVERSITY HTS. It added business courses, a graduate school, and an evening program in the 1950s. In 1968, the university moved from a full-time male enrollment to a coeducational institution.

The history of URSULINE COLLEGE parallels that of the URSULINE SISTERS who came to Cleveland in 1850 from France to establish the first religious teaching community in Cleveland. In 1871, Ursuline nuns founded the first chartered women's college in Ohio in a large house on EUCLID AVE., later moving to an Overlook Rd. campus from 1922–66, and following that to PEPPER PIKE. The SISTERS OF NOTRE DAME first established an academy in downtown Cleveland in the 1870s. Then in 1922 they founded a liberal-arts college for women, currently (1986) located in S. EUCLID. The college reflects the mission of the order's founder, Sr. Julie Billiart, the 18th-century pioneer in the education of women.

Another group that did not fit the traditional college-student mold was the part-time student. To meet these needs, the YMCA offered evening classes in downtown Cleveland in a variety of subjects, such as art, bookkeeping, and French, as early as the 1880s. By the beginning of the century, daytime classes were added. Enrollments kept increasing, and degree programs were developed in engineering and business by 1923. There were also a 2-year technical degree program called the Vocational Jr. College program, and a cooperative plan that was a unique feature of the curriculum. Students worked for half a term and then attended classes. Later, in 1929, the college was named Fenn College after a benefactor, SERENO P. FENN. WRU established Cleveland College to serve the adult learner in the 1920s. NEWTON D. BAKER, former Cleveland mayor and university trustee, helped to establish the college, which held classes in different parts of the community. It eventually moved downtown to PUBLIC SQUARE. In the early 1950s, Cleveland College moved to the Western Reserve campus, where it was eventually absorbed by the university.

Higher education continued to reflect the milieu in which it found itself, and as the Depression, followed by World War II, beset Cleveland, the colleges experienced some retrenchment and little growth. The applicant pool began to change, reflecting the World War II veterans who had discontinued or interrupted their college years and could now take advantage of the G.I. Bill of 1944, and many students from working-class families who were now beginning to see the value of a college education. There was also the anticipated growth in the college-age population resulting from the postwar baby boom. This group increased from 4% in 1900 to 40% in 1964. At this time the Cleveland area did not have any publicly supported colleges, and it appeared that the private colleges would be unable to absorb the anticipated increase in potential students. Private colleges seemed to make little effort to welcome and accommodate students with special needs, the married, part-time, or commuter students and those with diverse social or racial backgrounds. Cleveland's strong Democratic political tradition, different from the strong downstate Republican orientation, seemed to stand in the way of establishing a public (state) college system. Ohio State University dominated the public university scene, and Clevelanders had not demonstrated much interest in public higher education.

By the late 1950s, the community-college concept had still not been adopted in Ohio. Early efforts to establish public institutions of higher education in Cleveland emanated from the work of the Ohio Commission on Education beyond the High School in 1958. It issued a report, "Ohio's Future in Education beyond High School," recommending that the general assembly enact permissive legislation so that 2-year colleges or technical institutes financed by state and local funds and by student fees could be founded, and that these types of programs be established in Cleveland as soon as possible, with funds available by 1960. Ralph M. Besse, president of the CLEVELAND ELECTRIC ILLUMINATING CO. and also of the CLEVELAND COMMISSION ON HIGHER EDUCATION, served as a member of this commission and was a staunch supporter of establishing a 2-year public institution in Cuyahoga County. In 1959, Gov. Michael DiSalle held a State House Conference on Education, from which came relatively strong support for the comprehensive community college as a viable alternative for the direction of new efforts in higher education in the 1960s. Despite this strong support, there was much difference in opinion about the type and organization of public higher education in Ohio.

Meanwhile, locally, as early as 1952, the CLEVELAND FOUNDATION had supported the work of the Cleveland Commission on Higher Education, which was a coalition of local colleges composed of Baldwin-Wallace College, Fenn College, WRU, John Carroll University, and Case Institute of Technology. Its purpose was to coordinate planning among the colleges. At the time, the commission colleges enrolled over 90% of the college-age students in the area. In 1952 the commission issued a study, "These Will Go to College," which predicted a rise in the college population and found a sharp distinction among various socioeconomic groups attending college in the Cleveland area. At this time there were only 2 low-cost public universities in the area (at Kent and Akron), and they were located 30–40 mi. from downtown Cleveland. The private colleges seemed to have fixed abilities to expand, whereas the population was expected to increase 3-fold. A later commission report (1955) noted that general education and vocational education should be offered in 2-year institutions. It also suggested that less-able students attend such institutions where the programs would be more appropriate to them, thus preserving the elitism of the private institutions.

By 1959, the commission issued another report, "The Future of Higher Education in Cleveland." This report advocated more opportunities for part-time and adult students, with an emphasis on community-service courses, conferences, and specialized courses. It did not take into account the potential black and women students and predicted that these groups would not increase materially. The report also described a very active role for the commission in the creation of a community college. Two years following this report, the state of Ohio passed enabling legislation permitting counties to create a community college district, and in 1963, the state legislature provided state financial support for community colleges. All of that led to the establishment of CUYAHOGA COMMUNITY COLLEGE in 1963, which experienced the largest first-day enrollment of a community college in the nation's history. Its first home was at Brownell School, a 19th-century building leased from the Cleveland Board of Education in downtown Cleveland. Later it moved to its own downtown campus and established both an eastern campus in WARRENSVILLE TWP. and a western campus in PARMA, making it the largest college in Cleveland.

The expanding college population during the late 1950s and early 1960s led the Cleveland Commission on Higher Education to recommend the creation of public 4-year higher education. This time period saw classes offered at 2 local public high schools by Kent State University and Ohio University, which clearly documented the need for a new 4-year state university in Cleveland. CLEVELAND STATE UNIVERSITY was established by action of the Ohio General Assembly in 1964. In 1965, the trustees of CSU and of Fenn College formulated a contract to utilize Fenn as the nucleus of the new university. Fenn gave CSU its land and buildings and transferred its faculty and staff in 1965. This new university mainly served a commuter population with few residential students in downtown Cleveland. In 1986 its colleges included Graduate Urban Affairs, Arts & Sciences, Business Admin., Engineering, and Education. The Cleveland Marshall School of Law (est. 1897) merged with CSU in 1969 to become the CSU College of Law.

During the 1970s, the higher-education community continued to respond to the demands of the environment of a growing population by building and adding programs to meet the needs of an expanded student body. Some of the expansion, such as a series of dormitories constructed at CWRU in the 1960s, proved a liability as the college-age population shrank in the late 1970s. As local colleges and universities move into the 1980s and beyond, their thrust will once again need to be evaluated and changed because of the diminution of the potential pool of candidates. By the early 1980s, the colleges had already started to target the nontraditional-age student, including housewives and working men and women. With the era of rapid growth behind them, it was hoped that they might be better able to address the issue of quality curriculum offerings to meet the education needs of their many constituencies.

Sally H. Wertheim
John Carroll University

See also EDUCATION.

**HIGHLAND HEIGHTS** is a city located 18 mi. northeast of Cleveland and occupying 5.7 sq. mi. It is bounded by MAYFIELD VILLAGE on the east, MAYFIELD HTS. and LYNDHURST on the south, and RICHMOND HTS. on the west. Highland Hts. was originally part of Mayfield Twp., formed in 1819, together with GATES MILLS, Mayfield Village, Mayfield Hts., and a portion of Lyndhurst. Settlement in the area began in 1805, when several families migrated from New York. The first settler was Rufus Mapes. Development of the area was slow until 1877, when a plank road was built from E. CLEVELAND through Euclid and Mayfield townships along what is now Mayfield Rd. Another factor in the growth of Highland Hts. was the construction of the Cleveland & Eastern interurban railway between Cleveland and Chardon in 1899. By the 1920s, the automobile made the township even more accessible. Highland Hts. became a village in 1920 when the township was divided into the 4 villages. It became a city in 1967, operating under the mayor-council form of government. In the 1980s, as part of the Mayfield City School District, it had an elementary school, a junior high school, and a senior high school. Highland Hts. has several major businesses and industries, including the Allen Bradley Co., PICKER INTERNATL., and the COLE NATL. CORP., which produces controls for industrial computers and textiles. The city is home to the FRONT ROW THEATER, and provides its residents with 40 acres of parklands for recreational activities. Highland Hts.' slow growth has enabled it to maintain its residential character. It was the first community in Cuyahoga County to require all new subdivisions to have underground wiring and ornamental street lighting.

Nolfi, Peg, ed., *History of Highland Heights* (1976).

**HIGHWAYS.** Roads in Cleveland and other cities have served 2 main purposes. First, roads were built for commerce, including traffic movement and economic growth. Next, roads helped create and separate neighborhoods, allowing development of specialized districts for housing and business and an increase in property values. Inevitably, proponents of roads for traffic purposes came into conflict with those favoring the community and property interests of those living alongside. Officials in Cleveland and Cuyahoga County enjoyed only modest success in accommodating these conflicting goals. After 1900, state and federal officials financed part of the construction costs, leading to an upward shift in the level of conflict but no better luck in resolving it. The net result during the period between 1796–

1980 was creation of a vast and improved road network that never appeared affordable and adequate for traffic flow and local development. In 1796, MOSES CLEAVELAND and his survey party reached the site of the city and began marking off streets for future settlement. The grid idea with a couple of radial routes prevailed. Cleaveland's group sketched PUBLIC SQUARE, with Ontario running north and south and Superior east and west marking the center. Four additional streets bounded the outskirts of the area. In 1797, a second group of surveyors added 3 additional streets to the town plan. Actually, none of these streets existed; dense stands of trees covered the region. The marking of roads was simply a component in the division of land into lots for expeditious sale, the primary interest of the CONNECTICUT LAND CO. The net result of the 2 plattings, however, was to create a frame for Cleveland's development that emphasized expansion toward the east and south. From 1810–15, only Superior and Water streets were open for travel, but tree stumps and bushes remained as obstacles. Ontario was open south of the square but was equally undeveloped.

During the 1820s, growth of a warehouse and wholesale district in the FLATS along the CUYAHOGA RIVER encouraged officials to develop adjacent roads. On the far north, Bath St. ran between the river and Water St. Farther south, 4 lanes allowed traffic to descend into the Flats from Water and Superior streets. Construction in 1824 of 2 bridges across the river linked commercial and residential development around Public Square with river traffic and the smaller west side. But several routes authorized by council, such as W. and E. 3rd, remained undeveloped. Approval and completion of a route, it appears, rested on a petition presented by property owners along with the perception among officials that property values and trade would be enhanced. Streets constructed after 1820 often were named for leading businessmen and politicians who fostered commerce. Clinton Square, opened in 1835, honored Gov. De Witt Clinton of New York, who had visited the town in 1825 at the beginning of construction of the Ohio Canal. Case St. honored LEONARD CASE, a prominent real-estate developer. In 1836, council dedicated Clark St. for Jas. S. Clark, who had constructed the Columbus Bridge with a view toward development of his property in the Flats.

After 1840, leaders in urban America undertook the task of improving their streets. In 1880, Geo. Waring, an engineer active in street and sanitary improvements, conducted a survey of street conditions in the nation's cities. Half of the streets remained unpaved; only 2.5% of the paved roads were constructed of asphalt, a smooth, dust-free surface. During the 1870s, officials in cities such as New York, Cleveland, Chicago, and Washington, D.C., had installed wooden blocks, which muffled the noise of horses and carts. But wooden streets, soaked in creosote oil as a preservative, added to the fires that occasionally destroyed portions of major cities. Other surfaces included cobblestone and granite blocks, set on beds of sand, and gravel, the cheapest type of surface. Because abutters rather than the city usually financed improvements, the emphasis was on rapid extension of streets to houses and buildings in outlying districts rather than on securing the best surface. Street improvements, many hoped, would encourage a quick increase in property values, perhaps leading to the creation of exclusive residential districts such as Chicago's Union Park and EUCLID AVE. in Cleveland. By 1900, New York, Chicago, and Philadelphia had improved more than 1,000 mi., including asphalt surfaces. Officials in many cities, then, had developed a street system that was superior in many respects to counterparts in Europe and yet was regularly judged too costly, short, and bumpy.

The desire for miles of cheap roadway guided street designers in Cleveland. By the early 1880s, a lengthy network of streets, bridges, and viaducts had been constructed. The city had increased in size to 26.3 sq. mi., and the number of streets had jumped to 1,155, running 444 mi. in length. The CENTRAL VIADUCT was under construction to connect the city at Ohio St. with outlying areas south and west. The quality of surfaces varied; approximately 92 mi. had been graded, and another 32 mi. graded and curbed. During the 1840s, city officials had paved Superior St., and by the 1880s, paving, though still costly, had been applied to 58 mi. Altogether, 41% of the city's streets were improved. However popular these improvements, neither the costs nor the construction materials proved satisfactory. During the mid-1880s, officials installed block stone over several streets, including Broadway, Woodland, Superior, and Erie, a length of 13 mi. at a cost of $723,000. But the block stone was in fact the third type of improvement attempted; earlier pavements, including asphalt, had become "unendurable" and had generated a "long controversy." Nor was controversy limited to this particular project. During the early 1870s, property owners had petitioned council to open 17 streets, including Payne and Sheriff, the 2 largest projects. Approval rested on the legal requirement that petitioners would repay bonds issued by the city through tax assessments amounting to more than $1 million. Once the improvements were in place, however, several of the beneficiaries secured a court order preventing the city from collecting the taxes. The ability to avoid taxes for street improvements was a tentative matter legally and suggests the passion with which residents and officials in Cleveland sought to extend and upgrade streets.

Ca. 1900, rapid increases in auto sales began to highlight older problems and create new ones for those charged with road building. Competition between trolley operators and motorists for limited space added a fresh dimension to the traditional question of whether roads should benefit traffic flow or property values. Unable to satisfy diverse constituencies, road officials accelerated the pace of improvements and extensions. Between 1900–40, officials at every level paved more than 1.2 million mi. Local authorities proved unable to finance such costly improvements, forcing the level of highway funding (and decision making) up to the state and federal levels. In fact, the "battle for the streets" in cities such as Chicago, Los Angeles, Pittsburgh, and Cleveland prompted federal officials to contemplate funding the construction of a national expressway system. During the 1920s, road engineers and political leaders in the Cleveland region undertook major programs of extending and widening streets and roads. Federal and state funds were available for a number of these projects, which helped reduce the burden on local ratepayers and permitted more construction. Four-lane highways, replacing narrower and often twisty roads built prior to heavy traffic, were a popular design around Cleveland and many cities. On the far east, Kinsman, Euclid, and Lee roads were among those upgraded; and on the west, the 4-lane projects included West Lake Rd. from Blount St. to the west side of ROCKY RIVER. Widening of older streets inside Cleveland proved slower and more costly, but engineers widened and resurfaced a large number, especially where trolleys and automobiles competed for space on narrow brick pavements. Projects such as the widening of Chester from E. 13th to WADE PARK had to take place in sections of 8 to 10 blocks a year. In 1928, engineers counted nearly 1,800 mi. of roadway in the region constructed with federal, state, and county funds. Even more, they planned redevelopment and construction totaling 281 mi. in Cuyahoga County and another 312 mi. in the outlying areas at a cost of $63 million exclusive of rights-of-way and damages.

Widening and extending roads failed to solve the traffic mess. In 1934, the low point of the Great Depression, county engineers surveyed traffic volume on major streets. During a 12-hour period, they counted 43,000 vehicles crossing the Superior Bridge. More than 13,000 vehicles crossed Chester Ave. near 21st St. The outward movement of households and businesses added traffic along newer roads. Engineers counted 13,000 vehicles on Cedar Ave. west of Fairmount; 1,500 crossed Cedar at Warrensville, roughly the edge of suburban settlement. Leaders in politics and highway engineering added to the problem by spreading funds across numerous projects, partially satisfying demand and yet constructing roads that were below the standard of heavier and faster traffic. By the 1930s, engineers had begun to define the problems of constructing a highway system in political rather than technical terms. Road building always required the support of politicians, and the difference after the 1920s is one of emphasis. In brief, engineers lacked the financial resources and legal remedies required to construct a road network adequate to traffic. Demand for road improvements routinely outstripped resources. Not until additional funds were made available and direction of road building centralized, many argued, could engineers improve the road network. During harsh Depression days, moreover, automobile registrations jumped 16%, and travel increased 45%. Truckers and motorists contended with traffic jams; downtown businessmen faced declining sales; and all endured the waste and tragedy of accidents. "Our street systems," reported the Regional Assoc. of Cleveland in 1941, "belong to the horse-and-buggy era."

By the early 1940s, the construction of limited-access roads, known popularly as expressways, appeared to offer a solution to traffic jams and political stalemate. In 1939, the U.S. Bureau of Public Roads had offered formal articulation of a plan for constructing a national expressway system. Within a year or two, road engineers and city planners formed committees to fix local routes and secure the support prerequisite to a lobbying campaign with state and federal governments. In Nov. 1944, members of the committee in Cleveland published a plan for expressway construction consisting of an inner and outer beltway plus 7 radial routes. Expressways would eventually serve 20% of the region's traffic, or so ran the reasoning, drawing enough traffic from local roads to eliminate "need for many extensions and widenings." Fewer autos on local streets, in this scheme, would "ensure quiet in the neighborhood," encouraging residents not to seek " 'greener pastures' in the suburbs." Proponents of expressways in Cleveland, as elsewhere, also promised a reduction in the number of accidents and, of course, "quick movement of heavy traffic." Estimates of costs ran to $228 million during the course of 10 to 20 years, with the state and federal governments paying most of the bill. The plan overall expressed a conviction, widespread in highway circles, that expressways offered a technical fix for their own inability to untangle traffic, serve neighborhoods, and secure massive funding within the confines of urban political arenas.

The national expressway system was a popular idea. In 1944, members of Congress and Pres. Franklin D. Roosevelt approved construction of the Interstate Highway System. But they failed to vote funds for construction costs. Despite the widespread celebration of limited-access roads and faster traffic, leaders in the highway field, including truckers, economists, and the directors of farm and automotive groups, always sought to shift the financial burden of highway construction from themselves to general revenues, to taxes on other groups of road users, and to property owners. In cities such as Cleveland, debate and political tumult revolved around the potential of expressways for serving urban renewal, resuscitating the downtown, and speeding up traffic. Not until 1956 could members of Congress and Pres. Dwight D. Eisenhower approve dedication of the gasoline tax to rapid development of the federal highway systems, particularly the Natl. System of Interstate & Defense Highways. During the mid-1950s, engineers in Cleveland had spent $14 million to construct a section of the Innerbelt running 6/10 of a mile. In the future, federal officials would pay 90% of those costs, leaving the state responsible only for 10%. Free expressways proved no panacea in Cleveland. The scale of the interstate system, with its multiple lanes and wide interchanges, heightened the differences between those favoring traffic flow and others committed to property development. Conflict in the political arena began during the process of identifying routes. A route proposal submitted by a group of consulting engineers rested "solely on the basis of traffic," the planning director of Cleveland advised the county engineer on 1 June 1954, and "would result in so great a disruption of overall community plan that we cannot endorse it." By 30 Aug. 1954, the planning director was promoting the prospect that the report would serve only as an "invaluable reference document . . . (and) as a guide to transportation planning . . . through the future years." Route coordinates remained imprecise for several years pending the availbility of funds. By Dec. 1957, however, the report of another consulting firm had it that "the primary purpose of a freeway is to serve traffic. . . ."

Between 1958 and the mid-1970s, planning and construction of the interstate system emerged as routine items in local newspapers and public forums and as tangible facts on the landscape. Generally, those favoring traffic service predominated. The new Innerbelt, according to a report of 7 Oct. 1961 in the Cleveland *PLAIN DEALER*, "Loosens Downtown Traffic." Occasionally, proponents of local development and property values managed to secure changes in routings and the elimination of extensions. On 12 Dec. 1963, Mayor Paul Jones of SHAKER HTS. announced that he did not intend "to preside over the disfigurement of this city." In mid-1965, officials of the State Highway Dept. agreed to major changes in the location of interstate routes through the eastern suburbs. Observers noted that residents of these communities possessed wealth, which was imagined to translate directly into political protection, but unity and savvy were far more significant in the counsels of government. Traditional programs of road building and remodeling continued during the period of constructing the interstate system. The out-migration of households and businesses and a doubling of traffic during the first decade after WORLD WAR II guided highway planners. From 1946 through the late 1950s, engineering staffs emphasized removal of bricks and streetcar tracks and repaving with concrete and asphalt. Beginning in 1946, officials spent $80,000 a mile to remodel Cedar Ave. between E. 2nd St. and E. 109th. The interstate system never refocused traffic toward downtown, nor did it encourage residents to remain in the city. By the late 1960s, officials had to extend main roads far to the south, west, and east in order to serve traffic and property in numerous subdivisions around the region. During the 1970s, attention in the region and nation shifted to repair and rehabilitation. Cleveland exhausted its funds, and other levels of government had to contend with inflation, declining resources, and fierce competition for road improvements.

From the early 19th century through the late 1970s, engineers, politicians, and developers in the Cleveland region directed the funding and construction of a large and up-to-date highway system. Materials and design approximated national standards in each period. Equally, road builders in the Cleveland region served the conflicting interests of highway users and adjoining owners of property. During the period up to ca. 1900, property enjoyed the greatest attention; thereafter, the crush of traffic forced greater attention to the design and siting of roads with a view toward vehicular service. After 1900, moreover, the momentum of highway building encouraged the training of professionals in the fields of road construction and land-use planning. They were prepared to give active and articulate representation to these distinct points of view and to seek funding for them with state and federal officials. Professional status also conferred political and social legitimacy, allowing planners and engineers to interpret traffic and urban changes for politicians and residents. Engineers in the Cleveland region and nationwide held a larger influence and exercised a greater authority, especially because they had access to the revenues created by state and federal taxes on the sale of gasoline. Nonetheless, rarely could engineers in the Cleveland region—or in the nation as a whole—fund and construct the mileage demanded. During this entire period, road builders served the conflicting needs of a commercial civilization.

Mark H. Rose
Michigan Technological University

See also STREETS, URBAN TRANSPORTATION.

The **HILDEBRANDT PROVISION COMPANY,** a meat-processing firm established in 1893 by German immigrant Chas. R. Hildebrandt, was operated by members of the Hildebrandt family until it was forced to close in 1970. Arriving in the U.S. in 1883, 18-year-old Chas. Hildebrandt came directly to Cleveland and found work in the meat-packing house of Xavier Armbruster at 453 Sterling (E. 30th) St. When Armbruster died in 1887, Hildebrandt and his brother-in-law, August Habermann, bought the company, which they operated as Habermann & Hildebrandt. In 1893, Hildebrandt sold his portion of the business to Habermann and opened his own business at 532 Broadway. Employing 2 other people, he produced sausage and other meats. By 1897, his brother Julius had become a partner, and Hildebrandt Bros. had moved to 1104 (later 3620) Clark, where it remained until moving to its final location at 3619 Walton Ave. in 1929. Hildebrandt Provision was incorporated in Sept. 1906 with $65,000 in stock. By 1910, the company had grown to employ 65 people, with 8 salesmen working locally and 1 traveling salesman. By 1970 it employed 140 people. Since Hildebrandt sold its products only in Ohio, its operations were not subject to federal meat inspections. But the Wholesome Meat Act, passed by Congress in 1967, forced states to improve their meat inspections by hiring additional personnel, enforcing sanitary regulations regarding butchering and processing, assuring proper labeling of meats, and reviewing companies' plans to meet new, stricter standards and, on the other hand, a changing marketplace in which it had been losing money for the previous decade. Unable to afford the new equipment, Hildebrant Provision closed in late Jan. 1970.

The **HILL ACME COMPANY** is one of Cleveland's oldest firms engaged in the heavy manufacturing business. Jacob Perkins and Harry Hill founded and incorporated the firm in 1886 as the Hill Clutch Co., with a plant located close to Lake Erie, near present-day Edgewater Park. At first, the company manufactured only clutches. In 1906, Perkins established a foundry for Hill Clutch on W. 65th St. To signify its expanding facilities, it changed its name to the Hill Clutch Machine & Foundry Co. in 1920 and began to produce transmissions and various types of machine tools. In the 1930s, Hill grew further through acquisitions. In 1931, it purchased the Cleveland Knife & Forge Co. (founded 1891) on W. 113th St. Four years later, it acquired the Canton Foundry & Machine Co., a manufacturer of shears and cranes.

In 1940, Hill merged with another pioneer firm in the heavy manufacturing industry, the Acme Machinery Co., which had been started by Frederick W. Bruch, Claus Greve, and Daniel Luehrs in 1884 at the corner of Hamilton and Beiden (E. 45th) streets. The merged firm was incorporated as the Hill Acme Co. and made an expanded line of products, including special machinery and shears for the automotive, aviation, and steel industries. It was a pioneer in the manufacture of abrasive belt machines, used largely by automobile bumper manufacturers to polish metal. In 1952, Hill Acme moved its headquarters to 1201 W. 65th St. Adjacent to that plant, it opened a $250,000 research center in 1958. In the 1960s, it broadened its product line of machine tools by introducing material-handling equipment. Hill Acme also increased its foreign sales and acquired several firms. Through one of its acquisitions, it began to manufacture scuba-diving gear and compressed gas valves in the 1970s. In 1978, Hill Acme had 250 employees with $25–30 million in annual business. The firm also gained recognition over the years for its support of charitable and educational institutions.

**HILLCREST HOSPITAL,** located at 6780 Mayfield Rd. in MAYFIELD HTS., was opened in Nov. 1968 and is the successor to DOCTORS' HOSPITAL. The 230-plus-bed general hospital, which serves the eastern suburbs and parts of Geauga County, was built on land donated by D. A. and Anthony Visconsi, the builders of Eastgate Shopping Ctr. The hospital is owned and operated by the Cleveland Memorial Medical Foundation. In 1969, Hillcrest Hospital became involved in a controversy with the Renner Clinic Foundation over a new code of regulations that allegedly deprived the medical staff of management of medical functions, and levied a "bed tax" on physicians admitting patients to the hospital. Hillcrest continues the tradition of Doctors' Hospital and has research facilities for the study of cancer, cardiovascular diseases, and arthritis. By 1985, the hospital was part of STRATEGIC HEALTH SYSTEMS.

**HILLIARD, RICHARD** (3 July 1800–21 Dec. 1856), was an entrepreneur, a pioneer, and president of the village of Cleveland. Hilliard was born in New York State. The early death of his father left Hilliard, at age 14, to contribute to the general support of his family. He attended local schools for a few terms, then left to take an apprenticeship in Albany, N.Y. He left his apprenticeship to become a clerk and teacher. In 1824 he went to work for the mercantile business of John Daly. Hilliard quickly worked his way up to partner without capital. In the same year, the company relocated in Cleveland, and in 1827 Hilliard bought out Daly's interest in the firm. He then hired a resident partner in New York, Wm. Hayes. The two men stayed together as Hilliard & Hayes until Hilliard's death. Hilliard was an active member of the Trinity Church. He also helped finance the Erie Railroad. In the 1830s he and Courtland Palmer of New York and Edwin Clark of Cleveland began manufacturing and waterway development in the FLATS. Hilliard began his political career in 1830 when he served 2 terms as president of the board of trustees of what was the village of Cleveland. In the first city elections of 1836,

507

he was elected alderman. In May of that year, he served on a select committee for the common schools of Cleveland. He joined the Board of Trade in 1849 and became a commissioner on the Board of Water Works in 1853. He was also a member of the board of trustees for the Homeopathic Hospital College. In 1827, Hilliard married Sarah Katherine Hayes. The couple had 9 children.

**HINMAN, WILBUR F.** (b. 1841), was a volunteer Army officer in the CIVIL WAR. He enlisted in the 65th Ohio Volunteer Infantry for 3 years on 12 Oct. 1861, serving as 1st sergeant until promotion to 1st lieutenant of Co. E on 16 June 1861. He was wounded at the Battle of Chickamauga, Ga., 19 Sept. 1863 but recovered to be promoted to captain, Co. F, June 1864. He was mustered out as captain 30 Nov. 1865. Hinman returned to Cleveland after military service, where in 1878 he was a member of the Cleveland Board of Education committee organized to set up a school library system. He served as clerk of the Cuyahoga County Common Pleas Court, being elected in 1875 and reelected in 1878. Correspondence to JAS. BARNETT indicated that Hinman was either residing or employed in Washington, D.C., in 1887–88.

The **HIPPODROME THEATER** was located in an 11-story office building at 720 Euclid Ave. Designed by Cleveland architect John Elliot, the Hippodrome featured exceptionally good acoustics, a lavish interior, and a spaciousness that made it grandiose in appearance. Considered to be among the world's great playhouses, it attracted artists and performers of distinction. The theater featured every conceivable contemporary piece of equipment and lighting. The auditorium had boxes, 2 balconies with elevators, and seating for 3,548. There was a large orchestra pit, an orchestra room, a ballet rehearsal room, a 12,000 sq.-ft. steel fire curtain, and 44 dressing rooms on 9 floors. The stage was equipped to handle large-scale productions and spectacles such as operas. The world's 2d-largest next to the Hippodrome in New York, it measured 130' wide, 104' deep, and 110' high. The runways on either side of the stage were connected by backstage passages. The stage could be lifted to 4 different levels by hydraulic jacks. On one level was an 80x40x10-ft. water tank used for water spectacles. The theater was built by an operating company headed by Max Faetkenhauer at a cost of $800,000. After several years, theater operations were leased to B. F. Keith. In 1922 Walter Reasoner took over operations, followed by RKO in 1929. Among those who performed at the Hippodrome were Enrico Caruso, Sarah Bernhardt, W. C. Fields, Will Rogers, Al Jolson, and John McCormack. In 1929 the Hippodrome was renovated for the showing of motion pictures. Remodeling in 1931 made it the largest American theater devoted entirely to motion pictures. New seats and carpeting were installed. A large portion of the stage was removed, as were the orchestra pit and steel fire curtain. A huge arch replaced the proscenium boxes, while the main floor was lowered and a new mezzanine was added to increase the seating to above 4,000. In 1933 the theater went bankrupt, and operations were taken over by Warner Bros. In 1951 it became part of the Telenews chain. In 1972, the property was purchased by Alvin Krenzler. The Hippodrome was the last of the major downtown movie houses to close; its downfall came when the office space was closed and the theater's revenues proved insufficient to support the building. The Hippodrome was demolished in 1981 to make way for a parking garage.

**HIRAM HOUSE** Social Settlement was established in 1896 as an outgrowth of a class project initiated by a group of students from Hiram College. Following a brief tenure on the west side of Cleveland (June-Sept. 1896), Hiram House moved to the city's east side. It occupied several structures along Orange Ave. before constructing a permanent facility at 2723 Orange Ave. in 1899–1900. The neighborhood's population consisted primarily of East European Jewish immigrants in 1900. ITALIANS replaced the Jews in large part by 1914 and were replaced, in turn, by BLACKS in the post-World War I era. GEO. BELLAMY, one of the settlement's founders, served as its director from 1897–1946. He attracted substantial support to the institution from prominent families, such as the Mathers, Prentisses, and Hunts. The settlement used this support to expand its operations, purchasing a rural camp in MORELAND HILLS, Ohio, in 1902, and additional structures adjacent to its main building in 1906. In 1926, Hiram House began a series of branch operations at city school buildings in cooperation with the Board of Education. These operations continued when work at the Orange Ave. location ceased in 1941. The main settlement building was subsequently demolished. The branch operations ceased in 1948 upon recommendation of the Welfare Fed. Since 1948, Hiram House has operated only as a camping facility.

Grabowski, John J., "A Social Settlement in a Neighborhood in Transition, Hiram House, Cleveland, Ohio, 1896–1926" (Ph.D. diss., CWRU, 1977).
Hiram House Records, WRHS.

**HISPANIC COMMUNITY.** Members of Cleveland's Spanish-speaking community trace their heritage to Puerto Rico, Mexico, Cuba, various other countries in Central and South America and the Carribean, and Spain. All of these peoples can be called Hispanics, although in Cleveland the term *Hispanic* usually refers to the city's Puerto Rican residents, who make up the overwhelming majority of the local Spanish-speaking people. The Puerto Rican community of Cleveland is relatively new. Although a few Puerto Ricans settled in Cleveland following the SPANISH-AMERICAN WAR, and others arrived after WORLD WAR I, the largest influx to northern Ohio occurred between 1945–65. After WORLD WAR II, young unmarried Puerto Rican men were recruited to work in the factories of Lorain, Ohio, and in the greenhouses of northern Ohio. When their contracts terminated, many were attracted to Cleveland by its diverse job opportunities. Although most had not originally intended to stay in Ohio permanently, many changed their minds and sent for friends and relatives to join them. In 1955, Cleveland reported a total of 1,500 Puerto Rican residents. In 1960, Puerto Ricans accounted for about 82% of all Spanish-speaking residents in the city. Cleveland's Puerto Rican population increased dramatically owing to a high birth rate and migration from the island, New York, and Chicago. In 1983, approximately 25,000 persons of Puerto Rican descent lived in Greater Cleveland. As a group, Puerto Ricans were unique settlers in that they were already American citizens when they arrived in Cleveland, and they could easily travel back and forth to their homeland.

The majority of Puerto Ricans who came to Cleveland in the 1950s settled on the east side around Hough, Lexington, and, later, Superior avenues. These areas attracted Puerto Ricans because of their proximity to Our Lady of Fatima Catholic Church and St. Paul's Shrine, where Spanish-speaking Trinitarian priests were located. In 1958, an exodus of Puerto Ricans from the east side to the near west side began. Inner-city deterioration and a desire to be closer to jobs in steel mills and industrial mills in the FLATS area prompted the large-scale movement. Approximately

⅔ of Greater Cleveland's Puerto Ricans now (1986) live on the near west side from W. 5th to W. 65th streets, between Detroit and Clark avenues. On the east side, some Puerto Ricans are still found in the original settlement, from E. 30th to E. 77th and Wade Park to St. Clair. A growing number are settling in the N. Broadway area. Puerto Rican households are also scattered throughout Greater Cleveland's SUBURBS. In 1986, Puerto Ricans in Cleveland belonged to 3 different socioeconomic groups. Some were affluent, well-educated, fluent in English, and often members of professions. Others enjoyed a moderate income, worked in factories and mills, and lived in lower-middle-class neighborhoods. The third group worked as cheap labor, spoke little English, and lived in almost slum conditions on the near west side.

Historically, most Puerto Ricans are Roman Catholics, but unlike most Catholic people, Puerto Ricans did not bring their own priests with them. In 1954, the Cleveland Diocese established a Spanish Catholic mission, and Our Lady of Fatima Catholic on Quimby Ave. offered masses in Spanish. Other parishes often opposed Spanish masses and did not welcome new members from the Puerto Rican community. As a result of determined and sustained efforts by many of Greater Cleveland's Puerto Ricans, a church on W. 32nd St. near Lorain Ave. was purchased in 1975 and became SAN JUAN BAUTISTA CATHOLIC CHURCH. Though it is primarily Puerto Rican, other Spanish-speaking people are in the parish. Several Protestant churches in Greater Cleveland also have Puerto Rican followings, and a number of Catholic and Protestant churches offered special services and bilingual education programs for Spanish-speaking persons of all ages in 1986. The first Pentecostal church in Cleveland was the Spanish Assembly of God on W. 11th St., founded in 1952.

As a group, Puerto Ricans are fiercely proud of their traditions and customs. First-generation parents have attempted to maintain island traditions in their homes and clubs, which often bear the names of native island towns. Puerto Rican social, cultural, civic, and service clubs exist in Cleveland. The Spanish American Committee, a well-known social-service organization that serves primarily the Puerto Rican community, has been active since 1966. The Hispanic Community Forum sponsored the first annual Hispanic convention in Cleveland in 1984. Puerto Rican Friendly Day, an activity uniquely Puerto Rican, has been observed by Cleveland's Puerto Ricans each summer since 1969. Its purpose is to bring together the city's Puerto Rican residents and to educate the Cleveland community about Puerto Rican culture.

Mexicans constitute the 2d-largest Spanish-speaking ethnic group in Cleveland. The first Mexicans settled in Cleveland during the early 1920s, and a slow but steady stream of immigrants increased the city's Mexican population to 679 in 1920. During the following decade, the Mexican population fell to 162 as a result of the U.S. Immigration Act, which required many Mexicans to return to Mexico. During the 1940s, the steel industry in Cleveland and Lorain recruited large numbers of Mexican immigrants for war work. Some of those in Lorain eventually moved to Cleveland because of greater opportunities for employment in the larger city. Many Mexican immigrants decided to stay permanently in Cleveland. By 1983, approximately 4,000 people born in Mexico or of Mexican descent lived in the city. The early Mexicans were from rural areas. They came seeking economic opportunity and freedom from political instability and religious persecution. These early arrivals did not form ethnic settlements, as did many other immigrant groups. Instead, they settled in various parts of the city. In 1986, the majority of Mexican-

Americans lived on the west side around Lorain Ave., Detroit Ave., and Randall and W. 52nd St. Others are scattered throughout Greater Cleveland. One of the first cultural and social clubs started by Mexican people was the Azteca Club, founded in 1932. In 1951, the club purchased a store and suite at 5606 Detroit Ave. to serve as the center of social and cutural activities for Cleveland's Mexicans.

Most of Cleveland's Cubans came to the city following Castro's seizure of power in 1959. Prior to this time, only 200 Cubans had resided in Cleveland. The Cleveland Cuban Refugee Resettlement Committee, composed of Catholic, Protestant, and Jewish organizations, helped relocate refugees of the various faiths. Most of the new arrivals were families who intended to return to Cuba as soon as Castro was ousted. After the Bay of Pigs, many decided to stay permanently in Cleveland. In 1980, there were about 650 Cubans in Cleveland. The majority were well-educated and experienced business people. Some American industries with plants in Cuba offered jobs to the refugees. The Cubans quickly became self-supporting, acquired well-paying jobs, and moved into suburban neighborhoods. The Cubans of Cleveland organized the Circulo Cuban Assoc. of Cleveland, a cultural club for the purpose of preserving Cuban traditions, strengthening Cuban brotherhood, and preserving the dream of a free Cuba.

In 1980, roughly 5,000 Clevelanders hailed from various countries in Latin America other than Cuba, Mexico, and Puerto Rico. Most were fairly well-educated men who came after World War II. Some sought to continue their education in the Cleveland area; others sought jobs in the export and import business. Eventually many decided to stay in Cleveland permanently and married Clevelanders or sent for their families to join them. The new arrivals initially settled near each other and near the Mexicans and Puerto Ricans, with whom they shared bonds of culture and language. However, the immigrants never formed permanent settlements, because there were few people from any one nationality group. They are now (1986) scattered throughout the suburbs of Greater Cleveland. Many of the Latin American immigrants have become members of various professions. The only club that serves all Latin Americans is the Cleveland Pan American Cultural Society, an affiliate of the Pan American Union in Washington, D.C. The club was organized in 1960 by night students at Western Reserve University who felt a need for formal expression of Latin American culture and for programs to familiarize Greater Clevelanders with the distinctive culture and history of the various Latin American republics. Part of this effort is an annual folk festival in conjunction with the interhemispheric celebration of Pan American Day.

Relatively small numbers of Greater Cleveland's Spanish-speaking people trace their heritage to Spain. In 1983, there were approximately 900 Greater Clevelanders of Spanish descent. Most Spaniards came to Cleveland by way of Cuba; others migrated from the U.S. Southwest. They began arriving in Cleveland ca. 1910. Most came with the intention of staying here permanently. The immigrants tended to settle together. Initially, the English language posed a major obstacle, but once they learned the language, they integrated quickly and are now scattered throughout the area. Many new arrivals labored in the city's steel mills, factories, and foundries. Although the Spaniards readily adopted American customs, they preserved many of their social and cultural traditions. A society for Spaniards, Club Galicia, was established in 1926. It was active for many years until it disbanded as other associations took its place in the local Spanish community. Several media services are designed for the Spanish-speaking peoples of Cleveland. Spanish-language broadcasts for several hours a week are heard on local radio stations. Various newspapers and periodicals, including *LATINO MAGAZINE*, in Spanish are available, and the *Cleveland Plain Press*, a neighborhood newspaper, writes a few news articles in Spanish for the Hispanic community.

Nicholas J. Zentos
Lorain County Community College

See also IMMIGRATION & MIGRATION.

**HISTORIES OF CLEVELAND.** The histories of Cleveland provide evidence of different intentions on the part of their authors. A general, if imperfect, trend can be described, leading from celebratory, even "boomerish," full-scale general history to more limited analyses of specific segments of the city's past. There also has been difference in the authors' expectations of audiences, ranging from history that is sophisticated and likely to appeal principally to an educated elite, to history obviously intended for school use, to more popular accounts—with or without illustrations sufficient to merit ascription as "coffee-table" books. At the same time, attitudes and assumptions within the historical profession about the significance of local history have changed. In mid-19th-century America, when the first history of Cleveland was published, local and regional history was a respected field of endeavor. However, increasingly in the 20th century, local history came to be considered fit only for the attention of amateurs and antiquarians. Supposedly, serious historians needed at least the national canvas in order to frame significant questions about the past. Then, within the last few decades and the development of the "new" social history, another turning took place. Local arenas now seem particularly appropriate as testing grounds for many historical hypotheses.

The economics of publishing also have determined the nature of the city's histories. With sales usually limited to the interested residents of the place, local histories traditionally have had to depend on subsidies as well as sales. The vanity of subscribers to the older multivolumed sets is evidenced when some, if not most, of the pages are devoted to biographical sketches and/or photographs of significant subscribers. Then, too, corporate public-relations efforts are visible in more recent popular histories, in the sketches of commercial or industrial enterprises that have provided funding for the volume. In all, there appear to have been 3 more or less distinct eras of writing and publishing histories of Cleveland: (1) The "pioneer" period (the second half of the 19th century), in which talented men and women—writers who were not professionally trained as historians—laid down the basic political and economic narrative about the city's past. This period might be identified as the decades "between Whittlesey and Kennedy." (2) The first half of the 20th century, in which historians and others continued to produce general histories of the city, incrementally adding length to the narrative and increasing attention to cultural and social history. This period could be labeled the years "from Orth to Rose." (3) Since 1950—or "since Rose"—no full-scale documented general history of Cleveland has been published. Popular accounts continue to appear, as do monographs and studies of specific topics.

Before describing the histories and historians of these 3 eras, a note should be added about Cleveland history included in accounts with larger geographic dimensions. Although not generally included in this survey, sometimes very substantial information about Cleveland's past has been incorporated into these "larger-area" histories. Examples are histories of Cuyahoga County such as Crisfield Johnson, comp., *History of Cuyahoga County* (Philadelphia: D. W.

Ensign, 1879), and Wm. R. Coates, *A History of Cuyahoga County and the City of Cleveland* (3 vols., Chicago & New York: American Historical Society, 1924), which is described below. There also are histories of the WESTERN RESERVE such as Harriet Taylor Upton's 3-volume *History of the Western Reserve* (Chicago & New York: Lewis Publishing Co., 1910). Upton treats each of the 12 counties that make up the Western Reserve separately, but she provides topical chapters, too, and a special emphasis on the experience of women. Then there is a history of the "north coast," Randolph Downes, *History of Lake Shore Ohio* (3 vols., New York: Lewis Historical Publishing Co., Inc., 1952), and histories of the state, including the 6 volumes CARL WITTKE edited, *The History of the State of Ohio* (Columbus: Ohio State Archeological & Historical Society, 1941–44). There is information and sometimes ideas about Cleveland's past in all of these.

The undoubted "father" of Cleveland history was CHAS. WHITTLESEY, a professional geologist who published *Early History of Cleveland, Ohio, Including Original Papers and Other Matter Relating to the Adjacent Country. With Biographical Notices of the Pioneers and Surveyors* (Cleveland: Fairbanks, Benedict & Co.) in 1867. That same year, the WESTERN RESERVE HISTORICAL SOCIETY was founded; Whittlesey served as its first president. His history is exactly what one would expect of a talented professional whose interest in the past—especially archeology—coincided with his work on geological surveys. The volume begins with a description of "Pre-Adamite History"—or the geology of the Cleveland area—and ends, some 400+ pages later, with a section on "Fluctuations in the Level of Lake Erie." In between there is the substance if not the form of history, or, as another Cleveland historian described it: "disconnected facts collected from original and widely diverse sources." But that same critic asserted that "no history of Cleveland can be written, in all time to come, that is not primarily based upon . . . the intelligent labor of Col. Whittlesey." And, in the organization of his "disconnected facts," Whittlesey set down an embryonic chronological structure that his successors found useful, in whole or in part, to borrow.

Twenty years after *Early History of Cleveland* was published, W. Scott Robison, Whittlesey's immediate successor as historian of the city, produced a 500-page *History of the City of Cleveland: Its Settlement, Rise, and Progress* (Cleveland: Robison & Crockett-The Sunday World, 1887). Actually, the text measures a little less than 400 pages, for there are also 44 persons described in the biographical segment. This 1887 volume has Robison listed as "editor"; some chapters or parts thereof were written by other, identified, authors. The publishers' preface states their endeavor to present "a book that could be sold at a price considerably less than that of the average local work of this kind," explaining that "voluminous and elaborate local histories, with their proportionately high cost, have not proved commercial successes." To improve on that situation, in Robison's volume "prolix statements of facts, long comments, expanded theories and tedious discussions" are said to be avoided, as is "the history of the Indian tribes which inhabited this region. . . ." Robison's story extends from the organization of the CONNECTICUT LAND CO. to 1887; he shows concern for cultural and philanthropic endeavors as well as the usual politics and economic circumstances. In its time, the book must have been a welcome addendum to Whittlesey's earlier volume.

In 1896, Cleveland celebrated the centennial of its founding, and the occasion was marked by the publication of 2 histories. Clara A. Urann published a brief (120-page) *Centennial History of Cleveland* (Cleveland: J. B. Savage,

1896), undocumented but containing considerable primary-source quotations, with an emphasis on social and cultural developments in the city, less on economics, and very little political history. Considerably larger in scope and purpose was Jas. Harrison Kennedy's *A History of the City of Cleveland: Its Settlement, Rise, and Progress, 1796-1896* (Cleveland: Imperial Press, 1896). Seven years earlier, Kennedy, who was a Cleveland journalist, had collaborated with Wilson M. Day in producing *The Bench and Bar of Cleveland* (Cleveland: Cleveland Printing & Publishing Co., 1889). Day then was editor of *Iron Trade Review*; he later headed the Cleveland Chamber of Commerce and served as director-general of the city's centennial celebration. Kennedy's centennial-year history of Cleveland is documented, but addressed to the general reader; is illustrated and indexed; and contains some undigested information but also "real history" intended to explain Cleveland's rise and progress. During the first half of the 20th century, 5 "general" histories of Cleveland were published, each providing its own dimension and perspective on the city's past. Their authors were, in order of their publications, SAMUEL P. ORTH, Elroy M. Avery, Wm. R. Coates, Wilfred H. and Miriam Russell Alburn, and WM. GANSON ROSE. As a group, these histories are more comprehensive, more "scientific," and more satisfying than their predecessors. Yet despite their attractive qualities, all of them now seem old-fashioned and inclined toward rather naive faith in the march of Cleveland's progress. The first of the general histories to appear was Samuel P. Orth's *A History of Cleveland Ohio with Numerous Chapters by Special Contributors* (3 vols., Chicago-Cleveland: S. J. Clarke Publishing Co., 1910). This history followed standard format in division between the first volume (history) and the 2 that followed (biographical), although Orth distanced himself from the commercial aspects of the publication by informing his readers that he "has had no connection with the biographical volumes, and has no interest of any kind in them." Orth's attitudes about his endeavor are of interest. He asserted that his history was not to be "a mere narrative in chronological sequence of the city's achievements"; that it would "dwell particularly upon the sociological and the political city, rather than upon the commercial and industrial city." Orth divided his massive (815-page) historical volume into 10 divisions identified by labels such as "The Geographical and Physical Relations of the City," "Population," "Governmental and Political," and "Social Life." Each of these topical divisions was divided into chapters, in most cases chronologically ordered. Orth's collaborators included faculty members from the Cleveland Normal School, Case School of Applied Science, and Western Reserve University, as well as Cleveland-area physicians, dentists, engineers, and cultural, religious, and philanthropic leaders. Orth was an activist-scholar in the era of progressivism: lawyer, assistant U.S. attorney, school board president, lecturer at WRU, Oberlin, and the Case School of Applied Science. His broad definition of history is no less celebratory of Cleveland's "progress" than the centennial-year histories had been. But it is more inclusive, its elaborate structure reflecting its social-scientific creator. Three-quarters of a century later, it can still be consulted with profit.

Orth's successors faced the challenge of improving on his *History of Cleveland*. The first to try was Elroy McKendree Avery, a man who, like Orth, had combined academic and civic activities. School administrator, textbook author, city councilman, and Ohio state senator, he published *A History of Cleveland and Its Environs: The Heart of New Connecticut* in 3 volumes in 1918 (Chicago: Lewis Publishing Co.). Avery confides fewer concerns to his reader than did Orth, although he does explain the general lack of documentation with these words: "For the sake of the reader, I have made very sparing use of footnotes. . . ." Avery's first volume (the "history" part of his *History*) divides into 2 parts. The first 21 chapters (340 pages) are arranged chronologically; the rest of the 727-page volume is divided topically into chapters, some of which are contributed by others, especially H. G. Cutler, the general historian of Lewis Publishing, who, Avery explains, "came from Chicago to Cleveland and, for several weeks, was my genial and able assistant" "to enable me to complete the work on schedule. . . ." The chronologically arranged segment spans the 19th century; only 2 chapters describe Cleveland in the years 1896-1918. The topical chapters range across educational, professional, literary, and religious concerns, ending with a chapter on "Trade, Commerce and Industry." While the writing is generally direct and concise, much of the information is derivative. Avery seems to sense the circumstance, for he indicates that he found Kennedy's 1896 history especially helpful; that "as Mr. Kennedy and I were continually dipping our buckets into the same wells of information, identity of matter is not conclusive proof of plagiarism."

Wm. R. Coates offered his volumes of local history in 1924 ( *A History of Cuyahoga County and the City of Cleveland*, 3 vols., Chicago & New York: American Historical Society, 1924). Like Orth and Avery, Coates divided his work between 1 volume of history and 2 of biography. Coates seemed to have a romantic, nostalgic attitude toward his subject; he "anticipated it will be a pleasant task to review the past as well as to take stock of the present," but whether for him or his reader, he does not declare. Coates's *History* is a history of Cuyahoga County; the first 23 of 38 chapters cover the history of the townships other than Cleveland that constitute the county. They do so in prose that is full of specific, even trivial, detail. After nearly 300 pages, Cleveland's allotted space is reached; a brief excursion from township through village through city organization rapidly gives way to topical chapters on churches, schools, bench and bar, physicians, newspapers, colleges, etc. The volume ends with a chapter on Cleveland in the world war, one of the first attempts to record the impact of the war on the municipality.

In 1932, Wilfred H. and Miriam Russell Alburn, who operated a syndication service for newspapers, published *This Cleveland of Ours* (4 vols., Chicago-Cleveland-Indianapolis: S. J. Clarke Publishing Co., 1933). This "last of the dinosaurs" divided into 2 volumes (1,233 pages) of history and 2 volumes of biography. Almost as ambitious in structure as Orth's earlier work, this history of the city represents well its place in time—years punctuated by the collapse of the American economy. It is retrogressive in the manner that it emphasizes Cleveland's industries, although the Alburns recognize the bleakness of such celebration as of 1932 (the year their narrative ends), pointing out in their foreword that "if the 'Technocrats,' with their pitiless charts and graphs, are right in their conclusions, a new generation may find curious reading in this portrayal of a virile American community in the heyday of private enterprise. At the time of going to press, no immediate scrapping of the capitalistic system, or liquidation of the machine age, is anticipated. Nor, it may be added, any prompt entrance into a mechanized millennium." What the Alburns added to the earlier work by Orth and Avery and Coates was an emphasis on the industrial and commercial aspects of Cleveland's development, and an extension of the narrative of the city's development in the years after the 1896 centennial.

The final offering in this group of 5, and the last attempt to construct a general history of the city, was Wm. Ganson

Rose's *Cleveland: The Making of a City*. (Cleveland: World Publishing Co., 1950). This effort differed substantially from all others. Inspired by the city's sesquicentennial celebration in 1946, it is a single-volume (1,272-page) chronological compendium, relentlessly arranged by decades, with a 153-page triple-columned index that allows a user to locate information. Analysis and interpretation of the past are conspicuous by their absence; this is, in the words of another Cleveland historian, "a volume that is more a collection of facts than a history." These attributes make the book both frustrating and indispensable. The quantity of data is enormous, and, of course, the 2 decades that had intervened since the Alburns' history are canvassed here. Yet it is difficult to deny that it is "history" of this sort that gives the genre its reputation for inducing boredom. If Rose represents the culmination of almost a century of general histories of Cleveland, it may be that rejoicing rather than regret should mark the demise of the species.

There were, of course, other efforts expended during the first half of the 20th century. One of the more notable was ELBERT J. BENTON's *Cultural Story of an American City: Cleveland*; "During the Log Cabin Phases, 1796–1823," "During the Canal Days, 1825–1850," and "Under the Shadow of a Civil War and Reconstruction, 1850–1877" (Cleveland: Western Reserve Historical Society, 1943–46). A professional historian, director of the WRHS after his retirement from the WRU faculty, Benton retreads the familiar terrain of Whittlesey and successors, but with emphasis on the cultural development of the city. The boundaries were sometimes elusive, and Benton himself found that "a cultural history like a social history is difficult to define; both are fields less clearly established by custom than that of political or military history. Let us say that whatever contributes to refinement in manners and taste, whatever improves the moral and intellectual nature of man, is a cultural force or agency." So churches and libraries, newspapers and the lyceum, schools and colleges are described—as are such extracultural commodities as steamboats and railroads, banks and currency. Despite the definitional problems, Benton's study is carefully constructed, written with economy of words and considerable charm. The volumes provide a bridge of sorts between the older, comprehensive histories and the monographic literature that would come to characterize the writing of Cleveland's past in the decades ahead.

Since 1950, histories of Cleveland have differed markedly from what appeared earlier. The only attempts to treat the full narrative of the city's story have been "popular" in nature—undocumented, generally written by journalists rather than professional historians, intended to find a reading audience in the "lay public." The most successful of these, probably, have been those written by Geo. E. Condon: *Cleveland: The Best Kept Secret* (Garden City: Doubleday & Co., 1967) and *Cleveland: Prodigy of the Western Reserve* (Tulsa: Continental Heritage Press, Inc., 1979). At their best these are attractive, well-written, and reasonably reliable products. At their worst, they indulge in questionable historical explanations. There also have been histories designed for classroom use in public schools. F. Leslie Speir's *Cleveland: Our Community and Its Government* (Cleveland: Cleveland Public Schools, 1941) is a relatively informative overview of Cleveland's history and polity. In 1955, Harlan Hatcher (who had previously written a history of the Western Reserve) and Frank Durham published *Giant from the Wilderness: The Story of a City and Its Industries* (Cleveland: World Publishing Co., 1955). The principal interest in these publications is the choice of emphasis within the narratives presented. In this case, the authors present a hymn to urbanization and industrialization—as the title

implies—but also incorporate cultural and ethnic information about the city and its people.

Meanwhile, sophisticated monographs have appeared, providing us with institutional histories and analyses of the city's ethnic communities. The institutional histories have clustered for topic on the city's cultural and educational institutions, especially during anniversary years. Carl Wittke, *The First Fifty Years: The Cleveland Museum of Art, 1916–1966* (Cleveland: Cleveland Museum of Art, 1966), commemorates that institutions's golden anniversary; Donald P. Gavin, *John Carroll University: A Century of Service* (Kent: Kent State University Press, 1985), celebrates the centennial of John Carroll's founding; and CLARENCE H. CRAMER, *Case Western Reserve: A History of the University, 1826–1976* (Boston: Little, Brown & Co., 1976), marked that institution's sesquicentennial. All are admirable accounts by professional historians, as is Cramer's *Open Shelves and Open Minds: A History of the Cleveland Public Library* (Cleveland: Press of Case Western Reserve University, 1972). Edmund H. Chapman's *Cleveland: Village to Metropolis: A Case Study of Problems of Urban Development in Nineteenth-Century America* (Cleveland: Western Reserve Historical Society and Press of Western Reserve University, 1964) describes the city's built environment up to the mid-1870s, and Eric Johannesen's *Cleveland Architecture, 1876–1976* (Cleveland: Western Reserve Historical Society, 1979) carries the story into the 20th century.

The history of ethnic Cleveland has a history of its own. The first attempts to explain the varieties of Cleveland's polyglot population coincided with the melting-pot efforts of the World War I era. Brief accounts such as ELEANOR LEDBETTER's *The Czechs of Cleveland* and Chas. Wellsley Coulter's *The Italians of Cleveland* were produced in 1919 by the city's Americanization Committee. A second turning to ethnic Cleveland accompanied the New Deal Writers' Program of the Works Projects Admin. A compendium describing ethnic groups, from Albanians to UKRAINIANS, formed the unpublished manuscript "The Peoples of Cleveland," 1942. This alphabetically arranged survey offered a little Old World description, a little history, and an inventory of each ethnic group in Cleveland in the late 1930s and early 1940s. More recently, a more comprehensive and systematic survey of the ethnic communities of the city has been directed from CLEVELAND STATE UNIVERSITY by Karl Bonutti. The Cleveland Ethnic Heritage Studies Monograph Series began in 1975 with some early volumes concerned with general ethnic issues and information. These were followed by volumes devoted to particular ethnic groups, combining the history of the appropriate Cleveland community with native-land history, folk and art customs, and traditions.

Apart from these, directed to other audiences, of significance because of their methodologies and/or analyses are several monographs of high quality. Josef J. Barton's *Peasants and Strangers: Italians, Rumanians, and Slovaks in an American City, 1890–1950* (Cambridge: Harvard University Press, 1975) is sophisticated in its use of European-language sources and the way in which Cleveland statistics of social mobility (occupation, property) and structures are interpreted within the larger social-science literature. Lloyd P. Gartner, *History of the Jews of Cleveland* (Cleveland: Western Reserve Historical Society and Jewish Theological Seminary of America, 1978), is an able, fully documented account of Cleveland Jews from 1840–1945. Gartner's work was extended by Sidney Z. Vincent and Judah Rubinstein in *Merging Traditions—Jewish Life in Cleveland: A Contemporary Narrative, 1945–1975, A Pictorial Record, 1839–1975* (Cleveland: Western Reserve Historical Society and

Jewish Community Fed. of Cleveland, 1978). Kenneth L. Kusmer, *A Ghetto Takes Shape: Black Cleveland, 1870–1930* (Urbana: University of Illinois Press, 1976), analyzes the growth of the black ghetto in the city in intelligent fashion. Four years earlier, Russell H. Davis had published *Black Americans in Cleveland: From George Peake to Carl Stokes, 1796–1969* (Washington: Assoc. for the Study of Negro Life & History in cooperation with the Western Reserve Historical Society), a more general compilation of information about black Clevelanders.

History, of course, is everywhere. This survey has taken no notice of the ways in which the past is skillfully recreated by biographers and preserved by autobiographers; it has not included in its observations the history that exists in structures (landmarked or not) or in the extraordinary artifacts of the past faithfully preserved in institutions such as the Western Reserve Historical Society. Nor can the assessment end with sure-fire prediction of what will come next, for such prediction is not the role of the historian. Nonetheless, it does seem apparent that the current emphasis on social history and demography will continue to motivate historians in their efforts to understand the cosmopolitan nature of the Cleveland community. History is always implicitly comparative, but it is possible to imagine a more explicit recognition of that fact. Analysis that finds and explains similarities and differences among Midwest, Great Lakes, "Rustbelt," or "Snowbelt" cities should enhance our understandings of population shifts, economic changes, social policies, and similar phenomena of modern urban life. And in 1996, the bicentennial year of the city's birth, probably we will see again celebratory histories of the way Cleveland got to be the way it is.

Carl Ubbelohde
Case Western Reserve University

**HOADLEY, GEORGE** (1780–1857), was a politician and leading legal figure in mid-19th-century Cleveland. Hoadley was born in Connecticut. He graduated from Yale in 1801 and later studied law. As a young man, he held various jobs as a newspaper writer and tutored at Yale before embarking on a career in law. He also served a term as mayor of New Haven. Hoadley came to Cleveland in 1830, where he established a law practice. He was highly regarded for his erudition and was often consulted on matters of law. From 1832–46 he served as justice of the peace in Cleveland, and in 1846 he was elected mayor for a 2-year term. As justice of the peace, Hoadley purportedly decided over 20,000 legal cases during his 14-year tenure. He had a reputation for being firm but fair in the execution of this office; few of his decisions were reversed. He administered the oath of office to the first city council in 1836. As mayor of Cleveland, Hoadley was largely responsible for the establishment of the city's first high school. In his inaugural address, he sought support for a high school or "academic department" for qualified students from common schools. As a result of his efforts, the first high school for boys was opened in 1846; a department for girls was added the following year. The school was eventually closed because of opposition to its selective nature. Hoadley married Mary Woolsey in 1819. They had 3 daughters and 1 son. The son, Geo. Hoadly (he dropped the *e* from the family name), was elected governor of Ohio in 1883.

**HOBAN, EDWARD FRANCIS** (27 June 1878–22 Sept. 1966), was the sixth Catholic bishop of Cleveland. Hoban was born in Chicago, Ill., one of the 8 children of Wm. and Bridget O'Malley Hoban. He was educated at St. Ignatius Preparatory College in Chicago and St. Mary Seminary in Baltimore. On 11 July 1903, he was ordained to the priesthood in Holy Name Cathedral in Chicago. Hoban did pastoral work for several months before going to Gregorian University in Rome. When he graduated in 1906, he was named professor and treasurer of the Chicago seminary Quigley Preparatory College. He was then appointed to the Chicago Diocesan Chancery staff and became chancellor in 1906. Hoban was named auxiliary bishop of Chicago on 21 Nov. 1921. He coordinated and organized the 28th Internatl. Eucharistic Congress, held in Chicago in 1926. On 10 Feb. 1928, Hoban became the bishop of Rockford, Ill. In Rockford he opened many elementary and high schools, modernized the facilities of charitable institutions, and established a newspaper for the diocese. On 14 Nov. 1942, Hoban was named coadjutor bishop of the Diocese of Cleveland. He was to serve as administrator with the right of succession to the ailing Archbp. Schrembs. He became bishop of Cleveland when Schrembs died on 2 Nov. 1945.

Hoban took charge of the diocese during a time of rapid population growth. The diocesan population grew from 546,000 in 1942 to 870,000 in 1966, even though 6 counties were lost to the new Diocese of Youngstown, which was established in 1943. Hoban established 61 new parishes, 47 new elementary schools, and a dozen high schools to serve the needs of Catholics. In 1946 he launched a 2-year project to rebuild and remodel ST. JOHN CATHEDRAL. He also enlarged and expanded ST. JOHN COLLEGE (formerly Sisters' College) to meet the need for teachers in grade schools. Hoban centralized the child-care facilities at PARMADALE. Recognizing the growing number of infirm and aged people, he constructed additional nursing homes. HOLY FAMILY CANCER HOME was opened for terminal cancer patients. An undergraduate seminary, Borromeo, was opened in 1953; previously seminarians had been educated outside the diocese. Hoban actively promoted the Lay Retreat Movement at various diocesan retreat houses and expanded the Newman Apostolate for Catholic students attending public universities and colleges. In recognition of his services, Hoban was given the personal title of archbishop in 1951.

**HOCKEY (ICE).** Hockey has remained a sport of marginal popularity in Cleveland, despite periods of great success on the part of the city's professional teams. Ice hockey originated in Canada in the mid-1800s as a variation of the game of shinny. Shinny, played on foot with a ball and long-handled, bent sticks, allowed as many as 20 players a side. The object of the game, as in hockey, was to shoot the ball into a goal. Play was physically rough, with offensive players attempting to knock the defenders out of the way of the ball carrier, and defenders attempting to knock the ball carrier away from the ball. In fact, shinny was viewed as a sport of moral education for young boys, teaching the "manly discipline" required to overcome the difficulties of adult life. Shinny could be played year-round but was most commonly played by elementary school teams in the winter. By the 1830s, it had become a popular sport in the growing city of Cleveland. However, in the 1850s and 1860s, Canadians took to playing the game on skates, and ice hockey began to take shape. Physical necessities required changes in the rules. Large, open stretches of smooth ice were more difficult to find than open meadows. Also, skaters were faster than players on foot. Large teams proved impractical, and gradually 6 players were accepted as the standard.

Sometime in the 1890s, the new game was introduced to Cleveland. However, the sport seems to have remained a casual "pickup" recreation until 1929. In that year, Harry (Happy) Holmes secured $20,000 and formed a professional hockey team, naming it the Cleveland Indians. Holmes raised the final investment by touting the Indians as a diversion from the concern raised by the recent stock market collapse. He gained a franchise in the Internatl. Hockey League, a minor-league circuit. The team paid little more than the players' expenses. Holmes rented the ELYSIUM at Euclid Ave. and E. 107th St. for the Indians' home games. Despite the fact that the team had practiced together for only 2 weeks when the season opened, they went on to win the league championship for 1929–30. The star players for the Indians were Ken Doraty and Doug Young. Despite their initial success, the Indians were not able to repeat their triumph in succeeding seasons. The team fell steadily in the standings until the 1933–34 season, when they finished last in the Internatl. League. Declining fortune was accompanied by a fall-off in paid attendance. Not even "Happy" Holmes, noted for his public-relations skills, could convince a financially pinched public to support a losing team in the Depression years. Holmes himself had reached the end of his monetary resources. Still, he remained convinced of hockey's potential and began to search for a new backer to support the team. He brought in Al Sutphin, who would be responsible for the great years of hockey in Cleveland.

Sutphin bought the franchise, installed himself as president and treasurer of the club, and reorganized the team. They continued to play in the IL, but under the new name of the Falcons. Sutphin sought new players in order to build a winning team. He was not immediately successful, but gradually the team improved. By 1937, the team's finances were strong enough and the play good enough to move into the American Hockey League, the most important of the minor-league circuits. Sutphin renamed the club CLEVELAND BARONS and moved them into the newly completed CLEVELAND ARENA. The Barons proved themselves to be fully competitive in the AHL. Nevertheless, the AHL was not hockey's major league, and Sutphin wanted to move the team into the Natl. Hockey League. He worked for years to secure a franchise. In 1952, all requirements for entry seemed to have been met, until the NHL owners decided that television and radio contracts could not be counted as team capital. The franchise was denied. Sutphin continued to lobby for admission and received consideration again in 1968. The Barons were again denied entry. This time the NHL owners cited 2 reasons: the Arena was not large enough, seating 9,300 when 14,000 would be required, and Clevelanders had failed to attend the Barons' 1968 championship playoff series in substantial numbers. The NHL owners suspected that Cleveland was not a "major league town." Sutphin entertained the same suspicions. Attendance at Barons games had fallen in the late 1960s. While the team remained competitive, Sutphin began to look toward his retirement from hockey. In 1970, the Barons agreed to become the NHL Minnesota North Stars' primary "farm" team. That helped secure the team's financial base. In 1972, the club looked profitable enough to prompt sports entrepreneur Nick Mileti to buy it.

Mileti, seeking to build a major-league sports empire in Cleveland, immediately applied for admission to the NHL. His bid, underpinned by the new financial backing and the promise of a new home rink (the proposed Coliseum), seemed sure to finally gain NHL approval. However, at the last minute the Washington, D.C., bid received the new franchise. Mileti then turned to the recently organized World Hockey Assoc. The WHA was organized as a second major league to compete with the NHL, and generally located its teams in cities without NHL franchises. Mileti named his new team the Cleveland Crusaders. During the 1972–73 season, both the Barons and the Crusaders played at the Arena. Despite Mileti's hopes, the WHA could not win acceptance with the public as a proper major leauge. Although many NHL stars jumped to the WHA, the new teams were usually located in cities without a hockey tradition. During the 1972–73 season, the Crusaders found it difficult to attract a regular audience, and the Barons continued to lose patrons. The Crusaders' mediocre play did not help matters. During the off-season in 1973, Mileti shipped the Barons off to Jacksonville, Fla. This move, he hoped, would consolidate the Cleveland hockey market. Unfortunately for Mileti, the Crusaders did not significantly improve in the next 3 seasons. His final hope to move the team into the NHL was blocked by the league owners, who resented the WHA's player raids. At the end of the 1975–76 season, Mileti took the team to Hollywood, Fla., whereupon Cleveland finally received an NHL franchise. The California Golden Seals were an NHL expansion team that had not been able to establish itself in San Francisco. Mel Swig and Geo. Gund III bought the Seals and moved them to Cleveland. The team was renamed the Barons. The new club survived for only 2 years. Attendance failed to increase, and the team nearly went bankrupt at the end of their first season. A special appropriation by the NHL prevented their failure. The Barons did no better in 1977–78, and merged with the Minnesota North Stars, strengthening another weak team. The departure of the Barons spelled an end to 48 years of professional hockey in Cleveland.

Amateur hockey was played in Cleveland in the 1930s and 1940s, generally by teams sponsored by local companies. Typical teams were Thompson Prods. and Fisher Foods. However, those teams never organized in a formal league structure. League play began in 1951 with the Cleveland Midget Hockey League. Formed by Cleveland recreation director John Nagy and Police Dept. Juvenile Div. captain Arthur Roth, the CMHL was intended to occupy the time of boys who might otherwise have become involved in juvenile delinquency. Funds were provided by the CLEVELAND FOUNDATION and the ROTARY CLUB. In 1964, the Muny Leagues were organized by the Cleveland Recreation Dept. By the mid-1970s the Muny teams had evolved into teams playing at all levels in Midwest regional leagues. In 1986, numerous small leagues played at all Greater Cleveland ice rinks. Scholastic hockey began in 1940 with the organization of the Cleveland High School League. Most city high schools participated. However, the league dissolved in 1942. In 1969, the Greater Cleveland High School Hockey League was formed by Joe Prokop, a former Cleveland Baron. Beginning with 4 teams, the league grew to 20 participating schools in 1986. The highlight of the season is the Baron Cup tournament, in which the 8 best teams in the league play for a trophy donated by the Cleveland Barons in 1970. Collegiate hockey began in the 1940s when Western Reserve University, Case Institute, and JOHN CARROLL UNIVERSITY began fielding hockey clubs. The college teams have been arranged in several league formulations, generally on a regional basis. In 1986, most area colleges and universities hosted hockey clubs.

Michael McCormick
Western Reserve Historical Society

**HODGE, JOSEPH,** also known as Black Joe, was a hunter and trapper hired in June 1796 by the surveying party of MOSES CLEAVELAND to guide the group from Buffalo across the Pennsylvania border into the Western Reserve. He has thus been called the first black American to have contact with Cleveland, although he guided the party only as far as Conneaut Creek before returning to Buffalo in early July 1796. Little is known about Hodge's life. One recent investigator, Edith Gaines, has speculated that he was a runaway slave, escaped perhaps from a farm in the Hudson River Valley, where many slaves were owned until New York prohibited slavery in 1799. He was apparently captured by Seneca Indians in a raid during the Revolutionary War and lived with them until being returned to U.S. authorities at Ft. Stanwix in Dec. 1784. During captivity, he apparently became fluent in the Seneca tongue, for he later was a trader and storekeeper near an Indian settlement near Buffalo Creek. He was also married to an Indian woman. Hodge served as a guide and interpreter for Moses Cleaveland's surveying party from about 27 June 1796, when the party left Buffalo, until about 4 July 1796, when the surveyors crossed the Pennsylvania border. Little else is known about him, except that he died at an advanced age on the Cattaraugus Reservation.

**HODGE, ORLANDO JOHN** (25 Nov. 1828–16 Apr. 1912), was a politician and businessman involved in civic and humanitarian affairs in Cleveland; he organized the Cleveland Humane Society and wrote the bill that authorized the Federal Plan of government for the city of Cleveland. Hodge was born in Hamburg, N.Y. His father died when Hodge was 4, and Hodge came to Cleveland by himself in 1842 to work as a "roller boy" in a printing office. A volunteer in the MEXICAN AMER. WAR (1847–48), he was wounded twice. After his Army service, he attended Geauga Seminary from 1849–51; his classmates included Jas. and Lucretia Rudolph Garfield. Two positions Hodge held in the 1850s proved steppingstones in his career. He was elected as Cleveland's first police-court clerk in 1853, and in 1856 he became city editor for the *PLAIN DEALER*. In 1860, Hodge moved to Connecticut to supervise some business interests. There he continued actively in civic affairs, including serving as a member of Yale College's Board of Managers. He was elected to the Connecticut house in 1862 and the Connecticut senate in 1864. The senate elected Hodge as president in 1865.

Hodge returned to Cleveland in 1867. He was elected to the first of 4 terms on CLEVELAND CITY COUNCIL in 1873; during his last 2 terms, he served as council president in 1875 and 1885. While serving on the council, Hodge was elected to 4 terms in the Ohio house; he served as president pro tem in 1875–76 and as speaker in 1882–83. Ohio governor Foraker made Hodge a member of his staff and a colonel in the Ohio militia in 1889. In 1891, the general assembly authorized Hodge's proposal that the city of Cleveland implement the Federal Plan of government. The Republican party nominated Hodge for Congress in 1892, but he was defeated. After that, he retired from active politics. During his political career, Hodge also owned and edited the *Sun & Voice* from 1878–89. Other business activities included the presidencies of the Economy Bldg. & Loan Co. and the Lion Oil Co. He also was a real-estate dealer and owned extensive holdings. Hodge participated in many civic organizations. In 1873, he organized the Cleveland Humane Society; through his efforts, a state society was formed in 1874. He also served as president of the Sons of the American Revolution, the New England Society, and the EARLY SETTLERS ASSOC. He was made a life member of the WESTERN RESERVE HISTORICAL SOCIETY. He published genealogies of many Cleveland families, including his own. In 1892 Hodge published *Reminiscences*, his memoirs, which he reissued in 1910. Hodge married twice. His first wife, Lydia Doan, died in 1879; their son, Clark R., was born in 1867 and died in 1880. In 1882, Hodge married Virginia Shedd Clark.

Orlando J. Hodge Papers, WRHS.

**HOLDEN, LIBERTY EMERY** (20 June 1833–26 Aug. 1913), used a fortune amassed largely in western mining to revive the *Cleveland Plain Dealer*, invest heavily in local real estate, and promote the city's cultural life. Born in Raymond, Maine, he began teaching at the age of 16 and completed 2 years at Waterville College before moving west in 1856 to finish his education at the University of Michigan. While professor of literature at Kalamazoo College, he married Delia Elizabeth Bulkley, one of his students and the sister of Chas. H. Bulkley. After spending 2 years as superintendent of schools in Tiffin, Ohio, Holden moved to Cleveland in 1862 to study for a law degree. Holden invested in real estate and promoted improvements in the original E. Cleveland (UNIVERSITY CIRCLE) area, into which he soon moved. Serving as president of the board of education for several years, he was influential in the area's eventual annexation to Cleveland. In 1873 he began investing in mining properties, first iron in the Lake Superior region and later silver in Utah. It was the latter that multiplied his fortune and made him a leading spokesman in Washington for western silver interests.

When Holden purchased the *PLAIN DEALER* from WM. W. ARMSTRONG in 1885, rivals felt that his chief interest was the promotion of bimetallism. Holden's attentions to the Democratic daily went beyond political considerations, however. Shortly after taking over, he launched the morning *Plain Dealer* after buying out the *Herald* in association with the *Leader*. The *Plain Dealer* supported Bryan for president while under Holden's personal direction from 1893–98, but when he subsequently leased it to CHAS. E. KENNEDY and ELBERT H. BAKER, the *Plain Dealer* thereafter withheld its support from Bryan. Holden also owned the HOLLENDEN HOTEL, which he built in 1884. As president of the building committee, he was responsible for the construction of the CLEVELAND MUSEUM OF ART. Its adjacent setting of WADE and ROCKEFELLER PARKS was also pieced together largely through his efforts. Holden was also a trustee of Adelbert College, president of the WESTERN RESERVE HISTORICAL SOCIETY, president of the UNION CLUB, and mayor of Bratenahl Village, where he had his principal residence. Upon Holden's death at his Mentor farm, his estate was left in trust for his heirs. Besides his wife, these included 1 surviving son, Guerdon Stearns, and daughters Roberta Bole, Delia White, Emery Greenough, and Gertrude McGinley. Two sons, Albert Fairchild and L. Dean, had predeceased him.

**HOLLAND, JUSTIN MINER** (1819–24 Mar. 1887), was a black musician and composer, best known for his works on the guitar. He was also active in the antislavery movement and was a leader in black Masonic fraternities. Holland was born in Norfolk County, Va. He went to Chelsea, Mass., at the age of 12, where he received his early education. He entered Oberlin College in 1841 but left before graduation to pursue a musical career in Cleveland. Fluent in Spanish, French, and German, Holland was able to establish friendship links between black Masonic lodges in such places as Peru, Portugal, Spain, France, and Germany, thereby gaining an international reputation in that area. As a performing artist, Holland played the flute, piano, and guitar. On the guitar he is credited with 35 original works and 300 published arrangements. In 1874, *Holland's Comprehensive Method for the Guitar* was pronounced by critics as the best work of its kind in America. He also de-

515

veloped an international reputation as a teacher, composer, and arranger.

The **HOLLENDEN HOTEL,** once the most glamorous and colorful of Cleveland's hostelries, opened on 7 June 1885. It was the first large hotel for transients east of PUBLIC SQUARE and offered accommodations for permanent residents, as well. LIBERTY E. HOLDEN purchased the Philo Chamberlain property fronting on Superior, Bond (E. 6th), and Vincent streets and formed a corporation to construct a hotel. Associates in the venture included WM. J. GORDON and Chas. H. Bulkley. The Hollenden, which took its name from an early English form of the name Holden, was designed by architect GEO. F. HAMMOND. It boasted electric lights, 100 private baths, and fireproof construction. The massive 8-story hotel was noted for its lavish interior, with paneled walls, redwood and mahogany fittings, and crystal chandeliers. Politicians claimed the dining room and made it famous as a meeting place. The hotel grew in legend, too, as it hosted 5 presidents, industrial giants, and celebrities of stage and platform.

In 1926, a $5 million annex was built on the east side of the hotel, and the rear section of the main building was modernized. The hotel had several owners over the years. In 1960, the 600 Superior Corp. bought it. Only about 350 of the 1,000 rooms were in use in July 1962, when the hotel was closed to transient guests and permanent residents were asked to leave. The Hollenden was demolished the following year. The 600 Superior Corp., along with developer Jas. M. Carney, built a new hotel and parking garage on the site. Designed by architects Donald C. Snyder and Nicholas A. Tekushan, the new Hollenden House Hotel opened on 1 Mar. 1965. The 14-story, 400-room hotel cost $6 million. Its restaurant, Marie Schreiber's Tavern, was operated by long-time Cleveland restaurateur Marie A. Schreiber.

**HOLTKAMP, WALTER** (1 July 1894–12 Feb. 1962), was an internationally known organ builder and a leader in the reemployment of the traditional techniques of organ construction. Holtkamp was born in St. Marys, Ohio, the 5th of 6 children of Henry Holtkamp (1859–1931). In 1903, Henry Holtkamp moved to Cleveland to become a salesman for G. F. Votteler & Co., a small, regional organ builder. Eleven years later, the firm became known as the Votteler-Holtkamp-Sparling Organ Co. Walter Holtkamp attended school and began working in the company shop but did not study organ building. He joined the Army and toured Europe during WORLD WAR I. In 1919 he returned to the firm, then located at W. 14th St. and Abbey Ave. In 1922, the company moved to its present (1985) location on Meyer Ave., and Walter became artistic director of the firm in 1931, upon his father's death. Holtkamp had no outside affiliations. His entire life was dedicated to organ building. Indeed, after 20 years of marriage, he divorced his wife and took up residence over the shop to be nearer to his work. He did serve as first president of the Natl. Assoc. of Organ Builders in 1958 and represented America at an international convention in Amsterdam. Holtkamp could not play the organ, but according to Walter Blodgett, he had an extraordinary ear. He was convinced that the tone of the organs being built in the 1930s and 1940s was impaired because their pipes were being placed everywhere (the roof, the basement) except in the same room as the organ itself. In 1933, Holtkamp installed the innovative Rack positiv organ at the CLEVELAND MUSEUM OF ART. Albert Schweitzer, physician and noted organist, came to Cleveland in 1949 for the sole purpose of seeing it. Holtkamp also built organs for BALDWIN-

WALLACE COLLEGE, CASE WESTERN RESERVE UNIVERSITY, Oberlin College, MIT, Yale University, and the Air Force Academy, as well as for ST. JOHN CATHEDRAL and ST. PAUL'S EPISCOPAL CHURCH. His fame had spread so that in 1960, a group of students traveled 2,000 mi. to study his work. He was married to Mary McClure of LAKEWOOD, and their son, Walter, Jr. (born in 1929), still owned and operated the Holtkamp Organ Co. in 1985.

The **HOLY FAMILY CANCER HOME,** located at 6707 State Rd. in PARMA, was established in 1957 as a home for incurable cancer patients and is an early prototype of a "hospice" in the Cleveland area. Responding to a Cleveland Welfare Fed. survey (1954) on health needs for the chronically ill and incurably diseased in the Cleveland area, Archbp. EDWARD F. HOBAN asked the Dominican Sisters of St. Rose of Lima to staff a hospital for the incurably ill. The hospital, built with funds raised by the Catholic Charities, was opened in 1959. Terminally ill patients are accepted regardless of race, creed, or religion, and there is no fee for care at the home, which continues to be supported by the Catholic Charities' funds.

Archives, Diocese of Cleveland.

The **HOLY FAMILY CHILDREN'S HOME,** an orphanage, was established in June 1895 by Ellen Donovan, a young Irish Catholic woman. Donovan hoped to found a Roman Catholic religious community to serve the poor, recognizing that orphaned children, especially, were in need. With the assistance of her sister Theresa and several friends, she began caring for several orphans in a residence on E. Madison St. Though her plans for a religious community did not mature, the orphans came. With funds obtained from sewing and begging, Donovan was able to purchase a site for them at 645 Woodland Hills Ave. Her orphanage, the Home of the Holy Family, was officially incorporated on 8 Dec. 1896. Until 1918, the home existed precariously on the proceeds from benefits, dances, and card parties that had been organized for it. In that year Donovan applied for membership in the Cleveland Community Fund. Soon the home was receiving funds from both the Community Fund and the fledgling CATHOLIC CHARITIES CORP. Donovan was quite innovative in her management of children. She believed that brothers and sisters should be reared together rather than separately, as was the common practice of most orphan asylums. Her charges were sent to neighborhood schools and allowed to play with local children. Donovan sold the original site in 1911 and relocated her orphanage to 18120 Puritas Ave. on Cleveland's west side. She and her loyal helpers continued to staff the home until her death in 1939. Donovan had never succeeded in recruiting additional assistance for her home, so the diocese had to seek others to operate it. The Sisters of the Incarnate Word took charge of the facility and staffed it until 1952, when it was closed, and the remaining children were sent to PARMADALE.

Archives, Diocese of Cleveland.

**HOLY ROSARY,** the second parish established for ITALIANS in Cleveland, was begun in 1892. JOSEPH CARABELLI, a skilled marbleworker, was the first Italian to settle in the neighborhood of LAKE VIEW CEMETERY in 1879. Other Italian craftsmen settled there, and soon a thriving Italian community was established. The closest Italian parish was ST. ANTHONY'S CHURCH in downtown Cleveland. Fr. Joseph Strumia began offering Mass for this Italian community in 1891 at D'Errico Hall. At a public meeting held on 5 Jan. 1892, the community agreed to support a proposed church, and in a month, the people had collected $2,000 for their new church. A cornerstone was laid on 14 Aug. 1892, and 3 months later, the structure was completed. This new church of Our Lady of the Holy Rosary was to serve the Italians living east of Madison (E. 79th) St. Fr. Antonio Gibelli opened a school for his adult parishioners in 1895 to help them gain citizenship and acquire job skills. The URSULINE SISTERS began teaching religion to the children in 1896, because the parish was unable to afford a parochial school and various parish societies were also begun at this time to strengthen the faith of the parishioners and to preserve their Italian heritage.

Because of the growth of the parish, property adjacent to the old church was purchased in 1901, and a new church on that site, Mayfield at Coltman Rd., was completed and dedicated on 9 Nov. 1909, during the pastorate of Fr. Joseph Militello. His successor, Fr. Francis Haley, started athletic programs for the parish youth and opened a medical dispensary, which served parishioners. During the pastorate of Fr. Joseph Trivisonno, the church was extensively renovated, and he brought nuns from the community of the Maestre Pie Filippini to work in the parish. They provided religious instruction for the children and assistance to the elderly and needy parishioners. In 1945, during the administration of Fr. Ferdinand Tamburri, Holy Rosary opened its parochial school. In 1977 the religious community of the priests of the Congregation of St. Joseph was given charge of the parish.

Papers of Holy Rosary, Archives, Diocese of Cleveland.

**HOME RULE** freed Clevelanders from state-imposed restrictions on the management of local affairs, giving them the right to frame their own charter and to control their city government. This goal was accomplished by an amendment to the Ohio state constitution passed in 1912. From the time Cleveland was incorporated, the manner in which the city conducted its business was largely determined by the state. Lacking a general grant of local powers, the city could not deal with major local problems resulting from unprecedented growth during the 19th and 20th centuries. Led by Cleveland mayor NEWTON D. BAKER, a conference of cities drew up the home rule amendment, which was approved by a state convention called to redraft Ohio's constitution. Despite opposition from rural interests, the amendment was approved by a majority of Ohio's voters in 1912.

CLEVELAND CITY COUNCIL passed an ordinance authorizing the election of a charter commission to write a new city charter. Mayor Baker then appointed a nonpartisan committee of 9 to select 15 charter commissioners, and the committee's selections were announced in Dec. 1912. Meanwhile, a rival slate of candidates was proposed by the Progressive Constitutional League, 5 of whom were also on the nonpartisan "Baker" slate. The league's proposals included nonpartisan elections designed to eliminate machine politicans and a 9-member city council elected at large. Although the Baker group favored some of the league proposals, they did not want to commit themselves to a specific program before writing the charter. At a special election held in Feb. 1913, the voters approved both the ordinance passed by council and the Baker slate of charter commissioners.

It took more than 60 sessions and 4 months to produce Cleveland's first home rule charter. A major disagreement arose within the commission over the size of the city council. Those advocating a small council elected at large main-tained that it would be more efficient and less expensive and would eliminate the corruption associated with the political machines. Those favoring a large council elected by ward considered it more democratic, since it made councilmen answerable to the concerns of their wards. The new charter was basically modeled on the Federal Plan of city government, utilizing a council-mayor form of government. Both the mayor and the council were elected to 2-year terms on a nonpartisan ticket. A preferential voting system was established, giving voters the opportunity to vote their first, second, and other choices in elections. The mayor had control over the administration of city government and could appoint department heads without obtaining confirmation from city council. His veto of ordinances passed by council was extended to include an item veto. City council was reduced from 32 to 26 members elected by wards. Council was restricted to legislative matters; however, it could investigate the official acts and financial transactions of any city department. Initiative, referendum, and recall were adopted to give the people more control over their city government.

Once the charter was completed, the commissioners actively campaigned for its approval by the voters. Opposition came from a small group of Republican ward politicans led by former mayor ROBT. E. MCKISSON, who maintained that the new charter gave the mayor dictatorial power. Ward and precinct leaders of both major parties were unenthusiastic over the charter, fearing that they would lose their political influence. On 1 July 1913, the voters approved the charter by a 2-to-1 majority; however, only ⅓ of the electorate voted. The charter became effective 1 Jan. 1914. Charter provisions relating to nonpartisan primaries and elections and the preferential voting system were declared unconstitutional by Ohio's attorney general. His decision was overruled by the Ohio Supreme Court, and the charter went into effect. A year later opponents of nonpartisan elections tried unsuccessfully to amend the charter so that party affiliation of the candidates in both primary and general elections would appear on the ballot. The charter remained in effect until the city adopted the CITY MANAGER PLAN.

**HOMEOPATHY,** founded by German physician Samuel Christian Frederick Hahnemann, is a therapeutic drug specialty within the general field of internal medicine. Guided by the principle that that which causes a disease can also cure it, homeopathy had a profound effect on medical practice, ending "shotgun prescriptions" and introducing sorely needed elements of conservatism to the dominant medical theories of the day. Homeopathic physicians started to trickle into Ohio ca. 1836, selecting smaller cities in which to practice because of their poor reception in larger cities. Among the more well-known local homeopaths were Seth R. Beckwith, who had a large practice in Cleveland, serving as physician and surgeon to railroad company employees; Benjamin L. Hill, one of the founders of the Western Homeopathic College of Cleveland; and Hamilton Fisk Biggar, medical advisor with a national reputation and intimate friend of JOHN D. ROCKEFELLER. The first homeopathic pharmacy in Cleveland was opened in 1846, by B. H. Bartlett at the corner of Superior Ave. and PUBLIC SQUARE. In 1850, the Cleveland Homeopathic Medical College was founded in Cleveland, the second institution of its kind offering homeopathic instruction in the country. The Cleveland college operated from 1850-14, when it and the Pulte Medical College of Cincinnati passed to Ohio State University, creating the homeopathic department of the OSU medical school. The CLEVELAND HOMEOPATHIC HOSPITAL, the first organized hospital in Cleveland, was opened in May 1856 by Seth R. Beckwith. In 1873, it moved from Lake St. to Huron Rd. This hospital was the forerunner of the present-day (1985) HURON RD. HOSPITAL located in E. CLEVELAND. Homeopathy depended upon teaching institutions for its survival. In 1897, the Cleveland Medical College became known as the Cleveland Homeopathic Medical College. When the Pulte Medical College of Cincinnati closed, its operations were absorbed into the Cleveland college, which then changed its name to the Cleveland-Pulte Medical College. The formal instruction of homeopathy ended in Ohio in 1922, when the OSU board of trustees voted to discontinue the program. Since 1922, homeopathy has been taught by individual doctors on a graduate or postgraduate course basis. Today E. Cleveland's Huron Rd. Hospital is one of only 4 major homeopathic teaching institutions in the country. Homeopathy is now taught as a drug specialty within the general field of internal medicine, mostly in foreign countries.

**HOPE HOUSE,** founded in Nov. 1973, was the first rehabilitation home in Cleveland for alcoholic women. Hope House, Inc., was formed by Sr. Nancy Jean Tomcyak in 1972 in response to studies done by the METRO. HEALTH PLANNING CORP. and the FED. FOR COMMUNITY PLANNING showing the need for an intermediate-care facility within the city for women. The UNITED LABOR AGENCY a social-service organization, purchased a house for this purpose in 1973 at 7910 Lake Ave. The house was turned over to Hope House, Inc., and run by the sisters of the Order of the Holy Family of Nazareth under a $30,000 grant from the CLEVELAND FOUNDATION. Sr. Tomcyak was made executive director. With the help of organized labor, the house was renovated to accommodate 12 residents. At this time, similar facilities existed for men, but none for women. Hope House received women after they had undergone detoxification treatment in area hospitals. Women recovering from drug addiction were also accepted. The primary aim of the program was to help alcoholic women return to normal life, with a special emphasis on finding jobs. Many of the women during their stay worked at the Hope House Natural Bakery Store, which opened in 1975. The minimum stay at Hope House was 8 weeks. Throughout its existence, the facility was sustained by grants from local foundations. In Dec. 1978, with a small budget and staff assistance, the ULA turned over the care facility to an elderly self-help program.

The **HOPE MEMORIAL BRIDGE,** originally the Lorain-Carnegie Bridge, was opened in 1932. The second of the major high-level spans that cross the CUYAHOGA RIVER in downtown Cleveland, it was preceded by the DETROIT-SUPERIOR BRIDGE in 1918. A high-level crossing linking Lorain and Central avenues was envisioned as early as 1911, when it was proposed by H. D. G. Parsons and published in a map issued by the Carnegie Extension Assoc. In 1925, a special committee of the City Plan Commission recommmnded that a Central-Lorain Bridge should be built immediately, and an $8 million bond issue was approved in 1927. The realignment of the streets meant that Lorain and Carnegie, instead of Central, were actually connected. The new steel-and-concrete structure, nearly a mile long, consisted of 13 cantilever truss spans varying in length from 299' over the river to 132' at the ends. A lower deck intended to carry 4 lanes of vehicular traffic and 2 streetcar tracks was never completed.

The bridge was designed by engineers WILBUR J. WATSON & Associates, with FRANK WALKER as consulting architect. One of the variations from strict engineering necessity was the curving of the lower edge of the trusses to give a more pleasing arched appearance, and the major architectural feature was the 4 massive stone pylons with conventionalized figures representing Guardians of Traffic. The figures hold vehicles representing the spirit of progress in transportation: a hayrack, a covered wagon, a stagecoach, a passenger automobile, and 4 types of trucks. Designed by Walker and sculpted by Henry Hering, they are transitional between a stylized classicism and the Modernistic or Art Deco style. The sculptures are among the most remarkable in the country because of the integral character of the figures and their pylons, the appropriateness of the symbolism, the consistency of the style, and the scale of the figures. The bridge was closed in 1980–83 for the replacement of the concrete roadway deck. Upon reopening, it was renamed the Hope Memorial Bridge in honor of the family of entertainer Bob Hope, who were Cleveland stonemasons.

**HOPKINS, WILLIAM ROWLAND** (26 July 1869–9 Feb. 1961), was a lawyer, industrial developer, and member of city council and served as Cleveland's first city manager from 1924–29. Hopkins was born in Johnstown, Pa., one of 10 children of David J. and Mary Jeffreys Hopkins. The family came to Cleveland in 1874, settling in the Newburgh area. At the age of 13, Hopkins left school to work in the Cleveland Rolling Mills. With his earnings, he entered Western Reserve Academy, graduating in 1892 just before his 21st birthday. He continued his education at Western Reserve University, earning his A.B. in 1896 and an LL.B. in 1899. While in law school, he was elected to CLEVELAND CITY COUNCIL as a Republican, serving from 1897–99. He married Ellen Louise Cozad in 1903; they were divorced in 1926. Together with his brother Ben, Hopkins laid out districts for new industrial plant development, and in 1905 he promoted the construction of the Cleveland Short Line Railroad, also known as the Belt Line, which linked all the major industrial sections of Cleveland. He gave up his law practice entirely in 1906 and devoted himself to private enterprise.

Politics continued to interest Hopkins. He became chairman of the Republican county committee and a member of the election board. With the approval of both political parties, Hopkins was chosen by city council to be Cleveland's first city manager in Jan. 1924. As manager, he was removed from partisan politics, and during an honest and efficient administration, parks were developed, welfare institutions were improved, and the PUBLIC AUDITORIUM was begun. He is best known for developing the Cleveland Municipal Airport. Hopkins obtained options on 1,000 acres of land at Brookpark Rd. and Riverside Dr., upon which the airport was constructed and opened for business in 1925. Although as city manager he was administrative head of the city, he also took the lead in determining policy. City council felt that he had acquired too much control over city affairs and removed him from office by a 14–11 vote in Jan. 1930. In 1931 he returned to politics briefly as a member of council, where he fought unsuccessfully for the retention of the CITY MANAGER PLAN. In 1933 he returned to private life to look after his real-estate and business interests. The airport was named in his honor in 1951 (see CLEVELAND HOPKINS INTERNATIONAL AIRPORT). He died in Cleveland at age 91.

William Rowland Hopkins Papers, WRHS.

**HOPKINS AIRPORT.** *See* **CLEVELAND HOPKINS INTERNATIONAL AIRPORT**

**HOPWOOD, ERIE C.** (7 Feb. 1872–18 Mar. 1928), was one of the *Cleveland Plain Dealer*'s most honored editors. He was born in N. Eaton, Lorain County, Ohio. His youth was spent largely in Ashtabula County, which he left to attend Western Reserve University from 1897–1901. After a year of teaching in Middletown, Ohio, Hopwood returned to Cleveland as a police reporter for the *PLAIN DEALER*. By 1907 he had worked his way up through assistant city editor and city editor to night editor. In 1912 he succeeded to the position of managing editor, which gave him editorial control of the paper. With the retirement of ELBERT H. BAKER as general manager of the *Plain Dealer* in 1920, the title of editor was revived for Hopwood. Under the slogan "Justice in the news columns," he continued Baker's policy of unbiased news reporting. While confining himself largely to the administrative duties of his position, Hopwood continued to report on such occasions as a postwar tour of France and Belgium and the marathon 1924 Democratic Natl. Convention. Hopwood was widely recognized as a leader in professional and civic concerns. A founder of the American Society of Newspaper Editors in 1922, he helped draft that organization's idealistic "Canons of journalism," adopted the following year. He served as the society's secretary and had been its president for 3 years prior to his death. He was also a founding member of the Cleveland CITY CLUB and was elected its third president, 1914–15. Married to Ida Walter of New Philadelphia in 1903, Hopwood had 2 daughters and a son. He lived in CLEVELAND HTS. and SHAKER HTS., where he practiced his prize-winning hobby of amateur photography.

The **HORSBURGH AND SCOTT COMPANY** is a Cleveland firm that produces gears and industrial transmissions and has prospered over a century of operation. The company was founded in 1886 by millwrights Frank Horsburgh and Thos. Scott. Horsburgh, a Scottish immigrant, worked in various jobs, including installing line shafting in local flour mills, before joining with Scott. The firm operated a machine shop at 108 Canal St. that produced wire trolley switchovers, wire connectors, and allied parts for local streetcar companies. The company purchased equipment to branch out and make spur axle gears and pinions for the drives of electric streetcars. Scott left the firm in 1899, and the partnership was dissolved; the company, incorporated as the Horsburgh & Scott Co. in 1903, operated under Horsburgh's leadership until his death in 1933 at age 79. In 1903, H & S moved east from Canal St. to 5114 Hamilton Ave., with 20 employees and almost 6,000 sq. ft. of manufacturing space. As business grew, new buildings were constructed in 1913 and 1924. The product line was expanded to include spur, helical, bevel, and worm gears; a Sykes herringbone gear generator was added in 1927. Horsburgh's sons, Robt. G. and Thos. P., worked for the firm in their spare time while studying engineering at Case School of Applied Science; once they graduated, they guided the firm through the Depression and WORLD WAR II. The association with Case has continued into the 1980s. Robt. Horsburgh's 3 sons entered the family business after graduating from Case in mechanical engineering; in the 1980s, H & S worked with CWRU's engineering and metallurgy departments.

During World War II, the company continued producing gears and gear drives for heavy industry, especially steel mills; but growth was slow. H & S began to grow after the war as new products and services were developed, new markets were found, and the demand for industrial gearing increased. Plant size was increased 6 times to 400,000 sq. ft., with the most modern gear-cutting and heat-treating equipment. Most customers required special gears and transmissions for heavy industry. Sales reached $50 million in 1982 after a boom created by the 1974 oil embargo. During the 1980s, the firm was affected by the increasing obsolescence of the American steel industry and foreign competition. In 1985, still operating on Hamilton Ave., a new Horsburgh management transferred company ownership from a broad group of Horsburgh family and miscellaneous shareholders to an Employee Stock Ownership Plan, an employee retirement trust that owned 77% of the company in 1986; however, the firm was still managed by members of a 4th generation of the Horsburgh family.

**HORSTMANN, IGNATIUS FREDERICK** (16 Dec. 1840–13 May 1908), was the third bishop of Cleveland. Horstmann was born in the Southwark section of Philadelphia, Pa., the third child of 10 born to wealthy businessman Frederick and Catherine Weber Horstmann. He was educated at Central High School, the Jesuit College of St. Joseph, and St. Charles Borromeo Seminary, all located in Philadelphia. He became one of the first students to enroll in North American College in Rome in 1860, and he was ordained a priest on 10 June 1865 in Rome by Cardinal Patrizzi. Upon Horstmann's return to Philadelphia, he was named to the faculty at St. Charles Borromeo Seminary, where he taught philosophy, German, and Hebrew. In 1877 he became pastor of St. Mary Church in Philadelphia, where he gained a reputation as a careful administrator and an excellent preacher. In 1885 Horstmann was named chancellor of the Archdiocese of Philadelphia. He was known as an editor and writer on religious and scholarly themes, serving as assistant editor of the *American Catholic Quarterly Review*. He was one of the founding members of the American Catholic Historical Society.

On 29 Nov. 1891, Horstmann's appointment as the new bishop of Cleveland was announced. His consecration took place on 25 Feb. 1892 in the Cathedral of SS. Peter & Paul in Philadelphia. On 9 Mar. he was installed as bishop of Cleveland in ST. JOHN CATHEDRAL. He became bishop at a time when European immigration was swelling Cleveland's population. Horstmann recruited priests, seminarians, and religious to serve their countrymen. Of the 30 new parishes started in the Greater Cleveland area during his tenure, 22 were begun for the benefit of various nationalities. Horstmann faced crises with various nationalistic schismatic groups (e.g., the POLISH NATIONAL CATHOLIC CHURCH and others). Horstmann found resources to expand the existing Catholic hospitals and orphanages. He started both St. Anthony Home for Working Boys and the CATHERINE HORSTMANN HOME, a residential training school for girls. He endorsed the concept of compulsory parochial schools and demanded that high standards be maintained. In 1894 he encouraged the formation of the Cleveland Apostolate, a group of missionary priests under the direction of Paulist father Walter Elliott who went about speaking on Catholic doctrine and practices to non-Catholics. That did much to counter anti-Catholic prejudice. Horstmann had developed a heart condition, which caused his death in Canton, Ohio.

Lackner, Joseph, HSM, "Bishop Ignatius F. Horstmann and the Americanization of the Roman Catholic Church in the United States" (Ph.D. diss., St. Louis University, 1977).

**HORVATH, HELEN** (21 Jan. 1872–15 July 1943), was a Hungarian immigrant who promoted sensitive Americanization as a means of combating the intolerance of more established immigrants. Her "Speak United States," "See United States" philosophy encouraged newcomers to remember their own culture while learning enough about America to exploit its opportunities. Born Helen Zalavary, Mrs. Horvath came to Cleveland in 1897, where she was politicized by an incident in a store where a clerk mocked her accent. She studied English until her pronunciation was perfect and started language classes for other immigrants. In 1901 she opened a school for Hungarian newcomers, where she imparted a working knowledge of English and American ways with the goal of making her students self-confident hyphenated Americans. By WORLD WAR I, at the height of antiimmigrant hysteria, the Cleveland Board of Education brought Horvath and her adult education program into the city system and authorized her to open new schools. Horvath was also a pioneer in organizing Hungarian-American exchange programs; many events were sponsored by the Pro-Hungaria Society, which she set up here as a chapter of a worldwide organization. From 1925 onward, she took tours to Washington, D.C., which after 1928 were received at the White House by the First Lady; tour members presented Hungarian art, needlework, and books for display in the White House. Horvath Educational Tours also visited other parts of the U.S.

Papp, Susan, *Hungarian Americans and Their Communities in Cleveland* (1981).

The **HOSPICE COUNCIL OF NORTHERN OHIO** was formed in 1979 as the result of planning efforts by the CANCER CTR., INC., and later by the FED. FOR COMMUNITY PLANNING and local METROPOLITAN HEALTH PLANNING CORP. This effort was part of a larger national movement to establish hospices and hospice services for terminally ill patients in the U.S. during the 1970s. Hospice programs have been viewed as a type of health-care reform and as a challenge to the traditional delivery of health care to people with terminal illnesses. The goal of the Hospice Council was to coordinate the development of hospice programs in Greater Cleveland and the surrounding counties (Lake, Geauga, Lorain, and Medina). The programs for the care of the terminally ill were family-oriented and community-based; there was consumer representation on the board of trustees. Institutional providers (i.e., hospitals) of hospice services were not well represented on the board of trustees; hence, there was no sense of provider ownership. Initial funding for the Hospice Council came from the Cleveland, St. Ann, and Gund foundations. There were some corporate support and community contributions; however, there was no ongoing source of funds, as the council was not a provider of services. The council maintained and promoted a traditional view of hospice care, i.e., family-oriented home care-based services. They also tried to establish or adopt hospice standards of care. The Hospice Council was dissolved in June 1984; the reasons for its demise were varied and remain debatable. J. Kearney Shanahan and Frank Weakley, M.D., served as presidents of the board of trustees. Linda J. Proffitt served as its executive director.

A Plan for a Hospice System of Care for Cuyahoga, Geauga, Lake, Lorain, and Medina Counties (1979).

**HOSPITALS & HEALTH PLANNING.** In Cleveland, as elsewhere in the U.S., the hospital attained its "modern" institutional form by 1900–10, having passed through 3 more or less distinct stages. During the 19th century, the hospital began as an agency of social control and welfare, gradually became the principal provider of minimal medical care for the indigent and unfortunates of society, and emerged, ultimately, as the medical center for all classes of society, as well as the essential locus of training, research, and innovation in medicine. The institutional care of the sick originated in the incidental medical facilities provided for inmates of almshouses, jails, or, as in Cleveland, military posts. Here the first "hospital" was little more than a temporary barracks at FT. HUNTINGTON, situated near the mouth of the Cuyahoga on Lake Erie. A log structure built in 1813, it furnished sparse accommodations where sick or injured soldiers were treated by DAVID LONG, the sole physician residing in the village of Cleveland. After this makeshift hospital closed in 1815, no other institution aided the sick until 1826, when the township erected a poorhouse adjacent to the ERIE ST. CEMETERY. In 1837, following the incorporation of Cleveland as a city, the poorhouse became the "City Hospital." It was not, despite the change of name, a hospital in the accepted modern sense of the word; like other "hospitals" of the time, City Hospital functioned chiefly to relieve pauperism in the city of Cleveland.

In the second phase of their 19th-century development, hospitals became specifically medical institutions but limited their services to persons who could not afford the cost of treatment and convalescence in their homes. The opening of the U.S. MARINE HOSPITAL and ST. JOSEPH HOSPITAL in 1852 marked the beginning of this period in Cleveland. The U.S. Marine Hospital, financed and managed by the federal government, provided medical care for merchant sailors and their families and for civilian and military personnel of the government. St. Joseph, operated by the SISTERS OF CHARITY OF ST. AUGUSTINE, briefly served a growing community of Irish laborers in the city. During this period, the city and state governments also reorganized their medical facilities for the poor. The city of Cleveland tore down the poorhouse, or City Hospital, in 1851 and erected a new building, the City Infirmary, in 1855. In that same year, the state of Ohio opened the "Northern Ohio Lunatic Asylum," later known as CLEVELAND STATE HOSPITAL, in the nearby village of NEWBURGH. Despite these improvements, most people still viewed hospitals as refuges for the infirm poor. This negative image was, in fact, merited by the prevailing low standards of medical care. In this respect, the hospitals of mid-19th century Cleveland were little better than the dreaded "pesthouses" of the past.

During the last third of the 19th century, hospitals were transformed by a combination of scientific and technical advances that together amounted to a veritable revolution in medical thought and practice. The discovery of ether, chloroform, and nitrous oxide for anesthesia in the 1840s opened new realms for the surgeon, while the Germ Theory introduced by Louis Pasteur and applied to medical practice by Joseph Lister in the 1860s gave a clearer understanding of disease communication and prevention. These innovations could be implemented most successfully in the controlled environment of the hospital. In consequence, medical practice shifted progressively from the home to the institutional setting of the hospital. In Cleveland, the transfer of medical care from home to hospital accelerated in the closing years of the 19th century. At mid-century, as noted above, there were only 3 hospitals in Cleveland. Two decades later, in the period 1870–75, 7 were in operation: 3 under municipal, state, and federal management, 2 maintained by Catholic religious orders, and 2 voluntary hospitals under the control of lay trustees. By 1890–96 this number had more than doubled to include 8 hospitals under the care of religious denominations, 5 voluntary institutions, and the 3 existing public facilities. In addition, the Cleveland medical scene was also populated by a growing assortment of dispensaries opened by medical colleges in the city, small private hospitals operated as business ventures by enterprising doctors, and several private sanatoriums for the care of patients with emotional or drug- and alcohol-related health problems.

Notable qualitative changes accompanied the increase in Cleveland's hospitals. Most evident to the public was a changing physical form, as hospitals ceased to be merely dormitories for the destitute. The first hospital designed to serve medical needs and not just to perform custodial functions was St. Vincent de Paul Hospital (1865) (see ST. VINCENT CHARITY HOSPITAL & HEALTH CENTER). Its central section housed offices, a chapel, a pharmacy, and staff apartments, with kitchen, dining, and store rooms in the basement. This section was flanked by 2 wings, each occupied by separate male and female wards for 56 charity cases on the ground floor, while the 2d floor of both wings was divided into private rooms for 24 paying patients. Absence of separate surgical facilities was remedied by construction in 1872 of an amphitheater—the first in any hospital in Cleveland—at the rear of the main building. The general pattern set by St. Vincent, of wards linked by a contiguous block of administrative and service facilities, prevailed in the design of other hospitals built in Cleveland until the end of the 19th century. The first major change in the design of Cleveland hospitals came with the construction of Lakeside Hospital (see UNIVERSITY HOSPITALS). Like many hospitals in the city, Lakeside began its institutional life in a private residence converted to accommodate patient beds. Between 1876–96, Lakeside occupied the U.S. Marine Hospital; it was finally compelled to erect a new building upon expiration of its lease. In 1891 and 1895, trustees of Lakeside visited major hospitals in metropolitan centers east of the Mississippi and, subsequently, adopted a pavilion or "cottage" plan modeled on Johns Hopkins Hospital (1885) in Baltimore, then the most respected teaching hospital in America. The pavilion plan of the new hospital, located at E. 12th and Lakeside Ave., offered the execllent ventilation and drainage deemed essential for proper sanitation. Central administrative, kitchen, and laundry services were housed in separate buildings connected to wards, surgical buildings, and dispensary and nurses' quarters by long, seemingly endless corridors. The only structure that stood apart from the whole was the "autopsy building," which accommodated pathology and clinical microscopy laboratories after 1901. The overall layout of the hospital was dictated by the new appreciation of the role that germs played in disease, so that isolation and ventilation were thought to be the most important features of any hospital plan.

Hospitals in Cleveland first became educational institutions, helping to train physicians, when Dr. GUSTAV WEBER founded Charity Hospital Medical college in 1864. Weber, a prominent surgeon, launched the new school with the full cooperation of St. Vincent de Paul Hospital. Each party benefited from this relationship; Weber enjoyed privileged access to cases for clinical instruction, while St. Vincent engaged a competent medical staff at little or no cost. Although this exclusive arrangement ceased in 1870, when the college closed, St. Vincent had set a precedent in Cleveland; henceforth there would be close cooperation between hospitals and medical schools in the city. The first university hospital in Cleveland came into being in 1897–98 with the opening of Lakeside Hospital. At that time the trustees of Lakeside turned to the medical faculty of Western Reserve University to resolve its staffing problems. Since 1869, Lakeside had given WRU teaching privileges, but these were shared with the Wooster University Medical Dept. (1870–84), with each school holding its clinical sessions at different seasons of the year. After 1884, WRU acquired exclusive control of teaching privileges at Lakeside, and this affiliation was made still more extensive in 1898. By virtue of a contract between Lakeside and WRU, the Medical Dept. nominated resident staff, held exclusive teaching privileges, and furnished visiting physicians and surgeons. As a consequence of this agreement, Lakeside became the first university hospital in Cleveland and ranked among the first 10 such institutions in the US.

Hospitals constituted the sole training ground for nurses in Cleveland from 1884, when HURON RD. HOSPITAL opened the first training school for nurses in Ohio, until the establishment of a nursing degree by WRU in 1921. In the interval, several Cleveland hospitals, most notably Cleveland General (now ST. LUKE'S), Lakeside, and St. Vincent, created their own schools. In the early years of these programs, young women received in-service training in "practical nursing" and little formal instruction. Only at Lakeside, through the efforts of Isabel Hampton Robb, was nursing education put on a modern footing that emphasized instruction in the theoretical and scientific side of nursing as well as the practical. Scientific medicine, particularly the laboratory-based specialties of pathology, bacteriology, and physiology, entered the institutional setting of Cleveland hospitals after 1890. The most notable example of this influence was the establishment of a bacteriology laboratory at City Hospital. Dr. Wm. Travis Howard, a young pathologist trained at Johns Hopkins and professor of pathology at WRU, headed the laboratory and initiated scientific postmortem examinations at City Hospital. Years later Howard could claim, with justifiable pride, that "in Cleveland the systematic study of bacteriolgy, pathological anatomy and general pathology of autopsy and surgical material began at City Hospital."

By the turn of the century, many hospitals in Cleveland succeeded in attracting a "better," more affluent class of patients. Some hospitals actively courted paying patients by offering comfortable, if not luxurious, accommodations. While no Cleveland hospitals abandoned their original charitable obligations, the poor increasingly patronized outpatient dispensaries operated by the medical departments of WRU, the Cleveland College of Physicians & Surgeons (Ohio Weslyan University), and the CLEVELAND HOMEOPATHIC HOSPITAL College. Moreover, City Hospital was able to undertake a greater role in providing medical care for the indigent throughout the entire city following expansion and modernization of its facilities in 1889. Later, City Hospital also erected a tuberculosis sanatorium and a hospital for contagious diseases, and thereby relieved other hospitals of the burden of caring for patients with dreaded communicable illnesses. Henceforth, other hospitals in Cleveland could present themselves as "safe" havens for sick persons of all social classes. In addition to improving the attractiveness and safety of private rooms for paying patients, some hospitals permitted nonstaff doctors to visit and treat patients in the hospital setting. Lakeside Hospital, for example, relaxed its rules governing attending physician privileges to accommodate physicians who brought private paying patients. Lakeside also opened a specially designated operating room with flexible hours for use by physicians and surgeons not officially affiliated with the institution and also appointed a resident staff officer to provide special help in caring for patients of physicians and surgeons not on the regular staff.

The principal institutional developments in Cleveland hospitals between 1910–50 include the emergence of the group-practice hospital, the move of several hospitals to the suburbs, and the advent of health insurance programs. The CLEVELAND CLINIC FOUNDATION, incorporated in 1921, was the first and by far the most successful group-practice hospital in Cleveland. Its founders, particularly Drs. GEO. W. CRILE, FRANK E. BUNTS, and WM. E. LOWER, derived their inspiration from the example of the Mayo Clinic and from wartime experience working together as members of the LAKESIDE UNIT in WORLD WAR I. Their concept was to combine the practice of surgery and medicine with new diagnostic procedures, such as blood testing, x-rays, electrocardiography, and bacteriologic examinations, and ongoing medical research to develop new modes of treatment. Organized as a not-for-profit foundation staffed by salaried physicians, the Cleveland Clinic overcame the onus heaped on group clinics by individualistic private practitioners who perceived a threat to the free-market economy that prevailed in American medicine.

By 1920, as noted in the *Cleveland Hospital and Health Survey*, the hospitals of Cleveland could be categorized according to the strength of their community orientation. One group, comprising Fairview Park, St. John's, Glenville, Lutheran, Provident, GRACE, St. Ann's, and ST. ALEXIS, drew the majority of their cases from their own vicinity. Created to serve persons sharing a common faith or national heritage, these hospitals were rooted in a particular locale or neighborhood. A second group, which included Huron Rd., Lakeside, City, Mt. Sinai, St. Luke's, and St. Vincent's, no longer served just their immediate neighborhoods. Instead, they drew patients from all regions of Cleveland. Together these 6 hospitals contained 60% (1,812 beds) of the total capacity (3,088 beds) of the 20 hospitals belonging to the Cleveland Hospital Council (see CLEVELAND HOSP. ASSOC.) in 1920. Several hospitals in this second group led the move away from the center of Cleveland toward suburban communities in the 2 decades from 1915-35. In making this move, they were prompted by the need to renew aging physical plants and lured by the prospect of finding locations closer to a middle-class clientele better able to pay for hospital care. MT. SINAI initiated this relocation in 1916 by moving to the vicinity of what is today called UNIVERSITY CIRCLE. It was followed by Lakeside, Maternity (later MacDonald), and Rainbow hospitals, which all opened new buildings adjacent to WRU by 1931. This first wave of urban flight culminated with the relocation of St. Luke's on Shaker Blvd. (1927) and Huron Rd. in E. CLEVELAND (1935).

During the Depression, the hospitals of Cleveland confronted economic uncertainties by turning to a group medical insurance plan now known as Blue Cross (see BLUE CROSS OF NORTHEAST OHIO). Under early versions of Blue Cross, as first instituted in Dallas in 1929, individual hospitals concluded contracts with subscribing groups to provide hospitalization in return for a set annual fee. In Cleveland, no single hospital plan took hold. Instead, in 1934 the Cleveland Hospital Council initiated a citywide plan in which cooperating hospitals agreed to provide service on a prepaid basis. By this arrangement, Blue Cross enabled voluntary hospitals in Cleveland to maintain a steady level of bed occupancy while also preventing competition for patients among member hospitals. In 1938, Cleveland's Blue Cross became the first prepayment plan in the U.S. to reimburse hospitals on the basis of cost, a move made possible by the growth of its subscriber group to over 100,000. Over the following decades, Blue Cross emerged as the dominant form of hospitalization insurance in Greater Cleveland; on the eve of Medicare in 1965, 70% of hospital patients in Cuyahoga County were covered by Blue Cross of Northeast Ohio.

The economic stability provided by Blue Cross, combined with advances in surgery (open-heart surgery and kidney transplantation) and diagnostic technologies, encouraged considerable expansion of hospital facilities in Cleveland following WORLD WAR II. The number of beds in general medical-surgical and maternity hospitals in Cuyahoga County grew 20% between 1952-60 (from 5,197 to 6,636) and 30% between 1960-75 (from 6,636 to 9,666). The enlargement of existing facilities and the creation of new hospitals (Parma, BRENTWOOD, FOREST CITY, and SUBURBAN COMMUNITY) were financed by bond issues in the case of publicly supported hospitals and by individual, corporate, and foundation contributions and by reserve funds for depreciation in the case of voluntary hospitals. Federal grants, available chiefly through the provisions of the Hospital Survey & Construction Act (1946) [PL 79-725, Title VI of the Public Health Service Act], played only a supplementary role in hospital growth in Cleveland and Cuyahoga County before the mid-1960s. However, federal assistance in the form of Medicare and Medicaid did become an important source of general revenue for Cleveland hospitals after 1965; by 1980, Medicare and Medicaid constituted 41% of hospital patient revenues in the city of Cleveland and 38% in the suburban sections of the County. At the same time that hospitals underwent physical expansion, population growth slowed and then declined in Cleveland and the vicinity, Between 1960-70, population in Cuyahoga County grew only 4% (from 1,647,895 to 1,721,300); it then declined 7% in the decade 1970-80 (from 1,721,300 to 1,499,167). The net result of population loss was that the county, and especially the city of Cleveland, had a surplus of beds, and, hence, hospitals often fell below the 85% occupancy rate that was considered optimal for voluntary hospitals. Low occupancy, together with the financial burden of hospital construction or renovation and the cost of maintaining specialized services, led to a steady increase in per diem hospital costs to patients or their insurers. To be precise, the average cost per patient day in Cleveland hospitals rose from $28.40 in 1957 to $268 in 1980. The hospitals of Cleveland and related agencies confronted spiraling health costs in a number of ways. The chief means employed have been regional hospital and health planning, the imposition of cost ceilings by 3d-party insurers (Blue Cross and others), and the creation of health maintenance organizations (HMOs).

Regional hospital planning in Cleveland began with the formation of the Cleveland Hospital Council in 1916. This organization engaged Haven Emerson, health commissioner of New York City, to investigate and report upon the institutional network responsible for health care in Cleveland. His findings were presented in the *Cleveland Hospital and Health Survey* (1920), which was considered a landmark study in the field. However, this publication did not result in any coherent program of health care planning; the hospitals of Cleveland continued to pursue their own separate institutional goals without coordinating growth activities. The next major attempt to institute regional planning came in 1941, when HAROLD BURTON, mayor of Cleveland, appointed the Joint Hospital Committee. Created to consider the anticipated resurgence of hospital construction following World War II, the committee included members representing the city of Cleveland, the Cleveland Welfare Fed., and the Cleveland Hospital Council. Before this local body could undertake any planning, its role was effectively eclipsed by state agencies, which were given principal health-planning responsibilities under provisions of the Hospital Construction & Survey Act in 1946 (otherwise known as the Hill-Burton Act in honor of its legislative sponsors, Sen. Harold Burton of Ohio and Sen. Lister Hill of Alabama). The concept of regional planning was not revived until 1966, when the Comprehensive Health Planning Act returned planning responsibilities to local agencies. In northeast Ohio, this role was assumed by the Comprehensive Health Planning Agency, which served Cuyahoga, Lake, Geauga, and Medina counties. In its capacity as a planning body, the CHPA, later known as the METROPOLITAN HEALTH PLANNING CORP., commissioned studies of existing health-care facilities, determined the strengths and weaknesses of the region's hospital system, and assessed the validity of requests by area hospitals for expansion of facilities, particularly those seeking state and federal funding for new construction. Although the MHPC initially acted in a consultative capacity, its designation by the federal government as a Health Systems Agency increased its influence and power in the realm of regional health planning.

Imposition of cost ceilings upon Cleveland-area hospitals has come from 2 principal sources since the advent of Medicare in 1965. The first of these was Blue Cross, which had, since 1938, reimbursed hospitals upon the basis of cost instead of a schedule of negotiated rates. The basis for this arrangement was altered by the state legislation in 1972 and 1976 that prohibited hospitals from controlling the boards of Ohio Blue Cross plans and that admonished Blue Cross plans to create incentives to eliminate waste and unnecessary services, chiefly through negotiated reimbursement agreements. A second, more far-reaching challenge to hospital-determined costs for medical care came in Oct. 1983, when Medicare began the transition to a payment schedule based upon diagnosis-related groups, or DRGs, instead of actual costs incurred for hospital care of Medicare patients. The intent of the DRG program was to curb inflationary trends in hospital costs by basing payment upon the characteristics of the patient's illness rather than upon the specific demands of hospitals seeking reimbursement.

It is still too soon to assess all the consequences of these changes in hospital administration and finance, but one trend is already apparent: the shift to health maintenance organizations (HMOs) as a means for hospitals to introduce or cooperate with a prepaid group plan for payment of medical costs. HMOs were preceded by the prepaid group practice, which had its origins in health-care programs devised by industrial and railway employers. The employers engaged profit-making firms of physicians and surgeons to provide medical services at clinics and small hospitals financed by industrialists' subscriptions and deductions from workers' salaries. Corporate sponsorship of such prepaid programs began ca. 1910 in the Pacific Northwest and did not begin to spread in other regions until 1930. In Cleveland, employers did not have to resort to this form of "welfare capitalism," since there existed many hospitals ready to accommodate the industrial workforce under the Blue Cross plans. Organized labor felt differently, however, and saw the desirability of working men's enrolling in their own prepaid group plan. That came in 1964 when labor unions in Cleveland formed the Community Health Foundation. This HMO provided routine medical care in the offices of several private physicians and hospital care in cooperating institutions in the city. In 1969, the Community Health Foundation joined with the KAISER-PERMANENTE MEDICAL CARE PROGRAM to form the Kaiser Community Health Foundation. By 1974 the Kaiser-Permanente Medical Care Program had grown to comprise 3 separate hospital facilities in Cleveland. (A decade later, in 1985, the Kaiser-Permanente system had become the largest HMO in the U.S., encompassing some 4.6 million members in 9 geographic regions.)

Health maintenance organizations other than the Kaiser-Permanente Medical Care Program were slow to develop in Greater Cleveland until the late 1970s. (In 1970 there were only 33 HMOs nationwide; by 1977 the number

had grown to 183, with 6.85 million persons enrolled; by 1985 there were 323 HMOs in the U.S., with a total enrollment of 15 million.) In Cleveland and the immediate vicinity of Cuyahoga County, the number of HMOs had increased from 1 in 1970 (Kaiser-Permanente) to 8 in 1985. Finding an explanation for this sudden increase is no simple task, but one overriding factor seems to maintain a fee-for-service structure of payment beneath the shelter of a privately operated system of prepayment. In this manner, hospitals can escape either Blue Cross or federal DRG cost limitations and still render high-quality health service at what they (hospitals) consider to be a reasonable price.

James Edmonson
Howard Dittrick Museum of Historical Medicine

See also MEDICINE, NURSING.

**HOSTETLER, JOSEPH C.** (8 Aug. 1885–2 Dec. 1958), was considered one of Cleveland's finest lawyers. He was a senior member and a founding partner of the Cleveland law firm of Baker, Hostetler & Sidlo (see BAKER & HOSTETLER). Hostetler was born on a farm near Canal Dover, Ohio, in Tuscarawas County. His parents, Joseph and Caroline, were Amish. After graduation from high school in Canal Dover, Hostetler worked at various jobs to earn his tuition for Western Reserve University and law school. He followed his father, uncle, and cousin into the practice of law. During this period, he also worked as a police beat reporter in Cleveland. After he was admitted to the Ohio bar in 1908, Hostetler worked for 2 years in the law firm of WM. R. HOPKINS. While NEWTON D. BAKER served as mayor of Cleveland from 1910–16, Hostetler served as his assistant city law director. When Baker left office, Hostetler joined him in the newly formed law firm of Baker, Hostetler & Sidlo. He practiced law until his death at age 73.

Hostetler was one of the organizers of the NORTHERN OHIO FOOD TERMINALS and served as the chairman of its board of directors. He was elected a director of the Cleveland Trust Co. in 1938, succeeding to the vacancy created by the death of Newton D. Baker. He also served as a director of the Cleveland Welding Co. and the Consolidated Iron-Steel Mfg. Co. He headed the Chamber of Commerce-sponsored Playgoers of Cleveland, an organization that sought to have a legitimate theater season in Cleveland, presenting some of the best New York plays. He was a member from 1940–45 of the Distribution Committee of the CLEVELAND FOUNDATION, and in 1948 he was awarded an honorary Master of Law degree by Cleveland-Marshall Law School. Hostetler was elected the 36th president of the CLEVELAND BAR ASSOC. in 1947. He was secretary of the Cleveland Baseball Co. for 20 years and was counsel for the American League. He was an active member of the Cleveland Chamber of Commerce, and in 1938 he was chairman of its special committee to study building-code requirements. He also was a member of the MID-DAY and UNION CLUBS. Hostetler married Hazel Prior in 1917. One of his last public appearances was at the dedication of the Newton D. Baker Memorial Wing at WRU in Nov. 1958.

**HOTELS.** For nearly 200 years, the inns and hotels of Cleveland, from the oldest roadside taverns to early mercantile hotels, and from the modern convention hotels to the motels of the automobile age, have followed the developments characteristic of most cities of Cleveland's size and age. On the national scene, Cleveland's Hotel Statler (see STATLER OFFICE TOWER) was considered to be the first complete expression of the modern 20th-century hotel. The earliest inns in the region were typical 18th-century taverns, i.e., 2- or sometimes 3-story frame houses with public parlors and a kitchen on the ground floor and several bedrooms above. These appeared very early at places such as DOAN'S CORNERS (1799) and NEWBURGH (1811). The earliest in the village of Cleveland was Lorenzo Carter's tavern on Superior St. near the first settlement site (1802). Throughout the precanal era, Superior St. was the center of the retail business district. The Cleveland House, Mansion House, and Franklin House were all erected in the 1820s on Superior west of PUBLIC SQUARE. The enactment of legislation creating state roads in the 1830s encouraged stage lines, with a resulting increase in passenger traffic. Inns of the older type were built on the Pittsburgh, Buffalo, Columbus, and Detroit roads. As late as 1842, a tavern was built by Rufus Dunham on the Buffalo Rd. (Euclid Ave.); it was the only one in the city to survive into the 1980s.

With the rapid growth of Cleveland after the opening of the Ohio Canal in 1827, the expansion of business stimulated the building of many hotels in the city. They were of a new type, which remained dominant in the years before the CIVIL WAR: large brick structures with up to 200 rooms. The first hotel of this type was the American House, built in 1837 on Superior opposite the end of W. 6th St. It was followed in quick succession by the second Franklin House, the WEDDELL HOUSE, the Forest City House, and the Kennard House, all located in the vicinity of Superior and the Public Square. Each was 5 stories tall, the usual height limit before the general introduction of elevators. They had plumbing, bathrooms, and water closets, but these facilities were located in common areas instead of in every room. The buildings generally had retail stores and office space on the street level, and several had balconies overlooking the street on upper floors. The usual lifespan of an early-19th-century hotel under the same name and/or management was brief. The Franklin House operated only from 1845–55, and other hotels frequently changed their names under new owners. The notable exception was the Weddell House, which retained the same name from 1847–1961.

By the end of the Civil War, the need for accommodations in the flourishing industrial and commercial city was augmented by the ease of railroad travel. A large number of small 3- and 4-story hotels continued to be built in the downtown area. Two hotels were completed in 1884–85 that marked a significant change in the nature of hotel construction. Both were 8 stories tall, and both were of fireproof construction, built of iron, steel, tile, and cement, and faced with brick. The Stillman (1884) was the first residential hotel east of E. 9th St., and the HOLLENDEN (1885) was the first large commercial hotel east of Public Square. The Hollenden was erected by LIBERTY E. HOLDEN and Chas. H. Bulkley; it became Cleveland's legendary hotel for many years, visited by 5 presidents, heads of foreign governments, politicians, and entertainment celebrities. The interior was noted for its paneled walls, mahogany fittings, specially designed furniture, incandescent lights, and 100 private baths. The next stage in the development of the downtown hotel was even more significant. That was the large modern hotel, often with 1,000 rooms, each with bath, and a monumental suite of public rooms, all arranged to bring maximum income through the leasing of shops and concessions. According to the *Dictionary of American Biography*, the type "found its first complete expression" in Cleveland's Statler Hotel (1912), designed by Geo. B. Post & Sons. Other hotels of the same type were soon erected, including the Winton (later the Carter) in 1917 and the 1,000-room Hotel Cleveland in 1918. The

latter was built by the Van Sweringens on the corner of Superior and Public Square; the site had always held a hotel, being the location of the first Cleveland House and the Forest City House. Subsequently the Hotel Cleveland became an integral part of the Union Terminal complex in 1925–30.

In 1920 there were 76 hotels in Cleveland, with a total capacity of 5,000 rooms. By the end of the decade, there were 125. The changing character of the hotel business is illustrated by the Hotel Allerton of 1926 (later the Manger), part of a national chain. It was a 16-story building that featured extensive sports rooms, with a swimming pool and squash, handball, and tennis courts. The 300-room Auditorium Hotel, built in 1927 on E. 6th St. directly opposite the new PUBLIC AUDITORIUM, was especially attractive to conventioneers. All of these hotels made it possible for Cleveland to draw a flourishing convention business, and in the 1930s and 1940s, Cleveland was a leading convention center in the nation. Another important phenomenon of the 1920s was the construction of many luxury residential hotels. Containing both furnished and unfurnished apartments, most of them catered to residential and transient clients alike. At UNIVERSITY CIRCLE, 3 were constructed in 1923 alone: Wade Park Manor, Fenway Hall, and Park Lane Villa. The same year the ALCAZAR was built in CLEVELAND HTS., and on the west side the Westlake (1925) was built in ROCKY RIVER, and the Lake Shore (1929) in LAKEWOOD. These apartment hotels were fairly consistent in size, with a capacity of 400–450 rooms. Often their public rooms were furnished with specially designed pieces in historical styles in order to provide an atmosphere of luxury and exclusiveness.

During the Depression and WORLD WAR II, virtually no new hotels were built. After the war, the most important factor in the future of the hotel business was the automobile. It was no longer necessary to locate hotels in the center of the city near railroad and bus terminals. Yet the motels and auto courts, which were originally conceived as vacation or resort stops, did not expand into the field of the commercial hotel immediately. In 1960 there were still only 18 motels listed in Greater Cleveland. By the mid-1960s, however, the major national chains, such as Howard Johnson, Holiday Inn, and Sheraton, had constructed large suburban motels, and it is noteworthy that these were situated at first on the old Pittsburgh, Buffalo, Akron, and Detroit roads, where the early-19th-century taverns were located. In 1962 the Airport Holiday Inn opened, demonstrating still another radical change in traveling habits, and with the completion of the main federal interstate highways in the sixties, the interchanges to local connecting roads became the logical sites for major hotels. Whereas the motel was originally a clearly distinguishable type, characterized by the accessibility of each room from an outdoor parking space, by the 1970s less and less distinction could be made between the large suburban motor hotel, which began to include large meeting and banquet rooms, and the older commercial hotel.

At the same time, suburbanization and the declining population of Cleveland led to a decrease in the number of downtown commercial hotels. Moreover, other cities built newer, larger, and more spectacular convention facilities, and the major meetings that formerly had come to Cleveland went elsewhere. Most of the remaining 19th-century hotels were either closed or demolished, including the famous Hawley House (built 1882; razed 1976). The precedent-setting Hotel Statler became an office building. The Hotel Cleveland survived as the Sheraton, and later STOUFFER'S INN ON THE SQUARE. Two of the older hotels were razed and replaced by new buildings; the 1885

Hollenden was rebuilt in the modern style as the Hollenden House in 1964, and the Auditorium Hotel was torn down in 1970 and replaced by the Bond Court Hotel. In 1974 a new 400-room hotel, the Holiday Inn Lakeside, was built at the foot of E. 12th St. in the Erieview urban-renewal area. In the 1970s and early 1980s, several attempts were made by city development groups to promote the construction of a major new downtown commercial hotel, on the premise that the availability of new space would attract the lost convention business again, but none of these attempts was successful. During the same years, many of the residential hotels of the 1920s became retirement and nursing homes or were converted to condominiums. In 1985 there were 65 hotels and motels listed in the Cleveland area, of which 25 were operated by national chains.

Eric Johannesen
Western Reserve Historical Society

The **HOUGH** neighborhood is a 2-sq.-mi. area bounded by Euclid and Superior avenues and E. 55th and E. 105th streets. Originally part of E. Cleveland Twp., it takes its name from one of the neighborhood's major streets, Hough Ave., dedicated in 1873 and named for Oliver and Eliza Hough, early landowners in the district. Following the area's annexation in 1872, Hough became a fashionable residential neighborhood characterized by platted subdivisions of large single-family houses. It was still a predominantly white-working- and middle-class neighborhood in 1950. By 1960, however, it had undergone complete reversal—from 5% nonwhite in 1950 to 74% nonwhite in 1960. Long before this racial turnabout, however, Hough suffered from an aging housing stock, a decline in maintenance and in the percentage of owner-occupied dwellings, overcrowding (the result of families' doubling up or taking in boarders), and severely inadequate play space. Cleveland's black population increased sharply in the 1940s in response to the wartime demand for labor. Hough, close to the predominantly black Central neighborhood, became a natural area for change when the city's urban-renewal programs displaced many BLACKS in the mid-1950s. Realty companies fostered panic selling, and absentee landlords converted many single-family units into rooming houses and tenements. In 1951 the Hough Area Council led a campaign against the first signs of decay and in favor of better street lighting and police protection; 4 years later it fought against widespread blockbusting. In 1956 the neighborhood was an uneasy mixture of long-time residents, whites who had recently migrated from Appalachia, and blacks who had moved into Hough.

The $12 million Community Action for Youth program was begun in 1964 to address the problem of juvenile delinquency and bring cooperation among schools, public welfare organizations, and police. The University-Euclid urban-renewal project promised as early as 1960, however, lagged and still had not made significant headway 5 years later. Hough, the *Cleveland Press* reported in a series of articles in Feb. 1965, was in "crisis." Racial violence erupted on the night of 18 July 1966, marking the start of the devastating HOUGH RIOTS, with the widespread destruction of buildings and property. Since 1970, the Hough neighborhood has seen some modest commercial development, as well as the construction of major new public buildings. These developments include Martin Luther King Jr. Plaza, Giddings Elementary School, Martin Luther King Jr. High School, and the HOUGH NORWOOD FAMILY HEALTH CARE CTR. Lexington Village, a new residential development at E. 79th St. and Lexington Ave., was underway in 1985, although elsewhere the poor, deteriorated neighborhood remained pockmarked by abandoned buildings and vacant lots. The population of Hough declined from 65,694 in 1950 to 25,330 in 1980.

The **HOUGH AREA DEVELOPMENT CORPORATION** was a neighborhood development corporation concerned that redevelopment of the neighborhood after the HOUGH RIOTS be directed by local residents rather than outsiders. Formed in 1967, the HADC undertook several ambitious programs before losing federal funding and becoming inactive in 1984. DeForest Brown, a charismatic street minister turned social worker, took the lead in forming the HADC. Fearing that money poured into HOUGH by the federal government and local businesses after the riots would be used by outsiders for what he saw as the further colonialization of the black neighborhood, Brown put together a coalition of trusted professionals and neighborhood leaders to coordinate the redevelopment of the area. Formed in the spring of 1967 and known as the Machine, Brown's coalition included Hough leaders Daisy L. Craggett and Christine A. Randles, architect Julian C. Madison, and Burt W. Griffin and C. Lyonel Jones of the LEGAL AID SOCIETY. Brown's group formed the HADC in secret, fearing that publicity would attract attention from the local COUNCIL FOR ECONOMIC OPPORTUNITIES and other officials who would try to control it. HADC found support within the federal Office of Economic Opportunity and from Mayor Carl Stokes's CLEVELAND: NOW! program, which gave HADC an initial $62,000 grant. In July 1968, HADC received a $1.6 million grant from OEO to fund a shopping center, a housing development, and a factory.

Martin Luther King, Jr. Plaza, located at Wade Park Ave. and Crawford Rd., was envisioned as the center of new development in Hough. Promoted by HADC as "the first enclosed shopping center built to serve people living in a Black community" and opened in 1972, the $3 million shopping center with 26 townhouses on the roof had problems in its early years but served as a symbol of the ability of blacks to plan, build, and operate their own businesses in areas where traditional urban renewal had failed. Control of the plaza was turned over to a community board. HADC made lasting contributions to Hough in housing, providing 600 units of new housing. It also tried unsuccessfully to put together a 100-acre industrial park in the southwest corner of Hough between E. 55th, E. 71st, Chester, and Carnegie, but HADC's plan laid the groundwork for what became the Midtown Corridor development plan. Other HADC programs did not prove to be as successful. Its Community Prods., Inc. (inc. 1968), began manufacturing rubber parts for the auto industry in summer 1969. By the late 1970s, it employed more than 100 people, many of whom were former welfare recipients, and was making a small profit; but it was hurt severely by the recession in the domestic auto industry and closed in Dec. 1983. The Handyman's Maintenance Service, Inc., used federal funds to train unemployed workers but found little market in the area for its services. Perhaps its most controversial project was Ghetto East Enterprises, Inc., 2 McDonald's restaurant franchises HADC purchased in cooperation with the "Rabbi" David Hill; the negotiations for the restaurants involved picketing and boycotting by black Clevelanders who believed the stores' profits should remain in the area. Once HADC bought the stores, poor management led to financial losses, and the stores were later sold. Changes in federal policy in the early 1980s cut off federal funding for HADC; by Sept. 1982, its federal funds were spent, and it was dependent upon local foundation grants. In Jan. 1984, the Hough Area Development Corp. laid off its staff.

525

**HOUGH BAKERIES, INC.,** Cleveland's largest and oldest retail bakery, was founded on 25 (27) May 1903 by Lionel A. Pile. Located at 8708 Hough Ave., it was originally called Hough (Ave.) Home Bakery. The name was changed to Hough Bakeries in 1952 as branches opened all over the Greater Cleveland area. Lionel "Archie" Pile was born in Barbados on 29 Aug. 1879 on Plum Tree Plantation and was educated under the British system of private schools. On 7 July 1900, at the age of 21, he landed in New York City, where he obtained a job as a grocery clerk in Brooklyn. Having relatives in Cleveland, he came to the city on 22 Aug. 1902 and went to work at the Homeier Bros. Grocery at Hough Ave. and Crawford Rd. Saving pennies from his weekly salary, he soon accumulated $57 for the down payment on his business venture. He purchased a bake shop from his brother-in-law, Mr. H. O. Lewis, and opened for business with 4 employees.

The eldest of Pile's 4 sons, Arthur, joined his father at work in 1927, and both Lawrence and Kenneth Pile entered the family business after completing their educations. Robt. Pile began working full-time at the bakery in 1935. With all of the Pile men active in the business, it quickly began to grow. In 1913, Hough had unsuccessfully tried to expand their operation with 3 branch stores; however, in 1927 they were successful with a new branch store located in E. CLEVELAND opposite the Windermere car barns, and it was followed by more branch stores in CLEVELAND HTS. The Piles purchased the old Star Bakery plant at 1519 Lakeview Rd. in May 1941, and 4 years later the Hough Bakery Co. was incorporated. Today the Lakeview plant serves as the company's headquarters.

Hough's growing catering business was begun in 1930, featuring wedding cakes and canapes. In 1952 it catered the 5-day Supermarket Convention held in Cleveland's Public Hall, during which time 20,000 meals were served, including breakfasts, lunches, banquets, and midnight buffets. A subsidiary, Hough Caterers, Inc., was established in 1956 to handle this growing business. The firm also diversified into the production and distribution of frozen and prepared foods, forming Hough Foods, Inc., in 1955, and in the 1960s this subsidiary began to operate cafeterias at major plants. By 1973, Hough had reached annual sales of $12 million, with 1,000 employees. Today, Hough Bakery has grown to 28 separate branch stores in the Greater Cleveland area, 14 supermarket units, 6 outlets in May Co. stores, and 3 surplus-thrift outlets. Because the bakery has catered functions throughout the city, from small private affairs to city galas, including the banquets and festivities surrounding the visit to Cleveland by Britain's Prince Charles in 1977, it has earned the title of "Cleveland's Distinctive Caterers."

The **HOUGH RIOTS,** 18–24 July 1966, were a spontaneous outbreak of violence characterized by vandalism, looting, arson, and sporadic gunfire. There had been racial disturbances earlier that summer; however, these incidents proved to be more serious and widespread. The riots were sparked by an altercation at Hough Ave. and E. 79th St. on the evening of 18 July. Neighborhood people gathered at the intersection, and the police there were unable to deal with the situation. As the crowd grew larger, rock throwing, looting, and vandalism gradually spread throughout the Hough area. More police were called, there were reports of sniper fire, and it was not until early the next morning that the violence subsided. The following evening there were roving gangs looting, vandalizing, and setting fires in the area, as well as continuing reports of sniper fire. Firemen reported that they had rocks thrown at them as they answered fire alarms, and as a result they were ordered back to the station houses.

At the request of Mayor Ralph Locher, the Natl. Guard moved into HOUGH in the early morning hours of 20 July to restore order, and the mayor also ordered all bars and taverns closed. There was relative calm that evening; however, on Thursday the 21st, the violence spread to the fringes of Hough, with a major fire at Cedar and E. 106th St. Things gradually returned to normal, and on Monday, 25 July, those stores in the Hough area that had escaped serious damage were able to reopen. The Natl. Guard was gradually released from duty that week. During the riots, 4 people were killed, about 30 were injured, close to 300 were arrested, and approximately 240 fires were reported. There was no evidence that the riots had been planned or controlled by radical groups in Cleveland. However, once they began, extremists were in a position to exploit them. The underlying cause of the riots was blacks' frustration at not achieving their expectations of a better life. Efforts to rehabilitate Hough had been going on for 20 years with little success, and the infusion of $16.4 million dollars in urban-renewal funds from the federal government had produced no tangible results. The Hough riots were part of a national pattern of racial tension and frustration, which produced violence in many parts of the country in 1966.

Cleveland Citizens Committee on Hough Disturbances (1966).
Cuyahoga County Grand Jury Special Report Relating to the Hough Riots (1966).
Lackritz, Marc E., *The Hough Riots of 1966* (B.A. thesis, Princeton University, 1968).
Urban League of Cleveland Report on the Hough Riots.

The **HOUGH-NORWOOD FAMILY HEALTH CARE CENTER** was established in 1967 with an Office of Equal Opportunity grant to serve the needs of the inner-city poor. Designed for a public long neglected by the medical community, the clinic evolved from an object of suspicion on the parts of both neighborhood residents and professionals to a respected part of the local medical establishment. The center, at 1465 E. 55th St., offered primary care to any resident of the HOUGH, Norwood, or Goodrich area whose income fell below the $4,200 poverty line for a family of 4. The targeted population comprised 30,000 of the 76,000 who lived in Hough. Within the first year, hundreds of black and ethnic (Slovak, Spanish, and Croatian) patients registered at the center. By 1971, when the Hough-Norwood Ctr. celebrated its 4th anniversary, there were 16,000 on its active roles, and an average of 1,500 were served per week; the clinic estimated it served over half the neighborhood. The center opened satellite facilities at 8300 Hough in 1972 and at 12108 Superior in 1980. Although it encouraged appointments, the center maintained a walk-in service for minor emergencies and ties with Metropolitan General, University, and Mt. Sinai hospitals for major ones. The center was manned by pediatricians, dentists, internists, optometrists, medical assistants, dental technicians, and family-care workers. A night telephone center made referrals after hours. To entice the medically indigent to use the clinic's facilities, the center trained neighborhood residents for "outreach" and "health action" work, as well as other paraprofessional positions. The clinic offered transportation, child care, and a friendly waiting atmosphere.

The personalized service that drew patients to Hough-Norwood came under attack in a 1978 government report that accused the center of misspending. Of $1.1 million waste found at 6 neighborhood health centers throughout the nation, over half was concentrated at the Cleveland operation, which was found to have 1 extra doctor and 45 more support workers than needed. Director Jas. Turner, outraged at governmental insensitivity, made some staff cuts, the cost being some drug rehabilitation programs that required extra personnel. The center was also attacked for providing door-to-door transportation service where public transit was available. Ironically, the center was complimented on its preventive care. When the government transferred OEO funds to HEW in 1973, the center feared it would lose funding, since it would have to compete for dollars from the same source that funded hospitals, medical schools, and universities. With the support of the Cleveland ACADEMY OF MEDICINE, the clinic was successful in obtaining additional grants from the federal government. Also, the center solicited the business community to finance special projects, such as remodeling a building in GLENVILLE donated by AMERITRUST. The Hough-Norwood Family Health Care Ctr. and its branches continued to serve over 150,000 neighborhood residents in 1986.

The **HOUSE OF WILLS,** a funeral home established in 1904 as Gee & Wills, was, in 1986, one of the oldest and most successful black businesses in Cleveland. It was reportedly the largest black funeral home in the state. Gee & Wills originally opened their establishment at 2323 Central Ave. The partnership dissolved in 1907, at which time J. WALTER WILLS, SR., began to operate under the name of J. Walter Wills & Sons. Subsequent locations were at 2525 Central, 2340 E. 55th St., and its present (1986) main facility at 2491 E. 55th St. A second location operated at 14711 Harvard Ave. in the 1980s, serving the black community that had moved to that district in the 1960s and 1970s. In addition to its primary function, the House of Wills served as a facility for black community gatherings for many years. The auditorium at E. 55th St. was available for club activities and small programs for blacks, as they were barred from most comparable public facilities during the first half of the 20th century. The owner, J. Walter Wills, Sr., was an active leader and participant in community affairs for many years and was a respected figure in the black community.

**HOVORKA, FRANK** (5 Aug. 1897–9 Apr. 1984), was a Czech immigrant who became a chemistry professor at Western Reserve University and a leader in the field of electrochemistry. Hovorka was born in Cernicorvce, Bohemia, Austria-Hungary (presently Czechoslovakia), where he attended grammar school, learned the barbering trade, and later attended business school at night. In 1913, he came to the U.S. with his mother and settled in a Czech settlement in Amana, Iowa. Soon after, he began practicing barbering in nearby Waterloo, where a customer suggested that he attend an American grammar school to familiarize himself with American educational methods and eventually enter college. In 1915, Hovorka entered the Waterloo public schools; he finished all 8 grades in 1 year. He went on to the subcollegiate department at the State College of Iowa at Iowa City, 1917–19; he continued there and received a B.A., 1919–22. He received an M.S. in 1923 and a Ph.D. in 1925 from the University of Illinois. His dissertation on the properties of ionic solutions is still cited as a classic study in the electrochemistry of solutions. Hovorka was naturalized as a U.S. citizen in 1923.

In 1925, Hovorka joined WRU's chemistry department, where he helped establish a chemistry doctorate in 1930. He became a full professor and the director of the WRU chemistry labs in 1942 and served as chairman of the chemistry department 1950–58 and 1962–68. During his early years at Reserve, he served as a faculty advisor to the women

of WRU's Flora Stone Mather College. In 1954, Hovorka received WRU's Hurlbut Chair in chemistry. He retired in 1968 and was granted emeritus status. During his tenure, he served as the research director for 45 M.S.'s and 63 Ph.D.'s. In 1973, Hovorka and his wife, Sophie, and many of his former students donated over $1 million to establish the Frank Hovorka Chair in chemistry. Hovorka was nationally known for his work in electrochemistry and wrote over 100 technical papers. He was a pioneer in interdisciplinary research; in 1930, he was involved in joint projects with the WRU School of Medicine, the Institute of Pathology, and the CLEVELAND CLINIC. He perfected platinized graphite electrodes in the 1930s, which facilitated the development of modern fuel cells, which convert fuel gases into electricity without burning. In 1940, he broke new ground by developing a new technique for measuring acid concentrations of solutions by using porous graphite electrodes. Hovorka married Sophie Paul Nickel on 12 June 1926; she died in July 1979, after a marriage of 53 years. In July 1982, Hovorka married concert pianist and CWRU trustee Dorothy Humel. He had no children.

**HOWARD, NATHANIEL RICHARDSON** (23 Apr. 1898–23 Dec. 1980), was the last editor of the *CLEVELAND NEWS.* Howard was born in Columbus, Ohio. He began his newspaper career at the age of 14 as a reporter for the *Conneaut News Herald,* and while a student at Oberlin College he worked for the *Oberlin Tribune* and served as campus correspondent for the *Cleveland Plain Dealer.* He began working for the *Cleveland News* in 1918 but switched to the *PLAIN DEALER* a month later, where he rose through the ranks from police reporter to managing editor. In 1934 he wrote a series of articles entitled "I Fred Kohler" on Cleveland's former police chief and mayor. In 1937, Howard was appointed editor of the *Cleveland News* by the FOREST CITY PUBLISHING CO., which had operated both the *News* and the *Plain Dealer* since 1932. He maintained the staunch Republican identity of the *News,* which was vehemently opposed to the New Deal in the 1930s and warmly supportive of the Eisenhower administration in the 1950s. During WORLD WAR II, Howard served as assistant director of the U.S. Office of Censorship, where he aided in the formulation of a voluntary censorship program for the country's newspapers. Four months after the *News* ceased publication on 23 Jan. 1960, Howard rejoined the *Plain Dealer* as contributing editor until his retirement on 23 Apr. 1963.

In retirement, Howard published *Trust for All Times,* a history of the CLEVELAND FOUNDATION (1963), and *The First Hundred Years,* a history of the UNION CLUB (1972). He also served as editor of the *George M. Humphrey Basic Papers,* which were published by the WESTERN RESERVE HISTORICAL SOCIETY in 1965. Howard's professional and civic affiliations were numerous. He was president of the American Society of Newspaper Editors and the Cleveland CITY CLUB, a director of the Associated Press, chairman of the Sunny Acres Hospital Board, and a trustee of Oberlin College and ST. LUKE'S HOSPITAL. He also belonged to the Union, Advertising, and Natl. Press clubs and the Sons of the American Revolution. After the death of his first wife, Marjorie Norton, in 1928, he married Edith Moriarty, who survived him. He had 2 daughters, Mary Anne Amsbardy and Marjorie Johnson. Howard died in Cleveland.

Nathaniel R. Howard Papers, WRHS.

The **HOWARD DITTRICK MUSEUM OF HISTORICAL MEDICINE** is owned by the CLEVELAND MEDICAL

527

LIBRARY ASSOC. When the CMLA was founded in 1894, several of the member physicians felt that a collection of artifacts documenting medical history would be appropriate for the institution. Although a collection was begun at that time, a museum did not actually exist until 1926, when the CMLA built the structure at 11000 Euclid Ave. that it occupies today. Under the direction of Howard Dittrick, M.D., for whom the museum was named in 1945, the collections grew rapidly, but a limited budget precluded opening on a regular basis. During WORLD WAR II, the rare books belonging to the Surgeon General's Library (now the Natl. Library of Medicine) were moved to Cleveland for safety, and the space occupied by the museum was turned over to that library. The museum was moved into smaller quarters, and much of the collection was put into storage. It was not until 1960 that the museum was able to move back into its original quarters. At that time it was refurbished and opened on a regular basis with its own staff. In 1966, the CMLA joined with the health sciences libraries of Case Western Reserve University to form the CLEVELAND HEALTH SCIENCES LIBRARY, and the Dittrick Museum became the historical division of the Health Sciences Library. Its activities were expanded to include not only artifacts but also the rare book collection of the CMLA, books related to medical history belonging to the Health Sciences Library, and an archives documenting the medical history of northeastern Ohio. Since then, the museum has steadily grown; it currently provides both an exhibit museum emphasizing medical practice in the 19th and early 20th centuries and a research source for studies in medical history.

The **HOWARD WISE GALLERY OF PRESENT DAY PAINTING** was a privately owned gallery located at 11322 Euclid Ave. It was established in 1957 by Howard Wise, a member of the advisory council of the CLEVELAND MUSEUM OF ART, trustee and treasurer of the Institute of Music, and trustee of Western Reserve University, in an attempt to bring the works of contemporary European and American artists to Cleveland and to broaden the scope of art appreciation in the Cleveland area. The gallery opened on Sunday, 6 Dec. 1957, with an exhibition entitled "6 of Paris" featuring the works of 6 international artists then working in Paris. The gallery presented 16 1-man shows and 22 group shows and featured the works of over 200 outstanding painters, including Geo. Braque (1958), Hans Hoffman, and Jose Guerrero (1959), during its 3-year residence in Cleveland. The Wise Gallery's primary emphasis was on showing the works of the abstract-expressionist movement. It was, in addition, the first art room outside of New York City to show the artists of the Whitney Museum of Art's annual survey of contemporary American painting. In Sept. 1961, the Cleveland location was closed, and Wise moved the gallery to New York City.

**HOWE, CHARLES SUMNER** (29 Sept. 1858–18 Apr. 1939), was a college educator. As president of the Case School of Applied Science, 1902–29, he brought the school a national reputation through his insistence on high academic standards and was responsible for the construction of a number of new buildings on campus. Howe was born in Nashua, N.H., to Wm. and Susan Woods Howe. He attended elementary school in Boston and high school in Franklin, Mass. After graduation he worked in a print shop in order to earn money for college. In 1878 he received the B.S. in Agriculture degree from both the Massachusetts Agricultural College and Boston University. He received the Ph.D. degree in 1887 from Wooster University. Howe did postgraduate work at Amherst College the following

year. In 1879 he accepted first a high school principalship, then later a professorship at Colorado College. In 1881 he worked in the mining districts of New Mexico and Arizona. He entered Johns Hopkins University in 1882, doing graduate work in mathematics and physics. Accepting an appointment as adjunct professor of mathematics at Buchtel College in 1883, he became professor of mathematics and physics in 1884.

In 1889, Howe accepted an appointment to the professorship of mathematics and astronomy at the Case School of Applied Science. He brought the first German-made Riefler clock, then considered the world's best, to America, where he made his own modifications, making it in its day the most accurate timepiece in the world. Appointed acting president of Case in 1902, Howe was appointed president in 1903. He reinstituted freshman entrance examinations and maintained a class-rank status system for faculty. He was responsible for a number of new buildings on campus, including the physics and the mining and metallurgy buildings. Howe maintained a close relationship with a select group of influential Clevelanders, including JOHN ROCKEFELLER, WORCESTER WARNER, and AMBROSE SWASEY. Strongly believing that engineers had an obligation to participate in civic affairs, Howe was active in community affairs. He served as president of the Cleveland Chamber of Commerce and chairman of the Cleveland River & Harbor Commission and was prominent in the establishment of East and West Technical high schools.

**HOWE, FREDERIC C.** (21 Nov. 1867–3 Aug. 1940), was a prominent Progressive reformer who remained politically active from the Progressive Era into the New Deal. An expert on taxation and interested in urban planning, he began his reform career during the 15 years he lived and worked in Cleveland (1894–1909), allying himself with the Progressive mayor TOM JOHNSON. The son of a furniture manufacturer and retailer, Howe was born and raised in Meadville, Pa. He graduated from Allegheny College in 1889 but claimed in his autobiography to have learned little there, noting that his real education began during graduate studies at Johns Hopkins University (Ph.D., 1892). Unable to find a job in journalism in the depression of 1893–94, Howe entered law school in New York, then settled in Cleveland in 1894, working for the law firm of Harry & Jas. Garfield and becoming a full partner in 1896.

Howe's Methodist-Quaker upbringing ingrained in him a "sense of responsibility to the world," and he became active in the work of Goodrich Social Settlement, the Municipal Assoc. (see CITIZENS LEAGUE), and the CHARITY ORGANIZATION SOCIETY. He soon resigned from the latter, concerned that it was designed to keep the poor out of sight, and withdrew from the settlement, frustrated by its ineffectiveness. He then turned to politics in his efforts to reform society. In 1901, Howe was asked by members of the Municipal Assoc. to run for city council as a Republican. During the campaign, he was intrigued by Tom Johnson's ideas about Henry George's single-tax plan, the unjust powers of the privileged classes, and the possibilities for a cohesive urban community. Howe cooperated closely with the Democratic mayor after both were elected. Soon after, he was caught up in the controversy over the natural-gas franchise for the EAST OHIO GAS CO., which demonstrated to him that even members of the Municipal Assoc. had special interests that they expected their candidates to promote. Disillusioned, he ran for reelection in 1903 as an independent but lost. Howe continued in public office: he served as president of the Sinking Fund Commission in 1904–05. In 1905 he was elected to the state senate, serving (1906–08) as the leader of the reform forces and prompting an investigation of corruption in the state treasurer's office. In 1909, he was elected to Cleveland's 5-member Board of Quadrennial Appraisers and worked to increase the valuations on land and to lower the valuations on improvements. In 1910, Howe left Cleveland for New York City.

Howe was a studious commentator on national, social, and economic issues. He published a book on taxation in 1896 and the influential *The City: The Hope for Democracy* in 1905. He published 2 other books during his years in Cleveland: *The Confessions of a Monopolist* (1906) and *The British City: The Beginnings of Democracy* (1907). He lectured on corporate law at the Cleveland College of Law and on taxation and finance at Western Reserve University. In New York, Howe served as director of the People's Institute (1911–14) and was then the commissioner of immigration for the port of New York (1914–19). The latter was a particularly difficult post, and his work there during WORLD WAR I and the "red scare" of 1919 made Howe distrustful of the state, transforming him from a proponent of the welfare state to an advocate of cooperative democracy and pushing his thinking further to the left. He began to work with labor groups and to advocate the Plumb Plan for government control of the railroads. In 1921, he convinced the BROTHERHOOD OF LOCOMOTIVE ENGINEERS to open a cooperative bank in Cleveland. Howe returned to political life in 1932 to support Franklin D. Roosevelt. He was appointed consumers' counsel in the Agricultural Adjustment Admin.; there, he organized consumers against food profiteers. When the agency was reorganized in 1935, Howe was demoted to a special advisor to the secretary of agriculture. He resigned in 1937 but continued to study and write until his death. In 1904, Howe married Marie H. Jenney, a Unitarian minister and a prominent feminist. She died in 1934.

Howe, Frederic C., *The Confessions of a Reformer* (1925).

**HOWELL AND THOMAS** was an architectural firm active in Cleveland from 1916–30. Carl Eugene Howell (1879–17 June 1930) was born in Columbus, Ohio, and died in Monrovia, Calif. He attended Ohio State University and studied drawing at the Columbus Art School. He worked for a few years in the office of Frank Packard in Columbus and then studied further at the University of Pennsylvania, where he won the John Stewardson Traveling Scholarship in Architecture and spent a year traveling in Europe. He was a member of the Cleveland Chamber of Commerce, the Museum of Art, the University and Mid-Day clubs, clubs in New York and Columbus, the American Institute of Architects, and the American Academy of Rome. Jas. Wm. Thomas, Jr. (8 Nov. 1876–18 June 1973), was born in Wilkes-Barre, Pa., and died in Hudson, Ohio. He attended the University of Pennsylvania and graduated in 1904. He began his career in the New York office of the major architect Cass Gilbert. He became a member of the Cleveland Chap. of the AIA in 1911. Thomas married Pearl Delehunt and had 3 sons: Sherman, Vernon, and Gordon.

The firm of Howell & Thomas was formed in Columbus in 1908, where they designed a number of large residences and East High School. Beginning in the 1910s, they designed many homes in the Euclid Golf subdivision (Fairmount Blvd.) that was being developed by Barton Deming in CLEVELAND HTS. They soon moved their office to Cleveland and began designing homes throughout the Heights area. In 1922 they planned a group of 4 demonstration homes for the Van Sweringen brothers at Shaker and Courtland boulevards, and in 1924 they designed another 7 model homes for the Van Sweringen Co. on Parkland Dr. Some of their more important residences were built for Barton Deming, Isaac Joseph, Julius Feiss, and Albert Metzger. They designed additions to Shaker Hts. High School (later Woodbury Jr. High) and Lakewood High School, library and auditorium buildings for Ohio University at Athens, churches in Columbus, Canton, and Oxford, Ohio, and YWCA buildings in Cleveland and Zanesville. They also designed newspaper buildings in Pittsburgh, Rochester, Brooklyn, and Houston and Beaumont, Tex.

**HOYT, DUSTIN, & KELLEY** was a prominent turn-of-the-century law firm in Cleveland, specializing in business law. Its major partners served as counselors and directors of a number of steamship companies, RAILROADS, banks, and manufacturing firms. The partnership of Hoyt, Dustin, & Kelley existed as such from 1893–1908, but a 1943 history of its successor (McKeehan, Merrick, Arter & Stewart and George Wm. Cottrell) traced the firm's origins to the partnership of Geo. Willey and John E. Cary (1843–71), which became Willey, Cary, & Terrell (1871–74), and then Willey, Sherman, & Hoyt (1877–84) when Jas. H. Hoyt (10 Nov. 1850–21 Mar. 1917) joined Willey and Henry S. Sherman in 1877. Sherman and Hoyt operated on their own from 1884–89, before adding the name of Alton C. Dustin (1859–17 Nov. 1938) to the firm's title. Sherman, Hoyt, & Dustin (1889–93) became Hoyt & Dustin briefly in 1893 after Henry Sherman's death, but the two soon elevated to full partnership Hermon A. Kelley (15 May 1859–2 Feb. 1925), former assistant corporation counsel for the city of Cleveland, who had joined the firm in 1891. At various times, the company advertised itself in the city directories as specialists in patent and admiralty law. Jas. Hoyt was an organizer and counselor for the AMERICAN SHIP BUILDING CO., Pittsburgh Steamship Co., and GREAT LAKES TOWING CO.; was general counsel and director of the Hocking Valley Railroad; and served as a director for other railroads, steamship companies, banks, and manufacturers. Hermon Kelley served as secretary and general counsel for American Ship Building and Great Lakes Towing and was a director and general counsel for the Pittsburgh Steamship Co. Alton Dustin also served as general counsel for railroad companies and corporations. In 1909, Hoyt, Dustin, & Kelley added 2 new names to the firm's title, those of Homer H. McKeehan (27 June 1870–23 Apr. 1938) and Horace Andrews (21 Sept. 1861–27 Apr. 1939). With Dustin's retirement from practice in 1932, McKeehan became the senior partner in the new firm.

**HOYT, JAMES MADISON** (16 Jan. 1815–21 Apr. 1885), was a Cleveland lawyer and real-estate developer. He was instrumental in developing neighborhoods in both Cleveland and its SUBURBS. Hoyt was born in Utica, N.Y. Graduating from Hamilton College in 1884, he undertook the study of law, which upon his arrival in Cleveland he continued in the office of Andrews & Foote. Admitted to the Ohio bar in 1837, he was made a partner in the firm of Andrews, Foote & Hoyt until 1848, when the firm became Foote & Hoyt. In 1853, Hoyt withdrew from the practice of law and concentrated his interests on real-estate development in Cleveland and the vicinity. Hoyt developed new neighborhoods by purchasing large tracts of land, dividing it into lots, and selling them for homesteads. On his own or in combination with other investors, he subdivided almost 1,000 acres of city and suburban land and sold it for settlement. He alone was responsible for the opening and naming of over 100 streets. He was instrumental in developing the neighborhood on Prospect, east of Hudson, as well as large portions of St. Clair, Superior, and Kinsman avenues on the east side, and the neighborhoods of Madison Ave., Colgate, Lawn, and Waverly (W. 58th St.) on

529

the west side. Known as the "honest lawyer," Hoyt's reputation carried over to his real-estate dealings. He was generous toward those with whom he dealt, especially the poor and those in difficult circumstances because of unexpected illness or misfortune. In 1870 he was elected to the State Board of Equalization, and in 1873 he was appointed to the Cleveland Board of Public Improvement. Closely associated with first the Baptist and later the Congregational church, he was licensed to preach the Gospel but was never ordained. Hoyt married Mary Ella Beebe in 1836. The Hoyts had 6 children: Ella, Lydia Hoyt Farmer, Elton, Colgate, James, and Wayland. Hoyt is buried in LAKE VIEW CEMETERY.

The **HRUBY FAMILY,** leading musicians in Cleveland for 3 generations, was established in America by Frank Hruby, Sr. (IV) (1856–1912). Known as "America's foremost musical family," the family consisted of 8 children, who played several instruments each. Hruby was born in Cehnie, Czechoslovakia. His first musical job, at age 9, was with the Hagenbeck Circus. He stayed with the circus for 12 years, at the end of which time he was directing 3 bands. He traveled for several years, and while playing in England, he was hired to play 1st clarinet with a band at Brighton Beach. In 1884, seeking new horizons, he brought his wife and young son Frank (V) (1883–1974) to Cleveland. Here he learned that there was a need for experienced musicians and was told to contact Joseph Zamecnik, a Czech-born bandleader. Zamecnik introduced Hruby to John Faust, director of the old Opera House orchestra at E. 4th and Euclid. Hruby was soon offered a job there and held it for 22 years.

In 1889, Hruby organized the Great Western Band. The band played in every large Ohio city and was a favorite with the Republican party. It played for the dedication of the SOLDIERS & SAILORS MONUMENT in 1894 and the Republican Natl. Convention in St. Louis (1896), as well as in the city parks every summer. The Hruby family grew. Young Frank V, who played clarinet, piano, viola, and bass clarinet, was joined by brothers and sisters as soon as they were able to play an instrument. Alois (Louie) (1886–1968) played cello, trumpet, cornet, and cellophone (a cello-like instrument with a megaphonelike horn attached) and later taught at the CLEVELAND INSTITUTE OF MUSIC (1935–55). He played first the cello and later the trumpet in the CLEVELAND ORCHESTRA (1919–66). John (1887–1964) played cornet, trumpet, and violin with the Cleveland Orchestra (1918–26) and taught at Patrick Henry and Audubon junior high schools in the Cleveland school system and at CATHEDRAL LATIN HIGH SCHOOL (1930–50). Celia (Mazanec) (1889–1936) played flute and piano. Ferdinand (Fred) (1891–1978) played piano and clarinet. Charles (1893–1976) played cornet, trumpet, and violin. Mayme (Kolda) (1897–1984) played piano and cello. William (1899–1965) played percussion and trumpet with the Cleveland Orchestra and for many years was prominent as a prize-winning bandleader for various northern Ohio American Legion posts.

From 17 July 1907–27 Aug. 1922, the Hruby brothers played over 600 concerts throughout the country on the Lyceum and Chautauqua circuits. The family orchestra toured Europe, performing in Holland, Czechoslovakia, and Germany. As the family married, they traveled less, and in 1916 Frank V and Fred founded the Hruby Conservatory of Music at Broadway and E. 55th St. Eventually, all 8 Hruby children and 3 grandchildren taught there; each sibling had an assigned studio. The school had a branch on Detroit Ave. in the 1920s and one at the intersection of Euclid and Superior avenues from 1921–49, when it was

moved to Northfield Rd. and Euclid Ave. Both the Broadway and the E. Cleveland branches closed in 1968, upon the retirement of Fred and Frank from active teaching. Other fine musicians taught during the years at the Hruby Conservatory, including Cleveland Orchestra players Emil Sholle and Merritt Dittert. The 5 oldest brothers also formed a quintet known from coast to coast for their range of repertoire and skill. Between them they played 15 instruments. Frank (V), Mayme, and John were in the Cleveland Orchestra in its first year, 1918. All but Celia and Fred played for the orchestra at one time or another.

Three grandchildren of Frank IV became professional musicians. Frank (VI) (b. 1918), trained at Eastman School of Music, has had a distinguished career as a teacher, music director and conductor (Cain Park Summer Theater in CLEVELAND HTS., 1946–56), composer (several musicals for the Curtain Pullers), and writer (music critic and columnist, CLEVELAND PRESS, 1956–82). Richard Kolda (b. 1921), Mayme's son, played trumpet and taught in the Cleveland Hts. schools (1948–80). Joseph Hruby (b. 1922), son of Alois, has played trumpet with the Cleveland Orchestra and the Cleveland Philharmonic, as well as many stage, theater, and dance bands in Cleveland. He became vice-president of the CLEVELAND FED. OF MUSICIANS, LOCAL 4 AFM, in 1974.

**HUBBELL, BENJAMIN S.** (11 July 1867–21 Feb. 1953), was a prominent architect, active in Cleveland 1895–1930, who played a major role in the planning and development of the Wade Park area, now known as UNIVERSITY CIRCLE. With W. DOMINICK BENES, he was responsible for the design of several Cleveland landmarks, including the CLEVELAND MUSEUM OF ART (1916) and the WEST SIDE MARKET (1912). Hubbell was born in Leavenworth, Kans. He attended Cornell University, where as a senior he received a scholarship in architecture and was elected to the honorary society Sigma Xi. He graduated from Cornell with an M.S. in architecture in 1894. Within 2 years of graduation, Hubbell was made a partner in the firm of Coburn, Barnum, Benes & Hubbell (1896). A year later he established a partnership with Benes—Hubbell & Benes (1897–1939). It was as partners that both men completed their largest and most significant contributions. (See Benes, W. Dominick, for listing and dates of selected major projects.)

In 1916, when Hubbell & Benes were designing the Cleveland Museum of Art, they also exhibited locally drawings that sited proposed cultural buildings in the Wade Park Oval along formal, symmetrical axes in an informal park-like setting. The siting of buildings reflected the Beaux-Arts planning concepts utilized at the Columbian Exposition held at Chicago in 1893, as well as the Group Plan that placed public buildings around a formal mall on the lakefront in downtown Cleveland. While many portions of the 1916 Hubbell & Benes plan, including subsequent drawings shown in 1918 and 1919, were not developed in detail, they established the general character for the area. Hubbell is also credited with playing a leading role in the formation of the University Improvement Co. in 1918, a development company organized to preserve the neighborhoods and open spaces in the Wade Park area, and which eventually led to the construction of University Circle. He was a member of the Union, Rotary, Masonic, and Colonial clubs, the Cleveland Chamber of Commerce, and the the AMERICAN INSTITUTE OF ARCHITECTS CLEVELAND CHAPTER. Hubbell married Bertha M. in 1896 and had a son, Benjamin S., Jr., and a daughter, Virginia. They lived at their home, "Playmore," in Mentor, Ohio.

**HUGHES, ADELLA PRENTISS** (29 Nov. 1869–23 Aug. 1950), was best known as the founder of the CLEVELAND ORCHESTRA. Hughes was born in Cleveland, the daughter of Loren and Ellen Rouse Prentiss. She graduated from Miss Fisher's School for Girls in 1886 and from Vassar College in 1890 with a degree in music. She then took a grand tour of Europe, returning to Cleveland in 1891. Upon her return, she became a professional accompanist. Though successful in this role, she became interested in the broader aspects of musical promotion in Cleveland, and in 1898 she began bringing various performers and orchestras to the city. By 1901, she was one of Cleveland's major impresarios, regularly engaging orchestras to perform at GRAYS ARMORY. During the next 17 years she supplied the city with a series of musical attractions, including orchestras, opera, ballet, and chamber music. Seeing the need for a permanent orchestra, Hughes created the MUSICAL ARTS ASSOC. in 1915 from a nucleus of business and professional men to furnish support for her projects. It was through her influence that NIKOLAI SOKOLOFF came to Cleveland. In 1918, she, Sokoloff, and the Musical Arts Assoc. joined forces to create the Cleveland Orchestra. She served as its first manager, holding that position for 15 years. She also held administrative positions in the Musical Arts Assoc. for 30 years, retiring in 1945 only to continue her philanthropic work. Adella Prentiss married Felix Hughes in 1904. The couple was divorced in 1923.

Adella Prentiss Hughes Papers, WRHS.
Hughes, Adella Prentiss, *Music Is My Life* (1947).
Musical Arts Assoc. Archives, Severance Hall.

**HUGHES, (JAMES) LANGSTON** (1 Feb. 1902–22 May 1967), was a noted black poet, playwright, novelist, and lecturer. Considered a major 20th-century writer, he was one of the first blacks to write for a black as well as white audience. Born in Joplin, Mo., Hughes moved to Cleveland in 1916 to join his mother and stepfather. He had previously resided with various family members throughout the country. He initially began to write poetry while in the 8th grade in Lincoln, Ill. His serious writing began while he was a student at CENTRAL HIGH SCHOOL in Cleveland, where his efforts were encouraged by teachers, librarians, and Rowena and RUSSELL JELLIFFE of the Playhouse Settlement (see KARAMU HOUSE). Following high school graduation, he attended Columbia University for a year, but dropped out in order to travel the world. He worked his way through Spain, France, Italy, and Africa. Hughes's first poem, "The Negro Speaks of Rivers," was published in *Crisis*, the organ of the NAACP, in 1921. In 1922 he moved to Harlem, where he wrote *The Weary Blues* and became, along with Paul Robeson, Countee Cullen, and others, a noted member of the Harlem Renaissance. Following publication of *The Weary Blues* in 1926, Hughes wrote *Fine Clothes to the Jew* in 1927. Awarded a full scholarship for his poetry by Lincoln University in Pennsylvania, Hughes returned to school to receive his B.A. In 1930 he published his first novel, *Not without Laughter*. It was followed by *Scottsboro Limited* (1932) and *The Ways of White Folks* (1934). He received a Guggenheim Fellowship in 1935. In 1936–37, the Gilpin Players of Karamu House produced 6 of Hughes's plays. In 1939 he established the Negro Theater in Los Angeles and wrote a filmscript, *Way Down South*. He continued to write in a variety of formats up to the time of his death. In all, he produced 8 volumes of poetry, 4 of fiction, 6 books for young people, 3 humorous works, 2 autobiographies, a number of plays and essays, and several volumes relating to black history. He was a noted lecturer and one of the foremost figures in the movement for black civil rights and the search for black identity.

Dickinson, Donald C., *A Bio-Bibliography of Langston Hughes* (1972).

**HULETT, GEORGE H.** (26 Sept. 1846–17 Jan. 1923), was the inventor of ore-loading machinery that revolutionized the transportation of ore on the Great Lakes and at ocean ports. Hulett was born in Conneaut, Ohio, the son of Erastus and Amanda Norton Hulett. He attended local schools in Conneaut until the age of 12 and then moved to Cleveland, continuing his education in the public schools and at the HUMISTON INSTITUTE, from which he graduated in 1864. He became a merchant in Unionville, Ohio, conducting a general store until 1881. He then returned to Cleveland and was in the produce and commission business until 1890. In 1890, Hulett began manufacturing coal- and ore-handling machinery, which was to become his main field. In 1898 he was a construction engineer with the Variety Iron Works of Cleveland. He became an engineer with the McMyler Mfg. Co. in 1903, and it was with that company that he invented the Hulett unloader. In 1907 he was associated with Webster Camp & Lane in Akron, which merged in 1909 with Wellman Seaver & Morgan of Cleveland (see DRAVO WELLMAN CO.). Hulett was vice-president of the company until 1917 and a director until 1918. Hulett's most important achievement, however, was the invention of the Hulett car dumper machine (sometimes called the McMyler car dumper machine) and the Hulett unloader. The latter was a device with a cantilevered arm and a bucket for unloading iron ore and coal from lake vessels. Its importance is shown by the fact that while formerly it took 100 men 12 hours to unload 5,000 tons of ore, 4 Hulett unloaders could unload 10,000 tons from a lake vessel in less than 5 hours and required only 25 men for operation. The unloader became used universally on the Great Lakes, and also at various large ocean ports. The car dumper was used for unloading entire cars of ore, coal, and other materials at lake and ocean ports and blast furnaces. Hulett also invented the Hulett conveyor bridge for the handling of coal, iron ore, and limestone. Hulett married Addie Hutchings in June 1871 in Unionville, Ohio. They had 2 children, Frank E. Hulett and Mrs. H. J. Doolittle. Frank graduated from the Case School of Applied Science and became an engineer and contractor in Cleveland. Hulett died in Daytona Beach, Fla., and was buried in LAKE VIEW CEMETERY.

The **HUMILITY OF MARY SISTERS** were founded in 1854 by Rev. John J. Begel in Dommartin, France. Fr. Begel had recruited several women to serve as teachers to children of the poor. These women, under the direction of Antoinette Potier, later Mother Magdalen in religious life, would form the nucleus of the new community. The women dedicated themselves to the Blessed Virgin and resolved to serve the poor in a spirit of humility and love. In 1864, the community left for America to staff a parochial school at Louisville, Ohio. Mother Magdalen died shortly before departure, and the community was then under the direction of Mother Anna Tabourat. The sisters agreed to take charge of a farm at New Bedford, Pa. The donor of the property had given it to the Diocese of Pittsburgh, provided it was used for charitable purposes. The Pittsburgh bishop transferred it to the Cleveland Diocese because his diocese could not fulfill the agreement.

The Humility of Mary Sisters were not daunted by the farm's location or its rundown condition. Under the direction of Mother Anna, they cleared the land and started a school, ultimately establishing both an orphanage and a provincial house on the site. They taught at a number of PAROCHIAL SCHOOLS throughout the diocese. In 1892, they opened Lourdes Academy for girls in Cleveland on Lorain Ave. By 1897 they were able to move the academy into more spacious quarters on Franklin Ave. They continued their teaching apostolate but moved into the field of health care. They were given charge of St. Elizabeth Hospital in Youngstown in 1910. In 1922 they became the administrators of the Rosemary Home, a shelter for handicapped children. In 1924 and 1927 respectively, they took over the administration of St. Joseph's Riverside Hospital in Warren and St. Joseph Hospital in Lorain. The sisters continued their apostolate of service in many varied fields. In 1955 they staffed the new girls' high school, Magnificat, in ROCKY RIVER. Lourdes Academy was merged with St. Stephen High School in 1970. A year later, the merged school was transferred to the site of St. Peter High School on E. 17th and Superior Ave. and was reorganized as Erieview High School under the direction of the Humility of Mary Sisters. In 1985, the community pursued a varied apostolate in teaching and health care, along with community service.

Archives, Diocese of Cleveland.

The **HUMISTON INSTITUTE** was a private coeducational school for secondary education in Cleveland during the 1860s. It was also known as the Cleveland Institute. Prof. Ransom F. Humiston, an accomplished Cleveland teacher, founded the school in 1859. It was opened that year in the unused CLEVELAND UNIVERSITY Bldg. The sustaining purpose of the school was to offer a college preparatory curriculum as a superior alternative to the CLEVELAND PUBLIC SCHOOLS. It was both a boarding and a day school, attracting students from out of state as well as from the Cleveland area. In its final year, 1867–68, it had an enrollment of 196 pupils. The institute finally succumbed to public-school competition and in 1868 was taken over by the Western Homeopathic College.

**HUMPHREY, GEORGE MAGOFFIN** (8 Mar. 1890–20 Jan. 1970), was a lawyer, an industrialist, the long-time president of the M. A. HANNA CO., and secretary of the treasury in the Eisenhower administration, 1953–57. Humphrey was born in Cheboygan, Mich., to Watts Sherman and Caroline Magoffin Humphrey. He grew up in Saginaw, Mich., graduating from Saginaw High School in 1908. At the University of Michigan, he studied engineering but later switched to law, receiving his LL.B. degree in 1912. After graduation he practiced law in Michigan, becoming a partner in his father's law firm. Corporate law attracted him, and the M. A. Hanna Co. in Cleveland hired him as a general counsel in 1918. He became a partner in 1920 and was put in charge of iron-ore properties and operations. When Hanna incorporated in 1922, he was made vicepresident, and from 1929–52 he was president of the company. His managerial skills were credited with starting M. A. Hanna on the road to profitability after a $2 million deficit.

After WORLD WAR II, Paul Hoffman, head of the Economic Cooperation Admin., chose Humphrey to lead the Reparations Survey Committee to advise the Allied powers on the dismantling of German industry. On the recommendation of Hoffman and Gen. Lucius Clay, whom Humphrey had met during his Reparation Committee work, president-elect Dwight Eisenhower designated Humphrey his secretary of the treasury. As the Eisenhower cabinet's strongest voice of fiscal conservatism, Humphrey spear-

headed the administration's campaign to cut the federal budget in an effort to pare down the size of government, cut inflation, and stimulate private enterprise. He resigned in 1957; returning to private life in Cleveland, he resumed chairmanships in several of the companies he had previously been associated with. His philanthropic interests were in the medical field. In 1913 he married Pamela Stark, and they had 3 children, Pamela (Mrs. Royal Firman, Jr.), Gilbert Watts, and Caroline (Mrs. John G. Butler). Humphrey died in Cleveland at age 79.

George M. Humphrey Papers, WRHS.
Howard, Nathaniel R., ed., *The Basic Papers of George M. Humphrey as Secretary of the Treasury, 1953–1957* (1965).

**HUMPHREY FOUNDATION.** *See* **GILBERT W. & LOUISE IRELAND HUMPHREY FOUNDATION**

**HUMPHREY FUND.** *See* **GEORGE M. & PAMELA S. HUMPHREY FUND**

**HUNGARIANS.** Cleveland was at one time the city with the 2d-largest population of Hungarians in the world. There are several reasons why Cleveland was chosen by Hungarian immigrants to establish one of their most vibrant communities in the U.S.: job availability, accessibility, and, as more and more Hungarians settled there, the close proximity of countrymen. Hungarian immigration to Cleveland occurred in 3 distinct waves: turn-of-the-century immigration (1870–1924) the largest and most influential wave; postWorld War II "displaced persons"; and post-1956 refugee immigration. The Hungarians who arrived in the first wave settled around the easternmost edge of the city (which became the Buckeye Rd. Hungarian neighborhood) and formed a smaller settlement on the near west side. Significant Hungarian immigration to the city began in the 1870s. These Hungarians were part of a wave of approximately 1 million who came to the U.S. around the turn of the century: they came because land was scarce in their homeland, and cheap labor was plentiful. They initially intended to return to their homeland with enough saved capital to purchase land. The majority were single men or men who had left their families behind. They lived in boarding houses, run by the few women who had immigrated with their husbands. By 1900, there were 9,558 Hungarians in Cleveland.

A distinct Hungarian area of settlement came into being during the mid-1880s. The first families settled around the southeast edge of the city, close to the factories where they worked: around Madison St. (now E. 79th) and Woodland Ave. from E. 65th onward. Streets with particularly heavy concentrations of Hungarian residents included Bismarck, Rawlings, and Holton. These were the outskirts of the city; the streets were still unpaved and dark. The area was attractive because housing was cheap on the farthest edge of town, closeness to the factory meant they could walk to work, and their inability to speak English (especially initially) made them seek their countrymen. Reportedly, older, more established immigrant groups treated these newcomers with disdain, ridiculing their dress and Old World ways. Until there were a substantial number of their countrymen in the city, the Hungarians were wary of speaking their native toungue in the streets for fear of reprisals. The Hungarians initially found work at the Eberhardt Mfg. Co., the Mechanical Rubber Works, Natl. Malleable Steel Castings, the Ohio Foundry, the Standard Foundry, the Van Dorn Iron Works, old Glidden Varnish, Cleveland Bronze, and Carlin Bronze. Hungarians in Cleveland earned a reputation as hard-working and tolerant, and according to some sources, employers sought them out when hiring. They took any job available, even if it was backbreaking or dangerous. As increasing numbers of Hungarians found accommodation and employment in Cleveland and wrote about their gains in the New World to their relatives and friends at home, more Hungarians decided to immigrate to America, and specifically to Cleveland, where there were already fellow countrymen waiting to receive them. This process of "chain migration" was especially evident on the west side of the city, where several hundred immigrants from the same village in Hungary settled. They were lured by the sucess of one of their fellow villagers, THEODOR KUNDTZ, who established his own cabinetmaking company in 1876. By 1900, Kundtz Mfg. employed some 2,500 skilled workers, most of whom were Hungarian immigrants. Kundtz became one of Cleveland's wealthiest industrialists. He built the "Hungaria Hall" on Clark Ave. in 1890 for the community. However, the number of Hungarians on the west side was not large enough to support such a massive community center, and it was later sold to a Czech Sokol (Sokol Nova Vlast).

The first organizations established by the community were self-help/sick-benefit societies, formed in response to a need for security at a time when social security, unemployment compensation, and disability assistance were nonexistent. Other sick-benefit organizations were founded for the added purpose of establishing a church. Through the efforts of the King St. Ladislaus Roman Catholic Men's & Women's Sick Benefit Society, Rev. CHAS. BOEHM was sent to Cleveland; upon his arrival, he established the first Hungarian Roman Catholic church in North America, St. Elizabeth of Hungary. Cleveland was the first location of several Hungarian church denominations in North America, namely, the FIRST HUNGARIAN REFORMED (1891), Roman Catholic (ST. ELIZABETH'S CHURCH, 1892), and Greek Catholic churches (St. John's Greek Catholic, 1892). In the 1890s, these 3 denominations built churches on lower Buckeye Rd. By the early 1920s, 11 Hungarian churches representing 6 denominations had been established: 7 on the east side and 4 on the west side. In addition, there were 3 Hungarian Jewish congregations on the east side. Large-scale projects, requiring the support of all Hungarians living in Cleveland, stimulated a sense of community awareness and pride. A statue of the Hungarian patriot Louis Kossuth was erected at UNIVERSITY CIRCLE in 1902, when only 10,000 Hungarians lived in Cleveland. The founding of the UNITED HUNGARIAN SOCIETIES in 1902 also promoted unity and a sense of common purpose. This organization was, at the time of its founding, unique among Hungarian-American organizations in the U.S. Major movements of general interest to all Hungarian-Americans originated in Cleveland. The American Hungarian Fed. was founded in the city in 1906 to represent Hungarians living in the U.S. and to safeguard their rights as American citizens. The movement to erect a statue of Geo. Washington in Budapest was initiated and carried to fruition by TIHAMER KOHANYI, editor of the Cleveland-based SZABADSAG.

The Buckeye Rd. Hungarian community was a transient neighborhood until 1920. Immigrants came and went—visiting their families in Hungary, helping out at harvest time, and then returning to work in the factories during the winter months. They were known as "migrating birds." In Cleveland they lived in boarding houses and were generally not very concerned with establishing permanent ties. This situation was altered dramatically, however, by the results of WORLD WAR I and the Treaty of Trianon, which imposed harsh economic and political conditions on Hungary. The plight of the homeland had a dramatic effect on

Hungarian immigrants living in the U.S. Suddenly the decision to return or remain was imminent. Moreover, the U.S. imposed the quota system in 1921, which curtailed immigration in any year to 3% of the number of the nationality in the U.S. in 1900; later this number was further reduced to 2%. More than half of the 1 million Hungarian immigrants living in the U.S. returned to Hungary during and after World War I. In the case of the Cleveland Hungarian community, World War I and the effects of the Treaty of Trianon were the two most significant factors that decided the fate of the ethnic enclave. After 1920, an increasing number of residents purchased their own homes and became U.S. citizens. The original Hungarian neighborhood around E. 79th and Holton Ave. expanded from Buckeye Rd. to Woodland Ave. and E. 72nd St., and east along Buckeye from Woodhill Rd. to E. 125th St. Hungarian businesses soon dominated the entire span of Buckeye: around E. 79th and Holton Ave., on lower Buckeye, and from E. 79th to Woodhill, and on upper Buckeye from East Blvd. to E. 130th St. Clubhouses were built, and churches, which until then were wooden structures, were rebuilt in stone. In determining the stages of the development of the Buckeye Rd. Hungarian community, 1920–30 is known as the period of expansion, while 1930–60 is designated as the period of stability.

Cleveland's Hungarian immigrant population rose from 9,558 to 43,134 by 1920. Hungarians constituted 8% of the city's foreign-born population in 1900, and 18% in 1920. The Buckeye Rd. neighborhood became a dynamic ethnic community, self-contained and yet a part of the makeup of Cleveland. The facilities of the 7 churches and 8 clubhouses were in constant use. The community's social calendar included the following regular events (on the average): 12 grape harvest festivals, 11 New Year's Eve dances, 14 picnics, 12 plays, 20 banquets, and over 100 Hungarian weddings. In addition, lectures, forums, meetings (both civic and political), bazaars, and card parties were weekly events held at clubhouses and halls. Six Hungarian-language newspapers served the community. The largest, *Szabadsag*, reached a daily circulation of 40,612 in 1940. By 1920, there were more than 300 Hungarian-owned businesses and 81 Hungarian organizations in Cleveland.

By the 1930s, many Cleveland Hungarians were becoming acculturated to the American way of life, but many retained their native tongue and customs. At this time a substantial number of 2d-generation Hungarian-American youths were becoming active in the community, forming their own social and civic groups. During the Depression, a number of social and political organizations assisted the community through the hard economic times. These included charity committees, such as that established by the Women's Hungarian Social Club, homeowners' associations (to try to prevent evictions), and several labor organizations, among which was a Hungarian-language section of the IWW. The Hungarian community evolved into a political voting bloc during the 1930s, and from then on played a significant role in local and regional government. The community was overwhelmingly Democratic, as a result of the Depression and the politics of Pres. Roosevelt. Ward 29 was represented by Hungarian councilmen for nearly 45 years, starting in 1921 when Louis Petrash was elected. In Ward 16, Hungarian representation spanned 30 years, 1939–71. Approximately 26 Hungarian-Americans from the Buckeye community were elected or appointed to various offices on the city, county, and state levels of government. From 1931–74, there were usually 2 and oftentimes 3 Hungarian judges out of the 9 serving on the bench of the Municipal Court of Cleveland. Among these were Julius M. Kovachy, Louis Petrash, Joseph Stearns, and

Blanche Krupansky. Undoubtedly the most influential Hungarian-American politician in the history of Cleveland city government was JACK P. RUSSELL, who became president of city council in 1957 and held this position for 11 years.

WORLD WAR II disrupted the Hungarian community of Cleveland in a dramatic way: many Hungarian-American youths served and died overseas. Of those who returned, most did not return to the neighborhoods where they grew up, but moved to suburbs to start families. Thus, the disintegration of Buckeye as a Hungarian-American neighborhood began. Within 6 months following Pearl Harbor, 1,300 Hungarian men from Cleveland enlisted. In the predominantly Hungarian 29th ward, 4,305 men (13% of the population) served in the armed forces. Following the war, the community worked with and absorbed a new wave of Hungarian immigrants: the displaced persons. Despite more than 30 years of separation and relative isolation from the homeland, the community still gave support for the needs of Hungarians in displaced persons' camps in Europe. The Cleveland community was active in obtaining "Home and Job Assurances" needed by postwar immigrants to enter the U.S., and in searching for housing and employment once they actually arrived in this city. Between 1947–53, approximately 6,000 Hungarian immigrants arrived in Cleveland. Generally, they were from urban centers in Hungary and from the middle and upper-middle classes. Most were well-educated, emigrated with their families, and were established in their careers when they left. Most were handicapped by the fact that they were middle-aged: losing everything and having to start anew at this stage in their lives proved extremely difficult for many. The postwar immigrants left Hungary because of changes in the political system—not for economic reasons. They intended to return to Hungary when the Soviet occupation of the county ended, and were determined to work toward that goal while in America. As such they were emigres rather than immigrants. They were the most politically conscious among Cleveland's Hungarians, even when compared to the later Hungarian refugees of 1956. The organizations they founded aimed to maintain the traditions of the homeland, especially those undermined by the postwar government. They placed emphasis on educating the second generation in their language and heritage through Saturday language schools and the Hungarian Scouting movement. There were many writers and journalists among them: several new newspapers were founded in Cleveland during the 1950s and 1960s. This group published more books than any other wave of Hungarian immigrants.

The revolution in Hungary in Oct. 1956 brought another wave of immigrants to the U.S., approximately 41,000 refugees. The revolution was unexpected; the community only recently absorbed the postwar immmigrants. Hungarians in Cleveland reacted quickly. Within the first days of the crisis, mass rallies, attracting at times 5,000 people, were held, and organizations initiated relief programs. These refugees were the youngest wave of Hungarian immigrants and the group least prepared with future plans and goals. Unlike previous immigrants, these refugees had to leave Hungary suddenly and unexpectedly with the failure of the revolution. Many possessed a technical trade or had several years of university study. They evoked great public sympathy in the U.S. because of their fight against Communism, and numerous opportunities, such as scholarship programs, job placement, and financial assistance, were made available to them. It is difficult to determine the exact number of refugees who settled in Cleveland after 1956, because census data statistics between 1950–60 include many of the postwar immigrants as well. The number of refugees who settled in the Cleveland area has been estimated at 6,000–9,000. Moreover, it is impossible to ascertain how many stayed in the Cleveland area once they familiarized themselves with the English language and life in the U.S. Because of their relative youth and technical skills, and because many were single, they adjusted with greater ease than previous waves. As a direct result, the newcomers exhibited less attachment to community organizations and institutions.

For over 100 years, a distinct and unique Hungarian community has existed in Cleveland, one constantly rejuvenated by new waves of immigrants, new goals and ideas. However, the Buckeye Rd. neighborhood began to decline in the 1960s: the settlers who had established the community died, and the neighborhood failed to attract younger-generation Hungarian-Americans. The expectation that the postwar immigrants or 1956 refugees would rejuvenate the area never materialized. Buckeye experienced an alarming increase in crime during the late 1960s and 1970s. While many businesses and residents joined the "white flight" out of the neighborhood, hundreds of older residents refused to leave, and in the late 1970s, programs were instituted on the grassroots level as well as through government assistance to rejuvenate and stabilize the community. By 1980, the majority of Hungarians in Cleveland no longer lived together in the Buckeye Rd. neighborhood. However, the local Hungarian community was still viable. By the 1980s, there were 113,000 Greater Clevelanders of Hungarian birth or descent. Old organizations were replaced by a number of new ones founded by 2d- or 3d-generation Hungarian-Americans. These consisted mainly of folk-dance groups, cultural organizations, and civic clubs that attempted to preserve cultural traditions and to foster an awareness of ethnic background among the American-born children of the Hungarian immigrants.

Susan M. Papp
Canadian Broadcasting Corp.

---

Papp, Susan, *Hungarian Americans and Their Communities of Cleveland* (1981).

The **HUNKIN-CONKEY CONSTRUCTION COMPANY,** noted contractor for numerous public works throughout the U.S., was started in 1900 by Samuel and Wm. Hunkin as the Hunkin Bros. partnership and was incorporated in 1903. The Hunkins, who had been engaged in the building trades in Cleveland since 1870, traced their background in construction to 1558, when Elizabeth I granted one of their family a coat of arms for excellent masonry work on a church in Cornwall. A nephew, Guy E. Conkey, was put in charge of Cleveland operations after Sam Hunkin was killed in 1903 (1902?) and Wm. Hunkin left the city to oversee the rebuilding of San Francisco following the earthquake of 1905. In 1907, the firm name was changed to the Hunkin-Conkey Constr. Co. The Hunkins bought out the Conkeys in 1948.

In 1970, Hunkin-Conkey was the nation's 11th-largest construction firm, averaging $40 million in contracts annually and employing 2,000 people (500 in Greater Cleveland). The firm had an excellent reputation for competence, speed, and a creative approach to engineering. One excellent local example of its skill is the DETROIT-SUPERIOR BRIDGE (1918), at the time the longest double-deck bridge ever built. Its lower deck had room for 6 streetcars, while the upper deck had 45' of width for vehicles and 20' for pedestrian traffic. The new structure was arched to provide 92' clearance from the water to the underside of the center span. This feature provided a major construction challenge, which Hunkin-Conkey met successfully. Management at Hunkin-Conkey was kept within the family and was of the "hands-on" variety. Before agreeing to go into business with William, Sam, a stonemason, trained his brother in all aspects of construction and supervision, and later family members who joined the company likewise started at the bottom. Sam Hunkin, Jr., started his rise to the presidency and chairmanship as a water boy—and almost quit the first day when an angry bricklayer spat into 2 pails of water he had carried up a ladder to the top floor of a construction site—while future president Wm. Hunkin, Jr., held carpenters' and laborers' union cards and an ironworker's permit.

In the early days, capital finance in the heavy construction field was a gamble that cofounder Wm. Hunkin took more literally than most. When the firm was completing the Cleveland breakwater, Hunkin nearly lost a hand. He threatened to sue the surgeon who reattached it if he could not hold a good poker hand again. Later, when the firm needed capital for a big job, he went to a club where oil millionaires played poker and joined in, winning the game and his construction financing. The company prided itself on its expertise and specialized in the construction of BRIDGES, breakwaters, docks, dams, roads, factories, and hospitals. Its achievements span 7 decades and include many facilities that define the northeast Ohio area: the CLEVELAND MUNICIPAL STADIUM, the old post office, the Cleveland and Ravenna plants of the CLEVELAND WORSTED MILLS, the Ravenna Arsenal, the Corrigan-McKinney continuous strip mill of the old Republic Steel plant, the NASA LEWIS RESEARCH CTR., the East Ohio Twinsburg Pumping Station, the Twinsburg Stamping Plant, South and Shaw high schools, LAKEWOOD HOSPITAL, and the rubber plants of Akron. Among the company's national projects were the Arlington Memorial Bridge, the Pennsylvania Turnpike, and the Minnesota taconite plant of the Reserve Mining Co.

The company, which had its offices in the Hunkin Bldg. at 1919 E. 13th St., was a casualty of the recession of the 1970s; rising labor costs; the maze of red tape involved in contracting for public works; and, most of all, a decade of litigation over its last major projects. In the 1960s, Hunkin-Conkey became embroiled in several major legal battles with the city of Cleveland over excavation problems at the Convention Ctr.; with the Bratenahl Development Corp. over cost overruns; and with the unions over jurisdictional work stoppages. Though the company won the suits, the judgments awarded did not offset the expensive special equipment it needed (especially the pumping equipment needed to drain the Mall), the tie-up of personnel, equipment, and working capital, and the lost time. Before the suit with the city was settled, Hunkin-Conkey won a $6.1 million contract to expand the Easterly Sewage Plant, but this project too resulted in litigation after raw sewage poured into Lake Erie during construction. Although Hunkin-Conkey and the other principles in construction were exonerated when employee error was proved to be the cause of the rampant sewage, the suit was one more expensive aggravation. In an industry where the average life span is 10 years or less, the Hunkin-Conkey Constr. Co. closed in 1972 after more than 70 years.

**HUNTER, JANE EDNA HARRIS** (13 Dec. 1882–17 Jan. 1971), prominent black social worker, was the founder of the PHILLIS WHEATLEY ASSOC. The daughter of a sharecropper, she was born Jane Edna Harris at Woodburn Farm near Pendleton, S.C. She acquired her last name by a brief marriage. Hunter graduated in 1905 as a trained nurse from Hampton Institute, Va., and came to Cleveland, serving in various nursing jobs. Through her experiences in Cleveland, she became aware of the lack of institutions to serve the needs of unmarried, poor, homeless Negro

women and girls. She organized the Working Girls Assoc. in 1911 in order to find safe living quarters for such women. Later that year, a 2-story building at 2265 E. 40th St. was purchased, and the association's name was changed to the Phillis Wheatley Assoc. in honor of Phillis Wheatley, a Boston slave in the late 18th century generally considered to have been the first Negro poet in America. The programs of the association emphasized the teaching of service skills and provision of adequate housing, and served as a model for the organization of 9 similar institutions throughout the U.S. Hunter served as the association's executive secretary until 1948 and saw, with the support of prominent white Clevelanders, the agency grow into a 9-story structure at E. 46th St. and Cedar. Following retirement, she founded the Phillis Wheatley Foundation, a scholarship fund for Negro high school graduates, and later the foundation established the Jane Edna Hunter Scholarship Fund in her honor. Hunter earned a law degree from Marshall Law School and held honorary degrees from Fisk University, Allen University in Columbia, S.C., and Central State University in Wilberforce, Ohio. She founded the Women's Civic League of Cleveland in 1943, was a member of the NAACP, and served as vice-president and executive committee member of the Natl. Assoc. of Colored Women.

Hunter, Jane Edna Harris, *A Nickel and a Prayer* (1940).
Jane Hunter Papers, WRHS.

**HUNTING VALLEY** is an 11-sq.-mi. residential village of private estates, large farm acreage, and large suburban homes, located approximately 15 mi. southeast of downtown Cleveland. It lies on the CHAGRIN RIVER, bordered on the north by GATES MILLS, on the south by MORELAND HILLS, on the east by Geauga County, and on the west by the villages of WOODMERE and PEPPER PIKE. It was originally part of Orange Twp., which was settled in 1815 and established in 1820. Some of the first families laid out their farms and built their homes in the 1820s in the area where the Chagrin River and Fairmount Blvd. now intersect. During the 19th century, ORANGE was a thriving farming and dairy community. At the beginning of this century, some of Cleveland's industrialists began to purchase property in the area, including JEPTHA H. WADE II, who bought 455 acres on Fairmount Rd., calling it Valley Ridge Farm. In 1913 ANDREW SQUIRE bought 277 acres and developed them as a working farm and a horticultural and landscape gardening center. Students from Western Reserve University were invited to study the arboretum and the 95-acre pharmaceutical garden. In 1934 the Squire estate, known as Squire Valley View Farm, was bequeathed to WRU for continued educational and recreational purposes. Hunting Valley withdrew from Orange Twp. in 1924 and became incorporated as a village. Corliss E. Sullivan served as the first mayor, 1924–38. In 1940 the population was approximately 336.

In the 1920s, the VAN SWERINGEN brothers bought a large tract east of SOM Ctr. Rd. for their country home. The estate was named DAISY HILL after Louise "Daisy" (Mrs. Benjamin L.) Jenks, a friend and neighbor who often served as a hostess when the brothers entertained. After the deaths of the Van Sweringens and the subsequent liquidation of their holdings, the property was divided into more than 60 private estates. Although the character of the area has changed somewhat, it remains a close-knit, cohesive community. Many residents are descendants of families that originally lived on EUCLID AVE., later moving to WADE PARK, then to BRATENAHL, and finally to Hunting Valley. A greenhouse, located on the original Daisy Hill property, is the only commercial enterprise in the village. In 1970, UNIVERSITY SCHOOL for Boys established a 175-acre campus in Hunting Valley. The village is governed by an elected mayor and councilmen and is part of the Orange Local School District. Despite some new building in the postwar period, the population has remained quite stable. In 1950 it was 477, rising to 600 in 1960 and to 786 in 1980. In addition to their business enterprises, many of the residents participate in a variety of social and cultural projects and many volunteer activities, as well as sports, including foxhunting, polo, and riding on the trails that interlace the valley.

**HUNTINGTON, JOHN** (8 Mar. 1832–10 Jan. 1893), was an industrialist, inventor, philanthropist, and benefactor, one of the founders of the CLEVELAND MUSEUM OF ART, and the founder of the JOHN HUNTINGTON POLYTECHNIC INSTITUTE. He was born in Preston, Lancashire, England, the son of Hugh Huntington, professor of mathematics at Onuskirk (Ormskirk) in Lancashire and one of the founders of Trinity School (Episcopal) at Preston. Huntington was educated in England and at the age of 22 emigrated to America, coming directly to Cleveland on 10 Aug. 1854. First employed by Allen H. Hawley, a slate roofer, Huntington started his own slate roofing and contracting business in 1857. His work included the Mayflower St. School building and the roof of the UNION DEPOT. In Dec. 1863 he joined Clark, Payne & Co., an oil-refining business, and while there he patented many of his inventions for improving furnaces and methods of refining oil, as well as for the machinery used in manufacturing oil barrels. His inventions contributed to the rapid growth of the company, and it became one of the leading refineries of Cuyahoga County. In 1870 it consolidated with others, forming the Standard Oil Co. Huntington became part-owner of a large fleet of lake vessels in 1886 and subsequently became vice-president of the Cleveland Stone Co.

Elected to city council in 1862, Huntington initiated and helped to expedite many improvements for the city of Cleveland during his 13 years of service, including a paid fire department; the development of a municipal sewer system; the deepening of the river channel; the building of bridges; the reorganization of the waterworks department; the establishment of Lake View Park; and the construction of the SUPERIOR VIADUCT. On 8 Mar. 1889 (his 57th birthday), Huntington established the John Huntington Benevolent Trust for the benefit of charitable institutions of the city of Cleveland. His original gift of $200,000 in invested securities was placed in the hands of the following trustees, whom he selected: Edwin R. Perkins, John V. Painter, Samuel E. Williamson, CHAS. W. BINGHAM, John H. Lowman, Henry C. Ranney, and Jas. D. Cleveland. Through the years, over 40 charitable institutions benefited yearly through the trust.

Huntington married Mary Jane Beck in Dec. 1852 in Preston, England. The couple had 4 children who survived: Mrs. Francis P. Smith, Mrs. A. C. Hord, Mrs. Edward A. Merritt, and Wm. R. Huntington. Mary Huntington died in 1882, and later Huntington married Mariette L. Goodwin. Huntington died in London, England, while on a visit to reexamine the London Polytechnic schools—Regent St. and Battersea—prototypes of the kind of school that he envisioned for Cleveland and for which he left a substantial fortune. The John Huntington Polytechnic Institute was ultimately opened in 1918, and served the city until 1953, when it was discontinued. Huntington's gifts also helped to make possible the construction and maintenance of the Cleveland Museum of Art (1916). In 1926 the Cleveland Metropolitan Park System acquired property that had formerly been his summer home on the lakefront in BAY VILLAGE; it was named Huntington Park in his honor.

**HUNTINGTON, SAMUEL, JR.** (4 Oct. 1765–7 June 1817), was a prominent politician in early Cleveland. He led the conservative Jeffersonian movement in Ohio and served as the state's third governor. Huntington was born in Norwich, Conn., the son of Rev. Joseph Huntington. He was informally adopted by his uncle, Samuel Huntington, who subsequently became president of the Continental Congress and governor of Connecticut. Raised amid power and affluence, young Samuel studied at Dartmouth and Yale, graduating from Yale in 1785. After a grand tour of Europe, he became a Connecticut lawyer, politician, and land speculator. When his stepfather died, Huntington decided that his political opportunities in Connecticut were limited, especially since he had joined the minority Jeffersonian Republican party. In 1801, he moved to Ohio's WESTERN RESERVE, representing the land claims of his friends. He quickly prospered as a Cleveland land agent and hotel keeper. Huntington won instant political power in his new home, largely because he was already well known. Territorial governor Arthur St. Clair courted his support, but at Ohio's constitutional convention, Huntington formed a firm partnership with the Chillicothe Republican faction. He expected to be given a U.S. Senate seat, but his allies instead shunted him to the chief justiceship of the Ohio Supreme Court. Huntington felt frustrated in this post, and for several years he tried to win appointments in new territories.

In 1807–08, Chief Justice Huntington became involved in a power struggle between the legislature and the judiciary. Both Ohio's Federalists and conservative Republicans backed the judiciary, and in 1808 these groups supported Huntington's candidacy for governor. He won a 45% plurality in a 3-man race. Gov. Huntington did not have a successful term. He tried to become neutral in the legislative-judiciary struggle, and won only opprobrium. His appointment of a friend, ascerbic Stanley Griswold, to a vacant U.S. Senate seat was also condemned by all factions. In 1810, Gov. Huntington decided to seek a Senate seat himself. He won many votes in the legislative balloting but finished second to Thos. Worthington. In later years, Huntington served in the assembly, leading the anti-Chillicothe Republican faction, and he became an Army district paymaster in the WAR OF 1812. Seriously ill for years and injured in an accident, he died in June 1817. He was survived by his widow, cousin Hannah Huntington, and 6 of their children.

Samuel Huntington Papers, WRHS.

---

The **HUNTINGTON BUILDING**, when it was built in the early 1920s, was the 2d-largest office building in the world. It was then known as the Union Trust Bldg. and later became the Union Commerce Bldg. The Huntington Bldg. was erected between 1923–24 at a cost of $17 million. It was designed by the Chicago firm of Graham, Anderson, Probst & White. The Union Trust Co. owned the building until 1933, when the bank became insolvent. The State Banking Dept. took over the bank's affairs until 1939, when Union Properties, Inc., was organized to liquidate the assets of Union Trust. In 1949, the Union Bank of Commerce acquired the building at public auction through its subsidiary, the Union Commerce Bldg. Co., for $14.3 million. The building was again sold in 1961 to the First Union Real Estate Investments Trust for $25.5 million.

The 21-story building has frontage on Euclid Ave., E. 9th St., and Chester; it contains over 30 acres of floor space. Its structure was meant to evince the business character and financial ambitions of the 1920s. Its tenants during the 1920s represented railroads, iron and steel industries, shipping companies, the legal profession, and the insurance and securities business. From a low occupancy of 64% in 1934, the building maintained a nearly 100% occupancy after 1950. Its only major addition since 1924 was 7 stories added in 1961 to a part of the building that had been topped off at the 14th floor. The building's chief architectural feature is the *L*-shaped 3-story banking room, the largest in the country in 1924. The basilican halls with 38-ft.-high Corinthian columns and barrel-vaulted ceilings were intended to express grandeur and permanence. Also notable are the 4 large murals by Jules Guerin that fill the pediments at the ends of each hall. In 1973, the banking room underwent a $6 million restoration; Huntington Bank, which currently (1986) occupies the room, has completed further restoration since 1983. In 1983, the building was sold to a multipartnership that included Clevelander Carl D. Glickman and an affiliate of Leperq, de Neuflize & Co., Inc., New York investment bankers. The name was changed at that time, when Huntington Bancshares, Inc., of Columbus took over the Union Commerce Corp.

**HUNTINGTON FUND FOR EDUCATION.** *See* JOHN HUNTINGTON FUND FOR EDUCATION

The **HUNTINGTON NATIONAL BANK OF NORTHEAST OHIO** is one of Cleveland's major banks and a principal subsidiary of the Columbus-based Huntington Bancshares, Inc., Ohio's 5th-largest bank holding company. The development of Huntington in Cleveland was filled with mergers. The bank started in a period of consolidations, when 29 area financial institutions merged to form the Union Trust Co., which opened in the Citizens Bldg. at Euclid Ave. and E. 9th St. on 31 Dec. 1920 with $322.5 million in resources. Among the principal Cleveland banks included in the merger were the oldest unit in the consolidation, the Bank of Commerce Natl. Assoc. (founded 1853); the pioneer First Natl. Bank of Cleveland (1863), which merged with the Euclid-Park Natl. Bank (1886) in 1905 to form the largest national institution in Cleveland; the oldest and largest trust company in Ohio, the Citizens Savings & Trust Co. (1868); one of the nation's earliest neighborhood banks, the Broadway Savings & Trust Co. (1883 or 1884); and the Union Commerce Natl. Bank (1884). The new firm was the nation's 5th-largest trust company, primarily serving the business community.

In May 1924, Union Trust completed its new home, a $16 million 20-story building at E. 9th St. and Euclid Ave. At the time, it was the 2d-largest office building in the world, and it still contains the largest banking room in the country. The company continued to grow and had 21 branches by the early 1930s. However, the Depression forced the closure and liquidation of Union Trust with 70,000 depositors in Mar. 1933. Kenyon V. Painter, director of the Cleveland Union Trust Co., was convicted in May 1935 on charges of misapplying $2 million of Union Trust funds. Painter served 39 days in prison later the same year for perjury. Although he appealed his embezzlement conviction all the way to the U.S. Supreme Court, his plea was denied, and in June 1937 he entered the Ohio penitentiary to begin serving a 1-to–30-year sentence. He was given a full pardon by Gov. Martin L. Davey in October of that same year. On 16 May 1938, an entirely new financial firm, the Union Bank of Commerce, opened in the former home of Union Trust with $8 million in capital. Through its "Cleveland Plan," the bank was able to help Cleveland's businesses revive. Thus, Union Bank quickly became one

of the city's major financial institutions, with $109 million in deposits by 1946.

In the postwar period, the firm became more than just a "businessman's bank" as it broadened its services and pioneered in bringing new banking products to all segments of the community. In response to suburban development, it began branch banking in 1955. Three years later, it changed its name to the simpler Union Commerce Bank. The bank continued to support local businesses, especially in financing oil and natural-gas production in Ohio. Throughout the late 1960s and 1970s, Union Commerce was periodically in financial trouble because of poor management and bad real-estate loans. It was also weakened by numerous takeover attempts and many government inquiries and investigations. The bank's turmoil finally led to its purchase by Huntington Bancshares, Inc., in 1983. On 5 Dec. 1983, a national charter for the holding company's 43 Cleveland branch banks with over $1 billion in assets was granted under the name of the Huntington Natl. Bank of Northeast Ohio.

**HUNTINGTON POLYTECHNIC INSTITUTE.** *See* **JOHN HUNTINGTON POLYTECHNIC INSTITUTE**

The **HUPP CORPORATION** began as a car maker and then was revitalized as an appliance and heating-system manufacturer before becoming part of the WHITE CONSOLIDATED INDUSTRIES empire in the late 1960s. The company began as the Hupmobile Corp. in Detroit in 1908 to make the Hupmobile auto, but its Cleveland history started in 1928, when the company decided to make a low-priced version of the car in the factories once occupied by the defunct Chandler Cleveland Motors Co. From 2 factories at 131st St. and St. Clair and Euclid Ave. at London Rd., Hupp turned out 6,000 auto bodies and a variety of other parts per month, and assembled the cars. When the Depression hit, assembly and production of all parts but the bodies were moved back to Detroit, and the demand for bodies dwindled to a fraction of the early demand. By the late 1930s, the Hupmobile Corp. had not yet recovered from the Depression, and production of the auto was discontinued in 1940. Hupmobile, called the Hupp Corp. after 1946, maintained a contract machine shop in the Detroit area and moved its headquarters to Cleveland, where it produced freezers, air-conditioning units, and soft-drink dispensers at the former location of the Globe Stamp Works at 1250 E. 76th St., which it acquired in 1944.

After 1955, when the company was bought and managed by John O. Ekblom, Hupp began a program of selected diversification. Within a year, it had added 7 companies (including the Perfection Heating Co. of 7605 Platt and 1135 Ivanhoe) and increased its workforce from 400 to 4,000. By 1960, as a result of internal development and further acquisition of companies such as the Gibson Refrigerator Co., Hupp's business was 45% air-conditioning and heating systems, 35% appliances, and 20% aviation and auto parts and hydraulics. The company was considered a giant in the heat pump and industrial infrared heating and baking field. In 1967, the Hupp Corp. became part of the Cleveland-based White Consolidated Industries, a corporation with a similar philosophy of growth and development. Hupp's Hercules Engine Works became a part of another White, the late WHITE MOTOR CO. In 1985, Hupp maintained its offices on Ivanhoe, as well as in White Consolidated's headquarters at 11770 Berea Rd.

**HURON ROAD HOSPITAL,** 13951 Terrace Rd., traces its history back to May 1856, when Dr. Seth R. Beckwith opened the 20-bed CLEVELAND HOMEOPATHIC

HOSPITAL on Lake St. (Lakeside Ave.) at Clinton Rd., the first privately owned hospital in Cleveland. Beckwith, the surgeon for several area railroads, opened the facility to care for sick and injured railroad men. It soon became affiliated with the Homeopathic Hospital College of Cleveland, formed in 1850 as the Western College of Homeopathy; the medical school's faculty practiced and taught at the hospital. The Cleveland Homeopathic Hospital closed ca. 1860, when ST. VINCENT CHARITY HOSPITAL opened for both charity and paying patients. After several years, however, problems arose between the homeopathic and the allopathic doctors at St. Vincent, and the homeopaths withdrew. They joined the Willson St. Hospital, 83 Willson (E.55th) St., when it opened in 1866 with a board of trustees composed of both homeopaths and allopaths, but in 1867 difficulties again prompted the homeopaths to withdraw. In 1869, they bought the Humiston Institute building on the west side for $35,000 and formed the Cleveland Protestant Homeopathic Hospital; the 50-bed facility also served as a medical school, the Cleveland Homeopathic Hospital College. In 1873, the board of trustees bought the former Perry estate on Huron Rd., and on 6 Aug. 1874 the Huron Rd. Hospital was incorporated. In 1878, a joint fundraising exhibition of donated art objects and antiques raised $12,816 for Huron Rd. and City hospitals. Huron Rd. applied its half of the profits toward construction of a new facility, opened at 750 Huron Rd. on 29 Sept. 1880. In the new facility, the hospital embarked upon a period of growth and controversy. The Cleveland Training School for Nurses was established in 1884, the first nursing school formed west of the Alleghenies. In 1890, factionalism within the medical college prompted half the faculty to resign and form the Cleveland Medical College to rival the established school, which became the Cleveland University of Medicine; the two were reunited in 1897 as the Cleveland Homeopathic College, which was closed in 1922. During this period, the college formed the first homeopathic school of dentistry in the country, and staff members such as Dr. Hamilton F. Biggar cultivated ties with wealthy Clevelanders such as JOHN D. ROCKEFELLER that helped the institution prosper and expand.

Internal controversies continued, however; nurses went on strike in 1908, and in 1909 the hospital's homeopathic doctors successfully sued the trustees to prevent the admission of allopathic doctors to practice in the facility. Trustees then closed the hospital for repairs and kept it closed until negotiations resulted in a dual homeopathic and allopathic staff, which lasted until 1924, when the homeopaths again sued the trustees over the admission of allopathic doctors; the homeopaths again won in court, many board members resigned, and the homeopaths gained control of the hospital. By 1925, the hospital had outgrown its Huron Rd. facility; it sold the building to Ohio Bell and moved to temporary quarters at E. 89th and Euclid until fundraising efforts produced sufficient funds to build on land purchased from John D. Rockefeller. The Depression slowed fundraising, however; construction began in 1931 but was halted from 1932–34 for lack of funds. The 204-bed hospital was completed and opened in 1935. In a new facility with room for expansion, the hospital expanded and improved its staff and services: its Dept. of Anesthesia (est. 1935) was the first in the city to be staffed entirely by trained physicians; it opened the city's first hospital blood bank in 1942; and it established a course for x-ray technicians, a well-baby clinic, a sterility clinic, and a neuropsychiatric clinic in the 1940s and a cardiovascular laboratory in 1954. A $3.5 million, 100-bed expansion was completed in 1956, followed by a $4.25 million modernization program in 1968. A program to coordinate hospital

services in the county designated Huron Rd. Hospital a Metropolitan Ctr. Hospital; as such, it serves as a referral center for smaller hospitals and offers out-patient and ambulatory services as well as a wider range of specialties. It also has made various changes in services to match the changing medical needs of the community. By the celebration of its centennial in 1974, the 410-bed facility averaged 12,000 admissions and 23,000 emergency cases annually; it employed 1,200 people in 22 departments and had a medical staff of 200 physicians. In an effort to cut costs and improve services, Huron Rd. Hospital signed a merger agreement on 30 Oct. 1984 with HILLCREST HOSPITAL and EUCLID GENERAL HOSPITAL to form STRATEGIC HEALTH SYSTEMS to coordinate services and budgets; a year later, SUBURBAN COMMUNITY HOSPITAL announced plans to join the group.

Murphy, Nan, *A History of Huron Road Hospital* (1974).

**HUTCHINSON AND COMPANY,** though not founded until 1901, represented family Great Lakes shipping interests that dated back to ca. 1861, when John T. Hutchinson took partial ownership in a scow (schooner) as payment of a butcher bill. As he acquired income and secured loans, he purchased more vessels. In 1872–73 he had a schooner built and named it for his wife, Emma Camp Hutchinson. His son, Chas. L. Hutchinson, began his career on this sailing vessel as a cabin boy at the age of 16. He rose rapidly through the ranks and became its captain at age 20. Capt. Hutchinson sailed several more years, then came ashore to pursue the management of the scows. It was at this time that he and his partner, Walton McGean, started Hutchinson & Co. to operate the Pioneer and other Great Lakes fleets. The first steamship built by the company was named the *John T. Hutchinson* in honor of his father. During the early 1900s, the Pioneer Steamship Co. with Hutchinson as its president became a large and active business, carrying cargos of iron ore, coal, stone, and grain. It was at this time that he established the Rud Machine Co., a wholly owned subsidiary of Pioneer, for the purpose of making ship repairs. Hutchinson & Co. also operated vessels for the Inland Steel Co. and Internatl. Harvester from 1912 until the dissolution of the company. After a modest start with 3 wooden steamships and 2 wooden scows, the company grew to 38 ships and became the largest independent fleet on the Great Lakes by the 1920s, though by 1938 the fleet had shrunk to 22 ships.

In 1923, Hutchinson's son, John T. Hutchinson, established the Buckeye Steamship Co., and with its smaller vessels he was able to accept cargos and enter ports that the Pioneer boats were unable to service. This fleet carried the usual cargos of iron ore, coal, stone, and grain, as well as pulpwood, salt, sulfur, and an occasional deckload of autos. It grew steadily during the Depression years (1929–34) because of its wide variety of powered boats and barges and the aggressive business methods of its president, John T. Hutchinson. He served 4 terms as president of the LAKE CARRIERS ASSOC. Following the death in 1944 of Capt. Chas. L. Hutchinson, John T. Hutchinson became the senior partner of Hutchinson & Co. Gene C. Hutchinson and Dale L. Coy advanced to partnership and were also made directors of the Lake Carriers Assoc. Following the death of John T. Hutchinson, his younger brother Gene became president of Hutchinson & Co. and the Pioneer Steamship Co., with Chas. L. Hutchinson II (grandson of Capt. Chas. L. Hutchinson) named vice-president. With the exhaustion of high-grade iron ore in the Mesabi range, the opening of the St. Lawrence Seaway to ocean-going traffic, and increased costs of operation (mainly labor), the Great Lakes fleets suffered greatly diminished business opportunities. Gene C. Hutchinson, president of Hutchinson & Co. and Pioneer, presented a liquidation proposal to shareholders. It was accepted, and the firm ceased operation in late 1962.

**HYDE, GUSTAVUS A.** (15 Jan. 1826–26 Nov. 1912), was Cleveland's first official weatherman. Hyde was born in Framingham, Mass. He attended the Framingham Academy and then served an apprenticeship at the Boston Water Works in civil engineering and surveying. He became interested in meteorology at the age of 17 through the influence of Dr. Jas. P. Espy, who pioneered the scientific study of weather in America. Hyde, in 1843, became one of the original 120 volunteers who responded to Espy's call for a national network of weather observers. Hyde came to Cleveland in 1850, serving for 3 years. Between 1859–1907 he was engineer of the Cleveland Gas Light & Coke Co. Although he received no formal training as a scientist, Hyde enjoyed a modest scientific reputation in Cleveland. He was often called upon by the newspapers to explain local weather phenomena and other natural occurrences. In 1867 he was elected curator of the CLEVELAND ACADEMY OF NATURAL SCIENCES. As a volunteer weather observer, he also contributed weather information to several of the local papers. Hyde took daily weather observations in Cleveland continuously between 1855–1906. He recorded observations every day at 7 a.m., 2 p.m., and 9 p.m., noting the appearance of the sky, the wind direction, the beginning and ending of rain or snow, and the temperature. Each month a report was forwarded to Espy at the Smithsonian Institution. From data received throughout the U.S., Espy developed a synoptic chart, which he used to plot weather on a map. Hyde was the only official weather observer in Cleveland until 1870, when the signal corps established a weather station here. He conducted no scientific research himself, adopting Espy's theory of storms. Over the years he gave many lectures on storm movement to various professional and civic organizations in Cleveland. In 1896, Hyde wrote *The Weather in Cleveland Ohio, What It Has Been for 40 Years.* Published and distributed throughout Ohio, it was primarily factual rather than theoretical. Hyde sent his last report to the U.S. Weather Bureau in 1906. Of the 120 original observers, he kept the longest uninterrupted record. Hyde married Elizabeth R. Williams in 1852; they had 5 children.

**HYDROTHERAPY** was introduced in Cleveland in the 1890s as a treatment for typhoid fever. It was later applied in the treatment of various neuropsychiatric disorders. Developed in Germany, hydrotherapy was first used in the U.S. in the late 1880s. The method involved the immersion of the patient in a full tub of cold water for an extended period of time. Repeated treatment was thought to reduce the mortality rate among patients with typhoid fever. The first doctor to advocate hydrotherapy in this country was Dr. Simon Baruch of New York. Dr. Christian Sihler, a friend of Baruch's, was the first Cleveland doctor to advocate its use. Sihler was a neurologist and chief of staff at Lutheran Hospital, and later founded Windsor Hospital. During the 1890s, the use of hydrotherapy caused somewhat of a schism among Cleveland's medical profession. Opponents disapproved of its unpleasant aspects and questioned its effectiveness, while proponents used statistics to prove that it helped reduce the mortality rate in typhoid cases. It eventually became a fairly routine treatment in Cleveland-area hospitals. Hydrotherapy was later used to treat various nervous and psychiatric disorders, as many physicians believed that separation of nerve endings was a factor in disturbed emotional states. It was used for this purpose in some Cleveland area hospitals until mid-century.

The **IMMACULATE HEART OF MARY PARISH,** located at 6700 Lansing Ave. in Cleveland, was established on 3 May 1894 by Rev. ANTON F. KOLASZEWSKI, the former pastor of ST. STANISLAUS. Immaculate Heart began as a schismatic parish that served an ever-increasing number of Polish immigrants in the Warszawa district of Cleveland. Fr. Kolaszewski continued as pastor until 1908, when both he and his parishioners were formally reconciled with the church. A Franciscan priest, Fr. Methodius Kielar, OFM, was named administrator of the church. From 1909–12, Fr. Albert Migdalski, Fr. John Darowski, and Fr. Bronislaus Walter served successive terms as pastor. Fr. Marion J. Orzechowski was named pastor on 12 Feb. 1912. He proved a gifted administrator and an excellent pastor. He supervised the construction of a new church building in 1914. The people built the Romanesque structure themselves and donated the materials to save the cost. Immaculate Heart's first church building had also been used as a parochial school. Lay teachers staffed it until 1911, when the Sisters of St. Joseph of the Third Order of St. Francis took charge. In 1915, a temporary school building was erected. By 1925, a new school of 16 rooms was dedicated. Enrollment peaked at 1,350 children in 1932 but has since declined. Fr. Orzechowski remained at the parish until 1932, when he was named pastor of St. John Cantius. His successor, Fr. John Mlotkowski, continued his able work until his death in 1960. Mlotkowski's successor, Fr. Aloysius Dombrowski, remodeled the sanctuary so it would be in accord with the reforms of Vatican II.

Papers of Immaculate Heart, Archives, Diocese of Cleveland.

**IMMANUEL PRESBYTERIAN CHURCH,** located at 326 E. 156th St. in the COLLINWOOD area, began in Sept. 1903 as a mission Sunday school under the sponsorship of the Home Mission Committee of the Cleveland Presbytery. Dr. Frank N. Riale conducted the first services in an empty store on Waterloo Rd. near E. 156th St. CALVARY PRESBYTERIAN CHURCH assumed responsibility for the mission in 1903, and a constitution was written and bylaws were adopted. The store also served as a chapel. In 1905, Mr. and Mrs. Alexander A. Hunter gave property at the corner of Park Ave. and Maple (E. 156th St. and Macauley Ave.) to the mission for a chapel which was dedicated 2 Dec. 1906. Tragedy struck on 4 Mar. 1908 when 57 children of the Immanuel Church Sunday school perished in the COLLINWOOD SCHOOL FIRE; a marble tablet given by the Calvary Presbyterian Church Sunday school honors their memory. The Collinwood Mission was incorporated as an independent church on 23 Sept. 1909, and was named Immanuel by Rev. Edward Wright. During the pastorate of Rev. Geo. A. Mackintosh church attendance grew; a new church sanctuary of English Gothic design was erected, and it was dedicated on 20 Sept. 1925. The church, beset by financial difficulties, struggled during the Depression. Rev. Leroy C. Hensel, however, established many new programs, increasing church attendance, and the debt was eradicated. During the pastorate of Rev. Guy H. Volpitto the newly remodeled chapel was dedicated 17 Sept. 1961.

**IMMIGRATION AND MIGRATION.** The growth of major industrial centers such as Cleveland was made possible in large part by the migration of peoples of a variety of origins to provide the labor or entrepreneurial skills demanded by the changing economy. The nature of this migration (that is, what groups arrived during particular time periods) was determined not only by the opportunities available in the city but also by national and international factors that permitted, necessitated, or expedited the migration of various national groups. The nature of migration to Cleveland is not unlike that of similar midwestern industrial centers. In particular, it is very much akin to the experience of Chicago and, to a degree, Detroit, although the scale of immigration to Chicago was much greater than that to Cleveland. The situation in Cleveland was, however, quite different from that at major ports such as New York, which gathered larger and more diverse populations. During the area's formative period, 1796–1830, the lack of large-scale economic opportunity provided little attraction for migration to the region. Those who did come were largely Americans of English or BRITISH ancestry who had previously resided in New England or New York, although some individuals coming directly from England or Scotland settled in the region. Unique to the region was a substantial Manx migration to the NEWBURGH area in these early years. Toward the end of the period, some IRISH and a few GERMANS settled in the region, the former group being utilized, in part, to construct the OHIO & ERIE CANAL, while members of the latter group were farmers who had usually had a previous American residence. Following the completion of the canal in 1832 and of a rail network in the 1850s, the area's economic potential, par-

FOREIGN BORN POPULATION, CLEVELAND AND CUYAHOGA COUNTY, 1870–1980

| | 1870 Cleve. | 1880 Cuy. Co. | 1880 Cleve. | 1900 Cuy. Co. | 1900 Cleve. | 1910 Cleve. | 1920 Cleve. | 1930 Cleve. | 1930 Cleve.[1] | 1940 Cleve. | 1950 Cleve. Urban | 1960 Cleve. | 1970 Cleve. | 1980 Cleve. |
|---|---|---|---|---|---|---|---|---|---|---|---|---|---|---|
| Africa | — | — | 3 | — | 18 | — | — | — | — | — | — | 53 | 88 | — |
| Albania | — | — | — | — | — | — | — | — | — | — | — | 125 | 59 | — |
| American Black | 1,293 | — | 2,062 | — | 5,988 | 8,448 | 34,451 | 71,899 | — | 84,504 | 147,850 | 250,818 | 287,850 | 251,350 |
| Asia | 1 | — | 1 | 107 | 88 | — | 56 | — | — | 188 | 2,074 | 143 | 81 | — |
| Atlantic Islands | — | — | 54 | — | 1 | — | — | — | — | — | — | 12 | 14 | — |
| Australia | — | — | 15 | — | 37 | — | — | — | — | 41 | — | 178 | 94 | — |
| Austria | 2,155 | — | 258 | 5,004 | 4,630 | 42,059 | 58,321 | 6,774 | 7,488 | 9,931 | 11,451 | 8,274 | 2,557 | 3,675 |
| Azores | — | — | — | — | — | — | — | — | — | 1 | — | 12 | — | — |
| Belgium | — | — | 75 | 28 | 26 | 90 | 97 | 145 | — | 95 | — | 298 | 124 | — |
| Bohemia | 786 | 5,627 | 5,433 | 14,299 | 13,599 | — | — | 34,695[2] | 38,434 | 21,066 | 21,330 | 16,985 | 4,110 | 5,345 |
| Bulgaria, Servia, & Montenegro | — | — | — | — | — | 46 | 751 | 227 | — | 186 | — | 130 | 94 | — |
| Canada | 2,599 | 4,884 | 4,331 | 9,601 | 8,611 | 9,365 | 5,196 | 8,265 | 11,507 | 5,711 | 8,192 | 7,827 | 1,385 | 5,282 |
| Central America | — | — | — | — | 4 | — | — | — | — | — | — | 109 | 200 | — |
| China | — | — | 26 | 99 | 94 | 155 | — | — | — | — | — | 481 | 446 | 1,042 |
| Cuba | — | — | — | — | 17 | 71[3] | — | — | — | 77 | — | 212 | 168 | 378 |
| Denmark | 49 | — | 84 | 649 | 373 | 448 | 620 | 448 | 667 | 355 | 518 | 456 | 61 | — |
| England | 4,533 | 10,839[4] | 7,527 | 12,869 | 10,621 | 11,420 | 11,126 | 9,606 | 12,542 | 6,542 | 8,921[4] | 7,613 | 1,132 | 3,473 |
| Estonia | — | — | — | — | — | — | — | — | — | — | — | 221 | 30 | — |
| Europe (not specified) | 20 | — | 8 | — | 12 | — | 16 | — | — | 156 | 2,268 | 95 | 151 | — |
| Finland | — | — | — | 86 | 79 | 499 | 1,130 | 964 | 1,157 | 739 | 886 | 1,030 | 147 | — |
| France | 339 | 506 | 434 | 542 | 485 | 494 | 693 | 846 | 1,029 | 517 | 799 | 986 | 386 | 653 |
| Germany | 15,855 | 27,051 | 23,170 | 45,787 | 40,648 | 41,408 | 31,474 | 22,532 | 25,947 | 15,427 | 14,859 | 16,496 | 4,076 | 9,435 |
| Gibralter | — | — | 1 | — | — | — | — | — | — | — | — | — | — | — |
| Greece | 1 | — | 9 | 43 | 42 | 275 | 1,597 | 2,261 | 2,350 | 1,891 | 2,181 | 2,212 | 1,412 | 2,605 |
| Greenland | — | — | 1 | — | — | — | — | — | — | — | — | — | — | — |
| Holland | 495 | — | 830 | 946 | 804 | 1,076 | 1,055 | 800 | 930 | 547 | 635 | 800 | 145 | — |
| Hungary | 97 | — | 867 | 9,893 | 9,558 | 31,503 | 42,189 | 19,073 | 20,176 | 20,944 | 19,960 | 18,249 | 5,730 | 7,559 |
| Iceland | — | — | — | — | — | — | — | — | — | — | — | 31 | — | — |
| India | 4 | — | 9 | — | 30 | — | — | — | — | — | — | 170 | 307 | 2,447 |
| Ireland | 9,964 | 13,203 | 11,958 | 14,035 | 13,120 | 11,316 | 10,983 | 6,842 | 8,113 | 5,112 | 5,894 | 4,238 | 1,370 | 2,032 |
| Israel | — | — | — | — | — | — | — | — | — | — | — | 287 | 221 | — |
| Italy | 35 | — | 110 | 3,251 | 3,065 | 10,836 | 18,189 | 23,524 | 24,601 | 20,961 | 20,166 | 19,317 | 6,057 | 11,890 |
| Japan | — | — | — | — | 8 | 15 | — | — | — | — | — | 237 | 157 | 759 |
| Korea | — | — | — | — | — | — | — | — | — | — | — | 72 | 164 | 1,062 |
| Latvia | — | — | — | — | — | — | — | — | — | 346 | — | 1,477 | 482 | — |
| Lebanon | — | — | — | — | — | — | — | — | — | — | — | 767 | 214 | — |
| Lithuania | — | — | — | — | — | — | — | 4,698 | 4,824 | 3,890 | 4,093 | 3,755 | 923 | — |
| Luxembourg | — | — | 14 | — | 5 | — | 66 | — | — | 30 | — | 28 | 21 | — |
| Man (Isle of) | — | 40 | 38 | — | — | — | — | — | — | — | — | — | — | — |
| Mexico | 6 | — | 3 | — | 9 | 18 | 98 | 679 | — | 162 | 278 | 447 | 221 | 517 |
| New Zealand | — | — | — | — | — | — | — | — | — | — | — | 31 | 6 | — |
| N. Africa | — | — | — | — | — | — | — | — | — | — | — | 71 | 36 | 571 |
| N. Ireland | — | — | — | — | — | — | — | 1,372 | 1,859 | 825 | 224 | 791 | 178 | 169 |
| Norway | 6 | — | 37 | 297 | 249 | 512 | 601 | 516 | 682 | 424 | 575 | 523 | 43 | — |
| Pacific Islands | — | — | — | — | 5 | — | — | — | — | — | — | 8 | — | — |
| Pakistan | — | — | — | — | — | — | — | — | — | — | — | 38 | 26 | — |
| Philippines | — | — | — | — | — | — | — | — | — | — | — | 191 | 368 | 1,907 |
| Poland | 77 | — | 532 | 9,431 | 8,592 | — | — | 32,668 | 33,713 | 24,771 | 22,622 | 19,437 | 6,234 | 8,323 |
| Portugal | — | — | 3 | — | 8 | 3 | 14 | — | — | 22 | — | 60 | 33 | 102 |
| Romania | — | — | — | — | 39 | 761 | 2,945 | 6,672 | 7,135 | 3,997 | 2,882 | 3,540 | 1,000 | — |
| Russia | 35 | — | 66 | 3,685 | 3,607 | 25,477 | 41,969 | 15,193 | 16,910 | 11,967 | 12,118 | 11,487 | 2,383 | 7,250 |
| Scotland | 668 | 1,705 | 1,474 | 2,518 | 2,179 | 2,880 | 3,929 | 5,145 | 6,521 | 3,438 | 4,620 | 3,895 | 688 | 1,896 |

541

FOREIGN BORN POPULATION, CLEVELAND AND CUYAHOGA COUNTY, 1870–1980

| | 1870 Cleve. | 1880 Cuy. Co. | 1880 Cleve. | 1900 Cuy. Co. | 1900 Cleve. | 1910 Cleve. | 1920 Cleve. | 1930 Cleve. | 1930 Cleve.[1] | 1940 Cleve. | 1950 Cleve. Urban | 1960 Cleve. | 1970 Cleve. | 1980 Cleve. |
|---|---|---|---|---|---|---|---|---|---|---|---|---|---|---|
| S. America | 3 | — | 8 | — | 30 | — | 38 | — | — | 199 | — | 533 | 645 | 1,380 |
| S.W. Asia | — | — | — | — | — | — | — | — | — | — | — | 165 | 171 | — |
| Spain | 2 | — | 20 | — | 9 | 28 | 151 | 343 | — | 177 | — | 178 | 90 | — |
| Sweden | 26 | 248[5] | 180 | 1,145 | 1,000 | 1,657 | 2,299 | 1,922 | 2,674 | 1,389 | 1,850 | 1,425 | 175 | 432 |
| Switzerland | 704 | 935 | 732 | 1,555 | 1,288 | 1,373 | 1,209 | 972 | 1,181 | 618 | — | 467 | 124 | — |
| Syria/ Palestine | — | — | — | — | — | — | — | 1,180 | 1,247 | 1,068 | — | 237 | 119 | — |
| Turkey | 2 | — | 1 | 41 | 41 | 748 | 1,436 | 468 | — | 538 | — | 492 | 200 | — |
| Union of S. Africa | — | — | — | — | — | — | — | — | — | — | — | 43 | — | — |
| U.A.R. | — | — | — | — | — | — | — | — | — | — | — | 314 | 71 | — |
| Wales | 285 | — | 1,061 | 1,592 | 1,490 | 1,298 | 1,140 | 1,114 | 1,438 | 584 | — | 599 | 59 | 206 |
| W. Indies | 3 | — | 17 | 59 | 42 | — | 69 | — | — | — | — | 431 | 224 | 1,905 |
| Yugoslavia | — | — | — | — | — | — | — | 18,326 | 18,555 | 14,103 | 12,755 | 15,505 | 8,692 | 11,743 |

All data are taken from federal census schedules. The absence of a census figure for a particular group in a given year does not necessarily indicate that members of that group were not resident in Cleveland and or Cuyahoga County. Rather, the group may not have been counted separately and may be included with the figures for another group.
1. Figures given are for Cleveland, Lakewood, Cleveland Heights, Shaker Heights, and East Cleveland
2. Bohemia figures are for Czechoslovakia beginning in 1930
3. Includes West Indians
4. Includes Wales
5. Includes Norway

ticularly in mercantile endeavors, grew, and it proved more attractive to migrating groups. The predominant pool of immigrants in this period emanated from the German states, Great Britain, and, particularly, Ireland. The city attracted substantial representation from each of these groups in the 1830–70 period. In doing so, it reflected national trends that saw the German and Irish populations of many major cities grow. It did, however, lag behind certain cities, such as Cincinnati, where earlier and more rapid economic development resulted in an earlier and more substantial growth of these particular ethnic groups.

The most substantial and diverse migration to Cleveland occurred during the years 1870–1914, the period of the "new immigration," in which many Southern and Eastern Europeans came to the U.S. The exodus of large numbers of people from these areas of Europe was fostered by

IMMIGRATION TO CLEVELAND BY COUNTRY OF ORIGIN, 1874–1907

| | 1874 | 1875 | 1876 | 1877 | 1878 | 1879 | 1880 | 1881 | 1882 | 1883 | 1884 | 1885 | 1886 | 1887 | 1888 | 1889 |
|---|---|---|---|---|---|---|---|---|---|---|---|---|---|---|---|---|
| Arabia (Syria) | — | — | — | — | — | — | — | — | — | — | — | — | — | — | — | — |
| Austria | — | — | — | — | — | — | — | — | — | — | — | — | — | — | — | — |
| Belgium | — | — | — | — | — | — | — | — | — | — | — | — | — | — | — | — |
| Bohemia | 301 | 398 | 225 | 172 | 148 | 225 | 1127 | 1947 | 1896 | 868 | 1206 | 570 | 537 | 1406 | 1116 | 661 |
| Bulgaria | — | — | — | — | — | — | — | — | — | — | — | — | — | — | — | — |
| China | — | — | — | — | — | — | — | — | — | — | — | — | — | — | — | — |
| Croatia | — | — | — | — | — | — | — | — | — | — | — | — | — | — | — | — |
| Denmark | — | — | 4 | — | — | — | 14 | — | — | — | — | — | 8 | 33 | 30 | 28 |
| England | 242 | 203 | 126 | 103 | 97 | 124 | 335 | 667 | 829 | 479 | 183 | 141 | 160 | 321 | 515 | 434 |
| Finland | — | — | — | — | — | — | — | — | — | — | — | — | — | — | 1 | — |
| France | 3 | — | — | — | — | — | — | — | — | — | — | 3 | — | 7 | 2 | 7 |
| Germany | 667 | 402 | 270 | 273 | 202 | 379 | 1291 | 4709 | 4510 | 1875 | 3077 | 1473 | 806 | 1616 | 1256 | 1221 |
| Greece | — | — | — | — | — | — | — | — | — | — | — | — | — | — | — | — |
| Holland | 29 | 8 | 5 | — | 7 | — | — | 35 | 75 | — | 14 | — | — | 2 | — | — |
| Hungary | 74 | 108 | 61 | 69 | 44 | 98 | 218 | 573 | 817 | 323 | 182 | 121 | 236 | 436 | 455 | 420 |
| Ireland | 381 | 182 | 131 | 99 | 130 | 167 | 411 | 810 | 1010 | 994 | 499 | 134 | 167 | 686 | 448 | 431 |
| Italy | 87 | 12 | 15 | 23 | 10 | 7 | 52 | 23 | 60 | 16 | 42 | 30 | 130 | 71 | 191 | 194 |
| Man (Isle of) | — | — | — | — | — | — | — | — | — | — | — | — | — | — | 14 | — |
| Norway | — | — | — | — | — | — | — | — | — | — | — | — | — | 5 | 24 | 7 |
| Poland | — | — | — | — | — | — | — | — | — | — | — | 232 | 221 | 418 | 694 | 545 |
| Prussia | — | — | — | — | — | — | — | — | — | — | — | — | 10 | — | — | — |
| Romania | — | — | — | — | — | — | — | — | — | — | — | — | — | — | — | — |
| Russia | — | — | — | — | — | — | — | — | — | — | — | — | — | 4 | — | — |
| Scandinavia | — | — | — | — | — | — | — | — | — | — | — | 24 | — | — | — | — |
| Scotland | — | — | — | — | — | — | — | — | — | — | — | — | 4 | 40 | 35 | 49 |
| Slavonia | — | — | — | — | — | — | — | — | — | — | — | — | 32 | 198 | 159 | 570 |
| Sweden | — | — | 7 | — | — | 10 | 21 | 82 | 76 | — | — | 19 | 4 | 58 | 104 | 59 |
| Switzerland | — | — | — | — | — | — | — | — | — | — | — | — | — | — | — | — |
| Turkey | — | — | — | — | — | — | — | — | — | — | — | — | — | — | — | — |
| Wales | — | — | — | — | — | — | — | — | — | — | — | 3 | — | 36 | 17 | 54 |

Source: City of Cleveland Annual Reports

shortages of land in the home countries, more liberal emigration policies, increased military conscription, and particularly, in the case of the Jews (see JEWS & JUDAISM), persecutions. Pogroms against Jews living in the Pale of Settlement of the Russian Empire occasioned an emigration that vastly increased the Jewish settlements of cities such as Cleveland after the 1880s. The entire process was facilitated by the development of relatively cheap, regular ocean transport. As this situation coincided with the tremendous post-CIVIL WAR expansion of Cleveland's industrial base, the city received large numbers ITALIANS, Austro-Hungarians, and RUSSIANS. The influx was so great that by 1874, the city stationed members of the police force, designated as emigrant officers, at its various railroad stations to count and assist new arrivals in the city. However, while these groups represented a new source of population, immigration from the older sources, as detailed on the accompanying chart, continued unabated. Indeed, until 1893 more Germans arrived annually in Cleveland than did any other national group. By 1900, the city's German population of 40,648, was larger than that of any other foreign-born community. Because Cleveland's industries expanded at a slightly later date than those in Chicago or Detroit, it received its infusion of "new immigrants" somewhat later than did those cities. For instance, the Polish communities in these two cities had already established basic institutions such as churches and benefit organizations in the 1870s, while Cleveland's Polish community (see POLES) was still in a nascent state. While the city's representation of immigrants from these new sources parallels that in other cities, several groups did come to the city in extraordinarily large concentrations, most prominently the SLOVENES and SLOVAKS.

WORLD WAR I effectively ended the period of large-scale European immigration, as the conflict involved many potential immigrants and strangled the sea lanes. Restrictive legislation, such as the Literacy Act of 1917 and the Natl. Origins Act of 1921 (formalized in 1924), prohibited large-scale immigration after the conflict and provided quotas that discriminated against Southern and Eastern Europeans. Given the chaos in Europe following the war, it is justifiable to assume that the "new immigration" would have continued unabated had not restrictions been put in place. Despite problems in Europe, and particularly persecution in the Nazi German state, relatively little migration to the U.S. and Cleveland took place in the period 1914–45. However, the city's need for people continued during much of this time, particularly during the war and in the years before the Depression. New sources of migrants met this need, the most prominent of which was the American South, where thousands of BLACKS came north to work in wartime industries. Cleveland, which had had a black presence from its earliest history, had a relatively small black population of approximately 10,000 immediately before the war. By 1920 the figure had grown to 34,451, and 20 years later it stood at over 85,000. Other new sources of migrants opened during this period; it was, for instance, in the 1920s that the city received its first cohesive group of Spanish-speaking immigrants from Mexico. Although the Natl. Origins Act remained in effect after WORLD WAR II, special acts to permit the immigration of displaced persons from Europe helped to partially replenish some of the older European immigrant populations of the city. Again, Cleveland was typical of other industrial cities in receiving large numbers of displaced persons during the late 1940s and early 1950s. However, its share was somewhat smaller than that received by Chicago, New York, and other large cities. It was during this period that the city's UKRAINIAN population saw substantial growth, and following the 1956 revolution, the HUNGARIAN community was partially revitalized.

Of greater consequence during the 1945–65 period was the growth of non-European migrant groups, who, like the Europeans, were attracted by the area's still-growing post-

IMMIGRATION TO CLEVELAND BY COUNTRY OF ORIGIN, 1874-1907 (continued)

| 1890 | 1891 | 1892 | 1893 | 1894 | 1895 | 1896 | 1897 | 1898 | 1899 | 1900 | 1901 | 1902 | 1903 | 1904 | 1905 | 1906 | 1907 |
|---|---|---|---|---|---|---|---|---|---|---|---|---|---|---|---|---|---|
| — | — | — | — | — | 12 | 11 | 24 | 15 | 29 | 11 | 28 | 8 | 35 | 14 | 26 | 21 | 7 |
| — | — | — | — | — | 5 | 29 | 15 | 36 | 69 | 36 | 160 | 976 | 1110 | 225 | 421 | 1018 | 2064 |
| — | — | — | — | — | — | — | — | — | — | — | — | 5 | — | — | — | — | — |
| 1093 | 1292 | 508 | 465 | 69 | 264 | 247 | 105 | 185 | 202 | 352 | 336 | 547 | 892 | 371 | 709 | 1024 | 911 |
| — | — | — | — | — | — | — | — | — | — | — | — | — | — | 83 | — | 14 | — |
| — | — | — | — | — | — | — | — | — | — | — | — | — | 126 | 30 | — | — | — |
| 20 | 27 | 7 | 11 | — | — | — | 4 | — | — | — | — | — | 20 | 19 | 9 | 13 | — |
| 275 | 288 | 116 | 63 | 29 | 29 | 42 | 4 | 36 | 29 | 21 | 21 | 47 | 49 | 73 | 88 | 199 | 153 |
| — | — | — | — | — | — | — | — | — | — | — | — | — | 12 | 8 | 126 | 33 | 72 |
| 5 | 3 | — | — | 2 | 14 | 2 | 6 | 4 | — | — | — | — | 22 | — | 2 | — | 2 |
| 1486 | 1528 | 782 | 810 | 281 | 501 | 609 | 381 | 432 | 522 | 417 | 525 | 1128 | 1479 | 514 | 1168 | 1857 | 1703 |
| — | — | — | — | — | — | — | — | — | — | — | — | 9 | 6 | 4 | 16 | 2 | 32 |
| — | — | — | 1 | 1 | — | — | 1 | — | — | — | — | — | — | — | — | — | — |
| 1151 | 734 | 365 | 215 | 128 | 237 | 415 | 172 | 313 | 514 | 999 | 1257 | 1728 | 1824 | 1098 | 2678 | 2491 | 2468 |
| 144 | 245 | 131 | 92 | 69 | 117 | 155 | 136 | 208 | 261 | 175 | 312 | 160 | 171 | 73 | 334 | 345 | 360 |
| 103 | 125 | 83 | 121 | 54 | 146 | 286 | 226 | 301 | 555 | 439 | 981 | 1219 | 1932 | 1464 | 1918 | 2836 | 1963 |
| 10 | — | 5 | — | — | — | — | — | — | — | — | — | — | — | — | — | — | — |
| 8 | 4 | 3 | 10 | — | — | — | — | — | — | — | — | — | 5 | — | — | — | 47 |
| 794 | 1054 | 749 | 791 | 136 | 524 | 885 | 396 | 623 | 1192 | 1453 | 1900 | 2833 | 3211 | 1637 | 3082 | 2039 | 2514 |
| — | — | — | — | — | — | — | — | — | — | — | — | 1 | 234 | 133 | 274 | 677 | 995 |
| — | 70 | 103 | 28 | 10 | 152 | 131 | 60 | 179 | 301 | 340 | 485 | 634 | 1076 | 826 | 1552 | 1649 | 1519 |
| 29 | — | — | 13 | — | 3 | — | — | — | — | 11 | 25 | — | 2 | 12 | 17 | 53 | — |
| 489 | 603 | 256 | 694 | 3 | 74 | 255 | 94 | 166 | 157 | 342 | 330 | 1321 | 1246 | 390 | 1545 | 1912 | 2116 |
| 32 | 16 | 3 | 12 | 3 | 26 | 71 | 18 | 27 | 69 | 5 | 37 | 99 | 199 | 122 | 178 | 128 | 87 |
| — | — | — | — | — | — | 1 | — | — | — | — | — | — | — | — | — | — | — |
| — | — | — | — | — | — | — | — | — | — | — | 2 | — | — | — | — | — | — |
| — | 6 | — | — | 5 | — | 13 | — | — | — | — | 2 | 3 | 1 | — | — | — | — |

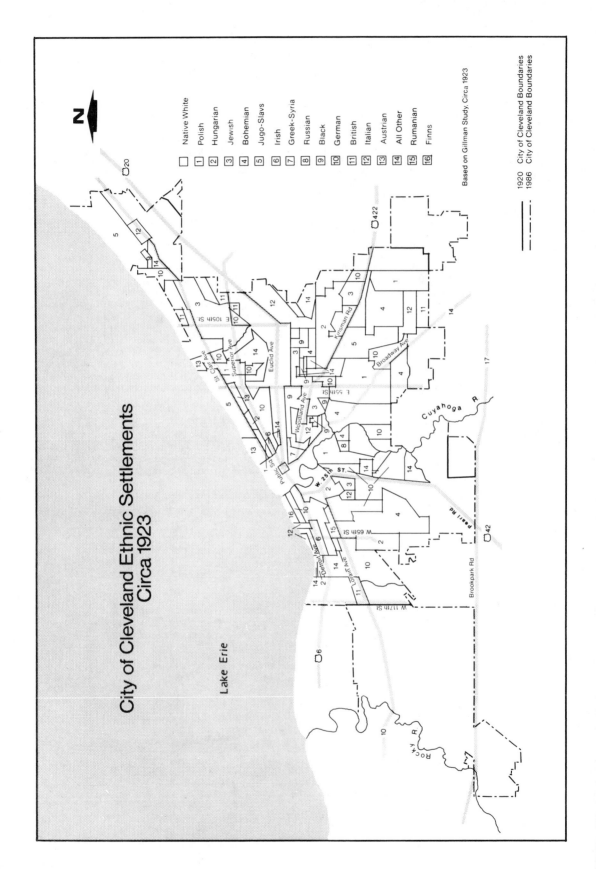

# City of Cleveland Ethnic Settlements Circa 1923

Lake Erie

Native White

1 Polish
2 Hungarian
3 Jewish
4 Bohemian
5 Jugo-Slavs
6 Irish
7 Greek-Syria
8 Russian
9 Black
10 German
11 British
12 Italian
13 Austrian
14 All Other
15 Rumanian
16 Finns

Based on Gillman Study, Circa 1923

1920 City of Cleveland Boundaries
1986 City of Cleveland Boundaries

war economy. It was in the immediate postwar period that the city's Puerto Rican population began to expand. Initially brought to work in the steel mills of Lorain during the war, Puerto Ricans began to move east to Cleveland in the late 1940s and by the early 1960s had formed a substantial community in the city. Mexican immigration also continued during this period, and following the Cuban revolution of 1960, the city received a substantial number of Cubans. Predominant in the period, however, was the continued movement of blacks into Cleveland. By 1960, the city's black population stood at over 251,000. The postwar period also saw the large-scale migration of people from the depressed areas of Appalachia to the Cleveland area. Though many Appalachians had earlier migrated to Akron to work in the rubber industry, it was not until after the war that a further move north to Cleveland was made in any great number. The repeal of the Natl. Origins (Quota) Act in 1965 and its replacement with regulations that restricted overall numbers of immigrants but gave no preference to any country or countries, formed the basis of the most recent period in the history of migration to Cleveland. During this period, the city's economy began to falter; it was not, therefore, as attractive a destination as before, but it still managed to gather one of the most diverse, if not substantial, groups of immigrants in its history. In particular, the relaxation of restrictions on Asian immigration brought numbers of CHINESE, Koreans, INDIANS, and Pakistanis to the city, many of them attracted initially by the area's colleges, and later by the growth of its medical and research industries. War and economic decline in Southeast Asia, Central and South America, and the Middle East brought the city its first groups of Vietnamese, Guatemalans, and Palestinians during the 1970s and 1980s. Though not as large as previous immigrant or migrant groups, these newer communities represented a complete shift in the pattern of migration to Cleveland.

The changing international situation and the economic position of Cleveland have shaped the nature of migration to the city in the past and will continue to do so as long as the area remains economically viable. It is important to note, however, that while the sources of migration have shifted innumerable times throughout the city's history, few of these have ever totally ceased to supply people to the city. English immigration to the area, for instance, continues into the 1980s, as does the movement of native-born white Americans. Nor does the city permanently retain those people that it attracts. While no major study of movement into and out of the city has been completed for Cleveland, it can be assumed that the city shares in the phenomenon of rapidly shifting population. Indeed, a limited study of the 25-block area around HIRAM HOUSE social settlement showed that during the early part of this century, over 90% of the residents in that area moved during a 10-year period. Cleveland, thus, is not an end point for movement but often a temporary haven in the pattern of national and international population movement.

John J. Grabowski
Western Reserve Historical Society

See also specific ethnic groups.

The **IMMIGRATION BUREAU** was a municipal agency established in Sept. 1913 to help and protect immigrants. Operated as part of the Public Safety Dept. in 1913, the bureau was transferred to the Dept. of Public Welfare in 1914. By 1922 it no longer existed. The bureau was established after an investigation by the Cleveland Immigration League demonstrated that immigrants arriving at Cleveland's train depots were "at the mercy of any who would misuse and misdirect them and such persons were found to be many." The "most atrocious" were chauffeurs and cabmen, but there were also "hangers-on and immoral men" who preyed upon young immigrant women. To protect the immigrants, the Immigration Bureau sent city immigration officers to the depots to meet trains carrying new arrivals to the city. Identified by their badges, these officers shielded the immigrants from those who wished to take advantage of their ignorance by making sure the friends and relatives who met them were, indeed, friends and relatives; they also helped immigrants find luggage, unscrambled garbled or vague addresses, and "tagged and grouped" the new arrivals according to their destinations within the city, either personally escorting them to their destinations or arranging passage there. Officers also registered immigrant children and turned their names over to the truant officers in order to ensure that the children were sent to school.

In addition to its "depot work," the bureau provided other services to immigrants to help them adjust to American life. Its small paid staff and many volunteers, under the direction of first Raymond E. Cole (1913–14) and then John Prucha, worked with the State-City Free Labor Exchange to help find employment for new arrivals, helped the Board of Education plan and then promoted English-language and citizenship classes, and assisted immigrants through the naturalization process. The bureau also published 9 foreign-language versions of *The Immigrant's Guide to Cleveland*, as well as the *Citizenship Manual for Cleveland*, with information about the naturalization process, national history, and national, state, and local government. The bureau also investigated complaints from immigrants, such as those about wage claims and industrial accidents, often resolving misunderstandings and mediating disputes. The bureau's services to the foreign-born population already in Cleveland increased in 1915, as the pace of immigration slowed considerably because of the war in Europe. By the 1920s, many other local agencies, such as the YWCA's Internatl. Institute (see NATIONALITIES SERVICES CTR.) and the Americanization Committee of the MAYOR'S ADVISORY WAR COMMITTEE, also were involved in providing services for the immigrant population. As private agencies increasingly took up service to the immigrants, the city apparently decided to disband its small bureau, whose directors had continually complained that its small staff and small budget frustrated their efforts.

City Immigration Bureau of Cleveland, *Citizenship Manual for Cleveland* (1916), WRHS..
————. *The Immigrant Guide to Cleveland, Ohio*. WRHS.
*Annual Reports of the Department of Government of the City of Cleveland*, 1913, 1914, 1915.

**INDEPENDENCE** is a residential and industrial suburb located on the west bank of the CUYAHOGA RIVER about 8 mi. south of Cleveland. Covering approximately 10 sq. mi., it is bounded on the north by BROOKLYN HTS., on the east by the river and VALLEY VIEW, on the west by SEVEN HILLS, and on the south by BRECKSVILLE. The origins of Independence are unknown, because the early township records were destroyed. The population was 354 in 1820, and in the same year the state road was opened from Cleveland to NEWBURGH (modern State Rt. 21). The character of the township changed when the Cleveland-Akron section of the Ohio Canal opened in 1827, and the population fell to 245 in 1830. During the depression years of 1837–40, Independence continued to be a farming and dairying community, using the canal to transport produce and dairy products to markets in Newburgh and Cleveland. In the 1840s, many skilled stonecutters from

Germany, Poland, Ireland, and Scotland were attracted by the commercial quarrying of sandstone and shale found in a vein extending from the river to Broadview Rd. By 1850, the population was 1,485, and Independence was one of the nation's foremost suppliers of building stone. In 1880 the population was 1,993, and the Valley Railroad (later part of the Baltimore & Ohio system) came through Independence. In the latter part of the 19th century, the quarries closed because of several factors, including the competition from larger Berea sandstone companies, use of emery or carborundum to replace grindstones, and the introduction of concrete as a building material.

In 1896, Independence Twp. east of the Cuyahoga River was annexed by the village of Newburgh. The village of Independence was incorporated in 1914. The section of the township remaining to the west became the village of Seven Hills in 1927. During WORLD WAR I, the agricultural character began to change as many residents went to the city to work in industry. The population in 1920 was 1,075. With the advent of the automobile and construction of highways, Independence began to become industrialized. The Willow Cloverleaf at Brecksville and Granger roads, completed in 1940, was one of the first highway interchanges in the country. New businesses included Pemco, Inc., the Thompson Ramo Wooldridge Replacement Div., the REPUBLIC STEEL Research Ctr., Goodrich, the Gulf Chemical Co., the Sperry-Univac Co., and the DAVY MCKEE CORP. A municipal charter was approved in Nov. 1958, and in Nov. 1960 Independence became a city. The population was 6,843. During the 1970s, new streets and homes were constructed, although the population peaked at 7,034 in 1970, dropping to 6,007 in 1985. A portion of the CUYAHOGA VALLEY NATL. RECREATION AREA lies within the city south of Rockside Rd. along the river. Elmwood Park also provides recreational facilities. Four churches, St. Michael's Roman Catholic (1851), Concordia Lutheran, Independence Presbyterian (1855), and Independence United Methodist (1862), still served the community in the 1980s.

The *INDEPENDENT NEWS-LETTER,* inaugurated by printer David B. McLain in July 1828, was Cleveland's third newspaper and the first to challenge the front-running *Herald* after the demise of the *Register* in 1820. It also contended with the *Herald* politically, supporting the Democratic Jackson administration and regularly printing U.S. laws, "By Authority." From 18 Apr.–4 Aug. 1829, McLain turned over the editorial direction of the *News-Letter* to Harvey Rice. It was a well-printed, attractive sheet of 4 pages of 6 columns, featuring numerous cuts and a variety of headline types. In May 1830, the name of Thos. J. McLain appeared on the masthead as publisher of the *News-Letter.* On 10 Aug. 1830, in hope of gaining better support, the *Independent News-Letter* announced its imminent removal to Warren, Ohio, where it began publication on 25 Aug. as the *Warren News-Letter & Trumbull County Republican.*

The **INDIA COMMUNITY CENTER,** 12412 Cedar Rd., Cleveland Hts., began in July 1976 as a temporary facility known as India House, located at 10819 Magnolia Dr. in UNIVERSITY CIRCLE. Established by the India Assoc. of Cleveland, India House was designed "to educate and expose the younger generation of Indians and their American friends to Indian culture and heritage." In Mar. 1977 the name was changed to the India Community Ctr. Using both India House and the First English Lutheran Church (2419 Euclid Hts. Blvd.) as its base until it could establish a permanent center, the India Assoc. offered courses in Indian culture throughout the late 1970s. By 1978 it offered courses in the Hindi and Tamil languages, dance, and music, demonstrations in Indian cooking, documentary films about India, and a speakers' bureau. In fall 1978, the India Assoc. spent $76,000 to buy the former branch office of Sun Newspapers at 12412 Cedar as a permanent community center for Cleveland's 2,200-member Indian community. The permanent center was established to serve the cultural needs of local Indians, to promote Indian culture and heritage among the young through organized educational and cultural activities, to channel the humanitarian efforts of the local community, and to foster among Americans a greater appreciation for Indian culture.

**INDIANS (AMERICAN).** *See* **AMERICAN INDIANS**

**INDIANS (ASIAN).** The history and current profile of the Asian-Indian community in Greater Cleveland reflects the pattern for the entire U.S. Indians first settled in Cleveland in the early 1920s; their numbers increased, gradually at first, and more rapidly after the replacement of the Natl. Origins Act in 1965. The demographic characteristics of individuals immigrating from India have changed significantly during this century. The number of students on visas, formerly a large proportion of the immigrants, has decreased drastically. Later immigrants were older, often coming to join family members who had settled in Cleveland after completing their educations at local colleges and universities. Statistics on Cleveland's Indian population for the years before 1960 are difficult to determine; from 1910–50, the U.S. Census grouped Indians together with a number of other nationalities under the headings "Others" or "Other Asians." The census records individuals of Indian origin in Cuyahoga County as early as 1880, but these individuals may have been ethnically British. However, it is certain that a small number of Indians, most of them university students, were living in Cleveland in the 1920s. Estimates set the size of the community at 100 in the 1930s. The censuses of 1960 and 1970 counted 170 and 307 Indians respectively; that of 1980 recorded 2,216 living in the county. These immigrants included a large number of physicians and engineers, drawn by Cleveland's hospitals, industries, and universities, as well as people in other professions and businesses. Indians joining family members already resident in Cleveland were also a significant factor in the growth of the Indian community. Many of the permanent residents became naturalized citizens; temporary residents were mostly students.

Individuals from all regions of India have immigrated to Cleveland. However, more have come from the state of Gujarat than from any other state. In the Cleveland area, the earlier immigrants lived primarily on the east side, in suburbs such as CLEVELAND HTS. and SHAKER HTS., near the major hospitals and educational institutions. In the 1970s and 1980s, Indians began settling in the western suburbs, as well, so that by the mid-1980s it was estimated that about 60% of the Indian population lived in the eastern suburbs, and 40% in the western suburbs. The community's first cultural organization was the India Students Assoc. It had its origins at a meeting called in Dec. 1962 to express concern over the Chinese invasion of India, and was attended by approximately 100 people. In 1964, the India Assoc. of Cleveland was officially established. As of 1986, there were 8 organizations in Cleveland dedicated to the regional, cultural, and social interests of the Indian population. The Fed. of India Community Associations of Northeastern Ohio, established in 1981, served as an umbrella organization for these groups and provided a unifying identity for Indians in Cleveland. Under FICA's coordination, the groups also did some lobbying in areas such as immigration and naturalization legislation, small-business development, and minority-status recognition. The INDIA COMMUNITY CTR. at 12412 Cedar Rd. in Cleveland Hts. began as the only institution of its kind in North America, wholly owned by the entire Indian community. In 1976, an executive committee of community members decided to purchase a permanent facility for social and cultural activities. They bought the Cedar Rd. building the following year and renovated it to create a hall, a kitchen, offices, and classrooms. Among the center's regular programs have been classes in language and Indian regional dance for young people and adults. The *Lotus*, a monthly newspaper, has become the principal vehicle of communication for Cleveland's Indian population, having in the mid-1980s a circulation of approximately 1,800 among families and libraries in Greater Cleveland.

Tansukh J. Salgia
Dyke College

The **INDUSTRIAL EXPOSITION OF 1909** was a massive exhibit of Cleveland manufacture that showcased Cleveland industries' end products. The exhibition, planned in 1908 by the Chamber of Commerce as an expression of civic pride, was held in a massive temporary building on the current site of City Hall. A bridge connected the imaginative canvas-and-pole structure with the CENTRAL ARMORY. Attendance records for expositions of this kind were broken as over 215,000 flocked to see the displays. Visitors, including many from abroad, left impressed with Cleveland's industrial strength. The exposition lured new industry to Cleveland and caused a surge in retail, convention bookings, and the real-estate market.

**INDUSTRIAL RAYON CORPORATION.** *See* **MIDLAND-ROSS COMPANY**

The **INDUSTRIAL WORKERS OF THE WORLD,** dedicated to the abolition of capitalism, were active in Depression-era Cleveland largely through the efforts of Frank Cedervall, chief organizer for the Metal & Machinery Workers Industrial Union, and his brother, Tor, the branch secretary. Organized in Chicago in 1905, the IWW espoused the belief that the working class and the employing class had nothing in common, and were destined to be locked in struggle until the workers organized, took over the machinery of production, and abolished the wage system. Though most successful in the West among miners, cowboys, immigrants, and lumberjacks, the IWW organized the stogie workers of Cleveland in 1908 and the rubber workers of Akron in 1912. Considered radical and un-American during WORLD WAR I, when cooperation between labor and management was deemed essential to the war effort, the Wobblies, as IWW members were called, were harassed into oblivion by the Espionage Act of 1917 and the Sedition Act of 1918.

In the 1930s, a new breed of IWW leaders were able to temper long-range goals with pragmatic immediate action that transformed the old image of the Wobblies as the "I Won't Works" to that of a responsible bargaining agent. Leaders such as the Cedervalls believed in the IWW version of "one big union" but saw the need to address more traditional trade-union concerns. A self-proclaimed "unattached radical" and a plasterer by trade, Frank Cedervall joined the IWW in 1931, then spent 3 years on the road organizing other workers. He then took over the leadership of Cleveland Local 440 of the Metal & Machinery Workers Industrial Union (organized 1918). With a nucleus of Hungarian tradesmen from the Buckeye neighborhood,

the Cedervalls spearheaded organizing drives in several plants in northeast Ohio: the Ohio Foundry Co., the Draper Mfg. Co., the Cochrane Brass Co., the American Stove Co. (Dangler Div.), Cleveland Wire & Spring, and Natl. Screw. While Cedervall proclaimed the IWW philosophy from the speaker's platform, he won support among tradesmen by bargaining for concrete benefits such as wages, hours, and union recognition, and over 6 years built local IWW membership to a peak of 3,000. At a time when the leadership of unions (especially those organized under Sec. 7A of the NIRA) was regarded as strident and confrontational, Cedervall was regarded even within the business community as firm but fair-minded. Though respected, Cedervall was accused (and acquitted) of charges that ranged from harassment to conspiracy. Despite setbacks, Local 440 became the most powerful IWW local in the country.

As the antileftist bias of the 1930s and early 1940s gave way to a full-blown anti-Communist movement in the late 1940s, Local 440 was faced with a dilemma that caused it to leave the international. Under a provision of the Taft-Hartley Act, union members were required to sign affidavits stating that they were not members of organizations dedicated to the overthrow of the U.S. government in order to qualify the local to compete with the AFL and CIO in plant elections. Though strongly anti-Communist, the international officers refused to sign the statements on principle. Cedervall maintained that signing was crucial to the survival of IWW locals, and when reasoning with the General Executive Board failed, he helped collect signatures from 440 members, which the NLRB refused to accept in the absence of official signatures from the international. Local 440 withheld dues, but when not even this action moved the body, Cedervall led the local out of the IWW. In 1950, the union became the independent Metal & Machinery Workers Industrial Union 440 of Cleveland, Ohio, and after a brief affiliation with the Congress of Independent Unions, it joined the MECHANICS EDUCATIONAL SOCIETY OF AMERICA, which in 1985 was still active.

Wortman, Roy T., "The IWW in Ohio, 1905-1950" (Ph.D. diss., Ohio State University, 1971).

**INDUSTRY.** Within 60 years of the founding of Cleveland, industry, especially the making of iron and its products, began to dominate the economy of the city and its vicinity. To a large degree, Cleveland's growth has been determined by its industrial base. The term *industry* in its economic and technical sense refers to the organized production of goods for the market. Historians also use the term *industrialization* to refer to the rapid increase in the size and number of industries in Europe and North America over the last 300 years. The U.S. was an early leader and Cleveland a major center of industrialization. Modern industry is associated with the factory system of production, in which workers are gathered in one place to work under centralized direction with the aid of powered machinery. Cleveland's factories have usually mass-produced standardized products such as clothing, iron shapes, or automobiles. Cleveland industry developed under favorable economic conditions. Primary among them was excellent TRANSPORTATION. The development of shipping on the Great Lakes, the completion of the OHIO & ERIE CANAL in 1832, the later construction of RAILROADS, and the more recent construction of major HIGHWAYS and airports have allowed Cleveland to receive a large flow of raw materials and to ship out finished products. In addition, exceptional businessmen and inventors have developed and promoted Cleveland's industry, and the city's workers have been recognized for their skill and productivity.

In its first 4 decades, Cleveland was an agricultural village and a regional center of commerce. Examples of manufactured items included farming tools, barrels for shipping salted meat, flour, and other food products, and household furnishings. These were made by craftsmen in small shops rather than in factories. In 1820, for example, a Cleveland newspaper contained advertisements for a wagonmaker's shop located near the courthouse on PUBLIC SQUARE, and a 2-story shop containing a shoemaker and a saddlemaker. With the coming of the canal, Cleveland's markets expanded. In 1837 the city was reported to have 4 iron foundries making steam engines and other products, 3 soap and candle works, 2 breweries, a window-sash factory, 2 ropewalks, a pottery, 2 carriagemakers, 2 millstone shops, and a large flour mill under construction. The CUYAHOGA STEAM FURNACE CO., just established, was probably the largest single industry. It had a blast furnace that made iron from ore, charcoal, and limestone brought by canal, and had a foundry to make the iron into usable products. Over the next 40 years, this company made a variety of goods, which were representative of Cleveland's flourishing iron trade: steam engines, locomotives, stoves, and iron for building construction. At the time of the U.S. manufacturing census of 1860, the most valuable industrial product of Cleveland was iron, while the manufacture of items made from iron was also very important. Like many other Great Lakes cities, Cleveland had a large flour- and gristmilling industry (ranking 2d in value of product), which served the productive Midwest farms.

Cleveland's history from 1860–1930 was mostly a record of heavy industrialization, not commerce in agricultural products. The Civil War gave immediate impetus to Cleveland's iron industry, and by 1880 the making of iron and steel represented 20% of the value of the city's manufactures. In part this growth was due to the enterprising Clevelanders who in the 1850s began exploiting the mineral resources of the upper Great Lakes and shipping the ores to Cleveland. Leaders in the iron industry after the CIVIL WAR included the Otis Iron & Steel Co. and the Cleveland Rolling Mill Co. in NEWBURGH. The latter began making Bessemer steel in 1868, and Otis instituted open-hearth steel manufacture in 1873: both technologies were importations of recent European innovations. Along with some other Cleveland companies, Otis and the Cleveland Rolling Mill eventually joined the U.S. STEEL CORP., formed in 1901. The making of machinery and other iron and steel products, such as ore vessels for the Great Lakes trade, continued to grow along with the production of iron and steel. Machine-tool companies such as WARNER & SWASEY and Cleveland Twist Drill made lathes, planers, drill presses, and similar devices or parts for them. Sewing-machine manufacturers (for example, the White Co.) and other machinery companies were major purchasers of machine tools. In turn, the Cleveland clothing industry, already the city's 3d-largest producer of goods (by value) in 1860, became a major consumer of sewing machines. This industrial interconnection (iron and steel, machine tools, sewing machines, clothing) is one example of how growing industries benefited by linking to one another. Such interconnections were crucial to the development of Cleveland's industries.

Another contribution to industrial growth in the later 1800s came in the form of entirely new industries. The petroleum-refining industry developed rapidly after the first American oil well was drilled at Titusville, in northeastern Pennsylvania, in 1859. Although Cleveland was no better located with respect to the new oil region than Pittsburgh or Buffalo, young Cleveland businessman JOHN D. ROCKEFELLER became the most resourceful organizer of the oil market. Bringing oil to Cleveland by railroad at low prices, Rockefeller built or purchased almost all of Cleveland's refining capacity in the 1870s and made the city the center of the American refining industry. By exercising a virtual monopoly in the industry, and attempting to control an enormous network of shipping, refining, and distributing enterprises, Rockefeller became a pioneer in modern corporate forms. He experimented by establishing in Cleveland the STANDARD OIL CO. of Ohio (1870), and then the Standard Oil Trust (1879). While Rockefeller's methods of business control were ruthless, and his industrial combinations were eventually broken up by court action, he was one of the first businessmen in the U.S. to recognize that rapid industrialization required new forms of organization.

Cleveland's CHEMICAL INDUSTRY arose in part out of the refiners' need for sulfuric acid. The Grasselli Co. of Cincinnati established a Cleveland works in 1866 specifically to supply sulfuric acid to refineries, but in succeeding years it supplied a wide range of industrial chemicals. Relying in part on petroleum products for their raw materials, Cleveland's large paint and varnish companies were founded in the 1870s. Henry Sherwin and Edward Williams joined in 1870 to form a paint-manufacturing company (SHERWIN-WILLIAMS), and 10 years later they introduced a ready-mixed paint, which found immediate success. Francis H. Glidden organized his company in 1875 and based its sales on varnishes and enamels. Electrical equipment was another new industry of the later 19th century. Although telegraphy had become the first viable electrical technology in the 1840s, its power and apparatus requirements were low and did not stimulate major industrial development. Clevelander CHAS. BRUSH pioneered in new electrical technology in the 1870s by developing an effective dynamo to generate large amounts of electricity, and an outdoor arc-lighting system to consume electricity. First put into continuous use on Public Square in Apr. 1879, Brush's dynamo and arc lights were soon installed in major cities throughout the world. In 3 years they could be found in San Francisco, London, and Shanghai, among others. Brush pushed his company into the production of batteries and streetcar equipment, as well, before it was absorbed by GENERAL ELECTRIC in 1891. Other electrical businesses were founded by persons trained in Brush's company, including Natl. Carbon and LINCOLN ELECTRIC, while Brush's personal influence continued to be felt at the Brush Laboratories. The success of Brush's business soon attracted numerous other firms to the electrical industry.

The AUTOMOTIVE INDUSTRY was the final major industry to emerge in Cleveland. The automobile was brought to a workable form by European inventors of the 1880s and early 1890s, but when Americans took to the "horseless carriage" after 1895, it was still not clear whether it would be gasoline-, electric-, or steam-powered. Cleveland boasted 3 of the earliest manufacturers of each type: ALEXANDER WINTON (gasoline), WALTER BAKER (electric), and ROLLIN WHITE and the White Co. (steam). A Winton sold in 1898 is often claimed to be the first American automobile made for the open market. The Cleveland automobile manufacturers mostly specialized in high-quality and luxury cars. Baker's electric vehicles, for example, were favored by wealthy women for quiet, pollution-free driving. White specialized in heavy touring cars, a tradition that served the company well when it decided to make only trucks. Other well-known Cleveland luxury cars included the Stearns, Jordan, and Peerless. In spite of having several hundred brands of automobiles made in Cleveland up to the 1930s, the city lost the leadership of the auto industry to Detroit as early as 1910. Henry Ford, whose vision of a car for the common man carried the day, chose to concentrate his efforts in what became the Motor City. However, Cleveland remained one of the most important assembly and parts-manufacturing centers in the U.S. Major automakers continued to build and operate new facilities in the Cleveland area after the mid-1900s. Several smaller industries arose in conjunction with automobile manufacture, including diesel engines, construction and industrial vehicles, and aircraft parts.

Cleveland's industry came to the end of its period of rapid growth by 1930. Cleveland was then second only to Detroit among American cities in the percentage of its workers employed in industry. This dependence affected society in a variety of ways. The public schools, for example, provided industrial training for their pupils, and in 1930 the city's Industrial Development Committee reported that industrial training could be found in all school grades. Moreover, thousands of workers were enrolled in the public schools' adult-education classes. Trade and industrial unions were also a means of accommodating industrialization. The city early acquired a reputation for strong trade and craft unions, which joined workers of similar skills to maintain or improve wages and working conditions. In the 1930s, Cleveland workers were also receptive to the formation of industrial unions, especially the UNITED STEELWORKERS and the UNITED AUTO WORKERS, which crossed over trade or craft lines. A sit-down strike at the General Motors Fisher Body plant on Coit Rd. in 1936 was a catalytic event in unionizing the automobile industry. The consistent training of Cleveland's workers, and the unionization of important industrial sectors, made the city attractive both to job-seekers and to businessmen, and did much to promote Cleveland's industrial growth. In 1931, the U.S. Census of the Cleveland metropolitan area (including Cuyahoga and Lorain counties) ranked it 8th nationally by the number of industrial employees, and 7th by value of its products. This ranking held essentially the same through the economic depression of the following decade, and through the ensuing war years. During WORLD WAR II, manufacturers and workers strained the city's productive capacity. Cleveland Twist Drill's outstanding record earned it the first Army-Navy Star Award in the nation. Several Cleveland firms, including HARSHAW CHEMICAL, Victoreen Instrument, Brush Beryllium, McGean Chemical, and H. K. Ferguson, contributed materially to the Manhattan (atomic bomb) Project. Nevertheless, the concentration of Cleveland industry on producers' goods, such as machine tools or construction equipment, which made it a wartime arsenal, also made it especially susceptible to economic fluctuations. Measured by national averages, Cleveland workers suffered more during depressions and recessions but did better in times of economic growth.

Cleveland's industry entered the 1950s with its boom years in the past and no obvious directions for change. The census of 1954 indicated that its traditional leading industries were essentially in the same positions as before the Great Depression. In terms of employment and value of products, the Cleveland area's leaders were transportation equipment (1st, 1st); machinery (2d, 2d); iron- and steel-making (3d, 3d); metal products (4th, 4th); and electrical machinery (5th, 6th). During the next 3 decades, these industries remained the leaders (though their rank order varied) and accounted for more than 60% of the city's industrial employment. By the 1980s, some sources of future change were visible. Most notably, the international iron and steel market was adverse to American industry as a whole and Cleveland in particular. The impact was symbolized by the dismantling of the U.S. Steel blast furnaces in Cleveland, and severe fluctuations in production levels at REPUBLIC STEEL, the JONES & LAUGHLIN CORP.,

and other iron and steel companies. Challenges from Japanese and European automakers and drastic increases in gasoline prices changed American automobile buyers' habits and required shutdowns or retooling of many Cleveland plants. On the other hand, increased military spending in the early 1980s had a positive effect on some Cleveland industries.

Few new industries seemed likely soon to take a major role in Cleveland, although the making of instruments and medical equipment grew significantly during the post-World War II years, and the manufacture of chemicals and plastics and the printing and publishing business remained strong. As Cleveland looked to the future, organized research seemed likely to assume a major role in new industrial development. From the establishment of the Natl. Electric Lamp Assoc. laboratories at NELA PARK (1911) and the Natl. Carbon industrial research facility at about the same time, Cleveland business supported research leading to new technologies. Later the federal government's Lewis Laboratory (1941) and the facilities of Case Institute of Technology became important sites for pioneering development. By the mid-1980s, the Cleveland area had over 200 corporate industrial research laboratories. Cleveland became a major American industrial center during the century after 1830 and has since maintained that position. Dependence upon an industrial economy has brought periods of high unemployment and air and water pollution, among other problems. But while participating in the general industrialization of the U.S. the industries of Cleveland generally have brought economic growth and prosperity.

Darwin H. Stapleton
Rockefeller Archive Center

See also AEROSPACE INDUSTRY, BREWING INDUSTRY, ELECTRICAL AND ELECTRONICS INDUSTRY, GARMENT INDUSTRY, TECHNOLOGY & INDUSTRIAL RESEARCH, and specific companies.

**INGALLS, DAVID S.** (28 Jan. 1899–26 Apr. 1985), was an aviator, lawyer, and politician. He was the U.S. Navy's only flying ace in WORLD WAR I. Ingalls was born in Cleveland. He attended UNIVERSITY SCHOOL, and then St. Paul's School in Concord, N.H. In 1916 he enrolled at Yale University as a premed student. When the war intervened, Ingalls enlisted in the 1st Yale Naval Aviation Unit. He graduated from Yale in 1920 and went on to study law at Harvard University, where he received a degree in 1923. From 1923–27, Ingalls was a member of the law firm of SQUIRE, SANDERS & DEMPSEY in Cleveland. He left the firm in 1927 to embark on a brief political career. That year he was elected as a state representative, and he was reelected in 1929. After an unsuccessful run for governor in 1932, Ingalls returned to Cleveland, where Mayor HARRY L. DAVIS appointed him welfare director, but he resigned in 1935 when Davis refused to install x-ray equipment in the former City Hospital. During the 1940s, Ingalls was variously involved in the military and aviation industries. In 1954 he became president and publisher of the *Cincinnati Times-Star*, after which, in 1958, he resumed his law practice in Cleveland.

As one of Cleveland's foremost aviation enthusiasts, Ingalls had a varied and notable career in that field. In World War I, he was assigned to a squadron of Sopwith Camels and shot down 4 enemy planes and 3 aerial balloons. He was awarded the British Distinguished Flying Cross and the U.S. Distinguished Service Medal. In 1929, Pres. Hoover appointed him assistant secretary of the Navy for aeronautics, which involved him in the development and testing of aircraft for the Navy and the establishment of air bases throughout the country. He returned to active duty in WORLD WAR II and in late 1942 served as chief of staff for the Air Ctr. Commander Forward Area on Guadalcanal. He was later awarded the Bronze Star and Legion of Merit. During the year preceding the war, in 1941, Ingalls had been general manager of Pan American Air Ferries. Following the war, until 1949, he was vice-president of Pan American Airways. Throughout the remainder of his life, he continued to fly private planes. In 1983 he was inducted into the Aviation Hall of Fame. Ingalls married Louise Harkness in 1922; they had 1 son and 4 daughters. After her death in 1979, he married Frances W. Wragg.

David S. Ingalls Papers, WRHS.

**INGALLS FOUNDATION.** See **LOUISE HARKNESS & DAVID SINTON INGALLS FOUNDATION, INC.**

**INGHAM, MARY BIGELOW (JANES)** (10 Mar. 1832–17 Nov. 1923), known as "one of Cleveland's most useful citizens," dedicated her life to teaching, missionary work, and temperance reform. Ingham was born in Mansfield, Ohio. She was the eldest daughter of Rev. John Janes, a Methodist minister, and Hannah Brown, a cofounder of the First Methodist Church of Ann Arbor, Mich. She was educated at Norwalk Seminary, Baldwin Institute, and later Western Reserve Seminary. Ingham arrived in Cleveland in 1846. After employment as a primary school teacher, she was appointed professor of French and belles-lettres at Ohio Wesleyan College for Women. Later she served as assistant principal at Norwalk North Grammar School and Rockwell School of Cleveland. Ingham retired from teaching in 1886 and began an active public career. In 1870, she coinaugurated the Women's Foreign Missionary in northern Ohio. She was also very involved in the Cleveland Chap. of the Natl. Women's Christian Temperance Union. She served as treasurer of the national union from 1874–75. She helped to establish reading rooms and Friendly Inns, one of which, the Pearl St. Inn, she headed for 7 years. Later Ingham turned her interests toward the arts. In Oct. 1882, she cofounded the Cleveland School of Art (later known as the CLEVELAND INSTITUTE OF ART). She served as secretary of the board of directors from 1884–94. Ingham combined her familial background with journalism by contributing to numerous church publications in Cleveland. She also wrote a 3-year series, using the pen name Anne Hathaway, on notable Cleveland women for the CLEVELAND LEADER. Other significant works included the book Notable Cleveland Women, a story entitled "Something to Come Home to," and a stage production, "Flag Festival, a Four Hundredth Anniversary Program," celebrating Columbus's founding of America and the fashioning of the flag. She married Wm. A. Ingham, a publisher and bookseller, in 1866. After her husband's death in 1898, Ingham moved to Los Angeles in 1908 and remained active in religious and missionary work until her death at age 91.

The **INNERBELT FREEWAY** was conceived by city planners in 1940 as a key to moving traffic around, rather than through, the downtown area. It was to be the largest road-building project in the city's history. Actual planning work for the Innerbelt Freeway began in 1944. The freeway was designed to connect the Shoreway, which ran along the lakefront, with the WILLOW FREEWAY, which ran due south from Broadway Ave., and also to link up with a new Medina Freeway to extend out to Cleveland Hopkins Airport. The basic route was from the E. 30th St.-Shoreway

area to Abbey Ave. and W. 14th St. on the near west side. A planning office was established in 1948, and first approval of the specific routing was granted in 1949. A total of 1,250 parcels of land had to be purchased for the highway's right-of-way. Land costs eventually totaled $22.5 million. When construction costs were added to land acquisition, it was estimated that the 3.24-mi. Innerbelt would cost taxpayers $75 million. Funding for the construction was 90% federal money, with 5% shares from the city and the state.

Construction on the project began 12 Dec. 1954, following groundbreaking ceremonies by Gov. Frank J. Lausche and Mayor Anthony J. Celebrezze. The first work centered on a new 8-lane bridge across the CUYAHOGA RIVER, located just south of the Lorain-Carnegie Bridge. The 4,233' span was the widest bridge built in the state, and it alone cost $26,066,000. It was also the first segment of the freeway to be opened; the first traffic was admitted on 18 Aug. 1959. The second segment to be opened , on 17 Dec. 1959, was from the Shoreway south to Chester Ave. near E. 24th St. The central portion, connecting these outer edges, did not open until 5 Dec. 1961, its progress having been slowed by the complicated land-acquisition efforts. More months were needed to open all 37 ramps that fed traffic onto and off of the freeway. The last of these was opened on 1 Aug. 1962. One part of the Innerbelt failed to live up to expectations. The curve bringing traffic to and from the Shoreway was soon discovered to be a major accident area. In 1969, the curve was rebuilt to change the degree of its bank, but despite the reconstruction, signs, flashing lights, and rumble strips, it continued to pose problems for vehicles which do not take seriously its 35 mph restriction. The Innerbelt Freeway took some 50,000 vehicles off the downtown streets and sped traffic around the downtown area. It became, in time, the vital connecting link with the area's 3 interstate highways, I-77, I-71, and I-90.

The **INSURANCE BOARD OF CLEVELAND** was founded in 1846 by Joseph C. Weatherly as the Cleveland Board of Underwriters to regulate the fledgling insurance industry. It also laid the groundwork for the Ohio Dept. of Insurance. Weatherly, who sold insurance for the North Western and Pelican Mutual companies, was the superintendent of the CLEVELAND FIRE DEPT., and founded the Board of Trade (see GREATER CLEVELAND GROWTH ASSOC.), met with 8 other agents who served Cleveland's 10,000 people. At a time when a company's agent quoted premiums based on his inspection of the company and then, according to one observer, hoped that a disaster did not "wipe out the company before collecting his commission," both the company and the public were dependent on the agent's integrity. The board recognized that the growth of the industry was based on public confidence in company agents. They met at Weatherly's office at Commercial and Exchange streets to regulate insurance agents and prices. Their first official task was to draft a standard list of fire insurance rates for dwellings, businesses, and factories; the rates for all Cleveland businesses could at that time be listed on an 8"x 14" sheet of paper.

The other purposes of the board were to interpret the fire insurance needs of the public to member companies; to safeguard the interests of policyholders; to generally improve the insurance business; and to promote fire prevention and other civic activities. Over the years, the board became a full-service organization, equipped to offer the public advice on all facets of auto, home, business, and general insurance. To prevent abuses, the board imposed strict standards on its members, which led to the levying of antitrust charges by the U.S. Dept. of Justice in 1951. The government claimed that the board practice of accepting as members only those agents of companies that wrote policies exclusively through board members amounted to restraint of trade and a monopoly over the fire insurance business in the county, as 85% of the insurance written was generated by the board's 175 member agents. Despite the board's assertion that it fostered competition through the system of agent-entrepreneurs, the government maintained that the board had a lock on the insurance business in Cuyahoga County. In 1956, U.S. District Judge Chas. McNama ruled that the Insurance Board in fact violated antitrust laws and harmed the public good by effectively boycotting agents who sold directly to the company. This ruling, observed by the insurance boards in other cities, opened up new marketing techniques in the insurance field at a time when the product lines were rapidly expanding. The board, whose membership now represented a small percentage of the insurance community, was still regarded as an influential spokesman on insurance issues. For this reason, the Cleveland community looked to the board for leadership in solving the insurance crisis of the mid-1960s and early 1970s: cancellation of insurance in inner-city areas and redlining.

At this time, home and business owners on Cleveland's east side complained that policies were being canceled, not renewed, or were being offered for renewal at extremely high rates. In response to criticism by housing and consumer groups, the board called for a study to document the complaints of cancellation but blamed the rates on the city's failure to maintain housing codes. The study concluded that most companies were trying to balance their sense of social responsibility with the economic realities of providing insurance in a decaying area where there was a high rate of code violations, vandalism, vacancy, and arson. Detractors condemned the study as a "whitewash" and claimed that especially after the HOUGH RIOTS of 1966–67, insurance companies made underwriting decisions based on race or perceived group characteristics of a postal zone. The board then called for a risk pool for Cuyahoga County, an idea that materialized, in broader terms, as the Fair Access to Insurance Requirements (FAIR) plan of 1968. Under FAIR, which was backed by the government as a provision of the Federal Housing Act of 1968, residents of high-risk areas were guaranteed the availability of insurance at rates in line with the condition of their property. This voluntary program was made mandatory by Gov. Jas. Rhodes in 1969 so that all companies writing insurance in an area were obliged to share the risk and administrative expense. In 1985, the Insurance Board continued its operations from offices in the STATLER TOWER.

The **INTERCHURCH COUNCIL OF GREATER CLEVELAND,** known as the Cleveland Church Fed. for most of its history, became a forum for ecumenical commitment in faith, service, and ministry in the early 1900s. It was a shared ministry of 780 local congregations, 12 denominations, and 5 interchurch agencies. The Interchurch Council was officially created on 11 June 1911 at FIRST PRESBYTERIAN (OLD STONE) CHURCH as the Federated Churches of Greater Cleveland. Leaders in its creation were Dean FRANK DUMOULIN, Dr. Thos. S. McWilliams, and Rev. Worth M. Tippy. The council's purpose was to safeguard all phases of church work—secular and religious activities, education, social welfare, and civic betterment, touching upon marriage and the home, industry, motion pictures, and social hygiene; phases of women's work, TEMPERANCE, world friendship, drama, and MUSIC. Sixty-seven churches initially sought to present a unified front on these common problems without conflicting with the creeds of the different denominations. Rev. Frank

DuMoulin served as the council's first president; Rev. Tippy as vice-president; Chas. E. Adams as treasurer; and Rev. N. M. Pratt as secretary.

The council encouraged Christian fellowship through 4 auxiliary organizations: the Ministerial Assoc. of Greater Cleveland, the Cleveland Council of Federated Church Women, the Cuyahoga County Youth Council, and the Churchmen's League. Its sources of revenue were churches and denominations, individuals and businesses, foundations, government, fees, and investments. The council became an all-Protestant church organization when it ended its affiliation with the Eastern Orthodox churches in 1975. Its name was changed in 1985 to the Interchurch Council of Greater Cleveland. Its president at that time was Rev. Harry V. Nevels, Jr., and the executive director was Rev. Thos. W. Olcott. Though the council continued to encourage interfaith and ecumenical dialogue, it began to place heavy emphasis on human needs. It became an advocate for the poor and undereducated through such programs as the Hunger Task Force. The 21 Hunger Centers, which supplied a 3-day ration of canned and dry food once every 2 months to families in need, was implemented in 1973. Project Learn, a volunteer tutor program, begun in 1974, was another major activity sponsored by the council. The Interchurch Council of Churches also promoted interracial understanding and advocated minority, peace, and justice issues. It was put in the forefront of the fight against apartheid with the development of the South Africa Coalition in 1983. Through the years, the council's focus remained on those people who shared hope, energy, and commitment so the Christian faith could be celebrated through effective cooperative ministry.

Cleveland Area Church Fed. Records, WRHS.

The **INTERNATIONAL ASSOCIATION OF MACHINISTS AND AEROSPACE WORKERS** began in 1888 in Atlanta, Ga., and was established in Cleveland in 1890. For nearly 100 years, it has served the needs of its members in the tool-and-die, machine-shop, service, and, more recently, aerospace industries, and has maintained a reputation as one of the most progressive unions in the labor community. Lodge 83, the first in Cleveland, organized machinists who worked in shops owned by Cleveland employers connected with the Natl. Metal Trades Assoc. At the time, machinists were versed in all shop operations and knew the owners personally. Though highly valued, machinists who joined unions were fired and blackballed among employers around the country, largely owing to information obtained by the Natl. Mfrs. Assoc. spies. Despite the risks, a small group of men met at Bland & Haler's Hall at Huron and Ontario and were chartered in Jan. 1890. A handful of other lodges were organized by 1896.

Following the lead of the national organization, which affiliated with the American Fed. of Labor in 1892, the local lodges affiliated with the Central Labor Union (later the CLEVELAND FED. OF LABOR). Clevelanders joined with other members of the "fighting machinists" in a general strike in 1901 for the 9-hour day. Its membership grew steadily, peaking after WORLD WAR I as a result of the growth in the machinery field created by the war. The union confronted the low wages ($.25 per hour for production workers) with strikes, unified under the slogan "A cent a minute, 8 hours a day." During the war, when no strikes were permitted, the group won raises for its members by systematically shifting them from one plant to another. Thereafter, the NMA attacked the labor movement by strengthening the blackball system and promoting the open shop, but Cleveland locals, organized into District 54 since

1913, fought back by regrouping for strength. In 1919, Lodge 83 and 4 others joined together to become Lodge 439, while Lodge 1363 was chartered as an Auto Mechanics Lodge; these 2 bodies supported the district in lean times. When the NRA was passed as part of the New Deal in 1933, District 54 was ready to organize. Between 1933–40, nearly a dozen new lodges were chartered. Some were composed entirely of workers at one plant (1108—Chase Brass & Copper, 1253—Warner & Swasey, 1228—Addressograph-Multigraph), while others cut across company lines to unite men employed in a particular industry (metal stamping) or job classification (tool-and-die makers). By 1934, more than 6,500 members were on the rolls, but many of the new lodges were unstable and collapsed in the face of employer opposition.

District finances faltered in 1938, when hundreds of machinists were out of work; revenues proved insufficient to support a staff of 5 and a series of strikes. Grand Lodge representative John J. Murphy was called in to aid the district by drafting new bylaws and revamping its financial base. In Oct. 1938, MATTHEW DEMORE led a reform slate of candidates pledged to streamline district affairs. Through his leadership and the success of a newly formed organizing committee, membership grew from 4,500 in 1939 to 15,000 by 1941. The IAM also entered into a closer relationship with the CFL, which provided assistance when needed. Over the years, the membership of the IAM changed with the declining fortunes of the machine-tool industry and the rising prominence of the aerospace industry. This change was reflected in the name, expanded to include these workers after 1966. Locally, lodges were gutted by the mergers, plant closings, and workforce reductions of major corporations such as WARNER & SWASEY, Chase Brass, and Addressograph. As of 1961, membership stood at about 19,000, as compared to 12,000 in 1986. While actively pursuing wages, benefits, and job stability for its members, the IAM has traditionally supported progressive social and political causes. That continues to be true under the national leadership of former Clevelander Wm. Winpisinger. In the 1980s, the union challenged military buildup on the grounds that dollars spent for defense did not create as many jobs as dollars spent for social ends. The machinists also criticized plant closings and robotics, while encouraging job retraining and commitment to workers.

The **INTERNATIONAL LADIES GARMENT WORKERS UNION** struggled to gain a foothold in Cleveland during the first 2 decades of the 20th century. Its early history was marked by sharp declines and rises in membership and several unsuccessful strikes. It did not fully establish unionism in the Cleveland garment trades until the Agreement of 1918–19. Toward the end of the 19th century, poor working conditions and low wages caused some workers to form small seasonal unions, and in 1899 the Cleveland Pressers' Protective Union was formed. But union organization did not increase until 1900, when the ILGWU was established in New York City. Shortly thereafter, several well-organized affiliates were created in Cleveland: the Cloak Cutters' Assoc.—Local 10, the Cloak Makers' Union—Local 13, the Cloak Pressers' Union—Local 14, the Ladies' Garment Workers' Union—Local 14, and the Ladies' Garment Cutters' Union—Local 48. In Aug. 1904, the Cleveland garment trade experienced its first major strike when the firm of PRINTZ-BIEDERMAN refused to renew its union agreement. Locals 13 and 14 called a general strike, against the wishes of the international. The strike ended in failure and disruption of the unions. Six years later, in an effort to organize strong unions outside New York, the international chose first to organize in Cleveland,

since Cleveland was second only to New York City in the cloak-and-suit trade and had a growing market. With 33 firms and 5,000 dissatisfied workers, Cleveland was ready for a strike (see GARMENT WORKERS STRIKE, 1911). In Apr. 1911, the General Executive Board met in Cleveland, where committees from Cleveland locals submitted lists of demands for employers, which the board sent to each employer on 3 June. On 6 June, a general strike was called, with the majority of workers turning out. The strike endured throughout the summer, but manufacturers were able to fill orders and opened shops in other Ohio communities. The length of the strike made it more and more difficult for the international to meet strike expenses; therefore, on 14–15 Oct. a special convention of the international was held in New York to assess the situation. Because of the financial difficulties, the strike was called off. From that time until 1918, the union could make no headway against the Cleveland Garment Mfrs. Assoc., and no local unions of any size or importance were established.

However, in 1918–19, one of the most important advances of the international was made in Cleveland. After campaigning to increase union membership in Cleveland, the international called a general strike on 23 July 1918. After 4 weeks of unsuccessful attempts to negotiate with employers, Secretary of War NEWTON D. BAKER established a board of referees to review the situation and prepare a settlement. The agreement that was finally accepted, in 1919, established a new relationship between workers and employers in the Cleveland garment trade and, after years of struggle, established collective bargaining in Cleveland. In the succeeding years, the decline in manufacturing in the garment trade in Cleveland contributed to the decline in union membership. In 1986, the Cleveland branch of the ILGWU counted approximately 1,200 members and 7 union affiliates.

The **INTERNATIONAL MANAGEMENT GROUP** began in 1960 when Cleveland lawyer and amateur golfer Mark H. McCormack became the agent representing professional golfer Arnold Palmer in his business and promotional affairs. By 1985, the pioneer firm in promoting athletes and sporting events had more than 500 clients, 400 employees, 13 divisions with offices in 15 countries, and annual revenues of $300 million. McCormack, the son of a prosperous Chicago publishing executive and an avid sports fan, was the star of the College of William & Mary's golf teams. It was at college tournaments that he first met Arnold Palmer. After attending Yale Law School and serving in the Army, McCormack joined the Cleveland firm of ARTER & HADDEN and continued to play golf, qualifying for the 1958 U.S. Open and playing in other amateur tournaments. He became friends with professional golfers and renewed his acquaintance with Palmer, becoming his agent in 1960. With McCormack as his agent, working to arrange product endorsements, Palmer saw his income increase from $59,000 in 1959 to nearly $500,000 in 1962. He also became one of the first athletes to appear in a television commercial, a cigarette ad in 1961. McCormack then became the agent for golfers Gary Player and Jack Nicklaus; by 1967 he had left Arter & Hadden to operate his sports-promotion agency from offices at One Erieview Plaza. McCormack and IMG were credited with being pioneers in the development of the modern sports agent, although McCormack felt he was not an agent but "an engineer of careers." He was the first to establish foreign offices and to sell the services of American athletes in Europe and Japan. By 1975, IMG no longer promoted only individual athletes but had also begun to arrange and promote sports events for other organizations.

In the next decade, IMG's number of clients, its revenues, and its range of activities grew dramatically. In addition to managing careers, IMG began to create and produce sports events for television, to offer investment advice to business executives, to publish, and to operate a Swedish amusement park. It also served as the business agent for the Wimbledon tennis tournament; for the London Symphony Orchestra; and for Pope John Paul II's 1982 tour of Great Britain, licensing the souvenirs sold during the visit and collecting royalties from their sale for the Catholic church. IMG brought several events to the Greater Cleveland area, including the World Series of Women's Golf tournament at the COUNTRY CLUB in 1980 and the the World's Championship of Women's Golf at the SHAKER HTS. COUNTRY CLUB in 1981. In 1981, the agency moved its headquarters from One Erieview Plaza to the Cuyahoga Savings Bldg. By 1985, Mark McCormack's Internatl. Management Group was considered the dominant force in the management and promotion of tennis and golf athletes and tournaments. It was also gaining strength in running and in the traditional American team sports: FOOTBALL, BASKETBALL, and BASEBALL. It charged 25% of an athlete's income to take care of his or her finances, make investments, secure endorsements, pay bills, and prepare taxes.

The **INTERNATIONAL SALT COMPANY,** with headquarters in Clarks Summit, Pa., is the largest salt producer in the U.S. and the only exporter of raw materials in Cleveland. The company began production in Cleveland in 1962. Located on WHISKEY ISLAND, it mines salt beneath Lake Erie in one section of a tremendous salt deposit extending over an estimated 70,000-sq.-mi. area under Michigan, New York, Pennsylvania, Ohio, West Virginia, and Ontario. The bed of salt beneath Lake Erie, of the Silurian Period, is more than 10' thick. Internatl. Salt conducted exploratory digging at 6 sites on Cleveland's lakefront in 1956. The following year, the company purchased 15 acres of land from the Pennsylvania Railroad and mining rights from the New York Central Railroad on adjacent property, which provided access to Lake Erie. The state of Ohio granted Internatl. Salt a 50-year lease to mine some 5,000 acres beneath the lake in return for payment of $.05 per ton of all salt mined. Construction of the mine began in 1958. It involved sinking a pair of 15-sq.-ft. shafts (one a service shaft, the other for hoisting the salt) 1,800' deep and tunneling out from their bottoms to reach the salt deposits. The company also constructed facilities for crushing, screening, handling, and shipping the salt. Construction of the mine was a joint project of the Frazier-Davis and HUNKIN-CONKEY construction companies.

Internatl. Salt uses the room-and-pillar mining method: 40-ft.-wide rooms are carved from the deposit, and 80' pillars of salt are left to hold up the mine roof and overburden. In 1985, the firm employed 255 persons (200 of these hourly workers) and had an annual output of 2.5 million tons. Products included rock salt in bags and bulk for highway, commercial, and industrial use, and farm products. Shipments are made by truck, rail car, or boat. A refinery built in 1966 to produce a high-purity evaporated salt used by the chemical industry proved unprofitable and was closed in 1974. By 1985, Internatl. Salt had mined 800 square acres, and its mine extended 1.5 mi. out under Lake Erie. Internatl. Salt had its origins in a mine established in 1884 at Retsof, N.Y. The company owns and operates mines at Retsof, Cleveland, and Avery Island, La.; a salt-evaporating plant at Watkins Glen, N.Y.; and a solar-process facility on Bonaire Island, in the Netherlands Antilles off the coast of Venezuela. The market area for products from its Cleveland mine is the eastern U.S. Since 1970, Internatl. Salt has been a division of Akzona, Inc., Asheville, N.C.

**INTERNATIONAL WOMEN'S YEAR, GREATER CLEVELAND CONGRESS,** was held 25–27 Oct. 1975 at the Convention Ctr. and attracted 45,000–50,000 people. The congress was organized in response to the United Nations General Assembly proclamation that designated 1975 as Internatl. Women's Year with the theme of "Equality, Development, Peace," and the Greater Cleveland Congress was hailed by its organizers as "the largest and most significant observance" of the year "in the United States and, in fact, the world." Planning for the local congress was initiated in 1974 by Evelyn Bonder, director of PROJECT EVE at CUYAHOGA COMMUNITY COLLEGE; chairperson was Gwill York, vice-chairman of the distribution committee of the CLEVELAND FOUNDATION, a major sponsor of the congress. Other contributors included the GEO. GUND FOUNDATION, the JR. LEAGUE, local industry, and individuals.

The free 3-day event included 150 workshops on such topics as women as consumers, women in unions, women as peacemakers, ethnicity, abortion, and rape. There were also 250 exhibition booths and addresses by First Lady Betty Ford and Jill Ruckelshaus, chairperson of the Natl. Commission on the Observance of Internatl. Women's Year. Organizers of the congress designed the event to be "apolitical, multi-racial and ecumenical"; after the congress, more political feminists attacked its apolitical nature in the local feminist newspaper *What She Wants,* and Marge Grevatt called it "Feminism for Sale" in an article in Roldo Bartimole's *POINT OF VIEW.* The congress produced a number of resources for local Cleveland women: a directory of existing social-service agencies serving local women, the *Women's Resource Directory;* a registry of women's organizations; and, most important, the women's center WOMENSPACE, which was developed during the planning stages of the congress and opened on 18 Mar. 1976. There was also a follow-up conference to the congress, "The Next Step," which attracted about 500 participants to 12 workshops and 2 addresses on 19 Apr. 1976 on the 10th floor of Higbee's.

**INTERURBANS.** Early in the 20th century, Ohio became the heartland of the electric interurban railway, and Cleveland emerged as one of its foremost centers. While the state's interurban network of 2,798 mi. knew no geographic bounds, the most heavily served areas skirted the shores of Lake Erie and followed the route of the old Miami Canal between Toledo and Cincinnati. The interurban was ideally suited for much of Ohio. The state's large number of relatively closely spaced cities and towns, its gentle landscape, and its well-developed, urban-oriented agriculture contributed to the growth of some of America's pioneer companies. Residents of Cleveland were riding electric intercity cars almost as soon as they appeared. In 1895, local promoters Henry A. Everett and Edward W. Moore, kingpins of the so-called Everett-Moore Syndicate, opened the 35.5-mi. Akron, Bedford & Cleveland Railroad Co., the "Alphabet Route," between the communities of its corporate name. The AB&C (later the expanded Northern Ohio Traction & Light Co.) prospered; the road did much to spawn interurban fever in the region, and, for that matter, in the nation as well. Indeed, its backers were so pleased that they launched several other interurban projects in Greater Cleveland. Electric interurbans developed quickly. By 1910, Cleveland boasted 6 separate systems. To the east there was the consolidated CLEVELAND, PAINESVILLE & EASTERN RAILROAD and the CLEVELAND,

PAINESVILLE & ASHTABULA RAILROAD, another Everett-Moore property. This 85-mi. network with its headquarters in Willoughby consisted of 3 parts: the 58-mi. main line from Cleveland to Painesville; the parallel "Shore Line Div." between Cleveland and Willoughbeach; and the 6-mi. "Fairport Div.," a branch that connected Painesville with Fairport. The CP&E-CP&A also provided a direct link between Ohio's interurbans and those of New York and New England. It connected at Ashtabula with the Pennsylvania & Ohio Railroad, which in turn met the Cleveland & Erie Railway at Conneaut, and that carrier interchanged at Erie, Pa., with the Buffalo & Lake Erie Traction Co. for various eastern points.

The Eastern Ohio Traction Co. (later reorganized as the Cleveland & Eastern Traction Co.) was another interurban that penetrated the countryside east of Cleveland. Its 33-mi. main line crossed the sparsely settled and at times hilly terrain between Cleveland and Chardon, a region with poor steam railroad service. The company also operated a 14-mi. appendage from "C&E Junction" (near Fullerton) southeast to Middlefield. Separate from the Eastern Ohio Traction Co., although operated jointly with it, was the Cleveland, Youngstown & Eastern Railway. Prior to 1910, however, this firm had been officially part of the Eastern Ohio, and for a decade the public commonly referred to it as the "Chagrin Falls & Garrettsville Branch." This 42-mi. interurban never reached Youngstown (although it had such plans), but it tied Cleveland with Garrettsville via Warrensville, CHAGRIN FALLS, and Hiram. To the south of Cleveland, the Northern Ohio Traction & Light Co. (originally the Akron, Bedford & Cleveland) provided extensive service. The original Cleveland-to-Akron stem soon grew into a nearly 150-mi. system. By 1910, lines ran from Akron through Canton and Massillon to Uhrichsville (projected to Wheeling, W.Va.), from Silver Lake Junction to Ravenna, from Akron to Wadsworth (projected to Seville and a connection with the Cleveland, Southwestern & Columbus), and from Massillon to E. Greenville (projected to Wooster). The NOT&L also provided Clevelanders with a connection with the Stark Electric Railway at Canton, a road that ran easterly to Alliance, Sebring, and Salem. And after Jan. 1913, Clevelanders could use the NOT&L to Ravenna for a more direct trip to Alliance via the newly opened Cleveland, Alliance & Mahoning Valley Railway, a company that by 1915 also reached Newton Falls and Warren.

Clevelanders enjoyed additional access to areas to the south, and they had a direct link to the southwest. The mighty CLEVELAND, SOUTHWESTERN & COLUMBUS RAILWAY provided these connections. Developed by F. J. Pomeroy and MAURICE J. MANDELBAUM, promoters similar in stature to Everett and Moore, the nearly 250-mi. CSW&C by 1910 consisted of 2 major units, the "Southern Div." and the "Western Div." The former ran from Cleveland through BEREA, STRONGSVILLE, Brunswick, and Medina to Seville. From this junction, a branch extended directly to Wooster, and the main line veered southwesterly through Lodi, Schland, and Mansfield to Bucyrus and an interchange with the Columbus, Marion & Bucyrus Railroad and the Columbus, Delaware & Marion Railway for Columbus. The Southern Div. also consisted of the Puritas branch, a 5-mi. line that linked the Lorain St. station in Cleveland with Puritas Springs. The CSW&C sported a close relationship with the 12-mi. Mansfield & Shelby Inter-Urban Railway, an interurban that tied the 2 communities of its corporate name. The Western Div. of the Cleveland, Southwestern & Columbus was not as large as the Southern, yet it served several sizable towns. Its principal route stretched from PUBLIC SQUARE for

42 mi. to Wellington, and passed through N. OLMSTED, Elyria, and Oberlin. A 25-mi. branch linked Oberlin with Berlin Hts. and Norwalk, and small appendages left Elyria north to Lorain and south to Grafton. The Western Div. even claimed a "twig," that is, a branch of a branch. For at Penfield Jct. on the Lorain branch, the company operated a short extension west to Amherst.

The LAKE SHORE ELECTRIC, one of America's premier interurbans, provided Clevelanders with direct access to Toledo and convenient connections with various midwestern electric roads, as well as another route to Norwalk. Organized by the Everett-Moore Syndicate in 1901 out of several small predecessor firms, the LSE ran 120 mi. from Cleveland through ROCKY RIVER, Lorain, Vermilion, Huron, Sandusky, and Fremont to Toledo. The company likewise operated a 42-mi. parallel route that left Ceylon Jct., 45 mi. west of Cleveland, for Berlin Hts., Norwalk, Bellevue, and Clyde and rejoined the northern artery at Fremont. The Lake Shore Electric's map also included the 18-mi. Norwalk-to-Sandusky branch and the 3.5-mi. Gibsonburg Jct.-to-Gibsonburg spur. Unlike the other Cleveland interurbans (with the exception of portions of the NOT&L), the LSE's core physically resembled its steam-road competitors. Yet the LSE faced considerable "street running," tracks in or along public roadways rather than on private rights-of-way. Still, the often direct approach to cities and towns proved to be one of the attractive features of this transportation form.

Cleveland's extensive interurban network seemed nearly universally popular, at least prior to WORLD WAR I. This enthusiasm was understandable. Unquestionably, these electric carriers offered the public clean and convenient service. Unlike the steam railroad, the electric car boasted "no cinders, no dirt, no dust, no smoke." Electric roads could be operated with greater frequency than steam ones, since interurbans enjoyed dramatically lower operating costs. Most interurbans ran on hourly or semihourly schedules and stopped (except for "limiteds") virtually anywhere, while steam trains commonly made only a few daily trips, pausing at only a few points. There also existed the attraction of cheaper rates. Typical charges for interurban travel in the Greater Cleveland area were substantially less than those of steam lines. In 1907, for example, the New York Central priced a 1-way ticket from Cleveland to Toledo at $3.25; the Lake Shore Electric, on the other hand, offered rides between these two cities for only $1.75.

There were additional attractions, particularly for those individuals who were drawn to electric interurbans as a business venture. An electric line could penetrate an area with inadequate or no railroad service (Medina County is a leading example), mainly because of lower overall construction costs. Most interurbans did not embrace the high construction standards of the steam roads. With the advent of traction routes, real-estate prices nearly always rose, often in a dramatic fashion, and at times to the personal benefit of these backers. Since all of Cleveland's roads furnished extensive package and express service, and several more moved carload freight (the NOT&L, CSW&C, and LSE led in this field), patrons could compete more successfully in the marketplace. Their dependence upon buggies or wagons traveling over primitive roads repeatedly made impassable by the vagaries of weather, had hindered full development of commercial activities, especially agriculture. The interurban effectively shattered the isolation for rider and shipper alike. A Seville resident, who knew well the CSW&C, explained this point nicely in 1913: "Shoppers can take advantage of Cleveland sales; farmers can expect their produce to arrive in city markets in good condition; and everybody can enjoy an outing to a motion-picture show." This individual might have noted, too, that a plethora of city goods flowed into the neighboring environs. They ranged from hardware to drugs. Wholesalers, of course, were found in Cleveland, and not the Sevilles of northeast Ohio.

Not all area residents applauded the coming of the interurban. In 1897, for example, Oberlin merchants distributed a handbill with the scare headline, "RUIN! Follows in the Wake of the Electric Railroads!" Included in the provocative copy were these statements: " *Elyria* has Three Steam Railways and Two Electric Roads. Result, Six Big Business Failures recently and Five of them within Three Days. *Oberlin* has one Steam Railway and no Electric Road. Result, One Small Failure in Twenty-five Years." The logic expressed was that railroads, especially electric ones, allowed residents to shop conveniently in other market towns, Cleveland in particular. That was true, for the interurban liberated the consumer. Naturally, Cleveland businessmen sensed how they might tap the hinterlands. Dry-goods merchants, for one, commonly paid the car fare if a patron bought a suit of clothes or made a similar purchase. Unquestionably, the region's interurbans aided Cleveland storekeepers more than they did those in surrounding places. Then, as the automobile and to a lesser degree the motor bus siphoned off riders, the principal source of revenue to the interurban, increased opposition to Cleveland's electric railroads materialized. Residents objected to excessive "street running" of passenger cars, and disliked even more the growing practice of freight trains operating through the ever-increasing congestion on area roads. In the public's mind, trucks, which could either skirt main avenues or maneuver more easily through traffic, appeared to be a better transportation alternative. Furthermore, repeated track repairs on streets sparked considerable disgust. By the late 1920s, rubber-tired competition largely explains why Cleveland-area interurbans had either died or were ailing badly. Already the weakest ones had folded: the East Ohio Traction Co. and the Cleveland, Youngstown & Eastern abandoned their operations in 1925, and the Cleveland, Painesville & Eastern quit a year later. But the devastating impact of the hard times that followed the stock market crash of 1929 killed the remaining 3 companies: the Cleveland, Southwestern Railway & Light Co. (formerly the CSW&C) closed in 1931; the NOT&L folded in 1932; and the Lake Shore Electric limped along until 1938.

Cleveland's 3 most robust interurbans (the last to be abandoned) responded to the challenges of the post-World War I era with considerable imagination. Both the NOT&L and the CSW&C bought better passenger equipment. The former acquired 30 attractive steel cars from the Cleveland-based G. C. Kuhlman Car Co. in 1920–21, and the latter purchased 6 steel Kuhlman-built cars in 1919 and a dozen lightweight ones from the Cincinnati Car Co. in 1924. The LSE together with the NOT&L pushed successfully for the development of a standard boxcar for interurban freight service, and by 1926 both roads operated this state-of-the-art rolling stock. Then in 1928, the NOT&L and LSE, joined by the neighboring Penn-Ohio Public Service (the former Mahoning & Shenango Railway & Light Co.), formed a joint venture known as the Electric Railways Freight Co. to operate a coordinated package and carload freight business. The firm provided joint billing, solicitation, and freight handling, but left car operations to the individual roads. And in a widely publicized burst of creativity, the LSE pioneered a form of modern intermodel service during the late 1920s. Called a "Banner Railwagon," this LSE creation consisted of a specially designed flatcar with inside-bearing trucks that rolled under 18-ft. motor-truck trailers. Innovation from even the spunkiest Cleve-

land interurban could not save this industry locally. Depressed times and keen competition led to the junking of the physical property and the sale, when possible, of rolling stock and other equipment to an admittedly limited used market. Those companies, such as the NOT&L, that produced excess electric power either moved exclusively into that economically viable field or profitably sold off these operations. After 1932, the Lake Shore Electric alone continued to place Cleveland on the region's rapidly shrinking interurban map. On 14 May 1938, the last car left Public Square for Toledo; only the CLEVELAND UNION TERMINAL, the Shaker Rapid, and the city surface lines still used electric traction. Then 10 years after the LSE stopped, Ohio's last interurban, the Youngstown & Southern, abandoned its electric operations. What was once viewed as the wave of the future in intercity transportation had collapsed totally; the state's interurban era had ended officially.

H. Roger Grant
University of Akron

Christiansen, Harry, *Northern Ohio's Interurbans and Rapid Transit Railways* (1965).

Hilton, George W., and John F. Due, *The Electric Interurban Railways* (1960).

The **INTOWN CLUB,** 1375 Euclid Ave., a private invitational ladies' luncheon club that meets for relaxation, fellowship, and enjoyment of the arts, was incorporated on 1 Nov. 1927. The club officially opened on 20 Jan. 1928 in clubrooms located at 3400 Euclid Ave. Mrs. John S. Sherwin was the first president. On 12 June 1934, the club moved to the 6th floor of the present Stouffer Bldg. (then the Kinney & Levan Bldg.) at PLAYHOUSE SQUARE, its present location. Through the years, the Intown Club has been the scene of a variety of activities, including musicals, traditional tea dances, wedding receptions, special luncheons and dinners, and private parties for family members and guests. Numerous speakers of social, political, literary, musical, and theatrical fame have presented programs for its members. The club's art gallery has displayed works by many artists and craftsmen, including those of Clevelanders and club members.

**IRELAND, JOSEPH,** was a New York architect who came to Cleveland and practiced between 1865–85, then returned to New York. Trained in the design of institutional buildings, Ireland was also a specialist in fireproof construction, a goal that engaged many architects in the post-Civil War period. His first Cleveland building was the Society for Savings on PUBLIC SQUARE (1867), later the home of the WESTERN RESERVE HISTORICAL SOCIETY. He also designed the Natl. Bank Bldg. on Superior Ave. at W. 9th St. in 1867. Its trustees, JOSEPH PERKINS, AMASA STONE, and Daniel Eells, were all instrumental in securing commissions for Ireland. In 1869, Ireland designed the Geauga County Courthouse in Chardon to replace the one destroyed by fire the year before. In 1870 he planned the home of Henry B. Perkins in Warren, which is still in use as the city hall. His Cleveland buildings included the Retreat, a women's institution donated by Joseph Perkins (1872); the Home for Aged Gentlewomen, built for Amasa Stone (1876); Daniel Eells's home on Euclid Ave. (1876); the Second Presbyterian Church on Prospect Ave. at E. 30th St. (1878); and Adelbert College of Western Reserve University (1882), also built for Amasa Stone. Only the Geauga County Courthouse, the H. B. Perkins home, and Adelbert Hall remained standing in the 1980s. Ireland worked in various phases of the Victorian Italianate and Eastlake styles, but his principal contribution was the introduction and development of fireproof construction in northeastern Ohio.

**IRELAND, THOMAS SEXTON, JR.** (16 Dec. 1895–26 Mar. 1969), was a Cleveland politician and writer known for his wide-ranging interests and colorful public image. Ireland was born in Cleveland's east end, the son of a manager of the GRASSELLI CHEMICAL CO. He attended Princeton and Harvard and graduated from Harvard Law School in 1927. He practiced law in New York for a time, returning to Cleveland later in 1927 after passing the Ohio bar. Following service in the Army, he began a weekly column for the Cleveland Italian newspaper *Corriere di Ohio*. He worked for a time as a laborer at the Republic Steel Corp. and became an active member of the Bridge, Structural, & Iron Workers Local 468, a membership he maintained throughout his life. By the 1930s he was a municipal court judge, and in the mid-1930s he ran unsuccessfully for the Ohio general assembly. He became a correspondent for the Cleveland *PLAIN DEALER* in 1948 and also wrote for papers in Columbus and the Pacific Northwest.

In 1959, Ireland ran for mayor of Cleveland in one of the most flamboyant political campaigns ever held in the city. One of his great campaign issues was the transit system's inadequacies, and he garnered tremendous publicity by personally chartering transit buses and providing service to underserved areas at off-peak times. Despite his flair for public relations, he lost the election. Ireland was widely read and an authority on many topics. He wrote books on the St. Lawrence Seaway (1934), the politics of the Far East (*War Clouds in the Skies of the Far East*, 1935), Ireland (*Ireland, Past and Present*, 1942), and industrial relations (*Child Labor as a Relic of the Dark Ages*, 1937). Ireland was married to Mildred Locke. They had 6 children: Patricia, Ruth, Thos. S. III, William, John, and Fred.

Thomas S. Ireland Papers, WRHS.

The **IRELAND FOUNDATION** was founded in 1951 by Margaret Allen Ireland (1894–1961). Ireland was the Ohio state director of public welfare under Gov. C. Wm. O'Neill, and in 1959 she became president of the NORTHERN OHIO OPERA ASSOC. She was born in Chicago in 1894, was raised in New York, and married R. Livingston Ireland in 1918. She became active in Cleveland's health-reform organizations, including the VISITING NURSE ASSOC., the Maternal Health Assoc., and the United Appeal, with particular interest in the aged and chronically ill. She was an alternate delegate to the Republican conventions of 1952 and 1956 and a recipient of the Chas. Eisenman Award for community service in 1954. R. Livingston Ireland, Jr. (1895–1981), was born in Cleveland. He studied mining engineering at Yale, then joined the Navy Flying Corps in WORLD WAR I. After the war he went to work for a subsidiary of the Hanna Co. in New York, and in 1920 he returned to Cleveland as assistant to the general manager of the Hanna Coal Co. He became manager in 1929 and president in 1931. When Hanna Coal was acquired by the Pittsburgh Consolidation Coal Co. in 1946, Ireland became chairman of the executive committee of Pittsburgh Consolidation, where he remained until 1962, when he was appointed vice-chairman of the Consolidation Coal Co. He held that post until his retirement in 1966. Ireland was also president of Hawken School from 1932–64. He and Margaret Allen Ireland had 4 children: Louise Humphrey Ireland, Kate Ireland, Robt. L. III, and Melville H. Ireland (d. 1981).

The foundation is broadly for educational and charitable purposes, with emphasis on nursing, higher and secondary education, and hospitals. Grants also go to MUSIC. No grants are given to individuals. In 1985, assets of the foundation were $5,599,000, with expenditures of $398,550 for 75 grants. Officers of the foundation included Kate Ireland, M. G. Mikolaj, Louise Ireland Humphrey, and R. L. Ireland III.

**IRISH.** Cleveland's Irish population, like that in many other cities, did not reach a significant number until the potato famine immigrations occurred in the late 1840s. Unlike those in many Eastern Seaboard cities, Cleveland's Irish never exerted influence beyond their numbers, though they have been part of the city's diverse ethnic community and activities since the first immigrants from Ireland arrived ca. 1820. The Irish continued to trickle into the city, and approximately 500 were in Cleveland in 1826, helping to build the OHIO & ERIE CANAL. But the Irish population did not reach significant proportions until 1848, when 1,024 immigrants were in Cleveland. Despite being agrarian in Ireland, they did not farm in the Cleveland area, instead becoming hard laborers, who unloaded ships or worked in the steel mills that were opening along the CUYAHOGA RIVER and in NEWBURGH. By 1870, the Irish population had grown to almost 10,000, which represented 10% of Cleveland's total population. Though still more Irish would come to Cleveland, Irish immigration would not keep up with the city's rapid growth, and by 1900, the 13,120 Irish composed only 3.5% of the total community. Most of the Irish clustered around the east and west banks of the Cuyahoga River's mouth, though a significant Irish community was located along Detroit St. on the west side. By 1930, only 8,113 Irish immigrants were living in the Cleveland metropolitan area, and in 1970, estimates of Irish descendants living in Cleveland ranged from 37,000 to 100,000, but no Irish neighborhoods remained. Most Irish were Roman Catholic, but some Protestant Scotch-Irish lived in the area from its founding. In Cleveland, as elsewhere in the country, the Scotch-Irish assimilated quickly into the mainstream population and lost their group identity, while the Roman Catholic Irish clustered together in recognizable communities. To encourage the continuance of Catholicism in northern Ohio, the state was divided into 2 dioceses, and in 1847 LOUIS AMADEUS RAPPE was appointed the first bishop of the northern third of the state. Rappe, a French missionary, had been in Ohio since 1840 and several times during the decade went to Cleveland, where he discovered the early victims of the Irish famine crowding in ghettos. He attracted money and help from his native France, bringing to Cleveland several priests and seminarians, along with needed funds.

Rappe began to build a community spirit with religion as the focal point. In 1848 he started a seminary, and in 1851 a convent, and an orphanage and children's hospital were opened. The latter cared for many Irish children whose parents had died either during passage or from the myriad diseases thriving in the Irish ghetto. Catholic sisters, whom Rappe had persuaded to come from France, staffed these enterprises. In 1852, the church of St. John the Evangelist at Erie and Superior was completed, the second Catholic church in Cleveland (the first was ST. MARY'S ON THE FLATS at Columbus and Girard, which was torn down in 1886). In 1853–54, Rappe established 2 parishes: St. Patrick on Bridge Ave. on the west side, and the Holy Name parish in the village of NEWBURGH, which was within walking distance of the steel mill where many Irish worked. These separate parishes led to a split in the Irish community in

Cleveland. In 2 generations, the east side Irish, led by Rappe, assimilated into the "Yankee" community, leaving their Irish neighborhoods and heritage for the developing suburbs. However, on the west side, Fr. Jas. Conlon, pastor of the St. Patrick parish and an Irish immigrant himself, encouraged the isolation of the Irish by helping form exclusive Irish societies, allowing the community to remain intact well into the 20th century. In 1877, Fr. Eugene M. O'Callaghan succeeded Conlon as pastor of St. Patrick's; he found that the parish had no funds and an uncompleted church that Conlon had started in 1871. During the next 2 years, O'Callaghan organized his parishioners to cut and transport limestone from a Sandusky quarry and finish building the A-frame church that still stands today. This effort appears to have solidified the parish community enough to sustain the Irish neighborhood right up to the end of WORLD WAR II. O'Callaghan left the parish in 1880 to found the St. Colman parish on Gordon Ave., between W. Madison and Lawn, which eventually became one of Cleveland's longest-lasting Irish parishes. In the 20th century, Catholic ethnic churches gave way to territorial churches, and by 1960, no distinctly Irish parishes remained.

The Irish were vigorous socially. In addition to many church-related activities, there were several secular groups to enjoy. The HIBERNIAN GUARDS, founded before 1850, were "a band of Irish soldiers" who paraded on St. Patrick's Day, had annual banquets, and during the CIVIL WAR actively recruited men who saw combat. In the early 1870s, the Irish Literary & Benevolent Society met weekly for social purposes and the promotion of Irish culture. While both groups are now defunct, the St. Patrick's parade continues, sponsored by the United Irish Societies of Greater Cleveland, an organization established in 1958 that represents 13 Irish organizations. Among them, the IRISH-AMERICAN CLUB, WEST SIDE, and the IRISH-AMERICAN CLUB, EAST SIDE, founded in 1931 and 1978 respectively, have 1,200 members. Temperance movements were active in Cleveland, too; an early society was the Knights of Fr. Mathew, which counted Bp. Rappe as a member. Today the Pioneers Total Abstinence Assoc. of the Sacred Heart, which was founded in 1956, totals approximately 300 teetotaling members. Irish nationalism in Cleveland found expression in the national Fenian movement during the 1860s. Dedicated to freeing Ireland from British rule, the Fenians organized support in America and trained men for an invasion of Canada. In 1866, 3 Fenians were arrested in Cleveland for their quasi-legal activity in the group.

The Irish were active in politics but did not build any durable political "machine" like those found in other large cities. Cleveland's diverse ethnic composition was reflected on the city council, and while certain districts and wards consistently elected Irish representatives, city council never had an unusually large proportion of Irish. The term of ROBT. E. MCKISSON, who served as mayor 1895–98, was the closest Cleveland came to having an Irish political machine. He was accused of using the spoils system for his own political gains. And near the end of the 19th century, JOHN FARLEY, mayor 1883–84 and 1899–1900, was active in Democratic politics and called a "boss" by some historians. Other notable Cleveland Irish politicians included JAS. J. MCGINTY (councilman 1913–30), WM. S. FITZGERALD (mayor 1920–21), Thos. McCafferty (councilman 1934–65), Margaret McCaffery (councilman 1948–63 and 1966–73), and Jas. Donnelly (councilman 1944–55). In addition to city politics, Cleveland Irish such as MARTIN FORAN, a congressman and judge, and MARTIN SWEENEY were involved in regional and national politics.

As in other cities in the 19th century, the Irish faced prejudice in Cleveland. The CLEVELAND LEADER consistently reported all barroom scuffles involving Irishmen and once claimed that 60% of all criminal activity had Irishmen at its roots. Ironically, also as in other cities, the police department had a disproportionate number of Irish on the force. In 1874, Cleveland's Irish population constituted 10% of the general population, but almost 20% of the force. By 1902, the Irish population represented only 3.5% of the city, but 12.5% of the police force. Today the Irish have assimilated into Cleveland's mainstream and are employed in all types of jobs.

Rev. Nelson J. Callahan
St. Raphael Church

Callahan, Nelson, and Hickey, William, *Irish Americans and Their Communities of Cleveland* (1978).

The **IRISH AMERICAN CLUB-EAST SIDE, INC.,** was officially chartered in the state of Ohio on St. Patrick's Day, 17 Mar. 1978. Its purpose is to promote Irish heritage and to sponsor social, cultural, educational, and athletic programs in Cleveland and around the state. Though the majority of members are of Irish descent, anyone may join under sponsorship from a member in good standing. The club purchased and remodeled a building at 22770 Lake Shore Blvd. for its headquarters in 1981. The building has a large meeting hall holding over 1,000 persons, a bar, and a kitchen. Its basement has a smaller bar, a hall for musical groups and dancing, and space for a library to be dedicated to Celtic reading. The club regularly holds raffles to help those in need. It sponsors trips for senior citizens (Golden Shamrocks), drives for charity, and "reverse raffles" and dinners to replenish funds. The club's main function is cultural. It highlights music and dancing from Ireland and teaches the Gaelic language and Irish cooking and handicrafts. It also publishes a newsletter, "The Shanachie." In 1985, there were over 1,200 members.

The **IRISH AMERICAN CLUB WEST SIDE** (est. 1931) maintains recreational facilities and meeting rooms and sponsors social and cultural events for members of Cleveland's Irish-American community. With 1,200 adult members at the time of its 50th anniversary in 1981, the club was the largest Irish organization in Cuyahoga County. The club developed from the work of 2 earlier organizations that promoted independence for Ireland: Clan na Gael and the Terence MacSwiney Club. The latter was named in honor of a martyr to Irish independence who died in 1920 after a 74-day hunger strike. In Oct. 1931, the West Side Irish American Club was formally organized to provide a social center for and to promote an interest in Irish history and culture within the local Irish-American community. Among the founders and influential early leaders were Jas. "Popsie" Kilbane, who hosted the first meeting in the basement of his Detroit Ave. home; Arthur McChrystal, the first financial secretary; and Patrick T. Lynch (1896–1975), the club's first and long-time president, serving in that capacity 1931–46 and 1948–67.

The annual St. Patrick's Day parade was a major event on the club's calendar, and 2 marching units were formed early in the group's history. In 1934, Tom Hastings and Marty Patton organized a fife-and-drum corps, complete with bagpipes, and in 1935, a ladies' drill team was formed by Colletta Masterson Jablonski. Until it moved to various locations between 1948–51, the West Side Irish Club was located on the 2d floor of a building at W. 64th and Detroit Ave. (6415 Detroit). It was located there when it was incorporated on 20 Sept. 1940. In 1950 the organization bought the former Madison Theater, 9613 Madison Ave., and remodeled it to include a hall, a bar, a library, a kitchen, and meeting rooms. The new home of the club opened on New Year's Eve 1951. In 1958, the club began to hold an annual Feis, a reunion designed to resemble the ancient Irish Feisanna, with competitions in sports, music, and oratory. During the 1960s, club events raised funds for a variety of projects, including the John F. Kennedy Memorial Library and the work of missionaries in the Philippine Islands. During the 1970s, the organization acquired additional facilities. In 1973 it bought 30 acres of land in Olmsted Twp., and in 1978 it purchased a recreational facility in Medina. Its hall on Madison Ave. continued to serve as a social center and meeting hall for a variety of Irish social, cultural, musical, and athletic organizations.

**IRISHTOWN BEND** is the area along the CUYAHOGA RIVER, south of Detroit and east of W. 25th, where Irish immigrants huddled in tarpaper shacks. Part of a larger area known as the ANGLE, and the earliest Irish settlement on WHISKEY ISLAND, Irishtown is centered around ST. MALACHI'S CHURCH at W. 25th and Washington. When the first Irish came to Cleveland in the early 1830s, they settled in the FLATS on Whiskey Island, a peninsula that extended from its mouth to W. 54th St. Mostly diggers and dockworkers, they lived near their work in what became 22 streets of tiny hovels. Though the area had been known as Whiskey Island before the coming of the Irish, the new inhabitants, hard-drinking after hard days of labor, gave a new meaning to the name; the area became the wildest, rowdiest section of Cleveland, home to at least 13 saloons, as well as houses of PROSTITUTION in Sin Alley west of Toledo St.

Throughout the 1830s and 1840s, the growing Irish community, bolstered by refugees from the Potato Famine, spread to both sides of the Cuyahoga. Though some Irish erected homes a step above tarpaper shacks, the settlements were characterized by extreme poverty and were ripe for 19th-century diseases: cholera, diphtheria, scarlet fever, and diarrhea infantum. In 1853, St. Patrick parish was established on Bridge Ave. to accommodate the growing west side Irish population. Irishtown residents traveled westward to the slightly more affluent area near the church; in 1868, neighborhood residents got their own church, St. Malachi's. As the Irish became more prosperous, the successful, known as "Lace Curtain Irish," looked down on the "Shanty" or "Pig in the Parlor" Irish, who resided in the Irishtown Bend area. These outcasts became extremely defensive about their territory; many a bloody battle was fought in the Angle to level uppity intruders. Irishtown Bend, a bastion of Irish frontier life, eventually became a warehouse area; after 1910 the city began revitalizing the area along the river. In the 1980s, St. Malachi's, however, remains a healthy parish, while the greater Angle area is a low-income residential area.

**IRWIN, JOSEPHINE SAXER** (1 Mar. 1890–15 Sept. 1984), was a noted suffragette who remained active in the women's-rights movement for more than half a century. Irwin was born in LAKEWOOD, Ohio. She received her college education at the School of Education at Western Reserve University, graduating in 1910. After graduation, she taught at Lincoln and McKinley elementary schools in Lakewood from 1910–19. Irwin was active in the peace movement before WORLD WAR I, was one of the first members of the LEAGUE OF WOMEN VOTERS, and was most noted for her participation in a massive suffrage parade staged on Cleveland's EUCLID AVE. in 1914. Her involvement in the women's movement also included her activities in behalf of the Equal Rights Amendment during the 1970s–

1980s, and she was a founding member of WOMEN-SPACE. From 1958–62, Irwin served as councilman-at-large in FAIRVIEW PARK, the first woman elected to the council in that city. She was a charter member of the CLEVELAND COUNCIL ON WORLD AFFAIRS and was inducted into the Ohio Women's Hall of Fame in 1983. In honor of Irwin's contributions, both the Natl. Organization for Women and WomenSpace have instituted a Josephine Irwin Award, which is conferred annually in Cleveland on the women who have contributed substantially to the cause of women's rights. Josephine Saxer married J. Preston Irwin in 1919. They had 2 sons, Wm. P. and John P., Jr., and a daughter, Elizabeth Irwin Harner.

Josephine Irwin Papers, WRHS.

The **ISLAMIC CENTER OF CLEVELAND,** 9400 Detroit Ave., serves as both a social center and a place of worship for its 300 registered members. One of the most important Islamic institutions in the city, the Islamic Ctr. began in 1963 when 7 area Moslems began meeting in the UNIVERSITY CIRCLE area to hold worship services. About 39 people formally established the Islamic Ctr. of Cleveland in 1967, drawing up a constitution and electing officers. In July 1968, the members of the center purchased the house at W. 94th and Detroit. Under the leadership of Hashem Hasan, president of the center, Selim Dervic, vice-president, and Igram Kalid, treasurer, members refurnished the building with a prayer room, a library, and classrooms for a school to teach the Islamic faith to their children. The center moved into its new home in the fall of 1969. In the spring of 1975, Saudi Arabian King Khalid, who had met members of the center during a stay in the CLEVELAND CLINIC the previous summer, paid off the $8,000 mortgage on the $26,000 building; part of his motivation was the religious teaching that prohibits Moslems from dealing with interest. During the 1960s and early 1970s, about 100 families were members of the Islamic Ctr. Members included American families as well as those from Algeria, India, Pakistan, Iran, Albania, Turkey, Bulgaria, Yugoslavia, and Hungary. During the 1970s and 1980s, membership in the center gradually increased as the size of local families increased, as more refugees from the Middle Eastern wars arrived in Cleveland, and as more Moslem students came to study in Cleveland-area schools. By Mar. 1986, the center had 300 registered members, and at times as many as 1,000 people attended its worship services. In the summer of 1985, members of the center paid $95,000 in cash for 36 acres of land in STRONGSVILLE, where they planned to build a multi-million-dollar mosque.

**ISSENMANN, CLARENCE G.** (30 May 1907–27 July 1982), was the 7th bishop of the Cleveland Diocese. He was born in Hamilton, Ohio, the only child of Innocent and Amelia Stricker Issenmann. He was educated at St. Joseph College in Rensselaer, Ind., before studying for the priesthood at St. Gregory Seminary and Mt. St. Mary Seminary, both in Cincinnati. Archbp. John T. McNicholas of Cincinnati ordained him on 29 June 1932. Issenmann received degrees in sacred theology from the University of Fribourg in Switzerland and in philosophy from the Angelicum in Rome. When he returned to the U.S., he was named to the staff of the *Denver Register.* During his 2 years with the *Register,* he acquired a doctorate in journalism from the Register College of Journalism. In 1938 he was appointed assistant editor of the *Catholic Telegraph Register* of Cincinnati, with additional duties as the archbishop's secretary. In 1942 he was named professor of theology at Mt. St. Mary Seminary in Cincinnati. He became chancellor of the archdiocese in 1945.

Issenmann was consecrated auxiliary bishop of Cincinnati on 22 May 1954. On 11 Feb. 1958, he was installed as the 6th bishop of Columbus. While bishop there, he served as episcopal chairman of the Press Dept. and assistant chairman of the Dept. for Lay Organizations of the Natl. Catholic Welfare Conference (a forerunner of the U.S. Catholic Conference) in Washington. On 7 Oct. 1964, Bp. Issenmann was named coadjutor bishop of Cleveland for the ailing Archbp. Hoban. When Hoban died on 22 Sept. 1966, Issenmann became the 7th bishop of Cleveland. As bishop, Issenmann restructured the school board and opened several new high schools. He had a special interest in the handicapped and developed special ministries to the deaf and mentally retarded. He opened St. Augustine Manor to provide skilled short-term nursing care. He established the COMMISSION ON CATHOLIC COMMUNITY ACTION to provide leadership in social-justice issues. Under Issenmann's direction, the Martin de Porres Ctr. was started to serve the poor of the Glenville area. The diocese also supported several low-income-housing projects and social-improvement activities in inner-city neighborhoods. Bp. Issenmann worked to make the decrees of Vatican II effective. He began a priests' senate, a clergy personnel board, and a senate of religious women. He established the Diocesan Pastoral Planning Office and endorsed the formation of parish councils in every parish. Issenmann's health began to deteriorate in the early 1970s, and he resigned from the diocese in July 1974.

**ITALIAN HALL** was one of the first buildings in Cleveland to house a theater. Built in the early 1830s on Water (W. 9th) St., it was one of the few brick buildings in Cleveland, with 3 stories and a theater on the top floor. During the 1830s, Italian Hall was the most fashionable theater in Cleveland, the stopping place for famous stars. John Mills was the proprietor during this period. Traveling companies were brought in by local backers. It was the first theater in Cleveland to feature raised seats. In the 1840s, newer theaters in the city began to compete for Italian Hall's fashionable audiences, and it eventually became a variety house.

**ITALIANS.** Although Italian names can be found in Cleveland city directories from the late 1850s, it was not until the CIVIL WAR that an Italian community began to form in the city. The 1870 census listed 35 Italians in Cleveland. The 50 years that followed saw the city become a magnet, drawing more than 20,000 Italian immigrants. Most of those who emigrated were *contadini* (peasants) from the Mezzogiorno (Southern Italy), where conditions of extreme poverty and government negligence brought unbearable hardship. The history of Cleveland's Italians comprises 3 separate stages: formation (1870–1929); transformation (1930–45); and realization (1945 to the present). By the late 1920s, the formative period was complete. Demographic patterns were established; 6 Italian neighborhoods had been established throughout the city. The largest was BIG ITALY, located along Woodland and Orange avenues from E. 9th St. to E. 40th St. LITTLE ITALY, centered at Mayfield and Murray Hill roads, proved the most enduring of the settlements. Nearby, at E. 107th St. and Cedar Ave., a community grew up around St. Marian Church. Also located on the city's east side was a substantial Italian settlement in COLLINWOOD. Two settlements were located on the west side, one near Clark and Fulton avenues and one on Detroit near W. 65th St., the latter being an offshoot of the former. Eventually, by the late 1920s, a 7th community was established by people moving out of the Big Italy area to the Woodland and E. 116th St. region. In each community, the Italians transplanted their institutions, including nationality parishes, hometown societies, mutual-aid organizations, and a multiplicity of family-owned businesses. Cleveland's Italians lacked any sense of national identity. Italy for them was the village from which they came. What the Italians brought to Cleveland were the traditions, values, patron saints, and dialects from the villages they represented. Their affinities and affiliations were largely with their *paesani* (fellow villagers).

The majority of Cleveland's Italian immigrants came after the turn of the century, when the city was expanding its streets and city services. Many, therefore, found work on BRIDGES, sewers, and streetcar tracks. They also provided cheap labor for the city's expanding factories and railroads. The clothing and garment industries were especially attractive to the Italians, many of whom were skilled in embroidering and needlework. The women as well as the men were employed in large numbers by PRINTZ-BIEDERMAN, JOSEPH & FEISS, H. Black, M. T. Silver, and other clothing factories of the city. The immigrant settlements often differed according to occupation. For example, Big Italy, the oldest colony and located close to the city's markets, became the center of the city's fruit industry, because many of the immigrants had come from Sicily, where fruits were grown. FRANK CATALANO, a pioneer settler of this area, introduced to the Cleveland area such cosmopolitan tastes as oranges, olive oil, figs, anchovies, garlic, bananas, nuts, and other delicacies. Catalano, with his Italian competitors, the Rinis, Geracis, Corsos, Schiappacassis, and C. V. Vettorio, made Cleveland the center of the produce industry in Ohio. In Little Italy, the chief occupations included tailoring, monument work, and gardening. While Italian landscapers tended the estates on the heights above Little Italy, the stonecutters applied their skills to the city's cemeteries, churches, and private homes. The pioneers in stonecutting were Jas. Broggini and JOSEPH CARABELLI. Broggini emigrated to Cleveland in 1870, establishing a monument works on Woodland Ave. Carabelli emigrated in 1880 at the age of 20. Seeing the opportunity for monument work in LAKE VIEW CEMETERY, he established what became the city's leading marble and granite works. Other Italian artists whose works adorned the city during the formative period included Raffaele Raineri, Vincent Belfi, Philip Garbo, and Antonio Mazzolini. Most of the frescoing and mosaic work in the city's public places and private homes was accomplished by Cleveland's Italian immigrants.

Cleveland's Italians were also active in the manufacturing industry during the formative period. For example, the Ohio Macaroni Co., established in 1910 by Joseph Russo & Sons, became the largest macaroni company in Ohio by 1920. The Roma Cigar Co., started in 1913 by Albert Pucciani, was producing 20,000 cigars weekly by 1920. Other companies founded by Cleveland's Italians included the Forest City Macaroni Co., the Foreign Prods. Co., the Giuseppe Botta Frozen Desserts Mfg. Co., the GRASSELLI CHEMICAL CO., DiCicco & Ranallo Dry Goods, the Monte Monumental Co., and the Incoraia Monumental Co. In banking, Nicola and Salvatore Gugliotta opened an office in 1904 on Woodland Ave. (Big Italy), while the leading banker in Little Italy was Vincent Campanella. By the end of the formative period, Cleveland's Italians made up 80% of its barbers and 70% of its cooks. Although only 4 of the city's restaurants were owned by Italians in 1920, one of these, the New Roma, was reputedly the largest and most attractive in Ohio. Italian chefs prepared meals at the Hotels Statler, Cleveland, Winton, and HOLLENDEN, and the SHAKER HTS. COUNTRY CLUB.

In the medical and dental professions, Cleveland's Italians increased progressively in number. Twenty medical doctors and dentists served the community by 1920. One of the most prominent was GIOVANNI A. BARRICELLI. These Italian-trained professionals followed the contadini to Cleveland and served the needs of the immigrants. The first Italian attorney in Cleveland, Benedetto D. Nicola, practiced law between 1904–64. He was the most prominent among Cleveland's 12 Italian attorneys during the formative period. Unlike the medical professionals, Italian-born attorneys did not follow the immigrants to Cleveland. Consequently, the community had to wait for the children of the immigrants to fill this void. Equally significant was the attitude of the immigrants toward politics. As long as the Italian community, the family, and the "old ways" were not threatened, the Italians did not show serious intentions in the political arena. In 1915, for example, only 1,423 were listed as "naturalized Italians voting" out of a foreign-born population of 13,570. It was not until the late 1920s that Cleveland's Italians took a more active interest in politics. Political leadership became dependent on the small nucleus of Italian-American attorneys who, like Nicola, Joseph Nuccio, and B. A. Buonpane, had already established their reputations by the end of the formative period.

One of the most effective means of ethnic expression that emerged from Cleveland's early community was the Italian-American press. In 1903, *LA VOCE DEL POPOLO ITALIANO* was founded by Olindo Melaragno. It was the first Italian newspaper in Ohio. By 1920 it claimed a circulation of 15,000 in the city and another 30,000 throughout Ohio and other states. *La Stampa* also emerged during the formative period. These papers interpreted American law, made clear economic and social rights, and emphasized the advantages of citizenship. They became an incentive for the illiterate to learn to read English and Italian, and they offered news from the homeland. By 1915, *La Voce* was the first Italian newspaper in the U.S. to publish articles in both Italian and English. Later, other newspapers, such as *L'ARALDO*, appeared and enjoyed limited success; eventually, as the reading skills of the second generation were lost, radio broadcasts with the "Italian Hour" became popular.

No other institution better reflects the uniqueness of Cleveland's Italian community than the hometown society. In these societies, the paesani were able to transplant the communal solidarity of their native villages to the New World. These societies did not emerge because Cleveland's Italians were uprooted; on the contrary, they were established to strengthen an identity the paesani already possessed. Each group of paesani feared being absorbed by Cleveland's greater Italian community. Meeting on a weekly basis, they reminisced in the dialect of their village, maintained family acquaintances so their American-born children would know each other, and continued ties with their Italian village. The paesani buried their dead, cared for widows and their children, and found employment for the unemployed and housing for those without shelter. The exploitation of the *padroni* so evident in New York City never became part of the Cleveland scene because of these societies. Among the societies founded in Cleveland were the Ripalimosani Social Union, Fraterna Sant'Agata, the Matrice Club, the TRENTINA CLUB, and the Noicattarese Club. By the end of the formative period, most of the hometown societies became affiliated with the Sons of Italy, which organized its first Cleveland chapter in 1913. By 1920, Cleveland's Italians had 9 lodges in the national organization. One of the major attractions of the Sons of

Italy was the mutual-aid or insurance benefits it provided. In case of death, grants of $400 as well as funeral expenses were paid to the family of the deceased. Cleveland's Italians established many organizations during the formative period; 80% of all the Italian males held membership in 1 or more of these societies.

The church was, perhaps, the major nonfamilial institution established during the formative period. Fr. Pacifico Capitani arrived from Rome in July 1886, and on 8 May 1887, the first Italian nationality church in Ohio was dedicated to St. Anthony. It served the Big Italy district. By the late 1920s, Cleveland's Italian-born exceeded 32,000. As the population increased, so did the nationality churches. Those established during the formative period were St. Marian (1905), HOLY ROSARY (1892) serving Little Italy, ST. ROCCO (1922), Holy Redeemer (1924) serving Collinwood, and Our Lady of Mt. Carmel West (1926). By 1937, enough Italians had moved from the Big Italy district to the Woodland-E. 116th area to warrant the establishment of Our Lady of Mt. Carmel East. Despite the overwhelming association of Italians with Roman Catholicism, several Protestant Italian churches were established, including Baptist, Congregationalist, and Presbyterian congregations. The most prominent and long-lived of these was ST. JOHN'S BECKWITH (1907) in the Little Italy neighborhood. The nationality churches acted as catalysts to unify the various paesani, as no single village group could build its own church. Still, the Italians did not forget their patron saints. Each group of paesani held a banquet and a street parade honoring its patron saint. The Italians of ST. ANTHONY'S CHURCH alone celebrated 22 feast days with a banquet; 12 of these were honored with street processions. By the 1980s, the Feast of the Assumption, sponsored by Holy Rosary Church, had become one of the sole surviving feasts and had grown into an enormous event, attracting Italians and non-Italians alike.

The end of the formative period came in the late 1920s, when events within the American experience challenged Cleveland's Italian community. The burdens created by Prohibition, the Depression, and the passage of restrictive immigration legislation served to place the Italians in a defensive position. That served to make the community politically active. The rise of Mussolini, which tended to gain international respect for Italy, had strong symbolic importance for immigrants. Prohibition seems to have provided the impetus for Italian political involvement as the community sought a means to redress slurs and discriminatory practices. While newspaper stories continually linked Italians to organized crime, the local police force engaged in questionable practices—at one point they stationed officers at all entrances to the Little Italy community and searched automobiles, without warrants, for illegal liquor. That led to the involvement of men such as ALESSANDRO DEMAIORIBUS in local politics. Although DeMaioribus, a city councilman, was a Republican, the majority of Italians became Democrats, and it was in this party that people such as FRANK CELEBREZZE and Anthony J. Celebrezze made their political careers. The career of Anthony Celebrezze as mayor, cabinet officer in the Kennedy administration, and federal judge epitomized the politicization of the local Italian community. By the 1980s, local Italians held a number of political posts as representatives, judges, and government administrators.

Cleveland's Italians also took great pride in the revitalized Italy. In 1935, Augusto Rosso, Italian ambassador to the U.S., came to Cleveland to participate in the dedication of the new Sons of Italy temple at E. 72nd St. and Euclid. That was the first time an Italian ambassador had visited the city. Rosso's participation in the dedication ceremonies was proof to Cleveland's Italian press that the Fascist regime followed with a vigilant and paternal eye the activities of Italian-Americans, and especially encouraged those initiatives that enhanced the Italian nationality in every corner of the globe. On 3 Oct. 1935, Mussolini ordered the invasion of Ethiopia. Cleveland's Italians responded with patriotic spontaneity. By Sept. 1936, the Italian community had donated $12,404.21 to the royal consul for the Italian Red Cross. At the height of hostilities with Ethiopia, more than 1,000 of Cleveland's Italians sent their wedding rings to Italy. In return, they received steel rings from Mussolini, who asked that they be worn as symbols of their faith in Italy. A year later, 4,000 Italians gathered in Little Italy to celebrate the first anniversary of the Italian empire. The local community's links to the homeland were abruptly upset in 1940 when Italy declared war on France and England. Between then and the entry of the U.S. into the conflict, almost all local support for the Mussolini regime melted. For a while, Cleveland's Italians did reap benefits from their association with the "Young Italy." Perhaps the greatest benefit was the ethnic maturity that resulted from an identity crisis they experienced when they found themselves classified as "enemy aliens." Ethnicity underwent a transformation as the Italian community redirected its energy toward the war effort. When the public schools dropped the Italian language, the Sons of Italy did not complain. Lodges that had been named after Italian royalty were renamed Abraham Lincoln, Betsy Ross, etc. Membership declined. The junior lodges were closed, and in 1945 the temple that Ambassador Rosso had dedicated was for sale.

WORLD WAR II was a watershed in the history of Cleveland's Italians. Many had relatives fighting on both sides. Cleveland's Italians led the city in scrap drives and bond drives. By 1942, they had sent 2,500 of their sons to the U.S. armed forces. One of these, Pfc. Frank Petrarca of Cleveland, was the first Ohioan awarded the Medal of Honor. Cleveland's Italians emerged from the war with a clear understanding of their place within the framework of American pluralism. Ethnic identity had survived the war, but it had been transformed. The Italians entered the postwar years with the realization that they were Americans of Italian descent. Much of the impetus for change after 1945 came from the returning veterans. Having been exposed to experiences outside the community, they sought advanced educational opportunities, more space, a higher income, and contact with non-Italians. What followed was an increase in intermarriage and a movement to the SUBURBS for better housing and educational facilities. Italians on the east side tended to move out along Mayfield Rd. to the suburbs of MAYFIELD HTS. and LYNDHURST. West side Italians moved along W. 25th St. to PARMA. Despite the outward movement, many of the old settlements, except Big Italy, remained viable into the 1970s. That was partly a result of the continuing migration of Italians into the U.S. and Cleveland. While eastern cities garnered more of the new immigrants, movement into Cleveland continued at a pace that helped maintain older communities. By 1960, there were still 19,317 foreign-born Italians in the city. However, within 20 years, deaths among the older generation and continued out-migration from the central city reduced Cleveland's Italian-born population to 11,890—though depleted, the Italian community was the largest European immigrant community in the city.

By the mid-1980s, it was apparent that Italian movement to suburban areas was continuing. Although the two west side settlements around St. Rocco and Mt. Carmel parish remained marginally viable, all that remained on the east side was Little Italy, which by that time had come to symbolize the Italian community in the minds of many Clevelanders through its array of restaurants, shops, and the annual Feast of the Assumption. However, the back streets of the area housed an increasing number of students from neighboring CASE WESTERN RESERVE UNIVERSITY and professionals working in nearby hospitals and craft shops, and it seemed at this juncture that the area's "Italianness" might become more symbolic than real. As was the case with many other immigrant groups, the suburbs seemed more attractive both to the descendants of immigrants and to new immigrants, and the future of Cleveland's Italians was, at this juncture, more firmly linked to regions outside of the city's corporate boundaries.

Charles Ferroni
Ashland College

Coulter, Charles, *The Italians of Cleveland* (1919).
Ferroni, Charles, "The Italians in Cleveland: A Study in Assimilation" (Ph.D. diss., Kent State University, 1969).
Veronesi, Gene, *Italian Americans and Their Communities of Cleveland* (1979).

The **IVAN CANKAR DRAMATIC SOCIETY** (Dramsko Drustvo Ivan Cankar) was considered the best-developed Slovenian theater ensemble outside of Europe. Cleveland's Slovenian immigrants had come from a strong literary tradition and enjoyed their language in any form. By WORLD WAR I, several short-lived drama groups were in existence. Stage productions were demanding and expensive. On 6 Feb. 1919, 36 young immigrants met at Birk's Hall on St. Clair Ave. They had participated in a benefit play performance and, buoyed by their success, sought to reestablish a theater group in the Cleveland Slovenian community. They named their club for the recently deceased Slovenian author and playwright Ivan Cankar, and purchased scenery, costumes, and scripts from a disbanding ensemble. Frank Cesen served as president, VATROSLAV GRILL as secretary, and Janko Rogelj as artistic director. The bylaws included a guarantee of equal treatment of women members. The society was incorporated in 1920. The group premiered within a month with *Deseti Brat*, adapted from a historical novel. The amateurs presented 50 different productions in the first 5 seasons. Many works had never been presented outside of Slovenia. Proceeds were divided between war-relief projects and construction of the SLOVENIAN NATL. HOME. The year 1924 marked a turning point for the society. The players moved into the new 1,500-seat hall in the Slovenian Natl. Home and were able to perform large-scale works on a spacious, fully equipped stage. Augusta Danilova, a doyenne of the Natl. Theater in Ljubljana, arrived for a year's residency, and the group blossomed under her tutelage. She organized drama classes, directed plays, and encouraged the presentation of more challenging works. A children's ensemble debuted in July. Membership grew to 75, with 2 plays per month in season.

The society became one of the most highly regarded Slovenian cultural organizations in the country. In its 35 active years, it gave 165 perfomances. Many were classics of the Slovenian theater, such as Cankar's *Kralj na Betajnovi* and Golar's *Vdova Roslinka*. Others were translations of works by Chekhov, Gorky, and Wilde. Original plays by immigrant authors Etbin Kristan and Katka Zupancic were part of the society's repertoire, along with a few comedies in English. Joseph Skuk, Louis Truger, and Antoinette Simcic were frequent directors, and featured players included Josephine Milavec, Olga Marn, Mary Ivanusch, John Steblaj, and Anton Eppich. Many players were chorus members, and musical numbers were added in later years. Some plays were taken to neighboring communities.

561

Proceeds were donated to the Slovenian Natl. Library, *CANKARJEV GLASNIK*, and unemployed workers in Cleveland, and for postwar reconstruction in Slovenia. The society's success spurred the formation of drama groups in other settlements, such as the Anton Verovsek Society at the Slovenian Workingmen's Home in EUCLID. Fewer available players reduced the number of presentations during the Depression. Young members were less fluent in the language, and new immigration slowed to a trickle. Performances were semiannual but were still well-attended. Membership declined sharply in nearly all Slovenian cultural groups in the postwar years. The Ivan Cankar Society gave its final performance in 1955 and was formally dissolved in 1962. Other theater ensembles followed suit. In 1986, only the Lilija Dramatic Society of the Collinwood Slovenian Home still gave sporadic plays.

**IVANUSCH, JOHN** (ca.1880–1 Sept. 1973), was a Slovenian composer, music teacher, and musical director. Born in Slovenia, Ivanusch began his musical education there at age 7; he later served in the Yugoslav navy under bandmaster Franz Lehar, composer of the opera *The Merry Widow*. Ivanusch came to Cleveland in 1919 and taught piano, strings, and brass instruments, as well as served as the director of the ZARJA SINGING SOCIETY. In 1928 he composed the opera *Rozamund of Tarjak* for the chorus. His wife, Mary Grill Ivanusch, was a singer and a teacher at the Slovene School of the SLOVENIAN NATL. HOME.

**I-X CENTER.** *See* **CLEVELAND TANK PLANT**

**IZANT, GRACE.** *See* **GOULDER, GRACE (IZANT)**

# J

The **J. B. ROBINSON COMPANY, INC.**, is one of the largest retail jewelers in the country. Joseph B. Robinson founded the business in 1946 as a 3-man wholesale diamond operation located on the 8th floor of the Schofield Bldg. on E. 9th St. With Robinson's death in 1959, his son, Lawrence, who had no experience in the jewelry business, tried to liquidate the firm. However, he could not find a buyer, and so he left some trusted employees and his mother in charge until 1962, when he decided to try his hand. He changed the company from a wholesale to a retail jewelry firm, specializing in diamonds and watches, with $200,000 in annual business. In the mid-1960s, the company started a radio campaign, with Robinson, who became known as the "Diamond Man," as spokesman. Robinson's initial attempts to expand from the downtown location were stymied because of the firm's small size; he had to settle for less desirable new locations across from major malls and shopping centers.

Robinson's first suburban store opened in Mentor in 1969. By 1975, it had 18 stores, 9 of them in Cleveland, with 240 employees and an annual business of $11 million. Numerous new branches opened in the Midwest and Washington, D.C., area in the late 1970s. In 1979, the $35 million business with 54 stores was acquired by the W. R. Grace Co. of New York (founded 1854), a diversified international corporation with interests in chemicals, natural resources, and consumer services. This merger allowed Robinson to carry a wider range of merchandise and improved the company's opportunity to expand further. In 1981, Grace placed its retail operations, including Robinson, into a joint venture with Vroom & Dreesman B.V., the largest retailing organization in the Netherlands. Robinson opened more stores, concentrating on Texas and the Southwest, and planned to diversify into other product areas. With headquarters in the STATLER OFFICE TOWER on Euclid Ave., the firm had 70 outlets with 650 employees by 1981.

The **J. SPANG BAKING COMPANY** was a retail bakery that operated on Barber Ave. for 70 years before closing in Mar. 1958. It was formed by German immigrant Julius Spang. Born in Germany in 1852, Spang learned the baking trade there, and in 1882 he brought his wife, Fredericka, and their 5 children to the U.S. After working at the Stillman Hotel and then for the Ohio Baking Co., Spang opened a small bake shop on Barber Ave. in 1888. He directed the baking operations himself, while Fredericka directed the

financial affairs of the business. He headed the company until his death on 31 Dec. 1950. The J. Spang Baking Co. was incorporated in 1909 and continued to expand its operations. By 1956, the company employed 433 people and operated 3 plants: the main plant at 2911 Barber Ave., another in Lorain, and a third in Akron. The Spang family maintained control of the company after the founder's death; the officers in 1956 included Arthur E. Spang, president; Chester Spang, vice-president and general manager; Wm. L. Spang, vice-president and secretary; and Harry Spang, treasurer. The Spang Baking Co. closed in Mar. 1958 and was sold to the LAUB BAKING CO. In 1908, Julius Spang's son Emil organized a second Spang bakery under his own name. The Emil Spang Baking Co. was a wholesale firm incorporated in 1913 and located at 1556 E. 24th St. Emil had managed his father's retail firm from 1900-08; he returned to his father's firm as a manager in 1922 but continued to operate his own bakery until he sold it in 1950.

**JACK & HEINTZ.** *See* **LEAR SIEGLER, INC. POWER EQUIPMENT DIVISION**

**JACKSON, PERRY B.** (27 Jan. 1896–20 Mar. 1986), a lawyer and a political and civic leader, became the first black to serve as a judge in Ohio when he was appointed to the municipal court bench in Aug. 1942 by Gov. John W. Bricker. Jackson was born in Zanesville, Ohio, the son of Brooks C. and Ida M. Jackson. After attending public schools there, he graduated from Adelbert College of Western Reserve University in 1919. In 1922 he graduated from the WRU Law School, was admitted to the bar, and began to practice law in Cleveland. Jackson quickly became involved in civic and political affairs in Cleveland. From 1923-27 he was editor of the *Cleveland Call*. Active in Republican politics, he was elected to the Ohio general assembly in 1928, serving 1 term there. He was responsible for the state's adoption of permanent voter registration forms that made no reference to race or color. Jackson's 2 years in the state legislature launched a long career of public service. In 1933 he was appointed to an unexpired term on CLEVELAND CITY COUNCIL. From July 1934-Aug. 1941 he served as assistant police prosecutor; from Aug. 1941-Apr. 1942 he was secretary to the director of public utilities. Jackson was appointed a municipal judge in Aug. 1942 but lost the election for his seat in 1943. In 1945 he won a 6-year term on the municipal court bench;

he was reelected in 1951 and 1957. In 1960 he was elected to the newly created Domestic Relations Div. of the common pleas court; he did not like his duties there, however, and in 1964 he was elected to an unexpired term in the General Div. of the common pleas court. He was reelected in 1967. He retired from the bench in 1973 but remained active as a visiting judge.

Jackson was a proponent of civil rights for BLACKS and was active in black political affairs. Refused service at a bar association meeting in the HOLLENDEN HOTEL in 1935, he sued the hotel and received $350 in damages. He was the Republican ward leader in the 16th ward in the 1930s, and in the late 1950s he was active in efforts to promote better political organization and leadership within the black community. He was a member of the executive committee of the local NAACP and a trustee of the local URBAN LEAGUE. Jackson was a national and state officer in the Elks and was an active Scottish Rite Mason. Active in the BOY SCOUTS and the YMCA, he was a trustee of the Cleveland Welfare Fed., Protestant Big Brothers, GOODWILL INDUSTRIES, and Ohio Boys' Town. A life member of the Family Service Assoc., Jackson was also a member of the advisory boards of the County Welfare Dept. and FRIENDLY INN SOCIAL SETTLEMENT, of several local mayor's committees appointed to investigate juvenile delinquency, and of the Natl. Council of Social Work. He served as president of the Cleveland Area Church Fed. and was a trustee of ST. JOHN'S AME CHURCH. Jackson was married on 22 Aug. 1933 to Fern Josephine Payne.

Perry B. Jackson Papers, WRHS.

*JACOBELLIS V. OHIO* was a case in which the U.S. Supreme Court reaffirmed its right to independently determine whether a particular work is obscene and therefore not entitled to the constitutional guarantees of freedom of expression. Overturning the conviction of Nico Jacobellis, manager of the Heights Art Theatre, for possessing and exhibiting an allegedly obscene motion picture, the court ruled that the film in question did not meet the obscenity test and could be publicly shown. The motion picture, *Les Amants* (The Lovers), was shown 13 Nov. 1959 at the Heights Art Theatre to a less than appreciative audience. Answering a complaint, Cleveland Hts. law-enforcement officials raided the theater, confiscated the film, and arrested Jacobellis. Waiving a jury trial, Jacobellis was tried before a panel of 3 judges and found guilty on 2 counts of possessing and exhibiting an obscene film. He was fined $2,500 and sentenced to the county workhouse if the fines were not paid. Jacobellis's conviction was affirmed by an intermediate appellate court, and in Jan. 1962 the Ohio Supreme Court agreed that applying local community standards, the film was utterly without redeeming social importance and, therefore, was not entitled to the constitutional guarantees of freedom of expression. The U.S. Supreme Court agreed to hear an appeal, and on 22 June 1964 the Court, in a 6–2 decision, reversed Jacobellis's conviction. The majority opinion, written by Justice Wm. Brennan, reviewed the test for obscenity, i.e., whether the average person applying contemporary community standards found that the dominant theme of a work appealed to lewd and lascivious interests, and added that the material must also be utterly without redeeming social importance in order to be denied constitutional protection. Noting that the charge against *Les Amants* was based almost entirely upon 1 explicit love scene shown near the end of the picture, the Court ruled that the film was not obscene and therefore was entitled to the constitutional guarantees of freedom of expression.

The Court also further defined contemporary community standards as being those of the nation as a whole rather than those of a particular local community. The majority concluded that Jacobellis's conviction violated the 1st Amendment and the due-process clause of the 14th Amendment and that there was no justification for making an exception to the freedom-of-expression rule.

**JANICKI, HAZEL** (19 Feb. 1918–1 Jan. 1976), a Cleveland artist, was one of the few American women to receive national recognition for painting in the decade following WORLD WAR II. Hazel Middleton was born in London to American parents and was raised in Paris. After her father's death, her mother married Joseph Janicki, and the family moved to Cleveland in 1929. Hazel Janicki attended Lakewood High School and enrolled in the Cleveland School of Art in 1937, where she received a Ranney scholarship and studied mural painting with Kindred McLeary. A postgraduate grant allowed her to travel to study murals in public places. She then worked for the CLEVELAND PUBLIC LIBRARY making posters and displays. Janicki first achieved attention in the 1944 Artists for Victory exhibition at the Metropolitan Museum of Art, where her mural for the USO Lounge in Cleveland's Old Federal Bldg. received honorable mention. Influenced by early Italian masters, Janicki was an accomplished portraitist, but became best-known for her meticulously crafted tempera paintings of realistic figures in dreamlike settings, a style then called magic realism or postsurrealism. She painted almost exclusively in egg and wax tempera on masonite. She ground her own pigments and prepared panels with as many as 8 layers of sizing. She was a frequent exhibitor, both nationally and locally, especially in the Cleveland Museum of Art MAY SHOWS, where, from 1943–51, she received 24 awards for painting and drawing. She was awarded a Tiffany Foundation grant in 1949, along with Sol Le Witt, and a purchase prize at the 1948 University of Illinois annual exhibition of contemporary painting, with Philip Guston, among others. She received the Clarke Prize for figure painting from the Natl. Academy of Design in 1951 and a grant from the Natl. Institute of Arts & Letters in 1955 for her "beautiful works of classical quality in a modern idiom."

Janicki continued to combine abstraction with detailed studies of rocks, shells, nests, drawers, and draperies into the 1960s. Actual draperies, knobs, and other objects began to emerge from the surfaces of her paintings, and tromp de l'oeil renderings covered the surfaces of enigmatic wooden constructions and assemblages from the late 1960s (*Children's Room Door*, 1969, Akron Public Library). In the 1970s she returned to painting, concentrating on photorealist depictions of boldly patterned draperies in fluorescent colors against stark backgrounds (*Triptych: Heaped, Stretched, Hanging*, 1972, Kent State University). Janicki taught design, drawing, and painting at Kent State University from 1952. She was active with the nonprofit Ten Thirty Gallery and was president of the WOMEN'S ART CLUB. Her works can be found in many American museums. Janicki was married twice to local painters. John Teyral (b. 1912) was one of her painting instructors, and they married in 1942 after her graduation. Wm. Schock (1913–1976) studied with Ben Shahn and Karl Zerbe in Boston and began teaching at Kent State University just before his marriage to Janicki in 1951. Schock, Janicki, and her stepfather were fatally injured in an automobile accident, New Year's Day, 1976.

Valencic, Joseph, *Hazel Janicki/William Schock: A Retrospective Exhibition* (1977).

The **JANUARY CLUB** was a small group of black writers, both men and women, who privately financed the publication of their own writing from 1930–33. Many such literary societies developed in other communities at this time as a result of the Harlem Renaissance, a cultural movement among Afro-Americans during the 1920s. The January Club claimed special inspiration from the first black novelist, CHAS. CHESNUTT, and the black poet LANGSTON HUGHES, both from Cleveland. In the foreword to an anthology of poetry published by the club, Jas. Robinson wrote, "Many of the writers of this volume have been motivated by the points laid down by the imagists which are: to use the language of common speech, to create new rhythms as the expression of new moods, to allow absolute freedom in choice of subject and to produce a clear unblurred poetry." The club was especially interested in providing an outlet for younger writers.

The January Club met initially at KARAMU HOUSE—then located at E. 38th St. and Central Ave.—and later at the Sterling branch of the CLEVELAND PUBLIC LIBRARY. During its 3-year existence, the club is known to have published at least 3 volumes of poetry. *Dundo*, published in 1931, claimed to be the "first anthology by the Negro youth of Cleveland" and the first of its kind anywhere in America. Many of the poems had previously appeared in other publications. Clarence F. Bryson coedited the volume with Robinson and was also a contributor; Bryson had visited Africa and often addressed the African theme. Five hundred copies of *Dundo* were published. The next anthology was *Shadows*. The club hoped to publish *Shadows* every spring, autumn, and summer (as it hoped to publish *Dundo* annually), although it is uncertain whether that was ever accomplished. The third publication was *Crispus Attacks*, a poem by Robinson, the club's best-known member. It was described as "A Patriotic Narrative of American Negro Heroism in the Boston Massacre"; 250 copies were printed. It was the last work to be published by the January Club.

*Dundo*, ed. Clarence F. Bryson and James H. Robinson (1931), WRHS.
*Shadows*, WRHS.

**JAPANESE.** The story of the Cleveland Japanese-American community has its real beginnings during WORLD WAR II, when significant numbers of the group began to settle in the area. Prior to this time, there were only a handful of isolated Japanese families who called Cleveland home. (The 1940 Japanese population of Cleveland was 18; and of the county, 24.) The vast majority lived on the Pacific Coast and in Hawaii. Nevertheless, to understand the nature of the relatively new Cleveland community, it is necessary to know something of the major dimensions of their pre-World War II lives on the West Coast. The majority of Japanese immigrated to the Pacific Coast between 1890–1924. That was because Japan did not legally allow emigration until 1885, and essentially, the U.S. halted immigration in 1924. The Japanese came to fill a farm-labor vacuum that had been created by the exclusion of Chinese laborers in 1882 and the movement of white laborers out of farm labor. At this time, California agriculture was rapidly expanding owing to the building of huge irrigation projects, the development of refrigerated freight cars, and the creation of efficient agricultural marketing organizations.

Crucial factors in explaining the development of all ethnic communities are the cultural and social organizational forms the original immigrants brought with them and the opportunities and constraints they faced here. In the case of the Japanese, these 2 broad set of factors resulted in highly collectivistic survival strategies. More specifically, because of the Japanese immigrants' experience with numerous voluntary organizational forms in the rural villages from which they came, the discrimination they faced from mainstream labor, business, and government, and their understanding of a money economy, they rapidly became small businessmen of various sorts. They were usually tied in with other Japanese businessmen so as to form an ethnic economy. For example, many quickly moved out of farm labor and began to lease or own their own farms. They also became shopkeepers, hotel owners, and other types of small businessmen in the cities, generally in one of the many "Little Tokyos" or "Nihonmachis" that were common in West Coast cities and towns. Pearl Harbor set in motion a series of events that would forever alter the fabric of Japanese-American life. In the spring of 1942, aliens and citizens alike were removed from their West Coast homes, first to temporary assembly centers on fairgrounds and racetracks and subsequently to 10 concentration camps located in desolate interior locations. Not only were individuals' economic and educational lives severely disrupted, but the Japanese communities were destroyed. By the fall of 1942, some college students, aided by the Natl. Student Relocation Council, which was spearheaded by the American Friends Service Committee, were allowed to leave the camps to resume their education. However, they could enroll only in institutions east of the Rockies, and even then only certain colleges and universities would accept them. For instance, in the Cleveland area, Japanese-Americans could not enroll in Western Reserve University until Sept. 1944, supposedly because a Navy research contract so specified.

The most common way the Japanese found their way to Cleveland and other midwestern and eastern cities was through the auspices of the War Relocation Authority, the civilian agency created to run the camps. An employer would send a job notice to the Cleveland office of the WRA, which would then relay it to the relocation centers. If interested workers did not have funds, they were given $25 and transportation. Once they arrived, they would go to a temporary residence such as the Baptist House Mission at 2429 Prospect Ave. Two fraternities at WRU were secured by the WRA to house single men. Many also lived in the less expensive downtown hotels, such as the Erie Hotel Annex on E. 9th St. and the Roosevelt Hotel. The newcomers took mostly industrial and clerical jobs. The Cleveland regional office of the WRA was run by Robt. N. Cullom. In addition, the Cleveland Resettlement Committee (1943–45), with offices at 1001 Huron Rd., facilitated the arrival of the Japanese. Local businessman Geo. Trundle was its chairman, and Beatrice Burr its executive secretary. A particularly active member of its board was Dr. Grace Coyle of WRU. This group designed and implemented a publicity campaign that attempted to increase the willingness of community members to accept the Japanese even before they arrived. Numerous private individuals, such as Robt. Meeks of LAKEWOOD, also opened their homes to help the evacuees get resettled.

Generally, the young American 2d-generation or Nisei males would leave the concentration camps first to "test the waters." That was because of the considerable amount of apprehension among internees about how they would be treated once outside. It should be noted that they were not permitted to return to their West Coast homes until 1945. Fortunately, most who came to Cleveland and other midwestern cities found the local communities generally receptive, at least in comparison to the much more hostile Pacific Coast they had left. The returnees' most serious problems were in housing. Because of the shortage created by the war, the effects of which were compounded by discrimination, many Japanese experienced difficulties in renting and buying property. In fact, the Cleveland Board of Realtors in July 1945 complained to Dillon Myer, head of the WRA, that the Japanese were taking up too much of the available housing. Myer replied that the Japanese had the right to move anywhere they desired, and the WRA's job was to help them. The majority of the Japanese initially settled in HOUGH in the vicinity of 79th St., principally because that is where they could find housing. A few others took up residence in GLENVILLE and on the near west side. It should be noted that the Japanese community in Cleveland never attempted to build a "Little Tokyo" like the ones found on the West Coast. That was a result partly of the official policy of the WRA, which was to spread families out to avoid creating a "visible target"; partly of the Japanese's own conviction that they would be better off avoiding recreating the pre-World War II enclaves; and partly of housing availability and nearness to employment forces. The size of the Greater Cleveland community reached its peak immediately after the war. In 1946, when the camps were finally closed, it is estimated that there were 3,000–3,500 Japanese-Americans living in the Greater Cleveland area. By 1959, this number was reduced to 2,000, and by 1978, to approximately 1,500. Most returned to the West Coast, particularly the growing Southern California region. Those who remained most often had their own businesses or were comfortably employed and thus did not wish to start their economic and social lives over yet another time. A significant number of female Japanese came to Cleveland as the brides of American servicemen. Many of them attended some of the Japanese-language functions held by the community, but most were never fully integrated, for a number of reasons, into the core ethnic community.

Almost immediately upon their arrival in Cleveland, the Japanese began, as they had before, to create numerous voluntary associations. For instance, by 1946, Les Debonaires (female), Keen Tyme, and the Young Buddhist Assoc. had been formed. The Issei Christian Fellowship (*Issei* is the Japanese geogenerational term for 1st-generation immigrant) began holding services in Japanese every other Sunday in the Old Stone Church on PUBLIC SQUARE. The Nisei Fellowship, most of whom were already members of neighborhood church organizations, gathered every Sunday evening at the First Methodist Church at Euclid Ave. and E. 30th St. The Young Buddhists met at the FIRST UNITARIAN CHURCH at Euclid and E. 82nd St. There was even a group, headed by an Anne Kunitami, that tried to "teach the Japanese-Americans the responsibilities of citizenship." Also, by this time numerous softball, basketball, and bowling leagues had been formed. The softball players used to play on the diamonds that were located on 30th and Chester Ave., the basketball teams at the Towne Club or CATHEDRAL LATIN HIGH SCHOOL, and the bowlers at Euclid 14th Lanes, Mercury Lanes, and Chester 30th Lanes. The Fairway Golf Club, still active in 1987, was also formed in 1946. For the more sedentary, there were also organized activities such as charter-boat outings on Lake Erie. Other groups that were formed were the Cleveland Nisei Tennis Club (still active), the Femway Golf Club (defunct), and the Young Buddhist Bowling League (still active). In order to inform people about community events and other useful information, a newsletter called the *Kaleidoscope* was started by volunteers utilizing borrowed equipment. Most of its functions were taken over by the *Cleveland JACL Bulletin*, which is still publishing monthly, still with volunteer labor.

Religious institutions are almost always important to ethnic communities. The Japanese community in Cleveland is no exception. One of the major religious institutions is the CLEVELAND BUDDHIST TEMPLE, which was dedicated on 7 Jan. 1945 at the Unitarian Church at 82nd St. and Euclid Ave. The Christian Issei did not purchase a church building. However, they did form the Japanese Christian Church, which affiliated with what is today Hough Ave. United Church of Christ on E. 65th St. The remaining handful of Christian Japanese speakers continue to meet as the Japanese Christian Fellowship at the CHURCH OF THE COVENANT at 11205 Euclid Ave. for religious and fellowship purposes. It should be noted that after some emotional discussions in community forums held soon after their arrival in Cleveland, the Japanese community decided not to form an English-oriented Japanese Christian church for the 2d- and 3d-generation Nisei and Sansei. The prevailing view at the time was that assimilation ought to be promoted by attendance at neighborhood churches.

The association that tends to act as an umbrella organization and best represents the community at large is the Cleveland Chap. of the Japanese American Citizen's League. The JACL is a national organization with over 110 chapters. It was started in 1930 by 2d-generation Japanese-Americans interested in both protecting the political rights of the Japanese and developing the capabilities of Japanese-Americans to contribute to the larger society. The Cleveland Chap. was organized in 1946. Its membership has been as high as 356 in 1959, and sometimes has dropped below 100. Some of the more significant of the organization's activities have been the operation of an antidiscrimination committee immediately after World War II, the late 1960s-early 1970s successful effort to repeal the Emergency Detention Act, and the current effort, in conjunction with the national JACL effort, to obtain redress for the World War II incarceration. The Cleveland JACL has always sponsored many conventional community activities, such as an annual scholarship dinner to honor all high school and college graduates of Japanese extraction (started in 1959) and the Holiday Fair, an ethnic food, crafts, and arts festival held at Euclid High School (initiated in 1970). This latter event draws some 500 people from both the Japanese and the larger community.

As the Nisei who were young adults at the end of World War II aged and their children, the Sansei, came upon the scene, the character of community activities changed. Many of the sports club disbanded, and few dances were held. Most of the special-interest groups, such as the 1st-generation, mutual-aid-oriented Shinwakai (which became the Cleveland Japanese Foundation), servicemen's brides' Fuji Club, female teen Debbyshires, Ten-Thirty Investment Club, Hui O Hawaii Club, Bridge Club, Japanese American Youth, Jr. JACL Boosters, and Jr. Matrons, have ceased to function. A culturally oriented group, the SHO JO JIs (which was started in 1955 by the JACL), continues to preserve the Japanese dance form, perform public-relations functions, and entertain people both within and outside of the community. An important function that brings together all elements of the Japanese community is the annual community picnic, which was started in Cleveland in 1947. It is currently held in July at Clay's Park in Massillon. The basic tradition goes back to the original Issei immigrants, who used to similarly gather with others from the same prefecture in Japan. Later it evolved to include all individuals living in the same local area. Not only is food highlighted, but "fun-type" adult and children's games are featured. A colorful and visible element in most ethnic communities is sources of ethnic foodstuffs. The Matsuya Co. was established at 81st and Hough in 1946 to fulfill this important need. Subsequently, Toguchi's at 3811 Payne Ave. took over this function. At the present time, the store is at the same location but is called Omura's.

The Japanese in Cleveland have never been a geographically identifiable ethnic enclave. Although there was some concentration in the 79th and Hough area immediately after World War II, the Japanese have spread out throughout the city and its surrounding suburbs. The model residence is a home in a white, middle-class, eastern suburb. There are about 6 elderly Issei living together on the same floor in the government-subsidized Euclid Villa complex. This arrangement, which was actively developed by Japanese community members in the mid-1960s, facilitates social interaction and alleviates language and cultural problems for some of the few surviving 1st generation. It remains to be seen whether the 2d generation will utilize this facility. As illustrated by the large number of voluntary organizations, the Cleveland Japanese community has been and continues to be well organized. This cultural pattern is consistent with that found in Japan as well as in the pre-World War II ethnic communities on the West Coast. In both contexts, the average Japanese belonged to numerous organizations. A good example is a new group of approximately 100 persons called the Cleveland Area Retired Persons, formed in 1985 to promote the interests of retired Cleveland-area 2d-generation Japanese-Americans. This active group, which sponsors picnics, dances, language, craft, and dance lessons, card parties, and other types of social functions, has no explicit instrumental purpose other than to support fellowship among its members. Thus, although the nature of the Cleveland Japanese community has changed dramatically since it was "created" immediately after World War II, it continues to be an important element in most members' lives.

Stephen S. Fugita
University of Akron

Henry T. Tanaka

Fugita, Stephen, et.al., *Asian Americans and Their Communities of Cleveland* (1977).

The **JAYCEES** (originally known as the Junior Chamber of Commerce) is a leadership-training organization for men and women ages 18–36. The Cleveland Jr. Chamber of Commerce chapter was organized in 1938 for men only, with Chas. J. Ford as the first president. Two years later, the group became affiliated with the Cleveland Chamber of Commerce. Although abbreviations had been used for the organization's name (such as J.C. or JayCees), the use of the word *Jaycee* became officially sanctioned in 1947. The organization began accepting women for full membership in 1984. After reaching the age of 36, a member can remain active as an associate member. The organization's original purpose was to offer new opportunities to Cleveland's young men by opening unlimited fields of civic participation. This purpose has expanded to include individual development through self-improvement programs as well as community-service projects, for both men and women. Training is available on 3 levels: individual development through leadership-training courses; management development through chapter management; and community development. Some of the annual community events sponsored by the Cleveland Jaycees have been the Holiday Shut-Ins Party for the elderly and handicapped, a Christmas shopping tour for underprivileged inner-city children, the Cleveland Easter Egg Hunt, and Parties-in-the-Park downtown Friday night events, held 10–15 times a year in the spring and summer months. Former community projects

of the group included a Teen-Age Road-e-o, oriented to making better drivers of the area's youngsters. The Jaycees at one time also sponsored an annual art show and the Miss Cleveland contest. In 1971, the Elderlot program was sponsored as a fundraising activity for a senior citizens' recreation program. The Cleveland chapter sponsored the Natl. Jaycees Convention here in 1980, which brought in over $15 million for the city. The Cleveland chapter annually selects a prominent Cleveland member to receive the Distinguished Service Award. The 1984 recipient of the award, Jose Feliciano, chief prosecuting attorney for Cleveland, was chosen as one of 10 Outstanding Young Americans in 1985. The first female Cleveland Jaycees president, Lauren Wintering, was elected for the year 1986–87.

Cleveland Jaycees Records, WRHS.

**JAZZ.** Cleveland began to participate in and contribute to the evolution and popularity of jazz music when the New Orleans jazz musicians moved to urban areas in the north and east after WORLD WAR I. The jazz form originally evolved in New Orleans in the early 1900s as an American hybrid of African rhythmic traditions improvised on the piano and upon instruments derived from the European marching band. Cleveland's participation has been lively and continuous since the 1920s, although initial development was along racially segregated lines. White jazz musicians were members of the American Fed. of Musicians Local #4, while blacks were in Local #550; only in 1962 was integration achieved by merging the black local into Local #4, with bandleader Caesar Dameron as the prime mover. In the 1920s, jazz sessions, at dance halls such as the Golden Slipper (later the Trianon Ballroom, Euclid-E. 100th St.) or at clubs and Prohibition speakeasies, were segregated by business establishment or sometimes, in a single establishment, segregated by hours (i.e., white musicians and clientele until midnight, black thereafter). Among artists active locally at the time who went on to national prominence were trumpeter Pee Wee Jackson and future bandleaders Artie Shaw, Guy Lombardo, and Woody Herman; while already nationally recognized figures such as Paul Whiteman and Bix Beiderbecke made Cleveland a regular major stop on their tours. The most prominent native Clevelander to achieve national recognition was NOBLE SISSLE, who teamed with the ragtime pianist Eubie Blake to create and stage a number of black jazz-based Broadway musicals.

In the 1930s and 1940s, racial integration of concerts and sessions became the norm, and one club, Val's in the Alley (Cedar-E. 86th St.), became nationally famous because of Art Tatum's presence there, until WORLD WAR II. His reputation gave prominence to jazz piano, and often induced such internationally famous figures as Duke Ellington, Ella Fitzgerald, and Benny Goodman, while on tour in Cleveland, to join in with Tatum and his group for some impromptu (and unpaid) sessions. Contemporaneous Clevelanders who contributed to the evolution of "be-bop" or "bop" jazz in the 1940s included Caesar Dameron, his brother Tadd, and Freddie Webster. Some relocated to New York City, while others, disillusioned by the continued national segregation of the musicians' locals, moved to Europe. The 1950s and 1960s witnessed the growth of "cool" jazz and the development of new instruments such as the jazz guitar, along with a general surge in popularity and intellectual respectability thanks to the rise of college-campus concerts and extensive commercial exposure by radio disc jockeys. An Oberlin College concert by Dave Brubeck inaugurated the college boom, and the recorded version inspired other jazz LP albums. These, in turn, were played and vigorously promoted by local radio personalities such as Henry Pildner (WGAR) and especially Bill Randle (WERE). At the time, such disc jockeys were their own musical programming directors, and Randle must be credited with being among the national leaders in popularizing recorded jazz (as well as pioneering in other forms such as early ROCK 'N' ROLL).

Among the most prominent local clubs featuring jazz were the Theatrical (Short Vincent St.), the Cotton Club (originally E. 4th St., then Quincy–71st St.), and the Smiling Dog Saloon (W. 25th St. at I–71 Interchange). In the 1970s, the Smiling Dog was the magnet for Cleveland jazz musicians.

Also notable is performer-educator Mark Gridley, whose book *Jazz Styles* is currently the largest-selling jazz-studies textbook in the U.S. The local growth of academic interest in jazz and resulting programs in jazz education have spawned a nationally-recognized spring jazz fest at CUYAHOGA COMMUNITY COLLEGE. Increasing commercial costs, however, have taken their toll on jazz music activity. While jazz concerts have become an established part of the popular repertoire at the Blossom Summer Music Ctr., jazz music on the radio has declined. The only full-time jazz station, WCUY-FM, dropped the format in 1971; only the Public Radio station, WCPN-FM, now devotes a significant proportion of its programming to jazz. In the mid-1970s, an umbrella nonprofit organization, the Northeast Ohio Jazz Society, was formed to assist local college stations and other institutions in promoting and presenting concerts not otherwise commercially feasible; additional enterprises of this sort may be required to maintain the vitality of the jazz tradition in Cleveland.

Christopher A. Colombi, Jr.

See also MUSIC, DANCE HALLS.

The **JEHOVAH'S WITNESSES** ministry is based on the understanding of Bible prophecies that Jehovah will soon replace the present political system with a divine government under the rule of Jesus Christ, who will restore paradisaical conditions on Earth. Among their controversial beliefs are their neutrality in politics, refusal to salute the flag, and refusal of blood transfusions. The "Truth" probably arrived in the Cleveland area in the late 1800s through visits of traveling speakers sent out by the Watchtower Bible & Tract Society to preach the "Good News of the Kingdom." These speakers presented free public talks on the Scriptures. Later, missionaries made follow-up calls, encouraging those who had displayed an interest to continue their Bible studies and to meet together. The Witnesses in Cleveland at first held their weekly meetings as small groups in private homes. By the 1920s, the Bible students were meeting as a single congregation in the Brotherhood of Locomotive Engineers building on St. Clair Ave., as well as at the Masonic Auditorium and the Whitely Printing Co. Individual local congregations began forming during the late 1930s, meeting in rented or purchased buildings, which they renovated into Kingdom Halls. The Lakewood Congregation was the first local congregation to organize, while the Brooklyn Kingdom Hall on State Rd. was the first hall in Cleveland to be built as a Kingdom Hall. In 1986, there were over 30 congregations in the Cleveland area. In 1946, the Witnesses held their "Glad Nations" Internatl. Assembly at the CLEVELAND MUNICIPAL STADIUM. Prior to 1971, they held their circuit and district assemblies in various rented private and public auditoriums throughout the area. In 1971, the Witnesses purchased the Vine St. Theater in Willoughby, which they renovated into a modern 1,600-seat auditorium. The most

distinguishing feature of the Witnesses has been their zealous preaching of the Kingdom, especially from house to house. Early local witnessing work was accomplished through the street-corner distribution of magazines and tracts, and the use of testimony cards in the house-to-house work. Later, sound cars and portable phonographs were used to present recorded messages. Although the Witnesses in Cleveland were not subjected to the violence experienced elsewhere, many were denied status as ministers by local draft boards during WORLD WAR II and were convicted for draft evasion.

**JELLIFFE, RUSSELL W.** (19 Nov. 1891–7 June 1980), was a social worker who, along with his wife, Rowena Woodham Jelliffe (23 Mar. 1892- ), came to Cleveland in 1915 and established an interracial settlement house that evolved into the nationally acclaimed KARAMU HOUSE. The Jelliffes contributed to black American theater and to race relations in Cleveland. Russell Jelliffe was born in Mansfield, Ohio, the son of jeweler Chas. W. and Margaret Ward Jelliff (Russell restored the final *e* to the family name in college). In 1910 he entered Oberlin College. There he studied political economics and met sociology and psychology major Rowena Woodham, the daughter of John Franklin and Minnie Saxe Woodham of Albion, Ill. The two were student leaders at Oberlin: Rowena served as president of the Oberlin Women's Suffrage League, and Russell was president of the senior class of 1914. After their graduation in 1914, the couple entered graduate school at the University of Chicago, where they studied sociology (receiving master's degrees in 1915) and spent time in the city's settlement houses, Graham Taylor's Chicago Commons and Jane Addams's Hull House. The couple were married on 28 May 1915 and made their home in Cleveland because of its ethnic composition, its wealth, and its progressive reputation. Russell was employed by the Men's Club of the Second Presbyterian Church, an elite church located in an increasingly ethnic neighborhood. The Jelliffes decided to live as well as work in the neighborhood and, with money from the church, bought 2 houses on E. 38th St. alongside the Grant Park playground. Using contacts with children as a means of entering the life of the area, the Jelliffes established their Playhouse Settlement as an important part of the community. As the migration of blacks from the South into Cleveland increased, the Jelliffes became teachers for the new migrants, instructing them in such daily urban tasks as using the streetcars.

In 1920, inspired by the comments of black actor Chas. Gilpin, who visited a play at the settlement, the Jelliffes decided that theater and the arts were the means by which they could both develop the potential of individuals served by their settlement and create a biracial community center. Rowena began directing a more serious theatrical group, the Gilpin Players; she studied theater in New York City in the 1920s, and from 1920–46 she directed about 100 productions at Karamu's theater. Her husband served as the technical director of the theater. By the time they retired as directors of Karamu House in 1963, the Jelliffes had built it into a cultural and educational instutution with 4,000 members, a facility worth more than $1 million, an endowment of $1.2 million, an annual budget of $250,000, and a full-time staff of 34 employees. Russell Jelliffe was also instrumental in the development of other institutions important to Cleveland's black community and to the improvement of race relations: the URBAN LEAGUE (1916) and the CLEVELAND COMMUNITY RELATIONS BOARD (1945); he also served on the executive committee of the local branch of the NAACP and was on the board of the Cleveland Council on Human Relations. He was involved in the creation of the Cleveland Metropolitan Housing Authority (1933), was president of the Group Work Council of the Welfare Fed. (1938–40), and was foreman of the Cuyahoga County Grand Jury in 1960. The Jelliffes received a number of awards and honors for their work, including the Chas. Eisenman Civic Award in 1941 and the 1944 Human Relations Award of the Natl. Conference of Christians & Jews.

**JENNINGS, ELIZABETH (ELIZA) WALLACE** (21 Dec. 1809–25 Sept. 1887), was a philanthropist and benefactress whose bequests helped establish the CHILDREN'S AID SOCIETY and the ELIZA JENNINGS HOME. Elizabeth Wallace was born in Belfast, Ireland, the first child of James and Margaret Hannah Chambers Wallace. In 1820 the family emigrated to Petersburg, Ohio, and on 16 Aug. 1829 Eliza married banker Simeon Jennings (b. 7 Nov. 1791) of Salem, Ohio, eldest son of Levi and Rebecca Everly Jennings. Eliza and Simeon lived in Salem for over 30 years and subsequently moved to West Virginia and Cleveland. The couple had no children. Jennings acquired wealth, bought 8 acres of hilltop land on the lakeshore, and built several mansions, including an Italianate villa at 10427 Detroit Ave., where the couple lived for several years. They leased farmland property to the newly incorporated Children's Aid Society, and after Mr. Jennings died on 30 Oct. 1865, leaving an estate of over $1.5 million, Eliza deeded the home and additional acres to the society in appreciation of the friendship between her husband and CAS founder Robt. Waterton.

The plight of an elderly, homeless, indigent, incurably ill friend, Miss Mary Love, inspired Eliza to donate property and funds to the YOUNG WOMEN'S CHRISTIAN ASSOC. for the purpose of erecting a home or hospital to care for the indigent and incurably ill women of the city. The home, constructed at 10603 Detroit Ave., opened in Oct. 1888, approximately a year after the death of Mrs. Jennings. Renamed the Eliza Jennings Home in her honor, it severed its affiliation with the YWCA, became an independent nonprofit organization in 1922, and built an enlarged structure on the same site, which was dedicated on 3 Dec. 1925. With the expansion of its facilities, it changed its scope to include a place for women (and men), not necessarily "indigent or incurably ill," to live out their lives in "comfortable elegance" and security. Mrs. Jennings also endowed the Jennings Institute, a Methodist Seminary in Aurora, Ill., and the Home for Aged Women in Salem, Ohio.

**JENNINGS FOUNDATION.** *See* **MARTHA HOLDEN JENNINGS FOUNDATION**

**JENNINGS HALL,** 10204 Granger Rd., was opened in Apr. 1942 to provide a home for elderly persons with small incomes. The home was established by Msgr. Gilbert P. Jennings, the founder of St. Agnes Catholic Church at E. 79th St. and Euclid Ave. Upon his death in Apr. 1941, Jennings left an estate, inherited from his brother and estimated at $120,000, for the establishment of the home. Construction began in Sept. 1941, and the facility was dedicated on 17 Mar. 1942. It had accommodations for 65 men and women and was operated by the Sisters of the Holy Ghost; the name of that order was changed to the Sisters of the Holy Spirit in Aug. 1968. Fire destroyed Jennings Hall on 2 Feb. 1946, taking the lives of 14 residents. The home did not have a surplus of money or enough insurance to construct a new, fireproof facility, but it was rebuilt nevertheless with the help of the CATHOLIC CHARITIES CORP. Construction began in the fall of 1947,

and the new facility, with accommodations for 106 residents, was dedicated on 8 May 1949. In Apr. 1956, a 2-story addition replaced the 8-bed infirmary with a 35-bed nursing facility. In Mar. 1985, 87 senior citizens lived in Jennings Hall.

The **JENNY LIND TOUR** visited Cleveland on 7 Nov. 1851. The noted Swedish soprano was making a grand concert tour of America, which had been arranged and promoted by Phineas T. Barnum. Lind initially arrived in Cleveland on Saturday, 25 Oct., on the steamer *Mayflower*; she stayed at the WEDDELL HOUSE through Sunday before leaving for a concert engagement in Cincinnati. She returned to the Weddell House 2 weeks later with a troupe of 14 performers for her Cleveland appearance. The performance was held in Kelley's Hall. A crowd of 1,300 had paid from $2 to $4 for tickets. The program began with clarinet and vocal selections by Signor Balletti. Lind then took the stage. Her program included such songs as "John Anderson, My Jo," "Gipsy Song," "Echo Song," and her famous "Bird Song." During her performance of Haydn's aria "Oh Mighty Pens," from *The Creation*, several onlookers who had been peering at the performance from a roof skylight broke through the skylight onto the interior dome. A momentary panic ensued, but the crowd was quickly calmed by another number by the Swedish Nightingale. During the performance, Lind's pianist, Otto Goldschmidt, was called upon to play a solo, as Lind apparently did not feel well. At the conclusion of the number, Goldschmidt was enthusiastically applauded, and Lind herself stepped from behind the curtain to join the accolade. She married Goldschmidt the following year. While in Cleveland, Lind made a trip to the Northern Ohio Lunatic Asylum in NEWBURGH to cheer the inmates.

The **JEWISH CHILDREN'S BUREAU,** a central children's social-services agency, was formally established in 1941 but traces its origins to 1898, when a group of women formed the Infant Orphan Mothers' Society with the goal of creating an orphan home for infants who were too young to enter the Jewish Orphan Home. A year later, the Jewish Infant Orphan Home was organized. A permanent facility was dedicated near Woodland on E. 37th St. in 1901. In 1904, the home became one of the Fed. of Jewish Charities' initial beneficiaries. Two years later, a new residence was purchased for $14,000 at 2200 40th Ave. The orphan home cared for an average of 60 infants at any given time during the 1910s, at an annual cost of $11,000. It also received assistance from the Mothers' Society, which in 1906 included over 900 members. The home was closed in Jan. 1922, when it merged with the Welfare Assoc. for Jewish Children, an organization established 2 years earlier as a division of the federation. The goal of the Welfare Assoc. was to place orphans in foster homes. In 1941, the Jewish Children's Bureau was created through a merger of the functions of the Welfare Assoc. and BELLEFAIRE, formerly the Jewish Orphan Home. The bureau handled all planning for the care of Jewish children who required assistance outside of the home. In 1945, the bureau assumed responsibility for the daycare functions of the JEWISH DAY NURSERY. At the same time, the nursery became an auxiliary agency of the bureau. Also in 1945, the bureau took over all casework activities of the Orthodox Jewish Children's Home. Three years later, the Jewish Big Brothers Assoc. and Jewish Big Sisters Organization services were transferred from the JEWISH FAMILY SERVICE ASSOC. to the bureau, with the Big Sisters program becoming a joint committee of the bureau and the NATL. COUNCIL OF JEWISH WOMEN. The growth of the bureau resulted in part from the consolidation of agencies' services that marked the post-World War II experience in Cleveland's Jewish community.

The **JEWISH CHRONIC RELIEF SOCIETY** was established in 1914 as the Cleveland Ladies Consumptive Aid Society, one of the dozens of charitable, relief, and benevolent societies founded in the Jewish community during the first 2 decades of the century. The society's initial aim was to provide care and assistance to indigent Jews suffering from tuberculosis. In 1923, the organization incorporated as the Cleveland & Denver Consumptive Ladies Aid Society, reflecting its extension of aid to individuals who had to enter a national Jewish tuberculosis hospital in Denver. Upon affiliation with the hospital, the society pledged $10,000 to the institution. In 1926, the society merged with the Los Angeles Consumptive Aid Society, which was founded in Cleveland in 1920 and became the Cleveland-Denver-Los Angeles Consumptive Aid Society. The society donated several thousand dollars to the Los Angeles Sanatorium, resulting in the construction of the Cleveland Bldg., a wing of the hospital. One of the goals of the society was the construction of a convalescent center for tubercular patients who were released from the Warrensville Sanatorium and City Hospital and who were not ready to return to everyday activity. In cooperation with the Bikur Cholim Ladies Sick Aid Society and the Fed. of Jewish Charities, the society raised the funds necessary to build a 19-bed center, which was dedicated in 1937. In 1945, the federation assumed control of the center and constructed a new hospital to meet the growing needs of the community. The society continued to donate $3,500 annually to the maintenance costs. In Nov. 1935, the society dropped its cumbersome name in favor of the Jewish Consumptive Relief Society. However, as the incidence of tuberculosis decreased, the organization again changed its name, to the Jewish Chronic Relief Society. It continued to aid the sick and needy and to contribute to the convalescent hospital. In the 1940s and 1950s, the society's membership was more than 1,000, including its auxiliary organizations. Currently, the society has less than 100 members, but it continues to provide aid to chronically ill Jews and contributes annually to the Rainbow Babies and Childrens Hospital.

The **JEWISH COMMUNITY CENTER** was formed in 1948 by a merger of 4 agencies committed to enriching Jewish life through recreational, social, and cultural programs. By centralizing and expanding the functions of the Jewish Young Adult Bureau, the Council Educational Alliance, Camp Wise, and the Cultural Dept. of the JEWISH COMMUNITY COUNCIL, the new organization aided the integration of Jewish immigrants into American life and offered community programs for every stage of the life cycle. The oldest component of the JCC, the Council Educational Alliance, was founded in 1899 at E. 20th and Woodland, where it offered citizenship, English, and craft classes to East European immigrants. It moved several times, finally locating at E. 135th St. and Kinsman (1928), when it dropped its Americanization programs in favor of cultural programs, recreational activities, and, during the Depression, vocational guidance for the American-born patrons. As the Jewish community spread geographically, the CEA established branches at E. 105th, E. 123rd, and Lee and Superior. Camp Wise was begun in 1907 as a fresh-air camp for poor and underprivileged children. Built on property in EUCLID donated by SAMUEL D. WISE, it was considered one of the best-equipped campsites in the country. Over the years, the camp attracted children of all backgrounds. The third agency that preceded the JCC was the

Jewish Young Adult Bureau. Formed in 1939 to coordinate some 50 citywide recreational and cultural programs, the JYAB became the Jewish Young Adult Services Div. of the JCC. Finally, the Cultural Dept. of the Jewish Community Council was organized in 1945 to revitalize Jewish cultural activities for adults. After a survey of adult cultural life, it was concluded that there was no central body to organize or coordinate Jewish art and culture. To meet this need, the Cultural Dept. sponsored a Jewish arts festival, committees for music and art, and a Yiddish Cultural Committee, which, among other things, prepared a yearly calendar that noted important dates in modern Jewish history, such as the uprising in the Warsaw Ghetto and the birth of the state of Israel.

After the merger of the 4 agencies in 1948 in a central office at 2059 E. 105th St., the JCC added a Golden Age Services Div., a new daycamp program, and a drama department. Programs for teens and adults offered in the branches now were centrally planned, with the building of the JCC at Mayfield and Taylor. In 1959, the programs were physically united as well. Meanwhile, extension programs were established to bring the services of the JCC to the Jewish community in the suburbs. Camp Wise and its sister camp, Camp Henry Baker, were relocated to Halle Park in Burton. In the 1960s and 1970s, the JCC expanded its services to meet current needs for senior lunch services, daycare, and the socialization of Soviet Jews. In 1981, a master plan recommended major renovation of the Mayfield building, immediate acquisition of a new site, the construction of a daycamp and family recreation area, and, at Richmond and S. Woodland roads, construction of a new site. Fifty-three acres of land were purchased in BEACHWOOD, and after assuring the city council there that its programs would not interfere with city programs, the JCC began construction in 1985 on a $13 million building.

Jewish Community Ctr. Records, WRHS.

The **JEWISH COMMUNITY FEDERATION** is the central policymaking and fundraising agency for the Jewish community. It was established as the Fed. for Jewish Charities in 1903 in an attempt to remove the chaos of charitable fundraising by the various Jewish welfare organizations and to allow them to concentrate more on service. The founders, among them EDWARD M. BAKER, CHAS. EISENMAN, Julius Feiss, Emil Joseph, and MARTIN A. MARKS, were merchants, manufacturers, and professionals drawn from the old German and Hungarian Jewish families that immigrated to the U.S. in the mid-19th century. The federation constitution called for the agency to collect and apportion contributions and donations among its constituent organizations. No affiliates that conducted their own fundraising could receive allocations; they had to campaign among their members during the federation fund drives, and only "mature" charities with proven fiscal track records could become affiliates. The organizations initially receiving federation funds included the Jewish Orphan Home, MONTEFIORE HOME, Council Educational Alliance, Infant Orphan Mothers' Society, NATL. COUNCIL OF JEWISH WOMEN, MT. SINAI HOSPITAL, and Hebrew Relief Assoc. Each organization provided assistance to the newly arriving East European immigrants but was run and operated primarily by the old German and Hungarian Jewish community. In addition to the 7 local agencies, the federation provided funds for the Natl. Jewish Consumptive Hospital in Denver.

As a product of the Progressive Era, the federation leadership sought efficiency, streamlining, and accountability in the operations of its affiliates. This attitude and the over-

570

whelming German Jewish dominance of the federation put it at odds with the largely working-class, often Orthodox, East European immigrants. Twice, the latter group attempted to establish umbrella organizations that would represent its interests and provide support for the rapidly proliferating immigrant charities. Both attempts, the UNION OF JEWISH ORGANIZATIONS (1906) and the Cleveland KEHILLAH (1913), ended in failure. In 1913, the federation helped establish the Welfare Fed. of Cleveland, and in 1919 it became a charter member and constituent agency of the Community Fund, the first such organization in the country. Edward M. Baker succeeded Chas. Eisenman as federation president in 1923 and ushered in an era of greater cooperation with the Orthodox community. A community survey in 1923 commissioned by the federation predicted that the Orthodox were the community of the future. Three years later, Rabbi ABBA HILLEL SILVER recommended bringing the Orthodox charitable and philanthropic organizations into the federation. In subsequent years it funded the Jewish Orthodox Home for the Aged, the Orthodox Jewish Orphans Home, YESHIVATH ADATH B'NAI IS-RAEL, and the Hebrew School (Talmud Torah), among other Orthodox institutions.

In 1926, the federation changed its name to the Jewish Welfare Fed. to reflect the expansion of its role in the community beyond providing funding for its charitable institutions. At the same time, the leadership recognized that a fundraising arm had to be created to provide aid to organizations that fell outside of the funding philosophy of the Community Fund, which did not allow its funds to go to religious education. The Jewish Welfare Fund was created in 1930, and after 5 rocky years it was reorganized, with Rabbis Silver and BARNETT BRICKNER as cochairmen. Ten years later, the fund raised $1 million for the first time. By 1984, the annual fund drive had reached $26 million. In 1935, the federation was instrumental in establishing the Jewish Community Council. The council was to act as the spokesman for the community and also to provide a policing function for internal conflicts. Among its primary tasks was working to combat anti-Semitism. In 1936, the federation affiliated with the council, and the latter soon represented over 80 local Jewish organizations. Fifteen years later, the council and the federation merged their functions to form the Jewish Community Fed. In 1965, as a symbolic commitment by the organized Jewish community to the future of Cleveland, even at a time when almost all Jews lived outside the city limits, the federation erected a new office building at E. 18th St. and Euclid Ave.

The **JEWISH DAY NURSERY** was established in Apr. 1920 by 15 women from the Woodland Ave. neighborhood. Gussie Teitelman and Mrs. Sam Brofman were the principals in creating this organization to care for the children of working, indigent, and sick parents; children of broken homes; and orphans. Charter members paid an initial $1, and dues were set at $.15 per month. Within 2 weeks of organizing, the Cleveland Jewish Day Nursery Assoc. had 200 members. In Nov. 1921, the officers of the yet-unopened nursery enticed Jeanette Sheifer, director of the Hebrew Day Nursery of New York City, to become director/superintendent of the Cleveland nursery. She remained in that position for 25 years. The nursery purchased a house near 55th and Hawthorne but was unable to open because it had failed to seek a license from the city's Dept. of Public Welfare. After an inspection in Apr. 1922, the nursery received permission to operate under the conditions that it affiliate with the Cleveland Day Nursery, investigate families before accepting children, and serve only the Orthodox community. The nursery opened on 8 May 1922 with 8

children. By the end of the year, 81 applications had been made. Tuition was $.10-$.50 per day, based on need, and children up to the age of 13 were accepted. The Jewish Social Service Bureau investigated the applicants' home life, and MT. SINAI HOSPITAL provided medical care and daily health inspections. In June 1927, the Jewish Day Nursery moved to a house on 102nd St. An adjacent house was subsequently purchased, providing room for 50 children.

Following WORLD WAR II, the Jewish Day Nursery merged with the JEWISH CHILDREN'S BUREAU, becoming an affiliate of the latter. That allowed implementation of a social-work component; made the bureau the policymaking entity; and changed the age range of the nursery to 2-to-5-year-olds. In 1951, Vita Lazarus became the first professionally trained director in the nursery's history. She was followed in 1956 by Miriam Shifrin, who was director until 1977. In 1956, the nursery sold the houses on 102nd St. and took up temporary residence on the grounds of BELLEFAIRE. After 5 years, a $200,000 building was constructed at Bellefaire for the nursery. Services provided to children and families during the 1950s included social work, child care, and educational and support aid to immigrant families. In the 1960s, the services expanded to include 6-year-olds, a kindergarten opened, family daycare homes became an off-site service, and medical, dental, psychiatric, speech, and hearing therapy were offered. The restriction concerning Orthodox children is no longer in effect.

Jeanette Sheifer Papers, WRHS.

The **JEWISH FAMILY SERVICE ASSOCIATION** is the principal family-counseling and social-work service agency for Cleveland's Jewish community. It was established in 1875 as the Hebrew Relief Society, originally to provide monetary and material relief to needy families and individuals. A Russian Relief Committee was established in 1882 to assist the large number of Russian Jews settling in Cleveland, and it merged with the Hebrew Relief Society in 1894. The society was a relatively small operation during the 19th century, never collecting more than $6,000 for aid in any one year. After joining the Fed. of Jewish Charities in 1904, it was able to dispense more than $10,000 in aid. The society hired its first professional superintendent in 1904, when A. S. Newman came to Cleveland from Chicago. He established the first rudiments of casework in 1906, replacing the traditional interview of the officers of the society. They were interviewed by the superintendent, who then investigated the family or individual need. Newman also established "friendly visits" by volunteers to recipients' homes to offer guidance. That was the society's first move toward comprehensive social service rather than simple material relief. As immigration slowed during WORLD WAR I and was restricted in the 1920s, the agency continued to move toward casework services. In 1924, it changed its name to the Jewish Social Service Bureau (JSSB), and later in the decade it affiliated with Western Reserve University's School of Applied Social Services in the training of social workers.

During the early years of the Depression, the bureau continued to dispense relief funds, but in 1933 it turned this function over to newly created governmental agencies. Following that change in services, the bureau expanded into homemaker services and refugee resettlement programs and established the Vocational Adjustment Dept., which later became the Jewish Vocational Service. In 1940, Rae C. Weil became director of the JSSB. Under her leadership, the agency instituted fee-based services to make the agency more accessible to those who hesitate to accept free aid

571

or charity. In 1943, the name was changed to the Jewish Family Service Assoc. Over the ensuing 4 decades, the association expanded its services to include a complete range of family and child welfare services. Among these are individual, family, and group counseling; mutual support groups for single parents, the widowed, and relatives of those with special problems, such as mental illness and handicaps; education and outreach; and referral services.

Jewish Family Service Assoc. Records, WRHS.

## JEWISH ORPHAN HOME. *See* ORTHODOX JEWISH CHILDRENS HOME

**JEWS & JUDAISM.** Jewish immigration to Cleveland, like the general pattern in America, can be divided into 2 distinct, overlapping periods. The German era (1837–1900) witnessed the settlement of Jews from Central Europe who spoke German and were imbued with a German cultural identity. The principal years of immigration ran to ca. 1875. The East European era (1870–1924) saw the community population grow from 3,500 in 1880 to approximately 85,000 in 1925 as Russian, Polish, Galician, and Romanian Jews settled in the city. The social and cultural character of the two groups was markedly different, and their institutional and communal development through the mid-1930s, though sharing some common threads, was more often parallel and separate. The first Jews to make their home in Cleveland arrived in the late 1830s from southern Germany. By 1840, there were 20 families and probably 20 single males residing in the city. The nascent Jewish community settled near the CENTRAL MARKET, generally west of the river. It was there that the community built its first institutions. In 1839, a religious body, the Israelitic Society of Cleveland, was established and soon evolved into ANSHE CHESED (now Fairmount Temple). The congregation erected a synagogue in 1846 on Eagle St. across from the market. Four years later, following a doctrinal dispute at Anshe Chesed, a second congregation, Tifereth Israel, was formed, and a synagogue at 6th and Miami was constructed in 1856. The occupational background of the Jewish immigrants was in the petty trades and artisan pools of Central Europe. The Jews who settled in Cleveland were primarily shopkeepers and peddlers, although a few were skilled craftsmen. Peddling, which required little skill and no capital investment, was a common avenue for entrance into a more stable commercial pursuit. By the 1870s, the community had grown and businesses expanded to the extent that young or newly arrived Jews no longer peddled goods, but received their business training as clerks or bookkeepers in the firms of relatives or landsmen. Jewish businessmen were involved in retail and wholesale dry goods, hides and furs, and grocery and clothing establishments; and to a lesser degree as commission merchants, shippers, and bankers. Still others, upon accumulating sufficient capital, became interested in manufacturing, especially clothing and textiles. By 1900, Cleveland's largely Jewish-owned GARMENT INDUSTRY was among the most important in America.

As the community's population increased and gained greater wealth, Jews abandoned the cramped quarters of the Central Market district and moved eastward along Woodland and Central. By 1875, many Jews already lived east of Perry St. (E. 22nd), with several residing in the fashionable neighborhoods around Case Ave. (E. 40th). During the 1890s, Willson Ave. (E. 55th) became the center of the German Jewish population. The German Jews created an array of organizations and institutions during the 19th century. The small cultural societies of the 1860s, such

as the Young Men's Hebrew Literary Society and the ZION MUSICAL SOCIETY, were short-lived, giving way in the 1870s and 1880s to the increasing social importance of fraternal organizations such as B'NAI B'RITH, and clubs such as EXCELSIOR and the Hungarian Benevolent & Social Union. In 1864, B'nai B'rith District Lodges Nos. 2 and 6 chose Cleveland as the site for an orphan asylum that would serve 16 states. Dedicated in 1868, the Jewish Orphan Asylum was located at E. 51st and Woodland, presaging the move of the community into that area. In 1882, the Order Kesher Shel Barzel established the Kesher Home for the Aged, which was renamed the Kesher Montefiore Home in 1884. Both agencies evolved into important large service institutions and eventually came completely under Cleveland Jewish community auspices.

The most important institutions for 19th-century Cleveland Jewry remained congregations Anshe Chesed and Tifereth Israel for the Germans, and to a lesser extent B'NAI JESHURUN for the Hungarian Jews. As their memberships increased and moved eastward, each erected new synagogues. Anshe Chesed relocated from Eagle St. to E. 25th and Scovill in 1887, and to E. 82nd and Euclid in 1912. Tifereth Israel moved farther, to Willson Ave. in 1894 and to Ansel Rd. in Wade Park in 1924. B'nai Jeshurun erected a large synagogue at Scovill and Willson in 1906 and, 19 years later, became the first established congregation to move into the Heights, building the Temple on the Heights at Mayfield Rd. east of Lee Rd. More important than the residential dimension of the congregations were the changes in appearance and ritual effected during the late 19th and early 20th centuries. The German Jews desired to minimize the differences between themselves and their non-Jewish neighbors. That was accomplished in religious practice by introduction of family pews, removal of hats and prayer shawls, hiring rabbis who could preach in English on secular subjects, and introduction of organs and choirs to the service.

In the 1870s, Reform Judaism began adopting a liberal theological view that was embraced almost immediately by Tifereth Israel, and somewhat later by Anshe Chesed. The former adopted a Reform prayerbook in 1866 and in 1873 joined the newly established Reform umbrella organization, the Union of American Hebrew Congregations. It was under the direction of Rabbi MOSES J. GRIES, however, that Tifereth Israel departed radically from traditional Judaism, and even from the mainstream of the Reform movement. During his tenure, the TEMPLE, as it was now popularly called, adopted the Union Prayer Book, eliminated Hebrew from the Sunday school curriculum and from religious services, substituted an English translation of the Torah to be placed in the synagogue's Ark, and changed Sabbath services from Saturday to Sunday. Although Anshe Chesed never espoused as radical a position, it embraced what became known as Classical Reform during the rabbinate of LOUIS WOLSEY (1907–25).

When East European Jews fled the pogroms, restrictive social legislation, and economic dislocation of Eastern Europe and immigrated to America, they discovered an affluent, entrenched German Jewish community that in most cases had more in common with its Protestant neighbors than with its newly arrived coreligionists. In Cleveland, the differences between the two groups were an embarrassment to the German Jewish leadership and an outrage to the new immigrants. A handful of East European Jews lived in Cleveland as early as the late 1850s, and by 1880, there were 4 or 5 Orthodox congregations. They were joined by thousands who immigrated to Cleveland, especially during the peak years, 1904–14. The new immigrants settled in the areas that had been abandoned by the German and

Hungarian Jews, and in the 1880s and 1890s resided side by side with other non-Jewish immigrants, particularly ITALIANS around Berg St., and HUNGARIANS and CZECHS along lower Broadway. Like their German predecessors, the early East European Jews moved out of the Central Market area at the first opportunity.

The German Jews made several attempts to address immigrant charitable needs in the 1880s and 1890s, but with limited success. The most important such agency was the Hebrew Relief Society (est. 1875), which provided case-by-case aid. German Jewish aid was a combination of self-interest, humane concern for fellow Jews, and paternalism. The foreignness of the East Europeans was seen as a threat to the social standing attained by German Jews, and efforts had to be made to Americanize the new immigrants. Foremost among these efforts was the creation of the Council Educational Alliance in 1899 by the local COUNCIL OF JEWISH WOMEN. Its purpose was to engage in educational and philanthropic work among the new immigrants. The CEA offered a variety of classes designed to help the immigrants' transition to an American way of life. It was, in addition, the meeting place for the plethora of clubs and societies created by East European Jews. Among the most important immigrant organizations were the social/benevolent societies usually formed as *landsmanshaften*. A *landsmanshaft* was a group of Jews from a common locale who banded together for social reasons, but also to provide aid and comfort to members when needed and to assist newly arrived *landsleit* in obtaining work. In addition to these functions, several of the *landsmanshaften* formed the nuclei for immigrant ethnic congregations such as Anshe Grodno and TETIEVER AHAVATH ACHIM ANSHE SFARD.

Between 1895–1920, at least 25 Orthodox congregations were established in Cleveland. However, none approached the importance of the older ANSHE EMETH. Before 1904, the Orthodox community had no rabbinical leader who could represent its interests. Rabbi BENJAMIN GITTELSOHN was internally important for his scholarship and spiritual guidance. However, it was Rabbi SAMUEL MARGOLIES, who came to the city in 1904, who became the most influential of the Orthodox leaders during the first quarter of the 20th century. His preeminence was based on his traditional Judaism, his appeal to Zionists, and his belief that Jews needed to Americanize as quickly as possible. The latter view led to the creation nationally of an American form of traditional Judaism—Conservative Judaism—that was embraced by Anshe Emeth in the 1920s and by B'nai Jeshurun somewhat earlier. Those two congregations by the mid-1920s ranked 3d and 4th in membership behind the two Reform temples. None of the Orthodox congregations, which were primarily ethnic or *landsmen* shuls, could approximate the size of these four until the era of mergers following WORLD WAR II.

The East European immigrants, like the Germans, tended to enter mercantile occupations when possible. However, the opportunities available in the wide-open economy of the 19th century did not exist to the same extent for the new immigrants. Over 15% of the East European Jews were engaged as peddlers or hucksters during the first decades of the 20th century, while 25–33% operated small stores or worked as clerks in Jewish-owned establishments. The single most striking occupational difference between East European and German Jews was that 40–50% of the former worked in the skilled and semiskilled trades, especially as cigarmakers and in the building and needle trades. Fully 20% of the employed Jews in Woodland were found in the clothing industry, generally with large Jewish manufacturing firms such as JOSEPH & FEISS, PRINTZ-BEI-

DERMAN, and D. Black & Co. Despite the lack of opportunity to accumulate wealth on the same scale as the German Jews, the frugal East Europeans did manage to attain enough money to move to newer and more commodious areas. At the turn of the century, Lower Woodland was a dilapidated, unsanitary, and unsafe section of the city. Most Jews had moved to the area around E. 35th St., and a decade later the center of the community had again pushed toward E. 55th St.

The Woodland district supported a vibrant Jewish culture during the late 1890s and the first 15 years of the 20th century. Yiddish and Hebrew literary societies and debating societies abounded, the Yiddish theater flourished at the Perry and then the People's theaters, and a long, successful Yiddish press began in 1908, when Samuel Rocker founded the Yiddishe *Tegliche Presse*, which was followed in 1911 by Rocker's Die *YIDDESHE VELT*, which survived until 1958. However, it lacked the size and insulation of communities such as New York's Lower East Side; Woodland's Yiddish life could not survive amid the pull and lure of Americanization or the eventual migration out of Woodland. One Americanizing influence was public education, which Jews supported almost without concession. Yet, Jewish education was recognized as the only way to ensure that children did not stray from Judaism. The afternoon school became the educational form the community would use during the first half of the 20th century for Jewish education. In 1883, the East European immigrants founded a Talmud Torah that offered traditional Jewish education in the cheder style. After 1904, it came under the influence of Rabbi Samuel Margolies, Joshua Flock, and Aaron Garber, who emphasized Hebrew and Jewish nationalism. In the 1920s and 1930s, the Talmud Torah, later known as the CLEVELAND HEBREW SCHOOLS, was directed by ABRAHAM H. FRIEDLAND, who infused it with an even more pronounced Hebraist and Zionist philosophy. In 1924, the BUREAU OF JEWISH EDUCATION was created with Friedland as director to provide direction and resource coordination for the community's schools.

The vast charitable and philanthropic need coupled with the fact that institutions competed with one another in fundraising led the German Jewish leadership in 1903 to establish the Fed. of Jewish Charities, an umbrella organization whose function was to raise and disburse funds to its beneficiary agencies, thereby freeing them to concentrate on providing services. The initial recipients were the MONTEFIORE HOME, Jewish Orphan Home, Council of Jewish Women, Infant Orphan Mothers Society, Hebrew Relief Society, MT. SINAI HOSPITAL, Council Educational Alliance, and Denver Consumptives Hospital. None of these were immigrant charities, reflecting the FJC policy of funding only "mature" organizations. This policy angered the East European Jewish leadership and led to the creation of 2 organizations that hoped to represent the entire community. The UNION OF JEWISH ORGANIZATIONS (est. 1906) operated for nearly 3 years and experienced some success in ridding the public school system of some anti-Semitic practices. However, the lack of adequate financial support and opposition from the FJC and the Reform congregations ensured its demise. In 1913, the shorter-lived Cleveland KEHILLAH was created by the former UJO leadership, but it suffered the same fate. Other immigrant institutions that paralleled those of the German Jews were longer-lived. The Orthodox Old Home, established in 1906 in reaction to the Montefiore Home's refusal to maintain a kosher kitchen, has evolved into one of the largest and most advanced Jewish homes for the aged in the U.S., MENORAH PARK. And the Orthodox Orphan Home, created in 1920, ran a small but successful program until 1959, when it merged with the JEWISH CHILDREN'S BUREAU.

The issue that most divided the two communities was Zionism. Small Zionist societies existed in Cleveland as early as 1897, but it was after the turn of the century, with increased immigration, that Zionism became the central force in the East European community. Zionist organizations proliferated in the early 1900s, running the spectrum from the Orthodox Mizrachi to the socialist Poale Zion and Farband. Rabbi Samuel Margolies was already a well-known Zionist when he arrived in Cleveland in 1904, and he and Rabbi Nachman Ebin and ABRAHAM KOLINSKY were among the principal leaders of Cleveland Zionism during the first 2 decades of the 20th century. Reform rabbis Moses Gries and Louis Wolsey opposed Zionism because it separated Jews from the rest of American society and contradicted the Reform ideology. However, in the 1920s, the old-guard Reform leaders began to change their attitudes as the Reform congregations came under the leadership of Rabbis ABBA HILLEL SILVER (the Temple) and BARNETT ROBT. BRICKNER (Anshe Chesed). Both rabbis were raised in the East European and Zionist milieu of the Lower East Side of New York, and both attained national and international stature in the Zionist movement—Silver became the leading figure in American Zionism by World War II.

As the 1920s approached, Jews began to desert Woodland and move eastward to GLENVILLE and to the Mt. Pleasant/Kinsman district. By 1922, 28.5% of Cleveland Jewry lived in or adjacent to the former area, and another 14% lived in the latter. By 1926, the Jewish population of Woodland decreased from 35,000 to 17,000, and 3 years later, the figure was further reduced to 1,400. The migrations to new neighborhoods had a slight class character. The Jews who moved to Glenville appear to have been the emerging European Jewish middle class. Although they were predominantly Orthodox, the focal point for Glenville Jews was the Jewish Ctr. (formerly Anshe Emeth), by the early 1920s a Conservative congregation and the most important social and recreational institution in the area. In addition, a few Glenville Jews were joining Reform congregations. The Jews of Mt. Pleasant/Kinsman have been characterized as proletarian, and indeed, those who settled in the neighborhood were heavily concentrated in the trades. Many of the Jewish unions relocated in Kinsman, and the Jewish socialists, most notably the WORKMEN'S CIRCLE, also moved to that area.

Glenville, a little over 1 mi. square, was far more densely populated than Woodland. Its main thoroughfares were lined with small shops, kosher butchers, and delicatessens. Mt. Sinai Hospital in 1916 was the first major social-service institution to relocate to the Glenville district, followed in 1921 by the Jewish Orthodox Old Home. During the same year, Anshe Emeth moved to Glenville and dedicated the Jewish Ctr. on E. 105th St. It was the center of intellectual ferment in Glenville and was a focal point for the community's Zionist activity. Just as Woodland served as the birthplace of several German Jewish fortunes, Glenville provided a similar setting for several East European Jews. LEONARD RATNER first entered business in Glenville and with his brothers eventually built FOREST CITY ENTERPRISES. Julie Kravitz helped create the Pick-N-Pay chain from a small grocery store on Superior Ave.

Kinsman was almost twice the geographic size of Glenville but held only about half as many Jews. John Adams High School in Kinsman was never more than 25% Jewish, compared to Glenville High School, which ran as high as 90%. The Jews who moved out of Woodland to Kinsman in the early 1920s settled between E. 118th and E. 123rd streets. By the early 1930s, the center of the population was between E. 135th and 147th, on the streets adjacent to Kinsman Ave. The Jews of Kinsman were relative newcomers to the city, as can be seen in the development of the area's congregations. Many of the religious institutions that moved into Kinsman had existed for only a few years in Woodland, and even more were established initially in Kinsman. Neveh Zedek on Union (est. 1920) was the largest of the congregations in this area of settlement, and the KINSMAN JEWISH CTR. (est. 1930, with a synagogue dedicated in 1933) at 146 E. 147th St. was smaller but of equal importance. With these two congregations, the most important institutions were the Council Educational Alliance, which began work in Kinsman in the 1920s, and the Workmen's Circle, the center of socialist and fraternal activity in the neighborhood. The alliance was originally at E. 118th St. but moved to E. 135th St. and Kinsman in 1928. It was across from the Carpenters Auditorium, which offered social activities for local residents. Workmen's Circle erected Workmen's Hall in 1927 at E. 147th and Kinsman, and it became the center for preservation of Yiddish culture, with lectures, entertainments, and a day school.

A small number of Jews lived on Cleveland's west side before the turn of the century, and by 1910 there were enough to form a congregation, B'nai Israel. In the 1940s, the congregation became known as the West Side Jewish Ctr. Most of the west side Jews owned small shops during this period. In 1954, a group of Jews formed Beth Israel, a Reform congregation. Three years later, it merged with the West Side Jewish Ctr. to form BETH ISRAEL—THE WEST TEMPLE. Several members of Beth Israel formed the CLEVELAND COUNCIL ON SOVIET ANTI-SEMITISM to conduct activities on behalf of Soviet Jewry.

The Fed. of Jewish Charities changed its name to the Jewish Welfare Fed. in 1926, reflecting its evolution beyond simply charity. It implemented recommendations of a 1923 community study and admitted several immigrant institutions to constituent status in a move to patch up differences with the East European Jews. A reorganization in 1930 created the Jewish Welfare Fund, and the Jewish Community Council was established in 1935. The former provided a more directed and systematic approach to fundraising for community programs, and the latter addressed the demands for democratization of community leadership originally raised by the creation of the UJO and the Kehillah. The council mediated internal community disputes, monitored anti-Semitism, and acted as the Jewish representative body to the general public. In 1951, the council merged with the Jewish Welfare Fed. to form the JEWISH COMMUNITY FED., which remains the fundraising and policy arm of the community.

Following World War II, the Jewish community engaged in a second major population migration as it began to depopulate Glenville and Kinsman and push into the Heights and eastern suburbs. A small number of Jews settled in the Heights during the first decade of the 20th century. In 1905, wealthy German Jews established the OAKWOOD CLUB on several acres of land near Mayfield and Taylor roads. A few Orthodox founded the Heights Orthodox Congregation (later the HEIGHTS JEWISH CTR.) in 1923, and B'nai Jeshurun dedicated the Temple on the Heights on Mayfield in 1925. Movement into the suburbs was often met with hostility from non-Jews, and court battles were fought to set aside restrictive covenants and to secure building rights for Jewish institutions, particularly in SHAKER HTS., BEACHWOOD, and PEPPER PIKE.

The fear that exposure to American culture and the lack of intensive Jewish education would estrange 2d- and 3d-generation Jews from traditional Judaism was well

574

founded. Although congregations often boasted large memberships in the 1930s and 1940s, synagogues were all but empty on the Sabbath, and few Jews took an active interest in the congregations. Reform Jews were more interested in the communal activities of their rabbis than in the religious aspects of congregational life. And Orthodox congregations, despite the dynamic and scholarly leadership of rabbis such as ISRAEL PORATH and DAVID GENUTH, were losing their hold on the children of members. However, following World War II, Orthodoxy in Cleveland, and America in general, experienced a resurgence that continued into the 1980s. In part, increased synagogue memberships and activity resulted from reaction to societal alienation felt by the young and a search for personal identity that led many Jews back to traditional Judaism. In Cleveland, the Young Israel, Chabad Lubavitch, and the religiously tinged Betar Youth appealed to young Jews on the dual religious and Zionist planes. In addition, the proliferation of Orthodox day schools, especially the growth and excellence of the HEBREW ACADEMY; the consolidation of congregations to build strength; and the fact that the Orthodox now had a body of wealthy philanthropists who freely spent money for religious causes, all contributed to the increasing strength of the movement.

The postwar migration introduced an era of consolidation, especially among the Orthodox congregations. The cost of relocating was more than the small congregations could afford. The federation worked with the Orthodox community to effect mergers that would increase memberships and treasuries, resulting in the creation of the Taylor Rd. and WARRENSVILLE CTR. SYNAGOGUES, and the Heights Jewish Ctr. The area between Coventry Rd. and S. Green Rd. in Cleveland Hts. became the heart of the Jewish community in the 1950s. Taylor Rd. by the late 1950s and early 1960s was the focal point and witnessed the greatest concentration of Jewish institutions in the community's history. Adjacent to Taylor Rd. were the JEWISH COMMUNITY CTR., PARK SYNAGOGUE, Montefiore Home, Council Gardens, Taylor Rd. Synagogue, Bureau of Jewish Education, Hebrew Academy, JEWISH FAMILY SERVICES ASSOC., and a host of smaller synagogues and institutions. Yet even with this concentration, the highly mobile Jews continued to move eastward, populating Beachwood, Pepper Pike, and even HUNTING VALLEY. The federation estimated conservatively that another wholesale move of institutions would cost the community $100 million. In 1969, the federation extracted promises from all major institutions to remain in the Heights. Only the Temple on the Heights, which had formulated plans for a move and purchased land near Brainard Rd., failed to agree. The federation established the HEIGHTS AREA PROJECT to encourage Jews to remain in the Heights and worked with community organizations, the police, and local government to ensure that the Heights remained socially, residentially, and politically stable. The federation also built new offices at E. 18th and Euclid to symbolize its committment to the welfare of the city.

The Reform movement also experienced a surge following World War II. In 1948, TEMPLE EMANU EL was created with the assistance of Anshe Chesed, the Temple, and the Union of American Hebrew Congregations to reach out to the unaffiliated. Under the direction of Rabbi Alan S. Green, the concept was immediately successful, and Emanu El in the 1980s was a large and growing congregation. Soon after Emanu El's founding, a group of Jews who were dissatisfied with Reform's return to Hebrew education and support of Zionism formed Suburban Temple along ideological lines common to Reform in the late 19th and early 20th centuries. Reform, nationally in the 1970s

and 1980s, established an aggressive outreach program to the unaffiliated intermarried Jews. Many of its tenets, particularly recent decisions on issues such as patrilineal descent as a determinant of whether one is Jewish, have brought Reform into direct and bitter conflict with the Orthodox. The divisions between the two are deep and are evident in the Cleveland Jewish community. In the 1980s, the Jewish community faces serious religious divisions but is probably organized and united better than at any time in its history. The JCF, which enjoys unprecedented financial support from the Orthodox, is the central fundraising and policy authority in the community. Cleveland's Jewish institutional structure is highly centralized compared to that of many other communities, and the JCF is per capita the most successful federation in the U.S.

Scott Cline
Seattle Municipal Archives

Gartner, Lloyd P., *History of the Jews of Cleveland* (1978).
Pike, Kermit J., ed., *A Guide to Jewish History Sources in the History Library of the Western Reserve Historical Society* (1983).
Vincent, Sidney Z., and Rubinstein, Judah, *Merging Traditions: Jewish Life in Cleveland* (1978).

**JICHA, JOSEPH W.** (1901–30 Aug. 1960), was a nationally known commercial artist and prominent watercolorist. He was born in Austria-Hungary and came to Cleveland with his family as an infant. His father, a skilled coppersmith who worked decorations for the CLEVELAND INSTITUTE OF ART, apprenticed 13-year-old Joseph to sculptor Walter Sinz at the institute. He graduated with a dislike for design classes but later realized that design was an important and integral part of commercial work, as well as painting. As a student, he was a member of the KOKOON CLUB. The Cleveland Community Fund commissioned him to design a poster for its campaign in 1928. In 1929, Jicha won the Frank Logan Medal, an international award, at the Chicago Art Institute for painting. He believed that the work he did as a commercial artist helped him as a painter, because of the careful planning that goes into design work.

Jicha worked for Fawn Art and Creative Artists on advertisments for the Hotel Statler, SHERWIN-WILLIAMS, and the Libbey-Owens-Ford Glass Co. His work appeared in the *Saturday Evening Post* and *Life* magazine. He won the Art Director's Show in New York City in 1936. He exhibited paintings in 1938 at the KORNER & WOOD BOOKSTORE and in 1941 at the Hotel ALCAZAR. These paintings included landscapes of the Florida Keys, Louisiana, Mexico, Panama, and Ohio. His paintings were described by critics as having great line strength and composition, with blazing colors. Jicha also exhibited in 1941 by invitation at the Natl. Watercolor Show in San Diego. His work is found in the San Diego Museum and at the Mexico Natl. Museum. He taught summer school at the Cleveland Institute of Art in 1950. Two years later, Jicha and his wife, the former Cora Jerry, and 4 dogs packed up their belongings to travel and paint across America for a year.

**JIROUCH, FRANK L.** (3 Mar. 1878–2 May 1970), was a sculptor known mainly for his sculpture in Cleveland's Cultural Gardens. Jirouch was born of a Czech father and a German mother in Cleveland. Little is known of his early life, but at the turn of the century he and Geo. Fischer worked together as woodcarvers on the Prudential Bldg. in New York City. In 1902, the two returned to Cleveland and started the firm of Fischer & Jirouch, mainly doing decorative architectural relief sculpture, a field the firm dominated for many years. During WORLD WAR I, Jirouch attended the Philadelphia Academy of Fine Arts. In 1921, he and his wife lived in Paris for 3 years, at which time he exhibited work at the Salon Francais and became a monitor at the Academie Julien. According to Jirouch in an interview in 1964, when he was 86, he returned to find the business of decorative relief sculpture on the wane. The Cultural Gardens were expanding, and it is thought that he did as many as 25 of the busts, statues, or commemorative plaques honoring a poet, educator, philosopher, etc. of the sponsoring group. There are 21 of these gardens, and Jirouch's contribution was greater than that of any other single sculptor. Among his pieces are Abraham Lincoln (1950), John Hay (1938), Artemus Ward (1948), and Ernest Bloch (1955, 75th birthday).

Campen, Richard N., *Outdoor Sculpture in Ohio* (1980).

## JOC-O-SOT, OR WALKING BEAR

**JOC-O-SOT, OR WALKING BEAR** (1810–3 Sept. 1844), was a Sauk chief in the Black Hawk Wars who achieved celebrity status in Cleveland. He came to the city in the 1830s as a hunting and fishing companion of Dr. HORACE ACKLEY. Attracting the attention of theater promoter Dan Marble, he agreed to go on tour to major cities, where curious crowds came to gape at the "savage" and view plays in which he starred about Indian life. When the traveling show went to England, Joc-O-Sot became the darling of the Royal Court; Queen Victoria even had a full-length portrait painted of him. While Joc-O-Sot was in Washington on a peace mission, an old bullet wound in the lung flared up and led to consumption. In a weakened state, he returned penniless to Cleveland, where he was aided by his old friend Dr. Ackley. Upon Joc-O-Sot's death, his friends arranged for his burial in the ERIE ST. CEMETERY. His epitaph, bearing an incorrect date, reads:

> Joc-O-Sot/ the Walking Bear/ a Distinguished/ Sauk Chief/ Died August, 1844/ Erected by ten citizens/ of Cleveland and a friend/ of Cincinnati.

**JOHN, HENRY J.** (5 Mar. 1885–28 Mar. 1971), was an internationally recognized expert in diabetes. He and his wife founded Camp Ho Mita Koda, the first nonprofit summer camp for diabetic children. John was born Jindrich Jeroslav to Czech parents in Olomouc, Moravia. Although his parents came to the U.S. when he was 5, he was unable to join them until he was 14. He entered the University of Kansas in 1907 to study pharmacy but changed to premed as a sophomore. He graduated in 1911 and then, through a research fellowship, attended the University of Minnesota, receiving an M.A. degree in 1912. In 1916, he received his M.D. from the Western Reserve School of Medicine and began an internship at ST. VINCENT CHARITY HOSPITAL in Cleveland. In 1917, John—by then a naturalized U.S. citizen—joined the Army Medical Corps. While serving as an Army doctor, he was the first to devise and make use of a plan to administer glucose intravenously after surgery. Discharged in 1919, he joined Dr. F. M. Allen in Morristown, N.J., where he began doing work on diabetes. While there, John met Dr. JOHN PHILLIPS, one of the founders of the CLEVELAND CLINIC FOUNDATION, and accepted an offer from Phillips to join the clinic's staff. At the clinic, John was given the task of organizing the hospital's laboratories. In 1924 he was the first physician in the U.S. to use insulin clinically. He left the clinic in 1935 and entered private practice. He served again as an Army doctor during WORLD WAR II, attaining the rank of lieutenant colonel. For most of the war he was chief of medical services at Atlanta's Lawson General Hospital. In 1928, John married Elizabeth (Betty) Beaman of Cincinnati.

In 1930 they founded Camp Ho Mita Koda, the world's first summer vacation camp for diabetic children. The Johns donated land and their summer cabin in Newbury Ctr., Ohio, to the camp and directed it for 20 years. John was also known for his literary and artistic talents. He was interested in Czech graphic art and possessed a large collection of it. A talented woodcarver, he made many fine pieces of sculpture and furniture. In addition to his many professional articles, he translated several Czech literary works into English. John was a founder of the American Diabetes Assoc. and cofounder of the Natl. Central Society for Clinical Research. In 1937 he received the Jewish Fed.'s Chas. Eisenman Award for outstanding work in the community.

Henry John Papers, WRHS.

## JOHN CARROLL UNIVERSITY

**JOHN CARROLL UNIVERSITY** was founded in 1886 as a liberal-arts college for men under the name St. Ignatius College. It was operated by priests of the Buffalo Mission of the German Province of the Society of Jesus who had accepted the invitation of Most Rev. RICHARD GILMOUR, second bishop of the diocese, to Cleveland to open a college here. The first classes were held in a temporary 2-story frame structure located on W. 30th and Jersey St. (Carroll Ave.). A 5-story brick structure that housed both high school and college was completed in 1890. The college was administratively separated from the high school in 1902 and was chartered to grant degrees in 1890. It was accredited by the North Central Assoc. of Secondary Schools & Colleges in 1922. In 1923, the school purchased land in UNIVERSITY HTS. for its eventual relocation, and in May of that year it changed its name to Cleveland University. In Sept. 1923, the present name was adopted. Construction began on the new site in 1931, but the buildings were not ready for classes until 1935. For a brief period, 1929–32, an attempt was made to bring all of the Catholic colleges and nursing schools of the diocese of Cleveland under the aegis of John Carroll University. From the late 1940s through the 1960s, extensive planning eventually added a library, a science center, a religious center, 3 dormitories, an athletic field, and a military-science building. Total enrollment peaked in 1966 at about 4,400 and by 1980 was approximately 3,800, with some 2,000 enrolled in noncredit programs, with a full-time equivalent faculty of 208. The undergraduate college became coeducational officially in 1968. The Graduate School had admitted women since 1934. Currently (1986) there are 3 major academic divisions, the College of Liberal Arts, School of Business, and Graduate School. Undergraduate-degree programs are offered in 28 major fields of the arts, social sciences, natural sciences, and business, as well as preprofessional studies for law, medicine, dentistry, engineering, and teaching. Administrative understandings make possible cooperative programs with the Loyola Rome Ctr. for Liberal Arts and with the Instituto Tecnologico y de Etudios Superiores de Monterrey in Mexico.

Gavin, Donald P., *John Carroll University* (1985).

The **JOHN F. AND DORIS E. ERNSTHAUSEN CHARITABLE FOUNDATION** was established in 1956 by John F. (1888–1974) and Doris E. (1891–1968) Ernsthausen. John Ernsthausen was president of the Norwalk Truck Line Co., one of the first truck companies in the country, which he founded in 1923. He began by transporting produce between farmers and the markets in Norwalk, Ohio, in 1912. He recognized the need for such a service, not only to farmers but as a more generalized service to producers and manufacturers. For his entrepreneurial success, Ernsthausen received the Horatio Alger Award in 1959. The foundation emphasizes support for the Methodist church, care of the aged, higher and secondary education, a community fund, and cultural programs. It gained a reputation for providing band uniforms to almost every high school band in the Cleveland area. In addition, the foundation supports Bowling Green State University, the First Methodist Church, and BALDWIN-WALLACE COLLEGE. It is primarily local in its giving. In 1981, assets of the foundation were $3,576,261, with expenditures of $351,160 for 23 grants. Managers included Paul L. Carpenter, Loyal L. Chaney, John F. Ernsthausen, Earle H. Lowe, and Cornelius J. Ruffing.

The **JOHN GILL & SONS COMPANY** was the firm of one of Cleveland's most important families of builders. The first John Gill came to the U.S. from the Isle of Man in 1854 and was one of the early masonry contractors in Cleveland. The first major structure undertaken by him was the Northern Ohio Lunatic Asylum (1875; demolished 1977). His son John T. Gill (1857-1927) served as a stonemason's apprentice and learned his trade working on the asylum. In 1881 he became a partner with his father, and the firm became John Gill & Sons. The firm built the Post Office building in Washington, D.C., the Baltimore Courthouse, the Jersey City Courthouse, and the Missouri State Capitol. After his father's death in 1911, John T. Gill became vice-president of the company. The firm built the Leader-News Bldg. (1912), the Hanna Bldg. and Theater and the Bulkley Bldg. and ALLEN THEATRE in PLAYHOUSE SQUARE (1921), the Federal Reserve Bank (1923), the Tifereth Israel Temple (1924), and, probably the most important building of its career, the Cleveland Terminal Tower (1927). After John T. Gill's death, his son Kermode F. Gill became president, and the firm went out of existence in 1953 following the death of K. E. Gill in 1951. In 1975, the Isle of Man issued 4 commemorative stamps recognizing the Manx pioneers of Cleveland, one of which portayed the Terminal Tower and the firm of John Gill & Sons (see CLEVELAND UNION TERMINAL).

The **JOHN HUNTINGTON FUND FOR EDUCATION** was incorporated in 1953 from the estate of JOHN HUNTINGTON (1832-1893). Huntington was born in Lancashire, England, and came to Cleveland in 1854 with his wife, Marietta Leek, and the first of their 5 children. He joined the firm of Clark, Payne & Co. in 1863, an oil-refining business, which then joined in the formation of the Standard Oil stock. He was an inventor, a member of the Cleveland City Council from 1862-75, and a philanthropist. In 1889, Huntington formed the John Huntington Benevolent Trust, now operated by the CLEVELAND FOUNDATION. In his will he established the John Huntington Art & Polytechnic Trust, which had 2 major purposes. First, in combination with the Horace Kelley Art Foundation, it provided the funds to build the CLEVELAND MUSEUM OF ART, begun in 1913 and completed in 1916. Second, it created the JOHN HUNTINGTON POLYTECHNIC INSTITUTE, which provided free evening classes on technical subjects beginning in 1918. In 1953, the institute was discontinued, with the proceeds going into the John Huntington Fund for Education. Following the Tax Act of 1969, an additional $9 million was paid from the Arts & Polytechnic Trust to the Fund for Education.

Grants from the foundation are uniquely for tuition and grants-in-aid available to residents of the Greater Cleveland area to study in scientific and technological fields on full- or part-time, day or evening schedules. Grants are made to and administered by educational institutions located in Cuyahoga County and are limited to individuals who live in the county. In 1985, assets of the fund were $14,381,000, with expenditures of $810,699 for 11 grants. Officers of the fund included Peter W. Adams, Oakley Andrews, Morris Everett, Earla Mae Inks, Ralph M. Besse, Susan Murray, Peter R. Musselman, R. Henry Norweb, Jr., Leigh H. Perkins, and Lewis Williams.

The **JOHN HUNTINGTON POLYTECHNIC INSTITUTE,** although no longer in existence, filled a gap in area educational needs for 35 years by giving tuition-free technical training to some 60,000 Cleveland residents. Since 1953 its successor, the John Huntington Trust Fund, has provided scholarship help to area students. Nearly a century ago—on his birthday in 1889—JOHN HUNTINGTON earmarked $200,000, mostly in Standard Oil stock, to fund a technical school to be known as the John Huntington Art & Polytechnic Trust. Impetus for the school came from Huntington's visits to his home country, England. He was particularly impressed with London's Battersea and Regent St. polytechnic schools. The polytechnic concept actually embodied a revolution in education at that time. Instead of the conventional liberal-arts programs—which emphasize contemplative studies—the aim of Huntington's institute was to prepare students for the real world by giving them vocational training. After Huntington's death in 1893, his hand-picked trustees—including Edwin R. Perkins, John V. Painter, Samuel E. Williamson, CHAS. W. BINGHAM, John H. Lowman, Henry C. Ranney, Jas. D. Cleveland, Geo. H. Worthington, and Huntington's wife, Marietta Leek Huntington—decided that the income from the estate earmarked for the institute was not enough to do anything meaningful toward starting the school. So for 25 years the money accumulated, until on 1 Mar. 1918, the school opened with a handful of students in a small upper room at 2032 Euclid. Following a number of moves around Cleveland, it finally found a home at the Otis-Sanders mansion at 3133 Euclid.

The stated purpose of the Huntington Institute was to provide "a night school for the promotion of scientific education for the benefit of deserving persons in said city who are unable to acquire a collegiate education." Students were required to be over 17 years of age, be employed in the city in one of the applied arts or an industrial occupation, and present satisfactory references from their employer. Courses covered a wide range of disciplines, including electricity, architecture, psychology, Spanish, painting, industrial design, and structural engineering. The institute did not offer degrees, but Alfred Mewett, dean of the school and a graduate of Regent St. Polytechnic, commented, "We're here to help the fellow on the job get an education." As a result, some students got what they wanted in a semester, and others took courses for years. Despite the undeniable success of the school—from a handful of students in 1918 to an enrollment of 2,000 in 1948 with a waiting list—in 1953 the trustees petitioned the Cuyahoga County common pleas court for permission to close the Huntington Polytechnic Institute in order to create the JOHN HUNTINGTON FUND FOR EDUCATION to aid deserving students to acquire scientific and technical training. The reason was that the rationale for the school had ended. Other technical and industrial schools in the area were serving the needs that had once made the institute unique.

The **JOHN P. MURPHY FOUNDATION** was founded by John Patrick Murphy (1887-1967). Murphy was born in Westboro, Mass., and graduated from Notre Dame University with a law degree in 1912. From there, he went on to practice law in Minnesota and Montana. It was in Montana that he came to the attention of the VAN SWERINGENs as a result of his work with railroad law. Murphy came to Cleveland in 1920 as the Van Sweringens' lawyer and represented them in their development of real-estate interests, RAILROADS, and PUBLIC SQUARE from 1920–37. He was named executor of the Van Sweringen estate after the deaths of the brothers. With his partner Chas. L. Bradley, Murphy took over the Van Sweringens' controlling interest in the HIGBEE CO. Bradley was named president, and Murphy secretary. Murphy took over the presidency in 1944 when Bradley retired, and he became chairman of the board in 1968. Murphy was married to Gladys Tate (d. 1968) and had no heirs. The majority of his estate, valued at $13 million, was added to the foundation upon his death. The foundation supports primarily local projects in the area of secondary and higher Catholic education (NOTRE DAME, JOHN CARROLL, and URSULINE COLLEGES), MUSIC, hospitals, and the Community Fund. In 1981, the foundation assets were $11,103,278, with expenditures of $415,881 for 32 grants. The foundation president was Frank E. Joseph, Murphy's personal attorney.

**JOHNSON, EARLE L.** (29 Jan. 1895–16 Feb. 1947), was an important figure in the early development of a national civil air defense system. During WORLD WAR II he served as national commander of the Civil Air Patrol. Johnson was born in Great Barrington, Mass. When he was 8, his family moved to Lake County, Ohio, settling on Old Orchard Farm near Painesville. He attended Painesville Sr. High School and in 1914 was admitted to Ohio State University, where he received a degree in chemistry. Johnson's career was varied. After graduating from OSU in 1917, he returned to Lake County to run the family farm. He soon became involved in the county's Republican party, and beginning in 1926 he served 3 terms in the Ohio house of representatives. In 1932, he managed DAVID INGALLS's unsuccessful campaign for governor of Ohio. During the 1920s and 1930s, Johnson started his own building and real-estate companies, eventually owning and managing a number of properties in Lake County, most notably in Painesville. As a businessman, he became vice-president of the LEISY BREWING CO. of Cleveland and vice-president of the Northern Ohio Insurance Corp.

Johnson was civically active in both Cleveland and Lake County. In the 1930s he was chairman of the Come to Cleveland Committee of the CLEVELAND ADVERTISING CLUB and was influential in drawing many large conventions to Cleveland during that time. Among his many civic commitments in Lake County, he continued his father's sponsorship of Camp Levan Johnson for underprivileged children. Johnson started flying in 1929, partly through the influence of his friend David Ingalls. In the early months of World War II, he urged the government to permit civilian pilots to help in the war effort. In 1941, Johnson organized many of Ohio's private pilots into a state wing of the Civil Air Defense. When the Civil Air Patrol was organized a year later, he left for Washington to become its assistant executive officer. He soon became national commander. Under Johnson, the CAP's responsibilities included air delivery of important supplies, aerial patrols—later expanded to include antisubmarine patrols—guarding small airfields, and an air cadet training program for the Army Air Corps. Serving with the army rank of colonel, Johnson was widely praised for his efforts and was awarded the Army's Legion of Merit. After the war, he worked temporarily with the Army-Navy Liquidation

Committee to dispose of surplus aircraft in North Africa. He then continued as national commander of the CAP until a fatal airplane accident in N. ROYALTON in 1947. He was buried in Arlington Natl. Cemetery. He was survived by his wife, the former Doris Doan, who died in 1974.

Earle L. Johnson Papers, WRHS.

**JOHNSON, LEVI** (1785–19 Dec. 1871), arrived in Cleveland in 1809 at the age of 24 from Herkimer County, N.Y. Johnson was a versatile man who built ships and constructed homes for some of the early settlers. He built Cuyahoga County's first courthouse and jail on the northwest corner of PUBLIC SQUARE (1812), an inn (Johnson House) in 1852, and Cleveland's first lighthouse (1830). One of the jury members at the trial of the legendary Indian O'MIC, Johnson also built the gallows on which the Indian was hanged. Johnson's skill as a shipbuilder contributed much to the growing demands of the city's expansion and lake trade. In 1813 or 1814, he built the schooner *Ladies Master* near his home in the woods. The vessel was then hauled to the river by oxen teams and launched. In 1814, he built the schooner *Pilot*, which required 28 yoke of oxen to move the craft to the river. He also constructed the 65-ton schooner *Neptune*, which was launched in the spring of 1816. In 1824, Johnson and the Turhooven brothers built and launched the *Enterprise*, a 220-ton steamboat, the first in Cleveland. It carried merchandise from Buffalo to Cleveland and towns along the lake. Also interested in real estate and building, Johnson owned 96 properties by 1838. In 1843, Johnson built his permanent family home, a stone mansion, at the corner of Water (W. 9th) and Lake streets. It was the city's first stone house and stood until 1909. A 65-ft. stone lighthouse was built by Johnson at Cedar Pt. in 1836. He also set the channel buoys in Sandusky Bay. In 1837, he built a 700-ft. stone pier east of the mouth of the CUYAHOGA RIVER. Johnson died of typhoid fever at the age of 86. At his death, he had continuously lived in Cleveland longer than any other person. He was buried in the ERIE ST. CEMETERY.

**JOHNSON, TOM L.** (18 July 1854–10 Apr. 1911), mayor of Cleveland and civic reformer, was one of the most noted figures of the American Progressive Era. Johnson was born in Blue Spring, Ky., near Georgetown, to Col. Albert W. and Helen Loftin Johnson. His family's support of the Confederate cause resulted in the destruction of their plantations and depletion of their fortunes during the CIVIL WAR. The family subsequently resettled in Staunton, Va., where Johnson earned enough money selling newspapers to finance his family's return to Kentucky, where they settled in Louisville. After working several months in a rolling mill, Johnson became an office boy in the Louisville Street Railway Co., which was owned by family friends Bidermann and Alfred V. duPont. Two years later, he became superintendent of the company. Johnson subsequently built a fortune through his invention of the see-through glass farebox for use in streetcars. Using the $20,000-$30,000 realized through this invention, and with assistance from his brother Albert W. and the duPonts, Johnson purchased, restored, and profitably sold the Indianapolis Street Railway. He then expanded his traction holdings to include lines in St. Louis, Detroit, and Brooklyn, N.Y., including the first traction line across the Brooklyn Bridge. In 1874, Johnson married a distant cousin, Margaret (Maggie) Johnson. Five years later they moved to Cleveland, where Johnson bought and eventually operated a street railway line after a long and bitter battle against MARCUS A. HANNA, who operated competing lines. In 1889, with the help of the duPonts, Johnson established a steel company, the Cambria Co., in Johnstown, Pa., and subsequently the Lorain Steel Co. in Lorain, Ohio. Both companies produced steel rails, including Johnson's own invention, the "trilby" rail for use in street railway applications. The Lorain Co. was eventually purchased by J. P. Morgan for incorporation into the U.S. STEEL CO.

Johnson's political career was sparked by his reading of Henry George's books *Social Problems* and *Progress and Poverty*. He became an advocate of George's philosophy of free trade and the single land tax, as well as his close personal friend. These ideas were in direct opposition to the principles that had made Johnson wealthy, and this dichotomy was to be the dominating contradiction for the rest of his political and social life. In 1890, Johnson ran and won as a Democratic candidate for the U.S. House of Representatives from Cleveland's 21st district. Reelected in 1892, he fought against the Republican protective tariff and for free trade. In 1901, Johnson was elected mayor of Cleveland, campaigning on the slogan of "home rule, 3-cent fare, and just taxation"; he was reelected for 3 terms. His tenure was characterized by friction and drama as he struggled to reform the city. Using tent meetings as a means of reaching the people and encouraging open discussions, he argued against monopolistic practices and for MUNICIPAL OWNERSHIP of public utilities. He initiated the Group Plan and the MALL, and with the assistance of cabinet members such as NEWTON D. BAKER and HARRIS R. COOLEY, he reformed and professionalized operations within city hall and various city departments. His 3-cent fare was achieved but lasted only briefly. HOME RULE for Cleveland was not achieved until after his death. Johnson's impact on the city was such that noted reformer Lincoln Steffens commented that "Johnson is the best mayor of the best governed city in America." Dissatisfaction with some of Johnson's reforms, particularly those dealing with street railways, led to his defeat in a bid for reelection against HERMANN C. BAEHR in 1909. His fortune depleted and his health destroyed by overwork and poor diet, Johnson died less than 2 years later. He was buried in Greenwood Cemetery, Brooklyn, N.Y., next to his idol, Henry George.

Johnson, Tom L., *My Story* (1913).
Murdock, Eugene, C., "Life of Tom L. Johnson" (Ph.D. diss., Columbia University, 1951).
Tom L. Johnson Papers, WRHS.

**JOHNSON, SIR WILLIAM,** (1715–11 July 1774), superintendent of Indian Affairs in North America, landed with his party on a beach "near to Cayahoga" on 26 Sept. 1761, thus becoming one of Cleveland's earliest prominent visitors. After the conclusion of the French & Indian Wars, rumors and intelligence of an impending Indian attack on Ft. Detroit prompted its commander, Capt. Donald Campbell, to seek aid. Upon request of Sir Jeffery Amherst, Johnson proceeded westward along the north shore of Lake Erie to Ft. Detroit with 140 Royal Americans and Indian scouts aboard 13 bateaux and canoes. His objective was to make treaties with the Indians and establish regulations for the fur trade. His return journey began on 19 Sept. by way of the south shore. It was on this part of the trip that he arrived, a week later, at Cleveland and encamped until departure the next morning.

The **JOINT VETERANS COMMISSION** was founded in the 1920s and consists of the following veterans' groups: the Army & Navy Union, USA; the United Spanish-American War Veterans (now defunct); the Jewish War Veterans; the Polish Legion of American Veterans; the Catholic War Veterans; the Marine Corps League; the Military Order of the Purple Heart; the Legion of Valor; and the GRAND ARMY OF THE REPUBLIC (now defunct). The purpose of the organization is to coordinate efforts of member organizations in discussing, surveying, and acting on legislation and institutions that affect the welfare of veterans. The commission was active in having the Veterans' Hospitals built on East Blvd. and in Brecksville, rather than in Akron; and in keeping the Defense Contract Admin. Services Region office in Cleveland when a move to Chicago was proposed. It also participates in parades and ceremonies on Veterans' Day, Flag Day, and Memorial Day. The commission is a member of the Memorial Day Assoc. of Greater Cleveland.

**JONES, DAVID I.** (18 June 1818–2 June 1891) and **JOHN** (ca. 1808–1870), were Welsh steelworkers who built the first steel mill in NEWBURGH in the late 1850s. Born in Monmouthshire, Wales, the two brothers worked in the Kowlais Mill in Glamorganshire, South Wales. They emigrated to the U.S. about 1845 and went to work for the Phoenix Iron Co. in Phoenixville, Pa. Along with several other Welshmen, they left Phoenixville early in 1856 to join the new Railroad Iron Mill Co. in Cleveland. The two brothers joined with J. W. Jones to form Jones & Co. and bought land in Newburgh in Apr. 1857 to build a rail mill. J. W. Jones, who was not related to the brothers, soon sold out, and the company changed names as new investors joined: it became Chisholm, Jones & Co. after HENRY CHISHOLM invested in the mill in 1857, and in 1858 Andros B. Stone joined, making the firm Stone, Chisholm & Jones. The Newburgh Mill became part of the Cleveland Rolling Mill Co. when the latter was incorporated in Nov. 1863. John and David Jones were not among the incorporators of the Cleveland Rolling Mill Co., but they were leading figures in its Newburgh mill. As the principal mechanic and draftsman, David was in charge of the mill until his death in 1891. John was manager of the rail mill and foreman of the puddle mill, the merchant trains, and furnaces. He suffered heavy financial losses as one of the founders of the unsuccessful Alliance Rolling Mill Co. in Alliance, Ohio. In 1858, the Jones brothers were among the worshippers who organized a Congregational church on Harvard St.: it later became the JONES RD. CONGREGATIONAL CHURCH. Each of the brothers died while visiting Wales. John was buried in his native soil; David was returned to Cleveland and buried in WOODLAND CEMETERY.

Pendry, William R., *A History of the Cleveland District* (1936).

**JONES, DAY, REAVIS & POGUE** is one of Cleveland's top corporate law firms and ranks among the 10 largest firms nationwide. In 1986, the Cleveland-based firm had offices in Washington, D.C., New York, Los Angeles/Orange County, Columbus, Dallas, Austin, London, Paris, and Riyadh, Saudi Arabia, and employed 650 lawyers specializing in trust and securities law. Among the firm's clients were industry leaders from America's top 500 corporations in such fields as tobacco, banking, computers, steel and natural resources, health care, and public services. The oldest forerunner of Jones Day was the law firm of Blandin, Rice & Ginn, which was founded in 1900. In 1911, Thos. Jones, the son of a former Ohio Supreme Court justice and a recent Ohio State University Law School graduate, joined the firm. During his career, Jones served as a director for many corporations, including the CLEVELAND RAILWAY CO., and was once counsel for the VAN SWER-

INGEN interests. In 1921, BR&G underwent organizational changes and emerged as Tolles, Hogsett & Ginn. When the firm needed a new head for their tax department, they hired John Reavis, a recent Cornell University graduate. Since 1919, Luther Day had been associated with the firm of Day & Day, practicing law with his brother, William, Jr. They came from a prominent legal family whose forefathers included their father, William, Sr., a U.S. Supreme Court justice, an Ohio Supreme Court justice, and a chief justice of the Connecticut Supreme Court. A skilled corporate lawyer, Luther numbered among his clients the REPUBLIC STEEL Corp. After William's death in 1936, Day helped form the firm of Day, Young, Veach & Leferer. The firm of Jones, Day & Reavis was created in 1939 by the merger of TH&G and DYV&L. With offices in the Union Commerce (Huntington Bank) Bldg., this new firm of 43 attorneys was one of the largest corporate law firms in Cleveland. In 1946, the firm added a new office in Washington, D.C., and a new partner, becoming Jones, Day, Cockley & Reavis. Richard Pogue, a University of Michigan graduate, joined Jones Day in 1957 as an associate specializing in antitrust law. In 1961 he became a full partner in the firm to which he lent his name. Since 1985, Pogue has been the firm's national managing partner.

**JONES, MYRTA L.** (ca. 1861–11 June 1954), was a social reformer dedicated to improving working conditions for women. She was a long-time member of the CONSUMERS LEAGUE OF OHIO and a central figure in the league's early history. A native of Cleveland, Jones was the daughter of Jas. M. Jones, a common pleas court judge in the 1870s and 1880s. Information about her early life is vague: after attending college, she moved to New York City and worked at the Rivington St. (Social) Settlement. By 1894, she had returned to Cleveland; she was a founding member of the FORTNIGHTLY MUSIC CLUB in Jan. 1894. In 1901, Jones began a lifelong membership on the executive committee of the Consumers League of Ohio. She served as president of the league from 1908–15 and again from 1918–20. Under her leadership, the league launched several campaigns to improve working conditions for women. Beginning in 1910, Jones led the league's public appeal for shorter hours for women working in department stores during the Christmas shopping season. She also presided over the transition of the league from a restrained group that supported legislation proposed by others to a more aggressive organization that proposed legislation itself. Jones also served as vice-president of the Natl. Consumers League in the 1910s and 1920s.

During WORLD WAR I, Jones chaired 2 committees on women in industry, one for the Ohio State Council of Defense and the other for the Ohio Div. of the Women's Committee of the Council of Natl. Defense in Washington, D.C. In this capacity she worked to recruit women to take the places of men in Ohio's wartime factories and sought to protect the health and safety of these women. In 1921, Jones came out of semiretirement to direct the Consumers League's unsuccessful campaign for a minumum-wage law in Ohio. Although she took a less active role in the league after 1921, she continued to correspond with its officers and contribute financially to its work. In addition to her work with the Consumers League, Jones helped organize ALTA HOUSE and served on its board of trustees; she was a member of the LEAGUE OF WOMEN VOTERS and active in the women's suffrage movement; and she supported the CLEVELAND MUSEUM OF ART. Jones married late in life. On 16 Sept. 1930, she married Henry W. Cannon, the 80-year-old former president of Chase Natl.

Bank. She lived in New York City from 1930 until 1952, when she returned to Cleveland.

Consumers League of Ohio Papers, WRHS.
Harrison, Dennis Irven, "The Consumers League of Ohio Women and Reform, 1909–1937" (Ph.D. diss., CWRU, 1975).

The **JONES AND LAUGHLIN STEEL CORPORATION (CLEVELAND WORKS)** is an important and innovative component of the 3d-largest steel producer in the country. The Cleveland plant began in 1873 when CHAS. A. OTIS with 2 associates formed the Otis Iron & Steel Co. It was the first firm in America formed exclusively to make acid, open-hearth steel. Under Samuel T. Wellman's guidance, the new Otis mill on the lakeshore at E. 33rd St. produced its first basic open-hearth steel in 1880. Six years later, the plant was one of the first to manufacture steel ingots by the basic open-hearth method. Otis's initial success was widely noted, and in 1889, British interests purchased the firm, leaving management in local hands. In 1912, it was incorporated as the Otis Steel Co. At that time, with business expanding, its Lakeside facilities became overcrowded, and Otis built a new plant along the CUYAHOGA RIVER near Jennings Rd. By 1919, the Riverside plant acquired the facilities of the adjacent Cleveland Furnace Co., organized in 1902 by David T. Croxton to produce pig iron. The postwar recession caused the British investors to sell Otis to a group of Clevelanders, headed by John Sherwin. By this time, Otis was a self-contained operation with interests in coal, stone, and ore properties. The postwar problem ended when Elroy J. Kulas became president in 1925. Under his direction, production expanded, reaching an annual capacity of 890,000 tons of steel by 1928. Kulas's efforts allowed Otis to weather the Depression, during which, in 1932, it constructed the widest continuous hot strip mill in the world.

Otis was involved in war production when it was purchased by Pittsburgh's Jones & Laughlin Steel Corp. in 1942. Established in 1853, J & L had become the nation's leading manufacturer of cold-rolled and drawn steels. Following World War II, J & L expanded the Riverside plant and dismantled the antiquated Lakeside plant. After the war, it expended more than $450 million to modernize the Cleveland Works, expanding it by acquiring a steel barrel company and various railroad and raw material companies. The Cleveland Works reached peak production in the early 1970s, producing 3 million tons of steel per year and employing 4,000. In 1974, Ling-Temco-Vought, Inc., later known as LTV, a diversified Dallas-based manufacturer of energy, shipping, and tool products, gained control of J & L. LTV's steel activities remained marginal until 1978, when it acquired the Lykes Corp., owner of Youngstown Sheet & Tube Co., making LTV the 3d-largest producer of steel in the country. In 1980, Youngstown's facilities were merged with J & L. During the early 1980s, J & L continued to prosper as LTV used its steel products for the oil industry. However, in 1982 it lost $299 million, resulting in massive layoffs and cutbacks. In 1984 the company merged with the REPUBLIC STEEL CORP to become LTV STEEL.

Morell, Admiral Ben, "J&L:" The Growth of an American Business (1953).
Otis Steel Co., The Otis Steel Company—Pioneer, Cleveland, Ohio (1929).
Otis Steel Co., A Photographic Presentation of the Otis Steel Company (1939?).

The **JONES HOME OF CHILDREN'S SERVICES,** 3518 W. 25th St., was an independent orphanage and foster-care home until it merged with Children's Services on 1 Nov.

1966. Known for many years as the Jones School & Home for Friendless Children, it was established in 1887 by Carlos L. Jones (18 June 1827–6 Feb. 1897) and his second wife, Mary B. Jones (d. 12 May 1898). A native of New Jersey, Jones came to Cleveland with his parents in 1831. He made his fortune as a manufacturer of farm implements and invested in real estate on Pearl St., moving to his farm there after retiring in the early 1880s. He also served as mayor of BROOKLYN. Two tragedies—the deaths of his first wife, Delia Brainard Jones, on 20 Apr. 1853, at age 34, and of his only son, John Marvin, in a drowning accident—led Jones to devote his efforts and property to the care of "friendless" children. Along with his second wife, he applied for a charter on 5 Nov. 1886, and on 22 Dec. 1886 they organized a corporation that included among its members Rutherford B. Hayes, J. M. Coffinberry, I. P. Lamson, and Samuel W. Sessions. Supported by gifts of clothing, food, and toys, the Jones home opened on 15 Dec. 1887 in the Joneses' frame cottage on Pearl at the corner of Library Ave.

The facility accommodated only 9 children; it was soon enlarged, with dormitories for 50 children. In June 1901, the trustees undertook a drive to build a new facility. The new 3-story brick building was designed by a nationally known local architect, SIDNEY R. BADGLEY. It could accommodate 75 residents, although it housed only 60 when it opened in Oct. 1903. It was modernized in the 1920s and again in 1944, and in 1960 2 cottages were added. The main building was completely renovated in 1971 at a cost of $400,000; in 1984 it was added to the Register of Cleveland Landmarks. Although Carlos Jones died 10 years after the home opened, his vision guided its operation for more than 50 years. When it celebrated its 50th anniversary in 1937, the home still adhered to Jones's policy that it admit only healthy, white, Protestant children, and none who possessed what were considered unfavorable hereditary traits; it also followed his decree that each child who left the home be given a Bible, and administrators still tried to follow his preference that children adopted from the home be placed in homes in the country. The Jones Home served 2,900 children in its first 50 years. Its budget for 1937 was $20,783, about ⅓ of which came from the Community Chest, which it had joined in 1920.

During Elizabeth W. (Mrs. Roy Ware) Littler's tenure as executive director from 1943–66, the operations were modernized. The words *Friendless Children* disappeared from the title, and the religious requirement was dropped; in 1957, the purpose of the home was described as providing "temporary group living for 45 white, dependent, boys and girls of any faith ranging in ages from 6 to 14," and its services included "a progressive program of casework, medical and mental health, recreation, education, and religion." By 1963 the racial requirement also had been dropped, and the budget had grown to more than $102,000, more than 75% of which came from the United Appeal. In 1966, the Jones Home was merged into Children's Services as a result of a recommendation by the Child Welfare League of America that the home become affiliated with a child-welfare agency in order to improve further its counseling and casework services. In 1982, funding difficulties forced the board of trustees to reduce the home's licensed capacity from 48 to 36 children.

Jones Home Records, WRHS.

The **JONES ROAD CONGREGATIONAL CHURCH** was founded by Welsh immigrants who settled in the Broadway and Harvard Ave. section of Cleveland (originally NEW-BURGH). The church was begun out of a Sunday school and prayer group held in the home of Wm. Jones on Harvard St. in 1857. The Welsh Congregational Society was organized, and a small church was built on Wales St. in 1860. The secretary of the congregation, Geo. M. Jones, served as preacher until a minister was hired in 1864. In 1876, a new building was built on Jones Rd. Dedicated on the 100th anniversary of the Declaration of Independence, the church was known for a time as Centennial Welsh Congregational Church. The building is a brick Gothic structure with a rear wing added in 1913. Among the founders of the church were DAVID I. AND JOHN JONES, who started the first rolling mill in Newburgh (which developed into the American Steel & Wire Co.) in 1857. The church was the center of the Welsh community and was a strong force in that community's religious and social life. By 1896, the church directory showed 211 members. While ecomomic conditions brought change to the neighborhood and the Welsh were dispersed, the Jones Rd. Congregational Church remained. Extensive renovations were made to the building from 1979–83, and by 1986 membership stood at approximately 75.

**JORDAN, EDWARD STANLAW "NED"** (21 Nov. 1882–30 Dec. 1958), was an automotive manufacturer who changed the style of American advertising. Born in Merrill, Wis., Jordan worked his way through the University of Wisconsin as a reporter. While a student, he disguised himself as a railroad yardman, boarded a presidential train, and managed to get an interview with Pres. Theodore Roosevelt. The next day he sold his interview for $20 to 150 newspapers, calling himself the "Wisconsin News Service." After college, NEWTON D. BAKER persuaded him to come to Cleveland, where he worked as a reporter for the *CLEVELAND PRESS*. Jordan left Cleveland to work as a press agent for the Natl. Cash Register Co. From there he went to the Thos. B. Jeffrey Co., an automobile manufacturer that was the forerunner of American Motors. By 1916, Jordan was determined to make his own car. Russell S. Begg (Jeffrey experimental engineer), Paul Zens (Jeffrey purchasing agent), and Jordan had little trouble raising $200,000 from some Chicago investors, but they needed another $100,000 to start their own car company. A friend invited Jordan to Cleveland, where, in a matter of hours, the additional money was raised. In June 1916, the JORDAN MOTOR CAR CO. opened. Jordan had a keen insight into merchandising, manufacturing, and advertising. He could sense that the public desired something new in an automobile. Appealing to that desire, he broke out of the mold of technological advertising and tapped into more basic desires: luxury and "snob appeal." His advertising campaign concentrated on equating models of automobiles with certain styles of living. Jordan's management innovations included a profit-sharing plan, and most employees owned stock in the company. Years later, when asked about the decline of his company (which closed in 1931), Jordan explained, "We were automobile manufacturers. We were pioneers of new techniques in assembly production, custom style sales, and advertising. . . ." Jordan dissociated himself from the company before it closed, separated from his wife, and left for the Bahamas. Eventually he went to New York and worked in advertising/public relations for several firms. From 1950–58, *Automotive News* carried his column "Ned Jordan Speaks." Jordan, married twice, was survived by 4 children.

Wager, Richard, *Golden Wheels* (1975).

The **JORDAN MOTOR CAR COMPANY,** last located at 1070 E. 152nd St., was founded by EDWARD S. (NED)

JORDAN in June 1916. The first cars were produced in August, and sales began in September; 1,788 cars were sold the first year. The Jordan Co. enjoyed spectacular financial success. For many years, a $500 profit was realized on each sale. Original stockholders received a 1,900% return on their investment. Some 30,000 cars were sold in the company's 16 years. The first cars were 4- and 7-passenger custom touring cars and a Jordan "60" Roadster, with a top speed of 29.4 mph. The 1918 line's new model was the Sport Marine that Jordan painted in colors named Briarcliff Green, Ascot Maroon, and Liberty Blue. A Friendly Three Coupe was introduced in 1920—"Seats two, three if they're friendly"! The company's most famous car was the Jordan Playboy. The Playboy's fame came not from the car itself but from its advertising; it was one of the first cars to be advertised in women's magazines. Breaking out of the mold of technological advertising of the period, the Playboy advertised a "style of living." In 1923, a new advertising campaign began. Realizing that a sales pitch based on technicalities reached only a small group, the campaign reached a much larger audience by basing itself on the suggestion that possession of the product would make the buyer happier. In 1924, the continental straight–8 engine was designed especially for Jordan (74 hp/75 mph). It was an immediate success. The company introduced one of America's first compact cars, the Little Custom Jordan, including the Little Tomboy (1927). But at $1,595, the price was too high. Some said the car was 30 years ahead of its time. The company made 10,527 cars; 6,258 were sold. The year ended with a deficit of $1,426,000. Production was suspended in Mar. 1931; Jordan went into voluntary receivership on 8 May 1931.

**JOSEPH, EMIL** (5 Sept. 1857–11 June 1938), practiced corporate, trust, and estate law in Cleveland. Devoting much of his life to public service and philanthropy, Joseph served as an officer or board member of numerous public and charitable institutions. He also enjoyed collecting, gathering a fine collection of books, artworks, photographs, and historical mementos. Joseph was born in New York; his family came to Cleveland when his father, MORITZ JOSEPH, joined the clothing-manufacturing firm of Goldsmith, Joseph & Feiss in 1873. Joseph graduated from Cleveland CENTRAL HIGH SCHOOL in 1875. Entering Columbia University, he earned an A.B. in 1879 and an LL.B. in 1881. Admitted to the Ohio bar, Joseph began practicing law in Cleveland as a partner with N. A. Gilbert in the Old Mercantile Bank Bldg. In 1883, he became partners with Gen. Edward Meyers in the Society for Savings Bldg. In 1885, he opened his own practice in the Union Commerce Bldg., performing executive as well as legal estate work. Joseph was a member of the Ohio State, Cuyahoga County, and Cleveland bar associations. On 10 Nov. 1936, the CLEVELAND BAR ASSOC. honored him for his 55 years in the legal profession with a framed resolution.

In 1912, Joseph was elected to the board of the CLEVELAND PUBLIC LIBRARY. Concerned with all aspects of the library's operations, he served as chairman of various committees. His special enthusiasm was for establishing branch libraries throughout the city. In 1932 he was elected president of the board. An active alumnus of Columbia University throughout his career, Joseph served as president of the Columbia Alumni of Cleveland. In 1932, Columbia honored him with a medal for conspicuous service to the university. In 1933, Joseph was named one of Columbia's 10 most distinguished living alumni. For many years, Joseph served as chairman of the board of the Jewish Orphan Home. In 1926, he was appointed a director of the Union Trust Co. He also served as president of the Town, EX-

CELSIOR, and OAKWOOD CLUBS. In his private life, Joseph collected an extensive, 5,000-volume private library. Portions of his collections of photographs of famous people, prints, and historical mementos were displayed throughout his E. 115th St. residence. Joseph married Fannie Dreyfoss in 1891. He was survived by his son, Frank, and 2 daughters, Mrs. Louis Bing and Mrs. Adrian Ettinger.

**JOSEPH, MORITZ** (9 Sept. 1834–7 June 1917), a German immigrant, came to Cleveland as a partner in the clothing-manufacturing firm of Koch, Goldsmith, Joseph & Co. As senior partner, he was responsible for making the JOSEPH & FEISS CO. one of the country's largest manufacturers of men's clothing. Joseph was born in Gauersheim, Rheinpfalz, Germany. At the age of 16, he left school and moved to Mainz, where he found employment as a clerk in a cloth business. Because of the greater opportunities, Joseph migrated to the U.S. in 1853, quickly securing a position as a bookkeeper and confidential man with a large New York mercantile house. When the firm shipped a large stock of merchandise to San Francisco in 1857, he went along in the same capacity. Seven months later, after the stock had been sold, he returned to New York and was admitted as a partner. Later, he was to accompany several large shipments of merchandise to both New Orleans and Mexico.

In 1863, Joseph became a partner in the New York company of Levi-Joseph, a subsidiary of Koch, Levi & Mayer of Cleveland. In 1867, when Levi-Joseph abandoned their New York business and went into other lines, Joseph returned to Europe, paying his parents a short visit. Upon his return, he became a partner in Simon, Loeb & Joseph, a New Orleans wholesale dry-goods firm. In 1872, Joseph sold his New Orleans interests to come to Cleveland, where in Jan. 1873 he became a partner in the wholesale clothing firm of Koch, Goldsmith, Joseph & Co. With the retirement of Koch in 1888, the firm became Goldsmith, Joseph, Feiss & Co., and with Goldsmith's retirement in 1907, it became the Joseph & Feiss Co. Dedicated to the business, Joseph was usually the first to arrive in the morning and the last to leave at night. As senior partner, he was as strict with himself as he was with his subordinates. He was also known for his acts of compassion and charity to the needs of the unfortunate. Believing that retirement meant that his days of usefulness were over, Joseph remained as the senior partner until his retirement on 1 Jan. 1917, when he became a part-time business consultant. Joseph married Jette (Yette) Selig on 6 Nov. 1853. The Josephs had 4 children, Issac, Siegmund, Fred, and EMIL JOSEPH.

The **JOSEPH AND FEISS COMPANY,** incorporated in 1907 under its present name, was established in Cleveland in 1845 as Koch & Loeb. The owners, who had operated a general store in Meadville, Pa., since 1841, set up a wholesale clothing store at 82 Superior St. that grew to become both a sales and a manufacturing operation. The company at first sold a general line of men's and boys' clothing and did a brisk business in white summerwear. It also sold piece goods to merchant tailors and retail clothiers who had tailoring departments. Though Joseph & Feiss sold its own brands of clothes, the manufacturing was not done on the premises under the direct supervision of the company. Rather, the cut parts of garments were contracted out to small ethnic shops on the outskirts of town. Joseph & Feiss wear represented an international effort, as Bohemians constructed the coats and overcoats, Hungarians and Germans the vests, and Germans the trousers. When the company began an internal manufacturing operation in 1897, the small units were absorbed, and the proprietors were brought in as foremen and their employees as operators.

The manufacturing operation soon outgrew its St. Clair St. location, and in 1920 a new factory was built on Swiss St. (now 2149 W. 53rd) at the intersection of the New York Central Railroad. To meet the new problems of managing production, the company introduced new methods, machines, and scientific management, including time and motion studies. The company was able to improve efficiency and cut costs through their efforts, but employees also benefited through higher wages and reduced hours. Caught up in the corporate paternalism of the times, Joseph & Feiss hired the superintendent's wife as a matron to look after the welfare of female employees, and designed extensive dining, recreation, and sanitary facilites for all. To further head off employee discontent, the company set up an employee relations department and pioneered in offering employee benefits, such as health and life insurance and retirement plans.

Joseph & Feiss was also innovative in its sales techniques. Because the firm name was lengthy and ever-changing until its stabilization as Joseph & Feiss in 1907, company advertising stressed its brand, Clothcraft, and the firm was a pioneer in promoting brand-name identification. It also heavily advertised its hottest-selling item, a $15 blue serge suit under its production number #5130, which reigned as the Model T of the clothing industry until 1925, and offered the company a steady base of sales. The company diversified its lines and brand names in subsequent decades, and in 1966 it attracted the attention of Phillips-Van Heusen, a century-old clothing firm. The two companies merged under the Phillips-Van Heusen corporate name, with Joseph & Feiss retaining its name as a division. For both companies, the merger was intended to permit expansion in retail and establish a better foothold in the growing dual-distribution system, where a manufacturer has retail outlets that are in direct competition with other stores to which it sells. Joseph & Feiss, which still retains its W. 53rd. St. factory, was, in 1985, a leading division of the Phillips-Van Heusen Corp.

Joseph & Feiss Co. Records, WRHS.

**JOSS, ADRIAN "ADDIE"** (12 Apr. 1880–14 Apr. 1911), was a major-league baseball pitcher for the Cleveland team in the American League between 1902–10. His career earned-run average of 1.88 per 9-inning game is the 2d-lowest in major-league history. Joss was born in Juneau, Wis., and graduated from Sacred Heart Academy at Watertown, Wis. He played for the Toledo Mud Hens for 2 years, and then his playing contract was sold to the Cleveland Blues. Joss began his major-league career on 26 Apr. 1902 by pitching a 1-hit shutout against St. Louis. From 1905–08, Joss won over 20 games a season, topped by 27 wins in 1907. His earned-run average for 1908 was 1.16, and on 2 Oct. of that year he pitched a perfect no-hit, no-run game against Chicago's Ed Walsh. On 20 Apr. 1910, he pitched another perfect game against Chicago. He completed a remarkable 90% of all games started in his career, with 160 wins and 97 losses. For several seasons, he was a sportswriter for the *Toledo News Bee*. Joss died of complications resulting from tubercular meningitis. His funeral was one of the largest in the history of Toledo, Ohio, and the noted ex-baseball player and evangelist Billy Sunday preached the funeral message. The Baseball Hall of Fame rules state that a player must appear in a minimum of 10 seasons to be considered for entrance. In 1978, the Committee on Veterans waived the rule for Joss, and the pitcher was voted into the Hall of Fame at Cooperstown, N.Y. Joss had a wife, Lillian, and 2 children, Norman and Ruth.

The *JOURNAL OF AESTHETICS AND ART CRITICISM* is a quarterly publication of the American Society for Aesthetics. Between 1945–80 it was published jointly with the CLEVELAND MUSEUM OF ART. In its first 4 years (1941–45), the *Journal of Aesthetics & Art Criticism* was published by the Philosophical Library, Inc., in New York. It was originally, and still is, "concerned with developments in the arts (i.e., art, literature, film, architecture, etc.), art history, and relations of the artist and the arts to society." During WORLD WAR II it was published at irregular intervals as funds permitted. In Sept. 1945, the American Society for Aesthetics (ASA) assumed sponsorship of the *Journal*, and Thos. Munro, curator of education at the Cleveland Museum of Art and professor of art at Western Reserve University, was made editor. Munro assembled an editorial staff primarily from WRU's faculty, and also from among the staff of the museum's Education Dept. Although the *Journal* was never published in Cleveland, under Munro within a few years both its editorial and business offices became centered at the art museum and the university.

For many years, Geo. E. Danforth, who headed the department of architecture at WRU, was the *Journal's* business manager. Jas. R. Johnson, an assistant professor of art, succeeded him in 1960. Another WRU faculty member, Remy G. Saisselin, an assistant professor of Romance languages, was an assistant editor along with Merald Wrolstad from the art museum. Ca. 1960, the *Journal* lost its affiliation with WRU, when both Johnson and Saisselin resigned from the faculty to accept positions at the museum's Education Dept. In 1963, Munro relinquished the editorship, and the editorial offices were moved to Wayne State University. The *Journal* remained a joint publication of the ASA and the Art Museum until 1980, when the business offices were moved to Long Island University.

**JUDAISM.** *See* **JEWS AND JUDAISM**

The **JUDSON RETIREMENT COMMUNITY,** a non-profit interdenominational agency consisting of 2 separate facilities, Judson Park and Judson Manor, functions as 1 institution that provides facilities for independent living, assisted living, and nursing care for retired men and women of independent means. It is descended from the Baptist Home of Northern Ohio. The idea for a permanent residence for lonely and aging Baptists (especially women who had no family or funds) originated on 1 Nov. 1904 when 6 members of the Women's Social Bible Class of the EUCLID AVE. BAPTIST CHURCH recognized the need for a home and decided to organize, raise funds, and invite other Baptist women to join their enterprise. On 9 Jan. 1905, 25 women met and named their society the Women's Social Club. Within a few months, over 120 women had volunteered and had contributed financial support. On 9 Jan. 1906, a meeting of women from other Baptist churches met at Euclid Ave. Baptist and formally organized the society, whose object was "the establishment and maintenance of a Baptist home" named the Baptist Home of Northern Ohio. It was incorporated on 17 Aug. 1906. On 27 May 1907, a board of trustees was formed. It included president, Alanson T. Osborn; vice-president, Isaac P. Chandler; treasurer, Wm. Urquhart; and secretary, Albert L. Talcott.

In June 1907, the group purchased the 19-room brick residence of Mr. and Mrs. Wm. P. Southworth, 3334 Prospect Ave., Cleveland. JOHN D. ROCKEFELLER contributed matching funds to complete the transaction. Churches of other denominations contributed money, furniture, and provisions. The first Harvest Ingathering, a fundraising function that continued for over 40 years, was held on 16 Oct. 1907 and marked the official opening of the home. In 1919 the group sold the Southworth home and purchased a residence at 8903 Cedar Ave. That home was sold in 1939, and the Baptist Home of Northern Ohio purchased the 7-acre estate of Warren G. Bicknell, Cleveland contractor. It included the brick-and-sandstone, multiple-gabled residence (built in 1919) at 1801 Chestnut Hills Dr. It was dedicated 7 Jan. 1940 and in 1941 was renamed the Baptist Home of Ohio. The original facilities of the residence were expanded by the addition of Moyat Hall (1950) and Milner Hall (1951) and by the construction of the 10-story Jordan Gardner Tower (1974), named in honor of Mrs. Grace Jordan Gardner, whose gift to the CLEVELAND FOUNDATION made the enterprise possible. Located at 2181 Ambleside Dr., it adjoined the other buildings as part of the Judson complex. The new apartment building was dedicated on 8 Dec. 1974, and the whole facility was named Judson Park in honor of the Baptist missionary Adoniram Judson. Also part of the Judson Community is Wade Park Manor, located in UNIVERSITY CIRCLE. It was built in 1921–22 and opened in Jan. 1923 as a luxury residential apartment hotel. It was purchased from David C. Lincoln in 1964 by the Christian Residences Foundation, a nonprofit, nonsectarian community organization composed of 7 area churches. The foundation operated Wade Park Manor as a retirement facility until 1983, when it became affiliated with Judson Park. It was completely remodeled in 1985, was renamed Judson Manor, and in 1986 continued to function as an integral part of the Judson Retirement Community. The community, which provides a wide range of services and activities for all its residents, is administered by a board of trustees, a staff of trained professionals, and many volunteers, including the Auxiliary and the Evening Auxiliary. It is financed by fees and donations from the residents, from other individuals, and from a variety of foundations and institutions.

The **JUNIOR LEAGUE OF CLEVELAND, INC.,** is an organization dedicated to training women volunteers for effective community participation. Volunteers receive leadership training through seminars and workshops and participate in projects that strengthen skills in research, development, and administration and benefit the Greater Cleveland community. The Jr. League was founded on 6 Sept. 1912. It was organized by a group of women who were members of the Brownie Club and the Babies Aid Society. The first meeting was at Mrs. Amasa Stone Mather's home. Initial membership was 67. The league's initial purpose, as stated in 1912, was "to foster interest in the social, economic, educational, cultural, and civic aspects of the community and to make efficient its voluntary service." The purpose of the league in 1985 was threefold: 1) to promote voluntarism, 2) to develop the potential of its members for voluntary participation in community affairs, and 3) to demonstrate the effectiveness of trained volunteers. The first president of the Jr. League was Mrs. Amasa Stone Mather (Katherine Hoyt, later Mrs. John Cross). She remained an honorary president after 1920.

The Jr. League has been managed by a board of trustees and an executive committee. The president and treasurer serve nonconcurrent 2-year terms, while the remaining trustees are elected annually. The categories of membership are active, provisional (probationary for a period of 1 year), sustaining, and honorary. Requirements of active membership include a regular weekly volunteer commitment or its equivalent in agencies, community organizations, or designated Jr. League committees; payment of dues; attendance at meetings; and support of all league fundraisers. During its early years, a major project was the establishment of the League House, located at 2344 Prospect Ave., as a low-rent residence for working women. It operated from 1919–46. During the Depression years, the league manned milk stations and brought theater to Cleveland children, when it sponsored the Jr. League Players. During WORLD WAR II, the league staffed Red Cross offices, handled Savings Bond drives, sponsored entertainment for servicemen, and helped to provide volunteers for civil defense. The "Wizard of Music," a radio series in Cleveland was sponsored by the league from 1949–52. In 1972, the group sponsored its first decorators' showcase, in which rooms of a prominent area residence were redecorated by selected local decorators and opened to the public. The following season, a national record of 24,718 people toured "Arrowhead Farm," the estate of the late ROBT. H. BISHOP, JR. A profit in excess of $90,000 was made, and the Cleveland public was exposed to the work of the best designers in northeast Ohio.

The league pledged $25,000 toward the redevelopment of PLAYHOUSE SQUARE and sponsored a gala preview party in Nov. 1973 when the PALACE THEATER reopened. It also put on an annual holiday festival to celebrate the beginning of Cleveland's holiday season; to raise funds for Jr. League projects; and to bring people downtown. In 1984, the 5th Annual Holiday Festival, held in the Skylight Concourse of the Terminal Tower, attracted 24,000 people. Membership in the Jr. League has grown steadily over the years, to over 1,100 in 1985.

Junior League of Cleveland Records, WRHS.

# K

**KAIM, JAMIL (JAMES)** (1892–21 Sept. 1971), was a leader in local Lebanese-American affairs and a prominent businessman. Born in Aitaneet, Lebanon, the home of many Cleveland-bound immigrants, Kaim graduated from American University in Beirut and served with the American Red Cross for 2 years before coming to Cleveland in 1920 to do some business for his father. He decided to stay in the city and open a confectionery at E. 17th and St. Clair. Knowing nothing about sweets, he patronized a popular PUBLIC SQUARE soda fountain, ordered a different treat each day, and wrote down the ingredients in Arabic. He later opened Kaim's Restaurant at 207 Frankfort NW and the Guardhouse at E. 6th, of which he was a part-owner. Kaim, always concerned with Syrian causes, established the AITANEET BROTHERHOOD, a charitable club to aid residents of his birthplace, in 1929. The next year, he organized the Cleveland-Lebanese Syrian Democratic Club in Cleveland, Akron, Canton, and Toledo, and was put in charge of all such clubs in Ohio by Franklin D. Roosevelt. A Cleveland correspondent for a Syrian paper in New York, he was announcer for local Syrian radio programs. He served as finance director of the Cleveland Lebanese Syrian Foundation, a member of the Cleveland Cosmopolitan Group, and a trustee of ST. ELIAS MELKITE CHURCH. During WORLD WAR II, Kaim was the chairman of a "Help Win the War" campaign that funded an entire mobile canteen for the American Red Cross and sent Christmas presents to soldiers of Lebanese and Syrian descent. Over the years, Kaim's main regret about leaving Lebanon was that his son Albert remained behind. Kaim and his wife, Shafiica, had left Albert and another son, William, with their grandparents. Kaim sent money for their passage to America, but the grandparents, desiring company in their old age, sent William but kept Albert. Since children of American citizens could enter the country without regard to quotas until age 21, Kaim, a citizen since 1926, felt there was time to retrieve Albert. When the war intervened and disrupted immigration, Albert passed his majority. After several failed attempts to enter the country, he finally qualified in 1949 under the Mexican quota, as his wife was a Mexican-born Lebanese. Kaim died at age 79, leaving 6 children.

The **KAISER PERMANENTE MEDICAL CARE PROGRAM** is a group-practice prepayment plan providing its membership comprehensive medical and hospital services. The Medical Care program is decentralized into 12 regions in 15 states and Washington, D.C. Each region is a federally qualified health-maintenance organization (HMO) managing its local operations through a structure of closely cooperating but separate health-care services and facilities. In 1986, the plan was offered by more than 2,500 companies in Greater Cleveland and had a membership of 155,000. Kaiser-Permanente evolved from industrial health-care programs for employees of the Kaiser companies. In 1933, Dr. Sidney Garfield established a small California hospital to provide health-care services for workers building the Los Angeles aqueduct. When the fee-for-service payments failed to generate sufficient revenues, Garfield developed a successful prepayment health-care plan that satisfied the needs of both the workers and the hospital. In 1938, the Kaiser company persuaded Garfield to establish for workers building the Grand Coulee Dam a similar plan that extended membership to include the workers' families. In 1942, Garfield organized his prepayment plan for West Coast shipyard workers. After WORLD WAR II, Kaiser officials and the plan's medical leaders opened membership to whole communities.

Operations in Cleveland began with the establishment of the Community Health Foundation in 1964, organized by the Meatcutters & Retail Store Employees Union (see UNITED FOOD & COMMERCIAL WORKERS). Structured similarly to Kaiser-Permanente, CHF provided services through east side ambulatory facilities and community hospitals and a west side medical center. In 1969, CHF merged with Kaiser-Permanente to form the Kaiser Community Health Foundation. That year Kaiser Foundation Hospitals purchased a skilled-nursing facility on Snow Rd. in PARMA for conversion into an acute general hospital. In 1971 another facility was purchased, at 11203 Fairhill Blvd., and a third hospital was purchased in 1973 across the street at 2475 Martin Luther King, Jr. Dr. (formerly Liberty Blvd.) to form the Cleveland Medical Ctr. In 1986, the Parma Medical Ctr. was complemented by medical offices in N. OLMSTED, ROCKY RIVER, and STRONGSVILLE. The Cleveland Medical Ctr. was supplemented by medical offices in Akron, BEDFORD, CLEVELAND HTS., and Willoughby. Because of increased competition for revenues, Kaiser-Permanente decided that its membership could better be served through a greater use of community hospital facilities. In 1986, the region decided to use the Cleveland Medical Ctr. only for out-patient services and affiliated with St. Luke's, Fairview General, Lakewood, and Akron

City hospitals and the Lake Hospital System to provide for specific services.

**KALISCH, ISIDOR** (15 Nov. 1816–11 May 1886), poet, journalist, and spiritual leader, was the first rabbi to serve the Cleveland Jewish community. He held the pulpit at ANSHE CHESED Congregation and Congregation Tifereth Israel. Kalisch was born in Krotoschin in the Duchy of Posen. He studied in the yeshivot of Posen and attended universities in Berlin, Breslau, and Prague. He became a journalist in the 1840s, writing articles that were considered radical for the period. He took an active part in the Revolution of 1848 in Germany, and after its defeat he was forced to flee. He immigrated to the U.S. in 1849. Once in America, Kalisch decided to enter the rabbinate. His first position was at Cleveland's Anshe Chesed Congregation, a post he assumed early in 1850. He was probably too liberal a thinker for the then-Orthodox congregation, and after only a few months, the congregation voted to dismiss him. Kalisch and 20 of his supporters from Anshe Chesed met on 26 May 1850 to establish a new congregation, Tifereth Israel (see The TEMPLE). Kalisch was hired as a rabbi, chazan, preacher, and teacher for 2 years at a salary of $400 per year. His principal duties were to teach in the elementary school and preach in German on the Sabbath. In 1853, Kalisch wrote and published a treatise entitled *A Guide for Rational Inquiries into the Biblical Writings, Being an Examination of the Doctrinal Difference between Judaism and Primitive Christianity, Based upon Historical Exposition of the Book of Matthew.* Originally published in German, the manuscript was translated into English in 1857.

Kalisch was one of the Jewish community's representatives to the CLEVELAND ASSEMBLY, which convened 17–20 Oct. 1855. The assembly was the first general conference of Jewish religious leaders ever held in America. Although it failed in its goal of uniting American Jewry under one spiritual platform, it did produce one tangible product: Rabbis Kalisch, Isaac Mayer Wise, and Wolf Rothenheim were appointed to prepare a new Jewish prayerbook. In 1857, they issued the *Minhag America,* which became the most popular prayerbook of moderate Reform congregations in the 1860s and 1870s. On 4 Jan. 1856, Kalisch delivered a sermon in English at the dedication of Tifereth Israel's newly erected Huron St. Synagogue. Because the congregation could not afford both the maintenance of the new building and the services of a full-time rabbi, he was subsequently relieved of his duties. After leaving Cleveland, Kalisch served congregations in Milwaukee (1857–60), where he presided over the merger of 3 congregations and the dedication of a new synagogue; Indianapolis (1870–72); Detroit (1864–66); Leavenworth, Kans. (1866–68); Newark, N.J. (1870–72); and Nashville (1872–75). In 1875, he settled in Newark and returned to a career of writing. He died there in 1886. Kalisch was married twice and was the father of 6 children. One of his sons, Samuel, became a justice of the New Jersey Supreme Court.

Kalisch, Samuel, "Rabbi Isidor Kalisch, a Memoir," in *Studies in Ancient and Modern Judaism . . . Selected Writings of Rabbi Isidor Kalisch* (1928).

**KALISH, MAX** (1 Mar. 1891–18 Mar. 1945), was a sculptor of national significance and local impact. Kalish was born Max Kalichik in Valozin, Lithuania. (The name was changed to Kalish in 1899). His father was a Talmudic scholar who came to Cleveland ahead of the family in 1896. Two years later, his wife came with Max and his brothers, Abe and Jack. A third brother, Arthur, was born in Cleveland. Kalish was educated at Harmon School and given an Orthodox Jewish education. A good student, he was interested in art at a very early age. He was encouraged by Jeannette Brown, an art teacher at the Council Educational Alliance. His interests were nurtured by several alliance staff members, and he was encouraged to try for a scholarship to the CLEVELAND INSTITUTE OF ART. He won that scholarship, which covered his first 2 years, as well as others that covered his schooling from that time on. He entered the art school at age 15, graduating at 19, winning the first prize for life modeling. Kalish's early religious training led him to create *Rebecca and Judas Maccabeus,* which was judged to be the best piece of sculpture ever exhibited by a student in the annual student show. It became his first sale, as well, when Rabbi LOUIS WOLSEY purchased a copy and encouraged other Reform rabbis to do so. In 1910, Kalish studied at the Natl. Academy of Design in New York, where his roommate was Billy Finkelstein, and later ALEX WARSHAWSKY. In 1912, he went to Europe for travel and study in Holland, France, and Italy. By 1913, he had been accepted at the Beaux-Arts—the French national school of fine arts. At the Paris Salon of 1913, he was one of 5 Americans exhibiting. Kalish returned to the U.S. via San Francisco, where he was a sculptor for the Pan-Pacific Exposition for 1½ years. When he returned to Cleveland in 1915, he tried a stint at dental school, which he abandoned, yet he benefited by gaining a mastery of body structure. From 1916–19, he was in the Army and assisted in reconstructive work on war-mutilated soldiers.

The years 1920–26 are undocumented, except that Kalish traveled to Europe and exhibited at the Korner & Wood Gallery in 1923, 1924, and 1926; his pieces tended to show "his love of the beauty of family life." Kalish concentrated on labor subjects. He won first prizes repeatedly at the Cleveland Museum of Art MAY SHOWS. He received excellent press here and across the country as he exhibited and elicited excited response to his labor figures from art critics. In 1923, Cleveland schoolchildren collected nickels and dimes to create a fund that would bring an Abraham Lincoln statue to the city. Kalish was commissioned to execute the design, which was installed on the west front of the School Admin. Bldg. Other commissions came from across the country. Newspapers and periodicals printed photographs of his works—statues of famous personalities in opera, music, medicine, religion, and other professional fields. Upon his death, CLEVELAND CITY COUNCIL enacted a tribute, a condolence letter came from Franklin D. Roosevelt, and the CLEVELAND MUSEUM OF ART gave a memorial exhibition of his work jointly with the paintings of Alex Warshawsky.

Kalish, Alice, *Max Kalish—As I Knew Him* (1969).

**KAMM'S CORNERS,** the intersection of Lorain and Rocky River Dr., was once the hub of the old West Park section of Cleveland. It is named for Oswald Kamm, who opened a grocery in 1875 and later a post office on the site occupied in 1986 by Tony's Restaurant. As postmaster of the Rockport post office prior to the creation of WEST PARK from Rockport Twp., Kamm walked daily to the Nickel Plate Railroad Station in Rocky River to fetch the mail; the postmark on the letters read "Kamm's Ohio." Kamm's Corners became an interurban transfer point from the Cleveland Green Line to the Southwestern that traveled to Lorain and Elyria. The area, absorbed into West Park in 1900 and annexed to Cleveland in 1922, remained a bustling shopping area in 1986.

**KAPPANADZE, JASON R.** (1874–15 Apr. 1962), was the pastor of ST. THEODOSIUS RUSSIAN ORTHODOX CA-

THEDRAL, serving from 1902–08 and again from 1922 until his retirement at the end of 1957. Kappanadze was born in Sviry, a village near Kutais, Georgia, in the south of Russia. The son of the village priest, he enrolled in the college of dentistry in St. Petersburg in 1890, but he soon decided to follow the profession of his ancestors, who were clergymen in the Orthodox church. He then studied at Tiflis Seminary, graduating in 1894. In 1895, the Russian government and the church administration sent him to Kodiak, Alaska, to take charge of a parochial school. There he met Mary Kashevaroff, the daughter of a local priest; they were married in the fall of 1896.

Consecrated into the priesthood in 1898, Kappanadze became the associate pastor of a cathedral in Sitka, Alaska, in 1899; in 1900 he was sent to Osceola Mills, Pa., where he took charge of several small parishes. He came to Cleveland in 1902 to take charge of St. Theodosius Russian Orthodox Cathedral, a parish then of about 15 families. There he directed the acquisition of the St. John's Convent building and property. In 1908 he returned to Russia, where he became a professor of theology at the seminary at Kutais and a ranking member of the local Sobor Cathedral. During WORLD WAR I, he served as a regimental pastor in the Imperial Russian Army at the Turkish front. In 1918 he went to Tiflis to take charge of the Slonsky Sobor, an ancient cathedral built in the 5th century. With help from the American Near East Relief and passports obtained for them by a high Communist official who was a former classmate of one of his sons, Kappanadze and his family escaped from Russia in 1921; they went first to Constantinople, then embarked on a 6-week trip from Turkey to the U.S. on board a small cattle boat, delivering the cattle to Algiers.

Kappanadze returned to St. Theodosius in 1922, where he remained until his retirement in 1957. There the "tall, strongly-built man with a silky-white beard and laughing eyes" established social centers in the parish, spoke strongly on American-Soviet relations, and developed the a capella choir that took its music out of the church to the community at large. He also helped form Russian Orthodox parishes in Detroit, Akron, and Lorain. Kappanadze advanced to mitred archpriest and then to protopresbyter, the highest office open to a married priest, and became an important leader in the Russian Orthodox church in Ohio. After he retired in 1957 (saying that it was time a native-born American who knew baseball took over) and became pastor emeritus at St. Theodosius, he traveled regularly to the Brotherhood of St. John Home for the Aged near Hiram, where he was chaplain. It was on one of these trips that both Kappanadze and his wife were killed in an automobile accident on 15 Apr. 1962. Rev. Kappanadze remains a daily presence at St. Theodosius, however; his likeness appears in one of the murals painted by Andrei Bicenko in the 1950s.

**KARAMU HOUSE** is a settlement house that became nationally known for its dedication to interracial theater and the arts. As a recreation center for area youth and an important cultural center for the area's black community, Karamu has encouraged and produced many students who went on to successful artistic careers. Karamu began in 1915 as the Playhouse Settlement, founded by 2 young white social workers, Rowena and RUSSELL JELLIFFE, with the support of the Second Presbyterian Church. Living as well as working in the ethnic neighborhood known as the Roaring Third, the couple bought 2 houses on E. 38th St. (2239 E. 38th) next to the Grant Park playground and used contacts with children as their entry into community life. The settlement provided a variety of services in the neighborhood and gradually earned acceptance from res-

idents. The Jelliffes soon turned to dramatics as an activity for channeling the children's energies, and in 1917 they produced *Cinderella* using a racially integrated cast. The Jelliffes hoped to create a biracial community center using theater, dance, and the arts. In Sept. 1919, the Jelliffes' affiliation with the church ended, and they incorporated the Neighborhood Assoc. They continued to provide a variety of services and became an important source of aid and instruction for southern black migrants arriving in Cleveland. But the arts became an increasingly important focus of the settlement. In 1920, the Dumas Dramatic Club was formed; it became the Gilpin Players in 1922 in honor of famed actor Chas. Gilpin, who had attended one of its presentations. Early productions were usually 1-act plays performed by interracial casts in school auditoriums or other rented halls; in 1927 the Gilpin Players acquired property adjacent to the settlement house, which they remodeled into a theater. They named their new theater "Karamu," Swahili for "a place of joyful meeting"; in 1941 the entire settlement adopted the Karamu name.

Karamu Theater burned in 1939; efforts to rebuild were interrupted by WORLD WAR II, but in 1949 the generosity of LEONARD HANNA, JR., the Rockefeller Foundation, and other wealthy whites financed construction of a new theater complex at E. 89th and Quincy. The new facility included the 223-seat Proscenium Theater, the 140-seat Arena Theater (Cleveland's first theater in the round), a visual-arts studio, clubrooms, a dance studio, lounges, and offices. In its new home, Karamu flourished: professionalized in the 1950s by staff members such as Reuben Silver, it gained a reputation as one of the best amateur groups in the country. In the 1920s and 1930s, Karamu had produced the works of then-unknown playrights such as LANGSTON HUGHES; it continued to encourage and develop new artistic talent, and many of its graduates went on to successful careers in acting, dancing, singing, and the visual arts. While the theater remained the keystone of Karamu's cultural program, it continued classes in painting, woodcarving, clay modeling, and jewelry making. The rise of Black Nationalism in the late 1960s presented a challenge to the interracial mission of Karamu House, and during the 1970s it embarked upon a controversial course of promoting black theater: theatrical presentations by blacks, about the black experience, aimed primarily at a black audience. Part of this experiment in black theater was the formation of a professional theater company in 1982. Although this period produced several critically acclaimed shows, the participation of whites at Karamu "diminished considerably." In 1982, Karamu's experiment in black theater came to an abrupt and controversial end, the professional troupe was dissolved, and the theater returned to its "multicultural" roots. In 1982, Karamu House had an $800,000 budget, and its operations included a daycare center and arts education programs in addition to the community theater.

Karamu House Records, WRHS.
Selby, John, *Beyond Civil Rights* (1966).

**KARLIN** was a Czech settlement established ca. 1890 near E. 55th St. and Fleet Ave. Named after a Prague suburb, Karlin reflected a common pattern of Bohemian settlement: a move to the outskirts of the city to form a new neighborhood rather than occupy an area abandoned by other groups. Originally Czechs who came to Cleveland in the first migration of the 1850s settled in the FLATS, while settlers of the 1870s and 1880s inhabited KINGSBURY RUN. This neighborhood, centered around Croton St. near E. 37th, spread toward Union and ultimately to E. 55th and Broadway, which led to the founding of Our Lady of Lourdes parish in 1883. The Czechs of the later 19th century found the Broadway area too crowded, and so they moved into the adjacent area near Fleet and E. 55th. Others located in Brooklyn around W. 41st St. between Clark and Dennison, though most settlement was on the east side; by 1911, Czechs settled south of Kinsman from E. 93rd to E. 131st streets. The residents of Karlin—so named by an early settler who opened a saloon and meat market in 1891—initially attended Our Lady of Lourdes parish, but they grew so numerous by 1902 that St. John Nepomucene Church was built in the neighborhood. This parish, named after one of the patron saints of the Czechs, became the religious hub of the area.

The **KEFAUVER CRIME COMMISSION** held hearings in Cleveland in Jan. 1951 as part of the U.S. Senate's probe into interstate crime. Under the direction of Sen. Estes Kefauver of Florida, 20 Clevelanders were subpoenaed to testify before the commission in the Senate's effort to review Cleveland racket relations with the rest of the country. Among those subpoenaed were bookies, gamblers, attorneys, and restaurant and motel owners. Several people went into hiding when they learned of the commission's intention. The commission hoped to document interstate rackets activity and control. Six states were named as having racket connections with Ohio: Michigan, Florida, Kentucky, Nevada, California, and Illinois. The commission sought information on the Kleinman-Dalitz-Rothdopf gambling syndicate, which had operated the Pettibone Club, once located in Cuyahoga County and Geauga County before settling in Covington and Newport, Ky., and in Las Vegas, Nev. The commission was also interested in discovering how Cleveland rackets had infiltrated into 100 legitimate businesses in the Midwest and elsewhere.

On 17, 18, and 19 Jan. 1951, the Kefauver Commission interrogated several racketeers, businessmen, and law officers. Sheriff Peter Burke of Lawrence County was questioned about his failure to conduct raids on gambling operations in his county. Cleveland millionaire ARTHUR "MICKEY" MCBRIDE was questioned about his connection with racketeer Alfred Polizzi and admitted having business dealings with Polizzi. Polizzi refused to discuss any activities before 1945 and was cited for contempt of Senate. Several others were also held in contempt for refusing to answer questions. Several points were made by the Cleveland hearings: interstate connections existed among criminals and organized gangs throughout the country; at least 6 states had Cleveland gang money in them; gambling had corrupted local government and law enforcement; and racket money had been invested in legitimate businesses. The commission intended to issue a report to Congress based on hearings in Cleveland and several other major cities in the hope of bringing new laws or a national crime commission into being. At the close of the Cleveland hearings, Sen. Kefauver hailed Cleveland and Cuyahoga County law enforcement, Mayor THOS. BURKE, Gov. Frank Lausche, and Alvin Sutton for their efforts at stopping CRIME.

The **KEHILLAH** was a second attempt by the East European Jews of Cleveland to establish a representative organization that would be a watchdog for Jewish interests. The first organizational meeting was held at B'NAI JESHURUN CONGREGATION in Feb. 1913. That meeting was called by the former leaders of the defunct UNION OF JEWISH ORGANIZATIONS, which had been formed in 1906. Henry Rocker and L. S. Desberg chaired the meeting, which was attended by 75 people. The first meeting

called for a convention of representatives to meet and form the Kehillah. In Oct. 1913, representatives from 30 organizations met. In early 1914, a second convention drew 300 delegates from 64 immigrant organizations. The spokesmen for the Kehillah were Rabbi SAMUEL MARGOLIES, Max Kolinsky, and Aaron Garber. The programs of the Kehillah were basically the same as those of the union 7 years earlier. It attempted to guard against encroachment on the rights of the Jewish community and tried to aid Jews in need both in Cleveland and abroad. Although based on the successful Kehillah experiment in New York City, the Cleveland Kehillah had neither the dynamic leader nor the financial support that aided the New York group. It could not attract representatives of the Reform community, and, in fact, it may not have tried. In addition, the Kehillah was criticized severely in the Yiddish press for its inability to financially support the CLEVELAND HEBREW SCHOOLS and for not responding sufficiently to the call for aid to Jews in Eastern Europe who were suffering during WORLD WAR I. Without a financial base and facing internal conflicts, problems that had caused the demise of the UJO, the Cleveland Kehillah could not function. It became inactive in late 1914 or early 1915, barely 1 year after its creation.

**KEITH'S EAST 105TH STREET THEATER,** which opened in Nov. 1921 as a vaudeville house, was built in UNIVERSITY CIRCLE to cater to the growing number of "suburban" residents who wanted entertainment closer to home. At a time when Cleveland's restaurants and theaters were located at PLAYHOUSE SQUARE, where the Keith chain was also building the PALACE, the corporation opened the E. 105th St. Theater. Although the location drew the desired crowds for 2 matinees and an evening performance on weekends, the actors felt secluded in a "theatrical outpost." Eventually, the theater was joined by the Park, Alhambra, University, and Circle theaters, plus Bailey's Dept. Store and popular Cleveland restaurants such as Clark's, the Tasty Shop, and Hoffman's Ice Cream Parlor. University Circle thus became the city's second major retail and entertainment district. To attract the public and to compensate the actors for their isolation, Keith's E. 105th St. was a showplace, with an ivory, rose, and gilt lobby and 3,000 rose-velvet seats. The public lounges featured ivory toiletry accessories, while the dressing rooms, all identical and named after states rather than numbered (thus minimizing ego battles among the stars), had long ivory dressing tables, well-lit mirrors, and connected tile showers. Keith's had a laundry room, billiard parlor, and nursery. While the opening performer, Jim Corbett, complained of no nail on which to hang his pants (there were hooks), most performers lauded the complete and thoughtfully laid-out facilities. The theater hosted the vaudeville greats and launched the careers of others, such as Bob Hope. With the decline of vaudeville, Keith's was converted to a movie theater. As the neighborhood changed, the theater was unable to attract patrons for first-run movies, and the quality of films and attendance deteriorated to the point that entrepreneurs sought other uses for the facilities. Keith's, however, continued to operate as a movie house until 1967, when it and several other buildings in the area were claimed for urban renewal.

**KELLER, HENRY GEORGE** (3 Apr. 1869–3 Aug. 1949), was characterized as the "dean of Cleveland artists" and the local artist who had brought more art honor to the Midwest than any other. He was both a good painter and a good teacher and spent all but 4 years in Cleveland implementing those aspects of his career. In 1950 (1 Feb.–19 Mar.) he was honored by the CLEVELAND MUSEUM

OF ART, which exhibited all of his known works in lithography and etching, and the Cleveland School of Art, which showed a selection of oils and watercolors done during the 40 years he taught on its faculty. Keller was born at sea as his parents came to America so that their child would never have to serve military duty. They came to Cleveland to join his father's brother Henry. In 1887, Keller entered the Cleveland School of Art, where he studied for 3 years. He went to Germany in 1890, studied at Karlsruhe for 2 years, and then returned to complete his 4th year at the Cleveland School. For 1 semester in 1898 he studied in Dusseldorf, Germany, which was followed by a 3-year course at Munich from 1899–1902. He finished there with honors, winning the silver medal at the Royal Academy. In between he attended the Art Students' League in New York and the Cincinnati School of Art. He returned and joined the teaching staff at the Cleveland School of Art, an engagement that lasted until 1945.

Keller had little sympathy with modernism in art; he saw his function to express nature as he saw it. He advised students to "trap a convincing reality." To put himself through art schools, Keller worked as a lithographer, mostly on circus and Buffalo Bill posters. During the summers, he and FRANK WILCOX experimented in lithography techniques. Keller exhibited outside of Cleveland as well as locally. In 1913, his *Wisdom and Destiny* was included in the famous Armory Show, N.Y. In 1928, he won the Davis Purchase Prize at the Witte Memorial Museum in San Antonio; in 1929, the Blair Purchase Prize at the Art Institute Internatl. Exhibition of Water Colors in Chicago. He made 11 Carnegie shows in Pittsburgh and had 1-man shows all over the country. In 1919, he won the Special Award for sustained excellence for entries in the first May Show at the Cleveland Museum of Art, and he won repeatedly in subsequent years. After 1926, he did not enter his work in competition. In 1929, he was elected into the Natl. Academy of Design.

One of Keller's best-known students, Chas. Burchfield, characterized Keller's success by noting that while he lived and worked in one locale, he reached out to the art, past and present, of the whole world for inspiration and background. But Keller's themes were American, and he felt the Midwest to be the great reservoir of the American Idea. Keller started a summer school at Berlin Hts., Ohio, ca. 1908 to allow some more progressive art ideas to be put forth. The locale gave ample opportunity to express nature in many forms, with its abandoned quarries, rich rolling farmlands, and country village. The dormitories were in a local farmhouse. The school entered into the local way of life, because the Kellers lived there half-time and because of Henry's pleasing personality. Keller married Imogene Leslie from Vermont. They had 2 sons, Henry Leslie and Albert Fay. Following his wife's death in 1948, Keller moved to San Diego, Calif. Both Keller and his wife are buried in the old burying ground at the edge of Berlin Hts. Village.

**KELLEY, ALFRED** (7 Nov. 1789–2 Dec. 1859), has often been called the "Father of the Ohio-Erie Canal." Kelley was born in Middlefield, Conn., and came to Ohio in 1810, where he was admitted to the bar and appointed prosecuting attorney for Cuyahoga County. He was educated in the common schools, at Fairfield Academy, and in the law offices of Judge Jonas Platt (Supreme Court of New York). A lawyer, Kelley was first president of the village of Cleveland (1815), a member of the Ohio house of representatives, a state senator, president of the COMMERCIAL BANK OF LAKE ERIE (1816), and president of several railroad companies. However, it was as a member of the State Canal Commission that he made his mark on the state. Once he

took up canal campaigning in 1823, the OHIO & ERIE CANAL dominated his life for the next several years. His leadership resulted in the canal's having the lowest cost per mile of any canal of comparable length in Europe or America. Before the canal could be built, however, Kelley had to fight to get the bill passed. After studying the record of voting on previous canal bills and education bills, he realized that the legislators who were voting for Nathaniel Guilford's education bill were voting against the canal bill, and vice versa. Kelley eventually convinced Guilford to piggyback the two issues so that both bills would pass, and that ensured success. Canal construction began in 1825, and Kelley personally supervised the work. In 1844, Kelley was elected to the state senate, where he originated the bill to organize the State Bank of Ohio and other banking companies. This bill, which he carefully drew up, eventually became the basis of the Natl. Bank Act of 1863. Kelley married Mary Seymour Welles of Lowville, N.Y., on 25 Aug. 1817. They had 11 children.

**KELLEY, DANIEL** (27 Nov. 1755–7 Aug. 1831), and his family of 6 sons were prominent among the early settlers of Cleveland. Kelley was born in Norwich, Conn., to Daniel and Abigail Reynolds Kelley. His grandparents, Joseph, a shipbuilder, and Lydia Caulkins Kelley were among the early settlers of Norwich. Kelley moved to Middletown, Conn., where in 1787 he married Jemina Stow, sister of Joshua Stow, a member of the Moses Cleaveland survey party that founded the city of Cleveland in 1796 and one of the 35 original members of the CONNECTICUT LAND CO. In 1787 Kelley moved to Lowville, N.Y., where he acquired considerable real estate and personal property. A conspicuous figure in the business and social life of Lowville, Kelley was elected the first judge of Lewis County. Through Jemina's brother, Silas, the Kelley family invested in the Western Inland Lock Navigation Co., which had a New York state charter to make improvements along the Mohawk River.

In 1810, Kelley's oldest son, Datus, left on foot for Cleveland. Later that year, Joshua Stow and Jared Kirtland persuaded Kelley's son Alfred to move there with them. Although the elder Kelley did not approve, sons Irad and Reynolds followed soon after, leaving only the 2 youngest sons, Thomas and Daniel, at home. Jemina's yearning for her absent sons resulted in the Kelley family's moving to Cleveland in the autumn of 1814. At the age of 59 and 51 respectively, Daniel and Jemina Kelley, for the second time in their marriage, assumed a life of privation in the wilderness to become pioneers in a new country. Kelley's reputation followed him, so that almost at once he became a man of importance in the community. Although they had little furniture after sacrificing most of their household items, the Kelleys were still in better financial condition than almost any other settler in Cleveland, being able to give $1,000 to each son to invest in land or business. In Mar. 1816, Kelley was elected to succeed his son Alfred as president of the village of Cleveland, and he was reelected in 1817, 1818, and 1819. In October, Kelley succeeded his son Irad as postmaster, serving until 1817. In 1816, Kelley and his sons Alfred, Datus, and Irad were among the incorporators of a company for the building of the first pier at the mouth of the CUYAHOGA RIVER. Upon his death, Kelley was interred in the ERIE ST. CEMETERY.

**KELLEY, IRAD** (24 Oct. 1791–21 Jan. 1875), was one of Cleveland's first merchants, a postmaster of Cleveland, a real-estate investor, and co-owner of Kelley's Island. Kelley was born in Middletown, Conn., and moved to the Cleveland area ca. 1812. He opened his first store in the first brick building in Cleveland, built in 1814 on Superior at Bank (W. 6th) St. by Joseph Reynolds and Kelley. When he became postmaster on 31 Dec. 1817, the post office moved into his store. Receipts for the year were $500, of which Kelley got 25% as compensation for rent, fuel, and hiring of a clerk. Kelley began replacing his first building in 1850 with another brick structure, the Kelley Block, also situated on Superior near Bank St. A store was on the 1st floor, and on the upper floor was Kelley's Hall, where concerts, lectures, and balls were held. In 1863, the name of the building was changed to the Athenaeum after the theater located therein.

Kelley also worked as a sailor. During his command of the ship the *Merchant*, he became acquainted with the Lake Erie Islands. In 1833, he and his brother Datus began purchasing land on Cunningham's Island at $1.50/acre. Eventually they owned the whole island, and the name was changed to Kelley's Island (1840). They opened the stone quarries and began cultivation, making Kelley's Island famous for limestone, red cedar, peach orchards, and vineyards. In 1833, Irad helped establish the CLEVELAND LYCEUM, which presented lectures, concerts, and other cultural events. Kelley joined his brother Alfred in the political arena in 1850, when he ran, unsuccessfully, against Joshua Giddings for the U.S. Congress. He also wrote about a number of political issues, including women's rights and railroad routes. He produced political songs for the 1840 presidential candidate Wm. Henry Harrison. Kelley married Harriet Pease on 5 Aug. 1819. They had 10 children.

Irad Kelley Papers, WRHS.
Kelley, Irad, "A Sketch of Irad Kelley" (WRHS), 1871.

**KELSEY, LORENZO A.** (22 Feb. 1803–13 Feb. 1890), was a steamboat captain and mayor of Cleveland from 1848–49. He was born in Port Leyden, N.Y., the son of a shipowner. He was educated in his local district. Kelsey moved to Youngstown to work in lumber. He moved to Cleveland in 1837 with his wife and became manager of the Cleveland House Hotel, a post he held for 1 year. He then became captain of the steamship *Chesapeake*, and later captain of the *General Harrison*. He also served as proprietor (1818–19) of the New England Hotel. With no political experience, Kelsey ran as a dark-horse mayoral candidate for the Democratic party in 1848. He defeated 2 other opponents, Chas. Bradburn and Milo Hickox. As mayor, Kelsey supported civic improvements and worked frequently with top members of the Democratic party. Throughout his career, he served as a delegate to Democratic conventions. In 1849 he returned to the hotel business until his retirement in the late 1850s. Kelsey married Sophia Smith (1806–1893) of Windsor, Conn., in 1825. The Protestant couple had 7 children.

The **KELVIN & ELEANOR SMITH FOUNDATION** was incorporated in 1955 by ALBERT KELVIN. Smith, president of the LUBRIZOL CORP., was born in Cleveland, Ohio. His father, ALBERT W. SMITH, was chairman of the departments of chemical engineering and mining engineering at Case School of Applied Science. Kelvin Smith married Eleanor in 1923, and they had 2 daughters, Cara Stirn and Lucia Nash. Most notable of Eleanor Smith's civic contributions was her 20-year association with the CLEVELAND SOCIETY FOR THE BLIND, of which she was president from 1952–57. She was recognized for her service to the society in 1960 with the United Appeal Distinguished Service Award. In 1961, Helen Keller presented Mrs. Smith with the highest honor offered by the American Foundation for the Blind.

The purpose of the foundation is to support the Greater Cleveland area, with emphasis on education, cultural affairs, hospitals, and conservation. The Smith family endowed a chair for a musical director of the CLEVELAND ORCHESTRA and contributed to the development and construction of Blossom Music Ctr. The foundation also supports the Sea Research Foundation, Inc., to study the effects of pollution on marine life. Other beneficiaries include the Cleveland Society for the Blind, the GARDEN CTR., and Mrs. Smith's alma mater, Smith College. No grants are given to individuals or for endowment funds, scholarships and fellowships, matching gifts, or loans. In 1982, assets of the foundation were $2,087,924, with expenditures of $190,596 for 56 grants. Officers of the foundation include Ralph S. Tyler, Jr., Mrs. R. Preston (Lucia S.) Nash, Jr., Douglas W. Richardson, and Mrs. Howard F. (Cara S.) Stirn, with Donald F. Seaburn, Jr.

**KENNEDY, CHARLES E.** (17 May 1856–12 June 1929), was a prominent Cleveland journalist. Born in W. Farmington, Ohio, Kennedy began his long career in Cleveland journalism as a reporter for the *Leader* in 1876. He moved to the *Herald* in 1880, serving as city editor and then advertising manager, and joined the *PLAIN DEALER* as advertising manager following the *Herald*'s demise in 1885. After 2 years of advertising work in New York, Kennedy rejoined the *Plain Dealer* in 1893 as general manager and a small stockholder. Although he was hired away by Joseph Pulitzer in 1897 to serve as business manager of the *St. Louis Post-Dispatch*, he returned the following year to assume direction of the *Plain Dealer* in conjunction with ELBERT H. BAKER, under an agreement signed with publisher LIBERTY E. HOLDEN. This dual arrangement lasted from 1898–1907, when Kennedy withdrew, leaving Baker in sole control as general manager. In view of the fact that he had served as editorial manager in the partnership, with Baker filling the position of business manager, Kennedy later claimed that he deserved a share of the credit that accrued to Baker as "founder of the modern *Plain Dealer*." Following his departure from the *Plain Dealer*, Kennedy became general manager of the CLEVELAND LEADER and then retired from journalism to devote himself to advertising work. He served as a member of the Cleveland Public Library board from 1903–20, and in 1925 he published a memoir entitled *Fifty Years of Cleveland*. He married Harriet L. Pratt of Warren in 1880, with whom he had a daughter, Winifred. Kennedy died in 1929 in his home on E. 115th St.

Kennedy, Charles E., *Fifty Years of Cleveland* (1925).

The **KENTUCKY STREET RESERVOIR** was the first reservoir and central pumping station to serve Cleveland. A special issue in the 1853 election asked citizens to approve a $400,000 expenditure for erection of a waterworks. It passed, and a board of waterworks trustees was established, consisting of HENRY B. PAYNE, B. L. Spangler, and Richard Hilliard. On 12 Oct. 1853, city council passed a resolution to locate the works on the west side of the CUYAHOGA RIVER. Land was purchased bordered by Kentucky St. (W. 38th) to the west, Duane St. (W. 32nd) to the east, Franklin Blvd. to the north, and Woodbine Ave. to the south. The 6-million-gallon-capacity reservoir opened on 24 Sept. 1856, after 2 years of construction. Final costs were $526,712.99. A celebration commemorating the event drew 30,000 visitors. A state fair in PUBLIC SQUARE at the time provided a showcase for the reservoir, which fed a fountain on the Square from which visitors could sample the drinking water. It was claimed to be the first fountain in Ohio. The reservoir covered 6 acres, rising 35 ft. above street level. Water was fed from the lake via a 300-ft.-steel tunnel that entered the lake near W. 58th St. Two large mains carried the water through the city. Steps up the side of the reservoir led to a promenade, called Reservoir Walk, which afforded a scenic view of the city. By 1860, omnibus service was established to carry visitors to the landmark, terminating on the Franklin Ave. side. The reservoir supplied Clevelanders with drinking water for 34 years. It was deemed inadequate by the early 1880s because of the city's growth. The old reservoir was abandoned and became known as Reservoir Park on 16 June 1890. The name was changed to Fairview Park in 1897. The site today contains homes, a baseball diamond, a city garden, and a county nursing home.

**KERN, FRANK J.** (18 Mar. 1887–4 Oct. 1979), was a family physician and leader in the Cleveland Slovenian community. His English-Slovenian dictionary helped 2 generations of immigrants adjust to a new language. Frank Jauh was the youngest child of a large peasant family from near Skofja Loka in the Austro-Hungarian province of Carniola (Slovenia in Yugoslavia). He studied for the priesthood in Ljubljana. In 1903 he left with a group of students for St. Paul Seminary in Minnesota to be ordained in the U.S. and to minister to Slovenian parishes. He did not complete his schooling, but moved to Cleveland in 1906 and worked for *Nova Domovina*. He became active in Slovenian affairs and was a founding member of the Slovenian Natl. Library. He moved to Calumet, Mich., briefly to edit a newspaper, but returned to Cleveland and taught English and penmanship. Frank entered Western Reserve Medical College in 1908, financing his education with translations and his own correspondence school for English. He added the surname Kern in 1911. After an internship at ST. VINCENT CHARITY HOSPITAL, he married Agnes Wertin from Calumet and opened an office on St. Clair Ave. He worked as a physician for 50 years, serving as a medical counsel for several fraternal insurance societies, including 2 based locally, the AMERICAN MUTUAL LIFE ASSOC. and the Serbian Beneficial Fed., "Unity." He also wrote medical columns for Slovenian newspapers in Cleveland and Chicago.

Kern was the first Slovenian-American candidate for councilman, running unsuccessfully on the Socialist ticket in 1913. In 1916, he and his brother-in-law, Paul Schneller, organized a neighborhood loan company that became the St. Clair Savings Assoc. He was the first president of the Slovenian Natl. Home Committee. During WORLD WAR I, he promoted the creation of an independent federation of South Slavic states, Yugoslavia, and was a representative of the Slovenian Natl. Union to the Jugoslav Natl. Council in Washington. He was also an executive board member of the SLOVENIAN AMERICAN NATL. COUNCIL formed to assist the homeland during WORLD WAR II. Kern first started work on an English-Slovenian dictionary as a seminarian when he found available books inadequate. His 1919 book, inspired by the Funk & Wagnalls *New Standard Dictionary*, was the most comprehensive available. He followed it with an English reader in 1926 that featured penmanship lessons. A 1944 edition of the dictionary served a new generation of immigrants after World War II. Kern and his wife had 3 children. An autobiography of his early life was published in Ljubljana in 1937.

Kern, Frank Jauh, *Spomni ob Tridesetletnici Prihoda v Ameriko* (1937).

**KIDD, ISAAC CAMPBELL** (26 Mar. 1884–7 Dec. 1941), was senior officer on board the battleship U.S.S. *Arizona* when it was attacked and sunk during the Japanese attack on Pearl Harbor. Kidd was the son of Isaac Kidd, a west side Cleveland merchant. He graduated from West High School in 1902 and entered the U.S. Naval Academy that same year, graduating in 1906. In 1911, he married Inez Nellie Gillmore of LAKEWOOD, Ohio. Kidd's first service was aboard the U.S.S. *Columbia* during the Panama Expedition in 1906. Further assignments took him on 6 other ships until 1925, when he served as executive officer of the U.S.S. *Utah*. His first command came the following year aboard the U.S.S. *Vega*. Kidd was named commanding officer of the *Arizona* in 1936. When the *Arizona* was attacked, Kidd, as commander, Battleship Div. I, went to the bridge, taking charge until the ship was hit and sunk, and he and much of his crew were killed. He was posthumously awarded the Congressional Medal of Honor for his part in the action at Pearl Harbor. A destroyer, the U.S.S. *Kidd*, and the Navy's Rear Admiral Isaac C. Kidd Computer Ctr. in BRATENAHL, Ohio, were named in his honor.

The **KIDNEY FOUNDATION OF OHIO, INC.**, is located at 2026 Lee Rd. in CLEVELAND HTS. Founded in Cleveland in 1950, it is an affiliate of the Natl. Kidney Foundation, Inc., which has its headquarters in New York. The creation of the Kidney Foundation in Cleveland resulted from the efforts of a small group of people who sought to provide services for patients suffering from kidney disease and to encourage and assist basic research programs. A series of educational programs were developed to create professional and public interest, and as that interest grew, so did the scope of services and activities. In 1964 the foundation incorporated under the name the Kidney Foundation of Ohio, Inc. Since its inception, the primary objective of the KFO has been to promote medical research in the field of kidney disease. Owing to the excellent facilities available in the area, northeast Ohio has become a medical and research center for many of the nation's leading renal experts. In addition, most of the funding for this research is concentrated in the metropolitan Cleveland area. To ensure quality research, the KFO created the Nephrology Fellowship for northeastern Ohio researchers. The KFO maintains a strong committment to professional education through area councils that regularly meet for information sharing and mutual support. It also sponsors and participates in numerous educational programs and health fairs designed to acquaint the public with the nature and effects of kidney disease. The foundation works in close cooperation with the Cleveland Eye Bank and Organ Recovery, Inc., to promote public awareness of the need for human organ donations. In 1986 the KFO served a 32-county area. It also supported other Ohio chapters in Lorain, Medina, Summit, Ashtabula, Lake, Mahoning, Trumbull, Columbia, and Wayne counties.

**KILBANE, JOHN PATRICK "JOHNNY"** (18 Apr. 1889–31 May 1957), was the world featherweight boxing champion from 1912–23. He was called the "most perfect fighting machine in the world" and Cleveland's "greatest champion." Kilbane was born in the area of Cleveland around W. 25th St., called the ANGLE. His father was a steelworker who went blind when Kilbane was only 6 years old. After completing the primary grades, Kilbane worked as a switch tender for the New York P & O Railroad. With some friends he traveled to Crystal Beach at Vermilion to watch Jimmy Dunn train for a fight. Soon Dunn was training Kilbane in the art of boxing. He related years later that "the first thing he (Dunn) started teaching a fighter was how not to get hit." Kilbane's first fight was in Dec. 1907, a 3-round decision for which he was paid $1.50 and carfare.

Boxing a series of bouts in California in 1911 led Kilbane to a title fight with Abe Attell, the featherweight champion, at Vernon, Calif., on 22 Feb. 1912. Called by *Ring* magazine a "fast, clever" boxer, Kilbane won a 20-round decision. Welcomed home on St. Patrick's day by 100,000 Clevelanders, the new champion, 5'5" tall and 120 lbs., was to retain the crown for 11 years, the longest reign in featherweight-division history.

Outside of Cleveland, Kilbane was not a very popular titleholder. After holding on to his championship with a disputed 20-round draw with Johnny Dundee on 29 Apr. 1913, Kilbane fought mostly no-decision contests for the next decade. During WORLD WAR I, he was a physical training instructor at Camp Sherman and Camp Gordon, Ga. On 17 Sept. 1921 at Cleveland's LEAGUE PARK, he knocked out contender Danny Frush in the 7th round. A crowd of 17,235 paid $97,239, a new Cleveland record for a boxing match. Kilbane received $60,000 for the fight. He did not box again until 1923, when he lost the title to Eugene Criqui, a French war veteran who knocked him out in 6 rounds. He ended his career 142–4. Although Kilbane received $75,000 for his last fight, he was almost broke by the time of the Depression. Kilbane worked for the CLEVELAND PUBLIC SCHOOLS as a physical instructor in 1934–35, but by the 1940s he turned to politics, serving in the Ohio senate and house of representatives for a time. In 1951 he was elected the clerk of municipal court, a post he held at the time of his death. He married Irene McDonald in 1910. His wife cooked all his training meals but never watched him box. They had 2 daughters, Helen, who died at the age of 6, and Mary.

## KING, MARTIN LUTHER JR. VISITS TO CLEVELAND. *See* MARTIN LUTHER KING JR. VISITS TO CLEVELAND

**KING, WOODS** (31 Jan. 1900–15 Jan. 1947), was a well-known Cleveland real-estate man, sports enthusiast, patron of the mounted police, and World War II hero elevated to the rank of brigadier general on 18 June 1945 by Pres. Harry S. Truman. Meeting an untimely death from heart disease at the age of 46, King devoted himself to military service and is best remembered for his duty and competence in the service. Born in Cleveland to Fannie T. and Ralph King, King received his early education at UNIVERSITY SCHOOL, where he attended classes from 1910–18. While a student at Williams College, he enlisted in the military, serving as a private from 1 Oct. 1918 until he was commissioned a 2d lieutenant on 29 Jan. 1919. After the close of WORLD WAR I, King's interest in horses led him to volunteer his time and money toward the development of the Cleveland Div. of Mounted Police. As a member of TROOP A, 107th Ohio Cavalry, King was awarded a gold badge as a special officer of the city in recognition of his friendship for the police department when, on Memorial Day of 1926, all police horses were ill and King, together with his brother Chas. G., lent the department 22 mounts from their private stables in Mentor for the day's parade. After his death, in 1948, Mrs. Fannie T. King was given a plaque dedicated by the mounted division for her son's 25 years of service.

Resuming active duty in 1940, King was appointed commander of the 107th Cavalry Regiment, based in Cleveland, which was a reconnaissance regiment attached to the 5th Corps. Upon mobilization, he took the troops to Camp Forrest, Tenn., for training and induction into service on 5 Mar. 1941. In 1944, King drew a highly responsible and important assignment in being sent to China to advise and train native troops. On 23 Feb. 1946, he received the Dis-

tinguished Service Medal for his work in retraining, reorganizing, and inspiring Chinese troops in South China during the time he was commanding general of the 4th Army Group Command. He was twice awarded the Legion of Merit for his liaison work in the Chinese Theater. In 1946, King was discharged because of a heart ailment he had contracted during his strenuous service in China. In private life, King was vice-president and treasurer of the Ventura Corp., a real-estate firm. He was also on the board of officers of the Realty Investment Co., with offices in the Colonial Arcade. He was a familiar figure in many sporting circles in Cleveland. King was survived by his wife, Louise Baldwin, and 3 children, Woods, Jr., Arthur, and Sally.

The **KING IRON BRIDGE & MANUFACTURING COMPANY** was the largest highway bridge works in the U.S. during the 1880s. The company played an important role in the development and construction nationwide of the metal truss bridge, a uniquely indigenous product of American engineering and construction technology. Although the King Iron Bridge & Mfg. Co. was not organized under that name until 1871, the company traces its origin to 1858, when Zenas King (1818–1892) began his work as a bridge builder. King's early years are obscure. He was born in Vermont but spent most of his early life in New York State before coming to Ohio about 1840. He pursued several different occupations before becoming an agent for a Cincinnati bridge company, Moseley & Co., in 1858. King's name first appears in the Cleveland city directory in 1861, when he is listed as a manufacturer of iron roofing and boilers. That year he established a short-lived partnership with Peter Frees to build boilers and bridges. By 1865, King had established his works on Wason (E. 38th) St. between Hamilton and St. Clair avenues. About 1888, the company moved to a larger plant on Ruskin (E. 69th) St.

King's business initially was confined to the manufacture of iron arch and swing bridges. But by 1878, he was building all types of truss, combination, and wooden bridges, including his famous patented tubular arch, as well as iron roof trusses, fencing, and jail cells. The company enjoyed a wide market, having by that year erected bridges in Topeka, Kans.; Binghamton, N.Y.; Ft. Laramie, Wyoming Territory; Bowling Green, Ky.; Santa Rosa, Calif.; and Macon, Ga. In addition to its office employees and a network of agents in Boston, Philadelphia, Des Moines, Kansas City, and other cities, from 150–200 men earned an average of $12 a week in the King shops. In 1875, the officers of King Iron Bridge & Mfg. were Zenas King, president; Chas. E. King, vice-president; Harley B. Gibbs, secretary; Wm. Vliet, engineer; and Thos. H. Brooks, superintendent. Serving as directors were Zenas King, Ralph Pratt Myers, H. D. Sizer, Andros B. Stone, Dan P. Eells, Chas. E. King, HENRY CHISHOLM, STILLMAN WITT, and Leverett Alcott. Jas. A. King assumed the office of vice-president in 1877 and became president in 1892. Upon Zenas King's death, the company's name was changed to the King Bridge Co. The company was disbanded in the 1920s. King-built bridges in Cleveland include the CENTRAL VIADUCT (1888; only the Abbey Ave. portion remains); the Center St. Bridge (1901), Cleveland's last remaining swing bridge; and the 591-ft. steel arch of the DETROIT-SUPERIOR BRIDGE (1918).

King Iron Bridge & Mfg. Co. Catalogs, 1875 and 1884, Ohio Historical Society Library, Columbus.

**KING MUSICAL INSTRUMENTS** has been responsible for redesigning and improving the tonal and playing quality of more than 28 instruments, including the slide trombone, cornet, trumpet, and clarinet. It also invented the Trombonium, the valve trombone used widely by high school marching bands. Its trumpets, trombones, and woodwinds were used by Big Bands and soloists such as Tommy Dorsey, Benny Goodman, and Paul Whiteman, as well as by instrumental groups of the 1960s and 1970s such as Blood Sweat & Tears and Chicago. King Musical Instruments was started in 1893 as the H. N. White Co. by Henderson White, a music engraver and printer and intrument repairman, whose sensitive ear was troubled by the imperfections of instruments of the day. With the urging and collaboration of Thos. King, a solo trombone player at the old LYCEUM THEATER in Cleveland, White perfected and marketed a trombone that was an overnight success. The instruments were immediately purchased by musicians who played in the then-popular park concerts, as well as the bands of minstrel shows and theater orchestras. White named it the King Trombone after Thos. King.

Later, White designed and patented a new silver cornet, followed by redesigned trumpets and baritone and double-bell euphoniums, each developed painstakingly through experiments conducted by White and his associates who were acoustic and metallurgical experts, at the factory located at E. 53rd St. and Superior Ave. In 1935, King Stringed Instruments were introduced with the big bass viol, followed in 1937 by the King cello and a silver-lined clarinet in 1938. White's dedication to quality included making working conditions as pleasant as possible. He sponsored a band that provided noon concerts for factory workers 3 days a week. Using newly manufactured instruments, he also used the concerts to detect imperfections. White died in Mar. 1940, leaving the business, which continued to grow, with his wife as president. Later, the company's name was changed to King Instruments when Nate Dolin became its new owner in 1965. To meet increased production demands, the company moved to a location at 33999 Curtis Ave. in Eastlake. In 1983, Daniel J. Henkin, owner of W. T. Armstrong, a manufacturer of musical instruments, purchased King Musical Instruments.

White, Mrs. H. N., *Fifty Years of Achievement in the Band Instrument Industry* (ca. 1943).

**KINSGBURY, JAMES** (1767–12 Dec. 1847), at the age of 29 was the first settler in the Western Reserve. He came to Conneaut, Ohio, from Alsted, N.H., with his wife, Eunice Waldo Kingsbury, and 3 children. In 1797, he and his family accompanied the surveyors of the CONNECTICUT LAND CO. and relocated in Cleveland in a log cabin near the CUYAHOGA RIVER. Later, they moved to higher ground away from the swamps, to a ridge southeast of Cleveland (Woodhill Rd.). That was the beginning of the Newburgh settlement. The Kingsburys became the parents of the first white child born in the Western Reserve. The birth occurred during a period when supplies were dwindling and there was an absence of game. Kingsbury had traveled east for supplies and was on his return trip. The child survived only a short while after Mrs. Kingsbury became ill and the cow died, cutting off the supply of milk for the baby. Kingsbury's appointment as judge by Gen. St. Clair in 1800 was part of the formation of the first governmental agency in the Reserve. Kingsbury was elected in 1803 to serve in various positions for the township: trustee, overseer of the poor, lister, and supervisor of the highways. In 1805, he was elected as a member of the legislature of the state of Ohio. He died in his Newburgh home at the age of 80.

**KINGSBURY RUN** is part of a winding, natural watershed carrying creeks and storm water from what is today WARRENSVILLE HTS. and MAPLE HTS. to the CUYAHOGA RIVER. East of E. 79th St. in Cleveland, the creek and creek beds are culverted and filled in many places, but from E. 79th St. west, Kingsbury Run forms a broad arc, and a deep, rugged valley remains. The area takes its name from JAS. KINGSBURY, one of the earliest settlers in the WESTERN RESERVE, who came with his family to Conneaut in 1796 and moved on to Cleveland a year later. On 11 Dec. 1797, Kingsbury moved from a cabin near what would later become PUBLIC SQUARE to a higher and more healthful location on the ridge southeast of Cleveland. That was the beginning of NEWBURGH. This ravine separating Cleveland from Newburgh became a route for railroads, beginning in 1857 with the Cleveland & Mahoning Valley line. In the 1860s it also became the site of industry, with John D. Rockefeller's crude-oil refinery and Wm. Halsey Doan's oil and naptha works. Spanning Kingsbury Run at Sidaway Ave. is Cleveland's only suspension bridge, the Sidaway Ave. Footbridge, built in 1930 to link the Jackowo and Garden Valley neighborhoods but no longer used. Kingsbury Run's fame, however, is due less to its role in the city's industrial growth than to the infamous Cleveland TORSO MURDERS.

The **KINNEY & LEVAN COMPANY** was one of the country's largest importers and wholesalers of crockery, glassware, and other home furnishings. Its predecessor, Geo. W. Kinney & Co., began in 1879 when Geo. W. Kinney opened a wholesale lamp goods and glassware business in the Atwater Bldg. at Water (W. 9th St.) and Superior Ave. He soon made friends with a young salesman, Aaron B. Levan, and in 1883, Kinney and Levan purchased the Bowman Bros. & Levan Co., for which Levan had worked, and opened it as their own store at 121 Superior Ave. The new partnership maintained a wholesale as well as a retail business in home furnishings. With the skillful buying of Levan and 6 other experienced salesmen, the firm prospered as new lines of housewares were introduced. In 1885, Kinney & Levan moved to Bank (W. 6th) St. By 1912, when the company was incorporated, Kinney & Levan realized that its business had grown so much, with trade covering 20 states, that a new building was necessary. The following year, the firm opened the largest exclusive store of its kind in the nation, a 6-story building in the new retail district at E. 14th St. and Euclid Ave. Kinney & Levan continued to grow, with over 300 employees by the late 1920s. In 1932, it enlarged and remodeled the store, making it a complete home-furnishing center. However, the company was a victim of the Depression. Kinney & Levan went bankrupt on 11 Apr. 1936, when creditors completed the sale of its goods.

Kinney & Levan Co., *Building to Better Serve, 1883–1913* (1913).

The **KINSMAN JEWISH CENTER** was one of the most important Orthodox congregations in Cleveland between 1930–60 and was also one of the first Orthodox congregations in the city to be organized along nonnational lines. The KJC was established in 1930 as B'nai Jacob Kol Israel Congregation and rented a house at E. 149th and Kinsman, where services were held for 3 years. Its founders had been members of the Kinsman branch of the Anshe Marmoresher B'nai Jacob Congregation. The branch was established in 1928. However, a group of men led by Dan Weiss and Pincus Newman determined to enlarge the congregation beyond its Hungarian character. In addition, they sought to create a community center that would serve the

Orthodox Jews of Kinsman and SHAKER HTS. In 1932, a building was dedicated at E. 147th and Kinsman that was to be the community center. It also served as the synagogue when plans for a place of worship were abandoned because of the exigencies of the Depression. It never became the focus of Jewish life in Kinsman as the Cleveland Jewish Ctr. did in GLENVILLE. However, as a congregation, it quickly grew in both size and importance. Beginning with fewer than 30 families, the KJC increased its membership to almost 400 families by 1940.

In 1933, the KJC established a Hebrew school that operated in the afternoon following public school. During the following year, a sisterhood was formed. In 1950, the KJC created one of the first synagogue-sponsored Jewish nursery schools in the city. During the 1950s, the synagogue also formed a Young Women's League, which provided a recreational program for boys and girls. In 1958, the movement of the Jewish population to the eastern suburbs led the center to sell its property and move to temporary quarters on Lee Rd. in Shaker Hts. With the cost of rebuilding prohibitively high, the center entered into a merger with TETIEVER AHAVATH ACHIM ANSHE SFARD Congregation and Congregation Neveh Zedek to form WAR-RENSVILLE CTR. SYNAGOGUE. Dan Weiss was the first president of the center and served for 20 years. Rabbi DAVID GENUTH was the congregation's first spiritual leader and held the pulpit from 1933–48. Rabbi Jacob Muskin was hired in 1948 and served as rabbi until the merger in 1959, when he became rabbi for the new Warrensville Ctr. Synagogue.

**KIRBY, JOSIAH** (16 May 1883–4 Feb. 1964), was a Cleveland businessman whose 50-year career in the city was plagued by controversy. Born in Wyoming, Ohio, he came to Cleveland in 1911 with $5.25 in his pockets following failure of a land-development plan in his home town, where he had also been mayor at age 21. In Cleveland, Kirby opened a life insurance business in the ROCKEFELLER BLDG. After some financial setbacks, he organized 3 mortgage companies, ultimately forming the Cleveland Discount Co., a $10 million mortgage corporation reported to be, at the time, the 2d-largest mortgage company in the world. Cleveland Discount was one of the few companies dealing in large construction loans. In 1920, the Rockefeller Bldg. was renamed the Kirby Bldg. when Kirby, through a lawsuit, forced JOHN D. ROCKEFELLER to fulfill an agreement to sell to Kirby. The building was bought back in 1923 by Rockefeller and the original name was restored. By 1921, Cleveland Discount had become the largest of its kind in the U.S., with capital listed at $37 million. Within the period 1921–23, Kirby built the 14-story Cleveland Discount Bldg. at 815 Superior Ave. But his company was taken over by receivers on 23 Feb. 1923, and an audit revealed a huge loss. Common stock was declared worthless, and the assets of the company were sold.

Other business failures included Kirby's involvement as commodore of the CLEVELAND YACHT CLUB (1918–20), during which time the club grew to 1,600 members. When he took command, the club was in receivership. During his term, 5 new buildings were constructed, and many improvements were made. However, when Kirby's delicately balanced financial structure collapsed, the Cleveland Yacht Club went into bankruptcy. Following several state court trials during the mid-1920s in which he was acquitted or released by failure of the jury to agree, Kirby was sentenced in a second federal trial to a 7½-year prison term in Atlanta, Ga. He was convicted of using the mails to defraud and also received 2 years for jury tampering.Kirby's troubles continued during his prison term. Suit

was brought against him by 4 stockholders of the Cleveland Discount Co. who charged that his mismanagement and misuse of funds had led to the company's insolvency. Kirby was released in 1932. He began life anew in Cleveland as a consulting sales engineer, but his main office was in Los Angeles, where he and his wife had purchased a home. By 1940, at age 57, he was reported to be living in New York and was indicted with 2 others by a federal grand jury on 14 counts, including conspiracy, mail fraud, and market rigging in the stock of the Automatic Prods. Corp. of Chicago. He was permanently enjoined from selling securities in 1949, which led to a 10-month term at a federal correctional institution at Milan, Mich. Upon his release, he returned to Cleveland. Kirby's last years offered him no reprieve from his troubles. In 1962, the Securities & Exchange Commission filed a contempt complaint charging that Kirby, at age 80, had been selling and buying stocks since 1954 in violation of a court injunction. He was placed on 5 years' probation when Judge Frank J. Battisti said that only Kirby's advanced age kept him from sentencing Kirby to prison. Little is recorded about Kirby's family life in Cleveland other than that during his 1962 trial it was reported that he was living with his second wife, Ruth, after "tragedy had deprived him of his [first] wife and all but one of his children."

**KIRTLAND, JARED POTTER** (10 Nov. 1793–18 Dec. 1877), was a leading naturalist and physician. He was one of the founders of the CLEVELAND ACADEMY OF NATURAL SCIENCES (the forerunner of the CLEVELAND MUSEUM OF NATURAL HISTORY) and the Western Reserve University School of Medicine. His father, Turhand Kirtland, was a general agent of the CONNECTICUT LAND CO. Born in Connecticut, Jared Kirtland received his early education and medical training there, first studying with Dr. John Andrews of Wallingford, Conn. In 1815, he graduated from Yale University's medical department. He married Caroline Atwater and practiced medicine for several years in Durham, Conn., before joining his father in Poland, Ohio, in 1823. Kirtland was elected to the Ohio House of Representatives for Trumbull County in 1828 and served for 6 years. While serving in the legislature as chairman of the Penitentiary Committee, he developed an interest in prison conditions and reforms and advocated the Auburn System for Ohio. For his efforts, Kirtland became known as the "Father of the New Penitentiary." In 1837 he received an appointment as professor of theory of medicine at the Medical College of Ohio and moved to Cleveland. In 1840–41 he accepted the chair in theory and practice and physical diagnosis at Willoughby Medical School (Willoughby University of Lake Erie). In 1844, along with JOHN DELAMATER, HORACE ACKLEY, and JOHN CASSELS, he founded the Cleveland Medical College—the medical department of Western Reserve College. As professor he taught medicine at Western Reserve University from 1844 until his retirement in 1864. Kirtland was active in local and state medical societies and frequently presented papers on various topics. In 1851 he served on a committee appointed by the mayor of Cleveland to secure safe drinking water for the city of Cleveland. In addition to his medical and teaching interests, Kirtland was one of America's leading naturalists in the 19th century and had a great interest in horticulture. He had an interest in and an extensive collection of sea shells. He published numerous natural history articles in *Gillman's Journal of Science*. Kirtland was elected to membership in the American Philosophical Society and was a founder and president of the Kirtland Society of Natural History and the Cleveland Academy of Natural Science. After 1843 he lived in

Rockport (ROCKY RIVER) and continued his experiments in horticulture. Kirtland was married twice, first to Caroline Atwater, then to Hannah Taucey of Rockport.

Kirtland and Morse Family Papers, WRHS.

The **KIWANIS CLUB,** a service organization founded in Detroit in Jan. 1915, was first organized in Cleveland on 19 June 1915, making Cleveland's the second-oldest club in what has become an international organization. Among the leaders in the formation of the Cleveland club were Ed C. Forbes, the club's first secretary, and Oscar F. Alexander, its first president. The purpose of the Cleveland club was to foster "the exchange of business and civic ideas [and] introductions of mutual benefit," and to aid the underprivileged. Cleveland was the site of the first national convention of Kiwanis Clubs, on 18 May 1916. At the meeting, the 16 clubs then in existence developed the idea of forming an international organizaton. In the Cleveland area, the service organization proved popular: by 1927, the Cleveland club had 210 members, and 9 other Kiwanis clubs had been formed in the suburbs and various sections of the city. The Cleveland club sponsored formation of a number of other clubs over the next several decades, including one in Vienna, Austria, in 1963. In mid-June 1942, Cleveland hosted the 27th Annual Kiwanis Internatl. Convention, which brought more than 6,000 delegates to the city; the city also hosted the 1955 convention. In 1951, the Greater Cleveland area had so many clubs that they were split into 2 divisions; by 1955, the 37 Cleveland-area clubs had 3,200 members, including the 320 members of the downtown club. Adhering to the motto "We Build," the area Kiwanis Clubs have been quite active in local charitable, civic, and service projects, especially to benefit the young and the underprivileged. Clubs sponsor Boy Scout troops, Little League baseball teams, and high school Key Clubs, and played a major role in the programs of the BOYSTOWN. They have also built and supported youth centers and recreation facilities, supported drug-education programs, provided scholarships, distributed toys to the underprivileged, raised funds to buy necessary items for handicapped people, and established awards to honor the good works of others.

**KLEIN NEWS CO.** *See* **GEORGE R. KLEIN NEWS COMPANY**

**KLONOWSKI, STANLEY J.** (29 May 1883–3 Feb. 1973), was a prominent Polish businessman and banker active in Cleveland civic affairs. Born and educated in Poland, Klonowski graduated from the University of Poland at Warsaw and was fluent in Russian, French, and English as well as Polish. After working as a postal clerk and telegraph operator and later serving in the Russian army, he came to the U.S. in 1904. He worked in a number of northern cities before settling in Cleveland in 1912. On 16 Jan. of that year, he married Stella Akuszewski. Klonowski worked for Polish businessman MICHAEL KNIOLA before starting his own business in 1913. Under his own name, he opened a private bank and foreign exchange, selling real estate, insurance, and steamship tickets as well. It was the first Polish bank in the city, and Klonowski incorporated it in 1920 as the Klonowski Savings Bank; the institution was reorganized in May 1921 as the Bank of Cleveland, located at 7100 Broadway. Klonowski guided the bank as its president until 1957 and then as chairman of the board.
Klonowski made headlines in 1931 when he wrote to Pres. Herbert Hoover and other government officials to suggest that the government create an agency separate from

the Federal Reserve to provide credit for banks and businesses on the brink of collapse during the Depression. When Hoover later announced a $500 million credit plan for banks, the *Plain Dealer* hailed Klonowski as the father of the plan, but Klonowski wisely refused to take credit for it. In 1933, Klonowski used $280,000 of his own money to pay his depositors and creditors all the money his bank owed them, rather than pay them a percentage. Active in civic affairs, Klonowski served on the board of the CLEVELAND PUBLIC LIBRARY for 25 years and was a member of the UNIVERSITY SETTLEMENT, the CITIZENS LEAGUE, the CITY CLUB, and the Natl. Conference of Christians & Jews. He was especially active in the affairs of the Polish and Catholic communities. He served as a member of the executive committee of the CATHOLIC CHARITIES CORP. and helped establish MARYMOUNT HOSPITAL. He was a member of the Knights of Columbus, the Cleveland Society of Poles, and 5 other local and national Polish organizations.

The **KNIGHTS OF COLUMBUS TRACK MEET** was an annual sporting event that brought national and international track and field athletes to Cleveland for competition between 1941 and its final meet in 1986. It was reportedly the 2d-oldest indoor meet in the U.S. when it ended for lack of a sponsor in Jan. 1987. The Catholic fraternal Knights of Columbus organized the first meet on 16 Mar. 1941; the proceeds went to the Catholic Youth Organization. The 15-event program, held at the the CLEVELAND ARENA, featured a number of world-record holders and was billed as the local debut of indoor track, then "a big-time sports attraction in the east." The 6,425 people who attended the 1941 meet watched competitors set 3 world records and tie another; among the record setters was local track star STELLA WALSH, who set a new world record for women in the 220-yd. dash. Records continued to fall over the next 5 decades as each March, world-class athletes, including many local track and field stars, competed in the event. The K of C meet was held at the Arena through 1971; in 1972, promoters moved it to Public Hall and moved the date to February, closer to the end of the indoor AAU championships, in hopes of attracting international athletes, who usually had returned to their native lands prior to the Cleveland meet. The event was moved to the Coliseum in Richfield a few years later. The 1986 meet appears to have been the last, however; in Jan. 1987, promoters canceled the 1987 event, having failed to find a sponsor and having raised only $20,000 of the $75,000 needed for the event.

The **KNIGHTS OF LABOR DISTRICT ASSEMBLY NO. 47** was an early local labor coalition that preceded the trade union bodies later formed by the AFL and the CIO. The assembly had its origin in the Industrial Council of 1874 but soon became affiliated with the Knights of Labor as the Trades & Labor Assembly. Within a decade, there were some 50 locals that constituted the district body, District Assembly No. 47. Reform unionists who sought to replace the wage system with a more equitable distribution of wealth, the local Knights got the support of activists such as LOUIS B. TUCKERMAN and MARTIN A. FORAN. Since anyone but lawyers and saloon keepers could join the organization, the meetings were fertile territory for local politicians and business promoters, who took the workmen further away from concrete workplace-oriented goals. Eventually, the idealistic goals supported by the Knights failed to gain the allegiance of workers, who abandoned the group for the newly formed Central Labor Union. Chartered by the AFL, the new body was organized by crafts and waged many jurisdictional fights with the Knights. By 1900, only 14 K of L locals remained, while the District Assembly No. 47 dropped from the city directory in 1903.

**KNIOLA, MICHAEL P.** (16 Sept. 1859–17 Sept. 1944), was a prominent businessman in Cleveland's Polish community and was influential in that community's civic and political affairs after 1890. Kniola was born in Samostrzel, Poland, one of 4 children of Peter and Anna Nowakowski Kniola. On 1 Apr. 1873, the Kniola family arrived in New York City; they settled in Spotswood, N.J., where Peter's older brother lived. There Michael attended night school; he worked for 2 years in a tobacco factory, and then in a brickyard in Sayersville. On 7 Feb. 1880 he married Mary Skarupski. At the suggestion of a friend, Kniola moved to Cleveland, arriving on 3 Apr. 1880 with his new wife and in-laws; his parents followed in September. He found work in the wire mill of the Cleveland Rolling Mill Co. and continued his education at the Broadway Night School. He eventually became a foreman in the wire mill. In 1886 Kniola went into business, opening a grocery store at 924 Tod (3690 E. 65th) St., his business and home address until his death. Using the store as a base, he provided other services to the Polish community. He advanced credit in the store, rented lodgings, sold insurance and real estate, and, working on commission as a labor broker for local firms and those in other cities, found jobs for recent immigrants. He also began selling money orders and arranging steamship passages. In 1890 he organized the latter two operations into the Kniola Travel Bureau, which had become such a success by 1900 that he sold his grocery stock and concentrated his efforts on the travel business, continuing in it until the late 1920s, when he turned it over to his son, Raymond.

Kniola was an important figure in the political and civic affairs of the Polish community. In 1892 he helped organize Cleveland's first Polish newspaper, *Polonia w Ameryce*. In 1893 he began the Polish Republican Club and helped bring Polish businessmen into the Republican party; he also served as a director of the Polish-American Chamber of Commerce, was an administrator of the probate court, and ran for city council in 1909. Kniola was also prominent in the fraternal, cultural, and religious affairs of the community. He helped organize the Knights of St. Casimir, a uniformed, semimilitary organization, and served as a director of both the Polish Alliance of America and the Polish Roman Catholic Union of the U.S. He was also a purchaser, incorporator, and president of the Polish Falcon Hall and served as director and treasurer of Polish Falcon Nest 141 (see SOKOL POLSKI). Kniola was also an organizer and trustee of ST. STANISLAUS CHURCH.

Coulter, Charles W., *The Poles of Cleveland* (1919).
Kniola Travel Bureau Records, WRHS.

**KNOBLE FLORISTS** was founded in 1906 by Herman P. Knoble near its present location at 1836 W. 25th St.; it became a leading member of the floral community. Herman Knoble was among the founders and charter members of the Floral Telegraph Delivery System (FTD), begun in 1912. In 1924 he founded the clearinghouse division of the organization, which centralized billing of FTD purchases. FTD and its clearinghouse represented a major marketing strategy for florists; it remained in place until the late 1970s, when FTD became computerized, using a system designed by the Chi Corp. of Cleveland. Over 15,000 florists throughout the country installed computer terminals to handle floral orders and billing, control inventory, and warn of local problems that might hamper delivery.

Knoble's son William entered the business in 1932 after studying floral culture at Cornell, and continued his father's role as an innovator in the profession. Seeing that delivery was an industrywide problem, since 90% of all floral customers wanted same-day delivery, Wm. Knoble started the Special Service Delivery Co. in 1953. Modeled after a similar service in Detroit, SSD used Knoble trucks as the nucleus of a fleet, and soon expanded to 15 vehicles that offered same-day delivery service. Some 60 local florists were using the service by 1956, but SSD became such a popular means of delivering small packages, documents, medicines, film, and small parcels that within 6 months of its founding, the service was making 2,200 deliveries a week. By 1969, SSD business outstripped that of the flower shop and made 10,000–12,000 deliveries per week within a 75-mi. radius. It had a corps of 150 regular customers to whom it could offer pickup or delivery within 15 minutes' accuracy. In 1985, it operated as SSD Distribution Systems at 9921 York-Alpha Dr., after many years at 2514 Bridge. Aside from his delivery innovations, Wm. Knoble was active in efforts of the local floral association to encourage people to buy flowers not only for special occasions but also to enhance their everyday lives. In the 1950s, he offered a monthly plant maintenance service to offices and industrial buildings and also started a school for floral design to train a supply of florists and floral assistants in current floral trends.

**KNOX & ELLIOT** was an architectural firm active in Cleveland from 1893–1925. Wilm Knox (1858–1915) was born in Glasgow, Scotland, and came to America in 1886. In the office of Burnham & Root in Chicago, he met John H. Elliot (ca. 1862–ca. 1925), who was born in Toronto, Canada. They formed a partnership and opened an office in Toronto in 1888, where they executed several large and important commissions. In 1892 they were invited to work with Henry Ives Cobb on the 1893 Columbian Exposition, and Knox became Cobb's office manager. Knox & Elliot set up practice in Cleveland in 1893. After Knox's death in 1915, the firm continued under Elliot until 1925. The work of Knox & Elliot consisted predominantly of commercial and industrial buildings, apartments, and some churches and private residences. Among the buildings still extant in the 1980s were the ROCKEFELLER BLDG., generally considered to be their Cleveland masterpiece; the Natl. Carbon Co. (Union Carbide) office building in LAKEWOOD; the Engineers Bldg.; the Standard Bldg.; the Carnegie Library on Lorain at W. 83rd St.; ST. JAMES AME CHURCH; the McKinley Terrace; and the Pelton Apts. One of their greatest buildings was the HIPPODROME THEATER, the largest remaining vaudeville theater in the nation at the time it was demolished in 1980.

Schofield, Mary-Peale, "Working File of Cleveland Architects . . ." WRHS.

**KOHANYI, TIHAMER** (d. 1913), was the founder of *SZABADSAG* (Liberty), the largest Hungarian daily newspaper in the U.S., and a prime mover in many organizations that aided Hungarian immigrants in their transition to America. After an unsuccessful attempt to practice law in Hungary, Kohanyi came to America at age 27. He held a succession of jobs as a coal shoveler, traveling book salesman, janitor, and clerk before settling in Cleveland in 1891. Here he immediately set upon organizing the Hungarian community; his first effort was the Cleveland Hungarian Young Mens' & Ladies' Society, which presented the first Hungarian drama presentation in Cleveland. Sensing a need for a Hungarian-language newspaper, he founded *Szabad-*

*sag* in Nov. 1891. To fund the effort, he secured $600 contributions from 2 Hungarian industrialists, Joseph Black and THEODOR KUNDTZ, and $15 pledges from 117 of his countrymen; out of fear that the effort would fail, only 50 pledges were paid, and the major donors refused to make additional contributions. Undaunted, Kohanyi managed, edited, and typeset the paper, as well as wrote many of the articles. *Szabadsag* became an important influence in the lives of Hungarian-Americans. It offered them news from their native land as well as useful information such as how to address letters and function in American society. It was a forum for readers and a clearinghouse for announcements of cultural, social, and religious events. *Szabadsag* promoted projects such as the creation of the KOSSUTH MONUMENT in Cleveland in 1902 and the Washington monument in 1906 in Budapest. Aside from its literary and cultural functions, the paper collected money for Hungarian widows, orphans, strikers, and disaster victims, and offered other personal services. Despite his generosity to immigrants through his paper, Kohanyi sustained himself on a meager income. After 20 years as editor of *Szabadsag*, he wrote that if one is truly cursed by fate, he will become a Hungarian journalist. Further sacrificing his health and personal life for the Hungarian cause, Kohanyi helped found the Catholic Hungarian Insurance Assoc. in 1897 and the American Hungarian Fund in 1906.

**KOHLER, FREDERICK** (2 May 1864–30 Jan. 1934), served as police chief of Cleveland for 10 years (1903–13) and was elected Cuyahoga County commissioner in 1918, mayor of Cleveland in 1922, and sheriff in 1924. Kohler was born in Cleveland, the son of Christian and Fredericka Kohler. He attended Outhwaite and Willson schools, leaving in the 6th grade to help his father in the Kohler Stone Works. After his father's death, the business failed, and Kohler worked at several laboring jobs. In 1887 he was appointed superintendent of WOODLAND CEMETERY. He married Josephine (Josie) Modroch on 15 Nov. 1888. The couple had no children. Kohler joined the police force in 1889 and became known as a zealous and effective police officer. He rose rapidly in the police ranks, becoming a captain in 1900.

In 1903, Mayor TOM L. JOHNSON appointed Kohler chief of police. Kohler was a strict disciplinarian who demanded a neat appearance and a full day's work from all policemen. He became involved in a scandal growing out of a divorce suit brought by a traveling salesman against his wife, and in Feb. 1913 the Civil Service Commission removed him as police chief on charges of neglect of duty and gross immorality. After several unsuccessful attempts at elective office, Kohler was elected county commissioner as a Republican in 1918, serving 2 terms. He served as mayor in 1922–24. During his 2-year administration, he emphasized economy in city government, cutting payrolls and city services. He also persuaded private agencies to take over the responsibility for families on relief. At the end of his mayoralty, the CITY MANAGER PLAN went into effect, and in 1924 Kohler was elected sheriff. As sheriff, he was accused of underfeeding the prisoners in the county jail. After a grand jury investigation of charges, the common pleas judges, who constituted the legal board of jail governors, ruled against Kohler. They ordered him to improve prison meals and return any unused money to the county. He left office in 1926. He died in Cleveland at age 69.

The **KOKOON ARTS CLUB** was one of Cleveland's most active artists' organizations between 1911–40. It was largely known for its unconventional activities and its espousal of "new art." Founded in 1911 by Carl Moellman and WM. SOMMER, the club was based on avant-garde artists' organizations in New York that sought new forms of artistic expression as alternatives to the conformity of academic art. The club also wished to cultivate in Cleveland the bohemian spirit found in the art centers of Europe. The Kokoon Club was selective in its membership, for many years refusing to admit women. From the beginning, dedication among the members was strong; many worked as commercial artists and used the club as a means to fulfill themselves as individual artists. Among the many Kokoon Club artists to achieve regional and, in some cases, national distinction were Wm. Sommer, HENRY KELLER, AUGUST BIEHLE, Rolf Stoll, Joseph Boersig, and JOSEPH JICHA. Hoping to keep the club intimate and serious, membership was limited to 30 (in later years it would exceed 75). The 13 original members met twice a week in a 1-room structure on E. 36th St., formerly a tailor's or dressmaker's shop. Models were recruited, and much of the time was spent painting. The club's first exhibition was in Nov. 1911, which one newspaper account described as "exceedingly daring in nature." The Kokoon Club's reputation was founded largely on its annual "Bal Masque." The first was held in 1913; like future Kokoon Club Balls, it was a celebration of Cleveland's bohemian community—artists, musicians, poets, etc., all took part. In 1915 the theme was "Parisian"; in 1918 it was "Persian"; and in 1929 it was the "Bal Dynamique" as an exotic tribute to the machine age. The ball featured unconventional costumes, exotic dances, opening processions, enormous props and clashing decorations, and unpredictable "stunts" throughout. With the exception of 1 year (1923), the ball survived the close monitoring of city hall and provided the club with the means to continue. In 1921, the club moved to larger quarters at 2121 E. 21st St. Among its activities, it invited to Cleveland leading art critics and artists, who frequently used the club's house for lectures or exhibitions. At least twice a year, the club held its own exhibitions, often drawing controversial reviews. Other activities included art instruction for the public, and various theme parties throughout the year—all of them artistically choreographed. By the late 1920s, the Kokoon Club had gained greater acceptance in the community. As "new art" also became more acceptable, it lost some of its original intellectualism and became more of a social organization. With the Depression, the club began a slow but steady decline. The last "Bal Masque" was held in 1946. The club managed to hold together with a dwindling membership for at least 10 more years.

The **KOL ISRAEL FOUNDATION** is an organization of Cleveland survivors of the Holocaust, the destruction of European Jewry by the Nazis during WORLD WAR II. Kol Israel, which means "All of Israel," was founded 15 Feb. 1959 to represent the Holocaust survivors in the area, while helping to secure special education, guidance and vocational training, and economic and social adjustment for people from foreign lands settling in Greater Cleveland, as well as to supply charitable support for the state of Israel. To those who had suffered in concentration camps, Kol Israel meetings became a refuge where they could get together with others who had a similar past. Founding officers were Wm. Miller, president, Simon Fixler, Herta Kuricki, Morry Malemacher, and Max Kuricki. Kol Israel helped newcomers who arrived after the organization was established by providing financial assistance and locating housing and jobs for those who had no relatives, friends, or agency to assist them.

An early project of the group was the erection of a monument to the memory of the 6 million victims of the Holocaust in Zion Memorial Park on 28 May 1961. Ashes of victims from 3 concentration camps were buried under the monument. In addition, both funds and ambulances were donated to the state of Israel in the 1960s and 1970s. The foundation has participated in the Warsaw Ghetto Uprising Memorial Service since 1978 and in the successor Community Holocaust Remembrance Day observance as the representative organization for survivors. In addition to the foundation, there is a Kol Israel Sisterhood and a Second Generation Kol Israel founded by a group of young people on 19 Mar. 1978 and dedicated to the continuance of the memory of the Holocaust victims. The Second Generation group has sponsored educational workshops for its members and the general public. On the 25th anniversary of the Kol Israel Foundation, membership was approximately 450, including the sisterhood. Officers in 1983 were Jack Wieder, president; Jack York, vice-president; Abbie Akst, treasurer; Jacob Hennenberg, secretary and historian; Bob Birnbaum, chairman; and Henry Miller, social chairman.

Hennenberg, Jacob, "A History of the Kol Israel Foundation" (n.d.)

**KOLASZEWSKI, ANTON FRANCIS** (5 Sept. 1851–2 Dec. 1910), was a dynamic Polish priest who constructed the present (1985) ST. STANISLAUS CHURCH and organized the parishes of Sacred Heart of Jesus and the IMMACULATE HEART OF MARY in the Warszawa district of Cleveland. Kolaszewski was born in Russian Poland to John and Catherine Gergens Kolaszewski. His family immigrated to America, where he began studies for the priesthood at the Franciscan College at Teutopolis, Ill. He was accepted by Bp. RICHARD GILMOUR for service to the Poles in Cleveland and completed his studies at St. Mary Seminary here. Bp. Gilmour ordained him on 1 July 1883. Kolaszewski immediately became pastor of St. Stanislaus Church on Forman Ave. His congregation numbered only 200 families, but it grew as thousands of Polish immigrants arrived seeking jobs in the steel mills. Their religion alone was familiar in the new land. Kolaszewski was not only their pastor but also their community leader, doctor, lawyer, mediator, translator, correspondent, and financial advisor as the occasion demanded. As his congregation outgrew its small church building, Kolaszewski envisioned a soaring brick Gothic church that would rank among the largest and most ornate churches of the diocese. Counting on the generosity of his poorly paid parishioners, he let out contracts, and the work was begun in 1886. When completed in 1891, St. Stanislaus Church cost $250,000. Earlier Kolaszewski had established a mission church under the title of Sacred Heart for the Poles who lived in the southern part of the district. He began holding separate services in private homes in 1888, and by 1889 he had already built a church for this new congregation.

Kolaszewski was unquestionably a zealous and hardworking priest; however, St. Stanislaus parish developed some factions. His optimistic appraisal of his congregation's financial resources was proved false. Kolaszewski had unwisely concealed both the cost of the church and the resulting debt from diocesan authorities. That, coupled with the dissension in the parish, caused Bp. IGNATIUS HORSTMANN, Bp. Gilmour's successor, to demand Kolaszewski's resignation in 1892. Kolaszewski left Cleveland and went to Syracuse, N.Y. There he began something of an association with the Polish nationalistic movement of dissident Roman Catholics. Kolaszewski professed both doctrinal orthodoxy and loyalty to papal authority, but he

reserved the right to question the authority of his bishop. In 1894, Kolaszewski returned to Cleveland. He was still popular with many of his former parishioners. A number of them joined the church of the Immaculate Heart, which Kolaszewski organized in the vicinity of St. Stanislaus. Kolaszewski emphasized both the orthodoxy of his congregation and its independence from diocesan control. He refused to concede and was undeterred by a formal excommunication. Various efforts at reconciliation failed until 1908. Kolaszewski reconciled with the church but resigned the pastorate.

**KOLLIN (KOLINSKY), ABRAHAM** (1879–4 Apr. 1968), attorney and communal leader, was born in Lithuania and came to the U.S. as a boy. He attended the CLEVELAND PUBLIC SCHOOLS and studied at the Cleveland and Western Reserve University law schools. He was admitted to the Ohio Bar Assoc. in 1902 and practiced law until his retirement in 1959. An ardent Zionist, Kollin was the first local writer to defend political Zionism in the Cleveland Jewish press. He argued that there had to be a territorial basis in a person's belief in Judaism, an argument that put him in direct conflict with the leaders of the Reform community. He was president of the Cleveland Zionist District for a period during the 1920s. Kollin was one of the leaders of 2 unsuccessful attempts to organize the East European Jewish immigrants' organizations into a single representative body. In 1906, he was among the founders of the UNION OF JEWISH ORGANIZATIONS, and in 1913, with his brother Max, he helped to organize the KEHILLAH, another umbrella organization. Kollin was a charter member of the American Jewish Committee and served as president of the Cleveland Lodge No. 16 of B'NAI B'RITH in 1910. He was also a member of ANSHE EMETH congregation, later known as the Cleveland Jewish Ctr. and then Park Synagogue. He was a charter member of the Cleveland CITY CLUB. In June 1917, Kollin was one of 5 men elected in a communitywide vote to represent Cleveland at the first American Jewish Congress, an attempt to create a democratically elected national Jewish organization with representatives from all sectors of the American Jewish community.

The **KOREAN ASSOCIATION OF GREATER CLEVELAND**, organized in 1966, is a cultural organization serving the Korean-American community. By 1976 the organization had grown to include 2,000 members and was sponsoring Korean Day Festivals to celebrate and publicize Korean culture. In addition to such cultural events for the community and outsiders, the association provides social-welfare services for members and holds ceremonies to commemorate important events in Korean history, such as the proclamation of independence celebration each March and the observance of the establishment of the republic each August. Membership in the association had grown to about 5,000 by 1986.

**KOREAN CHURCHES IN CLEVELAND** came into being after a modification in immigration quotas in 1970, when thousands of Koreans entered the U.S., many of whom found their way to Cleveland. While there were some with denominational preferences, many were either unchurched or unaffiliated. The primary resource center was the KOREAN ASSOC. to aid the newcomers to whom language and custom presented a most formidable barrier. During the next 15 years, the churches quickly augmented the services of the association and provided spiritual centers where the Korean language was employed in services and counseling. In 1985 there were 7 churches in the Cleveland area that served Korean congregations: the Cleveland Korean Church, a nondenominational church; the First Korean Church; Korean American United Methodist; the Korean American Presbyterian Church; Korean Presbyterian; Korean Central Baptist; and the St. Augustine Korean Catholic Church.

**KOREAN WAR.** The Korean War period marked the peak of Cleveland's rise as an industrial city and masked early signs of decline. Although the city's population rose slightly, 4.2%, between 1950–53, the flight to the SUBURBS was accelerating, and the county had grown by 11%. The economy had never been better. In 1952, Cuyahoga County was rated 5th in the country in productive capacity, but the city's infrastructure was beginning to decay. Slums were growing, and no major new buildings had been erected downtown since the Terminal Tower group on PUBLIC SQUARE. In Aug. 1951, the fire chief, Bernard W. Mulcahey, declared that 65% of 561 downtown buildings could be closed for fire violations. Unemployment was virtually nonexistent at 1.2%, but racial tensions were beginning to emerge as the black population, which had increased by 75% since 1940, was continuing to grow, constituting 16% of the city's population.

Clevelanders, with the rest of America, listened to the radio reports coming in all day Sunday, 25 June 1950, about the early morning invasion of South Korea by North Korean troops. They applauded with patriotic fervor Pres. Truman's 27 June order for air and naval support of the beleaguered troops of the Republic of Korea. It was a popular war at first, although Ohio's Sen. Robt. Taft immediately called for the resignation of Secretary of State Dean Acheson for instigating the war by his announcement of the exclusion of South Korea from our defensive perimeter. FRANCES PAYNE BOLTON, Republican congresswoman from the 22d district, seconded her fellow Ohioan's call in the House. Nevertheless, Republicans and Democrats alike supported the president's strong action against Communist aggression, including his call for increased military spending and the reinstitution of the draft, as well as price and wage controls. The city council even enacted rent controls through the spring of 1953. Large numbers of young Cleveland men and women were called to military service, some for the second time; 44,000 residents of Cuyahoga County saw service, 1,161 of whom died during the conflict.

On the home front, there appeared to be little evidence of the wartime conditions so familiar only 6 years earlier. The mayor appointed a woman, Elizabeth H. Augustus, as civil defense director. The *Plain Dealer* in Dec. 1950 complained of a manpower shortage and industry's need for 5,000 more workers, and the reinstated draft was taking its toll of Cleveland's young male population. The Natl. Production Act of Sept. 1950 put a ban on industrial hoarding of raw materials such as rubber, but that scarcely affected consumer goods. The county installed a $3 million air raid system, which included 59 alarms, 8,000 volunteers, and 2,000 Boy Scouts, and the whole system was set for testing on Saturday afternoon, 5 Dec. 1953, at 3 p.m. The alarms failed to go off. Clevelanders could afford to take such snafus in their stride, for the city's economy was booming. In 1952 the total payrolls of Cleveland's manufacturing industries exceeded the combined payrolls of the industries of 13 states. The Cleveland Army Ordnance District placed multi-million-dollar contracts with such Cleveland firms as LEMPCO INDUSTRIES, the WEATHERHEAD CO., the WHITE MOTOR CO., the Cleveland Welding Co., and many others. Bank loans soared to a new high. Steel production was at record levels, so that in Nov.

1951 REPUBLIC STEEL announced a $75 million plant expansion, and American Steel & Wire constructed a new $10 million blast furnace, which would be its last. The Community Chest reached successive all-time highs during the period, from goals of over $6 million in 1950 to over $7 million in 1952, reflecting the prosperous economy. The baby boom, too, was being felt, as 15,000 kindergarteners entered the school system in the fall of 1952, an increase of 4,000.

Meanwhile, local politics followed the fortunes of war. After MacArthur's brilliant coup on 15 Sept. 1950, with the amphibious landing at Inchon, behind North Korean lines, the rout began. On 3 Oct., as U.N. troops approached the 38th Parallel, the *Plain Dealer* cheered encouragement, echoing MacArthur's assurance that the Chinese would not enter the war, and urged a push for total victory in Korea, a decision Truman had already made. The initial purpose of the war was to restore the status quo, but with a total rout in progress, the prospect of uniting the two Koreas proved too tempting, and Truman allowed MacArthur's troops to cross the 38th Parallel and drive to the Yalu River. The full disastrous impact of this decision came 3 weeks after the November elections with the invasion of 4 Red Chinese armies. The election saw a Democratic defeat, but the former mayor of Cleveland, Frank Lausche, a conservative Democrat, maintained his hold on the governor's seat, and his hand-picked successor, THOS. A. BURKE, running a year later in 1951 as an independent Democrat, won his 5th term as mayor of Cleveland. The perennials, Republican Frances P. Bolton and the Democrat Stephen Young, returned to Congress, but Republicans won a stunning victory in the state legislature, capturing an overwhelming majority in both houses.

As the war grew worse, anti-Communist fervor mounted. "McCarthyism" had its origins during this period. It was a term given to a form of demagoguery practiced by Sen. Joseph McCarthy of Wisconsin, who, using his position on Senate committees, took advantage of public fear of Communism and Communist subversion by hurling charges of Communist affiliation or sympathy at liberal opponents. These charges were unproven and were often based on guilt by association but were sufficient in that climate of fear to brand the accused as guilty and in some cases ruin their careers. In reality, the Red Scare had its origins earlier, as the tensions between Russia and the U.S. grew in 1947 and 1948. For example, Calvin S. Hall, a psychology professor at Western Reserve University, as head of the Ohio Henry Wallace for President committee, had signed a petition in 1948 to get Wallace on the Ohio ballot, but the secretary of state of Ohio, Edward J. Hommel, denied the petition and accused Hall of being a Communist. President John Millis of WRU censured Hall for his activities. He, under pressure, resigned his position in the Progressive party. In May 1949, the Cleveland school board adopted a loyalty oath after a heated debate and compromise that included a denial of membership in Nazi or Facist, as well as Communist, organizations. Meanwhile, during the bitter FAWICK-AIRFLEX STRIKE (Apr. 1949), the company charged the United Electrical Workers' Union with being Communist, and later, in contempt-of-court hearings, union leaders were accused by the judge of having committed a "treasonous act" and of being party to a "Communist conspiracy."

With a conservative victory in the fall of 1950, the next session of the Ohio legislature established an Ohio Un-American Activities Commission; the Red Scare, fanned nationally by the activities of the House Un-American Activities Committee and Sen. Joseph McCarthy, now moved full-scale into Ohio. The commission held hearings in Columbus, Cincinnati, Akron-Canton, and Cleveland. Thirty-nine witnesses in the course of the investigations refused to testify about their political affiliations; 9 of these were Cleveland residents. For 3 days, 2–5 Dec. 1953, Common Pleas Judge Earl Hoover's courtroom was packed from 10 a.m. to 4:30 p.m. Among the 9 Clevelanders who were called as witnesses and refused to answer questions about their political affiliations was a Cleveland schoolteacher who taught science and driving at the Cleveland Trade School. He signed the school board's loyalty oath but was fired, not for violation of the oath but for "unbecoming behavior." A black man, Admiral Kilpatrick, former head of the Mine, Metal & Smelters' Union, lost his job at the Wellman Bronze Co. All 9 Clevelanders were cited for contempt of the commission but were not tried. The commission made a report at the end of its statutory existence, 31 Jan. 1954, and with the ending of the disgraceful televised Army-McCarthy hearings late that spring, the Red Scare abated, leaving in its wake shaken university and school faculties and faction-ridden library and school boards.

Cleveland had its share of natural disasters during the period. Two of the most notable were the blizzard of 1950 and the burning of the CUYAHOGA RIVER in 1952. On 24 Nov. 1951, a furious snowstorm blew into Cleveland, and it continued snowing for the next 3 days, dumping over 21″ on Cleveland, tying up the city for over a week, and necessitating calling out the Natl. Guard. In 1952, on Saturday afternoon, 1 Nov., a heavy oil slick on the surface of the Cuyahoga River caught fire, sweeping through the shipyards of the Great Lakes Towing Co., 201 Jefferson Ave., and also disabling the Jefferson Ave. bridge. The blaze formed a crescent around the shipyard, inhibiting the efforts of firefighters and eventually causing an estimated $1.5 million worth of damage. A sign of the city's ebullient self-confidence is suggested in the *Plain Dealer*'s characterization of the fire as, "if not the most disastrous, certainly the gaudiest." There was no public rejoicing when the final ceasefire was signed at Panmunjom 27 July 1953, just a general sigh of relief and an easing of tension. For Cleveland, the period marked the high tide of its industrial growth, with steel production records set in 1952 and 1953. Steel prices had doubled after a long strike in the spring of 1953, and all apparent signs presaged a bright future for the 7th-largest city in the nation. Its sports teams were at the top of their leagues. The impetus of the "forgotten war" had delayed the city's decline as an industrial and population center by a few years and thrust it to new levels of prosperity.

David D. Van Tassel
Case Western Reserve University

**KORNER & WOOD** was one of Cleveland's notable bookstores. It was an institution in downtown Cleveland and served as a gathering point for local writers and artists. The store was founded in 1900 by Harry V. Korner and A. Vinson and was located at 157 Euclid Ave., near PUBLIC SQUARE. Named Vinson & Korner, it was there for only a year. The store moved to the Barstow Bldg., where it remained until 1924. The owners, changing twice, wished to sell quality merchandise: books, stationery, office supplies, and art objects. Vinson left the store in 1904; John J. Wood joined Korner in partnership in 1905 but left in 1912. Harry V. Korner was left with the store and its corporate name, Korner & Wood. Korner (2 Jan. 1875–20 Oct. 1958) was considered the dean of local booksellers.

Even at its beginning, the bookstore was modern and progressive, with the latest works, including the avant-garde. However, it maintained a charming, subtle character and provided individual attention to its customers. Korner had

photographs as well as books lining the walls of his 1512 Euclid Ave. store. Houdini and Blackstone visited the store. Artists FRANK WILCOX and Grace Kelly exhibited works of art there. Sinclair Lewis stopped whenever he was in town. Elbert Hubbard, founder of the Roycrafters, sold his volumes at Korner & Wood. Korner's son, Harrison K. Korner, took over the family business when his father retired. Ernest F. Crummel was taken in as a partner and operated the decorative-arts section. A small fire in 1959 and a $5,000 theft in 1962, in which cash and valuable antiques were taken, dampened Korner's enthusiasm. He later announced that the downtown store would be closing because of a decline in sales. In 1963, following the closing of the downtown store, Korner still operated branches in Mayfield, Cedar-Fairmount, Cedar-Warrensville, Southland Plaza, and Kamm's Plaza. These remaining shops were also closed in 1965.

**KOSSUTH, LOUIS VISIT TO CLEVELAND.** *See* **LOUIS KOSSUTH'S VISIT TO CLEVELAND**

The **KOSSUTH MONUMENT** was erected on the northeast corner of East Blvd. and Euclid Ave. in 1902 (dedicated 27 Sept.) by the Magyar American Citizens to commemorate Hungarian patriot Lajos (Louis) Kossuth's visit to the U.S. in 1851–52. The Magyar group initially wished to place the monument on PUBLIC SQUARE but was prevented from doing so by the Slovak community of Cleveland; the Slovaks viewed the Magyars as their Old World oppressors and were resentful of any efforts to honor a Hungarian in the city's central square. Kossuth had visited Cleveland during his visit to the U.S. He arrived in the city on 31 Jan. 1852. He remained for 2 days, delivering several speeches and raising funds for Hungarian relief work. Cleveland citizens contributed over $1,500 to this cause.

**KOUDELKA, JOSEPH MARY** (8 Dec. 1852–24 June 1921), was the first auxiliary bishop of Cleveland and the second bishop of Superior, Wis. Koudelka was born in Chilstova (Bohemia), Czechoslovakia. His parents were Markus and Anna Jazousshek Koudelka. Koudelka began his studies at the Imperial College in Klattan, Bohemia. In 1869, his family immigrated to America and settled in Wisconsin. Koudelka began his studies for the priesthood at Mt. Calvary and then St. Francis Seminary in Milwaukee. In 1874 he transferred to St. Mary Seminary in Cleveland with the permission of the Milwaukee bishop John Henni. After his ordination as deacon, he was named administrator of St. Procop Church in Cleveland. Bp. Tobias Mullen ordained him to the priesthood on 8 Oct. 1875. After his ordination, he was named pastor of St. Procop's, where he spent 7 years. During that time, in addition to his pastoral duties, he published a set of Bohemian readers, a church history, and several prayerbooks.

In May 1882, Bp. RICHARD GILMOUR allowed Koudelka to go to St. Louis, Mo., to take charge of *Hlas*, an influential Bohemian publication. In 1883, Koudelka was called back to Cleveland to assist with the Bohemian congregations. On 15 July 1883 he was asked to take charge of a mission of the German parish of St. Mary. Under Koudelka's direction, it would become the parish of St. Michael, which served the Germans living in the Clark-Fulton area. During his 28-year pastorate, Koudelka established a school and built an impressive Gothic Cathedral-style church, which would become a national landmark. Koudelka's pastoral and linguistic skills were not confined to St. Michael parish. Bp. IGNATIUS HORSTMANN, Gilmour's successor, sent him to Europe to recruit priests and seminarians for work with the East European immigrants.

Koudelka served as a diocesan consultor from 1904–10. On 25 Feb. 1908 he was consecrated as the first auxiliary bishop of Cleveland. He served the diocese and St. Michael's Parish until 1911, when he was named auxiliary bishop of Milwaukee. On 6 Aug. 1913 he became the second bishop of Superior in Wisconsin. Despite his episcopal duties, he found time to preach and give missions to the Slavic peoples in the East and Midwest. He is buried in St. Mary Cemetery in Cleveland.

Houck, George F., *A History of Catholicity in Northern Ohio* . . . (1903).

Hynes, Michael J., *The History of the Diocese of Cleveland* (1953).

**KRAFT, EDWIN ARTHUR** (1883–15 July 1962), was a musician who held the position of organist-choirmaster of TRINITY CATHEDRAL for over 50 years. He was born in New Haven, Conn., and began his musical training and career early, becoming a church organist in New Haven at age 14. He studied at Yale and subsequently became the organist at St. Thomas Church (Episcopal) in Brooklyn, N.Y. He continued his studies in Berlin and Paris and returned to become organist-choirmaster of St. Matthew's Church (Episcopal) in Wheeling, W.Va. In 1907, the year of the consecration of Trinity Cathedral at E. 21st St. and Euclid Ave., Kraft was appointed organist-choirmaster. He played extensively around the Cleveland area over the following years, and gave recitals around the country. In addition to playing the cathedral organ, he directed the highly respected choir of men and boys. In 1914, Kraft left Cleveland to become municipal organist in Atlanta, Ga., but he returned to Cleveland and the cathedral the following year. In 1922 he played before an audience of 12,000 at the dedication of the Cleveland Municipal Organ at the PUBLIC AUDITORIUM.

Kraft participated in the founding of 2 chapters of the American Guild of Organists, in Cleveland in 1909 and in Atlanta in 1914. He transcribed a large number of orchestral and piano works for the organ and composed over 60 choral works. Many organ works of the time were dedicated by their composers to Kraft. Kraft married Nancy Lovis in Dec. 1909. They had 2 children, Nanetta and Edwin Arthur, Jr. Mrs. Kraft died in July 1925, and the following year Kraft married the head of the vocal department of the CLEVELAND INSTITUTE OF MUSIC, Marie Simmelink. Kraft retired from Trinity Cathedral in 1959. He died only minutes after playing one of his own organ transcriptions informally before a group of friends and former students.

Edwin A. Kraft Papers, WRHS.

The **KRONHEIM FURNITURE COMPANY** is one of Cleveland's leading furniture stores. The firm was founded as a 1-man upholstery shop by an Austro-Hungarian immigrant, Jacob Kronheim, in 1918. Kronheim, who arrived in Cleveland in 1902, had worked as an upholsterer for several companies before starting his own shop at Woodland Ave. and E. 37th St. He turned out 1 to 3 chairs or couches per day and built a reputation for honest workmanship and material. He developed several upholstering processes, which were patented and became distinctive features of the company's products. He then moved to a larger facility on Quincy Ave. near E. 77th St., where he started a factory with about 20 employees. The company further expanded when it opened its first retail store at 2043 E. 55th St. shortly after WORLD WAR I. In the early 1930s, Kronheim brought in 2 merchants, Emil M. Friedman and Max Amster, and an executive, Joseph J. Tronstein, to aid in further developing the company through their capital and merchandising skills. With the opening of a downtown store on Euclid Ave. in 1934, Kronheim had 2 stores, 2 factories, and a warehouse in Cleveland. The company became known for selling living-room furniture and odd pieces of upholstered furnishings directly from the factory to the consumer. In the 1950s, Kronheim had over 100 employees, and by the 1960s it began to establish more retail outlets with a large variety of home furnishings. In 1972, the firm bought a large warehouse at 1814 E. 40th St., which became its headquarters. By the 1980s, some of its inner-city stores had closed, but Kronheim still maintained 4 suburban stores.

**KUCINICH, DENNIS.** *See* **MAYORAL ADMINISTRATION OF DENNIS KUCINICH**

The **KULAS FOUNDATION** was founded in 1937 by Fynette Hill and Elroy John Kulas (1880–1952). Kulas was born in Cleveland and worked for the Natl. Electric Lamp Co. from 1900 to WORLD WAR I, when it was bought by General Electric. He went on to accumulate his wealth in the steel industry and organized the powerful merger of the Parish & Bingham Co. of Cleveland with the Detroit Pressed Steel Co. to form Midland Steel. He was also director of the Wheeling & Lake Erie Railroad, the Pittsburgh & West Virginia Railroad Co., and the American Iron & Steel Institute. While the stated purposes of the foundation are broad, the Kulas name is associated largely with music institutions and HIGHER EDUCATION in the Greater Cleveland area. The Kulases gave $50,000 for a music building at BALDWIN-WALLACE COLLEGE in 1938 and have since contributed widely to the enhancement of MUSIC and music education in the area. No grants are given to individuals or for endowment funds. In 1981, assets of the foundation were $10,341,850, with expenditures of $892,338 for 60 grants. Officers of the foundation are Richard W. Pogue, Allen O. Holmes, Frank E. Joseph, and Herbert E. Strawbridge.

**KUNDTZ, THEODOR** (1 July 1852–14 Sept. 1937), was a manufacturer of sewing-machine cabinets, bicycle wheels, church and school furniture, and automobile bodies. As president of the Theodor Kundtz Co. and an officer in other businesses, he became a prominent figure in Cleveland's Hungarian community. Born and educated in Unter-Metzenziefen, Hungary, Kundtz came directly to Cleveland when he arrived in the U.S. in 1873. He had learned the cabinetmaker's trade in his father's shop and found work in Cleveland with the Whitworth Co. at 28 St. Clair St. In 1875, Kundtz and fellow workers Geo. Gebhard, Chas. Simon, and Edward Genee gained control of John Whitworth's business, reorganizing it as the Cleveland Cabinet Co. By 1878, Kundtz had his own shop at 122 Elm St. Among his early customers was THOS. WHITE of the White Sewing Machine Co., for whom Kundtz made what became his chief product, sewing-machine cabinets. Kundtz soon expanded production to include bicycle wheels and, in 1890, church and school furniture. During WORLD WAR I, the firm made truck bodies for the Allied war effort. By 1900, Kundtz employed 2,500 skilled workers, many of them Hungarian immigrants. By the time the Theodor Kundtz Co. was incorporated on 1 Apr. 1915, it occupied 5 plants in Cleveland. Kundtz presided over the company until he retired in 1925 and sold it to White Sewing Machine.

Kundtz's business success made him a prominent citizen in the local Hungarian community. He gave employment and encouragement to many Hungarian immigrants, urging them to begin businesses of their own. He also helped build Hungarian Hall on Clark Ave. in 1890 and was the main speaker during its opening ceremonies on 19 May 1891. Kundtz had other business interests. He served as an officer in both the Forest City Bank and the United Banking & Savings Co.; he was president of both the Detroit St. Investment Co. and the Edgewater Bathing Beach Co.; and he served as a director of the Cleveland Tractor Co. He was a member of the Cleveland Chamber of Commerce, the Tippecanoe Club, and St. Rose Church. In 1884 he married native Clevelander Mary Balasch.

The **KURTZ FURNITURE COMPANY,** founded by Isadore and Rose Kurtz in 1905 at 4319 Lorain Ave., grew to become one of the largest furniture chains in Cleveland. Throughout its history, it remained family owned and operated. Isadore Kurtz operated his business with the help of his wife. He functioned as owner, furniture buyer, salesman, serviceman, handyman, and deliveryman. By 1914, he had moved to larger quarters at 4329 Lorain, and by 1919 he had bought up the entire block and converted it to one of the largest stores in the area. Kurtz sold his furniture primarily to the working man. At a time when only the socially prominent could get retail credit, Kurtz offered budget terms to the family man with a steady job. To promote electric refrigerators, he sold them with meters attached so that his working-class customers could pay for them as they did the iceman, at $.25 per day. Later, Kurtz stores were the first in the area to introduce innerspring mattresses and radios with batteries included. By 1968, the store had served 800,000 customers, many the 4th generation of their family to patronize Kurtz.

As his market grew, Kurtz increased the number of stores. His first branch was at 9312 Kinsman (1921), followed by a second at 310 Prospect (1927). Despite the Depression, Kurtz prospered. With the rise of suburban shopping centers, Kurtz followed the demographic trends and added branches: Parmatown (1959); 5059 Turney (1964); Shoregate (1968); SOUTHGATE (1975); Southland (1975); and Great Northern (1975). Some of the expansion ventures were of short duration; by 1979, only the Prospect and Lorain locations remained of the early stores, while only Shoregate, Southgate, and Southland remained of the later ones. In 1980, Kurtz drastically cut back its operations and remained only at the Southgate and Southland locations as Kurtz Living Rooms Plus. A victim of overexpansion and an abundance of discount furniture stores, Kurtz closed its doors in 1980.

**LTV STEEL,** the major subsidiary of the Dallas-based LTV Corp., grew out of the 1984 merger of JONES LAUGHLIN STEEL (acquired by LTV in 1974) and the REPUBLIC STEEL CORP. Talks began in Sept. 1983, and tentative agreement to combine the companies was announced at the end of the month. However, in Jan. 1984, the U.S. Justice Dept. rejected the plan as a violation of federal antitrust laws. Intervention by local, state, and federal officials, including Pres. Ronald Reagan and Vice-Pres. Geo. Bush, kept the plan alive, and in March the Justice Dept. approved an amended agreement requiring Republic Steel to sell its stainless-steel plant in Massillon, Ohio, and its rolling mill in Gadsden, Ala. After approval by the shareholders of both companies in May 1984, the companies became LTV Steel on 1 July, the nation's 2d-largest steelmaker behind U.S. Steel (USX). As the major subsidiary of the LTV Corp., Cleveland-based LTV Steel hoped to generate enough profit to get rid of its inefficient facilities and put together a highly competitive cost-effective steel company. Employing about 9,000 people in Greater Cleveland, its facilities included the general offices, steel plants, the steel-and-tube division, and a research center. Unfortunately, the nation's economy began to weaken about the time of the merger, and the deteriorating steel market forced the company to deeply discount its prices to remain competitive.

LTV suspended the payment of common stock dividends in Oct. 1984. By the end of Mar. 1985, most of the parent company's credit had been used, and it was able to cover its continuing losses only by selling assets to raise cash (LTV Steel lost over $600 million in 1985). In Apr. 1986, the UNITED STEEL WORKERS agreed to cuts in wages and benefits of about $3 per hour, although the Cleveland locals, which enjoyed full employment at that time, voted overwhelmingly against the reduction. In spite of the givebacks, 1,700 were laid off at the Cleveland works in May. The corporation's finances did not improve, and in June Standard & Poor lowered their debt rating, alerting investors to the increased risk of loans to LTV. S&P's action combined with the weakened economy apparently triggered a loss of confidence by suppliers in LTV's ability to pay its bills. With suppliers shortening credit terms, LTV ran out of cash, and on 17 July 1986, the corporation filed in federal court for protection from its creditors under Chap. 11 of the U.S. Bankruptcy Code. Its past debts frozen, LTV continued to operate, paying its suppliers from

current income while work was begun on the reorganization plan to restore its financial health. Although steel continued to be made in Cleveland, the bankruptcy adversely affected local city and county governments, schools, and libraries, whose income decreased as a result of LTV's inability to pay its taxes.

**L'ARALDO** (The Herald) gave Cleveland's Italian community its second newspaper when it began publication on 1 July 1938. A tabloid printed in both Italian and English, the weekly was put out by the L'Araldo Publishing Co. on Mayfield Rd. in LITTLE ITALY. Attorney J. H. Taddeo served as president and editor, while Emilio S. Ardito was business manager. While not unsympathetic to Mussolini in its early years, the paper called on its readers to be patriotic Americans after Pearl Harbor. A succession of editors kept the paper alive after WORLD WAR II, including Matteo Teresi, another attorney, and Dr. Claudio Ferrari, an assistant Italian counsel. One of the last was Alfonso D'Emilia, a former employee of the New York daily *Il Progresso Italo-Americano. L'Araldo*'s demise in 1957 left local Italian readers without a local organ.

**LA VOCE DEL POPOLO ITALIANO** (The Voice of the Italian People) was founded by cousins Olindo G. and Fernando Melaragno in 1904. Cleveland's first Italian newspaper, it was also published as *L'Italiano* and *Il Progresso Italiano in America* before assuming its permanent appellation on 2 Apr. 1910. Located on the fringes of BIG ITALY at Central Ave., the weekly was incorporated as the United Italian Publishing Co. By 1913, it was owned wholly by the Melaragnos, with Fernando handling the editorial chores and Olindo supervising the business side. One of the early officers, Dr. GIOVANNI A. BARRICELLI, remained a frequent contributor. In domestic politics, *La Voce* favored the Republicans and resisted Prohibition. Its interest in European affairs increased dramatically after Italy's entry into WORLD WAR I in 1915. In 1918, with the U.S. also in the war, *La Voce* began printing its editorials in English. Its opposition to Communism led *La Voce* to endorse Mussolini's postwar Fascist regime in Italy. Through the intercession of Il Duce himself, Italy's King Victor Emmanuel conferred the title of Chevalier of the Crown on Olindo G. Melaragno. Only after Italy's open entry into WORLD WAR II as Hitler's ally in 1940 did *La Voce* condemn the Mussolini government. With circulation under 2,000, *La Voce* suspended publication by some accounts in 1944. According to an article in the *CLEVELAND PRESS*, however, it was still being operated in 1945 by O. G. Melaragno's son, Columbus, as a largely newsless "phantom weekly," primarily interested in selling advertisements.

**LABOR.** The concept of a working class, distinct from farmers, small proprietors and professionals, or men of wealth, was of little use in the early years of the city's history; in these years an egalitarianism based on cheap land was reinforced by a relatively equal apportionment of the rigors of frontier life. The origins of many of Cleveland's earliest laborers can be traced to the OHIO & ERIE CANAL, which was begun in 1825 and immediately generated a demand for unskilled labor. As the first elements of a working class consisting of day laborers emerged, they were viewed with suspicion by their fellow citizens, who found Cleveland's frontier egalitarianism far superior to the class structure of eastern cities. In 1829, the *Herald* epitomized certain attitudes toward laborers, which would continue to be held by many Clevelanders into the 20th century: "laborers are much wanted upon the public works at this place. It is surprising to us why it should be so. At the wages paid for these jobs the young men of this vicinity could buy themselves a snug farm. How many hundreds of men and their families are there in the eastern cities, live from hand to mouth and drag out a miserable existence, educating their children for servitude, and perhaps the gallows, who, by industry and frugality in Ohio, might in a short time become comparatively able farmers...." Rather than attracting prospective additional farmers to Cleveland, the canal created the commercial and industrial basis for day labor by increasingly large numbers of skilled and unskilled workers. The dependence of the worker upon his employer in an inherently unequal relationship and the hostility of other social classes to laborers assured that they would come to view themselves as a distinct group with a need for unique organizations to represent them in the political and economic spheres.

Unskilled workers, who earned only $3 a week for 60 or more hours of work, were unorganized. Skilled workers, however, had the energy and interest and sufficient economic leverage to form unions. In 1834, journeymen printers formed the Cleveland Typographical Assoc. to bargain for improved hours and wages. The union was an auxiliary of the Typographical Auxiliary of Columbus, Ohio, and the New York Trades Union. Two years later, the carpenters organized a union to bargain with the master builders for a 10-hour day in order to "have time to attend to their domestic affairs." Neither of these organizations survived for any length of time, and with the Panic of 1837, attempts to organize ended for a decade. Cleveland workers did, however, follow the lead of eastern workers by attempting to organize societies of workingmen and mechanics to gain political influence. Despite these attempts, hard money and organized workers were in short supply in 1843, when 350 Cleveland and Ohio City workingmen paraded to protest the return of barter to the local economy. Considering that the cities' population was only slightly over 6,000 in 1840, it can be seen that that was a showing of considerable strength. The association they formed lasted a little over a year, providing a lyceum with lectures of interest to workingmen. Five years later, an Assoc. of United Mechanics again flourished briefly, providing speakers on political topics.

During the 1850s, an unskilled workingman continued to earn perhaps $4 or $5 a week for 60 or more hours of work. The *DAILY TRUE DEMOCRAT* editorialized for an increase in the pay of city street sweepers from $.75 per day to $1. Working women earned less. In 1850, after 15 years of declining wages and payment in "orders" rather than cash, the seamstresses formed the FEMALE PROTECTIVE UNION to secure better wages. Of the city's estimated 350 seamstresses (among 17,000 people), 50 formed a cooperative union store to better their lot. Despite these efforts, only 2 years later a seamstress felt compelled to "steal" a coat when her employer refused to pay her. The employer pressed charges, and the woman was brought into court looking "overworked and poorly fed," where a sympathetic judge dismissed the charge and ordered the merchant to pay court costs.

Efforts to organize continued throughout the 1850s; in this decade, workers organized, if only temporarily, in larger numbers and in more trades than ever before. The printers reformed their union in 1852 and went on strike in that year. Sixty men joined a carpenters' union, agreeing to a contribution of $.10 per week to support the union. Employers struck back in 1853 when the white waiters at the prestigious WEDDELL HOUSE struck and were replaced with black waiters. The painters organized and struck unsuccessfully, and 100 shoemakers protested wage reductions in 1858. In these same years, a Workingmen's Assoc. again started, and workers attempted to form a workingmen's party. In the depression of 1857–58, these organizations once again disappeared. The Typographical Union nevertheless enjoyed a rejuvenation, and in 1863, J. A. Spencer, president of the Cleveland local, hosted the Natl Typographical Union Convention in Cleveland. The hostility of many Clevelanders to labor organizations continued in these years, and EDWIN COWLES, editor of the *CLEVELAND LEADER*, celebrated the demise of the union in 1864. Despite this hostility, workingmen grew increasingly restive. The Typographical Union reformed, receiving its international charter in 1868, which it holds to this day (see TYPOGRAPHICAL WORKERS UNION #53). In these same years, the plasterers and the bricklayers would organize, and the coopers' union would play an especially prominent role in the union movement.

More general associations of workingmen likewise flourished. In 1868, a Workingmen's Assembly was organized, with 50 delegates from 5 Cleveland wards and several unions. The organization affiliated with the Natl. Labor Congress, and the congress's president, Richard F. Travellick, who espoused political action by workers, soon became a familiar speaker on Cleveland labor podiums. With political activity came factionalism; during the period, one newspaper account credited a meeting with creating enough noise "to honor a young earthquake!" While never a political force, the organization would survive into the 1870s, and many of its principles and members were later adopted by the Knights of Labor. As prosperity returned in the late 1860s, an unprecedented period of labor unrest opened. It began among the coopers in 1867 and was followed by the strike of 400 railroad shopmen in 1868 and a second strike by the coopers in 1869. In 1871, the Cleveland Ninth Circle Telegrapher's Protective League joined in a national strike against Western Union. The *Leader* editorialized that the spirit "of the English Trade Union" pervaded the entire working class, even as the Erie Railroad workers went on strike and the smoldering unrest in the cooperage trade broke into open riot. In this latter case, even the antilabor *Leader* noted that a reduction in wages from $15 per week to $13.50 provided some justification for the strike when rents in a working-class neighborhood ranged from $15 to $20 a month. A totally different, but equally important, role that the unions played at this time is revealed in the announcements of the iron moulders' picnic at HALT-

NORTH'S GARDENS in May and the 11th annual Iron Moulders Ball in Nov. 1870; a year later the Moulders raised $135 at their annual ball. The machinists and blacksmiths unions sponsored similar balls in these years.

In 1873, the Industrial Council of Cuyahoga County was formed, composed of 10 unions, including Typographical Local 53 and 3 coopers union locals. Robt. Schilling was president, and in 1873, the council successfully hosted a week-long convention of the Natl. Industrial Congress in Cleveland. By 1874, they had secured a· hall, and discussions were underway to develop a workingmen's newspaper. Many of Cleveland's major craft unions date from these years, a testimony to the permanence of the movement in Cleveland after the CIVIL WAR. As the recession of 1873-78 deepened, a series of unsuccessful strikes occurred in Cleveland. In 1874, a strike by 200 unorganized sailors became a riot, and a walkout by 800 coalheavers and dockworkers was successful despite a confrontation with police. In 1877, a key year in American labor history, Cleveland's workers continued to suffer from underemployment and low wages. Using Czech, German, and English, members of the coopers union organized a strike at the STANDARD OIL CO. The leaders, some of whom were Czech socialists, called for a citywide strike of all workers earning less than $1 per day and were joined by sewer masons, bricklayers, cigarmakers, and others. After this initial success, the strike disintegrated into violent confrontation when the strikers' wives attacked police, who began clubbing the women and ignited a riot in response. Three days later, the strike was over, but conservative Clevelanders were outraged and frightened by the call for a general strike. In July, when railroad workers across the nation began one of the most violent strikes in American history, Cleveland employers took a conciliatory approach, and the strike ended locally without significant violence. Despite the lack of violence, many Clevelanders feared for their lives during the railroad strike. Wealthy Clevelanders organized the First City Troop of Light Cavalry (see TROOP A) in 1877, and in June 1878, the CLEVELAND GATLING GUN BATTERY was recruited from the "best circles." In 1879, construction was begun on an armory complete with loopholes. In one of those anomalies of Cleveland's history, the building would never witness a shot fired in anger but would be the site for an 1882 meeting of the Fed. of Organized Trades & Labor Unions—destined to become the American Fed. of Labor.

Cleveland workers continued to strike in spite of these preparations, and with the return of prosperity, roughly 70-80% of strikes in Cleveland were successful in the years 1881-86. Rather than use guns and clubs, employers resorted to yellow-dog contracts and blacklists. However, in 1882, a major strike occurred at the Cleveland Rolling Mills. The iron- and steelworkers succeeded in organizing 80% of the plant's workforce and attempted to raise wages to the level prevailing in other cities. With the cooperation of the city, the company imported Polish and Bohemian immigrants to break the strike. Only 3 years later, however, the Polish and Bohemian workers struck and secured an increase in wages (see CLEVELAND ROLLING MILL STRIKES).

The 1880s were a period of gradual improvement for Cleveland workers. Real wages increased, work was plentiful, and 20% of all Clevelanders owned their own homes. Many workers looked to the Knights of Labor for leadership. The Knights ran candidates for public office, and nearly 50 assemblies were formed in Cleveland as the KNIGHTS OF LABOR DISTRICT ASSEMBLY NO. 47. In 1886, approximately 5,000 people attended the local Knights of Labor picnic. The present-day carpenters union

was organized in 1881 under Knights of Labor sponsorship. In 1887, the competing AFL chartered a Cleveland Central Labor Union. Organized by an immigrant German typesetter, ROBT. BANDLOW, this body was the forerunner of today's AFL-CIO. Working on his own time, Bandlow organized 26 locals between 1887-91. In 1886, MARTIN A. FORAN of the coopers union was elected to Congress with the support of labor; he later became a successful judge. As early as 1888, workers celebrated Labor Day, and by 1890 it was a legal holiday. Still another sign of the growing strength of labor was the founding of the CLEVELAND CITIZEN in 1891 by MAX S. HAYES and Henry C. Long. The Central Labor Unon assisted the fledgling newspaper, which presented trade-union and labor news while espousing a moderate socialism.

By 1900, there were 100 unions in Cleveland: 62 affiliated with the AFL, 14 with the Knights of Labor, and 24 were unaffiliated. At the same time, a more radical political movement was offering itself to the American working class—the American Socialist party. Given the overt hostility of capital to labor organizations and the harsh conditions of labor in 1900, one might expect a successful socialist movement—the opposite was true. During the first half of the 20th century, American workers would embrace trade unions while supporting the Republican and Democratic parties. A major factor mitigating the influence of socialism was the continued general prosperity of the working class. By 1900, 40% of Clevelanders owned their own homes, as opposed to 20% in 1880. In 1900, 10,000 men were employed in the building trades, more than a twofold increase over 1880. And new generations of workers' homes came equipped with electricity and indoor plumbing. Growth in unions slowed after 1904 in the face of hostile courts, continued immigration, and heightened employer opposition. The percentage of organized workers decreased as steel, petroleum, and other heavy industries expanded, creating large numbers of unskilled and semiskilled positions. Only during the war years 1917-18 did large numbers of workers join unions. During this brief period, which foreshadowed the growth of unions in the 1930s, immigration ceased, labor was scarce, and government policy favored unions. For black workers, who came to Cleveland in large numbers during the war to fill the gap created when immigration from Europe ended, union membership was especially a rarity, for, despite the central labor unions' endorsement of efforts to organize black workers, few BLACKS were ever accepted into craft unions.

Before WORLD WAR I, over 6,000 Cleveland women were involved in the GARMENT WORKERS STRIKE OF 1911. With the coming of the war, the trend to hire women in industry accelerated; however, they remained unorganized, and when the war ended, most women were summarily dismissed from employment. The women dismissed from the city streetcar lines went to court to keep their jobs but were unsuccessful in their suit. With the organization of the Cleveland-based CONSUMERS LEAGUE OF OHIO, attention came to be focused on working women. As women entered factories and other nontraditional areas, the percentage of women in the workforce rose from 15 in 1890 to 18 in 1920. By 1919, the Consumers League had developed a legislative program to protect working women. Portions of this program were enacted in the 1930s and remained in effect until protective legislation for women fell into disfavor in the 1970s.

By 1920, organized labor was concerned not about organizing new workers but rather with maintaining existing unions. Attempts to organize the steel industry in 1919 failed, and Cleveland witnessed the foundation of the American Plan Assoc., which aggressively promoted the open shop in Cleveland, importing strikebreakers and labor spies as needed. The outstanding experience of most workers in this decade, however, was increased prosperity. In Ohio, real wages rose from $672 annually in 1920 to $834 in 1929. The sacrifices of earlier generations bore fruit in a shift of emphasis from capital goods to consumer goods—the best example of which was the automobile, but which included housing, home appliances, and leisure-time activities. Black Americans did not benefit to the same extent from the increased prosperity. Many were new immigrants to the urban environment and lacked the necessary skills and education to compete for jobs. More important, they met with a perverse and extensive discrimination on the part of employers and unions, which relegated most of them to the expanding ghetto on Cleveland's east side. Nevertheless, the most gifted of these immigrants and many of the city's established black residents benefited from the prosperity of the 1920s, and extensive black homeownership in MT. PLEASANT and GLENVILLE dates from this era. The reactionary attitudes of the decade penetrated the working class as well as other segments of society. In many Ohio cities, the Klu Klux Klan became established not only in the middle class but among workers as well. Fortunately, the large number of ROMAN CATHOLICS and the overwhelming ethnic origins of Cleveland's working class prevented the Klan from playing a significant role in city politics or in the social life of workers.

Perhaps the most important trend, however, was the growing emergence of a class of workers who shared a sense of common goals which transcended the religious and ethnic identities that had been so important in earlier years. This common identity was the basis for the political realignment of the New Deal and the successful organization of the mass-production industries in the 1930s. The character of a generation of working Americans was shaped in the overwhelming depression of the 1930s. For all Americans, it was a period of tribulation and severe economic hardship. For American workers, however, the 1930s were the years in which they joined together to change the role of unions in the workplace. The instigation for this change came at a great price. A 1931 survey in Cleveland revealed that of the 234 families in a working-class neighborhood, 45 had no means of support, and 22 literally lived on garbage! A few depended on theft or PROSTITUTION, others on relatives, a working wife (at wages too low to support a family), or the earnings of children. Eight years later, the city physician reported frequent instances of malnutrition, while many individuals and families suffered beyond imagination. Those who continued to work successfully organized the mass-production industries. In Cleveland, the most important strike was the FISHER BODY plant sit-down in Dec. 1936, which served as the catalyst for the historic sit-down strike at General Motors in Flint, Mich. As the great mass-production industries were unionized, the Cleveland labor movement split into rival AFL and CIO factions—a split that would last until the 2 factions reunited in 1958 (see CLEVELAND INDUSTRIAL UNION COUNCIL and CLEVELAND FED. OF LABOR). The other great strike of these years, the LITTLE STEEL STRIKE OF 1937, was marked in Cleveland by an assault of strikebreakers and company police upon the steelworkers' soup kitchen and headquarters. Armed primarily with clubs, they beat men and hurled women out the windows of the building. In the early 1940s, the company lost a series of court decisions and was forced to recognize the union and to pay damages to workers injured in the assault.

The gains of the 1930s were consolidated and broadened during WORLD WAR II and the following years. Above all, the lines between workers and the middle class continued to blur as pensions, health-care packages, paid vacations, reduced hours, and higher pay brought workers a lifestyle similar to that of other Americans. Their children often attended college, and they moved to the SUBURBS, filling the open fields of GARFIELD HTS. and PARMA with new bungalows and ranch-style homes. Second and third cars became the norm; televisions, stereos, and boats became, if not necessities, then commonplace luxuries, and workers were accepted into a larger share of American life. Many blacks shared in these gains as a result of successful organizing drives in such mass-production industries as steel, automobiles, chemicals, and petroleum refining. The primary thrust of reform movements now came on behalf of minorities and women, who, in large part, simply wanted a fair share of what others were already receiving. The success of the labor movement in the postwar years brought a new sense of participation by all workers in the life of the city. Unions began to play a significant role in community and welfare organizations. An outstanding example was the introduction of the Kaiser Community Health Foundation into Cleveland by Sam Pollock and other members of the labor movement (see UNITED FOOD & COMMERCIAL WORKERS).

The position of workers in Cleveland began to erode in the 1970s and continued to do so into the 1980s. The movement of industry to the southern and western portions of the country and the shift to a service economy reduced wages and employment in Cleveland. The extent to which these factors are beyond the control of workers and their unions is underscored by the limited success of unions in meeting the problem simply by accepting lower wages. In a change from earlier years, the organized labor movement of the 1980s has been strong enough to support and even finance programs for the unorganized and unemployed worker. A second result of the decline in the local industrial base is a weakening of the once-powerful UNITED AUTO WORKERS and UNITED STEELWORKERS UNION. As a result, the role played by workers in service-oriented industries and the role of the unions that represent them—the TEAMSTERS UNION, the Communications Workers of America, and white-collar unions such as the American Fed. of Teachers—has increased correspondingly.

Dennis I. Harrison
Case Western Reserve University

See also GARMENT INDUSTRY, INDUSTRY.

The **LADIES HOSPITAL AID SOCIETY OF EAST CLEVELAND** (1868-78) was established on 27 May 1868 as an auxiliary society to aid the Cleveland City Hospital and promoted and supported the work of the Willson St. Hospital (forerunner of Lakeside/UNIVERSITY HOSPITALS). The society purchased or made items such as pillows, linens, and slippers for use in Cleveland City Hospital. Its efforts were subject to supervision by the hospital board of managers. Mrs. H. B. Tuttle, Jr., served as president until she was forced to resign because of her husband's association with the Homeopathic Hospital.

Record Book, Ladies Hospital Aid Society of East Cleveland, WRHS.

The **LADIES TRACT SOCIETY** was the local branch of the American Tract Society, organized in New York in 1825 to distribute Christian leaflets and pamphlets. The Cleveland organization was established on 30 Oct. 1830 by REBECCA ROUSE, an agent of the national organization and a leader in a variety of local moral-reform and benevolent efforts in the mid-19th century. Her husband, BENJAMIN ROUSE, was the local agent for the American Sunday School

Union & Tract Society, and their home was a depository for publications of that society. Little information is available about the work of the Ladies Tract Society in Cleveland, but as it was part of a large-scale, coordinated national tract movement, its work most likely resembled that of other societies in the distribution of religious material and the promotion of piety and general moral and social order in the changing community. How long the society existed is unclear, but it does not appear in the 1837 city directory.

**LAJOIE, NAPOLEON "NAP"** (5 Sept. 1875–7 Feb. 1959), was a BASEBALL player with the Cleveland team in the American League from 1902–14. Known also as "Larry," Lajoie was a graceful fielder and outstanding hitter as well as the popular playing manager of the Cleveland "Naps" during the first decade of the 20th century. Lajoie was born in Woonsocket, R.I., and worked in the cotton mills at a very early age. He completed the 9th grade. Playing semipro baseball in 1895, Lajoie signed with the Fall River team in the New England League. After only 80 games, his playing contract was purchased by the Philadelphia Phillies. When the AL was founded in 1901, Connie Mack persuaded Lajoie to sign with the Athletics in the new league. That year he batted .422, the highest average in AL history. In 1902, the Phillies obtained an injunction to keep Lajoie from playing with any other team in Philadelphia. On 1 June the AL permitted him to join the Cleveland Blues. In 1905, Lajoie was named the playing manager of the team soon called the "Naps" in his honor. He led the team in 1908 to a 2d-place finish but resigned as manager the next year with the team in 6th place. He continued to play for Cleveland until 1914, when he signed with the Philadelphia Athletics. In 1917 Lajoie managed Toronto, and in 1918 he was the manager of Indianapolis.

Certainly one of the greatest baseball players of the first half of the century, Lajoie was the 6th man voted into the Hall of Fame in 1937. With a lifetime batting average of .339, he had 3,251 hits in his 21-year major-league career. Lajoie led the AL in hitting during 3 of the first 4 years of it existence. On the last day of the 1910 batting season, he had 7 bunt singles and 1 triple in 8 times at bat in a doubleheader against St. Louis. A graceful second baseman, he led the league in fielding in his position 6 times. He ran an unsuccessful campaign for Cuyahoga County sheriff and served briefly as the commissioner of the Ohio & Pennsylvania League before moving to Florida in 1925. Lajoie married Myrtle Everturf on 5 Sept. 1907. They had no children.

The **LAKE CARRIERS ASSOCIATION,** with headquarters in Cleveland, is a trade organization serving companies operating U.S. flag bulk cargo vessels on the Great Lakes. It was founded in 1892 in Cleveland, although 2 direct predecessors—the Lake Carriers Assoc. in Buffalo and the Cleveland Vessel Owners Assoc.—were organized in 1885 and 1880 respectively. Morris A. Bradley was the first president of the new voluntary alliance of steamship companies, the purposes of which were to reduce navigation hazards on the Great Lakes; recommend improvements in harbors, channels, docks, and lighthouses; and aid in the recruitment and training of vessel personnel. In its early years, the Lake Carriers Assoc. maintained at its own expense certain navigation lights and financed important channel developments. The Livingstone Channel in the Lower Detroit River was named for Wm. Livingstone, association president 1895–96 and 1902–25, and the Livingstone Memorial Lighthouse at the head of Belle Isle was erected jointly by the Lake Carriers Assoc. and the city of Detroit.

The Lake Carriers Assoc. in 1985 represented 15 Great Lakes fleets, including those of the Cleveland-Cliffs Iron, M. A. Hanna, and Oglebay Norton companies. Its member fleets have a combined total of 98 vessels and transport more than 95% of the tonnage of U.S. Great Lakes vessels (chiefly iron ore, coal, limestone, and grain). In addition to its original aims, the association promotes the common interests of its members as they relate to legislative and regulatory matters. Beginning in 1952, the organization was served by its first full-time president, Adm. Lydon Spencer. Officers in 1985 were Geo. J. Ryan, president; Gordon D. Hall, vice-president and treasurer; and Carol Ann Lane, secretary. The association publishes the LCA *Bulletin* 3 times each year.

The **LAKE ERIE SCHOOL OF LAW** was incorporated in 1915 as the Rufus P. Ranney Law School, with power to grant degrees. It was named after Cleveland's leading lawyer of the 19th century, but Ranney, who died in 1891, had no connection with the school. It suspended operations in 1917, probably because of a decline in enrollment brought on by WORLD WAR I. It reopened in 1921 and amended its charter to change the name to Lake Erie Law School. Ranney's heirs had objected to the use of the family name in connection with a proprietary school, and had threatened legal action. The Lake Erie School was solely a night school. Classes were held in the late afternoon or evening on the assumption that all students were employed during the day. A student carrying a full load would attend 2–3 hours of class 3 evenings a week. Initially no college work was required for admission, and the program lasted 3 years. In 1923, in response to recommendations of the American Bar Assoc., the Ohio Supreme Court amended its rules on admission to the Ohio bar examination to require 4 years of part-time law school, and in 1925 to require 2 years of undergraduate education, and in both instances Lake Erie followed suit.

Unlike most night law schools, the Lake Erie School was affiliated with a part-time proprietary business school, the Spencerian School of Commerce, Accounts, & Finance. The relation between the law school and the college was not a formal academic affiliation. Technically, there was no affiliation. Both schools were proprietary and were owned by the same group of individuals. The law school used the administrative staff, buildings, and library of the college. The college also provided a source of admittees to the school and drew upon the law school for instruction in commercial law subjects for its students. Throughout the school's history, the faculty were exclusively part-time, the library grossly inadequate, and standards of scholarship and curriculum minimal. Nevertheless, the school made sweeping claims to academic respectability. Starting in 1927, it offered additional training, leading to a Master of Law degree, and in 1929 it offered a degree of Doctor of Juridical Science. In both cases, the advanced degrees were awarded for work that was an additional year of basic courses. Enrollment averaged 50–75 per year during the first half of the 1920s, and peaked at 196 in the academic year 1926–27. By the academic year 1929–30, the entering class had dwindled to 9 students. The decline was probably due to the economic depression and to public awareness of the lack of educational quality. Lake Erie School of Law forfeited its charter and closed its doors in 1933.

The **LAKE SHORE ELECTRIC RAILWAY COMPANY** was a major interurban electric trolley operated between Cleveland, Lorain, Sandusky, Norwalk, Fremont, Toledo, and Detroit. The interurban received its charter on 24 Sept. 1901 (sometimes given as 25 Sept.). It was created by consolidation of 4 interurban railways on 12 Oct. 1901. Edward W. Moore and Henry A. Everett, 2 Cleveland interurban magnates, were responsible for the merger of the Lorain & Cleveland Railway Co. and the Sandusky, Milan & Norwalk Railway. The Lake Shore Electric began offering through service from Cleveland to Toledo in Dec. 1901. Executive offices were located in Cleveland, and general offices were in Norwalk. Soon after service commenced, the depot from which all trains left was built at the intersection of Bolivar and Erie streets. Most of the line's characteristic orange cars were built at the Kuhlman Car Co. on Adams Ave. in COLLINWOOD. The interurban provided both passenger and package freight service. The Lake Shore sponsored excursions to the Lake Erie islands ferry docks and the lakefront resorts in an effort to build passenger traffic. In 1907, over 5 million passengers were carried. At this point the line operated 114 cars and 196.2 mi. of track. The Lake Shore Electric also organized the Illuminating & Power Co. in 1908 to generate electricity for its operations, as well as for sale to the public. In 1915, the line operated 8 limited trains per day between Cleveland, Toledo, and Detroit. Twenty additional mainline trains left Cleveland for Toledo every hour from 5 a.m. to 12 midnight. The Lake Shore Electric made its last profit in 1925. The increasing popularity of the private automobile and buses led to the interurban's downfall. Fred W. Coen, the first secretary and also the owner since 1927, was named receiver of the faltering interurban on 30 Jan. 1933. He remained in that capacity until the last car was run from Cleveland to Lorain on 15 May 1938. The company was the last to operate a non-suburban electric interurban line out of Cleveland.

Christiansen, Harry, *New Lake Shore Electric* (1978).
Morse, Kenneth S. P., *Cleveland Streetcars* (1955).

**LAKE TRANSPORTATION.** Cleveland has played a major role in the transportation scene on the Great Lakes over the years. Conversely, the Great Lakes transportation industry has had a major impact upon Cleveland. The south shore of Lake Erie provides the outlet for many rivers. Historically a town developed at the mouth of most of them. Only 3—Toledo, Cleveland, and Buffalo—emerged as major cities, with water transportation as the focus. For all 3, the catalyst was canal construction, with each serving as a terminal point. Ultimately the advantages of the canal would be offset by the inception of the railroad. This new factor enabled other communities along Ohio's north shore to compete successfully with Cleveland for the lake navigation business. With the advent of large-scale steel manufacturing, with its accompanying demand for large capital investment, the transportation scene again shifted. Special dockside equipment and specially designed ships capable of handling heavy bulk commodities such as iron ore and coal were introduced. Thus, the historical relationship between the Great Lakes maritime industry and the local Cleveland scene experienced 3 relatively distinct stages.

The first 4 decades of lake transportation in Cleveland (ca. 1800–40) were typical of the lake trade generally. Even though the steamboat made its first appearance off the mouth of the CUYAHOGA RIVER in 1818, any noticeable impact would have to wait until better harbor facilities were built. As late as Apr. 1830, the sidewheel steamer *William Penn* was lauded for entering the river while on its way to Detroit. A contemporary newspaper conjectured that it has "thus set an example, which, it is hoped, will be followed by its contemporaries." Cleveland would remain largely as a way port for the sidewheel steamers running between Buffalo and Detroit for another decade. The town basically was serviced by small 2-masted schooners, some of them locally built. They ranged in size from 44 to 90 ft. in length, the size of a modern tugboat or good-sized yacht. Their trade was locally oriented; they brought manufactured products to the community and took on locally grown produce for their outbound cargo. Many were owned on a percentage basis by local merchants and forwarding agents in consortium with their counterparts in Buffalo. Prominent among Clevelanders in this role were Chas. M. Giddings and Noble Merwin.

In 1841, the Ericsson screw propeller *Vandalia* revolutionized lake steam navigation. The propeller wheel, located at the stern, pushed the ship through the water. The positive features of the screw propeller ideally satisfied the physical limitations imposed by the undeveloped river and lakefront harbor conditions of Cleveland. The steam propeller was relatively cheap to build and to operate, presented an increased payload, was more maneuverable, and was of a shallow draft. All of these characteristics tied in nicely with the warehouses, grain elevators, and other docks that were built along the banks of the Cuyahoga and the Old River Bed to accommodate the prosperous canal years that preceded the coming of the railroad. Also, by the early 1850s, again with the screw propeller as the inspiration, the steam tug made its appearance. Now schooners could be towed through the narrow river entrance, along the winding river, past other vessels lying at docks, to their destination.

Under these conditions, and with the added benefit of strong stands of white oak in central and southern Ohio, the Forest City became one of the leading wooden-ship-building centers on the Great Lakes, rivaling even Buffalo. Both sailing vessels and propellers were built in large numbers in Cleveland. Production of new ships during the period 1846–70 was influenced by 3 factors: rising freight rates, particularly in the grain trade; construction of railroad-owned lake fleets to serve as connecting links in the carrying of passengers and freight; and the filling of voids in the lake fleets caused by extensive losses of ships through disaster. The emergence of Cleveland as a shipbuilding center, along with its canal advantage and, ultimately, the north-south railroad connection to southern Ohio coal fields, would usher in the prosperous lake-shipping period that followed the end of the CIVIL WAR.

The exploitation of the iron-mining districts of Michigan, Wisconsin, and Minnesota in the 1860s through the 1880s made Cleveland the "hub" of the Great Lakes maritime industry. Previously, Buffalo and Chicago, with their extensive grain interests, had occupied this position. During the late 1840s and 1850s, 4 Cleveland firms and their predecessors laid the seeds for this development. The CLEVELAND-CLIFFS IRON CO., PICKANDS-MATHER & CO., M. A. HANNA CO., and the Cleveland Rolling Mill Co. (later American Steel & Wire) brought the steel-manufacturing industry to Cleveland. That required huge capital expenditures, which developed a complete regional bulk transportation picture that included loading and unloading docks, river and harbor improvements, shipyards, fleets of specially designed bulk freighters, and RAILROADS. All were necessary to transport iron ore, coal, and limestone from the mines to the steel plants in the most cost-efficient manner possible. It would take 3 decades of technological improvements before a leveling-off stage would set in.

In 1869, the Cleveland shipbuilding firm of Peck & Masters built the first ship designed specifically for the iron-ore trade, the wooden propeller *R. J. Hackett.* It was followed a year later by a schooner barge, the *Forest City.* During the same period, Robt. Wallace, of Wallace, Pankhurst & Co. of Cleveland, built a portable steam engine to assist in unloading iron ore along the docks lining the Old River Bed. It replaced horses and cut unloading time in half. Now a 400-ton cargo could be unloaded in 1 day. By 1880, federal harbor-improvement appropriations had taken a dramatic upsurge for Cleveland, as a west breakwall was built into the lake to protect the river entrance from prevailing northwesterly winds and waves. In that same year, Cleveland docks received over 750,000 tons of iron ore. Alexander H. Brown, another Clevelander, devised an improved hoisting machine that enabled the heavy ore to be unloaded directly from ship to railroad cars or to dock storage areas. By the late 1890s, the Hulett ore unloader had been introduced (see GEORGE H. HULETT). With each innovation, the turnaround time was significantly reduced for ships, enabling them to head back up the chain of lakes for more cargo.

In 1892, a rivers and harbors act was passed by Congress that guaranteed a 20-ft. channel from Duluth to Buffalo. By that time, Cleveland had added a central breakwall and nearly had completed an east leg to provide protection for the growing maritime trade of the city. Also by 1890, Cleveland was well established as a principal builder of steel-hulled ships. Robt. Wallace and his associates had grown to become the Globe Iron Works and now boasted a steel shipbuilding yard and large dry dock. MARCUS A. HANNA and other Cleveland industrial leaders served on its board of directors and invested in ships built by the concern. In 1882, the Globe Works launched the iron-hulled *Onoko*, the prototype for the Great Lakes ore fleet. Four years later they built the first steel-hulled bulk carrier on the lakes, the *Spokane*. That same year, 1886, saw Cleveland ore receipts exceed 1 million tons. The closest rival in the ore trade was Ashtabula, whose rail connections fed the steel centers of the Mahoning Valley. Between 1886–90, the number of steel-hulled ships jumped from 6 to 68. Most were owned by Cleveland-based shipping companies.

Marcus A. Hanna very early in this movement began the Cleveland Transportation Co. Hanna Co. interests have continued to own or operate vessels in the ore and coal trades to the present. The same is true of Pickands-Mather & Co. and the Cleveland-Cliffs Iron Co. As a sign of the times, the Vermilion, Ohio, trio of shipbuilders/vessel owners Philip Minch, Isaac Nicholas, and Alva Bradley moved their operations to Cleveland during the early 1880s. They invested in steel-shipbuilding companies and steel-hulled ships. From that evolved the Kinsman Marine Transit Co. Other prominent independent vessel owners and operators, each of which controlled several ships by 1900, were the WILSON TRANSIT CO., the Gilchrist Transportation Co., the Hawgood Transit Co., W. C. Richardson, the Corrigan interests, the Bessemer Steamship Co., the Pittsburgh Steamship Co., Mitchell & Co., the Bradley Transit Co., and HUTCHINSON & CO. Thus the pattern was established that would last until after WORLD WAR II. Steel-hulled ships replaced wooden ones, and sailing ships disappeared. Corporate mergers occurred, names changed, and new companies appeared. But Cleveland would remain as the center of the Great Lakes bulk transportation industry.

At the same time as the ore trade increased in Cleveland, so too did the shipping of bituminous coal. Coal often meant a return cargo for vessels heading back up the lakes, especially to Milwaukee and Lake Superior ports. For many years, from 1890–1945, Cleveland averaged over 1 million tons of coal, most of it transported in Cleveland-owned hulls. Another important commodity to the Cleveland marine scene until shortly after the turn of the century was the receipt of lumber from the upper lakes. Although Cleveland could not compete with Tonawanda, N.Y., as a

lumber port, it reached its zenith in 1892 by receiving over 7 million board feet. After that, the trade dropped off rapidly as the timber resources disappeared.

Regular overnight passenger service was inaugurated between Detroit and Cleveland in 1868 by the Detroit & Cleveland Steam Navigation Co. It lasted until 1951. The huge sidewheel steamers were a familiar and popular sight, first as they docked near the old Main St. bridge in the Cuyahoga River, and later at the elaborate terminal constructed on the lakefront at E. 9th St. The CLEVELAND & BUFFALO TRANSIT CO. was incorporated in 1892 and also operated sidewheelers—to Buffalo, Toledo, the Lake Erie islands, and Cedar Pt. The C&B line ceased operations in 1939, the victim of the automobile. Over the years there were other connecting lines to various points on both sides of Lake Erie, as well as moonlight excursions out of Cleveland. But none had the longevity of the D&C and C&B lines.

As the Great Lakes shipping industry became more formalized and centralized in Cleveland toward the end of the 19th century, the city also became the regional headquarters of various support organizations. In 1880, the Cleveland Vessel Owners Assoc. was formed to protect and to forward the interests of the shipping companies. It became the LAKE CARRIERS ASSOC. in 1892. In 1984, the U.S. Coast Guard 9th District, covering all of the Great Lakes, has its headquarters in Cleveland. The U.S. Army Corps of Engineers also maintains a depot at the foot of 9th St. Cleveland also is the home of the Coal & Ore Exchange.

The period following World War II has seen many changes in the lake-shipping business. The St. Lawrence Seaway opened in 1959, and many agents maintain offices in Cleveland. The appearance of the lakefront docks changed as warehouses and coal docks were dismantled to make way for other dock facilities to better serve the ocean vessels. Less obvious to the observer, but perhaps more dramatic to the industry, has been the disappearance of all but one of the extensive independent fleets of bulk carriers with offices in Cleveland. Today only the Kinsman Marine Transit Co. remains. The other vessel operators are "captive" fleets, wholly owned subsidiaries of the mining and steelmaking complex. Only the Cleveland & Pittsburgh ore dock, which opened in 1912, still remains along the lakefront. The river has been "dekinked" to better handle the large self-unloading vessels that deliver taconite ore pellets to the few furnaces upriver. The only vestige of the once-prosperous shipyards in the Whiskey Island area is the tug-repair yard operated by the Great Lakes Towing Co. This firm was incorporated in 1899 and once held a near-monopoly on harbor towing throughout the American Great Lakes. The steam engine and large fleets have become victims of the diesel engine and technological efficiency. But Cleveland remains the hub of the lake-shipping industry—and undoubtedly will continue to as long as the Great Lakes serve as a commercial highway.

Richard J. Wright (dec.)
Bowling Green State University

Havighurst, Walter, *The Long Ships Passing* (1972).

**LAKE VIEW CEMETERY** is known for its hilly, manicured landscape graced by monuments of famous and humble Clevelanders and overlooked by Pres. Jas. A. Garfield's tomb. In Cuyahoga County, Lake View was not the first private, nonsectarian cemetery, nor was it immediately successful. Competition came from Cleveland's municipal cemeteries, and Lake View, although attractive, was associated with east side society. Thus, it had lean years before attaining the public favor it now enjoys. In July 1869, the

Lake View Cemetery Assoc. was formed with JEPTHA H. WADE as president. The name, Lake View, and the idea of such a vista appealed to founders before suitable land was secured. Several sites near E. Cleveland were considered before almost 200 acres were purchased for $73,000. Concern about the cemetery's distance from the city—almost 6 mi. from the courthouse and 2 mi. east of 55th St. (the city's limits)—weighed on the trustees' minds as the first lots were selected in July 1870.

Clevelanders appreciated the natural setting of Lake View, which became a place to visit on Sunday outings. When Geo. H. Keller's competition-winning GARFIELD MONUMENT was opened on Memorial Day 1890, more visitors came. By June 1891, separate admission tickets were issued to lot holders and to the public. This popularity, however, was slow to carry into lot sales. Frequent were reminders that sites could be purchased by those of "modest means." As Lake View matured, its architectural and historical presence complemented its natural setting. Esteemed Clevelanders were reinterred—LEONARD CASE, SR. and JR., were moved from ERIE ST. CEMETERY. Distinctive monuments honored CHAS. F. BRUSH and JOHN D. ROCKEFELLER, a former trustee. To remember Wade, the Wade Memorial Chapel, with a Tiffany-designed interior, was built in 1901. Others of note buried in Lake View are NEWTON D. BAKER, CHAS. CHESNUTT, MARCUS HANNA, and the VAN SWERINGENS. Not all honored are prominent individuals. Near the Euclid Ave. entrance is a monument to and a mass grave for 169 pupils and 3 adults who died in the Ash Wednesday 1908 COLLINWOOD SCHOOL FIRE. Lake View's peaceful setting of ornamental plantings and picturesque lakes created from Dugway Creek belies the largest dam in Cuyahoga County, which was built above the lakes in 1978 for flood control. From its heights, Lake Erie and Cleveland's skyline can be seen.

The **LAKESIDE UNIT, WORLD WAR I,** formally designated U.S. Army Base Hospital No. 4, was the first contingent of the American expeditionary forces to be transported to Europe after the U.S. entry into World War I. Based in a British army hospital near Rouen, France, it provided medical care for Allied troops from the spring of 1917 to the winter of 1918–19. The events that led to the formation of the Lakeside Unit began in 1915 when a surgical team from Lakeside Hospital headed by Dr. GEO. W. CRILE volunteered to serve a short stint at the American Ambulance Hospital in Paris. Upon his return, Dr. Crile, along with officials of the Red Cross, prepared a plan for making civilian hospital staffs available for military service. Base hospital units were organized under the auspices of the Red Cross at 25 hospitals across the country, with the stipulation that they would pass from the jurisdiction of the Red Cross to that of the War Dept. should the U.S. enter the war. Lakeside Hospital signed an agreement with the Red Cross in the spring of 1916, by pledging itself to assemble trained personnel to staff a 500-bed Army hospital. The Lakeside Hospital Unit was designated Base Hospital No. 4. Its medical officers received Army commissions, and its nurses were enrolled in the Red Cross (later, after the Army Nurse Corps was established, they became Army nurses).

Base Hospital No. 4 received the order for mobilization on 28 Apr. 1917. An enlistment office was set up to recruit the necessary nonmedical personnel, and Col. Harry L. Gilchrist assumed command. The Lakeside Unit departed Cleveland on 6 May 1917, with 26 medical officers, 64 nurses, 156 enlisted men, and 4 civilian employees (usually given as 27, 64, 155, and 4). Arriving in England on 18

May, the unit reached its destination, Rouen, on 25 May. It was based at the British Expeditionary Forces Hospital No. 9, a few miles outside of the city. During its 20 months of duty in Europe, the unit handled 82,179 cases. Most of the patients were from Great Britain and British Commonwealth countries. The hospital was 60 to 80 mi. from the lines of battle and was never a target of German shelling. The unit did, however, send surgical teams to British casualty clearing stations near the front, where they worked under fire.

In Aug. 1918, Mobile Hospital No. 5 was organized to assist in the care of seriously wounded patients on the American sector of the battlefront, staffed by 61 members of the Lakeside Unit. It was mobilized in September for the Meuse-Argonne offensive and opened on the 25th of that month in the Bois de la Placys. It cared for 994 patients, mostly American, French, and German, between then and the end of the year, when it was closed. Reinforcements sent to the unit during its tour of duty brought the total number of persons serving with it to 42 medical officers, 124 nurses, 356 enlisted men, and 5 civilians. Five officers commanded the unit in turn: Col. Gilchrist, Maj. WM. E. LOWER, Maj. Walter C. Hill, Maj. Allen Graham, and Col. FRANK E. BUNTS. Maj. Crile was the general clinical director of Base Hospital No. 4 and was frequently called upon to visit other of the Allies' medical facilities. The unit's first head nurse was Grace Allison; Elizabeth Folckemer succeeded her in late summer 1918. There were no fatalities among the personnel of the unit. Following the armistice, the hospital closed on 23 Jan. 1919; its personnel were demobilized during April and May.

Lakeside Unit, World War I, Papers, University Hospitals Archives.

**LAKEVIEW TERRACE,** internationally known as a landmark in PUBLIC HOUSING, was one of 3 Cleveland housing projects that were the first to be authorized by the federal government in the U.S. The other two were Cedar-Central and Outhwaite, and all were begun in 1935 and completed in 1937. Lakeview Terrace was especially notable because of its successful adaptation to a difficult site. The 22-acre site at W. 28th St. lies between the lake and the Main Ave. Bridge. It was an irregular hillside with an 80-ft. drop in elevation, an average slope of 10%, and a slope of 20% at the steepest parts. The scheme was adapted to the hillside by a curving road, with many of the housing units arranged in a fanlike pattern. There are 44 residential buildings of 3 types—apartments, row houses, and a combination of the two. The buildings are oriented as much as possible to provide daylight and views of the lake. They cover only 23% of the site area.

The architects were JOSEPH L. WEINBERG in association with Wm. H. Conrad and Wallace G. Teare. The building construction was entirely fireproof, consisting of masonry walls of brick on tile, with concrete roof and floor slabs. Interior partitions were of solid metal lath and plaster, and the windows had steel casements. The design of the buildings was clearly influenced by European precedent. The curved end walls, the windows arranged in horizontal bands, the iron railings, and especially the distinctive down-turned hoods over the doorways reflected the work of International Style architects. Lakeview Terrace also included the first community center in a public-housing project. It contained an auditorium, a nursery, a recreation room, and meeting rooms. A large central playground was provided adjacent to the Community Bldg. At the W. 28th St. entrance to the project, a building containing shops was replaced in 1973 by a high-rise apartment building for the elderly. The project was also innovative in its use of the decorative arts, made possible by the creation of the Treasury Relief Art Project in 1935. These included sculptured relief panels on the exterior wall of the community center auditorium and murals in the nursery. The liaison with the federal art agency was handled by WM. MILLIKEN, director of the CLEVELAND MUSEUM OF ART.

**LAKEWOOD** is a city on the shore of Lake Erie adjacent to Cleveland on the east and ROCKY RIVER on the west, and occupying 5.6 sq. mi. Originally part of Rockport Twp., created in 1819, Lakewood became a village in 1903 and was incorporated as a city in 1911. It was named for its natural setting on the lake. The development of Lakewood is closely tied with that of Cleveland and Rocky River. Early pioneer settlers such as Jas. Nicholson, Dr. JARED KIRTLAND, and Mars Wagar transformed the area between Detroit Rd. and Lake Erie from a wilderness into a settled community. By 1871, the area's population had reached 400, large enough for voters to create a separate school district east of Rocky River. The Detroit Rd. area became known as E. Rockport. Continued growth in population led to a movement for incorporation as the hamlet of Lakewood in 1885, but a legal dispute with the Rockport Plank Road Co. over ownership of Detroit Ave. delayed the formal use of the name Lakewood until 1889. The discovery of natural gas and oil wells in the Lakewood area and the Rocky River Valley greatly aided the area's development. Wells were drilled as early as 1883, with one yielding almost 22,000 cu. ft. of gas daily. Additional natural gas reserves were discovered in 1911. Unfortunately, they were exhausted within a few years.

The construction of a municipal light plant in 1896 and a streetcar line in 1903 facilitated the village's growth. By 1910, the population was more than 15,000. A real-estate boom occurred in 1917 with the opening of the DETROIT-SUPERIOR BRIDGE. The price of lakefront properties rose to $15,000 an acre. By 1920, the population exceeded 40,000. Over the years, Lakewood has prided itself on being a "city of homes." It is also a city of small businesses, numbering 1,100. The largest industry is the Carbon Prods. Div. of the Union Carbide Corp. on Madison Ave., which was established in Lakewood as the NATL. CARBON CO. in 1892. In 1916, Lakewood established its independent library system, which in 1980 had 2 buildings on Detroit Ave. and Madison Ave. The growth of the Lakewood School District paralleled the growth of its library system. In 1980, the system had 8,000 students and 10 elementary, 3 middle, and 1 public high school. In addition, 7 parochial schools served the city. Lakewood's facilities also included LAKEWOOD HOSPITAL, opened in 1907, swimming pools, tennis courts, ice-skating rinks, golf and boating facilities, municipal parks, and the Rocky River Reservation of the CLEVELAND METROPARKS SYSTEM. Lakewood's population in 1980 was 61,963.

Butler, Margaret, *The Lakewood Story* (1949).
Lindstrom, E. George, *Story of Lakewood, Ohio* (ca. 1935).

The **LAKEWOOD HISTORICAL SOCIETY** was established in 1952 specifically to restore and preserve the Old Stone House, the city's oldest (1832) residential structure. Located at 14710 Lake Ave., the house, furnished with artifacts dating from 1838–70, serves as the society's headquarters. In 1984, the society had 2 part-time staff and 500 members. In addition to sponsoring exhibits of textiles, tools, and dolls in its museum, it conducts oral-history interviews with older area residents and maintains an extensive slide library. Revenues are provided by memberships and through special programs such as the sale of herbs from the society's herb garden. A Jr. Women's Board of 35 members assisted the society by hosting tours and conducting various educational programs in local schools.

**LAKEWOOD HOSPITAL** (14519 Detroit Ave.) is a city-owned short-term nonprofit general hospital. It was the first hospital opened in a Cleveland suburb. Lakewood began as a private hospital founded by Dr. Lee Graber and located in a double frame house on Detroit and Belle avenues. It opened in Oct. 1907 with 15 beds and 3 doctors. A modern hospital was built in 1917, with remodeling and additions in 1940, 1950, 1967, and 1970–71. The city of Lakewood purchased the hospital in 1931. In 1986 there were 410 beds, and all customary diagnostic and therapeutic services, as well as some specialty services (including open-heart surgery and in-patient renal dialysis), were available. Lakewood had a school of nursing (1910–37), and later a school of practical nursing (1955). The hospital closed its obstetrical-maternity unit in June 1972 despite a lengthy and bitter public controversy, including a city referendum on the issue.

The **LAKEWOOD LITTLE THEATRE/BECK CENTER,** 17801 Detroit Ave., began as "The Guild of the Masques" under the leadership of Richard Kay (1929). It opened in 1930 with a production of Robt. Sherwood's *The Queen's Husband*. In 1933, the group incorporated as the Lakewood Little Theatre. During their early years, the theater group performed anywhere they could find space. It was not until 1938 that they found a home in the vacant Lucier movie theater at 17823 Detroit Ave. The building was remodeled for live performances (capacity 466). The theater leased the building until 1943, when it purchased the property with a $50,000 mortgage, which was paid off in 1957. In 1958 the theater studied potential sites for a cultural center and found its own site best. It purchased the adjacent properties, bringing the total area for the future center to 2⅓ acres.

In 1972, Kenneth C. Beck, Lakewood mayor Robt. Lawther, and the theater joined in planning a cultural center. A fundraising campaign netted $600,000, which was matched by Beck. Ground was broken for the Lakewood Little Theatre/Kenneth C. Beck Ctr. for the Cultural Arts in Dec. 1975. Opening the following year with a property value of over $3 million, the 42,000-sq.-ft. center was constructed around the original facility: additions included the 500-seat Karl A. Mackey Auditorium (named for the group's managing director since 1954), a museum, the Galleria, a large multipurpose room, a lounge, a general office, and dressing rooms. Besides the Lakewood Little Theatre's productions, the center's programs in the 1980s included educational programs (adult dramatic arts, dance, arts and crafts, and the Children's/Teen Theatre); the Museum/Galleria shows (3 produced in association with the CLEVELAND MUSEUM OF ART); and a special events/performing arts series, including touring dance companies and special concerts. Purchase of an adjoining Natl. Guard armory in 1979 for costume storage and rehearsal space and renovation of the original theater into a studio theater in 1984 further enhanced the center. The Beck Ctr. operated on a budget averaging $600,000 in the 1980s. Of that, 70% was earned income, and additional support came from such agencies as the Ohio Arts Council, Cuyahoga County, and the GEO. GUND FOUNDATION.

"50th Anniversary" (Lakewood Little Theatre brochure, 1979–80).
*Kenneth C. Beck Center for the Cultural Arts* (LLT publicity pamphlet, ca. 1984).

*The Lakewood Little Theatre/Beck Center* (LLT Publicity Pamphlet).

The **LAMSON AND SESSIONS COMPANY** was one of the nation's leading fastener manufacturers for over a century. In Oct. 1866, brothers Thos. H. and Isaac P. Lamson and Samuel W. Sessions formed a partnership to run a small Connecticut plant to make carriage bolts. Three years later, Cleveland's expanding markets and the availability of raw materials prompted them to move their plant to the city. In a joint venture, Lamson & Sessions helped to establish the Cleveland Nut Co. in 1872, which provided the partnership with a full line of fasteners. Lamson & Sessions prospered and in 1883 was incorporated. By 1900, the firm began to service Cleveland's growing AUTOMOTIVE INDUSTRY, which induced it to standardize its fasteners. The company continued to grow, and with military orders during WORLD WAR I, it surpassed the $2 million mark in sales. To maintain this level and broaden its production line, Geo. Case and Roy Smith designed and implemented an acquisition program during the 1920s. They purchased several local fastener manufacturers, the Kirt-Latty Mfg. Co., Foster Bolt & Nut Co., and Lake Erie Bolt & Nut Co. By 1930, Lamson & Sessions had grown from 1 plant to 8 plants nationwide, with a combined sales of $11 million. The Depression brought an end to expansion. During WORLD WAR II, the firm concentrated on engineering durable fasteners for military equipment. In the 1950s, it reinstated its acquisition program, not only aiming at further growth in the fastener industry but also entering new businesses, such as industrial equipment in the 1950s and aerospace components in the 1960s. In 1950, the firm built a new plant in nearby Brooklyn to consolidate most of its acquired Cleveland-area plants.

Beginning in 1976, the character of Lamson & Sessions began to change as it moved away from its fastener products and into the capital-goods industries. That year it acquired the Youngstown Steel Door Co. (founded 1924), the nation's leading producer of railway freightcar equipment. In 1979, Lamson & Sessions acquired the local holding firm Midso, Inc., which included the Midland Steel Prods. Co. (see MIDLAND-ROSS CO.), the country's chief manufacturer of mid-sized truck frames, and the Forest City Foundries Co., one of the oldest (1890) and largest gray iron foundries in the area, whose subsidiaries also produce aluminum and zinc castings. In 1980, Lamson & Sessions decided to divest itself of its ailing fastener business. Its emphasis on capital-goods industries was hampered by the recession of the early 1980s, which resulted in a net loss of $19 million in 1982 and the selling and closing of several of its acquired companies, including Forest City Foundries in 1983.

Case, George, Jr., *Lamson & Sessions—Starting a Second Century of Industrial Fastener Development and Production* (1965).

**LANGLEY, JOHN W.** (21 Oct. 1841–10 May 1918), was a chemist, an electrical engineer, and a teacher who taught at Case School of Applied Science from 1892–1907. Born in Boston, the son of wholesale merchant Samuel and Mary Sumner Langley, Langley was educated at Chauncey Hall School and Milton Hill High School. In 1861 he received a B.S. degree from Harvard University and joined the University of Michigan as a medical student and assistant instructor in chemistry. His brief medical training qualified him as an assistant surgeon in the U.S. Navy during the CIVIL WAR. He resigned in 1864 and spent the next several years traveling and studying in Europe and helping his brother, noted astronomer Samuel P. Langley, build refractors and a reflector telescope. Langley began his teaching career in 1866–67 as assistant professor of chemistry and natural science at Antioch College; he resigned for further travel and study. He returned to teaching as assistant professor of physics and mathematics at the U.S. Naval Academy from 1868–70. He resigned that post to accept a position in business and began a career of service as a consulting chemist and metallurgist for steel manufacturers. Langley's knowledge of the steel business was greatly enhanced between 1871–75 while he served as professor of chemistry and metallurgy at the Western University of Pennsylvania at Pittsburgh. In 1875 he accepted a professorship of chemistry at the University of Michigan, which he held until 1890, when he returned to Pittsburgh as a steel-industry consultant. In 1888–89 he organized the Internatl. Committee for Standards of Analysis of Iron & Steel. Langley moved to Cleveland in 1892 to accept the chairmanship of the new electrical engineering department of Case, serving as department head until 1905 and as a professor until his retirement in 1907. He directed the planning of and helped equip the new building erected for the department and developed the electrical engineering curriculum. He published articles on the chemistry of iron and steel in journals such as the *American Journal of Science*, and as Pres. Grover Cleveland's appointee, he served on the assay committee that inspected the processes and standard of metal used at the government mint in Philadelphia. On 12 Sept. 1871, Langley married Martica Irene Carret, the daughter of a Cuban planter. She survived him and died on 7 Mar. 1925.

**LATIN AMERICANS.** *See* **HISPANIC COMMUNITY**

*LATINO MAGAZINE* was the outgrowth of 2 previous Hispanic publications, all of them operated by Jose Pena. A graduate of Lincoln-West High School, Pena purchased a struggling tabloid named *El Sol* soon after its debut in 1972. Publishing at first out of his house on W. 38th St., Pena nursed it into a weekly of 8–16 pages and 3,000 circulation before it ceased publication in Aug. 1976. Pena introduced a second Spanish-language weekly, *Echoes de Cleveland*, in Aug. 1979. Published at 2144 W. 25th St., the 24-to-32-page tabloid had a full-time staff of 5 and a circulation of 5,000. Although it supported some Republicans, it leaned toward the Democrats politically. Down to 12 pages in size, its last number was issued in May 1981. *Latino* appeared in Aug. 1981, with a cover story questioning the murder conviction of Orlando Morales in the Tammy Seals case. Unlike its precursors, it assumed a monthly magazine format of from 16–62 pages. Although its 5,000 readers were concentrated in northeastern Ohio, it achieved statewide circulation as Ohio's only Hispanic publication. It was edited by Pena from offices on W. 25th St. before moving to the Terminal Tower. Steering away from political endorsements, *Latino* became involved in the production of Spanish radio programs as it continued to publish on a month-to-month basis.

**LATVIANS.** One of Cleveland's smallest ethnic groups is composed of men and women who trace their ancestry back to Latvia, a small land along the Baltic Sea that enjoyed political independence from 18 Nov. 1918 until invaded by the Soviet Union on 17 June 1940. Soviet occupation of the land and oppression of the people continue to be the subject of meetings and ceremonies sponsored by local Latvians. Latvian immigrants first arrived in Cleveland in the late 19th century. Because they were often counted as RUSSIANS and sometimes as GERMANS, it is difficult to determine exactly how many Latvians lived in the area at different points in time. Pioneering Latvian families in the area are considered to have been the Raufmanis (sometimes given as Kaulomonis) family, who arrived in 1887 and opened a printing shop, and the Krastins (sometimes Krostius) family, who arrived in 1902 and operated an automobile plant. By 1897, enough Latvian LUTHERANS lived in Cleveland for Rev. Hans Rebane, the pioneer Latvian Lutheran minister in the U.S., to visit Cleveland from his home in Boston and organize Immanuel Church with 50 members on 13 June 1897. These early immigrants came for economic reasons and were married men ages 25–40 who came alone and later sent for their families. The Russian Revolution of 1905 and the Latvian Revolution in 1906 sparked a brief period of Latvian immigration for political reasons after 1905. These immigrants found jobs in the steel mills, in automobile plants, and with the RAILROADS. Later immigration was slowed by WORLD WAR I, by federal legislation restricting immigration, and by the Depression. The local Latvian population remained small, about 1,000 in 1930, and no distinct settlements existed in the area, although some Latvians lived together near W. 25th and Memphis and in the Buckeye Rd. area. As late as the 1940s, Immanuel Church (Scranton Rd. and Seymour Ave.), then with 125 members, was being served by Chicago clergymen who visited Cleveland's Latvian Lutherans 4 times a year, and 2 church services were held at the Church of the Master (Baptist) at E. 79th and Euclid. Between 1925–41, the Latvian consulate for Ohio and Michigan was located in Cleveland. The largest local Latvian organization in Cleveland during the 1940s was the Latvian Singing & Cultural Society.

The greatest period of Latvian settlement in Cleveland occurred following WORLD WAR II. In 1949, the local community organized to help those displaced by the war and subsequent political upheavals, and an estimated 2,500 displaced Latvians settled in Cleveland in the 1950s and 1960s, largely on the west side and in the SUBURBS. Many new immigrants were highly educated and had professional training. Their arrival began the greatest period of social organization in the history of the small Latvian community. In 1951, the Latvian Evangelical Lutheran Church of Cleveland, Inc., and the Latvian Evangelical Church of Peace were formed; they merged in 1962 to form the Latvian Evangelical Lutheran Church of Cleveland, and in 1963 bought the Church of the Redeemer, the oldest church in LAKEWOOD, located at Detroit and Andrews. The remodeled church was dedicated on 5 Apr. 1964 as the United Latvian Evangelical Lutheran Church, which became a leading Latvian organization and in 1971 built a Latvian cultural center on its grounds. Also organized in 1951 was the 60-member Latvian Baptist Church, led by Rev. Geo. Barbins, former executive secretary of the Baptist Assoc. of Latvia. Barbins settled in North Carolina after coming to the U.S., but after a visit to Cleveland to attend the Baptist World Alliance in 1950, he moved his family there and worked to encourage other Latvian immigrants to settle in Cleveland. By May 1953, he had arranged local sponsorships for 200 people in European camps for displaced persons.

In addition, the Latvian community formed numerous voluntary organizations to preserve Latvian heritage and serve the needs of the community. Cultural organizations such as the Latvian Assoc. of Cleveland, the Latvian Folklore Club, and Boy Scout and Girl Scout troops were formed in the 1950s and 1960s, as were artistic groups such as the Latvian Theatre Group and the Pastalnieki Latvian Folk Dance Troop; service organizations such as the Latvian Credit Union of Cleveland and the Cleveland Chap. of the Latvian Welfare Assoc., Daugavas Venagi; and social and

veterans' organizations. Estimates of the Latvian population in Cuyahoga County in the 1970s ranged from 1,500 to 3,000. Major events in the local Latvian community have been those that have expressed a desire for renewed freedom for the homeland. The Cleveland community hosted the Latvian Song Festival in 1963, 1968, and 1973. The first song festival held in Riga in 1873 is considered to have been "the first organized countrywide manifestation of nationalism," giving later festivals strong overtones of patriotism and nationalism. The first Cleveland festival reportedly brought 10,000 Latvians to Cleveland; the centennial song festival celebration attracted an estimated 15,000 Latvians to Cleveland. Local Latvians also have held annual ceremonies to mourn the anniversary of the 1940 Soviet invasion and to commemorate Latvian independence. In 1980, the president of the Latvian Assoc. of Cleveland and 3 association members traveled to the Madrid meeting on the Helsinki Accord to press the delegates to consider the plight of the Baltic nations.

Kenneth W. Rose
Case Western Reserve University

The **LAUB BAKING COMPANY,** organized in 1889 by German immigrant Jacob Laub, grew to became the largest independent wholesale bakery in Ohio before closing in 1974. Born in Germany in 1861, Laub received a common-school education before coming to the U.S. in 1878. Shortly after his arrival, he became a baker's apprentice, and in 1889 he established his own business, baking rye bread, rolls, and coffee cake in his home at 1981 (later 4832) Lorain Ave. A loan from Samuel H. Halle enabled Laub to expand his operations by 1892; he maintained a store and office in his home and moved the bakery to larger facilities at 1092 (later 4919) Lorain. The Jacob Laub Baking Co. was incorporated in 1903, and by 1918 it had grown to employ 160 people. In 1929 the company became the first to sell sliced bread. Laub presided over the firm until his death in 1942; he was succeeded as president by his son, Herbert J. Laub, who directed the company until 1964. By 1953, Laub claimed to be the nation's largest house-to-house single baking company, with 82 home-delivery routes and 60 wholesale routes. Annual sales were about $5 million in 1953, and employment had increased to 465. The company grew by merger and acquisition in the 1950s. In 1954 it merged with the French Baking Co., owned by Maury Beyer and located at 1909 Scovill Ave. In 1958, it bought the J. SPANG BAKING CO., and in 1960 it acquired the Jersey Bread Co. of Toledo and the Sandusky Baking Co. of Sandusky. These acquisitions gave the firm combined annual sales of about $11 million. In 1965, the Laub family sold the baking company to a group of Cleveland investors headed by Edward Strang, Sr. On 8 Jan. 1974, the firm went out of business with no advance warning to its 300 employees or to its customers. Its old plants were too costly to operate and too inefficient to compete effectively with modern plants. The rising cost of flour also contributed to the demise of the company.

The **LAUB FOUNDATION** was founded in 1958 by Herbert J. Laub (1892–1967) and his sister Elsie K. Laub (1889–1969). Herbert Laub was the son of Jacob Laub (1861–1942), baker and founder of LAUB BAKING CO. (1889). Herbert went to UNIVERSITY SCHOOL and for 1 year to Western Reserve University before going to the Siebel Institute in Chicago to study baking, brewing, and milling. He joined Laub Bakeries in 1913 and took over the business when his father died. The purposes of the foundation are generally charitable, primarily for Cuyahoga and adjacent counties, with emphasis on private high school scholarship programs, cultural programs, and youth agencies. The Laub Foundation has funded a library at University School and the Malcolm D. Campbell III Library at the CHILDREN'S AID SOCIETY. No grants are given to individuals, for endowment funds, or for loans. In 1983, assets of the foundation were $1,997,117, with expenditures of $160,164 for 42 grants. Officers and trustees in 1985 included Malcolm D. Campbell, Jr., Amie Campbell, Robt. B. Nelson, Katherine C. Berry, and Thos. C. Westropp.

**LAUKUFF'S BOOKSTORE** was a leading source in Cleveland of books and other material relating to current movements in LITERATURE and the arts during the 1920s–1940s. Richard Laukuff, a German immigrant, opened his bookstore in 1916 at 40 Taylor Arcade. In an advertisement announcing the store's opening, Laukuff stated that it was his purpose "to present as they appear in this country and abroad, the noteworthy in literature and art, and to offer exceptional facilities both to keep in touch with modern movements in the literary and artistic world, and to obtain any book or work of art you may desire." Although the times changed, his purpose did not. As a bookseller, Laukuff also performed the various roles of moderator, patron, educator, and friend to the devoted among his customers. He reportedly ordered people out of his shop for mistreating books, and sent many others elsewhere to buy "ordinary" books. From his regular customers he expected reports on previously purchased books that he himself had not read. Laukuff's was open 6 days a week. The first years were rather slow, as Laukuff, like other German merchants, was the object of the anti-German sentiment that prevailed in this country following WORLD WAR I. During the 1920s, the store grew in popularity as Cleveland experienced a cultural awakening. Unlike other bookstores in Cleveland, Laukuff's appealed to a more liberal-minded clientele. Its reading room was often the scene of informal gatherings of artists, writers, poets, newspapermen, and other members of Cleveland's bohemian community. As a patron of local artists, Laukuff reserved one wall for the purpose of exhibiting paintings, including the works of WM. SOMMER, HENRY KELLER, Chas. Burchfield, and Wm. Zorach. Laukuff's specialized in books that were either banned or unavailable in other Cleveland bookstores. These included books by Jas. Joyce, Ezra Pound, Wm. Carlos Williams, HART CRANE, and Waldo Frank. Also featured were a variety of "little magazines" that kept abreast of current trends in literature. Artists visited the store to purchase the recent French and German publications on art. Various art prints were also made available. In addition to these diverse offerings, Laukuff's provided directors, stage designers, and actors from the CLEVELAND PLAY HOUSE with literature on the latest developments in European theater. As avant-garde movements in art and literature became more acceptable in the 1930s and 1940s, Laukuff's lost some of its original novelty, but it continued to offer a quality in books and atmosphere unavailable elsewhere in Cleveland. Laukuff died at the age of 81 in the early 1950s; his wife, Hermine, ran the store until its closing a few years later.

**LAUREL SCHOOL,** a private school for girls, was established by Jennie Warren Prentiss, a graduate of Lake Erie College, in 1896. The school was originally known as Miss Prentiss' School and was located in her home at 95 Streator Ave. (E. 100th St.). Seven girls constituted the first enrollment. Three years later, the school was incorporated with a board of trustees and renamed the Wade Park Home School for Girls. In 1899, Miss Prentiss's desire for a more distinctive name led to the choice of Laurel Institute; laurel

leaves, symbols of academic achievement to the Greeks, became the school's identifying motif. Miss Florence Waterman was named interim headmistress following Prentiss's retirement. In 1904, Mrs. Sarah E. Lyman was selected as principal, and an era began that was distinguished by growth and an increasing recognition of the school's excellence. Growth was stimulated, in part, by the closing of MISS MITTLEBERGER'S SCHOOL in 1908 and the subsequent transfer of many of its students to Laurel. In 1909, Laurel expanded into a new and larger building on E. 97th St. near EUCLID AVE. It remained in that location for 19 years. Laurel graduates were granted certificate privileges by leading colleges, a recognition not readily extended. Its English Dept. was invited to become a charter member of the School & College Conference on English, one of only 8 girls' schools in the country accorded that honor. By 1926, business and traffic had crowded the E. 97th St. location, and Laurel accepted an opportunity to move to a site at Lyman Circle in SHAKER HTS. Its move was part of O. P. and M. J. VAN SWERINGEN's plan to recruit the leading schools for location in their planned suburb. The cornerstone for the new building was laid in 1927, and the school opened in Sept. 1928. Mrs. Lyman retired in 1930, and Miss Edna F. Lake assumed the position of headmistress. During her tenure, a chapter of Cum Laude, a national honor society for high school students modeled on Phi Beta Kappa, was established in 1932. The period also saw growth in extracurricular activities, with emphasis on sports and arts. Miss Lake retired in 1958 and was succeeded by Miss Miriam Waltemyer, whose tenure continued to 1962.

In 1962, Daniel O. S. Jennings became the first, and to date (1986) the only, headmaster of Laurel. In 1963, construction began on a new primary wing. The old study hall was converted to a library. As demand for residential facilities declined, Laurel closed its dormitory, the last of the 4 Cleveland independent schools to do so. The 1st-floor space was remodeled and opened in 1968 as a science wing with facilities for biology, chemistry, earth science, and physics. In 1977, Barbara R. Barnes became head of the school. Physical growth continued: a new gymnasium was built, and the 2d floor of the old dormitory was converted to a middle-school wing. Under Mrs. Barnes, teachers' salaries increased dramatically, and the Hazel Hostetler Chair for Excellence in teaching was established, the first endowed faculty chair in an independent girls' day school in the nation. When Mrs. Barnes left in 1984, a second chair was endowed in her honor. Mrs. Leah S. Rhys became head in 1984 and brought a strong committment to curriculum updating and revision within the context of the liberal-arts tradition.

Andrews, Ethel, *Roots and Branches* (1971).

**LAUSCHE, FRANK.** *See* **MAYORAL ADMINISTRATION OF FRANK LAUSCHE**

**LAW.** Cleveland at the turn of the 19th century was a frontier outpost of American law. By the late 20th century it had become one of the most significant legal communities in the nation. The city gained, and retained, its prominence in the law because of a potent mixture of local variations of national trends and distinctive developments. This mixture is most clearly described by dividing the city's legal history into 3 major periods: the formative era, 1800–70; the industrial era, 1870–1930; and the modern era, 1930-present. The 3 periods correspond roughly to comparable eras in the nation's legal history. Within each era, the interaction of social, economic, and legal change can be examined by looking at courts, lawyers, and illustrative cases, laws, and individuals. In doing so, the industrial era stands out as the most important period in Cleveland's legal past. During those years, Clevelanders carved out a distinctive place for themselves in the American legal system.

The formative era (1800–70) in Cleveland's legal history began before statehood, when the community got its first legal officials. Beginning with JAS. KINGSBURY, local voters selected justices of the peace (hereafter jps). JPs, administrative and judicial officers who performed marriages, settled brawls, laid out roads, and signed pollbooks, established a foothold for a legal system that would increasingly become specialized and hierarchical. Similarly, SAMUEL HUNTINGTON, who arrived in 1801, and ALFRED KELLEY, who followed in 1810, are credited with beginning the Cleveland bar. Like the jps, Huntington and Kelley engaged in varied activities ranging across civil and criminal litigation, drawing of wills and other legal documents, collecting debts, and giving commercial advice.

In 1810, when Cuyahoga County was formed, the state legislature authorized the creation of a court of common pleas to be run by elected judges. The court, the city's most important legal forum throughout the era, had countywide authority in civil, criminal, and chancery jurisdiction. It consisted of 1 presiding judge and 3 associate judges until constitutional changes in 1851. Initially, the Colonial tradition of lay (non-legally trained) judges continued, as state law required only that the presiding judge be "learned in law." As happened so frequently in American towns of the era, the common pleas court quickly became congested. The docket filled with the troubles of a small agricultural community—drunkenness, violations of liquor license laws, land boundary squabbles, assault and battery complaints, and small business disputes. And after the completion of the Ohio Canal, commercial litigation added to the burden as the city's mercantile activity boomed.

Efforts at judicial relief came in 2 basic forms: more courts and more judges. Clevelanders seized upon these solutions in the 1830s and launched what would be recurrent efforts for judicial reform that would never quite ease the burdens thrust on the bench. After a successful experiment in Cincinnati, in 1847 Cleveland became the second Ohio city to get a superior court. Holding concurrent civil and chancery but not criminal jurisdiction with the common pleas court, the superior court was the city's first specialized tribunal. But it succumbed to statewide judicial reform in 1851. With the aid of Cleveland lawyer RUFUS RANNEY, a new state judicial structure was fashioned that significantly rearranged Cleveland's courts. The town was placed in one of 9 new common pleas court districts in the state. Judicial specialization began as well, with a constitutional authorization to confer the common pleas probate jurisdiction in a separate tribunal. The probate court, run by 1 elected judge, dealt with questions of inheritance, guardianship, incompetency, and other testamentary issues.

The reforms only temporarily eased civil litigation. Further judicial reorganization led to the creation of a police court in 1853 to deal with complaints about CRIME. Since 1836 the mayor had had jurisdiction over minor offenses. The mayor's court, along with jps, who continued to hear petty criminal cases and initiate criminal complaints, then formed the first layer of an increasingly intricate municipal legal order. Throughout the era, laypersons such as GEO. HOADLEY held these offices. But these traditional forms of dispensing criminal justice no longer sufficed. A city police court replaced the mayor's bench when voters selected John Barr as Cleveland's first police magistrate. Bar witnessed a steady stream of cases involving minor breaches

of criminal code, such as drunkenness and disorderly conduct. He also acted as the city's chief commercial regulator, since Cleveland, like other communities, used criminal laws to address problems such as selling unwholesome meat. Most cases began and ended in the police court, thus choking off one supply of cases to common pleas.

More changes came in 1855. By the early 1850s, Cleveland had become intertwined in webs of interstate trade and Great Lakes maritime commerce. Disputes flowing from these transactions landed traders in the jurisdiction of the federal courts. Litigation soon overwhelmed the state's lone federal district court, as it had Cleveland's courts. City attorneys, led by transplanted New Yorker HIRAM WILLSON, lobbied for a division of the state into 2 federal districts. They succeeded in 1853, and even secured the seat of the northern district for Cleveland. In 1855, Pres. Franklin Pierce rewarded Willson, who had practiced law in Cleveland since 1833, with appointment as the first judge of the Northern District of Ohio. Willson served until 1866, presiding over a docket dominated by admiralty cases.

Cleveland's increasingly intricate judicial structure reflected not only the city's rapid mid-century economic and social growth but also the fact that local courts and lawyers were making themselves indispensable parts of their communities. Although the city's first practitioner, Huntington, had left in 1807, Kelley seems to have demonstrated that a lawyer could survive in Cleveland. By 1814, the village had become home to about 7 attorneys. Out of necessity, lawyers and judges formed a separate community during these years. Traveling together "riding circuit," they ranged over the counties of the WESTERN RESERVE, stopping at county seats to hold court, with the lawyers dividing up clients and roles. As settlers streamed into northern Ohio, Cleveland attorneys could stay in town and earn a living. In fact, the city became a magnet for the bar as the canal-induced economic surge continued. By 1837, about 46 attorneys plied their craft there. The Cleveland bar's professional distinctiveness and confidence sprang from the era's legal training and practice. During this era, the vast majority of attorneys learned their craft as apprentices in the offices of established practitioners. Their training mixed clerical work, legal research, and client counseling. More significantly, in a period in which the bar (and the public) assumed that lawyers proved their professional competence in practice, not by meeting admission requirements, apprenticeship also encouraged young lawyers to use the market to test their abilities. The Cleveland bar was dominated by New Englanders until the middle of the century, when locally born attorneys became, and thereafter remained, a numerical majority. Attorneys tended to change firms frequently, and though a few of them concentrated on particular issues such as property transactions, most developed broad practices that mixed civil and criminal representation. The affinity of lawyers for politics, fast becoming a permanent feature of American political life in Cleveland and other communities, sprang from the bar's inherent understanding of governmental affairs and the professional and popular lawyerly model of the era. Drawn from the popularity of attorneys such as Massachusetts lawyer and senator Daniel Webster, the powerful courtroom advocate and entrancing orator stood as that lawyerly ideal. Connecticut native SHERLOCK ANDREWS was one such courtroom star in Cleveland. He won acclaim as an advocate with a compelling style that mixed logic, sarcasm, wit, ridicule, and pathos. For him, and others, courtroom appeal could be turned into political capital. Andrews held a range of offices: first president of the city council, county prosecuting attorney, member of the national House of Representatives, judge of the short-lived superior court, and member of state constitutional conventions in 1850 and 1873. In between each position, he practiced his profession. Most Cleveland lawyers did not quite have Andrews's range of activities or success. Even so, the bar thrived in Cleveland because lawyers succeeded in convincing their fellow citizens that they had unique abilities to tackle a range of problems involving business, government, philanthropy, and other vital issues of the day.

The strength of the Cleveland bar became evident in the crisis years of the CIVIL WAR and Reconstruction. Since 1820, when slavehunter Joseph Keeler had been convicted of kidnapping, the city had been drawn into the battle over fugitive slaves. The opening of the canal and the emergence of northern Ohio as a hotbed of ABOLITIONISM intensified the problem as local sentiment began to be at odds with national law. As so often happens, one case came to epitomize the tensions of the era. The 1858 OBERLIN-WELLINGTON RESCUE Case began when a band of Oberlin residents helped fugitive slave John Price flee a slavecatcher. They were indicted for violating the hated 1850 Fugitive Slave Law; their trial and conviction in Hiram Willson's federal district courtroom exposed concerns about law and justice that generally remained below the surface. When the defendants secured release in legal maneuvering, the *Plain Dealer*, a partisan Democrat paper, declared: "So the government has been beaten at last, with law, justice, and facts on its side; and Oberlin, with its rebellious higher-law creed, is triumphant." The bitter controversy suggested some broader implications of the bar's achievements during the era. Success brought with it high expectations that extended beyond mere demands that the law provide effective social and economic tools.

Though the war ended the threat of slavery, the turmoil of the conflict and its aftermath increased the problems thrust on the legal system. In part, the mid-century decades merely witnessed a continuation of earlier developments. Escalating litigation forced the addition of a third common pleas judge in 1869. The passage of a federal bankruptcy act in 1867 led to the appointment of Cleveland lawyer Myron R. Keith as registrar. Keith struggled with the aftershocks of the massive business failures of the war years until the act's repeal in 1878. But newer issues arose that signaled the end of the formative era of Cleveland's legal history. Postwar economic growth began to turn the city into an industrial, not merely a commercial, center. Attendant urban development and population growth did the same, particularly when the human stream into the city became more ethnically and racially diverse. In short, a new set of problems began to populate court dockets and attorney consulting rooms. Similarly, the presence of JOHN P. GREEN, a black from North Carolina who began to practice law in the city in 1872, indicated that pluralism would affect the profession as well as its cases. As changes accumulated in the 1870s, a new period began—the industrial era, 1870–1930.

Successful, at times pioneering, adaptation to industrialism made the Cleveland bench and bar an even more integral part of the city than they had been in the earlier era. It also ensured that, as before, the legal order would encourage Clevelanders to rely on judges and lawyers to deal with a bewildering range of problems.

Change simply outpaced the system. Bulging caseloads produced a new round of judicial reorganization. Initial solutions took the traditional form of increased judgeships and new intermediate tribunals. Emblematic was the recreation of a superior court in 1873 in yet another attempt to reduce the backlog in common pleas. Like its predecessor, the new court had a purely civil docket, and even that excluded divorce and insolvency. Even so, the 3-judge court heard over 2,500 actions in its brief 24-month existence. It succumbed to another tactic as bankruptcies, the economic wake of the vicious Panic of 1873, flooded the courts. Four additional common pleas judges joined the Cleveland bench in an 1875 attempt at relief. Yet neither the new judges nor complementary changes such as the 1884 creation of new intermediate appellate courts could keep up with the massive litigation generated by booming industrial Cleveland.

An 1886 attempt to professionalize the justices of the peace, though, does suggest an emerging approach to legal reform that would dominate the bench and bar throughout the industrial era. Since the city's founding, jps had held a kind of honorary office that did not require legal training and depended on fees for payment. There had been periodic complaints by Cleveland lawyers about the behavior and lack of expertise of certain jps. These concerns intensified as members of new political groups within the city won jp elections. Ethnic prejudice combined with an emerging sense of legal professionalism that equated competence with formal legal training to promote reform. When efforts aimed at creating a municipal court to replace the jps failed, critics secured legislation that abolished the fee system and replaced it with a yearly salary. Its supporters hoped the new arrangement would make the office less attractive, reduce the monetary incentives for jps to stir up business, and professionalize the disposition of petty disputes.

Industrialism had as transforming an effect on the practice of law as it did on its use. Lawyers found themselves confronted with an array of new questions, from the organization of giant national corporations such as the STANDARD OIL CO. to the rights of pedestrians injured by street railways. These and other issues strained the bar's knowledge and skill. At the same time, the earlier successes of attorneys made the law an inviting vocation for those who sought wealth, power, and change. The Cleveland bar swelled from 103 attorneys in 1870 to 610 by 1900, and these lawyers came from an expanding number of ethnic and religious groups and pursued increasingly diverse practices.

Specialization and organization dominated the the bar's adaptation to industrialism. A new professionalism significantly revised earlier notions of proper legal practice and training, as more and more leaders of the bar came to conceive of themselves as experts specially trained in schools of law to tackle specific industrial problems. The most dramatic examples come from the rise of a new legal actor and organization, the corporate attorney and the corporate law firm. Named after their main clientele, these lawyers assumed the leadership of their profession in cities like Cleveland. HOYT, DUSTIN & KELLEY was one such firm in Cleveland. When JAS. HOYT, Hermon Kelley, and Alton Dustin found themselves becoming business counselors to a permanent set of clients demanding continuous advice on issues such as corporate organization, stockholder rights, bond services, and patent law, the trio hired more attorneys and trained them in specific legal matters such as these. As a result, in a functional relationship of client and counselor, the law firms came to replicate their corporate clientele in terms of internal organization and specialization. The press for specialization permeated the city's bar. Other attorneys began to specialize in criminal practice, personal-injury cases, and admiralty law. Specialties emerged out of the technicalities of some areas such as patent law, and because some forms of practice, such as criminal law, were considered undesirable by many practitioners. Specialization thus brought with it a new professional hierarchy. Corporate attorneys emerged as the city's powerful legal elite. One such lawyer, FRANK GINN, was reported to be an officer or on the board of more companies than anyone else in Ohio. At the other end of the professional structure, solo practitioners, often from immigrant backgrounds, who engaged in criminal or personal-injury law, became the law's lower class.

Specialization thus also encouraged diversity in the Cleveland bar's styles of practice and its practitioners. Mary P. Spargo is credited with being Cleveland's first female practitioner. After apprenticing in the office of Morrow & Morrow, she gained admittance to the bar in 1885. Yet launching a practice proved difficult. A statute denied women the right to be notary publics, one source of fees for new attorneys such as Spargo. And most men apparently refused to accept a woman lawyer. Discrimination of various forms also greeted JEWS, CATHOLICS, POLES, BLACKS, and others who tried to join the ranks of the Cleveland bar. Many tried, and some, like Spargo, succeeded.

Ethnic and gender tensions within the bar also originated in a larger debate over professional standards. Lawyers and laypeople in Cleveland and other communities struggled to reconcile traditional views of the bar with the changes of the period. Elite lawyers took the lead. Their solutions took 2 main forms that drew on the professionalizing tendencies of the era: new bar organizations and new forms of legal training. Cleveland's lawyers were among the first to pursue both. The Cleveland bar had gathered at annual banquets and other meetings since before the Civil War, but the increasing emphasis on professionalization led to a new approach in 1869, when leading local attorneys formed the Cleveland Law Library Assoc. A repository for the city's first full collection of codes, decisions, and treatises, the association dedicated itself to promoting the "science of the law." Legal science, a professionalizing slogan of the era, came to stand for a vision of the law as a neutral, autonomous body of rules that could be mastered only by dedicated legal scientists. These attorneys took another step toward an emerging professional ideal in 1873, when they formed the CLEVELAND BAR ASSOC. One of the first local bar organizations in the country, the CBA pledged to maintain the "honor and dignity" of the profession, champion "legal and judicial reforms," and resolutely avoid religion and politics. The association quickly became the city's self-appointed arbiter of professional standards. It fought for reforms such as state bar examinations and codes of ethical practice. The CBA also policed the bench and bar for corruption. The city's legal elite took their campaign statewide in 1880 by taking the lead in the creation of the Ohio State Bar Assoc.

Education became a crucial issue in the organized bar's campaign to raise the standards of the profession. The university-affiliated law school became the new tool for raising professional standards. Based on scientific instruction through the study of appellate cases, law schools reinforced the professional image the organized bar sought. Though several proprietary schools had opened in Cleveland, the creation of a law school at Western Reserve University in 1892 signaled the start of modern professional education in the city. As the state and local bar began to demand college preparation, 3 years of legal training, and formal entry examinations, legal education became a means of regulating access to the bar.

At the turn of the century, courts and lawyers had become so vital to Cleveland that seemingly professional issues became public ones. In fact, debates over the bench and bar increased, because the law figured so prominently in community controversies ranging from crime control to taxation. At the heart of these concerns lay 2 fears: that Cleveland's courts were failing the city and thus exacer-

bating the traumas of industrialism, and that the replacement of the independent courtroom advocate by the corporate counselor as the bar's ideal had created an unrepresentative and unresponsive new legal elite. Ironically, but not surprisingly, the bench and bar were seen as both sources of problems and solutions. That is, as the reform effort called "progressivism" established a firm hold in Cleveland during the 1890s, law became both a target of and a tool for change.

Perhaps no issue so clearly reveals the contradictory impulses of the age than the great street railway fight of 1901-08. The battle began when Mayor TOM JOHNSON tried to gain municipal control of Cleveland's street railways and instituted a 3-cent fare. The companies resisted the seizure, claiming it violated their property rights. The resulting legal warfare pitted a team of reform attorneys headed by Cleveland law director NEWTON D. BAKER against a team of corporate lawyers directed by WM. SANDERS of SQUIRE, SANDERS & DEMPSEY. The tenor of the fierce legal confrontations was evident in Baker's characterization of opposing counsel as "case hardened, class conscious plutocrats, with splendid abilities but with human sympathy reduced to a minimum." The "traction war," as it was called, came to an end when federal judge ROBT. TAYLER engineered a compromise that gave Baker the victory. Tayler set up a sliding scale that limited trolley-line profits, ordered low fares, and gave CLEVELAND CITY COUNCIL jurisdiction over railway operations.

The traction war was merely one early-20th-century skirmish in a larger campaign to use law to adjust Cleveland and its citizens to the realities of industrialism. The era's burst of reform included a major overhaul of the city's courts that produced innovative new means of tackling urban problems. The city's juvenile-justice movement, one of the first in the nation, sprang from the conviction of reformers such as Baker and YMCA leader Glen Shurtleff that children needed special legal treatment not offered in the adult courts. First as part of the court of insolvency and then as a more and more independent tribunal, the juvenile court established special procedures that dealt with both neglected and delinquent youths. The addition of paid probation officers, extended jurisdiction, and statewide adoption of the reform in 1913 testified to the strength of the city's effort. The juvenile-justice movement's central assumption, that particular problems ought to be addressed by specialized courts, so symptomatic of the era's faith in expertise, spread as well. For example, alarmed at rising divorces, the city's common pleas judges created a special domestic-relations bureau in 1920. Similarly, new municipal boards arose to regulate health and safety matters formerly left to the criminal law (see CUY. COUNTY JUVENILE COURT & CUY. COUNTY DOMESTIC RELATIONS COURT).

Ever-present concerns about overcrowded common pleas courts, fears about police and judicial corruption, and determinations that jps were ill-suited to handle complex urban problems led to the creation of a municipal court in Cleveland. A successful campaign resulted in legislation in 1911 and limits on jps in the state's 1912 constitutional convention. Cleveland's municipal court began operation in 1912 as the city's main criminal-law trial court. It had jurisdiction over minor civil matters, as well. The court became a national model. Its probation unit, one of the first in the nation, pioneered in the use of psychiatric testing. The court's most significant innovation came in 1913 with the creation of the country's first conciliation procedure. Clevelanders embroiled in minor civil disputes could dispense with attorneys and have a judge work out a voluntary compromise. The reform soon spread to other major cities.

The municipal court proved such a success that its original 5 judges had expanded to 16 by 1924.

Newspaper stories on judicial corruption led local civic and professional organizations to request that the CLEVELAND FOUNDATION sponsor a study of the city's criminal-justice system. The result, the CLEVELAND SURVEY OF CRIMINAL JUSTICE directed by Harvard Law School's Roscoe Pound and Felix Frankfurter, became a national model for the study of urban criminal justice. A comprehensive investigation, the study revealed many of the legal costs of industrialism such as inefficient judicial administrative procedures, ill-trained court personnel, and a demoralized, low-status, and at times corrupt band of lawyers specializing in criminal defense. The stark findings led to prosecutions and a few reforms; yet, Clevelanders could take some solace from the American judicature's 1922 determination that the city had the best trial court in the nation. Moreover, the study had solidified the Cleveland Bar Assoc.'s determination to advise voters on the qualifications of those running for judgeships. The organization had experimented with various methods and in 1922 decided to endorse those candidates that met the association's criteria. Often controversial, the endorsements reinforced the organized bar's attempt to take politics out of law by convincing Clevelanders that a set of specific professional traits existed and could be measured by other lawyers.

Amid this burst of judicial reform, late-19th-century professional tendencies toward specialization, organization, and diversity continued unabated. A series of consolidations made these years the founding era for a number of firms that would dominate the city's bar late into the century. Born out of a 3-man partnership in 1890, Squire, Sanders & Dempsey epitomized the process. Bringing together a variety of skills from courtroom advocacy to business creation and office organization, the trio developed a law office that offered an expanding list of corporate clients a set of specific services. At one time, for example, the firm was credited with controlling virtually all of the municipal bond work in the state. By the late 1920s, the firm employed around 40 lawyers.

As successful adaptation kept corporate firms at the apex of the Cleveland bar, more and more attorneys began to band together. Those excluded from the corporate elite formed their own organizations. The firm of Hahn, Loeser had its origins in exclusionary policies that barred its Catholic and Jewish founders from jobs in major firms. By the 1920s, the city could count a number of black and ethnic law firms. Though they often mirrored the city's leading firms in their organization and in the business and cultural activities of their members, they generally occupied the lower rungs of the Cleveland bar's professional hierarchy. Diversity remained the order of the day in terms of practitioners and legal roles, as well. In 1904, Benjamin Nicola became Cleveland's first attorney of Italian ancestry. By 1919, the city's Italian newspapers listed 12 lawyers. In 1920, FLORENCE ALLEN won election as the city's first female judge. She went on to break the gender barrier at the state supreme court and in the federal courts. As the members of more and more groups joined the ranks of the Cleveland bar, the roles opened to lawyers grew as well. DANIEL MORGAN's career represented one of these new responsibilities. A Harvard-trained lawyer, Morgan grew disillusioned with practice in a major firm and turned his energies toward civic reform and politics. After serving in various offices, he capped his public career by becoming Cleveland's city manager in 1930. Such administrative positions in urban government became a new vocation for lawyers. Morgan's occasional reform colleague, WALTER T. DUNMORE, points to yet another new law job: law

school professor. Dunmore, trained at WRU's law school, joined its faculty in 1905 and became dean in 1911. He taught a variety of courses and became an expert in property law. A vocal critic of American legal education, Dunmore took on the role of professional critic that many law teachers assumed as he championed reforms from legal aid to more rigorous law school curriculums.

By the 1920s, Cleveland's courts and lawyers had successfully met the challenges of industrialism. Pres. Woodrow Wilson's selection of Newton Baker as his secretary of war and JOHN CLARKE as a justice of the U.S. Supreme Court was perhaps the most public evidence of the prominence of the Cleveland bar. Yet much of the bench and bar's success had grown out of the conducive environment of industrial Cleveland.

The Depression that began in 1929 changed all of that. It so significantly altered the city that it ended one period in Cleveland's legal history and began another—the modern era, 1930-present. Plant closings, layoffs, bank failures, and bankruptcies created a vicious downward economic spiral that had a disastrous impact on all Clevelanders. Except for the Civil War, the years 1930–40 are the only ones in the city's history in which the number of lawyers fell. The 1,219 lawyers and judges in 1930 saw their numbers dwindle to 985 in 1940. And as the city's economy crumbled, the courts overflowed. Foreclosures had risen so dramatically by 1935 that the common pleas judges had to hire a special referee to handle them. However, lawyers and judges had become so entrenched in the city's social and economic life that not even a depression could uproot them. Consequently, much of the local responsibility for dealing with its effects fell on their shoulders. As a result, the 1930s became an transition era of growth and change, not merely a calamity for the city's legal community.

Clevelanders turned to attorney HAROLD BURTON to guide them through the Depression as mayor. Like many lawyer-politicians before him, Burton found the law, electoral politics, and public office a successful combination. After a brief stint as acting mayor, he served 3 terms beginning in 1935. Burton took the lead in fighting for federal relief funds for impoverished Clevelanders and bringing labor and business to negotiating tables. Though he later entered national politics as a senator and Supreme Court justice, he reflected the larger tendency of Clevelanders and other urbanites to rely on the bar for political leadership. Lawyers tackled a host of problems in the troubled city. Attorneys EDGAR HAHN and Wm. Thomas took the lead in untangling the jumble of banking problems caused by closures and the national bank holiday, while lawyer HAROLD CLARK ensured the survival of the CLEVELAND MUSEUM OF NATURAL HISTORY. In each case, lawyerly skill and the bar's broad definition of its social and professional responsibilities ensured that attorneys would figure prominently in Cleveland's attempt to deal with the crisis.

Equally important, the Depression posed new challenges. HARRY PAYER, a renowned Cleveland trial lawyer, left his practice to serve in the administration of Pres. Franklin Roosevelt. He became one of the first of a new breed of lawyers who combined private practice with terms of service in the expanding national administrative system. Indeed, that growing federal bureaucracy had a direct impact on private practice itself in Cleveland, as in other leading industrial cities. The tendency of Roosevelt's New Deal to turn problems such as labor relations and the regulation of securities over to administrative agencies created new bodies of law and new roles for Cleveland corporate law firms. As a result, corporate practice became more varied, and federal regulatory law more important. WORLD WAR

II accentuated these trends. For example, when Jones, Day was formed in 1939, its 43 lawyers made it one of the largest firms in the city. Even so, the firm had to open a branch office in Washington in 1946 to handle its clients' regulatory matters. The label "Washington lawyer" arose to distinguish this new corporate practice from the now more traditional type that had earned the title "Wall St. lawyer."

Regulatory changes, in fact the very character of politics and policies in the 1930s, created professional tensions as well as opportunities. Newton Baker, for example, became a national leader of the professional opposition to the New Deal. The former Democratic officeholder and Wilson cabinet member had turned BAKER & HOSTETLER into one of the city's leading corporate firms by the early thirties. It represented General Electric, Goodyear, and other major national companies. When these corporations fell under the authority of New Deal agencies, Baker used the courts to fight the growth of federal business regulation. In cases such as *Tennessee Electric Power Company* v. *Tennessee Valley Authority*, an unsuccessful attempt to have the TVA declared unconstitutional, Baker tried to turn back the growing federal administrative state that was changing legal and business life. He even took his campaign to the pages of the *New York Times* in 1936. Though many lawyers shared Baker's views, the Cleveland bar had become too diverse to speak with one voice. Other leading lawyers, such as former justice John Clarke, defended the regulatory changes. And in 1937 a new professional association, the CLEVELAND CHAPTER OF THE NATL. LAWYERS GUILD, was begun by lawyers who sought an alternative to the corporate bar-dominated bar associations. The guild championed many New Deal measures and issues, such as civil liberties and civil rights.

Amid the changes of the era remained continuities. Institutional developments suggest the potent mixture of change and continuity that dominated modern legal history in Cleveland. More judges and more specialized courts continued to be the city's answer to the seemingly permanent problem of crowded dockets. Common pleas courtrooms multiplied as the number of judges rose from 15 in 1929 to 19 in 1955, 24 in 1965, and 34 in 1986. Common pleas judge Wm. Thomas, later appointed to the federal bench, even won a national reputation in the 1950s for his use of pretrial procedures to clear his congested court. Similar growth occurred in the municipal court, as did specialization. Predictably, a special traffic court came as the judicial response to the rise of a massive automobile-driving public. Often presided over by MARY GROSSMAN, who became the nation's first woman municipal court judge in 1923, the traffic court perpetuated the earlier conclusion that special problems needed special tribunals.

Judicial attempts to deal with family problems provide clear evidence of that continuing reality. Led from 1926–60 by Judge HARRY EASTMAN, a national authority on juvenile justice, the Cuyahoga County Juvenile Court became an ever more specialized institution. The court became an independent tribunal in 1934, created the nation's first juvenile court psychiatric clinic, and added a department of child support. When new theories of juvenile care emerged in the 1960s, undercutting the court's traditional therapeutic approach by emphasizing the legal rights of the young, the court added new branches dealing with probation and intake procedures. At the same time, the number of juvenile court judges had grown from 1 in 1930 to 5 in 1980. Parallel developments occurred in the courts that dealt with adult family problems. Though a bureau of the common pleas court oversaw divorces, by the 1950s Cuyahoga was the only large Ohio county without a spe-

cialized domestic-relations court. Legislative action in 1959 ended the anomaly with the creation of 2 judicial positions. By the 1980s, after a period of escalating divorces in Cleveland and the nation, the Div. of Domestic Relations had grown into 4 departments: the Family Conciliation Service, Legal Dept., Dept. of Investigation, and Bureau of Child Support. Moreover, one Cleveland judge, SAMUEL SILBERT, had become a national domestic-relations authority and one of the most popular judges in the city.

Specialization was also at work in the Cleveland bar as efforts continued to bridge the perceived gap between law and justice. In 1960, the city's LEGAL AID SOCIETY ceased relying on outside lawyers and hired its own staff. Federal policy affected this form of practice, too. The society's 2 divisions, civil and criminal, expanded rapidly as a result of funds made available through the Office of Economic Opportunity. Its staff mushroomed from 16 in 1966 to 66 in 1970. Legal aid also became specialized. The society had a Legal Reform Sec., and by 1978 its civil division included a Family Unit, an Older Persons Div., and a program that ran group homes for the mentally retarded. In 1976, the society finally won a 60-year-old battle to create a public defender's office. By 1983, the public defender's office employed 33 lawyers and handled 4,200 cases a year.

The most dramatic examples of successful specialization, and organization, during these years came from Cleveland's corporate bar. At a time when the city's business corporations suffered closures and contraction, its major law firms flourished as never before. They grew by retaining an internal organization that mirrored the needs of their corporate clientele. They hired more and more lawyers as internal departments grew to deal with increasingly intricate legal problems such as labor law, and new divisions were created to handle issues such as health law. The results were spectacular. CALFEE, HALTER & GRISWOLD ballooned from 10 lawyers in 1950 to 22 in 1962 and 100 in 1985. The pressure was intense, too. THOMPSON, HINE & FLORY, which had prided itself on growth from within, had to change its policy and absorb other firms to increase its numbers and corporate services. Cleveland firms also expanded geographically. Branch offices had first opened in Washington and Columbus to deal with client regulatory needs. But as businesses moved out of Cleveland, their law firms followed them. The firms created complex management systems that turned Cleveland into the headquarters of some of the nation's largest law firms. By 1985, Squire, Sanders & Dempsey had spread its 320 attorneys in offices across the nation and in several foreign cities. It had also created an internal bureaucracy that included a complex system of managers and committees that replicated the organization of the corporations it represented.

Successful adaptation enabled corporate firms to retain their leadership of the Cleveland bar. As they had since the 1890s, corporate attorneys dominated city practice in terms of status and imagery. Smaller firms copied their organization and vied to grow and join their ranks. Most law students considered corporate employment the measure of professional success, as did their law schools, which now had a monopoly on legal training. Even so, the modern bar's inherent diversity continued as well. In a reformist variation of the corporate model, Cleveland State law professors Jane Picker and Lizabeth Moody created the first law firm in the nation that specialized in sex-discrimination cases, the WOMEN'S LAW FUND. Another variant emerged in the 1970s with the legal clinic movement. These firms, like the national Hyatt Legal Services Co., were low-cost, high-volume offices that specialized in providing standardized services such as divorce representation and will drafting to middle-class clients.

The increasing range of legal practice, so characteristic of the bar since the advent of industrialism, also had sources in the explosion of attorneys in the late 1960s and early 1970s. Law schools in Cleveland and around the nation expanded as applications flooded in, and the national pool of law students grew from 68,562 in 1962 to a peak of about 126,000 in 1977. At the same time, racial, ethnic, and gender integration began in the bar. Corporate firms began to hire Jews, Catholics, and blacks. Jones, Day hired its first woman attorney, Naoma Stewart, in 1960; she also became the firm's first female partner. Similar changes occurred in all of the roles lawyers had assumed in the city. Thus, not surprisingly, Cleveland's first black mayor, Carl Stokes, came from the city's bar and later joined its bench.

At the same time that lawyers such as Stewart and Stokes integrated the city's firms and offices, clearer career tracks emerged within Cleveland's legal profession. Stokes's career, spent primarily in political office and the courts, itself points out that by the 1970s, the 19th-century tradition that had led leaders of the Cleveland bar such as Sherlock Andrews and Rufus Ranney in and out of practice and political office had given way to more fixed professional pursuits and profiles. The most graphic evidence in the modern era comes from a contrast between the lawyers who sat on the city's courts and those who worked in its corporate firms. Most common pleas and municipal court judges from 1940–67 were native Clevelanders, graduates of local law schools, members of an increasingly broad range of ethnic and racial groups, solo practitioners before becoming judges, and actively involved in local politics. In contrast, corporate firms tended to hire graduates of elite law schools, and to have a much higher proportion of non-Clevelanders and much less ethnic and racial diversity. Moreover, corporate lawyers tended to confine their public activities to professional, educational, and cultural affairs instead of electoral politics. Thus, while Jones, Day prided itself on being the first firm in the Midwest to actively recruit graduates of eastern law schools, only 1.89% of the city's judiciary had been trained in the Ivy League.

Similar patterns emerged in the various specialties of the bar. A professional calculus based on perception of difficulty, client status, and remuneration led to a pecking order that placed the corporate bar at the top and personal-injury work at the bottom. A couple of examples suggest the professional animosities and competition these developments engendered: in the early 1950s, a group of lawyers in the state tried and failed to secure legislation banning the use of deceased partners' names in a firm's masthead; in the 1970s, many lawyers and local bar associations opposed the use of professional advertising even after it had secured judicial approval. In short, specialization and diversity had strengthened the Cleveland bar as well as increased the tensions and conflicts that still swirled around the issue of professionalism.

Cleveland remained a conducive legal environment. Though hardly representative, a review of leading cases in the era suggests the range of issues that challenged the city's attorneys. Unlike in many American legal communities, in the late 1940s and early 1950s local attorneys from the Natl. Lawyers Guild and the Cleveland Bar Assoc. organized representation for those accused of subversion under the Smith Act. About the same time, the city's bar became embroiled in the SHEPPARD MURDER CASE, which ultimately led to rulings more explicitly defining press and individual rights. Similar decisions by the U.S. Supreme Court originated in Cleveland in cases such as *MAPP V. OHIO* (1961) dealing with the seizure of evidence, and the 1964 Heights Art Theatre Obscenity Case (*JACOBELLIS V. OHIO*). The mixture of a vibrant profession and conducive

environment continued to make the bench and bar one of the most significant elements of the city.

By the 1980s, Cleveland courts and lawyers had compiled a long and often illustrious history. Their past not only provides a telling chronicle of the importance of law in an American community; it also offers evidence of some of the sources of the city's uniqueness. Lawyers from Alfred Kelley to Naoma Stewart, judges from Samuel Huntington to Carl Stokes, and courts from the early jp tribunals to the later traffic court, have played a large role in shaping the city. Clevelanders have turned to the bench and bar to resolve disputes, furnish municipal leaders, and provide attractive vocations. The city, in turn, has had a dramatic impact on the bench and bar. A few decades after Cleveland's founding, the famous French commentator on American society, Alexis deTocqueville, concluded, "Scarcely any political question arises in the United States that is not resolved, sooner or later, into a judicial question." The complex interaction of Cleveland and its courts and lawyers offers dramatic evidence of the implications of Tocqueville's early-19th-century pronouncement.

Michael Grossberg
Case Western Reserve University

Brady, Thomas J., *The First 100 Years, A History of the Cleveland Bar Association* (1973).
Kennedy, James Harrison, and Day, Wilson M., eds., *The Bench and Bar of Cleveland* (1889).
Neff, William B., ed., *The Bench and Bar of Northern Ohio* (1921).

**LEACH, ROBERT BOYD** (1822–29 July 1863), was the first black physician in Cleveland. He was also one of the first BLACKS in Cleveland to advocate full rights as citizens for blacks. Leach was originally from Virginia. He moved to southern Ohio, and then to Cleveland in 1844. As a young man, he worked as a nurse on the lake steamers during navigation season. His preliminary knowledge of medicine came entirely from books. He entered the Western Homeopathic College in 1856 and in 2 years received a degree in homeopathic medicine. In 1858, after obtaining his medical degree, Leach established a practice in Cleveland, its black population then less than 800. He was a spokesman for blacks, and his name was frequently mentioned in news items relating to the struggle of blacks in Cleveland and Ohio. As a doctor, Leach had both white and black patients. He is credited with a specific remedy for the treatment of cholera, successfully used throughout the Great Lakes region. During the CIVIL WAR, Leach helped recruit black soldiers for the Union Army but was refused service himself; the army would not accept doctors trained in homeopathic medicine. Leach then began to study allopathic medicine, but within several months he died of a liver ailment.

The **LEAGUE FOR HUMAN RIGHTS** was organized in Cleveland in 1933 by Rabbi ABBA HILLEL SILVER and journalist Leon Wiesenfeld after they returned from a national convention in New York held by the League for Human Rights & against Nazism. The Cleveland league's initial purpose was to promote a boycott of goods produced in the newly created German Nazi regime and to disseminate accurate information about anti-Semitism and antiliberal activities of that regime. The Cleveland league had a 2-level internal organization. It maintained a letterhead committee of 60 individuals, mostly Gentile, who were in sympathy with the organization's purposes. This committee included prominent social workers GEO. A. BELLAMY, ALICE GANNETT, and RUSSELL W. JELLIFFE, and religious leaders such as Bp. WARREN ROG-

ERS and Rev. PHILIP SMEAD BIRD. Actual control of the organization, however, was vested in a "committee of fifteen." This group was made up of leaders from the Jewish community. The day-to-day functioning of the group was administered by a salaried director and a secretary. The group's first director, MILDRED CHADSEY, remained in the position for slightly more than a year. Her successor, GRACE MEYETTE, stayed with the organization until its dissolution in the mid-1940s and was a major force in the direction of its activities.

During the mid-1930s, the league began to expand its activities. Though it continued to promote enforcement of the boycott, it began to place heavy emphasis on exposing the activities of pro-Nazi and anti-Semitic groups and individuals in Cleveland. In this phase of its activities, the league investigated and denounced organizations such as the German-American Bund, the Silvershirts, and the United Mothers for Peace. Prominent individuals accused of anti-Semitic leanings were also investigated. These included the Cleveland publishers of Halt, a right-wing magazine, and national figures such as Chas. A. Lindbergh, Gerald K. Smith, and Rev. Chas. Coughlin. Because of his large following in the Cleveland area, which the league identified, Coughlin was a prime target of the organization. The league also worked against antiblack and other discriminatory activities in Cleveland. During this period, it cooperated with organizations such as the NAACP. During the initial phases of the European War, 1939-41, the league was a strong advocate of preparedness and aid to the Allies, condemning peace organizations as pro-Nazi. After America's entry into the war, the league watched for subversive activities and tried to aid the war effort in general. Among the final activities of the league was the publication of 6 issues of This Is Cleveland, a periodical that focused on different ethnic groups in Cleveland in an effort to promote mutual pride and understanding. Associate director Maria Halberstadt was active in this work and prepared the final complement, entitled "Heirs to Freedom," which emphasized the search for freedom and liberal ideals of Ohio's pioneers.

League for Human Rights Records, WRHS.

The **LEAGUE OF WOMEN VOTERS OF CLEVELAND** was formed in Apr. 1920 by a group of suffragettes who decided to disband the Woman's Suffrage Party of Greater Cleveland following an example set by the Natl. American Woman's Suffrage Assoc., which had organized the Natl. League of Women Voters at its 1919 Golden Jubilee Convention. In Cleveland, the league assumed charge of the Suffrage party's unfinished business, working to complete ratification of the 23d Amendment and to educate new voters. The league was nonpartisan and proposed to educate women, support improved legislation, and encourage engagement in politics by women. It was the first local chapter to send questionnaires to candidates and to hold public forums between opposing candidates. In tribute to its early achievements, the Cleveland organization was selected to host the 2d national convention for the league in 1921. BELLE SHERWIN, the Cleveland league's first president, served as vice-president from 1924-30. Much of the legislation endorsed by the league in the past concerned protective laws for female workers, child welfare legislation, and education bills. Today the league also conducts voter registration drives, provides assistance to election boards, and sponsors public demonstrations of registration and voting techniques.

Abbott, Virginia Clark, *The History of Woman Suffrage and the League of Women Voters in Cuyahoga County, 1911-1945* (1949).

League of Women Voters of Cleveland Records, WRHS.

**LEAGUE PARK** was built by the owner of the CLEVELAND SPIDERS, Frank DeHaas Robison. The first baseball game was played there on 1 May 1891 before approximately 9,000 fans. The park was located at E. 66th St. and Lexington Ave., just a short walk from the streetcar stop, on the line that Robison owned. The stands were wooden, on one level, and the only box provided was for the team's president. The press box was open; announcements were made from home plate with a megaphone. Though hosting baseball games was the park's primary function, football games were played there, and boxing events were held. It also served as a picnic ground for baseball fans who arrived early to watch batting practice. Baseball became increasingly popular in Cleveland, and by 1909 League Park's seating capacity was increased to 27,000 to accommodate the growing crowds. A second level of seats was added, and boxes became available. To prevent fires, a steel-and-concrete base replaced the wooden one. League Park was the scene of many baseball highlights during the 1920s and 1930s. The first and only unassisted triple play in baseball history and the first World Series grand slam occurred during the 1920 series at the park. Babe Ruth hit his 500th homer out of League Park in 1929. In 1936, Bob Feller pitched his first professional game there.

With the completion of CLEVELAND MUNICIPAL STADIUM in 1931, the CLEVELAND INDIANS played few games in League Park. In 1934, however, they returned to the park (except for Sunday and holiday games), in order to reduce costs and to improve the team's batting average, which had plummeted in the larger stadium. The Indians continued to play in League Park until Bill Veeck's 1947 Indians drew crowds that required the larger stadium. League Park also hosted black baseball in Cleveland. It was the home of the 1945 American Negro World Series champion CLEVELAND BUCKEYES. Over 10,000 spectators attended one championship game. The CLEVELAND RAMS played professional football games in League Park during the 1940s, including the 1945 championship game. After 1945, the CLEVELAND BROWNS used the park as a practice field until the city of Cleveland purchased it in 1951. The city tore down the deteriorating stands and converted the area into a playground. In 1979, the site was declared a Cleveland landmark.

Jedick, Peter, *Cleveland: Where the East Coast Meets the Midwest* (1980).

The **LEAR SIEGLER, INC., POWER EQUIPMENT DIVISION,** 17600 Broadway Ave., MAPLE HTS., is a major designer, developer, and manufacturer of electromechanical equipment for aerospace, missile, ordnance, and ground applications. The Power Equipment Div. has been based at this address since 2 Southern California-based corporations—Lear, Inc., and the Siegler Corp.—merged in 1962. The division was established when Lear's Romec Div. in Elyria and its Grand Rapids, Mich., Electro-Mechanical Div. were consolidated with Siegler's Jack & Heintz Div., located at the Maple Hts. address. Siegler acquired Jack & Heintz in 1961, a year after the death of its cofounder, Wm. S. "Bill" Jack, who had gained national recognition for his labor-relations policies in the 1940s. Born in Cleveland in 1888, Jack became a machinist in 1902, joined the Internatl. Assoc. for Machinists in 1911, and in 1913 became the union's business agent for the Cleveland district. He organized and then sold some successful businesses—the Accurate Machine Co., organized in 1917 and sold in 1921, and the Pump Engineering Service Co., organized in

1933 and sold in 1939—before founding Jack & Heintz, Ltd., in 1940 in Palo Alto, Calif., with chemical engineer and short-wave radio pioneer Ralph M. Heintz. In Nov. 1940 they moved their operations to Cleveland and changed the name to Jack & Heintz, Inc., manufacturers of precision parts for airplanes.

While Heintz directed the engineering and technical departments, Jack oversaw production, putting his union ideals into practice. Calling his employees "associates" and taking as a company motto "Labor and Management Associates in Progress thru Cooperation," Jack made his company a model of enlightened paternalism in the highly demanding and productive atmosphere of wartime: the company offered medical, accident, and life insurance and free medical care; free meals and vitamin pills were available around the clock in the cafeteria; steam baths and massages were available during breaks; and company-paid vacations in Florida were available for associates needing longer breaks. In return, Jack expected his associates to work 12-hour shifts, 7 days a week; they were paid time-and-a-half for working more than 40 hours. Such benefits, good pay, and appeals to workmen's pride paid off handsomely for the company. Beginning with 56 employees in 1940, the company grew to 7,600 in 1943 and 8,700 in 1944, with a list of 35,000 people anxious to become Jahco associates. In 1942, a Senate investigating committee praised Jack & Heintz for the cuts it had made in costs during its work on a defense contract; the extra profits were shared among all the associates.

After a postwar business slump in 1946, the company merged with the Precision Prods. Corp., becoming Jack & Heintz Precision Prods., with Byron C. Foy as president. The new company adopted a more conservative approach to business and labor relations. Siegler acquired the firm in 1961 and merged with Lear the following year, creating its Power Equipment Div. with K. Robt. Kahn as division president. In 1963 the division employed 2,200 people in the Cleveland area, including its plant in Elyria, 2 plants on Solon Rd., and the Broadway Ave. facility. By 1964, division sales reached $40 million annually, and the main plant had been remodeled to include a new aerospace engineering center, which employed 200 research and development personnel in 1967. By 1984, the Cleveland-based division was one of 39 divisions in a corporation that employed 30,860 people worldwide.

The Jahco News, 26 June 1942 and 24 July 1942 (WRHS).
Lear Siegler, Inc., Annual Reports, 1983 and 1984, Business Dept., Cleveland Public Library.

The **LEASEWAY TRANSPORTATION CORPORATION** is a holding company with over 110 subsidiaries in specialized highway transit, vehicle leasing, and distribution. Formed in 1960, the company was heir to a local cartage firm begun in 1899 by Hugh O'Neill and managed in subsequent years by his family. The company was unique because for many years vehicle leasing was its major product, and because it operated as a loose association of small companies. Before opening his business, Hugh O'Neill selected carriage horses for prominent Clevelanders, contacts he utilized when he set up his hauling operation. He earned the business of 2 Cleveland newspapers, local stores, and the Electric Package Freight Co. Later, he set up the trucking lines for the Van Sweringen brothers that later became U.S. Truck Lines. O'Neill oversaw the transition of the company from a horse-drawn fleet to a motorized one in 1912. O'Neill's sons, Hugh, Jr., William, and Francis, transformed the business into a complex of service, leasing, and trucking companies. In 1937, U.S. Truck decided to spin

off the Niagara Motor Express Co., which William bought and ran; he and his brothers accumulated companies that constituted a private empire. William then pulled more than 40 companies under a corporate umbrella, the Lease Plan Internatl. Corp., in 1959. Within a year, he arranged stock exchanges that loosely united the ownership of 79 companies primarily owned by him and his brothers. The decentralized organization of the new Leaseway Transportation Corp. reflected O'Neill's belief that a relatively small local company would better serve customer needs than a larger, more impersonal one could. He served as president for 15 years and built a $24 million company into a $475 million operation with annual growth of 23% in revenue and 21% in earnings.

The Leaseway family encompassed 150 companies by 1975, and the organization was the 3d-largest publicly held transit company and the 20th-largest transit company of any type. It offered its customers complete transportation—provision of the vehicles and drivers, hauling, storage, and management—without capital investment. About 75% of Leaseway business involved leasing of vehicles to a specific industry. Its Signal Delivery Service, for example, specialized in retail delivery, especially to Sears, while Anchor Motor Freight (the corporate protege of Hugh O'Neill, Jr.) delivered cars for GM, Ford, and Chrysler. Other subsidiaries hauled newspapers, gasoline and oil, cement, steel, and chemicals. Though the demand for Leaseway services followed the inflationary patterns of its client industries, the diversity of Leaseway holdings kept the company in a leading position. Contracts with customers were written with buy-back provisions that insulated Leaseway from financial loss if the customer canceled the order. The remainder of the businesses provided fleets of cars and trucks, as well as warehouse and distribution services. Leaseway engineering subsidiaries consulted on leasing and trucking problems with outside companies. In the 1980s, Leaseway remained profitable, despite inflation, extended recession in autos and other products it carried, and trucking deregulation. In 1982, it experimented with LTL (lighter than truckload) cartage, a labor-intensive undertaking, hoping to corner this market with low rates through the use of nonunion labor paid by incentives. The enterprise was seen as a direct challenge to the Teamsters, whose pay and work rules prohibited such activity. By 1986, the O'Neills, who owned 30% of the stock, and the management team, which was devoid of family members, decided to diversify the company and its holdings. The O'Neills led a group of dissidents (the Committee to Revitalize Leaseway) to challenge the current management of the corporate assets. Both sides desired to dominate the search for a buyer. In Nov. 1986, the proposed sale of Leaseway to Citicorp Capital Investors, Ltd., was announced, as was the proposed sale of the Full Service Leasing Div. That left the company with little of the leasing business that had been responsible for its growth. The O'Neills planned to retain their stock.

**LEBANESE.** See **ARAB-AMERICANS**

The **LEBANESE-SYRIAN JUNIOR WOMEN'S LEAGUE,** organized in 1929, is a social and charitable organization that sponsors fundraising events to support children's institutions overseas, scholarships for local students of Syrian-Lebanese descent, and donations to local welfare agencies. The league was founded with 23 charter members at a party for Syrian girls sponsored by the Internatl. Institute of the YWCA on 9 Dec. 1929. Known for its first several months as the Zenobia Club, it elected Linda George as its first president, Evelyn Bader as vice-president, and Sonia George as secretary and treasurer. On 15 July 1930, it changed its name to the Syrian Jr. League. The league sponsored socials, hikes, speeches, and plays; few members could speak Arabic, but they practiced the language to put on plays. At Christmas time the organization held a party for poor children and collected food to prepare food baskets for needy Syrian families. The social and cultural organization also helped establish the Syrian Cultural Gardens and sponsored the Capricornian Club for younger women. In the mid-1940s, the Syrian Jr. League adopted its present name in order both to acknowledge the independent state of Lebanon and to help satisfy the JUNIOR LEAGUE OF CLEVELAND'S concern about public confusion over the 2 organizations with similar names. Expansion of group activities and increased membership made it necessary for the group to leave the Internatl. Institute and move its activities to the Sheraton Cleveland Hotel. It met there until the hotel closed for renovations in 1977, then moved temporarily to the Plaza Hotel.

**LEDBETTER, ELEANOR EDWARDS** (1870–19 July 1954), was a branch librarian for the Cleveland Public Library system known for her pioneering work with immigrant groups and ethnic literature. Ledbetter was born in Holley, N.Y. She was educated at Brockport State Normal College and at Syracuse University. Her professional training was taken at New York State Library School in Albany. Ledbetter began her career as a cataloguer at Worcester, Mass., in 1896. In 1898 she accepted the position of librarian at the Buffalo Historical Society, remaining there for 3 years. In 1902 she took a position in South Bend, Ind., remaining there until 1903, when she became special cataloguer at the University of Texas. From 1907–09 she worked as a librarian in Newark, N.Y. Before coming to Cleveland in 1909, she worked for a brief period as assistant organizer for the Ohio State Library Commission. She was appointed a professional librarian at the Broadway Branch of the CLEVELAND PUBLIC LIBRARY in 1909, and the following year assumed the position of branch librarian. She retained that position until her retirement in July 1938.

Reflecting the surrounding communities of CZECHS and POLES, the Broadway Branch housed Bohemian and Polish collections. Ledbetter developed both an extensive knowledge of Polish and Czech literature and an affinity for and understanding of these immigrant groups. With the help of local priests and nuns from ethnic parishes, she earned the confidence of the local immigrants. During the strong AMERICANIZATION campaign during WORLD WAR I, Ledbetter ran citizenship classes and authored 3 books under the auspices of the Americanization Committee of the MAYOR'S ADVISORY WAR COMMITTEE. These volumes, *The Jugoslavs of Cleveland* (1918), *The Slovaks of Cleveland* (1918), and *The Czechs of Cleveland* (1919), not only evidenced her understanding of immigrant culture but, in the 1980s, also remained primary sources for the history of these communities in Cleveland. She also prepared another volume, *Winning Friends and Citizens for America* (1918), which was published by the Immigrant Publication Society. Following the ,war, Ledbetter prepared 3 additional works, *Polish Literature in English Translation* (1932), *The Polish Immigrant and His Reading* (1924), and a translation (1930) of Bozena Nemcova's Czech work *The Shepherd and the Dragon*, as well as articles for a variety of professional and ethnic journals. Her work in this area led to her election as chairman of the American Library Assoc.'s Committee on Work with Foreign Born. Ledbetter was honored for her work by the Polish government, which presented her with the Order of Haller's Swords, and the Polish Academy of Letters, which presented her a silver medal. The Czechoslovak government awarded her the Gold Medal of the Order of the White Lion. Ledbetter married Dancy Ledbetter on 30 Sept. 1903. They had 1 son, Dancy E. Ledbetter.

The **LEECE-NEVILLE COMPANY,** an important developer and manufacturer of electrical products for the AUTOMOTIVE INDUSTRY, was organized in 1909 by Cleveland inventor Bennett M. Leece and financier Sylvester M. Neville. Incorporated in 1910 with capital of $61,000, Leece-Neville opened at 2069 E. 4th St., moving to 5363 Hamilton Ave. by 1915. Formerly the manager of the Electrical Mfg. Co., Leece had become interested in electricity and electrical devices at an early age. He began Leece-Neville by developing a self-starting ignition system, for which he received the patent in 1918. By 1950, the company held 56 patents; 47 of these were registered in whole or in part to Bennett Leece. Leece-Neville operated for 3 years before obtaining a sizable contract in 1912. During WORLD WAR I the company grew, making generators, starter motors, gun sights, and other war materials. It flourished during WORLD WAR II, producing electrical starters, generators, and regulators for airplanes, trucks, and industrial and marine equipment. By war's end, Leece-Neville operated 2 plants on Hamilton Ave. After the war, the company pioneered the use of the alternator on municipal vehicles such as fire trucks, police cars, and buses. The introduction of the alternator on passenger cars in 1960 contributed to further company growth. In 1955, Leece-Neville purchased a plant at E. 51st St. and St. Clair to expand production, and in 1959 it established a plant in Gainesville, Ga. When Percy H. Neville became company president in 1951, annual sales were $6 million; in 1959, sales were $15 million, and the company employed 1,100 people. During Leece's direction of the company prior to his death in 1948, Leece-Neville grew largely as a result of the development of new products; in the 1960s, the company began to grow from acquisitions and mergers with other companies, as well, purchasing companies or establishing subsidiaries in Canada, Michigan, Pennsylvania, and Indiana. In 1967, sales topped $43 million. On 1 Feb. 1969, Leece-Neville merged with Victoreen, Inc., and became a subsidiary of the VLN Corp., which merged with the Sheller-Globe Corp. on 30 Sept. 1974, making the former Leece-Neville a division of Sheller-Globe.

The **LEGAL AID SOCIETY** of Cleveland was the 5th society in the U.S. organized, according to its charter, "to render legal assistance gratuitously or for a moderate charge to deserving persons not otherwise able to obtain the service of a competent attorney, and to promote measures for their protection." Praised as an innovative program by proponents of legal aid at various points in its history, the Cleveland organization was nevertheless typical of such societies, evolving from an agency for social control to one advocating social change in the 1960s. Two attorneys offering legal services to the poor through different agencies, Arthur D. Baldwin through the Day Nursery and Isadore Grossman through B'NAI B'RITH, joined forces to form the Cleveland Legal Aid Society, which was incorporated on 12 May 1905. Supported by private donations and later by the Community Fund, the society contracted with a specific lawyer to provide legal services for the indigent. Grossman was the society's first attorney (1905–12), followed by Robb Bartholomew (1914–18) and the firm of Chas. E. Clark & J. Milton Costello (1918–58).

In 1960, the society ended its practice of retaining outside lawyers and established its own civil and criminal divisions. The latter was especially controversial and met stiff opposition from judges and private attorneys, who challenged it in court. When the Ohio Public Defender Law was passed in 1976, the county took over much of the society's public defender services. The society expanded its services greatly in the late 1960s, when the Office of Economic Opportunity made available federal antipoverty funds. In Mar. 1966, it received $160,000 to establish 5 legal offices in low-income neighborhoods. Federal funds enabled the society to increase its legal staff from 16 in 1966 to 66 in 1970, when it served 30,000 people. Despite national political criticism of legal aid policies and budgetary uncertainties, the Cleveland society continued to expand the scope of its operations. By 1978, its civil division included a family law unit, an older persons' unit, and a program that operated 2 group homes for persons released from state mental hospitals after long-term commitments. Its legal reform section filed class-action suits and test cases on a variety of issues, and 2 other programs provided assistance and support to community organizations. In 1979, the Legal Aid Society moved into a renovated factory at 1223 W. 6th St. National budget cuts in 1981 and 1982 forced it to close several neighborhood offices, reduce its staff, and turn away clients, In 1983, the Bar Assoc. of Greater Cleveland began a special program to urge its members to work as volunteers for the society or to provide financial support for its work.

**LEHMAN AND SCHMITT** was a Cleveland architectural firm that designed many important public and institutional buildings between 1885–1935. Israel J. Lehman (1859–1914) and Theodore Schmitt (1860–1935) formed a partnership in 1885. The first 2 buildings of which there is a record were large covered public halls, the Sheriff St. Market (1891) on E. 4th St. at Bolivar and the CENTRAL ARMORY (1893). Their differences in style, the former classical and the latter medieval, epitomize the range of the eclectic architect. Lehman & Schmitt designed 2 large synagogues, Temple Tifereth Israel in 1894 (Friendship Baptist Church in 1985) and the Euclid Ave. Temple (ANSHE CHESED) in 1912 (Liberty Hill Baptist Church in 1985). In 1913 they planned a large Jewish social club in UNIVERSITY CIRCLE, the handsome Excelsior Club (Thwing Hall of CASE WESTERN RESERVE UNIVERSITY since 1929). Their public buildings included the old Central Police Station (1896) on Champlain St., an impressive classical edifice, and their major existing work (1985) is undoubtedly the CUYAHOGA COUNTY COURTHOUSE, completed in 1912, one of the chief Beaux-Arts monuments on the Mall. The firm also planned many public buildings outside Cleveland, including the Erie County Children's Home in Sandusky and courthouses in Peru, Ind., and Franklin, Pa. Lehman & Schmitt also designed commercial buildings, stores, and warehouses, of which the most important one remaining in 1985 was the Detroit-Warren Rd. Bldg. in LAKEWOOD (1923). After Lehman's death in 1914, Schmitt continued the firm as the Lehman-Schmitt Co. until his death in 1935.

The **LEISY BREWING COMPANY**, located at 3400 Vega Ave. on the near west side, was once Cleveland's largest independent brewery. It was established by Isaac Leisy (1838–1892), an Iowa brewer who learned that the Frederick Haltnorth Brewery was for sale while attending a brewers' convention in Cleveland. His brothers August and Henry joined him in the venture, and together they established Isaac Leisy & Co. in 1873. Leisy, with branch agencies in Ohio, western Pennsylvania, and Indiana, soon gained a reputation for its Premium Lager and Budweiser beers (Budweiser was not then a brand name). August and Henry left Cleveland in 1882, leaving Isaac Leisy as sole owner and manager. In 1884 he substantially enlarged the brewery,

replacing the old buildings with modern ones occupying 8 acres of land. Production rose from 12,000 barrels in 1873 to over 90,000 in 1890. Leisy employed 75 workers, the majority of whom were German-Americans. Isaac Leisy died in 1892, shortly after completing a baronial brownstone mansion next door to the brewery, and his son Otto I. (1864–1914) assumed control. Production climbed to 355,000 barrels by 1917. During Prohibition, the brewery was closed and its equipment sold, but with repeal Herbert F. Leisy (Otto's son and Isaac's grandson) reestablished the Leisy brewing dynasty. He reequipped and modernized the brewery with assistance from Carl Faller, the oldest active brewmaster in the U.S. when he died in 1939. In the 1950s, Leisy Black Dallas malt liquor and Leisy Light, Dortmunder, and Mello-Gold beer were distributed in Michigan, Pennsylvania, Kentucky, Indiana, New York, and Ohio. To increase capacity, in early 1958 Leisy purchased the Geo. F. Stein brewery in Buffalo. Geo. S. Carter, former Leisy sales manager who had propelled PILSENER's P.O.C. to a leading position in Ohio, returned to Leisy in June 1958 as president and a substantial owner, but all operations ceased the following year. The company later pointed to Ohio's $.36-a-case tax as a major factor in its demise. When it closed, Leisy was the oldest brewery in Cleveland and one of the longest surviving family-operated breweries in America.

Leisy Brewing Co. Records, WRHS.

**LELAND, JACKSON MILLER** (1818–20 Feb. 1896), was a music teacher and brass-band leader during the 19th century. Born in Holliston, Mass., he moved to Philadelphia, where he lived for years with an uncle. Upon returning to Holliston to live with his father, a music teacher, he developed proficiency in playing the violin, bugle, and clarinet. He arrived in Cleveland on 18 Dec. 1843 and shortly thereafter organized Leland's Band. On 21 Nov. 1844, the band played on the steamboat *Empire* and on other lakeboats that sailed between Buffalo and Chicago. Leland also toured the South with a theatrical group in 1846.

When the CIVIL WAR broke out, Leland and many band members enlisted in the 41ST OHIO VOLUNTEER INFANTRY, mustered in on 22 Oct. 1861 at Camp Wood in Cleveland. The band of the 41st Ohio was mustered out on 6 June 1862 at Corinth, Miss., after the War Dept. phased out regimental bands with General Order No. 90. Leland's Band returned to Cleveland, where it played at local Army camps of rendezvous and instruction. As troops left for the field, the band aired such favorite tunes as "The Girl I Left behind Me" and "Wait for the Wagon." Leland's Band played daily at the NORTHERN OHIO SANITARY FAIR on PUBLIC SQUARE between 22 Feb.–10 Mar. 1864. The band was without a leader when Leland again enlisted, as a private in Co. D, 150th OVI, at the age of 46 on 2 May 1864. He was promoted to principal musician and mustered out with the 150th in Cleveland on 23 Aug. 1864. In Apr. 1865, the band participated in Pres. Abraham Lincoln's funeral procession in Cleveland. As troops returned from Civil War service, Leland's Band greeted them as they detrained at UNION DEPOT and marched to Public Square for official welcoming ceremonies. The band serenaded Gen. Wm. T. Sherman on 29 July 1866 at the Kennard House. Leland's Band continued to participate in most major parades, events, and funerals of the period until Leland's death in 1896. He was survived by a second wife, Mary J., and 4 children. He had been a Mason and a member of the GRAND ARMY OF THE REPUBLIC.

Kimberly, Robert, and Holloway, Ephraim S., *The Forty-first Ohio Veteran Volunteer Infantry in the War of the Rebellion, 1861–1865*, (1897).

**LEMKO HALL,** located at 2337 W. 11th St. at the corner of Literary Ave., is owned by the Lemko Assoc. Home Branch No. 6, a branch of the Lemko Assoc. of the U.S. and Canada. The local branch was formed in 1929, and the larger group was formed in Cleveland in 1931. The organization was established to serve the people from Lemkovina, a Slavic area on the slopes of the Carpathian Mts. In the early 1930s, Cleveland had the largest Lemko community in the U.S. and was a center of Lemko activity before the Lemko Assoc. moved its headquarters to Yonkers, N.Y. The first Lemko Social & Civic Club in Cleveland was located at 1037 Starkweather Ave. in the mid-1930s. By 1937 the hall had been moved to 1205 Starkweather, where it remained before being moved to W. 11th St. in 1946. In 1977, the hall gained fame when it was used to film the wedding feast in the film *The Deer Hunter.*

**LEMKOS.** *See* **CARPATHO-RUSSIANS**

**LEMPCO INDUSTRIES, INC.,** started in 1918 as the Lake Erie Metal Prods. Co. to make axle shafts, became a leading local machine-tool producer and the umbrella corporation for 5 companies operating in the fields of auto rebuilding and replacement parts, import and export, die sets and supplies, and specialized machines. Begun in a Cuyahoga Valley garage in the ebbing days of WORLD WAR I, the company produced war material. After the armistice, Jas. F. Strnad and John Blazek, the owners, solicited orders by day and machined axle shafts and other small parts by night. As the infant auto industry expanded, demand for the company's product exceeded its productive capacity; as a result, the company incorporated under the acronym Lempco Industries, Inc., and sold stock to finance expansion first to a larger facility on the west side, and then, in 1923, to its present (1985) location at 5409 Dunham Rd. in BEDFORD.

In the 1920s and 1930s, the Lempco product line expanded to include brake drums and shoes, drum lathes, grinders, clutch plates, gears, and industrial machine tools and dies. Under the auspices of Dorothy Kimmel, Lempco moved into the import-export business. With the coming of WORLD WAR II, the company mass-produced shells using 2 converted boring machines in storage at the Chevrolet plant. Because of its size, the company was awarded contracts for 5% of the shells needed by the military, but as a result of its efficient and speedy production, Lempco turned out 38% of the national demand. The workforce, 500 strong, included 100 women and was encouraged to work hard by the example of owner Jas. Strnad, who worked alongside the workers in the early days of the war.

During the war, Lempco met civilian machine-tool needs through import, acquisition, and diversification, as the domestic machine-tool productive capacity was committed to the government. Dorothy Kimmel—who used "D. Kimmel" on the purchase order to draw attention away from her sex—arranged for the import of planers, turret lathes, drill presses, and milling machines from South America. Though Strnad worried about foreign competition, he felt that high tariffs would encourage American companies to buy American after the war. This initial foray into foreign trade prepared Lempco for broader expansion into import-export after the war; in 1949, Lempco and Thompson Prods., Inc., were the first Cleveland manufacturers to receive foreign orders for products purchased under the European Recovery Plan.

To plan for further domestic production, Lempco acquired the Evans Reamer & Machine Co. of Chicago in 1942, followed by the Cleveland Pressed Steel Co. in 1944 and the Webster Prods. Co. of Cleveland in 1948. These acquisitions firmly established Lempco in 3 main areas: industrial machine tools, auto shop equipment, and replacement auto parts. Beginning in the early 1940s, Lempco introduced a series of machines that revolutionized the industry with their speed and low cost. Throughout the 1950s, Lempco supplemented its product line with war material (land mines, fire bombs, shells); as a result of its diversification, the company was unaffected by the recession later in the decade. By 1963, the company had sales of over $35 million, and its catalog was regarded as an "industrial supermarket" of 66,000 items manufactured, bought, or sold by the company's divisions. Though affected by the decline of the machine-tool industry, Lempco remained strong, with 1984 sales of $23 million.

**LENHART, CARL H.** (1 Sept. 1880–8 Apr. 1955), was a Cleveland surgeon who participated in some of the most significant medical research conducted in Cleveland, including in the areas of shock and hemorrhaging, kidney studies, endemic goiter treatment, and surgical shock. Lenhart was born into the family of a country doctor in Wauseon, Ohio. He graduated with the A.B. degree from Adelbert College in 1901 and the M.D. degree from the Western Reserve University Medical School in 1904. During his residency and internship between 1904–06 at Lakeside Hospital, he did research with Dr. GEO. W. CRILE into the problems of shock and hemorrhaging. Between 1915–20, Lenhart worked closely with Dr. DAVID MARINE in investigating the etiology of simple goiters. As a teacher, he worked in the physiological laboratories of Dr. JOHN J. R. MACLEOD, the codiscoverer of insulin. In 1918, Lenhart was appointed demonstrator of surgery at WRU Medical School. He was appointed an instructor later in 1918, a professor of clinical surgery in 1930, and head of the school's department of surgery in 1932. In 1921, he was appointed head of the department of surgery at St. Luke's Hospital. Later he served as chief (1930–32) of the division of surgery at City Hospital and as director (1932–50) of surgery at Lakeside Hospital, where he maintained his private practice.

Lenhart was one of a number of physicians who devoted their lives to research in surgery and made Cleveland a pioneer area in the field. Together with Samuel O. Freedlander, he worked out the physiology of the pneumothorax and helped pave the way for open-heart surgery. He also worked with Dr. TORALD SOLLMAN on studies of the kidney. He retired from the practice of medicine in 1950. During his tenure at Reserve, Lenhart was devoted to the Dudley P. Allen Memorial Medical Library, serving as its head for many years. In 1952, he was named a trustee of WRU and established the Lenhart Memorial Lecture Fund at the university. Lenhart was survived by his wife, Ora.

**LEONARD, WILLIAM ANDREW** (15 July 1848–21 Sept. 1938), was the bishop coadjutor of the Episcopal Diocese of Ohio (1889) and the 4th bishop (1889–1930). He was a man of independent means who oversaw a diocese grown prosperous enough to afford the building of TRINITY CATHEDRAL (1903–07). Leonard was born in Southport, Conn. Both parents were from prominent Colonial families, and his father became a successful Wall St. banker. After a brief underage enlistment in the Union Army, Leonard graduated from St. Stephen's College (1866). He received his B.D. degree from the Berkeley Divinity School (1871). He married Sara Louisa Sullivan in 1873. Ordained deacon in 1871 and priest in 1872, Leonard began what became at the time the 2d-longest ecclesiastical career in the Anglican church with a rectorship in Brooklyn, N.Y. (1872–80). His popularity with national leaders and opinion makers such as JOHN HAY and Henry Adams while a rector in Washington, D.C. (1880–89), helped overcome a Tractarian-versus-evangelical dispute that caused the Diocese of Ohio to vote 5 times before electing him bishop coadjutor. Although an evangelical himself, Leonard used his personal wealth to adopt the lifestyle of his neighbors on Euclid Ave.'s Millionaires' Row as he successfully cajoled them into financial support of the diocese while gradually allowing the high-church adornments some of them desired.

Leonard founded the Free Library in Brooklyn, N.Y.; served on the board of trustees of Kenyon College; and took an interest in St. John's Home for Girls in Painesville. Among his several books is an interpretation of Herbert Spencer's philosophy. The ranks of the diocesan clergy doubled, and its membership quadrupled during Leonard's episcopacy. This growth was achieved during a period of prosperity, which Leonard managed in a way that consolidated and unified the diocese. He supervised the building of Trinity Cathedral and saved both Kenyon College and Bexley Hall from enrollment disasters caused by the long-running high church-low church dispute. He was a member of the Cleveland Park & Blvd. Assoc. as it engaged in the city's first efforts at modern urban planning (1891). His church offices included first president of Mid-West (1914–24) and twice presiding bishop of the church (1929 and 1930). He also supervised the American Episcopal churches in Europe for 9 years (1897–1906). While a rector in Washington, D.C., Leonard became a friend and advisor of Pres. Chester A. Arthur.

The **LEONARD SCHLATHER BREWING COMPANY** was begun in 1857 by Leonard Schlather and operated by him until 1902, when he sold out to the CLEVELAND & SANDUSKY BREWING CO. Schlather (1835–1918) was born in Ebenhausen, Wurttemburg, Germany. He emigrated to America in 1852, settling first in Altoona, Pa., before coming to Cleveland. In Cleveland, Schlather began his own brewery in 1857 with the aid of a loan from his brother Frederick. He built a brick building at Carroll Ave. and York (W. 28th) St., to which he successively added until 1885. Schlather also built a substantial Italianate house directly across from the brewery, on York St. Schlather sold the business to Cleveland & Sandusky in 1902. He retired from brewing but remained active in Cleveland financial affairs, serving as president of the People's Savings Bank and as a director of the Society for Savings and the Union Natl. Bank. Cleveland & Sandusky operated the Schlather brewery until Prohibition in 1919. During Prohibition, the company manufactured near-beer and carbonated beverages at the Schlather bottling plant (2600 Carroll Ave.). It did not reopen after Repeal in 1933. In 1985, the former bottling plant housed a Volunteers of America shelter and warehouse. The Schlather house was destroyed by fire in 1976.

**LEONARDS, JACK R.** (25 Feb. 1919–15 July 1978), was internationally known for his achievements in biochemical research. He was perhaps most prominently known as a world expert on aspirin. Leonards was born in Montreal, Canada. He graduated from McGill University in 1939, and 2 years later he received master's degrees in chemistry and nutrition from the Virginia Polytechnic Institute. He became associated with Western Reserve University in 1941 as a research fellow and received his doctorate there 2 years later. In 1957 he received a medical degree from the uni-

versity. In 1943, Leonards joined Ben Venue Laboratories, Inc., as a researcher. The firm in BEDFORD was one of the early manufacturers of penicillin, and Leonards did some of the original research on its production. From 1948 he was associated with Miles Laboratories as a consultant; he later operated his own laboratory, the Dr. Jack R. Leonards Medical Laboratory, in the Lakeland Medical Bldg. in EUCLID. From 1953 he was also an associate professor of clinical biochemistry at the Western Reserve School of Medicine. In the last 10 years of Leonards's life, most of his research efforts were concerned with aspirin. He testified as a leading expert at the FDA hearings on aspirin. During his career he had other notable achievements, including the development of glucola, a test for diabetes, and instant glucose as emergency treatment for persons in a diabetic coma. He also codeveloped one of the first mechanical kidneys. Leonards authored over 125 articles published in professional journals throughout the world.

**LEOPOLD BROTHERS FURNITURE,** established in 1859 by Henry Leopold, a German immigrant, has been continuously operated by the family. In 1985 it was one of the oldest furniture stores in America. Burdened by a $41 debt for his passage to Cleveland in 1853, Henry Leopold worked as a cabinetmaker for 6 years before opening a small furniture shop at Lorain and Green in 1859. Because he did not have the capital to invest in a stock of ready-made furniture, he made his own in the store basement—along with caskets, his staple item—and sold both to the immigrants who settled in the neighborhood. Leopold built furniture until his death, but by the 1880s, most of the stock was purchased from furniture companies as the needs of the growing city increased. After a fire in 1871, Leopold rebuilt the store nearby at 234–236 Lorain, where the business remained until 1926, when it moved to Lorain and W. 30th. In 1946 it occupied the old John Marshall High School building at 15149 Lorain. Though some of the institutional trappings were removed, the classrooms were left in place to permit showcasing the furniture in room arrangements. Additional floor space and parking were added in 1961. In 1985 the firm operated both the Lorain facility and a second store at 8149 Brecksville Rd.

The **LESTER M. SEARS FOUNDATION** was founded in 1949 by Lester Sears (1888–1967). Sears was born in Ravenna, Nebr., the son of a farm-implements dealer. In 1912, after moving with his family to Minnesota, he earned a B.A. from the University of Minnesota. Sears came to Cleveland in 1916 with his father to become assistant factory manager of the PEERLESS MOTOR CAR CO., making army trucks. In 1918, he was assigned to New Orleans by the secretary of war to evaluate truck production, and after the war he founded the TOWMOTOR CORP., manufacturing gas trucks and forklifts. By 1944, Towmotor made ⅓ of all the forklifts produced in the U.S. Sears sold his business in 1965 to Caterpillar, Inc. The next year he donated $1 million to Case Institute of Technology for a humanities center, and $1 million to Western Reserve University for a medical center. Sears was married to Ruth Parker in 1914 and had a daughter, Mary Ann. The purpose of the foundation is to support health, education, and environmental research. The foundation does not give grants to individuals, nor does it fund scholarships, fellowships, or loans. In 1983, the foundation assets were $1,996,333, with expenditures of $127,153 for 34 grants. Officers were Ruth Swetland Eppig, secretary, David Sears Swetland, and David W. Swetland.

**LEUTNER, WINFRED G.** (1 Mar. 1879–25 Dec. 1961), classical scholar, educator, and college administrator, was born in Cleveland, the 2d-youngest of 6 children of Frederick M. and Mary Ernst Leutner. He attended Zion Lutheran School (1885–92), where his father taught; later he went to Brownell School (1892–93). He graduated from CENTRAL HIGH SCHOOL (1897) and from Adelbert College in 1901, first in his class and a member of Phi Beta Kappa. He served as instructor in Greek at Flora Stone Mather College and Adelbert Colleges (1904), and he attended Johns Hopkins University, where he received a master's degree (1903) and a Ph.D. (1905). He was assistant professor of Greek at Wittenberg College from 1905–06 and an instructor of Latin and Greek at Adelbert from 1906–09. From 1907–08 he studied at the American School of Classical Studies at Rome and Athens. He then served as an instructor of Greek and Latin at Adelbert (1909–15) and became a full professor in 1915. In 1912 he was named dean of Adelbert College, and in 1925 he became dean of university administration. Dr. Leutner was instrumental in establishing Cleveland College, the downtown adult education college of Western Reserve University, and served as its acting director (1925–26). In 1933 he served as acting president of the university during Pres. Vinson's illness, and on 4 Dec. 1933 he was appointed president. He was inaugurated as the 8th president of WRU in June 1934. During his tenure (1934–49), Adelbert College, the School of Architecture, and the Case Reference Library, as well as Cleveland College, were absorbed into the university corporation. Dr. Leutner led the WRU through an economic depression, the war years, and the postwar increase in enrollment. Dr. Leutner received LL.D.s from the College of Wooster (1935); Wittenberg College (1935); and Oberlin College (1937); and an L.H.D. from Case Institute of Technology (1948). He served as trustee of UNIVERSITY HOSPITALS, the CLEVELAND CLINIC FOUNDATION, the MUSICAL ARTS ASSOC., the Cleveland YMCA, and HIRAM HOUSE; he was an honorary follow of the CLEVELAND MUSEUM OF ART and of the Cleveland School of Art. He was a member of the American Philological Assoc.; the Classical Assoc. of Great Britain; the Archeological Institute of America; the Classical Assoc. of the Middle West and South (founder and continuing member); the Cleveland Chamber of Commerce; the Assoc. of Urban Universities (vice-president, 1921–23; president, 1940–41); the English Speaking Union; the Ohio College Assoc.; the American School of Classical Studies in Rome and Athens; and the Ohio Society of New York. Dr. Leutner retired as president emeritus in 1949 and was named an honorary trustee of WRU. He married Emily Payne Smith of Detroit, Mich., on 30 June 1910. The couple had 1 son, Frederick S., and 2 daughters, Mrs. Mary (John L.) Willett and Mrs. Ruth (Geo. M.) Gantz.

**LEVINE, MANUEL** (25 May 1880–6 May 1939), was a Cleveland lawyer and judge. The liberal and energetic Levine sought to change social conditions that he perceived as causing hardships to immigrants and the underclasses and as causes of crime. Levine was born in Maresh, Russia, to David and Michele Levine. He immigrated to America and Cleveland in 1897. A star alumnus of the English-language and naturalization classes at HIRAM HOUSE, he graduated from Western Reserve University Law School with the LL.B. degree and was admitted to the Ohio bar in June 1902. Appointed assistant police prosecutor and assistant solicitor to NEWTON D. BAKER in May 1903, Levine targeted unemployment offices that bled foreigners seeking their first jobs of a large portion of their wages. Very much aware of the necessity for immigrants to learn

English, he returned to Hiram House to teach evening naturalization and English classes. Levine was elected police judge in 1908, municipal judge in 1911, and common pleas court judge in 1914, with reelection in 1920. In 1923, he became a judge on the Ohio Court of Appeals. Twice he was selected by his fellow Ohio jurists to serve as the chief justice of the appeals court. As a judge, Levine displayed understanding, great sympathy, and empathy for those in distress. His philosophy was to place human rights above property rights, and he sought to guard the individual against any unlawful intrusions. Levine seldom hesitated to strike out against social conditions that he saw as breeding grounds for CRIME. He instituted the Domestic Relations Bureau in common pleas court, established the state's first probation department, and pioneered in court-sponsored domestic conciliation efforts. Levine was married to Jessie Bialosky. The Levines had 3 children, Robt. M., Alfred D., and Mitzi.

Manuel Levine Papers, WRHS.

**LEVY, DARRYL ALLEN [d.a. levy]** (29 Oct. 1942–24 Nov. 1968), was a native Cleveland poet well known within the national counterculture of the 1960s. His poetry and other publications celebrated free expression and attacked social injustice and repression. Levy was a prolific poet whose work was widely published by the small presses of the counterculture. He was also a painter and a printer, publishing Cleveland's first underground newspaper, the *Buddhist Third Class Junkmail Oracle* (see UNDERGROUND PRESS). Locally, Levy gained notoriety less for his poetry than for his role in bringing the counterculture to Cleveland and his subsequent confrontations with police. His journal *Marijuana Quarterly* advocated the legalization of marijuana and was one reason narcotics agents raided Jas. Lowell's Asphodel Bookstore, which sold the journal, on 1 Dec. 1966. In Nov. 1966, a grand jury indicted Levy on charges of obscenity. On 28 Mar. 1967, he was arrested and charged with contributing to the delinquency of a minor during a poetry reading on 15 Nov. 1966. His arrest attracted much local publicity, and his supporters distributed "legalize levy" buttons and stickers. Afraid of going to jail, Levy pleaded no contest to the latter charge in return for probation and dismissal of the obscenity charge. The legal battle left him angry, increasingly paranoid, and despondent. His arrest made him a media star but deepened his disillusionment with society, which he attacked as fascist. After arguing with his companion, Dagmar Ferek, and burning much of his poetry, Levy committed suicide on 24 Nov. 1968. Stunned by his death, Levy's friends paid tribute to him by continuing his newspaper and publishing his remaining poetry periodically through 1976.

**LEVY AND STEARN** was the company from which was created Lane Bryant, Inc., the nation's foremost retailer of women's special-size apparel. Levy & Stearn was established in 1862 when Isaac Levy and Abraham Stearn opened a toy and novelty store on Superior Ave. near W. 9th St. Business grew rapidly, and it became the leading toy store in the region. In 1895, Levy left the firm; it then became known as Stearn & Co. and moved to a new store on Euclid Ave. By this time, it was both a retail and a wholesale business, and that year it introduced women's clothing. In 1914, the firm was incorporated as the Stearn Co. and moved to larger quarters at 1021 Euclid Ave. Stearn dropped its wholesale furniture and novelty departments and specialized in women's apparel and toys. By 1936, it dealt solely in women's clothing.

In 1946, Stearn was purchased by the Lane Bryant Co. of New York. Founded in 1900 by Lena H. Bryant, Lane Bryant was a pioneer in maternity and other special-size clothing for women. Stearn retained its name until 1950, when Lane Bryant completely absorbed it as its 10th branch store with about 250 employees. In 1965, the company moved its Cleveland downtown store into the renovated Taylor Bldg. (see WM. TAYLOR SON & CO.) at 696 Euclid Ave. By 1970, it had 8 stores in the Cleveland area. In the 1970s, Lane Bryant continued to expand nationally and locally, remodeling many of its Cleveland stores. However, its profits remained unchanged, and in 1982, the $370 million business was sold to a smaller firm, The Limited, Inc., of Columbus. After some organizational changes, Lane Bryant continued to operate as a division of The Limited with 4 stores in Cleveland. In 1983, Lane Bryant's downtown store became part of the corporation's new Sizes Unlimited, a chain of off-price stores for large women.

Mahoney, Tom, *Fifty Years of Lane Bryant* (1951).

**LEWIS, FRANKLIN ALLAN "WHITEY"** (18 Jan. 1904–12 Mar. 1958), was the sports editor of the *CLEVELAND PRESS* from 1939-58. He used his popular column to promote the interests of the ordinary sports fan. Lewis was born in Lafayette, Ind., but grew up on Cleveland's east side. He was a pool-playing partner of Bob Hope. A star athlete at Glenville High School, Lewis was an All-Senate halfback in football. He peddled ice in the summer and was the catcher for the Edelweiss Cream Cheese sandlot baseball team. After 1 year at Purdue University, Lewis moved to Florida, where he wrote for several newspapers. Leaving the Orlando *Reporter-Star* in 1929, he returned to Cleveland to be the boxing writer and assistant sports editor of the *Press*. Lewis left the *Press* in 1937 and worked for 2 years as a sportscaster at radio station WGAR, but he then was rehired at the *Press* as a sports columnist and editor. He wrote in the language of the typical fans, whom he called "Joes and Josephines." Two of his strongest campaigns were to build a baseball fence in the Municipal Stadium to make more home runs possible and to clean up the lakefront for more recreational use by the public. Lewis worked to keep the sports of boxing and horse racing honest in order to protect the ordinary sports fan who placed bets on the events.

Interested in finding out what average fans thought, Lewis watched baseball games from the bleachers. In 1945 he toured the Pacific war zones to inform servicemen from northeast Ohio what was going on in the sports world. His one book, *The Cleveland Indians*, published in 1949, the year after the team won the world championship, turned out to be a bestseller at $3 a copy. Earlier in the 1930s, he had written and published several popular songs. A person of great wit, Lewis placed trivia items in his column under the "Department of Agate Type." He was in great demand as a public speaker and master of ceremonies. Lewis was a member of the U.S. Attorney General Commission to Combat Juvenile Delinquency. He was at Tucson, Ariz., covering the Indians' spring training in 1958 when he died of a heart attack. He had married Helen Virginia Palmer on 8 Dec. 1939. The couple had no children.

Lewis, Franklin, *The Cleveland Indians* (1949).

**LEWIS RESEARCH CENTER.** *See* **NASA LEWIS RESEARCH CENTER**

The **LEZIUS HILES COMPANY** was a century-old commercial printing firm built by merger to regional promi-

nence. The company was started in 1888 as the Forest City Printing House with $600 capital and was located on Champlain St. near the present site of the Terminal Tower. In 1914, it was incorporated as the Lezius Printing Co., and in 1919 it bought out the Hiles & Coggshall Co., a small general printing firm started in 1883. The newly formed Lezius Hiles Co. Then acquired the Premier Co., a direct-mail advertising firm, thus becoming one of the top commercial firms in the city. The growth and new directions of the firm necessitated a bond issue in 1929 to buy more equipment and provide working capital—the first outside capital put into it. For many years the company was located on Rockwell; it then moved to E. 61st St. and Chester. It was strengthened by further acquisitions. In subsequent decades, the company developed an impressive reputation as a family-owned printing house that specialized in annual reports, catalogs, manuals, directories, and literature. The Lezius family sold its interest in 1977, while retaining a consulting role. Brought to bankruptcy by its management, it was sold again in 1986 to 3 investors, including John Arcuri, owner of Pioneer Business Forms in Wickliffe, and closed, putting 60 people out of work.

**LIBERTY ROW** is a stretch of oak trees, extending from Gordon, Rockefeller, and Ambler through Shaker Hts. Park, dedicated to local soldiers who died in WORLD WAR I. The Liberty Row trees were dedicated on Memorial Day 1919. Dedication plaques were located in front of each tree along the row, and for a time each tree was decorated by a small American flag each Memorial Day thereafter until the vandalism of the 1960s–1980s made that impractical.

Monuments File, Cleveland City Hall Library.

**LIBRARIES, ARCHIVES, AND HISTORICAL SOCIETIES.** In America, a variety of institutions collect, preserve, and disseminate recorded knowledge and information. Among these are libraries, historical agencies, and archives. In general, the development of these institutions in northeast Ohio has followed patterns experienced in other communities throughout the Old Northwest Territory. There are some differences, in part dictated by Cleveland's location, population trends, wealth, and good fortune in having creative men and women exerting their talents in these fields. During the first 70 years of its existence, Cleveland's libraries and historical societies offered little to indicate the national preeminence they would achieve in the 20th century. A variety of libraries, literary associations, and reading rooms were formed prior to the CIVIL WAR. In general, they were organized as stock companies or subscription libraries wherein members paid fees to belong. After initial bursts of enthusiasm, hard economic times or a lack of interest contributed to their demise. Only one, the CLEVELAND LIBRARY ASSOC. (f. 1848), left a lineal descendant that existed in the 1980s.

Of necessity, Cleveland's early residents focused their energies on surviving the environment and settling the land. Relatively little is known about their reading ability and habits. It is believed that only a few brought books with them. If anything, reading matter consisted of almanacs, home remedy and legal guides, farming manuals, and, when they could be obtained, newspapers. The first formal attempt to establish a library occurred in 1811, when 16 of Cleveland's 18 families joined to form the Cleveland Library Assoc. It lasted for approximately 2 years, a victim of the turmoil fomented by the WAR OF 1812. These were difficult times for many institutions. Cleveland's first newspaper, established in 1818, lasted only 2 years. In the 1820s, several state and national movements focused, in part, on the establishment of libraries. Interest in public education was growing. Calvin E. Stowe, Ohio disciple of Horace Mann, crusaded for the establishment of tax-supported schools and public libraries. Beginning in 1826, the American Lyceum Movement supported the development of libraries, in addition to lyceums, to provide intellectual stimulation and improvement through courses based on reading and discussion. More bookstores came into existence. They handled whatever the printing presses of the day produced—remedy books, almanacs, political and religious tracts, and, to a lesser extent, literary works. Despite these developments, the growing village of Cleveland took a back seat to neighboring communities in the area of library development. Through the efforts of 2 community-minded individuals, libraries were established in NEWBURGH and N. OLMSTED. In 1827, the Newburgh Library Society was founded, largely through the efforts of Daniel Miles. Its members paid an initiation fee and annual dues until the 1870s when the library's books were divided up among its members. Chas. H. Olmstead had a library of some 500 volumes, which in 1829 he offered to the community of Kingston (later Lenox) if the village would rename itself in honor of his father, Aaron Olmstead, an original shareholder of the CONNECTICUT LAND CO. Although some volumes were lost in transit from the East, the collection of books was probably the largest in Greater Cleveland at that time.

During the 1830s, Cleveland became a city. The canal, which had recently opened, brought people and goods, problems and opportunities. The increasing number of young people in the community stirred enterprising individuals to establish private schools. Practical training was emphasized, especially reading, penmanship, and bookkeeping. Young men, in particular, were the target of a variety of book-oriented associations that came into being in the mid-1830s. Members of the CLEVELAND LYCEUM gathered to hear lectures and exchange books and periodical literature. The Cleveland Library Co. operated for the benefit of its subscribers. Periodicals and newspapers were available to the members of the Cleveland Reading Room Assoc., whose facilities were open to members on a daily basis. The library of the YOUNG MEN'S LITERARY ASSOC. consisted of some 800 volumes. BLACKS, who constituted only a small percentage of the population, formed the Colored Men's Union Society, and could boast of a library of 100 volumes. By 1838, attempts to merge several of these failed, and none survived the 1840s, except the Young Men's Literary Assoc. In 1848, members of that association incorporated under the name the Cleveland Library Assoc. Although continuing its sponsorship of lectures, the association put more emphasis on the collection and dissemination of books for the benefit and use of its members. Among the leaders of this association were WM. CASE and CHAS. WHITTLESEY. Case, active in the city's cultural life since the 1830s, was the moving force behind the Arkites, an informal association of men interested in natural history and collecting specimens.

Whittlesey was one of the first residents to manifest an interest in collecting and preserving letters, diaries, maps, and other documents describing the experiences of the early settlers in Cleveland and the WESTERN RESERVE. A scholar and prolific writer on archeological and geological subjects, he published many of the documents he collected in his *Early History of Cleveland* (1867). Whittlesey also paid tribute to Judge John Barr, prominent Cleveland lawyer and jurist and former officer of the Cleveland Lyceum, who had begun collecting reminiscences from early residents of the city in the early 1840s. Barr corresponded with these principals, and in some instances their descendants,

gathering information relating to the period of exploration and settlement of northeast Ohio. By 1846, Barr, proud of the growth of Cleveland and optimistic about its future, published a short history of the city in *Fisher's National Magazine*. Despite the efforts and interests of Barr and Whittlesey in preserving original records and manuscripts, the pursuit of this objective was not the stated mission of any established institution. Preserving the records generated by the city and county governments was considered the responsibility of officeholders. The focus of libraries in the 1850s continued to be on printed books and lectures. The collection of the Bethel Reading Room was open to the public 2 evenings a week, and the Mercantile Library Assoc. offered a platform for the most prominent public speakers of the day. In 1854, the YOUNG MEN'S CHRISTIAN ASSOC. was organized to include a circulating library.

Prior to the Civil War, libraries were essentially one of many participatory pastimes available to the citizenry. Lectures, political speeches, and public meetings were the entertainment of the day. Privately funded libraries were gathering places where one could spend an evening discussing current events and issues. Educators, however, increasingly recognized books as essential in the process of disseminating knowledge. An 1853 state law provided tax funds for the purchase of books for school libraries. It was not, however, until after the Civil War that the city developed the institutions, both private and public, that could provide for the administration of library and archival collections for the public use on a wide-scale basis. The first public libraries in the U.S. were established in New England cities, beginning in Salisbury, Conn., in 1803. The first major city to have a public library was Boston, in 1852. Fifteen years later, an act of the Ohio legislature empowered local boards of education to establish libraries and provided financial support for these institutions from the general property tax. The Cleveland Public School Library, created by this 1867 law, did not formally open until 1869, some 16 years before the formation of the New York Public Library. The CLEVELAND PUBLIC LIBRARY's early years were characterized by controversy and financial crises as it struggled to define its mission and to gain cooperation from the community and its leaders. The year 1867 also witnessed the creation of the WESTERN RESERVE (and Northern Ohio) HISTORICAL SOCIETY as a department of the Cleveland Library Assoc. Several members of that association, steeped in the history of the Western Reserve and its Connecticut roots, felt it important that the history of this region, which was undergoing major changes, be preserved. The era of exploration was over. Increasing numbers of foreign-born were settling in Cleveland. The oil and steel industries' foothold on Cleveland was well established. Furthermore, more than 300,000 Ohioans had seen military service and more than 50,000 had died in the recently concluded Civil War.

The arrival of a tax-supported public library in the city did not stifle interest groups, which continued to sponsor special libraries to address specific social and intellectual needs. In 1870, the Cleveland Law Library was established for the benefit of its members and local government officials. Reading rooms, leisure-time alternatives to saloons, were opened by the Women's Christian Assoc. as part of its antialcohol program. The CLEVELAND MEDICAL LIBRARY ASSOC. was organized in 1894. The nucleus of its collection was the books and journals accumulated by the Cuyahoga County Medical Library over the previous decade. Most of these special libraries were organized for the benefit of their members, but most made their books available to the public. That was true of the ROWFANT CLUB, founded in 1892, an association of book lovers and collectors, whose collections were available to nonmembers by appointment. The libraries of Western Reserve College, which moved to Cleveland from Hudson, Ohio, in 1882, and the Case School of Applied Science, established in 1881, opened their reading rooms to the public.

The profession of library science considers the formation of the American Library Assoc. in 1876 as crucial in its history; in Cleveland, the year 1884 and the appointment of WM. H. BRETT as director are pivotal. Under Brett's leadership for the next 34 years, the library moved to the forefront of public libraries in America. Emphasis was placed on proper training of librarians. In addition, Brett embraced the concept of easy access to books by the public, which was manifest in the development of a network of branch and school libraries with comfortable surroundings and special accommodations for children. Operationally, the application of a decimal classification system permitted better control of a rapidly growing collection, which by 1900 consisted of more than 100,000 volumes and annually circulated more than 600,000 items. At century's end, the public library was poised for even more dramatic growth. A critical need was a permanent home, the library having occupied a succession of rented spaces in a variety of buildings, which included the Board of Education Bldg. and City Hall. The 4 branches that had been established were a beginning, but they, too, were in rented spaces, and their numbers were inadequate to serve all corners of the city, whose population was 381,000 in 1900. Among these residents were the many foreign-born and their children who looked to the library not only as a social center but also as a place to improve language skills and to learn more about their new homeland. During the 3 decades of its existence, the WRHS had accumulated significant collections of books, manuscripts, newspapers, and maps documenting the early history and settlement of northern Ohio. In 1892, the society ceased operating as a branch of the Cleveland Library Assoc. when its officers petitioned for and received a charter from the state of Ohio. In 1898, the WRHS exchanged its quarters on PUBLIC SQUARE for a newly constructed building on EUCLID AVE. at the western border of the UNIVERSITY CIRCLE area. Like the public library, the society was positioned to play an expanding role in preserving the heritage of the area.

In spite of the increasing resources committed to libraries and the efforts of private institutions, such as the historical society, an important aspect of local history was ignored. No effective plan was yet developed for the preservation of local government records. As early as 1836, CLEVELAND CITY COUNCIL addressed the importance of local records when it appointed a committee to obtain records from the former trustees of the village of Cleveland. Periodically thereafter, city officials bemoaned the lack of adequate storage facilities for the city's records, which continued to be the responsibility of individual department heads. In 1876, the city hall was moved to the Case Bldg., where a fireproof vault provided temporary protection for some city archives. This lack of attention to local historical documents was not unique. Few states took any steps to provide for the care of archives. In Ohio, the state historical society, founded in 1885, was more concerned with Indian relics and lore than with the voluminous documents produced by state agencies and local governments. Furthermore, most historians did not consider the study of local history to be a worthy endeavor. Great men, such as presidents and generals, war, foreign relations, and national politics commanded the attention of the academic community. Ironically, in a democratic society, where the public's access to the records of their government officials is crucial, government records were generally ignored.

The first quarter of the 20th century witnessed substantial growth and innovation for Cleveland libraries. Andrew Carnegie finally relented to years of solicitation by Brett and in 1904 provided a $100,000 endowment fund to initiate the Library School of Western Reserve University, the 4th school of library science established in the U.S. Several municipalities opened public libraries, including LAKEWOOD and E. CLEVELAND in 1916 and BAY VILLAGE, CHAGRIN FALLS, and CLEVELAND HTS. in 1921. The first special libraries sponsored by individual firms were established in 1912 by the *CLEVELAND PRESS*, the accounting firm of Nau, Rusk & Van Sweringen, and the Statler Hotel, whose collection was for the benefit of its guests. These were followed by libraries at the clothing firm of JOSEPH & FEISS (1913), the Federal Reserve Bank (1918), the WHITE MOTOR CO. (1918), the CLEVELAND CLINIC FOUNDATION (1921), and the CLEVELAND MUSEUM OF NATURAL HISTORY (1921). Numerous other public and private secondary schools and medical and educational institutions formed libraries. Nationally, in response to the rapid growth of libraries in museums, businesses, and financial institutions, the Special Libraries Assoc. was founded in 1909. By 1925, its published directory listed 975 special libraries in the U.S. Ohio ranked 6th among the states with 54 such libraries, 17 of which were in Cleveland. Despite the increasing number of libraries in Cuyahoga County, not all communities were served. In 1921, a state law authorized the formation of county library systems. A year later, residents of Cuyahoga County voted approval to such a system, the first in the state. Until 1942, the CUYAHOGA COUNTY PUBLIC LIBRARY had its headquarters in the Cleveland Public Library building.

In 1916, Cleveland's government offices moved into the new city hall, one of the buildings in the renowned Group Plan. The joy felt by those who welcomed the spacious quarters allotted for records storage waned in less than 2 decades as expanding staff levels relegated the records to the subbasement. The CPL also welcomed its new Group Plan building, which opened in 1925. With shelving capacity for 2 million books, a series of separate reading rooms, and a variety of provisions for special collections, the blind, and children, the magnificent building was, among other things, a manifestation of the high esteem in which the library was held, both locally and nationally. While Brett, his successor, LINDA EASTMAN, and board president JOHN G. WHITE led the CPL during its most expansive era, WALLACE H. CATHCART, director, and WM. P. PALMER, president, greatly enhanced the holdings and reputation of the WRHS during the 1910s and 1920s, a golden era for library collecting. The collections they amassed and those they solicited from wealthy Clevelanders provided the substantial basis on which the society's library and archival programs of the 1960s and later depend.

The Depression had a sobering effect on the city's libraries and cultural institutions. Most suffered serious reductions in financial support and staffing. In 1933, the source of funds for Ohio's public libraries was changed from the property tax to the newly created intangible property tax. That was no panacea, however, as revenues remained low in the face of increasing costs for books and services. Nevertheless, the public library, with its 69 branches and 2-million-volume collection, continued to lead the nation in per capita circulation. One highlight during these otherwise bleak years was the "discovery" of the city's and the county's government records. Under the sponsorship of the public library, employees of the WPA began in 1935 to inventory the records of Cuyahoga County as part of a statewide project. Teams of historians, teachers, and other professionals combed county offices and buildings to locate and describe records. Their inventories were condensed and published in 1937 in 2 volumes, which also contained a recommendation for the establishment of a central department of records to assure their preservation and accessibility by the public. Unfortunately, nearly 4 decades passed before the county government moved in this direction. A similar program was undertaken for the state's municipalities by the Historical Records Survey program of the WPA. The inventories of Cleveland's records were issued in 5 volumes over the years 1939–42. The workers found many records in poor storage conditions; City Hall was overcrowded and lacked sufficient space for the old records, let alone for the records that were being created by a government whose population was approaching 1 million. One small step to address this problem was taken in 1941, when a local ordinance required that copies of every printed city report and document be deposited in the Municipal Reference Library, a branch of the CPL at City Hall. No provisions were made for the voluminous unpublished records that are basic in the operation of the city and invaluable for historical research. Beginning in the 1970s, certain city records, particularly the surviving office files of mayors back to TOM L. JOHNSON, were transferred to the WRHS. In 1978, a city council ordinance created a city records commission to review records disposal.

The post-World War II years saw a substantial increase in the number of local historical agencies. In suburban communities, that was most evident as historical societies were established in Chagrin Falls (1946), SHAKER HTS. (1947), GATES MILLS (1948), Lakewood (1952), BEDFORD (1955), EUCLID (1958), STRONGSVILLE (1964), and ROCKY RIVER (1968), among others. Stimulated by community pride, each, in varying degrees, took steps to preserve records, papers, photographs, and other materials of a historical nature. Beginning in the late 1960s, the WRHS expanded its collecting policy to include urban, black, ethnic, Jewish, architectural, and labor history—all topics that were increasingly pursued by academic researchers as well as social and city planners. The success of these programs coupled with the growing community awareness of and support for these efforts culminated in the construction in 1983–84 of a modern library building with the necessary environmental controls to assure the preservation of these unique and irreplaceable collections. In 1959, a state law gave the Ohio Historical Society the responsibility for administering the records of Ohio's counties and municipalities. However, the state did not provide the funding to implement a records program until 1974. Field representatives began working in each of the 8 regions defined by the Ohio Network of American Research Ctrs., created in 1970 to provide a framework for the preservation of historically important government records, manuscript collections, newspapers, and audio/visual materials. In 1975, Cuyahoga County formed its own archives department to develop and implement retention and disposal procedures for its records.

The increasing attention to records was not limited to local governments. In 1974, the Society of Ohio Archivists, founded in 1968 as a professional association for archivists and manuscript curators, identified 953 manuscript repositories and institutional archives in the state. The 111 agencies listed in Cuyahoga County ranged from colleges and museums to banks, churches, businesses, newspapers, and professional associations. In the 1960s, genealogy became fashionable nationally as an increasing number of people took up the study of family history, which involves the use of local, as well as federal government, records. Some credit Alex Haley's *Roots* (1976) for stimulating this interest. In Ohio, the movement was evident years earlier. The Ohio Genealogical Society, with 6 chapters in the Greater Cleveland area by 1983, was founded in 1959.

The population decline in the city of Cleveland and the racial strife that surfaced in the mid-1960s affected Cleveland's libraries. The dramatic growth of personnel and facilities over the years left the CPL with little-used branches and operating expenses that threatened to exceed its annual income. Bold steps were taken to effect economies by closing some branches and bringing operating expenses into line by reducing the professional staff and other operating expenses. Of all the steps taken to streamline and modernize the operation of the library, none was more profound than the adoption of automation. In 1980, the CPL moved boldly into the computer age when it began to implement a systemwide on-line computerized catalog. By late 1983, the 975,000 bibliographic records that had been entered on-line at a cost of approximately $4 million were accessible to patrons and staff via terminals at the main library as well as at the 31 neighborhood branches. It was one of the first major public libraries in the U.S. to do so, thus providing a model system from which others could learn. Testimony to its success is the fact that by 1985, several other library systems, including those in Cleveland Hts.-University Hts., Shaker Hts., Euclid, Willoughby-Eastlake, and in Lorain, Medina, and Wayne counties tied into its on-line computer.

The growth of competing library systems in the Greater Cleveland area resulted in a duplication of services, as well as increased competition for tax support. The Library Council of Greater Cleveland, founded in 1969 and composed of directors of 16 library systems, explored areas in which libraries could cooperate. In 1975, the Cleveland Area Metropolitan Library System (CAMLS), an agency that grew to include 43 member institutions with 131 outlets and combined holdings of 7.4 million volumes by 1986, was established. It has published a variety of guides, directories, and lists to selected collections in the area, as well as facilitates a library loan among its members. Since the 1940s, consolidation of the independent public library systems has been a principal issue in Cuyahoga County. Institutional studies, community leaders, and some library officials have periodically called for merger and thus elimination of the apparent costly duplication of services. By 1952, 5 suburban systems did merge with the county library, but 9 continued to operate independently. In the absence of such a total merger, the competition heated among these systems for the intangible property tax and, after 1984, for the income tax proceeds that replaced the intangibles tax as the principal source of library funding. Into the mid-1980s, the Cuyahoga County Public Library, emphasizing the larger geographic area and population base it serves through its 26 branches, clung to its autonomy, as did the CPL. The failure to effect a merger, however, does not diminish the fact that residents of the Greater Cleveland area have access to a plethora of excellent library institutions and comprehensive collections for recreational and scholarly purposes.

Kermit J. Pike
Western Reserve Historical Society

**LIFE SAVERS,** the brightly colored ring-shaped candies, were developed by Cleveland chocolate manufacturer Clarence A. Crane, father of poet HART CRANE. The son of the owner of a successful maple-sugar cannery in Garrettsville, Ohio, Clarence Crane began making and selling chocolate candy in Cleveland in Apr. 1911. In 1912 he introduced "Crane's Peppermint Life Savers," which he hoped would bolster the usually slow sales of his chocolates during the summer. In 1913 he sold his Life Saver business and trademark for $2,900 to 2 New York businessmen, Edward J. Noble and J. Roy Allen, who formed the Mint Prods. Co. to market the peppermint candies Crane supplied. But Crane shipped the candies in cardboard tubes, which absorbed their flavor, and business was poor until Noble designed a new foil package. By 1915, Noble and Allen were producing Life Savers themselves and no longer used Crane as a supplier. Crane thus introduced Life Savers but did not benefit from their later success. His chocolate business, however, continued to expand. The Crane Chocolate Co. was incorporated in 1916, and by 1921 it had sales outlets in New York and Kansas City. Called "a near genius in business affairs" by one biographer, Crane embarked upon several other business ventures before his death on 6 July 1931.

**LINCOLN, ABRAHAM.** *See* **ABRAHAM LINCOLN'S VISIT TO CLEVELAND**

**LINCOLN, JAMES F.** (14 May 1883–23 June 1965), the head of the LINCOLN ELECTRIC CO. from 1914 until his death, was influential in promoting the arc-welding industry and was responsible for developing Lincoln Electric's famous incentive bonus system. He was also an outspoken critic of government intervention in business and industry and of the conduct of American foreign affairs during World War II and the cold war. Lincoln was born on a farm near Painesville, Ohio, the son of an English immigrant Congregationalist minister. Educated in the public schools in Painesville, he entered Ohio State University in 1902; there he studied electrical engineering and was captain of the undefeated football team in his senior year. Typhoid fever forced him to leave school without a degree in 1907, but he was awarded his degree in 1926. On 1 Apr. 1907, Lincoln joined his older brother John's Lincoln Electric Co. as a salesman. He became general manager when his brother retired in 1914, and served as president from 1928–54, when he became chairman of the board. An inventor himself, Lincoln received 20 patents; his training as an engineer enabled him to make the technological improvements necessary for arc welding to become a dependable and commercially viable process of joining metals.

Lincoln was much in the public eye in the early 1940s. He was a staunch defender of individualism and a harsh critic of the New Deal. During WORLD WAR II, the Lincoln Electric Co.'s incentive bonus payments from government war contracts raised the suspicions of government officials; in May 1942, the company's profits and incentive plan were investigated by the House Naval Affairs Committee, and in 1943 the Price Adjustment Board ordered Lincoln to return $3.25 million, which the board claimed was excessive profits from the war. Jas. Lincoln fought the charge, defended the incentive payments, and challenged the process by which wartime contracts were renegotiated. The Treasury Dept. later charged the company with tax evasion, as well; Lincoln was acquitted of all charges, however. Jas. Lincoln was a prolific author, writing numerous letters to the editor, pamphlets on political and social issues, and 3 books on industrial economics and the Lincoln incentive plan. He was also active in Republican politics, business and professional organizations, and higher education. He served on the Governor's Committee on Unemployment Insurance in 1932 and was elected president of the Cleveland Chamber of Commerce in 1942 and 1943.

He was a trustee of the Council of Profit Sharing Industries, a director of the Natl. Assoc. of Mfrs., and president of the Natl. Electrical Mfrs. Assoc. He also served as a trustee of the Cleveland Hearing & Speech Ctr. and of Ohio State University, Lake Erie College, Case Institute of Technology, Fenn College, and the Ohio Foundation of Independent Colleges. Lincoln was married in 1908 to Alice Patterson, who died in 1954. In 1961 he married Jane White, the dean of Lake Erie College.

James F. Lincoln Papers, WRHS.

The **LINCOLN ELECTRIC COMPANY,** established in 1895 to manufacture industrial motors and dynamos, began to manufacture welding machines in 1909 and became a pioneer in the development of the arc-welding industry. Under the direction of JAS. F. LINCOLN, it also developed a famous incentive system designed to induce employees to be more productive and efficient. John C. Lincoln (17 July 1866–24 May 1959), a Painesville, Ohio, native who studied electrical engineering at Ohio State University, founded Lincoln Electric to manufacture a motor of his own design. He patented the motor in 1895 and opened a shop at Frankfort and Seneca (W. 3rd) streets. On 9 June 1906, with 20 employees and $10,000 in capital, he incorporated the Lincoln Electric Co. The firm changed locations as it grew: after several locations, it moved to E. 38th St. and Kelley Ave. in 1908, then in 1923 to Coit Rd. and Kirby Ave., and again in 1951 to a new facility at 22801 St. Clair Ave. in EUCLID. The company experienced major changes in its operations in the 1910s. Jas. F. Lincoln, the founder's brother and a company salesman, became general manager in 1914 and was influential in promoting the welding industry. The need to repair Navy vessels during WORLD WAR I led to an expansion in the welding industry, and the manufacture of welding machines became a more substantial portion of Lincoln Electric's business. The company actively promoted the industry, establishing a welding school in 1917, publishing instructional technical materials, and later producing visual aids. In 1936 the firm established the Jas. F. Lincoln Arc Welding Foundation to promote scientific interest in and study of the welding industry.

Jas. Lincoln was also influential in developing a harmonious relationship between management and labor. In 1914 he established an advisory board of department representatives, with whom he met regularly and from whom he solicited suggestions. The company began offering its employees free life insurance in 1915 and paid vacations in 1923; the most efficient workers could buy stock in the company beginning in 1928; in 1935, cash bonuses were offered for useful efficiency suggestions; and in 1936, a pension fund was established. The most famous element of Lincoln's incentive plan, however, was its incentive bonus, instituted in 1934. With $4 million in sales in 1934, the company paid $131,800 in bonuses; in 1981, Lincoln's 2,684 employees shared a record $59 million in bonuses, an average of $22,008 per recipient. Another element of the Lincoln plan is the guaranteed-employment program begun in 1958. The company guarantees jobs for its workers, while the employees agree to accept necessary job and schedule changes. Lincoln has not laid off any employee since 1949. During the recession of the early 1980s, officials of the nonunion company were so convinced of the value of their labor-management system that early in 1983 they held a seminar to promote the Lincoln plan as one means to revive industrial America by lowering production costs, increasing worker productivity and efficiency, and improving product quality.

James F. Lincoln Papers, WRHS.
Moley, Raymond, *The American Century of John C. Lincoln* (1962).

**LINCOLN PARK** is a small, rectangular public park located between W. 11th and W. 14th streets and Kenilworth and Starkweather avenues in the TREMONT section of Cleveland. In 1850, Mrs. Thirsa Pelton purchased about 70 acres on Cleveland's south side with the idea of founding a girl's school. She died in 1853, and the school was never built. Mrs. Pelton's heirs surrounded "Pelton Park," as it was called, with a high fence and locked the gates. Local residents, however, had come to regard the park as a public recreation ground and repeatedly tore the fence down. The trouble stemmed from a map of the property filed in the courthouse in 1851. On it was a notation indicating that Pelton Park "is occupied as a pleasure ground and is to be so kept and used forever." That note paved the way for litigation and riot.

In 1868, the city council's committee on judiciary studied the problem and submitted a report declaring the park to be "under private control but yet a public playground." Bitter litigation followed, and the courts twice held that the park was wholly private. Feeling in the south side neighborhood ran high until, in 1879, the city finally purchased the property from John G. Jennings for $50,000. The house in the park and the fence around it were removed, trees were planted, and walks were laid. Bids for an "Oratorium" were awarded. Residents celebrated the opening of the park on 4 July 1880 with a barbecue. By 1896, the park had deteriorated and was restored with new walks, a fountain, and a music stand. A bicycle path was built, and the park was renamed Lincoln Square, later Lincoln Park. In 1913, brewer Otto I. Leisy donated $50,000 to the city to build a playground in the park, and in 1936 Lincoln Park was graded and landscaped under a WPA project. In the early 1950s, a swimming pool was installed on the grounds, and in 1981 a new "tot lot" was built. Even with these later additions, however, Lincoln Park retains the ambience of its early years because of its many beautiful mature trees.

The **LINDSAY WIRE WEAVING COMPANY** became one of the country's leading manufacturers of paper-mill wire cloth. It was established when Hamilton L. Lindsay, a mechanic at the wire-screening concern of the W. S. Tyler Co., invented an automatic power loom for weaving metal. Realizing the potential for his machine to revolutionize the papermaking process, Lindsay quickly secured a patent; and with the financial backing of ALEXANDER WINTON, Thos. Henderson, and Geo. H. Brown, he organized the Lindsay Wire Weaving Co. in 1903. Starting with only 6 employees at a plant at Aspinwall Ave. and E. 140th St., the company was an immediate success, selling $50,000 worth of wire cloth in its first year. Much of Lindsay's success was based on emphasis on research: constantly improving the wiremaking looms to meet the paper industry's needs for quality and efficiency.

To meet the demand for improved wire cloth, especially during WORLD WAR II, the company, under A. Fred Crossman, expanded its plant in the 1930s and 1940s. By 1951, it produced record sales of $5 million and employed over 300 people. Its wire cloth was also being used by the machine-tool, electronic, and communication industries. Under Crossman's sons, Fred and Robert, Lindsay continued to grow with the paper industry in the 1950s and 1960s. In 1957, the company built a branch plant in Mentor, and 5 years later, a new research laboratory in Cleveland. However, during this period papermaking technology changed as plastic cloth gradually replaced metal cloth. Lindsay

opened a plant in Mississippi in the early 1970s to adapt to this change. Since the Cleveland plant made only wire cloth, the company started to phase out its production. Finally, in 1978, the Crossmans sold their declining business to SW Industries, Inc., of Rhode Island, a North American subsidiary of a diversified British firm, BTR, Ltd.

**LINNDALE** is an incorporated village southwest of Cleveland and adjacent to BROOKLYN at the intersection of Memphis Ave. and Bellaire Rd. It occupies an area 6 blocks long and 2 blocks wide. At the end of the 19th century, Geo. Linn, a real-estate developer, sought independent status for the community, a part of Brooklyn Twp. He conducted official business in his home, and Linndale was incorporated in 1902. Located on the main line of the Cleveland, Columbus, Cincinnati & St. Louis Railroad, Linndale prospered briefly as a railroad town. During Prohibition it was a notorious gambling district. When the CLEVELAND UNION TERMINAL opened in 1930, Linndale was the western station where trains changed their steam locomotives for electric engines before entering the city. After WORLD WAR II, the use of diesel engines made the locomotive switchyards obsolete. With the construction of I–71 through the village, Linndale gained the reputation of making traffic fines its primary source of income by strictly enforcing the I–71 speed limit. In the 1980s, Linndale remained a small residential community. Operating under the mayor-council form of government, it had its own town hall and police, but contracted with Cleveland for fire protection and was part of the Cleveland City School District. There were no parks, recreational facilities, or commercial areas within the village limits. In 1985 the population was 129.

The **LION KNITTING MILLS** is one of a handful of knitting mills surviving in Cleveland, once the largest knitting center in the U.S. Founded in 1912 by Louis and Harold Ensten at the Whitney Power Block, the company produces sweaters, afghans, lap rugs, and throws for the private-label market. Lion's first product, the varsity or award-letter sweater, was knitted on hand-operated machines. By WORLD WAR I, the company had installed belt-activated flat-bed knitting machines. Lion did experimental work for the Quartermaster's Corp. and produced, on its new machines, a 100% wool watchcap, which soon became a regular issue for the U.S. Navy. When a machine malfunction produced a piece of jagged cloth, it was sewn together as a winter sports cap; patented and copyrighted under the name "Ace," it became part of the official uniform of the U.S. skating and bobsled teams. It became the largest-selling knitted cap in America and was exclusively produced by Lion until the patent expired in 1939.

To capitalize on the large skilled immigrant labor force living on the near west side, Lion moved to 3256 W. 25th St. near Meyer Ave. when it needed more room in 1921. It then added seamless circular machines to permit machine production of sweaters and other garments. The company's business expanded, and it survived the Depression by expanding its product line to include dog sweaters, which it sold through Sears. Based on the company's contribution to World War I and its work in outfitting the Byrd Antarctic expedition in 1932, Harold Ensten was called to Washington to review and create new items of combat knitwear. Among the Lion garments that became part of the armed forces' wardrobe were the wool knit cap, worn under the battle helmet, and the "fatigue sweater," made in a different color for each branch of service. During WORLD WAR II, Lion devoted 98% of its production to military orders and operated 3 shifts 6 days a week to produce 2 million of the 26 million sweaters made for the military. In 1948, Lion modernized its plant with newly designed circular knitting machines that could knit individual sweaters to size without seams, and with 110 machines, it operated the largest battery in the U.S. It also added washing and processing equipment that was new to the country so it could produce luxury sweaters of 100% cashmere, cashmere-wool blends, 100% lambswool, and 100% vicuna, which were previously produced in England and Scotland.

For 2 decades, Lion distributed its line to wholesalers, who sold the garments under high-quality brand names. By 1965 it was threatened by the importation of knitted garments from the Far East. Lion joined in calling for tariffs and quotas to compete against the foreign garments. It remained successful, however, by converting production to sweaters of 100% domestically grown cotton. When the new line was met with skepticism by its distributors, Lion bypassed them and began selling directly to specialty and department stores and mail-order houses. Continued foreign competition caused Lion to retool the mill with computer-controlled machines. In 1982, it set up a new division, North Bay Comfort Prods., which made afghans, lap robes, throws, and baby blankets. The diversified product line coupled with the increased capacity of the new machinery tripled sales in the early 1980s. The company expanded its W. 25th St. facilities for the 5th time in 30 years and built a new distribution center in STRONGSVILLE.

For 7 decades, the company remained a private corporation, held in 1985 by the Hibshman family. James and Norbert Hibshman, who came to Lion in 1932 and 1933 as coal stokers, acquired an interest in the company by 1946 that culminated in ownership in 1971. Since 1979, when James retired, Norbert and his son Lawrence have held major control. In 1985, Lion had a workforce of 240 skilled workers, who since 1981 have been represented by the INTERNATL. LADIES GARMENT WORKERS. Though the union had been unsuccessful in organizing the mill for 25 years when the workforce was more homogeneous, a shift in the composition to include more Hispanics and BLACKS led to victory for the ILGW.

**LITERARY SOCIETIES (BLACK)** were a much-favored form for social gatherings among the black middle class during the 19th century. Beginning with the Colored Young Men's Lyceum, organized ca. 1838 to discuss slavery and social justice, the city has hosted a large number of additional private and church-sponsored societies. Typical of the church organizations were the Cleveland Literary Society, organized at SHILOH BAPTIST CHURCH in 1873; the Tawawa Literary Society, an affiliate of the National AME Church organized at ST. JOHN'S AME CHURCH in 1893; and the Mt. Zion Congregational Church Lyceum, formed in 1885. Private societies included the Ideal Literary Society, which began in 1886; the Phillis Wheatley Society, organized in 1892; and the Wide Awake and Coral Builders societies, which are known to have existed in 1894. The societies provided a forum for debate on topics of interest to black citizens, and also fostered the art of elocution, an important skill for those race members who would become politicians and interpreters of black aspirations. The societies remained popular in some churches until the mid-20th century.

**LITERATURE.** Until the 1980s, Cleveland's literary life was wholly dominated by its literary societies and bookstores. The earliest bookstore on record appears in the 1820s; 4 more emerged in the 1830s as Cleveland began to generate commercial and population growth. These stores carried the standard books of the day, mainly the older classics. The first literary society, the Newburgh Literary Society, was founded in 1826. As a result of a national "lyceum" movement, several others developed in the 1830s and 1840s. The Cleveland Reading Room Assoc., with 200 subscribers, was founded in 1835, followed in 1836 by the Young Men's Literary Assoc., which later, in 1846, was consolidated with other literary societies to form the CLEVELAND LIBRARY ASSOC. These societies, open only to men, provided members with a reading room and small library (that included magazines and newspapers) and sponsored debates and lectures.

Illustrated weeklies and quarterlies increased in availability in the late 1830s. The earliest of these to appear in Cleveland, such as the *Edinburgh Review*, primarily served a narrow readership with developed literary tastes. The curiosity aroused by CHAS. DICKENS'S VISIT TO CLEVELAND in 1842 was due more to his status as "a famous English author" than to widespread familiarity with his works. Access to literature increased in the 1840s and 1850s as more bookstores opened and the repositories of the literary societies grew. Commercial libraries also began to emerge; in 1841, Sanford & Co., booksellers, advertised a circulating library of 500. In 1850, *Harper's New Monthly Magazine* came to Cleveland, bringing the novels of Dickens and other popular authors in serial form. Bestsellers in the 1850s included travel books, Emerson's essays, works by Washington Irving, and the poems of Longfellow, Bryant, and Whittier. Yearly lecture series, sponsored by the literary societies, were probably the most valuable sources of literary culture and general information. Lecturers such as Horace Greeley and P. T. Barnum were popularly favored over more literary figures. Although Emerson's first visit in 1857 was hailed as the most significant literary event ever to happen in Cleveland, on his second visit, in 1859, one Cleveland newspaper criticized him as "not the man to talk to the people of the west about the 'Law of Success.'" Into the 20th century, regional or "western-born" authors generally enjoyed a greater personal popularity in Cleveland than their eastern counterparts.

Between 1865–1900, the importance of the literary societies declined, while that of the bookstores grew. The city's bookstores benefited from improved transportation—easier access to eastern publishing houses—and the greater affordability of books due to cheaper printing costs. The emergence of the CLEVELAND PUBLIC LIBRARY (ded. 1869) was also a factor in the city's literary development. The domination of eastern cities in publishing and in American's literary life in general deprived Cleveland, at this time, of developing as a literary center. Before the CIVIL WAR, Cincinnati, because of its earlier development and relative isolation, enjoyed a regional distinctiveness in literature. By the time Cleveland experienced comparable development, it was no longer isolated.

Between 1865–1900, Cleveland was served by 6 major bookstores, as well as small stationery shops with limited supplies of books. As Clevelanders were largely dependent on the recommendations of these booksellers for what they read, the booksellers had an enormous influence in shaping their literary tastes. Cobb, Andrews & Co., the oldest and most fashionable, favored contemporary authors such as Henry James. BURROWS bought out Cobb, Andrews & Co. in 1888 and was the first store in Cleveland to come out with books by the Bronte sisters, Tolstoi, and Geo. Eliot. As the biggest advertiser, Burrows was also the most influential. Van Epps & Co., a smaller store, was the most conservative, primarily selling the works of established English authors. Bookstores, such as Ingham, Clark & Co., occasionally promoted books by local authors, sometimes publishing them as well.

Cleveland's literary tastes largely reflected national trends, as they always would. Romance, written by women for women, was the most popular; such stories were expected to be entertaining, yet tempered with morality. Local color (regional) stories were also popular. Historical romance and adventure stories came into vogue in the 1890s; *Ben Hur* was hugely popular in Cleveland. The realists, notably Henry James and Wm. Dean Howells, were slow to gain acceptance. Like other Americans, Clevelanders, wanting to be positive in self and future of the country, did not wish to read anything too disturbing. The reception of poetry in Cleveland, however, did not reflect national trends. Cleveland, situated in the "West" but with New England roots, patronized the older New England poets and the western poets of the "homespun" school—such as Jas. Whitcomb Riley. Many poets popular in the East, such as Walt Whitman and Emily Dickinson, were largely ignored in Cleveland. From its beginning, the Cleveland Public Library waged a campaign against Clevelanders' preference for current popular fiction, especially domestic romances. The CPL attempted to promote "educational and elevating" books, but as a public agency it had to succumb to public demands; out of 3,980 books purchased in 1874, 1,550 were novels. In contrast, several articles appeared in the *Cleveland News* during the 1880s that claimed that there was a lower percentage of "light reading" done in Cleveland than in any other city. It is, however, unclear how that was determined.

It was perhaps the best time to be an author in Cleveland; local pride was high, and publishing opportunities were at a peak. Despite the large number of "amateur" Cleveland authors to write books, there were several who did achieve national prominence. Of 11 Clevelanders to write romance, all women, only SARAH K. BOLTON received any sort of national acclaim. ALBERT G. RIDDLE and CONSTANCE WOOLSON, local-colorists, both attracted national recognition, Riddle for his sentimental novels about growing up in Geauga County. Although Clevelanders after the Civil War were under the national average in their patronage of the humorists, Artemus Ward (CHARLES FARRAR BROWNE)—largely a local product—was always popular in Cleveland. The type of fiction in which Cleveland authors excelled, in terms of both quantity and quality, dealt with socioeconomic issues. As a growing industrial center, Cleveland had its share of labor problems and growing social divisions between rich and poor. JOHN HAY's *The Breadwinners*, a national bestseller, presented a dim view of Cleveland's provincial society life. CHAS. CHESNUTT and Albion W. Tourgee, writing on race and Reconstruction, also added greatly to Cleveland's reputation in the socioeconomic category. Chesnutt was the first American writer to write about the Negro as a human being. Tourgee, whom Cleveland can partially claim, also achieved considerable success in this genre; his *A Fool's Errand* (1879) was a national sensation. Both authors were staunchly supported in Cleveland, where there had been strong antislavery sentiment prior to the Civil War. Although not the result of a unified literary movement, the socioeconomic novels that came out of Cleveland at this time form the only body of literature that can perhaps be uniquely linked to Cleveland.

Included in the abundance of nonfiction produced by Cleveland authors between 1865–1900 were 8 travel books, 6 volumes of war memoirs, 8 collections of essays, 6 sets of histories, 12 books on education, 45 biographies, and a plethora of religious literature. The best works were probably John Hay's *Castillian Days* (1871); *Abraham Lincoln, A History* (1890), by Hay and J. G. Nicolay; Riddle's *Recollections of War Times* (1895); and Jas. Ford Rhodes's 7-volume *History of the United States from the Compromise of 1850*. Cleveland was less distinguished in poetry. At least 30 volumes were published, most of it conventional verse espousing either moral sentiment or homey philosophy. Hay acheived some popularity as a poet, and Edmund Vance Cooke enjoyed considerable local acclaim toward the end of the century.

Cleveland's other literary aspects included a number of minor journals, development of new literary societies, and continued lecture-appearances by well-known authors. The *Magazine of Western History* was the only journal possibly ranked by literary and artistic excellence, although only a small portion was devoted to poetry and fiction. *Literary Life*, which started in Cleveland in 1884, later moved to Chicago. Cleveland became a popular city on the lecture circuit of famous authors that included Mark Twain and Oscar Wilde. The male-dominated literary societies that flourished prior to the Civil War were replaced by a multitude of literary groups with names such as East End Shakespeare and the Seventh Ward Literary Society. Most of the groups were composed of women and concentrated on reading and discussing established English authors. More scholarly societies, such as the NOVEL CLUB and ROWFANT CLUB, were founded in the 1890s.

During the first half of the 20th century, changes in the city's literary life were influenced by the development of leisure pursuits other than reading, the increased participation of women writers, and a growing preference for nonfiction over fiction. A less specific aspect was the diminishing of Cleveland's provincialism and its blending into the national literary picture. As Americans discovered other leisure pursuits, reading diminished as an entertainment. *CLEVELAND TOWN TOPICS*, the city's leading arts and entertainment magazine, in 1900 featured a full 2-page column, "In the Field of Literature," in which 15–20 books were reviewed weekly. Over the years, the column was shortened as coverage of other leisure interests, such as society, GOLF, AVIATION, etc., expanded. By 1928, only 1 to 3 books were being reviewed in a half-page column, "Book Review." Among Cleveland readers, novels with a moral were still popular, as were light romances. In nonfiction there was a growing interest in other lands, and a continuing interest in religion and pseudo-science. By 1920 there was a substantially greater interest in realistic novels, especially those dealing with family and labor issues. Novels dealing with "insignificant sex matters" were also popular, although they generally received poor reviews. These interests all reflected national trends. The CPL continued its fight to upgrade the public's reading tastes. In 1910, an experimental rack of "classed books" was set up to counteract the "universal cry for the latest modern novels." The attempt faltered, and as a compromise, old favorites in fiction were substituted. The CPL's annual report in 1935, however, reported a decrease in "desultory" reading, and an increased demand for technical and business books, books on current world affairs, and practical how-to-do-it books. Books classified under the broad category of sociology were also increasing in popularity.

As national literary reviews and bestseller lists became a dominant influence in shaping the nation's literary tastes, the influence of local booksellers decreased. In Cleveland, the major bookstores gave way to a proliferation of smaller, more diverse stores. The 2 most prominent of these were KORNER & WOOD and LAUKUFF'S. Both stores, considered very progressive, offered avant-garde literature, photographs, and the works of local artists. Artists and theater people relied on Laukuff's for information on the latest developments in art and theater in Europe. Cleveland department stores, such as HALLE BROS. CO., also entered into the book retail market. Bookstores serving

Cleveland's substantial ethnic population began to prosper, including N. P. Popp's, the largest Croatian bookstore in the country. In 1930, *Publisher's Weekly* claimed that Cleveland, in terms of its book-distribution agencies, was "one of the best served cities in the country."

By the 1920s, Cleveland in its literary tastes was considered on a level with eastern cities. In 1930, Harvey's, which operated a chain of bookstores throughout the West and Midwest, opened a store in Cleveland. The store was closely watched to determine whether or not openings should be attempted in Boston, New York, and other eastern cities. Despite this market classification, vestiges of Cleveland's western beginnings were evident in the frequent lampooning of eastern literary cliques, such as the Algonquin Round Table, in Cleveland literary columns. Smaller literary societies continued to form, many along social and economic lines. The CHESHIRE CHEESE CLUB was composed of male professionals who met weekly for lunch to discuss books. The Lincoln Literary Society was organized in an old settlement house on Woodland Ave. by young men from poor backgrounds who wished to improve their knowledge.

With fewer publishing opportunities, writers began to organize into mutual-support groups, the most active of these for women. The CLEVELAND WRITERS CLUB, which split from the Cleveland Women's Press Club in 1922, had a membership of 60. In 1928, the club introduced its first annual "Writers' Derby," providing a much-needed outlet for local writers. The League of American Penwomen (Cleveland chapter) was founded that year as a working group for those learning to write. In poetry, the Ohio Poetry Assoc. was founded in CLEVELAND HTS. in 1931. Several other groups published chapbooks. *American Weave*, founded in 1936, would later achieve national circulation. In the 1930s, 31 Cleveland writers published *The Life We Imagine*, consisting of 41 pieces of poetry and fiction. The works of established Cleveland writers received extra local support by being featured at book fairs or special displays at the CPL.

It was at this time that Cleveland made perhaps its greatest contribution to the national literary scene. Both HART CRANE and LANGSTON HUGHES received national attention, and are still regarded in the top rank of American poets. Crane's influence in Cleveland was negligible other than in bohemian circles. Hughes maintained ties with the KARAMU HOUSE, inspiring the formation of groups for young black poets such as the JANUARY CLUB. Among other Cleveland writers of note, Jake Falstaff, originally from Akron, refused New York offers and moved to Cleveland to write a successful column for the *CLEVELAND PRESS* and several books; at the time of his death in 1936, he was considered one of America's most promising poets. CARL WITTKE, a professor of history at Western Reserve University, published a number of significant studies on American culture. Dr. HARVEY CUSHING, a pioneer brain surgeon, won a Pulitzer Prize for his biography of Sir Wm. Osler.

Following WORLD WAR II, Cleveland's literary life was largely dominated by the CPL, Cleveland newspapers and department stores, and a number of new writers' groups. Another significant aspect was the emergence of Cleveland as a leading poetry center. In the bookstores, sales continued to be good and to mirror national bestseller lists. Books that made the bestseller list in Cleveland and nowhere else usually did so because of memorable personal appearances by authors. But beginning in the 1950s, there was a decline in the number of older, downtown stores in favor of national chains—usually located in suburban shopping malls—and an unusually high percentage of secondhand book-

stores. Laukuff's closed in the early 1950s, followed by Korner & Wood in 1965. Schroeder's, a Cleveland landmark on PUBLIC SQUARE, closed in 1979 after 71 years. One of the city's most popular bookstores, Publix, regionally known for its selection on art and the humanities, achieved another downtown comeback in 1986. Asphodel, a center for counterculture in the 1960s, moved to Burton. Most of these stores were family-run and provided informed service.

In the 1950s and 1960s, a number of annual book fairs became established in Cleveland. In 1952, the first Children's Book Fair was held under the sponsorship of the CPL, the *Cleveland Press*, and other organizations. In 1966, the *PLAIN DEALER* introduced its Midwest Fall Book Festival. Although the annual event was later terminated—mainly because it was never closely involved with book retailers—it served as a model for similar events in other cities, including Boston. For many years, the HIGBEE CO. was well-known to the publishing industry for its innovative promotion of books. The first Book & Author Luncheon series, for many years sponsored by the *Cleveland Press*, was held in 1956. The year's final luncheon was dedicated to Cleveland Authors' Day, so designated by Mayor Celebrezze. The luncheons have traditionally featured a wide range of authors, although celebrities-turned-author have generally drawn the highest attendance.

Since 1945, Cleveland has produced a number of notable novelists. Jo Sinclair received the Harper Award and widespread critical acclaim for her first novel, *Wasteland* (1947). Among the handful of noted novelists to come out of Ohio in the 1950s and 1960s, 5, Vance Bourjaily, Bentz Plagemann, Herbert Gold, Wm. Ellis, and Don Robertson, were Clevelanders. Both Ellis and Gold had books published in Cleveland by the WORLD PUBLISHING CO. Ellis's *Jonathon Blair* won a Pulitzer Prize. Chester Himes, a black writer, wrote several novels recognized as realistic and significant studies of race problems. Among Cleveland's contributions in nonfiction were notable works from professors at CASE WESTERN RESERVE UNIVERSITY. Thos. Munro wrote a number of noted books on aesthetics and the fine arts, and for many years was editor of the Cleveland-based *JOURNAL OF AESTHETICS & ART CRITICISM*. Bertram Wyatt-Brown was nominated for a Pulitzer Prize for *Southern Honor: Ethics and Behavior in the Old South*.

Notable poets from this period included Mary Oliver, and Richard Howard, who received a Pulitzer in 1970. Russell Atkins, perhaps Cleveland's most celebrated local poet, has been active in the city's poetry life since 1950 as editor of *Freelance*. Another well-known local poet was D. A. LEVY, who during the 1960s helped bring counterculture to Cleveland and established a sometimes controversial tradition of street poetry. Since 1961, Cleveland has emerged as a leading center for poetry. That year the poet Lewis Turco founded a poetry center at Fenn College, one of 5 such programs in the country at that time. Later, as the Cleveland State Poetry Ctr., the program was taken over by Alberta Turner. In 1971, the center expanded its outstanding program of readings and workshops to include an annual chapbook series featuring nationally known poets, and a series for local poets. The center's national reputation has brought many leading poets for visits to the city. CASE WESTERN RESERVE UNIVERSITY, under the leadership of English professor and poet Robt. Wallace, has produced a chapbook series, *Bits*, and an annual of light verse. Other forums for local poets include the readings and workshops of the Poets League and the more controversial PoetsBank, as well as occasional programs at CUYAHOGA COMMUNITY COLLEGE. Cleveland is also the center of a national poetry contest, sponsored by the Chester H. Jones Foundation. Because poetry is less dependent on the eastern publishing houses for its expression, it has been allowed to thrive in cities such as Cleveland where it has received significant encouragement from an enthusiastic minority.

As an industrial city, Cleveland has never been a place that attracts writers. The Cleveland Arts Prize, since 1961, has always included a category for literature, although many of the prizes have gone to former Clevelanders. There has also been occasional financial support in the 1970s—through the Cleveland Area Arts Council, for instance—given to some of the organized activities of writers' and poets' groups. Direct local support for writers has been almost nonexistent. Even so, writers, who are ultimately dependent on a national market for publication, have seldom depended on local support anywhere. Support for Cleveland writers does, however, exist in a number of writers' groups and workshops started in the 1970s. The Poets League, founded in 1974, is open to anyone interested in contemporary writing. It sponsors readings and other literary activities, and publishes a bimonthly newsletter; in 1984 it had a membership of 200 and a mailing list of 800. There is also a diversity of smaller groups that provide friendly criticism, an exchange of ideas, and mutual support. Workshops have also taken place under the auspices of Cuyahoga Community College, Karamu House, and *Writers' Digest*. Although never a leading literary center, Cleveland has had a full and active literary life. It has been traditionally well-served by its bookstores and public library system, and is a highly regarded retail market among publishers. A respectable number of notable authors have come from Cleveland, and both writers and those with other literary concerns have generally been able to find adequate forums for their common interests. And in one area, as a center for poetry, Cleveland has distinguished itself since 1961.

Nina Gibans
James Shelley

Coyle, Wm., ed., *Ohio Authors and Their Books* (1962).
Ford, Margaret P., "The Cleveland Literary Scene" (Ph.D. diss., WRU, 1957).
See also PRINTING & PUBLISHING INDUSTRY.

**LITHUANIANS.** The settlement of Lithuanians in Cleveland follows historical patterns similar to those of other East European nations. The first wave of immigrants came here at the turn of the century (1890–1910), and the second wave—more appropriately termed political refugees—arrived in the wake of WORLD WAR II (1948–50), after the USSR had forcibly annexed Lithuania, Latvia, and Estonia in 1940. Early Lithuanians, the first of whom are recorded here in 1871, were absorbed as cheap labor into thriving local industries. They concentrated around St. Clair and Oregon Ave. (now Rockwell) and ranged eastward to about E. 71st St. between Oregon and Cedar avenues. The overwhelming Catholic sentiments of the early community were evidenced in the establishment in 1895 of St. George's Lithuanian parish, which was housed at several locations until a cornerstone was laid in 1921 for the present structure at E. 67th St. and Superior Ave. That has witnessed the maturation of the parish and its associated social, civic, and community activity. Although the laissez faire system of the time exploited many immigrants, it also offered opportunities for success, and by the first decade of the 20th century, about 50 business establishments—many of them taverns that also served as informal community centers—boasted Lithuanian ownership. That was at a period when little more than 1,000 Lithuanians lived here. Successful entrepreneurs became natural community leaders and established institutional anchors for the further coalescence of the Lithuanian community—especially in the face of negative attitudes from the indigenous population. In 1906, civic and business leaders established the Lithuanian Bldg. & Loan Assoc. ("the Lithuanians' bank"), which evolved after World War II into the Superior Savings & Loan Assoc. Another core institution was the Lithuanian Hall Society, which bought a building in 1920 at E. 69th St. and Superior Ave. and which, as the Lithuanian Hall, became a center for the nurturing of cultural, civic, and artistic expressions of the Lithuanian heritage. Another mainstay of the community was the newspaper *DIRVA* (est. 1915). It was one of several publications current in the first part of the century but is the only one surviving to this day.

Among the early organizations were benevolent groups such as the St. George's Society (est. 1885). Other self-help groups sprang up as well, but eventually merged into the Lithuanian Alliance of America and the American-Lithuanian Roman Catholic Alliance, with posts in major cities. Other organizations, manifesting a need and a desire by the immigrants to maintain their culture and heightened by a national reawakening in Lithuania itself, which led to the independence of the country in 1918, thrived in the interwar period. By 1930, when approximately 10,000–12,000 Lithuanians lived in Cleveland, there were more than 15 civic, cultural, religious, sports, artistic, and political organizations centered here, and local chapters of more than 20 national organizations. The Lovers of the Homeland Society (Tevynes Myletoju Draugija) and the Knights of Lithuania (Lietuvos Vyciai) were among prominent groups in the early period of immigration. They were social and service organizations, with the Knights of Lithuania active to this day. The growing community had expanded eastward over the years, and by 1929 a second parish, Our Lady of Perpetual Help, was founded in the Collinwood area. A cornerstone for the present church was laid in 1952 at Neff Rd. and Sable Ave., and the church, school, and hall were completed in the early 1960s. Cohesiveness, thrift, diligence, and recognition of educational values were evident traits noted by observers of the Lithuanian immigrants, as were their long-standing contributions to the community by the establishment of the Lithuanian Cultural Gardens in ROCKEFELLER PARK.

The second wave of immigrants came after World War II, when approximately 4,000 Lithuanian refugees settled here. This influx comprised mainly educated, professional levels of society and included the last president of the Lithuanian Republic, ANTANAS SMETONA, who came here during the war and perished in a fire in 1944. Postwar refugees maintained a deep-seated feeling that their country would soon be freed from Soviet domination and that their stay here was temporary. For that reason, they tended to form their own organizations centered around institutions transferred here from the Old Country or formed anew, rather than join organizations established by the early immigrants, who had become not only acculturated to American ways but assimilated, as well. Some established institutions, such as St. George's and Our Lady of Perpetual Help parishes and the newspaper *Dirva*, were rejuvenated as a result of the new arrivals. Other organizations that had their roots in the homeland and were now forbidden under Soviet rule, proliferated. Thus, the scouting movement, university fraternities, religious organizations, professional societies, the Army Reserve of the Lithuanian Republic (Ramove), the former national guard (Siauliai), and other groups quickly reestablished themselves here and wherever other Lithuanian emigrants found themselves in the free world.

An all-encompassing cultural, educational, civic, and social organization, the Lithuanian-American Community of the USA, Inc. (Lietuviu Bendruomene), was formalized in 1952. On the political front, the Lithuanian-American Council (Amerikos Lietuviu Taryba), active in the U.S. since 1942, lobbied during the war and after on behalf of the plight of Lithuania under Soviet rule. The council embraced major organizations of the early immigrants as well as postwar organizations such as the Lithuanian Christian Democratic party, the Socialists, the Natl. Alliance, the Lithuanian Front, and others. Saturday schools for youngsters were an immediate priority for the preservation of the Lithuanian language, heritage, and culture. For that purpose, the Bishop M. Valancius School opened at ST. GEORGE'S CHURCH in 1949 and conducted classes into the mid-1960s. St. Casimir School started classes at Our Lady of Perpetual Help parish in 1952 and is in session to the present time. In 1949, the Lithuanian Voice Radio Program (Tevynes Garsai) was founded by a group of community activists. Boy and Girl Scout troops, a Catholic student federation (ATEITIS), a Lithuanian cultural fund, and a refugee society were all formed that same year. In 1950 an athletic club (Zaibas) was instituted, as was a theatrical society (Vaidila). In the cultural and artistic field, the Lithuanian Natl. Art Ensemble (CIURLIONIS) was reestablished upon its arrival here in 1949, followed by the formation in 1953 of the Folk Dance Group (Grandinele). Both these groups have achieved international acclaim through concerts in various countries.

The postwar period brought an added vitality to the Lithuanian community, whose members became acculturated quite readily and successfully, but who were more actively attuned to the preservation of the Lithuanian heritage in the face of the Russification occurring in Lithuania itself. A new community center, Lithuanian Village, was built and dedicated in 1973 along E. 185th St., and community activity shifted to that area and into the eastern suburbs, as the area around old St. George's parish went into decline. The Lithuanian community, which presently numbers about 16,000, remains active in civic, social, artistic, political, and community affairs, with a vast majority of the children of postwar emigrants holding degrees in higher education and well-situated in the professions. Cleveland's Lithuanian community is recognized as one of the most active and productive in terms of organizational activity, community consciousness, political and civic involvement in the general affairs of Greater Cleveland, literary activity and the arts, and folk art ensembles, and is the home community of numerous persons prominent in various fields among the Lithuanian nation worldwide. A notable measure of the Cleveland community's standing as a major anchor of the Lithuanian culture apart from the homeland is the Lithuanian Collection at Kent State University, a permanent archive of upwards of 15,000 volumes of historical documents, rare books, memoirs, publications, and papers chronicling the Lithuanian experience in immigration and exile.

Algis Ruksenas

Cadzow, John F., *Lithuanian Americans and Their Communities of Cleveland* (1978).
Coulter, Charles W., *The Lithuanians of Cleveland* (1920).

**LITTLE ITALY,** one of 5 major Italian settlements in Cleveland, is located from E. 119th to E. 125th streets on Murray Hill and Mayfield roads. In 1911, it was estimated that 96% of the inhabitants were Italian-born, and another 2% were of Italian parents. Many of these Italians were Neopolitan and were engaged in skilled lacework, gar-

mentmaking, and the embroidery trades. The largest group came from the towns of Ripamolisano, Madrice, and San Giovanni in Galdo, Campobasso Province, in the Abruzzi region. Established in 1885, this physically well-protected and well-defined ethnic enclave is bordered by the forested bluff of LAKE VIEW CEMETERY to the north and east and the Regional Transit Authority's Windermere-Airport Rapid Transit line and the Case Western Reserve University campus to the west. Often referred to as "Murray Hill" because of the street by that name intersecting Mayfield Rd., the center of the neighborhood, the Italian hilltown has a reputation as a closed community whose assets are historic, substantial, and original.

By the late 1890s, many Italian immigrants had settled in the Mayfield-Murray Hill area and worked in the nearby marbleworks, one of which was founded by skilled stonemason JOSEPH CARABELLI. Unlike the "typical" Italian immigrant, Carabelli was a northern Italian and a Protestant. Settling in Cleveland in 1880, he began the Lakeview Marble Works, becoming a major figure in the affairs of Cleveland's Italian community. While Murray Hill was developing during the early 1900s, other Italian settlements were forming, including one on the east side near E. 105th, Cedar, and Fairhill roads, and another on the city's west side in the vicinity of Clark and Fulton roads. Prior to WORLD WAR I, another Italian colony was formed in COLLINWOOD, and in 1910, when Collinwood was formally annexed to Cleveland, it brought another Italian settlement within the city limits. Little Italy in 1985 is the only city neighborhood attracting thousands of surburban shoppers in a rush to capitalize on its historical charm. Relatively crime-free, Little Italy is a trendy, upscale center for art, dining, and gracious living. In the community where the macaroni machine was invented in 1906, visitors will find the Little Italy Historical Museum, the ALTA HOUSE and Library, Murray Hill School, the HOLY ROSARY CHURCH, numerous restaurants, and artists' studios and shops.

The **LITTLE SISTERS OF THE POOR,** a Catholic religious order dedicated to helping the elderly poor, was founded in France in 1839. Since their arrival in Cleveland in 1870, the Little Sisters have operated a facility to care for needy senior citizens. Seven Little Sisters of the Poor came to Cleveland in May 1870 at the invitation of Bp. AMADEUS RAPPE. In June 1870 they opened a rest home on Erie (E. 9th) St. near the cathedral; it was one of 13 homes opened by Little Sisters in the U.S. between 1868-72. Their first Cleveland facility could accommodate only 12 people, and in Feb. 1871 the sisters bought land for a larger home at 281 Perry (E. 22nd) St. The building on the property was remodeled to accommodate 63 residents in Mar. 1871. The Home for the Aged was expanded in 1877 and again in 1890; in 1896, 16 nuns provided food, clothing, and nursing care for 100 male and 98 female "inmates."

The home accepted anyone, regardless of religion or race. To be admitted, one needed to be destitute, older than 60, and of good moral character. The home was supported by charitable donations in kind and cash. Using a "long black wagon," the sisters made daily visits to hotels, restaurants, and private homes to collect leftover food, old clothing, and other supplies. Non-Catholic Clevelanders provided much support for the work. With the exception of the City Infirmary, the home was the county's largest facility for the elderly for many years. No private rooms existed at the home, but 70 women and 130 men lived there in 1937; capacity in 1941 was 214 residents. The home traditionally accepted only the destitute, but as social security and pensions developed, it began to accept people with limited incomes of this kind.

In the late 1950s, the Little Sisters of the Poor were forced out of their E. 22nd St. neighborhood by urban-renewal efforts. Asked to move in 1957, the Little Sisters and Catholic Charities began to plan for a new home, which was built in 1960 and opened on 21 Apr. 1961. Located at 4291 Richmond Rd. in WARRENSVILLE TWP., the new Little Sisters' home for the aged—SS. Mary & Joseph Home—had accommodations for 235 residents. By the time the Little Sisters celebrated their 100th year in Cleveland in 1970, they had cared for 9,850 elderly poor Clevelanders. In 1971, the home received state certification as a nursing home as well as a rest home. It provided increasingly professional care as the number of lay employees increased from 30 to 85. In Mar. 1985, the home had 145 residents. In addition to its nursing-care and rest-home facilities, the Little Sisters' home offered residential facilities for independent elderly able to live on their own.

Archives, Diocese of Cleveland.

The **LITTLE STEEL STRIKE** began in Cleveland on 26 May 1937 when members of the Steel Workers Organizing Committee voted to strike REPUBLIC STEEL, Youngstown Sheet & Tube, and Inland Steel, the major independent steel producers, known as "Little Steel," after the independents refused to sign contracts that recognized the union. On 27 May, Gov. Martin Davey of Ohio announced an attempt to initiate negotiations between the committee and Republic Steel and Youngstown Sheet & Tube. By 12 June, Davey's efforts had been frustrated by the companies' refusal to accept the first condition of the proposed settlement. This clause recognized the committee as the representative of its members.

During the early days of the strike, a potentially explosive confrontation in Cleveland was averted when Mayor HAROLD BURTON revoked Republic's permit to operate an airfield on St. Clair Ave., which the company used to supply nonstriking workers in Republic plants at Niles and Warren. On 17 June, the federal government appointed a mediation board. By 21 June, the committee discussions had reached an impasse. The companies reiterated their refusal to enter into contract with the committee. Faced with the companies' determination to reopen the mills, Davey was asked to maintain the mills' status quo until the board could meet again. He responded by sending Natl. Guard troops to Mahoning Valley to keep mills there closed. Three days later, negotiations collapsed when company officials rejected the board's compromise settlement. Following the board's failure, Gov. Davey ordered the Natl. Guard to provide protection to employees who wished to return to their jobs.

While TOM GIRDLER of Republic Steel claimed the strike had been "licked" and Philip Murray claimed it was still 100% effective, Cleveland prepared for the reopening of Republic's mills. On 3 July, Mayor Burton and Sheriff Martin O'Donnell requested that Natl. Guard troops be sent for the 6 July opening of Republic's mills. O'Donnell declared military rule the day before the scheduled reopening. Despite the company claims throughout the stike, workers did not rush back to work; many chose to remain out on strike. Slowly the number of returning workers increased. Aside from occasional vandalism, Cleveland remained relatively quiet, and the Natl. Guard was removed by 16 July. Ten days later, Cleveland was rocked by violence between workers at Republic's Corrigan-McKinney plant and strikers outside the plant. However, by the end of Aug. 1937, the Little Steel Strike had faded in signifi-

cance. Gov. Davey's decision to use the Natl. Guard to keep the mills open had dealt it a serious blow. While the strike failed to gain recognition during the 1930s for the union among 3 of the major independents, these 3 would eventually sign contracts in the early 1940s, when the Natl. Labor Relations Board decisions would demand they comply.

**LOCAL CLEVELAND** was the Cleveland branch of the Socialist party. It was most active between 1910-20, during which time it advocated the rights of labor and took an antiwar stance during WORLD WAR I. The Socialist Party of America was formed in 1901, with a Cleveland branch organizing soon after under the name Local Cleveland. In 1909, Local Cleveland claimed 342 members; the party grew rapidly, and by 1917 its membership was approximately 3,000. In addition to fostering the basic socialist tenets, Local Cleveland also supported the labor movement and the rights of workers. It advocated the right of labor to demand better working conditions and also endorsed women's suffrage. In 1911, Local Cleveland proposed a new constitution for the state of Ohio. In it the party outlined its objectives with regard to labor. These included the collective ownership of industries, the prohibition of police power and injunctions against labor, and the subordination of military to civil authority. Their proposed constitution also supported organized labor's right to strike, to distribute information concerning industrial and labor disputes, and to boycott. Because of the Socialists' support of the rights of labor, the party and the labor movement were united.

However, as labor rallied to the American cause during World War I, the party's antiwar stand caused a break with labor. On 27 May 1917, Local Cleveland's party secretary, CHAS. RUTHENBERG, speaking in front of a large crowd on PUBLIC SQUARE, attacked the government and its involvement in the war and called for a general strike. The speech resulted in the imprisonment of Ruthenberg in the Stark County jail. Although Local Cleveland had approximately 3,000 members by 1917, it never became a threat to the established Democratic and Republican parties in Cleveland. Ruthenberg's subsequent adoption of Communist tactics, his support of the INDUSTRIAL WORKERS OF THE WORLD, and his election as the executive secretary of the Communist party sealed the fate of this party. That and the party's antiwar stand, as well as national measures against "subversive" organizations, caused it to wither into a minor, ineffectual body by the end of World War I.

*The Socialist News*, ed. Chas. Ruthenberg (1917).

**LOCHER, RALPH.** See**MAYORAL ADMINISTRATION OF RALPH LOCHER**

**LOESER, NATHAN** (1869–30 June 1953), was a founder of one of the city's largest and most prestigious law firms and a prime mover in the creation of MT. SINAI HOSPITAL. He was born in Cleveland but raised in Buffalo, where he attended public school. Loeser studied law and journalism at Cornell University and worked for a short time as a writer for the *Buffalo Express, Buffalo Courier, New York Herald*, and Associated Press. He returned to Cleveland in 1892 and took a position in the law office of Louis Grossman. He was admitted to the bar in 1896. Loeser and Grossman published the *American Lawyers Quarterly* for several years. In 1920, Loeser left the Grossman firm to establish Mooney, Hahn, Loeser & Keough, which in 1985 was Hahn, Loeser, Freedheim, Dean & Wellman.

Loeser was president of Mt. Sinai Hospital from the late 1890s until 1910. With JOHN ANISFIELD, he was instrumental in obtaining support from the Fed. of Jewish Charities for the construction of the hospital in 1916. Loeser was a long-time trustee of the federation. In 1901, he served 1 term as president of the Baron deHirsch Lodge of B'NAI B'RITH. As his father had before him, Loeser also served as president of the Euclid Ave. Temple. A close friend of Louis Beaumont, the principal owner of the MAY CO., Loeser was chosen by Beaumont to be among the first trustees of the LOUIS D. BEAUMONT FOUNDATION, a charitable trust that provided money for social welfare projects. For his leadership in citywide and Jewish community activities, Loeser was given the Eisenman Award by the JEWISH COMMUNITY FED. in 1949. In 1913, Loeser married Beatrice Moss. They had 2 children, Mary Ann and Dr. Chas. N. Loeser.

**LOESSER, ARTHUR** (26 Aug. 1894–4 Jan. 1969), was an internationally known pianist and head of the piano faculty at the CLEVELAND INSTITUTE OF MUSIC. Born in New York City, he studied at New York College, at Columbia University, and with Stojowski at the Institute of Musical Art (later part of the Julliard School). He began his concert career in 1913 and toured Europe, Australia, and the Far East. He joined the piano faculty of the Cleveland Institute of Music in 1926, becoming its head in 1953. In 1943 he was commissioned as an officer in the U.S. Army and became an interpreter of Japanese. He later became the first American musician to appear in Japan, with the Nippon Symphony, following WORLD WAR II. In Cleveland, Loesser not only taught but also was a writer on music. He was program editor and annotator for the CLEVELAND ORCHESTRA from 1937–42 and music critic for the *CLEVELAND PRESS* from 1938–56. His popular books *Humor in American Song* and *Men, Women, and Pianos* were published in 1943 and 1954 respectively. Loesser's later concert career included appearances with the New York Philharmonic, Minneapolis Symphony, Cincinnati Symphony, and Cleveland Orchestra. Loesser was married to the former Jean Bassett. He was the brother of Frank Loesser, well-known popular composer.

The **LOMOND ASSOCIATION** is a neighborhood organization formed to promote peaceful integration in the Lomond School District in SHAKER HTS. Like its counterpart, the LUDLOW COMMUNITY ASSOC., the Lomond Assoc. used education and communication, good organization, and an active campaign to maintain the stability and quality of the community during what for many area neighborhoods was a difficult period of racial change in the 1960s. In spring 1963, the Lomond school PTA formed a discussion group on "The Changing Neighborhood"; from it emerged a group concerned about maintaining a stable neighborhood while "facing the reality of integration in a mature way." These people, among whom were Dr. Chester Plotkin, Ruth Blumenthal, Stephen Alfred, Joseph A. Becker, and Stephanie Kulinski, were the early leaders in the development of the Lomond Assoc. The association held its first communitywide meeting in late Nov. 1963, and in early 1964 began to hold small discussion groups in which trained leaders sought to open communication among neighbors and destroy the myths related to integrated housing; more than 600 people attended such neighborhood discussions in 1964 and 1965. Also in early 1964, the association began to publish and distribute the *Lomond Newsletter* to publicize its goals and activities and to urge neighbors not to leave Lomond because of integration, and, if they must move, to avoid the use of "for

sale" signs, which were deemed psychologically harmful for the neighborhood. When a voluntary ban on such signs proved ineffective, the association effectively lobbied city council for an ordinance banning "for sale" signs.

As the Lomond neighborhood attracted increasing numbers of black homebuyers in the mid-1960s, leaders of the Lomond Assoc. noticed a decline in prospective white homebuyers. To prevent the area from becoming an all-black neighborhood, the association adopted a 2-fold plan: with funding from the CLEVELAND FOUNDATION in 1966, it hired a housing coordinator to promote the neighborhood to white buyers, and it began to promote open housing throughout the Cleveland suburbs in order to expand the available market of housing for BLACKS and reduce the high black demand for homes in Lomond. Between 1963–65, the annual percentage of Lomond home sales increased from 15% to 50%; through the efforts of the housing coordinator, the annual percentage of homes bought by blacks dropped from 51% to 39% from 1966–68. At the same time, the total number of homes sold in Lomond increased by 10% in 1967 and by 5% in 1968. In 1966, the Lomond Assoc. joined with other open-housing groups in Shaker Hts. to entice white real-estate brokers to show homes in integrated communities. In 1967 it founded and helped finance Suburban Citizens for Open Housing to help blacks gain access to housing in other suburbs. Also in 1967, the city council and the school board in Shaker Hts. agreed to finance and supervise the work of the housing coordinator of the Lomond and other Shaker Hts. neighborhood associations, forming the Shaker Communities Housing Office. Relieved of this responsibility, the Lomond Assoc. turned to neighborhood maintenance issues, forming a welcoming committee to greet prospective homebuyers and new residents, a program committee to organize social events, and a zoning and maintenance committee. It continued its efforts to prevent an all-black neighborhood in 1968 by establishing a financing program that loaned money for down payments to whites interested in buying homes on "heavily integrated blocks." By mid-1969, blacks owned 20% of the homes in the Lomond area.

**LONG, DAVID** (29 Sept. 1787–1 Sept. 1851), was Cleveland's first physician. He was also active in local politics and business ventures. Born in Hebron, N.Y., Long was the son and grandson of physicians. He studied medicine with his uncle, Dr. John Long, and attended medical school in New York City. He received his medical degree in 1810, at the age of 23, and moved to Cleveland. He was the first physician to settle permanently in the city and the only doctor in Cleveland for 4 years. He was joined in 1814 by Dr. Donald McIntosh. During the WAR OF 1812, Long served as a surgeon in the Western Army. At this time, Cleveland was in the 6th Medical District of the State of Ohio. Long was appointed one of 7 censors designated to regulate medical practice in the district. When the state was redistricted in 1824, Cleveland fell in the new 19th district. Long was elected the first president of the Society of the 19TH MEDICAL DISTRICT, the forerunner of the ACADEMY OF MEDICINE of Cleveland.

In addition to his private practice, Long was involved in commercial business enterprises. He operated a dry-goods and notions store on Superior Ave. for several years to supplement his income. In 1816 he was one of 8 incorporators of the COMMERCIAL BANK OF LAKE ERIE. He also was involved in the organization of the Cleveland Pier Co., which built the first pier into Lake Erie. With LEVI JOHNSON, he erected the first warehouse on the CUYAHOGA RIVER, in 1817. In later years Long concentrated more on his business affairs than on medicine.

When Cleveland was incorporated as a village in 1814, Long was elected a trustee. He served as trustee off and on until 1836. When Cleveland and NEWBURGH were fighting over which city was to become the county seat in 1826, Long was elected one of 3 county commissioners by a small margin, tipping the balance in favor of Cleveland. In 1829 he served as president of the village. Elected as a trustee again in 1832, Long was appointed to Cleveland's first board of health. He was also appointed, in 1835, to the committee charged with framing the first charter for the city of Cleveland. In 1811, Long became the first librarian of the Library Society of Cleveland, which he organized along with 15 others. He helped establish Cleveland's first church, Trinity Episcopal, in 1817. In 1820 he and his family became members of Cleveland's first Sunday school. In 1833 he was elected president of the CLEVELAND ANTI-SLAVERY SOCIETY. Long married Juliana Walworth, daughter of Cleveland's postmaster, in 1811. They had 2 children.

**LONG, WILLIAM FREW** (28 Apr. 1880–7 Jan. 1984), was an officer, pilot, civic leader, benefactor, and farmer, an authority on labor-management relations and on community zoning, one-time president of ASSOCIATED INDUSTRIES OF CLEVELAND, and retired mayor of the city of Macedonia (Summit County), Ohio. He was born in Allegheny, Pa., the son of Edward and Ella Edgar Long. Long, heir to the Frew oil fortune, spent his early days in affluence. His father, one of the founders of the Pittsburgh Stock Exchange, lost his oil fortune in a financial panic and died soon after, and William's plans to further his education and become a lawyer were thwarted. William left school at age 11, began selling newspapers, did clerical work in his uncle's factory, became an owner of a local laundry, and later was president of the Pittsburgh Laundry Assoc. Subsequently he became manager of the Pittsburgh, Pa., Mfrs. Assoc. (1913–20). Long joined the Signal Corps in 1917; was attached to ordnance depots in France, was commissioned a captain, and later transferred to the Army Air Corps—flying the early Jenny planes and commanding the 414 Pursuit Squadron. After the war, he was appointed manager of the American Plan Assoc. of Cleveland, which later became Associated Industries of Cleveland. As such, Long was noted for his strong stand against trade unionism, especially the closed shop and compulsory union membership. He was often called upon to debate labor relations with union leaders and to appear before congressional committees. He served as general manager from 1920–49.

In 1931, Long was promoted to colonel, serving as an Army Reserve officer attached to the War Planning Div. of the secretary of war. He was recalled to active service on 12 June 1941 and took a leave of absence from Associated Industries. He served as civilian personnel relations officer, and in 1944 he became general manager of the Natl. War Labor Board. At age 69, Long retired from Associated Industries; he was appointed to the Macedonia Twp. Board of Zoning, and in 1962 (when he was 82) he was elected mayor of Macedonia. He was instrumental in helping it achieve incorporation as a city in the early 1970s. After serving as mayor for 13 years, he retired on 31 Dec. 1975. He continued to live at his 350-acre working farm, Longwood. Col. Long died in Hudson, Ohio, at the age of 103 and is buried in Northfield-Macedonia Cemetery. He was survived by a son, Wm. Frew, Jr. His first wife, Martha, died in 1916; his second wife, Isabel Elizabeth (Patterson), died in 1956. He donated his Longwood Farm to the city of Macedonia for a park.

William Frew Long Papers, WRHS.

**LORAIN-CARNEGIE BRIDGE.** *See* **HOPE MEMORIAL BRIDGE**

**LORD, RICHARD** (1780–24 Jan. 1857), was a prominent early citizen and mayor of OHIO CITY. With JOSIAH BARBER, he is one of the earliest property owners on record. In 1807, Lord and Barber undertook to develop land extending along the west border of the CUYAHOGA RIVER in Brooklyn Twp. With his brother Samuel, Lord settled permanently in the area in 1818; his 320-acre farm included much of the lakeshore to what is now W. 117th St. In 1834, Lord became one of the 3 chief stockholders in the CUYAHOGA STEAM FURNACE CO., the first manufacturing concern in Cleveland. In 1840, he and Barber dedicated a parcel of land for a public square at the corner of Pearl and Lorain streets. It later became known as Market Square (now the WEST SIDE MARKET). Lord was the mayor of Ohio City in 1843; earlier he had served in various local government offices.

The **LOUIS D. BEAUMONT FOUNDATION** was established in 1949 from the estate of Louis D. Beaumont (1857–1942), cofounder of the MAY CO. Beaumont was born Louis Schoenberg in Dayton, Ohio, one of 6 siblings. With his brother-in-law David May and brother Joseph Schoenberg, he began the May Dept. Store chain, one of the most widely successful retail stores in the country. They were later joined by a 4th partner, Moses Schoenberg. Beaumont began his original trust in 1933, which then became the Commodore Beaumont Foundation under the terms of his will. Beaumont came to Cleveland in 1899. He was married twice. His first wife, and son, Dudley, died in the early 1900s. He moved to France before WORLD WAR I (where, because of intense anti-German feeling during the war, he changed his Germanic last name to its French equivalent). There he married Helene Beaumont. They had no heirs.

In accordance with the terms of Beaumont's will, the foundation was terminated in 1977, on the 35th anniversary of his death. Before final distribution of the principal began, the Beaumont Foundation was the largest private foundation in Cleveland, with over $30 million in assets. During its existence, the foundation made total grants of $67.9 million in 4 principal cities where the May Co. was located: St. Louis (headquarters, $18,035,000), Los Angeles ($7,184,000), Denver ($4,224,000), and Cleveland ($26,587,000), which was the largest recipient. The original purpose of the foundation, as noted in its papers of incorporation, was "to further and promote charitable, scientific, literary, educational and religious objects and purposes, including among them the prevention of cruelty to children and animals." Over the 35 years of the foundation, hundreds of organizations in Cleveland and the other May Co. locations were recipients of Beaumont support. Among the most notable Beaumont Foundation gifts are the Edgar A. Hahn Chair of Jurisprudence at the CWRU School of Law; Beaumont Hall on the CWRU campus, now housing the School for Applied Social Sciences; an endowed chair at the CLEVELAND ORCHESTRA; support for MT. SINAI HOSPITAL; and Camp Beaumont of the BOY SCOUTS. The original trustees of the foundation were NATHAN L. DAUBY, who prompted Beaumont's decision to create the foundation; Morton J. May; and NATHAN LOESER, who was succeeded by EDGAR HAHN.

**LOUIS KOSSUTH'S VISIT** to Cleveland in 1852 was part of a fundraising tour of U.S. cities undertaken by the

Hungarian patriot. It spawned the first Hungarian associations in a city that, at the time, had a small Hungarian population. Following the defeat of the Republican forces in the Hungarian War of Independence, Louis Kossuth fled into exile, and in hopes of raising money for a renewed battle against the Austrians, he accepted an invitation to visit America extended by Pres. Millard Fillmore. He arrived in New York on 4 Dec. 1851, where he was greeted by large crowds as the "Washington of Hungary." His speeches in perfect English (learned from his prison study of the English Bible and the works of Shakespeare) were well received by Americans, who identified the Hungarian struggle with their own war for independence. From New York City, Kossuth embarked upon a 16-state, 152-city tour, receiving the same glad welcome at each stop. Prominent Clevelanders invited Kossuth to the city. To prepare for his visit, the Hungarian Society of Cleveland and the Ladies Hungarian Society were established. Though the Hungarian population of Cleveland was small, the committees exploited the leader's universal appeal to mobilize community support. On 3 Jan., a band of Clevelanders met Kossuth in Pittsburgh and traveled back to Cleveland. When the train pulled into NEWBURGH, Mayor WM. CASE headed the welcoming committee, which boarded the train for the final short ride into the Cleveland depot. Kossuth's disembarkment in Cleveland at 11 p.m. was heralded by a round of cannon fire and an excited crowd. The German community accompanied Kossuth to the American House Hotel with a torchlight procession and music, and serenaded him outside.

After a 1-day rest, Kossuth spoke to a large crowd on the evening of 2 Feb. in front of the hotel on Superior Ave. In the afternoon, he spoke at the Cleveland Melodeon, after an introduction by the Friends of Hungary. Thousands paid the admission of $4 for reserved seats and $3 for general admission—a healthy sum when the average workman's wage averaged $1.50 a day. Kossuth spent 3 Feb. at private receptions and departed for Columbus on 4 Feb. with over $1,500. He left behind a public sensitized to the Hungarian cause, hucksters enriched by the sale of Kossuth cards, satin badges, and other souvenirs, and a market for the soft top hat he wore. As the "Kossuth craze" faded into history, the spirit of Louis Kossuth remained alive in the growing Hungarian community, enriched by veterans of the Hungarian War of Independence. Prior to the 50th anniversary of his visit, Hungarians decided to erect a commemorative statue. Though the idea won the support of Mayor TOM JOHNSON, some Slovak groups opposed the proposed erection of the statue on PUBLIC SQUARE.

The Kossuth Statue Committee commissioned Andras Toth to reproduce the Kossuth memorial he had designed for Nagyszalonta, Hungary, a feat he agreed to perform at no charge. They also sent requests to the commissioner of each county in Hungary for earth from famous landmarks in the homeland to be placed at the base of the statue. When the figure arrived, it was erected at UNIVERSITY CIRCLE on a foundation of native soil received from all but 2 Hungarian counties. On 28 Sept. 1902, 8,000 Clevelanders (including 600 ITALIANS in Kossuth hats) paraded from Public Square to University Circle and joined over 50,000 others for the unveiling of the statue. Lajos Perczel presented the statue to the city, and Mayor Johnson promised to guard it faithfully. At its base, Johnson placed a palm wreath sent by the mayor of Budapest, which contained 100 palm branches, 1 for each year since Kossuth's birth. Speeches by Hungarian leaders and a colorful pageant entertained the assembled dignitaries and the crowds. The Kossuth Statue Committee was the impetus for further or-

ganization of Hungarians around cultural and charitable concerns. Twelve organizations joined forces in 1902 as the UNITED HUNGARIAN SOCIETIES.

The **LOUISE HARKNESS AND DAVID SINTON INGALLS FOUNDATION, INC.,** was founded in 1953 by the Ingalls family. DAVID S. INGALLS, SR. (1898–1985), was born in Cleveland, the son of Albert S. Ingalls, vice-president of New York Central Railroad, and Jane Taft Ingalls, niece of Pres. Wm. A. Taft. Ingalls attended UNIVERSITY SCHOOL and Yale until the outbreak of WORLD WAR I. At that time he joined the first Yale naval aviation unit, launching a long career as a pilot and aviation executive. Ingalls distinguished himself as an ace pilot during World War I; he returned to graduate from Yale in 1920 and Harvard Law School in 1923. In 1927 he became state representative, a position he held for 2 consecutive terms. Shortly after, he was appointed by Pres. Hoover as assistant secretary of the Navy for aeronautics. In 1932, Ingalls ran unsuccessfully for governor. He returned to private law practice until 1941, when he became vice-president and general manager for Pan American Air Ferries to carry out World War II-related work. During the war, he re-enlisted in the Navy as a chief of staff on Guadalcanal, retiring after the war as a rear admiral. He was vice-president of Pan American World Airways until his resignation in 1949. In the ensuing years, he was president of the *Times Star* in Cincinnati, owned by the Taft family, and a lawyer in Cleveland. Ingalls married Louise Harkness (d. 1978) in 1922 and had 5 children: Edith Vignos, Louise Brown, Anne Lawrence, Jane Davidson, and David S., Jr. In 1979 he married his second wife, Frances W. Wragg.

The stated purpose of the foundation is "the improvement of the physical, educational, mental, and moral conditions of humanity throughout the world." Grants largely are given for higher and secondary education and for support for community funds and cultural programs in Ohio. Such support is mainly to organizations known to the trustees. In 1982, assets of the foundation were $7,264,366, with expenditures of $693,206 for 13 grants. Officers of the foundation included David S. Ingalls, Jr., Jas. Dempsey, Jr., Louise Ingalls Brown, Jane Ingalls Davison, Anne Ingalls Lawrence, and Edith Ingalls Vignos.

**LOVELAND, ROELIF** (31 Aug. 1899–20 Feb. 1978), is ranked with CHAS. F. BROWNE and HERMAN FETZER as one of Cleveland's greatest feature writers. Loveland spent 42 years on the staff of the *Cleveland Plain Dealer*. Born in Oberlin, Ohio, he saw combat in France as a U.S. Marine in WORLD WAR I. Following attendance at Oberlin College, he worked briefly for the *CLEVELAND PRESS* before joining the *PLAIN DEALER* in 1922. During the 1920s and 1930s, Loveland became a specialist in writing "color" pieces, as well as occasional verse. In 1944, he was sent to Europe to cover the coming invasion of France. He observed the invasion from a bomber piloted by a fellow Clevelander. His eyewitness account of the D-Day bombardment was later reprinted by Louis Snyder and Richard Morris in their anthology *A Treasury of Great Reporting*. Subsequently he landed at Normandy to cover Patton's 3d Army in its breakthrough across northern France. He was one of the first correspondents in liberated Paris. He then followed the 3d Army up to the borders of Germany before being recalled by the *Plain Dealer*. After covering the CLEVELAND INDIANS in 1948, Loveland was made an associate editor and editorial writer the following year. A year before his retirement in 1965, he was assigned to write a regular column. Celebrated for his extracurricular antics as well as for his writing, Loveland reportedly disappeared once for 3 days after being assigned by an editor to "go find spring," before filing a dispatch from Knoxville, Tenn.: "Spring is here." Following the death of his wife, Mildred, in 1951, Loveland married Wanda Arndt, a nursing supervisor at UNIVERSITY HOSPITALS, in 1953. After a long fight against bone cancer, he died of a stroke at University Hospital. He was survived by 2 sons from his first marriage.

**LOWER, WILLIAM EDGAR** (6 May 1867–17 June 1948), was one of the founders of the CLEVELAND CLINIC FOUNDATION and a pioneer in genito-urinary surgery. Lower was born in Canton, Ohio. After receiving his medical degree from Wooster University Medical School in 1891, he entered medical practice with his cousin, GEO. W. CRILE, SR., and FRANK E. BUNTS and served on the staffs of ST. ALEXIS HOSPITAL and Lakeside Hospital; he was chief of surgery at both Lutheran General (1914–38) and Mt. Sinai hospitals (1916–24). He served during the SPANISH-AMERICAN WAR and became commanding officer (1918) of the famed LAKESIDE UNIT during WORLD WAR I. In 1921, Lower joined Crile, Bunts, and JOHN PHILLIPS in establishing the Cleveland Clinic Foundation, patterned after the group medical practice model of the Mayo brothers in Rochester, Minn. Lower was president of the American Urological Assoc. and a member of numerous prestigious and specialized medical societies in the U.S. He wrote 2 books in collaboration with Crile and numerous papers on genito-urinary surgery. Lower married Mabel Freeman in 1909; they had 1 daughter, Mrs. W. J. Engel.

Bunts, Alexander T., and Crile, George W., Jr., eds., *To Act as a Unit* (1971).

The **LUBRIZOL CORPORATION,** 29400 Lakeland Blvd. in Wickliffe, was established in 1928 to manufacture and sell lubricants and lubricating machinery. By 1984, the company had grown into a diversified chemical company with 26 subsidiaries, annual sales of $831.6 million, and a net income of $67.7 million. It ranked 344th among the Fortune 500 companies in 1985. Lubrizol was founded on 28 July 1928 as the Graphite Oil Prods. Corp. It was established by Francis A. "Alex" Nason and Thos. W. James, both of whom were lubricant salesmen for a Chicago company; they were joined in their venture by 3 brothers: KENT H. SMITH, who became president of the company; Vincent K. Smith (4 June 1896–9 Mar. 1980), a lawyer who became the firm's secretary; and ALBERT K. SMITH, one of the directors. James also served as a director, Nason became vice-president and manager, and his father, Frank A. Nason, served as treasurer. Graphite Oil began production in a garage on E. 93rd St. but soon moved to 9016 Manor Ave. It changed its name to the Lubri-Graph Corp. in Apr. 1929 and in 1931 bought the former Clark Chemical Co. in Wickliffe to expand its production. The company employed 70 people in June 1934, when it became the Lubri-Zol Corp. In 1929, the firm established a research program supervised by CARL F. PRUTTON, which enabled it to introduce new products, to keep up with changes in the automobile industry during the 1930s, and to meet new demands for lubricants during WORLD WAR II. Lubrizol's earnings more than doubled between 1940–45; its revenues were more than $11 million in 1943. In 1942 the firm ended its retail operations to focus its efforts on research and production. It built a new chemical-research facility in 1946.

In 1950, Lubrizol's annual revenues were $18 million, and its net income was $2 million. The company then began to expand its operations. It built a new manufacturing plant near Houston, Tex., in 1950 and began to sell its products in Europe, Australia, New Zealand, and Latin America. Between 1951–62, Lubrizol subsidiaries in 5 foreign countries established production facilities. In 1960, Lubrizol held its first public stock offering, and its stock was placed on the New York Stock Exchange in 1966, when revenues reached $100 million and net income reached $10 million for the first time in company history. Lubrizol's annual revenues had grown to $200 million in 1970, with a net income of $23.4 million. Both sales and income increased annually throughout the 1970s, with the exception of a sharp decline in income in 1975. In 1977, Lubrizol began to invest in new technologies; over the next several years it bought partial interests in Genetech, Inc. (1979), and Creative BioMolecules, Inc. (1983), and bought the Lynnbille Seed Co. (1983), the Agrigenetics Corp. (1985), and the Merichem Co. (1985). Its acquisitions expanded its product line from chemicals for transportation and industry to include products for agribusiness and research into pharmaceuticals, animal vaccines, biotechnology, and oil recovery.

The **LUCILE DAUBY AND ROBERT HAYS GRIES CHARITY FUND** was founded in 1968 by Lucile Dauby Gries (1902–1968). Gries was the daughter of NATHAN DAUBY, executive of the MAY CO., and niece of Louis D. Beaumont (d. 1942). She was active on city boards and was particularly interested in the Cleveland Speech & Hearing Ctr. and MT. SINAI HOSPITAL. Robt. H. Gries (1900–1966) was a 4th-generation Clevelander, whose great-grandfather, SIMSON THORMAN, was the first Jewish settler in Cleveland, in 1837. He was also the son of Rabbi MOSES GRIES of The TEMPLE. Gries is noted for helping found the CLEVELAND RAMS in 1936, and then the CLEVELAND BROWNS in 1946 after the Rams moved to Los Angeles. He was an avid collector, whose specialty book collections, including his collection on tobacco, were given to the CLEVELAND PUBLIC LIBRARY. A portion of his large Oriental porcelain collection is displayed at the WESTERN RESERVE HISTORICAL SOCIETY. The fund gives primarily to local charities. It was the first foundation to sponsor a program for local public television (WVIZ), and the first private foundation to support the renovation of theaters in PLAYHOUSE SQUARE. It helped support the establishment of the Cleveland Jewish Archives at the WRHS; established a cancer fellowship at UNIVERSITY HOSPITALS; and commissioned the ballet Quicksilver for the CLEVELAND BALLET. It also provided early support for programs dealing with women's issues. In 1985, the assets of the fund were $1,867,034, with expenditures of $181,394 for 46 grants. The distribution committee included Ellen G. Cole and Robt. D. Gries.

**LUDLOW, ARTHUR CLYDE** (4 June 1861–16 Apr. 1927) was the long-time pastor of the Miles Park Presbyterian Church (1887–1923) and the author of several works on Presbyterian history in Cleveland. Born in Chardon, Ohio, he was the son of one of the first physicians in the area. He started his collegiate studies at Western Reserve College in Hudson, Ohio, moved with the institution to Cleveland, and graduated with a bachelor's degree (1884) and a master's degree (1887) from Adelbert College of Western Reserve University. He continued his education at Lane Theological Seminary (1884–85) and Union Theological Seminary (1885–87), where he received his divinity degree (1887). Ludlow's ministerial career was confined to the Miles Park Presbyterian Church; his long tenure there meant that much of the church's history and works were for almost 40 years a reflection of his activities and interests. While he was its pastor, Miles Park became recognized as a Presbyterian leader in northern Ohio. Ludlow coauthored a *History of Cleveland Presbyterianism* (1896) with his second wife, Rosa Elizabeth Roeder. He also wrote *The Old Stone Church: The Story of a Hundred Years, 1820–1920* (1920). At the time of his death, he was working on a centennial history of WRU, an institution to which he was devoted and where he had a retirement office in AMASA STONE CHAPEL. Service on the Cleveland School Board (1904–10) and support for the then-unusual idea of manual education characterized Ludlow's civic contributions. He served as stated clerk of the Cleveland Presbytery (1900–27) and also held the denominational offfices of permanent clerk and moderator of the Synod of Ohio. Ludlow married 3 times. Jennie Gould, his first wife, died in 1888. Rosa Roeder (d. 1918) was his second wife. Lillian S. Prall became his third wife, in 1923; she died in 1935.

The **LUDLOW COMMUNITY ASSOCIATION** is a neighborhood organization that began in the mid-1950s to ease racial fears and tension as black families moved into the Ludlow area of SHAKER HTS. It sought to maintain a stable, integrated community. The Ludlow community, which straddles the border between Shaker Hts. and Cleveland, extending southeast from SHAKER SQUARE, was a white community of about 500 homes valued at between $20,000–50,000 when black families began to move into the neighborhood in 1955. The home of one of the first black families was bombed, and there was some fear and panic among some white residents as the neighborhood became integrated over the next several years. By 1959, there were 80–90 black families in the area. The Ludlow Community Assoc. was begun by several homeowners who sought to preserve, in the words of its first president, a "happy, peaceful and prosperous" neighborhood during the process of integration. The association was formed in 1957 after 2 years of small meetings in block clubs to allow black and white residents to get to know one another. Leaders in its development were Irwin Barnett, Lewis Polster, and Gilbert Seldin; these men served as the trustees of the association when it was incorporated on 21 May 1959.

Block clubs, small meetings, and parties helped calm fears, eased tensions, and stopped the panic selling in the late 1950s, but by the early 1960s it was clear that more effort was needed to attract white homebuyers into the area in order to prevent the neighborhood from eventually becoming all black. The association received a $7,500 grant from the CLEVELAND FOUNDATION and early in 1960 established a real-estate clearinghouse to develop a white market for Ludlow homes. The Ludlow Co. was set up to help finance purchases of homes in the area by whites, since lending institutions often refused to lend money to whites seeking to buy homes in integrated areas. "Househunting parties" were organized to introduce prospective buyers to the area, and dinner parties were held with realtors to urge them to stop unethical, "blockbusting" tactics. Neighborhood maintenance committees were also established to maintain and improve sanitation, traffic, building codes, and recreation facilities. Such efforts were successful: in 1961, 9 white families bought homes in the area. By 1962, members of the Ludlow Community Assoc. not only were working to maintain the stability of their own integrated neighborhood but also were active in promoting integration in other suburbs. The association continued its efforts throughout the 1960s, and both BLACKS and whites continued to purchase homes in the area. By 1968, the organization was receiving national publicity for its program of neighborhood stabilization and integration. Between 1968 and the association's 25th anniversary in 1982, the neighborhood maintained a fairly constant racial balance, with 55% minority residents. The association had 300 members in 1982.

The **LUMIR-HLAHOL-TYL SINGING SOCIETY** is a Czech organization begun in 1867 in the Sawtell-Croton area of Cleveland as the Lumir Singing Society, which later merged with the Hlahol Singing Society and the Tyl Dramatic Society. The Lumir Singing Society was named after a famous Czech chorus in Prague. Founders of the Cleveland society included A. J. Roch, Vaclav Rychlik, Hynek Svarc, Vojtidek Svoboda, Frantisek Macourek, Joseph Struad, and Antonin Novy. The society was open only to men until 1880. In its early years, the society sang Czech choral works and songs, but its great love was opera, and in Feb. 1898 it presented *The Bartered Bride*, the first of what would become many performances of that work by the society. Edward Krejsa, a product of the Prague Conservatory of Music and who studied under Dvorak, became musical director of the society in 1907 and held that position for the next 35 years. In 1896, the Hlahol Singing Society was formed under the direction of Anton Machan. It merged with the Lumir group in 1918. In May 1940, the Lumir-Hlahol society merged with the Tyl Dramatic Society, which had been formed in 1881 (sometimes given as 1874). Known for a time as the Budivoy Dramatic Club Society, the organization in 1903 adopted the name of another Czech cultural leader, playwright Josef Tyl, who wrote the words to the Czech national anthem. By 1919, the society had 60 members and was producing a play a month during its season, which ran fom October to May. In the decade prior to its merger with Lumir-Hlahol, however, its productions had decreased to 1 or 2 each season.

Lumir-Hlahol-Tyl Singing Society Records, WRHS.

**LUNA PARK,** often called "Cleveland's fairyland of pleasure," was created by Fred Ingersoll, a famous builder of amusement-park rides. The park was the 34th such construction project undertaken by the Ingersoll Constr. Co. of Pittsburgh. It was located on a 35-acre site bounded by Woodhill Rd., E. 110th St., Woodland Ave., and Ingersoll Ave. Construction began in 1904, and the park opened on 18 May 1905. Many architectural styles (including Italian Renaissance, Egyptian, Gothic, and Japanese) characterized the midway, which was lit by thousands of incandescent lamps. A pool marked the center of Luna Park. In 1910, Ingersoll sold the very successful park to Matthew Bramley, a paving contractor and an original investor, who subsequently installed many new rides. The park had thrived on the availability of beer within the gates. However, with the beginning of Prohibition, its main source of revenue was removed. Despite Bramley's many innovative ideas, attendance continued to fall. With the onset of the Depression, Bramley was forced to close the gates of Luna Park in 1930. In 1931, wrecking crews began razing the park. The roller rink, a last vestige of Luna Park, was burned on 12 Dec. 1938.

The **LUTHERAN HOME** is a nonprofit residential and nursing facility for the elderly located on 20 acres of land at 2116 Dover Ctr. Rd. in WESTLAKE. Opened in 1936 in a small frame house that could accommodate 6 people, the facility had increased its capacity to 222 by 1985. The home was first expanded in 1939, when the house was replaced by a fireproof 3-story brick building, which was enlarged in 1944 and again in 1958; by 1959, the home could accommodate 70 residents. Beginning in 1961, the facility further increased its capacity and expanded its services by building 3 cottages, each containing 4 apartments. The cottages provided elderly residents greater independence but also gave them access to the home's nursing facilities as outpatients. The Lutheran Home is owned and operated by the Lutheran Home Assoc., which consists of 75 Lutheran churches in northeastern Ohio. Denominational and health restrictions for applicants were eliminated in 1957. The home has been certified by Medicare as an extended-care facility and by Medicaid as a skilled and intermediate nursing facility.

**LUTHERAN MEDICAL CENTER** (evangelical Lutheran Hospital), located at 2609 Franklin Blvd., was established in 1896 by the Evangelical Lutheran Hospital Assoc. of Cleveland. It was originally located in a private residence in FRANKLIN CIRCLE at W. 28th St. and Dexter Ave. In 1898, the Mark Hanna home was acquired and adapted for hospital use. It is a 221-bed, nonprofit, church-affiliated general hospital. The present hospital structure was built in 1922; additions and renovations were made in 1937, 1949, 1959, 1971, and 1975. In July 1986, Lutheran Medical Ctr. affiliated with FAIRVIEW GENERAL HOSPITAL in a joint venture called Health Cleveland, Inc. Health Cleveland is a holding company for Lutheran Medical Ctr. and Fairview General Hospital and their subsidiaries and foundations.

Brown, Kent L., ed., *Medicine in Cleveland and Cuyahoga County, 1810-1976* (1977).

**LUTHERANS.** When early Lutheran immigrants from Northern European countries settled in the WESTERN RESERVE as elsewhere, they formed branches of the church that were as diverse as their linguistic, ethnic, and political backgrounds; the religious tendencies prevailing in their homelands and among their leaders further contributed to the diversity of the church, as strains of the church differed according to orthodoxy, pietism, rationalism, idealism, and historical criticism. Such differing religious tendencies prompted one group of 45 worshippers to leave Cleveland's first German church, Zum Schifflein Christi (formed in 1835; see SCHIFFLEIN CHRISTI), in 1843 to form the city's first Evangelical Lutheran church, ZION EVANGELICAL LUTHERAN CHURCH.

As the history of the Zion Church suggests, the 19th century was one of institution building and religious and ethnic controversy for the Lutheran church in the Cleveland area, as elsewhere. Zion, known as the "Mother of Churches," was instrumental in forming other area churches, such as Trinity Evangelical Lutheran (1858) and ST. JOHN'S EVANGELICAL LUTHERAN CHURCH (1878); it also promoted Christian education, establishing its own Lutheran school by 1849 and in 1853 establishing a mission school in OHIO CITY, leading to formation of the Trinity congregation. Such mission-mindedness on the part of the Zion congregation went hand in hand with devotion to a particular vision of Lutheranism; in Sept. 1845, Zion hosted a meeting of pastors who were critical of the Joint Synod of Ohio for "ecclesiastical and confessional" and "moral" reasons; they were especially concerned with language, preferring German to English. The pastors, including Zion's Rev. August Schmidt, renounced connection with the Joint Synod; that was one of several meetings that led to the formation in 1847 of the Missouri Synod, which Zion joined in 1852 and which has always had more member churches in the Cleveland area than have other Lutheran synods. Language often became the battleground as German and other, later Lutheran immigrants who held dearly to tradition struggled to maintain their religious and cultural

identities in a foreign land against those who wished to "modernize" and Americanize their churches. While the Americanization forces often won out, occasionally the traditionalists triumphed, as did Zion's Rev. Henry C. Schwan when he introduced the German tradition of a lighted Christmas tree during the Christmas Eve service in 1851; despite much local criticism, Schwan maintained the Christmas tree, reportedly one of the first used in a church service in the U.S.

The growth of the Lutheran church during the city's industrial era (1870–1930) was the result of the arrival of Lutheran immigrants. Immigrant Lutheran churches formed during this period included First Scandinavian (1880), Bethlehem Church (Swedish, 1885), Holy Trinity Evangelical Lutheran Church (the first Slovak congregation in Ohio, 1892), Immanuel Danish-Norwegian (1894), Immanuel Church (Latvian, 1897), Gethsemane Lutheran Church (Finnish, 1903), First Hungarian Lutheran (1906), and Dr. Martin Luther Evangelical Lutheran Church (Slovak, 1910). These new Lutheran immigrant groups repeated much of the experience of the German Lutherans. For example, the Slovak SS. PETER & PAUL LUTHERAN CHURCH (est. 1901) began using English rather than Slovak in 1935 in order to maintain membership among its younger members; in addition to language, religious views and other issues prompted factions to establish the Pentecost Evangelical Lutheran Church in 1918 and the Gethsemane Lutheran Church in 1948. Also like the Germans, these Lutheran immigrant churches established their own schools and other institutions. First Hungarian Lutheran and its pastor, Rev. Steven Ruzsa, operated the Hungarian (Magyar) Orphans' Home on Rawlings Ave. from 1914–20. These churches also were mission-minded, helping to establish churches among their fellow immigrants in other parts of the county and in other cities.

With the passing of time, the descendants of the founders of these immigrant churches became Americanized, and the foreign tongues gradually disappeared from services. Divergences in viewpoints also disappeared, and several of the church organizational units, the synods, then merged. Thus, Greater Cleveland's 146 Lutheran congregations are now members of fewer synods; the 3 largest bodies in the area are the Lutheran Church-Missouri Synod (76 churches), the Lutheran Church in America (37 churches), and the American Lutheran Church (25 churches). The latter two plan to merge in 1988 with the Assoc. of Evangelical Lutheran Churches, of which Cleveland has 4 congregations. The Cleveland area also has 2 Wisconsin Evangelical Lutheran congregations, 1 independent church, and 1 congregation from the Latvian Evangelical Lutheran Church in America.

During the first half of the 20th century, local Lutherans continued their efforts to spread the word of God to unserved populations. On 3 Nov. 1914, representatives of 14 Missouri Synod churches in Cleveland formed the City Mission Society, which became the Lutheran Institutional Ministry in 1929; by 1964 it was providing ministerial services to 47 public and private institutions in the area, from private nursing homes to the Warrensville Workhouse. On 2 Oct. 1930, Dr. Walter H. Maier began broadcasting his "Lutheran Hour" radio program from the studios of WHK; the program, which was eventually broadcast worldwide, featured the Cleveland Bach Chorus (Greater Lutheran Chorus), which rekindled local enthusiasm for Bach's music in the 1920s–1930s. Pastor Horst Hoyer broadcast a radio program from 1958–78.

The post-World War II era witnessed the increased suburbanization of the Lutheran church. In 1948, plans were laid for a million-dollar construction program of Missouri

Synod churches in such communities as Fairview, EUCLID, CHAGRIN FALLS, Painesville, and MAPLE HTS. But as the church grew geographically, it also continued to expand its range of services. With the formation of Lutheran Hospital (later LUTHERAN MEDICAL CTR.) in 1896, the local Lutheran church began slowly to expand its work beyond religious and educational activities into the sphere of social welfare. The annual Lutheran Charities Campaign, begun ca. 1941, solicited funds to support various Lutheran institutions such as the LUTHERAN HOME, a nursing home opened in 1936. The church's social-welfare activities increased in the 1960s and 1970s in the wake of the 1967 Cleveland Summer Project, aimed at involving local congregations in racial and welfare programs. Led by Rev. Richard Sering, the 1967 project led in 1968 to the creation of the intersynodical Lutheran Metropolitan Ministry Assoc., which formed other agencies to meet local needs, such as the Lutheran Housing Corp.

In 1972, under the leadership of Pastor Horst Hoyer, the Lutheran Council of Greater Cleveland was formed to provide all branches of Lutheranism the opportunity to cooperate in support and promotion of Christ's ministry in the Cleveland area. This ministry extends to many Lutheran social agencies, including 8 centers for Crisis Ministry, the Housing Corp., 8 centers of the Urban Community Ministry, the Bethesda Group Home, the Community Reentry Program, the Immanuel Crisis & Hunger Ctr., the Nursing Home Ombudsman Program, and the Sexual Abuse Education & Assistance Program. The Lutheran Council, housed at 2031 W. 30th St., publishes the *Cleveland Lutheran Messenger*. In addition to sponsoring these social-welfare programs, area Lutheran churches continue to maintain a kindergarten, 16 elementary schools, and an East Side and a West Side high school.

John R. Sinnema
Baldwin-Wallace College

Allbeck, Willard D., *A Century of Lutherans in Ohio* (1966).
Meyer, J. H., *Early History of the Lutheran Church, Missouri Synod, in Cleveland, Ohio, and Vicinity, 1843–1893* (1960).
See also GERMANS.

The **LYCEUM THEATER** opened on 22 Oct. 1883 as the Park Theater. It became the Lyceum on 2 Sept. 1889. The Park Theater opened in the Wick Block on the northwest side of PUBLIC SQUARE next to the Old Stone Church. The Wick Block was built by the Wick family mainly to house the banking firm of Henry Wick & Co., but the Cleveland Board of Trade requested that a theater be included in the building plans. It was a large theater with an orchestra circle, a balcony, and a 3d-floor gallery. The stage was 38′ × 78′, with a proscenium opening of 36′. The newest in mechanical and electrical lighting was installed. The stage had 12 traps, a paint bridge, a movable scene frame, and 5 border lights with 50 gas jets each. There were also a prop room, a set storage room, a paint room, 3 fly galleries, and a rigging loft. The decor was in the Moorish style, with gold as the primary color. The Park Theater was under the management of AUGUSTUS F. (GUS) HARTZ. Opening night was a performance of *The School for Scandal*, with a reception at the home of Mr. and Mrs. Dudley B. Wick. On 5 Jan. 1884, a 3-alarm fire started after the audience had left a performance of *Humpty Dumpty*. The theater was rebuilt and reopened on 6 Sept. 1886 under the management of JOHN ELLSLER from the Opera House. The Park featured theater groups and opera companies. Ellsler made his last appearance as manager on 13 June 1887. On 2 Sept. 1889, the theater opened for its first season as the Lyceum Theater. The Lyceum had several managers until it was leased by the Ed Stair Syndicate. It featured a variety of popular attractions and summer stock in the early 1900s at lower prices than the EUCLID AVE. OPERA HOUSE. Its stars included Sarah Bernhardt and Lillian Russell, and the Cohan family. The Lyceum was torn down in 1913 to make way for the Illuminating Bldg.

Ezekiel, Margaret U., *The History of the Stage in Cleveland, 1875–1885* (Doctoral thesis, Dept. of Theatre Arts, WRU, Sept. 1967).
Wick, Warren Corning, *My Recollections of Old Cleveland* (1979).

**LYNCH, FRANK** (5 Nov. 1836–27 Feb. 1889), was a volunteer Army officer in the CIVIL WAR. Lynch was born in Canada. He had moved to Cleveland by the outbreak of the Civil War. On 14 Aug. 1861, he was commissioned captain, Co. G, 27th Ohio Volunteer Infantry, at Camp Chase near Columbus. In late Oct. 1862, he was ordered to open a recruiting office in Cleveland, which he established on Superior St. He later returned to the 27th Ohio, of Fuller's Ohio Brigade, which was heavily engaged throughout the Atlanta Campaign as part of the 4th Div., 16th Army Corps. During the Battle of Atlanta, 22 July 1864, Lynch was severely wounded during a charge; he never regained the full use of his arms. He was promoted to lieutenant colonel on 3 Mar. 1864 but never was mustered as such, being mustered out 20 May 1865. Lynch returned to Cleveland and became involved in Republican party politics in the 9th ward. His war wounds had debilitated his general strength, which plagued him for the rest of his life. In 1869, he was elected treasurer of Cuyahoga County; he was reelected in 1871. Lynch served on the committee for Decoration Day (now Memorial Day) ceremonies in 1871, chaired the Cleveland delegation to the Reunion of the Army of the Tennessee in Cincinnati, 6–7 Apr. 1872, and was a member of Creighton Post No. 69, Grand Army of the Republic. Lynch died from an apparent heart problem coupled with his war wounds. He is buried in LAKE VIEW CEMETERY.

**LYNDHURST,** incorporated as the village of Euclidville in 1917, was originally part of EUCLID TWP. It was renamed Lyndhurst in 1920. The name, chosen in a high school contest, was taken from Lyndhurst, N.J. The city was incorporated in 1951. It occupies 4.6 sq. mi. and is situated to the east of S. EUCLID, west of MAYFIELD HTS., north of BEACHWOOD, and south of RICHMOND HTS. and HIGHLAND HTS. The region had been settled by German immigrants and was principally agricultural before WORLD WAR I. Its population was 288 in 1920. The installation of water mains in 1922 and the increased availability of automotive transport caused the city to grow as a suburb. In 1940 its population stood at 2,391. In 1923, Lyndhurst residents strongly resisted a move to combine their schools with those of S. Euclid. In 1924, a landmark court decision ruled that the broad interests of education prevail over other considerations, and the schools were combined. The current combined school system has an enrollment of 4,926 in 9 elementary, 2 junior high, and 1 high school serving both communities. The major growth of Lyndhurst took place after WORLD WAR II. Principally residential, with a population of 18,092 in 1980, the city has no factories, though it has a number of retail businesses, many of which are centered at Richmond and Mayfield roads. In 1983, TRW constructed its world headquarters on the site of the former Chester and Frances Bolton estate. Recreational facilities include 2 swimming pools, 3 tennis courts, 1 public and 2 private golf courses, and 4 parks totaling 43.5 acres. Nine churches and 1 synagogue are located in Lyndhurst.

Keyerleber, Karl, *Hometown: The Story of Lyndhurst* (1950).

**LYRIC OPERA CLEVELAND** was founded by Anthony Addison, head of the Opera Dept. at the CLEVELAND INSTITUTE OF MUSIC, in 1974. In 1986 it was Cleveland's oldest ongoing opera company. It was founded as the Cleveland Opera Theatre Ensemble and became the Cleveland Opera Theatre in 1979. The name Lyric Opera Cleveland, announced on 2 Mar. 1985, was selected in an effort to clarify the company's identity in the community and to correct the growing confusion between the group and the CLEVELAND OPERA. In addition to presenting quality opera entertainment to summer audiences, the company has conducted outreach programs to provide opera education and entertainment to the young, elderly, and infirm. Lyric Opera Cleveland's main stage season has been from mid-July through early August, when 10 performances of 2 operas are sung in English, fully staged, employing a professional production staff and orchestra. Because of an outdoor picnic dinner available during an hour-long first intermission in most performances, the season was named the Al Fresco Festival. Lyric Opera Cleveland has played to approximately 5,000 patrons during its regular summer season, and to about 5,000 more through year-round outreach programs. It has performed at Kulas Hall of the Cleveland Institute of Music for all but 1 summer. The organization is governed by a board of trustees, headed in 1985 by Sam Sato, M.D. The executive director in 1985 was Michael McConnell.

# M

**MTD PRODUCTS, INC.,** a privately owned company, is a national leader in 2 industries—tool, die, and metal stampings and garden equipment. The company started as a tool-and-die shop in 1932 when Theodore Moll, Emil Jochum, and Erwin Gerhard founded the Modern Tool & Die Co. with a plant on W. 130th St. in PARMA. This company maintained a modest business for years; it then experienced great growth in the immediate postwar period. By 1952, it employed 500 people, with $7 million in business. About one-third of its orders were for tools and dies for various products, and the remainder were for metal stampings for the automotive and appliance industries.

The machine-tool business allowed the company to diversify. In 1954 it formed a garden-tool division. It began to manufacture mowers, tractors, and snow throwers and later moved into the production of recreational vehicles, such as bicycles, snowmobiles, and dune buggies. Demand for both product lines continued to grow. There were several expansions of the Parma plant, and in the 1960s, Modern built 3 other plants in the area, 2 in Medina County and 1 in Willard. In 1968, it changed its name to MTD Prods., Inc. MTD maintained its business in the 1970s but experienced some labor problems at its Parma plants late in the decade. In 1981, it strengthened its garden-line business by acquiring the reputable lawn and garden tractor line of the Internatl. Harvester Corp. and reorganizing it as the Cub Cadet Corp., a subsidiary of MTD. This acquisition greatly expanded MTD's market. By 1982 it had 12 engineering and manufacturing operations in the U.S., Canada, and W. Germany.

The **M. A. HANNA COMPANY,** one of the major iron-ore houses in Cleveland, is a leading company involved in mining, processing, and distributing minerals and in energy-related activities. Hanna Mining evolved from Rhodes & Co., a firm established in the 1840s by Daniel Rhodes. The firm initially mined coal in the Mahoning Valley area, but by the mid-1860s, it expanded into the mining and processing of iron in the Lake Superior region. The Hanna family's involvement in the company began when MARCUS HANNA married Rhodes's daughter in 1864. In 1885, Marcus, his brothers, Leonard C. Hanna and Howard M. Hanna, and Arnold C. Saunders took over the partnership and renamed it M. A. Hanna & Co. Under the Hannas, the company increased its fleet of bulk cargo vessels to 32 by 1917 and began to manage docks and blast furnaces.

In 1922, it was incorporated as the M. A. Hanna Co. with its offices in the Leader Bldg.

As a part of the trend toward mine-to-mill integration in steel production, Hanna placed its blast furnaces, its coke ovens, its vessels, and most of its iron-ore properties into the Natl. Steel Corp. in 1929 and in return received Natl. Steel stock. Hanna acted as a mining and shipping agent for Natl. Steel as it developed new iron-ore properties for itself and in joint ventures. By WORLD WAR II, Hanna managed the largest coal business in the Great Lakes region. Its Pennsylvania mines produced 12,000 tons of coal per day. In 1945, its bituminous-coal properties were put into the newly formed Consolidated Coal Corp. in return for Consolidated stock. GEO. HUMPHREY guided the company into a postwar period of diversification. Faced with the prospect of a critical shortage of iron ore in the early 1950s, the firm began production of high-grade iron-ore pellets and helped establish and manage the Iron Ore Co. of Canada, which undertook the development of the huge Quebec-Labrador iron fields with an annual production capacity of 30 million tons. The company also began to mine nickel in Oregon and silicon in Washington and acquired interests in mineral companies in Latin America.

In 1958, one of Hanna's subsidiaries, the Hanna Coal & Ore Co., emerged as an independent corporation, the Hanna Mining Co. The M. A. Hanna Co. continued as a mineral sales agent and an investment firm until it was liquidated in 1965. By the early 1970s, Hanna Mining was the world's second-largest producer of iron ore, after U.S. Steel. In the 1970s, Hanna entered the energy field, securing interests in petroleum, low-sulfur coal, and mineral-exploration companies. During the recession of the 1980s, the company suffered financial losses and periodically closed its 1 nickel and 4 iron mines. It has an annual production capacity of 53 million tons of iron and 26 million pounds of nickel. By 1985, Hanna Mining was active in 5 principal business areas: iron ore; oil and gas; nickel and silicon; coal; and management services. The firm believed that the name Hanna Mining did not reflect its diversified nature, which was international in scope, and in Mar. 1985 it elected to return to its original name, the M. A. Hanna Co.

F. S. Smithers & Co., *The Iron Ore Industry and the Cleveland-Cliffs Iron Company, the Hanna Mining Company, the M. A. Hanna Company* (1960).
Harvey H. Brown Papers, WRHS.

The M. A. Hanna Co., *Hanna Coal* (1945).

**MABERY, CHARLES F.** (13 Jan. 1850–26 June 1927), a chemist and a professor at Case School of Applied Science, was a leading researcher into the properties of petroleum. Born in New Gloucester, Maine, the son of Henry and Elizabeth Mabery, Charles received a public-school education, then spent 5 years teaching in various common schools and academies in Maine. In 1876 he earned a bachelor's degree from the Lawrence Scientific School at Harvard University, and in 1881 he received a Ph.D. from the Harvard Graduate School. From 1874–83 he served as an assistant in chemistry at Harvard and was the director of the Harvard Summer School in Chemistry for Teachers. Mabery came to Cleveland in 1883 to join the faculty at Case. He became a professor in 1884 and headed the chemistry department until he retired in 1911 because of ill health. Among his students were ALBERT W. SMITH and HERBERT DOW, founder of the Dow Chemical Co.

As a researcher in organic chemistry, Mabery was most interested in the composition of petroleum and published more than 60 papers on the substance. He was also interested in electrochemistry and worked with Alfred and Eugene Cowles to develop an electric furnace for smelting. He studied the metallurgy of aluminum, the extraction of bromine from brine, and the atmosphere of Cleveland. He was concerned about contemporary urban conditions and wrote papers on municipal water supplies and sanitation. Mabery was also a connoisseur of art and helped develop the CLEVELAND MUSEUM OF ART and the Cleveland School of Art. Upon his death, he left $65,000 to Case School of Applied Science. He stipulated that the money be held until it accumulated enough annual interest to endow a professorship. The first Chas. F. Mabery Professorship was awarded in 1969 to Geo. Olah. Mabery was married on 19 Nov. 1872 to Frances A. Lewis.

**MCAULEY, EDWARD J. "ED"** (24 Aug. 1903–25 Oct. 1961), was a sportswriter and columnist for the *CLEVELAND NEWS* from 1925–59. He also wrote for the *Sporting News* and, after 1959, syndicated a column in northern Ohio papers. Born in Hazelwood, Pa., McAuley grew up in Cleveland, attending St. Agnes Catholic School, Loyola (later St. Ignatius) High School, and JOHN CARROLL UNIVERSITY, graduating from the latter in 1925. He played both football and baseball in high school but chose to work on the school newspaper in college; that decision led to the journalistic experience that earned him a job at the *Cleveland News* in 1925. McAuley covered the Cleveland Rosenblums professional basketball team and college football in the area, but he became best-known in the 1930s and 1940s covering the sport he loved best: BASEBALL. From 1934 through the championship season of 1948, he covered the CLEVELAND INDIANS, and in 1939 he began writing a daily column in addition to his daily articles and features. He also served as the local correspondent for the *Sporting News*, later becoming its chief editorial writer. According to his *PLAIN DEALER* obituary, McAuley's baseball writings "ignored statistics and play-by-play to reflect the warmth of the human side of the game," and he became "one of baseball's foremost authorities." In the 1930s he led a successful campaign to have the hits and errors displayed on the scoreboard during the game. He was elected president of the Baseball Writers Assoc. of America in 1954 and in 1960 and 1961 served as the official scorer at Indians games. In 1952, the *News* editors decided to make greater use of the popular sportswriter and added to McAuley's duties a daily column on general and world affairs for the paper's first page; he continued the column for about a year. During his career, McAuley won 3 professional achievement awards from the CLEVELAND NEWSPAPER GUILD. He also won the 1958 Community Service Award of the Greater Cleveland Knights of Columbus. In addition to newspaper work, he lectured on journalism to high school and college classes and served as commissioner of the University Hts.-Cleveland Hts. Little League. McAuley was married in 1929 to the former Genevieve Quinn.

**MCBRIDE, ARTHUR B. "MICKEY"** (20 Mar. 1888–10 Nov. 1972), was a local businessman best known as the founder of the CLEVELAND BROWNS professional football team. His other business ventures included real estate, taxicabs, a radio station, and the controversial Continental Press Service, a nationwide distributor of racing news. McBride began selling newspapers on the streets of his native Chicago at age 6. After working for Wm. Randolph Hearst's newspapers in Los Angeles, San Francisco, Boston, and Chicago, he moved to Cleveland in 1913 to become circulation manager of the *CLEVELAND NEWS*. In Sept. 1930, with investments in local real estate, McBride resigned his post at the *News* to go into business for himself. In 1931 he bought a majority share of the Zone Cab Co., which later merged with the Yellow Cab Co. McBride's holdings steadily increased to include taxicab companies in Akron and Canton and real estate in Chicago and Florida.

McBride founded the Cleveland Browns in 1944. He had never seen a football game until his son entered Notre Dame in 1940; after watching the Fighting Irish, McBride became a dedicated football fan. He tried unsuccessfully to purchase the CLEVELAND RAMS in 1942, then joined the efforts of *Chicago Tribune* sports editor Arch Ward to organize the All-American Football Conference. When the 8-team league was announced on 3 Sept. 1944, McBride held the Cleveland franchise. He spent much of 1945 organizing and promoting his team, which did not begin play until 1946. After hiring the highly successful and popular Paul Brown as head coach, McBride turned his considerable promotional skills toward building fan support for the club, with a contest to name the team and advertisements on billboards, in newspapers, and on the back of his taxicabs. McBride owned the team during its years in the ill-fated AAFC and provided financial help to other owners in the league; when the AAFC collapsed in 1949, he arranged for the Browns to join the NFL. He introduced the concept of the "cab" or "taxi" squad for reserve players, so named because they drove cabs for McBride when not needed for actual play. In June 1953 he sold the team to a group of Cleveland businessmen for about $600,000, then the highest price ever paid for a pro football team.

Not everyone believed that all of McBride's ventures were entirely legal. In Jan. 1951, McBride was called to testify by Sen. Estes Kefauver's Senate Crime Investigating Committee, which questioned him about his ownership of the Continental Press Service and his alleged ties to organized crime, especially the Al Capone gang. McBride denied any such connections and claimed he had never broken the law. He was never charged with anything. Congress later passed legislation making wire services such as Continental illegal, and Continental Press was closed. McBride was preceded in death by his wife of many years, the former Mary Jane Kane, who died in Florida in Apr. 1971.

**MCDERMOTT, WILLIAM F.** (17 Feb. 1891–16 Nov. 1958), was the dean of Cleveland drama critics for nearly 40 years. McDermott was born in Indianapolis, Ind. After attending Butler College and working as a telegraph operator, he began his newspaper career on the *Indianapolis News* in 1914, and in 3 years he became its regular drama critic. Acting on the advice of numerous New York theatrical personalities, editor ERIE C. HOPWOOD brought McDermott to Cleveland as drama critic of the *PLAIN DEALER* in 1921. In addition to his customary critical jaunts to New York, McDermott persuaded the *Plain Dealer* to send him on annual tours of the European theatrical capitals, from where he sent back interviews with such luminaries as Somerset Maugham and Ferenc Molnar and accounts of visits to Max Reinhardt's castle and a Russian production of *Hamlet*.

With the decline of the legitimate stage in Cleveland after the 1930s, McDermott began writing columns on general topics. Moving farther afield, he covered the Detroit sit-down strikes of 1937 and the Spanish Civil War. During WORLD WAR II he covered the Italian front as war correspondent and subsequently described the formation of the United Nations in San Francisco. Following the war, McDermott continued to stand with one foot on the make-believe world of the stage and the other on the terra firma of world events. He took a strong stand against local censorship, which won the notice of *Newsweek*, and voiced some tentative concerns over the postwar growth of presidential power. Probably the high point of his critical career occurred during an illness in Dec. 1950, when Katherine Cornell brought the entire cast of her latest offering at the HANNA THEATER to his Bratenahl living room for a private performance. During his final illness, McDermott continued to send in his columns, dictating the last few to his second wife, the former Eva Pace of Newcomerstown, Ohio, whom he had married in 1938.

**MCDONALD & COMPANY SECURITIES** is a prominent Cleveland-based investment banking and brokerage house, which in 1985 was rated by *Forbes* magazine as one of the country's leading issues underwriters based on a survey of the performance of new issues over a 10-year period. The firm was formed in 1927 when Chas. B. McDonald and Jas. Callahan borrowed $50,000 to buy the Geo. W. York Co. Operating initially as McDonald & Callahan, the organization went through several name changes before becoming McDonald & Co. in 1944. The firm grew steadily, employing 200 people in 1964. In that year it purchased the assets of another Ohio investment firm, Field, Richards & Co. Employment increased to 250 in 1972 and to 440 in 1984. In July 1983, the company changed from a partnership to a publicly held corporation in order to maintain its independence at a time when other brokerage firms were being acquired by larger corporations. The stock offering raised its capital from $6 million to $26 million. The assets of the partnership were acquired for 5.25 million shares by the new McDonald & Co. Investments, Inc., incorporated in Delaware on 20 May 1983; 80% of the stock in the public corporation was held by former partners of McDonald & Co. The firm specializes in public and corporate finance. In addition to its 15 offices in Ohio, it operated 2 offices in Indiana and maintained other branches in Illinois, Massachusetts, Michigan, and New Jersey in 1985. Its total revenues that year were $43.9 million, yielding a net income of $2.85 million; both 1984 revenues ($51.16 million) and net income ($6 million) had been higher.

**MCFADDEN, JAMES A.** (24 Dec. 1880–16 Nov. 1952), was auxiliary bishop of the Diocese of Cleveland 1932–43 and the first bishop of Youngstown. McFadden was born in the Newburgh section of Cleveland. His parents were Edward and Mary Cavanaugh McFadden. He studied at the Cathedral and Holy Name grade schools and St. Ig-

natius High School and College before entering ST. MARY SEMINARY in Cleveland to study for the priesthood. He was ordained on 17 1905 by Bp. IGNATIUS F. HORST-MANN. From 1905–14, McFadden was associate pastor of St. Agnes Church in Cleveland. In 1914 he was named the founding pastor of St. Agnes Church in Elyria. He was called back to Cleveland in 1917 to serve as rector of St. Mary Seminary. In 1923, Bp. Schrembs named him the first diocesan director of the Society of the Propagation of the Faith, the diocesan mission office. Two years later, McFadden was named a domestic prelate, became chancellor of the diocese, and was given the title of monsignor. On 13 May 1932, he was named auxiliary bishop of Cleveland. His episcopal consecration took place on 8 Sept. 1932. On 15 May 1943, the formation of the Youngstown Diocese was announced. McFadden was appointed to head it on 22 July 1943. He continued to serve until increasing ill health forced him to ask for the appointment of a coadjutor bishop in Nov. 1949. His coadjutor bishop, Emmet Walsh, succeeded McFadden as bishop when McFadden died.

Archives, Diocese of Cleveland.

**MCGANNON, WILLIAM HENRY** (5 Oct. 1870–17 Nov. 1928), was a chief justice of the Cleveland Municipal Court who was twice acquitted of murder but was convicted of perjury in a third trial. McGannon was born in Willoughby but grew up in Conneaut and Geneva. After attending Geneva Normal School (1885–88), he taught for 2 years in Geneva and then moved to Cleveland. He attended Western Reserve Law School (1894–97). He passed the bar in 1898 and was soon appointed county examiner. He married Anna O'Donnell on 16 Oct. 1900. McGannon served as an assistant county prosecutor (1906–07) under Sylvester McMahon. In Nov. 1907, he was elected police-court judge. When the police court was abolished in 1911, McGannon was elected chief justice of the new municipal court, to which he was reelected to a 6-year term in 1915. McGannon was respected as a judge and was touted as the favorite for the 1921 Democratic mayoral nomination; many felt he could have been elected—at least until 8 May 1920. On that day McGannon hired mechanic Harold Kagy to fix his Cadillac; in late afternoon, they test-drove the car and ended up at a speakeasy on the city's far east end, where they met up with bondsman and saloon keeper John W. Joyce. Joyce joined them when they returned downtown. Stories conflict, but around midnight, Kagy was shot at E. 9th and Hamilton Ave. On his deathbed, Kagy stated that Joyce had shot him. Joyce denied the accusation, but Kagy maintained his story until his death.

Joyce was indicted for murder but was acquitted; the judge disallowed Kagy's claims. McGannon then was indicted. The first jury deadlocked despite the testimony of May Neely, who had followed McGannon's car and stated that McGannon had shot Kagy. At the second trial, Neely refused to testify on 5th Amendment grounds, and McGannon was acquitted. Neely had known McGannon for years, and rumors of an affair between them circulated. County Prosecutor Edward Stanton conducted a grand jury investigation; 15 people were indicted for perjury. McGannon, 2 reporters who had convinced Neely not to testify, and numerous witnesses who had supported McGannon's alibis were convicted. McGannon was sentenced to 1 to 10 years but served only 19 months because of diabetes. McGannon and his wife moved to Chicago in 1928, where he clerked for a law firm; he died after collapsing while boarding a trolley on his way to work. The McGannon trials, which occurred during a crime wave in Cleveland, are mentioned in the Cleveland Foundation's

CLEVELAND SURVEY OF CRIMINAL JUSTICE as an example of laxness in local justice. That led to reforms in the local justice system, such as the formation of a county probation department and the appointment of a chief justice for the common pleas court. The Assoc. for Criminal Justice was also formed to keep detailed records and issue regular reports suggesting further reforms of the local justice system.

**MCGEAN-ROHCO, INC.**, with offices in the Terminal Tower and a factory at 2910 Harvard, is a manufacturer of industrial and proprietary chemicals for the plating and metalworking industries. McGean-Rohco was established in the early 1980s when the McGean Chemical Corp. acquired another local firm, R. O. Hull & Co. The McGean Chemical Co. was founded in May 1929 by John A. McGean (1867–1958). Born in Cleveland, McGean served as president of the American Linseed Co. before returning to Cleveland in 1911 to become treasurer and later president of the Harshaw-Fuller & Goodwyn Co. With the founder as its president and his son Ralph L. McGean as vice-president and general manager, the company opened with offices in the B. F. Keith Bldg. at Euclid and E. 17th and a factory at 2910 Harvard. John McGean served as president of the firm until his retirement in 1955. During that time, the company became a leader in the manufacture of anodes and electroplating chemicals; it was also the original manufacturer of napalm and was the largest supplier of napalm to the U.S. government during WORLD WAR II.

By 1964, McGean had 300 employees; it operated a plant in Detroit in addition to its Cleveland facility, and its annual sales were more than $15 million. In 1965 McGean was bought by the Chemetron Corp. of Chicago; it operated as a division of Chemetron until 1968, when it was combined with Northwest Chemical in Michigan, Cee Bee Chemical in California, and Armalite Chemical in Toronto to form the new Inorganic Chemicals Div. of Chemetron. In 1974, a group of investors headed by division executive Dickson L. Whitney, son-in-law of Ralph McGean, purchased the division for $6 million and formed the new McGean Chemical Corp. By 1982, McGean Chemical had acquired another local firm, Rohco, Inc.

Rohco was founded as R. O. Hull & Co. in 1947 by local chemist Richard O. Hull. The company manufactured electroplating chemicals and equipment for plating zinc, cadmium, copper, and chromium, and by 1961 it had distributors in Los Angeles, Chicago, Toronto, and New Haven, Conn. The company had several locations before moving to 3203 W. 71st St. in 1963; it employed 20–30 people throughout the 1960s. It had sales of $5.3 million in 1972, and in July 1973 it was bought by the LUBRIZOL CORP. As a Lubrizol subsidiary, the company saw sales increase to $18 million in 1978; in May 1979, Lubrizol sold R. O. Hull & Co. to a group of private investors headed by Hull's management. By 1981 the company had changed its name to Rohco, Inc., and by 1982 it was part of McGean Chemical. In 1982, McGean-Rohco bought Du Pont Chemical's manufacturing rights to zinc, copper, and chromium plating agents; these and earlier acquisitions by McGean in 1978 (the formulated products venture from SHERWIN-WILLIAMS; technology and processes for plating on plastic from Borg-Warner; and the specialty chromium division of DIAMOND-SHAMROCK) helped boost McGean-Rohco's annual sales to $52 million in 1984.

**MCGHEE, NORMAN L. SR.** (20 Nov. 1897–20 July 1979), was the first licensed black stock dealer and broker in the Midwest and founded the first black-owned brokerage firm in the nation. He was active in city politics, serving as an appointed city council member in 1957. Born in Austell, Ga., McGhee was the son of an African Methodist Episcopal minister and a schoolteacher. Despite the limited education available to BLACKS in the South in the post-Reconstruction era, both of his parents were college-trained, and they encouraged their children to aspire beyond the 8 years of schooling available in Austell. McGhee therefore worked as a railway porter to earn his way to Howard University, where he completed high school (1916), college (1920), and law school (1922). After serving as private secretary and assistant to Emmett J. Scott, secretary-treasurer of Howard, McGhee came to Cleveland in 1925 to practice law. His association with Herbert S. Chauncey, a local black entrepreneur, led to his involvement as a legal consultant and shareholder in the EMPIRE SAVINGS & LOAN CO. and the Peoples Realty Co. He also became editor of the *Cleveland Post*, a weekly newspaper for Chauncey's insurance societies. When the *Post* merged with the *Call* to form the *CALL & POST*, McGhee became the new paper's first editor.

In order to supplement his income, McGhee became increasingly active in real estate. His success as a buyer, seller, and manager of his own properties established him as a model of black entrepreneurship. His organization of McGhee & Co. in 1952 was an extension of his determination to encourage blacks to gain a stronger foothold in the national economy through stock investment. Another innovation was his establishment of a mutual investment fund, Everyman's Fund, which was primarily aimed at the black community. A Democrat, McGhee was appointed to the City Planning Commission 1942–46. He also served as a ward leader in 1956. His civic activities included service as president of the Howard University Alumni, long-time fiscal advisor and board member of the PHILLIS WHEATLEY ASSOC., member of the board of FOREST CITY HOSPITAL, executive committee member of the Central Area Community Council, organizing member of the Glenville Area Community Council, and president of the Cleveland Chap. of Frontiers of America. McGhee never forgot his early religious roots and remained involved in the AME church as a trustee of ST. JAMES AME CHURCH and Wilberforce University. He was married 3 times. His first marriage, to Margery Vashon in 1925, ended with her death in 1933. He was married to Dorothy Cook from 1934 until her death in 1969. He married Rose Lewis Bulcher in 1970.

**MCGINTY, JAMES J.** (1882–11 Nov. 1937), a colorful Cleveland councilman from 1912–21 representing the Haymarket district, was a spokesman for both the poor and the powerful VAN SWERINGENS. McGinty attended Brownell School and CATHEDRAL LATIN, quitting at 14 to be a messenger for Western Union. He used his messenger days to expand his knowledge of the downtown area that would later be his ward. After a brief career as a demonstrator for a Lorain manufacturer, he turned to real estate, and by 1911 also to politics. Concurrently, he ran a bar below his Commercial St. home. Elected as councilman in 1911 for the newly redistricted downtown Ward 9, McGinty built support among his constituents through backslapping and entertainment that sometimes masked his concern for their well-being. He turned the annual ball of the Peerless Club, an organization of Haymarket youth, into the 9th Ward Ball. Until Prohibition, he brought in truckloads of sandwiches and beer for the annual event. When he could no longer serve beer, the balls failed, but he recouped by introducing ragtime concerts that attracted over 20,000 people. At his side was his wife, Mary (Lukacsko), who was known as the "Angel of the HAYMARKET" for her work among the poor. She died in 1921, and their only son died in infancy. In city council, McGinty was known as a hard worker who became the favorite of mayors and political leaders because of his affable nature and ability to get things done. He sponsored and often authored major city building legislation that included dock building for the lakefront; central heating plant ordinances to eliminate smoke and soot downtown; White Way downtown lighting; and zoning for orderly development. An ally of the Van Sweringens, he also promoted the legislation necessary to permit development of the Terminal Tower complex and the nearby Ohio Food Terminal. Since he also earned commissions from the Van Sweringens and owned stock in their ventures, he was accused of conflict of interest, but he claimed that he never compromised the good of the city or his constituents. In 1931, McGinty suddenly announced his resignation. He became a land and tax agent for the CLEVELAND RAILWAY CO. and was later (1936) named a vice-president. He died of a heart attack at age 54.

The **MCILRATH TAVERN** was a well-known hostelry located on the northwest corner of Euclid and Superior in E. Cleveland. Abner McIlrath opened the tavern in 1837, although some accounts state that his brother, Alexander, had earlier maintained a general store and tavern at the same location. The tavern distinguished itself as a local meeting place. People came from DOAN'S CORNERS and EUCLID TWP. to listen to candidates and vote. Abner, the owner of a pack of foxhounds, organized hunts, and shooting matches at Thanksgiving and Christmas. A garden was attached to the tavern and was considered a local meeting place for women. For children, a small menagerie was maintained that included an eagle, a wolf, and a bear. Abner McIlrath himself was locally celebrated for his size, purportedly 6′6″, 225 lbs. After his death, the tavern fell into neglect; it was torn down ca. 1890.

**MCILVAINE, CHARLES PETTIT** (18 Jan. 1799–14 Mar. 1873), was the second bishop of the Episcopal Diocese of Ohio (1832–73) and the second president of Kenyon College (1833–40). His travels about the state took him to Cleveland many times. His books and published sermons made him well known to the city's populace. McIlvaine was born in Burlington, N.J. He graduated from the College of New Jersey (1816), studied theology privately (1816–17), and entered a Presbyterian seminary for 2 years of study (1817–19). He married Emily Coxe in 1822.

McIlvaine's professional life, both in and out of the ministry (ordained deacon 1820 and priest 1823), was long and distinguished. He mixed his vocation and evangelical philosophy with a preference for society and power, while using his oratorical skills to advocate American religious freedom and warn about Catholic intrusion into Protestant America. His impressive physical qualities, strong opinions, and outspoken manner made for an iron-fisted administrator and a church philosopher not afraid to take up the cudgels in a pamphlet war against English Tractarians at Oxford or to ruffle the doctrinal sensitivities of his fellow American bishops. His prominence on both sides of the Atlantic led to honorary doctorates from Princeton and Brown (1832), Oxford (1853), and Cambridge (1858). He died in Italy, and his funeral was held in Westminster Abbey. Concerned about religious persecution, McIlvaine joined a deputation to Europe in 1871 to meet Czar Alexander II and protest Russian religious persecution in the Baltic area. Of his many writings, his most popular book was *Evidences of Christianity* (1832), which went into 30 editions.

McIlvaine organized one of the first Sunday schools in the nation while still a seminarian. His appointment as chaplain to the U.S. Senate (1822–25) came while he was still a young rector. At West Point, where he was chaplain and professor of ethics (1825–27), he revived interest in religion and influenced many students who became important leaders on both sides of the CIVIL WAR. As professor of religion at the University ov the City of New York 1831–32), he inaugurated a series of popular lectures. He declined the presidency of the College of William & Mary (1827). In Ohio, McIlvaine traveled constantly, confirming new members and consecrating new churches, including Cleveland's ST. JOHN'S (1836), Trinity (1854), and ST. PAUL'S (1858). At Kenyon he redeemed the college from bankruptcy and instituted its rebuilding. Pres. Lincoln appointed McIlvaine a special envoy to England to help salvage Anglo-American relations after the Trent Affair (1861).

Bishops of Ohio Records, Episcopal Diocese of Ohio Archives.

**MCKINNEY, WADE H.** (19 July 1892–18 Jan. 1963) and **RUTH BERRY** (24 Sept. 1900–4 Dec. 1966), were influential religious and civic leaders in Cleveland. As pastor of ANTIOCH BAPTIST CHURCH, Rev. McKinney was a powerful figure, especially among the city's black population. Ruth McKinney, an activist in church circles, was also important as a speaker and leader. Wade Hampton McKinney was born in White County, Ga. He attended Atlanta Baptist College Academy, Morehouse College, and the Colgate Rochester Theological Seminary. He also served in the U.S. Army in WORLD WAR I. In 1924, while serving as pastor of Mt. Olive Baptist Church in Flint, Mich., he married Annie Ruth Berry. She was born in Birmingham, Ala., and educated at Spelman College and Columbia University. The couple moved to Cleveland in 1928 to lead the fast-growing Antioch Church.

Rev. McKinney participated in local and national organizations. He served as president of the CLEVELAND BAPTIST ASSOC. and the Cuyahoga Interdenominational Ministerial Alliance. An outstanding orator, Rev. McKinney frequently served as spokesman for Cleveland's black community and was the first black foreman of the Cuyahoga County Grand Jury. Rev. McKinney was an organizer of the Quincy Savings & Loan Co. and of FOREST CITY HOSPITAL, and he led many voter-registration campaigns.

Annie Ruth Berry McKinney was a college teacher when she married. As the wife of Antioch's minister, she became active in the affairs of religious organizations in Cleveland and across the nation and was in great demand as a speaker. Beginning in 1952, she broadcast 1-minute radio "Thot-O-Grams" under the auspices of the United Church Women of Cleveland.

Wade Hampton McKinney Papers, WRHS.

**MCKISSON, ROBERT ERASTUS** (30 Jan. 1863–14 Oct. 1915), served as Republican mayor of Cleveland 1895–99. McKisson was born in Northfield in Summit County, Ohio, the son of Martin Van Buren and Finette Adeline Eldridge McKisson. The family came to Cleveland in the early 1870s, and McKisson attended Cleveland grammar school. The family moved to LaGrange, Ohio, in 1879, where he graduated from high school. He earned enough money to enroll in Oberlin Preparatory School in 1885. He came to Cleveland in 1887 to study law in the offices of THEODORE E. BURTON. Admitted to the bar in 1889, he practiced law with John Webster and Elgin Angell in 1891.

Politics attracted McKisson, and he was elected to the Cleveland City Council from the 3d district in 1894. During his year on council, he was an active critic of the Democratic administration of Mayor ROBT. BLEE, and he succeeded Blee as mayor in 1895. During his 2 terms in office, construction was begun on a new water and sewer system for the city. River and harbor improvements included the widening and straightening of the CUYAHOGA RIVER to facilitate steamer traffic, and 5 new bridges were built across the river. McKisson built a local political machine loyal to him and challenged MARCUS A. HANNA for control of the Republican party here. In 1898, he and Hanna were rival candidates to represent Ohio in the U.S. Senate. Senators were elected by the state legislature at that time, and McKisson came very close to defeating Hanna. McKisson was defeated for reelection as mayor in 1899, after which he retired from politics; he returned to the practice of law and became a partner in the firm of McKisson & Minshall in 1905. He married Celia Launette Watring in 1891, and they were divorced in 1900. He married Mamie Marie Langenau in 1901, and they were divorced in 1912. He married Pauline E. Reed of Buffalo 3 weeks before his death in Cleveland at age 52.

Campbell, Thomas F., "Background for Progressivism" (Master's thesis, Dept. of History, WRU, 1960).

**MACLEOD, JOHN JAMES** (6 Sept. 1876–17 Mar. 1935), headed the Physiology Dept. at Western Reserve University and was later awarded a Nobel Prize as a codiscoverer of insulin. MacLeod was born in Cluny, Scotland. He received a medical degree with honors from Marischal College in Aberdeen in 1898. After further study in Leipzig, he returned to England, where from 1900–03 he taught physiology and biochemistry at the London Hospital Medical School. In 1903, at the age of 27, he was appointed professor of physiology at WRU. While at WRU, MacLeod began research on the pathology of diabetes. His research and publications on diabetes and other subjects helped considerably to establish the reputation of the medical school. In 1918, MacLeod became professor of physiology at the University of Toronto, where he continued his work on diabetes. His collaboration with Dr. F. G. Banting led within a few years to the discovery of insulin. As a result, the two men were awarded the Nobel Prize in Medicine in 1922. MacLeod returned to Scotland in 1928 to become Regius Professor of Physiology at Marischal College. His last visit to Cleveland was in 1926.

**MCQUIGG, JOHN REA** (5 Dec. 1865–26 Oct. 1928), was a Cleveland banker, lawyer, and leader in military affairs; he served as captain of infantry in the SPANISH-AMERICAN WAR, lieutenant colonel of engineers during the Mexican border campaigns, and colonel of engineers during WORLD WAR I. From 1907–13, he served 3 consecutive terms as mayor of E. CLEVELAND, his place of residence. He is perhaps best remembered as the national commander of the largest veterans' organization in the U.S., the American Legion. Born to Samuel and Jane McKinley McQuigg on a farm near Hudson, Ohio, McQuigg was educated in Wooster at the local grammar school; he graduated from Wooster College, where he was a cadet captain, in 1888. Entering Cornell Law School for a term of 1 year, McQuigg transferred to the Natl. Law School in Washington, D.C., receiving his law degree in 1890. That same year he was admitted to the Ohio bar, and then he joined the Ohio Natl. Guard Infantry as a 1st lieutenant. From 1892–98, McQuigg was a member of the famous CLEVELAND GRAYS. During the Spanish-American War, he held rank as captain of the 10th Ohio Volunteer Infantry, and

from 1899–1916, he was lieutenant colonel of engineers of the Ohio Natl. Guard.

During World War I, on 5 Aug. 1917, McQuigg was promoted to commander of the 112th Engineers of the 37th Div.; he was responsible for mobilization of the regiment at Camp Sheridan, Ala. In June 1918 he was sent to France, serving on the western front; he received an honorable discharge from service on 17 Jan. 1919. On 28 April 1920, McQuigg was recommissioned colonel of engineers. Devoting considerable time, money, and energy to the development of the American Legion, McQuigg was commander of its Ohio Dept. from 1920–21 and was also an active member of legion finance and executive committees. On 10 May 1921, he was appointed brigadier general of the Ohio Natl. Guard of the 37th Div. This appointment, together with his committment to legion affairs, secured his election as national commander of the American Legion on 10 Oct. 1925 at the 7th Annual Convention in Omaha, Nebr. In private life, McQuigg was a keen businessman, helping to organize the E. Cleveland office of the Windermere Savings & Loan Co., which opened in 1915. With the main office located on EUCLID AVE., McQuigg worked for the east side branch, moving from director to vice-president, then to president and general counsel. In addition to his banking activities, McQuigg and former classmate Geo. B. Riley established the law firm of Riley & McQuigg for the general practice of law. McQuigg's special interest in municipal law aided in his successful bid for the office of mayor of E. Cleveland. McQuigg was survived by his wife, Gertrude W. Imgard, whom he married on 16 Feb. 1892, and their 2 children, Pauline and Donald.

**MADONNA HALL,** 106 E. 82nd St., is a nursing home that began as a Catholic-run boarding house for working girls and women. In 1926, the Daughters of the Immaculate Heart of Mary converted the large brick apartment building into a boarding home to replace the St. Mary's Home for Working Girls on E. 20th St., which the religious order had opened in 1895 in the remodeled building that had housed St. Mary's Orphanage (see ST. JOSEPH'S ORPHANAGE FOR GIRLS). Madonna Hall operated as a residence for business and professional women until 1946, when the Catholic Diocese of Cleveland acquired the 4-story brick building and converted it into a nursing home operated by the Franciscan Sisters of the Blessed Kunegunda. The building was remodeled to accommodate 105 elderly women. A separate chapel with seating capacity of 125 was dedicated on 26 June 1948. Catholic Charities and the Sisters of the Blessed Kunegunda operated the nursing home until the religious order became unable to staff it in 1970; that year the home was sold to a consortium of doctors. Their company, Scidem, Inc., headed by Dr. Edward L. Wilderson, continued to operate the facility as a nursing home. Residents who wished to remain in Catholic-run homes were transferred elsewhere, and Madonna Hall ceased to be a Catholic organization.

**MAGEE, ELIZABETH STEWART** (29 June 1889–14 May 1972), was active in Cleveland and nationally in securing labor-reform legislation. She was particularly instrumental in the passage of child- and female-labor laws. Magee was born in Des Moines, Iowa. In 1911, after graduating from Oberlin College, she taught in the Altoona, Pa., public schools. In 1916 she moved to Denver, Colo., where she served as the YWCA secretary. In 1918 she accepted a position in Detroit, Mich., as industrial secretary of the local YWCA, where she was responsible for planning and directing recreational and educational programs for the city's women industrial workers. From 1922–24 she served the YWCA in New York City as its national industrial secretary, organizing national concerns of female industrial workers. While in New York, Magee attended Columbia University, receiving a master's degree in economics in 1925.

From 1925 until she retired in 1965, Magee served the CONSUMERS' LEAGUE OF OHIO as its executive secretary. She immediately became active in the labor movement and began to develop a close relationship with labor leaders in state and federal government. Her study of unemployment in 1928 led to the Ohio Plan of unemployment compensation, which, as a form of unemployment insurance, stressed more secure funding and larger benefits. Magee played an instrumental role in the Consumers League as it campaigned for the passage of a minimum-wage law for women in 1933 and for Ohio's ratification of the federal child-labor amendment. Magee, along with the league, worked to prevent child labor; for a shorter work week for women; to improve the status of Ohio's migrant workers; and to support and improve various other social-welfare issues. Magee's work with the league attracted academics, religious leaders, and intellectuals to it and its purpose and goals. From 1943–58, she also served as the general secretary for the Natl. Consumers' League.

Consumers' League of Ohio Records, WRHS.
Elizabeth Stewart Magee Papers, WRHS.

The **MAISON FRANCAISE DE CLEVELAND** is an American organization whose purpose it is to promote Franco-American cultural activities. The group was founded by EMILE B. DE SAUZE in 1918. It was registered as a nonprofit organization by its first president, Paul D. Wurtzburger, and in 1923 it became affiliated with the French Alliances of the U.S. In 1980, the organization's membership stood at 260. Its main activities at the time centered about the encouragement of the study of the French language; this goal was fostered by the organization's gifts of monetary prizes to students in Cleveland secondary schools.

Maison Francaise de Cleveland Records, WRHS.

The **MALL** and the 7 public buildings surrounding it were constructed following the Group Plan of 1903, which probably constitutes the earliest and most complete civic-center plan for a major city outside of Washington, D.C. Since federal, county, and municipal governments were all planning to build large new structures, a Group Plan Commission was created in 1902 as a result of bills prepared by the American Institute of Architects and the Cleveland Chamber of Commerce and passed by the legislature. The members were Daniel Burnham, Arnold Brunner, and John Carrere. The Group Plan Report of 1903 recommended the 500-ft.-wide mall and the placement of the major buildings. The need for uniformity of style and building height was stated as the lesson of the Chicago Columbian Exposition of 1893. European precedents were cited, especially the Palais Royal and the Place de la Concorde in Paris. The Roman style was recommended, meaning the Beaux-Arts version of ancient classicism. The report was supported and its development promoted by Progressive mayor TOM L. JOHNSON. The significance of the conception was recognized across the country, and laudatory articles appeared in national journals.

The Federal Bldg. had already been planned, and was completed in 1910. It was followed by the CUYAHOGA COUNTY COURTHOUSE (1911), the CLEVELAND CITY HALL (1916), the PUBLIC AUDITORIUM (1922), the Public Library (1925), and the Board of Education administration building (1930). The last old structure within the

mall area was torn down in 1935, and the Mall was used for the GREAT LAKES EXPOSITION of 1936. At the south end of the Mall, the WAR MEMORIAL FOUNTAIN with a tall symbolic bronze statue by Marshall Fredericks was planned in 1946 but was not completed until 1964. In the early 1960s, the entire north mall was excavated to create a vast underground convention center connected to the Public Auditorium, and the Hanna fountains were installed on the surface and flanked with trees and plantings. The Mall is frequently used for various community celebrations and festivities.

**MALVIN, JOHN** (1795–30 July 1880), was an important leader of Cleveland's black community during the 19th century. He worked at various times as a cook, sawmill operator, carpenter and joiner, and canal-boat captain. He was also a licensed and ordained Baptist preacher, an active abolitionist, and a supporter of public education. Malvin was born in Dumfries, Prince William County, Va., of a slave father and a free mother. That made him free under the Slave Code. In his youth he was apprenticed as a carpenter. He was secretly taught to read by a slave who used the Bible as a textbook. He arrived in Cleveland in 1831, following a short stay in Cincinnati, where he became part of the antislavery movement.

Malvin is credited with organizing a black school committee in 1832 in Cleveland and a statewide committee in 1835, to find ways to finance educational opportunities for blacks in Ohio. Under the auspices of the School Fund Society, schools for black children were opened in Cleveland, Columbus, Springfield, and Cincinnati. At the same time, the state and local committees worked to change Ohio laws that prohibited municipalities from establishing even segregated schools for blacks. Efforts of black citizens in Cleveland resulted in some limited subsidy from city council for the privately supported black free school and abolishment of the clause in state law, in 1848, that limited access to public-school education to white children.

Malvin and his wife, Harriet, were 2 of the 17 charter members who signed the Covenant of Faith in 1833 to form the FIRST BAPTIST CHURCH. He led a struggle to prevent the church from building a "colored gallery," a popular means of segregating church members. At the onset of the CIVIL WAR, at age 66, he organized a black military company that offered service to the Union Army. The governor of Ohio turned down the offer, and the troops in Malvin's company joined the famous 54th and 55th regiments of Massachusetts. As a fighter for citizenship rights for blacks, Malvin participated in many local and state organizations and conventions. He served as a lecturer for the Ohio State Anti-Slavery Society and was reputed to be active in the Underground Railroad. Malvin vigorously worked in opposition to Ohio's BLACK LAWS, as well as to injustices and inequalities against blacks sanctioned by custom. He remained an active opponent of legislation that would limit the rights of Ohio's black citizens. Malvin, known to many as "Father John," died at the age of 85 at his Cleveland home.

**MANDELBAUM, MAURICE J. (MOSES)** (1863–16 July 1938), was a philanthropist, a Jewish communal leader, a banker, and one of Cleveland's most powerful interurban-railway magnates. Born in Cleveland, he was the son of Jacob Mandelbaum, a wealthy retail clothier who immigrated from Germany in 1852. After graduating from CENTRAL HIGH SCHOOL in 1880, he went to work for his father. Mandelbaum was involved in the creation of several business concerns during the latter part of the 19th century. He founded the Fisher Book Typewriter Co., which later became the Underwood Elliot Fisher Co., and was a founder of the Western Reserve Trust Co., which later merged with the Cleveland Trust Co. Following that merger, he served on the board of directors of Cleveland Trust. In 1896, Mandelbaum began his career in the railway business when he and his brother-in-law, Leopold Wolf, formed the Western Ohio lines. They also were interested in the Aurora-Chicago-Elgin line. Mandelbaum later became the principal owner of the Southern Ohio Traction Co.

Mandelbaum was a consummate fundraiser and was active in communitywide organizations, as well as being a leader in Jewish communal affairs. He was chairman of the Cleveland chapter of the Red Cross for 2 years, and he served on the board of directors of the CITIZENS LEAGUE. Following the death of his father in 1916, Mandelbaum became president of the board of the MONTEFIORE HOME. He served as director, treasurer, or president of Montefiore for 25 years. He was also on the board of trustees of the TEMPLE and served as vice-president of the Educational League, an organization established by Rabbi MOSES GRIES to ensure that alumni of the Jewish Orphan Home had the opportunity to receive college educations.

**MANNING, THOMAS EDWARD "RED"** (27 Sept. 1899–4 Sept. 1969), was the dean of radio sportscasting in Cleveland. He broadcast the first Indians game over radio station WTAM. Manning was born in the ANGLE, on the near west side of Cleveland. He attended St. Colman School and after classes sold afternoon newspapers. Winning a contest at Euclid Beach for the newsboy with the loudest voice led to his career as an announcer. Tommy McGinty hired him to introduce boxers at the Olympic Arena. A fine outfielder with the Telling team in Class AAA, Manning played before a crowd of 100,000 at BROOKSIDE PARK in 1917. The CLEVELAND INDIANS hired him to be the field announcer at Dunn Fld. (LEAGUE PARK). Using a 4′ megaphone, Manning shouted the lineups to the press box and the batteries to the fans. His voice was described as "the second loudest noise in Cleveland, the first being the foghorn off WHISKEY ISLAND."

Manning's first radio job came in 1926 when WJAY, located in the HOLLENDEN HOTEL, hired him to give the baseball scores. Manning moved to WTAM in 1928, and Billy Evans, Tribe general manager, hired him to be the first radio voice of the Indians. In 1931 another radio station got the baseball contract, and Manning's connection with the Indians ended. Years later, in 1956, he joined Jimmy Dudley to announce Cleveland baseball over station WERE, but he had to resign in 1957 because an ear infection made it painful for him to fly. For 6 years, beginning in 1929, Manning joined Graham McNamee to do network baseball and World Series broadcasting. The radio voice of the Ohio State University football team for 30 years, he was a cheerleader for the Buckeyes. An enthusiastic creator of word pictures, Manning did many dance-band "remotes" for WTAM and was the first to introduce singer Perry Como to a radio audience. The announcer for the famed "Gene & Glenn Show," he introduced many other radio programs. He announced for WERE, KYW, and WHK before retiring in 1967. Manning married his first wife, Amelia, on 11 Sept. 1924, and they were divorced in 1939. His second wife, Hazel, survived him.

**MANRY, ROBERT N.** (3 June 1918–21 Feb. 1971), sailed a 13½-ft. sloop named *Tinkerbelle* across the Atlantic from Falmouth, Mass., to Falmouth, England. At the time, it was believed to be the smallest boat ever to cross the Atlantic nonstop. Manry was born in Landour, India, the son of Presbyterian missionary-educator Dr. Jas. C. and Margaret Manry. He left India in Dec. 1936, and after studying briefly at Lingnan University in Canton, China, he enrolled at Antioch College in Yellow Springs, Ohio, in the fall of 1937. College was interrupted by service in Europe during World War II, after which Manry returned to Antioch, receiving an A.B. degree in political science in 1948. In 1950, he married Virginia Place of Pittsburgh. He worked as a reporter for newspapers in Washington Court House, Ohio, and Pittsburgh and Erie, Pa., coming to Cleveland in 1953 to work at the *PLAIN DEALER* as a copy editor.

Manry's enthusiasm for boating had begun in India when he sailed on the Jumna River. However, he was not able to afford to buy his own boat until 1958. Naming his second-hand boat *Tinkerbelle*, Manry, who described himself as a novice sailor, first sailed it on Lake Erie in 1959. In order to fulfill his dream of crossing the Atlantic, he improved his sailing skills and completed the necessary modifications so that *Tinkerbelle* could sail the Atlantic. After making thorough preparations for the voyage in 1965 and taking vacation time and a leave of absence from the *Plain Dealer*, he left Falmouth, Mass., on 1 June for Falmouth, England, 3,200 mi. away. The voyage took 2½ months, during which time he was knocked overboard 6 times and had to repair a broken rudder. As the news of his adventure became known, his progress was covered by the national and international news services. The *Plain Dealer* flew his wife and 2 children to England to meet him when he landed. Bill Jorgensen, WEWS newscaster, met and interviewed Manry on 9 Aug., when he was still about 270 mi. out at sea. He landed at Falmouth on 17 Aug. 1965, completing a 78-day voyage. Manry wrote a book about his adventure entitled *Tinkerbelle* and donated the sailboat to the WESTERN RESERVE HISTORICAL SOCIETY. In 1967–68, he, his wife, and their 2 children took a year-long cruise in a 27-ft. yawl, covering 5,000 mi. through the Great Lakes and down the Mississippi River, returning through the Atlantic and the St. Lawrence Seaway. After their return, Virginia was killed in an automobile accident in 1969. Manry then married Jean Flaherty, and shortly afterward he died of a heart attack at age 52.

Robert Manry Papers, WRHS.

**MANX.** *See* **BRITISH IMMIGRATION**

**MAPLE HEIGHTS** is a 5-sq. mi. residential and industrial community approximately 10 mi. southeast of downtown Cleveland. Bounded on the north by Cleveland and WARRENSVILLE HTS., on the south by BEDFORD and WALTON HILLS, on the east by BEDFORD HTS., and on the west by GARFIELD HTS., it was originally the northwest part of Bedford Twp., established in 1823. The early history of Maple Hts. is synonymous with that of Bedford. Benjamin Fitch of Connecticut was the first-known settler in 1813 of what was to become Maple Hts. John Dunham, who came in 1817, built the road known as Dunham Rd., which gave access to the Ohio Canal after 1827. The area grew and developed with the opening of the Cleveland & Pittsburgh Railroad (1849) and the Connotton Valley Railroad (1881). The Akron, Bedford & Cleveland interurban line was also completed through the area in 1895 and operated until 1932. By the turn of the century, immigrants from Bohemia, Slovenia, and Lithuania began to settle in the area to work in the industries of nearby NEWBURGH. The first Czech settlers were the families of Joseph Uhlik, Joseph Hodous, and P. N. Tresnicka. The first Slovenian families were those of Martin Potisek (1906) and John Rybak (1909). In 1914, the residents of the Maple Grove area, when annexation to Bedford Village seemed imminent, voted to form their own community. Maple Hts. Village was incorporated in July 1915 with a population of 1,000. It was named for the many maple trees in the area. The village continued to grow with immigrants from Southern and Eastern Europe, many of whom moved from Cleveland. Many Czechs moved from the old ST. WENCESLAS CHURCH at Broadway and E. 39th St. and founded a new St. Wenceslas Church on Libby Rd. In 1930, the population was 5,950. A city charter providing for a mayor-council form of government was adopted by voters in June 1930. Maple Hts. became a city on 1 Jan. 1932.

The city expanded industrially primarily along Dunham Rd. Plants included the Aluminum Smelting & Refining Co., Chas. Svec, Inc., LEMPCO INDUSTRIES, and the Dunham Industrial Park. Later companies located along Rockside Rd., including Kraft Foods, COOK UNITED, INC., the Lederer Warehouse Co., and the JONES & LAUGHLIN Steel Corp. Warehouse. Between 1934–40, the population grew from 5,950 to 6,728. It continued to grow during WORLD WAR II as major war-production plants opened in the city. During the postwar years, there was a building boom. Mapletown shopping center was built in 1947 at Libby and Broadway, and the giant shopping, recreational, housing, and medical center of SOUTHGATE was begun in 1951. The population grew from 15,586 in 1950 to 31,667 in 1960. In 1985, Maple Hts. had its own school system, a variety of churches, and many cultural, social-service, and recreational organizations. Much of the population was of Czech, Polish, Italian, or other Southern or East European ancestry. When the city celebrated its 50th anniversary in 1982, its population was 34,093.

*MAPP V. OHIO* was a landmark court case, originating in Cleveland, in which the U.S. Supreme Court ruled that under the 4th and 14th amendments to the Constitution, illegally seized evidence could not be used in a state criminal trial. This decision significantly changed law-enforcement procedures throughout the country. The case began on 23 May 1957 when police officers entered the Cleveland home of Dollree Mapp looking for a person wanted for questioning in a recent bombing and for illegal gambling paraphernalia. The police made a thorough search, and although neither the person nor the gambling materials were found, they did find obscene material, which Mapp denied owning. Under then-current Ohio law, possession of obscene materials was illegal, and Mapp was arrested. In the fall of 1958, she was tried, convicted, and sentenced to 1–7 years in the penitentiary for possessing obscene books, pictures, and photographs. No search warrant was produced at the trial, nor was the failure to produce one accounted for. Her lawyer, A. L. Kearns, appealed the decision to the Ohio Supreme Court on the basis that Ohio's obscenity law violated her right to privacy, and only secondarily that the conduct of the police in obtaining the evidence was unconstitutional. The court affirmed her conviction under the state obscenity law, and despite the absence of a search warrant, they also ruled that illegally seized evidence could still be entered in a criminal trial.

Kearns appealed the case to the U.S. Supreme Court on the same grounds, contending that Mapp's conviction violated her constitutional rights. At the invitation of the Court, Cleveland attorney Bernard Berkman, representing the American Civil Liberties Union, also submitted a brief. During the oral argument, he urged the high court to examine the constitutionality of search-and-seizure usage in state courts, since federal courts prohibited the use of illegally obtained evidence. On 20 June 1961, the Supreme Court in a 5–4 decision overturned Mapp's conviction on

the grounds that evidence seized without a search warrant cannot be used in state criminal prosecutions under the 4th Amendment to the Constitution, which protects people against unreasonable searches and seizures, and the 14th Amendment, which extends that protection to state jurisdictions, as well. This limitation changed state law-enforcement procedures by making it necessary to obtain a search warrant in most cases in order to avoid having evidence disallowed in court.

The **MARGARET WAGNER HOME,** a facility for the needy aged, was named after MARGARET WAGNER, former director of the BENJAMIN ROSE INSTITUTE. Wagner also founded the Golden Age Club, where aged members could practice their hobbies and enjoy various forms of entertainment. By 1945, there were 16 Golden Age Clubs, and membership had reached 850. The Margaret Wagner Home was built in 1960 and opened in 1961. It is owned and run by the Benjamin Rose Institute, which donates over $100,000 annually. It is located at 2373 Euclid Hts. Blvd. in CLEVELAND HTS. The home has 175 beds and is usually at full occupancy. It services both long-term and short-term patients who need only rehabilitation care for broken bones or strokes. These patients may use either the Medicaid or Medicare program or Rose Institute funds to pay for the treatment. The home is a nonprofit organization.

**MARGOLIES, SAMUEL** (1878–29 June 1917), educator, Zionist, and communal leader, was rabbi of ANSHE EMETH CONGREGATION from 1904–16 and during those years was the acknowledged spokesman for the Orthodox community in Cleveland. The son of Rabbi Moses Zebulon Margolies, Samuel was brought to America from his native Russia by his parents in 1882. In 1890 he returned to Russia to study at the Telshe Yeshiva. Eight years later he again came to the U.S.; he entered Harvard University, graduating in 1902. Margolies accepted the pulpit at Anshe Emeth in 1904 and was responsible for making it the most important Orthodox congregation in the city during the following decade. With an educational grounding in Talmudic studies and secular arts and sciences, Margolies introduced a modern element into Orthodoxy. He preached not only in Yiddish, which was the vernacular of immigrant Jews, but also in English, and he encouraged his listeners to discard their East European attire and mannerisms and to Americanize as quickly as possible. In 1912, he encouraged the creation of Congregation Beth Tifilah to serve Orthodox Jews who had moved into GLENVILLE. He was instrumental in arranging the merger between that congregation and Anshe Emeth in 1916. The merger and Margolies's leadership in increasing Anshe Emeth's membership were the foundation for the ultimate development of the Cleveland Jewish Ctr.

Margolies was the principal spokesman for the Orthodox in the Cleveland Jewish community. He was among the founders of the short-lived UNION OF JEWISH ORGANIZATIONS in 1906, an attempt to organize the proliferating immigrant organizations and societies. In 1913–14, he was president of the Cleveland KEHILLAH, a second attempt to organize the immigrant community. Margolies was a leader in the revitalization of Cleveland's Talmud Torahs and was founder of the Hebrew School & Institute on 55th St. He spearheaded the drive to insure that Mt. Sinai Hospital's kitchen would be kosher. Although CHAS. EISENMAN of the Fed. of Jewish Charities agreed to Margolies's demand, the hospital kitchen remained kosher for only 1 year. An ardent Zionist, Margolies served as president of the Ohio Fed. of Zionists, and in 1917 he received the largest number of votes to represent Cleveland Jewry at the first American Jewish Congress. He died prior to the convening of the congress. Margolies resigned from the Anshe Emeth pulpit in 1917 and entered the insurance business. He also was manager and an editor of the *YIDDISHE VELT*, a local Yiddish newspaper. He died at age 38 from injuries suffered in an automobile accident.

**MARIJIN SPOLEK** (the Marian Society), 1890-93, was Cleveland's first Slovenian organization, from which evolved several pioneering groups. Cleveland's fledgling Slovenian community was shocked in 1884 by the accidental death of one of its members, Peter Podrzaj. None of the men expected to stay in America. They worked to support their families in the Slovenian province of Carniola in Austria-Hungary. Few had any emergency funds. Joseph Turk, Cleveland's first Slovenian settler (1881), paid for the wake and burial to save Podrzaj from the potter's field. Turk ran the first boarding house, tavern, and grocery and had helped the new arrivals find jobs at the American Steel & Wire Co. Inspired by the fraternal societies of his Czech neighbors, he proposed a similar insurance group for SLOVENES to provide sickness, death, and burial benefits. There was initial disinterest, but by 1890, Turk got 7 men to form Marijin Spolek, utilizing the Czech term for "society." Turk was president and treasurer, with Joseph Strnisa as secretary. John Grdina, Anton Klinc, John Rus, Mihael Skebe, Jakob Turk, and Joseph Znidarsic made up the first membership, which was open to men ages 17-45. In 1892, Rev. STEPHAN FURDEK encouraged Turk to contact the bishop about the creation of a Slovenian parish. Turk gathered Spolek members to raise funds, and the following year, ST. VITUS CHURCH was established. Marijin Spolek was renamed Drustvo sv. Vid, the St. Vitus Society. Money was tight because of economic uncertainty. A depression in 1893 sent some men back to the homeland. Internal difficulties prompted several members to secede and form Slovensko Podporno Drustvo Slovenija (Slovenian Benefit Society Slovenija), presided over first by Strnisa and then Klinc. To protect the original society, Grdina and his officers requested affiliation with the newly formed national Kranjsko Slovenska Katoliska Jednota (Grand Carniolian Slovenian Catholic Union), based in Joliet, Ill.

Slovenija sponsored the first Slovenian men's chorus, Zora, directed by IVAN ZORMAN in 1897, which soon expanded into gymnastics and became the Slovenian Sokols led by Klinc. The St. Vitus Society supported the struggling parish and in 1895 sponsored the first Slovenian orchestra, the Austrian Cornet Band, with Zorman. KSKJ granted the society full membership in 1899, which caused yet another group to leave and form the Independent St. Vitus Society. By 1907, Slovenija had 529 members, and KSKJ 375. Marijin Spolek's founders became highly visible in the Slovenian community. Grdina was the first clothier and owned a large meeting hall. Skebe was founder of both St. Vitus Church and St. Mary's in COLLINWOOD. In 1899, Klinc started the first printery and newspaper, *Narodna Beseda*, today's *AMERISKA DOMOVINA*. Early groups were small, and few lasted more than a few years. Slovenija and the Sokols continued into the Depression, and KSKJ Lodge No. 25, St. Vitus, was still active in 1986.

Turk, Frank J., *Slovenski Pionir* (1955).

**MARINE, DAVID** (20 Sept. 1880-26 Nov. 1976), did research work on thyroid disorders during his tenure in Cleveland at the Western Reserve University School of Medicine and Lakeside Hospital, which subsequently led to the widespread iodization of salt to prevent goiter (a thyroid disorder). Marine was born in Whitleysburg, Md. He attended Western Maryland College and the Johns Hopkins School of Medicine, receiving his medical degree in 1905. Having decided to work in pathology, he came to Cleveland that summer to serve a year's stint as resident pathologist at Lakeside Hospital. Marine was also appointed to the faculty of the WRU School of Medicine, initially as demonstrator of pathology (1905-06), and eventually as associate professor of experimental medicine (1915-20).

Marine began his study of thyroid disorders immediately upon his arrival in Cleveland, at the university's Cushing Laboratory for Experimental Medicine. Cleveland was located in the nation's "goiter belt," a region extending from the Great Lakes states to both the West and the Southeast, and Marine noticed the swollen necks of dogs in the streets as he walked to his first day of work at Lakeside Hospital. He worked with a variety of animals in his investigation of the thyroid gland; his first study of the prevention and treatment of goiter in human beings involved pediatric patients at the Lakeside Hospital Dispensary. In 1917, Dr. Marine and one of his students, O. P. Kimball, published an article, "The Prevention of Simple Goiter in Man," which described the experimental goiter-prevention program they had set up in Akron, Ohio, involving nearly 4,500 schoolgirls. The final results, published in 1920, demonstrated the prophylactic efficacy of sodium iodine. Despite some opposition, the prevention of goiter through the use of iodized salt eventually became standard public health practice, both in the U.S. and throughout the world, largely as a result of Marine's work.

During and immediately after WORLD WAR I, Marine served as a medical officer with the U.S. Army in Europe. He returned briefly to Cleveland and then moved on to become director of laboratories at Montefiore Hospital in New York City, where he spent the rest of his career. He was also assistant professor of pathology at Columbia University's College of Physicians & Surgeons (1920-39). He continued his work on the thyroid gland, and much of his subsequent research involved it and other endocrine glands. Marine retired from his position as head of Montefiore's Dept. of Pathology in 1945. He spent the remaining years of his life in Sussex County, Del. He was married to Mary Elizabeth Nuttle; they had 1 son. Marine died at age 96.

David Marine Papers, University Hospitals Archives.

The **MARINE TOTAL ABSTINENCE SOCIETY**, a benevolent organization dedicated to combating intemperance, was first instituted on 6 July 1840. The society was affiliated with the Bethel Church, organized in 1835, and the WESTERN SEAMEN'S FRIEND SOCIETY, organized in 1830. Many sailors from Cleveland and around the world pledged their names to the society's roll, swearing never to participate in the drinking or selling of intoxicating liquid. The objective of the society was to make examples of sailors who had dedicated themselves to total abstinence to the rest of the community. Wm. H. Stanley, vice-president of the society in 1841, maintained that "sailors leave their names as an example worthy of imitation to the old man o' war's man, who having visited our inland seas, resolves to knock off the grog, and follow in the wake." Other prominent officers in 1840 included John G. McCurdy, president, and JOHN A. FOOTE and John Maplebeck, vice-presidents. The society met every Tuesday evening in an upper room occupied by the Bethel Church, located at 32 Superior St.

The Marine Total Abstinence Society continued to hold meetings until 21 July 1841, when, through nonattendance, it adjourned *sine die*. The pledge, which remained open for the signatures of seamen and others, continued to increase even after the regular meetings were discontinued. However, to raise the temperance tide "to weigh anchor, and hoist once more the glorious colors of the Temperance Ship," the society was reorganized in 1845. John G. McCurdy was reelected president, and Jas. Turnbell vice-president. The society retained a substantial following for several years after its reorganization; however, it is not mentioned in the *Directory of Cleveland Business* after 1856.

**MARITIME DISASTERS** were recorded in the waters of Lake Erie off Cleveland when the first explorers entered the area. The high rocky shore from just east of Cleveland west to Cedar Pt. combines with shallow water and sudden squalls to create one of the most dangerous stretches of water in the Great Lakes. However, not all the wrecks have been due to natural causes. Poor seamanship and mechanical failure have also claimed their toll. Before improvements in navigational aids and safety equipment and the professionalition of the sailor were effected in the 20th century, over 60 major wrecks came to litter the approaches to Cleveland. The North American Indians were fully aware of the danger of the southern shore of Lake Erie. Generally, they would traverse the lake along the Canadian coast. The French followed their example. Their caution spared them the embarrassment the English would suffer. The British inaugurated the modern era of shipwrecks in 1763 when Maj. Wilkins's fleet of 40 bateaux, en route to relieve besieged Detroit during Pontiac's Conspiracy, met a sudden squall off Rocky River. Only 3 of the boats survived, and the expedition was forced to walk back to Niagara. The following year, 1764, the troops that finally lifted the siege began their return to the East. Commanded this time by a Col. Bradstreet, this fleet, too, met a sudden squall somewhere in the same region. This force also returned to Niagara on foot. The British also lost the schooner *Beaver* between Bay Village and Lorain in 1771.

The early years of American settlement along the lake generated comparatively little lake traffic. The rush of immigration to the Great Lakes had not yet begun. There were 2 notable sinkings. In 1806, LORENZO CARTER rescued a fugitive slave named BEN from a schooner off Cleveland. In 1808, Cleveland's first fishing boat, captained by Joseph Plumb of Newburgh and crewed by AMOS SPAFFORD's son Adolphus, foundered in a storm off Bay Village. New settlement and technological innovations, including the canal and the steamboat, created a transportation industry that centered on Cleveland as a hub. However, these changes represented new dangers to the ships on the lake. Collision, fire, and explosion were added to weather as major hazards and quickly took their toll. The year 1850 proved to be particularly horrendous. On 23 Mar., off Cleveland, and 18 Apr., off Vermilion, the boilers of the *Troy* and the *Anthony Wayne* burst, killing 22 and 40. Then, on 17 June, paint stored near the firebox of the *G. P. Griffith* burst into a terrifying fire. Seven miles out from Willoughby, the captain ordered a desperate race for shore. Half a mile out, the *Griffith* struck a shoal. Hard aground, the wooden ship burned to the water, and 250 died. These disasters inspired new safely legislation that made lake navigation somewhat safer.

It proved, however, impossible to legislate good seamanship. On the morning of 21 June 1868, the steamer *Morning Star* and the schooner *Courtland* collided off Lorain. The *Morning Star* sank, with 23 aboard. It was later determined that the *Courtland* was running without lights while its lamps were being refueled. There were wrecks in the intervening years, of course, but the pace set after 1890 was remarkable. Rapidly expanding fleets of freighters and passenger steamers confronted the old hazards. Only the introduction of modern navigational aids and radio would give the sailors the advantage. Gales remained the most common cause for sinkings. Typical was the storm of 10–11 Aug. 1890. The schooners *Two Fannies* and *Fanny L. Jones* sank a short distance apart just west of Cleveland. On 28 June 1899, the steamer *Margaret Olwill* foundered in a wild squall near Lorain, taking the captain and his wife. Another storm, on 10 Sept. 1900, claimed the steamer *John B. Lyon* and the schooner *Dundee* and damaged 3 others. The steamer *Alex Nimick* arrived in Cleveland minus its wheelhouse. Surprisingly, neither of the Great Storms, 20–22 Nov. 1905 or 9–13 Nov. 1913, sank any ships near Cleveland, despite the staggering losses elsewhere. However, by this time a network of weather stations and early radio receivers were warning captains of approaching bad weather. Forewarned, ships could put in to harbor. Also, the ships had grown larger and stronger and were better able to face the storms. Nevertheless, bad weather accounted for most of the major losses. The last two notable sinkings, the sandsucker *Sand Merchant* on 16 Oct. 1936 and the tug *Admiral* and the barge *Cleveco* on 3 Dec. 1942, were both due to squalls.

However, foul weather was not the sole cause of catastrophe. From the early years, incompetence on the part of the crews played a significant part. Typical was the schooner *Wahnapitae*, which piled up on the Cleveland breakwall on 26 Oct. 1890. An unsecured deck cargo shifted when the steamer *Saint Magnus* was struck by the wake of a passing vessel in the CUYAHOGA RIVER on 7 June 1895. The vessel rolled over into the channel, blocking traffic until it could be raised. Fire remained a hazard, despite steel-hulled construction. The C&B Lines passenger steamer *City of Buffalo* burned at the E. 9th Street pier on 20 Mar. 1938. Sometimes mere happenstance would send a ship to the bottom, as when the sandsucker *Hydro* was holed by an unseen object in the river channel on 12 Sept. 1939. One other aspect of disaster on the lakes should be noted. Many ships built and operated by Cleveland companies and crewed by Clevelanders have been written off the registers in waters far from home. The steamer *Idaho* sank in a gale at the eastern end of the lake on 6 Nov. 1897. Two of its crew were rescued from the top of its mast, following a terror-filled night. Several of the ships lost in the Great Storms of 1905 and 1913 were out of Cleveland. Finally, the *Edmund Fitzgerald*, the most recent wreck on the lakes, on 10 Nov. 1975, was operated by the OGLEBAY NORTON CO., carried a load of iron ore for J&L Steel, and was largely crewed by Cleveland-area seamen.

**MARKETS AND MARKET HOUSES.** The public market is an institution in Cleveland, as it is in almost every large city in Europe and many in the U.S. It was conceived as a place where farmer and consumer could meet for the sale and purchase of farm products without the intervention of middlemen. If the commission merchant—the middleman—long ago took the farmer's place, prices were still lower than those of retail supermarkets, while quality was higher. The first public market in Cleveland was established in 1829 on Ontario St. south of PUBLIC SQUARE. Stalls were offered at auction to the highest bidder. The first ordinance regulating markets was passed the following year. Fresh meats could be sold every day except Sunday, while vegetables and "other articles" could be offered only on Wednesday and Saturday. By 1836, there were 4 open-air markets in a village of 3,080 inhabitants. A second food market had been established near the Canal Basin at the foot of Superior St., and 2 wood markets were operating, one on Public Square near Ontario and another at Superior and Water (W. 9th) streets. "No one thing does Cleveland more need, than a suitable public Market House, and regular market days," the *Cleveland Herald* pronounced on 23 Mar. 1839. That year, the city's first municipal market house was built on Michigan St. (behind the present Higbee Co. store). On market days—Tuesday, Thursday, and Saturday—long lines of wagons made their way there, and the surrounding area soon became a hay market, with farmers and hucksters selling directly from their vehicles. In OHIO CITY, FRANKLIN CIRCLE had been platted and dedicated to public use in 1836. It served as an open-air farmers' market until 1857, when it was refurbished as a city park. The market continued to operate nearby at Ann and Clinton streets until Sept. 1859, when it moved to the northwest corner of Lorain and Pearl (W. 25th) streets; there it occupied a small parcel JOSIAH BARBER and RICHARD LORD had set aside for public use in 1840. "Market Square," as it came to be known, was enlarged with subsequent donations of land in 1853 and 1864, and the city built a wooden market house there in 1868.

Despite the vehement opposition of market tenants and the public, in 1858 city council authorized removal of the Michigan St. Market and established a new Central Market near the banks of the CUYAHOGA RIVER and Pittsburgh St. The old market house on Michigan St. was torn down and rebuilt on the new site. Many objected to the CENTRAL MARKET as an "uncomfortable out-of-the-way place to buy," and it was slow to fill. Although farmers contended they had the right to sell their goods on any public ground they chose, an ordinance passed in 1859 regulated marketplaces and provided that all selling from wagons must be done from the market grounds. Although vendors defied the law, protest gradually subsided, and the Central Market became well established as the city's major marketing center. A new Central Market containing 100 stalls for fish, meat, and vegetables was completed on Ontario St. between Bolivar and Eagle streets in 1867. The same year, city council authorized construction of a small market house in the 5th ward, at the corner of St. Clair and Nevada streets. The Fifth Ward Market by 1874 was used only irregularly and was abandoned by 1900. The 45-stall Newburgh Market (later called the Broadway Market) operated at Broadway and Canton Ave. from Dec. 1879 until 1963.

Rapid urbanization and the rising cost of living after 1900 stimulated interest in efficient and economical markets and led to heightened activity in the establishment of city markets nationwide. In 1901, Mayor TOM L. JOHNSON appointed a market house commission. Among its first actions was the purchase of a site for a new WEST SIDE MARKET across the street from the old one. The new market, a fanciful interpretation of a Roman basilica designed by the firm of Hubbell & Benes, opened in 1912. Market Square continued to serve as a flower and produce market. The first annual report of the superintendent of markets, issued by Julius H. Schmidt in 1906, suggests that Cleveland was a leader in the establishment of municipal markets. Noting that such reports theretofore were "not customary," Schmidt said that "requests from other cities for information concerning Cleveland's markets have been so numerous that it is deemed necessary to have a printed report on file which may be sent to anyone seeking information. . . ." According to the report, all stalls and stands at the Central and West Side markets were rented, but the Newburgh Market was not well patronized. Under a new

ordinance regulating weights and measures effective 1 Jan. 1906, the Div. of Weights & Measures had inspected every weighing and measuring device used for the sale of commodities in Cleveland; and under the new health code, an inspector visited each market daily to examine all meat and produce. Receipts for market operations in 1906 equaled $37,511, while expenses were $14,379. Income was derived from renting stands, charges for cold storage at the West Side Market, licenses issued for the extensive farmers' curb market occupying Broadway and Woodland Ave. in the vicinity of the Central Market, and fees for inspecting weights, measures, and scales. In 1913 the superintendent of markets reported that an estimated 75,000 Clevelanders attended the public markets each week.

Cleveland's rapid population growth in the late 19th and early 20th centuries led to the opening of several privately owned and operated markets. The largest of these was the SHERIFF ST. MARKET, opened on Christmas Eve 1891. Occupying the entire block of Sheriff (E. 4th) St. between Huron and Bolivar roads, it competed—at first, unsuccessfully—with the nearby Central Market until it closed in 1936. Designed by LEHMAN & SCHMITT, it was an architectural wonder, with a great central iron-and-glass dome flanked by 2 cold-storage towers. The Euclid–105th St. Market, with 150 stalls, opened in 1917 at 10309 Euclid Ave. Built by the East End Market Co., it was strategically located to serve the prosperous suburbs of E. CLEVELAND, CLEVELAND HTS., and SHAKER HTS. The Euclid–105th St. Market was forced to relocate in 1941; it operated on a much-reduced scale at 1981 E. 105th St. until it finally closed in the aftermath of the HOUGH RIOTS. Other privately owned markets accommodating small stall operations were located at Euclid Ave. and E. 46th St.; Woodland Ave. and E. 55th St.; E. 106th St. and St. Clair; and Gordon Square at W. 65th and Detroit. The latter, opened in 1921 as part of the unusual multipurpose Gordon Square Bldg., closed in the 1950s. By 1900, it was no longer farmers who rented space at the public markets but commission merchants who bought their products from some 1,200 growers and producers occupying scattered quarters along Broadway, Woodland, and Central avenues. Beginning in 1917, farmers' cooperatives sold from trucks at 2 locations in E. Cleveland. A farmers' market at Coit and Woodworth roads, opened in 1932, was operated by the Northeastern Ohio Growers Cooperative Assoc., Inc. It consisted of 75 stalls occupied by farmers from Geauga and Lake counties. Open 2 days a week (3 days in summer), it was still doing business in 1980.

By the 1920s, dramatic changes in Cleveland were felt in the city's traditional marketplaces. Commercial expansion, especially the CLEVELAND UNION TERMINAL complex, had displaced thousands of people who had once lived on Orange, Prospect, and other streets rimming downtown. Refrigeration meant that consumers no longer had to buy their food fresh each day. And with the proliferation of automobiles and a reduced demand for hay, the HAYMARKET district at the south end of Ontario grew smaller. In 1929, Cleveland's wholesale food trade moved almost en masse into the new NORTHERN OHIO FOOD TERMINAL on Woodland Ave. But perhaps the most important changes were suburbanization and the advent of cooperative food stores and chain supermarkets. In 1929, 33 of Cleveland's largest food retailers combined to form United Food Stores, and 3 years later 200 grocers united to form Edwards Food Stores. Supermarkets, with their uniform merchandising and advertising and economies of scale, eroded business at the markets and put many small grocers out of business. So did a changing way of life. When Braman Grocery, in business at 9527 Madison Ave. since

1899, finally closed in 1955, Oliver Braman commented, "Fifty years ago when a housewife came in she'd buy flour, baking powder, lard and other things for a cake. Now she'll buy a cake mix." Although rentals became more difficult at the public markets ("because of the keen competition," reported the Div. of Weights & Measures in 1939), they remained busy and continued to earn income for the city while reducing the cost of living for its residents.

In the 1930s, the WPA assisted in repairing and painting the city's 3 markets. Despite criticism from downtown business interests that it was an eyesore, traffic bottleneck, and health menace, the Central Market continued to draw large crowds of shoppers and provide a livelihood for over 200 tenants until it burned to the ground in Dec. 1949. The following spring, all but 40 of its tenants reopened in the former Sheriff St. Market Bldg. Renamed the New Central Market and now operated privately, it was still doing business in 1986, though plans were underway for a new market house at E. 55th and Payne Ave. Woodland Ave.'s colorful farmers' curb market, meanwhile, was closed by the city on 8 Aug. 1950. "Chain stores and supermarkets are behind it," one vendor charged in the press. The city, however, considered the curb market a traffic and sanitary nuisance. When the Broadway Market was sold in 1963, the city was left with a single public market. The West Side Market, the ethnic center of Cleveland and a must-stop for politicians campaigning for office, continued to do a lively business in the 1980s, drawing city and suburban residents alike. Many stands there have remained with the same family for 4 generations. Although it no longer earned a profit in 1986, it succeeded in providing high-quality, fresh food at low cost.

Carol Poh Miller

See also BUSINESS-RETAIL.

**MARKS, MARTIN A.** (6 Feb. 1853–31 Aug. 1916), businessman and community leader, was born in Madison, Wis. He attended the public schools of Madison and at the age of 13 quit school to work in his father's dry-goods store. As a young man, Marks became active in B'nai B'rith. He was appointed to the board of trustees of the Jewish Orphan Home in 1885. While traveling to Cleveland on home business, Marks met Belle Hays, the daughter of KAUFMAN HAYS; he subsequently married her in Oct. 1885. Just over a year later, the couple moved to Cleveland. Marks initially purchased an interest in the wholesale clothing firm of Klein & Lehman; the name of the firm was changed to Klein, Marks & Co. In 1890, Marks went to work for the Northwest Life Insurance Co., and a year later he was hired as manager for northern Ohio for the Equitable Life Assurance Co. of New York. He remained with that firm for 14 years. In 1902, Marks became a director of the CLEVELAND WORSTED MILLS, a firm run by his father-in-law, Kaufman Hays. In Jan. 1906, he was elected secretary-treasurer of the mills, a position he held until his death. He also served on the board of directors of the First Natl. Bank and the GUARDIAN SAVINGS & TRUST CO.

Marks was president of the TEMPLE for 25 years, 1890–1904 and 1906–15. He served in that capacity when Rabbi MOSES GRIES was hired, and with Gries, who later became his brother-in-law, he oversaw the construction of a large synagogue at Willson Ave. in 1894 and the development of the Temple into an "institutional" synagogue. When Rabbi Gries suggested the creation of the Educational League to insure the possibility of higher education for orphans, Marks became the first president of the B'nai B'rith-sponsored organization. As a leader in the local B'NAI B'RITH, he was active in raising funds for the Consumptive

Hospital in Denver, which was founded in 1899. Marks was one of the 8 men who met in 1903 to establish the Fed. of Jewish Charities and was one of 3 people appointed to an FJC committee to review and report on all immigration bills proposed in Congress. He was a founder in 1913 of the Fed. for Charity & Philanthropy, a charitable organization in the general community. He also chaired the Committee on Benevolent Associations of the Chamber of Commerce.

**MARSH, W. WARD** (12 Aug. 1893–23 June 1971), chronicled half a century of motion-picture history, from *The Big Parade* to *Airport*, as the *Cleveland Plain Dealer*'s movie critic. Born in MacLean, Pa., Marsh attended Edinboro State Teachers College and Erie Business College, as well as Adelbert College at Western Reserve University. Joining the *PLAIN DEALER* in 1915, he began as a police reporter, religion editor, and copy editor. He married a coworker there, the former Mabel Boyes of New Brunswick, Canada, and took a leave of absence to serve as an infantry lieutenant in France during WORLD WAR I. Upon his return, Marsh began the first of 23,000 movie reviews for the *Plain Dealer* in 1919. During the films' silent era, he also doubled briefly as a pipe organist in a local movie house. During his long reign as dean of the nation's movie critics, Marsh numbered such notables as Joan Crawford and Ross Hunter among his personal friends in the industry. He made a cameo screen appearance in a Clark Gable vehicle entitled *Teacher's Pet* in 1957. As the area's undisputed movie trivia authority, Marsh wrote and produced a local television movie quiz program in the 1950s called "Lights, Camera, Question." He also taught a course, "The History, Enjoyment, and Criticism of the Movie," at Western Reserve's Cleveland College. In the twilight of his career, in the 1960s, Marsh fought a losing battle against the screen's increasing sexual permissiveness. His scathing review of a film called *The Lovers* in 1959 contributed to the prosecution of its exhibitor, Nico Jacobellis of the Heights Art Theatre, for obscenity. In a landmark censorship ruling in 1964, the U.S. Supreme Court declared the film was not obscene. Marsh died less than a year after his retirement. Long a resident of Hudson, he was survived by his wife, who died in 1974. Roger Marsh, their only child, had died in 1967. Marsh's collection of movie memorabilia, including 3 personally bound copies of scripts presented to him by Cecil B. De Mille, was donated to the CLEVELAND PUBLIC LIBRARY.

**MARSHALL, JOHN D.** (14 Mar. 1885–17 May 1961), served on city council for 12 years and as president of council was mayor of Cleveland under the CITY MANAGER PLAN from 1925–33. Marshall was born in Bucyrus, Ohio, the son of Daniel and Mary Gerster Marshall. After graduation from Bucyrus High School, he received an A.B. degree from Ohio Wesleyan University and an LL.B. degree from Western Reserve University in 1914. Marshall became assistant law director of the city in 1917 and 3 years later was appointed commissioner of franchises. He was elected to city council as a Republican in 1921. As president of council, he succeeded CLAYTON TOWNES as mayor in 1925 and remained until 1933, when the City Manager Plan was abolished. At that time, he retired from politics, resuming his law practice and serving as secretary of the Ohio Brewers Assoc. He died in Cleveland at age 76. In 1917, Marshall married Susan Ridell, and they had a daughter, Susan Marshall McDonald. His wife died in 1944. He was survived by his second wife, Irene.

**MARSHALL, LYCURGUS LUTHER** (9 July 1888–12 Jan. 1958), was a lawyer and the brother and law partner of Cleveland mayor JOHN D. MARSHALL. He served several terms in the general assembly in Columbus and 1 term in Congress as a representative. Marshall was born in Bucyrus and attended the local schools. He graduated from Ohio Wesleyan University in 1909. Afterward he taught at Emory-Henry College in Virginia and was principal of the high school at Crestline, Ohio. He went on to law school and, while studying for the bar, taught for the Nottingham and Euclid schools; in 1915, he graduated from the law department at Western Reserve University, was admitted to the bar, and began practicing law in Cleveland. A Republican, Marshall was elected as a state representative in 1920 and served 1 term (1921–22); after that, he ran for a seat in the Ohio senate and served 6 terms (1923–35). He also served as president of the Euclid Board of Education (1923–31) but resigned when he moved to Cleveland and unsuccessfully ran for a municipal judgeship. As a state senator, Marshall served as chairman of the Senate Judiciary Committee and was noted for introducing the bill that eliminated the legal restrictions against the presentation of motion pictures on Sundays. In 1931, he successfully steered into passage a new corporation code and a new probate code after years of effort to recodify these laws had failed. Marshall also authored the bill that allowed for the issuance of tax-anticipation warrants to pay county employees during the Depression; it was commonly known as "scrip money." In 1933, Marshall chaired the special banking committee that investigated the GUARDIAN SAVINGS & TRUST CO., the Union Trust Co., and other banks closed by the Depression; these hearings resulted in the eventual conviction and imprisonment of 2 bank presidents and several bank officers. In 1934 and 1936, Marshall ran unsuccessfully as the Republican nominee for congressional representative-at-large; however, he won in 1938 and was elected to the 76th Congress. In 1940, he was defeated for reelection. The same year, he was also defeated when he ran for a common pleas court vacancy. After these defeats, he returned to his law practice. In 1950, Marshall attempted a political comeback by running for Ohio secretary of state but was ruled off the ballot because of invalid petitions and a resulting lack of signatures in enough counties. Marshall was married to Minnie Martin; they had 2 sons, Hubert and Edward.

The **MARTHA HOLDEN JENNINGS FOUNDATION** was founded in 1959 by Martha Holden Jennings (d. 1962), from the estate of her late husband, Andrew R. Jennings (d. 1931), who was the European manager of the Internatl. Business Machines Corp. The foundation limits its giving to the state of Ohio, and Cuyahoga County especially. Its purpose is to improve the quality of teaching. It gives grants to primary- and secondary-education projects and the Tutor Corps and awards to outstanding teachers. The foundation also publishes a journal, which reports on educational programs funded by it. In addition, it publishes special reports on specific issues in EDUCATION. It gives grants to nonprofit institutions and to individuals.

Beneficiaries of the Jennings estate have included the CLEVELAND CLINIC, Case Institute of Technology, UNIVERSITY CIRCLE, and the CLEVELAND MUSEUM OF ART. No grants are given for capital funds, travel, operating budgets, annual campaigns, endowment funds, research, publications, or equipment. The original bequest of $5.5 million was in IBM stock. In 1983, the assets of the foundation were $29,906,203, with expenditures of $1,605,364 for 81 grants and 12 programs. In 1985, the board included Arthur S. Holden, Jr., chair; Geo. B. Chapman, Jr., president; Frank W. Milbourn, vice-president; John H. Gherlein, secretary; Claire D. Holden, assistant secretary; Allen H. Ford, treasurer; and Robt. M. Ginn, trustee.

The **MARTHA WASHINGTON AND DORCAS SOCIETY** was the first citywide poor-relief organization in Cleveland. Organized in 1843, the name of the society reflected its twin concerns: "Martha Washington" to indicate that it was a women's counterpart of the Washingtonian temperance movement then forming in the East, and "Dorcas" after the Biblical woman who was "full of good works and charity" (Acts 9:36–43). The society's officers and full members were women; men could join as honorary members. The Martha Washington & Dorcas Society concentrated on poor relief, leaving the major temperance work to other city organizations. By providing food, clothing, wood, and sometimes a job or a place in a concerned family, it filled a need for temporary at-home relief not met by the City Infirmary, which was essentially a poorhouse with little money to aid those outside its doors. The society disbanded in 1850, partly because its founder, most active worker, and "First Directress," REBECCA ROUSE, had turned her efforts to the formation and work of the Protestant Orphan Asylum. Thereafter the society found it increasingly difficult to aid the city's growing number of poor. It ended its efforts amid calls for "systematic" charity and suggestions that the city government take a more active role in addressing the problem of poverty.

**MARTIN, ALEXANDER H.** (8 Dec. 1873–1962), was a well-known black lawyer in Cleveland. He was civically active in the black community and was a leader among the city's black Republicans. Martin was born in Ironton, Ohio. He graduated from high school in Geneva at the age of 16, and then learned the barber trade. In 1891 he entered Adelbert College of Western Reserve University. He graduated as a Phi Beta Kappa in 1895 and received a scholarship to WRU law school. He qualified to take the state bar exam after only his second year and was admitted to the bar a year before graduating from law school. He married Mary Brown (see MARY BROWN MARTIN) in 1905. Martin practiced law in Cleveland for 65 years. For many years he was a perennial candidate for judge in various courts but was never elected. He also attempted to gain the Republican nomination for Congress in 1936. Martin helped organize the Attucks Republican Club Cleveland and served as its president. In 1900 he was instrumental in shifting black support in Cleveland to the Democratic nominee for president, Wm. Jennings Bryan. He later returned to the Republican party. Among his many civic involvements, Martin served on the executive committee for the CLEVELAND ASSOC. OF COLORED MEN and, in 1922, was one of the chief organizers of the Cedar Ave. Branch of the YMCA.

**MARTIN, MARY BROWN** (1877–19 Nov. 1939), was the first black elected to the Cleveland Board of Education. Brown was born in Raleigh, N.C. She came to Cleveland in 1886, where she attended Rockwell School and later CENTRAL HIGH SCHOOL. She graduated from Central in 1900 as the class vocalist and entered the Cleveland Normal Training School, graduating in 1903. Brown taught school for the next 2 years in Alabama and Arkansas. She then returned to Cleveland, where she married ALEXANDER H. MARTIN in 1905 and raised a family. In the 1920s, Martin became a teacher in the CLEVELAND PUBLIC SCHOOLS, and in 1930 she was elected to the Board of Education. She served 2 terms and declined to run for a third in 1937. In 1939, however, she was elected again.

Martin was also one of the few black women in Cleveland active in the women's suffrage movement. Mary B. Martin Elementary School at 8200 Brookline Ave. was named in her honor.

**MARTIN FIELD** was an airstrip located behind Glenn L. Martin's airplane-construction plant at 16800 St. Clair. Martin developed the airstrip and his airplane-construction company in 1918. When transcontinental air-mail service began in 1920, Martin Fld. served as the landing spot for planes delivering the mail to Cleveland. Martin continued to build aircraft in Cleveland until 1929, when he moved his operation to Baltimore; after his departure, the plant on St. Clair and the adjacent airstrip were used by the Great Lakes Aircraft Corp., which was dissolved in 1935.

**MARTIN LUTHER KING, JR., VISITS TO CLEVE-LAND** occurred frequently during his career as a civil-rights leader in the 1960s. His visits served to raise funds for civil-rights organizations, especially the Southern Christian Leadership Conference (SCLC), to urge voter registration and participation, and to bolster the nonviolent civil-rights movement in Cleveland. Rev. Martin Luther King, Jr., first visited Cleveland on 7 Aug. 1956 as the leader of the bus boycott in Montgomery, Ala. He reported on the progress of the boycott in a speech to the annual convention of the Natl. Negro Funeral Directors Assoc. at the HOLLEN-DEN HOUSE. A scheduled visit in Oct. 1960 to raise money for the southern civil-rights movement was canceled after King was arrested in a sit-in in Atlanta and refused bail, but on 26 Nov. 1961, King came to Cleveland and addressed 3,900 people in 2 church services at ANTIOCH BAPTIST CHURCH; later that afternoon he appeared on KYW-TV. King was met by much larger crowds when he returned to Cleveland from the protests in Birmingham, Ala., on 14 May 1963. He spoke to the Episcopal Society for Christian & Racial Unity at ST. PAUL EPISCOPAL CHURCH in CLEVELAND HTS. that afternoon, and that evening the car carrying King was mobbed by an enthusiastic crowd of 10,000–14,000 people as it made its way to his scheduled speech in CORY UNITED METH. CHURCH. The church could accommodate only 5,000 of those wanting to hear King's address, and additional appearances quickly were arranged at other churches. He returned to Cleveland on 29 Sept. 1963 and spoke for an hour at the installation of his friend Rev. Kelly Miller Smith as pastor of Antioch Baptist Church. A week after winning the Nobel Peace Prize, King was back in Cleveland on 23 Oct. 1964, in a "march on the ballot box" to urge Clevelanders to vote in the upcoming election. He appeared at 5 street-corner rallies, visited 2 schools, and spoke at Olivet Institutional Church. On 23 Mar. 1965, King left the march from Selma to Montgomery to appear at a Nobel Peace Prize dinner given in his honor at the Sheraton-Cleveland Hotel. The dinner was organized by local religious and civic leaders, and the proceeds went to the SCLC; the event was picketed by members of the local Natl. Assoc. for the Advancement of White People.

As part of his northern cities tour, King again visted Cleveland on behalf of voter registration on 27–28 July 1965. He met with local clergymen, held several community meetings, and spoke to large crowds in MT. PLEASANT and at the Arena, 3700 Euclid Ave. King was a regular visitor to Cleveland during 1967. He visited the city on 26–27 Apr. at the request of the United Pastors' Assoc. following several incidents of violence and vandalism in the city's black communities; in several appearances at schools, he urged students to learn, not burn, and to develop a sense of self-respect. King also traded barbs with Mayor Ralph Locher, who had called him an "extremist." King announced that he planned to develop a program of action to improve civil rights in Cleveland, and on 16 May he returned to the city to announce that he planned to lead a drive against "the evils of racial injustice and economic exploitation" in a city that, like others in the North, was "a teeming cauldron of hostility." In a 3-day conference in early June, King and his advisors developed a 4-point plan that would organize tenant unions, register voters, improve relations between police and citizens, improve black employment through negotiations, and, if needed, direct action protests. The latter program, Operation Breadbasket, led to boycotts against Sealtest and several other companies and was the most visible of the projects, although other events, such as the "ghetto grand jury hearings" on 28 June, served to dramatize the evils of life in the ghetto. King returned to the city regularly during the summer and fall of 1967 to help register voters and then to urge people to vote as Carl Stokes campaigned to become the first black mayor of a major American city. King's last public appearance in Cleveland was on 16 Dec. 1967, when he debated Cleveland Bar Assoc. president Jas. C. Davis on civil disobedience at the Human Rights Institute. King also spoke to a small east side group in early 1968. He was scheduled to return to the city on 10 Apr. 1968, to recruit marchers for the planned Poor People's Campaign.

**MARTINEK, JOSEPH** (23 Mar. 1889–21 Mar. 1980), was a Czech socialist who enjoyed a long and varied career as a newspaper editor, labor leader, gymnastic instructor, cooperative leader, author, and poet. Dedicated to socialism and Czech nationalism, he was an important leader locally, nationally, and in his native Czechoslovakia. Martinek was born in Podebrady, near Prague. He attended common school, high school, and technical school in Czechoslovakia, receiving training as a metalworker and working in Germany for 3 years. After his arrival in the U.S. in 1909, he settled with relatives in Cleveland, where he worked as a lathe operator and took courses in sociology at Western Reserve University.

In Cleveland, Martinek became involved in the labor movement and in Czech organizations. He was an early member of the WORKERS GYMNASTIC UNION, a socialist gymnastic and Czech nationalist organization, and served as a gym instructor for the group. He also became a valuable speaker at labor meetings, since he was able to speak German, Slovak, Russian, and Spanish in addition to Czech and English. His career as a newspaper editor began in 1912, when he became editor of the *AMERICKY DELNICKY LISTY* and a Czech labor weekly. He edited Czech-American publications until 1934. From 1918–34, he served as president of the Workingman's Cooperative, a chain of 7 co-op grocery stores; he also served on the board of directors of the Cooperative League of America. Martinek was active in politics in the 1920s and early 1930s. In 1924, he was part of the organization that carried Cuyahoga County for Sen. Robt. M. La Follette in the presidential primary. Martinek also ran for office, launching unsuccessful campaigns as a Socialist for county commissioner in 1926, state representative in 1928, and city council in 1929 and 1933.

Martinek displayed his interest in Czech nationalism through both his work in the Cleveland Czech community and his active struggle for Czechoslovakia in the 1910s and the 1930s. In Cleveland, he worked with the Workers Gymnastic Union, and in 1925 he was the founder of its summer camp, which became the cooperative village of Taborville. During WORLD WAR I, he fought with the Czechoslovakian Foreign Legion in Siberia, and in 1934, he returned to Czechoslovakia as the editor of the daily labor paper *Pravo Lidu*. Active in the anti-Nazi movement, Martinek was forced to flee the country to escape from Hitler's forces in 1938. He returned to the U.S. and served as the executive secretary of the Czechoslovak Natl. Council in Chicago from 1939–45. In 1947, Martinek moved to the desert near Tucson, Ariz. There he began to write scripts for Radio Free Europe and the Voice of America. He also began to write poetry, publishing 5 books between 1944–68. Sometime after his arrival in the U.S., Martinek was married to another native of Czechoslovakia, Marie Fiserova. She died in 1963.

Frank Bardoun Papers, WRHS.

The **MARY B. TALBERT HOME AND HOSPITAL**, operated by the SALVATION ARMY from 1925–60, provided assistance to pregnant unmarried black women and girls in Cleveland. The Salvation Army had operated a rescue mission for unwed mothers in Cleveland since 1892, but in 1925 the Council of Colored Women raised $1,000 for the extension of maternity care in the city and asked the Salvation Army to operate the home for them. The Talbert Home was designated specifically to help black women, and according to one Salvation Army historian, it was "the Army's only all-black maternity hospital." Located at 2215 E. 40th St. and managed by Artimeza Ward, the Mary B. Talbert Rescue Home, as it was originally called, moved to 5905 Kinsman Rd. in 1930 when the white rescue mission vacated that 25-year-old building for a new location on Torbenson Dr. The Talbert Home remained at this address until it was merged with the Maternity Home at BOOTH MEMORIAL HOSPITAL in Jan. 1961. The Mary B. Talbert Home & Hospital served 379 unwed mothers and their babies in 1958, and more than 4,300 people attended its classes in home economics and child care that year. When the maternity home closed in 1960, the Salvation Army continued to serve the Central-Hough-Kinsman areas with its Social Service Office and the Pre-Natal Clinic located at the same Kinsman address.

**MARYMOUNT HOSPITAL** is a nonprofit short-term general hospital in GARFIELD HTS. Operated by the Catholic church, it offers in-patient care in medicine, surgery, obstetrics, pediatrics, and psychiatry, as well as out-patient care through its emergency room and customary diagnosis and therapy services. In 1939, a group of area physicians noted an acute shortage of hospital beds and emergency treatment facilities in Garfield Hts. and the southeast area of Cleveland. They subsequently joined forces with the Sisters of St. Joseph of the Third Order of St. Frances, who shared the same concern. In 1945, the two groups combined to establish an advisory board, an organizational structure that led to the building and, in 1948, opening of a 100-bed hospital on McCracken Rd. in Garfield Hts. Among those instrumental in organizing Marymount Hospital were Mother Mary Theobold and Warren Chase. Chester Jablonski and Edmund Lewandowski were key figures in helping to obtain initial financial support from the Greater Cleveland Hospital Fund. The Sisters of St. Joseph of the Third Order of St. Frances primarily made up the staff. Within its first 10 years, Marymount more than doubled its bed count to 279. St. Joseph's Teaching Annex was added to house the School of Practical Nursing, which was established to deal with the area shortage of practical nurses. By the mid-1960s, Marymount was offering basic services of medicine, surgery, pediatrics, obstetrics, and psychiatry along with such ancillary services as the emergency room,

x-ray, and laboratory. Marymount was one of the first hospitals of its size to have a coronary unit (1967), an in-house nurse-training program, psychiatric beds in general care, and a clinical engineer. It was the first hospital in the Cleveland area to offer 24-hour emergency room service. In 1972, a new comprehensive Mental Health Ctr. was opened, financed mostly by federal and state funds. Additional expansion and renovations were started in the early 1980s. In Nov. 1983, however, 100 employees were laid off because of a decline in patient volume. To remain competitive in the health-care marketplace, Marymount introduced new programs in stress management, dieting, and exercise physiology.

**MASCHKE, MAURICE** (16 Oct. 1868–19 Nov. 1936), was the leader of the CUYAHOGA COUNTY REPUBLICAN PARTY for 35 years. Although he never was a candidate for public office himself, his support was vital to any Republican candidate seeking elective office. Maschke was born in Cleveland to Joseph and Rosa Salinger Maschke. He attended Central High School, graduated from Phillips Exeter Academy in Exeter, N.H., and attended Harvard University, where he studied law and political economy. After receiving his A.B. degree in 1890, he returned to Cleveland, studied law, and was admitted to the Ohio bar in 1891. While reading law, he earned money by searching titles at the CUYAHOGA COUNTY COURTHOUSE, and over a period of years he became an authority on title law. In 1914, he became a partner in the law firm of Mathews, Orgill, & Maschke. The firm later became Orgill, Maschke, & Wickham.

Maschke began his political activities in 1897 as a precinct worker for Republican Mayor Robt. E. McKisson's campaign. After McKisson's reelection, he was appointed a deputy county recorder. He formed a political alliance with ALBERT "STARLIGHT" BOYD and worked with Republican congressman THEODORE BURTON. He served briefly as county recorder in 1910 when County Recorder HERMAN BAEHR was elected mayor. In 1911 he was appointed collector of customs by Pres. Wm. Howard Taft. When Maschke left the customs office in 1914, he became the head of the county Republican party organization. The peak of his political power was from 1914–28. He was elected Republican national committeeman 1924–32 and actively supported the candidacy of Herbert Hoover for president. In Cleveland, he initially supported the appointment of WM. R. HOPKINS for city manager; however, as Hopkins's influence over city council grew, Maschke's support turned into opposition. The party leader was instrumental in persuading council to remove Hopkins from office in 1930. With the ascendancy of the Democratic party in the 1930s, his influence began to wane, and he retired as county Republican chairman in 1933. In addition to his political and legal work, Maschke was an outstanding bridge player, winning 3 national team championships. He married Minnie Rice in 1903, and they had 2 children, Maurice, Jr., and Helen Lamping Hanna. He died in Cleveland at age 68.

Maurice Maschke Papers, Ohio Historical Society.

The **MASONS** organized their first lodge in Cleveland in 1811. On 23 Aug. of that year, Free & Accepted Masons in the village of Cleveland held a "communication" and chose the name Concord Lodge. A charter was granted on 23 Aug. 1812 to make it officially known as Concord Lodge No. 15. Concord Lodge No. 15 met every Thursday preceding the full moon so that members, some traveling several miles, could make their way in the dark. For several years it met in the "long rooms" of various taverns, including the one owned by LORENZO CARTER, himself a Mason. Because most of the early pioneers belonged to the lodge, early social life in Cleveland was often centered there. Of 9 village officers elected in 1815, 5 were Masons, including Judge JAS. KINGSBURY, whose pretentious wood house became a favorite meeting place. Harvey Murray, the first master of the Concord Lodge, was appointed captain of the first company of militia formed in Cleveland in 1812. The first lodge in Cleveland was built in the 1820s but was leased to the Methodist Society in 1829. For the next 10 years, the charter of the Concord Lodge was allowed to lapse because of anti-Masonic sentiment prevalent throughout the country. In 1839, a number of prominent Cleveland Masons petitioned the Grand Lodge of Ohio for a dispensation "to resume our Masonic Labours." Cleveland City Lodge No. 15, "Old 15," was formed in Sept. 1841, although a charter was not granted until the following year. Earlier, in 1836, some members of the old Concord Lodge had separated to form Cleveland's second Lodge, Webb Chap. No. 14, Royal Arch Masons. The lodge was named after Thos. Smith Webb, founder of the American Rite of Freemasonry. Webb died in Cleveland in 1819 while touring western lodges. Like the Concord Lodge, the Webb Lodge lapsed into obscurity during the 1830s and did not resume activities until the 1840s. As Cleveland's population grew, other lodges formed. Iris Lodge No. 229 was organized in 1852 with 12 members. It was followed by Bigelow Lodge No. 243, named after its first worshipful master, A. D. Bigelow. The Iris Lodge, in 1868, was the first to put together a Masonic band in Cleveland. During the CIVIL WAR, many of Cleveland's Masons saw military action; all members of Cleveland City Lodge No. 15 in the Army and Navy were patriotically excused from paying dues.

In 1883, the first Masonic Temple was built on Superior Ave. and E. 6th. For many years it was primarily used by 4 Masonic bodies—Webb Chap. No. 14, Iris Lodge No. 229, the Cleveland Council, and the Oriental Commandery. During the final 3 decades of the 19th century, other lodges formed in Cleveland, many of which were based on Ancient Accepted Scottish Rite Freemasonry: the first in Cleveland was founded in 1859. Other lodges also began to form in communities just outside of Cleveland, such as the Dover Lodge, which was founded in Dover Ctr. (now WESTLAKE) in 1874. In 1915, Scottish Rite bodies and the Shrine (composed of 32d-degree Scottish Rite Masons or Knights Templar) organized the Masonic Bldg. Co. to build a new Masonic facility on EUCLID AVE. at E. 36th St. That resulted 4 years later in the construction of Masonic Auditorium; its dedication was one of the biggest events in the history of Masonry in Cleveland. Since its opening, the auditorium has served as the central facility for area Masons. It has also been used, particularly in the 1920s and 1930s, for many public events.

By 1934, there were 51 lodges of Free & Accepted Masons in Cuyahoga County, as well as 21 Royal Arch chapters, 5 councils, and 7 commanderies of the Knights Templar and Consistory. There were also 33 chapters of the Eastern Star, the women's auxiliary body, as well as the Grotto (composed of Master Masons) and the Shrine. Many of Cleveland's prominent business and civic leaders and politicians—including several mayors—were Masons. Among Cleveland's many lodges were several that were more specialized. These included Concordia Lodge No. 345 on the west side, which conducted all services in German; Service Lodge No. 658, exclusively for war veterans; and Meridian Lodge No. 610, which met in the daytime for the benefit of Masons employed at night. In addition,

blacks formed several lodges, one of the oldest of which is El Hasa Temple No. 28 of the Prince Hall Shriners. During WORLD WAR II, area Masons opened up a Masonic Service Ctr. with a library, recreation room, and writing desks for the benefit of all members of the armed forces. It was used by 80,000 between 1943–46. A program was also started that aided Masonic brethren in the war-torn countries of Europe. Since the war, 2 of Cleveland's most valuable Masonic bodies have been the Al Sirat Grotto and the Al Koran Shrine. In 1947, the Al Sirat Grotto was the largest grotto in the U.S., with 7,100 members. The grotto mainly serves as a social organization for Master Masons, but it is also known for its support of benevolence, including homes for crippled children. The Al Koran Shrine is the 4th-oldest shrine in the U.S. Over the years, it has been publicly known for its parade and musical units, as well as for its public services. The Al Koran Mosque, 3443 Euclid Ave., was completed in 1968 and has served as a hub for Shriners throughout northern Ohio. Between 1962–72, national membership in Masonry declined from 4.1 million to 3.8 million. The decline continued through the 1970s, mainly in urban areas such as Cleveland where there have been problems recruiting younger members. In 1972 there were 38,000 Masons in District No. 22 (Lorain and Cuyahoga counties), down from 42,891 in 1962. In 1986, there were 9 Masonic temples in the Cleveland area—in BROOKLYN, CLEVELAND HTS., LAKEWOOD, N. OLMSTED, and STRONGSVILLE, and in Cleveland on Lorain Ave., Kinsman, State Rd., and Franklin Blvd., as well as the Masonic Temple Auditorium on Euclid Ave.

The **MASSASAGOES** were native American Indians living in a village near the mouth of Conneaut Creek in the late 18th century. The surveying party led by MOSES CLEAVELAND encountered the Massasagoes in July 1796, and the tribe's chief, Paqua, summoned Cleaveland to a meeting to inquire about the white men's claim to the surrounding land. According to his journal, Cleaveland "assured them that they should not be disturbed in their possessions, [for] we would treat them and their families as our brothers." Paqua presented the surveyor with a "curious" pipe of peace and friendship, and Cleaveland gave the natives "a chain of wampum, silver trinkets, and other presents, and whiskey, to the amount of about twenty-five dollars." Cleaveland reports that the Massasagoes described themselves as poor and begged for more gifts, especially whiskey, but that a strong moral speech from him put an end to their begging. Although Cleaveland portrays the Massasagoes as beggars living "in indolence," P. D. Cherry's *The Western Reserve and Early Ohio* (1921) reports that the tribe's village, consisting of "some thirty well built cabins," was laid out regularly and systematically, presenting "an appearance of neatness and comfort unusual in the habitations of the red man."

**MASTER BUILDERS**, founded in 1909 by Sylvester W. Flesheim, is a supplier of cement additives to the construction industry and a leader in cement technology. In its early years, from its factory at 6511 Morgan Ave., the company smelted lead from old batteries to make a metallic floor hardener for improving wear resistance of cement floors, and then developed a nonshrink grout for installing heavy machinery. However, its major importance dates from its 1931 introduction of Pozzolith, a dispersing agent that promotes better hardening of concrete. The product also reduced the cost of concrete work; 5 lbs. of Pozzolith, worth $.30 in 1940 prices, added to a cubic yard of concrete reduced the amount of cement required by 15%, increased the durability and weather resistance, and speeded construction. Despite initial sales resistance, the sales of additives such as Pozzolith accounted for 10% of Master's sales before WORLD WAR II. After an intensive sales-education campaign in the 1940s, sales of Pozzolith quadrupled, accounting for ⅓ of the firm's business; it was used in 20% of the ready-mix concrete sold by 1950. The company's success made it a prime merger target, and in 1950 it was acquired by the American-Marietta Co. of Chicago, a manufacturer of paint, chemicals, and building products, to enhance its construction-materials line. The new owner retained the Cleveland headquarters of its new subsidiary at 7016 Euclid, though it closed the Morgan plant in 1952. American-Marietta, which had owned the Ferbert-Schorndorfer Co. (12815 Elmwood), a local paint and finish maker since 1942, followed its acquisition of Master with the purchase of the Arco Co. (7301 Bessemer), a maker of auto finishes, in 1951. In 1960, the company moved to Mayfield and Lee in CLEVELAND HTS.

Master Builders maintained its identity and prospered throughout the 1950s but contributed to American-Marietta's slow performance in the winter quarter of the fiscal year. To even out the year's operations and broaden its profit base, American-Marietta merged with the Martin Co., formerly a Cleveland-based airplane maker. As a major defense contractor, Martin offered American-Marietta an entry into the defense electronics business and new markets for its products. The resulting company, Martin-Marietta, based in Baltimore, established Master Builders as the lead company in the Martin-Marietta Chemical Group. Cleveland became the main office of the North Central Region of Martin-Marietta as the city was recognized as a world center of concrete technology. To provide for the company's research and development efforts, MM built a $10 million technical center at 23700 Chagrin in BEACHWOOD in 1977, reportedly the world's largest privately owned center of its kind for the concrete industry. Completely equipped for the chemical and physical analysis and testing of concrete, the facility also serves as the location of some 30 annual seminars for architects, engineers, and ready-mix executives; 10 training schools for new employees; and a consulting center on construction problems. In 1982, Martin-Marietta was involved in a 3-way takeover fight with Bendix and United Technologies that resulted in Bendix's being bought by the Allied Corp. As a result of its maneuvers to buy Bendix stock and prevent its own annihilation, Martin-Marietta emerged weakened and with $900 million more debt. However, its purpose in fighting for Bendix—to attain a larger share of the defense market—was realized; aerospace, over 60% of its business in 1982, was 70% in 1983 and 80% in 1984, while chemicals dropped. Though the company sold off most of its cement holdings, it reinforced its additives section by its purchase of another local firm, Set Prods.

**MASTERPIECES FROM THE BERLIN MUSEUMS** was the title of a traveling exhibition that came to Cleveland in 1948 and proved to be the most popular exhibition ever held at the CLEVELAND MUSEUM OF 'ART. In Apr. 1945, the 347th Infantry of Gen. Geo. Patton's 3d Army advancing into Germany discovered a cache of gold and works of art taken from Berlin treasuries and from Berlin's National-Galerie and the Kaiser Friedrich Museum; 207 of the most valuable masterpieces were shipped to the U.S. to be stored in the vaults of the Natl. Gallery until such time as they could be safely returned to Germany. The group of paintings included 15 Rembrandts, 6 Rubenses, 3 Raphaels, and 4 Titians, as well as numerous other works by acknowledged masters. Before returning the works to Germany, the Dept. of the Army allowed 97 of the works

to tour 13 cities in the U.S., including Cleveland. A $.25 admission fee was used for the German Children's Relief Fund. In each city, the exhibition drew record crowds. The Cleveland Museum of Art hosted the exhibition from 6–22 Oct. 1948. During that 16-day period, it was seen by over 100,000 visitors. On 21 Oct. the museum's 31-year attendance record was broken, as a record 18,120 people came to see the works of art. The Cleveland Museum of Art published the catalog for the exhibition for 8 other museums in several editions. A record 159,000 copies were published and sold.

**MASTERS, IRVINE U.** (1823–13 Nov. 1865), was an OHIO CITY politician and shipbuilder who became mayor of Cleveland. Masters was born in New York and moved to Ohio in 1851 with his first wife, Naomi. He soon became a trustee of Ohio City and helped WM. B. CASTLE negotiate the merger between Cleveland and OHIO CITY. After the merger, Masters served on CLEVELAND CITY COUNCIL from 1854–63, serving as council president 3 times from 1859–61 and 1862–63. As president, he officially welcomed Abraham Lincoln to Cleveland when the president-elect visited the city in Feb. 1861. In 1863, Masters, running for mayor of Cleveland as a Republican, defeated incumbent mayor EDWARD S. FLINT. As mayor, Masters was well liked by the public and the press and supported measures to improve the city's business. A Civil War mayor, he also felt that it was his patriotic duty to show the city's support for the national war effort; he held numerous public meetings and ceremonies for departing and returning soldiers. Masters suffered from tuberculosis and was forced to resign because of poor health in May 1864; the press reported that his excessive patriotism had ruined his already fragile health. While serving in politics, Masters was also a businessman. He was a partner with E. M. PECK in the Peck & Masters shipbuilding company: the firm's ships were among the larger on the Great Lakes. After resigning his mayoral office, Masters tried to maintain his business interests, but his declining health overwhelmed him, and he sold his interest in the business in 1865. Peck continued on in the shipbuilding business. Masters's first wife, Naomi, died in 1863. He then married M. Augusta Prull on 27 Oct. 1863. After his resignation from office, Masters went to New England and Nova Scotia in the summer of 1864 in hope of regaining his health; however, it did not improve. The next year, Masters tried another relocation to a healthier climate. He, his new wife, and his 3 children from his first marriage moved to Pine Island, Minn.; however, his health continued to decline, and he died several months later.

**MATHER, FLORA STONE** (Mrs. Samuel) (6 Apr. 1852–19 Jan. 1909), was a philanthropist, benefactress, and humanitarian whose dedication to the religious, educational, and social-reform activities of the city touched the lives of many Clevelanders and Cleveland institutions. Flora Amelia Stone, youngest daughter of wealthy industrialist AMASA STONE and Julia Gleason Stone, was born in the family mansion on Superior Ave. (site of the HOLLENDEN HOTEL), attended Cleveland schools, and graduated with honors from the CLEVELAND ACADEMY, a private school for young ladies, which was located on the south side of Huron Rd. In 1875 her sister, Clara, married JOHN HAY, diplomat and later secretary of state. In 1881, Flora married SAMUEL MATHER, iron-ore, steel, and shipping magnate. They shared and supported each other's charitable, educational, and varied church-related interests and philanthropies. Their children were Samuel Livingston, Amasa

Stone, Philip Richard, and Constance (later Mrs. Robt. Bishop).

In 1896, Mrs. Mather founded Goodrich House in honor of her childhood pastor, Rev. Wm. H. Goodrich. She also supported a variety of activities that were outgrowths of Goodrich House, including the LEGAL AID SOCIETY and the CONSUMERS LEAGUE OF OHIO. Throughout her lifetime, Mrs. Mather supported many of the activities of Western Reserve University, including the Advisory Council, the College for Women (renamed Mather College in her honor in 1931), and Adelbert College. In 1892 she was responsible for construction of Guilford Cottage (later Guilford House), a dormitory on the WRU campus named in honor of Miss LINDA T. GUILFORD, principal of the academy. She gave funds in 1902 for the construction of Haydn Hall, a multipurpose building named in honor of Dr. HIRAM C. HAYDN of Old Stone Church, to which Mrs. Mather belonged for her entire lifetime. Mrs. Mather died in 1909 at Shoreby, the family's lakeshore home in BRATENAHL. Her will included bequests to over 30 religious, educational, and charitable institutions, including funds for completion of the AMASA STONE CHAPEL on the WRU campus, which she and her sister, Mrs. John Hay, gave in memory of their father. In 1913, a women's dormitory, named Mather House in her honor, was given to the university by alumnae and friends. Standing adjacent to the CHURCH OF THE COVENANT, it now contains faculty and administrative offices.

University Archives, CWRU.
Mather Family Papers, WRHS.

**MATHER, SAMUEL** (13 July 1851–18 Oct. 1931), was a pioneer in the iron-ore and steel industries and a prominent local philanthropist. A descendant of the Mathers of Massachusetts on his father's side and Jas. Fenimore Cooper on his mother's, Mather was born to Samuel and Georgiana Woolson Mather, and educated in Cleveland. He planned to attend Harvard, founded by Increase Mather, and then to work at his father's business, the Cleveland Iron Co. While serving as a timekeeper apprentice at the mine, Mather had an incapacitating accident, which required a long period of treatment and recuperation that caused him to abandon his dreams of Harvard. However, the experience made him a lifelong supporter of educational institutions, UNIVERSITY HOSPITALS, and mine safety. In 1882, Mather affiliated with Col. Jas. Pickands and Jay C. Morse to form PICKANDS, MATHER & CO., a rival to Cleveland Iron. After 2 years of struggle, the company leased the Coulby mine in the Gogebic Range; it later acquired interests in the Mesabi Range in Minnesota and the Marquette Range in Michigan. Mather allied Pickands-Mather with the steel industry and built the company into a complete provider of resources and resource transportation. He made it the 2d-largest mining company in the Lake Superior district. When U.S. Steel was formed in 1902, Mather worked actively to facilitate the merger.

As his success in business compounded his inherited wealth, Mather devoted an increasing amount of time and money in the interest of his community and church. He was the senior warden and vestryman of TRINITY CATHEDRAL and president of the Federated Churches of Cleveland. He served as a trustee and major benefactor of HIRAM HOUSE. During WORLD WAR I he organized the War Chest and donated over $.75 million in his own name and that of his company; for his work he received a medal from the Cleveland Chamber of Commerce and the Cross of the Legion of Honor from the French government. Seeing the need to provide continuous help to the less

fortunate at home, he helped set up the Community Chest, to which he contributed $100,000 annually. In 1930, Mather set up a $1.6 million trust fund to insure that the fund would prosper after his death. A devoted family man, Mather married Flora Stone, daughter of AMASA STONE, in 1881, and fathered 4 children: S. Livingston, Phillip, Constance, and Amasa Stone. Mrs. Mather, active in local charity work, died in 1909, while Amasa died in 1922. When Mather died at age 80, he was the richest man in Ohio. His estate was divided among his children, grandchildren, and daughter-in-law, and various charitable causes. Major benefactors included Western Reserve University and University Hospitals, JOHN CARROLL UNIVERSITY, Kenyon College, the Episcopal Church, St. Luke's Hospital of Tokyo, Japan, and the Community Chest. Because of declining stock values in the Depression, the bequests could not be paid. As the value of the estate increased with market improvements, heirs contested the will, since Mather had changed the terms within a year of his death, and some bequests (notably one to WRU) were invalidated.

Mather Family Papers, WRHS.

**MATHER CHARITABLE TRUST.** See **S. LIVINGSTON MATHER CHARITABLE TRUST**

**MATHER FUND.** See **ELIZABETH RING & WILLIAM GWINN MATHER FUND**

The **MATHER GALLERY**, formally known as the Flora Stone Mather Gallery, is a student- and faculty-coordinated art gallery located in Thwing Ctr., the student union building of CASE WESTERN RESERVE UNIVERSITY, on Euclid Ave. The idea for a student/faculty gallery was first proposed by members of the Art Education Dept. of CWRU with the Student Union Board in early 1973. On Sunday, 21 Oct. 1973, after 6 months of planning, the Mather Gallery opened its doors, occupying a room that had once housed the campus paperback bookstore. The gallery was made possible by a generous gift of the Mather Alumnae Assoc. The opening exhibition presented works by members of the art department faculty, while the following show, "Photography and Sculpture of CWRU Students," drew responses from over 150 artists, who submitted 250 works of art. In Nov. 1973, the gallery hired a manager to aid the volunteer student committee; Mary Weiss, a student finishing her degree in art education, became the first gallery manager in 1974. Since 1973, in addition to presenting exhibitions of both local and national reputation, the gallery has hosted poetry readings, festivals, recitals, jazz concerts, and plant and print sales, and has become an integral part of campus life at CWRU.

The **MAY COMPANY OF CLEVELAND** is one of the area's largest retailers. It is a division of a national chain, May Dept. Stores, Inc., which has its headquarters in St. Louis. The national chain, which grew out of an operation initially established in Leadville, Colo., in 1877, was founded in Denver in 1888 by David May and his brothers-in-law, Louis, Joseph, and Moses Schoenberg. They decided to establish the third unit of this national organization in Cleveland in 1899 when the May Co. acquired the well-known clothing and furnishing store the E. R. Hull & Dutton Co. (founded 1873 as Mabley & Hull) at the southeast corner of PUBLIC SQUARE on Ontario St.

David May originally placed Louis Schoenberg (who later changed his last name to Beaumont) in charge of the May Co. in Cleveland. He worked at expanding the store so as to live up to its slogan, "May Company—Watch Us

Grow." In 1900, May erected a 3-story building as an annex. In the following years, it purchased additional buildings, making possible a Euclid Ave. frontage. In 1904, David May chose NATHAN L. DAUBY to manage the store. In the next 2 decades, Dauby oversaw further expansions, until a 1931 addition made May Ohio's largest store. During this time, the May Co. introduced several "firsts" to Cleveland, including free Eagle trading stamps, escalator service, a patrons' garage, air-conditioning facilities, and a playground for children. Dauby guided the firm for 6 decades, continually strengthening its reputation as a retail leader, and making it known for charitable and philanthropic work in the community.

In the 1950s, under Morton D. May, the national firm, which at that time had 6 branches, began a major expansion program, acquiring department-store chains across the nation. By 1983 it had 11 divisions, with 144 department stores in 15 states. The May Co. of Cleveland participated in this growth. As early as 1939, the store secretly acquired Taylor's Dept. Store, which it operated in downtown Cleveland until May decided to close it in 1961. In 1957, May started to establish suburban branch stores. By 1979, it had 9 branches in the Cleveland-Sandusky area. This expansion program bolstered sales, allowing the company to institute a multi-million-dollar modernization program in the 1960s. Nationally, in the 1970s, May diversified, acquiring and expanding chains of discount and shoe stores and becoming a major developer and operator of shopping centers. The May Co. of Cleveland remained strong into the 1980s. The downtown store consolidated its retail space by leasing several floors to a bank in 1980. By 1983, the company had over $212 million in sales in Cleveland.

The **MAY DAY RIOTS** occurred in Cleveland on 1 May (May Day) 1919. The Cleveland riots, which involved Socialists, trade-union members, police, and military troops, were the most violent of a series of similar disorders that took place throughout the U.S. The Socialists and trade unionists were participants in a parade organized by CHAS. RUTHENBERG to celebrate May Day, to protest the recent jailing of Socialist leader Eugene Debs, and to promote his own mayoral candidacy. Thirty-two labor and Socialist groups were scheduled to take part in the march. The line of march was organized in 4 groups, each with a red flag and an American flag at its head; many marchers also wore red clothing or red badges. While marching from Acme Hall on E. 9th St. to PUBLIC SQUARE, one of the units was stopped on Superior Ave. by a group of Victory Loan workers (see WORLD WAR I), who requested that the red flags be lowered. It was at this point that rioting began. Before the day ended, disorder had spread to Public Sqaure and to the Socialist party headquarters on Prospect Ave., which were ransacked by a mob of 100 men. Mounted police, Army trucks, and tanks were needed to quell the riots. Two people were killed, 40 injured, and 116 arrested in the course of the violence. Ruthenberg was arrested and charged with assault to kill a policeman. It is uncertain as to who began the riot. Most evidence shows that bystanders and police were primarily responsible. Other evidence indicates that the marchers taunted the onlookers. In either instance, the actions of those involved were largely shaped by the anti-Bolshevik hysteria that permeated the country during the "Red Scare" of 1919.

Johnson, Oakley C., *The Day Is Coming* (1957).
Murray, Robert K., *The Red Scare* (1955).

The **MAY SHOW** is an annual exhibition of the works of northeast Ohio-area artists sponsored every spring by the

**CLEVELAND MUSEUM OF ART.** The first Annual Exposition of Cleveland Artists & Craftsmen, as the show was called before it earned the popular nickname "May Show," was announced in the April CMA Bulletin of 1919. The idea for an exhibition featuring works of Cleveland artists was proposed by museum director Frederic Allen Whiting in his first address to the trustees of the museum as a means of spurring artistic growth and development in Cleveland by providing an annual review of artists' works and an opportunity for art patrons in Cleveland to buy works. The idea was suggested to Whiting by members of the Cleveland Art Assoc., then under the chairmanship of Mrs. Frank W. Wardwell. The first May Show allowed artists to display works created up to 10 years previous to the exhibition; beginning with the second show, however, only the previous year's work was eligible for submission. Mrs. Wardwell, Mrs. Harry L. Vail, and Mrs. S. Livingstone Mather served as chairmen for the early May Show general committees, and WM. M. MILLIKEN, then curator of decorative arts, was in charge of the exhibition, a position he was to hold until his retirement in 1958. He was helped by 2 assistants, Miss Helen S. Foote and Miss Louise H. Burchfield.

Mrs. Paul Smith supervised sales for the first exhibition, serving in that capacity for 33 years. She developed the format for sales and prizes that the show eventually adopted. It awarded cash prizes the first year, and then medals of merit for some years. It was then decided that an active sales program would be of more benefit to contributing artists than cash prizes or awards. Each artist was allowed to enter 10 items, up to 5 in any one category. In the first show there were 36 classes, including oil and watercolor painting, graphic arts, photography, sculpture, basketry, enamelwork, and garden design. During the Depression, Mrs. Benjamin P. Bole, Mrs. Malcolm L. McBride, and Miss Julia Raymond conceived the idea for the "Pick-Quick" Club, also known as the "Pickles" (Painting, Illustration, Carving, Ceramics, Lace, Etching, and Sculpture). Members committed themselves to buying at least 1 work a year from the May Show and in return were invited to a special preview showing of the works with first choice of purchase. This practice later led to the present-day custom of Patrons' Previews, an important social event in Cleveland.

In the 1940s and 1950s, the museum was inundated with bequests, culminating with the 1958 Hanna bequest that thrust the Cleveland museum into the mainstream of the world art market. As a result, members of the May Show committee decided that the standards of the May Show had to be raised, to the detriment of amateur artists and craftsmen. The number of categories was reduced to 12, and in 1961 the show was opened to the entire Western Reserve area, encompassing 13 counties. Later the number of categories was reduced even further, to 8, virtually excluding small crafts and aiming toward what the May Show Committee feels is their new purpose: the development of important art in Cleveland.

The **MAYFIELD COUNTRY CLUB,** an invitational golf club located on approximately 211 acres at 1545 Sheridan Rd., S. EUCLID, was originally part of the Euclid Club (1901). In 1908, some members withdrew from the Euclid Club and, under the leadership of Benjamin F. Bourne and Malcolm B. Johnson, organized the Mayfield Country Club (June 1909). W. H. (Bert) Way, a former professional at the Euclid Club, searched for, selected, and designed the golf course. The original clubhouse, designed by architect FRANK B. MEADE, which was opened 1 July 1911, was destroyed by fire on 10 Mar. 1914. It was rebuilt and reopened on Labor Day 1914. It was destroyed by fire a second time, 18 Apr. 1948, but was rebuilt on the same location and reopened a year later, in May 1949. In addition to GOLF, club activities include TENNIS, swimming, curling, paddle tennis, and social events for members such as receptions, dances, teas, and parties.

**MAYFIELD HEIGHTS** is a city located east of Cleveland and bounded by HIGHLAND HTS. and MAYFIELD VILLAGE on the north, LYNDHURST on the west, PEPPER PIKE on the south, and GATES MILLS on the east. The city covers an area of 4 sq. mi. Mayfield Hts. was originally part of Mayfield Twp., which was formed in 1819 and also included the modern communities of Gates Mills, Highland Hts., and Mayfield Village and a portion of Lyndhurst. Some of the city's early homes still stand as reminders of its early history. The strong residential design concepts adopted in a 1929 zoning ordinance are reflected in the modern design of most of the newer homes and in the city's street patterns. Approximately 58% of the city's residential development consists of single-family homes, while the remaining 42% consists of apartment dwellings. Mayfield Hts. was incorporated as a city in 1950 and adopted the mayor-council form of government. Following incorporation, its population grew to 13,478 in 1960, and 22,139 in 1970, then dropped to 21,550 in 1980. The city has little industry. Much of the commercial enterprise in this heavily residential area consists of 6 banks and 6 savings-and-loan associations. The city's 2 largest employers are HILLCREST HOSPITAL and the Mayfield Board of Education, with a senior high, 1 junior high, and 2 elementary schools. Recreational and public facilities include the Community Ctr. on Marsol Rd., a branch of the CUYAHOGA COUNTY PUBLIC LIBRARY, an outdoor swimming pool, a rollerskating rink, a bowling lane, 5 baseball fields, 4 lighted tennis courts, and 2 basketball courts. The city has more than 20 acres of parks and recreational land, including parks located on Chelmsford, Belrose, and Oakville roads.

The **MAYFIELD ROAD MOB,** so named because they met frequently in the Little Italy section of Mayfield Rd., was led by Tony and Frank Milano. Other members were reported to be John Angersola (alias John King), Chas. Colletti, and Alfred (Big Al) Polizzi. The mob was allegedly involved in a number of illegal activities during the 1930s, the most publicized being bootlegging. According to the news media, Milano's gang cornered the bourbon business, selling the liquor in case lots to licensed clubs and restaurants, which could make more profit from it than from licensed liquor. The gang emerged as leaders of the city's Italian syndicate during the 1930s.

Eliot Ness Scrapbooks, WRHS.

**MAYFIELD VILLAGE** is located east of Cleveland and is bounded by GATES MILLS on the east, MAYFIELD HTS. on the south, HIGHLAND HTS. on the west, and Willoughby Hills in Lake County on the north. It occupies just over 4 sq. mi. Mayfield Village was originally part of Mayfield Twp., which was formed in 1819 and also included the modern communities of Gates Mills, Highland Hts., and Mayfield Hts. and a portion of LYNDHURST. It remained part of the township until 1920, when a special election resulted in the division of the township into the 4 villages. Settlement in the area began in 1805, when several families migrated from Ontario County, N.Y., determined to create an ideal community in which to build homes and raise families. At the beginning of the 20th century, the area was still principally occupied with farming, dairy, and orchard-growing interests. A zoning ordi-

nance of 1935 secured the residential character of the area, even though it was surrounded by business and industry in nearby communities. The population has gradually increased from 1,977 in 1960, to 3,548 in 1970, and 3,577 in 1980. Mayfield Village has 3 schools and a branch of the CUYAHOGA COUNTY PUBLIC LIBRARY. Although a small community, the village is rich in beauty and recreational facilities, which include a golf course, a racquet club, and a portion of the N. Chagrin Reservation of the CLEVELAND METROPARKS SYSTEM.

The **MAYORAL ADMINISTRATION OF ANTHONY J. CELEBREZZE** (1953–62) came at a time when much of the Cleveland area was enjoying post-World War II prosperity and was looking forward to the economic benefits that would come from the opening of the St. Lawrence Seaway. With the heavy in-migration to Cleveland of people looking for jobs, however, there were increasing housing and employment problems that needed to be dealt with. After receiving his law degree in 1936 from Ohio Northern University, Celebrezze worked on the legal staff of the Ohio Bureau of Unemployment Compensation. He opened an office in Cleveland in 1939 and practiced law for 13 years. Interested in politics, he was elected to the Ohio senate in 1950 as a Democrat. Although reelected to the senate in 1952, Celebrezze chose to run for mayor of Cleveland in 1953 as an independent Democrat. Supported by Ohio Gov. Frank Lausche, *Cleveland Press* editor LOUIS SELTZER, and retiring mayor THOS. BURKE, he was elected to the first of 5 terms, easily defeating ALBERT PORTER, the regular Democratic candidate in the primaries, and Republican candidate Wm. J. McDermott in the general election. His popularity with the Cleveland voters increased with each election, and in 1961 he carried every ward in Cleveland, capturing about 73.8% of the total vote.

As mayor, Celebrezze organized the Cleveland Seaport Foundation to promote Cleveland as a world trade center, supported an $8 million Seaway bond issue, and helped initiate a $140 million urban-renewal program. Interested in rehabilitation, he participated actively in the development of the Cleveland Vocational Guidance & Rehabilitation Services, the successor agency to the Cleveland Rehabilitation Ctr. During his administration, major progress was made on a system of freeways designed to serve Cleveland and the rapidly growing suburbs, the population of which increased by about 62% from 1950–60. As white families moved to the surrounding SUBURBS, the population mix of the central city changed, with the proportion of BLACKS increasing from about 16.2% to 28.6% from 1950–60. Continuing in-migration to Cleveland of people looking for jobs during the 1950s contributed to housing and employment problems. The shortage of affordable housing caused overcrowding in the older neighborhoods, and a net decline in the number of available jobs in the area caused poor-relief costs to soar. To relieve pressure on the city budget, the mayor urged the county, which administered health and welfare services under contract with the city, to assume the financial burden of the relief costs, as well. By 1961, Cuyahoga County was contributing about $2.9 million and the city about $1.1 million toward the cost of poor relief. In addition, BLOSSOM HILL SCHOOL FOR GIRLS, the Hudson Boys Farm, and City Hospital (part of Metro General in 1986) were also transferred to the county during his administration. Celebrezze resigned as mayor in 1962 to become secretary of health, education, and welfare in the Kennedy-Johnson administrations. In 1965 he was appointed federal judge for the 6th Circuit Court of Appeals. He retired from active service on the bench in 1980.

Anthony J. Celebrezze Papers, WRHS.

The **MAYORAL ADMINISTRATION OF DENNIS KU-CINICH** (1977–79) was characterized by confrontation and turmoil as the mayor survived an attempted recall election and was faced with Cleveland's DEFAULT on its financial obligations. Kucinich's political career began with his election to Cleveland City Council in 1969 as a Democrat. While serving as councilman, he received his B.A. and M.A. degrees in speech communication from CASE WESTERN RESERVE UNIVERSITY. He was elected clerk of municipal court in 1975, serving in that position for 2 years, and then was elected mayor of Cleveland, the youngest big-city mayor in the country at that time. In spite of the urban populism he espoused and his genuine concern for the workingman, the mayor's confrontational style of politics and the quality of some of his appointments engendered opposition. With the public firing of his newly appointed police chief Richard Hongisto, those who felt that Kucinich was unable to effectively govern the city launched a movement to recall the mayor. By June 1978 they had acquired enough valid signatures to schedule a special election, and in August, the voters determined by a narrow margin that the mayor should remain in office for the balance of his term (see RECALL ELECTION OF 1978).

During Kucinich's administration, it became increasingly difficult for the city to meet its expenses, and those who considered the city's municipal light plant a continuing drain on the city treasury wanted it sold to the CLEVELAND ELECTRIC ILLUMINATING CO. Kucinich opposed the sale, believing that Muny Light's competition with CEI kept electric rates at a reasonable level. Furthermore, its sale would cancel the $328 million antitrust suit the city had filed against CEI, depriving the city of an opportunity to win the suit and collect the money. In Dec. 1978, the city was unable to pay off $14 million in notes owed to 6 local banks. Negotiations between the mayor, the city council, and the banks to roll over the notes reached an impasse, and Cleveland became the first major American city to default on its financial obligations since the Depression. To provide more income, the voters were asked in Feb. 1979 to increase the city income tax by .5% to 1.5% and to decide whether or not to sell Muny Light to CEI. They approved the income-tax increase but turned down the sale of the light plant. In Nov. 1979, Kucinich was defeated for reelection as mayor by Republican Geo. Voinovich. At a special election held in Aug. 1983, Kucinich was again elected to Cleveland City Council from Ward 12, where he served for 2 years. In 1985 he gave up his council seat to run for governor of Ohio, and later that year he moved to Mt. Vernon, Ohio. He withdrew from the gubernatorial race in Aug. 1986.

The **MAYORAL ADMINISTRATION OF FRANK J. LAUSCHE** (1941–44) governed Cleveland during WORLD WAR II and was characterized by its honesty and thrift. Lausche graduated from the John Marshall School of Law and was admitted to the bar in 1920. While he was working at the law firm of Locher, Green, & Woods, Cyrus Locher encouraged him to go into politics. In 1932, he was appointed and then elected judge in Cleveland Municipal Court; he moved over to the court of common pleas in 1937, where he was instrumental in closing several Cleveland gambling houses. Resigning from the court, Lausche ran for mayor in 1941, defeating acting mayor EDWARD BLYTHIN, and was reelected in 1943. Although nominally a Democrat, Lausche operated outside of the Democratic party organization throughout his political career. As mayor,

Lausche worked for lower taxes and was noted for having a clean and frugal administration. During his mayoralty, negotiations for the city to take over the Cleveland Railway system were finalized, and in 1943, he appointed the first transit board. Spurred in part by antipathy to Nazi racial doctrines, Cleveland's municipal government moved to address the needs of its black constituents. In 1943, the Cleveland Welfare Fed. began a 2-year study of racial and economic conditions in Cleveland's black community, and Lausche established the Committee on Democratic Practice, aimed at preserving minority rights during wartime and developing an educational program to combat discrimination and racial intolerance. Concerned about Cleveland's postwar development, the mayor organized the Postwar Planning Council in 1944 to identify major problems and coordinate future planning in areas such as traffic and public transportation, finance and taxation, public works, labor-management relations, and the needs of returning servicemen. Lausche successfully campaigned to become governor of Ohio in 1944, serving until 1946, when he was defeated by THOS. HERBERT. He was reelected in 1948, 1950, 1952, and 1954. He defeated GEO. BENDER to become U.S. senator from Ohio in 1957 and served until 1967.

Frank J. Lausche Papers, Ohio Historical Society.

The **MAYORAL ADMINISTRATION OF RALPH LOCHER** (1962–67) was characterized by progress in some areas, but also by racial turmoil, which accompanied agitation for social and economic change. Locher was admitted to the Ohio bar in 1939. After practicing law for 6 years and serving briefly as secretary to the Ohio State Industrial Commission, he became Gov. Frank Lausche's executive secretary in 1946. On Lausche's recommendation, Mayor Anthony Celebrezze appointed Locher city law director in 1953. As law director, Locher prosecuted several early antidiscrimination suits and testified before the Ohio general assembly in opposition to proposed utility rate increases. When Celebrezze resigned to become secretary of health, education, and welfare in 1962, Locher succeeded him as mayor of Cleveland. Support from the city's nationality groups formed his political base and helped elect him mayor in 1963 by a large margin. As mayor, he was instrumental in doubling the size of the city's port facilities and expanding CLEVELAND HOPKINS INTERNATIONAL AIRPORT. During Locher's administration, there was increasing tension between the growing black population and the white leadership of the city, particularly in the areas of minority employment, housing, and education. In Aug. 1963, Locher arranged mediation of a dispute between Plumbers Local #55 and the UNITED FREEDOM MOVEMENT over the admittance of black plumbers to the union. With successful resolution of the dispute, the threatened picketing of the Exhibition Hall construction site on the MALL by the UFM was averted. However, the problem of minority admittance to local unions remained. In 1964, the mayor supported the Cleveland school board's policy of building new schools in overcrowded neighborhoods, a move that cost him the support of many blacks who viewed this policy as a perpetuation of racial segregation. Locher was reelected mayor in 1965 by a narrow margin, and only after a recount. His leadership was not effective in improving conditions in the city—particularly in the Hough area. This lack of progress helped fuel the HOUGH RIOTS during the summer of 1966, when the mayor called in the Ohio Natl. Guard to restore order. The city's urban-renewal plan designed to relieve the housing shortage made little progress during his administration, and federal funds previously allocated to Cleveland's renewal program were frozen. Locher ran for mayor again in 1967 but lost in the primaries to Carl B. Stokes. He was elected judge of the court of common pleas in 1968 and probate judge in 1972, and currently (1976–86) is a justice of the Ohio Supreme Court.

Ralph S. Locher Papers, WRHS.

The **MAYORAL ADMINISTRATION OF RALPH J. PERK** (1972–77) came at a time when serious financial problems were developing in the city. The mayor was able to obtain federal funds to help meet current expenses and grants for a number of local programs. Perk began his political career in 1940 as a Republican precinct committeeman. He was appointed to the staff of the Ohio attorney general's office in 1950 and from 1953–62 was a member of Cleveland City Council, representing the Broadway-E. 55th area. He was elected county auditor in 1962 and remained there until 1971, when he became the first Republican elected mayor of Cleveland since HAROLD BURTON in the 1930s. Perk's political base was the heavily Democratic ethnic community, but he persuaded them to vote for him regardless of party label. As one of the few big-city Republican mayors at the time, he was successful in obtaining money from the Nixon administration in Washington. A grant of $22 million to help fight crime was awarded to Cleveland, and a new citywide emergency medical service and a community response unit for the police department were begun with the help of federal monies. During Perk's administration, the city took over the summer-jobs program for the disadvantaged from the Cleveland school board. Inflation and the 1973 recession contributed to a 30% increase in city expenses while Perk was mayor, and it was necessary to borrow almost $130 million to help balance the budget. Existing bond funds and general revenue-sharing funds from the federal government were used to help cover deficits. The city sewer system was sold to a regional authority for $32 million following litigation in 1972, and Cleveland's transit system was transferred to a regional agency in 1975 for $8.9 million, giving the city more operating capital. However, these proved to be only short-term solutions to the city's financial problems. Perk was reelected mayor twice, in 1973 and 1975, but he lost in a nonpartisan primary to Democrats Dennis Kucinich and Edward Feighan in 1977.

Ralph J. Perk Papers, WRHS.

The **MAYORAL ADMINISTRATION OF CARL B. STOKES** (1967–71) was marked by progress, controversy, and the unrest prevalent in many urban areas of the U.S. at the time. Stokes, a graduate of Cleveland Marshall Law School, was admitted to the Ohio bar in 1957 and served as an assistant prosecutor in the city's law department for 4 years. His political career began in 1962, when he was elected to the Ohio general assembly as a Democrat; he served there for 5 years. Entering the Cleveland mayoral race in 1965 as an independent, he narrowly lost to incumbent Democratic mayor Ralph Locher. When he ran again in 1967, as a Democrat, he defeated Locher in the primary and won the general election over Republican candidate Seth Taft. He was reelected to a second term in 1969. As the first black mayor of a major American city, Stokes attracted national attention. He persuaded the Dept. of Housing & Urban Development (HUD) to release urban-renewal funds frozen during the Locher administration. He was instrumental in persuading city council to increase the city income tax from .5% to 1% and to pass the Equal Employment Opportunity Ordinance requiring firms doing business with the city to have active programs to increase minority employment. During his administration, Cleveland voters increased spending for schools, welfare, street improvement, and the city zoo and passed a $100 million bond issue to help eliminate water pollution.

Stokes launched the CLEVELAND: NOW! program to rehabilitate the city. Over $5 million was raised and spent for a wide variety of community programs, and its momentum generated additional funds from federal, state, and local sources. However, contributions dried up in the aftermath of the GLENVILLE SHOOT-OUT, when it was discovered that Fred (Ahmed) Evans and his militant group had received some $6,000 from Cleveland: NOW! funds. The relationship between the mayor and the police department deteriorated after the shoot-out. Stokes attempted to reform the department, believing they were not responsive to the needs of the people, but he was unable to effect the changes he desired. He became embroiled in a controversy over his efforts to build public housing in the Lee-Seville area, a black middle-class neighborhood, and the voters twice refused to raise the city income tax again. As a result, he decided not to seek a third term in 1971. In 1972, Stokes left Cleveland to become a broadcaster at WNBC-TV in New York, but he returned to Cleveland in 1980 and established a private law practice, specializing in labor law. He was elected municipal court judge in 1983.

Stokes, Carl B., *Promises of Power* (1973).
Carl B. Stokes Papers, WRHS.

The **MAYORAL ADMINISTRATION OF GEORGE V. VOINOVICH** (1979- ) was successful in restructuring Cleveland's finances, allowing the city to escape from DEFAULT and remain solvent at a time when both the area's economy and federal funding of local programs were declining. After receiving his J.D. degree from Ohio State University in 1961, Voinovich began his political career as an assistant to the attorney general for the state of Ohio, 1962–63. A Republican, he represented Cleveland's mainly Democratic 53d district in the Ohio legislature from 1967–71. Voinovich ran for mayor of Cleveland in 1971 but lost to Ralph Perk in the Republican primary. Mayor Perk, however, appointed him county auditor, and he was subsequently elected to the position, serving from 1971–76. He then was elected Cuyahoga County commissioner, 1977–78, and served briefly as lieutenant governor of Ohio before running for mayor again; this time Voinovich defeated incumbent Dennis Kucinich in the 1979 election. At that time, the mayor and city councilmen served 2-year terms, but in Nov. 1980 their term of office was increased from 2 to 4 years. Voinovich was reelected to a 4-year term as mayor in 1981 and was reelected by a large majority in 1985. When Voinovich became mayor in 1979, Cleveland was in default. Voinovich initiated a complete audit of the city's books, which revealed past debts of approximately $110 million outstanding. He borrowed executives from private industry to study the city administration and recommend improvements. As a result, the city reorganized 10 city departments, and set up a new accounting system with internal auditing capability. In Oct. 1980, 8 banks agreed to buy $36.2 million in 14-year bonds to refinance the city's debt, and with this transaction, Cleveland escaped default, but the city's finances were still supervised by the state of Ohio. In the early 1980s, the city experienced a decline in receipts from the payroll tax as the local economy weakened and unemployment increased, and federal funding of local projects such as the summer-jobs program was cut back. However, aided by an increase in the city income tax from 1.5% to 2% approved in Feb. 1981, the Voinovich administration managed to avoid serious financial problems. The mayor continued to support the retention of the Municipal Light plant (renamed Cleveland Public Power), and during his administration, capital improvements were made to strengthen its operation.

The **MAYOR'S ADVISORY WAR COMMITTEE** (1917–19) was formed on 7 Apr. 1917, soon after the declaration of war by Congress. Mayor HARRY L. DAVIS appointed the committee of 50 religious, civic, and business leaders to plan ways in which Cleveland could assist the war effort. Officers included MYRON T. HERRICK, chairman; HARRY L. VAIL, executive secretary; FRED H. GOFF, treasurer; and Warren S. Hayden, secretary. In addition, the mayor appointed an executive committee of 10 to facilitate the committee's work, including the MAWC officers, himself, Richard F. Grant, CHAS. A. OTIS, Chas. E. Adams, Paul L. Feiss, G. H. Goff, Francis W. Treadway, M. P. Mooney, Otto Miller, Wm. A. Greenlund, Richard F. Grant, and ANDREW SQUIRE.

The mayor's committee and a network of various subcommittees coordinated, financed, and supervised almost all of the city's war-relief work, including fundraising projects of public and private institutions. It directed distribution of food and clothing; sponsored Americanization classes for immigrants; organized a speakers' bureau; supervised draft boards; and subsequently supervised rent control. This single cooperative effort designed to increase efficiency of money, time, and effort gained national recognition. During the early months of 1919, the Mayor's Advisory Committee held homecoming celebrations, opened neighborhood centers for returning soldiers, lobbied for veterans' compensation pay, and funded a city employment service. Efforts were focused on soldiers who were reentering civilian life. During the summer of 1919, the committee slowly disbanded the subcommittees, and in Dec. 1919 it ceased to exist.

Mayor's Advisory War Committee Records, WRHS.

**MEADE, FRANK B.** (6 Jan. 1867-Mar. 1947), was a prominent architect active in Cleveland from 1895 until the 1930s who designed more than 800 homes in historical revival styles, many of them in partnership with JAS. M. HAMILTON. Meade was born in Norwalk, Ohio, the son of Alfred N. and Mattie Morse Meade. Alfred was a captain in the 128th Ohio Infantry during the CIVIL WAR who later ran a lumber company in Cleveland. Frank Meade's grandfather, Wm. Gale Meade, was an architect-builder for 25 years in Huron County. Frank Meade was educated at public schools in Cleveland and graduated from CENTRAL HIGH SCHOOL in 1884. After graduation from MIT in 1888, he moved to Chicago, where he was employed as a draftsman in the firm of Jenney & Mundie (1889–93). He married Dora Rucker on 3 Nov. 1898. In 1894, Meade returned to Cleveland. He subsequently formed partnerships with Alfred H. Granger (Meade & Granger, 1896–97) and with ABRAM GARFIELD (Meade & Garfield, 1898–1904). Meade ran his own firm again until 1911, when he formed a partnership with Hamilton (Meade & Hamilton, 1911–41). It was during this latter 30 years that the two architects designed the great majority of residences for Cleveland industrialists and professional men who lived on EUCLID AVE. or in WADE PARK or in SUBURBS and villages such as BRATENAHL, Ambler and Euclid Hts. (now CLEVELAND HTS.), SHAKER HTS., Willoughby, and CLIFTON PARK (now LAKEWOOD).

(See HAMILTON, JAMES M., for partial list of residential clients.)

In addition to their residential practice, Meade & Hamilton completed 6 club buildings. Meade, an active club member (the Union, Roadside, Euclid, and Century clubs in Cleveland; the Erie and Lambs clubs in New York City), was also an organizer and first president of the HERMIT CLUB, and designed that group's clubhouse. He served as president of the Hermit Club. Meade also played a leading role in the development of the Group Plan in Cleveland. In 1911 he was appointed secretary of the Group Plan Commission, filling a vacancy created by the death of John M. Carrere. Meade's colleagues on the commission were prominent landscape architect Frederick Law Olmsted of Boston and sculptor Arnold Brunner of New York City. Meade was a member and past president of the AMERICAN INSTITUTE OF ARCHITECTS CLEVELAND CHAPTER and a member of the Cleveland Chamber of Commerce.

Johannesen, Eric, *Cleveland Architecture, 1876-1976* (1979).

**MEATCUTTERS UNION.** *See* **UNITED FOOD & COMMERCIAL WORKERS UNION**

The **MECHANICS EDUCATIONAL SOCIETY OF AMERICA** represented workers in the machine-tool, automotive, and steel industries as an independent union until it affiliated with the CIO in 1954. It was active in several Cleveland war-production plants, and conflicts with its then-rival CIO and strikes led to the military seizure of some plants. Founded in Detroit in 1933 for tool-and-die makers, MESA organized in Flint and Pontiac and then moved to Toledo and Cleveland, sites of automotive factories and job shops. Here, the union eventually became the bargaining agent at Cleveland Graphite Bronze, Eaton Axle, S. K. Wellman, Lees Bradner, Ohio Tool & Forge, Clark Controller, and several smaller companies. Under the leadership of Matthew Smith, MESA fought for recognition of the special skills of machinists through better wages and working conditions with radical tactics. Within months of its founding, it staged a walkout of its entire membership, which gained it recognition as an industrywide bargaining agent. MESA merged with the Associated Automotive Workers of America in 1935 but rejected a proposal in 1937 to merge with the CIO United Auto Workers. As the nation moved into war, labor was constrained from striking by the War Labor Board (WLB), which also mediated disputes. Unable to strike, MESA shared the fear of other union leaders that employers would use the war as an excuse to exploit workers. The many MESA strikes that erupted during the war thus had elements of suspicion toward government agencies and interunion strife that often exceeded the issue at hand. While some of the strikes started outside of Cleveland, the city's war production was still threatened by those because of the union's policy of calling out all members on any strike.

Major Cleveland war-material manufacturers such as Eaton, Graphite, Natl. Acme, and S. K. Wellman were at risk in Mar. 1942 when Smith threatened to call out the area's 42,000 war workers concerning its admission to local WLB negotiations involving the union and representation on the board. Mayor Frank Lausche attempted to name a MESA representative but was told that that would be unacceptable to the national body. Later that year, Cleveland workers were on the verge of a sympathy walkout over the allegedly CIO-inspired firing of 6 MESA workers at the Briggs Mfg. Co., Aircraft Div., of Detroit, who had previously withdrawn from the CIO. Plants such as Cleveland

Graphite Bronze were also affected by a series of strikes based on local issues and wages, work demands, and work rules. MESA activity also precipitated the seizure of 8 Ohio plants after an incident at the Electric Auto Light plant in Toledo. Workers who abandoned the CIO for MESA were fired, and Smith ordered a walkout in Oct. 1944 that affected all local affiliates except Cleveland Graphite Bronze. When Pres. Franklin D. Roosevelt ordered the seizure of the closed plants, the 5th Regional War Labor Board demanded the abandonment of further strike plans and arbitration of the strike issues, with Mayor Lausche to appoint arbitrators if the union and company could not agree. Smith claimed he would cancel strike plans if Lausche, viewed as antilabor, was not involved. The local chief of the WLB claimed he was powerless to change arbitration orders because of the seizure. Feeling that the survival of MESA was at stake, Smith called out more men in what was called the most serious strike of the war. When officials at Electric Auto Light offered to rehire the discharged men, the strike finally ended. After the war, MESA redefined strikes as incidents that momentarily disrupted worker peace rather than battles to the death, their previous definition. Officials signed the Taft-Hartley affidavits without incident. By 1954, the union merged with the Metal & Machinery Workers of America, an independent union representing 1,500 workers in 3 Cleveland plants. Later that year, after more than 100 representation fights with the CIO, MESA affiliated with that body and brought 12,000 local workers into the CIO fold.

**MEDICAL MUTUAL OF CLEVELAND, INC.**, offered Clevelanders prepaid physician care that complemented the prepaid hospitalization offered by its sister corporation, the CLEVELAND HOSPITAL SERVICE ASSOC. The need for prepayment for doctor care was long recognized by health planners, but pioneers in the Blue Cross field such as John Mannix, architect of the local plan, realized that protests from the medical profession would sabotage any hospital plan that included professional fees. Physicians maintained that payment of services to a third party interfered in the doctor-patient relationship (which involved the right to set fees) and represented the first step toward socialized medicine. Therefore, when the CHSA was set up, payment for doctors was not included. Mannix sold the Blue Cross plan to the medical community by emphasizing that patients would pay their doctor bills more quickly if they were relieved of burdensome hospital costs. By 1938, the ACADEMY OF MEDICINE acceded to the need for a medical service plan and formulated a preliminary proposal. It became the basis of 1941 legislation that established a state-approved plan. The Cleveland Medical Service Assoc. was created to provide complete medical care for persons with incomes of less than $1,800 for singles and $2,400 for families. Protests from physicians prevented the new organization from functioning. In 1945, trustees and officers of the CHSA and city hospitals borrowed $75,000 from the Welfare Fed. to found Medical Mutual of Cleveland, Inc., a separately managed company that would reimburse patients a set amount for surgery and obstetrical care. Though the Academy of Medicine protested, the plan clearly did not force physicians to accept a standard fee, as the contract was with the patient-subscriber, and not the doctor. Within a year, 100,000 people joined the plan. Premiums, rate increases, and expansion of benefits closely followed those of Blue Cross; in fact, only Blue Cross subscribers were eligible to purchase Medical Mutual. Within 2 years of its establishment, Medical Mutual coverage was broadened to include in-hospital care, while anesthesia coverage was added in 1956, diagnostic services

in 1956, and posthospital care in 1959. In 1966, Medical Mutual became a Medicare Part B intermediary. Later, programs such as catastrophic coverage, dental care, and vision care were offered by the company. In 1975 it set up the Medical Life Insurance Co. as a wholly owned subsidiary to generate income and offset Medical Mutual rates. Medical Mutual was affiliated from 1961 with the national Blue Shield system, which grants permission to use its logo only to those plans that maintain high standards of operation. In 1983, it incorporated the Blue Shield name when it merged with BLUE CROSS OF NORTHEAST OHIO (the old CHSA) to become BLUE CROSS & BLUE SHIELD MUTUAL OF NORTHERN OHIO.

**MEDICINE.** The development of medical care, science, and education in the Cleveland area is a microcosm of national developments in the U.S., as a frontier community evolved into a major industrial center. The growth of the population and the financial resources available were determining factors. Although the CONNECTICUT LAND CO. commenced to sell its WESTERN RESERVE lands in 1796, it was not until 1800 that a young Connecticut physician, Moses Thompson (1776–1858), went west, cleared his land, and took up residence in what is today Hudson, Ohio. For 10 years he was the only physician in the Western Reserve west of Warren. In 1810, DAVID LONG (1787–1851) from Massachusetts arrived in Cleveland, 25 mi. north on Lake Erie, which from its founding in 1796 had grown to 57 inhabitants. A recent medical graduate, Long came because of the personal solicitation of a local resident who suggested that his income could be supplemented at first by teaching school and selling merchandise, a pattern followed in all undeveloped areas in the expanding nation. Like PETER ALLEN (1787–1864) from Connecticut, who settled in Kinsman, Ohio, in 1808, Long and Thompson became prominent citizens in their communities, providing not only medical care over a large area but also leadership in local civic and cultural growth.

The completion of the OHIO & ERIE CANAL in 1832 made the area more accessible, and by 1837 Cleveland had over 5,000 inhabitants, including 27 medical practitioners. By 1848 the population had doubled to more than 10,000, which was quadrupled by 1860 as GERMAN and IRISH immigrants poured in. The medical practitioners reflected the varieties of medical practice then available in the U.S.: regular physicians (allopaths), homeopaths, botanics or Thompsonians, practitioners of electromagnetic medicine and mesmerism, and surgeon dentists. The practitioners treated the wide spectrum of human ailments that prevailed in a prescientific medical world in which the nature of disease was still poorly understood, and in which smallpox was the sole disease for which a preventive procedure, vaccination, was available. As emergencies arose, temporary hospitals were set up, such as the Army hospital created in 1813 in Cleveland to care for wounded soldiers of the WAR OF 1812, and the 1832 cholera hospital on WHISKEY ISLAND. For most mild illness, people treated themselves with home remedies, often obtaining their information from popular medical books. Patent medicines were widely advertised and often very profitable. Patients went to the doctor's "shop" only for minor surgery, tooth extraction, and medicines, which he compounded himself from drugs that he had purchased in Pittsburgh or other larger cities to the east. House calls occupied much of the physician's day, and often night, until well into the 20th century. Home delivery of infants was nearly universal until the 1920s.

In 1811, in order to regulate medical and surgical practice in Ohio, the state legislature set up a system of medical districts for the purpose of creating local societies whose function would be to certify and oversee practitioners. Because of the population growth, in 1824 the NINETEENTH MEDICAL DISTRICT, comprising Cuyahoga and Medina counties, was designated, and David Long was elected the first president. After a succession of name changes, in 1902 the present ACADEMY OF MEDICINE of Cleveland emerged. Late in the 19th century, the state became the licensing agency for Ohio practitioners. The earliest permanent HOSPITALS in the area were created as charitable institutions to give care solely to the poor and the homeless. In 1836, when Cleveland, with a population of 4,800, was incorporated as a city, the newly created Board of Health erected a city infirmary, the ancestor of the present Cleveland Metropolitan General Hospital, which has played a major role in the advance of medical science both locally and nationally.

Medical education quickly followed the population growth. In the early 19th century, most physicians were still being educated as house students of practicing physicians, Moses Thompson in Hudson having been such a preceptor. But gradually medical colleges, chiefly proprietary institutions organized locally by enterprising physicians, spread throughout the country. The first in northeast Ohio was established at Willoughby, 15 mi. from Cleveland, by a group of physicians who had migrated westward from New York State. Founded in 1834 as the Medical Dept. of Willoughby University of Lake Erie, the school at first attracted outstanding teachers such as JOHN DELAMATER (1787–1867) and JARED P. KIRTLAND (1793–1877), but internal dissension led shortly to their resignation and to their creation of a new school in Cleveland named the Cleveland Medical College. Originally chartered in 1843 as a department of Western Reserve College of Hudson, this school still exists today as the School of Medicine of CASE WESTERN RESERVE UNIVERSITY.

Cleveland also became an educational center for homeopathic physicians, who began to settle in Ohio in the 1830s. In 1846 a homeopathic society was founded and a homeopathic pharmacy opened on PUBLIC SQUARE, and 4 years later, in 1850, the second school of HOMEOPATHY in the U.S., the Western College of Homeopathic Medicine, opened. The Cleveland Homeopathic Medical College, as it was later called, remained in existence from 1850 to 1914, when it became a division of Ohio State University in Columbus. Since homeopathy had arisen as an attempt to reform the excesses of "regular" medical practices by opposing massive dosages and polypharmacy and advocating more conservative methods, it was viewed as a heretical medical sect by the regular physicians. Their bonds strengthened by opposition, the Cleveland homeopathic community in 1856 opened the first permanent hospital apart from the infirmary in the city. Named the CLEVELAND HOMEOPATHIC HOSPITAL, it treated mainly railroad employees who were sick or injured away from home. By 1879, since most other area hospitals that had been founded meanwhile would not admit homeopathic physicians or surgeons, a large new hospital (which established the first nurses' training school west of the Alleghenies) was built on Huron Rd., the antecedent of HURON RD. HOSPITAL today in E. CLEVELAND. Highly respected by the nonmedical community, a number of homeopathic physicians became community leaders, and at the turn of the 20th century, leading Cleveland citizens such as MARCUS A. HANNA, MYRON T. HERRICK, and JOHN D. ROCKEFELLER supported their institutions.

In the 19th century, the modern theories and practices of medicine began to emerge in Western Europe. The microscope revealed microorganisms that were demonstrated by Pasteur, Koch, and others to be disease-causing agents. It also revealed that the minute structure of the human body is composed of cells. In addition to the 2 new sciences of bacteriology (now microbiology) and cellular pathology, an innovation called anesthesia had been developed by American surgeons, and the English surgeon, Lister, had developed antiseptic surgical procedures. At the same time, the pharmacopoeia began to be enriched by a multitude of new chemical remedies produced by the new science of organic chemistry. All this new information was rapidly transmitted throughout the western world by European emigres, by an increasing number of medical and surgical periodicals, and by Americans studying abroad in the new centers of research.

Because of its strategic location in the center of the Industrial Crescent stretching from Buffalo to Lake Michigan, Cleveland gradually became a rich and growing center of intellectual and cultural resources and attracted talent from both home and abroad. By 1890 it had a population of more than 250,000, with 4 medical schools, 3 medical societies, and 335 physicians, 25% of them homeopaths. The medical community was quick to assimilate new medical knowledge and techniques, and to modify its institutions accordingly. Among the influential figures in Cleveland medical education during this period was GUSTAV C. E. WEBER (1828–1912), a German-born surgeon who came to Cleveland in 1856, having done postgraduate studies in Vienna, Amsterdam, and Paris. In 1864 he was one of the founders of ST. VINCENT CHARITY HOSPITAL, where he created a new medical school patterned after Bellevue Medical College in New York City, a hospital-college modeled upon Guy's and St. Thomas' in London, where students had access to clinical as well as didactic teaching. Nearly 20 years later, from 1883–93, after the consolidation of several medical schools, Weber served as dean of the Medical Dept. of Western Reserve University, as the former Cleveland Medical College had been renamed. His successor, Isaac N. Himes (1834–1895), who had also studied in Paris and Vienna and became Cleveland's first hospital staff pathologist, played the leading role in bringing the Medical Dept.'s faculty and curriculum up to the most advanced standards. A number of its faculty members, such as WM. THOMAS CORLETT (1854–1948), a dermatologist; John P. Sawyer (d. 1945), a physiologist; and Christian Sihler (1848–1919), a histologist, as well as the surgeons FRANK E. BUNTS (1861–1928) and DUDLEY P. ALLEN (1852–1915) had also studied abroad. The model for the Medical Dept. was the new Johns Hopkins University School of Medicine in Baltimore, Md., which admitted its first class in 1893 to a faculty and curriculum that embodied the most recent advances in medical education. It is not surprising that the Cleveland search committees turned to Hopkins for new faculty members, such as the pathologist Wm. Travis Howard, Jr. (1867–1953), and the gynecologist HUNTER ROBB (1863–1940). In 1909, after Abraham Flexner completed his famous survey of American medical schools, he wrote to the president of WRU: "The Medical Department of Western Reserve University is next to Johns Hopkins University . . . the best in the country."

No advances could have occurred if Cleveland hospitals had not become available for teaching and research. After the CIVIL WAR, every decade saw new hospitals established by private charitable corporations or churches, and some were the progenitors of present-day institutions: the Cleveland City Hospital Assoc., organized in 1866, gradually evolved into Lakeside Hospital, modeled on the Johns Hopkins Hospital (1889), and ultimately became a part of

UNIVERSITY HOSPITALS of Cleveland (1931); St. Vincent Charity Hospital opened its doors in 1865 and continued on its present site with continuous enlargement and transformation of its buildings; the city infirmary evolved in different locations into the Cleveland City Hospital in 1891, which in 1956 became the Cleveland Metropolitan General Hospital when its control was transferred to Cuyahoga County (see CUYAHOGA COUNTY HOSPITAL SYSTEM). These 3 hospitals and the Huron Rd. Homeopathic Hospital were at first the major teaching hospitals in the Cleveland area. With the shift of medical care from the home to the hospital following the introductions of new diagnostic procedures such as x-ray, bacteriological and chemical laboratories, and aseptic surgical techniques, from the 1880s onward more hospitals were founded to satisfy various needs, such as maternity, baby, and child care, racial groups, women physicians, and growing residential areas. By 1943 there were around 30 hospitals in Cleveland with more than 8,000 beds, and that did not include the neighboring communities. The patients were no longer the poor and homeless, but people of every financial status. Physicians making house calls became fewer and fewer.

With the advance of medical science, the disease picture in Cleveland, as elsewhere, gradually changed. As the causes of epidemic diseases became known, appropriate preventive or treatment methods were applied. A persistent problem had been typhoid fever, of which there were 3,460 cases in Cleveland between 1912–26. When Wm. Travis Howard, Jr., brought new pathological and bacteriological methods to Cleveland, he also became the city bacteriologist, a position created especially for him. Both he and his successor in 1912, ROGER G. PERKINS (1874–1936), suspected that the source of the typhoid bacilli was Lake Erie, from which the Cleveland water supply had been pumped since 1856. After extensive research, the problem was finally corrected by Oct. 1925, when complete filtration and chlorination of the lake water were attained. Infant mortality had also been very high, with deaths caused by diarrhea, dehydration, and malnutrition among the offspring of the uneducated immigrants from Southern and Eastern Europe. The Milk Fund Assoc., founded in 1899 as a private charitable organization, and the Babies' Dispensary & Hospital, incorporated in 1904 under the aegis of Edward Fitch Cushing (1862–1911) and HENRY JOHN GERSTENBERGER (1881–1954), provided care for poor children and freed them from milkborne pathogens. In 1912 the city Health Dept. established a Bureau of Child Hygiene, which set up 12 dispensaries throughout the city and oversaw the milk production and distribution from its own dairy farm, aided by volunteers. Also, the VISITING NURSES ASSOC. brought medical supervision and care into the homes of the poor. Not only were lives saved, but pediatrics began to develop as a strong medical specialty. Gerstenberger, with postgraduate training in Berlin and Vienna, was appointed professor of pediatrics at the WRU School of Medicine in 1913 when the first separate department was established. In addition to his teaching activities, he collaborated with a research chemist in developing SMA, a best-selling synthetic milk, the income from which helped to create the present Babies & Childrens Hospital of University Hospitals, which opened in 1925. Cleveland became a major center for the training of pediatricians.

With the advent of WORLD WAR I, a group of Lakeside Hospital physicians, surgeons, nurses, and enlisted men were organized by GEO. W. CRILE to serve in France. Sailing in May 1917, they were the first American group to serve in the war, and their Army General Hospital (Base Hospital IV) functioned for 20 months at Rouen. Because of their priority in World War I, when WORLD WAR II broke out, the LAKESIDE UNIT was invited by the surgeon general on Christmas Eve 1941 to be first again. A month later, the Clevelanders were again organized as the FOURTH GENERAL HOSPITAL, and together with supplies were on 2 ships headed for Melbourne, Australia, where they remained until the move in Mar. 1944 to Finschhafen, New Guinea, and in Aug. 1945 to Manila, finally disbanding in Oct. 1945 and ending 46 months overseas.

An indirect result of World War I was the creation of the CLEVELAND CLINIC in 1921. While working together in France, surgeons Geo. W. Crile, his cousin WM. E. LOWER (1867–1948), and FRANK E. BUNTS recognized the advantages of group clinical practice, and after returning they invited the internist JOHN PHILLIPS to join them in establishing the clinic. Crile had already distinguished himself nationally, by performing the first successful human blood transfusion in 1906, by his research on shock, and by his reputation for thyroid surgery. Noted for the development of strong specialty interests among its staff, the Cleveland Clinic rapidly assumed a position of leadership on the national and international health scene, sought by patients worldwide because of the quality of its care. A disastrous fire at the clinic in 1929 (see CLEVELAND CLINIC DISASTER) caused by burning x-ray films that produced deadly gas and many deaths (including founder John Phillips) was a temporary setback, but ultimately saved other lives worldwide, since it led to the development and use of nontoxic x-ray materials. The most rapid growth of the clinic began in the early 1970s and still continues. In 1974, the clinic acquired the fourth CAT scanner to exist, following the Mayo Clinic, Massachusetts General Hospital, and Montreal Neurological Institute. This computerized transverse axial scanning machine is one of those used for neurological diagnostic purposes, which is one of the major diagnostic advances of the 20th century.

After World War I, the affluent and growing city arranged to have a survey made of its hospitals in order to improve the quality of health care for its citizens. The 1,082-page *Cleveland Hospital & Health Survey*, printed in 1920, was carried out by an outside expert, Haven Emerson, and was one of the first in an American city. Cleveland has pioneered in many forms of cooperation and teamwork, such as the first Community Fund in the U.S., established in 1919 by community leaders combining both financial and social planning; the CLEVELAND HOSPITAL SERVICE ASSOC. (later renamed Blue Cross), which was established in 1934 as one of the first in the U.S. with all acute hospitals participating; and the founding in 1964 of the Community Health Foundation, the first health-maintenance organization in the Middle West, now the Kaiser Foundation Health Plan (see KAISER PERMANENTE). In addition, the CLEVELAND HEALTH EDUCATION MUSEUM, the first in the U.S., opened its doors in 1940.

In the 1930s, innovators such as JOSEPH T. WEARN at the School of Medicine and Russell L. Haden at the Cleveland Clinic brought laboratory-oriented medical science to the forefront, while obstetricians from Cleveland hospitals, led by A. J. SKEEL of St. Luke's, in 1932 formed the Cleveland Hospital Obstetric Society, which for 10 years collected data and analyzed the causes of maternal mortality, stimulating similar activity in other cities and influencing standards of the American College of Surgeons. Many cooperative medical events have occurred, such as the 1962 polio immunization campaign sponsored by the Cleveland Academy of Medicine and the Cuyahoga County Medical Foundation, when 2,400 physicians and other volunteers on Sabin Oral Sundays distributed sugar cubes containing polio vaccine and immunized more than 1.5 million people, more than 84% of the residents of Cuyahoga County, the best record in the U.S. This success was facilitated by cooperation and help from the nonmedical community, which provided advertising and public-relations expertise to mobilize the population. Earlier, in 1949, the Cleveland radiologists had cooperated with the Academy of Medicine, the Antituberculosis Society, and the Greater Cleveland Hospital Assoc. in a successful mass survey to detect tuberculosis among Greater Cleveland citizens.

One may finally ask, What are some of the unique contributions of Cleveland medicine? What, if any, major medical discoveries have been made? In addition to medical "firsts" such as Noah Worcester's first American treatise on dermatology, *A Synopsis of the Symptoms, Diagnosis, and Treatment of the More Common and Important Diseases of the Skin* (Philadelphia, 1845), or Abraham Metz's first textbook on ophthalmology, *The Anatomy and Histology of the Human Eye* (Philadelphia, 1869), or Samuel W. Kelley's first book on pediatric surgery, *The Surgical Diseases of Children: A Modern Treatise on Pediatric Surgery* (New York, 1909), 3 months to the day after Wilhelm Konrad Roentgen in Germany announced the discovery of x-rays, DAYTON C. MILLER, a professor at Case School of Applied Science, made the first x-rays in the U.S. on 8 Feb. 1896 and lectured 2 months later to the CLEVELAND MEDICAL SOCIETY. There were outstanding teachers, such as Wm. Thos. Corlett, who was appointed in 1901 as one of the few American physicians to test the new syphilis remedy, Salvarsan, at Lakeside Hospital, or CARL J. WIGGERS, who has been called the father of hemodynamics in the U.S. and was the first editor of *Circulation Research*, or TORALD H. SOLLMANN (1874–1965), who in 1901 published the leading American textbook on pharmacology, which went through at least 8 editions. Endemic goiter has disappeared because of the research between 1915–20 of DAVID MARINE and CARL H. LENHART that showed that it was caused by iodine deficiency in the diet.

During the past 50 years, the major contributions have been in cardiovascular diseases and their treatment: the studies of angina pectoris carried out by Harold Feil and Mortimer Siegel at MT. SINAI HOSPITAL and their pioneering work in electrocardiography; the classical experiments of HARRY GOLDBLATT associating the ischemic kidney with hypertension; the development of open-heart surgery by pioneer CLAUDE S. BECK, who gave the first course in cardiac resuscitation, and Jay Ankeney at University Hospitals (in 1956, Charity Hospital was the first in the world to have an intensive-care unit devoted exclusively to heart surgery); the development of kidney dialysis techniques by Willem Kolff at the Cleveland Clinic, where he also started to develop the artificial heart aided by research engineers at NASA in Cleveland; the contributions of the Cleveland Clinic as a "revascularization center" for coronary artery disease by means of bypass surgery, which depended upon the technique of cinecoronary-angiography developed by F. Mason Sones, Jr., which made the vessels visible. Many other Cleveland contributions to medicine, such as pioneering work in gerontology and the activities of the CLEVELAND MEDICAL LIBRARY ASSOC. (est. 1894), could also be mentioned. One can characterize medicine in Cleveland as equal and in many cases superior to that of other urban centers. In the 20th century, it has been especially distinguished by extensive cooperation among institutions and outstanding private and community support.

Genevieve Miller
Case Western Reserve University (emeritus)

Brown, Kent L., ed., *Medicine in Cleveland and Cuyahoga County: 1810–1976* (1977).
Dittrick, Howard, comp., *Pioneer Medicine in the Western Reserve* (1932).
Waite, Frederick Clayton, *Western Reserve University, Centennial History of the School of Medicine* (1946).
See also DENTISTRY, NURSING.

The **MEDUSA CORPORATION** began as the Sandusky Portland Cement Co. in 1892 with offices in Cleveland and the first plant at marl-rich Bay Bridge near Sandusky. Its founders were 3 brothers, Arthur, Spencer, and Wm. Newberry, who shared entrepreneurial and scientific skills. Arthur saw the potential in setting up a company based on the discovery by his brothers Spencer and William of a formula for Portland cement. He persuaded his father-in-law, DANIEL P. EELLS, SR., to be president for 5 years before assuming the post himself. Named for the Greek goddess Medusa, who turned all who looked at her to stone, the company was called the Medusa Portland Cement Co. from shortly after its founding until 1972, when it became the Medusa Corp.

In its first 50 years, the company expanded to 8 plants in 5 states as cement became a more popular, relatively low-priced building material, but its real prosperity did not occur until after WORLD WAR II. The cement business followed construction cycles, and during the war, nonessential construction was banned. After the war, pent-up demand for houses, schools, and hospitals brought prosperity to the cement business. In addition, business was increased by construction of the interstate highway system, as well as local HIGHWAYS. Medusa benefited from these building booms with record sales nearly every year during the 1950s. By 1959, the company had outgrown its offices in the Midland Bldg., and constructed a new headquarters at 3008 Monticello Blvd. in CLEVELAND HTS.

To keep ahead of the expanding cement market, Medusa expanded and modernized its facilities in the 1950s and early 1960s; in 1963, its plants produced twice as many barrels as it had in 1952. The company closed its original plant (the oldest in the U.S.) in 1961, since the marl supply in the area was exhausted; it opened new plants at York, Pa., Dixon, Ill., Manitowoc, Wis., and Charlevoix, Mich., and a plant and technical center at Wampum, Pa. The company sought to make cement competitively priced in traditional markets and also pursued new markets to utilize innovative cement products that were precast, prestressed, and pigmented. Unable to combat the seasonal nature of construction, which adversely affected its sales in the coldest quarter of the fiscal year, Medusa began diversifying in 1969 with its purchase of the Jas. H. Drew Co. of Indiana, a manufacturer of highway guardrails, signs, and traffic signals. Other acquisitions immersed the company in a variety of building-material and construction operations.

Medusa's efforts to create a forward-looking company made it an attractive candidate for takeover in the late 1970s. In 1977, Moore-McCormack, based in Stamford, Conn., made 2 bids for Medusa, but Medusa directors went to court to prevent an unfriendly takeover. Meanwhile, the company agreed to merge with another local mining and shipping company, OGLEBAY NORTON; but before the deal was consummated, Medusa realized that the alliance would dilute its own earnings, as Oglebay Norton was recovering losses from recent strikes in coal and iron, and also would plunge Medusa further into the seasonal business cycle. Medusa then considered merger with the Kaiser Cement & Gypsum Corp. of Oakland, Calif., but Kaiser changed the terms at the last minute. One day before the union was to take effect, the Crane Co. of New York announced that it held 20% of Medusa's stock and made a formal offer to merge. Though Medusa feared that Crane might be buying it as an investment to gut and resell, directors and shareholders approved the merger. Crane, a manufacturer of plumbing fixtures, steel, building products, and fluid-control devices, quickly acquired 96% of Medusa stock and made it clear that Medusa would be operated as a separate subsidiary, with headquarters remaining in Cleveland. Since 1981, Medusa has produced 15-20% of Crane's sales revenues. In 1985 it had 3 plants in Pennsylvania, Michigan, and Virginia, and employed about 150 locally.

**MELDRUM AND FEWSMITH,** an advertising agency founded in 1930 by Andrew Barclay Meldrum and Joseph Fewsmith, has created some of America's most influential and memorable advertising. Meldrum, a copywriter, and Fewsmith, an account executive, were creative partners for nearly 40 years, first in Philadelphia, then in Toledo, and then at Sweeney & James in Cleveland, before opening their own agency. At Sweeney & James in the 1920s, Fewsmith created the famous "Somewhere West of Laramie" ads for the JORDAN MOTOR CAR CO. This campaign is generally thought to have been the first use of sex to sell cars. Meldrum and Fewsmith were a creative team, sharing an office until Meldrum's death in 1947. M&F started with a staff of 4, no money, and no clients. Within 3 weeks, they had 3, including the newly formed REPUBLIC STEEL CORP. When THOS. GIRDLER, president of Republic, was too busy to see Meldrum and Fewsmith, they found out that he would be going to New York. They bought tickets on the same train, bribed a porter, and found Girdler's drawing room. When the train reached Grand Central Station, M&F had the Republic account, a relationship that lasted until Republic merged into LTV STEEL in 1984. During the Depression, M&F concentrated on newer companies that were trying to establish an identity. MARGARET BOURKE-WHITE took the photographs for the early Republic ads. M&F created the red jockey-cap logo for Carling's Red Cap Ale, and created a national market for the GLIDDEN CO. The Glidden account was opened in 1934 and in 1986 was still an M&F account, one of the longest agency-client relationships in America. M&F also excelled in creative advertising methods and services. In the 1950s, it was one of the first agencies to offer market research. In 1960, 6 million readers found half-page paint chips in the *Saturday Evening Post*, an early magazine-insertion mass sampling. BONNE BELL was a regional cosmetic company in 1961 when M&F created an ad for their astringent, Ten-O-Six Lotion, for the *New Yorker* that offered Ten-O-Six by the gallon. This unusual approach to selling cosmetics opened the New York and national markets to Bonne Bell. In the 1970s, M&F offered clients complete communication services, including advertising, public-relations, financial, and employee communications. In the 1980s, M&F had offices in Cleveland, Detroit, and Chicago and employed about 175 people. It also had affiliations with agencies in London and Brussels to handle European advertising for American companies.

The **MELLEN FOUNDATION** was established in 1963 by Edward J. Mellen (1910-1982). Mellen, a graduate of Lakewood High School and Cleveland College, began his career as a statistician for the Cleveland Stock Exchange and then went into business as an investment banker with Skall, Joseph & Miller. He was appointed executive vice-president, and in 1949 he went into partnership as Joseph, Mellen & Miller. In 1970 he was appointed chairman of the board. Over the course of his career, Mellen's investments spanned 20 companies. He was married to Louise Mellen, who died in 1977. The purposes of the foundation are generally broad, primarily for higher education, including fellowships for nursing education and critical-care nursing. Some support is given to churches and medical organizations. In 1982, assets of the foundation were $2,455,960, with expenditures of $474,202 for 13 grants. Trustees of the foundation include Edward J. Mellen, Jas. A. Cullen, Alan G. Rorick, and Stephanie Keane, with J. Raymond Barry, John Drinko, and Douglas L. Newell.

**MEMORIAL SHOREWAY** (officially called Cleveland Memorial Shoreway), originally a strip of road along the lakefront from E. 9th to E. 55th near GORDON PARK, was the first east-west freeway in Greater Cleveland. Built with WPA funds and labor, it was a local precursor to the interstate highway system. The road was planned as a work-relief program in the early 1930s, in fulfillment of a generation-long dream of linking both sides of town with a road with few stoplights. With $8 million from the WPA, an area along the lake often used for dumping was cleared and graded to make way for the 4-mi. stretch of road, which the city and county envisioned as part of a larger system of roads. Buildings were razed; piles of slag, industrial cinders, and debris were gathered and spread into the lake to create landfill; and the strip was paved. The city undertook the project on the assumption that it owned all affected land; when the cleanup was complete, corporations claimed the property as their own, which necessitated litigation. The 10,000 WPA workers completed enough of the preliminary road work for the city to host the GREAT LAKES EXPOSITION in 1936; within 2 years, the road reached the Illuminating Co. facilities. Requiring $6.5 million in labor and $1.7 in materials, the project was the largest WPA job in the nation. Though the indefinite state of lakefront planning prevented the WPA from laying a second strip of pavement and building grade separations from side streets, the roadway was opened to traffic in 1938. Referred to as the Shore Dr. or the Lakefront Rd., it was officially unnamed until WORLD WAR II, when it became the Memorial Shoreway in honor of the city's war veterans.

In conjunction with the construction of the Shoreway, the county commissioners built the Main Ave. Bridge and the E. 9th St. interchange (completed 1940) and planned the West Shore Dr. from EDGEWATER PARK to ROCKY RIVER. World War II interrupted further construction, but the Regional Assoc. of Cleveland, in conjunction with the city and county planning and engineering departments, as well as the State Highway Dept., developed a master plan for an express highway system. Since the Memorial Shoreway was only 4 lanes and had stoplights, it was slated for renovation almost from its opening. The plan, which defined a freeway as a limited-access highway, put downtown Cleveland at the hub of a half-wheel of expressways, parkways, and feeder roads. The spokes were to include the East Shoreway, the Lakeland Freeway, the Hts. Freeway, the WILLOW FREEWAY, the Medina Freeway, the Berea-Airport Freeway, and the West Shoreway; concentrically rimming the wheel were to be an innerbelt and outerbelt freeway, as well as a university freeway. A central interchange in downtown Cleveland would permit easy access to all freeways. Funding for the system was expected to come from the State Highway Dept. and the federal government, which after 1947 designated funds for an interstate highway system. In 1956, the Interstate Highway Act initiated an extensive $60 billion highway system, which insured that much of the 1944 Cleveland plan would become reality. The Memorial Shoreway itself, which had been extended to BRATENAHL at E. 140th in 1941, permitted crosstown traffic with some stops but was incomplete between E. 55th and E. 72nd. In 1953, a $7 million addition connected the two pieces of road and widened the original highway to make it an 8-lane, nonstop expressway. The wave of highway construction in the late 1950s joined the Memorial Shoreway to the new Lakeland Freeway, which by 1963 stretched eastward toward Painesville. Together the 2 freeways constituted the local section of I-90.

**MENOMPSY** (NOBSY) (d. 1802 or 1803), a Chippewa or Ottawa medicine man, was the victim of the first murder in Cleveland. Menompsy was treating the wife of Big Son, who was the brother of the Seneca chief STIGWANISH, or "Chief Seneca." Despite all his efforts, Big Son's wife died. Big Son, believing that Menompsy was responsible for his wife's death, sought retribution. According to Indian justice, Big Son had the right to retaliate, and he threatened Menompsy's life. Menompsy, who was a sacred priest as well as a medicine man, asserted that he was a charmed man and no bullet could harm him. While walking together one day, Big Son extended his hand as if to make amends and shake hands, but instead he drew a knife and stabbed Menompsy in the side. Despite all efforts, Menompsy died. The murder threatened the peace of Cleveland with Indian tribal warfare. Maj. LORENZO CARTER, friend to the Indians, negotiated a peace treaty between the two sides. The price for peace was 2 gallons of whiskey.

**MENORAH PARK,** the residential home and care center for Cleveland's elderly Orthodox Jews, was established in 1906 because the existing home for the aged, MONTEFIORE, did not satisfy the religious needs of the Orthodox aged. A house that provided room for 5 residents was purchased on Orange Ave. near E. 40th St. Residents, then called "inmates," were placed on a rigid daily schedule that included work in the kitchen, laundry, and garden. In 1911, under the leadership of the home's first president, Herman Peskind, a 46-bed building was constructed at 59th and Scovill. However, the new structure proved to be inadequate as demand for residence increased during the subsequent decade. In 1921, the home relocated in the Glenville neighborhood on Lakeview Ave.

The building on Lakeview cost $300,000. It could accommodate 80 residents, contained a synagogue that could seat 800, and for the first time provided the home with facilities to handle the sick. In 1928, an 80-bed, 2-story wing was added; and in 1948, a 55-bed wing, including occupational, recreational, and physical-therapy facilities, and a medical clinic were added. The name was changed in 1950 to the Jewish Orthodox Home for the Aged. Howard B. Bram became executive director of the JOHA in 1961 and has served in that capacity since. Also in 1961, a Women's Assoc. was formed. Its volunteers run the gift and snack shops, subsidize special events and activities, and sponsor outings. Today, the association includes over 2,000 members.

As Cleveland's Jews moved into the eastern suburbs after WORLD WAR II, the JOHA found it difficult to remain in GLENVILLE. Additionally, the demand for admission sorely taxed the facility. In 1968, the home moved to a new complex in BEACHWOOD on Cedar Rd. and adopted the name Menorah Park. The 4½-acre facility includes 11 residential units that provide housing for 265 residents and care facilities for an additional 130 daytime-care clients. Residents are grouped by medical, psychiatric, social, and nursing needs. Menorah Park has 240 staff and 150 volunteers and provides complete medical care for res-

idents. Among its other services is a meals for shut-ins program cosponsored with the JEWISH FAMILY SERVICE ASSOC. and B'nai B'rith Women. In June 1978, the R. H. Myers Apts., an independent-living center for the aged, opened adjacent to Menorah Park. It provides housing for over 240 elderly people in 207 1- and 2-bedroom apartments. Recreational, educational, cultural, medical, and household support services are provided for residents, including dinner 7 days a week.

Menorah Park Records, WRHS.

The **MERCANTILE NATIONAL BANK** was one of the early leading banks in Cleveland. The firm opened as the Merchants Bank on 24 June 1845 in the Atwater Block on Superior Ave. with capital of $112,500. It was one of the 2 state branch banks allotted to Cleveland under the new state banking system. Some of Cleveland's leading businessmen, such as SHERLOCK J. ANDREWS, THOS. M. KELLEY, and Geo. Mygatt, headed the bank in its early years and guided it through the Panic of 1857. By 1860, the bank was located at the corner of Superior and Bank (E. 6th) streets. With the establishment of a national banking act and the expiration of the bank's first charter, it was reorganized as the Merchants Natl. Bank on 27 Dec. 1864. Well-known banker TRUMAN P. HANDY led the bank the next 20 years, until its charter again expired in 1884, and it was reorganized as the Mercantile Natl. Bank with capital of $1 million. The bank ceased operation in 1905 when this charter expired.

**MERCHANT, AHAZ** (21 Mar. 1794–28 Mar. 1862), was a surveyor, builder, and civil engineer. He did much of the important surveying and engineering work for Cleveland prior to the employment of a city or county engineer. Merchant was born in western Connecticut and raised near Morristown, N.J. He was brought up on a farm and as a youth attended a common school. His skill in surveying was largely self-taught. After moving to Cleveland in 1818, Merchant acquired military experience in the state militia, where he eventually attained the rank of general. Like many of the early pioneers, Merchant applied himself to several occupations, but he was mainly distinguished as a surveyor. He served as county surveyor from 1833–35, and again from 1845–50. He was also Cleveland's first surveyor and street commissioner, a post he held from 1834–36. Merchant St. (W. 11th) was named after him. Merchant's work as a surveyor was quite extensive. He laid out most of the important allotments in OHIO CITY, supervised the first improvements to the old river bed, and graded many of the major streets in Cleveland. In 1831, he resurveyed many of the city's existing streets, and in 1835 he published a "Map of Cleveland and Its Environs," showing the entire street plan of the city. He also built several new roads, including Prospect Ave. and the road from Cleveland to Aurora (Rt. 43).

While county surveyor, Merchant constructed the first railroad in the county (the CLEVELAND & NEWBURGH RAILROAD CO.) in 1834. The railway consisted of wooden rails over which 2 horses pulled a flatcar. For several years it made 2 trips daily between Newburgh and Cleveland, used primarily to transport stone and lumber, and occasionally passengers. Merchant's son, Silas, was in charge of its operation. Merchant later constructed another horse railroad, which ran out Euclid Ave. to E. Cleveland. As a builder, Merchant built several structures in Cleveland. Notable among these was the Angier House, a fashionable 5-story hotel that opened in 1854. It was later known as the Kennard House. Merchant married Catherine Stewart in 1819.

Merchant Family Papers, WRHS.

**MERRICK, MYRA KING** (1825–11 Nov. 1899), was the first female physician in Ohio and one of the first in the U.S. She was born in Hinkley (Leicestershire), England, in 1825. She emigrated to the U.S. with her parents and settled in the Boston area. As a young child, she worked in the New England cotton mills. The family moved to the Cleveland area in 1841. After her marriage to Chas. H. Merrick in 1848, Myra and her husband moved to Connecticut. Her husband's illness prompted her to enter the medical profession as a means to support her family and care for her husband. She attended medical lectures at Hyatt's Academy in New York and later studied with Levi Ives in New Haven, Conn. She received her clinical training at Nichol's Hydropathic Institute. In 1852 she received her M.D. degree from Central Medical College in Rochester, N.Y. (There is some confusion and debate on Merrick's training and degree).

Returning to Cleveland in the 1850s, Dr. Merrick opened her medical office on fashionable Miami St. She developed a thriving medical practice, especially among the rich and influential members of Cleveland society. She was JOHN D. ROCKEFELLER's family physician and attended to other Standard Oil Co. executives. During the CIVIL WAR, while her husband served in the Union Army, she ran the family lumber business while continuing her medical practice. Since the Western Homeopathic College, like similar schools, was closed to female students, Dr. Merrick helped establish the Cleveland Homeopathic Hospital College for Women in 1867. She served as president of the college and professor of obstetrics and diseases of women and children. In 1878, Dr. Merrick, along with a former student, Kate Parsons, founded the Women's & Children's Free Medical & Surgical Dispensary, the forerunner of WOMAN'S GENERAL HOSPITAL. She served as president of the dispensary until her death in 1899. Myra K. Merrick had 1 son, Richard L. Merrick. Her daughter-in-law, Eliza K. Merrick, assisted her at the dispensary and continued to practice medicine at Women's General until it closed in 1984. She was a member of the Unity Church and of the Homeopathic Society. She is buried in Elyria, Ohio.

Chas. H. Merrick Papers, WRHS.
Gibbons, Marion N., "A Woman Carries the Caduceus—Myra K. Merrick." In *Pioneer Women in the Western Reserve*, ed. Howard Dittrick (1932).
Brown, Kent L. ed., *Medicine in Cleveland and Cuyahoga County, 1810–1976* (1977).

**MERRICK HOUSE SOCIAL SETTLEMENT** was founded in 1919 by the Natl. Catholic War Council and named for Mary Merrick of Washington, D.C., founder of the Natl. Christ Child Society. Located in TREMONT, an area of many nationalities, the settlement's programs accentuated citizenship and included cultural and recreational activities. In 1920, Merrick House was accepted as a member of the Welfare Fed. and the Community Chest. Three years later its first property was purchased, with funds from the CATHOLIC CHARITIES CORP. Programs during WORLD WAR II were revised in order to fit war demands. Nursery and daycare hours were extended, and civil-defense and first-aid programs were added, as were scrap drives and a victory garden. Following the war, Merrick House grew, carrying out extended nursery, recreational, and senior citizens' activities in as many as 6 locations and becoming

part of the institutional development program of the Catholic Charities Corp. POLES, SLOVAKS, RUSSIANS, and UKRAINIANS predominated in the neighborhood until the 1950s, when an influx of Puerto Ricans necessitated an increased focus on Spanish-speaking programs. Merrick House's resources were augmented in 1971 by the addition of a dental clinic, a gift from the Cleveland Chap. of the CHRIST CHILD SOCIETY. In 1980 its main properties included a Head Start house, the Settlement and Day Nursery, and its Senior Service Ctr.

Merrick House Records, WRHS.

**METHODISTS.** Methodists in Cleveland have had neither the numbers nor the prominence they have enjoyed in other areas of the country. Among Cleveland's Protestants, BAPTISTS have outdistanced them in the number of churches since the late 19th century, and CONGREGATIONALISTS and PRESBYTERIANS have surpassed them in political, social, and cultural influence. In 1865 there were 7 Methodist churches (or Methodist Episcopal, as they are formally known), the most of any Protestant denomination. Only Catholics, with 8 churches, had more. As Cleveland grew, Methodist churches failed to keep up the pace. By 1929, only 33 out of the almost 600 Cleveland churches were Methodist. Baptists outnumbered them, with 87 white and 23 black churches. Growth lagged even further toward the end of the century. In 1986 there were 67 churches, then known as United Methodist, compared to 337 Baptist and 157 Catholic, out of the approximately 1,300 Cleveland churches.

The relative lack of influence of Methodist churches stemmed from a number of factors. Methodists were never part of the transplanted New England leadership elite, as were Congregationalists and Presbyterians. Rather, they drew members from Pennsylvania and other mid-Atlantic states, from southern and eastern Ohio, and from Germany. These diverse groups account for much of the lack of unity in Cleveland Methodism. Divisions between English- and German-origin Methodists precluded common activities. Finally, schisms disrupted Methodist unity. Two early schisms from First Methodist Church, Protestant Methodist Church (1830) and Wesleyan Methodist Church (1839), indicated the potential for division. Methodist organizational patterns, too, hampered the denomination's influence. Well into the latter part of the 19th century, Methodists were supplied with different ministers each year, which made it difficult for a minister or church to develop the contacts and experience that would have led to more impact in the community. In addition, Methodists west of the river belonged to a different supervisory body (the North Ohio Conference) than those east of the river (the Erie Conference). Methodists formed the third religious body in the town of Cleveland. First Methodist Church was organized in 1827, but only after an initial attempt to establish a church had failed in 1822 (no one had paid the $.25 postage due on the recorder's fee on a deed mailed by a Boston man who had wanted to donate Cleveland land he owned to anyone who would build a Methodist church). Church St. Methodist (1833, now Hope-Wesley United Methodist Church) and Erie St. Methodist (1850, now EPWORTH-EUCLID UNITED METHODIST CHURCH) followed.

In the late 19th and early 20th centuries, many Methodist churches conducted missions aimed at arriving immigrants. Broadway Methodist Episcopal Church was the most prominent. The church became an "institutional church" with a wealth of activity in addition to worship. It offered an employment bureau, health care at ST. LUKE'S

HOSPITAL, English-language instruction, social gatherings, theater performances, and recreation. Services were conducted in a number of languages, and its religious-education work involved 17 different languages. Except for FIRST UNITED METHODIST CHURCH and a few others, churches of the denomination withdrew from downtown and the east side to move to the SUBURBS in the 20th century. Many of the west side churches remained. There were a number of mergers resulting from relocation, the end of bilingual work, and the joining together of the various branches of Methodism.

Methodists in Cleveland built institutions. The best-known is BALDWIN-WALLACE COLLEGE, the result of a merger in 1913 that combined German Wallace College (1864), a German Methodist institution established to promote scientific education and Biblical Christianity, and Baldwin Institute (1845), a college organized and controlled by the North Ohio Conference. St. Luke's Hospital was a creation of the Methodist church that began as Cleveland General Hospital (1894), affiliated with the College of Wooster and then Ohio Wesleyan. In 1906 the institution's name was changed to the St. Luke's Hospital Assoc. of Cleveland, Ohio, of the Methodist Episcopal Church. Benevolent institutions chartered by Methodists included the Methodist Deaconess Home (1890) and the Berea Children's Home. The Deaconess Home evolved into the WEST SIDE COMMUNITY HOUSE, a center sponsored by Methodists, community groups, and the United Way. The children's home was founded in 1864 as the German Methodist Orphan Asylum. During the 1960s, the children's home shifted from a residential orphanage to a facility offering a number of child-related services. It became a residential treatment center for emotionally disturbed children, and it ran foster-home and family-therapy programs. In addition to these efforts, Methodists joined in the work of the INTERCHURCH COUNCIL OF GREATER CLEVELAND, particularly its hunger centers.

A few black Methodist churches existed despite the early-19th-century formation of 2 black Methodist denominations (the AME and AME Zion) organizationally separate from the rest of the nation's Methodists. CORY UNITED METHODIST CHURCH, founded in 1875, became (in the 20th century) an influential church of the black middle and upper classes. Lane Memorial Colored Methodist Episcopal Church (1902) belonged to the jurisdiction created by southern Methodists in 1870 for their black churches. In 1919 it had 450 members. In 1968, additional German-origin churches joined the larger body of Cleveland's Methodists. Evangelical and United Brethren churches were brought into the Methodist fold in a merger that resulted in the creation of the United Methodist church. In Cleveland, that meant that German-origin Methodist churches increased their already substantial presence in the city's Methodist community.

Michael J. McTighe
Gettysburg College

The **METROPOLITAN HEALTH PLANNING CORPORATION** was, from 1968–82, an agency responsible for health-care planning in Greater Cleveland. In 1975 it was designated a health-systems agency. The MHPC was set up in 1968 as a regulatory agency to review hospital-expansion proposals in order to prevent duplication of services and help hold down consumer costs, and to assess health needs in Cuyahoga and adjoining counties. The impetus for the creation of such regional agencies came from the federal government under Pres. Nixon. With aid from the federal government, the MHPC initiated various new programs, including a city ambulance service and a dental education program in the public schools. In 1974, the MHPC commissioned a study of Ohio's Medicaid program. Many of the MHPC's responsibilities were previously under the jurisdiction of the Regional Planning Commission. The corporation was governed by a 49-member board of trustees, consisting of local government officials, health-care providers, and health-care consumers. Lee J. Podolin was the first executive director; Robt. E. Timko succeeded him in 1978.

In 1975, the MHPC was designated a health-systems agency by the Natl. Health Planning & Resources Development Act. It was one of 9 such regional agencies in Ohio; its geographic area consisted of Cuyahoga, Lake, Geauga, Lorain, and Medina counties. Its board of trustees was reduced to 30 but with essentially the same composition of providers (i.e., doctors, hospital officials, and health-insurance representatives) and consumers. Public officials in the 5 counties appointed 9 of the 17 consumers. The MHPC operated on conditional status until 1978, while the U.S. Dept. of Health, Education, & Welfare investigated discrepancies in the appointment of certain board members. The MHPC continued to have close control of health-facility construction and all phases of health planning. The agency was largely unpopular in the medical community, as it seldom approved hospital expansion; a surplus of hospital beds in the 5-county area was continuously cited. But the state repeatedly overrode the MHPC's decisions to turn down health-care projects, including a major renovation of MT. SINAI MEDICAL CTR., which did not decrease beds, and remodeling of SOUTHWEST GENERAL HOSPITAL, which added beds. In 1981, the federal government allowed the removal of regional planning groups. Ohio, under Gov. Rhodes, was one of the first states to do so. In 1982, the state withdrew the MHPC's reviewing authority, and on 30 Apr. it was dissolved. It was succeeded by the GREATER CLEVELAND VOLUNTEER HEALTH PLAN.

The **METROPOLITAN THEATER,** on Euclid Ave. at E. 49th St., opened on 31 Mar. 1913 with a performance of *Aida*, the first production in an 8-week season of opera in English. The opera house was planned by Max Faetkenheuer, musical director and entrepreneur sometimes called "the Oscar Hammerstein of Cleveland," who conducted the orchestra of the Lyceum Theater and presided over the openings of the Empire and Colonial vaudeville theaters in 1901 and 1903 respectively. He also promoted the construction of the HIPPODROME, second-largest theater in America in 1907. The Metropolitan was designed by Cleveland architects Fulton & Taylor. Its auditorium, approximately 75'x100' and seating nearly 2,000, was described in a contemporary account as "spacious yet cozy, modest yet elegant," and second only to the Hippodrome in beauty. The ornamental lobby, promenade, and wide aisles were especially notable.

The Metropolitan offered grand opera, musical comedy, orchestral concerts, and legitimate theater for several seasons, and soon it began showing films. In 1916 the premiere of *The Perils of Society* was held, a film made in Cleveland and enacted by the most prominent Cleveland citizens. However, the Metropolitan's location just west of E. 55th St. was not conducive to long-term success. Eventually the theater housed boxing matches and other special events. Between 1950–75 it became part of the radio station WHK Bldg. and served as its Studio I auditorium. Later the Metropolitan stood vacant for several years, showing movies on a sporadic basis. It was remodeled in 1985 for use by the AGORA.

MEXICAN-AMERICAN WAR. Many of the 10,000 people living in Cleveland in 1846, and citizens of northern Ohio generally, were not inclined to support the objectives of the U.S. in the War with Mexico or to volunteer for military service in that war. They viewed the conflict as a pure and simple plot to extend slavery, and they opposed both the war and its objectives as they perceived them. It is not surprising, then, that the war's consequences were much more dramatic in the world of politics than in military legend or economic effects. The war began with a skirmish between U.S. and Mexican army units in the disputed region between the Nueces and the Rio Grande rivers in Texas in May 1846. Congress approved the resolution for war on 13 May. Recruitment of volunteers for service proceeded very slowly in Cleveland, compared to other Ohio cities. A recruiting station and "Military Depot" was opened in late April; by early June, a contingent of volunteers had elected its officers: D. L. Wood, captain; Levi Rhodes, 1st lieutenant; Chas. Rhodes, 2d lieutenant. This unit expected to leave Cleveland for Camp Washington, near Cincinnati, via the canal, on 12 June, but orders arrived from Columbus for the corps to remain in Cleveland. It had been "organized too late to be accepted into the service of their company," and evidently it was soon disbanded. Regiments recruited from central and southern Ohio participated on different battlefronts. Gen. Zachary Taylor led American troops into northern Mexican provinces and to victory at Buena Vista near Monterey in Feb. 1847; another army moved along the Santa Fe Trail into New Mexico, captured Santa Fe in Aug. 1846, and then marched to and occupied California. If Cleveland men participated in either campaign, it was as individuals, not as a "Cleveland" contingent. Some men recruited from Cleveland were sent to the 5th Infantry at Newport, Ky., and from there to Mexico, but reliable information is lacking about their numbers or their experiences.

The city's organized militia companies—the Grays, the Light Artillery, and the newly formed German Guards—remained in the area. Their wartime activities extended no further than parades on the 4th of July and summer encampments at Camp Wayne, near Wooster, Ohio, in 1846 and in Chicago in 1847. The only organized unit formed from city volunteers was jointly raised in Cleveland and Cincinnati in the spring of 1847, after Gen. Winfield Scott had landed at Vera Cruz and begun his march inland toward Mexico City. On 21 Apr., Capt. John S. Perry led 84 men he had recruited into Co. H, 15th U.S. Infantry Regiment, to Cincinnati. There, they were joined by additional men and eventually arrived in Mexico to become part of Scott's forces. The statistics are far from exact, but it appears that Co. H rostered 103 privates, in addition to its 4 officers, 12 sergeants and corporals, and a musician. There were 33 deaths recorded (although only a few are identified as deaths in or from battle) in these identified places: Chepultepec, Cherubusco, Cuanaraca, Mexico City, Perote, Pueblo, and Vera Cruz. Twelve men were discharged for medical disabilities; 2 were discharged for unrecorded reasons; 4 were listed as absent after being sick. Military activities virtually ended in Oct. 1847. The peace treaty was signed 2 Feb. 1848 at Guadalupe-Hidalgo; the U.S. ratified the treaty on 10 Mar. The men remaining with Co. H were mustered out of service and returned to Ohio the following August.

In marked contrast with the Civil and the Spanish-American wars that followed, there was very limited city-based celebration of the participants or their exploits. Even before the outbreak of hostilities, during the time when annexation of Texas was a national political issue, it was apparent that Cleveland and northern Ohio generally viewed expansion of the U.S. into Mexican-claimed lands as a con-

spiracy of slaveholding southerners to increase their territory and national political power. When war came, most Democrats nominally supported the Polk administration (even if they did not enlist for service), while the Whigs divided into 2 antiwar groups: one group believed that opposition to the war should not continue once war was declared, no matter how misguided the president might be. The other, more radical, Whig group refused to support the war because of its "immoral" purposes. Led by such men as Congressman Joshua Giddings, they endorsed the Wilmot Proviso, which would have banned slavery in any territories gained as a result of the war. Giddings would find himself unable to support the Whig candidate for president in 1848 (Gen. Taylor, a slaveholder) and moved to the Free-Soil party.

A legacy of the war was the permanent shift in political sentiment away from the Democrats and Whigs toward the Liberty, the Free-Soil, and eventually the Republican parties. In 1848, the year the war ended, Cuyahoga County voted 1,776 for Whig Zachary Taylor, 2,368 for Democrat Lewis Cass, but—surpassing both in total votes--2,594 for ex-president Martin Van Buren, the candidate of the Liberty and Free-Soil groups. (Similar returns were recorded for Ashtabula, Geauga, and Lorain counties.) Politics was one arena for disputing the war and its aims; the city's religious groups also found themselves affected by the war. On 23 June 1846, a large meeting of citizens at the Wesleyan chapel approved resolutions condemning the war "with abhorrence and indignation," but extending thanks to the 14 congressmen who voted against declaring war. Most outspoken in opposition to the war were the Old School PRESBYTERIANS, CONGREGATIONALISTS, Unitarians, and Quakers. Unlike the WAR OF 1812, which preceded this conflict, or the CIVIL WAR, which followed closely afterward, the Mexican War seemed to have only adverse economic consequences in Cleveland. The war was especially blamed for the difficulties in securing financing for the Cleveland, Columbus & Cincinnati Railroad. Government borrowing for war purposes was believed to have drained risk-capital funds that otherwise might have been attracted to the venture. With no apparent economic "boom" resulting from the war, with divided churches and political parties, it is not surprising that the Mexican War enters the annals of the city's past in only minimal fashion. Cleveland residents viewed it as by far the least popular of the nation's 19th-century wars.

Carl Ubbelohde
Case Western Reserve University

*Official Roster of the Soldiers of the State of Ohio in the War of the Rebellion, 1861-1866, and in the War with Mexico, 1846-1848* (1895).

MEYER, EDWARD S. (10 Aug. 1843–26 Sept. 1920), was a volunteer Army officer in the CIVIL WAR and U.S. attorney. Meyer was born in Canton, Ohio. He graduated from Canton High School and St. Vincent's College. When the Civil War broke out, he enlisted as a private, Co. F, 4th Ohio Volunteer Infantry, and was later promoted to sergeant, Co. A, of the 19th OVI on 20 Apr. 1861. Appointed 1st lieutenant, 1 Nov. 1861, he resigned 27 Sept. 1862 to accept an appointment as captain, 107th OVI, 11 Nov. 1862, resigning on 1 Jan. 1865. He then served as major, 5th U.S. Veteran Volunteer Infantry, commencing 16 Feb. 1865. Meyer received brevets for war service at the Battle of Shiloh (6–7 Apr. 1862) and for the Battle of Chancellorsville (1–4 May 1862). He was awarded the rank of brevet brigadier general, U.S. Volunteers, dating from 13 Mar. 1865. After the Civil War, Meyer transferred to the Regular Army cavalry, served on the frontier, and retired 24 Aug. 1875 as a result of physical disability from wounds received in the service. He returned to Canton, where he studied law under his father; he was appointed assistant U.S. attorney, Northern District of Ohio, in Apr. 1877, and apparently moved to Cleveland. He then received an appointment as U.S. attorney from Pres. JAS. A. GARFIELD in 1881. After leaving the U.S. attorney's office in 1883, he worked to stop the manufacture and sale of alcoholic beverages by supporting the proposed 2d Amendment to the Ohio constitution. Meyer served on the advisory board of the *Second Amendment Herald*, but the amendment never became part of the state constitution. He then turned to the private practice of law in Cleveland. Upon his arrival in Cleveland, Meyer served as a 1st lieutenant in the 1st Cleveland Troop, 1877–78. He also finished 2 terms as president of the CLEVELAND GRAYS, 1885–87.

**MEYETTE, GRACE E.** (ca. 1890–9 Apr. 1967), came to Cleveland in 1927 to serve as industrial secretary of the YWCA. Educated at the London School of Economics, Columbia University, and the New York School of Social Work, she had previously worked for the YWCA in Philadelphia. Meyette was fired from her YWCA post in 1931, having allegedly tried to exert too much authority in other departments. The CONSUMERS LEAGUE OF OHIO objected to her dismissal, and Meyette remained active in the league for many years. She served on Mayor Thos. A. Burke's race relations committee and in 1931 was named local executive secretary to the Natl. Women's Trade Union League. Dedicated to defending the rights of women in industry, Meyette was appointed inspector for fair wages in the Cleveland district under the Natl. Recovery Act in 1934. She was fired from this post in 1935 in a move criticized by the press as a political maneuver by Gov. Martin L. Davey. In 1935, Meyette was chosen executive secretary of the LEAGUE FOR HUMAN RIGHTS, a Cleveland group founded to combat the influence of Nazism in America and expose Nazi propaganda. She served in the position until the dissolution of the league in the 1940s. Meyette died in CLEVELAND HTS. at the age of 77, after a long illness.

**MICHELSON, ALBERT ABRAHAM** (19 Dec. 1852–9 May 1931), was a physicist whose work with EDWARD W. MORLEY provided a foundation for the theory of relativity. Michelson was born in Strelno, Germany, and came with his parents to America in 1856 (some sources give 1854). The family first settled in Virginia City, Nev., but later moved to San Francisco, Calif. With a special nomination from Pres. Ulysses S. Grant, Michelson attended the U.S. Naval Academy in Annapolis, Md., graduating in 1873 in the top of his class in mathematics, optics, acoustics, and drawing. In 1875, while in the Navy, he conducted his first experiment to determine the speed of light. In 1881, after serving as a midshipman and an instructor in the Navy, Michelson went to Europe to study physics. He came to Cleveland in 1883 (some sources give 1882) to chair the physics department of the Case School of Applied Science, a position he held until 1889. Michelson's work interested Edward W. Morley, a chemist at Western Reserve University, which was adjacent to the Case School. The two decided to collaborate on an experiment to measure the motion of the earth through the "luminiferous aether." The Michelson-Morley experiments, contrary to the expectations of the 2 scientists, seemed to demonstrate the nonexistence of an aether; this result provided important support for Einstein's later special theory of relativity. The

partnership ended when Michelson went to Clark University in Massachusetts in 1889. In 1892, he went to the University of Chicago. In 1920, Michelson perfected a stellar interferometer, which was placed in the Mt. Wilson Observatory to measure the diameter of red giant stars. He also conducted 2 other experiments to determine the exact speed of light, producing more accurate figures in 1926 and 1931. During his career, he published 78 papers. He won the Rumford Medal of the Royal Society of London in 1889 and in 1907 became the first American to win a Nobel Prize in science, for his work in physics. Michelson married twice. His first wife bore him 2 sons and a daughter. He married his second wife, Edna Stanton of Lake Forest, Ill., in 1889; they had 3 daughters.

The **MID-DAY CLUB** opened atop the Union Trust (Huntington Bank) Bldg. in 1924 as Cleveland's largest private luncheon facility. Incorporated by 1928, the club reserved membership for businessmen and professional men who were members of other private clubs. In 1986, membership was automatically granted to all who are members of the GREATER CLEVELAND GROWTH ASSOC. Committed to the development of downtown Cleveland, the Growth Assoc., formerly known as the Cleveland Chamber of Commerce, sought to attract the "proper elements" to the city. As the social affiliate of the Chamber of Commerce, the Mid-Day Club provided fertile ground for the city's growth by bringing together men with political, business, and other interests who might not otherwise associate. The first officers of the club were Alex Brown, president; Elton Hoyt II, vice-president; Allard Smith, secretary; and Carl Osborne, treasurer. Like the private clubs originating in England, the Mid-Day Club originally was for men only, permitting women, accompanied by their husbands, by invitation only. As late as 1971, it was opened to women as guests only weekdays after 2:30 p.m. By the mid-1980s, the club was open weekdays to serve its members breakfast and lunch. Dinner was served in the evening for private parties of 100 or more. Still in its original location, the club is home to a number of antiques and artifacts depicting Cleveland's early history.

**MIDDLEBURG HEIGHTS,** occupying 8 sq. mi., is located 13 mi. southwest of Cleveland and is bounded by BROOK PARK on the north, PARMA on the east, STRONGSVILLE on the south, and BEREA on the west. Middleburg Hts. was originally part of Middleburg Twp., which received its name from the families migrating to the area from Middleburg, N.Y. The first settler in the area, Jared Hickox, arrived in 1809. The settlement grew slowly. Low, wet terrain and numerous swamps, breeding grounds for mosquitos, retarded development. AGRICULTURE was the mainstay of the early settlers, and cleared fields were mainly used for growing beans and as pasture. During the mid-1800s, 75% of Middleburg Twp. remained a dense, unsettled woodland. The construction of railroads in the late 1840s opened the area to neighboring communities, particularly OLMSTED FALLS and Berea. In 1842 the quarry industry began, attracting many German and later Polish families. The incorporation of Berea as a village in 1850 led to the partitioning of the township, and Berea took the quarry industry with it. An attempt by the village of Berea to annex Middleburg Twp. in the 1920s led to the incorporation of Middleburg as a village. In 1925, many farms were taken when the city of Cleveland developed the municipal airport. The Depression and the appropriation of 294 acres by the U.S. government in 1942 for a bomber plant further altered the course of development. During the postwar movement to the suburbs, Middleburg Hts.

grew from a village of 2,500 residents to a city of 7,282 in 1960. The city was incorporated in 1961 and adopted the mayor-council form of government. The population had increased to 12,367 by 1970, and to 16,218 by 1980. Middleburg Hts. contains small businesses and few industries. Southwest General Hospital and United Parcel Service were its largest employers in 1980, and the major business district was the Southland Shopping Ctr.

**MIDDLEBURG TOWNSHIP** was incorporated as a village in the 1920s and achieved city status as MIDDLEBURG HTS. in 1961. Occupying 5 sq. mi., it was situated 13 mi. southwest of Cleveland and was bordered on the south by the east branch of the Rocky River. Previously known as Twp. 6, Range 14, of the Connecticut WESTERN RESERVE, Middleburg Twp. also included the areas of BROOK PARK and BEREA. It acquired its name from early settlers migrating to the area from Middleburg, N.Y., who in 1820 voted for the incorporation of Middleburg as a township. The first white settler in the area, Jared Hickox, arrived in Aug. 1809 after accepting the offer of a free 50-acre tract from Gideon Granger, who owned substantial shares of the township. Emigration to Middleburg was slow because of the area's low, wet terrain and numerous swamps, an ideal breeding ground for disease-carrying mosquitos. Free land offers attracted only a handful of settlers. Those who settled cleared fields and densely wooded areas in order to farm. When Middleburg residents built the first post office, it was named Berea. The area surrounding the post office grew steadily until Berea developed its own identity. Located due west of Middleburg Hts., Berea distinguished itself through its quarry industry. Middleburg Twp. was dealt a blow when, in 1850, Berea incorporated as a village and took the quarry industry with it, leading to the first partitioning of the township. Middleburg continued as a farming community, concentrating upon land improvements in an effort to increase settlement. An iron-ore foundry, a factory, and a gristmill were the few industries built in the community. In 1914, the township met with a second setback when 10 sq. mi. of Middleburg were removed in order to create Brookpark Village. An attempt by Berea Village to annex the remainder of Middleburg Twp. led to its incorporation as a village during the 1920s.

Holzworth, W. F., *Men of Grit and Greatness* (1970).

The **MIDLAND-ROSS COMPANY** is a diversified manufacturer of consumer and industrial products, aerospace and electronic components, and capital goods. It began as the Parish & Bingham Co., founded in Cleveland in 1894, to produce bicycle, wagon, and trolley parts. With the introduction of the automobile, the company began to fabricate frames. On 21 Mar. 1923, Elroy J. Kulas merged Parish & Bingham, the Detroit Pressed Steel Co., and the Parish Mfg. Co. into the Midland Steel Prods. Co., with 2 Cleveland plants. It quickly became the largest producer of automobile frames. A brake division was established in 1928, producing mechanical and air brakes and air compressors. During WORLD WAR II, Midland manufactured jeep and truck frames and parts for shells and tanks.

In the mid-1950s, the board of directors initiated a program of diversification to provide the company with a broader base, aiming at a well-balanced variety of capital and consumer goods. That resulted in the formation of the Midland-Ross Co. on 7 Dec. 1957, when Midland Steel Prods. merged with the J. O. Ross Engineering Co., founded in 1921 in New Jersey as an engineer and builder of industrial heating, drying, and ventilating equipment. Under Wade N. Harris, Midland-Ross continued diversification by expanding into allied fields such as metal heat treating, casting, climate control, and transportation and aerospace. By 1960, the company had 12 divisions with 20 plants in 8 states and Canada.

In 1961, Midland-Ross acquired Cleveland's Industrial Rayon Corp., a manufacturer of automobile tire cord and rayon yarns. Organized in 1925, Industrial Rayon developed a continuous process for making viscose filament rayon in the 1930s but had suffered financially throughout the 1950s. Midland-Ross further expanded by establishing subsidiaries and providing licenses to foreign companies to market its products. In 1965, Harris purchased another major Cleveland firm, the Natl. Castings Co., a leading producer of railroad equipment, pipe coatings, grinding balls, and a variety of metal castings. Founded by 5 Clevelanders on 14 Aug. 1868 as the Cleveland Malleable Iron Co. and guided by Alfred Pope and his nephew, Henry, this local, pioneering firm became a nationwide organization by 1891 and thereafter developed into the world's largest producer of anchor chains and aviation castings.

Midland-Ross continued its acquisitions until 1969, when its new president, Harry J. Bolwell, realized that it had many disparate, marginally profitable operating units with little focus or direction. Bolwell restructured Midland-Ross by selling some of these companies, including Industrial Rayon in 1969, and focusing on 3 core areas—thermal processes, castings, and aerospace and electronic products. Throughout the 1970s and early 1980s, the firm consolidated by exiting declining areas, such as material handling, plastics, and automobile products. It sold its frame and brake divisions, which had constituted the original Midland Steel Prods. Co., and acquired sound firms in the core areas, especially in electronics. By 1981, Midland-Ross, with its international headquarters in Cleveland, had 19 divisions and subsidiaries operating 57 plants in 18 states and 9 foreign countries, with annual sales of over $900 million. In July 1986, the company was bought by Forstmann Little & Co. for about $450 million, and it was announced that the Cleveland offices would be closed early in 1987.

Harris, Wade N., *Midland-Ross Corporation* (1964).
Natl. Malleable & Steel Castings Co., *National Malleable and Steel Castings Company, 75th Anniversary, 1868-1943* (1943).
Pomeroy, Cleve H., *"85 Years!" National Malleable and Steel Castings (1868-1953)* (1953).
Rayon Corp., *Rayon Mile by Mile* (1947).

**MILES AVENUE CHURCH OF CHRIST,** located at 7166 Dunham Rd., WALTON HILLS, had its origins when DISCIPLES OF CHRIST joined in a meeting at Col. John Wightman's farm located on Harvard Ave. near Broadway in NEWBURGH in 1835. Preachers Alexander Campbell, Wm. Hayden, A. B. Green, and M. S. Clapp inspired many converts. Subsequently, 35 converts organized a church, which later became Miles Ave. Church of Christ. In 1835, brethren of the church assumed the duties of the congregation; John Hopkinson and Theodore Stafford were chosen first bishops, David L. Wightman and John Healy, deacons. In 1842 they moved from a tent to a log schoolhouse (the site of ST. ALEXIS HOSPITAL) on Broadway. They later moved to the Newburgh town hall, and in 1851 they purchased land from Mr. and Mrs. Eben Miles and erected their first church building at 9200 Miles Ave. Healy, Hopkinson, and Wm. Kelley served as lay ministers. J. D. Benedict became the first minister, in 1854, and served for 5 years. He was followed by JAS. A. GARFIELD, who had become a member of the Disciples church before he entered college. Although never formally ordained, he served from 1859–60 and participated in a series of evangelistic services entitled "Meeting of Days." In 1888, the original frame building was moved to the back of the lot on Miles Ave., and a larger worship area with classroom space was added. It was remodeled in 1919, and as the church continued to flourish, another remodeling program was begun in 1929 and completed in 1930. In 1979 the congregation sold the church and moved to temporary quarters at 750 Broadway in BEDFORD; in 1981 it purchased a 6.8-acre plot of land in Walton Hills. The new building was dedicated 12 Sept. 1982.

**MILES PARK** was originally the public square of the village of NEWBURGH. Created when county surveyor AHAZ MERCHANT plotted the village in 1850, the park and commons at Gaylord (E. 93rd) and Walnut (Sawyer) streets were the site of a town hall in 1860. When Newburgh was annexed to Cleveland in 1873, the site was christened Miles Park, in honor of Theodore Miles, who donated the land to the old village in 1850; the town hall was converted to a public library. In 1907, the old structure was demolished to make way for a new, larger library building. No longer a park, the site retains its historic name as the Miles Park branch of the CLEVELAND PUBLIC LIBRARY.

**MILL CREEK,** a tributary of the CUYAHOGA RIVER that formed part of the southern boundary of old Newburgh Twp., provided the area with the waterpower that made early NEWBURGH more prominent than Cleveland. Near the present Broadway and Warner roads, the stream dropped more than 40′ and abruptly turned to form 3 falls. In 1799, Wheeler W. Williams and Ezra Wyatt built the first sawmill in the area on one leg of the cataract, followed by a carding mill and flour mill. The gristmill featured 2 large millstones that could grind 20 bushels of wheat into smooth "bolted" flour. Its opening was marked by a grand celebration among the 10 early settler families of Newburgh and people from the surrounding area. The corn ground at the mill supplied a local distillery, the first industry established in Cleveland. As the business pulled to Newburgh by the mills grew, 2 famous hotels and eateries were built nearby in 1840—CATARACT HOUSE at E. 88th St. and Broadway above the falls, and Eagle House at Miles and Broadway. The former, which burned in 1850, was rebuilt with town money and prospered under a succession of owners as a hotel and popular local meeting place until 1905, when it was bought by the Pennsylvania Railroad for a right-of-way. Meanwhile, Eagle House attracted patrons in the 1840s with its nut cakes fried in bear grease and its famed "spring floor" ballroom. Mill Creek and its original falls were largely reoriented when the Pennsylvania Railroad built an overpass where the cataract fell.

**MILLER, DAYTON CLARENCE** (13 Mar. 1866–22 Feb. 1941), was a pioneer in the use of x-rays. Born in STRONGSVILLE, Ohio, and raised in BEREA, Miller graduated from Baldwin University (BALDWIN-WALLACE COLLEGE) in 1886. He received a doctorate in 1890 from Princeton. In 1890, he became a professor of mathematics and physics at Case School of Applied Science (CASE WESTERN RESERVE UNIVERSITY). From 1895–1936, he was head of the Physics Dept. Miller was a trustee of Baldwin-Wallace for nearly 43 years and chairman of the board for 5. As a consultant for the Aeolian Co., he was instrumental in developing the Webber piano.

Miller is best known for his pioneering work in surgical x-rays. When Konrad von Roentgen discovered the x-ray in 1895, the *Cleveland Plain Dealer* carried an account of the discovery. Miller gleaned enough information from that story to build an x-ray apparatus with a Crookes Tube and 12 wet-cell batteries. In 1896, he x-rayed his entire body section by section, producing the first full x-ray of the human body. The value of these x-rays became partially realized when Miller used the process to detect an improperly set broken arm of a patient of Dr. GEO. CRILE. Miller's other interests included sound (he developed a "phonodeik"—forerunner of the oscilloscope) and architectural acoustics. He was the acoustical designer of many buildings, including SEVERANCE HALL. He also performed and composed music; built a pipe organ; made a golden flute; and collected some 1,500 flutes, which he left to the Library of Congress—Music Division. In 1921, Miller met with Albert Einstein regarding his recreation of the Michelson-Morley experiments that had led to the development of the Theory of Relativity. Dayton married Edith Easton of Princeton, N.J., in 1893.

**MILLER, RAYMOND THOMAS** (10 Jan. 1893–13 July 1966), was a prominent lawyer, businessman, and politician serving as head of the CUYAHOGA COUNTY DEMOCRATIC PARTY for over 20 years. A native of Defiance, Ohio, he was one of 8 children born to Martin E. and Anne Riley Miller. He attended parochial and public schools in Defiance and continued his education at Notre Dame University, receiving his LL.B. degree in 1914. Miller then moved to Cleveland to practice law. As a member of the Ohio Natl. Guard, he was called to active service on the Mexican border in 1916, and during WORLD WAR I he saw active duty in France. After the war, he became interested in politics and was elected city prosecutor in 1928, where he played an active role in defeating the CITY MANAGER PLAN of government. With the return of the mayor-council form of government, Miller was elected mayor in 1932. During his 2-year term, he drastically reduced expenditures to cope with the growing Depression. He was instrumental in persuading the utilities to lower their rates. HARRY L. DAVIS defeated him in his bid for reelection in 1933.

The major portion of Miller's political career began in 1938, when, after a power struggle with W. BURR GONGWER, he was made chairman of the Cuyahoga County Democratic party. Lawsuits and countersuits followed until 1940, when the state central committee declared his appointment official. Under his leadership, the Democratic party was able to attract the black voters in Cleveland. Combined with its ethnic base, the party was successful in electing Democratic mayors for 30 years and consistently obtained a Democratic majority in council. Miller lost his chairmanship in 1964 to ALBERT PORTER. While leading the Democratic party, Miller also established a successful law practice, serving as legal counsel for the Cleveland-based BROTHERHOOD OF LOCOMOTIVE ENGINEERS and Brotherhood of Railway Trainmen. In the business world, he helped organize radio station WERE and was active in the formation of the CLEVELAND BROWNS. On 20 Apr. 1926 he married Ruth Hamilton, and they had 6 children, Mrs. Roseanne Perme, Ray T., Jr., Mrs. Ruth Mary Galvin, Richard, Robert, and Riley. Miller died in Cleveland at age 73.

Ray T. Miller Papers, WRHS.

**MILLIKEN, WILLIAM M.** (1889–14 Mar. 1978), was the second director of the CLEVELAND MUSEUM OF ART. Born in Stamford, Conn., of distinguished Scotch ancestry, he graduated from Princeton University in 1911. Prior to serving as a lieutenant in the U.S. Army between 1917–18,

Milliken was employed as assistant curator of the Dept. of Decorative Art in the Metropolitan Museum of Art in New York City. Following his discharge from the service, he was appointed curator of decorative arts at the CMA, a post that he held until his retirement from the museum in 1958. Milliken served briefly as curator of painting at the museum (1925–30) before his appointment as director in Aug. 1930 following the departure of the museum's first director, Frederic Allen Whiting. He served the museum in this capacity until Apr. 1958. The purchase of the Guelph Treasure in Aug. 1930 and the annual MAY SHOW are generally considered to have been his major accomplishments during his service to the museum. The Guelph Treasure, dating from a.d. 1000, provided the museum with international stature. The May Show, an exhibition of local art and crafts, was under Milliken's guidance from 1919–58. After leaving the CMA, Milliken served as advisor to the Natl. Gallery in Australia, presented lectures, organized the "Masterpieces of Art Exhibition" at the Seattle World's Fair in 1963, held the post of regent professor at the University of California in Berkeley, and authored 3 books. He served as trustee of the American Fed. of Arts (1929–62), as a board member of the American Assoc. of Museums and as president of that organization from 1953–55, and 2 terms as president of the Assoc. of Art Museum Directors (1946–49). He also served on numerous international museum councils and was presented many awards and honors by the European art world. Milliken is buried at Bridgeport, Conn.

Wm. M. Milliken Papers, WRHS.

**MILLS, JOSHUA** (1797–29 Apr. 1843), was a pioneer physician and served as mayor of Cleveland from 1838–39 and in 1842. Mills was a native New Englander educated in medicine. He came to Cleveland as a physician in 1827. Once established, he opened what was to be the most successful pharmacy in the city. Mills became a public figure in 1832, when his assistance in the CHOLERA EPIDEMIC of that year made him a member of the city's first Board of Health. In the first city elections of 1836, he became a Whig alderman. He soon became a member of city council and its president in 1837. He ran unopposed for mayor in 1838 and served 1 term. He was elected again in 1839. He was then defeated for reelection by NICHOLAS DOCKSTADTER in 1840 and by JOHN W. ALLEN in 1841. In 1842, he finally succeeded in being reelected to another term in office. Mills married Phoebe Stafford Higby in 1826. Their 2 children both died of scarlet fever in 1835.

**MINOR, NORMAN SELBY** (19 July 1901–15 May 1968), was a noted Cleveland criminal trial attorney. He possessed a bright and most ingenious legal mind and a magnetic personality that dominated the courtroom. A number of Cleveland's prominent black attorneys trained under him, including Merle McCurdy and Louis and Carl Stokes. Minor was born in Oak Park, Ill., to Wm. M. and Rebecca Walden Minor and came to Cleveland at the age of 4 with his family. Educated in the CLEVELAND PUBLIC SCHOOLS, he graduated from CENTRAL HIGH SCHOOL in 1921. A bout with pneumonia forced him to return home after 2 years at the University of Michigan. Enrolling at John Marshall Law School, he graduated with the LL.B. degree in 1927 and was admitted to the Ohio bar in 1928.

From 1928–30, Minor was associated with the law firm of Payne, Green, Minor, & Perry. During these years, he took the cases of men in jail in need of a lawyer free of charge in order to gain trial experience. Appointed assistant Cuyahoga County prosecutor in 1930, he recognized that he was the black prosecutor for black cases. He felt the pressure of being black in a system that had circumscribed stations for BLACKS. Knowing that there might not be anyone to follow him if he failed, Minor accepted his "missionary" role and gained a reputation as one of the city's best criminal trial lawyers. He prosecuted more than 5,000 felony cases and hundreds of trials, including 13 successful prosecutions for 1st-degree murder. His most famous case as prosecutor was that of Willie "The Mad Butcher" Johnson, who was convicted of murdering 12 women during the 1930s and 1940s. Actively involved in Democratic party politics throughout his career, Minor polled the largest vote of any black candidate to that time in a 1937 election defeat for a municipal court judgeship. In 1948 Minor returned to private practice, establishing law offices with Merle McCurdy. At the time of his death, he was practicing with John Carson and Floyd Oliver. As a criminal defense lawyer specializing in homicide cases, he was renowned for his abilities at cross-examination and choosing nonconvicting juries, and as a severe critic of Ohio's penal system. Minor's first marriage, in 1928, ended with the death of his wife, Novella, in 1937. On 28 Dec. 1938, he married Mary Christian. The Minors had 2 children, Valena and Harold.

**MISS MITTLEBERGER'S SCHOOL** (ca. 1877–1908) was one of Cleveland's most prominent schools for young women in the late 19th century. The school had its beginnings in Miss Augusta Mittleberger's home, where she began conducting private classes for young women. With the death of her father in 1877, Miss Mittleberger moved to larger quarters and accepted more students. In 1881, she was offered and accepted a house owned by JOHN D. ROCKEFELLER for her school. The house was moved approximately 1 block from its location on Rockefeller's land (he thought it obscured his view) to 1020 Prospect Ave. at E. 40th St. Soon after, Miss Mittleberger's students were called "the girls of 1020." Miss Mittleberger's became the school where prominent Clevelanders sent their daughters. It achieved a national reputation and boarded students enrolled at the school from other areas of Ohio and nearby states. The daughters of presidents Hayes and Garfield were both enrolled. In her catalogs, Miss Mittleberger stated her philosophy of education: "The aim, as in all good schools, is the training of the mind and the body and the development of character. Influence is developed in favor of higher education, pupils being sent to the best colleges open to women." (The schools mentioned were Vassar, Wellesley, Smith, Wells, and Cleveland College for Women.) Although nonsectarian, the school was rooted strongly in the Protestant moral tradition. "Above all," Miss Mittleberger stated, "it is considered of the greatest moment to place before our pupils right ideals of Christian excellence." Miss Mittleberger's School survived until 1908, when she retired. She quietly and simply announced to the students in late March of that year that the June commencement would mark the close of the school. As a tribute to her, she was given a gift of $1,000 in gold coins at the alumnae luncheon that followed that final commencement.

Miss Mittleberger's School Records, WRHS.

**MR. GASKET,** a company that manufactures automobile accessories for people who enjoy working on their own cars, began in a basement in the mid-1960s with a $5 investment; by the 1970s, its founder was a millionaire. In 1984, the company had sales of $97 million. Mr. Gasket was founded by Joseph F. Hrudka, the son of a west side bar owner and a graduate of John Marshall High School.

Hrudka left college after 1 semester, ran a car wash, and, with his brother Tom, raced cars. With a 1957 Chevrolet, Joe and Tom Hrudka won national drag racing championships in 1961 and 1962. At age 25, in 1964, Joe Hrudka invented a new type of gasket that would withstand high temperatures. He sold his 150-A gasket first to friends, then through a friend's store. In 1965 he went into business selling his own gaskets and other auto parts; in 1967 he sold $600,000 worth of auto parts and had moved his operations from 4468 State Rd. To 4569 Spring Rd. In 1969, Mr. Gasket had sales of $3 million and earnings of $375,000. The company went public for the first time that year; Hrudka sold ⅓ of the equity for $2.7 million. In Dec. 1971, W. R. Grace & Co. acquired all of Mr. Gasket for $17 million, $6 million of which went to Hrudka. Although Hrudka remained with the company as president and consultant, the new owner's style of management left little for him to do, and he left in 1976. By 1972 the company had moved to 4566 Spring Rd.; by 1981 it had 6 locations in the Brooklyn Hts. industrial park and employed 200 people in Cleveland, with another 300 working in plants in California and Mexico. Grace & Co.'s bureaucratic approach to management, however, failed to operate the business as well as Hrudka's less formal managers, who were truly interested in automobiles but who had been forced out by the new management style. Mr. Gasket's business declined as a result. As a part of the sale to Grace, Hrudka had agreed not to compete with Mr. Gasket for 10 years; as that period drew to a close, he and his former associates began to consider forming a new company. Grace then offered to return Mr. Gasket to its founder, and on 6 Apr. 1981, Hrudka bought the firm for $4 million. He fired 85 employees, reinstated his former associates, and embarked upon a campaign to acquire other auto-parts firms in an attempt to boost annual sales to $200 million and earnings to $20 million. Hrudka made Mr. Gasket a public company again in Oct. 1983, selling 23% of the company for $32 million. Between 1981–85, the number of Mr. Gasket products doubled from 4,500 to 9,000, and the company expanded its physical plant. In July 1984, the city of Brooklyn issued $2.5 million in industrial revenue bonds for Mr. Gasket to expand, and by 1985 the company had moved its headquarters to 8700 Brookpark Rd.

**MITCHELL, L. PEARL** (1883 [1890]–6 Sept. 1974), was a civil-rights activist, an officer of the NAACP, and a devoted member of Alpha Kappa Alpha, holding national offices in the sorority. Mitchell was born in Wilberforce, Ohio, one of 7 children of Dr. Samuel T. Mitchell, president of Wilberforce College. She attended elementary school and Wilberforce Academy and received a bachelor's degree from Wilberforce College. She also briefly studied music at the Oberlin Conservatory of Music and sociology at Kalamazoo College before turning to war-camp community service during WORLD WAR I. After her father's early death, she worked as a typist to help finance the education of her 3 younger siblings. In the early 1920s, Mitchell came to Cleveland. In 1926 she became a probation officer in the juvenile court, a position she held until ill health prompted her resignation sometime in the 1940s. In 1923 she joined the Cleveland branch of the NAACP; she eventually served as the organization's president in 1936–37, as its first executive secretary in 1945, and as national vice-president in 1959, and was a national director of membership campaigns, organizing such drives in Milwaukee, Birmingham, Dallas, Detroit, and Cleveland. As local president, Mitchell led protest drives against the school system's discriminatory operation of the Longwood and Outhwaite special-activity schools and against segregated public-housing projects. She

was able to mobilize support from local newspapers to gain employment for black nurses at City Hospital. Mitchell also organized and sponsored the local NAACP's youth council.

After her retirement in the 1940s, Mitchell continued her work on behalf of civil rights and expanded her range of civic involvement. In Sept. 1954, Gov. Frank Lausche appointed her to the board of trustees of the Ohio Soldiers' & Sailors' Orphans' Home; she was reappointed in 1959. During her tenure, she waged a successful struggle to integrate the Columbus facility. As mayor, Lausche had appointed her to the Women & Manpower Commission; she later served as executive secretary of the Greater Cleveland Fair Employment Practices Commission and was appointed by Mayor Carl Stokes to the Commission on the Aged. Pearl Mitchell also pursued her interest in drama. She was a member of the Gilpin Players and appeared in performances at the Play House Settlement. In 1950 she appeared in local playwright Jo Sinclair's *The Long Moment*, the first interracial play performed at the CLEVELAND PLAY HOUSE. Mitchell received many awards for her civil-rights and community-service activities. She never married.

L. Pearl Mitchell Papers, WRHS.
NAACP Cleveland Branch Records, WRHS.

**MITERMILER, ANDREW ROBERT** (27 Jan. 1840–10 Sept. 1896), was representative of the immigrant architects who were trained in Europe and practiced in Cleveland in the late 19th century. He was active in Cleveland from 1871–96 and designed business blocks, social halls, breweries, and churches for CZECHS and GERMANS. Mitermiler was born in Chocen, Czechoslovakia. He was educated at the University of Vienna, graduated as a civil engineer, and worked on the construction of the Innsbruck Tunnel in Austria. When he was about to be conscripted into the Austrian army, he escaped to America, arriving in Baltimore, Md., in 1861. He practiced engineering in Baltimore for several years and came to Cleveland ca. 1871. He worked as foreman in the office of architect J. M. Blackburn and then set up his own office in 1873.

By 1886, Mitermiler advertised the following list of buildings completed: churches on Superior and Jennings avenues, breweries for Leisy, Schlather, Gehring, and Baehr, the West Side Turn Hall, Tinnerman's, Maurer's, and Kundtz's commercial blocks, and the Leisy, Wiedeman, Loomis, and Junge residences. Among his buildings still standing in the 1980s were the Lohmann Block on Woodland Ave. at E. 84th St. (1885), the A. Zverina Block on Broadway near E. 55th St. (1889), the Rauch & Lang Carriage Works on W. 25th St. (1889), the Czech Sokol Hall on Clark Ave. (1891), and the Pilsner Brewery on W. 65th St. (1894). He designed the first building for ST. ELIZABETH CHURCH, the first Hungarian Catholic parish in the U.S., and worked on the church of St. Mary of the Assumption, a German Evangelical church on Scranton Ave., and the decoration of St. Michael Catholic Church. None of these works are extant. Mitermiler was associated with another Bohemian architect, John W. Hradek, on some commissions, especially the preliminary design for the BOHEMIAN NATL. HALL. DOMINICK BENES, later a partner in the important firm of Hubbell & Benes, worked as an apprentice in Mitermiler's office from 1872–75. Andrew R. Mitermiler married Elizabeth Staral, and they had 5 children, Mrs. Rose Zverina, Mrs. Elizabeth Kennedy, Andrew S., John A., and Anton.

**MITTLEBERGER'S SCHOOL.** *See MISS MITTLEBERGER'S SCHOOL*

**MIZER, CONRAD** (1857-1904), was a tailor whose chief contribution to Cleveland was his promotion of summer band concerts in public parks. Mizer loved the idea of picnic lunches on Sunday afternoons while listening to music. He asked the city of Cleveland for $5,000 to finance a season of music. At first he met with resistance, not only from the city but also from ministers who wished to keep the Sabbath free from nonreligious activities. The summer band concerts began in 1898. Band members were paid $3 per concert. Among the bands that performed were the Great Western, Natl. Military, and Cleveland Elks bands. In Sept. 1903, an all-Wagner program in Rockefeller Park was presented. The Great Western Band and a German chorus performed.

After the collapse of the CLEVELAND SYMPHONY ORCHESTRA in 1902, Mizer attempted to revive it with a winter concert series. He sought financial support from many prominent citizens and formed an executive committee with Edward Aylard and Archibald Klumph to handle the business arrangements. Mizer was the chairman. He had JOHANN BECK and EMIL RING alternate as conductors. On 4 Jan. 1903, at GRAYS ARMORY, the Cleveland Symphony Orchestra gave a well-attended production featuring the music of Bizet, Liszt, and Weber. These Sunday afternoon programs continued for 10 years with great success. They also helped to give local composers an opportunity for the performance of their works. Mizer's death was a severe blow to music in Cleveland. His funeral was held in Grays Armory, and he was buried in LAKE VIEW CEMETERY. A monument in his honor was erected in EDGEWATER PARK. Mizer was unmarried.

**MOLEY, RAYMOND** (27 Sept. 1886-18 Feb. 1975), was a political-science professor, a presidential advisor, a columnist, and a director of the CLEVELAND FOUNDATION who began as a progressive but grew more conservative as he grew older. Moley was born in Berea, Ohio, but grew up in OLMSTED FALLS; after graduating from the Olmsted Falls public schools, he attended Baldwin University in Berea, 1902-06. In 1906, he became superintendent of the Olmsted Falls public schools; he was elected village clerk in 1908 and mayor in 1911. While teaching at Cleveland's West High, 1912-14, Moley received an A.M. (1913) in political science from Oberlin College. In 1914, he began work on a Ph.D. in political science from Columbia University, which he completed under the tutelage of eminent political scientist Chas. A. Beard in 1918. In 1916, Western Reserve University hired Moley to teach political science—his first college position. Throughout his career, Moley was the academic who desired to be involved with practical politics. During WORLD WAR I, he also served as the head of both the local and state Americanization boards, which were formed to gain the cooperation, the respect, and eventually the naturalization of the thousands of foreign-born industrial workers in Cleveland and Ohio. His duties included making speeches, coordinating teachers' institutions, and writing articles. Moley also wrote a primer on American government for citizenship applicants, *Lessons in Citizenship.*

In Aug. 1919, Moley resigned from WRU to become director of the Cleveland Foundation. During his tenure, the foundation became noted for its surveys of city social problems. The criminal-justice survey attracted national acclaim; Moley hired Harvard professors Roscoe Pound and Felix Frankfurter to conduct it. Moley's duties included administering surveys, organizing publicity, making speeches, and publishing articles and summaries of survey results. He accepted a position teaching government at Columbia's Barnard College in 1923, remaining on the faculty until

1954. He soon attracted the attention of New York Gov. Franklin D. Roosevelt. In Jan. 1932, FDR asked Moley to assemble a group of advisors to help develop national programs for his presidential campaign by debating courses of action and alternative policies and drafting speeches. Moley selected a group of mainly Columbia professors, which became known as the Brain Trust.

Moley mainly wrote speeches for FDR during the launching of the New Deal in 1932-33. During the "Hundred Days," he served as assistant secretary of state, a position that gave him a salary to serve as FDR's top speechwriter and also as a policy advisor. He resigned in Aug. 1933 over conflicts with Secretary of State Cordell Hull. Moley continued advising and writing speeches for FDR on a part-time, nonpaid basis until 1936, but he grew disillusioned with New Deal hostility to business and FDR's increasing involvement in foreign affairs. By late 1935, he was reevaluating his beliefs in progressivism and becoming more conservative. In Oct. 1933, Moley became editor of the new *Today* magazine; he kept the position after *Today* merged with *Newsweek* in Feb. 1937. In 1941 he began a nationally syndicated triweekly newspaper column. Although he relinquished his administrative duties, Moley wrote for *Newsweek* until Dec. 1967. He also wrote 19 books and numerous articles on political affairs, which include 2 critical reviews of the New Deal, *After Seven Years* (1939) and *The First New Deal* (1966).

Moley's growing conservatism and his national journalistic reputation allowed him to become a senior advisor to Republican presidential aspirants Wendell Willkie, Barry Goldwater, and Richard Nixon. His highest honor came in 1970 when Pres. Nixon awarded him the Medal of Freedom. Moley married twice. He married Eva Dall in 1916 and had 2 sons, Malcolm and Raymond, Jr. The Moleys separated in 1933 and divorced in 1948. In 1949, Moley married Frances Hebard.

Moley, Raymond, *Realities and Illusions, 1886-1931*, ed. Frank Freidel (1980).
Raymond Moley Papers, Hoover Institution on War, Revolution, and Peace, Stanford, Calif.

**MOLYNEAUX, JOSEPH B.** (1 Jan. 1840-23 Apr. 1925), was a volunteer Civil War officer and secretary of the Cuyahoga County Soldiers & Sailors Monument Commission. Molyneaux was born in Ann Arbor, Mich. After working a variety of odd jobs in Elmira, N.Y., and Belleville, Ohio, he came to Cleveland before the CIVIL WAR and became a printer. He enlisted as a private in the 7TH OHIO VOLUNTEER INFANTRY in the spring of 1861 for 3 months' service. He reenlisted with the 7th OVI for 3 years' service and was promoted to captain on 1 Sept. 1862. At the Battle of Cedar Mountain, he was twice wounded and had 2 horses shot out from under him (9 Aug. 1862). He then took command of the regiment after all senior officers were either wounded or killed. He was mustered out as a lieutenant because of disability on 31 Dec. 1863.

Once recovered from his wounds, Molyneux accepted a commission as captain of Co. E, 150th OVI, then being raised in Cleveland in May 1864. He served in the defenses of Washington, D.C., at Ft. Thayer in the summer of 1864 with the 150th and was mustered out in Cleveland in August of that year. After the war, he returned to the printing business and served as deputy Cuyahoga County recorder, as assistant postmaster, and on the Board of Equalization & Assessment. He served on the Cuyahoga County Soldiers & Sailors Monument Commission from 1894-1925. At the time of his death, he was survived by his wife, Henrietta A., and 3 sons: Wm. V., Robt. T., and Raymond L. Molyneaux. He is buried in WOODLAND CEMETERY.

**MONA'S RELIEF SOCIETY.** *See* **CLEVELAND MANX SOCIETY**

*MONITOR CLEVELANDSKI* could trace its origins back to *Polonia w Ameryce* (Poland in America), Cleveland's first Polish newspaper, which was established in Jan. 1892. Located on E. 65th St., the original weekly was edited by John Malkowski and included among its incorporators such Warszawa businessmen as Stanley Lewandowski, MICHAEL KNIOLA, Telesfor Olstynski, and Matt Dluzynski. It was purchased by 1897 by Theodore Dluzynski, who installed L. S. Devyno as editor, purchased a new press, and erected a new building for the paper. He also succeeded in having a street parallel to the 6800–7100 block of Harvard Ave. named Polonia Ave., probably the only Cleveland street ever named after a newspaper. Upon its absorption of the Polish weekly *Jutrzenka* (Morning Star), *Polonia* commenced daily publication in 1918. It was sold in 1922 to the publishers of the *Detroit Daily Record*, who changed its name to the *Polish Daily Monitor* and resold it 3 years later to another local group. Wladyslaw J. Nowak, a wholesale grocer, emerged as the *Monitor's* new publisher. Selling off his grocery business, Nowak concentrated his attention on the newspaper, which was operated at 6875 Broadway Ave. in a building that also housed the United Publishing Co. Under Nowak and his editors, the *Monitor* attacked the growth of socialism in Poland and served as the unofficial organ of the Polish Catholic parishes of Cleveland. It continued until 13 June 1938, when it was sold to the city's other Polish daily, the *WIADOMOSCI CODZIENNE* (Polish Daily News), and suspended. Nowak retained United Publishing until 1946, when he sold it and the 6875 Broadway building to the TOWNSEND PLAN organization.

**THE MONROE STREET CEMETERY** has remained public under 3 jurisdictions: Brooklyn Twp., OHIO CITY, and Cleveland. Until the late 1890s, it was Cleveland's only west side public cemetery, despite the trustees' annual warnings about lack of salable lots. Brooklyn Twp. acquired its cemetery when Josiah Barber and his brother-in-law Richard Lord sold part of lot no 69 to them in Jan. 1836, for $160 to be used "forever as a public burying ground." When Ohio City was incorporated on 3 Mar. 1836, the township cemetery became the city cemetery, although perfecting its title was accomplished by another deed (1841). Ohio City gave its cemetery as close attention as Cleveland, on the Cuyahoga River's east bank, gave its cemetery, now called ERIE ST. The Ohio City council legislated rules and regulations, appointed a sexton, and arranged for systematic platting, as well as for the purchase and storage of a hearse. Amenities and necessities, such as shade trees, hitching posts, and fences, were added. When, in 1854, Ohio City was annexed to Cleveland, the cemetery became simply the west side cemetery. Scarcity of west side burial space spurred development of Riverside (1875) and Lutheran (1894) cemeteries on Pearl Rd. When Cleveland opened West Park (1900) on the old pest farm site on Chestnut Ridge Rd., the dearth was alleviated. Still, Monroe St., taking over 400 burials annually, went into the 20th century as the second-busiest municipal cemetery, after WOODLAND. Under Cleveland's charge, Monroe St. Cemetery, which became the more frequently used name, was ornamented with walks and plantings, protected by a patrolman, and fenced to keep out wandering hogs. A salesman was engaged to sell lots in this cemetery, which seemed to change dimensions frequently. Parcels were added one year, but footage was sold to the railroad the next year. When the proposed purchase of the neighboring Catholic Orphan Asylum was rejected, hope for significantly enlarging the site faded. Therefore, Monroe St. has remained the west side's plain and practical public cemetery.

The **MONTEFIORE HOME,** or the "Kesher Shel Barzel Home" for aged and infirm Israelites, was dedicated in June 1882. The home, originally costing $25,000, was located on Woodland Ave. and E. 55th St. At the start, it served approximately 40 residents, "preferably old and poverty stricken Israelites in physically good condition, free of contagious and mental diseases, with a lower age limit of 65. . . ." Its first president was Jacob Rohreimer, a leading Jewish citizen of Cleveland in the late 19th century. In 1884 the name of the home was changed to the Sir Moses Montefiore Home for the Aged & Infirm Israelites. Montefiore (1784–1885) was a famed Anglo-Jewish philanthropist widely known for his promotion of civil rights for Jews in England and a precursor of modern Zionism. In Nov. 1916, the Woodland property was sold for $155,000, and in Apr. 1917 the Dean property at 3151 Mayfield Rd. was acquired for the purpose of constructing a new home. In 1919, the new building was completed, with a capacity for 30 single residents and 12 couples. In 1923, the name of the home was changed to the Montefiore Home. From 1923 to the present, the Montefiore Home has modernized and expanded to become one of the best facilities in Cleveland in the area of geriatric care.

Montefiore Home Records, WRHS.

**MONTENEGRINS.** *See* **BALKAN IMMIGRANTS**

The **MONTESSORI SCHOOLS** in Cleveland offer an alternative education to children ages 3–14. Cleveland was one of the first cities in the U.S. To have a Montessori school. The schools are based on teaching concepts developed by Dr. Maria Montessori of Italy. In 1907, she established a school for disadvantaged (mostly poor) children in Rome, believing that they could learn more effectively through self-motivation. Her methods became popular in both Europe and the U.S. but faded into relative disuse following WORLD WAR I. During the 1950s, interest in her methods was revived in the U.S. The first Montessori school in Cleveland was founded by Mary Ruffing and a group of parents in 1959. It was the second, or third, such school to become established in the U.S. The first classes were held in a rented room in the basement of St. Patrick's Church. At that time only preschoolers were admitted; 40 were in the first class. The continuing purpose of the Montessori schools is to encourage self-discipline and allow students to learn at their own pace. Instruction is more individualized, and the relationship between student and teacher is less formal. Indeed, the teacher is not intended to be the central figure in the classroom. Classrooms also mix pupils of different ages to foster interaction. The Cleveland Montessori schools, like all others, are nonprofit and usually parent-owned. Each school is run by a board of trustees made up of parents, who also participate in building maintenance and upkeep. The first Cleveland school—now Ruffing West, in ROCKY RIVER, and Ruffing East, in CLEVELAND HTS.—received endorsement from the Catholic School Board.

By 1970, 7 Montessori schools had been opened in Cleveland. Within 5 years, 13 more had been added, with an attendance of over 1,000. By 1986 there were over 25 schools scattered throughout the Cleveland area, each independent of the others. At this time there were approximately 1,300 preschoolers and 1,800 elementary students enrolled. An annual tuition is required of each student, and in some schools there is strong competition for admission. Because of a reduced number of proficient Montessori teachers in Cleveland, in 1977 the Montessori Institute of Cleveland was founded as a teacher-training center, but it proved to be a short-lived affair. In the early 1980s, David Kahn, then principal of Ruffing East, applied to the Montessori centers in Italy and Holland for approval to institute a series of summer training sessions in Cleveland in the Montessori method. A national study funded by the CLEVELAND FOUNDATION supported the need for such a program. Despite some opposition, permission was granted, and a program—consisting of 3 summer sessions—was developed in conjunction with CLEVELAND STATE UNIVERSITY. The program, receiving applications from across the country, is the first to offer the A.M.I. Degree (Association of Montessori Internationale) through summer sessions in the U.S.

MONTRESOR, JOHN (22 Apr. 1736–26 June 1799), served as an engineer in the British Army in North America between 1754–78. As a member of the Bradstreet Expedition into the Lake Erie region, he conducted the first preliminary survey of the CUYAHOGA RIVER. Montresor was born in Gibraltar. He served as an assistant engineer under his father in the Engineer Corps of the British Army, and came to America in 1754 with Maj. Gen. Edward Braddock. After the French & Indian War, he conducted a partial survey of the St. Lawrence River and built redoubts around British forts in Canada. In 1764, Montresor accompanied Col. John Bradstreet's expedition to Detroit as the chief engineering officer and commander of a detachment of Canadian volunteers. On the expedition's return, most of its ships were wrecked in a storm near Rocky River. Montresor, using one of the few remaining boats, engaged in minor exploration of some of Lake Erie's tributaries. According to his *Journal*, one of the rivers he apparently visited was the "Cayahuga." Montresor went approximately 5 mi. up the river, measuring the depth and width of the channel in order to learn its potential for navigation. He then returned to Canada and later worked on British fortifications in the present northeastern U.S., and helped establish the long-disputed boundary between New York and New Jersey. During the Revolutionary War, until his retirement due to poor health in 1778, he was the principal engineer of the British.

*Journals of Capt. John Montresor*, Collections of the New York Historical Society (1881).
Webster, John, *Life of John Montresor* (1928).

MONUMENTS. What a city may think of itself is expressed, in large part, by the monuments it chooses to build. The emphasis, the mix of subject matter, the recurrence of themes establish a mood and convey a message to those who reside there and those who visit that give a city its particularity; in a word, its character. There are 4 themes evident in the principal monuments of Cleveland: tribute to individuals who served their nation and state, e.g., monuments to Commodore Perry and JAS. A. GARFIELD; the honoring, collectively, of groups either for their public service, as in the case of the SOLDIERS & SAILORS MONUMENT, or for contributions to the community's heritage, as in the case of the Cultural Gardens; the conscious attempt to create the essence of a monument through rational order as seen in the Group Plan of 1903; and, lastly, an unself-conscious celebration of the city's spirit, as revealed in the Terminal Tower, which, under careful analysis, seems to summarize the essential meaning of this industrial community in monumental terms.

From its inception as a village in the wilderness, Cleveland set aside a place in its plan for memorials. PUBLIC SQUARE appears in the 1796 plan, quite explicitly designed as a civic center around which the city would grow eventually in a roughly symmetrical fashion to the east and west. That ideal could not be realized with geometric purity because of the CUYAHOGA RIVER, the initial retarded settlement to the west, and the then-unforeseen industrial concentration that would occur in the upper Cuyahoga River Valley and on the near west side, forcing an ever-widening wedge between the implied unity of the plan that could not be knit together even by the extraordinary array of more than 20 wood, steel, and concrete bridges that have spanned the river. An attempt was made to reinforce the monumental character and focus upon the center city with the Group Plan of 1903, which was planned tangential to and east of Public Square. It could have made Public Square irrelevant, had it not been for the construction of the Terminal Tower in the 1920s, which, located at the southwest corner of the square, with its ancillary structures embracing the south and west sides, restored the Square's prominence and established a diagonal axial link with the southwest corner of the Group Plan.

In Sept. 1860, Clevelanders dedicated their first major monument, a 25-ft.-tall, Italian-marble statue of Commodore Oliver Hazard Perry to the memory of the hero of the Battle of Lake Erie, which had occurred in Sept. 1813, 47 years earlier. Their gratitude for his leadership had endured, but it was to be forgotten in the next 40 years. When it was dedicated, the statue occupied the geometrical center of Public Square, reinforcing its significance to the community. By 1867, however, commercial pressure caused the Square itself to be bisected on both the north/south and east/west sides, creating 4 park quadrants in place of the original single park, and the Perry statue was moved to the southeast quadrant, only to be displaced entirely from the Square with the construction in the early 1890s of the Cuyahoga County Soldiers & Sailors Monument. From Public Square, the PERRY MONUMENT traveled first to WADE PARK, then to GORDON PARK. Eventually the original statue left town altogether, to settle in Perrysburg, Ohio. Thus, Clevelanders, from one generation to another, shifted from veneration to ambivalence to disinterest with regard to the achievements of America's Great Lakes naval hero of the WAR OF 1812.

The GARFIELD MONUMENT honoring Pres. Jas. A. Garfield, Cleveland's second great monument, stands on the crest of a hill east of the city in LAKE VIEW CEMETERY. It was constructed in 1890, 30 years after the Perry monument. The architect was Geo. W. Keller of Hartford, Conn. The composition consists of a main cylinder 50-ft. in diameter and 165 ft. Tall, capped by a conical roof, and flanked on the west by a stolid rectangular portico to which are attached 2 small transitional cone-capped turrets that join it to the main tower. The local sandstone has soaked up considerable industrial smoke over the years and has weathered to a deep, almost acrid brown. Its overall feeling is medieval and morose, and vaguely unpleasant, as though its purpose were more to mourn the tragic death of the martyred president than to celebrate the achievements of his life.

The Cuyahoga County Soldiers & Sailors Monument of 1894 by LEVI T. SCOFIELD stands in the southeast quadrant of Public Square. Until the Terminal Tower was built, this memorial to the county's 6,000 veterans dominated the Square, its 125-ft.-high granite column supporting a 15-ft.-tall statue of liberty, rising from a 100-ft.-square mausoleumlike base and platform, all overlain with elaborate carvings in tribute to the principal branches of mil-

| Title | Artist | Location | Date |
|---|---|---|---|
| King Alfred the Great | Konti, Isadore | Cuy. Co. Court House | 1912 |
| Audrey I | Snelson, Kenneth | CMA, Sculpture Garden | 1965 |
| Austin International Fountain | Ingrand, Max | Severance Center | — |
| Awakening | McVey, William | Donald Gray Gardens | 1936 |
| Bacchanale | Hoffman, Malvina | CMA, South Terrace | — |
| Back | Matteson, Ira | CWRU, Juniper & Magnolia | 1981 |
| Baldwin Wallace Memorial Fountain | — | BW, Chapel Sq. Mem. Garden | 1956 |
| Bell Harp | Clague, John | Beachwood Library | 1984 |
| David Berger Monument | Davis, David E. | Jewish Community Center | 1973–74 |
| Bird Building Tower | Schreckengost, Victor | Cleveland Metro. Zoo | 1951 |
| Bird Fountain | McVey, William | Vocational Guidance & Rehab. Headquarters | — |
| The Book of Knowledge Given Man | McVey, William | Grasselli Library, JCU | 1961 |
| Boy and Panther Cub | Hoffman, Malvina | CMA, South Terrace | — |
| Boy Scout Memorial | — | South Chagrin Reservation | 1950 |
| Branching Out | Meadmore, Clement | CMA, Sculpture Garden | 1981 |
| Bridge to Knowledge | Davis, David E. | Beachwood Library | 1984 |
| Bruno the Bear—See Old Grizzly | | | |
| City Fettering Nature | Blazys, Alexander | CMA, East Side | 1927 |
| Moses Cleaveland | Hamilton, James G. | Public Square | 1888 |
| Clench | Meadmore, Clement | Developers Diversified, Moreland Hills | 1980 |
| Coastlines | Black, David | CWRU Medical School Plaza | 1983 |
| Commerce | French, Daniel Chester | U.S. Federal Building | 1911 |
| Hart Crane | McVey, William | CWRU, Freiberger Library | 1985 |
| Dansa | Ginnever, Charles | Edgewater Park | 1981 |
| Daylight and Darkness | Aitken, Robert | Nela Park | 1923 |
| Door | Kangas, Gene | CSU | 1986 |
| Simon DeMontfort | Adams, Herbert | Cuy. Co. Court House | 1912 |
| Desire to Heal | Tradowsky, Michael | CWRU Dental School | 1973 |
| Eagle War Memorial | McVey, William | E. 55th & Hamm Ave. | 1954 |
| Earth | Beach, Chester | CMA, Fine Arts Garden | 1929 |
| Eclipse | Shingu, Susumu | Signature Square, Beachwood | — |
| Edge | Kangas, Gene | Cuy. Co. Justice Center | 1977 |
| King Edward I | French, Daniel Chester | Cuy. Co. Court House | 1912 |
| Energy in Repose | Hering, Henry | Federal Reserve Bank | 1923 |
| Eternal Life—See War Memorial Fountain | | | |
| Euclid Square Fountain | Van Duzer, Clarence | Euclid Square | — |
| Flame | Rosenberg, Yetta | Temple Branch | 1976 |
| For D.C. | Smith, Tony | CMA, Sculpture Garden | 1969 |
| For P.N. | Smith, Tony | CMA, Sculpture Garden | 1969 |
| Fountain | Fiero, Emilio | CMA, Fine Arts Garden | 1928 |
| Fountain of Light | — | Nela Park | 1940 |
| Fountain of the Rivers | Beach, Chester | CMA, Fine Arts Garden | 1928 |
| James A. Garfield Monument | Keller, Geo. (Arc.) | Lake View Cemetery | 1890 |
| Global Flight | Van Duzer, Clarence | Cleveland Hopkins Airport | 1976 |
| Goats | McVey, William | Cleveland Metro. Zoo | — |
| Good Samaritan | McVey, William | CWRU, Baker Building | — |
| Goethe-Schiller Statue* | — | Cultural Gardens | 1907 |
| Pope Gregory IX | Matzen, Herman | Cuy. Co. Court House | 1912 |
| Grid 14 | Fordyce, Jon | University Hospitals | 1983 |
| Gulls | McVey, William | McVey Residence | 1955 |
| John Hampden | French, Daniel Chester | Cuy. Co. Court House | 1912 |
| Alexander Hamilton | Bitter, Karl | Cuy. Co. Court House | 1912 |
| Leonard C. Hanna, Jr. Mall Fountains | — | Mall | — |
| Marcus A. Hanna | St. Gaudens, Augustus | Euclid Ave. at Univ. Circle | 1908 |
| Happy Frog | McVey, William | Riverside Park, Chagrin Falls | — |
| Harmonic Grid #20 | Davis, David E. | Progressive Insurance Co., Mayfield Village | 1977 |
| Harmonic Grid #44 | Davis, David E. | Beck Center, Lakewood | 1976 |
| Head of Pierre De Weissant | Rodin, August | CMA, Sculpture Garden | 1886 |
| Integrity | Hering, Henry | Federal Reserve Bank | 1923 |
| Thomas Jefferson | Bitter, Karl | Cuy. Co. Court House | 1912 |
| Tom L. Johnson | Matzen, Herman | Public Square | 1916 |
| Tom L. Johnson Memorial Fountain | Binz, Philip | Library Park, Fulton Road | 1914 |
| Jurisprudence | French, Daniel Chester | U.S. Federal Building | 1911 |
| Justinian | Matzen, Herman | Cuy. Co. Court House | 1912 |
| Helen Keller | Scher, I. Alan | Cleveland City Greenhouse | — |
| John F. Kennedy Memorial | — | Brook Park, Kennedy Park | 1972 |
| Tadeusz Kosciuszko | Trentanove, G. | Wade Park, near CMA | 1905 |
| Louis Kossuth | Toth, Andreas | Euclid Ave. at Univ. Circle | 1902 |
| Stephen Langton | Adams, Herbert | Cuy. Co. Court House | 1912 |

| Title | Artist | Location | Date |
|---|---|---|---|
| Last | Smith, Tony P. | Lausche State Office Bldg. | 1979 |
| Abraham Lincoln | Kalish, Max | Cleveland Brd. of Educ. Bldg. | 1932 |
| Linndale Peace Memorial | Savish, Savo | Linndale | 1975 |
| Long March | McVey, William | Jewish Community Center | 1970 |
| *Maine* Relic Memorial | — | Washington Park | 1948 |
| Man Helping Man (fountain) | McVey, William | Cleveland Clinic | 1974 |
| Man, Woman and Earth | Trapp, Wayne | Mayfield High School | 1972 |
| Man's Reach | Rosenberg, Yetta | Suburban Temple, Beachwood | 1978 |
| Chief Justice John Marshall | Adams, Herbert | Cuy. Co. Court House | 1912 |
| William Murray, Lord Mansfield | Bitter, Karl | Cuy. Co. Court House | 1912 |
| Medusa Head | McVey, William | Medusa Cement Co., Cleve. Hts. | — |
| Merging | Tacha, Athena | CWRU, Mather Quad. | 1987 |
| Mermaids | Landi, F. (finished by Chester Beach) | CMA Fine Arts Garden | 1929 |
| Michelson-Morley Fountain | Behnke, William A. | CWRU | — |
| Conrad Mizer Memorial Fountain | Matzen, Herman & Streibinger, Frederic | Edgewater Park | 1913 |
| Morning Star | Hudson, Jon | CWRU, near Amasa Stone Chapel | 1982 |
| Moses | Matzen, Herman | Cuy. Co. Court House | 1912 |
| Moses | Mestrovic, Ivan | Temple Branch | 1966 (acq.) |
| Mother and Daughter | Lipschitz, Jacques | CMA, Sculpture Garden | 1929–30 |
| Mother Goose | McVey, William | Beachwood Library | 1984 |
| McDog | McVey, William | Cleveland Garden Center | 1985 |
| Night Passing Earth to Day | Jirouche, Frank L. | — | 1928 |
| Noah's Ark | Stackhouse, Robert | Bell Tower, St. Agnes Church | — |
| Old Grizzly | McVey, William | Cleve. Museum of Nat. Hist. | 1932 |
| Outdoor Office | McGuire | Progressive Insurance Co., Mayfield Village | 1984 |
| Jesse Owens | McVey, William | Huntington Park | 1983 |
| Oliver Hazard Perry** | Walcutt, William | Gordon Park | 1860 |
| Polar Bears | McVey, William | Cleveland Metro. Zoo | — |
| Portal | Noguchi, Isamu | Cuy. Co. Justice Center | 1976 |
| Ohio Chief Justice Rufus P. Ranney | Adams, Herbert | Cuy. Co. Court House | 1912 |
| Archbishop Amadeus Rappe | Serrao, Luella V. | St. John's Cathedral | — |
| Harvey Rice | Hamilton, James G. | East Blvd. near CMA | — |
| Ritual Tower 1 | Wines, James | CMA, Sculpture Garden | 1959–60 |
| Rock Forms: Passage of the Seasons | Noguchi, Isamu | CMA, north entrance | 1981 |
| St. John Bosco | — | Holy Rosary Church | 1941 |
| St. Luke Reading the Gospel | Sinz, Walter | St. Luke's Hospital | 1929 |
| St. Patrick | Deprato Studio, Chicago (designers) | Sisters of the Incarnate Word, Parma Hts. | 1953 |
| Security | Hering, Henry | Federal Reserve Bank | 1923 |
| Sentimental Scales and Wedge | Hunt, Richard | Cuy. Co. Justice Center | 1977 |
| Slovenian War Memorial | — | Slov. Workingmen's Home | 1946 |
| Snowfence | Kangas, Gene | CWRU, Euclid | 1981 |
| Soldiers and Sailors Monument | Schofield, Levi T. | Public Square | 1894 |
| John Lord Sommers | Bitter, Karl | Cuy. Co. Court House | 1912 |
| Spirit of Care | McVey, William | Community Health Foundation Center | — |
| The Spirit of Parmadale | Wintrich, John W. | Parmadale | 1926 |
| Spitball | Smith, Tony P. | CWRU, Sears Library | 1972 (inst.) |
| Squaw Rock | Church, Henry | South Chagrin Reservation | — |
| Start | Davis, David E. | CWRU, Bellflower & Ford | 1981 |
| Gen. Milan R. Stefanik | Motosna, Miroslav | East Blvd. near E. 105th | 1924 |
| William Stinchcomb Memorial | McVey, William | Rocky River Reservation | 1960 |
| Sun | Beach, Chester | CMA, Fine Arts Garden | 1929 |
| Sundial | McVey, William | CWRU, Mather Quad. | 1986 |
| Survivor | Kangas, Gene | Progressive Insurance Co., Mayfield Village | 1982 |
| Swan | McVey, William | University School, Hunting Valley | — |
| Tempus Pons (Time Bridge) | Floyd, Carl | Market Square | 1985 |
| Tension Arches | Tacha, Athena | Euclid Ave. at Huron | 1976 |
| Terminal | Kangas, Gene | Lausche State Office Bldg. | 1979 |
| The Thinker | Rodin, August | CMA, south entrance | 1917 |
| Three Figures on Four Benches | Segal, George | Cuy. Co. Justice Center | 1981 |
| Tonal Sculpture | Bertoia, Harry | CMA, Sculpture Garden | — |
| Triad | Miller, Leon Gordon | CSU | 1978 |
| Triple-L Eccentric Gyratory | Rickey, George | National City Bank | — |
| Turtle Baby | Parsons, Edith Baretto Stevens | CMA, Sculpture Garden | — |
| Twelve Signs of the Zodiac | Beach, Chester | CMA, Fine Arts Garden | 1928 |
| Twist | Tacha, Athena | CWRU, Bellflower Road | 1981 |
| Unstable Tables | Floyd, Carl | CWRU, Carleton Road | 1982 |
| Untitled | Floyd, Carl | Cleve. Pub. Library, Pearl Rd. | 1978 |
| Untitled | Stephan, Gary | Progressive Insurance Co., Mayfield Village | 1985 |
| Veterans War Memorial, Garfield Hts. | — | Garfield Blvd. & Turney Rd. | 1970 |

690

| Title | Artist | Location | Date |
|---|---|---|---|
| Victory Island War Memorial—See Eagle War Memorial | | | |
| Jeptha Wade Memorial | Hubbell & Benes (Arc.) | Lake View Cemetery | 1898 |
| Richard Wagner | Matzen, Herman | Edgewater Park | 1911 |
| Walrus | McVey, William | Cleve. Pub. Lib. Eastman Br. | — |
| War Memorial Fountain*** | Fredericks, Marshall | Mall A | 1964 |
| Warrior Borghese | Keller, Johann Bathasa | CMA Terrace | — |
| George Washington | McVey, William | Celebrezze Fed. Bldg. | 1973 |
| Waywood Walls | Tyrrell, Brinsley | CWRU, Dental School | 1983 |
| We Care | McVey, William | Kaiser Med. Center, MLK Blvd. | 1965 |
| Edward A. Wiegand Memorial | — | Lakewood Park | 1933 |
| Wings of Eternity, Memorial to Martha Holden Jennings | McVey, William | Euclid Ave. at Abington Rd. | 1968 |

This list describes outdoor statuary and monuments in the Greater Cleveland area, with the exception of busts and plaques contained in the Cultural Gardens and with the exception of most statuary located in cemeteries. It is not meant to be comprehensive, but rather to provide a guide to the types of statuary/monuments in the area and to the artists active in their creation over the years.

Locations given are those current in 1986. Several abbreviations have been used in the location description: BW—Baldwin Wallace; CMA—Cleveland Museum of Art; CWRU—Case Western Reserve University; CPL—Cleveland Public Library; CSU—Cleveland State University.

*The Goethe-Schiller statue was originally located in Wade Park.

**The Perry Statue located in Gordon Park is a bronze replica of the original by Walcutt. The original is now in Perrysburg, Ohio.

***The War Memorial Fountain is also titled Peace Rising from the Flames of War.

(Table compiled by Tina Musgrave)

itary and naval service. In iconographic comprehensiveness, encyclopedic reference, and sheer exuberance, this monument is typical of its time. Its very ornateness may be its greatest strength, as the buildings around the square base have, with the exception of the Terminal Tower's upper portion, become increasingy large and spare of detail. The Soldiers & Sailors Monument, despite its great column, is designed to be experienced at close range. It is a pedestrian's monument, and one is meant to walk up to it and study the bas-reliefs and free-standing figural groups.

There are numerous sculptures scattered about Cleveland, from Public Square's Tom Johnson to University Circle's Harvey Rice, and the Museum of Art's Noguchi stones, as the listing within this essay records. But these are, in most instances, either too small in scale or sited so discreetly, or so indifferently, that they can hardly be considered as monuments as they are perceived or presented. Rather, they are nuances in the cityscape. Cleveland does have some very fine monumental architecture. The CLEVELAND MUSEUM OF ART's Beaux-Arts Neoclassic original building (1916) by Hubbell & Benes may be the best example, in part because of its handsome siting west of the Fine Arts Garden Lagoon. Its neighbor to the southeast, SEVERANCE HALL (1931) by Walker & Weeks, commands a difficult triangular-shaped lot at the East Blvd. intersection with Euclid Ave. that offers a dignified entrance to the UNIVERSITY CIRCLE area. Certainly the buildings of the Group Plan: city hall, the old Cuyahoga County courthouse, the post office, and the Public Library, are superb examples of Beaux Arts urban structural monuments, exuding a sense of self-confidence and civic pride.

Also among Cleveland's monuments are its dedicated landscapes, particularly the Cultural Gardens and the Fine Arts Garden mentioned above. The former, located along Martin Luther King, Jr. Blvd. (originally Liberty Blvd., a memorial to Clevelanders who died for their country in WORLD WAR I), pay tribute to the ethnic origins of the area's residents. At the time these were created, Cleveland was a city of immigrants. The overall impact of the Cultural Gardens does not come from any individual garden; rather, it is the product of the total complex. The monumental effect of the Fine Arts Garden is created by its relationship to the Museum of Art, the Epworth-Euclid Church, and

SEVERANCE HALL, and the tight bounding of its periphery by streets along its border. However, it is the Terminal Tower that, in the end, is the undisputed, premier monument of Cleveland. Its tiered, richly detailed, classical fairytale turrets standing upon an understated, plain base of offices and hotel rooms, which in turn once capped a subterranean concourse filled with the sounds of trains and trolleys and hordes of commuters and transient visitors, sums up all that the city was in its thriving industrial age of the 1850–1930 period. The tower has strong reference to the funerary monuments of classical antiquity. There is no other city where this secular faith is so clearly expressed or so little perceived.

Theodore Anton Sande
Western Reserve Historical Society

See also ARCHITECTURE.

The **MORELAND COURTS** are a range of luxury apartment buildings without peer in the city of Cleveland. Occupying an entire block 1,500 ft. long on Shaker Blvd., they were conceived as part of the plan that eventually became SHAKER SQUARE. Construction was begun in 1922 by JOSIAH KIRBY of the Cleveland Discount Co. The enterprise failed in 1923, and the Moreland Cts. were completed by the VAN SWERINGENS as part of their Shaker Square development between 1925–29. The architect of the original concept was ALFRED W. HARRIS, who spent 14 months in the planning, and descriptions indicate that his intention was to write "the entire history of English architecture" on the 1,500-ft. facade. The stylistic details from successive English periods range from the Late Gothic and Tudor to the Jacobean and Georgian. The connecting links between the 8-story and 6-story towers are treated as screens, and the relationships between mass and ornament are surprisingly effective. The block connecting the original section to the Shaker Square buildings was designed by Philip Small for the Van Sweringens. The 147 apartments range in size from 6 to 12 rooms, and the cohesive theme of English architecture is reflected in the interior details of fireplaces, ceilings, woodwork, and lobby design. In 1978, the apartment building was transformed into condominiums.

691

The village of **MORELAND HILLS** is a 7.5-sq.-mi. residential suburb located approximately 14 mi. east of Cleveland. It is bounded on the north by HUNTING VALLEY and PEPPER PIKE, on the south by SOLON and BENTLEYVILLE, on the east by CHAGRIN FALLS, and on the west by ORANGE VILLAGE. Moreland Hills is one of 7 communities that were formed out of the original Orange Twp., which was established in 1820. The village was incorporated on 9 Sept. 1929, and a village charter was adopted on 7 Nov. 1972, defining the municipal corporation with a mayor-council form of government. Settlement began in 1815 in the areas where the road that became Ohio Rt. 87 crosses the CHAGRIN RIVER. The families of Serenus Burnett, C. L. Jackson, and Seth Mapes were among the early settlers. In 1837, JAS. A. GARFIELD, second son of Abram Garfield and 20th president of the U.S., was born in a log cabin near SOM Ctr. and Jackson roads. During the 19th century, Orange Twp. was known for its steam sawmills, cheese factories, and productive farms. Beginning in 1897, the Cleveland-Chagrin Falls Railway contributed to the suburban development of Moreland Hills, bringing residents back and forth to employment in Cleveland, and visitors to an amusement park built by John Stoneman and to the adjoining Crystal Lake. The village began to change from a predominantly residential suburb with the subdivision of homesites in 1935 by real-estate developer Robt. L. Stern. The population in 1930 was 141; in 1940, it was 561. By 1956, it had risen to 1,700, and in 1980 it stood at 3,083. The children of Moreland Hills attend school in the Orange School District or in the Chagrin Falls School District. In addition to containing recreational facilities, churches, service clubs, polo fields, and riding trails, Moreland Hills is the location of Hiram House Camp. The S. Chagrin Reservation of the CLEVELAND METROPARKS SYSTEM runs through the village along the Chagrin Valley. Abram Garfield Farmsite Park commemorates the birthplace of Pres. Garfield.

Schregardus, Robt. E., ed., *Things Remembered—Moreland Hills at 50 Years* (1979).

**MORGAN, DANIEL EDGAR** (7 Aug. 1877–1 May 1949), was a prominent politician whose long career included service as a Cleveland city councilman, Ohio state senator, Cleveland city manager, and Ohio Court of Appeals judge. He was also active in many social-reform movements in the city. Morgan was born in Oak Hill, Jackson County, Ohio, to Elias and Elizabeth Jones Morgan. He received his B.A. in 1897 from Oberlin College and an LL.B. from Harvard Law School in 1901. While practicing law in Cleveland, he took an interest in public affairs and was elected as a Republican to CLEVELAND CITY COUNCIL from 1909–11. Involved in the campaign for local government HOME RULE, Morgan was a member of the Home Rule Charter Commission set up in 1913 to write a new charter for Cleveland. In the commission deliberations, he led the fight to retain the large council based on small wards, believing that the people should have a neighborhood representative they could turn to for help. He supported the nonpartisan elections called for in the charter as a way to eliminate graft and corruption from city government. In 1928 he was elected Ohio state senator. In Columbus, Morgan earned a reputation for improving pending legislation to make it more effective, and for his work on the state's election codes.

Cleveland had adopted the CITY MANAGER PLAN of government in 1923, and city council elected Morgan city manager to replace WM. R. HOPKINS in 1930. During his tenure, he successfully negotiated the settlements of

disputes over the water and gas rates; opened up all staff positions at City Hospital to Negroes; and persuaded the Cleveland School Board and the county officials to put a $31 million bond issue on the ballot to pay for a 5-year program of public works. Morgan used the public-works projects to provide jobs for the unemployed as the city began to feel the effects of the Depression. However, the mounting unemployment outstripped the means available to Morgan to alleviate the problems. In Nov. 1931, the plan was abolished, and the city returned to the mayorward system of government. Morgan ran for mayor unsuccessfully in 1932, defeated by Democrat RAY T. MILLER. Gov. John W. Bricker appointed him judge on the Ohio Court of Appeals in 1939. He was subsequently elected judge and continued to serve until his death. When Morgan first came to Cleveland, he was a resident at Goodrich House, which resulted in a lifelong association with the social-settlement movement in Cleveland. He supported the programs of the CONSUMERS LEAGUE and the LEGAL AID SOCIETY, as well, serving as trustee for all 3 organizations. He was also a founder and first president of the Cleveland CITY CLUB. He married Ella A. Matthews 22 Apr. 1915. She had come to Cleveland in 1914 to work for women's suffrage, a cause that Morgan supported. They had a daughter, Nancy Olwen (Mrs. Armand B. Leavelle), born in 1923. In 1926 he married Wilma Ball, daughter of jeweler Webb C. Ball.

Campbell, Thomas F., *Daniel E. Morgan, 1877-1949, The Good Citizen in Policics* (1966).
Daniel Edgar Morgan Papers, WRHS.

**MORGAN, GARRETT A.** (4 Mar. 1877 [sometimes given as 1879]–27 July 1963), was an important inventor and businessman active in the affairs of Cleveland's black community. Among his inventions were the gas mask and the traffic light. Morgan was born in Paris, Ky.; his father was the son of a Confederate colonel, and his mother, a former slave, was part Indian. Morgan received 6 years of education before leaving home at age 14 for Cincinnati, where he worked and hired a tutor to continue his education. He came to Cleveland on 17 June 1895. After various positions as a sewing-machine adjuster for clothing manufacturers, Morgan went into business for himself in 1907, establishing a shop on W. 6th St. To repair and sell sewing machines. In 1909 he opened a tailoring shop; with 32 employees, he manufactured suits, dresses, and coats. In 1913 he organized the G. A. Morgan Hair Refining Co. to market a hair-straightening solution he had discovered by accident in 1905. This company soon offered a complete line of hair-care products.

By 1915, Morgan had several inventions to his credit. He had developed a women's hat fastener, a round belt fastener, a friction drive clutch, and, most important, a safety helmet designed to protect the wearer from smoke and ammonia. Morgan introduced his "Breathing Device" in 1912, improved it in 1913–14, and patented it in 1914. He demonstrated its value after the Cleveland Waterworks explosion on 25 July 1916. Using his device, Morgan descended into the gas-filled tunnel beneath Lake Erie to rescue several workers and retrieve the bodies of the dead. Unable to persuade black Clevelanders to invest in a company to produce his safety hoods, Morgan turned to the white community to help establish the Natl. Safety Device Co. in 1914. He served as general manager of the company; other officers in 1915 included Victor W. Sincere and WM. GANSON ROSE. During WORLD WAR I, Morgan's "Breathing Device" was further developed into the gas mask used by combat troops. Morgan's other major invention was the traffic light, for which he received a patent in Nov. 1923. His hand-operated signal was unique in its use of a third, cautionary signal between "stop" and "go." Morgan sold his traffic light to the General Electric Co. for $40,000 in 1923.

As a leader in Cleveland's black community, Morgan helped to develop institutions to serve the needs of local blacks. In 1920 he founded the *Cleveland Call*, a weekly newspaper that he published for 3 years. In 1908 he helped found the CLEVELAND ASSOC. OF COLORED MEN and served as its treasurer. He was also a member of the Committee for the Home for Aged Colored People, the PHILLIS WHEATLEY ASSOC., and the NAACP. In 1923, Morgan bought a 121-acre farm near Wakeman, Ohio; there he established the exclusively black Wakeman Country Club and attempted to sell lots to develop Wakeman Hts., "a village of our own," according to his promotional cards. In 1931, Morgan unsuccessfully ran for a seat on the CLEVELAND CITY COUNCIL as an independent candidate. He developed glaucoma in the 1940s, but his gradual loss of vision did not prevent him from designing new products: in 1961 he introduced a pellet to be placed in cigarettes to prevent a fire if the smoker fell asleep with the cigarette still burning. Morgan was married twice. His first marriage, in 1896 to Madge Nelson, ended in divorce after 2 years. In 1908 he married Mary Hasek, a Bohemian seamstress he met at work.

Garrett Augustus Morgan Papers, WRHS.

**MORITZ, ALAN RICHARDS** (25 Dec. 1899–12 May 1986), was an internationally recognized pathologist, known primarily for his role in establishing forensic pathology on a sound scientific basis. He was also a distinguished educator and administrator at CASE WESTERN RESERVE UNIVERSITY and UNIVERSITY HOSPITALS OF CLEVELAND. Born in Hastings, Nebr., Moritz received his B.S., A.M., and M.D. degrees from the University of Nebraska, the last in 1923. (He also received an honorary D.Sc. There in 1950, as well as an honorary A.M. from Harvard in 1945.) He first came to Cleveland as a house officer at Lakeside Hospital in 1923–24, and as a research fellow and then instructor in pathology at the WRU School of Medicine, 1924–26. After a year in Vienna, Austria, Moritz returned to serve as a resident in pathology at Lakeside Hospital from 1927–31, advancing to pathologist in charge at University Hospitals, 1931–37. At WRU he held appointments as assistant, then associate professor of pathology from 1930–37. In 1937 he left for Harvard, where he was appointed professor of legal medicine; from 1937 to 1939 he was also the travelling fellow of the Rockefeller Foundation for the study of legal medicine, and during the 1940s served as consulting pathologist to the Massachusetts State Police Force and the Massachusetts Department of Mental Health, and as chief pathologist at Boston's Peter Bent Brigham Hospital.

In 1949 Moritz returned to Cleveland as professor of pathology at the School of Medicine, Director of the Institute of Pathology of WRU and University Hospitals, and chairman of the Hospitals' department of pathology. He stepped down from the two latter positions in 1965, when he became provost of WRU, after a year as vice-president there, and subsequently provost of Case Western Reserve University, through 1968. In 1969 he took up administrative duties at University Hospitals, first as Director of Professional Affairs, and then as Chief of Staff, from 1970 until his retirement in 1971. Moritz authored, co-authored or edited 9 books on forensic pathology and published over 100 articles in scientific journals. He belonged to many professional societies and in 1968 became president of the American Board of Pathology. The greatest honor granted to a pathologist by his peers was given him in 1970 by the American Association of Pathologists and Bacteriologists to recognize great achievements in the field. When Moritz went to Harvard, he established the nation's first department of legal medicine there. In Cleveland he helped to set up the Law-Medicine Center at WRU. Early on in his career, his campaign to replace the antiquated and sometimes incompetent system of lay coroners with qualified medical examiners in all states made him nationally known. His own expert testimony in cases of questionable death over the years, ranging from domestic violence to the death of a prisoner in South Africa (in 1969), from Cleveland's notorious SHEPPARD MURDER CASE to the investigation of the autopsy of U.S. President Kennedy, tended to overshadow his continuing research work in other areas of pathology, including arteriosclerosis, as well as his excellence as a teacher. In his own estimation, his work on thermal trauma was his greatest scientific contribution. Moritz married Velma Lucina Boardman in 1927; they had 2 sons.

**MORLEY, EDWARD WILLIAMS** (29 Jan. 1838–24 Feb. 1923), was a scientist and professor at Western Reserve University whose work with ALBERT MICHELSON laid a foundation for Albert Einstein's later work. Morley was born in Newark, N.J., but his family moved soon afterward to Hartford, Conn.; in 1851 they moved again, to Massachusetts. Morley attended Williams College, graduating as valedictorian in 1860 and then receiving his master's degree in 1863 from the Andover Theological Seminary. In 1866, after working for the Sanitary Commission during the CIVIL WAR, he taught at the South Berkshire Academy in Marlboro, Mass. In 1868, Morley received 2 job offers from Ohio: a clergyman's position in Twinsburg, and the chair of natural history and chemistry at Western Reserve College in Hudson. Choosing the latter, he embarked on a career teaching botany, zoology, geology, mathematics, mechanics, human physiology, and astronomy, in addition to chemistry and natural history. From 1873–88, he was professor of toxicology in WRC's Medical Department in Cleveland.

From 1878–82, Morley studied the concentration of oxygen in the atmosphere, and from 1882–93, he worked to determine the relative atomic weights of hydrogen and oxygen. In 1884, Morley began work with Albert A. Michelson, at first building an accurate interferometer (1885), then later conducting the famous Michelson-Morley experiment (1887), which found that the supposed all-pervasive ether had no apparent effect on the speed of light. The latter work contributed significantly to the upheaval in late-19th-century physics that was essentially resolved by Einstein's Special Theory of Relativity. Morley was president of the American Assoc. for the Advancement of Science in 1895 and of the American Chemical Society in 1899. In 1902 he finished second in balloting for the Nobel Prize in chemistry. In 1907 he received the Rumford Medal from the Royal Society (London). During his life, he published 55 papers. Morley retired as a professor emeritus to West Hartford, Conn., in 1906 with his wife, Isabella Birdsall Morley. They were childless.

University Archives, CWRU.

**MORMONS.** The Church of Jesus Christ of Latter-day Saints (Mormon) has experienced 2 distinct periods of its history in northeast Ohio. The "Kirtland Era," which took place in the early 19th century, constitutes an important phase in Mormon history. A dominant theme in early Mormon history, including the "Kirtland Era," was that of the Saints gathering at a specifically identified geographic location in order to "build up the Kingdom of God." The later period, which has no distinctive name, has taken place in the era following World War II and is part of a larger historical development wherein the LDS Church has expanded its numbers and influence beyond the confines of the intermountain West. Joseph Smith, Jr., and 5 other men legally organized and incorporated the Church of Jesus Christ on 6 Apr. 1830 in Fayette, N.Y. (The phrase "of Latter-day Saints" was added in 1838.) The new church quickly attracted converts. Many of them became zealous missionaries, including Parley P. Pratt. Pratt, a former Campbellite preacher from Ohio, helped to introduce Mormonism into the WESTERN RESERVE, an area ripe for the restored religion. When Pratt returned to the Western Reserve from New York in Nov. 1830, he looked up a friend, Sidney Rigdon, a former Campbellite minister. Pratt and Oliver Cowdery were allowed to preach the restored doctrines of Mormonism to Rigdon's congregations in Mentor and Kirtland. Rigdon was so impressed that he read the Book of Mormon and admonished his congregations to carefully investigate the message presented to them. Conversion to Mormonism quickly followed for Rigdon and about 127 members of his flock. News of the success in the Kirtland area reached Joseph Smith, Jr., who still resided in western New York. In Dec. 1830, Smith received a revelation directing the Mormons in western New York to "assemble together in Ohio." In Jan. 1831, Joseph Smith, Jr., his wife, Emma, and their son, Joseph III, arrived in Kirtland. With the arrival of the Prophet and the New York membership during 1831, Kirtland became a physical and spiritual focal point for the Mormons.

Although Mormon activity was centered in the counties east of Cuyahoga County, proselytizing produced mixed results through the Western Reserve. In 1831, Mormon missionaries baptized John Murdock, a farmer who lived near Warrensville, Cuyahoga County. In turn, Murdock preached throughout the eastern portion of the county. Eventually 55 residents were baptized because of his efforts. Between 1831-38, 4 branches of the LDS Church were established in Mayfield, ORANGE, STRONGSVILLE, and Warrensville. The Shaker communities of northeast Ohio, including the one located at N. UNION (now SHAKER HTS.), also attracted the attention of the Mormons. In Mar. 1831, Joseph Smith directed Rigdon, Pratt, and Leman Copley to proselytize among the Shakers. The Shakers proved unreceptive to the Mormon message, and the effort was discontinued. Kirtland eventually lost its favored position. The attention of the Prophet as well as material goods and people were increasingly diverted to Jackson County, Mo., following a revelation in July 1831 that designated the area as the new Mormon Zion. Economic problems in Kirtland caused disharmony within the church during the mid-1830s. Dealings in land speculation provided quick profits for some, bankrupted others, and destroyed friendships. With the failure of the Kirtland Anti-Banking Safety Society, many in the church discounted Joseph Smith as a fallen prophet. He had helped to establish and run the institution for the Mormons to generate capital for the payment of debts. Finally, persecution from local residents outside the LDS Church increased over time. With the departure of the Prophet and many of the Saints from Ohio in 1838, the "Kirtland Era" of Mormon history came to a close. Over the next 10 years, the Mormons would be expelled from Missouri, build the city of Nauvoo, Ill., and consequently be forced to make their historic trek westward to the Great Salt Lake Valley, beginning in 1847. For nearly 100 years following the establishment of the Mormon Kingdom in Utah, the LDS Church administered to the needs of a scattered membership in northeast Ohio through administrative units known as missions.

In 1946, one branch of the LDS Church encompassed not only the city of Cleveland but also a large part of northeast Ohio. Members traveled from as far as the Pennsylvania border, Sandusky, and Hudson to attend Sunday services in a rented room in the Carter Hotel. The average attendance was 30. By 1986, the same boundaries housed 2 stakes comprising 15 wards, and 3 branches. Total membership stood at over 4,800. A Mormon stake and ward are analogous to a diocese and parish respectively. A branch is smaller in membership than a ward. At the stake level, 2 significant developments affected the LDS membership in Cuyahoga County. In Oct. 1961, a large portion of northeast Ohio was organized into the Cleveland Stake. The new stake administered to the needs of over 2,400 Latter-day Saints, who were organized into 8 wards and 3 branches. In 1983, the Kirtland stake was organized and took in the eastern portion of its mother stake. With the boundaries of the Cleveland and Kirtland stakes running north and south through PUBLIC SQUARE, each stake had within its geographic confines the western and eastern portions of Cuyahoga County respectively.

For nearly 20 years following the end of the war, the core of Cuyahoga County's LDS population consisted largely of transplanted westerners. Having moved into the Cleveland area because of job transfers, professional opportunities, and matriculations at local educational institutions, these relocated Latter-day Saints formed the nucleus of the local Mormon population. They helped strengthen a growing local body. Throughout the late 1940s and early 1950s, most of the local membership lived on the west side. During the years 1947-48, steps were taken to build a meeting house on Cleveland's west side. A parcel of land was purchased on Lake Ave. near Detroit Rd. A small 2-story structure was completed in 1950. As most of the members lived on the west side, consequently so did much of the priesthood and auxiliary leadership of the Cleveland Branch. Increasingly, a significant portion of the branch's population came to be composed of students attending Western Reserve University's School of Dentistry. These students, most of them having come east from Utah with their young families, were familiar, along with their spouses, with church government and the various auxiliary programs. Throughout the late 1940s and early 1950s, the dental students congregated in the LAKEWOOD area. When housing there became inadequate, the majority migrated to the east side and took up residence in CLEVELAND HTS. and Shaker Hts. Together with a small number of permanently relocated Mormons and a growing convert population, the student families helped to make up a viable Latter-day Saint population on the east side. In 1955, the Euclid Branch was organized. The majority of its leadership came from the student families residing within its boundaries.

The Euclid Branch, later renamed the Cleveland East Branch, stretched from Public Square to the Pennsylvania border. While most of its members resided on or near Cleveland's east side, there were families, mainly converts, scattered throughout the far eastern portions of the branch. All of the meetings and activities took place in the homes of members and in several community buildings, including the Brainard Community Ctr., the Mayfield YMCA, and various public schools. Inability to find a suitable site for a meeting house stymied construction attempts throughout the late 1950s. In 1962, a parcel on Cedar Rd. in Mayfield, just west of SOM Ctr. Rd., was purchased. The meeting house was begun in 1966 and completed in 1967. In 1969, after it had been fully paid for, the building was dedicated. The Cleveland East Branch became a ward in Oct. 1961 when the Cleveland Stake was organized. Since then, membership growth and ward proliferation have taken place east of Cuyahoga County, as well as within the boundaries of the county itself. A ward was established in Ashtabula in 1968; another in Kirtland in 1977. In 1986, 3 wards share the eastern portion of Cuyahoga County. They include the Mayfield, Shaker Hts., and Solon wards. Approximately 700 Latter-day Saints reside in eastern Cuyahoga County.

Following the student immigration from the west side, the population of the Cleveland Branch was reduced to 2 components, permanently relocated westerners and local converts. Both components grew, and by 1966, the Lakewood Chapel had become too small to house the west side branch. After selling the Lakewood building to a Lutheran congregation, members of the Cleveland Branch worshipped and held social activities in community buildings and private homes for 2 years. In 1968, a new building was completed on Westwood Rd. in WESTLAKE. The building housed 2 wards and the offices of the Cleveland Stake. A second chapel located on Rockside Rd. in SEVEN HILLS was completed in 1979. Individual branches of the Mormon church were established west of Cuyahoga County in Lorain and Sandusky in the 1950s. Consequently, the proliferation of the Cleveland Ward has occurred within the confines of western Cuyahoga County. In 1986, 4 LDS wards occupy the area. They include the Cleveland, N. Olmsted, Seven Hills, and Westlake wards. Approximately 1,200 Latter-day Saints now reside in western Cuyahoga County. The establishment of the Cleveland and Kirtland stakes and the subsequent organization of new wards within their boundaries were indicators of the numerical growth experienced by the LDS church throughout northeast Ohio, including Cuyahoga County, since the end of World War II. The average ward has 300 members. The creations of new stakes and wards are affirmations by LDS officials in Salt Lake City that a particular area is able to supply its own leadership and guidance to local church government and programs. This level of maturity is necessary to obtain before a stake and its wards can be organized as such since the LDS Church has no professional clergy and relies completely upon a lay priesthood and volunteer service. Within the broader picture of an expanding, 20th century LDS Church, the development of the Mormon Church in Cuyahoga County since 1946, has reflected the themes of numerical growth and continious maturing.

Harry F. Lupold
Lakeland Community College

Robert Psuik
Case Western Reserve University

Arrington, Leonard J. and Bitton, Davis. *The Mormon Experience: A History of the Latter-day Saints* (1980).
Backman, Milton. *The Heavens Resound: A History of the Latter-day Saints in Ohio, 1830-1838* (1983).

**MORRIS, CHARLES** (13 Aug. 1869–27 Jan. 1930), was one of Cleveland's most distinguished classical architects, active in Cleveland from 1902–05, and again from 1923–30. Morris was educated and received architectural training in New York. He was employed as an office boy by Carrere & Hastings in 1885, shortly after they first established their office. In 1891 he went to Paris to study at the Ecole des Beaux-Arts for 2 years. Returning to New York, he began an association with Richard Walker in Brooklyn, whose firm designed a number of Carnegie Library buildings. In 1902, Morris was invited to Cleveland to assist architects LEHMAN & SCHMITT in the design of the CUYAHOGA COUNTY COURTHOUSE. He became the principal designer, producing what has been called by a contemporary "one of the finest court houses in the country." In 1905 he planned the Broadway Free Library, a Carnegie library, on E. 55th St. He then returned to Walker & Morris and helped in the design of the 22d Regimental Armory, the Municipal Ferry Houses at S. Ferry, and the bridge and pavilions on Riverside Dr. After Walker & Morris broke up, Morris was appointed chief designer in the office of the supervising architect of the U.S. Treasury, where he designed a large number of post offices throughout the country during the 1910s. At the end of WORLD WAR I he moved to Cleveland, and in 1923 he joined JOSEPH WEINBERG to form the firm of Morris & Weinberg. They designed a number of successful commercial buildings, but their major work may be BELLEFAIRE (the Jewish Orphan Asylum) in UNIVERSITY HTS. Opened in 1929, it is a model residential campus based on the "cottage" plan. Morris was elected a fellow of the American Institute of Architects and served as president of the Cleveland Chap. in 1925–26. He was one of the founders of the Cleveland School of Architecture and served as its secretary until the school became affiliated with Western Reserve University in 1929. Morris married Jane Walker on 30 Apr. 1903 in Brooklyn, N.Y. They had 2 children, Jean and Robert.

The **MOSES CLEAVELAND STATUE**, erected in 1888 in honor of the 92d birthday of the city's founding, dominates the southwest quadrant of PUBLIC SQUARE. Erected by the EARLY SETTLERS ASSOC., whose members trace their heritage to pioneers of Cleveland, at a cost of $4,378, the statue was sculpted by J. C. Hamilton. It shows Gen. Cleaveland dressed as a surveyor, with Jacob's staff in his right hand and a compass in his left. The monument is 7'10" high and rests on a circular pedestal 7' high. Before casting the statue in bronze, the artist presented a plaster representation to the CLEVELAND CITY COUNCIL that was rejected because it was too tall. After a section was removed from Cleaveland's midriff and the halves were rejoined, Hamilton's work was accepted and cast in one piece, weighing 1,450 lbs. The statue was installed in the Square in a gala ceremony on 22 July 1888. The Early Settlers Assoc., accompanied by the CLEVELAND GRAYS, the Guard of Honor, marched from the Music Hall to Public Square for the unveiling. A. J. Williams read a speech by the ailing ESA president, HARVEY RICE. A program followed in the Music Hall, featuring an address by Samuel E. Adams. Throughout its history, the statue has withstood Public Square renovations, attempts to move it to UNIVERSITY CIRCLE, and rats in the base, and it remains a proud symbol of Cleveland.

The **MOSES CLEAVELAND TREES** were chosen from throughout Cuyahoga County as part of the sesquicentennial of Moses Cleaveland and his party's landing at the mouth of the Cuyahoga River on 22 July 1796. Each tree was of such an age as to have been part of the area's forests at the time of the landing. As part of Cleveland's 150th-anniversary celebration, the Cleveland Sesquicentennial Commission appointed the Committee on Moses Cleaveland Trees, whose objective was the discovery and labeling of 150 native trees over the age of 150 years growing in the county. Chair of the committee was Arthur Williams, curator of education at the CLEVELAND MUSEUM OF NATURAL HISTORY.

Each community in the county had the opportunity to nominate trees from its own neighborhoods. Through correspondence and publicity, the committee received nominations for 242 large trees. Each tree was inspected by the chairman and 1 or more committee members. Measurements of the trees' diameter were taken at a 4″ height with a steel tape, and the trees were critically judged as to the probability of their being 150 years or older. The desirability of each tree's location was also taken into account, as the committee sought as far as possible to select only those trees that were located along roadsides and park trails and in other places where they could be easily seen and appreciated by the public. Only a few outstanding trees located behind houses or considerably removed from the roadway were marked.

Local ceremonies accompanied the labeling of many trees. There were a total of 25 political subdivisions and 23 species represented, led by the white oak, sugar maple, American elm, and beech. Each tree's 5″x10″ aluminum label had a white lacquered background with etched lettering filled in with red enamel. The inscription read: "This is a Moses Cleaveland Tree. It was standing here as part of the original forest when Moses Cleaveland landed at the Mouth of the Cuyahoga River, July 22, 1796. Let us preserve it as a living memorial to the first settlers of the Western Reserve."

Williams, Arthur, *Final Report of the Sesquicentennial Commission's Committee on Moses Cleaveland Trees* (1946).

**MOSIER, HAROLD GERARD** (24 July 1889–7 Aug. 1971), served in the Ohio senate, in the U.S. Congress, and as lieutenant governor of Ohio. He made a reputation fighting against Communist influence in American life. Mosier was born to M. G. and Anna Hogsett Mosier in Cincinnati. Educated in the public schools of Highland and Clinton counties, he moved to Cleveland for his high school education, living with his uncle Thos. Hogsett. After graduating from East High School, he earned the A.B. degree from Dartmouth in 1912 and the LL.B. degree from Harvard University in 1915. He married Grace Hoyt Jones in 1918. Admitted to the Ohio bar in 1915, Mosier entered practice with the law firm of TOLLES, HOGSETT, GINN & MORLEY. He remained with the firm until 1920, serving 1 year during WORLD WAR I with the U.S. Ordnance Dept. In 1921, he helped form the law firm of Christopher, Mosier & Dover, leaving in 1930 to form the firm of Minshall & Mosier with Wm. Minshall.

Elected to the Ohio senate in 1932, Mosier authored the Ohio Liquor Control Bill and legislation ratifying the constitutional amendment repealing Prohibition. In the senate, he served as chairman of the Judiciary Committee and headed the Cuyahoga County legislative delegation. Elected lieutenant governor in 1934, he withdrew his candidacy for governor in 1936 to run for the U.S. House of Representatives. There he served as a member of the Dies Committee investigating "un-American" activities. Fighting to rid the country of Communist influence, he became known as the "Dies Red-Hunter." defeated in the 1938 primary, Mosier ran for governor in Ohio in 1940, but he was defeated. Admitted to the Maryland bar in 1943, he served as counsel to the Glenn Martin Co. in Baltimore, 1942–52, and as a legislative advisor to the Aircraft Industries Assoc. in Washington, D.C., from 1952–60, when he retired.

The *MOTHERS' AND YOUNG LADIES' GUIDE* was not only the first magazine believed to have been published in Cleveland but also the only women's periodical issued at the time in the West. Published by Timothy H. Smead, proprietor of the *OHIO CITY ARGUS*, it first appeared in June 1837. Throughout its 3-year existence, it was edited by Mrs. MARIA M. HERRICK. Although its subscribers ranged from New York to Illinois, the *Guide* circulated primarily in the Western Reserve. Sixteen pages in length, it resembled the early *Reader's Digest* in format and sold for $1 per year. The *Guide* devoted its columns almost exclusively to domesticity and sentimentality, with hardly a gesture toward militance or protest. Among its contents were such titles as "Treatment of Infants," "Female Education," "Evils of Tight Lacing," "Matrimony—A Great Mistake," "How to Ruin a Son," and "Ought Ladies to Write?" Most of its material during the first 2 years appeared to be original, some of it by males. A dearth of paying subscribers clouded the *Guide*'s last year of publication. Although expanded to 32 pages, it began to be filled almost entirely with long reprinted articles. After a combined issue for December-January, the *Guide* expired with the completion of its 3d volume, in May 1840.

**MOUNT HERMON BAPTIST CHURCH** was one of a number of major churches to come out of SHILOH BAPTIST CHURCH, the largest black church of that denomination in Cleveland in the mid-19th century. Organized in 1926, the church was the direct result of the merger of 2 small congregations, St. Paul and Mt. Carmel Baptist. After a series of ministers, 23-year-old Rev. Robt. Fuller became pastor in 1937; as of 1986 he was still serving in that capacity. Located at E. 38th and Woodland until 1939, the congregation moved to 2516 E. 40th St., where it was still located in 1986.

**MOUNT PLEASANT** is a section of southeast Cleveland bounded by Milverton, Abell, Griffing, and Parkhill on the north, Martin Luther King Blvd. on the west, E. 155th St. on the east, and Harvard on the south, with Kinsman as the main thoroughfare. Settled by successive immigrant groups, the section eventually became a stable area of black homeowners. Despite its changing composition, Mt. Pleasant has always been characterized by an attitude of neighborhood pride. The first residents of the area were Manx farmers who migrated there in 1826. It remained rural until 1921, when Joseph Krizek and his partners bought 20 acres southwest of Kinsman, where they mapped out streets and planted 248 maple trees along Bartlett St. The area received its name from its comely appearance. Among the immigrant groups who succeeded the Manx in Mt. Pleasant were GERMANS, CZECHS, RUSSIANS, JEWS, and ITALIANS. For many years the Jewish Council Educational Alliance at E. 135th and Kinsman drew 1,200 members for classes in citizenship, gym, sewing, photography, etc., while nationality clubs offered similar fare for their countrymen.

Unlike other areas of the city where BLACKS occupied housing abandoned by whites, Mt. Pleasant counted blacks among its earliest citizens. Reportedly, in 1893, a contractor who employed a large number of black workers was unable to pay wages in cash, so he gave them title to lots in the section north of Kinsman between E. 126th and E. 130th. The title holders built homes there; by 1907, there were 100 black families, and 100 other lot owners. The area was advertised in black newspapers as a suburban paradise, away from the smoke of the city, where blacks could buy a home, raise a family, and go to church. The section was noted for its high percentage of blacks who were homeowners. By the mid-1950s, more prosperous blacks moved to the Ludlow area of Shaker, adjacent to Mt. Pleasant. To prevent neighborhood deterioration, the Mt. Pleasant Community Council and block clubs fought delinquency, crime, and housing violations. In the 1960s, such efforts were intensified as the area was named a Neighborhood Development Project and received funds for small-scale urban renewal of housing; through the Mt. Pleasant Community Council Development Foundation, residents received financial and technical assistance to rebuild their homes. With the aid of CLEVELAND: NOW! and the United Appeal, the community-services center was relocated, and eventually the Murtis H. Taylor Multiservice Ctr. was built at 13422 Kinsman to provide recreation and centralize social services for residents. Programs such as the Mt. Pleasant Youth Action Council were set up to involve teenagers in off-the-street activities. Ever threatened by poverty and decay, the area was considered a target for large-scale urban renewal in 1983. To assist the professionals who donated time to create an enterprise zone there, residents contributed their time and efforts. The Red Berets were formed to fight crime with neighborhood patrols, and business owners undertook a major effort to clean up Kinsman.

The **MT. SINAI MEDICAL CENTER,** a nonprofit, university-affiliated medical center dedicated to a broad program of care, teaching, and research, grew out of the work of the Young Ladies' Hebrew Assoc. The association was founded for the purpose of providing "care for the needy and sick" in 1892. In 1902 the name was changed to the Jewish Women's Hospital Assoc., and a private residence on E. 37th St. was purchased and converted into a 29-bed hospital. The need for larger, improved facilities led to the formation of the Jewish Hospital Assoc. of Cleveland in 1912 and the opening in 1913 of the East Side Free Dispensary on E. 55th St. A board of trustees was elected, and later that year the name Mt. Sinai was adopted. Fundraising for a new building was authorized by the Jewish Welfare Fed., and in 1916 a new 160-bed hospital was completed on E. 105th overlooking WADE PARK. A survey by the Cleveland Hospital Council of area health facilities in the 1920s showed that Mt. Sinai had a greater diversity of cases than any other hospital, and that many of the cases came from outside its logical zone of service. From the beginning, half of its patients were non-Jewish. In 1927, $1.35 million was raised for new expansion that included a nurses' home for the Mt. Sinai School of Nursing, a research laboratory, and an out-patient dispensary. In terms of specialization, the hospital was well-known at this time for its fight against infantile paralysis.

During its first 3 decades, Mt. Sinai had only 2 presidents: Paul L. Feiss and Max Myers. The first director of medicine, Alfred S. Maschke, is credited as being the founder and developer of the hospital's Dept. of Medicine. Among Mt. Sinai's early eminent researchers was Dr. Benjamin S. Kline, who perfected a new slide test for disease and centered international attention on the hospital's laboratory. In the 1960s, Drs. HARRY GOLDBLATT and Erwin Haas, while working at the hospital's Beaumont Memorial Labratory, became internationally known for their work in biochemistry. Mt. Sinai became a teaching hospital in 1947 when it affiliated with the Western Reserve University School of Medicine. In 1951, bed capacity was increased to 390 through expansion and renovation, which included the Katy Sanders Laboratory for experimental surgery. With help from a community investment of $7 million, a 12-story building was added in 1960, increasing bed capacity to 524. Further expansion included a 10-bed kidney-dialysis center and construction of the Max Freedman Clinic for out-patient care. By 1967, Mt. Sinai, partly supported by funds from the United Appeal and the Jewish Welfare Fund, was one of the most heavily used area hospitals by poor families.

In the 1970s, Mt. Sinai continued to offer the basic services of medicine, surgery, obstetrics, pediatrics, psychiatry, and rehabilitation. Specialized services included open-heart surgery, renal transplant and dialysis, neonatal intensive care, and an organ bank. The School of Nursing graduated its last class in 1970. Continued expansion included the opening of a new laboratory facility for patient care and research, and the opening, in 1972, of an outpatient clinic in BEACHWOOD to serve the eastern suburbs. In 1978, Mt. Sinai officials floated a plan to reduce the 549-bed hospital to 150 beds and shift some of its services to the eastern suburbs. The plan was abandoned after criticism, led by city council president Geo. Forbes, that the facility was abandoning the black community. With the aid of tax-exempt hospital revenue bonds, a $95 million construction project was launched that resulted in the completion of a new wing in the early 1980s.

**MT. ZION CONGREGATIONAL CHURCH** came into existence in June 1864 when a small group of persons led by Edward Woodliff banded together as a prayer group. Former members of SHILOH BAPTIST CHURCH, they were soon joined by others and, after much discussion, decided that the Congregational order was best suited to their religious needs. The formal organization of the church took place at Plymouth Congregational Church. Thus, it became the first Congregational church organized by and for black worshippers east of the Mississippi. Guidance and encouragement came from all of the Congregational churches in the city. Rev. J. H. Meese was appointed as the first minister, and a church home was erected at Erie (E. 9th) St. and Webster Ave. Subsequent moves included occupation of church buildings at Maple (E. 31st) St., E. 55th St. and Central Ave. (in a structure formerly occupied by the TEMPLE), and 9014 Cedar Ave. In 1954, the congregation erected its current (1986) edifice at 10723 Magnolia Ave. Historically, Mt. Zion has offered its facilities and resources for a variety of social services. During the Depression, the church (then at the E. 55th location) became known as a clearinghouse for Negro problems. Later, the city's first black Girl Scout troop, a day nursery for working mothers, the URBAN LEAGUE OF CLEVELAND's Street Academy, and Friendly Town were among the social services centered in church-owned buildings. Membership in Mt. Zion has traditionally included many of the city's black leaders and professionals.

**MOVIES FILMED IN CLEVELAND** began with an educational version of *Snow White* (1916), the first of only 2 historically chronicled silent films made in Cleveland. The other was titled *The Perils of Society* (1916). The first "talkie" made in Cleveland was *It Happened in Cleveland* (1936). Locally financed and cast from students at John Marshall High School, the 2-reel film was shot at the school, the ballroom of the Hotel Statler, and also the Trianon Ballroom, then located at E. 93rd and Euclid Ave. *The Kid from Cleveland* (1949) is about a sportswriter who helps a kid go straight. It was filmed in Cleveland using the members of the 1948 World Series-winning Indians in scenes in and outside the Municipal Stadium and in other downtown locations (including the FLATS). Local actors, including former Play House director K. Elmo Lowe, were used for some supporting roles.

After realistic location shooting become more prevalent, moviemaking started to move out of Hollywood more often. The first effect was felt in Cleveland with *One Potato, Two Potato* (1964), about a divorced woman now remarried to a black man and fighting for custody of their daughter. Much of the film was made in Painesville. The first big commercial film made in Cleveland was *The Fortune Cookie* (1966), a comedy about a TV cameraman who is injured on the sidelines during a football game and decides to sue the CLEVELAND BROWNS with the aid of his lawyer brother-in-law. Staged scenes were shot in Municipal Stadium, where more than 10,000 Clevelanders gathered as extras to play the roles of fans. Additional footage was shot during a real football game on the following Sunday. Other scenes were filmed outside Public Square, outside St. Vincent Charity Hospital (called St. Mark's in the movie), and along side streets and other main traffic arteries.

*Up Tight* (1968) was a loose remake of the famous John Ford film *The Informer* (1935) about Irish revolutionaries, which used the black ghetto areas of Cleveland's east side to tell the story of militants betrayed by one of their own members. The crew spent 5 weeks shooting in the streets of Cleveland and heavily involved the black community, recruiting actors from the Karamu Theater. That same year, independent producers Roger and Gerald Sindell pooled their resources to make *Double-Step* (1968), a domestic tragedy involving the family of a cellist with the Cleveland Orchestra. Featured were scenes filmed in SHAKER HTS., at the Garfield estate in BRATENAHL, and in the Fine Arts Garden (where a murder takes place). The music score was played by the Cleveland Symphony Orchestra.

Hoping to capitalize on the success of the Broadway play *Hair*, producer John Pappas brought a crew to Cleveland to make cinema history's first full-length tribal rock musical movie, *Aquarius* (1970). Open auditions for singing and dancing parts for hippie and nonhippie types were held in facilities off PLAYHOUSE SQUARE. In one day, more than 2,000 lined up along Euclid Ave. hoping for a chance at a role. Scenes were filmed in places as diverse as the CLEVELAND MUSEUM OF ART and local bowling alleys. Interior scenes were set up in makeshift studios in a Playhouse Square building. *Aquarius* premiered in Cleveland at the Fox Cedar Ctr. Theater. Shaker Hts. native and local filmmaker Harold Cornsweet came home to make a comedy called *Return to Campus* (1973), about an older man who returns to college and winds up playing on the football team. Cornsweet used locales familiar to him in Shaker Hts., in addition to scenes on the campus of Ohio State University in Columbus.

Moviemaking in Ohio truly began to boom with the establishment of the Ohio Film Bureau in 1976. One of the first films to be made in Cleveland as a result of its efforts was *The Deer Hunter* (1977), which told of the effect of the Vietnam war experience on the lives of a group of regular guys. It was named Best Picture of the Year. ST. THEODOSIUS RUSSIAN ORTHODOX CATHEDRAL and nearby LEMKO HALL in Cleveland's industrial valley provided the setting for a fictional wedding and reception. Scenes were also filmed inside the blast furnaces of U.S. Steel and outside residential areas of the near west side. More than 400 Clevelanders were used as extras. *The Gathering* (1977) was a made-for-TV movie about a man dying of cancer who comes home to make amends with his wife. The entire movie was filmed on location in CHAGRIN FALLS, Hudson, and Cleveland, which was translated in the movie into a generic New England city. A special premiere showing for extras was arranged, prior to TV broadcast, at the Falls Theater in Chagrin Falls. Actress Natalie Wood strolled in front of the downtown MAY CO. department store and other storefronts along Euclid Ave. near Public Square for the made-for-TV movie *The Cracker Factory* (1979). Based on the book by Cleveland-area author Joyce Rebeta-Burditts, the Cleveland scenes amount to only these few exterior shots. The remainder of this film about a woman's struggle with alcoholism was made in Hollywood.

Cleveland in the 1950s was portrayed in the real Cleveland of the 1970s for the film *Those Lips, Those Eyes* (1979). Cleveland Hts.' open-air CAIN PARK THEATER was the setting for this story of a young premed student acting in summer stock while trying to decide about his future. Clevelander and Case Western Reserve University graduate David Shabar wrote the screenplay. Local actors, singers, and dancers were used in the scenes shot on the stage. The biggest benefit came for Cain Park itself, which underwent $100,000 worth of renovation paid for by the film company. The movie premiered at the Cedar-Lee Theatre. Singer Paul Simon, half of the folk-singing duo of Simon & Garfunkel, came to Cleveland to make *One Trick Pony* (1979), because he felt Cleveland was the rock 'n' roll capital of the world. Simon wrote the story and music for this tale of an aging rock star at the crossroads of his life. Auditions for local musical talent were held at the Agora nightclub near the campus of CLEVELAND STATE UNIVERSITY. Some interior scenes were also filmed there. The crew also went to BALDWIN-WALLACE COLLEGE to shoot some sequences. *The Escape Artist* (1980) told the story of a young magician who achieves success early in life and then has a difficult time adapting to an adult world. The crew spent more than $1 million in Cleveland and, along the way, filmed pieces of the movie downtown near City Hall and the county courthouse and in the Flats, OHIO CITY, and the Cedar Rd. and Fairmount Blvd. area.

The main floor of the Higbee Co. department store, as well as all of Public Square, was transported back in time through the addition of costumes, scenery, and old cars for the offbeat comedy *A Christmas Story* (1983), a tale told in flashback of a man remembering Christmas as a boy. In addition to the scenes filmed inside the transformed Higbee's 1st floor, outside, a resplendent Christmas parade, complete with floats and vintage cars, marched through downtown before the rolling cameras. In 1985, the Cleveland Film Festival featured *Stranger Than Paradise* (1984), directed by former Clevelander Jim Jarmusch. The highly lauded film premiered at the Cannes Film Festival in France. Shot on a petty-cash budget in black and white, the film follows 2 men and a woman on their way from New York City, through Cleveland, to Miami, Fla. Along the way are scenes shot on the 9th St. pier behind Captain Frank's landmark restaurant, on the west side, and along I-71.

*It Ate Cleveland* was the working title of a much-publicized mega-monster movie planned for Cleveland shooting by Cannon Films in 1985. However, the producers became embroiled in a legal battle with local Clevelanders with a script for a similar movie called *The Bloodthirsty Monster*. In the same year, local filmmakers representing Benchmark Productions garnered a lot of local publicity while filming a low-budget horror film, *The 33rd Night*, on location in a private residence in the theretofore quiet suburb of BRECKSVILLE.

In May 1986, Michael J. Fox, popular star of the TV sitcom *Family Ties*, spent a few days in the Cleveland area shooting the film *Just around the Corner to the Light of Day*. This story of a young factory worker (Fox) who also plays guitar in a rock band costarred film veteran Gena Rowlands and also rock singer Joan Jett, in her movie debut. Some scenes were shot at a Cleveland Hts. playground near the corner of Euclid Hts. Blvd. and Hampshire Rd. Other locations included the Euclid Tavern on Euclid Ave. near E. 116th St. and at Marshallan Prods., Inc. on W. 85th St. The film's director was Paul Schrader, screenwriter of *Taxi Driver* and director of *American Gigolo*. With the filming of *Just Around the Corner to the Light of Day*, the total number of films made in Cleveland (or the Greater Cleveland area) for theatrical release or expressly for television, was 16 in 1986. Omitted from the list are many movies made in other parts of Ohio, especially since the 1976 inception of the Ohio Film Bureau.

**MUELLER, JACOB** (10 Mar. 1822–31 Aug. 1905), was a German immigrant who became a civic leader in Cleveland's German-American community, active in local, state, and national politics. He was elected lieutenant governor of Ohio and served 1 term, 1872–74. Born in Alsenz, Bavaria, the son of a manufacturer, Mueller received a common-school education, then studied law and worked as a lawyer after 1845. He was active in the revolution of 1848 and served as a civil commissioner under the revolutionary government; when that government collapsed in 1849, he fled to the U.S. He later wrote an account of his experiences, *The Memoirs of a '48er.* Mueller joined his 2 brothers in Cleveland in Sept. 1849. He studied American law and English in the law offices of Geo. Willey and J. E. Carey. After being admitted to the bar in 1854, he practiced in partnership with Benjamin R. Beavis and Louis Ritter. That partnership was dissolved in 1859, and Mueller established the German Insurance Co., reportedly the first German-American insurance firm. He served as a director and secretary of the company until 1869, when he resigned to travel in Europe; the company was ruined as a result of the Chicago fire in 1871. While in Europe, Mueller joined the sanitary department of the German army during the war with France; his service was later rewarded with the Medal of Merit from the German emperor.

Mueller became active in politics and in the civic affairs of the local German-American community in the 1850s. Along with Louis Ritter, he formed a stock company in 1852 to establish a new German newspaper, *Waechter am Erie,* and was later an editor of *WAECHTER UND ANZEIGER.* He was also influential in establishing a number of German societies and political organizations. He served on the CLEVELAND CITY COUNCIL in 1857–58 as the representative from the 6th ward, and in addition to his election as lieutenant governor in 1871, he was elected as a representative from Cuyahoga County to the 1873–74 state constitutional convention. National politics also attracted Mueller's participation. He was a delegate to the Free-Soil party's national convention in 1855 and to the Republican national conventions in 1860 and 1872. In 1873 he broke with the Republican party over its policy on specie payments; joining the Democrats, he attended that party's national convention in 1876. In 1885, Pres. Grover Cleveland appointed him consul-general at Frankfurt am Main; he served there for 6 years. Mueller was married twice. His first wife, Charlotte Finger, died in 1858. He married Laura Schmidt in 1860; she died in 1886.

**MUNICIPAL OWNERSHIP.** Since 1890, when populist Dr. LOUIS B. TUCKERMAN first called for the city to build and operate an electric light plant, the question of municipally owned public utilities has provoked continuous and acrimonious debate. Charges of bribery and political corruption were common in the years before WORLD WAR I, and they have not disappeared in more recent times. The Progressive Era saw the full flowering of the demand to municipalize all public services, but mayors beginning with ROBT. MCKISSON campaigned for municipal ownership. TOM L. JOHNSON and NEWTON D. BAKER worked to implement their platforms with strong support from progressive councilmen such as FREDERIC C. HOWE, as well as more traditional politicians such as John Sultzmann. Early calls for municipalization thrust Cleveland into the forefront of the American reform movement. Mayors Johnson and Baker became influential national figures—heroes to some and dangerous radicals to others. While Cleveland's reputation as a beacon of hope for reformers faded at times during the next 5 decades, Mayor Kucinich's struggles to prevent the sale of Muny Light to its old enemy, the CLEVELAND ELECTRIC ILLUMINATING CO., again focused national attention on Cleveland in the 1970s.

The drive to introduce public services arose out of the need to provide essential services at a cost that poorly paid urban workers could afford. Under Mayors Johnson and Baker, facilities such as municipal markets and BATH HOUSES were introduced. Johnson municipalized the garbage collection and disposal system, as well as street cleaning. Equally important was the improvement of traditional municipal services whose operations were marked by inefficiency and corruption as a result of political spoilsmanship. It was Johnson's chief of police FRED KOHLER who transformed the department and earned a national reputation for reform. Prof. EDWARD W. BEMIS, a noted expert on utility rates, was placed in charge of the waterworks and had his department operating on a scientific, businesslike basis by 1910. His tenure resulted in the reduction of water rates, an end to political patronage, and a dramatic improvement in public health. Indeed, Cleveland's Water Dept. became a model for the nation and clearly demonstrated that a municipally owned service could be a success.

The political struggle for municipal ownership of streetcars and gas and electric power plants began in the 1899 mayoral election, when maverick Republican mayor Robt. McKisson, in the midst of a tough battle for political survival, called for public ownership of all public utilities. He contended that he was doing so as the defender of the wage earner against the privileged upper classes; he earned the praise of the city's radicals but lost the election. McKisson's advocacy of municipally owned public utilities reflected his political opportunism, but reformer Tom L. Johnson had a deeper commitment. Before he became mayor in 1901, he declared: "The public utility corporations are a bunch of thieves. I ought to know. I was one of them." As mayor he came to believe that privately owned utilities were dangerous bastions of privilege that would destroy democracy if they were not controlled. Johnson's most quoted declaration was made at one of his famous tent meetings. He told his audience: "I believe in municipal ownership of waterworks, of parks, of schools. I believe in the municipal ownership of these monopolies because if you do not own them they in turn will own you. They will rule your politics, corrupt your institutions and finally destroy your liberties."

The demand for municipal streetcars and power plants led by Johnson aroused the opposition of the owners of the private utilities and many other businessmen on the grounds of both ideology and self-interest. The Chamber of Commerce and the Municipal Assoc. dismissed the argument that public operation could provide electric power at a lower cost than private enterprise. A special committee of the Chamber of Commerce that studied Mayor Johnson's 1903 proposal to start a municipal electric light plant asserted that it was "a well known fact that municipal work is relatively more expensive than that done by private enterprise." The study found that low-cost rates would be limited to the small proportion of citizens served by the plant and concluded that "regulation not ownership is the safe policy for the city." The Municipal Assoc. pointed out the danger of inefficient operation as a result of political appointments and warned that "municipal ownership is socialism." The city's growing Socialist party, on the other hand, was contemptuous of what they termed "gas and water socialism," in lieu of radical change in the economic system. The Cleveland newspapers reflected the political stance of their owners. The independent *PLAIN DEALER* and the more radical *CLEVELAND PRESS* were generally supportive of Johnson and Baker's programs. The Republican-oriented *CLEVELAND LEADER* and the *CLEVELAND NEWS* condemned them.

It was during Johnson's 4 terms as mayor that the city witnessed the most intensive drive to achieve municipal ownership, but Johnson was not a rigid ideologue on the question. When the Rockefeller-controlled EAST OHIO GAS CO. offered to supply the city with natural gas at a price considerably below that charged by the existing franchise holders, Johnson was willing to negotiate a 10-year franchise that contained a clause permitting the city council to fix the price of gas when the franchise came up for renewal. When the artificial-gas companies and coal merchants tried to block the natural-gas proposal, Johnson claimed that they were using bribes to influence councilmen to vote against the ordinance and was able to secure passage of legislation authorizing the franchise. In response to criticism that he was doing business with the "notorious" Standard Oil Trust, Johnson pointed out that as a practical matter, the company had a monopoly of the natural-gas field with which the city could not compete.

Johnson's major utility fight was with the privately owned streetcar corporations. Although he was blocked by state law from establishing a municipal system, he sought to achieve low-cost urban transit by organizing a holding company that would operate city streetcars. Johnson was convinced, on the basis of his own experience in the streetcar business, that a 3-cent fare could replace the current 5-cent charge. When the streetcar company controlled by MARCUS HANNA merged with the Andrews-Stanley interests in 1903, this new monopoly intensified Johnson's determination, and his struggle to achieve a 3-cent fare polarized the city for the next 7 years.

While Johnson had some support from a broad spectrum of Clevelanders, it is clear from the voting patterns in city elections that the bulk of his political strength came from the working-class areas of the city. He used his famous tent meetings to explain his struggle against the forces of privilege that were using the power of monopoly to gouge the public. During this long, drawn-out fight, Johnson made skillful use of Prof. Bemis's technical knowledge and the brilliant legal skills of his law director Baker, but above all it was his own superb talents as a political leader that led to a partial victory over the streetcar interests in 1908. That year the private company agreed to lease their properties to a municipal traction company controlled by a 5-man board of directors appointed by the mayor. The municipal company was to charge a 3-cent fare, or cost-of-service fare, out of which was to be paid the operating costs plus a 6% profit to the holding company. All excess earnings were to go into the city's general funds. In celebration, Johnson designated 28 Apr. 1908 "Streetcar Day," with free rides for all. "It was like a holiday," he wrote in his autobiography.

But the holiday was short-lived. The new company was plagued with a bitter labor dispute, sabotage, and decreased revenues. Disillusioned voters in a referendum election rejected an ordinance that would have placed the city's backing behind the bonds of the municipal traction company. Unable to raise capital funds, the holding company was forced to return the streetcar properties to the former owners. In 1910, a new approach to end the decade-old struggle proved acceptable to all parties. An ordinance developed by Federal Judge ROBT. W. TAYLER in cooperation with Baker provided for private ownership, with a municipally

appointed traction commissioner acting as the overseer of the operation. The existing stockholders were guaranteed a 6% return on their investments. The first commissioner appointed by mayor HERMAN BAEHR was a failure, but Newton D. Baker selected PETER WITT for the position when he was elected mayor in 1911. Witt proved to be an excellent and creative administrator who not only achieved Johnson's dream of a 3-cent fare but also made improvements in service.

The question of municipalization of the CLEVELAND RAILWAY CO. (CRC) was raised periodically in the interwar years. During the 1920s, there was a general belief that the company, in the words of City Manager WM. R. HOPKINS, was securing "for Cleveland the best and cheapest street railway service enjoyed in any large city in the country." But the economic conditions of the 1930s brought decreased ridership, inability to meet fixed charges such as the 6% return, and the failure to replace aging equipment. In the late 1930s, Mayor HAROLD H. BURTON explored the idea of forming a competitive bus company using Public Works Admin. funds. His successor, Mayor EDWARD BLYTHIN, refused to accept a CRC proposal for an extension of its franchise, and countered with a call for municipal ownership as permitted under the franchise agreement. In 1941, city council passed an ordinance proposed by Blythin providing for the city to take over CRC property. Frank J. Lausche, who defeated Blythin in the mayoral race of 1941, completed the finance arrangements that consummated the $14 million purchase in early 1942. Another ordinance designated the mayor to appoint a 3-man board to operate the new Cleveland Transit System (CTS).

CTS prospered during WORLD WAR II and in the postwar period. In 1948 its future, according to several major studies, appeared promising. The management secured a $22 million loan from the Reconstruction Finance Corp. for rapid-transit construction, new equipment, and other capital improvements on condition that the board be increased to 5 members and given complete control over the system. Cleveland voters approved these conditions in Oct. 1949. Two years later, CTS secured another RFC loan for $29.5 million to complete the construction. On 4 Feb. 1952, ground was broken for the 13-mi. rail line. Service to the east side was started within a few months over existing lines, and by the mid-1950s, the west side line to the municipal airport was in operation. Another attempt to build a subway to serve downtown (the first one was in 1912) was blocked by county engineer ALBERT S. PORTER, a leading advocate of freeways.

But the rapid development of the outer ring of suburbs, supported by federal funds for freeways and federally financed loans for housing, led to the increased use of automobiles and a decline in CTS revenues. The substitution of buses for trolley cars and the building of high-rail rapid transit did not arrest the fall in ridership. Cleveland councilmen did not help matters by pressuring for reduced fares for several categories of riders while insisting that the system operate out of the farebox. Management, with neither local nor federal subsidies, had to reduce service to the point that those who could afford an automobile deserted public transit. As city neighborhoods and downtown shopping areas declined, the opening of new suburban shopping malls and industrial parks brought further dislocation to the system and insurmountable problems for central city residents, who were most dependent on public transit. Frequent breakdown of old equipment brought further decline in ridership.

By the late 1960s, the public transit system was in a state of crisis. When Mayor Carl B. Stokes and county commissioner Hugh Corrigan sought a solution by applying for federal funds, the federal agency UMTA (Urban Mass Transit Admin.) insisted upon a regional approach. The resulting 5-county Mass Transit Study Committee recommended a regional system to include CTS and all other systems within the county, but leaders of the emerging black majority in Cleveland and many white suburban politicians were afraid that their own power would be diluted under regional organization. In 1974, the Ohio state legislature, pushed by the Growth Assoc. of Cleveland, passed an enabling law to permit the creation of a GREATER CLEVELAND REGIONAL TRANSIT AUTHORITY with power to levy taxes subject to voter approval. But the situation did not look promising in the closing months of the year before the legislation was due to expire in December. Cleveland voters had just rejected a 1.5% income tax increase (the .5% was to subsidize CTS), and the political squabbling continued.

But the glaring need to get massive help from the federal government before the city's public transit was reduced to peak hour service or collapsed entirely brought about compromise. Mayor Perk gave up his demand that the central city have a majority on the proposed 9-person board when the county commissioners agreed that one of their 3 appointments would be a city resident. The shift in population and power in the county was reflected in the agreement that the Suburban Mayors & Managers Assoc. had the right to appoint 3 board members. Although the final legal agreements were signed in early 1975, further delays occurred when Cleveland's planning director Norman Krumholz insisted that the new system guarantee low fares for a number of years, free transfers for all riders, and better service for central city residents. On 22 July 1975, after a major countywide publicity campaign, the voters approved a 1% additional sales tax to finance RTA.

With massive federal aid and the local tax revenue that was available in the next decade, RTA rebuilt the decaying Shaker system, built major repair yards and sheds, bought scores of new rapid-transit trains and buses, and added new services such as Community Responsive Transit for the elderly and the handicapped. For a few years, the system thrived under the impact of heavily subsidized fares and the energy crisis, but by the mid-1980s, mismanagement, frequent breakdowns, fare increases, and the widespread use of political patronage resulted in growing public dissatisfaction and the decline of ridership. It was, however, the municipalization of electric power that created the most sustained and divisive controversy over the years. Although one of Mayor Johnson's major objectives was a city-owned power plant, his proposal to build a $2 million facility languished when he was defeated in 1909. Campaigning for mayor 2 years later, Newton D. Baker, who believed that all natural monopolies should be owned by the city, ran on a Johnsonian platform. He carried his campaign to the Chamber of Commerce, where he debated Samuel Scovil, vice-president of CEI, and asserted that public-service utilities had "consistently corrupted and depraved government for fifty years" and that public ownership was necessary for the "purification of city politics." After Baker became mayor, he cleared the legal obstacles erected by CEI so that the largest municipal light plant in the nation was able to begin operation in 1914.

From the beginning, the effectiveness of the Municipal Electric Light Plant, called Muny by Clevelanders, was a matter of dispute. Pointing out its dramatic increase in customers from 15,508 in 1915 to over 42,000 by 1927, Baker claimed that it had saved Clevelanders $14 million in its first 8 years of operation, but CEI expanded steadily by offering lower costs when the customer took into consideration the service charge added by Muny. During the 1920s,

the Kohler and Hopkins administrations were not committed to the expansion of Muny and adopted a policy of simply providing a yardstick for cost analysis rather than competing in areas already served by CEI.

In 1927, some councilmen who were concerned about the future of Muny asked utility director Howell Wright to study the plant's ability to increase its share of the streetlight system, to lower its rates, and to evaluate its need for new capital. Wright reported favorably on the plant's financial condition and its future, but asserted inaccurately that the state's constitution prohibited the issuance of bonds for extension or improvements of municipal enterprises. To match the private utility's lower rate, he proposed a new rate ordinance that reduced the city's profit by $30,000 a year. Three years later, Wright, who was ousted as director in 1930, wrote an article in a magazine underwritten by the private utility companies asserting that Muny was "an isolated and obsolete operation" and claiming that CEI, not Muny, had led the way in rate reductions. Ten years later, as a member of the public library board, Wright was found guilty of bribery and sent to jail.

The advent of the Depression brought devastating economic conditions that necessarily focused the attention of the city on survival. Not only did the profits from Muny go into the General Fund for relief programs, but the occupant of the city's chief executive position changed 6 times between 1930–36. Muny failed to expand and was the dumping ground for the political friends of various chief executives. The situation alarmed conscientious employees, who approached activist Republican lawyer Paul Walter about their concerns. In 1937, as a result of consultation with him, they formed an organization of key employees and supporters, the Cleveland Municipal Light Plant Assoc., with the purpose of lowering light and power rates for the community. The association was supported by Mayors Burton and Lausche, who were essentially conservative on social issues but recognized the potential political consequences of Muny's demise. The organization lobbied to prevent the plant's earnings from disappearing into the General Fund and to secure appropriations for new equipment and repairs. Paul Walter, who became president of the association, recalled that they faced "tremendous animosity" to these plans from CEI, which continuously lobbied councilmen against support for Muny. Walter claimed that when the federal government provided a grant of $3 million to aid in the reconstruction of Muny in 1938, CEI financed the referendum designed to block the improvement, but association members fought back in a door-to-door campaign, which carried the issue by a 94% majority.

In 1942, a coalition of reform-minded Republicans and Democrats were unsuccessful in passing a proposal to place public utilities—waterworks, sewer system, Muny, and CTS—under an independent commission. Later that year, when the Securities & Exchange Commission ordered the North American Co. To sever its relationship with several power companies, including CEI, the coalition proposed legislation authorizing the city to purchase CEI. Financier CYRUS EATON assured the council that he could secure the necessary financing and advised that municipal ownership of the company would be profitable for Cleveland. The measure aroused a furor within the conservative business community as well as from CEI, but supporters believed they had the votes for passage and were completely surprised when the legislation was defeated 19–13.

As the city came out of the Depression, the fortunes of Muny improved, but any major effort to expand its services was blocked by the lobbying of CEI. After World War II, at a time of tremendous expansion of electrical usage within the city and the rapidly growing suburbs, Muny

701

remained locked into serving about 20% of the electricity provided within the city boundaries. THOS. BURKE, mayor 1945–53, had little commitment to Muny. In fact, his law director became chief legal counsel for CEI in the early 1950s. Burke's successor, Anthony Celebrezze, managed to put through a $12 million plant expansion, and his successor, Ralph Locher, refused to talk to CEI when they proposed to purchase Muny. But by the mid-1960s, despite the infusion of some new money during the previous decade, the municipal operation was suffering from worn and unsuitable equipment, rigid union work rules, increasing costs of coal, and a fresh determination of CEI to put it out of business. Outages occurred frequently, and CEI, using what the Nuclear Regulatory Commission later denounced as unfair competition, blocked efforts of Muny to secure interconnection with the private utility, even for emergencies.

In 1965, Carl B. Stokes advocated the sale of Muny in his campaign for mayor, but when he was elected 2 years later, he lacked the political power in council to pass the legislation. His commissioner of power secured a temporary interconnection with CEI, but when the utility refused a permanent link, the Stokes administration asked the NRC to investigate CEI for possible antitrust violations. During the Stokes years, the city began to lose money on its power plant, which had to be subsidized out of the General Fund. Under increasing financial pressure, both Stokes and his successor Ralph Perk failed to pay for the power the city had secured from CEI. When Perk became mayor in 1971, he and council president Geo. Forbes secured passage of a $13 million bond issue, but the securities could not be sold. Perk accused CEI of sabotaging the issue, and Forbes threatened to drive the company out of the city. In 1975, the administration filed a $330 million antitrust suit against CEI. By this time, Muny's ability to produce electricity was seriously impaired, and it was increasingly relying on the purchase of power. Between 1971–75 it lost 10% of its customers because of poor service, frequent outages, and aggressive marketing by CEI. With $16 million in unpaid CEI bills and a generating plant that had ceased to operate in 1975, Perk and Forbes decided to sell the city's electric plant. CEI agreed to a package deal that included a $150 million purchase price and forgiveness for most of the debt, in return for the city's dropping its antitrust suit.

But the opposition to the sale of citizens' groups, the system's customers, and their council representatives was strengthened by the Jan. 1977 ruling of the Atomic Safety & Licensing Board that CEI had "deliberately rigged the interconnection policies to cause Muny Light's power failures." CEI was ordered to "wheel" cheaper power from the Power Authority of the State of New York (PASNY) over its lines. In the face of the political storm, city council refused to approve the agreement. CEI then turned to the courts to collect its debts. When the city offered to repay the money over a 14-year period, CEI president Karl H. Rudolph refused, saying, "We want our money. We're a business organization . . . we expect to be paid." In Apr. 1977, Clevelanders overwhelmingly voted down a property tax increase proposed by council to pay off the debt. Immediately, pressure mounted to sell the plant. The *Plain Dealer* editorialized that Muny Light was "outdated, inefficient and ought to be sold." Council subsequently voted to sell the plant, but Dennis J. Kucinich, clerk of courts, organized a Save Muny Light Committee, which secured sufficient signatures to put the question on the ballot. The election did not occur because of a dispute over the legality of the petitions, but Kucinich was elected mayor in Nov. 1977.

The sale of the Municipal Electric Light Plant was blocked, and Mayor Kucinich was determined to take advantage of the NCR's ruling that CEI had to wheel the cheaper PASNY power over its lines to Muny. CEI was equally determined to collect the city's $18 million debt in federal court, which issued judgment liens against city property and ordered Cleveland to pay its bill by Apr. 1978 or face a $5,000 daily fine. Kucinich attempted to issue bonds to raise the cash, but the Ohio Supreme Court blocked that avenue. When he resorted to taking money from operating funds, the city was left with a financial crisis that was further aggravated by Cleveland Trust's refusal to refinance $7.8 million in short-term city notes. During the summer of 1978, the Kucinich administration faced one financial crisis after another and survived a recall movement by only 236 votes out of 120,000 cast. By December, a federal court ruled that unless the city paid the remaining $5.7 million on its CEI debt, the $330 million antitrust suit initiated by the Perk administration would be thrown out—a suit that the city eventually lost. Rather than face the loss of the antitrust suit, the mayor depleted the city's treasury to the extent that there was no way to pay other short-term loans for $14 million that became due in Dec. 1978.

In a last-ditch effort to resolve the crisis, Kucinich met with the 6 banks that held the notes to seek a postponement for a special election in which he would ask an increase in the city income tax to pay off the debt, but Cleveland Trust's chief executive officer Brock Weir refused to accept the proposal. City council agreed to put an income tax issue on the ballot if the mayor would sell Muny. He refused but suggested a compromise of placing Muny under an independent board for an 18-month trial period to determine if it could survive financially. If it failed, he would agree to sell, but he was confident of the outcome of his proposal because a study by municipal experts issued in October had demonstrated that the plant was in the black and could make a profit as a distributor over CEI's interconnecting lines of the cheaper electrical power available from PASNY. City council turned down Kucinich's compromise. On 15 Dec. 1978, Cleveland went into DEFAULT. The decision not to roll over the short-term city notes was in the last analysis an exercise in power by the business establishment that had its roots in their historical hostility to public power as well as in the financial crisis facing the city.

Council chose a 2-pronged approach to the crisis by calling for a special election to authorize the sale of Muny Light and a 50% increase in the city income tax. Kucinich organized a powerful door-to-door campaign that persuaded voters not to sell Muny but to raise their taxes. He saved the light plant but not his office. In the fall of 1979, the Republican challenger Geo. Voinovich, backed by the city's business community notwithstanding his support for Muny, defeated Kucinich for mayor. The new mayor made clear his intention to revitalize Muny, which he renamed Cleveland Public Power (CPP). He, too, soon faced opposition from CEI, and like mayors before him accused the private utility of seeking to block legislation intended to make Muny better able to compete for customers. But in a surprise move in 1983, he authorized his utility director to enter into secret negotiations with CEI to try "to settle . . . long standing differences." When news of the proposed settlement leaked to the press, councilmen were shocked and angered by the proposed terms, which included CEI getting all of CPP's customers in return for $40 million and a promise that CEI headquarters with 1,000 employees would remain in Cleveland. Voinovich quickly repudiated the proposal and later stated that the political reality was that the plant could not be sold.

Results of the 1985 council election clearly indicated that those who supported CPP were a major force in city council. They pressed for a $50 million investment to make CPP more competitive and supported an aggressive marketing program that challenged CEI's hold on governmental and commercial accounts. A reluctant council president Forbes held council hearings on a $50 million improvement program that was part of a $100 million System Improvement Plan. For a time it appeared that the issue would become bogged down in racial politics. Because of an accident of history and geography, Muny had serviced predominantly white ethnic neighborhoods, but the 1979 referendum on the plant had demonstrated support in both black and white wards, and recent demographic changes brought an increasing number of blacks into CPP service areas.

In the fall of 1986, city council held extensive hearings on the multi-million-dollar expansion proposals. CEI, in what a *Plain Dealer* editorial characterized as a "crude approach to the city," threatened to pull its headquarters out of the city—with the implication of disastrous financial consequences for the city and its school system. But Forbes, whose approach was one of delay and divide, finally realized that if he continued to oppose the measure, he faced defeat. In Jan. 1987, city council voted 21–0 to expand CPP.

Over the years, Cleveland voters have continued to reflect a suspicion of the public-service monopolies that Tom L. Johnson attacked 80 years ago. Even when the light plant was badly managed as a result of political spoilsmanship, citizens remained true to the Johnsonian dream of providing cheaper power. Mayor Kucinich was an effective articulator of both the hostile feelings and the dream. It was Kucinich who rallied the people in the decisive referendum of 1979. But the success of the dream depends not only on the opportunity for expansion, but also on a system of businesslike administration unburdened by political appointments and supported by both the mayor and the city council. On the other hand, CEI spokesmen and their supporters in the business community have viewed municipal power not only as a kind of socialistic intrusion on private enterprise, but also as an unfair competitor. They point out that the municipal utility has never paid taxes, whereas CEI has paid millions of dollars to Cleveland and its school system. They claim that CEI has fought aggressively for expansion of industry in the Cleveland area, whereas the city did relatively little to promote business and industrial development. Many businessmen conclude that customers of public power who benefit from a 20% reduction in rates are being subsidized unfairly by the majority of taxpayers in the city. Cleveland Public Power is one of 2,200 public power systems that belong to the American Public Power Assoc. In 1984 it received the association's highest award for "outstanding improvements in service to customer/owners." In spite of strong opposition from a private competitor and periods of weak support from the city's own council and administration, Tom Johnson's dream of public power survives in Cleveland.

Thomas F. Campbell
Cleveland State University

See also URBAN TRANSPORTATION, WATER SYSTEM.

The **MURCH FOUNDATION** was incorporated in 1956 by Maynard Hale Murch (1874–1966). Murch was born in Chardon, Ohio, and graduated from Adelbert College of Western Reserve University in 1898. He was a reporter for the *Cleveland Plain Dealer* from 1903–09, until he began his own investment firm, Maynard H. Murch & Co.

Over the course of his career as an investment banker, he was also president of the Hampden Corp. and director of 12 others, including the WHITE MOTOR CO. From 1923 until his death at age 92, Murch was a trustee of the CLEVELAND MUSEUM OF NATURAL HISTORY. Another of his interests was the Cleveland Zoo, to which he donated two Kodiak bears in 1946. Murch, also a trustee and on the board of governors of WRU, received an honorary Ph.D. in 1960. He was married to Leah Daggett in 1905 (d. 1971) and had 2 children, Maynard Hale Murch, Jr., and Boynton Daggett Murch. The purposes of the foundation are generally for cultural programs, higher and secondary education, and hospitals. Grants are given locally. In 1981, assets of the foundation were $4,419,695, with expenditures of $383,985 for 46 grants. Officers include Maynard H. Murch IV and Jas. H. Dempsey, Jr.

**MURPHY, EDWARD F.** (15 July 1891–7 Mar. 1950), president of Teamsters Local 407, was a powerful figure in Cleveland labor circles and a policymaker in the CLEVELAND FED. OF LABOR for 4 decades. Born in the "Grove," an Irish settlement near the WEST SIDE MARKET, Murphy was the 6th of 11 children. Orphaned at 13, he first took a job driving a horsecart for the General Cartage Co., and then he became a drayman. His experience with long hours and low pay for truck drivers led him to become one of the first members of the Teamsters Local 407 when it was organized in 1911. By 1916, he was the vice-president of the local, and by 1924, the president. In 1929 he gave up truck driving to devote full time to union work.

With a former neighborhood friend, John Rohrich, Murphy founded the Teamsters Joint Council 41 with 3,500 members to coordinate the 7 Teamster locals in the area. He also took on a position as general organizer for the International (1931) and ultimately had jurisdiction over 125,000 drivers in Ohio, Michigan, western Pennsylvania, New York (except New York City), and Canada. Under Murphy's leadership, the TEAMSTERS UNION became powerful enough to stop deliveries at struck plants; from this position of strength, Murphy masterfully negotiated contracts that guaranteed better service to employers in return for fair wages. Skillful at bargaining, he believed that strikes should be used only as a last resort, and he was regarded by employers as trustworthy, fair, and tough. At a time when Teamster locals in other cities were blighted by violence, mishandling of funds, and corruption, Murphy kept area locals free of racketeering influence and strong-arm tactics.

Because of his integrity and the growing power of the union he represented, Murphy became increasingly important in the Cleveland Fed. of Labor. Though he accepted appointments to federation committees and councils, he wielded most of the power behind the scenes and never sought high position in the CFL. Seeing that a major barrier to local stability was the dominance of the building trades in the federation, he challenged their leadership. In 1938, the factions met in an election that resulted in the victory of Thos. Lenahan, the Teamster candidate, as executive secretary, and a truce whereby the Bldg. Trades Council and the Teamsters shared offices. The next year, Murphy was asked to resign his Teamster duties to work as a full-time organizer for the CFL. For nearly a decade, he maintained the balance of power in the federation.

In 1947, Murphy sensed that fresh leadership was needed to make the CFL more accessible to union leaders and the community to combat antilabor bias, and he advanced the candidacy of Wm. Finegan for executive secretary. After a bitter election, Finegan defeated Tommy "Mr. Labor" Lenahan. Less than a year after this demonstration of power, Murphy was badly injured in an auto accident while on a business trip. Because of his injuries, he was forced to cut back on his union activities. When Murphy died in 1950, he left a family of union activists (including Joseph Murphy of the Service Employees Internatl. Union) and a leadership vacuum in the Teamsters and the federation. His local and the Cleveland labor community constructed a monument to him at Calvary Cemetery and donated a floor at ST. VINCENT CHARITY HOSPITAL in his memory.

**MURPHY FOUNDATION.** *See* **JOHN P. MURPHY FOUNDATION**

The **MURPHY-PHOENIX COMPANY,** the family-owned manufacturer of Murphy's Oil Soap, was organized in 1889 as the Phoenix Oil Co. and incorporated in 1890 with $25,000 in capital. Capital was increased to $50,000 in 1893; officers that year included M. E. Murphy, president; D. M. Garvin, vice-president; and G. F. Zimmer, secretary and treasurer. The company, described by one business directory as "extensive dealers in petroleum and its products," manufactured oils for valves, cylinders, dynamos, machines, and harnesses under the Green Seal label; its plant was located in NEWBURGH along the Cleveland & Pittsburgh railroad line. By 1910, the company was under the direction of Jeremiah T. Murphy, who reportedly bought the idea for Murphy's Oil Soap from a German immigrant. Basically a potassium soap of vegetable oil, the soap proved easy to make. At first it was demonstrated and sold in hardware and department stores, and for years accounted for only part of the company's sales; the firm continued to manufacture metal-working oils and compounds for industrial uses. By 1939 the company had moved from 2554 W. 5th St. To a plant at 9505 Cassius Ave.; it employed about 30 people there in 1958. In 1966 it built another plant in Madison to manufacture concrete curing compounds used in road construction. Beginning about 1968 the company underwent several changes. That year the name of the company was changed from Phoenix Oil to the Murphy-Phoenix Company. In 1970 the company's business was about evenly divided between its household cleaner, which was sold only in the Great Lakes region, and its industrial compounds. But in the early 1970s, the company began losing household cleaner sales to national brand cleaners. To guarantee its own survival in the household cleaner market, Murphy-Phoenix devised a national marketing strategy built around its oil soap's loyal regional following, its ability to "clean everything," as its label proclaimed, and its lack of phosphates, making it environmentally safer than most other cleaners. The select national advertising campaign increased sales; by 1984 annual sales were $15 million with an annual growth rate of 20%; the household cleaner had expanded from a regional to a national product with 3 million regular customers and accounted for 80% of the company's business. By 1980 the company, which employed between 60 and 70 people, had moved its offices to 23811 Chagrin Blvd. in BEACHWOOD; in 1984 it expanded its manufacturing capacity by adding a plant in SOLON.

**MUSIC.** Music in Cleveland can date its present eminence from the first decades of the 20th century. By that time, population growth and business success had reached a plateau from which could emerge significant cultural events. It was during this era that the dedicated impresario ADELLA PRENTISS HUGHES (1869–1950), working through the FORTNIGHTLY MUSICAL CLUB and the Natl. Fed. of Music Clubs, brought the great names of western music to the city—Paderewski, Richard Strauss, Enrico Caruso; the orchestras from Boston, Chicago, Detroit, New York, Philadelphia, and others; the Ballet Russe, and more. During this time, music making by local ensembles of all kinds was at a new height. The CLEVELAND MUSIC SCHOOL SETTLEMENT (1912), the CLEVELAND INSTITUTE OF MUSIC (1920), and the CLEVELAND MUSEUM OF ART (1916) came into being. And at a benefit program for St. Ann Roman Catholic Church at GRAYS ARMORY on 11 Dec. 1918, the fledging CLEVELAND ORCHESTRA conducted by NIKOLAI SOKOLOFF (1886–1965) was born. From its earliest days, music making had sprung naturally from the Cleveland community. The earliest concert recorded in the *Annals of Cleveland* was a program of sacred music that took place at P. Mowrey's assembly room on 10 May 1821. Throughout the period before the CIVIL WAR, the *Annals* record an increasing string of events, including the formation of musical groups, including the CLEVELAND MOZART SOCIETY (from 1837), the CLEVELAND HARMONIC SOCIETY (1837), the Cleveland Sacred Music Society (1842), the CLEVELAND MENDELSSOHN SOCIETY (1850), and the ST. CECILIA SOCIETY (1852). Notable early opera was produced by the Cleveland Gesangverein.

For much of this period, Cleveland remained in the musical orbit of taste stemming from Boston. This influence was epitomized in the person of Lowell Mason (1792–1872), probably the most influential musician in 19th-century America, who conducted a seminal series of workshops in Cleveland during the 1840s. This tradition did not emphasize American resources but, rather, sought to propagate standards of "correct taste" as practiced in Europe. Mason's teachings had far-ranging implications for the development of music in Cleveland, particularly in the areas of sacred music and music education. Emphasis on sacred music here was particularly strong, and the church was early on a major supporter of the arts. The first full-time supervisor in the Cleveland public schools was a disciple of Lowell Mason by the name of N. COE STEWART (1837–1921), who held this post over a long tenure, 1869–1907. Band music was highly popular in 19th-century Cleveland, and for many was a principal source of musical exposure. Playing in parks, in concert halls, at lawn fetes, on lake steamers, in skating rinks, at conventions, at strawberry festivals, and at numerous special events, visiting and local BANDS seemed omnipresent. In Dec. 1837, the Cleveland City Band announced a public rehearsal at the courthouse. John Low gratefully acknowledged this organization the following year for its "exquisite performance at the Exchange Coffee House." The Cleveland Grays Band (1840), the Cleveland Independent City Band (1842), the Cleveland Brass Band (1844), and others quickly followed. The Hecker Band left Cleveland on the Detroit boat, 5 June 1861, to join the 4th Michigan Regiment during the Civil War. Band music for many years was to remain high on the list of Clevelanders' musical priorities.

Waves of immigrants coming from Europe reached Cleveland before the Civil War and continued after it, making the city the 7th-largest in the nation by 1900. Among these, the GERMANS were particularly skilled in music, and it was Cleveland's German community that was responsible for much of the music making during the 19th century. The first German singing society in Cleveland was the FROHSINN in 1848, followed by the Cleveland Gesangverein in 1854. The Gesangverein enjoyed an illustrious history, with activities extending well into the 20th century. German groups in America began to exchange visits, becoming more formally organized following a gathering of singers in Cincinnati in June 1849. From that time, regular

"SAENGERFESTS" took place, alternating between cities, over a long period of time. Five such saengerfests were held in Cleveland—in 1855, with 18 societies and about 300 singers; in 1859, with 24 societies and 400 singers; in 1893, with 85 societies and 2,200 singers; and the last, in 1927, with more than 100 societies and 4,000 singers (figures from the program books and press reports do not always coincide). These events combined social activities, including picnics, torchlight processions, dinners, and balls, along with the concerts. Hans Balatka (1855), F. Abel (1859), Carl Bergmann (1874), EMIL RING (1893), and Bruno Walter (1927) served as festival conductors. The 1927 festival honored Ludwig Beethoven, in celebration of the centenary of his death, but also recognized Cleveland composer Albert Gehring. Cincinnati served as a model for Cleveland in other ways. A saengerfest in May 1873 under the skillful leadership of Theodore Thomas (1835-1905), one of 19th-century America's best conductors, provided momentum for a series of May festivals to follow. Such large events were much a part of the American scene during these years, and one need only point to the peace jubilees in Boston in 1869 and 1872 and festival events in New York and Chicago during the 1870s and 1880s for other examples.

The impact of these events was not lost on Cleveland, and the person in a position to do something about it was Cleveland's most important choral conductor, ALFRED ARTHUR (1844-1918). Born near Pittsburgh, Pa., and trained in Ashland, Ohio, in Boston, Mass., and in Europe, Arthur moved to Cleveland in 1871. His career to that time had followed what might be considered a normal pattern for a midwestern native-born American musician. In Cleveland, Arthur was active as a composer, compiler, editor, educator, and conductor, his work spanning many facets in a way typical also of a less specialized world. His greatest achievement lay in his work with the CLEVELAND VOCAL SOCIETY, an organization that he conducted through 29 seasons through the spring of 1902. It was responsible for important first performances here, for entertaining renowned guests such as violinist Eduard Remenyi and composer Max Bruch, and for representing Cleveland with distinction at the World's Columbian Exposition in Chicago in 1893. Finally, Arthur was responsible for landmark orchestral concerts; 4 programs took place in Mar.-Apr. 1872 at Brainard's Piano Ware Rooms. A new ensemble, the Cleveland Amateur Philharmonic Society, came into being in 1881, with FERDINAND PUEHRINGER as its first conductor. Mueller Neuhoff succeeded Puehringer, to be replaced in turn by Franz Arens. In 1888 the Austrian oboist, composer, and conductor Emil Ring (1863-1922), who had first come to America in 1887 as a member of the Boston Symphony Orchestra, arrived to conduct the ensemble. Ring, a leader of obvious ability, gave programs of breadth, including works by Liszt, Wagner, Berlioz, Massenet, and Grieg. There were about 4 regular concerts each year, and the orchestra accompanied choral works for the Gesangverein, of which Ring was also the conductor, in summer programs at HALTNORTH'S GARDENS.

During the early 1900s, several local orchestras graced the growing scene, led by Emil Ring and a Cleveland-born colleague, JOHANN BECK (1856-1924). The short-lived CLEVELAND SYMPHONY ORCHESTRA with Beck as conductor represents an important venture in 1900-01. The 50-piece ensemble gave a total of 8 concerts at Grays Armory, 3 the first season the second, with important soloists a regular feature. After the demise of this ensemble, the CLEVELAND GRAND ORCHESTRA came into being, playing a series of "Citizens' Pop Concerts" through 1909 (the 1904-05 season prospectus advertised simply the

"Cleveland Orchestra"). Audiences evidently were large, and ticket prices low; deficits were met through timely contributions. Although the fare aimed first of all to entertain, the repertoire included its share of works by Beethoven, Mendelssohn, Schubert, and other established composers. The series continued from 1910-12 under the name People's Symphony Concerts, with the orchestra now called the Cleveland Symphony Orchestra, under the alternate direction of Ring and Beck. A certain emphasis upon local artists and local choral groups continued. The final program of the series, in Mar. 1912, included the SINGERS CLUB and contained music by Saint-Saens, Arthur Foote, and Edvard Grieg. A short-lived experiment then took place in the organization of the Cleveland Municipal Symphony Orchestra, the financial support for which was taken over by the city. Notable though the intentions were, the conductor brought here to lead the orchestra, Dutch violinist Christiaan Timmner, eventually proved unable to develop the ensemble, and it dissolved in Mar. 1915. The next step was the tenuous beginning of the Cleveland Orchestra itself, known in its first season as Cleveland's Symphony Orchestra. The press was enthusiastic. The ensemble of about 60 players, with Sol Marcosson as concertmaster, was recruited mainly from the best local talent. It performed a varied schedule of more than 2 dozen programs its first season, to June 1919. The time was right; Cleveland at last had an orchestra that would endure.

Cleveland had been developing its own musical resources during the period to 1918; yet the many musical visitors of importance who had come to the city to perform had helped shape standards of musical excellence and allowed Clevelanders to comprehend more clearly their emerging role on the national scene. From the very beginning, Cleveland had been on the touring circuit, and from everywhere they came. The Norwegian violinist "Ole Bull" made repeated visits beginning in the 1840s. The Manvers Operatic Co., probably the first opera company to come, in 1849, started a tradition that continues to this day in the regular series by New York's Metropolitan Opera. Jenny Lind, the Hutchinson family, Adelina Patti, Louis Moreau Gottschalk, Patrick Sarsfield Gilmore, John Philip Sousa, and many more gave programs. In the orchestral sphere, Theodore Thomas created a major impression, making Cleveland a regular stop after 1869. Chamber music also flourished. The Cecilian String Quartet, begun in 1875, was a pioneer. Back in Cleveland after a time of study in Leipzig, Johann Beck organized the SCHUBERT STRING QUARTET 2 years later; it gave numerous concerts during the 1880s. The successor to this group was the BECK STRING QUARTET, which made its debut on 16 Oct. 1890 in a concert in the chapel of Unity Church. On 6 Nov. 1890, the ensemble gave Beck's String Quartet in C Minor one of its frequent hearings. The PHILHARMONIC STRING QUARTET was an important presence, active in the mid-1890s and well into this century, and other groups followed. In Nov. 1918, the Chamber Music Society of Cleveland was formed, a precursor of the present CLEVELAND CHAMBER MUSIC SOCIETY, to present chamber-music concerts. The intimate art of chamber music, for many the distillation of music's ultimate values, has been dear to the hearts of Clevelanders over many decades.

Chronicler to Cleveland music events during the second half of the 19th century was the important firm of S. BRAINARD'S SONS. An organization of national prominence, the company regularly reported musical events and published actual music of the parlor music genre in the pages of its house organ, *Brainard's (Western) Musical World* (1864-95). Measured by circulation and longevity, this journal achieved remarkable success. *Musical World* reported fully the wealth of musical events that took place in Cleveland during the later 1800s. However, eventually Brainard's moved its business to the emerging center of Chicago. Nineteenth-century Cleveland composers shared the plight of their colleagues nationally of getting music published. The most likely possibilities were songs and piano music, and a number of local composers centered on these genres. Large orchestral works tended to remain unpublished, even those of experts such as Johann Beck. But Cleveland had its classically oriented composers of merit. Earlier composers of special talent born during the 1850s included Beck, JAS. H. ROGERS (1857-1940), and WILSON G. SMITH (1855-1929). Representative of a second generation were CHAS. V. RYCHLIK (1875-1962) and especially ARTHUR SHEPHERD (1880-1958), to many the "dean" of Cleveland composers, who came here in 1920 as assistant conductor of the Cleveland Orchestra and remained to compose and become long-time head of music at Western Reserve University. Other composers who have been a part of the Cleveland scene during the last half-century include VICTOR BABIN, Rudolph Bubalo, Marcel Dick, Dennis Eberhard, HERBERT ELWELL, Donald Erb, Edwin London, J. D. Bain Murray, Eugene O'Brien, Klaus George Roy, and BERYL RUBINSTEIN. Others, associated primarily elsewhere, who contributed include ERNEST BLOCH (who came to Cleveland in 1920 to lead the newly formed Cleveland Institute of Music), Douglas Moore, Quincy Porter, Roger Sessions, and Raymond Wilding-White. There is an active CLEVELAND COMPOSERS' GUILD, formed during the 1920s. Instrument building in Cleveland has played an important role. Significant among the builders are the Holtkamp Organ Co., an outgrowth of the firm founded here by Gottlieb Votteler in 1855, and the KING MUSICAL INSTRUMENTS CO., makers of brass instruments, founded near the turn of the century as the H. N. White Co.

Subsequent conductors of the Cleveland Orchestra who have fulfilled the promise are ARTUR RODZINSKI (here 1933-43), Erich Leinsdorf (1943-46), GEO. SZELL (1946-70), Lorin Maazel (1972-82), and newly appointed Christoph von Dohnanyi (1984). Pierre Boulez and Louis Lane also contributed immeasurably during the period 1970-72. SEVERANCE HALL (capacity 2,000) has been the orchestra's home since 1931. A Cleveland Orchestra Chorus was formed (continuous from 1955), reaching an early high point during the tenure here of Robt. Shaw (in Cleveland 1956-67) and continuing to high acclaim under its subsequent directors, now Robt. Page. A Children's Chorus, affiliated with the orchestra, was formed in 1967. The orchestra gives about 30 summer concerts annually at its summer home, the Blossom Music Ctr. (inaugurated 1968), where dance and "popular" concerts increase the number to approximately 70 yearly events during the June-September season. Important later contributors to the music scene have been the curators of musical arts at the Cleveland Museum of Art, Thos. Whitney Surette (1921-40), WALTER BLODGETT (1940-74), and Karel Paukert (1974- ). The McMyler organ (1922), the first in this country to be installed in a museum of art, and pace-setting in its design principles, was moved and rebuilt in a new auditorium in 1971. Currently (1985) David Cerone is president of the Cleveland Institute of Music, succeeding Victor Babin and more recently Grant Johannesen. Peter R. Webster became chairman of the Music Dept. at CASE WESTERN RESERVE UNIVERSITY in 1984, succeeding John Suess (chairman 1968-84). The Music Dept. of CLEVELAND STATE UNIVERSITY has been led by Edwin London since 1978, following a long tenure by Julius Drossin, who led

the department through a period of substantial growth. With branches and affiliates in several locations and a program of national prominence in music therapy, the largest community music school in the country with over 5,000 students, the Cleveland Music School Settlement, is headed by Malcolm Tait, who followed long-time director Howard Whittaker in 1984. Significant contributions are made by neighboring institutions BALDWIN-WALLACE COLLEGE, Oberlin College, and Kent State University.

Cleveland's numerous ethnic neighborhoods have added rich variety. Besides the Germans, mentioned earlier, whose contributions to musical life in Cleveland during the last century were most important of all, many other groups have also contributed. The CIURLIONIS Ensemble, of Lithuanian origin, came to the U.S. in 1949 after extensive concertizing in Europe. The Cleveland Kilty Band, founded in 1935 to preserve the art of Scottish bagpipers, has been important here. The Balmoral Dancers became a part of this organization. The GLASBENA MATICA, still active, has been important to the cultural life of the Cleveland SLOVENES over a long period of time. Representing the renowned Welsh singing tradition here have been the gatherings of the Gymanfa Ganu and, among others, the Cleveland Messiah Chorus. The HARMONIA CHOPIN SINGING SOCIETY, founded in 1902, was the first Polish male chorus in Ohio. The Hungaria Singing Society, our oldest Hungarian singing society, dates back to the 1890s. Ireland is represented by the Irish Musicians Assoc. of America, the Michael Keating Branch. The oldest Czech singing society in the U.S., the LUMIR-HLAHOL-TYL SINGING SOCIETY, was founded in Cleveland and in 1899 presented the first performance here of Smetana's *Bartered Bride*. The oldest and largest of the Yugoslav choirs in Cleveland has been the Serbian Singing Choir. Children's music has been represented in a number of directions, including the Zagreb Junior Tamburitzans. Although quite self-contained, the American Shakers and their music were part of 19th-century Cleveland. A Shaker colony known as NORTH UNION (in SHAKER HTS.) was formed ca. 1822 and saw its most prosperous days between 1840-58, dissolving in 1899 as its numbers dwindled. Devotional vocal music, sung in unison without instruments and written down for many years in letter notation, formed the core repertory for the Shakers' dance-oriented religious gatherings.

Cleveland has been a vital center of the more "popular" genres. Parlor music—that genre consisting mainly of piano music and songs aimed at the home market, particularly the ladies—was as widespread in 19th-century Cleveland as it was elswhere. Nearly half of the pages of *Brainard's (Western) Musical World* were filled with actual music of this sort, mainly by Americans. Music produced in *Musical World* was, of course, also readily available for sale. Moving ahead in time, popular song, JAZZ, Americanized POLKA, musical theater, and ROCK 'N' ROLL have all been important here. Famous songwriter ERNEST R. BALL (1878-1927) was born in Cleveland, and Art Tatum spent several seasons playing in Cleveland clubs during the 1930s. Tadd Dameron, Benny Bailey, Albert Ayler, and a host of others graced the local scene. A special Cleveland contribution lies in the inception here of rock 'n' roll, brought to prominence in the early 1950s in Cleveland before it achieved its phenomenal international popularity.

Evidence of Cleveland's continuing growth in the musical arts can be seen currently in a new emphasis upon local ensembles of merit. The CLEVELAND CHAMBER SYMPHONY (1980- ), Edwin London, conductor, and the OHIO CHAMBER ORCHESTRA (1971- ), Dwight Oltman, conductor, have joined older groups, including the

CLEVELAND WOMEN'S ORCHESTRA (1925- ), still under its original conductor, Hyman Schandler—the oldest women's orchestra in the nation—and the SUBURBAN SYMPHONY (1954- ), Martin Kessler, conductor, to greatly enrich the yearly spectrum of orchestral concerts. Various choral groups have contributed, including the William Appling Singers & Orchestra, founded in 1979. But especially opera and ballet have flourished in Cleveland during recent years. Two opera companies, CLEVELAND OPERA (1976- ) and LYRIC OPERA CLEVELAND (formerly the Cleveland Opera Theatre; autonomous since 1976), mount important productions. The CLEVELAND BALLET (1974- ) does excellent work. Concerts supported successfully at educational institutions and through such organizations as the Chamber Music Society, the Rocky River Chamber Music Society, and the Cleveland Museum of Art have been on the rise. Church music series often contribute in important ways. Good musical instruction at various levels, good library collections, and good newspaper reporting by Robt. Finn, Wilma Salisbury, Frank Hruby (of the musical HRUBY FAMILY), J. D. Bain Murray, and others have helped bring Cleveland concertgoers to new levels of sophistication. A model across the nation has become the program notes produced for Severance Hall by program-book annotator Klaus George Roy, and these, as well as other excellent notes for concerts throughout the community, have done much to educate Cleveland audiences. Young Audiences of Greater Cleveland, autonomous since 1977, has been increasingly active in bringing relevant programs of excellence into school situations. In the 1983–84 season, these totaled 663, including 5 residencies.

Patterns of funding for arts organizations have changed dramatically over the past 20 years. Particularly since the creation in 1964 of the Natl. Council on the Arts and in 1965 of the Natl. Foundation on the Arts & Humanities, with its components, the Natl. Endowment for the Arts and the Natl. Endowment for the Humanities, the federal government has come to play an increasingly important role. At the state level, the Ohio Arts Council, which has contributed much in support of music, was also founded in 1965. The amount of arts money received from foundations has decreased. Competition for funds, however, and "crisis financing" continue to hamper musical organizations as an increasing number of these vie for existing funds. As Congress debates the future of tax-exempt gifts to nonprofit institutions, as federal programs are cut because of the huge national deficit, and as funding in general becomes more elusive, musical organizations are finding they must learn better to manage their own affairs as well as to sharpen their focus and public image. Public relations has developed as an increasingly important field of professional concern. Indicative is the growth of arts administration as a professional field. The newly established and smaller musical groups have a particularly hard time, not only because of the problems of building constituencies but also because foundations and corporations have traditionally been cautious in supporting such groups, as they also show reluctance to fund experimental work or direct artistic costs.

Funding problems and opportunities, as well as the way demographic changes have occurred within the Greater Cleveland area, have brought about fundamental changes for Cleveland's musical enterprises. Support for major organizations remains strong but now rests necessarily upon a broader base. The dispersal of population into the suburbs has brought with it a rise in new musical groups associated with these areas. "Amateur" participation runs high. The base of audience support and musical undertakings is now more widespread. A number of foundations, including the CLEVELAND FOUNDATION, the KULAS FOUNDATION, and the Bascom Little Fund, have been receptive to these changes and willing to help. The hope is that, with a wider base, good musical standards may still be maintained. Music and music making are indeed recognized in Cleveland as an important part of life. Cleveland has built over the past century and a half a viable music-making and music-listening community and has gained for itself an international reputation for music. The signs are that that reputation will continue to deepen and grow.

J. Heywood Alexander
Cleveland State University

Alexander, J. Heywood, *It Must Be Heard* (1981).
Grossman, F. Karl, *A History of Music in Cleveland* (1972).

The **MUSICAL ARTS ASSOCIATION,** operating the CLEVELAND ORCHESTRA, Blossom Music Ctr., and SEVERANCE HALL in 1985, has existed since 1915 as an association to support music in the community. It is the largest association of its kind in the state of Ohio. The brainchild of impresario ADELLA PRENTISS HUGHES, who by 1915 had been managing the Symphony Orchestra Concerts in conjunction with the FORTNIGHTLY MUSICAL CLUB for more than 15 years, the Musical Arts Assoc. (inc. Oct. 1915) was operated for the first 10 years as a profit organization. The plural in the name was intentional, for the vision was for it to include dance, opera, chamber music, and the teaching of music at the CLEVELAND MUSIC SCHOOL SETTLEMENT and the public schools.

The founders reflected the members of the business community closely associated with the Symphony Orchestra Concerts. The incorporators were DAVID Z. NORTON, Paul Feiss, Otto Miller, Howard P. Eells, and Andrew Squire. Norton served as the first president. In 1947, Edmund S. Burke, Jr., Paul L. Feiss, Samuel H. Halle, Homer H. Johnson, Otto Miller, and Wm. G. Mather were patrons from among the original 30 directors. In 1985, the list of 60 trustees included Frank E. Joseph (president 1957–68), Herbert Strawbridge, Allen C. Holmes, Richard B. Tullis, R. Henry Norweb, Jr., Ward Smith (president), and Alfred Rankin (chairman of the board). Presidents included DUDLEY S. BLOSSOM (1936–39), THOS. SIDLO (1939–53), Percy W. Brown (1953–55), and Frank E. Taplin (1955–57), later president of the Metropolitan Opera Co. The activities of the Musical Arts Assoc. started with the sponsorship of the Diaghileff Ballet Russe (16–18 Mar. 1916), performed at the B. F. Keith HIPPODROME THEATER. The next event was a performance of Wagner's *Siegfried* by the Metropolitan Opera Co. at LEAGUE PARK, fitted with a new lighting system for that occasion and future events. An array of occasions such as these, with the major performers of the day—Fritz Kreisler, Schumann-Heink, Misha Elman—brought the finest musical opportunities to Cleveland. In Dec. 1918, the Executive Committee of the Musical Arts Assoc. authorized the organization of the Cleveland Orchestra on the basis of payment by rehearsal and concert of some 57 to 60 players. On 8 June 1919, the first season closed with 27 concerts total, 20 in Cleveland and 7 out of town. For the second year, 75 players under salary for 28 weeks gave 61 concerts, 44 in Cleveland and 17 out of town. This second season solidified the high commendation of peers and put the orchestra on the map with such older established orchestras as those of Chicago, Buffalo, and Pittsburgh. Severance Hall was the home of the Cleveland Orchestra after 5 Feb. 1931. Previously the orchestra had played at GRAYS ARMORY, the Masonic

Hall at 30th and Euclid Ave., and PUBLIC AUDITO-RIUM.

In the 1950s and 1960s, Cleveland was lagging behind the 5 major orchestras in both musicians' salaries and length of season. In order to guarantee 52 weeks of employment to the players, there was a need to add a summer festival program such as those in New York, Chicago, Philadelphia, and Boston. The construction of the Blossom Music Ctr. remedied this need. Peter Van Dijk was the architect, Pietro Belluschi the architectural advisor, and Christopher Jaffee and Heinrich Keilholz the acoustical engineers. Opened in 1968 and located on 800 acres in Cuyahoga Falls, Ohio, the center honored the long-time interest of the Dudley S. Blossom family in the Musical Arts Assoc. The Musical Arts Assoc. budget for 1984–85 was over $18 million, including costs of salaries, administration, travel, tours, music, and the maintenance of the orchestra's 2 homes, Severance Hall and Blossom Music Ctr. In order to meet these and future goals, the association established the Fund of the Future in 1984 to raise $10 million in permanent endowment funds and $2 million in capital funds.

Musical Arts Assoc. Archives, Severance Hall.

**MUSICARNIVAL** opened in the summer of 1954 as one of the first tent theaters in the U.S. It produced and staged musicals such as *The King and I* and *Oklahoma* until it closed in the summer of 1975 because of competition from the FRONT ROW THEATER and Blossom Music Ctr. The theater was located on the Thistledown Race Track grounds in the Warrensville Hts.-N. Randall area. Capital for its construction came from a group of prominent Clevelanders led by Robt. H. Bishop, the first president of Musicarnival. The theater seated approximately 1,500 people. In only its second season, it grossed over $245,000. Robt. A. Little, a Cleveland architect, designed the huge circular blue tent, which crowned a saucerlike arena with a round stage as its focal point. To eliminate view-obstructing poles and sagging canvas, the tent was supported by a central steel tripod with cables stretched out to the ground on all sides. The tent alone cost over $15,000. A blockhouse with dressing rooms and public restrooms was located next to the theater. In May 1956, a new and stronger tent was put up, and in 1957, an $80,000 blacktopped parking lot with a capacity for 1,000 cars was built. The original producer and director of Musicarnival productions was John L. Price. The original director of promotion was Marsh Samuel.

The **MUSTEROLE COMPANY,** manufacturer of a famous over-the-counter ointment, was begun in 1905 in a Cleveland drugstore. A. L. McLaren, a pharmacist at a drugstore at Cedar and E. 97th, developed a mustard ointment as a prescription drug. At first, he cooked up the remedy to order in a coffeepot on the prescription desk; as the popularity of the ointment grew, he stocked jars and was besieged with so many orders that he restricted sale of the medication to regular customers. The success of the mustard preparation caught the attention of Geo. Miller, who owned a nearby hardware store. Convinced of the "undoubted merits" of McLaren's product, he sold his store to back expanded manufacturing and packaging. After he and McLaren mobilized additional investors, the Musterole Co. was incorporated in 1907. Soon outgrowing its birthplace, the company was moved to 4612 St. Clair, and then to 1748 E. 27th St. Musterole, as the ointment was called, was used to relieve chest congestion, coughs, minor throat irritation, muscle aches, pains, sprains, and sore muscles. Within a decade after the company's founding, Musterole,

the convenient alternative to old-fashioned mustard plasters, was distributed throughout the U.S. and Canada; it went into worldwide distribution after WORLD WAR I. Throughout the years, the product remained a popular, locally produced proprietary medication. In 1956, Musterole was bought out by the Plough Corp. of Tennessee, and production facilities were moved to Memphis. Plough itself merged with the Scherring pharmaceutical company in 1970; the resulting Scherring-Plough Corp. handled prescription drugs and consumer products such as Dr. Scholl, Maybelline, Coppertone, and Musterole.

**MYERS, GEORGE A.** (5 Mar. 1859–17 Jan. 1930), was the owner of the Hollenden Barber Shop, which became his steppingstone into Republican politics in the 1890s. He became an influential black politician and civic leader. Born in Baltimore, Md., Myers was the oldest child of Isaac and Emma V. Myers. His father was an early black labor leader. Young George graduated from a grammar school for black children in Baltimore. Unable to attend Baltimore City College because of his race, he settled upon a career as a barber, against the wishes of his father, who urged him to study medicine. Myers arrived in Cleveland in 1879 and went to work at Jas. E. Benson's Weddell House Barber Shop. The foreman there for 9 years, he left in 1888 to open a shop in the new HOLLENDEN HOTEL; his new operation was financed by white friends such as LIBERTY E. HOLDEN and JAS. FORD RHODES. Among the innovations Myers claimed for his Hollenden Barber Shop were the use of porcelain fixtures and sterilizers and the installation of individual marble wash basins and telephones at each chair. Myers also made suggestions to a local barber-supply company that were helpful in developing the modern barber chair, and his was the first local establishment to offer the services of a manicurist. By 1920 his shop had grown to employ 17 barbers, 6 manicurists, 5 porters, 3 ladies' hairdressers, 2 cashiers, and 2 podiatrists.

The shop brought Myers into contact with many political figures, and he subsequently became a prominent black political figure in the 1890s, a close ally to MARCUS HANNA. In 1892 he served as a delegate to the Republican Natl. Convention and cast the vote that elected Wm. M. Hahn national committeeman from Ohio and made possible the creation of the McKinley-Hanna organization. Myers was a strong Hanna supporter throughout the decade; he even bribed a black state legislator in 1897 to insure Hanna's election to the U.S. Senate. He was an influential delegate at the Republican Natl. Conventions in 1896 and 1900 and served 3 terms on the Republican State Executive Committee around the turn of the century. His support for Wm. McKinley earned him a promise of a political appointment after the election; Myers refused appointment for himself but used his influence to gain government positions for 4 other blacks.

After the deaths of McKinley in 1901 and Hanna in 1904, Myers retired from national politics and devoted his attention to his family, his business, and local civic affairs. He was a leading Mason, an active Elk, and a member of the Social Circle. During the 1920s, Myers adopted a new tone of militancy in racial matters. This new militancy may have stemmed from the announcement by Hollenden Hotel management in 1923 that after Myers retired, all of the black barbers in his shop would be replaced by whites; that policy prompted the financially secure Myers to postpone retirement for 7 years. Among Myers's 1920s efforts on behalf of his race was a successful campaign to have local newspapers capitalize *Negro* and stop using such offensive

708

words as *darky*, and persuading authorities to place 2 black policemen near the Woodlawn Hill municipal swimming pool to prevent threatened violence over its use by BLACKS. On 17 Jan. 1930, Myers sold his barbershop to hotel management and bought a train ticket to Hot Springs, Ark., for a vacation to improve his heart condition, but he collapsed and died in the train ticket office. He was survived by both his first wife, Sarah, and his second wife, Maude E. Stewart, whom he married in 1896.

Garraty, John A., *The Barber and the Historian* (1956).
George Myers Papers, Ohio Historical Society.

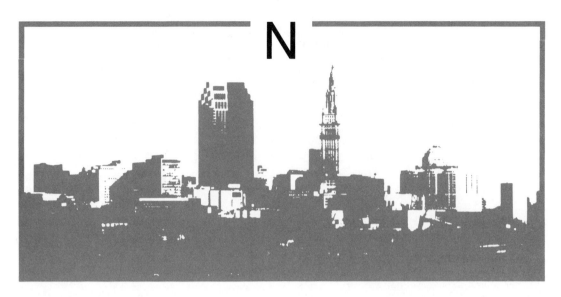

# N

The **NASA LEWIS RESEARCH CENTER**, a major component in the U.S. aerospace program, was established in Cleveland in 1940 as a laboratory of the Natl. Advisory Committee for Aeronautics, an institution responsible for encouraging the growth of American aviation through government research. The NACA convinced Congress that its laboratory at Langley Fld. in Hampton, Va., needed to be expanded. Congress authorized 2 additional laboratories, one on the West Coast, the other in Cleveland. Cleveland was selected because it was a center for the production of aircraft engine parts. Frederick C. Crawford, president of Thompson Prods., played an active role in attracting the government facility to Cleveland. The Aircraft Engine Research Laboratory was built at the western end of Municipal Airport on land that had formerly been used for the stands and parking for the NATL. AIR RACES.

During WORLD WAR II, the laboratory concentrated on the investigation of the problems of aircraft reciprocating engines, contributing to the solution of engine-cooling problems on the Super Fortress (B–29). Research on aviation fuels and icing problems also contributed to the war effort. When the Altitude Wind Tunnel was completed in 1944, it was considered the most advanced facility of its kind in the world. After the turbojet engine was developed in England and Germany, the tunnel was used for early testing of American-built jet engines, particularly those produced by General Electric and Westinghouse. After 1945, the laboratory was completely reorganized to work on jet propulsion, concentrating on advanced work on turbojets, rockets, and ramjets. In 1948 it was renamed the Lewis Flight Propulsion Research Laboratory after Geo. Lewis, the late director of research for the NACA. Throughout the 1950s, the laboratory did fundamental research in supersonic aerodynamics, particularly in relation to the flow of air into and through the turbojet engine. Its research also contributed to the development of new materials to withstand the extremely high temperatures necessary to operate turbojet engines. One of the most important areas of investigation focused on the axial flow compressor, which led to the development of the turbofan engine, a much lighter and quieter type of jet engine.

In 1958, in response to the launching by the Russians of the world's first satellite, the Lewis Research Ctr. became part of the Natl. Air & Space Admin. The center played an active role in the Mercury and Apollo programs under the leadership of director Abe Silverstein, one of the ar-

chitects of the American space program. Development work on upper-stage launch vehicles, such as the Centaur liquid-hydrogen rocket, was the center's most important contribution to the effort to land a man on the moon. Lewis engineers also did basic research on electric propulsion for space vehicles, and at the center's Plum Brook facility near Sandusky, they investigated the possibilities of nuclear propulsion for upper-stage rockets. In the 1970s, during the "energy crisis," attention turned to the investigation of ground-based energy systems, such as wind and solar power. After NASA's success with the space shuttle and renewed national interest in space in the 1980s, the Lewis Research Ctr. again took on an important role as the lead center for the development of a power system for a proposed space station and an advanced satellite communications system.

**NASSAU, JASON J.** (29 Mar. 1893–11 May 1965), was a noted scientist and a skillful popularizer. A leader in the field of astronomy, he possessed the rare ability to make himself understood by ordinary citizens. Nassau was born in Smyrna, Turkey, to Greek parents. He earned a Ph.D. from Syracuse University and did graduate study at Columbia University and Cambridge and Edinburgh universities in Great Britain. In 1921, he received an appointment as associate professor of mathematics and astronomy at Case Institute of Technology. In 1928 he became director of the Warner & Swasey Observatory on the Case campus. He held the position until his retirement as chairman of the Astronomy Dept. and director of the observatory in 1959, when he became professor emeritus.

Nassau was the first American astronomer to realize the benefits of the Schmidt-type telescope. It was on his recommendation that a 35″ Schmidt-type telescope was installed in the Warner & Swasey Observatory. Keenly interested in public education, Nassau made "public nights" a monthly feature at the observatory. When the smog and lights of the city made it necessary to move the telescope to a site near Chardon, the new observatory was named the Nassau Astronomical Station in his honor. Nassau's research on the structure of the Milky Way brought him international acclaim. He developed a technique for studying the distribution of red stars in the galaxy that was adopted by observatories all over the world. In 1957, he discovered a new cluster of 9,000 stars in the Milky Way. With Chas. Stephenson, he discovered 2 novae in Apr. 1961: Seutum–

60-Nassau-Stephenson and Serpens–60-Nassau-Stephenson.

A quiet, contemplative man rarely seen without a pipe, Nassau was one of the most popular professors on the Case campus and was always willing to lend a helping hand. In demand as a speaker at international conferences and at American and European universities, he was equally effective speaking before an area high school audience. Nassau published more than 80 research papers in principal astronomical journals. He was president of the Cleveland Astronomical Society and a fellow of the American and Royal astronomical societies. Nassau married Laura Johnson in 1920 and had 2 sons, Sherwood and James.

**NATIONAL ACME.** *See* **ACME-CLEVELAND**

The **NATIONAL AIR RACES** were first held in Cleveland in 1929. The Natl. Aeronautic Assoc. had sponsored the first Natl. Air Races in 1925. The 1929 races held at Cleveland Airport lasted for 10 days and included an exhibit of planes in Public Hall. There were 35 racing events and several cross-country derbies, including the Powder Puff Derby for women. Aviators participating in or attending the races included Chas. Lindbergh, the Navy "High Hats," and Amelia Earhart. Members of the 1929 board of directors included Alva Bradley, John T. Blossom, I. F. FREIBERGER, Wilbert Austin, Samuel Halle, and M. J. VAN SWERINGEN. It was this Cleveland meet that helped make the Natl. Air Races a major American event in the 1930s. With the exception of 1930, 1933, and 1936, the races were held in Cleveland until they ended in 1949. The races were important in establishing air travel as a viable means of transportation and in advancing research and development of better-designed planes, engines, equipment, and fuels. Races were often sponsored by specific companies. Two of the most famous were the Thompson Trophy Race, sponsored by Thompson Prods., and the Bendix Trophy Race, sponsored by the Bendix Corp. The Thompson race was a 55-mi. closed-course pylon race. The Bendix Race, a cross-country race from Los Angeles to Cleveland, traditionally opened the air races. While women aviators were allowed to enter the races, there was an unwritten law against their entering the Thompson Race. It was believed that they were too weak to handle this "no holds barred" race competently or safely. Disaster during the Thompson Trophy Race of 1949 led to the cessation of the races for many years. Pilot Bill Odom crashed his refurbished F–51 (P–51) into a Berea home on West St., killing himself, resident Jeanne Laird, and her 13-month-old son, Craig. That spurred a set of ordinances in Berea and other nearby communities to prohibit races over their cities. There was no national race in 1950. Between 1951–63, air shows/races were held throughout the country. A new CLEVELAND AIR SHOW began in 1964 at BURKE LAKEFRONT AIRPORT. Incorporated as the Cleveland Natl. Air Show, Inc., it continued the Natl. Air Race tradition, but without high-speed pylon racing.

Hull, Robert, *September Champions* (1979).
Natl. Air Race File, WRHS.

The **NATIONAL ASSOCIATION FOR THE ADVANCEMENT OF COLORED PEOPLE,** Cleveland Chapter, is an interracial organization originally formed to fight discrimination against BLACKS, particularly through legal action. The Cleveland branch was at one time among the largest in the U.S. and remained an avid proponent of moderate NAACP tactics in the 1980s. The group was responsible for the 1976 decision by the U.S. Federal District Court that led to busing to end school desegregation. On a national level, the NAACP was founded in 1909 by black radicals and white progressives critical of black leader Booker T. Washington's emphasis on self-help and accommodation, which implied Negro inferiority. The new organization, largely supported by a college-educated black elite, vocally denounced oppression and discrimination. Early Cleveland supporters of the national movement included CHAS. CHESNUTT and HARRY SMITH. The Cleveland chapter of the NAACP was established in the home of Frances E. Young in 1912 by 21 members concerned about discrimination in the post office. A mass meeting attracted 200 members, but the organization grew slowly and was so financially unstable that it lacked a headquarters until 1922. Under the first 3 chairmen, the NAACP was more of a discussion club than a force for social action. A renewed effort to attract members in 1922 attracted 1,600 people. More vigorous leadership by persons such as CLAYBORNE GEORGE, HARRY E. DAVIS, and Chas. W. White attracted action-oriented professionals and white-collar workers. The local got such a small percentage of its support from whites that it was advised to add whites to its board to attract more money from the white community. Prior to 1927, RUSSELL JELLIFFE of KARAMU HOUSE was the only white on the board. Though it had a somewhat middle-class emphasis, the Cleveland NAACP made a special effort to reach working-class blacks through meetings held in mills and factories, and derived some 40% of its funds from $1 memberships, presumably gathered from workers.

As a result of its growing membership after 1920, the NAACP successfully challenged theaters, restaurants, and public facilities with exclusionary policies, and stores such as Higbees's that refused to allow black women to try on clothing. In addition, the organization led the legal fight for black families refused housing in all-white neighborhoods and blacks extradited to the South on trumped-up charges. Despite its successes, the Cleveland branch of the NAACP faced a rising tide of northern racism. In the 1930s, the fight against discrimination was made more difficult by the Depression. By 1940, the branch was active enough to warrant a part-time secretary to manage its affairs; by 1945, a full-time executive secretary was hired. With a paid professional staff, the organization was able to take on more cases, actively recruit members, and better publicize its work. As a result, the branch had 10,000 members within a year, making it the 6th-largest in the nation. While major battlegrounds for national NAACP issues such as lynching, voting rights, and segregated schools were elsewhere, the Cleveland NAACP of the 1940s and 1950s was at the forefront of efforts to eliminate discrimination in AMUSEMENT PARKS and other public places. In response to a large black post-World War II migration, it countered increased discrimination in housing, employment, education, and public accommodations with vigorous efforts to include black citizens in all areas of American life.

By the 1960s, the NAACP tactics were labeled as too conservative by many blacks. For a time, the local group united with other groups in the more confrontational UNITED FREEDOM MOVEMENT and Operation Black Unity. These organizations picketed Cleveland Trust for its allegedly discriminatory mortgage practices and joined the boycott of McDonald's restaurants because of the lack of black-owned franchises. Ultimately, after disputes over leadership and tactics, the organization returned to its more traditional strategy of seeking change through the courts. Among its legal victories of the decade was the redistricting that led to the formation of the 21st Congressional Congress. Also, the organization challenged the building trades for their exclusionary policies. Despite criticism in an activist age, the local's membership of 12,000 made it the largest branch in the country. In 1973, Cleveland was chosen as a site for the NAACP's long-term battle against school segregation. The Cleveland chapter filed suit against the Cleveland Board of Education, which was found guilty of intentionally segregating the schools. When the court imposed busing as a remedy, the organization became so strongly identified with this tactic (unpopular among many blacks as well as whites) that membership dropped. In the 1980s, the NAACP tried to broaden public perceptions of its purpose, but continued problems in implementing the desegregation decision have demanded most of its organizational resources.

NAACP, Cleveland Branch Records, WRHS.

The **NATIONAL CARBON COMPANY** was organized by Washington H. Lawrence, a former associate of CHAS. F. BRUSH in the Brush Electric Co. In 1881, W. H. Boulton, a Brush foreman, formed a partnership to make electric-lighting carbons. Lawrence purchased an interest in the Boulton Carbon Co. in 1886 to form the Natl. Carbon Co. and acquired the Boulton plant on E. 55th St. MYRON T. HERRICK, Jas. Parmelee, and Webb Hayes, son of former president Rutherford B. Hayes, were associated with Lawrence. The carbon department of Brush was purchased by Natl. Carbon in 1891, and more than 20 other carbon and battery companies were acquired by 1906. The company had 2 Cleveland plants—at W. 73rd St. and the New York Central Railroad, and at Madison Ave. at W. 117th St. in LAKEWOOD. Its products included electrodes, brushes, radios, high-illumination carbons, Eveready batteries for flashlights, radios, and industrial and laboratory uses, Prestone antifreeze, and plastic products. In 1917 the company became a part of the Union Carbide & Carbon Corp. The Natl. Carbon office building on Madison Ave. (1896) is a handsome Romanesque-style building designed by Cleveland architects KNOX & ELLIOT. Natl. Carbon was instrumental in developing employee housing immediately west of the factory site in the Lakewood neighborhood known as the BIRDS NEST AREA because of the street names Thrush, Quail, Robin, Lark, and Plover. Washington Lawrence built himself a large mansion in BAY VILLAGE in 1898, which later became Bay View Hospital.

**NATIONAL CASTINGS COMPANY.** See **MIDLAND-ROSS COMPANY**

The **NATIONAL CITY CORPORATION** is Ohio's largest banking organization, and its principal subsidiary, Natl. City Bank, is the oldest bank in Cleveland. It started in 1845 when the new state banking act brought to an end the banking privileges of such organizations as the Fireman's Insurance Co. of Cleveland. Its leading officers, Reuben Sheldon and Theodoric C. Severance, sought a way out of liquidation by reorganizing the firm as a bank. The City Bank of Cleveland was one of the first banks to be granted a state charter, on 17 May 1845, with a capital of $50,000. It was opened on 1 July 1845 at 52 Superior St. in the Merchants Exchange Bldg. with 2 employees. Three years later, it moved to 21 Superior St. near Water (W. 9th) St. When its 20-year charter expired, it was reorganized as the Natl. City Bank of Cleveland on 12 Feb. 1865 with a capital of $100,000. The bank grew steadily during the late 19th century. By 1887, its capital had reached $250,000. The following year, it moved into the new PERRY-PAYNE BLDG. on Superior Ave. In 1902, the bank passed $2 million in assets. However, Natl. City was still considered a

relatively small bank, chiefly engaged in commercial banking. A reorganization of the bank's leadership in 1912 brought several changes. The following year, Natl. City moved to new and enlarged quarters in the Leader-News Bldg. on E. 6th St. and increased its capital to $500,000. The bank grew rapidly during WORLD WAR I through war-industry financing. In 1921, the firm moved into the renovated Garfield Bldg. (1895) at the corner of E. 6th St. and Euclid Ave. and renamed it the Natl. City Bank Bldg. In the 1920s and 1930s, Natl. City expanded its banking services; it entered the Depression in good financial shape. By 1936, capital had reached $7.5 million, at which time it began to function as a regional bank.

In the postwar period, Natl. City continued to expand. It secured the adjacent Guardian Bldg., initiated an extensive branch banking program, acquired several smaller, local banks, and introduced new customer services. By the early 1970s, it had 39 offices. In 1973, the Natl. City Corp. was formed as a holding company in anticipation of geographic and functional expansions. The following year, it began to acquire various banks in neighboring counties. In 1980, the company, with 111 statewide offices, 2,800 employees, and $4 billion in assets, opened its new headquarters, Natl. City Ctr., at E. 9th St. and Euclid Ave. The $6.6 billion multibank holding company also began to acquire various financial firms in the 1980s. A major acquisition occurred in 1984, when the Natl. City Corp. merged with the Columbus-based BancOhio Corp. Incorporated in Sept. 1929, BancOhio was the 3d-largest bank holding company in the state, with assets of $6 billion. The merger made Natl. City Corp. the largest banking institution in Ohio, with over $12 billion in assets.

Benton, Elbert J., A Century of Progress (1945).

The **NATIONAL CONVENTION OF BLACK FREEMEN** was a 3-day conference that began in Cleveland on 6 Sept. 1848. Presided over by Frederick Douglass, the convention brought together 50–70 free black leaders from the Old Northwest and Canada, men such as John Jones, a Chicago tailor and a prominent proponent of black rights; WM. H. DAY of Ohio; author, educator, doctor, and politician Martin R. Delany; escaped slave Henry Bibb; and Cleveland black leader JOHN MALVIN. Some convention sessions were held in the courthouse, and public sessions were well attended; all blacks who attended were accepted as members of the convention. Black delegates were reportedly treated well by Cleveland hotels and other facilities.

Resolutions passed at the convention favored business education, equality before the law regardless of color, affiliation with the antislavery cause, statistical studies on the status of Negroes, and frequent state and local conventions. Convention delegates were mostly self-made men, and this background influenced the debate over certain issues, such as business education and what kinds of work were considered honorable; an attempt to declare all work as honorable was defeated by those who looked down upon menial labor for blacks. Another hotly debated issue was the role of women at the convention. The women present at first were not allowed to participate, but after continued discussion a compromise was reached, which held that the general convention invitation of "persons" might be construed as including women. One historian has argued that while the Cleveland convention did not enthusiastically embrace women's participation, it was the first national convention to recognize that women had a right to participate. The presidential election of 1848 aroused heated debate over whether the convention should endorse Martin Van

Buren's Free-Soil party. The convention was highly critical of both the Whigs and the Democrats for having "betrayed the sacred cause of human freedom" with their stands on slavery, and only after much debate did the convention endorse the Free-Soil party.

Bell, Howard, "The National Negro Convention, 1848." *Ohio Historical Quarterly* 67 (Oct. 1958): 357–68.

The **NATIONAL COUNCIL OF JEWISH WOMEN, CLEVELAND SECTION,** is the oldest existing Jewish women's organization in the city. Established in Nov. 1894, 1 year after the national organization, it did not officially affiliate with the national until Feb. 1896. The Cleveland Sec. was formed by the merger of 3 older organizations, the Ladies Benevolent Society, the Ladies Sewing Society, and the Personal Services Society. Rabbi MOSES J. GRIES was one of the prime movers in the creation of the section and served as the organization's first president (1894–96), the only male officer in its history. He was followed by Flora Schwab, who served as president for the next 10 years.

Essentially a social-welfare and social-action agency, the Cleveland Sec. initially provided aid to the East European Jewish immigrants who were settling in the Woodland neighborhood. Among its early programs were English and citizenship classes, a public bath house, and day nurseries for working mothers. A fundraising bazaar in 1897 brought in $13,000, which provided seed money for the creation of the Council Educational Alliance. Established in 1899, the CEA, a settlement house, became the social and recreational center for the immigrant community and was the forerunner of the JEWISH COMMUNITY CTR. Although the CEA became an independent agency, the Cleveland Sec. maintained a majority membership on the board of trustees.

In 1897, the Cleveland Sec. established the city's first night school. Particularly popular among the city's new immigrants, the school was subsequently taken over by the city in 1900. In 1907 the Cleveland Sec. founded the Martha House, a home for young working girls who otherwise did not have a proper home environment. Many of the section's projects, such as CEA and the night school, have been taken over by other appropriate agencies once established and proved successful. The Vocational Counseling Bureau was taken over by the Jewish Welfare Fed.; and the Golden Age neighborhood clubs, created in the mid-1940s, became part of the Senior Adult Div. of the Jewish Community Ctr.

In Nov. 1963, Council Gardens, a nonsectarian, low-rent complex for healthy older adults who do not qualify for public housing, opened its doors. Conceived in 1953 by RUTH EINSTEIN, a long-time member of the Cleveland Sec., the complex received the section's endorsement in 1959, and loans from the federal government in 1962. Located on Taylor Rd. near Mayfield, it includes 130 units. The Cleveland Sec. offers a sophisticated volunteer training program for members who wish to participate in section-sponsored or -assisted community services. The section offers financial or volunteer assistance to community organizations and services such as Bellflower House, the Early Childhood Enrichment Ctr., Jewish Big Sisters, the Jewish Family Service Assoc., Project Hunger, and Women in Community Service, among others.

As one of the initial affiliated agencies of the Fed. of Jewish Charities, the Cleveland Sec. received an annual grant from the FJC. Other sources of funding included dues and special fundraising programs. In 1936, the first of the Council Thrift Shops was opened. The thrift shops became the largest source of income for the section, and soon after their creation, funding from the federation was discontinued by mutual agreement. For a period of 14 years, 1908–22, the Cleveland Sec. dropped its affiliation with the national organization in a dispute over local membership classifications and the amount of dues owed to the national. It became known as the Cleveland Council of Jewish Women. Differences were settled by 1921, and the Cleveland group voted to return to the national the following year.

Natl. Council of Jewish Women, Cleveland Section Records, WRHS.

The **NATIONAL EMIGRATION CONVENTION OF COLORED PEOPLE,** led by early black nationalist Martin R. Delany, was held in Cleveland from 24–26 Aug. 1854. The convention was called not simply to discuss the merits of emigration but also to develop a practical plan for blacks in the U.S. to emigrate to the West Indies or Central or South America. The controversial call for the convention unleashed a heated debate among black leaders, not only about emigration but also about strategies for improving the plight of blacks in general. One historian credits the Cleveland meeting with giving birth "to a new concept of black nationalism never before allowed expression in America." The call for the convention announced that discussions would be open "specifically by and for the friends of emigration and NONE OTHERS—and no opposition to them will be entertained." Such a strident announcement brought harsh criticism from some black leaders, particularly Frederick Douglass, but it attracted 106 delegates to the Congregational Church on Prospect St. The largest delegation was from the Pittsburgh area; others came from Louisiana, Missouri, Kentucky, and Canada, as well as from the northern states. Cuyahoga County was represented by Stephen Jones, R. M. Johnson, Wm. Dixon, MADISON TILLEY, and 5 women: Mary Davis, Nancy Williams, Sarah Graves, Louisa S. Brown, and Julia Williams; along with 24 other women delegates, these women took part in the first national convention open to women's participation. According to the proceedings, another Cleveland black, JOHN MALVIN, requested to speak in opposition to emigration but was denied the floor. Convention delegates approved a series of resolutions and a platform or a declaration of sentiments, which took a strident tone in commenting upon the political and social condition of black life in the U.S. They also approved a lengthy document entitled "Political Destiny of the Colored Race," which argued that "for more than two thousand years, the determined aim of the whites has been to crush the colored races wherever found" and urged emigration to areas such as Central and South America, which provided opportunity for "the enjoyment of civil and religious liberty." To make plans for such emigration, the convention established a board of commissioners, based in Pittsburgh; Delany was chosen as president of the commissioners, and along with fellow commissioners Wm. Webb and Chas. W. Nighten, he spearheaded the emigration movement until it peaked in 1861.

*Proceedings of the National Emigration Convention of Colored People* (1854), WRHS.

**NATIONAL HISTORY DAY** is a competition, directed from CASE WESTERN RESERVE UNIVERSITY, that encourages historical research and learning among secondary-school students. History Day, which occurs annually in June, is the culmination of a series of contests at progressive levels. Throughout the school year, students research and prepare papers, projects, dramatic performances, and media presentations based on an annual historical theme. Themes are broad enough in scope to encourage students to research topics ranging from family and community to world history. Participants assemble on a college or university campus, where their efforts are judged by professional historians. Winners in 6 categories in 2 age divisions then progress to a state contest; the state winners are invited to compete in a 4-day national event in the Washington, D.C., area. In addition to rewarding students, Natl. History Day also recognizes teachers for their efforts. Teachers of winning students receive memberships in various professional historical organizations.

The program was conceived and initiated in Cleveland in 1974 by history professor David D. Van Tassel of CWRU in response to numerous reports focusing on the decline in scholarship and inadequate teaching in American school systems. At that time, History Day was only a pilot project involving 129 secondary-school students in the Greater Cleveland area. By 1976, it had spread throughout the state. In 1977, the program began receiving funding from Youth Projects of the Natl. Endowment for the Humanities as start-up money to build a national program. In 1978, History Day programs began in Indiana and Kentucky. Iowa was added in 1979, and that same year the program incorporated into a nonprofit organization under the name Natl. History Day, Inc. The following year, 15 additional states were added, 19,163 students participated at various levels, and a national contest was held at Georgetown University in Washington, D.C. In 1981, the national contest was moved to the University of Maryland-College Park, where it has been held ever since. In 1986, 46 states and the District of Columbia held History Day contests. That year approximately 125,000 students, 35,000 teachers and 5,000 professional historians acting as voluntary judges and state and district coordinators participated in the program.

The **NATIONAL ORGANIZATION FOR WOMEN** (**NOW**), since the establishment of a chapter in Cleveland in 1970, has been a strong and effective advocate of women's rights and a promoter of women's issues. NOW was established in Cleveland largely through the efforts of Lois G. Adams, who served as president of the local chapter during its first several years. An initial attempt to organize NOW in Cleveland in the late 1960s faltered in 1968, when local organizer Betty Boyer and other members objected to the national organization's position on abortion; using the membership list of the local NOW chapter she had formed, Boyer established a new group, the Women's Equity Action League. Reestablished in Cleveland under Adams's leadership in 1970, NOW grew steadily to 300 members in 1978. Through mergers, the separate Cleveland, Lakewood, N. Olmsted, Hillcrest, and Heights chapters later were reduced to 2: Cleveland and Cleveland East.

Early in the 1970s, NOW established 26 Aug. as Women's Equality Day and celebrated it annually with conferences, workshops, and marches. The local group also established its activist orientation early in the 1970s. Much of its work went to support passage of the Equal Rights Amendment, both in Ohio and nationally. Cleveland NOW sponsored walkathons and other events to raise funds for the fight for the ERA. Work on behalf of the ERA led NOW to develop more of a political focus in the late 1970s. The chapters established a political-action committee to endorse and to work in support of candidates with appropriate stands on women's issues. One result of NOW's political activity was Sen. Howard Metzenbaum's recommendation of and Pres. Jimmy Carter's appointment of

Cleveland State University law professor Ann Aldrich to the federal bench in May 1980.

Many of NOW's actions were aimed at institutions such as local school systems and the media. NOW members successfully urged schools to discontinue the use of sexist textbooks and to offer greater athletic opportunities for girls; NOW protests also were responsible for changes in personnel policies that discriminated against pregnant teachers and for the creation of lunch programs in suburban schools. In 1976, Cleveland NOW filed informal complaints with the FCC, charging the 3 network-affiliated television stations and 6 radio stations in the area with sexual and racial discrimination in hiring. NOW leaders credit the action with helping to change hiring practices at the stations and making them more aware of their on-air treatment of women. Local NOW members also protested against sexist portrayals of women in advertising. In addition to public demonstrations to publicize women's issues and promote change, NOW also has provided educational services, sponsoring classes in home repairs and auto mechanics and using conferences and workshops to discuss and foster concern about a variety of women's issues, such as child care, abortion, and crime against women.

The **NATIONALITIES SERVICES CENTER** is a nonprofit social-service organization created in 1954 by the consolidation of 2 existing agencies, the Citizens' Bureau and the Internatl. Institute of the YWCA. The center helps recent immigrants adjust to life in a new land, provides technical assistance related to immigration and naturalization, and works to foster good relations between native- and foreign-born citizens. The Internatl. Institute of the YWCA was begun in New York in 1911 "for the protection and welfare of immigrant girls." The Cleveland YWCA undertook similar work in Sept. 1916 in its Dept. of Immigration, which became the Internatl. Institute in Dec. 1917. Its first center was in the Collinwood area, serving the SLOVENES, CROATIANS, SERBIANS, and ITALIANS there. Another office was opened in 1917 at 1620 Prospect Ave.; that building remained the institute's home throughout its history. By 1920, the institute had 14 nationality workers operating in 2 neighborhood centers—at 833 E. 152nd St. and 4816 Clark Ave.—and in settlements, libraries, churches, and even clients' homes, offering English classes at the convenience of immigrant women. In addition to teaching English, the institute's workers served as translators, helped immigrants with personal problems, and sponsored nationality clubs to encourage and foster "a distinct national consciousness" among immigrants. The institute also undertook efforts to educate Clevelanders about the various ethnic groups living in the city. Margaret Fergusson, who began as educational director in 1923, served as executive director of the institute from 1926 until it merged with the Citizens Bureau in 1954.

The Citizens Bureau developed as a result of the work of the Americanization Committee of the MAYOR'S ADVISORY WAR COMMITTEE. Financed by the board from 1917–19, the committee helped officials of the draft board in their dealings with immigrants, providing immigrants with information about the draft and processing exemption claims and affidavits. It also helped with naturalization cases and in 1917 began to offer naturalization classes, teaching 300 students that year. When the Mayor's Advisory War Committee ceased to exist in 1919, the Americanization Information Bureau received support from the Welfare Fed., which it joined in 1921; by 1922 its name had been changed to the Citizens Bureau. In 1920, attorney Geo. C. Green became the director of the bureau, a post he held until 1954. By 1921, the number of citizenship classes offered by the bureau had grown to 50, and more than 5,000 people enrolled in them; between 1917–21, the bureau provided aid and advice to 100,000 and taught 15,000 in its naturalization classes. In Apr. 1933, the agency moved its offices from the old courthouse at W. 3rd and Frankfort to the Marshall Bldg. on PUBLIC SQUARE.

After WORLD WAR II, the nature of the demand for services from the Citizens Bureau changed: services related to naturalization declined, while there was increased need for help in bringing friends and relatives to the U.S. These changes posed problems for the bureau, and in 1949 the Group Work Council of the Welfare Fed. began to explore whether it and the Internatl. Institute offered similar services and could be made to operate more efficiently. A recommendation to merge the two was adopted in 1952 and became effective in 1954. Located in the former headquarters of the Internatl. Institute from 1954 until moving to the Community Services Bldg. (1001 Huron Rd.) by 1966, the new Nationalities Services Ctr. continued the operations of its predecessors and began new programs, especially in publicizing the contributions of foreign-born citizens. It provided assistance to many new groups, such as Puerto Ricans in the 1950s, Hungarian and Cuban political exiles in the 1950s and 1960s, and both Lebanese and Vietnamese refugees in the 1970s. It compiled guides to local nationality groups in 1955, 1961, 1974, and 1981, and in 1962 began the annual All Nations Festival. In 1974 it created the Language Bank, a 24-hour translation service. By the mid-1970s, the center was helping more than 9,000 people annually and had an annual budget of $119,000.

Nationalities Services Ctr. Records, WRHS.

## NATIVE AMERICANS. *See* AMERICAN INDIANS

**NAVIN, ROBERT B.** (27 Apr. 1895–13 Feb. 1970), eminent sociologist and scholar, was dean and later president of ST. JOHN COLLEGE for 30 years. Merging his concern for academic excellence and his sensitivity to urban problems, he forged the downtown institution into an outstanding training ground for Catholic teachers and nurses. Born in Youngstown, Ohio, Navin studied for the priesthood in Rochester, N.Y., was ordained in 1923, and received a doctorate in sacred theology in Rome. Back in the states, he pursued graduate studies in education and sociology at Catholic University. His doctoral dissertation, "The Analysis of a Slum Area," was a study of Cleveland's E. 21st-E. 55th-Central-Woodland area, which became a pattern for studies in 34 other U.S. cities.

When Navin came to Sisters' College in 1929, the school was a newly formed college to train nuns for teaching in diocesan schools. Within a decade, he won its accreditation from the American Assoc. of Teachers' Colleges and developed a masters of education program. In planning curriculum, he stressed the development of well-rounded Christian teachers aware of the physical, spiritual, domestic, and social dimensions of their students. He oversaw the physical expansion of the school, which became St. John College in 1946 when it moved into a new building; Msgr. Navin became president at this time. With new facilities at E. 9th and Superior, the school was able to develop an accredited nursing program, offer adult-education classes, and open the auditorium and classrooms to community groups. Interested in the Catholic trade-union movement, Msgr. Navin encouraged labor-management and collective-bargaining workshops at the college.

Aside from his college activities, Navin was active in many civic organizations, his particular interest being housing and urban renewal. In WORLD WAR II, he was chair-

man of the Cleveland Area Rent Control Board and the Cleveland Area Rent Committee. Later, he served as president of the Better Homes & Neighborhoods Assoc. and was a member of the mayor's advisory boards of housing and urban renewal. His other affiliations included the Cleveland Welfare Fed., the URBAN LEAGUE OF CLEVELAND, the Council on Human Relations, the CONSUMERS LEAGUE OF OHIO, the Assoc. of Catholic Trade Unionists, and the Community Relations Board. Failing eyesight caused him to resign the presidency of St. John in 1960. As president emeritus, he made daily trips to the college, where he continued to advise his successor, Msgr. Lawrence Cahill. Additional health problems necessitated his move from his long-time home at St. Agnes rectory to an apartment at ST. VINCENT CHARITY HOSPITAL, where he overlooked the urban renewal of the E. 22nd-Woodland area—the fulfillment of a long-time dream.

**NAVY PARK,** located at Ridge and Clinton Roads, was one of 5 housing developments opened in 1946 for World War II veterans. During the war, the project housed itinerant war-industry workers. The developments were under the authority of the Cleveland Metropolitan Housing Authority. In the 1950s, the housing units were demolished. The property was then used for a U.S. Naval Reserve Training Ctr. for a number of years. In the 1970s, 1 large structure—the gymnasium—was the only building left standing. It was used for Golden Gloves boxing tournaments during that time.

**NELA PARK,** located at Noble and Terrace roads in E. Cleveland, is one of the earliest (if not the first) planned industrial research parks in the nation. It was conceived in 1910 by Franklin Terry and Burton Tremaine, officers of the Natl. Electric Lamp Co., which soon became the lamp division of GENERAL ELECTRIC. NELA is an acronym for Natl. Electric Lamp Assoc. A more effective working atmosphere, the economic advantages of a suburban location, and the development of a unique morale were among the reasons for the concept. The site was selected in 1910, a small plateau 234' above Lake Erie, with some dense woods and a picturesque ravine. The building program began in 1911 and was entrusted to one architect in order to achieve a consistent scheme. The architects for all the buildings begun before 1921 were Wallis & Goodwillie of New York. Frank E. Wallis was a student of English and Colonial architecture, and he did further studies of Georgian architecture in the south of England in preparation for the planning. The buildings were erected by the AUSTIN CO., pioneers in the concept of one organization integrating the design, engineering, and construction of a project; its work at Nela Park led directly to the standardization of construction methods in industrial building. The complex was very advanced in its handling of mechanical systems, with underground tunnels for all utilities, as well as some pedestrian subway connections.

The main conception of the campuslike park is a perfect representation of the early-20th-century academic ideal. The functional planning and architectural design of the individual buildings, as well as the ensemble, were carried out with great consistency and good taste. The office and laboratory complex includes 20 major buildings and several smaller structures located in a landscaped park of approximately 90 acres. The prevailing style is Georgian Revival, and all but 4 of the major buildings were built between 1911–21. Four of them are arranged around the Quadrangle, which dominates the architectural scheme of the park. The Engineering Bldg., on the north end, stands on the brow of the hill overlooking the north entrance lodge on

Terrace Rd. The Advertising Bldg., on the east side of the Quadrangle, has a classic portico of granite columns. The largest building is the Lamp Laboratory on the south end, and the west side is closed by the Institute (1921), which has a 72' bell tower and a Georgian facade facing a circular pool, with a bronze statuary group symbolizing the triumph of light over darkness. The entire area was landscaped according to plans developed at the outset. Winding roadways are lined with trees, and a great variety of plants and trees are represented. Public access to the park was encouraged at the beginning but was discontinued in later years. One of the best-known and most popular aspects of Nela Park has been its annual electrically illuminated Christmas display.

**NESS, ELIOT** (19 Apr. 1903–16 May 1957), nationally known for his leadership of the "Untouchables" in Chicago during Prohibition, spent a significant part of his law-enforcement career in Cleveland as one of the city's most effective safety directors. Ness was born in Chicago, the son of Norwegian immigrants. After graduating from high school, he attended the University of Chicago, where he studied political science, commerce, and business administration. Following graduation in 1925, he obtained employment in the insurance industry. He joined the U.S. Prohibition Bureau in 1929. His career with the bureau was highlighted by the formation of the "Untouchables," a group of agents who were beyond bribery and corruption. The most notable accomplishment of Ness and his unit was the conviction and subsequent incarceration of Al Capone on charges of income-tax evasion. Following the repeal of Prohibition, Ness was transferred to the Treasury Dept.'s Alcohol Tax Unit in Cincinnati, where he became responsible for locating and destroying illegal moonshine operations in the Appalachian backcountry. He arrived in Cleveland in 1935 as the head of the alcohol tax unit of the FBI. His reputation as an honest and capable law-enforcement officer brought him to the attention of Cleveland mayor HAROLD H. BURTON. Burton appointed Ness as the city's safety director later in 1935 in an effort to clean up the scandal-ridden police department. Ness quickly formed his own band of Cleveland "Untouchables," some of whom were private investigators. This unit was funded by an anonymous group of businessmen known as the "Secret 6." Ness quickly reformed the department, eliminating malfeasance through large-scale transfers of personnel and the conviction and imprisonment of others. He also upgraded the department, reorganizing the patrol system, motorizing it, and using radios in police cars to enhance communication. He established a separate traffic section and hired the city's first traffic engineer, enabling Cleveland, which had the worst traffic-fatality record in the nation, to twice win the Natl. Safety Council's award for reduction of traffic deaths. Ness also modernized the fire department, created the Police Academy and the Welfare Bureau, and helped found the local chapter of BOYSTOWN.

Ness's tenure saw a crackdown on labor-union protection rackets, illegal liquor suppliers, and gambling. His most spectacular moment in Cleveland came on 10 Jan. 1936, when he closed down the HARVARD CLUB, a notorious gambling house located just outside the city limits in NEWBURGH HTS. When Democratic mayor Frank Lausche took office, critics began to call for Ness's removal, citing his social drinking with members of the media, his divorce from his second wife, his outside work with the federal government, and a traffic accident in which he was involved that looked suspiciously like a hit-skip incident. Lausche, however, retained Ness, making him the first safety director to serve under both a Republican and a Democratic mayor.

Ness, however, left the city in 1942 to become director of the Div. of Social Protection of the Federal Security Agency. After the war he returned to Cleveland, where he ran unsuccessfully as Republican candidate for mayor in 1947. He devoted the remainder of his career to business endeavors, finally leaving the city for Coudersport, Pa., in 1956. Shortly before his death, Ness, suffering from financial reverses, began a collaboration with journalist Oscar Fraley that led to the immensely successful book *The Untouchables*, which detailed Ness's career in Chicago. Ness, however, died before the book was published.

Eliot Ness Scrapbooks, WRHS.

**NEW DAY PRESS** is a nonprofit publishing venture designed to eliminate stereotypes and distortions of history by printing new literature for black schoolchildren that presents the story of blacks in American history with dignity and from a black perspective. The idea for such a press developed in 1969, when CASE WESTERN RESERVE UNIVERSITY sponsored a conference on "Books That Don't Exist: Literature for Inner-City Children." As the result of 2 subsequent writers' conferences in the summers of 1970 and 1971, about 15 local writers, including Edith Gaines, formed a writers' group, Metro Writers, in late 1971. Material prepared by Metro Writers was field-tested by a group of E. Cleveland teachers who were in search of new material to use in a new curriculum for elementary schoolchildren. In Jan. 1972, New Day Press was formed to publish the new stories.

In Apr. 1972 the press issued 6 paperback books on pre-Civil War black history, and in 1974 it published a series of 5 stories on black history during Reconstruction. *Blacks in Ohio: 7 Portraits* appeared in 1976, and in 1980 New Day Press issued a volume of poetry by local schoolchildren entitled *If a Poem Bothers You* (ed. Nancy Woodrich). Located at KARAMU HOUSE, New Day Press had produced more than 50,000 copies of its 13 titles by its 10th anniversary in 1982 and had shipped orders to 45 states. Much of its work was financed by grants from such sources as the Presbytery of Cleveland and local foundations. In July 1980, a grant from the Ohio Arts Council enabled the press to hire a part-time coordinator to handle distribution and sales. In addition to publishing, the press encouraged creativity by sponsoring a short-story contest for children and holding monthly writers' workshops.

**NEW ENGLAND SOCIETY OF CLEVELAND & THE WESTERN RESERVE.** *See* **PATRIOTIC SOCIETIES**

The **NEW ORGANIZATION FOR THE VISUAL ARTS (NOVA)** was created in 1972 as an incorporated nonprofit professional organization dedicated to the promotion and development of the arts and ARCHITECTURE in the Cleveland area. In addition to promotion and development, NOVA's stated purpose is to increase and expand professional opportunities for Cleveland-area artists, and to work for the aesthetic improvement of the entire community. The organization also serves as a forum by which artists share ideas and opinions. The original organization from which NOVA developed was the Art Community Co-op. In late Oct. 1972, it voted to change its name to the New Organization for the Visual Arts. The new organization had approximately 80 members. In addition to special exhibitions, NOVA sponsors professional programs and "how to" workshops for area artists. It also provides a slide registry for members' works and a sales and rental committee, which is responsible for promoting sales of individual pieces and renting small exhibits to local businesses. Other core services provided by NOVA to its members include discount buying, legal referral service, a newsletter, exhibit opportunities, and access to trucking service. NOVA has been supported by grants from both government and private foundations, including the GEO. GUND FOUNDATION and the CLEVELAND FOUNDATION. Other funds derive from annual membership dues, commissions on sales of artists' works, and individual contributions. The members, under the guidance of the elected officers and trustee and advisory boards, run NOVA. It is administered by an executive director and staff. The original headquarters for NOVA were at 1240 Huron Rd. Mall. In Nov. 1976 it relocated to 1290 Euclid Ave. By 1976, 4 years after its inception, NOVA found itself with a $43,000 budget deficit, which led in 1977 to the development of a new directive for the organization, which established core services that would be covered by a basic budget. Among those who have served as NOVA's executive director are Cornelius Spring, Wm. Busta, Janet Spitz, and Janus Small.

**NEW YORK CENTRAL RAILROAD.** *See* **CONRAIL**

**NEWBURGH,** a township south of Cleveland, was an early population and economic center for the area. Bounded by Cleveland and E. Cleveland on the north, WARRENSVILLE on the east, INDEPENDENCE on the south, and BROOKLYN and the CUYAHOGA RIVER on the west, old Newburgh was on higher ground than Cleveland and thus avoided the outbreaks of malaria that hampered development to the north—but not wolves, which protested but did not stop settlement. In the early 1800s, with 10 families in residence, Newburgh was more prominent than Cleveland, described as "six miles from Newburgh." It was organized as a township in 1814.

As early as 1799, mills built at the cataract of MILL CREEK fostered economic prosperity, and soon a main coach road (later called Broadway) was cut through the area. Aside from the milled products, one of the earliest industrial products was burr millstone, quarried in Newburgh and cut by Abel Garlick. Some stone was shipped out of the region, but the majority was used locally. Newburgh's fertile soil and good pastureland encouraged farming, but the waterpower attracted heavy industry, which ultimately dominated the area economy. In the 1840s, the Cleveland & Pittsburgh (later Pennsylvania) Railroad was built through the township and provided easy access to shipping. The township's most famous industry, the Cleveland Rolling Mill, was started in 1857 by DAVID AND JOHN JONES to reroll iron rails. The Jones brothers were soon joined by Andros Stone and HENRY CHISHOLM, a Scottish immigrant who made the mill a preeminent steel producer. The coming of the mills changed the ethnic makeup of the community. New England and Manx settlers were outnumbered first by IRISH who came to build the nearby Ohio Canal, then by Welsh iron puddlers, and finally by Polish and Czech mill laborers.

Newburgh's early prominence made it a likely site for the county seat, but Cleveland, which finally overcame the mosquitoes, was selected in 1826 because of its location as a port of entry from Lake Erie at the Cuyahoga River. Cleveland's geographic advantages in time predetermined that much of Newburgh and surrounding townships would become part of the larger city. As a result, beginning in 1823, Newburgh was eroded through annexation to Cleveland, as well as to E. Cleveland and Independence townships. The heart of Newburgh—the area bounded by Union Ave. on the north, by E. 93rd St. on the east, and by current city borders on the west and south—became part of Cleveland in 1873. This section of town became Cleveland's 18th ward, dubbed "the iron ward." Many residents of the cohesive neighborhood protested the annexation. The remaining portions of the township were incorporated as the village of Newburgh in 1874, while keeping the township organization, as well. Additional annexations by Cleveland in 1878, 1893, and 1894 further compressed its size. In 1904, the village of NEWBURGH HTS. was incorporated, but this entity was further reduced in size with the organization of the Twp. of S. Newburgh (GARFIELD HTS.) in 1904 and the Twp. of Corlett in 1906 and final annexation of small parcels of land to Cleveland in 1913.

**NEWBURGH HEIGHTS** is a .5-sq.-mi. residential community located south of Cleveland between the industrial valley of the CUYAHOGA RIVER and the village of CUYAHOGA HTS. It was originally part of Newburgh Twp. The name was probably taken from Newburgh, N.Y. Newburgh Hts. was organized and incorporated as a village in 1904, with E. S. Peck as the first mayor (1904–08). The population in 1909 was 400. Newburgh Hts. was settled first by New England settlers, then by IRISH and Welsh immigrants, and subsequently by POLES, CZECHS, and GERMANS who worked in the nearby steel mills and factories of Newburgh. In 1917, Newburgh Hts. had a building boom; farms were subdivided into residential lots, taxes rose, and a group of residents seceded and formed the village of Cuyahoga Hts. The new boundaries left the residential area in Newburgh Hts. and the farmland and industrial area in Cuyahoga Hts. In 1930, the population of Newburgh Hts. was 4,152. It was 4,000 in 1940, 3,600 in 1953, and 4,000 in 1960. Raus Park in Newburgh Hts. was the setting for many gymnastic exhibitions, concerts, nationality dances, carnivals, and sporting events, including boxing and wrestling shows organized and promoted by the St. John's Club, the Polish Women's Progressive Aid Society, the Young Men's Progressive Club, the Hilltop Club, the Root Social Club, and the Governor's Club, as well as by many patriotic, political, and service organizations. In 1984 the population of Newburgh Hts. was 2,678.

The **NEWBURGH & SOUTH SHORE RAILWAY** operated a beltline railroad through the industrial region of the Cuyahoga Valley. A Class I, standard-gauge railroad, it operated only 7 mi. of main track and 78 mi. of branch tracks and sidings. Service to industry was its lifeblood. Connecting with all the major railroads serving Cleveland, it provided freight service to most of the industrial plants in the Cuyahoga Valley. Incorporated in 1899 by the American Steel & Wire Co., the N&SS became the wholly owned property of the newly created U.S. Steel Corp. In 1951, U.S. Steel moved ownership of the N&SS to its Bessemer & Lake Erie Railroad.

Completed in 1904, the N&SS was built primarily for hauling molten metal from American's Central Furnaces to its Newburgh Steel works. The main line started at the Central Furnaces near the CUYAHOGA RIVER and ran under Jefferson Ave. across the river, across Huston Ave., under Clark Ave., again across the river, across Campbell Ave., under Harvard Ave., across E. 49th St., bridging E. 71st St., and finally across Aetna Rd. During its early days, the N&SS operated side-saddled steam locomotives on roadbeds that were treacherous in anything wetter than a heavy dew and with a Morse-code system operated by erratic telegraph operators. At the railway's peak, the N&SS steam locomotives were gaily painted with large letters splashed against the black tenders and were among the last in the country to bear the engineer's name on the cab.

By 1927, the N&SS, operating 32 locomotives, did more business than any other 7-mi. stretch of railroad in the world. It introduced its first diesel locomotive in 1939. In 1947 the N&SS retired its remaining Baldwin locomotives, becoming the first Ohio railroad to abandon steam completely. In 1952 its offices were moved from their original location on Broadway to E. 71st St. adjacent to its terminal and railway shops. Reflecting the closing of many industries in the Cuyahoga Valley, business on the N&SS steadily declined after WORLD WAR II. After the closing of the Cuyahoga Steel Works in 1984 and the loss of almost all of its remaining business, the N&SS filed for abandonment with the ICC and sold 2.2 mi. of its main line to the Cuyahoga Valley Railway. The last train on the N&SS operated on 7 Mar. 1986, and the N&SS received final approval for closing on 30 June 1986.

The **NEWMAN-STERN COMPANY** was one of the nation's largest and best-known sporting-goods stores. The company gained note as a pioneer in the radio business. The firm began in 1915 when brothers Joseph S. and Arthur S. Newman and Arnold L. Stern opened the Electro-Set Co. for the manufacture of educational toys in a small store above a restaurant on E. 4th St. However, with Joseph Newman's interest in the infant radio industry, the company soon became Cleveland's first supplier of radio parts. RADIO was so new, though, that the firm pursued national business by way of mail-order catalogs. In 1917, the name was changed to the Newman-Stern Co. Its radio business was crippled during WORLD WAR I when the government banned the manufacture and sale of wireless equipment. Recognizing a growing trend in leisure and recreational activities, Newman-Stern turned to sporting goods to bolster dwindling sales.

After World War I, Newman-Stern went back into the radio as well as the toy and army surplus business, but its major product from then on was sporting goods. By 1920, it moved to larger quarters in the Leader Bldg. at E. 6th St. and Superior Ave. The following year, it moved into a new building at E. 12th St. and Walnut Ave. named after the company. After Arthur Newman died in 1950, Joseph Newman sold his family's interest in the business to department-store owner Nathan Marcus and Allan Kramer. Under their management, Newman-Stern expanded into the suburbs with 2 branch stores. In 1963, the Gateway Sporting Goods Co. of Kansas City, a national sporting-goods chain, acquired Newman-Stern. Four years later, its downtown store was moved to 634 Euclid Ave. By the early 1970s, Gateway was experiencing serious financial and management problems. To help relieve its debt, Gateway decided to close the 2 remaining Newman-Stern stores on 15 May 1973. However, the Newman name has continued to be connected with outdoor equipment. In 1967, the Newman family started its own separate retail firm to sell camping equipment. It became known as the Newman-Adler Co.

Joseph Newman Papers, WRHS.

**NEWSPAPERS.** *See* **PRINT JOURNALISM**

**NICKEL PLATE RAILROAD.** *See* **NORFOLK SOUTHERN CORPORATION**

The **NIGHT IN BUDAPEST,** a celebration with an ethnic flavor, was started in 1957 by flamboyant Cleveland councilman JACK RUSSELL to commemorate the Hungarian Freedom Fighters who defied Russian tanks in their homeland. The gala event, which became an annual one for 17 years, focused attention on Hungarian culture and on Hungarian-Americans. Named after a Buckeye Ave. nightclub

where Russell met his wife, the Night in Budapest offered a 7-course dinner prepared by neighborhood women and served by waitresses in native costume. The atmosphere for the evening was completed by Hungarian orchestras and strolling musicians.

The guest list for the Night in Budapest became a who's who of the Cleveland political community; Russell's friends and foes entered the hall under an arch of swords brandished by Hussar guards, but they were expected to sheath their political differences for the evening. In its first few years, the Night was held in the Bethlen Hall on East Blvd. and Buckeye, which was draped with native decorations, but the demand for the $12.50 tickets exceeded the size of the hall and squeezed out the neighborhood participants. As a result, in 1960 a second night was added, which featured a $6 dinner. By 1963, the evening was moved to the Hotel Sheraton, which could accommodate the 1,500–2,000 who wanted tickets, but the cooking was still done on Buckeye and transported downtown. Since the food was not kept at the proper temperature, some of the guests got food poisoning; in 1964, the managing director of the Sheraton oversaw the food preparation. Native wines accompanied the feast until 1967, when the city decided to enforce a long-ignored Ohio law against serving wine on Sunday.

Besides the food, music, and camaraderie, the Night in Budapest featured entertainment by a Hollywood star, usually of Hungarian origin, and a presentation of awards to 2 local and 2 nationally prominent persons. Chaired by movie producer Joe Pasternak, the cast of stars over the years included Tony Martin, Jimmy Durante, comedian Bill Davis, Zsa Zsa Gabor, and Paul Laka; the success Hungarians had found in films assured an annual supply of celebrities. The honored guests, chosen from a myriad of fields, included Browns tackle Lou (The Toe) Groza, MGM president Joseph Vogel, Judge Blanche Krupansky, Gray Drug president Adolph Weinberger, furniture dealer Louis Sobonja, former state representative Frank Pokorny, and *Press* editor LOUIS B. SELTZER. The Night in Budapest, begun at the onset of ethnic consciousness spurred by the civil-rights movement, started a trend toward ethnic celebrations in Cleveland. Neighborhood halls were the sites of nights in Warsaw, Zagreb, Ljubljana, and old Romania. The original fest, which always operated at a loss that was covered personally by Jack Russell, was discontinued in 1973.

**NIKE MISSILE BASES** were built at 7 sites in Cuyahoga County (with an 8th location in Lake County) during 1955–56. The bases, constructed at a cost of $12 million by the M. J. Boyle Cos. of Chicago, were part of a national network of air defense systems. The bases in Cuyahoga County were located at the following sites: Rocky River-Fairview Park (launch base near Westlake-Fairview Park border, control area at 21700 Westwood Ave.); Parma-Parma Hts. (launch base at 11000 York Rd., control area east of Parma Park Blvd.); Garfield Hts.-Independence (launch base at 733 Stone Rd., control area at 5640 Briarcliff); Warrensville Twp. (launch base at Richmond and Harvard roads, control area on Richmond Rd.); Willowick (launch base at 33605 Curtis, control area at 30100 Arnold); Bratenahl (launch base at 555 E. 88th St., control area at Gordon Park); and Lakefront Airport (launch base at the northeast corner of BURKE LAKEFRONT AIRPORT, control area at E. 40th and MEMORIAL SHOREWAY). Each launch base consisted of a battery of Nike-Ajax missiles, a missile-assembly building, a generator building, an acid-storage building, a fueling area, underground missile storage and launchers, barracks, and a launcher-control trailer. The control area, sited ½ mi. from the launch area, consisted of a mess hall, administration building, barracks, radar tower, and control van.

Built principally to counter an airborne threat from the Soviet Union, the bases and their equipment soon became obsolete because of technical advances. In 1959, the more sophisticated Nike-Hercules missile replaced the Nike-Ajax missiles at the Rocky River-Fairview Park and Bratenahl bases. By Aug. 1961, only the Warrensville and Parma-Parma Hts. Nike-Ajax bases remained operational; the 3 remaining sites had been closed. By 1971, all of the bases, including those equipped with the Nike-Hercules missile, were closed. The bases, once closed, were either razed or turned to other purposes. The Parma-Parma Hts. launch site became the location of the Western Campus of CUYAHOGA COMMUNITY COLLEGE; the Garfield Hts.-Independence bases were turned over to the boards of education of their respective communities, as was the Willowick launch site. The Bratenahl base eventually became the headquarters of the U.S. Navy Finance Ctr.

**NINE MILE CREEK** has its headwaters just south of Cedar Rd. between Green and Richmond roads, runs through E. CLEVELAND, and empties into Lake Erie some 9 mi. from PUBLIC SQUARE. The creek was the site of Cleveland's first church, the Plan of Union (later the First Presbyterian Church of E. Cleveland), in 1807. It later powered small mills and a tannery. A blue sandstone quarry was opened by the stream by 1867 and operated until 1900. Because of the steam's beauty, SAMUEL MATHER located his summer home (Shoreby) on its banks in BRATENAHL. Nine Mile Creek briefly gave its name to the village later called COLLAMER or E. Cleveland.

The **NINETEENTH MEDICAL DISTRICT OF OHIO,** the Greater Cleveland-Medina area, was one of 20 districts designated by the state of Ohio in 1824 for licensing doctors and supervising medical care. Though the original bill was passed in 1811, the number of districts changed as population shifted in the growing state of Ohio. On 24 May 1824, all qualified area physicians met at a hotel at Water and St. Clair to form the 19th District Medical Society. DAVID LONG, Cleveland's first physician, was elected president. The organization scheduled biannual meetings and set up formal licensing procedures for physicians. At first the meetings were held throughout the district, but Cleveland's better accommodations and transportation made the city the regular home base. Within 2 years, the society organized a medical library and set up a committee to purchase books. Little else is known about this organization which was reorganized in 1859 as the CUYAHOGA COUNTY MEDICAL SOCIETY.

The **NINETEENTH OHIO INDEPENDENT BATTERY,** 1862–65, Civil War service, was mustered into federal service at Camp Cleveland, Ohio, for 3 years on 10 Sept. 1862. It remained in Cleveland until movement to Kentucky on 6 Oct. In Lexington, Ky., the 19th Battery was assigned to the Army of Kentucky, Dept. of the Ohio, until Dec. 1862. Between Dec. 1862-Jan. 1863, it was assigned to the artillery of the 2d Div., Army of Kentucky, Dept. of the Ohio. From Jan.-June 1863, the 19th was assigned to the District of Central Kentucky, Dept. of the Ohio. Between June and July 1863, it was part of the 2d Brigade, 4th Div., 23d Army Corps. During July 1863, the battery was assigned to the 2d Brigade, 1st Div., 23d Army Corps, under which it aided in the operations and pursuit of Confederate cavalry forces under Gen. John H. Morgan to Steubenville, Ohio. From Aug. 1863-Jan. 1864, the 19th

was part of the Reserve Artillery, 23d Army Corps. Between Jan.-Apr. 1864, it was assigned to the 1st Brigade, 3d Div., 23d Army Corps. From Apr. 1864-Feb. 1865, it was assigned to the artillery, 2d Div., 23d Army Corps. The 19th Ohio Independent Battery completed the war assigned to the Dept. of North Carolina. It was mustered out, paid off, and discharged at Camp Cleveland, Ohio, 28 June 1865. Losses were listed as 1 officer and 5 enlisted men dead from hostile causes and 1 officer and 17 enlisted men dead from disease.

Tracie, Theodore C., *Annals of the Nineteenth Ohio Battery Volunteer Artillery* (1878).

The **NORFOLK SOUTHERN CORPORATION,** with headquarters in Roanoke, Va., was, by the mid-1980s, one of several major railroad systems serving Greater Cleveland. The descendant of the Norfolk & Western and the Southern railways, it was composed of several lines that were important in the history of Cleveland. Chief among these was the New York, Chicago & St. Louis Railroad which had merged with the Norfolk & Western in 1964. The NYC&SL was organized on 3 Feb. 1881. Its founders were Geo. I. Seney, Columbus R. Cummings, Alexander M. White, John T. Martin, Edward Lyman, and Walston Brown. Originally, the plan called for the construction of a main line from Cleveland to Chicago. A branch was planned to run from Fort Wayne, Ind., to St. Louis, Mo. By the time construction began in Apr. 1881, it had been decided to extend the eastern terminus from Cleveland to Buffalo. The founders of the NYC&SL never specified all the towns it would serve between Buffalo and Chicago. Localities lobbied to get the new railroad to serve them. A heated rivalry occurred between Norwalk and Bellevue, Ohio. In Mar. 1881, during the midst of the contest, the *Norwalk Chronicle* described the new road as a "double track, nickel-plated railroad." Soon, the New York & St. Louis became popularly known as the Nickel Plate. By the 1920s, the word *Road* had been added so that the nickname became the Nickel Plate Road.

Routing through Cleveland was made easier by the purchase of 2 small suburban railroads. One was the Rocky River Railroad, whose tracks gave the Nickel Plate a right-of-way through the city's west side. Chartered on 20 Feb. 1867, the Rocky River Railroad ran from Bridge St. and Waverly Ave. (W. 58th St.) westward to the east bank of the Rocky River, a distance of 5.53 mi. Among its promoters were Daniel P. Rhodes, Ezra Nicholson, Elias Simms, and John H. Sargent. The Nickel Plate acquired control of the Rocky River Railroad on 9 Sept. 1881 and suspended its operations in July 1881, after work crews coming eastward from Vermilion had completed an iron viaduct across the Rocky River and it became necessary to convert the tracks into the Nickel Plate's mainline. The right-of-way through the city's east side came through the acquisition of the CLEVELAND, PAINESVILLE & ASHTABULA RAILROAD. This road began operations on 1 May 1875 as the Lakeview & Collamer Railroad. Its tracks ran from Becker Ave. in Cleveland to Euclid Village. On 1 Sept. 1882, construction was finished. The main line ran from Buffalo, via Ft. Wayne, to Chicago, 521.89 miles. The branch line from Ft. Wayne to St. Louis had not been built. Operations began on 23 Oct. 1882. The chief office of the Nickel Plate was located in the Hoyt Block at Bank (W. 6th) St. and St. Clair Ave. In Cleveland, the Nickel Plate's tracks ran in basically a straight line from west to east. In the west, the tracks entered the city limits in the vicinity of Detroit Ave. and crossed Franklin, Lorain, Walworth, and Scranton avenues before coming to the CUYAHOGA

RIVER. Once over the river, the tracks ran through KINGSBURY RUN and crossed Willson, Kinsman, Adelbert, Mayfield, and Euclid avenues before leaving the city. Two small depots, one at EUCLID AVE. and the other at Pearl (W. 25th) St., were built to serve passengers until the mail station at Broadway and Cross Ave. was opened on 1 Oct. 1883. The Broadway depot served as the Nickel Plate's main passenger station in Cleveland.

On 26 Oct. 1881, the Nickel Plate was sold. Judge Stevenson Burke and JOHN DEVEREUX of Cleveland purchased a controlling interest in the road. Devereux and Burke were agents carrying out the wishes of Wm. K. Vanderbilt, who masterminded and financed the seizure. By acquiring control of the Nickel Plate, Vanderbilt prevented the railroad from being bought by Jay Gould, president of the Erie Railroad and Vanderbilt's arch rival, and eliminated a strong competitor to his own Lake Shore & Michigan Southern. Vanderbilt became president of the Nickel Plate and rewarded Burke and Devereux with seats on the board of directors. The chief offices remained in Cleveland. For the next 30 years, the Nickel Plate was controlled by the Lake Shore & Michigan Southern (which later became the New York Central Railroad) and subsequently led a meager existence, so as not to offer any serious competition to the Lake Shore. The Nickel Plate fell into receivership in 1885. It was reorganized as the New York, Chicago & St. Louis Railroad in 1887.

In 1916, the Nickel Plate was sold to ORIS P. AND MANTIS J. VAN SWERINGEN, who needed a portion of the downtown right-of-way to complete their transit line from SHAKER HTS. to downtown Cleveland. Accordingly, they established the Cleveland & Youngstown Co., which bought all the necessary property upon which to build the new transit line, except for the final 2-mi. section into downtown. The Nickel Plate (still controlled by the NYC) owned the last 2 mi. of land and refused to sell it to the Vans. Fortunately for the Van Sweringens, Congress had recently enacted the Clayton Antitrust Law, and the NYC was under pressure from the ICC to divest itself of the Nickel Plate. The Vans persisted, and eventually purchased the Nickel Plate for $8.5 million. Later, they acquired control of other roads, including the Lake Erie & Western and the Toledo, St. Louis & Western in 1922. The Vans united both of these railroads with the Nickel Plate. Unified operations began on 1 July 1923. The Vans also gained control of the Chesapeake & Ohio, Erie, Hocking Valley, and Pere Marquette railroads. Their proposal to merge these railroads with the Nickel Plate was rejected by the ICC in 1926. The center of the Van Sweringens' railroad empire was CLEVELAND UNION TERMINAL. The Nickel Plate's executive and general offices moved into the Tower on 1 Jan. 1928. After the dedication on 28 June 1930, the Nickel Plate began operating passenger trains from the Terminal and closed its old stations at Pearl St. and Euclid Ave. During the Depression, revenues from freight and passenger service plummeted. A share of Nickel Plate common stock that had sold for $240 in 1927 was worth $1.50 by 1933. Since the Vans had financed many of the improvements on the Nickel Plate with borrowed money, the road was heavily in debt during the 1930s and nearly went bankrupt. Only stringent economic measures and an $18 million loan from the Reconstruction Finance Corp. saved it from collapse. In 1935, Geo. Ball purchased the securities of the Nickel Plate from the Vans. Ball later turned over the securities to the Ball Foundation, his family's philanthropic institution. Later, these securities were purchased by Robt. Young and Frank Kolbe. Young soon bought out his partner and assumed sole ownership. Young controlled the Chesapeake & Ohio and tried several times

unsuccessfully to merge it with the Nickel Plate. In 1947, after his most recent merger attempt had been defeated, Young relinquished his control of the Nickel Plate.

After the Nickel Plate had achieved its independence in 1947, several steps were taken to improve its competitive position with other railroads. On 1 Dec. 1949, the road leased the Wheeling & Lake Erie Railroad. The W&LE was founded in 1871 and planned as a road running from the Ohio River through the coal fields of southeastern Ohio to ports on Lake Erie. A financial panic in 1873 discouraged government aid and private investment, and by 1877 only 13.5 mi. of track had been laid. In 1879, the W&LE ceased all operations and in 1880, agents of Jay Gould began buying large amounts of the Wheeling's stock, thereby allowing the company to restart construction. Gould's money helped the W&LE reach Martin's Ferry in 1891 and Wheeling by 1892. The road fell into receivership by Jan. 1897. The court-appointed receiver was Cleveland banker MYRON T. HERRICK. With the help of Wm. Mather and Earl Oglebay, Herrick formed a 99-year agreement with the Cleveland, Terminal & Valley Railroad that permitted the W&LE to run trains over the former's tracks into Cleveland. Herrick also managed the W&LE's purchase of the Cleveland, Canton & Southern Railroad in 1899. Both of these developments gave the W&LE access to Cleveland's industries and ports. The Cleveland, Canton & Southern had its origins in the Youngstown & Connotton Valley Railway, which was organized on 29 Aug. 1877 to construct a line from Bowerstown to Youngstown. In 1878, it purchased the bankrupt Ohio & Toledo Railroad, which ran from Carrollton to Oneida. On 16 Oct. 1879, the northern terminus of the newly formed Youngstown & Connotton Valley Railway was changed from Youngstown to Canton. On 29 Nov. 1879, the railroad's name was changed to the Connotton Valley Railroad Co. On 1 June 1882, the Connotton Valley formally purchased the Connotton Valley & Straitsville Railroad, which had been organized to build from Canton to Straitsville. After the merger, the Connotton Valley Railway continued to construct the line to Straitsville. By 1885, it had a total of 160.59 mi. of track in operation, consisting of a main line from Cleveland to Coshocton, and 2 branch lines. The tracks were narrow-gauge (3' wide).

The road's initial Cleveland terminus was a small depot on Commercial St. The tracks were later extended across Commercial St. and along Canal St. to the corner of Ontario and Huron avenues, where a new passenger depot was opened in 1883. Most of the road's freight tonnage was coal, which was delivered to the Cleveland Rolling Mill and the Union Rolling Mill companies. The Connotton Valley also operated a 2,200' wharf along the Cuyahoga River. The company went into receivership on 19 Jan. 1884. Samuel Briggs was named receiver. Following its sale under foreclosure to bondholders on 9 May 1885, it was reorganized and renamed the Cleveland & Canton Railway. The road's tracks were converted to standard-gauge by Nov. 1888. In May 1892, the Cleveland & Canton merged with 3 smaller railroads that the former had previously operated: the Waynesburg & Canton, which ran from Canton to Marks; the Coshocton & Southern, which ran from Coshocton to Zanesville; and the Cleveland, Chagrin Falls & Northern. The Cleveland & Canton was then renamed the Cleveland, Canton & Southern Railroad. It operated 209.59 mi. of track. The head office of the system remained in Canton. In Cleveland, the road's tracks entered the city in the vicinity of Calvary Cemetery on Miles Ave. They ran in a northwesterly direction, crossing Harvard Ave., E. 99th, E. 93rd, E. 91st, and Broadway and Union avenues before heading into Morgan's Run. After exiting Morgan's Run, the tracks ran along the Cuyahoga River Valley to the vicinity of Ontario and Huron avenues. The old Connotton Valley depot on Ontario St. continued to be used as the main passenger station.

In freight operations, the most significant development in the Cleveland area was the creation of a small beltline known as the Cleveland, Belt & Terminal Railroad. It was chartered on 13 May 1891, and the plans originally called for the construction of a line from the Cleveland, Canton & Southern tracks at NEWBURGH to the Nickel Plate tracks at Willson Ave. (E. 55th St.). It was hoped that this line would speed up the movement of freight through the Cleveland area. When the CB&T was opened for traffic in Jan. 1893, its tracks ran from the Cleveland, Canton & Southern in the Flats westward to the Big 4 (Cleveland, Cincinnati, Chicago & St. Louis Railroad) tracks near Denison Ave. In 1893, the Cleveland, Canton & Southern fell into receivership. On 15 Sept. 1893 J. W. Wardwell, the Cleveland, Belt & Terminal's superintendent, was appointed receiver. No plans of reorganization were ever filed, and the entire system was allowed to deteriorate until the purchase by the Wheeling & Lake Erie in 1899. In 1900, the W&LE had 435.7 mi. of track in operation. The majority of its earnings came from freight, particularly coal, coke, iron ore, stone, and sand. The management and board were heavily controlled by Clevelanders. Myron T. Herrick was board chairman, while fellow Clevelander Robt. Blickensderfer was the system's president and general manager. The W&LE used the tracks and facilities of the old Cleveland, Canton & Southern and the Cleveland, Belt & Terminal railroads. The chief passenger depot continued to be at Ontario and Huron.

In 1947, shortly before the Nickel Plate assumed control, the executive and general offices of the W&LE were located in Cleveland, the executive offices in the Union Commerce Bldg. and the general offices in the Huron Bldg. at Huron Ave. and E. 6th St. The W&LE's operations in Cleveland by 1947 centered entirely on freight. Among its customers were American Steel & Wire, the CLEVELAND WORSTED MILLS, Otis Steel, REPUBLIC STEEL, CLEVELAND PNEUMATIC TOOL, Champion Machine & Forging, Cuyahoga Stamping, and Grabler Mfg. The W&LE maintained a freight station at 3959 E. 93rd St. and a yard at Campbell Rd. All passenger service in Cleveland had been eliminated in 1938. In 1950, the Nickel Plate operated 2,266 mi. of track. The road's prosperity was based primarily on the rapid movement of freight. The Nickel Plate's passenger service in Cleveland was gradually reduced in the years from 1950–64. Aside from the main station in the Terminal Tower, the Nickel Plate operated passenger stations at Rocky River and E. CLEVELAND. In 1957, there were 6 passenger trains daily. The road's last passenger trains, the *City of Chicago* and the *City of Cleveland*, made their last runs on 9 Sept. 1965. In 1986, Cleveland was part of the Lake District of the Norfolk Southern's Pittsburgh Div. The district manager's office was at 1991 Crocker Rd. in WESTLAKE. Its operations in Cleveland in 1986 were devoted exclusively to freight. There were 5 major freightyards in the Cleveland area: the main yard at E. 55th St; and 4 other yards at Chardon Rd.-E. 200th St., Campbell Rd., W. 110th St., and Broadway. The Broadway yard was used chiefly for piggyback shipments. One of the road's largest customers in the Cleveland area in 1986 was the CLEVELAND ELECTRIC ILLUMINATING CO., for which it ran unit trains of coal to the Avon Lake, Eastlake, and Lakeshore generating plants (via the CONRAIL tracks). Another large customer was LTV Steel. Other notable customers in 1986 included American Can, Ajax Mfg., Cleveland Coal Storage. GENERAL ELECTRIC, LINCOLN ELECTRIC, Pitney Glass, and Parkwood Iron & Scrap, and the Crown Filtration and Nottingham Filtration plants, to which the road carried chlorine.

Rehor, John A., *The Nickel Plate Story* (1965).

**NORRIS BROTHERS,** a moving company located at 2138 Davenport NE, dates from 1867. The business, started by Thos. Norris, has remained a family operation. Throughout its history, Norris Bros. has maintained close links with the city of Cleveland. In the 1920s, the firm delivered loads of structural steel to the Public Hall construction site at E. 6th and Lakeside. Since that time, it has handled all exhibit and display materials and equipment to and from Public Hall. A power struggle among family members in 1976 resulted in internal organizational and ownership changes, but the company is still privately held and managed by direct descendants of Thos. Norris.

The **NORTH AMERICAN BANK** was incorporated in 1920 as the North American Banking & Savings Co. with $100,000 and 200 stockholders. One of the many businesses started by the "Little Father of the Slovenes," ANTON GRDINA, the bank, located at 6131 St. Clair, served the needs of the neighborhood until its absorption by Central Natl. Bank in 1959. Grdina entered the banking field with no knowledge of banking, just a desire to help Yugoslavian immigrants buy homes and establish themselves in America. Throughout the 1920s, the bank (along with Grdina's other financial enterprises, the Internatl. Savings & Loan and the St. Clair Savings & Loan) offered financial services to neighborhood people. As Slovenians penetrated other Cleveland neighborhoods, the bank opened branches at 15619 Waterloo and 3496 E. 93rd St.

North American Bank, as it was renamed in 1934 (after a brief tenure as the North American Trust Co. from 1929–34), was briefly closed as a result of the Bank Holiday of 1933, but it was the first Cleveland bank to reopen. Its reopening plan established the North American Mortgage Co., which managed the bank's frozen assets. In 1944, when the EAST OHIO GAS CO. EXPLOSION razed the E. 61st St.-St. Clair area, Grdina took charge of the rebuilding effort. To prevent industry from buying up the land, he set up the St. Clair-Norwood Rehabilitation Corp. to lend money to individuals to rebuild their homes on the original foundations. North American Bank was the depository for the money donated by neighborhood merchants to begin the building program. In 1959, the North American Bank was acquired by the expanding Central Natl. Bank, which promised to continue the "same friendly service" that had made the bank a successful neighborhood institution. Stockholders supported the merger to increase local access to capital funds; North American Bank assets were only $21 million, compared to Central Natl.'s $564 million. All employees and officers of North American became part of Central Natl., and the old offices remained branches.

The **NORTH AMERICAN COAL CORPORATION,** a major supplier of coal in the Great Lakes region, is one of the most important coal companies in the U.S. Much of the company's success can be credited to Franklin Taplin, long associated with the coal business as a sales manager for the local Youghiogheny & Ohio Coal Co., who founded the forerunner of North American Coal, the Cleveland & Western Coal Co., in 1913. It served primarily as a coal-selling agency. It subsequently established itself as a coal shipper, with large dock properties in Milwaukee, Duluth, and other Great Lakes ports by the 1920s. Following its reorganization in 1925 as the North American Coal Corp., the firm moved into coal mining, acquiring coal lands near Powahatan Point, Ohio, where its mine became the first in Ohio to be completely mechanized. It purchased additional mines in West Virginia in the 1930s, and later in Pennsylvania. Through the 1950s, the company primarily relied on its eastern mining and shipping operations for its lucrative business, selling much of its production to utility companies. In the late 1960s, under Otes Bennet, Jr., the firm began operations in the West, opening its first lignite coal mine in North Dakota in 1957. By the late 1970s, the company, in joint ventures, began to explore and mine the lignite fields of eastern Texas. Principal emphasis has been placed on these western operations since the 1970s, thus providing North American with a diversified base that has allowed it to remain highly profitable during even recessionary periods such as the early 1980s. It has over 5.3 million tons of minable coal reserves.

**NORTH AMERICAN SYSTEMS, INC.,** the manufacturer of the highly successful Mr. Coffee coffee-brewing machines, was started in the late 1960s by Cleveland shopping-mall and housing developer Vincent G. Marotta. Along with Samuel Glazer, a friend from high school, Marotta had entered the construction business in 1949, building homes and, after 1955, shopping malls such as the Richmond and Great Lakes malls. Marotta served as president of the Glazer-Marotta Co. from 1949–68; he resigned when money for mortgages became more difficult to obtain. He decided to diversify his business interests and entered the coffee-making business. In the fall of 1968, Marotta and 2 former Westinghouse engineers, Edward Able and Erwin Schulze, began work to develop a better coffee maker. For 3 years they worked in offices at 20515 Shaker Blvd., finally achieving success in 1971 after Marotta found that the ideal temperature for brewing coffee is 200 degrees F. They received 4 U.S. patents for the Mr. Coffee machine and began production in 1972 in a plant at 23750 Mercantile Rd. in BEACHWOOD. By Apr. 1974, the company had sold a million of its coffee makers and had captured 10% of the U.S. coffee-making business. It had 125 sales representatives and 300 employees.

In June 1974, the firm acquired the Fairfield Coffee Filter Div. of Tomlinson Industries, Inc., located at 5433 Perkins Rd. in BEDFORD HTS. By Feb. 1975, employment at North American Systems had increased to nearly 1,000, and the firm had moved to 24700 Miles Rd. in Bedford Hts.; it had also added a plant in California. North American Systems was called the biggest manufacturer of coffee makers in the U.S. by 1975, and Marotta received one of the Horatio Alger Awards that year. By 1977 his company employed 2,300 people. It employed 1,500 people in Greater Cleveland in 1981. The success of the Mr. Coffee machines spawned a number of imitations, which in turn forced North American Systems to spend much time in court, bringing suits for trademark violations against such rival products as Mr. Automatic and Mrs. Coffee. Other legal problems plagued the firm. In 1982 it was fined $750 by the Federal Elections Commission for its failure to bill the Carter-Mondale Presidential Committee for the use of office space; and in Oct. 1983, Vincent J. Menier, a former North American Systems executive, was convicted of embezzling more than $1 million from the company and sentenced to 5 years in jail. Menier contended that the funds in question were part of a corporate slush fund that he used with Marotta's approval.

**NORTH CONGREGATIONAL CHURCH,** organized in 1902, began as a Sunday school, which held its first services in a store on St. Clair Ave. near E. 70th St. The first church was built in 1902 with the help of the Cleveland Congregational Union, and especially that of H. Clark Ford. It grew to be a thriving institution under the leadership of its first pastor, Rev. Chas. H. Lemmon, who served 1902–16. When the neighborhood became commercialized, the members of North Congregational federated in 1945 with the Glenville Evangelical & Reformed Church located at E. 101st St. and St. Clair and worshiped with that congregation. In May 1954, the congregation of Glenville Evangelical & Reformed voted to sell their property and join the First Evangelical & Reformed Church. In June 1954, North Congregational merged with Glenville Congregational Church, located at Eddy Rd. and St. Clair. Glenville, which had also been established in 1902, was dissolved 17 Jan. 1962.

The **NORTH EASTERN OHIO TEACHERS ASSOCIATION,** a voluntary nonprofit service organization primarily for professional educators, located at 6500 Pearl Rd., PARMA HTS., Ohio, was formally instituted on 13 Nov. 1869 at the WEDDELL HOUSE by a group of administrators and teachers who had been meeting informally for several years to discuss their concerns about the educational situation in northeastern Ohio. The following officers were appointed: president, Thos. W. Harvey, superintendent of schools, Painesville; vice-president, Samuel Findley, superintendent of schools, Akron; secretary, H. B. Furness, superintendent of schools, Warren; and treasurer, Caleb S. Bragg, Cleveland. The Executive Committee included Andrew J. Rickoff, superintendent of schools, Cleveland; G. N. Carruthers, superintendent of schools, Elyria; and R. W. Stephenson, superintendent of schools, Norwalk.

The objectives of the NEOTA, as stated in the constitution (adopted in 1869), have remained essentially the same: professional improvement of its members; the advancement of educational progress of the schools in the northeastern section of Ohio; and the dissemination of correct educational ideas. The first meeting, held on 11 Dec. 1869 and attended largely by superintendents and teachers, discussed the improvement of country schools; a uniform classification of town and city schools; a course of study arranged with reference to classification; practical and disciplinary studies; new methods of instruction; moral and religious instruction; and the model teacher. Initially, 5 regular meetings were held each year. In Feb. 1886, these were reduced to 3; in Feb. 1907, to 2; and in 1924, to 1. Attendance soared so rapidly at first that 3 auditoriums were necessary: the HIPPODROME, the Opera House, and GRAYS ARMORY. Subsequently, annual meetings were held in the Cleveland PUBLIC AUDITORIUM, where a concert, often presented by the CLEVELAND ORCHESTRA, preceded an address by a nationally known educator. It was followed in the afternoon by a series of special-interest-group meetings held at various locations throughout the city.

Through the years, beginning in 1869, the NEOTA has made many proposals and recommendations that have been adopted at the district meetings, and which have resulted in legislation adopted by the General Assembly of Ohio, including the establishment of teacher-training institutions; the State Foundation Bill; teacher certification; teacher retirement laws and salaries; the organization of rural schools; better sanitary conditions in the schools; and subsequently the establishment of a State Board of Education. In addition to the annual meeting for the entire membership held in the fall, known as NEOTA Day, the association conducts numerous workshops through the year, planned by the following committees: Leadership Development;

Human Relations; Consumer Affairs; Public Relations; Economic Security & Retirement; Environmental Concerns; Legislative; and Instructional Improvement. Other committees have included Intra-Professional Political Action; Resolutions; Credentials; and Elections. The association is linked to the Ohio Education Assoc. and the Natl. Education Assoc. through the Representative Assemblies. In 1986, Wm. Noice of Mantua was president and Lowell E. Lutz the executive secretary.

The **NORTH ITALIAN CLUB** is a social and mutual-aid organization on Cleveland's west side, near ST. ROCCO PARISH. For many years, membership was open only to those with a northern Italian background. The club was founded in 1927. Its original purpose was to be a non-political fraternal and social organization. Within a few years, the articles of incorporation were amended as the North Italian Social Club; its members came from the northern regions of Italy—Venezia, Giulia, Tirolo, Veneto, Lombardia, Piedmente, Liguria, Emilia, Umbria, Marche, and Toscana. Only men were admitted. Among the charter members who signed the articles of incorporation were Wm. Alessandrini, Chas. S. Sasena, Frank Girardi, David Cozzarin, and Frederico Vettor. In 1934 the Women's Auxiliary was formed; Mrs. Palmira Sanvido and Mrs. Maria De Roia were among the early workers. Many of the club's early members were among the finest trade artists in Cleveland; many had worked on SEVERANCE HALL and other notable structures. A Venetian-styled 2-story building—built by members in their spare time—was completed in 1934 on W. 33rd, making the club one of the few such organizations to have its own house. It has been designated a historical landmark by the Cleveland Landmarks Commission. Although early meetings were conducted in Italian, the club encouraged naturalization among its members. For several decades, the club's average membership remained near 200, with a somewhat lesser number for the Women's Auxiliary. Between 1971-80, however, membership dropped from 200 to 108. That was partly because 2d- and 3d-generation northern Italians were moving out of the neighborhood and acquiring different interests. In the early 1970s, the North Italian Club opened membership to anyone with an Italian background, and an effort was made to attract younger members.

**NORTH OLMSTED** is a city on the western edge of Cuyahoga County 12 mi. southwest of Cleveland. It is bounded by WESTLAKE on the north, FAIRVIEW PARK and BROOK PARK on the east, OLMSTED TWP. on the south, and Lorain County on the west, and occupies 11.65 sq. mi. The village of N. Olmsted was formed in 1908 from portions of Olmsted and Dover townships. Jas. Greer was the first settler in the area, arriving in 1814. He was followed by other families from New England, who organized the village of Lenox in 1823. In 1829 the village was renamed after early settler Aaron Olmstead; in time the *a* was dropped from the name. Olmsted remained a small rural farming community until the 1920s. It then began to prosper as a truck-gardening and greenhouse center. Throughout the 1930s, N. Olmsted remained a quaint, neighborly village that reminded many of its New England origins. In 1931 the village, under the leadership of Mayor Chas. A. Seltzer, organized the N. Olmsted Municipal Bus Line to provide service that had been lost when the interurban lines were discontinued. The concept of a municipally owned bus line was opposed in the courts by some citizens and certain public utilities. The Ohio Supreme Court ruled in favor of the village, and it is claimed that N. Olmsted's bus line established a precedent for the entire nation. Today the bus line is operated by the Regional Transit Authority. N. Olmsted was incorporated as a city in 1960. In the 1980s, the city remained primarily residential, with almost no industry. Population increased from 3,487 in 1940 to 36,486 in 1980. Recreational facilities include a recreation center featuring 2 ice-skating rinks, indoor and outdoor swimming pools, indoor tennis, and a jogging track.

**NORTH PRESBYTERIAN CHURCH,** located at E. 40th St. and Superior Ave. NE, is one of the oldest Presbyterian churches remaining in Cleveland. It began in 1859 as a Sunday school mission of Old Stone Church. First located on the north side of St. Clair St. near Lyman (E. 41st) St., the Sunday school moved the following year to the south side of St. Clair. In the spring of 1867, the school moved to a new building constructed on Aaron (E. 36th) St. between Superior and St. Clair, a residential area where many members lived. The mission chapel, a particular project of the Young Ladies' Mission Society, was dedicated 10 Feb. 1867, and Rev. Aaron Peck began preaching regularly. Three years later, the mission Sunday school officially became North Presbyterian Church, organized by Dr. Wm. H. Goodrich (assistant minister at Old Stone) and elders Reuben F. Smith and Geo. H. Ely and named for the Old North Church, Boston, Mass.; 51 members from Old Stone Church were among the charter members, and Rev. ANSON SMYTHE, D.D., served as the first pastor from 1870-72.

Several Sunday schools that later became churches (Glenville, Boulevard, and Westminster) were started by North Church, and the new church building erected at Case Ave. (E. 40th St.) and Superior St. was dedicated 23 Oct. 1887. During Dr. William Gaston's pastorate, SERENO P. FENN, a member of Old Stone Church, served as superintendent of the Sunday school for over 17 years. It became one of the largest Sunday school groups in Cleveland during that time. Many of the North Church parishioners followed Rev. Robt. J. MacAlpine when he accepted a call from Boulevard Presbyterian Church in 1909. About 300 members remained.

During Dr. Harvey E. Holt's pastorate (1918-30), many community programs were initiated; they were continued through the Depression years by Rev. Arthur R. Kinsler, Jr., who came to North Church in May 1930. In addition to its many denominational programs, the church became a center for emergency food programs, clothing collection, and recreational and educational activities, including child care. Volunteers from other organizations helped the church staff with the administration of these supplementary programs. On 20 Sept. 1970, North Presbyterian Church celebrated its 100th anniversary. In Jan. 1981, Rev. Dr. Johanna Marie Baillie, a native of the Netherlands, assumed the pastorate of the church, which continues to serve its own predominantly industrial neighborhood.

*North Presbyterian Church—Celebrating 125 Years of Serving God and This Community* (Commemorative booklet, 23 Sept. 1984).
*One Hundredth Anniversary Brochure (1870-1970)* (Commemorative Booklet, 1970).

**NORTH RANDALL** is located 7 mi. southeast of Cleveland and is bounded by WARRENSVILLE HTS. on the north, east, and west and BEDFORD HTS. on the south. It occupies less than 1 sq. mi. It was incorporated as a village in 1908 and operates under the mayor-council form of government. Originally part of WARRENSVILLE TWP., N. Randall was known as Plank Road Station in the early 1800s. The construction of the Cleveland & Mahoning Railroad nearby in 1857 opened the farming community to neighboring areas and resulted in rapid growth and development for this portion of the township. In 1908, the N. Randall Park race track was opened; it soon became known as "the Saratoga of the West." From 1909–38, it was part of the Grand Harness Racing Circuit and gained a national reputation for its meets. Early in the 1900s, the village of N. Randall found its major industry to be the breeding and training of trotting horses. The Grand Circuit meets continued until 1938, when running races were introduced. Organized horseracing had come to Ohio in 1937 when Thoroughbreds were recruited from Kentucky to race in Cincinnati. As the demand for the sport increased, N. Randall provided an ideal site for northern Ohio racing enthusiasts at THISTLEDOWN RACE TRACK, which originally opened as Thistledown Park in 1925. The race track's reputation grew favorably, and it became home to the Ohio Derby, a major race held every June. In 1951, the Edward J. DeBartolo Corp. of Youngstown acquired the site of RANDALL PARK, and RANDALL PARK MALL, one of the largest shopping and commercial complexes in the country, was constructed in 1975. N. Randall had a population of over 1,100 in 1980. While it maintained its own fire and police services, it depended upon Warrensville Hts. to provide social, recreational, and educational facilities.

**NORTH ROYALTON** is a city located on the southern edge of Cuyahoga County. It occupies 21 sq. mi. and is bounded by PARMA on the north, BROADVIEW HTS. on the east, STRONGSVILLE on the west, and Summit County on the south. N. Royalton was originally part of ROYALTON TWP., created in 1818. Melzer Clark was the first settler, in 1811. In the 19th century, Royalton was a community of farmers. Many of the mid-19th-century farmhouses still remained in the 1980s. It became known as a dairy town, attracting a thriving business from surrounding communities. In 1866, Jas. Wyatt introduced the manufacture of cheese to the area. In 1880, Royalton Twp. was renamed N. Royalton. In 1927 the township was incorporated as the village of N. Royalton, with E. C. McComers as the first mayor. N. Royalton was incorporated as a city in 1961 and adopted the mayor-council form of government. Its growth progressed slowly from a population of 1,051 in 1840 to 2,559 in 1940. Following the postwar migration of Cleveland residents to the suburbs and the construction of the Ohio Turnpike in 1955, the population quickly rose to 9,290 in 1960, 12,807 in 1970, and 17,705 in 1980. In 1980, the city had 10 industries and over 200 small businesses, the major employer being the board of education. The N. Royalton schools include 3 elementary, 1 parochial, and 1 high school. N. Royalton has 30 acres of city parks, and recreational facilities include a tennis court, baseball and soccer fields, a fishing pond, and a branch of the CUYAHOGA COUNTY PUBLIC LIBRARY.

Marcus, T. Richard, ed., *North Royalton, Ohio, 1818–1968* (1968).

**NORTH UNION SHAKER COMMUNITY.** They called themselves "Believers," a shortened version of "the United Society of Believers in the Second Appearing of Christ," but they are better known as Shakers. Suffering persecution in England, a small band led by their founder, "Mother" Ann Lee, came to America in 1774. Ann Lee symbolized the second coming of Christ in female form, establishing the basis for the Shaker concept of sexual equality and the deity as a father-mother God. Assisted by a great religious revival, many Shaker colonies were founded in New York and the New England states. Missionaries brought Shakerism to the frontier in the early 19th century; N. Union

was one of the last of the 19 Shaker communities that were established. In 1811, Jacob Russell, a Revolutionary War veteran, purchased 475 acres of land in Connecticut's WESTERN RESERVE, situated in the upper DOAN BROOK valley. The following year, the Russell family of 20 traveled the 600 mi. from Connecticut to their new home in the wilderness. In 1821, one of Jacob's sons, Ralph, visited the Shaker community of Union Village near Lebanon, Ohio, where he was smitten by the Shaker beliefs and lifestyle into joining their faith. A Shaker elder persuaded him to establish a new colony on the Russell property, later given the religious name "the Valley of God's Pleasure."

The first N. Union meetings were held in the summer of 1822, attracting many visitors, some serious, others merely curious. The Russell family provided the first converts; others soon followed. The original landholdings increased to 1,366 acres, on which some 60 buildings were eventually constructed. Contrary to original expectations, the topsoil proved to be too thin to support wheat farming. Hence they turned to corn, flax, and hemp. Later, dairy cattle were introduced. Their kitchen gardens produced sweet corn, pumpkins, potatoes, and cabbage. Turnips were a luxury eaten in place of apples until the orchards matured. Committing oneself to Shakerism included taking vows of celibacy, confessing one's sins, turning any previously born children over to the Shakers to rear, donating all personal property to the community, and leading a simple life in a communal family where men and women were rigidly separated. At first there was only one Center Family occupying a large dwelling west of Lee Rd. between what are now Shaker and S. Park boulevards. Expansion soon led to the establishment of the East or Gathering Family on what is now Fontenay Rd., and the Mill Family at Coventry Rd. and N. Park Blvd.

N. Union reached its maximum growth by 1850 with 300 members. It was a thriving, almost completely self-supporting community, with a good income from the sale to the "world" of dairy products, canned fruits and vegetables, woolen and linen goods, medicinal herbs, garden seeds, brooms, and other handcrafted items. The high quality of the Shakers' products and their honest dealings won them an enviable reputation. Their industriousness represented the fulfillment of Mother Ann Lee's admonition, "Put your hands to work and your heart to God." Shakers were also known for their ingenuity. Inventions attributed to N. Union alone included the common clothespin, Babbitt metal, the rotary harrow, and an automatic spring. The last 3 were invented by Daniel Baird. To obtain waterpower, they dammed up Doan Brook at 2 locations, forming the Upper and Lower SHAKER LAKES. Near the former they built a brick woolen mill, and near the latter a sawmill and a massive stone gristmill, an engineering marvel. For many years farmers from the surrounding countryside brought their grain there to be ground. JAS. PRESCOTT was a well-known N. Union Shaker. Arriving in 1826, he remained until his death in 1888. He is best known for his journals describing daily events, faithfully recorded during his entire stay. Now possessed by the WESTERN RESERVE HISTORICAL SOCIETY, these records provide a detailed history of N. Union.

After the CIVIL WAR, Shakerism declined. The lure of free homesteads, railroading, gold and silver mining, and big corporations produced a more materialistic society. With religious revivals on the wane and communal societies losing their appeal, converts became fewer and fewer. Never turning away "lost souls from the other world," Shakers were frequently deceived by persons who pretended in the fall to aspire after Shakerism only to leave in the spring, after having enjoyed Shaker hospitality. They were called "Winter Shakers." Young people increasingly refused to accept a celibate lifestyle. The loss of the young forced the hiring of outside labor for the heavier tasks. This added expense exacerbated the increasing difficulty in selling handcrafted products in competition with industry's mass production. By 1889, only 27 members remained at N. Union, most of them old. They decided to disband. The surviving members moved to other colonies in southern Ohio. A syndicate bought the N. Union land in 1892. In 1905, the VAN SWERINGEN brothers purchased the land from the syndicate for $1 million and proceeded to develop it into the residential community of SHAKER HTS., the only city that can claim that a Shaker colony was located almost entirely within its corporate boundaries. All of the structures, by then derelicts, were torn down.

Although only 2 dams and a few stone gateposts remain as physical reminders of the N. Union Shakers, they have left a rich legacy: they were far ahead of their time in their practice of both racial and sexual equality; they were forerunners in taking care of orphans and homeless children; Shaker furniture is known for its strength, functionalism, simplicity, and beauty of form, a precursor of modern Danish; they invented hundreds of labor-saving devices, from which they did not profit financially because of their opposition to patents; they produced more folk music than any other group in America, with the exception of the Negroes, with their spirituals; in agriculture, their progressive methods of animal and plant husbandry influenced countless farmers; and their lifestyle, which embodied the ideals of simplicity, orderliness, pacifism, equality, perfectionism, cleanliness, and industriousness, evokes much admiration today. Shakerism may no longer be a viable religion, but its impact on our society has been considerable.

Richard D. Klyver
Shaker Historical Society

Piercy, Caroline, *The Valley of God's Pleasure* (1951).
Shaker Collection, WRHS.

The **NORTHEAST OHIO AREAWIDE COORDINATING AGENCY** was organized in 1968 after federal agencies began to require that applications for federal funds for certain kinds of local projects be reviewed by regional coordinating bodies to ensure that such projects were sound and were consistent with local and regional needs. Such agencies were mandated by the Model Cities Act of 1966 and were to be in place by 30 June 1967, but competition between Cuyahoga County mayors and the area's county commissioners for control of the agency delayed its formation for nearly a year. Such controversy over the agency's founding foreshadowed the political problems it would face in its operations. NOACA was finally organized in Apr. 1968 and received approval from the U.S. Dept. of Housing & Urban Development in June 1968. Its governing committee of elected officials agreed to emphasize 7 planning projects for the region: housing, econom'cs, parks and open spaces, water and sewer facilities, land use, information and data systems, and transportation. In July 1969, NOACA absorbed the Cleveland-Seven County Transportation-Land Use Study (SCOTS).

NOACA's authority initially covered the 7-county region of Cuyahoga, Lake, Lorain, Geauga, Medina, Portage, and Summit counties, but by 1970 some political jurisdictions had serious questions about participation in NOACA, which was supported in part by dues from local members. Withholding dues became a favorite method for members to use to dramatize disagreements with agency policies. By 1970, Medina, Portage, and Summit counties were exploring formation of their own coordinating group; in 1974, on orders from Gov. John Gilligan, Portage and Summit counties joined with Stark and Wayne counties to form a separate areawide agency, thus splitting the Cleveland and Akron planning areas and leaving NOACA with a 5-county area.

Several developments in the 1970s put NOACA on firmer ground financially and politically. One was the Dec. 1972 selection of Fred Pizzedaz, a former Cleveland urban-renewal and community-development official, as executive director; he provided the agency with strong leadership and a sense of direction as a planning agency. In 1974, NOACA was given the responsibility of coordinating transportation funds for the area, assuring it of an important function on the local political scene. In the environment-conscious 1970s, NOACA also took on an important role in coordinating and planning projects to deal with water and air pollution. From a staff of 35 in 1973, NOACA grew to employ as many as 102 people in the late 1970s, with a budget of more than $3 million. In the early 1980s, as the Reagan administration emphasized reducing the federal bureaucracy, NOACA experienced a reduction in its workload, but it remained an important regional agency; in Mar. 1984, Gov. Richard Celeste reaffirmed its role as a clearinghouse for area projects. By 1984 its staff had been reduced to 58 people, and its budget was $2.245 million. The reduction in business prompted the agency to market its information services to businesses and local governments, and it formed NOACA Data & Consulting Services.

The **NORTHERN OHIO FOOD TERMINAL** houses a large segment of northern Ohio's wholesale food industry. It covers an area of 34 acres, from E. 37th to E. 40th streets between Woodland and Orange avenues. To the terminal come carlot and locally produced fresh fruits and vegetables, wholesale meats, live and dressed poultry, butter, cheese, and eggs for the grocery, hotel, and restaurant trade. The terminal was built in 1929 by the Northern Ohio Food Terminal, Inc., an organization founded in 1926 specifically to build a new food terminal, and the Nickel Plate Railroad. Until it opened on 3 June 1929, Cleveland's wholesale food trade occupied scattered quarters along Broadway, Woodland, and Central avenues from E. 6th to E. 9th streets. This picturesque but crowded commission-house district moved almost en masse to the new terminal, which modernized Cleveland's handling of perishable foods.

The new terminal consisted of 4 reinforced-concrete buildings, each 485' x 100'; a 400' x 100' auction building; and a Growers Market, opened in 1930, with covered sheds covering 4½ acres. Other food interests, including major chain stores, located their warehouses nearby. Upon completion, the Nickel Plate Railroad retained ownership and operation of the terminal's 16-track delivery yard, which handled 18,000 cars annually. Officers of the Northern Ohio Food Terminal, Inc., in 1929 were Chas. F. Haas, president; Herbert Brandt, 1st vice-president; Joseph Sanson, 2d vice-president; Robt. F. Blair, secretary; and Donald Pocock, treasurer. In July 1952, an article in *Redbook* magazine cited Cleveland's Northern Ohio Food Terminal as one of the first modern markets built in this country and the nation's best example of a clean and efficient wholesale market. The terminal's silver anniversary in 1954 found it handling 40,000 carloads of food annually, with a value of $140 million. Through more than 100 food merchants, it provided employment to about 1,500 people. Russ Swiler had served as general manager since the terminal opened. The greatest change in 25 years, according to Swiler, was the growth of trucking. In addition to a constant flow of rail cars, more than 20,000 carloads were arriving by truck each year.

**NORTHERN OHIO LIVE** began publication on 22 Sept. 1980 as a biweekly guide to arts and entertainment events in the Cleveland area. It was created by Dianna Tittle, John Schambach, and Dennis Dooley, 3 former staff members of *CLEVELAND MAGAZINE,* who modeled it after *New York Cue.* Capitalization of $300,000 was raised from 27 local investors, incorporated as "M" Magazine, Ltd. Edited by Tittle, *Northern Ohio Live* picked up 12,000 readers during its first year and added the "WCLV Guide" to its contents, consisting of program listings for Cleveland's classical-music radio station. By Nov. 1981, however, it had cut back to a monthly publication schedule, and overall coverage began to place more emphasis on lifestyle features such as food and restaurants. *Live* has been edited in offices on Juniper Rd. in the University Circle area and printed in Akron. After assuming the title of associate publisher, Tittle was succeeded as editor first by Dooley and later by Mark Gottlieb. Schambach remained in his original position as publisher. Circulation in 1985 had grown to 30,000.

The **NORTHERN OHIO LUNG ASSOCIATION,** founded in 1904 as the Anti-Tuberculosis League, was active in combating tuberculosis before expanding its work in the 1960s to other respiratory diseases. Formally organized on 3 Mar. 1905, with Dr. John H. Lowman as president, it aimed to prevent and cure tuberculosis by coordinating the work of local agencies and individuals dealing with tuberculosis patients, by research into the nature and causes of the disease, and by educating the public about the disease's causes and prevention. Although not formally organized until 1905, the league had begun work in 1904, sponsoring a survey that revealed that tuberculosis was responsible for 10% of the deaths in Cleveland. To educate the public, the league organized a speakers' committee of public-health and social workers. This group gave 18 lectures in 1905.

Surveying the league's work in 1930, Yale public-health professor Ira V. Hiscock praised its impressive record of achievements. These included providing medical and support services for tuberculosis patients, lobbying the city government to expand its efforts to combat the disease, and continued public education. The league provided medical service through a dispensary it and Western Reserve University opened on 6 Oct. 1904 in the Medical College building at Erie (E. 9th) St. and St. Clair; this dispensary served 785 patients in 1908. Along with the city's Health Dept., the league opened a day camp for tuberculosis patients in July 1910. In 1924, it financed a dispensary staffed by black medical personnel and located in one of the city's growing black neighborhoods. In 1908 the league began to sell Red Cross Christmas Seals to support its work, and by 1918 the proceeds of these sales supported 7 dispensaries, an open-air school, and a tent colony for children with tuberculosis. The league also hired recreational workers to work with these children. At the league's urging, the city's Health Dept. made tuberculosis a reportable disease in 1907, and in 1911 it established its own Bureau of Tuberculosis. Together, the league and the Health Dept. launched a campaign for improved housing conditions, and in 1910 the league supported the successful $250,000 bond issue to finance construction of a sanatorium for tuberculosis patients.

During the 1920s, the league sponsored a number of health surveys in the Cleveland area. In 1935 it began to use mobile fluoroscopes to take chest x-rays of local residents. By 1948, it owned 3 mobile x-ray clinics and had discovered more than 4,500 cases of the disease in 5 years. By 1970, such x-ray surveys had been supplemented by a skin test. Between 1959, when 546 active cases of tuberculosis were reported in Greater Cleveland, and 1968, when 320 such cases were reported, the number of active cases declined annually. The league then expanded its interests to include other respiratory diseases, especially those related to smoking, such as emphysema, and air pollution. To reflect these new concerns, it changed its name, becoming the Tuberculosis & Respiratory Disease Assoc. in Apr. 1969; in 1973 it became the Northern Ohio Lung Assoc. By 1970 its activities included continued efforts to detect and eradicate tuberculosis, classes to educate medical professionals about respiratory diseases, efforts to educate the public about the dangers of smoking and air pollution, and grants to support medical research into lung diseases.

Northern Ohio Lung Assoc. Records, WRHS.

The **NORTHERN OHIO OPERA ASSOCIATION** was organized in 1927 to sponsor the annual visits to Cleveland of New York's Metropolitan Opera Co. Prior to the formation of the NOOA, the "Met" visited Cleveland sporadically, beginning with appearances in the EUCLID AVE. OPERA HOUSE in 1899 and GRAYS ARMORY in 1901. In 1910 and 1911, it played 2 4-opera "seasons" in the HIPPODROME THEATER. The Metropolitan tours acquired permanence in Apr. 1924, when an ad hoc group of sponsors headed by NEWTON D. BAKER arranged for performances in Cleveland's vast, newly opened Public Hall. By 1927 the season had expanded to a full week of 8 performances. Under the leadership of ROBT. J. BULKLEY, the Northern Ohio Opera Assoc. came into being that year to underwrite a newly signed 5-year contract with the Met. Thanks to the cavernous size of the local "opera house," Cleveland became the Met's most profitable tour stop, and its guarantors were never called upon to make up a deficit. In 1931, tenor Edward Johnson sang the title role in Deems Taylor's *Peter Ibbetson* before 8,483 operagoers, at that time the largest audience ever to witness a Metropolitan production—a fact that led Johnson habitually to refer to the company as "the Metropolitan Opera of New York and Cleveland" when visiting here later as the Met's general manager. Cleveland topped that record with 8,583 persons for a performance of *The Barber of Seville* in 1946, when a weekly attendance record of 72,690 was also claimed.

With the exception of the Depression years 1933–36, the Met continued its annual spring calls through 62 seasons by 1986. The week was shortened to 7 performances in 1966, and the experiment of a fall appearance was tried in 1974 and abandoned thereafter. Of the 89 different operas presented here, *Aida* was the perennial favorite, with 29 performances, followed by *Carmen* and *La Traviata,* with 24 apiece. Among its occasional ventures outside the standard repertoire, the Met also presented single performances here of Britten's *Billy Budd,* Humperdinck's *Koenigskinder,* Menotti's *The Last Savage,* Meyerbeer's *Le Prophete,* and Wagner's *Parsifal.* Answering the prayers of generations of music critics, the NOOA moved the Met seasons into the smaller STATE THEATER, which the Met reopened in 1984. The following year, however, the Metropolitan announced its intention of eliminating the tour upon the conclusion of the 1986 season. Even in that extreme eventuality, the Northern Ohio Opera Assoc. foresaw the possibility of enticing the Met to Cleveland on a single-city basis.

The **NORTHERN OHIO SANITARY FAIR** (22 Feb.–10 Mar. 1864) was organized by the SOLDIERS' AID SOCIETY OF NORTHERN OHIO to raise funds for their work in assisting Civil War soldiers. The fair was patterned after a similar event that had been staged in Chicago and had been visited by the officers of the society. The Cleveland fair, which was widely advertised in an effort to encourage attendance, was housed in a specially constructed building on PUBLIC SQUARE. The building, in the shape of a Greek cross, housed a series of exhibits, including floral, artistic, and war-souvenir displays. Single admission tickets to the fair cost $.25 each. No free passes were issued; even visiting dignitaries were required to contribute to the event. Local railroads cooperated with the Aid Society by selling tickets at their stations and promising free return rail fare to any visitor purchasing more than $1 worth of admission tickets. They also lifted freight charges for goods consigned to the fair. The fair, opened formally by Maj. Gen. JAS. A. GARFIELD, was more popular than expected and was extended beyond its planned closing date. At the end of the event, all goods not sold at the fair were auctioned off. The lumber and other building materials were also sold, bringing more than $10,000 in profit. Total proceeds from the event were $78,000.

U.S. Sanitary Commission Records, WRHS.

Brayton, Mary Clark, and Terry, Ellen F., *Our Acre and Its Harvest* (1869).

The **NORTHERN OHIO VIETNAM VETERANS OF AMERICA**, a local chapter of Vietnam Veterans of America, Inc., was formed in Dec. 1980 at a meeting of Vietnam veterans at the central YMCA in downtown Cleveland. The purpose of the organization was to bring attention to some of the problems that veterans of the VIETNAM WAR (fought 1965–75) were experiencing. The first concern was to obtain correct testing and evaluation from Congress for those veterans who had been exposed to "Agent Orange" and other chemical defoliants in Vietnam. Exposure caused illness in veterans and birth defects in their offspring. Another concern was to get help for the treatment of "delayed stress" symptoms for those veterans who underwent traumatic experiences in Vietnam that affected them years after military service had ended. A third concern was to support legislation for a sufficient GI Bill on the national and state levels. The GI benefits offered to Vietnam veterans were less than those awarded to World War II or Korean War veterans. The NOVVA officers elected in Dec. 1980 were Richard B. Masterson, president; John Wright, 1st vice-president; Joseph W. Zingales, treasurer; and Nick Early, Nick Orosz, Cathy Mauser, Timothy E. McMonagle, and Carl Luebking, directors. Active membership was approximately 300. The major project of NOVVA was the Vietnam War Art Exhibit, "The Vietnam Experience," held in Oct. 1981. The exhibit, although excellent, proved a financial failure, since foundations expected to underwrite it did not cover all of the costs incurred.

In Jan. 1982, NOVVA elections were again held, and disintegration set in. A majority of offices were won by "Vet Center" members and supporters. "Vet Centers" were Veteran's Admin.-funded service centers for Vietnam-era veterans. Because of numerous election and other bylaw violations, the new NOVVA board was not recognized by the Vietnam Veterans of America, Inc. One infraction was the acceptance of nonveterans on the board. Other grounds for disagreement centered around an incident in which a Vietnam Veterans of America delegation on an investigatory trip to North Vietnam was compelled to take part in the ceremonial laying of a wreath on the grave of Communist North Vietnam president Ho-Chi-Minh. These problems resulted in the formation of a local splinter group, the Northeast Ohio Vietnam Veterans. On 7 Aug. 1982, at Cuyahoga Community College, Metro Campus, former NOVVA and present NEOVVA members and officers met to determine if they could resolve their differences and resume their chapter Vietnam Veterans of America, Inc., duties and responsibilities.

**NORTHFIELD PARK** was opened on 23 Aug. 1957 as a harness-racing track to capitalize on a renewed interest in this aspect of horseracing. The track was built by Walter J. Michael, a Bucyrus industrialist, horse farmer, president of the old Grandview Race Track, and head of the U.S. Trotting Assoc. Located on Rt. 8, the half-mile track begins in Summit County and turns into Cuyahoga County before ending in Summit County. It soon hosted a yearly average of 150 nights of racing, divided among 3 meets: Northfield, Grandview, and Painesville. Northfield acquired the Grandview events after a fire at that track destroyed its grandstand and clubhouse in 1959. Northfield acquired the 84-acre property and used the facilities for training and stabling. Northfield inherited a tradition begun in Cleveland in the 1870s when gentlemen raced their sulkies at E. 55th and Euclid, and at the GLENVILLE RACE TRACK. After Glenville closed in 1908, the sport was relocated to RANDALL PARK RACE TRACK until 1939, when that track was converted to running races. After WORLD WAR II, a 35-day season of harness racing was held at the Painesville Fairgrounds and at the Bainbridge Race Track. Originally considered an old man's sport, harness racing attracted several generations of enthusiasts. In the track's first 10 years, the average age of the drivers dropped from the mid-40s to the high 20s, while college men (often the sons of older drivers) drove in the summer. Meanwhile, the number of fans in attendance increased along with the betting. By the 1970s, competition from running tracks such as THISTLEDOWN RACE TRACK led to money-losing meets. In 1972, Michael sold the track for $7.5 million to a group of investors that included Carl Milstein, Robt. Stakich, and Geo. Steinbrenner, who soon dropped out. Michael continued to operate the track's meets until 1974, when he sold the Northfield meet to Cleveland lawyer Wm. Snyder, Dr. Vic Ippolito, and others; in 1981 the new operators bought the Painesville meet from Homer Marshman, giving them control of all of the track's meets. In 1976, the new operators of Northfield expanded its season into winter for a total season of over 200 days; its winter meets were successful, since the fans viewed the race from a glass-enclosed clubhouse and grandstand. The winter races were called off only when the highways were too treacherous for travel. Despite new operators and winter racing, the track continued to lose money during the 1970s. In 1983, 458,000 people attended its races and bet $65 million, but the track lost $1 million; it reportedly was one of 2 tracks in the state on the verge of closing when the racing industry received a $12.4 million tax break from the state legislature in early 1984. In Nov. 1984, track owner Milstein evicted the operators from the track, claiming they were in arrears on lease payments and other bills. The Ohio Racing Commission gave the racing dates for the new season to Milstein, who promptly added Sunday racing to the winter season and made other improvements designed to improve business.

**NORTON, DAVID Z.** (1 June 1851–6 Jan. 1928), was a banker; a partner in the OGLEBAY NORTON CO., an iron-ore and lake-shipping company; and a noted philanthropist. Norton was born in Cleveland to Washington

Adams and Caroline Harper Norton. In 1840, his father established the first blast furnace in northern Ohio, at Clyde. Norton was educated in public schools. In 1868, he began his career in banking by becoming a messenger for the Commercial Natl. Bank of Cleveland, later known as the Guardian Bank. At age 21, he became cashier. In 1890, Norton, at the urging of his friend JOHN D. ROCKEFELLER, SR., resigned from the bank to join with Earl W. Oglebay in the organization of the firm Oglebay, Norton & Co. He retired from the company in 1924 but remained a director until his death.

Norton was a patron of the arts known for his quiet philanthropic interests. He actively supported the CLEVELAND ORCHESTRA and the CLEVELAND MUSEUM OF ART. He was a trustee of the Cleveland School of Art, Western Reserve University, Adelbert College, Kenyon College, UNIVERSITY SCHOOL of Cleveland, the WESTERN RESERVE HISTORICAL SOCIETY, HURON RD. HOSPITAL, LAKE VIEW CEMETERY, and the Society for Savings. He served as a director of the Natl. Commercial Bank, the Bank of Commerce, the Woodland Ave. Savings & Trust Co., the Bankers Surety Co., and the American Ship Building Co. He was also involved with the Commonwealth Iron Co., the Montreal Mining Co., the Castile Mining Co., and several lake-shipping companies. In 1910, Norton was elected president of the Citizens Savings & Trust Co. Upon its merger into the Union Trust Co., he became a director.

Norton was president of the Union, Country, and Rowfant clubs and a charter member. His personal interests included collecting Napoleana, which he left to the Western Reserve Historical Society, and Japanese art, which was given to the Cleveland Museum of Art. His historic family homestead, Shandy Hall, constructed by the Harper family in Unionville, Ohio, is now a property of the Western Reserve Historical Society. Norton married Mary Castle (the daughter of WM. B. CASTLE, the first mayor of Cleveland) on 11 Oct. 1876. They had 3 children, Miriam (Mrs. Frederick R. White), Robt. Castle, and Laurence Harper. Norton and his wife are buried in Lake View Cemetery.

Corporate Records, Columbia Steamship Co., Memorial to David Z. Norton, Jan. 1928.
*Oglebay Norton Company--125 Years, 1854-1979* (1979).
Taylor, Harrie S., *Oglebay, Norton: 100 Years on the Great Lakes* (1954).

**NORTON, LAURENCE HARPER** (8 May 1888-11 June 1960), mining and shipping company executive, was a director, 1927-60, and treasurer, 1957-60, of the OGLEBAY NORTON CO. His lifelong interests in history and the arts led to his involvement with numerous cultural organizations, particularly the WESTERN RESERVE HISTORICAL SOCIETY. Norton was born in Cleveland to David Z. and Mary Castle Norton. He graduated from UNIVERSITY SCHOOL in 1906 and from Yale University with the A.B. degree in 1910. From 1910-12, he studied at the Geo. Pierce Baker workshop at Harvard University, graduating with the M.A. degree. He served as secretary to the U.S. ambassador to France, MYRON HERRICK, between 1912-14. Returning to Cleveland in 1915, he started at the City Savings & Trust as a teller in order to learn the business.

Norton's banking career was interrupted by WORLD WAR I. He enlisted in the Ohio Natl. Guard; his unit was called for duty in Mexico. Discharged, he was called back to active duty 1 month later, serving in several campaigns in Europe with the 135th Field Artillery unit of the 37th Div. Discharged again in 1919, he returned to France as 3d

secretary and private secretary to the recently reappointed U.S. Ambassador Herrick, returning to Cleveland to assume family business interests when his father's health began to fail. Elected to 3 terms as a state representative, 1925-31, and 1 term as a state senator, 1931-33, Norton coauthored the Norton-Edwards Highway Bill, which recodified the state's highway laws, and authored legislation creating the Ohio Battle Monument Commission. Defeated for Cuyahoga County treasurer in 1932, he won election to 2 terms on the Cleveland School Board, serving as president 1935-37. In 1935, he was appointed to the Cleveland Ports & Harbor Commission and served as director of the Cleveland Crime Commission.

A lifelong bachelor, Norton's upbringing instilled in him a deep interest in history and the arts. He served as president of the Western Reserve Historical Society for over 25 years. During his tenure, the society erected a new wing to the building on East Blvd., part of which was made into the Napoleonic Room, housing his father, David's, collection of historical artifacts. Norton served on the board of the CLEVELAND PLAY HOUSE, 1925-60, and as its president, 1934-38. He also served as vice-president of the EARLY SETTLERS ASSOC. and on the board of directors of the Hinman Hurlbut Art Foundation and the John Huntington Foundation.

Laurence H. Norton Papers, WRHS.

**NORWEB, EMERY MAY HOLDEN** (30 Nov. 1895-27 Mar. 1984), was a benefactress, officer, and trustee of the CLEVELAND MUSEUM OF ART. She was largely responsible for establishing the museum's outstanding pre-Columbian and Oriental art collections. Norweb was the granddaughter of Mr. and Mrs. LIBERTY E. HOLDEN, early benefactors of the art museum. In 1917 she married R. HENRY NORWEB, who had joined the U.S. diplomatic service in 1916. Over the next 30 years, Norweb's diplomatic career took them to Japan, the Netherlands, Chile, Mexico, the Dominican Republic, Peru, and several other countries. During this period, Mrs. Norweb furthered her study of art and languages. While in Japan in the 1920s, she became interested in Oriental art and began to acquire pieces, which she eventually donated to the Cleveland Museum of Art. While living in South America during the 1930s, she began to collect pre-Columbian art at a time when there was little interest in that genre. Her acquisitions later formed the nucleus of the museum's pre-Columbian collection. The Norwebs returned to Cleveland in 1948. Mrs. Norweb became an active member of the museum's accessions committee, which was responsible for all new acquisitions, and in 1949 she joined the museum's board of trustees. In 1962 she became the first woman president of the art museum, one of only 2 women to hold such a position at that time in the U.S. Norweb's other interests included horticulture and coin collecting. She was well-known in Cleveland horticultural circles and was a trustee of the GARDEN CTR. She was a chairman of the American Numismatic Society of London, and donated many valuable English coins to the art museum.

**NORWEB, R. HENRY** (31 May 1894-1 Oct. 1983), was a Cleveland diplomat who held posts around the world. Born in England, Norweb moved with his family to Elyria, Ohio, in 1907. He received his B.A. from Harvard in 1916 and entered the diplomatic service that same year, taking the post of 2d secretary to France in Paris. Norweb was recalled to Washington in 1921, and between 1923-48 he was assigned to posts covering much of the globe: Japan, the Dutch East Indies, the Hague, Chile, Mexico, Bolivia

728

(as minister to that country), the Dominican Republic, Peru (as ambassador), Portugal, and Cuba. He retired in 1948. Throughout his assignments, Norweb's home remained Cleveland, and it was to his house in BRATENAHL that he retired. R. Henry Norweb married Emery May Holden, granddaughter of the founder of the *Cleveland Plain Dealer*, LIBERTY E. HOLDEN, in 1917 in Paris. They had 3 children, Jeanne, Albert, and Henry. Norweb was considered an authority on coins and coin collecting. He served as a trustee of Kenyon College and the WESTERN RESERVE HISTORICAL SOCIETY. Mrs. Norweb was an active socialite and was particularly identified with the CLEVELAND MUSEUM OF ART.

**NORWEGIANS.** *See* **SCANDINAVIANS**

**NOTRE DAME COLLEGE** is a Catholic women's college established by the SISTERS OF NOTRE DAME to develop women in the Christian humanist tradition. Its beginnings were in an academy erected by the sisters at Superior Ave. and E. 18th St. when they came to Cleveland from Germany in 1874 upon invitation of Bp. RICHARD GILMOUR; a branch academy with a boarding school was opened on Woodland Hills Ave. in 1877. On 18 Sept. 1922, the 4-year liberal-arts college for women was founded by Mother Mary Cecilia, 3d superior general of the Sisters of Notre Dame, in temporary quarters at 1324 Ansel Rd. A state charter was obtained in 1923. The college moved to its present 50-acre site in S. EUCLID at Green and College roads in 1928. Mother Mary Evarista was its first president. In the 1950s and 1960s, Harks Hall, an administration building, and Providence Hall were added to the campus. On the celebration of its 50th anniversary, in 1972, 3 additional buildings were dedicated: the Alumnae Hall dormitory, Connelly Student Ctr., and Clara Fritsche Library.

Notre Dame College offers B.A., B.S., and A.A. degrees. In 1969, it began to award dual secondary certification in special education and another field. The Catechetics Ctr. gives 2-year associate and 4-year bachelor's degrees as well as a 2-year Lay-Leadership in Ministry certificate to prepare part-time volunteer ministers called to serve the church. In 1984, the school was noted for the maintenance of its conservative tradition in Catholic women's education. Sister Mary Marthe was president; there were 171 full-time and 20 part-time lay teachers and 720 students, 405 full-time and 315 part-time. Some men were enrolled in the evening and on weekends. Notre Dame is accredited by the North Central Assoc. of Colleges & Secondary Schools and is a member of the Natl. Catholic Education Assoc., the Council on Education, the Assoc. of American Colleges for Teacher Education, the Natl. Conference of Church Related Colleges, the Ohio College Assoc., the Ohio Foundation of Independent Colleges, and American University Women.

**NOTTINGHAM** was a small village in EUCLID TWP. that once rivaled Euclid Village; both were carved out of old Euclid Twp. Three-fourths of a mile north of Euclid Creek, the area was bounded by Lake Erie on the north, Coit Rd. and the New York Central and New York, Chicago & St. Louis Railroad on the east-southeast, Akin Rd. on the west, and E. 170th St. on the southwest. Its main street was St. Clair. Organized in 1873, the village supported 2 stores, a stonemill, a grain mill, and 2 blacksmith shops in 1880. The incorporation lapsed but was renewed in 1899. In 1911 and 1912, the village was annexed to Cleveland, along with part of the village of Euclid. Nottingham remains part of the name of many small businesses and institutions in the area in the 1980s.

The **NOVEL CLUB** is a small and intimate group that serves as a forum for the discussion of both classic and contemporary works of fiction. The club was founded on 5 Dec. 1896 by Elizabeth Cutter (later Mrs. Dwight Morrow) and Wm. Torrance as the Classical Novel Reading Union; the exclusive emphasis on classics in literature—as the name implies—lasted only a few months. With the general purpose of providing Cleveland with an intellectually based literary club, its specific purpose was "to choose only novels of established excellence, and to consider them with something of the serious purposes of the student." Throughout the club's existence, its membership has consisted of both men and women from diverse backgrounds. In the post-World War II period, the club drew the majority of its members from CLEVELAND HTS. and SHAKER HTS. The maximum number of members was limited to 36 so that each could present a paper at least once every 2 years. Elizabeth Cutter, cofounder, was active in the club's leadership for over 40 years. Other early members active for many years were Annie Cutter, Grace Oviatt, Mrs. Philip Cobb, and Geo. Bierce. The club's activities have remained essentially unchanged since its founding. Nine novels are selected for discussion each year by vote from a list of proposals presented by the Program Committee. The club meets the first Tuesday of each month except during the summer. Two papers are presented at each meeting: a biographical study of the author, and a critical study of his or her work. Another member, designated as the evening's "Critic," submits 3 or 4 questions for discussion. Meetings take place in a different member's home each month; special meetings have, in recent decades, been held at the UNION CLUB.

Novel Club Records, WRHS.

*NOVY SVET* (New World) was organized on 16 Sept. 1950 to provide Cleveland with a Czech-language daily newspaper after the demise of the *Svet-American*. Edited by John Kratky and Anton Sustr, it was first located at 12020 Mayfield Rd. Later editors included Vaclav Matousek, former editor of the *AMERICKE DELNICKE LISTY* (American Labor News), Vaclav Hyvnar, Frank Novatny, and Milada Hyvnar. Although it continued daily publication through the mid-1960s, it was subsequently scaled down to a semiweekly, then a weekly, and finally closed in Jan. 1977. Three months later, *Novy Svet* was reorganized as a national Czech weekly. Although still edited in Cleveland by Jan Reban, it was printed by Universum Sokol Publications in Perth Amboy, N.J., and circulated from New York to California.

**NURSING.** The story of the advancement of nursing in Cleveland is one of multiple challenges as nurses have sought to improve nursing practice through upgrading standards for nursing education. Cleveland's nursing community has been in the forefront at the state, national, and international levels in providing the vision for many progressive innovations in nursing practice, education, and research and in public health. Many accomplishments could not have been attained without the support of others in the community who believed in nursing's mission and its contributions toward improving people's health. During the first 7 decades of Cleveland's development, ill people were cared for at home by their families or untrained nurses who also functioned as maids. The few existing HOSPITALS were primarily for the poor and homeless or for CIVIL WAR casualties. The public believed hospitals were places to die. Untrained men and women, with little or no general education and frequently considered undesirable, were employed to care for the sick. A few were dedicated caregivers and chose nursing as a vocation. The social consciousness of Cleveland's leaders in the late 19th century, however, led to the building of more hospitals following the development of anesthesia and aseptic techniques. The need for an organized system to improve patient care was recognized. This need led to the rise of modern nursing in Cleveland. Modern nursing had originated about 40 years earlier in England, when Florence Nightingale established a training school for nurses, which subsequently became the model for American schools.

Cleveland is recognized as the site for the origin of modern nursing in Ohio. The Cleveland Training School for Nurses (now Huron Rd. Hospital School) was established on the Nightingale model in 1884. As new hospitals were built, nursing schools were organized to provide a labor force for giving nursing care at little or no cost to hospitals. Each hospital controlled the financial operation of its school; therefore, the students' educational needs yielded to the needs of the hospital. Few graduate nurses were employed by hospitals. They sought employment primarily as private-duty nurses or in the public-health field. Hospital economics, lack of qualified candidates for admission, and the absence of an organized body for enforcing standards prevented the early Cleveland nursing schools from achieving the desired standards established by Florence Nightingale. Some nursing directors of schools became discouraged and left their positions. City Hospital had 4 directors in 5 years. Nurses employed traditional and nontraditional measures in meeting the challenge of upgrading their profession. They wrote to their legislators on matters of importance to nursing, even though most nurses could not vote because they were women. Nurses at CLEVELAND HOMEOPATHIC HOSPITAL went on a "sit-down" strike in 1908 to protest unsatisfactory conditions for providing nursing care. This strike may have been one factor leading to the closure of the hospital for a year.

Nurses also organized to accomplish goals. The nursing directors of the early Cleveland schools frequently were college-educated women who subsequently sought nurses' training. Many provided the leadership for upgrading standards for nursing education and practice in Cleveland and Ohio. These leaders recognized that as individuals they lacked the power to influence hospital administrators to accept minimum standards. To define plans for action that were both comprehensive and achievable, they established the Graduate Nurses' Assoc. of Cleveland (now the GREATER CLEVELAND NURSES' ASSOC.) in 1900 with the support of Isabel Hampton Robb, a national nursing leader. From its inception, the local association was instrumental in the promotion of high standards of health care and the advancement of nurses' professional, educational, and economic welfare. State regulation of nurses was one means by which these nurses sought to raise professional standards and improve nursing services to protect the public against incompetent and disreputable nurses. Many local hospitals and physicians opposed these efforts because they feared their cheap labor supply would be lost. By 1916, the first Ohio nurse-practice act had been enacted. The Cleveland nurses, however, opposed the act as passed because it was permissive and gave control of the profession to the state medical board. Women could not hold office on a state board at that time. The impact of this law was felt for years on nurses' income, living conditions, and status.

During the last decade of the 19th century, a few trained nurses had entered the public-health field. In 1901, the local nurses' association was instrumental in initiating the process to enlist the aid of prominent Clevelanders in establishing the Cleveland VISITING NURSES ASSOC. the following year. A scholarly journal developed by local VNA nurses in 1909 soon became the official publication of a national-public health nursing organization. In 1917, the VNA, the Cleveland Health Dept., Western Reserve University, and other agencies collaborated to establish the University Public Health Nursing District. Its purpose was to prepare well-qualified nurses for public-health service, provide nursing services in one city district, and set standards for public-health nursing. This district became recognized nationally and internationally as the model for public-health nursing programs. Nursing-care services included maternal and child health care, home visiting with instruction on the proper care of the sick and on how to stay healthy, school and industrial health care, and communicable-disease control.

According to the *Cleveland Hospital and Health Survey*, nurses' training in 1920 was "a rather sorry picture of mingled exploitation of willing labor and amateurish teaching." The report strongly supported the local nursing leaders' drive to upgrade the standards for nursing education. Many nurses, hospital administrators, and physicians, however, continued to oppose raising standards because of the perceived cost to hospitals and of fear that nurses would have too much knowledge and trespass on the province of the physician. In every major move by nurses to upgrade the profession in this century, opposition arose for these same reasons. As a result of the recommendations from the above survey, WRU established in 1923, in collaboration with the Lakeside Hospital school, the first collegiate nursing school in Cleveland, which eventually became the Frances Payne Bolton School of Nursing. This school was considered one of the outstanding schools in the country from the 1930s on. The establishment of a collegiate nursing program, however, did not reduce the exploitation of students in providing most of the nursing care in hospitals. The needs of hospitals for low-cost care continued to take precedence over education in most nursing schools until the 1950s. The Depression and the nursing shortage during WORLD WAR II were contributing factors. In 1934, for example, the local nurses' association deliberated a request for nurses to work without pay during the Depression. Their reply to a local medical society reflected the belief that if hospital administrators and physicians received pay, then nurses should not be expected to provide free services.

In the latter part of the 1930s, a shortage of nurses for full-time home care of invalids existed. To compensate, the Central School of Practical Nursing, the first such school in Ohio, was established as a 1-year training program. Later, practical nurses were trained to provide care for patients with stabilized conditions in a variety of health-care agencies under professional direction. Following World War II, an acute shortage of nurses existed. Nursing was not attractive to young adults because of its low pay and heavy demands, with minimal opportunity for job satisfaction. Drastic reforms in nursing education and practice were recommended. Higher education for nurses was becoming valued. Federal assistance for nursing education was introduced in 1956, thus facilitating the attainment of advanced education for many Cleveland nurses. With the establishment of a national accrediting body for nursing, standards for educational programs were developed and enforced. Local schools, therefore, were able to break their hospitals' dependence on student labor. Local hospitals employed more graduate nurses because they no longer could depend on student labor, and many hospitals were rapidly enlarging. The American Nurses' Assoc. and its local counterpart, the Greater Cleveland Nurses' Assoc., continued to work toward improving educational standards, nursing practice, and the economic welfare of nurses. The association became the collective bargaining agent for nurses in some Cleveland health-care agencies. Local nurses' salaries gradually improved. The University Public Health Nursing District was closed in 1962 when the knowledge and skills acquired through that course of study became a requirement within the curriculum of baccalaureate nursing programs. CUYAHOGA COMMUNITY COLLEGE established a 2-year nursing program in the 1960s and awarded an associate degree. With the opening of the Kent State University School of Nursing, some Cleveland hospitals closed their nursing schools the same decade. CLEVELAND STATE UNIVERSITY opened a program in the early 1970s for registered nurses to earn a baccalaureate degree in nursing. In 1979, CASE WESTERN RESERVE UNIVERSITY established the first professional doctoral program in the world for entry into nursing practice and awarded the N.D. degree. Although postgraduate education for Cleveland nurses existed during the first half of the century, its value was recognized only in recent years, when knowledge was expanding rapidly and many changes in health care were taking place. The opportunity to study toward a Master of Science in Nursing degree became available in 1938 at WRU. The focus of this degree was altered over the years to keep pace with changes in the complexity of health-care needs and treatments, in undergraduate nursing education, and in the need for nurse educators, supervisors, administrators, clinical specialists, and researchers. In the 1960s, Cleveland was the site of one of the first nursing research development programs in the country, and in 1972 a Ph.D. in nursing program was established locally. The first nurse midwifery graduate program in Ohio and the 14th in the country was established in Cleveland in 1983 to meet the increasing demands of women choosing nurse midwives as their major caregiver during normal childbearing experiences.

Nursing education in Cleveland in the 1980s presented a confusing picture. The American Nurses' Assoc. had taken the position in the mid-1960s that the preparation for entry into the practice of professional nursing should be at the baccalaureate level. Although mandatory licensure in Ohio was achieved in the 1960s, the nurse-practice act did not specify one type of rigorous, systematic educational preparation. Four types of nursing programs (hospital-based, A.D., B.S.N., and N.D.) existed in Cleveland, and each prepared nurses to take the same licensing exam. The lack of a standardized rigorous system of nursing education led some to believe that nursing had not yet reached the status of a profession, especially in the legal sense of the term. The outcome of 2 Cleveland studies conducted in the early 1980s revealed wide local support for the development of a state-supported baccalaureate program in Cleveland; Cleveland State University established such a program for entry into nursing in 1985. The high cost of maintaining hospital nursing schools resulted in some local hospitals' closing their schools in the 1980s. Nursing practice in the 1980s reflected improvements made in nursing education over the years. Although the tasks and procedures that nurses performed were considered important, they no longer were considered as ends by many nurses. These activities were becoming the means through which nurses achieved their goal of assisting people to attain their optimal level of health when they were well, ill, or dying—the goal of nursing originally envisioned by Florence Nightingale. More nurses became involved in health care in the community when patients began experiencing shorter hospitalizations and required professional nursing supervision at home through home health-care programs. In some local hospitals, nurses were assuming responsibility for the nursing care of their own caseload of patients, from admission to discharge. More Cleveland nurses were seeking advanced preparation and/or certification in specialty areas of practice. Nurses with master's degrees were assuming head-nurse positions in some agencies to provide the leadership necessary for improving nursing care. Some health-care institutions offered horizontal promotions for nurses to remain in direct patient care rather than move up the administrative ladder. Finally, some nurses became primary health-care providers, "nurse practitioners," in health-care centers. Several studies revealed that these nurses provided primary care that was cost-effective and did not jeopardize the quality of care. In fact, nursing care in general in the past 25 years has contributed immensely toward achieving positive outcomes for patients and the health of communities like Cleveland.

Evelyn M. Lutz
Kent State University

Greater Cleveland Nurses' Assoc. Records, WRHS.
Rodabaugh, James H., and Rodabaugh, Mary Jane, *Nursing in Ohio* (1951).
See also MEDICINE.

**NURSING HOMES.** *See* **OLD AGE/NURSING HOMES**

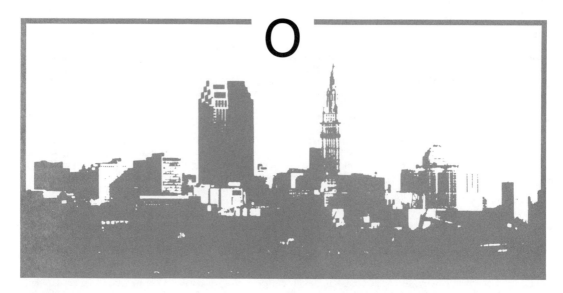

O

OAKWOOD is a village southeast of Cleveland, bounded on the north by BEDFORD, on the south by Summit County, on the east by GLENWILLOW, and on the west by WAL-TON HILLS. It occupies 3.87 sq. mi., making it one of the smaller communities in Cuyahoga County. Oakwood became the county's 58th municipality in 1951, when residents from the southeastern portion of Bedford Twp. voted for its incorporation as a village. The creation of BEDFORD HTS. and Walton Hills in the same year brought an end to the original Bedford Twp., formed in 1823. In 1962, as a result of postwar suburban migration, a number of residents petitioned to have Oakwood annexed to SOLON in an effort to thwart PUBLIC-HOUSING plans, but the movement was defeated. Oakwood's population grew slowly from 3,283 in 1960 to 3,759 in 1980. Financial problems threatened to halt the village's development. The Oakwood Village Boosters' Club was formed, which proved to be instrumental in raising funds through the sale of promissory notes and other projects, thus enabling the purchase of property to house the municipal offices. In 1955 a service building was constructed, and in 1960 a police department was created to serve the area with 1 part-time and 12 full-time police officers. Oakwood's fire department included 17 full- and part-time personnel. In 1985, the village operated under the mayor-council form of government. Oakwood Village is a member of the Bedford Branch of the CUYAHOGA COUNTY PUBLIC LIBRARY SYSTEM, and its primary and secondary schools are affiliated with the Bedford School District. The village is crossed by the CONRAIL and the NORFOLK SOUTHERN railroads. Oak Park Health Care Ctr. and Great Lakes Truck Equipment were among the largest employers in the community in 1982.

The OAKWOOD CLUB (est. 1905) was the first major Jewish organization located in the Heights. Founded specifically as a golf club for Cleveland Jewry's successful merchants and professionals, it later expanded to provide additional recreational and social facilities. Leopold J. Wolf, a partner in the banking concern of M. J. Mandelbaum & Co., leased 19 acres of land at the end of the interurban railway line at Mayfield and Noble roads in the spring of 1905, with the intention of establishing a country club. Julius Feiss subsequently deeded an additional 4 acres adjoining the site. By 1913, the club's land included over 159 acres. Oakwood was incorporated 1 July 1905 by Wolf,

MORRIS BLACK, EDWARD M. BAKER, Hascal Land, and MAURICE (MOSES) J. MANDELBAUM. At a meeting in November of that year, a $24,000 bond at 4% interest was proposed, and 70 subscribers to the bond became Oakwood's charter members. Along with the subscription, initiation fees were $100, and members paid $60 annual dues. Work began on the design and construction of a 9-hole golf course, which was officially opened on 10 Sept. 1906. In 1915, an additional 9 holes were dedicated. The course met professional championship standards and was chosen as the site of the 1921 Western Open Golf Tournament, which included golf greats Bobby Jones, Gene Sarazen, and Walter Hagen.

Beginning in 1910, the wives of Oakwood members entered the Cleveland Women's Golf Assoc.; Mrs. Louis Kane of Oakwood served as its president in 1930 and 1931. The Oakwood Women's Golf Assoc. was established in 1931. As Oakwood's membership grew, the facilities had to be upgraded and expanded. Extensive remodeling and new construction were undertaken in 1907, 1909, and 1915. However, the most extensive changes took place after 1930, following the merger of Oakwood and the EXCELSIOR Club. The latter, established in 1873, sold its club quarters to Western Reserve University in 1929 and considered building anew. However, approximately 200 men were members of both Oakwood and Excelsior, and a proposal to merge the clubs was raised. An Oakwood committee agreed to the merger, and the club membership was increased from 300 to 450, with classes of membership established to accommodate the nongolfers of the Excelsior. The merger was completed in Jan. 1931, and Oakwood was transformed into a social and recreational center for the members and their families. During that year, the clubhouse was expanded, and squash courts and bowling alleys were added. An outdoor pool was built in 1935, the facilities for women were enlarged in 1953, an entertainment and dining center was added in 1972, and indoor tennis courts were installed in 1973. In June 1943, Oakwood's clubhouse was taken over by the U.S. Army's 729th Military Police Battalion for use as a barracks. During the occupation, which lasted until Feb. 1944, club members used the Isaac Joseph home on Oakwood Dr. as an alternate clubhouse.

Oakwood Club Records, WRHS.

The OBERLIN-WELLINGTON RESCUE concerned a former slave, John Price, who had managed to escape from

732

his owner, John G. Bacon. He fled to the city of Oberlin, Ohio, a center of antislavery activity prior to the CIVIL WAR and a depot on the Underground Railroad. It was a refuge for slaves such as Price, who lived there peacefully for 2 years. Unfortunately, he was eventually recognized by a neighbor of his former master. Bacon sent a slave-catcher named Anderson Jennings to Oberlin. Jennings and his assistants lured Price out of town and captured him. The party went on to Wellington, 9 mi. farther south, and took refuge in the Wadsworth House, a local hotel.

John's abduction was discovered by the people of Oberlin, who marched in silent procession to Wellington with the intent of freeing him. By the time the crowd reached the Wadsworth House, an estimated 600 citizens were involved. They surrounded the hotel, removed Price through one of the windows, and returned him to Oberlin. He was hidden in the house of the future college president, Jas. H. Fairchild, and eventually escaped to Canada. On 7 Dec. 1858, 37 residents of Oberlin and Wellington were indicted for their part in John's escape, a violation of the Fugitive Slave Law of 1850. These men were subsequently arraigned in Cleveland by the U.S. District Court. The prisoners pleaded not guilty, and the trial was set for Mar. 1859. Public opinion was with the indicted; in January, a banquet was given at the Palmer House in Oberlin to honor the accused men who had helped Price escape. At this "Felon's Feast," letters of support were read to the accused.

The trial finally began on 5 Apr. 1859. The defense was represented by RUFUS P. SPALDING, ALBERT G. RIDDLE, and Seneca O. Griswold. The prosecution was represented by Geo. W. Belden. The first 2 men to stand trial, Simeon Bushnell and a black man named Chas. Langston, were found guilty, fined, and jailed. The rest of the cases were continued to the July court term. However, the prisoners were not left to languish alone in jail. Trainloads of people paraded around PUBLIC SQUARE in Cleveland, and dozens of speeches of encouragement were delivered to the prisoners from a platform erected for that purpose. The jailed men were also busy writing antislavery tracts and printing a newspaper, the *Rescuer*. The prisoners stayed in jail for 3 months. The indictments were finally dropped and the men released. The incident ended amid speeches, parades, and the presentation of flowers, and the prisoners returned home in triumph. A special ceremony was conducted in the First Church of Oberlin, where the "Marseillaise Hymn" and "Gathering of the Free" were sung.

**ODENBACH, FREDERICK L., SJ** (21 Oct. 1857–15 Mar. 1933), was a Catholic priest, a meteorologist, and a professor at JOHN CARROLL UNIVERSITY for 40 years. Called "the father of American seismology," he was responsible for the development of the nationwide Jesuit Seismological Service and other contributions to scientific study. The son of furrier John and Elizabeth Minges Odenbach, Frederick Odenbach was born in Rochester, N.Y. He received his early education in Rochester's Catholic schools and at the Collegiate Institute. After receiving a bachelor's degree from Canisius College in Buffalo in 1881, he joined the Society of Jesus in Sept. 1881 and was sent to the Netherlands for training. Although he returned to the U.S. to teach at Canisius for two years (1885–87), he spent much of the decade studying in Europe. He was ordained into the Catholic priesthood in England in 1891.

Odenbach returned to the U.S. in the fall of 1892 to become professor of physics and chemistry at St. Ignatius College (later John Carroll University) in Cleveland, where he remained until his death. In 1902 he became professor of astronomy and meteorology at the college. In addition to these teaching assignments, Odenbach taught a variety of other courses at various times, including botany, geometry, zoology, and Shakespeare. His teaching career extended into the mid-1920s; for the last 6 years of his life, he devoted his efforts to scientific research. In 1895, Odenbach, with the assistance of Geo. E. Rueppel, established a meteorological observatory. On 6 Dec. 1901, Odenbach became the sixth person to observe the rare Helvetian Halo. He was skilled in mechanics as well as science; in 1898 he took only 3 days to reassemble the 1,001-piece Secchi meteorograph offered to him by the Smithsonian Institution. He also made many of his own scientific instruments. In 1899 he invented the ceraunograph, an instrument that records the occurrence of thunder and lightning. He also developed an electrical seismograph after he established a seismological observatory in 1900. In 1909 he proposed a plan for a cooperative seismological program involving Jesuit schools throughout the U.S. and Canada, and he later became the director of the Jesuit Seismological Service.

The **OERLIKON MOTCH CORPORATION** is the largest distributor of machine tools in the U.S. and one of the nation's leading designers and builders of special machines. This firm originated in Cleveland in Sept. 1904 when brothers Stanley and Edwin R. Motch and Geo. Merryweather formed the Motch & Merryweather tool manufacturers in Ohio and eastern Michigan. Starting with 6 employees at its offices at 711 Lakeside Ave., the company originally represented 5 machine-tool builders. Under Merryweather and Edwin Motch, the company established branch offices, and later its service area expanded to include parts of Kentucky, Pennsylvania, and Maryland. In 1923, Motch & Merryweather moved into the new Penton Bldg. at W. 3rd and Lakeside.

In addition to distributing tools, Motch & Merryweather also rebuilt used ones. In 1924, it acquired and remodeled a plant on E. 70th St. for machine rebuilding. By WORLD WAR II, the firm had gained an international reputation for quality rebuilt machine tools. That allowed it to begin manufacturing machine tools, particularly circular sawing machines, in 1939. The need for saw blades led the company to produce cutting tools. In 1948, it built a plant on E. 222nd St. in Euclid specifically designed for its rebuilding business. By 1957, it had consolidated all its manufacturing and engineering operations at this plant. Edwin R. Motch, Jr., initiated a postwar period of expansion. Motch & Merryweather acquired machine-tool and cutting-tool companies nationwide, including a pioneer in the development of numerically controlled machines. Its distributorship continued to spread in the Midwest as well as on the West Coast, representing over 50 machine-tool builders nationally. In 1968, it became a publicly owned company.

Its record growth and proposed merger with a leading American machine-tool manufacturer in the late 1970s brought Motch & Merryweather international attention. In 1979, a Swiss firm, Oerlikon-Buehrle, owner of some of Europe's most prestigious machine-tool operations, entered the U.S. market by acquiring Motch & Merryweather. The Cleveland firm continued under local management as a subsidiary, renamed the Oerlikon Motch Corp. in 1981 with 1,500 employees nationwide, including 500 in Cleveland. Its association with the Swiss firm has allowed Oerlikon Motch to become more involved in international business; it formed its own import division in 1980 and moved into the Canadian market in 1982.

Motch & Merryweather Co., *50 Years of Service to Industry—1904–1954* (1954).

The **OGLEBAY NORTON COMPANY,** one of the oldest iron-ore houses in Cleveland, was established in 1851 as the firm of Hewitt & Tuttle. Cleveland commission agents Isaac Hewitt and Henry Tuttle became interested in the newly found iron deposits of the Lake Superior region. In 1852 they received the first cargo of Lake Superior iron to reach Cleveland, and 2 years later they became agents for the Lake Superior Iron Co. Henry's son Horace developed a 3,000-acre tract on the Menominee range, and a new partnership was organized in 1884 when Wheeling, W.Va., industrialist Earl W. Oglebay joined Horace A. Tuttle in Tuttle, Oglebay & Co. The firm sold a million tons of ore annually from a variety of mines, and also owned and operated the Montreal Mine in Wisconsin, which became the largest underground mine in the country, producing 30 million tons of ore from 1886–1962.

Upon the death of Horace Tuttle, Oglebay invited Cleveland banker DAVID Z. NORTON to join him. In 1890, Oglebay Norton & Co. began auspiciously, as Norton secured a contract to organize all of JOHN D. ROCKEFELLER's iron-ore properties in the Mesabi Range under the Lake Superior Consolidated Iron Mines and to act as manager and sales agent. In the next few decades, the firm broadened its area of business by becoming a sales agent for iron companies in Cuba and Canada. It acquired a fleet of 11 lake freighters, which became the Columbia Steamship Co. in 1921, later expanded and renamed the Columbia Transportation Co. in 1931. After its incorporation in 1924, Oglebay's nephew Crispin Oglebay led the company into a period of expansion. It became active in the sale of other raw materials for the steel, ceramic, and chemical industries. In the 1920s, the company branched into mining and selling coal, marketing fluorspar and ferro-alloys, and manufacturing insulation products for steel ingot pouring. During the 1930s, it began to manage 4 docks along the Great Lakes.

As early as 1939, the firm, aware of the depletion of high-grade iron ores, initiated a study of low-grade minerals and established the Reserve Mining Co. to develop taconite. Its largest venture was the establishment of a huge taconite mine in Eveleth, Minn., in the 1960s. In 1957, Oglebay Norton & Co. and its subsidiaries merged into a single unit, the Oglebay Norton Co., allowing for further growth and diversification. In 1959, it began operating 2 rail-to-barge coal-loading terminals on the Ohio River, and in the 1960s and 1970s it moved into the area of glass and foundry sand production and mining fracture sand for the petroleum industry. The company also absorbed Cleveland's Taylor & Boggis Foundry, which produced iron products. By the 1980s, its nonsteel earnings exceeded its steel-related revenues.

Ada Watterson Yerkes Papers, WRHS.
Oglebay Norton Co., *Oglebay Norton Company* (1979).
Oglebay Norton & Co., *Raw Materials for the Metallurgical, Ceramic, and Chemical Industries* (1947).
Taylor, Harrie S. *"Oglebay Norton": 100 Years on the Great Lakes* (1954).

**OGONTZ** (OGANTZ) was the leader of a band of Ottawa Indians encamped near the mouth of the CUYAHOGA RIVER during the first few years of Cleveland's settlement. The Ottawas usually spent the winter months on the west side of the river, migrating in the spring to the Sandusky area. Ogontz, although not known for his friendliness, was nonetheless tolerant of the white settlers and encouraged trade with them. As white settlement increased in the first years of the 1800s, the Ottawas resettled further west, mainly in the Sandusky area. Ogontz, by white accounts, was last seen there in 1811.

**OHEB ZEDEK** (Taylor Rd. Synagogue) is the largest Orthodox congregation in Cleveland. It is the product of mergers in the early 1950s of 6 small to medium-size Orthodox congregations following the Jewish migration to the Heights after WORLD WAR II. The original Oheb Zedek was founded in 1904 by over 40 Hungarian Jews, many of whom had left Congregation B'NAI JESHURUN in a dispute over mixed seating in the synagogue. In 1906, Oheb Zedek purchased a church at E. 38th and Scovill. Henry A. Liebowitz served as the first rabbi, 1906–22. By 1915, the congregation operated a branch in GLENVILLE near 107th and Superior for those members who had moved from the old Woodland neighborhood. A new synagogue was dedicated at Parkwood and Morrison streets in Glenville in Aug. 1922. Although Oheb Zedek's membership was less than 400, the new synagogue had seating for 1,200. Samuel Benjamin was the rabbi at the time of the dedication, serving from 1922–25. He previously had served 3 years at ANSHE EMETH, including the period in which the Cleveland Jewish Ctr. was dedicated. Rabbi Benjamin was followed by Rabbi ISRAEL PORATH, a Talmudic scholar who had been active in the civic life of Jerusalem prior to his arrival in Cleveland. He soon became the leading spokesman for the city's Orthodox community. Porath left Oheb Zedek in 1939 to assume the pulpit of Congregation N'vai Zedek. He was succeeded by Rabbi Louis Engelberg, who has served the congregation since that time. Engelberg also serves as chairman of the Orthodox Rabbinical Council of Cleveland. By 1950, approximately half the membership of Oheb Zedek lived in CLEVELAND HTS. near Taylor Rd. A branch was established in the Heights. In 1952, Oheb Zedek merged with Chibas Jerusalem to form the 500-member Taylor Rd. Synagogue. In 1953, the Parkwood property was sold, and in 1955 the present synagogue was dedicated. During that 2-year period, Taylor Rd. Synagogue completed mergers with Agudath B'nai Israel Anshe Sfard (1953), Agudath Achim (1953), Shaaray Torah (1955), and Knesseth Israel (1955).

Chibas Jerusalem was established in 1904 by 35 Jews who rented Crystal Hall at Woodland and E. 39th St. for services. In 1910, the congregation purchased a building at E. 39th and Scovill. However, as the Jewish population in Woodland moved eastward, the congregation built successive synagogues at E. 84th and Cedar Rd. (1917) and on Parkwood Dr. in Glenville (1926). It was the largest of the 5 congregations to merge with Oheb Zedek. Agudath B'nai Israel Anshe Sfard was established in 1914 and held services in a rented hall on E. 51st near Woodland. It was one of the last congregations to leave the Woodland neighborhood, dedicating a synagogue at 105th and Massie Ave. in 1934 or 1935. Agudath Achim was established in 1891, with Elias Rothschild serving as the spiritual leader. Services were held in a series of rented halls in the downtown area until 1904, when it purchased a building at E. 30th and Scovill. The congregation moved to Glenville in 1927, and in 1932 it remodeled a church at 104th and Adams St., where it held services until the merger with Taylor Rd. Synagogue.

Shaaray Torah was established in 1897 by Lithuanian Jews who met for services at the home of Isaac Crystal near E. 23rd and Orange. From 1912–29, the congregation worshiped in a small brick synagogue on E. 55th St. In the latter years, a building was purchased and remodeled on 105th in Glenville, adjacent to the Cleveland Jewish Ctr. Knesseth Israel was established in 1887 by 12 men who had left Congregation B'nai Jeshurun. The congregation held services in several locations until 1907, when it dedicated a synagogue on E. 46th between Woodland and Scovill. In the early 1920s, the congregation operated

3 branches, 1 in Woodland, 1 in Glenville, and 1 in Buckeye. In 1922, a synagogue was dedicated at 105th and Columbia, which served as its home until the merger with Taylor Rd. Synagogue.

Taylor Rd. Synagogue Records, WRHS.

The **OHIO AMERICAN** was conceived as an organ of the antislavery Liberty party. The paper made its first appearance in OHIO CITY on 19 Sept. 1844. Apparently subsidized by friends of the Liberty party, the 4-page weekly contained few ads and printed little local news other than political items and business notices. It was published by R. B. Dennis with the aid of various editorial associates, until L. L. Rice arrived the following summer to permanently fill the position of editor. Dennis moved the paper across the valley to Cleveland on 6 Mar. 1845, but withdrew as publisher at the end of the first year of publication. EDWIN COWLES was briefly listed as publisher on 28 Aug., when the paper was renamed the *Cleveland American*. Rice continued as editor, while the position of publisher was assumed repectively by M. W. Miller, Philander Whichester, and Wm. J. Tait. Sometime after the appearance of its last issue on 26 May 1847, the *American* was merged into the *DAILY TRUE DEMOCRAT*.

The **OHIO AND ERIE CANAL**, constructed by the state of Ohio between 1825–32, provided cheap transportation to promote the economic development of the state, connecting Lake Erie at Cleveland with the Ohio River at Portsmouth. Cleveland became the northern terminus through the efforts of attorney and state representative ALFRED KELLEY. Kelley supervised construction of the northern division of the canal as acting canal commissioner. The canal was a minimum of 40' in width at the water line, 26' at the bottom, and 4' deep. It was dug by laborers using picks, shovels, and wheelbarrows with oxen to drag heavy trees and stones. When construction began in 1825, wages were $5 per month plus temporary housing, board, and daily rations of whiskey.

The canal opened officially on 4 July 1827 between Cleveland and Akron as 3 canal boats arrived in Cleveland for an all-day celebration. Constructed at a cost of $4.3 million, the canal was 308 mi. long. It required 146 lift locks, 7 guard locks, 14 aqueducts, 153 culverts, 6 water supply dams, and 8 dams for slackwater pools. Wooden canal boats were limited by the size of the canal locks, which were 90' long in the chamber and 15' wide, with a pair of wooden gates at either end. Freight boats of about 85 tons' capacity were towed by mules in tandem. Passenger packets designed for faster travel were towed by horses, not to exceed a speed of 4 mph. The canal terminus in Cleveland was on the east side of the CUYAHOGA RIVER near Superior Ave. Two larger locks permitted lake ships of the era to enter the canal and a basin between the locks. In 1851, a weigh lock was installed near what is now W. 3rd St.

In 1872, the state of Ohio transferred ownership of 3 mi. of canal at the terminus to the city of Cleveland. The weigh lock was relocated to S. Dille St., and a guard lock was provided for an outlet onto the river by 1875. The abandoned canal bed was leased to the Valley Railroad in 1879. The original terminus was obliterated with the construction of the Detroit-Superior Viaduct. After 1850, canal use and maintenance declined as railroad mileage increased. Some sections were abandoned or sold to railroad interests by the 1870s, although there was extensive reconstruction from 1905–09. The state declined to rebuild the canal after many sections were destroyed by the spring flood of 1913.

A section south of Cleveland has been maintained for industrial use of the water, and a part within the CUYAHOGA VALLEY NATL. RECREATION AREA includes 3 locks and an aqueduct.

Kilbourne, John, *Public Documents concerning the Ohio Canals* (1828).
Scheiber, Harry N., *Ohio Canal Era* (1969).

**OHIO BELL.** *See* **AMERITECH**

The **OHIO CHAMBER ORCHESTRA,** founded in 1972, has been the assisting orchestra for the CLEVELAND BALLET, the CLEVELAND OPERA, and the Robt. Page Singers. That, together with its subscription concerts, educational programs, and community and summer concerts, made it the third-busiest orchestra in the state in 1984, surpassed only by the CLEVELAND ORCHESTRA and the Cincinnati Symphony Orchestra. The orchestra was established in conjunction with the 75th anniversary of BALDWIN-WALLACE COLLEGE. Its principal purpose was to perform the large and often neglected body of music written for small orchestras; to provide live orchestra music in institutions and cities that would be unable to sponsor concerts by major symphony orchestras; to accompany opera, ballet, and oratorio; and to provide a performance outlet for artists and professional performers with emphasis on Ohio-trained soloists and composers.

By 1984, the orchestra was governed by a 32-member board of trustees and administered by a full-time general manager and a staff of 8. Its founders were Dwight Oltman, the music director, Warren Scharf (head of the Baldwin-Wallace Conservatory of Music), Galen Kral, and John Darling. Between 1972–85, there were 3 executive directors: Lois Epp, Randall Rosenbaum, and Kathleen Evert. Its presidents have included Jas. Toedman, Henry Judson, Christine Gitlin, Lester Glick, and John Gibbon. During the 1983 and 1984 seasons, the orchestra received a subsidy from the CLEVELAND FOUNDATION to enable it to hold its concerts at PLAYHOUSE SQUARE, where the costs are much greater than those of other halls. It has never had a permanent home. The orchestra appeared regularly as part of the Baldwin-Wallace Bach Festival, played annual concerts at the Old Stone Church, was the official orchestra of the 5th Biennial ROBT. CASADESUS INTERNATL. PIANO COMPETITION in 1983, and accompanied the Cleveland Ballet on tours to New York, Florida, and Minnesota. It has performed in Jamestown, N.Y., Pittsburgh, and Findlay, Ohio.

**OHIO CITY (CITY OF OHIO),** one of Cleveland's older neighborhoods, was originally part of Brooklyn Twp., founded in 1818. On 3 Mar. 1836, 2 days before Cleveland's incorporation, the City of Ohio became an independent municipality; it remained so until 5 June 1854, when it was annexed to Cleveland. Although Cleveland had nearly 6,000 people to Ohio City's 2,000, the two cities became fierce competitors, especially in the area of commerce. With Ohio City's incorporation came a fight for shipbuilding and tonnage from the canal boats. This rivalry was best demonstrated in 1836, when Ohio City residents sought, violently, to stop the use of Cleveland's new COLUMBUS ST. BRIDGE, which siphoned off commercial traffic to Cleveland before it could reach Ohio City's mercantile district. The government of Ohio City consisted of a mayor, 12 councilmen, a city treasurer, a recorder, and a marshal. Mayors of the independent city were JOSIAH BARBER (1836), Francis A. Burrows (1837 and 1842), NORMAN C. BALDWIN (1838–39), shipbuilder and banker Needham M. Standart (1797–4 Dec. 1874, mayor 1840–41), RICHARD LORD (1843), saleratus manufacturer Daniel H. Lamb (1844–46), David Griffith (1847), tailor John Beverlin (1812–18 May 1891, mayor 1848), THOS. BURNHAM (1849–50), physician Benjamin Sheldon (1851–52), and WM. B. CASTLE (1853–54). The city's population grew from approximately 2,400 in the 1830s to 4,253 in 1850. There were 370 houses and 4 churches at the time of incorporation; at the time of its annexation, Ohio City had 3 school buildings, 3 more under construction, 2,438 school-age children, public school attendance of 800, and 11 teachers. Upon annexation, Ohio City became wards 8, 9, 10, and 11 of Cleveland.

After annexation, Ohio City became known as the near west side. A number of ethnic groups, including GERMANS, HUNGARIANS, and IRISH, lived in the area in the late 19th century. One of its focal points was, and is, the WEST SIDE MARKET, which was built by 1912 on the site that the first mayor of Ohio City, Josiah Barber, and another pioneer, Richard Lord, deeded to the city on the condition it be kept a marketplace. "Market Square," so designated since ca. 1840, was originally the site of the Pearl St. Market (built 1868) at the corner of Pearl (W. 25th St.) and Lorain St. Following WORLD WAR II, the area entered a period of decline. In 1968, the Ohio City Development Restoration Assoc. was chartered to stem the tide of neglect in the historic neighborhood. The association helped to strengthen a nascent trend of restoration that had begun in the early 1960s. From 1963–78, over 100 structures were refurbished, restored, or redeveloped, including St. Ignatius High School, the Carnegie Branch of the CLEVELAND PUBLIC LIBRARY, and the WEST SIDE MARKET, as well as numerous private residences. The cost of these projects was estimated at $30 million. As older structures were refurbished and occupied by upper-middle-class individuals and families, poorer groups were displaced, and charges of gentrification were made. By this time, Ohio City was home to over 15 ethnic groups representing 25,000 people in a 4.5-sq.-mile area. Among the newer immigrant and migrant groups were Hispanic-Americans and Asian-Americans. As of 1986, redevelopment was continuing in the area, although the issue of gentrification remained to be resolved.

Lewis, Joanne, *To Market/To Market* (1981).
Wheeler, Robert A., *Pleasantly Situated on the West Side* (1980).

The **OHIO CITY ARGUS,** Ohio City's first newspaper, appeared in time to promote the interests of west-siders in the famous Bridge War of 1836 (see COLUMBUS ST. BRIDGE). Established on 26 May 1836 by Lyman W. Hall and Timothy H. Smead, the 4-page weekly was Whiggish in its political affiliation. After 5 months, Hall dropped out of the partnership, leaving Smead to carry on alone as editor and publisher. The *Argus* led a precarious existence for 2 years, being burned out of one office and reduced to accepting payment in kind before its demise in the summer of 1838. The following September, Smead began a new Whig weekly in association with A. H. Lewis as editor. Named the *Ohio Transcript and Farmers' Register*, it evidently had an even shorter career than the *Argus*.

The **OHIO COLLEGE OF PODIATRIC MEDICINE** was in 1986 one of only 7 podiatric medical colleges in the country. Located at Carnegie Ave. and E. 105th St., it maintained a faculty of 36 full-time and over 200 part-time instructors and had a student enrollment of over 560. The college was originally founded in 1916 as the Ohio College of Chiropody, shortly after the Ohio legislature approved

the Platt-Ellis Bill, which provided for the regulation of medical specialties. Its founders, Cecil Beach, Max Harmlin, Oscar Klotzbach, Lester Siemon, Chas. Spatz, and Clerk McConnell, first located the school in the Republic Bldg. at 647 Euclid Ave. The college offered a 1-year course of study and graduated its first class of 20 students in 1917. Following a series of moves, the college in 1931 constructed its own building with 4 large amphitheaters, classrooms, laboratories, surgeries, clinics, and a library in UNIVERSITY CIRCLE at 2057 Cornell Rd. In 1976, the college moved into the Carnegie Medical Bldg. on Carnegie Ave. between E. 105th and 107th streets. The growth and development of the college and its educational program have reflected the advancements in the field of podiatry. Each move to new facilities has allowed for the further expansion of educational programs and increased opportunities for research and community service. In 1986 the college offered a 4-year curriculum concentrating on lecture and laboratory classes in the basic and applied medical sciences taught by M.D.s, Ph.D.s, and doctors of osteopathy. The college has a distinguished record of community involvement. Its operation of the Cleveland Foot Clinic and 16 local satellite clinics provides its students with practical clinical experience while giving needed podiatric care to the community. The college regularly provides free foot screening at area schools, daycare centers, senior citizens' organizations, businesses, and fairs. Faculty and students have assisted at major Cleveland road races such as the Revco-Cleveland Marathon and a Heart-A-Thon. The college has also worked closely with local neighborhood organizations to provide them with information and speakers about podiatric medicine.

**OHIO CRANKSHAFT.** *See* **PARK-OHIO INDUSTRIES, INC.**

The **OHIO MOTORISTS ASSOCIATION,** known as the Cleveland Automobile Club from its founding in 1900 until 1978, was the second automobile club formed in the U.S. and is the oldest still in existence. Founded to promote motoring as a sport, the association quickly became an information bureau and service agency for members and a lobbyist to promote what a 1912 publication called "sane legislation and highway improvement." The CAC was established by a group of local automobile manufacturers and motoring enthusiasts on 8 Jan. 1900, not long after the Automobile Club of America was established in New York City in June 1899. Although established as a social club, the organization was soon sponsoring a variety of contests so that manufacturers could display their new machines. It held its first annual race at the GLENVILLE RACE TRACK in 1902, and later in the decade held hill-climbing competitions and endurance runs.

In addition to sponsoring such competitions, the club began to provide services for its members. In 1902 it joined with 9 other auto clubs to form the American Automobile Assoc., and by 1903 it was publishing for its members traffic ordinances and a list of all registered car owners in the area. By 1916 it had begun lobbying efforts on behalf of motorists; published the monthly *Ohio Motorist*; offered an emblem for members' automobiles; and with 6,954 members was the largest auto club in the country. By 1928 its services included emergency road service, touring services, including maps, and a stolen car-department; also in 1928 it became the first U.S. auto club to offer bail bond service. During the 1930s and 1940s, the CAC introduced other services to members and the general public. In 1937 it opened a driver-training school; the following year it began to assist in high school driver-training courses, first at West Tech; and in 1946 it became the first auto club to equip emergency road-service vehicles with 2-way radios. When the Postwar Planning Council concluded its work in 1946, the council's panel on transportation, traffic, and transit continued to study highway development, parking, and other transit problems as a special department of the CAC.

Membership grew quickly after the war. With more than 65,000 members in the 1940s, the club surpassed 100,000 members in 1951; 200,000 in 1970; and 300,000 in 1975. Such increases allowed it to expand its services. Although some new services continued to promote safety, such as the sale of seat belts in 1962, in the mid-1970s new services included low-cost car rentals to members whose autos were stolen or being repaired, travel accommodations throughout the world, and discount merchandise and other low-cost services, such as insurance. Between 1903–40, the club had its offices at the Hollenden, 712 Superior; in May 1940 it moved into the former SAMUEL MATHER mansion, 2605 Euclid Ave., where it remained until it sold the building in 1967 to CLEVELAND STATE UNIVERSITY and in 1968 moved into new, $2 million headquarters at 6000 S. Marginal Rd. By 1978, members of the CAC were spread over 7 counties, and when it merged with the Oberlin Automobile Club (3,998 members; est. 1929) that year, the Cleveland club changed its name to the Ohio Motorists Assoc. The nonprofit organization had a net income of more than $252,000 in 1978.

The **OHIO POETRY ASSOCIATION** was established in the Cleveland Hts. home of Rachel Mack Wilson in 1931. Wilson, state president of the Natl. League of American Pen Women, served as the OPA's first president. The association's purpose was to promote the creation and appreciation of poetry by its members and throughout the community, state, and nation. Its motto, quoting Edmund Spencer, was "The poets' scrolls will outlive the monuments of stone." Founding members included Edmund Vance Cooke, Albert C. Fox, Harriet Gleason, Alice C. Redhead, Pearl R. Mountain, and Dr. EDWARD M. "TED" ROBINSON. Members met monthly for dinner, a forum discussion of submitted poems, and talks by guest speakers. The OPA sponsored annual peace poem, lyric poetry, Shakespearean sonnet, modern poetry, high school, and ballad contests. Scholarships were awarded for courses at Cleveland College. One of the association's members, Tess Sweazy Wills, was responsible for introducing the idea of an Ohio Poetry Day to the state legislature. A bill declaring the third Friday in October of each year as such was passed in 1937. Another distinguished member of the OPA was Loring Eugene Williams, a frequent speaker at monthly meetings and editor and publisher of the prestigious national poetry magazine *American Weave* (see PRINTING & PUBLISHING INDUSTRY).

There were 3 classes of membership in the Ohio Poetry Assoc.: active, associate, and honorary. Active members were those who joined as charter members and those recommended by the membership committee after a review of their work. Associate members were those who showed an interest in and appreciation of poetry. Applications were reviewed by active members. Honorary members were limited to those whom the society desired to honor. The association eventually formed more than 50 branches throughout Ohio. The Ohio Poetry Assoc. ceased to exist after giving out its last award for a peace poem contest, in 1975. Thereafter, other groups began in Cleveland, including the Poets' League of Greater Cleveland (1975) and the PoetsBank (1983), to further the creation and promotion of poetry.

The **OHIO SAVINGS ASSOCIATION,** incorporated in 1889, is one of Cleveland's oldest savings and loans. At the end of 1981 it had become the 49th-largest savings and loan in the U.S. In its first 9 years of existence, Ohio Savings operated as the Ohio Savings, Loan & Bldg. Co. In 1898 it became the Ohio Savings & Loan Co. Early officers included Dr. Elijah F. Davis, president, and Henry Grombacher, secretary until 1922. By 1904, Christian Schuele had become president. Until 1901, the main offices were located at 457 Pearl Rd.; in that year the office was moved to 517 Pearl, which later became 1866 W. 25th St. Ohio Savings maintained its headquarters there until moving to 515 Euclid in 1960; by 1977 it had moved to the Ohio Savings Plaza at 1801 E. 9th St.

Like other savings and loans in the area, Ohio Savings began to establish branch offices in the early 1950s. It had 1 branch in 1956, when it became the Ohio Savings Assoc., and 4 branch offices in 1960. A Cincinnati investment securities firm bought control of Ohio Savings in 1955. In 1961, Clevelander Leo Goldberg purchased control of the company. When he died 10 years later, his son Robert became president of the association. Ohio Savings grew rapidly in the 1970s, from 3 offices in 1970 to 40 in 1983. It established its own holding company, the Ohio Savings Financial Corp., in Oct. 1977; it had purchased Citizens Federal Savings & Loan of Akron in 1975 and acquired Shaker Savings in 1978. As of 30 June 1983, Ohio Savings' assets totaled $1.72 billion.

The **OHIO STATE AND UNION LAW COLLEGE,** commonly known as the Ohio State & Union Law School, was the largest, best-known, and longest-lived of the independent day law schools in Cleveland. Prior to the formation of the Law School at Western Reserve University in 1891, it was the major law school in northern Ohio and one of 2 viable law schools in Ohio. The college was founded in 1855 in Poland, Ohio, by the law firm of Judge Chester Hayden, Marcus King, and M. D. Leggett, as the Poland Law College. In 1857 it moved to Cleveland and was incorporated under its official name. Hayden served as dean, with 2 full-time instructors. Both instructors and most of the part-time faculty joined the Army during the CIVIL WAR, and Hayden had to run the school and teach all classes. In 1863, Hayden sold the school to a Cleveland lawyer, John Crowell. Crowell became president as well as sole shareholder of the corporation; he continued operation of the college until his retirement in 1876. Under Crowell, the college was located in the Rouse Block and was commonly referred to as the Crowell Law School, the Cleveland Law School, or the Cleveland Law College.

During the 24 years the college operated, approximately 500 students attended, and it awarded about 200 LL.B. degrees. It used the Dwight method of instruction, consisting of lectures and recitations, modeled on the Litchfield (Conn.) School. Initially, the course of instruction lasted a year, but it was changed to 2 years ca. 1870. The law school was apparently one of the few institutions of its day that did not discriminate on the basis of race. Noted black lawyer JOHN P. GREEN graduated from the school in 1870. Of the 278 living members of the Cleveland bar as of 1887, 34 were graduates of or had attended the Ohio State & Union Law College. The school closed upon the retirement of John Crowell in 1876.

Samad, S. A., "History of Legal Education in Ohio" (Ms. in law Libraries of Akron University School of Law and CWRU School of Law, 1972).

The **OHIO THEATER,** 1511 Euclid Ave., was opened on 14 Feb. 1921. Its architect was Thos. Lamb, and its interior decorator, Philip Garbo. Designed for stage plays, the Ohio was built for the Loew's chain by the Fleishman Constr. Co. of New York. Its opening consisted of *The Return of Peter Grimm*, starring David Warfield. The theater had a long and varied career. Originally designed as a legitimate theater, it was decorated in Italian Renaissance style in an elegant green-and-ivory color scheme. There were 3 murals on the walls of the foyer by Italian artist Sampitrotti. These were of the cycle of Venus: *Her Birth from the Waves* (west wall); *Her Triumph* (east wall); and *Her Consecration* (south wall). The paintings in the balcony were by P. Pizzi, representing scenes in Arcady depicting the joys of pastoral life. The auditorium itself was 14th-century Venetian.

In 1935, the theater was redecorated in the Art Deco style and reopened as the Mayfair Casino. The Casino was a supper club that featured assorted musical entertainment, including bands and musical revues. The redecoration included the addition of a mirrored circular bar in the lobby and tiers of tables in the old auditorium and a new circular stage. Though the Casino owners had big plans—including hopes that gambling would be allowed in the city—they were forced to close in 1936. The Ohio reopened in 1943 (with its original decor) as a movie theater. In 1964, a fire gutted the lobby, necessitating another redecoration. This time everything (including the auditorium murals) was painted red to hide smoke damage. Like other movie theaters downtown, it lost patronage and closed the first week of Feb. 1969. When the Playhouse Square Assoc. was formed in 1970, the Ohio was saved from destruction. In Oct. 1978, it was placed on the Natl. Register of Historic Places; and by 1981, restoration had begun. Renovated as the home for the Great Lakes Theater Festival, the Ohio reopened on 9 July 1982 after 9 months of renovation costing $4 million. The first show in the new theater was *As You Like It*, produced by the Great Lakes Theater Festival.

*Playhouse Square, Cleveland, Ohio* (The Red Book) (1975).
*Playhouse Square, Cleveland, Ohio* (The Blue Book) (1984).
"Playhouse Square Foundation Fact Sheet" (Volunteer Guide) (1981).

**OLD AGE/NURSING HOMES.** The origins of community responsibility for the elderly in Cleveland can be traced to the Northwest Territorial law for the relief of the poor enacted in 1795. This act placed the obligation for maintaining needy relatives upon "father and grandfather, and the mother and grandmother, and the children of every poor, old, blind, lame and impotent person." During the first half of the 19th century, assistance to Cleveland's needy, including the aged, continued to come primarily from the traditional sources—the family, private benevolence, and public relief. The course of benevolence in Cleveland, however, changed somewhat with the establishment in 1855 of the City Infirmary, which served as a melting pot of sorts where the poor, old, aged, insane, and handicapped were given a place to dwell and the requirements to sustain life. It was not until 1870 that the first home to provide particular care for the elderly was established in Cleveland by the LITTLE SISTERS OF THE POOR, a religious order founded in France in 1839. Between 1870–1908, 10 institutions, including the foundation of the Little Sisters, were established to provide shelter and care for elderly persons in Cleveland. The evidence suggests that a growing dissatisfaction with the City Infirmary as an appropriate facility for the care of the needy and infirm impelled religious leaders and social reformers to establish special homes for the aged. The Home for Aged Women and the ELIZA JENNINGS HOME, both managed by the Women's Christian Assoc., were established to provide shelter for elderly women whose only alternative was the City Infirmary.

Most of the private homes for the aged in Cleveland, including the asylum established by the Little Sisters and the homes created under the auspices of the Women's Christian Assoc., manifested the concern of "women of the church" for the dependent elderly. The Baptist Home of Ohio, the Dorcas Society's Invalids Home, and the A. M. MCGREGOR HOME were 3 other private institutions for the elderly established through the Christian good works of women or women's organizations. These 19th-century benevolent homes did not represent an exclusively Christian concern for the aged; Cleveland's Jewish community assumed responsibility for the care of its elderly members by establishing the Home for Aged & Infirm Israelites (MONTEFIORE HOME) in 1882, supported by the Kesher Shel Barzel, a Jewish fraternal organization, and the Orthodox Old Home in 1906. There was, however, a notable lack of activity on the part of other fraternal societies in Cleveland to establish homes for their elderly members. Also, despite Cleveland's large immigrant population, there were only 2 institutions, the German ALTENHEIM Home and the Home for Aged Colored People, established before 1909, that might claim affiliation with the city's ethnic groups. Those dependent and infirm elderly unable to meet the standards of the private and public institutions continued to find their only source of support in the City Infirmary; however, a complete transformation of the infirmary at the turn of the century resulted in a model facility known as the Cooley Farms, which attracted national attention. A unique feature of the colony farm, the new village for the poor, infirm, insane, and aged, was a separate building for elderly married couples that allowed them to continue to live together in a noninstitutional setting. The transformation of the City Infirmary's facilities for the elderly came at a time, however, when Clevelanders were beginning to express doubts about the usefulness of institutionalization as the sole solution to the increasingly complex needs of an expanding aged population. In 1909, for instance, the BENJAMIN ROSE INSTITUTE was organized to carry out the provisions of Mr. Rose's will, and its trustees adopted a policy of providing assistance to the elderly in their own households rather than providing support for them in institutions.

Other forms of noninstitutional support for the elderly evolved during the economic crisis of the Depression years. In 1933 the general assembly enacted the first Ohio law to provide public funds for the needy aged, and Title I of the landmark Social Security Act of 1935 appropriated $49,750,000 to enable each state to furnish financial assistance to needy older persons. One of the stipulations governing these grants-in-aid was that federal money could not be used to pay stipends to aged people living in public institutions. This provision led nationally to the decline of the poorhouse as an asylum for the elderly and contributed to the rise of the "proprietary home." Locally, the rapid growth of the proprietary home was evidenced by the establishment of 70 such institutions in Cuyahoga County by 1942 and was also marked by the passage of a state licensing law in that same year. The arrival of these new nursing homes in the Cleveland community was not universally welcomed, and Mary C. Jarrett, in her 1944 report "The Care of the Chronically Ill of Cleveland and Cuyahoga County," suggested that the existing proprietary nursing homes were close to a "public scandal." In Jan. 1946, Eugene S. Lindemann, chairman of the Coordinating Committee on the Chronically Ill, reported that in 1945 there were 34 nursing and rest homes, with 1,130 beds, licensed by the state to operate in Cuyahoga County, and that an additional 9 homes were operating without a license.

But although many of the proprietary nursing and boarding homes that developed in Cleveland during the 1930s and 1940s were the subject of criticism, they did serve a growing need for better health services for the elderly. Older persons were beginning to live longer, aided by dramatic improvements in medical knowledge and technology, and most of the private benevolent homes enforced policies that allowed them to accept as residents only those older persons who were able-bodied. Thus, new facilities had to be developed to provide the specialized treatment required by the increasing numbers of older persons who became chronically ill or mentally incapacitated. The first positive step to provide for the treatment and care of such persons came in 1932 with the construction of a 169-bed chronic hospital, on the colony farm, and in 1938 the Cuyahoga County Nursing Home was opened as a shelter for relief patients who were permanently and totally disabled. But the chronic hospital and the county nursing home were not equal to the task of caring for the large number of patients requiring care; in 1952, an agreement was entered into between the city of Cleveland and the board of Cuyahoga County commissioners, and the land and buildings on the Cooley Farms were transferred to the county to facilitate the construction of a new chronic hospital, later to be known as Highland View.

The 1950s witnessed some improvement in nursing-home care, as seen in the activities of the Welfare Fed.'s Chronic Illness Information Ctr. The center maintained contact with area nursing homes and provided information to the chronically ill of all ages, including the elderly, regarding the range of services offered by various institutions, and offered recommendations about the homes best designed to meet the needs of the individual patient. By Oct. 1957, there were 37 proprietary nursing homes licensed by the division of social administration of the department of public welfare to offer care in Cleveland and Cuyahoga County. The 1960s brought sweeping social changes to all areas of national life, including the implementation of some policies that directly affected the aged. For example, the enactment of the Medicare and Medicaid programs gave further impetus to the growth of commercial nursing homes, and this trend was clearly reflected in the Greater Cleveland community. The Cleveland city directory recorded the names of 26 city nursing homes in 1965, and 31 in 1972; and the east and west suburban directories included the names of 34 additional facilities. The vital role that the nursing home continues to play in providing shelter and medical care for the elderly in Cuyahoga County is best illustrated by the 8 pages of listings and advertisements, for approximately 116 such institutions, published in the most current Cleveland consumer directory.

Judith G. Cetina
Cuyahoga County Archives

## OLD STONE CHURCH. *See* FIRST PRESBYTERIAN CHURCH (OLD STONE)

**OLLENDORFF, HENRY B.** (1906–10 Feb. 1979), was a German-born and -trained lawyer who took up social work after coming to the U.S. to escape Nazi Germany. In Cleveland he founded and headed the Council of Internatl. Programs. Born in Esslingen, Germany, Ollendorff received a doctorate in law from the University of Heidelberg in 1929. He was imprisoned by the Nazis in 1937 and spent 13 months in solitary confinement. In 1938 he and his wife, Martha, came to the U.S. Ollendorff studied at the New York School of Social Work at Columbia University, graduating in 1940. He moved to Cleveland in Sept. 1940 and became a boys' worker at the FRIENDLY INN SOCIAL SETTLEMENT. He became head worker there in 1943 and in 1948 became the executive director of the Neighborhood Settlement Assoc., a position he held until resigning in 1963 to devote his full effort to the Council of Internatl. Programs. After his experience at the hands of the Nazis, Ollendorff had vowed never to return to his native Germany, but he did so in 1954 at the request of the U.S. State Dept., which asked him to teach a 5-month seminar for German youth leaders. While there he conceived of the idea for an exchange program to bring German social leaders to the U.S. for study and firsthand experience with American life and social work. The Council of Internatl. Programs, designed to promote international understanding, was formally established in 1956. In the next 22 years, the program brought to the U.S. representatives from 105 countries. Ollendorff's work for the Council of Internatl. Programs took him on annual trips abroad to interview applicants, and upon his return to Cleveland he frequently spoke before civic groups to relate his experiences and impressions about world conditions and about foreign attitudes toward the U.S. His efforts on behalf of mutual understanding and peace among the peoples of the world also earned him many honors, such as the 1959 Internatl. Services Award from the ROTARY CLUB of Cleveland and the 1971 Golden Door Award from the NATIONALITIES SERVICES CTR. He also received a bronze plaque from the State Dept. in 1976 and was honored with the West German government's Order of Merit and the French government's Order of Merite Social. In 1978, the trustees of the Council of Internatl. Programs established the Henry B. Ollendorff Foundation to continue his efforts toward world peace and friendship.

Henry B. Ollendorff Papers, WRHS.

**OLMSTED FALLS** is a city situated 14 mi. southwest of Cleveland and occupying 3 sq. mi. It is bounded on the east by BEREA, on the north by N. OLMSTED, and on the west by OLMSTED TWP. The early history of Olmsted Falls is closely tied to those of N. Olmsted and Olmsted Twp., all carved out of the original Olmsted Twp. The name was derived from early settler Aaron Olmstead in 1829; in time, the *a* was dropped from the name. During the 1820s, a sawmill and a gristmill were built at the falls of the west branch of the Rocky River. In 1843, the town of Norris Falls was created at the center of the township, and in 1845, the town was renamed Olmsted Falls after the larger falls used for the mills. In 1857, the village of Olmsted Falls was incorporated and adopted the mayor-council form of government. In 1849, the Cleveland, Columbus & Cincinnati Railroad was built through Olmsted Falls, and the village benefited significantly from the location of the railroad. However, expansion of the falls area slowed at the turn of the century and did not begin again until after WORLD WAR II. Highway development and suburban migration contributed to Olmsted Falls' postwar growth, and it became a city in 1961. Its population grew steadily from 2,144 in 1960 to 5,868 in 1980. Olmsted Falls provides a variety of public services, including police and fire protection. It had 1 elementary, 1 junior, and 1 senior high school in 1980. Recreational services included a summer program of baseball, basketball, tennis, swimming, and several parks and picnic facilities.

Offenberg, Bernice Weitzel, *Over the Years in Olmsted, Township 6, Range 15* (1964).
Olmsted Falls, "Community Profile" (1982).

**OLMSTED TOWNSHIP** is located in the southwestern corner of Cuyahoga County. It borders N. OLMSTED on the north and BROOK PARK and BEREA on the east, and surrounds OLMSTED FALLS on 3 sides. The township is governed by 3 trustees, who are elected at large. Originally part of Twp. 6, Range 15, of the Connecticut WESTERN RESERVE, the area was initially named Plum Creek Twp. Aaron Olmstead, a shareholder in the CONNECTICUT LAND CO., bid on and purchased the northern half of the area on 22 Apr. 1807, deeding it to his son Charles. In 1814 the Jas. Greer family became the first white settlers in the area, which they called Kingston in memory of their former home in Vermont. On 14 Apr. 1823, Kingston was organized as the village of Lenox in honor of settlers who had emigrated from New England. In 1829, village officials concluded an agreement with Chas. Olmstead to accept the name Olmstead in exchange for his library. It was not only the first library in the settlement but also the first west of the Allegheny Mts. The first elections in Olmstead were held in 1830. Olmsted Twp. grew steadily. In 1848, 2 general stores were built in the area. By 1950 the population reached 1,216. Different portions of the township developed sooner than others. That resulted in increasing discontent as residents in the more developed areas sought greater elective representation. As a result, both N. Olmsted and Olmsted Falls were created, leaving the township as a 10-sq.-mi. rural residential area. Township residents were traditionally concerned with zoning, as the area was one of the few in Cuyahoga County with open undeveloped land. The creation of the Columbia Trailer Park in 1954 was opposed by township residents, who feared the mobile-home park would upset the community's rural character. Subsequent disputes with land developers have led to several annexation attempts. Greenhouses were the township's largest industry in the 1970s. Together with Olmsted Falls, it was the 2d-largest area for greenhouses in the county. The township is part of the Olmsted Falls School District. In 1980 its recreational facilities included a golf course, horse farms, and Trolleyville USA, a museum featuring a working trolley line through the Columbia Trailer Park.

The **OLNEY ART GALLERY** was a privately owned and operated art gallery located on Jennings Ave. (W. 14th St.). It was established in 1893 by Prof. Chas. Fayette Olney and his wife, Edna, after the tremendous success of the ART LOAN EXHIBITIONS earlier that year assured the Olneys that Cleveland needed an art gallery. Objects from the Olneys' private collection were the basis of the gallery, although at times other prominent Cleveland citizens donated works for display, including Windsor T. White and CHAS. F. BRUSH. The gallery operated out of a long, narrow brick-and-stone building that housed over 200 objects, including oil and watercolor paintings, porcelains, and statuary. In 1896, the gallery was one of several in the U.S. that displayed Hungarian artist Michel Leib Munkacsy's *Christ before Pilate.* The following year, his *Last Moments of Mozart* was also featured there. The gallery closed in 1907, 4 years after Chas. Olney died; the bulk of the collection was left to Oberlin College.

**O'MALLEY, PATRICK** (1903–14 June 1983), was a long-term leader of the UNITED AUTO WORKERS and Cleveland AFL-CIO who forged both organizations into democratic, smooth-running bodies. A native of County Mayo, Ireland, O'Malley worked as a coal miner in England before migrating to Cleveland in 1924. After several jobs, he joined the WHITE MOTOR CO. in 1928 as an inventory checker and timekeeper, a position he would hold for 21 years. When the CIO organized White in 1932, he was among the first members; he quickly was elected union steward and bargaining-team member. Before moving on to higher

positions outside the local, he was to hold every office in Local 32. While at White, O'Malley studied accounting at night, but he abandoned hopes of becoming a CPA when the CIO turned its efforts toward ridding itself of Communists in the late 1940s. As president of the CLEVELAND INDUSTRIAL UNION COUNCIL after 1948, he helped purge the regional body as well as individual unions of leftists. When he became a UAW regional director in 1949, O'Malley quit his job at White. He was continuously reelected with minimal opposition until he reached 65, a mandatory retirement age he had pressed for years before. As the AFL and CIO tried to amalgamate on a national level, O'Malley forged the merger locally. When it was complete, he reigned as part-time president from 1958–68 and as full-time president from 1968–70. Ironically, O'Malley became full-time CLEVELAND FED. OF LABOR president at a time when the UAW was suspended over nonpayment of dues, a local manifestation of broader national conflict between the UAW and the AFL-CIO. To continue his eligibility to serve, O'Malley secured membership in the Internatl. Assoc. of Machinists. He resigned in 1970 to serve as foreman of the Cuyahoga County Grand Jury, and later served on the Cuyahoga County Commission on Aging. An Irishman possessed of the stereotypical Irish temper, brogue, and sense of humor, O'Malley was regarded as fair-minded and able to give and take in dealing with his constituency. Sensitive to the struggles in his native land, he led a group of Freedom for Ireland supporters who confronted Prince Charles when he came to dedicate the Cleveland State University Law School in 1977. O'Malley and his wife, Mary, had 2 children.

**O'MIC, JOHN** (ca. 1790–26 June 1812), an Indian, was the first person executed in northern Ohio. There is no agreement on the Indian's name, or how it was spelled. It is found spelled O'Mic (the most common version), O'Mick, Omic, and Omeek. It is also found as Devil Poc-con, Pochokow, Po-Kee-Kaw, Po-Ke-Kaw (probably the real name), or Poccon. His father was reportedly named O'Mic. O'Mic belonged to the Massasauga band of Chippewas. They resided near Pymatuning Creek, Jefferson County, until 1811, when they moved to the west bank of the Cuyahoga. On 3 Apr. 1812, 2 trappers named Buel and Gibbs were murdered in Sandusky. O'Mic and 2 other Indians were arrested. One committed suicide; the other was released because of his extreme youth. O'Mic was sent to Cleveland for prosecution (Sandusky was in the legal jurisdiction of Cuyahoga County).

The trial took place on 29 Apr. 1812, with judges Ethan Allen Brown and Wm. Irvin; SAMUEL BALDWIN, sheriff; ALFRED KELLEY, prosecutor; and Peter Hitchcock, defense. O'Mic was sentenced to death for the murder of Daniel Buel. Execution was set for 26 June. A large crowd gathered at PUBLIC SQUARE to watch the execution. At the gallows, Sheriff Baldwin tried to cover O'Mic's face, but the frightened Indian lunged for a platform post and clung to it. He told Lorenzo Carter that he would die courageously if he could have some whiskey. After several drinks were provided, O'Mic was executed. The day after they witnessed the execution, a group of Western Reserve physicians, led by Dr. DAVID LONG, reportedly took the body, intending to use it for medical studies. The skeleton was reportedly later taken to Hudson, Ohio, and then to Pittsburgh. O'Mic's death coincided with the outbreak of the WAR OF 1812. Many Indians fought on the side of the British, partly because of anger over O'Mic's hanging. When Gen. Hull surrendered Detroit to the British shortly after the hanging, settlers in the Sandusky area headed east for fear that the Indians would go on a rampage to avenge O'Mic's death. But the marauding bands never came.

Anonymous, "Partial Narrative of Murder Trial & Execution in the Public Square, Cleveland, June 24, 1812," WRHS.
Wright, Morgan, Ashtabula County, Ohio, "eyewitness" account of O'Mic's hanging, 17 Sept. 1908, WRHS.

The **ON LEONG TONG**, also known as the Chinese Merchants Assoc., is an organization that has provided the local Chinese-American community with the services of a bank, a welfare agency, a mutual benefit society, and a cultural preservation group, in addition to those of a trade association. The On Leong Tong was established first in New York in 1904; the Cleveland branch was formed in 1910. By 1911 the local group was meeting at a store at 1279 Ontario St., and by 1916 it had established its headquarters at 1307 Ontario in the midst of the city's Chinatown. When the demolition of the old buildings along Ontario began in 1927, the tong maintained its headquarters there as long as possible while it worked to construct a new facility at 2150 Rockwell Ave., which it completed and occupied in 1930. In 1944 it paid off the mortgage on its new building, and 4 years later it hosted the national meeting of the organization. The Cleveland association hosted the national convention again in 1961 and in 1973; the latter meeting was attended by 330 delegates from Hong Kong, Taiwan, and throughout the U.S.

Although the Chinese word *tong* means simply "meeting hall," the Chinese tongs operated as secret societies, and although *on leong* means "happiness and contentment," the local On Leong Tong in its early years became a controversial organization to many outsiders because of its association with violence and murder during the TONG WARS of the 1910s and 1920s, and because several of its leaders were reportedly linked to the strong-arm tactics used to coerce contributions to the Chinese war-relief fund in 1939. By the mid-1930s, however, the On Leong Tong and its former rival, the Hip Sing Tong, were cooperating in a program to raise money to transfer to China the remains of 120 CHINESE buried in the U.S. so that the dead could rest next to relatives and ancestors. By 1970, the tongs in general had lost much of their power within the Chinese-American community; Cleveland's On Leong Tong functioned mainly as a business association and a cultural-preservation organization. In 1968, its purpose was described as preserving Chinese traditions for the younger generations; in 1971 it was described as an agency that worked "to insure that Chinese businesses don't needlessly compete with one another."

The **150TH OHIO VOLUNTEER INFANTRY REGIMENT**, 1864, contained 801 Cleveland men during its 100 days' term of service in the Civil War. The 150th was raised in the spring of 1864. The CLEVELAND GRAYS took credit for raising 5 companies. The Grays enlisted for service as Co. A. After being organized and mustered in at Camp Cleveland on 5 May 1864, the 150th was ordered to the defenses of Washington, D.C., on 7 May 1864. It was assigned to the 1st Brigade, Haskin's Div., 22d Army Corps, from May-July 1864. During that period it was assigned to 7 of the forts, making up an 88-fort defensive network around Washington, D.C., to guard against Confederate attacks and possible invasion. From July-August, the 150th remained in the defenses on garrison duty, assigned to the 2d Brigade, Haskin's 22d Army Corps, Defenses of Washington. It was ordered back to Camp Cleveland in August, where it was mustered out on 23 Aug. 1864.

The regiment lost 2 enlisted men killed and 10 dead from disease.

Cannon, James, Memorial–150th Ohio-Co. K (1907). WRHS.
Gleason, William J., Historical Sketch of the 150th Regiment Ohio Volunteer Infantry (1899).

The **107TH OHIO VOLUNTEER INFANTRY REGIMENT**, 1862–65, was composed largely of German immigrants from Cleveland and Cuyahoga County. It was organized at Camp Taylor (see CIVIL WAR CAMPS) in the summer of 1862 and mustered into federal service on 9 Sept. The regiment was transferred to Covington, Ky., serving there until October. After a short period of duty at Delaware, Ohio, it was sent to Washington, D.C., where it was assigned to the 2d Brigade, 3d Div., 11th Army Corps, Army of the Potomac, in October. It served with this unit until December.

After December, the 107th was assigned to the following units: 2d Brigade, 1st Div., 11th Army Corps (Dec. 1862-July 1863); 1st Brigade, 1st Div., 11th Army Corps (July-Aug. 1863); 1st Brigade, Gordon's Div., 11th Army Corps, Dept. of the South (Aug. 1863-Jan. 1864); 2d Brigade, Gordon's Div., 10th Army Corps (Jan.-Feb. 1864); 1st Brigade, Ames' Div., District of Florida, Dept. of the South (Feb.-Apr. 1864); District of Florida (Apr.-Oct. 1864); 4th Separate Brigade, District of Florida, Dept. of the South (Oct. 1864); 1st Brigade, Coast Div., Dept. of the South (Nov. 1864); 4th Separate Brigade, Dept. of the South (Dec. 1864-Jan. 1865); 1st Separate Brigade, Northern District, Dept. of the South (Jan.-Mar. 1865); and 1st Separate Brigade, District of Charleston, Dept. of the South (Mar.-July 1865). The regiment participated in the Fredericksburg, Chancellorsville, and Gettysburg campaigns and assisted in the destruction of the Charleston & Savannah Railroad. The 107th was mustered out at Charleston, S.C., on 10 July 1865. Its men were discharged and paid off at Camp Cleveland shortly thereafter. The unit lost 57 men to hostile causes and 76 men to disease.

Smith, Jacob, Camps and Campaigns of the 107th Regiment Ohio Volunteer Infantry from August 1862 to July 1865 (ca. 1910).

The **177TH OHIO VOLUNTEER INFANTRY REGIMENT**, 1864–65, was organized at Camp Cleveland, Ohio, for 1 year's Civil War service on 9 Oct. 1864. The 177th was transported to Nashville, and then to Tullahoma, Tenn., for duty until Nov. 1864. Between Oct.-Dec. 1864, it was attached to the Defenses of the Nashville & Chattanooga Railroad, Dept. of the Cumberland. From Dec. 1864-Jan. 1865, it was attached to the 2d Brigade, 4th Div., 20th Army Corps. From Jan.-June 1865, the regiment was assigned to the 2d Brigade, 3d Div., 23d Army Corps, Army of the Ohio, Dept. of North Carolina. It was mustered out at Greensboro, N.C., on 24 June 1865. The 177th was discharged and paid off at Camp Cleveland, Ohio, on 7 July 1865. Losses were stated as 2 enlisted men dead from hostile causes and 82 dead from disease.

The **103D OHIO VOLUNTEER INFANTRY REGIMENT**, 1862–65, included approximately 460 men from Cleveland and Cuyahoga County during its 3 years of service. The regiment was raised at Camp Cleveland (see CIVIL WAR CAMPS) during the summer of 1862, leaving for Cincinnati on 3 Sept. It was assigned to the following units during its term of service: 2d Brigade, 1st Div., Army of Kentucky, Dept. of the Ohio (Sept.-Oct. 1862); 2d Div., 2d Brigade, Army of Kentucky (Oct.-Dec. 1862); 1st Brigade, 4th Div., 4th Army Corps, District of Central Kentucky,

Dept. of the Ohio (Jan.-June 1863); 1st Brigade, 1st Div., 23d Army Corps, Army of the Ohio (June-Aug. 1863); 2d Brigade, 3d Div., 23d Army Corps (Aug. 1863-Feb. 1865); and 2d Brigade, 3d Div., 23d Army Corps, Dept. of North Carolina (Feb.-June 1865). The regiment participated in the Knoxville, Atlanta, and Carolinas campaigns and the battles of Resaca, Armstrong's Hill, and Ft. Fisher. The unit was mustered out at Raleigh, N.C., on 12 June 1865, and its men were discharged and paid off at Camp Cleveland on 22 June. The 103d lost 139 men to hostile action and 109 men to disease. Veterans of the 103d OVI began holding annual reunions in 1867. Descendants of the veterans maintain a reunion campground in Sheffield Lake, Ohio. A Sons & Daughters Assoc. was formed in 1889, and in 1907 the veterans formed a corporation to maintain the campground. In 1972 a memorial foundation was established to maintain a museum dedicated to the history of the regiment.

Hayes, Philip C., *Journal-History of the Hundred & Third Ohio Volunteer Infantry* (1872).

Members of the 103d Ohio Volunteer Infantry, *Personal Reminiscences and Experiences* (1900).

The **128TH OHIO VOLUNTEER INFANTRY REGIMENT** served as the guard unit at the prison for captured Confederate soldiers at Johnson's Island during the CIVIL WAR. The first 4 units of the regiment—companies A, B, C, and D—were organized in Dec. 1861 and early 1862 and were known as Hoffman's Battalion in honor of commissary general of prisoners Lt. Col. Wm. Hoffman, the man responsible for establishing the prison on the island. These units guarded about 3,000 prisoners in the winter of 1863–64 and foiled a plot to free the prisoners in Nov. 1863. The companies in Hoffman's Battalion were transferred to the 128th on 5 Jan. 1864, joining 6 new companies—Companies E, F, G, H, I, and K—recruited and mustered into service at Camp Cleveland in Dec. 1863 and Jan. 1864. In all, 291 Cleveland men served in the 128th, including Lt. Col. Edward A. Scovill, Lt. Col. Thos. H. Linnell, and Maj. JUNIUS R. SANFORD. The unit was commanded by Col. Chas. W. Hill. Although its main duty was guarding the Johnson's Island prison, the 128th frequently provided detachments to serve elsewhere, such as for a short campaign against Rebel troops in West Virginia. The regiment was mustered out of service on 13 July 1865. In 1866, veterans of the unit joined with other veterans to form the 7th and 128th Regiments OVI to preserve monuments and memories of Civil War service and to hold annual reunions. The association had about 200 members in 1921.

The **124TH OHIO VOLUNTEER INFANTRY REGIMENT**, 1862-65, was organized at Camp Taylor (see CIVIL WAR CAMPS) in the fall of 1862 and mustered into federal service on 1 Jan. 1863. It moved to Elizabethtown, Ky., and remained there until Feb. 1863 as a part of the District of Western Kentucky, Dept. of the Ohio. The 124th was assigned to the following units during the remainder of the war: 1st Brigade, 3d Div., Army of Kentucky, Dept. of the Cumberland (Feb.-June 1863); 2d Brigade, 2d Div., 21st Army Corps, Army of the Cumberland (June-Oct. 1863); and 2d Brigade, 3d Div., 4th Army Corps, Army of the Cumberland (Oct. 1863-June 1865). The regiment participated in the Chattanooga-Ringgold and Atlanta, Ga., campaigns and was active in the relief of Knoxville, Tenn. The unit was mustered out at Nashville on 9 July 1865, and its men were paid off and discharged at Camp Cleveland shortly thereafter. The 124th lost 85 men to hostile action and 125 men to disease.

Lewis, George W., *The Campaigns of the One Hundred and Twenty-fourth Regiment, Ohio Volunteer Infantry* (1894).

**O'NEILL, FRANCIS JOSEPH "STEVE"** (18 Sept. 1899– 29 Aug. 1983), was a businessman who helped organize LEASEWAY TRANSPORTATION and was a principal owner of the CLEVELAND INDIANS baseball team. O'Neill was born in Cleveland and attended Loyola and St. Ignatius high schools. He went on to Campion Preparatory School in Prairie du Chien, Wis., and Campion College. He also attended Notre Dame University. Hugh O'Neill, Steve's father, had started a cartage business with horse-drawn wagons, which developed into several transportation companies; Steve started working for the Superior Transportation Co., and like his brothers, he worked for several of his family's multiple companies. O'Neill's special contribution to the family business was developing the home-delivery and cartage business. In 1961, 79 O'Neill family companies merged to form the Leaseway Transportation Corp., of which O'Neill became chairman of the board; he retired as chairman in 1969 but remained on the board of directors. He was also a part of the group that bought the Sheraton Cleveland Hotel on PUBLIC SQUARE and leased it to the Stouffer Corp., which renamed the hotel STOUFFER'S INN ON THE SQUARE.

O'Neill was always athletic and interested in sports. He played FOOTBALL, BASKETBALL, and BASEBALL in high school and basketball in college. During the 1930s, he and his brothers could often be found playing POLO. O'Neill was called by his initials, F. J., or more commonly Steve after his hero, Steve O'Neill, the Cleveland Indians catcher of the 1920 championship season and manager for over 2 seasons during the 1930s. O'Neill became an owner of the Indians in 1961 as part of the group led by VERNON STOUFFER. In 1973, he was forced to sell his Indians stock when he joined Geo. Steinbrenner's syndicate that bought the New York Yankees. In 1978, O'Neill sold his Yankees stock and put together a new ownership to buy the Indians and make the franchise solvent and keep it in Cleveland; he was the principal owner, majority stockholder, and chairman of the Indians—holding approximately 63% of the stock. Although he lost $10–12 million on the team, O'Neill refused many offers by groups wishing to move it elsewhere; he was determined to keep the Indians in Cleveland. When major-league baseball signed a $1 billion deal with NBC and ABC in Apr. 1983 that increased each team's share of television revenues, he announced that the team was not for sale. O'Neill married Anne Henry on 20 Jan. 1926; she died on 4 Jan. 1971. They had 3 children: Francis, Jr., Mary, and Elizabeth. O'Neill married his second wife, Nancy Marsteller, on 14 Oct. 1974.

**ORANGE** is a village located 15 mi. east of Cleveland. Bounded on the north by WOODMERE, on the east by MORELAND HILLS, on the west by WARRENSVILLE HTS., and on the south by SOLON, it occupies 4.5 sq. mi. It was originally part of Orange Twp., formed in 1820, which also included the modern communities of Moreland Hills, Woodmere, PEPPER PIKE, HUNTING VALLEY, and part of CHAGRIN FALLS. Serenus Burnett was the first settler in the township, arriving in 1815. The name Orange was chosen because several of the early settlers had migrated from Orange, Conn. The area grew into a thriving agricultural community, and by 1820 the population was nearly 300. Before 1850, log houses were replaced by framed homes, and steam sawmills and cheese factories were early industries that developed into major businesses by the turn of the century. The main road was SOM Ctr. Rd., which derived its name from Solon, Orange, and Mayfield as it ran through the centers of those townships. The VAN SWERINGEN brothers played an instrumental role in the division of Orange Twp. into separate governmental bodies in the 1920s. They began buying farmland as part of their comprehensive plan to develop the entire district from SHAKER HTS. to the CHAGRIN RIVER. As population increased, the apparent need for separate governmental representation led to the creation of the various communities. The village of Orange was incorporated in 1929. Although the original Orange Twp. now consists of 5 separate villages, local district schools were consolidated into the Orange School System. The Orange Branch of the CUYAHOGA COUNTY PUBLIC LIBRARY SYSTEM serves Solon, Pepper Pike, and their neighbors. The village of Orange had a population of 2,376 in 1980 and operated under the mayor-council form of government.

Fant, Kathleen Griffin, *Orange Township . . . Orange Community, A History from 1815-1824* (ca. 1982).

**ORDER OF FOUNDERS & PATRIOTS.** *See* **PATRIOTIC SOCIETIES**

**ORPHANAGES.** Colonial Americans, following the English poor laws, cared for dependent children as they did dependent adults: by providing outdoor relief that allowed recipients to subsist in their own homes, by boarding them out with the lowest bidder to be cared for and perhaps taught a trade at the expense of the town or county, or by placing them in public almshouses. In the first quarter of the 19th century, care of dependents in almshouses or poorhouses gradually replaced outdoor relief and boarding out, and institutions for children were segregated from those for adults. Cleveland's earliest public institution for dependent and neglected children was the almshouse or City Infirmary, built in 1837 to house the ill, crippled, insane, feeble-minded, and dependent of all ages. By 1858, public opinion and funds supported a separate House of Correction or House of Refuge for children under 17, intended to both shelter and reform them. From 1871–91, this institution operated in connection with the city workhouse, and its focus was delinquent and vagrant youth. From 1856–71, public funds also supported dependent children in the Cleveland City Industrial School, which had been founded as the "Ragged School" in 1853 by a Methodist home mission society, and which did not shelter but educated and trained vagrant children. The school was funded primarily by private contributions. During the second half of the 19th century, these public efforts were supplemented by private orphan asylums, sometimes aided by public funding but financed mostly through philanthropic gifts, church collections, or fundraising events such as bazaars and orphans' fairs. In Cleveland, for example, several church-related orphanages were established in which children were to receive a common-school education, vocational training, and moral and religious guidance. Since it was assumed that this training would take time, orphanages were designed for long-term care, although they occasionally provided only temporary shelter. Their stated goal for their inmates was return to the parental home, adoption, or release when the child was of legal age and could become self-sufficient.

The first Catholic orphan asylums were established in the 1850s during the administration of Bp. LOUIS AMADEUS RAPPE, partly in response to the Protestant proselytizing of institutions such as the "Ragged School." These orphanages were run by nuns but were under the direction of the Diocese of Cleveland. The Ladies of the Sacred Heart of Mary, brought from France by Rappe, opened ST. MARY'S Female Asylum in 1851, and in 1863 ST. JOSEPH'S ORPHANAGE for older girls; the two institutions merged as St. Joseph's in 1894. The SISTERS OF CHARITY, also from France, opened ST. VINCENT'S for Boys in 1853, and in 1873, in connection with St. Ann's Maternity Home, St. Ann's Infant Asylum, which cared for the smallest children, often foundlings or the infants of the unwed mothers sheltered in the Maternity Home. An orphanage for Catholic children but not under diocesan auspices was incorporated in 1896 as the Home of the Holy Family. Sectarianism was evident also in the Protestant orphanages. The Cleveland Protestant Orphan Asylum, for example, was first proposed at a meeting at the FIRST PRESBYTERIAN (Old Stone) Church in 1852. Funds for its support were collected from the local Protestant churches but were supplemented by monies from the city of Cleveland in recognition of the asylum's care for children from the City Infirmary. There is no record of Catholic institutions' receiving public funds. The Christian church (DISCIPLES OF CHRIST) opened the Cleveland Christian Home in 1901. The JONES HOME, opened in 1886, had no official ties with Protestant churches, but its inmates attended a Methodist Episcopal Sunday school and services. Also officially nonsectarian was the Lida Baldwin Infants' Rest, run by the Cleveland Humane Society from 1884 until its closing in 1915. The Independent Order of B'NAI B'RITH established the Jewish Orphan Asylum or Home in 1868 for the orphans of Jewish Civil War veterans, who came from all over the Midwest and parts of the South. Black children were apparently cared for by the Protestant Orphan Asylum; there are only scattered records of a short-lived black orphanage.

In the last quarter of the 19th century, this residential care of children was supplemented by the work of child-placing agencies, patterned after Chas. Loring Brace's New York Children's Aid Society. These provided only temporary shelter, and their goal was the placement of the child in a foster home or back with its family. The Cleveland CHILDREN'S AID SOCIETY, which grew out of the City Industrial School, provided both shelter and job training. The Cleveland Humane Society, like others across the country, was first a Society for the Prevention of Cruelty to Animals and began to serve children also in 1876, when it was entrusted with the enforcement of a new state law that prohibited cruelty to children. The society investigated cases of neglect, abuse, or abandonment and was empowered to remove a child from its parents and place it in an orphanage or foster home if necessary, although in most cases parents were simply admonished or forced to supply adequate financial support. In 1887, the Lutheran Children's Aid Society was established for children of that denomination. The proliferation of such social-welfare institutions prompted the Cleveland Chamber of Commerce to establish its Committee on Benevolent Associations in 1900, and in 1913 the Fed. of Charity & Philanthropy to systematize the fundraising and policies of these institutions. The federation's *Social Yearbook* (1913) reveals that the city's orphanages differed in their size and clientele. St. Vincent's Orphan Asylum, for example, admitted only boys ages 3–14, and St. Joseph's Orphan Asylum, only girls within the same age range. Both had a capacity of about 250. The Jones Home and the Protestant Orphan Asylum took both boys and girls. The Jones Home cared for 166 children in a year, and the Protestant Orphan Asylum, 369. The Jewish Orphan Home admitted both boys and girls and because of its regional constituency, took in about 500 inmates a year between 1890–1918. Although the active proselytizing of the 19th century had diminished, the links with the

743

major denominations ensured the orphanages' continued emphasis on religious and moral training.

In 1909, a White House Conference on Dependent Children signaled the vital interest of the Progressive Era in child welfare and helped to establish the 2 trends that would dominate child care up to the present: the shift from institutional to noninstitutional care and the increase in public funding and management. The conference took the official position that "home life" was best for children, and in 1910 the Western Reserve Conference on the Care of Neglected & Dependent Children reiterated that preference for family life over institutional life. This new emphasis on family life brought added importance to child placement. In 1921, the Children's Bureau was established to standardize placement procedures of Protestant and Catholic agencies. Foster-home placement of Jewish children was handled by the Welfare Assoc. for Jewish Children, organized in 1921 by the Jewish Welfare Fed. This trend, however, did not put the orphanages out of business. Two new institutions were founded. In 1909, the Episcopal Diocese of Ohio opened St. John's Orphanage for young girls, staffed by the Sisters of the Transfiguration; the facility was moved to Painesville in 1929. In 1921, the ORTHODOX JEWISH Orphan Home began operation. The largest Catholic, Protestant, and Jewish orphanages moved to the suburbs in the 1920s and expanded their facilities. In 1925, the Catholic Diocese opened PARMADALE in PARMA, which combined the boys from St. Vincent's and from St. Louis Orphanage in Louisville, Ohio. The Protestant Orphan Asylum moved to Orange Twp. in 1926, changing its name to BEECH BROOK. In 1929 the Jewish Orphan Home relocated to SHAKER HTS., becoming BELLEFAIRE. The noninstitutional names and the change from congregate housing to cottages indicated the desire to simulate home life. Referrals were made by the Children's Bureau or other child-placing agencies, by the juvenile court, or by parents. At least in principle, the institutions were designed for short-term care until children could be placed in foster homes or returned to their parents. The orphanages still retained their sectarian atmosphere, providing religious instruction and service.

Cleveland orphanages also relied increasingly on public resources. The county juvenile court (est. 1902) became responsible for making plans for dependent children, either in their own homes or in institutions, as well as for collecting support money from negligent parents. The haphazard regulation of existing county homes for children by the Board of State Charities was tightened in 1913 by a law that required the board to license all private and public children's agencies and institutions in the state. Private foster homes were also required to be licensed, and adoption procedures were more strictly controlled. Care of dependent children also received more public funding. Because there were no county children's homes in Cuyahoga County, the county in 1909 provided funds to the Humane Society so that it could place children in boarding homes, and in 1913 the society received city monies to establish a systematic child-placement system. In 1913 also, the state of Ohio passed a mothers' pension law, which provided funds for widowed or deserted mothers so that they could care for their children in their own homes. In 1930, the County Child Welfare Board took over the guardianship of more than 1,000 dependent children from the Humane Society and the Welfare Assoc. for Jewish Children when these agencies' financial resources were exhausted by the Depression. Beginning in 1935, the national Social Security Act provided for dependent children through the Aid to Dependent Children provision, based on the mothers' pension laws.

Other social-welfare legislation passed during and after the New Deal has lessened the need for orphanages as institutions for the care of dependent children. Old-age insurance and survivors' benefits, unemployment compensation, more adequate public-relief provisions, and the rapidly expanding AFDC program have lessened child dependency. Child dependency today is caused primarily by desertion, divorce, and illegitimacy, and dependent and neglected children have come increasingly under the care of the CUYAHOGA COUNTY DEPT. OF HUMAN SERVICES, which performs many of the services formerly provided by the orphanages, including adoption, temporary shelter, and placement in foster homes and residential institutions, including the orphanages themselves. Their original responsibilities diminished, the orphanages and other child-care agencies, spurred also by a greater emphasis in social work on psychiatric care, have shifted their focus to children with emotional or behavioral problems who cannot be cared for in private homes. For example, the Children's Aid Society, the Cleveland Christian Home, and the Berea Children's Home, which had opened in 1864 as the German Methodist Orphan Asylum, provide residential care for emotionally disturbed children.

Because of mergers and public funding, especially from the county and the federal government, many private institutions offer a wide range of services, including outreach programs for the larger community. In 1945, the Humane Society and the Children's Bureau combined to form Children's Services, which offers foster-home care, unmarried-parent counseling, and adoption placement. In 1966 this agency absorbed the Jones Home, which provides residential care for emotionally disturbed children. The Lutheran Children's Aid & Family Services also provides family counseling, adoption, and foster-home placement. A similar process of merger and diversification took place at Parmadale. In 1947, Parmadale received the girls from St. Joseph's-on-the-Lake, formerly St. Joseph's; in 1956, the small children from St. Edward's Home, founded in 1946; and in 1952, the children from the Home of the Holy Family, which had come under the control of the Cleveland Diocese in 1914. Parmadale now provides institutional services, primarily for the emotionally disturbed or handicapped child, but also sponsors outreach programs such as family counseling. Bellefaire's cottages house emotionally disturbed children who cannot be placed in foster homes or returned to their families. In 1941, the JEWISH CHILDREN'S BUREAU, formerly the Welfare Assoc. for Jewish Children, moved to the Bellefaire grounds, as did the Orthodox Jewish Children's Assoc. in 1946. The association, which had operated the Orthodox Jewish Orphan Home, became affiliated with the Jewish Children's Bureau and sponsored suburban foster homes for adolescents. Beech Brook, too, specializes in the residential treatment of emotionally disturbed children but also provides day treatment in an on-campus school as well as in the Cleveland public schools, out-patient care, and an adoption program for hard-to-place handicapped, emotionally disturbed, or racially mixed children.

Marian J. Morton
John Carroll University

Bing, Lucia Johnson, *Social Work in Greater Cleveland* (1938).
Polster, Gary E., "A Member of the Herd: Growing Up in the Jewish Orphan Asylum, 1868–1919" (Ph.D diss., CWRU, 1984.)
Fed. for Community Planning Records, WRHS.

The **ORPHEUS MALE CHORUS** was formed in 1921 by Chas. D. Dawe, a vocal teacher and choir director born in Port Talbot, South Wales (16 Mar. 1888), who came to

Cleveland in 1912 with his wife and son. The formation of the chorus began in 1921, when one day Dawe was giving a vocal music lesson and was interrupted by the hammering of a workman outside his studio. When Dawe complained about the noise, the carpenter explained that the noise didn't matter because the student had no voice anyway. Challenged by Dawe, the carpenter sang. Dawe was impressed and suggested that if the carpenter had friends who could sing as well, to bring them around. The carpenter, Robt. Walker, became the first member of the chorus and brought with him 18 carpenters, bricklayers, and plasterers. The first concert of the Orpheus Male Chorus was held in Mar. 1921.

Under the leadership of Dawe, the chorus grew to 90 members and won prizes in competition for small choruses in the Eisteddfod (competitive arts festivals) in Mold, Wales. In 2 trips abroad, it won the Second Male Voice prize (1923) and Chief Male Voice competition (1926). The latter was the first time the prize had been awarded to a chorus outside Wales. In 1935, the chorus traveled to Russia, a highlight of its existence. Upon his retirement and subsequent death in 1957, Dawe had conducted the chorus for 36 years and had missed only 2 or 3 rehearsals. Karl Mackey succeeded Dawe as conductor, followed by Wyn Morris in 1958, Howard Whittaker in 1961, and Cyril Chinn in 1963. The chorus disbanded in 1964, and many of its members joined the SINGERS CLUB, another Cleveland male chorus.

Grossman, F. Karl, *A History of Music in Cleveland* (1972).

**ORTH, SAMUEL PETER** (1 Aug. 1873–26 Feb. 1922), was an attorney, educator, lecturer, author, and historian. He was born in Capiac, Mich., the son of German Evangelical clergyman Rev. John and Katharine Troeller Orth. Orth accompanied Frederick A. Cook on his expedition to Greenland in 1894. In 1896 he graduated from Oberlin College with a B.S. degree. He later studied law and political science at the University of Michigan from 1896–97. He held the chair of political science and public law at Buchtel College, Akron, from 1897–1902. He was appointed honorary university fellow in political science at Columbia University and in 1903 received his Ph.D. degree in public law from Columbia. Later that year he came to Cleveland and began to practice law. He was elected a member of the Board of Education in 1904 and became president of the board in Jan. 1905. As president, Orth appointed an "Educational Commission" to investigate all departments of the CLEVELAND PUBLIC SCHOOLS. Their findings and recommendations led to the establishment of a technical high school, a high school of commerce, a comprehensive plan for playgrounds, a reorganization of school curriculum, and a normal school for teacher training.

During his stay in Cleveland, Orth also served as assistant U.S. attorney from 1905–06, and from 1906–08 he lectured on political science at Case School of Applied Science, Western Reserve University, and Oberlin College. He left Cleveland in 1912 to become the Goldwin Smith Professor of Political Science at Cornell University. He often spoke at civic and patriotic affairs in that city, was a director of the Ithaca Board of Commerce, and was very active in the local Republican party. In addition to writing many articles for professional journals, Orth wrote the following books: *Centralization of Administration in Ohio* (1903); *Five American Politicians* (1903); *A History of Cleveland* (3 vols.) (1910); *Socialism and Democracy in Europe* (1913); *Readings on the Relation of Governments to Industry* (1915); *The Imperial Impulse* (1916); and *The Boss and*

*the Machine* (1918). Orth married Jane Davis of Youngstown in 1899. The couple was en route to Egypt as part of a sabbatical leave when Orth died in Nice, France.

The **ORTHODOX JEWISH CHILDRENS HOME** was chartered in May 1920 as the Jewish Orphan Home following 2 years of discussion and fundraising among Cleveland's Orthodox Jews. It was created in reaction to another Jewish Orphan Home, which was for years under the direction of a Reform rabbi and whose board of trustees was dominated by members of the two Reform congregations of the city. The existing orphan home was considered an improper environment by the Orthodox community. The home's goals and objectives at its founding were to raise children in an "Orthodox Jewish spirit," to provide a school for teaching "Jewish trades and culture," and to place orphans in private Orthodox Jewish homes.

The home's first site, on E. 55th St., was opened in Aug. 1920 and accommodated 11 orphans. Three years later, the orphan population reached 28, making the home too small. In 1923, a building was purchased on Parkwood Dr. in Glenville, which included an adequate playground and ample living space. By 1925, the orphanage cared for 37 children, and by the end of the decade that total had increased to 60. Although a mid-1920s report on community institutions criticized the existence of 2 orphan homes, the Federation of Jewish Charities chose to fund the JOH. Federation affiliation allowed the home to expand to include a permanent superintendent, to begin casework services for children and families, and to erect a new wing to the Parkwood property.

In the late 1930s, the home began to include troubled children whose parents could not care for them. In 1944, reflecting this change, the home changed its name to the Orthodox Jewish Children's Home. In 1946, it moved to the grounds of BELLEFAIRE and formed an arrangement with the JEWISH CHILDREN'S BUREAU by which the latter provided psychiatric and social-work services. In 1956, the home recognized a need to change its orientation to focus on the operation of foster homes. Three years later, the home closed as an independent entity, became an affiliate of the Children's Bureau under the name the Orthodox Jewish Children's Assoc., and purchased 5 houses to serve as foster group homes for Orthodox children.

The **OSBORN ENGINEERING COMPANY,** Cleveland's oldest engineering firm, was founded on 1 July 1892 by Frank C. Osborn, formerly the chief engineer for Cleveland's King Bridge Co. Osborn's new company offered a wide range of services, including the designs, plans, estimates, and construction supervision for roofs, buildings, bridges, railways, and highways. Such diversity enabled the Osborn Co.-Civil Engineers to survive the severe economic depression of the 1890s. It was incorporated on 16 May 1900 as the Osborn Engineering Co. During its first 4 decades, Osborn built its reputation as the "stadium designers for the Nation." By the time of its selection as the project engineer for CLEVELAND MUNICIPAL STADIUM in 1928, the company had designed more than 75 sports facilities, including New York's Yankee Stadium, Boston's Fenway Park, and Chicago's Comiskey Park. Osborn has continued to design stadiums, working on projects for professional sports teams, major universities, racetracks, fairgrounds, high schools, and municipalities. As early as 1959, Osborn Engineering had completed a design for domed stadiums.

By 1958, the company was looking for a broader market for its services, particularly as domestic industrial construction and plant expansion decreased. It turned its attention toward domestic firms that were expanding their operations into international markets. The company designed factories for locations in South Africa, France, Saudi Arabia, and South America. This expansion enabled Osborn to recover from a postwar decline; in 1963 it began hiring additional employees. Business remained strong throughout the 1960s. As engineering became more competitive in the 1970s, Osborn expanded its range of services by forming partnerships. In 1971 it created Osborn Engineers Architects & Planners, and in 1974 both Osborn Co. Architects-Engineers and Osborn Co. Consulting Engineers. However, business and income still declined, forcing the company to reduce salaries, adopt a shorter work week, and lay off some employees in the mid-1970s. Sports facilities, which accounted for 20% of the firm's business in the profitable early 1970s, constituted only 4% of its business by mid-decade. Problems persisted through the recession of the early 1980s, during which Osborn continued to cut costs and drop unprofitable operations. It also adopted a more aggressive sales approach, concentrating on local business regardless of the size of the project.

The **OSBORN MANUFACTURING CORPORATION,** organized in the 1890s to make steel wire brushes, grew into the world's largest manufacturer of industrial brushes and foundry machines by the 1940s; in 1982 it employed 460 workers and had sales of more than $50 million. Little information is available about the company's early days. Located at 18 Huron Rd., it had been organized by 1891 by a group of investors, one of whom lent his name to the company before selling out. By the time of its incorporation on 3 Mar. 1892, the company had 8 employees and made several kinds of wire brushes and brooms.

The person most responsible for the firm's growth was Franklin G. Smith (23 Oct. 1867–13 May 1968). Born in Bellevue, Ohio, Smith came to Cleveland in 1887 and worked for the Wm. Bingham Co., a wholesale hardware firm. In 1892 he borrowed $3,000 from his uncle, Henry A. Sherwin (see SHERWIN-WILLIAMS CO.), and bought into the Osborn Mfg. Co. Smith was vice-president and general manager when the firm was incorporated; F. Wayland Brown was president, and Milton P. Brown secretary-treasurer. Smith became president of the firm in 1894 and served in that capacity until 1951, when he became chairman of the board, a position he held until his death at age 100. In 1902, after several years on High St., the company moved to its present location at 5401 Hamilton St. In 1908 Osborn began to manufacture molding machines; that became a more profitable operation after 1916 as the automobile industry grew. The company also picked up additional foundry business, expanding its brush-jobbing operation to include such foundry supplies as shovels. Osborn also began making power-driven industrial brushes in addition to hand-operated devices, and after 1918 it began selling its products abroad.

In 1938, Osborn Mfg. had annual sales of $2 million. Smith's son, Norman F. Smith, became vice-president and general manager that year and began to aggressively promote the company's engineering service to other manufacturers. During WORLD WAR II, Osborn made a conscious effort to secure new business by demonstrating ways in which the use of power-driven brushes could speed up defense production, especially in preparing metals for welding or riveting. By 1942 the firm employed 768 workers, and in 1950 sales were $8 million. Norman Smith was elected president in 1951; also that year the firm merged with Rubico Brush Mfrs., Inc., of New York, giving the company its third plant. By 1955, sales had reached $11.8 million, with earnings of $824,656. In 1967, Osborn had

700 employees, a subsidiary in France, net sales of $15.7 million, and a net profit of $1.3 million. With no children interested in taking over the business, Norman Smith sold it on 3 Sept. 1968, to the SHERWIN-WILLIAMS CO.; in Sept. 1975, Sherwin-Williams sold the subsidiary to machine-tool manufacturer Giddings & Lewis, Inc., which also operated Osborn as a subsidiary.

Street, Julian, *Men, Machines, and Morals* (1942).

---

**OTIS, CHARLES A., SR.** (30 Jan. 1827–28 June 1905), was a businessman and mayor (1873–74) of Cleveland. Otis was born in Bloomfield, Ohio, the son of a banker and railroad promoter. He attended local schools until his family moved to Cleveland in 1836. He worked in his father's ironworks until 1848 and then became a steamboat purser. In 1852, Otis founded the Lake Erie Iron Co.; he sold out his interest after the CIVIL WAR. He then spent a few months in Prussia (1866), where he studied that country's iron and steel mills. Upon his return he founded the Otis Iron & Steel Co., the first company in America formed solely to make acid open-hearth steel. He remained as president until 1899.

Otis ran on the Democratic ticket for mayor and defeated Republican JOHN HUNTINGTON. Although business interests prevented him from seeking a second term, he served on several boards, including the Board of Imprisonments (1878–79) and the House of Correction Board (1882–84). He established Cleveland's first Board of Fire Commissioners and BOARD OF POLICE COMMISSIONERS. Otis's later business pursuits included the establishment of the American Wire Co., the American Steel Screw Co., and the CLEVELAND ELECTRIC RAILWAY CO. In 1894 he became president of the New Commercial Natl. Bank, from which he retired in 1904. Otis married Mary Shepard in 1853, and they had 2 daughters before her death in 1860. In 1863 he married his sister-in-law, Anna Elizabeth Shepard, a union that produced 2 sons.

**OTIS, CHARLES AUGUSTUS, JR.** (9 July 1868–9 Dec. 1953), played a brief but pivotal role in the evolution of Cleveland newspapers, in the midst of a career devoted largely to industry and finance. A member of one of Cleveland's old, established families, he was a descendant of revolutionary firebrand Jas. Otis and the son of CHAS. A. OTIS, Sr., who served 1 term as mayor of Cleveland, 1873–74. The younger Otis tried his hand at ranching in South Dakota after graduation from Yale's Sheffield Scientific School. Returning to Cleveland in 1893, he entered business as a steel broker with Otis, Hough & Co.; in 1894 he married Lucia Edwards, daughter of Wm. Edwards, founder of the Edwards grocery firm. In 1899, Otis purchased the first seat held on the New York Stock Exchange by a Clevelander and formed the banking firm Otis & Hough to market steel securities. He subsequently helped organize and became president of the Cleveland Stock Exchange.

During the administration of Mayor TOM L. JOHNSON, the Republican Otis entered the Cleveland newspaper field and filled the role of the "Frank Munsey of Cleveland journalism." Beginning with the *CLEVELAND WORLD* in 1904, in 2 years he acquired 4 newspapers and merged them into 2. Purchasing the *CLEVELAND LEADER* and *News & Herald* in 1905, he merged the latter with the *World* and then added the *Evening Plain Dealer* to the consolidated afternoon paper, which he renamed the *CLEVELAND NEWS.* Within a few years, Otis disposed of both the *News* and the *Leader* to DAN R. HANNA, whose son later married Otis's daughter, Lucia.

In 1912, Otis reorganized Otis & Hough as Otis & Co. and became president of both Wm. Edwards & Co. and the Otis Terminal Warehouse Co. During WORLD WAR I, he served with the War Industries Board as a "dollar-a-year" man, and his firm reputedly led Ohio in the sale of Liberty Bonds. He sold his brokerage business in 1931 and largely retired, although he remained associated with the insurance firm of Lenihan & Co. Widely known as a club-man, Otis belonged to the UNION and CITY clubs and had a hand in the organization of the TAVERN, CLEVELAND ATHLETIC, and CHAGRIN VALLEY HUNT clubs. His interest in horses led to a paternal relationship with TROOP A of the Cleveland Mounted Police, whose goodwill trip to Mexico he financed in 1946. Referred to as "Mr. Cleveland" in his later years, Otis was a past president of the Cleveland Chamber of Commerce and was named, along with Wm. G. Mather, as cochairman of the Cleveland Sesquicentennial Commission. He died in Cleveland, survived by his daughter, Lucia Otis Hanna, and son, Wm. E. Otis.

Chas. A. Otis Papers, WRHS.

**OTIS, WILLIAM A.** (2 Feb. 1794–11 May 1868), was a Cleveland merchant, industrialist, banker, and civic leader. He was instrumental in the development of the WESTERN RESERVE as a trading partner with eastern markets and the development of the iron industry and railroads in Cleveland. Born in Massachusetts, Otis moved to Pittsburgh about 1818, where he worked in an ironworks. Two years later he moved westward again, to Bloomfield, Ohio, in Trumbull County. There he opened a tavern and established a mercantile business, furnishing settlers with goods in exchange for wheat, produce, and ash.

The completion of the Erie Canal in 1825 opened new possibilities for markets. Otis is credited with having shipped the first lot of Ohio wheat by water to New York City via Buffalo and the canal. He became a primary factor in utilizing the waterways in opening up the Western Reserve to the eastern markets. He later began shipping wool and pork, becoming for 20 years one of the leading shippers in the Western Reserve. Recognizing the advantages of Cleveland as a port, Otis moved his mercantile operations in 1836 to new headquarters in the city. He quickly became one of Cleveland's leading dealers in pork, flour, and potash. His extensive business concerns gave him cause to study the area's transportation problems. With the waterways opened to eastern markets, the major problem confronting trade involved getting inland goods to port. He became a strong advocate of the need for good HIGHWAYS, being influential in opening one of the area's earliest turnpikes. He also gave strong support to railroad building, being closely associated with the development of the Cleveland, Columbus & Cincinnati and the Cleveland & Pittsburgh railroads.

With the settlement of Ohio, Otis concentrated his interests upon iron manufacturing in Cleveland, becoming a pioneer in the industry. He also maintained close involvement with the city's financial growth as a member of the banking firm of Wick, Otis & Brownell. Along with others he helped organize the Commercial Branch Bank of Cleveland, the Commercial Natl. Bank, and the Society for Savings, of all of which he served as president. He was one of the founders of the Board of Trade and was one of the commissioners representing Cleveland in negotiations that resulted in the merger with OHIO CITY. Otis married Eliza Proctor on 22 Dec. 1825, and they had 3 children, Charles, Eliza, and William.

The **OTTAWA** were Algonkian-speaking hunters, gatherers, and fishers, with limited maize agriculture, when first encountered in 1634 as the *Cheveux Relevez* on Manitoulin Island in northern Lake Huron. Famed as the middlemen in the French fur trade, they fled west when the New York Iroquois dispelled the Huron Confederacy from Ontario. Living in mixed Huron-Wyandot villages at French posts in the western Great Lakes, many of the Ottawa settled at Detroit in 1713. While most of them returned to northern Michigan in 1715, some moved across the Detroit River, and after 1730 several groups relocated to Maumee and Sandusky Bay. The Ottawa continued to be active in the fur trade of northern Ohio, forming the largest group at Saguin's post on the Cuyahoga in 1742–43. Ottawa or Tawa villages are shown along the Middle Cuyahoga on several maps made between 1755–78, and Robt. Rogers encountered Ottawa hunters there in 1760. In 1786, Heckewelder established PILGERRUHE below TINKER'S CREEK on a recently abandoned Ottawa village, although he did not show any Ottawa settlement on his 1796 map. The journals of the CONNECTICUT LAND CO. survey party and subsequent accounts of early settlers suggest that there were groups living on the west side of the Cuyahoga until 1805, although most Ottawa families removed to the Sandusky (1797), and later (1813) to the Maumee River reservation. By 1838 these had left for Michigan or the Trans-Mississippi west. A few scattered Ottawa families were still reported to live in southern Summit County as late as 1842.

**OUR LADY OF FATIMA CENTER,** 6707 Quimby Ave., is a unique inner-city facility that serves all members of its community. While it is Catholic in origin, no doctrinal demand is requested. The staff of the center considers every member of the community to be as much a part of the parish as if he were a communicant of the church. The center grew out of Our Lady of Fatima Church, which was founded in 1949 by Bp. Begin, who determined that the parish of St. Agnes, located at Euclid and 82nd St., could better serve members who lived a considerable distance from the church with a branch, which was to be called Our Lady of Fatima. The Lexington Ave. area, where the branch was located, was a neighborhood in which change occurred rapidly. Four years from the time of the church's founding, Hispanics had replaced the original Slavic element, and within 4 more years the neighborhood had become predominantly black. The religious order that served the church and community was the Missionary Servants of the Most Holy Trinity, and it was from their ranks that Fr. Albert Koklowsky emerged. During the turbulent times of the HOUGH RIOTS, Fr. Albert, dubbed "the slum Priest" by the papers, was espousing black rights, trying to create peace and an end to the riots; he was perhaps the only person who could safely enter any zone of conflict. In 1970, Br. Anselm Deehr, another Missionary Servant from the Fatima Parish, opened the center, initially to feed the hungry and to handle material crises. By 1985, Our Lady of Fatima Ctr., in addition to hunger-crisis and food programs, had instituted a complete range of programs, from Head Start to crafts, tutoring, and counseling. Although the church has now remerged with St. Agnes, the center still looks on the community as the Fatima parish.

**OUR LADY OF MERCY CHURCH,** 2425 W. 11th St., began as an offshoot of ST. WENDELIN's PARISH. The SLOVAKS living in TREMONT objected to traveling through the industrial valley to St. Wendelin. They believed that they had enough people to establish their own parish. Though Bp. JOHN P. FARRELLY refused them permission, the Slovaks persisted. The Polish Nationalist pastor of Sacred Heart Church on W. 14th promised them a priest if they affiliated with the POLISH NATIONAL CATHOLIC CHURCH. They then organized the parish of St. John Baptist, which opened in 1915. The formal link with the Polish Nationalists drove many back to St. Wendelin's. The new parish held on for several years, but mounting problems forced them to approach the diocese for assistance.

Bp. JOSEPH SCHREMBS agreed to accept the repentant congregation. This reconciliation took place in 1922, when Rev. Francis Dubosh was named pastor of the church, which had been renamed Our Lady of Mercy. By 1927, the congregation had grown from 60 to 326 families. In that year, Fr. John W. Krispinsky became pastor. The congregation continued to grow during the prewar years. In 1942, the parish began a door-to-door collection for the necessary funds to build a new church. By 1945 they had realized $50,000 toward their goal. Construction was begun in 1948. The Romanesque-style church was dedicated on 23 Oct. 1949. The church's interior incorporates much of the Slovak peasant heritage. Its large mosaic has as its theme Mary, Our Sorrowful Mother, the patron of Slovakia.

Archives, Diocese of Cleveland.

## OUR LADY OF THE BLESSED SACRAMENT CHURCH

was the first parish established for black Catholics in Cleveland. A group of black Catholics had been meeting with the goal of evangelizing their fellow BLACKS. With the encouragement of the pastor of St. Philomena Church, Msgr. Joseph F. Smith (later rector of St. John Cathedral), the group petitioned Bp. JOSEPH SCHREMBS for the establishment of a parish specifically for blacks. On 11 Apr. 1922, the first mass was held at St. Bridget's Hall on E. 22nd and Woodland. Fr. Thos. McKenney was named pastor on 27 Apr. 1922. The congregation met at St. Joseph Franciscan Church on Woodland until they could find a permanent site. Msgr. Smith and his sisters donated $25,000 to the new congregation. A site was bought at 2354 E. 79th, and a brick Gothic-style church was built there. It was dedicated on 25 June 1923.

As the congregation was willing to make the necessary sacrifices for a school, Bp. Schrembs wrote Mother Katharine Drexel, founder of the Sisters of the Blessed Sacrament, and asked for teachers. In Sept. 1922 the sisters arrived, and the school opened. By 1925, there were 220 families in the parish and 156 students in the school. By 1930, the parish had grown to over 1,000 individuals. The Depression worsened the ever-present financial problems. Fr. McKenney received a new pastorate, and Fr. Michael L. Stevenson succeeded him in Aug. 1934. Despite everyone's best efforts, the parish faced foreclosure in Dec. 1936. With the assistance of Msgr. Smith, the church raised the needed funds for refinancing. In 1937, the religious community the Precious Blood Fathers of Cincinnati agreed to staff the church. Fr. Melchior Lochtefeld, C.PP.S., became pastor, and Fr. Henry Langhals was named associate.

Fr. Lochtefeld established programs to meet both the spiritual and material needs of his people. A vocational training program was begun in June 1938. An athletic program under the direction of the Catholic Youth Organization was started. On 11 Feb. 1940, the parish established a chapter of the Natl. Catholic Interracial Fed. Later that year the parish opened a credit union. The parish continued to grow even after its neighboring church, St. Edward's on Woodland Ave., was designated as Cleveland's second black Catholic parish. The growth made the physical limitations of the parish plant more evident. The neighboring parish of St. Adalbert at 2347 E. 83rd had a sound parish plant, but its Bohemian congregation had dwindled. The two parishes of Our Lady of the Blessed Sacrament and St. Adalbert's were merged on 6 Feb. 1961, and the facilities were combined.

Papers of Our Lady of the Blessed Sacrament, Archives, Diocese of Cleveland.

**OWENS, JESSE** (James Cleveland) (9 Sept. 1913–30 Mar. 1980), was a world-record-setting track-and-field athlete of the 1930s. He was voted by sportswriters in 1950 as the world's top track star of the century. Owens was born on a tenant farm in northern Alabama. He moved to Cleveland as a child. His athletic talent was first noted at Fairmount Jr. High School; his track coach, Chas. Riley, was amazed when Owens ran the 100-yd. dash in 10 seconds flat, a new junior high school record. As a high school senior at E. Technical, he equaled the world's record of 9.4 in the 100-yd. dash.

At Ohio State University, Owens was soon called the "fastest human." His greatest day came on 25 May 1935 at Ann Arbor, Mich., when he equaled or bettered 6 world records within 1 hour, in the 100-yd. dash, long jump, 220-yd. dash (also a record for 200 meters), and 220-yd. hurdles (also a record for the 200-meter hurdles). Owens was the only athlete to establish new track and field world records on the same day. His long-jump record of 26'8¼" stood for 33 years. Arthur Daley of the *New York Times* wrote of Owens, "He didn't run, he floated. He was the prettiest runner I ever saw." The Cleveland track star gained his greatest fame at the Berlin Olympic Games in 1936, when he won 4 gold medals. In the 100- and 200-meter sprints, he set records of 10.3 and 20.7 seconds respectively. In the long jump he set an Olympic record of 26'5⁵⁄₁₆". Owens then joined with Ralph Metcalfe, Floyd Draper, and Frank Wycoff to set a new world record of 39.8 seconds in the 400-meter relay.

After graduating from Ohio State University in 1937, Owens became a "professional entertainer" by tap dancing with Bill "Bojangles" Robinson. After he had tried several occupations, Owens's dry-cleaning business failed. From 1940–42, the office of Civilian Defense employed him as national director of physical education for Negroes. From 1942–46, Owens was the director of Negro personnel for the Ford Motor Co. in Detroit. In 1946 he moved to Chicago, where he became a sales executive. Noted for his inspirational addresses, Owens served on the Illinois Athletic and Illinois Youth commissions. An upbeat, optimistic individual, he was on the board of directors of Up with People, centered at Tucson, Ariz., where he lived at the time of his death. He married Ruth Solomon in 1931, and they had 3 daughters, Gloria, Beverly, and Marlene.

Baker, William J., *Jesse Owens* (1986).

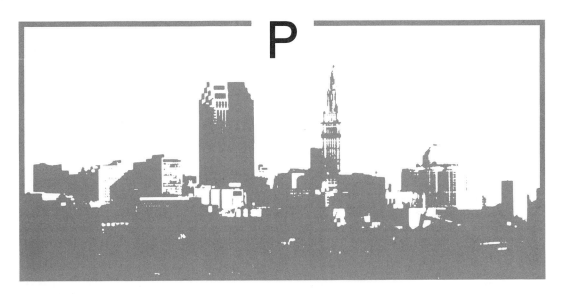

# P

The **PACE ASSOCIATION**—the Plan (or Program) for Action by Citizens in Education—was a foundation-sponsored local citizens' group that worked to help school systems improve the quality of education and to promote better race relations in the schools in the Greater Cleveland area between 1963 and early 1974. The association began on 22 Nov. 1962, when the Greater Cleveland Associated Foundation appointed a "blue-ribbon committee" to survey the "unmet needs" of public, private, and parochial elementary and secondary schools in Cuyahoga County and to develop a plan to meet those needs. The survey was prompted by increasing concerns about the quality of education in local schools and about whether the financial policies of local school boards, especially in Cleveland, were adequate to meet the needs for new buildings, new equipment, and new educational programs. Chaired by attorney Hugh Calkins, the 23-member PACE Committee issued its report in Apr. 1963. Among the problems discovered by the study were inadequate finances and other resources to meet educational needs and a lack of community support for the schools. The committee made 26 recommendations toward resolving these problems.

One recommendation was for the creation of a citizens' group to provide political support, civic leadership, and needed resources to local school systems. Calkins himself took the lead in organizing such a group—the PACE Assoc.—on 17 Sept. 1963. With a grant of $111,000 from the Greater Cleveland Associated Foundation to fund its operation for 3 years, PACE hired Robt. B. Binswanger as its executive director. Its priorities were to strengthen vocational and technical education, to develop neighborhood leadership in support of education in the central city, and to promote better race relations in the schools. Under Binswanger's leadership from 1963 to mid-1966, PACE also took the lead in establishing and financing school libraries, operated preschool programs, began a Summer Tutor Corps that used high school students to tutor children in elementary school, and launched a program to combat adult illiteracy. By Oct. 1965, the efforts of the PACE Assoc. had involved 20,000 volunteers.

Under the leadership of Robt. W. Jewell, Jr., between Aug. 1966 and Aug. 1968, PACE continued to develop new programs, such as the Early Reading Assistance program, using adult volunteers to help second-graders (1967); human-relations courses in the schools (1967); and an interdistrict summer-school program between urban, suburban, and Catholic schools, offering both remedial and enrichment courses (1968). By the early 1970s, PACE was working mostly with suburban schools because of what some observers saw as a lack of cooperation from Cleveland school administrators. By the end of 1973, the association was unable to find financial support for its work, and it ceased to operate in early 1974.

PACE Records, WRHS.

**PAIGE, LEROY ROBERT "SATCHEL"** (7 July 1906–8 June 1982), was a legendary professional BASEBALL pitcher in the Negro leagues who first pitched in the majors with the CLEVELAND INDIANS in 1948. Born in Mobile, Ala., Paige earned the nickname "Satchel" as a child carrying bags at the local railroad station; using a rope that allowed him to carry a number of bags and thus increase his tips, he was told that he looked like a "walking satchel tree." Paige was placed in an industrial school at age 12 after encountering truancy and juvenile behavioral problems. He credited the school with turning him from a life of petty crime. Paige became a semipro ballplayer at 17. Pitching in the Negro Professional Leagues from 1926–50, he was considered one of the best pitchers of his day. He could not play in the major leagues for most of his career because of the unwritten agreement that barred blacks. Paige was known as a drawing card and something of a jokester. Tall and lanky with a slow, deliberate gait, he was known for his trick pitches and colorful feats. A crowd-pleaser, he often called in his outfield while pitching and gave up no runs and would announce that he would strike out a certain number of batters and succeed. Paige and his teams often played and won exhibition games against white major-leaguers. Hall of Fame pitcher Dizzy Dean called Paige the best pitcher he ever saw.

Paige first pitched for a Cleveland team, the Negro Natl. League's Cleveland Cubs, in 1931. The team disbanded at midseason. With the elimination of baseball's color line in 1946, Paige got his chance to pitch in the majors, signing with the Cleveland Indians at midseason in 1948. He became the oldest rookie in major-league history at age 42. Paige was 6–1 as he helped the Indians to their first pennant in 28 years. To his disappointment, he pitched only ⅔ of an inning in the World Series. He was 4–7 for Cleveland in 1949 and was released. He returned to the majors with the old St. Louis Browns from 1951–53, and at age 59 he made a 1-game appearance with the Kansas City Athletics in 1965. Paige estimated that he pitched over 2,500 games and won about 2,000. He was elected to the Baseball Hall of Fame in 1971. Paige was married twice. His first marriage, to Janet Howard, ended in divorce in 1943. He married Lahoma Brown in 1947.

Paige, LeRoy (Satchel), as told to David Lipman, *Maybe I'll Pitch Forever* (1962).
Paige, LeRoy (Satchel), as told to Hal Lebovitz, *Pitchin' Man* (1948).

The **PALACE THEATER,** located at Euclid Ave. and E. 17th St. in the area known as PLAYHOUSE SQUARE, represented the high point of development in Cleveland's theater district when it opened 6 Nov. 1922. The house was originally named Keith's Palace Theater by owner/impresario Edward Albee in memorial to his friend and business partner B. F. Keith. Albee retained the architectural firm of Rapp & Rapp for the work. The architects presented Albee, at a cost of $3.5 million, with one of the grandest spaces ever devoted to the art of vaudeville. The Palace became the flagship of the Keith chain of theaters. Entering past brass box offices through bronze doors, patrons arrived in the mirrored inner lobby. The next room, the Grand Hall, glowed with the light of 154 Czechoslovakian cut-crystal chandeliers reflecting from golden ocher Carara marble. Dual white marble staircases swept up to the balcony. The room was hung with artworks valued in that day at over $1 million. The floral carpet was the largest ever woven by hand, with 9,000,272 knots. The atmosphere changed abruptly from Baroque exuberance to a vaguely Oriental effect upon entry into the auditorium. The room was supposedly modeled after an imperial palace garden in Beijing, China, but contained many Western decorative embellishments. The auditorium seated 3,100. The stage was immense: 59 ft. wide and 35 ft. high at the proscenium, and 90 ft. deep. The flies rose 7 stories above; 67 lines controlled the stage works. Backstage was every facility required for theatrical presentations. However, the Palace was most noted for the elegance of its 23 main dressing rooms. Moe Howard, of the Three Stooges, wrote that the Palace dressing rooms were the finest on the American vaudeville circuit. Each room was complete with full bath. The suites bore the names of states in the union. Also available to the performers were a beauty parlor, billiard room, and putting green.

During the Palace's first year, 1.7 million tickets were sold. However, tastes had begun to change. Though vaudeville continued to be popular, the era of the motion picture was beginning. By May 1926, 2-a-day vaudeville was dropped in favor of continuous live entertainment interspersed with motion pictures. In Dec. 1932, films became the main attraction, although vaudeville was staged periodically until the 1950s. Both Bob Hope and Red Skelton broke into the business on the Palace stage. Mae West, Eddie Cantor, Ethel Barrymore, Frank Sinatra, Sophie Tucker, Martha Raye, Sally Rand, Jimmy Durante, Fanny Brice, Gypsy Rose Lee, Gene & Glenn, and Sammy Kaye also entertained Clevelanders there. With the end of vaudeville, the Palace showed movies exclusively. However, at this time the long decline of the downtown area began. Ticket sales dropped steadily throughout the 1950s and 1960s. It seemed that the end had come when the air conditioning broke down on 20 July 1969 during a showing of *Krakatoa, East of Java.* The theater was boarded up, and the stage sat silent. In Feb. 1970, Ray Shepardson, an employee of the Cleveland Board of Education, investigated the Playhouse Square theaters as a possible site for a teachers' conference. Impressed, he spearheaded the formation of the Playhouse

Square Foundation, dedicated to the restoration and preservation of the theaters. By Nov. 1973, the association, with renovation assistance from the JR. LEAGUE, presented its first Palace Theater offering, *Ben Bagley's Decline and Fall of the Whole World as Seen through the Eyes of Cole Porter.* Other theatrical and concert performances followed. By Apr. 1982, the dressing rooms were restored in a joint project sponsored by the DIAMOND SHAMROCK CORP., the Jr. League, the Northern Ohio Design Community, and the building trades. In Mar. 1984, the state of Ohio appropriated $3.75 million for the restoration of the theater.

**PALESTINIANS.** *See* **ARAB-AMERICANS**

**PALMER, WILLIAM PENDLETON** (17 June 1861–17 Dec. 1927), spent his entire career in the steel industry, working his way through the corporate structure from an apprentice to become president of the American Steel & Wire Co., 1899–1927. An interest in history led him to become president of the WESTERN RESERVE HISTORICAL SOCIETY from 1913–27. Palmer was born in Pittsburgh, Pa., to Jas. Stewart and Eleanor Pendleton Mason Palmer. He graduated from Central High School there in 1878. Entering the steel industry as an apprentice, he started with Lewis, Oliver & Phillips in 1878. In 1881 he went to work for the Carnegie interests at Carnegie, Phipps & Co., becoming the company secretary in 1887 and the general sales agent in 1888. He was appointed assistant to the president of the Carnegie Steel Co. in 1894. In 1896, Palmer was appointed 2d vice-president of the Illinois Steel Co. He became general manager and president of American Steel & Wire, a subsidiary of the U.S. Steel Corp. in Cleveland, in 1899, serving until 1927. He also served as president of American's subsidiaries the NEWBURGH & SOUTH SHORE RAILROAD and the Trenton Iron Co. and as a director of the Cleveland Trust Co., the H. C. Frick Coke Co., and the Bank of Commerce. Palmer was elected president of the WRHS in 1913, serving until 1927. During his tenure, the society acquired the Wm. Palmer Collection, an extensive collection of books, manuscripts, and photographs relating to the American CIVIL WAR. Palmer married Mary Boleyn Adams on 14 Aug. 1898. The Palmers had 2 children, Jane and William, Jr. Palmer is buried in LAKE VIEW CEMETERY.

**PANKUCH, JAN "JOHN"** (1870?–28 Feb. 1952), was a Slovak newspaper editor and publisher active in national Slovak organizations. A native of Saris County, Slovakia, Pankuch came to the U.S. in either 1882 or 1889, most likely the latter. He worked as a laborer, grocer, and coal dealer in Cleveland while he tried to establish a publishing business. He tried first to establish newspapers that would appeal to Slovaks throughout the U.S. His first attempt was *Americky Slovak* (1892–94), which failed as a result of Pankuch's inability to manage the paper's business affairs. In 1894 he established a Lutheran weekly, *Cirkevne Listy* (Church Letters), which he published for 5 years, finally selling it in 1899 to a competitor, who moved it out of Cleveland. He then founded the *Lutheran* in 1900, publishing it until 1902; in 1904 the *Lutheran* was one of several papers that merged to form the *Slovensky Hlasnik* (Slovak Herald), the official organ of the Slovak Evangelical Union. Pankuch was more successful with publishing ventures directed toward the Slovak community in Cleveland. He published *Hlas* (Voice) from 1907–47 and *Denny Hlas* (Daily Voice) between 1915–25. Pankuch was also prominent in national Slovak organizations. He served as treasurer of the Slovak League of America during WORLD

WAR I, was a member of the American branch of the Czecho-Slovak Natl. Council, and in 1937 became president of the Natl. Slovak Society. A proud Republican, Pankuch was praised by one contemporary for his "sturdy Americanism and true patriotism."

Ledbetter, Eleanor E., *The Slovaks of Cleveland* (1918).
Megles, Susi; Stolarik, Mark; and Tybor, Martina, *Slovak Americans and Their Communities of Cleveland* (1978).

**PARAMOUNT DISTILLERS, INC.,** Cleveland's only distillery, is located at 3116 Berea Rd. The privately held company distills only cocoa and coffee essences for cordials but blends, bottles, and ships more than a million cases of liquor and liqueurs annually. Paramount Distillers was established in 1934 by Jacob F. Moessmer. Moessmer had established Federal Fruit Prods. (now Federal Flavors, Inc.), a manufacturer of flavoring extracts, in 1919. Originally located on W. 106th St., Paramount relocated in 1946 to a new building on Berea Rd. in Cleveland, which still serves as corporate headquarters. In 1957, Robt. G. Gottesman and Lewis L. Zeller, who previously were with the Schenley Import Corp. in New York City, purchased Paramount and Federal Flavors. Paramount then was a relatively small company making cordials and vodka, which it marketed to Iowa and Ohio. Gottesman and Zeller undertook an ambitious expansion program during the 1960s, enlarging Paramount's physical plant, product line, and market.

Today Paramount bottles its own brand of domestic and imported liquors and blends its own flavors to make cordials and flavored brandies. Its products include blended and bourbon whiskey, Scotch, gin, vodka, tequila, rum, and cocktails. These products are marketed primarily in the East and Midwest. Robt. Gottesman has been president and chief executive officer since 1957. Zeller died in 1971. In 1984 there were approximately 200 employees. In recent years, Paramount has enlarged its activities from the production of distilled spirits to other, associated enterprises. Subsidiaries include Paramount Brands, Inc., a wholesale liquor dealer in Mamaroneck, N.Y.; Meier's Wine Cellars, Inc., in Silverton, Ohio, the state's largest winery; and Mantey Vineyards, Mon Ami Winery, and Lonz Winery, 3 regional wineries whose products are sold primarily in Ohio.

**PARK-OHIO INDUSTRIES, INC.,** formed in 1967 by the merger of 2 Cleveland firms, is a conglomerate engaged in energy development and the production of forged and machined products, induction heating systems, containers, industrial rubber products, and metal abrasives. In 1984, Park-Ohio's sales totaled $195.3 million, with a net income of $5.7 million. Park-Ohio was created on 1 June 1967 by the merger of the Park Drop Forge Co. and the Ohio Crankshaft Co. Park, located at 777 E. 79th St., was incorporated on 27 May 1907, with Dwight Goddard as president. The firm made closed die forgings for crankshafts, camshafts, and other parts for diesel locomotives, trucks, and buses. By 1957 it had 600 employees and was reported to be "one of the largest custom forge shops in the world." By 1967 it owned 51% of Ohio Crankshaft Co.

The Ohio Crankshaft Co. was incorporated in 1920 by Wm. C. Dunn, president and general manager, and Francis S. Denneen, secretary-treasurer. First located in a garage at E. 152nd St. near St. Clair, the company manufactured crankshafts and camshafts for diesel engines. In 1922, the company moved into facilities at 6600 Clement Ave.; in 1934, it added a plant at 6600 Park Ave.; and in 1937, it built another at 4000 Harvard Ave. It built a fourth plant at 3800 Harvard Ave. during WORLD WAR II, reportedly the first emergency war plant built in the state. One factor

that contributed to the growth of Ohio Crankshaft was its development of a process that used high-frequency electrical current to heat, harden, or melt metals. In 1934 it established its TOCCO division to manufacture equipment used in this process. By 1967, the firm had 2,500 employees, $42 million in annual sales, and a net income of $1.8 million. Ohio Crankshaft and Park Drop forge merged in 1967; on 30 Nov. 1971, Park-Ohio merged with Growth Internatl., Inc., a Delaware corporation that operated as Discount Ctrs., Inc., from its beginning in 1961 until 1966. The entire organization took the name Park-Ohio Industries, Inc., on 31 May 1972. By 1975, net sales had increased to $115.7 million, and net income to $4.7 million.

The economic recession of the early 1980s meant difficult times for Park-Ohio's operations in the Cleveland area. In Oct. 1982, corporation officials warned that the union would have to make concessions at the TOCCO plant in Cuyahoga Hts. in order for it to remain in operation. Instead the union went on strike on 11 July 1983; the plant was closed and the work transferred to a more modern facility in Alabama. Because of increased competition, officials also planned work changes at the Ohio Crankshaft plant; workers there also walked off the job when their UNITED AUTO WORKERS contract expired on 11 July 1983, leading to a prolonged and sometimes violent strike. Other Park-Ohio operations proved more stable. In 1984 the corporation, with headquarters at 20600 Chagrin Blvd., employed 1,750 people and operated 5 plants in Ohio and facilities in 4 other states.

**PARK SYNAGOGUE** was built by the ANSHE EMETH CONGREGATION and the Cleveland Jewish Ctr. in 1947–50 and is generally regarded as a major work of 20th-century architecture. It was the largest and most ambitious of 4 synagogues and community centers designed by the world-famous architect Eric Mendelsohn (1887–1953) between 1945–53. Its design contributed to the emergence of a distinct style of synagogue architecture in the 1950s, which departed from the traditional Near Eastern eclecticism. The spiritual intent of Mendelsohn's plan is clearly explained in published statements by the architect, who worked closely with Rabbi Armond E. Cohen in its development. The main architectural form of the temple is a vast hemispheric dome symbolizing the unity of the heavens and the earth. At 100' in diameter, it was the third-largest in the U.S. in 1950; it was constructed of reinforced concrete sprayed in place over wooden forms. The roof is covered with copper. The drum of the dome is entirely glazed, as it was intended that the views of nature would bring the congregation closer to the spirit of God. The main sanctuary is connected to a fan-shaped assembly hall with folding doors, so that the size can be almost doubled for attendance on High Holy Days. A classroom wing is placed around a courtyard behind the assembly hall, and a bridgelike structure leads across a ravine to an auditorium wing, which was completed in 1969 under the direction of the firm of Bialosky & Manders.

The **PARKER HANNIFIN CORPORATION** is the world's broadest line manufacturer of fluid components for the aerospace and automotive industries. Arthur LaRue Parker founded the firm on the near west side in 1918 as the Parker Appliance Co. to market his newly designed pneumatic brake system for trucks and buses. To promote his product, Parker planned to drive a truck outfitted with his brakes across hilly roads, but in Pennsylvania, the truck went over a hill along with all of the fledgling company's capital. By 31 Oct. 1924, Parker had raised enough money to reorganize the company. By then, new uses had been discovered for Parker's pneumatic fitting products, and business prospered. One use was in the embryonic aircraft industry, centered in Cleveland. Parker aided early aircraft builders by developing compact, lightweight hydraulic systems that lessened aircraft weight. The aviation industry kept the firm solvent during the Depression, allowing it to purchase a plant at 17325 Euclid Ave. in 1935. By the late 1930s, Parker decided to concentrate its resources principally in the aircraft industry.

Parker Appliance became a public company in 1941. During WORLD WAR II, it devoted its entire resources, including over 5,000 employees in the Cleveland area, to producing hydraulic parts for airplanes for the government, becoming the world's largest manufacturer of such products. At the end of the war, the need for the company's products ceased. Employment dropped to 300, and the firm neared bankruptcy. Parker died in 1945. His widow, Helen, resisted liquidation of the company and recruited 2 proven executives, S. Blackwell Taylor and Robt. W. Cornell, to rebuild the company. As Parker recovered in the early 1950s, Taylor and Cornell set goals for corporate growth through product development and acquisitions in the fluid component field, especially for servicing the aviation industry. That led to its acquisition of the Hannifin Mfg. Co. of Illinois, the world's leading producer of hydraulic and pneumatic power cylinders, in 1957; the firm then became the Parker Hannifin Corp.

During the next 2 decades, Parker Hannifin acquired over 30 companies worldwide to broaden its industrial base. Through its technological developments and numerous acquisitions, the firm entered several related fields. In its attempt to seal fluid power components, the company developed standards for sealing devices in the 1950s. In the mid-1960s, it moved into the refrigeration field; in the early 1970s, the automobile replacement-parts business; and in the 1980s, the biomedical equipment field. It also became more involved in the aerospace industry as the space program developed. Parker Hannifin experienced gains throughout the postwar period until the recession of the early 1980s, but because of its balance of industries, it mitigated the effects of the financial downturn. In 1983, with the opening of a seal plant in the People's Republic of China, Parker Hannifin employed over 16,000 people in 123 plants in over 20 countries.

Parker, Patrick S., *Parker Hannifin Corporation* (1980).

**PARKS.** Not until the 1870s were public funds allocated to establish parks. Cleveland in its early years was surrounded by wilderness, and city leaders saw no urgency to secure parkland beyond the 10-acre PUBLIC SQUARE set aside as early as 1796. By the time they awakened to the need for public open space, areas near the center of the city had long since been appropriated to other uses, and the city was unable to establish parks convenient to the crowded neighborhoods that most needed them. A chain of parks envisioned in the 1890s—years before the "Emerald Necklace" of the Cleveland Metropolitan Park District was proposed—was never completed. In the 20th century, the encroachment of highways disfigured many of the city's finest parks, and lack of maintenance proved an enduring problem. In Sept. 1865, a city council committee was appointed to consider the establishment of public parks. The committee reported that Cleveland was "far behind most cities of its class" and urged the purchase of parkland to accommodate the city's "great future population." In 1871, by authority of a new state law, the city's first Board of Park Commissioners was created. The following year, park commissioners Azariah Everett, O. H. Childs, and

John H. Sargent reported that they had spent almost $29,000, principally on improvements to Monumental Park (as the Public Square was then known) and FRANKLIN CIRCLE. In 1874, the first park bond issues were sold to finance the purchase and improvement of Lake View Park. Other public parks established by 1880 included MILES, CLIFTON, and Pelton (see LINCOLN) PARKS—all relatively small parcels.

JEPTHA H. WADE's gift of 64 wooded acres in 1882 formed the first large park area in the city (see WADE PARK). In 1890, park commissioners reported that, in the development of parks, Cleveland stood "at the foot of the list" of cities in the U.S. having populations greater than 200,000. New York, Boston, Philadelphia, Chicago, Baltimore, Detroit, and Buffalo all had established well-planned park systems that had already resulted in "very material benefits." The park commissioners were "convinced beyond doubt" that public parks had "passed beyond the domain of luxuries" and cautioned that Cleveland's excellent natural park sites—among them the Doan Brook Valley, the lakeshore on the west side, and the Big Creek Valley south of Brooklyn Village—should be acquired before development encroached on them and put their purchase out of reach. Upon his death in 1892, WM. J. GORDON bequeathed to the city some 129 acres, already handsomely improved with winding drives and wooded groves. GORDON PARK answered part of the city's need for parklands, but it also underscored the need for a comparable park on the west side.

In 1893, the state legislature passed a park act granting park boards expanded authority to appropriate parkland and issue bonds. Cleveland appointed a new board of 5 commissioners "to provide for the Forest City a system of parks commensurate with her size and importance." The new board—consisting of Chas. H. Bulkley, Amos Townsend, John F. Pankhurst, Mayor ROBT. BLEE, and city council president A. J. Michael (soon succeeded by Chas. A. Davidson)—adopted the first general plan for park development in Cleveland and presided over the system's most critical decade. The plan's principal feature was the location of a large park on the outskirts of the city in each of 7 main sections. These would be connected by broad paved boulevards encircling the city. The board hired Boston landscape architect Ernest W. Bowditch to carry out the plan and issued $800,000 in bonds.

Acquisition of parkland accelerated dramatically. In 1894, the city purchased a large portion of the Doan Brook Valley between Gordon and Wade parks, the first 89 acres of EDGEWATER PARK, and 81 acres of Brooklyn (later BROOKSIDE) Park. The same year, park commissioners decided on 3 farms located between Turney Rd. and Broadway as the site for a south side park (see GARFIELD PARK). In 1895, the Shaker Hts. Land Co. donated 279 acres embracing the upper Doan Brook Valley and the SHAKER LAKES. At the city's centennial celebration the following year, JOHN D. ROCKEFELLER announced his gift of 276 acres along DOAN BROOK and $300,000 to cover the cost of land the city had previously acquired there. Rockefeller's gift completed the city's ownership of the entire Doan Brook Valley from the headwaters to Lake Erie. Other substantial additions to the park system during this period included the 86-acre WASHINGTON PARK in 1899 and the 100-acre Woodland Hills Park in 1900. The first parks in Cleveland, as elsewhere in the nation's cities during this period, were envisioned as "public pleasure grounds." Cleveland's park commissioners set out to create, in their own words, "a harmonious development of sylvan beauty to which all are welcome, rich and poor alike, where all may find rest and inspiration and pleasure." They viewed parks as places for passive recreation, where "pleasure parties and children might spend a few hours in enjoyment of rural conditions." Photographs show that they were indeed beautiful and, prior to WORLD WAR I, they were by far the most popular subject for penny postcards. The cards and the photographs show parks of pastoral beauty, with shaded glens, winding carriage drives, and picturesque lakes, ponds, and springs.

Cleveland's park board faced serious opposition in the late 1890s. The Park Board Reorganization Assoc., led by attorneys John A. Smith and JOHN ZANGERLE, charged that the board was "autocratic, dictatorial, irresponsible and unaccountable to the people." By establishing parks in SHAKER HTS., NEWBURGH, and BROOKLYN, the association charged, the board made them convenient for "people of leisure" but inaccessible to city residents who could not enjoy them without "the expense of transportation and considerable cost of time." The association further charged that city residents were paying to enhance the property values of adjoining townships, and even protested the renaming of Newburgh (Garfield), Pelton (Lincoln), and Brooklyn (Brookside) parks. ("Brookside smacks too much of a Boston flavor to suit the tastes of the citizens of Cleveland," one pamphlet complained.) After a sometimes bitter battle in the state legislature, the park board was abolished in 1900, and administration of the city's parks was vested in the new Div. of Parks & Boulevards of the Dept. of Public Works (later the Dept. of Parks, Recreation & Properties).

By 1896, Cleveland had laid the foundation for a park system that park commissioners claimed was "excelled by few [cities], if any, in the world." Within a comparatively brief period, some 1,200 acres had been assembled and improved. Fully ⅔ of the land had been donated, leaving the city to pay only the expenses of improvement and maintenance. But therein lay the problem that would plague the city's parks almost from the moment they were added to the system: bond funds could be used only for the purchase and permanent improvement of parkland, while maintenance costs had to come from taxes. The city increasingly found that it lacked the resources to maintain what it had built. As early as 1901, parks superintendent Robt. J. Kegg cautioned in his annual report, "You must bear in mind ... that every bit of new work added means greater maintenance expense the next year—more labor ... to keep these improvements and the parks themselves in proper condition. A proper appropriation should be set aside to take care of them, or they will soon deteriorate." Again, in 1902, the superintendent cited the constantly increasing cost of maintaining the city's park system and warned, "Without sufficient funds it will become an eyesore instead of a thing of beauty."

The Cleveland parks entered a new era under Mayor TOM L. JOHNSON, who initiated an effort to "bring the parks to the people." He ordered the removal of "Keep Off the Grass" signs, and during 1901, his first year in office, he set as a goal the establishment of playgrounds in the more crowded districts of the city. The impetus for building playgrounds in Cleveland mirrored the situation in other large industrial cities, where park-reform advocates argued for the location of new parks on sites more accessible to the working classes and for organized sports and other activities that would ensure healthful recreation. The Johnson administration's policy was to make the parks attractive at all times to all people. Thus, during the early 1900s, the city's Div. of Parks equipped new children's playgrounds, constructed athletic fields and basketball and tennis courts, and introduced Sunday and evening band concerts. Winter sports, especially ice skating, had gained popularity, and in 1901, the city established skating rinks at all the larger parks and hosted skating races at Brookside and Rockefeller parks. Park shelters at Edgewater and Woodland Hills parks were converted for use as municipal dancing pavilions. By 1904, 8 children's playgrounds were operating in the more congested areas of the city, and the Div. of Parks had embarked on the construction of the first of 5 free public BATH HOUSES. In 1916, with 2,160 acres of parkland, Cleveland ranked 12th in park area after New York, Philadelphia, Los Angeles, Chicago, Denver, Washington, D.C., Minneapolis, Boston, Cincinnati, St. Louis, and Baltimore.

By the 1920s, Cleveland's parks had begun to show the effects of intensive use and inadequate maintenance. The Community Betterment Council of the Welfare Fed. undertook a study of the problem and issued its report in 1923. "Cleveland's parks have required, and should have received better care and upkeep than has been given them," the council reported. According to the council, the city recently had cut 800 men from the payroll and had eliminated the positions of city forester and park engineer. Park buildings, the council charged, had been painted a garish orange and black to advertise work done by Mayor FRED KOHLER's administration, and the city was losing to disease what were conservatively estimated to be 4,000 trees a year. Meanwhile, a separate suburban park system had been carved out of the city's picturesque outlying districts, embracing some of Greater Cleveland's finest natural areas. As early as 1905, Cleveland park engineer WM. A. STINCHCOMB had urged that the city take advantage of its outstanding natural areas by creating an outer system of parks and boulevards to encircle the entire metropolitan area. The independent Cleveland Metropolitan Park District was created in 1917. Similar metropolitan systems already had been established in Boston, Westchester County, N.Y., and Cook County, Ill. CLEVELAND METROPARKS, as the metropolitan park district is known today, comprises 11 reservations in Cuyahoga and Medina counties; except for a portion of Big Creek, all are located outside the city limits. In a curious footnote to Cleveland park history, civic and business leaders in the 1930s urged the creation of a "Central Park" between Euclid and Chester avenues and E. 21st and E. 40th streets. The 65-acre park was seen as a counterpart of Manhattan's midtown park and as a means of arresting the erosion of property values along the city's once-fashionable Euclid Ave. Although the idea was endorsed by the Chamber of Commerce and surfaced time and time again in the city's dailies, it never materialized.

In many respects, the Depression may be said to have come to the rescue of the city's parks. With aid from the WORK PROJECTS ADMINISTRATION, Cleveland's parks were extensively rehabilitated and redesigned to accommodate automobiles and better withstand intensive use. In 1938, a force of nearly 9,000 men, divided into 2 shifts, worked 6 days a week building dams, bridges, culverts, bath houses, swimming pools, athletic fields, tennis courts, and playgrounds, and planting trees and shrubs. After 1940, the city's parks suffered from serious outbreaks of vandalism and theft, water pollution, and perpetually inadequate maintenance and security. Highway construction decimated large portions of Edgewater, Gordon, and Brookside parks. The parks department traditionally received the crumbs from the city's budget, and as the budget grew leaner in the 1960s, park personnel were continually reduced. The parks, once one of Cleveland's finest assets, were reduced to a deplorable condition. Mayor Ralph Perk's attempt in 1972 to address the situation with "Operation Turn Around" was ineffective, as was a $500,000 CETA program in 1975. No longer able to manage its extensive park system, CLEVELAND CITY COUNCIL in 1977 approved legislation to enter into a long-term lease agreement with the Ohio Dept. of Natural Resources. Edgewater, Gordon, and Wildwood parks became components of a new CLEVELAND LAKEFRONT STATE PARK. In recent years these parks have seen extensive capital improvements, as well as improved maintenance and security. In 1986, city council passed an ordinance authorizing the lease of Garfield Park to the Cleveland Metroparks for a period of 40 years; the action followed bitter and long-standing complaints by the city of GARFIELD HTS. that Cleveland failed to maintain it. With a few exceptions—notably the recently refurbished Public Square, Chester Commons, and the new Heritage Park in the Flats—Cleveland's parks bear witness to the great shift of the city's population in the last 40 years. With the flight of the middle class to the suburbs, the poor and working-class residents who took their place have inherited a greatly diminished park system that continues to suffer from inadequate maintenance.

Carol Poh Miller

**PARKVIEW VILLAGE,** now the southern portion of FAIRVIEW PARK, occupied a 1-sq.-mi. area west of the Rocky River Valley and north of Brookpark Rd. Originally part of Rockport Twp., the area was organized as part of ROCKY RIVER village in 1892. In Apr. 1910, the county commissioners granted the petition of the residents in the southern portion of the village to establish Goldwood Twp. In August, township trustees approved the incorporation of Fairview Village. That divided the township into 2 remaining portions. The northern portion was absorbed by Rocky River. The southern portion became the unincorporated Parkview Village. It was the hope of early officials that Parkview be annexed by Cleveland. In 1925, Parkview Village incorporated, primarily so that its residents could obtain city water and electricity. The first improvements were made as water mains were installed and connected with Cleveland's water system. During the period before WORLD WAR II, Parkview remained a rural farming community with an approximate population of 200; its children attended the Fairview public schools. The postwar years were a period of growth for Parkview as a residential community. By 1953, its population had increased to 1,100. In 1955, the first school in Parkview was built, and the first full-time police officer was hired in 1959. By 1960, Parkview's population was 93% residential, yet hindered by the lack of sewers, half the land remained undeveloped, and the village remained dependent upon Fairview for its fire protection. In 1961, Parkview residents rejected an attempt to annex the village to Fairview. The defeat was attributed to the older voters, who favored an autonomous municipality, plus a general feeling that taxes would be increased. In 1965, an annexation committee of 3 residents each from Fairview and Parkview was appointed to reach agreement on terms for annexation. Convinced by prospects of better municipal services and the fear of a proposed interstate "outerbelt" highway route through the heart of the village, Parkview voters approved the annexation agreement in 1965, as did Fairview voters in 1966. On 1 Jan. 1967, Parkview's 3,500 residents became Ward 5 in the city of Fairview Park.

Goebelt, Margaret S., *Fairview Park in Historical Review* (ca. 1978).

**PARMA** is an incorporated city southwest of Cleveland, 9th-largest in the state of Ohio. Occupying 19.7 sq. mi., it is bounded by Cleveland and BROOKLYN on the north, BROOKLYN HTS. and SEVEN HILLS on the east, N. ROYALTON and BROADVIEW HTS. on the south, and BROOK PARK, MIDDLEBURG HTS., and PARMA HTS.

on the west. Parma was originally part of Parma Twp., created in 1826. The first settlers were the Benajah Fay family from New York State, who settled along the Cleveland-Columbus Rd. in 1816. The name was taken from Parma, N.Y., where it was probably derived from the early-19th-century fascination with classical Italy. During the 19th century, Parma remained largely agricultural, with the sole manufacturer in the area being Dudley and Wm. Humphrey's clock shop. In 1912, a portion of the township seceded to form the village of Parma Hts. In 1924, Parma was incorporated as a village, and in 1926 it adopted the mayor-council form of government. In 1931 a proposition to annex it to the city of Cleveland was defeated, and Parma became a city. Parma's tremendous growth came after WORLD WAR II as young families began moving from Cleveland into the SUBURBS. Between 1950–80, its population soared from less than 20,000 to more than 110,000. The growth of business and industry in the area paralleled the increase in population. Parma is home both to many small businesses and to major industries such as General Motors, Modern Tool & Die, the Union Carbide Research Ctr., and Cox Cable Television. In addition, there are more than 25 smaller industries.

Parma, Seven Hills, and Parma Hts. make up the Parma School District. The system includes 14 elementary, 4 junior high, and 3 high schools. Parma also has 12 parochial elementary and 2 parochial high schools, with a student population of 8,253. CUYAHOGA COMMUNITY COLLEGE's Western Campus is situated at Pleasant Valley and York roads. Enrollment at the campus exceeded 12,000 in 1985. Parma is a member of the CUYAHOGA COUNTY PUBLIC LIBRARY SYSTEM, having 2 branch libraries. The city offers a wide variety of recreational facilities and services to its residents, including 26 park sites, swimming pools, an enclosed ice-skating rink, lighted tennis courts, a 150-acre golf course, baseball fields, 2 lakes, a senior citizen center, and the Gibbs Farm of the Parma Historical Society. The PARMA COMMUNITY GENERAL HOSPITAL, the KAISER-PERMANENTE Medical Ctr., Parmatown Shopping Ctr., and almost 90 acres of the Big Creek Reservation of the Metroparks System are also located in the city.

Kubasek, Ernest R., *The History of Parma* (1976).
Parma Chamber of Commerce, *Parma* (1984).
*Parma Sesquicentennial, 1826–1976* (1976).

**PARMA COMMUNITY GENERAL HOSPITAL,** located at 7007 Powers Blvd., Parma, is a 321-bed voluntary nonprofit general hospital. It provides in-patient care and medicine, surgery, obstetrics, and pediatrics. The original building was constructed between 1959–61. Additions were made in 1972–74 and again in 1976.

**PARMA HEIGHTS** is a city located southwest of Cleveland and bounded by BROOK PARK and MIDDLEBURG HTS. on the west and PARMA on the north, east, and south. It occupies 4.13 sq. mi. The early settlers were predominantly German and lived on family farms, with a few commercial establishments and country inns located along the Wooster Pike (Pearl Rd.), the main road from Cleveland to Columbus. The village of Parma Hts. was separated from the original Parma Twp. in 1911 because residents perceived a lack of representation. Natural gas and electric utilities were introduced into the area in 1915. Population growth was slow, and a rural atmosphere remained until after WORLD WAR II. The population was 300 in 1915, 900 in 1920, and only 1,330 by 1940. Like other suburbs, Parma Hts. benefited from the post-World War II exodus from Cleveland. Housebuilding boomed, and the population grew to 3,901 by 1950. In 1953 a new charter was adopted, modifying the mayor-council form of government and providing for a greater degree of home rule. Parma Hts. became a city in 1959. By the mid-1970s, 98% of the residential and 96% of the commercial acreage was developed. Parma Hts. has little industry, but serves as home to many businesses and has more than 200 office structures. It is included in the Parma School District along with the cities of Parma and SEVEN HILLS. There are 6 churches in Parma Hts., 97 acres of city parks, and recreational facilities, including a municipal swimming pool, an ice rink, and the Greenbrier Commons Community Theater. An additional 136 acres of the city are part of the Big Creek Reservation of the Metroparks System.

Turner, James, *Heritage of Parma Heights* (1969).

## PARMADALE CHILDREN'S VILLAGE OF ST. VINCENT DE PAUL,

**PARMADALE CHILDREN'S VILLAGE OF ST. VINCENT DE PAUL,** located at 6753 State Rd., PARMA, Ohio, is the result of a union of 2 organizations dedicated to caring for young people—Parmadale Children's Village of St. Vincent de Paul and St. Anthony's Home for Boys & Young Men. Parmadale, organized by the CATHOLIC CHARITIES CORP., was an outgrowth of St. Vincent de Paul Orphanage, originally operated by the SISTERS OF CHARITY beginning in 1853. Parmadale was dedicated at State and Ridge roads on 27 Sept. 1925 by Patrick Cardinal Hayes of New York City. Built as a series of cottages, the facility was designed to provide a homelike atmosphere for the boys. Additional cottages were dedicated by Bp. EDWARD FRANCIS HOBAN in 1947 to accommodate girls from ST. JOSEPH'S ORPHANAGE.

**PAROCHIAL EDUCATION (CATHOLIC).** When the Diocese of Cleveland was formed on 23 Apr. 1847, no parochial school existed within Cleveland's boundaries. The only schools were in Randolph, 12 mi. east of Akron, and in Avon. Bp. LOUIS AMADEUS RAPPE, first bishop of Cleveland, established 16 parishes and parish schools. On Christmas Day 1849, the first cathedral was opened, and a school was started in the nativity chapel. A Free School for Boys, and a year later a Free School for Girls, were begun at St. Clair and E. 6th streets. The influence of the parochial school from the earliest days of the diocese, for education in general and for the preservation of the Catholic faith, cannot be overemphasized. The tone of the public schools was very often hostile to the faith, and Catholic children were sometimes subjected to ridicule or abuse on account of their religion. The teachers in the public schools were almost invariably Protestant; quite often the public schools were operated in close cooperation with local Protestant churches. Ten years after the founding of the diocese, the State Teachers Assoc., being Protestant, urged the daily use of the Bible in the classroom. The only recourse was for the Catholic church to erect schools in which the children would be taught in a nonthreatening friendly atmosphere.

Even before 1847, anti-Catholic feeling was felt. When, in Cleveland, the Whigs had failed to gather in the "foreign vote," they had adopted a hostile attitude toward things Catholic, and the Republican party in the beginning was identified with the Know-Nothing movement and its anti-Catholic agitation. The 1st Plenary Council of Baltimore in 1852 made a powerful plea for parochial schools. Bp. Rappe responded to this educational request. St. Mary's School on W. 30th began in 1853 under Fr. John Luhr and in 1854 moved to a location on the corner of Superior and E. 17th St. A few years later, St. Peter parish became the

third Catholic church and school on the east side of the Cuyahoga. St. Joseph, at Woodland and E. 22nd, became the next parish and school in Sept. 1855. In 1854, Bp. Rappe began a parish in NEWBURGH, and a school was started in 1862. The Parish of Immaculate Conception had its beginnings in the old Cathedral Nativity Chapel, which Rappe moved out to the country, at the corner of Superior and E. 41st St. The URSULINES taught there, and priests from the seminary and cathedral assisted them. In 1871, Fr. Jas. O'Reilly organized the parish and school of St. Columbkille. St. Bridget's parish and school was established somewhat earlier, in 1857. The Bohemians, who had come to Cleveland earlier, established their parish and school in 1867, at E. 35th and Woodland. All parishes, ethnic or not, believed the parochial school necessary for the preservation of the Catholic faith. West of the Cuyahoga River, the veteran missionary Fr. Jas. Conlan set up ST. PATRICK'S PARISH and school in 1853. Twelve years later, in 1865, ST. MALACHI'S parish and school was formed on a section closer to Lake Erie. Earlier, in 1861, Bp. Rappe began at the corner of Tremont and Jefferson streets the first church and school of St. Augustine. For the French-speaking Catholics, a parish and school, St. Mary of Annunciation, was formed between St. Malachi's and St. Augustine. The German-speaking Catholics on the west side received their parish and school on 13 Sept. 1865. In Akron, Fr. Peter Donenhofer opened a school at St. Bernard's in 1863. At St. Vincent, the founding pastor, Fr. Matthew Scanlon, opened a school in 1866.

In this growing area of northeast Ohio, the invariable accompaniment of the church was the school building. Bp. Rappe had assisted at the 1st Plenary Council of Baltimore in 1852, at which an appeal had been made to establish a school with every parish. In the Cleveland Synod of 1857, Bp. Rappe pressed for this request. His tenure as bishop was significantly tied up with Catholic education. From Boulogne-sur-Mer, Bp. Rappe brought 5 URSULINES TO Cleveland, 2 Sisters of Charity, 4 priests, and 5 students, who landed at New York on 6 Aug. 1850. These persons would drastically affect Catholic education in Ohio. One year later came the Sisters of the Immaculate Heart of Mary. The Holy Humility of Mary Sisters arrived on 18 June 1864. The Sisters of St. Joseph, established in St. Louis in 1836, by the end of the century had 1,600 pupils in 8 parishes. The SISTERS OF NOTRE DAME were 101 sisters serving 6,407 students in 21 schools. The Immaculate Heart of Mary Sisters were teaching 5,000 pupils in 5 schools. In 1900, 85 Ursuline Nuns served 7,500 children in 20 parishes. The Humility of Mary Sisters were teaching 685 pupils in 9 parochial schools. Each of the bishops had to present his case for Catholic education to his people and to the many publics. Bp. RICHARD GILMOUR was known as a champion of Catholic schools. Most of his episcopacy was spent counteracting the attacks against Catholic schools and fighting the movement to tax nonpublic schools. In 1876, nearly 1/3 of the people of Cleveland were Catholics. In the period 1870–95, 32,401 GERMANS, 16,844 Bohemians (CZECHS), 7,943 IRISH, 7,000 HUNGARIANS and SLOVAKS, 6,457 English, 5,412 SLOVENES, 2,452 POLES, and 1,528 ITALIANS came to Cleveland. Most of these immigrants looked to the local parish school to preserve the faith for their children. On 28 Apr. 1887, a diocesan school board was begun, with the approval of Bp. Gilmour, who followed the directions of the 3d Council of Baltimore. The board was empowered to judge the qualification of new teachers and set up rules for guidance of district examiners, who inspected all the schools.

The Jesuit Fathers of the Buffalo Province came on 1 Aug. 1880 to St. Mary's on W. 30th St. to begin a college,

St. Ignatius, which was to become JOHN CARROLL UNIVERSITY, and with the decision, they began St. Ignatius High School. The college began on 6 Sept. 1886. In the first decade of its history, 72% of the graduates entered the seminary. During the administration of Bp. IGNATIUS F. HORSTMANN, the greatest school expansion of the diocese in the 19th century took place. A few parishes had a full 4-year high school curriculum by the early 1900s. Holy Name High School was one of the first coeducational high schools in the city. St. Vincent and St. Mary's in Akron and St. Mary's in Lorain supported full-scale high schools in the 1920s. St. Ignatius High School student attendance broke all records by 1911, when the college and high school celebrated its 25th anniversary. The Great Hall, previously used as a chapel, had to be divided into classrooms. In 1921, 341 students attended the high school, when 25 Jesuits taught. Bp. JOHN P. FARRELLY started the unification and standardization of the parish schools as well as the uniformity of teacher training on a diocesan scale. His great educational achievement was the establishment of CATHEDRAL LATIN HIGH SCHOOL. Dr. Edward Mooney was its first principal-director. In Sept. 1916, 160 young men began their first 2 years of high school in temporary quarters. The school was dedicated on 8 June 1918, a large tapestry brick, Renaissance style of architecture. Edward Graham of Boston was the architect. The increased enrollment, 740, after 1 year, forced the administration to have 2 half-day sessions. During Farrelly's 12 years of administration, 47 new churches and schools were erected. He considered Cathedral Latin High School his greatest accomplishment.

During Archbp. JOSEPH SCHREMBS's time, Catholic schools witnessed a great expansion in the development of innovative facilities and programs. In 1923, 45 acres were acquired in a new land development in UNIVERSITY HTS. John Carroll University began in July 1931. The Ursulines had a charter for a college from their earliest days in the diocese. The Sisters of Notre Dame began a college in the early 1920s. In 1933, Gov. White asked the state legislature for relief for all schools in the state. Powerful interests, including the open opposition of the CITIZENS LEAGUE of Cleveland and the Jr. Order of American Mechanics, blocked any concession. Dr. JOHN HAGAN, superintendent of Catholic schools, continued to lead the crusade for state aid for nonpublic schools, but to no avail. Archbp. EDWARD F. HOBAN's accomplishments for Catholic education were outstanding. By 1952, 33 new Catholic elementary schools opened, and 31 existing schools were remodeled, enlarged, or rebuilt. Catholic education had reached 112,357 elementary children and 26,600 high school students when Bp. CLARENCE ISSENMANN became bishop. The mid-1960s witnessed a trend of consolidations at the elementary and secondary levels. St. Agnes, Blessed Sacrament, St. Edward, and Holy Trinity elementary schools had amalgamated or consolidated. Attempts of consolidation were made on the near west side. The elementary attempts failed, but because of suggestions by high school principals, Lourdes' Central High School, St. Stanislaus, St. John Cantius, St. Michael's, and St. Stephen's consolidated into Cleveland Central Catholic, which opened in Sept. 1969. This new high school concept stressed updating and modernization to widen the scope of Catholic secondary education, especially in areas of modern vocational needs. By 1970, Cleveland proper witnessed a 28% decrease in enrollment in parish schools with religious teachers, who composed 56% of the elementary faculties. That would decrease to 21% by 1980.

Bps. Jas. Hickey and Anthony Pilla strengthened the Catholic schools through a combined process of financial

subsidy, education trust, and various forms of consolidation. The 1970s saw the Cleveland Public School Desegregation Act of 1976. The federal court-appointed monitor kept reports on public and Catholic school enrollments. The nonnormal enrollment change from Cleveland public schools in 1978 to Catholic schools was 629 students, but in that same year 540 Catholic school students switched from Catholic schools to Cleveland public schools. The nonnormal figure in 1982 was 289 Cleveland public students changing to Catholic schools. Never was the percentage of change greater than .005%. Financial ramifications had a significant impact on the Catholic School Board and schools in the 1970s. The diocesan school office had been operated by royalties on textbooks and student fees until 1970, when the diocese started to subsidize the operation. In 1973, the average tuition of a high school was $500, which by 1980 had increased to $1,700. At the elementary school level the average tuition was in 1971, $100; 1973, $346; 1978, $543. The increase affected all parishes, so by 1980 every parish subsidized its elementary school by 59%. The offertory collection was 74% of that subsidy. Catholic school enrollment in the 1980s has leveled off. Cathedral Latin, Bp. Farrelly's great accomplishment, closed its doors in 1979 because of a lack of enrollment, not a lack of deeply dedicated alumni. Perhaps that is an indicator for Cleveland's history of Catholic education. Today, 166 elementary schools and 26 high schools with 76,802 students and 3,698 teachers represent the church's continuing intense interest in its future history and that of this nation.

Rev. John A. Leahy
Church of St. Bartholomew

**PARSONS, RICHARD C.** (10 Oct. 1826–8 Jan. 1899), was a prominent Cleveland lawyer and politician. He was active in local and state government, and was twice elected to Congress. Parsons was born in New London, Conn. His family later moved to New York City, where his father was a merchant. Parsons came to Cleveland in 1849 and studied law with Chas. Stetson. He was admitted to the Ohio bar in 1851. Parson's political career spanned the years 1852–77. It was not until 1880 that he was able to establish a full-time law practice. After retiring from politics in 1877, he served for 3 years as editor-in-chief of the CLEVELAND HERALD, of which he was also co-owner. In 1852, Parsons was elected to CLEVELAND CITY COUNCIL, and the next year he was chosen council president. He was elected to the Ohio legislature in 1857 and was reelected in 1859. The following year he was made speaker of the House of Representatives, the youngest person, perhaps, ever to hold that position. In 1861, Pres. Lincoln asked him to be the U.S. minister to Chile, but Parsons declined. He subsequently, however, was appointed consul at Rio de Janeiro, and accepted. Parsons returned to Cleveland in 1862 as the new collector of internal revenue. He was removed from that office 4 years later for refusing to support Pres. Johnson. In 1866 he procured another federal appointment, as marshal of the Supreme Court. In 1872, Parsons was elected to the 43d Congress as a Republican from the 20th congressional district. As a congressman, he was largely credited with bringing about major improvements to Cleveland's harbor. He secured the first appropriation for a breakwater to aid the commercial value of the city, and was also instrumental in securing a lifesaving service and a lighthouse. Later in life, Parsons served as a president for the EARLY SETTLERS ASSOC., and in 1896 he was active in the city's centennial celebration.

PATRIOTIC SOCIETIES, organizations formed to honor early American settlers, their deeds, and their legacy, are composed of men or women whose ancestral lineage meets strict eligibility rules. The purposes of these organizations generally are to perpetuate the values and institutions of the early American settlers, to commemorate particular historical events, and to preserve historical records. The earliest of these patriotic societies in Cleveland was the New England Society of Cleveland & the Western Reserve, organized on 22 Dec. 1853 at the Plymouth Congregational Church's celebration of Forefathers' Day to commemorate the Pilgrims' landing at Plymouth Rock. The society was formally organized and incorporated in Dec. 1855, with BENJAMIN ROUSE, president, and Geo. Mygatt and Orlando Cutter, vice-presidents. Its purpose was to perpetuate the memory, principles, and spirit of the early settlers of New England, especially "their heroic self-denial, invincible courage, enlarged views and wise policy." The society met annually on Forefathers' Day through 1859, but the CIVIL WAR disrupted its annual meetings; the society was dormant until reorganized in 1894–95, when its annual meeting on New Year's Day and its festival around Forefathers' Day were renewed. As celebration of the Christmas holidays made it increasingly difficult to hold its festival so close to Christmas, the society in 1912 moved its festival to 21 Nov., Mayflower Anchor Day. Membership, open to "any person of good character" who was a "native or descendant of a native of a New England State," grew from the 55 charter members to include 250 people in 1935.

Several local branches of national patriotic organizations were formed to celebrate Anglo-Americanism during the highly nationalistic 1890s. The Western Reserve Chap. of the Natl. Society Daughters of the American Revolution was organized on 19 Dec. 1891 by Catherine Hitchcock Tilden Avery, former teacher and school principal and wife of historian and educator Dr. ELROY M. AVERY. On a visit to Washington, D.C., soon after the national DAR was formed (11 Oct. 1890), she became a member of the District of Columbia Society; upon her return to Cleveland, she interested a group of eligible friends in forming the Western Reserve Chap., which received its charter on 18 Feb. 1892. Other area chapters were formed later: the Molly Chittenden Chap., organized 22 May 1912; the Moses Cleaveland Chap., 7 Mar. 1913; the Lakewood Chap., 18 Apr. 1937; the Shaker Chap., 21 Oct. 1931; the Martha Devotion Huntington Chap., 10 Oct. 1940; and the Ann Spafford Chap., 23 May 1946. Chapters hold monthly meetings to vote on various resolutions passed by the national society and to plan and implement national and local projects, which have included some of the earliest AMERICANIZATION programs in Cleveland; essay and poster contests in schools; loan and scholarship programs for students; service to patients in veterans' hospitals; working with youngsters in BOY and GIRL SCOUT troops and through sponsorship of Jr. American Citizens Clubs; work with genealogical records; maintenance of schools in several rural areas; and the provision of nursing care and emergency relief to victims of wars and floods. The DAR is perhaps the most active and widely known of the various patriotic societies. Membership is open to women 18 or older who are descended from a man or woman who, with unfailing loyalty to the cause of American independence, served as a sailor, soldier, colonial or state civil officer, or recognized patriot, or rendered material aid thereto.

On 5 May 1892, just 5 months after his wife formed the local DAR, Elroy M. Avery helped found and became president of the Western Reserve Society of the Sons of the American Revolution. The national organization had been formed in New York on 30 Apr. 1889; membership was open to men 18 and older who were lineal descendants of ancestors who were "at all times unfailing in . . . loyalty to, and [who] rendered active service in, the cause of American Independence." The Western Reserve Society numbered 23 charter members in 1892 and grew to about 400 members in the mid-1940s. Two local patriotic organizations were formed in 1896. One was the Order of Founders & Patriots, membership in which is open to men 18 and older "of good moral character and reputation" who are lineally descended from an ancestor who settled in an American colony prior to 13 May 1657, and whose later ancestors during the American Revolution "adhered as patriots to the cause of the Colonies." Another was the Natl. Society of the Colonial Dames of America, formed nationally in 1891 but organized in Ohio on 30 Apr. 1896 and chartered on 1 July 1896. By 1946 the "Cleveland Circle" of the society numbered 23 members, women who were "descended in their own right from some ancestor of worthy life who came to reside in an American colony prior to 1750" and whose ancestor, or one of his descendants, founded an important institution, held government office, or otherwise rendered distinguished service prior to 5 July 1776 that "contributed to the founding of this great and powerful nation." The Cleveland Circle had 34 members in 1961.

The Society of Mayflower Descendants, organized in Ohio in 1898, did not become active in northeast Ohio until the 1920s and 1930s. The Western Reserve Colony was chartered on 28 June 1927 and held its first meeting on 2 Nov. 1927. In 1930, Mrs. Walter D. Meals organized the Cleveland Colony, with 15 members. Membership in the Cleveland Colony grew to 156 by 1940 and 290 in 1984. Formed "to perpetuate to a remote posterity the memory of our Pilgrim Fathers" and "to maintain and defend the civil and religious liberty as set forth in the Compact of the Mayflower," the society distributes copies of the Mayflower Compact to schools, performs genealogical research on the descendants of the Mayflower passengers, and holds annual Thanksgiving celebrations. The Natl. Society of Colonial Dames of the XVII Century, founded nationally in 1915 and in Ohio in 1960, is the most recent addition to the patriotic societies in the Cleveland area. Open to women who are lineally descended from an ancestor who lived in one of the 11 British colonies of America prior to 1701, the society works to preserve historical records and sites, to foster interest in Colonial research, and to promote education. Cleveland-area chapters include the Henry Brooks Chap. in BAY VILLAGE, organized on 26 July 1978, and the Richard Cutting Chap. in SHAKER HTS., founded on 31 Jan. 1980.

**PAYER, HARRY FRANKLIN** (3 July 1875–12 Oct. 1952), was a Cleveland lawyer, government official, and linguist. His ever-present formal attire, wing collar, ascot tie, bushy sideburns, and cherubic cheeks and his oratorical skills made him one of Cleveland's most flamboyant and unforgettable figures. Payer was born in Cleveland to Frank and Mary Cross Payer. Educated in the Cleveland public schools, he graduated from CENTRAL HIGH SCHOOL in 1893. Working his way through Western Reserve University, he graduated with the A.B. degree in 1897 and from the Cleveland Law School in 1899. Payer was admitted to the Ohio bar in 1899. In 1900 he managed TOM L. JOHNSON's first mayoral campaign. From 1901–07, he served as assistant city solicitor for Cleveland under NEWTON D. BAKER. In 1907, he became the senior member of the law firm of Payer, Winch, Minshall, & Karch, later Payer, Bleiweiss, Mollison & Crow. Nicknamed "Demosthenes" because of his acknowledged oratorical abilities, Payer earned a reputation as one of the area's top criminal lawyers and renown for the huge awards he gained in personal-injury cases.

In 1933, Pres. Franklin D. Roosevelt appointed Payer as assistant secretary of state. Serving from June-November, Payer became known as "Mr. Pickwick" because of his resemblance to the Dickens character. In December, Payer was made special counsel to the chief of the Foreign & Export Div. of the Reconstruction Finance Corp. He resigned in Apr. 1934 to return to private practice. Payer was one of the founders of the CUYAHOGA COUNTY BAR ASSOC. and served 3 terms, 1929-31, as its president. As chairman of the association's Committee on Judicial & Legal Reforms, he supported the common pleas courts' psychiatric clinic, bail-bond reform measures, and the three-fourths jury laws. Known as a linguist, Payer was a student of foreign languages, speaking Czech, Polish, Italian, French, and German and reading classical Greek and Latin. During WORLD WAR I, Payer, of Czech background, served on the Czechoslovakian Relief Commission. Payer indulged in a style of life as he thought it should be lived. He owned a beautiful home in CLEVELAND HTS. with a library of 10,000 books, intricately carved furniture, and oil paintings. Believing that an alert body was the necessary complement to an alert mind, he did physical workouts daily. Most of all, Payer believed that joy was not in possessions or money but rather in immersing oneself in an active life, and that by helping others one helps himself. Payer married Florence L. Graves in 1903. They had 3 children.

Harry F. Payer Papers, WRHS.

**PAYNE, HENRY B.** (30 Nov. 1810-9 Sept. 1896), had a long, active, and eminent career in the fields of law, politics, and business. A conservative Democrat, he held numerous public offices, nearly gaining the 1880 Democratic party nomination for president. Payne was born in Hamilton, N.Y., to Elisha and Esther Douglass Payne. He graduated from Hamilton College in 1832 and began studying law in the office of John Spencer. He moved to Cleveland in 1833, where he continued his law studies in the office of SHERLOCK ANDREWS; he was admitted to the Ohio bar in 1834. After 12 years of building a prosperous law practice with HIRAM WILLSON, Payne was forced to retire from legal practice as a consequence of a hemorrhage of the lungs.

Payne served as Cleveland's first solicitor under its municipal charter. Elected to city council in 1847, he assisted in effecting financial reforms and the reconstruction of the fire department. In 1856 and 1860 he served as a delegate to the Democratic party's national conventions. In 1849 he was elected to the state senate, and in 1851 he was an unsuccessful candidate for the U.S. Senate. In 1857, Payne ran unsuccessfully for governor. That year he joined with Sen. Steven Douglass in opposing the Lecompton constitution, and he assisted Douglass in his 1858 campaign against Abraham Lincoln. In 1849, Payne, along with JOHN ALLEN, RICHARD HILLIARD, John Woolsey, and others, worked for the completion of the Cleveland & Columbus Railroad; he served as its president from 1851-54. During the CIVIL WAR, Payne joined other prominent politicians in making speeches encouraging Union Army enlistments and advancing monies as a guaranty for the advance of county funds to equip new regiments. In 1862 he became head of the newly created Board of Sinking Funds Commissioners in Cleveland.

Payne headed the Ohio delegation to the 1872 Democratic Party Natl. Convention. Elected to Congress in 1874, he served on the committees on banking and currency and civil-service reform. Following the 1876 elections, he was named chairman of the congressional portion of a joint House-Senate committee that created the Electoral Commission (upon which he also served as a member) that determined the electoral votes. A candidate for the presidential nomination in 1880, Payne served 1 term, 1885-91, in the U.S. Senate. Payne married Mary Perry in 1836. The Paynes had 5 children, including Flora, Oliver, and Nathan. Payne is buried in LAKE VIEW CEMETERY.

**PAYNE, LAWRENCE O.** (11 Oct. 1892-26 Sept. 1959), was a black Cleveland lawyer, politician, and newspaper publisher. He was prominent among the new group of black political leaders elected to Cleveland city council in the 1930s that moved away from the traditional black support of the Republican party to a more independent political stance. Payne was born and educated in the public schools of Columbus, Ohio. During WORLD WAR I, he enlisted in the Army, serving in France, where he was awarded the Purple Heart. Coming to Cleveland after the war, he continued his education, graduating from the Cleveland Preparatory School in 1922 and receiving the LL.B. degree from John Marshall Law School in 1923. Admitted to the Ohio bar that year, Payne secured an appointment as Cleveland's first black assistant police prosecutor. On 21 Oct. 1924, he married Maybelle Payne.

Payne's election to city council in 1929 came at a time when the power of the old black leadership was on the wane. Winning election as ward leaders as well, the black "Triumvirate" of councilmen LEROY BUNDY, CLAYBORNE GEORGE, and Payne significantly increased their own political power and the amount of political patronage available in the black community. Holding the balance of power in the selection of a new city manager in 1930, the three councilmen received for their support of DANIEL MORGAN the admission of blacks to the School of Nursing and as interns at City Hospital, as well as appointment of blacks to city offices. In 1932, the councilmen withheld support for the Republican candidate for council president until all three were given committee chairmanships.

During the mid-1930s, the black councilmen continued to use their voting leverage to wring concessions from city hall and increase their power within the Republican party. In council, Payne served as chair of the welfare committee and supported a larger police force, a permanent police-women's bureau, the separation of first-time and habitual offenders, the enlargement of the Blossom Hill and Hudson correction farms, and development of the lakefront. Appointed to the State Parole Board in 1938, Payne showed his political strength in the 1939 council elections, helping to elect Augustus Parker, WM. O. WALKER, and HAROLD GASSAWAY. In 1940, Payne and Walker formed the P. W. Publishing Co., publishers of the weekly *CLEVELAND CALL & POST*, setting up operations on E. 55th St. and expanding the paper to 12 pages. Payne resigned from the Parole Board in 1945, returning to private practice, except for an unsuccessful bid for the 21st congressional seat in 1952.

**PAYNE, NATHAN PERRY** (13 Aug. 1837-11 May 1885), was born in Cleveland, the eldest son of HENRY B. and Mary Perry PAYNE. He attended CLEVELAND PUBLIC SCHOOLS and then the Pierce Academy in Middleborough, Mass. He then returned to Cleveland to become an accountant in a coal firm. In 1860, he helped to form a coal company, Cross, Payne & Co., which later became Payne, Newton & Co. Late in the Civil War he became a "100 day" volunteer, although he had enlisted at war's outbreak in the CLEVELAND GRAYS. He served 2 terms on the local board of education and 6 years on city council at several times between 1862–72. He was elected mayor of Cleveland on the Democratic ticket in 1875 but served only 1 term, declining to be renominated for the sake of his business activities. He was, at various times, a park commissioner and vigorously promoted the development of public PARKS. Payne never married. He lived in his later years with his grandmother, Mrs. Nathan Perry, Jr. (Paulina Skinner Perry).

**PAYNE, OLIVER HAZARD** (21 July 1839–27 June 1917), was born in Cleveland, the son of Henry B. and Mary Perry Payne. Educated at Phillips Academy and Yale, he left the latter in 1861 to serve in the CIVIL WAR. Initially joining an Illinois regiment, he later served in the 124th Ohio Volunteer Infantry, in which he became a colonel in Jan. 1863. Wounded at the battle of Chickamauga, he convalesced in Cleveland; he returned to his regiment in 1864 and later earned the brevet of brigadier-general. In Nov. 1864 he resigned his commission and returned to Cleveland, where he entered the refining business and iron industry. He organized Clark, Payne & Co., which became the largest Cleveland competitor of Rockefeller, Andrews & Flagler and the largest single refiner in the city. In 1872, his interests were merged into the STANDARD OIL CO., and he became one of the principal officers of that firm. He served as treasurer until 1884, when he moved to New York; Payne's holdings in Standard Oil were exceeded only by those of Rockefeller, the Chas. Pratt estate, and the Harkness Family. In New York, Payne began to invest in other enterprises, most notably the American Tobacco Co. and its subsidiaries. Also active in politics, he was a major contributor to the Democratic party in both New York and Ohio. His influence was probably partially responsible for the appointment of his brother-in-law, Wm. C. Whitney, as secretary of the Navy in the Grover Cleveland administration. A noted philanthropist, Payne established the Cornell Medical College and anonymously donated more than $8 million to that institution in his lifetime. Other gifts and bequests were made to Lakeside Hospital, Yale, the Jewish Orphan Asylum, Hamilton College, Western Reserve University, ST. VINCENT CHARITY HOSPITAL, and the University of Virginia. A bachelor, Col. Payne (so called because of his war rank) was a noted yachtsman; his ship, *Aphrodite*, a 300′ steam yacht, was the largest such ship in the country when completed in 1898. When Payne died in New York, his estate, estimated to be as large as $190 million, was distributed, after bequests, among most of his nieces and nephews, including Wm. Bingham II, Elizabeth Bingham Blossom, FRANCES PAYNE BOLTON, and Harry Payne Bingham of Cleveland. He is buried in LAKE VIEW CEMETERY.

**PEAKE, GEORGE** (1722–Sep. 1827)—last name sometimes spelled Peek or Peak—was the first black to settle permanently in Cleveland. He was also something of an inventor, developing a new hand mill for grinding grain. A native of Maryland and a former resident of Pennsylvania, Peake came to Cleveland with his wife and 2 sons in Apr. 1809. They were apparently well-off financially when they arrived; Peake's wife reportedly possessed a half a bushel of silver dollars, a remarkable sum at a time when most commercial activity involved barter and trade. Peake himself was also rather wealthy, it appears; on 31 Dec. 1811 (sometimes cited as 1812), he purchased 103 acres of land in Rockport. Peake's initial wealth was apparently ill-gotten; as a British soldier in the French & Indian War, he had served under Gen. Jas. Wolfe in the battle of Quebec, but he later was reported to have deserted the army, taking

with him the money he had been given to pay the other soldiers. Peake endeared himself to his Cleveland neighbors by the invention of a new hand mill, which was easier to use than the crude "stamp mortar and spring pestle" that they had adapted from the Indians' process for grinding grain. Peake's mill used stones that were 18–20″ in diameter and produced a much better quality of ground meal. Geo. Peake was reportedly "a highly respected citizen."

**PEASE, SETH** (9 Jan. 1764–12 Sept. 1819), was an early surveyor in the WESTERN RESERVE. The son of Joseph and Mindwell Pease, he was born in Suffield, Conn. He married Bathsheba Kent on 21 Dec. 1785. Pease first came to the Western Reserve as an astronomer and surveyor for the expedition led by MOSES CLEAVELAND for the CONNECTICUT LAND CO. in 1796. Under the direction of Augustus Porter and along with fellow surveyor AMOS SPAFFORD, he began to survey the area around Cleveland in Sept. 1796. Both Pease and Spafford produced maps of the town. Although the cabin the surveyors lived in was known as "Pease's Hotel," Pease was a resident of the area only long enough to complete his work, then returned to his Connecticut home. In the spring of 1797, he again returned to the Western Reserve as an employee of the Connecticut Land Co. He served as the principal surveyor in a 9-member party that laid out all of the townships east of the CUYAHOGA RIVER. In 1797, Pease produced the first published map of the Western Reserve. His field notes, journals, and letters provide a detailed description of his experiences in the Reserve. Pease also carried out surveys of a township in present-day Maine in 1795 and of the Holland Purchase in New York in 1798–99. In 1806–07 he was U.S. surveyor general in the Mississippi & Orleans Territory and ran the government survey of the southern boundary of Western Reserve lands west of the Cuyahoga River. He also served as assistant postmaster general.

Seth Pease Papers, WRHS.

**PECK, ELIHU M.** (14 Sept. 1822–8 May 1896), along with his partner IRVINE U. MASTERS, was an important mid-19th-century shipbuilder who left the business in the early 1870s to pursue other business interests. Born in Butternuts, Oneida County, N.Y., Peck had come to Ohio by the fall of 1845. He married Susan Ettling Rogers in Bedford on 28 Sept. 1845. He worked as a ship carpenter until the mid-1850s, when he went into business for himself. By 1854 he and Masters had formed a partnership, building 1 bark, 1 brig, and 1 schooner that year for 1,380 tons in total construction. In 1857 they built 3 propellers and 3 schooners, one of which was the 200-ton *E. M. Peck*. During the decade in which they were partners, Peck & Masters built about 50 steam and sail vessels and ranked as one of the leading shipbuilding firms in the city. By mid-Feb. 1865, the partnership had been dissolved because of Masters's poor health. Peck continued in the business alone, designing and building about another 50 barks, steamers, and tugs in the next 7 years or so. He increasingly devoted his time to other matters, however, and ca. 1872 he withdrew from shipbuilding in favor of other business endeavors, eventually leaving Cleveland for Detroit in the mid-1870s. Among his other interests were politics—he served as a delegate to the county Republican convention in 1855 and was elected a waterworks commissioner in 1867—and other business ventures, including the Citizens Savings & Loan Assoc. (vice-president, 1868–71), the Peoples Savings & Loan Assoc. (vice-president, 1872), and the Peoples Gas Co. (president, 1872). Peck also engaged in a variety of transportation enterprises on the lakes. He was reportedly the first to employ a tow boat in the ore-carrying business, using a steamer to tow a schooner filled with ore from the upper to the lower lakes and thus revolutionizing the ore trade. He also organized the Northwestern Transportation Co. and built for it the *Amazon*, then the largest steamer on the lakes; it was as president of this company that he left Cleveland for Detroit, where he died. At the time of his death, he was the principal stockholder in Northwest and was president of the Swain Wrecking Co.

The **PEERLESS MOTOR CAR COMPANY** was established in Cleveland in 1889 as the Peerless Wringer & Mfg. Co. The company's first location was on the city's east side at the junction of the Cleveland & Pittsburgh and the New York, Chicago & St. Louis railroads. Originally a producer of washing-machine wringers, the firm also began manufacturing bicycles in the late 1890s. In 1895 it moved to a new location at 2654 Lisbon St. and changed its name to the Peerless Mfg. Co. In 1901, the company began manufacturing automobiles and parts, and in 1903, it again changed its name, to the Peerless Motor Car Co. After expanding the business to include parts for French-made automobiles in 1909, Peerless obtained a license to manufacture De Dion-Bouton automobiles, taking over that firm's Brooklyn plant. It began modifying the De Dion cars and within a year was manufacturing its own designs.

Louis P. Mooers was Peerless's most successful automobile designer. He joined the firm in 1902 and designed the first completely original Peerless. He began entering his designs in automobile races that year, without much initial success. Nevertheless, before Mooers left the company in 1906, Peerless became a very successful name in racing. The Peerless slogan was "All that the name implies," and Peerless cars were known for their luxury. Many of their models, based on Mooers's racing cars, also promised high performance. The interiors of the cars were outfitted in expensive materials. In 1905, for example, the 3 Peerless touring car models were priced at $3,200, $4,000, and $6,000. Peerless originally manufactured 2-cylinder cars, gradually adding 4- and 6-cylinder engines. By 1915, it was making only 6- and 8-cylinder engines. In 1915, the control of the company changed when Peerless merged with the General Vehicle Co. of New York. The Cleveland concern became a subsidiary of the resulting Peerless Truck & Motor Co.

By the 1920s, it became clear that large, luxurious "touring" cars reached too small a market. Even though Peerless lowered its prices and tried to promote medium-sized cars, the Depression hurt the company badly. Jas. A. Bohannon, who at age 33 became president of Peerless in 1929, tried to save it from the business depression. New, innovative ideas were introduced under Bohannon. In 1930, the management hired Count Alexis de Sakhnoffsky, a European auto designer, in one last effort to sell luxury, but the effort was unsuccessful. In 1931, Peerless engineers collaborated with the Aluminum Co. of America and developed a prototype for an all-aluminum automobile. The model was put through a series of tests in California but was never manufactured. The Peerless Motor Car Co., the last Cleveland-based company to manufacture automobiles in the city, closed its operations in 1931. Bohannon made a careful study of the Depression-era market and decided to convert the car plant into something more profitable—a brewery. By 1933, the factory buildings housed the CARLING BREWING CO., with Bohannon still president.

Wager, Richard, *Golden Wheels* (1975).

**PEIXOTTO, BENJAMIN FRANKLIN** (13 Nov. 1834–18 Sept. 1890), journalist, lawyer, communal leader, and diplomat, was born in New York City and was brought to Cleveland at the age of 13 when his father, DANIEL LEVY PEIXOTTO, accepted a position at Willoughby University Medical School. Peixotto entered the retail clothing business in the mid-1850s in partnership with his friend Geo. A. Davis. At the same time, he was an editorial writer for the *PLAIN DEALER*, a position he assumed in 1856. He quit the newspaper in 1862 when its editorial policy sympathized with the Copperhead movement.

In 1855, Peixotto and Davis founded the Hebrew Benevolent Society, with Peixotto serving as secretary. In 1863, Peixotto began his long career as a leader of the Independent Order of B'NAI B'RITH when he helped found Solomon Lodge, the first lodge in the city. In 1860, he founded the Young Men's Hebrew Literary Society, the first Jewish cultural organization in Cleveland. Four years later, he convinced the membership to affiliate with B'nai B'rith as Montefiore Lodge. At the age of 29, Peixotto was elected leader (Grand Saar) of the national B'nai B'rith, a position he held for 4 years. He was instrumental in the decision by B'nai B'rith District #2 to establish the Jewish Orphan Asylum in Cleveland. He successfully pushed for a $1 capitation tax on members and helped organize women's groups in 9 cities to raise funds for the orphanage. Peixotto was a member of Tifereth Israel and served as its treasurer and trustee. He established the congregation's Sunday school in 1858 and served as its superintendent until 1861, when he resigned in a dispute over the introduction of an organ and family pews, but he rejoined the congregation in 1864 and restarted the school. Peixotto left Cleveland in 1866 for New York City, where he established a law firm. In 1870, he was named American consul to Romania, where he experienced some success in relieving disabilities against the Jews of that country. In 1877, Peixotto was appointed American consul in Lyon, France; he remained in that position until 1885, when he returned to New York. He was married in 1858 to Hannah Strauss of Louisville, Ky.

**PEIXOTTO, DANIEL LEVI** (1800–1843), was the first Jewish doctor to teach medicine in Ohio, and one of the first to establish a practice. Peixotto was born in Amsterdam of Spanish-Portuguese parents. He received his medical degree from Columbia University. He later became secretary of the New York Academy of Medicine and president of the *New York Medical & Physical Journal*, to which he contributed many scientific articles. In 1835 he moved his family to Cleveland in order to accept a position at the new Willoughby Medical College. In 1836 he gave the introductory address for the college. Also that year he was elected to the newly established Chair of the Theory & Practice of Medicine & Obstetrics. Peixotto resigned from the troubled college in 1838. He continued his practice in Cleveland and occasionally lectured on hygiene at the CLEVELAND LYCEUM. In 1839 he appeared on the science program at the Ohio Medical Convention meeting in Cleveland. He returned to New York in 1841, where 2 years later he died of consumption.

**PELTON, FREDERICK W.** (24 Mar. 1827–15 Mar. 1902), was a banker, soldier, pioneer, and mayor of Cleveland, 1871–73. Pelton was born in Chester, Conn., and came with his father to BROOKLYN in 1835. There he grew up on a farm and attended public schools. Having completed his work at the Brooklyn Academy, he entered into business with the office of Wheeler, Chamberlain, & Co. in Akron, which later relocated in Cleveland, bringing Pelton back to the city. From 1858–67, he worked in the ship chandler business. During the CIVIL WAR, Pelton served as a captain in Co. E of the 1st Ohio Artillery and in the

8th Independent Battery. After the war, he became secretary of the Buckeye Insurance Co. He also joined the Halcyon lodge and became a 33d-degree Mason. In 1865, Pelton was elected to city council; he served as its president from 1866–69. He also served as county treasurer. In 1871 he was elected mayor and as such headed a committee to find a bridge site for the SUPERIOR VIADUCT.

After his term as mayor, Pelton retired to private life. He became president of the Citizen's Savings & Loan Assoc., which he had founded in 1868. He also was a founder of the RIVERSIDE CEMETERY Assoc., of which he became director in 1876. He was later a director of the People's Savings & Loan Co., as well as the president of the Masonic Mutual Life Insurance Co. In 1886 Pelton returned to office, serving on the board of the House of Correction (1886–89) and as a director on the board of the city's workhouse (1889–91). After serving these terms, he retired completely from public life. Pelton married Susan Dennison on 26 Aug. 1848. The couple had 7 children.

**PENNSYLVANIA RAILROAD.** *See* **CONRAIL**

**PENTON/IPC, INC.,** a publisher of business and technical trade magazines, directories, and handbooks, is descended from 2 old-line Cleveland firms, the Penton Publishing Co. and the Industrial Publishing Co. Founded by John A. Penton in 1904, Penton Publishing brought together 3 local trade magazines: *Iron Trade Review, Foundry,* and *Marine Review.* Through the years, Penton grew with Cleveland to become, during the 1920s, one of the nation's largest business magazine publishers. Two of its most influential magazines, *Steel* (now *Industry Week*) and *Machine Design,* first appeared at that time. In 1930, Irving B. Hexter founded the Industrial Publishing Co., issuing its first monthly magazine, *Industry & Welding* (now *Welding Design & Fabrication*). Like Penton, IPC grew with the times, establishing other trade magazines, such as *Hydraulics & Pneumatics* and *Precision Metals.*

In 1964, the Pittway Corp., a conglomerate with interests in real estate and the manufacture of home fire alarms, acquired Industrial Publishing. Used by Pittway as the nucleus of a publishing empire, IPC expanded greatly from 1964–75 by adding other business publications. In 1976, Pittway acquired Penton, then merged its operations with those of IPC to create Penton/IPC, Inc. Since 1976, Penton/IPC has moved into other activities, all related to business communications. They include Saddlebrook, a Florida condominium-convention center complex; Curtin & Pease, direct-mail marketers; Rick Reinert Productions, a film animator in California; and Penton Learning Systems, which offers courses and seminars for business and professional people. Company headquarters are at 1111 Chester Ave., Cleveland, Ohio 44114.

**PEOPLES-HOPE UNITED METHODIST CHURCH** had its origins in 1845 as the First Methodist Episcopal (German) Church, and through merger with several other historic churches, it remained a vital west side congregation in 1986. As the German Mission Society, 13 congregants met in homes until 1848, when the church acquired a lot on Prospect between Erie and Ontario and built a church at a cost of $2,000. In 1860, Erie St. or German Methodist Episcopal Church, as it was then called, sold its building and constructed a new church at Erie and Prospect with the proceeds. To distinguish itself from another German ME church that it founded on the west side (with which it would later merge), the church changed its name to First Methodist Episcopal (German) in 1870. The church moved again in 1878, to Scovill and Sterling (E. 30th), and then

to E. 71st and Cedar in 1906. The First ME Church (German) merged with St. Paul's at Bridge and Harbor in 1922. This congregation traced itself to the Ohio City Mission at Lorain and McLean (W. 26th), begun in 1853 by the Methodist Episcopal Society from the east side church. Within 5 years, the congregation split off from the mission to become the German ME Church, its name until 1881, when it became St. Paul's ME Church (German). When the German Methodist Conference dissolved in 1933 and became part of the Northeast Ohio Conference, St. Paul's was one of 5 affected German ME congregations in the area. (The others were Bethany, Church of the Cross, Zion, and Emanuel in Berea.)

As its neighborhood changed and congregants moved away, St. Paul's merged with the Franklin Blvd. Methodist Church to become WESLEY METHODIST CHURCH in 1947. Also a well-established congregation, Franklin was begun in 1833 as the Hanover St. Church; after a merger with the York St. Methodist Church in 1866, it experimented with names but settled on the name Franklin Blvd. Methodist in 1867. The church building at W. 32nd and Franklin featured a 2-ton replica of the Liberty Bell that once crashed through 2 floors to the basement. It was rehung in time to announce the armistice ending WORLD WAR I. Wesley merged in 1973 with the Hope United Methodist Church, an amalgam of the First United Brethren Church (founded 1854) and Emanuel Evangelical Church (founded 1865). Hope, at W. 42nd and Orchard, was noted for its work with the Puerto Rican and Ukrainian communities, and at Christmas, carols were sung in Spanish, English, and German. The church also provided facilities for a Puerto Rican congregation under Rev. Daniel Rodriguez. When he became the assistant pastor at Wesley United Methodist, that church became the site of social services and worship for the Spanish-speaking community. Though both Hope and Wesley adapted to changes in the neighborhood, both lost members with freeway construction and were beset with leadership and financial problems. The product of their merger, the Hope-Wesley United Methodist Church, was further strengthened by a final merger in 1985 with the Peoples United Methodist Church (est. 1894 as the Gordon Ave. Methodist Church). The Peoples-Hope United Methodist Church is located at 1880 W. 65th St.

Hope-Wesley United Methodist Church Records, WRHS.

**PEPPER PIKE** is a city located 13 mi. east of Cleveland and bounded by LYNDHURST and MAYFIELD HTS. on the north, HUNTING VALLEY on the east, WOODMERE, ORANGE, and MORELAND HILLS on the south, and BEACHWOOD on the west. Incorporated as a city in 1970, Pepper Pike operates under the mayor-council form of government. It occupies 7 sq. mi. In 1815, the first pioneers began settling in Orange Twp., formally organized in 1820, which included the area comprising the modern communities of Pepper Pike, Orange, Moreland Hills, Hunting Valley, and Woodmere. Orange Twp. developed during the first 100 years primarily as a farming community. By the late 1880s, cheesemaking had become the primary industry of the area. Although the community was still heavily rural at the turn of the century, the operation of the Chagrin Falls-Cleveland interurban railway made it accessible to many suburban residents. Most of the automobile roads in the area remained unimproved until the 1930s. During the 1920s, the VAN SWERINGEN brothers began purchasing farmland in the township as part of their comprehensive plan to develop the entire district from SHAKER HTS. to the CHAGRIN RIVER. The Van Sweringens' plan to subdivide the area laid the groundwork for changes affecting the area for the next 50 years. As the population increased, so did the need for more local government representation. In 1924, residents of northern Orange Twp. voted to separate, and the village of Pepper Pike was incorporated. That was the first separation action of what was eventually to lead to the creation of 5 different communities. An emphasis on the rural and residential character of the community led to the development of Pepper Pike as a city of upper-middle-income residents. The population was 5,933 in 1970, increasing to only 6,177 in 1980. Pepper Pike is part of the Orange School District, with 2 elementary, 1 junior high, and 1 senior high school. The school district is the city's largest employer. Pepper Pike is home to URSULINE COLLEGE and BRENTWOOD, SUBURBAN, and ST. LUKE'S hospitals. Recreational facilities include racquetball clubs, a golf course, the Pepper Pike Club, and the Orange Branch of the CUYAHOGA COUNTY PUBLIC LIBRARY.

Fant, Kathleen Griffin, *Orange Township . . . Orange Community, a History from 1815 to 1924* (1982), Orange Community Historical Society.

**PEPPERCORN, BERYL** (25 Apr. 1892–28 May 1969), was one of Cleveland's most progressive, competent, and respected labor leaders. As manager of the Cleveland-area Amalgamated Clothing Workers of America, he greatly aided the workers in the men's clothing industry to organize and lift themselves out of the sweatshop conditions. On the way to establishing one of the stronger unions in Cleveland, he also developed good relations with management, other unions, and the community. Peppercorn became aware of the sweatshop conditions in the clothing industry at the age of 9 when he went to work in a tailor shop in his native Austria. His family migrated to America a few years later and eventually settled in Cleveland ca. 1906. Peppercorn soon became active in the labor movement. He joined the union at his tailor shop at 15 and shortly after that was chosen shop manager. In 1914, he assisted in bringing the newly formed ACWA into Cleveland to organize the industry. He was rewarded for his early work in this local union by assuming its leadership, as manager of the Cleveland Joint Board, in 1924.

Successes were few and far between for the ACWA and Peppercorn in those early years. However, Peppercorn's persistent organizing efforts finally paid off in 1934 when one of the most formidable nonunion firms, JOSEPH & FEISS, recognized the ACWA after a strike by its workers. This victory inspired other clothing workers in nonunion shops, and by 1935, Peppercorn had negotiated contracts between the ACWA and almost all of the men's clothing companies in the Cleveland area. Encouraged by his success in the ACWA, Peppercorn became more involved in the general labor movement. He and the ACWA had always advocated an industrial union, and thus they were quick to leave the AFL in 1935 and to help in establishing the CIO in Cleveland. In 1937, Peppercorn was one of the organizers of the local, central body of the CIO, the CLEVELAND INDUSTRIAL UNION COUNCIL, and became its first president.

As CIUC head, Peppercorn showed his integrity and leadership qualities. Not only did he have to struggle with the rival AFL unions in the early years of the CIO, but, more important, he also had to purge the CIO of the Communist leaders and unions that had infiltrated it. Peppercorn played an integral role in organizing other nonunion industries for the CIO. He also encouraged the ACWA and other CIO unions to commit themselves to political activ-

ities. He aided them in the formation of the Labor's League for Political Action. With WORLD WAR II, Peppercorn became involved in various community affairs in support of the war effort. In 1958, after 34 years of service, Peppercorn resigned as manager of the Cleveland Joint Board. His reputation as a fair and responsible labor leader was reflected in the fact that not only did the ACWA honor him several times in his later years, but other labor unions and the clothing trade employers also did so.

Beryl Peppercorn Papers, WRHS.

**PERK, RALPH.** *See* **MAYORAL ADMINISTRATION OF RALPH PERK**

**PERKINS, ANNA "NEWSPAPER ANNIE,"** was a fixture on PUBLIC SQUARE in the 1890s. She acquired the sobriquet "Newspaper Annie" from her occupation of selling the *CLEVELAND PRESS*. She was also conspicuous for her advocacy of women's dress reform, which she exemplified in a self-devised costume of tennis cap, cropped hair, men's jacket, knee-length white duck trousers, and cotton stockings. Although she came to Cleveland from Berlin Hts., Ohio, one account placed her birth in Green Springs, Ohio, sometime in the late 1840s. She was the daughter of a carpenter and joiner known as "Boss" Perkins, who moved the family to Berlin Hts. It was there that she developed her ideas on feminism and selected poetry as her vocation.

Finding her unconventional lifestyle incompatible with small-town life, Perkins came to Cleveland sometime in the late 1880s. She brought with her privately printed copies of a self-explanatory poem entitled "What Is It?", apparently the only example of her work that has survived outside of occasional local newspaper contributions. She earned a living by selling the *Press* on the southeast corner of Ontario and Public Square. Living alone, she occupied a sparsely furnished room in the Bradley Block downtown, and later on Detroit Ave. on the near west side. Among her other idiosyncrasies were vegetarianism, hydrotherapy, and spelling reform, to which she conformed by spelling her name "Ana Purkin."

After an initial period marked by ridicule and harassment, Perkins seems by most accounts to have earned the tolerant respect of Clevelanders. She became a kind of elder statesman among the city's newsboys and a frequent speaker at such clubs as the Franklin and the Sorosis. A favorite piece of Cleveland folklore related how grocer W. P. Southworth, seeing her shivering in the winter cold in front of his store, escorted her across the street into Hull & Dutton's to outfit her with a men's overcoat. Anna Perkins died of typhoid fever in St. Alexis Hospital on 1 Feb. 1900. After a simple service arranged by local clubwomen, her body was returned to Berlin Hts. for burial in accordance with her wishes.

**PERKINS, JOSEPH** (5 July 1819–22 Aug. 1885), a businessman and philanthropist, was one of the leading benefactors of Cleveland charities in the late 19th century. During the last 2 years of his life, he served in the U.S. House of Representatives. Perkins was born in Warren, Ohio, to a wealthy family. He graduated from Marietta College in 1839 and returned to Warren to work for his father in the railroad business. He came to Cleveland in 1852 to become president of the Bank of Commerce; he served in that position until 1872. He was also president of the Cleveland & Mahoning Railroad and had interests in several other companies and banks. Perkins was one of the city's most active citizens. He was one of the founders of the WESTERN RESERVE HISTORICAL SOCIETY;

was the first president of the Cleveland City Hospital (later Lakeside), in 1866; and contributed $5,000 toward the purchase of the Holden property for the Case and Western Reserve campuses. He served as a trustee for Western Reserve College from 1846–85. A founder of LAKE VIEW CEMETERY, he served on the public committee to raise funds for the GARFIELD MONUMENT. As a philanthropist, Perkins's gifts to city charities were extensive, particularly to homes for orphans and the aged. He gave large amounts of money to the convent of the Good Shepherd (a Catholic home for girls) and to the Protestant Orphan Asylum. In 1869 he donated a house for use as a retreat for "unfortunate" women. A few years later, he funded the building of a house for aged women. While on the Ohio Board of Charities, Perkins devised a system of classifying prisoners and developed a plan for controlling the state's infirmary system. He married Martha Steele of Marietta in 1840.

**PERKINS, ROGER GRISWOLD** (17 May 1874–28 Mar. 1936), scientist and professor at the medical school of Western Reserve University, was responsible for the filtration and chlorination of Cleveland's water supply. Born in Schenectady, N.Y., Perkins was the son of Maurice Perkins, a professor of chemistry at Union College. He graduated Phi Beta Kappa from Union in 1893 and received an A.B. from Harvard in 1894 and a medical degree from Johns Hopkins in 1898. That year he came to Cleveland for his residency in pathology at Lakeside Hospital. He began his teaching career in 1899 as a demonstrator in pathology at WRU. He remained until 1930, appointed to professorships in pathology, bacteriology, and preventive medicine. In 1914 he became head of the newly established department of hygiene and bacteriology.

Perkins's most important contribution was the investigation of the city's water supply in order to eradicate typhoid. He began work in 1901 upon receiving a fellowship grant from the Rockefeller Foundation to study bacteria. At that time the incidence of typhoid in Cleveland was very high, in some years approaching 5,000 cases. Appointed city bacteriologist in 1906 and 1913, Perkins conducted experiments in the diagnostic and sanitary laboratory set up at WRU. He established, and became chief of, the Bureau of Laboratories of Cleveland's Div. of Health. He held this post from 1914–23. The result of his studies was the isolation and identification of the streptococcus mucosus, which Perkins was the first to describe, along with Wm. T. Howard. Filtration of Lake Erie water was established under his advice and guidance. During the winter of 1910–11, Perkins conducted experiments to determine the possibility of chlorinating the city's water. The Water Dept. considered chlorination only as an emergency measure until full filtration could be achieved. Chlorine treatments began in 1911, only after much convincing of the Water Dept. and the general population. When citizens complained that the water tasted bad, erroneously blaming the chlorine, the treatments were reduced, and the incidence of typhoid escalated. Full chlorination and filtration was achieved in 1925.

Although ineligible for active service, Perkins served in WORLD WAR I as scientific attache at the U.S. embassy in Paris. He became director of the Sanitation Div. of the American Red Cross Commission to the Balkan States. He was awarded the Order of the Crown of Romania and the Order of the Serbian Red Cross. Perkins was also interested in the purification of milk and food, and in his capacity as director of laboratories for the city, he introduced and maintained efficient food inspection and helped suppress the sale of patent medicines. He formed the Cleveland

Health Council in 1925 and was a member of the American Public Health Assoc.'s Committee on Research & Standards. In this capacity he contributed heavily to the adoption of bacteriological methods for examining milk and water. Perkins was also a member of the ACADEMY OF MEDICINE in Cleveland, the American Assoc. for the Advancement of Science, the Society of American Bacteriologists, and the American Assoc. of Pathologists & Bacteriologists.

Married in 1905 to Edna Brush, the daughter of CHAS. F. BRUSH, Perkins became a trustee and activities planner for the BRUSH FOUNDATION. He was interested in anthropology and human growth patterns and helped develop the Hamann Museum, which contained human and anthropoid skeletons for study. A book collector, he bequeathed his large library to the Cleveland Medical Library in 1936. Perkins retired to Providence, R.I., in 1930, where he died.

Roger Griswold Perkins Papers, Allen Memorial Medical Library Archives.

The **PERRY MONUMENT** commemorating the victory at the Battle of Lake Erie by Commodore Oliver Hazard Perry (1785–1819) was sculpted by Wm. Walcutt and dedicated on 10 Sept. 1860 in the center of Cleveland's PUBLIC SQUARE. Figures of a midshipman and a sailor boy, also sculpted by Walcutt, were placed on either side of it in 1869. In 1878, the statue was relocated to the southeast section of Public Square. It remained there until 1892, when the SOLDIERS & SAILORS MONUMENT replaced it. The Perry Monument was placed in storage until ca. 1894, when it was relocated at a small lake in WADE PARK near UNIVERSITY CIRCLE. The monument was moved again in 1913 to make way for the construction of the CLEVELAND MUSEUM OF ART, to a location in GORDON PARK on Lake Erie. In 1929, the EARLY SETTLERS ASSOC. commissioned the casting of 2 bronze replicas to replace the deteriorated original monument; one was sold to the state of Rhode Island, and the second replaced the original in Gordon Park. The Walcutt original was given to the city of Perrysburg, Ohio, where it was positioned to overlook a main thoroughfare of the city.

Perry Monument Commission Records, WRHS.

The **PERRY-PAYNE BUILDING** at 740 Superior Ave. W. was built in 1888–89 by HENRY B. PAYNE, prominent lawyer and railroad executive, who named it for himself and his wife, daughter of Nathan Perry, Jr. The building was occupied primarily by shipping and iron-ore company offices. The Perry-Payne represents the climax of a stage in commercial office construction before the introduction of the all-steel structural frame. The transition from masonry to iron construction, generally explained in terms of the work of the Chicago School, developed independently in several cities. In Cleveland it is seen primarily in the work of FRANK E. CUDELL (1844–1916) and J. N. Richardson (1837–1902). Three of their key buildings were still standing in the 1980s—the Geo. Worthington Bldg. at 802 W. St. Clair (1882), the Root & McBride-Bradley Bldg. on W. 6th St. (1884), and the Perry-Payne. In each one the ratio of window area to supporting masonry wall was increased, made possible in part by the use of interior iron columns. Where the two earlier buildings have wooden floors, the Perry-Payne has floors of tile and concrete. In addition, the Perry-Payne had an 8-story interior court with a glass roof, but it was floored over at a later date. Builders, architects, and other visitors came to Cleveland from considerable distances to inspect the building, its structure, and its light court during the early years of its existence.

**PERUSEK, HARVEY GREGORY** (1888–7 June 1940), was a Slovenian artist and art teacher who came to Cleveland from Yugoslavia at age 14. Several of his paintings won prizes at art shows in Chicago in 1930 and 1932, and his *Slovene Village* is in the permanent collection at the CLEVELAND MUSEUM OF ART. In Cleveland, Perusek founded the Yugoslav School of Art and served as its director and instructor. He also became director of the city's Crafts & Art Ctr., 10013 Detroit Ave. Showings of Perusek's and his students' work were held at the SLOVENIAN NATL. HOME in the 1930s.

**PETTIBONE CLEVELAND** (a division of the Pettibone Corp.) existed for many years as the Cleveland Frog & Crossing Co., which was started in 1884 by Geo. C. Lucas to implement his idea for making railroad frogs from steel rails instead of cast iron. He approached N. P. Bowler, owner of a small foundry in the FLATS, and suggested forming a company to manufacture the frogs. Bowler agreed, and within a few years, the patented product that permitted a train traveling on one track to pass over an intersecting track was so popular that the partners built a new factory on an acre of land at 6917 Bessemer. Cleveland Frog & Crossing had some of the most specialized frog-making equipment in the country. By 1893, the company employed 250, counted as its customers all the major railroads, and used over 2,000 tons of steel and wrought iron annually. Meanwhile, its product line had expanded to include switches, switch stands, guard stands, guardrails, and special track and curves. The factory covered 10 acres by 1924.

After Bowler died in 1909, Lucas, the general manager, brought in Washington W. Balkwill, who had been involved in the founding of the company, to help operate it. In 1949, Balkwill's son and heir, George, enmeshed the business in a 3-year legal battle over his attempted sale of the controlling stock to a Chicago agent for the Pettibone Milliden Corp. of Illinois. The court ruled that his sale was legal. The new owners set up the Pettibone Ohio Corp. as a successor to Cleveland Frog & Crossing, which was called Pettibone Cleveland after 1983. The subsidiary quickly established itself as the country's second-largest producer of switches, crossings, frogs, guardrails, switch stands, and rail braces. Among its leading products is the "Pettibone Speed Swing Loader," a piece of equipment used by many railroads during construction and maintenance of track right-of-way. Other subsidiaries of Pettibone (since 1969 the Pettibone Corp.) manufactured equipment for metals and chemical processing; construction; foundry operations; materials handling; and logging. The corporation had sales revenue of $200 million for 1984 and employed 2,200 worldwide and 100 locally.

**PHILANTHROPY.** Philanthropy in Cleveland sprang from a strong religious impulse. In the 20th century there has been more of an effort to develop the modern professions, especially MEDICINE and social work. But in the 19th century, the religious influence was direct. The fledgling lake port's first relief agency, the WESTERN SEAMEN'S FRIEND SOCIETY, was organized in 1830 by BENJAMIN ROUSE, an agent of the American Sunday-School Union. Rouse's desire to promote moral values as well as to provide emergency food and shelter gave his efforts a philanthropic, and not merely a charitable, purpose. The MARTHA WASHINGTON & DORCAS SOCIETY (1843) was also organized for the broader purpose of "retarding intemperance," as well as for the relief of poverty; its successors, including the Cleveland Women's Temperance Union (1850) and the Ladies Bethel Aid Society (1867), all offered Protestant forms of "Christian philanthropy." REBECCA CROMWELL ROUSE and several of the other Protestant churchwomen who led these organizations raised nearly $1 million through the SOLDIERS' AID SOCIETY OF NORTHERN OHIO between 1861–68, not only to meet the needs of Union soldiers but also to support the strict social and moral discipline advocated by the U.S. Sanitary Commission. The religious basis of philanthropy led to complementary and sometimes competing efforts, not only among the Protestant denominations but, more significantly, competition among Protestants, CATHOLICS, and JEWS. With their strong religious emphasis, few of the 19th century's benevolent institutions transcended the inward-looking purposes of a mutual-benefit society. To complement Protestant poor-relief efforts, in 1852 Bp. LOUIS AMADEUS RAPPE called to Cleveland the SISTERS OF CHARITY, who provided philanthropy in a Catholic spirit; as the Jewish population grew, a Hebrew Benevolent Society appeared in 1855. Although the city government provided a larger share of the meager assistance deemed necessary to sustain the very poor after 1855, religious participation in this field continued; as late as 1901, Mayor TOM L. JOHNSON appointed the pastor of the Cedar Ave. Church of Christ, HARRIS R. COOLEY, as the city's director of charities.

After the CIVIL WAR, private philanthropy emphasized the creation of more specialized institutions. Orphan asylums appeared first. Bp. Rappe established ST. VINCENT'S for boys and ST. MARY'S for girls as early as 1851; the Protestants who had created the SOCIETY FOR RELIEF OF THE POOR founded the Cleveland Orphan Asylum in 1852. The German Methodist Orphan Asylum and the Jewish Orphan Asylum, originally intended in part for the children of soldiers killed in the Civil War, followed in 1864 and 1869. When hospitals and homes for "foundlings"—abandoned infants—appeared in the 1870s and 1880s, they, too, were allied with the major religions. The courts, which were the key government agencies of the period, supported this pattern by assigning foundlings and orphans according to their parents' known or supposed religious affiliation. After 1876, the state government also empowered the Cleveland Humane Society to remove children from cruel or neglectful parents and to place them in ORPHANAGES or foster homes; but the society's funds came from private contributions. Like the orphanages, new facilities intended to encourage morality and good health among the young people who flocked to the small but rapidly growing industrial city on the lake were also founded by wealthy merchants who acted through religious associations. Protestants started the YOUNG MEN'S CHRISTIAN ASSOC. in the mid-1850s; they revived it in 1867 and added the YOUNG WOMEN'S CHRISTIAN ASSOC. a year later. Benefactors quickly provided dormitory and recreation halls that were unusually large for a city of Cleveland's size, but not large enough to discourage the WOMAN'S CHRISTIAN TEMPERANCE UNION (WCTU) from establishing a network of alcohol-free "friendly inns" in the 1870s and a Training Home for Friendless Girls in 1893.

Despite the best efforts of the YMCA and the WCTU, Cleveland had its full share of unwed mothers, prostitutes, alcoholics, and enfeebled old people who were unable to earn a living. Pious and wealthy citizens tried to meet the needs of these people through an ever more diverse array of special institutions. Homes for "unfortunate women" who had fallen into PROSTITUTION or become pregnant outside wedlock included the Catholic House of the Good

Shepherd (1869) and the Stillman Witt Home attached to the Protestant Orphan Asylum (1873). The private, general-purpose relief organizations of the antebellum years were reorganized to provide employment advice and (largely religious) family counseling. The Catholic LITTLE SISTERS OF THE POOR (1870), the Protestant YWCA (1868), and the Jewish Home (1877) all provided homes for some of the elderly. Several Protestants, concerned about the living conditions, the educational opportunities, and the political views of Cleveland's rapidly expanding immigrant communities, established HIRAM HOUSE (1896), Goodrich House (1896) (see GOODERICH-GANNETT NEIGHBORHOOD CTR.), ALTA HOUSE (1898), and other social SETTLEMENT HOUSES. The Jewish Council Educational Alliance, forerunner of the JEWISH COMMUNITY CTR., offered comparable facilities after 1897. During the 19th century, local governments played a much smaller role in these fields in general relief. Individual towns did, on occasion, provide tuition and other support to private schools, ranging from the Methodist mission's Cleveland City Industrial School to E. CLEVELAND's Presbyterian-sponsored Shaw Academy, but this practice came to an end as public school systems developed. In a pattern that was to become much more common in the 20th century, kindergartens pioneered in the 1880s by the private Day Nursery & Free Kindergarten Assoc. were adopted by public school districts in the 1890s.

Faced with the expanding population of a rapidly growing, polyglot industrial city and with a larger and ever more varied set of benevolent institutions, Cleveland's philanthropists began to introduce new forms of organization after 1880. They established a CHARITY ORGANIZATION SOCIETY to discourage mendicancy and promote efficiency, in 1881, just a year after Buffalo adapted the English Charity Organization Society idea to American conditions. Three years later, the Charity Organization Society merged with Cleveland's leading Protestant counseling group to create the Bethel Associated Charities. But the charity organization emphasized efficiency and promoted a comprehensive concern for the region's entire population, which included growing proportions of Catholics and Jews. For these reasons, it did not mix easily with traditional religious benevolence. "Charity cannot be organized like the Steel Trust, or run by paid clerks," an evangelical Protestant wrote indignantly at the end of the century. "Charity means love; it is a personal thing. Can you picture Christ organizing love, card-indexing the good and the bad?"

Religious influence was less marked in the field of cultural philanthropy—a field that was little cultivated in 19th-century Cleveland. The private associations that brought Western Reserve University from Hudson, Ohio, to Cleveland and created Case Institute of Technology at the beginning of the 1880s emphasized secular rather than religious purposes. They also received important support from the city government when they located on the attractive grounds of WADE PARK, created by JEPTHA H. WADE with private funds but developed and maintained by the city. Yet religious influence did persist in the field of higher education. Case Institute and WRU were amply supplied with chapels, Protestants gave generously to a wide variety of denominational colleges in Ohio and elsewhere, and in Cleveland, Catholics started several institutions of higher learning to complement their system of parochial elementary and diocesan secondary schools (see PAROCHIAL EDUCATION). A more tightly organized, more professional, and in some ways less religious organization of philanthropy dominated Cleveland after 1900. By 1920, Greater Cleveland had taken advantage of the opportunities opened by its rapid growth into a modern metropolis and was earning a national reputation for the innovative and unusually efficient organization of its philanthropy. Business leaders, especially bankers, corporate lawyers, and the leaders of the very large corporations that made steel, oil, paint, machine tools, and clothing and that had suddenly become such large employers in the city, took the lead. These leaders created 3 new institutions, the charity federation, the community chest, and the community foundation, that transformed philanthropy not only in Cleveland but also throughout the U.S.

In 1900, a Committee on Benevolent Associations of the Chamber of Commerce began to look for ways to rationalize the raising and distribution of funds and to evaluate and monitor the work of the many specialized institutions that had been created in the decades after the Civil War. Following the example of the Fed. for Jewish Charities (1903), the suggestions of insurance executive MARTIN MARKS, and the advice of iron ore magnate SAMUEL MATHER, this committee proposed the creation of a Fed. for Charity & Philanthropy. In 1913 the federation carried out the first campaign in the U.S. designed to raise funds for a large number of separate homes, clinics, and family services, regardless of Protestant, Catholic, or Jewish sponsorship. The campaign was so successful—it increased the number of contributors to these institutions from a few hundred to over 6,000—it became the model for the Red Cross and Victory Chest drives carried out across the nation to meet the needs created by WORLD WAR I. Cleveland's Community Chest (which evolved into the UNITED WAY), also the first in the U.S., continued to run unified fund-raising campaigns after the war. In 1919, more than 148,000 donors responded to its appeal.

Four factors account for the success of Cleveland's united fundraising campaigns. From the beginning, they represented a truly united effort, because the wealthy individuals who had traditionally supported particular institutions were willing to allow them to become part of a communitywide federation, evaluated and funded by a highly professional central agency. Also from the very beginning, the united campaigns were mounted by some of the most highly skilled fundraisers to be found in the U.S. These fundraisers worked in an unusually supportive environment. Cleveland, like Detroit, Pittsburgh, and other manufacturing cities that grew rapidly between 1890 and 1930 (and unlike New York, Boston, or Philadelphia), had a small number of large integrated manufacturing corporations, including GENERAL ELECTRIC, UNITED STATES STEEL, JONES & LAUGHLIN STEEL, FORD, and General Motors, that employed a large portion of its labor force; these corporations strongly supported the Community Chest through the rapidly developing personnel departments. Finally, although the new organization of philanthropy reduced the influence of organized religion, religious leaders of all faiths gave the unified drives their wholehearted support.

Within the new philanthropic system, the Fed. for Charity & Philanthropy continued to evaluate individual institutions, study the city's needs, and distribute the funds raised by the Community Chest. In studying the city's needs, it was quickly joined by the CLEVELAND FOUNDATION. Organized by FREDERICK GOFF, president of the Cleveland Trust Co. (now AMERITRUST), the Cleveland Foundation was the nation's first community foundation. Between 1914–24, it made remarkably effective use of the survey idea originated in charity organization societies in England and New York and applied with great fanfare in the Pittsburgh Survey of 1909. The Cleveland Foundation hired prominent experts—Chicago welfare director Sherman C. Kingsley, Leonard P. Ayres of New York City's

Russell Sage Foundation (which had pioneered the social survey), WRU's RAYMOND A. MOLEY, Roscoe Pound and Felix Frankfurter of the Harvard University Law School—to evaluate Cleveland's provisions for welfare, education, criminal justice, and recreation. The resulting studies attracted widespread attention, and Cleveland's community foundation, like its Community Chest, was copied in many other large cities.

The highly professional studies sponsored by the Cleveland Foundation effectively set priorities for the city's private institutions. They played a role, for example, in WRU's 1916 decision to raise funds to support a School of Applied Social Sciences to train the professional social workers who were rapidly replacing the pious, temperance-minded ladies who had carried out "friendly visits" to the homes of the Protestant and Jewish poor since the 1840s. They encouraged the creation of the Metropolitan Park System (see CLEVELAND METROPARKS) and, less effectively, called attention to the needs of the city's rapidly expanding population of BLACKS. From time to time, the foundation's reports also shaped public policies in such fields as EDUCATION, criminal justice, and recreation. By increasing the influence of corporate leaders and of the distinguished professionals they admired, Cleveland's new philanthropic institutions reduced the influence of religious congregations on poor relief, family counseling, and youth-service activities. Protestants and Jews responded by creating new, more centralized organizations to formulate and express their common views on social questions. Catholics joined Protestants and Jews in creating new centrally managed campaigns to raise funds for specifically religious educational, chaplaincy, and outreach activities.

A preliminary effort to create a Christian Fed. of Cleveland in 1900 had accompanied the decision of the Bethel Associated Charities to lay aside its traditional Protestant identity and change its name to Cleveland Associated Charities. By 1911, Cleveland's Protestants had worked out a more permanent form of association, the Federated Churches of Cleveland (now known as the INTER-CHURCH COUNCIL OF GREATER CLEVELAND). Its purpose was to "improve the social and religious life of the growing city," in part by promoting "comity in religious work among the foreign populations of the city" and encouraging "united and aggressive action upon religious and social questions." In the 1920s, the Protestants added a concern for Christian education to its agenda, and in 1911 it returned to the roots laid down by Benjamin and Rebecca Rouse in the 1830s when the Federated Churches merged with the Cuyahoga County Sunday School Assoc. and undertook to train and equip Sunday school teachers in many Protestant churches. The JEWISH COMMUNITY FED., begun in 1903 and later expanded to accommodate Cleveland's growing Orthodox community, was still more effective in raising and allocating funds for Jewish educational and cultural institutions, ranging from Hebrew schools to the Jewish Community Ctr., as well as for benevolent institutions that included MT. SINAI Hospital and JEWISH FAMILY SERVICES. In 1919, the CATHOLIC CHARITIES CORP. was organized to carry out a similar unified drive for funds for specifically Catholic agencies and institutions.

After 1920, Cleveland philanthropy also reorganized old charitable institutions to make use of the new expertise. As social workers, psychologists, and other child-development specialists gained prominence, for example, the old orphanages were reorganized to care for handicapped, retarded, and disturbed children. Most Catholic orphanages were consolidated into the expanding facilities of PARMADALE after 1925; the Protestant Orphan Asylum

(BEECH BROOK) moved to Orange Twp. in 1926; and the Jewish Orphan Asylum moved into the new buildings of BELLEFAIRE in SHAKER HTS. in 1929. By the 1940s, most of these institutions were distinguished more for the particular character of their professional services, as evaluated by the FED. FOR COMMUNITY PLANNING, than for their religious affiliations, and many of them accepted children regardless of religious background. Funds for child protection and family counseling that previously had gone to the Humane Society and the Bethel Associated Charities, by 1940 went to organizations that styled themselves after the Children's Services agency and Family Services. In this manner, explicitly religious, counseling, and chaplaincy programs were separated.

The Depression and the New Deal reinforced the continuing tendency toward the specialization and professionalization of charitable organizations. When the Depression threw over ⅓ of Cleveland's labor force out of work, it was clearly impossible for private charity even to address the need for general relief. Municipal and state institutions had long supplemented the work of private orphanages and institutions for the mentally handicapped; these were considerably expanded after 1900, and again in the 1930s. Even more decisively, the New Deal established the policy of using government agencies, supplied with federal and state funds, to provide direct relief through Social Security, Aid to Dependent Children, and other programs. In 1935, over 1,000 of the social workers employed by the Family Service Society were moved, in a body, to the Cuyahoga County Welfare Dept., which now became responsible for administering Social Security, ADC, and other federally funded social-welfare programs. Private philanthropy's long-dominant role in the provision of counseling and the management of relief was permanently curtailed. Many traditional charitable organizations were thus forced to define new, more specialized and professional roles for themselves. And the Fed. for Community Planning found itself working with union and political leaders as well as with major donors and professional social workers to coordinate the work of *public* as well as *private* social agencies.

"Since 1900," one religious leader would observe in 1956, "the specialists have taken over, and the clergyman finds himself unable to communicate with the criminologist who runs the jail, the administrator who manages the hospital, the social worker who counsels. . . ." Cleveland philanthropy, thoroughly persuaded of the value of professional expertise, supported the triumph of the specialists in the professions and the arts as well as in what came to be known as the social services. It provided significant additional facilities and endowments for the private universities, both in Cleveland and elsewhere, whose graduate and professional faculties sought knowledge for the new professions and trained the new specialists. And it created, in UNIVERSITY CIRCLE, an extraordinary set of cultural institutions that appeal particularly to the city's managerial and professional workers.

In Cleveland itself, private philanthropy played an important role in the creation of unusually distinguished professional communities in the fields of medicine, engineering, LAW, social work, and MUSIC. Following the recommendations of the nationally influential *Cleveland Hospital & Health Survey* conducted under private auspices by Dr. Haven Emerson in 1920, the city's major donors moved several private hospitals to University Circle, built up the extraordinary facilities of UNIVERSITY HOSPITALS, Mt. Sinai Hospital, and ST. VINCENT CHARITY Hospital, and established a large endowment for Western Reserve University's Medical School (begun in 1843; University Circle bldgs. from 1924) and Frances Payne Bolton School of Nursing (1923). These facilities in turn made for the rich medical environment that allowed the private, independent CLEVELAND CLINIC to achieve great success by the 1960s. Private philanthropy also provided the funds needed to create the Case Institute of Technology and WRU's schools of Law and of Applied Social Sciences, which train many of the specialists employed by the city's notable engineering and law firms and social-work agencies. Many Clevelanders also made notable gifts to universities and colleges elsewhere in Ohio, the Midwest, and the Northeast. They established traditions of academic rigor and innovation at both WRU and Case Institute of Technology. Nevertheless, by 1986 they had not yet provided CASE WESTERN RESERVE UNIVERSITY (created by merger in 1967) with quite enough support to allow it to realize its full potential as a major comprehensive private research university serving both the metropolitan region and the nation at large.

Between 1880 and the 1960s, private philanthropy also sponsored much of the basic higher education available in Greater Cleveland. The Methodists maintained BALD-WIN-WALLACE COLLEGE in surburban BEREA, and Catholics supported the educational work that flowered into JOHN CARROLL UNIVERSITY and NOTRE DAME and URSULINE colleges. WRU sponsored a downtown branch, Cleveland College, and the YMCA set up Fenn College to provide night-school and business courses. With the transformation of Fenn College into CLEVELAND STATE UNIVERSITY in the mid-1960s, and the creation of CUYAHOGA COMMUNITY COLLEGE, private philanthropy saw this field become the responsibility of government. Apart from supporting a nationally distinguished School of Library Science at WRU from 1903 until its closure in 1986, private philanthropy similarly left libraries to public agencies, notably the great CLEVELAND PUBLIC LIBRARY.

In the cultural field, the highly organized character of Cleveland philanthropy is reflected in the extraordinary set of institutions gathered in University Circle. Priority there has long been given to music and art, and the result is 2 of the best institutions in the U.S., the CLEVELAND ORCHESTRA and the CLEVELAND MUSEUM OF ART. The symphony has been supported by endowments, by SEVERANCE HALL (on land made available by WRU), and by the Blossom Music Ctr. for summer concerts. Its musicians, together with others who teach and study at the CLEVELAND INSTITUTE OF MUSIC, WRU's Dept. of Music, Baldwin-Wallace College's programs for church musicians, and the CLEVELAND MUSIC SCHOOL SETTLEMENT, give Cleveland an unusually large and distinguished musical community. Extraordinary gifts have also provided the Cleveland Museum of Art with one of the 3 or 4 most distinguished comprehensive collections of painting and sculpture—and, over the years, with one of the most highly professional curatorial staffs—in the U.S. University Circle houses other cultural institutions, as well as CWRU and the University Hospitals and Cleveland Clinic medical complexes. By the 1970s, the CLEVELAND MUSEUM OF NATURAL HISTORY, the CLEVELAND HEALTH EDUCATION MUSEUM, and the GARDEN CTR. OF GREATER CLEVELAND had established national reputations for excellence in their fields, and the WESTERN RESERVE HISTORICAL SOCIETY had put together unusually strong collections of books, manuscripts, and automobiles. In 1957, Cleveland philanthropy created still another centrally managed, innovative organization, the University Circle Development Foundation, to provide land acquisition and real-estate management. Later, parking, and police services to all the private cultural

and educational institutions located in the area were established. Supported entirely by private funds, University Circle has carried out urban redevelopment and policing functions ordinarily assigned to public officials. Even more than its counterparts in the Hyde Park-Kenwood area near the University of Chicago and the Morningside Hts. area around Columbia University in New York, UNIVERSITY CIRCLE, INC., has served as a model for university and cultural institutions in other cities.

By the early 1950s, most large donors and fundraisers believed that Cleveland had about the right mix and the right number of private charitable, educational, and arts institutions and coordinating organizations. The challenge, they believed, was to keep those organizations operating according to the highest professional standards. When new tax laws encouraged the possessors of large fortunes to make large gifts after 1949, most of them chose to add to the endowment of existing institutions or to create new general-purpose foundations. Several new foundations, of which the largest was the GEO. GUND FOUNDATION, joined with the Cleveland Foundation in a continuing effort to direct philanthropic funds to the areas of greatest current need. By 1985, the combined endowments of these foundations amounted to nearly $750 million and provided the Cleveland area with one of the largest and most flexible sources of support for philanthropic activities available in any city in the U.S.

The demand for funds from foundations and annual fund drives alike rose abruptly after the mid-1960s. Many demands paralleled those of the past. Medical advances had created new needs for research and treatment facilities. The desire for first-rate THEATER and dance organizations increased the competition for the funds available for cultural philanthropy. Continuing efforts to sustain the highest standards in higher education, in the arts, and in counseling and medical services required funds that were difficult to find. But Cleveland's new problems—overt racial conflict, suburbanization, and the decline of the central city's population, the decline of heavy industry, and economic stagnation in general—presented the most difficult new challenges. The population and the tax base of Cleveland declined sharply, leaving the city's government incapable of maintaining all the activities it had taken on. PARKS fell into a sorry state for lack of routine maintenance; schools were disrupted by racial conflict and petty political squabbles; STREETS, BRIDGES, and sewers began to disintegrate. The Cleveland Public Library found it increasingly difficult to maintain its great research collections as the city's middle-class population moved to the suburbs. Its branch libraries struggled to meet the needs of their increasingly impoverished users, and new state funding formulas cut sharply into its revenues. Pressure to move these activities into private hands, especially the hands of philanthropic agencies, mounted.

Several long-established organizations moved vigorously to meet these challenges. The Protestant Fed. of Churches reorganized itself as the Greater Cleveland Interchurch Council and gave increasing emphasis to its efforts to promote interracial cooperation and to feed the hungry. The Fed. for Community Planning sought new ways to bring together the disparate agencies that were dealing with related problems, and to establish a common welfare agenda for the region. The Interchurch Council, the Fed. for Community Planning, and several individual religious congregations and private social agencies undertook to carry out new programs established and funded by the federal government. By the late 1970s, the Interchurch Council of Greater Cleveland was once again a major supplier of food and other direct material relief to the poor, just as its pred-

767

ecessors had been in the 19th century. The United Way, which had developed a large and highly professional staff of its own, in turn moved to take over many of the allocation and evaluation activities formerly carried out by the Fed. for Community Planning. In the 1980s, new government policies posed still more urgent questions. Government funds that had met more and more of the cost of social services, medical care, and education from 1964–75, had freed private funds for investment in research, specialized care, and the arts. When federal expenditures for domestic social purposes were capped after 1976 and cut after 1980, private philanthropy was pressed to replace them. The private institutional pattern established between 1900–20, like the pattern of government support begun in the 1930s and greatly expanded in the 1960s, met with new criticism. Once again philanthropic institutions, in Cleveland as throughout the U.S., were forced to reconsider their priorities and their methods of operation.

David C. Hammack
Case Western Reserve University

See also specific foundations.

The **PHILHARMONIC ORCHESTRA** was the first substantial orchestra in Cleveland drawing its members from the community. The orchestra was founded in 1881 by FERDINAND PUEHRINGER. Originally called the Philharmonic Society, it consisted of 30 amateur musicians. Professionals were added later. The Philharmonic was designed to combine musicians of all nationalities to form an orchestra with a permanent conductor. It was chiefly concerned with playing orchestral pieces. Puehringer was succeeded by Prof. Mueller Neuhoff, who expanded the orchestra's repertory to include opera productions. Franz X. Ahrens followed Mueller in 1889 and expanded the size of the orchestra from 40 to 60 musicians. Finally, under EMIL RING, the programs were enhanced and the performances improved. The orchestra became heavily indebted in 1893. Despite a reorganization in 1894, it was forced to disband in 1899.

The **PHILHARMONIC STRING QUARTET** was founded in 1886 by Geo. Lehman, A. Reinhardt, Julius Hermann, and Chas. Heydler (from the newly organized PHILHARMONIC ORCHESTRA). Its purpose was to bring to life the classics of music and to contribute to the cultural development of Cleveland. Concerts were given in Cleveland, Akron, Oberlin, Tiffin, and Erie. In 1888, Lehman went to Europe to continue his studies in music, and he was replaced by John Marquardt. EMIL RING, Franklin F. Bassett, and JAS. H. ROGERS assisted the Philharmonic String Quartet on piano for the works of Schubert and Schumann. In 1897, Sol Marcosson came into the quartet at their invitation from the FORTNIGHTLY MUSICAL CLUB. They were then considered to be the leading chamber music group in the city, not only because of their collective abilities but also because they added to the standard quartet repertory with works by Borodin, Faure, Franck, and Wolf. Chas. Heydler was the remaining original member in 1900. He also played cello with the Schubert or BECK STRING QUARTET. Sol Marcosson and Carl Dueringer played violins, and Jas. Johnston played the viola. CHAS. V. RYCHLIK replaced Dueringer as second violinist in 1908. In May 1917, the quartet was joined by JOHANN BECK (viola) and Oscar Eiler (violincello) to play Brahms's Sextet in B Flat, Opus 18 and Beck's Sextet in D Minor. The Philharmonic String Quartet dissolved in 1928.

Alexander, J. Heywood, *It Must Be Heard* (1981).

**PHILLIPS, JOHN** (19 Feb. 1879–May 1929), was a physician and member of the faculty of the Western Reserve University School of Medicine. He was also a founder and director of the CLEVELAND CLINIC FOUNDATION. Phillips was born in Welland, Ontario, Canada. He received his medical degree from the University of Toronto in 1903 and then moved to Cleveland, where he served as an intern at Lakeside Hospital until 1905, and as a resident in medicine until 1906. He joined the WRU faculty in 1906, becoming an assistant professor of therapeutics. His tenure at WRU was briefly interrupted between 1917–18 when he served as a captain in the medical corps of the U.S. Army. As a practicing physician, Phillips was mainly concerned with internal medicine and diseases of children. Phillips was one of the founders, with Drs. GEO. W. CRILE, FRANK E. BUNTS, and WM. E. LOWER, of the Cleveland Clinic Foundation, under the auspices of which the Cleveland Clinic was opened in 1921, and the Cleveland Clinic Hospital in 1924. With the other founders, Phillips established an endowment, enlarged by public donations, for care of the sick and for medical research. Although he continued as an assistant professor at WRU, he relinquished his duties as a practicing physician to devote time as a director of both the Cleveland Clinic and the Cleveland Clinic Hospital. As a physician, Phillips was variously associated with Lakeside Hospital, Babies Dispensary & Hospital, and St. John's Hospital. He contributed about 70 articles on subjects relating to internal medicine to various medical journals. He was a member of many medical societies, including the American College of Physicians; he was also a trustee of the CLEVELAND MEDICAL LIBRARY ASSOC. Phillips was married to the former Cordelia Sudderth. He was killed in the CLEVELAND CLINIC FIRE at age 50.

The **PHILLIS WHEATLEY ASSOCIATION,** a member of the GREATER CLEVELAND NEIGHBORHOOD ASSOC., offers social services and recreational opportunities to the residents of the E. 44th and Cedar area. It began in 1911 as a home for black working girls where vocational skills were taught. The home began as a dream of JANE EDNA HUNTER, who came to Cleveland in 1905 after nursing training at the Hampton Institute. While trying to accumulate the funds to open such a home, Hunter attended law school and passed the Ohio bar examination. By 1911, she had $1,500, which she used to open a boarding home for 10 women at E. 40th and Central. The number of residents soon strained the capacity of the 23-room house. By 1917, after an extensive fundraising effort, the association purchased a 3-story building to house 75 at E. 40th and Central. An adjoining building was purchased in 1919 to house social and educational activities and the Stephen School of Music. As Hunter envisioned, the home provided a wholesome atmosphere for working girls. Often from the rural South, the newcomers were the prey of con men, as well as employment agencies that lured them to Cleveland with free transportation in return for several months' salary. To make the girls feel at home, cafeteria food was prepared with a southern flair. Residents could improve their job skills through cooking and vocational classes offered at the association.

At the time of the founding of the PWA (which was named after America's first black woman poet), Hunter faced opposition from many blacks who objected to the establishment of a segregated institution. Some who felt themselves accepted in white society saw it as a "jim crow

768

hotel for black girls." Hunter finally won the approval of black ministers. However, she secured the broad financial backing she needed only through concessions to whites. She pursuaded Henry Sherwin, of the SHERWIN-WILLIAMS CO., to contribute to the enterprise but had to accept his condition that prominent white women be named to the board. Black leaders, including Hunter, realized that the association, by providing a black alternative, allowed whites who supported it to maintain a white-only YWCA. Keeping in mind the greater goal of establishing a refuge for black migrants, Hunter continued to secure white contributions. She was also criticized for the emphasis on training the girls in domestic skills, which would qualify them for positions that corresponded to the white stereotype of what black women should do. In 1927, the substantial support of the PWA allowed it to build a new 9-story building at 4450 Cedar Ave. As the philosophical debates of the early years subsided, the PWA was seen as an exemplary black self-help organization that permitted young girls to maintain their heritage and their self-respect. With the diminished need for group housing, the association concentrated on its recreation and cultural programs, and added daycare and neighborhood outreach services. The organization, at 4450 Cedar, provided child-development and daycare services to promote strengthened family living, group work among youth, nutrition programs, and support services for the elderly in the 1980s.

Phillis Wheatley Assoc. Records, WRHS.

The **PHILOSOPHICAL CLUB OF CLEVELAND** is an exclusive organization whose members convene biweekly for dinner and the reading and discussion of papers. The themes, authored in turn, address a variety of personal interests but concentrate on the topics of sociology, business and economics, arts and humanities, government, and science. The prototype of the club was the Cleveland Council of Sociology (later named the Chamber of Commerce Club), the roster of which expanded from 30 to approximately 100 as guests attained membership. Feeling that their participation was inhibited and that the informal atmosphere was declining, several members decided to develop a new society that would reestablish and stabilize the origins of the council; thus, by the efforts of Case School professors CHAS. H. BENJAMIN and CHAS. S. HOWE, the Philosophical Club was instituted during the summer of 1902, its first official meeting called in November of that year. The club's constitution (adopted Apr. 1911) specifies an active body of 30. New candidates are nominated upon the death or resignation of a member; memberships are confirmed by popular vote (with 2 blackballs necessary for denial) and do not exceed 30 days (unless extended, unanimously, in writing). Members of the Philosophical Club, like the original 20 men invited to its organizational session, are primarily east side residents engaged in college instruction, business, and other professional occupations. Affiliates have been identified predominantly in fields of medicine, law, banking, publishing, administration, science, industry, and trade; some, if not renowned in their practices at their times of admittance, occasionally have gained recognition during their terms of association. A representation of accomplished clubmen includes all Case School presidents since 1902; NEWTON D. BAKER; WHITING WILLIAMS; Chas. S. Brooks, traveling author and cofounder of the CLEVELAND PLAY HOUSE; and MEREDITH COLKET. Guest speakers have included Dr. John Stockwell, astronomer and author; Dr. Edward Dewey, savant and author on cycles; and EDWARD BLYTHIN. The latter two visitors ultimately were elected to membership. In 1985, the

purpose of the Philosophical Club of Cleveland remained to provide members the occasion for leisurely discourse of social perceptions.

Philisophical Club of Cleveland Records, WRHS.

## PICK-N-PAY. *See* FIRST NATIONAL SUPERMARKETS

**PICKANDS, JAMES S.** (15 Dec. 1839–14 July 1896), was a volunteer Civil War officer and cofounder of the PICKANDS MATHER & CO. of Cleveland. Pickands was born in Akron, Ohio, the son of Rev. Jas. D. Pickands. The family moved to Cleveland prior to 1860. He left a job as a cashier to enlist in Co. E, 1st Ohio Volunteer Infantry, on 16 Apr. 1861. He was promoted to corporal on 29 Apr., sergeant on 1 June, and 1st sergeant on 2 July. Pickands was mustered out with his company on 1 Aug. 1861. Hoping eventually to serve in the Regular Army as a career officer, he accepted an appointment in another volunteer unit—as major of the 124TH OVI, on 25 Oct. 1862. He was promoted to lieutenant colonel on 1 Jan. 1863. During the Atlanta Campaign, he was seriously wounded at the Battle of New Hope Church, Ga. (fought 25 and 27 May 1864), but recovered in time to be present at the battle of Nashville, Tenn., 15–16 Dec. 1864. He was promoted to colonel after the war ended on 20 June 1865.

In 1867, James and his brother, Henry S. Pickands, moved to Marquette, Mich., to seek their fortunes. James, in partnership with another Clevelander, Jay C. Morse, opened a hardware store, supplying goods to iron ore-mining companies. In 1870, James added a coal-fuel business to his moneymaking endeavors. By 1875, he had been elected mayor of Marquette, and in 1880 he formed the Taylor Iron Co. with Jay Morse. His wife, the former Caroline Martha Outhwaite of Cleveland, whom he had married in 1870, died of pneumonia on 17 May 1882, at Marquette. Grieving deeply, James moved back to Cleveland and formed the Pickands Mather & Co. in partnership with SAMUEL MATHER in 1883.

James later married Seville Hanna, sister to MARCUS HANNA, in 1887. His health began to fail in 1895, and he died at his home on Kennard (E.46th) St. a year later at age 57. He raised 3 sons with his first wife: Joseph, Henry S., and Jay M. Henry S. took over his father's partnership. Jay M. worked for the company until his sudden death in 1913. During his lifetime, Pickands had been president of the Western Reserve Natl. Bank, the Cleveland Chamber of Commerce, the Army-Navy Post of the Grand Army of the Republic, the military Order of the Loyal Legion of the U.S., and the Military Committee in charge of the dedication of the SOLDIERS & SAILORS MONUMENT, 4 July 1894.

Havinghurst, Walter, *Vein of Iron* (1958).
Lewis, George W., *The Campaigns of the One Hundred and Twenty-fourth Regiment* (1894).

**PICKANDS MATHER & COMPANY,** one of 4 major ore houses in the U.S., has its headquarters in Cleveland. A chief supplier of raw materials to the steel industry, it manages one of the largest fleets of freight carriers on the Great Lakes. Pickands Mather & Co. started in 1883 when SAMUEL MATHER joined Jay Morse and Col. JAMES PICKANDS in a partnership to deal in pig iron and coal. The company's initial interests were limited to 2 small mines in upper Michigan and a wooden steamer. Under senior partner Mather, the firm became a sales agent in the new iron ranges of Wisconsin and Minnesota during the 1880s and 1890s. To facilitate its business, Pickands Mather began to manage Great Lakes docks and acquire steamship companies. In 1913, the firm organized all of its vessel companies into the Interlake Steamship Co., the second-largest fleet operating on the Great Lakes, with 39 carriers.

In the early 1900s, the company broadened its services by securing interests in blast furnaces on the Lower Lakes. By the 1920s, it had become the second-largest producer of iron ore in the country. In 1929, the firm combined its 4 blast-furnace companies into the Interlake Iron Corp. It was at this time that the company expanded its interest in coal, having originally purchased coal mines in southwestern Pennsylvania in 1909 and later in West Virginia and Kentucky, which produced a total of 9 million tons annually. Over the years, Pickands Mather formed an alliance with the Youngstown Sheet & Tube Co., making a large investment in that steel firm. When CYRUS EATON attempted to take over Youngstown Sheet in 1929 as part of his plans for a huge conglomerate, the Midwest Steel Co., Pickands Mather intervened to protect its interests. The steel company was preserved, but at a severe cost to Pickands Mather. Henry Dalton and Elton Hoyt II guided the firm through the Depression and into the pressing demands of WORLD WAR II.

Pickands Mather was one of the first firms to research taconite in the late 1930s. In the 1940s, it formed its own company, the Erie Mining Co., in Minnesota to develop taconite pellets; it became a commercially successful venture by the mid-1950s. Simultaneously, Pickands Mather gained interests in the iron fields of Canada. By the 1980s, the firm produced 20% of all iron pellets in both countries. In 1960, Pickands Mather was incorporated. Thirteen years later, it became part of Moore McCormack Resources, Inc., a shipping company. Under Moore McCormack, Pickands Mather continues to manage 5 iron and 7 coal mines in North America as well as Australia and transports 12.5 million tons of cargo annually on the 11 vessels of its Interlake Steamship Co.

Dalton, Henry G., *Luncheon Commemorating the Fiftieth Anniversary of Pickands, Mather & Company* (1933).
Havinghurst, Walter, *Vein of Iron* (1958).
Pickands Mather & Co., *M/V James R. Barker* (1974?).

**PICKER INTERNATIONAL, INC.,** one of the world's leading manufacturers of medical diagnostic systems, began in New York in 1916. Jas. Picker, a druggist who came to the U.S. from Russia in 1901, supplied Kodak x-ray film and supplies to Mt. Sinai Hospital from his nearby drugstore. In 1916 he established the Jas. Picker Co., and in 1921 the Picker X-Ray Corp. began to manufacture x-ray units. Seeking to expand his line of diagnostic products, Picker expanded his production facilities into Cleveland in 1929, purchasing the Waite & Bartlett Co. and making it the Waite-Picker Mfg. Div., with 25 employees in 1930. During WORLD WAR II, Picker X-Ray was the only company producing portable field x-ray units for the Allied forces; after the war, Picker returned to the government $4 million that he believed was profits the company should not receive from the tragedy of war.

In addition to producing x-ray units for medical uses, Picker developed units for use as inspection tools in industry. The corporation employed 700 people in 1958 when the Picker family sold the business to the CIT Financial Corp. of White Plains, N.Y. In June 1959, the manufacturing division at 17352 Euclid Ave. was joined by another Picker facility, a million-dollar research center at 1020 London Rd. Picker's business had expanded beyond x-rays to include such new diagnostic procedures as nuclear medicine, ultrasound, and computer tomography. The name Picker X-Ray Corp. was shortened to the Picker Corp. in 1967 to reflect this diversity of operations.

The Picker Corp. moved its manufacturing division to a new facility at 595 Miner Rd. in HIGHLAND HTS. in 1967 and in 1970 announced that its corporate headquarters also would be moved to that location. Picker was an industry leader in the 1950s and 1960s, but its business declined in the 1970s as a result of poor marketing, poor research and development, and general disorganization within the corporation. In Jan. 1980, the CIT Financial Corp. sold Picker to the RCA Corp.; on 1 Apr. 1981, RCA sold Picker to the General Electric Co. of England, which combined Picker with several of its subsidiaries—the Cambridge Instruments Co., the GEC Medical Co., and American Optical—to create Picker Internatl., Inc. With its world headquarters on Miner Rd., Picker Internatl. employed 2,000 Greater Clevelanders in 1984, including 400 scientists.

**PILGERRUH** (or Pilgrim's Rest) was the first organized settlement in the Cleveland area. Located in the Cuyahoga Valley, Pilgerruh was established in Aug. 1786 by Moravian missionaries and their Indian converts. Rev. John Heckewelder and Rev. David Zeisberger led the group. They had been involved in the settlements of Schoenbrunn (the first organized settlement in Ohio) and Gnadenhutten. The Moravians came to the Cuyahoga Valley after having been continuously driven out of previous settlements by hostile Indian tribes and the British. They established Schoenbrunn and Gnadenhutten (1772) in the Tuscarawas Valley. But with the outbreak of the Revolutionary War, the pacifist Moravians were in a precarious situation sitting on land between the Americans and the British. In 1781, the British accused the Moravians of being spies for the Americans and forced them out of the Tuscarawas area and into the Upper Sandusky area (Wyandot County). From there they went to the Detroit area and established New Gnadenhutten on the Huron River. They left that settlement in 1786 and headed east across Lake Erie to the Cuyahoga. On 24 Aug. 1786, Congress awarded them their lands in the Tuscarawas Valley. However, warnings of continued hostilities from neighboring tribes thwarted their return to that area, and they settled in the Cuyahoga Valley on the ruins of an old Ottawa village, where they constructed 28 buildings.

There is controversy over the exact site of Pilgerruh. Although Rev. Heckewelder drew a map of the village, the topography of the area has changed over the years, making the exact site difficult to pinpoint. Archeological studies by David Sanders Clark (1936) placed the village near the present Canal and Schreiber roads. However, subsequent studies of the artifacts from this work date some of the items as prehistoric and others from the period 1810–30. Excavations and ground searches (1980) by David Brose of the CLEVELAND MUSEUM OF NATURAL HISTORY place Pilgerruh between the present Stone and Schreiber roads between the OHIO AND ERIE CANAL and the Cuyahoga. Other interpretations of the map place it closer to the junction of TINKER'S CREEK and the Cuyahoga. However, since it was a village, it is reasonable that the actual site could have covered the entire area. The Moravians were on the move again by 19 Apr. 1787 and left Pilgerruh and headed west to establish New Salem near Milan, Ohio.

Heckewelder, John, "Settlement der Indianer Gemeine an-der Cayahaga" (map of Pilgerruh) (ca. 1794), WRHS.

The **PILSENER BREWING COMPANY,** once located at the southwest corner of Clark Ave. and W. 65th St., was established by Bohemian brewer Wenzel Medlin (1849–1912) in 1892 and was incorporated the following year. The name Pilsener comes from the city of Pilsen in western Czechoslovakia, where Pilsener, a light Bohemian lager beer, was first made. In 1917, Pilsener produced 4 different brews: P.O.C. (which stood for "Pilsener of Cleveland"), Gold Top, Extra Pilsener Beer, and Pilsener Dark Lager; consumers received coupons for the return of empty bottles and exchanged them for premiums in a Pilsener catalog. Brewery operations were interrupted by PROHIBITION, but bottling resumed on 2 May 1933. The Cleveland-based City Ice & Fuel Co. took control of Pilsener in 1935. City Ice & Fuel later diversified its line to include cold storage, dairy products, and ice appliances in addition to brewing, and in 1949 it became the City Prods. Corp.

In 1960, Pilsener employed 300 and had an annual capacity of 375,000 barrels. Louis F. Garrard was president, and Jack E. Berno was general manager. In Jan. 1963, the Duquesne Brewing Co. bought the brewery and the P.O.C. label, and all brewery operations ceased. The last equipment was auctioned in Aug. 1963. P.O.C., which now stood for "Pleasure on Call," was brewed by Duquesne in Pittsburgh. Ironically, when Duquesne went out of business 10 years later and sold its brand names and certain assets to C. Schmidt & Sons, P.O.C. was again made in Cleveland until Schmidt, the city's last brewery, closed in 1984. The corner site of the Pilsener Brewing Co. was once known as Pilsener Square. Much of the red-brick brewery complex was still standing in 1984.

The **PLAIN DEALER** was founded as a weekly newspaper on 7 Jan. 1842 by JOSEPH WM. GRAY (1813–62) and became an evening daily on 7 Apr. 1845. Its name was probably inspired by a weekly Jacksonian paper published in New York from 1836–39 by Wm. Leggett. Among its early staff members was CHAS. FARRAR BROWNE, who served as commercial editor from 1857–60 and introduced his alter ego, "Artemus Ward," in the *Plain Dealer*'s local column in Jan. 1858. In the turbulent years leading up to the CIVIL WAR, the *Plain Dealer* occupied the often unenviable position of the local Democratic organ in what was regarded as a rabidly Republican city and region. During the Democratic Buchanan administration, however, Gray loyally supported his political mentor Stephen A. Douglas on the Lecompton controversy of 1858. For this heresy, the administration deprived Gray of the local postmastership, a political appointment he had held since 1853, and sponsored a short-lived Democratic rival, the *National Democrat*.

From the firing on Ft. Sumter until his death on 26 May 1862, Gray held the *Plain Dealer* to the loyal Democratic policies outlined by Douglas. The paper was then taken over by the administrator of his estate, John S. Stephenson, who turned it into a virulent Copperhead organ. The *Plain Dealer* condemned Lincoln and his emancipation policy and lent its support to the arch-Copperhead Clement L. Vallandigham in his unsuccessful campaign for governor in 1863. Because of the unpopularity of these stands, Stephenson was removed as Gray's administrator, and the *Plain Dealer* suspended publication for several weeks beginning 8 Mar. 1865. It reappeared on 25 Apr. 1865, under the editorship of WM. W. ARMSTRONG, who restored it as a responsible, but not too profitable, Democratic organ.

On 2 Jan. 1885, the *Plain Dealer* became the property of LIBERTY E. HOLDEN, a Cleveland real-estate and mining magnate, who came out with a morning edition on 16 Mar. 1885, after purchasing the Cleveland *Herald* and dividing its assets with the CLEVELAND LEADER. With circulation rising to nearly 30,000, the *Plain Dealer* also

began a Sunday edition at about the same time. The evening edition coexisted with the new morning edition until it was finally merged into the *World-News* in 1905. After personally operating the paper from 1893–98, Holden arrived at an arrangement to place its control in the hands of veteran Cleveland newsmen ELBERT H. BAKER and CHAS. E. KENNEDY. Baker became the principal partner in the arrangement and solely directed the *Plain Dealer* as general manager from 1907–20. Among the changes instituted by Baker were the introduction of a leased wire service and the rigid exclusion of editorial bias from the news columns. Politically, the paper supported Cleveland's Progressive Mayor TOM L. JOHNSON and participated in the muckraking movement with exposes of corruption in state government. An advocate of Cleveland architect FRANK E. CUDELL's Group Plan, Baker had the Plain Dealer Bldg. at E. 6th and Superior (now part of the Cleveland Public Library) enlarged and rebuilt after a fire in 1908 to harmonize with the public buildings surrounding the Mall.

With the death of Liberty Holden in 1913, ownership of the *Plain Dealer* was placed in trust for his heirs for 25 years. It eliminated its oldest rival by the purchase of the 6-day *Leader* in 1917, while the *Sunday Leader* was acquired by the CLEVELAND NEWS. The *Plain Dealer* and the *News* in 1932 merged their stock into the FOREST CITY PUBLISHING CO., which was dominated by the *Plain Dealer* but continued to operate both papers independently. Breaking with its 98-year Democratic orientation, the *Plain Dealer* attracted national attention in 1940 when it endorsed Wendell L. Willkie for president. Since then, it has endorsed the Republican nominee in every presidential election except 1964, when it chose Lyndon Johnson over Barry Goldwater. Editorial cartoonist Ed Kuekes brought Cleveland its only Pulitzer Prize, in 1953, for a cartoon that had appeared in the *Plain Dealer*.

In 1960, Forest City Publishing sold the *News* to the CLEVELAND PRESS, and the *Plain Dealer* moved into the former *News* building on Superior at E. 18th, where it publishes today. One of Liberty Holden's heirs, great-grandson Thos. Van Husen Vail (1926- ), assumed personal direction of the *Plain Dealer* in 1963 as publisher and editor. Vail initially promoted an aggressive, investigative spirit in the newsroom, which won the notice of *Newsweek* magazine in 1965 and the nation in 1969, when the *Plain Dealer* was the first U.S. newspaper to print Ronald Haeberle's pictures of the My Lai Massacre in Vietnam. In 1967, however, the Holden trustees decided to sell the *Plain Dealer* to the Samuel Newhouse chain for a record price of $54.2 million. Vail was retained as salaried publisher and editor by Newhouse, who left full editorial discretion in his hands. The *Plain Dealer* finally surpassed the *Press* in circulation in 1968 to become Ohio's largest daily newspaper (1980 figures: 392,688 daily; 454,922 Sunday). Other notable *Plain Dealer* staff members have included editors ERIE C. HOPWOOD and PAUL BELLAMY, executive editor PHILIP W. PORTER, reporters Benjamin F. Allen and Jas. Naughton, columnists CARL TROWBRIDGE ROBERTSON, Wes Lawrence, and Geo. Condon, drama critic WM. F. MCDERMOTT, music critic Robt. Finn, sports editor GORDON COBBLEDICK, and cartoonists JAS. H. DONAHEY and Ray Osrin.

Shaw, Archer H., *The Plain Dealer* (1942).

**PLANNED PARENTHOOD OF CLEVELAND.** *See* **FAMILY PLANNING**

**PLAYHOUSE SQUARE** is a district at Euclid Ave. and E. 14th St. comprising 5 theaters, office buildings, stores, and restaurants. The possibility of making the portion of Euclid Ave. east to 17th St. into a street of fine shops and vaudeville, movie, and legitimate theaters was envisioned by Joseph Laronge after WORLD WAR I. Together with Marcus Loew of the New York theater syndicate, Laronge and others formed Loew's Ohio Theatres, and as the concept developed, the planned entertainment district was created between 1920–22. The first two theaters to open were built by the Loew Theatres on a lot on Euclid Ave. only 85' wide but 500' deep. The STATE and OHIO theaters were built at the back of the property, with unusually long lobbies, giving them the desired frontage on Euclid. They opened in Feb. 1921. According to Thos. W. Lamb, architect of both theaters, the State's Italian Renaissance lobby, 45' x 180', was the longest of any theater in the world. The auditorium seats 3,400. The Ohio Theater, reached by a lobby parallel to the State's, has a smaller auditorium of 1,400 seats and was used for legitimate drama.

The ALLEN THEATER opened 2 months later in the Bulkley Bldg. next door. The 8-story commercial and office building contained an innovative enclosed parking garage behind the theater. Both building and theater were designed by C. Howard Crane. The Allen, planned specifically for motion pictures, was longer and narrower and had no backstage space. Compared to other exotic movie palaces of the 1920s, the relatively early Playhouse Square theaters were in a restrained classical style, with lavish use of marble, expensive woods, murals, tapestries, and gilded plaster relief. The PALACE THEATER, built to house the performances of the Keith vaudeville circuit, opened in Nov. 1922. It is set in front of Loew's State on E. 17th St., and above the lobby and foyer rises the 21-story B. F. Keith Bldg. The building and theater were designed by Geo. and C. W. Rapp, Chicago theater architects. Conceived as a palace for ordinary people, the theater has a 3-story lobby with 2 curving marble staircases. The Palace auditorium seats 3,680. Connections between the 4 theaters make it possible to go from the Palace stage into Loew's State, and thence into the Ohio, and finally into the Bulkley Bldg. and the Allen Theater. This connected plan is one of the most unusual features of the Playhouse Square development.

In Mar. 1921, the HANNA THEATER opened in the annex of the Hanna Bldg. across Euclid Ave. The 16-story office building was erected by DAN R. HANNA in memory of his father, MARCUS A. HANNA. The buildings were designed by New York architect Chas. A. Platt, architect of Hanna's Leader-News Bldg. The Hanna was a legitimate theater seating 1,535 and was operated by the Shubert theater syndicate of New York. Compared to the other theaters, the Hanna has a diminutive lobby, and the auditorium is Pompeian in its decorative treatment. After more than 40 successful years of vaudeville, motion pictures, stage plays, and even Cinerama, the Allen, State, Ohio, and Palace were all closed in 1969. A plan to save the theaters—which have a combined capacity and flexibility greater than that of Washington's Kennedy Ctr.—was conceived by Ray Shepardson. In 1970 a nonprofit group, the Playhouse Square Assoc., was formed. With support from the JR. LEAGUE, a cabaret theater was created in the lobby of the State. *Jacques Brel Is Alive and Well and Living in Paris*, the first major performance offered there, went on to become the longest-running show in Cleveland history.

In 1973, the Playhouse Square Foundation was created to carry out the restoration, operation, and management of the theaters. Grants from the Natl. Endowment for the Arts and local foundations made planning studies possible. By 1977, the foundation obtained long-term leases for the Palace and also the State and Ohio in the Loew's Bldg., which was purchased by the Cuyahoga County commis-

sioners. A combination of funding from government, the local foundations, and private corporations was committed to the project. In 1982, the CLEVELAND FOUNDATION purchased the Bulkley Bldg. complex, in the first such action in the nation in which a community-based foundation bought real estate crucial to a downtown development. The Ohio Theater was rapidly renovated in 1982 for the Great Lakes Shakespeare Festival, which moved from Lakewood to Playhouse Square. In 1984, the State's stage house was greatly enlarged to accommodate ballet, opera, and large-scale musical productions, and it was the scene of the Metropolitan Opera tour in 1984 and 1985. The revival of Playhouse Square as a performing-arts center in the 1970s and 1980s was the largest project of its kind in the nation.

**POINT OF VIEW** began as an attempt to explain the causes behind the urban unrest of the 1960s and became Cleveland's foremost example of alternative or advocacy journalism. Although issues were undated for the first few years, the first number appeared in June 1968. It was the creation of Roldo Bartimole, a native of Connecticut and former reporter for the *PLAIN DEALER* and the Cleveland office of the *Wall Street Journal*. Bartimole's objective was to uncover stories that were being ignored by the mass media, particularly those that exposed the behind-the-scenes operations of the power structure. Ignoring canons of objectivity, he openly took sides on issues but avoided making endorsements. His most consistent beat was reporting what he perceived as the transgressions of the establishment media, particularly those of his former employer, the *Plain Dealer*. Other targets of Bartimole's muckraking included local foundations, public utilities, and even the fundraising tactics of the UNITED WAY. During the Kucinich mayoralty, *Point of View* attacked both the administration and its business opposition with impartial invective. From its inception, *Point of View* remained a 1-man operation, "fiercely independent," in the words of the proprietor. A sheet of 4 letter-sized pages, it appeared biweekly except for single issues in July and August. It was sold primarily by subscription; its circulation rose from 300 in the first year to over 1,000 in the 1980s. Local politicians and outside observers agreed that *Point of View* exerted an influence far out of proportion to its size and circulation, however. It was called the country's sharpest media critique by media watcher Jas. Aronsonk, and an "invaluable pain in the neck" by the *Nation*. Bartimole viewed his principal accomplishment as providing the facts and information whereby community groups might defend their own interests.

**POLES.** Poles formed one of Cleveland's largest nationality groups in the 20th century. Although not as old or large as the Polish communities in Chicago and the Greater Detroit area, the local community had an important demographic and economic influence on the city, particularly during its period of heavy industrial growth. It is impossible to name the first Pole to settle in Cleveland or Cuyahoga County, although isolated individuals may have visited or temporarily settled in the city before the CIVIL WAR. The first cohesive settlement of Poles occurred in BEREA in the late 1860s, where they found employment in the stone quarries. At about this time, isolated groups of Poles arrived in Cleveland; 77 were counted in the 1870 census. The Cleveland Poles did not form a specific neighborhood at this time but appear to have settled within the Czech community around Croton St. Several factors combined in subsequent decades to greatly increase Polish migration to Cleveland. Chief among these was an exodus from the then-divided Polish nation caused by German cultural pressures in Prussian Poland and poverty and repression in Russian Poland. Combined with relatively safe and inexpensive ocean transport and the need for workers in Cleveland's rapidly growing industries, these factors caused the city's Polish population to grow to 35,024 by 1920, with most of this growth occurring between 1900–14. Travel brokers, such as MICHAEL KNIOLA, in the city's Polish neighborhoods made all necessary arrangements for the transport of people from Poland to join relatives already resident in the city. All immigration after WORLD WAR I was inconsequential, and it is from this great pre-World War I influx that the neighborhoods and organizations of Cleveland's Poles are largely derived.

Distinct Polish neighborhoods began to form by the late 1870s as immigrants chose to work in specific industries and lived nearby. By the late 1870s, a number of Poles worked in the Cleveland Rolling Mills in NEWBURGH, sharing jobs there with CZECHS, IRISH, Scots, and Welsh. Although initially resident with the Czechs in the Broadway-E. 55th St. area, the Poles eventually created their own settlement adjacent to Tod (E. 65th) St. and what became Fleet Ave.; their choice of location was influenced as much by its proximity to the mills as by their selection of a site at Tod and Forman Ave. for their church, ST. STANISLAUS. With the construction of a church building in 1881, the settlement, soon to be known as Warszawa, began a period of growth that continued into the 1920s. It continued to be viable into the 1980s, by which time it was more generally known as SLAVIC VILLAGE. By the late 1880s, another Polish settlement, known as Poznan, had become established in the vicinity of E. 79th St. and Superior Ave. Settled as early as 1878, this neighborhood was close to industries that eventually stretched along the railroad lines on the lakefront to the north. A third major settlement, Kantowa, arose in the TREMONT area in the late 1880s and 1890s as steel-mill activity grew in the Cuyahoga valley immediately to the east of the neighborhood. By World War I, several smaller neigborhoods had also been settled. Josephatowa was settled in the late 1890s near E. 33rd St. and St. Clair Ave. and was close to the Otis Steel works; Barbarowa, which grew after 1900, was located on the western edge of the river valley at Denison Ave. and was near to the GRASSELLI CHEMICAL CO. plant in the valley below; and in the early 1890s, Poles, along with other groups, including SLOVAKS, began settling along Madison Ave. near W. 117th St. in order to be close to jobs at the NATIONAL CARBON CO.

Though the immigrants began a number of small enterprises to serve their neighborhoods—by 1900 there were 32 Polish grocery stores and 67 saloons in Cleveland, as well as a number of other small enterprises—the economic base of each neighborhood was strongly linked to its adjacent industry. Indeed, it was the first of the CLEVELAND ROLLING MILLS STRIKES in 1882 that was responsible for a sizable growth in the area's Polish population as Polish immigrants were recruited in New York to break the strike. By 1919, Poles constituted over 50% of the large workforce of the U.S STEEL'S American Steel & Wire Div. (formerly the Rolling Mills). Other enterprises in the Warszawa area that had large numbers of Poles in their workforces included the Kaynee Blouse Co., CLEVELAND WORSTED MILLS and Grabler Mfg. Co. Until the coming of age of the second and, primarily, third generations, Cleveland's Poles were largely linked to heavy industry and labor; such entrepreneurial ventures as were founded were directed largely toward members of the nationality, and not the community at large.

Whereas industry provided the economic base for the immigrants, the Roman Catholic church proved the cul-

tural center of each neighborhood. St. Stanislaus (est. 1873) was the mother parish for Cleveland Poles. Serving the Warszawa neighborhood, it served as the basis for 2 other congregations, Sacred Heart of Jesus (1889) and St. Hyacinth (1907). St. John Cantius (1897) served, and gave its name to, the Kantowa region, and St. Casimir (1893) served Poznan. Other parishes established in Cleveland were St. Hedwig (1914) in LAKEWOOD; St. Barbara (1905), after which the Barbarowa neighborhood was named; and St. Josaphat (1908), after which Josaphatowa was named. As Poles migrated to the suburbs, nationality parishes were established in the new locations. St. Mary of Czestochowa (1914) served Poles who moved to the Corlett area around E. 131st and Harvard; Sts. Peter & Paul (1925) served the growing GARFIELD HTS. Polish population; and Corpus Christi (1936) at Biddulph and Pearl Rds. served Poles migrating to that area.

Because of the importance of the church, it often proved to be the center of controversy as priests assumed great influence in communities and often came into conflict with diocesan authorities. Indeed, the major internal conflict in Cleveland's Polish community came about when Fr. ANTON F. KOLASZEWSKI was removed from St. Stanislaus parish by the diocese in 1892. Though the exact charges against Kolaszewski are still unclear, it is apparent that his enormous expenditures to construct a new church for St. Stanislaus created a debt that alienated many of his parishioners as well as the bishop. Sent to Syracuse, N.Y., Kolaszewski returned to Cleveland in 1894 at the request of some his former parishioners and established IMMACULATE HEART OF MARY PARISH. Having defied diocesan authority, he and the members of the parish were excommunicated; they were received back into the church and diocese only after Kolaszewski resigned his pastorate in 1908. The rancor between the pro- and anti-Kolaszewski factions in the Warszawa neighborhood was extreme and led to the establishment of separate fraternal organizations and newspapers and influenced the outcome of elections. Its stigma remained well into the 1930s. It was not, however, unlike similar instances in Detroit and Chicago. Continued dissatisfaction with a diocese directed by German and Irish interests eventually led some Cleveland Poles to join the independent POLISH NATL. CATHOLIC CHURCH. The first parish, Sacred Heart of Jesus (1913), was established in the Kantowa neighborhood. Eventually 4 additional parishes would be established in the city.

Despite the overwhelming influence of the Roman Catholic church, several non-Catholic churches have served Cleveland's Poles. These included Trinity Baptist (ca. 1910), eventually located at Broadway and Fullerton. In 1943 its building was sold to the Catholic Diocese and used for Transfiguration Church, the last Polish Roman Catholic parish to be established in Cleveland. In the 1980s, a second Baptist church was begun. Located on E. 59th St., it occupied a building that had once housed the Mizpah Mission Church for Poles and Bohemians, a Congregational body established by the Schauffler Missionary Training School in the late 1880s.

Outside of the church, the fraternal insurance organization claimed a large hold on the Polish immigrant neighborhood. The 2 major national fraternals, the Polish Roman Catholic Union and the Polish Natl. Alliance, had established their first branches in the city by 1880 and 1886 respectively. The former was closely linked to the church, while the latter was more secular and was a principal advocate of Polish national independence. While the PRCU often met in church facilities, the PNA constructed meeting halls in each of the 3 major neighborhoods; the one serving Kantowa was the Polish Library Home, which housed a notable collection of Polish literature until it was closed in 1982. Religious factionalism also had its effect within the fraternals. The UNION OF POLES IN AMERICA, a locally based fraternal, began in 1894 as the Polish Roman Catholic Union of the Immaculate Heart of Mary to serve members of the schismatic Immaculate Heart parish. Another local fraternal, the ALLIANCE OF POLES OF AMERICA, was established in 1895 by a group of Clevelanders who were unhappy with the Polish Natl. Alliance's decision to admit non-Catholic Poles to membership. As many of the early fraternals prohibited membership by women, local Polish women established the ASSOC. OF POLISH WOMEN in the U.S. in 1911; it grew out of the Polish Women's Alliance.

The Poles also established a number of cultural organizations, many of which had ties to the fraternals or to the church. Among the more important to be established in Cleveland were the HARMONIA CHOPIN, a choral group founded in 1902, the Polish Natl. Choir of the Polish Natl. Alliance, and the Halka Singing Society of the Assoc. of Polish Women. More than a dozen choral and drama groups were active by the 1920s. The Cleveland Society of Poles, formed in 1923 from a branch of the Polish Natl. Alliance, consisted largely of Polish businessmen. Active into the 1980s, it held annual debutante balls for the daughters of members and donated funds to Polish colleges and other organizations dedicated to perpetuating Polish culture. A similar women's group, the American Polish Women's Club, was also established in 1923 and shared the Cleveland Society's goal of perpetuating Polish culture. Of great importance in the community's history was the SOKOL POLSKI, or Polish Falcons. This national organization fostered Polish nationalism through gymnastics. The local branch, Nest 141 (est. 1911), served as the base for the recruitment of Polish volunteers to fight with the Allies against the Germans in World War I. The nest later became known largely for its athletic program with one of its most prominent members being Olympic gold medal winner STELLA WALSH.

The local community reached its peak in 1930 with a population of 36,668 foreign-born Poles. At that time the city supported 2 Polish-language daily newspapers, *WIADOMOSCI CODZIENNE* and the *MONITOR CLEVELANDSKI*, the latter being a descendant publication of *Polonia w Ameryce*, which, established in 1891, was the first Polish paper to be published in the city. The community also supported a number of banks and savings and loans, including the Warsaw Savings & Loan (1916), the Bank of Cleveland (1913), and, later, THIRD FEDERAL SAVINGS & LOAN (1938). Despite the size and apparent prosperity of the community, it was still fragmented and already in decline. Though the St. Stanislaus-Immaculate Heart of Mary rift had largely healed, it was replaced by differences over the political situation in the new Polish state. Poles in Kantowa, who had come largely from Russian Poland, tended to be socialist and supported the regime of Marshal Joseph Pilsudski, while those resident in the large Warszawa section had supported Ignace Paderewski, the first premier (1919) of an independent Poland. Pilsudski, Poland's first president (1918), became its premier and dictator in 1926. The split, reflected in the newspapers, with the *Wiadomosci* being pro-Pilsudski and the *Monitor* anti-Pilsudski, completely stifled any attempts to unify Polish organizations or opinion in Cleveland. Only the German invasion of Poland ended the problem, but a similar problem arose after WORLD WAR II, with the community divided in its opinion of the Communist Polish state. Such division within the community could well be the chief reason for the almost total lack of achievement by Polish

politicians beyond the ward level. Although the Warszawa district has almost always been represented on city council by someone of Polish background since 1905, no Polish-American has seriously contended for the mayoralty despite the size of the community. Predominantly Democratic in outlook since the Depression, Cleveland's Polish community has produced only a small number of notable political figures. Perhaps the most important was JOSEPH SAWICKI who was elected to the state house in 1906 and the municipal court in the 1920s and 1930s.

By 1930, however, the community had also begun to wane. With no new immigration, the number of foreign-born Poles began to decline. Not even the influx of displaced persons after World War II did much to reverse the trend. By 1970, only 6,234 Poles resided in Cleveland. In 1980, the number had risen to 8,323; however, these immigrants were scattered throughout the standard metropolitan statistical area. All of the old neighborhoods, except that around Fleet Ave., had severely shrunk or disappeared as the 1st-generation immigrants died and their offspring moved away. Indeed, the movement to suburban areas began as early as 1910, when Poles followed the streetcar lines out of Warszawa to the Corlett district. Other streetcar lines and automobiles permitted additional movement into GARFIELD HTS. and the fringe areas near PARMA in the 1920s. Halted by the Depression and war, movement began again in the 1950s as the old neighborhoods emptied into Garfield Hts., WARRENSVILLE HTS., MAPLE HTS., and Parma. Further exacerbating the situation in the old neighborhoods was the decline of the industries around which they had been built. Many of the basic industries around the Fleet Ave. area, such as the American Steel & Wire Plant, the Cleveland Worsted Mills, and Grabler Mfg., had closed by the end of the 1960s.

Despite the decline of the pioneer Polish neighborhoods in the 1970s, all of the city's Polish Catholic churches remained active as of 1980, a testament to the central position of the Roman Catholic church in the culture. However, many of those attending some of the churches came from suburban homes to do so; whether their offspring continue the tradition is very much in doubt, and it is likely that all of the old neighborhoods, except that along Fleet Ave., will have disappeared by the next century. The continued life of Warszawa—Slavic Village—cannot, however, be dependent on the restricted immigration from Poland or upon nearby industrial opportunities; the area's residents must make their heritage a viable attraction for tourists, middle-income home buyers, and the nostalgic descendants of the area's founders.

John J. Grabowski
Western Reserve Historical Society

Coulter, Charles W. *The Poles of Cleveland* (1919).
Grabowski, John J. et al., *Polish Americans and Their Communities of Cleveland* (1976).
U.S. Works Projects Admin., "The Poles of Cleveland" (Unpublished manuscript, 1941, WRHS).

The **POLICE ATHLETIC LEAGUE,** founded in 1956 by patrolman Joseph Zarlenga, was organized to combat juvenile delinquency by providing Cleveland children from low- to moderate-income families with centers for organized recreational activities. Zarlenga originally wrote the charter of the Cleveland PAL by adapting the bylaws and constitution of the charter of the New York City PAL chapter and the charter of the BOY SCOUTS. The Cleveland chapter was incorporated on 28 May 1956, by Zarlenga, patrolman Joseph Mazzarella, and Frank Shaeffer. The administrators are all city police officers. A board of trustees consisting of 18 police officers and 18 civilians oversees the nonprofit organization. Support from the community was initially slow, but by PAL's second year, over 300 youths were active in activities such as baseball, basketball, and boxing. Community leaders, prominent sports figures, and other persons offered their support and time to assist PAL in the development of its many programs. The first PAL center was located at 8119 Wade Park Ave. Over the years, depending on available funding, the number of centers has fluctuated. PAL once had 10 centers, but the cost of maintaining the buildings and programs has brought the current (1985) number of centers to 4. Rather than serving the immediate community, these 4 centers have adopted an "outreach" philosophy and offered their programs to youngsters from throughout the city.

PAL centers were usually located in low-income, high-crime areas of Cleveland. At these centers, PAL provided a wide range of recreational activities for over 5,000 members ages 8–18. Getting youngsters off the streets and involved in the variety of activities offered by the program has been only part of the organization's work. PAL has also undertaken personal counseling and made referrals to existing community programs, and has sought to establish links between the juvenile court, the Police Dept., and other social-service agencies to aid in the referral of youth to the PAL programs. Over the years, PAL has served thousands of boys and girls through its offering of such activities as cooking, arts and crafts, table games, boxing, weightlifting, football, bowling, ice hockey, special outings, and other programs. A drill team, the "Royal Dynasty," begun in 1983, has participated in statewide competition. Many of the organized sports activities provide local, statewide, and national competition. Cleveland PAL was strengthened under the leadership of Frederick J. Stauffer, appointed director in 1968, and Lt. Geo. Trammell, PAL's president in 1969. Stauffer helped Cleveland PAL to become affiliated with the Natl. Police Conference on PAL & Youth Activities in 1966, and in 1973 he was elected national chairman of the Education Committee for the Natl. Police Conference, a post Trammell subsequently held.

The **POLISH NATIONAL CATHOLIC CHURCH** began in Scranton, Pa., in Mar. 1897, when Fr. Francis Hodur (1866–1953) led his new church out of the Roman Catholic church as the result of a dispute over control of local church property. The Polish Natl. Catholic church was established formally in Sept. 1904 at its first synod; by then it had 20,000 members in 5 states. In addition to having the local congregation own and control church property, the Polish Natl. Catholic church differed with the Roman Catholic church in that the mass was said in Polish rather than Latin, and in 1921 the new denomination abolished the rules of celibacy for priests. POLES in Cleveland established 5 Polish Natl. Catholic parishes between 1910–60. The first was the Sacred Heart of Jesus, 2310 W. 14th St., established in 1913. The second, Our Lady of Czestochowa, was established in 1915; it later became St. Mary's and had 660 members in 1955, when it moved from 3510 Broadview Rd. to a new $300,000 church at Wexford and Broadview Rd. in PARMA. The Church of the Good Shepherd, 7301 St. Clair Ave., was established in 1931, and Holy Trinity, 7460 Broadway, was established in 1940. All Saints Polish Natl. Catholic Church, 3736 E. 59th St., was established ca. 1954. In 1962, Bp. John Misiaszek announced that the main masses would be said in English rather than in Polish in the Polish Natl. Catholic parishes in northeastern Ohio. By 1970, the 5 area parishes had a total membership of 4,000.

**POLITICS.** For most of its history, Cleveland has been governed much like other American cities. A mayor elected at large and a council chosen by wards have usually constituted the formal instruments of administration and legislation, while a multiplicity of private groups have sought to influence the direction of public policy. With few exceptions, Cleveland's mayors before WORLD WAR II were business and professional men of old-stock Protestant ancestry. Even those who were 2d-generation Americans, such as HARRY L. DAVIS and FRED KOHLER, were Protestants whose fathers came from Wales and Germany respectively. The election of Frank Lausche in 1941 brought the first person of "new immigrant" background to the mayoralty. Since Lausche, Cleveland's mayors have come from a variety of ethnic backgrounds and from the black community. Ward elections made council reflect the ethnic diversity of the city much earlier. In 1903, councilmen separated into the "Irish" and the "Germans" for purposes of playing baseball. The quotation marks indicate that some players, at least, were members of that group for one day only; still, surnames indicate that the team titles made sense. By the 1920s, people of Southern and Eastern European origins, along with an occasional black, began to win seats on council and increasingly to play leadership roles. By the 1930s, the general ethnic makeup of the ward and the background of the councilperson corresponded fairly closely. Council was thus something of a representative democracy, in that the larger groups in the city could have at least one of their own on the municipal legislature. Only a minority of council members were workers; most were small businessmen and professionals, especially lawyers, who were often from, but no longer necessarily of, the working class. These developments were not always pleasing to the city's economic elite. They did not like having to bribe councilmen to get what they thought they were entitled to as a matter of right; individual council members lacked the time, staff, or expertise to deal with complicated matters of physical development or the city's relationships with its privately owned public-service corporations. Council, then, was reactive rather than proactive.

Yet it was not corruption or incapacity that most concerned leading businessmen, but council's inescapable parochialism. Cleveland's legislature was a living embodiment of the dictum that all politics are local politics. Council members were products of particular wards with their individual mixtures of ethnicity and class, and they approached proposals primarily from the perspective of "What's in it for my ward?" Even if they rarely formally articulated their views, most believed that the city was primarily a collection of neighborhoods, that people lived most of their lives in a limited spatial area, and that they did not want to be taxed for the sole benefit of downtown business or some ward on the other side of town. The elite, on the other hand, saw the city as an organic whole, with its various parts organized in a functional and spatial division of labor under the direction of downtown business and professional leaders. These men, overwhelmingly of old-stock Protestant origins, wanted public policies that would promote economic growth and maintain an orderly and efficient city. To them, what was good for major industry and downtown business was good for the city as a whole. From this perspective, council's insistence on cutting it up or cutting it out, that is, ensuring that each part of town benefited equally from spending on grade-crossing eliminations or other capital improvements, simply promoted inefficiency or wasteful duplication.

Parochialism came from the voters as well as members of council. Ohio's stringent limitations upon cities' taxing and borrowing power meant that additional levies and many bond issues for capital improvements had to be approved by the voters. Council could issue bonds only to a stipulated percentage of the city's tax duplicate, the total of assessed valuation of property in Cleveland. After 1902, council had to secure a 60% "for" vote on any bonds that it wished to issue that would raise the total face value of bonds outstanding beyond the 4% of the duplicate. The total permitted of such voter-approved bonds was an additional 4% of the duplicate. Proposals to build bridges or eliminate grade crossings usually required voter approval, and the 60% majority meant that any organized opposition could defeat a bond issue. Thus, any grade-crossing elimination had to package sites from western, eastern, or southern portions of the city or face certain defeat. Sometimes council tried to leave the proposed location of a bridge off the bond-issue ballot to minimize opposition from those who wanted the bridge somewhere else. The most important spatial separation in Cleveland was that between east and west sides, divided by the broad valley of the CUYAHOGA RIVER. The central business district is east of the river, so west-siders have much more reason to cross over than east-siders, many of whom could see little reason to approve bond issues for bridges that they would rarely, if ever, use. NEWTON D. BAKER once proposed redrawing political boundary lines on a north-south basis to reduce the east-west division within the city. Nothing came of this idea. The division between east and west sides long precedes the racial separation of the city into a predominantly black east side and a predominantly white west side.

Outside the formal structure of government, the most important political players were the party organizations, and such groups as the Chamber of Commerce (GREATER CLEVELAND GROWTH ASSOC.) and the Chamber of Industry, an association organized in 1907 to promote west side interests. In addition, there were a number of locally oriented improvement associations. As in other cities, the party organizations were most concerned with organizational maintenance and the avoidance of divisive issues. Those who wished something from the city could find it useful to have friends in both major parties. Major businessmen were overwhelmingly Republican, but the VAN SWERINGENs' man in council was Democrat JAS. J. MCGINTY. The Chamber of Commerce, an outgrowth of the earlier Board of Trade, was extremely influential in the city's political life. In the early 20th century, it had a paid staff and could command the time and attention of the most important men in the city. Its committees consisted of leading industrialists and their commercial and professional allies. These committees prepared well-researched and -written reports on items of interest to the chamber. These resources were precisely what council lacked, so that in many instances, the chamber could control the agenda and frame the terms of debate. The chamber's style was to seek agreement among all the economic interests involved in a particular policy area. Where such agreement was possible, as in the Group Plan of public buildings, the projects were moved forward. Where it was not, such as lakefront development, nothing much happened.

Conspicuously absent from the deliberations of the chamber were small businessmen, workers, and those of recent immigrant origin. They were "the people" whose function it was to man the factories, do the domestic chores, and approve at the polls the initiatives of the chamber. Still, so long as most business and professional leaders lived within the city limits, the chamber maintained a general interest in the functioning of the city. A city that promoted the well-being of its workers would be an economically efficient unit. By the mid-1920s, most of its leaders no

longer lived in the city, and the chamber expressed less interest in the general welfare and focused more exclusively upon economic development and keeping taxes down. The census of 1930 indicated that the suburbs taken together were of higher socioeconomic status than the city. The reverse side of the coming of age politically of the ethnics was the removal of affluent old-stock Americans into suburbs such as SHAKER HTS. In 1929, perhaps ⅔ of the teachers and administrators in Cleveland's school system lived in the suburbs. The political impact of suburbanization was highlighted in 1931 when the 3 leading candidates for the mayoralty all had to move back into the city to establish legal residences.

Leaders of civic organizations such as the chamber and the good-government CITIZENS LEAGUE remained in the suburbs. They were thus vulnerable to attacks by Cleveland's elected officials that people who lived elsewhere should not try to govern the city or even advise the locals on how it should be done. As an organization, the Citizens League believed in the concept of Greater Cleveland and that even though its members' residence might be beyond the city limits, they still had the right, indeed the obligation, to promote the cause of good government in Cleveland. The league was an outgrowth of the Municipal Assoc. formed in 1897. Like good-government organizations in other cities, it sought to promote better candidates for public office and fiscal responsibility on the part of city government. One of those principles was nonpartisanship, which Cleveland at least nominally adopted in its charter of 1913. This charter was first adopted after Ohio voters had approved a HOME RULE amendment to the state constitution the previous year. The home rule amendment came after a decade of agitation from urban reformers around the state to have Ohio join the other states that gave cities the constitutional power to direct their own destinies. This autonomy did not extend to financial matters.

A commission under the leadership of Mayor Newton D. Baker wrote the 1913 charter. It included the initiative and referendum provisions, nomination by petition, and election of a nonpartisan, preferential ballot. This last provision was designed to weaken the role of the party organizations and to ensure election by majorities. In most but not all cases, candidates who had the support of the party organizations fared much better than those who did not. In the late 19th century, Republicans won more elections in Cleveland than Democrats did. TOM JOHNSON and Newton Baker reversed this pattern in the early 20th century, but from 1916–41, Cleveland again was a primarily Republican city, at least for the mayoralty. Since the 1940s, Democrats have far outnumbered Republicans within the city, although there have been some Republican mayors, such as Ralph Perk and Geo. Voinovich. In the 1920s, Cleveland departed from the mayor-council form to adopt the CITY MANAGER PLAN. The experiment, promoted by such groups as the real-estate board and the Citizens League, was supposed to limit even further the role of the political parties. The reality was that the parties learned how to use this new arrangement almost as well as the mayor-council form. By 1931, the city manager form of government was abandoned in favor of a return to the mayor-council pattern.

Whether mayors or managers, Cleveland's chief executives have found themselves chronically short of money. Before 1909, Ohio permitted reassessment of property for purposes of taxation only every decade. Thus, Cleveland's government could not take advantage of the rapid rise in property values in the prosperous first years of the century. When Cleveland was able to more than double its tax duplicate, the legislature in Columbus severely limited the rate of taxation. By the Smith Act, property for all purposes combined, city, county, schools, and state, was limited to a total of 10 mills, or 1% of the duplicate. By referendum, the voters could approve an additional 5 mills. This legislation crippled municipal operating budgets. By 1919, Cleveland had accumulated operating deficits totaling $7 million and had to issue "revenue deficiency bonds" to cope. In the early 1920s, the legislature did grant some relief, not transfer payments from the state to the city, but by giving more latitude to city officials and voters in setting higher tax limits for themselves. For a brief period in the 1920s, the city could finance its activities without undue strain. The Depression shattered Cleveland's economy, and with it its fiscal stability. Because of the city's concentration of capital-goods production, it suffered terribly from unemployment, lower tax collections, and high relief needs throughout the 1930s. World War II restored Cleveland's prosperity, and the 1950 census recorded the largest population in the city's history, 914,000. In ensuing decades, the combination of accelerated suburbanization and a decline in the economic base of the metropolitan area led to population losses of more than 300,000 and brought Cleveland to DEFAULT by the late 1970s. Cleveland could no longer provide basic services out of its own resources; only intergovernmental transfer payments such as revenue sharing allowed it to stay afloat.

The city's fiscal crisis, occasioned now not by legislative restrictions upon its ability to tax itself adequately but by a long-term decline in its economic and population base, is one of many reasons why some people have promoted REGIONAL GOVERNMENT. In the early 20th century, Cleveland was still growing territorially as well as in population, but it could not annex populous and then prosperous SUBURBS such as LAKEWOOD and E. CLEVELAND. Only those areas that could not finance a desired level of public services and capital improvements sought union with the city. Within the city, some boosters wanted annexation so that Cleveland could enhance and maintain its position as the Fifth City, reached in the census of 1920. A sufficient number of both suburbanites and city dwellers opposed metropolitan government, supposedly more palatable to the suburbs than outright annexation, to defeat it in referendums from the late 1920s to the late 1950s.

By the 1970s, Cleveland officials coped as best they could with declines in population, in the capital infrastructure, and in the economic base. Complicating these problems was the central fact and the central cleavage of race. In the 1920s, Cleveland's BLACKS, then concentrated in 2 wards on the near east side, constituted an important component of the Republican organization and received some minor patronage in return. During the 1930s, the city's blacks shifted from being overwhelmingly Republican to being strongly Democratic and became a significant proportion of the city's emerging Democratic majority. The war economy of the 1940s and the pent-up civilian demand of the postwar years induced thousands of southern blacks to migrate to Cleveland, swelling the black population from 9.7% of the total in 1940 to 38.3% in 1970. Just as the increasing cosmopolitanism of the city speeded the suburbanization of old-stock Americans in the 1920s, the larger black population after 1945 intensified the out-migration of white ethnics. For example, the HOUGH area on the east side went from 95.1% white in 1950 to 74.2% black in 1960. Ethnic and racial identifications and antipathies, always significant in Cleveland politics, increased in importance as sources of political decision making.

For a brief moment in the late 1960s, it looked as if Mayor Carl Stokes had succeeded in forging a coalition of downtown business leaders and blacks. Whatever hopes existed evaporated after the GLENVILLE SHOOT-OUT in 1968 between black nationalists and Cleveland police, which led to 7 deaths and destroyed Stokes's credibility among a majority of whites. Stokes was followed by 2 white ethnics, Ralph Perk, a Republican and dedicated defender of the status quo, and Dennis Kucinich, a maverick young Democrat and self-styled urban populist out to defend the interests of the neighborhoods against the excessive demands of downtown business. Kucinich combined reasonable policy perspectives with an abrasive and confrontational style that made difficult any cooperation between the city's economic and political leadership. Kucinich's successor, Geo. Voinovich, conducted a more decorous administration, one that has restored civility to the city's political discourse (for recent mayors, see MAYORAL ADMINISTRATION OF).

There was also one major structural change in the postwar period. When Cleveland returned to the mayor-council form in 1931, the city established 33 wards, each with a representative in council. Legislative and developmental proposals thus required 17 yes votes for passage, a difficult number to obtain for any project whose benefits were targeted to a limited area of the city. Structural reformers have long urged a small council. The most extreme version presses for at-large elections of a small council, a provision that almost assures elite domination. Clevelanders recognized that this proposal would not allow for the social diversity of the city. But the LEAGUE OF WOMEN VOTERS and other such groups wanted a council with few members and larger districts, one that would avoid the parochial limitations of small wards. Earlier proposals for reduction in size of council had foundered on racial divisions and animosities. Finally, in 1981, the voters approved a charter amendment reducing council from 33 to 21 members. Such structural changes, no matter how well founded, can do only so much. To be well governed, cities need adequate resources, competent officials, and an electorate supportive of quality. Cleveland has sometimes, but not always, had all these good things at once. At this time, it seems as if the decline of the city's economic position means that such favorable periods will be less common in the future than in the past.

James F. Richardson
University of Akron

See also GOVERNMENT.

**POLKAS.** American polka music evolved as a hybrid of folk songs and dances brought by European immigrants, with influences from other musical expressions. The term has come to encompass waltzes, schottisches, quicksteps, mazurkas, and other ethnic dances. Cleveland has been called "America's Polka Capital" and was identified with a particular style of polka music that has been widely copied. The polka was a European sensation before it swept America in the 1840s. The dance and its variations were already in the repertoires of local musicians by 1845, when Jack Leland penned a quickstep for his Cleveland Brass Band. Lively polkas and romantic waltzes were popular throughout the Victorian era. Two typical titles by area composers were "The Put-in-Bay Polka" (1871) and "The Irresistible Schottische" (1885). The city's orchestras presented such songs in parades, recitals, and summer concerts at ROCKEFELLER PARK, Kelley's Hall, and HALTNORTH'S GARDENS. GERMANS and CZECHS played their own versions at social events and performances of groups such as the St. Cecilia Society Orchestra, the Cleveland Gesangverein, the Lumir Chorus, and Frank Hruby's

Great Western Band. European folkloric themes were the rage at the turn of the century, and mandolin clubs flourished. The first tamburitza groups were established among Cleveland's CROATIANS and SLOVENES at this time.

Accordions probably came to Cleveland the same time as polkas. Early accordions were button-operated, with diatonic tonality capable of only major scales. These were often called *button boxes* or *cheese boxes*, a term thought to have originated in Cleveland. Chromatic and piano models with greater ranges and key mechanisms were prevalent by 1900. Accordionists were in demand among nationality groups for weddings, dances, and parties. Rudimentary bands were gradually formed with the addition of a piano, strings, brass, or woodwinds. Some groups added banjo and drums, and by 1920 the first polka bands appeared. Each nationality had its own musical style, and most bands were talented enough to play for different audiences. Czechs and Germans preferred rousing oom-pah beats; Slovenians, smooth, gliding renditions; and ITALIANS, staccato rhythms. POLES emphasized wind instruments; Croatians used more guitar and tamburitza; and HUNGARIANS highlighted violins and the cimbalom. Parish and community halls opened as cultural and entertainment centers. Dances were held regularly at places such as Our Lady of Lourdes Hall on Broadway and Knaus' Hall on St. Clair. Nick Shkorka, Anton Mervar, and John Mikus manufactured accordions, and John Bencic specialized in tamburitzas. Instruments were also ordered from Europe.

The phonograph and the RADIO created an unprecedented boom in popular music in the 1920s. Polkas and waltzes were still played, but the ethnic bandleader might be called upon to perform an occasional turkey trot or Charleston to please younger dancers. Second-generation ethnic Clevelanders were able to appreciate commercial music as well as their own culture's sounds. New York record companies catered to ethnic audiences with imported discs and nationality music series. Records were promoted and distributed nationally via catalogs, neighborhood music shops, such as those lining Broadway, and even furniture stores and jewelers. Anton Mervar contacted record companies to issue Slovenian series with Cleveland artists. The Matt Hoyer Trio became the first Slovenian ensemble to record in the U.S. From 1919–30, the group made 100 instrumental arrangements for the Victor and Columbia labels. Hoyer reworked old polkas and folk songs and updated them with banjo accompaniment. Songs such as "Jack on St. Clair" set the tone for Slovenian bands in America. The Victor Lisjak and Louis Spehek orchestras also recorded for the labels. Dick Mates performed for Czech series, and Jan Kapalka for Polish series.

By 1930, nearly every major nationality had a regular broadcast on Cleveland stations WGAR, WHK, WJAY, and WTAM. Several producer-announcers, including John Lewandowski, Henri Broze, and Martin Antoncic, remained popular well into the 1960s and 1970s. These programs also served as showcases for polka musicians. At the insistence of local musicians' unions, live music was used almost exclusively, giving performers valuable exposure for bookings. Radio favorites during the 1930s and early 1940s included accordionists Frank Novak, Eddie Simms, and Lou Trebar, bassist Geo. Wisneskey, Joe Sodja on the banjo, Emil Hronek on the vibraphone, and pianists Art Broze and Wm. Lausche. Instrumentalists frequently worked on several different nationality shows. Lausche made numerous recordings with Victor and Columbia, sometimes joined by a studio orchestra and his sister Josephine and Mary Udovic as vocalists. He "Americanized" Slovenian tunes with contemporary dance-band arrangements and pioneered the polka sound that would become associated with Cleveland. Lausche's original compositions, such as "Cleveland, the Polka Town," became polka classics.

The Depression dashed the nationality record industry, but musicians were kept busy. Dancers were willing to part with a quarter to forget their troubles at neighborhood halls, taverns, and the nationality villages at the Great Lakes Exposition. Cleveland bands rushed to record, especially when radio restrictions were eased after the start of WORLD WAR II. Joe Kusar continued the Hoyer button-box style, and Emery Deutsch performed Hungarian melodies. Jerry Mazanec and Jerry Pobuda gave Czech numbers a fresh sound. Joe Sodja's orchestra tried for American listeners. Boys who grew up with records, radio, and neighborhood musicians were forming bands and playing for weddings, church socials, and lodge picnics.

Frankie Yankovic was a bandleader while still a teenager in Collinwood's Slovenian settlement. His early releases, engineered at Czech announcer Frederick Wolf's Cleveland Recording Co., sold rapidly to polka fans and earned him a contract with Columbia in 1946. Dancers welcomed Yankovic's approach of fluid waltzes and slower polkas that were simpler than the Chicago Polish style and less foreign than the Milwaukee German sound. The Yanks hit the charts in 1948 and 1949 with 2 million-selling arrangements of "Just Because" and "The Blue Skirt Waltz." Yankovic toured extensively, sometimes giving 300 performances a year, including in Cleveland. He was crowned "America's Polka King" in Milwaukee in 1948. He staffed his band with experienced musicians, such as Johnny Pecon, versatile enough to play for any audience. Many Yanks alumni formed their own successful bands. Johnny Pecon's orchestra was considered the leading exponent of the Cleveland polka style. He is thought to have established the dance sequence of 3 polkas, followed by 3 waltzes and 3 other numbers. Record deals were offered to Cleveland-style groups led by Pecon, Johnny Vadnal, Kenny Bass, Georgie Cook, Eddie Habat, Pete Sokach, and others. The Polish-style bands of Chester Budny and Ray Budzilek also signed with major labels.

Polka fever broke nationally ca. 1950. Cold-war America wanted hearty, wholesome songs reminiscent of old values. Major entertainers scored polka hits. The absorption of the polka into popular music showed an acceptance of the multicultural identity of America. Polka fans packed music spots such as the Golden Goose on E. 123rd, the Rendezvous Bar on W. 25th, the Gaiety Inn in Collinwood, the Bowl Ballroom on E. 93rd, Grdina's Twilight Ballroom on St. Clair, and the Metropole Cafe on E. 55th. Parish halls and centers, such as the SLOVENIAN NATL. HOME, the Polish Women's Hall, and Karlin Hall, sponsored weekly dances where teens could mingle with "their own kind." Outlying recreation grounds, GERMAN CENTRAL FARM in Parma, the Slovene Natl. Benefit Society Farm in Kirtland, and others, attracted Sunday crowds in the summer. America's first polka radio and television shows made their debuts in Cleveland in 1948, and other shows proliferated throughout the 1950s, often hosted by bandleaders. "Polka Varieties" premiered in 1958 on WEWS and became a Sunday tradition for 25 years. Each hour-long program starred a local orchestra, led by names such as Art Perko, Lenny Zadel, Mary Champa, and Ed and Gilda Cifani, with additional music from up-and-coming bands, singers, and folklore societies. The Pol-Kats Social Club was organized in 1957, with members from the CLEVELAND FED. OF MUSICIANS, and promoted polka music.

ROCK 'N' ROLL and increased TELEVISION viewing were blamed for the polka's decline, but the big labels were dropping polka performers as early as 1953 because of overexposure. Neighborhood youth dances practically disappeared after 1955. Polka music maintained followers in strongly ethnic cities such as Cleveland, where bandleader bars were popular. Polkas reached a low point in the early 1960s, when a wide-scale scorn for working-class ethnicity prevailed, particularly in the media. Yankovic's comic hit "Who Stole the Kishka?" was ridiculed as a prime example of ethnic low culture. Several factors led to a polka revival after 1965. FM radio provided more air time for nationality programming, and 2 stations, WXEN and WZAK, presented all-ethnic formats. Announcers such as Joseph and Betty Bauer, Leslie Dus, and Frank Pitrone produced shows 7 days a week. Tony Petkovsek, Jr., began an expanded daily polka program in 1961 and emerged as an important figure in the revitalization of Cleveland's polka scene. He included album premieres, opinion call-ins, on-location shows, interviews, contests, and even a polka history segment by Don Sosnoski. The recordings of 2 groups from Europe introduced a fresh, commercialized folk sound and new melodies to Cleveland airwaves. The Avsenik Bros.' Alpine renditions inspired bands such as that of Duke Marsic. Lojze Slak's folksy diatonic accordion touched off a button-box craze. Both ensembles made appearances in Cleveland.

John Gayer's Delta Internatl. was Cleveland's leading polka record label. Over 40 albums were released from 1963–78, featuring Pecon, Lou Trebar, Al Markic, Al Tercek, and a new generation of entertainers such as Richie Vadnal, Hank Haller, Wally Chips, Joe Oberaitis, and vocalist Cecilia Valencic. Some bands produced their own albums and, for a small investment, had them pressed and packaged. The days of million-selling hits were over, however. Most releases were for 1,000 albums, and sell-outs were rare. Distribution was limited because chain stores no longer handled polka recordings. Yankovic was the last Cleveland polka figure on a major label.

Polkas made a strong comeback in the 1970s. The fans of the 1940s and 1950s were middle-aged, and polka music offered a pleasant, nostalgic refuge. Ethnic pride was growing in Cleveland, and well-organized, innovative polka events became important, including the All Nations Festival on Hanna Mall, Oktoberfests, and Old World celebrations. The Polka Mass was first presented in Lowellville in 1972, with polkas and waltzes rewritten as hymns. A dozen polka broadcasts emanated from stations in northeast Ohio. Anthony Zebrowski alone hosted 33 hours a week. Timko's Polka Place on E. 156th St., the Hofbrau House on E. 55th, and the Brookstate Inn in Parma were the top-drawing polka nightclubs. Two polka monthlies were published, *Polka News & Events*, by Peter Cassara, and *Polkarama*, by Jack O'Breza, Jr., plus a newspaper, *Polka Scene*, by Eddie Andres. The button-box mania among Cleveland's Slovenians spread to ethnic communities as distant as Alaska. The instrument could be learned by rote, and contests and festivals boosted participation. By 1985 there were 16 clubs in Cleveland.

Polka music suffered setbacks in the 1980s. WXEN and WZAK had bumped ethnic programming in favor of disco formats, and polka disc jockeys were forced onto low-powered stations or into retirement. WEWS canceled "Polka Varieties." Rising orchestra prices forced small establishments to drop live music. Yet Cleveland was still called "Polkatown, U.S.A." There were over 100 polka bands in the area by 1985, plus button-box clubs, tamburitza ensembles, choruses, folk dancers, and brass bands. Cable television's Nationality Broadcasting Network held promise. Yankovic received the first Grammy award for best polka album in 1986. Polka events were fewer, but musically strong and well-attended. New bands were being organized by the youngsters that were raised in the polka-

charged 1970s, ensuring the continuation of this uniquely American musical form into the next century.

Joseph Valencic

Dolgan, Cecilia V., "Button Box Clubs in the United States." In *Slovenski Koledar '86* (1985).
Dolgan, Robert, and Yankovic, Frankie, *Polka King* (1977).
See also MUSIC.

**POLO** was a popular sport in the Cleveland area during the 1920s and 1930s. Disrupted by WORLD WAR II, it was revived in the 1950s by enthusiasts who formed the Cleveland Polo Club. Polo was introduced in the area in 1911 by Edmund S. Burke, Jr., known as the father of Cleveland polo. Burke and another early Cleveland player, Corliss E. Sullivan, learned the game while wintering in Camden, S.C. Burke laid out a polo field on his estate in Wickliffe, hired polo expert Earle Hopping to come to Cleveland to teach the game and serve as coach, and bought several Texas ponies to provide mounts for area players. By 1914, Burke had put together a champion team: Burke, A. D. Baldwin, Ben Hitchcock, THOS. H. WHITE, and Robt. C. Norton, who won the Mid-Western Championship that year. As the sport grew in popularity, other players mounted up, and other local fields were laid out in the 1910s and 1920s. The CHAGRIN VALLEY HUNT CLUB formed a polo team and laid out a regulation field in 1916; 2 were laid out at the Kirtland Country Club, and 1 each at the Circle W Farm of Walter C. White, at the Waite Hill estate of John Sherwin, Jr., and at the Halfred Farms of Windsor T. White. In 1931, play began on the Hunting Valley Polo Field on Chagrin River Rd. During the 1920s, Cleveland teams regularly won the championship of the U.S. Polo Assoc.'s Central Circuit, formed in 1925. In 1927 and 1931, the Chagrin Valley Hunt Club team won both the Central Circuit title and the Natl. Intercircuit Championship. In 1928, the Natl. Intercircuit Championships and the 12-Goal Polo Tournament were held on the field at Walter White's Circle W Farm in GATES MILLS, the first time in American polo history that the national championships were held in the Midwest. About 8,000 people attended the 19 games played during the championship matches. The championship returned to the Cleveland area in 1936 and 1940. Special matches, such as the series of games played by the Mexican Army team against local teams in 1939, helped maintain interest in the sport. By the time local polo enthusiasts celebrated the 25th anniversary of the sport in Cleveland in 1936, crowds of 2,000–3,000 were attending the outdoor games on weekend afternoons. Of the $10,300 budget of the local polo committee in 1937, $7,000 was derived from the $.50 cent admission fee, and the rest from fees assessed to the 24 local polo players.

In addition to outdoor polo, indoor polo became popular in the 1920s and 1930s. TROOP A began playing polo indoors in the winter in 1922; by 1933, the indoor season was running from November-April, with 14 3-player teams and 43 players taking part. An estimated 54,000 people attended indoor matches that season. In addition to teams such as Troop A, the Pessimists, and the Cleveland Riding Club, businesses such as FISHER FOODS sponsored indoor polo teams in the 1930s. Like their outdoor counterparts, indoor teams often competed against teams from other cities, including college teams from Harvard and Yale. The growth of local polo was interrupted by World War II. Mechanization of the cavalry put an end to teams sponsored by the U.S. Army, and business-sponsored teams also disappeared. The outdoor sport was revived in the early 1950s, but on a much smaller scale. A team was organized in 1950 by Wm. Herbert Greene; by 1953, it was playing an 8-game schedule in the Penn-Ohio league. Early in 1953, Greene established the Cleveland Polo Assoc., with membership of more than 200 enthusiasts willing to help support the team. By 1960, average attendance was about 200; that year the Mid-States Polo League was organized. About 3,000 people attended the club's games in 1964, and by 1965 Cleveland had 2 complete 4-player polo teams. The Cleveland Polo Club had 10 playing members in 1978, and its games attracted 500 persons. By 1978, winter indoor polo had been revived at the Circle Emerald Riding Stables in BEDFORD. By the 1980s, Cleveland had only 1 outdoor polo team, the Cleveland Shamrocks, whose games at the S. Chagrin Metroparks Reservation field at Chagrin Blvd. and Chagrin Rd. continued to attract hundreds of observers. In 1980, the Shamrocks won the Mid-State Championships, the first polo title for a Cleveland team in 20 years, but expenses prevented the team from traveling to the national championships in Arizona.

**POLYCLINIC HOSPITAL,** located at 6606 Carnegie Ave., was opened on 3 Feb. 1930. Organization of the hospital and clinic was based on the "Cornell Plan," which provided for maintenance of several small buildings and services outside the main hospital. Polyclinic Hospital began as a clinic staffed by a group of physicians from the staff of ST. LUKE'S HOSPITAL, and the old hospital's old building on Carnegie was purchased and renovated by Polyclinic. In 1971, Polyclinic established the first health center operated by a hospital to serve inner-city residents. Polyclinic's satellite clinics specialized in treating urologic and venereal diseases. Plans to move to SOLON, Ohio, and/or merge with St. Luke's Hospital or Bedford Municipal Hospital were proposed and abandoned. Polyclinic closed its facilities in Apr. 1978 and merged with WOMAN'S GENERAL HOSPITAL.

Archives, Howard Dittrick Museum of Historical Medicine.

The **POOR CLARE (COLETTINE) RELIGIOUS** established their first American convent on 10 Aug. 1877 in a former school at McBride and Broadway in Cleveland. Two Italian Poor Clare sisters, Mother Mary Magdalene Bentivoglio and her sister, had originally hoped to establish a monastery in Minnesota, but that proved impractical. They traveled to Cleveland at the request of their religious superior, Fr. Gregory Janknecht, OFM. This nucleus was expanded with the arrival of 5 Poor Clare nuns from Germany: Sisters Josepha, Margaret Mary, M. Hyacinth, Theresa, and Veronica, who would become the first abbess of the community. Their convent in Duesseldorf had been disbanded by the orders of the Bismarck government in 1875 during the Kulturkampf era. They had fled to Holland, where they received an invitation to come to Cleveland to establish a contemplative community. They arrived in Cleveland in Dec. 1877 and began a monastic life of prayer and sacrifice. The Italian sisters left in 1878 to establish a community in New York. The German sisters then maintained the monastery.

Despite its austerity, many young women were attracted to the life of the Poor Clare nuns. In 1879 the sisters bought property on Perry (E. 22nd) St. just north of St. Bridget Church for a new convent. By 1885 they had finished the monastery and had established their growing community there. A still larger convent located farther away from the congested downtown area was needed. Ten acres of property on Rocky River Dr. were purchased, and construction was begun under the direction of the Franciscan brother Leonard Darschied. The building was completed, and it was blessed on 14 June by Bp. IGNATIUS F. HORST-MANN. Living a life of prayer and poverty as decreed by both St. Francis of Assisi and St. Clare, the Poor Clares supported themselves by manual labor and alms. Blessed with a number of vocations, the sisters were able to send nuns to found communities of Poor Clare nuns in Chicago and Rockford, Ill.; Oakland, Calif.; Newport News, Va., and Brazil.

Papers of Poor Clares, Archives, Diocese of Cleveland.

**POORHOUSES.** See **OLD AGE/NURSING HOMES**

The **POPULIST POLITICAL PARTIES** were independent third parties active in Cleveland in the last half of the 19th century. Known variously as the Greenback party, the Union Labor party, and the People's or Citizen's party, they advocated reform through political action to improve the quality of life in American society. At a convention held in Cleveland in 1875, local labor leader Robt. Schilling tried unsuccessfully to unite urban workers with the farmer-oriented Greenback party, which favored the free circulation of paper money. Organized in Oct. 1887, the Union Labor party, led by Dr. LOUIS B. TUCKERMAN, called for city ownership of public utilities and a moratorium on city bonds except to buy up private utilities. They chose a slate of candidates for the 1887 county and state elections and received about 7% of the county vote. Although they nominated a full ticket for the 1888 municipal elections, their vote fell short of the previous year's.

The People's party, organized in 1891, also advocated municipal ownership of utilities, as well as direct election of U.S. senators, an 8-hour day, initiative, referendum, and direct primaries. They believed in gradual change by enacting a limited practical program of reform. In 1893, mayoral candidate EDWARD S. MEYER, choice of both the People's and Citizen's parties, received about 16% of the vote, but the rest of the ticket did not do as well. Thos. Fitzsimmons, People's party candidate for mayor in 1895, received 5.5% of the total vote. The party's most successful campaign was conducted in behalf of Toledo mayor Samuel R. Jones, who ran for Ohio governor in 1899. Jones carried the county by 15,036 votes but received only about 12.5% of the statewide vote. The organized party disbanded when Democrat TOM L. JOHNSON, who supported many of their reforms, was elected mayor in 1901.

**PORATH, ISRAEL** (3 July 1886–11 Apr. 1974), spiritual leader and scholar, was the "dean" of Cleveland's Orthodox rabbis for almost 5 decades. Born in Jerusalem, Palestine, Porath received a traditional Talmudic education, graduating from Etz Chaim Yeshiva in Jerusalem. He became a Zionist as a disciple of Rabbi Abraham Isaac Kook, the chief rabbi of Palestine. Porath was active in the public life of Palestine as an educator and local administrator. He was responsible for negotiating with the Turkish rulers of Palestine regarding school affairs, and he administered relief efforts for Jews suffering various hardships during and after WORLD WAR I. In 1923, he immigrated to the U.S. and accepted a pulpit at Congregation B'nai Israel in Plainfield, N.J. Two years later he became the rabbi at Cleveland's Congregation OHEB ZEDEK, a position he held for 14 years. Following his tenure at Oheb Zedek, Porath served 6 years as rabbi of Congregation Neveh Zedek. In 1945, he left Cleveland to become dean of the Salanter Yeshiva in New York City. However, within 1 year he returned to Cleveland to become rabbi of the HEIGHTS JEWISH CTR.; he remained in that position until his retirement in 1972.

Porath was active in Cleveland's Jewish community, representing the interests of the Orthodox. He served on the board of trustees of the ORTHODOX JEWISH CHILDRENS HOME and the Orthodox Old Home and was chairman of the education committee of YESHIVATH ADATH B'NAI ISRAEL. He was a founder and chairman of Cleveland's Orthodox Rabbinical Council, the community's agency for the interpretation of religious law and its application to daily life. Porath was also active in the life of the general Jewish community, serving on the executive council of the Jewish Community Council, the board of the Jewish Welfare Fed., and the advisory board of B'NAI B'RITH. In 1960, he was elected an honorary life trustee of the JEWISH COMMUNITY FED. and was also named honorary president of Cleveland Histadrut Ivrit. An ardent Zionist, Porath was a member of the Religious Zionists of America and of the executive board of the Natl. Mizrachi. For his work in the area of Jewish education and promotion of Hebrew language and culture, he received the first A. H. Friedland Award presented by the BUREAU OF JEWISH EDUCATION in 1968. A Talmudic scholar, Porath compiled an 8-volume outline of the Talmud in Hebrew titled *Mavo Ha-Talmud*. Porath married Miriam Tiktin in Jerusalem in 1905. They had 6 sons and 1 daughter.

Rabbi Israel Porath Papers, WRHS.

**PORTER, ALBERT S.** (29 Nov. 1904–7 Jan. 1979), served as Cuyahoga County engineer for 29 years and as county Democratic party chairman for 6 years. He was born in 1905 in Portsmouth, Va., to Albert S. and Lena Edmonds Porter. The family moved to LAKEWOOD, where he attended Lakewood High School, graduating in 1922. He attended Ohio State University, receiving his B.S. degree in civil engineering in 1928, and the following year he joined the Cleveland Highway Research Bureau. He became chief assistant to county engineer John O. McWilliams in 1933, where he remained until 1947, with time out for 5 years of Navy service during WORLD WAR II. After McWilliams's resignation in 1947, Porter became county engineer and served in that capacity for almost 30 years. During his tenure, much of the freeway system linking Cleveland to its suburbs was built. Porter was active in Democratic politics. He became county chairman of the Democratic party in 1963 upon the resignation of RAY T. MILLER and served until 1969. He was defeated for reelection as county engineer in 1976. As a result of a grand jury investigation in 1977, he pleaded guilty to 19 counts of theft in office, was fined $10,000, and was placed on probation for 2 years. He died in 1979. Porter married Genevieve Shaveyco on 29 Dec. 1949; they had 2 sons, Lee and Alan, and a daughter, Carol.

**PORTER, PHILIP WYLIE** (7 Aug. 1900–20 May 1985), was a reporter, columnist, and editor at the *PLAIN DEALER* for 44 years and the author of 2 books. He was born in Portsmouth, Va., to Albert S. and Lena Edmonds Porter. The family left Virginia in 1911, going first to Columbus, and then to LAKEWOOD in 1913. As a junior at Lakewood High School, Porter got a summer job as an office boy at the *CLEVELAND LEADER* in 1917, and after graduation in 1918, he attended Ohio State University, majoring in journalism. He was the OSU campus correspondent for the *Plain Dealer* during the academic year and worked as a staff police reporter in the summer. He joined the *Plain Dealer* staff after graduation in 1922 as a general-assignment reporter. Promoted to city editor in 1929, Porter began the "Inside the News in Cleveland" column, which he continued when made news editor in 1936. After 3½ years of military service during WORLD WAR II, he re-

turned to the *Plain Dealer* as Sunday editor, managing editor, and, in 1963, executive editor. He retired at the end of 1966 but continued to write a column for the SUN NEWSPAPERS until 1983.

Porter is the author of 2 books, *The Reporter and the News*, a textbook of practical guidelines for journalism students coauthored with Norval N. Luxon in 1935, and *Cleveland: Confused City on a Seesaw*, published in 1976, based on his recollections of the Cleveland scene during his years as a newsman. In 1979, he also edited *The Best of Loveland*, a compilation of pieces by his *Plain Dealer* colleague, ROELIF LOVELAND. Porter had helped found the City Club Forum Foundation in 1941 and was made a charter member of the City Club Hall of Fame on 3 May 1985. He was married 3 times, to Annanette Blue in 1922, Helene Betschart in 1945, and Dorothy Rutka Kennon in 1960. He had 3 daughters, Phoebe Ann, Susan Wood, and Molly Schaeffer. He and his third wife were victims of a double homicide in May 1985, when Porter was 84.

Porter, Philip, *Cleveland* (1976).

**PORTER, SIMEON C.** (1807–6 May 1871), was an architect active in Cleveland between 1848–71. He was born in Waterbury, Conn., the son of Lemuel Porter, a woodworker and joiner. The family moved to Tallmadge, Ohio, in 1818, and later to Hudson. Porter erected several of the buildings of Western Reserve College (now Western Reserve Academy) and many houses in Hudson before moving to Cleveland in 1848. From 1849–59, Porter was the partner of CHAS. W. HEARD, and the firm of Heard & Porter was the leading architectural company of the decade in Cleveland. They planned the Second Presbyterian Church (1852), Old Stone Church (1855), CENTRAL HIGH SCHOOL (1856), several commercial blocks, and numerous other schools and residences, including those of Hinman B. Hurlbut and Chas. Hickox. Porter separated from Heard in 1859 and continued to practice independently. He designed Cleveland's West Side High School in 1861, but he was most active outside of Cleveland, erecting buildings in Akron, Brecksville, Kent, Hudson, and Alliance. When Porter died in 1871, he was buried in the new LAKE VIEW CEMETERY.

**POTTER AND MELLEN, INC.,** is one of Cleveland's prominent jewelry and silverware stores. Horace Potter, noted jeweler, teacher, designer, and master craftsman, founded the firm as the Potter Studio in a small room at E. 115th St. and Superior Ave. in 1900 (sometimes given as 1899). Potter designed and created jewelry, silverware, and other artwork. In 1921, he employed Louis Mellen in his shop, which had occupied various buildings in its early years. The Potter studio was incorporated in 1924. In 1928, Potter joined with Guerdon W. Bently, a creator of prints and bronzes, to form the Potter Bently Studios, Inc., which moved into a new building at 10405 Carnegie Ave. near E. 105th St. The new store, managed by Mellen, displayed the works of both artists. In 1933, Bently withdrew from the business, and the store's name was changed to Potter & Mellen, Inc. The firm then started to expand its line of products to include fine china and glassware. It also operated a garden-and-flower shop for a short time. The facilities were later expanded to provide more space for creative work, restoration and repairing of silverware, and redesigning of old jewelry. Potter & Mellen has always remained small, averaging around 10 artisans and clerks in its store, but it has won many national and international awards for its craftsmanship.

The **PREFORMED LINE PRODUCTS COMPANY,** manufacturer of hardware and accessories for electrical and telephone transmission cables, was organized in 1947 to produce armor rods for protecting and reinforcing overhead electrical transmission lines. Both the product and the company were the invention of Thos. F. Peterson (12 Dec. 1902–24 Aug. 1962), the New York-born son of an immigrant Norwegian sailor. Peterson came to Cleveland in 1941 as director of electrical cable engineering and research for the American Steel & Wire Co. Ca. 1934 he developed a preformed spiral armor rod for reinforcing or splicing overhead high-tension cables, but he did not begin to promote his invention until 1947. By 1944 he had perfected the rod and licensed others to manufacture and sell it, but business was poor. Peterson formed his own production and sales effort in mid-1947 with 4 employees. Located at 1051 Power Ave., Preformed Line Prods. had sales of $250,000 its first year. In 1950 sales reached $1 million, employment had risen to 20, and the company purchased new facilities at 5349 St. Clair Ave. The company grew steadily and by 1962 enjoyed sales of $9 million, had grown to employ 500 employees, owned 3 manufacturing plants in Cleveland and another in Palo Alto, Calif., and had established overseas affiliates in Australia and India (1957), Great Britain and Germany (1958), Canada and Spain (1960), and Japan (1961). Peterson continued to develop new products as well, holding more than 30 patents by the time of his death. The company began to expand by acquisition in the 1960s. In 1964 it acquired the assets of Ship Services, Inc., of Brooklyn, and formed a subsidiary, Ship Rigging & Testing Services, Inc.; in 1968 it acquired the California-based Smith Co., which produced accessories for underground construction in the telephone and community television industries. It continued such acquisitions and expansion into the 1980s, acquiring a controlling interest in a Canadian maker of fiberoptics systems, Foundation Instruments, Inc., in 1980. That year the company employed 2,000 people worldwide, including 150 at 2 Cleveland plants, and dedicated its new $3 million corporate headquarters and research and engineering center at 660 Beta Dr. in Mayfield. In 1981 the company's net sales of $77.9 million brought it a net income of $7.956 million.

**PREHISTORIC INHABITANTS.** Following the northward melting of the last glacial advances ca. 15,000 years ago, northeast Ohio was an area of slow, gravel-choked rivers, high bogs, and ice-ponded lakes. Vegetation was a mixture of near-Arctic tundra, with birch and willow or cedar and spruce forests on the lower ground, and most upland forests of oak, maple, and pine. Across this landscape roamed herds of caribou, as well as mastodon, giant beaver, moose, bear, lynx, and wolves. While it is quite probable that the Paleo-Indians, early ancestors of the American Indian, had already arrived in the New World, there is no convincing evidence of their presence in northern Ohio at this early date. With the draining of western Lake Erie in the period after 12,500 years ago, watersheds throughout the area were affected. Bogs and marshes were drained with the falling water tables, and the rejuvenated rivers and streams began sweeping out their valley sediments and rapidly eroding into the uplands, capturing other streams that formerly had drained south to the Ohio. Caribou herds were restricted to the fringe of grassland and spruce forests along the older lakeshore, while upland forests of beech, maple, oak, and hemlock supported large groups of elk, white-tailed deer, turkey, and raccoon, as well as smaller numbers of wolves, bobcats, and cougars. The only Paleo-Indian campsites documented in northern Ohio occur on the bluffs overlooking the Vermilion and

Black rivers. However, over 60 examples of their characteristic "fluted" spearpoints, finely chipped of high-quality flint and chalcedony, recovered from plowed fields scattered across Medina, Summit, Cuyahoga, Lake, and Geauga counties, testify to the presence of small groups of these ancient hunters and gatherers utilizing, if not occupying, the Cleveland region between 12,500–9,500 years ago. There are 2 older collections of such "fluted" spearpoints, which might have been obtained from multifamily campsites. A Western Reserve Historical Society report for 1876 described a number of similar spearpoints acquired from the western edges of the Mill Creek Valley in old Newburgh Twp. (now GARFIELD HTS.), while a series of 1930 photographs in the Natl. Archives illustrate 9 identically made fluted spearpoints from a garden along the western bluffs of the Rocky River in what may now be FAIRVIEW PARK.

Beginning some 9,500 years ago, the onset of a continental pattern of warmer and drier weather, coupled with a slow rise in Lake Erie and the changes thus created in the rivers that flowed into it, initiated significant and rapid changes in the region's climate and ecology, and in the technology and society of its prehistoric populations. Sometime between 9,000–6,500 years ago, essentially modern natural environments had become established throughout the region. The aboriginal inhabitants of this period, termed Early Archaic, appear to have increased in density as they became more efficient in exploiting the resources from the forests and lakeshore of what would become Greater Cleveland. Living in larger groups of several related families that congregated in locations of seasonally abundant resources, along the river bottoms and lakeshore, the populations broke into single-family hunting and gathering groups dispersed into the uplands for the winter and spring. The fluted spearpoints of fine chipped flint had been replaced by a variety of less-well-wrought stemmed or notched spearpoints and knives, usually of low-quality flints. These styles reflected the local blending of larger regional traditions as seen in the Great Lakes/Prairie states and the eastern Appalachians. There was also a sudden increase in chipped and partially ground adzes and axes, mortars, and pestles made of igneous and metamorphic rock, all suggesting increased woodworking and seed or nut harvesting.

While Early Archaic chipped-stone spearpoints, knives, and stone axes have been found in most of the townships within Cuyahoga and adjacent counties, few Early Archaic campsites have been fully explored or adequately reported. There was a significant concentration of small Early Archaic material recovered from areas surrounding the old Lake Abraham bog in MIDDLEBURG HTS., and Early Archaic tools have been found at springs near the headwaters of Big Creek in PARMA, Cahoon Creek in WESTLAKE, MILL CREEK in MAPLE HTS., and TINKER'S CREEK in BEDFORD. One major Early Archaic campsite existed where Hilliard Blvd. crossed the Rocky River in LAKEWOOD, and a series of stratified Paleo-Indian to Early Archaic deposits existed along Furnace Run in northern Summit County. A well-preserved Early Archaic site has been excavated in a rockshelter along the Aurora branch of the CHAGRIN RIVER in Solon Twp. But it is likely that the major Early Archaic sites in the Cleveland region now lie under the central city itself, or have been destroyed by the industrial developments of the Cuyahoga flats. A further possibility is that many sites located along the lower portions of the rivers have since been buried by the rise of Lake Erie nearly 130 ft.; several Early Archaic points have been recovered *in situ* from deep stratigraphic trenches dug in the first terrace of the Cuyahoga River in the southern portions of Cuyahoga County.

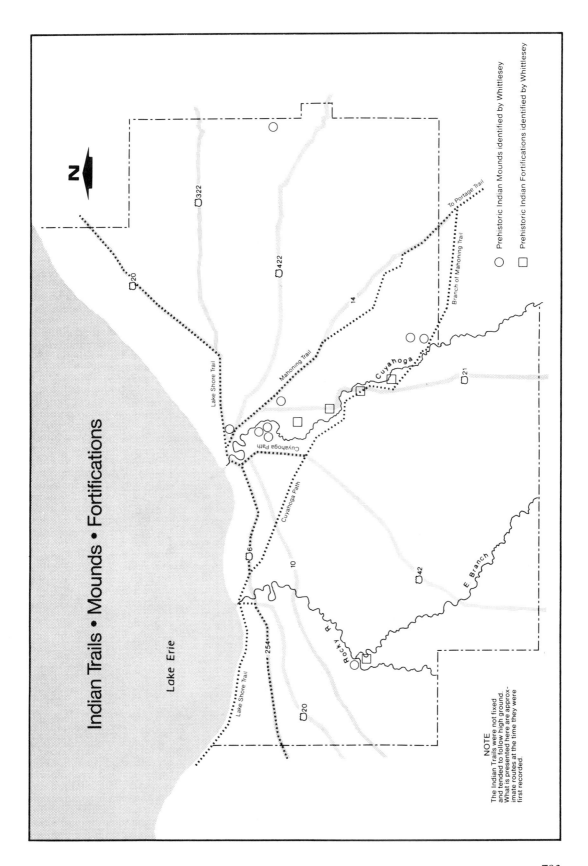

# Indian Trails • Mounds • Fortifications

Lake Erie

N

Lake Shore Trail

Lake Shore Trail

Mahoning Trail

Cuyahoga Path

Cuyahoga Path

Cuyahoga

Branch of Mahoning Trail

To Portage Trail

E Branch

ROCKY R.

322

422

20

6

254

20

10

14

21

42

○ Prehistoric Indian Mounds identified by Whittlesey

□ Prehistoric Indian Fortifications identified by Whittlesey

NOTE
The Indian Trails were not fixed
and tended to follow high ground.
What is presented here are approximate routes at the time they were
first recorded.

In the Middle Archaic period (6,500–4,000 years ago), population density increased and regional territories began to be more expertly and intensively utilized for scheduling the seasonal movements of family groups to obtain the available natural resources. The aboriginal technology reflects this specialization with a proliferation of ground and polished stone tools and ornaments and a significant increase in the standardization of a greater variety of specialized chipped-stone notched points and knives, as well as scrapers and drills. There is some archeological evidence at seasonally well-endowed locations that an increased number of groups came together and stayed longer. In northeastern Ohio, such locations appear to have been at the Lake Erie mouths of the major streams. While in Cleveland those areas have been lost to erosion, past collections of Middle Archaic artifacts have come from Vermilion, Lorain, Painesville, Ashtabula, and Conneaut. A collection from the Buckeye-Woodhill area of Cleveland suggests a Middle Archaic occupation of that area. Smaller sites have been located along the old terraces of upstream portions of the Cuyahoga from NEWBURGH HTS. to INDEPENDENCE. They also exist along the East Branch of the Rocky River in Berea and STRONGSVILLE, along Chippewa Creek in BRECKSVILLE, Tinker's Creek in Bedford, and Griswold Creek in HUNTING VALLEY. There appears to have been little Middle Archaic occupation of such upland areas of Greater Cleveland as Parma, to the west, or the several heights, to the east. From those scattered sites along the lake ridges east of Cleveland or on the Cuyahoga River terraces in northern Summit County, as well as from the single eroded late Middle Archaic level of the Aurora Branch Rockshelter in Bentleyville, have come the earliest evidence of burial practices in the region. Where data are reliable, the burials in shallow circular pits were of individuals somewhat casually accompanied only by 1 or 2 chipped-stone points or by a single ground-stone axe or pendant.

The Late Archaic period of the eastern U.S., from ca. 4,000–2,500 years ago (2000–500 B.C.), coincides with a period of much warmer climate than presently exists. Late Archaic sites yield the first unambiguous evidence for regionally specific and spatially restricted aboriginal territories within which aboriginal groups scheduled their seasonal movements to obtain natural resources, especially nuts. It also shows clear evidence for limited gardening of squash and a number of native seed plants, and for long-distance trade of raw material and finished artifacts destined to mark ceremonial status differences within the cemeteries of those aboriginal groups. Although there were few changes in the styles or functions of chipped-stone tools, new artifacts of ground and polished stone and of shell appeared during the Late Archaic. Among these were hollow tubes used as handles and smoking pipes; geometric and zoomorphic carved weights and hooks for spear throwers (Atlatls); and ritually shaped pendants and plummets of a variety of rock and native ores. Points, knives, axes, beads, and bracelets hammered out of the native Lake Superior copper were exchanged from group to group as far south as the Gulf Coast, while beads, dippers, cups, and pendants cut from Gulf Coast conch shell were traded into northern Ohio. In Ohio, many of the Late Archaic burials were of single individuals in circular pits covered with red ocher. They were often accompanied by a number of such traded artifacts or by caches of unused chipped-flint spearpoints, or the preforms from which such points could be finished. Groups of such burials occurred in high gravel or sand knolls, and occasionally layers of sand or loam were mounded over the pits. Locally, the largest known Late Archaic burial area was located on the point at the junction of the East and West branches of the Rocky River in Berea.

Several smaller burial groups were reported long ago: in the OHIO CITY area, from the bluffs over the lower course of Chippewa Creek, in Brecksville; near Mill Creek, in the Lee-Seville area of Cleveland; and across from Brandywine Creek in northern Summit County. While collections yielding Late Archaic artifacts are known from every township within the Greater Cleveland area, the greatest concentration appears to have been along the ancient lake beach ridges and upon the wider upper terraces along some of the major rivers.

In Ohio, the following Early Woodland and Middle Woodland periods, from 500 B.C.-A.D. 100, and from A.D. 100-ca. A.D. 700, are characterized by increasing elaboration of the ceremonial exchange and mortuary rituals of the Late Archaic. In the Ohio Valley, the Adena culture, with its small circular earthworks and ritual burial mounds of varying sizes, is the local Early Woodland expression. Several new artifact types mark this period, including the manufacture of crude but elaborately decorated pottery of several types. While seasonal economic activities are not well known, the frequency of charred seed, squash, and pumpkin and the limited ceremonial presence of some maize suggest the beginnings of limited village horticulture, although it was not of great economic importance at this time. Certainly the most visible, and one of the most diagnostic, remains of this period are the large and small earthen mounds used in the aboriginal mortuary ceremonies. Distributions of the known mounds were concentrated on high bluffs and terraces overlooking the major waterways, but that may be a preservation phenomenon. It is difficult to reconstruct the exact lifestyles of these early inhabitants. The low density of known Early and Middle Woodland sites is probably a result of the still somewhat mobile subsistence-settlement patterns and of the alteration and destruction of the land surface over the past few centuries.

The mound reported by Whittlesey from the western portion of the Eagle St. Cemetery appears to have been an Early Woodland Adena mound, although none of the materials excavated from that site have been reported in detail. Whittlesey investigated several apparently Adena mounds within the Cuyahoga Valley east of Tinker's Creek, and recovered a tubular stone pipe from a large Adena mound just east of the Cuyahoga River. Parts of this mound still exist under Mound School at E. 55th St. and Eliza Ave. One other test excavation beside a small mound in the southwestern portions of VALLEY VIEW Twp. has yielded Early Woodland pottery and a geometric pendant. Although no artifacts have been recovered from that mound itself, the landowner's description of its method of construction is also suggestive of the Early Woodland-period culture. Additional Early Woodland materials in this general region have been recovered by professional and amateur archeologists, but all such components appear to represent small, seasonally specialized campsites. However, characteristic projectile points assignable to this period have been found as surface materials on the fossil Lake Erie beach ridges behind EDGEWATER PARK, and 1 broken point was recovered from a recent construction trench dug in the first terrace of Giddings Brook in the area just west of UNIVERSITY CIRCLE.

The Middle Woodland period represents the continuation of tendencies developing through the Early Woodland period. There is some trend for more nucleated settlement, and there is evidence of increasing importance of horticulture, especially with maize, although the economy still appears to have been based on semisedentary hunting and gathering. In this period, there is a culmination in Ohio for the Hopewellian culture, whose mortuary ceremonialism used elaborate geometric earthworks containing large multiple burial mounds, with status-differentiated burials and artifacts from as far as the Rocky Mts. The elaborate earthworks characteristic of southern Ohio are not known outside of this region, although a number of what may be Middle Woodland earthwork sites are being investigated in northern Summit County. Within the Cleveland area, some local collections have revealed Hopewellian projectile points, flint-blade knives, and ceramics, although few well-documented exotic artifacts have been found other than copper axes and conch-shell cups from the few Middle Woodland mounds that once existed. One Middle Woodland mound, located just south of Brecksville, contained a large cache of such Hopewellian trade goods within a 6-sided stone crypt. Another smaller mound between Willowick and Eastlake has yielded several large ceremonial spear points of chert from southwest Illinois. A small group of Early to Middle Woodland mounds, excavated in 1878 from what seems now to be the polo fields in the S. Chagrin Reservation, yielded a very unusual cache of "duck-billed" points made of an Arkansas flint.

There were some conical burial mounds along the Middle Cuyahoga River, just south of Independence, which when excavated in the last century yielded material similar to that associated with southern Ohio Hopewellian ceremony. In BROOK PARK and Dover Ctr., several mounds yielded a few similar grave goods, but these were reported long ago and were poorly recorded. Whittlesey's mention of stone-covered graves along the river bluffs overlooking the lower portions of the Cuyahoga River from CUYAHOGA HTS. to Ohio City may also pertain to this period. While a few characteristic tools of this period have been recovered in earlier survey work in what is now Cleveland, the urban and industrial developments of the last century have probably destroyed many actual sites that existed. A few stray items in the WESTERN RESERVE HISTORICAL SOCIETY are from collections spread over a century; however, even at these sites the majority of cultural materials were demonstrably later, suggesting that the majority of seasonally occupied sites were more common in other river valley locations. In the adjacent uplands, the Early and Middle Woodland period is represented by the disturbed remains of what seem to be a number of small, ridge-top hunting camps. Several of these sites have been investigated in Brecksville, BROADVIEW HTS., and EUCLID, and similar materials are known for many townships in the county (Brose 1976), although there is no evidence to support the persistent myths of burial mounds in Cleveland's RIVERSIDE or WOODLAND CEMETERIES. As in the earlier periods, many sites may be buried under valley sediments, or on older, drowned Lake Erie beaches off river mouths, now lost to erosion.

In the period after A.D. 400 throughout the Midwest, there was a decline of the Hopewellian exchange systems and of mortuary ceremonialism. That does not indicate cultural disintegration, however. No evidence for invasion or population replacement exists. While local sites did not yield elaborate ritual artifacts, populations in fact increased in density. There was a consistent economic shift to reliance on maize agriculture and on rescheduling other subsistence activities toward this end. Small Late Woodland villages represent substantial and increasingly self-sufficient groups between A.D. 400 and A.D. 700. However, the material remains of the early Late Woodland period are rather unspectacular and show a general sameness throughout most of the northeastern U.S. Subtle variations in projectile points and ceramic style demarcate local cultural groups. This period of the "Gray Cultures" is of critical importance in understanding the shift from the Hopewellian complex to the Historic period in this area. Unfortunately, most of the archeological sites of this period in the general region are small rockshelter campsites along the edges of the major river valleys to the south and east of Cleveland. However, 2 small rockshelters were investigated near the Fairhill Reservoir, and a series of pottery vessels of this period were recovered in the relocation of Rockside Rd. Because of the preservation factors at these sites, the ceramics and the projectile points are all that are normally recovered. Their plain or cordmarked grit-tempered ceramics, which had straight or slightly curved rims with flat lips, some with interior cordmarking, are usually decorated with fingernail impressions. These show a gradual change from styles widespread throughout the Ohio Valley to styles more typical of sites of the Great Lakes region. Occasionally, as at the small sites located in Lorain, Portage, and Geauga counties, charred plant and animal remains have revealed the increasingly cultural control in economic and dietary changes that took place during this period.

The early Late Woodland corresponds to a period of relatively mild climate, with lesser but still adequate summer precipitation, and with relatively long, warm summers. Winters appear to have been changing from somewhat cooler and drier than the modern "normal" (1930–60) throughout the period from ca. A.D. 750-A.D. 950. The local weather then appears to have become rather warmer than modern weather. Summers grew somewhat moister than today, while the increasing dryness and mildness of winters from A.D. 950-ca. A.D. 1100 would have lessened snowfall along the lakeward Allegheny Plateau escarpment, while it extended (especially along the lakeshore) the frost-free growing period. Archeological sites in northeast Ohio that date between A.D. 700-A.D. 950 show few differences in the size or composition of the groups that occupied them, although these sites seem to have been occupied at different seasons and for different purposes. None of them are permanent agricultural villages, although corn and squash are present at several. Most sites occupied from late summer to early spring sat on steep ridges overlooking valleys of the Cuyahoga, Rocky, or Lower Chagrin rivers. Small, circular houses contained 1 or 2 fire hearths and a few shallow storage pits. Most projectile points were notched, but a few were triangular, and there were a variety of tools and ornaments made of antler and bone. During springtime, populations lived in large plant-collecting and fishing camps located along the lakeshore ridges or around the shores of small ponds and bogs, or near the headwaters of creeks and tributaries to the major rivers. Early collections from E. CLEVELAND, BRATENAHL, and Lakewood include examples of their chipped-stone projectile points, both corner-notched and triangular types, and their ceramics, which were grit-tempered, with cordmarked exteriors and plain interiors. Some ceramic rims were slightly in-curving and had folded collars. Decoration on the exterior neck and rim included incising and various types of stamped impressions.

Between A.D. 1000-A.D. 1200, there were several summer villages on the terraces of the Cuyahoga and Lower Chagrin rivers in Independence, BROOKLYN, and MAYFIELD. These had oval houses of single-post construction. The cordmarked ceramics of this period were often grit- and shell-tempered, with slightly flared rims and flat or rounded notched lips. A few ceramic vessels show a folded collar. All of the recovered projectile points are triangular. Similar stone tools and ceramics have been encountered in the refuse-filled hearths and postholes of circular single-post structures occupied along banks of the Cuyahoga River from Bath Twp. in Summit County, downstream to the Big Creek junction. While no direct dates are available, the artifacts, features, and possible structures encountered in sites on the lower Tinker's Creek floodplain in BEDFORD HTS., along Morgan Run in the Union area of Cleveland, and along Big Creek near the present Cleveland Zoo, are nearly identical.

Beyond those relatively thoroughly explored sites within the region, similar ceramic and lithic artifacts have been encountered at relatively large agricultural sites located on the second terraces of the Cuyahoga, Chagrin, and Grand rivers. Along the smaller tributaries of these rivers, well into the uplands, in RICHMOND HTS., BEACHWOOD, Strongsville, N. OLMSTED, GATES MILLS and WARRENSVILLE, and CLEVELAND HTS., there were a number of very small reoccupied fall and winter hunting camps. Some of these were in rockshelters. It is likely that the sporadic recovery of similar artifacts underlying some early-19th-century canal-building activities on the Cuyahoga River floodplain represents even smaller, more seasonally limited single-family activities, possibly collecting tubers and greens during the early spring, usually called "the starving moon" by Indians throughout this area. There were also a few aboriginal sites of differing sizes occupied during the fall. At Euclid, at Cahoon, under the Cleveland Greenhouse at Doan Creek, and at the mouth of the Rocky River in BAY VILLAGE were sites, located on sand ridges cut by streams entering Lake Erie. These sites seasonally were reoccupied as small fishing camps. Throughout this period, the social emphasis on burial ceremony declined. Most individuals appear to have been placed in simple shallow graves located within the area of the campsite or small village at which they had died. Grave goods are rare, and those that exist appear to have been mundane personal tools, utensils, or ornaments. There is nothing to indicate ranked social status.

In eastern North America from A.D. 1200-A.D. 1600, a "Mississippian" culture with unspecified MesoAmerican influence became increasingly urbanized and agricultural, with major population growth. Their planned communities, with monumental multistage platform mounds and the development of sophisticated and increasing craft specialization, indicate quasi-theocratic control of stratified populations. Warfare and defensive fortifications appeared, as did a new elite mortuary cult. While this complex did not spread far up the Ohio Valley or into the Great Lakes area, its influences can be seen in Cleveland after A.D. 1200 in new ceramic and house styles, in the introduction of new crops (common beans), and in the occasional presence of materials traded into the region from more southerly centers. In southern Ohio, this Mississippian-influenced Woodland population is called Ft. Ancient, and where Ft. Ancient survived into the early Historic period (A.D. 1600–1680), it represented some portion of the Shawnee. In New York and Ontario, this period saw populations similar to those in northeast Ohio diverge into the various Iroquoian tribes encountered by the French. It was at this time that the distinct archeological complexes of the Cleveland area began to show a strong difference from sites between the Black River and the Sandusky Bay/Lake Erie Islands region to the west.

Within northeastern Ohio, the phases of the Late Woodland/Mississippian culture were named the Whittlesey Tradition, after Col. CHAS. WHITTLESEY, who first reported many of their major late sites. Major climatic changes occurred throughout the Whittlesey Tradition. From A.D. 1150-A.D. 1280, summer precipitation gradually decreased to modern normal throughout the region. However, the period around A.D. 1250 represented a dramatic shift to summers of considerable dryness until A.D. 1350–1380. However, there was little change in summer precip-

itation patterns along the Lake Erie shoreline from Cleveland east to Erie, Pa. During this same period, from A.D. 1150-A.D. 1250, there was a winter warming trend, with longer growing seasons with briefer but locally heavier winter precipitation. After A.D. 1250, winters grew slightly drier and cooler, so that by A.D. 1350 the weather from fall through spring was similar to the normal modern pattern. There was some local lessening of the general summer aridity by ca. A.D. 1400, but even this portion of northeast Ohio displayed some "dustbowl" effect from A.D. 1250-A.D. 1350. Nearly modern winters appear to have continued up to ca. A.D. 1450, at which time a massive and rapid shift occurred to the very cold, dry, long winters of the "Little Ice Age" characteristic of the 16th century.

From A.D. 1200-A.D. 1350, sites of the earliest Whittlesey phase reflect an economy that still balanced hunting, fishing, and gathering, with limited gardening. From spring through fall, small villages, probably occupied by 3 or 4 related families, were located along the major rivers, either on the lakeshore or at tributary junctions 3–5 mi. upstream, where mixed forests grew on the broad floodplain terraces. During winters, small family groups hunting deer, turkey, raccoon, and elk camped at springs or in upland rockshelters. All of these sites have grit- and shell-tempered pottery, usually with plain or cordmarked surfaces; occasionally there were incised lines or stamped rows of tool impressions below the lip. Although there were certainly seasonal and functional differences between them, most sites are characterized by similar tool types and styles. These were made of chipped and ground stone, and less commonly of bone and antler. Few tools of any type are found at many sites, except for flake scrapers, with a few small triangular projectile points and stemmed knives. Within Cuyahoga County, village sites of this period have been investigated along the lower portions of the Chagrin River in Mayfield and Willoughby, and along the Rocky River in Brook Park and Berea. Similar material has been found on the Cuyahoga floodplain near the mouth of Big Creek, Mill Creek, and Chippewa Creek; and along the lakeshore in Bay Village, Westlake, Bratenahl, and Eastlake. Small upland hunting camps existed in Bedford, Berea, Independence, Northfield, and Warrensville. Occasional projectile points of these same styles have been found scattered in the previous plowed fields of farms everywhere throughout the area.

Between A.D. 1350-A.D. 1500, the Whittlesey Tradition underwent a shift to increasing reliance on agriculture with the introduction of beans and new varieties of maize. The larger villages were at first occupied from summer into the fall, and were on the low terraces near secondary stream mouths, either on the lake plain or well up the major rivers. Small autumn and winter fishing stations and hunting camps were located on the edge of the lake plain, occasionally associated with group cemeteries. Some were found upon the upland plateau at springs and bogs. But throughout these phases, as the summer villages grew larger and were occupied from earlier in the spring to later in the fall, the society became more and more dependent on agriculture. The specialized hunting and fishing campsites on the lakeshore became smaller, restricted to particular types of forest openings, and grew far more scattered. And by ca. A.D. 1400, the summer villages were generally found on protected promontories overlooking the interior river valleys. Through this period, most of the plain-surfaced pottery vessels became thinner. Many jars have a thickened strip or handles below the rim, and some have a series of parallel or opposed incised lines below the lip. Both Ft. Ancient and New York Iroquoian trade ceramics occur in a few village sites. The number, quality, and variety of bone and antler tools increased, while the workmanship and variety of many chipped- and ground-stone tools decreased, especially in the larger summer villages. The small, narrow, triangular projectile points are certainly arrowheads, while the large stemmed knives were replaced by broad curved triangular knives. There were changes in domestic architecture, as well. The earlier houses, randomly scattered across the sites, were simple circular to oval "wigwam" structures about 250 sq. ft., made of saplings lashed together at the top. The later, rather squared houses, with areas around 400 sq. ft., were regularly spaced and oriented, some with dug trenches for setting the wall posts.

Throughout the earlier portions of the Whittlesey Tradition, the simple burial rites of the preceding Late Woodland period were maintained. Some indication of a greater social hierarchy appears in the Mississippian influences, locally adopted after A.D. 1350. Multiple burial and occasional reburial of family members in larger graves at specific village sites probably represents the social recognition of family- or lineage-controlled territory. Although the grave goods accompanying the departed are still rather mundane, some family groups were accompanied by far more ornamental goods than were other groups. By the later phases of the Whittlesey Tradition, nearly all burials were in single graves located in rather large cemeteries close to, but not within, the large permanent villages. Grave goods are quite rare, and no individuals have more than 1 or 2 items. These are invariably personal ceremonial property rather than symbols of group ritual.

The final Whittlesey phase of northeast Ohio began in the period ca. A.D. 1500. There is clear evidence for year-round occupation in large fortified villages growing maize, beans, and squash. Within these villages were dense rows of multifamily "long houses," and at one site in Independence, there was a circular semisubterranean ceremonial pit house used as a sweat lodge. Several recently investigated village sites of this Late Whittlesey phase were located in Newburgh, Brecksville, Independence, and WALTON HILLS. They were located at about 8-mi. intervals on isolated promontories of steeply dissected bluffs along the Cuyahoga Valley. But the village sites that Whittlesey reported in southern Cleveland and Cuyahoga Hts. are now gone, and any large sites farther downstream were probably destroyed by the mid-1800s. It is possible that these few large villages of the final Whittlesey phase represent 10- to 20-year village movements of a single "tribe" within the Cuyahoga Valley. The subsistence-settlement system had apparently shifted to reliance on a focused, if not intensive, agricultural economy like that of the Iroquois. Nonagricultural resources were subordinated to scheduling at periods of nonintensive agricultural efforts. While there were obviously some attempt to exploit seasonally differing resources, the location of special-purpose activities was controlled by the transportation technology and the need for close articulation with central agricultural villages within restricted territories. The location of these major agricultural villages does not, however, appear to be correlated only with the limited fertile bottomland for resource procurement. The frequency of palisades, earthen walls, and ditches and the village locations on narrow-necked, steep-sided promontories commanding a view of their valley suggests that the earlier authors were essentially correct in their "defensive" interpretation. There were, at the same time, more cases of traumatic injury, nutritional deficiency, and disease. At a few of the large village sites, refuse pits contained butchered and charred fragments of human bone.

These large village sites had as neighbors small special-purpose campsites located on nearby river bluffs, in the mixed-oak forests. Within the area of Cleveland, such sites

have been tested in Brooklyn, Brook Park, Fairview Park, Newburgh, Bedford, Valley View, and Garfield Hts. More distant still were a number of small, sometime fortified, winter elk- and/or deer-hunting stations near streams draining the upland plateau in N. RANDALL, S. EUCLID, PARMA HTS., Brooklyn, Euclid, Cleveland Hts., and ORANGE Twp., and from the BUCKEYE-WOODLAND neighborhood in Cleveland itself. A few small fishing camps and waterfowl-hunting sites were located during the spring and fall on the beachridges or lakebluffs, often near marshes, fens, or bogs. Such sites have been reported in E. Cleveland, Middleburg Hts., HUNTING VALLEY, SOLON, Bedford, Bay Village, and N. ROYALTON, and similar archeological materials were reported from the Brooklyn, HOUGH, and TREMONT neighborhoods of the city, as well as from early recovery within the lower Cuyahoga River flats. Finally, a few small groups, probably hunting for bear and raccoon, occupied rockshelters in narrow valleys well into the interior hills of the Appalachian Plateau or camped on small ridges that were sometimes fortified. Two of these small ridge-top sites overlooking Chippewa Creek were excavated just east of BROADVIEW HTS. several years ago.

If the Whittlesey settlement pattern approximates that of the Iroquois, their sociocultural behavior seems closer to such Algonkian groups as the Shawnee. That such a combination may not have been advantageous is suggested by the fact that despite the increased agricultural economy, prior to the disappearance of local aboriginal groups ca. A.D. 1640, the entire region of northeastern Ohio displays a more highly concentrated but lower overall population than existed in A.D. 1400. It may be significant that the latest Whittlesey phase, from A.D. 1500-A.D. 1640, corresponded with the "Little Ice Age," a period of much moister and very long and cold winters (with average conditions approximating those of the 1976–77 winter of recent notoriety). It is possible that frost-free seasons were so shortened and irregular during the climatic episode that the agricultural economy became a disadvantage. While summer precipitation and temperatures along the northeast Ohio Erie shoreline were apparently rather warm and wet, late-spring and early-fall frosts would have placed a premium on areas of well-drained and sheltered arable soils. Indeed, the latest aboriginal population density is estimated to have become increasingly clustered after A.D. 1500, and by the end of this period, increasing archeological evidence exists for lower populations for internal demographic stress, warfare, torture of captives, and limited cannibalism. These factors may explain the failure of Late Whittlesey populations to compete successfully for a role in the early European fur trade, or to survive the territorial competition that it created. At any rate, the latest Whittlesey sites have been dated to ca. A.D. 1640. They contain no evidence of deliberate destruction or of even indirect European contact. Following the abandonment of these sites, the area of northeastern Ohio appears to have been unoccupied on any permanent basis until the mid-1740s, when groups of Wyandot or OTTAWA moved west into the area from Detroit.

Specific ethnic identification for late archeological manifestations of the Whittlesey Tradition is, unfortunately, speculative. Radical population displacements are documented in contemporary European accounts of the 17th century. Thus, we cannot assume that within this region the groups historically reported in the early 18th century are ethnically related to those responsible for the archeological components of the early 17th century. Within the Cleveland area, this issue looms large for several reasons. There has been a history of uncritically accepting the Erie as a precontact tribe that occupied the entire south shore of Lake Erie. Documentation supporting such a position is, at best, minimal. Based upon the earliest French documents, there were a number of distinct aboriginal groups along the south shore of Lake Erie in the early 17th century. The best candidates for prehistoric Erie villages are sites between Erie, Pa., and Buffalo, N.Y., and it would appear that the Erie were never located farther west than the present New York/Pennsylvania state line. To the south and/or west of the Erie, the Wenro also were said to speak an Iroquoian language, while further west were Algonkian-speaking groups. Many of the latest prehistoric sites in Erie County, Pa., display ceramics stylistically related to those of the Niagara region, and occasionally contain early-17th-century European trade goods. If any ethnic identity can be assigned to those sites, it may well be the little-known Wenro as distinct from the Erie. It was once claimed that sites of the Whittlesey Focus were found along the entire south shore of Lake Erie. This term had the disadvantage of imposing what seems to be uniformity on a number of very different archeological manifestations.

Late prehistoric ceramics recovered from sites in the area between Lorain and Conneaut are distinct from those from more eastern or western Lake Erie sites of the same period. Those late prehistoric sites in southeastern Michigan and northwestern Ohio, previously assigned to the Whittlesey Focus, possibly represent the proto-Algonkian occupation that early maps place at the west end of Lake Erie. Certainly, the latest occupations in the Toledo area reflect considerable influence (if not some actual population movements) from late Ft. Ancient groups in central Indiana and Ohio. These groups (at least part of which were the central Algonkian populations) appear scattered south to north across the pages of early history as Shawnee, Miami, Mascouten, Sauk-Fox, or Kikapoo. While it is true that the latest prehistoric Whittlesey culture of the Cleveland area had a ceramic tradition more closely related to that of the Algonkian-speaking cultures to the south and west than to that of the Iroquoian speakers to the north and east, there is at present no clear evidence for the names by which their historic descendants (if any) were known.

David S. Brose
Cleveland Museum of Natural History

The **PREMIER INDUSTRIAL CORPORATION** is a multi-million-dollar distribution company with its headquarters at Euclid Ave. and E. 43rd St. It specializes in the distribution of electronics equipment, maintenance products, and firefighting equipment. Products ranging from lubricants, welding supplies, fasteners, and electronic components are marketed to over 100,000 customers around the world. The current corporation grew out of the purchase of Premier Automotive Supply, an automotive-parts distributor, by Joseph C., Jack N., and Morton L. Mandel in 1940. In 1946 the company was incorporated as Premier Autoware, and in 1954, Premier Fastener was formed as a subsidiary company. Stock in the Premier Industrial Corp. was first offered for public sale in 1960.

The company grew extensively during the 1960s and 1970s. The purchase of Newark Electronics in 1968 brought Premier into the lucrative electronics distribution business; by 1984, electronics constituted half of the company's sales and 60% of its profits. In 1977, Premier opened a $1.6 million corporate research and development center, which assisted the company in tailoring its products to customers' needs. The Mandels have remained the chief officers of the company. In 1984, Morton served as chairman of the board, with Jack and Joseph serving as finance committee chairman and executive committee chairman respectively. Robt.

Warren, who joined the company in 1955, was appointed president in 1970. In 1984, the company consisted of 18 divisions and had sales of $330 million.

**PRENTICE, WALTER M.** (1824–2 June 1864), was a Cleveland physician and Army surgeon in the CIVIL WAR. Prentice was one of 3 sons of N. B. Prentice, a saddler in Unionville, Lake County, Ohio. In 1850–51, Prentice was practicing medicine in Canfield, Ohio. There, a younger brother, Noyes Billings Prentice, studied medicine under him. By the time of the Civil War, the two brothers had formed a partnership and were practicing medicine in Cleveland with an office at 11 Pearl St. on the west side. Walter entered the Army "on the staff of General Frye and became recognized as a surgeon of rare ability." He died of disease at Stanford, Ky., while serving as commandant, Medical Corps, at the hospital at Pt. Burnside, Tenn. He is buried in the MONROE ST. CEMETERY. Noyes Billings Prentice served on the medical staff at the U.S. GENERAL HOSPITAL at Cleveland on University Hts. during the Civil War.

**PRENTISS, FRANCIS FLEURY** (22 Aug. 1858–1 Apr. 1937), was a founder and president of the Cleveland Twist Drill Co. and a major Cleveland philanthropist. Foremost among his many civic and charitable endeavors was his support of ST. LUKE'S HOSPITAL. Prentiss was born in Montpelier, Vt. In 1869 his father, a lawyer and banker, moved the family to Winona, Minn., where Francis attended the public schools. At 16 he became a clerk in his father's Second Natl. Bank in Winona. In 1879, Prentiss moved to Cleveland and formed a partnership with Geo. C. Davies to manufacture locks in a shop on Center St. The following year he formed a new partnership with Jacob D. Cox, the forerunner of the Cleveland Twist Drill Co. Prentiss served as president of the company from 1904–11, then became chairman of the board of directors, holding that post until his death. He had other business interests, serving as a director of the Lake Shore Savings & Trust Co., the Cleveland Life Insurance Co., the Superior Steamship Co., the Cleveland Graphite Bronze Co., OSBORN MFG., and the Youngstown Steel Co.

In the early 1900s, Prentiss took an active role in the civic, cultural, and charitable affairs of the city. He was president of the Chamber of Commerce (1906) and chairman of the Cleveland INDUSTRIAL EXPOSITION (1909), the Cleveland Committee of the Natl. Education Assoc. Convention (1908), and the City Planning Commission (1915). Between 1901–19, Prentiss was among the financial backers of the visiting orchestra series, the forerunner of the CLEVELAND ORCHESTRA. He was instrumental in forming the MUSICAL ARTS ASSOC. and served as one of its trustees. He served as a trustee of the CLEVELAND MUSEUM OF ART, the WESTERN RESERVE HISTORICAL SOCIETY, Western Reserve University, Case School of Applied Science, and Andrews School for Girls in Willoughby.

Two projects received much of Prentiss's attention: the HIRAM HOUSE social settlement and St. Luke's Hospital. He was an officer in and a leading donor to both institutions for 30 years. He served as president and chairman of the board of Hiram House. He also served as president of the St. Luke's Hospital Assoc., beginning in 1906, when he gave the Cleveland General Hospital $30,000 to finance its move from Woodland Ave. to Carnegie and loaned it another $88,000. He later donated $2 million to help finance construction of a new facility, and in 1933 he personally assumed the institution's $337,557 debt. It has been estimated that Prentiss gave a total of more than $6 million to the hospital. Upon his death, he left 70% of his estate to St. Luke's. In Apr. 1934 he received the Cleveland Chamber of Commerce's Medal for Public Service. Prentiss was married twice. On 3 Jan. 1900, he married Delight Sweetser; she died in 1902. On 19 Sept. 1917, he married Elisabeth Severance Allen, the widow of Dr. DUDLEY P. ALLEN, a surgeon. Because of her own support for St. Luke's, she was chosen to succeed Prentiss as its president in 1937.

**PRENTISS FOUNDATION.** *See* **ELISABETH SEVERANCE PRENTISS FOUNDATION**

The **PRESBYTERIAN UNION,** originally named the Cleveland Presbyterian Church Union, is a voluntary association of Presbyterian pastors and officers from various churches in Greater Cleveland and was organized to extend and strengthen Presbyterianism in the city by establishing a network of mission churches, Sunday schools, and other religious and humanitarian enterprises throughout the city. The preliminary planning meeting, held on 13 Nov. 1869 in the chapel of Westminster Church, Prospect and Huntington streets, was attended by officers of the FIRST, Second, Euclid St. (Third), and Westminster churches. It established goals and planned for further meetings. The next meeting, held on 10 Dec. 1869, enjoined a committee to draft a constitution; Joseph B. Merriam was appointed treasurer.

At their meeting on 10 Jan. 1870, also in Westminster Church, 16 representatives attended from the following Presbyterian churches: East Cleveland, Old Stone, Miles Park, Parma, Second, Euclid St., and Cleveland West. A constitution was adopted binding the churches together in a united effort in the work of church extension. The first officers included: president, Rev. Wm. Henry Goodrich, D.D.; vice-president, Rev. Jas. Eells, D.D.; secretary, Caleb S. Bragg; and treasurer, JOSEPH PERKINS. The executive committee included Reuben F. Smith, SOLON L. SEVERANCE, and Geo. H. Wyman. For the next 20 years, the union, meeting quarterly, assumed the financial responsibility for helping many Presbyterian churches and/or mission Sunday schools get started, assisted with financing building programs, helped churches finance repairs and maintenance, and contributed to pastors' salaries. Funds came from substantial individual donations and from church contributions.

On 24 Apr. 1891, the Presbyterian Union was incorporated. Property could henceforth be held in the union's name. Dr. Hiram C. Haydn of Old Stone Church was instrumental in the founding and sustenance of the union, serving as president from 1874–75 and from 1908–13. TRUMAN P. HANDY, who served from 1873–74 and from 1875–93, guided the union during critical years. The union helped to plan and expedite the centennial celebration, held 12–14 Nov. 1911, honoring 100 years of Presbyterianism in Cleveland. At this time, the union extended opportunity for membership to all Presbyterians, and in 1928 it developed a new constitution, making it possible for all Presbyterian churches to be represented on the board of trustees. During the Depression, the union provided emergency funds for many churches that were in danger of closing. It also established and maintained Harkness Camp, a coeducational camp on 15 acres of Lake Erie shoreline near Willoughby, Ohio. The camp provided opportunities for children from the suburbs as well as from the inner city from 1919–45.

During its latter years, the Presbyterian Union endeavored to be seen as a social organization where all Presbyterians could meet and unite for fellowship and service. Many of its activities overlapped with those of other Pres-

byterian organizations; consequently, in 1948–49 the Endowment Fund of the Cleveland Presbytery, the Church Extension Committee of the Presbytery of Cleveland, and the Presbyterian Union consolidated into a single corporation, entitled the Board of Trustees of the Presbytery of Cleveland, to extend and promote the growth and activities of the Presbyterian church. The first meeting of the combined organizations was held on 20 Feb. 1949.

**PRESBYTERIANS.** The Presbyterian church was among the first of the Protestant denominations to establish itself in the Cleveland area; it was brought along with some of Cleveland's earliest settlers and subsequently achieved rapid growth and development. Presbyterianism as a form of church polity originated in the 16th-century Protestant Reformation and the teachings of John Calvin of Switzerland and John Knox of Scotland. Calvin saw the church as a community with equally apportioned membership under the single head of Christ. This view begat a representative form of government that incorporates a "priesthood of all believers," in which clergy and laity differ only in function; there is equality of all clergy; and governance is carried out equally by clergy and laity through elections at all levels: the session (individual local church), presbytery (a group of local churches), synod (a regional group of presbyteries), and General Assembly (the highest legislative body, elected by presbyteries). The present mainline denomination, the Presbyterian Church (USA), dates its beginnings to New England Puritans who preferred a representative form of government to the Congregational form. By the beginning of the 18th century, the church was a mixture of New England Puritans, Scots-Irish, Welsh, and other immigrant Presbyterians. Schisms from the mid-18th century to the mid-19th, engendered by various differences of doctrine, worship, practice, and social stance (particularly with regard to slavery and temperance), and subsequent expansion of the offshoots of the church made the later 19th and the 20th centuries a time for mergers in an attempt to bring the many pieces back into a whole. The most recent of these mergers, in 1983, brought together the 2 major branches of the Presbyterians, the Presbyterian Church in the U.S. (historically the southern branch of the church) and the United Presbyterian Church (historically the northern church), both of which had been created from numerous earlier mergers, into the Presbyterian Church (USA).

The early history of the Presbyterian church in Cleveland and the WESTERN RESERVE is inextricably linked to that of the Congregational church (see CONGREGATIONALISTS), by a scheme known as the Plan of Union, adopted in 1801 by the Presbyterian General Assembly and the Congregational General Assoc. in an effort to establish new churches. Churches were to be organized under the plan, served by missionaries secured for the most part by the Connecticut Mission Society (Congregational), and administered by the Presbyterian General Assembly and its synods in the east. Wm. Wick and JOSEPH BADGER were the first circuit missionaries for the region under the Plan of Union. The so-called Presbygational churches generally took one denomination name or the other based on prior relationships of the members or the preferences of the preacher, and often switched alliances when congregations had grown and the original aim of founding new churches in the frontier was achieved. This pooling of resources was highly successful in achieving that aim in new communities in the Reserve and in western New York State. By the 1830s, however, differences had developed, principally over questions of polity and practice as well as the slavery question, and the Plan of Union was officially abrogated in 1837. As late as the 1850s, churches founded under the plan realigned their relationships with the denominations to suit the opinions and convictions of the membership. First Presbyterian of E. Cleveland ("Old First"), founded in 1807, is a Plan of Union church, as are FIRST PRESBYTERIAN (OLD STONE), EUCLID AVE. CONGREGATIONAL, Archwood Congregational, and others. Disputes within the larger Presbyterian church played a large role in the dissolution of the Plan of Union and also caused a split in the denomination itself. The Utica, Geneva, and Genesee synods in New York state, and the Western Reserve were "exscinded" by the General Assembly in 1837, and in 1838 the assembly itself was split into "Old School" and "New School" branches, the latter of which assumed responsibility for northern Ohio churches.

In Cleveland, the earliest Presbyterian church was First Church, E. Cleveland (see FIRST UNITED PRESBYTERIAN CHURCH OF E. CLEVELAND), founded in 1807, followed by First Presbyterian (Old Stone), in 1820. Much of the growth of the Presbyterian church in the 19th century was as a result of the emphasis the church placed on educating its membership. The Presbyterian ideal of a lay membership governing the church on equal footing with clergy called for a literate membership. In the early and mid-19th century, the Sunday school movement was taking root in the U.S., and its concepts fitted the Presbyterian ideal well. First Church, Cleveland (Old Stone), is said to have been unable to organize a Sunday school in 1833 because none of the children could read. Thus, a free school was organized and was eventually housed in the Bethel Church on Eagle St. It was adopted as the first school when the public school system was instituted in the 1870s. In the day of itinerant preachers, churches often began as Sunday school classes rather than as worshipping congregations and remained so until they gained a sufficient size and wealth to retain a preacher. This practice continued as the city grew, and city churches often opened Sunday schools in new neighborhoods, which later became independent congregations. First Church (Old Stone), Second Presbyterian, First, E. Cleveland, and NORTH PRESBYTERIAN each propagated new churches in this way.

Among the early acts of the Presbyterian church in the Western Reserve was to begin an academy at Hudson in 1826 to provide candidates for the ministry in the hope of satisfying the pressing need for clergymen in new communities and churches. Western Reserve College remained in Hudson until 1882, when, through the efforts of Rev. HIRAM C. HAYDN, pastor of First Church (Old Stone) and a trustee of the college, it was moved to Cleveland and became, through the donation of AMASA STONE, Adelbert College of Western Reserve University. Western Resrve Academy, a preparatory school, was operated for a time in Hudson by WRU and was later privately reconstituted. WRU was later merged with the Case School of Applied Science to form CASE WESTERN RESERVE UNIVERSITY. Later in the 19th century and well into the 20th, the Presbyterian committment to education manifested itself in the many programs conducted as mission projects of various churches, among them the several settlement houses that ultimately became the Garden Valley Neighborhood Ctr., started by the Woodland Ave. Church in 1913 on Woodland Ave.; KARAMU HOUSE, originally known as the Playhouse Settlement, begun at E. 38th and Central in 1915 as a project of Second Presbyterian; and Goodrich House (see GOODRICH-GANNETT NEIGHBORHOOD CTR.), a project of FLORA STONE MATHER and First Church (Old Stone) begun in 1896.

Since Calvinism had spread widely in Europe, the influx of immigrants to Cleveland in the late 19th and early 20th centuries brought the founding of several ethnic Presbyterian congregations. Among these were First Magyar Presbyterian, Slovak Calvinistic United Presbyterian in Lakewood, Lake Shore Welsh Presbyterian (later E. 55th St. Presbyterian), and ST. JOHN'S BECKWITH MEMORIAL CHURCH in LITTLE ITALY, a mission to Italian immigrants. A Korean church, Korean Central Presbyterian, was established on the west side in 1983. Much of the work of Presbyterians as a body was directed to other types of missionary activity in the community, as well. In addition to settlements and schools, the WESTERN SEAMEN'S FRIEND SOCIETY, a mission and shelter for destitute sailors, was founded by the church. Begun in 1830 and reorganized in 1867 as the Cleveland BETHEL UNION, it constructed a building at Superior and Union Ln. in 1867, providing shelter and other social services, including employment, to the needy. The Bethel Union later developed into the Associated Charities.

The Presbyterian church is a strongly institutional church, and much of its extension after pioneer times was accomplished in a cooperative fashion within the denomination. The PRESBYTERIAN UNION, founded in 1869, provided planning and financing for the founding of at least 40 churches in the Western Reserve between 1869–1933. Cleveland had been a headquarters of the various presbyteries governing area churches since the founding of First Church, E. Cleveland, in 1807, which was the center of the Grand River Presbytery and later the Cleveland Presbytery. The present (1986) Presbytery of the Western Reserve dates from 1973, and was preceded by one of the same name constituted from a merger in 1958. The present presbytery embraces 60 churches in Cuyahoga, Lake, Geauga, Ashtabula, Lorain, and parts of Medina, Portage, Summit, and Trumbull counties. By the 1930s, much of the mission concern of the church was directed toward the maintenance of congregations and to social concerns. The local presbytery in 1937 passed resolutions opposing what it considered to be objectionable enlistment methods for the state militia, and in 1938 passed a resolution condemning the treatment of Jews in Germany.

Following WORLD WAR II, the church shared in the national experience of rapid population growth. From 1948–62, 15 churches were established in the Western Reserve. The pattern of steady growth of Presbyterianism in the Cleveland area is reflected in membership figures drawn from the minutes of the various presbyteries centered in Cleveland. While boundaries were changed several times within the time period shown, the trend of steady increase mirrors the growth of the Cleveland-area population: 1818, 599 members; 1900, 9,108 members; 1920, 15,724 members; 1950, 30,929 members; 1965, 49,317 members (figures include Cuyahoga and surrounding counties); 1975, 29,326 members (after a boundary realignment that removed the Akron area from the Presbytery of the Western Reserve). Other projects of the church have included participation in the Inner City Protestant Parish, begun in 1955 on the near west side, which served a diverse and changing neighborhood; the establishment of an Office of Religion & Race (June 1963, the first such office in the country); a Hunger Program (est. 1976); and a peacemaking project, Swords into Plowshares, created in 1980 to explore options for peaceful solutions to world conflicts. In 1986, the Presbytery of the Western Reserve was composed of 60 churches, of which 40 were in the immediate Cleveland area, and its membership was 22,710.

George D. Barnum
Case Western Reserve University Libraries

Ludlow, Rev. and Mrs. Arthur C., *History of Cleveland Presbyterianism* (1896).

See also RELIGION.

**PRESCOTT, JAMES SULLIVAN** (26 Jan. 1803–3 Apr. 1888), was a stonemason, educator, and historian whose autobiographical account of the history of the NORTH UNION SHAKER COMMUNITY provides a major source for the history of Cleveland Shakerism. Born in Lancaster, Mass., Prescott was a descendant of John Prescott, one of the first settlers of Lancaster, who had immigrated in 1640 from Lanshire, Lancashire, England. Prescott received his early religious training from his Congregationalist mother. After her death in 1813, he went to W. Boylston, Mass., to live with his uncle, Brigham Prescott, a well-educated man who tutored his young nephew. At the age of 16 he moved to Springfield, Mass., where he joined a stonemason, Chas. Stearns, to learn the trade. After serving a year as an apprentice, he joined Dunforth Rogers, a stonemason in Hartford, Conn. During this time he affiliated with the Baptist religious revival movement, and in 1821 he became a teacher in the African Sunday School. While serving his apprenticeship, he attended Literary School & Female Academy (a high school), and in 1824 he entered Westfield Academy, Mass., where he completed his education.

After spending a year (1825) teaching the Oneida tribe of Indians for the Baptist Missionary Convention of New York, Prescott emigrated to Cleveland in July 1826, where he worked as a journeyman stonemason. Later in the summer, Elisha Russell, an elder in the N. Union Colony of Shakers, persuaded Prescott to come to N. Union to assist in building the foundation of a dwelling house. After working for several months in the colony, Prescott, "having found the faith he had been seeking," was admitted to the Shaker Society in the fall of 1826. In 1827, he was appointed an elder, and the following year he became a teacher in the colony, beginning a lifetime of service and devotion to the development and promotion of the Shaker Society. He served as a farmer, educator, headmaster, stonemason, and craftsman (especially furniture) and in positions of leadership, including presiding elder, deacon, and legal trustee. He became the spokesman for the Shakers at national spiritualist conventions held in Cleveland in 1852 and in 1871. He spent some time in 1870 with the Tuscarora Indians in Tonawanda, N.Y., as a teacher and missionary and in 1876 went to Boston to visit a distant cousin, Wm. H. Prescott, the historian. In 1870, Prescott wrote the history of N. Union expressly for the WESTERN RESERVE HISTORICAL SOCIETY at the specific request of John Barr, a member of the society and ex-judge of the police court. Barr then had the account published in a series of articles in the *Cleveland Herald*. Subsequently, Prescott corrected, revised, and updated his manuscript, and on 22 July 1881, he dedicated it to the EARLY SETTLERS ASSOC. Prescott died about a year before the dissolution of the N. Union Colony.

MacClean, John P., *Shakers of Ohio* (1907).
Piercy, Caroline P., *The Valley of God's Pleasure* (1951).
Shaker Manuscript Collection, WRHS.

**PRESCOTT BALL AND TURBEN, INC.**, considered the largest regionally based investment firm between New York and Chicago and ranked the 33d-largest in the U.S. in 1982, is perhaps the most innovative investment firm in Cleveland. Prescott Ball & Turben is the product of several mergers. Merrill, Turben & Co. was organized in 1924 by Chas. B. Merrill and Claude F. Turben. In 1934, Edward P. Prescott and Morton J. Stone formed Prescott & Co., located in the Natl. City Bank Bldg. Both firms began to acquire and merge with other firms in the 1960s. Merrill, Turben &

Co. absorbed Beadling & Co. of Youngstown (1962), C. J. McCloy & Co. of Cincinnati (1966), and Wawkins & Co. of Cleveland (1967); Prescott & Co. absorbed the First Cleveland Corp. (1963) and Stranahan, Harris & Co. of Toledo (1964). In Oct. 1967, Prescott & Co. and Merrill, Turben & Co. merged to form Prescott, Merrill, Turben & Co. The new organization had capital of more than $7 million, 325 employees, and 113 registered representatives in 11 branches throughout Ohio.

By 1973, Prescott, Merrill, Turben & Co. had grown to employ 525 people. That year it merged with Ball, Burge & Kraus, which had 210 employees. The new firm, Prescott Ball & Turben, had a net worth of more than $14 million, 175 registered representatives in 18 branches in Ohio, and 60 more in 6 branches in New York, Pittsburgh, Indianapolis, and Louisville. In 1981, the firm expanded into realty financing with the acquisition of the Pittsburgh-based Zappala & Co. By 1982, PB&T had annual revenues of more than $100 million and employed 275 registered representatives in more than 30 offices in Ohio, New York, Michigan, Pennsylvania, Kentucky, Massachusetts, Florida, and California. That year PB&T was one of several regional securities brokers purchased by the Kemper Corp. of Chicago. Kemper paid $64 million in cash and stocks for an 80% interest in the Cleveland firm, which became a subsidiary of Kemper's Lumbermens Mutual Casualty Co. In the early 1980s, Prescott Ball & Turben made headlines for several innovative moves. In 1980 it bought and began restoration of the former Bonwit Teller building at 1331 Euclid Ave., which had been built in 1915 as a department store. The brokerage firm moved its headquarters there in Nov. 1981. In 1979 the firm began a free monthly newspaper, *Investor News*, which had a circulation of 50,000 by Aug. 1982 and was hailed as the largest Ohio business publication in circulation and perhaps the 3d-largest nationally distributed business paper. In 1984, PB&T entered into a joint venture with the Lazarus Dept. Stores of Columbus, establishing full-line brokerage houses in Lazarus stores and offering stocks for sale and educational programs on investment and financial planning.

The **PRESCOTT HUNTER/JUMPER CLASSIC** is the major equestrian sporting event in Greater Cleveland. First held in 1965, the competition was the first major equestrian grand prix in the Western Hemisphere. In 1980, the Cleveland-based investment, banking, and brokerage firm PRESCOTT, BALL & TURBEN, INC., undertook local sponsorship of the event. In 1981, the Cleveland Grand Prix became part of a series of 30 North American competitions overseen by the American Grand Prix Assoc. and sponsored, generally, by Mercedes-Benz of North America, Inc. By 1985, prize money for the 30 events exceeded $1.2 million. The Cleveland Grand Prix has been held annually toward the end of July and consists of 1 week's worth of competition at the Cleveland Metroparks Polo Field in the S. Chagrin Reservation in MORELAND HILLS. Attendance for the event in the 1980s has exceeded 10,000 each year.

The second **PRESIDENTIAL DEBATE OF 1980,** sponsored by the League of Women Voters, was held in Cleveland on 28 Oct. 1980. This debate between Democratic Pres. Jimmy Carter and Republican presidential candidate Ronald Reagan was the last held prior to the 1980 election. The Cleveland Chap. of the LEAGUE OF WOMEN VOTERS, led by Pres. Mildred Madison and Grace Kudukis, public-relations spokesperson, together with the *CLEVELAND PRESS*, the Cleveland Convention Bureau, and the GREATER CLEVELAND GROWTH ASSOC., worked actively to insure that Cleveland would be the site of a nationally televised presidential debate. Cleveland civic leaders raised approximately $193,000 to cover debate expenses and make a donation to the league. Negotiations with the candidates' staffs were finalized 21 Oct. At that time, it was agreed that a 90-minute debate would be televised nationally from the Music Hall at the Convention Ctr. on 28 Oct. The debate went off without incident as the candidates answered questions concerning domestic and foreign policy from a panel made up of Harry Ellis of the *Christian Science Monitor*, Wm. Hilliard of the *Portland Oregonian*, Barbara Walters of ABC News, and Marvin Stone of *U.S. News & World Report*, with Howard K. Smith as moderator. Press analysis afterward indicated that while Carter focused on detail and Reagan had a relaxed and genial style, there had been no clear winner.

The **PRESS CLUB OF CLEVELAND** was originally organized on 1 Feb. 1887 as the Cleveland Press Club. Presided over by John C. Covert, editor of the *CLEVELAND LEADER*, the group established headquarters in the former home of HENRY CHISHOLM, picked up over 100 honorary members, and apparently faded from view within a year. A second attempt to organize was made on 31 May 1895 in the Tippecanoe Club, but this assemblage also seems to have been quickly disbanded. A third attempt to incorporate a press club was made on 25 Mar. 1947. Under the leadership of Milton J. Lapine and with the support of the CLEVELAND NEWSPAPER GUILD, it proved to have more permanence. Established in palatial quarters in the Olmsted Hotel, it became a meeting place for visiting celebrities and the host of the annual "Page One Ball." It also sponsored a local radio program patterned after "Meet the Press," called "The Press Club Presents."

Unable to afford the upkeep on its Olmsted Hotel suite, the Press Club entered a nomadic period of existence in the mid-1950s. Among other places, it occupied quarters in the HOLLENDEN HOTEL, PLAYHOUSE SQUARE, and the Merchandise Mart before straitened finances left it homeless in 1970. Indicative of the members' frustration during this peripatetic existence was the protest staged in 1961 by a group of "Roundtable Regulars," who hired a flatbed truck to transport them undisturbed while seated at a table from an abandoned lodging on Walnut St. to the Hollenden Hotel. The most recent reincarnation of the Press Club occurred in 1977, when Stanley J. Modic engineered its affiliation with the Communicators Club in the Statler Office Tower. Open to anyone with a vested or casual interest in the media, the Press Club of Cleveland has maintained its strength at over 200 members in 5 categories: active, associate, student, nonresident, and retirees. Current activities of the club include seminars on media-related issues and the annual Northeastern Ohio "Excellence in Journalism" awards for outstanding work in newspaper, magazine, radio, and television journalism. In 1981 it inaugurated the Cleveland Journalism Hall of Fame with 11 charter members.

**PRESSER, WILLIAM** (14 July 1907–18 July 1981), was a noted Cleveland labor leader. He gained particular attention during his involvement with the TEAMSTERS UNION between 1950 and his death in 1981. Presser was born in Cleveland into a staunch union family. At the age of 15 he was apprenticed as a hatmaker, and at 17 he became a journeyman. His first known union activity occurred in 1926, when he campaigned to organize fish and poultry workers in Cleveland. He was later a prominent leader in the dry-cleaning, vending, and electrical unions. In 1950, Presser became a Teamster organizer, and in 1952 he be-

came president of Joint Council 41. For the next 30 years he kept in close contact with top Teamster bosses. He was a strong supporter of Jas. Hoffa.

Presser's union activities caused him to become a very controversial figure in Cleveland. During his leadership, the union was the focus of a number of federal investigations, including several labor racketeering probes. In 1953, Presser was fined $1,500 for conspiring to eliminate competition in the sale and distribution of vending-machine products. In 1955, a House special antiracketeering subcommittee found him responsible for the existence of rackets corruption and violence concerning Teamster operations in Ohio. Presser served 6½ months in 1960 for obstructing justice after he destroyed records to be used as evidence, and later he served 50 days for contempt of Congress when he refused to say whether he had destroyed certain records. In 1970, Presser pleaded guilty to 8 counts of a federal grand jury charge of 24 counts of conspiracy that charged a plot to shake down employers to advertise in a union publication; he was fined $12,000. Despite his controversial activities, Presser played a large, benevolent community role. He was responsible for raising large sums of money on behalf of various charities and was honored by civic and political members of the Cleveland community. In 1967, a dinner in his honor raised money for schooling retarded people. In 1969 he was honored for leading a drive to sell bonds for Israel to unions.

**PRETERM, INC.,** is a nonprofit medical clinic run by women for women that provides abortion counseling, abortions, contraceptives, and educational and outreach programs relating to reproductive health. Preterm was established on 15 Mar. 1974, largely as a result of the legalization of abortion by virtue of the U.S. Supreme Court ruling of 1973. Its founders wished to provide information about the recently legalized procedure, as well as to offer abortions and other medical procedures for women with a degree of care and sensitivity. In 1975, Preterm offices were open 3 days a week and offered abortion counseling, abortions, breast examinations, and Pap smears. In 1976, branch pregnancy-testing centers were established in ROCKY RIVER and BEDFORD. The Bedford office was subsequently closed because of community pressure. In 1978, the organization offered premarital blood tests and became an observation center for local schools. By 1982, it also offered testing for venereal diseases, modernized early pregnancy testing, and ultrasound testing. Patient fees and Medicaid for indigent patients covered many of Preterm's services. The prohibition on the use of Medicaid payments for abortions in 1981 caused the organization to lower its fees in order to make the procedure available to poorer women. Foundation grants and individual contributions assisted in supporting Preterm's programs. In 1984, Preterm's offices were located at 10900 Euclid Ave.

*Preterm Newsletter* (Summer 1984).

**PRICE WATERHOUSE** is one of the most influential of the "Big 8" public-accounting firms in the U.S. First established in England in the 1800s, PW opened its first American office in 1890. In 1986 the firm maintained nearly 300 offices in more than 80 countries, including some 1,500 partners and a support staff of over 22,000. The U.S. firm had over 70 offices, with almost 600 partners and a total staff of 8,000. The PW Cleveland office operates with a staff of 14 partners, 90 senior managers and senior consultants, and 69 staff accountants. In 1986, its main Cleveland offices were located in the SOCIETY NATL. BANK (formerly the Central Natl. Bank) BLDG. at 800 Superior

Ave. NE; it also operated a satellite office on Chagrin Blvd. in BEACHWOOD. Shortly after WORLD WAR I, PW considered opening new offices in cities where it did substantial volumes of work. That had the dual purpose of satisfying the requirements of existing clients and extending the practice to meet the rapidly shifting demands of the postwar years. Influenced heavily by the recommendations of Samuel Bool, a partner in PICKANDS, MATHER & CO., PW chose Chas. Cullen Roberts to open the office in the Williamson Bldg. in Cleveland in 1919. The Cleveland office struggled during its first years in order to establish itself in a city dominated by practitioners who had been established since early in the century. Early accounts such as the CLEVELAND ELECTRIC ILLUMINATING CO., the White Sewing Machine Co., and Pickands, Mather & Co. were transferred from other PW offices in New York and Pittsburgh. Later, accounts in Cincinnati were also transferred to Cleveland. By 1923, the Cleveland staff had grown to 23, and offices had been moved to the Union Trust (Huntington Bank) Bldg. at 925 Euclid Ave. During the early Depression, the permanent staff remained fairly constant at 10 men. The period 1935–45 was one of steady growth, with the permanent staff increasing to more than 40. In the late 1960s, PW moved its main office to its present (1986) location.

Price Waterhouse, *A Tradition and a Future* (1985).

The **PRINT CLUB OF CLEVELAND** is an invitational organization of connoisseurs of prints and printmaking. It was founded by Ralph R. King (1855–1926), print enthusiast and benefactor, along with a group of charter members and was incorporated as the Print Club on 20 Dec. 1919. Among the incorporators were Wm. G. Mather, John S. Newberry, WM. B. SANDERS, Thos. L. Johnson, Willard M. Clapp, Ralph T. King, LEONARD C. HANNA, JR., Ralph M. Coe, Malcolm L. McBride, H. A. Hauxhurst, H. M. Hanna, Jr., Salmon P. Halle, E. L. Whittemore, F. Allen Whiting, Elton Hoyt, and Chas. T. Brooks. The first meeting, held at the UNION CLUB on 5 Jan. 1920, elected trustees and adopted the following purposes: "to assist the Cleveland Museum of Art to acquire a print collection of high excellence" (later amended to "enhance that collection by consistently generous gifts") and "to stimulate interest in prints and print collecting." Chas. T. Brooks was the first president, 1920–21; King and his family were lifelong supporters and benefactor members. In 1922, the Dept. of Prints & Drawings was established at the CLEVELAND MUSEUM OF ART with the stimulus and support of the Print Club, and since that time "the fortunes, needs and goals of the two organizations have been closely intertwined." The reciprocal relationship has enriched both institutions. Since 1923, the Print Club has allocated funds for the museum to purchase prints and drawings of the annual MAY SHOW artists. Also, in 1923, the executive committee decided to issue an annual "presentation print" exclusively for the museum and for Print Club members. Accordingly, HENRY G. KELLER, Cleveland artist, was commissioned to make the first etching in 1924. This traditional annual gift to the museum and to each of the 250 Print Club members for their own private collections, along with other bequests, has helped the museum to develop a collection of prints. In conjunction with the publishing of the prints, the club has held special exhibitions and lectures and has printed specially illustrated catalogs. Through the years, the curatorial staff of the museum's print and drawings department (notably Ralph King, Theodore Sizer, Henry S. Francis, and Leona E. Prasse) and the Accessions Committee of the Print Club have coordinated the club's gifts, reflecting the changing needs of each organization. Several funds have been established by the Print Club of Cleveland Fund (1969) to enable members to make significant contributions to the museum collection, as well as to collections in other cities. On 9 June 1950, the club became the Print Club of Cleveland, and in 1965 members began taking a series of trips to visit museum collections, often enriching both their own individual collections and that of the museum.

**PRINT JOURNALISM.** Like many of civilization's amenities, journalism came late to the Cleveland area. The settlement waited more than 20 years for its first newspaper, Andrew Logan's *CLEAVELAND GAZETTE & COMMERCIAL REGISTER*, founded on 31 July 1818. Although the *Gazette* lasted less than 2 years, Eber Howe's *Cleveland Herald* (1819) appeared in the meantime to keep the town supplied with a weekly newspaper. Frontier publishing was not an easy business. Logan had to bring his own hand press and type with him from Beaver, Pa. Howe had to manufacture his own ink and make his own deliveries on a circuit extending to Painesville and back. Even paper had to be imported from Pittsburgh until 1823, when a mill was opened in BROOKLYN. Cleveland's third newspaper, David McLean's *INDEPENDENT NEWS-LETTER* (1828), moved to Warren within 2 years in search of readers. In Cleveland, as elsewhere, this early period of journalism was the era of the partisan press. In return for subsidization by one of the political parties, newspapermen customarily followed the party line and shared in the victory with postmasterships and city printing contracts. Most of the 2 dozen papers attempted in the 36 years after Logan's *Gazette* were founded on that basis. Six appeared in 1841 alone, of which none lasted more than 2 years, although the *EAGLE-EYED NEWS-CATCHER* achieved an immortality of sorts by virtue of its name. Editors survived by accepting payment in kind and, reluctant to lose even subscribers who were behind on their payments, continued to send papers until arrears were paid. An agreement signed by Cleveland's 4 papers in 1836 attempted to control competition by establishing standard advertising and subscription rates.

Newspapers shared in the local boom brought by the completion of the Ohio Canal. The *Herald* became the city's first daily, on 30 May 1835, followed shortly by the *CLEVELAND ADVERTISER* (est. 1831) and the newly founded *CLEVELAND DAILY GAZETTE* (1836). Although the *Advertiser* reverted to a weekly and the *Gazette* merged into the *Herald* (see CLEVELAND HERALD & GAZETTE), they were ultimately replaced by the *PLAIN DEALER* in 1842 (daily, 1845) and the *True Democrat* in 1846 (daily, 1847). Specialized papers also made their debuts, including 2 German publications (*GERMANIA*, 1846, and *Waechter am Erie*, 1852), a black organ (*ALIENED AMERICAN*, 1853), and even a high school paper (Central's *School Boy*, 1848). Competition often descended to the personal level, as when the editor of the *Herald* sued those of the *Daily True Democrat* for accusing him of plagiarizing the *Plain Dealer*. Between the Mexican and Civil wars, technological changes improved the city's newsgathering and production potential. A steam press was installed by the *Herald* in 1845, and the telegraph arrived from Pittsburgh in 1847. By 1854, both the *Herald* and the *Plain Dealer* were receiving dispatches over it from the Associated Press. Cleveland's first "star reporter" materialized in the lanky form of humorist CHAS. F. BROWNE, who used the *Plain Dealer*'s local column for the development of his "Artemus Ward" character from 1857–61. With the conversion of the *Forest City Democrat* into the

CLEVELAND LEADER by EDWIN COWLES in 1854, Cleveland journalism entered a 30-year period of stability. Three attempts to found new dailies failed against the dominance of the 3 established dailies. Cowles boldly staked out a radical antislavery position for the Leader, leaving the moderate ground to the Herald and the Democratic cause to the Plain Dealer. The CIVIL WAR was fought fiercely but by proxy in the city's papers, as none engaged the services of an exclusive war correspondent.

By the end of the war, the Leader had a clear edge over its rivals. It was the first newspaper in the city to incorporate (1865) and the first to install a perfecting press (1877). In the 1870s, the dailies reduced their pages in size but doubled their number from 4 to 8. The Sunday Morning Voice was the first to publish on Sunday, in 1871; the Leader and Herald did not follow suit until 1877. The equilibrium on Newspaper Row was finally upset on 2 Nov. 1878, with the appearance of a small, 4-page news sheet named the Penny Press. Greeted as a joke by the competition, EDWARD WYLLIS SCRIPPS's paper nevertheless had revolutionary implications, combining the concise news formula of his brother's Detroit News with his own sympathy for the underdog. Not only was it the city's first genuinely liberal crusader since the early days of Cowles's Leader, but it was also the first in its era to court Cleveland's growing population of laborers and immigrants with a price of 1 cent. As the Press quickly built up a circulation lead over its rivals, the Herald found itself squeezed out of the race. It was purchased and divided by the Leader and Plain Dealer in 1885. LIBERTY E. HOLDEN, the Plain Dealer's new owner, used his half to break into the morning field. Seen at the time as a concession to the afternoon supremacy of the Press, it was a move that ultimately, if unwittingly, insured the Plain Dealer's survival as the city's lone newspaper a century later.

Toward the end of the 19th century, stimulated by industrialization and urbanization, the personal journals of the past were converted into organs of mass circulation. While profits were potentially higher, the amount of capital required by a new newspaper had also increased. Newspapers in this period, therefore, came to be regarded as more business than political enterprises. Four Cleveland dailies were attempted in 1889, of which the CLEVELAND WORLD survived to become the local exemplar of "yellow" journalism. A strike and boycott by local printers failed to halt the introduction of the linotype at the Plain Dealer in 1892. Realizing the increased value of their properties, owners began placing them in the hands of professional editors and managers. Scripps, who had left Cleveland in 1880 to found what became the Scripps-Howard chain, left the Press under the capable direction of Robt. Findley Paine. Holden gave complete control over the Plain Dealer to CHAS. E. KENNEDY and ELBERT H. BAKER in 1898. With 6 established dailies publishing in 1900, it was the golden age of Cleveland journalism. By 1905, Press circulation had reached 141,314, while the Plain Dealer (77,856) had finally overtaken the Leader (53,000). Ads disappeared from the front page, replaced by daily editorial cartoons and halftones. Ethnic newspapers proliferated to serve their foreign-speaking constituencies, some on a daily basis. Reporters were losing their anonymity, as the bylines of columnists JOHN "JACK" RAPER and EDWIN MEADE ROBINSON appeared respectively in the Press and Leader, and that of critic ARCHIE BELL in the World.

Led by the Plain Dealer in 1896, the dailies began leaving their cramped quarters in the Warehouse District to establish a new Newspaper Row along the axis of E. 6th and Rockwell Ave. After the appearance of industrialist CHAS. A. OTIS on the publishing scene, there were fewer

to move. Purchasing the Leader and the World, Otis combined the World and the Leader's afternoon edition, the News & Herald, into the CLEVELAND NEWS in 1905. In related moves, he also killed the Evening Plain Dealer and the Sunday World, leaving the city with 2 morning, 2 evening, and 2 Sunday newspapers. Unable to overcome a long decline since the death of Cowles, the Leader left the morning field to the Plain Dealer in 1917. At the price of the Leader, stability returned once more to the Cleveland journalism scene. Elsewhere it was the age of the tabloid, but none appeared in Cleveland. When the CLEVELAND TIMES attempted to challenge the Plain Dealer in the morning (1922–27), it was as a "business man's paper," and it failed. After the death of Holden and the retirement of Baker, the Plain Dealer seemed content to settle into the role of "grey lady," one it often performed with distinction. It acquired radio station WHK in 1934 but, in a secret arrangement made with the Press, refrained from using it to promote the Plain Dealer in exchange for a dependable supply of newsprint from Scripps-Howard. It acquired the News in 1932 but, instead of developing it into a serious competitor with the Press, merely killed its Sunday edition and eventually sold it to the Press in 1960. At the Press, the Scripps era ended and the age of LOUIS B. SELTZER began. Although the liberalism of the Scripps-Howard chain was buried with the founder, Editor Seltzer compensated locally by promoting clean government and community service. The Press called the shots in local politics and was named one of America's 10 best newspapers by Time magazine in 1964.

A notable generation of writing talent was introduced in Cleveland papers between the wars. It included such names as critic WM. MCDERMOTT and sportswriter GORDON COBBLEDICK at the Plain Dealer and society writer WINSOR FRENCH and columnist HERMAN FETZER at the Press. DAVID DIETZ, science editor at the Press for the entire Scripps-Howard chain, won a shared Pulitzer Prize in 1937, while cartoonist Ed Kuekes of the Plain Dealer brought Cleveland its only outright Pulitzer in 1953. Writers at the Press and News formed the nation's first local chapter of the Newspaper Guild in 1933. A new era in journalism was heralded after WORLD WAR II by the arrival of TELEVISION, which came to Cleveland in 1947. Newspapers were squeezed between this new rival and the increased power of labor unions, which had brought Cleveland its first newspaper strike in 1946. Afternoon dailies became especially vulnerable to a syndrome compounded of suburban lifestyles and the growing impact of television. At first the Press continued its hegemony under Seltzer, opening a new plant on Lakeside Ave. in 1959 and then eliminating the afternoon competition of the News. The tide began to turn in the 1960s, however, as the Press bore the brunt of criticism for the media circus of the SHEPPARD MURDER CASE. It began to lose its circulation lead after the newspaper strike of 1962–63. After Seltzer's retirement in 1966, the Press was generally neglected by Scripps-Howard in favor of its more profitable Cleveland television property, WEWS. When Liberty Holden's great-grandson Thos. Vail took personal charge in 1963, the Plain Dealer showed signs of reviving the crusading tradition in Cleveland. The Holden estate trustees decided to sell the paper to the Newhouse chain in 1967. Thereafter the Plain Dealer exploited its morning advantage over the declining Press. With the closing of the Press in 1982, the Plain Dealer became the lone survivor of Cleveland's journalistic wars. As was the case with local business in general, the city's only daily was no longer locally owned. Under the management of the Newhouse organization, the Plain Dealer seemed to many to be heir to the city's dominant conservative tradition. There were no clear contenders for the locally more sporadic tradition of the liberal crusader.

Although Cleveland had become a "one-newspaper town," it did not lack alternative viewpoints. Besides the television and radio stations, there were numerous suburban weeklies, most of them consolidated into the SUN NEWSPAPERS chain. Two monthlies had made their appearance in CLEVELAND MAGAZINE (1972) and NORTHERN OHIO LIVE (1980). Neighboring dailies such as the Akron Beacon Journal edged into the Cleveland market, as well as national dailies such as the New York Times and USA Today. But by the mid-1980s, it remained to be seen whether a viable alternative to the Plain Dealer would eventually coalesce from this fragmentation of the local media.

J.E. Vacha

Hooper, Osman Castle, History of Ohio Journalism, 1793-1933 (1933).
Kennedy, Charles E., Fifty Years of Cleveland (1925).
McCabe, Charles R., ed., Damned Old Crank (1951).
Porter, Philip W., Cleveland (1976).
Seltzer, Louis B., The Years Were Good (1956).
Shaw, Archer H., The Plain Dealer (1942).
Storkan, Charles Joseph, "Cleveland Newspapers, Magazines, and Periodicals from Its Beginning to 1900" (Master's thesis, WRU, 1950).
See also PRINTING & PUBLISHING IN CLEVELAND; RADIO; UNDERGROUND PRESS; and specific ethnic and other specialty publications.

**PRINTING AND PUBLISHING IN CLEVELAND.** The 1880s were a pivotal decade in the cultural history of Cleveland. It was a period that saw the founding of Case School of Applied Science, Western Reserve University, and the institutes of art and music. It was also a period of growth for the local printing and publishing industry, although the product of the press (including periodicals) for the most part served the commercial and industrial communities. It was not until the 1940s and the flowering of the WORLD PUBLISHING CO. that Cleveland could boast a first-class trade publisher. Although Cleveland was discovered and settled in 1796, by 1810 it had only 57 inhabitants. The WAR OF 1812 further impeded population growth, and as late as 1820 there were only 606 people. There were good reasons for the slow growth: westward movement was mostly via Pittsburgh and the Ohio River, for the Lake Erie route was little used until the opening of the Erie Canal in 1825. Also, land in southern Ohio was cheaper than that being sold in the WESTERN RESERVE by the CONNECTICUT LAND CO. The completion of the OHIO & ERIE CANAL in 1833, linking the Ohio River and Lake Erie, proved a stimulus to Cleveland's growth, and by 1840 the population stood at 6,071. The press had arrived in 1818 to print the village's first newspaper, and Cleveland's first book, advertised in the newspaper that allegedly printed it as Catherine Brown, the Coverted Cherokee, appeared in 1820. But publishing in Cleveland, except for newspapers, did not really begin until 1837, when Sanford & Lott issued the first business directory. That same year they obtained a license to print 10,000 copies of Webster's Spelling Book. The following year their press issued an anonymous work entitled Yorick and Other Poems. Wm. T. Coggeshall's The Poets and Poetry of the West (1860) identifies the author as Jas. Warren Ward and calls Yorick "the first volume of poems published in northern Ohio." In 1838, MOSES. C. YOUNGLOVE, a bookseller, acquired a press and issued the Western Reserve Almanac and Webster's Spelling Book. Thus, by the end of the 1830s, Cleveland had 2 publishers.

The centers of American publishing, as might be expected, were in the old Colonial cities. Philadelphia early on became the leader. A directory states that in Philadelphia from 1742-1820 there were 133 publishers, 60 printer-publishers, 21 bookseller-publishers, and 11 printer-publisher-booksellers, for a total of 225. A similar directory issued for New York, covering the years 1725-1820, lists 67 "printers and publishers" and 41 "printers and booksellers," for a total of 108. Later, as a result of its phenomenal growth as a commercial center, New York would outstrip Philadelphia and all other cities to become America's publishing capital. Closer to home, as Cleveland was struggling to grow, Cincinnati was developing into America's 4th-largest publishing center, after New York, Philadelphia, and Boston. Geography had blessed Cincinnati; it grew on the banks of the Ohio, the main artery of early western travel, and by 1850 it had a population of 116,000. There were 12 major publishing houses, employing 700 people. By contrast, the U.S. Census of 1850 reported a Cleveland population of 17,034, and there were 5 printer-publisher-booksellers. Although not large compared to Cincinnati's, Cleveland's population in 1850 had increased by 10,963 (180.6%) since 1840. Cleveland had by this time become the center of a network of roads, stage lines, and, increasingly, railroads. The city's population would double with each census over the next several decades, not only because of the improvement in transportation but also because of the attraction of the new industries, steel production and oil refining.

Because printing and publishing were mostly commercial and local government-oriented, they tended to locate in close proximity to those functions, in Cleveland's old commercial core area, now called the Warehouse District. That is the region bounded on the east by W. 3rd St., on the west by the CUYAHOGA RIVER, on the south by Superior Ave., and on the north by the lakefront. In 1857, of 10 printers, 9, or 90%, were located in this area; in 1875, 70% of Cleveland's 33 printers were to be found there; and in 1885, 60% of Cleveland's 54 printers were still to be found in the area. By 1905, as Cleveland's commercial core spread southward and eastward, only 22% of the city's 129 printers were still in the area west of PUBLIC SQUARE. Numerically that amounts to 28 firms, not far removed from the 32 of 1885 and the 22 of 1875, which indicates that printing was a locationally stable industry and an intensive user of commercial space. The 1905 figures also show that of those firms located downtown, 5% were in the ARCADE, and 12% were in the CAXTON BLDG., which was specifically designed to accommodate the printing trades.

While Cleveland owes much to the RAILROADS for stimulating its population growth, it is probably because of them that a large book-publishing industry did not develop there. Thanks to the railroads, the products of eastern publishers were made more readily available to western cities. Cincinnati's publishing industry declined steadily following the Civil War, as it found itself bypassed by the railroads. Chicago owed its rapid growth to the railroads, but, although it became the nation's 2d-largest city, its publishing industry never equaled that of antebellum Cincinnati. The improvement of east-west transportation was probably a factor in the opening of Jewett, Proctor & Worthington in Cleveland in 1851. The firm, billing itself as "publishers, booksellers and stationers," was an affiliate of the John P. Jewett Co. of Boston. Historians of American publishing know Jewett as the firm that agreed to issue Uncle Tom's Cabin after Mrs. Stowe's usual publisher, afraid of southern reaction, refused. It was because of this connection that both "Cleveland: Jewett, Proctor and Worthington" and "Boston: John P. Jewett and Co." appear on the title page of *Uncle Tom's Cabin*. There was little else of note in antebellum and immediate post-Civil War book publishing in Cleveland, save for a succession of city directories. In 1857, the Jewett firm and its Boston parent published *Mount Vernon and Other Poems* by HARVEY RICE, a Cleveland educator and man of letters. In the 1860s, Fairbanks, Benedict & Co. published 2 volumes of local history, Chas. Whittlesey's *Early History of Cleveland, Ohio* (1867) and Maurice Joblin's *Cleveland, Past and Present* (1869). These were Cleveland's first local histories, locally published, and they began a trend that has continued, sporadically, to the present day (see HISTORIES OF CLEVELAND).

The 1880s were a watershed decade in the growth of Cleveland publishing. The city's educational and cultural institutions were being formed, and as if in response to an atmosphere of increasing sophistication, 4 new publishing houses came into being: Burrows Bros., the Imperial Press, Wm. W. Williams, and the American Publishing Co. All were, for the most part, devoted to book publishing. Cleveland's most successful publishing house during the last two decades of the 19th century was BURROWS Bros. At first their list consisted of educational or self-help works, e.g., shorthand texts. Then in 1889 they published a "fine" edition of R. D. Blackmore's *Lorna Doone*. The book was acclaimed for its paper, binding, and typography, and especially for its illustrations, of which there were several hundred, executed by a number of well-known artists of the time. Burrows' most successful imprint was *The Jesuit Relations and Allied Documents*, a translation of the writings of Jesuit missionaries who came with the early French explorers of the Ohio Valley-Great Lakes region. The finished work ran to 73 volumes, including a 2-volume index. *The Jesuit Relations*, like *Lorna Doone*, was praised for its beauty as a physical object as much as for its content. Chas. Burrows and his printer, the Imperial Press, may possibly be credited with starting a minor trend toward the production of bibliophile treasures. About this time (1892), the ROWFANT CLUB was founded, and as Cleveland's bibliophile society, one of its activities has been the publication of fine editions of literary works. One of the club's early members was Chas. Burrows. Burrows's love of fine books may have contributed to his eventual abandonment of the book trade. In collaboration with his friend ELROY M. AVERY, Burrows spent lavishly in trying to produce a monumental history of the U.S. The first volume of *A History of the United States and Its People* appeared in 1904; in all, 7 of a projected 12 volumes were published. Burrows never fully recouped his expenses, and in 1912 he sold the company to a local partnership. Meanwhile, in 1902 Arthur H. Clark, a former partner of Burrows, started his own company and began publishing works on American history. Between 1902–29, Clark published 68 titles in Cleveland and achieved national renown as a publisher of western Americana. In 1930 he relocated to Glendale, Calif., where the company remains in business.

Cleveland's most successful and best-known publisher was the World Publishing Co. Formed in 1929 when the Commercial Bookbinding Co. bought the World Syndicate Co., a reprint house that specialized in Bibles and dictionaries, the firm began to prosper in the late 1930s under the direction of Ben Zevin. Zevin introduced mass-production methods, which produced inexpensive lines of hardbound and paperback books. While retaining the Bible and dictionary lines, Zevin turned World into a trade publisher, with such titles as MacKinlay Kantor's *Andersonville*, Simone de Beauvoir's *The Mandarins*, and Harry Golden's *Only in America*. World was sold to the Times Mirror Co.

of Los Angeles in 1962. It continued as a publishing concern until 1974, when the Bible and dictionary lines were sold to Wm. Collins of Great Britain (the trade list having been sold to T. Y. Crowell the year before).

Scholarly publishing on a more or less regular basis began in Cleveland in 1870, when the WESTERN RESERVE HISTORICAL SOCIETY began its Tract Series. The series ceased publication in 1929, with Tract No. 110. After a 13-year hiatus, the society started its Publication Series in 1943, which, as a continuation of the Tract Series, began with No. 111. Some notable works in the Publications Series are ELBERT JAY BENTON's *Cultural Story of an American City: Cleveland*, 1943 (no. 112–14), and Edmund H. Chapman's *Cleveland: Village to Metropolis*, 1964 (no. 116). The Western Reserve Historical Society pursues a policy of scholarly publishing, often issuing as many as 4 titles a year. Cleveland's other major scholarly publisher was the Press of CASE WESTERN RESERVE UNIVERSITY. Founded in 1938 as the Press of Western Reserve University, it produced only 1 or 2 titles a year until the university merged with Case Institute of Technology in 1967. The merger provided the stimulus toward creating a high-quality university press. During the period 1965–70, the press thrived; its sales increased tenfold, and it was renowned for its translations series, its literary criticism, and its medical publishing. But when hard times struck higher education in the 1970s and academic libraries lost their grants, scholarly presses suffered, including the Press of CWRU. Citing an unmanageable deficit, the university board of trustees voted on 9 Feb. 1973 to close the press. Although CLEVELAND STATE UNIVERSITY does not have a press as such, it has issued scholarly works under the university imprint. An example is the Ethnic Communities in Cleveland series.

Throughout the 19th century, periodical publishing thrived in Cleveland. From 1818, the year the first newspaper appeared, until 1900, over 800 periodicals—newspapers and magazines—were published. Some magazines were of a practical bent, such as *House & Garden*, or nationalistic, such as the *Irish National Magazine*. Others sought a more learned or specialized readership, such as the *Journal of Science & Art* and the *Magazine of Western History*. Both of these were of a high quality, especially the *Magazine of Western History*, which contained authoritative and well-documented articles, as well as book reviews and "historical notes." A noteworthy journal of the arts was *Brainard's Musical World*, which was established in 1864 and until 1869 was called the *Western Musical World*. Published by S. Brainard & Sons, local sheet-music publishers, the magazine was devoted to the cause of "music and fine arts in the Great West." The first edition was of 2,000 copies; by 1871, they were issuing 25,000 copies. Along with articles and news items, each issue carried several pieces of music. *Brainard's Musical World* ceased publication in 1895. As transportation continued to improve, western markets were flooded with the products of eastern periodical publishers, and it became more difficult for local publishers to compete, especially in the areas of cultural and general-interest magazines. But Cleveland has done well in business, technical, and industrial publishing. From the mid-19th century onward, the number of business, technical, and agricultural magazines grew steadily. By the 1880s there were 39 titles covering such various fields as farming, engineering, and railroading. There were labor magazines, too, e.g., *Labor Chronicle*, *Independent Labor Press*, and the *Bakers' Union*. Works such as these, and others, reflect the growth of industry and commerce in Cleveland late in the century.

One of the most successful of 20th-century Cleveland publishers was the Penton Press. Founded in 1901, it prospered over the years, issuing such titles as *Industry Week*, *Foundry*, and *Machine Design*. In 1976 Penton merged with the Industrial Publishing Co. (est. 1930) to form PENTON-IPC. The new company publishes 27 titles, including *Progressive Architecture*, *Air Transport World*, and *Modern Office Technology*. Penton-IPC has offices in 15 American cities and in London, Tokyo, and Verviers, Belgium. The firm's longevity and continuing success are maintaining the Cleveland tradition of service to industry, begun a century ago. The arts have not been entirely neglected in 20th-century Cleveland, however. Some interesting literary or "little" magazines have appeared over the years, beginning with *American Weave*, which published from 1936–71. Its first editors were Loring and Alice Crane Williams (she was Hart Crane's aunt). At first an outlet for northern Ohio poets, *American Weave* became a national magazine in the 1960s, publishing many poets whose reputations were to grow. One of these was the controversial D. A. LEVY. Along with writing, levy turned to publishing, producing several magazines in the sixties, the best-known being the *Buddhist Third Class Junkmail Oracle*, which aired the works of some nationally known poets (see UNDERGROUND PRESS). *Free Lance* first appeared in 1950, an outgrowth of the Free Lance Poets & Prose Workshop. By 1955 it was receiving national attention and submissions from such poets as Robt. Creeley and Marianne Moore. Financial difficulties caused its eventual demise in 1980.

Small-press publishing in Cleveland has been an integral part of the little-magazine movement. For instance, the editors of *American Weave* produced an anthology series, *America Singing*, as well as full-length collections of the works of individual poets. Under the imprint of the Renegade Press, d. a. levy turned out 2 chapbooks of his own work in the 1960s along with the collected works of some of his friends. Cleveland's most active small-press publisher of recent years is the Poetry Ctr. at Cleveland State University. It has produced anthologies of national and regional poets, including *Poetry: Cleveland*, which appeared in 1971. The center also publishes the *Gamut*, a partly literary and partly general-interest magazine. Another active press is Bits, which is presided over by Robt. Wallace of the faculty of Case Western Reserve University. Bits has produced a chapbook series, a magazine called *Bits*, and an annual of light verse. There are probably hundreds of small presses in the U.S., in small towns and big cities. In all cases they serve a limited clientele with a special interest: the short novel, the essay, poetry, the art of making beautiful books. The small presses of Cleveland have nurtured, and in turn have been nurtured by, the poets of the Western Reserve. It is a symbiosis that should continue.

Russell Duino
Cuyahoga Community College

## The **PRINTZ-BIEDERMAN COMPANY**, one of the oldest American manufacturers of women's apparel when it closed in 1978, was organized in Dec. 1893 by master tailor Moritz Printz. A native of Austria, Printz came to Cleveland in 1872 to work for his brother-in-law, cloak manufacturer David Black. The head designer for D. Black & Co., Printz decided to stay in Cleveland when Black moved his company to New York in 1894. Along with his sons, Alexander and Michael, and his son-in-law, Joseph Biederman, Printz established the Printz-Biederman Co. as a partnership. The company was incorporated in 1904 with Alexander Printz as president, a position he held until 1954.

Operating from a loft at 102 St. Clair, Printz-Biederman grossed $100,000 in its first year of operation. In 1903 the company moved to 71 Bank St. (1213 W. 6th St.); it remained in the W. 6th-Lakeside area until 1934, when it built a new plant at 1974 E. 61st St. In 1917, the company sold $3 million worth of merchandise; sales reached $6.44 million in 1922, and the firm employed 800 people. It employed 1,000 workers in 1931, and by 1933 it had sales offices in New York, Boston, and Chicago, in addition to Cleveland. In 1943, it supplied garments to 1,200 retail stores nationwide. In 1954, the firm was taken over by Max Reiter, a cofounder in 1939 of the Ritmor Sportswear Co., now known as BOBBIE BROOKS. The company employed 1,000 people that year, two-thirds of them in Cleveland, and annual sales were $8 million. During the 1960s, the payroll included only 350 employees, and by 1969 the company had moved to 2230 Superior Ave. In the late 1970s, the line of products was limited to ladies' suits and coats, and the firm employed only 40 Cleveland workers. The Printz-Biederman Co. was closed completely in 1978.

Printz-Biederman Company Records, WRHS.

**PRIVATE SCHOOLS.** The public-school movement in the U.S. did not really begin until the 1830s and 1840s. Consequently, schools established in the early 19th century were, of necessity, private schools. The line between public and private, however, was not as rigid as it most often is today. The people believed that education benefited the community at large and that the costs should be borne by all. In 1817, the trustees of Cleveland passed a resolution ordering that those who had contributed toward the erection of a private school building should be reimbursed. This kind of government support was common throughout the country before the development of public schools. These early private schools died out soon after 1836, when CLEVELAND CITY COUNCIL first established a free school in the city. The next period of growth of private schools began in the late 19th century. Urban public schools nationwide were experiencing a time of growth and turmoil. An influx of immigrants meant that public schools were losing much of their Anglo-Saxon, English-speaking singularity, and it was believed that the quality of education and moral instruction was suffering. That led to the development of private schools that were more in tune with an older ideal of education. The mission of the BROOKS SCHOOL, founded in 1877, was to fulfill "the need of a classical and English school in Cleveland . . . a church school which should afford the highest order of instruction . . . whose chief aim would be for all pupils to become truthful, courteous, Christian gentlemen." Other schools, e.g., LAUREL SCHOOL, founded in 1896, followed newer models, such as John Dewey's Progressivism. These schools came to share a number of important characteristics: they were single-sex, emphasized a high-quality college preparatory education and Protestant moral values, and prepared students to take a role in upper-class society.

The most successful private schools that developed at this time were MISS MITTLEBERGER'S SCHOOL FOR GIRLS, HATHAWAY BROWN, UNIVERSITY SCHOOL, Laurel School, and HAWKEN SCHOOL. They were all founded by strong individuals who convinced wealthy industrialists such as the Mathers, Herricks, Wades, and Boltons that they had a better way to educate their children. These schools looked to New England for direction. The heads of the schools tended to be from eastern schools. A primary goal of the schools was to prepare students for acceptance to the best colleges and universities: Vassar, Wellesley, and Smith for the girls; Harvard, Yale, and Princeton for the boys. Another important characteristic of these schools is that they were developed as, or came to be called, country day schools. The best setting for education was thought to be away from the central city. Initially, the schools were located in the area of upper Euclid Ave. As the city spread, though, they moved east. With encouragement from the VAN SWERINGEN brothers, Hathaway Brown, Laurel, and University schools moved to SHAKER HTS. in the 1920s. Hawken moved to S. EUCLID. (Miss Mittleberger's School became defunct in 1908 when she retired.)

The period from the 1930s to the 1950s saw little change in Cleveland's private schools. Hathaway Brown, Laurel, University, and Hawken schools had established themselves with solid reputations. The Depression of the 1930s, the war years of the 1940s, and the prosperity of the 1950s posed challenges, but they led to no dramatic changes in the schools. Beginning in the 1960s, however, there was a new spirit of reform, which saw dramatic changes in the older, established schools as well as the inauguration of new private schools. Some of the changes at the older schools were cosmetic. Uniforms became less stringent or were replaced by dress codes. Gone was the girls' uniform of long skirts, stiff corsets, high linen collars, and tight belts, replaced by more casual skirts, sweaters of various colors, and slacks in the cold winter months. The schools closed their dormitories, which had always housed a few students from out of town or from the remote Cleveland areas. Other changes were more substantive. The most important one involved reaching out to new constituencies. An attempt was made to break down the stereotype of elitism and snobbery of the private schools. The preferred name became independent schools, not private schools. The WASPish, elitist heritage did not disappear; but increasing numbers of blacks, Jews, and Catholics were accepted. Scholarship funds, while not new to the schools, were strengthened to enable a few middle- and lower-income students to attend. The issue of coeducation was addressed. Hawken became coeducational in 1974. Talks were held to consider the merger of Hathaway Brown or Laurel with University School. After much consideration, the value of single-sex education was reaffirmed, and no merger occurred.

As the older, established schools experienced a resurgence, new private schools were founded to meet the increasing dissatisfaction with public schools. Confidence in public schools reached an all-time low. Desegregation was unsettling and often inflamed the crisis in public schools. Ruffing Montessori and the Griswold School were founded at this time to meet the newly perceived crisis. Montessori schooling came to the U.S. in the 1950s. Ruffing Montessori was the first school of this type founded in Cleveland, and the second in the U.S. The attraction of Montessori schools was that learning took place without external rewards and grades. This alternative form of education soon became popular with upper-middle-class families. Wealthy supporters were found, and the school was able to move from its early quarters in a west side Catholic church to 2 campuses: one in Cleveland Hts. and one in Rocky River (see MONTESSORI SCHOOLS). (Interestingly, one of the prime supporters of the school was the descendant of a founder of University School.) The Griswold High School, originally founded as a private, proprietary school in 1924, was purchased to serve as an alternative to the upheaval that took place in the Cleveland public school system in 1979 as a result of court-ordered desegregation. An elementary school, the Freedom Academy, was added to the high school to provide an option for younger children. In a short period, the schools came to be seen as an alternative for those dissatisfied with public schools for a variety of reasons, not only desegregation. By 1985, 1/3 of the students came from

school districts other than the city of Cleveland. In contrast to other private schools, Griswold's clientele is largely lower-middle-class, and no wealthy patrons were found to support the school, as was true of Cleveland's other private schools.

Timothy C. Connell
Laurel School

The **PROFESSIONAL MEN'S CLUB OF CLEVELAND,** an invitational organization for men, was preceded by the Cleveland Chap. of the Internatl. Assoc. of Torch Clubs, Inc. At a preliminary meeting held at the Wade Park Manor on 3 June 1927, attended by over 50 professional leaders of Cleveland, the purposes of the national organization (started in 1919) were described as "to provide an open forum for discussion of interprofessional ideas and to promote culture as a counter balance to the narrowing tendencies of specialization." Probate Judge Geo. S. Addams of Cleveland was nominated temporary chairman, and Dean WINFRED G. LEUTNER of Western Reserve University was nominated temporary secretary. The following men, representing a variety of professions, were selected to nominate members, propose a list of officers, and draw up the bylaws: BENJAMIN S. HUBBELL, SR., architect; Robt. Hoffman, engineer; Dr. John P. Stephan, dentist; Dr. Lewis C. Wright, clergyman; Ted O. Thackrey, editor; JAS. H. ROGERS, music critic; Dr. Henry Turner Bailey, artist; Prof. Hippolyte Cruener, educator; Chas. K. Arter, attorney; Paul M. Rea, scientist; and Dr. CARL A. HAMANN, physician. The club officially came into being at a dinner meeting held at the UNIVERSITY CLUB several weeks later. THOS. L. SIDLO, attorney, was the first president.

In 1930, the group withdrew from the Internatl. Assoc., formed its own independent organization, and changed its name to the Professional Men's Club of Cleveland, Ohio. Dr. Harry A. Peters, headmaster of the UNIVERSITY SCHOOL for boys, served as first president of the new club (1930–31). The stated purposes of the new organization were "to unite in good fellowship and understanding men engaged in the practice of recognized professions; to afford them a means of expressing themselves on civic, social and scientific matters; to give them a larger view of each other's professional problems and to make possible an interchange of knowledge and understanding gained from their own experience." Membership, which in 1985 was limited to 125, was based on invitation and selection by members. Meetings, held monthly from autumn to spring, usually consisted of an address given by an authority in one of the professions followed by an open-forum discussion period.

The **PROGRESSIVE CORPORATION** is a Cleveland-based insurance holding company that in 1985 owned 22 subsidiaries and had 2 mutual insurance company affiliates. Its companies specialize in nonstandard high-risk automobile insurance and other forms of specialty insurance. Progressive began in 1937 when 2 young attorneys formed the Progressive Mutual Insurance Co. Joseph M. Lewis and J. H. Green began with $10,000 in capital and, although licensed to write all types of automobile and casualty insurance, limited themselves to auto insurance. By 1940, they were writing about $100,000 worth of insurance a year and had a surplus of $1,600; after a difficult period during the war, business grew in the postwar period. From 3 employees in 1937, the company grew to 45 employees, more than 25,000 policyholders, and assets of $2 million in 1951; by the time it opened new offices at 3600 Euclid Ave. in Jan. 1951, it had branch offices in Akron and Youngstown. Progressive's business continued to grow during the 1950s; by 1959, assets were $6.5 million. In 1947, the company began to offer its "one-shot adjustment service," appraising damaged autos at its company headquarters and reducing time and paperwork. In 1959, it initiated its "Safe Driver Award," and in 1956, the business was expanded into another company, Progressive Casualty Insurance. On 8 Feb. 1965, the Progressive Corp. was incorporated in Ohio and acquired all shares of Progressive Casualty and 3 related insurance companies. By 1970, Progressive Casualty, which accounted for 75% of the Progressive Corp.'s business, was writing its nonstandard high-risk auto insurance in Ohio and 8 other states and was licensed in 20 others. In 1971, Progressive held its first public stock offering, and in 1972, to help keep the company in the Cleveland area, the Cuyahoga County commissioners issued industrial-development bonds to help finance construction of a new corporate headquarters at 6300 Wilson Mills Rd.

During the 1970s and 1980s, Progressive continued to grow. The company moved to decentralize its operations by establishing branch offices in such places as Austin, Tex., and Sacramento, Calif. By 1981, one industry analyst rated Progressive as the leading property-casualty firm in the U.S. Its success was attributed to strong, demanding management, headed since the mid-1960s by Peter B. Lewis, and to its unorthodox attitude toward the insurance industry, emphasizing profitability over volume and relying on specialized markets and short-term investments. In 1984, Progressive thwarted a potential takeover by agreeing to pay $34 million for the 900,000 shares of its common stock held by the American Financial Corp. In 1985, Progressive had $456.5 million in total revenues and a net income of $35.6 million. It ranked 55th in size among property-casualty insurance-company groups in the U.S that year.

The **PROGRESSIVE GOVERNMENT COMMITTEE** was organized on 4 July 1929 to save the CITY MANAGER PLAN from charter amendment. Over the next 2 years it fought for an independent council, and against party-machine politics. The City Manager Plan—the first to be introduced in a large municipality—was instituted in 1924. Public support for the plan gradually weakened, and by 1929 its continuance was seriously threatened. The Progressive Government Committee, composed of 1,400 workers and office staff under chairman Clarence J. Neal, was formed as an independent party to help defeat an amendment that would revert city government back to the Federal Plan. In the August election, the amendment was defeated, and the committee decided to continue as an active party in order to put into the council race in November a slate of qualified candidates supportive of the manager plan and proportional representation. The Progressive Government Committee was run by a committee of 10 key members. If it carried the November election, it planned to continue as a third political party. But the upset failed to fully materialize, partly because the committee failed to define its aims to a public that never did fully understand the manager plan. Of the committee's full slate of 25 nonpartisan candidates, 12 were elected, which—although a partial victory—was not enough for a majority. Although the committee continued to work for city management rule and proportional representation, public enthusiasm waned, and in 1931 the Federal Plan was reinstituted.

**PROGRESSIVE (POLITICAL) PARTIES** were active in Cleveland at 3 different times: from 1911–14 in the Natl. Progressive (Bull Moose) party supporting Theodore Roosevelt for president; from 1922–24 as the Conference for Progressive Political Action; and in 1948, when the Progressive party was again organized to participate in Henry Wallace's campaign for president. Although the issues varied, the Progressives generally were concerned with reform through peaceful change to improve American society.

In 1910, insurgent Republican John Fackler, with support from DANIEL MORGAN and JAS. R. GARFIELD, organized the East Cleveland Progressive delegation to the Republican County Convention, and in Nov. 1911 at a dinner meeting held in Cleveland, the state Progressives organized the Ohio Progressive Republican League. These two groups, which later formed the nucleus of the local and state Bull Moose movement, opposed conservative Republicans committed to Wm. Howard Taft's reelection as president. In Cleveland, Fackler and his group favored Robt. M. La Follette as an alternate candidate, and the faction led by CLEVELAND LEADER owner DAN R. HANNA supported Theodore Roosevelt. With La Follette in poor health temporarily, the two factions united in support of Roosevelt. When the Republicans nominated Taft for president in June 1912, the Natl. Progressive (Bull Moose) party was organized as a third party with Theodore Roosevelt as its presidential candidate. The new party favored direct primaries, initiative, and referendum and was opposed to monopoly, favoring the supervision of all corporations by a state commission. The Ohio Progressive party was formed in Sept. 1912, with Garfield elected state chairman. In Cleveland, the Progressives nominated a full slate of candidates for county offices in 1912. The election returns showed that the Democrats won both the county and state offices. However, the Progressive candidates received more votes than their Republican counterparts. In 1914, Garfield was the Progressive candidate for Ohio governor; however, both he and the party did poorly.

The Progressives were not a significant force again until 1922, when a coalition including unions, Progressives, the nonpartisan league, and Socialists formed the Conference for Progressive Political Action. Financed largely by the Railway Brotherhoods, the CPPA endorsed candidates for the congressional elections in the fall of 1922. CPPA Secretary FREDERIC HOWE and his committee campaigned for the endorsed candidates, including their acknowledged leader, Robt. La Follette, who was reelected to the U.S. Senate from Wisconsin. At the CPPA meeting in Cleveland on 12 Dec. 1922, Wm. Z. Foster and the Marxist-Leninist Workers party appeared. The Progressives, however, refused to seat them as delegates, citing their disruptive tactics and rejection of democracy. The CPPA agreed that the major Progressive issue was the excessive power of corporate monopoly, but they also advocated public ownership of utilities and prohibition of the use of injunctions in labor disputes. They continued to temporize over the formation of a third political party to promote their concerns. However, at their convention in Cleveland on 4 July 1924, the CPPA nominated La Follette as their presidential candidate, and 2 days later the Socialist Convention also meeting in Cleveland (see SOCIALIST CONVENTION OF 1924) nominated him for president, as well. Both the Socialists and the CPPA actively campaigned for La Follette in the election of 1924. The city of Cleveland gave him a majority of 7,675 votes; however, Republican Calvin Coolidge carried the county, the state, and the nation.

The party again became active when the Progressive Party of Ohio State was founded on 19 June 1948 to support Henry Wallace's candidacy for president. Wallace opposed universal military training and the "war-like policy" of the government. He sought to curb the power and profits of monopoly and favored increased civil rights for minorities. The national party was organized in July, and in August, at a 2-day convention held in Cleveland, the Cuyahoga

County party was formed, with Herschel G. Holland elected chairman of the Central Committee. In addition to its support of Wallace, the local party platform called for a Cleveland Transit Board elected by the people, expansion of the Municipal Light Plant to supply power for the transit system, and a municipal fair-employment-practices law. In the 1948 presidential election, Wallace received about 3.4% of the total vote in the county. After 1948, the Progressive party exerted little influence on the local political scene.

Benjamin Gray Papers, WRHS.

**PROGRESSIVE SLOVENE WOMEN OF AMERICA** (Progresivne Slovenke Amerike) is a national women's humanitarian organization dedicated to educational, social, and welfare work and maintaining ties with the Slovenian homeland in Europe. On 4 Feb. 1934, a group of 21 women and men, all active in Slovenian-American organizations, met at the LYNDHURST home of VATRO GRILL and his wife Anna to plan an independent society of women to assist families in Cleveland's Slovenian community afflicted by the Depression. The society was tentatively named American Daughters of America. Anna Grill served as the first president, with Mary Durn as secretary. An organizational banquet was held 21 Dec. at the SLOVENIAN NATL. HOME, with a new name for the society, Progressive Slovene Women of America, reflecting the founders' liberal tenets. The first circles were formed in the St. Clair, COLLINWOOD, and EUCLID communities. Early activities included programs with speakers from welfare agencies and institutions of higher learning providing financial aid. The AMERICAN RED CROSS provided home-nursing classes. The PSWA also helped promote Louis Adamic's book *The Native's Return*, an account of his trip to Yugoslavia with a visit to his birthplace in Slovenia and the first book to create an awareness of one of America's smallest nationalities. Funds were raised with monthly dues, bake sales, and handicrafts. The PSWA was incorporated in Ohio in 1938, and the first circles were established outside the state. The first convention was held in 1939 at the Slovenian Workmen's Home in the Collinwood neighborhood.

As hard times eased, the PSWA introduced cultural activities such as exhibits, stage performances, and lectures by speakers such as Adamic on Slovenian and general issues. The women also extended support to local and national groups, including the CLEVELAND PUBLIC LIBRARY and the American Red Cross. The PSWA ran blood-donor and defense-bond drives during the war years and were particularly involved with the Yugoslav Relief Committee and the SLOVENIAN AMERICAN NATL. COUNCIL to assist the occupied homeland. They formed their own relief committee in 1944 and purchased 2 jeeps and medical supplies for Slovenian partisans. Clothing collections were held for the Yugoslav Red Cross in Slovenia, and $38,000 was raised for food and medicine. In the postwar reconstruction period, the women aided hospitals and clinics in Ljubljana, including medical equipment for the Children's Hospital and learning tools for deaf and blind children. A book campaign benefited Slovenian schools and libraries. A 1950 conference proposed the creation of a Ljubljana-based information bureau to act as liaison between Slovenian emigrants and their homeland. Slovenska Izseljenska Matica was established, and in 1952, in conjunction with the first PSWA tour to Slovenia, it sponsored the first annual Emigrants Picnic, attracting Slovenians from around the world. A cookbook and cooking classes enhanced fundraising in the later 1950s and 1960s. The SLOVENE HOME FOR THE AGED in Cleveland and the American Museum of

Immigration in the Statue of Liberty complex were primary beneficiaries. The PSWA was also instrumental in obtaining Louis Adamic's manuscripts for the Princeton University Library and arranging Adamic symposiums in 1977 and 1981. Membership peaked in the mid-1950s with 1,500 women in 18 circles, 7 in northeastern Ohio, and others in Pennsylvania, Illinois, Wisconsin, Mississippi, and Florida. Past presidents included Frances Candon, Paula Klinc, Cecilia Subelj, and Josephine Zakrajsek. Mary Ivanusch served as editor for 40 years, and Zakrajsek as national secretary for 36 years. In 1978, the PSWA received the Order of the Silver Wreath from the Yugoslav government for their relief assistance and for promoting mutual understanding between the two countries.

Candon, Vera A. et al., *Progressive Slovene Women of America 50th Anniversary* (1984).

The **PROHIBITION AMENDMENT,** outlawing the manufacture, transport, and sale of alcoholic beverages, was in effect in Cleveland 27 May 1919–23 Dec. 1933—nearly 8 months longer than the 18th Amendment to the U.S. Constitution and its enforcing Volstead Act. In Nov. 1918, voters passed a state Prohibition amendment promoted by the Westerville-based Anti Saloon League. In Jan. 1919, the general assembly ratified the 18th Amendment. November voters kept state Prohibition but rejected state Prohibition enforcement, the 18th Amendment, and 2.75% beer. State Prohibition began 27 May 1919, enforced by local police only. Most Cleveland liquor dealers sold or stored their stocks and closed, or sold nonalcoholic drinks. About 50 of 1,028 bars stayed open. Workers said they would drink as long as the rich kept liquor cellars. A policeman said, "Hell, I'm not going to arrest nobody for doing what I like to do myself." Liquor could be easily purchased. Alcohol stocks in Cleveland declined when the Prohibition Bureau sent an administrator and federal agents as the Volstead Act and the 18th Amendment became law on 16 Jan. 1920. Voters upheld state Prohibition enforcement in a Nov. 1920 referendum; a State Enforcement Dept. was formed in 1921. The general assembly allowed local magistrates to raid private homes and be paid from conviction fees. State agents joined Law Enforcement League officers to raid Cuyahoga County homes; agents accused police of interference and took cases to suburban justices of the peace and mayors, expanding jurisdictions by opening Cleveland offices. Constables and various local officials were convicted of bribery and other crimes. Raiding ended with the Mar. 1927 U.S. Supreme Court ruling that officials had illegal financial stakes in obtaining convictions; voters in November rejected reestablishing the raids. Cleveland kept all municipal court alcohol fines until ordered to pay the state half in 1926. The city could not keep all fines until a city Prohibition act, passed in Nov. 1928 to raise revenue, was accepted by the Ohio Supreme Court in Nov. 1929.

Despite 3 enforcing levels, liquor was usually available in most neighborhoods. Blind pigs, or speakeasies, sold liquor behind lawful businesses. An anti-Prohibition group found 2,545 in 1931 in Cleveland, compared with 1,028 saloons in 1919; Phil Selznick's Club Madrid on Euclid Ave. and Geo. Young's Stage Door Club at E. 9th and Chester were notable. As initial stocks dwindled, forged permits to legal warehouses, bootlegging, and area stills provided new sources. An estimated 30,000 Clevelanders were selling liquor in 1923; 10,000 stills were operating; and 100,000 were violating the law at home. Diversion schemes attracted national attention. Abraham and Louis Auerbach were convicted for using alcohol from their Million Dollar Hair Tonic Co. to produce liquor. Between 1923–26, 112 were convicted nationwide as the Superior Industrial Alcohol Co. distributed denatured alcohol without the required poisons. Alcohol was bootlegged to Cleveland from Canada or local stills. Cars made daily trips to Canada, and rumrunners brought supplies across Lake Erie. Boaters, druggists, government agents, and the police participated, but bootlegging soon attracted crime; by 1925, bootleg operations were hierarchical organizations owned by "barons." Poor workers made liquor from corn sugar and materials the barons supplied. John and Joseph Lonardo controlled much of the corn-liquor bootlegging in the city, but they were killed in a 1927 bootleg war. Bootleg murders were common. When hijackers began muscling into various fields of the industry, "protectionists" gradually controlled each field. One group dominated the entire industry; the MAYFIELD RD. MOB had operations in Little Italy, on E. 105th St., and near E. 55th St. and Woodland Ave. Bootleg barons included the 7 Porello brothers (4 of whom were killed), Joe Tonardo, Nathan Weisenburg, Moses Donley, Paul Hackett, and J. J. Schleimer. These and the names Milano, Furgus, and O'Boyle held the same connotation as the name Capone in Chicago.

Prohibition was never popular in Cleveland; repeal sentiment grew in the late 1920s as enforcement waned. The public resented liquor wars and raids. The 1929 stock market crash and the Depression killed the idea that Prohibition stimulated prosperity. Juries were acquitting alcohol violators brought to the criminal courts. JOHN L. SEVERANCE, BENEDICT CROWELL, and Elton Hoyt III led the Assoc. against the Prohibition Amendment's (AAPA) Cleveland branch and argued throughout Prohibition that the law violated state and local self-government and reduced the authority of law. In 1929, 2 other anti-Prohibition groups formed in Cleveland. In April, Katherine Hoyt (Mrs. Amasa Stone) Mather helped found the Women's Organization for Natl. Prohibition Reform. The WONPR denied that women had a special interest in Prohibition. In 1930, the first WONPR national convention was held in Cleveland. Mrs. Mather served as state director, regional director, and a national WONPR vice-chairman; under her leadership, Ohio membership rose from 2,500 to over 70,000 by 1932. She publicized letters exchanged with Sen. Simeon D. Fess in which the dry Ohio senator refused to commit himself to a referendum on the 18th Amendment. The WONPR first suggested that state conventions repeal the 18th Amendment, a method not used since the ratification of the U.S. Constitution.

After Cleveland and Chicago gang wars, businessman Fred G. Clark founded a group, the Crusaders, against gang wars and Prohibition, which attracted LEONARD C. HANNA, Philip R. Mather, and CHAS. A. OTIS. The Crusaders formed "battalions" of "militant young men" into chapters nationwide—soon claiming 4,000 members. Cleveland hosted the Crusaders' first national meeting, in Jan. 1930, and became national headquarters. By 1932, they claimed 1 million members. The Crusaders listed the 1930 election of Clevelander ROBT. J. BULKLEY as U.S. senator as a triumph. Bulkley shocked Democratic leaders by promoting repeal in dry areas of Ohio; he soundly defeated a dry incumbent appointed by the governor. Many attributed Bulkley's victory to his repeal stance, but an anti-Republican reaction to a poor economy also helped; however, the issue aroused statewide interest to attract national attention.

Franklin D. Roosevelt's 1932 presidential victory boosted the repeal movement. Cleveland City Council called for repeal or modification of the 18th Amendment in Dec. 1932. Congress submitted on 20 Feb. 1933 a repeal amendment to the states containing the ratifying conventions requested by the WONPR. On 7 Apr., sales of 3.2% beer were permitted under the Volstead Act; Ohio licensed brewers, retailers, and wholesalers. On 28 May, the AAPA, the WONPR, the Crusaders, and other repeal groups formed the Ohio Repeal Council; the council, based in Cleveland, nominated a convention slate and promoted a law calling for at-large convention delegates. Enforcement shrank by 1932, and bootleg fines dropped by half; almost 50% of all violations never reached police court. Once beer was legalized, Cleveland police did not check violations without a complaint. The Prohibition Bureau closed on 8 Aug. 1933; federal agents left the city. That November, voters repealed state Prohibition, approved at-large convention seats, and elected only repeal delegates to the constitutional convention. As Sen. Bulkley presided, the convention ratified repeal on 5 Dec.; national Prohibition ended that day when Utah ratified. State Prohibition ended on 23 Dec.; the general assembly replaced enforcement with a state monopoly on hard liquor sales and licensed sales by the drink. Licensed pharmacies sold alcohol until 4 Cuyahoga County state liquor stores opened on 6 Apr. 1934.

The **PROHIBITION PARTY** in Cleveland began when local Republicans who advocated TEMPERANCE nominated a slate of candidates for the municipal election in Mar. 1869. These included Grove Abbey for mayor; Jay Odell, city treasurer; Geo. P. Burwell, cemetery trustee; and Horace Benton, waterworks trustee. Abbey received 1,049 votes, approximately 9% of the total vote. It was believed to be the first distinctively Prohibition ticket offered to the voters anywhere in the country. In subsequent local elections, Prohibition party candidates attracted very few votes.

The State Temperance party was formed at a meeting in Crestline on 24–25 Apr. 1869, with Burwell elected president of the Cleveland party. A national party was then organized in Sept. 1869 at Chicago. Initially, the party identified itself with several types of reform. At its second national convention, held in Cleveland on 17 May 1876, the platform called for the prohibition of the importation, exportation, manufacture, and traffic of all alcoholic beverages, the suppression of lotteries, the abolition of polygamy, universal suffrage, and prison reform. Green Clay Smith of Kentucky was nominated for president at this convention. In 1877 the state party nominated a full slate of candidates for state office. In Cuyahoga County, however, Geo. Jenkins, candidate for lieutenant governor, received the most votes (198). In 1880, the national convention was again held in Cleveland, at which time it nominated Neal Dow of Portland, Maine, for president. This time the platform advocated only the prohibition of alcoholic beverages and universal suffrage. Although the party's influence grew in Ohio, it was not a significant force in Cuyahoga County. In both national and local elections in the 1880s and 1890s, the county gave the party's candidates only 1–1.5% of the vote. The party continued to nominate candidates for local office until the end of the century.

Case, George L., *The Prohibition Party, Its Organization, Growth, and Purpose* (1889), pamphlet, WRHS.

**PROJECT EVE** was a pioneer effort to bring women into the workforce. Originated by Evelyn Bonder, prime mover of INTERNATL. WOMEN'S YEAR programs in Cleveland, it was the basis of the DISPLACED HOMEMAKERS and WomenFocus programs at CUYAHOGA COMMUNITY COLLEGE. Project EVE, which stands for Education, Volunteerism, & Employment, was founded in 1976 to provide educational and vocational counseling to women regardless of education, economic background, lifestyle, age, or marital status. Its programs offered counseling to help participants examine and evaluate the changing roles of women in a changing society, as well as individual and group personal and vocational guidance. Seminars on careers, goals, values, aptitudes, and life planning were set up to aid the process of self-assessment. Project EVE was the first program to originate in Cleveland to confront the issues later outlined as crucial for women during Internatl. Women's Year. The program, part of the Div. of Continuing Educational Services at CCC, evolved into women's programs there; by 1979, the major thrusts of Project EVE were channeled into either the Displaced Homemakers or the WomenFocus curriculum. Displaced Homemakers, directed toward divorced and separated women, was fostered by a grant from the Ohio legislature. The first pilot project gathered 15–20 women at each CCC campus for sessions to examine career goals and decide, through counseling, whether to enroll at CCC for courses, take noncredit courses, or seek on-the-job training or guided job placement. In 1986, the Displaced Homemakers program attracted over 300 women each quarter. WomenFocus offers workshops and noncredit courses directed toward personal development and job enrichment for working women. The courses are taught at CCC campuses and throughout the community.

**PROSSER, DILLON** (2 July 1813–11 Apr. 1897), was a prominent leader in Cleveland Methodism and an early pioneer in social relief work. He was founder of the so called Ragged School. Prosser was born in Otsego County, N.Y. He became involved in Methodism early in his life, and at the age of 17 he was licensed to "exhort." After 2 years at the Western Reserve Seminary, Prosser in 1833 received a license to preach. His religious background greatly influenced his lifelong participation in charitable causes. From 1830 until his death, Prosser served in various offices in the Methodist Episcopal church. As a licensed preacher, he worked in various churches in Pittsburgh between 1834–36. He was ordained a deacon in 1836 and moved to Erie, where he assumed full ministerial duties. At the age of 25 he was made an elder, the highest office he would achieve.

Prosser came to Cleveland in 1850. In 1853 he opened a mission school for poor children, one of the earliest of its kind in Cleveland. The "Ragged School" originated as an outreach effort of a young men's prayer group, a forerunner of the YMCA. Relief work was directed toward "the rescue of destitute children." With the assistance of women volunteers, Prosser visited homes in the city reported to have malnourished, abused, or "idle" children. At the school, these children received classroom instruction, clothes, food, and shelter. Prosser himself reportedly preached to them from an overturned flour barrel. The school was reorganized in 1856 as the City Industrial School and in later years changed names several times as it came under the management of different charities. Prosser was extremely active in the Methodist Episcopal church and was responsible for the organization of 9 churches in Cleveland and several others outside the city. He made money from real-estate investments in Cleveland and contributed a considerable part of it, including land, to both religious and charitable work. Prosser was married 3 times. In 1840 he married Caroline Blakeslee of Austinburg, Ohio. After her death in 1849, he married May Holloway of Cuyahoga Falls in 1850. She died only a few years later, and he then married Cornelia McFarlane of Chagrin Falls in 1856.

**PROSTITUTION** has flourished in Cleveland since its founding, despite periodic outbursts of civic outrage and police activity directed toward its elimination. Such activities have served only to change its location. From Cleveland's earliest history as an important shipping point on the Great Lakes until the CIVIL WAR, the city had segregated districts in the HAYMARKET where women attended to the needs of sailors and shipping men. A second district sprang up in the CENTRAL VIADUCT area for farmers and food merchants. After the war, the district moved up the hill from the waterfront, and by the 1880s it was concentrated in the area bounded by Ontario, Lakeside, Superior, and E. 12th in homes abandoned by the wealthy, who had moved farther out. Another district developed at Chester and Walnut between E. 9th and E. 12th. The houses operated openly; police raided the premises monthly but did not close them down. By the turn of the century, the police sought tighter control over the vice districts and an end to streetwalking, and an elimination of all districts but the E. 6th and Superior area. The monthly raids were discontinued.

In 1914, Mayor NEWTON D. BAKER closed down the segregated district under protest from his safety director and house owners alike on the grounds that eliminating an open red-light district would spread uncontrollable prostitution over the city. Working girls who lived in the houses appealed to local clergy for help in finding new living quarters as landlords, fearful of immoral entrepreneurship on their premises, refused to rent to the women. Reformers advocated that the city find jobs for the prostitutes, but the girls asserted that their work provided a more adequate living than would low-paying clerical or retail work. True to the predictions of Baker's critics, unauthorized prostitution districts developed around the city, notably "Little Hollywood" on E. 73rd between Hough and Lexington; E. 9th and Superior; E. 30th and Cedar; E. 19th and Euclid; E. 17th and Prospect; and E. 105th and Euclid. Downtown Cleveland was a haven for streetwalkers. Young girls came to dances to meet men and go off to hotels. In an era when hotel operators insisted that check-ins have luggage, the girls toted tiny but empty suitcases to dances; suitcase renting was a big business. In contrast to the 27 houses and 300 known prostitutes operating in the segregated district at its shutdown, an estimated 5,000 vice resorts (including speakeasies and gambling joints) flourished by 1930. Sporadic crackdowns in the 1920s gave way to major raids in 1932–33. The Roaring 3rd Central precinct was cleaned up as police visited every known den of sin on Short Scovill (E. 9th–E. 14th), Charity Ave., and Orange Ave., and closed down the houses. Suggestions to reopen the segregated district were rejected because of opposition from a city council committee headed by Newton D. Baker.

By 1940, downtown hotels along Prospect and Carnegie did such a brisk business that police had to break up traffic jams at 3 a.m. Vigorous raids by safety director ELIOT NESS in 1940 reduced known prostitutes to 100 by 1941, but the trade remained viable. During WORLD WAR II, the activities of the professionals were supplemented by "pickup girls" and "kacki wacki" girls. Yet, Cleveland was rated by the 5th Service Command and the 9th Naval District as having the best moral tone of any major city in the region. In subsequent decades, prostitution moved in response to urban renewal, highway construction, and suburbanization. With the razing of buildings at E. 9th and Short Vincent and E. 105th and Euclid, 2 legendary vice districts closed. East side prostitution remained concentrated along Prospect. Police efforts to suppress activity, such as through Mayor Ralph Perk's Smut Squad (1973), were successful until police manpower was deployed elsewhere. Since the 1960s, prostitution has been called a victimless crime by some, but according to critics, patrons of prostitutes are frequently robbed and beaten up, while passersby are harassed. Those who hoped to renovate areas such as Upper Prospect for downtown living pointed out that prostitutes brought a criminal element to the neighborhood and discouraged legitimate business activity. Opponents of prostitution have sought mandatory sentences for prostitutes and exposure of their clients to discourage activity.

**PRUTTON, CARL F.** (30 July 1898–15 July 1970), was a chemical engineer and an educator. He taught at the Case Institute of Technology from 1920–48 and served as a research consultant to the LUBRIZOL CORP. Prutton was born in Cleveland, the son of John and Julia Seelbach Prutton. He was educated in the Cleveland public schools, then attended Purdue University for the 1915–16 academic year before serving in Mexico in 1916 with the Indiana Natl. Guard. After military service, Prutton entered Case School of Applied Science, and after graduation in 1920 he joined the school's faculty as an instructor in chemistry. He received a master's degree in chemical engineering from Case in 1923, and in 1928 he earned a doctorate in physical chemistry from Western Reserve University. He married Marie Agatha Saunders on 2 June 1919.

As a member of the Case faculty, Prutton advanced to assistant professor in 1925 and associate professor in 1929. In 1936 he became a full professor and was named chairman of the Dept. of Chemistry & Chemical Engineering, a position he held until he left the school and Cleveland in 1948. During his years at Case, Prutton developed new courses and laboratory programs. He oversaw the construction of a new laboratory for chemical engineering and physical and organic chemistry in 1938, and was responsible for the creation of a program in graduate study in chemistry. In addition to his academic work, Prutton served as a consultant to several companies, among them Dow Chemical (1921, 1928–41) and Lubrizol (1929–51). In 1944–45, he took a leave of absence from Case to serve full-time as the director of research. Working both on his own and with ALBERT KELVIN SMITH, Prutton was responsible for more than 100 patents, known in the oil and chemical industries as "the Prutton patents."

Prutton enjoyed teaching, but by the late 1940s he was bored with the increasing number of administrative responsibilities that fell to him as department chairman. He resigned from Case in 1948 to join the Olin Mathieson Chemical Corp. in Baltimore as director of research; he became a vice-president there in 1949. In 1954 he joined the Food Machinery & Chemical Corp. in San Jose, Calif., as its vice-president and director of the chemical division. He retired in 1960. Prutton wrote about 40 technical papers and in 1944 was the coauthor of a textbook in physical chemistry. In 1942–43 he served as the chief of the Process Development Branch of the Office of the Rubber Director; he was also a consultant to the War Production Board. Among the honors he received were the 1940 Modern Pioneer Award of the Natl. Assoc. of Mfrs. and honorary degrees from Case (1954) and WRU (1964).

The **PUBLIC AUDITORIUM** was opened in 1922, the fourth building completed in the MALL area. At the time it was the largest such convention hall in the country. The auditorium was an important factor in bringing the REPUBLICAN NATL. CONVENTION to Cleveland in 1924 and 1936. In the 1930s and 1940s, its facilities made Cleveland a leading national convention center, and it continues to host numerous industrial shows every year (see also FAIRS & EXPOSITIONS). The Public Auditorium was planned before WORLD WAR I, when the need for large public

exhibition spaces was already apparent. It was financed by a bond issue in 1916, but construction was not begun until 1920. The classic Renaissance-style building was designed by city architect J. H. MacDowell, with FRANK R. WALKER as consulting architect.

The combined seating capacity of the main floor and galleries of the complete hall was 11,500. The basement exhibition hall contained over 28,500 sq. ft. of space. The circulation plan was designed so that 13,000 people can be evacuated from the building in 4½ minutes. The building contained the most advanced mechanical systems of the 1920s for heating, ventilating, cooling, and fire prevention. The stage at one end of the hall is 60 x 104 ft., with a proscenium opening 72 ft. wide and 42 ft. high. One of the largest pipe organs in existence is installed on the stage. In 1929 the Music Hall, seating 2,800, was added to the south end of the building; its stage is placed back-to-back with the auditorium stage house. An underground exhibition hall was constructed beneath the north end of the Mall and connected to the auditorium in 1932. In 1964 the entire Mall area was excavated for additional convention space and automobile parking, and a grand entrance lobby in the modern style, designed by Outcalt, Guenther, Rode & Bonebrake, was built onto the west side of the auditorium.

**PUBLIC HEALTH.** The underlying responsibility of the CLEVELAND BOARD OF HEALTH, to promote a healthy environment and improved quality of life through community action, has not changed since the first board was constituted in 1832. Municipal health professionals, with the help of civic and social reformers and often supported by federal grants, formulated and instituted beneficial municipal health programs in spite of state and local political machinations, public apathy, insufficient funding, and socioeconomic changes that hampered their efforts. The isolated and sparsely populated Cleveland frontier settlement of 1796 had little need for medical or public-health services. The first physician to practice in Cleveland was Dr. DAVID LONG in 1810. The early settlers contended with arduous living conditions and malarial fever, but suffered few deaths from the ravages of epidemic or endemic diseases or the problems associated with urban living. By 1821, there were more than 600 people in the village, and the trustees adopted simple rules and regulations to control sanitary conditions. Cholera, the first serious epidemic to strike Cleveland, was brought to the city in 1832. Aware of the dangers from this dreaded disease, the trustees, which included Dr. Long, established a board of health. The board erected a quarantine station and hospital and prescribed sanitary measures to control the spread of the disease. Cleveland was chartered in 1836 and granted the right to organize a permanent board of health, but in spite of periodic epidemics of cholera (see CHOLERA EPIDEMIC), yellow fever, influenza, and typhoid, the city did not establish a permanent health organization. On 7 Mar. 1850, the state legislature authorized the CLEVELAND CITY COUNCIL to form a board of health with powers to abate the nuisances and to enact measures to combat the spread of infectious diseases. Since the state laws did not make it mandatory to create the board, and because the population remained passive to the potential dangers, no real effort was made by municipal officials to implement the legislative acts until 10 Jan. 1856, when an ordinance was passed that created a permanent board of health. Dr. Fred W. Marseilles was appointed the first health officer. For the next 20 years, the city slowly developed a public-health organization, enacted health ordinances, and provided some sanitary services (see SANITATION).

As early as 1826, the city poorhouse furnished rudimentary hospital care for the indigent, elderly, and chronically ill. Some improvements in hospital services were made in 1836 and 1855; however, it was not until 1889 that a modern city hospital was built. It opened several years later. In the interim period, health care was provided by private hospitals operated by medical schools and benevolent and religious organizations. Out-patient medical care for the neighborhood poor began in 1856 with the appointment of Dr. Thos. G. Cleveland as the city physician. Following the CIVIL WAR, the increased population and numbers of poor made it necessary to restructure the health-care system and to appoint additional physicians in 1871, and thereafter as the need arose. In 1986, 4 health centers provided care, training, and inspection services to the city, and in some cases to county residents. In the last quarter of the 19th century, the campaign for public-health reform accelerated, and sanitary reformers throughout the nation embarked on a crusade in behalf of improved public health and personal hygiene. Dr. Frank Wells, the Cleveland health officer, approved their aims, although he did not join their ranks. In the annual report of the Board of Health for 1876, Dr. Wells attributed the high death rate to poor sanitation, germs, and adverse socioeconomic conditions. Wells argued that the leading cause of disease was the filth that accumulated in the city. Health ordinances enacted up until 1875 dealt almost exclusively with the problem of unsanitary conditions, the prevention of noxious odors, and the sale of adulterated milk and food. Since it was believed that the main function of the Board of Health was that of sanitary policeman, authority for its activity was mistakenly vested in the Board of Police Commissioners on 2 separate occasions--1876-80 and 1892-1902. The results fell far below bureaucratic expectations, and the city was forced to return control to an independent board of health.

The preoccupation with filth as the main source of disease caused the then-emerging germ theory of disease to be disregarded. The importance of pathogens in disease causation was acknowledged by city officials in 1901, when Wm. Travis Howard, a professor at Western Reserve University Medical School, was placed in charge of a newly established municipal bacteriological laboratory. The laboratory was employed to routinely examine potential sources of disease in water and food supplies, and to establish and approve standards by which to safeguard the health of the city. Dr. Wells added another dimension when he warned of the destructive effect upon health of overcrowding, poor ventilation, and improper food and clothing—problems that had been neglected and ignored. His views were upheld by future Cleveland health officers and public-health employees, who, without negating the danger that arose from an unsanitary environment, proposed that greater attention be paid to the socioeconomic issues that were at the core of many of the health problems that faced the city. The medical profession's acceptance of pathogens as a source of disease and the influence of social conditions on illness released the Cleveland Board of Health from its task as a provider of sanitary services and allowed it the opportunity to concentrate its efforts on new areas in the prevention of illness and disease.

The accelerated industrial growth that occurred in the Greater Cleveland metropolitan area in the last 4 decades of the 19th century made the city an attractive place to work and live, in spite of environmental shortcomings that arose when native and foreign workers seeking employment opportunities poured into the city. The changing demographics, lack of planning, economic upheavals of the period, housing shortages, municipal fiscal conservatism,

and a pervasive social Darwinism compounded the public-health problems that existed. To prevent Cleveland from being inundated by filth, to prevent the spread of epidemic and contagious diseases, and to encourage continued growth, the municipal authorities took steps in the last quarter of the 19th century to provide a sanitary infrastructure, and reaffirmed their right to enforce the sanitary laws. In spite of the progress, in 1910 the Board of Health reported that expenditures for the city's health programs had not kept pace with those in other major cities of the U.S. Dr. C. E. Ford, secretary of the Board of Health, warned that since public health was a purchasable commodity, Cleveland could "determine its own death rates."

The first serious effort to educate and involve the social and civic leaders in public-health programs was made as early as 1875. In that year the Board of Health published and made public its first annual report. It detailed the work of the department for the year and allowed the health officer and the various department supervisors the opportunity to air their concerns and to recommend institutional changes designed to improve the work of the department. The participation of civic and social reformers in health matters began slowly but accelerated sharply in the first decade of the 20th century. Their achievements included public-school sanitation and student hygiene; social settlement-house educational programs to inculcate civic pride and proper sanitation in the ethnic communities; visiting-nurse services; child and maternal welfare; mental hygiene; nutrition; and the control and prevention of contagious diseases. Almost all of these programs were incorporated into departments of the Board of Health, and by 1921, the voluntary efforts of a handful of civic-minded residents had dramatically altered the composition and the purpose of the municipal health department. In spite of the advances that were made, there were those health officials who indicated the need for greater progress. On 1 Oct. 1919, the Cleveland Hospital Council appointed the Committee on Hospital & Health Survey of Cleveland to examine and recommend methods to achieve "better public health and fewer preventable deaths." The study included 4 broad areas—medical education, nursing education, care of the individual sick, and the advancement of public health and preventive medicine. The survey was undertaken with the cooperation of national, state, and local health and civic organizations. The report, made public on 22 Sept. 1920, emphasized the city's health and sanitation deficiencies and offered constructive recommendations to correct those weaknesses. Not all of the recommendations were adopted. Nonetheless, progress was evident, not only in the increased per capita cost for health care between 1920-30 but also in the reduced death rate. However, the improved conditions did not apply to all segments of the population. The death rate for the black population increased for the same period from 8 to 14.9% ≈ 15%.

By the turn of the century, the county no longer was a series of isolated communities. Suburbs became burdened with the same health problems that faced Cleveland. Referring to the adverse conditions that existed throughout the state, the *Ohio Public Health Journal* stated in Dec. 1918 that local health organizations were notoriously inadequate. State efforts resulted in the appointment of a full-time health commissioner in Cuyahoga County in 1920. The county was granted the authority to provide health care to those communities that previously had supplied only minimal services. From humble beginnings, the Cuyahoga County District Board of Health grew to 107 full- and part-time employees who provided services to some 736,628 residents in 1984, although Cleveland, E. CLEVELAND, CLEVELAND HTS., SHAKER HTS., and LAKE-

WOOD continued to furnish their own but similar health services. To improve the overall health system, recommendations to combine all municipal department activities of the county into one central agency had been made at various times but had been rejected for political and economic reasons. The recommendations made by the 1920 survey were never fully realized, and many were finally aborted by the Depression. Fortunately, the federal government, with the cooperation of private welfare agencies, intervened and provided funding for the overhaul and improvement of the sanitary infrastructure and for the continued support of municipal health agencies.

As a result of WORLD WAR II, for a 10-year period from 1940–50, little attention was paid to the city's health problems. However, it was evident to many health professionals that the course of public health had to be redirected once again; that new problems had arisen—paradoxically, many as a result of a better health-care system and a higher standard of living. A study prepared by the Cleveland Metropolitan Service Commission in 1956 confirmed that preventive medicine and the control of contagious diseases, ordinances to improve sanitary conditions in the home and factory, tighter food and drug inspection laws, accurate vital statistics, and a higher standard of living had increased life expectancy as well as the incidence of diseases associated with old age. The emphasis shifted to expensive long-term chronic illnesses such as hypertension, diabetes, heart disease, arthritis, mental health, and drug and alcohol abuse.

In the late 1950s, the city began a steady and precipitous decline in population, and the loss of tax revenues resulted in a sharp reduction in its health services. The problem became exaggerated with time. In June 1972, Dr. J. C. Robertson of the Mayor's Health Advisory Committee, in a statement of *Proposed Health Program Priority*, wrote that the city was at the brink of self-destruction. He warned that the Board of Health was "grossly inadequate" to the challenge, because it was underfinanced, understaffed, and deficient in certain key skills; a common complaint of health officers for more than 100 years. Dr. Robertson proposed drastic measures, which included limiting the activity of the staff to those tasks that would prevent epidemic catastrophes. Fortunately, federal programs and funds were available, and the city was able to continue the more important health services. From the 1960s, the Dept. of Health & Public Welfare was no longer the sole guardian of environmental health, sharing responsibilities with the federal, state, and county governments, but it was still responsible for some 48 health and sanitation functions, ranging from animal bites to vending-machine inspections. The problems of public health that confronted the municipal health workers of the 19th century were still present in the 1980s, but to them had been added the problems created by the technological revolution of the post-World War II period. Cleveland's response to them would most likely be dictated by the changes in medical technology and the availability of federal funding to purchase and implement such medical advances.

Sam Alewitz

See also HOSPITALS, MEDICINE.

**PUBLIC HOUSING.** As early as the 1810s, visitors to Cleveland were commenting upon the wretched housing conditions. After the CIVIL WAR, as thousands of European immigrants were attracted to the city by the demand for workers in expanding industrial and commercial enterprises, Cleveland's slums grew along with its population. Despite turn-of-the-century conditions that resembled a medieval town, there is no evidence that city administrations responded with programs to eradicate housing problems. Even reformer TOM L. JOHNSON paid little attention to the housing question, although his fellow reformer, FREDERIC C. HOWE, hoped that the adoption of the single-tax plan of Henry George would provide the money to clean up the slums of the city. The men who envisioned the Group Plan in 1895 and those who implemented it gave no thought to the question of housing the hundreds who had to move as their slum dwellings were demolished to make way for stately civic buildings. A Cleveland Chamber of Commerce investigation in 1904 concluded that a whole litany of social and moral evils were caused by poor housing conditions and spurred passage of the city's first comprehensive building code. This code followed the pattern already established by housing reformers such as Lawrence Veiller, one of the most influential experts in the country, who firmly believed the housing field should be left to private enterprise. He opposed municipally built housing on the grounds that such programs were socialistic. Codes, however, did not provide housing for low-income people. So firmly entrenched were the views held by the majority of social reformers and public officials that nothing constructive was done to alleviate the housing plight of the urban masses. Even Cleveland's first home rule charter of 1912 did not go beyond conventional wisdom when it provided for a city plan commission "to encourage a more orderly and attractive development of Cleveland."

Between 1900–20, Cleveland's population doubled, from 381,768 to 796,841, with the arrival of Eastern and Southern European immigrants, as well as increasing numbers of black migrants from the South. Inadequate housing conditions were made worse by this influx of mostly unskilled workers. While there is a record of the city's purchasing a parcel of land in 1913 for low-cost housing, none ever materialized. In 1917 the Cleveland Real Estate Board secretary claimed that there was need for an additional 10,000 houses, and another investigation by the Chamber of Commerce revealed that living conditions needed immediate remedy. This time the chamber acted by funding a real-estate firm for housing BLACKS in the old Central area and trying to secure a million dollars from the federal government's Wartime Emergency Housing program, but the war ended, and the scheme was dropped.

During the postwar period, housing problems increased, especially for the growing black population. While there was much attention paid to postwar plans in England to build houses for returning soldiers, in the U.S. only a few dreamed of such a governmental program. It was not until the 1930s that progress began to be made in public housing. A number of national reformers introduced the concept of limited-dividend housing. Investors would receive only a 6% return, but the housing would be tax-exempt. Gov. Alfred E. Smith enacted such legislation in New York. ERNEST J. BOHN, a young Cleveland lawyer serving in the Ohio legislature, traveled to New York to learn more about the program. Subsequently, as a councilman representing the HOUGH district, he became aware of the financial and social costs to the community of the housing situation. In 1932, former city manager DANIEL E. MORGAN joined forces with Bohn to press for passage of the State Public Housing Act, which authorized the creation of a semiprivate Public Housing Corp. to build low-cost housing for people with limited incomes. While the legislation secured the right of eminent domain, the law failed to work because the reformers were unable to secure tax exemption to attract private investment. Undaunted, Bohn persuaded his colleagues on city council to appoint a committee to investigate housing conditions. In 1933, Cleveland sponsored the first national slum-clearance conference, attended by experts from across the nation, who formed the Natl. Assoc. of Housing Officials and named Bohn, age 32, to be president of the new organization.

In Cleveland, Bohn continued to press for legislation that would provide tax incentives for investment in low-cost housing. His pragmatic approach was attractive to the ailing construction industry, as well as to social reformers. In 1934, a limited-dividend housing bill with tax exemption came into operation. Its sponsors thought that limited-dividend housing could be built using funds from the Reconstruction Finance Corp., but the plans failed because Cleveland sponsors could not raise the 15% matching money that was required. Bohn concluded that "slum clearance and the construction of housing for poor people would have to be taken on as a direct public responsibility without private investments." To persuade Clevelanders that slum areas were an economic liability to the city, he launched a study with the assistance of Rev. ROBT. B. NAVIN, a sociologist, and HOWARD WHIPPLE GREEN, a demographer. Their examination of a section of Cleveland located between Central Ave. and Woodland Ave. from E. 22nd St. to E. 55th St. demonstrated that the decrease in tax revenue, relative to the cost of city services, in this slum area amounted to the city's subsidizing each resident in the amount of $51.10 per year. This study was replicated in other cities. Bohn believed that the results were largely responsible for public acceptance of public-supported low-income housing. With the New Deal, $150 million of the Public Works Admin. budget was set aside for housing. Because of the earlier work done by architects and contracting firms on limited-dividend schemes and Bohn's work, Cleveland got the first 3 PWA Housing Div. projects. Members of the Cleveland Metropolitan Housing Authority served as informal members of the Cleveland Housing Committee, which was established as the PWA advisory body, and worked with the directors of the limited-dividend company that had options on the Cedar-Central land. PWA financed the construction of projects at Cedar-Central, Outhwaite, and LAKEVIEW TERRACE, which were built between 1935–37. They were described by Wallace G. Teare, one of the Lakeview Terrace architects, as setting "entirely new standards of site planning and building design."

When the Wagner-Steagall Housing Act of 1937 created the U.S. Housing Authority, with power to make loans and grant subsidies to local housing agencies, CMHA ceased its advisory role and took on responsibility for planning, construction, and operation of low-rent housing development, under the direction of Bohn. The federal statute required that local communities contribute 20% of the federal subsidy, which could take the form of municipal tax exemption. In 1938, CMHA and Cleveland signed an agreement for cooperation in "equivalent elimination" of substandard dwellings. For every new dwelling unit built by the housing authority, one substandard dwelling would be demolished or brought up to housing code by the city. In addition, the city agreed to provide city services without charge. In later years, CMHA did contribute a percentage to the cost of city services. An agreement was also signed between CMHA and Cuyahoga County. CMHA's first housing projects were Valleyview, Woodhill, Carver Park, and extensions to Outhwaite. In 1940 the authority took over the operation of the PWA Housing Div. estates of Cedar, Outhwaite, and Lakeview Terrace. In 1940, Bohn resigned as city councilman and became the first paid director of CMHA, a job he had been performing since 1933. He served in that position for the next 28 years and became one of the most influential men in the public-housing field

in the U.S. He had helped write the Wagner-Steagall Act and is credited with persuading Sen. Robt. A. Taft to sponsor the 1949 housing bill. Both presidents Eisenhower and Johnson asked him to serve on their housing advisory committees. Although Bohn was technically an employee of his board, he skillfully controlled the operation of successive boards, as well as exerted strong control over the management of the housing estates. His imprint was on every policy established by the board or executed by the management. As housing problems became acute after World War II, his modus operandi came increasingly under attack, particularly in relation to screening procedures.

In the early years, the selection of estate residents was carefully screened and their behavior monitored to prevent antisocial behavior. Recreation facilities were provided and staffed by the WORK PROJECTS ADMINISTRATION, and the same New Deal agency employed artists and musicians to provide cultural performances. Families on relief were not initially allowed into the estates because they were not able to pay the fixed rents, but in 1949 such discrimination was prohibited by the Taft Housing Act. While there was no formal policy of segregation, blacks and whites were clearly separated into different estates. Despite extensive picketing by the NAACP in the late 1940s and early 1950s and the passage in 1949 of a city ordinance banning racial discrimination in public housing, policies remained unchanged until the late 1960s. At the 1966 U.S. Civil Rights Commission hearings in Cleveland, the staff report noted that public-housing tenants were over 47% black by 1965, but they were still concentrated in a few east side estates. By the 1950s and 1960s, the city had witnessed enormous demographic and social changes. The federally subsidized FHA and GI building programs made it possible for middle-class white families to move into the suburbs. The black population of Cleveland increased from 85,000 in 1940 to 148,000 by 1950. In the next decade, approximately 100,000 southern blacks migrated into Cleveland as over 170,000 whites left the central city. Urban renewal and highway construction displaced over 11,000 by 1966. The impact on the central city was devastating. The HOUGH area, which had a population of 40,000 in 1940, had over 82,443 mostly black residents by 1956. Throughout the city, housing stock deteriorated.

CMHA under Bohn continued pioneering projects: high-rise buildings for the elderly, with medical clinics operated by nearby hospitals with federal funds and "meals on wheels" programs. The first public housing for the elderly in the nation was a 14-story building built as a part of the Cedar extension. But the changing face of Cleveland, the increase of slums around deteriorating housing estates, and the rise of a militant civil-rights movement called for imaginative leadership to focus on new approaches to the city's housing crisis. Although Bohn was managing 11 projects housing 26,000 people by the mid-1960s, many reformers and planners were critical of his refusal to consider rehabilitation of existing houses or new concepts of scattered-site housing. It was the election of Carl B. Stokes that spelled the end of Bohn's long reign. Stokes, like many young black politicians and some white civic leaders, felt that CMHA needed fresh blood. As mayor he controlled 2 of the 5 appointments to the board of CMHA, and he was able to secure Bohn's resignation within a year of his election. Bohn's successor, Irving Kriegsfeld, had been executive director of PATH, a nonprofit housing group. He was an aggressive administrator who began to push for programs that would end racial discrimination in west side estates, promote scattered-site housing throughout the city, and build new integrated housing estates on the west side. Unlike Bohn, who had been a skillful politician, Kriegsfeld relied solely on the mayor's support to advance his programs. New housing on the west side was opposed by the white area's powerful councilmen, Jas. M. Stanton and Dennis Kucinich, while black councilmen protested the attempts to build scattered-site housing in their black middle-class neighborhoods. Stokes backed Kriegsfeld completely despite the political fallout and later wrote that the building of 5,496 units in his 4 years as mayor was one of "his true and lasting achievements."

Stokes's successor, Ralph J. Perk, was a strong opponent of expanding public housing into white and black middle-class areas. The new director of CMHA, Robt. Fitzgerald, who had been the authority's chief engineer, was a low-key individual who found his problems almost insurmountable. Federal housing policy favored private-sector approaches—giving rent supplements and providing low-interest loans to private developers who would build or rehabilitate houses for the elderly and families of low and moderate incomes. The programs started with low-interest loans and later changed to deep subsidy through the Sec. 8 Program of the 1974 Housing Act. Increasingly, housing estates were occupied by single women heads of households on welfare. The 1968 Brooke amendment to the 1949 Housing Act put a ceiling of 25% of a family's income that could be collected, and rents no longer provided sufficient funds for maintenance. CMHA became increasingly dependent on federal money, but HUD provided only 90% of funds required for maintenance and less than half of other expense requests. The result was tragic. Deterioration that had already begun on older east side estates spread. Older estates became infested with drug pushers and juvenile crime. In Valleyview on the west side, living conditions became so deplorable that residents abandoned their units as arson and vandalism plagued the estate. In July 1978, police officers refused to enter the estates unless they had 2-men patrols. When ordered to resume their single-man patrols, police went on a strike, which ended only after bitter confrontations between Mayor Kucinich and the union. Confrontations among CMHA board members and with activist tenants, the continual victimization of the elderly in and around inner-city estates, and reports of inadequate security, poor maintenance, and lack of heat in the estates made daily headlines in newspapers and on television.

Progress in the early 1980s was overshadowed by a new conventional wisdom expressed by the architect Peter Blake, who said, "Public housing has got to be the very worst way of solving our housing problems." But in the midst of despair, it was the tenants themselves who organized to forge a new, positive approach to their problems. They fought to secure representation on the CMHA board, better security, and improved facilities. Local councilmen obtained community block grants to help finance additional security forces and community improvements. The CLEVELAND FOUNDATION funded grants for tenant-management training programs. In the new spirit of seizing the estates back from the vandals and drug pushers, Lakeview Terrace's tenant council invited Bertha Gilkey, a noted and successful tenant activist from St. Louis, to help them organize self-management of their estate. During 1976–86, housing for the elderly continued to spread, with high-rises scattered throughout the metropolitan area. Because most of them are not located in slum areas, they have not been plagued with the problems that have afflicted Cedar Extension and Riverview. The downtown high-rise for senior citizens was named the Ernest J. Bohn Bldg. In the 1980s, executive director Geo. M. James changed policy regarding rehabilitation. Proposals for demolition of Cedar and Lakeview Terrace apartments were rejected in favor of res-

toration and improvement. In the summer of 1985, the restoration of the Cedar estate had begun, and model suites were presented to the public at an open house in honor of the 50th anniversary of its construction. With all its faults and shortcomings, the public-housing movement in Cleveland has fought public indifference and outright hostility in order to bring decent housing to hundreds of thousands of low-income people in the past 50 years. With "proper care," adequate funding, good site selection, and good management, the dream that moved Cleveland's housing pioneers need not crumble.

Thomas F. Campbell
Cleveland State University

Ernest J. Bohn Housing & Planning Library, CWRU.

Navin, R. B., "Analysis of a Slum Area" (Master's thesis, Catholic University of America, 1934).

PUBLIC SAFETY. When Cleveland received its first city charter in 1836, it had only about 6,000 people, and its leaders did not see any great need for elaborate instruments to preserve public safety. In general, Cleveland, like its neighbors Buffalo, Detroit, Chicago, and Milwaukee, followed the lead of eastern cities such as Philadelphia in matters of governmental structure and services offered. Innovations such as the establishment of organized, bureaucratic police began in the older and larger eastern cities and then diffused down to newer and smaller communities. Boston, New York, and Philadelphia established modern police forces in the late 1830s and 1840s, after Cleveland had become a city, and it was not until the 1850s that Cleveland followed their lead. In the 1850s and 1860s, Cleveland's police acquired uniforms and a bureaucratic structure. Its members worked 12-hour shifts with only an occasional day off. Up to 1866, an elected marshal directed the police, so theoretically the voters exercised indirect control over the department. In that year the state legislature intervened to establish a police board for Cleveland, with members appointed by the governor. That arrangement lasted until 1872, when the legislature gave control of the department to a board consisting of the mayor and 4 elected members. In 1891, Cleveland's "federal charter" established a department of public safety under a director appointed by the mayor. This structure survived until 1902, when the Ohio Supreme Court declared existing municipal charters contrary to the constitutional provision that all laws affecting cities must be uniform in their operation. The legislature, dominated by Republicans, adopted a uniform municipal code. The code called for a bipartisan board of public safety. If the mayor and 2/3 of city council could not agree on the members of the board, then the governor of the state would make the appointments. In the case of Cleveland, TOM L. JOHNSON frustrated the scheme by having sufficient support in council to get the board he wanted. In 1908 the legislature substituted a single safety director for the board, and in 1912 the voters approved a constitutional amendment permitting cities to draft their own charters.

One problem that has never been satisfactorily resolved in Cleveland is the overlap and sometimes confusion between the powers of the safety director and those of the chief of police. In some matters, the chief reports to the safety director; in others the chief has independent authority. In disciplinary matters, orders for suspension or removal of officers approved by the chief and safety director could be revoked by the civil service commission. These administrative peculiarities aside, Cleveland's police developed much like those of other cities. Political influence was certainly useful in initial appointment, desirable assignments, and promotion, and MASONS were on faster tracks than CATHOLICS. The opposite situation prevailed within the CLEVELAND FIRE DEPT., which became, and long remained, heavily Irish. Despite the constant jockeying for personal and partisan advantage, the CLEVELAND POLICE DEPT. was not a totally demoralized, ineffective organization in the late 19th and early 20th centuries. It could and did maintain order, provide services, catch some criminals, and periodically sweep the streets of beggars and drunks. It was an especially formidable force in labor disputes, usually directed against the interests of striking workers, as in the STREETCAR STRIKE OF 1899.

Individual administrators could exert considerable influence on the operations of the department and the general public life of the city. The most newsworthy was the tempestuous FRED KOHLER, chief of police 1903-13. Kohler exercised substantial and sometimes erratic control over the police during his tenure. He insisted on a neat appearance, discriminated against Irish officers, brought his favorites downtown, and exiled his opponents to the "woods." He also initiated some substantive changes in Cleveland's policing. The most famous was the Golden Rule policy substituting waivers for formal arrests in the case of minor infractions. Police in Cleveland and other cities made a large number of arrests for drunkenness and disorderly conduct. These arrests took up a great deal of police time and clogged the lower courts and correctional facilities. The Kohler policy saved time and resources for both the authorities and those accused of these low-level misdemeanors.

Kohler's policy toward vice was one of "repression." If "resorts" (houses of PROSTITUTION) were orderly, they were not bothered with raids; if they were not, a policeman stood outside taking names and addresses of those entering. Saloons that kept things quiet were allowed to operate on Sunday despite the state law against Sunday sales. Both of these policies met with the approval of Mayor Johnson, who thought that municipal government had more important items on its agenda than satisfying the Civic Reform Union and other moralistic groups. Johnson's law director, NEWTON D. BAKER, rejoiced in the shrinking size of the city's red-light district and considered it the result of sensible law enforcement policies. Baker also saw no point in trying to enforce the Sunday closing statute so out of touch with a majority of the city's people. Following Baker's tenure as mayor, the next mayor, Republican HARRY L. DAVIS, had little interest in the details of his job or in any sort of police repression of illicit enterprise. His safety director, Anton Sprosty, sought to prevent police raids without city hall approval, a move that opponents regarded as tantamount to protected vice within the city. Davis generated another group of opponents when in the great steel strike of 1919 he warned strikebreakers not to come to Cleveland. Employers fumed, but the more numerous workers appreciated his threat to use the police to keep the scabs out.

Cleveland's police and court system received national attention with the publication of *Criminal Justice in Cleveland* in 1922. This comprehensive survey, financed by the CLEVELAND FOUNDATION, was anything but complimentary. The section on the police appeared under the byline of Raymond Fosdick, but the work was done by Leonard Harrison. Fosdick-Harrison found the police to be disorganized, of low morale, and poorly led. Cleveland's police continued to function as it had when Cleveland was a much smaller community, not the 5th-largest city in the country, as it was in 1920. In keeping with an emerging consensus among scholars and interested civic groups that the police were primarily a crimefighting organization, the chapter devoted considerable attention to the detectives and, not surprisingly, was negative in tone and findings. Detectives should be separately recruited; too many able and ambitious people either refused to join police departments or left soon after appointment rather than spend long years doing routine patrol duty. Similarly, administrators should also be either separately recruited or chosen on some basis other than the ability to pass civil-service exams or membership in the right political clubs.

*Criminal Justice in Cleveland* advocated a reformed police department and court system, one that would be efficient, incorruptible, free from partisan and councilmanic interference, and dedicated to rigorous law enforcement. Cleveland was too diverse a community, socially and politically, for this program ever to be adopted in full. In 1921, to many people's surprise, the voters did approve a charter amendment instituting a city manager form of government; but the party organizations soon made their peace with this structure, and political business proceeded more or less as usual, with council members continuing to intercede in disciplinary matters and on assignments and promotions for favored police officers. Certainly Geo. Matowitz survived as chief of police from 1931-51, in part because of civil-service protection and by concentrating more on keeping the plants in his office well watered than in providing strong leadership to the department. There was one instance of decisive leadership during his tenure; that came during the early years of ELIOT NESS's period of service as safety director in the 1930s. Ness came to Cleveland at the behest of Republican mayor HAROLD BURTON when he was only 32. He reorganized the department extensively by eliminating many precinct houses and concentrating on motor rather than foot patrol. He divided the city into 38 zones, each of which would be patrolled by its own car. Changes of shift were to take place within the cars to eliminate time lost going to and from district headquarters

Ness seemingly lost interest in the job after the first few years and was less active for some time before he left Cleveland in 1942. His reorganization did bring Cleveland fully into the motor age. As in other cities, the automobile and the motor truck had brought major changes to Cleveland before 1920. These changes intensified during the 1920s as the inner wards of the city lost population; only the rapid growth of peripheral wards kept Cleveland from losing population. Suburbs such as SHAKER HTS. grew even more rapidly. Many of the people in the outer wards and the suburbs commuted to their jobs in automobiles. The police responded to this upsurge by allocating 15% of its officers to traffic duty by the mid-1920s. Other policemen spent a portion of their day as school crossing guards. More of the department's budget had to go to equipment so that crooks in cars could at least be chased by cops in cars. By the end of the decade, the department had its own radio frequency, although it was not until the late 1930s that all of its cars were equipped with 2-way radios.

Despite Ness's reorganization and the technological changes, Cleveland never became a "reformed" city. In an unreformed city, the police took a tolerant view of vice in certain sections of town, while political and personal connections were crucial to career development. In a reformed city, one usually characterized by social homogeneity and above-average income, the police emphasized service to the affluent and a legalistic approach to wrongdoing. Law enforcement in Cleveland, as in other unreformed cities, did not always follow the procedural purity so central to the reformed tradition. The operative principle of the city's political life was more "What have you done for me lately?" than "How can I fulfill all of the legal responsibilities of my position?" A Cleveland police officer's career depended on the clout and concern of his "quill," department jargon for a powerful patron, as well as the officer's own competence.

Police officers were not just passive pawns of their political masters. They could and did organize to protect their own interests. In 1935, Cleveland policemen started a local chapter of the Fraternal Order of Police. This action was contrary to the rules of the department and the specific orders of the chief. Matowitz failed to enforce his own order, and by 1945 the FOP had about 750 members out of a department total of 1,300. The FOP at this point was concerned mainly about pension rights and in assuring elaborate due process and appeals procedures in disciplinary cases. Civil-service rules and the FOP helped the police resist any demands for change coming from outside the department, or even their own leadership. There were not many such demands. Tradition and bureaucratic inertia ruled in many American police organizations in the 1940s and 1950s, Cleveland's included, in large part because there was not much public controversy over the nature of the police role during these decades. Police agencies could be criticized for their action or inaction in specific cases, but few people publicly questioned their conception of their functions or their basic mode of operation. The 1960s were different. Cleveland has been a cosmopolitan city throughout the 20th century with a rich ethnic mixture. From 1940 on, the black portion of the city's population grew rapidly, until it reached 29% in the 1960 census. The combination of a white exodus and a black influx in the 1950s meant that the HOUGH area on the east side went from 95% white to 74% black within the decade. While the city experienced this explosive demographic transformation, the police department remained much the same. In the late 1960s, BLACKS were less than 10% of the police force and about 40% of the city.

Like many other cities, Cleveland experienced the "long, hot summers" of the 1960s. In 1966, the federal Civil Rights Commission took extensive testimony about the police department's much slower response time to calls from blacks than those from whites. In that same year the HOUGH RIOTS occurred, and in 1968, 7 people, including 3 police officers, died in the GLENVILLE SHOOT-OUT between black militants and Cleveland police. Mayor Carl Stokes, a black, dealt with the disorder by removing all white police from the area and having it policed by black officers and civilians. The police radio that night was filled with racist epithets against the mayor. Stokes's relationship with the police had never been easy; after Glenville they were impossible, because the black group involved in the fatal conflict with the police had been financially supported by his CLEVELAND: NOW! program.

In 1967, the same year Stokes was elected mayor, the CLEVELAND LITTLE HOOVER COMMISSION reported its recommendation to improve the city's operating efficiency. The section on the police was extremely critical, so much so that the commission as a whole refused to accept it. It offered 65 recommendations, of which the department rejected 34 major points while accepting 31 minor ones. Perhaps these tense relations accounted for the bluntness of the commission's language. "Its state of development, in the context of knowledge now available, is a generation behind modern police management concepts and technology." Cleveland's crime rate, bad enough as it was, would rise substantially with accurate and complete reporting. The commission dealt with the perennial cries for a larger force by asserting that "the mere addition of personnel to a poorly organized and managed department solves no basic problems." The commission's most serious criticisms came in the area of community relations. "The

department is defensive, isolated and parochial, and mistrustful of the public it serves." Part of the reason was demographic. The police reflected the immigration of earlier generations, not the in-migrants of this one. Perhaps more important was the prevailing conception of police work and the place of community relations within it. The police viewed themselves as crimefighters and community relations as a social-work approach to policing incompatible with crime control. The police had to use community relations for public relations, to limit criticism and promote positive public feelings. Anything beyond that involved contaminating contact with radicals and others out to embarrass the police rather than to help them in the suppression of crime. Civil-rights groups favored police-civilian review boards, an institution anathematic to the police, who believed that no one outside the department could ever properly judge decisions made on the streets under conditions of extreme stress.

By the 1970s, another problem came to the fore: money. In 1967, Cleveland's safety forces succeeded in putting through a charter amendment that guaranteed them salaries 3% higher than those of any other Ohio city of 50,000 or more persons. This provision was only one of several factors causing the city fiscal distress. The basic problem was that the city's revenue needs were outstripping its resources. Population declined and factories closed, while calls for police and fire service mounted. Transfer payments from the federal government became ever more important in meeting the bills. In 1969, the police department had a budget in excess of $32 million. At that time, nothing came from the federal government, but by 1975, 42% of the more than $45 million budget came from Washington. At the beginning of the 1970s, Cleveland had more than 2,400 police officers; by 1984 the department had shrunk by 1/3.

In the 1960s, the fire department underwent a dramatic increase in workload without a corresponding increase in personnel. In 1960 Cleveland had 10,796 alarms and 1,272 firefighters; in 1971 the city had 30,084 alarms and 1,292 firefighters. Moreover, firefighters on east side runs found themselves targets of rocks and other missiles, perhaps because blacks made up an even smaller percentage of the fire department than they did the police. Cleveland's firefighters also had to struggle with outmoded equipment and stations closed because of lack of resources. By the 1980s, Cleveland's safety forces were stretched thin and heavily dependent upon transfer payments from the federal government for basic operating expenses. How well they will be able to meet the needs of the city in the future depends upon decisions made in Washington as well as city hall.

James F. Richardson
University of Akron

**PUBLIC SQUARE** marks the center of the city of Cleveland. The "Original Plan of the Town and Village of Cleaveland," prepared in 1796 by the CONNECTICUT LAND CO., laid down a 10-acre public square bisected by 2 wide streets, Superior and Ontario. It was conceived as the open space of a traditional New England town plan, intended to serve as a common grazing area and meeting place. In 1810 the Public Square was a cow pasture still studded with tree stumps, but it already had begun to attain importance as the center of settlement. Around its periphery, fine residences had given way to business blocks, and the square was a commercial center.

In 1857, Superior and Ontario streets were vacated at Public Square, and a white double-railed fence enclosed the grounds, which were landscaped. But some viewed the fence as an obstacle to progress. Representing property owners and merchants, LEONARD CASE and HENRY B. PAYNE took the matter to court and won; the fence was removed, and Ontario and Superior were reopened to traffic in 1867. In 1861, city council passed an ordinance changing the name of Public Square to "Monumental Park" in recognition of the memorial to Commodore Perry unveiled there the previous year (see PERRY MONUMENT), but "Public Square" continued in popular use. The city's new Board of Park Commissioners adopted the Square for its first improvement project in 1872. It was landscaped and ornamented with a waterfall and artificial pond in the southwest section, a large rustic pavilion in the northeast, and a basin and lily fountain removed from FRANKLIN CIRCLE in the northwest. Later in the decade, on 29 Apr. 1879, Public Square was the site of the first successful demonstration of electric streetlights. In the late 19th century, 2 memorials were erected that were still prominent features of the Square in 1986: a statue of MOSES CLEAVELAND unveiled by the EARLY SETTLERS ASSOC. in 1888, and the Cuyahoga County's SOLDIERS & SAILORS MONUMENT, dedicated on Independence Day 1894.

In 1930, a wave of modernization wiped out the rustic character of the Square. Moses Cleaveland took his place in front of the new Terminal Tower, a geyser fountain was installed in the northeast quadrant, and large shelters accommodated the city's streetcar travelers. Over the next several decades, the Square grew shabby and neglected, functioning more as a transit hub than a public park. In 1976 the Downtown Cleveland Corp. and the city of Cleveland, with grants from local foundations and the GARDEN CTR. OF GREATER CLEVELAND, commissioned Sasaki Associates of Watertown, Mass., and Cleveland architects M. Hisaka & Associates to prepare a redevelopment plan for Public Square. Their plan called for the restoration of "Cleveland's front room" by reducing the impact of Superior and Ontario with landscaping and pedestrian amenities, planting shade trees around the perimeter, and giving a new emphasis to the quadrants as 4 distinct urban plazas and gardens. Construction, funded by the city of Cleveland, Cuyahoga County, and the state of Ohio, was still underway in 1984.

**PUBLISHING.** See **PRINTING AND PUBLISHING IN CLEVELAND**

**PUCKETT, NEWBELL NILES** (8 July 1898–21 Feb. 1967), was an educator, sociologist, and renowned folklorist. He was born in Columbus, Miss., the son of Willis Niles and Mathilda Boyd Puckett. After attending local schools, he received his B.S. degree in 1918 from Mississippi College at Clinton, and his Ph.B. in 1920, his A.M. in 1921 (Page Fellow), and his Ph.D. in 1925 from Yale University. He served a year as hospital apprentice in the Navy in 1919, joined the sociology faculty of Western Reserve University in 1922, was appointed professor of sociology in 1938, and served as chairman of the Sociology Dept. from 1954–62.

Puckett was president of the Ohio and Cleveland folklore societies, was elected a fellow of the American Folklore Society (1959), and was active in the American Anthropological Society, the American Name Society, the American Assoc. of University Professors, and other professional organizations. Through his studies of naming practices, superstitions, folk beliefs, wit and humor, and religious beliefs rooted in folk tradition, Puckett made valuable contributions to understanding the history of our nation, the "black experience" in America, and our traditional culture. His involvement in the history and culture of black Americans began long before black-studies programs became part of the college curriculum. His research led to

several publications, including *Folk Beliefs of the Southern Negro*, first published in 1926. In 1937, his initial findings on "Names of American Negro Slaves" was published in *Studies in the Science of Society*, edited by Geo. Murdock (Yale University Press). Frequently repeated field trips took him from the Deep South, through the counties and metropolitan areas of Ohio, to the Canadian wilderness. His natural ability to establish a rapport with all sorts of common folk enabled him to gain their trust and respect. His life was devoted to the study of traditional folk cultures, spanning the spectrum of American folk experience from black studies to ethnic traditions, rural and urban.

Puckett offered a pioneering course in black studies at WRU, organized the Cleveland Folklore Society, utilized the mass media for collection of information on folk beliefs in Ohio, researched pre-Civil War population and plantation records in the South, and published the preliminary findings of his research in professional journals. Through 4 decades of field research, he compiled detailed, accurate, and extensive collections of authentic data on "Black Names," "Religious Life of the Southern Negro," "Canadian Lumberjack Songs," and "Ohio Superstitions and Popular Beliefs." His papers, tapes, transcripts, and photographs are part of the Newbell Niles Puckett Memorial Gift, established by his wife, Ruth N. Puckett, in 1968, and deposited in the John G. White Collection of the CLEVELAND PUBLIC LIBRARY. Puckett was married twice, to Marion A. Randall in 1923 and, following her death in 1959, to Ruth Neuer in 1960. He died at the age of 65 and is buried in Knollwood Mausoleum.

**PUEHRINGER, FERDINAND** (1841–15 Sept. 1930), was an impresario, conductor, composer, and teacher. Puehringer came to America in 1863 from Austria, after having studied music with Franz Von Suppe. He became a professor of music at Wittenberg College in Springfield, Ohio, and came to Cleveland in 1872. As an impresario, Puehringer was affiliated with many local musical societies, such as the GERMANIA ORCHESTRA. He organized and directed many of his own groups, such as the Boys Band. He also produced many operas, including Lortzing's *Der Waffenschmied* in 1874, and at the ACADEMY OF MUSIC in 1876 he produced *The Czar and Zimmerman*, *The Bohemian Girl* with EFFIE ELLSLER, and Offenbach's *Orpheus in the Underworld*. Puehringer put the Germania Orchestra on a sounder financial basis by beginning subscription concerts. That same year, he started a singing and orchestra school to improve his own performers. It also enabled him to later organize the PHILHARMONIC ORCHESTRA. Consisting of 30 amateurs, then later professional musicians, with rehearsals being held at the YMCA Bldg. on Prospect Ave. and E. 9th., the Philharmonic Orchestra gave its first performance on 31 Oct. 1881 to benefit the Society for Organizing Charities. They were assisted by a soprano singing an aria from *Rigoletto*, the Arion Male Quartet, and a pianist, Clara Strong, playing Chopin. Puehringer later became director of the Park Theatre Orchestra. In 1887, his light opera *Captain Cupid*, with libretto by Wm. R. Rose of the *PLAIN DEALER* and Wm. E. Sage of the *CLEVELAND LEADER*, was produced there. His other works include *The Hero of Erie* (about Oliver Hazard Perry's battle on the lake in 1813) and *Anna Liese*. Puehringer was married to Mary Emich and had 1 child.

**PUERTO RICANS.** See **HISPANIC COMMUNITY**

**PURITAS SPRINGS PARK,** a popular west side amusement resort for 60 years, was built in 1898 by John E. Gooding of Painesville. It was located on the north side of Puritas Rd., overlooking the Rocky River Valley. On the same site, a group of Clevelanders 4 years earlier had erected a bottling plant to meet demands for the spring mineral water found there—hence the name of the park and the streetcar line that served this section of southwest Cleveland. Puritas Springs Park featured a roller rink, a dance hall, picnic spots, and a ball field. But the 80-acre park was best known for its fast, thrilling rides, especially the famous (and dangerous) Cyclone roller coaster. Gooding, who lived with his family in a house on the park grounds, is credited with introducing the first horse-drawn and steam-powered carousels in Ohio. When LUNA PARK closed in 1929, Gooding acquired its famous carousel of 72 hand-carved steeds and installed it at Puritas Springs. Gooding died in 1938. His daughter, Pearl Visoky, became president of the Puritas Springs Park Co. Later, Gooding's grandson James continued operations until he sold the park in 1958 to a land-development company. A fire the following spring caused extensive damage, and the park was razed for a housing development and shopping center.

**PYKE, BERNICE SECREST** (22 Mar. 1880–10 May 1964), was the first woman ever elected a delegate to a national political convention and the first woman to serve in a Cleveland mayor's cabinet. She was born in Frankfort, Ross County, Ohio, the daughter of Samuel Frederick and Mary Jane Miller Secrest. After graduation from high school in Chillicothe, Ohio, in 1898, she attended Ohio Wesleyan University and received her A.B. degree from Smith College in 1902. She taught mathematics in Illinois schools until her marriage in 1905. She and her husband then came to the Cleveland area. Pyke was active in the women's suffrage movement in Cuyahoga County and in 1920 was elected a delegate to the Democratic Natl. Convention, where she was in charge of the women's effort to promote the candidacy of Gov. Jas. M. Cox of Ohio for president. She was elected a delegate to 4 more national Democratic conventions. Mayor RAY T. MILLER appointed her director of public welfare in 1932; she served through 1933. In 1934, Pres. Franklin Roosevelt appointed her collector of customs for the Cleveland district, a position she held until 1953. She died at her home at age 84. She had married Arthur B. Pyke on 4 Jan. 1905, and they had a son, John Secrest Pyke.

# Q

**QUAYLE, THOMAS** (9 May 1811–31 Jan. 1895), along with his partner John S. Martin, was an important mid-19th-century shipbuilder in Cleveland who turned his business over to his sons upon his retirement in the early 1880s. He was also a Democratic city councilman in the 1860s. Quayle was born on the Isle of Man, where he learned ship carpentry. After coming to the U.S. with his parents in 1827, he became an apprentice ship carpenter. He entered into his first shipbuilding partnership in 1847 with John Cody; in 1850 he took on a new partner, Luther Moses, and the business prospered, with sometimes 7 ships under construction at once. But it was the partnership of Quayle and John S. Martin (June 1814–8 Mar. 1874), formed by 1855, that enjoyed the greatest success. Between 1855–74, Quayle & Martin was one of the leading shipbuilding companies in the city, building as many as 12 or 13 ships a year. By 1865 the firm was turning business away. Quayle continued to build ships after Martin's death, taking on 2 of his sons, Thos. E. (26 July 1836–15 Aug. 1896) and Geo. L. (d. 22 Feb. 1927), as partners in Quayle & Sons. Quayle's firms built some of the largest wooden ships on the lakes—such as the 2,082-ton *Commodore* in 1875, reportedly the largest ship on the lakes at the time—and were considered pioneers in the development of the large wooden propellers. When the elder Quayle retired from shipbuilding in the early 1880s, a third son, William (1838–25 June 1893), joined the firm, and the business continued as Thos. Quayle's

Sons for the next decade, until steel vessels replaced wooden ships on the lakes. Thos. Quayle was married twice. He was first married in 1835 to Eleanor Cannon, also from the Isle of Man, who bore 11 children before her death in Sept. 1860. In 1867 he married Mary Proudfoot.

The **QUINCY SAVINGS & LOAN** was built on the remains of a Czech savings institution to become the 19th-largest black-owned savings and loan in the country. In 1953, insurance and real-estate entrepreneur M. C. Clarke of the Dunbar Insurance Co. raised $185,000 from the black community to buy the assets of an ethnic savings and loan. Convinced that blacks could own and operate successful businesses to meet needs that whites would not meet, he paid increasing dividends each year and built the business into a strong local enterprise. The Quincy Savings & Loan enabled many blacks to get home mortgage financing. Under Clarke's leadership, assets grew from less than $400,000 at the time of purchase to $2 million by 1955, $8 million in 1969, and $10 million in 1978. When the company outgrew its original location at 8309 Quincy, it moved to 7609 Euclid, the building owned by the Dunbar Life Insurance Co. Despite its success, the company's name was dropped from the telephone directory in 1980. The Cleveland Community Savings Co. briefly occupied the premises.

# R

**RADIO.** In Cleveland, the development of radio went through 3 distinct phases: an initial period when the medium was largely experimental and gradually became commercialized; a second when radio flourished as a commercial medium; and the third following WORLD WAR II, when radio strove to cope with television and increasing competition within its own industry. Cleveland's first radio station was WHK, which went on the air early in 1922. Later that year, WJAX began broadcasting, followed in 1923 by WTAM, sharing time on the same 390-meter frequency. By 1925, WJAX had been sold to the Goodyear Tire & Rubber Co., Akron, which changed the call letters to WEAR. Not long after, it was again sold, to WTAM's owner WILLARD STORAGE BATTERY, insuring WTAM a clear channel at 390 meters. WEAR was phased out before the end of the decade. In 1927, WJAY began to operate under a sunup-to-sundown license. WGAR joined the Cleveland group late in Dec. 1930. During these early years, it appeared that radio might havearrived at the wrong time. The 1920s saw an entertainment boom in downtown Cleveland, and at E. 105th St., with the construction of palatial new theaters featuring vaudeville, Broadway shows, and Hollywood films. Restaurants provided social dancing during lunch, dinner, and after-theater hours. Such competition proved a dilemma for the city's pioneering stations. However, local stations countered by broadcasting from restaurants, hotel dining rooms, and even theater stages, building audiences both at home and in the various venues. Listings for 1925–26 show broadcasts from the Hotel Cleveland, the Rainbow Room Orchestra at the Hotel Winton, the STATE THEATER, the Hotel Statler, the Bamboo Gardens Orchestra, and the Hotel Hollenden Orchestra. In almost all of these instances, name bands, such as those headed by Guy Lombardo or Maurice Spitalny, were the focus of the broadcast as they performed in the various hotels' ballrooms.

During this formative period, 3 realities emerged: advertising was necessary for income; planned, exciting programming was imperative; and a professional approach to sales and promotion—like that of local theater managements—was an immediate need. Radio advertising was a controversial subject, opposed by many, who believed the new medium should be used to educate and cultivate higher levels of taste. Broadcasters also had to prove to potential advertisers that their dollars were actually accomplishing something. The use of well-known entertainers and per-

sonable hosts on the airwaves proved the answer that would draw both audiences and advertisers. Two such widely favored entertainers in Cleveland were Cartwright "Pinky" Hunter, a singer, long identified with Emerson Gill's Orchestra; and "Ev" Jones, popular bandleader, whose WTAM programs brought him and the station a loyal following.

By 1926, radio was no longer a novelty; and many held the view that local stations were not equipped financially to sustain quality programming. They felt that New York, with its exemplary stations, WEAF and WJZ, should share their excellence with listeners everywhere. In Sept. 1926, the Radio Corp. of America announced the formation of the Natl. Broadcasting Co. for that purpose. Within 3 months came the announcement of a second, rival network, which by autumn of 1928 had been purchased by Wm. Paley. He renamed this network the Columbia Broadcasting System. NBC elected to initiate not 1 but 2 networks, to comply with government pressure that broadcasters should inform and educate, as well as entertain. Sarnoff chose WEAF to entertain as the Red Network, and WJZ as the Blue Network to inform and educate. Almost immediately the "Red" Network courted WTAM to become its Cleveland affiliate, while CBS approached WHK in the same manner. NBC's "Blue" Network was picked up by WGAR when it debuted in Dec. 1930. WJAY, because of its sunrise-sunset license, remained independent until its purchase by the *PLAIN DEALER* in 1937, with the new call letters WCLE. In its 10 years (1927–37), under Monroe F. Rubin and general manager Grant C. Melrose, WJAY made a strong impact on Cleveland radio, as a proving ground for aspiring local and area talent. It also provided an outlet for Cleveland's large ethnic population. From the ranks of its ethnic programmers came Frederick C. Wolf, who, with ethnic business and professional associates, would later found WDOK in 1950.

As the 1930s opened, competition at both local and network levels increased as the market grew. Every strategy was used. Announcers began to vary their deliveries, from "hard sell" to "intimate." Stations promoted themselves with billboards and public appearances of station personalities. Better microphones, speakers, and amplifiers made the medium more effective. Advertising agencies were retained to promote stations in the print media. That led to agencies' representing sponsors. In the 1930s, both networks and local stations fine-tuned programming to match certain audiences. Audiences were studied, from sign-on to

# CLEVELAND RADIO AND TELEVISION STATIONS

| Year | AM Stations | FM Stations | TV Stations |
|---|---|---|---|
| 1922 | WHK<br>WJAX | | |
| 1924 | WHK<br>WTAM<br>WJAX | | |
| 1926 | WTAM – 770<br>WEAR – 770<br>WHK – 1100<br>WDBK – 1320 | | |
| 1930 | WJAY – 610<br>WEAF – 660<br>WJZ – 760<br>WABC – 860<br>WTAM – 1070<br>WHK – 1390 | | |
| 1935 | WJAY – 610<br>WTAM – 1070<br>WHK – 1390<br>WGAR – 1450 | | |
| 1940 | WCLE – 610<br>WTAM – 1070<br>WHK – 1390<br>WGAR – 1450 | | |
| 1945 | WJW – 850<br>WTAM – 1100<br>WGAR – 1220<br>WHK – 1420 | | |
| 1950 | WJW – 850<br>WTAM – 1100<br>WGAR – 1220<br>WDOK – 1260<br>WERE – 1300<br>WHK – 1420<br>WSRS – 1490<br>WJMO – 1540 | WBOE – 90.3<br>WSRS – 95.3<br>WERE – 98.5<br>WHK – 100.7<br>WCUO – 103.0<br>WJW – 104.1<br>WTAM – 105.7 | WNBK – 4<br>WEWS – 5<br>WXEL – 9 |
| 1955 | WJW – 850<br>WTAM – 1100<br>WGAR – 1220<br>WHK – 1420 | WBOE – 90.3<br>WSRS – 95.3<br>WGAR – 98.5<br>WERE – 99.5<br>WHK – 100.7<br>WDOK – 102.1<br>WJW – 104.1<br>WTAM – 105.7 | WNBK – 3<br>WEWS – 5<br>WXEL – 8 |
| 1960 | WJW – 850<br>KYW – 1100<br>WGAR – 1220<br>WDOK – 1260<br>WERE – 1300<br>WHK – 1420<br>WJMO – 1490<br>WABQ – 1540 | WBOE – 90.3<br>WCUY – 95.3<br>WERE – 98.5<br>WGAR – 99.5<br>WHK – 100.7<br>WDOK – 102.1<br>WCRF – 103.3<br>WJW – 104.1<br>WSOM – 105.1<br>KYW – 105.7<br>WNOB – 107.9 | KYW – 3<br>WEWS – 5<br>WJW – 8 |
| 1965 | WJW – 850<br>KYW – 1100<br>WCUE – 1150<br>WGAR – 1220<br>WDOK – 1260<br>WERE – 1300<br>WELW – 1330<br>WSLR – 1350<br>WHK – 1420<br>WPVL – 1460<br>WJMO – 1490<br>WABQ – 1540<br>WAKR – 1590 | WKSU – 89.7<br>WBOE – 90.3<br>WCUY – 92.3<br>WZAK – 93.1<br>WDBN – 94.9<br>WCLV – 95.5<br>WCUF – 96.5<br>WAKR – 97.5<br>WGAR – 99.5<br>WHK – 100.7<br>WDOK – 102.1<br>WCRF – 103.3<br>WJW – 104.1<br>KYW – 105.7<br>WXEN – 106.5<br>WEOL – 107.3<br>WNOB – 107.9 | KYW – 3<br>WEWS – 5<br>WJW – 8<br>WVIZ – 25 |

# CLEVELAND RADIO AND TELEVISION STATIONS (continued)

| Year | AM Stations | FM Stations | TV Stations |
|---|---|---|---|
| 1970 | WJW – 850<br>WKYC – 1100<br>WGAR – 1220<br>WIXY – 1260<br>WERE – 1300<br>WELW – 1330<br>WHK – 1420<br>WJMO – 1490<br>WABQ – 1540 | WBWC – 88.3<br>WUJC – 88.9<br>WBOE – 90.3<br>WCUY – 92.3<br>WZAK – 93.1<br>WDBN – 94.2<br>WCLV – 95.5<br>WCUE – 96.5<br>WERE – 98.5<br>WNCR – 99.5<br>WMMS – 100.7<br>WDOK – 102.1<br>WCRF – 103.3<br>WCJW – 104.1<br>WKYC – 105.7<br>WXEN – 106.5<br>WBEA – 107.3<br>WNOB – 107.9 | WKYC – 3<br>WEWS – 5<br>WJW – 8<br>WAKR – 23<br>WVIZ – 25<br>WUAB – 43<br>WKBF – 61 |
| 1975 | WJW – 850<br>WSUM – 1000<br>WWWE – 1100<br>WGAR – 1220<br>WIXY – 1260<br>WERE – 1300<br>WELW – 1330<br>WSLR – 1350<br>WLRO – 1380<br>WHK – 1420<br>WPVL – 1460<br>WJMO – 1490<br>WKNT – 1520<br>WABQ – 1540<br>WBKC – 1560 | WBWC – 88.3<br>WUJC – 88.9<br>WKSU – 89.7<br>WBOE – 90.3<br>WRUW – 91.1<br>WLTY – 92.3<br>WZAK – 93.1<br>WDBN – 94.9<br>WCLV – 95.5<br>WCUE – 96.5<br>WREO – 97.1<br>WAEZ – 97.5<br>WTOF – 98.1<br>WGCL – 98.5<br>WNCR – 99.5<br>WKNT – 100.1<br>WMMS – 100.7<br>WDOK – 102.1<br>WCRF – 103.3<br>WQAL – 104.1<br>WWWM – 105.7<br>WXEN – 106.5<br>WBEA – 107.3<br>WELW – 107.9 | WKYC – 3<br>WEWS – 5<br>WJW – 8<br>WAKR – 23<br>WVIZ – 25<br>WUAB – 43 |
| 1977 | WMGC – 1260 | | |
| 1980 | WJW – 850<br>WEOL – 930<br>WSUM – 1000<br>WWWE – 1100<br>WGAR – 1220<br>WBBG – 1260<br>WERE – 1300<br>WOBL – 1320<br>WELW – 1330<br>WSLR – 1350<br>WLRO – 1380<br>WHK – 1420<br>WPUL – 1460<br>WJMO – 1490<br>WKNT – 1520<br>WABQ – 1540<br>WBKC – 1560 | WBWC – 88.3<br>WUJC – 88.7<br>WCSB – 89.3<br>WKSU – 89.7<br>WBOE – 90.3<br>WRUW – 91.1<br>WLYT – 92.3<br>WZAK – 93.1<br>WDVN – 94.9<br>WCLV – 95.5<br>WKDD – 96.5<br>WREO – 97.1<br>WAEZ – 97.5<br>WTOF – 98.1<br>WGCL – 98.5<br>WKSW – 99.5<br>WKNT – 100.1<br>WMMS – 100.7<br>WDOK – 102.1<br>WCRF – 103.3<br>WQAL – 104.1<br>WZLE – 104.9<br>WWWM – 105.7<br>WZZP – 106.5<br>WBEA – 107.3<br>WDMT – 107.9 | WKYC – 3<br>WEWS – 5<br>WJKW – 8<br>WAKR – 23<br>WVIZ – 25<br>WUAB – 43 |
| 1984 | WQLS – 1460 | WRQC – 92.3<br>WDBN – 94.9<br>WNIR – 100.1<br>WMJI – 105.7<br>WLTF – 106.5 | |

| Year | AM Stations | | FM Stations | | TV Stations | |
|------|-------------|---|-------------|---|-------------|---|
| 1985 | WJW | – 850 | WBWC | – 88.3 | WKYC | – 3 |
| | WEOL | – 930 | WUJC | – 88.7 | WEWS | – 5 |
| | WSUM | – 1000 | WCSB | – 89.3 | WJKW | – 8 |
| | WJTB | – 1040 | WKSU | – 89.7 | WOIO | – 19 |
| | WWWE | – 1100 | WCPN | – 90.3 | WAKR | – 23 |
| | WGAR | – 1220 | WRUW | – 91.1 | WVIZ | – 25 |
| | WBBG | – 1260 | WRQC | – 92.3 | WUAB | – 43 |
| | WERE | – 1300 | WZAK | – 93.1 | WCLQ | – 61 |
| | WOBL | – 1320 | WDBN | – 94.9 | | |
| | WELW | – 1330 | WCLV | – 95.5 | | |
| | WSLR | – 1350 | WKDD | – 96.5 | | |
| | WRKG | – 1380 | WONE | – 97.5 | | |
| | WHK | – 1420 | WTOF | – 98.1 | | |
| | WQLS | – 1460 | WGCL | – 98.5 | | |
| | WJMO | – 1490 | WGAR | – 99.5 | | |
| | WKNT | – 1520 | WNIR | – 100.1 | | |
| | WABQ | – 1540 | WMMS | – 100.7 | | |
| | WBKC | – 1560 | WDOK | – 102.1 | | |
| | | | WCRF | – 103.3 | | |
| | | | WQAL | – 104.1 | | |
| | | | WZLE | – 104.9 | | |
| | | | WMJI | – 105.7 | | |
| | | | WLTF | – 106.5 | | |
| | | | WBEA | – 107.3 | | |
| | | | WDMT | – 107.9 | | |
| 1986 | WHLO | – 640 | WNCX | – 98.5 | | |
| | WRMR | – 850 | | | | |
| | WBKC | – 1460 | | | | |
| | WCDN | – 1560 | | | | |

sign-off time, with programming altered according to who was listening. That resulted in daytime dramas (soaps) to meet the desires of housewives. Evening programming came to feature variety shows, hosted by established stars such as Rudy Vallee, Bing Crosby, and Al Jolson. Quiz shows, born in the 1930s, also found a niche in evening programming. These influences quickly reached the local level, where they engendered a trend toward a more conversational "everydayness" on the air. Two-person shows began, such as "Ethel and Ben" (homemakers) on WGAR, "Mildred and Gloria," a women's show, on WTAM, and "Just Married" on WJAY (a dramatic show that foreshadowed the improvisational skits of the 1970s). All dialogue was ad-libbed from a synopsis sheet prepared by creator Edyth Fern Melrose.

In 1937, CBS named WGAR as its local affiliate, whereupon WHK accepted the NBC "Blue" affilation and that of the newly arrived Mutual Broadcasting System. The year before, WHK had completed the first full season of radio coverage of Cleveland Indians BASEBALL games. In that year it also sent a radio newsman to cover a flood disaster on the Ohio River. Both actions were made possible by the increasing technical sophistication of the medium. WGAR staged a call-in disaster-relief broadcast for the same emergency. The growing role of radio in local and national life was best attested to by its place in the GREAT LAKES EXPOSITION in 1936. PUBLIC AUDITORIUM was transformed into a studio, where network prime-time programs were invited to perform, throughout the summers of 1936–37. By the end of the 1930s, 5 principal areas of programming had evolved; their development extended through the 1940s. They were: news; remote broadcasts; sports; ethnic programming; and in-house scripted and produced productions of major size. This last category, by most stations, was relegated to special and infrequent status, because of its large demands on station budgets and personnel.

Because a fully departmented approach to news involved considerable costs for staff, equipment, and main-

tenance, radio stations deferred from such activity in the 1930s. They could not compete adequately with newspapers on in-depth coverage. However, radio's one peculiar strength was in its immediacy; and that was what stations exploited. They developed the headline style of succinct reporting, and, when possible, brief interviews with witnesses or participants. Stations recognized the importance of regularly scheduled newscasts throughout each day: several between 6 and 8 a.m.; at noon; between 6 and 7 p.m.; and at 11 p.m. In each case, weather reports and traffic and road conditions were standard auxiliaries.

Remote broadcasts required, normally, 1 announcer and 1 technician, responsible for gear and setup. The 1930s witnessed regularly scheduled broadcasts from the major downtown hotel dining rooms, the Mayfair Casino, the Alpine Village, and nightclubs in the E. 105th St. area. In the late 1930s, concert pickups from SEVERANCE HALL and summer concerts at Public Auditorium were routinely made. Sports broadcasting always implied the need for remote work, although studio sports programs were as common as newscasts. The earliest references to sports came in 1922, when WHK and WJAX included scores and brief highlights in their local newscasts. WTAM soon became ascendant in sports, however, with TOM MANNING as the announcer best known in the area. His association with the CLEVELAND INDIANS began in the late 1920s, and by 1930 he was doing play-by-play from LEAGUE PARK, with Bert Pruitt customarily the technician in charge. Other notable local sportscasters have included JOHN "JACK" GRANEY, Jimmy Dudley, Bob Kelly, Bob Neal, and Van Patrick in the 1930s and 1940s, and in the 1960s and later, Gib Shanley, Joe Tate, Nev Chandler, Bruce Brennan, and Jim Donovan. Ethnic programming, begun at WJAY, was eventually taken up by other stations (usually on Sunday mornings), including WGAR, WHK, and WERE. In 1950, WDOK picked up where WJAY and WGAR had left off. In the early 1960s, 2 other stations, WXEN and WZAK, devoted most of their schedules to ethnic broadcasting. Such activity declined in the 1970s, and by 1985, Cleveland's Public Service station, WCPN, was the major purveyor of ethnic programming.

The growth and sophistication of radio during the 1930s placed it in an excellent position to cover World War II, both internationally and domestically. On the domestic front, in 1943 the FCC enforced a long-deferred antimonopoly action against NBC, resulting in the immediate sale of the "Blue" Network to Edward J. Noble, who renamed it the American Broadcasting Co. He chose as its Cleveland affiliate the city's newest radio station, WJW, owned By the O'Neill family of Akron. The edict also forced the closing of WCLE by the *Plain Dealer* as a Cleveland station. The ruling would therefrom forbid any person or group to own more than 1 radio station in a single market (later to include television). To assist the war effort, WHK, under writer-producer Leslie Biebl, produced "Victory Time," a series of variety programs employing a 20-voice chorus, and 28-piece orchestra under Willard Potts, and sponsored by Thompson Prods. (see TRW). At WGAR, SIDNEY ANDORN wrote and produced a major variety production featuring soloists, chorus, and orchestra for Jack & Heintz (see LEAR SIEGLER), depicting the company's geared-up efforts in war production. "Sam at War" was another featured production at WHK by Biebl, in behalf of CIVIL DEFENSE, employing CLEVELAND PLAY HOUSE actors. WGAR's award-winning "Serenade for Smoothies," sponsored by Ohio Bell in the interests of recruiting women as key personnel, featured soloists, a girls' quartet, and staff orchestra; it debuted in 1943 over an Ohio network of 3 stations, playing before audiences in the Little Theater of

Public Hall. Wayne Mack was writer and producer. In 1942, "Bondwagon" broadcasts were produced by WGAR from the stage of the PALACE THEATER, urging the purchase of war bonds with entertainment by the nation's finest dance bands. Local stations sent correspondents to both the European and Pacific war theaters, to interview Cleveland men and to send back their greetings. Local stations also sent representatives to USO depots around the city.

As World War II ended, in 1945, interest in sports rose to fever pitch, as both the new CLEVELAND BROWNS and the Cleveland Indians fielded teams of exceptional quality. The Tribe's Hooper rating in the world championship year of 1948 was 60%; and the fortunate station was WJW, the flagship of a special Ohio network (WAKR, Akron; WHBC, Canton; WWST, Wooster; WICA, Ashtabula; and WNCO, Ashland). The full games were carried on WJW-FM, while WJW-AM, with its "Blue" Network commitments, was available only part of the time; in that year there were more FM radio sets sold in Cleveland than in any other market in the country. Licenses for Edwin Armstrong's "static-free" frequency modulation (FM) concept of radio transmission were first granted in 1940–41. Most Cleveland stations began making applications over the decade.

Television came to Cleveland in 1948 and ushered in the third period of local radio history. By 1950, 3 television stations (WEWS, WXEL, and WNBK) were operational in Cleveland; plus radio newcomers WDOK, WSRS, and WABQ. During the transitional 1950s, the medium began to evolve into the multifaceted, loosely structured industry that it became by the 1980s. The networks remained intact during the decade, providing standard services, but independent local stations introduced, from motives of economy, a new and somewhat different type of announcer, the disc jockey. He was given a 3- or 4-hour block of air time to do with pretty much as he pleased. By a curious coincidence, the DJ and ROCK 'N' ROLL music arrived at about the same time; they were clearly meant for each other. The disc jockey and rock music would dominate American music for the next 20 years. Two other forces were present as radio headed into the 1960s. One was the proliferation of new stations whose formats were quite individual and different, such as WCLV-FM, devoted entirely to the fine arts and concert music; WCRF, a religious station; and WSUM, devoted to community service. That all pointed to considerable fragmentation of the listening audience.

The other force was the imposing effect of rapidly developing technology. For instance, the development of flexible, reusable plastic tape equipped the industry with a tool that had uses impossible to overestimate. The development of transistorized portable radios and stereophonic broadcasting gave new flexibility to the medium. Perhaps the greatest effect locally was the ascendance of FM broadcasting. In 1965, WDOK was purchased by the Westchester Radio Corp., which immediately transferred its established format entirely to the FM frequency and revamped the personality of the AM property and its call letters into that of a rock 'n' roll station, WIXY. The resulting outrage was great, but subsided when listeners discovered FM to be superior in quality. The experiment gained national attention, and considerably influenced the emergence of FM into a dominant role in radio. In the late 1960s, the FCC decreed that FM stations could no longer be written off as duplicators of AM programming, but must provide a responsible share of their own creative product. That helped push FM toward center stage; as did the rather rapid accommodation of stereo to FM by "splitting" the FM wave. Another boon

of that technology was the subcarrier (SCA), which was used in "storecasting" by the Muzak Corp., and in special hookups for ethnic broadcasting, requiring modified receivers, as well as "schoolcasting," in use in some schools (parochial) outside the WBOE service of the Cleveland Board of Education. It was made available by Seaway Radio, Inc. (which owns WCLV).

In the 1960s and 1970s, there was a turnaround in which radio reversed its original purpose of serving all its audience with a wide swath of variety to the role of specialist, ready with a certain kind of entertainment by each station for the interested listener. The majority of stations elected to provide rock music, which created a problem: it led to a feverish hunt for listeners. Promotions to gain audience by the various stations became, at times, juvenile and indiscreet. The FCC came in for sharp criticism for its laxity in surveillance of program content; but it held adamantly to its position of neutrality, stating that it could not possibly "police" 10,000 radio stations. This policy led to a gradual deregulation of radio, beginning in the mid-1970s and completed early in the 1980s. The 1970s witnessed the maturing of both contemporary radio and the teen and preteen audiences of 1950s. The number of stations in Cleveland and northern Ohio climbed to more than 40. Formats were no longer sacrosanct; a losing format was simply changed. Station after station underwent format changes. For example, WIXY became WBBG in the 1970s, when the station decided to program the Big Band music of the 1940s for the 50-and-over segment of the population. As rock 'n' roll aged, other local stations began to exclusively play rock "oldies" for the baby-boom generation.

Perhaps Cleveland's outstanding example of intrepid programming during this volatile period was that of WCLV-FM, the fine-arts station, which stayed with its format and, despite a relatively small share of the listener market, remained one of the area's most profitable ventures. On the other side of the musical spectrum, WMMS-FM managed to hold a consistent rock format for a number of years and to achieve national stature for its programming and audience size. By the mid-1980s, Cleveland's radio industry was still largely in turmoil, with programming shifts, personality changes, and the rapid purchase and sale of stations. As such, it reflected general national trends; the stability of stations WCLV and WMMS was so outstanding that it transcended local boundaries and served to make these 2 components of local broadcasting nationally noteworthy. If any major theme has evolved from the seeming confusion of the radio industry, both locally and nationally in the posttelevision period, it is the continued viability of the industry. Unlike television, radio is not visually intrusive, and the medium can be effective as an entertainer or advertiser even when its audience is engaged in other activities. If anything, the miniaturization made possible by technology has made radio a greater part of the lives of Greater Clevelanders in the 1980s than ever before.

Wayne Mack

See also specific stations by call letters.

**RAILROADS.** While water traffic, on both Lake Erie and the OHIO & ERIE CANAL, did much to develop Cleveland, it took the appearance of the railroad to make the community's industrial takeoff a reality. From the 1860s to the 1960s, railroads served as the principal transporter of goods and people to and from the Forest City. Not long after the steam locomotive made its 1829 American debut, Clevelanders realized the potential for this novel transportation form. In 1836, area promoters organized what proved to be one of the most bizarre construction schemes in the annals of American railroad history, the Ohio Rail Road Co. Enthusiasts sought to create a transstate route that would run westerly from the "paper" community of Richmond on the Grand River in Lake County through Cleveland to another "paper" settlement, Manhattan, on the Maumee River in Lucas County. Rather than employing a dirt grade, the Ohio Rail Road planned to operate on strap rails attached to a 100-ft.-wide bridgelike structure, which would be supported by massive stakes driven into the ground. Although the project received substantial financial backing from the state legislature, hard times, triggered by the Panic of 1837, did much to kill it. But before the end, workers had installed about 63 mi. of the wooden superstructure, including a section near the CUYAHOGA RIVER, and for years the rotting timbers reminded residents of this unusual and unsuccessful railroad project.

Fortunately, Clevelanders had the good sense to select conventional railroad technology for their future projects. The economic dislocations that fatally crippled the Ohio Rail Road initially prevented backers of the proposed Cleveland, Columbus & Cincinnati from turning the plans expressed in their company's 1836 charter into reality. Eventually, though, a stronger economy led to line surveys, acquisition of rights-of-way, and then actual construction of a railroad in the late 1840s. Cleveland's railroad era officially began on 3 Nov. 1849, when the CC&C's lone engine coupled onto a string of flatcars near River St. Commented the *Cleveland Herald*, "The whistle of the locomotive will be as familiar to the ears of the Clevelander as the sound of church bells." The CC&C opened its first segment, 36 mi. to Wellington, in July 1850, and completed the remaining mileage into Columbus the following February. Its first Cleveland depot stood on the lakefront near W. 9th St. That same month, the Cleveland & Pittsburgh, a road that traced its corporate origins back to the 1836 charter of the Cleveland, Warren & Pittsburgh, dispatched trains over its new 26-mi. line between Cleveland and Hudson. Within a year, that carrier entered Pittsburgh. Also, a 62-mi. branch, initially organized in 1851 as the Cleveland, Mt. Vernon & Delaware Railroad, opened in 1852 between Hudson and Millersburg via Akron.

Railroad building in the Cleveland area continued at a brisk pace. The developing network of independent roads from New York to Chicago touched Cleveland in the early 1850s. Using the 1848 charter of the Cleveland, Painesville & Ashtabula, Cleveland promoters embarked upon a project between the Forest City and the Ohio-Pennsylvania state line, and they succeeded in 1852. The next year the Cleveland & Toledo, an amalgamation of several "paper" companies that dated back to the mid-1840s, received permission to link these two Ohio communities. Soon the firm reached the west bank of the Cuyahoga River. In 1869 these separate companies, together with the Michigan Southern & Northern Indiana and the Buffalo & Erie, became the Lake Shore & Michigan Southern Railway Co., a firm dominated by eastern interests. This merger gave a single management control of passenger and freight operations between Buffalo and Chicago. Also included in Cleveland's first wave of steam railroad construction was the Cleveland & Mahoning Valley Railroad. Chartered in 1848 and spearheaded by Western Reserve promoters, this "hot-air" road languished because its backers could not attract either domestic or foreign capital. Finally, these men, led by Jacob Perkins, pledged their own fortunes to the scheme, and this future component of the Erie took shape. By 1857, rails linked Cleveland with Warren and Youngstown. The C&MV not only provided Cleveland with another railroad, it also opened up the rich Mahoning Valley

coal fields to local industries and to the Great Lakes export trade.

The devastating impact of the Panic of 1857, coupled with the outbreak of the CIVIL WAR 4 years later, virtually halted railroad building in northeast Ohio. Even with peace in 1865 and a relatively healthy economy, railroad construction in the Cleveland area languished except for the 101-mi. Lake Shore & Tuscarawas Valley Railway. This predominantly coal-hauling line opened on 18 Aug. 1873, between Lorain and Uhrichsville. The LS&TV faced subsequent reorganizations and expansions until at the turn of the century it became the Cleveland, Lorain & Wheeling Railway, part of the Baltimore & Ohio system. The end of the war also saw the opening of a new UNION DEPOT on the city's lakefront near W. 9th St. The LS&TV enjoyed good timing, for the Panic of 1873 produced exceedingly difficult times for most in that decade. Depressed conditions understandably stymied railroad expansion. But an upturn in the economy after 1878 sparked a second wave of railroad building, in both northeastern Ohio and the nation. Included in this second wave was the Valley Railroad. Started on the eve of the Panic of 1873 by several Cleveland businessmen, including JEPTHA H. WADE I and NATHAN P. PAYNE, this company had to wait out the depression. Finally, it completed its Cleveland-to-Canton main line, via Akron, and service commenced in 1880. Although the Valley Railroad transported considerable coal as the result of extensions south of Canton, the hard times that came in the wake of the Panic of 1893 plunged it into receivership. Reorganization in late 1895 as the Cleveland Terminal & Valley Railroad brought new vitality. Like the Cleveland, Lorain & Wheeling, the CT&V belonged in the orbit of the B&O.

Another second-wave road was the Cleveland, Canton & Southern, also a coal-hauler. An outgrowth of the Ohio & Toledo and the Youngstown & Connotton Valley railroad companies, this line reached Cleveland from Canton and Kent in Jan. 1882, under the flag of the Connotton Northern Railroad. Like the Lake Shore & Tuscarawas Valley and the Valley railroads, this road was not especially robust, and it was susceptible to economic downswings. The recession of 1884-85 threw the Connotton Northern into a receivership that produced the Cleveland & Canton Railroad. The Panic of 1893 prompted further corporate reshaping when the Cleveland & Canton became the Cleveland, Canton & Southern. Ultimately in 1899, the property, which gave Cleveland convenient access to east Ohio coal fields, found a financially healthier home within the Wheeling & Lake Erie system.

By far the most significant development of the second-wave period for Cleveland was the creation in 1881 of the New York, Chicago & St. Louis Railway, better known as the Nickel Plate Road. Spearheaded by a combination of easterners and Ohioans—the so-called Seney Syndicate—this firm quickly emerged. The Nickel Plate's promoters built a nearly 600-mi. road in less than 600 days. By 1882, the company connected Buffalo, N.Y., with Chicago, Ill., via Cleveland; in fact, the road's officials selected Cleveland as its headquarters site. Entry into the city from both the east and the west involved purchase of 2 independent short lines, the CLEVELAND, PAINESVILLE & ASHTABULA RAILROAD (Cleveland to Collamer) and the Rocky River Railroad (Cleveland to ROCKY RIVER). Within a week after the Nickel Plate's official opening, its owners sold out to the Vanderbilts, a business family that controlled numerous railroads, including the Lake Shore & Michigan Southern. The Vanderbilts understandably desired to protect their position in the LS&MS, and so under their stewardship the Nickel Plate languished until the New York

Central, successor to the Vanderbilt empire, sold it on the eve of WORLD WAR I. The sale of the Nickel Plate was the preeminent example of how control of many local roads rapidly gravitated toward New York or other eastern corporate centers during the 19th century.

Builders of the Nickel Plate Road had the good sense to recognize that by the 1880s, the country's railroad enterprise was headed in a new direction. Companies would be more than short lines such as the LS&TV or the Valley Railroad that wandered into the hinterlands; they would link large urban centers. This desire for regional "system building" led to the formation by 1910 of several powerful roads in Cleveland. The New York Central controlled 3 firms: the LS&MS, the Cleveland, Cincinnati, Chicago & St. Louis Railway (the "Big 4," including the former Cleveland, Columbus & Cincinnati), and the Nickel Plate Road; the B&O operated the CL&W and the CT&V; the Pennsylvania dominated the Cleveland & Pittsburgh; and the Erie acquired what originally had been the Cleveland & Mahoning. Only the Wheeling & Lake Erie lacked the status of being a major regional concern. Ultimate control of all of these roads, as noted above, was held outside of Cleveland.

Cleveland's railroads reflected other national trends in the industry. As in virtually every large American city after 1900, the rapid increase of freight traffic led to expanded facilities, including belt and industrial switching lines. The New York Central, for example, built the Cleveland Short Line Railway between 1906–12. When finished, this 20-mi. belt road carried freight not bound or originating in Cleveland south around the city, thereby relieving the congestion at the lakefront facilities. And private manufacturers also owned and operated their own switching lines. For instance, the UNITED STATES STEEL CORP. controlled the NEWBURGH & SOUTH SHORE, chartered in 1899, which consisted of 10 mi. of main line between Cleveland and Newburgh and another 20 mi. of spurs and sidings.

But in the 1920s and 1930s, Cleveland differed from other communities when it rightfully laid claim to being America's railroad capital, as control of several of the roads began to come home. The city contained the headquarters of the ALLEGHANY CORP., a business superpower that controlled approximately 30,000 mi. of track worth an estimated $3 billion. This railroad combine was the handiwork of ORIS P. AND MANTIS J. VAN SWERINGEN, known commonly as the Vans. These Clevelanders, who originally were not involved in railroads, had prospered as the result of suburban land development. Yet, to insure the fullest returns on the SHAKER HTS. properties, the Vans needed direct transit service into downtown Cleveland. Since the city's streetcar system failed to satisfy their needs, they launched in the summer of 1911 an interurban, the Cleveland & Youngstown Railroad, to build initially from Shaker Hts. to downtown Cleveland, and later to Youngstown. While they solved part of their right-of-way needs with acquisition of real estate along KINGSBURY RUN, they needed direct entry into the city's heart. The Vans decided that the right-of-way of the Nickel Plate from E. 34th St. into the downtown offered the best solution. Fortunately, they made valuable contacts with officials of the New York Central, the carrier that controlled the Nickel Plate; and they benefited, too, from the federal government's desire to force the New York Central to divest itself of this potential competitor. In a highly leveraged buyout, the Vans got the Nickel Plate in early 1916. Not only did they win access for their traction line (later the Cleveland Interurban Railway and then the SHAKER HTS. RAPID TRANSIT) into Cleveland's central business district, but

they also found themselves in control of a "Class 1" steam railroad.

The Vans upgraded a rather shabby Nickel Plate Road. Soon it turned a handsome profit. In the early 1920s, the Vans won ICC approval to expand their railroad holdings; the ICC permitted the Nickel Plate to acquire 2 midwestern roads, the Toledo, St. Louis & Western ("Clover Leaf") and the Lake Erie & Western. Subsequently through holding companies, most notably the Alleghany Corp., the Vans assembled their business colossus. By the time of their deaths in the late 1930s, they controlled 9 major roads, the Chesapeake & Ohio, Chicago & Eastern Illinois, Denver & Rio Grande Western, Erie, Missouri Pacific, Nickel Plate, Pere Marquette, Texas & Pacific, and Wheeling & Lake Erie. Depression and death threw the Van Sweringen combine into a tailspin. While restructuring diminished the power of the Alleghany Corp., the legacy of the Vans in Cleveland remained. For example, the closeness between the Nickel Plate and the Wheeling & Lake Erie led to the former company's official takeover of the latter in the late 1940s. But the more obvious and in some ways the most lasting Van Sweringen gift to the city was CLEVELAND UNION TERMINAL. The brothers orchestrated construction of a nearly true union terminal project (the Pennsylvania never joined and continued to operate out of the old Union Depot and eventually out of its E. 55th and Euclid station) that began in Sept. 1923 and opened in June 1930.

Cleveland Union Terminal helped to meet the extraordinary demands placed on the area's railroads during WORLD WAR II. Thousands of travelers poured through the structure, for more than 60 passenger trains paid daily calls, as did the cars of the Shaker Hts. Rapid line. But then in the postwar era, the popularity of intercity train travel waned. Carriers at first cut back their local runs, but by the late 1950s even name trains such as the Mercury became only memories. While the diesel-powered streamliners of the New York Central, in particular, attracted patrons, increased automobile and air travel could not save them. By the early 1970s, most of the nation's railroads gladly turned over their remaining passenger trains to the federal government. A vastly pared-down intercity rail passenger network, Amtrak, debuted on 1 May 1971; Clevelanders were left with only 1 daily passenger train each way between New York and Chicago, and an independent commuter run to Youngstown, and that service lasted only a few years longer. Soon after Amtrak entered Cleveland, it suspended operations. The trains, however, returned, although they did not stop at the Union Terminal but rather on the lakeshore, first at a temporary building, popularly dubbed an "Amshack," and after 1977 in a modern, albeit modest, permanent station at the same location, which ironically was located within a mile of the site of the city's first station.

Not only have there been spectacular changes in the overall nature of rail passenger travel, but the corporate structure of the railroad industry itself has also changed dramatically. The 1960s witnessed "merger madness," a force that evolved into the mega-merger craze of the late 1970s and early 1980s. Clevelanders saw both phenomena. During the 1960s, every major Cleveland railroad participated in a corporate merger. The industry believed that consolidation was the best avenue to savings and long-term propriety. The Erie and the Delaware, Lackawanna & Western fused in 1960 to produce what became the ill-fated Erie-Lackawanna; the Chesapeake & Ohio acquired the Baltimore & Ohio in 1963 (B&O-C&O); the Nickel Plate Road entered the Norfolk & Western's system in 1964; and in the nation's most spectacular union, the New York Central and the Pennsylvania united in 1968 to create the Penn Central Transportation Co., a firm that collapsed within 2 years. While railroad officials may have had some misgivings about mergers, especially after the Penn Central bankruptcy, they turned to creating huge interregional systems. All of Cleveland's major railroads were involved. The ailing Penn Central became the quasi-public Consolidated Rail Corp. (CONRAIL) in 1976. The federal government forced this new carrier to include the hapless Erie-Lackawanna. Then in 1980, the ICC gave the green light for the C&O-B&O, the "Chessie System," and the Seaboard Coast Line to form CSX, and in 1982, regulators granted the Norfolk & Western permission to merge with the Southern, creating the NORFOLK SOUTHERN. Thus, each of 3 giant railroads that dominated freight traffic east of the Mississippi River—Conrail, CSX, and Norfolk Southern—operate into Cleveland. Local railroads have gone through all the stages of growth—from their inception as puny pikes to their maturity as enormous entities.

H. Roger Grant
University of Akron

A **RAILWAY HOSPITAL** was created in 1856 when Cleveland railroad companies cooperated in renting an abandoned water-cure establishment on Lake St. and converting it into a hospital for employees injured in accidents. Some private patients were admitted, usually gynecological cases. Dr. Seth R. Beckwith, a well-known Cleveland homeopathic physician and professor of surgery at Western Homeopathic College, was permitted to treat his private patients at the "railway" hospital. The hospital was closed after 3 years for an undisclosed reason. The Railway Hospital was one of a small series of temporary hospitals in Cleveland prior to the CIVIL WAR, and it is an example of an early industry-sponsored health-care facility.

George A. W. Crile, Sr., Papers, WRHS.

The **RAINEY INSTITUTE,** located on E. 55th St. south of Superior, is a prominent settlement house serving the HOUGH area of Cleveland. It has provided recreational and educational services for adults and children and has served as a gathering place for community organizations. The institute was founded in 1904 by Eleanor B. Rainey to support the activities of Anna Edwards. Miss Edwards had been providing physical, industrial, and moral training, as well as wholesome recreational facilities, for the people in the community around E. 55th St. and St. Clair. Rainey approved of these goals; she built a house to accommodate these activities and also promised financial support for the enterprise. Rainey died in 1905, and the building was named the Eleanor B. Rainey Memorial Institute in her honor. During the next 20 years, the institute was supported by the Rainey family, whose gifts were dispersed through the Women's Philanthropic Union. The daily management of the institute was under the care of Anna Edwards. Following her death in 1923, her sister, Flora Edwards, became director. In 1949, Flora Edwards was succeeded in her duties as director by Jessie L. Peloubet, the daughter of an early associate of the institute. Mrs. Peloubet remained as director until 1959. In 1959, the trustees of the institute decided to join the Neighborhood Settlement Assoc. and hired a full-time social worker to direct the institute. In 1960 Shirley Lautenschlager became the director. A board of managers was organized in 1961. Since then, Rainey Institute has joined the Welfare Fed. and the GREATER CLEVELAND NEIGHBORHOOD CTRS. ASSOC. Since 1967, the institute, under the direction of Zandra Richards, has attempted to achieve its goals through music, doing so in cooperation with the CLEVELAND MUSIC SCHOOL SETTLEMENT. Classes are offered in music theory, music therapy, and dance. Private lessons for various musical instruments are also offered.

"Rainey Institute, 60th Anniversary, 1904–1964" (Xerox pamphlet, 1964).
Rainey Institute Records, WRHS.

**RAMMELKAMP, CHARLES HENRY, JR.** (24 May 1911–5 Dec. 1981), scientist and teaching physician, won international acclaim for the discovery of streptococcus bacteria as the cause for rheumatic fever. As medical director of City/Metropolitan General Hospital, he was credited with much of the excellence of care developed at the hospital and its national reputation as a medical center. Rammelkamp was born in Jacksonville, Ill., to Chas. Henry and Jeanette Capps Rammelkamp. He graduated from Illinois College in Jacksonville with the A.B. degree in 1933 and from the University of Chicago with the M.D. degree in 1937. He was appointed an assistant in medicine at Washington University in St. Louis, 1939; research fellow in medicine at Harvard University, 1939–40; and instructor of medicine at Boston University, 1940–46. During WORLD WAR II, he was a consultant to the secretary of war and a member of the Army's commission on acute respiratory diseases. In 1946, Rammelkamp was appointed assistant professor of medicine and preventive medicine at the Western Reserve University Medical School. He was associate professor of preventive medicine, 1947–60; professor of medicine, 1950–60; and professor of preventive medicine, 1960–80. In 1950 he was appointed research director at City Hospital, and he was director of medicine 1957–80. At his retirement he was named professor emeritus of epidemiology and community health. In 1948, Rammelkamp became a member of the Army's streptococcal-disease commission and the field director of the streptococcal-disease laboratory at Ft. Francis E. Warren in Cheyenne, Wyo. There he and his team of researchers studied men who had sore throats and discovered that streptococcal bacterium infecting the throat can lead to rheumatic fever. This discovery led to the corollary discovery that adequate doses of penicillin at the time of strep throat prevented rheumatic fever. In 1952, Rammelkamp and Dr. John Dingle identified the specific strain of streptococcus bacteria that was the cause of the kidney disease acute nephritis. In 1954, Rammelkamp was awarded the Lasker Award for his discoveries.

**RANDALL PARK RACE TRACK,** since 1976 the site of one of the world's largest malls, was, for 60 years, a noted horse track for runners and trotters. With its neighbor, THISTLEDOWN RACE TRACK, Randall Park provided the village of N. RANDALL with its major industry and raison d'etre. Formerly located in an area bounded by Northfield, Harvard, Warrensville Ctr., and Miles roads, the track was originally part of the Forest City Farm, established in 1883 as a horse-breeding farm by C. F. Emery. The land was bought in 1905 by Youngstown entrepreneurs; it was then acquired by Bert Shank, who sold 100 acres north of Emery Rd. to Wm. B. Chisholm for his Thistle Down Farms. Part of the remaining land became the village of N. Randall, created in 1908 to provide a site for harness racing after the closing of the GLENVILLE RACE TRACK in that year. Shank was the first mayor of the village, while HENRY K. DEVEREUX was treasurer. The new track, built at a cost of $250,000, hosted the Grand Circuit in 1909, won by Emery's trotter Carroll, driven by Mayor Shank before a crowd of 17,000. The location of the N. Randall Track (as it was originally called) was too distant for many fans. Although Devereux, who selected the site, was eventually proved correct in his assertion that the widespread use of automobiles would lessen the impact of the distance, patronage fell off by WORLD WAR I and did not improve until after WORLD WAR II, by which time the track was converted from a harness track to a field for running races. The track was owned by Devereux's Forest City Livestock & Fair Co. until 1944; it was closed in 1935 and then in 1939 was leased to a group of Cleveland sportsmen organized as the Cleveland Jockey Club, Inc., which modernized it and converted it for running races in 1939 and 1940. The venture proved unprofitable, and no races were run in 1941 or 1942, but in 1943 and 1944, Sam Lombardo, John Masoni, and associates reopened it for both harness and running races. After the track changed hands several times, Lombardo and Masoni's Randall Park Racing Associates purchased it in 1946 for $180,000; they sold it for $950,000 in 1950 to Saul Silberman and Ralph DeChiaro, who were credited with improving the facility, the quality of racing, and attendance before selling the track in 1956 for $3.6 million. The new owners, a Pittsburgh syndicate that included Dan Parrish, Art Rooney, and Edwin Moon, sold it for $4.2 million in Oct. 1960 to shopping-center magnate and Thistledown owner Edward DeBartolo. It was expected that he would immediately raze the premises to build a shopping center, but the continued prosperity of the track kept it operating. Despite its proximity to Thistledown (viewed by many as the better track), Randall was preferred by many for its friendliness, the ease of placing a bet, and the proximity of the fans to the track. In 1968, Randall Park's races were transferred to Thistledown; in 1969 the site, home to auto racing in the 1910s and in subsequent years site of the Buckeye Handicap and 8 other stakes races, was rezoned for retail uses. Demolition of the facility began in 1973; in 1976 RANDALL PARK MALL opened on the property.

The **RANDALL PARK MALL** is one of the world's largest enclosed shopping malls. It was built by the Edward J. DeBartolo Corp. of Youngstown, a major developer of shopping centers. DeBartolo bought the old RANDALL PARK racetrack in N. RANDALL and WARRENSVILLE HTS. in 1961; he first announced plans to develop the 117-acre site as a single-level mall with over 100 stores and adjoining office buildings in 1964. The next several years brought zoning problems, costly court battles, market changes, and 360 revisions of the mall blueprint. It was not until Mar. 1973 that the racetrack was torn down and construction began on the mall. By this time, the plans had tripled in size. The $175 million project would be a 2-level mall with over 200 stores in 2.2 million sq. ft. of retail space.

DeBartolo took charge of all phases of development of the mall, from concept to its completion on 11 Aug. 1976, when 4 department stores and over 100 specialty stores opened. One department store and many other smaller stores opened in the following months. The interior of the mall was unique, with tiled floors, marble columns, exotic landscape, various stage areas, sculptured ceilings, and decorative ramps and crossovers. Owned and operated by DeBartolo, the mall was a success, with collective first-year sales of $140 million. Almost all the stores' sales were higher than anticipated. Randall Park did siphon off business from other area shopping centers, as expected, but it did not cause any to close. Instead, most of them continued to thrive, as did Randall Park. By 1984, the mall, with over 5,000 employees, attracted over 30,000 shoppers during the week and 300,000 on weekends.

**RANNEY, RUFUS P.** (30 Oct. 1813–6 Dec. 1891), was one of Ohio's greatest lawyers and jurists. He was respected by his contemporaries for his profound legal knowledge, his devotion to the right and just, the integrity of his public and private life, and his charming personality and quiet dignity. Ranney was born in Blandford, Mass. In 1824, the family moved into Ohio, settling in Freedom, Portage County. Most of Ranney's early training came from his family, as public schooling was limited on the frontier. Ambitious and determined to secure an education, Ranney enrolled at Nelson Academy and later Western Reserve College, but he was unable to finish because of lack of means. In 1835, Ranney entered into the study of law in the office of Joshua Giddings and Benjamin Wade in Jefferson. His progress was so rapid that he passed the requisite examination and was admitted to the bar in 1836. When Giddings entered Congress in 1838, Wade and Ranney formed what became the leading law firm in northeastern Ohio. In 1845, Ranney opened a law office in Warren, where he immediately took a prominent position in the Trumbull County bar. In 1846 and 1848, he made unsuccessful bids for that district's congressional seat. In 1850, Ranney was elected a delegate to the convention to revise the Ohio constitution. There he gained recognition as one of the convention's leading figures while serving in the judicial department and on the revision, enrollment, and arrangement committees.

In Mar. 1851, Ranney was elected by the general assembly to the Ohio Supreme Court. Later that year, at the first elections held under the newly revised state constitution, he was chosen as one of the judges of the new supreme court, being assigned the longest term. In 1856, Ranney resigned from the supreme court and moved to Cleveland, where he resumed the practice of law as senior member of the firm of Ranney, Backus & Noble. In 1857, he was appointed U.S. attorney for northern Ohio, but he resigned from the position after only 2 months. In 1858, Ranney made an unsuccessful bid to become governor. Against his expressed desire, Ranney was nominated for the state supreme court again in 1862, and to his surprise, he was elected. He resigned in 1865 and resumed his Cleveland law practice. In 1881, he was elected unanimously the first president of the Ohio Bar Assoc. Ranney was married to Adeline W. Warner. They had 4 sons and 2 daughters.

**RANSOM, CAROLINE L. ORMES** (1838–12 Feb. 1910), was a distinguished pioneer woman portrait painter. Little information on her early life is available. Her place of birth is even disputed; however, Newark, Ohio, is deemed the likely place. Her education in art began in New York. She was instructed by A. B. Durand, Thos. Hicks, and Donald Huntington in landscapes, figure painting, and portraits. She then studied for 2 years with Wilhelm von Kaulkoch in Munich. Ransom returned to America in 1860, setting up a studio in Cleveland on 236 Superior Ave. and W. 3rd St. Her specialty was portraits. Her subjects included Col. CHAS. C. WHITTLESEY, the first president of the WESTERN RESERVE HISTORICAL SOCIETY; Gen. Jas. B. McPherson (reported to be the best likeness of him); Benjamin Franklin Wade, lawyer and statesman; and Gen. JAS A. GARFIELD in military dress. Ransom was paid an extraordinary amount of money for the time for her portraits. In 1867, Congress allowed $1,000 for a portrait of Joshua R. Giddings, and in 1875, $15,000 for one of Gen. Geo. H. Thomas. Both likenesses were hung in the Capitol in Washington. In 1876, Ransom was unanimously elected an honorary member of the Army of the Cumberland, the only woman to be elected. She was also one of the founders of the Daughters of the American Revolution. She moved to Washington, D.C., in 1884. Her studio and living quarters there were combined so she could paint constantly. The walls were covered with copies of the masters' works and her own work in progress. Ransom also founded the Classical Society and was its leader for 15 years.

**RAPER, JOHN W. "JACK"** (20 Feb. 1870–12 Dec. 1950), a self-styled "hick from Hicksville," came in time to be acclaimed as "Cleveland's most effective citizen." Born in McArthur, Vinton County, Ohio, he was raised in Chillicothe, where his father edited Ohio's oldest extant paper, the *Scioto Gazette*. Raper began newspaper work himself at age 19 in Springfield and worked in a succession of cities before joining the *CLEVELAND PRESS* in 1899. Beginning as drama critic, he caused a 2-year boycott of *Press* advertising pages by theater managers for such barbed reviews as his 3-word classic "Burn a rag." Asked by editor Harry N. Rickey to try his hand at a daily column, Raper complied with "Most Anything" in 1900. "Most Anything" was defined by several recurring trademarks. At the head of the column usually appeared a down-to-earth philosophical observation by Raper's rustic alter ego, "Josh Wise." Once a week, events in an imaginary small town were chronicled in "All the News from Hicksville." The column's most avidly followed department was the famous "bullpen," which first appeared in 1907. There, some of the most pompous and pretentious pronouncements by various public figures were simply reprinted verbatim, alongside a bold, black cut of a bull, which ultimately came in 3 sizes, according to the egregiousness of the offense.

Raper became a familiar public figure himself, frequently speaking to groups ranging from students to bankers. At the Cleveland CITY CLUB, he was one of the chief votaries of the "Soviet Table," a faction consisting of PETER WITT and others of radical or progressive bent. Raper's own annual appearances on the rostrum were eagerly awaited by members for their irreverent slants on the contemporary scene. A faithful New Dealer, Raper continued to support Franklin Roosevelt in speech and print long after Scripps-Howard and the *Press* had abandoned him to perdition. During WORLD WAR II, Raper brought back from his vacation in New Mexico a detailed description of the Army's "Forbidden City" of Los Alamos, which was printed in the *Press* more than a year before the bombing of Hiroshima. In 1945, he compiled a book from his "Josh Wise" sayings under the title *What This World Needs*. Retiring in 1947, he died in Pueblo, Colo. He was survived by his wife, Marie A. Delahunt of Buffalo, and a daughter, Mrs. Wick R. Miller of Albuquerque, N. Mex.

**RAPPE, LOUIS AMADEUS** (2 Feb. 1801–8 Sept. 1877), was a missionary and first bishop of the Diocese of Cleveland. Rappe was born in Audrehem, District of Saint-Omer, Pas-de-Calais, France, one of 10 children of Eloi and Marie-Antoinette Noel Rappe. Deciding on the priesthood, Rappe studied at the college of Boulogne-sur-Mer and the seminary at Arras. He was ordained in Arras on 14 Mar. 1829 by Cardinal de la Tour d'Auvergne-Langereis. Rappe served as a parish priest at Wismes before he was named chaplain of the Ursuline nuns at Boulogne-sur-Mer. There he met Cincinnati bishop John B. Purcell, who was in France recruiting priests for work in Ohio. Rappe decided to join Purcell and arrived in America in Oct. 1840. Purcell named Rappe the first resident pastor of St. Francis de Sales Parish in Toledo and gave him the added duty of caring for Catholics along the canal routes. Rappe established a school and an academy and soon became known as an advocate of the Total Abstinence Movement (see FATHER MATHEW TOTAL ABSTINENCE SOCIETY). He also built several churches in the neighboring towns. On 23 Apr. 1847, Pope Pius IX officially established the new Diocese of Cleveland, which took approximately half of the territory held by the Diocese of Cincinnati. The new diocese contained counties now under the jurisdiction of the Toledo and Youngstown dioceses. Rappe was consecrated bishop of the new diocese on 10 Oct. 1847 in St. Peter in Chains Cathedral, Cincinnati.

Rappe journeyed to Cleveland, where he began work on the new church that would become ST. JOHN CATHEDRAL. New congregations for Irish and German groups were soon created. Rappe made several trips to Europe, where he recruited priests and nuns. The Ursulines from Boulogne-sur-Mer came to teach in the schools, and the Daughters of the Immaculate Heart of Mary opened 2 orphanages for girls: ST. MARY'S in 1851 and ST. JOSEPH'S in 1863. Rappe organized the SISTERS OF CHARITY OF ST. AUGUSTINE, who started orphanages and opened the first general hospital in Cleveland, ST. VINCENT CHARITY, in 1857. Concerned about priestly training, Rappe began St. Francis de Sales Seminary, which became ST. MARY SEMINARY. His administration was troubled by conflicts with German and Irish priests. Rappe resigned from the Diocese of Cleveland in mid-July 1870 and spent his last years as a missionary in Vermont and Canada. His death occurred at St. Albans, Vt. He was buried in St. John Cathedral in Cleveland.

**RATNER, LEONARD** (1896–30 Dec. 1974), business executive, Jewish community leader, and philanthropist, was born Leiser Ratowezn in Bialystok, Poland. Ratner received a Jewish education in Poland and upon finishing school entered the weaving trade. He immigrated to the U.S. in 1920 and settled in Cleveland in 1921. Ratner's first occupation in Cleveland was as a weaver, but he soon quit and opened a creamery on 105th St. His sister Dora and brother Max also worked there, and subsequently they established a second creamery. The family sold its creameries in 1926 to concentrate on the lumber and building business. Chas. Ratner, another brother, had established the Forest City Lumberyard in 1922 and in 1924 helped Leonard open Buckeye Lumber on St. Clair. In 1929, Leonard turned the lumberyard over to his brother Max and established the B. & F. Bldg. Co. He specialized in the construction of 3-bedroom homes, erecting houses primarily in E. CLEVELAND, EUCLID, and along Lake Shore Blvd. In 1934, Leonard joined Forest City Lumber (see FOREST CITY ENTERPRISES).

Leonard was active in Jewish communal affairs. In 1931, he began volunteer work with the Jewish Welfare Fed.; he served as treasurer and vice-president during the 1960s, and was elected honorary life trustee in 1966. In 1961, he was elected honorary trustee for life of MT. SINAI Hospital after serving on the board of trustees for 2 decades. The Ratner family was instrumental in the drive to build the huge PARK SYNAGOGUE complex in CLEVELAND HTS. in the late 1940s and early 1950s. Leonard served as the congregation's president from 1952–55. Nationally, Ratner was a member of the board of trustees of the Jewish Joint Distribution Committee, the Council of Jewish Federations & Welfare Funds, the American Committee for the Weizman Institute, the Jewish Theological Seminary, and the American Friends of Hebrew University, and a member of the campaign cabinet of the United Jewish Appeal. On 16 Nov. 1924 he married Lillian Bernstein, a community leader and founder of the Lillian Ratner Montessori School at Park Synagogue. The Ratners had 2 children, Albert and Ruth.

RAUCH & LANG CARRIAGE COMPANY. *See* BAKER MATERIALS HANDLING COMPANY

REAL ESTATE. *See* CLEVELAND AREA BOARD OF REALTORS

The **REAL PROPERTY INVENTORY OF METROPOL-ITAN CLEVELAND**, begun in 1932 and incorporated in 1937 by local statistician HOWARD WHIPPLE GREEN, collected detailed statistics and issued reports about population trends, housing, manufacturing, retail business, and other aspects of life in the Cleveland area. Green's inventory of real property in Cleveland by census tracts became the model promoted by the Civil Works Admin. in the 1930s and adopted by other cities. RPI was initiated by the Cleveland Real Estate Board, which organized the Committee on Real Property Inventory. The economic depression of the period played a crucial role in defining the purpose of the Real Property Inventory, as committee chairman Raymond T. Cragin acknowledged when he called the collection of statistical information a tool "to aid in formulating sound business judgment" and lamented "that we did not temper our enthusiastic optimism during the boom period [of the 1920s] with a sane view of the facts." The committee chose as the director of the project Howard Whipple Green, who enlisted the help of mail carriers and later workers from the Civil Works Admin., the Federal Emergency Relief Admin., and the WORKS PROJECTS ADMIN. to help collect detailed information about the population, buildings, and businesses in the Cleveland area. The material was published in both summary and raw form, providing a census tract-by-census tract portrait of the city. The detailed, descriptive reports, the first of which was issued in 1933, strictly avoided analysis, leaving interpretation of the figures and trends to individual users.

Until 1936, RPI included information from only Cleveland and a few large suburbs; after 1936 its surveys included all of Cuyahoga County. In 1937 RPI became an independent nonprofit organization supported by local banks, daily newspapers, public utilities, the county, and other business and service organizations who subscribed to its services. In 1933 it had begun publishing *A Sheet-a-Week*, a weekly 2-page publication that gave different statistical reports each week. In addition to annual reports (which by the mid-1950s included *Family & Housing Characteristics* and *Retail Stores & Shopping Centers*), the organization published a number of special reports, such as those on standard of living (1935), substandard housing (1941), housing (1947), and manufacturing (1951). The heyday of RPI was the period between 1933 and Green's death in July 1959. During that time it was an important source of information to local business, government, and social planners trying to meet various local needs during economic hardship and wartime economic adjustment. Its reports continued to be of value throughout the 1960s, but by the mid-1970s, the Real Property Inventory had fallen on hard times. It failed to publish its annual reports for 1975 and suspended publication of weekly reports until late 1976, when increased contributions from its nearly 100 subscribers and a $20,000 grant from the CLEVELAND FOUNDATION enabled it to resume work briefly until 1977.

*A Sheet-a-Week*, WRHS.
Green, Howard Whipple, "The Cleveland Real Property Inventory." In *Homes and Growth*, Cleveland Real Estate Board (ca. 1951).
Real Property Inventory of Metropolitan Cleveland, Reports No. 1–21, 1933–34, WRHS.

**REASON, PATRICK HENRY** (1816–12 Aug. 1898), was a prominent black engraver and lithographer who came to Cleveland from New York in 1869. Reason had been an abolitionist and a leader in fraternal orders in New York, but in Cleveland he apparently concentrated his efforts on his work. Born in New York City and baptized Patrice Rison, Reason was the son of Michel Rison from St. Ann Island, Guadeloupe; his mother, Elizabeth Melville Rison, was from Saint-Domingue. Young Patrick was educated at the New York African Free School, where he exhibited his talent at an early age when he made an engraving of the school that was used as the frontispiece of Chas. C. Andrew's *History of the New York African Free Schools* (1830). In 1833 he was apprenticed to an engraver; in 1835 he became interested in portraiture, and over the next 15 years he became a widely published artist whose works appeared in periodicals and as frontispieces in books, especially slave narratives. Reason worked for Harper's and other New York publishers and did some engraving for the government, but firms often refused to hire him; their engravers would not work with him because of his race. Reason received several offers of employment from firms in Cleveland, and by 1869 he had moved there with his family. By 1872 he was working for jeweler Sylvester Hogan, who had a shop on Superior. He worked for Hogan through the early 1880s; by 1886 he had his own shop on Superior, later moving it to Euclid Ave. While in New York, Reason had been a founding member of the Philomatheon Society in 1830; in 1842 the society became the first lodge of the Negro Grand United Order of Odd Fellows, and Reason became a prominent member of the Odd Fellows, active in lodge affairs into the 1860s. He also lectured on the educational, social, and economic condition of black Americans. On 22 June 1862, Reason married Esther Cunningham of Leeds, England.

The **RECALL ELECTION** of 1978 was a special election held to determine whether or not Mayor Dennis Kucinich would be removed from office. The recall movement was sparked by the public firing of police chief Richard Hongisto by the mayor in Mar. 1978. Using the media, Hongisto charged that Kucinich interfered with the operation of the police department, and the mayor in turn accused Hongisto of insubordination. Capitalizing on the mayor's confrontational style of politics, those opposed to him began circulating petitions for his recall. Although Kucinich had been consistent in his populist philosophy and his support of workingmen's concerns, those petitioning for his removal believed that his aggressiveness and inability to compromise, as well as the youth and inexperience of some of his appointees, impeded his ability to govern the city.

According to the city charter, to recall an elected public official it is necessary to submit petitions containing valid signatures representing 20% of the total vote in the last municipal election. The city council clerk checks their validity and certifies them. The official then has 5 days to resign from office. If he does not, a special election is held. The official is removed from office if a majority of the voters approve the recall. Unlike in the impeachment process, it is not necessary to accuse an official of any specific wrongdoing. When petitions to recall Mayor Kucinich were submitted to city council clerk Mercedes Cotner in early May, they were some 3,355 signatures short of the 37,552 required. The recall proponents had 20 days to obtain more signatures, and on 1 June, petitions with 5,321 additional signatures were turned in. Kucinich challenged the validity of the petitions on the grounds that only those who had voted in the last municipal election could sign them. Judge John Angelotta ruled that the signatories had only to be registered voters. Kucinich pursued his case to the court of appeals and to the Ohio Supreme Court, both of which upheld Angelotta's decision. The petitions were certified. That marked the first time a Cleveland mayor had faced a recall election. Since Kucinich did not resign from office, the election was scheduled for 13 Aug. 1978. The vote was extremely close, but after 2 recounts, it was established that Kucinich remained mayor by 236 votes out of 120,300 cast. After the failure of the recall, the city continued to be governed in much the same way as it had been before. At the next election in 1979, Kucinich was defeated for reelection. See MAYORAL ADMINISTRATION OF DENNIS KUCINICH.

The **RECREATION LEAGUE OF CLEVELAND**, a private, invitational organization representing many of Cleveland's "founding" families, was formed in 1927 by a group of parents who wanted "to provide supervised recreation and wholesome entertainment" for their own sons and daughters. A constitution was adopted, and the following officers were elected: FRANCES P. (Mrs. Chester C.) BOLTON, president, 1926; Mrs. Arthur Shepard, secretary; and Edward B. Greene, treasurer. Among the members of the first executive committee were Mr. and Mrs. DUDLEY BLOSSOM and Mr. and Mrs. BENEDICT CROWELL. In its early years, the league sponsored coasting parties, afternoon tea dances, and other entertainment for the children (juniors, ages 14–16, seniors, 16–18). In Dec. 1937, the league held its first Assembly Ball for the members' college-freshmen daughters. Patterned after the Philadelphia Assembly Ball (1748), the Christmas holiday festivity where approximately 50 young ladies are formally introduced to Cleveland society has been described as a "family affair" as the debutantes ("hostesses") are led down the UNION CLUB staircase by their fathers in the traditional Grand March, greet their families and friends at a formal reception, and conclude the evening with a dinner and dance with their escorts. The Union Club, variously decorated in accordance with a theme for the evening, has become the usual setting for this annual event. The Recreation League also sponsors a Bachelors' Ball, a party for their members' sons who are college sophomores. Begun in the early 1960s, the Bachelors' Ball is also held during the holiday season, often on New Year's Eve.

**RED JACKET'S SPEECH** took place in Buffalo, N.Y., on 23 June 1796. Red Jacket, the great orator of the Six Nations (Iroquois), delivered this speech during a 3-day council with MOSES CLEAVELAND to negotiate a settlement of Indian claims to the WESTERN RESERVE. In a treaty signed at Ft. Stanwix in 1784, the Six Nations yielded to the U.S. claim to their lands west of the western boundary of Pennsylvania. The Indians, however, continued to voice certain nominal claims to this land, which included much of the Western Reserve. In order not to create an unnecessary liability in opening these lands for settlement, the proprietors of the CONNECTICUT LAND CO. thought it prudent to play a conciliatory role with the Indians. Moses Cleaveland, therefore, while enroute to the Western Reserve in 1796, met with the principal chiefs of the Six Nations and with representatives from western tribes outside Skinner's Tavern in Buffalo. The council fire was uncovered, and the first 2 days were spent feasting and drinking; the more serious negotiations occurred on the third day.

Among the representatives of the Six Nations was Red Jacket (ca. 1751–1830), a sachem of the Senecas. Red Jacket was well known for his eloquence, memory, and wit. Throughout his life he was a sagacious defender of his people's values and customs against the intrusion of white civilization. His speech to Cleaveland was delivered through an interpreter and recorded by John Milton Holley, a member of Cleaveland's party.

You white people make a great parade about religion, you say you have a book of laws and rules which was given you by the Great Spirit, but is this true? Was it written by his own hand and given to you? No, says he, it was written by your own people. They do it to deceive you. Their whole wishes center here (pointing to his pocket), all they want is the money.... He says white people tell them, they wish to come and live among them as brothers, and learn them agriculture. So they bring on implements of husbandry and presents, tell them good stories, and all appears honest. But when they are gone all appears as a dream. Our land is taken from us, and still we don't know how to farm it.

The council ended with the Six Nations' acquiescing to white settlement of their land in the Western Reserve. As recompense they received from Cleaveland 2 beef cattle and 100 gallons of whisky.

**REED, JACOB E.** (1852–9 Oct. 1935), called by one historian "the black version of the Horatio Alger myth," came to Cleveland with very little but became a wealthy businessman who moved comfortably in both the elite black and white communities. Reed was born in Harrisburg, Pa., and came to Cleveland in the late 1880s. He worked as a waiter, a streetcar conductor, and a janitor before forming a partnership with Mathias Reitz to open a fish market in 1893; both Reed and Reitz are listed as janitors in the 1892 city directory. Located at the SHERIFF ST. MARKET and specializing in fish, oysters, and other seafood, their business did very well, supplying some of the city's leading hotels, restaurants, and families. Ca. 1914, Reed bought out his partner, and Reitz & Reed became the Jacob E. Reed Co. Reed's extremely successful business made him a member of the small black elite at the turn of the century; he owned a Peerless touring car and was a member of the Cleveland Automobile Club. He could also afford to own his own home, moving between 1900 and 1916 from 865 Giddings Ave. to 2193 E. 36th to 2575 E. 130th St. Reed was also active in civic and fraternal affairs in the black community. He was the first vice-president of the CLEVELAND ASSOC. OF COLORED MEN, a founding member of ST. ANDREWS EPISCOPAL CHURCH, a 33d-degree Mason, a member of the Elks, and an officer in the Odd Fellows. Upon his death in 1935, Reed was survived by his second wife, Rena.

**REGIONAL GOVERNMENT.** The movement for regional government in Cuyahoga County was an effort by middle-class progressive reformers to solve metropolitan problems more efficiently by giving a restructured county government effective power to deal with areawide concerns. They believed that the conflicting interests of the city's diverse population encouraged political separatism and helped create a corrupt and inefficient government controlled by political bosses. Consolidating numerous jurisdictions into a metropolitan government would produce better municipal services and lower taxes; differences between the levels of urban society could be reconciled under the aegis of a politically influential middle class. Cleveland progressives argued that good government was essentially a matter of keeping politics out of the governing process. Among the political innovations they advocated were election of the legislative body at large to raise the class level of the policymakers, nonpartisan elections to reduce the power of political parties, and the separation of government administration from the political process to provide a more rational, businesslike approach to governing. At the same time they were supporting a regional government movement, local progressives were applying their ideas to Cleveland's HOME RULE charter, and later to a CITY MANAGER PLAN.

Campaigning for regional government before WORLD WAR I, reformers sought to achieve their goal by annexing SUBURBS to the central city while it still contained about 85% of the county's residents, and before serious problems of urban growth occurred. By that time, however, the larger suburbs were prosperous enough to provide their own services and had little interest in joining Cleveland. Failing that, the reformers turned to restructuring county government; however, the state constitution had to be amended to give the county power to act independently. Since 1810, Ohio's counties had been considered an administrative arm of the state, exercising only those powers granted to them by the state legislature. Allowing counties to write their own home rule charters would free them from many state-imposed limitations. Led by the CITIZENS LEAGUE and the LEAGUE OF WOMEN VOTERS, with major support from local businessmen, reformers campaigned vigorously for county home rule, which would permit the implementation of a metropolitan government. Several times during the 1920s, constitutional amendments were submitted to the Ohio legislature, but the opposition of rural interests and city and suburban officeholders who feared the loss of their jobs prevailed. Another proposed amendment permitting a federated form of metropolitan government protecting the right of local self-government was submitted to the state legislature in 1931, but even with the backing of powerful farm organizations, the Ohio general assembly was unwilling to open the door to the creation of a megagovernment. Frustrated by their defeat, amendment supporters began a petition drive to force a statewide vote on the issue. They were successful in securing the required signatures (10% of Ohio's voters), and the constitutional amendment was approved in 1933, with Cuyahoga County giving it a 66% majority.

The central problem facing the Cuyahoga County Home Rule Charter Commission, elected in 1934, was how much and what kind of power the county government should have. The fervent reformers in the League of Women Voters and MAYO FESLER, head of the Citizens League, wanted a strong metropolitan authority with sharply restricted powers for the municipalities, and they presented a borough plan that was a true city-county consolidation to the commission. Its introduction crystallized opposition to a strong regional government. Alarmed at the threat to suburban autonomy, a Suburban Charter League made up of western and southwestern suburbs was formed. Encouraged by the league, several outlying communities talked of seceding from Cuyahoga County and asking the state legislature to allow them to join adjacent counties. The realists on the commission advocated a simple reorganization of county government—one that did not disturb municipal functions—believing it would be more acceptable to the voters. According to the Ohio constitution, a simple reorganization required approval of a majority of the county's voters, but any transfer of municipal functions required a more substantial consensus, the so-called 4 hurdles, which specified that a majority of votes had to be obtained in Cleveland, in the areas outside the city, in the entire county, and in more than 50% of the cities and villages in the county.

The moderates prevailed, and the county home rule charter submitted to the voters in 1935 called for a simple reorganization with a central administrator appointed by a 9-man legislature elected at large. The number of elected officials would be reduced, with existing county offices headed by appointees of the county administrator. As chairman of the Charter Commission and popular Republican candidate for mayor, HAROLD H. BURTON promoted both his candidacy and passage of the home rule charter as a cost-cutting measure. Clevelanders gave both Burton and the charter a majority, and countywide, it received a 52.9% majority made up of voters in Cleveland, the eastern suburbs adjacent to Cleveland, and outlying enclaves of wealth such as HUNTING VALLEY and GATES MILLS. Opposition came from municipal officeholders, the semi-rural middle tier of eastern suburbs, together with all the southern and western municipalities in the county. In spite of the county majority, the charter's validity as a simple reorganization was tested in the case of *Howland* v. *Krause*. The Ohio Supreme Court ruled in 1936 that the charter was not a reorganization but did give the county municipal functions; therefore, approval by the 4 separate majorities was required.

A county home rule charter continued to be an elusive goal, with voters asked to approve charters in 1950, 1959, and 1980; and an alternative form of government providing some changes short of home rule offered in 1969 and 1970. All failed to win even a simple majority, and with each successive attempt, voter approval dwindled. All the charters called for an elected county administrator; the legislative bodies varied in number and were elected either from districts or at large, or a combination of both. The 1950 and 1959 charters provided for the transfer of the Cleveland water- and sewage-treatment facilities to the county, a proposal actively opposed by central city officials, who in 1959 alleged that the charter would "rip up the assets of the community." Clevelanders had further reason to be protective of their interests in 1959, as the makeup of the 19-member county assembly appeared to favor suburban representation at a time when their population was approaching that of the central city.

County home rule was finally achieved in Ohio after a state constitutional amendment had been passed allowing county charters to be put on the ballot by initiative petition. Utilizing the new option in 1979, Summit County reformers submitted a county charter to their voters, many of whom had become disenchanted with the secret deliberations of the 3 Summit County commissioners and the cost overruns on the renovation of the county administration building. Since the charter did not affect municipal powers and had strong support from the *Akron Beacon Journal* and little determined opposition, it was approved by a 62.5% majority of the voters. Encouraged by Summit County's success with the initiative option, Cleveland reformers followed suit, placing a home rule charter on the Nov. 1980 ballot; however, a 1976 survey of local attitudes toward regional government had shown that 61% of the people opposed it—an opposition that cut across social, economic, and political lines. The prognosis for the 1980 charter was not good, and it went down to defeat, gaining approval from only 43.3% of the electorate. Major opposition came from Cleveland's BLACKS, unwilling to dilute their recently achieved political power by sharing it in a broader-based government.

In spite of their persistent efforts, the largely middle-class regional government adherents were unsuccessful in presenting a persuasive case, even though they argued that regional government made fiscal sense in view of the ongoing decline of the city's economic base. A majority of the voters appeared to care little about overlapping authorities; they were not convinced that more efficient management or cost savings would be forthcoming. They did fear, however, that proposed county reorganizations would ultimately result in the takeover of municipal functions, and they would lose both access to and control of any government that embraced the larger geographic area. Suburbanites, anxious to guard their community prerogatives, and Clevelanders who viewed metropolitan government as a threat to their political power preferred a "grassroots" governmental pattern with political power dispersed among numerous social, economic, and ethnic groups. This fragmented political power characteristic of Cleveland's urban scene since early in the century constituted a formidable obstacle to metropolitan integration. Nationally, city-county consolidations had occurred in major urban areas such as Boston, Philadelphia, New York, and San Francisco during the 19th century. In the 20th century, merger efforts fell short in most places until the post-World War II era, when successful consolidations occurred in smaller, more homogeneous urban communities such as Davidson County (Nashville), Tenn. (1962), and Marion County (Indianapolis), Ind. (1969).

In the absence of metropolitan government, other avenues were available to deal with areawide problems. With a general trend toward more county local control and independence, Cuyahoga County was able to expand its ability to provide significant services, particularly in the fields of public health and welfare. However, there were still unmet needs that existing local governments were unable or unwilling to undertake—needs that were filled by special metropolitan agencies formed to manage specific public services. These agencies had substantial administrative and fiscal autonomy and were not subject to control by the electorate. Although special agencies had existed in the county as early as 1851, the real growth came after World War II. An increasing number of them were formed to manage pollution control, airport zoning, conservation, tax collection, health planning, port authority, vocational education, and the countywide transit system and the sewer district. These agencies were governed by policymaking boards or commissions, most of which were appointed or elected indirectly and were funded by federal, state, and county grants or from taxes, and several had multicounty authority. Local critics maintained that the agencies, using assets created with public funds, were run by virtually independent professional managers, making decisions outside of public scrutiny with no accountability to the electorate. The proliferation of these agencies was a national as well as a local phenomenon, an inconspicuous government providing an ad hoc solution to regional problems. Cuyahoga County remained fragmented, with independent, self-contained municipalities pursuing ethnic and social separatism and successfully resisting all efforts to introduce metropolitan government. Problems needing regional cooperation could be administered within the county government framework or by an agency created for that purpose. However, the progressives' hope of providing a comprehensive approach to areawide problems through metropolitan government did not appear to be feasible unless a substantial crisis developed in the administration of a vital public service.

Mary B. Stavish
Case Western Reserve University

**REGIONAL TRANSIT AUTHORITY.** *See* **GREATER CLEVELAND REGIONAL TRANSIT AUTHORITY**

The **REINBERGER FOUNDATION** was established in 1968 by Clarence T. Reinberger (1898–1968). Reinberger, a native Clevelander, began his career as a pioneer in the auto parts business in the 1920s. He was manager and then president of the Automotive Parts Co., a statewide chain of retail stores. He later was chairman of the Genuine Parts Co., parent organization of the NAPA auto parts retail stores. He was married to Louise Fischer. The purposes of the foundation are generally for the arts, social welfare, Protestant church support, and medical research. The Reinberger Foundation has been particularly generous to the CLEVELAND ORCHESTRA, donating $1 million in 1985 for the Reinberger Chamber Music Hall at Severance. Grants are primarily given in the Ohio area, with some support in Central Florida. No grants are given to individuals. In 1985, assets of the foundation were $16,515,140, with expenditures of $891,996 for 39 grants, making it one of the largest private foundations in the Greater Cleveland area. Officers of the foundation included Louise Reinberger, president; Richard H. Oman, secretary; Robt. N. Reinberger; and Wm. C. Reinberger.

The **RELIANCE ELECTRIC COMPANY,** founded in 1905 by Cleveland industrialist Peter M. Hitchcock and John C. Lincoln, became a leading manufacturer of electrical products for industry. Growing dramatically after WORLD WAR II, the company was sold in 1979 for more than $1 billion. Reliance was established as the Lincoln Electric Mfg. Co., with an office at 1409 the Schofield Bldg. at Euclid and Erie (E. 9th) streets. The company, incorporated in 1906 as the Lincoln Motor Works Co., produced variable-speed motors designed by John Lincoln. Peter Hitchcock, Lincoln's cousin and partner, died in 1906, and Lincoln sold his interest in the firm, which was continued by Chas. and Reuben Hitchcock, Peter's sons. Clarence L. Collens became president in 1907. The company became the Reliance Electric & Engineering Co. in 1909 and operated under that name until shortening it to the Reliance Electric Co. in 1967.

From 1906–11, Reliance operated from the CAXTON BLDG. in the 800 block of Huron Rd.; in 1911 the company moved into a new facility at 1088 Ivanhoe Rd. During World War II, Reliance built 2 new plants in Cleveland, both on E. 152nd St., and in 1951 it began construction of another plant on a 62-acre site in EUCLID. In 1957, Reliance consolidated with the Dayton-based Master Electric Co.; it began a new subsidiary in Canada in 1959 and formed a partnership with a Swiss firm in Oct. 1961. Sales reached $118.9 million in 1966, and the mergers and acquisitions continued: Reliance merged with the Toledo Scale Co. and the Dodge Mfg. Corp. of Indiana in 1967; it purchased the Atlanta-based Custom Engineering Corp. in 1968 and the small computer manufacturer Applied Dynamics, Inc., in 1969. Reliance had annual foreign sales of $30 million in 1969, and that year it bought 2 more European companies. In 1973 it merged with the Lorain Prods. Corp.

Reliance posted record earnings of $64.6 million on sales of $966.2 million in 1979. In Dec. 1979 the Exxon Corp. purchased Reliance for $1.23 billion. In 3 of the next 4 years, Reliance lost money: $6 million in 1980, $50 million in 1982, and $59 million in 1983. It made a $31 million profit in 1981. Its sales totaled more than $1.5 billion in 1983. With headquarters at 29325 Chagrin Blvd., Reliance employed 30,000 people worldwide in its 9 divisions in 1983. In Feb. 1984, the 320 workers at the Reliance plant on Ivanhoe Rd. in Cleveland learned that the plant was being closed and its operations moved to more modern facilities in Ashtabula and Shelby, N.C., because of low demand, excess production capacity, and intense competition in the industry. Other local Reliance operations continued to provide employment for 1,500 Greater Clevelanders.

Moley, Raymond, *The American Century of John C. Lincoln* (1962).

**RELIGION.** Among the nation's communities, only a few other northern industrial cities match the variety that marks

Cleveland's religious life. What had been a religiously homogeneous settlement dominated by white Protestants from New England in the early years of the 19th century fragmented beginning in the 1840s, when Catholics and Jews arrived to create a pluralistic town. Black Protestant and Orthodox Christian churches were added in large numbers at the turn of the century. In the years after WORLD WAR II, the religious landscape broadened even further to include groups as diverse as JEHOVAH'S WITNESSES, Bahais, Buddhists, and Muslims. The religious traditions themselves, following a pattern common to all American religions, have adapted, sometimes creatively and willingly, sometimes painfully and reluctantly, to the pluralistic, urban environment. Through all the changes, churches and synagogues in Cleveland persisted in addressing not only the spiritual needs of the city's residents but also their social concerns through activity in education, PHILANTHROPY, moral reform, and social action. The city's early years were marked by religious homogeneity. New England Protestants, especially CONGREGATIONALISTS and PRESBYTERIANS, were the earliest white settlers. Other Protestant groups—BAPTISTS, EPISCOPALIANS, and METHODISTS—were also well-represented. The first organized religious body within the then-existing town was Trinity Episcopal Church, organized in 1816. The "first churches" of the other New England denominations followed: FIRST PRESBYTERIAN (1820), First Methodist (1827), and FIRST BAPTIST (1833). Theologically, these churches were moderately evangelical. Their beliefs resembled those of the traditional New England churches far more than they did those of the enthusiastic, revival-oriented churches of the Burned-Over District of Upper New York to the east or those holding to Oberlin perfectionism to the west. The Protestant churches and their members promoted an extensive network of voluntary organizations dedicated to TEMPERANCE, antislavery, poor relief, orphans, and home and foreign missions. Among these groups was the WESTERN SEAMEN'S FRIEND SOCIETY (1831), organized as an auxiliary of the American Seamen's Friend Society. The society, based in Cleveland with branches throughout the Great Lakes, was dedicated to mission work among the seamen. Presbyterians played a leading role in the society and the society's Bethel Church (1835).

Toward the 1850s, the religious landscape began to diversify as Irish Catholics became a substantial religious presence (see CATHOLICS, ROMAN). They were joined by German Catholics and Protestants, German Jews, and black Protestants. ST. MARY ON THE FLATS (1839; also known as Our Lady of the Lakes) was the first Catholic church. The Catholic Diocese was established in 1847. Other groups were represented by smaller numbers. The first German Protestant church was SCHIFFLEIN CHRISTI (1834). A handful of German Jews organized the Israeltic Society (1839; it merged with ANSHE CHESED in 1842). Black Protestants founded ST. JOHN'S AME CHURCH in 1830. The Shakers, officially known as the United Society of Believers in Christ's Second Appearing, began their N. UNION SHAKER COMMUNITY just east of the town in 1822. At the time of their greatest strength, from the 1840s to the CIVIL WAR, they numbered about 200. When the community dissolved in 1889, there were only 27 members, who dispersed to other Shaker communities. The land of the N. Union Shakers was purchased by the VAN SWERINGEN brothers in 1905 for their own vision of a utopia, which took the name SHAKER HTS. Another of the new religions of the early 19th century, the MORMONS (Church of Jesus Christ of Latter-day Saints), settled in nearby Kirtland for a time. Some stayed, while others continued the Mormon pilgrimage to Nauvoo and Salt Lake City.

By 1865, the city directory listed 50 churches; 21, including 1 black church, 2 Jewish synagogues, and 8 Catholic and 5 Lutheran churches were exceptions to the dominance of New England-derived white Protestantism. In the years after the Civil War, religious diversity became the norm. By 1929, after over half a century of large-scale immigration and migration, New England-derived Protestant churches had lost their numerical dominance. Black Protestant (52), German Lutheran (65), Reformed Protestant (20), Catholic (87), Jewish (32), and Orthodox (9) religious bodies accounted for 265 churches, compared to 215 for the traditional New England denominations. (That undoubtedly undercounts smaller churches, including many black storefront churches.) Coming to grips with the implications of the proliferation of religious groups occupied the attention of many religious Clevelanders during these years. Pluralism became the pattern not just in the city at large, but also within each religious tradition. Denominations found themselves divided between long-time residents and new arrivals and between those who sought to preserve old-country traditions and those who sought to Americanize or modernize. In general, the longer-established groups, such as Irish Catholics and German Jews, were eager to adapt to their new society's ways. In contrast, newer arrivals tended to be resistant to the idea of abandoning their familiar cultures and religions. The result was a splintering along ethnic, racial, and class lines. Individual churches and synagogues tended to be homogeneous, generally made up of a single ethnic or racial group, or even of those who had come from a specific country, city, or town. Conscious that they were the minority, and perceiving that the broader society was closed to them, each of the minority ethnic and racial groups relied on religion to preserve familiar languages and customs and to serve as cultural centers, relief agencies, employment bureaus, and providers of education.

Each of the city's major religious groups responded to the religious pluralism in its own fashion. Protestants attempted to establish missions in areas where there was no Protestant presence. Existing Protestant churches expanded their activities to include recreation, instruction in English, and training in job skills. The best-known of such churches, often referred to as institutional churches, was Pilgrim Congregational. Social-settlement houses, although not officially associated with specific churches, were largely the creations of socially concerned Protestants anxious to deal with urban problems and guide the adjustment of newcomers to the city. The most prominent interdenominational effort of Protestants was the Greater Cleveland Council of Churches (1911), now (1986) the INTERCHURCH COUNCIL OF GREATER CLEVELAND. The YOUNG MEN'S CHRISTIAN ASSOC. (1854) and the YOUNG WOMEN'S CHRISTIAN ASSOC. (1867) were other joint efforts of Protestants across many denominations. The SALVATION ARMY, an outgrowth of mission work in England, established its first American mission in Cleveland in 1872. A rural colony, the Army's third in the U.S., was formed in 1898 on land a few miles east of the city.

In these years, many New England Protestants moved to the city's fringes and beyond, beginning a process of suburbanization that was to characterize Cleveland religion for the next 100 years. A few flagship churches, such as First Presbyterian, Trinity Episcopal, and First Methodist, remained downtown, while most of the old central city became the home of Catholics, Jews, and black Protestants. The Catholics, Jews, Orthodox, and black Protestants who moved to the city were not converted in large numbers by the white Protestant mission efforts. They retained their original faiths, but not without serious disagreement about what forms that faith should take in urban and industrial America.

For Catholics, the years from the end of the Civil War to World War II were marked by the church's emergence as a substantial force in the city. By the start of the 20th century, there were more Catholics than Protestants in Cleveland. The growth of Catholic fraternal organizations, religious orders, schools, charities, and hospitals testified to the maturing of the immigrant church. Maintaining a cohesive church made up of diverse ethnic and nationality groups proved difficult. Irish and German Catholics had arrived in the 1840s. The Irish established themselves in the hierarchy after the Civil War, and the resulting friction with German, and later Polish and Italian, Catholics was not easily resolved. Officially, the hierarchy insisted on uniformity and territorial parishes. In practice, it settled for diversity and nationality parishes (parishes dominated by a specific ethnic group). As a result, Cleveland Catholicism came to reflect the variety of the cultures from which it had come. Old-country languages, saints, holidays, and customs left their distinctive stamp on each of the various groups of Catholics. Catholic schools, established within most parishes because of distrust of the Protestant-dominated public schools and the desire to preserve old traditions, paralleled the ethnic divisions.

Jews, though not so numerous as Catholics, also established themselves as a significant presence in the city in the years after the Civil War (see JEWS AND JUDAISM). They made up approximately 10% of the city's population in 1920. Jews, too, like Catholics, faced internal divisions in these years. Among Jews, the split between earlier and later immigrants took the form of the development of Reform synagogues, which largely represented German Jews and the desire to modernize and Americanize, and Orthodox synagogues, the effort of East European Jews to preserve older traditions. The leading Reform synagogue was Tifereth Israel (later the TEMPLE), which even went so far as to adopt Sunday as the day for worship services. The Temple, under Rabbi MOSES J. GRIES, was the first example in America of the Open Temple, a Jewish counterpart to the Protestant institutional church. Reform synagogues were more influential and visible to the city at large, but Orthodox synagogues were more numerous. They were formed by Jews from Romania, Lithuania, Hungary, Poland, and Russia who had developed a deep-felt piety little influenced by the currents of the Enlightenment that had shaped German Judaism. In the 1920s, Conservative Judaism, an effort to chart a middle ground between the Reform and Orthodox branches, established itself in Cleveland. It was represented by B'NAI JESHURUN and ANSHE EMETH.

Jews mounted their own charitable and educational efforts. The Cleveland branch of the Council of Jewish Women established the Council Educational Alliance (1899), a largely German-Jewish effort to influence and serve the newer Jewish immigrants. In 1903, the Fed. of Jewish Charities was formed to mount a single benevolent campaign each year for all Jewish projects. Hebrew schools, designed for much the same purposes as Catholic schools, were also established in these years. The suburbanization of the Jewish population came in a number of steps. Many moved in the 1910s and 1920s to the GLENVILLE area. The move to the SUBURBS, especially to CLEVELAND HTS., came in the 1920s and after. In 1925, B'nai Jeshurun (Temple on the Heights), a Hungarian-Jewish synagogue, became the first to move. Jews, especially those of Reform synagogues such as Rabbi Gries and ABBA HILLEL SILVER, were active in ecumenical movements in these years. Through the Associated Charities and Euclid Ave. (later Fairmount) Temple's Institute on Judaism, Jews kept in contact with the city's Protestant community. The major ecumenical effort, the Natl. Conference of Christians & Jews, was organized in Cleveland in the late 1920s.

In the city's early years, black Clevelanders had attended integrated churches. JOHN MALVIN and his wife, Harriet, were among the 17 original members of First Baptist Church in 1833. Many of the old-line Protestant churches remained integrated, but increasingly in the years after the Civil War, the majority of black churchgoers attended black churches. The forerunner of these black churches was St. John's African Methodist Episcopal Church (1830), the town's 4th-oldest church. Cleveland's first black Baptist church, SHILOH, was founded in 1851 after mission work by First Baptist Church. Two other early churches, MT. ZION CONGREGATIONAL and ST. ANDREW'S EPISCOPAL, were known for their upper-class membership. Many newer migrants from the South, searching for a more congenial church than the restrained middle- and upper-class churches, joined smaller churches. Many of these were storefront churches, of which there were 109 in 1928. By the beginning of the 20th century, churches, like other urban institutions, were segregated by race. A few BLACKS from established families attended white Episcopal and Methodist churches, and the Catholic church, with only a few black members, continued to be integrated. Catholics adopted the pattern of segregation in 1922 by formally establishing a black Catholic church despite protests from black Catholics.

Besides Catholics, Jews, and black Protestants, a fourth group, the EASTERN ORTHODOX, began to establish itself as part of the city's religious landscape in the years from the Civil War to World War II. Although they were Christian like white and black Protestants and Catholics, years of separate religious, social, and cultural development (the Orthodox and Catholic branches of Christianity had formally split in 1054) left the Orthodox a decidedly different religious tradition. Immigrants from Russia, Poland, Romania, and other areas of Eastern Europe brought the Orthodox church with them. The most prominent Orthodox church, the multi-onion-domed ST. THEODOSIUS RUSSIAN ORTHODOX CATHEDRAL, was founded in 1896. ST. MARY'S ROMANIAN ORTHODOX CHURCH was the first Romanian Orthodox building to be constructed in the U.S. (1904). Of all the churches, the Orthodox were the least visible in the broader social, cultural, and political life of the city. They tended to continue to perform their original function as guardians of traditional culture long after other churches had started to participate in other areas of the city's life.

By the years after World War II, the ferment within the denominations had subsided, and a pattern of religious diversity was cemented into place. Not only the city but also each denomination would be pluralistic. The infusions of new religious traditions, or variations of existing ones, continued. Some of the new traditions were brought by immigrants—Hispanic, Korean, and Vietnamese Catholics, Russian Jews, and Bahais from Iran. Other traditions, some spurred by immigrants familiar with original forms, such as Buddhism, Hinduism, and Islam, took their place in the ever-diversifying religious culture of the city. Many black Clevelanders responded to religious alternatives to the dominant Baptist and AME traditions by joining the Nation of Islam, Orthodox Islam, or a variety of black religious nationalist faiths.

The sheer number and variety of Cleveland's religious organizations was striking. The 1986 phone book listed 1,301 churches in the metropolitan area. These included

14 AME and AME Zion churches, 157 Catholic churches, 28 Eastern Orthodox churches, 30 Jewish congregations, and 98 Lutheran churches. Of the remaining churches, approximately 320 were descendants of the traditional New England Protestant denominations—Baptist, Congregationalist (incorporated into the United Church of Christ), Methodist, and Presbyterian. Some groups that formerly had had little religious presence had sizable representations: the Jehovah's Witnesses listed 18 centers, while CHRISTIAN SCIENTISTS counted 14. Continuing a trend that began early in the 20th century, smaller black and white Protestant churches proliferated in the city and suburbs. These were often nondenominational. The 1986 listing included 23 Apostolic, 17 Assemblies of God, 40 Church of God, 7 Holiness, 63 Pentecostal, and 44 "nondenominational" churches, approximately 15% of the area's churches. Noninstitutional forms of religion also attracted Clevelanders. TV ministries, tent revivals, mass revivals, and meetings in the Coliseum in nearby Richfield, and representatives of religious groups selling goods, passing out literature, or admonishing passersby in the downtown area were all part of the city's religious life.

The clerical ranks increased in diversity in the 1970s. A scattering of women served as ministers in denominations ranging from the Methodists to the United Church of Christ. One Reform Jewish synagogue had a woman rabbi. Black-white integration at the clerical level was minimal. Black clergy usually served all-black churches. The trend toward suburbanization continued. Inner-city Catholic parishes dwindled as their members moved to the suburbs. The city exhibited a recognizable religious geography. In general, the city's west side was white Protestant and white and Hispanic Catholic. The southern suburbs and pockets of the east side were white Catholic. Black Protestants dominated most of the east side. Suburbs offered more diversity, although here, too, some groups coalesced, such as Jews in the eastern suburbs.

Cleveland's religious organizations came to accept and applaud the religious pluralism that had been so disruptive in earlier years. Ecumenical efforts multiplied. The Natl. Council of Churches held its founding meeting in Cleveland in 1950. At the local level, the Greater Cleveland Interchurch Council led these efforts. Orthodox churches withdrew in the late 1970s, wishing to take a stronger stand against Communism and a more conservative approach to social issues. The Orthodox clergy maintained an informal link with the council even after their departure. The Catholic Diocese and the Jewish Community Fed. sent observers. Other ecumenical efforts included the West Side Ecumenical Ministry and the Inner City Renewal Society (earlier the Inner City Protestant Parish). Benevolent and social-reform efforts were often conducted under ecumenical auspices. The Interchurch Council and a loose coalition of churches organized through the West Side Ecumenical Ministry created an extensive network of food-distribution and meal centers. A number of churches backed construction projects for the elderly and handicapped. White Protestant churches remained highly visible. The downtown churches served as focal points of the city's religious life, often being used for interdenominational and memorial services, and for general religious and civic occasions. Suburban churches, many of which had been small offshoots of the city churches, were now independent and of considerable size and longevity.

For the Catholic church, the years after World War II were a time for catching up with the growth in the suburbs and for building an extensive parochial school system. The reforms of Vatican II were welcomed with little visible disagreement. The hierarchical organization of the diocese diminished as a style based more on consultation emerged. In 1969, a program of permanent deacons was begun. Participation in conducting services and liturgy was widened, but the unwillingness of the church to ordain women still provoked controversy and discontent. New groups played an increasing role in the church. By the 1980s, Hispanics represented 25–30% of the 1 million members of the diocese. The numbers of black, Korean, and Vietnamese Catholics increased. The symbolic affirmation of Catholicism's ethnic diversity came in 1980 with the appointment of Anthony Pilla as bishop. Pilla became the first local priest to become bishop, as well as the diocese's first bishop from the ranks of the "new immigrants." Among social issues, abortion and American policy in Central America became prime concerns. The diocese established a Salvadoran mission in 1964. A Clevelander, Grace Donovan, was one of the 4 women whose brutal killings in El Salvador captured national attention and contributed to the disillusionment of many with the American policy in Central America. The Commission on Catholic Community Action participated in a variety of peace and other social issues, both national and local.

For Jews, the years after 1945 were dedicated to becoming established in new suburban locations and maintaining religious and cultural identities amid the challenges of suburbia. Divisions between Reform, Orthodox, and Conservative branches continued, although the tensions between groups lessened in the face of common concerns such as the survival of Israel. Jews continued to be members of a minority tradition, making up an estimated 5% of the population of the Cleveland area. Umbrella organizations, such as the JEWISH COMMUNITY FED. OF CLEVELAND and the JEWISH COMMUNITY CTR. in Cleveland Hts., coordinated philanthropic, religious, recreational, and cultural activities. HADASSAH, Pioneer Women, and Mizrachi Women continued their own benevolent efforts. Cleveland's Jews became actively concerned in these years about Soviet Jewry. As early as 1954, a CLEVELAND COUNCIL ON SOVIET ANTI-SEMITISM was formed. In the 1970s and 1980s, Cleveland's Jews campaigned for the release of Soviet Jews. Synagogues and the Jewish Community Ctr. sponsored immigrants and offered help in adjusting to America and learning English. Often, instruction in Judaism was necessary for Soviet immigrants, a group for which Judaism had become more of a cultural identity than a religious commitment.

In the years after World War II, black Protestant churches began to be recognized as a substantial force in the city. Leading ministers exercised informal political influence, and candidates, black and white, used the church to provide access to black votes. Black churches furnished much of the impetus for civil-rights activities in the city and were instrumental in the election of the city's first black mayor, Carl Stokes. Large inner-city churches of the Baptist and AME denominations remained the most pervasive form of black religious life. In the suburbs, nondenominational churches, many attracting substantial numbers of young members, flourished. Black churches maintained their strong commitment to social service in familiar forms, such as providing food and benevolent help of all kinds, and in new forms, such as sponsoring, with the help of government financing, senior citizens' housing and jobs programs. Black churches began to become heavily involved in many of the projects of the Greater Cleveland Interchurch Council, especially its Hunger Ctr. and the Inner City Renewal Society. Black religion diversified significantly in the years after World War II. The Nation of Islam was represented by Muhammad's Temple No. 15, and traditional Islam by Masjid Bilal. A variety of Black Nationalist and black Jewish groups, such as the Original African Israelites, attracted followers disenchanted with mainstream Baptist and AME churches.

Orthodox churches prospered in these years, yet they still lacked the civic responsibility of other religious groups, and they remained somewhat separate from the ecumenical and social efforts of white and black Protestants, Catholics, and Jews. In numbers, they were a substantial presence, outnumbering Jews. In the mid-1950s, there were 23 Orthodox churches, including 5 Russian, 5 Greek, 4 Ukrainian, 2 Serbian, 2 Romanian, and 1 Albanian, and 4 all-English churches formed mainly in the suburbs, where there were not enough of one ethnic group to constitute a church. Because of the post-World War II immigration from Eastern Europe, the Orthodox churches were among the fastest-growing of the city's religious groups. Although not as active as other denominations in social activities outside their own religious community, Orthodox churches supported hunger programs and some of the other activities of the Interchurch Council. In 1977, the Ukrainian Orthodox Church established a shelter, St. Herman's House of Hospitality. Orthodox churches have also been active participants in MERRICK HOUSE and the Tremont Development Corp.

What had been a religiously homogeneous city in the early 1800s was by the 1980s the epitome of heterogeneity and on the way to becoming more so. New arrivals kept adding to the city's diversity. The denominational, ethnic, and racial divisions that marked the formal institutions of the city's religious life seemed little likely to change. Yet there was a general recognition of the strengths of diversity and cultural distinctiveness. Cleveland's Protestants, Catholics, Jews, Orthodox, Muslims, and other religious communities pursued their spiritual, charitable, educational, and social activities in an atmosphere of widespread tolerance and often, informal cooperation.

Michael J. McTighe
Gettysburg College

See also various ethnic groups.

The **REPUBLIC STEEL CORPORATION,** with its headquarters in Cleveland, was the 5th-largest steel producer in the U.S. at the time of its merger into LTV Steel in 1984. Republic was established on 8 Apr. 1930 through an amalgamation of several steel companies manipulated by CYRUS EATON and Wm. G. Mather. Before 1930, Eaton and Mather had used Youngstown's Republic Iron & Steel Co. to acquire numerous small steel firms, including Cleveland's Steel & Tubes, Inc., founded in 1902 as the Elyria Iron & Steel Co. Republic then merged with 3 other companies, including Cleveland's Bourne-Fuller Co., to form Republic Steel, at that time the 3d-largest steelmaker in the country. Bourne-Fuller, founded in 1881, was a steel warehouse operator and sales agency, but had 2 important holdings, the Union Rolling Mill Co., which had manufactured iron in Cleveland since 1866, and the Upson Nut Co., one of the country's oldest and largest bolt and nut companies, which had originated in Connecticut in 1854. Republic pioneered in manufacturing light, alloy, and stainless steels, becoming the world's largest producer. However, the firm suffered financially during the Depression. By 1935, its president, TOM GIRDLER, stabilized the company by acquiring 2 major steel firms, Corrigan-McKinney and Truscan. Cleveland-based Corrigan-McKinney, founded by JAS. W. CORRIGAN in the early 1880s as an iron-ore and lake-shipping business, had developed into a pig-iron and steel producer. Its extensive iron-ore and coal reserves and a strategically located plant along the CUYAHOGA RIVER

improved Republic's position. Youngstown's Truscan, which had acquired a pressed-steel plant in Cleveland in 1927, assured Republic a broad outlet for steel in a variety of construction and industrial products. With 3 major plants in Cleveland, Republic moved its headquarters there from Youngstown in 1936. Republic continued to grow in the late 1930s, building a new continuous strip mill in Cleveland in 1937. However, it was plagued with labor problems. Hundreds of workers were injured attempting to unionize Republic facilities during the LITTLE STEEL STRIKE of 1937. Two deaths occurred in Cleveland. After Senate investigations and federal pressure, Republic recognized the CIO in 1942. By then it was one of the largest employers in Cleveland, with 9,000 workers.

Republic continued to grow in the postwar period. In 1959 it opened a research center in INDEPENDENCE, which achieved improvements in steelmaking processes, especially for bar, sheet, and tubular products. The firm spent $1.2 billion on modernization efforts during the 1960s, bringing total production to over 10 million tons annually. By 1965, the Cleveland works was the largest of Republic's 8 steel plants. The 1970s witnessed the restructuring of Republic as it consolidated its steel holdings and sold some of its declining businesses, such as the merchant iron and nuts-and-bolts divisions. It also diversified, becoming more involved with natural resources and moving into the shipping, petroleum, insurance, and aviation industries. However, with the rest of the American steel industry, Republic's steelmaking operations began to suffer from increased competition from foreign producers. Republic's share of the U.S. steel market slipped to 7% by 1982. These effects were compounded by the business recession of 1981–83. Attempting to stem the losses, Republic closed older, inefficient plants and laid off thousands of workers. In addition, the company invested in the newest steelmaking technology. At the Cleveland plant, blast furnaces were upgraded, and a continuous caster was installed. These changes helped to lower operating costs. In another response for survival, smaller steelmakers faced the choice of merger or failure. Republic began to search for a merger partner, and found one next door in Jones & Laughlin Steel. See also LTV STEEL.

Frank A. Scott Papers, WRHS.

Girdler, Tom M., *Bootstraps* (1943).

Marvin Clinton Harrison Papers, WRHS.

Republic Steel Corp., *A Trip through the Cleveland District Plant of Republic Steel Corporation* (1949).

Republic Steel Corp., *Republic Goes to War* (1944).

Republic Steel Corp., *World's Largest Continuous Strip Mill* (1939).

The **REPUBLICAN NATIONAL CONVENTION OF 1924** was held 10–13 June in the newly built Public Hall in Cleveland to select the Republican presidential and vice-presidential candidates for the 1924 election. It was the first national political convention held in the city and the first ever to be broadcast on the radio. Led by Congressman THEODORE BURTON, Cleveland civic leaders offered the Republican Natl. Committee free use of the Public Hall, a $125,000 expense fund, and a written pledge that current hotel and restaurant prices would prevail throughout the convention. Arrangements were made to broadcast the convention to 9 cities simultaneously, using long-distance telephone wires. Locally the convention was carried on WTAM and WJAX.

During the week before the convention, supporters of Calvin Coolidge set up headquarters at the Hotel Cleveland. There was little doubt that Coolidge, who had become president on the death of Warren G. Harding, would be the party's nominee for president. The Federal Reserve Bldg. was the site of the convention headquarters, where final arrangements were made, including a program of entertainment for the attendees. The convention opened on Tuesday, 10 June, with 1,109 delegates. Congressman Burton delivered the keynote address. On the second day, committee reports were read, deliberations on the platform began, and permanent chairman Frank W. Mondell spoke. Musical entertainment was provided by John Philip Sousa and his band. The main business of the convention was transacted on the third day, with the nomination of Calvin Coolidge on the first ballot by a vote of 1,065 to 44. In the contest for vice-president, former Illinois governor Frank O. Lowden received the required majority on the second ballot but sent word that he declined the nomination. At a special session late that evening, Brig. Gen. Chas. G. Dawes was chosen on the third ballot as the vice-presidential nominee. A brief session was held on Friday, at which time Wm. M. Butler, Coolidge's campaign manager, was elected chairman of the Republican Natl. Committee. Neither Coolidge nor Dawes was at the convention when he was nominated. Coolidge stayed in Washington and listened to the proceedings on the radio.

The **REPUBLICAN NATIONAL CONVENTION OF 1936** was held 9–12 June at the Public Hall in Cleveland to select the Republican presidential and vice-presidential candidates for the election of 1936. Cleveland was chosen by the Republican Natl. Committee over St. Louis, Chicago, and Kansas City. Led by Congressman CHESTER BOLTON, Cleveland civic organizations and businessmen raised $150,000 in expense money to help persuade the committee to hold the convention here. The Public Hall was repainted and remodeled to accommodate the equipment and wiring necessary for the delegates and the media. Special musical programs were arranged, and major speeches were scheduled for the late evening hours, so that the radio networks' commercial programming would not be preempted. The city hosted about 13,000 visitors, including 1,001 delegates, their alternates, campaign workers, reporters, and committeemen.

A week before the convention, headquarters for the presidential hopefuls were set up. Kansas Gov. Alfred Landon's supporters were at the Hotel Hollenden; those of Sen. Wm. Borah and Col. Frank Knox were at the Hotel Cleveland; and Sen. Arthur Vandenberg's followers were at the Hotel Statler. As the delegates began to arrive, an unsuccessful Stop Landon movement was initiated, and platform deliberations were begun. The convention began 9 June with the certification of credentials and the seating of delegates. Oregon Sen. Frederick Stiewer was the keynote speaker the first day. On the second day reports were read, and Herbert Hoover delivered an address. The main business of the convention was transacted on the third day, with Alfred Landon nominated as the Republican presidential candidate on the first ballot. On 12 June, the last day of the convention, Col. Knox was selected as Landon's running mate, and John Hamilton, Landon's campaign manager, was elected chairman of the Republican Natl. Committee. Neither Landon nor Knox was in Cleveland when he was nominated. Knox had been here for the first 3 days of the convention but left, believing that Sen. Arthur Vandenberg would be the vice-presidential candidate. Vandenberg refused the nomination, and Knox was selected. Landon stayed in Kansas throughout the proceedings, although he was in constant telephone contact with his supporters here.

**REPUBLICAN PARTY.** *See* **CUYAHOGA COUNTY REPUBLICAN PARTY**

The **RETAIL MERCHANTS BOARD, INC.,** began in 1898 as a committee of the Chamber of Commerce. It was formally organized in 1900. Seeing the potential of cooperation to achieve mutual aims, downtown merchants agreed to meet weekly to discuss the state of retail trade in Cleveland. Part of the board's thrust over the years was to promote buying and influence buying patterns. A perennial concern was business hours, with the issue in 1907 being whether to close 1 half-day a week and early on Saturday evening, and that in the 1950s and 1960s being whether to agree to Sunday openings of "nonessential" businesses. In an effort to encourage early buying to prevent a Christmas Eve rush of shoppers, the board members contributed to a joint advertising fund as early as 1907, and over the years decided when the official advertising campaign would begin. Noting a slack in Friday business, they decided to offer incentives to shoppers—an idea that was used again in 1911 to enliven midweek shopping. Enlisting the cooperation of the street rail companies, they advertised special Wednesday sale items aimed at suburbanites, and also offered rate rebates to the riders. Besides coordinating hours and sales practices, the board tried to keep pace with nationwide trends. To obtain the answers to questions such as "Do stores offer free delivery?" it conducted research among out-of-town retailers. When local merchants became convinced, on the basis of national data, that patrons expected free delivery, they set up a joint delivery service in 1912 that remained viable until United Parcel took over in the 1950s. The board was concerned with broader issues that affected retail concerns. Often that involved lobbying for better downtown parking or keeping transit fares low for shoppers. During the Depression, local merchants used their influence, through the board, to keep credit flowing to Cleveland.

Plagued with shoplifting and forgery in the early 1900s, the board offered suggestions to minimize loss and encouraged the hiring of store detectives. It set up a Protective Services Div. in 1922 that verified checks and ran employment checks on prospective retail employees and credit checks on consumers; in the 1930s, the board offered a forgery clinic to retailers. Among its most notable (and long-standing) achievements was the creation of the Retail Men's Credit organization, which operates the Credit Bureau of Cleveland, one of the largest and earliest such operations in the U.S. In 1968, when the Chamber of Commerce merged with the Greater Cleveland Growth Board to become the GREATER CLEVELAND GROWTH ASSOC., the Retail Merchants Board decided to incorporate separately, moving into space leased by the Credit Bureau of Cleveland at 666 Euclid. In its 1969 articles of incorporation, the board articulated the blend of business, civic, and protective service functions that the prior board had established. After splitting from the Growth Assoc., the board began to operate at a loss. By 1973, the purpose of the Retail Merchants Board was less clear, as the focus of retailing had moved from downtown. Also, the rising strength of national chain stores such as Penney's and Sears took many merchandising and executive policy decisions out of local hands. In an attempt to get better promotion of the Cleveland area, the board then ceded its promotional activities back to the Growth Assoc. (See also BUSINESS-RETAIL.)

**REVCO D.S., INC.,** is the world's largest drugstore chain and a pioneer in the discount drug field. Revco was founded in 1956 by a Detroit drugstore operator, Bernard Shulman, who saw an opportunity to apply high-volume, low-margin merchandising to the drug business and converted his conventional drugstore into a discount drugstore. By the following year, Shulman had a chain of 4 stores, which he named Regal D.S., Inc. The company was an instant success, with $300,000 in annual sales. By 1961, it had 20 stores in the Midwest, 3 of them in Cleveland. That year, Regal made its first acquisition, the 41-store chain of the Standard Drug Co. of Cleveland. Standard had begun in 1899 when 2 drug salesmen, Chas. A. Goodman and Perin Shirley, opened a small drugstore, Gem Pharmacy, at E. 9th St. and Superior Ave., with C. Edward Roseman as manager. Roseman's success at that store led to other stores and its incorporation as Standard Drug in 1906. By the 1940s, Standard had become Cleveland's largest drugstore chain. Regal converted most of the Standard stores into discount operations, limiting sales to drugs and health and beauty aids. In 1962, the name of the company was changed to Revco D.S., Inc. Two years later, the firm moved its headquarters from Detroit to Cleveland, because over half of its 59 stores were now in the area, and the city was an ideal distribution point for the Midwest.

During the late 1960s and early 1970s, Revco acquired numerous drugstore chains in the Midwest, Middle Atlantic, Southeast, and Southwest. By 1978, when it opened its 1,000th store, its expansion program was concentrating on the South and Southwest. As it grew, Revco also expanded its services. The company pioneered in the establishment of discount plans for senior citizens and small children in the 1960s. Throughout the 1970s, Revco built larger stores, increased the line of products it carried, including its own private-label products, and introduced new health-care services, such as optical departments and dental centers. In 1972, Revco began moving into the drug-manufacturing business through the acquisition of several firms. Revco's growth has not been without problems. In 1977, the company pleaded no contest to a charge of fraudulent welfare prescription billings by the state of Ohio, and was fined $532,000. In 1984 Revco was forced to recall a vitamin supplement, E-Ferol, manufactured by the company, when the product was implicated in the deaths of 38 premature infants. Even so, these incidents have not injured the company's growth. To operate this dynamic firm, Revco built a $4.5 million headquarters in Twinsburg in 1974. By 1984, Revco had 1,763 stores in 28 states, with $1.8 billion in annual sales and over 17,000 employees. In 1986, the board of directors approved a $1.5 billion plan to convert the shareholder-owned company to one privately owned.

The **REVCO MARATHON AND 10K,** actually a 26-mi. marathon and a separate 10-km run, is considered one of the major races for runners in the country. It is annually sponsored by the REVCO DRUG STORE chain and is cosponsored by various Cleveland-area companies. Revco first sponsored the Revco-Western Reserve Marathon in May 1976; it was run in Hudson and attracted only 250 runners. The race was moved to Cleveland in May 1978, and the number of participants grew rapidly. The race was ranked among the top 25 road races in the nation by *Runner's World* magazine in the 1980s. The marathon begins and ends on EUCLID AVE. at CLEVELAND STATE UNIVERSITY. The route winds through PUBLIC SQUARE, over the DETROIT-SUPERIOR BRIDGE, and then follows Detroit Ave. to Lake Ave. through LAKEWOOD and ROCKY RIVER to a turnaround in BAY VILLAGE. The course is fast and relatively flat and does not include a major difficulty like the Boston Marathon's infamous "Heartbreak Hill." The number of runners rose to over 3,000 in 1986; runners have come from 40 states and countries, including Great Britain, Kenya, Mexico, New Zealand, and Finland. The race has attracted Olympic runners Lasse Viren, Grete Waitz, Anne Audain, Bill Rodgers, Dr. Tony

Sandoval, and others. Tom Fleming won the first men's marathon in 1978 in 2:15:02; Kim Merritt won the women's race in 2:48:59. Dr. Tony Sandoval set the men's record, 2:14:36, in 1982; Jane Wipf set the women's record of 2:40:42 in 1981. Runners in both races are classified into 7 age groups, ranging from those 14 and under to those 60 and above. In 1984, many Olympic hopefuls used the 10K race as a warmup for that year's Olympic trials. The 10K run was even more popular than the marathon and attracted over 13,000 runners in 1986. The 10K followed the marathon route to W. 64th and back until 1983; after that, the route was changed to follow Euclid Ave. to Ontario St. and then out St. Clair Ave. to E. 46th and back. Winners in various classes receive a wreath of laurels and a gold medallion. No cash prizes are awarded, although Revco has paid travel expenses to bring world-class runners to Cleveland.

**RHODES, JAMES FORD** (1 May 1848–22 Jan. 1927), was a scholar, historian, author, and businessman. He was born at his family's home on FRANKLIN CIRCLE in Cleveland. His father, Daniel Pomeroy Rhodes, a native of Sudbury, Vt., had come to Cleveland as a young man and made his fortune as one of the city's first entrepreneurs in the coal-mining industry. His mother, Sophia Lord Russell Rhodes, a native of Connecticut, was the granddaughter of JOSIAH BARBER, first mayor of OHIO CITY (1836). James Ford Rhodes, the couple's second son, received his early education in Cleveland's private and public schools; he graduated from West High School in 1865. He attended the University of the City of New York as a special history student from 1865–66, and the University of Chicago from 1866–67; he never graduated. In 1867, Rhodes traveled abroad, where he studied history and French literature in Paris and iron metallurgy at the Berlin School of Mines. He visited iron and steel mills in western Germany, England, and Scotland, and when he returned to the U.S. (1868), he visited the iron and coal deposits in Georgia, North Carolina, and Tennessee. He joined his father's business in 1870, and in 1874 he founded Rhodes & Co., producers and commission merchants in the iron, iron-ore, and coal business, along with his older brother, Robert, his brother-in-law, MARCUS A. HANNA, Chas. C. Bolton, Arnold Saunders, and Geo. H. Warmington. The firm flourished, and Rhodes became a wealthy man. In 1881 he began to write monthly trade circulars for his company; they were widely circulated and well received. In 1884, Rhodes decided that he was financially secure enough to retire from his lucrative business and devote the rest of his life to studying and writing history. The firm was dissolved (Apr. 1885) and was later reorganized as M. A. Hanna & Co.

Rhodes published several articles in the *Magazine of Western History* (1885–86), and from 1888–91, he wrote the first 2 volumes of his 7-volume *History of the United States from the Compromise of 1850*. He moved to Cambridge, Mass., in 1891 and to Boston in 1895, where he was accepted into the political and literary circles. By 1906 he had completed vol. 7 of the history. In 1909, his book *Historical Essays* was published, and in 1917 his series of lectures about the American Civil War, which he had presented at Oxford (England) University, were published. In 1918 he received the Pulitzer Prize in history for his *History of the Civil War, 1861–1865*. He also wrote *History of the United States from Hayes to McKinley, 1877–1896* (1919) and *The McKinley and Roosevelt Administrations, 1897–1909* (1922). Rhodes received many honors and honorary degrees, including LL.D.s from Western Reserve University (1893); Yale University (1901); and Harvard College

(1901). He also received the Loubat Prize from the Berlin Academy of Science in 1901; and Litt.D. degrees from Kenyon College (1903), the University of Wisconsin (1904), New York University (1908), and Oxford, England (1909). He was elected a fellow in the American Academy of Arts & Sciences and a member of the American Academy of Arts & Letters. In 1898–99 he was president of the American Historical Assoc.

On 4 Jan. 1872, Rhodes married Ann Card of Cleveland, daughter of Jonathan F. Card, a former business partner of his father's. The couple had 1 son, Daniel Pomeroy Rhodes II (b. 20 Jan. 1876). Rhodes died in Brookline, Mass. His ashes are buried in RIVERSIDE CEMETERY. On 23 June 1932, the recently completed high school building located at 5100 Biddulph Ave. was named James Ford Rhodes High School in his honor by the Cleveland Board of Education.

Cruden, Robert, *James Ford Rhodes* (1851).

**RICE, HARVEY** (11 June 1800–7 Nov. 1891), was the leading force behind the reorganization of the common schools of Ohio in 1853 and was active in the political and literary life of Cleveland. He is considered the "Father of the Common Schools of Ohio." Rice was born in Conway, Mass. He studied classics at Williams College, graduating in 1824. That year he traveled west to the settlement of Cleveland, where he secured a position as instructor at the Academy on St. Clair St. In 1826, Rice studied law, eventually entering into a partnership with REUBEN WOOD— later governor of Ohio. Rice was elected justice of the peace in 1829 and served as Democratic representative from Cuyahoga County to the Ohio legislature in 1830. In 1831, he was appointed by that body as agent for the school land sales of the Connecticut Western Reserve, a tract of some 56,000 acres. The lands were sold through public auction and private sales over approximately 3 years. The $150,000 received from the sales was deposited into the state school fund for the exclusive benefit of educating children of the Western Reserve.

In 1834, Rice was appointed clerk of the common pleas and supreme courts, a position he held until 1841. He was elected in 1851 to the Ohio senate as a Democrat. As senator, he introduced a bill that called for the reorganization and centralization of the common schools of Ohio. The bill created a uniform district structure and established an equitable system of taxation to benefit all the common schools in the state. He also introduced a bill to establish reform farms for criminal youth. As a result, the reform farm at Lancaster, Ohio, was created. Both bills passed in 1853. As a member of the Cleveland city council in 1857, Rice secured the passage of a resolution that consolidated 2 benevolent institutions, the Industrial School and the CHILDREN'S AID SOCIETY. That year he also introduced a resolution that resulted in the erection of a monument (1860) to Commodore Oliver H. Perry (see PERRY MONUMENT). In 1861, Rice served as the president of the Cleveland Board of Education, a position he held until 1863. He became the director of the CLEVELAND WORKHOUSE in 1871. From 1879 until his death, he was the president of the EARLY SETTLERS ASSOC. In addition to being an educator and legislator, Rice was a prolific author. His publications included *Pioneers of the Western Reserve*, *Nature and Culture*, and a book of poetry, *Mount Vernon and Other Poems*. Rice was married twice. His first wife, Fanny Rice, died in 1837. In 1840, he married Emma Marie Wood, sister of Reuben Wood.

Akers, William J., *Cleveland Schools in the Nineteenth Century* (1901).

Freese, Andrew, *Early History of the Cleveland Public Schools* (1876).
Harvey Rice Papers, WRHS.
Rice, Harvey, *Leaflets of a Lifetime* (1895).

The **RICHMAN BROTHERS COMPANY** is a manufacturer and retailer of men's suits, furnishings, and hats. The company-owned retail outlets supply a cross-country network of stores from a 23-acre tailoring plant and offices at 1600 E. 55th St. Richman Bros. was begun in 1879 when Henry Richman moved his small wholesale clothing-manufacturing concern to Cleveland from Portsmouth, Ohio. In 1907 the company took its present form when the founder's sons, Nathan, Charles, and Henry, opened retail outlets with an innovative merchandising approach—"factory to consumer"—thus eliminating the costly middleman. Richman's was the first maker of men's clothing to sell directly to customers through a combination of mail order and company-owned retail stores. All suits were sold at the single price of $10 until the program was dropped when men's furnishings and hats were added to the line in 1939.

A pioneer in innovative employee relations, the company encourages a family atmosphere: employees' birthdays are remembered; executives greet employees by name at the door each morning and evening; there are no time clocks; and service awards acknowledge superior work performance. Richman's was the first industrial organization in the country to grant a 2-week (later 3-week) paid vacation to all employees. In addition, company-paid insurance and benefits programs and no-cost loans set an industry precedent in industrial relations. During the 1950s, Richman Bros. grew to be the largest clothing chain in the nation, with 119 retail outlets by 1959. Geo. Richman, a distant cousin of the three Richman brothers, directed the company at this time. Major expansion programs undertaken by the company included opening boys' departments in selected stores; the acquisition of Stein stores in 1959, a chain of 91 menswear stores operating in the South and Southwest; the formation of the General Men's Wear Corp. in 1962 to operate leased menswear departments in 3 major discount-store chains; and a mid-1960s experiment, Adam's Row stores, in which the trendier fashions of the time were marketed. In 1969 the Richman Bros. Co. merged with the F. W. Woolworth Co. of New York.

**RICHMOND HEIGHTS** was the last portion of Euclid Twp. to be incorporated as a village. Originally incorporated as the village of Claribel in 1917, it became Richmond Hts. in 1918. The suburban city of 4.7 sq. mi. is located 15 mi. east of downtown Cleveland and is bounded on the north and west by EUCLID, on the east by HIGHLAND HTS., on the south by LYNDHURST, and on the southwest by S. EUCLID. The area developed slowly. It was principally a farming community, the only major early industry being a series of charcoal pits that provided fuel for the growing iron industry in Cleveland. Its population was 265 in 1920, growing to only 891 in 1950. Major expansion followed the installation of gas and water mains in 1953. When the population reached 5,000 in 1960, Richmond Hts. became a city. In 1980, the population reached 10,096. The city is served by the Richmond Hts. Local School District, which currently has an enrollment of 883 in an elementary, middle, and high school on one campus. The GENERAL ELECTRIC CO. Lamp Glass Dept., located on Highland Rd., is the city's only substantial industry. Richmond Hts. is primarily residential, with 1 hospital, RICHMOND HTS. GENERAL HOSPITAL, 8 churches, and a number of retail stores, many of which are located at the Hillcrest Square Shopping Ctr. at Richmond and Wilson

Mills roads, or in the Richmond Mall at the same intersection. The city is governed by a mayor-council system. It maintains 2 parks providing 32 acres of recreational facilities. The CUYAHOGA COUNTY AIRPORT, located on Richmond Rd., is partially situated in the city.

Keidel, Helen, ed., *Richmond Heights, Ohio, 1917–1967* (1967).

**RICHMOND HEIGHTS GENERAL HOSPITAL,** located at 27110 Chardon Rd., is a 220-bed osteopathic community hospital. It was opened in 1961, with major additions in 1970. Dr. Jerry A. Zinni, an osteopathic physician, established the hospital and served as its president. By 1986, Richmond Hts. General was accredited for osteopathic interns and residents and was a training site for the Ohio University College of Osteopathic Medicine. It has a school of radiologic technology and serves as a training site for paramedics in eastern Cuyahoga County. It has an outpatient facility in Madison, Ohio. Richmond Hts. General Hospital is formally affiliated with SAINT VINCENT CHARITY HOSPITAL.

*The Northeast Ohio Health Services Area and Its Hospital Needs* (1976).

**RIDDLE, ALBERT G.** (28 May 1816–16 May 1902), was a well-known criminal lawyer in Cleveland and a politician. He was active in county and state government and served 1 term in Congress. Riddle also distinguished himself as a public speaker and writer. He wrote several novels and a series of historical works on the Civil War. Throughout his life, he was an ardent promoter of equal rights for BLACKS. Riddle was born in Monson, Mass. His family moved to Newbury in 1817. Although he received training in carpentry, he came from an educated family and obtained a thorough education. He commenced the study of law under Seabury Ford in 1838 and was admitted to the Ohio bar in 1840. Riddle established a practice in Chardon and Painesville. He was elected Geauga County prosecuting attorney within a year and served a 6-year term. In 1848, his political career began when he was elected to the state legislature as a representative of the FREE SOIL PARTY. His speaking ability enabled him to mediate, as a Free-Soiler, between the Whigs and Democrats. In 1850 he moved to Cleveland and resumed his law practice, forming a partnership with SAMUEL WILLIAMSON. He was soon largely engaged in criminal court—for lack of civil business—and was elected the prosecuting attorney of Cuyahoga County. In the highly publicized OBERLIN-WELLINGTON RESCUE case in 1859, Riddle was the principal defending lawyer. A few years later, he was asked to be the defending lawyer for John Brown, but because of the late message, he was unable to arrive until the trial had already begun.

In 1861, Riddle was elected to Congress, representing Cuyahoga, Lake, and Geauga counties. When the CIVIL WAR broke out, he was the first in Congress to argue in favor of arming the slaves. The war, however, also brought about the end of his promising career in politics. Hoping to view the first battle of the war at Bull Run, Riddle was among the many politicians who were conveyed in carriages to the scene of the battle. After the confused retreat back to Washington, he wrote a letter to his wife describing the day's events. Parts of the letter were somehow published in the *CLEVELAND LEADER* without Riddle's knowledge. The *Cleveland Herald*, the *Leader*'s rival and politically opposed to Riddle, published another account of his adventures at Bull Run that depicted him as a coward. Although probably libelous, the account was enough to cause Riddle's defeat for reelection in 1863. After the war,

Riddle moved permanently to Washington and became a lawyer in military cases. In 1865, he also prosecuted John H. Suratt for his part in the assassination of Pres. Lincoln. Later he became the attorney for the District of Columbia. In one case he defended a black woman accused of murdering a white man and won her acquittal. During his life, he either prosecuted or defended in 40 homicide cases. In 1873, Riddle achieved some success as a novelist with *Bart Rigby*, an autobiographical novel. In the 1880s he completed a series of books on the Civil War and American leaders of the time. Riddle was married to Caroline Avery of Chardon.

Albert G. Riddle Papers, WRHS.

**RIDNA SHKOLA,** "Native School" in Ukrainian, is a school that has operated since the early 1950s to teach the language, history, and culture of the Ukraine to Cleveland-area youngsters of Ukrainian descent. The school was organized in 1950 by members of the association Prosvita and supporters of the Ukrainian youth organization Plast (Boy Scouts). Opened under the direction of Mrs. Mychajlyna Stavnycha at SS. Peter & Paul Parish on W. 7th St., it had 27 students and a limited curriculum in 1950. The school moved to MERRICK HOUSE in 1952 and later followed its students' families to the suburbs, moving to Thoreau Park Elementary School in Parma in 1959 and to Schaaf Jr. High School in 1960. By 1973, the history, literature, music, and geography classes taught on Saturday mornings at Schaaf Jr. High School had an enrollment of 340 students in grades 1–11 and a faculty of 19. Described as "one of the largest and best organized nationality schools" in the area, Ridna Shkola had an annual budget of $18,000 and charged $50 tuition in 1973. It also received support from the Ridna Shkola Assoc.

**RING, EMIL** (21 Nov. 1863–1 Feb. 1922), was a Czech oboe player, pianist, teacher, conductor, and composer prominent in Cleveland's musical development. Ring was born in Fetchen, Czechoslovakia, and trained at the Prague Conservatory of Music. He played in orchestras in Leipzig, Berlin, Vienna, Holland, and England. His first exposure to Cleveland came with a fateful meeting with Cleveland soprano Rita Elandi at a royal command performance for Queen Victoria. The two formed a fast friendship that would eventually lead Ring to the singer's city. Ring went to Boston when he moved to America in 1887. He played in the Boston Symphony Orchestra for 1 year. He came to Cleveland in 1888 to become the conductor of the PHILHARMONIC ORCHESTRA, which had been organized 7 years before and then had 55 members. Ring immediately demonstrated his ability as a conductor by his knowledge of a range of music, including works by Liszt, Grieg, Berlioz, Wagner, Hartman, Massenet, and Volkman. The orchestra held summer concerts in HALTNORTH'S GARDENS and had 14 regular programs. From 1888–95, Ring served as a piano instructor at the Cleveland Conservatory of Music at E. 6th St. and Euclid. In 1898, the FORTNIGHTLY CLUB under Ring united with the SINGERS CLUB in a remarkable performance of Rossini's *Stabat Mater* at TRINITY CATHEDRAL. In 1902, Ring and his friend JOHANN BECK were selected to lead the Cleveland Grand Orchestra. For 10 years Ring and Beck alternated as conductors, with the standard music repertoire as the primary draw. Among his other musical pursuits, Ring was a long-time director of the Gesangverein and festival conductor of the 27th Saengerfest in July 1893 (see SAENGERFESTS). The Gesangverein premiered his *An die Tonkrenst*, a short oratorio work that was published in 1900.

Ring composed in almost every form. He left the Emil Ring Memorial Collection to the CLEVELAND PUBLIC LIBRARY, where it stands as one of the largest collections of music in the area. Ring was a member of the Musicians' Club from its inception. He never married.

**RINGWALL, RUDOLPH** (19 Mar. 1891–26 Jan. 1978), was a violinist and conductor. Born in Bangor, Maine, he studied at the New England Conservatory, graduating in 1913. From 1913–15 and 1917–20 he was a violinist with the Boston Symphony Orchestra under the direction of Karl Muck. Between 1914–17 he played in a string quartet in San Mateo, Calif., with NIKOLAI SOKOLOFF. He also taught at the New England Conservatory from 1916–20. From 1920–21 he played with the Natl. Symphony Orchestra in New York City under the direction of Willem Mengelberg. He took a year off to study with Arnold Rose in Vienna in 1924. Ringwall began his affiliation with the CLEVELAND ORCHESTRA in 1926. He served as assistant conductor from 1926–34 and became associate conductor in 1934. He remained in that position until he resigned in 1956. He performed as either assistant or associate conductor with Sokoloff, ARTUR RODZINSKI, Erich Leinsdorf, and GEO. SZELL. Ringwall also started and directed the twilight and summer pops concerts with the Cleveland Orchestra. In addition to his orchestra duties, Ringwall played in the CLEVELAND STRING QUARTET with Josepf Fuchs and others until 1936. He also hosted a radio program of classical and semiclassical records on WHK and WJW before and after his retirement. A witty and articulate speaker, he was often on the podium at local musical events. He married Lucy Adams in 1915. They had 1 daughter, Rosamond.

**RISKO, JOHN "JOHNNY"** (18 Dec. 1902–13 Jan. 1953), was a popular heavyweight boxer from Cleveland during the 1920s and 1930s. Between 1925–34 he gained fame as a "spoiler" of the dreams of aspiring heavyweight champions. Risko was born in Austria-Hungary in what is now Czechoslovakia. Arriving in Cleveland at the age of 6, he attended Brownell School on the west side until he was 8. He was soon working at a bakery. Years later, a friend introduced the "Baker Boy" to "Dapper Danny" Dunn (see DANIEL A. DUNN), who had a gym on W. 14th St. With Dunn as his trainer and manager, Risko soon became a local hero as he fought 59 amateur bouts and scored 39 knockouts. FRANKLIN LEWIS of the *Press* wrote that Risko "had the most devastating punch of all the big fellows." The famed New York fight promoter Tex Rickard, after seeing a Risko knockout, said, "I never seen such a fellow."

After turning pro in 1925, Risko was soon a contender for the championship. In his fourth professional bout, against Homer Smith in Elyria, he injured his right shoulder. From then on he counted on his aggressive style, his competitive heart, and a devastating left hook to win fights. Nicknamed "Cleveland's rubber man" because of his ability to absorb opponents' blows, Risko was called the "Trial Horse of Champions." He fought Gene Tunney in Cleveland on 18 Nov. 1925 and lost a close 12-round decision. He defeated both Jack Sharkey and Max Baer, later heavyweight champions of the world. Trailing Baer beginning the 9th round, Risko's windmill style overpowered his young opponent to win the decision. Only Max Schmeling knocked him out in an important fight in 1929. In 17 years as a professional fighter, Risko fought 137 times, won 44 decisions, scored 22 knockouts, lost 36 decisions, and was knocked out 3 times. Risko did not train hard for every bout and was a big spender of his prize-fight earnings. His manager, Danny

Dunn, forced him to invest part of his income in a $100,000 trust fund. Risko joined the Army in 1942 at the age of 40. He married Margaret E. Yoder on 4 May 1930. They were later divorced, and he married Mildred Weber. He had no children.

The **RIVER TERMINAL RAILWAY COMPANY** is a class I "switching" or "belt" line that has been a vital link between Cuyahoga River Valley industries and the main-line railroads into Cleveland. Over the years, approximately 90% of its service has been to steel industries. The River Terminal Railway was incorporated in 1909 as a subsidiary of the Corrigan-McKinney Steel Co. Its original purpose was to serve 2 small blast furnaces on the west side of the CUYAHOGA RIVER. In 1935, Corrigan-McKinney was consolidated into REPUBLIC STEEL, and the River Terminal Railway became a subsidiary of that company. In 1937, the railway's main track was 1.5 mi. long, connecting Republic's blast furnaces with 2 open hearths on the opposite side of the river. It continued to add sidings, locomotives, and freight cars and expanded its service to pick up iron ore from Republic's docks and move it to interchange points with other railroads for movement to plants in Warren and Youngstown; from these points it would pick up coal and move it back to the mills. By 1972 it was moving 120 carloads of coal a day, and 1.5 million tons of iron ore. The railway also hauled huge quantities of iron ore, molten steel, and finished products from one section of Republic's plant to another. During this period, it continued to serve chemical plants and other industries along the Cuyahoga River.

In 1936, the River Terminal Railway was the first railroad in Cleveland to purchase a diesel locomotive. By the late 1950s it had completed the switch from steam to diesel. It was also the first line in Cleveland to install a radio telephone communications system between its main switching tower and all trains. In 1944, 140 workers went on strike over Republic's suspension of a conductor in a dispute over safety regulations. The week-long strike forced the total shutdown of Republic's mills, which employed 4,600 people. Shorter strikes in 1950 and 1957 caused similar shutdowns. Since the 1950s, the company's growth has stabilized, although the number of employees has been reduced approximately 33% by labor contracts and reductions, and various technological improvements that require smaller crews. Its function, however, has remained essentially the same. In 1983, the River Railway Terminal Co. became a subsidiary of the LTV Corp.

**RIVEREDGE TOWNSHIP** occupies a narrow 48-acre strip of land bounded by the Rocky River, CLEVELAND-HOPKINS INTERNATL. AIRPORT, the NASA LEWIS RESEARCH CTR., and I-480. The township was created in 1926 when residents in the western section of BROOK PARK Village, dissatisfied with the results of a bitterly fought election, decided to form their own township. Its name was taken from its location at the edge of the river. In 1932, additional land was added to the township in an effort to obtain federal funding for the construction of the Brookpark Rd. Bridge across the Rocky River. The township was divided in two shortly thereafter, when the city of Cleveland annexed land for the airport. Through the mid-1950s, Riveredge was little more than a truck farm. In 1956, John Baluh purchased the Fischer family land for $70,000. A grocer, Baluh moved into real estate, promoting trailers as affordable housing. Riveredge became a township on wheels, a privately owned trailer park with 243 mobile homes and a population of 477. Its population grew 40-fold after 1960. Riveredge provided residents with fine services, including a volunteer fire department and a police department with a reputation for strict enforcement. When the township went into default in 1978, its fire department was replaced by service from Cleveland and FAIRVIEW PARK. In 1985, the fate of Riveredge Twp. was being disputed in a battle between the cities of Cleveland and Fairview Park over annexation, the expansion of the airport runways, and changes in flight patterns on the airport approaches.

**RIVERSIDE CEMETERY,** a private association organized in Nov. 1875, fulfilled a need, because on the west bank of the CUYAHOGA RIVER, cemeteries were small and few; until the late 1890s, the MONROE ST. CEMETERY was the only Cleveland municipal cemetery there. The Riverside Cemetery Assoc. purchased the Brainard farm's 102.5 acres in Nov. 1875. E. O. Schwaegerl, landscape architect and engineer, prepared a plan. Ground was broken in Apr. 1876, and the area was ready for the 11 Nov. 1876 centennial memorial service featuring president-elect Rutherford B. Hayes, during which eminent persons ceremonially planted trees along the main drive.

Riverside contained over 5 mi. of roads, and 6 acres of lakes spanned by rustic wooden bridges. It was easily available by public or private transit, only 3 mi. from PUBLIC SQUARE. The trustees emphasized the "park" in this park cemetery concept. Each year the superintendent reported that more visitors were attracted to the shady drives and fine views of the Cuyahoga Valley from bluffs reputed to be the burial site for Chief Blackhawk's mother. By 1883 this influx was a problem. Riverside was the cemetery for the the the west side aristocracy, including the Brainards, the Lamsons, the Sessions, and the Rhodeses (historian JAS. FORD RHODES was buried in the family plot). Its devoted support from the community assured its solvency. By 1902, however, the trustees reminded themselves that Riverside was not indifferent to the humble. "It is and ever must be distinctively a cemetery of the masses." In this century, Riverside's acreage has been trimmed by expressways, and its lakes have been drained. It is still attractive; its expansive views of the Cuyahoga Valley remain to be enjoyed.

*Historical Review of Riverside Cemetery Association* (1889).

**ROBB, HUNTER** (30 Sept. 1863–15 May 1940), professor of gynecology at Western Reserve University, was the first physician in Cleveland with special training in gynecology and gynecological pathology. He was a proponent of aseptic surgical techniques. Born in Burlington, N.J., Robb was the son of Thos. and Caroline Woolman Robb. Educated at the Episcopal Academy of Philadelphia, Burlington College, and the University of Pennsylvania, he received his medical degree in 1884 from Pennsylvania. Between 1884–86 he was in residence at the Presbyterian and Episcopal hospitals of Philadelphia. In 1886 he became the assistant of Dr. Howard A. Kelly, who had established what would be known as the Kensington Hospital for Women. When Kelly accepted a post as professor of gynecology and obstetrics at Johns Hopkins in 1889, Robb joined him as an associate in gynecology.

While at Johns Hopkins, Robb began to investigate the contamination of wounds via hands and abdominal drainage tubes. He was interested in the newly developing field of aseptic surgical techniques and published a book on the subject in 1894. One of Robb's associates, Dr. Wm. Steward Halsted, professor of surgery, had introduced rubber gloves for his assistants in surgery. He had contracted with the Goodyear Co. to manufacture 2 pairs of thin experimental gloves for his favorite nurse, who had complained

that the sterilizing solutions used on the hands caused a rash. The gloves proved so satisfactory that Halsted ordered them for all of his assistants. He did not consider them as a preventive device, but Robb began to see the possibilities as he studied infection.

Robb came to Cleveland in 1894 to accept a post as professor of gynecology at WRU. He was also attached to Lakeside Hospital as visiting gynecologist. Robb limited his private practice to this specialty. He continued studies in abdominal surgery and infection, experimenting on animals to study hemorrhage and shock. He advocated rubber gloves and sleeves for operators and assistants, as complete sterilization of the hands was nearly impossible. He was the first physician in Cleveland to use them. He was also the first surgeon in Cleveland to use a gas-ether combination in anesthesia. Robb was a member of the CLEVELAND MEDICAL SOCIETY and the Gynecological Society of Paris and a fellow of the American Gynecological Society. He published scholarly papers on surgical techniques and diseases of women. Retiring in 1914, Robb served as a major in the Medical Corps during WORLD WAR I. He was stationed in the U.S. Robb was married in 1894 to Isabel Adams Hampton, the superintendent of nurses at Johns Hopkins and the author of a standard book on nursing. They had 2 children. Upon her death, Robb remarried in 1929. His second wife was Marion Wilson of New York.

The **ROBERT CASADESUS INTERNATIONAL PIANO COMPETITION** was organized by the Casadesus Society in collaboration with the CLEVELAND INSTITUTE OF MUSIC to honor the memory of Robt. Casadesus (d. Sept. 1972), the great French pianist, composer, and teacher. Cleveland was selected as a site for this biennial event because of the close tie between Casadesus, GEO. SZELL, and the CLEVELAND ORCHESTRA. Organized in 1975, the competition encouraged contestants, all pianists ages 17–32, to attain the finest elements of pianistic excellence, clarity of expression, and the fullest possible commitment to the attributes of Casadesus, while urging their reach into repertory not generally regarded as standard. The initiative to create the competition was taken by his wife, Gaby Casadesus.

The final round of the competition, limited in 1985 to 42 contestants (in 1983, there were 600 applicants), includes the execution, with orchestra (see OHIO CHAMBER ORCHESTRA), of a Mozart concerto. It is an appropriate homage to Robt. Casadesus, an interpreter, without equal, of these concerti. Since 1975, an increasing number of gifted young musicians have been attracted to the competition because of the high standards required. Several past winners are internationally recognized performers. The prizes have also increased in number and prestige over the years. For example, the 6th international piano competition in 1985 offered the following prizes and engagements: 1st prize—$5,000 (presented by Mme Robt. Casadesus and the Robt. Casadesus Society); 2d prize—$2,000 (presented by Miss Alice Tully in memory of Geo. Szell); 3d prize—$1,500 (presented by Mrs. Kenyon C. Bolton in memory of her husband); 4th prize—$1,000 (presented by Mr. and Mrs. Alfred M. Rankin); 5th prize—$750 (presented by Mr. and Mrs. Reynolds Morse); 6th prize—$500 (presented by Mr. and Mrs. Harold Fallon in memory of VICTOR BABIN). There were several special prizes: the S.A.C.E.M. prize—$1,000, offered for the best presentation of a 20th-century French work; the Chopin prize—$500 donated by Mr. Chas. Rybacki; and the Mozart prize—$350 donated by Mrs. Alfred G. Brooks.

The 1st- or 2d-prize winner was invited by the Robt. Laurent Vibert Foundation to stay during the summer of 1986 at the Chateau de Lourmarin (near Aix-en-Provence), France, and to give a recital at the foundation during the stay. The 6 finalists receive the Robt. Casadesus Commemorative Medal. In the 1985 competition, the following engagements were offered with the 1st prize: appearance as a soloist with the Cleveland Orchestra; recital at the Maison Francaise, New York University, New York City; recital at the CLEVELAND MUSEUM OF ART; solo performance with the Orchestre Pasdeloup, Paris, France; solo performance with the Orchestre Philharmonique de Lille, France; broadcast at Radio-France, Paris, France; recital at the Societe Chopin, Lyon, France; recital at the Theatre Nouvelle France, Le Chesnay, France; and recital at the Vendredis Musicaux de Rueil-Malmaison. In 1983, the jury was headed by Elie Siegmeister, an eminent American composer. The jury was international, with Hans Leygraf from the Mozarteum, Salzburg, Austria; Madame Kazuko Yasukawa of the Tokyo University of Arts & Music; Jean-Paul Sevilla of the University of Ottawa, Canada; and Mesdames Lucette Descaves and Gaby Casadesus from Paris. Americans included Grant Johannesen, Vitya Vronsky Babin, and Eunice Podis of the Institute of Music, Cleveland; and John Owings, 1st-place winner of the 1975 Robt. Casadesus Competition.

ROBERTSON, CARL TROWBRIDGE (31 Jan. 1876–2 June 1935), was the central figure of Cleveland's most distinguished journalistic dynasty. He was the son of Geo. A. Robertson, founder and editor of the *Cleveland Morning Recorder*. Born in N. Bloomfield, Trumbull County, Ohio, Robertson graduated from Cleveland CENTRAL HIGH SCHOOL in 1894. In 1898 he graduated from Harvard with majors in chemistry and Semitic languages. After a year as a graduate teaching assistant in chemistry, he returned to Cleveland to begin a career in journalism. Following a short apprenticeship on his father's *Morning Recorder*, Robertson moved to the *PLAIN DEALER* in 1901. He began on the city hall beat, where he remained through the TOM L. JOHNSON era. Promoted to editorial writer and associate editor, he took a pro-Allied position during WORLD WAR I and won decorations for his editorials from the governments of Poland and Greece. Robertson also became a widely recognized authority on contract bridge. The Cleveland Whist Club was the only club he ever joined, and he was a member of its teams that won the national championship in 1902 and 1903 and second place in 1901 and 1904.

Another hobby of Robertson's was exploration. In 1920 he directed an expedition that resulted in the discovery of a previously unknown section of Mammoth Cave, Ky., which was subsequently named Robertson Ave. in his honor. Three years later he crossed the Atlantic in a 3-masted schooner with the CLEVELAND MUSEUM OF NATURAL HISTORY's Blossom expedition to Cape Verde. Robertson's love of travel and exploration led to many *Plain Dealer* articles, including series on Mammoth Cave, the Indiana sand dunes, Portugal, and "Cities of Old Romance." From 1920 until his death, he also contributed a widely followed "Outdoors Diary" to the paper. Married twice, Robertson had a daughter, Jane, from his first marriage, to Maizie Bushea, whom he divorced in 1924. Later that year he married Josephine Wuebbon, a *Plain Dealer* reporter, who accompanied him on his final travel, a tour of North Africa. He is buried near Rabat, Morocco, where he died suddenly. Josephine Robertson enjoyed a distinguished career on the *Plain*

*Dealer*, achieving widespread recognition as a medical reporter. Their son, Donald (Don) Robertson, became a reporter for the *Plain Dealer*, a columnist for the CLEVELAND PRESS, and a noted regional novelist, best known for his fictional account of the East Ohio Gas disaster, *The Greatest Thing since Sliced Bread*.

Shaw, Archer H., *The Plain Dealer* (1942).

ROBINSON, EDWIN "TED" MEADE (1 Nov. 1878–20 Sept. 1946), conducted Cleveland's most prestigious contributors' column in the pages of the *PLAIN DEALER*. He was born in Lima, Ind., which was later renamed Howe after the secondary academy he attended there. After graduating from Wabash College in 1900, he worked briefly for the *Indianapolis Sentinel* and *Indianapolis Journal* before coming to Cleveland in 1905. Joining the CLEVELAND LEADER, Robinson began a column called "Just by the Way," which was characterized by spontaneous wit and comment. He moved to the *Plain Dealer* in 1910, a year after his marriage to Clevelander Martha Coon. Their only child, Ted Robinson, Jr., later was a contributing editor for *Time* magazine.

Under the heading "Philosopher of Folly," Robinson perfected a format in the *Plain Dealer* similar to that being developed simultaneously in the *New York World* as "The Conning Tower" by Franklin Pierce Adams. Robinson's own light verse and wry commentary were complemented by an outpouring of similar fare from regular contributors writing under such noms de plume as "Prof. Si N. Tific," "Homo Seidel," "N. Deavor," and "Sue Burbanite." Eventually more than 600 volunteer writers saw their contributions printed in Robinson's column. Their only other reward was an invitation to an annual contributors' dinner hosted by Robinson from ca. 1912–38. Most of them were gifted amateurs, such as Joe S. Newman, Edward Bushnell, Ernst Altschul, and Helen Ives Gilchrist. Their numbers also produced a few professionals, however, such as Jim Tully, HERMAN FETZER, and Eleanor Clarage.

Robinson's poetry won him renown independent of his role as columnist. His publications included 2 volumes of verse, *Mere Melodies* (1918) and *Pipings and Pannings* (1921), and the novel *Enter Jerry* (1922). Members of the CLEVELAND WRITERS' CLUB voted him their favorite local author in 1930. At the *Plain Dealer*, he became an associate editor as well as the paper's literary editor after 1922. Throughout the 1930s, he lectured on language and philology at Cleveland College. Besides serving as president of the CITY CLUB and the American Press Humorists, Robinson was a vice-president of the CLEVELAND PLAY HOUSE and a member of the ROWFANT CLUB and the American Dialect Society. He died suddenly at the end of his annual summer vacation at Provincetown, Mass. A poem he had written to appear in his column the following morning bore the recurring refrain, "The Autumn comes—and I must go!" He was buried with his parents in Brooklyn, Conn.

ROBINSON, J. B. CO. *See* J. B. ROBINSON COMPANY

ROCK 'N' ROLL. The history of rock 'n' roll music in Cleveland is framed by 2 superbly promoted and successful public-relations coups: the Mar. 1952 "Moon Dog Coronation Ball" created by disc jockey Alan Freed, and the May 1986 announcement that Cleveland has been chosen as the permanent home of the Rock 'n' Roll Hall of Fame & Museum. Far more than New York City, Los Angeles, or any other major commercial and entertainment center,

Cleveland has been the flagship city of the nation in the popularization, growth, and current domination of rock music in American popular culture. Rock 'n' roll music (more commonly and simply called rock) evolved from the black traditions of blues and rhythm 'n' blues music that had developed in urban America in the earlier and mid-20th century. After WORLD WAR II, Freed played rhythm 'n' blues music on Akron station (WAKR), and soon after, as part of the process of opening such music to white performers and for a white audience, he coined, with record retailer Leo Mintz, the expression "rock 'n' roll." By 1951, at his new Cleveland station (WJW-AM) and under his sobriquet "Moon Dog," Freed had generated an enormous audience, both black and white, for this new form. The "Moon Dog Coronation Ball" was the logical extension of his promotion. It gave instant national celebrity to theretofore obscure rhythm 'n' blues (or rock) performers; filled the CLEVELAND ARENA with over 25,000 partisans; and put rock 'n' roll music—and Cleveland as its birthplace—firmly on the map.

Freed himself left for New York City a few years later, but by the mid-1950s, a host of new disc jockeys (including Bill Randle, a central figure also in the popularization of jazz music on radio) and radio stations (including WJW and WERE, all in ferocious competition for audience and ratings) collectively sustained and built the momentum. By the late 1950s, with Elvis Presley, and the early- to mid-1960s, with the Beatles, rock music had begun to evolve into more complex and differentiated subforms, and superseded its black origins. As it grew to overwhelm other types of popular music, Cleveland again was at the forefront, with radio programming innovations on WHK, WGAR, and WIXY in the '60s, and by refining the link between live concerts and radio promotion and airplay. The superior sound quality available on FM stations meant a shift away from AM to FM stations such as WMMS, which has won awards continuously in the 1970s and 1980s as the best rock music station in the country; most of the pioneering AM rock stations have changed both their call letters and their formats, largely to a mix of "soft rock" and standard sentimental ballads or "oldies," the type of music predominant before the rock revolution.

The takeover by FM stations has aided and in turn been aided by the development of LP rock albums (as distinct from separate recordings of individual pieces) and by strengthening the radio-live concert connection, for which the "Moon Dog" event had been the model. Preeminent in this field have been the local promoters Jules and Michael Belkin. Their concerts have regularly filled such arenas as Blossom Music Ctr., the Akron Rubber Bowl, the Richfield Coliseum, the Convention Ctr. Music Hall, and the FRONT ROW THEATER. Most spectacular of all were their "World Series of Rock" annual concerts, which drew crowds in excess of 75,000 to CLEVELAND MUNICIPAL STADIUM in the 1970s and early 1980s. Radio exposure and large-scale concerts in Cleveland have launched many of the most famous and commercially successful individual and group rock performers. Most notable among native Clevelanders were Eric Carmen and in particular the Michael Stanley Band; those whose careers were guaranteed by initial Cleveland exposure include Bruce Springsteen (the 1980s heir to Elvis Presley's title "King of Rock"), Hall & Oates, and even such British heirs to the Beatles as David Bowie and Duran Duran. It is therefore fitting on its merits, even without the massive lobbying by local promoters and political and civil groups, that Cleveland is the home of the Rock 'n' Roll Hall of Fame & Museum.

Christopher A. Colombi, Jr.

**ROCKEFELLER, JOHN D.** (8 July 1839–23 May 1937), an important industrialist and philanthropist, rose from his position as an assistant bookkeeper for a Cleveland commission merchant to become one of the wealthiest men in the U.S. through his efforts in developing the STANDARD OIL CO. Born on a farm near Richfield, N.Y., Rockefeller was the son of Wm. A. and Eliza Davidson Rockefeller. It was his frugal, religious mother from whom he took the moral values that later led him to lead a relatively simple life for a man of such wealth. He came to the Cleveland area with his family in 1853, settling in STRONGSVILLE. Boarding in Cleveland, he attended CENTRAL HIGH SCHOOL from 1853–55. After additional courses at a business college, he became assistant bookkeeper for commission merchants Henry B. Tuttle and Isaac L. Hewitt in Sept. 1855. In Mar. 1859, Rockefeller and Maurice B. Clark established their own commission business, which prospered during the CIVIL WAR.

In 1863, Rockefeller entered the oil business, and in 1865 he left the commission business to work full-time in oil. He organized the Standard Oil Co. and became its largest stockholder when it was chartered in 1870. He directed the company until retiring in 1896, but he retained the title of president until 1911. The oil business made him one of the richest men in the country, worth about $18 million by 1880. He was also involved in other local business ventures: an attempt to develop a sanitarium on his FOREST HILL property and to build a railroad to service it failed in 1875; he held stock in the Cleveland Arcade Co., and in 1905 he built the million-dollar, 16-story ROCKEFELLER BLDG. at Superior Ave. and Bank (W. 6th) St. Rockefeller's business dealings meant that he spent increasingly more time in New York; he bought a home there in 1884 and eventually made that city his legal residence. He nevertheless maintained 2 homes in Cleveland and until 1915 continued to spend summers at the Forest Hill estate with his wife, Laura Celestia Spelman, whom he married on 8 Sept. 1864.

Just as Rockefeller's business success began in Cleveland, his practice of donating to charity began there as well. In 1856 he donated $19.31 to local charities; his charitable donations grew to $250,000 in 1887 and $1.35 million in 1892. Many institutions to which he belonged received donations, including the Erie St. Baptist Church (later the EUCLID AVE. BAPTIST CHURCH), the WESTERN RESERVE HISTORICAL SOCIETY, the EARLY SETTLERS ASSOC., and the YMCA. Rockefeller also provided crucial support for many of Cleveland's benevolent institutions, including the Ragged School (later the Industrial School and the CHILDREN'S AID SOCIETY), BETHEL UNION, the WOMEN'S CHRISTIAN TEMPERANCE UNION and its "friendly inns," ALTA HOUSE, the VISITING NURSES ASSOC., the DORCAS Invalids' Home, and the Children's Fresh Air Camp. He also gave money to the Western Reserve University School of Medicine and the Case School of Applied Science, and he donated to the city more than $865,000 worth of land for use as PARKS, including the SHAKER LAKES and his Forest Hill estate. To insure that his donations went toward worthwhile projects, Rockefeller established several organizations to handle his charitable giving. The Rockefeller Institute for Medical Research was established in 1901, the General Education Board in 1902, and the Rockefeller Foundation (worldwide in its scope) in 1913; the Laura Spelman Rockefeller Memorial was created in 1918 to promote social studies.

Izant, Grace Goulder, *John D. Rockefeller* (1972).

The **ROCKEFELLER BUILDING** is a 17-story office building erected by JOHN D. ROCKEFELLER in 1903–05. The historic WEDDELL HOUSE hotel (1847) previously stood on the site on the corner of Superior and W. 6th St. The Rockefeller Bldg. housed offices of iron, coal, and lake-shipping concerns. The original structure consisted of 7 bays along Superior Ave. at the W. 6th St. corner, and in 1910 an additional 4 bays in the same design were added to the west. In 1920 JOSIAH KIRBY acquired the building, and the name was changed to the Kirby Bldg. Rockefeller was angered by the change and bought the building back, restoring the name in 1923. The Rockefeller Bldg. was designed by KNOX & ELLIOT. The resemblance of its design to that of the Guaranty Bldg. in Buffalo (1885) by Louis Sullivan has often been pointed out. The building is the best example in Cleveland of the "Sullivanesque" style. The characteristics of the style are the emphasis on the vertical columns to express the steel frame underneath, and the interlacing organic-geometric cast-iron ornament on the lower stories. The latter is an especially fine feature of the Rockefeller Bldg. The building is listed in the Natl. Register of Historic Places and was included in the Historic American Bldgs. Survey published in *The Architecture of Cleveland: Twelve Buildings, 1836–1912.*

**ROCKEFELLER PARK** is located on 270 acres on the city's east side. It is actually 3 links in a long chain of parks extending from GORDON PARK on the lakefront to Shaker Hts. Park in SHAKER HTS. The northernmost and largest section, designated the Brookway Div., lies between Gordon Park and WADE PARK; the Cedar Div., in the middle, lies between Euclid Ave. and Ambler Park; and the Fairmount Div. connects Ambler and Shaker Hts. parks. The park and its principal thoroughfare, Martin Luther King, Jr., Dr. (originally Lower East Blvd., and later Liberty Blvd.), follow the meandering course of DOAN BROOK for a distance of about 7 mi.

By deed dated 5 Apr. 1897, JOHN D. and Laura Spelman ROCKEFELLER conveyed to the city of Cleveland parcels of land valued at $270,000 for use as a public park. Rockefeller provided additional gifts for the park and boulevard and the construction of a bridge across the park and boulevard at Superior Ave. Cleveland architect CHAS. F. SCHWEINFURTH designed the bridge, as well as 3 others spanning the boulevard at St. Clair and Wade Park avenues, and at the tracks of the Lake Shore & Michigan Southern Railway. The park was a succession of picturesque walks, picnic spots, playgrounds, and winding drives. Rockefeller Park Lagoon, a large artificial pond stretching from E. 105th St. nearly to Ansel Rd., was stocked with fish, and rowboats could be rented at the boathouse. In winter, skating and curling were popular pastimes. A natural spring near Wade Park Blvd. was frequented by those seeking to avoid unpalatable city water.

On 30 July 1939, 35,000 people attended the dedication of the Cleveland Cultural Gardens, which covered 35 acres in the park. The park was also the site of the Rockefeller Park Greenhouse, built in 1905, and in 1984 continued to supply plants for the parks and other city-owned properties. By reason of the language in the 1897 deed, after Rockefeller's death in 1937, the use of any part of the parkland for other than park or boulevard purposes required the ratification and approval of all of the Rockefeller heirs. In 1958, the living heirs conveyed all right, title, and interest, including reversionary interests and rights to enforce restrictive covenants in the land, to the Rockefeller Bros. Fund, Inc., a New York charitable corporation.

Since 1979, the CLEVELAND FOUNDATION has served as trustee for the Rockefeller Bros. Fund, with a residual interest in the event that the city of Cleveland should violate the terms of the original deed. The decision to pass control to a local watchdog was precipitated by the improper sale of a portion of the parklands in 1969 and the misspending of $10,000 of the Rockefeller Park Capital Improvement Fund to build the HAROLD T. CLARK TENNIS Stadium in 1977. As the surrounding neighborhoods deteriorated over the years, so too did Rockefeller Park. The Cultural Gardens became the frequent target of vandals. The meandering boulevard came to function as a 4-lane highway. In 1960, the once-popular lagoon was partly drained and filled because of complaints about stagnant water; by 1978, what remained was a "waterless, weed-filled eyesore," according to one reporter. Only in the early 1980s was the lagoon rebuilt, to about half its original size.

**ROCKPORT,** one of the northwestern townships of the WESTERN RESERVE, was created on 24 Feb. 1819. Its 22 1-sq.-mi. sections were divided by the Rocky River. In the ensuing years, the cities and villages of LAKEWOOD, ROCKY RIVER, FAIRVIEW PARK, and LINNDALE would be created out of the township. The township's fertile soil encouraged the creation of farms, orchards, vineyards, greenhouses, and nurseries. Clay deposits fostered the production of brick and tile. Datus and Sarah Dean Kelley were the township's first permanent residents. In 1891, the area west of the river was organized as the hamlet of Rocky River; it later became a village (1903) and a city (1930). The area east of the river became the hamlet of Lakewood in 1885; it later became a village (1903) and a city (1911). In 1910, Fairview Village was created out of the southern portion of Rocky River. By the 1980s, the former township was given over principally to suburban residential communities.

**ROCKY RIVER** is a city on the shore of Lake Erie 9 mi. west of Cleveland. It occupies 4.2 sq. mi. and is bounded by FAIRVIEW PARK on the south and BAY VILLAGE and WESTLAKE on the west. The eastern boundary with LAKEWOOD is marked by the deep gorge of the Rocky River. First explored in 1805, the mouth of the Rocky River was envisioned as a site with a great future. Development of the area was directly related to improvements in transportation. In the early 19th century, it was necessary to ford the river or rely on ferries in order to cross the Rocky River Valley. In 1821, the first bridge across the river was completed. An iron bridge replaced the wooden toll bridge in 1890. In 1910, the 700-ft.-long DETROIT-ROCKY RIVER BRIDGE was constructed. With a central arch of 280 ft., it was the longest unreinforced concrete arch in the world. In 1964, the Clifton-Westlake Bridge, a 1,139-ft. span, was opened north of the Detroit-Rocky River Bridge. The latter was demolished and replaced in 1980. Rocky River was originally part of ROCKPORT Twp., created in 1819. Rocky River was established as a hamlet in 1891, and in 1903 it was incorporated as a village. The area remained predominantly rural, with farms flourishing until the early 1920s, when the transition to a suburban city of homes began. The village became a city in 1930, and the mayor-council form of government was adopted. Throughout the 1940s, greenhouses and truck farming remained profitable businesses; there is little industry. Retail and commercial establishments are concentrated along Detroit Rd. and Center Ridge Rd. The population was 11,237 in 1950, and increased to 21,084 in 1980. Recreational facilities include the Rocky River Reservation of the Metroparks System, a swimming pool, an ice-skating rink, tennis and basketball courts, and a fishing pier.

**RODZINSKI, ARTUR** (2 Jan. 1892–27 Nov. 1958), was the second conductor of the CLEVELAND ORCHESTRA. Rodzinski was born of Polish parents in Dalmatia, Yugoslavia. He was naturalized an American citizen in 1933. Following his father's wishes, he studied law at the University of Vienna and graduated as a Doctor of Law. While studying law, he also studied music at the renowned Vienna Academy of Music. When WORLD WAR I started, his father, a general, was seperated from Rodzinski. That allowed Rodzinski to pursue his first love, music. Throughout the war, he continued to study music at the Vienna Academy, and piano with Saur and Lalewicz. Once in the U.S. he received his Doctor of Music degree from Oberlin College.

When the war ended, Rodzinski was appointed conductor of the Lemberg Opera. In 1925, he accepted a position as assistant conductor of the Philadelphia Orchestra. Before coming to Cleveland in 1933, he directed the Los Angeles Philharmonic Orchestra. With the departure of NIKOLAI SOKOLOFF, Rodzinski became the new conductor for the Cleveland Orchestra in 1933. Under his direction, the orchestra flourished. He initiated opera productions. His direction of the Cleveland Orchestra impressed a national audience. He helped select and train the NBC Symphony Orchestra, coconducted with Arturo Toscanini, and was the first American conductor to be selected for the Salzburg Festival. He conducted the Cleveland Orchestra from 1933–43, leaving because of strained relations with the management. He briefly conducted the New York Philharmonic Orchestra but spent the rest of his life guest-conducting. Rodzinski was married twice. His first marriage, to Mme Ilse, a concert pianist, ended in divorce in 1934. In July 1934, he married Halina Lilpop Wieniawski.

Marsh, Robert C., *The Cleveland Orchestra* (1967).
Musical Arts Assoc. Archives.

**ROGERS, JAMES HOTCHKISS** (7 Feb. 1857–28 Nov. 1940), was a composer, music critic, organist, and teacher (see CLEVELAND INSTITUTE OF MUSIC). He was born in Fair Haven, Conn., the son of an Episcopal clergyman. He began to take piano lessons at the age of 12, then later organ lessons, while being educated at the Lake Forest Academy. From 1875–80, Rogers studied in Europe. In Berlin, he had Erlich and Loeschorn for piano teachers, plus Haupt and Rhode for organ. Two years later, he moved to Paris, studying piano with Fissot, organ with Guilmant, and organ and composition with Widor. In 1883, Rogers moved to Cleveland and became organist at the Euclid Ave. Temple, playing until his retirement in 1932. He also served as organist for the Shaker Hts. Neighborhood Church, and later the FIRST UNITARIAN CHURCH. He was music critic for the *PLAIN DEALER* from 1915–32. He composed over 550 works and taught at the Cleveland School of Music. He was a member of the SINGERS CLUB of Cleveland and the American Society of Composers, Authors & Publishers.

It is said that Rogers in his capacity as music critic was never harsh. Even when Isadora Duncan danced in an outrageous red costume in 1922, Rogers simply wrote after the talk had died down, "all things considered, the orchestra did very well." Rogers himself explained that his role was not to discourage but rather to encourage and advise. He was honored in 1931 by being named organist emeritus of the Euclid Ave. Temple. Upon his retirement, he was again honored, this time by 500 musicians and friends at a farewell dinner. He moved to Pasadena, Calif., that year and resided there until his death. Rogers won international fame as a composer. Besides writing for Catholic and Jewish services, he wrote over 50 compositions for the organ, 5 cantatas, over 130 songs, and instruction books for both piano and organ. His composing style was late Romantic and tended toward the sentimental. One of his best-known works is "In Memoriam," a 6-song cycle centering on Walt Whitman's poems. The composition was written for his son, Henry, who was killed in WORLD WAR I. His Sonata for Organ in E is considered brilliant. The Mass in F, composed much later, shows his respect for more traditional forms. In 1946, the CLEVELAND ORCHESTRA dedicated a program to Rogers, and a portrait, painted by Mary Seymour Brooks, was presented to the WESTERN RESERVE HISTORICAL SOCIETY. Rogers married Alice Abigail in Cleveland. They had 2 children.

Alexander, J. Heywood, *It Must Be Heard* (1981).

**ROGERS, WARREN LINCOLN** (14 Nov. 1877–6 Nov. 1938), was the bishop coadjutor of the Episcopal Diocese of Ohio (1925–30) and the fifth bishop (1930–38). In contrast to his predecessor, WM. LEONARD, Rogers was a person of no independent means charged with administering a diocese during the Great Depression. Rogers was born in Allentown, N.J. His mother was a distant relative of Abraham Lincoln, and her death when Rogers was a young boy forced his move to Michigan to reside with relatives. He converted to Episcopalianism while a student at the University of Michigan, from which he graduated in 1907. He received Bachelor of Divinity degrees from both Union Seminary (1911) and the General Theological Seminary (1912).

Service as a Baptist lay preacher preceded Rogers's Episcopal conversion. After being ordained deacon and priest in 1911, he served as a rector in Detroit (1911–13), Pittsburgh (1913–16), and Jersey City (1916–20) before starting a tenure as dean of Detroit's St. Paul's Cathedral (1920–25). A belief in low-church practices, a selfless character, a likable personality, and a talent for preaching combined to make Rogers a popular churchman who twice was almost elected to the Michigan bishopric. These characteristics attracted the Ohio diocese to him. After assuming the episcopacy, Rogers faced the problems of economic depression, demonstrating an appreciation for both a balance sheet and a balanced budget. Rogers was a member of the Cleveland YMCA board. He was on the boards of trustees of Kenyon College, Western Reserve University, and Lake Erie College and was president of the Harcourt School for Girls in Gambier, Ohio. He was also a member of the American Peace Society.

The Depression meant Rogers had to deal with reduced parish and episcopal circumstances. He cut his salary by half and subjected all other diocesan salaries to 3-month reviews and adjustment. He raised $400,000 for a capital fund and gave up the bishop's home, which was converted into a crippled-children's shelter. He published a diary of his official activities in the issues of *Church Life* to present the membership with a picture of active leadership to keep up morale. His eloquence made him a popular speaker in both the U.S. and England. Rogers's Detroit radio sermons were the first in the country; he was known as the Radio Dean and had a popular nationwide hookup. Helen Clingen Speakman married Rogers in 1911; she died in 1919.

Bishops of Ohio Records, Episcopal Diocese of Ohio Archives.

The **ROGERS EXPEDITION,** led by Maj. Robt. Rogers, crossed the south shore of Lake Erie in Nov. 1760 by boat and on foot with the objective of taking command of Ft. Detroit, following the French & Indian War. Existing journals indicate that the Cleveland area furnished at least 1 landing site. Rogers and his bold but rowdy and rather undisciplined troops were ordered by Brig. Gen. Monckton to take possession of Ft. Detroit. With Presque Isle as a starting point, the main group under Rogers traveled by bateaux, stopping at various locations along the way. Simultaneously, Rogers ordered Capt. David Brewer to travel by land, driving a herd of 40 oxen. Accompanying Rogers was GEO. CROGHAN, a trader and deputy superintendent of Indian affairs under Sir Wm. Johnson. His familiarity and friendship with the Indians aided the safe passage of the expedition and eased tensions upon their arrival at Ft. Detroit. Journals of both Rogers and Croghan relating this journey exist. Included in them is a description of a meeting with a group of Ottawa Indians from Detroit. Some historians maintain that the location of this meeting was the CUYAHOGA RIVER. However, the journals fail to concur upon dates and locations and contain uncertain names of rivers and creeks. Recent opinion favors the CHAGRIN RIVER as the location of this meeting.

Rogers, Robert, *Journal of Robert Rogers* (1933).
Thwaites, Ruben G., *Early Western Travels, 1748–1846* (1904).
Volwiler, Albert T., *Geo. Croghan and the Westward Movement* (1926).

**ROMAN CATHOLIC CEMETERIES** are integral to the religion's practice. Under canon law, Catholics should be buried in cemeteries established by a parish, several parishes, or the diocese. Lacking that, the consecrated section of a non-Catholic one may suffice, or each grave may be blessed at entombment. In 1847, when LOUIS AMADEUS RAPPE came to the new Diocese of Cleveland, he found many Irish and German Catholic immigrants who had few supporting institutions, such as cemeteries. ST. MARY'S ON THE FLATS established in 1839, may have had a burying ground nearby for those unable to afford ERIE ST. CEMETERY. However, until Bp. Rappe purchased 16 acres on Kinsman (now Woodland) Ave. for St. Joseph (1849), Cleveland's first Catholic cemetery, most faithful, such as the first pastor, Fr. John Dillon, were buried at Erie St. Later he and others were reinterred in Catholic cemeteries. Bp. Rappe also established St. John Cemetery near the public WOODLAWN CEMETERY. In Cuyahoga County, 10 cemeteries are parochial, and 4 are diocesan in origin. Seven parish cemeteries were formed during Bp. Rappe's tenure (1847–70). Bp. RICHARD GILMOUR (1872–91), discouraging individual parish plots, promoted consolidated cemeteries. Bp. IGNATIUS HORSTMANN (1892–1908) and Archbp. EDWARD HOBAN (1945-1966) pursued this policy by opening, respectively, Calvary (1893) on Cleveland's southeast side and Holy Cross (1950) in a western suburb, BROOK PARK.

Parish cemeteries evoke a ministry to diverse groups. St. Mary's of the Assumption (1851), Brook Park, provided a burying ground for neighboring German Catholic farmers. St. Lawrence mission church (1851), INDEPENDENCE, began a cemetery that remains under the care of St. Michael Parish. Tucked beside the church, St. Patrick's plot reportedly began in 1853. In OLMSTED FALLS, St. Mary of the Falls parish (1854) has death records that may date the cemetery to 1856. E. Cleveland St. Paul, EUCLID, began its church and cemetery in 1860; 35 children, victims of the COLLINWOOD SCHOOL FIRE, are buried there. Berea's St. Mary, an Irish parish, formed the Depot St. cemetery (1861). St. Mary (1854), on Cleveland's Carroll Ave., established its cemetery (1861) on W. 41st and Clark. Most buried were German Catholics, but some were CZECHS from St. Procop, and others ITALIANS from ST.

ROCCO. The last 3 parish cemeteries to have been established were outside of Cleveland. Holy Family (1872), PARMA, opened a cemetery in 1873. St. Adalbert (1873), BEREA, ministering to Polish quarry workers, established a cemetery east of town in 1875. IMMACULATE HEART OF MARY (1894) has its church in Cleveland's Polish neighborhood, but its cemetery is in CUYAHOGA HTS.

**ROMANIANS.** Among the new Southern and East European immigrants coming to Cleveland in the late 1800s were an increasing number of ethnic Romanians. Most of them emigrated from the province of Transylvania, which at that time was a part of Austria-Hungary. Other Cleveland Romanians came from the province of Bucovina on the Polish and Russian borders, which was also a part of Austria-Hungary before WORLD WAR I. There were also a number of JEWS from the Old Kingdom of Romania. The first Romanians in any significant numbers came to Cleveland as solitary immigrants, usually at the urging of Hungarian, Saxon, Swabian, and Jewish acquaintances from back home, who had emigrated earlier. The flow of Romanian immigrants grew steadily and continued unabated until the outbreak of World War I. By that time, there were about 12,000 ethnic Romanians in Cleveland. The overwhelming number of them were of peasant stock who found immigration an alternative to the restrictive social, political, and economic possibilities in their homeland. The Romanians settled near their places of employment, so they could walk to and from work. The largest concentration was on the west side, between W. 45th and W. 65th streets, immediately north and south of Detroit Ave. There they gradually replaced the Irish and Germans. Most worked in nearby commercial and industrial businesses, such as WESTINGHOUSE, GENERAL ELECTRIC, AMERICAN SHIPBUILDING, Hill Clutch, Walker Mfg., the ore docks, the stockyards, meat-packing houses, and knitting mills. A sizable group was also located in the E. 65th-St. Clair area prior to and after World War I. There were also pockets of Romanians farther east in the COLLINWOOD area, in the Buckeye Rd. section among the HUNGARIANS, in BEDFORD, and in the eastern part of LAKEWOOD. Nearby, the city of Lorain had its own Romanian community, which was in contact with the Romanians of Cleveland. Even though most of the Romanians were farmers from small villages, few settled in rural areas. They had no capital to buy land or farming tools. Eventually, when they had some money, a few did venture to buy farms nearby.

In the early years of Romanian immigration, fraternal, cultural, and social clubs, small businesses, and other organizations were established in each neighborhood. None of the neighborhoods, except that on the west side, was large, stable, or strong enough to become self-sufficient and maintain such enterprises for any length of time. Many of the isolated Romanians traveled to the larger and better-organized neighborhood on the west side to attend church services and other important Romanian functions. Many of those scattered throughout Greater Cleveland eventually moved to the west side, and their former neighborhood communities gradually died out. By the time of WORLD WAR II, most Romanians lived on the west side. Initially, most of the Romanians were males who had no intention of remaining. They ranged in age from their late teens to about 40 and lived in boarding houses run by enterprising Romanian families from the same districts as the boarders. Since most intended to return to their homeland, they made no serious effort to learn English. Those who had steady jobs and foresaw their future in this country started to bring over their families. Others went back to marry and returned with their brides to Cleveland. Before World War I, permanent settlement in Cleveland appeared to be the choice of a minority of the immigrants.

After the war, when the provinces of Transylvania and Bucovina, from which most of the Cleveland Romanians had emigrated, became a part of Greater Romania, nearly half of the immigrant population returned to their native land. In the 1920s, only about 6,000 Romanians were left in Cleveland. After the Quota Act of 1921 and subsequent restrictive immigration legislation, few Romanians were able to get visas for this country. At the same time, some Cleveland Romanians moved to other American cities during the postwar boom. Those who remained organized parishes and other Romanian organizations on a more permanent basis. By 1940, there were only 4,000 Clevelanders who identified themselves as Romanians and participated, even sporadically, in Romanian-organized activities. In the years following World War II, beginning ca. 1948, about 2,000 Romanians arrived in Cleveland. These latest immigrants were mostly political refugees, displaced persons, and expatriates. Unlike their predecessors, many were intellectuals, professionals, and skilled tradespeople who had fled Romania primarily because of their disagreement with the Communist regime that had been installed there after World War II. They came not only from the current province of Transylvania, as did most of the earlier immigrants, but also from all parts of Romania and elsewhere. A considerable number of Romanians from the Yugoslav province of Banat also settled in Cleveland during this post-World War II period. The compact west side Romanian community started to break up after World War II, when the American-born offspring moved farther west to the suburbs. The old neighborhood was slowly resettled by Appalachians, Hispanics, and, more recently, Arabic and Asiatic peoples. At the same time, some of the newly arrived Romanian immigrants settled in this area. Only a few old-time Romanians, mostly elderly people, remained in the original neighborhood in the 1980s.

The formal organization of Romanian life in Cleveland closely followed the pattern of other ethnic groups. In the earliest period, before adequate safety regulations, there were numerous industrial accidents and no hospitalization plans, workmen's compensation, social security, or other governmental welfare programs to meet emergencies, so each ethnic group relied largely upon its own resources. This situation gave birth to the organization of fraternal and mutual-benefit societies to aid contributing members in case of illness or death. On 2 Nov. 1902, 42 Romanian Clevelanders founded the Carpatina Society, among the first such mutual-benefit organizations in America. Similar fraternal and cultural societies were soon organized in other sections of Cleveland having a Romanian population. With the breakup of some of the neighborhoods, the societies joined the larger and stronger Carpatina Society. The society built a hall, offices, and facilities in 1917 at 1303 W. 58th St., which became the center of many Romanian social, cultural, family, civic, and patriotic activities. The society sponsored a youth organization, sports teams, ladies' auxiliaries, and other groups. With the change of the neighborhood, the hall was sold in 1973; 24 acres were purchased in WESTLAKE with the view of constructing new facilities. In the meantime, meetings and activities continued to be held in existing Romanian church halls.

Shortly after organizing mutual-benefit societies, Romanians founded parishes and built modest churches, parish houses, educational classrooms, social rooms, and other facilities. The Romanian parishes not only carried out religious services and programs but also planned nonreligious cultural and social activities to help preserve and perpetuate Old World traditions. The majority of the Romanians in Cleveland belong to the Orthodox Christian church. Most of the others are BYZANTINE RITE CATHOLICS, known also as Greek Catholics or Uniates. There are also a number of Romanian Baptists, and recently, in the 1970s and 1980s, other smaller Protestant groups, such as Pentecostals, Nazarenes, Adventists, and JEHOVAH'S WITNESSES, became active in the community. Initially, Romanians belonging to the Orthodox church attended services in other ethnic Orthodox, Catholic, or Protestant churches. On 15 Aug. 1904, they organized ST. MARY'S, the first Romanian Orthodox church in America. The metropolitan of Transylvania sent Fr. Moise Balea in 1905, who held services in rented quarters until a church was built in 1907 at 6201 Detroit Ave. In 1960, the church moved to 3256 Warren Rd. In 1936, a faction broke away from St. Mary's to found the Buna Vestire parish on W. 57th St. The parish later moved to ROCKY RIVER. Three Byzantine Rite Romanian churches were established in Cleveland. The oldest parish, ST. HELENA'S, was founded on 19 Nov. 1905. In 1986 it was still located at its original site at 1367 W. 65th St. The other remaining Byzantine church is Most Holy Trinity, located in Chesterland. Six Romanian Baptists in 1911, with the help of Rev. L. A. Gredys, established a parish, and in 1922 they built a church at 1416 W. 57th St. Their numbers increased considerably after World War II with an influx of many coreligionists from Romania.

Cleveland is the national headquarters of the majority of Romanian mutual-benefit societies in America and Canada. The 2 existing national organizations merged into the Union & League of Romanian Societies in 1928 and in 1930 built a headquarters at 5703 Detroit Ave. The building was sold in 1984, and another one was purchased in N. OLMSTED. Cleveland has also been a center for the preservation of Romanian culture. The local societies and churches have regularly sponsored many cultural events, such as lectures, plays, folk dancing, and art exhibits. There were always a number of Romanian folk dance groups. The Sezatoare group, founded by Nicolae Smarandescu in 1959, remained active in 1986. Another group, the Miorita, was associated largely with the post-World War II emigres. Theodore Andrica, former nationalities editor of the *CLEVELAND PRESS* for over 40 years, founded the Cultural Assoc. of Americans of Romanian Descent in 1940, with branches in a number of cities. The association published the *New Pioneer* to disseminate information and deal with general cultural subjects of interest to Romanians. A number of Romanian newspapers, with a national circulation, were published in Cleveland, including *Romanul*, *Solia*, *Unirea*, *Foia Poporului*, and *America*, the official organ of the union and league, which has appeared uninterruptedly since 1906. Though the Cleveland Romanian community has lost its physical cohesiveness in the post-World War II period, the sizable influx of postwar emigres and the strong position of the Orthodox church, particularly St. Mary's, have helped the community maintain a variety of traditional programs and events into the 1980s.

Rev. Vasile Hategan

The **ROOT AND MCBRIDE COMPANY** was one of the leading pioneer wholesale dry-goods firms in the Midwest. The company started in 1849 as a general store, called the City Mills store, on the corner of Superior and Seneca (W. 3rd) streets. City Mills was operated by A. M. Perry & Co., a partnership of 2 local merchants, Ashbel M. Perry and Ralph R. Root. In 1857, Root and another local retailer, Edmund P. Morgan, purchased Perry's interest in the City Mills store, changing its name to the Morgan & Root Co. That same year, Leander McBride came to Cleveland to work at the store as a clerk. By 1864, Morgan & Root saw an opportunity for greater expansion and invited McBride and several other individuals to become partners in the firm, reflected in its new name, Morgan, Root & Co. The store also moved to a bigger location, at the corner of Frankfort and Bank streets (now W. 6th). In 1868, Morgan, Root & Co. sold its retail division and concentrated its energies on the wholesale distribution of dry goods and notions, including floor coverings, curtains, blankets, toys, and men's clothing. In the meantime, Leander McBride's brother, John H., joined the firm. In 1884, Edmund Morgan retired, and the McBride brothers purchased his interest in the business, which then became the Root & McBride Bros. Co., located in a new 6-story building at 1250 W. 6th St. Eleven years later, it was incorporated as the Root & McBride Co.

The McBride family managed the firm in the early 20th century. Leander, John, and Malcolm McBride were very active in civic affairs. Under Malcolm McBride, the company gained national recognition in the 1930s. By 1949, its 150 employees were supplying dry goods to many retail merchants in 6 midwestern states. In the early 1950s, the dry-goods and textile businesses underwent a recession. Although the industries began to recover in 1953, Root & McBride did not experience that upswing in business. In March of that year, a group of investors took control of the firm under the name of the Natl. Investment Co. By the end of 1953, Root & McBride was liquidated. It officially went out of business on 21 May 1954. The corporate name of Root & McBride was retained and acquired in 1958 by the Meskin-Davis Co., a distributor of surplus stock.

**RORIMER, LOUIS** (12 Sept. 1872–30 Nov. 1939), was a teacher, an artisan, a decorator, and a businessman who was a pioneer in interior decorating and its utilitarian use. Rorimer, the son of a wealthy tobacco dealer of German descent, was born in Cleveland. He was educated under sculptor Henry Matzen at the Manual Training School. When he was 16, he went to Europe to study. He attended the Kunstsgewer in Munich and the Academie Julien in Paris for decorative arts. While in Paris, Rorimer met Oscar Wilde and was impressed with the way in which beautiful language could be used in everyday speech. He also met and befriended Gertrude Stein and told her that her collection of Picassos would be worthless. Upon returning to Cleveland in 1893, Rorimer established a studio in the ARCADE. He later merged with the Brooks Household Arts Co., a consultant firm in interior design. They became the nationally known Rorimer Brooks Co. The company moved to the Garfield Bldg. after the merger, then, with constant growth and expansion, relocated to 2232 Euclid Ave. Their clientele included the Statler Hotels, the Chamber of Commerce Clubs, and the Van Sweringen offices.

Rorimer stated that he was an artist first, a teacher second, and a businessman third. He believed that art was an essential ingredient in daily life. With this philosophy, he vigorously promoted and used the cleaner, more utilitarian designs of modern art, as opposed to Victorian styles. From 1918–36, Rorimer taught architectural design at the Cleveland School of Art. He exhibited drawings, sculpture, and furniture at the CLEVELAND MUSEUM OF ART. His studios were stocked with treasures from Spain, Britain, and France. Rorimer was a past vice-president and on the board of directors of the American Institute of Decorators until his death. He was president of the CLEVELAND PLAY HOUSE from 1932–34. He was a member of the 1925 Hoover Commission from the U.S. to the Paris Industrial Arts Exposition. Rorimer married Edith Joseph in 1903 and had 2 children, Louise and Jas. J. James became a curator at the New York Metropolitan Museum of Art.

Pina, Leslie Ann, "Rorimer-Brooks: Interior Design in Cleveland, Ohio 1896–1957," Ph. D. dissertation, CWRU, 1986.

**ROSA, STORM** (18 July 1791–3 May 1834), was a pioneer doctor in the Western Reserve and one of the first to advocate homeopathic medicine in Ohio. Rosa was born in Coxsackie, N.Y. He attended and later taught at the village school. At the age of 22 he entered into medical studies under various local doctors, and in 1816 he received a license to practice from the Medical Society of Seneca County, N.Y. Soon after, he established a practice in Madison, Ohio. After 2 years, Rosa moved to Painesville. He developed a good practice and had a substantial house built there. Between 1834–35, he taught at the new Medical College of Willoughby University as adjunct professor of materia medica. At the college's first commencement, he received an honorary degree.

A man of diverse interests, Rosa served as an associate judge of the court of common pleas in Geauga County, and as secretary for the Geauga County Agricultural Society. He also, from 1838–39, was editor of the *Painesville Telegraph*. In 1843, Rosa turned to homeopathic medicine. He promoted its principles against attacks from the local medical profession and helped found the Homeopathic Society, which met in Burton in 1847. In 1840 the faculty of the Eclectic Medical Institute in Cincinnati established a chair of HOMEOPATHY; Rosa was unanimously elected to fill the position at a convention of homeopathic doctors in Cleveland. The chair was abolished after the first semester, when Rosa converted too many students and other professors to the principles of homeopathic medicine. He returned to Painesville and in 1850 became professor of gynecology and obstetrics at the Cleveland Homeopathic Medical College. He held this position for many years despite numerous invitations to teach elsewhere. In 1852, Rosa, with Dr. Horatio Gatchell, built a stone bath house at Little Mountain for water cures. A gymnasium was also built to provide the benefits of exercise. The experiment faltered, lasting only a few years. Rosa married Sophia Kimball on 4 Aug. 1818. They had 2 children, Catherine and Lemuel.

Biographical File, Howard Dittrick Museum of Historical Medicine.

**ROSE, BENJAMIN** (1828–28 June 1908), was a Cleveland businessman noted particularly for his philanthropic interest in the care of the aged. Rose was born in Warwickshire, England, coming to the U.S. at the age of 10 and settling in Cincinnati with his family. At the age of 12 he got his first job as a laborer in a Cincinnati slaughterhouse. The following year he moved to Cleveland and went into the provision business with his brother. After a partnership with Chauncey Prentiss, Rose organized the CLEVELAND PROVISION CO. in 1877. Cleveland Provision became the largest meat packer in Cleveland, its success based largely on Rose's innovative practices, most of which centered about the use of refrigeration both in his packinghouse and in rail and ocean shipping of his products. In 1908, Rose used some of his capital to build the Rose Bldg. at E. 9th St. and Prospect Ave., the largest office building in Ohio at that time. He died while on a trip to England in 1908. Rose left a permanent memorial to Cleveland by bequeathing his fortune of $3 million to charity. The funds made possible the establishment of the BENJAMIN ROSE INSTITUTE, which provides relief and assistance to the needy aged and to curable crippled children.

**ROSE, WILLIAM GANSON** (29 Oct. 1878–16 Aug. 1957), was an author, historian, lecturer, advertising executive, and civic promoter. He was born in Cleveland, the son of Wm. R. and Eliza E. Ganson Rose. He attended Cleveland public schools, graduating from CENTRAL HIGH SCHOOL and in 1901 from Adelbert College of Western Reserve University. Following graduation, he served as dramatic editor of the *PLAIN DEALER* from 1902–07. He became an advertising and business counsel to several banks and private industries, and in 1915 he formed his own advertising and public-relations firm, Wm. G. Rose, Inc. During his career, Rose managed fairs and expositions, including the Cleveland INDUSTRIAL EXPOSITION (1909); the Detroit Industrial Exposition (1910); the Newark, N.J., Industrial Exposition (1912); the Cleveland ART LOAN EXPOSITION (1913); and the first Cleveland Electrical Exposition (1914). In 1930 he managed the Internatl. Gordon Bennett Races held in Cleveland, and in 1936–37 he promoted and directed the GREAT LAKES EXPOSITION. He directed 5 4th of July FESTIVALS OF FREEDOM, often held in the Cleveland Stadium, and served as chairman and director of the cultural, educational, and entertainment features of the Cleveland Sesquicentennial in 1946.

Rose also served on the City Planning Commission in 1915, and in 1916–17 he chaired the Committee of 100 Organizations, which promoted and ultimately secured passage of the $2.5 million Public Hall Bond Issue. He was president of the CLEVELAND ADVERTISING CLUB from 1914–16; president of the Advertising Affiliation of Buffalo, Cleveland, Detroit, and Rochester in 1915; and vice-president of the Financial Advertisers Assoc. of Advertising Clubs of the World from 1918–19. He was program chairman of the Cleveland Chamber of Commerce from 1927–57 and an organizer of the Better Business Bureau in 1913. He served on the boards of HIRAM HOUSE, the Welfare Fed., and the Community Fund. He was director of the American Red Cross Campaign of Ohio, Indiana, and Kentucky in 1917 and in 1931 was chairman of the Cuyahoga County Emergency Relief Committee. He belonged to the American Press Humorists, Delta Tau Delta, the ROTARY, and the CLEVELAND ATHLETIC CLUB. Often described as "Cleveland's number one booster," he was a raconteur and toastmaster at many public and private celebrations.

Rose wrote numerous articles for newspapers and magazines, as well as several books, including *The Comic History of Cleveland* (in collaboration with his father, 1901); *The Ginger Cure* (1911); *Putting Marshville on the Map* (1912); and *Success in Business* (1913). On 10 Apr. 1950, the WORLD PUBLISHING CO. of Cleveland published 10,000 copies of his comprehensive 1-volume history of Cleveland, entitled *Cleveland, The Making of a City*, a chronologically arranged narrative account of the community from its founding through 1946. Rose died in Cleveland and was buried in LAKE VIEW CEMETERY. His wife, the former Julia Miller, whom he had married in 1927, died on 19 May 1976. The couple had 1 daughter, Mrs. Walter R. (Nancy) Jones.

Wm. Ganson Rose Papers, WRHS.

**ROSE, WILLIAM GREY** (23 Sept. 1829–15 Sept. 1899), a successful businessman and real-estate developer, served as Republican mayor of Cleveland 1877–78 and 1891–92. Rose was born in Mercer County, Pa., the youngest of 11 children of James and Martha McKinley Rose. He attended public schools, Austinburg Grand River Institute in Ohio, and the Beaver Academy. He studied law in Mercer, was admitted to the Pennsylvania bar in Apr. 1855, and prac-

ticed law there. He served in the Pennsylvania legislature 1857–58. Rose came to Cleveland in 1865 and became a member of the Cuyahoga County bar. He helped found the CLEVELAND PROVISION CO., prospered in the oil-refining business, and developed real estate subdivisions east and south of the city. By the age of 45 he was independently wealthy.

Elected mayor during a depression resulting from the Panic of 1873, Rose cut the administrative expenses of the city government. As mayor, he helped to prevent violence during the strike against the Lake Shore & Michigan Southern Railway in 1877 and the coopers' strike the same year. His second term as mayor was the first under a new charter granted by the state known as the federal plan of government. He was an able administrator, providing the city with cleaner streets and better enforcement of city contracts, and he supported lower gas rates to consumers. He married Martha E. Parmelee in Mar. 1858, and they had 4 children, (Alice) Evelyn (Mrs. Chas. R. Miller), Hudson, Frederick Holland, and Wm. Kent. Rose died in Cleveland at age 69.

**ROSE-MARY, THE JOHANNA GRASSELLI REHABILITATION AND EDUCATION CENTER,** began as a home for crippled children and currently (1986) provides residential evaluation and treatment for multihandicapped children ages 3–12. The home was opened in 1922 by the Catholic Diocese of Cleveland on 7 acres of property in Euclid donated by CAESAR GRASSELLI in memory of his wife, Johanna, an invalid for many years. The former Grasselli summer home was named for its first patron, a crippled orphan found shortly after her birth in Youngstown. Prior to the establishment of this facility, Catholic crippled children were cared for at the Holy Cross Home, an Episcopal agency. However, a change in policy limited services to Episcopal children, and in response Grasselli offered the summer house to the Diocese of Cleveland. The Sisters of the Holy Humility of Mary staffed the home with its capacity of 24. The Catholic Daughters of America maintained and raised funds for the home, and Mr. Grasselli, who visited each week, filled every need for medical equipment and furnishings. Rose-Mary Home was the first treatment center of its kind in the world, where modern treatment methods were employed to correct physical handicaps of children with strong, healthy minds. Through physical therapy, disabled children were taught to reeducate weak muscles to achieve as close to normal function as possible. The treatment took place in a homelike setting, with furnishings and utensils especially designed for the children. In 1943, the adjacent Wm. Delaney house and property were acquired and used for staff sleeping quarters. To provide additional space for treatment, a new building was completed in 1949 with Catholic Charity funds on the same site at 19350 Euclid. The facility concentrated all activities of the home under one roof and permitted care of up to 50 children. In 1967, the home redefined its mission to become a residential evaluation and training center for retarded children. It admitted children in the 30–50 IQ range, 3–12 years old, for a 14-to-18-month stay. The goal was to prepare them to enter existing programs in the community. In addition, Rose-Mary worked with parents, teaching them how to manage a retarded child. Rose-Mary, which currently (1986) has 40 residents, is still staffed by Holy Humility sisters and is funded by CATHOLIC CHARITIES and the UNITED WAY.

**ROSENBLUM, MAX** (5 Dec. 1877–5 Sept. 1953), owned the Rosenblum-Celtics professional BASKETBALL team and was known as the father of sandlot BASEBALL in Cleveland. One of 6 children, Max was born in Austria-

Hungary, the son of Adolph and Esther Rosenblum. His family came to the U.S. when he was 6 years old and settled in Cleveland ca. 1885. He attended public schools but left school after the 6th grade. Later, he enrolled in Canton Business College to study bookkeeping. When he was 17, he worked as an errand boy for a clothier, and by 1902 he was manager of the Enterprise Credit Clothing Co. at 32 Public Square. In 1910, he opened his own clothing store at 2014 Ontario, selling clothes on credit. In 1919, Rosenblum's, Inc., moved to 321 Euclid Ave. His slogan was "It's easy to pay the Rosenblum Way."

When the American Basketball League was founded in 1925, Rosenblum, owner of the Cleveland Rosenblums, was one of the leaders in establishing the league. His team, managed by I. S. (Nig) Rose, won the league championship in 1925–26, averaging 10,000 attendance in the 2 playoff games at the Public Hall. Seats ranged in price from $.75-$1.65. With the breakup of the championship New York Celtic team at the end of the 1927 season, Rosenblum signed ex-Celtic players Joe Lapchick, Dutch Dehnert, and Pete Barry to play for the Rosenblums, and they regained the league championship in 1928–29 and 1929–30. With the onset of the Depression, attendance at ABA games dwindled. At the beginning of the 1930-31 season, manager Nig Rose, wrote Joe Lapchick that they could guarantee his $1,000-a-month salary for only 4 months of play. Financially unable to finish the season, the team folded in Dec. 1930. Rosenblum continued to arrange independent games with other professional and collegiate teams in Cleveland during the 1930s.

In 1917, Rosenblum ventured into the local sports scene, organizing a softball team; later he was one of the organizers of the Cleveland Amateur Baseball Assoc. and backed numerous sandlot teams. Throughout his life, Rosenblum recognized the value of sports for young people and tirelessly promoted amateur baseball, basketball, FOOTBALL, BOWLING, and soccer teams. He also served as president of the Welfare Assoc. for Jewish Children for 15 years. Rosenblum married Sallie Weiss on 11 Nov. 1900. They had a son, Harvey, and 2 daughters, Mrs. Thelma Sobel and Mrs. Pearl Hartman. After her death in 1938, he married Ann Whitney in 1943. He died in Cleveland at age 75.

**ROSENTHAL, RUDOLPH M.** (7 May 1906–19 June 1979), served 46 years as rabbi and rabbi emeritus at Cleveland's Temple on the Heights, one of America's largest Conservative congregations. Rosenthal was born in Cleveland and studied at Hebrew Union College in Cincinnati. In 1928, following 4 years at Hebrew Union and the University of Cincinnati, where he received a B.A. degree in 1928, he moved to New York City, where he studied at Rabbi Stephen Wise's Jewish Institute of Religion and concurrently at Columbia University's Teachers College. In 1932, he received a Master of Hebrew Letters from the former and a Master of Arts degree from the latter. Rosenthal was ordained by Wise in 1932. On the day of his ordination, he married Bertha Becker. He accepted a position in Louisiana, serving several small congregations along the Mississippi River. In 1933, he accepted a call to the pulpit from Congregation B'NAI JESHURUN, the Temple on the Heights, in Cleveland. During his rabbinical tenure, Rosenthal was active in Jewish communal affairs, civic activities, and civil-rights work. An ardent Zionist and supporter of Stephen Wise, Rosenthal established the Heights Temple Zionist District, making the congregation the first in America to become affiliated with the Zionist Organization of America. In 1936, he was selected as a delegate to the first World Jewish Congress, held in Geneva. He also served as

president of the local chapter of the American Jewish Congress.

Rosenthal was imbued with the social activism of his mentor Rabbi Wise and was active in the struggle for civil rights. He was cochairman of the NAACP Membership Campaign in 1960 and received the Freedom Plaque given by the NAACP in 1975. He worked on behalf of the United Negro College Fund and was a board member of Wilberforce University, as well as served as treasurer of the Wilberforce University Foundation. In 1959, Rosenthal was appointed to the GREATER CLEVELAND SAFETY COUNCIL, and in 1974, he served on Mayor Ralph Perk's Crime Commission. Among his other civic activities were membership on the city's Commission on Juvenile Delinquency, on the board of trustees of the NATIONALITIES SERVICE CTR., and in the Ohio Grand Jury Assoc., and appointment in 1952 as the first Jewish chaplain of the CLEVELAND FIRE DEPT. During his career, Rosenthal received a dozen honorary doctoral degrees and several citations for his humanitarian work. In 1964, he was named "Humanitarian of the Year" by the City of Hope, and in 1977 he received the "Distinguished Son of Ohio" award from the Civic Recognition Committee of Ohio.

Rabbi Rudolph M. Rosenthal Papers, WRHS.

**ROSENWASSER, MARCUS** (4 Oct. 1846–4 Sept. 1910), was an eminent physician and teacher of medicine. Born in Bohemia, Rosenwasser was one of 8 children brought to Cleveland by their parents in 1852. He attended Cleveland's public schools and graduated from CENTRAL HIGH SCHOOL in 1864. He then returned to Europe to study medicine at the universities of Prague and Wurzburg. He worked in European hospitals and completed postgraduate work at Wurzburg and the University of Vienna before returning to Cleveland in 1868. Rosenwasser specialized in obstetrics and gynecology. He served many years as an obstetrician at St. Ann's Maternity Hospital in Woodland, where he was in great demand by the immigrant community. He was also a resident gynecologist at MT. SINAI Hospital and served as a consulting gynecologist at ST. JOHN HOSPITAL and City Hospital. He was a visiting surgeon at Cleveland General Hospital. Rosenwasser was a professor of gynecology at the Cleveland College for Physicians & Surgeons and a professor of obstetrics at Wooster University Medical School. He served as dean at both institutions.

In 1901, Mayor TOM L. JOHNSON appointed Rosenwasser president of the CLEVELAND BOARD OF HEALTH, a position he held for 2 years. Rosenwasser belonged to several medical societies and was a fellow of the Assoc. of Obstetricians, vice-president of the American Society of Obstetricians & Gynecologists, and president for 1 term of the CUYAHOGA COUNTY MEDICAL SOCIETY. Although not an active Jewish communal leader, Rosenwasser rendered service to the community as volunteer physician for the JEWISH ORPHAN HOME for 42 years. He was also a board member of the TEMPLE and was a member of B'NAI B'RITH and the EXCELSIOR CLUB.

The **ROTARY CLUB OF CLEVELAND** has been a prolific civic-service club since its formation by 25 charter members on 1 Dec. 1910. Chas. R. Miller served as the first president of the Cleveland club, and Wm. Downie as secretary. By 1935 the club had 400 members and was second in size only to the 550-member original club in Chicago (est. 23 Feb. 1905). Established for "the promotion of the business interests of its members," for "the promotion of good fellowship," and for "the advancement of the best interests of Cleveland, and the spreading of civic pride and loyalty among and between her citizens and her commercial enterprises," the Rotary Club accepted as a member "any person who is engaged as proprietor, partner, corporate officer, manager or representative of any concern in any legitimate business or professional undertaking the City . . . provided that . . . he is [not] engaged in a line of business already represented by a member of this club." The overt promotion of members' businesses soon gave way to the larger goal of community service. In 1914, the Rotarians began a "big brother" program to help worthy boys, but of greater significance was their aid to crippled children. The Cleveland Rotarians, along with their colleagues in Elyria, pioneered and originated Rotarian work on behalf of crippled children; the Cleveland club helped form the national and Ohio branches of the SOCIETY FOR CRIPPLED CHILDREN, promoted legislation to provide services to the disabled, and aided crippled children locally through its sponsorship of surveys of medical needs and its provision of funds and material assistance in founding clinics and such facilities as Camp Cheerful. By 1954, club donations to the Society for Crippled Children totaled $200,000. In 1945, the Rotary Club of Cleveland received the Rotary Internatl. President's Award for its "significant achievements in promoting the ideal of service" in its work for crippled children and on behalf of military inductees and veterans during WORLD WAR II.

In May 1941, Cleveland Rotarians established the Cleveland Rotary Foundation to continue to finance charitable projects. By 1953 it had spent $150,000 on various projects and had $90,000 in principal. During the 1950s, 1960s, and 1970s, the club continued its work on behalf of the disabled, but its activities also reflected the changing concerns of the times. In 1957 it established its "good neighbor" awards to recognize efforts to improve Cleveland-area neighborhoods; in 1962 it enrolled its first black member, Albert C. Stewart, assistant research director at Union Carbide; and in 1966 and 1967 it contributed funds for a program to buy poisons, equipment, and trash cans to exterminate rats in HOUGH. Its Medal of Valor awards to honor policemen for heroism in the line of duty began in 1966; in 1968, firemen were included in the awards. The club repeatedly has worked on behalf of troubled youngsters, from its sponsorship of leadership development summer camps in the 1930s, to its project to help find jobs for youths returning from state correctional schools in 1956, to its early 1970s project to help find jobs for school dropouts in cooperation with the public schools' work-study program. During both the 1920s and 1980s, the club regularly honored the area's top high school students. By 1980, the Northeast Ohio District contained 52 Rotary clubs, and the Rotary club of Cleveland had more than 700 members, making it still the 2d-largest in the world. Cleveland hosted Rotary Internatl. conventions in 1925 and again in 1939.

**ROUSE, BENJAMIN** (23 Mar. 1795–5 July 1871), was an honored, influential citizen of Cleveland, considered to be one of the city's pioneer philanthropists. Rouse was born in Boston, Mass. Losing both his parents at the age of 6, he was unable to secure a formal education. He compensated for this inadequacy through common sense and fanatical determination. At the age of 17, he served in the WAR OF 1812. After the war he became a building contractor in association with Peter Osgood. On 12 Aug. 1821, he married Rebecca Elliott Cromwell (see REBECCA ROUSE). They moved to New York in 1824. A strong interest in and devotion to Christianity characterized Rouse's new career as a successful real-estate developer. While in New York, he became deeply interested in the establish-

ment of Sunday schools for the poor of that city. He was so successful in this task that the American Sunday School Union asked him to become their agent in Cleveland, with a commission to open a depository and organize Sunday schools in the Western Reserve. Rouse accepted this appointment and moved to Cleveland with his wife in Oct. 1830.

Cleveland was then a small village of about 1,000 people, with little indication that it would develop into an industrial metropolis. In this "small-town" environment, Rouse established his residence at the northwest corner of Superior St. and PUBLIC SQUARE. He opened a depository of Sunday school books in his home. Rouse spent many years spreading the Gospel both literally and figuratively throughout areas in northern Ohio. In addition, he founded a Tract Society, a Seamen's Friend Society, and several other organizations. He was active in organizing the FIRST BAPTIST CHURCH of Cleveland, in 1833, and for nearly 40 years served as a leading member and deacon. In 1852 he erected the Rouse Bldg. at the corner of Public Square. Rouse died at the age of 76 and was survived by his wife, Rebecca, for 16 more years.

Adella Hughes Family Papers, WRHS.

**ROUSE, REBECCA CROMWELL** (30 Oct. 1799–23 Dec. 1887), was a leading 19th-century social-services organizer and reformer in Cleveland. She is regarded as the founder of the MARTHA WASHINGTON & DORCAS SOCIETY and the organizer of the SOLDIERS' AID SOCIETY of Cleveland. Born in Salem, Mass., Rouse is described by Mary Ingham in *Women of Cleveland* as the "founder of woman's work in Cleveland." Educated in religion and the classics, Rouse also acquired worldly knowledge through her extensive travels abroad. In 1821 she married BENJAMIN ROUSE; they lived in Boston and New York before moving westward to Cleveland in 1830. As a member of the LADIES TRACT SOCIETY, Rebecca Rouse became well known by making personal visits to every home in the village of Cleveland and exchanging pioneer experiences. Religiously inclined, she was one of the original members of the FIRST BAPTIST Society. In 1842, she founded and became the president of the Martha Washington & Dorcas Society, one of the first benevolent organizations in the city, from which originated the Protestant Orphan Asylum, of which she served for many years as the director. Interested in and dedicated to reforming the baneful effects of alcohol, she helped organize the CLEVELAND LADIES TEMPERANCE UNION in June 1850.

Rouse's organization of the Ladies' Aid Society on 20 Apr. 1861, 5 days after Pres. Lincoln's first call for troops, was perhaps her most notable benevolent activity. The Ladies' Aid Society, later to become the Soldiers' Aid Society of Cleveland, U.S. Sanitary Commission, was a precursor to the AMERICAN RED CROSS. She served as its president and was personally responsible for raising vast amounts of money through sanitary fairs. The society collected and distributed supplies of inestimable value and offered nursing to military men and their families throughout northern Ohio. This crucial "home-front" effort, which Rouse directed on the local level, lasted for the duration of the CIVIL WAR. In her honor and in grateful memory of her services and devotion, Rebecca Rouse's figure is reproduced in one of the bronze panels on the SOLDIERS & SAILORS MONUMENT located in Cleveland's PUBLIC SQUARE. Rebecca Rouse lived 88 years, outliving her husband, Benjamin, by 16 years.

Adella Hughes Family Papers, WRHS.
*World's History of Cleveland* (1896).

The **ROWFANT CLUB** (1892), located at 3028 Prospect Ave., is an organization of book and print collectors. The club was organized on 29 Feb. 1892 by Chas. Orr, librarian at Case School of Applied Science, Reuben A. Vance, Wm. H. Gaylord, Thos. Walton, Paul Lemperly, Francis A. Hilliard, Chas. A. Post, and Clifford F. King. Meetings were originally held in the Case Library Bldg.; they moved in 1893 to 255 Erie (E. 9th) St., and in 1895 to permanent quarters in the Merwin House at 3028 Prospect Ave. (formerly the old Doubleday House and the home of actors JOHN and EFFIE ELLSLER). The club's officers included John Cutler Covert, president; Chas. W. Burrows, vice-president; Paul Lemperly, secretary and librarian; and Albert Lee Withington, treasurer. The club chose to identify itself with Frederick Locker-Lampson by adopting the name of his Sussex County, England, estate, "Rowfant." Membership, by invitation only, is limited to men of diverse business and professional interests whose bond is a love of books, book collecting, and the art of bookmaking. Topics for weekly discussions originally focused solely on books and literature. Subsequently a variety of topics, including art, history, travel, and economics, have been discussed at the club's regular meetings. The club insignia, groundhog and candles, are used in initiation and election procedures. The Rowfant Club maintains a library consisting of volumes acquired by members or donated to the club. It includes a diverse collection of books, manuscripts, first editions, and specially printed manuscripts, and the club's own imprints, including its annual yearbook. Reminiscent of the Grolier Club (Society) of New York and Benjamin Franklin's Junto, the Rowfant Club has been called a "bookman's shrine."

The **ROXY THEATER** was the best-known burlesque house in Cleveland. It attracted the major touring burlesque acts and achieved a national reputation. The roots of the Roxy date from 1906, when Truman M. Swetland leased the property, located at 1882 E. 9th St., from Levi E. Meachum for 99 years. In 1907, the Family Theater opened at that location. A movie house by 1909, it was renamed the Orpheum Theater in 1913 and continued to show movies until it closed in Feb. 1929. As the Roxy, it again opened as a movie theater in 1931. By 1933, under new owner Geo. Young, the Roxy became a nationally known burlesque house. Throughout its heyday, the Roxy was a stop for entertainers such as Abbott & Costello, Phil Silvers, Red Buttons, Ann Corio, and, later, Tempest Storm and Busty Russell.

The theater was remodeled in 1956 by new owners Frank Engel and Frank Bryan, and they brought their Eastern Burlesque circuit to Cleveland. Headliners at that time were Blaze Starr and Rose LaRose. From 1968 until its final closing and razing in 1977, the Roxy alternated between live entertainment and X-rated movies. The theater and property were sold in 1971 to Kope Realty for $150,000. It was necessary to break both the 1906 lease agreement between Swetland and Meachum and Swetland's will, which had stipulated that after his death, the property should be continuously leased, with the income to be divided between Oberlin College, Case School of Applied Science, and Western Reserve College (the latter two now part of CASE WESTERN RESERVE UNIVERSITY). With the approval of the remaining Meachum heirs, the $150,000 sale price was evenly split between the two institutions. Interestingly enough, the property had been appraised at $70,000 the year before the sale. In Sept. 1972, the lobby of the theater was bombed, but the Roxy reopened in Feb. 1973, showing X-rated films. Later that year, manager Tommy Flynn was arrested on obscenity charges for showing "Be-

hind the Green Door." The Roxy closed permanently 6 Nov. 1977. The Natl. City Bank bought the property and tore down the theater to make way for the Natl. City Ctr.

**ROYALTON TOWNSHIP** was originally part of Brecksville Twp. in Twp. 5, Range 13, in the Connecticut WESTERN RESERVE. On 27 Oct. 1818, county commissioners set aside Twp. 5, Range 13, as a separate township called Royalton. It was formally voted into existence on 6 Nov. 1818. Bounded on the north by PARMA, on the south by Medina County, on the east by BRECKSVILLE, and on the west by STRONGSVILLE, Royalton Twp. was known as the highest territory in the county, as it stood 1,238 ft. above sea level and 375 ft. above Lake Erie. In 1811, Melzer Clark became the first white settler in the area. The first settlement was located in the southeastern part of the township, where bear, deer, and turkey were plentiful. In 1816, Robt. Engle founded the area's second settlement. The election creating Royalton Twp. was held at Engle's home. Growth came slowly but steadily to the community. In 1821, Jonathan Bunker erected the first single-framed dwelling. By 1827, several frame homes had been built. The only village in the township, called Royalton Ctr., contained a town hall, 3 general stores, 3 churches, a cemetery, and an Odd Fellows lodge. Soon the area developed into a busy trading center. Road improvements aided the development of the southeastern portion of Royalton Ctr. Farm wagons and carriages were forced to use dirt roads until plank roads were built. York Rd. and State Rd. were the first two plank roads laid out, all with the help of public contributions. Royalton Twp. developed into an important dairy center. In 1866, Jas. Wyatt opened a cheese factory, which allowed Royalton to manufacture dairy products and supply them to neighboring communities on a regular basis. When the cheese industry slowed, farming continued as the mainstay of the area (see AGRICULTURE). Education was initially provided by lessons taught in individual homes. In 1829 the first school was built; by 1830, 3 more schools were added, and the township was divided into 4 school districts. By 1902 there were 9 1-room schools, and in 1907, the first high school was built with public funds. Royalton Twp. was named after Royalton, Vt., the home town of 2 early settlers, David and Knight Sprague. In 1881 the township name was changed to N. Royalton because of the existence of a town in Ohio bearing the name Royalton. Royalton Twp. was incorporated as the village of N. ROYALTON on 4 Apr. 1927. In 1961 the village was incorporated as the city of N. Royalton.

*History of North Royalton*, North Royalton Pamphlet File, North Royalton Public Library.

Marcis, T. Richard, ed., *North Royalton, Ohio, 1818-1968* (1968).

**RUBINSTEIN, BERYL** (26 Oct. 1898–29 Dec. 1952), was a prominent pianist, composer, and teacher. He was director of the CLEVELAND INSTITUTE OF MUSIC from 1932-52. Born in Athens, Ga., the son of a rabbi, Rubinstein began his career as pianist as a child performer touring the U.S. from 1905-11. He made his debut with the Metropolitan Opera Orchestra in 1911 and subsequently went to Europe to study with Jose Vianna De Motta and Ferrucio Busoni. He made his professional debut in New York in 1916 and appeared with the New York Philharmonic, Cleveland, Detroit, Philadelphia, San Francisco Symphony, and London Symphony orchestras. In 1921, Rubinstein joined the piano faculty of the Cleveland Institute of Music; he became head of the piano department in 1925, dean of faculty in 1929, and director in 1932, in which position he remained until his death. During his tenure at the institute, he brought world-renowned musicians to the faculty. He continued his active concert and recital career. As a composer, he produced works for orchestra, piano, violin, string quartet, and voice, and an opera, *The Sleeping Beauty*, premiered in New York in 1938. He served in the U.S. Army 1942-44 and gave over 75 concerts for servicemen. Rubinstein died of cancer. He was survived by his wife, Elsa, and a son, David.

The **RUBINSTEIN CLUB** was a local women's chorus. Organized in Feb. 1899, the club was led by Mrs. Royce Day Fry, who had studied voice and conducting with Carl Zerrahn in Boston. It gave its first public performance in May 1899 with a chorus of 16 voices at a musical presented at Plymouth Church. Under Fry's direction, the club developed into a fine choral group and joined the Natl. Fed. of Music Clubs. In 1905 the club's organist and choirmaster, JAS. ROGERS, became its conductor. Concert programs under his direction featured classical choral works by such composers as Wagner and Debussy. Mrs. Seabury Ford became the club's new music director in 1907. A noted singer, she brought further distinction to the club with her musical training and knowledge of voice. Emphasizing tone quality, articulation, and pronunciation, she sought to get the best results from her singers. Her success was noted in the critical reviews of the club's 2 annual concerts. Under Ford's guidance, the club came to number 85 voices. It would often invite soloists to perform and frequently performed the compositions of such Cleveland composers as Homer Hatch and Fanny Snow Knowlton. Mrs. Ford resigned in 1910, citing the demands of her own solo career and her duties as a mother. She was succeeded by composer Chas. Sommer. A concert of works by Bruch and Schubert in 1912 was the club's last, and in 1915 it was officially disbanded.

**RUETENIK, HERMAN J.** (20 Sept. 1826-22 Feb. 1914), was an educator, an author and editor, and a leader in the development locally of the German Reformed church. Ruetenik was born in Demerthin, Brandenburg, Germany, the son of minister Karl A. and Charlotte Woldman Ruetenik. He graduated from the Joachimsthal Gymnasium in Berlin and studied divinity at the University of Halle from 1846-48. After the failure of the revolution in 1848, he came to the U.S. as a political refugee. In 1852, Ruetenik entered the ministry in the Reformed church in the U.S. and was named the principal of the English Classical School in Easton, Pa. He was ordained into the ministry while in Easton on 17 July 1853, and later that year he came to Ohio as a missionary. After serving as a missionary in Toledo and as a professor at Heidelberg University in Tiffin, Ruetenik came to Cleveland in 1859 as a missionary and became the pastor of the independent Congregation of Brethren, which eventually became the First Reformed Church. He later established the Second Reformed Church and in 1868 founded the Third Reformed Church, which he led until ca. 1871; in 1886 he established the German Sunday School Mission, which became the Eighth Reformed Church on 17 May 1889. He also worked to establish the deaconess's home on Scranton Rd., and in 1913 he organized an Italian mission in the HAYMARKET district.

Ruetenik also established institutions to support the Reformed church. Soon after his arrival in Cleveland, he began publishing religious periodicals for the Reformed church faithful; this enterprise evolved into the Central Publishing Co. of the Reformed Church, located on Pearl Rd. (2969 W. 25th St.). A more ambitious undertaking was Calvin College. Founded by Ruetenik in 1866 with $600

he raised in Germany, the college was located on 5½ acres of land (purchased for $500) in the village of BROOKLYN. Modeled after the German gymnasium, the school was to give instruction in German and to teach Greek and Latin. Ruetenik's plans apparently received little support from Reformed church officials, and the college's educational goals were revised in later years to follow more closely American educational practices.

Ruetenik was a scholar and an author. Besides serving on the faculty at Heidelberg, he served as professor of theology at Mission House in Franklin, Wis. He was the author of 7 published works, including *German Grammar* (1900) and *Pioneers of the Reformed Church in America* (1902). Ruetenik was married on 11 Oct. 1853 to Amelia Clara Martin in Easton, Pa. She died on 13 Jan. 1905. Of their 5 sons, Martin L. Ruetenik (17 May 1868-23 Sept. 1947) continued his father's interest in gardening and became a pioneer in greenhouse gardening, and Gustave A. Ruetenik (9 Aug. 1857-13 Sept. 1926) was a teacher and administrator in the CLEVELAND PUBLIC SCHOOLS.

**RUETENIK GARDENS** has been an innovative leader in the greenhouse vegetable-growing industry in northeastern Ohio since its founding in the 1880s as the first greenhouse in the Cleveland area. Martin L. Ruetenik (17 May 1868-23 Sept. 1947), son of Rev. HERMAN J. RUETENIK, was a young truck farmer on Schaaf Rd. when he built Cleveland's first greenhouse and began raising leaf lettuce in 1885; he began growing tomatoes the following year. Ruetenik's use of scientific methods of cultivation made him an industry leader both locally and nationally; he was a pioneer in combating celery blight, and many of his farming techniques were adopted widely. In 1907, Ruetenik had an entire acre of his Schaaf Rd. land under glass; his total greenhouse acreage expanded to 3½ acres by 1924. The financial success of his business enabled him to initiate a profit-sharing plan with his employees in 1902.

Ruetenik was influential in establishing several industry organizations and other enterprises. He helped organize and was a 2-year president of the Natl. Vegetable Growers Assoc.; and he was a founder of the Growers Basket Co., the Growers Marketing Co., and the Schaaf Rd. Coal Co. He was president of the ,incoln Savings & Banking Co. and was the first mayor of BROOKLYN HTS. after its incorporation. Ruetenik also helped his sons establish farming enterprises outside of Cleveland. He and Howard J. Ruetenik established a 240-acre vegetable and Christmas tree farm at Orwell in 1926, and with Paul B. Ruetenik he established 25 acres of gardens and greenhouses in Vermilion. Following Martin Ruetenik's death, ownership of the Cleveland business passed to his daughter, Dorothea, and her husband, Walter F. Pretzer, who gained a national reputation for his farming methods and was a 4-term president of the Vegetable Growers Assoc. of America. After Pretzer's death in 1959, his son Richard became the owner of Ruetenik Gardens.

Ruetenik Gardens gained a reputation as a leader in experimenting with new techniques and ideas. Paul Ruetenik experimented with hydroponics in the 1940s and 1950s, and Richard Ruetenik experimented with the plastic bubble in the 1960s. High energy costs in the 1970s, which reduced profits and sharply reduced the greenhouse acreage in the Cleveland area, forced Pretzer to experiment with growing and marketing crops other than the traditional hothouse tomato and lettuce. In the fall of 1984, he and his son Walter, manager of the business, stopped growing tomatoes and concentrated their efforts on raising herbs and greens for local restaurants and gourmet cooks.

847

RUMBOLD, CHARLOTTE MARGARET (28 Dec. 1869–2 July 1960), was active in the civic affairs of 2 cities: St. Louis, Mo., and Cleveland. In her native St. Louis, this daughter of a respected physician espoused progressive municipal measures. Her achievements as the city's superintendent of playgrounds and recreation (1906–15) caused a successor to declare that "the public recreation system in Saint Louis remains as a monument to Charlotte Rumbold." In Cleveland, where she worked for the Chamber of Commerce (1917–38), her promotion of PUBLIC HOUSING and urban planning was no less significant. In St. Louis, Rumbold advocated civic and suffrage issues. Through involvement in the national Playground Assoc. of America (1906), she widened her acquaintances to include those, such as FRANCIS F. PRENTISS and Munson Havens, who championed the "city efficient." By summer 1915, her St. Louis tenure ended when the Board of Aldermen, ignoring women's and children's pleas, refused to raise her salary. On the principle of equal pay, she resigned.

Expert in social surveys, Rumbold, at the request of the CLEVELAND FOUNDATION, undertook one in 1916 that became vol. 31, *Commercial Recreation*, in the foundation's recreation study series. By Apr. 1917, she joined the Chamber of Commerce as secretary of its City Plan Committee. She was that and the chamber's assistant secretary until her retirement. Nationally and locally, as a member of the WOMEN'S CITY CLUB as well as an employee of the chamber, Rumbold advanced arguments for the planned city: land-use ZONING (see *VILLAGE OF EUCLID* V. *AMBLER REALTY CO.*); the Group Plan; and provision of public housing, PARKS, and HIGHWAYS. She served as secretary and a board member for several chamber-initiated groups, e.g., the Euclid Ave. Assoc. (1920). WM. HOPKINS appointed Rumbold to the Cleveland City Plan Commission (1924–42). In concert with the chamber, Rumbold sparked the Ohio Planning Conference (1919), thereafter serving as its president, secretary, treasurer, and statehouse lobbyist. In 1933, as the secretary of Cleveland Homes, Inc., she worked diligently in Cleveland and Washington, D.C., to secure New Deal funds for the Cedar-Central housing project. Slight of stature, vivacious in conversation, Catholic in interest, Charlotte Rumbold was described in 1945 by an appreciative LOUIS B. SELTZER: "Tiny Woman Never Shrinks from Storms."

**RUSINS.** *See* **CARPATHO-RUSSIANS**

**RUSSELL, JACK PAUL** (2 Feb. 1915–7 June 1979), served as councilman from the 16th ward of Cleveland from 1943–71, during which time he was Democratic majority leader for 8 years and council president for 8 years. Russell was born Paul Ruschak in the Buckeye Rd. area of Cleveland, the son of Stephen and Mary Ruschak, who had immigrated from Hungary. His first political experience came as a campaign manager for Joseph Stearns, who ran for council in 1933. He built up his influence in the Buckeye area by publishing neighborhood newspapers, including the *Buckeye Press*. When he decided to enter politics in the late 1930s, he changed his name to Jack Paul Russell, and in 1943 he was elected to city council. He served as Democratic majority leader from 1944–52 and president of council from 1955–63. After losing the council presidency to Jas. V. Stanton, he continued to represent the 16th ward until 1971. Russell was a flamboyant and influential ward politician who used his political base in the Buckeye area to rise to a position of power in city government. He supported a number of projects aimed at improving the city and was noted for keeping his word. His trademarks were his white Stetson hat, a Cuban cigar, and a large black

Cadillac. In 1957, he lectured at Harvard on municipal government; and a year later, he was the subject of a national CBS television documentary dealing with urban machine politics. During his years in council, he operated several businesses, including the Ohio Fire Protective Systems. In 1935 he married Irene Maguary, and they had 3 children, Richard, Marilyn Richards, and Elaine Thomas. He died in Cleveland at age 64.

**RUSSIANS.** Cleveland's Great Russian community has never been very large. Even in the 1980s, it was difficult to accurately estimate the number of Great Russians in the area, because many ethnic groups, such as the BYELORUSSIANS and CARPATHO-RUSSIANS, have derived from regions under the control of Tsarist Russia or the Soviet Union and have thus been enumerated as Russians or are popularly considered as Russians by the general populace. Even the city's preeminent "Russian" symbol, ST. THEODOSIUS RUSSIAN ORTHODOX CATHEDRAL, was built not by Great Russians but by Carpatho-Russians. Indeed, in the 1980s, all of the Russian Orthodox churches in the region had mixed congregations that probably included Great Russians. Great Russians began arriving in the city in small numbers during the late 19th and early 20th centuries. Those who came before WORLD WAR I were largely political refugees, often of a radical bent, who were at odds with the tsarist government. Following the Russian Revolution of 1917, the nature of Russian immigration to Cleveland reversed entirely as former supporters of the tsar came to constitute the major portion of local Great Russian immigration. Even with the impetus of the revolution, the city's Russian community is estimated to have consisted of only 5,000 persons at most by 1932.

No real Great Russian neighborhood evolved in Cleveland, although a small community could be found near E. 30th and Woodland Ave. by 1912. Its focal point was the radical Russian Workingman's Club. The tendency of the Russians to scatter throughout the community was strengthened by the nature of the postrevolutionary immigrants, who tended to be skilled and highly literate and therefore able to assume employment and residence in various sections of the city. Organizations within the new group of immigrants were few. Some did gather at HIRAM HOUSE social settlement. A Russian Circle was begun at the Internatl. Institute of the YWCA in the 1930s; the 64 Russians enrolled at the YWCA lived in areas as diverse as LAKEWOOD, PARMA, and CLEVELAND HTS. In the 1930s, the city did have a branch of the liberal national organization the Russians Consolidated Union of Mutual Aid. Several local organizations started by the Soviet Union in Cleveland during the 1930s, including the Friends of the Soviet Union at E. 55th and Euclid and the Russian American Institute in the Erie Bldg., may have appeared Russian to the general onlooker, but they failed to garner any membership from the local Russian community. Instead, they, like the radical Ukrainian Labor Temple in the TREMONT area, tended to attract American radicals or those from ethnic groups such as the HUNGARIANS and UKRAINIANS. Given the difficulty of emigration from the Soviet Union, Cleveland's Great Russian population received little replenishment until the 1970s, when, by virtue of international pressure and agreements between the USSR and U.S., a number of Russian Jews migrated to the U.S. and to Cleveland. Many of them took up residence in the Jewish community of Cleveland Hts. and, because of their numbers and language, formed what could be considered as a Russian-speaking community, with much of its activity centered in the COVENTRY VILLAGE BUSINESS DISTRICT. As of this writing, there is little expectation of any substantial migration from the Soviet Union, by either Great Russians or other national groups subject to its rule. It can therefore be assumed that the pre-World War I radicals, the postwar political emigres, and the Russian Jews will, for some time to come, constitute the main streams of Russian migration to Greater Cleveland.

John J. Grabowski
Western Reserve Historical Society

Telberg, Ina, "Russians in Cleveland" (Master's thesis, WRU, 1932).

**RUTHENBERG, CHARLES** (9 July 1882–3 Mar. 1927), was a prominent member of the Socialist and, later, Communist parties in Cleveland, holding leadership positions in both organizations and running for political office as their representative. Ruthenberg was born in Cleveland to German immigrant parents. His father, August, a longshoreman, had been a cigarmaker and an active member of the German Democratic party in Germany. Educated at German Lutheran Hign School and DYKE COLLEGE, young Ruthenberg intended to pursue a career in the Lutheran ministry. Instead, he began working in business as a salesman and bookkeeper for the Cleveland district office of the Selmer Hess Publishing Co. of New York. Ruthenberg at first considered himself a Progressive, backing the policies of Cleveland mayor TOM L. JOHNSON. However, after reading Marx's *Das Kapital*, he became committed to the Socialist cause. By 1912, he was a militant member of the party, rejecting all ideas of economic reform and insisting instead on the inevitable class struggle between wage earners and capitalists. As the leader of the local chapter of the Socialist party, Ruthenberg proved to be an effective organizer and a perennial political candidate. He ran for mayor 4 times, in 1911, 1915, 1917, and 1919; for governor of Ohio in 1912; for the U.S. Senate in 1914; and for the U.S. House of Representatives in 1916 and 1918. By 1917, Ruthenberg had given up his job in order to devote more time to his political work. He had also moved to the radical left of the party, and after the Bolshevik Revolution in Russia, he switched his allegiance to the COMMUNIST PARTY. After the formation of the Communist Internatl. in 1919 and the left-wing schism within the U.S. Socialist party, Ruthenberg became executive secretary of the immigrant-dominated Communist Party of America. Ruthenberg's last major political action in Cleveland was his leadership of the May Day Parade of 1919, which resulted in a riot and his arrest on a charge of assault with intent to kill (see MAY DAY RIOTS). Ruthenberg died suddenly in 1927 at the age of 44 of a ruptured appendix. His body was cremated in Chicago, and his ashes were sent to Moscow, where they were interred in the Kremlin Wall. Ruthenberg and John Reed were the only American Communists so honored by the Soviet Union.

**RYCHLIK, CHARLES V.** (26 June 1875–6 Dec. 1962), was a Cleveland-born composer and violinist, whose *Encyclopedia of Violin Technique* helped rank him as one of the top authorities and teachers in his field. Of Czech descent, Rychlik at age 14 was the youngest member of the Cleveland Musicians Union. In 1891 he began studies at the Prague Conservatory. While still enrolled, he joined the Bohemian String Quartet, which performed in all the major cities in Europe. Rychlik was suspended from the conservatory for performing in public with the quartet but was later reinstated. He graduated in 1895. While traveling with the Bohemian String Quartet, Rychlik met Brahms and Bruckner in Vienna. In fact, Brahms played viola with the group on a piece he had written. Rychlik boarded at the home of Anton Dvorak. In 1896 he returned home to

Cleveland, and the following year he joined the Chicago Symphony Orchestra under Theodore Thomas. In 1901, Rychlik's father died, and he came home to stay. He played violin in the forerunner of the CLEVELAND ORCHESTRA under JOHANN BECK and then EMIL RING. In 1908, he replaced Carl Dueringer as 2d violinist in the PHILHARMONIC STRING QUARTET. He played with the group until its demise in 1928. Rychlik also played with the infant Cleveland Orchestra from its inception in 1918 for 2 years. During this time, Rychlik began teaching and composing. He wrote numerous works for violin that are still widely performed. His *Rhapsody* in 4 contrasting movements (1923) was given its premiere in 1933 by the Detroit Orchestra. He composed and taught at his home/ studio on 5611 Fleet Ave. His students included author-musician F. KARL GROSSMAN and child prodigy Erni Valasek. In 1940, 400 pupils, friends, and colleagues gathered in the Hotel Cleveland ballroom to pay him tribute. Some 40 of his pupils went on to become members of the Cleveland Orchestra, and they honored him by performing some of his works. Rychlik contributed much to the musical life of Cleveland and internationally through the publication of his 25-volume *Encyclopedia of Violin Technique*, which took some 20 years to complete. He also compiled *Supplement to Sevcik, Opus One.* Rychlik was unmarried.

**RYDER, JAMES F.** (1826–2 June 1904), was a pioneer photographer responsible for introducing the technique of retouching negatives to American photography. In Cleveland he is best known for encouraging ARCHIBALD WILLARD to paint The *SPIRIT OF '76*, and as the man primarily responsible for the distribution and popularity of Willard's works through the medium of chromolithography. Born in Ithaca, N.Y., Ryder began work in a book-printing office in 1844. While there he met the local daguerreotypist, who encouraged Ryder to purchase a camera and join his establishment in Ithaca in 1847. In 1849, Chas. E. Johnson, a daguerreotypist from Cleveland, met Ryder and invited him to visit his studio. Ryder soon left Ithaca and became a traveling daguerreotypist, working his way toward Cleveland. He worked in Kirtland, Painesville, CHAGRIN FALLS, and BEDFORD before settling for the winter months in Elyria in 1850. Johnson visited Ryder in Elyria in 1850 and asked him to become, for a time, manager/operator of Johnson's studio in the Merchants' Bank Bldg. in Cleveland. Ryder left his own Elyria studio in the hands of his assistant, Mr. Park, and moved to Cleveland. For the next 2 years he divided his time between Cleveland and Elyria. In 1852, he married one of Park's sisters. When the CIVIL WAR began, Ryder offered the citizens of Elyria free photos of their young men who were going off to serve in the war.

In 1868, Ryder introduced negative retouching to the U.S. He paid for the passage to the U.S. of Prof. Karl Leutgib from the Munich Academy to teach him the new process. As a result, Ryder received an award at a photography show held in Boston in 1869. In 1872, Ryder moved his operations to a studio/gallery at 239 Superior St. His offices were there until his retirement in 1894. Also in 1872, the artist Archibald Willard sent 2 paintings to Ryder's shop to be framed. Ryder displayed the paintings in his storefront windows, and they became so popular with passersby that he decided to make chromolithograph copies of the works, which became bestsellers across the U.S. Ryder and Willard worked closely together from that time, and it was at Ryder's instigation that Willard worked up the painting The *Spirit of '76* for the Centennial Exhibition in 1876. Ryder is also known for his photographs of several U.S. presidents, most notably Pres. Garfield, who sat for him several times both before and after his election to the presidency. In 1902, following retirement, Ryder produced his autobiography, entitled *Voightlander and I*, an account of his fascination with all the techniques and forms of photography. It is one of the few biographical accounts produced by a 19th-century photographer. Ryder died in his home at 3586 Euclid Ave.

Ryder, James F., *Voightlander and I* (1902).

# S

**S. BRAINARD'S SONS** was Cleveland's leading 19th-century musical-instrument dealer and music publisher. Silas Brainard founded the company in 1836 and opened a piano store in the American House hotel on Superior Ave., selling Chickering pianos shipped from the factory in Boston. In 1845 he purchased Watson's Hall, which had been built in 1840, and renamed it Melodeon Hall. In 1860 the name was changed to Brainard's Opera House, and in 1875 to the GLOBE THEATER. In 1864, Brainard began publishing *Western Musical World*, a monthly journal of articles, hints to musicians, and sheet music. In 1869 the name was changed to *Brainard's Musical World*. Brainard took his sons Chas. S. and Henry M. into the business, and in 1871 the company became S. Brainard's Sons. In 1876 they built a new 4-story building on Euclid Ave. near E. 4th St. to accommodate the store and publishing house. Its interior was fitted with massive woodwork, gas light, and a steam-driven elevator. In the 1870s and 1880s, Brainard's published vocal and instrumental music, songbooks, and especially political and patriotic songs. In 1878 S. Brainard's Sons established an office in Chicago; the company left Cleveland altogether in 1889, moved to Chicago, and continued to publish *Brainard's Musical World* until 1895. Henry M. Brainard remained in Cleveland to operate his own store, an outlet for Steinway pianos.

## S. K. WELLMAN COMPANY. *See* BRUSH-WELLMAN CORPORATION

The **S. LIVINGSTON MATHER CHARITABLE TRUST** was founded in 1953 by Samuel Livingston Mather (1882–1960). Mather was born in Cleveland, the son of Flora Amelia Stone (d. 1909; see FLORA STONE MATHER) and SAMUEL MATHER (1851–1931). He graduated from University School in 1901 and received his A.B. from Yale in 1905. He then entered his father's business, the Cleveland Cliffs Iron Co., where he was vice-president all his life. In 1906, Mather married Grace Fleming Harman (d. 1931), with whom he had 4 children: Samuel Harman, Grace Flora (Mrs. Robt. C. Hosmer, Jr.), Elizabeth Harman (Mrs. S. Sterling McMillan), and Samuel Livingston, Jr. (d. 1931). Mather's second marriage, in 1932, was to Alice Nightengale Keith (d. 1950).

The purposes of the trust are broadly for education, child welfare, youth programs, mental health, social services, cultural programs, the environment, and natural re-

sources. The largest grant ever given by the trust was to the CHILDREN'S AID SOCIETY. Other recipients have been the CLEVELAND MUSEUM OF NATURAL HISTORY, PLAYHOUSE SQUARE, and the CLEVELAND INSTITUTE OF ART. Support is given for both general operations and specific projects. No grants are awarded to individuals or for endowment funds, scientific and medical research programs, matching gifts, annual campaigns, deficit financing, land acquisition, areas "appropriately" supported by the government and UNITED WAY, or loans. Gifts are primarily given locally. The assets of the trust in 1985 were $2,313,800, with expenditures of $118,200 for 49 grants. The distribution committee included S. Sterling McMillan, Elizabeth M. McMillan, and Madeleine M. Offutt.

The **SACRED MUSIC SOCIETY** was an early musical organization devoted to the performance of religious works. It was established in 1835 at Trinity Church on Seneca (W. 3rd) St. The group consisted of choir members of the church and was augmented by nonmember professional outsiders. It sang the works of Bach, Haydn, and Handel. The society dissolved in the late 1840s.

**SAENGERFESTS,** national gatherings of German singing societies, were a major vehicle for the development of music in Cleveland. The first Saengerfest (Singing Festival) in Cleveland took place 28–30 May 1855; it was the 7th such event in America. The purpose of the Saengerfest was to exchange visits among the various German singing societies so they could hear one another and celebrate their German heritage. A total of 5 Saengerfests were held in Cleveland. Hans Balatka, a resident of Milwaukee, was the conductor of the 1855 festival. Clevelanders Fritz Abel and EMIL RING conducted the 1859 (14–17 June) and 1893 festivals respectively. Carl Bergan of the New York Philharmonic was leader of the 1874 (22–27 June) Saengerfest. The last Saengerfest (June 1927) held in Cleveland was the most spectacular. With famed conductor Bruno Walter, the 36th Natl. Saengerfest (of the North American Saengerbund) hosted 100 societies and 4,000 singers. In addition, 2,000 schoolchildren drawn from Cleveland public schools sang under the direction of Russell V. Morgan. Their program featured works by Schubert. The 1874 and 1893 festivals also used schoolchildren, under the direction of N. COE STEWART. Some 12,000 people jammed Public Hall to hear the last concert. Walter and concertmaster Josepf Fuchs received a standing ovation for Wagner's *Die Meistersinger von Nurnberg*; Lawrence Tibbett, baritone of the Metroplitan Opera, sang *In Mai*, composed by former Clevelander Albert Gehring. The concert was dedicated to Beethoven, upon the centenary of his death.

**SAFE AND SANE FOURTH OF JULY** was a movement started in Cleveland in 1908 to stop the annual holiday carnage. Motivated by a tragic accident, the city passed an ordinance prohibiting fireworks in the city. Every year Cleveland, like many other cities, enumerated the dead and wounded from fireworks. The city had experienced a dramatic explosion in a fireworks factory, the Thor Mfg. Co. on Orange Ave., in May 1903; 200 buildings were damaged and 12 demolished, while 3 persons were killed. More devastating in terms of threat to life were the yearly accidents; nationally from 1902–08, 1,300 were killed and 28,000 seriously injured, with blindings and loss of limbs and fingers leading the list of injuries.

Despite yearly outrage at the statistics, no action was taken until an incident occurred in a local Kresge store. A woman and her son were looking at a counter of fireworks when the boy grabbed a mechanical sparkler labeled "absolutely harmless" and practiced snapping it. A spark alighted on the flag that waved over the display, and it blew to a counter of explosives. Skyrockets and Roman candles shot across the room, as hundreds of firecrackers exploded at once. The tremendous noise caused a stampede among 2 floors of shoppers. In the rush to escape, scores were burned, while 5 clerks, a woman shopper, and the small boy whose fascination with the sparkler had led to the explosion lay trampled to death.

The next day, the Cleveland Congress of Mothers (see CLEVELAND COUNCIL OF PARENT-TEACHER ASSOCS.) mobilized all women's organizations in the city to influence Dan Pfahl, a Cleveland councilman, to introduce legislation banning fireworks in the city. Despite the opposition of 1 councilman who was a fireworks dealer, a law was passed that made Cleveland the first "safe and sane" city in America. The Cleveland law, which made the neighborhood more peaceful, ladies less afraid to walk past mischievous youths, and horses calmer, was a model for similar laws in other cities. In 1909 Washington, D.C., banned fireworks, followed by New York, Boston, Baltimore, Toledo, Chicago, and Kansas City in 1910 and Detroit in 1911. By 1939, 380 other cities forbade private fireworks displays, while 200 others restricted their use.

**ST. ALEXIS HOSPITAL MEDICAL CENTER** is a 303-bed acute-care hospital that provides a full range of services; specialized areas include respiratory care and industrial health. It was the second Catholic hospital founded in Cleveland. St. Alexis was founded in 1884 by 2 sisters of the Order of St. Francis, Sisters Leonarda and Alexia. With the aid of the Franciscans, the hospital opened at Broadway and McBride avenues in a brick 8-room house. Its initial purpose was to serve the workmen and manufacturing concerns that were beginning to locate in the NEWBURGH area. The hospital's interest in industrial health has continued into the 1980s. Among the distinguished physicians who have served on the medical staff of St. Alexis were Drs. FRANK E. BUNTS, GEO. W. CRILE, and WM. E. LOWER, 3 of the 4 founders of the CLEVELAND CLINIC. In 1906, Dr. Crile performed at St. Alexis the world's first direct blood transfusion between humans. New construction began the year after the hospital was founded. The sisters raised $5,500 to build a new wing, which added 32 beds. A main building was constructed in

1885. In 1925, an addition to the main building was completed and named the Leonarda Memorial Bldg. A building for the nursing school, established in 1918, was erected in 1930. The first maternity department was constructed as an addition to the Leonarda Memorial Bldg. in 1945. The next major expansion program was completed in 1955, when the 10-story main building was erected at a cost of $3.5 million. A new service wing with an x-ray department, enlarged surgical division, new maternity suite, modern emergency area, and office space was added in 1959.

In its early years, St. Alexis primarily served area industries; most of its emergency cases were workers involved in industrial accidents. The hospital also served the families of workers, who usually lived near the factories. By the late 1890s, 75% of its patients were charity cases, and fewer than 25% of the patients treated were Catholic. Special wards were maintained for employees of certain companies, especially those working for the RAILROADS. Almost the entire nursing staff at this time was composed of sisters. In the early 1920s, the hospital's out-patient department became the first such department in the country to offer chemotherapy. Since the 1920s, St. Alexis has offered all the basic services found in most community hospitals of its size. The inhalation therapy department, later known as Pulmonary Disease Services, was established in 1954; the coronary-care unit in 1968; and a respiratory-care unit in 1980. To remain viable in an increasingly competitive health-care field, in the early 1980s special programs were introduced that included a stroke rehabilitation team, occupational health services for area businesses, a pastoral care team, and home health care. Like other area hospitals, St. Alexis branched out into the SUBURBS; the construction of an urgent-care center in BROADVIEW HTS. was started in 1983. In 1986 the hospital changed its name to St. Alexis Medical Ctr.

**ST. ANDREW'S ABBEY** is a Benedictine monastery located at Buckeye Rd. and East Blvd. It represents the oldest Roman Catholic monastic community in the world. The Benedictines came to Cleveland in 1922 when 2 monks from the Slovak community at St. Procopius Abbey in Lisle, Ill., responded to Bp. Schrembs's request. They assumed the pastorate of St. Andrews Parish on Superior Ave., which served a Slovak congregation. In 1927, the community established Benedictine High School, with an initial enrollment of 27. In 1929, the high school moved to the quarters of the old Notre Dame orphanage at 10510 Buckeye. In 1929, the Benedictines were given charge of St. Benedict Parish on East Blvd. On 12 Aug. 1929, the monastery received the status of an independent Benedictine community.

The Vatican declared the monastery an independent abbey on 13 July 1934. Fr. Stanislaus Gmuca, OSB, was elected the first abbot. Under his direction, the community completed the construction of a new high school building on East Blvd. in 1940. In 1946, Rev. Theodore Kojis, OSB, succeeded Abbot Stanislaus as head of the community. During his administration, ground was broken for a new abbey in 1950. The building was constructed and dedicated in 1952. Jerome Koval was elected third abbot in 1966. In 1985, under the direction of Abbot Roger Gries, the Benedictine priests and brothers fill a variety of apostolates in the Cleveland community. Both the abbey and Benedictine High School are prominent institutions in the Buckeye-Woodland area of Cleveland. The abbey also serves as a major center of Slovak culture.

Archives, Diocese of Cleveland.

**ST. ANDREW'S EPISCOPAL CHURCH** was the most elite black church in Cleveland at its founding in 1890. Formerly a mission that grew out of Trinity and Grace Episcopal churches, St. Andrew's was accepted as a parish by the Diocesan Convention in 1892. After meeting in homes and then in the chapel of Trinity Church at Superior and E. 6th St., the congregation bought an old church at E. 24th and Central. It occupied this building until 1915, when ST. VINCENT CHARITY HOSPITAL expansion forced its move. By 1916, the church was settled in its present (1986) building on E. 49th and Cedar. The parish was incorporated in 1926. The parishioners at St. Andrew's were the old elite of the black community, not the black working class or the rising group of businessmen, politicians, and professionals with economic roots in the emerging ghetto. Prominent among the founders were JOHN P. GREEN (state representative and lawyer), JACOB REED (seafood merchant), and Richard A. Jones (editor of the Negro *Globe*.) St. Andrew's currently operates a neighborhood ministry next to the church.

The **SAINT ANN FOUNDATION** was established in 1973 when, as a result of the declining birth rate and financial strain, St. Ann's Hospital, located at 2475 Martin Luther King, Jr. Dr. (formerly East Blvd.), was sold to the KAISER PERMANENTE System. The foundation uses the income gained from the sale of the hospital for grants to support programs for charitable, religious, educational, and scientific purposes related to health and health care. It is a subsidiary of the Sisters of Charity of St. Augustine Health & Human Services, a Catholic multihospital system sponsored by the SISTERS OF CHARITY OF ST. AUGUSTINE. St. Ann Hospital (also known as St. Ann Maternity Home & Infant Asylum) was Ohio's oldest maternity hospital and developed the first formal social-services program for unwed mothers in Cleveland. It also took care of abandoned infants. Opened in 1873 in rented frame houses on Garden St., the maternity home was established by the Sisters of Charity of St. Augustine at the request of Bp. RICHARD GILMOUR. In 1901, the hospital moved to the old Severance mansion at 3409 Woodland Ave. In 1910, it began accepting private patients. The infant formula Similac was tested at St. Ann in cooperation with Cleveland's first milk lab. With the purchase of the Otto Leisy estate in 1947 and the construction of a new St. Ann Hospital, the hospital and infant home were separated in management supervision. The infant home became the St. Ann Infant Home and Loretta House, and in 1950 the name was changed to the DePaul Infant Home and Loretta Hall. The Leisy mansion was renovated, and a new wing was added to St. Ann in 1951. The hospital provided obstetrical, gynecological, medical, and pediatric services. A new hospital was constructed in 1965, and the Leisy mansion was razed in 1969. St. Ann Hospital was sold to the Kaiser Permanente System in 1973, and the St. Ann Foundation was established with the funds from the sale.

**ST. ANTHONY'S CHURCH** was the first Roman Catholic parish to serve the Italian immigrants who had settled in the HAYMARKET area, a downtown neighborhood bounded by Central, Broadway, and Ontario streets. The church's origins date back to 1886, when Fr. Pacifico Capitani began holding services for Italian immigrants at ST. JOHN CATHEDRAL. A search was begun for a suitable church, and a frame hall on Ohio St. (now Central Ave.) was purchased from a German turners' society. Bp. RICHARD GILMOUR dedicated this hall on 8 May 1887 and placed it under the patronage of St. Anthony. This building served the ever-increasing numbers of Italian immigrants who came to Cleveland from Italy and the Termini Imerse vicinity in Sicily. The congregation was too impoverished

to afford a school, but the URSULINE SISTERS provided religious instruction for the children. In 1904 the congregation was able, under the direction of its third pastor, Fr. Humbert Rocchi, to build a Romanesque red-brick church at E. 13th and Carnegie.

By 1929 the original neighborhood had begun to disperse, but St. Anthony's still remained the center of religious and cultural life for the Italian community. On 18 Sept. 1938, St. Anthony's parish was merged with the nearby Irish church of St. Bridget's located at 2508 E. 22nd near Woodland Ave. Its parishioners had moved to newer neighborhoods farther to the east. The Italian congregation took over a well-made parish plant complete with a Gothic church and school. The congregation now had a school for its children. The original St. Anthony's Church was transferred to ST. MARON congregation, which served Maronite Rite Catholics of Syrian or Lebanese background. The combined parish continued serving the Central area until 1961. Shifts in population had caused the parish enrollment to drop below 200 families. Urban renewal and the proposed INNERBELT FREEWAY threatened to further reduce the parish. The diocese decided to close the church and school. The last mass was held in the church on 11 June 1961. Later that summer the parish structures were demolished to accommodate the freeway. The remaining neighborhood parishioners joined St. Joseph's Parish on Woodland Ave.

Papers of St. Anthony. Archives, Diocese of Cleveland.

The **ST. CECILIA SOCIETY** was the first orchestra in Cleveland. The society grew out of the German Singraf Society. While an exact date of establishment is uncertain, it was actively operating in the 1850s and 1860s. The society presented waltzes and polkas, and in later years it accompanied the Gesangverein in a variety of operatic and choral pieces. The date of dissolution for the group is also uncertain, though the society probably survived to the late 1860s, at which time its membership may have been absorbed by the GERMAN CONCERT ORCHESTRA.

The **ST. CLAIR SAVINGS AND LOAN HOLDUP** took place on Friday, 12 Apr. 1957. It was the first bank robbery in history filmed by a hidden camera. The bank, located at 6235 St. Clair Ave., had been robbed twice during the previous 18 months. As a result, Cleveland policeman Thos. Story, superintendent of communications, chose the St. Clair Savings & Loan to use a camera on a trial basis. Story conceived the idea of a hidden camera and, with the help of a New York camera expert, perfected it so that it would start when the bank alarm was sounded. The camera was installed on Thursday, 11 Apr. 1957. The next day, a man and a woman, both carrying pistols, robbed the St. Clair Savings & Loan of $2,376. As the newly installed police camera was rolling, Steven Ray Thomas, wearing a handkerchief around his face, held the customers and employees at gunpoint while Wanda DiCenzi scooped the money into a bag. They escaped in a stolen car driven by Rose O'Donnell. After dividing the money, the three parted.

The police quickly had the pictures of the robbery printed in the newspapers. By Friday evening, the news of the robbery and use of the new police camera had spread across the country. DiCenzi saw the pictures in the paper and heard about them on the radio. Thomas fled to Indianapolis after the robbery but returned on Saturday after hearing about the police pictures. He and DiCenzi gave themselves up on Saturday; O'Donnell was apprehended after a neighbor phoned police concerning her whereabouts. All of the money was recovered except $800, which was spent on clothes and motel bills. Police from across the country came to Cleveland to study the robbery and learn more about the hidden camera. Its use proved to be a major breakthrough in apprehending criminals and deterring robberies.

**ST. ELIAS CHURCH** was established in 1905 to serve a number of Syrian, Lebanese, and Palestinian immigrants who were Catholics of the Melkite Rite, one of the eastern rites of Catholicism. In 1901 a Basilian Salvatorian priest, Fr. Basil Marsha, came to Cleveland to minister to them. Their first liturgy was at St. Joseph's Church on E. 23rd St. on Christmas Day 1901. They met in St. Joseph's and later at the Cathedral for Masses. By 1906 they were able to remodel a building at 2231 E. 9th for a church. This new church was the first Melkite parish outside of New York and the third in America. By Nov. 1907, the parish needed larger quarters. Two homes, at 1225 and 1227 Webster Ave., were purchased and remodeled for a church and rectory. Bp. JOHN P. FARRELLY officially dedicated the church in Apr. 1908. It was at this time that the church was officially placed under the patronage of St. Elias.

Fr. Marsha resigned in 1921 and returned to Lebanon. Bp. JOSEPH SCHREMBS appointed Fr. Malatios Mufleh as his successor. The parish grew, and the congregation dispersed through the city, making the Webster site unsatisfactory. The parish decided to relocate, purchasing the building of the SOUTH PRESBYTERIAN CHURCH on Scranton Rd. and Prame Ave. in June 1937. The church was remodeled and dedicated on 27 Feb. 1938. In 1955, Rev. Ignatius Ghattas, who had served as an associate, succeeded Fr. Mufleh as pastor. In June 1961, the congregation bought property at 8023 Memphis Ave. in Brooklyn. The construction of the present (1985) church there was completed in Nov. 1964. It was formally dedicated on 2 May 1965.

Archives, Diocese of Cleveland.

**ST. ELIZABETH'S CHURCH,** located on Buckeye Rd. in Cleveland, was the first church established for Hungarian Roman Catholics in the U.S. Hungarian immigrants came in great numbers to the Cleveland area during the late 1880s and early 1890s. At first they worshipped at ST. LADISLAUS CHURCH with the SLOVAKS, but disagreements caused them to petition for their own parish. Bp. IGNATIUS HORSTMANN wrote Cardinal Kolozs Vaszary of Hungary for a missionary priest. Fr. CHAS. BOEHM was sent, and he arrived in Cleveland on 1 Dec. 1892. He celebrated mass for the first time on 11 Dec. 1892 in ST. JOSEPH'S ORPHANAGE on Woodland Ave. for the new congregation of St. Elizabeth's. A brick structure was built on Buckeye Rd. just west of Woodhill by Sept. 1893. A school was opened for the children a month later. It was subsequently expanded and put under the direction of the URSULINE SISTERS. In 1944, the Ursulines were replaced by the religious community of the Daughters of the Divine Redeemer. They taught in the school until it was closed in 1964.

Fr. Boehm remained as pastor until 1907, when he left to work with other Hungarian communities in America. His successor was Fr. Julius Szepessy. Under Fr. Szepessy, the present stone Romanesque church was completed in 1922. Bp. JOSEPH SCHREMBS dedicated it on 19 Feb. 1922. After Fr. Szepessy's death in 1922, the now Msgr. Boehm took charge of the parish. Msgr. Emory Tanos became pastor in 1927 and served until his retirement in 1971. His successor was Fr. Julius Zahorsky, who was succeeded by Fr. John J. Nyeste in 1977. St. Elizabeth's Church has been placed on the Natl. Register of Historic Places and has been designated a local landmark.

**ST. GEORGE ORTHODOX CHURCH,** 2587 W. 14th St., was established by the United Syrian Orthodox Society, which was formed on 16 Nov. 1926 to organize a church for Syrians of the Orthodox faith in Cleveland. Meeting in the home of Abraham Sahley, the Orthodox members of the Syrian community elected Geo. Gantose as president of the society, Mery Salim as vice-president, Joe Hanna as treasurer, and Wady Borgaily as secretary. Prior to the purchase of a church site, the society arranged for services to be conducted by visiting priests, using as one temporary meeting place the billiards room of the GRAYS ARMORY on Bolivar Rd. The society later arranged to use the facilities of a Seventh-Day Adventist church. In Dec. 1927 the society appointed Fr. Elias M. Meena as pastor of the church; he became the guiding force in its development for the next 24 years.

In June 1928, the society spent $38,000 to buy the Lincoln Park Methodist Episcopal Church at W. 14th and Starkweather. Five years later the church interior was redecorated, but shortly thereafter, fire destroyed the church in early May 1933. Under Fr. Meena's direction, the 200 families in the parish worked to rebuild the church, raising the necessary $40,000 by subscription. On 9 June 1935, the rebuilt church was dedicated; designed in Byzantine style, it featured a crystal chandelier designed by Fr. Meena and a hand-inlaid altar screen crafted by a Damascus native, David Deeb. In 1954 Deeb, then 79 years of age, designed and constructed the Bishop's Throne for the church. In 1950 and 1957, St. George hosted the annual conventions of the Syrian Antiochian Orthodox Diocese. By 1959, "practically all" of the liturgy was being spoken in English, as church leaders attempted to attract younger members of the faith back into the church. A 2-story, $250,000 educational and cultural center, including classrooms and a gymnasium, was added to St. George in May 1964. During the 1970s, the church offered courses in Arabic and hosted an annual summer festival highlighting Middle Eastern culture.

St. George Orthodox Church, *40th Anniversary Commemoration, 1928–1968.*

**ST. GEORGE'S LITHUANIAN CHURCH** was the first church established for Lithuanian Catholics in the Diocese of Cleveland. Though the immigration of Lithuanian Catholics into the Cleveland area dated from the 1880s, the official establishment of St. George's parish did not occur until 1901. Before that time, Lithuanian Catholics usually affiliated with Polish churches. Fr. Joseph Maszotas, a Lithuanian seminarian ordained by Bp. RICHARD GILMOUR in 1889, served briefly at ST. STANISLAUS. He organized a Society of St. George for his countrymen, but there were not enough families to support a congregation. Visiting Lithuanian priests provided services for several years. In 1895 Fr. Joseph Delinikaitis organized a mission congregation, which met at St. Peter's Church. A year later he left for an assignment outside the diocese.

In 1901, the community had increased to the point where a parish could be maintained. Fr. Joseph Jankus, the first pastor, built a small wooden church at E. 21st St. and Oregon (Rockwell) Ave. Fr. Jankus remained as pastor until 1905, when he was succeeded by Rev. M. Plausinaitis, and then Msgr. Victor Pauksto. Fr. Joseph Halaburda became pastor in 1907. He acquired additional property at E. 65th and Superior Ave., where the present church building stands. He also began a parochial school staffed by the Notre

Dame Sisters for the parish children. Fr. Halaburda was succeeded in 1919 by Rev. Vincent G. Vilkutaitis, who remained as pastor for 40 years. The Sisters of St. Francis of the Providence of God replaced the Notre Dame Sisters as teachers in the school in 1932. They staffed the school until its closing in 1970. The parish of St. George's was divided in 1929, and the parish of Our Lady of Perpetual Help was established to serve the Lithuanians living in the COLLINWOOD and EUCLID areas.

**ST. HELENA'S ROMANIAN CATHOLIC CHURCH** is one of 16 Romanian Byzantine Rite (Uniate) parishes in the U.S. The parish was established on 19 Nov. 1905 through the efforts of Fr. Epaminonda Lucaciu, the first Romanian priest sent to the U.S. by the Bishop of Transylvania. The congregation met at ST. MALACHI'S CHURCH on W. 25th St. until their own church was completed at 1367 W. 65th St. Dedicated in Oct. 1906, the building was erected at a cost of $6,500. The frame structure was remodeled in 1939 and extensively rebuilt in 1965 at a cost of $72,000. A church hall was erected in 1942 and replaced in 1975 by a new social center, which in turn was expanded in 1981. Following Rev. Lucaciu's departure in 1907, the parish was ministered to by Rev. Dr. Alexandru Nicolescu (1907–09), Rev. Aurelius Hatiegan (1909–19), Rev. Dr. Geo. Babutiu (1934–50), and Rev. Mircea M. Toderich (1950–84). Fr. Hatiegan, the third parish priest, was also responsible for the establishment of an east side Romanian parish, Most Holy Trinity, on E. 93rd St. in 1916. The church has a Sunday religious school and a ladies' auxiliary (est. 1922).

*1906–1981, 75th Anniversary of Saint Helena Church in Cleveland* (1981).

**ST. JAMES AFRICAN METHODIST EPISCOPAL CHURCH** evolved from a small prayer meeting in 1894 to become one of the city's leading black churches. St. James AME developed from the small East End Prayer Meeting organized and hosted by Rosa Johnson and her husband, James, in their home at 44 Frank St. in Feb. 1894. The congregation had grown to 16 members by Mar. 1894, when it was reorganized as the East End Mission of ST. JOHN'S AME CHURCH. The congregation met in the Republican meeting place the Wigwam, at Cedar near Streator (E. 110th), from late Apr. 1894 until its own church building on Hudson Ave., begun in June 1896, was completed in Nov. 1899. The church had been incorporated a few months earlier. Beginning with Rev. W. W. Ponton in 1894, St. James AME was served by 6 pastors between 1894–1900. By Oct. 1903, it had 94 members and was out of debt. The succession of ministers continued in the early 1900s, with none serving more than 5 years until Rev. Joseph M. Evans (1919–26), whose tenure is called the "Progress Regime" in one church history. By 1925, the church had 516 members and Sunday school enrollment of 465; that year the congregation paid $57,000 for the former Trinity Congregational Church, 8401 Cedar Ave., a site the church has occupied since Jan. 1926.

Progress continued under the leadership of Rev. D. Ormonde Walker (1926–37), who became active and prominent in the civic and political affairs of the community as well as its religious life. On 27 Apr. 1927, he founded the St. James Literary Forum to "furnish a platform for the discussion of public questions by competent men and women." The forum became an important local institution and gained a national reputation. An occasional political candidate himself, Walker aggressively urged local BLACKS to abandon the Republican party and vote for Democrats. Rev. Joseph Gomez (1937–48) successfully rebuilt St. James

AME Church after it suffered $100,000 in damages from a fire on 2 Jan. 1938. The rebuilt church was dedicated on 4 May 1941 but was destroyed by another fire on 16 Mar. 1950. Rev. Hubert N. Robinson (1948–55) led the efforts to rebuild the church, which was dedicated again on 12 Apr. 1953. During the tenure of Rev. Donald G. Jacobs (1955–68), a $180,000 Education Annex was added. Jacobs led the church during the tumultuous civil-rights movement, giving it greater involvement in the problems of the inner city and making it a center for projects related to community issues. Jacobs's successor, Rev. Alvia A. Shaw, led a congregation of about 1,300 members in the mid-1970s and presided over the church's 85th-anniversary celebration in July 1979.

**ST. JOHN, SAMUEL** (1813–9 Sept. 1876), was a science professor, a proponent of natural history, and a newspaper publisher during his short time in the Cleveland area in the mid-1800s. Born in New Canaan, Conn. (where he also died), St. John was educated at Yale, where he studied chemistry and was valedictorian in 1834. In 1839 he began his teaching career at Western Reserve College in Hudson, becoming professor of chemistry, geology, and mineralogy, and teaching biology as well. When the college established its Medical Dept. in Cleveland in 1843, St. John was appointed to oversee the awarding of degrees by the medical faculty. He became professor of chemistry, natural history, and medical jurisprudence at the Medical College. St. John was active in several scientific endeavors in Cleveland. When the CLEVELAND ACADEMY OF NATURAL SCIENCES was organized on 24 Nov. 1845, he was one of its original curators and served as secretary. He also served as secretary of the controversial publication committee for the 1853 meeting in Cleveland of the American Assoc. for the Advancement of Science. In 1851 he and Prof. Jehu Brainard published a geology text, *Elements of Geology*. St. John also tried his hand at newspaper editing, joining Dr. JARED P. KIRTLAND and O. H. Knapp in 1850 as coeditor of the new weekly the *Family Visitor*, which was published until ca. 1858. In 1852, St. John resigned from Western Reserve College in a dispute with the administration over back salary owed him. He stayed in Cleveland, reportedly becoming principal of the CLEVELAND FEMALE SEMINARY in 1854. In 1856 he accepted a chair in chemistry at the College of Physicians & Surgeons in New York.

**ST. JOHN AND WEST SHORE HOSPITAL** (29000 center Ridge Rd.) is a 200-bed voluntary nonprofit general hospital. It serves as the core facility of the Westlake Health Campus Assoc., which in 1986 had as its major goal the development of a community-oriented health campus on 64 acres with a broad range of health and human services. The hospital, a 4-story stucture, was opened in 1981 and is coowned by ST. JOHN HOSPITAL and the West Shore Osteopathic (formerly Bay View) Hospital. Bay View Hospital (formerly located at 23200 Lake Rd.) was a 111-bed voluntary nonprofit short-term osteopathic hospital. The original structure was the Washington H. Lawrence mansion, built in 1899–1900. In 1948, Richard A. Sheppard, the founder and chief of staff of the Cleveland Osteopathic Hospital, established Bay View Hospital in the old mansion. A 60-bed addition was made in 1963, and a modernization program was completed in 1966. Dr. Stephen A. Sheppard became medical director in 1959. Bay View was one of a series of osteopathic hospitals (e.g., BRENTWOOD HOSPITAL, RICHMOND HTS. GENERAL HOSPITAL) that were established when osteopathic physicians were not allowed or found it difficult to practice medicine in allopathic hospitals. In 1981, Bay View was

855

closed, and its beds were transferred to St. John & West Shore Hospital. The hospital structure was converted into condominiums and named Cashelmara.

**ST. JOHN CATHEDRAL** was established by the first bishop of Cleveland, AMADEUS RAPPE, shortly after his appointment in 1847. He recognized that the Catholic population needed a more centrally located church than ST. MARY'S ON THE FLATS. Property on Erie St. (E. 9th) and Superior that had been purchased in 1845 by Fr. Peter McLaughlin was selected as the site for the new church. Bp. Rappe bought additional land on Superior and opened a temporary church, the Chapel of the Nativity, on Christmas Day 1848. This building also served as a parochial school during the week. The cornerstone for the new cathedral, which had been named for St. John the Evangelist, was laid on 22 Oct. 1848. Patrick Chas. Keeley designed the interior and much of the exterior in an Ornamental Gothic style. Keeley would later gain national prominence as a church architect. Financial difficulties postponed the completion of the church building until late 1852. In 1853 Bp. Rappe took over the pastorate of the cathedral when Fr. Louis de Goesbriand, its first pastor, was named bishop of Burlington, Vt. Bp. Rappe remained as pastor until his resignation as Cleveland's bishop in 1870.

The growing cathedral parish needed larger school facilities. A separate school for boys was opened in 1857 under a lay staff, most of whom were seminarians. The URSULINE SISTERS instructed the girls near their Euclid Ave. convent. In 1888 a new school building was constructed for the children. The cathedral school was closed in 1943 because of declining enrollment. Both Bp. IGNATIUS HORSTMANN (1892–1908) and Bp. JOHN P. FARRELLY (1909–21) considered transferring the cathedral to locations on the east side of Cleveland. Bp. JOSEPH SCHREMBS (1921–45) decided to keep the Superior Ave. location. He opened Sisters' College, a normal school for training the religious who would teach in the diocesan schools, in 1928 at the cathedral location. Between 1946–48, his successor, Bp. EDWARD F. HOBAN, extensively rebuilt and remodeled the buildings that made up the cathedral plant. A new building for Sisters' College, now renamed ST. JOHN COLLEGE, was included in the construction. In 1977, Bp. James A. Hickey renovated the sanctuary area of the cathedral, so it would be in conformity with the liturgical changes required by the Second Vatican Council.

Houck, George F., *A History of Catholicity in Northern Ohio and in the Diocese of Cleveland from 1749 to December 31, 1900* (1903).
Hynes, Michael J., *The History of the Diocese of Cleveland* (1953).
Papers of St. John Cathedral, Archives, Diocese of Cleveland.

**ST. JOHN COLLEGE** began as Sisters' College in 1928 to train teachers to staff the elementary schools of the Catholic Diocese of Cleveland. It later expanded its mission to preparing nurses for Catholic hospitals. A pioneer experiment in Catholic education, St. John was one of the few diocesan colleges in the U.S. In 1922, Archbp. JOSEPH SCHREMBS desired to unify the 9 normal schools operated by religious communities to train their young sisters. His plan, which took 6 years to accomplish, resulted in Sisters' College, set up in the old Cathedral School Bldg. at 1027 Superior. Within 4 years of its opening in 1928, it was granted full college status and the power to confer degrees; by 1935 it was accredited by the American Assoc. of Teachers Colleges. The first president was Bp. JOHN R. HAGAN. The college was set up to accommodate re-

ligious teachers who taught with provisional certificates while completing their education. As a result, enrollment was particularly heavy in the summer and Saturday sessions; the first summer session in 1928 had 274 students, while the fall Saturday enrollment was 427, as compared to the 38 full-time day students. Representatives of 28 religious orders attended the college; each order had a member on the faculty who oversaw and handled any problems involving her sisters. Lay students were welcome at the college so long as they were willing to be placed in a diocesan school after graduation. In its early years, Sisters' College offered a B.S. in education; though it expanded its offerings to include a B.S. in nursing (1947) and an M.A. in education (1939), the college never lost sight of its historical mission: to provide young women with an excellent education grounded in Catholic values. Education majors received 2 years of liberal-arts classes before their final 2 years of preparation for specific grade levels or subject areas. To give the students field experience, the diocese designated St. Stephen, St. Phillip Neri, St. Colman, Immaculate Conception, and Immaculate Heart as practicum schools.

By 1947, the college moved into new quarters in Cathedral Square at E. 9th and Superior, while the old facility became the Chancery. To reflect the broader range of students it now sought, Sisters' College became St. John College at the time of the move. Under the direction of Msgr. ROBT. NAVIN, the dean of students, the college acquired a high scholastic rating, a reputation for excellence, and a growing student body. St. John added new noncredit adult education classes to its curriculum and was the site of frequent seminars on labor-management relations and meeting of clergy and laity. In the 1950s, the college became owner and curator of the valuable art collection of Archbp. EDWARD F. HOBAN. Because of growing financial problems over the years, the college could not properly maintain the works, and in 1973 it auctioned off the religious paintings, ivories, bronzes, and artifacts for $250,000. An enrollment boom in the 1960s necessitated a new addition; as the demand for teachers dropped off by the early 1970s, the college pondered its future as enrollment slid and the diocese threatened to withhold its subsidies. A trustees' committee led by Richard DeChant of the GREATER CLEVELAND GROWTH ASSOC., the first Catholic layman on the board, explored alternative courses of action: merger with another Catholic college, operation as a self-sustaining college, or closing. Ultimately, the nursing program, which accounted for the majority of the school's undergraduates, was moved to URSULINE COLLEGE so as not to lose program accreditation, and the remainder of school closed in June 1975 amid student protest.

**ST. JOHN HOSPITAL** (St. John of God Hospital), located at 7911 Detroit Ave., was opened in 1890 by the Sisters of St. Francis of Lafayette, Ind. Land was purchased by Bp. RICHARD GILMOUR with a gift from W. J. Gordon, and a hospital was constructed to serve Cleveland's west side Catholic community. In 1916, Bp. JOHN FARRELLY asked the SISTERS OF CHARITY OF ST. AUGUSTINE to take over administration of the hospital and establish a school of nursing. The first department of physical therapy in Ohio was established at the hospital in 1920. In 1940, St. John installed a million-volt x-ray unit, which was the second of its kind in the U.S. Along with facilities in Seattle, New York, and Chicago, St. John provided advanced radiotherapy for cancer patients. St. John Hospital School of Nursing closed in 1971. Extensive renovation of the hospital buildings occurred in 1980 and 1982. In 1986, St. John was a 200-bed general acute-care hospital. Clifton Care (W. 115th St. and Clifton Blvd.) and Brooklyn Care Ctr. (4370

Ridge Rd.) were 2 urgent-care centers of St. John Hospital. It was a coowner, with the West Shore Osteopathic Hospital, of ST. JOHN & WEST SHORE HOSPITAL (29000 Center Ridge Rd., WESTLAKE), and a subsidiary member of the Sisters of Charity of St. Augustine Health & Human Services, a Catholic multihospital system with its headquarters in Richfield, Ohio.

**ST. JOHN'S AME (AFRICAN METHODIST EPISCOPAL) CHURCH** was the first and only permanent black church to be established in Cleveland during the antebellum period. The original charter was issued to the African Methodist-Episcopal Society, a group of 6 persons who had been recruited in 1830 by Fr. Wm. Paul Quinn, Western Section missionary for the new black denomination. Originally, the society met in the homes of members, but as the group grew, services were held in the Apollo Hall located on the 3d floor in Merwin Square. The first church building was located at the southwest corner of Bolivar and Prospect Ave. and was dedicated on 6 Jan. 1850. The congregation was known at that time as the Bolivar St. AME Church. Subsequent moves were to Ohio St. (part of Carnegie Ave. in 1986) in 1863, where the name was changed to the Ohio Street AME Church; then to Erie (E. 9th) St. in 1878, when the name was changed to St. John's AME Church. In 1908 the congregation erected a new church at E. 40th and Central Ave., where it remained located in 1986. The congregation grew from the small band of ex-slaves who were issued the first charter in 1836 to later represent every stratum of the city's black community. The AME denomination originated as an expression of northern black dissatisfaction with a trend toward segregation inside mainline Protestant churches. However, during the 19th century, many local blacks retained membership within white institutions. When Cleveland attracted a larger black population after WORLD WAR I and the city became more divided, the church attracted a larger membership. Its location within the Central community made it a natural focus for recreational and social activities for BLACKS from the 1920s.

**ST. JOHN'S BECKWITH MEMORIAL CHURCH** was a Protestant mission to the Italian immigrant community that developed in the late 19th century in the east end known as LITTLE ITALY. A Sunday school was started in the summer of 1888 for Italian children and adults in an orchard near LAKE VIEW CEMETERY by Louise Woodward and Florence Cozad, members of the EUCLID AVE. CONGREGATIONAL CHURCH. A mission was established in 1890 by Euclid Ave. Congregational with the assistance of the Congregational City Mission Society, which assumed sole responsibility in 1901. The mission was based at Lakeview Congregational Church until 1904 and subsequently used a rented hall. In 1904, an Italian pastor, Rev. Pietro Monnet, was called. Rev. Monnet, faced with financial difficulties, went to the Second Presbyterian Church (later a part of CHURCH OF THE COVENANT), and in 1906, with the permission of the founding organizations, responsibility for the mission was assumed by the Session of the Second Presbyterian Church, with funds from the bequest of T. Sterling Beckwith. A building was dedicated on 27 Feb. 1907 at the corner of Murray Hill Rd. and Paul St. as St. John's Beckwith Memorial Church. Much of the work of constructing and finishing the building was contributed by members. In 1907 the church had 36 members.

The church had an independent session (governing board) until 1922, when, faced with internal difficulties and financial problems, the session was dissolved, and the church was placed in the charge of the Italian Mission Committee

of the Church of the Covenant. The congregation grew steadily from 38 members in 1926 to 125 in the early 1960s. During the long pastorate of Rev. Fiore D'Isidoro, services continued in both English and Italian, and renovations were made to the building in 1953–54. In 1955, Church of the Covenant severed its connection with St. John's Beckwith, and the mission was constituted as an independent church. In late 1961 or early 1962, the Presbytery of the Western Reserve officially dissolved the church, and in 1963 the property was sold and the members dispersed into other congregations.

Rev. Fiore D'Isidoro Papers, WRHS.

**ST. JOHN'S EPISCOPAL CHURCH,** which claims for its founding date and place the same meeting at the home of Phineas Shepherd in BROOKLYN as TRINITY Parish, survives as the congregation with the oldest church edifice standing in the Cleveland area. The claim to the common founding date stems from Trinity Parish's having been organized in 1816 in Shepherd's home on the west side of the CUYAHOGA RIVER. When that parish returned to the east side in 1826, several Brooklyn families left it, and in 1834 they founded St. John's, meeting in the Columbus Block in OHIO CITY until occupying the basement of their new church on the corner of Church and Wall (W. 26th) streets. A founding member of the parish, Hezekiah Eldredge, architect and master builder, contracted to construct the building of gray sandstone in the Gothic style, completed in 1838. It features a square central tower and octagonal turrets at the 4 corners. The interior was on a rectangular plan, with a raised projecting chancel at the front and choir gallery to the rear.

A fire in 1866 left only the exterior walls standing. The reconstruction steepened the pitch of the roof and arranged the interior on a cruciform plan. In the late 19th century, a Gothic Revival parish house was added to the west of the building. In 1953 a tornado destroyed the roof and chancel, and in this restoration the interior was returned to its original rectangular plan. Finials were removed from the turrets and the tower in 1965. The church is said to have been a key point on the Underground Railroad. Fugitive slaves holed up in the tower until signals were seen from the lake, calling them to the last leg of their escape. Two parishes were organized in the 1870s out of missions of St. John's: All Saints and St. Mark's. By the 1960s, the older, wealthier element in the parish was gone. A group known as the Inner City Protestant Parish was formed and met at St. John's. Two congregations, an older, conservative Episcopal one and a more active interdenominational one, existed side by side until the late 1960s, when the Inner City Parish was merged into St. John's. In 1981, structural deterioration forced the congregation to stop meeting in the building. A portion of the building was restored by an outside tenant; plans are being made and funds raised throughout the diocese to restore and maintain the building and the parish in the 1980s.

St. John's Episcopal Parish Records, WRHS.

**ST. JOHN'S EVANGELICAL LUTHERAN CHURCH** is located at 5830 Cable Ave. One of the largest congregations in the Missouri Synod at one time, it was organized as a daughter parish of ZION EVANGELICAL LUTHERAN CHURCH, E. 30th St. and Prospect Ave. On 1 Sept. 1878, approximately 15 families, many from Zion Lutheran Church, formed the congregation and selected the name St. John's German Evangelical Church. Rev. August Dankworth, the congregation's first pastor, was installed 20 Oct.

1878 and conducted services temporarily at Engel's Hall at the corner of E. 49th St. and Broadway Ave. Henry Hoppensack, one of the founders, donated land on Bessemer St. near Tod (E. 65th) St. for a new church building. It was erected, quickly furnished, and dedicated on 24 Nov. 1878. Later that year, it joined the Evangelical Church Lutheran Synod of Missouri. Many German Lutheran families who had come to the old NEWBURGH area to work in the steel mills joined the congregation, and the membership increased. During the pastorate of Rev. Karl Kretzman (1887–97) the neighborhood became increasingly industrialized, and consequently the 1,000–1,500-member congregation decided to relocate. A new church was constructed at 5830 Cable Ave. near Broadway and E. 55th St., and was dedicated on 9 Mar. 1902. Church membership increased until it became one of the largest in the Missouri Synod, and St. John's Day School, the largest in the synod, had over 500 pupils. In 1939 the word *German* was dropped from the church's name. In the 1950s membership began to decline as more and more church members moved to the suburbs. The school closed on 9 June 1958, and by 1964 it had become St. John's Inner City Church, with a membership of 350 communicants. The congregation voted to close the church, and on 30 June 1985, Pastor Richard Gahl, executive director of the Ohio District's Missouri Synod, conducted the final worship service for the 60-member congregation. In 1986 the building was demolished, and the land became a parking lot.

**ST. JOSEPH HOME FOR THE AGED,** located at 6431 Woodland Ave., provided care for its ambulatory elderly residents from Jan. 1944 until it closed in Jan. 1966. The Franciscan Sisters of the Blessed Kunegunda, newly arrived in Cleveland from Chicago, opened the home on 6 Dec. 1943 in the building formerly occupied by ST. JOSEPH'S ORPHANAGE, which had moved to 18485 Lake Shore Blvd. The first resident was admitted on 2 Jan. 1944, while the building was being renovated. Officially dedicated on 18 Feb. 1945, the home had the capacity to serve 100 residents; however, it soon had 108. The building that housed the home was built in the late 1870s, and with little renovation other than that done in 1944 to transform it from an orphanage into a home for the elderly, the structure was in poor condition by the late 1960s. Urban-renewal projects in the surrounding neighborhood made expensive renovation unwise, since the building could have been lost to urban-renewal efforts at a later date. As a result, the St. Joseph Home for the Aged was officially closed on 1 Jan. 1966, and the remaining 55 residents were transferred to JENNINGS HALL, the LITTLE SISTERS OF THE POOR, and the St. Edwards Home in Akron.

**ST. JOSEPH HOSPITAL,** the first general public hospital in Cleveland, was established on 5 Aug. 1852 in a 2-story frame house at Willett and Monroe streets in OHIO CITY. The SISTERS OF CHARITY OF ST. AUGUSTINE were invited by BP. AMADEUS RAPPE of the Catholic Diocese of Cleveland to come to Cleveland and undertake the management of a hospital in the diocese. The hospital building was purchased from a railroad company with funds derived from the sale of sand and gravel from diocesan-owned property. A public fair was held in Kelly's Hall (Superior St.) to raise money for the hospital. Two Sisters of Charity, Sr. Bernadine and Sr. Francoise, and 2 novices (Louise Brouillat and Cornelia Muselet) came from the Hospital of St. Louis in Boulogne-sur-Mer, France, to staff the new facility. In addition to caring for indigent patients, St. Joseph served as an orphanage. Boys were taught carpentry and tailoring and made suits and cassocks for Cleveland's

Catholic clergy. The hospital was closed in 1856, but the building continued to be used as an orphanage until St. Vincent Orphanage was completed in 1859. The facility's location away from the central city and its emerging identity as an orphanage may explain the demise of St. Joseph Hospital. In 1865, the Sisters of Charity of St. Augustine again established a hospital, ST. VINCENT CHARITY HOSPITAL, to serve the poor in Cleveland.

Gavin, Donald R., *In All Things Charity* (1955).
Hynes, Michael J., *History of the Diocese of Cleveland (1847–1952)* (1953).

**ST. JOSEPH'S ORPHANAGE FOR GIRLS** was a Catholic institution that existed from 1863–1947, when its residents were transferred to PARMADALE CHILDREN'S VILLAGE. St. Joseph's had its beginnings in Oct. 1851 with the organization of ST. MARY'S Asylum for Females. St. Joseph's was organized officially in 1863, when 12 of the younger girls from St. Mary's were moved to a large brick building in a "country location" on Woodland near E. 60th St. (6431 Woodland). St. Joseph's was operated by the Daughters of the Immaculate Heart of Mary. A chapel was added to St. Joseph's in 1866, and in 1871 the institution had 160 young residents. The addition of a 3-story brick building in 1879 increased the asylum's capacity, so that by 1881, St. Joseph's and St. Mary's had a combined total of 195 residents. For years, St. Joseph's served as the home for young orphans under the age of 8; at age 9, the girls were sent to St. Mary's for education and training. That changed in the 1890s with the merger of the two asylums into St. Joseph's; the addition of another 3-story brick residence in 1894, financed by the sale of some adjoining land, further increased capacity, and the girls from St. Mary's were transferred to St. Joseph's, which was incorporated in 1889. The old St. Mary's property on Harmon (E. 20th) was reopened in 1895 as St. Mary's Home for Working Girls. The 1907 *Cleveland Charities Directory* listed capacity at the orphanage at 250, but according to Cleveland Diocese historian Michael Hynes, St. Joseph's was home to 245 girls in 1908. In 1923, the orphanage had 42 staff members and a budget of $46,533 and was a member of the Welfare Fed. By 1937, the staff had been increased to 53, and the average number of residents had fallen to 120–140. In Mar. 1944, the 108 girls in St. Joseph's were transferred from Woodland Ave. to the former CUNNINGHAM SANITORIUM at Lake Shore Blvd. and E. 185th St. (18485 Lake Shore Blvd.), which had been acquired by the Cleveland Catholic Diocese and renamed St. Joseph's-on-the-Lake. The former St. Joseph's on Woodland was remodeled and reopened as the ST. JOSEPH HOME FOR THE AGED. The girls remained at St. Joseph's-on-the-Lake until 1947, when they were moved to Parmadale.

Hynes, Michael, *History of the Diocese of Cleveland* (1953).

**ST. LADISLAS CHURCH,** the first church for Slovak Catholics in Cleveland, dates from 1885. In that year Fr. STEPHAN FURDEK began holding services at St. Joseph's Church on Woodland Ave. for SLOVAKS living in the downtown neighborhood bounded by Berg, Commercial, and Hill streets. In 1889, Fr. Furdek bought property on Corwin St. and Holton Ave. and began constructing a church. Bp. RICHARD GILMOUR consecrated the new church of St. Ladislas in December of that year. The new parish had originally been composed of HUNGARIANS and Slovaks. By 1890, Fr. John Martvon was its first pastor. In 1892 the Hungarians withdrew to establish their own parish, ST. ELIZABETH'S. The parish grew so large that Bp. IGNATIUS F. HORSTMANN established the parish of St. Martin to serve the Slovaks living in the downtown area. Fr. Martvon's successor, Fr. V. Panuska, became St. Martin's founding pastor in 1894. The following priests served as pastor of St. Ladislas between 1894–1904: Fr. J. Jiranek, Fr. Peter Cerveny, Fr. John Tichy, and Fr. F. Horvath. Fr. John Svozil was named pastor in 1904 and began planning a new church; it was designed by architect Emil Uhlrich and was dedicated by Bp. Horstmann on 7 Oct. 1906. In 1907, the Notre Dame sisters replaced the Ursuline nuns as teachers in the parish school. The next pastor of St. Ladislas was Fr. Ladislas Necid, who served 1907–42. The school had become crowded, and many parishioners now lived farther east in the Buckeye Rd./Woodland area. Fr. Necid built a new school at Lamontier and East Blvd. for them; it became the nucleus of the new St. Benedict parish in 1928. The original St. Ladislas School in the Holton neighborhood closed, but was reopened in 1931 under the direction of the Vincentian Sisters of Charity. Shifts in population caused it to close for good in 1967. A fire destroyed the church building on 8 Aug. 1970. A decision to close the Holton site and relocate the parish was made. The new parish of St. Ladislas was established at 2345 Basset Rd. in Westlake in 1973.

Papers of St. Ladislas, Archives, Diocese of Cleveland.

**SAINT LUKE'S HOSPITAL,** one of Ohio's largest private hospitals, is a 500-bed general and teaching hospital, providing services in general and special surgery, general and special medicine, obstetrics and gynecology, pediatrics, psychiatry, radiation therapy, and diagnostic radiology. St. Luke's was founded on 30 Jan. 1894 as Cleveland General Hospital. On that day, the articles of incorporation of the College Bldg. & Hospital Assoc. were signed, and in the fall of the same year, Cleveland General was opened with 75 beds on Woodland Ave. near E. 20th. The hospital's main purpose was to provide clinical training for students from the Medical Dept. of Wooster University, and a training school for nurses. The incorporators were Dr. GUSTAV WEBER, Leonard Schlather, Jas. B. Parker, and Drs. MARCUS ROSENWASSER, Henry W. Kitchen, and Chas. B. Parker. All were variously connected with the Medical Dept. of Wooster University. Many notable doctors, nurses, and administrators have been connected with St. Luke's. Important figures in its early development included Sister Caroline Kirkpatrick, superintendent of the Training School for Nurses; FRANCIS F. PRENTISS, one of the first presidents; and his wife, Elisabeth Prentiss, who provided vital financial support. In 1906, under the leadership of Francis Prentiss, Cleveland General was renamed St. Luke's Hospital. The year before, the medical staff had become affiliated with the medical department of Ohio Wesleyan University, a Methodist institution. As St. Luke's, its purpose was amended to "conduct a general hospital and school of nursing." In 1908 the hospital moved to a new 120-bed facility on Carnegie Ave. near E. 66th. By 1910, the bed capacity had been increased to 180, and the Cleveland Maternity Dispensary was added to the hospital. It remained at the Carnegie location until 1927, when it moved into a new hospital, largely financed by Mrs. Prentiss, on Shaker Blvd. near E. 116th St. At this time there were approximately 40 physicians on the medical staff, 12 on the house staff, and 125 nurses.

Following the Depression, St. Luke's embarked on a periodic program of expansion that continued until the early 1980s. In 1942 a central service wing was added, housing Medical Research, Surgical Research, the Dietary Dept., Purchasing, and Accounting. Completion of the Nurses' Residence in 1948 freed the East Wing and enabled the hospital to increase its bed capacity. Two other buildings were completed in 1963 and 1975. St. Luke's also increased its affiliations with area nursing schools, including CUYAHOGA COMMUNITY COLLEGE (1964) and Kent State University (1968); its own school of nursing closed in 1970. Over the years, St. Luke's achieved distinction through several of its departments. Early graduates of the Training School for Nurses were the first to practice public-health nursing in the city. Under Dr. ARTHUR SKEEL, the Obstetrics Div. from 1910–38 was the most advanced and innovative unit of its kind in Cleveland. The Dept. of Research, organized in 1952, originated studies in emphysema and cardiocirculatory problems and went on to develop the first heart-lung machine. Since 1975, St. Luke's has placed emphasis on developing specialty areas such as ophthalmology. Through the ST. LUKE'S HOSPITAL ASSOC., it has also attempted to acquire or affiliate with other hospitals for shared services and special programs.

The **SAINT LUKE'S HOSPITAL ASSOCIATION** is a multi-institutional system consisting of hospitals that ST. LUKE'S has acquired or affiliated with for shared services and special programs. The SLHA was founded in 1904 as "Saint Luke's Hospital Association of Cleveland, Ohio, of the Methodist Episcopal Church." A corporation, it had previously been known as the College Bldg. & Hospital Assoc., which operated Cleveland General Hospital. The articles of incorporation were amended to state a new purpose, "to maintain and conduct a general hospital and school of nursing in Cleveland, Ohio, under the control of the Methodist Episcopal Church and acquire by gift or otherwise the necessary real estate, buildings, property and funds, and do all other things incident thereto." Until 1980, the history of the SLHA was largely that of a single hospital site, St. Luke's. In 1980, the association adopted a long-range plan of acquisition and new programs. The plan included placing physicians in suburban medical buildings to create greater accessibility for patients; to build a 24-hour emergency center in SOLON to serve Chagrin Valley residents; to acquire or affiliate with other hospitals; and to create a for-profit corporation that would be a new source of revenue. By 1983, the SLHA held leases on 5 medical buildings, observed the growth of the Emergency Ctr. of Solon, acquired SHAKER MEDICAL CTR. HOSPITAL, founded Medical Outreach Services—a for-profit venture for diversification and profitability, and negotiated affiliations with the Northeast Ohio Family Practice Ctr. in Solon and BRENTWOOD HOSPITAL for residency programs. That year it became a parent company with control over St. Luke's Hospital, Shaker Medical Ctr. Hospital, and Medical Services Outreach Services, Inc. That allowed the assets and liabilities of all the corporations to be consolidated under the association so that the best interests of the entire system could be served. Each subsidiary corporation, however, maintained its own board of trustees and control over operating decisions.

**ST. MALACHI'S CHURCH,** located on Cleveland's near west side, was organized to partition the large Irish ST. PATRICK'S parish and to place a parish closer to residential sections near the lake on the near west side. The parish was organized and a building site purchased in 1866. The congregation met at ST. MARY'S ON THE FLATS until their brick Gothic building was completed on the corner of Washington Ave. and Pearl (W. 25th) St. The dedication was held in Mar. 1871. The building was well known for its tall spire and illuminated cross, visible to sailors on Lake

Erie. It was also notable for its statuary. In 1867 the first parish school was built, and a former public school was purchased soon after for a separate boys' school. A new school building was built in 1885. The URSULINE SISTERS taught girls only until 1914, when they took over all classes on the departure of the Christian Brothers. A new building for the church was built of stone in a Gothic style in 1945–46 and was dedicated at the original site in 1947.

After a one-time high of 2,000 families early in the century, membership had fallen to 60 families by 1928. A rebirth took place with the construction of the LAKEVIEW TERRACE public-housing project, which added 620 families, half of which were Catholic. By 1938 membership had climbed to 400 families, and the school was enlarged. The parish school became the Urban Community School in 1968 and continued under the direction of the Ursulines. Eventually both ST. PATRICK'S and ST. WENDELIN parish schools were incorporated into Urban Community School. One parish was merged with St. Malachi's, the French-speaking Annunciation parish, in 1916. No divisions have taken place.

Ohio Historic Records Survey Project, Works Projects Admin., *Parishes of the Catholic Church, Diocese of Cleveland* (1942).

**ST. MARON** congregation dates from 1914, when approximately 10 immigrant families from Syria and Lebanon formed the St. John Maron Society. They were Catholics of the Maronite Rite who had worshipped in Latin Rite churches but wished to preserve their religious heritage by establishing their own Maronite church. The St. John Maron Society raised the necessary funds, and a house at 2214 E. 21st St. was bought for use as a church in 1915. Bp. JOHN P. FARRELLY blessed the remodeled home on 2 Apr. 1916. Rev. Peter Chelala was the first pastor. In 1939, the parish acquired the church building of ST. ANTHONY'S parish at 1245 Carnegie. That congregation had vacated the structure because of its merger with St. Bridget's Church. The parish was named St. Maron and has since become a center of Lebanese culture. A number of church societies effectively preserved both the religious heritage and the culture of the church. The church building was extensively remodeled and renovated in the 1980s.

Archives, Diocese of Cleveland.

**ST. MARTIN OF TOURS PARISH** was one of Cleveland's nonterritorial ethnic Catholic parishes, serving Slovak families on the east side. St. Martin was established in 1893 by Bp. IGNATIUS F. HORSTMANN to permit a large number of members of ST. LADISLAS parish (E. 92nd St. and Holton Ave.) to worship nearer their homes. It was attended as a mission until 1894, when the first pastor, Rev. Wenceslas Panuska, was appointed, and a building was purchased on Henry (E. 23rd) St. near Scovill Ave. from an Evangelical Lutheran congregation. This church, enlarged in 1896, served until 1907, when a stone building of French Gothic style was built at Scovill Ave. and E. 23rd St. In 1894, a frame building on the church property was remodeled into a school, and a convent for the Sisters of St. Joseph, who taught in the school, was provided. The school was enlarged in 1896.

The original communicants of St. Martin's were Slovak. Of the 30 Cleveland parishes organized between 1892–1908, only 8 were territorial; the rest served various nationalities. Of these, 5 were Slovak. By the 1950s, population had radically declined in the parish; membership had dropped from a high of 2,500 families at the turn of the century to 55 families by the mid-1950s. The parish school

was closed in 1950, and the church itself closed in 1958. Furnishings and appointments were sent to the new St. Martin's parish at 14600 Dunham Rd. in GARFIELD HTS. The final mass was said 11 Sept. 1960, with the Te Deum sung in Slovak. The building was razed the same week. Three parishes were formed out of St. Martin: St. Andrews (1906), SS. CYRIL & METHODIUS (1902), and OUR LADY OF MERCY (1922).

**ST. MARY SEMINARY,** the Diocese of Cleveland's graduate school of theology, opened in 1848. In that year Bp. AMADEUS RAPPE remodeled a stable at Bond (E. 6th) St. and St. Clair for the education of students for the diocesan priesthood. This seminary was originally known as St. Francis de Sales Seminary, but the name was changed to St. Mary Seminary after a short time. At various times in its history, the seminary also carried the subtitle of Our Lady of the Lake. By 1850, the seminary needed more space. Bp. Rappe bought the former Spring Cottage Bath House at Lake and Hamilton streets. Even with the addition of new buildings in 1853 and 1856, still more space was needed, and Rappe built a larger structure on that site in 1859.

In 1922, Bp. JOSEPH SCHREMBS decided to restrict the seminary to an undergraduate college program and sent the Cleveland seminarians to Mt. St. Mary Seminary in the Cincinnati archdiocese for their theological studies. He also purchased a plot of land at Superior and Ansel roads and began the construction of the present (1985) Spanish mission-style building in 1924. By 1929 Schrembs decided that Cleveland should once again provide graduate theological training for its future priests. Until 1954, St. Mary Seminary provided both undergraduate and graduate theology programs for Cleveland students. In that year a separate college program was established at the Borromeo campus in Wickliffe. St. Mary Seminary became a fully accredited member of the Assoc. of Theological Schools in 1971. In 1985, the curriculum of the seminary was designed to give students a broadly based preparatory experience. Its 5-year program offered courses in theology and other subjects necessary for successful ministerial work.

Archives, Diocese of Cleveland.

**ST. MARY'S ON THE FLATS,** the colloquial name of the parish of Our Lady of the Lakes, was the first Catholic church in Cleveland. It was organized in 1826 when Irish Catholic immigrants arrived to work on the construction of the Ohio Canal. Before its closing, it was also the parent of many west side parishes and ST. JOHN CATHEDRAL. Masses were first said in Cleveland by visiting priests, including Very Rev. Stephen Badin, the first priest ordained in America. The first resident pastor was a Clevelander, John Dillon, appointed in 1835, under whose pastorate the parish met in the Masonic Hall, Shakespeare Hall, and Mechanics Hall. Fr. Dillon died the following year at the age of 29, but before his death he managed to raise $1,000 toward a church building. In 1837, property at the corner of Columbus and Girard streets in the Flats was sold on land contract for the purpose of establishing the parish of Our Lady of the Lakes, although this name was eventually replaced by the more common St. Mary on the Flats. The first mass was said in the frame building in 1839. Dedication followed in June 1840, and the building was completed later that year. It was a mixture of Greek Revival details. In 1847 the Diocese of Cleveland was established, and Most Rev. AMADEUS RAPPE became the first bishop. St. Mary on the Flats became his cathedral and served until St. John Cathedral was completed at Superior and Erie (E. 9th) streets in 1852. Upon completion of the cathedral, St. Mary's began its life as the mother of west side churches. German-speaking Catholics worshipped there from 1847–65, when St. Mary's of the Assumption was complete. ST. MALACHI'S (1865), ST. WENCESLAS (1867), Annunciation (1870), and ST. STANISLAUS (1872–79) parishes all met at St. Mary's until their own buildings were built. The first Catholic church in Cleveland was the first to be closed; the last mass was said in the decaying building in Jan. 1886. The building was razed in 1888.

Ohio Historic Records Survey Project, Works Projects Admin., *Parishes of the Catholic Church, Diocese of Cleveland* (1942).

**ST. MARY'S ORPHAN ASYLUM FOR FEMALES** was organized in Oct. 1851 on St. Clair near E. 6th to provide shelter and other aid to homeless girls ages 2–8. A home for older girls, on Harmon (E. 20th) St., was organized in 1854. Both homes were founded by Bp. AMADEUS RAPPE and were staffed by an order of nuns known as the Ladies of the Sacred Heart of Mary (of the Sisterhood of France), the first of that order to become established in the U.S. The home for younger girls received primarily orphans, but also girls from impoverished homes and "weak minded" girls. At the age of 9, the girls were sent to the home on Harmon St., where they received a basic education and were trained in general household duties in order to become self-supporting. In the early 1860s, the home for younger girls moved to Woodland Ave. and became ST. JOSEPH'S Orphan Asylum. St. Mary's Orphan Asylum on Harmon St. was a 3-story brick structure that could accommodate 150 girls ages 9–16. It was supported by general collections, fairs, donations, and earnings of the older girls, who, when old enough, found employment in private homes. In 1894, St. Joseph's Orphan Asylum was enlarged to accommodate the older girls from St. Mary's. The home on Harmon St. reopened the following year as St. Mary's Home for Young Women. It was intended as a temporary home for girls and young women seeking employment. Later it became known as St. Mary's Home for Working Girls. It continued under that name until its closing in the early 1930s.

**ST. MARY'S ROMANIAN ORTHODOX CHURCH** was established on 15 Aug. 1904 by a constitutive assembly of 101 members of Cleveland's Romanian immigrant community. The church's first structure, at 6201–05 Detroit Ave., cost $10,000 and was dedicated in Aug. 1905. It was struck by fire twice, first in June 1918 and again in Dec. 1932. In Jan. 1927, the church dedicated a church hall, known as "the National Home": the dedication was attended by Prince Nicholas of Hohenzollern, son of Queen Marie of Romania. In Aug. 1960, the church moved to a new structure at 3256 Warren Rd. Situated on a 7.5-acre site, the building, designed by Haralamb Georescu of Los Angeles, was constructed in the style of the wooden churches of Transylvania. The original church hall at the new site was destroyed by fire in July 1973. It was subsequently replaced in 1975 by a social hall that includes meeting space, a library, and a permanent Romanian ethnographic museum, the largest nationality museum in Greater Cleveland. The congregation's first priest, Rev. Fr. Moise Balea, served from 1905-Nov. 1907. Active in the Romanian community, Fr. Bales eventually established 20 parishes throughout the U.S. and was the founder of *America*, the first Romanian Orthodox newspaper published in the U.S. Six priests served the church between 1907–28. They were followed by 2 priests, Rev. John Trutza (1928–54) and Rev. Vasile Hategan (1954–82), who were very much responsible

for the growth of the church and the resolution of various financial difficulties. Rev. Richard Grabowski of California succeeded Rev. Hategan in 1982. In addition to its museum, the church also supports classes in religious education and a number of clubs and societies, including a ladies' auxiliary and a church mothers' club.

Hategan, Vasile, *St. Mary's Romanian Orthodox Church* (1979).

**ST. PATRICK'S PARISH**, referred to as the mother church of the west side, is one of the oldest parishes of the Cleveland Catholic Diocese. It originally served a largely IRISH population, but eventually served a variety of nationality groups in the area. St. Patrick's was founded in 1853, 6 years after the Cleveland Diocese was established. Two lots on Whitman Ave. were purchased, and a brick church was dedicated on Christmas 1853 and consecrated in 1857. The present (1985) building on 3602 Bridge Ave. west of Fulton Rd. was begun in Aug. 1871 and built slowly over the next several years. Sanctuary, sacristy, tower, and stained-glass windows were added in 1913, and the church was finally consecrated on St. Patrick's Day 1931. It is of stone, in the Gothic style, with a square central tower and steeply pitched roof. During the first year of the parish, the church housed a boys' school, and a girls' school, taught by the URSULINE SISTERS, was opened at Franklin Circle. In 1863, a new hall on Whitman Ave. housed the girls' school; a new, larger school was opened in Aug. 1891. At one point near the beginning of the 20th century, St. Patrick's was reported to be the largest parochial school in the U.S. The school ceased operation in 1976, when it was merged into the Urban Community School at ST. MALACHI'S parish. The building was razed in 1978. St. Patrick's has been divided many times, thus gaining its "mother church" status. Among the parishes formed from it are St. Augustine (1860), St. Mary's of the Assumption (1865), St. Malachi's (1865), Annunciation (1871), St. Stephen (1873), St. Procop (1874), St. Colman's (1880), St. Michael (1883), St. John Cantius (1899), St. Rose of Lima (1908), and Blessed Sacrament (1903). The parish has survived the changes in its neighborhood and in the early 1980s was the object of renovation and restoration to the church and parish hall.

**ST. PAUL'S CHURCH** is the only parish serving Latin Rite CROATIANS in the city of Cleveland. The first Croatians in Cleveland attended religious services at ST. VITUS CHURCH. However, the immigrants desired a priest conversant in Croatian. By 1901, the Croatian community was large enough to support a church. On 21 July 1901 they purchased the present parish site on E. 40th just south of St. Clair Ave. Fr. Milan Sutlic, newly arrived from Croatia, became St. Paul's first pastor in 1902. The cornerstone of the church was laid on 2 Aug. 1903. The first church services in the new building were held on Easter Sunday in 1904. In 1904, Fr. Sutlic was succeeded by Fr. Nicholas Grskovic. A parochial school was begun under his direction in 1910. Fr. Michael Domladovac became pastor in 1917. In 1920 he hired the Sisters of the Third Order of St. Francis of Christ the King to teach in the parish school. Fr. Joseph Misich became pastor in 1937. It was during his administration that the mortgage was paid off. He encouraged a number of vocations to the priesthood and religious life. An influx of Croatian refugees occurred after WORLD WAR II. The parish was instrumental in helping many of them find permanent homes and employment. In 1986, the parish was the center of Catholic Croatian culture in Cleveland.

Papers of St. Paul's Parish, Archives, Diocese of Cleveland.

**ST. PAUL'S EPISCOPAL CHURCH**, organized at a time of rapid development among Cleveland churches, has followed the path of its parishioners' migration from central city to suburban locations. The parish was organized with 45 members at the American House Hotel on 26 Oct. 1846, with Gideon B. Perry as the first rector. Services were held in rented rooms until a frame church was built on the southeast corner of Euclid and Sheriff (E. 4th) streets in 1848. This building burned before its completion, and the entire city contributed to the construction of its replacement, a brick Gothic building opened in 1851 and consecrated in 1858. As the area became more commercial, St. Paul's sold the Euclid and Sheriff site and met in temporary quarters until a new church at Euclid and Case (E. 40th) St. was completed in 1876; the first services were held there on Christmas Eve. The building was Victorian Gothic, faced in sandstone and designed by Gordon W. Lloyd of Detroit. This new site placed St. Paul's in the center of the fashionable Euclid Ave. "Millionaires' Row," and the church became identified with the district. Several churches were started from St. Paul's, including EMMANUEL (1876), St. Philip the Apostle (1894), Christ Church (1909), and Grace Church, South (1869). By the 1920s, the population of the parish was shifting to the suburbs, and the St. Paul's vestry elected to move the church to CLEVELAND HTS., joining with St. Martin's parish. A new building was begun at the corner of Fairmount and Coventry roads, designed by the Cleveland firm of Walker & Weeks. The parish hall was erected in 1927-28, the 125-ft. tower in 1929; and after many delays and changes, the church was completed in 1949-51. The style is an adaptation of English Gothic idioms. The building at Euclid and E. 40th St. was sold in 1931 to the Cleveland Catholic Diocese and was rededicated as St. Paul's Shrine of the Blessed Sacrament. Several noted clergymen have served the parish, including Dr. WALTER R. BREED, Dr. Theodore H. Evans, and Dr. Chave McCracken. Additionally, 2 curators of music at the CLEVELAND MUSEUM OF ART have served as organist/choirmaster: WALTER BLODGETT and Karel Paukert, both widely known as recitalists.

Jarvis, F. Washington, *St. Paul's Cleveland, 1846-1968* (1968).
St. Paul's Episcopal Church Records, WRHS.

**ST. PETER'S CHURCH** was the first German congregation formed in the Diocese of Cleveland. In 1984 it maintained the diocese's oldest church building in continuous use, at 1533 E. 17th St. at Superior. The origins of St. Peter's Church, the first parish established for German-speaking Catholics, date to 1853. Fr. John H. Luhr began to minister to the Germans who met in the church of ST. MARY ON THE FLATS located on Columbus Rd. hill. The location was inconvenient, and property was bought at E. 17th and Superior on 10 Mar. 1854. This location was considered out of the way by the west side Germans, who worshipped on Columbus Rd. until their Church of St. Mary on Carroll Ave. was completed.

By the fall of 1854, a combination church-school building was completed. To meet the needs of his growing congregation, Fr. Luhr opened a second school, St. Bernhardt's, on Irving (E. 25th) St., which would become the nucleus of St. Joseph's Parish on Woodland Ave. Construction began on the second (present) church in 1857. It was finished and dedicated on 23 Oct. 1859. The total cost was $36,000, which had been raised in small donations. The school, originally staffed by lay teachers, soon had religious as teachers: the Brothers of Mary, who began teaching the boys in 1863, and the Daughters of the Immaculate Heart of Mary, who arrived to teach the girls in 1864. It was up to Fr. Luhr's successor, Fr. Francis Westerholt, to plan a larger school. By 1874 it was completed, and the Notre Dame Sisters replaced the Daughters of the Immaculate Heart as teachers. In 1922, the Notre Dame Sisters took complete charge of the school. A 2-year commercial high school was begun in 1924. During the 1940s it became a 4-year high school. The parish lost members as the surrounding area became commercialized. The grade school closed in 1962. In 1971, St. Peter High School was merged with the combined schools of Lourdes Academy and St. Stephen's High School and was renamed Erieview High School, with the new school situated in the former St. Peter's building.

Papers of St. Peter's Parish, Archives, Diocese of Cleveland.

**ST. ROCCO'S PARISH** was the first west side Italian parish and grew from colorful and unusual traditional beginnings. The parish was organized out of celebrations of St. Rocco's Day. These celebrations became a kind of street fair and featured a procession and pageant, and sometimes a mass. Eventually the spirit of the celebrations engendered the desire for an Italian church on the west side, and an "independent" chapel (without clergy or recognition of the Catholic church) was built on Trent Ave. This congregation was eventually received into the Roman Catholic church, and St. Rocco Parish was established in 1922. In 1926, a combination church and school was built at 3205 Fulton Rd. The school was opened in Sept. 1927 in the charge of the Sisters of the Order of the Most Holy Trinity. A parish house was built in 1927, and a convent in the same year. The school was enlarged in 1933. The parish was considered quite large, since it was the first and for a time the only Italian parish on the west side. In 1932 a mission, Our Lady of Mt. Carmel, was established farther west on Detroit Rd. A new church building was built at the Fulton Rd. site in 1952. The church and school continued to operate in 1985 in what was still a neighborhood of Italian-American families.

The **ST. SAVA SERBIAN ORTHODOX CHURCH CONTROVERSY** (1963-75) split the Cleveland Serbian community. It demonstrated the deleterious and divisive effects of combining politics with religion. The controversy concerned not only control of church property but also the right of an episcopal form of church government to control an organization when the majority of its members oppose that hierarchy. An administrative dispute between the patriarch of the Serbian Orthodox church in Belgrade, Yugoslavia, and the church's popular American bishop in 1963 resulted in the bishop's being deposed. As in other parts of the country, the Serbians in Cleveland were divided in their support between the two sides. When the deposed bishop called for an annual meeting, the congregation split over the issue of attending. Later supporters of the deposed bishop objected to a church dues increase, and the matter ended up in court. The controversy escalated, quickly becoming a struggle to control the church's real property, including the recently constructed St. Sava's Serbian Orthodox Church on Broadview Rd. and Ridgewood Dr. in PARMA. Throughout the dispute, accusations flew, tensions mounted, feelings worsened, and lawsuits proliferated as all hopes for reconciliation dissipated. Control of St. Sava's changed hands several times. Police were called upon numerous times to quell disturbances between the factions inside as well as outside the church. For a time, the courts closed the church, and no one was allowed to use it. In Cleveland, the breakaway faction was composed mainly of former members of the professional and upper classes of Serbian society who had emigrated because of the Communist takeover. They viewed the patriarch as a puppet of the Yugoslav government. The mother-church faction consisted of mainly native-born Americans of Serbian ancestry who did not share the concern for the politics of their ethnic homeland. The mother-church faction counted 400 members—half as many as the breakaway faction. A court-negotiated settlement between the two groups in 1975 granted the mother church ownership of the church and parish house. The breakaway faction received the church's 38-acre picnic grounds, property on Ridgewood Dr., and property on Wallings Rd. in Broadview Hts., on which they constructed the St. Sava Serbian Eastern Orthodox Religious Social & Cultural Ctr.

**ST. STANISLAUS CHURCH,** established in 1873, is the mother parish for Polish Roman Catholics in Cleveland. Established to serve the growing number of Polish immigrants in Cleveland, the parish had no permanent structure until 1881. Until that time, the congregation met in either ST. MARY ON THE FLATS or St. Joseph's (German) on Woodland Ave., and was ministered to by several priests, including Fr. Victor Zareczny of St. Adalbert in Berea. In 1881, under the direction of the Franciscan community of St. Joseph's Church, the St. Stanislaus congregation purchased property at Tod (E. 65th) St. and Forman Ave. near the Cleveland Rolling Mills, where many of the POLES worked. By late 1881, the congregation had erected a wooden structure that housed both a church and a school. On 23 July 1883, Fr. ANTON F. KOLASZEWSKI became pastor. Dynamic and charismatic, he came to the parish when the surrounding neighborhood was beginning to develop into the city's major Polish settlement, Warszawa. Kolaszewski oversaw the construction of a new, Gothic church edifice, which was completed in 1891 at an estimated cost of $250,000. Located at Forman and E. 65th St., it still served the community in 1985. The huge debt incurred in the church's construction, as well as a variety of other charges, led to Kolaszewski's removal from the parish in 1891. He was replaced by Fr. Benedict Rosinski, whose efforts centered on erasing the debt and coping with the community divisions engendered by Kolaszewski's removal. In 1906, the parish was returned to the administration of the Franciscan community, and Fr. Theobald Kalamaja, OFM, was named pastor. The Franciscans continued to administer the parish in 1985.

The church school, initially supervised by Franciscan nuns from Stevens Pt., Wis., was given over to the Sisters of the Holy Family of Nazareth in 1907. In that year, the parish built a new brick school building to accommodate 1,500 pupils. Enrollment peaked at 2,686 in 1933. In 1944, the church opened a high school, which in 1969 was merged with 3 other parochial high schools to form Cleveland Central Catholic. Though a number of families left the neighborhood after WORLD WAR II, St. Stanislaus still remained a viable parish into the 1980s. Its strong association with the neighborhood's beginnings worked to its benefit during efforts to revitalize the community as Cleveland's SLAVIC VILLAGE in the 1970s and 1980s.

**ST. THEODOSIUS RUSSIAN ORTHODOX CATHEDRAL** (733 Starkweather Ave.), with its central cupola and 12 surrounding cupolas symbolizing Christ and the Apostles, is considered to be one of the finest examples of Russian church architecture in the U.S. Begun in 1911 and redecorated in 1954, the cathedral is the third structure to serve its parish. The St. Theodosius Russian Orthodox parish was organized by a small group of Russian immigrants in 1896. The immigrants had worshipped at the Uniat Church, but conflicts with that church led 23 men to form the St. Nicholas Society on 28 Sept. 1896; that society spearheaded the organization of the parish. The first church was a frame building erected at McKinstry (W. 6th) St. and Literary Rd.; the first resident pastor was Fr. Victor Stepanoff, who also helped establish the school. At the end of 1902, the parish bought the St. John's Convent and the surrounding land for $30,000, largely through the efforts of John Ferencz, who mortgaged his own property to raise part of the money. Under the leadership of Rev. JASON R. KAPPANADZE, the parish divided the land into 80 individual lots and sold these to parishioners for $125 apiece. In 1909 the parish acquired land in Brooklyn Twp. for use as a cemetery.

The former convent served as the church until parishioners decided in May 1911 to build a cathedral. With the assistance of Fr. Basil S. Lisenkovsky, local architect Frederick C. Baird designed the church, using features adopted from the Church of Our Savior Jesus Christ in Moscow. The cathedral, which cost $70,000 to build and was decorated with paintings imported from Russia, was dedicated on 19 July 1913. Under guidance of Rev. Kappanadze from 1902–08 and again from 1922–57, St. Theodosius became an important fixture in the life of the Russian Orthodox immigrant community. By the mid-1930s, the church's a capella choir was receiving much praise for its concerts at the CLEVELAND MUSEUM OF ART, and non-Russian Clevelanders were attending the church to see and hear special services. By the time of its 50th anniversary in 1946, St. Theodosius counted 1,200 member families. In Jan. 1953, Andrei Bicenko, at age 78 a noted artist who had decorated many European churches and developed the neo-Byzantine style of art before being expelled from Yugoslavia in 1951, was commissioned to cover the walls and ceilings of St. Theodosius with religious murals. Bicenko and his assistants completed the task after 18 months at a cost of more than $100,000, and the redecorated cathedral was rededicated on 3 Oct. 1954. Following the retirement of Rev. Kappanadze in 1957, priests began to offer the liturgy in English as well as in Slavonic. By 1974, parish membership had fallen to 600 families, but the church continued to be an important religious and cultural institution, sponsoring an exhibition of Russian artwork in 1980 and offering regular choral concerts. St. Theodosius was placed on the Natl. Register of Historic Places and in 1974 was also named a Cleveland landmark. It attracted much attention when portions of the film *The Deer Hunter* (1978) were filmed there in the summer of 1977.

**SAINT VINCENT CHARITY HOSPITAL AND HEALTH CENTER,** a 492-bed nonprofit general acute-care hospital located at 2351 E. 22nd St., opened on 10 Oct. 1865 and was Cleveland's first permanent general hospital. Bp. AMADEUS RAPPE secured land for St. Vincent at the corner of Perry, Gordon, and Marion streets, and the hospital was staffed and managed by the SISTERS OF CHARITY OF ST. AUGUSTINE. It served both poor and private paying patients. Cleveland's first surgical pavilion and amphitheater was constructed in 1872, and a free medical dispensary for the poor was opened in 1894. The School of Nursing, Cleveland's first Catholic diploma school of nursing, was established in 1898. Rosary Hall, one of the first hospitals in the U.S. to offer special services and a program for alcoholics, was dedicated in 1952. The first open-heart surgical procedure in the Midwest was performed at Charity Hospital in 1956. In 1985, St. Vincent

Charity Hospital & Health Ctr. formally affiliated with RICHMOND HTS. GENERAL HOSPITAL. Woodruff Hospital closed in 1986 and transferred its beds and programs to Charity Hospital as the Woodruff Pavilion. Major subsidiaries of Charity included the Chagrin Valley Medical Ctr. in S. Russell and the Cleveland Research Institute, located at the hospital. Along with CLEVELAND STATE UNIVERSITY and CUYAHOGA COMMUNITY COLLEGE, St. Vincent Charity Hospital & Health Ctr. is a member of the St. Vincent Quadrangle, which was an organization trying to improve the physical surroundings and safety of the areas around the member institutions. St. Vincent Charity Hospital & Health Ctr. is a subsidiary of the Sisters of Charity of St. Augustine Health & Human Services, a Catholic multihospital system sponsored by the Sisters of Charity of St. Augustine based in Richfield, Ohio.

Archives, Sisters of Charity of St. Augustine, Richfield, Ohio.
Gavin, Donald P., *In All Things Charity* (1955).

The **ST. VINCENT DEPAUL SOCIETY,** formed in Paris in 1833, is an international association of volunteer Catholic laymen dedicated to serving the poor. By 1983, the international group had more than 50,000 members in 112 countries. The first American branch of the Vincentians was established in St. Louis in Nov. 1845; the St. Vincent DePaul Society in Cleveland was formed at ST. JOHN'S CATHEDRAL in June 1865 by Bp. AMADEUS RAPPE. Basing their welfare and spiritual work on belief in the dignity of the individual, the Vincentians have carried out their relief efforts on an individual basis at the parish level since the beginning of their work in Cleveland. A 1914 directory of Cleveland charities described the society's aims as the promotion of religious instruction, the distribution of books among the poor, visits to the sick, and the provision of food, clothing, and fuel to the needy. In the 1920s and 1930s, the parish-based, individualized approach of volunteer laymen was augmented by more coordinated efforts among the independent parish councils, by the use of professional social-work methodology, and by greater cooperation with other social-service agencies. The society hired its first paid staff worker in 1921. In 1931, it opened its first thrift store to provide inexpensive clothing and furniture for the impoverished during the Depression and organized its Institutional Visitation Committee to carry out its visitation program in hospitals and other institutions; both the thrift store and the visiting committee were still in operation 50 years later. In addition, the Vincentians have been responsible for the development of other agencies. They were involved in Big Brother work in the 1920s and helped organize the Catholic Big Brothers; they also promoted the Scouting program and laid the groundwork for the Catholic Apostolate to the Blind (1948), the Catholic Resettlement Council (1949), and Catholic Counseling (1965). Other services have included free scholarships for children at PARMADALE, legal advice for the poor, and proper burials for poor people who have died in public institutions. The St. Vincent DePaul Society spent more than $51,000 to aid 907 families in 1949; in 1982, its 1,100 volunteers in the 1,435 churches in the 8-county Cleveland Catholic Diocese distributed nearly $2 million in aid and helped 28,699 families. It also operated 44 hunger centers in the area, which served 444,000 meals in 1982.

**ST. VINCENT'S ORPHAN ASYLUM** was a Catholic home for boys ages 4–14. It was founded by Bp. AMADEUS RAPPE in 1852 and run by the SISTERS OF CHARITY OF ST. AUGUSTINE. St. Vincent's was opened with funds from a fair that was patronized by all denominations. In

May 1853, a frame house was completed, and 11 orphans were admitted. By the end of that year, 46 had been admitted. In 1858, construction of a large brick house began at the corner of Monroe Ave. and Fulton Rd. on the west side. Completed in 1865, the building housed 100 orphans. A chapel was added in 1867. By 1879, 1,272 boys had been received and cared for. In addition to orphans, St. Vincent's also received boys from poor families. At the age of 13 or 14, the boys were placed in private homes, often to take work. St. Vincent's was entirely supported by donations and fairs. It remained at the Fulton Rd. location until its closing in the early 1920s.

**ST. VITUS CHURCH,** located at E. 61st St. and Glass Ave., was the first Catholic church in Cleveland designated for Slovenians. The beginnings of St. Vitus date to the 1880s, when a contingent of Slovenian millworkers came to the NEWBURGH area. Within a few years, the nucleus of the colony had shifted to the St. Clair-Superior area. The Slovenians approached Bp. RICHARD GILMOUR for a parish of their own. The first priest appointed was the newly ordained Vitus Hribar. He first held services for his new congregation on 6 Aug. 1893 at ST. PETER'S CHURCH in Cleveland. By 1894, the new congregation had purchased lots on Norwood and Glass avenues. The first liturgy in a wooden church at this site was held on 4 Nov. 1894.

By 1902, the church had to be expanded. The Notre Dame nuns were hired to instruct the ever-increasing number of children in the parish school. An attempt to divide the parish into 2 churches proved unsuccessful. The new parish of Our Lady of Sorrows, located in the western section of St. Vitus, could not sustain itself. In 1907, Rev. Bartholomew Ponikvar became the second pastor of St. Vitus. Under his direction, a new 3-story school building was started in 1912. Plans were made for a new church, which was to become one of the largest Slovenian churches in America. It was completed and solemnly consecrated on 20 Nov. 1932. It was designed in the Lombard-Roman style. In 1952, Msgr. Ponikvar died, and his successor was Msgr. Louis Baznik, a priest-son of the parish. In 1984, St. Vitus was still the home of many Slovenian cultural and fraternal organizations. One of its priest-sons and former pastors, Most Rev. A. Edward Pevec, became an auxiliary bishop of Cleveland.

Papers of St. Vitus Church, Archives, Diocese of Cleveland.

**ST. WENCESLAS CHURCH** was the first parish established to serve Bohemian (Czech) Catholics in Cleveland. Services for the first Bohemian immigrants were held in ST. PETER'S, St. Joseph's, and ST. MARY'S ON THE FLATS. In 1867, Bp. AMADEUS RAPPE established the congregation of St. Wenceslas and placed it under the direction of Fr. Anthony Krasny. Property was bought on Arch (E. 35th) St. at Burwell, and building started. The cornerstone was laid on 20 Oct. 1867, and the first liturgy was held on 22 Dec. 1867. By 1870, a rectory had been built and a school established. The first teachers were the Daughters of the Immaculate Heart of Mary. In 1876 they were replaced by the Sisters of St. Joseph (CSJ). These sisters would staff the school until its closing in 1962.

In 1886, the parish needed a larger site. Land was purchased, and the church relocated to E. 37th and Broadway. The cornerstone for the new church was laid on 5 June 1892, and though not complete, it was ready for use later that year. Financial problems prevented the completion of the church until 1899. By the early 1920s, many of the parishioners had left. The Broadway neighborhood had become increasingly polluted and congested. A number of parishioners had settled in MAPLE HTS., and tentative plans were made to move the church there. From 1923–26, services were held in a mission church in Maple Hts. On 15 Oct. 1926 it was decided to retain the Broadway church and establish the Maple Hts. church as a new, separate congregation. The Cleveland parish continued to serve its parishioners, though its size dwindled. Plans for building I-77 encompassed the church site and sealed its fate. In July 1963, the parish was closed and its building demolished. Besides the Maple Hts. parish, the following churches are considered daughter parishes of St. Wenceslas: St. Procop, St. Adalbert, and Our Lady of Lourdes.

Papers of St. Wenceslaus Parish, Archives, Diocese of Cleveland.

**ST. WENDELIN PARISH,** one of Cleveland's several Slovak Roman Catholic churches, was the first Slovak church on the west side. The parish was formed in May 1903 by Bp. IGNATIUS F. HORSTMANN out of ST. MARTIN OF TOURS parish at E. 23rd St. and Scovill Ave. St. Martin's was a long distance away from west side Slovak families settled in the area south of Lorain Ave. and east of W. 25th St. Masses were first said in the parish in private homes and a rented hall. A frame church was built along with a sisters' home on Columbus Rd. near W. 25th in Dec. 1903, serving 200 families. Between 1915–21, the parish was "independent"; that is, it operated without clergy, as no Slovak priest could be found. The church served first-generation immigrants, and bilingual priests were required. A school was begun along with the church, housed in an existing building on the property. In 1925, a combination church and school in a Romanesque idiom replaced the wooden buildings. Another Slovak parish, OUR LADY OF MERCY, was started out of St. Wendelin, serving families farther west, beginning in 1921. Despite changes in the surrounding neighborhood, St. Wendelin continued to serve many first- and second-generation Slovak families, as well as newer residents in the neighborhood in 1985. The school was merged into the Urban Community School at ST. MALACHI'S Parish in 1978.

**SS. CYRIL AND METHODIUS PARISH,** 12608 Madison Ave., was established to serve the Roman Catholic Slovak immigrants who had settled in the southeastern neighborhood of LAKEWOOD, popularly termed the BIRD'S NEST. In the early 1900s, these immigrants had come to Lakewood seeking jobs in the cluster of mills and factories around the Berea Rd./Madison Ave./W. 117th St. area. A number of them met and decided to petition Bp. IGNATIUS F. HORSTMANN for a parish. The closest church for Slovak Catholics was ST. MARTIN'S, located on E. 23rd and Scovill Ave. The first mass in this new parish was celebrated on 3 Aug. 1903 by Rev. Chas. J. Ouimet in a home located on the future church site. SS. Cyril & Methodius was declared a mission of ST. WENDELIN Church, and St. Wendelin's pastor, Rev. OLDRICH J. ZLAMAL, was named its administrator. A small frame building was constructed in 1905 as the first church. Fr. Zlamal ministered to his growing congregation until Sep. 1905, when Fr. Thos. Balloon was named first resident pastor.

A school was also opened in 1905. Originally staffed by lay teachers, the school was placed under the jurisdiction of the Notre Dame Sisters in 1908. A new school was begun in 1915 during the pastorate of Fr. Adalbert Masat. Neighbors secured an injunction halting its construction, but it was lifted and the work completed in 1916. Fr. Francis J. Dubosh succeeded Fr. Masat in 1927 as pastor. Within 2 years, the parish began its present (1985) church. It was constructed in the Lombard Romanesque style. The church

was dedicated by Bp. JOSEPH SCHREMBS on 7 Sept. 1931. For economic reasons, the exterior of the church was left largely undecorated. In 1948 the parish gained the services of Dr. Joseph G. Cincik, a Slovak artist and scholar. The bishops of Slovakia had commissioned Dr. Cincik to design a national shrine in honor of SS. Cyril and Methodius, the saints who Christianized the Slovaks. The Communist regime halted this plan. Dr. Cincik's work was transferred to the Lakewood church in a series of murals adorning the walls. These murals display the life stories of SS. Cyril and Methodius and the history of the church in Slovakia. They are enhanced by motifs drawn from Slovak culture.

Archives, Diocese of Cleveland.

**SS. PETER AND PAUL LUTHERAN CHURCH,** 13030 Madison Ave., was established to serve the Slovak Lutherans in Cleveland. The congregation began in 1901, and the first church was built on the corner of Thrush and Quail avenues in LAKEWOOD, where services were held until 1927, when a new edifice was dedicated on the corner of Madison and Grace avenues. From its beginning in 1901 to 1935, the predominant language was Slovak. In 1935, however, the membership decided that in order to keep its younger generation intact, it was necessary to conduct some services and classes in English. Two issues split the congregation, in 1918 and again in 1948. The first was a majority vote of the congregation to withdraw from the Missouri Synod. The dissenting members established the Pentecost Lutheran Congregation. The second dissension involved the issue of Freemasonry, and the departing faction established Gethsemane Lutheran Church. In 1985, SS. Peter & Paul Evangelical Lutheran Church continued to serve a growing membership and thrive in its early Lakewood neighborhood.

**SALEN, CHARLES P.** (5 Dec. 1860–23 June 1924), was a leader in the CUYAHOGA COUNTY DEMOCRATIC PARTY who managed the congressional and mayoral campaigns of TOM L. JOHNSON. Salen was born in Portsmouth, N.H., the son of Peter and Frederick Wyx Salen. The family came to Cleveland ca. 1866, where Charles, the youngest of 4 children, attended public schools. After graduating in 1878 and attending Concordia College in Ft. Wayne, Ind., for 1 year, he returned to Cleveland and began working for the *West Side Sentinel*. Politics attracted his interest, and he established a weekly Democratic newspaper, as well as organizing the Young Men's Democratic League of Cleveland.

Salen's first elective office was that of city clerk, where he served from 1883–85, and again from 1887–89. In 1890 Salen was appointed secretary of the Board of Elections, and with the adoption of the Australian ballot in 1891, he initiated the use of metal election booths to insure voting secrecy. He managed Tom L. Johnson's successful campaigns for election to Congress in 1890 and 1892, as well as his mayoral campaigns in 1901, 1903, and 1905. When the local Democratic party split over the nomination of Wm. Jennings Bryan for president in 1896, Salen led the faction that supported Bryan. He was director of accounts from 1899–1901, and his investigation of the previous McKisson administration resulted in a return of $20,000 to the city treasury. He served as director of public works under Mayor Johnson for 1 year, and was elected county clerk in 1902, serving until 1910. He was also a member of the State Executive Committee of the Democratic party for a number of years and was its chairman in 1903.

As a promoter of amateur sports in Cleveland, Salen supported Sunday baseball, organized the Ohio Skating As-

865

soc., and maintained a free skating rink at West Blvd. and Detroit known as Salen's Rink. He operated refreshment stands at PUBLIC SQUARE, LUNA PARK, and Gordon Gardens in association with Jacob Mintz. He was married to Mamie Schwab, and they had 2 daughters, Aimee (Lowensohn) and Lorna (Giffin). He died in Lakewood at age 63.

Chas. P. Salen Papers, WRHS.

**SALISBURY, JAMES HENRY** (13 Oct. 1823–23 Aug. 1905), physician and medical researcher, was an able microscopist and a painstaking investigator who researched the germ-causation theory of disease. Salisbury was born in Scott, N.Y., to Nathan and Lucretia Babcock Salisbury. After receiving his early education at the Homer Academy, he graduated with the Bachelor of Natural Science degree from Rensselaer Polytechnic Institute in 1846, the M.D. degree from Albany Medical College in 1850, and the M.A. degree from Union College in 1852. In 1844 he was appointed assistant chemist with the Geological Survey of the State of New York. In 1849 he was promoted to principal chemist, serving until 1852. During 1851–52 he also served as a lecturer on elementary and applied chemistry at the New York Normal School in Albany, after which he applied himself to private practice and research. After serving as a physician during the CIVIL WAR, Salisbury came to Cleveland to assist in starting the Charity Hospital College, where he lectured on physiology, histology, and microscopic anatomy between 1864–66. In private practice in Cleveland until ca. 1880, when he moved to New York City, he specialized in the treatment of chronic diseases, especially those previously considered fatal. Salisbury had begun research into the study of germs as the cause of diseases as early as 1849. Severely criticized in Europe and America, it was not until 1865 that his findings were proved correct. However, Salisbury had moved on to other areas of research and did not share in the credit for the discovery. In 1860 he began studying the origin and functions of blood. Later, Salisbury turned his attention to the relation of food and drink to the occurrence of disease and advocated dietary measures as a cure. He is remembered for a beef dish used in his cures, to which he lent his name: the Salisbury steak. His other areas of study included the chemical analysis of plants, the role of spores, fungi, and parasites as causes of diseases, and studies of ancient rocks and earth writings. Salisbury married Clara Brassee on 26 June 1860. The Salisburys had 2 children, Minnie and Trafford.

The **SALVATION ARMY,** formed in England in 1865 by Rev. Wm. Booth and known as the Christian Mission until 1878, is an evangelical Christian denomination organized along military lines. The first Salvation Army outpost in the U.S. was located in Cleveland from 1872–76. It was established by an unemployed British cabinetmaker and lay preacher, Jas. Jermy, who had worked with Booth in England before bringing his family to America. Jermy and local preacher Jas. Fakler founded the Christian Mission in 1872; they held regular open-air meetings in front of saloons in the HAYMARKET district and published a paper, the *Mission Harvester*. Fakler left Cleveland in 1874, Jermy returned to England in 1875, and the mission closed in 1876.

The Army came to Cleveland again on 29 Oct. 1883; 4 soldiers attracted an audience of 200 at an open-air meeting in the Haymarket district that Sunday. They soon established their headquarters at the corner of Hill and Commercial streets and began to offer Saturday night dinners to the needy. Open-air meetings to preach the Gospel and charitable services for the needy were mainstays of the Army's work during its years of struggle to gain acceptance in the U.S. By the late 1890s it had gained acceptance in Cleveland and began to grow in membership and to expand its services. The Army had 3 divisions in the city in 1891, and 8 in 1897. It conducted its first fundraising campaign in 1889, soliciting funds by mail to construct a women's training center; in 1892 it opened the first of its many specialized institutions in the city, a rescue home for unwed mothers, located on Kinsman Ave.

By 1907, the Army had 5 corps in Cleveland and was involved in a variety of projects. It began prison visitations as early as 1893; it operated an employment bureau, a missing-persons department, an "anti-suicide" bureau, the rescue home, a day nursery, a salvage and industrial department, and 2 workingmen's hotels. Sharing the common belief that there were both worthy and unworthy poor, the Army also had slum officers who investigated requests for assistance before applicants were given any of the coal, clothing, bedding, or furniture distributed by the Army. It also had a young people's orchestra, sponsored outings for children, and at Christmas distributed food baskets and put on a program of entertainment. These were in addition to its religious activities in open-air meetings, evening services, and Sunday school.

The Army continued to expand its services to meet pressing social needs. It opened a maternity home for black women in 1925 (see MARY B. TALBERT HOME), the Evangeline Residence for young business and professional women in 1942, the Family Emergency Home for homeless women and children in 1955, and the Hough Multi-Service Ctr. in 1969, and in 1978 it opened a rehabilitation center for teenagers convicted of first or second offenses. It also began the Tremont Coordinated Service Program for the Elderly in 1973. Older programs were updated and supplemented with new ones; the industrial and salvage department became the Men's Social Service Ctr. in 1936, was completely transformed after WORLD WAR II using Alcoholics Anonymous programs, and became the Adult Rehabilitation Ctr. in 1977. In 1949 it was supplemented by the Harbor Light program to provide a more systematic approach to alcoholic-rehabilitation efforts. The Salvation Army provided special services during times of economic crisis and war, providing support services for the soldiers at the front and offering emergency food and shelter to Clevelanders in need during the economic declines in the 1930s and in 1982–83. In 1983, the work begun in Cleveland 100 years earlier involved 32 officers and 750 soldiers, and cost $12 million.

**SAN JUAN BAUTISTA,** Cleveland's first HISPANIC parish, was established in 1975. However, the Hispanic Apostolate in the Cleveland Diocese predates it. A ministry to the Hispanic-speaking was begun in 1952, with Msgr. Thos. Sebian serving as its first director. A radio program called "Ecos Latinos" was also begun. The Conversion of St. Paul Shrine, which was adjacent to the Hispanic settlement in the Hough-Norwood area, served as its headquarters. The Spanish community grew rapidly, increased by both immigration and births. The Hough-Norwood area was overshadowed by a growing concentration of Hispanics in OHIO CITY, TREMONT, and the Clark-Fulton areas on the west side of Cleveland.

From 1958–70, the Trinitarian Fathers coordinated the ministry, and services were held at a number of east and west side churches. By the early 1970s, St. Stephen's Church on W. 54th in Cleveland had become the headquarters of the Hispanic ministry, but Spanish liturgies and outreach programs had been established at a number of churches bordering on Hispanic areas. On 15 Oct. 1975, Bp. Jas. A. Hickey established the parish of San Juan Bautista, whose purpose was to serve the Hispanics, in particular those on the west side. Fr. Antonio Pagan, who had been ministering to the Hispanic community, was named its first pastor. A search was begun for a suitable building and site; in 1976, the West Side Hungarian Reformed Church at 1946 W. 32nd was purchased. In 1984, parish pastors were Fr. Domingo Rodrigues and Fr. Vincent A. Pasqualetto, both members of the Trinitarian community.

Papers of San Juan Bautista, Archives, Diocese of Cleveland.

**SANDERS, WILLIAM BROWNELL** (21 Sept. 1854–25 Jan. 1929), was a Cleveland corporate lawyer, a judge, and a founding partner of the law firm of SQUIRE, SANDERS & DEMPSEY. Sanders was born in Cleveland to William and Cornelia Smith Sanders. The family moved to Jacksonville, Ill., when he was 1 year old. Educated in the Jacksonville public schools, Sanders entered Illinois College, graduating with the A.B. degree in 1873 and later the A.M. degree. He attended the Albany (N.Y.) Law School, graduating with the LL.B. degree in 1875. Admitted to the New York bar in 1875, Sanders soon returned to Cleveland, joining the law firm of Burke, Ingersoll & Sanders. In Feb. 1888, he secured an appointment as a Cuyahoga County common pleas court judge. In Jan. 1890, he resigned the bench to assist in the formation of the firm of Squire, Sanders & Dempsey, of which he continued as a partner until his death. At the turn of the century, Sanders became embroiled in one of Cleveland's most spectacular legal and political battles when Mayor TOM L. JOHNSON tried to gain municipal control of the Cleveland street railroads and institute a 3-cent fare. With Sanders directing the opposition, the intense legal battle lasted 7 years with almost no letup. The result, known as the Tayler Grant, was worked out by Sanders and Federal Judge ROBT. W. TAYLER; it gave an exclusive street railway franchise to the CLEVELAND RAILWAY CO. and stipulated low fares and municipal oversight of the system. The strain of battle was disastrous to both Johnson and Sanders. Johnson was defeated for reelection and died in 1911, while Sanders's health was wrecked. Thereafter Sanders devoted less time to his law practice, spending most of his time traveling and at his New England summer home. Sanders was instrumental in establishing the CLEVELAND MUSEUM OF ART on a firm financial foundation. Three Clevelanders, JOHN HUNTINGTON, Hinman Hurlbut, and Horace Kelly, had each left trust funds for the establishment of an art museum. Believing that 1 museum would be better than 3, Sanders arranged the incorporation of the 3 separate funds into 1 trust. Sanders was selected as the first president (1913–20) and a trustee of the museum. He was also a trustee for the Society for Savings and a director of the Guardian Trust Co. and the Kelly Island Line & Transport Co. Sanders married Annie Otis in 1884. They had 1 daughter, Mary Ermina.

**SANFORD, ALFRED S.** (5 Mar. 1805–23 Dec. 1888), was the antebellum captain of the CLEVELAND GRAYS. He was Cleveland fire chief in 1845. In 1863 he became an incorporator of the St. Clair Street Railroad Co. At Pres. ABRAHAM LINCOLN'S FUNERAL in Cleveland, Sanford served on the General Committee, the Sub-committee on Location of Remains, and the Sub-committee on the Military. By the time of the 1865 funeral, Sanford was referred to as "General Sanford."

**SANFORD, JUNIUS R.** (1836–16 May 1904), was a Clevelander who was active in military organizations during the CIVIL WAR. Sanford was active in the Ohio Militia before the Civil War; he was a 3d sergeant, CLEVELAND GRAYS, 1856, and lieutenant colonel, Cleveland Battalion. He was elected lieutenant colonel, Cleveland Battalion, Ohio Militia, 15 June 1858. After the Civil War broke out, Sanford served as adjutant, 41ST OHIO VOLUNTEER INFANTRY Regiment, beginning on 23 Aug. 1861. He was promoted to 1st lieutenant on 25 Aug. He resigned 5 Jan. 1862. Apparently returning to Cleveland, he taught military tactics at Cleveland Institute (formerly CLEVELAND UNIVERSITY), R. F. Humiston, proprietor, on University Hts., across the street from Camp Cleveland, between 1862–65. Sanford also reentered military service as captain of Co. E, ONE HUNDRED TWENTY-EIGHTH OHIO VOLUNTEER INFANTRY, beginning in Nov. 1863. He was later appointed acting assistant inspecting general on the staff of Gen. Samuel P. Heintzelman, commander of the Northern Dept. On 25 Mar. 1865, he was promoted to major; he was mustered out on 13 July 1865. Sanford died suddenly at his residence at 1279 Cedar Ave. on 16 May 1904. He had worked as a clerk during the latter part of his life. He is buried in LAKE VIEW CEMETERY.

**SANITATION.** Progress in Cleveland sanitation followed the classical patterns of those cities in the U.S. that experienced rapid industrial and urban growth, where sanitary reforms were often initiated one step ahead of potential disasters. The city's earliest sanitary measures were based upon New England's experiences, which centered around noxious miasmas, filth, and sin as causative agents of disease. Many of the reforms that were adopted were based on fear and faith, supported by insufficient medical knowledge. For a short time after incorporation in 1814, the village authorities relied upon individual social concern to keep the community clean. As commerce developed and the community grew, and as social relationships changed, it became necessary to impose legal restrictions in order to reduce the dangers that arose from the more crowded and unsanitary conditions. When the village had reached a population of approximately 600 in 1820, the authorities enacted the first sanitary regulations. Animals were confined, and slaughter was restricted to areas that were to be kept clean and free of unhealthy odors. To insure compliance, a village inspector was appointed, and fines were levied. However, during its formative years, the city did little to provide any hygienic amenities. Public works were almost nonexistent; some public water pumps were provided, and streets were laid out, but they were not graded, properly paved, or cleaned. No effort was made to collect and dispose of solid wastes. The cholera epidemics that struck Cleveland in 1832, 1849, and 1854 were attributed at first to sin, and later to the accumulated filth in the city (for 1832 case, see CHOLERA EPIDEMIC). Recognizing the imminent dangers that could arise from unsanitary conditions, on 10 Jan. 1856, the state legislature granted Cleveland the right to establish a permanent board of health in the city. Sanitary ordinances were enacted to abate nuisances, but it was not until 10 Apr. 1866 that the city council approved a number of regulations that served as the foundation for the city's sanitary code. In spite of its rapid growth, Cleveland remained a provincial city. Efforts to enforce existing ordinances and to build public works were not readily accepted by a population that objected to the cost for civic improvements, and to sanitation ordinances in general as an infringement of civil rights. In spite of a lack of public support, by the mid-19th century, the city began a series of public works to improve the quality of

Cleveland life, including the construction of a public WATER SYSTEM, drainage sewers, and the paving of STREETS.

In 1876, Dr. Frank Wells, the city health officer, argued, as did sanitarians throughout the nation, that pure water, a sanitary environment, pure air, and pure food were prerequisites for good health. Potable water, the primary ingredient for a healthy community, was provided by springs, wells, and cisterns, or in barrels until 19 Sept. 1856, when a newly built public water system supplied unfiltered Lake Erie water to a small portion of the city. Within 20 years, the sewage and filth of the city, which was discharged into the CUYAHOGA RIVER and Lake Erie, transformed the water supply into a health hazard. In the hopes of curtailing the high incidence of typhoid fever and enteric diseases associated with contaminated water, on several occasions the intake pipes were moved farther away from the shoreline and sewer outlets. These changes yielded limited and temporary results. Progress in the science of bacteriology, the experiences of other cities, and the data on water purification obtained by Drs. Howard Haskins and ROGER G. PERKINS of the Western Reserve University Medical School convinced the city officials in 1911 to chlorinate the city's water supply, and in 1917 part of the supply was filtered. Each improvement produced a notable drop in the incidence of water-borne diseases. The filtration and chlorination of the city's water supply were completed in Oct. 1925, and except for the use of contaminated well water, plumbing mishaps, or unsanitary food, diseases caused by impure water virtually disappeared. Water for the greater metropolitan area was supplied in part by local communities and the city of Cleveland. As the area population increased, it became evident that it was more economical for the city to become the principal supplier. At the present time, Cleveland provides an average of 320 million cu. ft. of water each day to INDUSTRY and to 1.75 million residents in 75 communities covering approximately 545 sq. mi. However, with a reported 20% leakage in 1984, the system has reached critical limits. According to the Urban Institute, a Washington, D.C., think tank, the water and sewer systems have "outlived their expected service lives," become "functionally obsolete," and placed the purchasers of these services in imminent danger.

The history of pure water in Cleveland cannot be studied without a realistic appraisal of environmental conditions, since Lake Erie served as both a reservoir for fresh water and a depository for the household and industrial wastewater and sewage. Culverts, which were built in 1840 to provide some relief for the removal of ground water, to enhance property values, and to reduce the threat of miasmatic diseases, soon became a health menace when used as sewers. The city's accelerated growth in the 1850s made a sewer system mandatory and encouraged the hasty installation of poorly designed sewers. Without a well-engineered sewer system and wastewater-treatment facilities, the separate sewers served as conduits of sewage into the Cuyahoga River and Lake Erie. In 1881, Cleveland mayor RENSSELAER R. HERRICK was forced to declare the Cuyahoga River a sewer that ran through the heart of the city. The following year, measures to rectify the dangerous condition were initiated, but it was not until 1896 that funding for an engineered sewer system was approved. As late as 1914, 50 separate sewer lines continued to pour millions of gallons of raw sewage into the Cuyahoga River and Lake Erie. By 1920, with 791 mi. of sewers in place, it was evident that if the city intended to use Lake Erie as a source of potable water, the treatment of sewage was necessary.

In 1911, the city council approved an ordinance authorizing the Dept. of Public Service to operate an experimental sewage-treatment plant. Tests were conducted from 1912–13. On the basis of these tests and the positive results obtained in other cities, the Dept. of Public Service recommended the construction of a wastewater-treatment plant. The Westerly Wastewater Treatment Plant was completed in 1922. The Easterly Plant was erected soon after, and the Southern Plant in 1928. Funds supplied by federal works programs in the 1930s were used to upgrade the performance of these plants. Improvement in water quality was limited until the enactment of federal pollution-control and water-quality laws in the late 1960s. The passage of the Natl. Environmental Policy Act in 1969 granted the federal and state governments authority to establish environmental-protection agencies to compel compliance with the newly adopted and stricter water-quality standards. Although short on funds, the city was forced to make additional expenditures to meet these mandated programs, to the neglect of the system as a whole. In Apr. 1972, a Cleveland Regional Sewer District was formed by judicial fiat after the city was unable to comply with the required clean-water standards. Between 1973–81, the sewer district spent approximately $500 million on improving the wastewater-treatment plants, with more improvements in the sewage-treatment facilities planned. No longer accountable for wastewater treatment, the Cleveland Dept. of Public Utilities continues to be responsible for maintenance of 4,500 mi. of sewer lines, portions of which are in need of immediate replacement. The problem of supplying drinking water and clean water for recreational purposes remains an ongoing task that has transcended state and national boundaries and, as in the problem with acid rain, is of international concern.

A heightened awareness of water pollution came in 1969 when the Cuyahoga River burned (see CUYAHOGA RIVER FIRE) and Lake Erie was declared sick because of premature aging. These events were the consequence of years of neglect, indifference, and scientific misconceptions. For almost 100 years, all manner of household and industrial wastes were thrown into the streets and culverts, left to clog the sewer basins, disposed of in the city's waterways, dumped into the lake, left to rot in backyards and open lots, incinerated, or used as swill and fertilizer, a portion of which eventually entered the area's water supply. In 1860, the private collection and disposal of solid waste was begun, but it was restricted primarily to the commercial areas of the city. With a population of almost 44,000, Cleveland was an unsanitary and unsavory place to work and live. In 1895, the city of 208,673 people produced an average of 100 tons of solid waste per day, of which only a small portion was disposed of safely. The problem of solid-waste collection and disposal went beyond aesthetics, and the garbage, refuse, and ashes threatened to inundate the city. To help ease the burden, in 1897 the city contracted for the private construction and operation of a reduction plant, which separated the garbage into disposable and salable products, and in 1905 the city assumed the management of the operation. That same year the city began the systematic collection of household garbage, and in 1906 the collection of ashes and refuse.

In 1923, attempts to put an additional reduction plant into operation were met with neighborhood resistance, and the proposal was abandoned. In 1935, the first incineration plant was made operative; the following year the reduction plant was closed. Additional incinerators were placed in various locations throughout the county. Incinerators remained in use until the 1970s and were shut down when the plants no longer could meet the required federal air-quality emissions standards. In spite of the sharp increase in solid wastes in the county, disposal is not now considered a major problem in the Cleveland regional area. The solid wastes are collected regularly and taken to sanitary landfills in outlying counties. There is competition for landfill space, and increased costs, but there are options open to the city and county: to ship the waste by rail to be used as landfill in abandoned open pit mines, or to employ the more environmentally speculative coincineration of solid waste to produce energy and to reduce the amount of landfill space. Responsibility for the safe disposal of hazardous wastes, the by-product of a technological society, is under the jurisdiction of federal and state environmental-protection agencies, and county and municipal participation is limited. Progress in city sanitation is evident, especially when comparison is made to sanitary conditions that exist during periods of labor unrest, or when the city services are curtailed. However, improvement is not evident in all neighborhoods. In 1981–82, the city spent $3 million to clean up garbage and refuse that had been dumped on approximately 3,500 open lots. Unsanitary conditions in slum areas, aggravated by the garbage and refuse dumping, required the city to provide a full-time staff in the Div. of Rat Control of the Dept. of Public Health & Welfare for rat eradication. In the 1880s and 1890s, garbage was considered a threat to the health of the city. In the 1980s, garbage, according to Cleveland mayor Geo. Voinovich, is a "political bargaining chip and a demogogue's delight."

Clean streets have always been looked upon as an indicator of the sanitary state of a municipality. For most of the 19th century, Cleveland streets remained unpaved or poorly paved, poorly cleaned, and poorly lighted. In 1895, the city began a street-paving program using improved construction materials that made street cleaning practicable. Advocates for clean streets prevailed in their campaign, and in 1902, during the administration of reform mayor TOM L. JOHNSON, "White Wings" were employed to clean the principal streets of the city at least twice a week. In 1906, street-flushing machines were employed. In 1913, a Bureau of Street Cleaning was established under the jurisdiction of the commissioner of streets; in 1916, solid-waste collection was taken from the jurisdiction of the Bureau of Street Cleaning and placed under the supervision of the Dept. of Public Service. Street cleaning has been vastly improved by the introduction of new technologies, but Cleveland streets are cleaned only during the period when snow-removal equipment is not in use, and only in the more visible districts of the city. Today, the lack of proper street cleaning may occasionally attack one's sensibilities, and in some cases may be deleterious to a healthy environment. However, it does not present the same problem of 100 years ago, when garbage and refuse were ground into the unpaved streets and mixed with overflowing cesspools, and thousands of horses deposited hundreds of thousands of tons of manure on the streets, which served as a breeding ground for millions of flies, each a potential disease carrier.

Pure air has been a long-sought wish of Cleveland health workers since the first load of coal was sold with some difficulty in 1828. Improvements in the design and manufacture of household and industrial equipment, and the expansion of the transportation and power industries rapidly increased the use of polluting soft coal. By 1855, a pall of grime and soot covered the city. However, complaints about dirty air were challenged as an attack on industrial progress. State intervention in 1885 and subsequent local ordinances were largely ignored and proved ineffective. Efforts to clean up the air were slow and difficult. By 1900, it was determined that the air in Cleveland was no longer fit for human consumption, but the lack of

law enforcement made it impossible to control further pollution. Throughout the 1920s, individuals and civic organizations campaigned for smoke abatement, emphasizing the economic costs to city residents and businesses. A reduction in pollution did occur in the 1930s, but only as a result of an economic depression, and not through the efforts of an aroused citizenry. In 1941, it was estimated that approximately 50,000 tons of soot were removed from buildings, at an annual cost of $20 million. In spite of these figures, the Cleveland press and manufacturers' associations continued to argue against enforcement measures. It was not until the passage of federal and state legislation in the 1950s and the amended Clean Air Act of 1967 that the city could effectively move to reduce air pollution. The city, funded by the federal and state environmental-protection agencies, provides air-pollution services for Cuyahoga County and has the responsibility of enforcing state and federal regulations. Concern about costs, interference with private industry, and the loss of 69,000 jobs between 1979–83 nonetheless have given way to anxiety about the effect of air pollution on good health. Sewer gas, the great bugbear of the late 19th century that distressed Geo. Anderson, the Cleveland sewer inspector, gave way to the tons of soot that showered the city, which in turn has given way to the dangers from indoor air pollutants produced by high-energy homes, hazardous gases, and automobile emissions, all of which require attention.

The relationship between disease and unsanitary food has been known empirically for thousands of years. It is not surprising that attempts were made by municipal officials in urban settings to prevent the sale of adulterated or tainted foods. A Cleveland ordinance of 1875 required dealers of milk, meat, and vegetables to open their premises for inspection by authorized personnel. Inspection was not permanent or conducted by qualified personnel until 1888, when the city appointed Dr. Joseph Mellor as the first full-time milk inspector. However, the lack of standards for purity made it difficult for him to carry out his assignment. For the remainder of the century, the role of the Board of Health was that of guardian against adulterated and deteriorated foods, with particular attention paid to milk, meat, and bread, although city ordinances included the surveillance of a wide variety of food products and establishments manufacturing and dispensing these products in Cleveland. The opening of the city bacteriological laboratory in 1901 and the passage of the Federal Pure Food & Drug Act and the Meat Inspection Act in 1906 allowed the city to impose stricter sanitary standards on the manufacturing and distribution of food and drug establishments and institutions. Today, the responsibility to inspect food-dispensing and -manufacturing establishments to insure the sale and distribution of pure and wholesome products lies within the jurisdiction of municipal and county boards of health. Unlike 100 years ago, when inspection was dependent on the limited knowledge of untrained people and unscientific methodology, today the responsible agencies use modern scientific test procedures, employing trained personnel who, within the limits of available technology, can detect noncompliance with the food and drug ordinances.

Sam Alewitz

The **SAVEL CHOIR** was one of the most prominent Finnish organizations in Cleveland for almost 30 years. It was organized in 1937; the word *savel* means "melody" in Finnish. The choir's purpose was to preserve the Finnish culture through music. Dr. Waino A. Mackey was the first director. An accomplished pianist and instructor of piano, he arranged many of the selections sung by the choir. Dr.

Mackey retired in 1954. Arthur Saarinen, director of orchestral activities in the FAIRVIEW PARK schools, became the director of the choir and served in that capacity until 1966. The Savel Choir performed an annual concert each spring. In addition, it sang at various nationality functions and Finnish festivals in Cleveland and in neighboring communities such as Fairport Harbor. In 1957, the choir performed in the annual U.S.-Canadian Finnish Music Festival in Ontario, Canada. It also made an appearance on WEWS-TV in the early 1960s. The choir sang Finnish folk music and compositions by Finnish composers, such as Jean Sibelius. Many of the charter members were still with the Savel Choir when it disbanded in 1966.

**SAWICKI, JOSEPH F.** (18 Mar. 1881–30 Oct. 1969), was a Cleveland lawyer, legislator, politician, and judge. His career included extensive involvement with the Polish-American community in Cleveland. Sawicki was born in Gorzno, Poland, the oldest of 14 children of Peter and Bogumila Jurkowska Sawicki. The family immigrated to America and Cleveland when Sawicki was 5 years old. He received his early education at St. Stanislaus School and the CLEVELAND PUBLIC SCHOOLS. He worked his way through St. Ignatius College, BALDWIN-WALLACE, Western Reserve University Law School, and Cleveland Law School, where he received the LL.B. degree in 1904.

Sawicki was admitted to the Ohio bar in 1904 and began the general practice of law. He was elected 3 times to the Ohio legislature, 1905–08 and 1911–12. He was appointed by Gov. Jas. Cox as judge of municipal court on 1 Jan. 1919 and won his first election to the post that November. In 1932, Sawicki was forced into involuntary bankruptcy, with over $200,000 debt from real-estate investments and campaign expenses. When court records made public the numerous loans made to Sawicki from practicing lawyers, the executive committee of the CLEVELAND BAR ASSOC. demanded his resignation. Faced with an ouster movement, Sawicki retired from the municipal court bench on 1 July 1933 and returned to private practice. In 1953, Sawicki served as a member of the Cleveland Charter Commission. In 1959, he was appointed as a special counsel for the Ohio attorney general.

Active in the Polish-American community in Cleveland all his life, Sawicki was honored by the Cleveland Society of Poles as the "Good Joe of 1967" for his work in numerous Polish relief groups and as past president of the Polish-American Chamber of Commerce. An avid coin and art collector, he was president of the Western Reserve Numismatic Assoc. and a member of the American, Krakow, and Warsaw numismatic associations and the Polonaise Art Club. Sawicki married Elizabeth Veronica Sadowska on 24 June 1908. The Sawickis had 2 daughters, Mrs. Edward Gilbert and Mrs. Jas. Wager, and 2 sons, Eugene and Edwin.

**SCANDINAVIANS.** Scandinavian migration to North America, relatively insignificant prior to 1850, increased rapidly after the CIVIL WAR because of successive crop failures and unemployment in the homeland and the reported opportunities for a better life in the New World. By 1920, more than 2 million Scandinavians had settled in the U.S. and Canada, chiefly in states bordering the Great Lakes and in the central and northern Great Plains states. Smaller groups were attracted to large East Coast cities, New England, Texas, Canada, and the Pacific Northwest. Relatively few Danes, Norwegians, or Swedes chose to settle in Cleveland or elsewhere in Ohio. Attracted by opportunities for work as longshoremen on the docks, Scandinavian immigrants began to arrive in northeast Ohio ca.

1869, mainly at first at the port of Ashtabula. By 1873, some 30 Swedes had settled east of that city's harbor. Specially helpful to newcomers in finding work and a suitable place to live was a dock foreman, Andrew Swedenborg. For almost 40 years, he worked supervising longshoremen. The harbor community grew rapidly, and in 1890, the U.S. government granted it its own post office, named Sweden, and appointed an early Swedish settler who owned the local grocery, Edward P. Brodin, to be its postmaster. In the 1870s, Danes, Norwegians, and Swedes in steadily increasing numbers came to Cleveland and settled both east and west of the CUYAHOGA RIVER. Some were experienced seamen or longshoremen; a few were farmers. A considerable number were skilled carpenters, blacksmiths, or tradesmen. Among the women, some were seamstresses or cooks; many sought work as domestic servants. Cleveland, with its many construction firms and factories, steel mills, huge docks for unloading iron ore, and shipping, offered many possibilities for employment for these immigrants. In 1880, there were 84 Danes, 37 Norwegians, and 180 Swedes in Cleveland. By 1910, the numbers had increased to 448, 512, and 1,657 respectively. As these figures do not include American-born spouses, children, or grandchildren, the community may be judged as more substantial than indicated.

Although Scandinavians settled on both sides of the Cuyahoga, Danes and Norwegians, whose languages are more closely related to each other than either is to Swedish, preferred to live on Cleveland's west side. Although their number was never sufficient to dominate any neighborhood, prior to 1920 their homes were located mainly between W. 25th and W. 65th and between Lorain Ave. and the lake. As Cleveland's population increased, some Danes and Norwegians moved farther south to Memphis Ave., but by 1950 many families had moved out to the far west side, settling in ROCKY RIVER. By this time, however, ethnic Scandinavian ties had largely disappeared as families were assimilated into mainstream America. Swedes also settled on both Cleveland's west and east sides, but the majority preferred to live east of the Cuyahoga River. By 1900, when there were 1,000 Swedes in Cleveland, most lived in a neighborhood bounded on the north by Superior Ave. and on the south by Lexington Ave. between E. 55th and E. 90th streets. Although the area was not exclusively Swedish, there were a number of Swedish stores, professional offices, and business establishments there.

Since the Lutheran church is the state church in all 3 Scandinavian countries, most immigrants were inclined toward attending Lutheran services (see LUTHERANS). Beginning in 1874, Norwegian Lutheran missionary pastors from time to time held Sunday services in NEWBURGH Twp. and in Cleveland. In 1878, Rev. J. I. Welo organized a Norwegian congregation in the German Zion Lutheran Schoolhouse on Bolivar Rd. on Cleveland's east side. This congregation later evolved into Our Savior's Norwegian Evangelical Lutheran Church, located across the Cuyahoga River at 1433 W. 57th St. Between 1883–92, pastors Olaf E. Brandt and J. H. Lunde conducted Danish and Norwegian services at Trinity Lutheran Schoolhouse on W. 30th St. In 1893, a Danish Lutheran congregation was organized in Rocky River, which in 1897 built Immanuel Lutheran Church at 19151 Eastlook Rd. From 1885–1915, Danish and Norwegian services were conducted on Cleveland's east side at First Scandinavian Evangelical Lutheran Church on Outhwaite Ave. and E. 63rd St. Pastor Oscar Strom served these two churches between 1907–33, and, for a time, also Our Savior's Lutheran Church. In 1951, Immanuel and Our Savior's churches merged to form Our Savior's Rocky River Lutheran Church, 20300 Hilliard Rd.

Outstanding among Swedish missionary pastors in the early 1880s was Rev. Gustav Nelsenius, who in 1885 organized the Swedish Evangelical Lutheran Bethlehem Congregation, which met for several years in Olivet Chapel, a vacated Bohemian mission at Hill and Commercial streets, overlooking the east bank of the Cuyahoga River. Moving to Cleveland in 1888, he served as pastor of this congregation until 1891, during which time Bethlehem built its first church, on Central Ave. near E. 24th St. In 1899 the congregation moved to 7505 Wade Park Ave., remaining there for 50 years. In 1953 it moved to 3740 Mayfield Rd. in CLEVELAND HTS.

On 7 Mar. 1920, Immanuel Lutheran Swedish Congregation was organized on Cleveland's west side. For several years, Sunday school and Swedish worship services were held at Emmaus Lutheran Church on W. 36th St. at Mapledale Ave., conducted by Rev. J. Alfred Lundgren, who was then pastor at Bethlehem Church. At first numbering only 25 families with 40 children, this congregation built its own church on Forestdale Ave. near W. 25th St., where the first service was held on Christmas Day 1924. In 1933, the congregation disbanded. Later, the members reorganized, forming the Gloria Dei Evangelical Lutheran Congregation. Housed for a time in a temporary building, in 1940 it dedicated its first permanent structure, located at 5801 Memphis Ave. Competing for members among Cleveland's Swedes during the first half of the 20th century were several other Swedish churches within just a few blocks of each other. Organized in 1889, the Swedish Baptist Congregation built its first church in 1894 on White Ave. and E. 57th St., and its second church in 1913 at 1418 Addison Rd., near Wade Park Ave. In 1940 the congregation changed the name of its church to Bethel Baptist, and in 1952 it moved to Cleveland Hts., where in 1957 it dedicated its church at 2706 Noble Rd. Also organized in 1889, the Swedish Congregational Church (later Swedish Evangelical Mission Covenant) for some years held services in Olivet Chapel. Assisted by Plymouth Congregational Church, it built its first church in 1892 at 5803 Lexington Ave. In 1910 it moved into its second church, at 7411 Decker Ave., near Addison Rd. In 1955 the church divided into 2 congregations, First Covenant and Bethany Covenant, which eventually built churches, one at 1985 Green Rd. amd the other in LYNDHURST at 5120 Ridgebury Blvd. The Swedish Methodist Congregation was organized in 1892. Upon receipt of a large gift from an American Methodist, F. W. Walworth, the congregation in 1906 built Walworth Swedish Methodist Church at 1337 Giddings, 1 block south of Superior Ave. In 1969 the congregation disbanded, and its members joined other Methodist churches.

In Sept. 1905 at a meeting of 35 persons at E. 71st St. and Lexington Ave., the Swedish Corps of the SALVATION ARMY was organized. It served in many ways as a church, conducting Sunday school and worship services. It also functioned as a social organization, sponsoring concerts and recreational programs, some of which attracted as many as 100 people. In the early 1920s, the Swedish Corps moved its headquarters to 1309 E. 90th St., and in 1969 it merged with the Wade Park Corps to form the Addison-Superior Corps, which consisted predominantly of black members. Although the Scandinavian community in Cleveland was never large, 2 Swedish cooperative organizations were formed to provide assistance at time of illness and death. The Gustavus Adolphus Sick Benefit Society (org. 1890) held its monthly meetings for many years at Bethlehem Lutheran Church. The Harmony Relief Society (founded 1892) met first at the Swedish Covenant Church and subsequently at the Swedish Methodist Church. For many years the Danish Brotherhood, the Swedish Nobel-

Monitor Lodge #130, and the Swedish Central Union provided modest assistance in times of need to their respective members and others. In 1970 there were 175 Swedes, 61 Danes, and 43 Norwegians in Cleveland proper. Altogether there were 6,200 members of these nationalities and their American offspring in Greater Cleveland in that year. By this time, however, the Scandinavian community had been assimilated into the mainstream of life in Cleveland. Use of the Scandinavian languages disappeared by the 1920s and 1930s in the nationality churches. The Danish Brotherhood, Swedish Cultural Society, and Nobel-Monitor Lodge #130 of the Vasa Order of America do, however, remain active as social organizations striving to maintain Scandinavian cultural ties and traditions.

Paul A. Nelson
Cleveland Clinic

**SCHAEFER BODY, INC.,** evolved from the Gustav Schaefer Wagon Co., incorporated in 1917 and established in 1880 as Schaefer & Eckhardt. Gustav Schaefer, an immigrant, had learned the skill of wagon-wheel making from his father and was a blacksmith. Arriving in Cleveland with his trunk and 50 cents, he worked first as a stonecutter in the Berea Quarries and then as a cooper making barrel hoops for JOHN D. ROCKEFELLER. The Gustav Schaefer Wagon Works began on Lorain Ave. with $800 working capital. It specialized in custom-made, hand-striped wagons and carriages. By 1913, the company's ad in the Cleveland directory reflected its adaptation to the changing transportation scene: "Builders of all kinds of heavy and light wagons. Commercial Auto Bodies of all types. Auto Wheel building and repairing. Auto Painting and Trimming." By the mid-1920s, the company was still listed as the Gustav Schaefer Wagon Co. Directory ads stressed quality and indicated a continuing adaptation to the needs of automobiles and trucks. Full-page ads proclaimed that it was "Cleveland's Complete Body Shop." Custom truck body building was a specialty; pictures of armored trucks and delivery trucks were featured.

The company was first listed as the Schaefer Body Co. in 1926. The following year, its logo became "Schaefer Cleveland" and its motto "Call the Schaefer Man." A fire destroyed the plant in 1927, and the company was further crippled by the Depression. It was unable to recover, and its assets were sold at pubic auction in 1935. Following bankruptcy proceedings, the company was reorganized as Schaefer Body, Inc., financed with Cleveland capital with Henry G. Schaefer, Gustav's son, as the president. At this time it relocated on the east side on Superior Ave. Gustav Schaefer died in Nov. 1936 at age 92. He had been active in Trinity Lutheran Church and was one of the first members of the Natl. Chamber of Commerce, Washington, D.C. He was an influential lobbyist for electric arc lights on Lorain Ave. and bridges over the Cuyahoga. In 1964, Schaefer Body was described as the "city's largest and most complete body shop." It not only repaired truck, trailer, and auto bodies and provided contract maintenance for fleets, but it also was a major sales and service outlet for new equipment. A new management took over the operation in 1972. It planned an expansion of service, the addition of new lines of truck equipment products, and the phasing out of manufacturing operations. Expectations were that the firm would become stronger in the areas of distribution and service. President Arthur Kruse, grandson of Gustav, stated, "We fully expect Schaefer Body to be an industry leader here for the next 93 years, just as it has for the past 93." Despite the optimism this reorganization engendered in Schaefer Body, the company ran into a variety of problems that resulted in its closing in 1977. All assets, including equipment and machinery, were liquidated.

The **SCHAUFFLER COLLEGE OF RELIGIOUS AND SOCIAL WORK,** located at 5115 Fowler Dr. SE near Broadway, was an interracial, international, and interdenominational undergraduate college initially founded for the purpose of training young Slavic women as Christian missionaries to the Czech community of Cleveland. In 1882, Henry A. Schauffler, a former missionary in Turkey and Bohemia, accepted an invitation from Chas. T. Collins, pastor of Plymouth Congregational Church, to become pastor of Olivet Chapel (a mission of Plymouth Church) and to work with the Czech community. In Oct. 1883 the Congregational Home Missionary Society appointed him superintendent of Slavic missions in the U.S. to organize Christian work among the immigrants under the auspices of the Bohemian Mission Board of Cleveland. The Bohemian Board secured land on Broadway in 1884 and erected BETHLEHEM CONGREGATIONAL CHURCH (ded. Jan. 1885).

Schauffler, believing that there should be an undergraduate school that would provide an opportunity for young Slavic women to receive specialized training to help (and to evangelize) immigrants in Cleveland from Bohemia, persuaded Clara Hobart to establish the Slavic Bible Readers' Home (School) next door to the Bethlehem Church. The school began on 23 Jan. 1886 with 1 teacher, Miss Hobart, and 1 pupil, Miss Anna Belsan, in a wing at the home of Miss Hobart's parents, 1254 Broadway Ave., where it remained for over 2½ years. In 1888 it became known as the Bohemian Bible Readers' School and moved to a private residence at 1572 Broadway. Mrs. Clara Hobart Schauffler, who had become the first principal, served until 1889. Two years later, on 19 May 1890, a cornerstone was laid at 5115 Fowler Dr. near Broadway for their own building; it was dedicated on 31 Dec. 1890. At this time, qualified young women of all nationalities were admitted; admission no longer was limited to women of Slavic descent. The name was changed in 1892 to the Bethlehem Bible Readers' School & Home, and in 1897–98 to the Bethlehem Bible & Missionary Training School. After Dr. Schauffler's death on 15 Feb. 1905, the school was renamed the Schauffler Missionary Training School. An administration building, several dormitories, and a chapel were constructed. During the administration of Dr. Raymond G. Clapp, who served as principal from 1924–41, Schauffler changed from a 3-year training school to a 4-year college. In 1930–36 it was known as the Schauffler School—A College of Religious Education, Missionary Training, & Social Work. Students came from many states and foreign countries, took a wide range of academic subjects, and did supervised fieldwork in a variety of social-work agencies and in many local churches.

The school was supported by endowments, by contributions from many churches, and by individuals, as well as by the Daughters of the American Revolution, who provided scholarships through their Americanization Committee. In 1943, Schauffler was recognized by the Amer. Assoc. of Schools of Social Work and became a charter member of the Natl. Council on Social Work Education. Under the leadership of Dr. Geo. P. Michaelides, Schauffler continued to expand and to demonstrate its philosophy: "To give social direction to religion and religious motivation to social work." In 1953, men were accepted as degree candidates by the college. As the neighborhood became more and more industrialized, enrollment began to decline, and in June 1954, Schauffler moved to the Oberlin College campus and became the Div. of Christian Educa-

tion. The last students graduated from Schauffler in 1957, and it ceased to exist as a separate entity. Subsequently, in 1967, the endowment funds were transferred to Defiance College, Ohio, where Schauffler Hall (completed in 1981) and specialized courses in religious education and social work continue the work Dr. Schauffler began.

**SCHIFFLEIN CHRISTI** was the first Evangelical Protestant congregation in Cleveland, formed in 1835. Through schism, it spawned what was to become the first German Lutheran church in the city. According to tradition, Zum Schifflein Christi (the Little Boat of Christ) was begun by German sailors who had promised to found a church if they were saved from a storm. Church records, however, indicate that a small group of families banded together to found the First Evangelical Protestant Congregation under Rev. Johann F. Tanke, in 1834. Within a year, dissension caused the congregation to break off and hold meetings in empty storerooms, while the original group, still without a permanent home, met at the Masonic Temple. After the schism was ended through the selection of a new pastor, the church constructed its first building, at Erie and Hamilton. It remained at this location until 1876, when it built at Superior and Dodge. The name was changed to Schifflein Christi at this time. By 1842, some families broke away to found ZION EVANGELICAL LUTHERAN CHURCH, from which sprang most other Evangelical Lutheran churches in the area. Throughout the 19th century, internal troubles were a constant threat to the existence of the church. In 1923, Schifflein Christi merged with the Ebenezer Evangelical Church, which had just lost its pastor, to become the First Evangelical Church, at 841 Thornhill Dr. With its merger with Trinity Evangelical Protestant Church in 1929, it became the First Evangelical & Reformed Church. In 1953, it merged with the Glenville Evangelical Reformed Church, while a final merger in 1969 joined it with the Fellowship United Church of Christ of Wickliffe, at 30040 Ridge Rd.

Schifflein Christi Records, WRHS.

The **SCHMELING-STRIBLING FIGHT** was the first heavyweight championship match waged in Cleveland, and the first sporting event to take place in the newly completed Cleveland Stadium on 3 July 1931. It matched Max Schmeling, German-born heavyweight champion, with Wm. L. "Young" Stribling, a seasoned veteran of 300 bouts. Dubbed the "second battle of Lake Erie," the fight built Stribling's credibility and proved to be his only chance at the title. Schmeling had fought 53 bouts with only 4 losses. Previously, he had fought Jack Sharkey for the heavyweight championship of the world winning on a foul. His opponent, known as "Young" Stribling because he had entered the ring at age 14, was a popular fighter known for his gentlemanly conduct and his good punch with either hand. The Georgia-born son of vaudeville performers, Stribling was trained to be a boxer by his father, who promoted his career. On the night of the fight, former champion Jas. Corbett proclaimed the Cleveland Stadium a wonderful place for the fight to spectators, who bought tickets that ranged from $3–25. (Even in the Depression, over 5,300 $25 tickets were sold.) Schmeling was slightly favored to win by East Coast bookies, but "Willy the Whacker" was the popular favorite. For the first 4 rounds of the match Schemeling bided his time. In the 5th round, Schmeling got his chance as Stribling slowed up, and after 3 more rounds, Schmeling delivered a staggering right-handed punch. In the 10th round, Schmeling decked his opponent, who regained his footing by the 9 count, but the referee declared Schmeling the victor. The Cleveland fight proved to be the summit of Stribling's boxing career, as he died from injuries received in a motorcycle accident in 1933.

**SCHNEIDER, CHARLES SUMNER** (1874–10 Mar. 1932), was one of Cleveland's most brilliant eclectic architects from 1901–32. Schneider was born and educated in Cleveland. He received his first architectural training in the office of Meade & Garfield, after which he studied at the Ecole des Beaux-Arts in Paris. Returning to Cleveland, he joined the office of Wm. Watterson in 1901. While in the firm of Watterson & Schneider, he designed the ornate Italian Renaissance-style Rockefeller Physics Bldg. at Case School of Applied Science in 1905. He also planned the office building of the Cleveland Baseball Co. at LEAGUE PARK; both were still standing in the 1980s.

Schneider began his own independent practice in 1908. In 1912 he was associate architect with Geo. B. Post in the construction of the Hotel Statler, which has been called the "first complete expression of the modern hotel." In the 1920s, Schneider was associated with architects Edward J. Maier and Francis Hirschfeld. Working in both the classical and medieval idioms, he became a prolific designer of private residences in CLEVELAND HTS., SHAKER HTS., LAKEWOOD, and other cities. They included houses for Ernest S. Barkwill and for Mrs. Sophia S. Taylor, president and chairman of WM. TAYLOR SON & CO., and the splendid classic revival residence for Edwin Motch on S. Park Blvd. However, Schneider's residential masterpiece was the Tudor mansion for the estate of F. A. Seiberling in Akron, Stan Hywet (1915), which was based on a study of several great English country houses.

Schneider's versatility is demonstrated by comparing Stan Hywet with Plymouth Church in Shaker Hts. (1923), which is the most accomplished example of a Georgian Colonial-style church in the region. He also planned the Shaker Hts. City Hall (1930) and several public schools. He designed Quad Hall on Euclid Ave., a residential hotel for men (1925), Austin Hall at Ohio Wesleyan University in Delaware, Ohio, and 1 major classical office building in Cleveland, the Brotherhood of Railroad Trainmen Bldg. (1921). Schneider was a member and served as president of the Cleveland Chap. of the AMERICAN INSTITUTE OF ARCHITECTS, and was elected a fellow of the AIA in 1923. He married Georgia P. Leighton, and they had 3 children, Margery, Frederick, and Leighton.

**SCHOENFELD, FRANK K.** (7 Dec. 1904–29 Dec. 1984), was a chemical engineer who became an executive in the B. F. Goodrich Co., serving as the director of the company's research center in BRECKSVILLE in the 1960s (see B. F. GOODRICH CO.-RESEARCH & DEVELOPMENT). Born in Pittsburgh, the son of George and Rose Koch Schoenfeld, Schoenfeld received his undergraduate degree in chemical engineering in 1927. He received a master's degree from Western Reserve University in 1933 and a doctorate from WRU in 1937. He joined B. F. Goodrich as a chemist in 1927 and worked on vinyl resins. In 1939 he became manager of Koroseal Research & Development, and in 1942 he was named director of this group, which worked on the development of manufacturing processes for vinyl chloride and polyvinyl chlorides. In 1943 he became a technical superintendent in the newly formed B. F. Goodrich Chemical Co., a division of B. F. Goodrich. He advanced to vice-president of technology in 1946; in 1954 he became vice-president of research for the parent firm, and in 1959 he was named vice-president of research and development. He held the latter position until he retired in 1968. Schoenfeld wrote a number of technical papers and earned patents in the fields of pigments, adhesives, rubber derivatives, polymerization, manmade rubbers, and plastics. He received several awards for his work, including the 1959 medal from the Industrial Research Institute and the Cleveland Technical Societies Council's Annual Distinguished Service Award for 1966. He was a member of the American Chemical Society, the American Institute of Chemical Engineers, the Industrial Research Institute, the Society of the Chemical Industry, the Directors of Industrial Research, and Alpha Chi Sigma. In addition to his work for Goodrich, Schoenfeld served as a director of British Geon, Ltd. In Dec. 1957 he became a member of the board of governors of WRU; he was elected its chairman in Nov. 1963. Schoenfeld was married on 10 Oct. 1930 to Helen Mars Wood of Beorgen, N.Y. She died in Mar. 1970.

The **SCHOOL FUND SOCIETY** was a state organization of black citizens originally called together by a concerned group of Clevelanders in 1835. Its main objective was to find ways to insure educational opportunities for black children in the state. The society grew out of the fledgling efforts of a small group of Cleveland's black citizens to finance their own school because a state law, passed in 1829, specifically prohibited the attendance of black or mulatto children in public schools. Though the law provided for taxes collected from the property of colored persons to be appropriated for instruction for BLACKS, in practice funds were seldom used for this purpose. The society was successful in opening schools in Springfield, Cincinnati, Columbus, and Cleveland. It also petitioned the state legislature to change exclusionary laws. The statewide convention to address educational concerns led to future meetings of black Ohioans, which came to be known as Conventions of the Colored People of Ohio. The conventions addressed many issues of concern, not the least of which were slavery in the South and repressive laws in the North that deprived blacks of their rights of citizenship. Among Clevelanders active in the convention movement were JOHN MALVIN, John L. Watson, WM. H. DAY, ROBT. B. LEACH, and John Brown.

**SCHREMBS, JOSEPH** (12 Mar. 1866–2 Nov. 1945), was the fifth bishop of the Diocese of Cleveland. Schrembs was born in Wurzelhozen (Regensburg), Germany, the 15th of 16 children of Geo. and Mary Gess Schrembs. He came to America at age 11 and studied at St. Vincent Archabbey in Latrobe, Pa., before going to Louisville, Ky., as a teacher. He studied for the priesthood at seminaries in Quebec and Montreal. He was ordained to the priesthood in St. Andrew Cathedral, Grand Rapids, Mich., on 29 June 1889. Schrembs served at parishes in Saginaw, Bay City, and Grand Rapids, and in 1903 he was named vicar general of the Grand Rapids Diocese. On 22 Feb. 1911, he was consecrated auxiliary bishop of Grand Rapids. He was named first bishop of the newly organized Diocese of Toledo on 11 Aug. 1911. As bishop, Schrembs combated the anti-Catholic prejudice of the city. He was one of the 4 bishops on the administrative committee of the Natl. Catholic War Council set up during WORLD WAR I. After the war, he successfully lobbied in Rome for its continuance and became one of the members of the permanent committee that supervised its operation. (It was then known as the Natl. Catholic Welfare Council.) Schrembs was instrumental in organizing the Natl. Council of Catholic Men and the Natl. Council of Catholic Women.

Schrembs succeeded the late Bp. JOHN P. FARRELLY as bishop of Cleveland on 8 Sept. 1921. He followed Farrelly's plans in the expansion of the Board of Catholic Charities. He consolidated the boys' orphanage and opened a model institution on the Parmadale site. He began ROSE-MARY HOME, a rehabilitation center and shelter for handicapped children. He relocated ST. MARY SEMINARY to its Ansel Rd. site and opened the new complex in 1925. In 1931 he began Sisters' College in an effort to provide standardized teaching preparation for religious teaching in diocesan schools (see ST. JOHN COLLEGE). Schrembs guided the diocese through the rigors of the Depression and its crushing financial burdens. He was keenly interested in social justice and actively supported the trade-union movement. He was one of the first clerics to use RADIO as a means of evangelization and instruction. The high point of Schrembs's administration was his hosting the SEVENTH NATL. EUCHARISTIC CONGRESS in Cleveland in 1935. As a mark of honor, Schrembs was given the honorary title of archbishop in 1939. A diabetic condition proved to be increasingly disabling, and a coadjutor bishop, EDWARD F. HOBAN, who was to handle the administrative matters of the diocese, was appointed on 14 Nov. 1942.

The **SCHUBERT QUARTET** was an early Cleveland chamber music group, part of a growing late-19th-century interest in forms other than choral music. The quartet was organized in 1878 by JOHANN BECK (1st violin), with Julius Deiss (2d violin), Chas. Reinhart (viola), and Chas. Heydler (cello). Concerts were given at Brainard's Parlors, at Heard's Hall, and with German singing societies. Early performances included a zither club (a popular fad). Concerts were given until 1890, when the group became known as the BECK STRING QUARTET. In Feb. 1891, with a new cellist, Max Droge, it gave the first Cleveland performance of Schubert's Piano Trio in B-flat Major. After this time, the players performed in various combinations under various names.

The **SCHUHPLATTLER AND TRACHTENVEREIN BAVARIA** was formed in 1972 from the remnants of the Schuhplattler & Costume Club, a singing and dancing club. The group specializes in the form of dancing known as Schuhplattler, or shoe slapping. The Schuhplattler & Trachtenverein Bavaria, under the direction of president Reinhold Rock and dance coordinator Rudy Hermes, accumulated top honors in a number of annual competitions held throughout North America. It won the traveling trophy donated by the Bavarian government in 1973, 1975, 1977, 1979, 1983, and 1985. In 1985, the group had over 50 dancers and a support staff of 125 members. It performed locally at German Day celebrations, folk festivals, Oktoberfests, and private functions. The Schuhplattler & Trachtenverein Bavaria rehearsed at the Banater Club on Lorain Ave.

**SCHWEINFURTH, CHARLES F.** (3 Sept. 1856–8 Nov. 1919), was one of Cleveland's most active and distinguished architects, who designed many of the city's finest residences, churches, and educational buildings. Born in Auburn, N.Y., Schweinfurth attended public schools there and graduated from Auburn High School in 1872. He subsequently worked at architectural offices in New York City (1872–74), at the office of the supervising architect of the U.S. Treasury in Washington, D.C. (1874–80), and in Cleveland as the architect of a great stone mansion (since demolished) on Euclid Ave. for financier SYLVESTER T. EVERETT. By 1910, Schweinfurth had completed at least 15 residential designs for prominent and wealthy Clevelanders on Euclid Ave. between E. 12th and E. 40th streets, when the thoroughfare was called "Millionaires' Row." Still standing is the SAMUEL MATHER house (1910) at 2605

Euclid Ave., now used as a conference center by CLEVELAND STATE UNIVERSITY. Schweinfurth also designed Samuel Mather's residence "Shoreby" (1890) on Lakeshore Blvd. in BRATENAHL; the MARCUS A. HANNA house (1890) on Lake Ave. (demolished); his own home on E. 75th St. between Chester and Euclid avenues; and the Gordon Morrill residence (1915) on Magnolia Dr. in UNIVERSITY CIRCLE. Significant church commissions included the remodeled interiors of the Old Stone Church (1884) on PUBLIC SQUARE; CALVARY PRESBYTERIAN (1890) at E. 79th St. and Euclid Ave.; the Ursuline Convent (1893, since demolished) at E. 55th St. and Euclid Ave.; and TRINITY CATHEDRAL & Parish House (1907) at E. 22nd and Euclid Ave., which many critics and historians believe is his finest work. Schweinfurth had a long and productive relationship with SAMUEL and FLORA STONE MATHER, which led to designs for the UNION CLUB (1905) in downtown Cleveland, as well as several buildings on the early Adelbert and Mather college grounds. Three of these structures are still present on the CASE WESTERN RESERVE UNIVERSITY campus, including the Florence Harkness Chapel (1902) and Haydn Hall (1902) on Bellflower Rd. and the former Backus Law School (1896) on Adelbert Rd. Four landmark stone bridges (1896–1900) that cross Rockefeller Pkwy., now Martin Luther King Blvd. in University Circle, are Schweinfurth designs.

Johannessen, Eric, *Cleveland Architecture, 1876–1976* (1979).
Perry, Regenia, "The Life and Works of Charles Frederick Schweinfurth" (Ph.D. diss., WRU, 1967).

**SCIENCE.** In America during the 1800s science grew from the level of dilettantes to large-scale research performed by university-trained professionals. Financial support for science matured, as well, outgrowing the individual's pocketbook to tap the coffers of government, corporations, and public and private institutions. In the 20th century, science and TECHNOLOGY produced a powerful combination of knowledge about the world and the ways to manipulate it for personal and public benefit. This knowledge permeated the culture and changed the very way that human society thought about itself and the surrounding natural environment. Even with the diminishing role of the amateur in science, the power of science and technology to affect the society resulted in a continued and growing public interest in scientific topics. The pattern of scientific work in Cleveland in the early days of its history was largely that of amateur, though serious, naturalists. These "scientists" were actually a group of young men from the city's well-to-do leadership, headed by WM. CASE, son of LEONARD CASE, SR., an early settler and landowner in Cleveland. During the 1830s, William and several friends created what was then a typical cabinet of natural curiosities, with specimens of flora and fauna from around the Cleveland area. This collection of birds, fish, and botanical and geological samples was kept in a small house, named the "Ark" because of its assorted contents, located on PUBLIC SQUARE next to the Case residence. The "Arkites" met on a regular basis to present formal and informal papers on various scientific topics. As the members of this local group grew older, the meetings grew less frequent and eventually stopped, and the collections fell into disuse and disorganization.

With the opening of the full length of the Ohio Canal in 1832, Cleveland became a commercial "boom town" that offered great opportunities to professionals in all fields. One of these was JARED P. KIRTLAND, a doctor trained at Yale, who had moved to Ohio at the age of 30 in 1823 to practice medicine. By 1843 he was on the faculty of the medical school of Western Reserve College. Although the college was located in Hudson, Ohio, about 20 mi. from Cleveland, the medical school was in the city. Kirtland bought land in Rockport (later called Lakewood), just west of Cleveland, and took an active role in stimulating the development of intellectual interests in the city. In 1845, he led a group of professional men, many of whom taught science and medicine at the colleges and medical schools being started in the city at the time, in forming the CLEVELAND ACADEMY OF NATURAL SCIENCES. The primary reason for the founding of the academy was to create in Cleveland a fine museum of natural history. To house this museum, rooms in the medical school of Western Reserve College had been offered by the faculty, many of whom were founding members of the academy. Kirtland's national reputation as a man of learning and creativity brought to the city in the summer of 1853 the annual meeting of the American Assoc. for the Advancement of Science. This meeting of the AAAS, the first but not only such meeting in Cleveland, is often cited by historians of science in America as a watershed meeting of the early 19th century. It was during and after that meeting that issues regarding the role of amateurs in professional scientific work were raised. While many members of the Cleveland Academy of Natural Science were amateur naturalists, not a great many papers read at the meeting were in the field of natural history, reflecting the changing nature of American science toward the physical sciences. Also, several of the papers presented by local amateurs were not well received by the visiting professionals and eventually were deleted from the published proceedings. A version of the proceedings of this meeting of the AAAS was published in Cleveland in *Annals of Science*, a short-lived (1853–54) journal edited by Hamilton Smith, a Yale graduate, an astronomer, and a Cleveland resident. The *Annals* were an attempt to present scientific papers and information at a level understandable to the local and, hopefully, a larger amateur audience.

While the Cleveland Academy of Natural Science (renamed the Kirtland Society for its founder) focused on natural history and involved the various teachers of the medical schools in Cleveland, at Western Reserve College in Hudson, Elias Loomis, professor of natural philosophy, established the first permanent observatory west of the Allegheny Mts. in the late 1830s. Loomis, trained at Yale, remained at the college only until 1844, but the observatory still exists on the grounds of the old college campus in Hudson. After the Civil War, scientific activity in Cleveland increasingly became concerned with the physical sciences of astronomy and physics. In 1881, the new machine-tool company of WARNER & SWASEY moved to Cleveland from Chicago. The two founders of this company were deeply interested in astronomical telescopes and during the 1880s and 1890s built the largest such telescopes in the world. Cleveland became the source for the world's finest astronomical instruments, such as those provided for the Lick Observatory of the University of California, the U.S. Naval Observatory, the Yerkes Observatory of the University of Chicago, the MacDonald Observatory for the University of Texas, and others.

Cleveland's first scientific and technical college, the Case School of Applied Science, opened in 1880 on Public Square. College-level technical schools such as Case were started throughout the U.S. in the years after the CIVIL WAR, many with money made available through the federal Morrill Land Grant Act, but also many privately funded like Case. The U.S. was quickly becoming a world leader in technology and INDUSTRY, and it was hoped that schools such as Case, MIT, Cornell, and the state universities would be able to provide the kind of practical engineering education needed for the economic growth of the nation. Although a self-educated scholar and astronomer, Ohioan JOHN STOCKWELL, was appointed the first professor of mathematics and astronomy, the new Case School attracted well-trained professionals to its faculty. In the 1880s, the physicist ALBERT A. MICHELSON, who in the early 20th century would be America's first Nobel Prize winner, joined the faculty and together with the chemist EDWARD MORLEY conducted one of the most famous of 19th-century physical experiments. The Michelson-Morley experiment tested the question of the existence of an all-pervasive "ether" in the universe through which electromagnetic radiation, such as light, propagated. Classical physics theorized the existence of such an ether in order to account for the observed properties of light. The Michelson-Morley experiment, repeated several times in the late 1880s and for which Warner & Swasey provided some of the equipment, showed that the ether did not exist. One of the great negative-solution experiments in the history of science, the Michelson-Morley results pointed the way toward Einstein's work on the theory of relativity at the turn of the 20th century. Another prominent physical scientist at Case was DAYTON C. MILLER. Miller conducted many experiments in acoustics, establishing that tradition in experimental and theoretical work in the Case physics department. In 1896 he was one of the first Americans to follow up on the x-ray work of Wilhelm Roentgen in Germany. Miller took some of the first x-ray pictures in America at Case and published early accounts of his experiments.

While the faculty at Case continued to research the physical world, science in the early 20th century was finding a new home in municipal government. The city of Cleveland's sanitation, water, and public health departments were involved in numerous studies of the environmental changes brought on by urban growth. In the first years of the new century, TOM L. JOHNSON, one of the great Progressive mayors of the era, formed an administration that aggressively sought solutions to the problems of a tainted water supply, typhoid fever outbreaks, and smoke pollution. The city's water department, dating back to the building of the first pumping station and reservoir in the 1850s, had grown into a large, technological system, supplying water to not only city residents but suburban dwellings, as well. Studies done by city workers in conjunction with physicians teaching at the medical school at Western Reserve College showed the connection between water pollution and typhoid fever. Chlorination of the water began in 1911, after many tests, and the typhoid threat was eliminated (See WATER SYSTEM). One of the earliest scientific studies of the polluted air of a major industrial city was done by CHAS. F. MABERY, a chemist working at the Case School in 1895. The city of Cleveland, plagued with coal-smoke pollution since the years just before the Civil War, joined the "smoke abatement" movement of the early 20th century, hired smoke inspectors, and attempted to combat the increasingly dirtier skies. City smoke inspectors became experts on the physical and chemical properties of smoke. The natural sciences received public attention in 1920 when the CLEVELAND MUSEUM OF NATURAL HISTORY was founded. Interestingly, 2 years later a forgotten bank account of the old Kirtland Society (Cleveland Academy of Natural Sciences) was discovered, and the one surviving member of that 19th-century group, living in 1920 in Washington, D.C., voted to allow the transfer of the funds, totaling $750, to the new institution. The museum thrived and continues to serve the Greater Cleveland area with a program of exhibits and school-group and public programming.

In the 1920s, an extensive research program in human anatomy, eugenics, and children's-health statistics was conducted by 3 Cleveland physicians: CARL HAMANN, ROGER PERKINS, and THOMAS WINGATE TODD. Perkins headed the city's Div. of Health and assisted Hamann, who brought Todd to the city from England, in planning and executing a long-term investigation into public health through the study of anatomy. Using cadavers obtained legally from the city's workhouse and morgue, thousands of human skeletal remains were collected into one of the largest and finest such collections in the world. The collection is now housed at the Cleveland Museum of Natural History. In the late 1920s, Todd was selected to head a new organization, the BRUSH FOUNDATION, which had been created by CHAS. FRANCIS BRUSH, electrical-industry pioneer in Cleveland and member of Cleveland's wealthy business community. Brush had lost his only son and his son's daughter to blood poisoning in a dramatic battle to save the young girl's life. In his sorrow, the elder Brush created the Brush Foundation to promote research to improve the overall genetic stock of the human race. The foundation's research program involved the systematic compilation of vast amounts of medical data on a select group of 1,000 school-age children in the Cleveland area. The data collected on these children included regular full-length x-rays of the whole body, and precise x-rays of facial and dental structure as they aged. Between 1929–42, over 22,000 physical exams and over 90,000 psychological exams were conducted, and more than 250,000 x-rays were made. Although the study concentrated on 1,000 of the children, the total number of subjects by the end of the project was more than 5,000. Todd died in 1938, and the study was continued on a much-reduced scale until the shortages of WORLD WAR II brought it to a close. After the war, other researchers questioned the radiation damage to the subjects from such extensive and regular exposure to x-rays, but recent studies do not show any increase in cancer rates or other diseases among this group. The records from this study remain intact at CASE WESTERN RESERVE UNIVERSITY.

The Case School of Applied Science, renamed Case Institute of Technology, continued to be the focus of scientific work in the city, especially in the postwar years of the 1950s and the post-Sputnik era of the early 1960s. Astronomy at Case flourished under the direction of JASON J. NASSAU, working at the Warner & Swasey Observatory, established with money from the Cleveland machine-tool firm and equipped with Warner & Swasey telescopes. Nassau developed techniques using wide-field Schmidt and other kinds of telescopes for obtaining spectrographic information on large numbers of stars at one time and for identifying a type of star called a "Red Giant" because of its size and spectral color. The Astronomy Dept. at Case went on to specialize in galactic structure, establishing a new observatory in Chardon, Ohio, to escape the growing artificial light pollution of the city and then eventually joining a shared-time facility in the Southern Hemisphere, in Chile.

In the 1960s, important work in particle physics was done at Case Tech. Frederick Reines, who had worked at Los Alamos on the Manhattan Project to develop the first thermonuclear bomb during World War II, became head of the Case Physics Dept. in 1959. Reines developed an extensive program of research in atomic particles, developing underground observation chambers in salt mines under Lake Erie just east of Cleveland that were designed to shield experiments from cosmic rays emanating from outer space. Experiments to study the cosmic rays themselves from high-altitude balloons were conducted by Reines and his team in Texas. In 1965, working in conjunction with a team of researchers deep in a gold mine in South Africa, Reines and Thos. Jenkins (also of Case) were the first to detect the presence of the elementary subatomic particle the neutrino from a source in nature. It had been theoretically predicted that the neutrino, found until that time only in manmade nuclear experiments, should be observable as part of the natural radiation streaming down onto the earth from outer space. Engineering science at Case expanded into new fields in the 1960s. Materials research, polymer science, electronics, and systems analysis became the focus of various centers of research at the school. With the formation of Case Western Reserve University in 1966, Case's science and engineering departments became linked to the biochemical and medical researches at Western Reserve University, creating a large institution involved in biomedical engineering research. Government-operated research has been conducted in Cleveland since World War II at the NASA LEWIS RESEARCH CTR. at Cleveland Hopkins Airport on the city's far west side. This facility, begun by the Natl. Advisory Committee on Aeronautics in the 1940s, was continued by its successor, NASA. It remains a national center for research into propulsion systems for space exploration.

Anthropological research received worldwide acclaim in the 1970s with the work of Donald C. Johanson at the Cleveland Museum of Natural History. Doing fieldwork in the physical anthropology of early man in Africa, Johanson discovered the remarkably complete skeletal remains of a female, which he dated back more than 3.5 million years. This early human, named "Lucy" by Johanson and his team of researchers, represented a major find in anthropology, pushing the beginnings of mankind back farther than formerly imagined. Although his findings were challenged by such noted researchers as the Leakeys, Johanson's find withstood scientific scrutiny. Important, too, was the great amount of public interest in Johanson's work that was generated by the announcement of Lucy's discovery. For although amateurs now rarely play an important role in the work of science, public intrigue with the latest findings grows as society becomes increasingly more dependent on research in science and engineering.

Edward J. Pershey
Edison National Historic Site

SCOFIELD, LEVI T. (9 Nov. 1842–25 Feb. 1917), was an important late-19th-century Cleveland architect, specializing in institutional structures and public monuments. He served in the CIVIL WAR from 1861–65 and became chief engineer on the staff of Gen. Jacob Cox. After the war he designed several large state institutions, including the asylums for the insane at Athens (1868) and Columbus (1869), the North Carolina State Penitentiary at Raleigh (1870), and the reformatory at Mansfield (1884). Because of his war service, he was one of the chief proponents of the Cuyahoga County SOLDIERS & SAILORS MONUMENT, which he designed and supervised between 1886–94. Scofield designed many private residences, of which the R. K. Winslow house (1878) on Euclid Ave. was representative, and Cleveland public schools, such as Central High (1878) and Broadway (1881); in 1893 he received the commission for the Ohio Monument at the 1893 World's Columbian Exposition, a standing figure symbolic of the state surrounded by bronze sculptures of her most distinguished sons. In 1901 he designed the Schofield [sic] Bldg., a 14-story office building on the southwest corner of Euclid and E. 9th St. Most of Scofield's architectural designs were in the massive, picturesque, Late Victorian manner, with Gothic or Romanesque details. Mrs. Levi Scofield was active in

Cleveland social affairs, president of the YWCA, and also first president of the board of the PHILLIS WHEATLEY ASSOC. The Scofield residence (1898) stands at 2438 Mapleside, Cleveland.

Gleason, William J., *Soldiers and Sailors Monument* (1894).

**SCOTT, FRANK A.** (22 Mar. 1873–15 Apr. 1949), was a distinguished Cleveland businessman and civic leader. During WORLD WAR I, he served under Secretary of War NEWTON D. BAKER. Scott was born in Cleveland. He attended Cleveland public schools and received additional tutoring from John H. Dynes of Western Reserve University. At the age of 18, he began working for a railroad company, moving into increasingly responsible positions. He served from 1899–1905 as secretary of the Cleveland Chamber of Commerce, and from 1905–09 as secretary and treasurer of the Superior Savings & Trust Co. In 1909 he joined the WARNER & SWASEY CO., and within a few years he rose from secretary to vice-president. From 1920–28, he served as president and chairman of the board at Warner & Swasey. Prior to the involvement of the U.S. in World War I, Scott was an outspoken advocate of military preparedness. In 1916 he became a member of the Naval Consulting Board of the U.S. When the U.S. entered the war the following year, Scott was appointed chairman of the Munitions Standards Board by the Council of Natl. Defense. He had to resign later that year because of poor health, but he maintained his rank of colonel in the ORC of the U.S. Army and was appointed as honorary advisor to the Army Industrial College. In 1919 he received the Distinguished Service Medal. After the war, Scott resumed his active participation in various Cleveland civic, cultural, charitable, and educational institutions. He served for many years as vice-president of Associated Charities, and as treasurer and vice-president of Lakeside Hospital. He played a leading role in the building fund drive for UNIVERSITY HOSPITALS, and became president of that institution in 1928. As a trustee of WRU and a member of the Corp. of Case Institute of Technology, Scott attempted to achieve a merger between the two institutions. During the Depression, he served as a financial director for WRU. Scott married Bertha B. Dynes, who died in 1909. His second marriage, to Faith Alice Fraser, ended with her death in 1936. He later married Dulcie Schiflet.

Frank A. Scott Papers. WRHS

The **SCOTT AND FETZER COMPANY**, organized in 1914 as a machine shop and later a vacuum-cleaner manufacturer, had grown by 1984 into a major conglomerate, with 12 subsidiaries operating 42 plants that employed more than 16,000 people in the U.S. and Canada. Scott & Fetzer began as the Geo. H. Scott Machine Co., a partnership between Geo. H. Scott and Carl S. Fetzer. Located at 118 Noble Ct., the company was incorporated on 30 Nov. 1917 as the Scott & Fetzer Machine Co. Scott served as president and Fetzer as vice-president and treasurer. By 1918 the company had moved to the corner of Locust Ave. and W. 114th St. On 19 July 1919, the firm became the Scott & Fetzer Co. By 1922, it had begun to manufacture the vacuum cleaner designed in 1918 by Cleveland inventor Jas. B. Kirby.

Under Scott's leadership until 1961, Scott & Fetzer grew steadily. By 1951 it had moved to a new location at 1920 W. 114th St. In 1956, Kirby vacuum cleaners were sold door-to-door by 4,000 salespeople; sales that year were $9 million, and net income was $665,902. Sales in 1964 were $18.8 million, and that year the company began a major

expansion program by acquiring other companies. Over the next 20 years, Scott & Fetzer acquired 38 companies and sold 15. Among its acquisitions were PLM Prods. of Cleveland and Quikut of Fremont, Ohio, in 1964; the Adalet Co. of Cleveland in 1966; the Halex Die Casting Co. of Bedford Hts. in 1967; and the Cleveland Wood Prods. Co. in 1970. In 1978 Scott & Fetzer acquired World Book-Childcraft Internatl. Company sales were a record $697 million in 1979.

Scott & Fetzer had 1,915 employees in Greater Cleveland in 1982 when it began a restructuring program after its earnings declined by 6.8%. It refocused operations to concentrate on home and family products. By 1984 it had pared down its operations to 3 product groups: the Education, Information, & Training Group produced encyclopedias, reference books, and software; its Household Prods. & Services Group manufactured Kirby vacuum cleaners and industrial and institutional floor-maintenance equipment; and the Commercial Industries Group made a variety of connectors, fittings, medical regulators, and flow meters. Scott & Fetzer's sales totaled $695 million in 1984, with a net income of $40.6 million. After 2 years of effort by the management of Scott & Fetzer to sell the company, it was taken over in Jan. 1986 by Berkshire Hathaway of Omaha, Nebr., an insurance holding company.

**SCOVILL, PHILO** (30 Nov. 1791–5 June 1875), was a pioneer, contractor, and merchant. Scovill was born in Salisbury, Conn. His family moved several times during his youth, and in 1816 Scovill came to Cleveland, where he established himself as a merchant in the drug and grocery business. Disenchanted with this line of work, he moved into a lumber venture with Thos. O. Young. Once a local sawmill was completed, Scovill & Young entered into building and house contracting. At that time their only competition was LEVI JOHNSON, and because the town was growing rapidly, both businesses prospered. In 1825, Scovill built Franklin House, a popular tavern, which he managed until 1848. In 1938 the tavern was torn down, and the site became a parking lot. During his career, Scovill purchased over 110 acres of land in and around Cleveland. The popularity achieved through his entrepreneurial developments gained him seats as county commissioner, 1827; as Whig representative to the state legislature, 1835–36; and on CLEVELAND CITY COUNCIL, 1841–42. Scovill was content to serve only single terms in office. During his later career, he became director of the Cleveland & Pittsburgh Railroad Co. and one of the founders of the First Natl. Bank (1863), and later its president. Scovill and his wife, Jemima Bixby Scovill, were married in 1819; she was the founder of the Old Women's Home of Cleveland. The Scovills had 2 sons and a daughter.

**SCRANTON, IRENE HICKOX** (1800–15 Mar. 1858), was an educator, churchwoman, and benefactor. Born in Durham, N.Y., she came to Kinsman, Trumbull County, Ohio, in 1817 and taught school there for 3 successive summers. She returned to the East in 1820 and attended Female Academy in Litchfield, Conn. She subsequently returned to Kinsman and opened a boarding school for young ladies. Later, after coming to Cleveland, she became principal of a school for girls near the American House, and afterward on Superior St. near Public Square. She was one of the founders of the FIRST PRESBYTERIAN (OLD STONE) CHURCH. On 27 June 1828 she married JOEL SCRANTON, a leather and dry-goods merchant whose store was located at the corner of Superior and Water (W. 9th) streets. In 1833 they moved to a farm known as Scranton's Flats. Mrs. Scranton was considered one of the most benevolent of Cleveland women at the time, caring for many poor and ill people in the city. The couple had 5 children, but only 1, Mrs. Mary Bradford, survived. Mrs. Bradford was one of the founders and main benefactors of the Cleveland School of Art. She became second president (1885–1904) and was later named a trustee of the CLEVELAND INSTITUTE OF ART. She died 11 July 1918 at the age of 85.

**SCRANTON, JOEL** (5 Apr. 1793–9 Apr. 1858), was an early resident of Cleveland who arrived in 1819 and became a prominent merchant and landowner. Scranton was born in Belchertown, Mass., the son of Stephen and Asenath Scranton. His father, a manufacturer in iron and steel, was responsible for introducing the manufacture of cut nails in the state of New York. Joel Scranton spent his childhood in Otsego County, N.Y., and settled in Cleveland in 1819. Most accounts of his life report that he arrived in Cleveland with "a schooner load of leather" to sell to residents. Primarily a leather merchant in the early 1820s, Scranton opened a store in Sept. 1827 at the corner of Superior and Water (W. 9th) streets, selling leather, dry goods, groceries, crockery, and machine cards. In the early 1830s, J. Scranton & Co. also advertised its interest in buying corn and rye. By Jan. 1833, Scranton had sold the store. With the proceeds from his retail enterprises, Scranton bought land at low cost. Among his purchases were the flats on the west side of the CUYAHOGA RIVER, along what became Scranton Ave. There he operated a farm. That area was known by 1847 as "Scranton's Flats"; in the 1840s and 1850s it became a business and sporting center, with everything from railroads to shooting contests to circuses located there. As more businesses located next to his property, Scranton's land grew in value, and he left a large estate upon his sudden death from apoplexy in 1858. In 1838 Scranton was elected a director of the Bank of Cleveland. He was a member of the Presbyterian church and was a Mason. He and his wife, IRENE HICKOX SCRANTON, were married on 27 June 1828.

The **SCRANTON ROAD BAPTIST CHURCH** was begun in 1869 as a Free Will Baptist mission, and despite many changes, it has endured to the present day. Luther Doolittle, one of the founders, raised money for the first church at Putnam (E. 38th) and Scovill by begging door to door and among friends. After the first minister chosen by the congregation created a serious split that hindered the growth of the parish, a new leader was chosen. By 1874, the church relocated to the south side of town, to the present site at Clark and Scranton. The new church, erected in 1893, was not dedicated until 1900, when all debt was cleared. In 1917, the Scranton Rd. Free Will Baptist Church united with the BAPTISTS and was admitted to the CLEVELAND BAPTIST ASSOC. as the Scranton Rd. Baptist Church. Aside from the doctrinal implications, this move aided the church financially. Because of a membership decline due to death of parishioners and people moving from the area, the church was unable to support itself. As a result, it conveyed title to the property to the CBA and held meetings with Czecho-Slovak Baptists until 1942, at which time the parish voted to be self-supporting. The church retained its ties with the Czechoslovak Baptist Convention, as well as the Cleveland Baptist Assoc. As the west side neighborhood changed, Scranton Rd. Baptist began to minister to the newer Appalachian residents. In 1986 it was located at 3095 Scranton Rd.

Cleveland Baptist Assoc., *150 Years of Mission to Greater Cleveland, 1832–1982* (1982).

**SCRIPPS, EDWARD WILLIS** (18 June 1854–12 Mar. 1926), noted newspaper publisher and founder of the *CLEVELAND PRESS*, was the youngest in a family of 13 children. Scripps was born near Rushville, Ill. His grandfather, Wm. A. Scripps, had been part-owner of the London (England) *Literary Gazette*, and a cousin, John Locke Scripps, had helped Joseph Medill found the *Chicago Tribune*. Largely self-educated, Scripps helped his older brother James start the *Detroit News* in 1873. Scripps came to Cleveland after a European tour in 1878, where he started the *Penny Press* on 2 Nov. with the assistance of his cousin, John Scripps Sweeney, as business manager; 60% of the $10,000 capital had been provided by his brothers James and George in Detroit. Copying the success formula of the *Detroit News*, which featured a condensed format and strict operating economies, Scripps himself discharged the duty of editor of the *Penny Press* at the age of 24.

By his own account, Scripps spent a total of 23 months in first-hand direction of what became the *Cleveland Press*. After a breaking-in period of 16 months, Scripps left Cleveland to start the *St. Louis Evening Chronicle* in Mar. 1880. A year later he returned to Cleveland for another 6 months, leaving for Europe on the third anniversary of the *Press*'s birth. Brief as was his actual Cleveland residence, it was marked by a major confrontation with HENRY CHISHOLM, principal owner of the Cleveland Rolling Mills. When a *Press* reporter mistakenly identified Chisholm's son as a participant in a street brawl, Chisholm instigated an attack on the reporter by his employees and started civil and criminal proceedings against Scripps and the *Press*. Scripps retaliated by preparing a special edition of the *Press* headed "The Crime of Chisholm" (referring to the attack on his reporter) and running a condensed version of the same on a daily basis until he had won the criminal libel suit and Chisholm had dropped the libel suit and paid damages of $5,000 to the reporter. Chisholm's subsequent death was attributed partly to the *Press*'s attacks, for which Scripps acknowledged responsibility but averred that he would not have changed his course in any event.

After 1881, Scripps spent a total of about 30 days in Cleveland while conducting a peripatetic existence founding and running the other papers that eventually were merged into the Scripps-Howard organization. While still in Cleveland, he purchased the *Cincinnati Post*, the first paper in which he held controlling interest, although he subsequently gained control of the *Press* from his brothers ca. 1890. Among the other newspapers that he started or bought were the *Columbus Citizen*, *Toledo News-Bee*, *Pittsburgh Press*, and *San Francisco News*. He also founded or organized the United Press Assoc., the Newspaper Enterprise Assoc., the United Features Syndicate, the Scripps Institute of Oceanography, and the Science News Service. Retiring from active business to his Miramar Ranch near San Diego in 1890, Scripps died on his yacht *Ohio* in Monrovia Bay, Liberia.

**SCOTS.** *See* **BRITISH IMMIGRATION**

**SCULPTURE.** *See* **MONUMENTS**

**SEAWAY FOODS, INC.,** is a major wholesaler of food and grocery products in northern Ohio. A consolidation of 4 Cleveland wholesale grocery companies, it was formed on 6 Jan. 1956 as the Seaway Whsle. Co. The 4 firms were the Eagle Whsle. Grocery Co. (founded 1905), owned by the Bronstein family; the grocery division of the J. F. Sansons & Son Co. (1906); the Economy Cash & Carry Co. (1928), headed by the Garson family; and the David Lombardy Co. (1928). The name Seaway was chosen because of the talk at the time about the opening of the St. Lawrence Seaway and its impact on the Great Lakes. The 4 companies continued to operate individually until 17 Aug. 1957, when Seaway opened its $1.5 million warehouse and headquarters at 22801 Aurora Rd., BEDFORD HTS. At that time, it was the largest wholesale grocer in Ohio.

Seaway originally distributed dry groceries to independent grocers in the area. It later added fresh fruits and vegetables, baked goods, frozen foods, and dairy products. In 1958, it established a group of independent retail stores, known as Food-Way-Market. Five years later, the firm formed a new voluntary group of supermarkets, called Pic-Rite Markets. Seaway provided independent grocers with aid in arranging finances and equipment for new stores, and for capital-improvement programs and acquisitions. It also provided office space for them in its headquarters. By 1959, the firm had more than 1,600 customers in northern Ohio, including 6 voluntary grocery groups. In 1961, its name was changed to Seaway Foods, Inc., to reflect the introduction of its own line of private-label products. By 1964, Seaway had tripled both its warehouse space and its sales from its original $30 million. Through acquisitions in the late 1960s, Seaway broadened its wholesale services to institutional customers and operated retail and convenience stores in Ohio and Pennsylvania. In the late 1970s, it conducted a $4 million expansion program at its warehouses in Bedford Hts. and at E. 40th St. and Woodland Ave. By 1981, the company had reached $300 million in sales, with 650 employees and 13,000 items in stock. It remained a privately owned firm, operated by its 4 founding families.

The **SECOND OHIO VOLUNTEER CAVALRY,** 1861–65, was organized at Camp Wade (see CIVIL WAR CAMPS) during Aug.-Sept. 1861. The regiment, which contained 317 Cleveland men, was mustered into federal service on 10 Oct. 1861. It was initially transferred to Camp Dennison near Cincinnati, where it remained until Jan. 1862. During January and February the regiment was on scout duty along the Missouri border. It was then attached to Doubleday's Brigade, Dept. of the Missouri (Feb.-June 1862). The regiment was assigned to Ft. Scott, Kans. (June-Aug. 1862); Solomon's Brigade, Dept. of Kansas (Aug.-Oct. 1862); and the 1st Brigade, 1st Div., Army of the Frontier (Oct.-Dec. 1862). Shortly before the end of the year, the 2d Cavalry was ordered back to Columbus, Ohio, where it remained until Mar. 1863.

The unit's subsequent assignments were: 1st Cavalry Brigade, District of Central Kentucky, Dept. of the Ohio (Mar.-June 1863); 3d Brigade, 1st Div., 23d Army Corps (June-Aug. 1863); 3d Brigade, 4th Div., 23d Army Corps (Aug.-Nov. 1863); and 1st Brigade, 2d Div., 23d Army Corps (Dec. 1863-Feb. 1864). Following a veterans' furlough that lasted until Mar. 1864, the regiment was assigned to: 9th Army Corps, Army of the Potomac (Apr. 1864); 1st Brigade, 3d Div., Cavalry Corps, Army of the Potomac, Middle Military Div. (May 1864-May 1865); and Dept. of the Missouri (June-Oct. 1865). The 2d was involved in the pursuit of Gen. John Hunt Morgan, Burnside's East Tennessee Campaign, the battles of the Wilderness, Spottsylvania, and Cold Harbor, Sheridan's Shenandoah Valley Campaign, and the Appomattox Campaign. It was mustered out and its men discharged and paid off at Camp Chase, Columbus, on 11 Sept. 1865. The 2d Cavalry lost 7 officers and 76 enlisted men to hostile causes and 5 officers and 179 men to disease.

**SELTZER, LOUIS B.** (19 Sept. 1897-2 Apr. 1980), longtime editor of the CLEVELAND PRESS, was one of the most notable figures in Cleveland journalism. Seltzer was born and raised on Cleveland's near west side, the oldest son of popular Western-adventure writer Chas. Alden and Ella Albers Seltzer. He quit Denison School in the 7th grade and at the age of 12 got a job as an office boy at the CLEVELAND LEADER. Although he quickly worked his way up to reporter and writer of a Sunday column ("Luee the Offis Boy"), he was fired 2 years later and took a job with an advertising agency. A year later, Seltzer was back in newspaper work as police reporter for the *Cleveland Press.* He married Mary Elizabeth Champlin in 1915, and a year later he became city editor of the *Press.* Feeling his lack of experience at 19, he voluntarily resigned the post after 3 months and took the position of political editor. Acting on a tip from a Youngstown Democratic leader, Ed Moore, Seltzer scored a national beat at the 1924 Democratic Convention by predicting the deadlock between the Smith-McAdoo factions and the eventual emergence of John W. Davis as a compromise nominee.

Appointed editor of the *Cleveland Press* by Roy W. Howard in 1928, Seltzer held that position for 38 years, during which time he was acknowledged as one of the country's leading newspaper editors. Stressing the public-service role of the newspaper, Seltzer sought to establish close ties with the city's neighborhoods by personal involvement in civic and charitable endeavors. He became known as "kingmaker" in Ohio politics, notably through the *Press*'s successful sponsorship of the careers of Frank J. Lausche and Anthony J. Celebrezze. In the last years of his tenure, he held the largely honorific post of editor-in-chief of the Scripps-Howard Newspapers of Ohio, and the *Press* was included in *Time* magazine's 1964 selection of the nation's 10 best newspapers.

Seltzer's ineffaceably optimistic autobiography, *The Years Were Good* (1956), was cast in the classic Horatio Alger mold. Seltzer emphasized his rise through application and industry from a disadvantaged background and stunted formal education to a position of professional preeminence. His sympathies were more with the children of the rich than with those of the poor, he said, because "struggle is good for the soul. I have had my full share of it." Seltzer accepted personal responsibility for the *Press*'s coverage of the SAMUEL SHEPPARD MURDER CASE of 2 years before. Although the U.S. Supreme Court would eventually order the case to be retried, Seltzer made no exception for the Sheppard case when he stated that, given the chance to relive his life, he wouldn't change "a solitary thing."

Stepping down as editor of the *Press* in 1966, 1 year after the death of his wife, Seltzer wrote occasional columns in retirement for suburban newspapers. He also published a short collection of character sketches, *Six and God* (1966). He was affiliated with more than 50 organizations; he was director of the American Society of Newspaper Editors and chairman of the Greater Cleveland Bicentennial Committee. As a member of the Pulitzer Prize Advisory Board from 1956-68, he delivered an attack on obscenity and poor taste on the stage at the time that the board voted to withhold the Drama Award from Edward Albee's *Who's Afraid of Virginia Woolf?* in 1963. Seltzer died in the Medina County home of his daughter, Mrs. Shirley Cooper. His son, Chester E. Seltzer, also a newspaperman and writer, had died in El Paso, Tex., in 1971.

Seltzer, Louis, *The Years Were Good* (1956).

**SENTER, GEORGE B.** (1827–16 Jan. 1870), served as councilman, mayor, and military leader during the CIVIL WAR. Senter was elected to Cleveland city council from the 1st ward in 1858. He served as the city's mayor from 1859-60. When the Civil War broke out, Senter, for whom no military record can be found, probably served in an honorary capacity as assistant commissary-subsistence officer at Camp Taylor (see CIVIL WAR CAMPS) on Woodland Ave. during Apr.-May 1861. He was elevated to the position of commandant of Camp Cleveland on University Hts. in Brooklyn Twp. on 16 July 1862, a post at which he served until 20 Apr. 1864. In 1864 the Cleveland city council elected Senter to serve the remainder of the mayoral term of IRVINE MASTERS, who had died in office. Senter, a staunch supporter of the Union cause, had, in 1861, invited president-elect Abraham Lincoln to visit Cleveland, which he did (see ABRAHAM LINCOLN'S VISIT). In 1865, as mayor, Senter performed the sad task of proclaiming a day of mourning on 15 Apr. to honor the assassinated president. Senter apparently spent the period after the war practicing law and holding part-interest in a wholesale wine and liquor business. He died at his home on Euclid Ave. He is buried in WOODLAND CEMETERY. His 2-story brick mansion, built in 1842, was purchased for $60,000 in 1872 by the UNION CLUB and converted into its first headquarters.

Geo. B. Senter Papers, WRHS.

**SERBS.** Although the Serbs are not one of Cleveland's largest ethnic groups, they have made themselves widely known throughout the city. Serbian immigration to Cleveland came in 2 main periods: from the beginning of the 20th century to the beginning of WORLD WAR I, and from the end of WORLD WAR II to the present. In the 1980s, Serbs continue to migrate to the city from Yugoslavia, and with other Yugoslavs form a significant body of recent immigrants to the area. Serbs as a group maintain a strong ethnic identity, and while they adapt readily to American life, they do not quickly assimilate into American society. Many, although they may be 3d- or 4th-generation American Serbs, maintain traditional beliefs and customs. Lazar Krivokapic, a Serb from Montenegro who settled in Cleveland in 1893, is considered the city's first Serb. It was not until after the turn of the century, however, that significant numbers of Serbs came to Cleveland. Virtually all of these Serbs were not from Serbia but from the Austrian Military Frontier in Croatia; consequently, they were part of the enormous migration from the Austro-Hungarian Empire. The largest group came from the area called Lika, while many others came from Banija, Kordun, Backa, and the Banat. There were also a significant number from Dalmatia and some from Montenegro, which at that time was an independent kingdom. Most intended to come only to earn enough money to pay debts at home or to earn enough to ensure a more comfortable life in their native regions. They were virtually all of peasant origin. They worked in factories in Cleveland, especially in steel mills such as Otis Steel or American Steel & Wire. Many Serbs did return to their native regions, but most stayed and established new lives in the U.S. Few women came in the early migration, and most of those who did ran boarding houses where large groups of Serbs lived.

Most Serbs lived in the area from the E. 20s to the E. 40s north of Superior Ave. Hamilton and St. Clair avenues were particularly dense areas of Serbian settlement. Many CROATIANS, especially Greek Catholics from the area of Zumberak, had also settled in this area. Serbs felt especially friendly toward the Zumbercani, as these Greek Catholics were called, because their religious customs were similar to those of the Serbian Orthodox religion and because the dialect they spoke was similar to that of the Serbs from the Croatian Military Frontier. Roman Catholic Croats also lived in this area, and slightly farther to the east began the large settlement of SLOVENES, with whom the Serbs felt some kinship as fellow South Slavs from Austria-Hungary. It is estimated that at the time of the WORLD WAR I, approximately 1,000 Serbs lived in Cleveland. A small group of Serbs began St. Sava Lodge in 1904 as a mutual-benefit society to aid members who were ill or injured or to provide death benefits for those far from their families. More women gradually came to the settlement, usually wives or sisters of Serbs already here. As children began to be born to the immigrants, the need for other organizations began. In 1909, St. Sava Lodge organized St. Sava Church so that Cleveland Serbs could observe their religious and ethnic customs. A succession of houses served as churches until 1919, when the community purchased a German Lutheran church on E. 36th St. between Superior and Payne avenues. World War I stopped immigration; and with Serbia playing a key role in that war, Cleveland Serbs, in cooperation with other Slavs in the city, became involved in anti-Austrian demonstrations. Some returned to Europe to fight for the Serbian cause.

Stabilization and AMERICANIZATION were the key factors affecting the Cleveland Serbian community until the second period of immigration, which began following World War II. New lodges were formed and were united under one large fraternal organization called Jedinstvo, or Unity, which had its headquarters in Cleveland until 1963, when it merged with the Serb Natl. Fed. Many Serbs began to move from the original St. Clair Ave. settlement, often called Centrala, to other areas closer to their work. The COLLINWOOD area in particular, because of available jobs at the COLLINWOOD RAILROAD YARDS and FISHER BODY, attracted many Serbs. Other settlements were in the E. 55th and Broadway area for those who worked at REPUBLIC STEEL; Madison Ave. on the west side; and an area near the WEST SIDE MARKET, where many Serbs from Dalmatia settled. Americanization became a stronger force as the number of American-born Serbs increased and as many of the early settlers died. The restrictive immigration policies enacted during the 1920s prevented a new influx of immigrants, so that the community stopped receiving the influence of new immigrants.

The migration that immediately followed World War II was markedly different from the earlier one. Nearly all the immigrants were displaced persons, people who had been prisoners of war in Germany and did not want to return to a Communist Yugoslavia, or political refugees such as Chetniks who fled Yugoslavia after their military defeat. Many were from Serbia proper and were schooled professionals from urban backgrounds. With their strong commitment to Serbian culture and their large numbers (over 700 came to Cleveland between 1949–52), they instilled new life into Cleveland's Serbian community. They formed new organizations, cultural, fraternal, and political, and strengthened the St. Sava Serbian Orthodox parish. Many of them received employment at Republic Steel and settled in the E. 55th and Broadway area. Tensions and resentments between many members of the two migrations arose, with many American-born Serbs not inclined to understand the strong political commitments apart from the American mainstream that the "DPs" held. Many newer immigrants felt that the earlier migration had lost much of its Serbianness and that its members were reluctant to share power in organizations with the newcomers. These tensions were not exclusive to the Cleveland Serbian community, but were common to all communities in the U.S. where the two migrations coexisted.

These tensions grew particularly strong in the 1960s, when it was decided to build a new facility for the St. Sava congregation at the corner of Ridgeview Dr. and Broadview

Rd. in PARMA. The new St. Sava church facility, completed and consecrated in June 1963, immediately became the object of legal, religious, and political arguments between the two groups. Each side had its own board and priest, held services separately, and claimed to be the legitimate holder of parish property. From 1963–75, the contention between the two factions, expressed through litigation in courts and public demonstrations, filled the Cleveland news media. Eventually the controversy was solved, with each group maintaining its own St. Sava Church (See ST. SAVA SERBIAN ORTHODOX CHURCH CONTROVERSY). The church schism created a deep rift in the entire Serbian community. Some families and friends were split on the issue, and many Serbs felt uncomfortable having to take a stand for either side. Since the settlement in 1975, there has been a continuation of separate Serbian communities, although rancor had begun to subside by the 1980s. Both sides have attracted recent immigrants from Yugoslavia, although many Serbs remain unaffiliated. Both parishes still maintained cultural organizations and sponsored programs to uphold Serbian consciousness. The locations of both churches have had a pronounced effect on the housing patterns of Serbs in Greater Cleveland. Although they are found throughout Cuyahoga County, the preponderance of Serbs in the 1980s was in the southwestern suburbs, particularly Parma, PARMA HTS., SEVEN HILLS, and BROADVIEW HTS. A reduced settlement remained in the E. 55th and Broadway area.

The Serbian population has continued to grow because of the relaxation of Yugoslav immigration laws. Since the early 1960s, there has been a continuous stream of Yugoslav immigrants to Cleveland, with a high percentage of Serbs. Because they are not counted separately, but as Yugoslavs, it is impossible to give their number. These new immigrants, many of them educated professionals, have strongly influenced the maintenance of Serbian cultural values. In the 1980s, the Serbian language was still widely spoken throughout the community, and radio programs in Serbian continued to be popular. The Serbian community thus maintained a high ethnic consciousness, in contrast to many other ethnic groups in Cleveland, where that consciousness had waned.

Donald A. Tipka
Cleveland Public Library

Georgevich, Dragoslav et al., *Serbian Americans and Their Communities of Cleveland* (1977).
Ledbetter, Eleanor, *The Jugoslavs of Cleveland* (1918).

**SETTLEMENT HOUSES.** Cleveland, along with Chicago, Boston, and New York, was one of the centers of the settlement-house movement in America. Settlement work began in the city in the late 1890s. Within a decade, a half-dozen settlements operated in neighborhoods throughout Cleveland. Several of the city's settlement houses achieved national recognition for their programs. KARAMU HOUSE (formerly Playhouse Settlement) has long been regarded as one of the centers of black theater in the U.S. Similarly, the musical training programs of the CLEVELAND MUSIC SCHOOL SETTLEMENT have served as a model for other programs across the nation. Settlement houses constituted one of the major and most enduring reform movements of the late 19th century. They were a response to the overcrowding, impoverishment, corruption, and disease caused by the rapid industrialization and growth of many cities during the latter half of the century. The unique aspect of the movement was its attempt to produce change by working from within those areas of the city and the segments of its population affected by such urban problems. The movement began in England in 1884 when a group of students from Oxford University established a residence within the slums of London. At this residence, Toynbee Hall, they attempted to share their knowledge and skills with the area's residents and, in turn, learn firsthand of the problems of the slum. Through such sharing, they strove to create a means of understanding and solving the problems of urban life. Foremost in their working philosophy was the concept of the urban village, wherein the network of sharing and mutual aid perceived to be effective in a small village would be transplanted to the urban neighborhood. The establishment of the Neighborhood Guild in New York City in 1885 marked the importation of the settlement movement to the U.S. Three years later, Jane Addams began work at Hull House, the most famous settlement in America. By 1900, over 100 settlement houses existed across the nation.

The social settlement is closely identified with the various reforms of the Progressive Era in America. Not only was the American settlement house a singular aspect of reform during this period, but the individual programs sponsored by the settlements addressed a variety of reform concerns identified with progressivism. These programs and activities included educational work, such as evening classes for adults, kindergartens, and vocational training; citizenship programs and voter education; the creation of playgrounds and urban open space; the establishment of visiting-nurse networks and health-inspection programs; a concern for child labor, unions, and working standards; and the establishment of housing codes. Many of these programs later became standard features of public education and governmental service. Support for many early settlement houses came through independent boards of directors or affiliation with a religious or educational organization. The supporters of the early settlement houses in America, as well as the settlement workers, were largely native-born and Protestant. They came from middle- or upper-middle-class families and, primarily, from small towns and cities. Conversely, the settlements operated mainly in Catholic or Jewish immigrant neighborhoods. It is this aspect of cultural difference between the settlement worker and neighborhood resident that most clearly set the American settlement movement apart from its English model. It is worth noting that the movement forms not only a part of American reform history, but also an important aspect of immigrant and ethnic history.

The first settlement house established in Cleveland was HIRAM HOUSE (1896). By WORLD WAR I, a variety of such houses existed in Cleveland, each serving a distinct neighborhood. While Hiram House served the Jewish (later Italian and then black) community along lower Woodland Ave., ALTA HOUSE (1900) served the Italian population of Mayfield Rd. EAST END NEIGHBORHOOD HOUSE (1907) worked with the HUNGARIANS and SLOVAKS of the Buckeye-Woodhill district, and Goodrich House (1897; see GOODRICH-GANNETT NEIGHBORHOOD CENTER) served the various South Slavic groups resident along St. Clair Ave. Other settlements active in Cleveland by the 1920s included WEST SIDE COMMUNITY HOUSE (1922), MERRICK HOUSE (1919), the RAINEY INSTITUTE (1904), UNIVERSITY SOCIAL SETTLEMENT (1922), the Playhouse Settlement (1915), the Council Educational Alliance (1899), the FRIENDLY INN (1897), and the Cleveland Music School Settlement (1912). The 1920s and 1930s saw tremendous changes in the operation of settlements in Cleveland and throughout the nation. Chief among these was the professionalization of settlement staff. Increased emphasis was placed on the hiring of social workers trained in college-level programs such as those offered by the School of Applied Social Sciences of Western Reserve University.

Professionalism on the staff level was matched by a more scientific approach to methodology and program. Organizations within the settlement movement did much to foster such change. On the national level, the Natl. Fed. of Settlements (est. 1911) provided a professional forum. Locally, the Cleveland Settlement Union and later the GREATER CLEVELAND NEIGHBORHOOD CTRS. ASSOC. provided a means for a coordination of effort and information exchanges.

The second major change to affect the settlement houses in the period following World War I was the increased centralization of all social work and philanthropic activities within major American cities. While settlements had enjoyed autonomy in terms of fundraising and allocation during the first decades of the century, many came to be dependent on centralized welfare campaigns by 1930. Such central funding formed only one aspect of the loss of settlement autonomy. Funding agencies could frequently dictate the areas in which a settlement would spend monies received from general welfare solicitations. That often hampered a settlement's latitude in program development. In Cleveland, the Fed. for Charity & Philanthropy, and later the Welfare Fed., solicited and allocated funds for charitable work. Despite this loss of autonomy and attendant changes such as the curtailment of immigration and the decline of urban populations in general, many of the settlement houses established during the Progressive Era endure. The new emphasis placed on the neighborhood through various city, state, and federal funding programs during the 1970s has provided a renewed vitality for these institutions.

John J. Grabowski
Western Reserve Historical Society

See also PHILANTHROPY and specific institutions and reformers.

**SEVEN HILLS** is a city in central Cuyahoga County 13 mi. south of Cleveland, bounded by BROOKLYN HTS. on the north, INDEPENDENCE on the east, BROADVIEW HTS. on the south, and PARMA on the west. It occupies 4.86 sq. mi. Seven Hills was originally part of Independence Twp. Its early history was closely tied to the development of 2 neighboring communities, Independence and BROOKLYN. Independence was known early for its orchards, vineyards, and stone quarries. The "stone business" was prominent in the area before the CIVIL WAR. Later, large areas of land were cleared and used for farming. In 1914, the eastern portion of Independence Twp. was incorporated as the village of Independence. In 1927, the remainder of the township became the village of Seven Hills and began operating under the mayor-council type of government. The hilly terrain and natural setting probably gave rise to the name, but the early residents may also have referred to the 7 hills of Rome. Through the years, Seven Hills has remained primarily a residential community. Because of early suburban development, only 12 farms remained by 1938. The population grew from 333 in 1938 to 555 in 1940, 1,350 in 1950, 5,708 in 1960, 12,700 in 1970, and over 16,000 in 1980. Seven Hills became a city in 1961. The city is distinctive in having no central business district or town square. Seven Hills, Parma, and PARMA HTS. make up the Parma School District. There are 5 elementary schools in Seven Hills. The CLEVELAND ELECTRIC ILLUMINATING CO. is the major employer. Calvin Park and several picnic grounds provide recreational facilities.

The **SEVENTH NATIONAL EUCHARISTIC CONGRESS,** held in Cleveland 23–27 Sept. 1935, was one of a series of Eucharistic Congresses that have long been held by the Roman Catholic church. The purpose of these gatherings was to increase devotion to Jesus Christ present in the Eucharist. Bp. JOSEPH SCHREMBS, Cleveland's fifth bishop, was very active in the Eucharistic Congress movement. Cleveland was selected as the site of the 7th Natl. Eucharistic Congress in 1935. A committee under the direction of Msgr. Floyd L. Begin, including numerous priests, worked for months coordinating all the details.

Patrick Cardinal Hayes of New York, Archbp. Cicognani, the apostolic delegate, and Archbp. John McNicholas of Cincinnati were several of the many dignitaries who attended opening ceremonies in the Cathedral. Thousands of people, including U.S. Postmaster Jas. Farley, representing Pres. Franklin D. Roosevelt; the governor of Ohio; and Mayor HAROLD BURTON attended the civic reception the evening of 23 Sept. A choir of 3,000 singers drawn from local parishes sang the mass in the PUBLIC AUDITORIUM that morning. That evening 50,000 people crowded into the Municipal Stadium to listen to speakers ranging from Alfred E. Smith to Bp. Fulton J. Sheen. The talks centered around the theme of how Catholics could change society by living the principles of their faith. Public masses and devotions filled the schedule. A midnight mass originally scheduled for Public Hall was switched to the stadium to accommodate thousands of pilgrims from Pittsburgh.

On Thursday, 27 Sept., the final day, declared a civic holiday by Mayor Burton, 20,000 Catholics who were members of fraternal and religious societies, the safety forces, and other organizations and students marched to the stadium. The bishops and the apostolic delegate were at the end of the parade. As the marchers entered the stadium, they created the formation of a monstrance, a vessel used for the display of the Eucharist. In the stadium they heard Pope Pius XI speak by radio from Italy. He praised the devotion of the people and asked them to live lives worthy of the beliefs they professed. The Eucharistic Congress drew many Catholics not only from Cleveland but also from around the nation.

The **SEVENTH OHIO VOLUNTEER INFANTRY REGIMENT,** 1861–64, was the first Civil War regiment rendezvoused and organized in Cleveland. Three companies were composed solely of Clevelanders, while Clevelanders served as officers in other companies, giving the unit a total of 610 local men. The 7th was raised at Camp Taylor (see CIVIL WAR CAMPS) on 22–25 Apr. 1861 and mustered into federal service on 30 Apr. It spent May-June at Camp Dennison near Cincinnati. Afterward it was assigned to the following units: Railroad District, W.Va. (June-Dec. 1861); 3d Brigade, Lander's Div., Army of the Potomac (Jan.-Mar. 1862); 3d Brigade, 2d Div., 5th Army Corps, Dept. of the Shenandoah (Mar.-May 1862); 3d Brigade, Shield's Div., Dept. of the Rappahannock (May-June 1862); 2d Brigade, 1st Div., 2d Corps, Army of Virginia (June-Aug. 1862); 1st Brigade, 2d Div., 2d Corps, Army of Virginia (Aug.-Sept. 1862); 1st Brigade, 2d Div., 12th Army Corps, Army of the Potomac (Sept. 1862-Oct. 1863); Army of the Cumberland (Oct. 1863-Apr. 1864); and 1st Brigade, 2d Div., 20th Army Corps, Army of the Cumberland (May-July 1864). The 7th participated in the battles of Winchester, Antietam, Chancellorsville, and Gettysburg and was sent to help quell the New York City draft riots in Aug.-Sept. 1863. The regiment was mustered out and its men paid off and discharged at Camp Cleveland on 8 July 1864. The unit lost 10 officers and 174 men to hostile action and 2 officers and 87 men to disease during its term of service.

Wilder, George L., *The History of Company C, Seventh Regiment, O.V.I.* (1866).

Wood, George L., *The Seventh Regiment* (1865).
Ohio Volunteer Infantry, 7th Regiment Records, WRHS.

**SEVERANCE, CAROLINE M.** (12 Jan. 1820–10 Nov. 1914), an early feminist activist in Cleveland, is known as America's first clubwoman. Born Caroline M. Seymour in Canandaigua, N.Y., she came to Cleveland with her family, and at age 20 married Theodoric C. Severance, a banker. While raising 5 children, she pondered the inferior status of women before the law and became the first woman to lecture in Cleveland on behalf of women's suffrage. In 1851 she was influenced by the convincing rhetoric of Sojourner Truth at a women's-rights convention in Akron, and helped lay the framework for the Ohio Women's Suffrage Assoc. When Antoinette Brown from Oberlin, later the first ordained female minister, was refused entrance to a New York City temperance convention where she was a delegate, Caroline Severance retorted with a paper called "Humanity"; the speech so aptly voiced the sentiments of the infant women's movement that it was repeated at other gatherings. In 1854, following a session of the Natl. Women's Assoc., Severance addressed the Ohio legislature on the rights of women to hold inherited property and their own earnings. When her husband's career led him to Boston in the mid-1850s, Severance directed her growing awareness of women's rights toward club work. With Julia Ward Howe, she organized the New England's Women's Club, "a social center for united thought and action" for intellectual women. From this club, whose interests ranged from infant mortality to the admission of women to higher education, grew many other clubs organized to develop women's growing sense of themselves. Severance resided in Boston until 1875. She then moved to Los Angeles, Calif., where she formed the first kindergarten and continued her suffrage work. Occasionally she came back East to lecture on suffrage, abolition, peace, birth control, and morality. In 1869, she was among the signers of the first national suffrage convention in Cleveland. Active in California suffrage work, she was the honorary president of the California Equal Suffrage Assoc. when the Los Angeles Equal Suffrage Assoc. joined the state body (1905) and was president of the Women's Suffrage League. Her continued activities for women's rights made her a recipient of greetings from suffrage conventions until her death.

**SEVERANCE, JOHN LONG** (8 May 1863–16 Jan. 1936), was a noted industrialist. Born in Cleveland, Severance was the son of Louis Henry Severance and Fannie Benedict Severance. He attended CLEVELAND PUBLIC SCHOOLS and graduated from Oberlin College in the class of 1885. After graduation, he returned to Cleveland to work for the STANDARD OIL CO. for the next 7 years. In 1891 he married Elizabeth Huntington DeWitt, who died in 1930. In 1892 Severance left Standard Oil to work with the Cleveland Linseed Oil Co., a pioneer paint and varnish industry. In 1899 he was instrumental in founding the American Linseed Co., into which Cleveland Linseed was merged. In 1901 he organized and became president of the Colonial Salt Co., and about the same time he assisted in the organization of Linde Air Prods. His other business connections included serving as chairman of the board of the Cleveland Arcade Co. and the Youngstown Steel Door Co. He was also director of the Cleveland Trust Co. and the Youngstown Sheet & Tube Co. His philanthropic interests included holding the office of president of the CLEVELAND MUSEUM OF ART and of the MUSICAL ARTS ASSOC. Besides being a liberal benefactor to the art museum during his life, at his death he left it a collection valued at over $3 million. In 1929 he gave the city $1.5 million to build a concert hall for the CLEVELAND ORCHESTRA; in 1930 he increased his donation to $2.5 million in memory of his wife. Severance was one of the initial members of the Cleveland Community Fund. In addition, he was a trustee of Oberlin College, Western Reserve University, and Nanking University in China. He was also a sponsor of the Severance Medical School & Hospital at Seoul, Korea, an institution founded by his father. Severance was a member of the UNION CLUB, the TAVERN CLUB, the MID-DAY CLUB, the UNIVERSITY CLUB, and the ROWFANT CLUB.

**SEVERANCE, SOLON LEWIS** (8 Sept. 1834–8 May 1915), was born in Cleveland, the son of Solomon Lewis and Mary Long Severance and the grandson of Dr. DAVID LONG. Educated in the district and private schools of Cleveland, he became an office boy in a banking firm at the age of 14. He rose in the firm and later organized the Euclid Ave. Natl. Bank, in company with several other investors. That bank merged with the Euclid Park Bank and, later, became part of the First Natl. Bank. He was a director of the latter bank and also of the First Trust & Savings Bank. Severance's great interests were in religion and philanthropic work and in travel. He was a charter member of the Woodland Ave. Presbyterian Church and one of the first directors of the Fresh Air Camp. He married Emily Allen, younger sister of Dr. DUDLEY P. ALLEN (who married her cousin, Elisabeth Severance). One child was born, Julia Severance, who later married Dr. Benjamin L. Millikin. Like his brother, Louis, Solon Severance tried to encourage sympathy for foreign missions. A world traveler, he made illustrated lectures of his journeys and presented them to friends and groups in Cleveland.

**SEVERANCE CENTER,** located at the corner of Mayfield and S. Taylor roads in CLEVELAND HTS., was hailed as Ohio's first indoor shopping mall and the third-largest mall in the U.S. when it was built in the early 1960s. The mall was erected on the former site of "Longwood," the 161-acre estate of JOHN L. SEVERANCE (1863–1936) and later the residence of his nephew, Severance Millikin, who lived on the property until 1960. In 1953 Millikin hired the AUSTIN CO. to develop plans for the future use of the property, and in 1954 the site was rezoned for commercial, residential, and office use. The following year the Austin Co. acquired the land from Millikin. A Seattle development firm, Winmar Co., Inc., became a joint developer in the venture in 1955 and acquired a controlling interest in the project in 1960. After years of planning, ground was broken for construction on 27 Feb. 1962. The 2 anchor stores at either end of the mall, Halle's and Higbee's, opened officially on 17 Oct. 1963. Other original occupants of the mall included Gray Drugs, Fisher Foods, Winkelman's, the Society Natl. Bank, and an investment securities firm. By Mar. 1964, 52 shops and stores were open for business in the mall, and the center was doing $1 million in business a week.

During the 1970s, Severance Ctr. faced increasing competition from newer malls built throughout the Greater Cleveland area. Severance was remodeled in 1972 and underwent several major changes in the 1980s. In Mar. 1982, one of the mall's major department stores, Halle's, went out of business, creating a major vacancy at one end. In 1981 Gold Circle built a new discount department store at the mall, adding another wing to Severance's existing facilities, but by early 1985 sales at the store were not meeting the expectations of Gold Circle management, and the store was closed. In 1984 the Winmar Co., the owners of Severance as well as malls, office buildings, and condominium developments in 7 other states, announced a $20 million remodeling project which would enlarge Severance from 71 to 120 shops and would transform the mall into a "regional town center" linked to the new Cleveland Hts. city hall building under construction nearby.

**SEVERANCE HALL** was built as the home of the CLEVELAND ORCHESTRA just 12 years after its formation in 1918. The concert hall was given by JOHN L. SEVERANCE, prominent businessman and a member of a distinguished Cleveland family, as a memorial to his wife, Elizabeth DeWitt Severance. He announced his gift in 1929, on the condition that funds would be raised locally for a permanent endowment and maintenance fund. The campaign to raise such funds was led by DUDLEY S. BLOSSOM, and one of the major contributors was John D. Rockefeller, Jr. The concert hall was erected in 1930–31 from designs by Cleveland architects Walker & Weeks and cost $2.5 million. The building contained the concert hall seating 1,844, a chamber-music hall on the ground floor seating 400, and a radio-broadcasting studio. On either side of the auditorium were triangular wings that contained circulation areas, a green room, a lounge, offices, and a library. Onstage were an elevator for the orchestra, a cyclorama, and a skydome for operatic productions, as well as a large E. M. Skinner pipe organ. The hall had a unique system of colored spotlights operated by a clavilux or "color organ" for constantly changing lighting effects. In 1958, the stage of the hall was completely rebuilt, with a new acoustical shell to improve the projection of the orchestra's sound. The architecture of Severance Hall was transitional between the classical style represented by the CLEVELAND MUSEUM OF ART across the Wade Park Lagoon and the Art Deco or Art Moderne style that had developed in the late 1920s. The main entrance is a Renaissance portico, the elliptical 2-story grand foyer is transitional in style, and the auditorium is modern in its stylized ornament and color. At the opening, the exterior was called "Georgian" and the interior "French modernistic" by the critics. An unusual feature of the building was an internal automobile driveway beneath the entrance, allowing concertgoers to be let off at the lower lobby. In 1971 the driveway was closed, and the space was converted into a restaurant.

**SHAKER HEIGHTS** is an incorporated city on the eastern edge of Cleveland, 8 mi. southeast of downtown. It occupies 6.5 sq. mi. of gently rolling wooded land and is bounded on the north by CLEVELAND HTS. and UNIVERSITY HTS., on the east by BEACHWOOD, and on the south by WARRENSVILLE HTS. and WARRENSVILLE TWP. The name was derived from the Shakers, the celibate sect who settled on the land, originally part of Warrensville Twp., in 1822. The N. UNION SHAKER COMMUNITY ceased to exist in 1889, and the lands were purchased by various speculators. Development did not begin until 1905, when ORIS P. AND MANTIS J. VAN SWERINGEN began purchasing land and developing a comprehensively planned "Garden City" suburb. The ideal community plan included the maintenance of natural topography and lakes, curving roads, and specific locations for apartments, commercial areas, public schools, churches, and 3 private secondary schools. A large tract originally designated for a municipal park was transferred to the SHAKER HTS. COUNTRY CLUB, which became a focal point at the end of Courtland Blvd. and opened in 1915. In 1911, the development was detached from the village of Cleveland Hts. and incorporated as the village of Shaker Hts. The population was estimated at 250. Through strict ZONING and building restrictions, deed restrictions, and

architectural design guidelines managed and enforced by the Van Sweringen Co., the plan for a lasting model residential suburb was achieved in the 1920s and 1930s. The population was 1,700 by 1920, and in 1931, when Shaker Hts. became a city, it was 17,783. The city charter provided for a mayor-council form of government, with council members elected at large. The third mayor, WM. J. VAN AKEN, served 1917–50. The growth of the suburb was made possible by the Van Sweringens' construction of the SHAKER RAPID TRANSIT line directly to downtown Cleveland. First opened in 1920, the line had 2 branches, one on Shaker Blvd. to Green Rd., the other on Van Aken Blvd. to Warrensville Ctr. Rd. The lines were acquired by the city from the Cleveland Interurban Railroad Co. in 1944 and transferred to the GREATER CLEVELAND REGIONAL TRANSIT AUTHORITY in 1975.

In 1949, the population of Shaker Hts. was 23,393. The Van Sweringen Co. ceased to operate as a real-estate firm in 1959, but continued to oversee the deed restrictions for several years, after which the authority was vested in the city. Shaker Hts. has provided a model for many other cities in transportation, education, government, housing, recreation, and landscaping. Its school system is reputedly one of the finest in the country. There are 38 churches and synagogues of all denominations. The Shaker Hts. Public Library operates a main library and the Bertram Woods branch. The public Horseshoe Lake Park is situated on the asternmost of the 2 lakes formed where DOAN BROOK was dammed by the Shakers and later improved by the Van Sweringens. The population of Shaker Hts. was around 36,000 in 1960. The original vision of a planned "Garden City" suburb was maintained into the 1980s through the active efforts of a landmarks commission, an architectural-design review board, design-standards publications, commercial revitalization projects, and local community associations. Whereas the Van Sweringen Co. land agreements in the 1920s included racial and ethnic restrictions, intensive efforts to achieve an integrated community were successful in the 1970s and 1980s (see LOMOND ASSOC. and LUDLOW COMMUNITY ASSOC.). Between 1970–80, the population declined from 36,306 to 32,487.

The **SHAKER HEIGHTS COUNTRY CLUB**, 1300 Courtland Blvd., SHAKER HTS., a private, invitational organization, was founded in 1913 as a result of dissension among the members of the Euclid Golf Club over long-range goals, possible relocation plans, and the restrictions on Sunday golf. One group remained with the original club, a second group formed the MAYFIELD COUNTRY CLUB, and a third group, spearheaded by Jerome B. Zerbe (Euclid Club president) and Judge Ducane E. Tilden, organized the Shaker Hts. Country Club. It was incorporated on 18 Aug. 1913. The first officers included: president, Zerbe; 1st vice-president, Wm. E. Wall; 2d vice-president, Judge Tilden; treasurer, W. H. Baldwin; secretary, Carl S. Russell; and chairman of the House Committee, Chas. L. Bradley. The VAN SWERINGEN brothers deeded land on the upper Shaker Lakes Territory in fee simple to the club. Subsequently it acquired additional property. It encompassed over 155 acres in 1986. FRANK B. MEADE, head of the architectural firm Meade & Garfield, designed the 16th-century English-style brown-brick clubhouse, which features a replica of a Tudor Grand Hall. It was opened on 29 May 1915 and has been redecorated and refurnished several times. The golf course was designed by Donald J. Ross and Grange Alves. The first 9 holes were ready 31 May 1915, the second 9 on 4 July 1915. Geo. Chalmers, the first caddymaster, later became golf pro at the CHAGRIN VALLEY COUNTRY CLUB. Robt. McDonald, the first golf professional, was succeeded by Alves, and later by Dave Livie, who served Shaker for over 30 years. In 1916, president Harry Gillett appointed E. Miller France (one of the founders) a "one-man club forester"; he selected and planted over 3,500 trees to replace those destroyed by Dutch elm disease. He was responsible for the action to preserve the Dave Livie Memorial Elm. Many memorial trees, with accompanying commemorative plaques, have been donated by club members. In addition to golf, the club provides many other recreational activities for its members, including swimming, tennis, paddle ball, and bowling. Many social events are held at the club throughout the year.

The **SHAKER HEIGHTS RAPID TRANSIT** is the sole vestige of Ohio's once-mighty traction network. The electric streetcar debuted in the state in 1887, and by the 1920s its tracks crisscrossed the countryside and provided the predominant form of transit in all its major cities. By 1954, however, the Shaker Rapid was all that remained of Ohio's trolley heyday. The Shaker Rapid, originally the Cleveland Interurban Railroad, commenced service on 11 Apr. 1920. Its 2 branches, Moreland (later Van Aken) Blvd. and Shaker Blvd., connected SHAKER HTS. with downtown Cleveland. The transit lines had been built by the VAN SWERINGEN brothers to provide a convenient transportation link from the residential properties they were developing in the suburb to the downtown commercial center.

The major reason for the Shaker Rapid's survival was its traffic-free right-of-way. From its eastern termini to SHAKER SQUARE, its tracks were located in the boulevards' median strips. From Shaker Square to E. 93rd St., they were laid in a cut blasted from solid rock. Westward from there to E. 34th St., they entered KINGSBURY RUN leading to the steam railroads' corridor. The line had been engineered to keep its cars segregated from traffic and immune to the problems that plagued street-bound trolleys. The Shaker Rapid promised and delivered quick and dependable transit service. At E. 34th St., the rapid cars were forced to climb from their private right-of-way and follow public streets to their loop at Public Square. In July 1930, however, the final leg of their traffic-free route was completed, and the cars continued on private right-of-way to a station in the newly completed CLEVELAND UNION TERMINAL. Two extensions were also constructed. In 1929 the Moreland line was extended eastward from Lynnfield (its original terminus) to Warrensville Ctr. Rd. In 1937 the Shaker line was extended from Warrensville Ctr. Rd. to a new loop at Green Rd.

Following the collapse of the Van Sweringens' financial empire, the Shaker Rapid was placed into bank receivership in 1935. The banks operated the system for 9 years and then sold it to the city of Shaker Hts. Municipal operation commenced on 6 Sept. 1944. The lines were transferred to GREATER CLEVELAND REGIONAL TRANSIT AUTHORITY ownership on 5 Oct. 1975. In 1980 the Authority began an 18-month, $100 million renovation of the system, which saw the lines entirely reconstructed. Service on the rebuilt system, renamed the Blue (Van Aken) and Green (Shaker) lines, was inaugurated on 30 Oct. 1981. The original Shaker trolley line had been upgraded to contemporary light rail standards, an example of a mode of urban transit making a comeback throughout America in the 1980s.

The **SHAKER HISTORICAL SOCIETY** was founded on 21 Oct. 1947. During the preceding years, a few individuals had been interested in preserving the heritage of the Shakers, but it was Mrs. Caroline Piercy, author of *The Valley of God's Pleasure*, who served as the catalyst in the establishment of the society. The first meeting was held on 13 Oct. in the Shaker Hts. Sr. High School, when the charter, drawn up by attorney Cary Alburn, was read and approved; a nonprofit corporation was formed. The first president was Wm. Slade, superintendent of schools. People who had been close neighbors of the NORTH UNION SHAKERS donated many artifacts to a permanent collection. Some were purchased at the auction held in 1889 at the time the community was disbanded. These early artifacts were stored until 1956, when the society was able to establish a museum in a room of Moreland Elementary School. Increasing school enrollment forced the museum to look elsewhere. After several moves, the itinerant museum was finally able to move into its present quarters at 16740 S. Park Blvd. Frank Myers, long-time trustee and benefactor, donated his home at 16740 S. Park Blvd., built in 1910, to the society in Sept. 1970. The property was immediately transferred to the state of Ohio, giving it a tax-exempt status and some financial assistance for capital improvements. Financial support for building maintenance, a professional curator, purchase of artifacts, and operational expenses is provided by the society's board of trustees and a dedicated women's committee through dues from about 400 members, an endowment fund, book sales, garage-on-the-ground sales, and profits from a boutique known as "The Spirit Tree." The museum's collection of Shakeriana is the largest in the state except for manuscripts. There are also many artifacts reflecting the heritage of SHAKER HTS. and early WARRENSVILLE TWP. On the 2d floor is the Nord Library, named in memory of Mrs. Elizabeth Nord, the dedicated volunteer curator during most of the society's early years. The preservation of the Shaker heritage and the heritage of the local area remains the chief objective of the society. It is accomplished through free museum tours and monthly programs open to the public, marking of century homes and local historic sites, and cooperating with the Shaker Hts. and other school systems in providing museum tours for classes and curriculum units on Shakerism and local history.

Klyver, Richard, "History of the Shaker Historical Society" (1980).
Piercy, Caroline, *The Valley of God's Pleasure* (1951).

The **SHAKER LAKES** in Shaker and Cleveland Hts. are part of the Doan Brook Watershed. The 2 lakes were created in the mid-19th century by the NORTH UNION SHAKER COMMUNITY. By damming DOAN BROOK, the Shakers provided waterpower for a woolen mill at Upper Lake (also known today as Horseshoe Lake) and a sawmill and gristmill at Lower Lake. The Shaker colony flourished through the CIVIL WAR, but by 1880 its membership was aged and dwindling. The colony leased its lands in 1889 to the Shaker Hts. Land Co., a Buffalo real-estate syndicate headed by H. W. Gratwick, and merged with another Shaker colony.

Geographic obstacles, including poor roads and the area's remoteness from interurban lines, at first made development difficult. Realizing that the new Rockefeller Parkway (see ROCKEFELLER PARK) would make its property more accessible, the Shaker Hts. Land Co. in 1895 donated 279 acres, including the upper Doan Brook Valley and both lakes, to the city of Cleveland. The deed was for a period of 99 years and stipulated that the land be used "for park purposes only." Landscape architect Ernest W. Bowditch laid out winding roads following the terrain, the lakes were rebuilt, and the Shaker farm and mill buildings were demolished. In 1913 the Shaker Hts. Land Co. conveyed to the Van Sweringen Co. such reversionary interests as it had in the parklands, together with other properties. In 1933–34, the Shaker Lakes parklands were further developed for public recreation by CWA workers, who improved roads, built trails through the woods and along the lakeshores, and drained swampland. In 1947, the city of Cleveland leased the parklands to the city of SHAKER HTS. for a period of 20 years and consideration of $1. Shaker Hts. agreed to occupy, use, and at its own expense improve and maintain what had become known as Shaker Hts. Park. The lease was renewed in 1967.

The Shaker Lakes were threatened in the 1960s by the construction of I–290 (the Clark Freeway). Cuyahoga County engineer ALBERT S. PORTER, espousing the plan, called the lakes a "two-bit duck pond," but the highway was never built. The lakes have been plagued by the inflow of sewage, high levels of sediment, and the depletion of oxygen and aquatic life. In 1974 a symposium was held on the water quality of the Shaker Lakes and Doan Brook, but pollution of the watershed remains a problem. The Shaker Lakes, together with the Shaker Lakes Regional Nature Ctr. at 2600 S. Park Blvd., have been designated a Natl. Environmental Education Landmark.

The **SHAKER MEDICAL CENTER HOSPITAL** was a small, community-oriented hospital that served as a lower-cost alternative for patients who did not require the highly specialized services of larger hospitals. Shaker Medical Ctr., as it was commonly known, was founded in the early 1950s by Dr. Victor D. Ippolito as a voluntary, short-term general hospital. In 1963 it was established as a not-for-profit corporation. The original building on Shaker Blvd. was erected in 1954; a 3d floor was added in 1962, and further expansion was completed in 1971. The hospital provided inpatient care in medicine and surgery, an emergency department, and an out-patient department that provided customary diagnostic therapy and services. Considered a proprietary hospital, it did not qualify for Blue Cross payments until it acquired not-for-profit status. During the 1960s, the facility consisted of 31 beds, a laboratory, and x-ray, surgery, and emergency services. The 1971 expansion added 8 beds, 2 coronary intensive-care units, and 6 general step-down beds. In 1982, the ST. LUKE'S HOSPITAL ASSOC. purchased the Shaker Medical Ctr. Hospital. It continued to offer specialties in noninvasive cardiology, urology, general surgery, family practice, sports medicine, and podiatry. In 1984, however, the association closed Shaker Medical as part of a plan to eliminate beds from its multi-institutional system.

**SHAKER SQUARE** is an early suburban shopping center in Cleveland, built in 1927–29 in conjunction with the development of neighboring SHAKER HTS. The intersection of Shaker Blvd. and Moreland Blvd. had been laid out as a traffic circle in the teens. It was also the junction of the 2 branches of the SHAKER RAPID TRANSIT, the Green Rd. and Van Aken lines. Plans for a shopping center were originally conceived in 1923 as part of the MORELAND CTS. project. The commercial buildings were planned to be Tudor in style to harmonize with that development. When it failed a year later, the VAN SWERINGEN brothers decided to build Shaker Square and engaged Philip Small and Carl Rowley as architects (see SMALL & ROWLEY). According to Rowley, the circle was changed to an octagon in order to accommodate automobile parking. The octagonal plan then suggested 18th-century European royal squares as a design source, and the central pavilions flanked by lower wings can be seen in each quadrant. The style and detail, however, are American Colonial to conform with the domestic vision and style of the planned suburb of Shaker Hts. The COLONY THEATRE was added to the square in 1937. Designed by John Eberson, the master

of the atmospheric movie palace, it has one of the finest Art Moderne interiors in the city.

The Shaker Square stores were planned to appeal to the upper-class clientele of Shaker Hts. and housed a great variety of businesses over the years, from realtors and markets to men's and women's specialty clothing, banks, professional offices, service stores, restaurants, and coffee shops. In the 1970s there was a concerted effort to preserve the original character of the shopping center, and a non-profit development group, the Friends of Shaker Square, was formed to oversee this effort. In 1976, Shaker Square was listed in the Natl. Register of Historic Places.

**SHAKERS.** *See* **NORTH UNION SHAKER COMMUNITY**

**SHAPIRO, EZRA Z.** (7 May 1902–14 May 1977), attorney, Jewish community leader, and international Zionist figure, was born in Volozhin, Poland, and brought to Cleveland by his parents in 1906. The son of a rabbi, Shapiro received his Jewish education in the CLEVELAND HEBREW SCHOOLS. He received a law degree from Northern University in 1925 and established a private practice in Cleveland that same year. He left private practice for 2 years to serve as the Cleveland city law director from 1933–35. Shapiro became interested in Zionism as a youth and was elected president of the Cleveland Zionist District in 1924. Ten years later he was appointed chairman of the Natl. Executive Committee of the Zionist Organization of America. He was national vice-president of the United Israel Appeal from 1955–70 and was a founder in 1957 and first president (1957–60) of the American League for Israel. In 1960 he was honored with the title honorary president of the league. Shapiro served as a delegate to several World Zionist Congresses beginning in 1937. In 1951 he chaired the Committee on Fundamental Problems at the WZC. He was instrumental in drafting the Jerusalem Platform that defined the direction for Zionism following the creation of the state of Israel.

Another of Shapiro's abiding interests was Jewish education. He was president of the Cleveland Hebrew Schools from 1939–43 and of the BUREAU OF JEWISH EDUCATION from 1953–56. In 1959, he became vice-president of the American Assoc. for Jewish Education, a position he held until 1966. Shapiro was active in other community organizations, serving on the board of the JEWISH COMMUNITY FED. from 1934–70, and as president of the Jewish Community Council from 1942–45. He sat on the board of PARK SYNAGOGUE from 1950–70 and served on the CLEVELAND COMMUNITY RELATIONS BOARD from 1963–70. In 1971, Shapiro immigrated to Israel, where he became the world chairman of the Keren Hayesod-United Israel Appeal. He married Sylvia Lamport on 27 Nov. 1932. They had 2 children, Daniel and Rena (Mrs. Michael Blumberg).

Ezra Z. Shapiro Papers, WRHS.

**SHEPHERD, ARTHUR** (19 Feb. 1880–12 Jan. 1958), served as the linchpin of Cleveland's musical community for nearly 30 years. He was born of Mormon parents in Paris, Idaho. Graduating from the New England Conservatory of Music by 1897, he rejoined his family in Salt Lake City, where he became organizer and conductor of the Salt Lake City Symphony Orchestra. An early composition, *Overture Joyeuse*, won the Paderewski Prize in 1902. Returning to Boston in 1910, Shepherd taught at the New England Conservatory and conducted at the St. Cecilia Society. His cantata *City by the Sea* won a prize from the Natl. Fed.

of Music Clubs in 1913, and in WORLD WAR I he went overseas as bandmaster of the 303d Field Artillery.

Called to Cleveland in 1920 by NIKOLAI SOKOLOFF, Shepherd became assistant conductor and program annotator for the CLEVELAND ORCHESTRA. Although the "pops" and children's concerts were his primary responsibilities, illness on the part of Sokoloff gave Shepherd the opportunity to conduct the orchestra's first performance of Beethoven's Ninth Symphony in 1924. Shepherd resigned from his conducting chores in 1927 to become lecturer in music at Western Reserve University. He remained as the orchestra's annotator until 1930, however, and also was music critic for the *CLEVELAND PRESS* from 1928–31. When music was raised to departmental status at WRU in 1928, Shepherd was appointed chairman. Notable under his tenure was a 20-year program of experimental opera at the university.

Shepherd's music was fairly traditional in technique and strongly flavored with the folk idiom of his native West. Eight of his orchestral compositions, including his 2 symphonies, were programmed over the years by the Cleveland Orchestra. Probably his most characteristic piece was the First Symphony (1927), actually a "Western" suite of 4 movements subtitled *Horizons*. It was rivaled in popularity by the *Overture to a Drama* (1919). Also prominent in his output of over 100 works were a violin concerto, 4 string quartets, 2 piano sonatas, and numerous songs and choral pieces. An honorary doctorate from WRU and membership in the Natl. Institute of Arts & Letters both came to Shepherd in 1937. After his retirement from teaching in 1950, he continued to compose until his death in Cleveland. Surviving him were his second wife, the former Grazella Puliver of Cleveland, 3 sons, and a daughter.

Koch, Frederick, *Reflections on Composing* (1983).
Marsh, Robert C., *The Cleveland Orchestra* (1967).

The **SHEPPARD MURDER CASE** (1954–66) was notable because the U.S. Supreme Court set aside Dr. Samuel Sheppard's 1954 conviction for the murder of his wife, Marilyn, on the grounds that the defendant was not sufficiently protected from the excessive publicity surrounding the case, and this circumstance caused him to be denied a fair trial in the Cuyahoga County Common Pleas Court. The high court's decision helped define the protections from adverse media coverage necessary to guarantee a fair trial under the 14th Amendment to the Constitution. On 4 July 1954, Marilyn Reese Sheppard was found murdered in her BAY VILLAGE home by her husband, Dr. Samuel H. Sheppard, who said that a bushy-haired intruder had killed his wife, beaten him unconscious, and ransacked their home. Despite repeated questioning by officials, who focused their investigation on him, Sheppard maintained that he was innocent of the crime. During this period, the Cleveland newspapers, particularly the *CLEVELAND PRESS* and its editor, LOUIS SELTZER, alleged that the Sheppard family had conspired to shield Sam from the authorities, emphasized his refusal to take a lie-detector test (which was his right), and published gossip regarding his family life. The publicity intensified with Sheppard's arrest on 30 July and continued through his 9-week jury trial, beginning 18 Oct. with Judge EDWARD BLYTHIN presiding. Evidence presented by the prosecution team of John J. Mahon, Saul D. Danaceau, and Thos. C. Parrino included analysis of bloodstains found in the house, speculation on the nature of the murder weapon by Coroner Samuel R. Gerber, and a recounting of Sheppard's relationship with Susan Hayes, a former lab technician at Bayview Hospital, in order to establish a possible motive for the murder. In what was

later called a "carnival atmosphere," the defense, made up of attorneys Wm. J. Corrigan, Sr., Wm. J. Corrigan, Jr., Fred Garmone, and Arthur E. Petersilge, was unable to convince the jury of Sheppard's innocence. He was convicted of 2d-degree murder on 21 Dec. 1954 and given a life sentence. His defense attorneys immediately appealed the decision to the Cuyahoga County Court of Appeals and the Ohio Supreme Court, but they were unable to overturn the verdict. The U.S. Supreme Court refused to review the case.

Sheppard began serving his prison sentence first in the Ohio Penitentiary, and later at the Marion (Ohio) Correctional Institution. After several more attempts to secure his release, Sheppard and his new attorney, F. Lee Bailey, finally met with success in July 1964 when Judge Carl A. Weinman of the U.S. District Court of Southern Ohio issued a writ of habeas corpus to release Sheppard on the grounds that Judge Blythin had failed to grant a change of venue or postpone the trial; had failed to disqualify himself, although his impartiality was uncertain; and had permitted improper introduction of lie-detector testimony and unauthorized communications with the jury during their deliberations. The state of Ohio challenged Weinman's decision in the 6th Circuit Court of Appeals in Cincinnati and won a reversal in May 1965. Bailey petitioned the Supreme Court for a review of the 6th Circuit's decision, and on 6 June 1966 the Court sustained Weinman's decision, citing Judge Blythin's failure to protect Sheppard from the inherently prejudicial publicity that had saturated the country. They instructed Weinman to issue the writ of habeas corpus releasing Sheppard from prison but gave the state the option to retry him within a reasonable time. Sheppard was retried in the fall of 1966, and the jury found him not guilty of murdering his wife. Two days after his release from prison in 1964, he married Ariane Tebbenjohanns, with whom he had begun corresponding when he was in prison. After his second trial, he was readmitted to the practice of osteopathic medicine but was involved in a malpractice suit. He left medicine to become a part-time professional wrestler, and after he and Ariane were divorced in Oct. 1969, he married Colleen Strickland, the daughter of his wrestling partner. He died 6 Apr. 1970 of liver failure at the Columbus home of his wife's parents. He was 46 years old.

Holmes, Paul, *The Sheppard Murder Case* (1961).
Sheppard, Samuel, *Endure and Conquer* (1966).

**SHERA, JESSE HAUK** (8 Dec. 1903–8 Mar. 1982), was an internationally respected librarian and library educator who was dean of the School of Library Science at Western Reserve University (subsequently CASE WESTERN RESERVE UNIVERSITY). Shera was born in Oxford, Ohio, and received an A.B. in English literature from Miami University (Ohio) in 1925, an A.M. from Yale in 1927, and a Ph.D. from the University of Chicago in library science in 1944. He became dean of the Library School at WRU in 1952, having served as bibliographer for the Scripps Foundation for Research in Population Problems (1928–40), and having worked at the Library of Congress (1940–41), in the Office of Strategic Services (1941–44), and as associate director of the library and associate professor of library science at the University of Chicago. As dean of the WRU Library School, Shera was instrumental in the founding of the Ctr. for Documentation & Communication Research, of which he was appointed director in 1959. The center did pioneering research in the field of automated information storage and retrieval and machine literature searching, interests of Shera's since his days at the Office of Strategic Services.

Shera served as president of the Ohio Library Assoc. and on advisory commissions to the Census Bureau, Education Office, and Natl. Science Foundation. In 1957 he gave lectures in Brazil, and at various times he represented the U.S. government in Europe and Latin America at international conferences on documentation and librarianship. He served on the President's Commission on Employment of the Handicapped and the Cleveland Mayor's Commission on Employment of the Handicapped. Shera received the Beta Phi Mu award for contributions to library education and the Melvil Dewey award for contributions to librarianship, both from the American Library Assoc. He was Ohio Library Assoc. Librarian of the Year and received numerous other awards and honors throughout his long career. Shera served as dean of the Library School until 1970, when he stepped down but continued to teach. In 1972 he was appointed dean and professor emeritus. Shera was married to Helen M. Bickham. They had 2 children, Mary (Baum) and Edgar B.

The **SHERIFF STREET MARKET** opened its doors on Christmas Eve 1891. Located downtown on Sheriff (E. 4th) St. between Huron and Bolivar roads, it was the largest food market in Cleveland until completion of the WEST SIDE MARKET in 1912. For 45 years it was the trading place of thousands of Clevelanders, most of whom lived within walking distance. Lack of refrigeration meant that meat and vegetables had to be purchased fresh each day. The market was built and operated by the Sheriff St. Market & Storage Co., a stock company incorporated in July 1890 by Jas. M. Jones, John M. Henderson, Joseph Hays, Edwin T. Hamilton, Leonard Schlather, and Wm. H. Gaylord. Jones was the first president. Homer McDaniel served as market manager from 1894 until his death in 1928.

Designed by the partnership of LEHMAN & SCHMITT, the Sheriff St. Market consisted of a large central aisle bridged by slender iron trusses, with light admitted from a clerestory, roof skylights, and a great domed skylight in the structure's central pavilion. It was flanked by 2 6-story towers, the upper floors of which were used for cold storage. Outside, a wide veranda sheltered the produce stalls. The market boasted its own electric power plant. In 1929 the market house was sold to the Realty Corp. of Cleveland, which announced that it would be redeveloped for another use. A portion of the building was being remodeled as a bus terminal and garage when it was badly damaged by fire on 9 May 1930. The north wing and central pavilion were torn down, but the south wing continued to house the Sheriff St. Market until it closed in 1936. The building was used for storage from 1936–50. It reopened on 30 Mar. 1950 as the New CENTRAL MARKET, which was still in business in 1985.

**SHERITH JACOB CONGREGATION,** one of Cleveland's principal Orthodox congregations during the 1920s and 1930s, was established on 20 Oct. 1899 by 18 Hungarian Jews who lived near E. 20th St. and Orange Ave. in the Woodland neighborhood. Services were initially held at Bernstein Hall on Perry and Orange streets. In 1904, Sherith Jacob purchased and remodeled a building at E. 25th St. and Orange, which became known as the Irving St. Shul. As Cleveland's Jews began migrating to new neighborhoods, Sherith Jacob left Woodland. A synagogue was established at E. 76th St. and Cedar Rd. in 1914, but it was destroyed by fire on Kol Nidre night in 1919. In March of the following year, the congregation purchased a church at Parkwood and Olivet Ave. in GLENVILLE. Sherith Jacob operated a branch synagogue in Woodland until the late 1930s for those members who could not or would not move out of that neighborhood.

In 1932, the congregation acquired a building at Arlington Ave. and Eddy Rd. to use as another branch in order to meet the needs of members who lived at the eastern edge of Glenville. A new synagogue was erected on the site and dedicated in Mar. 1944. Sherith Jacob subsequently sold its Parkwood property and held services exclusively at the new Eddy Rd. Synagogue. The congregation's first rabbi was Julius Joel Klein, one of the charter members, who served until 1917. The congregation had no rabbi for 5 years, then hired Klein's grandson, Ormond Klein, who remained in the pulpit only 4 years. In 1928, Sherith Jacob hired Hugo H. Klein, another grandson, who served for over 30 years. He organized the first Hebrew and Sunday schools at the congregation, and in 1930 he established the Young Men's Culture Club, which sponsored Friday-evening lectures at the synagogue.

Following WORLD WAR II, as Cleveland's Jewish community continued its eastern migration, Sherith Jacob was forced to abandon the Eddy Rd. site. The building was subsequently used by the Kaliver Yeshiva. The congregation could not afford to purchase a new building or erect a synagogue in a new location. Services were held thereafter at several sites, including Milliken School, the Jewish Community Ctr., and YESHIVATH ADATH B'NAI ISRAEL. In the spring of 1962, Sherith Jacob merged with Sherith Israel to form Sherith Jacob Israel congregation. Sherith Israel was organized in May 1922 by Orthodox Jews living in the Mt. Pleasant area. Services were held in a rented building at E. 114th and Lock Ave. until 1926, when the congregation purchased a building on E. 119th St. Seeling Ginsburg served as rabbi from 1925–38. When Ginsburg left Sherith Israel, there were only 42 members. The congregation grew smaller over the next 2 decades until the members decided the 1962 merger would be in their best interest. Despite the merger of the two congregations, their combined resources were not great enough to overcome the prohibitive cost of building a new synagogue in the Heights. In 1970, Sherith Jacob agreed to merge with WARRENSVILLE CTR. SYNAGOGUE.

Sherith Israel of Mt. Pleasant Records, WRHS.

**SHERWIN, BELLE** (20 Mar. 1868–9 July 1955), was a noted reform and feminist leader. She was born in Cleveland to Henry Alden and Frances Mary Smith Sherwin. Her father, a noted manufacturer, was a founder of the SHERWIN-WILLIAMS CO. Sherwin attended public schools in Cleveland and received a B.S. degree from Wellesley College in 1890, where she was chosen Phi Beta Kappa. She added to her formal education with a year of study in history at Oxford University from 1894–95. Returning to the U.S., she taught for 4 years in Boston at St. Margaret's and Miss Hersey's School for Girls. In 1900 she returned to Cleveland, where she served as the first president of the CONSUMERS LEAGUE OF OHIO. During the period before WORLD WAR I, Sherwin was active in numerous Cleveland welfare organizations, serving as director of the Public Health Nursing Assoc. and a member of the Fed. for Charity & Philanthropy and the Council for Social Agencies. Following World War I, she was director of the Cleveland Welfare Fed. (1900–14), and from 1921–24 she was vice-president of the Natl. League of Women Voters. She served as league president from 1924–34. Sherwin was a founder of the WOMEN'S CITY CLUB in Cleveland. She received honorary degrees from Western

Reserve University (1930), Denison University (1931), and Oberlin College (1937).

Belle Sherwin Papers, Radcliffe College.

The **SHERWIN-WILLIAMS COMPANY,** a pioneer in the development of the paint industry, was established in Cleveland in 1866 by Henry A. Sherwin (27 Sept. 1842–26 June 1916). By 1983 the company's operations included 1,417 paint stores, 402 drugstores, a chemical division, and subsidiaries in 5 foreign countries. Sales of $1.973 billion in 1983 ranked Sherwin-Williams 184th among the Fortune 500 corporations. In July 1866, Sherwin invested $2,000 in Truman Dunham & Co., 118 Superior St., importers and dealers in paints, oils, varnishes, and window glass. By 1870, the original partnership had dissolved: Dunham and Geo. O. Griswold took over the linseed oil works, and in Feb. 1870, Sherwin, Alanson T. Osborn, and new partner Edward P. Williams formed Sherwin, Williams & Co., located at 126 Superior and 44 Long streets. In 1873, Sherwin's group bought the Standard Oil Co. cooperage building, 601 Canal St., for its first factory and began manufacturing paste paints, oil colors, and putty. At first, Sherwin-Williams continued the normal practice of selling paint ingredients that the customer then mixed together, but the company soon began experiments to develop a reliable ready-mixed paint. It revolutionized the industry in 1880 when it began to market such a paint. Its success led the firm to dispose of its retail sales operation in 1882 to concentrate on manufacturing. By the time Sherwin-Williams was incorporated in Ohio on 16 July 1884, it had sales agents in New York and Chicago. In 1888 it bought the Calumet Paint Co. in Chicago to better serve its growing market there among the railroad, farm implement, and wagon industries. The firm enjoyed its first million-dollar sales year in 1890 and began to market its products from Boston to San Diego and into Canada. In 1901 it opened a manufacturing plant in Newark, N.J., and in 1903 a branch office in England. It expanded its holdings to include raw materials, buying lead, zinc, and copper mines in New Mexico in 1904. In Dec. 1905 it organized the Ozark Smelting & Mining Co.

Sherwin-Williams acquired other firms in the 1910s, and it also expanded its operations in new directions. Shortages of German-made colors during WORLD WAR I forced Sherwin-Williams to begin manufacturing its own dyestuffs and chemicals in 1915, thus opening up new markets for its products among textiles and printing inks. In 1922 it also began to produce new, faster-drying lacquers. In the 1940s, the company turned to product development to create growth. In the early 1940s, it introduced both Kem-Tone paint, a fast-drying water-based paint for interior home use, and the "Roller-Koater," a roll-on painting tool to replace the brush. The firm also introduced Kem-Glo paint, a porcelainlike enamel paint, in 1948; Super Kem-Tone, a washable latex, in 1950; and A-100, a latex paint for exterior use, in 1960. By 1960, net sales had reached $282 million. Sherwin-Williams acquired a brush-manufacturing company in 1956 and in the 1960s acquired 4 other companies, including Cleveland's OSBORN MFG. CO. in 1968. In 1969 it consolidated its chemical operations into a chemical division. In the 1970s, however, the company was hurt by intense competition within the paint industry and was forced to sell some of its operations, including Osborn Mfg. in 1975; portions of its chemicals division in 1972 and 1977; its European, Indonesian, and domestic coating facilities in 1977; and about 100 company-operated stores in 1978. The firm lost $8.2 million in 1977 and was the subject of an unsuccessful takeover bid. By 1980, Sherwin-Williams was again profitable and acquired other firms, including parts of Dutch Boy, Inc. On 3 Oct. 1981, Sherwin-Williams bought GRAY DRUG STORES for $55 million. Although the company closed its 109-year-old Canal Rd. plant in 1982, eliminating about 70 jobs, it still employed 3,000 of its total 23,000 workers in Cleveland-area facilities. Since 1930, its main offices have been located in the Midland Bldg., 101 Prospect Ave.

Sherwin-Williams Co., *The Story of Sherwin-Williams* (1955).

**SHIELDS, JOSEPH C.** (10 May 1827–21 Dec. 1898), was a Civil War artillery officer and Cuyahoga County treasurer. Shields was born in New Alexandria, Westmoreland County, Pa. By trade he was a tanner and furrier. Between 1845–52, however, he worked as a mechanic in Pittsburgh before moving to Cleveland in 1852. Shields was employed in 1852 and 1853 by the Cleveland Transfer Co., and then by the Cleveland & Toledo Railroad, 1853–58. For 2 years, working for Judah Benjamin, future Confederate leader, he superintended the building of a stage line across the Isthmus of Tehuantepec in Nicaragua. In 1860 he worked for the Adams Express Co. in New Orleans, La. In Apr. 1861, he was back in Cleveland with the Cleveland & Toledo Railroad. During the first 3 months of the CIVIL WAR, Shields served in Battery D, FIRST OHIO VOLUNTEER LIGHT ARTILLERY, also referred to as the Cleveland Light Artillery. In July 1862, he recruited the 19TH OHIO INDEPENDENT BATTERY. His recruiting office was located on Bank (W. 6th) St., close to the WEDDELL HOUSE hotel. He achieved the rank of captain on 28 July 1862. Shields resigned his commission on 15 Sept. 1864, shortly after the close of the Atlanta campaign, to tend to business matters in Cleveland. As a military leader he was described as being physically strong, courageous, energetic, and resourceful. During the postwar years, Shields was a passenger conductor on the Lake Shore & Michigan Southern Railroad, owned a grocery store, and ran a paving contracting business. He served as Cleveland city councilman, 1867–68. In Aug. 1886, he served as deputy treasurer, Cuyahoga County, and in 1889 he was elected county treasurer, serving to 1894. Shields was a member of the Forest City Post, Grand Army of the Republic; the Cuyahoga County Soldiers & Sailors Union; the Military Order of the Loyal Legion of the U.S.; and the Cleveland Light Artillery Assoc. In 1862, he married Ellen S. Crawford. They had no children. At the time of his death, he resided at 2542 Euclid Ave. He is buried in LAKE VIEW CEMETERY.

**SHILOH BAPTIST CHURCH** is the oldest congregation of black BAPTISTS in Cleveland and the 2d-oldest black church in the city. The exact date of its founding is not certain, but evidence indicates that the nucleus of the early membership consisted of a group of recent migrants from the South who regularly gathered for prayer at a small grocery store at 245 Erie (E. 9th) St. They were led by Michael Gregory, the store's proprietor. In 1850, C. C. Willis, minister of FIRST BAPTIST CHURCH, was appointed to head a mission that included the Gregory group along with a few black church members. The mission followed a pattern in northern cities that encouraged separate race ministry, despite objections by some established black citizens who preferred an integrated worship experience. The first mission was located on Brownell (E. 14th) St. Rev. W. P. Brown served as the first minister. Under his leadership, the membership grew and eventually moved to larger quarters on Central Ave. near Perry (E. 22nd) St. Shiloh was officially recognized as a regular Baptist denominational church in 1869. By then it had moved once again, to Sterling (E. 30th) St. near Scovill Ave. As BLACKS migrated to Cleveland during WORLD WAR I, the membership continued to grow. A campaign for funds for a new church building resulted in the purchase of the former synagogue of B'NAI JESHURUN congregation at E. 55th St. and Scovill in 1925; the church still occupied this structure in 1986, maintaining a large membership. Congregations that grew out of Shiloh Baptist Church's membership include MT. ZION CONGREGATIONAL CHURCH (1924), Messiah Baptist Church (1927), ANTIOCH BAPTIST CHURCH (1893), and Mt. Herman Baptist Church (formed as a result of a merger between Mt. Carmel and St. Paul Baptist churches in 1926).

The **SHO-JO-JI DANCERS** are a JAPANESE dance group consisting of young girls who are 2d-, 3d-, and 4th-generation Americans of Japanese ancestry. The group was organized in 1955 under the sponsorship of the Japanese American Citizens League, Cleveland Branch. Its purpose was to preserve the traditional dances of Japan. The group's first performance was held on 27 Oct. 1956 at the Children's Festival of the Chrysanthemum in Rm. 36 of the Cleveland Public Library's main branch. The library's director contacted Mrs. Vi Takahashi, a professional dancer from Japan then residing in Cleveland, and asked her to organize a children's dance group for the festival. Takahashi assembled 7 young girls, ranging in age from 7 to 9, and readied them for the festival, instructing them in the delicate Japanese dances.

The Sho-Jo-Jis' first performance was such a success that they received many invitations to perform at other city functions. They have performed at every folk festival of the CLEVELAND FOLK ARTS ASSOC. from 1956–85, in addition to a large number of cultural, civic, educational, service, and veterans' organization functions. Vi Takahashi stepped down as the group's director and instructor after only 1 year of service, because of her husband's acceptance of a job in another state. Mrs. Peggy Tangi, her successor, stayed in the position for 10 years. In 1985 the group was under the direction of Mrs. Sally Taketa. The instructors included Mrs. Yoshiko Baker, classical-traditional dance expert; Mrs. Linda Orura, classical dance expert; and Mrs. Dolly Semonco, folk dance expert. Although the group remained in existence in 1985, recruiting had become increasingly difficult, a result of the decrease in Japanese families living in Cleveland. To compensate for this decline in membership, the group was no longer all Japanese, but accepted children of mixed ancestry, as well.

**SHORT VINCENT,** a street 1 block in length between E. 9th and E. 6th streets NE, was once a colorful center of downtown Cleveland after-hours nightlife, gambling, and B-girls. Officially named Vincent Ave. NE, the street crossed farmland once held by John Vincent, an early Cleveland settler. After 1885, when the HOLLENDEN HOTEL was built, the street filled with restaurants and taverns to accommodate guests of the hotel, the back door of which faced Short Vincent. By the late 1920s, the local saloons, eateries, barbershops, cleaners, and other small businesses became a gathering place for gamblers, bookies, sports figures, racketeers, lawyers, and newspapermen. Short Vincent offered good food, underworld gossip, and the odds on anything.

Short Vincent was home to such Cleveland landmarks as the Theatrical, the Taystee Barbeque, Frank Ciccia's Barbershop, the Grogshop, and Kornman's Restaurant. Some of the district's most colorful characters were owners of popular establishments. Morris "Mushy" Wexler opened the Theatrical in 1937, but he also ran the Empire News Service, a telegraph operation that simultaneously informed

bookies around the state of changes in the line for horseracing and layoffs in football. While the federal government eventually closed down the gambling hotline, the Theatrical continued to serve high-quality food and offer big-name jazz entertainment. When the restaurant was destroyed by fire in 1960, the owners rebuilt it for a thinner, older, but still devoted crowd.

While the north side of the street featured legally parked cars and "respectable" businesses, the south was studded with illegally parked cars and girlie shows; the street between was referred to as the Gaza Strip. Although the ROXY, the madame of female strip joints, was not actually on Short Vincent but near the street's junction with E. 9th, this establishment and others—Freddie's Cafe, the French Quarter, the 730 Lounge Bar—offered onlookers (particularly tourists) the opportunity to observe, and later be fleeced by, shapely bar girls. When the shows ended, heavily made-up "dancers" violated the neutrality of the Gaza Strip via an alley leading from the Roxy onto Short Vincent.

In its heyday in the 1930s and 1940s, Short Vincent was patronized by the late Bill Veeck, former Indians owner, and a band of newspaper reporters known as the Jolly Set. This group, led by *Cleveland Press* columnist WINSOR FRENCH, organized Fun for Funds, a charity bazaar, in 1953. The street was closed off, booths were set up, and a flagpole was installed for, and occupied by, Racehorse Richard Tuma, a bartender at Mickey's Show Bar. For a month Tuma advertised the fair from his perch; on the day of the event, he hurriedly shinnied down the pole when a tornado was spotted. The tornado made a shambles of Short Vincent; though Tuma was faulted by locals for not going on record as the first man to endure a tornado from atop a flagpole, he later (1958) gained fame by outrunning a racehorse at Cranwood Parkway.

Despite the popularity of the street, Short Vincent was the frequent target of civic outrage and law-enforcement-agency surveillance. The federal government crackdown on gambling made bookie operations and crap games less open. The Ohio State Liquor Control Commission periodically tried to close down or suspend the licenses of the bars, while the newspapers ran exposes on the B-girls. Former safety director ELIOT NESS once retaliated against a padded bill in a Short Vincent establishment by closing down the place because it had only 1 door. By the early 1960s, the south side of Short Vincent was dark, and much of the north side was razed to make way for the Central Natl. Bank Bldg. The demolition of the south side was completed in 1978 to make way for the Natl. City Bank Bldg.

**SHOREWAY.** *See* **MEMORIAL SHOREWAY**

**SIDLO, THOMAS L.** (10 Mar. 1888–27 May 1955), was a lawyer and a founding partner of the Cleveland law firm of Baker, Hostetler, Sidlo & Patterson (see BAKER & HOSTETLER). Sidlo was born in Cleveland to Czech immigrants Thomas and Anna Sidlo. His father was a master mechanic at the American Steel & Wire Co. Sidlo attended public schools in Cleveland, graduating from South High School. He started as a freshman at Western Reserve University but transferred to the University of Wisconsin at Madison for 2 years. He returned to WRU in 1908 for his senior year. He graduated in 1909 and continued at WRU, receiving his M.A. in 1910 and his LL.B. in 1912. He was admitted to the Ohio bar in 1912. Sidlo supported NEWTON D. BAKER in his campaign for mayor of Cleveland, and when Baker took office, Sidlo was made chief deputy under PETER WITT, the street railway commissioner. In 1913, Sidlo became the commissioner of franchises, and shortly thereafter the commissioner of information and publicity. In 1914 he was made the director of public service. When Baker left office in 1916, Sidlo helped him form the law firm of Baker, Hostetler, Sidlo & Patterson. Sidlo was a member of the Cleveland, Ohio State, and American bar associations. He also was a member of the COURT OF NISI PRIUS. He was the financial director, controller, and general counsel for the Scripps-Howard Newspapers, the United Press Assoc., and the Newspaper Enterprise Assoc. from 1924, resigning in 1936. After Sidlo resigned as general counsel of the E. W. Scripps Co., he devoted a great deal of his time to his numerous outside interests, which encompassed more than 200 organizations. His chief interests were in music, theater, foreign affairs, and science. He was chairman of the NORTHERN OHIO OPERA ASSOC.; president and a member of the executive committee of the MUSICAL ARTS ASSOC.; president of the CLEVELAND PLAY HOUSE; president of the Foreign Affairs Council in Cleveland; chairman of the Cleveland Committee for Relief in Czechoslovakia; and a trustee of Science Service, Inc. He was also a member and officer of many local organizations, including the Cleveland Chamber of Commerce, the Community Fund, the Cuyahoga County Citizens Tax League, the CLEVELAND MUSEUM OF NATURAL HISTORY (president and trustee), the CITIZENS LEAGUE OF CLEVELAND, the CLEVELAND MUSEUM OF ART, and the WESTERN RESERVE HISTORICAL SOCIETY. Sidlo married Winifred Morgan of Cleveland on 27 June 1914. She died on 11 Mar. 1932. He later married Elizabeth Avery of Grand Rapids, Mich., on 22 June 1935.

**SIEUR DE SAGUIN** (variations Seguin, Seguein, Shaguin; no given name is known), a French trader, was the first recorded resident of Cuyahoga County to construct a permanent residence. During his stay, the locality was under the control of France, to whom the Indians gave their allegiance. A trader such as Saguin was needed to trade with and maintain the good will of the Indians, as well as to relay intelligence of Indian attitudes and English influence and deployments. That Saguin stayed near Cleveland is affirmed in the memoirs of Robt. Navarre, intendant of Detroit from 1730–60, who in 1743 was sent to visit the trading post that had been established on the CUYAHOGA RIVER by Saguin. The exact length of Saguin's short tenure, beginning by 1742, is uncertain, but he had constructed at least 2 buildings and apparently cultivated corn before being instructed by Sieur Pierre Joseph Celoron De Blainville in 1743 to depart his post.

Saguin's growing fur trade brought 1,800 lbs. of furs in 1743, but the fear of losing their own Ottawa trade to him made the authorities at Detroit reluctant to send the gunpowder that the Indians needed and requested in trade. This attitude made his position increasingly untenable. It is unlikely that he returned. Saguin's presence on the Cuyahoga River is also confirmed by reference to the river as the Riviere a Seguin (de Lery, 1754) and River de Saguin (Montresor, 1764) and Lewis Evans's 1755 map notation of the "French House." Estimates of Saguin's location on the Cuyahoga River range from the junction of TINKER'S CREEK to BROOKLYN HTS.

**SIFCO INDUSTRIES, INC.,** is a major international metalworking firm. Five Cleveland men formed the company in 1913 as a small heat-treating operation on Chester Ave. to improve the physical properties of metal, accordingly naming the firm the Steel Improvement Co. In 1916, it expanded into forging when it acquired the neighboring Forest City Machine Co., a producer of pole-line hardware, and was renamed the Steel Improvement & Forge Co. During

WORLD WAR I, the company serviced the automobile, arms, and naval industries. It suffered a drop in business after the war.

In the 1920s, Chas. H. Smith began to strengthen the company by addressing its production and sales problems. He first moved the firm away from dependence on the AUTOMOTIVE INDUSTRY, entering the valve, pneumatic tool, mining, and material-handling industries. Smith was also able to gain a competitive advantage for the firm by experimenting with materials that were previously not considered forgeable. It had substantial success with monel metal and other special alloys, which were forged into "steel plugs" utilized by the petroleum industry. To facilitate increased sales, the firm moved into larger quarters at Addison Rd. and Metta Ave. in 1928. As it struggled through the Depression, the company entered the aviation industry. Smith quickly prepared his company for wartime business to manufacture large volumes of forgings for both British and American aircraft. Constantly researching new methods of improving metals by forging, the company made significant innovations with torpedoes and developed the turbines and blades for the first American jet engine.

Although business dropped after the war, Chas. H. Smith, Jr., continued his father's expansion of the company, forging the new metal titanium in 1949 and opening an airplane-parts plant in Canada in 1951. Three years later, the company sold its Canadian firm when it had the opportunity to acquire the forging division of the Champion Forge Co. Champion, founded in 1903 by Claus and Louis Greve, was Cleveland's oldest forging company, whose well-known large forgings were used for airplane landing equipment. The merger made Steel Improvement one of the nation's largest commercial forging shops. In the late 1950s and early 1960s, the company expanded abroad, developing significant forging operations in Argentina, Brazil, Japan, and India. By acquiring several small companies, in the 1960s and 1970s the firm entered related areas, such as custom machining, electroplating services, large-diameter bearings, and cold forging. In 1969, it changed its corporate name to SIFCO Industries, Inc. Despite some cutbacks during the recession of the early 1980s, SIFCO continues to grow, constructing a plant in Ireland to repair aircraft parts and establishing joint ventures to remanufacture turbine components and to form an export trading company.

**SILBERT, SAMUEL** (15 Apr. 1883–18 Feb. 1976), was a lawyer and long-time common pleas court judge. The eldest of 4 children, Silbert was born in Riga, Latvia, and came to America at the age of 6 with his widowed mother. Living in Newark, N.J., he worked selling newspapers on street corners and in an ink factory. By the age of 16, he was a state champion amateur boxer. Moving to Denver with his family, he worked as a train news butcher before coming to Cleveland in 1902. Working days and attending high school and law school on alternate nights, he graduated from Cleveland Law School with honors and was admitted to the Ohio bar in 1907. He married Anna Weinstein in 1909 and that year met defeat in the Ward 12 city council election. Silbert's public career started in 1912, when he was appointed an assistant police prosecutor by Mayor NEWTON D. BAKER; he served until 1915. Within 3 years, Silbert had established a conciliation system credited with settling over 29,000 disputes. In the 1915 municipal court elections, he led a field of 28 candidates. On the municipal court bench, he introduced several judicial novelties, including a water cure for alcoholics by which defendants could avoid the workhouse by downing 10 glasses of water each day. His second and last defeat at the polls came in 1923, when he was defeated in the election for chief justice of the municipal court. Elected to the common pleas court in 1924, Silbert continued to serve at that post, also serving as chief justice, 1955–63, until his retirement on 1 Jan. 1969. Most of the time he served in divorce court, handling almost 100,000 cases in his career. As a nationally recognized authority on domestic relations, divorce, and marital problems, Silbert used his knowledge, experience, understanding, and patience to reconcile thousands of couples. Silbert's popularity was so great and his vote-getting ability so formidable, he often ran for reelection unopposed, and even when opposed he often led the entire judicial ticket.

Samuel Silbert Papers, WRHS.
Silbert, Samuel, *Judge Sam* (1963).

**SILVER, ABBA HILLEL** (28 Jan. 1893–28 Nov. 1963), religious leader, Zionist, educator, orator, and social-welfare activist, was born in Neinstadt, Lithuania. Brought to America in 1902, Silver grew up on the lower east side of New York City, where he learned English, Yiddish, and Hebrew. In 1904, with his older brother, he founded the Herzl-Zion Club, a Hebrew-speaking Zionist youth organization. In 1911, Silver enrolled at the Hebrew Union College and the University of Cincinnati. He graduated from both in 1915 and was ordained a Reform rabbi in the same year. Silver served as rabbi at the Eoff St. Temple in Wheeling, W.Va., from 1915–17. He was a founder and board member of the Wheeling Associated Charities. While in Wheeling, he met Virginia Horkheimer, whom he married in 1923.

Silver succeeded MOSES GRIES as rabbi of the TEMPLE in Cleveland in 1917 at the age of 24. Under his leadership, the congregation erected a magnificent new synagogue in 1922 at Ansel Rd. in the WADE PARK district. Although trained in the Classical Reform tradition, Silver differed from the more radical Gries on several issues. Silver turned the emphasis at the Temple from the concept of the "institutional synagogue" to one that was more religiously and culturally centered. He reinstituted Hebrew in religious education and openly espoused political Zionism, in opposition to a large element of the congregation. Under his leadership, the Temple became the largest Reform congregation in the country by 1927, with a membership of over 1,700 families.

Silver was among the leaders of the Zionist Organization of America as early as 1920 and gradually became more powerful nationally and internationally during the 1920s and 1930s. In 1938 he was chairman of the United Palestine Appeal, and later he was cochair of the United Jewish Palestine. In the late 1930s and early 1940s, Silver stood in opposition to the leadership of Rabbi Stephen Wise, head of the ZOA, reflecting a schism that existed in the Zionist movement internationally. In 1943, Silver wrested control of the newly founded American Zionist Emergency Council from Wise. The AZEC was the most important Zionist organization of the war years and was devoted to the creation of the state of Israel as a means to save world Jewry. Following WORLD WAR II, Silver served as president of the ZOA, and in that capacity he spoke to the United Nations in May 1947 demanding a vote on the partition of Palestine. He also served as chair of the American Sec. of the Jewish Agency in 1947.

In local Jewish affairs, Silver was the first president of the BUREAU OF JEWISH EDUCATION, serving from 1924–32. In 1935, he and Rabbi BARNETT BRICKNER served as cochairs of the newly reorganized Jewish Welfare Fund, the fundraising arm of the Jewish Welfare Fed. In 1933, Silver was the prime mover in the creation of the

LEAGUE FOR HUMAN RIGHTS, an organization that monitored and investigated anti-Semitism and racial injustice in Cleveland. Silver was active in social-welfare issues, particularly those that touched the working person. In 1919, he denounced the concept of the open shop, and in 1921 he resigned from the Cleveland Chamber of Commerce because it supported open shops. He argued that trade unionism was the only road to social justice and industrial peace. In 1928, he was appointed chair of the Cleveland Committee on Unemployment Insurance, and soon thereafter he was appointed by Gov. Geo. White to serve on the state Commission on Unemployment Insurance. Silver worked hard to see the passage of the state's unemployment-insurance law in 1936.

Silver was one of the true rabbinic scholars in Cleveland's history, ranking with BENJAMIN GITTELSOHN and ISRAEL PORATH. He published 6 major works during his lifetime and 1 posthumously. They include *The History of Messianic Speculation in Israel from the First through the Seventeenth Century* (1927); *The Democratic Impulse in Jewish History* (1928); *Religion in a Changing World* (1931); *Where Judaism Differed* (1956); *Moses and the Original Torah* (1961); and *Therefore Choose Life* (1967). When Silver died in 1963, he was succeeded in the Temple pulpit by his son Daniel Jeremy Silver.

Rabbi Abba Hillel Silver Papers, the Temple.
Silver, Rabbi Daniel Jeremy, ed., *In the Time of Harvest*, (1963).

The **SINGERS CLUB,** a male chorus, was begun informally in 1891 at the Central YMCA by Homer B. Hatch and Carroll B. Ellinwood. Both men were active in local music and choral activities. Auditions were held to select young men with better-than-average voices. The club rehearsed at the YMCA and offered Sunday afternoon programs in exchange for use of its space. In 1893, the organization formally became known as the Singers Club of Cleveland. Its debut was at the chapel of the FIRST BAPTIST CHURCH on 19 Apr. 1894, conducted by Ellinwood, who served as conductor for 7 years. Chas. Clemens, an organist, led the group from 1901–06, followed by Albert Rees Davis (1907–19). Other conductors were Harvey B. Gaul, J. Van Dyke Miller, BERYL RUBINSTEIN, Boris Goldovsky, Goe. Strickling, Robt. Stofer, Frank Hruby (see HRUBY FAMILY), Lawrence Stevens, and Thos. J. Shellhammer.

The **SINGING ANGELS** are a world-famous singing group composed of children ages 5–18 and representing 8 Ohio counties and approximately 45 northern Ohio cities. The group performs under the auspices of the nonprofit Ohio Children's Performing Music Foundation, and its repertoire includes spiritual music, classicals, show tunes, and barbershop harmony. The Singing Angels perform throughout the year at various civic and business events and hold an annual spring benefit concert. The group was founded in 1964 by Bill Boehm, a professional singer, director, and producer. Originally an 80-member chorus, it now includes 100 singers in the reserve training chorus and 150 in the performing chorus. The Singing Angels average approximately 80 shows a year on stage, on television, and in churches. They have traveled to many foreign countries, including Europe in 1974 and China in 1983. In Cleveland, they have performed at MUSICARNIVAL and the Blossom Music Ctr. Among the many honors the singing group has received are the 1970 Emmy Award for their "Songs of Christmas" television special produced by WEWS-TV and the 1974 Distinguished Award from the Freedom Foundation of Valley Forge. Boehm is the director of the Singing Angels. Geo. F. Strickling is the choral director, and Mrs.

Leonnore Vannice is the publicity director. The Singing Angels practice at the Cleveland Fire Training Academy.

**SISSLE, NOBLE** (10 Aug. 1889–17 Dec. 1975), was a black composer, bandleader, and vocalist. He is best remembered for his songs composed in collaboration with Eubie Blake, including "I'm Just Wild about Harry" and "Love Will Find a Way." Born in Indianapolis, Sissle as a child sang in his father, George's, church. Educated in the public schools of Indianapolis and Cleveland, where his family moved in 1909, he graduated from CENTRAL HIGH SCHOOL in 1911 and continued his studies at DePauw University in 1913 and Butler University in 1914–15. Sissle began singing professionally in 1908, touring with the Edward Thomas Male Quartet. After high school he toured with Hahn's Jubilee Singers. In 1915 he organized his own short-lived group in Indianapolis, also singing with Joe Porter's Serenaders and Bob Young in Baltimore. There he met Eubie Blake and formed a songwriting team, with Sissle as the lyricist; they achieved success with their first publication, "It's All Your Fault." Sissle joined a New York society dance orchestra in 1916. In 1917 he joined the 369th Infantry Regimental Band as a drum major and served overseas, touring with the orchestra until 1919. During 1919–20, Sissle and Blake toured the vaudeville circuit. In 1921 their production of "Shuffle Along" opened an 18-month run on Broadway, followed by another 2 years on tour. Their other collaborations included "Elsie" (1923), "Chocolate Dandies" (1924), and "Shuffle Along of 1933." Sissle and Blake toured the vaudeville circuit again in 1925, and Europe in 1926. After dissolving the partnership, Sissle performed both as a soloist and with his own band in Europe before returning to New York in 1931. From the mid-1930s to the mid-1950s, Sissle led his own Noble Sissle Orchestra, extensively touring the U.S. In 1937 he helped found the Negro Actors' Guild, serving as its first president. During WORLD WAR II he toured with a USO troop, staging "Shuffle Along" for servicemen in Europe. Throughout the 1940s, Sissle wrote columns for the *New York Age* and the *Amsterdam News*. In 1952 he was a disc jockey on radio station WMGM in New York. During the 1960s, he continued managing his own publishing company and nightclub, as well as leading his own orchestra. He retired to Florida in the 1970s.

The **SISTERS OF CHARITY OF ST. AUGUSTINE** were a community organized by Bp. AMADEUS RAPPE to care for the sick. Originally 4 Augustinian nuns had come to Cleveland to carry out this work. The 2 older nuns returned to France, and Bp. Rappe, wanting the community to continue, asked an Ursuline novice, Catherine Bissonette, who had been both a teacher and a nurse, to take charge of the younger sisters. She took the name of Mother Ursula and served as the first superior. The nuns cared for the sick in their homes until ST. JOSEPH HOSPITAL, located in OHIO CITY, was opened in 1852. They also cared for the orphaned children of their patients. By 1856, St. Vincent Orphanage superseded the hospital. Plans were made for a more centrally located hospital, and ST. VINCENT CHARITY was opened in 1863. It was officially dedicated on 10 Oct. 1865.

Bp. RICHARD GILMOUR recognized the need for a maternity hospital and foundling home. In response to this need, the sisters opened St. Ann's Hospital in 1873. A new building for St. Ann's, adjacent to Charity Hospital, was opened in 1876. By 1892 the community itself needed larger quarters, and a new motherhouse was opened on Lake Ave. The Sisters of Charity of St. Augustine, skilled nurses themselves, began educating other nurses when they opened

their school of practical nursing at St. Vincent Charity Hospital in 1898. The sisters opened hospitals in Sandusky and Canton and took charge of St. John Hospital in 1916. Later they would open hospitals in Akron and Columbia, S.C. They entered the education apostolate when they opened St. Augustine Academy in LAKEWOOD in 1925. The same year found them carrying out child-care and educational programs at PARMADALE, the diocese's new consolidated orphanage. In 1984, with their motherhouse at Mt. Augustine in Richfield, the sisters pursued wide-ranging apostolates of service.

Gavin, Donald P., *In All Things Charity*, (1955).
Hynes, Michael J., *The History of the Diocese of Cleveland*, (1953).

The **SISTERS OF NOTRE DAME** trace their roots to the original Congregation of the Sisters of Notre Dame in Namur, founded in France by Julie Billiart in 1804. The congregation of sisters in the U.S. is the third branch or offshoot of this original group, and was cofounded in Germany by Aldegonda Wolbring and Lisbeth Kuhling. European political events were the impetus for the order's arrival in Cleveland—its first location in the U.S. Bismarck abolished and closed all Catholic convents and schools in Germany in 1870. In 1874, 21 sisters arrived to teach at ST. PETER'S, which had the first German-speaking school in Cleveland. They were invited by Bp. RICHARD GILMOUR at the request of Fr. Westerholt of St. Peter's. In 1877, the first Provincial House and Notre Dame Academy were established at the corner of Superior and E. 18th St. By 1915, more space was needed, and the academy moved to Ansel Rd. In 1928, the first unit of NOTRE DAME COLLEGE for Women was dedicated on 4545 College Rd. in S. Euclid. Subsequent buildings included an additional wing, 3 student resident buildings, and a library. The college's mandate was to prepare high school and elementary teachers for certification, as well as to confer degrees in the arts and sciences. The college focused its programming and attributed its success to its "educational program centered in religion and the cultural subjects," which emphasized "the essential dignity and worth of human personality," while not neglecting vocational skills. Early graduating classes had around 20 students; in 1985, enrollment was 765.

Other facilities of the order moved to Chardon in 1957. Constructed there were Notre Dame Academy, the Notre Dame Education Ctr., which includes the Provincial House and an infirmary for the ill and elderly sisters, and Notre Dame Elementary School. In 1970, Notre Dame Montessori opened across from the Education Ctr. The academy's first building was torn down and in 1985 was the site of Erieview Catholic High School. The academy's Ansel Rd. building became Lulu Diehl Jr. High of the CLEVELAND PUBLIC SCHOOLS. In 1985 there were over 1,000 sisters in Cleveland and the surrounding area teaching at the college, the academy, Regina High School, Central Catholic High School, and 21 elementary schools, including the Julie Billiart School for Slow Learners. in 1985, the order had 4 provinces or administrative centers in the U.S. and 12 others around the world. The U.S. provinces in addition to Cleveland were Toledo; Covington, Ky.; and the state of California. Over 5,000 sisters were in the U.S. in the 1980s, most of them teaching.

The **SISTERS OF THE GOOD SHEPHERD** have worked among homeless and delinquent women and girls in Cleveland since 1869. In 1986, their school, Marycrest, remained a residential treatment center for teenage girls in need of discipline and rehabilitation. The sisters were called to the

Diocese of Cleveland by Bp. LOUIS AMADEUS RAPPE, who saw a need to establish a home for "wayward girls and fallen but penitent women." The Sisters of the Good Shepherd, heirs of the Refuge movement founded in France in 1835 and organized in a generalate in 1835, were known for their work with such unfortunate women. Five sisters came from the Cincinnati province to set up a residence at 347 Lake St. Six orphans were taken into the Class of the Guardian Angel (also called the Preservate), and 6 "wayward girls" were admitted to the Sacred Heart (or Penitent) Class. Although the average age of the residents did not exceed 18 in the Preservate and 29 in the Penitents, women of advanced age without a place to go were welcomed into the House of the Good Shepherd while they searched for a permanent home. The classes grew steadily during the 1870s as the court system sent the orphans, homeless, and troubled there. By 1875, the sisters relocated their apostolate to larger quarters at Sterling and Sibley (E. 30th and Carnegie). The work of the sisters was financed by benefactors, including JEPTHA WADE, JOHN HUNTINGTON, WM. GORDON, and JOSEPH PERKINS. A contemplative branch of the order, known as the Magdalenes, supported the work of their active sisters through prayer and commercial sewing after 1876. The House of the Good Shepherd, a founding member of the Community Fund, was also partially funded by this body in the 20th century. The House of the Good Shepherd accepted orphans well into the 1940s, but as the trend toward foster placement reduced the need for orphanages, the sisters directed all their efforts toward delinquent girls and those considered too disruptive for foster homes. The last orphan left the home in 1950.

Girls and women who entered the Sacred Heart Class were given a new name to help them make a new start. Their goal in coming to the Good Shepherd home was to reevaluate their lives and learn values to help them live better-adjusted lives in society. Often this process resulted in making peace with their alienated families or in finding a "situation" (employment as a domestic) or other employment. Some women chose to remain in the home as live-in assistants, while some entered the Magdalenes. Because of the difficult nature of the work, however, residents were permitted to enter the Religious of the Good Shepherd (the official name of the active branch of the order). In 1946, the House of the Good Shepherd changed its name to Marycrest and relocated to Wickliffe, an ill-fated move that put the home out of Cuyahoga County and too far away to be used by the courts for placement. As a result, Marycrest diminished its 200-resident facility to a 100-bed home at 7800 Brookside Rd. in INDEPENDENCE, where it was located in 1986. In the 1980s, Marycrest served up to 70 delinquent and predelinquent girls ages 10-18, who are referred by courts or social-service agencies or are privately admitted. The facility has a staff of 60, including 11 sisters trained in administration, recreation, social work, psychology, and domestic arts. Marycrest offers an accredited academic and vocational high school program as well as a program to educate graduates in skills such as comparative shopping, money management, cooking, and job hunting. Marycrest is also home for 17 Contemplative Sisters of the Good Shepherd, formerly called the Magdalenes and then the Sisters of the Cross. The local Good Shepherd community is part of a worldwide order of 6,000 sisters who serve on 6 continents.

The **SIXTH OHIO VOLUNTEER CAVALRY** was organized at Camp Hutchins in Warren, Ohio, on 7 Oct. 1861. Composed of recruits drawn mostly from the Western Reserve, it was authorized by the War Dept. as the second regiment in Wade's & Hutchins' Cavalry Brigade. In Jan. 1862, the regiment moved to Camp Dennison for drill instruction. In March it was assigned to Camp Chase to aid in guarding Confederate prisoners. After receiving sabers and belts, the 6th Ohio moved to Wheeling, W.Va., on 13 May 1862, where it was equipped with horses, carbines, and pistols. It entered Union field service, joining Fremont at Strasburg during his pursuit of Jackson down the Shenandoah Valley. During a skirmish at Strasburg, 6 men of the 6th Ohio were wounded, and on 7 June at the battle of Cross Keys, several Ohio cavalrymen were killed. After a brief encampment at Strasburg, the regiment moved under Gen. Sigel, who had replaced Fremont, to continue fighting the Confederates in the region. Coming under Gen. Pope's command, the 6th Ohio faced Confederate fire at Rappahannock for 4 consecutive days. On 29 Aug., after the Second Battle of Bull Run, the 6th Ohio, along with the Union Army, retreated to Alexandria. Having passed the 1862-63 winter campaign guarding the passage of the Rappahannock, the 6th Ohio was reorganized for the spring campaign under the command of Gen. Hooker. In March the regiment engaged in the battle of Kelly's Ford. Later that spring it confronted Gen. Lee's Confederate forces as they moved toward Maryland. Following their engagement at Gettysburg, the 6th Ohio pursued Lee's retreating army and engaged in a series of battles before the winter campaign. While spending winter quarters at Warrenton, several hundred members of the 6th Ohio reenlisted. During the 1864 campaign, the regiment was engaged almost daily in the field, always in the advanced-guard position. The 6th's campaign opened in May with a series of skirmishes leading up to the Battle of the Wilderness, followed by Gen. Sheridan's raid on Richmond and the Battle of Yellow Tavern. The 1865 spring campaign again brought the unit in pursuit of Lee's Army. On 9 Apr., as part of Gen. Smith's regiment, they opened the Battle of Appomattox Court House. Later the 6th Ohio had the honor of escorting Gen. Grant from Appomattox to Burkesville Station. In August it was mustered out of service in Cleveland.

The **SIXTIETH OHIO VOLUNTEER INFANTRY REGIMENT** (Reorganized), 1864-65, was composed of a number of men from Cleveland and Cuyahoga County. This unit should not be confused with the 60th OVI, which served 1 year in 1862. The reorganized 60th Regiment was mustered at Cleveland and Columbus, Ohio, between Feb.-Apr. 1864. During the war, the regiment was assigned to the following units: 2d Brigade, 3d Div., 9th Army Corps, Army of the Potomac (Apr.-Sept. 1864); and 2d Brigade, 1st Div., 9th Army Corps (Sept. 1864-July 1865). The unit participated in the battles of the Wilderness, Spottsylvania, and Cold Harbor, and was active in the siege of Petersburg and the James River Campaign. The 60th was mustered out in the District of Columbia on 28 July 1865, and its men were discharged and paid off at Camp Chase, Columbus, Ohio. The unit lost 3 officers and 110 men to hostile causes and 130 enlisted men to disease.

**SKEEL, ARTHUR J.** (1874-7 Dec. 1942), was nationally known for his efforts in the advancement of obstetrics. Between 1910-38 he served as director of the Obstetric Div. of ST. LUKE'S HOSPITAL. Skeel attended Cleveland schools and studied medicine at the University of Michigan. He began to practice medicine in 1897 under an older brother who was an obstetrician and gynecologist. From 1907 he specialized in obstetrics and diseases of women. During his 40 years of practice, great strides were made in the field of obstetrics. Skeel himself was especially concerned with new ideas in prenatal and postnatal care that minimized the mortality rate among mothers and newborns. He founded the St. Luke's Obstetric Dispensary (for out-patient services), one of the earliest such organizations in Cleveland. He also founded the Cleveland Hospital Obstetric Society and was active in similar organizations in Ohio and other states. Among his various honors, he was made a fellow of the American Assoc. of Obstetricians. In addition to his work at St. Luke's, Skeel was professor of obstetrics at the Cleveland College of Physicians & Surgeons, which later merged with Western Reserve University.

**SLAVIC VILLAGE,** located on the southeast side of Cleveland, is primarily an East European neighborhood extending southward from Union Ave. to Harvard Ave. between I-77 and Broadway Ave. Formerly known as Warszawa, the neighborhood officially became Slavic Village on 28 Apr. 1978 through the efforts of Neighborhood Ventures, Inc., which was itself founded in Oct. 1977 as a grassroots renovation project. The village has 11,000 residents and has involved over 75 businesses in remodeling commercial portions of the old neighborhood. Slavic Village was begun by young Polish-Americans who had decided to return to the neighborhood and restore to it new life while emphasizing their ethnic heritage. Their design was to transform many of the dreary and deteriorated buildings along Fleet Ave. between E. 49th and E. 65th streets into a uniform Polish "Hylander" style of architecture. The design uses rough-hewn wood to give a rustic appearance to the building facades.

Although the area was primarily Polish-American and Czech-American, sponsors decided to call the nongovernmental project Slavic Village in order to attract other ethnic groups to the area. Their goal was to encourage and inspire residents in the Polish Warszawa neighborhood to begin fixing and painting their homes and businesses as part of a general neighborhood-improvement plan. The Neighborhood Ventures, Inc., program was started by Teddy and Donna Sliwinski and architect Kaszimier Wieclaw. The project received no city or federal government monies. Instead, it has been funded by private investments and donations, including a $1,000 donation from the Cleveland Society of Poles and a $3,800 grant from the Ohio Arts Council for the creation of murals depicting Polish and Bohemian life. Initial renovation began with 8 buildings along Fleet Ave. between E. 59th St. and E. 65th St. to ST. STANISLAUS CHURCH. By 1980, 31 buildings had been renovated in the chalet-like style. The nonprofit Slavic Village Assoc. (inc. July 1978) helped to preserve residential and commercial buildings constructed at the beginning of the century by sponsoring an annual Harvest Festival, the proceeds of which were donated to the building fund. The recession of the early 1980s, coupled with high unemployment, slowed the renovation's progress. Also, organizers have had to contend with another major drawback: the pollution from nearby steel mills and other industrial plants west of the area results in the area's having the dirtiest air in the city. Crime has also been a problem to the area's development. Yet, the prohibitively high cost of suburban housing has attracted young couples to the area to buy and renovate many older single- and 2-family homes.

**SLOVAKS.** At one time in the early 1900s, Cleveland was reputedly the city with the largest number of Slovaks in the world. As of 1970, an estimated 48,000 persons of Slovak birth or ancestry resided in the Greater Cleveland community, making Slovaks one of the city's major immigrant groups. However, it is impossible to deduce the exact number of Slovaks resident in the city at any one time, since, except for a brief period during WORLD WAR II, the Slovak state has not existed in modern times. Slovak immigrants were therefore listed as Austrian or Hungarian prior to WORLD WAR I or as Czechoslovakian following the war. This lack of official identity forms, perhaps, the main aspect of the local community's history; one of its chief goals has been the recognition of its ethnic distinctiveness as well as of its cultural contributions. Immigration to Cleveland began in the late 1870s, at which time the city's immigrant officer began counting a large number of "Slavonians" (perhaps Slovaks and SLOVENES) arriving in the city. It is estimated that there were 35,000 Slovaks in the city by 1918. The first area of settlement was on E. 9th St. near the CUYAHOGA RIVER. As numbers increased, some Slovaks began to reside along Buckeye Rd. and parallel streets from about E. 78th St. to Woodhill Rd. Some of these came to live near their place of employment, the NEWBURGH plant of American Steel & Wire. Other Slovaks moved to the west side, and even farther to LAKEWOOD. There, in the "Birdtown" area (Quail, Thrush, Plover streets), they lived near the Union Carbide Co., then the NATL. CARBON CO., where they worked.

Like many other ethnic groups, Slovaks established churches once the population in various neighborhoods had grown large enough to support them. The first Catholic Slovak parish was ST. LADISLAS (1889), located on E. 92nd St. In 1974, a new St. Ladislas was built in WESTLAKE, but it was not composed exclusively of families of Slovak descent. In 1892, Slovak Lutherans organized their first Cleveland and third U.S. congregation, HOLY TRINITY. The church was originally located at 2506 E. 20th St.; in 1959, a new parish was established in PARMA, where in the 1980s a small minority of the members were of Slovak ancestry. Eventually, Slovaks founded some dozen churches—Catholic, Lutheran, and Calvinist. Among those still in existence in the 1980s were the Catholic parishes of NATIVITY of the Blessed Virgin Mary, ST. WENDELIN, St. Benedict, and SS. CYRIL & METHODIUS. Protestant churches included SS. PETER & PAUL LUTHERAN in LAKEWOOD, Holy Trinity Lutheran, Pentecost Evangelical Lutheran, Gethsemane Lutheran, and Dr. Martin Luther Evangelical Lutheran. By this time, most of the Protestant churches were located in the city's western suburbs, reflecting the move of the population to those areas.

In addition to individual churches, several major Catholic religious orders in Cleveland have been closely associated with the Slovak community. The most prominent have been the Benedictines. In 1922, the dependent priory of St. Andrew was created from the Benedictine Abbey of St. Procopius in Lisle, Ill. It eventually became the first and only Slovak abbey in the U.S. In 1922, these Slovak Benedictines also assumed pastoral responsibility for St. Andrew (Svorad) parish on Superior Ave. and E. 51st St. In 1927, the Benedictines established a high school that was attended mostly by Slovak young men. In 1986, Benedictine High School was located on Dr. Martin Luther King Blvd. and Lamontier Ave. and was staffed by the Benedictines. The Benedictines also staffed Nativity of the Blessed Virgin Parish in 1986 and have served as chaplains at the Ladies' Assoc. retirement home, VILLA SANCTA ANNA. In 1929, the Benedictines assumed publication of the monthly religious magazine *Ave Maria*. In the mid-1930s, a delegation from the Slovak cultural institution Matica Slovenska visited Cleveland; they later presented a large number of publications to ST. ANDREW'S ABBEY. These became part of the large library of the Cleveland branch of today's Slovak Institute, a resource center for the study of Slovak culture and literature; the institute was first founded in

Cleveland in 1952, and then in 1963 became affiliated with a newly established one in Rome. The institute publishes a bimonthly, *Most* (The Bridge, 1955- ); it and *Ave Maria* are 2 of 3 publications for Slovaks that remain of some 30 once printed in Cleveland. Notable among the early Slovak publishers in Cleveland was JAN PANKUCH.

Slovak fraternal-benefit societies were established as the community grew. Two not only were established in Cleveland but also became national in scope, with the city serving as headquarters for the organizations. In 1890, Rev. STEPHAN FURDEK of Cleveland proposed a union among various independent fraternals. In September of that year, the FIRST CATHOLIC SLOVAK UNION, originally only for men, was founded at a meeting of 8 such societies from 4 states. Then there were 400 members; in the 1980s, membership had grown to over 79,000. The national offices were still in Cleveland. In 1891, Rev. Furdek established a weekly newspaper for this union called *Jednota* (Union); in 1911, the union relocated its printery to Middletown, Pa., from where it continues publication of *Jednota* in an English-Slovak version. The second such Cleveland organization was in response to the need to insure women and children. In Aug. 1892, delegates of various independent societies from 4 states founded the FIRST CATHOLIC SLOVAK LADIES UNION (now ASSOC.). Then there were fewer than 100 members; in the 1980s, membership was over 90,000. Its national offices have remained in the Cleveland area. Since their beginnings, both unions have supported Slovaks with more than insurance. The Slovak Ladies Union established Villa Sancta Anna, a retirement home on Chagrin Blvd., in 1960 and annually subsidized it with $100,000. A third national Slovak organization founded in Cleveland that continued to have national and even international importance is the Slovak League of America, an umbrella group of all major Slovak societies. In the early years of this century, Slovaks in Austria-Hungary were the object of laws and regulations that discriminated against the use of their language and attempted to stifle their native culture. In response, there was a call among Slovaks in America for an All-American Slovak Congress, the first of its kind. It was held 26 May 1907 in GRAYS ARMORY, with some 7,000 participants. Rev. Furdek presided over this meeting and became the first president of the Slovak League formed at this gathering.

As the early Slovak immigrants became assimilated into American society, they began to use the American political process to achieve some of their national or ethnic goals. As early as 1893, Slovaks formed a Republican Club. In 1902, Slovaks, along with other Slavic groups and Romanians, successfully opposed the erection of a statue in PUBLIC SQUARE of Louis Kossuth, who was considered an enemy of the non-Magyar nationalities in Austria-Hungary. The statue was subsequently erected in UNIVERSITY CIRCLE (see KOSSUTH MONUMENT). In 1911 and 1914, Slovaks again rallied the other groups to protest visits of officials from Austria-Hungary. With the outbreak of World War I, Cleveland Slovaks became more concerned with the fate of Slovaks in Austria-Hungary. On 22 Oct. 1915, in the BOHEMIAN NATL. HALL on Broadway, the Cleveland Agreement was signed by the Slovak League for U.S. Slovaks and the Bohemian Natl. Alliance for U.S. Czechs. This agreement called for the formation of a federal state of Czechs and Slovaks, Czechoslovakia. On 15 June 1918, the Cleveland branches of the Slovak and Czech groups that had signed the agreement hosted Thos. G. Masaryk, the first president of Czechoslovakia after World War I, just 2 weeks after he had helped realize the Pittsburgh Agreement that even more affirmed the spirit of the Cleveland Agreement. During the 1920s and 1930s, Cleveland Slovaks joined other Slovaks in agitating for the realization of the Pittsburgh Agreement; many Slovaks felt that the Czechs had not fully shared power with the Slovaks in the new Czechoslovak state.

The intense national consciousness of Cleveland Slovaks was also reflected in their artistic and cultural activities. Gen. Milan Rastislav Stefanik, an aviator and national hero during World War I, served as the focal point for such activity. In 1921, the Stefanik Circle was formed not only to promote Slovak dramatic art and entertainment but also to raise funds for the erection of a statue to Stefanik, who had been killed in an airplane crash in 1919; this group still had some 70 active members in the 1950s and staged several productions in the mid-1970s. In June 1924, the statue, by the noted Slovak sculptor Frico Motoska, was unveiled at a site in WADE PARK at the intersection of Dr. Martin Luther King Blvd. and East Blvd. Other drama and choral societies were established throughout the history of the community. One of the earliest was Krivan, founded in Cleveland in 1906 by Dr. Miloslav Francisci. Dr. Francisci, who was the son of a famous Slovak writer, emigrated to Cleveland in 1886. Besides being director of Krivan, he composed a number of dramas and operettas in Slovak. Besides Krivan and the Stefanik Circle, there were 5 other societies in Cleveland affiliated with Catholic or Lutheran parishes. In 1986, none remained active.

During the 1920s and 1930s, Slovak immigration decreased significantly. After World War II and even the many events of 1968 in Czechoslovakia, such immigration to Cleveland was negligible. By the 1980s, most individuals of Slovak ancestry in Cleveland had moved to the suburbs of Parma, BEDFORD, or GARFIELD HTS. Despite the aging of the 1st-generation population and its general dispersal, an annual Slovak Festival was still being held on Labor Day in the 1980s. In 1983, in recognition of the continuing Slovak presence and spirit in the Cleveland area, a Slovak language-and-culture lectureship was created at JOHN CARROLL UNIVERSITY and subsidized by a Fulbright agency, the Council for the Internatl. Exchange of Scholars. It may well be that such continuing activity in the face of a dearth of new immigrants reflects the Slovak community's persistent longing to assure the establishment of its ethnic distinctiveness, a goal that has been the focal point of much of their local activity in the past 100 years.

Gerald Sabo
John Carroll University

Barton, Josef J., *Peasants and Strangers* (1975).
Ledbetter, Eleanor, *The Slovaks of Cleveland* (1919).
Megles, Susi; Stolarik, Mark; and Tybor, Martina, *Slovak Americans and Their Communities of Cleveland* (1978).

The **SLOVENE HOME FOR THE AGED,** 18621 Neff Rd., is a nursing home for elderly Slovenian-Americans. Built in 1962, it was the second nursing facility in the U.S. built to serve the Slovenian-American community; the first was in California. Organizational efforts to establish the home began in the late 1950s. By June 1958, a board of directors had been organized with Blas Novak as president. Construction of the home began with groundbreaking ceremonies on 30 June 1962. The original structure contained 12 double rooms, giving the home the capacity to care for 24 residents. An addition in 1971 more than tripled its capacity. This $600,000, 2-story addition contained 31 double rooms and facilities for physical and occupational therapy. In Oct. 1980 the Slovene Home for the Aged had 87 residents and employed 42 nursing assistants.

**SLOVENES.** The Slovenes, a South Slav people whose homeland today is the northwestern part of Yugoslavia, began to settle in Cleveland in the 1880s. Immigration from Slovenia to Cleveland was heaviest in the periods 1890–1914, 1919–24, and 1949–60. Prior to WORLD WAR II, the principal cause for emigration from Slovenia was a desire for economic betterment. The economically most underdeveloped rural areas of Slovenia provided most of the emigrants. The Slovenes who came to Cleveland after World War II were mainly political refugees and included a larger proportion of well-educated and professional individuals than had been part of the earlier waves of immigrants, who had come from a peasant or agricultural background. The community was augmented by the arrival of the U.S.-born generations, and also by immigration from Slovene settlements elsewhere in the U.S. Cleveland became a magnet for Slovenes because of its rapidly expanding industrial base, which required large numbers of unskilled and semiskilled laborers. Word of Cleveland and its attractiveness spread rapidly in the homeland through family correspondence, while Slovenes elsewhere in the U.S. learned of the city through either family ties or the rapidly expanding network of Slovene-language newspapers. Census data for 1910 listed 14,332 Slovenes in Cleveland, making it at the time the 3d-largest Slovene city in the world. The 1970 census listed 46,000 Slovenes in the Cleveland metropolitan area as being foreign-born or of mixed parentage. By the early 1900s, Cleveland attained the status of being the largest Slovene settlement in the U.S.; it retained this status into the 1980s.

The first Slovenes to arrive in Cleveland settled in the NEWBURGH area of southeast Cleveland. They found employment in the nearby steel industry. By the later 1880s and early 1890s, a much larger Slovene community began to form along St. Clair Ave., and at its greatest extent in the 1920s and 1930s, it reached from E. 30th to E. 79th St., north to the lake, and south to Superior Ave., and even beyond. By the early 1900s, another sizable Slovene community emerged in the COLLINWOOD area of northeastern Cleveland and into EUCLID. Relatively few Slovenes settled on the west side of Cleveland. Two small communities did develop, however, one in the WEST PARK area and the other in the Denison neighborhood. All of these Slovene settlements were still identifiable in the 1980s, although they were in various stages of decline, as the U.S.-born generations had both largely assimilated and also moved into adjacent, more affluent suburbs. By the 1980s, the Lake County cities east of Cleveland and Euclid had sizable Slovene populations, as did MAPLE HTS. and GARFIELD HTS.

As ever-larger numbers of Slovenes settled in the Newburgh, St. Clair, and Collinwood areas between the 1880s and early 1900s, a sense of community began to develop. There is no evidence to indicate that these early arrivals, who were predominantly young males, considered themselves permanent residents of the city. There was no interest in Americanization, or in acquiring citizenship. the first institutions to emerge were responses to immediate needs. Enterprising individuals began to open taverns, which soon became social centers, with the owners assuming a prominent social and economic role among their fellow countrymen and often expanding into other business ventures. Over time, some of the immigrants sent for wives and children and fiancees; family units began to appear. Most of the Slovene immigrants came from a strongly Roman Catholic religious tradition. One of their earliest desires was to have their spiritual needs attended to by Slovene-speaking priests. This attitude led to the emergence of Slovene national priests. ST. VITUS parish, serving the St. Clair community, was organized in 1893; St. Lawrence parish appeared in 1901 in the Newburgh area, while St. Mary parish

was founded in Collinwood in 1906. All three remained national parishes into the 1980s. Slovenes in Euclid were inclined to attend St. Christine parish. Each of the Slovene national parishes also established a parochial school, although by the 1980s the St. Lawrence school had been closed. Other organizations common to a Roman Catholic parish were also established.

The early Slovene immigrants felt a need for organized economic self-protection against illness, injury, and death. That prompted them to form a broad range of mutual insurance societies, some local and short-lived, others eventually affiliating into national or statewide Slovene fraternal insurance societies. Among Cleveland Slovenes, the first such organization was known as MARIJIN SPOLEK (Society of Mary) and appeared ca. 1890; in 1894 it became a branch of a national Slovene fraternal. Many of these societies also promoted organized singing, literary, and other cultural activities. By the later 1890s, more and more new organizations were being formed, as were business ventures. On 3 June 1897, the Slovenski Sokol (Slovenian Sokol) was formed; in addition to gymnastics, it promoted literary and musical activity among its members. Its immediate precursor was a singing club. In all, Cleveland Slovenes have founded more than 40 singing groups alone during their presence in Cleveland. In 1899, the first Slovene-language newspaper to be printed in Cleveland appeared. *Narodna Beseda* (National Word) survived only briefly, but it was followed by a number of successors. *AMERISKA DOMOVINA* (The American Home), still published twice weekly in the 1980s, could trace its history to the early 1900s. Also significant for the Cleveland community was *ENAKOPRAVNOST* (Equality), a liberal newspaper that appeared from 1918–57 and was in constant ideological conflict with the conservative and Catholic-oriented *Ameriska Domovina*. The formation of national parishes, mutual insurance societies, singing and drama clubs, newspapers, and scores of businesses by the early 1900s indicated that for a large number of the Cleveland Slovenes, a return to the homeland was increasingly unlikely. Most now had a new homeland. The newspaper that succeeded *Narodna Beseda* in Nov. 1899 significantly was titled *Nova Domovina* (New Homeland). Another confirmation of this ever-stronger commitment to the U.S. was acquisition of U.S. citizenship. It is estimated that by 1912, about 3,000 Cleveland Slovenes were already citizens, and another 6,000 could meet the requirements. Acquisition of citizenship surged especially during WORLD WAR I (1914–18) and the 1920s.

Already by 1914, a basic and permanent ideological cleavage had emerged within the Slovene community, both in Cleveland and in other major settlements. Reduced to essentials, this cleavage had religiously oriented Slovenes on one side, buttressed by the Slovene-American Catholic clergy, while liberal, "freethinking," and socialist Slovenes were on the other side. In the Cleveland community, this cleavage resulted in the formation of parallel sets of institutions. Many of the singing societies, for example, comprised in the main Slovenes from one or the other side of the community, and this differentiation applied as well to the audience. The Lira singing society, formed in 1912, appealed primarily to Catholic Slovenes resident in the St. Clair community, for example, while the ZARJA SINGING SOCIETY was founded in 1916 under the sponsorship of a socialist club. There were many exceptions to this pattern, of course, but it is not possible to understand the history of the Cleveland Slovene community without recognition of this ideological separation.

The onset of World War I in 1914 effectively stopped immigration to Cleveland from Slovenia. The community continued to grow rapidly, the increase coming primarily from the expanding U.S.-born generation, but also from the arrival of Slovenes from other parts of the country. The fact that Slovenia, as a part of Austria-Hungary, was involved in the war from the beginning intensified interest in foreign affairs within the community, and that increased with direct U.S. involvement in 1917. The war years seem to have been a watershed for many of the immigrants, as they came fully to realize the permanence of their commitment to America. One result was an intensification of activity within the Cleveland Slovene community itself. Among the goals expressed by community leaders in the pre-World War I period was that of building Natl. Homes, which would be centers of social and cultural life in the Cleveland Slovene settlements. Efforts began in 1903 but did not succeed until 1919, when 4 such homes were dedicated. The largest, the SLOVENIAN NATL. HOME at 6417 St. Clair Ave., with a seating capacity of more than 1,000, was constructed in 1924. Financed through the sale of shares to Slovene organizations and individuals, operated by boards of trustees elected by the shareholders, the Natl. Homes served as anchors in the settlements, in company with the Roman Catholic national parishes. By the 1940s, each of the major Cleveland and suburban settlements had its own Natl. Home, and 8 such homes continued to exist in the city in the 1980s.

The appearance of the Natl. Homes was a seminal event for the Cleveland Slovene community. Each of these facilities, in fact, became a social and cultural center. Concerts, plays, dances, and banquets were regular features, and never more so than during the 1920s and 1930s. A large number of singing societies were formed, and they became permanent fixtures in the community. Following Zarja (1916) came Jadran (1920) and GLASBENA MATICA (1930), to name but 3 of the most prominent from that era that still flourished in the 1980s. Full-scale opera productions were mounted regularly from the later 1920s until the 1950s; among the many productions, for example, was Verdi's *La Traviata* in Slovene translation. The IVAN CANKAR DRAMATIC SOCIETY was founded in 1919 and remained active until the 1950s. Also appearing in 1919 was the Lilija Dramatic Society, which remained active into the 1980s, thanks to the participation of Slovenes who emigrated to Cleveland after World War II, and their U.S.-born children.

The period between the world wars saw the arrival of a professional class in the Slovene community, with attorneys and physicians, including dentists, especially prominent. During these years, some Slovenes began to be prominent in professional sports, especially baseball and boxing, while others launched successful political careers. Most conspicuous was Frank J. Lausche, who served as mayor of Cleveland, governor of Ohio, and U.S. senator, among other public offices. Frank Yankovic gained national recognition in the 1950s as a polka-band leader; known as the "Polka King," he was awarded a Grammy for his recordings of polka music in 1986 (see POLKAS). The Cleveland Slovene community provided a substantial role for women to express themselves from a very early period. They were admitted to membership in the mutual insurance societies, as well as the singing and drama societies. Cleveland Slovene women established their own society, the PROGRESSIVE SLOVENE WOMEN OF AMERICA, in 1934. Catholic-oriented women generally affiliated with the Slovene Women's Union, founded in the 1920s and based in Joliet, Ill.

World War II affected the Slovenes in 2 major ways. First, many Slovenes served in the armed forces, and a number were killed or wounded. The Axis occupation of Yugoslavia and thereby Slovenia was followed by the rise in the original homeland of rival resistance groups. One, the Partisans, was controlled by the Communist party under Josip Broz Tito. The other was Catholic and anti-Communist. Cleveland Slovenes divided sharply over which of these resistance groups to support. Some opted for the Partisans; they were influenced by Louis Adamic, a nationally prominent Slovene-American writer of the 1930s and 1940s. These Slovenes organized material and moral support for the Partisans and continued their efforts into the postwar years, and indeed into the 1980s. One result of these efforts was the eventual establishment in Cleveland of an official Yugoslav consulate, which has always been led by an ethnic Slovene.

Catholic-oriented Cleveland Slovenes largely distanced themselves from the pro-Partisan Slovenes and eventually found reinforcement for their views with the arrival in the U.S. of several thousand Slovene political refugees. Many of these newer immigrants found their way to Cleveland. As a rule, they were better educated than their predecessors, and politically very conscious. Although accepted by most of the Catholic community, they were viewed with suspicion and hostility by the liberal, or "progressive," wing of the Slovenes. These newest arrivals soon became active in the cultural life of the community and provided reinvigoration for it. In the 1950s they founded the Korotan Singing Society and the Kres Folklore Dance Group. In the later 1970s, their U.S.-born offspring established the Fantje Na Vasi men's chorus and were the backbone of the Lilija Dramatic Society. At St. Vitus and St. Mary parishes, Saturday Slovene-language schools remained active into the 1980s. Since the 1960s, the largest single project of the Cleveland Slovene community has been the SLOVENE HOME FOR THE AGED, a 150-bed skilled-nursing facility located on Neff Rd. in northeastern Cleveland. Opened in 1962 as a rest home with 24 beds, the home has since been expanded twice. Funds for construction came in the form of voluntary donations from the community.

By the 1980s, the Slovene community in the Cleveland area numbered well over 50,000, although many of these were no longer ethnically conscious. Yet the community vigorously continued to support literally hundreds of organizations that reflected their ethnic heritage and traditions. The *Ameriska Domovina* is unique in Cleveland as an ethnic newspaper still published twice weekly; the daily radio programs of Tony Petkovsek, begun in 1961, retain a substantial audience; concerts and other cultural performances still commonly fill the auditoriums of the Natl. Homes. While use of the Slovene language has all but disappeared in large parts of the community, there seems little doubt that Slovenes in Cleveland will remain a coherent entity for decades to come.

Rudolph M. Susel
American Home Publishing Co.

The **SLOVENIAN AMERICAN NATIONAL COUNCIL** (Slovenski Ameriski Narodni Svet) attempted to unite Americans of Slovenian heritage to assist the occupied homeland during WORLD WAR II. In 1941, the Slovene lands were occupied by German and Italian forces. Cleveland's Slovenian population had shown active concern for their homeland's fate in the previous war by forming groups such as the Slovenian Republican Alliance and sending messages to leaders in Washington. Leaders from Slovenian-American fraternal societies organized under the Yugoslav Relief Committee to collect funds for shipments of food, clothing, and medicine. Many felt that a stronger effort was necessary, and on 5 Dec. 1942, the Slovenian Natl. Congress convened in the SLOVENIAN NATL. HOME on St.

Clair Ave., with 528 representatives from organizations across the nation. It was the largest show of Slovenian-American solidarity ever witnessed. Members were urged to put their differences aside and work together for the welfare of the Slovenian nation. They formed the Slovenian American Natl. Council to develop activities and to work for the liberation of Slovenian territories and their union as a state within a free, federated Yugoslavia. Author Louis Adamic was made honorary president, with Clevelanders Janko Rogelj and Rt. Rev. John Oman among the executive board members. Telegrams were sent to Pres. Roosevelt, Cleveland mayor Frank J. Lausche, and other officials in Washington and Europe.

SANC tried to remain politically neutral, but eventually had to decide which liberation faction to support. Adamic argued for the backing of Titoist partisan forces, and many conservative and Catholic members withdrew from the council. Adamic's influence extended into the White House, and his involvement with SANC and other Yugoslav-American organizations may have had some effect on the U.S. government's eventual recognition of Tito. SANC worked with Croatian and Serbian groups to cooperate with larger entities such as the American Committee for Yugoslav Relief and the United Committee of South Slavic Americans. Over 100 SANC branches were established in the U.S. and Canada to collect funds. Fraternal and cultural societies also helped. Periodic conventions were held, with resolutions passed on issues such as civil rights for Slovenian minorities in Italy and Austria. In the postwar years, SANC and similar committees were criticized for their direct dealings with a Communist government. Matt Cvetich, a SANC member from Pittsburgh, active in other Slavic-American organizations, revealed himself as an FBI informant. In 1948, several relief groups, including SANC, were cited by the House Committee on Un-American Activities. In Slovenia, SANC's efforts were met with appreciation. Over $1 million in cash, food, clothing, and medical supplies and equipment was distributed, with the Ljubljana Children's Hospital as the primary recipient. In its final years, SANC was run mostly by Clevelanders from an office in the Natl. Home complex. Frank Cesen was the last president, with John Pollock as secretary. Funds were disbursed by 1951, and the council formally disbanded in 1953.

The **SLOVENIAN NATIONAL HOME** on St. Clair Ave. is the largest and most significant social and cultural center for local Slovenian-Americans. Ideas for a national hall based in the St. Clair community to accommodate meetings, rehearsals, and gatherings had been discussed as early as 1903, when the Slovenian sokols sought to build a gymnasium and library. The opening of Knaus' Hall that year, followed by other privately owned halls, slowed the plans for a publicly held center for more than a decade. Interest was renewed in 1914 when 105 delegates from 42 lodges and organizations met to undertake the sales of $10 shares. By 1916, $10,000 had been collected; a second conference established bylaws and a board presided over by FRANK J. KERN. In 1918, the board of directors purchased the Diemer estate on St. Clair between E. 64th St. and Addison Rd. for $45,000. Member societies of the Club of Associations then began meeting in the Italianate Victorian mansion. Other Slovenian neighborhoods were also planning their own halls, and 2 opened in 1919 in EUCLID and COLLINWOOD. Efforts to build a St. Clair hall continued with contests and shares sold door to door. The Cleveland lodges of the Slovenian Natl. Benefit Society bought over ¼ of the shares. The cornerstone was laid in 1923, and on 1 Mar. 1924, the Slovenian Natl. Home was opened with

a parade and 50 speakers, including Mayor CLAYTON C. TOWNES. The final cost was $106,240.

The new building, constructed around the old residence, could handle large and small affairs simultaneously in 2 auditoriums and several meeting rooms. The brick facade was designed in a commercial vernacular style with a flat cornice and simple classical ornamentation in white terra cotta. The arched central doorway, framed by Tuscan columns supporting an entablature, leads to the original structure and stairs to 2d-floor offices. Seven storefronts line the facade. The main auditorium is entered right of center through a lobby with marble details. The lobby stairs continue to the Slovenian Natl. Library on the mezzanine level, and the sokol gymnasium and a meeting room on the 2d floor. Up to 1,000 can be seated on the main floor of the hall, and another 324 in the balcony. The large proscenium stage is 65 ft. high and can accommodate more than 100 performers. The Artcraft Co. painted classical decorations for the interior. Illustrator Maksim Gaspari from Slovenia sent an allegorical depiction of Mother Slovenia holding court before figures representing the region's literary greats; Shirley Braithwaite transferred this sketch onto the fire curtain in 1941. Eleven offices provided space for doctors, lawyers, and other neighborhood professionals. A spacious, skylit studio apartment was home, successively, to the Bukovnik photo studio, painter Henry Prusheck and his Yugoslav School of Modern Art, the Slovenian Natl. Museum, and musical director Anton Schubel.

The home was the scene of numerous social events, such as weddings, banquets, lectures, performances, and weekend dances. Nearly 100 fraternal, political, social, cultural, and sports societies, mostly Slovenian-American, have used the facility. These have included the PROGRESSIVE SLOVENE WOMEN OF AMERICA, the SLOVENIAN AMERICAN NATL. COUNCIL, the ZARJA SINGING SOCIETY, GLASBENA MATICA, and the IVAN CANKAR DRAMATIC SOCIETY. Activities at the home were revitalized in the 1960s with groups such as the Korotan singers and Kres dancers, established by a new generation of young Slovenian immigrants. The children of older immigrants returned to the hall for meetings and special occasions such as debutante balls. Thanksgiving Day polka festivals attracted upward of 2,000 each year. The hall was also the site of political rallies and visits by various local and state candidates.

Dolgan, Robert, *50 Year History of the Slovenian National Home* (1974).

**SMALL AND ROWLEY** was an architectural partnership that specialized in traditional Colonial and English architecture in the 1920s. Although the firm existed only from 1921–28, and both partners pursued individual careers, they are inseparably linked because of their work for M. J. and O. P. VAN SWERINGEN. Philip Lindsley Small (18 July 1890–18 May 1963) was born in Washington, D.C., and raised in Springfield, Ohio. He moved to Cleveland in 1904, was educated at Adelbert College of Western Reserve University, and graduated from MIT in 1915. He married Grace Hatch on 31 Dec. 1920. He opened his first office in Cleveland the same year. Chas. Bacon Rowley (1890–17 Dec. 1984) was born in Springfield, Ohio, where Rowley and Small met as children, and attended high school in Jackson, Mich. He also attended MIT, graduating in 1912. Rowley married his wife, Elizabeth, on 14 Feb. 1914. He came to Cleveland in 1920, and the firm of Small & Rowley was formed in 1921.

Small & Rowley designed a group of 5 demonstration homes for the Van Sweringens' SHAKER HTS. development in 1924. During the partnership, they completed more than 40 Georgian- and Tudor-style homes, as well as residences for the Van Sweringens on S. Park Blvd. and in HUNTING VALLEY (see DAISY HILL). They also planned the CLEVELAND PLAY HOUSE (1926-27) on E. 86th St. and created the plan for SHAKER SQUARE (1927-29), as well as completed the MORELAND Cts. Apts. At its height, the firm employed more than 50 people. Small and Rowley separated in 1928, and Small formed the new firm of Philip Small & Associates. He worked almost exclusively for the Van Sweringens at first, designing interiors for Higbee's Dept. Store, additional work on the Terminal group, the Country Club of Pepper Pike, and railroad projects. He did the planning and design for JOHN CARROLL UNIVERSITY. In 1934, Small was associated with Walker & Weeks on the design of the U.S. Post Office in the Terminal Group. In 1936 the firm became Small, Smith & Reeb, and in 1956 Small, Smith, Reeb & Draz. The firm designed the KARAMU HOUSE Theater and Community Service Bldg. (1949-59) and several buildings for WRU and Case School, including the science center, the student activities building, 2 dormitories, the physics building, and the Freiberger Library. Rowley formed the firm of Chas. Bacon Rowley & Associates in 1928. He designed public schools for BEDFORD, the Shaker Hts. Public Library, and the MAYFIELD COUNTRY CLUB, and 4 buildings for Kenyon College. During the Depression, in 1932, he designed experimental houses of steel sheathed with porcelain enamel shingles. After WORLD WAR II, the firm became Rowley, Payer, Huffman & Caldwell. Rowley retired in 1961 and served as consulting architect for TRUE TEMPER until 1968. He died in Harwichport, Mass.

**SMETONA, ANTANAS** (10 Aug. 1874–9 Jan. 1944), came to Cleveland in Apr. 1942 as the exiled president of Lithuania. He lived "a quiet and unostentatious life" in Cleveland but continued to travel to various Lithuanian communities throughout the U.S. and to write and speak on behalf of his Soviet-controlled homeland. Born of peasant parents in Uzulenents, Smetona became an ardent promoter of Lithuanian nationalism as a youth. His zeal for the nationalist cause earned him expulsion from college and later from law school in St. Petersburg, where he was also jailed. Upon his release from prison, he settled in Vilna, where he worked in a bank and later edited a small periodical.

Persisting in his support for Lithuanian freedom, Smetona was one of 3 ministers chosen to head the provisional government after Russia renounced its claim to the country in 1918, and he served as president of the country from 1919-22; he was again elected president in 1926 and was reelected in 1930. He and his wife were forced to flee the country on 15 June 1940, during the Soviet invasion. They escaped first to Germany, then to Switzerland, and traveled to other countries before arriving in the U.S. in Mar. 1941. Smetona was greeted by Pres. Franklin D. Roosevelt upon his arrival in the U.S. In Cleveland, Smetona and his wife, Sophie, lived in an attic suite above the apartment of their son, Julius, a grinder for the Standard Tool Co. Smetona used the home at 11596 Ablewhite Ave. as the base for his political operations until his death in a house fire.

Cadzow, John F., *Lithuanian Americans and Their Communities of Cleveland*, (1978).

**SMITH, ALBERT KELVIN** (5 Jan. 1899–15 Nov. 1984), was a founder of the LUBRIZOL CORP. and a philanthropist whose charity benefited a number of local musical, educational, health, and social-service agencies. Smith was born in Cleveland, the youngest son of ALBERT W. SMITH,

chairman of the chemical engineering and mining engineering departments at Case School of Applied Science; the elder Smith, an associate of HERBERT DOW, helped found the Dow Chemical Co. Kelvin shared his father's interest in chemistry. After graduation from East High School in 1916, he entered Dartmouth College, graduating with a bachelor's degree in physics in 1920. He then entered Case, receiving a bachelor's degree in chemical engineering in 1922. He spent the next 4 years working as a chemist for Dow before becoming research director of France Mfg., and later a chemical engineer for the McGean Chemical Co. He married Eleanor Armstrong in 1923.

In 1928, Smith and his brothers KENT H. and Vincent K. (4 June 1896–9 Mar. 1980) joined with Alex Nason to form the Graphite Oil Prods. Co., the predecessor to Lubrizol. Smith became a leading stockholder and was also the company's director of research. He founded Cleveland Industrial Research, Inc., in 1935 and served as its president until 1945. He became president of Lubrizol in 1951, serving until retiring in 1962. During that time, the company established manufacturing subsidiaries in 5 foreign nations, expanded its domestic operations, became a publicly owned company, and more than doubled its sales and earnings. Smith also served as the chairman of the board of directors from 1964–66 and was a director of the company until Apr. 1971.

Smith amassed a fortune, much of which he donated to institutions and agencies in whose works he had an interest. He endowed a chair for the music director of the CLEVELAND ORCHESTRA, was a major contributor to the development and construction of Blossom Music Ctr., and was also a trustee of the MUSICAL ARTS ASSOC. He was a trustee of Case Institute of Technology, where he funded the Albert W. Smith Merit Scholarships, and of Lake Erie College, where he helped establish an equestrian program. He endowed a professorship in physics at Dartmouth and, with his brothers, established a professorship in chemistry there. Smith College, his wife's alma mater, also received his support. Smith gave to the CLEVELAND SOCIETY FOR THE BLIND Sight Ctr., the CLEVELAND CLINIC FOUNDATION, and the GARDEN CTR. OF GREATER CLEVELAND, and served as a trustee of UNIVERSITY HOSPITALS and the Cleveland Health Museum. In 1977 he established the Sea Research Foundation, Inc., to acquire and operate 2 aquariums in Niagara Falls, N.Y., and Mystic, Conn.; he had helped finance construction of each. Smith served as an officer in the Ohio Mfrs. Assoc. and the Chemical Industrial Council of Ohio, and held memberships in the American Chemical Society and the Franklin Institute.

Smalheer, Calvin V., *The Story of Lubrizol* (1972).

**SMITH, ALBERT W.** (4 Oct. 1862–4 Mar. 1927), was a chemist, a professor at the Case Institute of Technology, and one of the founders of the Dow Chemical Co. Smith was born in Newark, Ohio, the son of carpenter and contractor Geo. H. and Mary Smith. He graduated from the University of Michigan in 1885 with a degree in chemistry; he received a B.S. degree from the Case School of Applied Science in 1887 and his Ph.D. in 1891 from the University of Zurich. Smith returned from Europe to join the faculty of Case, serving as professor of metallurgy and chemistry there from 1891-1907, when he became head of the metallurgical engineering department. He served in that capacity until 1911, when he succeeded CHAS. F. MABERY as head of the chemistry department. Smith headed that department until his death. He gained a reputation as an informal but dedicated teacher who sometimes lent students money to enable them to remain in school.

As a student at Case, Smith became friends with another chemistry student, HERBERT DOW, whom he helped to establish the Dow Chemical Co. Smith provided not only his knowledge of chemistry but also part of the initial funding for the venture. He was one of the original directors of and served as a chemical consultant for the firm. Smith also helped establish the Midland Corp., a subsidiary of Dow, to explore the possibilities of developing products from the deep-well brines from which Dow produced bromine. At Midland, Smith developed processes for the manufacture of chloroform and carbon tetrachloride. Midland was eventually absorbed by Dow. During WORLD WAR I, Smith helped Dow and the war effort by developing the machinery needed to produce mustard gas in large quantities.

Smith clearly was interested in the practical applications of scientific knowledge; that interest extended to public affairs as well as business. Under Cleveland mayor NEWTON D. BAKER, Smith served on the city's water purification commission and was influential in having the west side water-filtration plant approved and built. Smith belonged to a number of professional societies. He was a member of the Franklin Institute, the American Chemical Society, the American Assoc. for the Advancement of Science, the Society for the Promotion of Engineering Education, the American Institute of Mining Engineers, the American Electro-Chemical Society, the American Institute of Chemical Engineers, and both the French and the English Society of Chemical Industry. He also served as the president of the Case Athletic Assoc. until 1900. Smith was married on 5 June 1890 to Mary Wilkinson. Their 3 sons were among the founders of the LUBRIZOL CORP.

Smalheer, Calvin V., *The Story of Lubrizol*, (1972).

**SMITH, ALLAN JR.** (1810–1890), was an American portrait and landscape painter. He was born in Dighton, Mass. He worked in Detroit for 6 years before moving to Cleveland in 1841, where he practiced for over 40 years. Smith embarked on his artistic career as a youth by copying prints and drawings. His first practical experience as a painter was working in the scene-painting department of the Bowery Theater. His formal academic training came while he was a student at the Natl. Academy. In 1835, Smith moved west to Detroit, where he worked for 6 years. In 1841, he moved to Cleveland. While there he painted some of his most famous portraits: Gov. Tod of Ohio, Gov. Fairchild of Wisconsin, and the presidents of Western Reserve and Kenyon colleges. He also painted Leonard Case, Jr.'s, formal portrait. In 1848, he won an Art Union Prize for his portrait entitled *Young Mechanic*. In 1883, Smith moved to Painesville. He later moved to Concord, Ohio, where he died.

**SMITH, CHARLES H.** (23 Nov. 1837–13 Aug. 1912), was a Cleveland attorney, merchant, banker, and volunteer Civil War officer. Smith was born in Taunton, Mass. He lived in Fall River, Mass. (1845–50), with his parents and then in Jamestown, N.Y. (1850–56), before moving to Cleveland in 1856, where he went into the furniture business. When the CIVIL WAR broke out, he enlisted in Co. A, SEVENTH OHIO VOLUNTEER INFANTRY, composed of the Cleveland Light Guard Zouave Co., of which he was a member. After 3 months' service, Smith returned to Cleveland and helped to recruit a company for 3 years' service as Co. G, 27th OVI. He was appointed sergeant on 27 July 1861 and orderly sergeant on 12 May 1862; and he was commissioned 2d lieutenant on 2 Nov. 1862 for meritorious conduct on 4 Oct. 1862, at the Battle of Corinth, Miss., in which he led a charge against the position of the 9th Texas Infantry, capturing its flag and color guard.

Smith was subsequently assigned to Co. A; he was commissioned 1st lieutenant on 9 May 1864 and captain on 3 Nov. 1864, being assigned to Co. K. His final promotion, to major, was dated 3 May 1865. He served in a variety of capacities on detached duty by special order. Smith was mustered out at Louisville, Ky., 11 July 1865 and was discharged at Camp Chase, Ohio, 20 July 1865. He received a law degree from Ohio State University in 1871, but did not practice. Instead, he spent 33 years in the grain trade. He also served as a director and treasurer of the Equity Savings & Loan Co. He married Louisa M. Johnson in Cleveland on 26 Nov. 1868. They raised 3 daughters and a son. He participated in the following organizations: Military Order of the Loyal Legion of the U.S.; Society of the Army of the Tennessee; Grand Army of the Republic; Fuller's Ohio Brigade (lifetime president); and the Masons. He died at his residence at 11803 Kinsman Rd., Cleveland, at the age of 74. He is buried in LAKE VIEW CEMETERY.

Chas. H. Smith Papers, WRHS.

Smith, Charles H., *The History of Fuller's Ohio Brigade, 1861–1865*, (1909).

**SMITH, DOROTHY** (26 Apr. 1892–30 Dec. 1976), was a prominent social worker in Cleveland and, later, Mentor, Ohio. Smith was born in Springfield, Mo. She attended Vassar College on a scholarship and entered the field of social work upon her graduation in 1914, assuming a position with the YWCA in Pawtucket, R.I. Named general secretary of the Pawtucket YWCA in 1916, she established vocational programs in nursing and child care and placed her organization in the forefront of the local war effort. Smith came to Cleveland in 1921 and a year later became the general secretary of the Cleveland YOUNG WOMEN'S CHRISTIAN ASSOCIATION. Under her guidance, the YWCA built a new headquarters, established a program to aid senior citizens, added recreation programs, and strongly supported Prohibition. Smith resigned her post on the eve of the Depression to enter the insurance business. During her 13 years in the insurance field, Smith served as an advisor to many programs instituted to assist people crippled by the Depression. WORLD WAR II and the resulting shortage of skilled adminstrators brought her back to the field of social work. In 1943 she accepted the job as an adult worker at the EAST END NEIGHBORHOOD HOUSE; she became director in 1944 and in the next 12 years led it to national prominence. She instituted various volunteer programs that allowed the settlement to cut its adminstrative costs by 40% and oversaw the construction of a new recreation building in 1947. Smith resigned as executive director in 1955 but continued to serve as an advisor to East End for 10 more years. During this period she also became active with the Mentor Community Fund, serving on its board of trustees from 1957–64. Smith spent her last 10 years in quiet retirement in Mentor.

East End Neighborhood House Records, WRHS.

**SMITH, GEORGE HORATIO** (1849–8 Apr. 1924), known principally as one of the collaborators in the design of the ARCADE, was an important Cleveland architect with an active practice from 1881–1918. Little is known of Smith's upbringing, training, family, and early career. He appeared on the Cleveland scene in 1882 with the design for Samuel Andrews's great Victorian Gothic baronial mansion (ANDREWS'S FOLLY). Immediately thereafter he designed the

Euclid Ave. mansion of CHAS. F. BRUSH (1884), which was nearly as pretentious. Both houses already showed a complete confidence in handling European styles. In 1890 Smith's Hickox Bldg. at E. 9th and Euclid (Bond Store and Natl. City Bank site) and the Arcade were both completed. From the similarities in the facade composition of the two buildings, it is assumed that Smith's responsibility in the collaboration on the Arcade was the design of the Superior and Euclid Ave. office buildings, and that JOHN EISEN-MANN planned the structural engineering for the interior arcade. After the success of the Arcade, Smith also designed the Colonial Arcade between Euclid and Prospect in 1898.

When the trustees of the Cleveland City Hospital Society decided to leave the old Marine Hospital in 1895, Smith was chosen as architect of Lakeside Hospital, which opened on the lakefront in 1898. Consisting of a group of separate administrative, ward, nurses' residence, and dispensary buildings, it was used until the hospital moved to UNIVERSITY CIRCLE in 1931. In 1900 Smith designed the Rose Bldg. on Prospect and E. 9th St.; in 1906–10 the new plant of the White Sewing Machine Co. (later White Motor) on St. Clair at E. 79th; and in 1908–11 the new Plain Dealer Bldg. on Superior at E. 6th St. (Cleveland Public Library Business & Science Annex) to harmonize with the Group Plan buildings. Smith retired in 1918. He died in Bethlehem, Pa., and was buried there.

**SMITH, HARRY CLAY** (28 Jan. 1863–10 Dec. 1941), one of the pioneers of the black press, was brought to Cleveland 2 years after his birth in Clarksburg, W.Va. Shortly after graduating from CENTRAL HIGH SCHOOL, he and 3 associates founded the *CLEVELAND GAZETTE* in 1883. Beginning as managing editor, Smith soon became the sole proprietor of the weekly newspaper, which he kept alive for the next 58 years. A disciple of MARCUS HANNA, Smith entered politics as a deputy state oil inspector from 1885–89. He was elected as a Republican to 3 terms in the Ohio general assembly, where he sponsored 2 significant laws benefiting the state's black population. The Ohio Civil Rights Law of 1894 provided for penalties against discrimination in public accommodations, while the Mob Violence Act of 1896 served as a model for antilynching laws subsequently passed in several states and introduced in the U.S Congress. Even out of office, Smith managed to make his presence felt in state politics. For years, he conducted a crusade to block the showing in Ohio of the classic but racist film *The Birth of a Nation*. When a miscegenation bill was proposed for Ohio, Smith personally led a delegation to Columbus to lobby for its defeat. His further efforts to win state office were less successful, however. Running for the Republican nomination for secretary of state in 1920, he defeated an attempt to remove his name from the ballot because of its similarity to that of another candidate, but lost the nomination nonetheless. Though he also lost bids for the Republican nomination for governor in 1926 and 1928, he felt that he had broken ground as the state's first black candidate for that position. Somewhat reclusive during the last decade of his life, Smith still managed to get his *Gazette* out regularly on time. With the approach of war in 1941, he was named to serve on Local Draft Board No. 13. Three days after Pearl Harbor, he died suddenly in his office at 2322 E. 30th St. He had no wife or children, and his property was left ultimately for the benefit of the Negro blind.

**SMITH, KENT H.** (9 Apr. 1894–26 Mar. 1980), was a founder and long-time president of the LUBRIZOL CORP. and a leader in charitable and educational institutions in the Cleveland area. Born in Cleveland, Smith was the eldest

son of ALBERT W. SMITH. He graduated from East High School in 1911 and attended Dartmouth College, receiving a B.S. in 1915. He then enrolled in Case Institute of Technology and earned a degree in chemical engineering in 1917. During WORLD WAR I he served as a 2d lieutenant in the aviation section of the American armed forces in France. After the war, Smith worked for the Dow Chemical Co. (1919–21) and then became president of the Ce-Fair Development Co. (1921–28), which built the ALCAZAR HOTEL and the Fairmount-Cedar Bldg. in CLEVELAND HTS. It also built and operated miniature golf courses. In 1928 Smith joined his brothers ALBERT KELVIN and Vincent in founding the Graphite Oil Prods. Corp., which later became the Lubrizol Corp. Smith was the firm's first president (1928–29), then served as vice-president (1929–32) before resuming the presidency (1932–51). During his presidency, the company grew from 5 employees to 590, and sales increased from $8,000 to $26 million. He also served as chairman of the board (1951–59) and was a director from the firm's founding until his retirement in 1967. Smith had other business interests as well and served as a director of several local companies.

Smith was active in the leadership of charitable and educational institutions, especially Case Institute of Technology. He became a trustee of Case in 1949 and was active in fundraising and administration, serving as acting president from 1958–61 while its president, T. Keith Glennan, headed NASA. Smith also promoted the idea of the merger between Case and Western Reserve University; he became an honorary trustee of the institution in 1967. He donated large sums of money to Case and to other universities, often in honor of his father. Smith also helped establish the Corporate 1% Program for Higher Education, Inc., and was a cofounder of the Greater Cleveland Assoc. Foundation, serving as the chairman of its board (1961–69). He was a member of the Council of Foundations, serving as president of that national organization in 1967–68. Smith served as a trustee for the CLEVELAND INSTITUTE OF ART, the Cleveland Zoo, the CLEVELAND COUNCIL ON WORLD AFFAIRS, Holden Arboretum, and the CLEVELAND MUSEUM OF NATURAL HISTORY. He was a life trustee of Euclid-Glenville Hospital and a director of the GREATER CLEVELAND GROWTH ASSOC. His leadership earned him many awards, including the 1962 public-service award from the Cleveland Chamber of Commerce and the 1969 Chas. Eisenman Award from the Jewish Community Fed. Smith was married on 3 Jan. 1946, to Thelma Gertrude Sampson.

Smalheer, Calvin V., *The Story of Lubrizol* (1972).

**SMITH, WILSON G.** (19 Aug. 1856–27 Feb. 1929), was a composer, writer, and major music critic in Cleveland during the early 20th century. Smith was born in Elyria and attended public schools. He graduated from West High School, but health problems prevented him from going to college until 1876. He graduated from the University of Cincinnati and went directly to Berlin in 1880, where he studied music under Scharwenka, Kiel, Moszkonski, and Oscar Raif. Upon returning to Cleveland, Smith opened a studio and taught organ, piano, voice, and composition. He joined the staff of the CLEVELAND PRESS in 1902. Smith was known and admired for his honest critique, which was both intelligent and laced with humor. The musical stars of Cleveland and others who performed sought his approval of their talents.

The author of many musical texts used in the U.S. and Europe, Smith's most popular work was *Thematic Octave Studies: In the Form of Variations on Original Theme:*

*Opus 68*, published in 1902. Smith wrote over 1,000 compositions, including piano solos and suites, songs and technical studies for the piano, dances, and waltzes. His piano suites, such as *The Bal Masque*, have been orchestrated and played by the CLEVELAND ORCHESTRA. His work is considered to be thorough and faithful to the "laws" of music. Smith's compositions also include the popular songs "If I But Knew," "Heart Sorrow," "Humoresque," and "Mazurka." His major work was *Homage to Edward Grieg*, a 5-part piece dedicated to the Scandinavian music master. Grieg himself commended Smith on this work. Smith was married to Mez Brett, a writer and an artist. They had a daughter, Edna.

**SMITH FOUNDATION.** *See* **KELVIN & ELEANOR SMITH FOUNDATION**

**SMITHKNIGHT, LOUIS** (16 Dec. 1834–27 Mar. 1915), was a volunteer artillery officer during the CIVIL WAR and a postwar militia artillery officer. Smithknight, born in Saxony (northwest Germany), came to the U.S. in 1845. He lived in Columbus, Ohio, before arriving in Cleveland in 1850. He became a naturalized citizen on 3 Sept. 1855. After an unsuccessful gold-hunting journey to Colorado in 1858, he returned to Cleveland and opened a drugstore.

When the Civil War broke out, Smithknight enlisted as a private in the FIRST OHIO VOLUNTEER LIGHT ARTILLERY for 3 months' service. Returning to Cleveland, he was appointed captain, TWENTIETH OHIO INDEPENDENT BATTERY, which was being organized in Cleveland, on 2 Aug. 1862. The battery spent the winter of 1863 at Murfreesboro, Tenn., where Smithknight was forced to resign on 23 Apr. 1863 from disability after falling from a horse. Returning to his drugstore, he reorganized the CLEVELAND LIGHT ARTILLERY in 1872 and remained its captain until 1887. Smithknight also served as colonel of a battery of statewide artillery. He was active in Republican politics and a member of the Grand Army of the Republic. He served on 3 committees for the dedication of the SOLDIERS' & SAILORS' MONUMENT. He married Nettie Kingsley of Cleveland in 1866. They raised a daughter, Julia, and a son. Smithknight died of bronchitis and was buried next to his wife in WOODLAND CEMETERY.

Cleveland Light Artillery Assoc. Records, WRHS.

**SMYTHE, ANSON** (1 Jan. 1812–2 May 1887), is often referred to as "the Father of the Cleveland Public Library." An educator and Presbyterian minister, he was also an important figure in the reorganization of Ohio's public schools in the 1850s. He later served as superintendent of the Cleveland public schools and as the first pastor of the NORTH PRESBYTERIAN CHURCH in Cleveland. Smythe was born in Franklin, Pa. He attended Milan Academy and then Williams College. After teaching for a few years, he entered the Yale Theological Seminary, graduating with honors. Smythe's early pastorates included a home missionary assignment on the "frontier" of Michigan, where he suffered the privations of a pioneer life. His next pastorate was the Congregational Church of Toledo, where he became interested in the improvement of the city's public schools. He then served successively as superintendent of the Toledo public schools and state commissioner of the Common Schools of Ohio (1856–62). He came to Cleveland in 1863 to become superintendent of the CLEVELAND PUBLIC SCHOOLS (1863–66). In 1872 he resumed the ministry, becoming pastor at North Presbyterian Church. In Toledo, Smythe was given broad powers to reform the

school system. His reputation as an educational administrator led to his election as state commissioner. During his term, he visted schools in every county of the state. Along with HARVEY RICE, H. H. Barney, Thos. Harvey, and other professional educators of the period, Smythe worked on the restructuring of Ohio's public schools. Later, as superintendent of Cleveland schools, his emphasis on strict classification by age and ability led to overcrowding in some grades, and many objections. That, however, led to the creation of 10 new primary and secondary schools within 2 years. Smythe declined reelection in 1866. Smythe, in 1867, was the key figure in the creation of the CLEVELAND PUBLIC LIBRARY. Largely through his efforts, the legislature on 3 Apr. passed an enabling act that authorized the support of libraries through taxation. Smythe remained the pastor at North Presbyterian until the loss of his voice forced his retirement.

**SOCIAL PLANNING AREAS,** geographic units of about 3,500 persons designed to coincide with accepted geopolitical boundaries, played an important role in Cleveland social-welfare programs for nearly 30 years. First utilized in 1951 by the Cleveland Welfare Fed. to coordinate existing social-service and health projects on the neighborhood level, SPAs served as the primary basis for local social analysis and established the criteria for much of the neighborhood development and change evident in the city to the present day. In the late 1970s, the effectiveness of these areas was undermined by changing needs. Social Planning Areas were developed as the changing social, economic, and demographic nature of Cleveland gave rise to the need for more specific analytical tools in the planning of health and social-welfare services. The establishment of the Fed. for Charity & Philanthropy in 1913, the Welfare Council in 1914, and the Welfare Fed. of Cleveland in 1917 represented initial attempts to develop a coordinated program of social welfare, but the Great Depression in the 1930s forced reformers to change the scope and direction of their activities. They began to use statistical analysis of neighborhood social needs to understand mounting pressures.

Led by HOWARD WHIPPLE GREEN, local researchers began to use census tracts to determine neighborhood social-welfare needs. The census tract, a small geographic area within a municipality, contained anywhere from 2,500 to 8,000 persons. First suggested by Dr. Walter Laidlaw of New York in 1906 as a way to simplify the data-collecting process, the new census tract offered the kind of specific social, economic, and demographic information lacking in more conventional, widespread neighborhood or city ward studies. The Census Bureau allowed Cleveland and certain other cities to experiment with census tracts from 1910–40. This statistical analysis became the model for national census studies in 1940. From the early 1930s to the early 1950s, the Cleveland Welfare Fed. increasingly relied on census tract data as a way to anticipate local needs. In particular, various social agencies, settlement houses, and recreation groups used such statistics to justify their annual funding requests from the Community Chest. The Welfare Fed. also employed these statistics during the 1930s and 1940s to study specific social problems and needs on the larger neighborhood level. Unfortunately, census tract data failed to deal with such new neighborhood problems as the growing juvenile delinquency rate in Cleveland during WORLD WAR II. A new way to measure social-welfare needs and the effectiveness of local programs was needed.

Under the leadership of Chas. E. Gehlke, the Welfare Fed. expanded upon these earlier census tract areas to create larger, more readily defined Social Planning Areas in

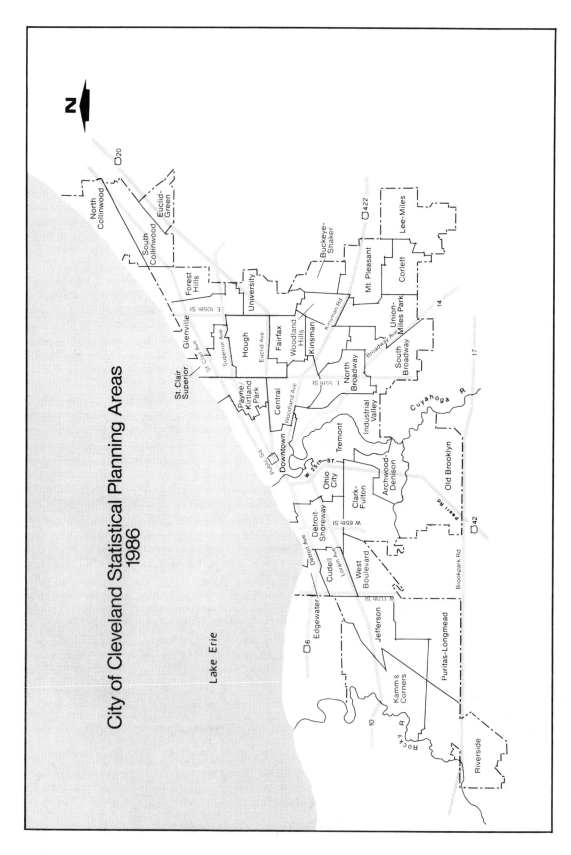

City of Cleveland Statistical Planning Areas 1986

Lake Erie

the early 1950s. These newly formed SPAs were for the most part a direct outgrowth of historical neighborhoods. Federation officials believed that these areas would better serve the community on an individual basis, since neighborhood concerns increasingly outweighed smaller block-by-block census tract analysis. With that in mind, the federation's research department created 28 different SPAs within the city and 14 in the remainder of the county. Their boundaries remained constant from the early 1950s to the late 1970s, providing the federation with a constant geographic base in which to measure changes and aiding it in determining yearly allocations for the various social agencies. The federation tried to create homogeneous planning areas wherever possible, since neighborhood homogeneity, along with local identity, was considered essential if these planning areas were to be effective.

By the early 1960s, the initial purpose of Social Planning Areas had been expanded to encompass a number of new concerns, including illegitimate-birth rates, household makeup, population changes, suicide rates, crime figures, housing stock conditions, income level, racial components, and ethnic background. Statistical findings and the overall approach to yearly federation reports became far more sophisticated and detailed by the late 1960s and early 1970s. Unfortunately, SPAs as such no longer served the pressing needs of local welfare organizations, the federal government, or city officials. In the late 1970s, the effectiveness of SPAs was undermined by increased federal involvement in social-welfare activities, the changing socioeconomic makeup of contemporary neighborhoods, the expanding responsibilities of UNITED WAY, and the reevaluation by the Cleveland Planning Commission and the Welfare Fed. of their own roles within the community. With Pres. Johnson's Great Society Programs in the mid-1960s, federal officials became more directly involved in local social-welfare and health programs and demanded new, more specialized statistical data not provided by traditional SPA studies, which frequently overlooked such contemporary issues as habitual unemployment, hunger, disease, overcrowded housing, racial discrimination, and lack of educational and job training for minorities. The federation's inability to provide such information forced federal officials to turn to other public-sector groups for the needed statistical research and analysis.

One group to which federal officials turned was the City Planning Commission, which had remained outside the sphere of social planning before the 1960s, preferring instead to concentrate its efforts on various urban-renewal projects. But urban social turmoil during the 1960s, more sophisticated approaches to urban planning in general, and increased federal involvement in local social-welfare efforts encouraged the commission to expand its role. By the late 1970s, supported by federal officials and other community leaders, the CPC had assumed the primary role as city planner. By the late 1970s, federation leaders were forced to reconsider the value of Social Planning Areas and their role in this direct research process. Changing social-welfare needs, a shrinking population base, an uncertain local economic climate, and a reorganization of United Way itself compelled the federation to scrap earlier-established SPAs and to redirect its own welfare efforts away from local planning objectives and general data collecting toward specific neighborhood programs designed to gain available federal funding directly. The CPC quickly filled the void created by the sudden withdrawal of the federation. In conjunction with the Dept. of Community Development & Community Relations, it expanded the 28 original SPAs to 39 new, smaller subdivisions that seemed to reflect the changing contemporary Cleveland neighborhood scene better than the earlier, more rigidly defined Social Planning Areas.

Richard Klein

The **SOCIALIST CONVENTION** of 1924 was held in Cleveland on 6–7 July at the Hotel Winton. The delegates' major objective was to decide whether to endorse Sen. Robt. M. La Follette for president of the U.S. and to adhere to the principles of the Congress for Progressive Political Action, which had endorsed him on 4 July. The delegates' main concern was the formation of a third party dedicated to the interests of farmers and workers. Although La Follette was not a Socialist, the delegates to the Cleveland convention voted to support him by an overwhelming majority. And although they voted to adhere to the program of the Progressives, the Socialists also adopted a resolution of their own. In a statement of principles, the Socialists announced that theirs was a party of labor and urged workers to unite and take economic and political power away from capitalists and abolish class rule. They then claimed that it was the duty of the Socialist party to aid all unions in working toward better wages and working conditions. The convention also issued a statement against imperialism and war, and in favor of a child-labor amendment and the removal of legal discrimination against women.

The **SOCIALIST LABOR PARTY** of Cleveland had its greatest influence in the 1890s, when it supported Cleveland's labor movement and was active in the internal politics of the national SLP. The SLP advocated direct revolutionary struggle by the workers to overthrow the capitalist system, eliminate the forces of exploitation, and organize the means of production to social needs. They believed that no country was truly socialist, and that workers suffered basically the same exploitation in the USSR as in the U.S. The SLP was founded in Philadelphia as the Workingmen's Party of the U.S. in July 1876. In 1877 the local branch of the SLP was formed, and Clevelanders Leopold J. Palda and Frank Skarda founded the Czech-language *Delnicky Listy* (Workingman's News), the first SLP newspaper in America. In the Ohio state elections held in Oct. 1877, the Workingmen's party nominated a full slate of candidates, headed by Lewis Bond and Frank Skarda of Cleveland for governor and lieutenant governor respectively. They garnered about 6% of the Cuyahoga County vote. The SLP changed its name to the Socialistic Labor party in Dec. 1877 and to the Socialist Labor party in 1890.

In the 1890s, the Cleveland SLP, led by MAX HAYES and ROBT. BANDLOW, split with the New York faction led by Daniel DeLeon on the question of whether or not to cooperate with the trade unions. The New York group endorsed the SPL-based Socialist Trades & Labor Alliance, founded in 1895, while the Cleveland SLP supported alliances with the populists and the Central Labor Union in order to increase its political strength. By joining with the populists as part of the Independent Labor party, the Cleveland SLP had contributed about 20% of the total vote given to populist mayoral candidate Thos. Fitzsimmons in 1893 (see POPULIST POLITICAL PARTIES). The local group was finally suspended from the national SLP for its continued support of trade unions. In an effort to compromise, the suspension was overturned, and in 1896 the SLP created a Natl. Board of Appeals, with its headquarters in Cleveland, to adjudicate intraparty disputes. With Hayes and Bandlow on the board, decisions favored SLP members who cooperated with trade unions rather than the ST&LA, and the split between the Cleveland and New York factions became final in 1899. Led by Hayes, many SLP members joined the Socialist party when it was formed in 1901. With the defection of a large part of its membership, the local SLP was destined to remain a small doctrinaire group of Marxist "purists." In the local election of 1915, Richard Koeppel, SLP candidate for mayor, received only .4% of the vote, while the Socialist candidate polled almost 6%. In 1922, John D. Goerke of Cleveland visited SLP branches in the eastern U.S. and reported a lack of enthusiasm, a fear of being labeled "red." Most of the branches opposed any meddling by the Russian-based Comintern, which promoted international Communism. The party continued to decline in the 1930s and gradually died out.

The **SOCIETY CORPORATION** is one of Ohio's major financial-services companies, with one of the nation's oldest mutual savings banks, the Society Natl. Bank, as its major subsidiary. The idea of a mutual savings society in Cleveland was suggested by businessman Chas. J. Woolson and lawyer Samuel H. Mather in 1849. With the support of 17 leading businessmen, they procured the passage of a state act to incorporate such an organization on 22 Mar. 1849. The Society for Savings in the city of Cleveland opened on 2 Aug. 1849 in the rear of the Merchants Bank (see MERCANTILE NATL. BANK) at Superior and Water (W. 9th) streets. At first Society struggled as a financial institution. By the end of its first year, it had $9,500 from 130 depositors. Despite the Panic of 1857, the firm began to flourish and had to move to larger accommodations in the WEDDELL HOUSE on Bank (W. 6th) St. By 1859, it had reached $490,000 in deposits.

Society's deposits quadrupled during the CIVIL WAR, and by 1867, it was necessary to erect its own office building on the northeast corner of PUBLIC SQUARE. The number of depositors steadily grew, as did additions to its headquarters. Under Mather's guidance, Society opened a grander, 10-story bank building, designed by Chicago architect John W. Root, at 127 Public Square in 1890 (see SOCIETY NATL. BANK BLDG.). By that time, Society had $19.3 million from over 41,000 depositors. Within 20 years, 1 out of 6 Clevelanders had their savings at Society. During both world wars, the firm was instrumental in the war bond drives. The Depression had little effect on Society, as its deposits continued to grow. It was during these years that it began one of the nation's first school savings programs.

Despite deposits of over $200 million by the early 1950s, the Society for Savings was legally limited in its growth, as it could not offer certain services. Thus, on 16 Jan. 1956, it formed a subsidiary, Society Natl. Bank of Cleveland, to provide commercial banking services. For 2 years, these 2 institutions conducted business together in 9 offices. However, the operations proved costly and inefficient. So, on 31 Dec. 1958, Pres. Mervin B. France orchestrated the unification of the Society for Savings into Society Natl. Bank. The bank was then placed under the ownership of a new holding company, the Society Corp. Starting in the late 1960s, Society began to acquire various banks throughout Ohio, established international banking services, and introduced various new banking products. In 1984, it broadened its line of financial services with the purchase of the Interstate Financial Corp. of Dayton. In 1985 Society restructured its Ohio banking subsidiaries into 3 regions and officially acquired the CENTRAN CORP. in September of that year. With the completion of the Centran merger in Feb. 1986, Society was Ohio's third-largest bank holding company, with $8.7 billion in assets.

*Society National Bank of Cleveland, 1849-1974* (1974), WRHS.

The **SOCIETY FOR CRIPPLED CHILDREN OF CUYAHOGA COUNTY, INC.**, is a nonprofit agency that provides out-patient rehabilitation services for disabled individuals from birth through age 21. Founded nationally in 1907, the local organization began work in 1940; by 1979 the local society's programs had grown to include a social-service department to coordinate services to meet family needs; an early childhood education program for disabled youngsters under age 5; physical and occupational therapy; speech pathology; and the 72-acre Camp Cheerful in STRONGSVILLE to help disabled youngsters learn social skills and independence during camping sessions. The society was begun in Elyria by industrialist Edgar F. Allen, whose only son was killed in a streetcar accident on Memorial Day 1907. His son's death and the injuries to others led Allen to dedicate his life to helping disabled children; he headed campaigns to build 2 local hospitals and founded the Society for Crippled Children, which maintained its headquarters in Elyria until moving to Chicago in 1945.

The Cleveland branch of the society evolved from the work of the Assoc. for the Crippled & Disabled, an organization led during the 1930s and 1940s by BELL GREVE, who was also active in the Internatl. Society for Crippled Children. Early in 1934, the association established a Curative Playroom for disabled children in its facilities at 2233 E. 55th St.; the Cleveland Society for Crippled Children shared this address when it began to offer services on 7 July 1940. Instrumental in founding the local chapter were Frank T. McGuire and Wm. B. Townsend. Both men remained society officers into the mid-1960s, McGuire as president, Townsend as director.

In 1945, an auxiliary was formed as a community support group for the society's work, and by 1951 the society had opened Camp Cheerful and a child-treatment center at 2239 E. 55th St. By 1953 the West Side Treatment Ctr. at 14587 Madison Ave. had also been opened; it served as the local society's headquarters until 1965, when the million-dollar Heman Rehabilitation Institute was opened at 1101 Buckeye Rd., replacing the E. 55th St. facility. The new building was named for Homer D. and Antoinette M. Heman, whose $300,000 contribution had helped finance construction. In 1966, the society served 1,400 disabled children. For many years the society was associated with and supported by the Natl. Easter Seals campaign, but in 1959 the local group disaffiliated itself from the national group to join the community-oriented Health Fund. The society later left the Health Fund and since 1968 has been a member of the UNITED WAY. In 1979, the Heman Rehabilitation Institute was renamed to honor the society's long-time director, Wm. B. Townsend. By 1982, the society was serving 70 children a week.

The **SOCIETY FOR THE RELIEF OF THE POOR,** formed at a meeting of the city's leading citizens at Empire Hall on 26 Dec. 1850, first advocated public measures to aid the poor, then began its own relief efforts. The society was formed a month after the MARTHA WASHINGTON & DORCAS SOCIETY ceased its private relief efforts because of increasing poverty in the city and the lack of government assistance. At its initial meeting, presided over by Mayor WILLIAM CASE, the Society for the Relief of the Poor approved resolutions calling upon the city to erect a poorhouse, a workhouse, and a house of refuge that would permit its residents to maintain themselves by raising their own food. It also urged all religious denominations to provide assistance to their poor members. A year later, the leaders of the society apparently believed that their requests had not been met sufficiently, for at a meeting on 18 Dec. 1851, the society took more direct measures. The meeting formally established "a Society for the Relief of the Poor," to be known as the "Cleveland Relief Association"; adopted a plan proposed by Wm. Slade, Jr., for "systemizing" the charitable efforts of Clevelanders; and raised $500 to aid the poor. The society's work was supported by subscriptions from its benefactors, by the proceeds from entertainments sponsored by its ladies' committee, and by donations of wood and clothes. BENJAMIN ROUSE and his wife, REBECCA, a veteran of the Martha Washington & Dorcas Society, served as agents of the Relief Assoc. and carried out its daily work, distributing more than $2,000 in the winter of 1851–52. Officers of the society were JOHN A. FOOT, president; JAS. A. BRIGGS, vice-president; H. F. Brayton, treasurer; and R. C. Parsons, secretary. The work of what the *Daily True Democrat* hailed as "a permanent organization for the Relief of the Poor" proved to be only temporary. In Dec. 1852, the executive committee of the society decided that "a voluntary relief fund" was not necessary for the upcoming winter; the previous year's effort had been demanded by "the extreme severity of the weather." Moreover, the committee argued, the railroads had relieved the city "of a large class of persons who are liable to need assistance," labor shortages existed, church efforts and benevolent associations were numerous, and the city had made "judicious and efficient arrangements" to help the poor. Members of the society thus turned their energies to other charitable efforts after 1852.

The **SOCIETY NATIONAL BANK (SOCIETY FOR SAVINGS) BUILDING,** located on the north side of PUBLIC SQUARE, is the most important remaining building in Cleveland by John Wellborn Root of the influential Chicago firm of Burnham & Root. The officers of the Society for Savings included Samuel H. Mather, SAMUEL ANDREWS, and MYRON T. HERRICK, and they made a special attempt to bring together the industrial and decorative arts in the building. It was erected in 1889–90; its design combines elements of the Gothic, Romanesque, and Renaissance styles, of which the most prominent are the short granite pillars of the ground-story Gothic arcade, the arches of different styles in the upper stories, and the massive corners with their turrets reaching to 152 ft. The structure was conceived by Root as representing a medieval keep or fortified tower. While the red sandstone outer walls are load-bearing and self-supporting, the interior structure was built of steel columns and diagonally braced floors, in effect independent of the outer walls.

The interior is one of the most gorgeously decorated spaces in the city. The banking room is 26 ft. high, and its ceiling is a stained-glass skylight in the tradition of the Arts & Crafts movement. The Gothic decorative scheme was planned by Chicago decorator Wm. Pretyman, and the murals were designed by Wm. Crane, the English painter and illustrator who was the leader of the Romantic movement in decorative art and an associate of Wm. Morris. Above the 1st floor, one of the most important features of the building was a 9-story light court surrounded with balconies that provided access to the offices. It has been covered over at several floors, so that the glass ceiling is illuminated artificially.

The **SOCIETY OF MEDICAL SCIENCES** was formed in Dec. 1887 by dissident members of the CUYAHOGA COUNTY MEDICAL SOCIETY who wanted their professional organization to be a serious forum for scientific and medical topics and who felt that the county organization was out of step with medical research. Unlike the county group, which met quarterly in the afternoon, the new society met more frequently and in the evening, so that busy young doctors could attend after a long day at the hospital or office. To achieve the goal of improved access to medical literature to all, the group levied an admission fee of $25 and annual dues of $10 to sustain purchases of medical books and journals. The Society of Medical Sciences handled its business outside regularly scheduled meetings, so that entire meetings could be devoted to questions of medical importance. Unlike the more secretive Cuyahoga County Medical Society, it published its proceedings in the *Cleveland Medical Gazette*. With the formation of the CLEVELAND MEDICAL LIBRARY ASSOC. in 1894, the need for the Society of Medical Sciences lessened as academic resources, as well as a place for discussion, were available to all. After a short tenure as the Cleveland Clinical Society, the group ceased to exist in 1896.

**SOCKALEXIS, LOUIS FRANCIS "CHIEF"** (24 Oct. 1871–24 Dec. 1913), was a Penobscot Indian who played professional BASEBALL with the Natl. League CLEVELAND SPIDERS from 1897–99. He is said to be the person for whom the CLEVELAND INDIANS baseball team is named, making him the only individual to have a major-league baseball team named after him. Sockalexis was born on the Penobscot Indian Reservation in Old Town, Maine. A gifted athlete, he excelled in track, gymnastics, polo, skating, and baseball. He attended Holy Cross College in Worcester, Mass. He played on the college's baseball team, hitting .436 in 1895 and .444 in 1896. He also played amateur baseball in Maine's Knox County League.

Sockalexis turned professional in 1897, joining the Cleveland Spiders as an outfielder. He hit home runs in his first 2 at-bats for Cleveland and turned in an excellent season, batting .338 over 66 games. Unfortunately, he became addicted to alcohol, and his career waned after just 1 year. He appeared in only 21 games for the Spiders in 1898, hitting just .224. He finished his major-league career after only 7 games in 1899, released by the team and unwanted by any other. Sockalexis is said to have lived the life of a drifter after leaving baseball. He died in Burlington, Maine, at the age of 42. In 1915, the Cleveland American League baseball team was in need of a new nickname. They had been known since 1905 as the Naps, in honor of popular player-manager NAPOLEON "NAP" LAJOIE. But LaJoie had been sent to the Philadelphia Athletics following the 1914 season, prompting the need for a new name. A newspaper contest was held, and the winning entry Indians was chosen. It was submitted by a fan who said he was doing it in honor of the Chief, Louis Sockalexis.

**SOHIO.** *See* **STANDARD OIL COMPANY**

**SOKOL CLEVELAND** was a Czech gymnastic, cultural, and educational organization founded in 1895. It absorbed another Czech Sokol unit (Sokol Cech-Havlicek) in 1960 to become one of only 2 remaining units in the city before being disbanded in 1985. The Czech Sokol movement was begun in Prague on 16 Feb. 1862 by Dr. Miroslav Tyrs, who provided the ideology for the movement, and Jindrich Fuegner, who provided financial support for its growth. The Sokol (Falcon) movement was named for the bird native to Czechoslovakia and known for its strength and freedom. These were the qualities the movement's founders believed their program of gymnastics and physical training would cultivate among the Czech people. They saw it as a means to develop a sense of national and racial pride and unity among CZECHS. Their movement was taken up by other Slavic groups in Europe, as well as by immigrants in the U.S. The first Czech Sokol in the U.S. was founded in St. Louis on 14 Feb. 1865.

The first Sokol formed in Cleveland was Sokol Cech, organized in 1879 (sometimes given as 1869 and mentioned as the second-oldest Sokol in the U.S.). Among its founders were Frank Sluka and Joseph Blaha. Named for poet Svatopluk Cech, Sokol Cech had its own gymnastics hall at 4820 Wendell Ave.; by 1919 it had 148 men and 46 women members. In 1921 it merged with another group, Sokol Havlicek, founded in 1905 and named for journalist Chas. Havlicek, which met in the BOHEMIAN NATL. HALL. In 1919 Sokol Havlicek had 132 male and 105 female members; by 1935 the combined Sokol Cech-Havlicek was the largest Sokol in Cleveland, with 500 adult and 250 junior members.

Sokol Cleveland was organized in Aug. or Sept. 1895; its first meeting was held in a hall on Plymouth (Central) Ave. Frank Hrubecky served as its first president, and gym classes were held in his storeroom. At the end of the first year, the group had 94 members, and on 31 Mar. 1896, it was incorporated. In 1910 it built a hall at 8932 Quincy and organized a women's auxiliary. By 1919, Sokol Cleveland's members numbered 172 men and 122 women; by 1935 it had about 400 adult and junior members. It sold its hall on Quincy in May 1943 and in 1946 opened a new one at 20110 Harvard Ave. Membership declined from 127 in 1955 to 111 in 1959. In 1960, Sokol Cleveland merged with Sokol Cech-Havlicek; membership in the latter group had declined from 129 in 1955 to 99 in 1959. Between 1960–64, membership in the new Sokol Cleveland Cech-Havlicek increased from 208 to 216. In 1985, however, the organization was dissolved and its hall put up for sale; many of its members joined SOKOL GREATER CLEVELAND.

Ferdinand Jirsa Papers, WRHS.
Frank J. Bardoun Papers, WRHS.
Ledbetter, Eleanor E., *The Czechs of Cleveland* (1919).

The **SOKOL GREATER CLEVELAND GYMNASTIC AND EDUCATIONAL ORGANIZATION, INC.,** was formed in May 1976 by the merger of 2 Czech Sokols, Sokol Nova Vlast and Sokol Tyrs. The Czech Sokol movement once had 5 organizations in the Cleveland area, but by Aug. 1985 Sokol Greater Cleveland was the only remaining Czech Sokol in the area (see SOKOL CLEVELAND). Of the 2 groups that merged to form Sokol Greater Cleveland, Sokol Nova Vlast (the New Fatherland) was the older. Formed on 19 Feb. 1892 (sometimes given as Jan. 1893), Sokol Nova Vlast met in the Bohemian Sokol Hall at 4314 Clark Ave. By 1919 it had 133 male and 95 female members; its membership had grown to nearly 600 adult and junior members by 1935. In the 1950s and 1960s, its membership was about 170. Sokol Tyrs was formed in 1919 in the new Czech settlement in the Mt. Pleasant area. It was organized on 20 July 1919 by John Sebek and John Fencl as Sokol Jan Amos Kamensky. (That its charter members had been members of other Sokol units may account for the discrepancies in various accounts of the origins of Sokol Tyrs. See, for example, Ledbetter, *The Czechs of Cleveland*.) On 22 May 1920, the group joined the national American Sokol Organization, and in 1926 it became Sokol Tyrs. It dedicated its new hall at E. 131st St. and Melzer Ave. on 27 Apr. 1927. By 1969, Sokol Tyrs had 348 members and 191 gymnasts.

Before their formal merger in 1976, Sokol Tyrs and Sokol Nova Vlast joined forces in a fundraising effort in the mid-1960s, forming American Sokol, Inc., in an attempt to raise money to build a new Sokol hall and community center for use by a new, combined organization. Sokol Tyrs had organized several clubs, which needed meeting facilities: a sewing club, formed in 1928; a concert band, established in 1957; a junior hobby club, created in Mar. 1959; and the Little Theatre Group, also organized in 1959.

Efforts to build a new hall failed, however, and in June 1975 American Sokol, Inc., bought the BOHEMIAN NATL. HALL and deeded it to Sokol Tyrs. After the merger, members of both Sokol Tyrs and Sokol Nova Vlast worked to renovate the hall. By 1985, Sokol Greater Cleveland had 550 adult members and about 250 children who regularly took part in the group's activities. Cleveland has played host to several important Sokol events. A major field competition, or *slet*, was held here in 1900, and in 1935 the city hosted the American Sokol Organization's slet; the national organization also held its 1970 convention in Cleveland.

Ferdinand Jirsa Papers, WRHS.
Frank J. Bardoun Papers, WRHS.
Ledbetter, Eleanor E., *The Czechs of Cleveland* (1919).

**SOKOL POLSKI,** the Polish Falcons of America, is a cultural and recreational society with its local headquarters at 7146 Broadway. Similar to the Czech Sokol, or Falcon, movement (see SOKOL CLEVELAND), the Polish Falcons began as a movement to foster national pride and patriotism among POLES in Poland in 1867. The first American nest of Polish Falcons was organized in Chicago in 1887, and a national organization was incorporated in 1894. The first nests in Cleveland appeared during the first decade of the 20th century. The first organization in Cleveland was formed in 1902 on the city's south side and became Nest 23 of the national group. Its founders included Paul Kurdziel, Joseph Mikalski, and Boleslav Racinowski. It appears to have been a short-lived group. By 1904, many of its members found it too far to travel to attend Nest 23's meetings and decided to establish another group, Nest 50, on the east side. Nest 50 met at 8315 Kosciusko Ave.; its first president was Joseph Lewandowski, and Wladyslaw Karolczak served as its first instructor. In 1909, a third Cleveland nest was organized; it eventually became the major local branch of the Polish Falcons of America. Nest 141 was established by MICHAEL P. KNIOLA, Walter Owczarek, John Legucki, Wm. Halter, Paul Wrobel, Joseph M. Rutkowski, and Frank Januszcwski. In 1911, the group bought the former United Presbyterian Church building at 7146 Broadway, and in 1912 it became a member of the national Polish Falcons of America.

In addition to gymnastic training and language classes, the local Polish Falcons supported efforts to liberate their homeland. As the "Free Poland" movement developed in the U.S., the Sokol group took on a military character and began programs in military training; by 1914, 1,000 men were taking such training. After the U.S. entered WORLD WAR I, the hall on Broadway was turned into a recruiting and induction center for Polish army personnel, raising an army of immigrants to return to Europe to fight. The Sokols abandoned the military policy once the war ended. During the 1920s, the Sokols expanded their activities beyond gymnastics to include American sports. In 1923, instructor Felix A. Siclatycki introduced basketball, baseball, track, and folk dancing, and in 1927 boxing was added. Among the youngsters taking advantage of the Sokols' programs in the 1920s was STELLA WALSH, later a track star who returned to the nest as an instructor. The Polish Falcon Hall was remodeled in 1935–36. Members of Nest 141 again rallied to help the homeland in the late 1930s and 1940s. The group sent clothing and medical supplies and helped Poles displaced by the war. When prosperity returned after the war, the organization again expanded its sports offerings, organizing a bowling league for men in 1957 and one for women the next year. By 1965, Nest 141 was one of 184 Polish Falcons nests across the U.S., and that year it elected its first woman president, Bertha Modrzyinski, who continued to lead the organization into the 1980s. The group had 300 members in 1969; by 1979 its gymnastics classes were being held at South High School, and the hall served as a meeting and social center.

Polish Falcons of America District IV, *42nd Biennial Convention. 40th Biennial Track and Field Meet. 60th Anniversary Nest 141* (1969), WRHS.

## SOKOLOFF, NIKOLAI (28 May 1886–25 Sept. 1965), was the first conductor of the CLEVELAND ORCHESTRA. Sokoloff was born in Kiev, Russia. At the age of 13, he and his family moved to New Haven, Conn., where he enrolled at Yale University's music school. After graduation, he studied music with Chas. Martin Loeffler in Boston. Later in his life, he studied with Vincent d'Indy in Paris. At the age of 17, he became a violinist in the Boston Symphony Orchestra. He left Boston and, after studying in Paris, became the conductor of the Manchester Orchestra in England. In 1918, he returned to America, where in Cincinnati he met ADELLA PRENTISS HUGHES and was persuaded to accept a position from the MUSICAL ARTS ASSOC. to make a survey in Cleveland's public schools and outline an instrumental music program. He accepted the position on the condition that he would be able to organize and conduct his own orchestra.

Sokoloff conducted the Cleveland Orchestra for 14 years, 1918–32, and in that time initiated highly acclaimed national and international tours. He established a unique series of educational concerts for schoolchildren, which became the model for other orchestras, and introduced recording and broadcasting concerts to Cleveland. Upon leaving Cleveland, Sokoloff was appointed as the director of the Federal Music Project in 1935. Through this organization, he channeled money into Cleveland for unemployed musicians. Because of this support, Cleveland heard more opera and orchestral music than it had in many years. When he left the Federal Music Project in 1937, he became the conductor for the Seattle Orchestra. Later he organized an orchestra in LaJolla, Calif., where he remained until his death. Sokoloff was survived by his wife, Emma.

Marsh, Robert C., *The Cleveland Orchestra* (1967).
Musical Arts Assoc. Archives.

## The SOLDIERS' AID SOCIETY OF NORTHERN OHIO, 1861–68, part of the U.S. Sanitary Commission, was organized to provide assistance for soldiers serving in the CIVIL WAR. The society was initially organized as the Ladies Aid Society by a group of women from various Cleveland churches. The group first met on 20 Apr. 1861, at which time it organized a "blanket raid" to collect quilts and blankets for troops being mustered at Camp Taylor (see CIVIL WAR CAMPS). The first officers of the society were REBECCA ROUSE, president; Mrs. John Shelley and Mrs. Wm. Milhinch, vice-presidents; Mary Clark Brayton, secretary; and Ellen F. Terry, treasurer. On 16 Oct. 1861, the society joined with other benevolent groups to form the Soldiers' Aid Society of Northern Ohio. Financed by private donations, the organization cared for the sick and wounded, provided ambulance and hospital service, solicited clothing and medical supplies, and sent parcels of food to soldiers in the field throughout the Civil War. The society established a distribution center at 95 Bank (W. 6th) St. to handle the quantities of material it received. In Feb. 1864, it organized a Sanitary Fair on PUBLIC SQUARE, which raised over $100,000. These funds allowed the society to establish a depot hospital in Cleveland. Following

the cessation of hostilities, the society conducted an Employment & Free Claims agency for the benefit of returning veterans. The society ceased operations in Nov. 1868, when the need to serve veterans had diminished.

U.S. Sanitary Commission Records, WRHS.
Brayton, Mary Clark, and Terry, Ellen F., *Our Acre and Its Harvest* (1869).

The **SOLDIERS AND SAILORS MONUMENT,** situated on the southeast quadrant of Cleveland's PUBLIC SQUARE, is the city's major Civil War memorial. Designed by LEVI T. SCOFIELD, the monument was dedicated on 4 July 1894, after nearly 15 years of planning. The initial drive to build a local monument began on 30 Oct. 1879, when a group of more than 12,000 Civil War veterans met at CASE HALL in Cleveland to advocate such a project. Actual planning and funding of the monument were handled by a 3-man commission appointed under an act of the state legislature passed on 16 Apr. 1888.

The monument consists of an elevated base containing a tablet room. The base is surmounted by a column capped with a 15-ft.-high Statue of Liberty, bringing the total height of the structure to 125 ft. Surrounding the exterior of the base are 4 groupings of bronze sculpture (cast approximately one-third larger than life) depicting various battle scenes. These groupings are titled *The Color Guard, At Short Range, The Advance Guard,* and *Mortar Practice.* The first of these groups, *The Color Guard,* is based on the actual defense of the regimental flag of the 103D OHIO VOLUNTEER INFANTRY at the battle of Resaca, Ga. The tablet room contains lists of Cuyahoga County residents who served in the CIVIL WAR, as well as 4 bronze reliefs, entitled *Emancipation of the Slave, Beginning of the War in Ohio, Sanitary Commission, The Soldiers' Aid Society and the Hospital Service Northern Ohio Soldiers and Sailors Aid Society, Sanitary Commission and Hospital Service Corps,* and *The End of the War—The Peacemakers at City Point.* The total cost of the monument was $280,000, all but $10,000 of which was raised through public taxes. Scofield, however, donated all of his architectural services to the project.

Gleason, William J., *A History of the Cuyahoga County Soldiers' and Sailors' Monument* (1894).

The **SOLDIERS' HOME** (opened 12 Dec. 1863-closed June 1866) grew out of the need to ease and facilitate the transportation of sick, wounded, or disabled men during the CIVIL WAR. Homes, or "rests," as they were often called, were established in all major American cities along the popular routes of travel. All soldiers of the national army on furlough or honorable discharge could avail themselves of temporary lodging in the Soldiers' Home as needed. The home in Cleveland was situated on the lakefront pier upon which the Union Railroad Depot was located. This location facilitated the movement of injured soldiers, allowing them to be carried quickly and directly from a train to the beds in the home.

Randall Crawford was chief architect of the facility. He fashioned it much like the one located in Louisville, Ky. There were 2 wards at the south end of the building, which contained 25 beds. The rooms were well ventilated, and the walls brilliantly whitewashed. Flags and patriotic regalia were in evidence everywhere. In the middle ward or reception-room area, numerous pictures of landscapes, patriotic emblems, and a library could be found. The gas company donated all the gas to operate the lights. That was a significant contribution, as the home remained lighted most of the time, to the benefit of those entering it at night. The water company allowed free usage of its pipes, and a local doctor donated all of the beds and rope mattings found in the ward. Some 56,645 men received aid through the Soldiers' Home. Eventually an employment agency grew from this facility, which assisted disabled soldiers to secure gainful employment. Another free service was the collection of bounty and pension claims to soldiers. Over 112,000 meals were served to soldiers during its 3-year period of existence.

**SOLLMAN, TORALD HERMAN** (10 Feb. 1874–11 Feb. 1965), physician, medical educator, researcher, and technical advisor, was the dean of American pharmacology. A noted authority on drugs, he was a major force in the development of American pharmacology for more than 60 years. His writings laid the groundwork for a number of major discoveries. Sollman was born in Colberg, Germany, to August and Adelhaid Eckhardt Sollman. He attended the gymnasium in Colberg, 1884–88, before coming to America at the age of 13 to live with his brother, Luitpold, a druggist in Canton. While working in Luitpold's store, Sollman studied English medicine in his spare time. At the age of 17 he became the youngest person to receive a pharmacist's license from the state of Ohio. Within 2 years of opening a branch store in Canton, he had saved enough money to finance a year's study in pharmacology at the Val de Grace Military Hospital in Paris, France, 1893–94. After he graduated from the Western Reserve University Medical School with the M.D. degree in 1896, he did additional studies in Strasbourg in 1899.

Sollman served as a demonstrator in physiology at WRU, 1895–99; lecturer in pharmacology, 1898–1901; assistant professor of pharmacology and materia medica, 1901–04; and professor, 1904–44. A professor who exacted thoroughness from his students, he was responsible for building up the pharmacology department, training many future leaders in the field. During WORLD WAR I, he was a consultant to the U.S. Army on poison gas and did numerous experiments in the treatment of mustard-gas burns. In 1917, he authored *Laboratory Experiments in Pharmacology*, the first laboratory manual in pharmacology written in English; the oft-revised manual became "the book" in its field. In 1928, Sollman was appointed dean of the WRU Medical School. As dean he instituted higher standards for the selection of students and insisted on a balance of students desiring to be practitioners with those who wished to enter research. Upon his retirement in 1944, he was named professor emeritus and dean emeritus. Sollman married Alice Sersall in June 1902 and had 1 daughter, Mary Alice. Sollman was honored when the Wyeth Laboratories in Philadelphia established the Torald Sollman Award in Pharmacology. International in scope, the Sollman Award was considered comparable to the Nobel Prize.

**SOLON** is a city located 18 mi. from Cleveland in the southeast corner of Cuyahoga County, occupying 22 sq. mi. It is bounded by Geauga County on the east, Summit County on the south, ORANGE, MORELAND HILLS, and BENTLEYVILLE on the north, and BEDFORD HTS., OAKWOOD, and GLENWILLOW on the west. Solon was incorporated as a village in 1917 and became a city in 1961, operating under the mayor-council form of government. The earliest settlers in Solon Twp. arrived from Connecticut in 1820. The township was named after Lorenzo Solon Bull, son of Isaac Bull, one of the first settlers. Swampland and drainage problems confronted the pioneers. Once the land was cleared and drained, corn and wheat became the staple crops. In addition, 5 cheese factories were built, cre-

ating a profitable dairy business. In 1850 the population was 1,034. The coming of RAILROADS contributed to Solon's growth; in 1857, the Cleveland-Youngstown section of the Cleveland & Mahoning Railroad opened through Solon. The main road was SOM Ctr. Rd., so named because it passed through the centers of Solon, Orange, and Mayfield townships. The first industrial firm to locate in Solon was the Bready Cultimotor tractor company, formed in 1929. Since then, more than 150 businesses have located there, ranging in size from small shops to industries employing over 1,000. Industry has traditionally contributed more than 50% of the tax base. The largest employers in 1985 were TECHNICARE, STOUFFER FOODS, and WESTERN ELECTRIC. With its commercial district concentrated at the centrally located intersection, Solon maintained its small-town appearance. In 1980, 60% of the land remained undeveloped. Solon has 2 elementary, 1 junior high, 1 senior high, and 1 parochial school. The city's population increased from 6,333 in 1960 to 11,519 in 1970, and 14,341 in 1980. Recreational facilities include a 402-acre park with 2 lakes, picnic areas, hiking trails, and a golf course.

The **SOLON HISTORICAL SOCIETY** is an organization devoted to the discovery, preservation, and dissemination of knowledge about SOLON and its vicinity; its exploration, settlement, and development. The society was founded 1 July 1968, following meetings of an interested group of citizens and a membership drive that enlisted over 1,000 persons. It was incorporated as a nonprofit organization under the laws of Ohio. The Solon Historical Society Bldg., owned by the city of Solon, is located on Bainbridge Rd. across from Solon City Hall. This building has housed the society's collections since 1969, when it was vacated by the Pioneer Memorial Church. The original stained-glass windows across the front are in memory of the founders of the Twp. of Solon, and the Garfield window, which graces the small attached chapel facing west, honors the 20th U.S. president, JAS. A. GARFIELD, who lived and taught in Solon and preached in the church. The museum is open before meetings, Sunday afternoons, May through September, and on election days. The Solon Historical Society and museum are administered by a staff of volunteers; the society has an executive board of 15 members. In 1985, there were over 300 paid members. The society holds 6 meetings each year, with programs that are open to the public at no cost, and 1 or more field trips.

**SOMMER, WILLIAM** (18 Jan. 1867–20 June 1949), was a Cleveland artist whose work gained national recognition shortly after his death. Sommer was born in Detroit to German parents. From age 11 to 16, he studied drawing, and that, except for a year in Europe, including Munich (1890–91) under Prof. Herterich, was his only formal art training. His Detroit teacher Julius Melchers was a church woodcarver and trainer of talent for the Detroit Calvert Lithograph Co. From 1881–88, Sommer served as an apprentice with the company. Returning from a year abroad, he worked for some lithograph companies in New York and became a member of the Kit Kat Club. He then moved to Cleveland at the invitation of Wm. Brewer of the Otis Lithograph Co. and lived in LAKEWOOD (1371 Westlake Ave.). Sommer worked for the W. J. Morgan Lithograph Co. until 1929, when he was laid off as they adapted the offset press. After that time, he painted full-time and accomplished such works as the murals in Public Hall, Cleveland; Brett Hall, Cleveland Public Library; the post office, Geneva, Ohio; and the Board of Education Bldg., Akron, Ohio. These were done as an employee of the WPA Artists program, an assignment he secured through the assistance of WM. MILLIKEN, then director of the CLEVELAND MUSEUM OF ART. In the 1920s and 1930s, he regularly won prizes in drawing and watercolor at the Cleveland Museum of Art's MAY SHOWS. Sommer helped to found the KOKOON CLUB in 1912 and in 1918 did costumes and decor for the Play House production of *Everyman*.

Sommer purchased a house at Brandywine, Ohio, and an old school for a studio. These served as a meeting place for local artists, including ABEL and ALEX WARSHAWSKY and Wm. Zorach when they were in town, and poets HART CRANE (whom Sommer met in 1921), Hazel Collister Hutchison, and Peter Keisogloff. The meetings with Crane are noted in Crane's poem "Sunday Morning Apples." The two were in the habit of spending an evening together once a week, when they would retire to the "ivory tower" to play records or read. Crane, when he moved to New York, took Sommer's paintings and drawings with him. Among others, Wm. Carlos Williams bought some and wrote Sommer in gratitude. However, it was only after Sommer's death that the Metropolitan Museum of Art and the Whitney in New York, the Natl. Collection of the Smithsonian Institution in Washington, and the Nelson-Adkins Gallery in Kansas City purchased his work and that films, books, and articles began to recognize the full measure of his art. Sommer married Martha Obermeyer in 1894; she lived until 1945.

Cleveland Museum of Art, *The William Sommer Memorial Exhibition Catalogue* (1950).

The **SONS OF TEMPERANCE** was a national semisecret fraternal mutual-benefit society, which came to Cleveland in the wake of the evangelical Washingtonian TEMPERANCE movement in the 1840s. The highly centralized order of the Sons of Temperance was organized nationally in 1842 in New York; its members pledged not to "make, buy, sell, nor use as a beverage, any spirituous or malt liquors, wine or cider." In addition to protecting its members from "the evils of intemperance," the organization was designed to "afford mutual assistance in case of sickness" and to improve members' characters. The first Cleveland lodge of the Sons of Temperance was formed on 27 July 1847; branches of the order existed in the city for nearly 40 years before dying out by 1886. Lodges met weekly; the first lodge, Div. No. 275, met at first over Bingham's hardware store in the post office building, but moved its meeting place several times in the course of its history. The number of lodges in the Cleveland area and membership in the order remained modest until the late 1860s. There were 2 lodges in 1848, but by 1857, Div. No. 275 was the only lodge in Cleveland; it had 150 members that year. Between Oct. 1866 and Aug. 1867, however, 4 new lodges were organized. Among them was a special division for BLACKS, who were not permitted to join regular lodges; the Lincoln Div. was organized in July with 41 charter members. Women were associated with the local Sons of Temperance by 1859.

A Jan. 1868 article in the *Leader* noted that the purpose of the organization was "to rescue from the cess-pools of intemperance, the miserable victims of a depraved appetite." While it did work to reclaim drunkards and prevent others from falling prey to the evils of drink, the local Sons of Temperance also joined in the unsuccessful efforts of the Cleveland Temperance Alliance in 1852–53 to promote state and local legislation prohibiting the sale of liquor. When such efforts proved fruitless, the Sons apparently turned to other measures; a June 1858 *Leader* article noted that the Sons had formed "a vigilante committee . . . to

prosecute illegal dealers in spirituous liquors." When the Sons of Temperance celebrated their 20th anniversary in Cleveland in July 1867, the order counted 500 local members. Most of its members appear to have been tradesmen and middle-class professionals. Among the officers in 1857 were furniture dealer Wm. Hart, clerk Jas. Denham, and bookkeeper Edward E. Powers; lodge heads in 1874 included molder John McLeish, real-estate agent Samuel Foljambe, and carpenter Jeremiah A. Brown (who headed a "colored" division). The number of Cleveland-area Sons of Temperance lodges declined gradually in the late 1870s and 1880s, from 11 in 1874 to 7 by 1880, 5 in 1881, 3 in 1883, and 2 in 1884. By 1885 only the Broadway Div. remained, meeting in a church at Broadway and Gallup streets; by 1886 it too had disappeared.

**SOUTH BROOKLYN,** centering around the intersection of Pearl and Broadview roads, is a part of Cleveland's west side that was once the village of Brighton. Along with OHIO CITY, W. Cleveland, Old Brooklyn, LINNDALE, BROADVIEW HTS., and BROOKLYN, Brighton was created from Brooklyn Twp. Originally part of Warren Young's farm, Brighton was organized as a village in 1836 to capitalize on an expected land boom. In 1837, Nathan Babcock was elected mayor. When the expected growth did not occur, the residents lost interest in the village organization, refused to hold an election, and let the general assembly revoke its charter in 1839. Brighton reverted to the township, although the name stuck. In 1889, the community was organized under the name S. Brooklyn, amid protest by area businesses who feared new regulations. One company, the Cleveland Dryer Co., a manufacturer of superphosphates on MILL CREEK, obtained an injunction against the village, which they lost in the local court of appeals and the supreme court. The village, which had 800 people at its inception, was viewed as a haven from the soot of Cleveland. Cleveland, however, eyed the territory as annexable prey. In an election held in 1905, S. Brooklyn citizens voted 411–198 to become part of the city. Despite the vote, a vocal minority staged a desperate fight for independence. The mayor and proannexation councilmen ousted their opponents or pressured them to resign, and appointed similar-minded replacements for the last hour of the village's life as an independent entity. With the opposition quelled, S. Brooklyn joined Cleveland.

**SOUTH EUCLID,** originally a part of Euclid Twp., was incorporated as a village in 1917. The city occupies 4.7 sq. mi. and is bounded by CLEVELAND HTS. on the west, LYNDHURST on the east, RICHMOND HTS. on the north, and UNIVERSITY HTS. on the south. The original Euclid Twp. was named for the Greek mathematician by one of the surveyors of the CONNECTICUT LAND CO. During the 19th century, farming was the predominant occupation, with a scattering of small businesses that served the farming community. In 1867, Duncan McFarland opened a quarry along Euclid Creek, providing the area with its first and best-known industry. Access to the region was improved by the construction of a plank toll road along Mayfield Rd. in 1877 and the construction of an interurban railroad in 1899. The village grew slowly after 1917. The installation of utilities in the years after WORLD WAR I attracted some suburban growth, and the population rose to 6,146 by 1940. In June 1941, S. Euclid was incorporated as a city, with a mayor-council form of government. Major growth of the area occurred after WORLD WAR II. In 1980, the population stood at 29,000. The predominant ethnic groups were Jewish and Italian; together they constituted 68% of the population. The postwar growth saw the establishment of major shopping districts at the intersections of Cedar and Warrensville Ctr. roads and Green and Mayfield roads. Some light manufacturing firms located near the Green and Monticello Rd. area. A branch of the CUYAHOGA COUNTY PUBLIC LIBRARY was located in the old Wm. Telling mansion in 1950. The city's school system is combined with that of Lyndhurst. There are also 3 parochial elementary schools and 1 high school. NOTRE DAME COLLEGE is located in S. Euclid, as are 6 churches and 1 synagogue. Recreational facilities in the 1980s included 3 parks totaling 33 acres, 3 swimming pools, a private golf course, the OAKWOOD CLUB, and tennis courts.

South Euclid Golden Jubilee Book Committee, *Golden Jubilee, 1917–1967, South Euclid* (1967).

The **SOUTH EUCLID HISTORICAL SOCIETY** was incorporated on 2 Mar. 1966 to preserve historical data and mementos relating to S. EUCLID, Ohio. In 1967 the society published an 80-page history of S. Euclid on the occasion of the community's 50th anniversary. In 1975–76, it helped restore a schoolhouse in LYNDHURST as part of the national Bicentennial activities. In 1975 the society acquired quarters in the west wing of the former Telling estate, then owned by the CUYAHOGA COUNTY PUBLIC LIBRARY, at 4645 Mayfield Rd. Within this facility, the society established a series of display rooms that exhibited period furniture and artifacts or that highlighted important aspects of local history, such as the BLUESTONE QUARRIES. In 1984, the society had 125 members and functioned with a totally volunteer staff. In addition to operating its museum, the volunteers arranged sightseeing trips and hosted a monthly meeting of the membership. Dues and periodic fundraising projects provided operating revenues.

**SOUTH PRESBYTERIAN CHURCH** was located at 3166 Scranton and Prame streets. It began in the fall of 1890 as a mission Sunday school organized by Rev. Dr. Wm. Gaston, pastor of NORTH PRESBYTERIAN CHURCH. In October the PRESBYTERIAN UNION rented a hall for the Sunday school and engaged Rev. Alonzo Michael, who conducted classes from 19 Oct. 1890 until 1 Jan. 1891. In May 1891 the Presbyterian Union engaged Rev. Jas. D. Corwin as the group's leader. As membership in the Sunday school grew, a decision was made to construct a sanctuary. Accordingly, the Presbyterian Union purchased property at the corner of Scranton and Prame St., a church building was erected, and the first service was held on 1 Jan. 1892. On 21 Jan. 1892, the Presbyterian Committee (from the Presbytery of Cleveland) and elders Reuben F. Smith and Jas. A. Robinson organized South Presbyterian Church. It was incorporated on 4 Mar. 1892. Rev. Corwin served briefly in May 1892, and Rev. John L. Roemer was installed 19 Apr. 1893. During the pastorate of Rev. Geo. A. Mackintosh, the original frame structure was moved to an adjacent corner; a building campaign was launched; and the cornerstone for the new sanctuary was laid. It was dedicated on 1 Oct. 1905. As the neighborhood had become predominantly Roman Catholic, St. Elias Syrian Catholic Church purchased South Presbyterian Church, and on 11 July 1937, South Presbyterian merged with the Parma Presbyterian Church to form the PARMA-SOUTH PRESBYTERIAN CHURCH.

The **SOUTH WAITE FOUNDATION** was incorporated in 1953 by Francis M. (1906–69) and Margaret H. Sherwin. Francis M. Sherwin was a director of the HALLE BROS. CO. and former president and chairman of the board of the Brush Beryllium Co. From 1932–42, he was assistant treasurer of the Cleveland Trust Co. He was educated at Hotchkiss School and Yale University. Sherwin married Margaret M. Halle and had 3 sons, Peter, Brian, and Dennis. He was a trustee of the Cleveland Health Museum and mayor of Waite Hill. Grants are usually given to organizations with whom the foundation is familiar, with emphasis on community funds, the arts, secondary education, and medical research. No grants or scholarships are given to individuals. In 1982, assets of the foundation were $1,442,968, with expenditures of $111,237 for 30 grants. Officers included Brian Sherwin, Margaret H. Sherwin, and Donald W. Greuttner, with Sherman Dye and Geo. Karch.

The **SOUTHGATE SHOPPING CENTER** was one of the nation's first large shopping centers. It was built by A. Siegler & Sons, Inc., of Cleveland, which had been in the development business since the 1910s. In 1951, the firm announced the building of a $17 million community development in MAPLE HTS. to be called Southgate, with a shopping center, 500 homes, and 450 apartment units. With several other construction firms, Siegler began developing the 200-acre site along Libby Rd. between Warrensville Ctr. and Northfield roads in 1953. By the fall of 1954, 6 stores had opened in the center. The formal dedication was in 1955, when 44 stores opened. During the first several years of operation, the stores totaled annual sales of $7–8 million. Siegler owned and operated the shopping center through the Southgate Management Co.

As the center grew, with new stores opening each year, so did the surrounding community. The center provided 2,500 jobs in 1955. By 1961, Southgate had grown to 86 stores, with over $70 million in sales. Maple Hts.' population had almost doubled during the 1951–61 period. Expansion continued in the 1960s, with more stores, supermarkets, banks, residences, restaurants, and hotel, office, and medical facilities added to the complex, which employed nearly 2,500 persons. Southgate remained the largest shopping center in the area until the opening of the nearby RANDALL PARK MALL in 1976. Many believed Southgate might close, as the new mall immediately drew away the center's business. It lost 2 department stores to the mall and experienced a $42 million decrease in sales in 1976. But Southgate was able to hold on to many of its specialty stores and the largest supermarket outlets in the state. By late 1978, it experienced a resurgence with the opening of Ohio's largest K-Mart. Annual sales rebounded to the $125 million level as stores and customers started to return to Southgate. The center was able then to begin a $5 million remodeling program in 1980. By that time, it had 150 stores, with 30,000 shoppers daily.

**SOUTHWEST GENERAL HOSPITAL** operated one of the most active emergency departments in Cuyahoga County in 1986. A short-term, nonprofit general hospital, it has, for 60 years, received community support through a capital-improvements levy. Southwest General was founded in 1921 by 6 doctors. The need for a hospital in the BEREA area came during the influenza epidemic of 1919, when residents of the southwestern corner of the county realized that Cleveland hospitals were too far away. Residents of the area raised $100,000 to fund the hospital, originally known as Sprague House, the former home of M. A. Sprague. Impetus for its founding came from Dr. H. B. Kirtland. With 8 beds, it was one of the first community hospitals in the U.S. founded by public subscription. A new hospital, with 32 beds, was built on Bagley Rd. in Berea in 1925. Until 1959 it was officially known as Berea Community Hospital. The hospital was and continues (1986) to be supported by 6 communities: BROOK PARK, STRONGS-

VILLE, MIDDLEBURG HTS., Berea, OLMSTED FALLS, and OLMSTED TWP. As a general hospital, it provided basic medical services to residents in this area. The original structure was slowly added to, and by 1971 bed capacity had been increased to 180. The name was changed in 1959 to Southwest Community Hospital, and in 1968 to Southwest General Hospital. Construction of a new 235-bed hospital began in 1973 on a 20-acre site in Middleburg Hts. The new hospital, which opened in 1975, was supported by 1-mill levies voted by the 6 communities. Costing $15 million, the new hospital had beds for medical, surgical, obstetrical, and pediatric patients, as well as intensive- and coronary-care units. It also operated an out-patient clinic and professional building. In 1980, the hospital was filled to capacity several times, and there was an increased demand for services. An expansion project was proposed and approved by the state health department. Begun in the early 1980s, expansion was planned to include a new 3-wing addition that would increase bed capacity by 61, including 25 new beds for patients in a new psychiatric department.

**SPAFFORD, AMOS** (1753–1816), was a surveyor for the CONNECTICUT LAND CO. and an early settler of Cleveland. He performed one of the earliest surveys of Cleveland and made the first map detailing its original plan. Spafford was born in Vermont. He was known as "Major" Spafford, indicating a military connection and possible service in the Revolutionary War. He was a surveyor in both parties sent to the WESTERN RESERVE between 1796–97. During Cleveland's initial years of settlement, Spafford was given authority for fixing lot and street lines and determining land titles. He was also active as a public official, serving as a township trustee in 1802, and as township chairman in 1803. In 1802 he applied for and received a license to keep a tavern in Cleveland. In 1796, under the superintendence of Augustus Porter, Spafford and SETH PEASE surveyed a square-mile area for the future site of Cleveland. Both men made maps of the survey, but "Spafford's Map" is considered to be the first. It was endorsed in Spafford's hand as the "Original plan of the town and village of Cleaveland, Ohio, October 1, 1796." Several sheets of foolscap were pasted together to make the map. Spafford resurveyed the village in 1801 and planted 54 oak posts at the principal corners.

Spafford himself was one of the original lot owners in Cleveland. He was partly responsible for persuading the Connecticut Land Co. to reduce the higher price it had attached to city lots. In a letter written to the company in 1801, Spafford threatened to leave the Western Reserve altogether if the price was not lowered. He reportedly continued to have problems with real estate, as he acquired more land than he could pay for or resell. In 1809 he was elected to the lower house of the state legislature from Geauga County. Soon afterward he was appointed collector for the new port of entry on the Maumee River, and in 1810 he departed Cleveland to assume that post near Perrysburg, Ohio. He was married to Olive Barlow. Their daughter, Anna, was reportedly the first schoolteacher in Cleveland.

**SPALDING (SPAULDING), RUFUS** (3 May 1798–29 Aug. 1886), was a lawyer, judge, and congressman; he was a vocal opponent of slavery and the Fugitive Slave Law. Spalding was born on Martha's Vineyard, Mass., the son of a successful doctor. He was educated in Presbyterian schools and studied at Yale, 1813–17. He moved to Cincinnati in 1818, and the following year to Little Rock, Ark., to practice law. In 1821 he returned to Ohio, settling in Warren, then Ravenna and Akron. He originally visited Cleveland

in Mar. 1823, moving there permanently to practice law in 1852. Spalding led Cleveland lawyers against southern slaveowners who came North to claim fugitive slaves throughout the mid-1800s. In 1859 he defended Underground Railroad supporter Simeon Bushnell from charges that he had tried to obstruct a slaveowner from returning a captured runaway to the South. Bushnell was found guilty, but public opinion was moved by the efforts of the abolitionists (see ABOLITIONISM). Politically, Spalding had been a Democrat until the party turned proslavery. He then joined the Free-Soilers and later became an organizer for the Republican party. On this ticket he was elected Ohio congressman in 1863 after having served as state representative from Portage (1839) and Summit (1841) counties. He had also served as Ohio Supreme Court judge (1852). Spalding was active in community affairs in Cleveland. He assisted in building the collection of the Cleveland Law Library and in 1883 was named to a committee to erect a monument to Gen. MOSES CLEAVELAND. Spalding married Lucretia Swift, daughter of his friend Judge Zephaniah Swift, in 1822. The couple had 7 children.

**SPANG BAKING CO.** *See* **J. SPANG BAKING COMPANY**

**SPANGLER, BASIL L.** (1822–19 Jan. 1876), was a Cleveland dry-goods merchant who served as assistant quartermaster in the U.S. Army during the CIVIL WAR. Spangler was the son of Michael Spangler, who came to Cleveland from Stark County in 1816 and entered the tavern, hotel, and real-estate business. Another son, Miller M. Spangler (1813–5 May 1897), served as Cleveland fire chief (1842, 1844, 1847, 1850–55) and county sheriff. Basil L. Spangler served on the Cleveland Board of Water Works in 1853. He began his military service as quartermaster, with the rank of captain, at Camp Cleveland (see CIVIL WAR CAMPS) in July 1862. In Sept. 1863, he was in charge of the commissary at Camp Cuyahoga, a militia drill and training camp located at Willson's Grove in Cleveland for the 7th Military District, Ohio Militia. Spangler served as quartermaster at Cleveland until July 1865. He is buried in LAKE VIEW CEMETERY.

The **SPANISH-AMERICAN WAR.** Clevelanders were active, enthusiastic supporters of U.S. foreign policy as practiced by Ohioans Wm. McKinley, the president; Wm. R. Day, the secretary of state; and his successor, JOHN HAY. They lamented the national loss when the battleship *Maine* exploded in the harbor of Havana, Cuba, in mid-Feb. 1898; they were attentive to the diplomatic efforts to end Spanish control in Cuba in the weeks that followed. When war came, following McKinley's War Message to Congress on 11 Apr., they demonstrated their commitment to the "cause" by volunteering in large numbers for active service in what John Hay later called the "splendid little war." Despite the rapid response, the Cleveland contingents recruited for service were denied an opportunity to demonstrate their bravery in battle; the war was so short in duration, there was neither time nor transport facilities enough to move eager troops to the battlefields.

Approximately 1,000 Cleveland-area volunteers responded to the 26 Apr. "first call" for troops; an additional 1,400 volunteered with the second call in June. Most of these men were rostered in the 5th Regiment of the Ohio Natl. Guard. Until the war came, the regiment's duties had been confined to peacekeeping in labor conflicts such as the Massillon coal strike in 1894 and the 1896 Brown Hoist strike. Now, on 29 Apr. 1898, the 5th (845 men) left Cleveland for "Camp Bushnell" (an improvised rendezvous named for then-Ohio governor Asa Smith Bushnell, near Columbus), "the first of Cleveland's offering in the war for humanity . . . on their way to duty." Geo. A. Garretson, a Civil War veteran who was president of the Bank of Commerce in Cleveland, was commissioned brigadier general of volunteers. Majors Chas. F. Cramer and Arthur K. A. Liebich served with Garretson in command of the 5th Regiment. Battery A, with 103 men, commanded by Capt. Geo. T. McConnell, followed after the 5th on 30 Apr. The regiment was mustered into U.S. service on 11 May and was sent to Camp Thomas, Ga. Col. Courtland L. Kennan would command the unit during war operations. From Georgia, the regiment was moved to Tampa, Fla. Other Cleveland units were troops A, B, and C of the 1st Ohio Volunteer Cavalry (265 officers and enlisted men), commanded by Maj. Webb C. Hayes, which left Cleveland on 6 May, and Co. "D," 9th Battalion (colored), commanded by Capt. John C. Fulton (eventually 107 officers and enlisted men), which was mustered into the Natl. Guard on 27 May. Ten officers and 206 enlisted men of the Naval Reserves, and the 1st Battalion Engineers (the Grays), with 12 officers and 309 enlisted men, in mid-June were incorporated into the 10th Ohio Volunteer Infantry Regiment, commanded by Maj. Otto M. Schade. It is estimated that an additional 15 officers and 531 enlisted men from Cleveland volunteered independently and served in various other units during the conflict.

While the Cleveland contingents formed and were sent to training camps, the war went forward rapidly. American troops in Cuba captured the heights of El Caney and San Juan in the first 3 days of July; on 3 July, the American fleet commanded by Adm. Wm. T. Sampson destroyed the Spanish fleet under Adm. Pasqual Cervera, blocked the entrance to Santiago Harbor, and effectively sealed off the island's defenders from external support. On the other side of the world, Commodore Geo. Dewey had captured Manila, and the U.S. occupation of the Philippine Islands proceeded. Some Cleveland men volunteered for service with outfits that did get to Cuba, Puerto Rico, or the Philippines. Some of these were physicians and surgeons. But for Cleveland-based contingents, it was a different story. The 5th Regiment arrived by train in Tampa on 21 May, "travel stained and weary from a three days' journey through dust and smoke and heat." There the men established camp and waited for their supplies to be issued and transport assigned. On 1 June they were told to be ready to move at an hour's notice; their equipment, including the officers' horses and outfits, was on board the transport *Florida*. They expected to board ship on Monday, 6 June, but the *Florida* was struck by Transport No. 11 (the *Miami*) and partly sank in Tampa Bay with the 5th Regiment's equipment aboard. When Gen. Wm. R. Shafter sailed for Santiago on 8 June, the Cleveland contingent was left behind. The Peace Protocol was signed and hostilities ceased on 12 Aug.; the formal treaty ending the conflict would be negotiated at Paris (signed on 10 Dec.) and, after a bitter debate concerning acquisition of the Philippine Islands as part of the negotiated terms, ratified by the U.S. Senate on 6 Feb. 1899. By then, many of the Cleveland soldiers had already returned to civilian life. The 5th Regiment had come back to the city in September; it was mustered out on 5 Nov. Twenty deaths had occurred among the men in its ranks. TROOP A of the 1st Ohio Volunteer Cavalry was mustered out in Cleveland in October; Co. D of the 9th Battalion would remain in service until Jan., 1899, and the 10th Ohio Volunteer Infantry until March of that year.

The churches of Cleveland had held Thanksgiving services on 10 July for "glorious American victories" in the War with Spain. In his sermon at Old Stone Church, Dr.

HIRAM C. HAYDN asserted that wars seemed "necessary now and then to bring out the qualities of courage and bravery" among the people, adding that peace also offered "daily opportunity for heroism." What a contrast with the Mexican War, when churches were particularly involved with antiwar efforts. In both episodes, however, the concern about oppressed people—enslaved blacks, or Cubans, or Filipinos—helped shape attitudes toward the conflict. The War Emergency Committee of the Western Reserve Chap. of the Daughters of the American Revolution opened a collection point for contributions of pillow slips, pajamas, and nightshirts, as well as money for military hospitals. Located first in the Garfield Bldg. on E. 6th St., it later was moved to the Lennox Bldg. at the corner of Euclid Ave. and E. 9th St. As the "veterans" from the Florida embarkation camps returned, parades in their honor escorted them to feasts in the CENTRAL ARMORY, with "well-drilled young ladies, dressed in white and carrying flags," and the band playing "The Girl I Left behind Me." After the peace treaty was concluded, celebration of the nation's effort continued. A Spanish cannon, trophy of the war, was mounted on the Public Square. The United Spanish War Veterans formed a permanent organization in Cleveland and soon built up a substantial membership. The first "camp" was named for Gen. Geo. A. Garretson. Under the direction of Maj. Otto M. Schade, the first commander, the organization's activities flourished. Each camp was supported by a "White Escort" or women's auxiliary, especially in its Decoration (Memorial) Day commemorations. As late as the 1940s, there were 7 camps in the Cleveland area and a membership of 700. Although the war with Spain had paled in significance compared to the enormities of 2 world wars, it is obvious that some Clevelanders were dedicated to keeping alive memories of the short but (in their perspective) "splendid" conflict.

Carl Ubbelohde
Case Western Reserve University

Revere, Paul, *Cleveland in the War with Spain* (1900).

**SPEAKER, TRISTRAM "TRIS"** (4 Apr. 1888–8 Dec. 1958), was a baseball player for the CLEVELAND INDIANS from 1916–26. A peerless centerfielder, he was the player-manager of the city's first American League World Championship team, in 1920. Speaker was born at Hubbard City, Tex. A natural right-hander, he broke his arm as a youngster and learned to bat and throw left-handed. After high school, Speaker attended the Ft. Worth Polytechnic Institute for 2 years before beginning his professional baseball career. By 1909, he was the centerfielder for the Boston Red Sox, and with Harry Hooper and Duffy Lewis he made up what is still considered baseball's greatest defensive outfield. He was selected as the AL's Most Valuable Player when Boston won the 1912 World Championship.

After a salary dispute with the Boston ball club, Speaker's playing contract was traded to Cleveland in 1916 for $50,000. Speaker refused to report to the Indians until he received $10,000 of the purchase price. In his first year with Cleveland, Speaker hit .386 to win the AL batting championship. His salary of $40,000 was the highest in baseball at that time. On 19 July 1919, Speaker was named manager, replacing Lee Fohl, and the team finished 2d that year. In 1920 Speaker hit .388 and set a record of 11 consecutive hits as Cleveland won the league and world championships over the Brooklyn Dodgers. Unjustly accused of fixing a game with Ty Cobb, Speaker resigned as manager and player for the Indians in 1926. He was cleared of the charge and played his last 2 years with Washington and Philadelphia.

Speaker holds the AL outfield record for the most lifetime putouts of 6,706 and 449 assists (also a major-league record). Somewhat overshadowed by his contemporaries Ty Cobb and Babe Ruth, Speaker had a lifetime batting average of .345, and his 3,515 hits in 22 seasons rank him in the top 10 hitters of all time. He was the 7th player selected for the Baseball Hall of Fame in 1937. Popular in the city of Cleveland, he was called "Spoke" and the "Grey Eagle" because of his prematurely gray hair. Community-minded, Speaker helped found the SOCIETY FOR CRIPPLED CHILDREN and Camp Cheerful. For a time, Speaker was part-owner of the Kansas City team in the American Assoc. During the 1930s, he was in the wholesale liquor business and served for a time as the chairman of the Cleveland Boxing Commission. From 1947 to the time of his death, Speaker was an advisor, coach, and scout for the Indians. He married Mary Frances Cudahy in Cleveland in 1925.

**SPENZER, JOHN GEORGE** (6 Sept. 1864–28 July 1932), was an early expert in forensic medicine; he introduced the latest European toxicological techniques to the Cleveland area. Spenzer was born in Cleveland. He attended CENTRAL HIGH SCHOOL and in 1880 entered Western Reserve University, where he studied chemistry and toxicology under Dr. EDWARD MORLEY. He received his medical degree in 1884 but continued to study under Morley until 1887. After 5 years of additional study at the University of Strassburg and in Paris, Spenzer returned to Cleveland to teach at the College of Pharmacy, and later at the Cleveland College of Physicians & Surgeons. In 1910 he joined the faculty at WRU to teach legal chemistry and medical jurisprudence. Spenzer's course at WRU covered such topics as medical evidence and testimony, and criminal acts determined by medical knowledge. He became a regional expert on blood and poison analysis and was often called upon for blood identification. He also testified in numerous court cases that required medical evidence (e.g., whether or not a person was poisoned; or if certain spots were human blood). In 1917, Spenzer became director of the Medical Chemistry Laboratory, located in the Rose Bldg. Much of his research was devoted to vitamins and vitamin treatment for malnutrition. Because of his work in toxicology, in 1926 Spenzer was called upon to do an analysis of the CUYAHOGA RIVER to determine how harmful the discharge of acids and alkalines was to the water supply. Spenzer married Minnie Elizabeth Kittelberger on 10 June 1898.

Biographical Files, CWRU Archives.
Student Paper, Howard Dittrick Museum of Historical Medicine.

The **SPIETH, BELL, MCCURDY & NEWELL CO., LPA,** is a law partnership of 23 attorneys located in the Huntington Bldg. at EUCLID AVE. and E. 9th St. Incorporated in 1975, Spieth Bell is a medium-sized law firm with 17 partners, 5 associates, and 1 "of counsel." In 1986, the firm's managing partner was Richard Watson. Spieth Bell's principal areas of practice are commercial, corporate and securities, estate planning, domestic relations, mergers and acquisitions, probate, trusts, real estate, labor, tax, litigation, and entertainment and sports. Representative clients of the firm have included the CLEVELAND CAVALIERS, WCLV-FM, WOIO-TV, BALDWIN-WALLACE COLLEGE, RELIANCE ELECTRIC, WARNER & SWASEY, and the Milbar Corp. Spieth Bell's origins date back to 1867, when the law partnership of Mix & Noble opened at 150 Superior Ave. In 1870 the firm became Mix, Noble & White when JOHN G. WHITE was added as a partner.

White's greatest contribution was in bringing continuity to the young firm. The donor of the White Collection at the CLEVELAND PUBLIC LIBRARY, he remained with the firm until his death in 1930. In 1883, the firm moved to the Blackstone Bldg. In 1887 it changed its name to Mix & White. In 1890 it added 2 partners, becoming White, Johnson & McCaslin. The firm became White, Johnson, McCaslin & Cannon in 1896. In 1900 it moved its offices to the Williamson Bldg. Until its move into the Huntington (Union Trust) Bldg. in 1924, the firm underwent further changes by becoming White, Cannon & Johnson (1910); White, Johnson, Cannon & Neff (1913); White, Johnson, Cannon & Spieth (1919); and White, Cannon & Spieth (1923).

Lawrence Caleb Spieth (1883–1963) received his law degree from Western Reserve University and was admitted to the Ohio bar in 1907. He joined the firm as a corporate attorney and was made a partner in 1919. In 1929 the firm changed its name to Cannon, Spieth, Taggart, Spring & Annat. In 1939 it became Spieth, Taggart, Spring & Annat. In 1947, Harold K. Bell became a partner in the firm of Spieth, Spring, Annat & Bell. Bell received his law degree from WRU and was admitted to the Ohio bar in 1919. By 1948 the firm was known as Spieth, Spring & Bell. Everett D. McCurdy (1905–1986) joined the firm as an associate in 1952, and was made a partner in the firm of Spieth, Bell & McCurdy in 1958. In 1964 the firm became Spieth, Bell, McCurdy & Newell, reflecting Sterling Newell, Jr.'s, elevation to partnership. The only remaining active partner in 1986, Newell received his law degree from New York University and passed the Ohio bar in 1949.

**SPIRA, HENRY** (1863–10 Apr. 1941), was a banker whose principal customers came from among the thousands of immigrants who settled in Cleveland during the first 3 decades of the century. Spira was born and educated in Richwald, Hungary, and immigrated to the U.S. in 1879. He worked as a laborer for a steamship company upon his arrival in America, but he soon migrated to central Ohio, where he worked as a peddler and shopkeeper. In 1885, he returned to Hungary for 5 years, where he established a liquor business. In 1890, he returned to America, settled in Cleveland, and opened a saloon in the Woodland neighborhood.

In 1891, Spira became involved in a foreign-exchange and steamship ticket sales business, thus catering to the immigrant community in Woodland. By 1916, he had expanded into general banking with the creation of the Bank of Henry Spira. The bank's name was changed some years later to the Spira Savings & Loan Assoc. He maintained the foreign-exchange business through a new company, the Spira Internatl. Express Co., which was also an investment firm. In 1932, Spira retired from banking, and Spira Savings & Loan was taken over by the Guardian Trust Co. Spira was president of the Temple on the Heights for 12 years. Beyond that, his involvement in Jewish community organizations seldom included a leadership role. However, at his death, a large portion of his estate was willed to Jewish institutions, including the HEBREW FREE LOAN ASSOC., the Temple on the Heights, the Jewish Orthodox Home for the Aged, the MONTEFIORE HOME, MT. SINAI Hospital, the JEWISH ORPHAN HOME, and the Jewish Welfare Fed.

The **SPIRIT OF '76,** depicting a flag bearer, drummer boy, and fifer marching across a battlefield during the American Revolution, is perhaps the most famous painting to have been produced in Cleveland. The painting, by ARCHIBALD WILLARD, was created at the suggestion of Cleveland photographer JAS. F. RYDER in 1875. Ryder felt that a semihumorous, patriotic painting would be appropriate for showing at the Internatl. Centennial Exhibition to be held in Boston in 1876, and that chromolithographs of such a piece would be popular items at the forthcoming U.S. centennial exhibition in Philadelphia. Willard began work on the painting, originally entitled *Yankee Doodle*, in an upstairs bedroom of his home in Wellington, Ohio. In Feb. 1876, the work was moved to Willis Ame's studio in the old Union Natl. Bank Bldg. at 308 Euclid Ave. to facilitate modeling sessions. Hugh Moser, a Civil War veteran and friend of Willard's, posed as the fifer; HENRY K. DEVEREUX, son of Gen. JOHN H. DEVEREUX, served as the model for the drummer; and Willard's father, Rev. Samuel Willard, served as the inspiration for the flag bearer. The death of Willard's father before the completion of the painting led Willard to create a serious rather than humorous work.

Ryder's chromolithographs of the painting were quite popular at the centennial celebration and led to demands that the painting be brought to Philadelphia. After the exhibition was over, the painting was shown in several large cities. While it was in Boston, the name *Spirit of '76* was suggested and adopted to avoid confusion of the painting with the bumbling Boston yokel Yankee Doodle. The painting was then exhibited in the Old South Church in Boston for several years before being returned to Ryder's gallery, where it was purchased by Gen. Devereux. The painting's popularity led Willard to paint 6 successive "original" versions. Two copies are held in Cleveland, one at the WESTERN RESERVE HISTORICAL SOCIETY and the second at Cleveland City Hall, this copy having been commissioned by Mayor NEWTON D. BAKER in 1912. Much controversy and speculation surround the current location of the original version. It is widely held that that version is now in Marblehead, Mass.

**SPITALNY, PHIL** (7 Nov. 1890–11 Oct. 1970), was a composer, conductor, and clarinetist. Spitalny was born in Odessa, Russia. He attended the Odessa Conservatory and toured Russia as a child clarinet prodigy. His family migrated to the U.S. in 1905 and settled in Cleveland. Spitalny played in and directed local bands in Cleveland and Boston. He directed a 50-piece symphony orchestra in one of Boston's larger movie houses. He conducted his own orchestra on radio, in hotels, and on recordings and made a successful New York debut in 1930. In 1934, Spitalny organized an all-girl orchestra, which made its debut at the Capital Theater in New York. The orchestra performed on the radio program "The Hour of Charm" beginning in Jan. 1935. It continued performing on the radio, in concerts, and eventually on television. It received the Achievement Award of 1937 of the radio committee of the Woman's National Exposition of Arts and Industries for the most distinguished work of women in radio for that year. Spitalny composed such songs as "Madelaine," "Enchanted Forest," "It's You, No One But You," "Save the Last Dance for Me," "The Kiss I Can't Forget," and "Pining for You." He was married to Evelyn Kaye Klein, who was a member of the all-girl orchestra.

**SPORTS.** The earliest inhabitants of the WESTERN RESERVE lacked the time, energy, and resources for any but the most basic recreations. Hunting and fishing were too vital to the survival of the homestead to be enjoyed solely for the drama of the chase. Too few people were available for team sports. Special equipment, such as ice skates or bats for cricket or rounders, would have consumed space on the western trek better given to tools. For many people,

such time as could be spared away from agriculture was spent on Sabbath devotions. Even so, the severity of life on the frontier required some tempering. Rudimentary swimming was popular in the summer months, although few people could swim in the modern sense. Foot and horse races were common, generally with wagers riding on the results. These usually resulted from impromptu encounters in town or on the trails. Other competitions would pit individual muscle and skill in woodchopping or furrow plowing; however, these contests were part of larger social events, such as fairs or barnraisings, which would draw the families in from their lonely farms. The contests, then, served 2 purposes. Not only would a champion, skilled in the arts that the pioneers valued, be chosen, but significant amounts of work would also be performed. In the meantime, communal activities would bind the group as a society, in the guise of recreation. Quilting and cornhusking bees, which required the cooperative effort of a number of people, provided the opportunity for social discourse and gossip. The products of such bees were turned to practical use. While early Clevelanders enjoyed their recreations, they did not play games in the modern sense. Such sports, with no discernible outcomes aside from the final score, were extravagances for the pioneers.

That began to change with the construction of the canals of the 1820s. Waterborne transportation, which facilitated the movement of people and goods, began to reshape Cleveland's economic role. While the city continued to service the needs of the surrounding farms, it increasingly became a center for industry and a transshipment point for trade. The population grew, from approximately 600 in 1820 to just over 1,000 in 1830. Greater wealth and lowered transportation costs allowed the importation of items that had previously been considered luxuries. It is in this period that organized team sports make their first appearances in the historical record. While the older recreations remained popular, opportunities for participation in the agriculturally oriented activities began to diminish in the city center. At the same time, the new industry and commerce introduced additional leisure time for greater numbers of Clevelanders. Therefore, sufficient numbers of players could be gathered at a set time to stage matches of rounders or old-one-cat (early forms of BASEBALL) or shinny (an early form of HOCKEY).

This period marks a transitional point in the city's economy and culture. The rugged individualism of the pioneer grew less important for survival. Instead, the new industrialism required an ethic of group cooperation, necessary for the management of complex, interrelated tasks. The new sports taught that ethic. Even the older creations were, in part, marked by this change. Hunting and fishing, once crucial as economic activities, now became recreational, to be scheduled into leisure time. Of course, the harvests of these expeditions were welcome additions to the family larder. However, the tradition of individualism did not disappear. Horseracing, BOXING AND WRESTLING, and shooting matches continued to pit individual competitors against one another. Society and culture still placed a high value on personal achievement. Thus, by the 1830s, the 2 enduring themes of American sports were in place. Cooperative team sports and solitary performance sports mirrored the competing social ethics of individual community and liberty. Significantly, both shared the goal of accomplishment through victory, of the defeat of an opposition. These themes remained unchallenged for years. The trends begun in the 1830s continued relatively unchanged into the 1850s. Then, the industrial takeoff of Cleveland financed an expansion of sporting activities.

The decade before the CIVIL WAR saw the systemization of sporting events. Whereas previously, matches of all descriptions had been scheduled on a casual basis, with such participants as were available, now organizations set dates and advertised venues. One of the city's perennial favorites, horseracing, was among the first to be so treated. In 1850 the Cleveland Jockey Club was established. The club hosted an annual 5-day meet of pacing and trotting events (horseback racing was considered vulgar). The next year, the Gymnasium opened on Superior Ave. The facility provided acrobatic and calisthenic equipment. In addition, it sponsored track-and-field meets, boxing, and wrestling. Recreational BOATING had been growing in popularity, and in 1855, the Ivanhoe Boat Club was created. The club was devoted to rowing and sculling, but became the model for the yachting clubs to come. In another aspect of gamesmanship, the Cleveland Chess Club was organized in 1858. In the meantime, casual sports remained popular. A craze for mass winter sleigh riding swept northern Ohio in 1856, and huge meets were held throughout the Reserve. Ice skating also became fashionable for winter recreation. The older games continued to be played. However, a revelation had been made that would affect sports in both Cleveland and the nation: the games required money. Financial reward both enabled and attracted the highest levels of competition. The great age of sports in America was about to begin.

Of course, the first 5 years of the 1860s were dominated by another contest: the Civil War. Most organized sporting activities drew to a standstill as men were called away to the Army. However, the tremendous economic growth in Cleveland created by the war generated new impetus and opportunities for sportsmen with the return of peace. Certainly, the most important of these changes was the advent of modern professional sports. In Cleveland, it began with the formation of the FOREST CITY BASEBALL CLUB, an amateur baseball team, in 1865. Baseball was emerging as the "national pastime," and such clubs were springing up across the country. In short order, the influences of money (through gambling) and community rivalry caused abuses against the amateur status of the game. "Ringers" (skilled players posing as local citizens) and "fixed" games came to light. In 1869, the Cincinnati Red Stockings became the first club to turn from amateur to professional status. The most innocuous of the abuses, the importation and payment of talented players, was legitimated. The more serious offenses, such as the manipulation of game results by corrupted players on behalf of gamblers, were policed by the club's internal discipline. Immediately following the Cincinnati announcement, the Forest City Club reorganized itself on a professional basis.

Many important trends came to fruition with this transformation. Sports became an industry, providing a livelihood for players and profits for owners and facility operators. The increasingly heterogeneous population of the city found a common rallying point in the performance of "their" team. The manufacturing economy found an apt symbol in the cooperative competition of professionalized sports. Sports became a microcosm of, and metaphor for, free-enterprise capitalism. However, an important new theme was introduced, in direct competition with the older ones of individualism and team play. In 1867 the German community founded the Socialer Turn-Verein, a combined athletic club and social center. The GERMANS, more communitarian in thought than the individualistic Anglo-Americans, deemphasized the competitive aspect of sport. The "Turners" valued the aesthetics of gymnastics and the social bonding of group activities. This new theme would be reworked by succeeding East European immigrants in the Sokol movement to provide a familiar reference in a bewildering culture. The political aspect of sports was now overtly displayed.

Other sports continued to organize. Another horseracing track, the Cleveland Driving Club, was founded in 1867. Also that year, the Forest City Skating Rink, the area's first indoor rink, was built; it became a hub of wintertime social gatherings. Fads swept through the city. Long-distance walking changed from an onerous chore to a recreation under the inspiration of Edward P. Weston, a nationally renowned pedestrian, again in 1867. In 1869 the bicycle craze rode into town in the guise of the uncomfortable Velocipede. The 1870s generally continued these trends. In 1871, the Forest City Club joined the Natl. Assoc. of Professional Baseball Players. Although neither organization lasted out the decade, the structure of industrialized sports was becoming set. In 1872, the first bowling alley was built on Bank (now W. 6th) St. BOWLING was popular among workingmen, as it was inexpensive, could be played individually or as part of a team, and usually featured a saloon on the premises. On the other end of the social spectrum, the UNION CLUB was also founded that year, for the promotion of "physical training and education." However, across the years, the club's role as an "old boys" network came to predominate its function. Professional baseball was reintroduced in 1878, with the Cleveland Baseball Club of the Natl. League. The communal sports movement grew with the foundation of the Sokol Czech in 1879.

The 1880s brought not only increased participation in sports, but also expansion in the variety of games played. TENNIS, roller skating, and bicycling were adopted by the social elite in the first half of the decade. The first FOOTBALL game was played in 1887, when CENTRAL HIGH SCHOOL defeated Case School of Applied Science. The modern era of Cleveland sports can be said to begin with the last decade of the 19th century. In 1891, the first great sports stadium, LEAGUE PARK, opened. Three notable, and ultimately profitable, games were introduced: BASKETBALL in 1894 by the YMCA; GOLF in 1895 by SAMUEL MATHER; and hockey at an indeterminate date by amateur sportsmen. The cult of the star player was established in the career of DENTON TRUE "CY" YOUNG, who led the CLEVELAND SPIDERS baseball team to the Temple Cup national championship. Finally, Cleveland fans were surprised to learn another feature of the sports industry: teams could be relocated in search of greater profitability. The very competitive Spiders were purchased, then transferred to St. Louis. When a less talented team was fielded under the old name, the city found that loyalty was transient in the business of athletics.

Sports were essentially divided into 3 categories: the spectator-sports business; elite participatory sports; and amateur participatory sports. The first included baseball, boxing prizefights, and exhibitions in a variety of games. Representative selections of all social classes could be found at these events. The second included horse and sleigh racing, tennis, golf, yacht racing, bicycling, and whist (bridge). These games demanded either a large capital outlay, or an equal commitment of leisure time. Finally, the less-well-off could find recreation through amateur clubs, organizations, schools, or casual games, in which the financial burden was spread across a large number of people. This pattern remains true, with modifications, into the 1980s. However, the modifications would prove to have important social, economic, and political ramifications.

Cleveland entered its most expansive years with the turn of the century, and sports shared in the growth. Stars were found who were made to symbolize the city's industrial strength. NAPOLEON LAJOIE, the best baseball player

917

of the period, was imported to bolster the sagging Cleveland team. He performed so well that the team was renamed the "Naps" in his honor. More important, he restored attendance, which prevented the removal of the team from Cleveland. The city retained its "major-league" status. Amateur leagues in all sports were founded at the municipal, collegiate, and high school levels. Progressive Protestantism, inspired by the example of Theodore Roosevelt, declared that physical education was concomitant with mental and moral development, and necessary for the security of the nation. (Nonetheless, football for some ministers was beyond the pale.) The city's first professional football and basketball games were played during the 1900s as exhibition matches. Auto racing and rallying began with the Cleveland Auto Club's Century Runs in 1901 and the Glidden Tours in 1905.

Two interesting sidelights occurred in the decade. First, Cleveland's BLACKS invaded the previously all-white domain of major sports when Ted Green led Case School to the state football championship in 1902. Next, the growing political and economic power of sportsmen was displayed when horse racers and players created the town of N. RANDALL in 1908. Cleveland had annexed the independent village of GLENVILLE, the old center of racing, in 1905, and made gambling illegal. The GLENVILLE RACE TRACK was abandoned, and the horsemen reestablished operations miles to he south. Women's involvement in sports also increased during the 1900s. While women had been enthusiastic participants in the bicycle craze of the 1880s and 1890s, most other sports were deemed unfeminine. The newer sports, golf, tennis, and badminton, were seen as sufficiently decorous to allow female players. This partial enfranchisement in the sporting world reflects the larger issues of suffragism and feminism under discussion in general society at the time.

The major innovation in Cleveland in the 1910s was the introduction of professional football. A team called the Cleveland Indians was organized in 1916, but proved a financial failure. (The organizers may have hoped to trade upon the name recognition of the baseball team, which had also become the Indians the previous year.) In 1919 the CLEVELAND TIGERS were created and proved a success, which convinced the investors to buy into the American Professional Football League. This league would grow into the modern Natl. Football League. In addition, the growth of amateur-league structures continued. These often served specific constituencies, such as the Old Boys Workers Group basketball league of 1915, the Cleveland District Golf Assoc. of 1917, or the Cleveland Women's Bowling Assoc. of 1918. These groups were often clearly defined along class, racial, or sexual boundaries.

The 1920s are often represented as a great turning point in the history of sports. The years 1850–1920 have been called the "Age of the Player," in which the athletes controlled the rules of the games. The years after 1920 have been styled the "Age of the Spectator." Business interests are thought to have taken charge, particularly in the wake of the 1919 Chicago "Black" Sox scandal. Play was standardized, control was tightened (with the intent of preventing further public disillusionment with corrupt players), and inducements were offered (promotional events, doubleheaders, and the like), all with the intention of providing a predictable product to the buying public. That seems to have been particularly true in Cleveland professional sports. The decade saw the greatest expansion of professional sports in the history of the city. Golf clubs and courses sprang up throughout Cuyahoga County, and the first major golf tournament, the Western Open in 1921, was held. Three football teams represented the city, in sequence, in the

APFL. The baseball Indians won the World Series in 1920. The basketball Rosenblums won the first championship of the American Basketball League in 1925, and repeated in 1928 and 1929. The hockey Indians also debuted with a championship, in 1929. The NATL. AIR RACES were launched that year. The great expansion created a buyer's market for athletes' services by flooding the field with opportunity. General prosperity gave the spectators dollars to spend, and the owners rushed to service the fans. Other considerations than the bottom line were also served. Ethnic Clevelanders found athlete heroes whose skills and success marked them as typical Americans. The IRISH had boxer JOHNNY KILBANE, the JEWS, football quarterback BENJAMIN (BENNY) FRIEDMAN, the POLES, STELLA WALSH, and the SLOVAKS, the Benedictine High School football team. The Newman-Stearn Co. team won the World Women's Basketball Championship in 1926. The Air Races presented science in action. Sports, more than ever, symbolized the city's growth, civic cohesiveness, and technological prowess.

The economic catastrophe of the Depression was uneven in its effects on American society in general. While at times unemployment reached 30%, those who retained work usually did not suffer from the Depression's effects. That proved to be true for Cleveland sports in the 1930s in 2 ways. First, while some professional sports enterprises went bankrupt (the basketball Rosenblums and the football Indians), others drew enough spectators to continue profitable operations (the baseball Indians and the hockey Indians/Falcons/Barons), and still others found new demand for their services (the football Rams). Second, the upperclass recreations continued a leisurely expansion. The Cleveland Open golf tournament of 1938 offered a purse of $10,000. The city continued to produce national and international bridge champions.

Nonetheless, undercurrents of the social turmoil were evident. JESSE OWENS came out of Cleveland into legend by shattering Nazi theories of racial superiority at the 1936 Berlin Olympics, only to discover in later life that athletic triumph did not guarantee success in white society. The great unionizing drives led the city's bowling pinboys and billiard racksetters to organize as Local 48A of the Bldg. Service Employees. Finally, the communal sports movement reached its peak with the 1936 Workers' Olympiad. The event, sponsored by the Czech Socialist WORKERS GYMNASTIC UNION, drew hundreds of Sokol-style gymnasts to protest the competitive nature of both traditonal sports and capitalist economics. Some of the danger of that turmoil was allayed by sports as entertainment and employment. Two improved sports facilities were constructed, CLEVELAND MUNICIPAL STADIUM in 1931 and the CLEVELAND ARENA in 1937. Baseball began radio broadcasts over WHK in 1931. The federal WPA constructed nearly $12 million of recreational improvements in the CLEVELAND METROPARKS, providing jobs in the process. The spectacle of the Air Races provided hope in the inevitability of progress.

Sports always stagnate during wartime, as the manpower pool is called to other concerns. WORLD WAR II was no exception. Teams played, but no innovation occurred. That changed dramatically with the end of the war. Wartime experiences had forced a new sophistication on all segments of American society. Members of widely varied ethnic and class groupings had been forced into close proximity by military service or civilian employment. Pent-up demand and a reinvigorated economy were poised for a great economic boom. Changes in work standards, labor laws, and productivity had released time for leisure uses. RADIO and, more important, TELEVISION needed material to fill air time. All of these worked on sports, beginning almost immediately with the end of the war.

It is difficult to determine which was more significant, the advent of the black athlete in the professional major leagues, or the impact of electronic media on the operations of sports. Each proved to have profound social ramifications. In Cleveland the "color line" was broken when Bill Willis and Marion Motley debuted with the CLEVELAND BROWNS in 1946. Like previous minority ethnics, blacks hoped to use athletic success to legitimate themselves. The strategy seemed to succeed, perhaps too well. An athletic career increasingly came to be viewed as the only ticket out of the ghetto. Still, in these early years of the civil-rights movement, the 2 football players, track's Harrison Dillard, and baseball's Larry Doby seemed the embodiment of desegregation. The electronic media brought athletes directly into the home. Enthusiastic commentators raised their status to the heroic. Their comments were sought on every subject, from the utility of consumer products to the general social situation. Even more than that, athletes were held as role models for the country's young people. The late 1940s were Cleveland's moment of supreme civic confidence. INDUSTRY boomed as never before, providing goods and services to a prosperous domestic public and a war-ravaged world. The succession of championship professional teams was viewed as positive proof of the city's enduring vitality and central role in the national economy. However, those very same social changes that had produced the postwar wealth were about to spur the long decline of the core city. Increased income and fear of black integration created the white flight to the suburbs. The urban center came to be a destination, rather than a residence, and one of increasingly alien and fearful mien. The decay of the urban core began in the 1950s. The process was mirrored in professional athletics, although the two were not causally linked. Still, the frustration created by mediocre sports performances contributed to the erosion of the city's image and confidence. This effect was particularly pronounced among the working class, whose civic involvement tended to be limited to support of the teams. The decay was a gradual process, in both the city and the professional sports teams. The Indians won 1 last American League pennant (1954) before lapsing into long years of ineptitude. The Browns remained a contender in the NFL in the 1960s. However, the hockey CLEVELAND BARONS were denied entry into the Natl. Hockey League in 1952, in part because the NHL owners suspected that Cleveland did not have "major league potential."

These social changes also affected amateur and scholastic sports. The rapidly growing suburbs quickly established recreational programs for both classes of participants. Again, general prosperity allowed new options in leisure pursuits. Within the city limits of Cleveland, a similar expansion occurred, but with some important differences. Municipal leagues were funded in several sports, with an expressed intention of providing diversion to school-age children and combating juvenile delinquency. High school games became racial, ethnic, or neighborhood contests, underlining the tension of the perceived economic competition between races, and cultural breakdown within classes. Even the sports generally regarded as upper-class, such as golf or tennis, gained fewer well-to-do adherents. All of these trends accelerated in the universal unrest of the 1960s. Unparalleled national wealth contrasted sharply with center-city poverty. Locally, the decline of the city's economic power had become evident. In a time when sports were an obsession as never before, Clevelanders were afraid to attend athletic events because of crime or racial violence. The materialism and mercenary motivations of the well-paid professional athletes were denounced by social critics. Nationally, the failure of the city's professional sports team contributed to Cleveland's increasingly poor reputation. The career of the Browns' great fullback, Jim Brown, is a study in the tensions and contradictions of the period. Brown is considered by many to have been the greatest athlete in the history of football. Graceful, powerful, and talented, he set many records in his 9-year tenure (1957–65). He was a complex man whose motivations ran deeper than those of the typical football player. His racial pride as a black was strong, he was aware of the larger issues such as civil rights and Vietnam, and he reacted strongly to slights. While at the height of his skills, he gave up football to take up acting. It could be said that, like the rest of the country, Brown chose to pursue illusions in the later years of the decade.

On all levels, the 1960s proved to be a reprise of the 1950s. The Barons were again denied entry into the NHL, for the same reason. Suburban athletic participation grew as new sports, such as skiing, were introduced. Inner-city programs staggered along, beset by a declining financial base, as games were played under police supervision. Local colleges and universities began to experience problems maintaining student sports in the face of competition from the major "sports factory" schools. It seems that Cleveland's long decline hit bottom in the 1970s. The series of economic recessions and energy shocks severely wounded the city's manufacturing economy. Municipal finances were in disarray. The city was strongly polarized along racial and class lines. Fittingly, the professional athletes, advanced in the past as the symbols of industrial might, now appeared as the models of futile efforts. Attendance began to fall steadily at Indians games. Instances of crowd violence were reported at Browns games. The establishment of major-league hockey (the Crusaders and the revived Barons), basketball (the CLEVELAND CAVALIERS), and soccer (the Cobras) proved a source of amusement, astonishment, and anger for fans. Even the great sports "palaces," the Stadium and the Arena, were now seen as aged and decrepit embarrassments. A new facility, the Coliseum, was built miles from the center city, specifically to service the more affluent suburbs. Even the city's scholastic athletic league, the Senate, had to be reorganized in North and South groupings, in order to minimize the visibility of the east-west racial division.

Another symbol appeared in the person of Frank Robinson, the great baseball outfielder and the first black hired as a manager for a major-league team (1974). In an industry that thrives on symbols, Robinson was a natural choice. He was to represent a new beginning, a recognition of skill and accomplishment. In addition, it was hoped that he would draw larger numbers of black Clevelanders to Indian games. However, his contentious personality and the team's lack of ability forced his dismissal after less than 3 seasons. Robinson became a victim of misdirection and misunderstanding, much like the city he was to supposed to inspire. Sports participation, as usual, grew in the suburbs. In fact, increased popularity of soccer among the affluent caused the formation of a major-league team, the CLEVELAND FORCE, which played in the Coliseum. While styling itself a Cleveland team, the Force recognized that it attracted a metropolitan audience.

Cleveland seems to have decided to have a renaissance in the 1980s. Investment in downtown, the medical complexes, and the neighborhoods was high, although the industrial economy remained depressed. Similarly, the sports establishment attempted to revive itself, although not without a few pratfalls, caprices, and catastrophes along the way. Ted Stepien's ownership of the Cavaliers (1980–83) was regarded as the byword in how not to run a sports franchise. In 1983–84 it was learned that several Browns players were undergoing treatment for cocaine addiction. For many fans, the understanding that the heroes of the playing field were subject to the problems of the larger society came as a shock. The Indians lost 102 games in 1985, the worst record in modern baseball. Finally, the cocaine overdose of the Browns' Don Rodgers renewed questions about the role of sports and athletes in society. Nonetheless, the sudden success of all the city's sports operations in 1986 assisted the renaissance spirit. Indeed, early in the 1986 season, when it seemed that the Indians would be purchased and moved from the city, Clevelanders turned out at the Stadium in numbers that had not been seen in years. The Browns, the Cavaliers, the Force, and the Cleveland State University Vikings basketball team all contended for championships. The Indians fielded their strongest team in decades, and finished out of last place. The teams provided a topic of conversation other than closed factories, racially divided politics, crime, a tottering school system, and diminishing municipal services. Perhaps, as in the past, the athlete-symbols were leading indicators of better times ahead. Underneath all the discussions of the varied purposes of sport, it must never be forgotten that the games remain primarily business. It is a business of monumental proportions. In the 1980s, the city government and leading citizens hoped to use a $250 million domed stadium as a linchpin in a major downtown redevelopment program. While all of the major professional teams refused to reveal their internal figures or net worths, it was estimated that the Browns could be valued at $50 million, the Indians at $35 million, the Cavaliers at $15 million, and the Force at $7 million. Overall, it was estimated that nearly $1 billion was spent in the 5-county metropolitan Cleveland area on sports equipment, admissions, and memorabilia every year in the 1980s.

Michael McCormick
Western Reserve Historical Society

**SPORTS MEDICINE** became established in Cleveland in 1969 with the creation of a Sports Medicine Sec. in the Dept. of Orthopedic Surgery at the CLEVELAND CLINIC. It was one of the first units of its kind in the country. The idea for a section devoted to sports medicine was conceived by a group of orthopedic surgeons at the clinic. Since the early 1960s, interest in sports medicine had been on the rise nationally because of a growing belief that injuries to athletes required special attention, and also because more people from all age groups were participating in athletics. The major points of the clinic program were early diagnosis, early treatment, rehabilitation, and ultimately prevention. The section's first director was Dr. H. Royer Collins, followed in 1975 by Dr. John Bergfield. From the beginning, emphasis at the clinic was on school athletics. In 1970, the first annual symposium on sports medicine was held, attended by doctors, trainers, coaches, and sports officials. Other school and community programs for the prevention and treatment of athletic injuries followed. The Sports Medicine Sec. introduced a training program for arthroscopic surgeons in in-depth sports medicine, including wide clinical research into the process of wound and cartilage healing, and proper use of diets, fluids, drugs, protective gear, and exercises. By 1977, the Sports Medicine Sec. was seeing an average of 45 athletes per day. An exercise room with Nautilus machinery had been added, and also a workshop for the making of special pads and braces. The section also expanded its treatment to include medical problems that arose from milder activities such as bike riding or dancing. Similar sports-medicine programs, although less comprehensive than the clinic's, were instituted at Shaker Hts. and LUTHERAN medical centers, and at Rainbow Babies & Childrens Hospital during the 1970s.

**SQUIRE, ANDREW** (21 Oct. 1850–5 Jan. 1934), as a corporation lawyer was instrumental in planning the organizational structure of numerous local companies during the period of Cleveland's growth as a national industrial center. Squire was born in Mantua, Ohio, to Andrew Jackson and Martha Wilmot Squire. Educated in the Mantua public schools, he began studying medicine, but he chose instead a career in law. He graduated from Hiram College in 1872 with the LL.B. degree. Coming to Cleveland with a letter of introduction from Congressman JAS. GARFIELD, Squire worked in the law office of Caldwell & Marvin while reading the law. Having never attended a law school or a lecture, Squire passed an oral examination and was admitted to the Ohio bar in 1873. He became a member of the firm of Hart & Squire in 1876. He withdrew in 1878 to form what was to become the firm of Estep, Dickey & Squire. In 1890, Squire and JAS. DEMPSEY, a junior partner in the firm, united with WM. SANDERS to form SQUIRE, SANDERS & DEMPSEY.

Squire's subsequent specialization in corporation law led him to handle the affairs of many of Cleveland's largest and most important businesses. His precept was "The harder the conflict, the greater the triumph." He carried the thought like a banner through all his legal battles. In the courtroom Squire was capable of presenting the facts in a case with such conviction and force that the jury generally was convinced. Recognized as a man of unfailing courtesy and candor and infinite kindness, Squire became the close friend and advisor to many of Cleveland and Ohio's business and political leaders of his day, including MARCUS HANNA, Wm. McKinley, SAMUEL MATHER, and MYRON HERRICK. Yet, he also found time to listen to and advise young and upcoming lawyers on their problems. Squire served as a trustee or officer of numerous Cleveland businesses, including Union Carbide & Carbon, the CLEVELAND QUARRIES, Corrigan-McKinney Steel, the CLEVELAND UNION STOCKYARDS, and the Cleveland & Pittsburgh Railroad. During his later years, Squire spent considerable time at Valleevue, his Chagrin Valley estate, growing rare plants and herbs. Squire married Ella Mott, who died in the early 1890s. In 1896, he married Eleanor Seymour. Squire had 1 son, Carl.

White, Jack, Esq., "Biography on Andrew Squire" undated.

**SQUIRE, SANDERS AND DEMPSEY** is a Cleveland-based law firm with a national reputation as one of the foremost firms in corporate and municipal law. In 1986, its practice spanned a broad range of specialties, including international, environmental, labor, and public law. Employing over 320 attorneys, it maintained offices in Washington, D.C., New York, Columbus, Miami, Phoenix, and Brussels in addition to Cleveland, and had one of the largest group of trial lawyers of any American firm. Born out of a 3-man partnership formed in 1890, SS&D was, in 1986, one of the few major Cleveland law firms operating under its original name. ANDREW SQUIRE, WM. B SANDERS, and JAS. H. DEMPSEY constituted the founding trinity of what is often referred to as Cleveland's oldest law-firm partnership, and Ohio's largest. Squire was one of the great corporate lawyers of his day and maintained numerous political connections throughout the city and state. Sanders, recognized as one of the finest legal minds of his times, is best remembered for creating the trust arrangements that made the CLEVELAND MUSEUM OF ART a major world museum and for leading the legal opposition against the attempt by Mayor TOM L. JOHNSON to gain municipal control of Cleveland's traction lines. Dempsey, Squire's law partner in the firm predating SS&D, was the organizational genius who managed the firm's everyday affairs. SS&D experienced tremendous growth during that period when large corporations and giant mergers were the order of the day during the industrial age, and at one time it handled nearly all of the municipal bond work in Ohio. In 1967 the firm merged with McAfee, Hanning, Newcomer, Hazlett & Wheller, making SS&D the largest law firm in Ohio, with 115 lawyers. In 1976, the firm opened its first foreign office, in Brussels. A single partnership unites all offices, and the firm is directed by a 7-member management committee elected by the partners. SS&D became enmeshed in controversy in 1975 when as bond counsel for the city of Cleveland it faced a conflict-of-interest situation when it also represented CEI, which then had problems with the Cleveland Municipal Light Plant. As a result, the firm ceased representing the city as bond counsel. SS&D, still maintaining a commitment to the growth and development of Cleveland, encourages public-service work at all levels from its staff of attorneys.

**SQUIRE'S CASTLE** is a picturesque castellated and turreted ruin located on Chagrin River Rd. in the N. Chagrin Reservation of the Cleveland Metroparks System. The irregular stone structure was originally built as part of the estate of Feargus B. Squire (1850–1932), vice-president and general manager of the STANDARD OIL CO. until 1909. Attracted by the beauty of the Chagrin Valley, Squire purchased 525 acres there in the 1890s. He engaged a New York architect and planned 2 buildings in the style of English or German baronial halls. The existing structure was erected to serve as a gatehouse and caretaker's quarters, and the estate was improved with groves of trees, ponds, bridges, and miles of gravel roadway. The main residence was never built, and Squire built his principal home in Wickliffe. In 1922 the property was sold to a private land developer, and it was acquired by the Metropolitan Park Board in 1925 as the beginning of the N. Chagrin Reservation. The gatehouse was seriously vandalized and deteriorated; it is now only a shell, consisting of the stone and brick walls. Popularly known as "Squire's Castle," it is used as a shelterhouse and picnic area by park visitors.

Cavalier, Julian, *American Castles* (1973).

**STAGER, ANSON** (20 Apr. 1825–26 Mar. 1885), was a pioneer in the field of telegraphy. He was born in Ontario County, N.Y., and reared in Rochester, N.Y., where his father manufactured tools. At the age of 16, Stager worked on the *Rochester Daily Advertiser*, owned and published by Henry O'Reilley, who also had a contract to construct a line of Morse's electromagnetic telegraph from Philadelphia to the Midwest. Stager learned telegraphy and in 1846 became an operator on and later manager of the first line between Harrisburg and Philadelphia. In 1847 he became general superintendent of the Pittsburgh, Cincinnati, & Louisville Telegraph Co. In 1852, he was appointed general superintendent of the New York & Mississippi Valley Printing Telegraph Co. Stager came to Cleveland as general superintendent of the Western Union Telegraph Co. in 1856. He had assisted JEPTHA H. WADE in the consolidation of various lines into that company earlier in the year.

Following the outbreak of the CIVIL WAR, Stager entered military service as assistant quartermaster of volunteers. In Feb. 1862 he was appointed colonel on the staff of Gen. Henry Halleck, Pres. Lincoln's chief military ad-

visor and general-in-chief at the War Dept. In this position, Stager served as chief of the U.S. Military Telegraph, and as such he is credited with devising and implementing the military cipher system used throughout the war. Stager returned to Cleveland during the war, continuing to serve as military superintendent of the telegraph. His mansion on Euclid Ave. later became the headquarters of the UNIVERSITY CLUB. He continued to serve as general superintendent of Western Union until 1869, at which time he became vice-president of the company's Central Div. and moved to Chicago. Stager remained in Chicago until his death, but his remains were returned to Cleveland for burial at LAKE VIEW CEMETERY. Stager had married Rebecca Sprague of Buffalo, N.Y., in 1847. She died in 1883.

Thompson, Robert Luther, *Wiring a Continent* (1948).

The **STANDARD BREWING COMPANY** was founded in 1904 by Stephen S. Creadon and John T. Feighan. In 1905 they located their plant in an old flour mill at 5801 Train Ave. on Cleveland's near west side, where they produced Old Bohemian beer and, later, Erin Brew. (A friend is said to have suggested the latter name in 1914 because Standard was headed by men of Irish descent.) During Prohibition, Standard manufactured near-beer, soft drinks, and ice cream. With repeal, it became one of the fastest-growing brewing companies in the country. Although Standard confined its market to a 50-mi. radius of Cleveland, its profitable trade caused it continuously to expand plant capacity. The *Brewers Journal* in 1939 cited Standard as "a great believer in persistent, consistent, and original methods of advertising"; in the 1930s Standard sponsored a radio program featuring commentator SIDNEY ANDORN 6 days a week and used billboards liberally. "Erin Brew . . . In Perfect Taste," was the company's long-time slogan.

After WORLD WAR II, Standard initiated a 6-year, $5 million expansion program. It added a new cold-storage and fermentation plant, and in 1950 it opened a new bottling and canning plant, raising capacity to more than 550,000 barrels annually. Standard claimed to be the first brewery in Ohio to introduce flat-topped cans. "The current trend toward small homes and apartments has increased the demand for smaller containers," company president John T. Feighan, Jr., was quoted as saying. In 1950 the brewery employed 400 persons and had broadened its market to include southern Michigan, western Pennsylvania, and New York in addition to northern Ohio. In 1961, Standard sold out to the F. & M. Schaefer Brewing Co. of New York, then 7th nationally in sales volume. With the sale, Schaefer, which commanded a huge regional market with annual sales of 3.5 million barrels, made a move toward the national market. Only 3 years later, however, the New York brewer found production in Cleveland uneconomical, as Schaefer recently had acquired the Theo. Hamm brewery in Baltimore and now found itself with excess capacity. In 1964, Schaefer sold the Train Ave. brewery to C. Schmidt & Sons, Inc., of Philadelphia. Schmidt continued production there until 1972, when it relocated to the CARLING BREWING facility on Quincy Ave.

The **STANDARD OIL COMPANY (OHIO)**—SOHIO—is the original among several companies that operated under the Standard name. Chartered on 10 Jan. 1870, Ohio Standard was the state's first million-dollar corporation; it had assets of $6.6 million in 1911. These had grown to $8.3 billion in 1979. With sales of $11.6 billion in 1983, Sohio ranked 25th among American companies in sales, and 10th by net income ($1.5 billion). The major figure behind the establishment and early growth of Standard Oil was JOHN

D. ROCKEFELLER, who founded the company in 1870 along with his brother William, HENRY M. FLAGLER, SAMUEL ANDREWS, and STEPHEN V. HARKNESS. Rockefeller entered the oil business in 1863 as a financial supporter for Samuel Andrews, an Englishman and self-taught chemist whose idea it was to establish a firm to distill kerosene from crude oil. The new Andrews, Clark & Co. opened the Excelsior refinery at the juncture of KINGSBURY RUN and the CUYAHOGA RIVER; in 1865 Rockefeller entered the oil business full-time, buying the company and maintaining a partnership with Andrews. The company changed names several times as it took on the partners who eventually chartered Standard Oil.

Standard Oil owned 2 refineries in Cleveland when formed in 1870 and had offices in the Cushing Block on PUBLIC SQUARE. It accounted for 10% percent of the business in a chaotic new industry. Rockefeller and his associates proposed to stabilize the industry by combining refineries and centralizing their management. Accordingly, they offered cash and Standard Oil stock to buy other refineries. By 1872, Standard Oil controlled 21 of Cleveland's 26 oil refineries, as well as major refineries in New York, Philadelphia, and Pittsburgh. By 1882 the company controlled 90% of the nation's refining capacity. Continued expansion required a new system of organization to circumvent the company's Ohio charter, which prohibited company activity outside the state. In 1879, 3 trustees were given control of all the stock of Ohio Standard's affiliates; in Jan. 1882, the Standard Oil trust agreement gave 9 trustees all the stock of 40 companies, including Ohio Standard.

A successful lawsuit by the state of Ohio in 1892 forced dissolution of the trust in Ohio and prompted the 1899 reorganization of Standard Oil (New Jersey) as a holding company to receive the stocks previously held by the trustees. In 1911, the U.S. Supreme Court found this holding company to be a monopoly in violation of the Sherman Antitrust Act and ordered it broken up. As a result, Standard Oil of Ohio became an independent company. New president A. Palmer Coombe took charge of a company that controlled marketing operations in Ohio and owned an outmoded 3,400-barrel-a-day Cleveland refinery, but which owned no crude oil reserves and no pipelines, depending upon other companies to supply it with oil. In 1907 Ohio Standard moved its offices from their 33-year location in the Standard Block to a new building on E. 55th St.

Standard's business soon began to increase with the growing use of automobiles. In 1901 the company had begun to sell both gasoline and kerosene directly to householders in 1-gallon cans. The company was in a position to capitalize on the new demand for gasoline: when gasoline sales surpassed the sale of kerosene for the first time in 1911, Ohio Standard controlled 85% of the gasoline business in the state. Wallace T. Holliday became company president in 1928 and directed the firm through WORLD WAR II, initiating major changes and new growth. The "Sohio" sobriquet was introduced in 1928; Sohio began building its own crude-oil pipelines in 1934, extending them into Texas in 1949. Refinery production increased dramatically during the 1940s, and sales rose from $45 million in 1928 to $140 million in 1943.

The company expanded its marketing operations into other states and diversified its activities in the 1950s and 1960s. It entered the petrochemical business in 1954, plastics in 1962, and coal and uranium in 1968. By 1970 the company had 21 subsidiaries in the transportation, marketing, chemicals and plastics, and food and lodging industries. In 1969, Sohio acquired the BP Oil Corp., the U.S. subsidiary of the British Petroleum Co., Ltd., of London,

in exchange for Sohio stock. The exchange gave Sohio oil leases on the rich North Slope of Alaska, as well as marketing and refining properties on the East Coast. By 1979 the British firm's stocks had grown to a 52% share of Sohio. In 1984, Sohio no longer operated a refinery in the Cleveland area but maintained a research center and corporate headquarters there. The $2.4 million Warrensville Research Ctr. opened in 1957, and in Sept. 1980 a $20 million expansion program was begun there. In 1982, construction began on a major new Sohio building on Public Square to house the corporation's main offices, located in the Midland Bldg. since 1930.

Hidy, Ralph W., and Hidy, Muriel E., *Pioneering in Big Business 1882-1911* (1955).
Izant, Grace Goulder, *John D. Rockefeller* (1972).
Standard Oil Co. (Ohio), *Sohioan* (Jan. 1970).

The **STANDARD PRODUCTS COMPANY,** founded in Detroit, Mich., in 1927, is now a world leader in the manufacture and production of rubber and plastic parts for the AUTOMOTIVE INDUSTRY. In addition, it currently operates an additional 21 manufacturing facilities in 5 countries, along with a large public distribution facility in Dearborn, Mich. The company began to grow from its position as a small manufacturer of window channels for automobile bodies when Jas. S. Reid, M.D., a physician turned inventor, purchased an interest in the company in order to manufacture his invention of a better gasoline tank cap, in 1922. Reid founded the Reid Prods. Co. in 1930 to manufacture automotive door checks and supports. Under Reid's direction through their first 3 decades, Standard Prods. and Reid Prods. developed and patented the first flexible window channels and weatherstrips for automobiles and the equipment to manufacture his other new products. The operation prospered on Power Ave., now Erieview Plaza, and a second plant was opened at Port Clinton, Ohio, in 1934. Standard Prods. and Reid Prods. continued to work cooperatively until they merged in 1946 and moved the companies' world headquarters to the Cleveland location of 2130 W. 110th St. This location is presently the location of Standard's plastic-trim plant.

Although automotive window seals continued to be the principal product, Standard also began to make metal stampings, door locks, rubber moldings, and other plastic products. During WORLD WAR II, it was also involved in the manufacture of Springfield rifles. It has continued to grow by developing additional products, such as electrostatically flocked rubber channels, and weatherstrips, which later became a standard in the automotive industry. Part of the company's growth also enabled it to establish a large product-development facility in Dearborn, Mich., near the engineering departments of its largest customers. Standard has continued to grow through the years. For example, in the 1960s it expanded its Canadian subsidiary through the purchase of 4 plants in Ontario. These plants primarily manufacture extruded sponge-rubber seals. During the 1970s, the company acquired controlling interest in several foreign companies. Among these acquisitions are Silent Channel Prods. of Great Britain, Tecniauto of Spain, and Itatiaia Standard of Brazil. The acquisition of Silent Channel Prods. provided full ownership in that company, of which Standard Prods. previously only had a minority interest. The late 1970s brought about the acquisition of the Oliver Tire & Rubber Co. (1977) and the Dixie Cap Rubber Co. (1979). The former has become the nation's 2d-largest independent manufacturer of tread rubber. In 1982, Standard continued its growth by acquiring the Harrelson Rubber Co. of Asheboro, N.C. The various acquisitions and licensing agreements in other countries have literally allowed Standard Prods. to be involved with every automobile on the road through its product usage.

**STANDARD TRUST** was a short-lived bank that was created from the Brotherhood of Locomotive Engineers' Cooperative Natl. Bank of Cleveland, the first labor bank in the nation. The brotherhood planned the bank as early as 1912, but WORLD WAR I delayed its opening. Warren S. Stone, head of the brotherhood, guided the bank's formation. On 28 June 1920, it received a federal charter, with $1 million capital, and on 1 Nov. 1920, it opened for business, with 10 employees and $700,000 in resources, in a former restaurant at St. Clair Ave. and Ontario St. Although the bank served everyone as a commercial savings and trust company, it lent funds principally to members of the brotherhood. With Warren Stone as president, the bank prospered in its first 5 years. In 1922, it moved part of its business to larger quarters at 308 Euclid Ave. Three years later, the brotherhood erected one of the finest and largest banking structures in the country, a $7 million, 21-story building at its original location. It then had 157 employees and resources of more than $28 million. In 1928, it shortened its name to the Engineers' Natl. Bank of Cleveland.

However, by 1925, the bank was experiencing financial difficulties, and the brotherhood considered withdrawal from the banking business. Problems increased in the late 1920s, and it consolidated some of its 15 national branches with private banking interests. On 11 Mar. 1930, the bank was reorganized as the Standard Trust Co., when C. Sterling Smith, former executive vice-president of Engineers' Natl., merged Engineers' with 3 smaller firms, the Nottingham Savings & Banking Co. (inc. 1901), the Guaranty State Savings & Loan Co. (1916), and the Commonwealth Savings & Loan Co. (1919). Standard Trust had 7 offices with $23 million in resources. Although the brotherhood relinquished all its banking interests, its members continued to give their business and support to the new bank. Standard Trust, though, commenced at the beginning of the Depression and, less than 2 years later, on 21 Dec. 1931, went into liquidation. An investigation by the State Banking Dept. found that large loans had been made to friends of Pres. Smith with inadequate security. Smith was indicted for embezzlement and sentenced to prison in 1933. By 1941, the liquidators were able to return about 50% of the $13.2 million in deposits to 22,000 people.

**STARKWEATHER, SAMUEL** (27 Dec. 1799–5 July 1876), was a Cleveland lawyer and politician. He served as judge of the common pleas court and as mayor of Cleveland. Starkweather was born in Pawtucket, R.I. He worked on a farm until the age of 17, when he entered Brown College, graduating second in his class in 1822. After his graduation, he was appointed a tutor at Brown, remaining until 1824, when he left to study the law with Judge Swift in Windham, Conn. Starkweather was admitted to the Ohio bar in Columbus in the winter of 1826–27. He soon after moved to Cleveland, and joined the CLEVELAND GRAYS in 1837. He also quickly assumed a prominent position in Cleveland politics. He was a staunch Democrat and a strong supporter of presidents Jackson and Van Buren. During their administrations, he served as collector of customs for the Cleveland district and superintendent of lighthouses.

In 1844, Starkweather was elected mayor of Cleveland, winning reelection in 1845, and again in 1857 for a 2-year term. In 1852 he was the first judge of the court of common pleas for Cuyahoga County elected under the new state constitution, serving for 5 years. Starkweather took a special interest in the CLEVELAND PUBLIC SCHOOLS. Along with ANDREW FREESE and Chas. Bradburn, he helped establish the first high school in Cleveland and the first in the west established in connection with common schools. He was active in promoting the development of the RAILROADS in Cleveland, helping to establish the Cleveland, Columbus & Cincinnati Railroad. Starkweather married Julia Judd on 25 June 1825. The Starkweathers had 4 children. Starkweather is buried in LAKE VIEW CEMETERY.

The **STATE SAVINGS AND LOAN COMPANY,** the 9th-largest savings and loan institution in the Cleveland area, was established in 1909 as the Tatra Savings & Loan Co. A Slovak immigrant, John A. Sotak, contractor Joseph Dovalosky, and merchant Michael Phillips pooled $20,000 and opened the first office at Scovill Ave. and E. 23rd St. Named after the Tatra Mts. in Czechoslovakia, the savings and loan provided local workingmen with a safe place for their savings with a liberal interest return. By 1917, with $120,000 in assets, Tatra needed more space and moved to Scovill Ave. and E. 25th St. In the early 1920s, the firm relocated to the Sotak family store at 2437 Scovill Ave., and opened a west side branch. By 1925, Tatra assets had topped the $1 million mark, and it erected its own office building at Woodhill Rd. and Sophia. While many area savings and loans collapsed during the Depression, Tatra had a sound foundation and remained in business, emerging with $435,000 in assets. In 1946, as some ethnic communities disappeared, the name of the firm was changed to the State Savings & Loan Co. Six years later, State, with $11.5 million in assets, moved its main office to S. EUCLID. In recent decades, it has continued to grow, and by 1983, it had 10 offices with 170 employees and almost $400 million in assets. State Savings has been part of Statewide Financial corporation, a holding company owned mainly by Joseph E. Sotak, Jr. By 1986, the firm had run into difficulty as a result of unwise loans to area construction companies and developers. The Federal Home Loan Bank Board determined that State Savings was unsolvent, and in June 1986 it was taken over by First Nationwide Bank of San Francisco.

The **STATE THEATER,** 1519 Euclid Ave., opened on 5 Feb. 1921. It was designed by architect Thos. Lamb. Designed for movies and vaudeville, the State was the flagship theater of Marcus Loew's Ohio Theatres. Built by the Fleishman Constr. Co. of New York, it cost $2 million. Described as Italian Renaissance, the State actually combined Roman, Greek, and European Baroque designs. The original auditorium seated 3,400. The theater contained 2 sets of marble staircases to the mezzanine; the longest lobby in the world serving a single theater--320 ft.; and 4 murals by Jas. Daugherty in the lobby: *The Spirit of Pagentry—Africa, The Spirit of Drama—Europe, The Spirit of Cinema —America*, and *The Spirit of Fantasy—Asia*. The State opened with a movie, *Polly with A Past*, and a Buster Keaton short, *Neighbors*. In 1967, the State was modified for cinerama. But like other downtown theaters, it lost patronage, and it closed in Feb. 1969. After the closing, the treasures in the building were sold and the seats removed and sold at auction. A mural was removed, and holes in the roof caused more damage. The State seemed doomed to become a parking lot. Then the 27 Feb. 1970 *Life* magazine featured the mural *Spirit of Cinema—America*. That helped start a movement to save the theaters in PLAYHOUSE SQUARE. By July 1970, the Playhouse Square Assoc. was formed to save the OHIO, the PALACE, and the State from destruction. Their first attempt at putting theatrical life back into the old theaters was a production of *Jacques Brel Is Alive and Well and Living in Paris.*

Opening in the State lobby on 18 Apr. 1973, it ran until 29 June 1975. That ushered in an era of cabaret-style shows in the lobby, slow fundraising, and beginning renovation work. After a number of donations from organizations and individuals, including the JR. LEAGUE and the CLEVELAND FOUNDATION, the State was restored to become home to the CLEVELAND BALLET and CLEVELAND OPERA. The newly restored theater reopened on 9 June 1984 with a new $7 million stagehouse.

The **STATLER OFFICE TOWER** at E. 12th St. and Euclid Ave. was for many years a prominent Cleveland hotel, which was converted to office space because of falling occupancy rates. The Hotel Statler was built in 1912 as a magnificent addition to the Statler chain. Its Playhouse Square location was next to the STILLMAN THEATER, itself the former site of the Stillman Hotel, an ill-fated hostelry built in 1884 and razed in the 1890s because of lack of patronage. The hotel, which opened on 12 Oct. 1912, was built of steel, concrete, and fireproof tile, while the exterior was granite, Indiana limestone, red brick, and white terra cotta. The luxury of the furnishings and appointments was supplemented by practical innovative touches: an electric dishwasher in the kitchen, an antiscalding mixer in the shower in each room, and a sophisticated cash-register system that recorded transactions throughout the hotel. Decorated with an Italian classical influence by New York designers, the Statler contained 700 rooms (later expanded to 1,000); some, considered closet-sized by later standards, rented for only $1.50 per night.

The land underneath the Statler was originally leased from the Stillman Amusement Co.; in 1928, the hotel acquired this and adjoining property occupied by the theater, with the intention of converting the Euclid Ave. frontage into more lucrative hotel stores. By 1937, the hotel expanded and modernized, adding a new ballroom, lounge bar, and dining room. The new bar was supposed to be christened with a bottle of champagne by CHAS. A. OTIS, the hotel's first guest in 1912. To prevent the danger of flying glass, the bartender had replaced the bubbly with ginger ale; when the bottle bounced across the bar several times instead of breaking, Otis suggested drinking the contents. To that end, the bartender brought out real champagne for the toast. The ballroom and the Terrace Dining Room offered Big Band entertainment.

In 1954, the Hilton Hotel chain bought out the Statler hotels, and the Cleveland property was considered to be one of the finest in the chain. Yet, it was both showing its age and suffering the fate of other downtown hotels throughout the country in the motel age. To combat sliding occupancy rates (40% in 1965), Hilton management poured $3.3 million into the facility, refurbishing rooms, remodeling the lobby, adding a corridor to the newly built Stillman Parking Garage that replaced the old theater, enlarging the ballroom, and adding a large coffee shop. Before renovations were complete, the Statler-Hilton was sold to New York investors under the name the Ohio Hotel Co. Hilton continued to manage the hotel until 1967, when the new owners signed it as a Hilton franchise and took over the operation. In an effort to make the venture more profitable in a city that had the lowest hotel occupancy among the 10 principal U.S. cities, they converted several floors to office space by 1971. Within a year, the Statler-Hilton appealed to Cuyahoga County for a 30% reduction in taxes because of its 34% occupancy rates.

When Ohio Hotels ascertained that association with the Hilton corporation was not generating the desired profits, the owners dropped the franchise and changed the name to the Cleveland Plaza in 1973. Later that year, Ohio Hotels sold the property to the Mercantile Mortgage Co. of St. Louis. Manager Wm. J. Burns, a veteran hotel man, spearheaded a $2.5 million renovation project that reduced the number of rooms to 560 by combining some of the smaller rooms and renting out more space. When the latest round of improvements did not produce the desired rise in occupancy, the hotel was sold to developer Carl Milstein, who planned to convert the remaining rooms to offices. Engaging Jim and Nick Swingo to manage the food and beverage service, Milstein offered banquet space for 3,000. Unfortunately, the 1,140 who lost their jobs when the hotel closed were replaced by only 200 full- and part-time food workers. In 1980 the name reverted to its historical roots: the Statler Office Tower.

The **STATUE OF TADEUSZ ANDREZEJ BONAWENTURA KOSCIUSZKO,** Polish army officer and statesman, was unveiled and dedicated in WADE PARK on 8 May 1905. The 8-ft. statue, situated on a 20-ft.-high pedestal, was sculpted by Gaitano Trentanove at a cost of $9,000. Funding of the statue was sponsored by Clevelanders of Polish descent.

**STEARNS, F. B. CO.** *See* **F. B. STEARNS COMPANY**

**STEFFENS, SEARLES AND HIRSH** was the firm name from 1897–1905 of a partnership of 3 architects responsible for many notable buildings in Cleveland and northeast Ohio. Geo. H. Steffens (1871–1928) and Paul C. Searles (1870–1947) formed a partnership in 1896 and took Willard Hirsh (1872–1920) into the firm later the same year. Their most important commission was the BOHEMIAN NATIONAL HALL on Broadway, built by a group of Czech societies as a social center and gymnastic hall. Completed in 1897, it was completely restored in the 1970s. In 1905, the partners split into 2 firms, Searles & Hirsh and Steffens & Steffens, the latter partnership of Geo. Steffens and his brother John F. Steffens (1880–1943). Steffens & Steffens designed commercial buildings such as the Miller Block on Lorain Ave. at W. 32nd St., apartments such as the Stockbridge, the luxury hotel on Euclid Ave., and the Hruby Conservatory of Music, the school on Broadway founded and operated by the Frank J. HRUBY FAMILY from 1917–68. Searles & Hirsh also designed commercial buildings of all kinds and apartments such as the Alhambra on Wade Park Ave. Their masterpiece was probably the residence built in Alliance, Ohio, for Col. Wm. H. Morgan, founder of the Morgan Engineering Co. and inventor of the electric overhead traveling crane. The house, Glamorgan (1905–08), is a brilliant exercise in eclecticism, with a Tudor exterior of Vermont marble, and stands on a 25-acre site in Alliance.

The **STELLA MARIS DETOX CENTER,** an alcohol and drug treatment and rehabilitation center located at 1320 Washington Ave., was founded on 10 May 1948 by several people led by Fr. Otis S. Washington, assistant pastor at ST. MALACHI'S CHURCH. The project began as "a home for drunks," as long-time director Harry Ryan described it in 1968. The facility was first located in a rented abandoned building at 1306 Winslow Ave.; in Oct. 1953, its officers broke ground for a new 2-story building on Washington Ave. capable of accommodating more men. By 1968, the facility had 2 buildings, a hospital, and a dormitory where 73 men lived during rehabilitation; by 1981 it had grown to 3 buildings, and a drive was underway to modify the detoxification center. The facility was given the name Stella Maris, the Latin phrase meaning "Star of the Sea," in honor of the Mother of God. Although one of its founders was a Catholic priest, the home was nonsectarian and was not connected with CATHOLIC CHARITIES; although its program followed the guidelines of Alcoholics Anonymous, it was not directly affiliated with AA. Stella Maris was funded by donations and by the sale in its west side stores of used furniture renovated by its residents. One visitor described the center as "ruggedly individualistic and ruggedly non-sectarian," referring to its insistence on individual responsibility both in its rehabilitation program and in its own policy of refusing to take advantage of government grants. In 1981, Stella Maris was operating on a monthly budget of $35,000 and was in the process of renovation of its detoxification center in order to meet state requirements for certification to receive insurance payments for medical care. By 1986, Stella Maris's around-the-clock nursing staff and 2 physicians offered in-patient treatment for both alcohol and drug addiction, including detoxification, counseling, and aftercare, and operated a halfway house to shelter former addicts while they continued their rehabilitation.

The **STERLING-LINDNER COMPANY** was an important department store in downtown Cleveland. It was a combination of 3 smaller stores—the Sterling & Welch Co., the W. B. Davis Co., and the Lindner Co.—each of which was a leading retailer in its own specialty. The oldest of these firms was Sterling & Welch, Cleveland's first carpet and interior-decoration house. It began in 1845 when Thos. S. and Wm. Beckwith opened a dry-goods store on Superior St. With changes in partners, T. S. and W. S. Beckwith & Co. changed its name and address several times. In 1857, the store dropped its dry-good products and added floor coverings and curtains. Both Frederick A. Sterling and Geo. P. Welch joined the company in its early years. By 1889, they had control of the partnership, which was incorporated in 1902 as the Sterling & Welch Co. By 1874, the firm had moved to Euclid Ave. by PUBLIC SQUARE. In 1909, it moved to 1215 Euclid Ave., where it built one of the largest and finest home-furnishings stores in the country. In 1927, Sterling & Welch started the tradition of installing in its store the largest indoor Christmas tree in the country.

The W. B. Davis Co. was a pioneer menswear store in Cleveland, one of the largest in the U.S. It started in Jan. 1879 as a custom-shirt factory, operated by Wm. B. Davis and Edwin Parsons at Superior and Bank (W. 6th) streets. By 1880, Davis had changed the business into a men's-furnishings store, which was incorporated on 5 May 1888. It served presidents Garfield, McKinley, and Harding. By 1896, the store moved to Euclid Ave., and in 1917 it acquired the Davis Bldg. at 325 Euclid. The Lindner Co. was once the largest women's specialty store in Cleveland. Max Lindner, Max Hellman, and MORRIS BLACK founded the store in Apr. 1908 on E. 9th St. It was such a successful business that by 1915, Lindner built a larger store on PLAYHOUSE SQUARE at 1331 Euclid Ave.

In 1947, one of the nation's largest operators of department stores, the Allied Stores Corp. of New York, acquired Lindner & Davis. Two years later, it purchased Sterling & Welch. In Aug. 1949, the Lindner-Davis general department store opened in the remodeled old Higbee Bldg. at Euclid Ave. and E. 13th St., adjacent to the Sterling & Welch store. The following year, the 2 companies were merged into the Sterling-Lindner-Davis Co. *Davis* was dropped from the name in 1958. In the early 1960s, the firm felt that it was in a prime location downtown and decided not to establish suburban branch stores. Allied Stores then realized that without outlying stores, Sterling-Lindner was not profitable. On 21 Sept. 1968, the store was closed.

Feather, William, *Milestones* (1929).

**STEWART, N. COE** (d. 28 Feb. 1921), was a conductor, composer, and music intructor. As director of music in the CLEVELAND PUBLIC SCHOOLS, he was responsible for implementing a highly successful music program in the 1870s. Stewart studied music under Lowell Mason, a nationally recognized expert on that subject from Boston. Stewart, like Mason, was a pioneer in his emphasis on the value of music education in public schools. He took charge of music in the Cleveland schools in 1869 and instructed the system's 160 teachers on how to teach music. Stewart himself taught choral music in Cleveland high schools. He later served as president of the Music Teachers Assoc. and was credited with conceiving the idea for that organization. Stewart was also quite active in other areas of the city's music life. In 1881 he organized the Central Musical Assoc., a large choral group, and for 7 years he served as its conductor. In the 1890s, he became director of the Star Course concert series. As part of the series, in 1892, Stewart was responsible for the New York Symphony's first performance in Cleveland. Stewart conducted a combined chorus from the Cleveland schools on many occasions. In 1874, he directed a chorus of 1,600 children at the SAENGERFEST. At the 27th Saengerfest in 1893, he directed 4,000 schoolchildren in a selection from *The Creation*. He presented a similar performance the following year for the dedication of the SOLDIERS & SAILORS MONUMENT. He also published widely circulated songbooks for children and systematic courses of elementary instruction in music. Stewart's wife was active in music circles, mainly as the organizer of a series of winter concerts at the Music Hall. His daughter, Gabrielle, assisted him in the management of the Star Course series.

**STIGWANISH**, also known as Stigwandish or Stigonish, was a prominent Indian chief in the Cleveland area in the early years of settlement; his name translates into English as Standing Stone, but area settlers called him Seneca, after his tribe. Stigwanish was the chief of the Seneca Indians remaining in Ohio after "Mad" Anthony Wayne's 1794 victory at Fallen Timbers. He was called a "noble specimen of Indian character" after he helped the first survey party of the WESTERN RESERVE in 1796. He remained in the settlement of Cleveland and helped JOB STILES and his wife, Tabitha Cumi, and others survive the winter of 1796–97. Edward Paine, Jr., whose family settled Painesville, wrote, "Seneca has the dignity of a Roman Senator, the honesty of Aristides, and the philanthropy of William Penn." Stigwanish continually traveled the Western Reserve to Cleveland, Painesville, Ashtabula, and his annual wintering residence near the CUYAHOGA RIVER in Streetsboro Twp.

Stigwanish moved to Seneca County (which was named after him) in 1809. Before the start of the WAR OF 1812, most Indians in northeast Ohio left for Canada to aid the British and plan raids along Lake Erie's south shore. Stigwanish warned that the British were inciting the Indians. When the British finalized their plans, Stigwanish returned to warn settlers; most women and children were evacuated from lakeshore settlements. However, spies alerted the British, who canceled their plans. Stigwanish died in 1816. Three versions of his death exist; in all three, a white man whose family had been murdered and scalped by Indians killed him. The Northeast Ohio Council of the BOY SCOUTS OF AMERICA named their camp in Madison Stigwandish in the chief's honor.

925

STILES, JOB PHELPS (ca. 1769-ca. 1849), was the first settler of Cleveland. He and his wife, Tabitha, accompanied the MOSES CLEAVELAND party to the WESTERN RESERVE in 1796 and were the first residents of Cleveland with the intention of permanent settlement. Stiles was born in Granville, Mass. He and his wife were purportedly both schoolteachers and lived in Vermont prior to coming to Cleveland. As Stiles was never officially listed as being a member of the surveying party, it is unclear whether he was ever an employee of the CONNECTICUT LAND CO. It is probable, however, that he had some sort of arrangement with the company, or at least with Cleaveland. Before leaving Cleveland in the autumn of 1796, the surveying party erected a cabin for Stiles and left him in charge of their supplies.

The Stiles cabin was located on Lot 53 at the present corner of Superior and W. 3rd St. They were joined by Jacob Landon, who was to remain as a boarder, but Landon left for unknown reasons 2 weeks after the surveying party's departure. Another man, Edward Paine, replaced him and traded with the Indians encamped for the winter near the mouth of the Cuyahoga. On 23 Jan. 1797, Tabitha gave birth to a son, Chas. Phelps Stiles, the first white child born in Cleveland. Tradition states that Indian squaws attended Tabitha during childbirth. She was 17 years old at the time. The Stileses apparently survived the winter without any serious deprivation. They remained in the cabin until 1798, when they moved to higher ground southeast of the city in NEWBURGH, ostensibly to escape the unhealthful conditions prevalent near the stagnant water that formed at the river's mouth. They lived there until 1800, when for unknown reasons they returned to Vermont. Stiles's wife was formerly Tabitha Cumi Elderkin of Hartford, Conn. For being the first white woman to settle in Cleveland, the proprietors of the Connecticut Land Co. awarded her 1 city lot (2 acres), 1 10-acre lot, and a 100-acre lot. Stiles died in Branford, Vt., ca. 1849; Tabitha survived him for several years. Their son, Charles, died in Beaver, Ill., in 1882.

The STILLMAN THEATER was among the most elaborate motion-picture houses in the U.S. It opened in 1916 on the former estate of STILLMAN WITT, a railroad builder. It was located at 1115 Euclid Ave. and had a seating capacity of 1,800. The Stillman closed on 28 July 1963 and was converted into a parking garage.

STINCHCOMB, WILLIAM ALBERT (5 June 1878–17 Jan. 1959), was the father and directing genius of the CLEVELAND METROPARKS SYSTEM. As the park system's engineer, he purchased and developed thousands of acres of land, creating an "emerald necklace" park system encircling the city that was unequaled in any part of the country. Stinchcomb was born in Cleveland and educated in the CLEVELAND PUBLIC SCHOOLS. In 1895 he went to work as a surveyor for the city engineer. Appointed chief engineer of the City Parks Dept. in 1902, he laid out detailed plans for the future development of the city's park system. Stinchcomb was elected to the first of 3 successive terms as county engineer in 1912. As engineer, he was responsible for the construction of the DETROIT-SUPERIOR BRIDGE and the planning for the Lorain-Carnegie Bridge. He drafted the first comprehensive plan for public development of the lakefront and almost single-handedly convinced the Ohio legislature to block a city deal turning over $30 million worth of shoreland to the railroads.

In 1913, Stinchcomb got the Ohio legislature to revise the state constitution to permit legislation authorizing conservation of Ohio's natural resources. When the Ohio Supreme Court ruled Cuyahoga County's park law unconstitutional in 1913, Stinchcomb drafted new legislation and lobbied it through the legislature. This legislation laid the groundwork for the Metropolitan Park System, of which he was appointed first engineer. Stinchcomb mapped out a great circle around the city from Lake Erie, up the Rocky River Valley to STRONGSVILLE, east to the CUYAHOGA RIVER watershed in BRECKSVILLE, up TINKER'S CREEK to BEDFORD, over the divide to the CHAGRIN RIVER, and down again to Lake Erie. Using the proceeds from a 0.1 mill levy, Stinchcomb started buying land: ravines, gullies, and rough terrain that were little good for farming or building. During the Depression, Stinchcomb used Civilian Conservation Corps and Public Works Admin. grants to advance the park system's progress by a quarter-century. Thousands of unemployed were put to work clearing, draining, grading, and paving roads through rugged terrain. They built shelterhouses, parking lots, bridges, fords, dams, nature trails, ball fields, playgrounds, and museums, and reforested thousands of acres of wasteland. Plans to erect a memorial recognizing his accomplishments and long service were started with Stinchcomb's retirement in 1957. The site chosen was on a high point jutting out onto the Rocky River's east bank. Here, in a park area designed by Ernst Payer, a 30-ft.-high carillon tower of curved white concrete, designed by Wm. McVey, was erected shortly before Stinchcomb's death. Stinchcomb and his wife, Anne, had 2 children, Thomas and Betty.

STOCK EQUIPMENT, a world leader in the designing and building of bulk material flow-control equipment, supplies coal-feeding and -handling equipment, radioactive waste-disposal systems, and incineration-energy recovery systems to the power and energy industry. The Stock Engineering Co. was founded on 1 Oct. 1929 by Arthur J. Stock. Early products were specifically for stoker-fired coal application. Until the late 1960s, the company's major specialty was feeding, measuring, and controlling the flow of coal from the coal bunker to pulverizers or stokers. As the demand for electricity increased in the 1950s, Stock developed a gravimetric feeder to permit accurate control of combustion in the boiler and minimize stack emissions. The Stock gravimetric feeder has been the standard for the power industry for many years; 5,000 Stock feeders are currently in operation.

In 1967, Stock started development of radioactive waste-disposal equipment for use in North American nuclear-power plants. In 1986 the company offered solid radwaste systems, dry waste compactors, remotely operated material-handling equipment, cartridge filter handling systems, liquid radwaste tankage, sampling stations, and volume-reduction system interface equipment. Equipment has also been sold that utilizes cement and Dow polymer for waste solidification. In 1982 Stock added a modular incinerator for the disposal of solid, sludge, and liquid wastes with effective energy recovery. Applications include general and pathological hospital wastes, special hazardous wastes, shipboard and offshore wastes, and municipal wastes. In 1986, Stock Equip. offered its radioactive and nonradioactive waste systems to a world market. The company's headquarters and main manufacturing plant were in CHAGRIN FALLS, with additional facilities in Lynn Haven, Fla.; Funabashi, Japan; and Johannesburg, South Africa. Since 1980 Stock Equip. has been a unit of General Signal.

STONE, AMASA (27 Apr. 1818–11 May 1883), was a prominent local contractor, railroad manager, financier, and philanthropist. Born the son of a farmer in Charlton, Mass.,

926

he eventually moved to Cleveland, where he made his fortune by accepting stock in partial payment for his construction jobs. As a youth of 19, he was apprenticed to his older brother in the construction trade, and soon superintended the building of houses and churches. After buying out the remaining year of his apprenticeship, he worked with his brother-in-law Wm. Howe to perfect and construct the Howe truss bridge—a wood-and-iron bridge designed for transporting heavy loads over short spans. Howe and Stone installed the first Howe truss over the Connecticut River at Springfield for the Western Railroad Corp. In 1842, Stone and a partner, Azariah Boody, bought the patent rights to the Howe truss. Stone eventually constructed hundreds of them, using his own improved version of the design.

Stone's reputation as a competent contractor and excellent project administrator grew to the point that he was offered the superintendency of the New Haven, Hartford, & Springfield line, a position he held only a year because of the pressures of his construction business. After building the Cleveland-to-Columbus spur of the Cleveland, Columbus & Cincinnati Railroad, in 1851 he came to Cleveland to assume the superintendency of the road and to build the Cleveland, Painesville & Ashtabula. By 1852, he was a director of both roads, and by 1857 he was the president of the CP&A. He built the Chicago & Milwaukee Railroad and served as its president, as a director of the New York Central, and as the managing director of the Lake Shore & Michigan Southern Railroad (1873–75).

Stone's wealth grew as he took part of his pay in stock at a time when railroads were booming. He put part of his wealth into the rising steel industry and was a major stockholder in the Cleveland Rolling Mill and several related mills throughout the country. He was also a stockholder and director of several local banks that financed railroad, oil, and steel ventures. On 29 Dec. 1876, an iron Howe truss bridge of the Lake Shore Rd. collapsed at Ashtabula, and a train carrying 159 people plunged into a ravine 69 ft. below; 92 people died in the wreck. A subsequent investigation criticized the rescue effort and implicated Stone, who had ignored the advice of professional engineers in designing the bridge, and had insisted on using an overly long Howe truss span. Following the release of the findings, the chief engineer of the road, Chas. Collins, committed suicide, and Stone's professional and personal reputations were attacked. Despite Stone's confident posture throughout the investigation, he was plagued by the tragedy to the end of his life. As business pressures mounted, he found some relief through PHILANTHROPY. His most noted donation was $500,000 to Western Reserve University in 1881, to be used to establish Adelbert College, in memory of Stone's son, who had died in a swimming accident at Yale in 1866. Among other conditions, Stone requested a leading role in designing and constructing the buildings.

Stone, a self-made man with a Puritan temperament, suffered from insomnia, dyspepsia, depression, and eczema, which worsened as his business dealings grew more complex. In 1883, still saddened by his son's death and by the Ashtabula tragedy, he was further vexed by William H. Vanderbilt's plan to consolidate the Lake Shore Rd. with the Nickel Plate. On 11 May 1883, after the failure of several steel mills in Chicago, Kansas City, and Youngstown in which he had a controlling interest, he committed suicide. At his death, Stone left a wife, Julia Gleason Stone, 2 daughters, Clara Stone Hay and FLORA STONE MATHER, and a multi-million-dollar estate that included an additional $100,000 bequest to WRU.

Dow, Burton Smith III, "Amasa Stone, Jr.: His Triumph and Tragedy" (Master's thesis, WRU, 1956).

**STOUFFER, VERNON BIGELOW** (22 Aug. 1901–26 July 1974), was a Cleveland businessman who as president of the Stouffer Corp. built his family's lunch-counter restaurant operation into a national chain of restaurants, motor inns, and food-service operations. Stouffer was born in Cleveland to Abraham and Lena Mahala Bigelow Stouffer. He attended Medina public schools and graduated with a B.S. in 1923 from the Wharton School of Business of the University of Pennsylvania. He investigated several types of businesses before settling upon the food industry. In 1922, Abraham Stouffer opened a stand-up dairy counter in the Arcade featuring buttermilk, cheese sandwiches, and Lena Stouffer's Dutch apple pies. Young Stouffer joined his father in 1924. Seeing the need for a restaurant serving quick, tasty meals at moderate prices, they opened Stouffer's Lunch in Apr. 1924. Located in the Schofield Bldg. at E. 9th St. and Euclid, it was the first of a chain of restaurants featuring Lena's style of cooking. In 1929 the Stouffers went public, and the Stouffer Corp. was founded. Eventually it became part of Litton Industries. Stouffer often said that he felt more at home in the kitchen than at the office. Throughout the years, he would personally test his company's new products, and while traveling he would keep his identity secret and personally check the quality of the food and service at his restaurants and inns.

In 1966, Stouffer purchased controlling interest in the financially struggling CLEVELAND INDIANS baseball franchise. He later said it was the longest 5 years of his life, as the club suffered from poor teams, low attendance, and a poor economy. In 1972, Stouffer was forced to sell the franchise to a group headed by Nick Mileti. Stouffer established the Vernon Stouffer Corp. to support worthwhile activities in medicine, education, and public welfare. In 1966, he established the Stouffer Prize to give recognition for research in controlling hypertension and arteriosclerosis. Stouffer was interested in the development of a modern zoological park in Cleveland and served as president of the Zoological Society. He was awarded the Cleveland Medal for Public Service in 1964 and was named the *Plain Dealer*'s 1968 Businessman of the Year. He was a trustee for Litton Industries, United Airlines, REPUBLIC STEEL, and Society Natl. Bank, as well as a founder of the Natl. Recreation & Park Assoc. Stouffer married Gertrude Dean in Feb. 1928. The Stouffers had 3 children, Marjorie, Deanette, and James.

**STOUFFER FOODS** is a Cleveland-based corporation whose operations include a nationwide chain of restaurants, motor inns, frozen prepared foods, and food-service management. Stouffer's began in 1922 as a stand-up milk counter in the Arcade, owned and operated by Abraham E. Stouffer. The addition to the menu of his wife Lena's homemade apple pie is credited with the company's instant success. Her motto—serve the same kind of food in the stores that you would at home—remained a company policy. In 1924 and 1925 respectively, the Stouffers' sons, VERNON and Gordon, joined the business and opened the first Stouffer restaurant—a sandwich shop—in the Schofield Bldg. In 1931 the restaurant and the company headquarters moved to the Citizens Bldg., and an active program of expansion was launched, lasting some 40 years, whereby restaurants were opened in Detroit, Pittsburgh, and Philadelphia. Stouffer restaurants were known for serving high-quality food and drink at an acceptable price in attractive surroundings. The success of the operation was due primarily to the continual efforts to eliminate unnecessary costs: menus were scientifically planned; each executive was a food expert; kitchens were equipped with the most modern and efficient facilities; and little waste was produced.

When A. E. Stouffer died in 1936, the presidency of the company was taken over by his elder son, Vernon, while Gordon served as president and general manager. Gordon was elected chairman of the board in 1953, but after his death in 1956, Vernon filled the position. In the early 1960s, Vernon's son James and son-in-law, Jas. Biggar, rose to executive positions within the company. By the mid-1950s, the company had grown into a nationwide industry. In addition to the expansion of the restaurant chain (17 restaurants were in operation in 1953), Stouffer's began to sell prepared foods. In 1946 a store adjacent to the Stouffer restaurant at SHAKER HTS. began to sell partially cooked take-home meals that reduced the preparation time of an entire meal to 30 minutes. By 1952, frozen meals and picnic lunches were sold to take out. A pioneer in the production of frozen foods, Stouffer's opened a plant on Woodland Ave. in 1953 for this purpose. By 1956 the operation was expanded, and frozen food was distributed throughout the East and West coasts. In 1966 this operation was moved to SOLON. In 1967, Stouffer Foods merged with Litton Industries, a $100 million California-based conglomerate, whose Atherton Div. was a major supplier of microwave ovens for commercial food service. Litton was then sold to Nestle S.A., the Swiss-based food-processing giant, in 1980.

**STOUFFER'S INN ON THE SQUARE** is the most recent hotel to occupy a historic PUBLIC SQUARE site at the intersection of Superior Ave. at the Square. Originally apportioned by the CONNECTICUT LAND CO. to SAMUEL HUNTINGTON, soldier and later Ohio governor, the land was sold for $100 in 1812 to Phinney Mowery, who constructed a popular tavern there. In 1820, Mowery sold the premises to Donald MacIntosh, who operated it as the Cleveland Hotel until it was destroyed by fire in 1840. Rebuilt, it operated as the Dunham House for 5 years, until it was renamed the Forest City House, the name it bore until 1915. For 6 decades, the Forest City House was a social, commercial, and historical center of Cleveland and was host to the city's most important guests. By 1915, the landmark structure was a shabby reminder that much downtown activity had moved farther uptown. In an attempt to revitalize the Public Square area, investors closed the old hotel and rebuilt a magnificent new 1,000-room structure at a cost of $4.5 million. The Hotel Cleveland, as it was then called, joined the new Illuminating Co. Bldg. and the May's store in the lower Superior-Public Square area, and was seen as a spur to further rebuilding.

By the mid-1920s, the 10-story white brick edifice, heralded a few years earlier as a precursor of downtown development, was seen as a thorn in the sides of the VAN SWERINGEN brothers, who built the Terminal Complex. Though the developers envisioned a hotel as integral to their plans for an improved railroad terminal, rapid-transit station, and interlocking series of buildings, they felt that the Hotel Cleveland was too small; a 2,000-room, 18-20-story structure was necessary to maximize the land use. Also, they claimed that the building was architecturally inappropriate in style and color to the proposed new buildings and was incapable of being structurally underpinned to permit rapid tracks to run underneath it from the west from the High Level Bridge. The Van Sweringens, who acquired ownership of the hotel property on a 99-year lease renewable in perpetuity, planned an addition to the hotel and talked of razing it to construct a more fitting structure. Faced by rising costs, the brothers settled for reinforcement of the hotel and digging a tunnel underneath it.

During the Depression, the fortunes of the hotel sagged, along with those of the Van Sweringen brothers. The Hotel Cleveland remained under the control of the Cleveland Terminal Bldg. Co. until 1947, when the Cleveland Hotel Co. was established as a subsidiary of the larger company. The operation then fell under the control of the 60 Trust of Boston, a pension trust owned by Textron, Inc. By 1950, the Hotel Cleveland was leased by Arthur M. Sonnabend of the Childs Co., a nationwide restaurant chain that had recently moved into the hotel management business. Though its occupancy rates were falling, and its premises were showing their age, the hotel was viewed as the number 2 hotel in Cleveland; it was bought in 1958 by ITT to be part of its Sheraton chain. Operating as the Sheraton-Cleveland, the hotel featured a new $5.2 million grand ballroom and other improvements, but its success faltered in the 1960s along with downtown hotels throughout the country. The advantages of its central location were offset by traffic problems in the Public Square area.

After warnings from the Cleveland health inspectors to "clean up or close down," and tax problems with the IRS, the hotel was sold in 1975 as a Sheraton franchise to Thos. Lloyd of Cambridge, Ohio; within a year, it was put into receivership because of its continued tax delinquencies. As part of a downtown revitalization effort, an investor group, STS, Inc. (Save-the-Square, Inc.), was formed by the EATON CORP., HIGBEE'S, the Cleveland Stadium Corp., Chessie Systems, TRW, LEASEWAY TRANSPORTATION, and Stouffer's. The group proposed to invest $14 million—$7 million from the STS members, and $7 million from local banks—to pay off the creditors and refurbish the hotel. Restored to its former elegance, the hotel was reopened in 1978 as Stouffer's Inn on the Square.

**STOUT AIR SERVICES, INC.,** was an early airline that provided transportation between Detroit and Cleveland in the late 1920s and 1930. The service was initiated by Wm. B. Stout, an engineer, a designer of toys, motorcycles, and automobiles, and an associate of Henry Ford. Stout founded the Stout Metal Airplane Co. in Detroit in 1922 to develop an aircraft capable of reaching greater speeds and able to carry a greater load. Ford later bought the aircraft-production company, and Stout organized the passenger service in 1925, beginning with service between Detroit and Grand Rapids. Stout began service between Cleveland and Detroit in Nov. 1927, using metal 14-passenger trimotor monoplanes built by Ford's aircraft division. Manager of the Cleveland office was Glenn G. Jury. Located in the Marshall Bldg. at Broadway and Hamlet in 1928, the office was moved to PUBLIC SQUARE in 1929 and to Rocky River Dr. in 1930.

Passengers making the 100-minute trip in the early weeks of service were attracted by the novelty of the experience, but by Apr. 1928 the flights were attracting primarily business travelers. In the first 5 months of service, the company transported 2,000 passengers between Detroit and Cleveland "without the slightest accident to persons or property." By May 1929 Stout had added flights to Chicago to its schedule. That same month the Thompson Aeronautical Corp. announced that it would begin over-the-lake air passenger service to Detroit; Stout countered the competition by reducing the flying time between Cleveland and Detroit from 100 to 90 minutes. Air service in Cleveland under the Stout name continued into 1930, but in 1929 Stout Air Services was purchased by Natl. Air Transport, which later became United Airlines.

Stout, William B., *So Away I Went* (1951).

**STOW, JOSHUA** (1762–1842), was an original shareholder in the CONNECTICUT LAND CO. He accompanied the

MOSES CLEAVELAND party as its commissary manager and later helped to develop land for settlement in Summit County. Stow was born in Middlefield, Conn. Although he is commonly associated with early settlement in the WESTERN RESERVE, like Moses Cleaveland, Stow never actually settled there himself; for the duration of his life he remained a resident of Connecticut. Stow was a practical man, and also literate. As commissary manager for the surveying party, he was given charge of the company's provisions. After the party returned to Connecticut, he relinquished this post and spent the rest of his life attempting to encourage development of his land tracts in Summit County. In this respect he was both a promoter and a businessman. In cases where he was unable to make use of land in the Western Reserve, he traded it for land in Connecticut.

In Connecticut, Stow was involved in both local and state government. He is primarily responsible for having a freedom-of-religion clause, which he authored, included in that state's constitution. Among the public offices he held were postmaster in Middletown and judge of the county court. When the surveying party set out from Schenectady in the spring of 1796, Stow, with several men, was to transport the company's supplies by water and meet up with the main party in Buffalo. At Oswego, the British detained Stow and for a while prevented him from entering Lake Ontario. He was eventually allowed to pass, only to lose 1 of the 4 boats in a storm. As commissary manager, Stow was resourceful and had a professed desire for rattlesnake meat. When the surveying party reached Conneaut Creek, a crude structure was erected to house supplies and was referred to as "Stow's Castle," in his honor. In his lifetime, Stow purportedly made 13 trips between Connecticut and the Western Reserve. He managed his affairs in Ohio through his business partner, Wm. Wetmore. In 1809 these two men, along with Henry Newberry, founded Cuyahoga Falls. Stow Twp. in Summit County was named after Stow. Several of his relations did eventually settle there.

**STRATEGIC HEALTH SYSTEMS** (767 beta Dr., MAYFIELD VILLAGE) is a multihospital system composed of HURON RD. HOSPITAL, HILLCREST HOSPITAL, EUCLID GENERAL HOSPITAL, and SUBURBAN COMMUNITY HOSPITAL. It was formed in 1982 and represents an example of the trend toward the development of multihospital systems. In contrast to the national and regional systems, Strategic Health Systems' subsidiaries are all located in the Greater Cleveland area. Robt. Moss was president of the system in 1986.

The **STREETCAR STRIKE OF 1899** began in Cleveland in June against the Big Consolidated Line of the CLEVELAND ELECTRIC RAILWAY CO. It led to large-scale rioting, which continued until early fall. On 10 June 1899, over 850 employees of the Big Consolidated voted to strike for better wages and working conditions, and union recognition. Rioting broke out on Prospect St., at the Lake View Car Barns, and across the city as the company made attempts to operate cars with nonunion men. Large numbers of police were assembled and attempted to keep the mobs from damaging cars and attacking conductors. Although suburban traffic was severely handicapped and riders inconvenienced, the sympathies of the public remained with the strikers throughout the first phase of the strike, as Pres. SYLVESTER EVERETT of the railway company refused the strikers' demands and continued to hire strikebreakers. A state board of arbitrators arrived in Cleveland on 12 June, but Everett refused to meet with them.

On 20 June, the worst riot since the beginning of the strike occurred on the city's south side when a crowd of 8,000, including strikers and sympathizers, attacked the company's Holmden Barns, threatening the lives of non-union men and wrecking cars. Police were able to disperse the crowd without bloodshed, however. Smaller riots also took place in other parts of the city. A committee of city councilmen was formed to arbitrate the case. On 21 June the union presented its demands for recognition, the reinstatement of all employees, and written cause for all dismissals. On 24 June it appeared that the strike had ended; the company took back 80% of the strikers and promised to restore the old work schedules. For the next 3 weeks, however, intermittent rioting continued on the south side, where nonunion men continued to run the cars.

On 17 July, the employees struck again, claiming that the company had disregarded its promises concerning work schedules. Everett immediately began hiring strikebreakers, and rioting again ensued, but more violently, as explosives were used to demolish cars and tracks. On 21 July Mayor JOHN FARLEY called upon state troops for help. Everett, however, was able to restore a number of lines to operation. On 21 July he announced that he would rehire men only as individuals, not as union members. By 26 July, state troops controlled much of the rioting, and by the end of the month they began to withdraw from the city, although violent incidents continued to erupt. During the month of August, additional men began to apply for reinstatement with the company. The union then attempted to enforce a boycott of businesses and individuals who patronized the Big Consolidated lines. On 6 Aug., over 500 businessmen signed an antiboycott resolution, and the boycott and strike were doomed to failure. As more employees returned to work, Everett was able to run additional lines. Outbreaks of violence continued into the fall of 1899. However, the strike failed, and the initial gains the union made vanished after the second, more violent phase of the strike.

**STREETS.** In 1796, AMOS SPAFFORD and SETH PEASE plotted the first lots in the early "walking city" of Cleveland, with town lots west of Erie (E. 9th) St., 10-acre lots eastward to Willson (E. 55th) St., then 100-acre lots. Three main thoroughfares existed: the North Highway (St. Clair), Center Highway (Euclid), and South Highway (later Kinsman, then Woodland). Streets were platted with rights-of-way at 99 ft., with the exception of Superior St., with its 132-ft. width. Because of Indian lands and the barrier presented by the CUYAHOGA RIVER, lands immediately adjacent west of the river awaited later development. Twenty years later, in 1815, the following downtown streets were noted: St. Clair, Bank (W. 6th), Seneca (W. 3rd), Wood (E. 3rd), Bond (E. 6th), and Euclid. As populations grew, streets were laid out apace, though in much of the downtown area paving was considered unnecessary, as native sands and gravels afforded drainage. By 1832, an ordinance was in place calling for sidewalks 12 ft. wide on ordinary streets, and 16½ ft. wide on Superior. Walks were financed with a tax levy, and the ordinance provided fines for vehicular trespass on sidewalks. Late in 1833, Jas. S. Clark, Edmund Clark, and RICHARD HILLIARD laid out Cleveland Centre in the first curve of the Cuyahoga, known as the Ox Bow Bend. A geometric pattern of streets bearing foreign names such as German, French, and China radiated from Gravity Place.

By 1837, MacCabe's directory of Cleveland noted that the city could boast of 88 streets, lanes, and alleys. These streets were maintained at least in part by citizen corvees, each able-bodied male being expected to contribute "with a good and sufficient shovel to perform two days labor required . . . by law." Though highways (often with tolls) leading to Cleveland were beginning to be paved, pavement within the city seems to have begun only ca. 1842, with the planking of Superior St. Heavy planks were laid crosswise, making a smooth surface until the planks began to wear, rot, and loosen. Local flooding often carried off planked street surfaces with the freshets. By Cleveland's 50th anniversary in 1846, Superior was planked from the river to PUBLIC SQUARE, but adjacent streets were noted to be deeply rutted and often muddy, presenting barriers to use by wagons, stagecoaches, rigs, and victorias. New forms of transportation began to become prominent on Cleveland's streets. Beginning with the advent of railroad service to the city in 1849, increased commerce encouraged the development of omnibus horse-drawn routes within the city and between the city and outlying settlements—Kinsman, E. CLEVELAND, DOAN'S CORNERS, and the west side. The 1850s brought the beginnings of horse-drawn street railways in addition to omnibuses, and the 1860s saw a period of rapid expansion of street railway routes (see URBAN TRANSPORTATION). By 1851, Superior St. was paved with stone and plank, which, when in good condition, was considered fine for travel. In 1852, the term *Avenue* was applied to several streets, including Case (E. 40th), Sawtell (E. 51st), Willson (E. 55th), Sterling (E. 30th), and Superior, signifying population growth and the importance of the streets so designated. In 1854, OHIO CITY was annexed, and additional linking bridges were built at Main St. and Seneca (W. 3rd).

Street maintenance is a constant problem, and the city authorities began ca. 1860 to experiment with use of petty offenders (of all social classes) in a chain-gang system to clean the streets. In the mid-1860s, street-cleaning sprinklers were used to lay down dust, particularly in the hot summer months. By 1860, Cleveland could claim 182 streets, more than 5 avenues, and 3 alleys, but a prominent street such as Superior extended only to Erie (E. 9th) St. until 1865, when it began to be extended farther eastward. The 1860s brought rapid expansion of the horse-drawn streetcars, with the first route to the west side established in 1863. By 1870, Cleveland's streets included more than 10 mi. of stone pavement and nearly 9 mi. of Nicholson or wood-block paving. An experiment in McAdam (macadam) pavement was begun near Public Square in 1871, and the city purchased a steamroller in 1872. The city engineer preferred, however, to utilize Medina sandstone for street surfacing—a material used to pave Euclid as far as Willson Ave. (E. 55th) by 1875. Growing population and enlarged commerce across the Cuyahoga River put increasing pressure on the "drawbridges . . . [reached from the West side] by a perilous walk or drive down a slippery hill over a group of railroad tracks." Demanded by citizens' groups as early as 1870, the magnificent stone SUPERIOR VIADUCT was opened with great fanfare in Dec. 1878. The stone approaches on the west side, still visible near the DETROIT-SUPERIOR BRIDGE, were joined, with Superior leading to Public Square with an iron swinging span and additional east side approaches. Some 3,200 ft. long and 42 ft. wide, it symbolized Cleveland's rapid growth in this period.

By 1880, Cleveland could boast 975 streets, 183 avenues, 113 lanes, alleys, and places, and 5 roads. Wood or Nicholson pavements, popular earlier, were rapidly being replaced with Medina sandstone, though the latter was a pavement material found to be hard on riders' bones! Geo. Waring, who compiled in the 1880s a remarkable account of the status of American cities' facilities in 1880, reported that Cleveland had 2.2 mi. of asphalted streets, and 1.2 mi. of asphalt combined with stone—then a new material that later would become, along with concrete, one of the most prominent surfacing materials. At the same time, New York City was experimenting with concrete pavement, and was reported to have half a mile of the street material in 1880. Attempts at the development and enforcement of street ordinances marked the 1880s in response to earlier street developments, which often were haphazard, with poor grading and foundations, frequently leading to bottlenecks in increasingly dense traffic flows. The 1-mi. Garden St. (Central Ave.) electric railway in July 1884 heralded the end of horse-drawn streetcars. The first electric streetcars were powered by underground cables energized with a Brush arc-light generator. Soon, however, overhead wires with trolleys (hence the name trolley car) were found to be more suitable than the troublesome, hard-to-maintain underground cableways. Only the later development of the automobile really would enable the filling in of the interstices in the starfish pattern created by rail-bound transit systems.

In 1888 were reported the first streets (Carroll and Bolton [later E. 89th]) utilizing brick pavements, later a very popular material that could be noted on local streets until well after World War II (only a rare few examples still remain uncovered by asphalt in 1986). In 1889, Cleveland was reported to possess 440 mi. of streets and alleys; yet paving was proceeding at less than 2 mi. per year, lagging badly behind perceived needs. A 1-mill levy imposed in 1889 was seen as a "progressive step." By 1890, Euclid Ave. was compared favorably with Berlin's Unter den Linden and Paris's Champs Elysees, adorned with stately trees lost later as a result of automobile and industry-generated pollutants and commercial development. On the west side, Franklin Ave. was a fashionable area for many leaders in the iron and steel, coal, and shipping industries. By now, many streets lacking hard surfaces were partially planked, leading to controversies about who should give way when vehicles met. Already, the city was criticized for its failure to provide adequately for north-south traffic movement (a problem that still existed in some parts of Cleveland in 1986). Bulkley Blvd. was commenced, joining EDGEWATER PARK with Detroit near the Superior Viaduct, and forming a roadway precursor to the present MEMORIAL SHOREWAY West along the Erie lakefront.

The automobile's appearance in the 20th century was undoubtedly a predominant influence in the direction of the paving of streets. However, even before the appearance of the automobile in large numbers came a massive invasion of "safety" bicycles in the 1890s. Bicycles accommodate muddy, bumpy streets far worse than do horses, and prior to the arrival of the 20th century, bicyclists' demands for smoother thoroughfares had some effect. In 1897, it cost $2 per month to hire a sprinkler to lay the dust in front of a Euclid Ave. mansion. However, existing law demanded that a 2-ft. strip along the curb be kept dry for the convenience of "wheelmen," or cyclists. Following demands from bicyclists, auto drivers began early in the 20th century to add their voices demanding better street pavements. Total traffic volume by the 1910s led to demands for broadened arterial streets leading from downtown to residential city and suburban areas. Chester Ave., finally completed to the UNIVERSITY CIRCLE area only after World War II, was opened as far as E. 21st St. in 1919 and to E. 40th St. in 1926. By 1920, Cleveland could report 2,204 streets totaling 886 mi., of which 601 were paved; 384 mi. of street railways remained, of which only the off-street "Rapid" lines remained in 1986.

Late in the 1920s, a major survey was made of roads and streets in the Cleveland region by the Bureau of Public Roads. Some of its findings suggest that by the late 1920s, Cleveland was firmly in the grasp of the automobile, and that future changes in the city typically (as in most American cities) would be made to suit the convenience of the automobile rather than responding to other needs to keep the city on a human, accessible scale. Buses were introduced, and their number grew rapidly. By 1927, many motorists were not taking the most direct routes from the eastern suburbs to downtown, noting that problems with the most direct routes included poor pavements, narrow streets, streetcars and their loading platforms as impediments, slow and faulty traffic control devices, parking, and bus and truck traffic. Auto traffic was predicted to increase by 45% in the 1927–32 period, and a full 100% from 1927–42. Though the Depression intervened, it appears that auto traffic did not diminish significantly during that economic slump. Lakefront road development was predicted and recommended in the report, with traffic flow at the low-level Main Ave. bridge already at 7,000 cars per day in 1927. Other density data included the Detroit-Superior High-Level Bridge (56,000 cars/day), Carnegie Ave. at E. 55th St. (38,000 cars/day), and Superior and E. 55th St. (33,000 cars/day). Suburb-to-city traffic was the focus and the problem, in contrast to the present-day stress upon resolving traffic flows from suburb to suburb. Road conditions remained a problem, the survey rating nearly half the paved regional roads as being in condition to be serviceable for less than 10 years. Interestingly, weekend automobile traffic in city and suburban areas greatly exceeded average weekday flows. Sunday counts were 145% of weekday averages, and Saturday traffic was 122% of average Monday-Friday numbers. Motorists appear to have taken streetcars and buses to work, saving their driving and joyriding for weekends.

The beginnings of the present freeway-beltway system appear in the 1930s, with the planning and building of the Main Ave. high bridge (completed 1939) with WPA assistance, along with the first segments of lakefront freeways in the form of Lakeland Freeway east to GORDON PARK (completed 1938) from the bridge and a revised Bulkley Blvd. extending westward. Parts of the system growth eastward were related to the 1936 GREAT LAKES EXPOSITION, for which much east side lakefront land was filled and leveled. Hence, major street projects proceeded even during the Depression. If the 1930s was a decade of surprisingly great roadbuilding activity despite the Depression, the 1940s was a decade for planning, combined with delays ensuing from the American involvement in World War II. Willow Cloverleaf (a part of what is now I–77) was opened in 1940, as part of the WILLOW FREEWAY planned to reach from the southern part of Cleveland to downtown; and in 1940, the voters approved a large bond issue to include work on the Lakeland Freeway, Rocky River Bridge, Willow Freeway, and continuation of Chester Ave. toward University Circle. The latter project was most contentious since it involved the destruction of many large residences; this Chester Ave. extension process explains the absence of dwellings facing Chester from E. 55th St. eastward. Plans were developed for the INNERBELT FREEWAY system designed to reduce traffic congestion downtown, but serious attention to that set of projects had to await the conclusion of World War II and the arrival of massive amounts of federal funding in the form of interstate highway and other road subsidies related to the purposes of the Federal Highway Act of 1956.

The Innerbelt was completed from the shoreway (Lakeland Freeway) to Chester Ave. in 1959 and to W. 14th St. in 1961; it was connected to the Willow Freeway (I–77) in 1965. I–71, stretching southwestward toward Columbus, was put into place. The massive extension of I–90 westward from the Innerbelt was undertaken with enormous destruction to established neighborhoods, prior to the present period in which impact analyses and statements are required prior to approval of the environmental and social incursions often occasioned by major roadbuilding activities. Outside Cleveland itself, more interstate segments were put into place, such as I–271 to the east and parts of I–480 to the south; in 1986, the latter was still in the process of extension westward to the neighborhood of the CLEVELAND HOPKINS INTERNATL. AIRPORT. By 1970, the bulk of the interstate system links had been completed, and since that time few new increments have emerged. Plans for very substantial additional intracity freeways were strongly pushed by county engineer ALBERT PORTER. Citizen opposition to these plans, particularly to a proposal for a freeway that would have eliminated or diminished the SHAKER LAKES area in SHAKER HTS., ended in their being abandoned. What has emerged, however, is a new set of traffic problems with implications for both downtown Cleveland and its suburban surroundings. Paired with a decline in Cuyahoga Valley steel-related heavy industry has been a movement of residential population outward from Cleveland itself, along with the resettlement of many firms to outlying suburbs as part of a flight from the city occasioned by a complex of factors including crime and perceived decline in city services and general environmental quality. One result has been a decline in commercial activity in the central city. Another is the growth of traffic jams related not to suburb-to-city but rather to suburb-to-suburb intercourse, as drivers move from residence to shopping area to job, largely ignoring the older shopping and work environments downtown. Since roads were built in response to historical data about traffic flows, new directions in flows were difficult to anticipate and often baffled the most competent of highway engineers and designers. To paraphrase a wise philosopher, "We must know and predict the future, but we can only know the past."

Willis E. Sibley
Cleveland State University

Bluestone, Daniel M., ed., *Cleveland* (1978).
Cleveland City Planning Commission, *Cleveland Today ... Tomorrow* (1950).
Watson, Sara Ruth, and Wolfs, John R., *Bridges of Metropolitan Cleveland* (1981).

**STREIBLER, MARTIN** (10 Feb. 1825–14 May 1864), was a sergeant in Co. E, 103D OHIO VOLUNTEER INFANTRY, during the CIVIL WAR. He is one of 2 local men depicted by name on the sculpture titled *The Color Guard* on the SOLDIERS & SAILORS MONUMENT. Streibler was born in France to Mary and Geo. Streibler. After his father died in 1844, Streibler reportedly served with the French dragoons for 6 years. Sometime before 1862, he, his mother, and a younger brother, Joseph, emigrated to the U.S. and settled in Cleveland. Streibler enlisted in the 103d regiment on 11 Aug. 1862. He was enlisted by Capt. LEVI T. SCOFIELD, who would eventually sculpt his figure for the Soldiers & Sailors Monument. Streibler was a "thoroughly disciplined" soldier who was much admired by his comrades. After being promoted to corporal, he was made sergeant on 9 Feb. 1863. On 14 May 1864, Streibler was killed while leading the 9-man color guard at the battle of Resaca, Ga. Scofield, an engineer for the regiment, viewed this action from his position in the rear and later used it as his inspiration for the monument sculpture.

**STRICKLAND, BENJAMIN** (19 July 1810–21 Feb. 1889), was Cleveland's first permanent dentist. Strickland was born in Montpelier, Vt. He received an M.D. degree from an eastern school and practiced medicine for a short time before coming to Cleveland in 1835. He opened an office in the Central Bldg. and advertised his services as a dentist; in the morning he made house calls, and in the afternoon he received patients in his office. In 1841, Strickland was admitted to the American Society of Dental Surgeons. Two years later he received an honorary D.D.S. degree from the Baltimore College of Dental Surgery. Strickland was later quite active in the development of state and local dental associations. He was a charter member of the Ohio State Dental Society and served as president (1858–65) of the Ohio Northern Dental Assoc. He also organized the Forest City Society of Dental Surgery, which later became the Cleveland Dental Assoc. Strickland advertised through the newspapers the painless extraction of teeth with the use of cold application; he also, for this purpose, was one of the first dentists in the state to use Morton's Letheon. A source for dental supplies, Strickland manufactured porcelain teeth and sold gold, tin, foil, and various instruments. Regionally, he was considered an authority on pulp treatment, fillings, and root-canal work. In 1875, Strickland retired. He died 14 years later of pneumonia. His wife was the former Hannah Walworth, whom he married in 1841.

Gellin, Milton E., *Cleveland Dentists before 1856* (1946).

**STRIEBINGER, FREDERIC WILLIAM** (22 Apr. 1870–30 Sept. 1941), was an architect active in Cleveland from 1898–1940. Striebinger was born in Cleveland to Martin and Anna Raparlie Striebinger. He attended the Cleveland public schools until 1888. He studied painting for 1 year with Wm. Merritt Chase in New York in 1889. He is said to have been the first Clevelander to study at the Ecole des Beaux-Arts in Paris (1891–96). Striebinger was an accomplished classical architect. His major buildings include the Second Church of Christ, Scientist, 1916 (later the 77th St. Cleveland Playhouse); the Harry Coulby residence, 1912 (Wickliffe City Hall); the Cleveland Gesangverein Hall, 1900 (HOUSE OF WILLS Funeral Home); the Woodward Masonic Temple, 1907 (Call & Post Bldg.); the Heights Masonic Temple, 1915; the Third Church of Christ, Scientist, 1906; and the Tremaine-Gallagher House in Cleveland Hts., 1914. Striebinger was known among his peers as the epitome of the eclectic architect, one with the broad knowledge necessary in the appropriate handling of historical sources, but without great creative originality. This judgment is refuted by the buildings themselves, especially the Coulby and Tremaine mansions, which are superb examples of the Renaissance Revival of the early 20th century. Striebinger was married twice. His first wife, Elizabeth Maude Smythe, died in 1938. He married Alice M. Rabensdorf on 12 June 1939.

**STRONGSVILLE** is a city located 15 mi. from Cleveland in the southwestern corner of Cuyahoga County, bounded by Lorain County on the west, Medina County on the south, BEREA and MIDDLEBURG HTS. on the north, and N. ROYALTON on the east. It was incorporated as the village of Strongsville in 1927 and became a city in 1960, operating under the mayor-council form of government. The city was originally Strongsville Twp., organized in 1818. Occupying 25 sq. mi., it has the 2d-largest area of the cities in Cuyahoga County. The township was named after John Stoughton Strong, an early pioneer and land agent from Vermont. Strong purchased several thousand acres in the township, which he later sold to other settlers. By 1820, the population reached 297, and the first roads were constructed. Until WORLD WAR II, farming was the chief occupation. Early industries included 2 sawmills, sandstone quarries, and a brick-manufacturing company,

but their presence never detracted from the predominantly agricultural character of the township. In 1955 the Ohio Turnpike was opened through Strongsville. Real-estate developers bought much of the land, and by the early 1960s only a few full-time farmers remained. With the construction of I–71, the city became a crossroads linking major east-west and north-south highways. It began an aggressive program to attract industry to the area, and in 1966 the Strongsville Industrial Park was opened. Consisting of 2,700 acres and comprising 17% of the city's total land area, the park attracted the Glidden-Durkee Research Ctr. in 1967, and shortly thereafter 10 other companies located in the industrial park. In 1961, Strongsville withdrew from the Cuyahoga County School System and established the Strongsville Board of Education, with 7 elementary, 2 junior, and 1 senior high school. The school system is the largest employer in the city, followed by the Van Dorn and Glidden-Durkee corporations. Part of the CLEVELAND METROPARKS SYSTEM is located in Strongsville, and the city offers recreational activities, including baseball, BASKETBALL, swimming, ice skating, golf, and country club membership. In 1980 the population was 28,577.

**STUDENTS FOR A DEMOCRATIC SOCIETY** was a national organization of radical college students attempting to build a new, broad-based left during the 1960s. Loose ties between the national organization and local chapters permitted much local autonomy. In Cleveland, SDS promoted civil rights, welfare rights, draft resistance, and opposition to the war in Vietnam. SDS came to Cleveland in the summer of 1964, when 2 Western Reserve medical students, Charlotte Phillips and Ollie Fein, founded an SDS Economic Research & Action Project at 2908 Jay Ave. Called the Cleveland Community Project, this organization aimed to build an alliance between poor whites and black civil-rights groups based on economic issues. Frustrated in its attempts to work with public-housing residents and the unemployed, the CCP succeeded in reviving a dormant organization of welfare mothers, Citizens United for Adequate Welfare. In the winter of 1965, CUFAW agitated successfully for a free-school-lunch program and later joined efforts to gain representation for the poor on the Cleveland COUNCIL FOR ECONOMIC OPPORTUNITIES.

SDS's work with welfare recipients laid the foundation for the Cleveland Welfare Rights Movement and served as the training ground for future leaders of the antiwar and women's movements, such as Paul Potter, Sharon Jeffrey, Carol McEldowney, and Kathy Boudin. As the VIETNAM WAR escalated, Cleveland SDS took a prominent role in the local antiwar movement. It participated in demonstrations and in the spring of 1967 established the Cleveland Draft Resistance Union to provide counseling and support for young men wishing to avoid the military draft. The union worked with local high school students and with some men in the armed forces who opposed the war effort. SDS's leadership role in the antiwar movement led to the development of SDS chapters on local campuses. Western Reserve University formed a chapter in the spring of 1965; by the summer of 1969, chapters existed at CLEVELAND STATE, CUYAHOGA COMMUNITY COLLEGE, and JOHN CARROLL UNIVERSITY. Local SDS activities reflected the increasing militance of national SDS in the late 1960s. Cleveland SDS demonstrated at the 1968 Democratic Convention in Chicago and heckled campaign speeches by presidential candidates in Cleveland that fall. In May 1970 there were violent antiwar protests on the campuses of CASE WESTERN RESERVE, John Carroll, and Cleveland State. The national organization disintegrated into feuding factions in 1969–70, and by 1971 no active SDS chapter existed in Cleveland.

**SUBURBAN COMMUNITY HOSPITAL** (4180 Warrensville Ctr. Rd., WARRENSVILLE HTS.) is a 180-bed voluntary nonprofit short-term general hospital. It was built in 1957, and additions were made to the structure in 1968 and 1975. Suburban Community Hospital is a member/subsidiary of STRATEGIC HEALTH SYSTEMS.

The **SUBURBAN SYMPHONY ORCHESTRA** is made up of people from all walks of life, housewives, doctors, businessmen, students, and semiprofessionals, who have blended their common hobby of music into a viable community experience. The symphony was founded in 1954 with Robt. C. Weiskopf, a salesman for a cotton firm, as conductor. Started with the blessings of the Cleveland Hts. Joint Recreation Board, the ensemble performs classical music at an affordable price; most concerts are free. Costs are met by members, friends, and sponsors. In 1959, the Suburban Symphony gave Leonard Bernstein's *Jeremiah Symphony* its Cleveland premiere. The symphony has, through the years, given Cleveland composers a chance to hear their music played, such as HERBERT ELWELL's piece *The Forever Young* for solo voice and orchestra, which was performed in 1971. That same season the local premiere of Mendelssohn's *Concerto for Violin* with Bernard Goldschmidt, violinist for the CLEVELAND ORCHESTRA, and Eunice Podice, pianist, was presented. In their home auditorium at Beachwood High School, the symphony, accompanied by Akron composer-pianist Pat Pace of the Pace Jazz Trio, performed new interpretations of Gershwin's *Rhapsody in Blue* and portions of *Porgy and Bess* in 1976. Jose Greco, the dancer, joined them for a concert the following year. Robt. Weiskopf died in May 1979. He had been ill for a year, and Yoel Levi had conducted during the 1978 season. In 1980, Martin Kessler (composer and music director of the Opus One Chamber Orchestra) was named new conductor and business manager. Since then Leonid Grin, associate conductor of the Moscow Philharmonic Orchestra, has guest-conducted. In 1984, the Suburban Symphony Orchestra celebrated its 30th anniversary with concerts of Mozart and Haydn. In 1985 the symphony had 85 members and a projected 5 concert series.

**SUBURBS.** The history of suburban development is long and complex. While some Cleveland suburbs are nearly as old as the city, they range from industrial (LINNDALE) and entertainment centers (N. RANDALL) to small, exclusive residential villages (HUNTING VALLEY) and large blue-collar cities (PARMA). As a result, defining suburb and suburbanization is difficult at best. Suburbs lie within commuting distance of a city and initially housed urban workers. While often dependent on city amenities, they remain administratively separate. In contrast to cities, most suburbs have more middle-class residents, lower densities, and higher rates of homeownership; residents have longer work commutes. Several forces encourage suburbanization (growth at the city's edge); including individual decisions by residents influenced by the rural ideal, urban flight, transportation technology, overcrowded and environmentally unpleasant conditions in the city, and private and public policy at local, state, and federal levels. Despite the diversity of Cuyahoga County suburbs, each community is inextricably tied to the history of the core city. From this relationship, it is possible to trace the history of Cleveland suburbs in 4 periods: horse-drawn streetcar suburbs—the urban ring, 1850–90; streetcar suburbs and the first suburban rings, 1890–1930; the beginnings of urban decen-

tralization, 1930–50; and automobile suburbs and suburban supremacy—outer rings, 1950–80. These periods witnessed the development of particular types of suburban communities. However, neither suburbs of the same time period nor the 3 major regions (east, west, and south) are all alike; local geography, immediate historical context, and residents themselves account for these differences.

Before 1850, Cleveland had several rivals, in addition to being surrounded by a series of independent rural townships, villages, and settlements. Lacking a transportation system to disperse its population, it remained a walking city—a dense settlement in which residents walked to work and shop. With continued population growth, Cleveland approached its geographic limits by the 1850s. Changes in legal requirements for annexation and transportation technology removed the barriers limiting its spatial expansion. The 1851 state constitution gave local communities the power to make annexation decisions; eventually that permitted the city to absorb its first ring of suburban development. In 1859, the E. CLEVELAND RAILWAY began construction of a horse-drawn streetcar line, which provided the start of a cheap, reliable transportation system to disperse the congested urban population. During the 1860s and 1870s, other companies laid tracks to undeveloped outlying areas, while dummy railroads such as the Lakeview & Collamer on the east and Rocky River on the west brought urban residents to rural retreats where they could experience the benefits of country living. In the 1880s, the Nickel Plate Railroad purchased and upgraded the dummy lines and began limited commuter service. (See URBAN TRANSPORTATION and specific streetcar companies.) The horse-drawn street railways opened up for residential development nearby suburban land adjacent to the tracks and up to about 3 mi. from downtown. The 5-cent fare permitted more affluent urbanites to escape to the country, where they constructed large homes in a wide variety of popular architectural styles.

New suburbanites wanted to keep the urban services they had enjoyed, but township and county governments could not match the city's educational facilities, paved and lighted streets, and fire and police protection. To gain these amenities, suburbanites formed villages: the first E. CLEVELAND (1866), GLENVILLE (1870), W. Cleveland (1871), COLLINWOOD (1883), BROOKLYN (1889), S. BROOKLYN (1889), and NOTTINGHAM (1899). They, too, found the costs staggering. Ultimately, most 19th-century suburbanites chose to join Cleveland to gain the best of both worlds: the bucolic suburban ideal and urban services. Expansion-minded Cleveland sought these mergers, initially absorbing the remainder of Cleveland Twp. (1850), its leading rivals, OHIO CITY (1854) and NEWBURGH (1873), and parts of neighboring townships (Brooklyn, Newburgh, and E. Cleveland). Cleveland then annexed its neighboring villages: the first E. Cleveland (1872), Brooklyn (1890), W. Cleveland (1894), Glenville and S. Brooklyn (1895), Corlett (1909), Collinwood (1910), and Nottingham (1913).

The development of electrified streetcars in the late 1880s provided a dynamic force for the transformation of the metropolis. Three times faster than horse-drawn streetcars (5 vs. 15 mph), the invention permitted radial suburban development up to 10 mi. from the city center. The new technology arrived as Cleveland confronted a series of immense problems: huge migrations from Southern and Eastern Europe seemed to "overrun" the city; fine residential neighborhoods succumbed to industrial and business expansion; pollution from new industries blotted out the skies, choked the lungs, and fouled rivers; while urban government appeared increasingly corrupt. As the city used segregation by function to bring order to this apparent chaos,

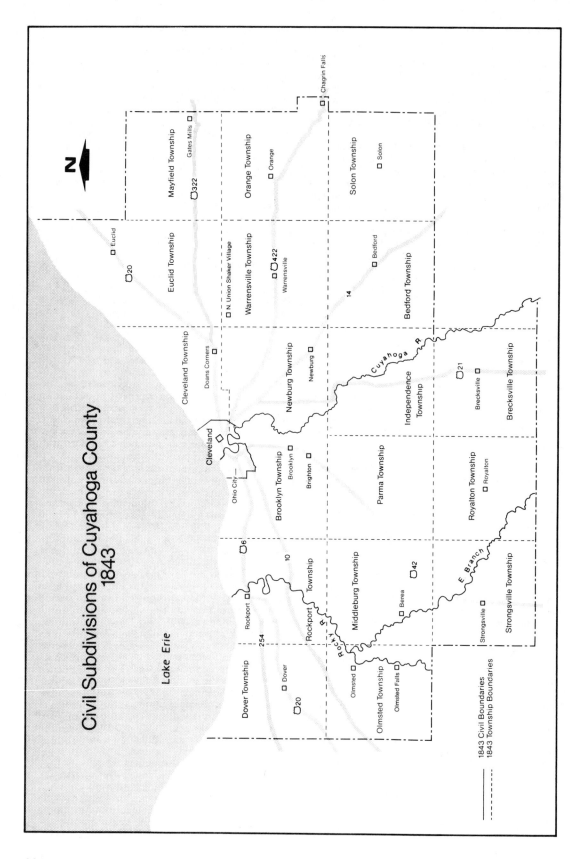

Civil Subdivisions of Cuyahoga County 1843

Lake Erie

N

Dover Township
☐20 Dover

Rockport Township
☐ Rockport
10
254

Olmsted Township
☐ Olmsted
☐ Olmsted Falls

Middleburg Township
☐ Berea
☐42

Strongsville Township
☐ Strongsville

Cleveland Township
Doans Corners ☐
Ohio City ◇ Cleveland

Brooklyn Township
☐ Brooklyn
☐ Brighton
☐6

Parma Township

Royalton Township
☐ Royalton

Euclid Township
☐ Euclid
☐20

Warrensville Township
☐ N Union Shaker Village
☐422
☐ Warrensville

Newburg Township
☐ Newburg

Cuyahoga R.

Independence Township
☐21

Brecksville Township
☐ Brecksville

Mayfield Township
☐ Gates Mills
☐322

Orange Township
☐ Orange

Solon Township
☐ Solon

Bedford Township
☐ Bedford
14

Chagrin Falls
☐

E Branch

ROCKY R.

———— 1843 Civil Boundaries
– – – – 1843 Township Boundaries

934

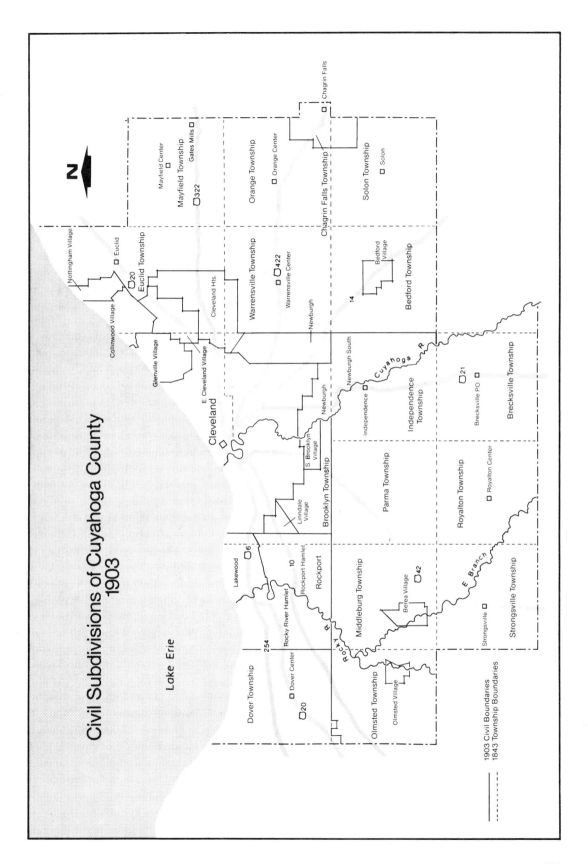

## Civil Subdivisions of Cuyahoga County 1903

Lake Erie

N

Nottingham Village
Euclid
Collinwood Village
20
Euclid Township
Glenville Village
E. Cleveland Village
Cleveland Hts.
Cleveland

Mayfield Center
Mayfield Township
Gates Mills
322

Orange Township
Orange Center

Chagrin Falls
Chagrin Falls Township

Solon Township
Solon

Warrensville Township
422
Warrensville Center
Newburgh

Bedford Village
14
Bedford Township

Newburgh
S. Brooklyn Village
Brooklyn Township
Linndale Village

Newburgh South
Independence
Independence Township

Cuyahoga R.

Parma Township

Brecksville Township
Brecksville PO
21

Lakewood
6
Rocky River Hamlet
Rockport Hamlet
10
Rockport

Royalton Township
Royalton Center

Dover Township
Dover Center
20
254

ROCKY R.

Middleburg Township
Berea Village
42

Strongsville
Strongsville Township

E. Branch

Olmsted Township
Olmsted Village

1903 Civil Boundaries
1843 Township Boundaries

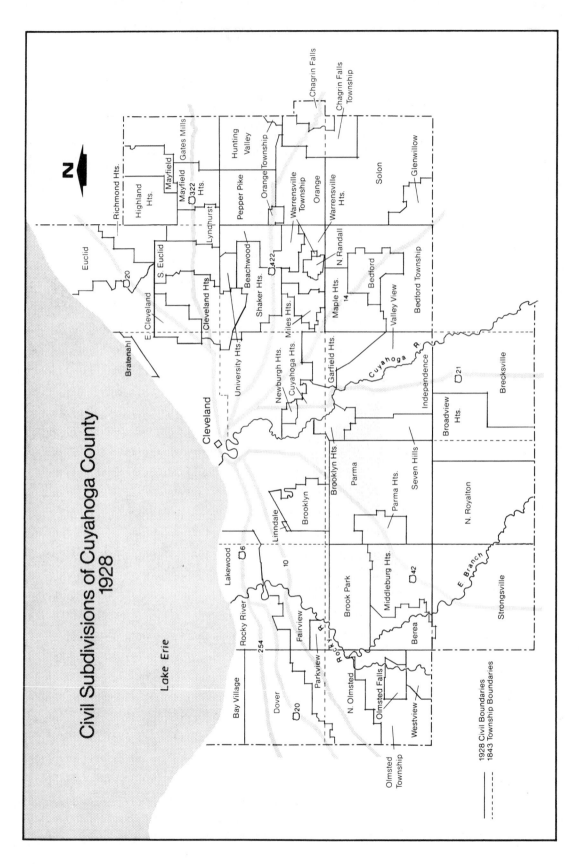

# Civil Subdivisions of Cuyahoga County 1928

Lake Erie

1928 Civil Boundaries
1843 Township Boundaries

936

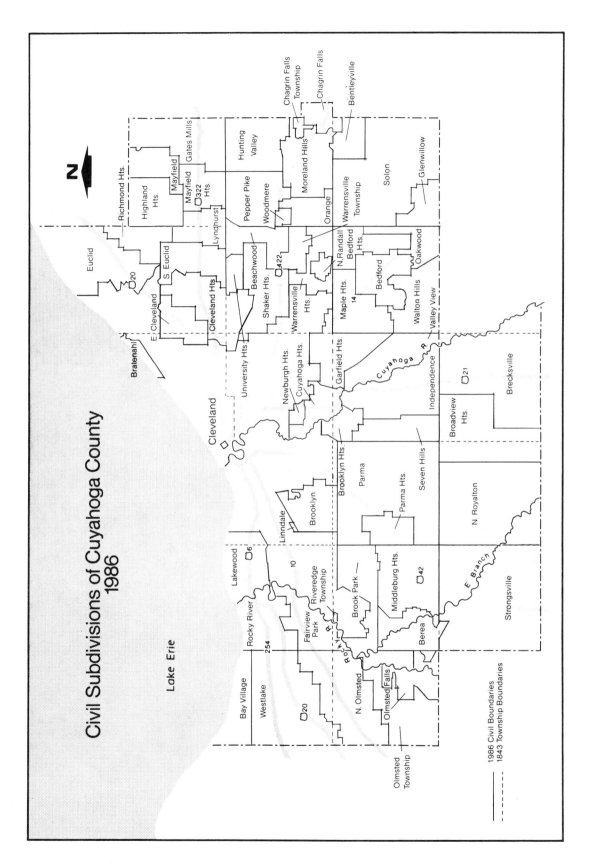

# Civil Subdivisions of Cuyahoga County 1986

Lake Erie

1986 Civil Boundaries
1843 Township Boundaries

937

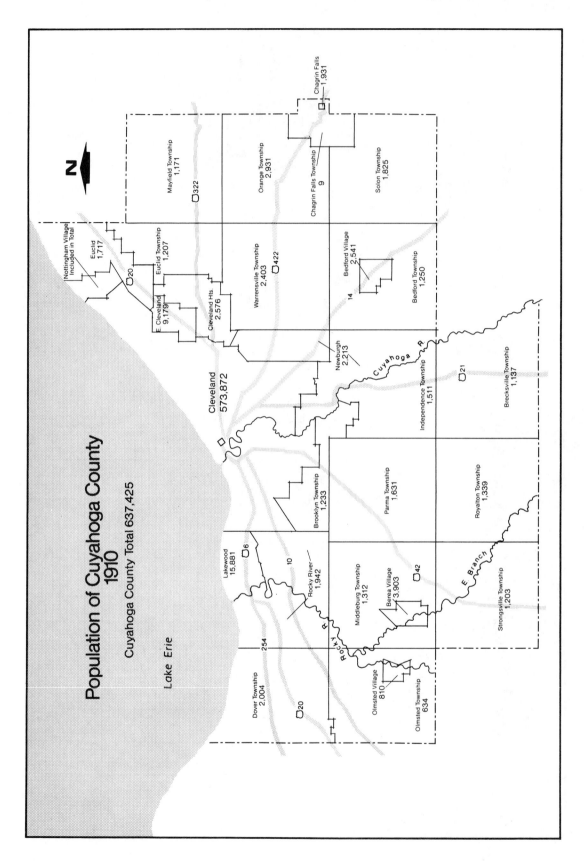

# Population of Cuyahoga County 1910

Cuyahoga County Total 637,425

Lake Erie

Nottingham Village Included in Total

Euclid 1,717

E Cleveland 9,179

Euclid Township 1,207

Cleveland Hts 2,576

□20

Mayfield Township 1,171

□322

Warrensville Township 2,403

□422

Orange Township 2,931

Chagrin Falls Township 9

Chagrin Falls 1,931

Solon Township 1,825

Cleveland 573,872

Newburgh 2,213

Bedford Village 2,541

Bedford Township 1,250

14

Cuyahoga R.

Independence Township 1,511

□21

Brecksville Township 1,137

Brooklyn Township 1,233

Parma Township 1,631

Royalton Township 1,339

Lakewood 15,881

□6

Rocky River 1,942

10

Middleburg Township 1,312

Berea Village 3,903

□42

E Branch

Strongsville Township 1,203

Dover Township 2,004

□20

254

ROCKY R.

Olmsted Village 810

Olmsted Township 634

N

938

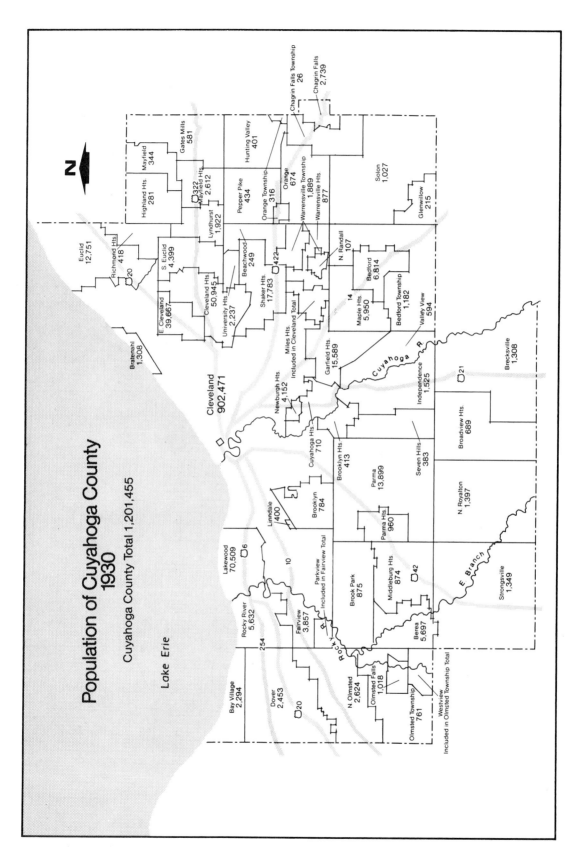

# Population of Cuyahoga County
## 1930

Cuyahoga County Total 1,201,455

Lake Erie

Cleveland
902,471

Euclid
12,751

Richmond Hts
418

20

S. Euclid
4,399

E. Cleveland
39,667

Cleveland Hts
50,945

University Hts
2,237

Bratenahl
1,308

Highland Hts
281

Mayfield
344

Gates Mills
581

322
Mayfield Hts
2,612

Lyndhurst
1,922

Beachwood
249

Shaker Hts
17,783

422

Hunting Valley
401

Pepper Pike
434

Orange Township
316

Orange
674

Warrensville Township
1,889

Warrensville Hts
877

Chagrin Falls Township
26

Chagrin Falls
2,739

Solon
1,027

Glenwillow
215

N. Randall
107

Bedford
6,814

Maple Hts
5,950

14

Bedford Township
1,182

Valley View
594

Independence
1,525

21

Brecksville
1,308

Broadview Hts
689

Seven Hills
383

N. Royalton
1,397

Strongsville
1,349

Miles Hts
Included in Cleveland Total

Garfield Hts
15,589

Newburgh Hts
4,152

Cuyahoga Hts
710

Brooklyn Hts
413

Parma
13,899

Parma Hts
960

Cuyahoga R.

Lakewood
70,509

6

Linndale
400

Brooklyn
784

Parkview
Included in Fairview Total

10

Rocky River
5,632

Fairview
3,857

254

Brook Park
875

Middleburg Hts
874

42

Berea
5,697

Westview
Included in Olmsted Township Total

E. Branch

Bay Village
2,294

Dover
2,453

20

N. Olmsted
2,624

Olmsted Falls
1,018

Olmsted Township
761

N

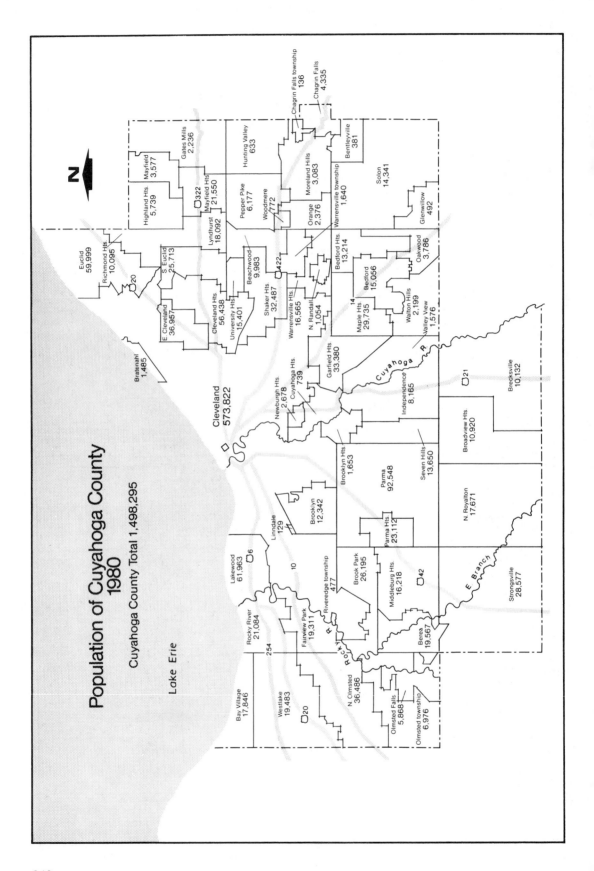

# Population of Cuyahoga County 1980

Cuyahoga County Total 1,498,295

Lake Erie

Cleveland 573,822

Bratenahl 1,485

Euclid 59,999
Richmond Hts. 10,095
S. Euclid 25,713
E. Cleveland 36,957
Cleveland Hts. 56,438
University Hts. 15,401
Shaker Hts. 32,487

Highland Hts. 5,739
Mayfield 3,577
Gates Mills 2,236
Mayfield Hts. 21,550
Lyndhurst 18,092
Beachwood 9,983
Warrensville Hts. 16,565
N. Randall 1,054

Hunting Valley 633
Pepper Pike 6,177
Woodmere 772
Orange 2,376
Moreland Hills 3,083
Warrensville township 1,640
Bentleyville 381
Solon 14,341
Glenwillow 492

Chagrin Falls township 136
Chagrin Falls 4,335

Bedford Hts. 13,214
Bedford 15,056
Maple Hts. 29,735
Walton Hills 2,199
Valley View 1,576
Oakwood 3,786

Newburgh Hts. 2,678
Cuyahoga Hts. 739
Garfield Hts. 33,380

Cuyahoga R.

Independence 8,165

Brooklyn Hts. 1,653
Seven Hills 13,650
Broadview Hts. 10,920
Brecksville 10,132

Parma 92,548
Parma Hts. 23,112
N. Royalton 17,671

Linndale 129
Brooklyn 12,342
Brook Park 26,195
Middleburg Hts. 16,218
Strongsville 28,577

Lakewood 61,963
Riveredge township 477
Berea 19,567

Rocky River 21,084
Fairview Park 19,311

Bay Village 17,846
Westlake 19,483
N. Olmsted 36,486
Olmsted Falls 5,868
Olmsted township 6,976

E Branch

14

422
322
20
6
10
254
20
21
42

N

middle-class urbanites looked to the suburbs as both rural haven and escape from urban disorder. Unlike previous suburban developments that turned to the city for salvation, streetcar suburbs deliberately distanced themselves. Privately owned, franchised electric streetcar companies often controlled by land developers laid out tracks on EUCLID AVE. (to Lee Rd. by 1893); Euclid Hts. Blvd. (to Edgehill by 1897); and Detroit Ave. and Clifton Blvd. (to the Rocky River by 1894 and 1904 respectively). Almost immediately after completion of the first streetcar lines, residents of these outlying areas took advantage of Ohio's permissive incorporation laws and established villages: E. Cleveland (1895), LAKEWOOD and CLEVELAND HTS. (1903). Rapid population growth quickly raised them to city status: E. Cleveland and Lakewood in 1911, and Cleveland Hts. in 1921. Nevertheless, Cleveland's first streetcar suburbs grew most quickly between 1910–30; E. Cleveland added 30,488 new residents, while Lakewood's population increased by 55,328, and that of Cleveland Hts. by 47,990. A second suburban ring, linked to the downtown by streetcar or rapid transit, also began to form. Made up of the older independent villages (BEDFORD and BEREA) and new suburban developments (EUCLID, GARFIELD HTS., MAPLE HTS., Parma, ROCKY RIVER, and SHAKER HTS.), these communities obtained city status by 1931. In addition, 52 new villages incorporated.

Unlike earlier suburban communities, streetcar suburbs chose to remain independent from Cleveland. While the new suburbs attracted residents with their pastoral landscapes, urban migrants remembered the conditions that had driven them from the city. With Cleveland overwhelmed by its own population growth, the new suburbs benefited from additional time and the scale of their own growth to establish services expected by urban dwellers. Having escaped, new suburbanites sought to keep unwanted urban elements out; antiannexationists often painted city government as corrupt despite muckraker Lincoln Steffens's claims that Cleveland was one of the best-run cities in the country. E. Cleveland rejected merger with Cleveland in 1910 and 1916, because "saloons might be established...we could not endure bar-rooms next to our homes" and because of the fear of immigrants and their institutions. A dry Lakewood rejected annexation in 1910 and 1922 because it already had "ample school facilities, police, fire, city planning, zoning, and sanitary protection." Shaker Hts. developers went further by strictly controlling access to community property and through explicit deed restrictions prohibiting new immigrants and BLACKS. After 1910, few suburban communities save WEST PARK and Miles Hts. chose to join the city. Despite a population growth of almost 2.5 times between 1900–30, Cleveland's share of the county population dropped from 87% to 75%.

While the Depression of the 1930s and WORLD WAR II greatly slowed the pace of urban and suburban growth, events during the period set the stage and direction for an even greater transformation of the metropolitan area. Cleveland's population grew by less than 13,000, and Lakewood lost population, while that of Cleveland Hts. grew by 9,000. The newer cities of Bedford, Garfield Hts., Rocky River, and Shaker Hts. all experienced substantial growth. By 1950, Cleveland's share of the county population had slipped nearly another 10%. Second, substantial street and highway construction along with the increased use of automobiles during the 1920s and 1930s began to free suburban development from the geographic limits imposed by the linear streetcar, while greater use of trucks and electricity freed industries from older city sites. These developments made accessible the large tracts of cheap, low-taxed lands outside the city; both private and public decisions on industrial and institutional location added to this growing pattern of decentralization. Industrial corridors expanded along Brookpark Rd. and in Euclid. In retailing, Sears, Roebuck stores on Lorain and Carnegie avenues represented the beginning of decentralization; the development of SHAKER SQUARE as Cleveland's first suburban shopping center provided a clearer model for the postwar period. (See BUSINESS, RETAIL.)

Third, in its efforts to aid the Depression-devastated housing market, the New Deal Federal Housing Authority and later the Veterans Admin. developed programs for homebuyers that provided the means and patterns for the suburban explosion; these patterns differed greatly from the more dense, urban rebuilding of postwar Europe. Instead, they targeted FHA and VA home-loan guarantees for newly constructed single-family homes in new suburban areas; they also adopted guidelines from real-estate and banking industries that required racial segregation (enforced through developer-instituted restricted covenants). By reinforcing existing segregation practices, these programs effectively blocked black access to suburban housing. Although the U.S. Supreme Court struck down restrictive covenants in 1948, the FHA continued to require covenants; they were common in suburban tracts of the 1940s and 1950s, especially in Garfield Hts., Parma, PARMA HTS., and Maple Hts. By supporting existing banking, real-estate, and development practices, government programs subsidized white, middle-class residents to leave the city, but effectively locked black residents into the emerging ghetto. Finally, the Depression and World War II slowed housing construction, resulting in overcrowding and a severe housing shortage. When prosperity returned during and after the war, Clevelanders who had rented or doubled up with relatives sought homes of their own. The pent-up demand, along with public policy, helped create the suburban housing explosions of the late 1950s, 1960s, and 1970s. Unlike streetcar suburbs, which housed mostly skilled and white-collar workers, the post-World War II developments provided homes for industrial workers. During the 1930s, these workers founded new unions, especially the UNITED AUTO WORKERS and UNITED STEEL WORKERS; under the banner of the Congress of Industrial Organizations, industrial workers gained the power to claim both livable wages and job security. These efforts made owning a new suburban home possible for a whole new group of Clevelanders.

While the rise of independent suburbs and the automobile can be traced to the start of the 20th century, they did not begin to dominate the metropolitan area until the post-World War II period; combined, they led to the development of a new suburban landscape. By 1940, when 64% of all Cuyahoga County families owned an automobile, a significant majority of the working residents of streetcar suburbs had abandoned the streetcar for a car to get to work. Most striking, in Shaker Hts., where the pioneering off-grade rapid-transit system provided the best public transportation in the county, nearly 75% of principal income earners used automobiles for the journey to work. Although some streetcar routes continued until the 1950s, overexpansion, congested routes, declining ridership, financial problems, and competition from automobiles clearly doomed the streetcar.

As the automobile gained ascendancy, the stage was set for the most massive residential construction and suburban growth in Cleveland history. The boom was fueled by the housing shortage, the broad base of families who could now afford a home of their own, and the FHA/VA support for new home construction. While significant population increases in the second ring of streetcar suburbs (Bedford,

Euclid, Garfield Hts., Maple Hts., Rocky River, and Shaker Hts.) made these communities transitional automobile suburbs, the most spectacular growth took place outside older suburban communities. The first ring of automobile suburbs included the new cities of BAY VILLAGE (1950), LYNDHURST, and FAIRVIEW PARK (1951). The most spectacular growth took place in Parma. Its population of nearly 14,000 residents in 1931 had nearly doubled by 1950, and its postwar growth clearly established it as one of the new automobile suburbs. The 1950s alone produced 54,000 new residents; another 17,000 followed in the 1960s. Parma easily surpassed Lakewood, the largest streetcar suburb, to become the county's second city. A second ring of automobile suburbs experienced their greatest growth during the 1960s and 1970s; all save MAYFIELD HTS. (1950) gained city status at the beginning of the period: Parma Hts. (1959); BROOK PARK, N. OLMSTED, WARRENS-VILLE HTS. (1960); and BEDFORD HTS. and SEVEN HILLS (1961). While Cleveland's suburban cities either lost population or experienced minimal growth from 1970 on, at the edge of the county, aided by interstate highways, a final ring of suburbs emerged. N. ROYALTON, SOLON, STRONGSVILLE, and WESTLAKE all registered significant growth from 1960–80; suburban development also spread beyond the county. Population figures clearly reveal the dynamics of suburban growth from 1949 to its peak in 1970; while Cleveland lost 127,457 residents, the county exclusive of the city grew by 631,042. Despite a loss of 45,000 in the 1970s, the suburban share of the county's population jumped from 28% in 1940 to 62% in 1980. The county's suburban population passed Cleveland's during the 1960s, and the gap widened in the 1970s and 1980s.

While new suburban growth exploded on the periphery, older streetcar suburbs and the inner ring of automobile suburbs began to undergo aging and transformation. The population base declined and changed as the more affluent left for newer homes and less affluent residents moved in; as older communities, they began to confront some of the problems of the core city: aging population and infrastructure, increased need for social programs, and an eroding tax base. At the same time, new construction began to alter the face of these communities; high-rise apartments and office buildings replaced older homes and business structures. As businesses increasingly chose suburban locations for their offices (high-rise in older suburbs/campus-style in newer ones), streetcar suburbs such as Lakewood began to merge their older function of bedroom community with that of specialized satellite city for the metropolitan area. The suburban explosion left a fragmented governmental structure in its wake. By 1956, 1 county, 20 cities, 38 villages, 4 townships, 32 school districts, 9 library districts, and regional authorities such as the CLEVELAND METROPARKS SYSTEM governed some aspect of the area. Since at least 1919, some Clevelanders, urban and suburban, had expressed concern about this growing fragmentation, disorder, and waste. During the 1920s and early 1930s, reformers working largely through the CITIZENS LEAGUE pressed a variety of issues to provide some form of city-county consolidation. Nevertheless, voters failed to approve county charter reform proposals in 1934 and 1959. Ironically, streetcar-suburb residents who had opposed annexation overwhelmingly supported both reform measures; resistance to metro government came from the newer suburbs.

The automobile revolution dramatically changed the metropolitan landscape; in contrast to the streetcar's linear focus on downtown, the more flexible automobile encouraged decentralization. It permitted suburban development to fill in areas between streetcar settlements and opened up land beyond the streetcar's reach. While streetcar lines pioneered commercial strip development, postwar developers added new auto-oriented businesses and vernacular architectural styles to suburbia; gas stations, drive-in restaurants, and motels lined new suburban arteries. Beginning in the 1950s, they recreated late-19th-century arcades, placed them on vacant suburban lots, surrounded them with huge parking areas, and renamed them shopping malls; in the process, they refocused attention from downtown to the new suburban developments. The automobile revolution also produced a new residential landscape. Streetcar suburbs are small, densely built environments of single-, double-, and multifamily housing; they contrast sharply with the more spacious automobile suburbs. In size, Cleveland's 3 streetcar suburbs average only ¼ of the newest automobile suburbs: 5–21 sq. mi. In 1960, E. Cleveland and Lakewood were as densely packed as Cleveland, with about 12,000 residents per sq. mi. In contrast, the transitional streetcar-auto suburbs ranged from 3,000–6,000 residents per sq. mi. Population density of automobile suburbs declines as the distance from town increases; most first-ring suburbs ranged between 3,000–4,000; the second ring between 800–3,000; the third ring between 300–750. Similarly, while 62% of Lakewood's 1980 housing units were multifamily, single-family homes made up nearly 75% of N. Olmsted's housing. Subdivision scale, house building, and style also changed dramatically. Streetcar-suburb landowners subdivided small parcels into lots and sold them to individuals or speculative builders; their modern counterparts subdivide large tracts of land and design and construct all houses. Streetcar-suburb builders constructed homes in a variety of styles (Colonial Revival, Homestead, American Four Square, Bungalow, and Cleveland Double); recent developers use 2 or 3 basic house forms on their entire tract. These homes are often single-story or split-level ranch-style. Unlike the older, multistoried homes, they lack front porches and appear more uniform and monotonous, although residents personalize their property by embellishing their yards and house facades.

While suburban history fits generally into the above typology, this approach provides little insight into the sharp differences between communities of the same time period. Cleveland suburbs each have their own identities, some assiduously cultivated and others imposed by outsiders. More important, Cleveland suburbs can be grouped in another series of interlocking categories, including: east vs. west vs. south; white-collar vs. blue-collar; or by ethnic groups attracted or kept out. Clearly, one of the longest-standing differences in Cleveland is the one between the east and the west sides; it dates at least to the 1836–37 Bridge War, which pitted rivals Cleveland and Ohio City against each other (see COLUMBUS ST. BRIDGE). Suburban communities have taken up this battle with east and west suburbs each united to denigrate the other; a rich suburban folklore has grown up around this schism. Important differences do exist between east and west; Cleveland Hts. and E. Cleveland quickly adopted the city manager form of government in the early 1900s, while Lakewood overwhelmingly defeated the reform measure. Not surprisingly, this white-collar battle between east and west ignores the south side, which has its own unique history. In contrast to east and west suburbs, which are largely white-collar, southern suburbs were surrounded by the expansion of industrial employment centers and housed predominantly blue-collar workers.

Cleveland suburbs vary considerably by their population's ethnic origins; ethnic clusters have shaped suburban landscapes and lifestyles, as well as those of Cleveland. Since groups tend to migrate out of the city along major arteries, various ethnic groups have moved along one or more radials out to the suburbs. The first Jewish migrants to 19th-century Cleveland settled in central city neighborhoods; eventually the center of Jewish population moved successively into Woodland, Glenville, and Kinsman. Despite restrictive covenants, Jews (see JEWS & JUDAISM) eventually transported their communities to the eastern suburbs. By 1980, they made up 20% of Cleveland Hts. and Mayfield Hts., and almost ⅓ of Shaker Hts., S. EUCLID, and PEPPER PIKE, while UNIVERSITY HTS. and BEACHWOOD (about 60% and 85% respectively) are predominantly Jewish suburbs. Moreover, Jews have developed a rich infrastructure of institutions that help set the tone for the larger communities; these include a weekly newspaper ( CLEVELAND JEWISH NEWS), commercial areas at Cedar Ctr. and Beachwood Pl., and other institutions clustered along Taylor Rd. In contrast, there are 26 synagogues/temples on the east side; the west side has only 1 fledgling congregation. Black migrants also entered the city's central districts and moved east through Kinsman and HOUGH. Both within the city (Collinwood and Broadway) and in the suburbs, blacks confronted more significant barriers than Jews and other ethnic groups. As late as 1970, black suburbanites made up a majority of only 1 suburban city (E. Cleveland--59%), and a significant minority in one other (Shaker Hts.--15%). The black population in Cleveland Hts., Euclid, and Maple Hts. was less than 3%, while other suburbs had virtually none: Parma (50 blacks), Parma Hts. (4 blacks), Lakewood (21 blacks), and N. Olmsted (18 blacks). Ten years later, blacks made up 25% of the population of Shaker Hts. and Cleveland Hts., 14% of Garfield Hts., and 8% of Euclid, while white flight from E. Cleveland created a nearly all-black suburb. Access to most white suburbs continued to be restricted in the 1980s.

In contrast to the more concentrated Jewish and especially black residence patterns, Americans of Polish descent are widely scattered across the county. While some remain in SLAVIC VILLAGE, many have reaggregated in the southern suburbs of Garfield Hts., Maple Hts., and Parma, as have some of the key institutions of Cleveland Polonia. Slovak-Americans and their institutions have also played important roles in Parma and Lakewood. Similarly, nationality halls, once common to inner-city ethnic enclaves, have begun to appear on the suburban landscape; recent additions include the German Society of Danube-Swabians in Olmsted Twp. and the East Side Irish-Americans in Euclid. The presence of these institutions on suburban landscapes suggests the continuing importance of ethnicity to both suburbanites and suburbia.

While suburbs are less heterogeneous than Cleveland, no suburb is homogeneous. Most have discrete neighborhoods, but few are as diverse as Lakewood. From its suburban beginnings, Lakewood drew residents from every class level; in 1930 the city had census tracts in the lowest to the highest income groups. Lakewood residents have created a complex social geography of different landscapes based on economic status; these range from a working-class, Slavic urban village in the southeast (the BIRD'S NEST AREA); to a skilled and white-collar middle-class landscape of single- and double-family homes in central Lakewood; and an upper-class resort/yacht club residential area (CLIFTON PARK). Apartments along Clifton, Lake, and Edgewater in eastern Lakewood have added a fourth landscape, housing singles and childless couples (including gays), whose lifestyles contrast sharply with the other three. Suburbs also differ from each other in terms of layout, social class, and various demographic factors. Perhaps the most obvious difference is in physical form. While all suburbs exercised some form of planning, the VAN SWERINGEN brothers'

development of Shaker Hts. is unique for extensive control over virtually every aspect of the emerging community. In contrast to Shaker's carefully laid-out curvilinear streets, segregated shopping district, and off-grade rapid-transit system, libertarian suburbs, such as Lakewood, reflect more utilitarian concerns, with grid street patterns, high densities, and mixed land uses. Suburban history, however, is very dynamic, and such characteristic conditions can rapidly change. Changing technologies, housing costs, and area-wide economic development will continue to shape Cleveland's suburban history in the coming decades.

James Borchert
Cleveland State University

Schauffler, Mary, "The Suburbs of Cleveland: A Field Study of the Metropolitan District outside the Administrative Area of the City" (Ph.D. diss., University of Chicago, 1941).

**SULLIVAN, JEREMIAH J.** (16 Nov. 1844–2 Feb. 1922), was a businessman, and later a prominent banker who founded the Central Natl. Bank and Superior Savings & Trust. Sullivan was born on a farm near Canal Fulton, Ohio, where he attended local schools. In 1879 and 1885, he was elected a state senator representing Wayne, Knox, Holmes, and Morrow counties. He helped establish the Soldiers Home in Sandusky and served as a trustee. In 1887, Pres. Grover Cleveland appointed him national bank examiner for Ohio. He came to Cleveland and in 1890 helped organize the Central Natl. Bank of Cleveland; in 1900 he became its president. In 1905 he organized the Superior Savings & Trust, where he also served as president. The two banks merged in 1921 into Central Natl. Bank Savings & Trust Co., and Sullivan became chairman of the board of directors. Sullivan was involved in local and national banking organizations. In 1899, he became the Cleveland Assoc. of Credit Men's first president. He was the first president of the Bankers' Club of Cleveland and served as president of the Ohio Bankers' Assoc. In 1905–06, he served as president of the Natl. Board of Trade. In 1914, he was president of the CLEVELAND CLEARINGHOUSE ASSOC. Sullivan was among a few prominent American bankers who favored the Federal Reserve Act of 1913. He also helped bring to Cleveland the 4th FEDERAL RESERVE BANK. He served as president of the Cleveland Chamber of Commerce in 1905. He was a member of the Ohio Society of New York and the MAYFIELD COUNTRY, Colonial, and Roadside clubs. The Ohio Natl. Guards' 5th Ohio Regiment elected him colonel in 1893. He was active in the Ohio Democratic party. Sullivan married Selina J. Brown in 1873. They had a son and 2 daughters.

**SUN NEWSPAPERS** grew from a single weekly into the dominant suburban newspaper chain of metropolitan Cleveland. Its nucleus was the *Shaker Sun*, founded by Harry Volk in 1946. Within 6 years, Volk had purchased the *Heights Press*, which he merged with the *Sun* as the *Heights Sun Press*, and the *Hillcrest Messenger*, which was renamed the *Sun Messenger*. He expanded his operations to the west side by acquiring half-interests in the *Lakewood Post* and the *Fairview-Rocky River Herald*, which were rechristened the *Sun Post* and *Sun Herald* respectively. Regarding the SUBURBS as "the new frontier of journalism," Volk published on Thursdays in order to effectively cover their prevalent Wednesday council meetings. Extensive cultural coverage was provided by knowledgeable art critics, and a series on inadequate suburban sewage treatment brought Volk a national award. By the time he sold

943

out in 1969, he had built the Sun chain up to 6 newspapers with a combined circulation of over 140,000.

Volk's holdings were purchased for a reported $2 million by ComCorp, a venture owned by Howard Metzenbaum and David Skylar. Already owners of the *Parma Post* and the *West Side News*, the new publishers continued purchasing established properties and inserting the prefix *Sun* into all the chain's nameplates. After ComCorp went public in the early 1970s, Sun Newspapers experienced a succession of new owners. Acquired by Booth Newspapers of Ann Arbor, Mich., a subsidiary of the Newhouse chain, they were placed in trust to avert a potential conflict of interest with the *PLAIN DEALER*, another local Newhouse property. They were sold in 1977 to the Post Corp. of Wisconsin, which in turn was purchased by Geo. Gillette of Nashville, Tenn. Local growth was maintained, as the *Euclid Journal* and *Collinwood Scoop Journal* were added to the chain. Following the death of the *CLEVELAND PRESS* in 1982, Sun papers introduced a television magazine and a new lifestyle section, but summarily dismissed the possibility of daily publication. In 1986, Sun Newspapers were sold to a group of local and out-of-town investors organized as the SunMedia Corp. Included in the package was Gowe Printing of Medina, where the weeklies were printed. The chain had grown to 18 community newspapers with a combined circulation of 243,000. Its publications included the *Sun Observer* (SHAKER HTS.-BEACHWOOD), *Bedford Sun Banner, Garfield-Maple Heights Sun, Herald Sun* (SOLON-ORANGE), *Sun Courier* (BRECKSVILLE-INDEPENDENCE), *Brooklyn Sun Journal, News Sun* (BEREA-BROOK PARK-MIDDLEBURG HTS.), and *Strongsville Sun Star*. In Medina County, the chain also published the *Sun Times Sentinel* (Medina-Brunswick) and *Sun Banner Pride* (Wadsworth).

The **SUNDAY POST** was probably first issued on 26 Sept. 1875. By 4 June 1876 (No. 37), it was a 4-page sheet of 7 columns each, selling for $.05. Expansion to an 8-page, 6-column format took place by 8 Apr. 1877. Published by the Post Printing Co., the paper had its offices on Seneca St. ORLANDO J. HODGE was its owner when the *Sunday Post* was merged with the *Sunday Morning Voice* as the *Sunday Voice & Post* on 16 June 1878 (see *SUNDAY VOICE*).

The **SUNDAY VOICE** was Cleveland's first successful Sunday newspaper, remaining on the scene for 30 years as a weekly publication. It was founded 15 Oct. 1871 by 4 partners; W. Scott Robison emerged as sole owner during the first year. Edited for a time by HARRY L. VAIL, the *Sunday Morning Voice*, as it originally was called, survived the calumny of local clergymen and in its turn campaigned against some of the city's lingering Sunday laws. Within 3 years, it had expanded in size from 4 to 8 pages. The *Voice* also survived a growing field of competitors spawned by its own success. Both the *CLEVELAND LEADER* and the *Herald* added Sunday editions in 1877, while the *SUNDAY POST*, begun by ORLANDO J. HODGE in 1875, was merged with the *Voice* on 16 June 1878. Hodge became editor and Robison business manager of the combination, which for a few months was known as the *Sunday Voice & Post*.

Eventually Hodge became sole proprietor of the *Voice*, as he and Robison had a falling out over distribution of the paper's profits. Robison left to start his second Sunday paper, the *Sunday Sun*, on 10 Oct. 1880. It was merged into the *Voice* on 15 Nov. 1885, about the same time that the *PLAIN DEALER* finally entered the Sunday field. At 14,200 copies, the combined *Sun & Voice* claimed to have Cleveland's largest Sunday circulation. Hodge continued to operate the *Voice* through a succession of managing editors that included Jas. H. Kennedy and Geo. Hoyt. Though once on the verge of being renamed the *Sun*, the paper went through a period as the *Ohio Sun-Voice* before settling on the *Sunday Voice* with some degree of finality.

Always Republican in political affiliation, the *Voice* nevertheless sublimated its partisanship to the feature material deemed appropriate for a day of leisure. Among such items introduced in the *Voice* were fiction, literary reviews, a chess column, and a question-and-answer box. Some of Cleveland journalism's first readers' contests were conducted by the *Voice*, beginning in 1885. For a time in the 1880s, there was also a column devoted to social coverage of the city's black population. Although its circulation gradually eroded to around 5,000, the *Sunday Voice* managed to survive until shortly after 1900. By that time its publisher was Wm. E. Godfrey. Other staff members had included Geo. A. Robertson, Wm. R. Rose, and Wm. E. Sage.

The **SUPERIOR AVENUE BAPTIST CHURCH** was one of the most prosperous places of worship along old Superior St., called the "street of churches" because of the 12 churches concentrated between E. 9th and E. 55th. Founded in 1848 as the Cottage Baptist Sunday School on St. Clair, it moved to E. 25th and Superior, where a wooden structure was erected in 1852. By 1878, the name was changed to the Superior Ave. Baptist Church to reflect its location. A new stone building, erected in 1892, was destroyed by lightning in 1901 but was rebuilt to serve its 700 member families. As the parishioners abandoned the church for new neighborhoods, the building became surrounded by commercial enterprises. In 1941, when only a handful of members remained, the church sold its building to the State Chemical Co. and relocated to E. 58th and Hough, until the parish acquired the old Hough Ave. Church at 5708 Hough. In 1954, it changed its name to Faith Baptist Church, and in 1958 it relocated to 4117 Rocky River Dr.

The **SUPERIOR STREET TABERNACLE** was begun as the City Mission by the Methodist churchman Rev. DILLON PROSSER. It was noted for its striking octagonal building opened on Superior St. in 1877 and for the size of its congregation, over 2,000 in its heyday in the late 1870s. Originally located on St. Clair, the mission changed its name to the Waring St. Methodist Episcopal Church with its move to that location in 1871. The church became the Superior St. Tabernacle when it dedicated its new building at Superior and Aaron (E. 36th St.) in 1877. In 1886, the name was modified to the Superior St. Church, a name it used until 1894, when it disappeared from the city directory.

The **SUPERIOR VIADUCT** was the proposed solution for improving transriver commuting in the years following Cleveland's 1854 annexation of OHIO CITY. Pressure began to be felt to build a new bridge connecting the east and west sides, one that would be adequate to the steadily increasing traffic. The river bridges up to that time had been "low-level," necessitating being opened for every river craft that needed to pass. City voters approved construction of the new bridge in Apr. 1872. It was to extend from Superior Ave. and W. 10th St. on the east to Detroit Ave. and W. 25th St. on the west. Despite opposition from some citizens' groups and even from city council, public support for the undertaking did not waver, and planning for the bridge went forward. Bridge plans called for a western approach consisting of Berea sandstone arches built on piles driven

20 ft. into the muddy subsoil. A total of 10 arches carried this portion of the viaduct, a total of 1,382 ft., 72 ft. above the foundations. Connecting the masonry arches to the eastern portion of the bridge was a 332-ft. pivoting center span. The eastern end of the viaduct was of girder design, 936 ft. long. With approaches, the viaduct totaled 3,211 ft., with a 64-ft. roadway. Construction began in Mar. 1875, and the bridge was completed and opened to traffic on 28 Dec. 1878. Costs, including land purchases, totaled $2.17 million. The bridge carried both private traffic and streetcars.

There were drawbacks, however. Because of the center drawspan, traffic still had to halt to permit river vessels with tall superstructures to pass. In 1909, the center span was opened approximately 300 times each month. Each opening took 4 to 6 minutes, then the river boat had to pass through, and finally the drawspan had to be closed. These delays became increasingly annoying. The opening and closing procedure itself began to take a toll on the bridge structure. Voices were raised once again for a new bridge, one that would be completely high-level. In 1918 the DETROIT-SUPERIOR BRIDGE was opened to traffic, and the Superior Viaduct became redundant. It was closed to traffic in 1920, and its eastern portion and center span were demolished in 1922. In 1939, the easternmost 3 arches of the remaining sandstone segment were blasted away to allow for a widening of the river. Seven arches, a total of 600 ft., remained in place. Efforts began in the 1970s to transform this vestige of the viaduct into a historical park, with spasmodic progress up to the 1980s.

**SUPERMAN,** the popular comic book superhero, was created by writer Jerry Siegel and artist Joe Schuster in 1933 while both attended Glenville High School. Their creation became known worldwide, inspired numerous imitation superheroes, and brought fortune to many, but Siegel and Schuster enjoyed none of that fortune between 1949–75. Native Clevelander Jerome "Jerry" Siegel (17 Oct. 1914- ) was writing mystery stories and vignettes for the school newspaper when he created the Superman character. His collaborator, Toronto native Joe Schuster (10 July 1914- ), worked up the initial drawings for the comic. Together they published their own science-fiction fan magazines as teenagers and entered the new comic-book business in 1936, not with their Superman character but by writing and drawing other adventure strips for New Fun Comics, Inc., which later became Detective Comics, and still later, Natl. Periodicals. For 6 years Siegel and Schuster tried unsuccessfully to find a publisher for their Superman comic strip. In 1938, publisher Harry Donnenfeld paid $135 for their strips, which he repasted into a 13-page comic-book story. Superman first appeared in the premier issue of *Action Comics* in June 1938. The great popularity of the character soon led to *Superman* magazine, a syndicated newspaper comic strip (1939–67), a show on the Mutual Radio Network, animated cartoons (1941–43 and 1966–67), a 15-episode movie serial featuring Kirk Alyn (1948), a full-length Columbia movie, *Atom Man vs. Superman*, again with Alyn, and Lippert Pictures' *Superman and the Mole Men* (1951). The star of the latter, Geo. Reeves, also played Superman on the 104 episodes of the TV show "The Adventures of Superman" in the 1950s. Superman also took center stage in the Broadway play *It's a Bird . . . It's a Plane . . . It's Superman!*, as well as in a 1942 novel by Geo. Lowther.

With Superman appearing everywhere, his creators slipped into obscurity and poverty. By signing a release form when they sold their strips to Donnenfeld, Siegel and Schuster had lost all rights to their character. When the McClure Syndicate purchased the strip for newspaper syndication in 1939, Siegel and Schuster, with few options left, agreed to work exclusively for Donnenfeld for 10 years at $35 per page and half the net profit. When their contract ran out in 1948, they sued to recover the copyright; although they received a $100,000 settlement, they lost the court case, their jobs, and any further involvement with Superman comics. Siegel continued to work on various newspaper comics but had little success; Schuster had great difficulty finding work. About 1963 they sued again; after 12 years, the courts again ruled against them. By 1975, both were living in or near poverty and decided to publicize their plight. With public support from the Natl. Cartoonists Society and the Cartoonists Guild, they pressured Warner Communications, Inc., owner of Natl. Periodicals, for financial compensation. In Dec. 1975, the corporation agreed to pay each man $20,000 a year for the remainder of his life and to include their bylines on all future productions featuring Superman. Their creation and their names returned to the screen in the highly successful Warner Bros. film *Superman* (1978) and sequels *Superman II* (1981) and *Superman III* (1983).

The **SUPREME LIFE INSURANCE COMPANY OF AMERICA,** a national black-owned insurance company formed in 1929, acquired Cleveland's black-owned insurance company, Dunbar Life Insurance, in 1960. Dunbar Life had its origins in 1936 when M. C. Clarke formed the Dunbar Mutual Insurance Society. Clarke, an examiner for the state insurance department, was sent to Cleveland in 1935 to look into the business affairs of Cleveland's struggling fraternal insurance societies. Rather than liquidating those with problems, Clarke consolidated the assets of the Midwestern Insurance Co., Pyramid Insurance Co., and 2 groups formed in the 1920s by Herbert S. Chauncey, Crusaders Mutual Insurance Society and Modern Crusaders of the World. The new company, the Dunbar Mutual Insurance Society, named for Dayton poet Paul Laurence Dunbar, had $500,000 worth of insurance in force in 1936; by 1940, insurance in force had increased to $1.47 million. In Apr. 1943, Clarke incorporated the new Dunbar Life Insurance Co. and set out to sell 10,000 shares of stock at $16.50 per share. By 1 Apr. 1945, all the stock had been sold, and the company was licensed to begin business. All of the policyholders of Dunbar Mutual were reinsured by Dunbar Life, which in Jan. 1948 reported $6 million worth of insurance in force and assets of more than $400,000. The company also had more than $300,000 in first-mortgage loans to more than 100 families. Dunbar Life was the city's largest black-owned business, employing 26 people in Cleveland and 85 people statewide. In Aug. 1945, Dunbar Life moved its headquarters from 5705 Woodland Ave., which Dunbar Mutual had occupied since 1939, to 7609 Euclid Ave. Following Clarke's death in 1956, Dennis C. Chandler became president of the company, which in 1957 had offices in Akron, Youngstown, Toledo, Dayton, Columbus, and Cincinnati. By the end of 1958, Dunbar's assets had grown to nearly $2 million, and its insurance in force was more than $12 million. Dunbar Life's stock was valued at $46 per share for the merger into the Supreme Life Insurance Co., which became effective on 1 Jan. 1960. The Chicago-based parent company had been formed in 1929 by the merger of Liberty Life of Illinois, Supreme Life & Casualty of Columbus, and Northeastern Life of Newark, N.J. After the 1960 merger, Dunbar Life became the Ohio Div. of Supreme Life and was responsible for about 30% of Supreme's business.

*SVET-AMERICAN* represented a merger of 2 newspapers that dominated Cleveland's Czech-language press for the first half of the 20th century. The senior partner was the *American*, established as a daily in 1899 by FRANK J. SVOBODA, a Czech immigrant and former typesetter for the *Penny Press*. Svoboda kept his paper going for 40 years, most of which he spent as sole owner. During its last decade, it was incorporated as the American Bohemian Publishing Co., with Svoboda serving as president and general manager. Inaugurated on 22 Feb. 1911, the daily *Svet* (World) soon thereafter absorbed Vaclav Snajdr's weekly *DENNICE NOVOVEKU*. Published by the Svet Printing & Publishing Co., it was managed in the 1920s by John A. Stukbauer and edited by Frank J. Kutak. It opened its silver-anniversary year by issuing a 32-page edition on Washington's Birthday in 1935. On 5 June 1939, the *American* was absorbed into the *Svet* as the *Svet-American*. Under the direction of John L. Payer, the combined daily was published in the *Svet* office at 4515 Broadway. As a consequence of its pro-Communist stance following WORLD WAR II, the *Svet-American* ceased publication in July 1950. It was soon replaced by a new Czech daily, *NOVY SVET* (New World).

**SVOBODA, FRANK J.** (1 May 1874 [occasionally given as 1873]–1 Mar. 1965), was a prominent Czech newspaper publisher from 1899–1939 and a state legislator from 1943–60. Born in Bohemia, Svoboda came to the U.S. in 1884 with his parents, John, a laborer, and Mary, a midwife. He attended Our Lady of Lourdes school and took evening classes in the public school. He left school at age 14 to become a printer's helper. By 1894 he had opened his own printing office at Broadway and E. 55th St. In 1899 Svoboda began to publish a Czech daily newspaper, the *American*, which was especially popular among Czech Catholics. In 1908 the *American* absorbed the weekly paper *Volnost* (Freedom). Svoboda was the sole owner of the *American* until the Depression forced him to take on partners in 1932. He then became the president and general manager of the American-Bohemian Publishing Co., located at 5377 Broadway. Svoboda continued to publish the *American* until June 1939; the paper was then bought by the *Svet* (World) (see *SVET-AMERICAN*), and Svoboda retired from publishing.

During the 1930s, Svoboda became active in politics. He served on the City Planning Commission for 10 years and was a local leader in the Townsend movement for an old-age pension (see TOWNSEND PLAN), serving as president of the Fleet Ave. Townsend Club, a member of the district board, and a representative on the Ohio Townsend advisory board. He resigned from his positions in the Townsend movement in Feb. 1936 when he announced his candidacy for the U.S. Congress, running against incumbent ROBT. CROSSER in the May primary. In 1942, running as a Democrat, Svoboda won election to the Ohio house of representatives. He served 2 terms there (1943–44, 1945–46) and was then elected to 6 terms in the Ohio senate, winning his last 2 terms without the endorsement of the local Democratic party. When he retired from the state senate in 1960, he was the oldest person ever to serve in the senate and had served the longest of any state legislator elected from Cleveland. In addition to publishing and politics, Svoboda was active in local religious and fraternal societies. Besides being a director of the American Assoc. of Foreign Newspapers and active in the Czech Democratic Club, he was a member of Sokol Tyrs, the First Catholic Central Union of the U.S., the Knights of Columbus, the Catholic Order of Forresters, the Ben Franklin Club, the CITY CLUB, and the Chamber of Commerce. Svoboda was married on 30 June 1896 to native Clevelander Josephine Holpuch. She died on 25 Oct. 1961.

**SWASEY, AMBROSE** (19 Dec. 1846–15 June 1937), mechanical engineer, manufacturer, and philanthropist, was born in Exeter, N.H., where he served as apprentice machinist from 1865–69. There he first met WORCESTER WARNER, with whom he formed a partnership in 1880 to build and sell machine tools. The partnership grew into the WARNER & SWASEY CO. of Cleveland. Swasey held several patents on gear-cutting machinery and, influenced by his partner, became a designer of astronomical instruments, for which their company became world-famous. He was a founding member of the American Society of Mechanical Engineers in 1880 and served on several government agencies, including the Natl. Research Council during WORLD WAR I. A generous benefactor of higher education and Baptist missionary work, between 1914–31 Swasey gave a total of $890,000 to the United Engineering Society in New York for the establishment of an "Engineering Foundation" to promote research. In 1900 he was decorated by France for his work on astronomical instruments. Swasey was president of the Cleveland Chamber of Commerce in 1905. On 19 Dec. 1936 he received the Hoover Medal of the Engineering Societies of America. In 1930 he received the Cleveland Medal of Service from the Chamber of Commerce. On 14 Nov. 1923, Dr. Otto Struve named a newly discovered asteroid Swasey in his honor. In 1871, Swasey married Lavinia Marston of Exeter; they had no children. The Swaseys moved to Cleveland when the company relocated there from Chicago in 1881. Swasey died at Exeter.

**SWEDES.** *See* **SCANDINAVIANS**

**SWEENEY, MARTIN L.** (15 Apr. 1885–1 May 1960), was a colorful and outspoken Cleveland-area congressman and politician. He waged numerous campaigns for public office, was a crusader for the repeal of Prohibition, and was involved in several political feuds that split the county Democratic party. Sweeney was born in Cleveland to Dominic and Anna Cleary Sweeney. At the age of 12, he had to find work to support himself while attending St. Bridget's Parochial School. Later, while working as a longshoreman and construction worker, he attended Cleveland Law School part-time, graduating and being admitted to the Ohio bar in 1914. After serving 1 term (1913–14) in the Ohio legislature, Sweeney entered private practice until 1923, when he won election as a Cleveland Municipal Court judge. On the bench, he was a vocal opponent of the 18th Amendment, calling Prohibition a crazy law enacted by fanatics and impossible to enforce.

In 1931, Sweeney won election to fill an unexpected vacancy in the 20th congressional district. Attending the 1932 Democratic Natl. Convention as a delegate pledged to Al Smith, Sweeney instead supported Franklin Roosevelt. That resulted in a split with the county Democratic party chairman BURR GONGWER. The split widened further when Sweeney supported the Republican candidate after losing the 1933 Democratic Cleveland mayoral primary. Still in Congress, Sweeney continued his opposition to Prohibition. In mid-1936, he turned against the policies of Pres. Roosevelt, becoming a political supporter of the Catholic priest Chas. Coughlin. Reelected in 1934 and 1936 without Democratic party support, Sweeney considered his victories as mandates for independent action. During the late 1930s, he became an increasingly ardent isolationist in foreign policy and gained a reputation as the leading Anglophobe in Congress. Sweeney patched up his differences with Gongwer in 1937. But RAY T. MILLER broke with Sweeney and Gongwer and won the county party leadership. Sweeney failed to oust Miller as county chairman in

1940 but successfully defended his congressional seat against the Miller-supported Michael Feighan. In 1941, Sweeney once again lost in the mayoral primary. In 1942, he was defeated for Congress by Feighan. After failing to win the governor's nomination in 1944, Sweeney returned to private practice with his son Robert. Sweeney married Marie Carlin on 21 Aug. 1921. They had 4 children, Martin, Jr., Anne Marie, Robert, and Eileen.

## SYRIANS. *See* **ARAB-AMERICANS**

*SZABADSAG* (Liberty) became in time the largest as well as oldest Hungarian-language newspaper published in the U.S. It was founded in Cleveland by TIHAMER KO-HANYI with the financial backing of local Hungarian citizens in 1891. Kohanyi ran the weekly pretty much as a 1-man operation before seeing his way clear to the commencement of daily publication in 1906. During its first 2 decades, *Szabadsag* raised $50,000 for the aid of Hungarian immigrants and helped collect funds to raise the KOSSUTH MONUMENT in Cleveland and a statue of Geo. Washington in Budapest. Pres. Wm. Howard Taft attended the paper's 20th-anniversary banquet in 1911. Following Kohanyi's death in 1913, *Szabadsag* continued with the aid of such contributors as caricaturist Louis Linek and novelist Joseph Remenyi. In an attempt to rectify the perceived injustices of the Treaty of Trianon between Hungary and the World War I Allies, it collected and delivered 1 million signatures to Pres. Franklin D. Roosevelt in 1936. Upon the purchase of its Huron Rd. plant by the Ohio Bell Telephone Co. in 1928, *Szabadsag* effected an arrangement with the German daily *WAECHTER UND ANZEIGER*, whereby the two papers would both be printed by a new Consolidated Publishing Co. in the latter's plant on E. 12th St. Herbert L. Kobrak, who had managed *Szabadsag* for various periods both before and after this partial merger, later gained notoriety when he fatally shot *PLAIN DEALER* executive John S. McCarrens and himself in the former's office in 1943. *Szabadsag* regained its independence in 1939, when a group of local HUNGARIANS purchased it following the bankruptcy of Consolidated Publishing. Managing editor ZOLTAN GOMBOS gained control of the paper, which reached its peak circulation of 40,612 in 1942. Under Gombos, *Szabadsag* leaned toward the Democrats politically and remained generally opposed to the Communist regime established in Hungary after WORLD WAR

II. Gombos organized the Liberty Publishing Co. to publish *Szabadsag* and several other papers he acquired, including the New York daily *Amerikai Magyar Nepszeva* (American Hungarian People's Voice). In a diminishing market, Gombos maintained *Szabadsag* on profits from the war years as one of the city's last foreign-language dailies. By the end of the 1960s, however, even *Szabadsag* had returned to its original weekly status. It was sold by Gombos shortly before his death in 1984 and was reorganized as Liberty Media, Inc. A biweekly English-language supplement was introduced in 1986.

**SZELL, GEORGE** (7 June 1897–30 July 1970), was an internationally renowned conductor and music director of the CLEVELAND ORCHESTRA. Szell was born in Budapest and grew up in Vienna, where he studied with Mandyczewski (theory), J. B. Foerster and Max Reger (composition), and Richard Robert (piano). He made his debut as pianist at age 10, playing his own music. His conducting debut came at age 16 with the Vienna State Opera Orchestra. Two years later, following an appearance with the Berlin Philharmonic Orchestra, Szell was engaged by Richard Strauss for the staff of the Berlin State Opera House. He subsequently held other conducting posts, primarily in German opera houses, and was general musical director of the German Opera and Philharmonic of Prague and director of the Scottish Natl. Orchestra. He became music director of the Cleveland Orchestra in 1946 and continued in that position until his death. With the orchestra, he toured the U.S. and Canada, Europe in 1957 and 1959, and the Far East just before his death in 1970. Philip Hart wrote in the *New Grove Dictionary of Music and Musicians* that Szell and the Cleveland Orchestra "developed a superb ensemble that embodied his strict notions of discipline in producing an orchestral sound with the clarity and balance of chamber music." He was known as a stern taskmaster, bordering at times on the tyrannical, but was greatly respected by fellow musicians. At the time of his death, the Cleveland Orchestra had gained its stature as one of the finest in the world. Szell held honorary degrees from Western Reserve University and Oberlin College, and was a Chevalier of the French Legion of Honor. His recordings with the Cleveland Orchestra are among the best symphonic documents of their era. He married Helene Schulz in 1938, a second marriage for both.

Grossman, F. Karl, *A History of Music in Cleveland* (1972).

# T

**TRW, INC.,** with its headquarters in Cleveland, is a major international corporation recognized for its technological expertise, innovative spirit, and leadership in the AUTO-MOTIVE, AEROSPACE, and electronics (see ELECTRI-CAL AND ELECTRONICS) industries. The company originated in Cleveland. On 28 Dec. 1900, 5 men formed the Cleveland Cap Screw Co. to produce connectors and fittings primarily for automobiles and light machinery. The company's first technological innovation was the production of automobile valves in 1904. It soon became the recognized leader in the manufacture of such valves and remains the world's largest independent producer. In 1905, the WINTON MOTOR CARRIAGE CO. bought controlling interest in the firm. The company's principal development began under the leadership of CHAS. E. THOMPSON. He reorganized the firm in 1908 as the Electric Welding Prods. Co., started to produce chassis parts, and acquired plants in other automobile-producing cities. In 1915, he was able to purchase the company's independence from Winton and changed its name to the Steel Prods. Co.

During WORLD WAR I, the firm entered the aeronautical industry when it began to manufacture airplane engine valves. In 1926, the business was renamed Thompson Prods., Inc. It was by then a well-established manufacturer of finished automotive and aviation goods. As an innovative and dramatic sales promotion, the company initiated the Thompson Trophy Air Races in 1929. Thompson's development of an effective replacement-parts system during the 1920s also served to keep it functioning during the Depression. Upon Thompson's death in 1933, Frederick C. Crawford took over the firm. Crawford was primarily responsible for the company's encouragement of corporate civic-mindedness and its novel program of labor relations. To quell several unionizing efforts by the CIO through the Natl. Labor Relations Board in the 1930s and 1940s, Crawford fostered the establishment of a company union, the Automobile & Aircraft Workers of America, a company newspaper, and frequent meetings with and reports to the employees. With the approach of WORLD WAR II, the federal government aided Thompson Prods. in increasing its production of aircraft engines by building a new plant, TAPCO, in EUCLID in 1941. During World War II, it applied its aircraft technology to fuel booster pumps, which enabled the first high-altitude flights.

Following the war, Thompson Prods. began to diversify more into the aerospace industry, manufacturing parts for jet engines as well as radio and radar hardware. It also started investing in related overseas companies, especially in the automotive-parts industry, with present interests in some 22 countries. During the 1950s, it entered the growing fields of electronics and ballistic-missile development, principally through investing in a new electronics and system-engineering enterprise, the Ramo-Wooldridge Corp. of California, in 1953. Five years later, the two companies merged into Thompson Ramo Wooldridge. In 1965, the company changed its name to TRW. As a pioneer in the design and manufacture of unmanned spacecraft, TRW has had a prominent role in the U.S. space program, producing the Apollo lunar module descent engine and a third of the U.S. satellites, including the Pioneer series. With a decline in the aerospace industry in the early 1970s, TRW entered new markets—bearings, fasteners, tools, oil-field equipment, and alternative energy sources. Its biggest customer remains the federal government.

TRW, Inc., Records, WRHS.

The **TAVERN CLUB,** located on the southwest corner of E. 36th St. and Prospect Ave., is one of Cleveland's oldest private social organizations. It was founded in 1892–93 by a group of young men, primarily from the UNION CLUB, who wanted a meeting place "uptown" surrounded by open spaces. The founders and first officers included HENRY K. DEVEREUX, president; Wm. C. Rhodes, vice-president; Addison H. Hough, secretary; and Perry W. Harvey, treasurer; as well as Harry R. Edwards and CHAS. A. OTIS, JR. At that time, membership was limited to 50. From 13 May 1893–14 May 1898, the club occupied the Goodman residence on the northeast corner of Case Ave. (E. 40th St.) and Prospect Ave. The club was incorporated in 1898 under the name the Tavern Co.; membership increased to 75, later to 150, and subsequently to 200. From May 1898–31 Dec. 1904, the club leased premises at 968 Prospect St. On 1 Jan. 1905 it moved to its present building, designed by J. MILTON DYER, club member and Cleveland architect. The exterior construction and the traditional interior decor of the building, as well as the main purpose of the club—fellowship in a congenial setting—have essentially remained the same since the club's beginning.

948

TAYLER, ROBERT WALKER (26 Nov. 1852–26 Nov. 1910), U.S. federal judge, was the author of the Tayler Grant, which ended Cleveland's traction war and regulated the operations of the reorganized street railways in Cleveland. Tayler was born in Youngstown, Ohio, to Robt. Walker and Louisa Maria Woodbridge Tayler. Educated in the Youngstown public schools, he spent 3 years at Georgetown University before entering the Western Reserve University Law School and earning the LL.D. degree in 1872. Following graduation, he taught 1 year at Lisbon (Ohio) High School and for 2 years was superintendent of schools. During 1875–76, he edited the *Buckeye State*, and while engaged in teaching and journalism, he continued his study of law. Tayler married Helen Vance on 18 May 1876. Admitted to the Ohio bar in 1877, he opened his law office in E. Liverpool, practicing there until 1880, when he won election as prosecuting attorney of Columbiana County. In 1894, he won election to Congress for the first of 4 terms. He retired from Congress in 1903, joining the law firm of Arrel, McVey & Tayler in Youngstown. In 1905, Pres. Theodore Roosevelt appointed Tayler to the federal judgeship of northern Ohio with courts at Cleveland and Toledo. Among the cases heard in Tayler's court were the trial of CASSIE CHADWICK and the reorganization actions arising from the "traction war," and the attempt by Mayor TOM L. JOHNSON to take public control of Cleveland's railway systems. The resulting court action, authored by the judge, became known as the Tayler Grant. Becoming effective on 18 Dec. 1909, the grant provided for a sliding scale that limited trolley lines' profits to 6% and gave jurisdiction over railway operations to the CLEVELAND CITY COUNCIL, thereby returning peace and stability to Cleveland's streetcar operations.

TAYLOR, ALBERT DAVIS (8 July 1883–8 Jan. 1951), was a landscape architect and town planner active in Cleveland from 1914–51. Taylor, born a twin, was raised and educated in Carlisle, Mass. He studied for 1 year at Cornell University and received his A.B. from Massachusetts College in 1905. He began his career in the office of Warren Manning in Boston. While there, he prepared the topographic survey for the new campus of the Ohio State Normal College (Kent State University) in 1911. He accompanied Manning to Cleveland in 1914, where Taylor immediately established his own office. He is credited with introducing many principles of European landscape design to the U.S. His landscape projects in the Greater Cleveland area included residential, institutional, and public properties. Among them were the gardens and grounds of many private homes, especially on the Heights, in which he used both formal and informal planning principles. Taylor designed the garden of Trinity Cathedral House in 1930 and planned some of the later additions to LAKE VIEW CEMETERY in the 1930s.

Taylor's public works included the site plan for the Baldwin Filtration Plant in 1920, plans for the development of Ambler Park from the Baldwin plant to Coventry Rd. in the 1930s, the retaining walls along Cedar Glen in CLEVELAND HTS., a plan for the completion, landscaping, and extension of the Mall in 1931, and a development plan for FOREST HILLS PARK in 1938. Finally, Taylor was the landscape architect for the site of the Pentagon, the new office building of the War Dept., completed in 1943. Like other architects of the period, Taylor found sources and inspiration for his work in European precedents such as the Ecole des Beaux-Arts and English estates and gardens. He wrote numerous pamphlets and articles on landscape design and home gardening for such publications as *American City* and *Landscape Architecture*. Tay-

lor married Genevieve Brainard in 1917. They had a son, Chas. B. Taylor.

TAYLOR, WILLIAM SON & CO. *See* WILLIAM TAYLOR SON & COMPANY

The **TAYLOR CHAIR COMPANY**, located in BEDFORD, originated in 1816 when pioneer Benjamin Franklin Fitch, who had come to the Western Reserve with his family in 1801, began making split-bottom, slat-backed chairs by hand at his cabin located at what is now the corner of Libby and Warrensville Ctr. roads. Fitch's chairs were superior to others, partly because he used preshrunk materials combining green and dry lumber so that they would not creak. Nearby settlers often traded farm produce and/or labor for the chairs. Increasing demand forced Fitch to move his chairmaking from his home to another cabin. Later he invented the strap lathe, which speeded up the work and increased production; subsequently it became a standard machine in the furniture industry. Fitch chairs, including armchairs, side chairs, rockers, and highchairs, gained a reputation for being durable, compact, and comfortable. As demand increased, Fitch added workmen to his staff, including Wm. O. Taylor, who had come to the WESTERN RESERVE from Charlemont, Mass., in 1831. Taylor became Fitch's assistant and in 1841 married his daughter, Harriet, thus beginning a long succession of continuous family ownership. The company became known as the W. O. Taylor Factory. Fire destroyed the Libby Rd. sheds in 1850, and the factory was moved to its present location in Bedford, adjoining TINKER'S CREEK, which provided water for steam power and was next to the Cleveland & Pittsburgh Railroad, providing transportation to markets beyond the Western Reserve. Two sons, Joseph Fitch Taylor and Vincent A. Taylor, joined the company, and it became Wm. O. Taylor & Sons. In 1871 Joseph Fitch Taylor died, and the company became Wm. O. Taylor & Son. By 1879, the company was making 40 different styles of single- and double-seated cane chairs.

The company was incorporated in 1885 as the Taylor Chair Co.; incorporators included Wm. O. Taylor, president; Andrew W. Hensey, vice-president; Vincent A. Taylor, treasurer; and Cyrus P. Flick, secretary. The company produced over 48 different types of chairs, concentrating on a variety of rockers. By 1907 it had expanded to over 102 designs and began to specialize in office furniture. Cleveland's growth created a demand for both home and business furniture. In the 1920s, the company established an alliance with the Horrocks Desk Co. of Herkimer, N.Y. These two companies, each separately owned, functioned as a team and featured coordinated styling of office furniture. Mrs. Moselle Taylor Meals assumed the presidency in 1953 after the death of her husband, Gordon, vice-president, and of her father, Joseph F. Taylor. She introduced the company's first "high style" designer chairs, receiving patents for her contemporary furniture design in the 1950s and 1960s. This trend represented a change for the company as it embarked on designer lines for business offices. In 1968 it added 15,000 sq. ft. to the 120,000-sq.-ft. plant in Bedford. In 1973 it built a new 40,000-sq.-ft. manufacturing facility in Clarksdale, Miss. By 1986, the company had become known for the manufacture of designer office furniture of various woods, leather, upholstering fabrics, and metal.

Arthur, Allan, *Sesquicentennial: The Taylor Chair Company* (1966).

TAYLOR ROAD SYNAGOGUE. *See* OHEB ZEDEK CONGREGATION

**TEACHER EDUCATION.** The history of teacher education in Cleveland reflects earlier national and state movements to begin normal schools; these efforts were responsive to needs created by the establishment of the common school during the first half of the 19th century (1789–1860). Previously there had been little or no interest in or need for teacher education. Teacher education in Cleveland can be traced to the 1830s. As early as 1836, Edward Deering of Mansfield lectured on the qualifications of teachers before the College of Professional Teachers at Cincinnati. He noted 3 topics: subject matter, mode of teaching, and personal character. These same themes undergirded discussions about teacher education not only in Cleveland but on national and state levels as well. Specifically, discussions, reflective of Deering's statements, have revolved around the relationship and the importance of the liberal and the technical or professional coursework in the teacher-education curriculum. To this day, the issues do not seem to have been resolved, and the discussions continue at varying levels of intensity.

Specifically, teacher-education efforts in the Greater Cleveland area resulted from the Common School Law of 1836. Nelson Slater founded the Western Reserve Teacher's Seminary and Kirtland Institute in 1839. Many prominent citizens, such as Seabury Ford, served on the board of directors. The school was divided into 2 sections, the Teacher's Seminary and the Institute for Scholars who wished to follow other pursuits. There was a model school, forerunner of laboratory schools, for children under 14, where prospective teachers of both sexes could gain some practical experience. The 2-year course of study consisted of critical reading, orthography, penmanship, arithmetic, and English grammar. In addition, there were lectures on management of schools, on teaching methods, and on Ohio laws regulating the schools. The course attempted to provide students with both the liberal and the technical attributes they would need to function well as teachers. To accommodate the student, the fall terms closed in time for them to teach winter school, the winter term in time to teach summer school, and the summer term in time for the commencement of haying and harvesting. Fees were $18 per year. After the first year, Slater left the seminary and was replaced by Ada D. Lord, who had been a teacher. The school moved from its original site in the Kirtland Mormon Temple to the Methodist Church for a 10-year period. In 1847, Lord was succeeded by Dr. John Nichols, who supervised the building of a new facility in 1850. There were then about 200 students enrolled. Dr. Nichols resigned in 1853, and following his departure, the school declined and finally closed because of competition from other new schools and financial problems.

Normal schools were a major initiative in the education of teachers for the Cleveland schools. In 1869, Cleveland school superintendent Andrew J. Rickoff inaugurated a week-long training institute. Then he established the Cleveland City Normal School in Aug. 1872. However, it did not officially open until Sept. 1874. It was located in the central part of the city on Eagle St. Alex Forbes was its first principal. It was felt that normal schools were necessary because they furnished a pool of trained persons for the schools of Ohio and added a professional dimension, thus raising the standards for teachers. Requirements for admission included a Cleveland high school diploma or the equivalent. Only females attended this first Cleveland normal school, which was free to all residents of the city ages 16–21. Nonresidents and those over this age paid an annual tuition of $20. Support came from the public school fund, and control was vested in the Board of Education. Enrollment, mostly from Cleveland high schools, numbered

about 40 students, the first class graduating 26. The curriculum included a review of material studied in the common schools and methods of teaching. The students also practiced in actual school settings, where they were supervised by "critic teachers." The students were then hired to teach in the Cleveland schools.

The period 1860–1910 was a transitional period when normal schools were being scrutinized and other approaches to educating teachers considered. Many normal schools were transformed into professional schools and departments in liberal-arts colleges or into 4-year colleges, largely because educators defended the importance of educating potential teachers in the "science" of pedagogy and organized their efforts in the 1890s with the establishment of the Natl. Society for the Scientific Study of Education in 1901, originally the Herbart Society. Coupled with the growth of the child-study movement and the development of the field of psychology, that caused educators to advocate a "science of education." The response on the part of liberal-arts professors was negative, emphasizing the art of teaching. These discussions led many to conclude that education did not deserve the status of a university discipline since it was inconsistent with the university aim of scientific research, lacked a body of literature that was acceptable, and relied on a weak faculty. There were also perennial comments about the caliber of the student attracted to the field, particularly as it moved from a 2- to a 4-year curriculum. At that time, teacher-education curriculums and standards reflected both liberal and technical aspects.

Elements of these issues and movements could be found in what was occurring in Cleveland during this period. When Dr. Burke A. Hinsdale became superintendent of the CLEVELAND PUBLIC SCHOOLS in 1882, he reorganized the normal school. By 1893, kindergarten training was added to the curriculum. In 1905, SAMUEL P. ORTH, president of the Cleveland Board of Education, appointed an education commission to study all aspects of the schools. It recommended that the normal school be redesigned. During the period from ca. 1910 on, public school enrollments and curriculum expanded. That increased demand for teachers in new roles and also required that more stringent standards be set. Ca. 1914, the state legislature passed legislation providing that teacher-training institutions be involved in improving teaching. So confident were they that that would lead to the desired changes, they made this training prerequisite to certification without any type of examination. Expectations surpassed results, causing the legislature to pass a law that made it necessary for all students entering teacher-training institutions to take statewide examinations in the use of English, general ability, and subject matter. As part of their high school preparation, they were to have taken American history and government, arithmetic, geography, physiology or biology including laboratory work, physics, or general science.

From 1915–20, a joint committee of the Cleveland Normal School, Western Reserve University, and the Cleveland Board of Education offered courses for practicing teachers who wished to qualify for salary increases and for a bachelor's degree. The next major initiative focused on the role of colleges in the education of teachers. Wm. A. Bagley, a noted educator, chaired a CLEVELAND FOUNDATION commission on the professional training of teachers in Cleveland, which issued a report that led to a reorganization into the Cleveland School of Education. The commission report noted concern about the quality of teachers and addressed the necessity of meeting the need for additional teachers, noting that once that was achieved, a qualitative standard should be added that would be applied to admission, as well as curriculum. There was also much discussion about the requirements for the baccalaureate degree and the differences from the normal school background. Quality and salary of staff were also addressed. The commission noted that in the advanced education of elementary-school teachers, it was important that teachers have a clear understanding of the basic function of elementary education and its importance, and knowledge of materials and educational practices. In 1928, WRU organized its own school of education, into which were merged the Cleveland Kindergarten Primary Training School, a private school founded in 1894 to train teachers, and the Senior Teachers College, which was the name under which the joint committee of the school board and WRU had previously offered some preparation for secondary teachers in the College for Women (later Flora Stone Mather College) and Adelbert College. Later a department of education was established in Mather College, where both Mather and Adelbert students could take professional education courses for certification. In 1928, the university's School of Education was managed by a board of representatives of the Board of Education and the university. In 1945, the School of Education was disbanded, and its full-time women students were transferred to Mather College, its men students to Adelbert College. Courses for practicing teachers were transferred to Cleveland College. All professional education courses required for state certification were taken through the new Div. of Education.

Other colleges and universities in the Cleveland area also prepared teachers. Programs could be found in departments or divisions of education at BALDWIN-WALLACE COLLEGE, JOHN CARROLL UNIVERSITY, NOTRE DAME COLLEGE, and URSULINE COLLEGE. ST. JOHN COLLEGE also educated teachers, mainly for Catholic parochial schools, until it closed in 1974. When CLEVELAND STATE UNIVERSITY was established in 1967, a college of education was included. It was the first state-sponsored teacher-education facility in Cleveland. All of these colleges and universities continued to educate teachers in the 1980s, with the exception of CASE WESTERN RESERVE UNIVERSITY, which phased out its education department in 1979 at the undergraduate, graduate, and doctoral levels, except for a limited program in art and music education. Baldwin-Wallace College, John Carroll University, and Ursuline College continue to offer graduate programs in education, and Cleveland State University began a doctoral program in 1987.

Moving into the 1960s and 1970s, teachers became involved in an effort to take over the responsibility for their training at the in-service level through the establishment of teacher centers, reflective of a national teacher-center movement. The movement took on many forms, with some centers sponsored by school systems, others by institutions of higher education, others by independent agencies, and still others by combinations thereof. However, collaboration in program development was an important ingredient, and a somewhat new idea in teacher education. Basically the centers were places where teachers could gather to engage in dialogue about teaching, obtain resources, and take workshops from each other and/or university and other educational personnel. They had their own governance boards, often composed of representatives of the profession. Cleveland's efforts reflected what was happening nationally. The city had one of the early centers, which was established in 1973 and was originally housed in the Cleveland Hts.-University Hts. School District. It was funded by the Rockefeller Foundation and 3 local foundations. It provided services by and for teachers until its demise in 1979 because of loss of continued funding. Federal funds

became available for the teacher-center movement in the late 1970s, allowing a coalition of educators to establish Teacher Ctr. 271 in 1976. This center was governed by a board of educators and operated until 1979, when it refocused its efforts into the Educational Computer Consortium of Ohio.

Other endeavors that provided professional development for both teachers and administrators continued in the form of the Ctr. for Professional Development instituted by John Carroll University and several local school districts in 1981, and the Educational Development Ctr. begun by Cleveland State University and local school districts in 1983. These organizations were representative of the movement to upgrade the professional development of educators in a collaborative effort using practitioners in the planning and implementation of the programs. Early debates over the liberal and technical in teacher education still continued in the 1980s, though the scientific basis for teacher education had become more established through an emerging knowledge base, which has grown out of major research efforts. Though teacher education has seen much progress from its early days, many of the same discussions and debates continue as to its substance and content. Concerns about teaching and teachers still reflected much of the rhetoric of the early common-school days in Cleveland, focusing on the importance of qualitative aspects and the need for well-educated teachers. The state department of education, through its new standard initiatives and teacher-education institutions, through curriculum revision and the rigor of entry and exit criteria, continued to try to alleviate these concerns, while engaging in the philosophical discourse of what is good teaching and its requisite preparation.

Sally H. Wertheim
John Carroll University

The **TEAMSTERS UNION,** officially the Internatl. Brotherhood of Teamsters, Chauffeurs, Stablemen, & Helpers, is one of the largest and most powerful labor unions operating in Cleveland. Organized locally in 1912 when Local 407 was chartered, the union quickly attracted 500 men employed as draymen and teamsters for hauling and delivery services. Two of the early members, Edward Murphy and John Rohrich, guided the union in its first few decades and kept it free of the racketeering that characterized Teamster locals in other cities. By 1932, Local 407 was the largest in the country. Murphy and Rohrich organized all locals in the area into District Council 41. When union organization was spurred by the NIRA, the Teamsters were the largest beneficiaries; membership grew from 3,500 in 1933 to 15,000 in 1935 to 24,000 in 1940. The new Teamsters included such groups as laundry, dry-cleaning, beverage, and newspaper drivers. The union became so strong that it soon challenged the power of the Bldg. Trades Council, the dominant force in the CLEVELAND FED. OF LABOR. In 1938, Murphy masterminded the election of 2 Teamster-backed candidates for CFL office. Local Teamster history was marred by the assassination of business agent Arthur Whitlock in the 1930s, but under Murphy's leadership, the Teamsters were regarded as a tough, honest union willing to bargain. After Murphy died in 1950, union power was usurped by WM. PRESSER and N. Louis (Babe) Triscaro. Allies of Dave Beck and Jimmy Hoffa, national leaders known for their brawn and mob ties, the new leaders oversaw a new era in which Cleveland Teamster activities were accompanied by violence and threats. Corruption and reported ties with the underworld resulted in a federal probe of the union in 1957 and suspension of the Teamsters from the newly formed AFL-CIO. Cleveland leader Presser was called before a grand jury, the finances of 20 Teamster leaders were investigated, and 3 officers and the books of the Cleveland AFL-CIO were subpoenaed. In line with national directives, the Teamsters were expelled from the federation, a loss of 40,000 members that threatened both finances and nonraiding agreements among member unions.

One key to Teamster power has been the group's ability to strengthen its internal organization. In 1953, Ohio and 11 other Midwest states banded together to form the Central States Conference of Teamsters, and also consolidated their pension funds. In 1964, the union negotiated the Master Freight Agreement with 2,000 trucking companies that governed wages and working conditions for the general freight haulers that constituted the bulk of union members. When contract negotiations on the Master Freight Agreement broke down in 1970, 1976, and 1979, wildcat strikes incapacitated trucking, as well as other industries dependent on supplies delivered throughout Cleveland. Over 6,000 of the area's 10,000 Teamsters were affected; truckers who ventured onto the highway during the strike were attacked. The power of the Teamster local is also felt in its billion dollars of deposits in Cleveland banks, donations to charity, backing of political candidates, and domination of employment in many industries. Since 1957, the union has sought to organize diverse groups of workers such as nurses and public-service employees, and prior to major changes in the trucking industry brought by deregulation in 1980, it continued to increase its numbers at a time when other unions lost members. Since deregulation, over 20,000 drivers have lost their jobs as small firms have been forced to close down or cut rates to remain competitive. Teamster leaders have tried to salvage jobs through concessions. In 1986, truck drivers made up a smaller percentage of union membership. Locals operating in Cleveland included 407 (general freight hauling), 507 (industrial—the power base of Wm. Presser and his son Jackie), 416 (vending-machine service), and 436 (racetrack employees and concession drivers).

Cleveland Teamster leaders have figured prominently in the national movement. The late Wm. Presser, former president of Teamsters Joint Council 41 and the Ohio Conference of Teamsters and an international vice-president, appeared in federal investigations of corruption, especially in relation to improper loans made by the Central States Pension Fund. His son Jackie, who succeeded his father in local offices and who is (1986) the president of the international, allegedly turned FBI informant in an effort to deflect corruption charges. Leadership of the Pressers and others at all levels of the union has come under criticism by factions within the union for excessive salaries paid to officials and strong-arm tactics. Critics have maintained that this dissatisfaction was a factor in the wildcat walkouts of the 1970s and the violence that accompanied them. Within Local 407, disgruntled steelhaulers threatened to defect from the Teamsters, but ultimately retained their membership while forming the Brokers & Steelhaulers Assoc. This local was also the seedbed of Teamsters for a Democratic Union, a faction that later established its headquarters in Detroit, and which is dedicated to getting better contracts and promoting more effective union representation. The group merged in 1979 with the Professional Drivers Council, formed in 1971 to win better safety conditions for truckers.

TEBELAK, JOHN MICHAEL (1949–2 Apr. 1985), was the composer of the hit musical *Godspell*. Tebelak was born in Berea and became active at the age of 9 in the Berea Summer Theater. He was a choirboy at TRINITY CATHEDRAL, where he became fascinated with the pa-

geantry and drama of religion. At the age of 21, he directed productions of *Macbeth* and *Cabaret*. He later attended Carnegie-Mellon University in Pittsburgh, where he wrote *Godspell*, a musical based upon the Gospel according to St. Matthew, as his thesis. With music by Stephen Schwartz, *Godspell* was first produced in 1971 by the Cafe La Mama in New York City. The show moved to Off-Broadway and won the Natl. Theater Conference Award for best production. Several honors were bestowed on *Godspell* from *Variety* magazine's 2d annual poll of New York drama critics. Leonard Bernstein later consulted with Tebelak for a presentation of the musical mass *Godspell*, and it opened at the John F. Kennedy Ctr. for the Performing Arts in Washington, D.C. Tebelak himself conducted its opening at Cleveland's Great Lakes Shakespeare Festival. The show was then moved to Broadway and thereafter became the basis of a movie. Even though Tebelak stated that he loathed organized religion because it "missed the point," he became a postulant in the Episcopal church in 1978. He was also dramatist in residence at the Cathedral of St. John the Divine in New York City and staged several plays, including his own play about the Americans held hostage in Iran in 1979–81. In 1981, Tebelak dropped out of the seminary and began full-time work in the theater once again. He never married.

The **TECHNICARE CORPORATION,** located at 29100 Aurora Rd. in SOLON, is a leading manufacturer of medical diagnostic imaging equipment. By 1982, Technicare and another Cleveland-based firm, PICKER INTERNATL., were among the 3 leaders in adapting nuclear magnetic resonance technology for medical uses. Technicare had its beginnings in July 1970, when a Massachusetts-based investment firm purchased Ohio-Nuclear, Inc., a Cleveland-area manufacturer of medical diagnostic equipment. Ohio-Nuclear had been incorporated in Oct. 1958 by Donald W. Steel. Known in its early years as Nuclear-Ohio, Inc., and located at 27105 Knickerbocker Rd., BAY VILLAGE, the company employed 6 people in the manufacture of equipment and instruments for the nuclear industry. By May 1962 it had begun to construct gamma irradiators for medical, biological, and engineering uses. By 1964, the company had changed its name to Ohio-Nuclear, Inc., and had moved to 1725 Fall St. In 1970, Ohio-Nuclear employed 55 people and had sales of $3 million. In July 1970 it was acquired by the Boston Capital Corp., an investment firm headed by former Clevelander Joseph W. Powell; the Cleveland investment firm of Saunders, Stiver & Co. owned 10% of the stock in Boston Capital. Over the next year and a half, Boston Capital acquired other companies in the medical field: Mobilaid, Inc., of Elyria, Ohio; the Invalex Co. of Long Beach, Calif.; and the Chayes Dental Corp. Boston Capital changed its name to BCC Industries, Inc., in June 1971 and moved its headquarters to Cleveland. In Oct. 1971 it ceased to be an investment firm and became an operating company, with 60% of its products manufactured for the health-care industry. On 5 Dec. 1972, it again changed its name, to BCC, Inc., which it dropped in July 1973 to become Technicare. Net sales of $35.6 million in 1973 produced a net income of $3.5 million.

Technicare moved its headquarters in 1976 from Investment Plaza, 1801 E. 9th St., to Solon. Net sales in 1976 were $103 million and net income $7.6 million; sales rose to $107 million in 1977, and income jumped to $16.4 million. A large increase in net sales in 1978 to $150 million did not produce a proportionate rise in income, which in fact fell to $3.6 million. In Feb. 1979, Technicare merged with a major manufacturer of health-care products, Johnson & Johnson of Brunswick, N.J., and operated as its subsidiary. Technicare began to develop nuclear magnetic resonance equipment in 1979 and over the next 3 years invested about $20 million to develop a commercial program using the new medical technology. By 1981, Technicare employed 2,900 people worldwide, 1,600 in Greater Cleveland. The increasing complexity of the equipment used in medical diagnostic imaging involved higher costs at the same time that the drive for health-care cost containment was surfacing. The company continued to lose money, and in Apr. 1986, Johnson & Johnson announced that Technicare and its diagnostic imaging business would be sold to General Electric. Johnson & Johnson, however, retained the Solon plant, and operations there were phased out.

**TECHNOLOGY AND INDUSTRIAL RESEARCH.** Early Cleveland's household, agricultural, and industrial processes and devices were simply transfers or adaptations from elsewhere. The earliest settlers borrowed the 18th-century technologies of Europe and North America, including water-powered saw- and gristmilling, blacksmithing, brewing and distilling, textile manufacture, and intensive farming with plows and other iron implements. The Cuyahoga Furnace, established in 1834 in the Flats, reproduced the iron-smelting technology used in the U.S. for over a century, though it added the recent innovation of blowing the blast with a steam engine. Similarly, the Cleveland Paper Co. began operations in 1860 with well-known technology, and the Kuhlman Furniture Co. relied upon traditional craftsmen when it was established in 1867. Cleveland's entry into the steel industry began in 1868 when the Cleveland Rolling Mills Co. opened a Bessemer works, which was based on British patents of a decade earlier as well as important American modifications developed in New York and Michigan.

By the mid-19th century, however, Cuyahoga County farmers had become innovators in beekeeping, the use of hay mowers, and silo construction. And in the last third of the century, Clevelanders invented a number of significant devices and processes that laid the foundation for further industrial growth. Some Cleveland inventions were the result of individual inspiration and insight. For example, both John McMyler and A. N. Simmerly invented and patented derricks for loading and unloading ships, and in the 1880s founded Cleveland companies to manufacture them. But other inventors were professionals who obtained technical training or formal education, and then devoted their careers to creating new devices or attacking critical problems in developing industries. An early inventor of this type was Elisha Gray. Educated at Oberlin (Ohio) Preparatory School and Oberlin College, Gray became enthralled by electricity and experimented regularly with it at the college's laboratory in the early 1860s. His first patent (1867) was for a telegraph apparatus, and he successfully demonstrated it at the headquarters of Western Union in Cleveland. In 1869 he sold Western Union an interest in a telegraph printer he had designed, and with the cash he purchased a half-interest in a telegraph-instrument shop in Cleveland. By the time Gray moved his business to Chicago in 1871, he had a close and regular relationship with Western Union. The next year the company took a ⅓ interest in Gray's business, and it was transformed into WESTERN ELECTRIC, the manufacturing and development arm of the telegraph giant.

Another professional inventor, and one who carried out his life's work in Cleveland, was CHARLES F. BRUSH. Born in EUCLID, Brush completed engineering training at the University of Michigan in 1869 and subsequently set up a consulting chemical laboratory in Cleveland. Privately he carried on experiments in electricity, an emerging field of industry, and in 1875–79 he developed and patented crucial elements of the first central-station arc-lighting system in the world. Brush established the Brush Electric Co. in 1880 with the help of local capitalists, and marketed his system worldwide for street lighting. At his factory at 45th St. and what is now Commerce Ave., he established a laboratory in which he did fundamental work on storage batteries, securing the basic American patents on what eventually became a vital part of the automobile. He continued to carry out technical research in Cleveland until his death in 1929. Brush's pioneering innovations in the electrical industry attracted to him a number of Clevelanders who later founded important companies. Alexander E. Brown, a Scottish immigrant, worked for Brush, then designed a hoist for unloading iron ore from Great Lakes vessels. It was first used in 1881; by 1893 an estimated 75% of Great Lakes ore was handled by hoists made by Brown's Cleveland company. Brush stimulated 2 other enterprises even more directly. Washington H. Lawrence worked with Brush in developing workable carbon points (from petroleum refinery residue) for arc lights, and in 1886 was a founder of the NATL. CARBON CO., of which he became president. Lawrence participated in and promoted further research, which developed the use of carbons for batteries, dynamo and motor brushes, and telephone transmitters. By ca. 1900, Natl. Carbon had a laboratory specifically for battery development. LINCOLN ELECTRIC was founded in 1896 by another former Brush employee, John C. Lincoln. He pioneered in the development and manufacture of arc-welding equipment, and by the 1930s his company was known worldwide for its products.

Other innovators found the Brush laboratory and shops congenial for research and development projects. Walter Knight and Edward Bentley began their experiments on electric trolleys there, and although their work was not commercially successful, they are credited with making the first working installation of an electric streetcar line in the U.S. Eugene and Alfred Cowles first operated their electric furnace at the Brush site in 1883. Elmer Sperry, an enormously successful professional inventor, carried out his work at the Brush shops from the time of his arrival in Cleveland in 1893 until 1905. He had begun a career of consultation in electrical engineering in New York State and later in Chicago, but became firmly established as one of the outstanding consulting engineers in America during his Cleveland years, when he focused on electric vehicles and batteries. Much of his time here Sperry spent working closely with GENERAL ELECTRIC, but he carried out numerous investigations on his own, notably in electrochemical processes.

Certainly Brush and the cluster of inventions and innovations that spun off of his work are the most dramatic examples of the surge in technical change associated with the industrialization of Cleveland in the late 19th century, but there were many others. AMBROSE SWASEY and WORCESTER WARNER, for example, applied their machine-tool skills to telescope and instrument manufacture with great success, completing the great Lick Telescope in 1889. That telescope's worldwide publicity brought them numerous telescope contracts thereafter. The automobile industry in Cleveland also had leaders who were innovative. ALEXANDER WINTON introduced the 2-cylinder automobile engine in 1901, and later turned his attention to developing the diesel engine. WALTER BAKER was a leading manufacturer of electric vehicles, and ROLLIN WHITE patented a semiflash boiler for steam automobiles. The steel industry benefited enormously from Samuel Wellman's work at the Otis Steel Co., where he introduced the open-hearth process in 1874, and first produced basic open-hearth steel in 1886.

Through this late-19th-century age of rapid innovation and invention, the companies that remained in the forefront of their fields relied upon the energy and initiative of talented individuals for new or adapted technology. Sometimes the company's founder, or sometimes a professional inventor kept as a consultant, these individuals seldom had more than a personal laboratory and 1 or 2 assistants, and their approach to patenting was often haphazard, leading to costly litigation when opportunities to patent were missed. By 1900, however, research and development of new industrial technology had begun to be institutionalized and systematized, in order to anticipate and control the course of invention and innovation. Modern industrial research began as companies hired professional researchers as permanent employees and created well-supplied laboratories for them. Early steps in that direction were taken by the STANDARD OIL CO., which began its program of research in 1877 by employing HERMAN FRASCH, a pharmaceutical chemist, to work on refining problems in Cleveland. In 1889, Standard Oil established a permanent research department, which is usually regarded as the first such department in the petroleum industry. The SHERWIN-WILLIAMS CO. hired its first full-time chemist, Percy Neyman, in 1884, and its second in 1892. The outstanding pioneering research laboratory in Cleveland was NELA PARK. The Natl. Electric Lamp Assoc. (NELA) was founded in 1901 by a group of lightbulb manufacturers competing with General Electric. Soon NELA established a research and development laboratory in Cleveland in order to standardize and upgrade its product, an effort that was so successful that NELA more than doubled its share of the market in the next decade. That success, and the laboratory director's desire to remove research from the gaseous pollution, vibrations, and electrical disturbances of a city location, led NELA's leaders to build a larger research center in suburban E. CLEVELAND. The new site, Nela Park, was begun in 1911 and eventually comprised 20 buildings on 90 acres. In 1912, GE absorbed NELA, and the site became GE's Lamp Development Laboratory. GE created an outstanding team of engineers and scientists who carried out a series of major inventions and innovations in lighting technology. In 1917, Dr. Aladar Pacz completed work on a workable tungsten wire filament, and in the 1930s the Nela Park staff did fundamental investigations of sodium-vapor and fluorescent lamps. Throughout the 20th century, the NELA team was expected to solve GE's lightbulb-manufacturing problems, and they often conducted basic scientific research on light emission and transmission. During the first decade of the 20th century, other corporate giants, such as AT&T, Eastman-Kodak, and Du Pont, established massive research divisions, and GE had an even larger laboratory in Schenectady, N.Y. But, as symbolized by Nela Park, Cleveland was one of the leaders in industrial research, and it remained a major center in succeeding years. A survey by the Natl. Research Council in 1930 revealed that the city had 41 laboratories, concentrated in the CHEMICAL, metallurgical, paint, and machinery industries. Cleveland then had the 5th-largest concentration of industrial research laboratories in the U.S. Fifty years later, the Cleveland metropolitan area had over 200 industrial laboratories, including major research centers for such diverse corporations as Sohio, Durkee Foods, and Union Carbide.

From about the time of WORLD WAR II, the federal government and higher education became the rising stars of industrial research. In Cleveland that was symbolized by the establishment of the NATL. AERONAUTICS & SPACE ADMIN. LEWIS RESEARCH LABORATORY and the growth of Case Institute of Technology. The Natl. Advisory Committee for Aeronautics founded Lewis in 1941 on a site adjacent to Cleveland's airport, and commissioned it to test aircraft engines. As one of NACA's test facilities, Lewis conducted important wartime research on piston engines and their fuels, lubricants, and coolants. After the war, its attention turned to developing the jet engines invented by British and German engineers, and in the 1950s and the 1960s (when NACA became NASA), Lewis pioneered in rocketry. Both of these research and development programs remained strong through the 1980s, although energy conservation and fuel efficiency also entered Lewis's agenda.

Case Institute of Technology regarded scientific research and industrial development as tasks compatible with education from the beginning of classes in 1882. Over its first 50 years, Case professors contributed to the understanding of petroleum chemistry and electrochemistry, and helped to develop the technologies on which the Dow Chemical and LUBRIZOL corporations were founded. By 1930, Case was one of about 20 institutions of higher learning that could be identified as regularly conducting industrial research. Yet the research depended upon individual efforts. With the presidencies of Wm. Wickenden (1924–47) and T. Keith Glennan (1948–67), Case established closer relationships with industry and government. By accepting long-term contracts, and committing its faculty, graduate students, and laboratories to industrial research, Case dealt regularly with the iron and steel, metal fabrication, and chemical industries. During World War II, federal contracts became increasingly important, and by the 1950s, 70% of Case's research income came from government research, mostly for the Defense Dept. Notable research during the institute's second 50 years occurred in polymers, strength of materials, complex systems design, computers, and biomedical engineering. Classified military projects, such as the multi-million-dollar "Doan Brook" enterprise of the 1950s, cannot yet be assessed by historians.

By the 1980s, industrial research laboratories in Cleveland fostered invention and promoted technical innovation on behalf of industrial corporations, government agencies, and higher education. Many Clevelanders looked to such laboratories as the source of the new ideas that would stem or reverse the decline of Cleveland's industrial base. Others viewed with concern the increasingly military orientation of research, and the integration of military, academic, and industrial institutions, which was most visible in research laboratories. In any case, though a relatively small part of Cleveland's economy and workforce, the laboratories will continue to play an important role in the future.

Darwin H. Stapleton
Rockefeller Archive Center

See also INDUSTRY, SCIENCE, and specific companies and individuals.

**TELEGRAPHY AND TELEPHONES.** Cleveland's connection to the rest of the U.S. by telegraph line was a communications breakthrough essential to the city's commercial and industrial development. During critical years in the formation of the U.S. telegraph industry, pivotal officials resided in Cleveland. The telephone, arriving in Cleveland 3 decades after the telegraph, altered the way Clevelanders conducted business and social intercourse. Cleveland's first telegraph line began operation between Cleveland and Pittsburgh in Aug. 1847, 3 years after Samuel F. B. Morse completed the first American line, connecting Baltimore with Washington. The Lake Erie Line, a *T*-shaped line extending from Buffalo via Cleveland to Detroit and from Cleveland to Pittsburgh, was in full operation by spring 1848. It was built by the Lake Erie Telegraph Co. as part of Henry O'Rielly's Atlantic, Lake, & Mississippi Telegraph system. By summer 1848, the Lake Erie Line faced competition from the Erie & Michigan Telegraph Line extending from Buffalo to Milwaukee through Cleveland, Detroit, and Chicago. John J. Speed and Ezra Cornell built the line under contract to F. O. J. Smith. Speed, in turn, subcontracted parts of the line to JEPTHA H. WADE. The telegraph, called the magnetic telegraph or lightning line, was hailed as a communications breakthrough. Its most important service was to bring news, especially business news such as stock market quotations and political news such as election returns. But in the beginning, expectations were disappointed by poor service. Like most early telegraph lines, the Lake Erie and Erie & Michigan lines were built hastily, using cheap materials and poor insulators. The telegraph news columns frequently contained apologies instead of the latest news.

Soon after completing his section of the Erie & Michigan telegraph, Jeptha Wade organized a connecting line between Cleveland and Cincinnati, in operation by 1 Jan. 1850. Telegraph lines proliferated in Ohio as in the rest of the U.S.; by 1852, 14 companies operated 3,210 mi. of telegraph wire in Ohio. There was too little business, however, to support all the rival companies. Speed, Wade, and Cornell were among the first to see the need for consolidation. The western section of the system they created appeared in the 1853 Cleveland city directory as the Speed & Wade Telegraph Lines, consisting of the Erie & Michigan along with 4 other telegraph companies. Lake Erie Telegraph was by then part of the Natl. Telegraph Cos. system. House's Printing Telegraph, a third party, arrived in Cleveland in 1851 under the auspices of the New York & Mississippi Valley Printing Telegraph Co., operating a line from New York to St. Louis. In Mar. 1854, the New York & Mississippi Valley Co. gained control of Lake Erie Telegraph. A month later they bought out Speed's and Wade's interests in the Cornell-Speed-Wade system. Ezra Cornell held out until Nov. 1855, when the Erie & Michigan merged with the New York & Mississippi Valley. In spring 1856, the company was reincorporated as the Western Union Telegraph Co. Although Western Union headquarters were in Rochester, ANSON STAGER, general superintendent for the company, and Jeptha Wade, general agent or negotiator, relocated to Cleveland. Western Union dominated telegraphy in the West and until 1864 was the only telegraph company serving Cleveland.

During the 1850s and 1860s, Stager and Wade negotiated contracts between Western Union and the railroads. Telegraphic train dispatching, attempted first in 1851, gradually came into general use during the next 10 years. The railroads came to rely on the telegraph for speed and safety. The telegraph companies, in turn, gained rights-of-way and other benefits through contracts with the railroads. During the CIVIL WAR, Anson Stager was appointed military superintendent of all telegraph lines and offices in the North. He continued to serve simultaneously as general superintendent of Western Union, and before the war's end he left Washington for Cleveland, where he performed both duties. As president of Western Union in 1866 and 1867, Wade negotiated its merger with its 2 main rivals, the U.S. Telegraph Co. and the American Telegraph Co. Both Wade and Stager encouraged inventor Elisha Gray's experiments in telegraphy, giving him work space in Western Union's Cleveland repair shop. In 1869, Stager loaned Gray money to establish the telegraphic instrument-manufacturing firm of Gray & Barton, forerunner of WESTERN ELECTRIC.

Gray & Barton moved to Chicago in 1870; Gray later became Alexander Graham Bell's chief rival claimant as inventor of the telephone. Local telegraph systems began to appear in Cleveland during the late 1860s. By 1869, Cleveland's first fire-alarm telegraph system was in operation. District telegraph companies were organized during the 1870s to send messages within the Cleveland metropolitan area. Subscribers to the American District Telegraph Co. (ADT), organized in Cleveland in 1876, could signal the central station for police, fire, a messenger, a physician, or even a carriage. In June 1877, just 1 year after Alexander Graham Bell demonstrated his telephone at the Centennial Exhibition in Philadelphia, Cleveland's first telephone was installed between the yard and office of Rhodes & Co. coal dealers on Water (W. 9th) St. More private lines followed, but telephone service in Cleveland properly begins with the first telephone exchange, opened 15 Sept. 1879 by the Western Union Telegraph Co. In Nov. 1879, Western Union, in an agreement with Bell Telephone, withdrew from the telephone business, and the Cleveland exchange was sold to a local group with a Bell license. The Cleveland Telephone Co. was incorporated in Jan. 1880. Until the 1890s, it was the only successful local telephone company in Cleveland.

The introduction of the telephone posed little threat to the telegraph, generating far less excitement than the introduction of the telegraph 30 years earlier. Well into the 20th century, the telegraph remained more popular than the telephone for long-distance use, and continued to dominate the news business. Cleveland was served by Western Union and a variety of competitors. Meanwhile, the telephone gradually gained popularity for local communication. The 76 subscribers of Sept. 1879 grew to nearly 300 by Mar. 1880. In 1890 there were 2,979 telephone subscribers in Cleveland, a city with a population over 261,000. The great majority of subscribers during this period were businesses. Telephone service was expensive: $72 per year for a business, $60 for a residence in 1885. At pay stations (there were 5 in 1881), the cost was 10 cents for a call of 5 minutes or less, except at the Newburgh station, where the cost was 20 cents. Technical problems encountered by the first subscribers included irregular ringing of the phone when the subscriber was not wanted, failure to get a response from the central office or from a subscriber, interruption of a conversation, and difficulty in hearing. The Midland Telephone Co., a Chicago-based Bell organization, brought Cleveland its first long-distance telephone line in 1883, connecting the city with Youngstown. That same year Midland was taken over by the Central Union Telephone Co., also based in Chicago and organized to develop Bell telephone service in Ohio, Illinois, and Indiana. Central Union operated long-distance lines in cooperation with Cleveland Telephone's local lines. By 1893, the long-distance lines of the American Telephone & Telegraph Co. reached Ohio, and Clevelanders, in theory, could telephone cities on the East Coast. Actually, long-distance service remained unreliable until the late 1890s, when metallic 2-wire circuits were introduced in Cleveland. Even after that, the vast majority of telephone calls were local (approximately 98% in 1905), with the telegraph still used for long distances.

When the Bell patents expired in 1893 and 1894, competing telephone companies appeared throughout the U.S. The Home Telephone Co. was organized in Cleveland in 1895, then reorganized as the Cuyahoga Telephone Co. in 1898. By the end of 1904, Cuyahoga Telephone was serving 12,194 subscribers with 13,711 phones, while Cleveland Telephone was serving 14,442 subscribers with 18,688 phones. Cuyahoga Telephone's low rates encouraged more people to lease telephones and forced Cleveland Telephone to lower its rates, as well. As a result, by 1905 approximately 1 in 14 Clevelanders had a telephone, and the number was growing rapidly. Through Cuyahoga Telephone, in cooperation with the independent U.S. Telephone Co., Clevelanders could telephone many cities and towns in Ohio that were neglected by the Bell companies. The existence of 2 separate phone companies, however, meant that subscribers to Cleveland Telephone could not telephone subscribers to Cuyahoga Telephone. Businesses had to subscribe to both companies until 1910, when the two began to exchange services. In 1914, Cuyahoga Telephone and U.S. Telephone became part of the Columbus-based Ohio State Telephone Co., the largest independent telephone company in the U.S. In 1920, Cleveland Telephone became the Ohio Bell Telephone Co. and purchased the Ohio property of the Central Union Telephone Co. In 1921, Ohio State Telephone merged with Ohio Bell. Over the next 4 years, Ohio Bell, based in Cleveland, unified telephone service throughout the state. In 1927, Ohio Bell began introducing dial telephones in Cleveland. Although telephone use declined early in the Depression, recovery during the late 1930s brought the total for Greater Cleveland up to 199,400 subscribers with 296,400 phones by 1940. By 1942, all of Greater Cleveland was converted to dial telephone service, entailing the elimination of 4-party lines. In 1954, direct long-distance dialing was introduced to the Cleveland area in Willoughby. Post-World War II growth in telephone use can be seen in the increase in the number of telephones in Ohio Bell's Cleveland service area, from 590,629 in 1950 to 1,046,991 in 1965 to 1,478,418 in 1980. Following divestiture of AT&T on 1 Jan. 1984, Ohio Bell became part of the Chicago-based AMERITECH CORP.

Jane Busch
Western Reserve Historical Society

**TELEVISION.** The first television station in Cleveland was also the first in Ohio. WEWS, channel 5, went on the air the night of 17 Dec. 1947. Possibly 6 other TV stations had preceded WEWS on the air, and 3 of those had held experimental licenses from the Federal Communications Commission dating to 1941. These were located in New York City and in Schenectady, N.Y. The FCC began granting other TV licenses at the end of WORLD WAR II, and commercial television stations began lighting up the small screens in 1946 and 1947. WEWS thus was at the forefront when it televised its first program from Cleveland's PUBLIC AUDITORIUM in the heart of downtown. The program was the annual Christmas Show, sponsored by the *CLEVELAND PRESS*. It was a logical opening program, because the new station and the *Press* were owned by the Scripps-Howard newspaper chain. In fact, the station call letters came from the initials of the founder of the *Press*, EDWARD WYLLIS SCRIPPS. Channel 5 had its studios and offices on the 2d floor of the old Women's City Club building on E. 13th St., just north of EUCLID AVE. The transmitter site was in PARMA, south of Cleveland, where the high elevation helped produce a widespread signal. It was nearly a year later before the Natl. Broadcasting Co. began service on channel 4, on Sunday evening 31 Oct. 1948. The first program was an NBC network show, "Television Playhouse," which was filmed from an original telecast in New York and fed into the NBC Midwest network from Chicago. This second station used the letters WNBK and operated from what was then the NBC Bldg. on Superior Ave. at E. 9th St. NBC was already a fixture in the Cleveland broadcasting picture, because it owned and operated radio station WTAM. Cleveland's third commercial TV station, WXEL, began service on channel 9 on 19 Dec. 1949. Its

first program was a Dumont Network production from the Metropolitan Opera. Channel 9 was owned by the Empire Coil Co. of White Plains, N.Y., and its president, Herbert Meyer. The station had its studios and transmitter in Parma, at Pleasant Valley and State roads.

Until Jan. 1949, TV programs in New York or any other East Coast city could not be seen live west of the Allegheny Mts., because TV required coaxial cable. The American Telephone & Telegraph Co. completed a coaxial cable network over the mountains on 11 Jan. 1949, and a special program marking this historic occasion originated in Cleveland on that date. The first major live news event on this network was the inauguration of Pres. Harry Truman on 20 Jan. In the early years of Cleveland television, the stations transmitted little more than their test patterns during the morning hours, followed by programs for children. Programs aimed at women in the home were scheduled in the early afternoon, followed by programs for school-age children. It was not uncommon for a station to sign off at 6:00 p.m., announcing that service would resume at 8:00 p.m. In the interim, the test pattern was back on the screen. When programming resumed, the schedule offered old movies or kinescope films of network programs, usually of inferior quality. At 11:00 p.m., an announcer read the news that had come off an AP or UP teletype circuit.

In 1952, WXEL was bought by the Storer Broadcasting Co., along with radio station WJW. Storer changed WXEL to WJW-TV to match the radio station letters, and in a matter of months, negotiated for channel 9 to become the exclusive CBS-TV station in Cleveland, leaving channel 5 with ABC. The Dumont Network had gone out of business by this time. Apr. 1954 brought another major change, part of a national revamping of the TV spectrum by the FCC. Channel 4 was moved to channel 3, and channel 9 became channel 8. It was part of a plan to improve transmission and avoid the possibility of interference with other stations. In those early days, a few performers carried most of the programs, and many of these people had previous experience on the RADIO, which gave them a following. At channel 5, GENE CARROLL did children's programs as Uncle Jake, and later conducted an hour-long program on Sunday, which was little more than a TV version of a local amateur hour. At channel 4, Linn Sheldon, a well-known entertainer, donned an elflike costume, added big ears, and built quite a following with his character known as Barnaby. Another ex-radio performer by the name of Ron Penfound dressed in railroad overalls and was known as Captain Penny on several children's shows. Many of these early local children's shows relied heavily on film cartoons or old Hollywood 1-reelers such as the "Our Gang" comedies and the Three Stooges. The first telecast of a CLEVELAND INDIANS Baseball game was on channel 5 on a Saturday afternoon in May 1949, with Bob Feller pitching. In later games, the station added to the program by picking up sound with a parabolic microphone aimed at the players. That was dropped after a game in which angry Indians manager Lou Boudreau had shouted his profane opinion of an umpire's call at home plate.

News coverage began mainly as visual radio newscasts, with the stations using newscasters who had established themselves in radio. Channel 4, even before it moved to channel 3, used the popular Tom Field, who was well known for his newscasts on WTAM, the NBC radio station. Channel 9 hired Bob Rowley, who had been a newscaster on radio station WJR in Detroit. However, in 1951, channel 9 put its prime 11:00 news in the hands of a speech professor from Western Reserve University, Dr. Warren Guthrie. Guthrie's sponsor was the STANDARD OIL CO., long a sponsor of newscasts on radio, now anxious to achieve a similar reputation in TV news. As the Sohio reporter on channel 9, Guthrie became an instant success. His newscast was 10 minutes long, and he did it all himself, including weather and sports. Later, sports became a separate segment done by John Fitzgerald, and soon weather was made another segment handled by Ken Armstrong, who had succeeded Bob Rowley as news director. One of Guthrie's students, Jack Perkins, was hired as a newscaster at channel 5, and he came on the screen at 11:00, competing with his professor. Perkins, from Wooster, Ohio, had won a scholarship to the university in competition sponsored by WGAR radio and had acquired several years of experience in WGAR news before he was hired by channel 5 and teamed with a nationally known newscaster brought in from New York, John B. Hughes. Perkins remained at channel 5 until 1963, when he joined the NBC news organization in New York. He often was on the NBC morning "Today" show, subbing for regulars such as Tom Brokaw. Guthrie remained the Sohio reporter on channel 8 for 12 years. In 1963, the station management decided it wanted a new personality, and Guthrie was succeeded by a 2-man team of Doug Adair and Joel Daly on the 11:00 news. Adair would later move to channel 3 and then to Columbus. Daly moved on to Chicago, where he enjoyed a long tenure in TV news.

Through all the changes in the TV news operations in Cleveland, a red-haired woman, Dorothy Fuldheim, became a dominant figure. A journalist and lecture-circuit speaker originally from Milwaukee, Fuldheim was hired by channel 5 in 1949 when she was 55 years old. She had also worked as a book reviewer and radio news commentator. Scripps-Howard had hired her originally to be on their FM radio station, which had preceded their TV station on channel 5. It was a logical move to the new TV station, where she became a huge success with her news reports and candid commentaries on national as well as local events. Fuldheim traveled the world, reporting on major events and interviewing prime ministers and kings. Any major figure visiting Cleveland would seemingly always be on channel 5 with Dorothy Fuldheim. She continued on the station almost to her 91st birthday, until she suffered a stroke in June 1984.

Cleveland television had another major change between 1956 and 1965. NBC persuaded Westinghouse Broadcasting in Philadelphia to trade stations, with NBC moving its Cleveland WNBK radio and TV operations to Philadelphia, and Westinghouse moving its KYW radio and TV to Cleveland. Westinghouse changed channel 3 to KYW-TV and quickly gained a reputation for live, innovative programming. The news operation was expanded beyond what NBC had been doing in Cleveland. A variety show hosted by Mike Douglas was so successful that it was taped and syndicated to many other TV stations across the country. The "Mike Douglas Show" was actually a copy of a local program running on channel 5, "The One O'Clock Club." This show featured a live band and interviews and humor by 2 unlikely partners, commentator Dorothy Fuldheim and Cleveland radio disc jockey Bill Gordon. It was an open secret that this pair did not get along well, and barbed remarks often passed between them on the air, even with smiles. With celebrity guests, the program was quite popular on Cleveland TV. The Westinghouse program used Mike Douglas as host. He was a former vocalist with the Kay Kyser orchestra. KYW gave the program a sizable budget and went all-out to bring in big stars each week to cohost the show. Westinghouse won this competition. Channel 5 saw its audience for the "One O'Clock Club" decline to the point that it was discontinued. The Douglas show remained on the Westinghouse schedule until 1982. Despite its success, Westinghouse had not wanted to move

to Cleveland. The company filed a lawsuit, contending that NBC had used improper pressure to force the move. Westinghouse won its case, and in 1965 moved its operations back to Philadelphia, and NBC returned to Cleveland. NBC modified the call letters to WKYC and later sold off the radio station, which changed its letters to WWWE. The NBC-Westinghouse trade had some interesting side effects. When NBC moved to Philadelphia, newscaster Tom Field was not happy in his new location. At channel 5, John B. Hughes wanted to return to New York. So Field returned to Cleveland in 1961 as the prime news reporter on channel 5 at 6 and 11 and enjoyed high ratings. Westinghouse, while in Cleveland, had hired a young meteorologist named Dick Goddard to do the weather reports. Goddard did not like moving to Philadelphia with KYW; so he quit Westinghouse and came back to Cleveland, but on channel 8, not channel 3.

By 1965, other TV channels were coming onto the screen in Cleveland. After a long effort at raising both money and interest, educational station WVIZ went on the air on channel 25 on 7 Feb. 1965. WVIZ scheduled many classroom-type educational programs during school hours and coordinated these with Cleveland and suburban schools. Many programs were tape recorded and made available for the schools to use at a time of their own choosing. WVIZ affiliated with the Public Broadcasting Network and was able to offer such programs as "Sesame Street" and "The Electric Company" for children, as well as many high-quality dramatic and musical programs, including the Metropolitan Opera. Channel 25's general manager, Betty Cope, has held that post from the station's beginning in 1965 to the present (1986). She gained her television experience in production and programming at channel 5 in the late 1940s.

The next TV station to go on the air was WKBF, owned by the Kaiser Broadcasting Co., a unit of the old conglomerate Kaiser Industries. It began service in Aug. 1968, offering a limited schedule of local programs, an evening newscast at 10:00, and a heavy schedule of old movies. As channel 61, WKBF was an ultra-high-frequency station, and most TV sets of that time could receive only the "very high-frequency" stations, such as channels 3, 5, and 8. The audience for the new station was small despite the supposedly innovated 10:00 newscast. It finally went off the air in Apr. 1975. However, it resumed broadcasting on 3 Mar. 1981 as WCLQ, owned by the Channel Communications Co. of Ohio. By this time, all TV sets were required to receive the UHF as well as the VHF signal, and the market in Cleveland seemed large enough to support additional stations. In Sept. 1968, channel 43 went on the air as a "Lorain-Cleveland" station. The FCC had assigned the channel to Lorain, a city west of Cleveland. The Gaylord Broadcasting Co., the licensee, provided some programs that catered to Lorain, but the station was located in Cleveland. On 19 May 1985, another UHF station, channel 19, came on the screen. The station was headed by Hubert Payne, who had been a sales manager at channel 3. Its program schedule was heavy with movies and reruns of former network programs.

Cable television came into the Cleveland area in 1974, with franchises granted by many suburban cities. The larger systems were Cox Cable, serving west side communities, and Viacom, serving the east side areas. Cable TV was also provided by Space Cable, Continental Cable, Complexicable, Shamrock Cable, West Shore Cable, and others who entered the market month by month. However, a cable franchise was not authorized by the city of Cleveland until July 1985, with programming not scheduled until the fall of 1987. For many years, cable operators did not regard the city of Cleveland as a profitable market compared to the potential in the residential suburbs. The arrival of the video tape recorder in the mid-1980s also had an impact on the Cleveland TV viewing market and its audience ratings. By the end of the 1980s, the Cleveland audience was becoming fragmented, as was the situation elsewhere in the nation. The 3 network-affiliated channels, 3, 5 and 8, were still drawing the larger share of the viewing audience, but these were smaller, as TV viewers tuned to the independent, nonnetwork stations or the cable stations, or used their VCRs to record and view programs at a time of their own choosing; or they bought or rented video tape programs and did not watch one of the transmitting stations at all. The diversity of options available to viewers in the 1980s seems to have permanently locked Cleveland television into following a myriad of national trends to attract viewers, rather than providing impetus for local experimentation.

Charles Day

See also specific television stations.

The **TELLING-BELLE VERNON COMPANY** was the first dairy company in Cleveland to deliver milk in glass bottles. The company was created on 29 Jan. 1915 by the merger of the Telling Bros. Co. and the Belle Vernon Farms Dairy Co. Telling Bros. began as a 1-man milk route operated by Wm. E. Telling from 1891–93; by 1895 he and his brother Chas. B. Telling had opened a confectioners' shop at 2826 Euclid Ave., across from LAKE VIEW CEMETERY. In Dec. 1895 he and another brother, John C., organized the Telling Bros. Ice Cream Co. and opened another shop at 953 Willson Ave. (E. 55th St.). By 1899 they had relocated to 397 (3833) Cedar Ave. The firm was incorporated in 1905, and in 1913 Telling Bros. sold 4.2 million quarts of ice cream.

The Belle Vernon Farms Dairy Co. began as the Maple Grove Farm Dairy Co., organized by Addison S. Drake and Addison G. Nickerson ca. 1891. By 1895 JACOB A. BEIDLER had become president of the company, and he reorganized it as the Belle Vernon Farms Dairy Co. in Feb. 1897. By the turn of the century, Congressman Beidler's company had gained a reputation as one of the "progressive spirits in the milk business." Located at 957 Willson Ave., the company was next to Telling Bros. for several years, and the two firms shared a telephone in their adjoining storerooms. By 1901 Belle Vernon was located at 1312 (5812) Euclid, remaining there until moving to 3821 Cedar in 1915. By 1903 the company had merged with the milk company of John P. and Perry E. Mapes. The new Belle Vernon-Mapes Dairy Co. had 40,000 daily customers by 1913 and was supplying 25% of the milk sold in Cleveland.

Wm. E. Telling became president of the new Telling-Belle Vernon Co. in 1915. General offices of the firm were located at 3821–3835 Cedar, with a wholesale office at 706 Eagle St., until the company moved into new quarters at 3740 Carnegie in 1935. Telling-Belle Vernon became a division of the Natl. Dairy Prods. Corp. in 1928 and in 1935 began to market its milk using the Sealtest symbol to indicate that it met the quality specifications of Natl. Dairy. By 1946 the company had 70,000 customers, 1,400 employees, and milk-bottling plants in Ashtabula and Painesville, as well as Cleveland. It also had ice cream plants in Cleveland, Akron, Columbus, and Wheeling, W.Va., and a butter plant in Cleveland. The company claimed to be the largest distributor of dairy products in Cleveland and the largest dairy in Ohio. From 1951–57, Natl. Dairy once again split Telling-Belle Vernon into 2 separate companies, the Belle Vernon Milk Co. and the Telling Ice Cream Co. The two were again merged in 1957 as part of the Sealtest of Ohio Div. of the Natl. Dairy Prods. Corp., which became

the Sealtest Foods Div. of the Kraftco Corp. in 1969. Sealtest operated a plant at 3740 Carnegie until 1980.

**TELLO, MANLY** (1842–4 Apr. 1905), was a lawyer and journalist. He was prominent among Cleveland Catholics as editor of the *Catholic Universe*, and nationally was considered a power in Catholic journalism. Tello's father was Spanish, and his mother Irish. He was educated at Holy Cross College in Worcester, Mass., and St. Charles Seminary in Maryland. An ardent Southerner, Tello served in the Confederate Army until his capture by Union forces while carrying secret dispatches. He later escaped from the Rock Island prison camp and fled to Canada, where he married Anna Sales, the daughter of another Confederate refugee. After the war, Tello practiced law in Louisville, Ky., until he was offered the editorship of the *North West Chronicle*, a Catholic newspaper, in St. Paul, Minn. His work attracted the attention of Bp. RICHARD GILMOUR, who brought him to Cleveland in 1877 to assume the editorial management of the *Catholic Universe* (see *CATHOLIC UNIVERSE BULLETIN*). He managed the paper until after the death of Bp. Gilmour in 1892. Tello was editor of the *Universe* at a time when other Cleveland newspapers, most notably the *CLEVELAND LEADER*, were espousing anti-Catholic sentiment. As a mouthpiece of the church hierarchy, the *Universe*, under Tello, was enlarged and became one of the most influential Catholic papers in the country. Tello was a stalwart defender of church authority; his archaic but trenchant style of writing made him one of the leading figures in Catholic journalism in the U.S. The *Universe* was not a financial success under Tello, as he was known more for his literary sense than for his business acumen. He was also criticized, even by Bp. Gilmour, for occasionally using the paper to promote Southern interests. In an attempt to broaden the paper's appeal, Tello introduced coverage of the emerging sport of BASEBALL, which led to some controversy within the diocese. For his outspoken views, Tello—even within the diocese—attracted as much negative attention as he did positive. Tello spent the remaining 13 years of his life practicing law in Cleveland. He was remarried in 1892, to Anna Boylan of Cleveland.

**TELSHE YESHIVA**, an internationally prominent center for traditional Jewish scholarship and learning, was established in Cleveland in 1941 after being forced from its original home in Lithuania. Established in 1875 in the town of Telz, Lithuania, it became by 1900 one of the 3 largest yeshivot in Russia. Under the leadership of Rabbis Eliezer Gordon (1883–1910) and Joseph Leib Bloch (1910–30), the yeshiva instituted new methods for Talmudic study, including dividing the pupils into 5 classes based upon their level of knowledge and requiring periodic testing. With the German invasion of Russia, it was closed, and many of the students and teachers were killed. Elijah Meyer Bloch, who had studied at Telshe Yeshiva and had been on the faculty since 1917, escaped to the U.S. and established the yeshiva in Cleveland. In Apr. 1942, the yeshiva dedicated a remodeled house on East Blvd. However, by 1944 it had moved to a new location on E. 105th. By 1947, Telshe Yeshiva had over 150 students, many from outside the U.S. Bloch remained dean until his death in 1955. He maintained as a central element in the yeshiva's educational philosophy a system of learning known as "The Way of Telz." It teaches the skill of logical analysis based on inductive reasoning, a system established at the yeshiva in the late 19th century.

In 1956, the yeshiva acquired the 53-acre Jas. B. Kirby estate in Wickliffe; it began construction of a large complex in 1964. In 1965, Mordechai Gifter became the dean of the yeshiva. Born in Portsmouth, Va., in 1916, Gifter received his advanced education at Telshe Yeshiva when it was still located in Lithuania. He served as rabbi at congregations in Baltimore and Waterbury, Conn., before taking a post at the yeshiva teaching Talmud, religion, and ethics. Telshe Yeshiva has created an extensive education network similar to that which existed in Lithuania. In 1959, it established the Yavne Teachers Seminary, a 2-year program for women that offers a teacher's diploma and the opportunity to transfer credits to local colleges for pursuit of a bachelor's degree. A teacher's seminary for men was created in 1961 for graduates of the yeshiva. Qualified graduates of Telshe receive rabbinical ordination and may choose to enter the kollel, or postgraduate religious studies. The yeshiva also sponsors an Orthodox high school called Telshe High. It is for grades 9–12 and is accredited by the Ohio State Board of Regents. It prepares students for entrance into either the yeshiva's college courses or advanced secular studies.

**TEMPERANCE.** Temperance reform in Cleveland illustrates the wide appeal and the diverse tactics of the national temperance movement from the mid-19th century until the passage of the 18th (Prohibition) Amendment in 1919. Reformers and conservatives, wealthy and working-class, Protestant and Catholic, women and men, young and old, participated in temperance activities. Cleveland's early temperance organizations had their roots in the temperance agitation of the first decades of the 19th century, when improvements in distilling techniques, the unavailability of other beverages, and the need to ease the tensions created by the period's rapid social changes raised alcohol consumption to unprecedented heights. The city's first recorded groups were the CUYAHOGA COUNTY TEMPERANCE SOCIETY, formed in 1830 and later renamed the Cuyahoga County Total Abstinence Society, and the CLEVELAND CITY TEMPERANCE SOCIETY, founded in 1836. Both were patterned after the first national temperance organization, the American Temperance Society, and both preached total abstinence from alcohol. These reformers blamed poverty and immorality on drinking and argued that these problems could be solved through moral pressure upon the drinker and political pressure upon local officeholders to pass regulatory legislation.

Cleveland's first benevolent society, the WESTERN SEAMEN'S FRIEND SOCIETY, founded the MARINE TOTAL ABSTINENCE SOCIETY in 1840, which survived almost 2 decades. Its clientele were the men who sailed Lake Erie and the newly built canals upon which the city's thriving commerce rested. Many of these workingmen, along with the well-to-do founders, signed the lengthy roll of those who had taken the "pledge" to abstain from alcohol. In the 1840s, temperance reform in Cleveland and elsewhere was swept up in the enthusiasm of the Washingtonian movement, which relied upon revivalistic techniques in lectures, plays, and literature to achieve the spiritual reclamation of drunkards by their conversion to total abstinence. Established temperance groups expanded their memberships, and several new groups were formed, such as the Young Men's Washingtonian Total Abstinence Society and the MARTHA WASHINGTON & DORCAS SOCIETY, which also distributed poor relief.

The Washingtonian movement sustained its emotional energies only through the 1840s, but it broadened the base upon which Cleveland's next significant temperance groups, the SONS OF TEMPERANCE and the Independent Order of Good Templars, capitalized. The national Sons of Temperance was formed in 1843, and the Templars in 1851. Both were fraternal orders with secret rituals and degrees

and ranks of membership. By 1848 the Sons had 3 divisions in Cleveland, and a decade later, the Good Templars had several lodges. Both groups also advocated political action to end the liquor menace. In 1852–53, Cleveland groups formed a political alliance to support a third-party gubernatorial candidate who endorsed the total prohibition of the sale and manufacture of alcoholic beverages. The election was lost, but prohibition through the passage of such a "Marine Law" became an important goal from that time forward, and independent political activity became an attractive strategy.

Catholic temperance groups also flourished in the 1840s and 1850s in urban areas such as Cleveland, inspired by the preaching of the Irish priest Fr. Theobald Mathew, who visited Cleveland in Aug. 1851, at the invitation of Bp. AMADEUS RAPPE. The Fr. Mathew Mutual Benevolent & Total Abstinence Society (see FATHER MATHEW TOTAL ABSTINENCE SOCIETY) grew out of this visit, the first of many Catholic temperance groups, reflecting the growth in the city's Catholic population. During the CIVIL WAR, Americans turned their attention from temperance and other reforms, but at the war's end, temperance advocates pushed forward with the political tactics with which they had experimented in the 1850s. In 1869, at the meeting of the Ohio State Temperance Alliance, a small group, with its base in Cleveland's vigorous temperance movement, endorsed the formation of a third political party; and in Mar. 1869, it nominated a slate of prohibition candidates for Cleveland city office. By September, the national Prohibition party had been formed. In 1876 and 1880 the party held its presidential nominating conventions in Cleveland, calling in 1876 for a constitutional amendment providing for national prohibition and in 1880 endorsing women's suffrage, the first national political party to do so. The PROHIBITION PARTY continued to run candidates for city office in Cleveland in most elections until the end of the century.

The WOMAN'S CHRISTIAN TEMPERANCE UNION also had its official beginning in Cleveland in 1874. Women had earlier participated in temperance activities, as in the Martha Washington & Dorcas Society and in auxiliaries to the Sons of Temperance and the Good Templars. In 1850, a Ladies Temperance Union had also been established in Cleveland. Tactics of these groups reflected the 19th-century belief that women were more pious and moral than men, which encouraged women to join reform efforts such as temperance, designed to improve male behavior, but limited them to moral suasion or other appropriately feminine strategies. Inspired by the "crusades" of praying and exhorting women who descended upon local saloons in small Ohio towns, Cleveland women in 1874 formalized the establishment of their new temperance group, the Women's Temperance League of Cleveland, which had already begun its own crusading and which affiliated with the national WCTU in 1880. The league's goal was conversion of the drinker both to temperance and to Protestant Christianity. To achieve that, the women founded "temperance inns" where "gospel temperance" was preached and where inexpensive lodgings and meals were also available.

In 1885, when the national WCTU endorsed the Prohibition party, a group within the Cleveland WCTU withdrew from the national and formed the Woman's Christian Temperance Union of Cleveland, Nonpartisan. Cleveland women who remained loyal to the national coalesced around the Cuyahoga County WCTU. The "loyals" also endorsed women's suffrage, but the Nonpartisan did not, although it did support the temperance and school ballots for women. Cleveland became a center for the national and state Nonpartisan movement and organizations, and the Nonpartisan WCTU was the more active of the city's 2 WCTU groups, with the financial support of JOHN D. ROCKEFELLER and other prominent Cleveland businessmen. The Nonpartisan built and maintained several social-welfare institutions, including the Training Home for Friendless Girls, the Mary Ingersoll Club for Working Girls, the Eleanor B. RAINEY INSTITUTE, now part of the CLEVELAND MUSIC SCHOOL SETTLEMENT, and Central Friendly Inn, which became a settlement while still under the Nonpartisan's management (see FRIENDLY INN). In 1927 the Nonpartisan became the Women's Philanthropic Union, which administered the funds that partially sustained these institutions. The county WCTU worked for scientific temperance education in the Cleveland public schools and campaigned actively for women's suffrage, Prohibition party candidates, and the passage of a state prohibition amendment.

The national Anti-Saloon League was born in 1893 in Oberlin. Its strength lay in the evangelical Protestant churches, which provided funds and pulpits for league speakers and lists of registered voters, but the league was also a national political pressure group staffed by paid professionals and utilizing the new techniques of mass communication. It was almost solely a single-issue group, its stated goal being simply an end to saloons. In Cleveland, the Ohio league shared the headquarters of the Nonpartisan WCTU, whose members also served on the league board.

The league had its own publishing company, which produced millions of pages of temperance materials, including an annual yearbook with information on the national consumption of alcohol, state and federal liquor laws, all the dry counties and cities in the country, and a list of all national temperance groups. The league also endorsed candidates for local and state office and worked for state prohibition amendments in Ohio in 1914, 1915, and 1917. In 1918 Ohio did pass a state prohibition amendment, and in Jan. 1919 it passed the 18th (Prohibition) Amendment to the federal Constitution, which became law a year later. This national victory had been made possible by the decades of education, agitation, and political pressure by the temperance forces since the mid-19th century. The passage of the amendment was also facilitated by the United States' entrance into WORLD WAR I in 1917, which made the prohibition of the sale and manufacture of alcoholic beverages an attractive means of saving manpower, money, and grains. (See PROHIBITION.)

Temperance reformers hailed their triumph and claimed that prohibition had brought prosperity, morality, health, and happiness, as they had claimed it would, but also remained active to consolidate their gains. The Prohibition party ran presidential candidates throughout the 1920s, each platform demanding vigorous federal enforcement of the amendment. The national WCTU continued to emphasize temperance education and held its Golden Jubilee in 1924 in Cleveland, its birthplace. The Cuyahoga County WCTU increased its membership. The Anti-Saloon League continued to stress the benefits of prohibition and in 1928 endorsed Herbert Hoover for president over Alfred Smith, who was known to favor repeal of the Prohibition Amendment.

By the mid-1920s, when federal enforcement of the amendment became less effective or less determined, the opponents of prohibition were articulate and well organized. In the forefront was the Assoc. against the Prohibition Amendment, which drew its membership especially from Ohio and Cleveland. In 1929 the Women's Organization for Natl. Prohibition Reform was established by wealthy

and socially prominent women such as Clevelander Mrs. Amasa Stone Mather, and in 1930, the organization held its first convention in Cleveland. Also active in efforts to repeal the amendment were the Cleveland Crusaders, formed in 1929 by a group of young businessmen led by Fred Clark. These groups maintained that the amendment was an unwarranted intrusion of government into the lives of individuals and that its haphazard enforcement eroded the legitimacy of all government, encouraging crime and corruption.

With the onset of the Depression, supporters of repeal also argued that it would bring back prosperity by creating jobs for workers and tax revenues for state and federal governments. In 1933 Ohio voted for repeal of both the state and federal prohibition amendments, with Cleveland endorsing repeal enthusiastically. The repeal of the 18th Amendment, like its passage, was made possible by well-planned, well-financed action, combined with fortuitous circumstances. Repeal also symbolized the repudiation of the 19th-century lifestyle and value system that had fostered the temperance movement in small towns such as Cleveland, where benevolence, evangelical religion, and self-discipline had been preached and practiced. As the city's population grew and became more ethnically diverse after the turn of the century, and as its reform efforts became secular and professionalized, the temperance associations, which had their roots in the 19th-century context, lost their appeal for urban Americans. The Prohibition party and the national WCTU remained active in the 1980s, and the Anti-Saloon League became part of the American Council on Alcohol Problems. But in 1934 in Cleveland, only the Ohio Anti-Saloon League survived.

Marian J. Morton
John Carroll University

See also BREWING & DISTILLING and PROHIBITION.

The **TEMPLE,** Cleveland's second-oldest existing congregation, was established as Tifereth Israel on 26 May 1850 by several members of ANSHE CHESED who had left that congregation in a dispute over the ritual used in religious services. Rabbi ISIDOR KALISCH, who had assumed the Anshe Chesed pulpit a few months earlier, was hired and remained at Tifereth Israel through 1855. The congregation received a $3,000 bequest from the estate of New Orleans philanthropist Judah Touro on 2 Mar. 1854. The money served as the foundation of a fundraising campaign that culminated in the erection of a synagogue at Huron and Miami streets in 1855. The building was dedicated on 14 Dec. of that year.

Like many German-Jewish congregations of the mid-19th century, Tifereth Israel began instituting reforms in ritual and decorum soon after its formation. Family pews (ending the traditional separation of the sexes during religious services) and installation of an organ were part of the remodeling and enlargement of the synagogue in 1861. At the same time, a choir was formed, and 5 years later the congregation adopted the Minhag America, a distinctly American Reform prayerbook. During the rabbinical tenures of Jacob Mayer (1867–74) and Aaron Hahn (1874–92), Tifereth Israel adopted reforms and discontinued many traditional practices. In 1873, the congregation joined the Union of American Hebrew Congregations, the newly formed lay organization of the Reform movement.

MOSES J. GRIES became rabbi in 1892, and during his 25 years in the pulpit, he led Tifereth Israel into the forefront of Reform Judaism. In 1894, the congregation dedicated a new synagogue at Willson Ave. (E. 55th St.). Tifereth Israel became known as the Willson Ave. Temple, but more commonly was called the Temple. Rabbi Gries introduced the concept of the open synagogue to the Temple. Under his leadership and that of MARTIN MARKS, who served as president of the congregation for 23 years, several new programs and activities were established, including a Women's Assoc. (1897), a library (1898), a gymnasium (1901), and an orchestra (1916). During Gries's tenure, the congregation adopted the Union Prayer Book, Hebrew was dropped from the Sunday school curriculum, almost all Hebrew was deleted from the religious services, and Sabbath worship services were moved from Saturday to Sunday.

Rabbi ABBA HILLEL SILVER succeeded Gries in 1917 and served the congregation until his death in 1963. Silver altered the focus of the Temple's activities, discontinuing the purely recreational and social programs in order to concentrate on cultural and religious activities. By 1920, most of the Temple's membership had moved east from the Willson Ave. neighborhood to WADE PARK and the Heights. A large parcel of land was purchased at Ansel Rd. and E. 105th St. Architect Chas. R. Greco, who had designed the Temple on the Heights, designed a new $1.5 million synagogue, which was dedicated in Sept. 1924. The sanctuary of the new structure seated 2,000. By 1945, the Temple's membership was so great that on the High Holy Days, branch services were held in SEVERANCE HALL. Silver, whose stature was international because of his leadership of the American Zionist movement, was succeeded at the Temple by his son Rabbi Daniel J. Silver. Following World War II, the Temple's members again moved east. In 1969, the congregation dedicated the Temple Branch in PEPPER PIKE. Most services and a number of activities are presently (1986) held at the branch.

**TEMPLE EMANU EL** was the third Reform congregation established in Cleveland. It was organized in 1947, nearly 100 years following the creation of ANSHE CHESED CONGREGATION and Tifereth Israel-The TEMPLE. Recognizing that half of Cleveland's Jews were unaffiliated following WORLD WAR II, the Union of American Hebrew Congregations asked Rabbi Alan S. Green, a native of Cleveland, to form a congregation specifically to attract the unaffiliated. Anshe Chesed and the Temple each provided 6 members from their respective boards of trustees to assist in the initial planning for the new congregation. Green's goal was to establish a family-centered, nonformal, "singing congregation." Cantor Irvin Bushman was hired, and from the first service in Aug. 1947, he created an atmosphere of participation in religious services. By the end of its second year, Emanu El had a membership of 500 families and 550 students in its religious school under the direction of Sophie Herman.

Emanu El's services were initially held at Plymouth Church and BELLEFAIRE; religious school classes met at Moreland Public School; and the congregation's band praticed at Sol & Joe's Garage. In the early 1950s, a site was purchased on Green Rd. near Cedar Rd., and a synagogue was designed by SIGMUND BRAVERMAN and Moses Halperin. The new structure was dedicated on 4 June 1954, and an addition, the Rabbi Alan S. Green/Frances Green Religious School, was dedicated on 6 Feb. 1977. Rabbi Green's desire to create an activist congregation was given expression through the formation of its many affiliate groups. The Sisterhood (est. 1947) made contributions to and provided volunteers for the JEWISH COMMUNITY FED., UNITED WAY SERVICES, and Ben Shemen Children's Village in Israel. The Brotherhood, formed in 1948, sponsored a blood bank and cultural programs for the congregation and the community. A Couples' Club was established by the Greens and 8 couples in 1950 to integrate new and prospective members; by the mid-1970s, the club had grown to over 150 couples. Finally, the Young People's Congregation, established in 1963 for members 35 years old and under, encourages the study of and adherence to Reform Judaism's practices.

Temple Emanu El Records, WRHS.

**TEMPLE ON THE HEIGHTS.** *See* **B'NAI JESHURUN CONGREGATION**

**TENNIS.** Tennis clubs were organized in Cleveland during the 1880s. The first identifiable location for the sport was on the Billings' front lawn on the south side of Euclid and what is now designated E. 88th St. Hosting the games were Chas. and Frank Billing, joined by Henry Wick, Harry Judd, Orlando Hall, and Sterling Beckwith. Shortly thereafter this group moved over to Geo. Worthington's front lawn. Organized tennis, however, began with the formation of the East End and Buckeye clubs in the Euclid-Willson Ave. (E. 55th St.) area. Cleveland's first tennis tournament was launched in 1880 at the East End Tennis Club under the direction of GEO. WORTHINGTON, assisted by Chas. B. Post and T. Sterling Beckwith. The East End Club eventually moved to Euclid Ave. and Kennard (E. 46th) St. It continued to flourish, adding new courts on Carnegie west of E. 77th St. The Ohio State Open was held there prior to 1914, as were the Intercity tournaments. Local women were slower to take up the game because of the style of dress they were forced to wear in the 1890s. Elizabeth Dean Sprague won the Women's City Championship 3 straight years (1899–1901). Mary K. Brown was pronounced women's tennis champion of the U.S. for 3 straight years from 1912–14, and captured the women's doubles championship in 1921 and 1925 with Helen Wills as a partner. In 1916, the Natl. Clay Courts were played at the Lakewood Tennis Club, with nearly 2,000 in attendance. Willis Johnson defeated Conrad Doyle in the singles, while Molla Bjernstedt and Geo. M. Church won the mixed doubles trophy. Over 90% of Cleveland tennis players in the WORLD WAR I era belonged to racquet clubs (outdoor tennis only), which included the Edgewater, Nela Park, East End, General Electric, Lakewood, University, and Cleveland Yacht clubs. An outgrowth of the East End Tennis & Racquet Club in 1923 was the Cleveland Tennis & Racquet Club, which was established at Kemper and Fairhill Blvd. It was taken over in 1937 by the CLEVELAND SKATING CLUB. Public courts became important during the 1920s and 1930s. All courts, public and private, had a "blue" clay surface. The MAYFIELD COUNTRY CLUB had, and in 1986 still has, the only two grass courts in the area.

Tennis conditions changed considerably following WORLD WAR II with the introduction of all-weather courts, new rules such as the "tie break," larger racquets, and yellow tennis balls. As the residential and commercial areas of the city expanded, most of the public and semi-private outdoor clubs disappeared. In their place "indoor suburban" clubs appeared. Additional tennis activity occurred on golf-club courts, but never as intensively as at the racquet clubs. Most of the country clubs separated themselves from the interclub "A" league that flourished in the 1970s and 1980s, establishing a "B" league that permitted many additional players to compete. From the 1920s to 1980s, Cleveland tennis tournaments varied greatly from junior, public-park, and amateur to professional. The city tourneys were called "the munis" and were sponsored by the *CLEVELAND PRESS*. The *PLAIN DEALER* for many years sponsored the junior tournaments, which led to the development of many fine players. During World War II, the city championships were played at the Cleveland Skating Club; previously they had been held in GRAYS ARMORY. John March, owner of the Shaker Racquet Club, originated a series of tournaments for professionals starting at the CSC in 1950 where Pancho Segura won the singles title over Frank Kovacs, who teamed with Webley van Horn to win the doubles. He repeated the successful pro contest in 1953 and 1954 at the Lakewood High School courts.

In 1960, Cleveland achieved national status when Robt. Malaga brought the DAVIS CUP finals "challenge round" to the city. "The Green Coats" were a large group organized in 1960 by Malaga, Jos. Nook, and Henry Trenkamp to handle all details of the Davis Cup. This event in Sept. 1964 was the pinnacle of tennis locally as the top tennis representatives of the U.S and Australia came together in the final "challenge" round, which was not settled until American Dennis Ralston lost in 5 sets to Australian Fred Stolle. The success of the Davis Cup matches assured continuity of significant tournaments in Cleveland. The city leadership, the Greater Cleveland Tennis Assoc., and the business community of Cleveland cooperated in a joint effort to carry on the tradition established at the Cleveland Skating Club from 1960-63, and thereafter at the HAROLD T. CLARK TENNIS COURTS. As of 1986, Cleveland had sponsored 10 Davis Cup, 6 Wightman Cup, 3 Bonne Bell, and 20 other national open and amateur championships. The Cleveland area produced fine players such as Clark Graebner, who ranked among the top 10 nationally for 8 years, winning 3 U. S. Men's natl. singles titles in the 1960s. Other local players of note were John Dorr and Monte Ganger who won the U.S. doubles championship, Edw. DiLeone, Kirk Reid, and Robt. Malaga, who later became executive director of the United States Lawn Tennis Assoc. Notable local women players have been Edna Shalala and Gwyneth Thomas who ranked among the top 15 women in U.S. amateur tennis from 1957-63. In 1974, Joe Zingale brought team tennis to Cleveland when he bought the CLEVELAND NETS franchise for $50,000. World Team Tennis, originated by tennis star Billie Jean King, her husband, Larry, and sports entrepreneur Dennis Murphy, was short-lived (1973-78). It fielded 16 teams to play a schedule of 44 contests each; large salaries were offered to lure top players away from traditional tournament tennis. Since 1973, the youth of the central city and adjacent suburbs have benefited from the Natl. Jr. Tennis League formed by Jas. and Sally Young. It brings together local young tennis aspirants wishing to learn the sport during the summer months. Applying the team format of 2 singles and 1 doubles in 3 age groups (12, 14, and 18), teams play for 4 days at Gordon and Rockefeller parks, then compete against other teams on the fifth day. Financial support comes from the private and public sectors, with supervision on a voluntary basis. Through 13 successful years, the NJTL has grown to include 5,000 tennis enthusiasts in the Cleveland area.

Ted E. Worthington
Presidents Counsel, Inc.

The **TENTH OHIO VOLUNTEER CAVALRY,** 1862-65, was organized at Camp Cleveland (see CIVIL WAR CAMPS) in 1863. Companies A through L were mustered into federal service from January through March, but Co. M was not mustered in until July at Camp Chase in Columbus, Ohio; 55 Clevelanders served in this unit. The 10th Cavalry left for Nashville, Tenn., on 27 Feb. 1863, where it was assigned to the 2d Brigade, 2d Cavalry Div., Army of the Cumberland, until June. The unit was subsequently as-

signed to the 3d Brigade, 2d Div., Cavalry Corps, Army of the Cumberland (June-Aug. 1863); the 2d Brigade, 2d Div., Army of the Cumberland (Aug.-Nov. 1863); the 2d Brigade, 3d Div., Cavalry Corps, Army of the Cumberland (Nov. 1863-Oct. 1864); and the 2d Brigade, 3d Div., Cavalry Corps, Military Div. of the Mississippi (Oct. 1864-June 1865). During its term of service, the 10th participated in battles and campaigns at Murfreesboro, Tenn., Chickamauga, Ga., and Atlanta, Ga., as well as took part in Sherman's "March to the Sea." The regiment was mustered out on 24 July 1865 in Lexington, N.C., and its members were formally discharged and paid off at Camp Cleveland shortly thereafter. During its term of service, the 10th lost 3 officers and 34 enlisted men to hostile causes and 1 officer and 60 enlisted men to disease.

Daniel D. Hopper Papers, WRHS.

**TERMINAL TOWER.** *See* **CLEVELAND UNION TERMINAL**

The **TETIEVER AHAVATH ACHIM ANSHE SFARD** congregation was typical of the nationality-based Orthodox Jewish congregations that flourished in Cleveland during the pre-World War II years. Around 1900, a small group of Russian Jews from Tetiev established the Tetiever Verein, later to be known as the Tetiever Social & Benevolent Society. In 1909, members of the society joined with other Tetiever Jews to form a congregation. In Sept. 1910, the congregation incorporated as the Tetiever Ahavath Achim Anshe Sfard Congregation, formally under the leadership of Louis Goldberg, Jacob Weinman, and Kolman Kasner, among others. The Benevolent Society became an affiliate of the congregation. Congregants met for religious services in the homes of members until 1911, when a house was purchased at E. 40th near Woodland. In 1914, a synagogue was erected on the property, and the congregation worshipped there until 1927, when a new synagogue was dedicated on Linn Dr. in the Glenville neighborhood.

Rabbi Mordecai Landa was the first full-time religious leader hired by the congregation. He assumed the pulpit in 1931 and served for 22 years. Faced with the migration of Jews out of GLENVILLE into the eastern suburbs, the congregation was forced in 1954 to consider building at another location. Property was purchased on Warrensville Ctr. Rd., and the Linn property was sold. Services were held in a house on the property until a new building was completed in 1957. Two years later, the congregation merged with the KINSMAN JEWISH CTR. and Congregation N'vai Zedek to form the WARRENSVILLE CTR. SYNAGOGUE. Frank Tavens (Tavensky) was instrumental in effecting the merger. He was president of the Tetiever Congregation from 1940-59 and then served as the new congregation's first president. He was the son of Abraham Tavensky, one of the founders of the Tetiever Congregation. The congregation had several active affiliate groups besides the Benevolent Society, including the Tetiever Ladies Aid Society & Young Women's Relief Society. Its function was to encourage and assist new immigrants from Tetiev in settling in Cleveland. A Tetiever Ladies Auxiliary was established as a fundraising and support group for the congregation. During WORLD WAR II, the United Tetiever Service Organization was established to keep in contact with Tetievers who were serving in the armed forces.

Tetiever Ahavath Achim Anshe Sfard Congregation Records, WRHS.

**THAYER, LYMAN C.** (1821-23 Dec. 1863), was a Cleveland attorney and volunteer cavalry officer. Thayer was born in Berkshire, Mass. He was admitted to the bar in 1845 and became a well-known attorney in Boston. Moving to Cleveland in 1853, he formed a partnership in law with Geo. H. Wyman, with whom he was affiliated until 1856. In 1856 he formed a partnership with David Kellogg Cartter. After the outbreak of the CIVIL WAR, Thayer enlisted in the SECOND OHIO VOLUNTEER CAVALRY on 19 Aug. 1861. He served as regimental quartermaster during campaigns in Missouri, Kansas, and the Indian Territory before resigning because of ill health on 22 Mar. 1862. Once recuperated, he was commissioned a major in the TENTH OHIO VOLUNTEER CAVALRY on 10 Nov. 1862 at Camp Cleveland. Ill health again beset Thayer while he was campaigning in Tennessee. After a medical furlough, he returned to Tennessee, only to resign because of ill health on 6 Oct. 1863. He returned to Cleveland, succumbing to pleurisy at his residence at 20 Huron St. On 26 Dec. 1863, the Cleveland bar held a meeting at which appropriate resolutions were passed and speeches read in Thayer's honor.

Proctor Thayer Papers, WRHS.

**THEATER.** In a frontier situation, where the settlers must be self-sufficient, entertainment is usually a home-grown product. So it was in the village of Cleveland early in the 19th century, when amateur theater manifested itself. Play-readings and amateur performances, mostly in the schools, appear in the record with sufficient frequency to suggest that considerably more of the activity went unrecorded. Such activity eventually led to the forming of the first recorded community drama group. They called themselves the Theatre Royal Society, performed in a hall called the Shakespeare Gallery in the early spring of 1819, gave the proceeds to the village, and vanished from the record. The first known visit of a professional acting company to Cleveland was in 1820, when Wm. B. Blanchard and his troupe performed in the dining room of Mowery's Tavern, under conditions little more adequate than the elemental prescription for theater, "a passion and a plank."

The census of 1820 showed that Cleveland ranked 14th in population among settlements in the Reserve. The little village with the great potential had to wait 5 more years before a second company visited it. But in the long run, 1825 was significant to Cleveland for something much more important. It was the year that marked the opening of the Erie Canal and the beginning of work on the Ohio Canal. The Erie Canal was responsible for more shipping on the lake, and when the Ohio Canal was completed in 1832, with Cleveland as its northern terminus, the time had arrived for the explosion of growth that made it the chief city of northern Ohio, with far more people to be entertained (see OHIO & ERIE CANAL). Since the lake and the canal were the principal avenues of travel to and from the outside world, it followed that the theater season would be a summer one, coinciding with open season of transportation on those freshwater routes. Seeing this opportunity, in 1834, 2 enterprising actor-managers, Edwin Dean and David McKinney, put together a company of players to perform on a lake circuit formed by the triangle of Buffalo, Cleveland, and Detroit, with intermittent extension south on the canal to Columbus. In Cleveland, ITALIAN HALL served as the showplace for their productions for 4 seasons from 1834–37. With local backers, they were planning a fine new theater building for the city when the financial Panic of 1837 intervened. In 1810 J. W. Watson built a small theater on the 2d floor of a building on the north side of Superior Ave., between Bank (W. 6th) and Seneca (W. 3rd) streets. After 6 different names and ownership changes, as the GLOBE THEATER, it was razed in 1880.

The coming of the RAILROADS to Cleveland in the early 1850s precipitated another period of rapid growth. Joseph C. Foster continued the struggle to establish a permanent stock company in Cleveland. His effort found its focus at the Cleveland Theater on Center (Frankfort) St. By 1853, he had been successful enough to set about building a new, more satisfactory theater in the vicinity. In 1859, after a quick succession of names, that new theater became the ACADEMY OF MUSIC, and under that name it began its nearly 24-year tenure as Cleveland's premier legitimate theater. The man responsible for the lasting name and ascendancy of the "Old Drury," as it came to be known, was JOHN A. ELLSLER, who with his wife and daughter solidly established the stability and reputation of the stock company there as one of the finest in the country. As Cleveland entered the 1870s, a consensus gradually developed that the academy was becoming inadequate for the changing times. Ellsler took the lead, and the result in 1875 was a new first-rate theater for the city, the luxurious EUCLID AVE. OPERA HOUSE. Better times in the 1880s led to more theater building as the city continued to grow. In 1883, the Park Theater opened on the northwest quadrant of PUBLIC SQUARE, and in 1889 it became the LYCEUM THEATER. It was first managed by AUGUSTUS F. HARTZ. The CLEVELAND THEATER, another playhouse named for the city, opened in 1885. A tent theater, the Cleveland Pavillion Theatre, flourished that summer in the city. HALTNORTH'S GARDENS had popular alfresco entertainment at that time also. The COLUMBIA THEATER opened in 1887, presenting vaudeville, melodrama, and eventually burlesque. In the 1890s, theater became more flamboyant and sensational, striving for a surface kind of realism. In 1896, as the 10th-largest city in the nation, Cleveland celebrated its centennial. There were parades, pageants, and various amateur entertainments. An original opera was presented at the Euclid Ave. Opera House.

In the 19th century, the plays and the stagecraft, in terms of originality and innovation, were pretty much imported products, created and often packaged in New York. The reversal of this order in the case of "Uncle John Essler's School" at the Academy of Music, which contributed such performers as Clara Morris and EFFIE E. ELLSLER to the national acting scene and Abe Erlanger to management, was uncommon. Up to mid-century, the repertoire offered was typical enough; melodrama and spectacles, tragedies and comedies were all popular. Particularly popular on Cleveland stages also, and probably connected to the New England heritage in the Western Reserve, was the stage Yankee, that Down-Easter character, rustic, shrewd, and comic, and descended in numerous plays from Royall Tyler's Jonathan in *The Contrast* (1787). The effect of New England Puritanism on theater in Cleveland is more difficult to assess. John Ellsler, writing in his memoirs and reflecting on a lifetime of theater activity in Pittsburgh and Cleveland, and a fortune lost in Cleveland theaters, ruefully concluded that Pittsburgh was the better theater town, a conclusion that, if true at the time, would certainly be reversed in the next century. After mid-century, strong abolitionist sentiment gave stage adaptations of *Uncle Tom's Cabin* a unique popularity beyond their artistic merit. The existence of this fervent abolitionism alongside Jim Crow seating in some Cleveland theaters was an ironic fact of the times.

More new theaters came in with the century. The Empire Theater opened in 1900 on Huron Rd. with more vaudeville, as did the COLONIAL THEATER in 1903. Then in 1908 came the mighty HIPPODROME THEATER. This immense playhouse was awe-inspiring and in

963

many ways typified the ebullient spirit of the times. It was built to accommodate the realistic action-spectacles that the movies would soon be doing massively and more successfully. These national trends toward the colossal and superficial in entertainment were soon to be challenged by a counterforce: the Little Theater movement that began in Europe in the 1880s and spread to America in the new century. It was a movement that would soon profoundly and permanently affect the course of theater in Greater Cleveland. The year 1915 has to be noted as special in the annals of Cleveland theater history, for that is when 2 great and enduring theater organizations had their tentative beginnings: the CLEVELAND PLAY HOUSE and KARAMU. Both grew in different ways from the ideals and ferment of the Little Theater movement. While formal dramatic activity at Karamu did not begin until a few years later, 1915 was the year that 2 practical idealists, Rowena and RUSSELL JELLIFFE, came to Cleveland with their galvanizing beliefs that the cultural arts could make a significant contribution to race relations in an urban setting. The first full-fledged City Club ANVIL REVUE, which had evolved from its earlier stunt nights, was held in 1917. The 1920s witnessed the rapid rise of local theater organizations as the important tastemakers and educators of audiences. In addition to the Cleveland Play House and Karamu, another important force for the "new theater" was gradually coming into being at Western Reserve University. Barclay Leathem, working to overcome faculty prejudice against academic credit for theater studies, formed the Dept. of Speech there in 1927. By 1931, it had become the Dept. of Drama & Theater and was offering graduate study in the field. It was part of Leathem's vision to promote a working relationship between his department, the Play House, and Karamu, in which his students would gain practical experience working with seasoned actors and technicians in professional-level productions. On campus, his department's own pioneering productions helped to introduce students and local audiences to such important playwrights as O'Neill, Strindberg, Brecht, and Sartre.

The "wonderful year" for theater openings in Cleveland had to be 1921. In that year, PLAYHOUSE SQUARE sprang into being seemingly overnight. As a foreshadowing, the STILLMAN THEATER had opened for motion pictures 5 years earlier. But beginning 5 Feb. 1921, Loew's State opened as a million-dollar motion-picture palace. About a week later, the OHIO THEATER opened as the first legitimate house in the area, followed by the HANNA THEATER in March as a replacement for the Euclid Ave. Opera House, which closed permanently the following year. In April, the ALLEN THEATER made its bow as another million-dollar showplace for films. Then, toward the end of 1922, Keith's PALACE THEATER opened as the capstone of this remarkable grouping. Elsewhere in the city, at E. 6th and Lakeside, PUBLIC AUDITORIUM was dedicated on 15 Apr. 1922, with its huge stage and impressive architectural style. The Public Music Hall and the Little Theater were added in 1929 to form the complex.

The fall of 1929 brought the stock market crash, which became at once a jolting epilogue to the 1920s and a sobering prologue to the 1930s. The talkies and RADIO really came into their own as inexpensive entertainment. One amazing local phenomenon in radio was GENE CARROLL and Glenn Rowell doing their show "Gene & Glenn with Jake & Lena," heard on radio station WTAM. It attracted national attention. The Theater of Nations, beginning in 1930, boosted ethnic pride as a 3-year series of plays, presented in the Little Theater of Public Hall by nationality groups from around the city. Karamu's entry in the first series, *Roseanne*, brought the group additional citywide

attention when it was subsequently booked for a special week's engagement at the Ohio Theater. Indeed, the 1930s continued to bring them ever-widening recognition. Later in the decade, one of their own, LANGSTON HUGHES, turned to them as the group best suited to produce his plays. The collaboration that followed remains a rare example of what a playwright and a producing organization working together, over a period of time, can accomplish. The effort saw 6 plays by Hughes presented at Karamu in 4 years, 5 of them world premieres, and the 1930s are remembered with pride in Karamu lore as the "Hughes Decade."

As the Little Theater movement of the 2 previous decades began to fade into the less avant-garde community-theater trend of the next 2 decades, a group in LAKEWOOD espousing Little Theater ideals was organized and presented its first play in 1931 as Guild of the Masques. It soon became the LAKEWOOD LITTLE THEATER, which remains one of Cleveland's distinguished theater organizations. The GREAT LAKES EXPOSITION helped bolster the depressed spirits of the area in the summers of 1936–37. Of theater interest were abbreviated productions of some of Shakespeare's plays, presented in a reproduction of the Globe Playhouse, and in the second summer, Billy Rose's lavish swim spectacle, *Aquacade*. In CLEVELAND HTS. on 10 Aug. 1938, CAIN PARK THEATER, an open-air, community theater, was dedicated, having evolved from modest beginnings 4 years earlier. Under the direction of Dina Rees Evans, it made a unique and lasting contribution to theater here for both adults and children.

The 1940s and the total war effort pushed many peacetime activities aside; but youngsters were not neglected, with children's theater programs not only at Cain Park but also at the Cleveland Play House and, in the late 1940s, at the Lakewood Little Theater's School and the Children's Theater-on-the-Heights. At the college and university level, there were growing theater traditions at BALDWIN-WALLACE COLLEGE and JOHN CARROLL UNIVERSITY. The KOREAN WAR and McCarthyism set the anxious tone of the early 1950s. And the growth of TELEVISION accelerated the vogue for "home entertainment." But the appetite for live theater survived, as witnessed in 1954 by the establishment of MUSICARNIVAL, one of the first tent theaters in the U.S. In 1960, the Dobama Players put on their first play (see DOBAMA THEATER). Under the vigorous and imaginative leadership of Don Bianchi, they have carved a special niche for themselves in the area. Also in 1960, the drama group of the JEWISH COMMUNITY CTR. moved into their model new home, the Blanche R. Halle Theater, to continue a tradition of excellence in production that began in the latter 1940s. In an exciting example of community effort on many levels, the Great Lakes Shakespeare Festival, later the GREAT LAKES THEATER FESTIVAL, was established in 1962 in LAKEWOOD. On the other hand, the situation in Playhouse Square was far from inspiring. By the end of the 1960s, all the theaters in the area were closed except the Hanna, and the fine though battered old buildings were facing demolition. But in the early 1970s, the Playhouse Square Assoc., led by Ray Shepardson, began its battle to save the theaters and the area. Joined by business, other community allies, and the vigorously creative theater department at CLEVELAND STATE UNIVERSITY, it achieved a renaissance, and the future of the theaters has been assured.

In HIGHLAND HTS., the FRONT ROW, a large arena-style theater, opened in 1974, staging performances by national as well as local celebrities. In the early 1980s, significant developments in Cleveland theater included the revival of the 3 downtown theaters under the Playhouse

Square Foundation, and the moving of the Great Lakes Theater Festival from Lakewood to Playhouse Square. Another important development was the founding of the Cleveland Public Theater in 1984. A nonprofit corporation, it offers much-needed development opportunities to local playwrights, actors, and directors, and new and relevant ways to present the theatrical experience. Thus, from the perspective of the 1980s, the prospects for theater in Cleveland look good, especially for its local product. This has become more important as road shows continue to dwindle. The city is fortunate to have the Cleveland Play House looking forward to even greater accomplishment as one of the country's fine regional theaters, together with Karamu Theater, the Lakewood Little Theater, and the Great Lakes Theater Festival, each carrying on its own distinct tradition within the community.

Herbert R. Mansfield
Cleveland Public Library (retired)

The **THIRD FEDERAL SAVINGS AND LOAN ASSOCIATION OF CLEVELAND** has been a stable lending institution with headquarters in the Broadway area since 1938. Since then its assets have grown to more than $1 billion. Founded by Benjamin S. Stefanski with $50,000 in capital, Third Federal opened for business on 7 May 1938 at 6875 Broadway. By 1940 it had 3 offices, including a main office at 7007 Broadway, which was still its headquarters in 1983. Wladyslaw J. Nowak, publisher of the Polish newspaper *MONITOR CLEVELANDSKI*, served as Third Federal's first president; Stefanski began as its secretary-treasurer and was president by 1948, directing a company whose assets had grown to $9 million. The greatest period of growth in Third Federal's history came in the 1970s, when 6 mergers increased its holdings by $200 million. Still under Stefanski's direction, Third Federal had 16 branch offices and $1.08 billion in assets as of 30 June 1983.

The **THIRTY-SEVENTH OHIO VOLUNTEER INFANTRY REGIMENT**, 1861-65, was one of 3 Ohio CIVIL WAR regiments consisting primarily of German immigrants. Approximately 152 Clevelanders served in this regiment. The 37th was organized at Camp Brown (see CIVIL WAR CAMPS) during Aug. and Sept. 1861. It left for Camp Dennison, Ohio, at the end of September and was mustered into federal service on 2 Oct. 1861. During its term of service, the 37th was assigned to the following units: Benham's Brigade, District of the Kanawha (Oct. 1861-Mar. 1862); 2d Brigade, Kanawha Div., Dept. of the Mountains (Mar.-May 1862); 2d Brigade, Kanawha Div. (May-Aug. 1862); District of Kanawha, Dept. of the Ohio (Aug.-Dec. 1862); Ewing's Brigade, Kanawha Div. (Dec. 1862-Jan. 1863); 3d Brigade, 2d Div., 15th Army Corps, Army of the Tennessee (Jan.-Oct. 1863); 2d Brigade, 2d Div., 15th Army Corps, Army of the Tennessee (Nov. 1863-May 1865); and Dept. of Arkansas (June-Aug. 1865). During its period of service, the regiment took part in the following battles and campaigns: Logan Court House, Vicksburg, and Sherman's "March to the Sea." The 37th was mustered out on 7 Aug. 1865 at Little Rock, Ark. Its members were discharged and paid off at Camp Cleveland, Ohio, after 12 Aug. 1865. The regiment lost 9 officers and 102 enlisted men to hostile causes and 1 officer and 94 enlisted men to disease during its period of service.

37th Ohio Assoc., *Ninth Reunion of the Thirty-seventh Regiment, O.V.V.I.* (1890).

**THISTLEDOWN RACE TRACK** (est. 1925) was the area's major running track in 1986. Built by John H. McMillen

on land owned by Wm. B. Chisholm in the Village of N. RANDALL, Thistledown was opened for 1 racing season beginning 20 July 1925. However, legal complications and quarrels among the management led to its closing in 1926. A primary cause was State Attorney General C. C. Crabbe's campaign against corporately owned betting tracks. In 1928, Edward B. Strong purchased the track from receivers for $900,000 in the hope that Ohio would repeal its law against trackside betting. Until betting was legalized at state-controlled tracks in 1933, betting at Thistledown took place under the "contribution" system, whereby patrons could "invest" in or "contribute" to the ultimate success of a horse; that permitted bettors to make their own odds without the intervention of bookies or racetrack employees. Racing continued at Thistledown through the 1944 season, but a $500,000 fire on 29 Oct. 1944 wrecked the grandstand and clubhouse. Plans to rebuild and reopen were delayed by wartime restrictions on construction. In Aug. 1950, Cleveland Raceway Inc., a group of investors that included Cary Boshamer, M. B. Lesnick, Henry Gottfried, and Louis Pondfield, bought the track from Strong's estate. After a $3 million rebuilding program, it finally reopened on 11 Sept. 1953. The 1954 season, offering racing purses totaling $800,000, attracted horsemen from as far away as Rhode Island and Florida. By the 1980s, the racing season at Thistledown (set by the Ohio Racing Commission) averaged 190 days per year and included the Summit, Randall, Thistledown, and Cranwood meetings. The most prestigious race held is the Ohio Derby for 3-year-old runners. Begun in 1876 but not run 57 times, it is the 8th-oldest race in the U.S. and, with a $150,000 purse, one of the richest for 3-year-olds. By 1986 it had been held 52 times at Thistledown; it also had been run at Chester Park in Cincinnati, Bainbridge Park, Cranwood Park, and RANDALL PARK RACE TRACK. In 1959, Edward DeBartolo purchased Thistledown for $5 million and made slight improvements in the facility. Despite protests from employees and horsemen about the poor condition of the barns, no major renovations were undertaken until 1981. By this time Sunday racing, begun in 1974, had been canceled, as the generally poor economic climate affected racing. In 1983, the Thoroughbred track, the state's largest, attracted 895,689 customers who wagered $114.8 million on the races, but the track lost nearly $1 million. After the state legislature gave the racing industry a $12.4 million annual tax break in 1984, Thistledown launched a $25 million modernization and renovation program to elevate the track from its average status to "one of North America's premier racetracks." Its average "handle" of $643,785 in 1985 ranked it 33d among the 54 major tracks in the U.S.

The **THOMAS H. WHITE CHARITABLE TRUST** was founded in 1913 by THOS. HOWARD WHITE (1836-1914). White, a manufacturer of sewing machines during the CIVIL WAR, moved to Cleveland from Orange, Mass., in 1865. He formed the White Sewing Machine Co. in 1876. One of his sons, ROLLIN H. WHITE, invented the White Steamer automobile in 1906, and along with 2 other sons, Walter and Windsor, Thos. White formed the WHITE MOTOR CO., which manufactured trucks. Rollin White formed the Cleveland Tractor Co. in 1914. Thos. White donated a sculpture studio to the Cleveland School of Art, and he was a trustee of the Case School of Applied Science. He was also a patron of the WESTERN RESERVE HISTORICAL SOCIETY. White was married to Almira Greenleaf White and had 4 sons, Windsor T., Clarence G., Rollin H., and Walter C., and a daughter, Ella White Ford.

The White estate was first divided among the children, and then went into trust. The estate was first distributed for charitable purposes in 1939. The purposes of the trust, administered by AMERITRUST in 1985, are for education and charitable purposes for the city of Cleveland only. Such purposes include scholarships, scientific research, care for the sick, aged, and helpless, and recreation for all classes in Cleveland. The trust awards $150,000 annually in minority-student college scholarships. No grants go to individuals or for endowments, operation budgets, annual campaigns, deficit financing, land acquisition, research, publications, or conferences. In 1983, the assets of the trust were $4,793,545, with expenditures of $338,250 for 59 grants.

**THOMAS W. EASTON'S SONS, INC.,** was established in 1870 as an industrial moving concern by Thos. W. Easton. The firm's services included the rigging and hauling of heavy machinery and equipment, as well as steel erection, crane and equipment rental, and warehouse services. It is located at 8915 Crane Ave. While continuing to move major equipment, Easton's has responded to the changing high-technology economy by specializing in the transportation and installation of medical diagnostic equipment and automated systems. The company, which operates locally and in the northeast quadrant of the U.S., is now a division of Forest City Erectors, Inc., the local company that installed the computerized scoreboard at the Cleveland Stadium. However, it is managed by the 4th generation of Eastons.

**THOME, JAMES A.** (20 Jan. 1813–4 Mar. 1873), was a prominent Presbyterian minister in Cleveland. In the years preceding the CIVIL WAR, he was an activist in the antislavery movement. Thome was born in Augusta, Ky. He was raised in a strict Presbyterian home that provided him with a strong religious background. He confronted the issue of slavery early in his life, as his own father was a slaveowner. Thome attended school, and later college, in Augusta. In 1833 he entered the Lane Seminary in Cincinnati, where he studied theology under Dr. Lyman Beecher. Between 1835–36 he attended Oberlin College, where he received a degree in theology. He married Anna S. Allen of Fairfield, Conn., in 1838.

From 1838–48, Thome filled the chair of rhetoric and belles lettres at Oberlin College. During this period he was actively involved in the antislavery movement, then centered in Oberlin. He later turned to the ministry, serving as minister of the First Presbyterian Church of Brooklyn (Ohio City) from 1848–71. Thome first came under the influence of northern abolitionists while attending the Lane Seminary. Along with several other students, he was ousted from the seminary for his extreme views. Many of these students, including Thome, matriculated at Oberlin, an institution more supportive of their beliefs. In 1836, Thome became actively involved with the American Anti-Slavery Society. That year, its officers chose Thome to go on a 6-month tour of the West Indies to report on the progress of emancipation there. The society published an account of his travels in 1838. In 1840, Thome jointly authored a paper, "Slavery and the Internal Trade in the United States," that was submitted to the General Anti-Slavery Convention held in London.

As minister of the First Presbyterian Church of Brooklyn (founded in 1834), Thome continued to espouse the cause of freedom for black slaves. Throughout this period, he was active in raising funds to support black education. After the Civil War, in 1867, he took a year-long sabbatical from his ministry and went to England to seek aid from benevolent societies for the purpose of helping freed slaves. Thome's church united with the Congregationalists in 1857 and became the First Congregational Church of Cleveland.

He resigned as minister in 1871, ostensibly for health reasons. A few years later he died of pneumonia in Chattanooga, Tenn., where he had gone to continue his ministry.

**THOMPSON, CHARLES EDWIN** (16 July 1870–14 Oct. 1933), was a pioneer in the Cleveland automotive industry. His development of the Thompson Valve made possible high-powered automobile and aircraft engines. Thompson was born in McIndoe Falls, Vt., to Thomas and Mary Ann Young Thompson. He attended elementary school in Lynn, Mass., and the Boston Preparatory School. He came to Cleveland in 1892 as an inspector and branch manager for the Cleveland Telephone Co. In 1898, he was promoted to district manager with the Bell Co. in Dallas, but for family reasons he returned to Cleveland in 1900. With the help of J. A. Krider and W. D. Bartlett in 1901, Thompson organized the Cleveland Cap Screw Co. In 1905, he became the general manager, and the name of the company was changed to the Electric Welding Prods. Co., specializing in the welding of automobile chassis and bicycle parts. In 1916, Electric Welding merged with 2 Detroit firms, the Michigan Welding Prods. Co. and the Metals Welding Co., to form the Steel Prods. Co. A major problem with the early automobile engines was the need for engine valves that could withstand tremendous stress. Thompson helped devise a method of increasing the durability of the engine valve by electrically welding the head to the stem. In 1917, he developed a method of forging a solid 1-piece valve from steel alloy. Inspired by a magazine article on a nickel steel alloy developed in Germany, Thompson, in 1920, perfected a method of fabricating a high-resistance steel engine valve composed of a chromium, nickel, and silicon alloy. This process gave Steel Prods. such a lead in the field that by the latter part of the 1920s, almost all American cars used the Thompson Valve, as did Chas. Lindbergh on his transatlantic solo flight in 1927. In 1924, Steel Prods. entered the replacement-parts business, building an organization of 800 distributors. In 1926, in recognition of Thompson's leadership in the field, the name of the company was changed to Thompson Prods. (see TRW INC.). In 1929, Thompson began sponsoring the Thompson Trophy Race at the NATL. AIR RACES in an effort to further American leadership in the development of high-speed land planes. Thompson married Maora Hubbard (d. 1900) in 1889, Alberta Brown in 1919 (div. 1927), and Gloria Hayes Hopkins in 1927. He had 6 children, Edwin, Howard, Kenneth, Thomas, LaRene, and Mrs. Philip Farley. Upon his death, Thompson's body was cremated, and the ashes were released over PUBLIC SQUARE from a plane piloted by his friend Jas. Doolittle.

TRW Records, WRHS.

**THOMPSON, HINE & FLORY,** one of Cleveland's most respected law firms, has been engaged in the general practice of law under its present (1986) name for over 70 years. Beginning with its principal office in Cleveland, the firm expanded, opening offices in Columbus, Washington, D.C., and Palm Beach. In 1986, TH&F employed 175 lawyers, who in addition to their practice are involved in various professional activities and community and government service. In 1907, Amos Burt Thompson, the firm's founding member, formed a partnership with Chas. P. Hine. In 1912, Walter L. Flory joined both Thompson and Hine in the Society for Savings Bldg., where the firm advertised as Thompson, Hine & Flory. The firm moved to temporary offices in the Old Arcade, then to the Brotherhood of Locomotive Engineers Bldg. until Oct. 1925, when it took up office at the old Natl. City Bank Bldg., its present (1986) location. Greater Cleveland's prominence as a national law center nurtured TH&F's rapid growth. Up until 1942, the firm maintained a policy of "growth from within." Hiring only the most qualified graduates out of law school, the firm soon expanded to take over 5 floors of the NCB Bldg. With the proliferation of specialty areas in law after WORLD WAR II, TH&F found it necessary to "grow from without" through mergers with smaller firms and partnerships. That enabled it to expand its practice to include areas such as admiralty law and increase administrative-agency business by opening offices outside the Cleveland area. In 1986, TH&F's Cleveland office employed 134 lawyers and a staff of 242, including paralegals. The Columbus office had 22 lawyers, and the Washington, D.C., office 17. Given the firm's strong committment to public service, its lawyers have traditionally held prominent roles in the community, professional, and corporate life of Greater Cleveland. Amos Thompson served longer than any other individual as a director of the Cleveland Trust Co. (AMERITRUST). Walter Flory was a key organizer and supporter of the CLEVELAND PLAY HOUSE. Other members of the firm have served as Ohio attorney general, justice of the Ohio Supreme Court, and president of the Ohio Bar Assoc. In setting legal precedent, Jerome Fisher argued the first case in Ohio in behalf of Planned Parenthood, upholding the organization's right to distribute birth-control literature.

**THORMAN, SIMSON** (1811–12 June 1881), businessman and Jewish community leader, was the first permanent Jewish resident of Cleveland. Born in Unsleben, Bavaria, Thorman immigrated to the U.S. by the late 1820s. He passed through Cleveland in 1832, purchasing land at Erie (E. 9th) and Woodland streets. He then continued west as far as Donaphin, Mo., where he was a trapper and also purchased land that remained in his family for 150 years. Thorman returned to Cleveland in 1837 and settled in the FLATS on Mercer St. He continued in the hide and fur business, making periodic trips to St. Louis, where he purchased pelts from trappers and Indians. Although he remained in this business until his retirement, he also owned a grocery for a short period of time, and in the late 1850s he owned a cattleyard and slaughterhouse at Case (E. 40th) and Croton streets. In 1839, several friends and acquaintances from Unsleben settled in Cleveland. During that year, Thorman and his cousins Aaron Lowentritt and Isaac Hoffman established the Israelitic Society of Cleveland, the city's first Jewish congregation. The following year, Thorman was one of the incorporators of the WILLETT ST. CEMETERY, the city's first Jewish burial ground, which he gave to the city. He was among the founders and served as first president (1853–59) of the Solomon Lodge No. 6 of B'NAI B'RITH, the first chapter of B'nai B'rith in Cleveland. In 1867, he served 1 term on CLEVELAND CITY COUNCIL. Thorman married Regina Klein (1816–1885) in 1840, the first Jewish marriage in the city. During that same year, a son, Samuel, was born, the first Jewish child born in the city. In all, the Thormans had 11 children.

The **331ST INFANTRY REGIMENT** was in service during WORLD WAR I as part of the U.S. Army 83d Infantry Div. Composed entirely of Clevelanders ages 21–31 who were drafted into the Army, the regiment included companies A, B, C, D, H, and L and a supply company. Basic training of the new recruits was conducted at Camp Sherman, located 2.5 mi. northwest of Chillicothe, Ohio.

The **332D INFANTRY REGIMENT** was in service during WORLD WAR I as part of the U.S. Army 83d Infantry Div. It was composed of Clevelanders ages 21–31 who were drafted into the Army. Commanded by Capt. John Dempsey, the 332d saw action during the war in Italy, and shortly after the armistice marched into conquered Austria.

**THROCHMORTON, ARCHIBALD HALL** (28 Mar. 1876–20 May 1938), was a legal scholar and educator. He earned the reputation of giving unsparingly to his students and every good cause. Throchmorton was born in Loudon County, Va., to Mason and Annie Humphrey Throchmorton. Educated in Loudon County public schools, he spent much of his time as a youth in the courtroom of his father, a Virginia justice of the peace. He received the A.B. degree from Roanoke College in 1896, the A.M. degree from Princeton University, where he studied jurisprudence with Woodrow Wilson, in 1897, and the LL.B. degree from Washington & Lee University in 1900. He was admitted to the bar in Virginia in 1900, in Kentucky in 1905, in Indiana in 1912, and in Ohio in 1917. From 1900–02, Throchmorton practiced law in Leesburg, Va. From 1902–11, he was dean of Central University of Kentucky in Danville. From 1911–14, he was professor of law at Indiana University. From 1914 until his death, he was a professor of law at Western Reserve University Law School, teaching torts, constitutional law, and pleadings. Noted as a legal scholar, Throchmorton wrote extensively. His *Ohio General Code* (1921) became the authoritative text. As editor of *Cooley on Torts*, Throchmorton rewrote the original text of the legal classic to bring it up to date. His other works included *Cases on Contracts* (1913), *Cases on Evidence* (1913), *Cases on Equity Jurisprudence* (1923), and *Cases on Code Pleadings* (1926). He was coeditor of *Clark on Contracts* (4th ed., 1937) and *Cases on Contracts* (2d ed., 1931). A strong advocate of individual liberties, Throchmorton frequently denounced what he saw as efforts to establish state socialism in America. He felt America needed more common sense, less legislative and bureaucratic interference with business, less suppression of the individual, and more encouragement of individual initiative. He opposed the ratification of a child-labor amendment to the U.S. Constitution and Pres. Franklin Roosevelt's attempt to increase the number of justices on the U.S. Supreme Court. Throchmorton was a member of the Cleveland Hts. Charter Commission in 1921. He served on the Cleveland Hts. Board of Health, as president of the Cleveland CITY CLUB (1926), and as a director of the Cleveland Hts. Savings & Loan Co. and the Cleveland and Ohio bar associations. Throchmorton married Julia Elizabeth Painter on 29 June 1899.

**THUNDERWATER, CHIEF.** *See* **CHIEF THUNDERWATER**

**THWING, CHARLES FRANKLIN** (9 Nov. 1853–29 Aug. 1937), author, lecturer, educator, university president, and clergyman, was born in New Sharon, Maine, the eldest of 5 children of Joseph Perkins and Hanna Morse Hopkins Thwing. He was educated at Phillips Academy, Andover, Mass., graduating in 1871 with honors. He entered Harvard College (1872), was elected to Phi Beta Kappa at the end of his sophomore year, and graduated with honors in history and philosophy (1876). He attended Andover Theological Seminary, graduating in 1879, and was ordained to the Congregational ministry in 1879. On 8 Sept. 1879 he married Carrie F. Butler of Farmington, Maine. The couple had 3 children: Mary Butler (Mrs. Jas. M.) Shallenberger; Francis Wendell Butler-Thwing, who made his home in England; and Apphia (Mrs. Roy K.) Hack. Carrie Thwing died on 24 Apr. 1898. Thwing was pastor of the North Ave. Congregational Church of Cambridge, Mass., from

1879–86, and pastor of the Plymouth Congregational Church of Minneapolis, Minn., from 1886–90. On 11 Nov. 1890 he became president of Adelbert College and Western Reserve University. On 11 Mar. 1891 he was inaugurated as WRU's 6th president. At that time, Reserve consisted of Adelbert College, the College for Women, and the School of Medicine. During Thwing's 31-year administration, the School of Library Science (1904), the School of Applied Social Sciences (1916), the School of Law, the School of Dentistry, the Graduate School (1892), the School of Pharmacy (1919), and subsequently the Dept. of Religious Education and the School of Education became part of WRU. Over 26 new buildings were erected; enrollment increased from 246 to 2,000–5,000, and instructors from 37 to 415. On 22 Dec. 1906, Thwing married Mary Gardiner Dunning of Auburn, N.Y. An 1897 graduate of Vassar College, she was the first president of the Cleveland WOMEN'S CITY CLUB and a founder of the School of Nursing and was active in social, educational, and philanthropic affairs. She died 8 Oct. 1931.

Thwing received innumerable honors, including a Doctor of Divinity degree from Chicago Theological Seminary (1889); the LL.D. from Marietta College (1894), Illinois College (1894), Waynesburg College (1901), and Washington & Jefferson University (1910); the Doctor of Literature from the University of Pennsylvania (1917); and the Doctor of Literature & Humanities from WRU (1926). He received the Cleveland Chamber of Commerce Medal for Distinguished Public Service (1925); was a life senator of United Chapters of Phi Beta Kappa (national president 1922–28); and was a member of the Society of Arts & Sciences, the American Historical Assoc., the Author's Club of London, the British-American Club at Oxford, the Century Club of New York, and the American Academy of Arts & Sciences. He was a trustee of the CLEVELAND CLINIC, the HIRAM HOUSE Social Settlement, and the Carnegie Foundation for the Advancement of Teaching (1905–21). Dr. Thwing, affectionately known as "Prexy," resigned on 11 Nov. 1921 at age 68; he was made president emeritus and was given his home on Bellflower Rd. as a permanent residence. He continued to travel and to write, publishing over 400 articles for professional journals and over 50 books, including *Guides, Philosophers, and Friends* (1927) and its sequel, *Friends of Mine* (1933). Thwing died in Cleveland and was buried in LAKE VIEW CEMETERY.

Cramer, Clarence H., *Case Western Reserve* (1976).

The **TIEDEMANN HOUSE**, located at 4308 Franklin Ave., is the most noted and one of the most architecturally distinguished residences on Franklin Ave., the west side equivalent of famous Euclid Ave. Its notoriety as a haunted house came as it was called "Franklin Castle" in the late 20th century. Its builder, Hannes Tiedemann (1832–1908), was a wholesale grocer in the firm of Weidemann & Tiedemann beginning in 1864. In 1883 he was a founder and vice-president of the Savings & Trust Co., one of the first institutions organized in Ohio under the law permitting the formation of trust companies. The family lived continously at this address from 1866–95, and the present Queen Anne-style house was erected in 1881. The house's architects, Cudell & Richardson (identified by a carved stone on the house), were Cleveland's most important architectural firm in the 1880s. The style of the house, a large rock-faced sandstone mansion with a round corner tower, was exactly contemporary with architectural developments in Chicago and New York. Tiedemann died in 1908 at the age of 75. In the 20th century the house was occupied by a German singing society, the Deutsche Socialisten, and later by the Bildungsverein Eintracht club. The spurious haunted-house stories do not seem to predate 1965.

**TIFERETH ISRAEL CONGREGATION.** *See* **TEMPLE** (The)

**TILLEY, MADISON** (1809–30 Oct. 1887), was an early black political leader and a successful businessman. Born in slavery, Tilley escaped to Ohio as a young man, and ca. 1837 he came to Cleveland, where he worked as a boatman and later as a teamster. According to his *PLAIN DEALER* obituary, Tilley "obtained a fair education and accumulated considerable property" in Cleveland. By 1840, he was one of only 5 blacks in the city who owned taxable property. He worked as an excavating contractor with 20 wagons and 40 horses and employed an integrated workforce that at times numbered 100 men. His business success enabled him to acquire property in the old Haymarket district and to leave an estate estimated at $25,000-$30,000 at the time of his death. Although reportedly illiterate, the politically active Tilley became an aggressive leader in the city's black community, using his forceful personality and public-speaking ability to promote the value of the ballot to blacks. He changed political views several times during his career, beginning as a Whig, later becoming a Republican, and finally switching to the Democratic party. In 1885, he was an unsuccessful candidate for the state legislature. He was also one of the local delegates to the 1854 NATL. EMIGRATION CONVENTION held in Cleveland. By the time Tilley died at his Hill St. home after a long bout with dropsy, he had gained the respect of both blacks and whites in Cleveland. The *CLEVELAND GAZETTE* noted the "vast attendance of both white and colored" at his funeral, and the *Plain Dealer* praised him as "a man of unusual force of character, of rare judgement, and of great moral courage." Tilley's wife, Rachel, whom he had married in Chillicothe, died on 26 Apr. 1879 at age 60.

*TIME MAGAZINE* was published in Cleveland from 1925–27 in an effort to improve its delivery time to the West Coast. Begun in New York by Britton Hadden and Henry R. Luce in 1923, the fledgling "Weekly Newsmagazine" was often reaching western subscribers 3 days behind schedule. Luce made the decision to relocate in Cleveland during his partner's absence in Europe. In order to save the company from responsibility for moving expenses, editorial employees were dismissed in New York on 17 Aug. 1925 but were promised reemployment if they applied in Cleveland on 19 Aug. *Time*'s first Cleveland issue appeared on 31 Aug. 1925, printed at the Penton Press at W. 3rd St. and Lakeside Ave. (see PENTON-IPC). One windfall from the move was approval of the magazine's application to the U.S. Post Office for reclassification as a weekly newspaper, which made it eligible for priority handling; it had been unsuccessful in its attempt to win this favor in New York. *Time*'s renewed application was helped by the sponsorship of the Cleveland Chamber of Commerce and Congressman THEODORE E. BURTON.

*Time*'s founders were divided in their feelings toward their new home. Cleveland provided the China-born Luce with an American hometown he had never had, and he comfortably settled with his young family in CLEVELAND HTS. To the bachelor Hadden, Cleveland was a bastion of Babbittry only slightly ameliorated by the opportunity it afforded him to organize his own sandlot baseball team. Citing Cleveland's remoteness from news sources, Hadden took advantage of a European vacation by Luce to move the editorial staff back to New York in the summer of 1927. Cleveland had been good to *Time*, nevertheless. Circulation climbed from 70,000 to 111,000 during the Cleveland years, and the magazine's cover also acquired its distinctive red border at the Penton Press. During a cash-flow crisis at the end of 1925, an overdraft granted by Central Natl. Bank had enabled the magazine to meet its payroll until holiday subscriptions replenished its coffers. Although *Time* moved its printing facilities to Chicago shortly after returning the editorial department to New York, it continued to deposit its circulation receipts at Central Natl. through 1983.

Elson, Robert T., *Time Inc.* (1968).

**TINKER'S CREEK,** a powerful stream that dissected old Bedford Twp., was responsible for early economic development in the area, and remains a beautiful park spot in the Metroparks system. Named for Capt. Joseph Tinker, one of MOSES CLEAVELAND's surveyors, Tinker's Creek originates in Streetsboro as a lazy stream and becomes stronger as tributaries supplement its flow northward. Entering Cuyahoga County at GLENWILLOW, the creek flows for 7 twisted miles through Bedford Twp. east to west through OAKWOOD, BEDFORD, BEDFORD HTS., and WALTON HILLS. Before exiting into VALLEY VIEW, where it empties into the CUYAHOGA RIVER, the creek flows through a deep, narrow gorge and erupts into a waterfall at Bedford. As early as 1815, entrepreneurs tapped the waterpower of the falls for manufacturing and for milling flour, logs, cider, and textiles; for a time, the falls even powered a rolling mill, which later moved to Massillon. The most prominent mill was the Waters & Son Mill, which ground feed for farmers and produced 4 different grades of wheat, buckwheat, and graham flour, including the regionally prominent Pansy brand. The last of the mills ceased operation in 1908. The sheerness and rockiness of the Tinker's Creek gorge made much of the land along the creek bed inaccessible and useless for homes and farming, and insured its preservation as a wilderness area. Its many scenic points, including Lost Meadow, Dearlick, the Arch, and Red Bridge, offered excellent fishing and good sites for picnicking. Part of this area was opened in 1902 as a resort for open-air dancing and picnicking; by 1924, an elegant dance hall and bowling emporium were built for year-round use. Until it was destroyed by fire in 1944, this pavilion attracted streetcar loads of people who danced to Ed Day and the 10 Knights (also called the Bedford Glens Orchestra). In 1926, the park board added 1,000 acres of Tinker's Creek Glen to its growing Metropark system; as Bedford Reservation, the park was improved with roads, bridle paths, and shelters. Currently, the park remains a vital link in Cleveland's Emerald Necklace. Its gorges were recognized as Registered Natl. Natural Landmarks by the U.S. Park Service in 1968.

**TOD, DAVID** (21 Feb. 1805–13 Nov. 1868), was a pioneer in developing the coal and iron-ore deposits in the Mahoning Valley, and was governor of Ohio during the CIVIL WAR. Tod was born near Youngstown, Ohio, to George and Sarah Tod. He received his early education in the nearby common school and later attended Burton Academy in Geauga County. After studying law in the office of Powell Stone in Warren, he was admitted to the Ohio state bar in 1827, entering private practice with Matthew Burchard. A supporter of Andrew Jackson, Tod was appointed postmaster in Warren in 1832. He was elected to the state senate in 1838, returning to private practice in 1840. After being narrowly defeated for governor in 1844, he started the project of developing the coal and iron-ore deposits in the Mahoning Valley, shipping the coal to Cleveland and

other lake markets. In 1847, Pres. Jas. Polk appointed Tod as ambassador to Brazil. Serving 4½ years, he helped to restore normal relations between the two countries and succeeded in recovering claims of American citizens amounting to $300,000. In 1852, he returned home to Youngstown and his coal and iron interests, meanwhile serving as the second president of the Cleveland & Mahoning Railroad. A delegate to the 1860 Democratic Natl. Convention, Tod later became an ardent supporter of Abraham Lincoln. With the support of the Union party, a combination of Democrats and Republicans who supported the war effort, Tod won the Ohio governorship in 1862. That year he moved his family to Cleveland. Living in a home at St. Clair Ave. and Bond (E. 6th) St., he quickly became one of the city's most prominent citizens. Tod spent most of his term as governor dealing with the problems of the Civil War, but because of some poor decisions and appointments, the Union party chose not to renominate him. After leaving office in 1864, he returned to Youngstown to tend to his numerous business interests. Poor health forced him to decline Lincoln's offer of the position of secretary of the treasury. Chosen to serve as a presidential elector in 1868, Tod died before the Electoral College selected the new president. Tod married Maria Smith on 4 June 1832. They had 7 children.

**TODD, THOMAS WINGATE** (15 Jan. 1885–28 Dec. 1938), professor of anatomy at the Western Reserve University Medical School, was internationally known for his studies of the growth and development of children. Todd was born in Sheffield, England, to James and Katharine Wingate Todd. He completed his secondary education in Nottingham and graduated with the M.B. and Ch.B. degrees from Manchester University and London Hospital in 1907, having attained honors in the study of anatomy, physiology, and surgery. He served at Manchester as a junior and senior demonstrator of anatomy, 1907–08, and lecturer on anatomy and clinical anatomy, 1910–12; and at the Royal Infirmary as house surgeon and lecturer, 1909. During WORLD WAR I, Capt. Todd served as surgical medical officer with the 110th Canadian Regiment base hospital in London, Ontario. Appointed Henry Wilson Payne Professor of Anatomy at WRU by Dean CARL HAMANN, Todd came to America in 1912. In 1920, he became director of the Hamann Museum of Comparative Anthropology & Anatomy. In teaching, Todd was an innovator, using roentgenology and fluoroscopy extensively, and devising a stereoscopic slide projector for his lectures. With the opening of the new WRU School of Medicine facilities in 1924, he created a modern department of anatomy, which included a medical librarian, a statistician, a medical illustrator, a machinist, a photographic staff, animal facilities, and an embalmer and assistants. He continued to build the Hamann Museum, adding a curator and assembling a comprehensive osteologic collection, including the world's largest collection of anthropoid skeletons and the largest collection of documented human skeletons. He authored *The Atlas of Skeletal Maturation*, a study that enabled doctors to determine the health and maturation of children by examining the bones of their hands. Todd married Eleanor Pearson on 9 Nov. 1912. The Todds had 3 children, Arthur, Donald, and Eleanor.

**TOLL ROADS** were once common in Cuyahoga County. They were a means of advancing transportation for commodity goods and services throughout the county to its large market centers. The first toll road in Cuyahoga County, the Wooster Turnpike, was built by land developers Lord & Barber in 1824. Its route began in Cleveland and ended in Wooster. It followed what is now Pearl Rd./Rt. 42. It ceased operations ca. 1843, when the toll gates were destroyed by a mob over excessive toll charges. By 1827, few toll roads existed in the old Brooklyn area. The State, Pleasant Valley, Broadview, and Schaaf roads were privately constructed. A plank road called Fullerton was a toll road at Schaaf and Rose (Pleasant Valley) roads until 1890. In 1830, a turnpike was built from BEDFORD by way of TINKER'S CREEK through NEWBURGH to Broadway Ave. In 1835, the Parma Independence Plank Road was completed. Its exact route is not clear. It ceased operations after 1900.

In 1845, a new, second toll road along what is now Pearl Rd. was proposed; it was established in 1849 as the Wayne, Medina, & Cuyahoga Turnpike Co. It ceased operations ca. 1852, when a railroad built a depot in BEREA, which diverted the traffic to it. In 1848, the Lorain St. Plank Road ran from Puritas Springs Rd. to W. 98th St. Tollgate houses were at Lorain and W. 98th, Highland Ave., W. 117th, Triskett Rd., and Wooster Rd. in what is now FAIRVIEW PARK. In 1849, a toll plank road was completed from Cleveland to CHAGRIN FALLS. Other plank toll roads ran from Cleveland to Willoughby and ROCKPORT. In Cleveland, Euclid Ave. was a state road covered with planks from Perry (E. 22nd) St. to the city limits.

By 1870, most of the plank roads had disappeared because of exposure to the sun, rain, and snow. With the heavy loads and shod horses, the planks quickly crumbled, since they were not kept in repair. Many turnpike companies failed because of declining revenues on the routes or mismanagement. About 1872, the Linndale Plank Road Co. was established. It began at Pearl Rd. and Memphis Ave. in Cleveland, went west past W. 73rd St., and ended at W. 117th and West Blvd. near LINNDALE Village. In 1875 it merged to become the Cleveland, Linndale & Berea Plank Road Co. The route to Berea began at Purtis Corners along Rocky River Dr. south to Berea. A date for the end of operation for this road cannot be determined. In 1876, a third toll plank road along what is now Pearl Rd. was established by the Brighton & Parma Toll Road Co. Its route was 5 mi. long, beginning at what is now Pearl and State roads in Cleveland and ending at Pearl and York roads in PARMA HTS. It ceased operations in 1907, and was replaced by a brick road in 1908. In 1885, the State Road Plank Road Co. was established. It began at State Rd. and Brookpark Rd. in Cleveland and extended south about 5 mi. No date for cessation of operation can be determined. The Ohio Turnpike, which was begun in 1949, is the most recent toll road to have been built in Cuyahoga County.

**TOLLES, HOGSETT, GINN & MORLEY** was a prominent Cleveland law firm of the 1910s–1920s specializing in business law. Much of its work was for railroads and utilities. The firm was formed in 1913 by the merger of 2 established Cleveland firms: Kline, Tolles, & Morley and Blandin, Hogsett & Ginn. Sheldon H. Tolles (1 Oct. 1858–14 July 1926) had been involved in a number of partnerships with Virgil P. Kline since beginning his Cleveland practice in the early 1880s; ca. 1901, John E. Morley (13 Jan. 1874–8 Jan. 1947) joined their staff in Kline, Carr, Tolles, & Goff. Ca. 1908, they formed Kline, Tolles, & Morley. Blandin, Hogsett & Ginn had its origins in 1892, when FRANK H. GINN (25 Feb. 1868–16 Feb. 1938) was admitted to the Ohio bar and joined the practice of E. J. Blandin and Wm. L. Rice; by 1898, they had formed the partnership of Blandin, Rice, & Ginn. In 1912, Thos. H. Hogsett (1858–17 July 1931) joined the firm, which then became Blandin, Hogsett, & Ginn. When it was created in 1913, Tolles, Hogsett, Ginn, & Morley established offices in the Williamson Bldg. The partners in the firm provided

legal counsel for a number of local business institutions, such as the Union Trust Co. Sheldon H. Tolles was active in the street railway disputes, served as counsel for the EAST OHIO GAS CO. and American Telephone & Telegraph, and was division counsel for both the Ohio Bell Telephone Co. and the Baltimore & Ohio Railroad. John Morley was also a specialist in corporate law before leaving the firm in the 1920s to manage real-estate interests. Frank Ginn was an associate of the VAN SWERINGEN brothers and served as a director of both the Chesapeake & Ohio and Pere Marquette railroads. On 18 Nov. 1938, with Tolles, Hogsett, and Ginn dead and Morley in business elsewhere, the partners of Tolles, Hogsett & Ginn announced plans to merge with the firm of Day, Young, Veach, & LeFever to create the firm of Jones, Day, & Reavis effective 1 Jan. 1939 (see JONES, DAY, REAVIS & POGUE).

The **TONG WARS** were outbreaks of violence between rival societies within Cleveland's Chinese community in the 1910s and 1920s. Such violent outbursts were not unique to Cleveland's Chinatown but reflected the hostilities and rivalry between tongs nationally. Violence between the ON LEONG TONG and the Hip Sing Tong first occurred in Cleveland not long after Chinese businessman Dar Game formed the latter organization in the city in early 1911. The Hip Sing Tong, which met at the Hep Lin Wah Co. at 1287 Ontario St., soon challenged the On Leong Tong's power within the Chinese community, and on 20 Nov. 1911, 30-year-old Woo Dip, a member of the On Leong Tong, was shot 3 times in his tong's meeting room in the basement of a grocery store at 1279 Ontario. Witnesses identified the gunman as Leong Young, a member of the Hip Sing Tong.

At first the shooting was explained as part of a dispute over a $2 gambling debt, but it was later alleged to be the penalty assessed against Woo Dip by the Hip Sing Tong for his refusal to pay $2 in protection money. Police launched a massive search for Young; according to the *Plain Dealer*, they "raided every Chinese restaurant and laundry" in the city and "pulled Chinese from their beds and searched their quarters, but made no arrests." Young escaped the search, but, with the assistance of national representatives from the On Leong Tong and the testimony of 2 disaffected local members of the Hip Sing Tong, 2 other members of the Hip Sing Tong were convicted in the attack on Woo Dip. Members of the Hip Sing Tong charged that its convicted members were victims of a conspiracy on the part of the On Leong Tong.

No tong-related killings were reported in Ohio between 1913–24, but by the summer of 1924 tensions between the 2 rival tongs again were running high in Cleveland. On 29 May 1924, a former president of the On Leong Tong, 58-year-old Yee Hee Kee, was shot 5 times while standing in front of his store at 1295 Ontario. The shooting was explained initially as the result of generational differences within the tong, but later that summer 7 Hip Sing Tong members were convicted of participating in a $70,000 extortion scheme. Relations between the tongs remained tense throughout the summer. Rumors of open warfare between the two groups led Cleveland police to search tong members for weapons; police also provided special protection for the On Leong Tong convention in July amid reports that the Hip Sing Tong planned to raid the convention to steal its rival's treasury.

The tong wars came to a climax in a confusing series of events the following year. On 23 Sept. 1925, Tee Chock, a 26-year-old waiter and member of the On Leong Tong, was found brutally murdered in his room at 1283 Ontario. Using information supplied by an elderly "Celestial," Mark Ham (sometimes reported as Mock Hem), police arrested

3 Hip Sing Tong members at their tong's headquarters near E. 55th and Prospect. Safety Director Edwin D. Barry, however, was angered at the constant tension and periodic violence between the tongs and was determined to end the hostilities once and for all. He ordered the arrest of every Chinese male in the city, closed Chinese businesses, and took steps to have the Ontario St. Chinese settlement condemned as a health and fire hazard and razed. Those arrested were photographed, fingerprinted, and questioned by immigration officials. More than 700 people were arrested in the roundup, and the mass arrest soon proved to be an embarrassment to the city. Among those arrested were students visiting the U.S. from China; when it learned of their arrest, the Chinese government filed an official protest with Secretary of State Frank B. Kellogg, who in turn passed the complaint to Ohio Gov. A. V. Donahey, who notified City Manager WM. R. HOPKINS. Additional protests from the Cleveland Chinese community led city officials to issue an official apology to those arrested.

The murder case itself, meanwhile, took a confusing turn. The main witness for the police, the elderly Mark Ham, changed his story and confessed that the murder had been committed by members of the On Leong Tong in order to discredit the rival tong and to punish 3 recent defectors. Ham himself had served as the lookout during the murder and was charged as an accomplice. On Leong Tong members claimed that Ham's confession had been made through a Hip Sing translator and was not true. During the trial, Ham claimed to have received death threats. He hanged himself in his jail cell before the trial was over. By 1930, local newspapers were reporting that the tong wars were "a thing of the past," and by the middle of the decade the former rivals were cooperating on various projects within the Chinese community.

**TOOMEY, JOHN A.** (28 May 1889–1 Jan. 1950), physician, professor of pediatrics at Western Reserve University Medical School, and head of the Contagious Ward at City Hospital (Metropolitan General), pioneered one of the most effective methods in aiding the recovery of polio patients through physical rehabilitation. Toomey was born in the NEWBURGH area of Cleveland to Hugh and Mary Jane Burr Toomey. He attended St. Ignatius High School and graduated from JOHN CARROLL UNIVERSITY with the B.A. degree in 1910 and the M.A. in 1912, and from Cleveland Law School with the LL.B. degree in 1913. While in school he worked as the assistant superintendent at MT. SINAI Hospital and as steward at City Hospital. Admitted to the Ohio bar in 1913, Toomey entered private practice but found the legal profession "too cold-blooded." Returning to school, he graduated from WRU Medical School with the M.D. degree in 1919. While interning at City Hospital, he was appointed medical superintendent. When the hospital opened a ward for contagious diseases in 1924, he was placed in charge. Toomey held numerous posts at WRU, including demonstrator of anatomy and medicine, 1920–22; instructor of pediatrics, 1922–24; senior instructor in contagious diseases, 1924–28; assistant professor of contagious diseases, 1928–31, and of pediatrics, 1931–33; associate professor of pediatrics, 1933–40; and professor of clinical pediatrics, 1940–50. Toomey's views on poliomyelitis and the treatment of infantile paralysis involved him in numerous controversies with other medical professionals. He disliked the use of plaster casts in treatment, arguing that the cardinal points in polio treatment were early detection and vigorous massage. Also involved in the controversy over the entry site of polio into the human system, he was among the first to realize that polio entered not through the respiratory system but rather through the gas-

trointestinal tract. Toomey possessed a brilliant ability to detect the earliest signs of polio. Although he was well-known for his brusque manner and pungent language, he had a personality that made people like and trust him. Toomey married Mary Louise Baget in 1918. After her death in 1947, he married Helen Katharine Toomey in 1949. Toomey had 4 children, Charles, John, Mary, and Francis.

The **TORSO MURDERS** were committed over a period of 3 years between Sept. 1935 and Aug. 1938. Most of the bodies were discovered in the KINGSBURY RUN area—a creek bed that ran from E. 90th St. and Kinsman Rd. SE to the CUYAHOGA RIVER. Seven men and 5 women were killed; most were dismembered, and all were decapitated. The murderer was never discovered. On 23 Sept. 1935, the headless and emasculated torso of a man was found in Kingsbury Run. A search turned up the missing head and another torso, also headless and emasculated. The first victim was never identified. The second was identified as Edward Andrassy. Leads about Andrassy's drinking and brawling habits turned up nothing.

On 26 Jan. 1936, portions of a woman's torso were found on E. 20th St. in 2 baskets covered with burlap bags. The rest of the body, identified as Florence Polillo, was found 12 days later a few blocks away. Chicken feathers were found in the bags, and coal was imbedded in the torso. A search of local poultry and feed stores turned up nothing. Polillo was known among the low-lifes in the Kingsbury Run area, several of whom were questioned and released. Polillo and Andrassy were 2 of only 3 victims who were identified. Most victims were transient individuals whom no one would miss. In early June 1936, the head of a man was found in the Run; the body, tattooed in various areas, was found between railroad tracks where E. 55th St. crosses the Run. A mask cast from the head was displayed at the Northwest Territorial Exposition (held to promote Cleveland as an idyllic place to live and work) but was never identified.

Between July 1936-Aug. 1938, 8 more victims died at the hands of "the butcher"; 4 were men, and 4 were women, one of whom was identified as Mrs. Rose Wallace. Over a 6-year period, Detective J. Peter Merylo questioned over 5,000 individuals. However, all leads ended in failure. On 18 Aug. 1938, Cleveland Safety Director ELIOT NESS burned the shantytown of Kingsbury Run to the ground. The refugees were taken to jail or to the Wayfarer's Lodge. That ended the torso murders. On 5 July 1939, Frank Dolezal, known to have carried knives, to have drunk with Andrassy, and to have fought with Polillo, was arrested. On 7 July he confessed to Polillo's murder, but his description of the disposal of her body was inaccurate. On 12 July his counsel claimed that he denied the confession. Dolezal hanged himself before he could be tried. Coroner Samuel Gerber found that 6 of Dolezal's ribs had been fractured, probably at the time of his confession. Gerber speculated that someone had put pressure on Dolezal to force a confession. The real murderer, believed to be a powerful man with some knowledge of anatomy (the slicing of the bodies was done very neatly), to be known among the low-lifes of the Run, and to be of higher social standing, was never discovered.

The **TOWMOTOR CORPORATION** was founded in 1919 by Lester M. Sears when, after a year of planning, he unveiled the prototype of the gasoline-powered industrial tractor that revolutionized materials handling. After some initial sales, Sears's father capitalized the enterprise, and until his death in 1934, he ran it with his son from Bliss

Ave. in EUCLID. The plant later moved to 1226 E. 152nd St., and then to 16100 Euclid. In its first 14 years, Towmotor made small tractors that pushed or towed heavy loads through manufacturing plants; in 1933, it introduced a major innovation—the first forklift industrial truck. Over the years, the design was streamlined to produce a compact basic unit that featured a short turning radius, high-speed reverse and forward speeds, a pair of forward forks on hydraulic lifts, and a carefully balanced rear end. Though many companies built variations, Towmotor's "one man gangs" were so popular that all industrial forklift trucks were generally referred to as "Towmotors." Towmotors were considered essential cost-saving equipment even in hard times; 1 Towmotor performed the work of 30 men with hand trucks. Thus, during the Depression, the company's sales doubled. During WORLD WAR II and the KOREAN WAR, sales of Towmotor units to unload ships were brisk. In the 1950s and 1960s, Towmotor set out to capture a greater share of the market by introducing new models and acquiring companies with product lines that expanded capacity. The gasoline, diesel, LP gas-powered, and electric units for general and specialized use that enhanced the line won the company both defense and civilian business and entrenched its position as the leader in the 1,500–15,000 lb. capacity range. With the purchase of the Gerlinger Co. of Dallas, Oreg., Towmotor's lift capacity was increased to 60,000 lbs. While the market for such powerful trucks had traditionally been western logging, Towmotor developed new markets in steel and other heavy industry in the East and Midwest. The company's only other acquisition was Ohio Gear (1333 E. 179th St.) in 1963, which gave it instant expertise in gears, sprockets, shafts, and speed production units.

By 1963, when the Caterpillar Tractor Co. of Peoria, Ill., completed a merger with Towmotor, Towmotor was a stable company with established worldwide markets and local employment of over 1,500. Caterpillar maintained that Towmotor would keep its production, sales, and service integrity, but immediately the "Caterpillarization of Towmotor" began. Caterpillar built a new facility at 7111 Tyler Rd. in Mentor, as Towmotor had planned earlier, and began building other plants worldwide. Vehicles produced at Mentor and elsewhere carried both the Caterpillar and Towmotor names at first, but by the early 1970s, the Towmotor name was removed. Towmotor's position in the lift-truck field slipped as a result of its affiliation with the equipment giant. It benefited from Caterpillar's automated parts system and worldwide sales and service organization but was hurt by some of its sales techniques. Towmotor, which had seen minimal labor trouble throughout its history, was also hurt when Caterpillar was chosen as a strike target for the UAW in 1967, 1971, and 1983. Throughout the 1970s, Caterpillar, faced with foreign competition, slumping demand, and recessions, became an outspoken advocate of moving production to its most cost-effective worldwide facilities. One of the first subsidiaries affected by such conditions and policies was Towmotor; from 1978–82, employment at the Mentor plant dropped from 2,800 to 622. When workers at Towmotor and 18 Caterpillar installations in 6 states went on strike in 1983, the company threatened to shift production to Korea; before a settlement was reached, Towmotor workers learned that Caterpillar was seriously considering closing the plant unless workers would agree to a 45% wage and benefit cut that would permit the plant to break even. A month after workers signed an agreement that froze wages, Caterpillar contracted with a Seoul manufacturer to produce lift trucks. In Aug. 1983, Caterpillar announced that the plant would close in 1985.

**TOWN HALL OF CLEVELAND,** a subscription lecture series, was founded by Mrs. Wm. C. (Alice Katherine Newton) Wallin when she came to Cleveland from Detroit, Mich., with her husband in 1930. Mrs. Wallin, a former newspaperwoman, college-admissions officer, insurance executive, and participant in Detroit Town Hall, started the Town Hall of Cleveland (the 4th city in the country to have a Town Hall) as "courses designed for intelligent thinking." She initiated the series with the encouragement of Mrs. Wm. G. Mather, Mrs. Geo. M. Humphrey, Mrs. Eugene Grasselli, Mrs. Louis B. Seltzer, and Mrs. Richard H. Cobb. In addition, 50 other Cleveland women purchased 4 tickets each for the first subscription series. Dr. Will Durant, philosopher and author, spoke at the first meeting of Town Hall, 21 Oct. 1931 at the OHIO THEATER on "A Program of National Progress," in which he advocated an Academy of Political Science as a means to obtaining better government. Mrs. Newton D. Baker presided as hostess at the first subscription luncheon, held at the Hotel Statler, where Dr. Durant was guest of honor. Other speakers in the first series included Winston Churchill, Don Blanding (Hawaiian poet), Will Irwin (journalist), Mr. and Mrs. Martin Johnson (African explorers), and Mark Sullivan (author). Mrs. Wallin, assisted by Mrs. Richard H. Cobb and Mrs. Celeste (Beckwith) Chapman Williams, secured over 400 speakers of note through her 32-year tenure as director of Town Hall.

In Feb. 1962, Mrs. Wallin retired and sold Town Hall to Mrs. William G. (Peggy Wisner) Meldrum, a newspaper photographer, who continued the traditional format of a monthly morning lecture, followed by a luncheon including a question-and-answer period. The lectures, held from autumn of one year through late winter of the next, cover a wide variety of subjects and are presented by authorities on world and/or international affairs, educators, humorists, politicians, columnists, editors, publishers, musicians, poets, playwrights, psychologists, actresses, and diplomats and statesmen from both the U.S. and abroad. In 1962, there were 400 memberships (paid subscriptions); in 1969, 700 persons purchased season tickets, and in 1971 over 800. In 1972, over 1,000 series tickets were sold, and in 1984–85 over 1,200 tickets. Town Hall met in the Ohio Theater at first, later at the Cleveland Hotel and then Higbee's Auditorium. In 1985 the lectures were held in STOUFFER'S INN-ON-THE-SQUARE. In 1980, Mrs. Theodore W. Jones, founder of the Quintessence Series at the CLEVELAND PLAY HOUSE, joined Mrs. Meldrum as a partner. Although the Town Hall audience has been predominantly female, including many whose families were among the early founders of the series, an increasing number of men joined the morning lecture audience in the 1980s.

**TOWNES, CLAYTON C.** (30 Jan. 1888 [1887?]–24 Feb. 1970), served as president of city council and the first mayor of Cleveland under the CITY MANAGER PLAN. Townes was born in Cleveland, the son of Wm. C. and Kate Hoyt Townes. He received his LL.D. degree from Western Reserve University Law School in 1911, and the same year, he took over his father's seat in city council when his father died. Although he lost the seat in the next election, he was elected to council as a Republican 2 years later and served there for 6 terms, 4 of them as its president. When the City Manager Plan went into effect in Jan. 1924, Townes, as council president, became mayor. He resigned as mayor in 1925 and resumed his law practice as a partner in Townes & Portmann. He married Grace Dix in 1917, and they had 3 children, Betsy Townes Abbey, Jean Townes Weaver, and Rachel Townes Hale. After his wife's death in 1932,

972

he married Rose Bud. He moved to Florida in the 1930s, where he died at age 82.

**TOWNSEND, AMOS** (1821–17 Mar. 1895), was a businessman and politician who took an active interest in Cleveland's public and political matters. Townsend was born in Brownsville, Pa. He attended the local common schools until the age of 15, when he became a clerk in a Pittsburgh retail establishment. At the age of 19 he moved to Mansfield and formed a partnership with N. D. Hogg for the transaction of general mercantile business under the name of A. Townsend & Co. The firm lasted 5 years, until the partnership was dissolved and the business closed. It was during Townsend's residence in Mansfield that violence over the slavery issue erupted in Kansas. The U.S. House of Representatives appointed a special committee to proceed to the area, investigate, and report back on the exact causes. Townsend accompanied the committee in the office of marshal, a position of some danger that he filled in a manner that gained him the respect of all parties.

Townsend arrived in Cleveland in 1858, accepting a position with Gordon, McMillan & Co., wholesale grocers. He remained there until 1861, when he became a junior partner in the wholesale grocery firm of Edwards, Iddings & Co. With the death of Iddings in 1862, the firm became Edwards, Townsend & Co. Over the years the firm was successful in establishing an extensive business and a reputation for stability and enterprise. During the CIVIL WAR, Townsend served with the 1ST OHIO VOLUNTEER LIGHT ARTILLERY. Elected to CLEVELAND CITY COUNCIL in 1866, Townsend served for 10 years, the last 7 of which he was president. Elected in 1873 as a member of the state constitutional convention, he served on the committee for finance, taxation, and municipal affairs. In 1876 he won election to Congress, being reelected in 1878 and 1880. While in Congress he served as a member of the Post Offices & Post Roads Committee and the Commerce Committee, where he was instrumental in securing the passage of large appropriations for the building of the breakwater at Cleveland. Townsend died in St. Augustine, Fla., and is buried in LAKE VIEW CEMETERY.

Amos Townsend Papers, WRHS.

The **TOWNSEND PLAN**, the proposal made in Jan. 1934 by California physician Dr. Francis E. Townsend for a $200-a-month guaranteed income for each senior citizen, found strong and long-lasting support among certain Greater Clevelanders. The Cleveland area provided such support for the plan that Townsend located the national headquarters of his organization in the area from 1946–56; after the national organization disbanded in 1966, the Ohio headquarters at 11102 Detroit Ave. were "generally regarded as the national office." The first Townsend Club in Cleveland was formed at a meeting in the ballroom of the Hollenden Hotel on 4 Nov. 1934; its 100 charter members were gathered by 2 organizers from California, Dr. Frank Dyer and Chas. M. Hawks. Dr. Townsend himself visited Cleveland 3 times in the next year, speaking to 3,000 people at Public Hall on 18 Nov., to 3,500 there on 6 Jan., and to 15,000 at EUCLID BEACH PARK on 15 Aug. According to area manager Rev. Alfred J. Wright, 150 clubs were organized in the Cleveland area that year.

Townsend's plan was much in the public eye locally; in Nov. 1935 the CLEVELAND PRESS published a series of articles by both its proponents and its opponents. From 15–19 July 1936, the national convention of the Townsend organization met in PUBLIC AUDITORIUM; the convention brought 8,000 delegates to the city. By Mar. 1938 there was still much local enthusiasm for the Townsend Plan; there were 80 active Townsend clubs in the Cleveland area, and their weekly Sunday rallies at Public Hall attracted an audience of about 1,500. There were still 42 local groups, with a membership of 1,500–2,000, as late as 1947. The national convention returned to Cleveland in 1953, meeting at the Masonic Auditorium.

From 1946–56, the national headquarters of the Townsend Plan were located at 6875 Broadway Ave. In early 1946 the organization acquired the old United Publishing Co. building, and in May it began publishing the *Townsend National Weekly* at that address. The organization remained there until the fall of 1956, when financial problems prompted the leaders to move the headquarters to Washington, D.C. They left behind a strong local organization headed by long-time Townsend supporters Chas. "Harry" Wendorff and his wife, Rose. Active in the movement since 1936, the couple had managed Lakewood Club #2 since 1938. A retired driver for both the CLEVELAND RAILWAY CO. and the Cleveland Transit System and a tax consultant, Charles served on the Metropolitan Council (1943–46) and as deputy state director (1947–58) before becoming state director in 1959 and holding that post until his death at age 82 in May 1977. He was the driving force behind the state organization, and his death brought the end of meaningful action on the part of the organization.

Ohio Townsend Plan, Inc. Records, WRHS.

The **TRANSOHIO SAVINGS BANK** was formed on 1 May 1980 with the merger of 3 savings associations affiliated with the Transohio Financial Corp. The merger of the Union, United, and Akron savings associations made the new Transohio Savings Assoc. the largest member of the financial corporation, then the largest savings and loan holding company in Ohio and 8th-largest in the U.S. Akron Savings, founded in 1888, was the oldest of the 3 companies. Of the 2 Cleveland companies involved, Union Savings was the older. Incorporated as the Union Building & Loan Co. on 22 June 1891, it began operations at 149 the ARCADE, then moved to 60 PUBLIC SQUARE in July 1893. In 1896, with assets totaling $900,000, the company changed its name to Union Savings. Construction of the Terminal Tower forced the company to move in 1919 to the CUYAHOGA BLDG. at 232 Superior Ave. In 1947, Union Savings' assets were more than $10 million. The other Cleveland component of the Transohio merger, United Savings, began operations in 1916 as the Warsaw Savings & Loan Assoc. Organized by Clevelanders of Polish descent, Warsaw Savings changed its name to United Savings in 1952 to emphasize its service to the larger community. Leo W. Schmidt, one of its founders, headed the association from 1949–80. The new Transohio Savings Assoc. was hit hard by the recession of 1981–82, losing more than $43 million but maintaining its position as the state's largest savings and loan. By 1 July 1983, Transohio had 69 branch offices and $1.98 billion in assets. That month, to guard against the vagaries of the residential housing market and to reflect its broad range of services, the Transohio Savings Assoc. became the Transohio Savings Bank, changing from a savings and loan with a state charter to a federally chartered bank. Transohio Savings is the largest subsidiary of the Transohio Financial Corp. Formed in Dec. 1970, the holding company purchased the Cincinnati Savings Assoc. in 1973 and County Savings of Ravenna and Newark Savings in 1979. At the end of 1982, the corporation's assets of $2.175 billion placed it 48th among U.S. diversified financial companies ranked by assets.

**TRANSPORTATION.** SAMUEL P. ORTH, author of *A History of Cleveland, Ohio* (1910), sensed the vital importance of transportation to Cleveland: "[It] is the life of the modern city." Indeed, a principal factor that explains why Cleveland grew into a major metropolis involves geography. Initially, that meant access to water; a town site located along the mouth of the CUYAHOGA RIVER made real sense. Much of the community's early history involved LAKE TRANSPORT, with scores of sailing schooners, brigs, and barks that transported intercity cargos. Eventually steam-powered vessels appeared, and quickly took over much of the carrying trade. The first steamboat on the Great Lakes, the 330-ton *WALK-IN-THE WATER*, made its maiden voyage in 1818; by 1840 more than 60 steamboats of considerably advanced design served the lakes, and many called at Cleveland's docks. These vessels were faster, and in most cases could carry bigger payloads, than their wind-driven counterparts. The value of the Great Lakes to Cleveland increased because of factors other than improved boats. Internal improvements to these waterways—lighthouses, deeper harbors and channels, and the like—made them more useful to shipping interests. The opening in Nov. 1829 of the Welland Canal between Lake Ontario and Lake Erie enhanced the overall value of the Great Lakes to Cleveland, and construction in the 1850s of the Sault Canal around the falls of St. Mary's River at the foot of Lake Superior had an even more pronounced effect. Most of all, the city's iron and steel industry blossomed. The basic components of these metals—iron ore and limestone—could be transported to sites along the Cuyahoga River by an inexpensive all-water route from the Lake Superior country.

While heavy cargos dominated Lake Erie commerce, especially after the CIVIL WAR, boats also carried people. Daily passenger service between Buffalo and Detroit via Cleveland began in 1830. And the Forest City became home port to several of the leading Great Lakes passenger carriers. As late as the first quarter of the 20th century, the Detroit & Cleveland Navigation Co. and the CLEVELAND & BUFFALO TRANSIT CO. boomed the merits of pleasure and overnight business trips by water: "Spacious staterooms and parlors combined with the quietness with which the boats are operated insures refreshing sleep." But by WORLD WAR II, the automobile and airplane—the same transportation forms that would greatly reduce intercity rail passenger travel—virtually killed lake passenger service, and the piers at the foot of E. 9th St. became quiet. In the case of the Cleveland & Buffalo Transit Co., a fire that destroyed its *City of Buffalo* on 30 Mar. 1938 produced the crippling blow. Although one firm introduced the short-lived AQUARAMA cruise ship, it met with far less success than did the railroads' introduction of diesel-powered streamliners about the same time. Modernization also affected freight-carrying vessels on the lake. Great "fresh-water whales"—the long bulk carriers—appeared early in the century. They continued the tradition of transporting raw materials to Cleveland plants. By the 1960s, these distinctive boats shared water space with oceangoing ships. Completion of the manmade channels and locks of the St. Lawrence Seaway project in 1959 made the latter's entry possible, and thus Cleveland became an ocean port. The mariner's map of the world had been altered significantly.

While an evolutionary process was at work on the Great Lakes, Cleveland's other important water route, the OHIO & ERIE CANAL, eventually stopped being a transportation artery, but not for several generations after its opening. Even though Cleveland's population in 1820 totaled only 606, it could still rightfully claim to be a premier lake port. Therefore, state officials wisely selected the community during the early 1820s to be the northern terminus of the projected 308-mi. canal. When completed in 1832, the "Great Ditch" linked Lake Erie at Cleveland with the Ohio River near Portsmouth. A usage pattern somewhat resembling the one seen for lake commerce characterized the Ohio Canal. At first both "hogs and humans" traveled this waterway; the latter boarded specially fitted packets. This means of transportation reached its zenith in the 1840s, but declined dramatically with the advent of railroads. Canal travel was extremely slow and unavailable during cold weather. Admittedly, it was smoother than the ride provided by the various stagecoach lines. Freight, which likely included wheat, flour, whiskey, pork, salt, limestone, and coal, continued to move by canal long after packets disappeared. Even as late as 1900, the low rates charged by boat owners still attracted bulk cargos, mostly coal, from east-central Ohio into the Cleveland FLATS. But eventually railroads, in particular the Cleveland Terminal & Valley, conquered the venerable Ohio Canal.

Steam RAILROADS revolutionized Cleveland transportation. By the outbreak of the Civil War, only a dozen years after the arrival of the first steam locomotive, this means of intercity transport was firmly established. The vast majority of people selected railroads for personal travel and to meet their shipping needs. All recognized that water competitors were slow and were universally susceptible to the vagaries of the weather, especially thick winter ice. Furthermore, the railroad offered convenience; businesses tended to choose a railroad rather than a water location. By the post-Civil War era, the flanged wheel had become virtually synonymous with transportation. Yet the Railroad Age did not last forever. The first major challenge to the dominance of steam trains came with the introduction of the electric INTERURBANS. Clevelanders in 1895 could brag that they had one of the country's first intercity traction lines, the Akron, Bedford & Cleveland Railroad. Within a decade, residents had the services of a half-dozen interurban systems that radiated out of the city to the east, south, and west. Interurbans, with their frequent runs, attractive rates, and noticeable cleanliness, siphoned off tens of thousands of potential steam railroad patrons, and they captured much of the highly profitable package express and less-than-carload freight business. At times, the Cleveland-area steam roads slashed charges or increased trips, but usually they let the interurbans have much of the traffic.

Just as steam railroads showed their vulnerability to interurbans, the latter proved to be even more susceptible to competition. Gasoline-powered vehicles speedily replaced those propelled by compressed air. After the dawn of the 20th century, Cleveland emerged as a major center of the AUTOMOTIVE INDUSTRY, and per capita ownership of the horseless carriage soared. In 1916, for example, Cuyahoga County's automobile registrations totaled 61,000; 10 years later the figure stood at 211,000. Cleveland's long-standing ties to the automobile are represented nicely in the career of resident Frank B. Stearns (1878-1955). In 1898, Stearns launched a manufacturing concern, the F. B. STEARNS CO., to build automobiles of his own design. With skill, hard work, and access to pools of capital, he established himself as an important American automobile maker. Before his company closed in 1929, it produced more than 10,000 cars, and they ranked with the nation's best. But Stearns had other automobile-related interests. He participated in several road races, mostly to show the superiority of his car and the enormous potential of the automobile. In Jan. 1900, he helped found the Cleveland Automobile Club, the nucleus of the powerful and influential American Automobile Assoc. (see OHIO MOTORISTS ASSOC.). And he wrote for the club's publication, the *Cleveland Motorist*. Stearns, like thousands of

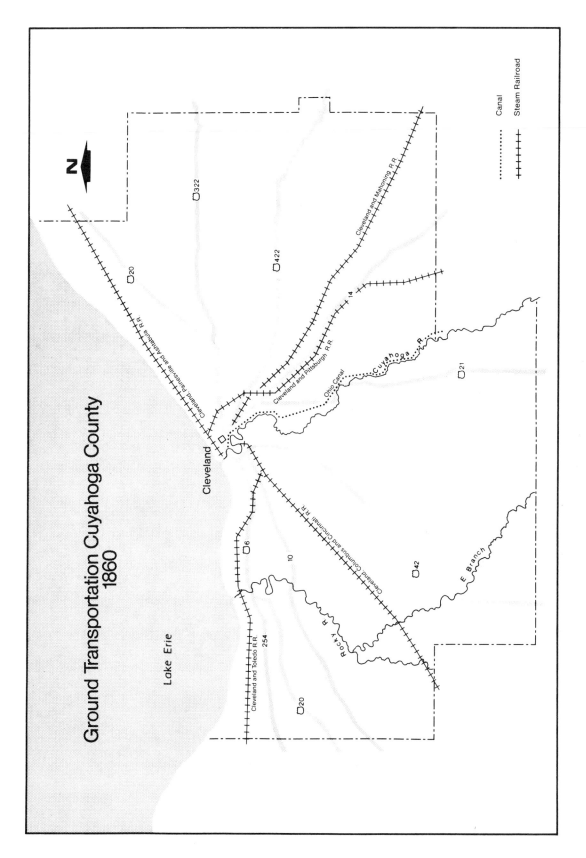

# Ground Transportation Cuyahoga County 1860

Lake Erie

Cleveland

Cleveland, Painsville and Ashtabula R.R.

Cleveland and Pittsburgh R.R.

Cleveland and Mahoning R.R.

Cleveland Columbus and Cincinnati R.R.

Cleveland and Toledo R.R.

Ohio Canal

Cuyahoga R.

Rocky R.

E. Branch

N

| Canal | Steam Railroad |

322  422  20  14  21  6  10  42  254  20

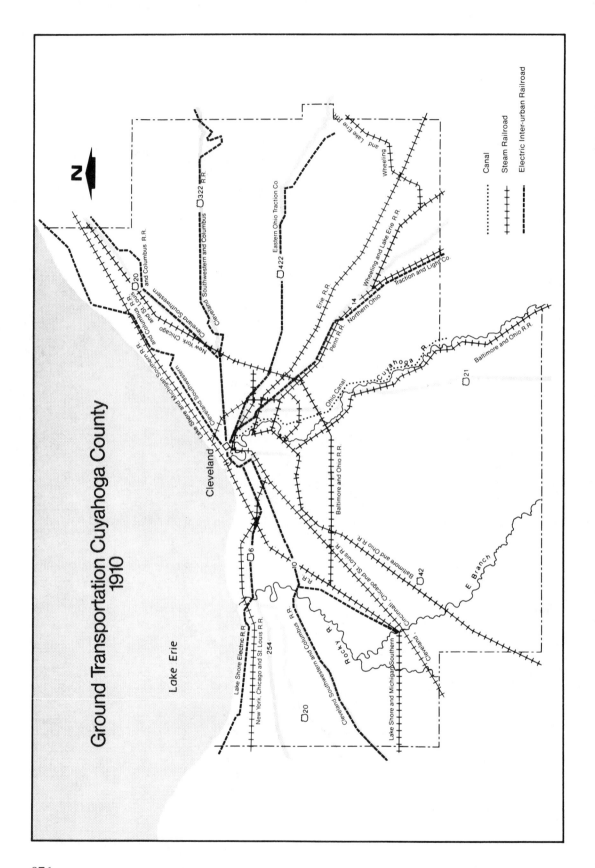

# Ground Transportation Cuyahoga County 1910

Lake Erie

Cleveland

**N**

Canal
Steam Railroad
Electric Inter-urban Railroad

Cleveland and Columbus R.R.

Cleveland Southwestern and Columbus R.R.

Eastern Ohio Traction Co

Lake Erie R.R.

Wheeling and

Wheeling and Lake Erie R.R.

Northern Ohio Traction and Light Co.

Erie R.R.

Penn R.R.

New York, Chicago and St. Louis R.R.

Cleveland Southwestern

Lake Shore and Michigan Southern

Cleveland Southwestern

Cuyahoga R.

Ohio Canal

Baltimore and Ohio R.R.

Baltimore and Ohio R.R.

E. Branch

Baltimore and Ohio R.R.

Cincinnati, Chicago and St. Louis R.R.

Rocky R.

Lake Shore and Michigan Southern

Cleveland

Lake Shore Electric R.R.

New York, Chicago and St. Louis R.R.

Cleveland Southwestern and Columbus R.R.

322

422

20

6

254

20

21

42

976

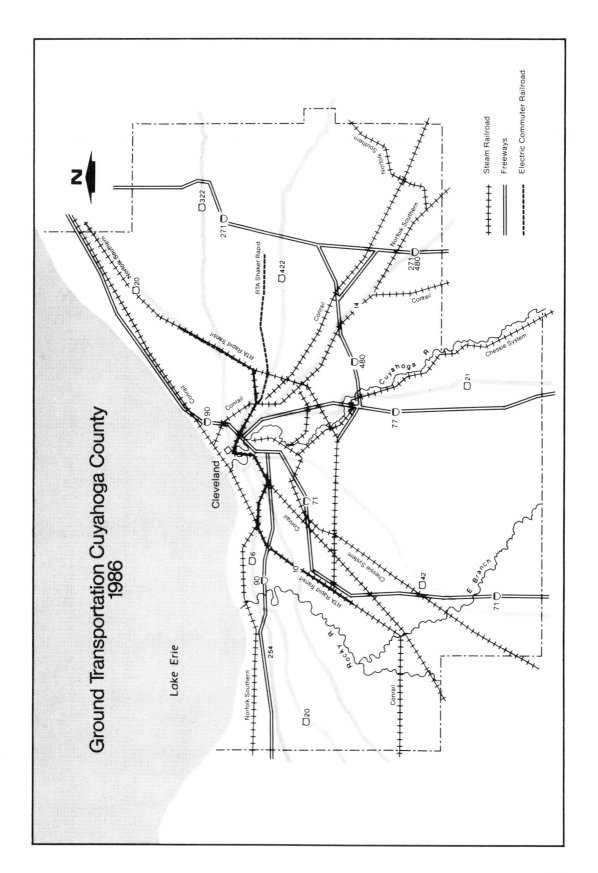

# Ground Transportation Cuyahoga County
## 1986

Lake Erie

Cleveland

Steam Railroad

Freeways

Electric Commuter Railroad

Norfolk Southern

Conrail

Chessie System

Cuyahoga R

Rocky R

E Branch

RTA Rapid Transit

RTA Shaker Rapid

N

977

Clevelanders, wanted to expand automobile usage. It would be in part through the labors of the Cleveland Automobile Club that the area lifted itself out of the mud by the 1930s.

Better roads not only stimulated automobile sales, they also did much to encourage expansion of bus and trucking operations. Cleveland's early intercity bus companies operated relatively short routes; in fact, their system maps closely resembled interurban maps. In 1925, for example, travelers could board vehicles of the Cleveland- Ashtabula-Conneaut Bus Co. on PUBLIC SQUARE for these communities and numerous intermediate points; they might select a run of the Cleveland-Akron-Canton Bus Co., a carrier that followed much of the route of the Northern Ohio Traction & Light Co., or they could opt for buses of the Cleveland-Warren-Youngstown Stage Co. or the Cleveland-Elyria-Toledo Bus Co. In the 1930s, these smaller firms gave way to larger ones. The Cleveland-based Buckeye Stage System sent its 45 passenger coaches to Columbus, Cincinnati, Elyria, and Sandusky; and Central Greyhound, associated with Greyhound Lines, also based in Cleveland, operated extensively throughout the eastern Midwest. While some smaller operators remained, they eventually either folded or merged with Greyhound or its major rival, Continental Trailways.

Although Cleveland never evolved into the region's leading motor-carrier center, it benefited enormously from the steady growth of this transportation form. But in terms of truck production and truck transport, Cleveland still held importance. As early as 1902, the city's newly established WHITE MOTOR CO. sent 5 experimental trucks on a successful round-trip run from New York City to Boston, and that company, which for several decades was Cleveland's largest independent manufacturer in any field, remained in the forefront of truck development and production. The White firm also sported a sizable bus-building division. Small trucking concerns, often equipped with White vehicles, appeared before WORLD WAR I; most provided intracity cartage. But with the triumph of the state's goodroads movement in the 1920s and early 1930s, and subsequent heavy spending by Congress on federal highways, firms became regional and even interregional in scope. Soon, though, the massive construction of the interstate highway network (after 1956), the growing power of the Brotherhood of Teamsters, and other factors gave rise to motor-carrier consolidation. Cleveland had the services of the industry's "Big 5": Roadway, Consolidated Freightways, Pacific-Intermountain-Express, Yellow Freight, and McLean Trucking. These companies and their competitors took advantage of the Cleveland market through such improved roadways as the Ohio Turnpike and interstates 71, 77, 90, 271, and 480.

The presence of a vigorous motor-carrier enterprise and, to a much lesser degree, buses, meant that Clevelanders were no longer utterly dependent on water and rail. Even though rubber-tired vehicles freed the shipper, local businesses commonly confronted stiff competition from those in other communities, whether in Ohio or elsewhere, that had lacked access to a sophisticated Cleveland-type transportation infrastructure. The truck, more than any other transportation form, challenged Cleveland's claim as the "best location in the nation." Clevelanders, though, could smile about their good fortunes with AVIATION. Throughout the life of commercial aviation, the city benefited from virtually unequaled air service. Even prior to regularly scheduled passenger operations, Cleveland and a select number of other places enjoyed access to airmail flights. When the public began to travel by air after the mid-1920s, the local terminal never lacked sufficient carriers. In the 1930s, a number of companies provided service,

but by World War II only 3 dominated: American, Pennsylvania-Central (subsequently Capital) and then United. Regulators, however, in the late 1940s opened the city to other strong firms, and the number of carriers remained stable. But deregulation in 1978 ushered in a plethora of companies, mostly small commuter ones. Cleveland, too, became more of a "hub" operation. United, Cleveland's largest airline, dramatically reduced its service into Akron-Canton Regional Airport, concentrating instead on its Hopkins operations.

Passengers who used CLEVELAND HOPKINS INTERNATL. AIRPORT after the early 1960s enjoyed easy access to Public Square and other east and west side locations. For Cleveland could claim to be the city with the first rapid-transit line to its airport. The Cleveland Transit System (later the GREATER CLEVELAND REGIONAL TRANSIT AUTHORITY) was merely the latest operator of Cleveland's surface rail network. Like most sister cities, Cleveland experienced all types of intracity transportation (see URBAN TRANSPORTATION). The earliest rolling stock to appear on its streets was the horse-drawn omnibus, the 19th-century forerunner of the taxi. Omnibus runs started in 1857 and connected the railroad station and lake docks with various public houses. Soon, though, the horse (and occasionally the mule) pulled an omnibus-type car on flanged wheels over light rails fixed in the streets. By the Civil War, these "streetcars" rolled on EUCLID AVE. as far as Erie (E. 9th) St., turning south on Prospect Ave. and east to the corporation limits. While horse lines flourished in the postwar period, they disappeared in the 1890s. Most communities that had horsecars converted to the much more efficient and economical electric trolleys introduced in 1887.

While this transformation likewise occurred in Cleveland, an intermediate phase took place, the cable car phenomenon of the 1880s and early 1890s. Cleveland joined such places as Chicago, Cincinnati, Kansas City, and St. Louis with cable cars; in fact, there were once 62 firms in 28 communities that embraced this type of public surface transport. While inferior overall to the future trolley, the cable car was more desirable than the horsecar, largely because of its greater speed and lower operating cost. In 1890, Cleveland's 261,000 citizens could ride the cars that belonged to the Cleveland City Cable Railway from Union Station up Water (W. 9th) St., and then east on Superior Ave.; or they could change to the Payne Ave. line that continued toward the east onto Lexington and Hough avenues. In 1893, the CCC became part of MARCUS HANNA's expanding street railway holdings, the WOODLAND AVE. & WEST SIDE STREET RAILROAD. The cable lines continued to run throughout the 1890s, even though electric cars spread quickly throughout the city. But the higher costs of operations, the difficulty of expansion, and the faster speeds and better reliability of electric cars led to conversion of the Superior line to trolleys in 1900; the remainder of the system met a similar fate a year later.

Not only did Cleveland's developing electric streetcars spell doom for the horse and cable cars, but the substantial profit potential and the high capitalization requirements led to the unification of various electric lines in 1893. The result was creation of 2, at times competing, systems, the CLEVELAND ELECTRIC RAILWAY CO. and the Cleveland City Railway Co. The local press called the former the "Big Consolidated" and the latter the "Little Consolidated," which common parlance soon shortened to "Big Con" and "Little Con." The urge to form a private monopoly led to merger of the "Big Con" and "Little Con" in 1903, thus creating "ConCon." Although the city finally had its streetcar lines under a single management, that did not necessarily please residents. Consumers wanted a 3-cent fare, and not the prevailing charge of 5 cents. Progressive mayor TOM L. JOHNSON led the battle for a permanent solution to the "streetcar problem"—MUNICIPAL OWNERSHIP. But true public control did not occur until 1942, when the CLEVELAND RAILWAY CO. became the Cleveland Transit System. Yet during the Johnson years, reformers repeatedly fought "ConCon" over the fare issue through such consumer-sensitive alternative car lines as the Forest City Railway Co. (1903), Municipal Traction Co. (1906), Low Fare Railway Co. (1906), and Neutral Street Railway Co. (1908). These uplifters won for riders a brief lease of "ConCon" by the city after 1908, and the establishment of a prolonged period of reasonable rates.

The same technological change that affected the nature of 20th-century intercity travel likewise affected urban transit. "Jitney" buses invaded Cleveland streets before World War I, but they usually could not compete with the 3-cent trolley fares. And conventional buses joined the Cleveland Railway Co.'s transportation fleet during the 1920s and after. Eventually, the trolley disappeared from Cleveland's streets; the last streetcar rattled into its carbarn from its Public Square-to-Madison run on 24 Jan. 1954. Yet the use of rail transit did not end. The SHAKER HTS. light rail line, the legacy of the partially completed Cleveland & Youngstown interurban, had since 1914 carried thousands of patrons daily (see SHAKER RAPID TRANSIT). Then in 1948, Mayor THOS. A. BURKE obtained a commitment from the federal government's Reconstruction Finance Corp. to buy city of Cleveland revenue bonds to build a cross-town rapid-transit network. After a charter amendment that gave an expanded transit board the necessary authority to manage such an operation, the Reconstruction Finance Corp. made the loan for $29 million in July 1951. Ground was broken at the Windermere station yard on 4 Feb. 1952. By the mid-1950s, the "rapid" connected Windermere on the east side with W. 117th St. and Madison on the west side, through Terminal Tower on Public Square, and it entered the airport a decade later. In 1977, a revamping of the city's transit system produced the Regional Transit Authority, which included the Shaker Hts. Rapid; thus, the area's rail and bus operations came under one governmental body. Clevelanders enjoyed a well-integrated public transportation system; they had an alternative to automobile travel.

While competition between the various modes had characterized much of transportation in Cleveland, the complete picture reveals striking examples of coordination and cooperation between transport forms. Obviously, intracity transit operations historically have united local stations and terminals. Trucks and buses, too, have served as vital links in the transportation chain. Less apparent have been the ties between the intracity water, rail, and air carriers. Steam railroads almost from their inception have made connections with lake vessels, especially those that hauled bulk commodities such as coal. In time, interurbans offered interchange arrangments with passenger boats. The Northern Ohio Traction Co. before World War I established through tariffs for travelers on its system who were bound for Great Lakes cities on the Cleveland & Buffalo or Detroit & Cleveland transit lines. In the same vein, the Nickel Plate Road, virtually alone among Cleveland steam roads, promoted steam-electric railroad interchange of freight. A company advertisement of the late 1920s announced proudly: "A physical connection is made with the Nickel Plate Railroad at Cleveland, which permits the movement of Electric Railway Freight Cars into the Nickel Plate Freight terminal for the interchange of both carload and less carload freight." Like the Nickel Plate, the interurbans were hungry for any type of revenue business, and they com-

monly established remarkable creative relationships with other types of transport. The most fascinating are 2 traction companies' dealings with the infant airline industry. In Feb. 1926, officials of the Northern Ohio boasted of the inauguration of "Freight Aeroplane Service." Package freight (largely automobile-related) moved by interurban to Cleveland, and then was trucked to the airport for a flight via the "New Ford Air Mail Service" to Detroit. Two years later, on 28 May 1928, the Cleveland & Southwestern claimed to be the first railroad in the nation to offer a through coordinated rail-air service plan. Interurban passengers could purchase a Cleveland-to-Detroit airplane ticket on STOUT AIRLINES from any of 10 stations: Oberlin, Elyria, Wellington, Medina, Wooster, Ashland, Mansfield, Crestline, Galion, and Bucyrus.

Ultimately, the automobile and the motor truck reduced the service given by most of the incumbent forms of public transportation. Since the 1930s, these have been the modes that have altered dramatically the landscape of Cleveland and America; they have truly made the 20th century "the age of the rubber tire." Still, of course, the city has continued to benefit from those old 19th-century traffic arteries, Lake Erie boats, and the railroads. Moreover, it has exploited well the advantages of air service. Cleveland, Ohio, remains one of the best-served places in the nation.

H. Roger Grant
University of Akron

The **TRAVELERS AID SOCIETY** is a free nationwide service for people in difficulty away from home. Services are provided through community social agencies, which work closely with societies in other cities. No charge is made for the service, but reimbursement for out-of-pocket expenses is expected from those able to pay. Services include contacting the traveler's family, arranging overnight stays, and making short-term loans. The society was established in Cleveland in 1920, and as a member of the Welfare Fed., it was supported by the Community Chest. Its establishment followed that of a Natl. Travelers Aid Society in 1917. The Travelers Aid Society was originally the idea of Brian Mullanphy, mayor of St. Louis, who died in 1851, leaving 1/3 of his million-dollar fortune for the aid of immigrants going west during the days of the Gold Rush. Services such as those provided by the society had been initiated by the Cleveland Catholic Diocese and the deaconesses of the Methodist Church as far back as 1890, when both churches employed workers in the old UNION DEPOT to protect and assist young girls on their arrival.

In its early days, Travelers Aid operated 7 days a week, 24 hours a day, at 5 railroad stations, an interurban station, and a boat dock. Ten workers assisted travelers, taking a protective role toward young and inexperienced newcomers. In 1925, this function was taken over by the newly established WOMEN'S BUREAU OF THE CLEVELAND POLICE DEPT. That same year, the society began doing casework. The Depression saw an increased need for aid to travelers as people traveled extensively in search of employment. Because of the strain on its funds, the society was taken over by the Federal Transient Program and the Cuyahoga County Relief Admin. in 1933. This change meant a reduction to a 16-hour day and a concentration on the special problems of youth, emotionally disturbed newcomers, and stranded travelers.

In 1937, the society began accepting social-work students from Western Reserve University's School of Applied Sciences as a field-instruction unit. In 1939 a field office was established at the Greyhound Bus Station, as large numbers of travelers began to use buses. Services were provided in the 1940s to mobilized defense-plant workers and the armed services. A new wave of immigrants at the end of WORLD WAR II, consisting of displaced persons and refugees, were served by the society. In the 1950s, the society worked with black migrants from the Deep South and Appalachian newcomers. Often ill-equipped to deal with urban life, these groups were aided and counseled by the society. In 1956, it opened an office at CLEVELAND-HOPKINS INTERNATL. AIRPORT. In 1970 the Travelers Aid Society became part of the newly established CTR. FOR HUMAN SERVICES, but it severed that connection in 1985 to join the American Red Cross Emergency Services.

Center for Human Services Records, WRHS.

**TRAVIS, PAUL B.** (2 Jan. 1891–23 Nov. 1975), was an artist, teacher, and adventurer well known to the Cleveland artistic community from the time of a noted African art expedition in the 1920s to his death. Travis was born in Wellsville, near Lisbon in Columbiana County, Ohio, and spent his childhood on a farm there. He thought he wanted to be an engineer and won an engineering scholarship to Washington & Jefferson College, but he started teaching instead in the country school. On coming to Cleveland, he entered the Cleveland School of Art in 1913 and studied with teachers such as FRANK WILCOX and HENRY KELLER. Following graduation in 1917, he served a year with the American Expeditionary Forces in France, and after the armistice he spent 6 months as an instructor in life drawing at the AEF University in Beaune, France. He began teaching full-time at the Art Institute in 1920, continuing until his retirement in 1957. He also taught at the John Huntington Polytechnic Institute.

In 1927–28, Travis made a much-celebrated and widely publicized African expedition. The Gilpin Players (active at KARAMU HOUSE) and the African Art Sponsors, a group of black citizens interested in African art, financed his 7-month collecting and painting trip to Africa. The art and artifacts he collected as assigned were received by the CLEVELAND MUSEUM OF ART, the CLEVELAND MUSEUM OF NATURAL HISTORY, and Karamu House. This trip motivated Travis to prolific production, spurred on by his fascination with the colors of African art. Travis was equally at ease with oil, watercolor, the etcher's needle, and the lithographer's crayon. Many of his works are in private collections and museums throughout the country, including the Brooklyn Museum, Cleveland Museum of Art, and New York Public Library. Making his permanent home in Cleveland, he lectured at various museums and universities and served as a trustee of Goodrich House, Karamu, and the Cleveland Council on Human Relations. Travis once remarked that his career would not have been possible without the Cleveland MAY SHOW. When the Museum of Art held its 52d show in 1971, he had exhibited and won regularly in every show. Travis was married to Marjorie Penfield and had 1 son and 2 daughters.

Paul B. Travis Papers, WRHS.

**TREMCO, INC.,** a manufacturer of sealants, protective coatings, and weatherproofing compounds, was established in 1928 by WM. C. TREUHAFT and operated as an independent company until 1979, when it became a subsidiary of B. F. Goodrich. Tremco was incorporated as the Tremco Mfg. Co. on 11 Feb. 1928, with $100,000 in capital. Treuhaft was its president, Ronald Brown its secretary, and Elmer C. Hann the treasurer. The former president of a distributor of industrial construction products, Treuhaft wanted his new firm to emphasize its sales service for the customer. In 1942 the company moved from its first location at 393 E. 131st St. to 8701 Kinsman Rd. Between 1948–58, the firm doubled its number of products to 250; sales in 1957 were nearly $7 million. In 1958, Tremco was reported to be the nation's largest maker of maintenance materials for industrial, institutional, and commercial buildings. By June 1959, Tremco had moved into a new $1.5-million administration and technical center at 10701 Shaker Blvd.

In the early 1960s, Treuhaft sought to expand the company's annual sales to $20 million and make it a publicly owned operation. Sales of $8.8 million and earnings of $564,395 in 1961 were new records for the firm. In Aug. 1961, Tremco acquired Jamestown Finishes, Inc., of Jamestown, N.Y., which it operated as a subsidiary until selling it in Dec. 1970. Between 1961–63, Tremco acquired 96% of the stock of Armalex Glass Industries of Canada; it sold it in Dec. 1969. In Mar. 1965 Tremco bought a Cleveland firm, the Glastic Corp., which it sold in Nov. 1968 for $5 million. Tremco's annual sales rose to more than $23 million in 1965, with a net profit of nearly $2 million. In 1972, Tremco had grown to 2 factories in Cleveland, 1 in Canada, and another in England, employing 1,029 people; net sales that year were $36.7 million, and net income $2.2 million. Tremco added a plant in Barberville, Ky., by 1974 and transferred 150 of its 250 Cleveland workers to the new facility; the transfer of jobs out of Cleveland prompted the first strike in the firm's history by the remaining workers, who feared all of the company's Cleveland operations would be closed. On 17 May 1974, the Tremco Mfg. Co. changed its name to Tremco, Inc. By 1979 the company had grown to 1,200 employees worldwide. Faced with the possibility of acquisition by the Chemed Corp., which had bought 5.2% of its stock, Tremco agreed in Sept. 1979 to become a subsidiary of B. F. Goodrich for $106 million. By mid-Jan. 1980, B. F. Goodrich had acquired 100% of Tremco, Inc.

**TREMONT** is an industrial/residential neighborhood located on Cleveland's near west side. Its boundaries include the CUYAHOGA RIVER to the east and north, and Clark Ave. or Harvard, Harvard-Denison Bridge to the south (depending upon source of information). Originally part of BROOKLYN Twp., the area was a section of OHIO CITY from 1836–54. In 1850, a group of prominent citizens, including Rev. Asa Mahan, former president of Oberlin College; Wm. Slade, later governor of Vermont; and WM. CASE and SAMUEL STARKWEATHER, former and present mayors of Cleveland, founded CLEVELAND UNIVERSITY in what was to become Tremont. The institution lasted only until 1855 but left a legacy of streets that would constitute at one time a very fashionable neighborhood: College Ave., Jefferson Ave., Literary Rd., Professor St., and University Rd. These streets formed the center of University Hts. during the years in which the buildings of Cleveland University were used by 3 other educational endeavors, including the HUMISTON INSTITUTE, Cleveland Protestant Hospital, and Western Reserve Homeopathic Hospital, predecessor to HURON RD. HOSPITAL, 1896. Lincoln Hts. succeeded University Hts. as the name for the neighborhood. Although Tremont was used as far back as 1837 in advertisements, only with the construction of Tremont School in 1910 did the neighborhood officially get its most recent name. Tremont's industrial base began with the establishment of the LAMSON-SESSIONS CO. in 1869 on Scranton Rd. near the Cuyahoga River. It and numerous later enterprises, including steel mills in the Cuyahoga Valley, provided employment to many new immigrants who settled in the area. These included IRISH and

GERMANS in the 1860s; POLES, 1890s; and GREEKS and Syrians (see ARAB-AMERICANS), 1900s. Other nationalities that came to Tremont include displaced UKRAINIANS in the 1950s and Puerto Ricans (see HISPANIC COMMUNITY) in the 1960s. A total of 30 nationalities have lived or were living in Tremont as of 1985.

Complementing the neighborhood's ethnic variety is its architecture. Many churches are on state and/or national historic landmark registers, including ST. THEODOSIUS RUSSIAN ORTHODOX CATHEDRAL (1912), Pilgrim Congregational (1893), St. Michael the Archangel (1888), and St. Augustine Roman Catholic (1896). Other buildings of landmark status include Cleveland Fire House #8 (1870), Sindy's Tavern (Kroger Grocery Store, ca. 1875), and the Wm. Holzhauer house (ca. 1870). By the 1980s, Tremont was a run-down, isolated neighborhood in which 68% of the housing was built before 1900. The population shrank from 36,686 in 1920 to 10,304 in 1980. Two bridges (Abbey Road and Clark Ave.) that connected Tremont to the rest of Cleveland were closed. The geographic isolation was completed by the cliffs rising from the Cuyahoga River, Walworth Run, which dissected the area, and I-71, which also cut through the neighborhood. MERRICK HOUSE, founded in 1919 as a neighborhood settlement, is a community focal point for Tremont. The Tremont West Development Corp. is one neighborhood organization trying to revitalize the area through rehabilitation of housing, seeking to help many Appalachians, who formed the latest wave of immigrants to settle in Tremont.

Hendry, Charles, *Between Spires and Stacks* (1936).

The **TRENTINA CLUB** was one of many "hometown" societies formed by Italian immigrants in Cleveland to provide financial assistance to members in need and to offer a friendly refuge in a new and different world. The club was founded as Instituzione Mutuo Beneficenza Trentina in 1930 by 12 natives of Trento, Italy. In 1935 the club, led by president Chas. S. Sasena, vice-president John Belfi, and secretary Leo Batoki, had 100 members; by then the qualifications for membership in the organization had been expanded to include immigrants from Italy's northern and central provinces. Like its sister organization the NORTH ITALIAN CLUB, the Trentina Club paid sick and death benefits, had no political affiliations, and used Italian as its official language during meetings. By the 1950s, the club had established its headquarters at 3401 Clark Ave., which was still its location on its 50th anniversary in 1980.

**TREUHAFT, WILLIAM C.** (21 Oct. 1892–24 Dec. 1982), was a Cleveland industrialist and a civic leader quite active in the affairs of philanthropic, cultural, educational, and health organizations. Treuhaft was born and educated in Cleveland. From 1910–14 he attended both Case Institute of Technology and Adelbert College, enrolled in a 5-year combined course of engineering and humanities. He left the program after 4 years to go into business. His rise in the business world was rapid. In 1916 he became president of the Sterling Prods. Co., a distributor of industrial construction products. That firm consolidated with the Arco Co. in 1927; Treuhaft served as a vice-president of Arco in 1927, but along with other Arco executives and technicians, he left in 1928 to form his own company, Tremco Mfg. (see TREMCO, INC.), where he was president until 1966, then chairman of the board until 1973.

Treuhaft's career of service to others also started early. He played piano for teenage dances at ALTA HOUSE, and in college he served as a supervisor and instructor at Camp Wise in Painesville. His civic and philanthropic work was divided between welfare, cultural, health, and educational institutions. He served as president of the Community Chest campaigns in 1956 and 1957 and of the United Appeal (see UNITED WAY) in 1966 and 1967. He was an officer in BLUE CROSS OF NORTHEAST OHIO, MT. SINAI Hospital, and the JEWISH COMMUNITY FED.; and was a trustee of the CLEVELAND HEALTH MUSEUM and president of the CLEVELAND MUSEUM OF ART. He was also chairman of the board and an executive committee member of UNIVERSITY CIRCLE, INC. Treuhaft also served as a trustee of BALDWIN-WALLACE and URSULINE COLLEGES and CASE WESTERN RESERVE UNIVERSITY; as president of the trustees at the latter institution in 1968, he endowed 2 chairs, 1 in humanities and another in the school of management. In 1914 Treuhaft married Elizabeth Marting, a language teacher at HATHAWAY BROWN SCHOOL. For their joint efforts in philanthropic and civic affairs, they shared the 1950 Chas. Eisenman Award of the Jewish Welfare Fed. and the 1972 Natl. Human Relations Award of the Natl. Conference of Christians & Jews.

The **TREUHAFT FOUNDATION** was founded in 1955 by WM. C. TREUHAFT (1892–1982) with Eugene H. Friedheim. Treuhaft was born in Cleveland and graduated from Case Institute of Technology in 1928. He was a founder of the Tremco Mfg. Co., a construction firm (president 1928–66), and of Armalux Glass Industries of Toronto. He was also actively involved in welfare in Cleveland, as president of the Community Chest, vice-president and trustee of the JEWISH COMMUNITY FED. for 30 years, and president of the United Appeal. He was also a trustee of CASE WESTERN RESERVE UNIVERSITY and chairman of UNIVERSITY CIRCLE, INC. Treuhaft married Elizabeth Marting, a graduate of HATHAWAY BROWN SCHOOL and Smith College and later a teacher at Hathaway Brown. Elizabeth Treuhaft received her master's degree from Western Reserve University and was on the boards of BALDWIN-WALLACE COLLEGE and University Circle, Inc. She and Wm. Treuhaft were cowinners of the Eisenman Award for Civic Achievement in 1951, and of the Natl. Human Relations Award of the Natl. Conference of Christians & Jews in 1972. The couple had no children. The purposes of the foundation are to support higher education and Jewish welfare. The foundation has supported Baldwin-Wallace College, Hathaway Brown School, Smith College, URSULINE COLLEGE, and University Circle, Inc. In 1979, the foundation donated $1.5 million for an endowed chair in EDUCATION and the humanities at CWRU. No grants are given to individuals, nor will grants be made for matching gifts or deficit financing. In 1983, the assets of the foundation were $13,549,061, with expenditures of $1,004,957 for 154 grants. Trustees of the foundation include Irwin M. Feldman, Elizabeth M. Treuhaft, and A. W. Treuhaft.

**TRINITY CATHEDRAL** and its parent Trinity Parish constitute not only the present-day seat of the bishop of the Episcopal Diocese of Ohio, but also one of Cleveland's original religious organizations. Trinity Parish was organized at the house of Phineas Shepherd in BROOKLYN on 9 Nov. 1816, although EPISCOPALIANS had been present from the time of MOSES CLEAVELAND's arrival, and occasional services were performed. A constitution was drawn up at this November meeting, and at a subsequent meeting in 1817, the parish was officially founded. The first rector was Connecticut clergyman Roger Searle. Between 1820–25, the parish worshiped in Brooklyn, where many of the members lived. With the decision to move to the east side of the CUYAHOGA RIVER in 1826, a frame building was built on the corner of St. Clair and Seneca (W. 3rd) streets and consecrated in 1829. It was the first church building within the Cleveland village limits. The move east precipitated the founding in 1834 of St. John's Parish in OHIO CITY, made up primarily of former Trinity parishioners who lived on the west side.

By 1846, the parish began to plan for a larger and more central building. A lot was purchased 2 blocks east of PUBLIC SQUARE on Superior St. The building, completed in 1854–55, was of Gothic design. Shortly before the new structure was completed, the older church on St. Clair St. burned to the ground. In the second half of the 19th century, St. John's (1834), Grace Church and St. Paul's (1845 and 1847 respectively), St. Peter's (1867), Christ Church (1869), and St. Mary's (1870) were formed out of or as missions of Trinity. Trinity Parish had maintained a close relationship with the espiscopate of the Diocese of Ohio since 1836, when the bishop had been invited to reside adjacent to the church. In 1890, Trinity Church was offered to Bp. William A. Leonard as a cathedral to be maintained by the parish. Plans were begun by CHAS. F. SCHWEINFURTH in 1890 for a building at Euclid Ave. and E. 22nd St. Sketches were presented for both a Romanesque and a Gothic design and, although the vestry initially leaned toward the less costly Romanesque plan, the plan eventually evolved to the English Perpendicular Gothic structure, built between 1901–07 and consecrated on 24 Sept. 1907. The cathedral is cruciform in plan, with a square central tower rising above the crossing. The exterior is of Indiana limestone, and the interior is finished in vitrified brick, stone, and dark oak. It is attached by an ambulatory to a parish house containing a parish hall, meeting rooms, and offices, completed in 1895. Trinity Parish has had many notable Clevelanders on its membership rolls, including several generations of Mathers and Boltons, CHAS. F. BRUSH, and JAS. R. GARFIELD. The parish has been involved in various work within the community, ranging from the Church Home for the Sick & Friendless (ca. 1855) and the Children's Home (1865) to hunger and daycare programs in the 1980s.

Pierce, Roderick Hall. *Trinity Cathedral Parish* (1967).

**TROOP A,** also known as the 1st City Troop, the 1st Cleveland Cavalry, and the Black Horse Troop, was an independent military organization established after the Railroad Strike of 1877 raised fears about the ability of the militia to maintain law and order. The unit was called into action several times in its history. Led by Dr. Frank Wells, Augustus G. Stone, DAVID Z. NORTON, John Tod, and Col. Wm. H. Harris (captain, 1877–84), the 1st Troop, Cleveland City Cavalry, was organized on 10 Oct. 1877 as an "independent military company" whose 41 charter members were "desirous of perfecting ourselves in Horsemanship, in the Use of Arms, and Military Exercises." Initial members included such figures as Chas. Bolton, Henry S. Blossom, EDWIN H. COWLES, DAN P. EELLS, SAMUEL MATHER, and Geo. W. Worthington.

The company began weekly drills on 3 Dec. 1877. In 1878 construction began on the company's first armory, at 927 Euclid between Sterling (E. 30th) and Case (E. 40th), but the $3,100 armory lacked stables and was replaced in 1885 with a $31,000 structure at Willson and Curtis (1919 E. 55th), which in turn was replaced in 1923 by a $310,000, 2-story brick-and-steel armory in SHAKER HTS. at Fairhill and Kemper roads. During its first several years, the company's activities were mostly drills, encampments, social occasions, and appearances at public ceremonies. On 29

Aug. 1887, after having staved off in 1886 a bill in the legislature that would have abolished independent military units, members of the cavalry troop voted unanimously to become a unit in the Ohio Natl. Guard.

Troop A was placed on alert several times during the 1880s and 1890s but was not called into action. During the SPANISH-AMERICAN WAR, the troop formed the nucleus of the 1st Ohio Volunteer Cavalry and went to Lakeland, Fla., but again saw no action. Reorganized after the war by members of its Veterans Assoc., which had been formed in 1891, Troop A did see action in the streets of Cleveland during the STREETCAR STRIKE OF 1899, escorting 2 cars down Broadway from the Miles Ave. barns and standing guard at various locations around the city. Strikers and their sympathizers threw firecrackers, boiling water, bricks, and cans at the mounted troops, who made 1 arrest and were under orders to fire if necessary. Troop A again was called to service during the tobacco wars in southern Ohio in 1908 and a streetcar strike in Columbus in 1910, and after floods in Fremont in 1913 and a tornado in Lorain in 1924. In 1916, 98 members of Troop A patrolled the border between Texas and Mexico during the border dispute.

During WORLD WAR I, Troop A and the Ohio Regiment of Cavalry became a field artillery unit and saw action in France, losing 5 members in combat. The troop left federal service in Apr. 1919 and rejoined the Ohio Natl. Guard as Troop A, 107th Cavalry. At its 48th-anniversary celebration, Troop A received from John Philip Sousa the original score of his "Black Horse Troop March," which he had written in its honor. In 1940 the troop was reorganized as a Horse Mechanized unit, and during WORLD WAR II it saw action as the 107th Cavalry Reconnaissance Squadron; it returned to the Ohio Natl. Guard in 1947 and continues service as the 107th Armored Cavalry Regiment. In 1962, the Veterans Assoc. sold the Shaker Hts. armory to the Ohio Natl. Guard, which in 1971 moved to new quarters at 4303 Green Rd.

Cavalry Veterans Assoc., *First City Troop. Eightieth Anniversary* (1957).
Cleveland Military Units Papers, WRHS.
Mewett, Alfred R., *A Brief History of Troop A* (1923).
Patty, Clay W., and Ball, William B., *A Brief History of First Cleveland Cavalry* (1937).

**TROSKY (TROJOVSKY), HAROLD ARTHUR "HAL"** (11 Nov. 1912–18 June 1979), was a BASEBALL player for the CLEVELAND INDIANS from 1933–41. A power-hitting first-baseman, he had over 200 home runs during his 9 seasons with the Indians. Trosky was born in Mansay, Iowa, and grew up in nearby Norway. After completing high school, he signed in 1931 to play baseball with the Cleveland Indians farm team at Cedar Rapids. By the fall of 1933, Trosky was a member of the Indians after hitting 33 home runs for Toledo that season. In a newspaper interview he remarked, "Out here [LEAGUE PARK] I figure I can hit the wall at least once in a while." From 1934–39, Trosky hit on and over the wall as he averaged over 100 RBIs each season. His greatest year was 1936, when he hit safely in 28 consecutive games, drove in a team-record 162 runs, slugged 42 home runs, and had a batting average of .343. In games played on 30 May 1934 and 5 July 1937, Trosky hit 3 consecutive home runs. During the late 1930s, Trosky began to suffer from migraine headaches; he did not play for the Indians after the 1941 season. He returned to baseball in 1944 with the Chicago White Sox, remained out of the game in 1945, and finally retired after playing 88 games for Chicago in 1946. In retirement,

Trosky became a successful hog and dairy farmer. He married Lorraine Glenn on 15 Nov. 1933, and the couple had 4 children, Hal, Jr., James, Lynn, and Mary Kay. Hal, Jr., pitched during the 1958 season for the Chicago White Sox.

The **TRUE TEMPER CORPORATION** dates from 1808, when Lyman Batchelder of Wallingford, Vt., established a shop to make forks and hoes. In 1902, Batchelder & Sons Co. and 16 others, including 2 firms in Geneva and Ashtabula that made hand tools, merged and were incorporated in New Jersey as the American Fork & Hoe Co. The company had its general offices in Cleveland in the Keith Bldg. at 1623 Euclid, and in 1910, it was reincorporated in Ohio. By 1930, when the company was enlarged by a $20 million merger of small corporations to become the largest hand-tool company in America, it supplied about 90% of the hand tools used by U.S. farmers. Not all of its constituent companies made the same tools, but all used a similar manufacturing process.

The American Fork & Hoe facilities east of Cleveland at Geneva made rakes and pitchforks and in the 1920s developed other products rolled the same way as fork tines: a 1-piece solid fishing rod, followed by a tubular fishing rod, a golf-club shaft, and later ski poles. This plant remained the corporate tubular-products-manufacturing site until the mid-1950s, when part of the fishing-rod operation was moved to Anderson, S.C. Meanwhile, the Ashtabula plant prduced forged components. During WORLD WAR II, it was famous for steel shell casings and a newly designed bayonet. In the postwar period, farm tool sales fell, but residential sales soared. To reflect this market shift, AF&H changed its name to the True Temper Corp. in 1949. In anticipation of the expected sales increase in the 1960s, the company began a program of plant construction and consolidation, with the local result being that the Ashtabula plant was closed, the Geneva plant was centralized, and a major new 88-acre, $3.5-million plant was constructed at Saybrook in 1957 between the other two Ohio sites.

The Saybrook plant, designed for a 50% greater productive capacity than the 6 plants it replaced, featured an on-premises sawmill for cutting and forming the tool handles, an electrical substation, and a sewage-disposal plant. Because of the amount of hand work required to produce the tools, the plant was not highly automated. Over 300 varieties of rakes, shovels, hoes, and other tools were made there, while the company golf-shaft and tubular-products division remained at Geneva. In 1970 the plant employed 400, while some 700 others worked at Geneva and in downtown Cleveland; thus, about ⅓ of the company's worldwide workforce was centered in Cleveland. The corporation was plagued by scandal in the late 1940s. In 2 separate cases, the company, along with other major tool and sports-equipment manufacturers, was fined for antitrust violations and price fixing. After a federal judge ruled that the conspiratorial actions of 5 companies had resulted in a 30% increase in hand-tool prices in the late 1950s, 2 True Temper executives and 7 others were sentenced to 90-day jail sentences—a first in American corporate history. True Temper sales were unaffected, and its sales soared to over $50 million by 1966.

In 1967, the corporation was acquired by the Allegheny-Ludlum Steel Co. of Pittsburgh, a merger that had few negative local implications until the late 1970s, when the effects of recession and foreign hand-tool competition caused the firm to reassess its productive capacity. The company gradually cut employment at Saybrook and Geneva and planned to move its administrative operations to Pittsburgh. Before the move took place, however, Allegheny-Ludlum struck a deal with the Wilkinson Match Ltd.

Co. of London that resulted in True Temper becoming a wholly owned subsidiary of the British company and Allegheny-Ludlum a 44% owner of Wilkinson. In 1981, True Temper was reorganized and divided into True Temper Hardware and True Temper Sports, and the previously canceled move to Pittsburgh was accomplished. True Temper operations at the manufacturing plants were trimmed and consolidated. In 1985, the Saybrook plant employed about 250, and its reduced operations occupied a fraction of the plant, making it a potential candidate for closing.

**TUCKER, BEVERLEY DANDRIDGE** (4 Feb. 1882–4 July 1969), was bishop coadjutor of the Episcopal Diocese of Ohio (Sept.-Nov. 1938) and the sixth bishop (1938–52). His interest in missionary work helped revive a diocese hard hit by the Depression. Tucker was born in Warsaw, Va. His distinguished family included Episcopal clergymen, and Tucker shared this profession with his father and 2 of his brothers. His mother was related to Geo. Washington. Tucker received a B.A. from the University of Virginia (1902). He also graduated from the Virginia Theological Seminary (1905) and earned a B.A. (1908) and M.A. (1912) at Oxford University, which he attended as a Rhodes Scholar. He married Eleanor Carson Lile in 1915.

Ordination as a deacon (1908) and priest (1909) was followed by Tucker's assumption of a number of rectorships in Virginia (1908–20 and 1923–38) and a professorship at the Virginia Theological Seminary (1920–23). In Virginia and Ohio, Tucker worked to improve interracial harmony and the spirit of ecumenicalism. He also fostered the interests of small churches and encouraged the development of schools, colleges, and welfare organizations. After retirement, he continued diocesan work, taking confirmations and giving sermons. Service on numerous boards and an interest in education were hallmarks of Tucker's career. In Ohio, these combined in his membership on the boards of trustees of Kenyon College, Lake Erie College, and Western Reserve University.

Tucker reversed a tradition of forbidding Ohio rectors who had not graduated from the Bexley Hall seminary in Gambier, Ohio, and thus allowed the recruitment of rectors with different backgrounds. He also kept up with the shift of Cleveland's population to the suburbs and made sure churches were established to accommodate the movement from the city. He served as president of the Cleveland Church Fed. (1947), an institution interested in interchurch cooperation in Greater Cleveland. His fundraising efforts resulted in an increase in diocesan giving to the missions from $13,000 to $150,000 annually. He also worked to achieve Bexley Hall's first accreditation by the American Assoc. of Theological Seminaries. Tucker early on recognized the importance of Martin Luther King, and in July 1963 he introduced King to a Cleveland audience by comparing him favorably with Pope John XXIII.

Baker, Wallace J., *Bishops of Ohio, 1819–1968* (1968).

**TUCKERMAN, JACOB E.** (1876–27 Feb. 1967), son of social reformer Dr. LOUIS B. TUCKERMAN, was an eminent physician and public-spirited Clevelander in his own right. Born in Austinburg, Ohio, he received his medical degree in 1902 from the Cleveland College of Physicians & Surgeons and interned at ST. ALEXIS. While managing a growing private practice, he served many civic causes, including the 1913 Cleveland City Charter Commission, the CLEVELAND MEDICAL LIBRARY ASSOC., and the Negro Welfare Assoc. He was also active in the local and national medical academies, serving as president of the American Academy of Medicine 1917–18 and president of the Cleveland ACADEMY OF MEDICINE after it was incorporated in 1924. Eventually joining the staff of Euclid-Glenville Hospital, he was chief of surgery and chief of surgery emeritus for many years. Tuckerman, whose father, uncles, and brothers were doctors, raised a family of doctors and nurses. Interning at St. Alexis and working at Euclid-Glenville became a family tradition. Tuckerman was an accomplished figure skater to within 2 years of his death.

**TUCKERMAN, LOUIS BRYANT** (1850–5 Mar. 1902), was the progenitor of a prominent family of Cleveland doctors and a dominant personality in local reform activities in the late 19th century. Born of an old-line Protestant family, he was a social reformer who saw the evils of industrialization as violations of human rights. He was dubbed the "Father of Cleveland Liberalism" by TOM L. JOHNSON. Born in Rome, Ashtabula County, Ohio, Tuckerman graduated from Amherst College, attended Yale Theological Seminary, and received his medical degree from Long Island in 1877. He was the prime organizer of the FRANKLIN CLUB, a forum that met on Sunday afternoons to discuss current events, and was the catalyst for the discussion of such issues as municipal affairs, public ownership of utilities, and public health. He claimed that the club, through the petitions that resulted from its forums and the delegations that lobbied city officials, was responsible for the reduction of gas rates in 1891 and other progressive reforms.

Under Tuckerman's guidance, the club trained participants in the weekly discussions in disciplined thinking. Because the sessions were reported regularly in the *Citizen* and the conservative dailies as well, Tuckerman and his allies spread their message far beyond the Sunday soapbox. By 1894, when progressivism had taken hold, the club attracted 150 participants each week and spurred the formation of other groups organized around the single tax, public ownership of utilities, and political reform. The club fell into public disfavor after the assassination of Pres. McKinley in 1901, when it was learned that his assassin, LEON CZOLGOSZ, had attended a supposedly inflammatory speech by Emma Goldman at the club.

An idealist and a moderate, Tuckerman promoted third-party campaigns of the Greenbacks Citizen party and various working-class parties before throwing his support to the Populist party in the 1890s (see POPULIST POLITICAL PARTIES). In 1885, he ran for local office on a platform that was typical of his concrete approach to social reform; he campaigned for better hospital facilities, more adequate health services, labor representation on the Police Board, public ownership of utilities, and an improved school system. Though he got few votes, he generated public interest in the issues. In 1889, when he was again a candidate, his speech outside the hall where a Democratic candidate was speaking attracted a bigger crowd than the man inside.

Beginning in 1885, Tuckerman edited the *Workman*, a labor journal priced at $.01 a copy, to discuss important issues before the state legislature that related to labor. The weekly, whose masthead bore the slogan "Arbitration, Cooperation, and the Rights of the Homestead," critiqued the changing relations between labor and capital in the industrializing society. Viewing the labor movement as an excellent vehicle for promoting the social, political, and industrial reforms dear to his heart, he supported the KNIGHTS OF LABOR. After 3 years, he sold the *Workman* in order to devote more time to his medical practice; in the absence of his crusading spirit, the paper collapsed after a few months. Though Tuckerman's roots were in rural Ohio, he became absorbed in the public-health issues of urbanizing Cleveland. As a pioneer member of the Cleveland ACADEMY OF MEDICINE, Tuckerman stirred up his colleagues on such matters, and as the head of the organization's committee on legislation, he lobbied in Columbus for public-health laws.

**TURNBULL, RUPERT B. JR.** (3 Oct. 1913–18 Feb. 1981), was a colon and rectal surgeon and a pioneer in making Cleveland and the CLEVELAND CLINIC a world center for colon and rectal surgery. Born in Pasadena, Calif., Turnbull received his undergraduate degree from Claremont College (1936) and his medical degree from McGill University, Canada (1941). He did his postgraduate training at the South Pacific Hospital (San Francisco) and served at the Gorgas Memorial Hospital, Panama Canal Zone. He served as a field surgeon with the 1st Marine Div. in the South Pacific, Okinawa, and Tientsin. He came to Cleveland to complete his surgical training at the Cleveland Clinic upon the recommendation of Geo. (Barney) W. Crile, Jr., and trained with Dr. Tom Jones in abdominal surgery. Turnbull developed a surgical technique to make a stomach opening for the intestines (ileostomy/colostomy). With the development and refinement of colon and rectal surgery techniques, he became the world's authority on ulcerative colitis and was the first colon and rectal surgeon to recognize the importance of postsurgical therapy for colostomy and ileostomy patients. As the "father of enterostomal therapy," Turnbull along with Norman Gill founded the world's first school of enterostomal therapy, and later the Internatl. Assoc. of Enterostomal Therapists.

In collaboration with Drs. Geo. Crile, Jr., Bryan Brooke, and others, Turnbull developed and refined numerous other colon and rectal surgical techniques. He published over 185 scientific articles on various aspects of colon and rectal surgery and cancer. Along with Frank L. Weakey, Turnbull wrote the standard atlas of surgical techniques in the construction of stomas, *Atlas of Intestinal Stomas*. He was a member of numerous American and international medical societies, including the American College of Surgeons, the James IV Assoc. of Surgeons (president, 1974), and the Royal Australian College of Surgeons. He served on the editorial boards of various scientific publications, including *Disease of the Colon and Rectum*. In 1976, the Rupert B. Turnbull Surgical Society was formed by the numerous former residents and fellows who had trained under him. Turnbull was head of the Dept. of Colon & Rectal Surgery at the Cleveland Clinic until 1976, when he was named senior surgeon. In 1978 he left Cleveland to take a staff position at the Santa Barbara Medical Foundation in California. He was an active member of the Christ Episcopal Church and held membership in the Mentor Yacht Club and the ACADEMY OF MEDICINE's Pasteur Club. Rupert and Dougal Turnbull had 2 sons, Robert and John, and a daughter, Dae. Turnbull died while vacationing in Honolulu at the age of 67.

Rupert B. Turnbull Papers, Archives, Cleveland Clinic Foundation.

**TURNER, RACHEL WALKER** (1868–12 Nov. 1943) was a black soprano who began her career in Cleveland and later toured the U.S. and Europe. Her repertoire included classical selections as well as songs such as "The Last Rose of Summer" and "Swanee River." Little reliable information is available about the young Rachel Walker. She was a graduate of Cleveland's CENTRAL HIGH SCHOOL, entered Cleveland Normal Training School, and became a teacher in 1889, teaching in the city schools until sometime in the mid-1890s, when she went to study in New York, apparently after JOHN P. GREEN secured for her the financial assistance of JOHN D. ROCKEFELLER. In late

1895 or early 1896, she toured California as the prima donna of the white Henry Wolfsohn Musical Bureau, and in July 1896 she made her debut as "the creole nightingale" in New York City at the Olympia Roof Garden, where the "unusual compass and excellent quality" of her voice made her "an extraordinary hit." A correspondent for the CLEVELAND GAZETTE who saw her New York performance complained about her "palm[ing herself] off as a 'creole'" rather than stressing "the Afro-American connection." She later sang in Washington, D.C., as a member of the Robt. Downing Co., then went to London to study and made frequent appearances in Europe. She remained in Europe until the outbreak of WORLD WAR I, when she returned to Cleveland and married Robt. Turner. Although she made a few concert appearances, opportunities were few, and her singing career came to an end.

The **TWELFTH OHIO VOLUNTEER CAVALRY,** 1863–65, was organized at Camp Cleveland (see CIVIL WAR CAMPS) and mustered into federal service on 24 Nov. 1863. From Dec. 1863-Feb. 1864, the 12th was on duty at Camp Chase in Columbus, Ohio. Half of the regiment was on detached duty at Johnson's Island near Sandusky, Ohio, during that period. In Feb.-Mar. 1864, the 12th was on duty at Camp Dennison near Cincinnati, Ohio. Seventy-five Clevelanders served in the regiment. During the remainder of the CIVIL WAR, the 12th was assigned to the following units: 2d Brigade, 5th Div., 23d Army Corps, District of Kentucky (Apr.-July 1864); 4th Brigade, 1st Div., District of Kentucky, Dept. of the Ohio (July 1864-Feb. 1865); and the Cavalry Brigade, District of East Tennessee (July-Nov. 1865). The 12th Cavalry participated in the following battles and campaigns: the opposition to John Hunt Morgan's invasion of Kentucky, the Southwest Virginia Expedition, and Stoneman's raids into southwest Virginia. The 12th was mustered out on 14 Nov. 1865 in Nashville, Tenn., and its members were discharged and paid off at Camp Chase shortly thereafter. The regiment lost 50 enlisted men to hostile causes and 112 to disease during its period of service.

Henry C. Jones Papers, WRHS.

The **TWENTIETH OHIO INDEPENDENT BATTERY,** 1862–65, was mustered into federal service at Camp Cleveland (see CIVIL WAR CAMPS) on 29 Oct. 1862. From Dec. 1862-Feb. 1863, the battery was in movement toward Murfreesboro, Tenn. During its period of service, the 20th was assigned to the following units: 2d Div., 20th Army Corps, Army of the Cumberland (Feb.-Oct. 1863); 1st Div., Artillery Reserve, Dept. of the Cumberland (Oct. 1863); 3d Div., 4th Army Corps, Army of the Cumberland (Nov. 1863); Garrison Artillery, Chattanooga, Dept. of the Cumberland (Dec. 1863-Nov. 1864); Garrison Artillery, Nashville, Tenn., Dept. of the Cumberland (Nov. 1864-Feb. 1865); and Garrison Artillery, Chattanooga, Dept. of the Cumberland (Feb.-July 1865). It participated in campaigns and actions at Murfreesboro, Tullahoma, and Atlanta. The 20th Battery was mustered out and its men were discharged and paid off at Camp Cleveland on 19 July 1865. The battery lost 1 officer and 8 enlisted men to disease during its period of service. One source indicates that the 20th sustained 14 casualties at the Battle of Franklin, Tenn., on 30 Nov. 1864.

The **TWENTY-NINTH OHIO VOLUNTEER MILITIA** was created in 1863 after the passage of a state militia law requiring all white male citizens ages 18–45 to enroll for 5 years' service. It was composed primarily of men from each of Cleveland's 16 wards. Little is known about the personnel or organization of this unit, although the following individuals were listed as officers in Aug. 1863: WM. H. HAYWARD, colonel, JOHN FRAZEE, lieutenant colonel, and J. Dwight Palmer, major. Companies A and B of the militia were composed solely of members of the CLEVELAND GRAYS. The Grays also provided equipment to the 29th in Nov. 1863. The unit's functions were primarily social and ceremonial. It provided an honor escort for regiments returning from the CIVIL WAR, and participated in funeral ceremonies, such as Pres. ABRAHAM LINCOLN'S FUNERAL in Cleveland in Apr. 1865. Individual companies of the militia held balls and masquerade socials until the end of the Civil War along with maintaining a regular schedule of drill. However, the militia was mustered in for 100 days of federal service in the Washington, D.C., area on 7 May 1864, at which time it was apparently redesignated as the 150TH OHIO VOLUNTEER INFANTRY. The militia drifted into inactivity after the end of the war and by Dec. 1865 seems to have disbanded.

The **TWENTY-THIRD OHIO VOLUNTEER INFANTRY REGIMENT,** 1861–65, was organized at Camp Chase in Columbus, Ohio, and mustered into federal service on 11 June 1861. Though organized in Columbus, the regiment contained 341 Cleveland men during its 4 years of service. The 23d was assigned to the following units during its term of service: Cox's Kanawha Brigade (July-Sept. 1861); Scammon's Brigade, District of the Kanawha, W.Va. (Sept.-Nov. 1861); 3d Brigade, Kanawha Div. (Nov. 1861-Mar. 1862); 1st Brigade, Kanawha Div., Dept. of the Mountains (Mar.-Sept. 1862); 1st Brigade, Kanawha Div., 9th Army Corps, Army of the Potomac (Sept.-Oct. 1862); 1st Brigade, Kanawha Div., District of West Virginia, Dept. of the Ohio (Oct. 1862-Mar. 1863); 1st Brigade, 3d Div., 8th Army Corps, Middle Dept. (Mar.-June 1863); 1st Brigade, Scammon's Div., Dept. of West Virginia (June-Dec. 1863); 1st Brigade, 3d Div., Dept. of West Virginia (Dec. 1863-Apr. 1864); 1st Brigade, 2d Infantry, Div. of West Virginia (Apr. 1864-Jan. 1865); 1st Brigade, 1st Infantry, Div. of West Virginia (Jan.-April 1865); and 4th Provisional Div. of West Virginia (Apr.-July 1865). The 23d participated in the following battles and campaigns: Antietam; the pursuit of John Hunt Morgan's Raiders; General Cook's raid on the Virginia & Tennessee Railroad; and Gen. Sheridan's Shenandoah Valley Campaign. The regiment was mustered out at Cumberland, Md., on 26 July 1865. Its members were discharged and paid off at Camp Cleveland (see CIVIL WAR CAMPS) on 28 July 1865. The 23d lost 5 officers and 154 enlisted men to hostile causes and 1 officer and 130 enlisted men to disease. Two future U.S. presidents, Rutherford B. Hayes and Wm. McKinley, served with the unit, and 5 of its members, Hayes, James M. Comly, Russell Hastings, E. P. Scammon, and William S. Rosecrans, rose to the rank of general.

Adelaide Rudolph Papers, WRHS.
John S. Ellen Papers, WRHS.
Williams, T. Harry., *Hayes of the Twenty-third* (1965).

The **TYPOGRAPHICAL WORKERS UNION LOCAL NO. 53** is the oldest existing trade union in Cleveland. Local No. 53 received its charter on 26 July 1860 from the Natl. Typographical Union (later renamed the Internatl. Typographical Union—ITU). After an unsuccessful strike in 1865, it disbanded, but it was reorganized in 1868. The local's initial purpose was to improve the wage earnings and working hours and conditions of newspaper and commercial printers. In 1860, printers were working 12-to-14-hour days and were paid on a piece-system rate of $.30 per 1,000 ems of type. Through arbitration and strikes, the rate was gradually increased to $.40 for the day shift and $.43 for the night shift. In 1892, the union won for its newspaper printers an 8-hour day and a flat weekly rate of $21 for the day shift and $24 for the night shift, which gradually increased to $53.55 and $58.95 by 1928. The book-and-job branch of the industry also found its days shortened, from 10 hours in 1864 to 8 hours in 1905, and its wage rate raised from $9 per week in 1864 to $49 per week in 1929. As an active member of the ITU, the local sent delegates to the union's conventions and played host to the conventions of 1863, 1912, 1947, and 1968. One of the local's presidents, Jas. Hoban, was elected 2d vice-president of the ITU in 1912; local No. 53 member Jack Gill was elected to serve a term as the ITU's secretary-treasurer in 1944. As the 20th century progressed, the union expanded it activities. It began providing financial assistance to its members through a loan fund and sickness and mortuary benefits. In 1917, following the example set by the ITU, it instituted pension benefits for members. Local No. 53 was the first typographical local to own and operate its own apprentice training school. The school opened in 1926 and provided training on all types of printing machinery. In 1928 the local inaugurated its own newsletter, *Typographical News*. This organ kept members up to date on union activities, provided information concerning members, and offered helpful advice relating to the printing trade.

International Typographical Union, Local No. 53 Records, WRHS.

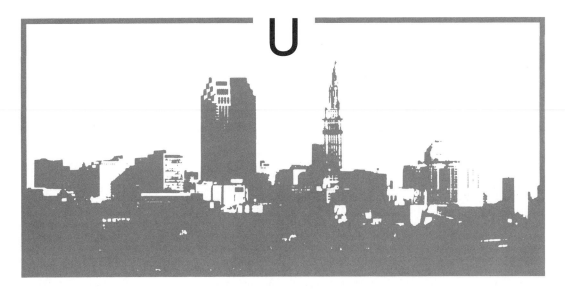

U

**URS DALTON,** formerly Dalton-Dalton-Newport, was acquired by the URS Corp. in 1984 and adopted its present (1986) name in Apr. 1985. Among the top architectural firms in the country, Dalton offers such professional services as architectural design, mechanical, electrical, structural, civil, and environmental engineering, city planning, urban renewal, and computer services. The firm emphasizes individual specialization in specific fields of design and engineering and a team effort designed to provide the benefits of the combined knowledge of all its disciplines. In 1947, Byron Dalton established Dalton-Dalton Associates in Cleveland as a partnership with his sons, Robert, James, and Calvin, and his nephew, George. The firm's early years were devoted to commercial and institutional architecture: stores, banks, schools, hospitals, and churches. The firm's first planned diversification was into the design of manufacturing and research facilities for industry. By the early 1950s, the firm recognized the need to engage in all phases of engineering, so it added structural, mechanical, and electrical engineering services. By 1956 it offered the first total architectural and engineering service under 1 roof in the city. During the late 1950s, it instituted plans to achieve a national and international practice, secure governmental contracts, and expand its principals beyond the family. In 1959, Robt. Yoder, Arthur Welker, and Richard Newport were elected to partnership. Following the acquisition of a professional services corporation in 1964, the firm became a corporate practice, Dalton-Dalton Associates, Inc. The acquisition of the Akron firm of Beiswenger, Hoch & Arnold in 1965 expanded Dalton's services to include highway, bridge, heavy civil, and sanitary design. The merger also resulted in the firm's first computer section, which remained among the most advanced in the architectural and engineering fields. In 1969, the firm became Dalton-Dalton-Little following the merger with the firm of Robt. A. Little. In 1970 it merged with Loewer & Associates of Washington, D.C. By 1972 the firm had changed its name to Dalton-Dalton-Little-Newport. During the 1970s it engaged in numerous city planning studies, especially in the areas of transportation and the environment. Among the firm's major Cleveland projects are the North Pt. Office Complex, the Ohio Bell General Office Bldg., MT. SINAI MEDICAL CTR., and the interiors for the headquarters of STANDARD OIL, the EATON CORP., and NATL. CITY CORP.

The **U.S.S. COD (S.S. 224),** a submarine permanently moored on Cleveland's lakefront, was built by the Electric Boat Co., Groton, Conn., during WORLD WAR II. The *Cod* is a Gato-class submarine and was launched on 21 Mar. 1943. It operated in the Pacific and made 7 patrols against the Japanese from American bases in Brisbane and Fremantle, Australia, and the Philippines after the American invasion. While on active duty, the *Cod* sank 10 Japanese warships and 30 merchant ships and damaged 7 others. It was depth-charged, was strafed, and survived a major fire in the torpedo room. The *Cod* also did search-and-rescue missions off Luzon in preparation for the invasion of the Philippines. On 9–10 July it rescued a Dutch submarine, taking on all hands and destroying the Dutch vessel so it would not fall into enemy hands. The *Cod* sank a total of 26,985 tons of Japanese shipping. Upon commissioning in 1943, the *Cod* was commanded by LCDR J. C. Dempsey, USN. Command of the *Cod* also came to LCDR J. A. Adkins, USN, and LCDR E. M. Westbrook, USN. The *Cod* was placed in storage on 22 June 1946 and remained so until the KOREAN WAR. In late 1950 it was moved to Cleveland to act as a training ship for naval reservists. However, when the Navy shifted to nuclear submarines, the *Cod* became obsolete. On 1 Jan. 1972 the *Cod* was decommissioned, and some heated discussion ensued as to what was to be done with it. On 25 Jan. 1975 it was donated to the Cleveland Coordinating Committee for *Cod*, and is now used as a historical display, open to the public from May to September.

**UKRAINIANS.** The first large groups of Ukrainians arrived in America in the 1870s from the Lemko, Carpatho-Ruthenia, and Galitsian (Halycchyna) regions. Their numbers are difficult to determine, because they were counted as Austrians, HUNGARIANS, POLES, or RUSSIANS, the groups that at one time or another occupied Ukraine. Most were known as Ruthenians after the name of their former state, Rus-Ukraine. Their motives for emigration were mainly socioeconomic; their objective, as a rule, was to work, get wealthy, return home, and buy land. WORLD WAR I, however, caused them to settle as permanent residents. The first Ukrainians arrived in the Cleveland area in the mid-1880s. They and others settled mainly on the west side in the TREMONT area. Subsequent waves of immigrants arrived between World War I and WORLD WAR II and consisted of former fighters for Ukrainian independence.

987

They, like those who came after World War II, were mainly political emigres and gave the older immigrant community a new ideological direction. They provided a motivated leadership that was geared to definite political and economic goals. After the Helsinki accords of 1975, a small number of Ukrainians came from the Ukrainian SSR and Poland. In 1986, the local community numbered over 35,000 and served as the nerve center for 34 other Ukrainian communities in Ohio. By this time the center of local Ukrainian settlement had shifted largely to PARMA and its adjacent communities.

Ukrainians are Greek or, more recently, Ukrainian-Byzantine Catholics. In 1902 they began their first local church activity in a Tremont-area trolley garage. By 1910 they had constructed the mother church of SS. Peter & Paul in Tremont, from which sprang the parishes of St. Mary (1952), now in Salem, St. Josaphat (1959), St. Andrew (1972), and St. Pokrova (1973), all of which are in Parma. St. Josaphat Church, located in the largest Ukrainian settlement area in Parma, became first the deanery for all Ukrainian Catholic churches in Ohio, and in Feb. 1984 the seat of the Parma Eparchy with its first bishop, R. Moskal. The Parma Eparchy is the center of religious life for much of the central U.S. and extends south to Florida. It is under the jurisdiction of the metropolitan of Philadelphia, S. Sulyk, who in turn is under the control of the cardinal and patriarch of Ukraine, M. Liubachivsky of Rome and formerly a parish priest of SS. Peter & Paul Church in Cleveland. The Ukrainian Catholic church in Cleveland established an orphanage (1902), which was later moved to Philadelphia in 1923; it operates a school in Parma (1947) and has its own picnic grounds, cemetery, and other properties. The Ukrainian Orthodox church had its beginnings in Cleveland with St. Volodymyr Church (1926), which later moved to Parma. Other Orthodox churches, St. Nicholas of Lakewood (1916), Holy Trinity in N. Royalton (1952), and St. Andrew in Cleveland, were organized and, with the exception of St. Nicholas and St. Andrew, fall under the jurisdiction of Metropolitan Mstyslav. The churches operate a Saturday school (1952), where the Ukrainian language, culture, and catechism are taught. Also active in religious life are 2 small Ukrainian Baptist communities that have parishes on the near west side.

Early Ukrainian settlers in Ohio were mostly apolitical. Politics became important after World War I. The end of the war saw the influx and growth of adherents of Ukrainian Hetmanate (royalist), progressive, and nationalist causes. Competition, sometimes hostile, left the pronationalist forces in control. The royalists declined with the death of their leader, while the progressives (socialists) fell into disrepute when post-World War II emigres told about the horrors of Stalin's manmade famine of 1932–33, concentration camps, and the Communist domination of Ukraine. That, and the struggle of the Ukrainian Insurgent Army against both the Nazis and the Russians, unified the Ukrainian community and placed in disrepute groups sympathetic to hostile ideologies. Structural unification of the community in the Cleveland area began in 1928 with the creation of the UNITED UKRAINIAN ORGANIZATIONS (UZO), which in 1940 became a member of the newly formed Ukrainian Congress Committee of America, which in turn became affiliated with the World Congress of Free Ukrainians, created in 1967. In 1986, the UZO represented over 50 member organizations. It coordinated many political, cultural, and social activities, including the creation of a Ukrainian garden in the Cleveland Cultural Gardens; the erection of the monument of T. Shevchenko, Ukraine's bard, in Washington, D.C.; the commemoration of Stalin's famine, which destroyed 10 million Ukrainians; the yearly celebration of Ukrainian independence of 22 Jan. 1918; and the Captive Nations Week. Its affiliates (religious, humanitarian, political, women's, and youth organizations) had independent projects that resulted in the building of the Lesia Ukrainka monument in the Cultural Gardens, the memorial to World War II Ukrainian-American veterans, and a monument to Ukrainian Insurgent Army fighters. Two affiliates, the Committee Against the Use of Soviet Evidence in American courts and Americans for Human Rights in Ukraine, promoted activities that sought to defend Ukrainians and dissidents in the Soviet Union. Two others, the Organization for the Rebirth of the Ukraine (1931) and the Organization for Defense of the Four Freedoms of Ukraine (1947), engaged in similar activities. Two organizations that actively aid Ukrainians abroad are the Ukrainian Gold Cross (1935) and the United Ukrainian-American Relief Organization.

American-Ukrainians have been active in local politics, serving as mayors of Parma and Middleburg, councilmen, solicitors, and law directors, and in other capacities. Those Ukrainians whose parents went through the Depression have a tendency to support the Democratic party, while children of those who came after World War II tend to be Republicans. Initially, Cleveland Ukrainian community life revolved around the church and fraternal organizations. The latter evolved out of the need to insure workers and to finance their projects, businesses, churches, national homes, etc. The largest fraternal organization is the Ukrainian Natl. Assoc., which began in 1902 and presently has 14 branches. Others include the Ukrainian Natl. Aid Assoc. with 5 branches, the Ukrainian Workingmen's Assoc. with 7 branches, and the Providence Assoc. with 5 branches. Banking began with the organization of the Ukrainian Bank in 1915 on the west side, and later a branch in Parma and N. Royalton. Two credit unions, the Cleveland Self-Reliance Union and the "Osnova," were organized in the 1950s. Businesses were also numerous. In 1934 there were 71 businesses, 1 of which employed over 40 people. The number of businesses has remained steady over the years. One of these, the "Dnistrova Khvylia," produces Ukrainian records, which are distributed nationwide. Before World War II, small business dominated the Cleveland Ukrainian-American Businessmen's Assoc.; today it is the professionals that are in the majority in this organization. The professionals include lawyers, teachers, professors, writers, doctors, engineers, etc. The last two have organizations of their own, with 65 members in a medical association.

Cultural education has remained a focal point of community life, with the churches providing much of the leadership. The priests and deacons originally ran Saturday schools for the young. In the 1980s, Saturday schools continued to exist but went under the name RIDNA SHKOLA (Native School) (1950), with professional lay teachers and a program prepared by the Educational Council of the Ukrainian Congress Committee of America, centered in New York. The local Ridna Shkola received accreditation from the Parma Board of Education. In addition to teaching the Ukrainian language, history, geography, and culture, the school organizes debutante balls and other events that financially support the program. Ukrainian professors at local and state universities have contributed to the creation of large Ukrainian collections in the local and university libraries (Kent State Univ., JOHN CARROLL UNIV., Youngstown State Univ., Ohio State Univ., and the Univ. of Dayton). A Ukrainian museum and archives, located at 1202 Kenilworth Ave., was organized in 1952. The Ukrainian Chair at Harvard was the brainchild of the 3d Congress of the Ukrainian Students' Assoc. of America, meeting here in Cleveland. This student organization, with branches throughout the U.S. and its "Harvard Project," captured the imagination of the older generation of Cleveland, which by the 1980s had contributed close to $1 million. The local student organizations of Adam Kotsko, TUSM (the Ukrainian Student Organization), and Zarevo worked on the project. Also locally active in academe is the Shevchenko Scientific Society (1956) branch, with its center in New York. Three local Ukrainian printing presses published area authors and newspapers.

Other local organizations are dedicated to preserving aspects of Ukrainian culture. Youth organizations such as the Ukrainian Youth Assoc. (1950) and "Plast" (the Ukrainian Scout Organization) (1949) own property outside of Cleveland and sponsor summer camps where Ukrainian arts as well as sports are emphasized. All youth organizations, including the Organization of Democratic Ukrainian Youth (1951), have had dancing ensembles. In the 1980s, the Kashtan (1979) dancing ensemble and school was one of the most active in the area. Church choirs and later the Homin (1949), Shevchenko (1960), and DNIPRO (1955) choirs have dominated musical activities. Also active were the Ukrainian Musical Institute (1951) and the School of Bandura (a national instrument) (1968). Percussion bands, mandolin ensembles, and private orchestras have also been active since the founding of the community. Local Ukrainians view the construction and dedication of the Ukrainian Garden in the Cleveland Cultural Gardens in 1939 as one of the community's major achievements. The commission of A. Archiperko, one of the founders of cubism, to prepare the bronze busts of T. Shevchenko, I. Franko, and St. Volodymyr was accomplished during the Depression. The statue of L. Ukrainka, a Ukrainian poet, was created by M. Chereshniovsky, who was commissioned by the Ukrainian Women's Assoc. (Soiuz Ukrainok) (1930) and its 6 branches. It was dedicated in 1969 and remains a symbol of the community's commitment to art and heritage.

George P. Kulchytsky
Youngstown State University

Bachynsky, Leonid, *Ukrainski drukovani Vydannia v Klivlendi, 1915-1958* (1958).
K., V., "Istoria 8-ho Viddilu UZKh u Klivlendi, Ohio," in *50 Littia Ukrainskoho Zolotaho Khresta v ZSA, 1931-1981* (1981).
Kulchycky (Kulchytsky), George P., "Ukrainians in Greater Cleveland," in *Ukrainian Festival of Songs and Dances* (1976).
Wynnytsky, Z., *The Clevelanders of Ukrainian Descent*, Clevelenad: The Ukrainian United Organization (1961).

The **UNDERGROUND PRESS** developed to serve the communication needs of political and cultural radicals in the 1960s and early 1970s. Its salient features were its opposition to the VIETNAM WAR and its promotion of drug use, rock music, and free sexual expression. Underground papers also experimented with new styles of type and layout and rejected traditional notions of journalistic objectivity as false. Two publications dominated Cleveland's underground press. The *Buddhist Third Class Junkmail Oracle* appeared in June 1967. Published by poet D. A. LEVY and distributed free, the *Oracle* reflected the interests of the emerging hippie counterculture. The paper resembled a collage in its layout, appearing as a jumble of poetry, artwork, announcements, advertisements, and essays and poems reprinted from papers in other cities. Levy published the *Oracle* until his death in Nov. 1968; it was continued by his friend Steve Ferguson until Mar. 1970. Ferguson then began his own *Great Swamp Erie da da Boom*, which lasted until the summer of 1972. It was succeeded by Nelson Moore's *Cuyahoga Current* (1972).

The other dominant paper in Cleveland's underground was more overtly political. The *Big Us* began publishing in 1968. Edited by Carol McEldowney and Carole Close, the *Big Us* reflected the views of the STUDENTS FOR A DEMOCRATIC SOCIETY, a leading radical organization. In its more traditional layout, the *Big Us* published news of the local radical movements, political analysis, letters, announcements, essays from other underground papers, and music reviews. With its 28 Oct. 1969 issue, the *Big Us* changed its name to the *Burning River News*. In Mar. 1970, the *Burning River News* and the *Oracle* combined forces to publish the *Burning River Oracle*, but soon the union was dissolved. Although *Burning River* continued into the summer, it was one of the many short-lived underground publishing ventures. Other short-lived efforts from the 1960s include the 1-issue *Swamp Erie Pipe Dream* (May 1967); Matthew Shulman's *Cleveland Tribunal*; and *Cleveland after Dark*, an entertainment weekly owned by a group in Boston that suspended publication in June 1970.

In Dec. 1970, students and staff members at CLEVELAND STATE UNIV. began publishing *Bread, Peace, and Land*, which continued as late as 1973. Other alternative publications appearing in 1973 included *Modern Times*, from a west side collective and aimed at workers; the *Plain Press*, a near west side community paper published partly in Spanish; and the *Star*. As radicalism waned in the early 1970s, the underground press became more respectable in style and tone. The best example of the greater success of the alternative press in Cleveland is the free weekly entertainment-oriented paper *Scene*, begun by Richard Kabat in July 1970. On the other hand, Roldo Bartimole's muck-raking *POINT OF VIEW* (June 1968- ) has continued its serious criticism of the political and corporate powers-that-be in the Cleveland area.

The **UNION CLUB OF CLEVELAND**, located at E. 12th St. and Euclid Ave., is a private organization composed of many of the city's industrialists, businessmen, and professional citizens and is one of the oldest social organizations in Cleveland. It was incorporated on 25 Sept. 1872 as the Union Club of Cleveland; a group of 60-70 men who had originally belonged to the Cleveland Club formed the new group for the purpose of having a place "for reading, for discussing the topics of the day, for entertaining and for promoting physical training and education." The founders included WM. J. BOARDMAN, Chas. A. Brayton, Chas. B. Pettengill, HENRY B. PAYNE, Wm. H. Waite, Lucien Hills, Waldemar Otis, WM. BINGHAM, SAMUEL MATHER, Harvey H. Brown, GUSTAV C. E. WEBER, Geo. Westlake, AMOS TOWNSEND, and Geo. E. Armstrong. The first officers were Bingham, president; Payne, 1st vice-president; Otis, secretary; and SYLVESTER T. EVERETT, treasurer. The club purchased the home of GEO. B. SENTER near E. 6th St. and Euclid Ave. for its headquarters. On 25 June 1901, the club was incorporated for profit; it became the Union Club Co. and subsequently purchased the Castle property at E. 12th St. and Euclid Ave. A clubhouse, designed by Cleveland architect CHAS. F. SCHWEINFURTH, was constructed to accommodate the increased membership (700-1,000) and remains the club's home. A dedication ball was held on 6 Dec. 1905. The purposes of the reincorporated body included "promoting friendship, culture and intellectual improvement and means of entertainment, amusement, recreation, enjoyment and pastime for stockholders and members." On 23 May 1961, the Union Club Co. amended its 1901 articles of incorporation, becoming an Ohio corporation not for profit. It continued to "conduct a club which provided facilities for its members and their guests for dining and meetings." Although traditionally membership has been limited to men, several women have become members, and since 1882, ladies have had their own dining room and lounge. Many lectures, political meetings, concerts, and private social functions have been held at the Union Club, and its members have contributed leadership and funds to many civic causes through the years—through both their individual and collective benefactions.

**UNION COMMERCE BANK.** *See* **HUNTINGTON NATIONAL BANK**

**UNION COMMERCE BUILDING.** *See* **HUNTINGTON BUILDING**

**UNION DEPOT** was the name given to the 2 major railroad stations erected in Cleveland before the Terminal Tower. The first Union Depot was built in 1853 at a cost of $75,000. It consisted of a group of wooden sheds at the foot of the hill where Bank (W. 6th) and Water (W. 9th) streets met the lakeshore. It was significant in that it was the first central rail depot in the city; prior to its construction, the railroads that served the city had each maintained their own small depots. The first Union Depot burned in 1864. An elaborate replacement was planned for the same site. The second Union Depot was opened in 1866. At the time of its construction, it was the largest building under 1 roof in the world, measuring 603′ × 180′. The depot was among the first buildings to utilize structural iron, with its roof supported by 49 iron trusses. Berea sandstone formed the walls. A 96′ tower dominated the building's southern facade. The cost of construction was $475,000. The new depot was dedicated on 10 Nov. 1866. A formal banquet to celebrate its opening was held in the depot. The depot designer and president of the Lake Shore Railroad dedicated the new building and prophetically predicted that while the depot might seem too large at the time, it would someday be too small. By the 1890s, the depot was indeed too small for the number of trains and people coming into Cleveland daily. It grew grimy and dingy and was an embarrassment to many citizens. Plans for a new depot, part of the Mall Bldgs. Group, were begun, but WORLD WAR I halted them. Eventually the VAN SWERINGEN brothers, owners of the Nickel Plate Railroad, persuaded the city and the other passenger railroads (except the Pennsylvania) to allow construction of a depot as the basis of the Terminal Tower, providing a Public Square station. The Terminal Tower opened in 1930, relieving Union Depot of the bulk of its traffic. The Pennsylvania Railroad, however, continued to use the old station until Sept. 1953. Union Depot stood abandoned until it was razed in 1959. Parts of the stone retaining walls overlooking the area of the station remained on the hill between W. 6th and W. 9th streets in 1985.

The **UNION OF JEWISH ORGANIZATIONS** (est. summer 1906) was the first attempt by East European immigrant Jews to organize a central authority in the community. In 1903, the Fed. of Jewish Charities had been established by the old-line German and largely Reform Jewish community of Cleveland. The cultural differences between those who supported the federation and the East European Jews were great. The union was an attempt to unite the large number of immigrant organizations that had been established in Cleveland during the previous decade. The first meeting of the union was attended by 100 delegates representing 45 organizations. The leaders of the movement were Rabbi SAMUEL MARGOLIES of ANSHE EMETH congregation, Abraham Kolinsky, Adolph J. Haas, Max E. Katz, and Max Meisel. The union carried out several successful lobbying activities, including forcing postponement of a mu-nicipal bond vote that had been scheduled for the Jewish New Year, elimination of *The Merchant of Venice* from the required reading list for high school, and the exclusion of Christmas carol singing from predominantly Jewish public schools. Additionally, it raised funds for Romanian Jews who were victimized during the peasant uprisings in 1907. The union suffered 2 notable failures in attempting to influence internal Jewish community affairs. It was unable to force the MONTEFIORE HOME to introduce kosher food for its residents, and its demand that the federation make the small immigrant charities beneficiaries of its funds was rejected. Problems facing the union could not be overcome; its constituent organizations all had separate agendas, which created turmoil in any attempt to reach consensus, and were very poor, thus keeping the union from obtaining monetary strength. Additionally, the Reform congregations and organizations controlled by the Reform community had not been asked to join, and the B'NAI B'RITH dropped out of the union soon after its creation. The weaknesses of the union left the organization moribund and led to its quiet demise during 1909.

The **UNION OF POLES IN AMERICA** is a fraternal insurance organization created in 1939 by the merger of 2 local Polish Roman Catholic unions. With its headquarters located at 6501 Lansing Ave. since 1940, the union had assets of $4.6 million in 1983. The oldest of the 2 organizations that merged to form the UPA was the Polish Roman Catholic Union of the Immaculate Heart of the Blessed Virgin. Founded on 21 July 1894, this organization was affiliated with the schismatic parish of the IMMACULATE HEART OF MARY, established by Rev. ANTON KOLASZEWSKI in 1894, and apparently offered benefits to parish members. Most of its 90 charter members were members of the parish. The purpose of the group was to unite Poles, Lithuanians, and other Slavic groups into one Roman Catholic organization and to perpetuate the faith. It also provided death benefits to members. The organization attracted members from other towns and parishes, and in 1915 it received a charter from the state to operate as a formal insuring agency. By 1933, it had 6,000 members and opened its headquarters at 6503 Lansing Ave. By 1935, membership had fallen to 4,000 in 45 Cleveland branches and 7 others elsewhere in Ohio. The union had assets of $261,000, maintained a school to teach gymnastics and physical culture to young people, and published its own newspaper, *Zjednoczeniec*.

The Polish Roman Catholic Union of Our Lady of Czestochowa, the other partner in the merger that created the UPA, was formed in Mar. 1898 by 148 charter members. Its purposes were similar to those of the slightly older organization. By 1938 it had 100 branches in the Cleveland area and assets of $500,000. When it merged with the Union of the Immaculate Heart of the Blessed Virgin on 20 Apr. 1939 to create the Union of Poles, its newspaper, the *Kuryer*, became the official paper of the new organization. In 1940, the new UPA had 12,000 members and built a new headquarters at 6501 Lansing. In 1941 there were 70 groups of the society in Cuyahoga County, and its historian described it as primarily a local rather than a national group. By 1974, its 167 lodges had 25,000 members, 15,000 of whom lived in Ohio and 55% of whom were women. By 1978, the union's assets were more than $5 million. In addition to insurance, the union offered home loans and provided social and cultural activities for its adult and juvenile members. In 1979 it awarded scholarships of $100 to 14 students entering Catholic high schools.

Grabowski, John, et al., *Polish Americans and Their Communities of Cleveland*, (1976).

U.S. Works Project Admin., "Poles of Cleveland" (1941), WRHS.

**UNIONS.** *See* **LABOR**

**UNITARIAN-UNIVERSALISM.** Both the Unitarian and Universalist movements started in England. Each was considered liberal and unorthodox by traditional Christians, as both were founded as protests against strict Calvinism. They advocated freedom of thought and conscience. The American churches began in the eastern states: Unitarianism in New England with the Transcendentalists, and Universalism in Pennsylvania with John Murray. The 2 denominations came to the Cleveland area separately early in the 19th century. The first Universalists to arrive were independent rural settlers. There were Universalist societies in Newbury ca. 1820; in Aurora by 1822; in Chardon as early as 1829; in N. OLMSTED in 1834; and in BEDFORD, Burton, Auburn, and Willoughby by 1850. These were small societies, mostly served by occasional visits from traveling preachers. In 1836, a church was organized in OHIO CITY, and a building was erected. Its 2 early pastors were Jacob Whitney and Alvin Dinsmore. Dinsmore was principal of the Universalist Institute at Ohio City, 1838–42. During the 1820s and 1830s, Cleveland was frequently visited by traveling preachers; in 1846 a church was purchased, but by 1852 it had passed into other hands. There was a reawakening of zeal ca. 1862, but by the mid-1870s, factional differences divided the church, and by 1880 Cleveland again had no formal Universalist presence. In 1891, All Souls Universalist Church was organized, and 2 years later a chapel was dedicated at E. 55th and Thackeray Ave. In 1922 the church moved to a building at Superior and Melbourne avenues in E. CLEVELAND. In 1932, All Souls merged with the First Unitarian Church of Cleveland. During its life, All Souls' ministers were Carl French Henry, Chas. Ellsworth Petty, Rufus Dix, Ray Darwin Cranmer, and Tracy Pullman. Of all the small Universalist congregations proliferating in the remainder of the Cleveland area through most of the 19th century, only one, the North Olmsted Church, organized in 1836 by Rev. Harlow P. Sage, was still viable in 1986. Its building, completed in 1838, is the 2d-oldest surviving church structure in Cuyahoga County in 1987. The church belfry was reportedly used as a station on the Underground Railway. This congregation was distinguished by having called a woman, Abbie Danforth, to be its minister in 1878.

The Unitarian experience in Cleveland was different. Among the early settlers in the WESTERN RESERVE were many who had been inspired by the New England founders of American Unitarianism. These independent thinkers formed a society in 1836. They met sporadically with occasional visiting ministers until 1867, when a minister was called and the group was incorporated as the First Unitarian Society of Cleveland. In 1878 the minister, Frederick Hosmer, inspired the congregation, which had been meeting in CASE HALL, to build a church, and in 1880 a building on Bolivar Rd. was dedicated, and the name was changed to Church of the Unity. Two women, Revs. Marian Murdoch and Florence Buck, served jointly as ministers from 1892–99. The church on Bolivar housed one of the first free kindergartens in Cleveland and domestic science classes for immigrant women. A new church was built at E. 82nd and Euclid in 1904, and the name was changed to First Unitarian Church of Cleveland. In the following years there was great growth in Cleveland Unitarianism. Outstanding ministers Minot Simons, Dilworth Lupton, Everett Moore Baker, and Robt. Killam fostered this expansion. Other Unitarian churches in Cleveland sponsored by First Church were West Shore Unitarian Church on Hilliard Rd. in Rocky River, East Shore in Mentor, and the Unitarian Society. The society was organized to keep a Unitarian presence in the inner city when First Church moved to SHAKER HTS. in 1951. In 1969 the Unitarian Society moved to a former synagogue on Lancashire Rd. in CLEVELAND HTS. In 1967 the 2 denominations merged nationally, and the churches became Unitarian-Universalist. In 1986 the denomination was represented in Greater Cleveland by 5 churches: First Unitarian, West Shore, East Shore, Unitarian Society, and the Universalist Church of N. Olmsted.

Lillian F. Brinnon
Archivist, First Unitarian Church of Cleveland

Robinson, Elmo Arnold, *The Universalist Church of Ohio* (1923).

**UNITED APPEAL.** *See* **UNITED WAY SERVICES**

The **UNITED AUTO WORKERS,** the full name of which is the United Automobile, Aerospace, & Agricultural Workers, represents over 60,000 workers in Greater Cleveland. The UAW was organized nationally in 1934 as a federal union by the AFL. The AFL, a craft-oriented body, half-heartedly incorporated the diverse auto industry into its ranks, but did little to organize the workers. By 1936, the UAW joined the CIO, along with several other unions frustrated that the AFL was ignoring the vast potential of industrial workers. The first president was Homer Martin, a Baptist minister who conducted union meetings like revivals. The UAW became a battleground of left- and right-wing factions, and after 2 years, Martin was replaced by R. J. Thomas, a representative of the rank and file. Martin, meanwhile, formed a short-lived rival union that affiliated with the AFL. In Cleveland, the basis of what was to become the UAW began in 1934 with the formation of the Cleveland District Auto Council. Its members included federal unionists at FISHER BODY, Hupmobile, NATL. CARBON, Baker Raulang, Bender Body, WILLARD STORAGE BATTERY, and WHITE MOTOR. Though the AFL ordered the council disbanded, the council under president Wyndham Mortimer operated without a charter, published a paper, the *United Auto Worker*, and called a national conference of all federal unions in the auto industry, which resolved to establish a national union under AFL auspices. The AFL responded by calling Mortimer and his allies Communists, but after several conferences, the AFL relented. The Cleveland District Auto Council sponsored mass meetings to win worker support, and the fledgling auto union realigned with the CIO. UAW organization proceeded quickly at White Motor, Fisher Body, TOW-MOTOR, and about 40 other factories. By 1942, the union had 40,000 members in Cleveland and was the largest union in the CIUC. From the beginning of the UAW, Cleveland was a major site of union activity; workers from Local 45 at the Coit Rd. Fisher Body plant participated in the sit-down strike of 1937 that resulted in a contract with General Motors.

Union activities in Cleveland were shaped by the ideology and vision of Walter Reuther, who later became UAW president. A Democratic Socialist who disavowed the Communists after working in a Soviet auto factory from 1933–35, Reuther wanted to equalize the power of the auto companies and that of the workers. He hoped to form an organization that would insulate its members from economic fluctuation. To this end, he formulated a continuous stream of plans that were the basis of contract talks over his years in power and of UAW social action plans. One thrust of UAW activity throughout the 1930s–1940s was aimed at ridding the union of Communist influence. The primary Cleveland battleground was Local 45, where

Reuther waged a running battle with Communist sympathizer LEO FENSTER, the recording secretary, and Chas. Beckman, the president. The other emphasis was to win contracts that improved the standard of living for auto workers. In addition to wage improvement, early contracts sought pensions, cost-of-living increases, hospitalization, and improved vacation benefits. By the mid-1950s, the UAW fought for a guaranteed annual wage to stabilize hours and wages even in times of lessened demand for cars; this demand was met in 1956 in the form of SUB pay (Supplemental Unemployment Benefits), funded by the auto companies.

Reuther balanced the workers' concern for bread-and-butter improvements with his own concern for social justice. As a result, he promoted public health insurance and job retraining to meet the rising threat of automation. By 1961, the union advocated a 30-40-60 plan to achieve full auto industry employment in the face of automation: 30 hours' work for 40 hours' pay and retirement at 60. While this plan was never adopted, the sensitivity of the auto industry to automation and other damaging trends was reflected in falling UAW membership and showed the wisdom of Reuther's plan. The Parma Chevy plant Local 1005, which once had 6,500 members, had only 3,500 active members with 1,500 laid off in 1982. At the Brook Park Ford plant, the UAW's 2d-largest local (Local 1250), with over 8,000 workers, was threatened by a proposed move of engine operations to Mexico and the transfer of UAW members from closed plants in Michigan who would displace local workers. In the 1980s, the UAW challenges were concessions, accompanied by threats of plant closings. The Coit Rd. Fisher Body plant closed in 1982 despite worker approval of concessions. Workers at GM, Ford, and Chrysler locals voted against the givebacks but were forced to accept them. The UAW became part of the Cleveland AFL-CIO after the two organizations merged in 1958. However, because of disagreements at the national level over foreign policy, civil rights, organizational drives, and other union and political issues, the local UAW followed Reuther's lead and resigned from the CLEVELAND FED. OF LABOR. The union remained outside the AFL-CIO despite discussion of rejoining it in 1981 to maximize labor's impact in the Reagan era.

Barnard, John, *Walter Reuther and the Rise of the Auto Workers* (1984).

Mortimer, Wyndham, *Organize!* (1971).

## UNITED CHURCH OF CHRIST. See CONGREGATIONALISTS

The **UNITED FOOD AND COMMERCIAL WORKERS** was formed nationally by the 5 June 1979 merger of the Amalgamated Meat Cutters & Butcher Workmen of America and the Retail Clerks Internatl. Assoc. The national merger was followed locally by the 5 Sept. 1983 merger of 3 locals—Retail Clerks Local 880 in Cleveland, Retail Clerks Local 698 in Akron, and Meat Cutters District Union 427—to form Local 880 of the UFCW, one of the largest locals in the nation with 32,000 members. By the time of the 1983 merger, Meat Cutters District Union 427 had gained a reputation as an innovative and progressive organization. Amalgamated Meat Cutters & Butcher Workmen was chartered by the AFL in 1897 and gradually consolidated into 1 organization the separate unions that represented various workers involved in the preparation and sale of food. Locally, District 427 was chartered in Sept. 1933, but it appears in city directories as early as 1929. Initial concerns were attracting members, signing contracts with independent store operators, and reducing store hours, including Sunday closings. The union soon began to organize meat cutters working for chain stores, and in Oct. 1934 it struck the A&P stores and warehouses in Cleveland. Under the guidance of Eugene Rich, the Meat Cutters grew from a small local in the retail field to 1,100 members in 750 markets in 1938. Organizing in the Cleveland area moved from the retail field into the poultry trade and the packing industry.

The union was plagued by scandal and internal mismanagement in the 1940s and early 1950s. Rich was removed as secretary in 1944, and the union was placed in receivership by the international's executive board; in 1951, it was again placed in receivership. Election of new leaders in 1953 elevated veteran organizer Sam Pollock (1909-1983) to the presidency. A political progressive active on a variety of social issues, Pollock led the union to a period of growth and innovation. In 1952, a 9-day strike by the 2,300-member union produced a 2-year pact that called for a 40-hour, 5-day workweek in the second year, and included a health and welfare program financed by the employer. Health care became an important issue for Pollock and other leaders. In 1964, District 427 formed the Community Health Foundation, "the first, pre-paid, direct-service, medical care program in northeastern Ohio"; it merged with the Kaiser Health Plan of California in 1969 to form the Kaiser Foundation Medical Health Care Plan of Ohio. In 1964, Pollock and Frank Cimino, who succeeded Pollock as president in 1973, proposed creation of a centralized, "portable national pension plan" for union members, and the idea became part of the national organization's bargaining program. In the late 1970s, District 427 began to offer members low-cost legal services through Hyatt Legal Clinics. District 427 also formed an independent political club to educate members and the public about issues, candidates, and legislation. The union made available its offices and equipment to other groups, such as those opposing the VIETNAM WAR, for meeting places and newsletter preparation. After the HOUGH RIOTS of 1966, District 427 and Bldg. & Service Maintenance Union 47 joined forces to establish the Community for Better Living, which helped finance construction of the Park Village Apts., "the first rent supplemented apartment complex in the country." Throughout its history, District 427 has merged with other locals in sometimes unrelated industries. By the 1980s it had branched out to include barbers, cosmetologists, and nursing-home employees. Its major merger into UFCW Local 880 was designed to consolidate services in health and welfare and to produce greater efficiency of operations.

United Food & Commercial Workers Internatl. Union, District 427, Records, 1937-73, WRHS.

The **UNITED FREEDOM MOVEMENT** was a coalition of more than 50 civic, fraternal, social, and civil-rights organizations formed to bring the civil-rights revolution to Cleveland in the early 1960s. Inspired by the southern civil-rights movement, leaders of the UFM brought about an uneasy alliance between local militants and moderates. The local chapter of the NAACP issued invitations to the meeting at which the UFM was established on 3 June 1963. Some militant leaders have argued that the NAACP effort was an attempt by the moderates to gain control of Cleveland's civil-rights movement by stealing their plan to form a coalition of militant groups committed to direct-action protest. Skeptical of what a civil-rights group led by moderates would be, militant leaders joined in hopes of influencing its direction. Harold B. Williams, executive secretary of the local NAACP, was the coordinator of the UFM;

other leaders included 4 cochairmen: Carriebell J. Cook, Rev. Isaiah Pogue, Jr., Rev. Paul Younger, and Clarence Holmes. Commissions were established to examine the education, housing, employment, health and welfare, and voting and political participation of BLACKS in Cleveland. Using negotiations first and then direct-action protests if necessary, the UFM planned to pressure local leaders in business, industry, and politics to improve the plight of blacks in these areas. The movement's first actions involved employment. In late June and July 1963, UFM leaders threatened to picket the MALL to protest discrimination in hiring tradesmen to work on the expansion of Public Hall; negotiations between the UFM leaders, city officials, and representatives from industry and labor unions produced an agreement late in July. The UFM also sponsored the Freedom March on 14 July 1963, which culminated in a rally that drew about 20,000 people to the Stadium to hear national leaders Roy Wilkins of the NAACP and Jas. Farmer of CORE.

In Aug. 1963, the UFM turned its attention to the Cleveland school system, charging that there was de facto segregation in the schools, discrimination in the assignment of black teachers and principals, and segregation in the largely white schools that received black students from overcrowded schools in black neighborhoods. The school controversy was heightened in the spring, when UFM pickets, including liberal whites and clergymen, moved from the Board of Education Bldg. to the neighborhood receiving schools in late January and were met by hostile crowds of whites, resulting in violence at the Murray Hill school. Sit-ins at the school board building followed in early February. By Mar. 1964, the movement argued that the school board was pursuing a policy of building new schools that would continue the segregation of black students. Picketing and other protests to halt work at the construction sites led to the accidental death of Rev. Bruce Klunder on 7 Apr. 1964 at the Lakeview school site. Later in April, the UFM sponsored a boycott of schools to protest the board's policies. It also went to court in an unsuccessful attempt to halt new construction. Much of the work of the UFM was aimed at getting school officials and political leaders to acknowledge the grievances of the city's black residents. Thus, school board president Ralph McAllister's constant refusals to meet with UFM leaders were seen as an insult to the black community, as were similar refusals by Mayor Ralph Locher in the summer of 1965. By the fall of 1965, tensions had increased between moderates and militants within the movement. The group was divided over whether it should endorse candidates seeking political office, especially the candidacy of Carl Stokes for mayor. When the UFM steering committee voted to allow political endorsements, 3 of its leaders resigned. Although the UFM did not endorse any candidates, the controversy so split the organization that it brought about its demise. As militants increased their power within the coalition, the NAACP withdrew in Feb. 1966.

The **UNITED GERMAN SINGERS** began in 1854 with the formation of the Cleveland Gesangverein. An informal singing group, the FROHSINN, had been formed as part of the Freimaenner Band in 1848 by a man named Heber. In Oct. 1854, a dispute arose within the Bund about whether Cleveland should succeed Canton as host of the Saengerfest of North America and sponsor the 1855 event. Fritz George and Carl Adam, leaders of the faction that favored hosting the event, led their group out of the club and formed the Gesangverein with 34 members under the musical direction of Fritz Abel. Eighteen societies with 118 voices represented the Gesangverein at the May 1855 Saengerfest in Cleveland; Cleveland again hosted the Saengerfest in June 1859, and the Gesangverein was represented by 400 voices in 24 societies (see SAENGERFESTS). A hall at Willson and Scovill (2491 E. 55th) was built for the Saengerfest in 1893 and continued to function as the Gesangverein's meeting place. The Gesangverein celebrated its 50th anniversary in 1904 with a concert featuring EMIL RING conducting a chorus of 100 voices. By ca. 1912, the Gesangverein was no longer listed separately in the city directory but continued as the United German Singers, presently (1986) located at 4515 State Rd.

The **UNITED HUNGARIAN SOCIETIES** brought together 12 Hungarian organizations when it was formed in 1902 to "coordinate the cultural, charitable and welfare activities of the member societies" and the local Hungarian community. The organization grew out of the Kossuth Statue Committee, which was formed in July 1901 and erected the statue in the patriot's honor in Sept. 1902. Under the leadership of the UHS, the local Hungarian-American community undertook many major projects to commemorate and promote its heritage and to help fellow HUNGARIANS and others in need in both Europe and the U.S. To honor Hungarian history and culture, the organization began holding annual ceremonies to recall the 1848 war for independence and sponsored Magyar Day Festivals in July; in 1924, it established the Baracs Library at the CLEVELAND MUSEUM OF ART to honor the contributions of Dr. Henrik Baracs; in 1930 it presented a bust of Hungarian poet Alexander Petofi to the CLEVELAND PUBLIC LIBRARY; and in 1933 the organization took charge of the Hungarian Cultural Gardens, adding busts to the gardens over the years. The United Hungarian Societies also provided financial assistance to the people of Hungary in times of crisis. It sent aid to famine victims in 1923, to those expelled from homes in Yugoslavia in 1935, and to flood victims in 1936, and also sent funds to hospitals, orphanages, and veterans' homes. In the U.S., the organization sent aid to striking Pennsylvania miners in 1928, established a job-placement service in Cleveland during the Great Depression, and donated to AMERICAN RED CROSS relief efforts in 1936. The UHS also coordinated relief and resettlement efforts for refugees after the 1956 revolution in Hungary. At the time of its 35th anniversary, the United Hungarian Societies had 61 affiliated organizations; by its 75th anniversary in 1977, the number of member organizations had declined to 50.

Papp, Susan M., *Hungarian Americans and Their Communities of Cleveland* (1981).

The **UNITED LABOR AGENCY** is the direct outgrowth of the Cleveland AFL-CIO community-service department in Cleveland. It has operated since 1970 as a labor-based, multiservice social-service agency. In 1968, the community-service department of the Cleveland AFL-CIO sent 3 representatives to the UNITED WAY to act as labor liaisons as part of a national program of labor participation with the United Way. That same year, and as a result of such contacts, the problem of kidney failure among individuals in 3 union families was discovered; no coverage had been provided for kidney dialysis for union members. In response, members of 2 union affiliates formed the Community Dialysis Ctr., Inc., to provide kidney dialysis for union members. To administer the center, an executive committee was formed, which acted as a board of directors. The members of the original committee were Sebastian Lupica, executive secretary of the AFL-CIO in Cleveland; Frank Valenta, president of the Cleveland AFL-CIO; Bill

Castevens, director of Region 2 of the UNITED AUTO WORKERS in Cleveland; and Jackie Presser, president of Joint Council 41 of the Cleveland TEAMSTERS UNION. Mell Witt served as the first executive director of the center.

In 1970, the name was changed to the United Labor Agency, and it was expanded as a multiservice agency to develop a program to meet the various needs of the Cleveland community. The agency was designed to provide services for the elderly and daycare, and to address the problems of ex-criminal offenders back on the streets. It also provided traditional services to labor in the event of strikes and layoffs, as well as educational services not only to union members but also to the community at large. The ULA also sponsors the ULA Culture & Arts Education Committee, founded by the committee's chairman, Ben Shouse. The committee is the only standing broad-based labor committee in the country that is dedicated to supporting cultural and arts programming. By combining social service and cultural service, the agency provides cultural and arts programming to unemployed workers through its Unemployed Workers' Discount Arts Program. Through the program, unemployed workers can continue to take their families to cultural and arts programs in the city for a minimal cost, thus maintaining the family unit during a time of crisis. The committee helps bring labor into city cultural life. The agency also helps develop cultural programs concerning labor in the form of plays, concerts, and exhibits.

The **UNITED STATES COAST GUARD** was created in 1915 when the federal government combined the U.S. Revenue Cutter Service and the U.S. Life Saving Service with the Steamboat Inspection Service into 1 organization. In 1939 the Lighthouse Service was added. In 1986, the Cleveland 9th District Office is located at 1240 E. 9th St. The Lighthouse Service started operations in Cleveland with the building of the first lighthouse in 1829. Located at Main and Water (W. 9th), the lighthouse stood on a bluff near the mouth of the CUYAHOGA RIVER. In 1859, the tower was refitted with a gas light. When the tower was demolished in 1892, the house became the lighthouse keeper's residence. The house was subsequently demolished in 1937 for construction of the Main Ave. High-Level Bridge. In 1892, a new 63-ft.-high lighthouse was constructed on the recently constructed breakwall along the west side of the harbor entrance. The lantern, built in Paris in 1884, had a 6-in. lens that emitted a 32,000-candlepower beam that could be seen 16 mi. out on the lake. Its foghorn could be heard 20 mi. away. During the late 1930s, the lighthouse began transmitting radio signals to further aid navigators. The U.S. Revenue Cutter Service was created to regulate the collection of duties on ships and vessels and goods imported into the country. The first revenue cutter to visit Cleveland was the *Erie* in 1833. The most prominent cutter to serve in the Cleveland area was the *William P. Fessenden*. Built in Cleveland by Kirby & Peck, the 180-ft. sidewheel steamer served from 1865-85. The U.S. Life Saving Service started Cleveland operations in 1876. Its purpose was to aid mariners who wrecked along the coast. Part of the Lake Erie & Ontario District, the Cleveland station was located at the harbor entrance. For their work during the busy 1873-74 shipping season, including the rescue of the crew of the schooner *Sophia Minch*, the Cleveland station keeper and crew all received Gold Lifesaving Medals. During Prohibition, the Coast Guard had the responsibility of preventing the smuggling of illicit liquor along the lake's shoreline. When the Coast Guard began icebreaking operations on the Great Lakes in the 1930s, the Ice Navigation Ctr. was located at Cleveland's 9th District Headquarters. In 1978 the Coast Guard turned their abandoned station

on WHISKEY ISLAND over to the city. In the 1980s, the Coast Guard's major responsibility on the Great Lakes is search-and-rescue missions.

The **UNITED STATES COAST GUARD STATION** was located on the West Pier at the mouth of the CUYAHOGA RIVER for exactly a century from 1876-76. The first government appropriation providing life-saving boats on the Great Lakes was made in 1854, but the U.S. Life-Saving Service was not established until 1876. The Life-Saving Service became the U.S. COAST GUARD in 1915. Its services included rescuing the shipwrecked and those endangered by storm and flood, carrying food and supplies to isolated communities, and eliminating navigation hazards. The Cleveland Life-Saving Station began operation on 29 Sept. 1876. The boat station at the West Pier occupied a series of wooden structures until 1940, when a new modernistic station was erected. The concrete structure consists of a 60-ft. observation tower (not a light), the operations building and boathouse, and a garage. It is a rare utilitarian building conceived and executed as a work of art; the design is derived from the streamlined shapes of a ship. The architect was J. MILTON DYER, designer of the classical CLEVELAND CITY HALL 30 years earlier. The station served until 1976, when the building was occupied by the water quality-control laboratories of the City of Cleveland Div. of Water. The building was then put up for public auction in 1984. The Coast Guard continued to operate a boat station at the foot of E. 9th St.

The **UNITED STATES CUSTOMS SERVICE** is responsible for enforcing customs and tariff laws and collecting the revenues from imports. Ohio is included in the Customs Service's Midwest region. The Cleveland District Office, located at 55 Erie View Plaza, is responsible for Ohio and parts of Indiana, Kentucky, and West Virginia, as well as 200 mi. of Lake Erie shoreline. In 1986, the Cleveland office had a staff of about 35 inspectors and investigators to monitor the traffic between Canada and the U.S. Customs inspection was provided at CLEVELAND HOPKINS INTERNATL. and BURKE LAKEFRONT airports. During the Great Lakes shipping season, inspectors were assigned to the Cleveland dock. The Customs Service has undergone a number of organizational and name changes since Congress authorized the collection of duties and tariffs. Customs became a division within the Treasury Dept. in 1875 and a bureau in 1927. It became the U.S. Customs Service in 1973 and remains a branch of the Treasury Dept. During the 1800s, Customs was aided by the U.S. Revenue Cutter Service. Created in 1789 to be a floating police force, the RCS employed boats for the collection of revenues. Official records contain little information concerning revenue cutters assigned to the Great Lakes before the Civil War, probably because of the service's practice of chartering local vessels for use as cutters rather than building or procuring their own fleet. The first revenue cutter to visit the port of Cleveland was the *Erie*, during its initial voyage in 1833 (see UNITED STATES COAST GUARD). In 1829, the Custom House in Cleveland was located behind the post office in Miller's Block on the north side of Superior St. between Seneca (W. 3rd) and Bank (W. 6th) streets. It moved to the new government building on Superior at the northeast corner of PUBLIC SQUARE in 1859 and into the new Federal Bldg. at Superior and PUBLIC SQUARE in 1911.

The **UNITED STATES DEPARTMENT OF COMMERCE** (Cleveland District Office) has regional and/or district responsibility to foster and promote domestic and international business. It assists and supports area firms in developing exporting capability by providing business leads and advice on export control matters. Although the emphasis has been mainly on international trade, the department has taken on other responsibilities in answer to national needs. After WORLD WAR II, the District Office counseled returning veterans on opportunities in business ownership, utilizing the department's publications on establishing and operating a business. During the KOREAN WAR (1950–53), the office administered the federal program to allocate critical materials to industry. A minority business opportunity program begun by the Cleveland office in Mar. 1969 was one of several prototype programs established in the nation. During the energy crisis in the mid-1970s, the office participated in the program for national industrial energy conservation until it was taken over by the newly created Dept. of Energy. In the 1980s, organizational changes and direct telecommunications have improved the services available to the business community. The Dept. of Commerce was first represented in Cleveland by Foreign Secretary Fred Roberts in 1915, followed by Joseph VanderLaan in 1920, Mary Woods, and Col. Quinn. In the early 1930s, the department representative was housed in the Cleveland Chamber of Commerce. In 1932, a separate office was established as one of 34 in the U.S. VanderLaan returned to Cleveland as manager from 1934–42, and Fred Roberts from 1942–45. Regional and district managers have been Geo. A. Moore, 1946–56; Edwin C. Higbee, 1956–64; Chas. B. Stebbins, 1964–80; Zelda W. Milner, 1980–1986, and Toby Zettler, present (1986). The principal advisory body on export expansion was called successively the Cleveland Regional Export Expansion Council, 1960–74; the Cleveland District Export Council, 1974–75; and the Northern Ohio District Export Council, 1975-. There are 2 district offices of the U.S. Dept. of Commerce in the state, 1 in Cincinnati and the Cleveland office, which services 48 counties in northern Ohio.

**UNITED STATES GENERAL HOSPITAL AT CLEVELAND** was a pavilion-style, 320-bed Civil War Army hospital, located on University Hts. in Brooklyn Twp. from 1862–65. Construction began on 14 Nov. 1862, on the southeast corner of Hershal (W. 5th) St. and Franklin St. opposite Camp Cleveland. The 7-ward complex was one of many such general hospitals built throughout the North and occupied South. It was located on 3.76 acres of property apparently leased to the government by its owner, Cleveland merchant and real-estate investor Silas S. Stone. John R. McClurg, U.S. Army surgeon-in-charge, announced that the hospital was officially opened on 13 Jan. 1862. He served until 21 May 1864. Surgeon Geo. N. Sternberg, U.S. Army, assumed "command" on 25 May 1864 and served until the hospital was closed on 17 July 1865. Approximately 3,020 Union soldiers convalesced there during its entire existence. Most were from Ohio regiments, although a good number were members of non-Ohio units. Two Confederate prisoners were also treated. Only enlisted men and noncommissioned officers were admitted. Commissioned officers were treated in separate hospitals, as were black enlisted soliders in units of the U.S. Colored Troops. Of the patients, 103 were the victims of gunshot wounds that had necessitated amputations, resections, or excision, usually in hospitals closer to the front. A total of 89 patients died. The most frequent causes of death were diarrhea, measles, and pneumonia. The dead were buried in West Side (now MONROE ST.) CEMETERY. Some were reinterred after the war in WOODLAND CEMETERY. Most patients survived disease and infection to be sent back to duty or to be discharged from the Army for medical reasons. Soldiers who were not able to return to their original

units were put into an invalid corps called the Veteran Reserve Corps to serve as guards wherever needed or as stewards and male nurses in general hospitals.

The **UNITED STATES MARINE HOSPITAL,** located on Erie (E. 9th) and Murrison streets, was opened in 1852 to provide medical care for sailors in the U.S. Merchant Marine, the Coast Guard, the U.S. Lighthouse, and U.S. veterans. It was part of a network of 26 government-owned hospitals for seamen. In 1837, Congress passed a bill to authorize the president to establish hospitals for seamen on western rivers and lakes. Three hospitals were built on the Mississippi, 3 on the Ohio River, and 1 in the Lake Erie region. Land for the Marine Hospital was purchased from LEVI JOHNSON and his wife for $12,000. Construction was begun in 1844 but was not completed until 1852. The hospital, a 3-story Ionic-style building, had 8 wards and could accommodate 150 patients. It was financed by a tax ($.40 per year) on sailors coming into port, and later a tax on tonnage, but in 1905, Congress voted an appropriation to support its marine hospitals rather than taxing sailors. After the CIVIL WAR, the Marine Hospital took in soldiers as well as sailors, but the care of soldiers ended in 1870, and the demand for services for sailors declined. In 1874, the city of Cleveland petitioned Congress to lease the hospital for medical purposes. In return, the city pledged to provide care for sailors at the fixed rate of $.50 per day. This effort failed because of the question of property rights of a railroad that ran between the hospital and the lakefront. In 1875, Cleveland City Hospital (the Lakeside Hospital Corp.) succeeded in leasing the building and grounds for 20 years. Physical improvements were made, including an amphitheater for clinical lectures and a children's ward. With the termination of the lease in 1895 and the completion of the new Lakeside Hospital, the Marine Hospital reverted to government control (U.S. Marine Hospital Service, Public Health Service). In 1929, the building and site were sold to the Pennsylvania Railroad, and a new hospital was built at E. 124th and Fairhill Rd., on a portion of the Otto I. Leisy estate. With the establishment of the Veterans Admin. Hospital System, the Marine Hospital was closed on 30 June 1953 and declared surplus government property. The hospital was given to the state of Ohio and was used as FAIRHILL MENTAL HEALTH CTR.

The **UNITED STATES STEEL CORPORATION** is the largest producer of steel in the country and one of the nation's major manufacturers of wire and wire products. For many years, all of its Cleveland plants were part of the corporation's American Steel & Wire Div., which made Cleveland the wire center of the world. One of the Cleveland-based firms that eventually became part of U.S. Steel dates back to the beginning of the city's iron and steel industry. In 1857, 2 brothers, DAVID AND JOHN JONES, founded Jones & Co. in NEWBURGH, where they erected one of the first rolling mills in the area. By the following year, HENRY CHISHOLM and Andros B. Stone had bought into the firm; it became the Stone, Chisholm, & Jones Co., which produced iron rails. The firm built the first blast furnace in Cleveland in 1861. On 9 Nov. 1863, the company was reorganized and incorporated as the Cleveland Rolling Mill Co. Five years later, one of the country's first "blows" of Bessemer steel occurred at the Newburgh mill. The firm began to produce various types of wire products in the 1870s. In 1881, with the erection of the Central Furnace near the CUYAHOGA RIVER, it expanded its facilities. But it also experienced some violent strikes in the 1880s, caused by ethnic differences and the various skill levels of its workforce (see CLEVELAND ROLLING MILL STRIKES).

By this time, several other companies were in operation that would become part of U.S. Steel—the H. P. Nail Co., founded in 1877 by Henry Chisholm at the foot of Case Ave. (E. 40th St.) to make wire nails; the American Wire Co., incorporated by CHAS. A. OTIS in 1882 at the foot of Marquette Ave. to produce all types of wire products; and the Baackes Wire Nail Co., started by Michael Baackes in 1889 at the foot of E. 67th St. to manufacture nails and wire. Baackes was acquired by the Chicago-based Consolidated Steel & Wire Co. in 1895. As part of an effort by Elbert Gary and John Gates to pool the wire rod market, all these Cleveland firms became part of the newly formed American Steel & Wire Co. of New Jersey by 1899. Two years later, U.S. Steel was established, and American Steel & Wire became its subsidiary. Under U.S. Steel, the Cleveland plants continued to expand, producing a variety of wire and steel products for numerous customers. Its main facilities were the American Works, comprising the old American Wire Co. plant; Central Furnaces & Docks, which had been established by the Cleveland Rolling Co.; and the Newburgh Works, which was started by the Jones brothers in 1857. These plants were joined by the Cuyahoga Works in CUYAHOGA HTS. in 1907 and the Cleveland Coal & Chemical Works, located between the Cuyahoga Works and the Central Furnace, in 1916. At its height, American Steel & Wire had 9 divisions in Cleveland. In 1924, its national headquarters were consolidated in the ROCKEFELLER BLDG. in Cleveland.

The Depression in the 1930s highlighted the antiquated state of many of U.S. Steel's Cleveland plants. In 1933, much of the historic Newburgh plant was closed, and its operations moved to Lorain. By 1937, American Steel & Wire had 8,000 employees in Cleveland. Throughout the 1940s and 1950s, the remaining plants were expanded and modernized. The 1960s were marked by streamlining efforts and legal battles over pollution controls. In 1962, the American Works was closed because its equipment was obsolete. In a reorganizational move, the American Steel & Wire Div. was dissolved in 1964, and the Cleveland offices were moved to Pittsburgh. In 1968, the remaining facilities of the Newburgh Works were closed. With 2,000 employees in the Cleveland area, U.S. Steel began to experience more financial problems by the late 1970s. Its Central Furnace Docks & Cleveland Coke Works were closed in 1978. U.S. Steel was crippled by the recession of the early 1980s, losing $361 million in 1982. That resulted in massive layoffs in the Cleveland plants and the announcement of the closing of its last major operation in Cleveland, the Cuyahoga Works, in May 1984. In July 1986, U.S. Steel sold the Cuyahoga Works to the American Steel & Wire Corp.; and it reopened 2 months later, producing wire and rods from steel billets.

Holloway, J. F. Henry Bessemer and His Inventions... (1884).
Pendry, William R., A History of the Cleveland District... (1936).
United States Steel Corp., American Steel and Wire Div., People, Progress, and Products... (1956).

The **UNITED STATES SUBMARINE VETERANS OF WORLD WAR II, NORTHEAST OHIO CHAPTER,** was founded in 1968 to help preserve the memory of 3,505 U.S. submarine sailors who lost their lives during WORLD WAR II on the 53 U.S. Navy submarines lost in the Atlantic and Pacific theaters of war. Members must have served on a U.S. Navy submarine between 7 Dec. 1941 and 31 Dec. 1946. The first president of the Northeast Chap. was Ted Poelking of Cleveland. The motto of the Submarine Veterans is "Pride Runs Deep." Meetings are held at the homes of members. A sons' and daughters' organization was formed in 1977. A ladies' auxiliary provides trays and favors for the Holy Family Cancer Home in Parma, Ohio. The Northeast Chap. was represented at the launching of the nuclear submarine U.S.S. Ohio in Groton, Conn., on 11 Nov. 1981. Members participate in local commemorative ceremonies on Memorial Day and on Veterans' Day. Some members are active in the preservation of the U.S.S. COD (S.S. 224), a World War II submarine that is open to the public.

Bastura, Bernard, History of the United States Submarine Veterans of World War II (1981).

The **UNITED STEELWORKERS OF AMERICA,** organized in the late 1930s, were formally established at a convention in Cleveland in May 1942. Efforts to organize steelworkers in Cleveland began with the formation of local branches of the Amalgamated Assoc. of Iron, Steel & Tin Workers beginning ca. 1877. The Amalgamated was involved in the CLEVELAND ROLLING MILL STRIKES of 1882 and 1885. It remained active locally until 1892. Other unions apparently were also active: in 1898, American Steel & Wire employees struck from 1 Aug.–21 Oct. for higher wages, finally settling for a compromise; and in Jan. 1900, 200–300 members of the Natl. Assoc. of Rod Mill Workers struck the 4 Cleveland plants of American Steel & Wire in an unsuccessful attempt to increase wages. In 1902, at least 2 locals of the Amalgamated Assoc. of Iron, Steel & Tin Workers were formed; it had locals in Cleveland in 1902–04, 1907–10, and 1915–17. In 1917–18, the AF of L began planning an effort to organize the steel industry nationally and formed a federation of 24 unions in the industry to coordinate the effort. When U.S. Steel refused to negotiate, the leaders called a national strike for 22 Sept. 1919. More than 18,000 workers in 16 Cleveland unions struck, closing 16 Cleveland mills. By mid-October, both American Steel & Wire and Otis Steel had plans to reopen. On 17 Oct., 2 pickets outside American Steel & Wire's Cuyahoga coke plant were shot, reportedly by machine gun fire from inside the plant as they tried to intercept workers going into the plant. As plants reopened, striking unions began to disintegrate as some found reason to send their men back to the mills. The national strike was ended officially on 8 Jan. 1920, with no concessions from U.S. Steel.

The next major organizing effort in the steel industry was that undertaken by the Committee (later Congress) for Industrial Organization in the late 1930s. It was spearheaded by the AFL, beginning in 1936; an agreement between the Amalgamated Assoc. and the CIO led to formation of the Steel Workers Organizing Committee. When the AFL expelled the CIO, the latter reorganized as an independent rival to the AFL and continued its organizing drives. Organizations of Cleveland's steelworkers began on 7 July 1936, as delegates representing 25,000 workers met at Maennerchor Hall to plan their strategy. In the spring of 1937, the SWOC scored a major victory when U.S. Steel recognized the union as the bargaining agent for its employees who were members of the Amalgamated. The SWOC's inability to secure recognition from independent steel producers prompted the violent LITTLE STEEL STRIKE OF 1937. Senate investigations and federal pressure eventually forced even the most adamant independent, REPUBLIC STEEL, to recognize the union in 1942. From 19–22 May 1942, 1,700 delegates met in Cleveland's Public Hall in the constitutional convention that reorganized the SWOC as the United Steelworkers of America.

The union in Cleveland was plagued in its early years by internal problems. Local organizers in the 1930s included Jas. C. Quinn, Jas. C. Adams, Mike Yanak, Jack Ferline, Wm. F. Donovan, and Dave and Alex Balint. In Mar. 1939, Donovan was appointed district director; he led the Cleveland-area district until Nov. 1953. Known as an "arch foe of Communists in the CIO," he expelled the Balint brothers for their leftist tendencies, and was an "outspoken critic of wildcat strikes," which plagued the young union in the 1940s. He helped formulate the agreement between local CIO unions and the CLEVELAND FED. OF LABOR, according to which the CFL agreed not to organize in the steel and auto industries and the CIO agreed to stay out of the building trades and trucking industries. The union engaged in a national strike in July-Aug. 1956, and in 1959, 28,000 Cleveland-Lorain-area steelworkers were idle during a 116-day national strike. The period 1945–80 was a time when "the name of the game was tonnage" for producers, and the union succeeded in winning "greatly improved pay and benefits." Some members were not pleased by the peaceful labor/management relationship during this period, and in the late 1970s the Chicago-based insurgent forces of Edward Sadlowski found strong support in the Cleveland area. During the 1980s, local membership in the USW decreased dramatically as foreign competition and other forces prompted a massive reorganization of the American steel industry. Between 1981–85, membership in District 28 fell from 47,000 to 26,000. The industry's need for lower production costs resulted in closed plants and laid-off workers, and the union consequently worked for job preservation and wage maintenance.

Anthony J. DiSantis Papers, WRHS.

**UNITED TORCH.** See **UNITED WAY SERVICES**

The **UNITED TRANSPORTATION UNION** was formed in 1969 from 4 railroad unions, the most prominent of which was the Brotherhood of Railroad Trainmen; its headquarters were in Cleveland for most of its 86-year history. The brotherhood was the largest of the railroad brotherhoods, a substantial power within both the railroad industry and national labor affairs. Founded in 1883 by 8 brakemen of the Delaware & Hudson Railroad in Oneonta, N.Y., the fledgling brotherhood was assisted in its earliest development by Eugene V. Debs, then an officer with the Brotherhood of Locomotive Firemen & Enginemen. In 1899, the national headquarters (Grand Lodge) of the Brotherhood of Railroad Trainmen were moved to Cleveland by a decision of the national convention held in New Orleans; its previous headquarters had been in Oneonta, N.Y., Chicago, Galesburg, and Peoria, Ill., respectively. The brotherhood was to remain in Cleveland until 1969, during which time it both influenced and was influenced by local Cleveland political and economic affairs. Because the national offices were located in Cleveland, many of the brotherhood's national affairs were litigated within the local Cleveland state and federal courts. Generally supportive of Democratic party candidates, the brotherhood was well connected to the Democrats through its one-time chief legal counsel, RAY T. MILLER.

The brotherhood was founded primarily as a mutual-aid and benevolent society; it was not until well into its existence that it began to assume the role of collective bargainer on behalf of its members. Like the other railroad brotherhoods, it continued to act as both a benevolent society and a trade union and relied heavily upon legislative lobbying for passage of favorable state and federal laws regulating the railroad industry. The brotherhood repre-

sented both "roadmen" and "yardmen" within the industry and first successfully organized interstate bus operators in the 1930s. Membership peaked in 1956 with 217,000 trainmen in the U.S. and Canada. Fiercely independent for most of its history, the brotherhood finally joined the newly merged AFL-CIO in 1957 after both organizations unsuccessfully wooed the Trainmen for mergers in 1940s. Upon first moving to Cleveland, the brotherhood was housed in the American Trust Bldg. It moved to the newly erected Brotherhood of Railroad Trainmen Bldg. at the corner of W. 9th St. and Superior Ave. in 1922 but outgrew the building's space and in 1944 sold it to local investors. Brotherhood headquarters next occupied 3 floors of the Standard Bldg. (erected by the BROTHERHOOD OF LOCOMOTIVE ENGINEERS), eventually moving its offices to 666 Euclid Ave., where it remained until 1969.

From its founding, the brotherhood had only 6 leaders, among whom Alexander F. Whitney was probably the most famous and colorful. The brotherhood was noted for the bitter and often vicious intrafraternal feuding that characterized governance of its national affairs. The struggle for leadership and control of the powerful organization often boiled over during the long and fractious national conventions, many of which were held in Cleveland. When, during the particularly obstreperous 1939 convention, the Cleveland newspapers continued to print "unauthorized and untrue" stories concerning brotherhood proceedings, a resolution was introduced to authorize the brotherhood to move its headquarters to Chicago. In 1969, responding to pressures created by a declining railroad industry, the Brotherhood of Railroad Trainmen merged with the Switchmens Union of North America, the Order of Railway Conductors & Brakemen, and the Brotherhood of Locomotive Firemen & Enginemen to form the United Transportation Union. The Brotherhood of Railroad Trainmen's president, Chas. Luna, assumed the leadership of the newly merged organization of 230,000 members. In 1985, the United Transportation Union headquarters were located at 14000 Detroit Ave. in LAKEWOOD.

**UNITED UKRAINIAN ORGANIZATIONS,** 5566 Pearl Rd., was formed in 1928 to coordinate the social, cultural, and charitable work of the various Ukrainian-American organizations in Cleveland. Its first president was Omer E. Malytzky. By 1935, 40 local groups were members of the UUO, then located at the Ukrainian Natl. Home, 2253 W. 14th St. In 1940, the organization undertook the formation of a national Ukrainian organization, the Ukrainian Congress Committee of America, Inc.; in 1966, the local UUO began to function as the local branch of the national organization. During the course of its history, the local group regularly has sponsored celebrations of Ukrainian culture, paid tribute to Ukrainian heroes such as poet and patriot Taras Shevchenko, commemorated Ukrainian independence day (1 Nov. 1918), raised funds for various charitable projects, and rallied to protest oppression of the Ukrainian people by various foreign powers, especially the Soviet Union. The United Ukrainian Organizations had 48 member organizations in 1981.

**UNITED WAY SERVICES** of Greater Cleveland, led by local corporate and business leaders, directs the annual fundraising drive to support its member health and welfare agencies. In the early 1900s, Cleveland business leaders developed the budgeting and fundraising procedures that have evolved into United Way campaigns across the country. The first united charitable fundraising drive in Cleveland was "Good Will Week," 2–9 June 1913, sponsored by the Fed. for Charity & Philanthropy. The mail solicitation represented a conscious effort to make charity more efficient and to expand the number of donors beyond the usual few large contributors. Organizations receiving monies from the federation's campaign agreed not to solicit additional funds from people contributing to the federation and to allow the federation to oversee their finances. Until 1918 these annual fundraising drives were mail solicitations. Inspired by the successful $5 million Red Cross campaign in June 1917 and the Nov. 1917 YMCA fundraising drive, the Cleveland War Council conducted a well-publicized Victory Chest campaign in May 1918. Surpassing its $6 million goal by $4 million, the Victory Chest set the pattern for future annual fundraising drives.

The Community Fund campaign began in 1919 with SAMUEL MATHER as chairman. It raised $4 million from 148,234 donors. With a campaign slogan to inspire contributors and a competitive organization of volunteers, the fund steadily increased its goal to $5.65 million in 1931, which it surpassed with 471,319 donors. The fund drive fared poorly during the Depression, but during WORLD WAR II, the goals, pledges, and numbers of donors increased. Renamed the War Chest in those years, the Community Fund became the Community Chest from 1947–58. Failure of the 1970 United Appeal campaign to match the total raised in 1969 led to the establishment in Sept. 1970 of the Commission on Health & Social Services, which recommended that the annual drive be reorganized to include the 3 main health groups not then represented in the annual solicitation. After much debate and negotiation, the Health Fund joined the new United Torch campaign in 1972; the Cancer Society joined in 1973, and the Heart Assoc. in 1974. In 1978, United Torch Services changed its name to United Way Services in order to identify itself more clearly with its national organization. United Way distributed more than $40 million to 170 local agencies in Cleveland in 1984.

The **UNIVERSAL NEGRO IMPROVEMENT ASSOCIATION (UNIA)** was a branch of a national movement that stressed black pride, racial unity of all BLACKS, and the need to redeem Africa from white rule. Dubbed the "back to Africa" movement, the UNIA promoted limited recolonization. Marcus Garvey, a Jamaican, founded the organization in 1914 in Jamaica, and between 1916–22 opened branches in 30 cities. He established the Black Star Steamship Line, the Negro Factory Corp., and a newspaper. Through the *Negro World*, he articulated the frustrations of lower-class blacks in white urban society. By exalting blackness, he underscored the fact that blacks had dignity before God and an intrinsic status that would lead them to form separate institutions out of pride, and not because they were shut out of white ones. Garvey emphasized racial unity between American and African blacks, and made Afro-Americans feel that they shared a heritage with their African brothers even though they surpassed them in economic success and well-being. While the broadest appeal of the UNIA was to the lower class, the movement corresponded with surging pride among middle- and upper-class blacks.

In Cleveland, a branch of the UNIA was organized in 1921. The parent body, searching for a local leader, looked to Dr. LEROY BUNDY, a dentist and political activist indicted in the race riots at E. St. Louis, Ill. Bundy, politically ambitious, oversaw the 1,000-member local while promoting himself as Garvey's $6,000-a-year assistant president. When Bundy realized that the salary was not forthcoming and professional losses became substantial, he did little to promote the organization, and ignored Garvey on his visits to Cleveland. Eventually, the organization was

headed by S. V. Robertson, sanitation worker and supporter of black party boss THOS. W. FLEMING. The message of the UNIA in Cleveland was diluted by factional rivalry and by its ties to establishment politics. However, here as elsewhere, the real significance of the movement was in the hope and sense of unity it gave to blacks who populated Cleveland's east side ghetto. UNIA members met at Liberty Hall and had a brass marching band that performed on Central Ave. The local welcomed Garvey 3 times before he was convicted of fraud in 1924. After Garvey's indictment, exile, and death in 1940, the organization he had founded remained commited to Pan-Africanism. For a time, the movement had its headquarters in Cleveland, and it had an office at 2200 E. 40th until 1980. In its later years, the organization was headed by Mason Hargrave.

Kusmer, Kenneth, *A Ghetto Takes Shape* (1976).
UNIA Records (microfilm), WRHS.

**UNIVERSITY CIRCLE,** located in the city of Cleveland near the eastern boundary, is a 488-acre complex that includes many of Cleveland's major cultural, educational, religious, and social-service institutions in a parklike setting. It is the only cluster of its kind in the world. The area was first settled in 1799 with the establishment of NATHANIEL DOAN's tavern at what is now E. 107th St. and Euclid Ave. The small community that grew up around the tavern was named DOAN'S CORNERS. University Circle began to take shape in the 1880s. Western Reserve University moved its campus from Hudson, Ohio, to Euclid Ave. in 1883. Case School of Applied Science (Case Institute of Technology) moved from downtown Cleveland to a site next to WRU in 1885. In the same decade, JEPTHA H. WADE donated to the city of Cleveland a large tract of land that adjoined the WRU campus. The gift stipulated that the land be used as a public park with an art gallery. Other land donations, including gifts from Patrick Calhoun, a developer of CLEVELAND HTS., and JOHN D. ROCKEFELLER of STANDARD OIL, and land purchases by the colleges completed the Circle by 1900. The name of the area was taken from a streetcar stop. The line ran on Euclid to a turnaround at E. 107th. The name of the stop, University Circle, became the name of the area.

The presence of the colleges, the land-use stipulations, and the beauty of the area attracted other cultural, educational, religious, and social-service institutions. In 1897, the WESTERN RESERVE HISTORICAL SOCIETY moved from PUBLIC SQUARE to the Circle. By the 1940s, the WRHS moved to a second Circle location, occupying the adjoining Hay and Hanna houses on East Blvd. An addition, built in 1965, houses the Crawford Auto-Aviation Museum. In 1916, the CLEVELAND MUSEUM OF ART, with its broad front steps leading to the Wade Park Lagoon, was built in a corner of WADE PARK. The GARDEN CTR. OF GREATER CLEVELAND was located at the edge of the lagoon from the 1920s until the 1960s. A new facility was constructed over the Wade Park ravine, once the home of the bears at Cleveland's first zoo. The ravine is now a nature walk that leads from the Garden Ctr. to the grounds of the CLEVELAND MUSEUM OF NATURAL HISTORY. Two major additions were made to the Circle in 1931. SEVERANCE HALL, the home of the CLEVELAND ORCHESTRA, was constructed at the corner of Euclid and East Blvd. on land purchased from WRU. UNIVERSITY HOSPITALS on Adelbert Rd. was dedicated that same year.

Between 1900–18, the Wade family developed the remaining Wade land into a residential area. The people who moved to the area included the Wades, Hannas, and Binghams. Many were trustees of Circle institutions, and generous benefactors. That was perhaps the most important factor in the development of the Circle's unique character. The close but informal ties between the trustees and supporters of the institution led to a spirit of cooperation. After WORLD WAR II, the next generation of Circle benefactors and directors moved to the suburbs, and some of the surrounding neighborhoods began to deteriorate. Mrs. Wm. G. Mather donated the seed money to form the University Circle Development Foundation (UCDF) and to commission a Boston urban-planning firm, Adams, Howard, & Greeley, to design a development plan for the Circle.

The Adams, Howard, & Greeley Plan of 1957 laid down guidelines for Circle institutions to work together to provide for future needs that would be harmonious with the Circle's character. UCDF was not an unqualified success. While institutions supported the plan, many who worked and lived in the Circle, especially WRU students and faculty, were opposed to parts of it. A particularly contentious issue was a proposed road that would carry traffic along the perimeter of the Circle. Supporters claimed that the road would divert through traffic to the Circle's edge, keeping the core for local traffic and pedestrians. Detractors said that the road would be a freeway that would destroy the Circle's integrity. The issue was fought on and off through the 1960s, with only a small portion of the road constructed. In 1970, UCFD was reorganized as UNIVERSITY CIRCLE, INC. UCI had many of the same functions as UCDF, and the Adams, Howard, & Greeley plan was still in effect in 1986. However, the emphasis since 1970 was less on new construction and more on adopting use of older structures. Many of the homes in the Circle have been used to house agencies such as the Arthritis Foundation, the Gestalt Institute, and the CLEVELAND MUSIC SCHOOL SETTLEMENT. In 1986, UCI had approximately 60 different member organizations in University Circle or close by that served the physical, cultural, and spiritual needs of Greater Cleveland.

**UNIVERSITY CIRCLE, INCORPORATED,** in the form of its predecessor, the University Circle Development Foundation, was created in 1957 as the result of a planning study sponsored by a citizens' committee and funded by Mrs. Wm. G. Mather. The purpose of the plan was to reinforce the commitment of the cultural, educational, medical, and social-service institutions of the UNIVERSITY CIRCLE area and to carry out a long-range development plan. The 20-year master plan, created by planning consultants Adams, Howard & Greeley of Cambridge, Mass., provided for the orderly growth of the member institutions and the development of the entire physical environment. The plan emphasized the aesthetic qualities of the area and proposed the means to create "a unified, beautiful cultural center." The foundation was strongly endorsed by the various institutions, each of which assigned a part of its individual autonomy to the corporation, giving it the authority to do the things that could be done better jointly than separately.

More than 35 institutions belonged to UCI by 1985. In carrying out its main objective of maintaining the physical environment, UCI served as a "land bank" for its members: purchasing, leasing, and maintaining properties in the Circle. Land acquired by the corporation was partly resold to member institutions to further their development and was partly used for common purposes. Among the common facilities developed were parking areas and multilevel parking garages, landscaping and new roadways, a free shuttle bus, and a private police force, which was established in 1959 and works in full cooperation with the Cleveland police. UCI also acts as a consultant in matters concerning land use and development; initiates and oversees construction and environmental projects; and promotes the preservation of some of the area's historic houses for institutional use. Stimulating and strengthening the relationships between its members and the communities bordering the University Circle area were also accomplished by means of urban revitalization projects and through cultural, educational, and medical programs for the community. Some actions of an institution with such broadly based powers were bound to be subject to debate. Local protest groups, among other factors, delayed the execution of one of the primary long-range projects, a circumferential road around the University Circle area. The road was completed only between Adelbert and Mayfield roads as Circle Dr. The recycling of some residential areas for institutional and athletic uses was also controversial, especially the erection of a cluster of university dormitories at E. 115th St. and Magnolia and Juniper drives in 1968.

The **UNIVERSITY CLUB,** 3813 Euclid Ave., located in a restored historic Cleveland mansion on "Millionaires' Row," is a social club for business and professional men and women. In 1896–97, Drs. Chas. Harris, Samuel Ball Platner, and Abraham Lincoln Fuller, professors at Adelbert College, organized the original University Club as an invitational social club, with membership limited to men having a college degree so that they would have a place for congenial companionship among men of like minds and interests. The group met at the Hollenden Hotel at first; was incorporated as the University Club on 8 June 1898 with 31 incorporators; and held its first stockbrokers' meeting on 15 June 1898, with a membership of 140 men representing 40 different colleges and universities. CHAS. W. BINGHAM was the first president. On 27 Mar. 1899, the club moved into its first headquarters, the John Tod house at 692 Prospect St. Membership increased, necessitating larger quarters, and the club arranged to purchase the Beckwith mansion (its present location) from Dr. CHAS. F. BRUSH, who also owned the adjoining property. The mansion became the clubhouse on 20 Dec. 1913. Through the years, the home was a permanent residence for many Cleveland men, as well as the setting for a variety of social, intellectual, and athletic activities, including private parties, dances, college reunions, receptions, lectures, and the traditional tennis and squash tournaments. The club celebrated its golden anniversary 24–25 Sept. 1948, with almost 1,000 in attendance.

In the 1950s and 1960s, membership decreased, and various financial plans were effected by its members to restore economic security to the club. As membership continued to decline, the club was in danger of dissolution. On 6 July 1980, it was sold to Thos. H. Roulston, founder and president of Roulston & Co.; Harvey Oppmann, real-estate investor; and a group of associates, who promised to renovate the historic clubhouse. In May 1980 the Cuyahoga County commissioners approved the sale of $1.5 million in tax-free industrial revenue bonds to help preserve the University Club. The redecorated club reopened in Nov. 1980 with membership limited to 1,000 business and professional men and women of all ages and races for meetings, entertainment, sociability, and recreation. Many social events and civic meetings have since been held there. Roulston is president, and Mrs. Rosanna (Collins) Sprague, vice-president. The clubhouse is entered in the Natl. Register of Historic Places.

**UNIVERSITY HEIGHTS** is a city located 8 mi. east of Cleveland, occupying 2 sq. mi. and bounded by S. EUCLID on the north, BEACHWOOD on the east, SHAKER HTS. on the south, and CLEVELAND HTS. on the west. Originally part of WARRENSVILLE TWP., University Hts. was incorporated as Idlewood Village in 1908. The present name was adopted in 1925 when JOHN CARROLL UNIVERSITY moved to the Heights. During the 19th century, the township's primary occupation was farming. Around WORLD WAR I, farming began to give way to residential growth. The population grew from about 500 in 1925 to 2,237 in 1930 and 5,981 in 1940, when University Hts. was incorporated as a city. Among the factors contributing to the city's success as a residential suburb has been its aesthetic appeal. The community of tree-lined streets twice earned the "Tree City, USA" award. Legislation adopted in 1967 authorized an inspection program that promoted not only mechanical and structural soundness but external appearance, as well. BELLEFAIRE, the new home of the JEWISH ORPHAN HOME (1868) when it moved to University Hts. in 1929, exemplifies the campus concept of institutional planning. The city is part of the University Hts.-Cleveland Hts. School District, which included 11 elementary, 3 junior high, and 1 senior high school in 1985. The population of University Hts. in 1980 was 17,055.

**UNIVERSITY HOSPITALS OF CLEVELAND** is a nonprofit teaching institution, comprising an incorporated group of hospitals with historic ties to the CASE WESTERN RESERVE UNIVERSITY School of Medicine. The hospitals' origin dates from 1863. Victims of the CIVIL WAR, primarily refugees from the South, had found their way to Cleveland and were stranded without homes. A group of men and women, meeting in the FIRST PRESBYTERIAN CHURCH, established the "Home for Friendless Strangers" to provide assistance, including medical care, for which they rented a house on Lake St. (Lakeside Ave.). After the war, the need for a refugee shelter declined, but there still was not adequate medical care for Cleveland's poor. The home's founders and others set up a committee to investigate the situation in 1865. That led to the incorporation of the Cleveland City Hospital Society in 1866. The society bought a house at 83 Wilson St., which it operated as a hospital from 1866–76; in 1870 a board of trustees assumed responsibility for its direction. During the early 1870s, the hospital cared for 150–200 patients a year, mostly charity cases. In 1873 it recorded 8,146 days of care and had an operating budget of $6,500. By 1874, conditions were so crowded that the trustees decided to move the hospital to another location, and in 1875 they obtained a 20-year lease from the federal government for the U.S. MARINE HOSPITAL on Lake St. The hospital was renamed Cleveland City Hospital. During 1875, 240 patients were admitted, 57 of them seamen. In 1889, Cleveland's city government built its own hospital, and the name of the older, privately run hospital was changed again to Lakeside Hospital. Lakeside's 1890 statistics showed 1,035 patients admitted (395 pay, 228 charity, and 412 seamen), 27,549 days of care, and an operating budget of $37,488.

During this period, the hospital was administered by its board of trustees, officers, board of managers, and several committees responsible for special areas; the members of all these groups served voluntarily. Lakeside's first professional superintendent was not hired until 1897. Just as the hospital depended on the voluntary efforts of community members for management and operation, so it depended on donations to meet expenditures. Some money was received from the city government for care of the indigent, some from the U.S. government (during the Marine Hospital lease) for the care of sailors, and a nominal fee was charged those patients able to pay it, but these funds did not nearly cover the hospital's expenses. Aware that new facilities would be needed when the lease on the Marine Hospital ran out, the trustees purchased 5 acres, also on Lake St., upon which to build a new hospital. It was planned as an 11-building complex, using the pavilion concept of hospital design. Depressed financial conditions delayed construction, and the new hospital was not yet completed when the lease on the Marine Hospital expired in 1896. During the 16 months that Lakeside Hospital was closed, it entered into formal affiliation with Western Reserve University (the university's medical school was located near the new hospital building) in 1897. The agreement gave the school faculty responsibility to supervise the clinics in the new hospital and to teach in its wards, and made official Lakeside's status as a teaching hospital.

In 1898, the new complex began operation. In 1900 it admitted 2,154 patients (473 private, 638 pay, and 1,043 free) for 49,372 days of care; 20,529 visits were made to its dispensary; its operating budget was $1,106,691. The Lakeside Hospital Training School for nurses had also opened in 1898. Initially, students paid no tuition but took an active part in caring for patients almost as soon as they arrived; indeed, the hospital was heavily dependent upon them. In 1899, the entire nursing staff of the hospital numbered 61, of whom 35 were students. In cooperation with the VISITING NURSES ASSOC. and various dispensaries and schools, students were trained in district nursing and the care of out-patients. The school closed in 1924, superseded by WRU's nursing school. In 1914, the trustees purchased land in UNIVERSITY CIRCLE for the construction of a new hospital; WRU was planning to expand in this area, an expansion that would include the construction of a new medical school. With the beginning of WORLD WAR I, all plans for construction were temporarily put aside. Lakeside Hospital assembled a group of medical officers and nurses, which went into active service overseas as the LAKESIDE UNIT following the U.S. declaration of war. Following the war, the WRU School of Medicine was the first structure of the new medical center to be built; the next were Maternity Hospital and Babies & Childrens Hospital, both of which were also affiliated with the medical school, and which would join Lakeside as the first members of the University Hospitals complex.

The Maternity Home of Cleveland Assoc. opened a hospital in a house at 58 Huron St. in 1891, which was incorporated in 1892 as the Maternity Hospital of Cleveland. The hospital subsequently moved to 134 E. Prospect in 1898, then to 2364 E. 55th St. in 1906, and finally to 3735 Cedar Ave. in 1912. The older buildings could house only a few beds; the Cedar Ave. structure increased capacity to about 60 beds. Like Lakeside Hospital, Maternity Hospital was an independent institution that depended on private donations and subscriptions. It accepted both charity and pay patients, although in practice there were few of the latter, as most women who could afford a private physician preferred to deliver at home. Initially, it cared for in-patients. In 1906 a separate service was organized under the auspices of the medical school in conjunction with Lakeside Hospital to offer home deliveries to charity patients. The medical school rented a house at 2509 E. 35th St. as headquarters for the service in 1909; it became known as the Maternity Dispensary of Lakeside Hospital and WRU, and also worked informally with Maternity Hospital. In 1917, by formal agreement, the dispensary became the Outpatient Dept. of Maternity Hospital and WRU. In 1914 the Maternity Hospital, in need of a larger and more modern building, also decided to move to University Circle. As was the case with Lakeside Hospital, war interrupted the plans, but in 1923, a campaign was begun to raise money for the construction of a new Maternity Hospital, and also Babies & Childrens Hospital, at neighboring locations in the medical center on Adelbert Rd.

The precursor of Babies & Childrens Hospital was the Infant's Clinic of the Milk Fund Assoc., opened in the Central Friendly Inn in 1906. It was reorganized in the winter of that year and incorporated as Babies' Dispensary & Hospital; land was purchased on E. 35th St. for the construction of its buildings. The dispensary began operating in the summer of 1907, housed in a residence extant on the property; a new dispensary building opened there in 1911. Its work centered on the reduction of Cleveland's infant mortality rate and the promotion of babies' health through proper nourishment and care. Mothers could bring sick infants to the dispensary to be examined by physicians; milk was bottled there under sanitary conditions; and, most important, the nurses who visited in neighborhood homes had their headquarters there. Babies' Dispensary also opened several branch dispensaries in neighborhoods throughout the city. Eventually, the Cleveland Health Dept.'s BUREAU OF CHILD HYGIENE assumed responsibility for the branch dispensaries. The dispensary's patients consisted of babies from families unable to afford the standard fees of the day for medical care, and at first physicians' and nurses' services were free. In 1915 the dispensary began to charge some families according to their ability to pay. Another change came in 1921, when the age limit for patients was raised from 3 to 14 years, and the dispensary became a children's, as well as an infants', clinic. This step pointed the way toward the opening of the dispensary's successor, the Babies & Childrens Hospital. Even during the dispensary's earliest years, its founders had looked forward to the establishment of a pediatric hospital as their eventual goal. Having affiliated with Lakeside Hospital and the School of Medicine to form the University Medical Group in 1913, the dispensary's trustees also decided to build in University Circle, and joined Maternity Hospital in raising funds for the purpose. Babies & Childrens Hospital and Maternity Hospital were dedicated in 1925. Maternity Hospital was renamed MacDonald House in 1936 (in tribute to its first superintendent, nurse Calvina MacDonald), by which time it was caring for gynecological as well as obstetrical cases; it continued providing home-delivery services until 1953. (In 1984 the hospital's name was changed to MacDonald Hospital for Women.) In Sept. 1925, the two hospitals joined with Lakeside Hospital and Rainbow Hospital for Crippled & Convalescent Children, each hospital becoming an official member of the University Hospitals Corp. as of 1 Jan. 1926.

The next unit of the center to open was the Institute of Pathology of WRU and UHC, dedicated in 1929; in addition to its research and educational functions, it also handled clinical laboratory services for the hospitals. The campaign to raise funds for the construction of a new Lakeside Hospital did not begin until 1927; it raised $6,534,355 for the construction of the hospital, and 2 special contributions of $750,000 each provided for the construction of a private pavilion (the Leonard C. Hanna House) and nurses' residence halls, as well. The hospital was dedicated in 1931. In 1940, to effect greater economy and more efficient operation, the administration of the individual hospital units was formally consolidated, and all the boards of trustees except that of Rainbow Hospital were merged. In that year, UHC had 22,081 in-patients (more than 12,000 of whom were private patients), for a total of 247,875 days of care; 184,177 out-patient visits; and, in the maternity service, 1,373 deliveries and 12,382 home visits. Operating expenses were $2,067,102.

Upon the entry of the U.S. into WORLD WAR II, a Lakeside Unit, as part of the FOURTH GENERAL HOSPITAL of the U.S. Army, again saw overseas service. In the decade following the war, ties between UHC and the WRU School of Medicine were strengthened when the hospitals granted the school nearly $1 million, approximately 75% of which was actually used. During the 1950s, 2 more units became part of the medical center complex. As early as 1925, a hospital for the treatment of mental disease had been proposed. In 1946, UHC and the medical school created departments of psychiatry, and in 1956 the Howard M. Hanna Pavilion was opened for the care of psychiatric patients. Benjamin Rose Hospital became a member of UHC in 1957, although it continued to be overseen by the trustees of the BENJAMIN ROSE INSTITUTE. The hospital had been opened by the institute in 1953 as part of the latter's mission to assist the elderly, and specialized in geriatric care and rehabilitation. Located next to the hospitals and the medical school, Benjamin Rose Hospital had close ties with both from the very beginning. UHC assumed total responsibility for Benjamin Rose in 1969, at which time its name was changed to Abington House; it was closed in 1983 and converted to office space.

In 1960, UHC's operating expenses were $12,466,100. The in-patient total was 29,007, more than 1/3 of whom were staff patients; the hospital provided 260,391 days of care and had 167,880 out-patient visits. In 1962, a joint trustee committee representing UHC and WRU announced plans for an 8-year, $54.8 million expansion program known as the University Medical Ctr. Development Program to construct new facilities and renovate existing buildings. In 1967, a new addition to Lakeside Hospital, the Robt. H. Bishop Bldg. (named after a former director of University Hospitals), was completed. The culmination of the program came in May 1972 when the CWRU Health Sciences Ctr., the Mabel S. Andrews wing of the Institute of Pathology, and UHC's Rainbow Babies & Childrens Hospital were dedicated.

Rainbow Babies & Childrens Hospital combined in one hospital the services of Babies & Childrens Hospital and the Rainbow Hospital for Crippled & Convalescent Children. The latter had its beginning in 1887, when a group of young women who called themselves the Rainbow Circle of King's Daughters decided to concern themselves with the needs of the children of the poor. In 1891 they established Rainbow Cottage on a farm near Lake Erie in the GLENVILLE area as a facility where convalescent children could regain health and strength. In 1900, a new Rainbow Cottage was built on Mayfield Rd. After it was destroyed by fire in 1904, Rainbow Circle decided to lease, and then to purchase, Novak Villa on Green Rd. in S. EUCLID. In 1913, a new hospital was built on the site, and the name was changed to Rainbow Hospital for Crippled & Convalescent Children. It cared for children with bone infections, rickets, poliomyelitis, and rheumatic fever, as well as other crippling diseases and illnesses. It closed in 1971, and its patients moved to the new hospital in University Circle, which had been built on the old site of Babies & Childrens Hospital. Babies & Childrens Hospital had been moved 80 ft. to allow for the construction of the new hospital in 1969, after which time it continued to operate until Rainbow Babies & Childrens Hospital was ready to receive patients in 1971; subsequently, the old building was demolished. The University Suburban Health Ctr., a medical office building, was built on the site of Rainbow Hospital in 1973. Statistics for 1985 showed an institution with 874 beds, 242,597 patient days, 5,260 equivalent full-time staff, and an operating budget of $208.3 million. As of 1986, UHC's units included, in addition to those enumerated above, the Joseph T. Wearn Laboratory for Medical Research, a joint project of UHC and WRU, dedicated in 1962; the Geo. M. Humphrey Bldg., opened in 1978, housing admitting, ambulatory surgery, and emergency-room facilities; the University Hospitals Health Ctr./East, a satellite facility in Lake County, added in 1983; and the Harry J. Bolwell Health Ctr., devoted to ambulatory health services, opened in 1984. Moving out into the changing health-care current of the mid-1980s, UHC added new programs, including helicopter transport and home-care services, to maintain its position in the swelling medical-care sector of Cleveland's economy.

UNIVERSITY SCHOOL, a private college preparatory school for boys, was founded in 1890. Newton M. Anderson, in a speech on 20 May 1890, was able to convince several prominent Clevelanders, including MYRON HERRICK, SAMUEL MATHER, ANDREW SQUIRE, and JEPTHA WADE II, that a new type of school was needed for their sons. Schooling for boys had been based on the classical model, with almost exclusive emphasis on training the mind. Anderson believed that this aproach was not fitted for the practical life, especially given the rapid development of industry. The young men who would become leaders of industry needed firsthand experience with machines. University School sought a thorough mixture of the theoretical and practical. In addition to traditional classrooms, the school contained a machine shop, forge shop, carpenter shop, swimming pool, and gymnasium. The school had 100 applications for admission even before a building could be erected. This original structure, designed by CHAS. F. SCHWEINFURTH, was located at Hough and Giddings Ave. (E. 71st St.), at the time a sparsely populated, almost rural area. That was important to Anderson, who believed that boys needed to get away from the city for their education. This type of school came to be called the country day school, and University School was the first in the Midwest, if not in the entire U.S. Originally the school trained boys from grades 5–12. The lower grades were added a few years later. Despite the emphasis on manual training, college preparation was still a primary consideration. Of the first graduating class in 1891, 3 members went to Yale, and the others went to Case, Adelbert, and MIT. The pattern of placing graduates in the best colleges, especially Ivy League ones, has been consistent in the school's history. University School's success has been due in large part to its headmasters. Just 5 men have served in that capacity; only 3 from 1908 to the present. The first of these, probably the one who most clearly defined University School, was Harry A. Peters. Peters began teaching at the school in 1902 and was headmaster from 1908–47. He urged his charges to work diligently and espoused maxims such as "Waste not, want not." It was common for him to take a trip to the East each fall to see that the recent graduates were adapting well to life at college.

During his tenure at University School, Peters saw the school through a number of difficulties. The first was WORLD WAR I. The boys were encouraged to join the war effort, and an infantry battalion was formed, training regularly on the school football field. In 1926 he oversaw the school's move to SHAKER HTS., a prodigious undertaking. During the Depression, faculty salaries decreased significantly, but the school's enrollment dropped only slightly. During WORLD WAR II, Peters again urged his students to support the war effort; classes were offered in navigation and engine mechanics. In 1947, Peters retired. His replacement, Harold Cruikshank, saw the school through less trying times. He left in 1963 as a new era of change and challenge greeted University School. The changes

were overseen by the current (1986) headmaster, Rowland McKinley. The racial barrier was broken in 1963 when Carl Stokes's son was accepted. Uniform requirements were lessened. Coeducation was considered but after lengthy discussion was rejected. As enrollments increased, expansion occurred, and a second campus for grades 9–12 was added in HUNTING VALLEY in 1970. In 1986, University School was the only all-male independent school in the Cleveland area.

The UNIVERSITY SOCIAL SETTLEMENT was one of the last major settlement houses founded in Cleveland. It was organized in 1926 as the University Neighborhood Ctrs. by the School of Applied Social Sciences (SASS) of Western Reserve University as an experimental program to provide training for graduate students and services to the community. The Broadway Ctr. House, located in a Polish neighborhood at 7214 Broadway, opened in Jan. 1926, and the Harvard Ctr. at Harvard Ave. and E. 72nd St. opened the following September. Six full-time employees and 11 graduate students conducted recreation and health programs at these centers and carried out surveys of community life histories. The centers operated on a decentralized basis and rented as many as 5 buildings at a time during the next 10 years. University Neighborhood Ctrs. was administered by the faculty of SASS and was financed by a fund at WRU endowed by Mrs. Dudley Blossom. Wilbur I. Newstetter served as director from 1926–36. University Neighborhood Ctrs. incorporated and became a member of the Cleveland Welfare Fed. in 1936, dropping its affiliation with WRU and changing its name to University Settlement. A board of directors was formed consisting of selected members of an advisory committee of local residents and selected faculty members of SASS. Wm. Joseph became the new director. Mrs. Blossom's financial backing of the settlement decreased during the next 5 years, and greater support came from the Community Chest and the Welfare Fed. University Settlement continues to offer a wide range of community services and activities; however, the number of settlement locales has been reduced. Its main office at 7310 Fleet Ave. was completed in 1953.

University Social Settlement Records, WRHS.

The URBAN LEAGUE OF CLEVELAND, founded in 1917 as the Negro Welfare Assoc. of Cleveland, is an interracial organization formed to confront barriers to economic opportunities. Its early focus on finding jobs for black workers has been supplemented with concerns with housing, education, and research. The organization was incorporated in Dec. 1917 at the behest of the Welfare Fed. of Cleveland to aid the adjustment of black workers coming to Cleveland and other northern cities during the Great Migration after WORLD WAR I. In the absence of social agencies to absorb the cultural shock of this move, the Negro Welfare Assoc. was set up in Jan. 1918 under the direction of Wm. R. Conners, who would lead it for 25 years. The organization worked with the new arrivals to acclimate them to the city and the factory, and with employers to gain acceptance for BLACKS. Conners lined up job openings in local industry and operated an employment agency to recruit suitable applicants. A long-time housing advocate, he also aided newcomers in finding a place to live. By the 1930s, improved housing was a primary goal of the association. In addition to specific programs to find housing for people, some programs were directed toward promoting racial understanding that would end employment and housing barriers. Meanwhile, other efforts aimed at the black community urged better sanitation and provided counseling in domestic relations. Affiliated with the Natl. Urban League since its founding, the Negro Welfare Assoc. changed its name to the Urban League of Cleveland in 1940. With the passing of Conners and the appointment of Sidney Williams, the organization concentrated on war-time labor relations, and local employers, convinced by the league that blacks could perform war work, looked to that agency for a supply of qualified workers. After the war, when Williams left, the group concentrated on vocational counseling to help youth prepare for the job market.

In the 1950s, the league continued its direct service research and self-improvement programs, but through conferences and community planning, it appealed directly to the public to bring about racial understanding. Its concerns and programs included open housing and the hiring of blacks in public contact positions in department stores and banks. By the 1960s, the league, considered a conservative body, nonetheless participated in Operation Black Unity, the boycott against McDonald Hamburger Systems to achieve more black ownership of inner-city franchises. It set up a skills bank with the cooperation of the Dept. of Labor, organized Operation Equality to facilitate integration in housing (see FAIR HOUSING PROGRAMS), and worked for fair-housing laws. The league opened a street academy for youth disaffected by public education. Throughout the 1970s and 1980s, the league continued to promote equal opportunity in employment and housing. As of 1986, the Urban League offered 5 major programs in employment counseling, office systems training, minority business development, elderly services, and housing counseling. Its offices were located at 12001 Shaker Blvd. in 1986.

Urban League of Cleveland Records, WRHS.

**URBAN TRANSPORTATION.** During the last 150 years, transit in Greater Cleveland has gone from the horse and buggy to modern, diesel-powered buses and electric-rail coaches. Ownership has gone from small, privately owned, and minimally regulated systems (prior to 1910), to private corporations with tight public controls (1910-41), to city programs governed by a small board (1942-75); and to an autonomous regional authority (1975- ). Cleveland's urban transit programs have run the gamut of problems and opportunities faced by metropolitan systems. Their histories have been complex and often stormy. Few populations have had such deep and continuing interests about mass transit. While some cities have watched their systems atrophy, a relatively small number of dedicated and able persons have dreamed about transit improvements and have had the courage to effectuate many of them in northeast Ohio.

The first urban transportation system established in the Cleveland area was the CLEVELAND & NEWBURGH RAILROAD, incorporated in 1834 by prominent Clevelanders. Operated by Silas Merchant, this line ran from a quarry atop Cedar Glen via Euclid to PUBLIC SQUARE, with passenger service commencing at the Railway Hotel at what is now E. 101st and Euclid. The line went bankrupt in 1840 and received a nearly $50,000 subsidy from the county, but continued losing money and ceased operations in 1842. Ca. 1857, omnibuses, or "urban stagecoaches," appeared on Cleveland's streets. At first they ran between the downtown hotels and the railroad stations and saved patrons the trouble of carrying bags through "rutted, quagmire streets," but they later extended service to "residential sections, remote business locales, and parks and water cures." But omnibus travel, while more convenient than walking, was itself uncomfortable and unreliable. Horse-drawn carriages had difficulty on muddy streets, and om-

nibuses often did not operate in such conditions. Cleveland omnibus operator Henry S. Stevens sought a solution to this early urban transit problem and found it in the horse-drawn streetcar: rails secured in the streets made it easier for the horses to pull the cars in all sorts of weather. The first "oat-powered railway" in Ohio was introduced in Cincinnati in 1859; that year CLEVELAND CITY COUNCIL granted 2 of Stevens's companies—the E. CLEVELAND RAILWAY CO. and the Woodland Ave. Street Railroad Co. (later the Kinsman Street Railroad Co.)—franchises to lay rails in the streets. Service began regularly on 5 Sept. 1860; between 1863-76, 8 other companies were formed to operate lines along other streets.

To extend service from the end of these lines into the countryside, 3 suburban steam lines were organized in the late 1860s and 1870s. The CLEVELAND & NEWBURGH "DUMMY" RAILROAD, organized in 1868, ran from the Woodland-E. 55th St. barns to Broadway and Miles Ave.; its steam locomotives were disguised as passenger cars to fool horses, thus earning it the name "dummy" railroad. It operated until numerous accidents forced it into receivership in 1877. The Rocky River Railroad, organized in 1867, began at W. 58th and Bridge and ran to a resort called Cliff House; this line, instrumental in the development of LAKEWOOD, operated until 1882. The third such line was JOHN D. ROCKEFELLER's Lakeview & Collamer Railroad Co., in operation from 1875-81. In the 1870s, complaints about streetcar service were frequent. The uncoordinated transportation system required riders to take several different lines to reach their destinations and to pay a new fare on each. In 1879, a veteran street railway businessman new to Cleveland sparked the beginning of a prolonged struggle that would affect not only intracity transportation but local politics as well. TOM L. JOHNSON fought to enter the Cleveland street railway business, then worked to develop a single-fare ride from the west side into downtown. The CLEVELAND RAILWAY FIGHT OF 1879 pitted Johnson against banking, coal, iron, and shipping tycoon MARCUS ALONZO HANNA and had profound implications for the future of local transportation.

Between 1879-93, the Cleveland transportation system was electrified and consolidated. As early as 1872, when the EPIZOOTIC epidemic struck area horses and brought most street railways to a halt (a few lines used mules, which were unaffected by the epidemic), street railway owners had sought other forms of power. The first local attempt to use electricity to power the cars came in July 1884 but proved unsatisfactory. Electrical power was used successfully by the E. Cleveland Street Railway Co. on 18 Dec. 1888; it began running 4 electrical cars the next day and extended its electric service to Public Square on its Euclid line in July 1889. The first electric car to reach the Square, however, had been on the South Side Railroad's Jennings Ave. (W. 14th) line on 19 May 1889. By 1894, all but 2 lines in Cleveland had been electrified; these were the Payne Ave. and Superior St. lines of Frank Robison's Cleveland City Cable Railway Co. Cars on these lines were powered by cable ropes pulled through concrete tubes by large flywheels located in powerhouses. The city's first cable car appeared on 17 Dec. 1890 on the Superior line; the change from horse-drawn cars to cable cars was gradual, but Robison had adopted cable cars after they had been outmoded by electricity. The Superior line was electrified in July 1900, the Payne line in Jan. 1901, but the latter carried the last cable car in Cleveland on 19 Dec. 1901.

Prior to 1893, Cleveland had 8 different companies operating 22 different lines. Consolidation of these scattered lines began in the 1880s. In 1885, the Kinsman Street Rail-

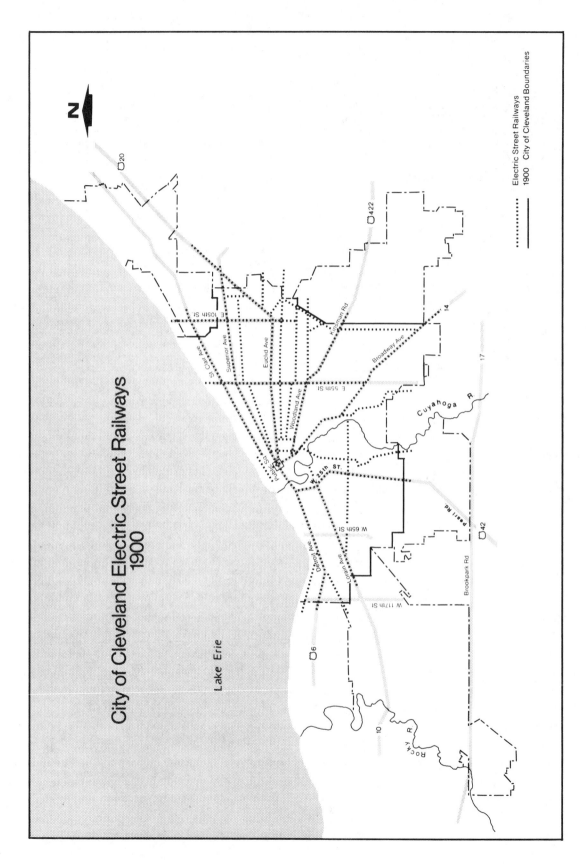

City of Cleveland Electric Street Railways
1900

Lake Erie

N

Electric Street Railways
1900   City of Cleveland Boundaries

1004

road Co. (operating the Woodland and Kinsman lines) merged with Hanna's West Side Railway Co. (Detroit, Lorain, and Franklin-W. Madison lines) to form the WOODLAND AVE. & WEST SIDE STREET RAILROAD. In 1889, Frank Robison's Cleveland City Cable Railway Co. was formed by the mergers of the St. Clair Street Railroad Co. with the Superior Railroad Co. (Payne and Superior lines). In Mar. 1893, the CLEVELAND ELECTRIC RAILWAY CO. was formed by the merger of Azariah Everett's E. CLEVELAND RAILWAY CO. (Euclid, Cedar, Wade Park, Garden [Central], Quincy, and Mayfield lines) with Joseph Stanley's BROADWAY & NEWBURGH STREET RAILROAD CO. (Broadway and Belt lines); in April, the Cleveland Electric Railway added Tom and Al Johnson's Brooklyn Street Railroad Co. (Pearl, Scovill, and Abbey lines) and their South Side Street Railroad Co. (Jennings [W. 14th], Scranton and Clark, and Fairfield lines). The Cleveland Electric became known as the Big Consolidated, and shortly after its mergers were completed, the Little Consolidated—more properly the Cleveland City Railway Co.—took shape in May with the mergers of the Cleveland City Cable Co. and the Woodland Ave. & West Side Street Railroad.

Cleveland Electric suffered through a violent strike in 1899 (see STREETCAR STRIKE OF 1899), but for the most part it did battle with the Little Con until it acquired its competitor in July 1903. For the rest of the decade, Cleveland Electric did battle with reform mayor Tom L. Johnson, who argued for a 3-cent fare and MUNICIPAL OWNERSHIP of the lines. Using the battle to educate the people about the evils of "privilege" and the benefits of municipal ownership, Johnson gave the streetcar wars great emphasis during his administration. The railway disputes eventually were brought before the U.S. District Court, Northern Ohio. The determined efforts of Judge ROBT. WALKER TAYLER to resolve the issue were praised by friends and skeptics. Paradoxically, he acted as neither a judge nor a transit specialist, but as a superb conciliator and mediator. His "Cost of Living Service" was released on 15 Mar. 1909. In summary, his theory was that "the community never pays more than the cost of service rendered; that the owners of the property never, by any device, get more than 6% on the agreed amount of their investment; and that the community will at all times know just how the property is being operated and have the power to correct any abuse either of management or of service."

After more than 50 hearings by council's Committee of the Whole, the Tayler Franchise was adopted by council on 18 Dec. 1909, approved by Cleveland voters on 10 Feb. 1910, and made operational on 1 Mar. 1910. It inaugurated a new era in Cleveland's transportation history. Franchises of the former competing companies were given to the CLEVELAND RAILWAY CO. Appraised value was $14,675,000. Guidelines for costs and changes were prescribed. Innovations provided for the position of city street railroad commissioner (appointed and removed only by the mayor but paid by the company), for boards of arbitration, and for municipal ownership, when such was permitted under Ohio's constitution. Cleveland's system caught the attention of the nation. One of Tom Johnson's bright young men, also a single-taxer, was appointed by Mayor NEWTON D. BAKER as railroad commissioner. PETER WITT not only scrutinized every move of the company, he also was an innovator. He pioneered the "skip-stop" plan, under which inbound cars stopped at every other street and outbound ones at the other. Because each patron walked 1 additional block per day, service was faster. He developed and patented the "Pete Witt Car," which had front and rear doors for entrance and exit.

The system that brought Cleveland some of the best and cheapest service in the nation was not immune to the Depression of the 1930s. Decreased patronage, inability to meet fixed charges, including the 6% return, and continued use of depreciated equipment spurred interest in public ownership. Under powers granted him by the Tayler Ordinance, commissioner Edward J. Schweid, with the assistance of consultants, prepared an *Analytical Survey* in 1937. Based upon a microscopic examination of the economic facets since 1910, it carried overtones of the inevitability of public transit ownership, which finally arrived in 1942. Twenty years after the Ohio constitution had permitted a city to purchase a transit system, Cleveland's council passed Ordinance No. 86-A-42. Transportation revenue bonds were to be issued in the amount of $17.5 million. At midnight 23 Apr. 1942, Cleveland took possession of the system, acquiring assets with a book value of $39,394,233 for a base consideration of $14,127,480. Operation and management became a part of the Dept. of Public Utilities. The new commissioner was Walter J. McCarter, former vice-president of operations of the Cleveland Railway Co. On 3 Nov. 1942, voters approved a charter amendment establishing an independent transit board "to supervise, manage and control the transportation system." The 3-member board began to function on 1 Jan. 1943; its first chairman was Wm. C. Reed, former director of public properties. Some decisions, however, were still subject to approval by city council. Other voter-approved charter amendments increased the membership to 5 and gave the mayor, with council approval, the power to appoint members and to remove them after a public hearing. All other decisions, including the establishment of its merit system, were given to CTS. The Transit Board followed the model of the directors of a private corporation—to determine policies and to give us a general manager the responsibility for operations. Walter McCarter continued in that position and hired Donald C. Hyde as personnel director. Having had excellent training and experience in Milwaukee's transit, Hyde served as general manager from 1947 until his retirement in 1966.

The city's performance with public transit was amazingly successful until the early 1970s. WORLD WAR II had brought rapid increases in ridership. Automobile manufacturing ceased; gasoline was rationed; employees, including many more women, worked more days per week. The 1942 debt, which was scheduled for repayment in 20 years, was redeemed in half the time. A 1957 Reconstruction Finance Corporation loan of $29.5 million was for the purchase of vehicles, for improvements in surface facilities, and for assistance with the construction of a rapid rail system. Operation of the rapid transit between Public Square and Windemere began on 15 Mar. 1955; service to the west side began on 14 Aug. 1955 and was extended to the airport in 1968, making Cleveland the first city in the Western Hemisphere to have rapid-rail transit from the center city to the airport. Opening of the crosstown rapid transit marked another milestone in the city's transportation history and served to measure progress. Buses, first introduced in 1914 and used briefly, then reintroduced with greater success in Aug. 1925, proved more flexible, if less glamorous, than rail-bound streetcars, which were gradually phased out, the last one running on 24 Jan. 1954. CTS was a "profit-making" venture between 1942–69, but it lost $1,774,861 in 1970, and the annual deficit increased to $6,893,571 in 1974. Council approved an $8.8 million loan to CTS. Charged with operating from the farebox, Cleveland could no longer hold fares to $.50 for local rides without additional sources of income. Federal, state, and local legislation offered possibilities. In 1973, the Northeast

Ohio Coordinating Agency commissioned a feasibility study by a 21-member Five-County Transit Task Force chaired by Robt. T. Pollock, CTS's general manager and chief executive officer. The 1974 report provided a framework for transit developments and expansions. The GREATER CLEVELAND REGIONAL TRANSITY AUTHORITY was created on 30 Dec. 1974, when it was approved by the Cleveland council and the Cuyahoga County commissioners. Agreements were reached by the governing bodies for the transfer of 7 systems operating in Cuyahoga County to RTA. On 22 July 1975, residents of Cuyahoga County overwhelmingly approved a 1% sales tax to finance operations. RTA was inaugurated on 5 Sept., and 1 month later a new fare structure ($.25 local and $.35 Express Rapid) became effective. By the end of the first year of operation, total system ridership had increased 65% over pre-RTA levels for all transit in Cuyahoga County.

RTA's revenue sources and amounts had changed dramatically by 1985. Total revenues were $136.4 million in 1985; passenger fares brought in only $36.8 million. Much of the system's income came from public sources: the sales tax contributed $77.9 million, the state chipped in $6.8 million, and Federal Operational Assistance provided $11.3 million. In addition, sizable amounts of money were made available from the federal government on a matching basis. The results were that new rolling stock replaced a large percentage of that owned by the predecessor companies. Roadbeds and rails were built or renovated. New bus routes were started, and others were extended. New centers for maintenance and repairs were constructed; others were renovated. To better serve senior citizens and the handicapped, RTA developed Community Response Transit, a service utilizing special buses. Significant differences developed between the RTA trustees and the old CTS board. The restriction against people in public positions serving on the CTS board was not continued under RTA. CTS board members received a salary and were required to meet once a week; RTA trustees received a fixed fee for attendance at any RTA meeting, including committee sessions. Turnover was small for CTS but comparatively heavy for RTA: in 1986, only 1 of the initial RTA trustees, Harry Alexander, was still a member. One practice was continued, however: the use of final and binding decisions by an arbitration board or an arbitrator of labor disputes. Since the first agreement was entered into by the Cleveland Railway Co. and the Amalgamated Transit Union (and its predecessors) in 1910, fewer than 30 days had been lost because of strikes. Such a record had brought Cleveland worldwide recognition. Important issues faced RTA by 1986: whether to expand from basically a single-county to a multi-county system, whether to change the number of trustees to an odd number to avoid paralyzing voting deadlocks, and where else to turn for financing in the face of reduced federal capital and operating grants. Answers to these and numerous other queries remain to be seen.

Dallas Young

Christiansen, Harry, *Northern Ohio's Interurbans and Rapid Transit Railways* (1965).
Christiansen, Harry, *Trolley Trails through Greater Cleveland and Northern Ohio* (1975).
Morse, Kenneth S. P., *Cleveland Streetcars* (1955).

**URSULINE COLLEGE** is a Catholic liberal-arts college for women located at 2550 Lander Rd., PEPPER PIKE. The school was founded on 17 Nov. 1871 when Mother Mary of the Annunciation Beaumont applied for and received a charter to confer college degrees (see URSULINE SISTERS). In 1922, the Ursuline nuns were authorized by the bishop to start a separate college, which began classes at 50 Euclid Ave. In 1927, the college moved into 2 large remodeled residences at 2234 Overlook Rd. It graduated its first class in 1925 after receiving approval from the state department of education the previous year for the training of high school teachers. Ursuline was admitted into the North Central Assoc. of Colleges in 1931 and was accredited between 1937–39 for training teachers in home economics, art, and music. The college expanded in 1944 through the acquisition of the John Sherwin estate. In 1952, the Ursuline nuns announced plans to move to the present 112-acre site in Pepper Pike; they had purchased a portion of it in 1928 and the remainder in 1949. The first building on the new campus was opened in 1959. During the 1960s, enrollment at the college doubled, and residence facilities tripled. Significant administrative changes were made with the establishment of a separate corporation of the college and the appointment of a board of trustees, which for the first time included laymen. In addition, the first faculty senate was founded, as were an office of continuing education and a 2-year course in retail and merchandising. In 1970, the property on Lander was divided between Ursuline Academy and the college. St. John College's nursing program was transferred to Ursuline in 1975. The 1970s saw the introduction of courses for women in management, fashion design and fashion merchandising, and business management. The first off-campus courses were offered. In addition, the campus grew with the construction of the Matthew J. O'Brien Campus Ctr. and the Florence O'Donnell Wasmer Art Gallery, which augmented the Mullen Academic Bldg., the Dauby Science Ctr., the Fritzsche Student Ctr., Grace Residence Hall, the Ralph M. Besse Library, and Gladys Murphy Residence Hall. In 1984, Ursuline had a faculty of 9 priests, 37 Ursuline nuns of Cleveland, and 98 lay professors; 1,337 students were enrolled, and 26 bachelor's majors were available.

The **URSULINE SISTERS OF CLEVELAND** are members of an international Roman Catholic religious community dedicated to Christian education, founded by St. Angela Merici. Bp. AMADEUS RAPPE recognized the need for religious to staff the parish schools. He had become familiar with the work of the Ursuline nuns of Boulogne-sur-Mer, France, when he served as their chaplain. In 1850, in answer to his request, 5 Ursuline nuns were sent to Cleveland. Mother Mary of the Annunciation Beaumont was the superior of this community. Upon arrival, the sisters took charge of the Catholic girls' school on Euclid Ave., the forerunner of the Cathedral school. By 1853 they were staffing an academy and St. Patrick's school in OHIO CITY. Since their rule of life required a cloistered environment, any travel outside the convent required a special dispensation from the Vatican. It was given, and the Ursulines expanded their apostolate to outlying schools. Besides the PAROCHIAL SCHOOLS, the sisters maintained boarding schools. In 1871 they opened URSULINE COLLEGE for women. By the mid-1870s, they had outgrown their Euclid site and decided to purchase property located on the shores of Lake Erie at the mouth of Euclid Creek. There they opened Villa Angela, a boarding school and academy. In 1876 the Ursulines opened a school for boys, St. Joseph Seminary, at the Villa Angela location. They sold the Euclid Ave. property in 1890 and began negotiations for land at Scovill and Willson Ave. (E. 55th). The transaction was completed, and the cornerstone was laid on 8 Aug. 1892. The new Ursuline motherhouse was an imposing English Gothic structure. The Ursulines continued to staff additional parochial schools in Cleveland. Their apostolate was not restricted to teaching. When the influenza epidemic closed the schools in 1918, the sisters made themselves available as nurses. In June 1922 the sisters transferred their college to the building of the former diocesan preparatory seminary located adjacent to Western Reserve University. The college remained there until it was relocated to PEPPER PIKE. The E. 55th property was sold in 1941, and the motherhouse was relocated to Villa Angela. The next year saw the purchase of the Painter estate on Fairmount Blvd. at Lee Rd. in CLEVELAND HTS., which became the new BEAUMONT ACADEMY. By the 1950s, the community had outgrown Villa Angela, and the motherhouse was transferred to its present location next to Ursuline College in Pepper Pike.

Francis, Sister M. Michael, OSU, *The Broad Highway* (1951).

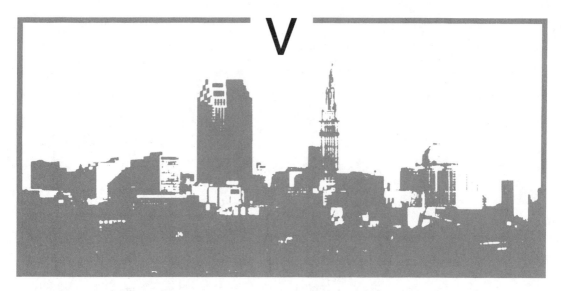

# V

**VAIL, HARRY L.** (11 Oct. 1860–27 Feb. 1935), was a prominent Cleveland journalist, lawyer, and politician. He served as a Cuyahoga County commissioner during one of Cleveland's most ambitious periods of urban development. Vail was born in Cleveland. His father had been a presiding judge of the Cleveland Police Court, and later died in the CIVIL WAR. Vail attended CENTRAL HIGH SCHOOL and at the age of 19 received his B.A. from Ohio Wesleyan. Over the next 5 years, he studied law at intervals; he was admitted to the bar in 1884, although he did not begin to practice law until 1888. Following college, Vail embarked on a reporting and editorial career in Ohio, working for the *Cleveland Herald*, the *Cincinnati Enquirer*, and the *Cincinnati Times*, where he was managing editor. In Cleveland, he was also the city editor of the *SUNDAY VOICE*, which, as the first Sunday paper in Cleveland, drew a storm of criticism from local clergymen. Vail entered public service in 1894 as clerk of the court of common pleas and circuit courts, a position he held until 1900. He then served as a county commissioner, 1904–13. While holding that office, Vail was instrumental in initiating some of the city's largest public building projects. Notable among these were the new courthouse and the DETROIT-SUPERIOR BRIDGE. After 1913, Vail served in various public offices for both the state and local governments. In 1917, Mayor HARRY L. DAVIS appointed him secretary of the War Advisory Board, and in 1921, the governor of Ohio appointed him to serve on an advisory committee for the state's Div. of Americanization. Vail devoted much of his later life to his real-estate interests. He was director of the Lawmer Land Co., and vice-president of the Warner Land Co. He continued to be active in the Republican party, and as a member of the UNION CLUB and CITY CLUB. Vail's wife, the former Sarah Wickham, was an organizer of the YWCA in Cleveland and a founder and president of the Cleveland Art Assoc., which sponsored the first MAY SHOW.

**VAIL, HERMAN LANSING** (6 July 1895–7 Jan. 1981), was a lawyer and newspaper publisher who combined a balance of talents and contributions to the areas of law, politics, business, and cultural, civic, and educational institutions. Vail was born in Cleveland to HARRY L. and Sarah A. Wickham VAIL. He was nicknamed "Dutch" for his blond hair and Dutch grandmother. He graduated from UNIVERSITY SCHOOL in 1913. He earned an A.B. from Princeton University in 1917 and an LL.B. from the Harvard University Law School in 1922. He was admitted to the Ohio bar in 1922. For many years Vail was a partner in the law firm of Sayre, Vail, Steele & Renkert and later was senior partner in the firm of Vail, Steele, Howland & Olson. A lifelong Republican, Vail served 2 terms, 1929–33, in the Ohio legislature, where he was chairman of the House Tax Committee, and in 1934 and 1935 was a member of the Ohio Special Joint Taxation Commission. He served on the BRATENAHL Village Council from 1933–51, as its president from 1940. Vail became involved in the FOREST CITY PUBLISHING CO., the publisher of the *PLAIN DEALER*, as a trustee representing the Holden family. His first wife, Delia, was a granddaughter of LIBERTY E. HOLDEN, owner of the newspaper. In 1941 Vail was named a director of Forest City, and on 1 June 1962, he succeeded Stanley E. Graham as president serving until July 1970. He was also president of the Art Gravure Corp. of Ohio. In the cultural and civic field, Vail served as chairman of the NORTHERN OHIO OPERA ASSOC., president of the WESTERN RESERVE HISTORICAL SOCIETY, the CITIZENS LEAGUE, and the CLEVELAND COUNCIL ON WORLD AFFAIRS. Vail married Delia B. White on 22 June 1922. The Vails had 2 sons, Herman, Jr., and Thomas. Delia Vail died in 1952. In 1965, Vail married Mary Louise Gleason. Vail was also a distinguished book collector, specializing in items relating to the Hudson Bay Co.

**VALLEY VIEW** is a small village located 7 mi. south of downtown Cleveland along the Ohio Canal in the Cuyahoga River Valley. It is 7 mi. long and 1.5 mi. wide and is bounded by GARFIELD HTS. and Walton Hills on the east and INDEPENDENCE on the west. Valley View was originally part of Independence Twp., but the origins of Independence are unknown because the early township records were destroyed. In the early 19th century, the area prospered as an agricultural community. When construction began on the OHIO & ERIE CANAL, local valley residents contracted with their teams to construct and maintain the canal. The opening of the Akron-Cleveland section of the canal on 4 July 1827 opened a new era of transportation, and local farmers and tradesmen found cash markets for their crops and services. In 1894, the portion of Independence Twp. east of the CUYAHOGA RIVER was annexed to NEWBURGH Twp. In 1896 the southern

1008

portion of Newburgh detached itself to form the Twp. of S. Newburgh, and in 1919 it was further divided into the villages of Valley View and Garfield Hts. Valley View adopted the mayor-council form of government and has maintained its own police and fire departments since 1937. Valley View's modern growth began in the 1950s. Five industrial and commercial parkways were established, which housed businesses such as GRAY DRUG, Big 4 Lumber, and the Norton Constr. Co. With the creation of the CUYAHOGA VALLEY NATL. RECREATION AREA in 1974, a large portion of Valley View south of Rockside Rd. and east along Tinker's Creek Rd. was incorporated into the park. In 1985, the Valley View schools were part of the Cuyahoga Hts. School System. The population of the village in 1980 was 1,550.

**VAN AKEN, WILLIAM J.** (29 Oct. 1884–28 Dec. 1950), was a prominent real-estate magnate and mayor of SHAKER HTS., 1915–30 and 1931–50. Van Aken was born in E. Cleveland Twp., where he attended public schools. He graduated from CENTRAL HIGH SCHOOL in 1903. He immediately took a position as an office boy for the Natl. Malleable Castings Co. He later rose to the position of accountant. In 1916 he entered the real-estate profession, joining the firm of Green, Cadwallader, & Long. Within the year, he left that firm and became an independent broker. In 1915, Van Aken, a Republican, became mayor of what was then the village of Shaker Hts. He had previously served as trustee (1911) and councilman (1912). When the village became a chartered city in 1930, Van Aken became the first mayor of the city in the 1931 elections. He continued to serve in that position until his death. Van Aken was active in many community organizations, including the Cleveland Chamber of Commerce and the Knights of Columbus. He was also the director of the Cooperative Investment Co. Van Aken married Florence Swallow in Oct. 1911. The couple had 6 children.

The **VAN DORN COMPANY** has an international reputation as an innovator and expert in the forming of metals and plastic. By 1985 it had 19 plants in 7 states, Puerto Rico, and Canada. The company started in Akron in 1872 when Jas. H. Van Dorn established a small fence business. Six years later, he moved to Cleveland to be nearer major supply and transportation sources and named his firm the Cleveland Wrought Iron Fence Co. Van Dorn quickly moved into related areas, its plant at E. 79th St. manufacturing all types of ornamental iron works and, within a few years, became the world's largest producer of jail cells. To note this expansion, it was renamed the Van Dorn Iron Works Co. in 1884. In 1897, Van Dorn's son, Thos. B., developed the company's structural-steel business, which led to its work on various structures in Cleveland. With the emerging automobile industry, Van Dorn's 1,100 employees began to supply frames, fenders, and automobile parts for local companies. The firm pioneered in developing the mechanical dump-truck hoist. It then turned to special railroad equipment, metal furniture, and mailboxes. During both world wars, Van Dorn produced tanks and armor plates for cars and aircraft.

The company suffered severely during the Depression, as most of its products were expensive capital equipment; only its production of prison and mailing equipment allowed it to survive. Pres. Norton T. Jones recognized the firm's vulnerability and began to revive Van Dorn by outlining a program of selective diversification, moving into consumable-products industries, which would offer greater growth potential. In 1944, Van Dorn entered the container business by acquiring the Davies Can Co. In 1945 it pur-

chased the newly formed Colonial Plastics Mfg. Co., a manufacturer of plastic pipes. That same year, Norton organized a plastics machine division to produce induction molding presses. By selective, nationwide acquisitions during the 1950s and 1960s, Van Dorn was a leader and innovator in the container and plastic fields; it became the largest producer of drawn aluminum cans for processed foods and of injection molding machines. To emphasize its diversity, its name was shortened to the Van Dorn Co. in 1964. By the late 1960s, few vestiges of the old Van Dorn Co. remained. It sold its prison business in 1967. It maintained a steel heat-treating facility, although that constituted only 1% of sales. Van Dorn had moved into a related area in 1959 when it started to manufacture heating systems. During the 1970s and 1980s, Van Dorn consolidated and reorganized its container and plastic subsidiaries into 8 divisions, employing 2,200 people and maintaining its headquarters and 4 plants in Cleveland. The company's diversity has helped it through recent economic downturns. It experienced record sales in 1981.

Van Dorn Co., *100 Years at Van Dorn* (1972).

**VAN HORN, FRANK R.** (7 Feb. 1872–1 Aug. 1933), a mineralogist and geologist, was a professor at Case School of Applied Science, where he also provided valuable service as head of the athletic association for 26 years. Known as "the Count," he had amassed what was called "the largest mineralogical collection in the country" at the time of his death. Van Horn was born in Johnsonburg, N.J., the son of Geo. W. and Ellen Robertson Van Horn. He attended the State Model School at Trenton (1886–88) prior to enrolling at Rutgers, where he received a B.S. in 1892 and a master's degree in mineralogy in 1893. He then studied at the University of Heidelberg, earning a Ph.D. in 1897. Returning to the U.S. in 1897, Van Horn became an instructor in geology and mineralogy at Case School of Applied Science. He advanced to assistant professor in 1899 and to professor in 1902, holding that rank at the time of his death. He traveled widely in pursuit of his profession, making 5 trips to Europe, 1 to Alaska, 1 to Africa, and 15 to the Pacific coast to study geology and collect minerals. His collection included 10,000 specimens at the time of his death. Van Horn lectured on his travels and was the author of 2 textbooks—*Lecture Notes on Systematic Zoology* (1902) and *Lecture Notes on General and Special Mineralogy* (1903)—and 26 technical papers. He was also the coauthor of a U.S. Geological Survey report in 1931, *Geology and Mineral Resources of the Cleveland District.*

In addition to his teaching and scientific duties at Case, Van Horn was instrumental in developing the school's athletic program. Made head of the poorly organized athletic association in 1900, he gave structure to the organization's informal financial policies and paid off its debt, built a new athletic field that became one of the best in the city, and increased the school's athletic assets to $155,000. Called "the father of Case athletics," Van Horn is credited with saving the football program and encouraging other athletic endeavors at the school. Van Horn was a member of several professional organizations. He was a charter fellow and later secretary of the Mineralogical Society of America; he was a fellow and counselor of the Geological Society of America, and a fellow of the American Assoc. for the Advancement of Science and of the Ohio Academy of Science. He was also a member of the American Institute of Mining & Metallurgical Engineers and of the Seismological Society of America. On 8 June 1898, Van Horn married Myra Van Horn, his first cousin. Part of their wedding trip was a mineral-collecting expedition to Wyoming.

VAN SWERINGEN, ORIS PAXTON (24 Apr. 1879–22 Nov. 1936) and **MANTIS JAMES** (8 July 1881–12 Dec. 1935), were real-estate developers and businessmen responsible for the development of SHAKER HTS., SHAKER SQUARE, the SHAKER RAPID, and the Terminal Tower complex. The brothers also put together a railroad empire in the 1920s that collapsed during the Depression. Born near Wooster, Ohio, O. P. and M. J. were the youngest of the 5 children of Jas. T. and Jennie Curtis Van Sweringen. Their father was a Civil War veteran whose wounds limited his ability to work; the brothers grew up in poverty and did not attend school beyond the elementary level. Ca. 1890 the family moved to Cleveland, and by 1897 both brothers were working for the Bradley Fertilizer Co. At the turn of the century, they entered business on their own in real estate; a venture in LAKEWOOD failed, and they were forced to turn temporarily to other occupations before resuming their real-estate ventures. By 1905, the brothers had become interested in the old Shaker property east of the city (see NORTH UNION SHAKER COMMUNITY) and began buying options on the land. Over the years they increased their holdings there, improved the property, and developed the exclusive Shaker Hts. community. Needing transportation between the new suburb and downtown, they convinced the city street railway to extend lines to some parts of their property, but in 1909 they were forced into the decision to build their own transportation line and began acquiring the necessary property along KINGSBURY RUN. The New York Central's Nickel Plate (the New York, Chicago & St. Louis Railroad) owned part of the lands the brothers needed; in July 1916 they paid $8.5 million to buy the Nickel Plate, which they turned into a profitable line. The Nickel Plate became the centerpiece of the rail empire the Van Sweringens built: they acquired the Toledo, St. Louis & Western, the Lake Erie & Western, and the Chesapeake & Ohio and its subsidiary the Hocking Valley in 1922, and later added the Erie, the Pere Marquette, and the Missouri Pacific systems. On 11 Apr. 1920 they put into operation their Shaker Rapid, for which they had acquired their first rail line.

To provide a new central rail terminal downtown, the Van Sweringens proposed a massive development near PUBLIC SQUARE. Their proposal challenged plans for a lakefront terminal but won the approval of city council and the voters; construction began in 1923, and the Terminal Tower complex officially opened on 28 June 1930. In 1926 the brothers received the Cleveland Chamber of Commerce's Medal for Public Service. By 1929 the Van Sweringens had put together a $3 billion, 30,000-mi. railroad empire and had significant holdings in such corporations as Midland Steel, Goodyear Tire & Rubber, and WHITE MOTOR. But their financial empire was heavily dependent upon stock values, and after the stock market crash in 1929, the brothers' holdings quickly lost value. As the business depression spread, their operations failed to bring in sufficient income to cover their heavy debts. On 1 May 1935, the Van Sweringens defaulted on $48 million in loans from J. P. Morgan & Co., which ordered the collateral sold at auction in September. The brothers arranged financial backing, formed another holding company, and were able to buy back their holdings for just over $3 million, but neither brother lived to rebuild the empire. Away from work, the Van Sweringens were very private men. Neither ever married, and they avoided Cleveland society, taking their only pleasure from their HUNTING VALLEY estate, DAISY HILL.

Haberman, Ian S., *The Van Sweringens of Cleveland* (1979).

The **VETERAN'S ADMINISTRATION MEDICAL CENTER** in Cleveland comprises 2 facilities: the Cleveland Veteran's Admin. Hospital (WADE PARK), a 780-bed general medical and surgical hospital, and the Brecksville Veteran's Admin. Hospital, a 999-bed psychiatric hospital. The two hospitals merged their services in 1971. The Cleveland VA Hospital developed from the CRILE HOSPITAL, which had opened in PARMA HTS. during the early 1940s. Crile was originally intended as a temporary Army hospital to care for sick and wounded military personnel. It was taken over by the VA in June 1946 and converted into a 1,000-bed general medical and surgical hospital to serve all veterans. It became known as the Crile VA Hospital (also as Crile General Hospital), named after Dr. GEO. CRILE, a Cleveland surgeon who led the first American hosptial unit in France during WORLD WAR I. In 1946, the year of its establishment, the hospital became affiliated with UNIVERSITY HOSPITALS; later it became affiliated with Western Reserve University's medical school. Specialized services included an ophthalmology department, a ward and rehabilitative program for paraplegics, and reconstructive hand surgery. Many of the hospital's early patients were long-term.

In 1948, the VA acquired a 20-acre site on East Blvd. near Wade Park, where it planned to build a new 500-bed general hospital. The plan was variously shelved and revived until 1960, when it was approved by the House Appropriations Committee. Congresswoman FRANCES P. BOLTON was instrumental in winning support for the new hospital. When it opened in June 1964, the old hospital was vacated; it was later sold to Cuyahoga County. The first director of the new hospital was Dr. Benjamin Wells. In addition to its primary function as a medical and surgical hospital, the hospital also maintained an out-patient clinic for veterans. Specialized services continued to be added, including an artificial-kidney center in 1965 and an intensive-care unit in 1969. Problems occasionally developed from overcrowding and lack of registered nurses. A $2.3 million wing was added in 1974 that increased the number of beds and also housed a new research facility. In 1971, the Cleveland VA Hospital merged many of its services with the Brecksville VA Hospital. One result was the transfer of all surgical cases from BRECKSVILLE to Cleveland. The overall purpose of this merger was to improve patient care, make better use of expensive and specialized medical equipment and scarce medical personnel, and lower costs. The two hospitals combined into a regional operation that encompassed most of northern Ohio. During the 1970s, the Cleveland hospital began to accept nonveterans for the first time, primarily patients suffering from spinal-cord injuries.

The Brecksville VA Hospital opened in 1961 in a new $23 million facility on Brecksville Rd. In contrast to the Cleveland VA Hospital, it was essentially intended as a neuropsychiatric hospital. It also assumed the administrative duties of the BROADVIEW HTS. VA Hospital, a 324-bed tuberculosis hospital that had opened in 1940. Because of declining occupancy, the Broadview Hts. facility closed in 1965 and was transferred to the Ohio Dept. of Mental Hygiene. The Brecksville Hospital opened with 999 beds and a full-time workforce of 950. During its first year of operation, 944 patients were admitted, and 260 were discharged. The "unit care" concept was adopted, and the hospital was organized into independent 300-bed units, each with its own staff, services, and programs. As a modern facility, it was equipped with a gymnasium, swimming pool, and bowling alley. In the late 1960s, the hospital gained national recognition through its program to successfully return veterans to employment. A program to rehabilitate alcoholics was introduced in 1969, and a Drug Abuse Ctr. in 1971 in order to treat Vietnam veterans suffering from drug addiction. Treatment for compulsive gamblers—linked to combat stress—was also started. A program to treat Post-traumatic Stress Disorder in Vietnam veterans was unveiled in 1984. Following the merger of the Cleveland VA Hospital in 1971, the Brecksville hospital handled supply storage for the 2 facilities and also laundry. It continued to accept patients, although those with disorders more neurologically related were transferred to the Cleveland hospital. In 1975, the hospital was forced to reduce its use of psychotherapeutic drugs when a government report revealed that many patients were receiving excessive doses.

**VETERANS OF FOREIGN WARS,** a national organization for military veterans formed in a small tailoring shop in Columbus, Ohio, in Apr. 1899, first appeared in the Cleveland area in 1920 with the formation of Post No. 84, commanded by Geo. Collyer. Soon there were 3 posts in the area, with about 800 members dedicated to the perpetuation of the memory of those who had died in service abroad, to assisting their widows and orphans and veterans in poor health, to promoting legislation of benefit to veterans, and to fostering "true patriotism" and loyalty to the U.S. government. During 1931 and 1932, the Cuyahoga Council of the VFW participated in the national organization's campaign to gather signatures in support of immediate payment of war veterans' bonuses. The local VFW remained "comparatively small" prior to the end of WORLD WAR II, but in 1945 and 1946 its membership increased greatly; by late 1946 the VFW had 13,000–14,000 members in Cuyahoga County, and several local posts reported memberships of more than 1,000. The county council had established a Rehabilitation & Service Headquarters in 1944 to help veterans determine their rights under the law and to provide assistance in filing claims for disability and allowances. The services offered by the VFW, as well as its social function, contributed to its popularity. During the 1950s, issues in local VFW circles included the legality of bingo games and slot machines in VFW halls and the issuance of state liquor licenses to posts. In 1950 the VFW had begun to sponsor annual Loyalty Day parades and ceremonies to counteract the May Day celebrations in Communist nations, and such events became popular attractions downtown before moving to the SUBURBS in 1978. The Voice of Democracy competitions, with scholarships as prizes, became another popular program sponsored by the VFW to promote patriotism and loyalty among the young. Cleveland hosted the national VFW conventions in 1947 and 1964. Between 1953–67, the number of VFW posts in the area increased from 54 to 65, with 42 ladies' auxiliaries operating in the county. By 1984, there were about 25 VFW posts in the area.

**VIETNAM WAR.** The Vietnam War, an undeclared war in Southeast Asia in which the U.S. was engaged heavily from Aug. 1964 until signing a peace agreement in Jan. 1973, affected Clevelanders much as it did other Americans. As a political issue, the war contributed to the ideological polarization and increased cynicism of the citizenry; in its effect on the economy, the war benefited the city's industries before producing major economic disruptions in the late 1960s and early 1970s. But the war was first and lastingly a human tragedy, for in disrupted, scarred, and lost lives, individuals bore its greatest burdens. The war most directly affected those young men called into military service by the Selective Service System. Between 1965–72, about 154,000 men of draft age lived in Cuyahoga County. Local statistics for military service are not available, but from 1970 census figures and percentages derived from national figures, it appears that of the county's draft-age men,

about 50,000 enlisted, 12,000 were drafted, and about 92,000 never served in the military. Of those who never served, about 88,000 were deferred, exempted, or disqualified from service, while about 4,000 were apparent draft offenders. Of the estimated 62,000 Clevelanders who served in the military during the Vietnam era, probably 47,000 never went to Vietnam, 3,000 served in Vietnam but saw no combat, and 12,000 experienced combat.

Thus, approximately 15,000 men from Cuyahoga County served in Vietnam. The State Adjutant General's Dept. reports that 403 county men died there; obituaries and the lists of those killed published annually in Memorial Day editions of local newspapers suggest that about 427 county men died in Vietnam. Probably another 2,000 were wounded. Casualty figures reflected the pattern of American involvement in the war. One local man, Navy flight surgeon Bruce C. Farrell of WESTLAKE, died in Oct. 1963, before the beginning of what is commonly defined as "the Vietnam era," 5 Aug. 1964. No local men died in Vietnam in 1964, but as American involvement increased, so did the number of dead from Cuyahoga County: 17 in 1965, 48 in 1966, 89 in 1967, and 127 in 1968. The "Vietnamization" of the war and a phased withdrawal of American troops lowered county deaths to 87 in 1969, 39 in 1970, 15 in 1971, and 4 in 1972. Women also served in Vietnam, and one nurse from Cleveland, Ruth Whiting, was killed in early 1968; no figures are available to suggest how many other women from Cuyahoga County served in the war. Published obituaries and addresses, while not available for all of those who died from Cuyahoga County, are available for enough men to present a rough profile of area men who fought in Vietnam. Statistically, this profile suggests that the men sent to war from Cuyahoga County came disproportionately from the poorer areas of the county. Young men from the upper-income neighborhoods were more likely to avail themselves of deferments or to serve in less hazardous roles.

Cuyahoga County soldiers went to war with varying attitudes about their task. Many were enthusiastic about the war and their military service; some even left high school to enlist. Others exhibited a strong sense of duty and purpose in volunteering for combat, sometimes going to great lengths to guarantee themselves service in Vietnam. Others fought despite misgivings about the war. For others, military service presented an obstacle to be cleared before proceeding with life: desiring "to get it over with" before going to college or getting married, these men often enlisted or volunteered through the draft. Local antiwar activists were similarly varied. From political action in support of negotiations, to direct-action protests against American involvement in a "civil war," to the belief that the war issue held possibilities for revolutionary change in America, the Cleveland antiwar movement reflected the variety of motivations, strategies, and political philosophies present in the national movement. But if anything distinguished Cleveland from other cities in regard to the war, it was the role played by local antiwar leaders such as Dr. Benjamin Spock, Dr. Sidney M. Peck, and attorney Jerry Gordon in efforts to create a popular, broad-based national movement.

Antiwar sentiment was apparent in Cleveland even before the Gulf of Tonkin incident in Aug. 1964. On 18 June 1964, the *PLAIN DEALER* published as an advertisement an open letter signed by 69 Clevelanders urging American officials to negotiate a settlement rather than increase U.S. involvement. The letter was initiated by local attorney Sheldon D. Clark, a Quaker who had served as assistant state attorney general (1950) and assistant county prosecutor (1951–57), and who in 1966 was the Democratic nominee in an unsuccessful bid to unseat Wm. E. Minshall in the 23d congressional district. Clark entered the race to give voters the opportunity to vote for a "negotiated settlement" of the war and came out in favor of including the Natl. Liberation Front in negotiations. Expansion of the American military role in Vietnam in 1965 increased the activity of local as well as national antiwar forces. The University Circle Teach-in Committee, formed in Mar. 1965, held its first teach-in the following month. As the teach-in suggested, educational activities and rallies to publicize opposition to the war were prominent in the efforts of such early local antiwar groups. But antiwar sentiment was not widely shared in these early years, and a midnight vigil and rally on PUBLIC SQUARE on 15–16 Oct. 1965 drew jeering counterprotesters.

Prior to mid-1967, a number of local antiwar groups had been formed in Cleveland, but their efforts were ineffective and largely uncoordinated. After mid-1967, Cleveland's antiwar forces coordinated their efforts more closely, led by the Cleveland Area Peace Action Coalition under the direction of sociology professor Dr. Sidney Peck. In June 1967, the Vietnam Resolution Committee was formed to gather signatures on petitions in support of placing on the ballot an antiwar resolution urging the president to "bring all American troops home from Vietnam now so that the Vietnamese people can settle their own affairs." The resolution garnered the necessary signatures but was kept off the ballot by city council; it nevertheless provided a means of organizing antiwar support. Jerry Gordon, attorney for the Resolution Committee, later became a leader in Get Out Now!, formed in Oct. 1968, an educational group advocating immediate American withdrawal. Some antiwar groups were more radical in their outlook and more militant in their approach to organizing. The Direct Action Committee, formed in the fall of 1967, confronted "hawks" such as Geo. Wallace during their appearances in Cleveland and helped organize protests against the Dow Chemical Co. at CLEVELAND STATE UNIVERSITY. One of the most active of the radical groups was the Cleveland Draft Resistance Union, formed in spring 1967. A project of the STUDENTS FOR A DEMOCRATIC SOCIETY, this Marxist group saw the draft as an effective tool in politicizing white students and workers. The group worked closely with Blacks against the Draft and provided draft-counseling services and organized rallies in support of draft resisters reporting to the Induction Ctr.

Cleveland hosted several important antiwar conferences that promoted local antiwar leaders into national leadership roles. Three of these conferences in 1966, chaired by widely respected veteran peace activist A. J. Muste, brought together the most active local organizations in the country under Muste's policy of not excluding groups on the basis of politics. The first 2 Cleveland conferences—called national leadership conferences and held on 22 July 1966 and 10 Sept. 1966—were "tenuous and groping," but at the third meeting on 26 Nov. 1966, Sidney Peck proposed what movement historians have described as a "visionary plan for a huge national mobilization" in New York City and San Francisco on 15 Apr. 1967. His plan launched the important national Spring Mobilization Committee to End the War in Vietnam, and the success of these demonstrations, along with continued escalation of the war, gave the national and local antiwar movements new momentum. Cleveland again gave rise to an important national organization in 1970; in the aftermath of the invasion of Cambodia, the CAPAC, then led by Gordon, hosted the Natl. Emergency Conference against the Cambodia-Laos-Vietnam War on 19–21 June 1970 at CUYAHOGA COMMUNITY COLLEGE. That conference gave rise to the

Natl. Peace Action Coalition, a nonexclusive group dedicated to the organization of massive opposition to the war.

Beginning with the increased draft calls and inductions in 1965, draft avoidance became an important element in the antiwar movement. As the draft quotas and inductions increased, the possibility of serving in a war became real for many Cleveland-area men. The *Plain Dealer* reported "a marked increase in draft dodging in Northeastern Ohio" in Oct. 1965, with legal officials reporting 25 cases that month alone. By Feb. 1973, about 500 draft-evasion cases were pending trial in the Cleveland federal district; several of these defendants were known to be in Canada. The Draft Counseling Assoc., formed in 1968, and other draft-counseling services counseled many men about their rights under the law, advising them of available deferments and other options and guiding them through the selective-service system. Lawyers specializing in draft cases provided additional assistance. In addition to conscientious objection, medical exemptions, and student deferments, service in the Natl. Guard or military reserve units provided refuge from the draft, refuge that on occasion was bought and sold illegally. In the spring of 1966, the FBI broke up a Cleveland draft-evasion ring that sold forged Air Force and Natl. Guard papers; in Apr. 1970, 3 civilian employees of the Lakewood Ohio Natl. Guard Armory were charged with soliciting bribes from potential enlistees in exchange for placing their names closer to the top of the waiting list for enlistment. By May 1970, the average wait on these lists was 3–4 months.

By 1970, support for the antiwar movement was coming from Mayor Carl Stokes's office. Antiwar sentiment increased with the invasion of Cambodia and the killings of students at Kent State University, events that created turmoil on normally quiet college campuses such as that of CASE WESTERN RESERVE UNIVERSITY. Also contributing to the increasing unpopularity of the war were stories of American atrocities against the Vietnamese. In 1967, David Tuck, a Cleveland post office employee, returned from a 13-month tour of duty in Vietnam and began speaking out against the war; in Nov. 1967 he traveled to Copenhagen and testified at the Internatl. War Crimes Tribunal about atrocities he had seen and was ordered to perform. On 20 Nov. 1969, Clevelanders awoke to find Ronald K. Haeberle's shocking and disturbing photographs of the My Lai massacre published exclusively in the *Plain Dealer*. In 1970, Clevelanders followed the trials of Samuel G. Green, Jr., a Clevelander court-martialed for participating in the killings of 5 Vietnamese women and 11 children.

Such stories contributed to an unfair stereotypical image of murderous American soldiers that made it difficult for people to deal with the realities of the war and the soldiers who fought it. As in other cities, Cleveland-area Vietnam veterans waited a decade for a measure of recognition for service rendered in a trying time. One commentator noted that the stereotype of "the crazy druggie" had obscured the fact that the "majority of veterans [had] returned home to marry, have kids, seek jobs and go on with their lives," putting the war behind them. In 1980, Cuyahoga County had about 66,200 Vietnam-era veterans. The celebration afforded the returning Iranian hostages that year sparked in some veterans a desire for recognition, and when it came, it was largely of their own making. In 1984, the Greater Cleveland chapter of the Vietnam Veterans of America established "a small flower garden" in front of the War Memorial on St. Clair. The dedication ceremony on 30 Sept. 1984 was "one of the first official tributes to Vietnam veterans in Cleveland" and signaled the emergence of area Vietnam veterans. The local VVA chapter, formed in 1980 as an alternative for Vietnam veterans who felt

1012

unfairly treated by federal agencies and other veterans' groups, was one of several organizational efforts undertaken by local Vietnam veterans to deal with the problems of unemployment, inadequate benefits, Agent Orange, and other issues. An informal group known as "'Nam Vets Helping 'Nam Vets" successfully battled the local VA for a treatment program for Posttraumatic Stress Disorder. Aiding the campaign for treatment was Cleveland State University psychologist John P. Wilson, a leading authority on PTSD and counseling troubled veterans, who had been involved in developing the training program used for counselors in Veterans Outreach Ctrs., 2 of which opened in Cleveland in Dec. 1979. The political battle to fund these federally sponsored centers, as well as the Agent Orange issue, contributed to the organization of local veterans.

While Vietnam veterans were battling their veterans' agencies for adequate treatment, Cleveland's established social-service agencies were busy helping a new population adjust to American life. The fall of Saigon in Apr. 1975 brought a new immigrant population to Cleveland. Vietnamese refugees began arriving in Cleveland in May 1975, as Clevelanders adopted orphans airlifted out of the country and sponsored refugee families. The influx of Vietnamese families created a crisis for area social-service agencies. Led by Joseph Meissner of the LEGAL AID SOCIETY, 10 such agencies quickly formed Vietnamese Information Services to coordinate relocation efforts. The NATIONALITIES SERVICES CTR. organized social and legal services and job-training and placement programs for the newcomers, and sponsored classes in English and home economics. By Nov. 1975, the Vietnamese Community had been formed as a nonprofit group to help the refugees with social activities and to aid in the preservation of Vietnamese culture and tradition. In Oct. 1976, a Vietnamese grocery opened; by 1985, about 1,000 Vietnamese called Cleveland home. Displaced against their will, the Vietnamese refugees served as a final reminder of the lasting impact and human costs of the Vietnam War.

Kenneth W. Rose
Case Western Reserve University

The **VILLA SANCTA ANNA HOME FOR THE AGED,** 25000 Chagrin Blvd. in BEACHWOOD, was built in 1959 and dedicated in early Jan. 1960. The home was built and sponsored by the FIRST CATHOLIC SLOVAK LADIES ASSOC., a national organization, and operated by the Daughters of St. Francis of Assisi, who came to Cleveland as refugees in 1947. The million-dollar, 3-story structure had accommodations for 75 elderly men and women when it opened; by June 1974, it was home to 100 senior citizens.

The *VILLAGE OF EUCLID V. AMBLER REALTY CO.* was a landmark court case that established the zoning rights of municipalities. On 22 Nov. 1926, the U.S. Supreme Court, led by Chief Justice Wm. Howard Taft, reversed a lower federal court ruling, 6–3, to establish the principle and practice of land-use zones in the U.S. Until then, zoning land in municipalities for specific uses had been a popular "city efficient" technique receiving lukewarm support in the nation's state courts. *Euclid* v. *Ambler*, the first federal test, established legal precedent and constitutional justification for ZONING and, implicitly, "comprehensive" land-use planning. Before EUCLID considered zoning in May 1922, the idea and practice were promoted by Cleveland businessmen and progressives. The Chamber of Commerce, especially its City Plan Committee under the secretaryship of CHARLOTTE M. RUMBOLD, advanced zoning as a land-use control enhancing real-estate values. Robt. H. Whitten, a committee member and a drafter of the 1916

New York City ordinance, served as advisor to the Cleveland City Plan Commission (1917–22), and later as a city plan consultant (1922–24). His assistance was sought; in 1920 he drafted a LAKEWOOD zoning ordinance. The committee advanced ideas through subcommittees that later became semiautonomous, e.g., the University Improvement Co. (1918). Another, the Euclid Ave. Assoc. (1920), promoted developing the avenue within and beyond Cleveland's limits as a noble business and ceremonial thoroughfare. Fearing that the Ambler Realty Co., which owned 68 acres between Euclid Ave., the Nickel Plate Railroad, E. 196th St., and E. 204th St., might encourage industry, village officials and committee members corresponded about protection by zoning. On 13 Nov. 1922, Euclid adopted an ordinance that prohibited Ambler's developing the Euclid Ave. frontage as industrial, an ordinance remarkably similar to New York City's.

Ambler Realty sued Euclid in state court and lost. Claiming its land had been "taken" without due process, Ambler went to federal court. Jas. Metzenbaum, village counsel, defended zoning, while NEWTON D. BAKER, a City Plan Committee member, prosecuted Ambler's case before his friend Judge David C. Westenhaver. The committee filed an amicus curiae brief for Euclid. In Jan. 1924, the judge ruled for Ambler. The village appealed to the Supreme Court. Ambler might have been sustained, but Alfred Bettman of Cincinnati sought a rehearing, at which time he filed a persuasive *amicus curiae* brief with the Court led by his friend Chief Justice Taft. Thereupon Justice Sutherland redrafted the opinion to reverse the lower court's decision. Although the decision had landmark effects on U.S. law and land use, the contested land, ironically, became the site of a plant of the FISHER BODY DIV. OF GENERAL MOTORS.

Simpson, Michael, *People & Planning* (1969).

The **VISITING NURSES ASSOCIATION** is a nonprofit, voluntary health organization dedicated to assisting homebound, mainly indigent patients in their health-care needs. It is one of the oldest organizations of its type in the U.S. The Cleveland VNA developed from a volunteer group of young women, mainly from wealthy backgrounds, who called themselves "the Baker's Dozen." Medically untrained, the women would visit the homes of needy families where there was an illness and furnish what comforts they could. The association was officially organized in 1901 when a graduate nurse, Alice Page, was hired as superintendent to recruit other nurses. Its initial purpose was "to provide graduate nurses to visit those otherwise unable to secure skilled assistance in time of illness, to teach cleanliness and the proper care of the sick, and to prevent the spread of disease." The VNA was modeled after a similar organization in Chicago. An office was opened, and nurses were initially placed in 3 settlements—Goodrich House, ALTA HOUSE, and HIRAM HOUSE. As the staff increased, nurses—wearing blue-and-white-striped gingham dresses—were sent out to homes in the community. Each visit lasted no more than 45 minutes; although a donation of $.25 was accepted, there was no required charge. During the first few years, care was largely devoted to typhoid victims.

By 1939, the Cleveland Community Fund was providing most of the financial support. Seven stations had been established throughout the city, with headquarters on Fulton Rd., and the nursing staff numbered 74. Over the years, care had shifted to infants with measles, chicken pox, and diphtheria, and also tubercular patients. The nurses continued to offer basic medical services and to evaluate the need for expert services. Although a standard charge for services was introduced, it was generally scaled to the patient's ability to pay. Oftentimes, there was no charge. The VNA inspired the establishment of preschool centers and child dispensaries, and was largely responsible for having nurses placed in schools. Between 1940–80, care shifted from acute illness, such as bronchitis, pneumonia, and communicable diseases, to heart disease, strokes, cancer, and diabetes. Programs for the elderly and former mental patients were added in the 1970s. Other developments included the total-care concept, in which services are coordinated with social- and mental-health consultants, nutritionists, and home health aides. Since the 1960s, Medicare and Medicaid have made 33% of the payments; other money has come from fees, United Appeal, and various government programs. Because of rising health costs in the 1980s, the VNA was forced to reduce its staff and number of visits.

The **VIXSEBOXSE GALLERY** is one of Cleveland's oldest and most prominent art galleries. It was established by Wm. Vixseboxse in 1922. Vixseboxse, a painter as well as an avid collector himself, had come to the U.S. from his native Rotterdam in 1904 and taken a job as a designer with the interior design firm of Webber-Lind & Hall. The first gallery opened in 1922 in the Vickers Bldg. at Euclid and E. 65th St. In 1935 the gallery moved into the Howe mansion at 2258 Euclid Ave., which had just been vacated by the GAGE GALLERIES, a few doors east of TRINITY CATHEDRAL. It remained at that location until 1979, when the gallery was moved to its present location in CLEVELAND HTS., at 12413 Cedar Rd. and Fairmount Blvd. The gallery specializes in the sale and appraisal of fine paintings and prints, as well as provides the services of framing and restoration. Wm. Vixseboxse died in 1974, after which the gallery operated under his son Bernard (d. 1982) and daughter Jeanette Vixseboxse Yeagle, as well as Bernard's daughter Ellen Kloppman.

The **VLCHEK TOOL COMPANY** (in 1985 part of the Pendleton Tool Industries Div. of Ingersoll-Rand) was started in 1895 as a blacksmith shop by Frank Vlchek, a Czech immigrant. The company became a leader in the hand-tool and plastics fields. Vlchek came to Cleveland in 1889; after a few years as a blacksmith and toolsmith, he opened the Vlchek Tool Co. on E. 83rd and Central Ave. The company shod horses and made and sharpened tools for stonecutters and masons; by 1909, it was shipping hammers, wrenches, and stonecutters' tool all over the country. As the auto industry grew, manufacturers included Vlchek tool kits as standard equipment in their cars. Soon, special Cleveland-produced kits were included with tractors and airplanes; in WORLD WAR I, Vlchek was the exclusive producer of tool kits for the Liberty Airplane Motor. The rising prosperity of the company led to the building in 1918 of a new, larger facility on E. 87th St., near the New York Central Belt Line, fitted with equipment largely designed by the owner. By 1930, the operation had expanded 8 times to meet a 70% increase in business since 1920, but owing to Vlchek's pursuit of labor-saving machinery, the firm used 17% fewer men. Vlchek was praised for his streamlining efforts as the "Henry Ford of the tool industry." In 1930, the company introduced a new screwdriver with a shock-proof handle made by a "secret process" that eliminated several manufacturing steps and utilized a rudimentary plastic material. This development made Vlchek a major producer of screwdrivers and a pioneer in plastics technology. By 1938, Vlchek set up a plastics division, which was soon (1945) located in Middlefield.

During WORLD WAR II, Vlchek produced hardware for the military, but unlike many other industries, it was able to devote a considerable amount (25%) of its productive capacity to civilian tool production, as tools were necessary to maintain vehicles and machinery. When civilian vehicle production resumed after the war, the company supplied 85% of all tool kits included in new cars, plus an additional 20,000 tools per day for distribution to hardware stores, mail-order companies, and tool suppliers in the automotive and agricultural-implement fields. As a sideline, Vlchek also produced 8 of the 16–25 hardware parts used in parachute manufacture. In 1949, Vlchek and the Natl. Screw & Mfg. Co., another Cleveland firm, were among a group of 9 tool companies charged with restraint of trade by the Justice Dept. for their domination of the screwdriver industry. The charges were dropped when the local firms and 160 others nationwide signed an agreement to stop practices considered in violation of antitrust laws. Despite the corporate growth throughout the 1950s, in 1958, minority stockholders challenged the firm's reporting policies and executive compensation practices; the insurgents lost their proxy fight, although the company agreed to issue more adequate reports and, if possible, common stock dividends. In the wake of this internal battle, Vlchek was bought out by the Pendleton Tool Industries Co. of California, the world's largest producer of hand service tools. Both parties claimed that the merger would provide new marketing opportunities; locally, the expectation was that both the tool and plastics divisions would be expanded. In 1964, Pendleton itself merged with Ingersoll-Rand. Vlchek became the Challenger Tool Co. in early 1969, but ironically, a month later, Ingersoll-Rand announced that the obsolete E. 87th St. plant would be closed and tool operations moved to one of the Pendleton Tool Div.'s other 9 tool-production sites throughout the U.S., Canada, and Mexico. The 275 employees represented by Local 640, UAW, and the Internatl. Die Sinker Conference were laid off with the promise that they would be given preference at other Pendleton plants. The Vlchek Plastics Co. was unaffected by the tool plant closing.

**VOINOVICH, GEORGE.** See **MAYORAL ADMINISTRATION OF GEORGE VOINOVICH**

The **VOJAN SINGING SOCIETY,** a prominent Cleveland cultural organization, was founded in 1924 as one of the cultural bodies under the aegis of the WORKERS GYMNASTIC UNION (Delnicke Telecvicne Jednoty, DTJ). The DTJ Karl Marx Dramatic Society had disbanded in 1923. A group of CZECHS interested in dramatic arts and in preserving the Czech culture founded the new society. It was named after the Czech character actor Eduard Vojan, who was well known for his portrayals of the actual lives of the peasants in Central Europe. Its first presentation was a play called *Zlate Casy*, which was performed in Feb. 1925 at the BOHEMIAN NATL. HALL. Later a choral group was organized, with Joseph Krabec as its music director. He served in this capacity until his death in 1961. Krabec with Rudolph Sliva composed *The Vojan March*, which was sung at all events in which the society participated. All plays were performed in Czech, with the exception of *The Golden Trail*, which was performed in English in 1932. Internationally known plays such as Karel Capek's *R.U.R.* were performed by the society. The most successful production of the Vojan Society was Smetana's *The Bartered Bride*. First presented in 1934, it was repeated many times until 1959. In addition to presentations in Cleveland, it was also performed in Pittsburgh, Detroit, and Chicago. The Choral Society participated in many local cultural events and performed on local radio and television stations. During WORLD WAR II, it sang at the USO and bond drives. The Vojan Society stopped performing plays in the late 1960s. As of 1985, the Singing Society was still performing.

Frank Bardoun Papers, WRHS.

The **VOLUNTEERS OF AMERICA,** an American offshoot of the SALVATION ARMY, is a national volunteer agency organized along quasi-military lines. The Volunteers have provided relief for Cleveland's poor since 1896. Part of the institutional church movement concerned with both the religious and the social welfare of the urban poor, the Volunteers of America were formed in New York City in Mar. 1896. By May, 3 Volunteer posts existed in Cleveland under the direction of Capt. John Denton. Both the leadership and the location of the posts changed frequently in the early years, but by 1907 the Volunteers offered a variety of services. The People's Mission and the Sunday school provided spiritual uplift, and the Relief Dept. helped the poor with rent payments, groceries, and medicine. On 19 May 1906, the Working Girls' Home opened at 2556 E. 14th St. (moved to 1214 Woodland, 1909–15); and in Dec. 1906, the men's home opened at mission headquarters, 131 Prospect Ave. Meals were available regularly, with a special dinner at Thanksgiving and presents for the children at Christmas. In 1911 the Volunteers opened their Fresh Air Camp, a summer vacation spot for urban children, in Eagle Cliff.

By the end of WORLD WAR I, the efforts of the Cleveland Volunteers were focused on the gospel mission and relief activities. In 1927 all the Volunteer facilities were located at 8021 Wade Park, where the chapel and men's lodge remained until Mar. 1952, when the Volunteers moved to 2 buildings on Carroll Ave. After WORLD WAR II, the Volunteers expanded their activities to provide employment and rehabilitation for the poor and disabled. Discarded household items were collected, repaired, and resold. The new facilities on Carroll Ave. contained carpentry and paint shops, electrical and upholstery repair, and baling and sorting rooms. From 1958–66, the Volunteers operated 15 branch stores to sell merchandise repaired by employees. Beginning in the late 1960s, the number of branch stores declined, partly because of the recession of 1981–82; in 1982 only 3 were in operation. The popularity of garage sales reduced the number of items donated to the Volunteers, and thus the group's budget. With its major source of income diminished, the organization looked elsewhere for funds and considered closing. In 1981 and 1983, foundation grants enabled the Volunteers to expand their shelter for the homeless, and in 1982, only last-minute donations allowed them to serve their traditional Thanksgiving dinner.

The **VORWAERTS TURNER HALL** was built at Willson and Harlem streets (1622 E. 55th) in 1893 by members of the Turnverein Vorwaerts, a German cultural and gymnastic group established on 18 May 1890. Led by Ernst Mueller and Bernhard Hoehner in its early years, the group met at 83 Aaron (E. 36th) St. before moving into its new hall. After the Turnverein Vorwaerts merged with the Germania Turnverein in 1908, the hall became known as the Germania Turnverein Vorwaerts Hall and continued to host gymnastic and German cultural events. By 1941 the Germania Turnverein Vorwaerts had become the Cleveland East Side Turners; they continued to use the hall until the early 1970s.

**VOSMIK, JOSEPH FRANKLIN "JOE"** (4 Apr. 1910–27 Jan. 1962), was a baseball player for the CLEVELAND INDIANS from 1930–36. Considered by baseball experts the best hitter to come from the Cleveland sandlots, he averaged over .300 in his major-league career. Vosmik was born in Cleveland. A local idol of the fans in the Broadway-E. 55th St. neighborhood, he was befriended by Bill Kuchta, a Harvard and E. 71st St. druggist who kept him supplied with bats and baseballs. Signed by the Indians after an All-Star Class A game at LEAGUE PARK in 1928, Vosmik began his professional career the next year with Frederick of the Blue Ridge League. He reported to the Indians in Sept. 1930, after batting .397 with Terre Haute of the Three-I League. Vosmik's debut as a regular outfielder in 1931 was spectacular. Against the White Sox, he went 5 for 5, including 3 doubles off the right-field wall. His greatest season was 1935, when he lost the batting title to Buddy Meyer of Washington, who hit .3490 to Vosmik's .3483. If the Cleveland outfielder had sat out the final day of the season, he would have tied Meyer for the batting crown. In 1935, Vosmik led the league in base hits (216), doubles (47), and triples (20), driving in 110 runs. Vosmik was traded to St. Louis in Jan. 1937. In 1938 he was sent to the Boston Red Sox, where he led the league with 201 base hits. Finishing his major-league career with Brooklyn in 1942 and Washington in 1944, Vosmik compiled a lifetime batting average of .307. During the late 1940s and early 1950s, he managed teams at Tucson, Dayton, Oklahoma City, and Batavia and scouted for the Cleveland Indians in 1951 and 1952. Later he worked as an automobile and appliance salesman. Vosmik married Sally Joanne Okla on 4 Nov. 1936; the couple had 3 children, Joseph, Larry, and Karen.

**VOTIPKA, THELMA** (20 Dec. 1898–24 Oct. 1972), was an opera singer with the Metropolitan Opera Co. Votipka was born in Cleveland, the daughter of Emil and Jessie Votipka. She was a student at the Oberlin Conservatory, and also studied with Lila Robeson in Cleveland and Anna Schoen Rene in New York City. Her operatic debut was as the singing countess in the *Marriage of Figaro* for the American Opera Co. in 1927. She sang with the Chicago Opera from 1929–31, the Stadium Opera in 1930, and the Philadelphia Opera in 1932. In 1935, Votipka joined the roster of the Metropolitan Opera Co. She remained with the Metropolitan for 28 years. She specialized in small roles, never wanting to become a prima donna. Her most notable roles were Marianne in *Der Rosenkavalier*, Mamma Lucia in *Cavalleria Rusticana*, Flora in *La Traviata*, and Marthe in *Faust*. Her favorite role was that of the witch in *Hansel and Gretel*. After retiring in 1961, she made a brief return to the stage of the Metropolitan for the 1962–63 season. During her years with the Metropolitan, she also sang in San Francisco, Hartford, Conn., Cincinnati, and Puerto Rico. She married John C. Groth on 24 Dec. 1947.

The **VOYAGE OF THE BLOSSOM** was a 20,000-mi. anthropological expedition sponsored by the CLEVELAND MUSEUM OF NATURAL HISTORY in the 1920s. Its purpose was to make natural-history collections and surveys on the islands of the South Atlantic. Dr. Leonard Sanford, medical examiner for the Yale athletic teams in 1922, had a dream of a collection of birds of the world, to be shared by museums of the world. He presented the idea to Paul Rea, then director of the Cleveland Museum of Natural History. Mrs. Dudley Blossom, prominent Clevelander and museum trustee, developed an interest in this project and provided her financial support for a voyage to the South Atlantic islands. At the same time, the American Museum of Natural History in New York had a similar plan for the

South Pacific. That expedition was financed by Harry Payne Whitney, Mrs. Blossom's cousin. The two museums expected to exchange discovered data and specimens. The vessel, originally named the *Lucy R.* and renamed the *Blossom* as a compliment to its benefactor, was built in 1920. A 3-masted sailing ship of the old-fashioned windjammer type, it had no auxiliary power. The vessel's length was 109 ft., with a weight of 103 tons, and a 22-ft. beam. Smaller than Christopher Columbus's *Santa Maria*, it had no centerboard and thus tended to drift leeward or backward. The ship sailed from New London, Conn., on 29 Oct. 1923, with a crew of 18. After a stop at Gardiner's Bay, Long Island, for additional work on the ship, the expedition departed 10 Nov. 1923, with an assurance of good weather ahead. Eight days later, the vessel encountered severe storms, which lasted for 2 weeks, with winds of 80–90 mph on one day. The *Blossom* reached the Cape Verde Islands on 10 Dec., and the crew began their collecting. At this time the ship was 200 mi. off course, and their wireless was dead. Back home, the *Blossom* was reported lost. Despite a troubled start, the expedition did achieve success. Some of the stops included Dakar, Gambia, St. Helena, Ascension, the Sargasso Sea, and Trinidad. After its last stop in Rio, the *Blossom* sailed north, where it docked at Charleston, S.C., on 4 June 1926. The 2½-year expedition resulted in the collection of 12,000 specimens, 4,000 photographs, and thousands of feet of film. The total cost of the expedition was $75,000.

# W

**WBOE,** for 40 years the Cleveland Board of Education radio station, was later resurrected as WCPN, the local outlet of Cleveland Public Radio. As WBOE, it was the first federally licensed educational broadcast facility in the nation. Broadcasting originally from Lafayette School on Abell Ave., it went on the air as an AM station on 21 Nov. 1938. Two months later WBOE moved to the Board of Education Bldg. on E. 6th St., where it had 4 studios and a control room on the 6th floor. In 1941 the station was the first educational broadcaster in the nation to convert to FM, with 1,000 watts on 42.5 megacycles. Programming, which initially was confined to the elementary levels, was also expanded by 1941 to incorporate junior and senior high school grades. Under the direction of Dr. Wm. B. Levenson, the station won national recognition for its use of radio broadcasts synchronized with lantern slides and playscripts, speakers on such topics as health and science, and student-produced programs on current events and student etiquette. WBOE joined forces with the CLEVELAND PLAY HOUSE in 1947 to allow students to hear and read along with Shakespearean plays. In 1948 the station increased its power to 10,000 watts at 90.3 megacycles. Chas. E. Siegal became its director from 1962–78, when Board of Education financial cutbacks took WBOE off the air. During the next 6 years, WBOE was silent save for the sideband broadcast of CRRS, the Cleveland Radio Reading Service, with specialized offerings for the blind read by a volunteer staff at the Sight Ctr. Several groups contended in the meantime for the Board of Education's radio license. It was finally awarded by the FCC to Cleveland Public Radio, whose board included members of the Board of Education, the CLEVELAND PUBLIC LIBRARY, and CUYAHOGA COMMUNITY COLLEGE. Its primary objective was to provide a local outlet for programming of the Natl. Public Radio network. With a remote broadcast of a jazz concert featuring vocalist Mel Torme, the station returned to the air as WCPN-FM on 8 Sept. 1984. Located in Cleveland Centre at 3100 Chester Ave., WCPN offered a full schedule of news and public-affairs programming, produced locally as well as nationally. Also featured was jazz programming under the direction of Chris Columbi.

**WCLV** began its career as Cleveland's principal fine-arts radio outlet on 1 Nov. 1962, when it first aired as WDGO-FM. Founded by partners C. K. Patrick and Robt. Conrad of Radio Seaway, Inc., it broadcast at 95.5 megacycles and

acquired its permanent call letters 4 days after its debut. As program manager, Conrad supervised the station's "mix" of classical music, jazz, folk singing, and poetry. He also hosted a lighter potpourri of comedy and music called "WCLV Saturday Night," which actually had originated as "WDGO Saturday Night" on 1 Oct. 1962, and went on to become the longest-running program on a single Cleveland radio station. Originally located in the Eastgate Shopping Ctr., WCLV moved studios and transmitter to the Terminal Tower in 1968. It began broadcasting CLEVELAND ORCHESTRA concerts in 1965 and picked up the Metropolitan Opera broadcasts several years later. As other area stations underwent identity crises, such locally familiar voices as those of SIDNEY ANDORN, Bud Wendell, Betty Ott, and Wayne Mack found outlets at WCLV. The "CITY CLUB Forum," previously carried by WGAR and WJW, also came to WCLV; it was actually Cleveland's longest-running radio program regardless of station.

As a by-product of its own programming, WCLV also began producing taped broadcasts for syndication to other stations. Foremost among these were the Cleveland Orchestra broadcasts, which were distributed to nearly 300 radio stations plus the British Broadcasting Corp. and Australian radio. Other programs that went into syndication from WCLV included "Music from Oberlin," "CIM Recital Hall," "Adventures in Good Music," and the "City Club Forum." Another sideline emanating from the station's close relationship with the Cleveland Orchestra was the annual fundraising "marathon," which WCLV began in 1970. Its record of $2.5 million raised from listeners for the orchestra by 1986 led to imitators in numerous other cities. Other local arts organizations have since benefited from their own marathons on WCLV. Among the numerous awards garnered by the station were 2 Governor's Awards from the Ohio Arts Council and a Gabriel Award from the Natl. Catholic Broadcasting Assoc. It was named Classical Music Station of the Year in 1981 by *Billboard* magazine. Annual commercial revenues totaled $1.5 million by 1986, when WCLV employed a staff of 25. That year also marked its move to a new studio-transmitter complex in WARRENSVILLE HTS., where it broadcast at 37,000 watts. Translator stations in Wooster and in Erie, Pa., also extended the station's range.

**WEWS** (Channel 5), the first television station in Ohio and only the 16th in the nation, went on the air officially on

17 Dec. 1947. It is owned by the E. W. Scripps Co., publishers of the CLEVELAND PRESS; its call letters were chosen to represent the initials of the company's founder, EDWARD WYLLIS SCRIPPS. From the first, WEWS has been the flagship station of the Scripps-Howard Broadcasting Co., which has had its headquarters in the station's facilities on Euclid Ave at E. 30th since 1975. Originally located behind the Sterling-Linder-Davis department store on E. 13th St., WEWS signed on with a variety show hosted by actor Jas. Stewart. Jas. C. Hanrahan was its first general manager, aided by chief engineer J. Harrison Epperson. In the early days they tested the boundaries of their new medium by such experiments as the reenactment of a mugging in nearby Dodge Ct.

Although first affiliated with CBS, WEWS became an ABC outlet in the 1950s, when CBS in Cleveland jumped to WJW. Locally, WEWS was responsible for one of the nation's longest-running variety shows in the "Giant Tiger Amateur Hour," later known as the "Gene Carroll Show" after its master of ceremonies, GENE CARROLL. Dorothy Fuldheim appeared on the station for 37 years as news commentator and host of the "One O'Clock Club." WEWS was the first local station to win the Geo. Foster Peabody Award for public-service programming. Another WEWS show, "Morning Exchange," is acknowledged in the industry as the model for the national "Good Morning America" program. Its format of talk and guest personalities was hosted by Fred Griffith and was later reproduced in an equally successful "Afternoon Exchange." In the local news field, Channel 5's "Eyewitness News" pioneered in the use of mini-portable cameras and helicopters in the 1970s. Its uplink satellite was the first of its kind in Cleveland and was used by the Ohio Lottery Commission in its telecommunications. With only 3 managers during its 4 decades, WEWS has enjoyed unusual stability of direction. Hanrahan was followed in 1964 by Donald L. Perris, who was promoted to president of Scripps-Howard Broadcasting in 1975. Edward D. Cervenak ran the station from then to his retirement in 1986, when he turned over the controls to Jas. H. Knight.

WGAR radio was founded in 1930 by Geo. A. Richards, a millionaire from Michigan and owner of WJR in Detroit. His action carried risks, as the Cleveland market seemed saturated, with 3 other stations already in operation. Richards, however, wanted to prove that the area could sustain another station and thereby give listeners a wider choice in dialing. After an hour of congratulatory messages on 15 Dec. 1930, WGAR switched over to "Amos 'n' Andy," a popular show on the NBC Blue Network. Operating from a penthouse studio in the Hotel Statler, WGAR broadcast on 500 watts at 1,450 kilocycles. Under general manager John F. Patt, it billed itself as the "Friendly Station," concerned with Cleveland's future. WGAR became a CBS affiliate in 1937. It acquired its familiar frequency of 1,220 kilocycles in 1944 and 3 years later raised its signal to a powerful 50,000 watts. Patt made WGAR a major part of Cleveland life, as the station became the first in the country to receive the Geo. Foster Peabody Award for its outstanding programming. Such luminaries as Jack Parr (who worked as a reporter at the station), Gene Autry, and W. C. Hardy could be heard on WGAR. SIDNEY ANDORN, a prominent reporter and interviewer, became famous for on-location interviews conducted over WGAR. The station was purchased in 1953 by the Peoples Broadcasting Corp., which became Nationwide Communications, a subsidiary of Nationwide Insurance, the following year. Carl George, a staff member since 1935, became general manager, and WGAR switched network affiliation from CBS to ABC. With the

hiring of Bill Clock in 1969, it became the first general station in Cleveland to employ a black disc jockey. During the 1970s, it moved from the STATLER OFFICE TOWER to a studio-transmitter facility in BROADVIEW HTS. In 1984, WGAR switched its music format from "adult contemporary" to "country." Its FM installations, inaugurated at 99.5 megacycles in 1982 for better frequency response, began simulcast programming with the AM mother station in 1986, under general manager Bill Weller and program director Tom Barney.

WHK, Cleveland's pioneer radio station, was one of the first 6 broadcasting stations in the nation. Started under the call letters 8ACS in 1921, it was owned by Warren R. Cox and operated from his home at 3138 Payne Ave. Although its original purpose was to serve as a hobby for the members of the Cleveland Radio Assoc., the Cleveland Press and the Plain Dealer reported that an estimated 15,000 people had heard of it by Nov. 1921. However, the transmitting of entertainment by amateur radio stations came to an end in Feb. 1922, when the U.S. Dept. of Commerce made it unlawful to broadcast any information from amateur radio stations without a limited commercial license. Cox immediately applied for one, and soon afterward 8ACS became WHK. Assigned the frequency of 1,420 kilocycles, the new WHK aired for the first time on 5 Mar. 1922, from the rear room of a Radiovox store located at 5005 Euclid Ave. By 1925, Cox sold the station to the Radio Air Service Corp., which appointed Leighton Caldwell as manager. A year later Eric Howlett and Harry Howlett were appointed sales manager and program director respectively. Increased in power to 5,000 watts for both day and night operations, WHK joined CBS in 1930, linking it with stations all over the country for network programs. Its original program format of largely recorded music was changed and expanded into a larger format that included speeches, sermons, news, concerts, interviews, and weather reports. Purchased by the PLAIN DEALER in 1934, WHK became a part of the FOREST CITY PUBLISHING CO., which owned both the Plain Dealer and the CLEVELAND NEWS. K. J. Carpenter became manager, and Carl E. Smith was promoted to chief engineer. Although Forest City also acquired 4 other stations in Ohio, no attempt was made to operate them with WHK as a unified network, or to promote Forest City's newspapers over the air. By the 1940s, WHK had switched its network affiliation from CBS to the Mutual Broadcasting System. Forest City finally sold WHK in 1958 for approximately $750,000 to the Metropolitan Broadcasting Corp. (Metromedia). In 1972 it was purchased by the Cleveland-based Malrite Communications Group, Inc., which also owned local station WMMS-FM. Long located at 5000 Euclid Ave., in 1976 WHK moved to studios in the STATLER OFFICE TOWER.

WJW radio for over 40 years was a staple of the Cleveland airwaves and an important contributor to the community. It was started in Mansfield, Ohio, in 1926 with a license issued to John F. Winer, who placed a "W" before his own initials for the call letters. Two years later he increased the station's power from 50 to 100 watts, making WJW a viable product. The station did not come to Cleveland until 13 Nov. 1943, when Wm. M. O'Neil bought into it and then purchased all of the stock. He moved WJW to Rm. 1336 of the Guardian Bldg., where it operated as Cleveland's 5th radio station at 850 kilocycles and 5,000 watts. As the local affiliate of ABC, formed from the old NBC Blue Network, WJW brought soap operas, sports, and the Metropolitan Opera broadcasts to Cleveland. During its history, WJW also featured programs with comedian Jack Benny, news commentary by Dorothy Fuldheim, and Alan Freed's "Moondog" rock 'n' roll show. Bruce MacDonald, a drafted employee of WJW, served as the station's armed forces contact during WORLD WAR II. The first airwaves strike at WJW occurred over pay in 1951; it lasted 20 days. O'Neil sold WJW on 17 Nov. 1954 to Storer Broadcasting, which teamed it with its local television operation, WXEL, and 2 years later moved both into a remodeled Georgian building at 1630 Euclid Ave. as WJW Radio & TV. Storer dropped the ABC radio affiliation in 1957 to become independent, although the station later had a brief affiliation with NBC before becoming independent again. During the 1960s, the "Ed Fisher Show" was immensely popular during a 10-year run, as was the station's adult contemporary format of news, talk, and jazz. Also active in community affairs during the 1960s, WJW helped to raise money for hospitals and gave support to servicemen in Vietnam and to the Jr. Olympics. Sold to Erie Broadcasting in the fall of 1976, WJW then began to highlight talk shows (news, commentary, psychology, etc.) and adult popular music. It had begun separate FM programming in 1965 on a station that eventually passed into separate ownership as WGCL. WJW was sold again in 1985, this time to Booth Broadcasting, at which time its long-familiar call letters were exchanged for WRMR.

**WJW-TV** (Channel 8) became the last of Cleveland's 3 VHF television stations when it signed on over Channel 9 as WXEL on 17 Dec. 1949. Built by the Empire Coil Co. of New Rochelle, N.Y., it originally occupied quarters at Pleasant Valley and State roads in PARMA. Franklin Snyder was its first general manager, and Russell Speirs was program director. The station switched network affiliation from ABC to CBS and simultaneously moved to Channel 8 in 1955, following its purchase by the Storer Broadcasting Co. of Miami, Fla., which occupied a seat on the CBS board. Its call letters were changed to WJW in 1956, after the purchase by Storer of the local radio station of the same designation. Both radio and television studios moved into remodeled Georgian headquarters in the old Lake Theater at E. 17th and Euclid Ave in the same year. One of WJW's early programming successes was the "Sohio Reporter" news program, which featured the chairman of Western Reserve University's speech department, Warren A. Guthrie, from 1951–63. Equally popular was "Adventure Road with Jim Doney," which began serving its daily blend of exotic travel and sports fare in the late 1950s. In order to market Channel 8's library of old horror films, staff announcer Ernie Anderson created his "Ghoulardi" personality in the mid-1950s. After Anderson's departure to become ABC's principal "voiceover" announcer, his Friday night time slot was filled by other staff personnel in the guises of "Hoolihan and Big Chuck" and "Big Chuck and Little John." Another WJW institution was meteorologist Dick Goddard, who provided more than 2 decades of continuity in a position of normally high turnover. News programming in the 1970s came under the direction of Virgil Dominic, who also served as news director for the entire Storer operation. WJW also picked up the local end of the popular syndicated "PM Magazine," providing a full-time staff for the production of the show's Cleveland segments. Following Storer's sale of the radio station, the television station was given the call letters WJKW to emphasize its separate identity. It moved into a new facility at 5800 S. Marginal Rd. in 1975 and reclaimed its old call letters in 1985, when WJW Radio became WRMR. A dual tower in Parma provided WJW with the strongest television signal in the area.

**WKYC** (Channel 3), for all but 10 years of its existence, was one of 5 network-owned television stations of NBC, as originally allowed under Federal Communications Commission regulations. It first went on the air 31 Oct. 1948, as WNBK over Channel 4. A move to Channel 3 was mandated in 1954, when its erection of the most powerful antenna in the Midwest caused interference with other local channels. In a 1955 trade between NBC and the Westinghouse Broadcasting Co., Westinghouse took over NBC's Cleveland outlets, while NBC acquired the former's facilities in Philadelphia. With Westinghouse came the call letters KYW, which were applied to both Channel 3 and its sister radio station, WTAM. Before the exchange was nullified by the FCC a decade later, KYW had moved its studios from the Superior (formerly NBC) Bldg. to the former E. Ohio Gas Bldg. on E. 6th St. Westinghouse also launched the "Mike Douglas Show" in Cleveland, from where it acquired a national following before leaving with Westinghouse. When NBC returned to Cleveland as a station proprietor in 1965, it brought the call letters WKYC for the former KYW monogram, which returned to Philadelphia with Westinghouse. Within a few months, WKYC had become Cleveland's first all-color television station. WKYC Radio, however, was sold off by NBC at the end of the 1960s and resurfaced under various ownerships as WWWE. Locally, the station inherited "Barnaby," one of the city's most popular children's shows, from the KYW era. Actor Linn Sheldon had created the leprechaun title character, who was joined later by a sidekick called "Woodrow the Woodsman." The show aired live 7 days a week at its peak and made Sheldon the city's highest-paid celebrity. Only 2 years after hiring Paul Schiera as its first full-time news reporter, the station introduced one of the nation's first half-hour newscasts in 1959. Live telecasts from SEVERANCE HALL of the CLEVELAND ORCHESTRA under GEO. SZELL were also featured during that era. Programming in the 1980s included "Feagler!", one of Cleveland's longest-running public-affairs shows, which was moderated by former *CLEVELAND PRESS* columnist Dick Feagler. "Hickory Hideout," a WKYC-produced children's show, was also aired by the NBC-owned stations in New York, Chicago, Washington, and Los Angeles. In 1986, WKYC became the city's first VHF channel to broadcast in stereo.

**WMMS** began as WHK-FM in 1946 when WHK received one of the first experimental FM licenses. By the early 1950s, the FM station, broadcasting at 100.7 megacycles, was playing adult-oriented music. In Aug. 1968 it switched to underground progressive and contemporary ROCK 'N' ROLL, which was more creative than profitable. At the same time, the station owner, Metromedia, changed the call letters to WMMS (MMS meaning Metromedia Stereo). After briefly returning to its adult format, in Sept. 1970 it settled permanently on rock 'n' roll as its primary music form and slowly began to build its audience. When Malrite Communications bought WHK and WMMS for $3.5 million, a small but loyal audience protested the purchase, believing the new owners would change the station's format. After studying the Cleveland market, Malrite chairman Milton Maltz decided to stay with rock 'n' roll, and the sale became final at the end of 1972. With John Gorman as program director (1973–86), a cohesive staff developed a rock-centered radio station that came to dominate the Cleveland radio market and gain a national reputation as a forum for new rock 'n' roll acts. It was an early showcase for Bruce Springsteen's music and has been active in promoting local rock 'n' roll music as well. By the late 1970s, the station was regularly besting its Cleveland competition in the Arbitron ratings. In the 1980s it was dominant in this market and was one of the highest-rated radio stations in the country. From 1979–86, the readers of *Rolling Stone* magazine voted WMMS the "Radio Station of the Year" award.

**WTAM** was the realization of the dreams of Theodore Willard and S. E. Lawrence, as they inaugurated radio broadcasts on that station in Sept. 1923. Broadcasting originally at 750 kilocycles and 1,500 watts, WTAM offered a 3-hour schedule of evening programs. During the next 5 years its power was increased to 3,500 watts, the programming day was expanded, and the station was moved to the Union Trust Bldg. WTAM was incorporated in Mar. 1928, and in May, Willard sold the station to the CLEVELAND ELECTRIC ILLUMINATING CO. and the VAN SWERINGEN brothers, who viewed it as a community asset to be used for spreading the fame of Cleveland. WTAM's request to become the first station in Cleveland to increase power to 50,000 watts was approved by the federal government in 1928. With construction of a new transmitting tower in BRECKSVILLE and new studios in the Auditorium Bldg., WTAM's new clear-channel 1,070 frequency reached from northern Canada to the Gulf of Mexico and from the Atlantic seaboard to the Rocky Mts. A gala celebration broadcast on 6 Nov. 1929 heralded the most powerful regularly licensed radio station in America. As part of a major nationwide reorganization of radio stations to eliminate crosstalk interference, WTAM shifted to 1,980 kilocycles in Feb. 1930. In October, NBC took over operations and made WTAM a major link in its "Red" Network. Station operations moved in Apr. 1937, to the Guarantee Title & Trust Bldg. at 850 Superior Ave., renamed the NBC Bldg. Its broadcasting frequency moved once again in 1941, to 1,100 kilocycles, where it remained. Some of the early artists who performed live on WTAM included Guy Lombardo and the Royal Canadians, Fred Waring and His Orchestra, Lum and Abner, and sportscaster TOM MANNING. Notable broadcasts included a 3-way 1923 broadcast between Cleveland, Akron, and a dirigible, and the first radio network coverage of a national political convention, the REPUBLICAN CONVENTION OF 1924 from Cleveland's Public Hall. In Feb. 1956, WTAM and WNBK-TV were purchased by the Westinghouse Broadcasting Co., which dropped WTAM's NBC affiliation and changed its call letters to KYW. The station rejoined NBC as WKYC in 1965, then became WWWE when it was sold to Ohio Communications in 1972. Sold to the Pacific & Southern Co. in 1977, WWWE again dropped its network affiliation and acquired an FM outlet with the purchase of station WDOK. Since then, the two stations have been owned by the Gannett Co. and, after 1985, Lake Erie Broadcasting.

**WVIZ** (Channel 25) was inaugurated on 7 Feb. 1965 to bring noncommercial, educational television to the last major city in the U.S. without it. It finally materialized through the efforts of a committee of civic and educational leaders appointed by Mayor Anthony J. Celebrezze, with seed money provided by the CLEVELAND FOUNDATION. Studios were established in Cleveland's Max Hayes Vocational School under the general management of Betty Cope, formerly the producer of Dorothy Fuldheim's news commentary and "One O'Clock Club" programs on WEWS. Programming originally was weighted heavily toward the daytime educational schedule, funded primarily by annual pledges of $1 per pupil from city and suburban boards of education. Eventually these payments were assumed by the state of Ohio and supplemented by royalties from national syndication of educational shows produced by WVIZ's Instructional Classroom Programming unit. Expansion of the station's evening and weekend schedule, primarily from the cultural offerings of the Public Broadcasting System, was financed by individual membership pledges from viewers as well as proceeds from an annual benefit auction. Since 1967, WVIZ has operated from its own studios at 4300 Brookpark Rd., where it broadcasts as Channel 25 on the UHF band. A new transmitter was installed in 1973, followed a year later by a building expansion. Its enlarged staff of 85 remained under the direction of Betty Cope, who also served as president of the Educational Television Assoc. of Metropolitan Cleveland, the station's licensee. Besides its classroom schedule, WVIZ has produced such local public-affairs shows as "Medi-Scene," "North Coast Report," and high school sports events. It has also created monthly documentaries on subjects ranging from literacy to the photography of MARGARET BOURKE-WHITE. Nationally, WVIZ has provided public television with several CLEVELAND ORCHESTRA performances, 2 plays from the FAIRMOUNT THEATRE FOR THE DEAF, and the Great Lakes Shakespeare Festival production of Synge's *The Playboy of the Western World*. It has also served as the local outlet for such PBS network shows as "Masterpiece Theater," "Nova," "Live from the Met," "Sesame Street," and "The MacNeil/Lehrer News Hour."

The **W. BINGHAM COMPANY** was one of the Midwest's largest hardware concerns. The firm was founded by WM. BINGHAM, who had worked as a clerk in GEO. WORTHINGTON's store for 5 years. On 1 Apr. 1841, Bingham and a partner, Henry C. Blossom, purchased the hardware stock of a failing company, Clark & Murfey, and opened their own store, W. Bingham & Co., at the corner of Superior and Water (W. 9th) streets. In 1855, it expanded its services by erecting a new building near its original location. It was incorporated as the W. Bingham Co. in 1888. In 1915, Bingham discontinued its retail business. The architectural and engineering firm of Walker & Weeks then designed for Bingham one of the finest and most serviceable wholesale warehouses in the nation, at 1278 W. 9th St. Bingham expanded its line of goods, but its major business always remained hardware supplies. By the 1940s, the company's trade extended over 12 states. On 15 June 1961, Bingham closed its warehouse, citing the rise of discount stores and trading-stamp premiums as reasons for the firm's low net profits. The closure idled 300 employees in Cleveland and 100 in other cities. Before its closing, some of the officers of Bingham, headed by Victor E. Peters, acquired the company's industrial division and continued to operate it as a new firm, Bingham, Inc., which handled tools and operating supplies for industrial plants, railroads, and mines. Bingham remained at W. 9th St. until 1980, when it moved to 1068 E. 134th St. Although it has employed fewer than 100 people, it has remained one of the leading distributors of industrial supplies in the region.

**WADE, EDWARD** (22 Nov. 1802–13 Aug. 1866), was a lawyer and a member of the U.S. House of Representatives, 1853–61. Wade was born in W. Springfield, Mass., where he was educated locally. In 1827 he was admitted to the bar, after which he moved into practice in Jefferson, Ashtabula County, Ohio. In 1831 he became justice of the peace for the county, a post he held for 1 year. He moved to Unionville in 1832 and worked as a prosecuting attorney. In 1837 Wade came to Cleveland, where he continued his law practice and became one of the area's leading abolitionists. In 1837 he became the president of the CUYAHOGA COUNTY ANTI-SLAVERY SOCIETY, often defending fugitive slaves in court. In 1842 he organized the Liberty party. It was Wade's reputation as an abolitionist that gained him a seat in Congress as a Free-Soiler in 1853. He held that position until 1855, when he was again elected, but on the Republican ticket. He remained as congressman until 1861. He was on the first boards of trustees of the Homoeopathic Hospital College (1849) and CLEVELAND UNIVERSITY. Wade was married twice. His first wife, Sarah Louise Atkins, died shortly after their marriage. His second marriage was to Mary P. Hall.

**WADE, JEPTHA HOMER I** (11 Aug. 1811–9 Aug. 1890), was a financier and a leader in erecting telegraph lines in the mid-19th century. He settled in Cleveland in 1856 and became a civic leader. Wade was born in Romulus, Seneca County, N.Y., the son of a surveyor and civil engineer. He pursued several careers before settling on the new telegraph business; he operated a sash and blind factory and was an itinerant portrait painter in the late 1830s and early 1840s. He became interested in the telegraph, and in 1847, as a subcontractor for J. J. Speedy, he began constructing a telegraph line from Detroit to Jackson, Mich. Wade soon added lines from Detroit to Milwaukee and to Buffalo by way of Cleveland. In 1849–50 he built lines from Cleveland to Cincinnati and St. Louis. In 1854 he consolidated his lines with those of Royal E. House to create a network of lines across the Old Northwest, and in Apr. 1856 their network was part of the 13-company consolidation of telegraph lines that created the Western Union Telegraph Co. Wade served as the general agent for Western Union, and he continued to develop new lines and telegraph companies in the West, forming the California State Telegraph Co. and the Pacific Telegraph Co.; the latter was connected to St. Louis and San Francisco by wire in Aug. 1861. Wade became president of Western Union in 1866, but poor health forced him to resign the following year.

Wade moved to Cleveland in 1856 and played a leading role in the city's business and civic affairs. He was a director of 8 railroad companies; was a leader in the organization of the Citizens Savings & Loan Assoc. in 1867 and its first president in 1868; served as president of the Natl. Bank of Commerce; was an incorporator of the Cleveland Rolling Mill Co. in 1863; became a sinking-fund commissioner in 1870 (serving for 20 years); and was an organizer and the first president of the LAKE VIEW CEMETERY Assoc. He was also a director of the CLEVELAND WORKHOUSE and the House of Correction; a member of the public park commission; a member of the Natl. Garfield Monument Assoc.; and one of the incorporators of Case School of Applied Science in Apr. 1880. In June 1881, Wade offered the city 75 acres of land along Doan Brook to be used as a park; the city accepted the gift, and the land was deeded to the city in Sept. 1882 (See WADE PARK). He also donated land to Western Reserve University. Wade was married in Oct. 1832 to Rebecca Loueza Facer, who died in Nov. 1836. He was remarried in Sept. 1837, to Susan M. Fleming. She died in Aug. 1889.

Jeptha Homer Wade Family Papers, WRHS.

**WADE, JEPTHA HOMER II** (15 Oct. 1857–6 Mar. 1926), was a financier and philanthropist who played an important role in the development and growth of the CLEVELAND MUSEUM OF ART. Wade was born in Cleveland, the only son of Randall P. Wade and the grandson of JEPTHA HOMER WADE. Randall Wade (26 Aug. 1835–24 June 1876) followed his father into the telegraph business before becoming a bank executive in 1857. He served in the U.S. Military Telegraph Dept. during the CIVIL WAR, then had a variety of business interests in Cleveland before his early death. Jeptha Wade II was educated by tutors and in private schools as his family prepared him to inherit its various business and philanthropic interests. He graduated from Mt. Pleasant Academy in Ossining, N.Y., and later received a master's degree from Western Reserve University. Wade developed a close relationship with his grandfather after his father died. Like his grandfather, the younger Wade took an active role in business and civic affairs: he served as an executive in 45 companies, including railways, mining companies, manufacturing firms, and banking institutions; and he was a trustee and supporter of the Cleveland Art School, the Protestant Orphan Asylum, the WESTERN RESERVE HISTORICAL SOCIETY, and WRU. He also contributed to the Children's Fresh Air Camp, Lakeside Hospital, and the CLEVELAND MUSEUM OF NATURAL HISTORY. Wade shared his grandfather's interest in art and became a leading supporter of the Cleveland Museum of Art. He was one of its incorporators in 1913 and served as its first vice-president, becoming president in 1920. His many contributions to the museum included a collection of rare lace, textiles, jewels, enamels, and a number of paintings. He also established a purchasing fund, which grew to more than $1 million. In Oct. 1878, Wade married Ellen Garretson. Upon her death in 1917, Wade established a memorial fund in her name to aid charities in which they were interested.

Jeptha Homer Wade Family Papers, WRHS.

**WADE PARK,** which joins the southern end of ROCKEFELLER PARK at E. 105th and extends south of EUCLID AVE. along East Blvd., encompassing much of UNIVERSITY CIRCLE, was originally the private estate of JEPTHA H. WADE, a Cleveland industrialist who began to develop his farmland and natural woodland as a public park in 1872—permitting the public to use sections as they were completed. Wade donated over 63 acres to the city on 15 Sept. 1882, one of the first large gifts of open space to the city. Subsequently, additional acres were purchased by the city, and in 1892, Wade Park became a major recreational area for many years, with picnic facilities, tennis courts, a lagoon, and ball fields. Later, it became the setting for many of Cleveland's cultural institutions, including the CLEVELAND MUSEUM OF ART, the Fine Arts Garden, and the GARDEN CTR. OF GREATER CLEVELAND.

**WAECHTER UND ANZEIGER** (The Sentinel & Advertiser) is Cleveland's longest-lived ethnic daily and one of the city's major newspapers in its own right. It began life on 9 Aug. 1852 as *Waechter am Erie* (Sentinel on the Erie), a German weekly founded by 3 "48ers," Heinrich Rochette, Louis Ritter, and JACOB MUELLER. To edit it, they sent to Buffalo for August Thieme, who not only ran it but soon purchased it as well. Under the progressive Thieme, *Waechter am Erie* became a force in the young Republican party. During the 1856 Fremont campaign, it temporarily boosted the Republican standard-bearer on a daily basis. It supported Lincoln in 1860 and endorsed the Emancipation Proclamation, but flirted with the radical Fremont movement in 1864 before returning to the regular fold. In 1872 it bolted to the Liberal Republican ticket of Greeley and Adams, while a newly founded rival, the *Anzeiger* (Advertiser), supported Grant and the regulars. Prior to his death in 1879, Thieme had converted the *Waechter* to a daily on a permanent basis in Sept. 1866. By 1880, when it was published once again by Mueller, it had also added a Sunday edition. In 1893 it was merged with the *Anzeiger* by the German Consolidated Newspaper Co., capitalized at $100,000.

Although WORLD WAR I temporarily pumped circulation to a record 34,000, it proved ultimately disastrous for the *Waechter und Anzeiger* after the U.S. entered the conflict against the mother country. Two of its editors were interned as enemy aliens, while ownership of part of its stock by a German resident placed the paper under the direction of the Custodian of Enemy Alien Property. Locally, it had to endure advertising boycotts, attacks from English competitors, and even the burning of newspaper bundles bound for would-be readers by the BOY SCOUTS! While managing to survive the war, the *Waechter und Anzeiger* had lost more than half its circulation by 1924, when it supported the isolationist Robt. La Follette for president. In 1928 it effected a limited merger with the Hungarian-language *SZABADSAG* under the aegis of the Consolidated Press & Printing Co., but its Sunday edition was dropped during the Depression. *Szabadsag* and the *Waechter* went their separate ways in 1939, when the German paper was reorganized by the Press & Plate Co. It published its last daily issue on 10 May 1954, when Press & Plate went out of business. Its assets were subsequently purchased by a recent immigrant, Stefan Deubel, who revived the *Waechter und Anzeiger* as a weekly in Sept. 1954. Since then its circulation has leveled off at around 3,500, and it has leaned politically toward the Republicans.

**WAGNER, MARGARET W.** (19 Oct. 1892–19 Aug. 1984), was an early social worker in Cleveland who gained a national reputation for her innovative work with the elderly during her 29-year tenure as director of the BENJAMIN ROSE INSTITUTE. A native Clevelander, Wagner was the daughter of financier Frank B. Wagner. She graduated from HATHAWAY BROWN SCHOOL in 1910 and later studied at Miss Spence's School in New York, Finch College, and the School of Applied Social Sciences at Western Reserve University. Her career in social work began in 1912. As a member of the JR. LEAGUE OF CLEVELAND, Wagner volunteered to work in the children's division of Lakeside Hospital. Through her work there, she became interested in working with handicapped children and was the first social worker hired by the Assoc. for the Crippled & Disabled. Her experiences working with the disabled led her to urge the city's director of public welfare, DUDLEY S. BLOSSOM, to establish a social-service department at City Hospital. Wagner joined the hospital in 1924 to administer the new program.

In 1930, Wagner became the executive secretary of the Benjamin Rose Institute and began to transform it into a professional social-service institute. She made the institute an advocate for the needs of the elderly and expanded the scope of the services it offered. It undertook studies of the needs of the elderly in the community and established new institutions to meet those needs, such as the Golden Age Clubs Wagner initiated in 1937, and the Benjamin Rose Hospital, founded especially for the elderly in 1953. In the 1940s and 1950s, the institute acquired and operated residential and nursing homes to meet the housing needs of senior citizens. After her retirement in 1959, Wagner helped design the modern nursing home the institute built and named for her in 1961 (See MARGARET WAGNER HOME). Wagner was active in social-work organizations both locally and nationally and lectured throughout the nation. She was a member of the Natl. Committee on Aging of the Social Welfare Assembly in New York and a member of the Natl. Assoc. of Social Workers. She also initiated the Cleveland Welfare Fed.'s first committee on the elderly. Wagner received many awards for her service to the elderly. She received the Community Chest's award for distinguished community service in 1955, the Inter-Club Council's Women of Achievement Award in 1958, the Cleveland Welfare Fed.'s award for outstanding service in 1959, and the WOMEN'S CITY CLUB's Margaret A. Ireland Award in 1964. In 1984 she was honored as an outstanding alumna of Hathaway Brown School.

**WAITE, FREDERICK CLAYTON** (24 May 1870–30 Mar. 1956), founded the Dept. of Histology & Embryology at the Western Reserve University Medical & Dental Schools. A medical educator, he helped establish higher standards for medical and dental schools in the U.S. Waite was born in Hudson, Ohio, to Nelson and Cynthia Post Waite. He took to learning naturally. His mother taught him until the age of 6. Upon entering the first grade, he was promoted in 2 hours. Waite earned his way through the Western Reserve Academy by doing odd jobs, graduating in 1888. He also earned his way through WRU by working in the college library and painting campus buildings. He graduated with the B.Litt. degree in 1892 and the A.M. degree in 1894. In 1892, he took a job at WRU as Dr. Francis Herrick's first assistant in biology. Waite entered Harvard in 1895, earning the A.M. degree in 1896 and the Ph.D. in 1899. From 1898–1900, he taught biology at Peter Cooper High School in New York. He taught at New York University, 1899–1900, and spent 1900–01 as an assistant in anatomy at Rush Medical College in Chicago. In 1901, Waite was appointed assistant professor of histology and embryology at Reserve's Medical & Dental Schools. He was promoted to associate professor in 1904 and professor in 1906. He remained chairman of the department until his retirement in 1940, when he was appointed professor emeritus. Before WORLD WAR I, Waite devoted much time to administrative duties and working with the American Medical Assoc. He visited and inspected virtually every U.S. medical school several times. During WORLD WAR I he served as a captain in the U.S. Surgeon General's Office. After the war he worked at raising standards at both medical and dental schools throughout the country. Working for the Natl. Dental Education Conference, Waite inspected almost every dental school in the U.S. He provided key testimony that closed down 2 Missouri schools that sold diplomas. Waite was a prolific author, especially after his retirement, when he wrote books on the history of the WRU Medical & Dental Schools and the Hudson Academy years. Waite married Emily Fisher Bacon in 1916.

**WAITT, MAUDE COMSTOCK** (11 Aug. 1875–13 Dec. 1935), was the first woman elected to the Ohio senate, from Cuyahoga County, where she served for 4 terms. Waitt was born in Middlebury, Vt., the daughter of Orvis and Mary Comstock. She graduated from Middlebury High School and attended the Normal School at Vermont College. After graduation, she taught school in Rockland, Mass. Shortly after her marriage, she and her husband came to Cleveland, living here from 1902–04 and then moving to Fremont, Ohio. They returned to Cleveland in 1916. Waitt became active in the woman's suffrage movement and served as a member of Lakewood City Council in 1921 and 1922. In 1922 she was elected to represent the 25th Ohio senatorial district as a Republican. After being reelected 3 times, she retired from the senate in 1930 because of poor health. She died in Lakewood at age 60. She married Walter G. Waitt ca. 1901, and they had a daughter, Doris Ida.

*WALK-IN-THE-WATER* was the first steamboat on Lake Erie. Built at Black Rock, N.Y., in 1818, it was a paddle-wheel-driven boat, 132′ long and 32′ across the beam. It displaced approximately 240–342 tons. Noah Brown supervised the building of the ship, and Robt. Fulton supervised the mechanical installations. It was built by Joseph B. Stuart, Nathaniel Davis, Asa H. Curtis, Ralph Pratt, Jas. Durant, John Meads, Robt. McQueen, Samuel McCoon, Alexander McMuir, and Noah Brown. Its first captain was Job Fish. The boat's smokestack was 30' high and was set between 2 sails that were used when wind was good. Ladies' quarters were in the fore deck, and gentlemen's were aft, below deck. The boat also had a smoking room, a baggage room, and a dining room. The cabins were said to be fitted in an elegant and convenient style. The steamer could accommodate 100 cabin passengers and a large number of steerage passengers. There are 2 versions about the naming of the steamer: it may have been named for a Wyandot Indian Chief, Walk-in-the-Water, or, according to Capt. Baton Atkins of Buffalo, N.Y., after an Indian's exclamation upon seeing Fulton's first boat, the *Clermont*, in 1807, "walks in the water." *Walk-in-the-Water*'s maiden voyage began on 25 Aug. 1818, with 29 passengers bound for Erie, Grand River, Cleveland, Sandusky, and Detroit. When it arrived in Cleveland, most of the village's inhabitants came to greet it. During this trip, it went from Buffalo to Detroit in approximately 9 days, traveling about 8–10 mph. Cost was $18 for cabin and $7 for steerage. On 27 Sept., the boat sustained damage after running aground near Erie. It was repaired and in 1819 became the first steamboat in Lake Michigan when it went to Mackinaw and Green Bay. It was wrecked during foul weather on 1 Nov. 1821 near Buffalo while carrying 18 passengers and a full cargo. All on board survived. The loss was estimated at $10,000–12,000. After the wreck, its engine was placed in the *Superior.*

**WALKER, FRANK RAY** (29 Sept. 1877–9 July 1949), was a prominent architect who with HARRY E. WEEKS founded Walker & Weeks, Cleveland's foremost architectural firm during the 1920s. Walker was born in Pittsfield, Mass., and educated at public schools there. He graduated from MIT in 1900, then traveled to Europe, where he studied at the Atelier of Monsieur Redon in Paris and lived for a year in Italy. Upon returning to the U.S., Walker practiced architecture in the Boston, New York City, and Pittsburgh offices of Guy Lowell. At the suggestion of John M. Carrerre, a member of the Cleveland Group Plan Commission, Walker moved to Cleveland in 1905 and joined the firm of J. MILTON DYER, which had been commissioned to design a city hall for Cleveland as part of the Group Plan. Both Walker and Weeks worked for Dyer; they left his office in 1911 to establish their own practice. Walker & Weeks were known as specialists in bank buildings, completing 60 throughout Ohio. In Cleveland, however, they were better known for their design of major commercial, public, and religious structures in classical revival styles. A partial list of major projects includes the Bingham Co. Warehouse (1915); the Guardian Bldg. renovation (Natl. City Bank) (1915); PUBLIC AUDITORIUM (1922); the 4th District FEDERAL RESERVE BANK of Cleveland (1923); the CLEVELAND PUBLIC LIBRARY (1925); the United Banking & Trust Co. (Central Natl. Bank), W. 25th St. and Lorain Ave. (1926); EPWORTH-EUCLID METHODIST CHURCH, with architect Bertram Goodhue (1928); First Baptist Church in Shaker Hts. (1929); ST. PAUL'S EPISCOPAL CHURCH in Cleveland Hts. (1929); Pearl St. Savings & Trust (AmeriTrust), W. 25th St. and Clarke Ave. (1929); and CLEVELAND MUNICIPAL STADIUM with the OSBORN ENGINEERING CO. in 1931.

Walker also played a major role in establishing design and planning standards for the city of Cleveland. He was the first professional advisor to the City Planning Com-

mission and a member of that body for 10 years. He was an advisor to the University Development Commission, a member of the Cleveland Chamber of Commerce City Plan Committee, a critic and patron of an atelier that became the John Huntington Polytechnic Institute, a trustee and faculty member of the Western Reserve University College of Architecture, and an advisor to the Cleveland School of Art. Walker was associated with the development of GATES MILLS, serving as president of the Gates Mills Improvement Society (1917–19) and as the village's first mayor (1920–24). He was a trustee of the CLEVELAND MUSEUM OF NATURAL HISTORY, a member and past president of the Cleveland Chap. of the AMERICAN INSTITUTE OF ARCHITECTS, a director of the Cleveland Chamber of Commerce, and a trustee of the CLEVELAND ENGINEERING SOCIETY, the Community Fund, and St. Christopher's Episcopal Church of Gates Mills. Walker was married in Oct. 1915, to Katharine Tollett Stone.

**WALKER, HAZEL MOUNTAIN** (16 Feb. 1889–16 May 1980), was the first black to be appointed as a school principal in Cleveland. She was also among the first black women admitted to the practice of law in Ohio. A native of Warren, Ohio, Walker graduated from the Cleveland Normal Training School, then received bachelor's and master's degrees in education from Western Reserve University, earning the latter in 1909. That year she began teaching 3d-graders at Mayflower Elementary School for $45 per month. She taught at Mayflower until 1936, during which time she became known for her ability to teach reading to children whose families either could not read or spoke no English. Walker's duties as a teacher left her with free time in the summer, which she used to study law at BALDWIN-WALLACE COLLEGE. She received her degree in 1919 and passed the bar examination the same year, but she had no intention of practicing law; she simply wanted to prove that black women were capable of becoming lawyers. She then worked with the juvenile court, providing tutorial help to black children from the South who were having problems adjusting to the Cleveland schools. In 1936, Walker became principal of Rutherford B. Hayes Elementary School; she was the first black to head a school in the city. She was appointed principal of the new Geo. Washington Carver Elementary School in 1954 and served in that capacity until she retired from the school system in 1958. She was elected to a 6-year term on the Ohio State Board of Education in 1961 but resigned in 1963 when she moved out of the state. Walker was an early member of and actress at the KARAMU HOUSE and is credited with choosing the theater's name in 1924. She played leading roles in many of its productions and also appeared in radio skits. Karamu honored her for her work in 1951. Walker was also active in politics, serving on the CUYAHOGA COUNTY REPUBLICAN PARTY executive committee in the 1930s. She was a member of the URBAN LEAGUE and the local NAACP and was one of the first blacks to become a member of the WOMEN'S CITY CLUB. She held memberships in the BUSINESS & PROFESSIONAL WOMEN'S CLUB, Delta Kappa Gamma, and Alpha Kappa Alpha. The Cleveland Urban League honored her for her work in 1958. Walker was married twice. Her first husband, Geo. Herbert Walker, died in 1956; in 1961 she married Joseph R. Walker of Everett, Mass., who died in 1973.

**WALKER, WILLIAM OTIS** (19 Sept. 1896–29 Oct. 1981), not only was a powerbroker in the local community and the state Republican party, but was also regarded as the "dean of black publishing" in America. Born in Selma, Ala., he went to work for the Pittsburgh Urban League after studying at Wilberforce University and Oberlin Business College. Entering the field of black journalism, he was first a reporter for the *Pittsburgh Courier*, then city editor of the *Norfolk Journal & Guide*, and finally cofounder of the *Washington* (D.C.) *Tribune* in 1921. Walker had temporarily left newspaper work for a position in a Baltimore department store when he was invited to come to Cleveland in 1932 to manage the *CALL & POST*. Within a few years, he restored the recently merged black weekly to profitability and acquired majority ownership. Possibly the only black newspaperman to interview the Scottsboro boys in their Birmingham jail, Walker was also a founder of the FUTURE OUTLOOK LEAGUE. By and large, however, Walker's loyalty to the Republican party identified him as a conservative in black politics. As a Republican, he served as councilman for Ward 17 from 1940–47. As Ohio's director of industrial relations from 1963–71, he was the first black to hold a cabinet-level position in the state government. In his weekly *Call & Post* column, "Down the Big Road," he critized expenditures for relief and called instead for policies that would create more jobs in the private sector.

Despite his conservatism, Walker often took radical stands when he thought blacks would benefit. He supported Democrat Carl Stokes for mayor in 1967, though he later fell out with both Carl and Louis Stokes. When several black councilmen were accused of taking kickbacks in the operation of carnivals, Walker helped organize a fund to provide for their legal defense. In the 1960s, he joined forces with "Rabbi" David Hill in a boycott to force McDonald's Restaurant to grant franchises to blacks. He helped organize black self-help groups such as Operation Alert and the Surrogates. He was president of the local chapters of the Negro Business League, URBAN LEAGUE, and NAACP. He was on the boards of the Cuyahoga Community College Foundation, the NATIONALITIES SERVICES CTR., the Cleveland Zoological Society, and the CLEVELAND CONVENTION & VISITORS BUREAU. Before his death, Walker arranged for the transfer of title to the *Call & Post* into the hands of his associates. He died of a heart attack in the Call & Post Bldg., even as he was being considered for appointment as chairman of the U.S. Civil Rights Commission. He was survived by his second wife, Naomi, whom he had married following a divorce from his first wife, Theresa, in 1955. Within a year of his death, Walker was elected to the Gallery of Distinguished Newspaper Publishers at Howard University.

**WALLACE, GEORGE ALEXANDER LEROY** (22 Feb. 1848–3 Aug. 1940), was a member of the CLEVELAND FIRE DEPT. for 62 years, serving as chief of the department from 1901–31. Wallace was born in Erie, Pa., to Geo. A. and Margaret Hendrickson Wallace. He came to Cleveland with his family in 1854 and attended school downtown in the Rockwell Bldg. At the age of 14, he left school and got a job as a railroad brakeman. Wallace joined the Cleveland Fire Dept. as a 2d-class fireman in June 1869. He rose rapidly through the ranks, acquiring a reputation as a fine hoseman and troubleshooter. Working with Co. No. 2 on Champlain St., Wallace rose to hoseman, then hosecart driver. He became captain of Hook & Ladder Co. No. 4 in 1873 and of Hook & Ladder Co. No. 1 in 1874. In 1883, Wallace was appointed 5th assistant chief. In 1901, after rising to 4th and then 3d assistant, he was appointed chief by Mayor JOHN FARLEY, commanding 1,040 officers and men at 63 engine houses and stations. Throughout his tenure as chief, Wallace fought to keep out politics and make the department's operations a matter of fitness and faithfulness. As chief, he displayed a high degree of executive and leadership ability, his strength due to the love of his subordinates and the admiration of civilians. Wallace projected a hard-boiled exterior that hid a sensitive inner self. He possessed judicial qualities, always maintaining discipline and inspiring the respect of his men; he treated his men as if they were his own sons. At the scene of a fire, Wallace was the absolute boss. Dressed in a white hat, coat, and boots, the chief demanded strict obedience from his men and any crowds standing by. Nicknamed the "Old War Horse," Wallace was always to be found amid the thickest flames and smoke, shouting out orders intermixed with expletives hotter than the fire. Courageous and tough, Wallace issued no orders that he himself would not have obeyed. Many times he risked his life entering burning buildings to save victims, family pets, or heirlooms. Among the memorable fires at which Wallace directed firefighting efforts were the COLLINWOOD SCHOOL FIRE of 1908 and the CLEVELAND CLINIC FIRE of 1929. Wallace married Emma Stanhope in 1874. The Wallaces had 2 sons, George and Stanhope.

**WALSH, (WALASIEWICZ), STELLA (STANISLAWA)** (3 Apr. 1911–4 Dec. 1980), was a noted woman track star from Cleveland. She was named by the Helm Athletic Foundation in 1951 as the greatest woman athlete of the first half of the 20th century. Walsh was born in Wierzchownin, near Warsaw, Poland. Her parents brought her to Cleveland when she was 10. She attended South and Notre Dame high schools and was enrolled for a time at the University of Warsaw in 1933. She became famous during the summer of 1926 when she tied the women's record of 6 seconds for the 50-yd. dash. By 1928, Walsh was prepared to represent the U.S. in the Olympics, when it was discovered that she had never become an American citizen. With her naturalization process nearly completed, she was laid off from her job with the New York Central Railroad. Walsh was then offered a job by the Polish consulate in New York if she would represent Poland in the Los Angeles Olympics in 1936. She did not become an American citizen until Dec. 1947 and because of an Olympic rule never ran for the U.S. in Olympic competition. Representing Poland, Walsh won the 100-meter dash at the 1932 Olympic games, setting a world record in the event. In 1936, she finished 2d at the Berlin games to Helen Stephens of the U.S. By 1946 she held 65 world and national track and field records and had won 33 events in the women's national AAU championships. Still competing in her fifties, in 1967 Walsh won a 60-yd. dash in 7.7 seconds, less than a .5 second slower then her 7.3 world record time in 1934. She won over 5,000 track and field events during her career. An accomplished all-around athlete, Walsh was a noted basketball and softball player. In 1948 she founded the San Fernando Valley Women's Athletic Club, the first women's track club on the West Coast. In the 1970s she coached the Polish Falcons (see SOKOL POLSKI) track club in Cleveland. She was married for a short time during the 1950s and continued to use Stella Walsh Olson as her legal name thereafter. She was shot to death during an attempted robbery in an Uncle Bill's parking lot on Broadway.

**WALTERS, REUBEN W.** (22 Aug. 1838–19 Apr. 1918), was a CIVIL WAR soldier, physician, and Cuyahoga County Soldiers & Sailors Monument Commission member. Walters was born in Russell, Ohio (Geauga County). He began to study medicine in 1861 but halted his education to enlist as a private in Co. D, 7TH OHIO VOLUNTEER INFANTRY, on 15 Aug. 1864. When the 7th was mustered out in the summer of 1864, Walters was transferred to the 5th

OVI to complete his enlistment. Appointed hospital steward on 16 Mar. 1864, he was mustered out of the Army 17 Mar. 1865. After the war, Walters studied at and graduated from Jefferson Medical College in Philadelphia; Cleveland Medical College; and Cleveland Homeopathic Hospital College. Gov. Bishop of Ohio appointed him surgeon of the 15TH OHIO NATL. GUARD REGIMENT on 17 July 1878. Walters practiced medicine in Chagrin Falls beginning in 1867. He also served on the original building commission of the Cuyahoga County SOLDIERS & SAILORS MONUMENT, dating from 20 June 1884. He was buried in Evergreen Hills Cemetery, Chagrin Falls, Ohio.

**WALTON, JOHN WHITTLESEY** (1845–19 Nov. 1926), was a prominent Cleveland businessman and philanthropist. In 1871, Walton formed a partnership with J. E. Upson and started a business as ship chandlers and grocers in the Winslow Bldg. The ship chandlery business grew and led to the incorporation of the Upson-Walton Co. in 1893. Walton was the second president of the company after Upson. Upson-Walton eventually achieved worldwide distribution and was the only company in the country to combine the manufacturing of wire rope, tackle blocks, and rope fittings. It also operated the only rope mill in Ohio. Walton used his wealth and influence to aid various civic and charitable causes in Cleveland. In 1867 he was one of the men responsible for the revival of the YMCA in the city. From 1874–1926, Walton was actively involved in charity, serving during this period as treasurer of the Bethel Associated Charities. He also headed the section on philanthropy for the city's Centennial Commission. Throughout his life, Walton was keenly interested in the emerging scientific approach to social work. He donated many books to the CLEVELAND PUBLIC LIBRARY relating to this field and sociology, and other books of educational value.

John Whittlesey Walton Papers, WRHS.

**WALTON HILLS** is a village southeast of Cleveland bounded on the north by MAPLE HTS., on the east by BEDFORD and OAKWOOD, on the west by VALLEY VIEW, and on the south by Summit County. It occupies 5.5 sq. mi. Walton Hills was created from the southwestern part of Bedford Twp. In 1937, real-estate developer Ludwig S. Conelly bought the J. C Walton farm and laid roads following the natural contours of the land. Several homes were built on the new Walton Rd., and the isolated location of the homesites led to the growth of a community zoned primarily for spacious country homes. Walton Hills was incorporated as a village in 1951. Efforts to create an exclusive country village were not completely successful. Since zoning required residential lots to have a minimum of 40,000 sq. ft., while neighboring Maple Hts. had a minimum requirement of only 6,000 sq. ft., some residents and developers sought the annexation of all or part of Walton Hills to Maple Hts. The annexation issue was a continuing legal battle for the mayor and council of Walton Hills. Walton Hills schools are part of the Bedford School System, with 5 elementary, 1 junior, and 1 senior high school. There are also 1 parochial and 1 vocational school. The village is part of the Bedford Branch of the CUYAHOGA COUNTY PUBLIC LIBRARY SYSTEM. There is significant industry in the area, including the FORD MOTOR CO. Stamping Plant, Normandex, Universal Paint, and the FERRO Chemical Corp. Recreational facilities include 2 golf courses and the nearby Bedford Reservation of the CLEVELAND METROPARKS SYSTEM. The population in 1980 was 2,199, a decrease of 400 since 1970.

**WALWORTH, ASHBEL W.** (1790–24 Aug. 1844), was the son of JOHN W. WALWORTH, an early settler of Cleveland. Like his father, he was a farmer and a holder of public office. He was largely responsible for bringing about the improvements to Cleveland's harbor area. Walworth was born in Croton, Conn. At a very young age he moved with his family to New York State, and then to the Painesville area in 1800. Although he received no formal schooling, like his father he was considered an educated man. The family came to Cleveland in 1806. After his father's death in 1812, Walworth assumed his duties as postmaster of Cleveland. He also succeeded his father as collector of the District of Erie (i.e., the port of Cuyahoga), an office he held until 1829. Between 1815–26, with the exception of a few years, Walworth was annually elected to city offices. These included township clerk (1815–17), treasurer (1821–26), and justice of the peace (1823–26). He was also the proprietor of a 300-acre farm in Cleveland that he inherited from his father. Later in 1835, he was treasurer of the Tippecanoe Club of Cuyahoga County, which evolved into one of the country's first Republican clubs. He was also a member of the committee for the First Presbyterian Society of Cleveland, which purchased land for the FIRST PRESBYTERIAN CHURCH (Old Stone Church).

As collector, Walworth was concerned with lake shipping and improving Cleveland's commercial possibilities as a port city. One obstacle that needed to be rectified was a sandbar that continuously formed over the mouth of the CUYAHOGA RIVER; Walworth and other Clevelanders in 1815 formed the Cleveland Pier Co. for the purpose of constructing a pier out into the lake. A pier was built but soon was wrecked in a storm. Continuing his efforts for the development of an outer harbor, Walworth received $5,000 from Congress in 1824 for the construction of another pier, which also proved ineffective in keeping the mouth of the river clear. At this time, Cleveland was receiving only 30–40 ships a year, and Congress was unwilling to grant additional funds for its harbor improvement. As a result, Clevelanders raised $150 in order to send Walworth to Washington to promote Cleveland's potential for commerce. He argued his case before a congressional committee, which resulted in an appropriation of $10,000 and the assistance of the U.S. Engineer Corps. That initiated a series of improvements on Cleveland's harbor, which extended into the 1840s. In 1820 Walworth married Mary Ann Dunlop of Schenectady, N.Y. They are both buried in ERIE ST. CEMETERY.

**WALWORTH, JOHN W.** (1765–10 Sept. 1812), was an early settler of Cleveland. He held various government offices on the local, county, and federal levels. Walworth was born in Croton, Conn. After spending several years at sea, he left Connecticut in 1792 and settled near Lake Cayuga, N.Y. He spent the winter of 1799 near Painesville, Ohio, where the next year he purchased 2,000 acres of land. He settled his family there on 8 Apr. 1800. Walworth was reportedly an educated man, a distinction supported by the number and types of government offices he held. In 1802, Gov. St. Clair appointed Walworth as justice of the peace for Trumbull County, which at that time included Cleveland. Two years later he was made postmaster of Painesville. When the CUYAHOGA RIVER was made a port of entry into the U.S. in 1805, Pres. Jefferson appointed Walworth to be the inspector of revenue (collector of the District of Erie). As this office required his presence in Cleveland, he resettled there in 1806. The move almost cost him his life; his family's boat was wrecked on the shore of Lake Erie. He received 2 other appointments in 1806, as postmaster of Cleveland and as an associate judge of Geauga

County. When Cuyahoga County was organized in 1810, he was made county clerk and recorder. Also that year, he was appointed clerk of the Supreme Court of Ohio. Walworth was primarily a farmer, having exchanged his land near Painesville for 300 acres in Cleveland. The "Walworth Farm" extended southward from Huron Rd., with the Cuyahoga River as its western boundary. Among Walworth's other involvements, he was one of the founders of the first Masonic Lodge in northern Ohio, established in Warren in 1803. He was also a member of the Board of Commissioners for the Improvement of the Cuyahoga & Tuscarawas Rivers, a project conceived to provide an improved connection between Lake Erie and the Ohio River. Walworth was married to Julianna Morgan. She was one of 3 women who refused to leave Cleveland at the outbreak of war in 1812; she chose to remain with her husband, who was dying of tuberculosis.

The **WAR MEMORIAL FOUNTAIN** is Cleveland's major memorial to those citizens who served in WORLD WAR II. It was designed by sculptor Marshall Fredericks and dedicated 30 May 1964. The building of the memorial was initiated and promoted by the *CLEVELAND PRESS*, which raised $250,000 in donations from citizens and organizations for the project. The centerpiece is a 35-ft. bronze figure representing man escaping from the flames of war and reaching skyward for eternal peace. The bronze sphere from which the figure of man rises is 10½' in diameter and represents superstitions and legends of mankind. Four granite carvings, each 12' long, 4½' wide, and 4½' high, surround the sphere and represent the geographic civilizations of the world. The polished rim surrounding the fountain is of granite. On the surface are bronze plates bearing the names of 4,000 Greater Clevelanders who perished in World War II and in the KOREAN WAR.

**WAR OF 1812.** When Congress declared war against Great Britain on 18 June 1812, the village of Cleveland consisted of 100 or fewer souls huddled near the mouth of the CUYAHOGA RIVER. Except for their geographic location, they had no reason to be either especially interested or principal actors in the war. However, situated on a significant Lake Erie harbor and attuned to American ideas of possible acquisition of British lands on the lake's northern shore, the villagers were affected in significant ways by the War of 1812. Cleveland served as a base for supplies, a rendezvous for military units, and the location of a military fort and hospital. The war also provoked alarms and invasion scares, which were quieted only with Perry's naval victory on Lake Erie and the subsequent demolition of a British and Indian force by Gen. Wm. Henry Harrison at the Battle of the Thames in the autumn of 1813. American activities were centered on Lake Erie and its connecting waterways for 3 primary reasons: to inflict damage on British military units garrisoned in Upper Canada (today's Ontario), to end the alleged British instigation of Indian depredations on American frontier settlements, and, if possible, to acquire Canadian lands by invasion and occupation. However, the early endeavors were disastrous for America, especially the humiliating surrender of Detroit by Gen. Wm. Hull in Aug. 1812. That particular event opened the waterways for invasions of northern Ohio. After a report from the Sandusky-Huron area falsely informing Clevelanders of enemy boats proceeding down the lake, many residents abandoned their homes and sought refuge farther inland. However, the "hostile marauders" turned out to be Americans paroled from Hull's disaster. New England Federalists might be antiwar, but transplanted Western Reserve Federalists recognized the need for defense. Their initial effort cen-

tered 2 militia companies at Cleveland, soon augmented by additional militiamen, all commanded by Gen. Elijah Wadsworth. Most of these troops moved out of the village within a short time, on their way westward to the Sandusky and Maumee valleys. In the spring of 1813, Capt. Stanton Sholes and a company of regular army troops arrived. Sholes put his men to work building a hospital, and then a small fort (FT. HUNTINGTON) and a breastworks of logs and brush near the bank of Lake Erie. From that vantage point, soldiers and civilians could view a part of the British fleet that appeared off harbor on 19 June 1813. A period of calm beset the fleet when it was a short distance from shore; then a thunderstorm drove the potential raiders from the Cleveland area.

Americans had come to realize that control of Lake Erie was requisite to any penetration of Upper Canada by way of the Maumee and Detroit route. In anticipation of challenging British control of the lake, Lt. Oliver Hazard Perry constructed a fleet at Erie, Pa. Additional vessels, the *Porcupine* and the *Portage*, built in the upper waters of the Cuyahoga River, would join with his force before he sailed westward to engage the British. On 10 Sept. 1813, Perry accomplished his objective in magnificent fashion. Moving from his flagship, the *Lawrence*, when it was destroyed, he continued command from the deck of the *Niagara*, reporting his destruction of the British fleet in unforgettable prose: "We have met the enemy and they are ours." Americans, starved in this second year of warfare for words of cheer, had found a worthy naval hero. And by virtue of the victory, the way now was cleared for Gen. Wm. Henry Harrison's invasion of Upper Canada. He annihilated a British-Indian force on 5 Oct. 1813 at the Battle of the Thames, ending warfare on Lake Erie and its shores. Clevelanders long reported stories of having heard gunfire from the vessels engaged in Perry's Battle of Put-in-Bay; they adopted Perry as a civic hero, erecting a statue of him on Public Square in 1860 (see PERRY MONUMENT). Less newsworthy, perhaps, but no less significant in the life of the embryonic city, was the way in which supplies for troops, mustering of militia and regular army units, and medical and hospital care for sick and wounded soldiers came to be centered at Cleveland. By the time the war ended with the Treaty of Ghent (24 Dec. 1814), the residents of the village could congratulate themselves on their brave defense against invasion (that did not occur), their logistical contributions to the nation's military and naval efforts, and the way in which their village's natural resources of river and harbor had become recognized as advantages for regional supply and support.

Carl Ubbelohde
Case Western Reserve University

The **WAR VETERANS BAR ASSOCIATION,** composed of WORLD WAR II veterans, was formed in 1946 to assist former servicemen in legal matters. Its first president was future U.S. senator Stephen M. Young. The association expanded its services in 1947 to provide legal assistance at reasonable fees to persons of moderate means. A subsidiary, the Cleveland Lawyers Referral Plan, was formed, and a full-time office was established in the Engineers Bldg. The main objective was to provide preventive law through consultation. Although legal assistance to veterans remained the WVBA's priority, in the 1950s it further expanded its public services. Through a speaker's bureau, members addressed public groups, answering legal questions on wills, real estate, accidents, etc. The association also began to endorse judiciary candidates. In 1956 it made a demand to the chief of police that lawyers be allowed to see prisoners in jail before they were charged with a crime. Throughout the 1960s and 1970s, the WVBA continued to operate its referral service, which grew to include nonveteran lawyers, as well. Its veterans' services were enlarged to accommodate veterans of the VIETNAM WAR. The association also introduced annual monetary awards for law students at John Marshall and CASE WESTERN RESERVE UNIVERSITY law schools with the highest grade-point average. The WVBA continued to operate its public services until its dissolution in the early 1980s.

The **WAREHOUSE DISTRICT** is an area north and west of Superior Ave. and W. 3rd St. which is the remnant of the late-19th-century Victorian wholesale commercial area. Before 1850, the 8-block district was part of the original residential area of the city, but by the mid-1850s rows of commercial blocks began to dominate it. While the oldest of the remaining buildings are from the 1850s, the majority were built in the 1870s and 1880s. The post-Civil War buildings housed wholesale grocers and dry goods, tool suppliers and ship chandlers, and an early department store. In the 1880s, the offices of American Express, the Worthington Hardware Co., and the Cleveland Rolling Mill were located in the district. The Grand Arcade on St. Clair Ave. had many different occupants, including the North Electric Telephone Co., manufacturers of switchboards and telephones. The large warehouse and commercial blocks housed hardware distributors, marine suppliers, and garment manufacturers. Other tenants included tailors, clothing merchants, and dealers in spice, tobacco, shoes, and printing. Formerly there were several hotels, and the *PLAIN DEALER* occupied more than 1 building in the district. Toward the end of the century, several major office buildings were erected for the iron, coal, oil, railroad, and shipping industries, including the PERRY-PAYNE, WESTERN RESERVE, and ROCKEFELLER BUILDINGS. The last major building to be erected was the Brotherhood of Railroad Trainmen Bldg. (1921), later an Ohio Bell Telephone building. Some of the buildings remaining in the 1980s are outstanding examples of architectural design, including the Hoyt Block (1875), the Root & McBride-Bradley Bldg. (1884), the Perry-Payne (1889), the Western Reserve (1891), the Rockefeller Bldg. (1903), and the Bingham Co. Warehouse (1915). Since WORLD WAR II, a third of the district has been razed and replaced by surface parking lots. In the 1980s, many of the buildings in the Warehouse District began to be rehabilitated for purposes ranging from residential loft use to professional offices, and new condominiums were erected at the western edge of the district in a style compatible with the 19th-century warehouse structures.

WARNER, WORCESTER REED (6 May 1846–25 June 1929), a founder of the WARNER & SWASEY CO., was a pioneer in the machine-tool industry, an inventor of telescopes, and a benefactor to science. A farmer's son, Warner was born in Cunningham, Mass., and apprenticed in his youth as a machinist. By 1869, he was a foreman in the Pratt & Whitney shop in Hartford, Conn., where he met his future partner, AMBROSE SWASEY. In 1880, Warner and Swasey decided to leave Pratt & Whitney to open a machine-tool business of their own. Using their savings of $10,000, the pair first settled in Chicago but relocated in 1881 to Cleveland, a better source of skilled mechanics. From a small shop along the Cleveland & Pittsburgh Railroad tracks on E. Prospect, the tiny Warner & Swasey Co. expanded on the same site near the present E. 55th and Carnegie. The firm became a leader in the design and building of turret lathes, which were first used to make brass plumbing parts, but its early reputation was really built on

telescopes. Fascinated by astronomy, Warner was sent by Pratt & Whitney to take charge of their exhibition at the Centennial Exhibition in Philadelphia in 1876. His continued interest in the stars led to his experimentation with new types of telescopes. In 1880, the purchase of a telescope built at the Chicago plant by Beloit College put the company in the telescope business. The firm soon became a major builder of equatorial mounts and refractor telescopes; the mounts were noted for their accurate and reliable drive mechanisms. After 1900, the company concentrated production efforts on machine tools, but it continued to build telescopes until 1970. In 1918, Warner donated a 9″ refractor telescope, a first-prize winner at the Panama Pacific Exhibition of 1915, to Case School. Later, he and Swasey donated money for an observatory to house this telescope and many other scientific instruments. In addition to his role as an inventor, scientist, and businessman, Warner was active in many scientific and professional societies, in addition to the Cleveland Chamber of Commerce. Warner died in June 1929, while on a trip to Germany. He left his wife, the former Cornelia Blakemore, and 1 daughter, Helen Blakemore Warner.

The **WARNER AND SWASEY COMPANY** is a leading manufacturer of machine tools, with a worldwide reputation for its telescopes and precision instruments. Its founders, WORCESTER R. WARNER and AMBROSE SWASEY, were New England machinists who decided to form their own machine-tool partnership in Chicago on 5 May 1880. Because of Chicago's distance from manufacturing centers and its lack of skilled mechanics, they decided to move east to Cleveland, opening a shop on 5 Aug. 1881 on Carnegie Ave. near E. 55th St. At first, the company built all types of machine tools, but with the advent of the sewing machine, bicycle, and automobile industries, it began to concentrate on producing turret lathes. The company also produced telescopes, primarily because of Warner's avocation of astronomy. The techniques and machinery used to make machine tools were also used to manufacture telescopes. The firm designed and built its first telescope in 1880. It gained international fame in this area in 1886 when it was awarded the contract to build the largest telescope up to that time for the Lick Observatory in California. After its completion in 1888, orders for other large telescopes came in, including from the U.S. Naval Observatory in 1893 and the Yerkes Observatory in Wisconsin in 1897. During the Spanish-American War, Warner & Swasey received contracts for military optical goods. The company was able to use its astronomical instruments to gain publicity, while most of its profit came from machine tools. After 1900, when Warner & Swasey was incorporated, it began to place more emphasis on its profitable business in turret lathes, introducing several new types. By 1928 the company was the world's leading manufacturer of turret lathes. To accommodate its growing business, Warner & Swasey expanded its Carnegie plant several times. The firm remained active in the optical field, producing panoramic sights, binoculars, and other military optical equipment during WORLD WAR I. It continued to build telescopes, including one for the Case School of Applied Science. It became the leading producer of equatorial and reflector telescopes. After it became a public company in 1940, management gradually withdrew from the telescope business. It produced its last one in 1971.

A decrease in the demand for machine tools affected Warner & Swasey immediately after World War I and during the Depression. It recovered by 1937, and employment reached 1,350. During WORLD WAR II, the company employed 7,000 people and produced half of the turret lathes manufactured in the U.S. To prevent another depressed market after the war, it diversified into the textile-machinery, construction-equipment, and electronics industries through internal growth and acquisitions. By 1965, Warner & Swasey employed 2,000 people and began to spread beyond its Carnegie plant, moving several operations to Solon, Ohio, and its headquarters to UNIVERSITY CIRCLE in 1968. In 1980, Warner & Swasey was purchased by the Bendix Corp. of Michigan, a manufacturer in the automobile, aerospace, and electronics industries. During the business recession of the early 1980s, Bendix closed several Warner & Swasey plants in the Cleveland area and implemented large-scale layoffs. Warner & Swasey then began to concentrate on customizing machinery originally made in Japan and entered the robotics industry. In 1983, Bendix was taken over by the Allied Corp. of New Jersey, an industrial firm in the chemical, aerospace, and automobile industries. Allied was unable to revitalize Warner & Swasey (by then referred to as the Bendix Automation Group), and it lost $63 million in 1983. In 1984, Allied sold Warner & Swasey to the Michigan machinery firm of Cross & Trecker.

Pershey, Edward J., "The Early Telescope Work of Warner and Swasey" (Ph.D. diss., CWRU, 1982).
Warner and Swasey Collection, CWRU.
Warner and Swasey Co., *The Warner and Swasey Company, Cleveland, Ohio. U.S.A.* (1916).
*The Warner and Swasey Anniversary Celebration* (1920).
*The Warner and Swasey Company, 1880–1930* (1930).

**WARREN, DANIEL** (1786–13 Oct. 1862), was an early pioneer in Cuyahoga County, the first to settle in WARRENSVILLE TWP. Warren was born in New Hampshire. He was both a farmer and a brickmaker, and also served in the township government of Warrensville. In 1808, he left Acworth, N.H., for Painesville, eventually settling in Jefferson. The following year, he moved to NEWBURGH to claim property, sight unseen, that he had received in exchange for $300 owed to him for making the first brick courthouse at Jefferson. In the spring of 1810, Warren bought a farm in the western part of Twp. 7, Range 11. He built a cabin and cleared the land for a small farm. As a brickmaker, he was often away from his family for several days at a time to pursue his trade. His wife, Margaret (Prentiss), purportedly gave the township her husband's name at a housewarming party held in their first cabin. In the first township election, Warren was elected chairman. In 1817 he was elected justice of the peace; he later served in various township offices, including trustee in 1827 and 1828. As another form of public service, he established a tavern in Warrensville, on the northeast corner of Milverton and Kinsman roads.

**WARRENSVILLE CENTER SYNAGOGUE** is the 2d-largest Orthodox congregation in Cleveland. It was established in May 1959 from the merger of TETIEVER AHAVATH ACHIM ANSHE SFARD CONGREGATION, the KINSMAN JEWISH CTR., and Congregation N'vai Zedek. Additional mergers were effected in 1970 and 1972 as smaller Orthodox congregations joined Warrensville Ctr. The 1959 merger creating Warrensville Ctr. Synagogue was consummated in large measure through the efforts of Frank Tavens, president of the Tetiever congregation from 1940–59. He served as Warrensville Ctr.'s first president (1959–62) and in 1962 was elected honorary president for life. Sigmund Schuster and Chas. Segall, presidents of the Kinsman Jewish Ctr. and N'vai Zedek respectively prior to the merger, became vice-presidents of the new congregation.

Jacob Muskin, who previously had served the Kinsman Jewish Ctr., was elected rabbi and remains in that position today. The present central building of the synagogue was erected in 1957 by the Tetiever congregation, 2 years after it purchased the land on Warrensville Ctr. Rd. near Mayfield Rd. The structure served the congregation until the mid-1960s, when the Youth Education Ctr. was constructed. Dedicated on 19 Mar. 1966 the new center included classrooms, a library, and a gymnasium.

Warrensville Ctr. Synagogue is in reality the product of 8 Orthodox congregations. Besides the Tetiever Congregation, which was founded in 1909 by Jews from Tetiev, Russia; the Kinsman Jewish Ctr., established in 1930; and N'vai Zedek, a congregation established by Lithuanian Jews in 1922, the congregations that form Warrensville Ctr. include SHERITH JACOB and Sherith Israel, established in the Kinsman neighborhood in 1923, which merged in 1962 to form Sherith Jacob Israel. This latter congregation merged with Warrensville Ctr. in 1970. Ohel Jacob was founded by Russian and Sephardic Jews in lower Woodland in 1915. In 1926, the congregation built a synagogue in Kinsman, where it remained until 1956, when it purchased a lot on Lee Rd. in SHAKER HTS. Ohel Yavne was established in 1919 in Kinsman, meeting initially in the home of Shmuel Levine, then erecting a synagogue on a portion of Levine's property. In 1959 Ohel Yavne and Ohel Jacob merged to form the Shaker-Lee Congregation. Rabbi Isaac Krislov served Ohel Jacob and Shaker-Lee for almost 35 years. In 1962, Congregation Tifereth Israel joined Shaker-Lee. Tifereth Israel was founded by Polish and Austrian Jews in 1920 and became known as the shochetim shul because of the large number of ritual slaughterers who worshipped there. Shaker-Lee, which dedicated a synagogue in 1961, sold its building in 1970 and in 1972 merged with Warrensville Ctr. Synagogue. Warrensville Ctr. kept intact all of the auxiliary groups from the merged congregations (e.g., the N'vai Zedek Free Loan Society and the Tetiever Ladies Aid Society). A sisterhood was established by combining the sisterhoods of the Tetiever Congregation and the Kinsman Jewish Ctr. Soon after the creation of the Warrensville Ctr. Synagogue, several congregational groups were established, including the Minyonaires (1960), a teenage boys' organization; a men's club (1961); and the Adult Institute for Jewish Education (1962). In 1965, a weekday Hebrew school was instituted. Frank Tavens received the 1961 President's Award from the Union of Orthodox Congregations for his leadership in arranging the merger that created the Warrensville Ctr. Synagogue. In 1962, in recognition of its growth and programming, the UOC presented the Pioneer Congregation Award to Warrensville Ctr.

Sherith Israel of Mt. Pleasant Records, WRHS.
Tetiever Ahavath Achim Anshe Sfard Congregation Records, WRHS.

**WARRENSVILLE HEIGHTS** is a city located southeast of Cleveland and occupying 4.5 sq. mi. It is bounded by WARRENSVILLE TWP. and SHAKER HTS. on the north, BEDFORD HTS. and MAPLE HTS. on the south, Cleveland on the west, and ORANGE on the east. It was originally part of Warrensville Twp., named after one of the earliest settlers, DANIEL WARREN. Incorporated as a separate village in 1927, Warrensville Hts. became a city in 1960, operating under the mayor-council form of government. During the late 1920s and early 1930s, the village was recognized as the "Geranium Center of the United States." Eight large greenhouses located on Emery Rd. and Richmond Rd. supplied businesses and individuals with the popular flower. In 1985, only 2 greenhouses remained. The city experienced its most rapid growth between 1948–57.

The postwar migration to the suburbs turned the once predominantly agricultural region into a modern residential suburb. Between 1940–60, the population increased 20 times, from 1,175 in 1940 to more than 23,000 in 1960. Warrensville Hts. is a well-rounded community offering a variety of social, recreational, and economic services. The Warrensville Hts. School System, which also includes Warrensville Twp. and N. RANDALL, consists of 4 elementary, 1 junior high, and 1 senior high school. The Eastern Campus of CUYAHOGA COMMUNITY COLLEGE is located in adjacent Warrensville Twp. Other public services include police and fire protection, 2 hospitals, a municipal swimming pool, and a community library. In the 1980s, Warrensville Hts. had approximately 100 light commercial and industrial concerns along the Emery Industrial Pkwy. The firms were engaged primarily in the fabrication of metal alloys, chemical and oil derivatives, plastics, electronics, and food services. Other major enterprises included the Standard Oil Research Ctr. The population of Warrensville Hts. in 1980 was more than 16,000, of which 75% were black and 25% white.

**WARRENSVILLE TOWNSHIP** is located southeast of Cleveland and bounded on the north by BEACHWOOD, on the west by SHAKER HTS., on the east by ORANGE, and on the southwest by WARRENSVILLE HTS. The original Warrensville Twp. covered 25 sq. mi., and portions of the present Shaker Hts., UNIVERSITY HTS., and Warrensville Hts. were all formed from the original township. Warrensville was named for settler DANIEL WARREN, who arrived in 1810, and the township was established in 1816. Throughout the 19th century, the township was a rural agricultural community. Between 1904–15, the cluster of progressive city and county institutions was located in the present township. The County Infirmary, now part of Highland View Hospital, was located there in 1904. In 1906, the county tuberculosis sanatorium opened on the Cooley Farms, and the expanded Sunny Acres Sanatarium opened in 1913. The CLEVELAND WORKHOUSE and House of Correction were moved to Warrensville Twp. in 1912. In addition to these public institutions, the township contains only the Highland Park Cemetery, the Highland Park Golf Course, and the Eastern Campus of CUYAHOGA COMMUNITY COLLEGE.

**WARSHAWSKY, ABEL "BUCK"** (28 Dec. 1883–30 May 1962) and **ALEXANDER "XANDER"** (29 Mar. 1887–28 May 1945), were artists with international ties and reputations and with close Cleveland roots. Abel was perhaps "the most phenomenally successful artist Cleveland has ever produced." The brothers, 2 of 9 children of Ezekiel and Ida Warshawsky, Jewish immigrants from Poland, had somewhat parallel early lives and artistic training. The family came to Cleveland from Sharon, Pa. The children went to Brownell School, and both attended the Cleveland School of Art (now Institute) and the Natl. Academy of Design in New York. Among Alex's classmates were other Cleveland artists who would attain national reputations, including Wm. Zorach and MAX KALISH. Both brothers seem to have gone right to Europe after their New York training. Abel went to France in 1908, and between then and 1938 he divided his time equally between Paris and Brittany. He seems to have known many of the important members of the intellectual and artistic community of the time, including Jo Davidson, John Marin, Paul Signac, Thos. Hart Benton, and Wm. Zorach. He was given his first opportunity to go to Europe through LOUIS RORIMER, his former Cleveland Art School sculpting instructor, who saw his potential. Abel once described himself as a classic Impres-

sionist and was one of the 2d-generation American Impressionists who matured at the turn of the century. Alexander, like his older brother, spent a good part of his career in France. He came to Paris in 1916 and occupied the former studio of Gustav Courbet. His style was distinctly different from Abel's; his subjects were Breton peasants and landscapes—with flat surfaces and clear outlines, smoothly brushed surfaces, and highly keyed colors. The brothers shared several experiences. Both pacifists, they served together behind the French lines in WORLD WAR I decorating soldiers' huts with murals and organizing sports events/programs. The French government recognized them for this work and asked them to exhibit in the Luxembourg Gallery. They returned once a year or more to renew Cleveland ties to friends and family. Several times, they exhibited jointly.

Abel claimed that if he stayed in Cleveland, he would "sink down to the level of the local artist and possibly be forced to take a job in Commercial art." It was the threat of WORLD WAR II that eventually forced him to leave France. His works were shown in many local and national galleries and were acquired by the French government and 13 American art museums. He was named Chevalier of the Legion of Honor by the French government for his contributions to painting. Upon permanently returning to America, Abel settled in Monterey, Calif., where the craggy coast reminded him of Brittany. He was married 3 times: to Vantine Laudell (divorced 1926), Minny (died), and Ruth Tate, whom he married in 1939. Alex was a world traveler, as opposed to his Paris-based brother. One of his most notable achievements was the organization of an exhibition in Cleveland of Postimpressionism in 1914. Although several local artists were included, most of the work was by New York artists promoted by Alfred Steiglitz, well-known photographer and champion of modern art. Although the show was controversial, Alex was credited with arranging the opportunity for Cleveland to view modern art. Alex lived in Paris over a 25-year period. Upon his frequent journeys to the U.S., he exhibited his paintings. His works have hung in galleries in New York, Chicago, and San Francisco. He lived in Los Angeles for 12 years before his death. He was married to Berthe, a designer of children's clothes, and they had a son, Ivan.

**WASHINGTON PARK,** located at E. 49th St. and Washington Park Blvd., straddles the boundary of NEWBURGH HTS. and the city of Cleveland. It was bought by the city in 1899, after a local amusement park was closed down. Originally a natural area of dense woods and deep ravines, particularly that of Burke Run, a tributary of the Cuyahoga River, it was transformed into a public recreation area with tennis courts, baseball diamonds, and picnic grounds. After years of neglect, it was somewhat restored in the 1930s by the WPA but later deteriorated. Construction of the WILLOW FREEWAY in 1949 and industrial encroachment on the park's southern boundary destroyed much of this woodland park. In the late 1960s the Burke Run ravine was filled, and in 1969 the park was leased to the Cleveland Board of Education for construction of a horticulture center as part of their ecology program.

The **WATER STREET THEATER** was built by John S. Potter in 1848. Located on Water (W. 9th) St., it seated over 1,000 and included 2 tiers of boxes and 4 private boxes. The theater was destroyed by fire in 1850.

**WATER SYSTEM.** The production, purification, and distribution of potable water constitutes what may be called a "hidden system" in the infrastructure of the modern city.

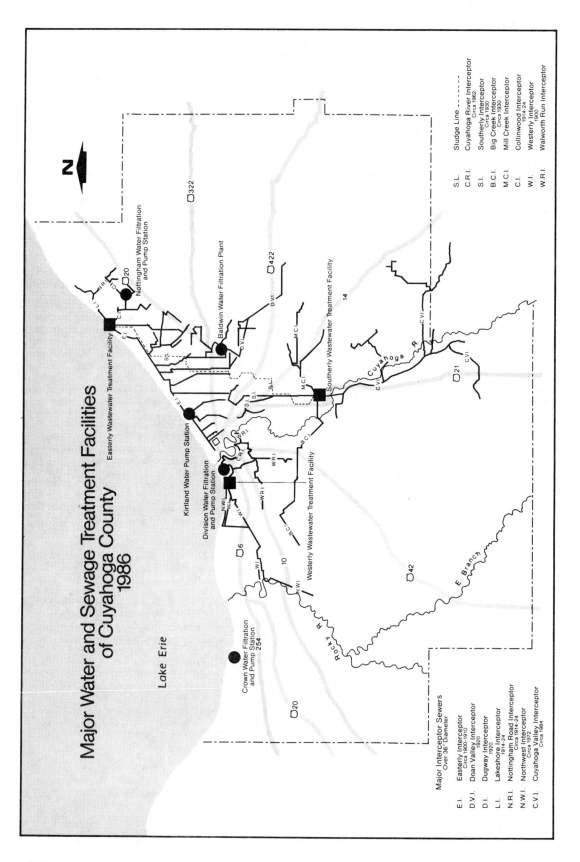

# Major Water and Sewage Treatment Facilities of Cuyahoga County 1986

Lake Erie

Easterly Wastewater Treatment Facility

Nottingham Water Filtration and Pump Station

Baldwin Water Filtration Plant

Southerly Wastewater Treatment Facility

Kirtland Water Pump Station

Division Water Filtration and Pump Station

Westerly Wastewater Treatment Facility

Crown Water Filtration and Pump Station

Cuyahoga R.

Rocky R.

E Branch

Major Interceptor Sewers
Over 36" Diameter

E.I.    Easterly Interceptor
      Circa 1900-1910
D.V.I.   Doan Valley Interceptor
      1920
D.I.     Dugway Interceptor
      1920
L.I.     Lakeshore Interceptor
      1914-24
N.R.I.   Nottingham Road Interceptor
      Circa 1914-24
N.W.I.   Northwest Interceptor
      Circa 1972
C.V.I.   Cuyahoga Valley Interceptor
      Circa 1984

S.L.    Sludge Line -------
C.R.I.   Cuyahoga River Interceptor
      Circa 1982
S.I.     Southerly Interceptor
      Circa 1930
B.C.I.   Big Creek Interceptor
      Circa 1930
M.C.I.   Mill Creek Interceptor
C.I.     Collinwood Interceptor
      1914-24
W.I.    Westerly Interceptor
      Circa 1900
W.R.I.   Walworth Run Interceptor

Until faucets run dry, or reservoirs are exhausted, citizens tend to remain unaware of the nature and condition of the complex technological, social, and political attributes of the water system.

Early settlers in Cleveland were dependent upon surface-water supplies from ponds, lakes, rivers, and streams, and upon dug wells, the latter becoming more prevalent as population density increased in the early walking city. A town pump located on PUBLIC SQUARE is reported to have been in operation in 1812. Ca. 1820, a well existed at Bank (W. 6th) and Superior with a diameter of 8 ft., designated mainly for firefighting. At the same time, "every family had a well; however, Benhu Johnson hauled lake water when droughts set in . . . [for] twenty-five cents for two barrels." In mid-1833, PHILO SCOVILL and some associates organized the Cleveland Water Co. to supply water for the village, but the city council continued its involvement, ordering the expenditure of $35 for the sinking of public wells in Public Square in 1840. By 1852, water was being drawn from springs, wells, canals, and the CUYAHOGA RIVER, with storage cistern-based pumps utilized in the business district for firefighting and public uses. With expansion needs in mind, and in the absence of sufficient private capital, a popular vote (1,230–599) in 1853 authorized the city to spend $400,000 to build a waterworks, and water was pumped from Lake Erie in 1856, nominally ending the "long and useful career of the well on the Public Square." The KENTUCKY ST. RESERVOIR, located at Kentucky (W. 38th) and Prospect (later Franklin) streets, was opened in Sept. 1856 to store water pumped by 2 Cornish steam engines, the first west of the Alleghenies. Water was brought from the lake via a 50-in. boilerplate pipe tunnel extending 300 ft. into Lake Erie to an intake submerged 4 ft. and touching shore at about W. 58th St. Two distribution mains totaling 44 mi. were established, along with a water fountain in Public Square. In its first year of full operation, 127 million gallons of water (38,000 gallons per day) were distributed (in 1900, distribution was about 20 billion gallons—about 5.5 million gallons per day; in 1970, about 129 billion gallons—about 35.3 million gallons per day).

One often unanticipated result of new piped-water supplies in American cities was a rapid increase in usage, especially in kitchens and for flushing new indoor toilets. Traditional privies, storage cisterns, and other means for disposing of sewage rapidly became inadequate, leading to an early requirement for sewage-disposal systems. The first sewer in Cleveland is reported to have been built for surface drainage of Euclid St. in 1856, but the river, lakes, and brooks continued to receive much varied and untreated drainage until nearly 1900. During the latter part of the 19th century, periodic complaints surfaced concerning the intolerable condition of wells and cisterns as a result of inflows of garbage and sewage. City health officials protested in 1881 that some 25 sewers, factories, oil refineries, and other industries were polluting the Cuyahoga River and adjacent Lake Erie, though only about a third of Cleveland citizens were using "city water." The water utility continued to expand, such that by 1864, most of the 75 cisterns placed around the city for firefighting water supplies were supplanted by piped water. In 1870, a new water-intake crib was anchored by tons of stone 36 ft. deep and some 6,600 ft. offshore to gain access to water outside the boundaries of growing lake-edge pollution. In the process of building this intake pipe and subsequent cribs, intakes, and tunnels in the 19th and 20th centuries, some 6 major accidents costing the lives of 58 men have occurred (see WATERWORKS TUNNEL DISASTERS). In 1870, water meters began to be introduced to enable more accurate

billing for water services and usage, and by 1880, 125 mi. of water mains had been completed in Cleveland, the capacity of the system being about 10 million gallons per day. By the mid-1880s, the original Kentucky St. Reservoir already had become inadequate, requiring the building of the Fairmount and Kinsman reservoirs. The location of the new reservoirs also was responsive to substantial population growth in the direction of the Heights east of downtown Cleveland.

In 1890, a new 7-ft.-diameter, 9,117-ft.-long water-inlet tunnel was completed. Nearly 1,500 private wells still existed on streets with city piped water, with thousands of wells still extant where city pipes had not yet been put into place. Yet a further tunnel was begun in 1896, this one destined to feed water to the Kirtland water-pumping station located on the lakefront between downtown Cleveland and BRATENAHL. The intake structure for this tunnel, which at a distance resembles a freighter, is known as the "5 Mile Crib," that being the distance from the actual lake intake to the Kirtland pumping station. The first water to reach the Kirtland station arrived in 1904, following numerous accidents, some involving tunnel gas explosions during the period of construction. The intake pipe was one of the longest in the world at the time, some 26,000 ft. in length and 9 ft. in diameter, with a daily capacity of 170 million gallons. In 1911, Cleveland again exhibited its leadership by introducing water chlorination, at first through the use of bleaching powder. However, at times the chlorinated, but largely unfiltered, water was found unpalatable, and in 1915, it was reported that on at least one occasion, thousands patronized springs in places such as WADE PARK and ROCKEFELLER PARK, requiring police to keep order. Ca. 1916, an additional intake tunnel was built, with a submerged intake west of the "5 Mile Crib," and destined to feed water to the Division Ave. Filtration Plant, which became operative in 1918. Extending lakeward from an older onshore crib, the total combined length of the old and new intake tunnels is about 26,000 ft. By 1920, the system of water mains had grown to 985 total mi.

The system continued to grow in reponse to Cleveland's growth and expanded water needs. The Baldwin Filtration Plant on the border of CLEVELAND HTS. was completed in 1925, with a reservoir capacity of more than 135 million gallons (see BALDWIN RESERVOIR). The facility is capable of pumping up to 200 million gallons per day. The plant incorporated an underground storage reservoir gouged out of rock, which may be the world's largest. Expansion and alterations begun much earlier on the Kirtland station were completed in 1927, giving Cleveland wholly filtered and chlorinated water. By the 1940s, Cleveland's water system included cribs, 4 lake tunnels, 2 filtration plants (Division Ave. and Baldwin), 3 major pumping stations (Kirtland, Fairmount, and Division), and 2,700 mi. of water mains. Growth did not cease at that point, however. A new 3.5-mi., 10-ft.-diameter tunnel was built into the lake to supply water to the new Nottingham Filtration Plant and pumping station in northeast Cleveland. This project was completed in 1951, with a capacity of about 150 million gallons per day. A fourth, 2.5-mi., 8-ft.-diameter tunnel extends northward into Lake Erie from the Crown Filtration Plant, completed in 1958 in WESTLAKE. This plant had a daily capacity of 50 million gallons, making the nominal total capacity of the system on the order of 225 billion gallons annually. In 1970, the system's water mileage exceeded 4,000 mi., serving 75 sq. mi. in Cleveland and an additional 450 sq. mi. in Cuyahoga, Medina, Lorain, and Lake counties. Since 1854, when Cleveland's public water supply was established, annual consumption has increased an average of 12 billion gallons each decade—much of the increase coming in the 20th century.

By 1986, the mileage of mains in the Cleveland system had grown to about 5,800 mi., serving some 400,000 accounts. Some changes also had occurred in the distribution system, such that in 1986, direct service existed in Cuyahoga, Medina, and Summit counties, with master-metered bulk service to Lake County, and to the municipalities of Cleveland Hts., BEDFORD, E. CLEVELAND, and LAKEWOOD. Each of the later municipalities purchased water in bulk, and redistributed it to customers with its own rate structure. Purification and filtration have continually been improved. In 1986, purification processes included, in addition to settling and filtration, the use of aluminum sulfate for impurities coagulation, potassium permanganate for oxidation, chlorine for disinfection, and activated carbon for taste and odor control. In addition, since 1965 sodium silicofluoride has been added to the water to control tooth decay. In 1970, a water utility publication indicated that as much as 545 million gallons per day were consumed by customers of the Cleveland water system. In 1986, that figure is closer to 320 million gallons per day (about 118 billion gallons annually), a substantial decline. Much of the decline in demand may be accounted for by demographic changes.

Cleveland's water system, through direct and bulk sales, serves the water needs not only of the city of Cleveland but also of 68 surrounding suburbs and municipalities located in Cuyahoga, Lake, Summit, and Medina counties. In the 1970s, dissatisfied with the level and quality of water services provided, coalitions of suburban officials initiated litigation directed toward making Cleveland's water system a regional one, similar to the slightly earlier regionalizing of the water pollution control system into the organization known today as the Northern Ohio Regional Sewer District. In order to avoid the loss of control of the system, the city of Cleveland agreed to undertake a massive program of renovations, rehabilitation, and improvement of the water system—a program that in 1982 was projected at a total cost of roughly $918 million. Cost projections were revised regularly as interest rates and projected demand for water changed, and the projected investment in repairs and improvements for the 1986–92 period was calculated at about $380 million. It is expected that the capital-repair and improvements program will extend into the 1990s before completion. Funds for the capital-improvement program were acquired through increases in water rates to repay bonds sold for construction purposes, and did not require specific voter approval. These increases caused some political furor in city council, however, despite the fact that Cleveland's water rates remained among the lowest of any major American city, while water quality remains very high.

Willis E. Sibley
Cleveland State University

Bluestone, Daniel M., ed., *Cleveland* (1978).
City of Cleveland, Water Div., *The Cleveland Water Story* (ca. 1970).

**WATERFIELD, ROBERT "BOB"** (26 July 1920–25 Mar. 1983), was a star player during his 8-year professional FOOTBALL career with the Cleveland and Los Angeles Rams (see CLEVELAND RAMS). In his rookie season he led the Cleveland Rams to the 1945 championship of the Natl. Football League and was unanimously elected the Most Valuable Player in the league. He was inducted into the Pro Football Hall of Fame in 1965. Born in Elmira, N.Y., Waterfield played college football for UCLA in 1941,

1942, and 1944. He spent his entire professional career with the Rams organization, helping to transform the lowly Cleveland Rams of the late 1930s and early 1940s into league champions. The 6'2" 200-lb. quarterback completed 51% of his passes in 1945, threw 16 touchdown passes, and scored 5 touchdowns himself that season. He was a versatile player; in addition to playing quarterback, he was the punter and placekicker, making 31 of 34 field goals in 1945. During his first 4 years in the league, until the rules were changed to allow unlimited substitutions, he also played defense; he intercepted 20 passes during his career. Waterfield led the NFL in passing twice (1945 and 1951), and he led the league in field goals in 2 seasons (1949 and 1951). During his career he completed 813 of 1,617 attempted passes (50.3%) for 11,849 yards and 98 touchdowns. His passes were intercepted 127 times. Waterfield himself scored 573 points on 13 touchdowns, 315 points after touchdowns, and 60 field goals. As a punter he kicked for a 42.4-yard average. He led the Rams to 3 Western Div. crowns after the team moved to Los Angeles, and to the NFL championship in 1951. He made the All-NFL team 3 times. After retiring from the game, Waterfield returned to coach the Rams in 1960, 1961, and part of 1962. He then became a scout for the team and a rancher near Van Nuys, Calif. During his 1 season in Cleveland, Waterfield attracted more than the usual attention afforded professional athletes: his wife, actress Jane Russell, spent the football season with him in Cleveland. Married in 1943, the couple was divorced in 1968.

**WATERWORKS TUNNEL DISASTERS** have occurred 6 times during the development of Cleveland's water system, killing a total of 58 men. Five of the disasters occurred as a result of work on the Kirtland St. (east side) tunnel and cribs, which began on 8 Oct. 1896. Upon its completion in 1903, the 9-ft.-diameter tunnel was one of the largest in the world, extending over 4 mi. into the lake to Crib No. 3. It had a daily capacity of 170 million gallons. The first disaster took place on 12 May 1898. A work crew digging 6,300 ft. from shore hit a gas pocket, resulting in an explosion that killed 8. A second explosion, killing 11 more workers, took place on 12 July 1898. As work progressed, a temporary wooden crib, No. 2, was erected as an access point to the tunnel. It served as a temporary home for 42 workers and was to be joined to the No. 3 crib via a tunnel extension. The workers were isolated at the crib; no boats were kept there. A daily supply boat shuttled food and construction supplies. At 2:30 a.m. on 14 Aug. 1901, cinders from the No. 2 crib's boiler stack landed on the roof, starting a fire. The fire hose and pump were in the tunnel at the time, being used to help drain seepage. Eleven men were working in the tunnel; most of the others were asleep in the crib. Five men were burned to death, 4 while still in their bunks. Three men drowned trying to escape. A fire tug arrived and put out the fire by 4:30 a.m. One rescuer, Plummer Jones, was killed trying to reach the men in the tunnel. Of the 11 men working in the tunnel, 9 were rescued. The other 2 were given up for dead. Five days later a work crew heard a faint tapping in the tunnel; the 2 were found at the far end, barely alive. While the disaster was still under investigation, work continued. Just 6 days after the fire, on 20 Aug., a gas explosion in the tunnel at the No. 3 crib ripped the lining out of the shaft, killing 5. Another gas explosion on 14 Dec. 1902 killed an additional 4 men. The first water was pumped through the tunnel to the Kirtland St. Pumping Station in Feb. 1904.

The final waterworks tunnel disaster took place 14 years later, on 24 July 1916. Eighty men were digging in a 10-ft.-wide tunnel when they hit a pocket of natural gas. A spark triggered an explosion, killing 11 men. Two rescue parties entered the pressurized tunnel, but neither returned, having been overcome by the gas. Ten would-be rescuers died. The hero of the event was black Clevelander GARRETT MORGAN, the inventor of a gas mask. He was called by police and asked to attempt a rescue. Morgan, his brother Frank, and 2 others made 2 expeditions into the gas-filled tunnel, sustained by the masks. They rescued 2 men and recovered 4 bodies. Officials from the U.S. Bureau of Mines stopped further rescue and recovery efforts.

**WATSON, WILBUR J.** (5 Apr. 1871–22 May 1939), was a civil engineer who established a national reputation and was especially eminent in bridge design. Watson developed a carefully stated philosophy of the relationship between engineering and aesthetics, and his pioneering use of structural and reinforced concrete produced some of the most beautiful BRIDGES in northern Ohio and helped to set standards for bridge construction across the country. While employed by the OSBORN ENGINEERING CO. in Cleveland, he was designing bridges as early as 1898. He founded his own firm, Wilbur J. Watson & Associates, in 1907. His achievements include the recognition of the possibility of using precast concrete beams for bridges (1908); the pioneer design of steel centering for erecting concrete bridges (Rocky River Bridge, 1910); early experiments with mushroom-and-slab floor construction (1911); the design of the Howard St. Bridge in Akron, highest bridge of its kind in 1912; concrete bridges for the Cleveland & Youngstown Railroad (SHAKER RAPID TRANSIT LINE) (1916); construction of the unique Akron Goodyear Zeppelin Airdock (1929) covering 8½ acres, the largest uninterrupted interior space in the world; the engineering of the Lorain-Carnegie (1932) and Main Ave. (1939) bridges in Cleveland; and the bascule bridge in Lorain (1940). His publications included *Bridge Architecture* (1927), *A Decade of Bridges: 1926-1936* (1937), and *Bridges in History and Legend* (1937), the latter written in collaboration with his daughters Sara Ruth and Emily.

**WEARN, JOSEPH T.** (15 Feb. 1893–24 Oct. 1984), was a physician and dean of the Western Reserve University School of Medicine. While serving as dean, he implemented a new curriculum that brought universal recognition and preeminence to the school. Wearn was born in Charlotte, N.C. He received his B.A. from Davidson College in 1913 and his medical degree from Harvard Medical School in 1917. He served 2 years as a resident at Peter Bent Brigham Hospital in Boston, and then 2 years as an instructor in pharmacology at the University of Pennsylvania before joining the faculty of the Harvard Medical School. He joined the medical faculty of WRU in 1929, serving as dean of the School of Medicine from 1945–59. He served as an officer in the Medical Corps of the U.S. Army for a brief period following America's entry into WORLD WAR I in 1917. Prior to 1929, Wearn published many articles on the kidney and heart. While at the University of Pennsylvania, he performed classical experiments in the direct puncture of the glomerular space and tubules of frogs' kidneys, which made possible much of the present understanding of renal function. During WORLD WAR II, he served as medical consultant to the secretary of war and traveled extensively in the Pacific Theater. For his service he was awarded the Medal of Freedom.

Under Dr. Wearn's guidance, the faculty and financial position of the WRU School of Medicine were strengthened. A vigorous fundraiser, Wearn brought the school from near bankruptcy to a reasonably sound financial position. In 1952, he introduced the first major change in medical school curriculum in more than half a century. Under it, medicine was taught as a whole concept rather than as a series of unrelated disciplines. That involved teaching of subject areas by committees of faculty members rather than strictly by department. The purpose was to develop and maintain in the student a sensitivity to the social and economic as well as medical problems of all patients, and to stimulate initiative to continue the educational process throughout the professional career. Since its implementation, medical educators from all over the world have come to Cleveland to study the curriculum. After retiring in 1960, Wearn served both CASE WESTERN RESERVE UNIVERSITY and Harvard Medical School as a consultant on medical affairs. He was a member of many medical societies, including the American Medical Assoc. and the Assoc. of American Medical Colleges; he was president of the latter, 1953–54. He was honored by CWRU in 1973 when he was given the first University Medal for outstanding service. In 1961, the $5.3 million Joseph Treloar Wearn Laboratory for Medical Research on Abington Rd. was dedicated to the former dean. Wearn was married to the former Susan Lyman.

The **WEATHERHEAD DIVISION OF THE DANA CORPORATION** was founded in Cleveland in 1919 as the Weatherhead Co. and soon became an important parts supplier for the automobile industry. By 1977 the company manufactured components for the control and transmission of fluids in steering, braking, fueling, lubricating, and cooling systems of various kinds. The Cleveland-based company employed more than 3,900 people in 9 plants in 1977 and was acquired that year by the Dana Corp. The firm was established in Nov. 1919 by Albert J. Weatherhead, Jr. (26 June 1892–13 Dec. 1966). A native Clevelander, he was the son of the inventor and manufacturer who owned the Cleveland Faucet Co., manufacturer of bar and soda-fountain accessories. Using $1,000 he had saved during his service in WORLD WAR I, Weatherhead set up a shop at 706 Frankfort St. to make radiator drain cocks for automobiles. By 1922, the plant produced much of the auto industry's supply of drain cocks and priming cups. By 1926 Weatherhead employed 35, and it had established a research department to enable it to keep pace with changes in the auto industry.

On 6 June 1933, the Weatherhead Co. was incorporated in Ohio, and by 1936 its operations had grown to occupy 7 buildings on Frankfort St. That year it bought the Chandler-Huppmobile plant at 300 E. 131st St.; it consolidated its operation there in 1937. It established a Canadian subsidiary in 1936, built an auto-parts plant in Columbia City, Ind., in 1937, and also in 1937 began to manufacture precision aircraft components for the Navy. WORLD WAR II expanded the company's work for the defense industry; it produced the compressors used to open the bomb bay doors in the B-29 airplanes. Weatherhead began its postwar expansion program by building a $250,000 research facility in Cleveland. It also acquired companies in other cities, buying 6 between 1948–73. It formed a new aviation and missiles division in 1958; by 1969, products such as rifles, mortars, and antitank shells accounted for 10% of its business. Sales and income grew steadily during the 1960s. Sales of $57 million in 1964 produced a net income of $1.582 million; by 1969 sales had grown to $107 million and income to $3.5 million. But 1970 proved to be a difficult year; the company suffered a net loss of $3.6 million. During the 1970s it diversified into industrial applications of fluid systems and into sales to truck manufacturers. In 1976 the company had sales of $131.7 million and a net income of $4.7 million. The Dana Corp. bought Weatherhead on

19 Sept. 1977, for $14 million in cash and $32.9 million in stocks. The company continued to operate in its E. 131st St. facilities for several years, but by 1982 it had moved its general offices and factory to 767 Beta Dr. in Mayfield. By 1983 it was operating no longer as the Weatherhead Co. but as a division of the Dana Corp.

Grabner, George J., *The Weatherhead Company* (1970).

The **WEBB C. BALL COMPANY** was one of Cleveland's major jewelry retailers. The business was established in 1881 by Webb C. Ball, who pioneered in establishing and maintaining the requirements and rate of proficiency of watches used in railroad service. Ball was born in Knox County, Ohio, on 6 Oct. 1846, and as a young man learned the jewelry business. In 1879 he bought an interest in the Cleveland firm of Whitcomb & Metten Jewelers, and by 1881 he had become the sole owner. His first location was at Superior and Seneca streets, where he sold timepieces, diamonds, sterlingware, and jewelry. Ball's association with the railroads grew out of the 1891 collision of 2 Lake Shore & Michigan Southern trains, caused by an engineer's watch being 4 minutes slow. The tragedy, which cost 11 lives, prompted Lake Shore officials to ask Ball to develop specifications for an accurate, dependable railroad watch and to establish a time-inspection system. The requirements he established for the standard-grade railroad pocket watch included a minimum of 17 jewels and the ability to maintain accurate time in 5 positions within a temperature range of 30–95 degrees F. An open-face watch with a clear white dial, arabic figures, and 5-minute dots was specified. It had to be inspected for accuracy every 2 weeks, with a tolerance of 30 seconds allowed, and cleaned once a year (later once every 18 months), all for a fee. Trainmen were required to carry a watch meeting these standards, together with a complete record of its performance signed by an authorized time inspector.

The first Ball railroad watch was made in 1893 by the E. Howard Watch Co., and subsequent models were manufactured by the Hamilton, Waltham, and Elgin Natl. watch companies. Before any watch with Ball's name on it was sold, it was thoroughly checked by his watchmakers to be certain it met the specifications. Ball eventually became general time inspector for more than 125,000 mi. of railroad in the U.S., Canada, and Mexico. The sales, service, and inspection system he designed brought substantial growth and prosperity to his company, which was now organized into 4 divisions: the Ball Railroad Standard Watch Co., the Ball Watch Co., the Ball Retail Jewelry store, and the Ball System of Watch Inspection. In 1911 the company moved to larger quarters at 1114 Euclid Ave., and the business further expanded with branches in Chicago, San Francisco, and Winnipeg. Webb C. Ball became the largest wholesale distributor of standard railroad watches in the country. Ball died 6 Mar. 1922 at the age of 75; however, the firm remained in business for many more years. After WORLD WAR II, the company was adversely affected by declining railroad business and changing times. It continued to sell fine jewelry at the Euclid Ave. location until 1962, when it went out of business.

**WEBER, GUSTAV C. E.** (26 May 1828–21 Mar. 1912), was a nationally known surgeon and professor of medicine. He was instrumental in the founding of ST. VINCENT CHARITY HOSPITAL and Medical College and held positions at the Cleveland Medical College and later Western Reserve University. Weber was born in Bonn, Germany, in 1828. His father, Moritz Ignaz Weber, was an author and professor of anatomy at the University of Bonn. Weber

was educated in Europe. He came to the U.S. in 1848 and settled in St. Louis, where he intended to become a farmer. Unenthusiastic about farming, he entered the St. Louis Medical College and received his degree in 1851. He returned to Europe to continue his studies and intern in Amsterdam. In 1853 he joined his elder brother in practice in New York City. Upon the retirement of HORACE ACKLEY from the Cleveland Medical College in 1856, Weber applied for the posts of professor of surgery and professor of principles and practices of medicine. He was appointed and remained on the faculty until 1863, when he was dismissed by the trustees because of differences of opinion. He then joined with the Catholic bishop of Cleveland, AMADEUS RAPPE, who wished to establish a Catholic hospital in the city. The hospital was founded, and Weber became chief of staff in 1864. He also founded the medical school attached to Charity Hospital, where he was professor of surgery, dean, and treasurer of the faculty. Charity Medical College was absorbed into the University of Wooster in 1870, and Weber continued to serve as dean of the faculty.

Weber remained at Wooster until 1881, when he returned to the Cleveland Medical College. When WRU was newly incorporated in 1884, he became a trustee and a member of the executive committee of the Medical Dept. He also became dean, serving until 1893. In addition to teaching and private practice, Weber served in the CIVIL WAR as surgeon of Ohio. He was Cleveland's city physician from 1857–60. In 1859 he established the *Cleveland Medical Gazette*, the first medical journal in the city. He was editor for 2 years. In 1896 he was appointed by Pres. McKinley to the post of U.S. consul in Nurnberg, Germany. He remained in Europe for 4 years. A skillful surgeon, Weber performed many different types of surgery. He invented surgical and gynecological instruments and developed new techniques. His extensive library and armamentarium were donated to the CLEVELAND MEDICAL LIBRARY ASSOC., of which he was an honorary member, upon his retirement. Weber was also a member of the Ohio State and Cuyahoga County medical societies. He was active in German social and charitable organizations and published scholarly articles on surgery. Upon his return from Nurnberg, Weber was honored at a welcome dinner at the UNIVERSITY CLUB, where he suffered a stroke as he rose to respond to congratulatory remarks. He spent his remaining years in retirement in Willoughby with his wife, Ruth Elizabeth Chaney Weber, whom he had married in 1854. The Webers had 2 children.

Gustav Weber Papers, Allen Memorial Medical Library Archives.

**WEDDELL, PETER MARTIN** (1788–1847), was a prominent early merchant and hotel owner in Cleveland. He began the construction of the WEDDELL HOUSE, Cleveland's most fashionable hotel during the mid-1800s. Weddell was born in Westmoreland County, Pa. When he was 14, his family moved to Paris, Ky., where he found work in a general store, becoming a partner within 5 years. When the senior partner died, Weddell moved to Newark, Ohio, and opened his own general store. While in Newark he met his future wife, Sophia Perry of Cleveland, who was attending school in Newark. They were married in 1815. In 1820, Weddell moved to Cleveland and opened a general store on Superior St. He opened a larger store in 1823, at Superior and Bank (W. 6th) St., which soon became one of the largest stores in Ohio, making him one of Cleveland's most prominent businessmen. Through the 1830s, Peter M. Weddell & Co. was one of Cleveland's leading merchandising firms, offering dry goods, carpets and rugs, and groceries. In 1827, Weddell joined Edmund Clark and Geo. Stanton in organizing the Cleveland & New York Line, a commission storage and transportion firm. He served as a director for the COMMERCIAL BANK OF LAKE ERIE from 1832 and later headed its successor, the Merchants Bank. He was also one of the incorporators of the Ohio Railroad Co., which struggled for several years before collapsing in 1843. Weddell served on the board of the Cleveland Medical College, and contributed funds to Western Reserve University in Hudson. With others, he also contributed money for the purchase of land on PUBLIC SQUARE for the Old Stone Church. In 1845, Weddell tore down the store that had made him wealthy to begin construction of a hotel. Two years later he laid the cornerstone of the "Astor House of the Lakes" (later, Weddell House). He intended to make it the finest hotel in Cleveland, purchasing most of the lavish furnishings in the East. He died shortly before its opening.

Weddell Family Papers, WRHS.

The **WEDDELL HOUSE,** located at Superior Ave. and Bank (W. 6th) St., was the best-known of the early hotels built in Cleveland in the first half of the 19th century. The Franklin House, the American House, and the forerunner of the Forest City House were in existence when the Weddell House was opened in 1847, but it was destined to become the most illustrious of all. Early settler and businessman PETER M. WEDDELL built the hotel on the site of his successful mercantile store, with Geo. P. Smith as his builder. The Weddell House was the first Cleveland hotel approaching the luxury of eastern ones; it was compared with Boston's Tremont House of 1828, which is sometimes called the first modern American hotel. A 5-story brick-and-sandstone structure with about 200 rooms, the Weddell House contained offices, stores, several parlors, and a large dining room on the first 2 floors. The demand for rooms was so great that the hotel was enlarged in 1853 by a 4-story addition on W. 6th St. The corner at Superior and W. 6th had a recessed porch supported by 5 2-story Greek Doric columns. The most historic occasion associated with the hotel was the appearance and address of president-elect Lincoln on this corner balcony on 15 Feb. 1861, during his inaugural trip to Washington (see ABRAHAM LINCOLN'S VISIT). In 1904 the original portion of the hotel was razed and replaced by the ROCKEFELLER BLDG. The addition on W. 6th St. remained until 1961.

**WEEKS, HARRY E.** (2 Oct. 1871–21 Dec. 1935), was a prominent architect who with FRANK R. WALKER founded Walker & Weeks, Cleveland's foremost architectural firm during the 1920s. Weeks was born in W. Springfield, Mass., and attended public schools there. He graduated from MIT in 1893 and worked for several prominent Massachusetts architectural firms before owning his own firm in Pittsfield, Mass., for 3 years. It was in Pittsfield, Walker's birthplace, that Weeks first met his future business partner. At the suggestion of John M. Carrere, a member of the Cleveland Group Plan Commission, Weeks moved to Cleveland in 1905, the same year as Walker. Both men joined the firm of J. MILTON DYER. In 1911, Walker and Weeks left Dyer's office and established their own practice. Their new firm was known as a specialist in financial buildings, and it completed 60 banks throughout Ohio. In Cleveland, however, Walker & Weeks were best known for their design of major commercial, public, and religious structures, most of them in classical revival styles. (See Walker, Frank R., for lists of major projects.) Weeks was

a member of the Euclid Ave. Baptist Church and president of its board of trustees in 1926. He was also a member of the Cleveland Chamber of Commerce, the CITY CLUB, the CLEVELAND ATHLETIC CLUB, the Cleveland Chap. of the AMERICAN INSTITUTE OF ARCHITECTS, and the CLEVELAND ENGINEERING SOCIETY. He married Alice B. Tuggey in 1896.

**WEIDENTHAL, LEO** (23 Apr. 1878–8 May 1967), was a long-time editor of the *Jewish Independent* and founder and honorary president of the CLEVELAND CULTURAL GARDENS FED., a federation of patriotic educational and nationality groups dedicated to cultural enlightenment and mutual understanding. Often described as a one-man cultural force, he was active in Jewish welfare circles and in civic affairs of the city. Weidenthal's chief interest was a battle for more parks and playgrounds and more cultural and recreational opportunites for Cleveland residents. He was a quiet, constructive contributor to civic advance whose collections relating to literature and the stage were of great value. Born at 63 Ontario St., about halfway between Lakeside and St. Clair avenues, Weidenthal began his newspaper career as a reporter for the CLEVELAND WORLD, and then the CLEVELAND LEADER. In 1906, he became a reporter for the PLAIN DEALER and was assigned to the city hall beat. Leaving the *Plain Dealer* in 1917, he became editor of the *Jewish Independent*, a weekly founded by his brother Maurice on 9 Mar. 1906. As one of Cleveland's ablest and best-known newspapermen, Maurice was a former *Plain Dealer* reporter and former reporter for the *Press* before the *Jewish Independent* seated him in the editor's chair on 25 May 1906. Leo shared the newspaper field with another brother, Henry, who once was managing editor of the *Press* and the *News*, of which he was also a staff writer, and sports editor of the *Plain Dealer*.

Weidenthal spent a great deal of time cataloguing his large collection of books, autographs, and letters marking the history of the theater since the early 19th century. In addition to his theater interests, he was an amateur painter, and author of the book *From Dis Waggon*, which was about Shakespeare and the Cultural Gardens of England. Active in civic affairs, Weidenthal was one of 3 founders of the Cleveland Chap. of the Natl. Conference of Christians & Jews, organized in 1933. He was also vice-president of the EARLY SETTLERS ASSOC. He is credited with suggesting that Cleveland support a mounted police patrol, and he was an outspoken critic of the modern freeway. Until his retirement from the *Jewish Independent* in 1964, it was said that Weidenthal never took a vacation and worked 6 days a week, 52 weeks a year. His only diversion was an occasional weekend in New York City to attend plays with his nephew, David Sperling, with whom he had lived. His honors were many, starting on 24 Sept. 1917, when he was given an unusual honor by the city council through the passing of a resolution praising his splendid service to the city during his 10 years as city hall reporter for the *Plain Dealer*. Other honors included the CLEVELAND FOLK ARTS ASSOC. Award (1958) and the Brotherhood Award of the Natl. Conference of Christians & Jews (1961). Weidenthal died a bachelor, leaving no immediate heirs.

**WEINBERG, JOSEPH LEWIS** (12 Nov. 1890–14 Jan. 1977), was an architect who pioneered in American urban-renewal and slum-clearance efforts with his design of the LAKEVIEW TERRACE project in 1934. Weinberg was born in Omaha, Nebr., to Lewis and Mollie Lazar Weinberg. At age 10, he and his brother and 2 sisters came to Cleveland to live at the JEWISH ORPHAN HOME on Woodland

Ave. after the death of their father. When he was 15, he brought his mother to Cleveland and attended CENTRAL HIGH SCHOOL while working for the city as a lamplighter. After graduation from Harvard University in 1912, he trained in architects' offices in New York, Detroit, and Cleveland, where he worked for Walker & Weeks and J. MILTON DYER. After a year in the Army Signal Corps during WORLD WAR I, Weinberg entered private practice in Cleveland in 1919. In 1923 he became a partner in the firm of Morris & Weinberg, but he returned to private practice in 1930. From 1928–41 he taught architecture at Western Reserve University and the John Huntington Polytechnic Institute. During WORLD WAR II, he was the chief architect in the 5th construction zone for the U.S. Quartermaster Corp, 1941–42, and chief engineer (architect) working at the Holston Ordinance Works project for the Kingsport Tennessee District Engineer Office, 1942–44. He also served as a planning consultant to the Cleveland Neighborhood Constr. Project, 1945–46. Weinberg was a partner in the firms of Weinberg, Laurie & Teare, 1946–49; Weinberg & Teare, 1949–65; Weinberg, Teare & Fisher, 1965–72; and Weinberg, Teare & Herman, 1972–77. His architectural designs include portions of the interior of CLEVELAND CITY HALL and Lakeside Courthouse; Lakeview Terrace, 1934; Lakeview Towers, 1975; BELLEFAIRE, 1929; and the Community Chest Headquarters Bldg., 1957. Weinberg married Edith Lazarus on 28 May 1933. The Weinbergs had 2 children, Judith and Daniel.

**WELFARE FEDERATION.** *See* **FEDERATION FOR COMMUNITY PLANNING**

**WELFARE/RELIEF.** The relief of destitution has been a responsibility of local government since American Colonial times. Territorial laws for the relief of destitution existed before Cleveland's founding and settlement. Changes in the laws have always preserved the original purposes and methods of the English laws of 1601. The purpose was to prevent extreme suffering and death, not to relieve poverty. Relief was kept low and unattractive, lest low-paid workers be lured into dependency, requiring more taxes from the remaining workers. The unattractiveness of relief was found in all 3 forms: indoor relief (admission to the poorhouse or infirmary), outdoor relief (aid to sustain independent living), or in-kind relief (material goods such as food, coal for heating, etc.). Provision was always well below levels of adequacy, and the relief recipient was usually made to feel demeaned by dependence. The universal poverty of relief recipients occurred even in Cleveland, the nation's most generous large city (measured by electoral willingness to be taxed for relief and per capita donations to UNITED WAY SERVICES and Catholic, Jewish, and other charities). Cleveland's reputation for generosity was established early in its first century. In a centennial publication, former relief director Lucious Mellen wrote that the people of Cleveland had always shown their willingness to be taxed for public charity and to give money and service to the less fortunate. The willingness was reaffirmed in 1986, when 80% of the voters approved renewal for one of 2 health and human service tax levies.

The first poor law affecting Cleveland was that of the Northwest Territory (1790, later amended). Township justices of the peace appointed unpaid overseers of the poor, who reported to the justice of the peace on the needs of the poor, and who received instructions as to grants of aid and type and amount. The justice had to levy taxes to support the program. The township was required to maintain "proper houses and places, and a convenient stock of hemp, flax, thread and other ware and stuff, for setting to

work" the able-bodied. Poor children could be apprenticed. Those who cared for the poor were paid twice a year. The territorial poor law was retained by the state of Ohio until 1805, when Ohio enacted its first poor law, making minor changes but retaining essential features of the 1790 law. Overseers were responsible for the care and management of the township poor but could give aid only with the approval of the trustees. Contracting was retained, but not responsibility of relatives for their dependent kin. The Ohio law also allowed payments for overseers. An 1807 law required black settlers to post a $500 freehold bond, in case of dependence on relief. The bond was eliminated in 1829.

A decade-long economic slump began in the WAR OF 1812. In 1816, Ohio enacted a law permitting county commissioners to operate poorhouses for all destitute persons. Cleveland was able to set up a poorhouse because Cuyahoga County did not. Cleveland's wooden 1½-story poorhouse went up in 1827, conveniently located near the city's ERIE ST. CEMETERY. Ohio's canals vitalized the limp economy, allowing change in the requirement that overseers wait for trustee approval before giving aid. Canal enterprise attracted many. In 5 years (1832–37), the population rose from 1,500 to 9,000. In 1836, the Ohio legislature gave Cleveland the status of a city. But 1837 brought another episode of national depression. The Cleveland poorhouse housed about 2 dozen poor, sick, and insane. Underpaid local physicians also cared for about 200 other poor persons. In 1849, under a new state law, CLEVELAND CITY COUNCIL voted to levy a tax to pay for a hospital and a new poorhouse. Nearby villages and townships paid Cleveland for infirmary care for their paupers, making Cleveland the relief center for the county. Ohio law changed *poorhouse* to *infirmary* in 1850. An 1853 law eliminated the overseer, whose duties were assigned to township trustees. Trustees issued relief and signed annual contracts for care of paupers. In 1855, the decrepit poorhouse behind Erie St. Cemetery was finally replaced by an infirmary built near the location of its descendant, Cleveland Metropolitan General Hospital. The gathering clouds of depression brought another panic in 1857; 25–50% of the workers in the city lost their jobs. In 1858, the City Infirmary housed 187 inmates aged 1 month to 80 years; 15 were insane. Economic problems persisted until the economic stimulus of the CIVIL WAR revitalized Cleveland's economy.

The number of dependent survivors of dead, disabled, and missing Civil War soldiers led to a new burst of institutional development. Ohio's 1865 poor-laws recodification broadened and improved relief. The new law required election of infirmary directors (for 3-year terms), bringing political values into infirmary operations. The infirmary board made rules for infirmary management, signed contracts, and allowed purchases. The directors received up to $2.50 a day for official duties. The appointed superintendent managed the infirmary under their authority. The infirmary housed paupers, the insane, "idiots," and children too young to be apprenticed. Cleveland's population doubled between 1860–70, and the growing economy rewarded many with material plenty. Still, poverty was visible, and sympathetic persons established nongovernmental agencies to relieve the poor. Concern about the care of the poor led Ohio to become the second state to establish a board of state charities (1866) to study such institutions. The board's first annual report (1867) presented a bleak picture. Five years later, the Ohio legislature enacted new requirements, such as a performance bond of $2,000–30,000; itemized bills for all labor and purchases; and the superintendent's signature on every bill. Decisions of the directors were opened for public inspection.

Hard times started again in 1873 and continued. By mid-Jan. 1875, soup lines were needed. By April, over 7,000 gallons of soup and 10,000 loaves of bread had been given out in Cleveland. Recovery began to be felt in 1878. In 1886 the Ohio general assembly enacted a relief program for Civil War veterans and their dependents. Local commissions administered the program. In the depression of 1893–97, local unemployment estimates ranged from 15,000–25,000. In the winter of 1893–94, about 9,086 persons received $37,365 in relief, or $4.11 per person. Some cleaned horse droppings from Cleveland streets at $.10 an hour. A Citizens' Relief Committee raised relief funds. Cleveland relief costs rose, arousing fear that the city's generosity had attracted "a horde of paupers from neighboring cities." Each case was investigated before aid was given. In 1898, Ohio became the second state to establish public aid for the blind. Late in 1907, an economic panic occurred, and unemployment again rose. On the initiative of voluntary relief agencies, Cleveland officials hastened planned construction and ordered wagons, boilers, and other products early, to stimulate business. An estimated ⅔ of the common laborers were destitute.

The celebrated Ohio Children's Code (1913) established a program of public relief for mothers of children under 16, if the breadwinner was dead, had deserted, was in prison or a state hospital, or was disabled. The juvenile court administered the program. By 1914, Cuyahoga County's mothers' pension budget of $75,000 enabled many children to remain with their mothers. The 1914–15 depression was more serious than a Mayor's Committee on Unemployment believed. The Labor Exchange, which helped find jobs, in just 1 week registered 11,000 jobless persons willing to work at any job at any pay. In Mar.-Apr. 1915, a canvass of 16,851 families found 11.6% unemployment; 2,358 jobless workers, who with their families totaled 67,787 dependent people. Mayor NEWTON D. BAKER's Cleveland Citizens' Relief Commission tried to find work for men through "Hire-a-Hand." The commission's effort to raise $100,000 for work relief drew opposition from a private agency, which feared it would lose charity donations as a result. The campaign raised $86,000. Harmony was restored by giving private agency clients priority service.

The Depression of 1920–21 was felt in Cleveland in the fall of 1920, and it continued through a second winter until more than 125,000 workers were out of work at the end of 1921. The City of Cleveland Div. of Outdoor Relief granted only in-kind relief (coal, shoes, and groceries). The private family-relief agencies let their clients take public aid to reduce the burden on the private agency budget. In 1921, the voluntary Welfare Fed. allocated some charity funds from the Community Fund to the public State-City Free Labor Exchange, because the service was badly needed and the public funding was insufficient for effective operation. The city hastened to carry out 6 large (public) construction projects costing $15 million. Again, however, private agencies tried to cope with the situation with minimal governmental involvement.

Volunteer and professional opposition to governmental relief weakened, then vanished, under the relief burden of the Depression of the 1930s. The same agencies that, in 1923, had persuaded Cleveland to stop giving outdoor relief came back in 1931 to ask for city funds for their relief programs. Funds were provided. Cuyahoga County's first public-relief endeavor, the Cuyahoga County Relief Admin., was planned by a committee of voluntary agency representatives and put into operation only after the very last day private agencies were permitted by federal law to distribute federal relief funds. On 1 Aug. 1933, the entire voluntary agency relief staff became county employees, performing the same roles in the same locations as earlier. The dollar cost of relief in the Depression was estimated by HOWARD WHIPPLE GREEN at $200 million, about 1/6 of the $1.2 billion the unemployed would have earned. From 46,000 to 219,000 were without work during each month of the 1930s. Pres. Franklin Roosevelt's temporary relief and work relief programs were followed by the Social Security Act of 1935, which created the country's first national system of welfare assistance, a system that would persist and take precedence over all others by the 1960s. Within a few years, larger numbers of destitute Americans received larger amounts of welfare aid than had been received before by recipients of local relief. After 1935, the poor law was the only major assistance program left under state jurisdiction.

After 1946, state law allowed consolidation of relief and welfare functions in county agencies. Cuyahoga County established a county welfare department on 1 Jan. 1948. Ten years later, studies urged consolidations that had not yet occurred. In Feb. 1958, relief cases of the Soldiers' & Sailors' Relief Commission (see CUYAHOGA COUNTY SOLDIERS' RELIEF COMMISSION) were transferred to the county. Ohio government has not always been sensitive to the decline of the local economy. Between 1953–63, Cuyahoga County experienced a net job loss of 40,000. During the latter part of this period, state welfare payment levels were reduced, and the state failed to adopt federal program improvements that would have reduced the welfare burden on county taxpayers and helped more destitute persons. State inaction resulted in the loss of more than $1 million for aged, blind, and disabled aid programs alone.

When the U.S. declared war on poverty in the 1960s, it seemed that Ohio enlisted on the enemy side. A 1966 U.S. Civil Rights Commission study found that payments were too small to support children in health and decency. In 1966, a Cleveland Welfare Rights Organization was created to protect the rights of the poor; among its leaders was LILLIAN CRAIG. In the winter of 1967–68, Mayor Carl Stokes appointed a Commission on the Crisis in Welfare in Cleveland, in part because of the growth of poverty among Cleveland children. Its report described serious problems in the welfare system. The years since the report on the Crisis in Welfare have not brought improvement. Changes in the industrial needs of the nation have affected the economy of the Cleveland area. Many jobs vanished in the 1960s and 1970s, leaving lifelong workers without employment. By 1980, ⅓ of Cleveland's children lived in poverty. Changes between 1980–86 enlarged the Cleveland poverty population (all ages) by 40%. The withdrawal of the federal government from "safety net" and other programs also contributed to the problem. Relief rolls grew by 6% from Jan. 1984 to June 1986 (42,629 to 45,234 persons). Relief costs rose by $1.2 million (from $4,115,857 to $5,354,461). Cleveland's genius for generosity and civic know-how were well established at the time of the centennial of the city's founding, but the declining regional economy and growing poverty pose unprecedented challenges for the years ahead, threatening bleakness for the city's bicentennial in 1996.

Earl E. Landau

See OLD AGE/NURSING HOMES, PHILANTHROPY, and specific charitable and welfare organizations and agencies.

**WELSH.** See **BRITISH IMMIGRATION**

The **WELSH HOME,** 22199 Ctr. Ridge Rd., is a national rest home for the elderly founded in 1911 to serve natives of Wales, people of Welsh descent, and their spouses. The home was established by Mrs. Mary Jane Hasenpflug and other members of the Cleveland Welsh Club, the founding organization of the Women's Welsh Clubs of America, which operates the home. The first Welsh Home, located on Mayfield Rd. in S. EUCLID, was opened on Thanksgiving Day in 1919; it had accommodations for 15 senior citizens. In 1921 the Women's Welsh Clubs bought 7½ acres of wooded land on Ctr. Ridge Rd. in ROCKY RIVER, and by 1924 they had established the home at this new site. Twenty-nine elderly men and women lived at the home in 1929; its capacity remained constant until 1953, when the older home was replaced by a new $250,000 structure able to accommodate about 34 residents. The annual budget of the home was $20,000 in 1953, and the endowment fund, started in 1925, had grown to $235,000. A project to enlarge the home was begun in the spring of 1985.

**WESLEY METHODIST CHURCH,** located on the near west side at Bridge Ave. and W. 44th, was organized and incorporated on 11 May 1947. It was a merger of 2 historic Methodist congregations: Franklin Ave. Methodist Church and St. Paul's German Methodist Church. Rev. Wilbur B. Meiser, pastor of the Franklin Church, became pastor of the united congregations, which worshiped at the site of St. Paul's Church. Franklin Ave. Methodist, the older of the two, also resulted from 2 churches: Hanover Ave. Methodist and the York St. Church. In Sept. 1833, 10 members of the Cleveland Methodist Society living in OHIO CITY formed a class at the home of Nathaniel Burton on the east side of Pearl St. The class, first led by Rev. John P. Smith, later met for services in a school building on Hanover St. (sometimes given as Vermont St.). In 1834, under the leadership of Wm. Warmington, a lot was purchased on the northeast corner of Church and Hanover streets. Ground was broken on 30 June 1836 by Diodate Clark, and construction began. A severe storm in Nov. 1836 leveled the walls. With the generosity of Samuel Tyler, the walls were rebuilt, and the congregation, led by Rev. Horatio N. Sterns, worshiped in the basement from Nov. 1837 until the sanctuary was completed in 1846.

In Apr. 1866, it was resolved that a new church was necessary. In May 1866, York St. Church, located at the corner of York St. and Bridge, merged with Hanover, and the merged church was named Union Centenary Methodist Episcopal Church. On 16 Apr. 1867, after property was purchased at the corner of Franklin and Duane streets, the name was changed to Franklin Ave. Church. The cornerstone was laid 27 Aug. 1867. For a brief time, the name was changed to Christ Church, but in Dec. 1867, it became Franklin Ave. Church again. After a final service in the Hanover Church (Dec. 1869), the new church was dedicated on 30 Jan. 1870, with Bp. Matthew Simpson and Rev. B. I. Ives preaching the dedicatory sermons. Rev. Jas. Erwin served as first pastor. In 1850, Methodist prayer meetings were being held in German homes in Ohio City. In 1853, the Methodist Conference sent Rev. John N. Baldhuf to organize the Ohio City Mission. Property was purchased at the corner of W. 26th and Lorain Ave., and a brick church was constructed. In 1880, land was purchased at the corner of Bridge and W. 44th. A new church was completed in 1882 and was completely rebuilt in 1912. For over 60 years, services were conducted in German; gradually English was introduced, and German was discontinued. When fire completely destroyed the Franklin Ave. Church on 26 Mar. 1947, St. Paul's invited the congregation to worship with them, and the congregations subsequently merged and became Wesley Methodist Church.

**WEST PARK,** the west side neighborhood and the last large suburb to merge with Cleveland, occupies a 12.5-sq.-mi. area between W. 117th St. to the Rocky River Valley and from LAKEWOOD's southern boundaries to Brookpark Rd. Throughout the years, West Park has maintained a reputation as a stable neighborhood with well-maintained homes and strong neighborhood businesses. The Cleveland Planning Commission divides West Park into 4 subneighborhoods: Warren-Munn, the area's "elite" suburban area; Riverside and Jefferson, areas of well-kept homes and middle-class families; and Puritas-Bellaire-Longmead, with a fair-sized black population and some lower-income areas. Originally part of ROCKPORT Twp., West Park was named for Benjamin West, an early settler and the owner of one of 3 large farms between W. 117th St. and KAMM's CORNERS. During the mid-19th century, the area was a community of isolated homes and rutted wagon paths. Lorain Ave., the only major thoroughfare, was a wooden plank toll road that ran past the Sherman House and the Old Lorain St. House, rest stops for travelers. Ca. 1875, Oswald Kamm opened his grocery, and later a post office on the southwest corner of Lorain and Rocky River Dr. across from a stagecoach stop and toll gate. The area became known as Kamm's Corners and developed into West Park's major commercial district. In 1900, the county approved the formation of the Twp. of West Park. The township's major concern was transportation. With unimproved roads covered by snow in the winter and lost in a sea of mud in the spring, many residents found themselves isolated. West Park became referred to as the "lost city." Relief for its standard residents came only with the arrival of INTERURBANS and the streetcar. Before 1900, the area's only public transportation was a horse-drawn omnibus operating between W. 98th St. and Kamm's Corners. During the early 1900s, the Cleveland & Southwestern Interurban operated to E. 98th St., connecting with the WOODLAND AVE. & WEST SIDE RAILWAY. In 1913 the CLEVELAND RAILWAY CO. ran cars east to W. 117th St., extending the line to Kamm's Corners in 1923 and to the airport in 1931. Elections on annexation were held in West Park and Cleveland in 1922. Proponents pointed to West Park's unimproved roads and higher tax rates and Cleveland's better schools and natural gas rates. Opponents argued against Cleveland's machine politics and big-city debt. Annexation was approved by large majorities and occurred on 1 Jan. 1923.

The **WEST SIDE COMMUNITY HOUSE,** 3000 Bridge Ave., a settlement house serving the near west side, opened in May 1922, consolidating the various institutions organized after 1890 as part of the Methodist Episcopal Deaconess Home. The home, organized by the Women's Home Missionary Society of the Methodist Episcopal Church, first opened at 1058 E. Madison Ave. (E. 79th St.) on 21 Apr. 1890 and was incorporated in Jan. 1892. Work at the home followed the broad responsibilities given the church's deaconesses "to minister to the poor, visit the sick, pray with the dying, care for the orphan, seek the wandering, comfort the sorrowing and save the sinning." The home was moved to 268 (later 1904) Woodland in 1895; in 1907 its services included mothers' meetings, a girls' sewing school, and a "kitchengarden" designed "to teach little girls the first essentials of good home-keeping—order, cleanliness and well-cooked meals." On 16 Jan. 1904 the deaconesses opened the West Side Cottage at 78 Hicks St.; the cottage was moved to 626 Pearl (2045 W. 25th St.) in 1905. Services there soon included a day nursery, kindergarten, evening clubs for boys, and industrial and sewing classes for older girls and women. Increased demands for services, overcrowding, and temporary leases prompted moves to new quarters. In 1908 land on the northwest corner of Bridge Ave. and W. 30th St. in OHIO CITY was purchased and the West Side Cottage moved there. Construction of a new building there permitted consolidation of all Deaconess Home facilities in the new West Side Community House in 1922. In its new facility, the organization began broadening its services; free of the constraints of too little space in previous facilities (usually converted dwellings) and constant fundraising (because of support from the Welfare Fed.), attendance and programs grew. Shortly after the building was opened, the house offered 26 classes for girls and 40 for boys; classes in AMERICANIZATION, English, and citizenship were popular with the immigrant residents of the surrounding area. Christian education continued to play a significant role as well. Combined attendance reached 70,000 annually by 1927 and grew to 88,000 by 1934, when the Depression brought greater demand for community services. During and after WORLD WAR II, the emphasis and direction of the programs changed. Many earlier services such as nursing and domestic and industrial training classes were taken over by other organizations, and population had shifted in the neighborhood from largely middle-income European immigrants early in the 20th century to lower-income Appalachians and Puerto Rican migrants. In 1944, the charter of the house was altered to make the institution a nonsectarian, professional, community-oriented concern. Professionally trained social workers replaced the deaconesses, and in 1946 the first nondeaconess director was hired. Ties to the Methodist church (later to the United Methodist church) remained. In the 1980s, the West Side Community House continued to offer a wide range of community programs and services, including daycare, youth programs, senior citizens' activities and services, and hot meal programs to those in need. It is administered by an executive director and trustees from the community.

West Side Community House Records, WRHS.

## The WEST SIDE FEDERAL SAVINGS AND LOAN ASSOCIATION was founded in 1886 as the Cleveland West Side Bauverin Co., a building association. It was representative of a type of banking institution authorized by the state legislature in 1867 to enable associations of persons to raise funds among their members to build homes. This institution, which soon assumed the functions of a savings and loan, was one of the oldest savings and loans in Cleveland. For its first 15 years, the association, founded by German immigrants with $439,000 capital, floundered with low assets; in 1911, assets climbed to $1 million, and the savings and loan prospered as an independent institution until it was absorbed by Cardinal Federal Savings & Loan in 1976 (see CARDINAL FEDERAL SAVINGS BANK). The original office of the West Side Savings & Loan was at 2621 Lorain Ave. in the current numbering.

## WEST SIDE IRISH AMERICAN CLUB. See IRISH AMERICAN CLUB WEST SIDE

The **WEST SIDE MARKET** is one of the outstanding city-owned markets in the country, with 185 stands offering an assortment of fruits, vegetables, meats, fish, poultry, dairy products, baked goods, ethnic foods, and delicacies. This marketplace began in 1840 when JOSIAH BARBER and RICHARD LORD gave OHIO CITY a tract of land at the corner of Pearl (W. 25th) and Lorain streets with the stipulation that it always be kept as a public market site. This

corner became known as Market Square, where farmers living west of the Cuyahoga River gathered to sell their produce along the street. With additional gifts of land, the marketplace expanded, and in 1868, a wooden 1-story structure known as the Pearl St. Market was erected on the site. As the city's population increased, the small markethouse proved inadequate for the needs of the west side. In 1901, Mayor TOM L. JOHNSON established a market commission, which issued bonds to acquire property for a new market. The following year, they purchased a site across the street from the old market. In 1908, the architectural firm of Hubbell & Benes began building the new $680,000 markethouse. When dedicated in 1912, the massive yellow-brick building was heralded as the most modern and beautiful municipal food market in the world. There were 3 major parts to the markethouse—the interior concourse, which provided room for 100 stalls; the outdoor arcade, with 85 stands; and the clock tower. In 1915, many of the vendors joined in forming the West Side Market Tenants' Assoc. to promote the new markethouse and to lobby for tenant needs. The association was instrumental in implementing improvements to the markethouse. In 1953, it aided the city in financing a $1.1 million modernization program for the market. The historical and architectural significance of the building was recognized when it was designated a Natl. Historic Landmark in 1973. Another $.5 million renovation project occurred in the late 1970s. Many of the stands have been operated by the same families for 2 or 3 generations, serving many of the same customers and their descendants 4 days a week.

Cleveland Landmarks Commission, *West Side Market* (1973).
Kyle, Phyllis Richards, "Ohio City, West Side Market, the Near West Side and Shakespeare in Early Cleveland" (1971), WRHS.
Lewis, Joanne M., *To Market to Market* (1981).

The **WESTERN ELECTRIC COMPANY,** the manufacturing and supply subsidiary of AT&T, was founded in Cleveland in 1869 but soon moved to Chicago. The company evolved from a modest telegraph supply shop owned by Geo. W. Shawk, a former telegraph repairman who had bought the shop in 1856. Shawk's Cleveland shop was one of 2 established by the consolidation of the various small shops doing business with Western Union. In 1869, Shawk sold half of his interest in the shop for $900 to Enos M. Barton, a young telegraph operator from Rochester, N.Y. Later that year, Shawk sold his remaining interest to inventor Elisha Gray, and on 18 Nov. 1869, the partnership of Gray & Barton began. The company manufactured fire and burglar alarms and telegraph equipment at 93 St. Clair (498 W. St. Clair). The partners soon brought in a third investor, Gen. ANSON STAGER, a Western Union vice-president. Stager invested $2,500 in the company and persuaded his new partners to move their operations to Chicago. The company and its owners are not listed in the 1870–71 Cleveland city directory. Gray & Barton was reorganized and incorporated in Illinois with $150,000 in capital in 1872; it was controlled by Western Union after 1872, until the Bell Co. bought a majority interest in it in 1882. Western Electric returned to Cleveland in 1912, when it opened an electric supply house at 724 Prospect; that was its 29th distribution center in the U.S. By the 1920s, the distribution center had moved to larger quarters at E. 65th and Carnegie, and the company had an installation department at 4300 Euclid. By the late 1930s, the distribution center had moved to 10101 Woodland Ave.; by 1952, that plant was renovating more than 18,000 telephones and 25 switchboards a month and stocked 11,000 telephone-supply items, including telephone poles and cable. In Nov. 1957, the company opened a new distribution center at 32000 Aurora Rd. in SOLON, employing more than 600 people. After the 1982 settlement of the Justice Dept.'s antitrust suit against AT&T and its operating companies, the Western Electric Co. was reorganized as AT&T Technologies, Inc., a wholly owned subsidiary of the American Telephone & Telegraph Co.

The **WESTERN FRATERNAL LIFE ASSOCIATION** is a Czech-American fraternal-benefit society based in Cedar Rapids, Iowa. Known until 1971 as the Western Bohemian Fraternal Assoc., the organization was founded in 1897 by lodges of the Czech-Slavonic Benevolent Society that left that organization to form a new association that admitted women as equal members and based insurance premiums on the age of the policyholder. Cleveland branches of the Czech fraternal group were organized in the 1920s and 1930s; Rad Cleveland, whose organizers included Joseph Marotta, was founded ca. 1924; another local lodge, Rad Husova Pravda, was established ca. 1933. In 1971, these two lodges and a third Cleveland lodge—Rad Miroslav Tyrs—hosted the national organization's convention, which brought 325 delegates from 20 midwestern and western states to Cleveland. By 1971, the association had 60,000 members and was open to all people regardless of ethnic heritage; to reflect its broader appeal, the Cleveland convention voted to change the name of the organization to the Western Fraternal Life Assoc. The organization continued to promote Czech culture through sponsorship of language programs at the university level and support for other Czech institutions. It had 2,000 members in the Cleveland area in the early 1970s.

The **WESTERN RESERVE** encompassed approximately 3,333,699 acres of land in what is now northeastern Ohio. Bounded on the north by Lake Erie, on the east by Pennsylvania, it extended 120 mi. westward. On the south, the Reserve's line was set at 41 degrees north latitude, running just south of the present cities of Youngstown, Akron, New London, and Willard. The state of Connecticut exempted the land from the 41 degrees as far north as 42 degrees 2 minutes (western extensions of its own boundaries) when it ceded its western claims to the U.S. in 1786.

In its 1662 royal charter, Connecticut's boundaries were established as extending "from sea-to-sea" across North America. Long before Connecticut became interested in her western lands, royal grants also had created New York and Pennsylvania, both of which intruded on Connecticut's lands. In the 1750s, a group of Connecticut speculators organized the Susquehanna Co. and began to sell lands and settle families in the Wyoming Valley near present-day Wilkes-Barre, Pa. In 1771, Connecticut extended official sanction to the speculators' settlements; when Pennsylvania protested, appeals were made to the British Privy Council to determine the issue. The War for American Independence broke out before a decision was made, and the issue was transferred to the American Congress. (Meanwhile, in 1778, a bloody massacre took place in the Wyoming Valley; British, Tories, and Indian allies wiped out almost the entire male population.) In 1782, under the complicated system for resolving interstate disputes provided by the Articles of Confederation, a federal court at Trenton, N.J., determined that the Wyoming lands belonged to Pennsylvania. At the same time, Congress was encouraging states that claimed western lands to cede them so that it could regulate their sale and governance. After Virginia's cession in 1784, Connecticut felt impelled to act. Virginia had exempted lands promised to war veterans; Connecticut now reserved lands roughly equal in dimension to the Wyoming Valley lands

from her cession. Congress took 2 years before reluctantly accepting the Connecticut cession, and then only because the Pennsylvania delegation championed Connecticut's offer. It is assummed that threats to reopen the Wyoming Valley case motivated Pennsylvania's support of Connecticut.

The Western Reserve came into being not by what was done but by what was not done. Connecticut ceded to the U.S. all her western lands claims, except the area of the Reserve, on 14 Sept. 1786. Indian title to the lands east of the CUYAHOGA RIVER was extinguished in the Treaty of Greenville in 1795. That same year, the state of Connecticut sold most of the reserved lands to the CONNECTICUT LAND CO., and established a school fund with the proceeds from the sale. The actual survey and division of the lands would be directed by the company. Connecticut had exempted the "Firelands," some 500,000 acres in the western part of the Reserve, in order to compensate citizens whose property had been destroyed in British raids during the Revolutionary War. What was not immediately determined was the governmental jurisdiction. The year after the Connecticut cession, Congress created the Northwest Territory, but it was assumed that Connecticut, not the territory, was empowered to exercise political jurisdiction over the Reserve. The ambiguity lasted until 1800, when Congress passed the "Quieting Act"; Connecticut surrendered all governing authority, and shortly thereafter, Arthur St. Clair, governor of the Northwest Territory, designated the Western Reserve as Trumbull County, fixing the county seat at Warren.

The **WESTERN RESERVE BUILDING** is one of 3 tall office buildings by the firm of Chicago architect Daniel H. Burnham built in Cleveland between 1889–93. Built in 1891–92, its structure is transitional between that of the other two buildings, the SOCIETY NATL. BANK (1889–90) and the CUYAHOGA BLDG. (1892–1893). The exterior structure consists of masonry load-bearing walls, the interior supports include cast- and wrought-iron members, and the floors are of tile arch construction. Because of its adaptation to the sloping triangular site at Superior Ave. and W. 9th and W. 10th streets, the 8-story building has design features that the others do not, including the placement of the bay windows and the treatment of the sandstone piers of the 2 lower levels. The cornice design, a simple curve of corbeled bricks, is similar to that of the firm's masterpiece, the Monadnock Block in Chicago. The Western Reserve Bldg. was constructed for SAMUEL MATHER (1851–1931), noted Cleveland civic leader and industrialist in the iron-ore and coal-mining industries. It was rehabilitated by the Higbee Development Corp. in 1975–76, and the Romanesque entrance arch, which had been altered with granite facing in the 1940s, was restored.

The **WESTERN RESERVE HISTORICAL SOCIETY** is Cleveland's oldest existing cultural institution. Founded on 28 May 1867 as the Western Reserve & Northern Ohio Historical Society, it was initially a branch of the CLEVELAND LIBRARY ASSOC. The society's stated purpose was the collection and preservation of materials relating to the history of Cleveland, the WESTERN RESERVE, Ohio, and the "great west." During its early decades, such activity usually centered around the accumulation of manuscripts, books, and other library materials relating to the early history of the community. However, the institution also began to acquire a variety of artifacts relating to local history; these eventually formed the basis of its museum. Leadership and funding were provided by a number of prominent citizens, among which were CHAS. WHITTLESEY and

CHAS. C. BALDWIN. The society was originally located on the 3d floor of the Society for Savings Bank building on PUBLIC SQUARE. By 1871, the institution had garnered enough support to open to the public. However, the increasing size of the collections created a space problem. With the support of a series of wealthy trustees, including JOHN D. ROCKEFELLER and Rutherford B. Hayes, the society was able to purchase the bank building in 1892 and expand its operations to all 3 floors. The library alone occupied the upper 2 stories. On 7 Mar. 1892, the society was incorporated as an institution independent of the Library Assoc. In 1898, the society moved to a new structure at E. 107th St. and EUCLID AVE., a 3-story facility that permitted expansion of both the museum and library collections and an increased number of public lectures. Under the direction of WALLACE H. CATHCART, president of the society 1907–13 and director 1913–42, the society's library expanded greatly, acquiring extensive new collections of local material, CIVIL WAR records, and material relating to the Shakers. Beginning in the 1960s, the library instituted special collecting programs in fields such as black, ethnic, Jewish, and labor history, which added significant amounts of material to its holdings. By 1986, its collections included over 250,000 books, 25,000 bound volumes of newsprint, and nearly 6 million manuscript items.

In the late 1930s, the society expanded its facilities, acquiring Lawnfield (1936), the home of Pres. JAS. A. GARFIELD in Mentor, and Shandy Hall, a home constructed by the Harper family in Unionville in 1815. In 1939 and 1940, the institution's main operations were moved to 2 mansions on East Blvd. The museum was relocated in the Hay House, constructed by Mrs. John Hay in 1910, and the library into the adjacent Hanna House, which was constructed by the Harry Payne Bingham family in 1918. By this point the museum's holdings had become extensive and contained the nuclei of the costume and American furniture and decorative-arts collections that would grow to national importance by the 1970s. Further facilities expansion occurred in the 1950s and 1960s. Under the administration of director MEREDITH B. COLKET, JR. A central addition joining the 2 mansions and a 3-floor library stack facility were opened in 1959. In 1963, TRW, INC., donated its collection of historic automobiles and aircraft to the society. An adjoining structure, the Frederick C. Crawford Auto-Aviation Museum, was opened in 1965 to house these new collections, which had formerly been exhibited at the Thompson Auto Album at E. 30th St. and Chester. In 1957, the society acquired the Jonathan Hale homestead in Bath, Summit County, a facility that it developed as an operating early-19th-century farm and village. An additional operating farm, Loghurst, in Mahoning County, was acquired in 1978. By the 1980s, WRHS had evolved into one of the largest privately-supported historical societies in the country. Its 4 main divisions, the History Library, History Museum, Auto-Aviation Museum, and outlying sites, employed over 80 full-time employees. In 1984, the society opened a new 68,000-sq.-ft. library building at its East Blvd. headquarters, the initial phase of a facilities-expansion program envisioned for the East Blvd. headquarters.

Benton, Elbert Jay, *A Short History of the Western Reserve Historical Society, 1867–1942* (1942).
Knowles, Margaret K., *The First Hundred Years* (1967).

The **WESTERN RESERVE PRESBYTERIAL ASSOCIATION** is the descendant organization of a number of Presbyterian missionary groups, one of the earliest of which was the Woman's Foreign Missionary Society. The Woman's Foreign Missionary Society of the Presbyterian Church of Cleveland was organized on 12 June 1872 at a meeting at the Second Presbyterian Church. It was an outgrowth of the much earlier Parlor Missionary Society, which had been organized in 1833 at Old Stone Church (see FIRST PRESBYTERIAN CHURCH). The group originally met in the homes of the members as they prepared boxes for the missionaries who had been sent to foreign fields by the Board of Foreign Missions of the Presbyterian church. At its first annual meeting, held on 10 Sept. 1873, the group reorganized and became the Woman's Presbyterial Foreign Missionary Society, an association composed of representatives from various women's auxiliaries of Presbyterian churches in and around Cleveland. It directed and coordinated the activities of these auxiliaries as they gave spiritual and financial support to various Presbyterian missionary projects in foreign fields. In 1893, the name was changed to the Women's Foreign Missionary Society of Cleveland Presbytery. Its purposes continued to be to provide information about missionary projects, to stimulate interest in the foreign fields, to promote the formation of local Foreign Missionary Societies (auxiliaries), and to aid the Women's Foreign Missionary Society of the Pennsylvania Church with headquarters in Philadelphia, Pa. The society was merged with the Woman's Home Missionary Society in 1914 and became part of the United Society of Woman's Home & Foreign Mission Societies of Cleveland Presbytery.

The Woman's Presbyterial Home Missionary Society, an organization composed of representatives from the various local Presbyterian church auxiliaries, was established on 10 Apr. 1881 at the Euclid Ave. Presbyterian Church, for the purpose of coordinating and supporting the activities of the individual mission groups. Through the years, the society organized additional auxiliaries in local Presbyterian churches in order to provide prayerful and financial support to the projects established by the Woman's Executive Committee of Home Missions (with headquarters in New York City); it systematized and united the efforts made by these local associations and sent out boxes to Presbyterian Home Missionary families and schools throughout the country.

The decision to merge the Woman's Foreign Missionary Society and the Woman's Presbyterial Home Missionary Society was made at their annual meetings in 1914. Accordingly, on 3 Mar. 1915, the first annual meeting of the United Society of Woman's Home & Foreign Missionary Societies of Cleveland Presbytery was held at CALVARY PRESBYTERIAN CHURCH, E. 79th St. and Euclid Ave. The reorganized united society served as a liaison between the auxiliaries in the various local churches and the Natl. Mission Boards and continued to support Presbyterian missionary activities throughout the world, including medical schools, world service, overseas hospitals, missionary education, and local Presbyterian social-service agencies. In 1924, it became known as the Presbyterial Missionary Society of Cleveland Presbytery, and in 1942 as the Cleveland Presbyterial Society for Missions. In Aug. 1956, with the cooperation of the CUYAHOGA COUNTY JUVENILE COURT, the society established Project Friendship, Inc., an organization whose program was particularly designed to help adolescent girls referred by the court. Mrs. Chas. Adams Hall served as its first president. In 1972, Project Friendship became an independent ecumenical agency. In Apr. 1973, the name of the society was changed to the Western Reserve Presbyterial Assoc. Its first annual meeting was held at FAIRMOUNT PRESBYTERIAN CHURCH; Mrs. W. Dean Hopkins was the first president of the newly named organization. The association continued to plan and coordinate the activities of over 47 local Presbyterian Woman's Mission Associations through a varied program of meetings as well as financial and prayerful support to a wide variety of mission projects in Cleveland and throughout the world.

**WESTERN RESERVE UNIVERSITY.** *See* **CASE WESTERN RESERVE UNIVERSITY**

The **WESTERN SEAMEN'S FRIEND SOCIETY,** the western branch of the American Seamen's Friend Society, was organized on 10 Nov. 1830 and chartered in Ohio in 1850 "to promote the Intellectual, Social, Moral, and Spiritual condition of Sailors and Boatmen employed on the Western Waters." Rev. Gordon Winslow, an agent of the American Seamen's Friend Society, brought the society's evangelical mission to Cleveland in Oct. 1830 and soon established the city as the headquarters of the western society. In 1833 a chapel was erected near the canal basin; the Bethel Church was organized on 25 Oct. 1835 and incorporated on 20 Mar. 1841. By 1850 its original 9 members had grown to 137; by 1852 its Sunday school had an attendance of 120–150 children and 15–20 teachers. Leading Clevelanders such as Samuel Cowles, JOHN FOOTE, and TRUMAN P. HANDY served as officers and directors of the society. Between 1830–50, the main work of the society was "itinerant missionary service" carried on by such devices as the Gospel Ship. From 1850–67 it established chapels in various western cities; in 1858 it had chapels in Toledo, St. Louis, Pittsburgh, Detroit, Cincinnati, Sandusky, and Chicago, and a budget of $15,820, which included donations from 10 states, including Iowa and Missouri. Such publications as the *Boatman's Magazine* (begun Oct. 1834), *Spirit of the Lakes & Boatmen's Magazine* (1849–52), and the *Western Pilot* (begun in Jan. 1853) helped spread the society's message. The work was directed and financed by headquarters in Cleveland until more localized control was instituted. For much of this time (1848–67), Raymond H. Leonard guided the society's work.

In 1867 the society adopted several new policies designed to enhance efficiency and provide greater strength for its work in small cities. In large cities such as Cleveland, Bethel work was placed under the complete control of a local board of directors who were empowered to hold property and to oversee the work of chaplains and agents. That coincided with the building of large "Institutional Bethels," which combined the religious work of the church with more secular services such as the provision of shelter and poor relief. The Cleveland BETHEL UNION was organized in 1867, opened its own Bethel Bldg. at Superior and Spring (W. 10th) in 1869, and by 1896 had a temperance society, a relief society, a sewing society, a coffee and lunch room, and a visiting committee to serve the sick and the poor. The society worked in Cleveland until ca. 1923. The final superintendent of the Cleveland mission at 1024 Superior Ave. was Clara E. Fall, widow of Rev. John O. Fall, who served as superintendent until his death in June 1912. Clara Fall apparently continued her missionary work among sailors after the Cleveland mission closed; she died in the Canal Zone in 1925.

The **WESTINGHOUSE ELECTRIC CORPORATION,** an early manufacturer of electrical equipment that has grown into a multipurpose engineering firm, was established by Geo. Westinghouse in 1886. Known as the Westinghouse Electric & Mfg. Co. in 1898, it established a sales office in the HOLLENDEN HOTEL and purchased the Walker Mfg. Co. Westinghouse became a manufacturer in Cleveland partly as the result of a lawsuit against the competing Walker

Mfg. Co. Established in 1883 by machinist John Walker, Walker Mfg. produced power-transmitting machinery, cable railway networks, and other machinery. The company had prospered sufficiently by 1890 to build new plants on its site on the lakeshore at the foot of Waverly Ave. (W. 58th St.). Both General Electric and Westinghouse, however, charged that some Walker products infringed upon patents they held, and they sued Walker in 1894. Walker lost the case and later found it difficult to continue to operate under the restrictions the court placed on its manufacturing activities; in 1898 the company was sold to Westinghouse for about $1 million. Westinghouse operated its new Cleveland plant as its casting division, making aluminum and brass castings. During the 1930s, the plant at 1216 W. 58th St. manufactured a variety of lights, including those used at airports, along highways, and in industry. By 1960, more than 560 people worked at the plant, which had become the headquarters for the Westinghouse Lighting Div. Employment increased to more than 600 in 1964, and in 1968 the company ceased its sandcasting work at the plant, using die-cast molding machinery to manufacture lights until the facility was closed in 1979. From 1980–82, Westinghouse's lighting-division plant in Cleveland was located at 5901 Breakwater Ave. As it closed its manufacturing operations in Cleveland, Westinghouse expanded its sales and service operations in the area, making evident the corporation's diversified activities. By 1951, in addition to its lighting-division plant, Westinghouse operated in Cleveland branches of its sales and engineering, elevator, and manufacturing and repair divisions, as well as sales offices. By the mid-1970s its operations included architectural systems, computer instrumentation sales and services, and construction-industry sales. By 1978, many of these operations were located at 4600 Rockside Rd.

**WESTLAKE** is a city located 12 mi. west of Cleveland on the western edge of Cuyahoga County. It is bounded by Lorain County on the west, BAY VILLAGE on the north, ROCKY RIVER on the east, and N. OLMSTED on the south, and occupies 16.5 sq. mi. Originally part of Dover Twp., organized in 1810, it was incorporated as Dover Village in 1911, adopting the mayor-council form of government. The first settlers in the area arrived in 1810 from Connecticut. German immigrants began to arrive in the middle of the century. Pioneer industries included mills, shops, 2 potash asheries, and an iron furnace. The vineyards of Dover Twp. established its position as America's 2d-largest grape-producing region in the late 19th century. During the post-Civil War era, the lakeshore of Dover Twp. attracted affluent Clevelanders as an ideal location for summer homes. In 1901, residents in the northern part of the township voted to form Bay Village. During the first half of the 20th century, Dover Village remained essentially rural, and farms, truck gardens, and flower gardens continued to flourish. The name Westlake was chosen in 1940 to avoid confusion with Dover in Tuscarawas County, and in 1957 Westlake became a city. Unlike neighboring communities to the north and east, Westlake still retained a significant percentage of undeveloped land. Population grew from 3,200 in 1940 to 5,500 in 1950 and 15,989 in 1970. The completion of I-90 promoted growth by making Westlake more accessible. By 1980 the population reached 19,483. The city has its own school system with 7 schools, and recreational facilities include a swimming pool, baseball fields, and picnic areas. Clague Park was the former property of the Clague family, pioneers from the Isle of Man, and the Clague house is a museum of the Westlake Historical Society.

WESTROPP, CLARA E. (7 July 1886–25 June 1965), was a cofounder and executive of the WOMEN'S FEDERAL SAVINGS BANK, and a leader in the support of missions of the Roman Catholic church. One of 9 children of Thos. P. and Clara Stoeckel Westropp, Clara graduated from West High School and the Dyke School of Commerce. Later, to meet the responsibilities of bank management, she studied at the Savings & Loan Institute in Mercersburg, Pa. Convinced that women could bring to the business world an appreciation of home ownership plus a recognition of the value of regular saving, Westropp responded with enthusiasm when her sister, LILLIAN M. WESTROPP, proposed that they establish a savings and loan association to be directed and run by women. This venture, begun in 1922, was the first savings institution in the country to be organized, managed, and chiefly staffed by women. Originally organized under a state charter, it was reorganized under a federal charter in 1935 and renamed the Women's Federal Savings & Loan Assoc. of Cleveland. Clara Westropp personally sold over half the initial stock capitalization of $85,000. Beginning in modest quarters, for which it paid a monthly rent of $40, the association relocated in 1937 to larger offices at 320 Superior Ave., in a 5-story building that it subsequently acquired and renamed the Women's Federal Bldg. By 1954, the association was the 3d-largest savings and loan in Cuyahoga County, with assets exceeding $38 million. Serving the general public and no longer exclusively operated by women, it started its branching operation in 1957 in UNIVERSITY HTS. and since then has opened numerous branches in Cleveland neighborhoods and suburbs. In 1952, the Cuyahoga Savings & Loan League chose Clara Westropp as its president, the first woman to hold that office. She was the founder and for 20 years the chairman of the St. Xavier Mission Assoc. of the Cleveland Diocese and was also diocesan mission chairman of the Natl. Council of Catholic Women. In 1965 she was awarded posthumously the Mission Secretarial Award from Washington, D.C., making her Catholic Woman of the Year. Also posthumously, the Cleveland Board of Education named Clara E. Westropp Jr. High School in her honor. Westropp died in 1965 at the home at 16711 Southland Ave. that she shared with her sister, Judge Lillian M. Westropp.

WESTROPP, LILLIAN MARY (9 May 1884–15 Aug. 1968), was a judge in the Cleveland Municipal Court, and cofounder and president and later chairman of the board of the WOMEN'S FEDERAL SAVINGS BANK. She also led in the establishment of the psychiatric clinic that still serves the municipal and common pleas courts in Cuyahoga County. Westropp was born in Cleveland, one of 9 children of Thos. P. and Clara Stoeckel Westropp. She graduated from West High School in 1903 and the Dyke School of Commerce. A brief theatrical career, which included a role in *East Lynne* with a traveling company and study at the Haroff School of Expression, was followed by enrollment in the law school of BALDWIN-WALLACE COLLEGE in a class of 100 men and 3 women. Working as a stenographer by day and studying law at night, she completed a 4-year course in 3 years, graduating in 1915 with the degree of LL.B., magna cum laude. Entering private practice with emphasis on real estate and finance, Westropp was one of the first women admitted to the CLEVELAND BAR ASSOC. and the first woman to be elected to its executive committee. In 1929 she became assistant county prosecutor. In this office she instituted a bail-bond system insuring 100% collection. In 1931, Gov. Geo. White appointed her to fill the municipal judgeship made vacant by the election of MARTIN L. SWEENEY to Congress. Westropp was reelected for an unbroken series of 6-year terms until she retired from the bench in 1957. During her tenure, she initiated a court psychiatric clinic, securing the aid of the BUSINESS & PROFESSIONAL WOMEN'S CLUB, plus backing from 30 other organizations in obtaining passage of enabling legislation in the state legislature. The psychiatric clinic (est. 1937) was a prototype for similar facilities in other cities, and still serves the municipal and common pleas courts here.

In collaboration with her sister, CLARA E. WESTROPP, Westropp organized and helped to direct the Women's Federal Savings & Loan Assoc. of Cleveland, the first such enterprise in the world to be owned, directed, and chiefly staffed by women. The association was originally under state charter (1922); its federal charter dated from 1935. Judge Westropp served as president from 1936–57, and as chairman of the board of directors until her death. She stated that her objective in starting Women's Federal was to give women confidence in their own ability in matters of finance and to prove they could succeed in the financial field. Westropp was active in the Democratic party, organizing Democratic Women, State of Ohio, in 1920, and being chosen a member of the executive committee of the CUYAHOGA COUNTY DEMOCRATIC PARTY in 1923. She was a member of the Cleveland, Cuyahoga, Ohio State, and American bar associations; the Natl. Probation & Parole Assoc.; and the Natl. Assoc. of Women Lawyers. She was an organizer and charter member of the Women Lawyers' Club of Cleveland; the WOMEN'S CITY CLUB; the LEAGUE OF WOMEN VOTERS; the Catholic Daughters of America; the Cleveland Diocesan Council of Catholic Women; and the Business & Professional Women's Club, and an organizer and life member of the board of directors of Woman's Hospital in Cleveland.

WEYGANDT, CARL (14 June 1888–4 Sept. 1964), was a lawyer and state legislator and a prominent judge in Ohio courts for 38 years. He was chief justice of the Supreme Court of Ohio for 30 years, an office he held longer than any other person in the state's history. Weygandt was born near Wooster, Ohio, the son of a common pleas judge. He atttended Wooster public schools, and later Wooster College, from which he graduated in 1912. For the next 3 years he taught at Wooster High School. He then entered the Western Reserve University Law School and graduated in 1918, that same year being admitted to the state bar. Remaining in Cleveland, Weygandt entered into practice with the firm of THOMPSON, HINE, & FLORY. In 1920 he was elected to the Ohio general assembly, one of 2 Democrats to survive the Harding landslide. During his 2 years as a state legislator, Weygandt introduced several bills to help reform the state judiciary; he also fought for a minimum wage for women. He returned to practice in 1923 as counsel for the Cleveland Automobile Club. An outstanding college athlete, Weygandt continued his interest in sports as a football referee. Until 1932, he officiated in games from Massachusetts to Nebraska, and was considered a national expert on the game.

Weygandt began his long and successful career in Ohio courts when, in 1924, Gov. Donahey appointed him to the common pleas court bench to replace a retiring judge. In 1930, Weygandt was elected judge of the Court of Appeals of Ohio, 8th Appellate District, and in 1933 he was elected chief justice of the Supreme Court of Ohio. During his first term as chief justice, Weygandt was largely credited with quelling personal feuds within the Ohio Supreme Court and in improving its efficiency. He was reelected to 5 more terms; his greatest victory was achieved in 1956, when he was reelected by a record 500,000 votes. Weygandt often advocated higher salaries and a better retirement plan for judges in order to keep competent men on the bench. For various reasons, including unhappiness with his own yearly salary of $12,000, Weygandt almost resigned in 1954, but appeals from the governor and the Ohio Bar Assoc. changed his mind. During his 30 years as chief justice, Weygandt heard over 20,000 cases and swore in more Ohio governors than any of his predecessors. He was defeated for reelection by Kingsley A. Taft in 1962. Weygandt was married to Jessie M. Silver and lived in Lakewood.

**WHEELBANKS, DAVID M.,** was chiefly responsible for establishing the foundation for the first permanent religious organization among BLACKS in Cleveland. A prominent black minister in Cleveland from 1830, Wheelbanks organized the effort to build the first African Methodist Episcopal church in Cleveland—ST. JOHN'S—in 1848.

Hicks, Josephus Franklin, *St. John African Methodist Episcopal Church* (1959).

The **WHIG PARTY** was a diverse group of former Federalists, anti-Masons, and national Republicans who opposed the Democratic party and president Andrew Jackson during the 1830s. Although both parties favored economic expansion, the Democrats sought it through limited government, while the Whigs favored an activist national government that would support internal improvements within the nation. The Whigs also promoted humanitarian reforms, including public schools and temperance. The Whig party of Cuyahoga County appealed to the merchants and businessmen who stood to profit from the building of the OHIO & ERIE CANAL, and Evangelical Protestant reformers. Locally, the *Cleveland Herald* supported the Whig cause, and prominent party members included JOHN W. ALLEN, SHERLOCK ANDREWS, ELISHA WHITTLESEY, and NICHOLAS DOCKSTADTER. Although party lines were quite fluid in local elections, by 1834 the Whigs were a recognizable political party in Cleveland and hosted several gatherings of Whigs from other areas.

In 1836, the local Whigs favored Wm. Henry Harrison over Martin Van Buren for president, and the county gave Harrison a majority, although Van Buren prevailed nationally. Whigs also dominated the village election in 1837. A high point for the local party was the successful campaign of Harrison for president in 1840. Cleveland delegates supported his nomination at the state party convention in Feb. 1840 and conducted an energetic campaign for both Harrison and Thos. Corwin, the Whig candidate for governor of Ohio. Reflecting Harrison's campaign slogan of "Tippecanoe and Tyler Too," Cleveland and OHIO CITY each organized its own Tippecanoe Club in Mar. 1840. Political campaigns were a major source of community entertainment, and each group built a log cabin to serve as a meeting house for political rallies. When Harrison and Corwin won their elections, both cities held large victory celebrations. A number of Whig candidates were also successfully elected to local office in 1840 and 1841. Supporting Henry Clay over Democrat Jas. K. Polk for president in 1844, the local Whigs established the "Clay Club House" on Water (W. 9th) St. near Superior as campaign headquarters, and for the first time made an effort to win over the immigrant vote. Clay won a small majority in both the city and the county but lost the national election to Polk. In local elections, Whig rivalry with the Democrats continued, as the Whigs were able to obtain their fair share of the local offices. However, Whig party influence on the electorate gradually weakened, and by the early 1850s, Cleveland Whigs were supporting Free-Soil and "people's" candidates in local elections.

**WHISKEY ISLAND** is a triangular piece of land 1 mi. long and 1/3 mi. at its widest. Located on the near west side of Cleveland, the peninsula is bounded by Lake Erie to the north; (approx.) W. 54th St.; and the CUYAHOGA RIVER to the south and east. This land was located nearly 1/4 mi. down the Cuyahoga when MOSES CLEAVELAND visited the area in 1796. It was the first piece of solid land amid the swamps lining the river. LORENZO CARTER built his family farm on Whiskey Island (so named when a distillery was built on the land in the 1830s). With the construction of the Ohio Canal in 1825 and the rechanneling of the Cuyahoga River in 1827, the area was settled, largely by Irish immigrants. In 1831 the Buffalo Co. and the New Harbor Co., representing investors from Buffalo and Brooklyn, purchased the Carter farm and divided the 80 acres into small allotments with 22 streets. Docks were built, and some manufacturing plants were constructed, including the Lake Erie Iron Works, makers of steamboat shafts and railroad axles. Thirteen saloons were located in the area. Cleveland's second hospital, the "pest house," was built on Whiskey Island in 1832, following an outbreak of Asiatic cholera that was carried on a troop ship from the Black Hawk Wars that stopped in the city (see CHOLERA EPIDEMIC). Fifty people were killed. The year after CHAS. OTIS started the Lake Erie Iron Works (1852), the Cleveland & Toledo Railroad (later the New York Central) was chartered. The railroad ran its northern division through Whiskey Island, stopping at the river to ferry its passengers across the Cuyahoga because the city refused permission for the railroad to connect to the eastbound line. The Irish moved from Whiskey Island when better employment and housing opportunities became available. The exodus of human residents from the swampy area continued into the 20th century, leaving Whiskey Island to the railroads, hoisting machines, and eventually a salt mine; the docks were built elsewhere. By the mid-1980s, only the footers from some Whiskey Island houses and remnants of River Bed St. remain as reminders of Whiskey Island, 1830–1900.

**WHITE, JOHN GRISWOLD** (10 Aug. 1845–27 Aug. 1928), was a noted lawyer, chess historian, bibliophile, and philanthropist. Born in Cleveland, he was the son of Bushnell White, lawyer, U.S. commissioner, and U.S. district attorney, and Elizabeth Brainard White, both from New England. He attended Canandaigua Academy in New York and CENTRAL HIGH SCHOOL in Cleveland. In 1865 he graduated from Western Reserve College at Hudson, where he was a member of Phi Beta Kappa and the Philozetian Literary Society and salutatorian of his class. White was admitted to the bar in 1868. In 1870 he went into partnership with Robt. E. Mix and Judge Conway W. Noble. The firm subsequently became White & Mix; it is still active in the Union Commerce Bldg. as the SPIETH, BELL, MCCURDY & NEWELL CO. White was a brilliant lawyer and dean of the Cleveland bar; his largest practice was in real estate. He was also well-versed in maritime, church, and municipal law. He acted as special counsel for the CLEVELAND RAILWAY CO. in the fight with TOM L. JOHNSON over the Municipal Railway; was attorney for the Catholic Diocese of Northern Ohio; and participated in litigation between 2 factions of the Evangelical church. His advice was sought on major problems arising as Cleveland became a metropolis.

White was a member of the CLEVELAND GRAYS, the Ohio Natl. Guard, the UNIVERSITY, ROWFANT, Castalia Travel, and Rockwell Springs Travel clubs, and the

Cleveland Law Library; charter member of the UNION CLUB; and with R. E. Mix, founder of the CLEVELAND YACHT CLUB. He served on the CLEVELAND PUBLIC LIBRARY board of trustees from 1884–86 and 1910–28, as president for 17 of those years. He was instrumental in selecting WM. H. BRETT and LINDA EASTMAN to head the library. Largely through his efforts, the CPL grew to national prominence, established a branch library system, was the first large municipal library to introduce the open-shelf policy, and was the first to implement an employee retirement plan. During his lifetime, White personally selected and donated over 60,000 books on Orientalia, folklore, and related subjects to the library; upon his death he bequeathed his 12,000-volume chess and checker collection to it. He left the bulk of his estate as an endowment to maintain and develop the John G. White Collection of Folklore, Orientalia and Chess, now part of the special collections of the CPL.

Cleveland Public Library, *The Open Shelf. Memorial Number: John Griswold White, Citizen of Cleveland, Lawyer, Scholar, Bookman, Donor of the White Collection* (ca. 1929).
Cleveland Public Library Round Table, *Tribute Presented to Mr. White by the Round Table on the Occasion of his Eightieth Birthday* (1925).
Reece, Motoko B. Yatabe, "John Griswold White, Trustee, and the White Collection in the Cleveland Public Library" (Ph.D. diss., University of Michigan, 1979).

**WHITE, MOSES** (25 Feb. 1791–1 Sept. 1881), was an early settler of Cleveland and, although a layman, was very active in the city's early religious life. He was a deacon of the FIRST BAPTIST CHURCH for almost 50 years. White was born in Warwick, Mass. He was trained as a tailor, and with his wife, Mary (Andrews), he operated a tailor shop for several decades in Cleveland. They came to Cleveland in 1816 from Mendon, Mass. Discouraged by the absence of organized religion in Cleveland, White, with ALFRED KELLEY and Noble H. Merwin, worked to promote Christianity in the early settlement. White himself had publicly professed his faith in Christ in 1816. The three men retained visiting ministers or, in the absence of clergy, conducted their own services. As part of the Sunday school movement, in 1819, White helped organize the first religious school in Cleveland and served as its secretary. In 1833, he was a charter member of the First Baptist Church of Cleveland. White's daughter, Minerva, was the first to be buried in the ERIE ST. CEMETERY.

**WHITE, ROLLIN HENRY** (11 July 1872–10 Sept. 1962), was a pioneer in the Cleveland automobile industry and a founder of the WHITE MOTOR CORP. and the Cleveland Tractor Co. White was born in Cleveland to Thos. H. and Almira Greenleaf White (see THOS. H. WHITE). Educated in Cleveland public schools, he graduated from Cornell University in 1894 with bachelor's degrees in both mechanical and electrical engineering. Returning to Cleveland, White went to work for his father's White Sewing Machine Co. The 1890s were a period of expansion, as the company added roller skates, kerosene lamps, bicycles, automatic lathes, and screw machines to its production line. The father, however, decided that the "horseless carriage" was just a fad and left the automobile-manufacturing portion of the business to his sons, Windsor, Walter, and Rollin, who were experimenting with early automobile designs. In 1899, Rollin invented a flash boiler that could safely be used on steam automobiles. In 1900, the Stanhope model, the first of the White Steamers, was introduced. To demonstrate that White automobiles were safe, Rollin took to racing them on the old GLENVILLE RACE TRACK. As

a race driver, he excelled in hill-climbing competitions, and in 1902 he set a world's land speed record for steam carriages. In 1906, White became vice-president of the newly formed White Co., later the White Motor Corp. White continued the production of the White Steamers until 1909, when it was decided that the gasoline engine was superior to steam. In 1910, the first White trucks were produced. In 1911, Rollin conceived the idea of developing a small farm tractor. However, demand for the White truck kept the company from undertaking production. In 1914, Rollin left the White Co., and in Jan. 1916 he organized the Cleveland Motor Plow Co. to begin production of the tractor. In 1917, the name of the company was changed to the Cleveland Tractor Co., or CLETRAC. As president, White did most of the designing for the tractor. From 1921–23, Cletrac produced the Rollin, an automobile named after White. In 1930, White became chairman of the board; his son, W. King White, became president. White retired in 1944 when Cletrac merged with the Oliver Farm Equipment Co. White married Katharine King on 2 Sept. 1896. The Whites had 3 children, Rollin Henry, Jr., Wm. King, and Elizabeth King.

**WHITE, THOMAS H.** (26 Apr. 1836–22 June 1914), was the founder of the White Sewing Machine Corp., one of Cleveland's largest manufacturing concerns in the late 19th and early 20th centuries. It was the parent company of the WHITE MOTOR CO. and the Cleveland Automatic Screw Machine Co. White was born in Phillipston, Mass., the son of a manufacturer. After receiving a common-school education, he devoted himself to mechanical studies. By 1857, he had invented a small hand-operated single-thread machine. Urged by friends to concentrate on sewing-machine production, with initial capital of $500, White started his own business and began making "The New England Sewing Machine," retailing for $10. Wm. Grothe was his partner. Seeking a central location near markets and materials, in 1866, White moved his company—the White Mfg. Co.— from Templeton, Mass., into a small factory on Canal St. in Cleveland. In 1876, the White Sewing Machine Corp. was formed, with White as president and treasurer. Within 10 years of coming to Cleveland, production had increased from 25 to 2,000 units per week, making Cleveland the center for the making of sewing machines. Branch dealers were opened across the country and in England. Civically active in Cleveland, White gave generously to various charities and educational institutions. Among the latter, in 1908, he financed the building of a separate studio for sculpture at the Cleveland School of Art. He also served on CLEVELAND CITY COUNCIL, 1875–76. White married Almira L. Greenleaf of Boston; they had 6 children, 4 boys and 2 girls.

**WHITE, WILLIAM J.** (7 Oct. 1850–16 Feb. 1923), was a chewing-gum manufacturer who was active in politics, serving 1 term in Congress. White was born in Rice Lake, Ontario. His parents moved to Cleveland when he was 6. He first entered business by operating a candy store. In 1884, a grocer who knew White received a barrel of what was thought to be nuts; White purchased the barrel, which turned out to be Yucatan chicle. He and his first wife then experimented in their kitchen and found that the chicle could be softened and made chewable; they added mint to make the mixture appealing. White soon began selling the new product under the name "Yucatan" in his own candy store and to local merchants. In 1890, he established and was the first president of the AMERICAN CHICLE CO.; he became known as the chewing-gum king of America. White put Dr. EDWIN E. BEEMAN's pepsin into his gum to create Beeman's Pepsin Gum. By 1893, the company had sold over 150 million sticks of gum. During the 1880s, American Chicle built a 4-story gum factory at W. 51st and Detroit Ave.; much of this structure remained standing until 1968.

White was also interested in politics. He moved to W. Cleveland and was elected its mayor in 1889. In 1892, he accepted the Republican nomination for Congress and was elected to represent the 20th district in the U.S. House of Representatives. In 1894, White declined reelection and returned to business. As American Chicle prospered, White's personal tastes became extravagant. In 1889, he purchased 455 acres at Lorain and Wooster roads, which he called "Two Minute Villa," for a stock farm and racetrack; that same year, he built Thornwood, a 52-room mansion at Lake Ave. and W. 110th St. Thornwood was a showplace for paintings, tapestries, Oriental rugs, and antique and imported furnishings. He also owned a yacht, the *Say When*. He was noted for giving Ziegfeld Follies queen Anna Held a $120,000 diamond necklace. Some of White's paintings are now located in the CLEVELAND MUSEUM OF ART. White divorced his first wife, Ellen, the daughter of an Ontario welldigger, on 2 Oct. 1906; the next day, he married divorcee Helen Sheldon. The two moved to Riverside Dr. in New York. Probably in 1916, White became penniless after business difficulties, and he was removed as president of American Chicle by his associates. Four years later, White was again the "gum king" with the prosperous Wm. J. White Chicle Co. in Niagara Falls. His second fortune was lost because of litigation with his original company. He returned to Cleveland in 1922, penniless again, but trying to regain his former stature. He built a new factory at Madison and W. 112th. In Jan. 1923, White injured himself when he slipped on a sidewalk on W. 110th St.; he never recovered from his injuries and died a few weeks later. He is buried in LAKE VIEW CEMETERY.

**WHITE CHARITABLE TRUST.** *See* **THOMAS E. WHITE CHARITABLE TRUST**

**WHITE CITY** was an amusement park located on Lake Erie at E. 104th St. Established in 1900, it was first known as "Manhattan Beach." The name was changed to White City soon afterward. The former manager of Euclid Beach Park was the owner of Manhattan Beach. Among the park's attractions were Bonavita the lion trainer and Madame Morelli the leopard trainer. The amusement park burned on 26 May 1906, and later in 1907 it was severely damaged by wind and rainstorms. It was closed soon afterward.

**WHITE CONSOLIDATED INDUSTRIES** was founded by THOS. H. WHITE. Armed with a sewing-machine patent, White came to Cleveland to be closer to his potential market and his suppliers and set up the White Mfg. Co. with $350 capital in 1866. Ten years later, he changed the name to the White Sewing Machine Co.; in a 5-story factory on Canal St. with 600 employees, a White Rotary Bobbin sewing machine was made every 4 minutes. By 1878, sales were $2.5 million. Under the influence of White's sons, ROLLIN, Windsor, and Walter, the company diversified; by 1903, White made automatic lathes, screw machines, roller skates, bicycles, kerosene lamps, and White cars and trucks. Thos. White thought the car was a passing fancy that the company should not produce; his sons thought otherwise. In 1906, the sons split off from their father as the White Motor Car Co. (see WHITE MOTOR CORP.), and White Sewing Machine again concentrated on its original product. In 1924, White assured a steady demand for its product by contracting with Sears, Roebuck & Co. to

supply their private-label machines, and in the following 2 years, it acquired the Domestic Sewing Machine Co., the King Sewing Machine Co., and the Theodore Kundtz Co. White moved into the Kundtz plant at 2120 Elm, where it remained until 1949, when it moved into a new plant and headquarters at 11770 Berea Rd. This facility was designed to permit straight-line production. White could then produce 2,000 machines a day. Ironically, White improved its production at a time when imported sewing machines began to flood the U.S. market. Though sales averaged nearly $20 million a year in 1954, White was suffering the effects of being a one-product company in a changing industry.

The company was revolutionized in 1956 when 3 executives from the White Motor Co. came to White Sewing Machine. Dubbed the "Flying Squadron," the three, led by Edward Reddig, instituted a program of ruthless cost-cutting, analysis, merging, and reorganization. Recognizing that the domestic sewing-machine business was dying, especially after Sears (40% of White's business) gave its manufacturing to the Japanese, Reddig vacated the main plant, cut production, fired a third of the employees, and reorganized the sewing-machine business as an import business. While Singer, the number-one manufacturer, fought for import restrictions, White arranged to have machines made abroad to its specifications. Formerly the number-two manufacturer, White became (to Sears) the number-two importer. Reddig reoriented White's manufacturing strength to other products and aimed for diversity. He acquired a small appliance manufacturer, the Apex Electrical Mfg. Co., and several industrial supply houses, including Strong, Carlisle & Hammond of Cleveland (which White held until 1985), its subsidiary, the H. P. Weller Co., and Boyer Campbell. Among the major appliance acquisitions under Reddig were Tessler Industries of Cleveland, an importer (1964); Standard Sewing (1965); the HUPP CORP. (1967); the Blaw-Knox Co. (1968); the Franklin Appliance Div. of Studebaker (1967); the Kelvinator Appliance Div. of American Motors (1968); and the appliance division of Westinghouse (1975). Other major purchases included Murray W. Sales & Co. (1960); Leland-Gifford (1965); the White Machine Works (1966); and the Lees-Bradner Co. of Cleveland (1967). In planning acquisitions, Reddig developed a formula for success: buy a faltering company at book value and turn it around by slashing overhead and enforcing stringent cost controls. His purchases created a White that was profitable, diversified, and integrated in the sense of having a complementary product line. To reflect the company's comprehensive line of household appliances, tools, valves, and machinery, the corporate name was changed to White Consolidated Industries in 1964.

The former White Motor Corp. executives of White Consolidated proposed a merger with WMC in 1970 and in 1976. The 1970 merger was prevented by the Justice Dept. on the grounds that the new corporation would have a monopoly in the farm market, as White Consolidated's Allis-Chalmers division controlled 22% of the market, while White Motor controlled 15%. WCI tried to sell its Allis-Chalmers stock (and eventually did so at a loss), but not before merger negotiations with WMC were abandoned. By 1976, WMC was failing badly, and the Justice Dept. assured WCI executives it would not oppose the merger. Unconvinced and unable to get satisfactory financing, the 11 nonmanaging directors voted down the merger 11–5, to the chagrin of Reddig, who was hospitalized and unable to engage in last-minute persuasion. When Reddig retired in 1976, he was replaced by a management team led by Roy Holdt. White continued its policy of judicious acquisition and streamlined operations, with more emphasis on marketing, more concern with stockholder relations, and a new emphasis on civic involvement. The company acquired several major appliance competitors (Philco, the Ford Appliance Div. line, in 1977 and Frigidaire from GM in 1979), as well as tool companies such as the Sunstrand Corp. (1977) and the American Tool Co. (1980). In the years 1975–85, White sales increased from $1.2 billion to more than $2 billion.

In 1985, White Consolidated Industries had 3 divisions. The Home Prods. Div. accounted for 76.8% of sales; it manufactured such brand names as Kelvinator, Gibson, Hamilton, Frigidaire, Bendix, Philco, and White-Westinghouse, and distributed the Swedish-made Elna sewing machine. Its machine and metal-castings division (12.1% of sales) produced machine tools, graphic-arts machinery, and equipment for the steel industry. Its general industrial and construction equipment division produced asphalt pavers, road wideners, food- and chemical-processing machinery, industrial refrigeration, and valve controls. With its headquarters on Berea Rd., White operated in 22 states, Canada, Mexico, Europe, and the Far East and employed 23,000 people. White Consolidated signed an agreement to merge with AB Electrolux of Sweden in Mar. 1986.

The **WHITE MOTOR CORPORATION** was created out of the White Sewing Machine Co. (see WHITE CONSOLIDATED INDUSTRIES), begun by THOS. H. WHITE in 1876. One of White's sons, ROLLIN, invented the auto flash boiler in 1899, and with the aid of his 2 brothers, Windsor and Walter, he enhanced the company's line with trucks and the White Steamer in 1900. Between 1902–06, White vehicles won many prizes in cross-country competitions in the U.S. and in reliability trials in Europe. Though White outsold its nearest auto competitor 2 to 1, Thos. White dismissed the importance of the car, which led his sons to organize the White Motor Car Co. across the street from their father's enterprise on Canal St. in the Flats in 1906. In 1909, the company made its first vehicle under its own name. Cars led sales, but in WORLD WAR I, the company shifted to trucks; it stayed with the product after the war, becoming the number-one maker of trucks and custom vehicles.

During the Depression, sales plummeted, which led White to merge with Studebaker in 1932. Two years later, Studebaker was reorganized, and White emerged independent as the White Motor Corp. Under Robt. Black, the company became a major producer of heavy-duty trucks and buses. During WORLD WAR II, production facilities at the plant at 842 E. 79th St. were converted to make scout cars, half-tracks, tank destroyers, and personnel carriers; to maintain its prewar business, the company set up a program to service old trucks and buses until customers could buy new equipment after the war. In addition, it devoted itself to postwar production planning and market analysis, which proved wise as major auto manufacturers entered the light-truck field in the late 1940s. To prevent the failure that had consumed some 1,800 other truck companies nationwide (and 85 other car and truck makers in Cleveland), Pres. Black and later CEO and chairman John Nevin Bauman led the company into the heavy-duty-vehicle field. In an era before acquisitions were common, White bought a position of leadership in both the heavy-truck and the farm-equipment fields. By purchase of small truck makers such as Auto Car (1953), Reo Motors (1957), and the Diamond T Motor Car Co. (1958) and small farm-machinery companies such as the Oliver Corp. (1960) (see CLETRAC), Cockshutt Farm Equipment, Ltd., of Canada (1960), and Motec Industries (1960), it increased sales from $130 million in 1950 to $770 million in 1967.

While the mergers produced growth, they did not reflect sound management. The result was that the company could not make inroads in any market because it lacked integration in its product lines, consolidated leadership, and corporatewide planning. To get into the off-road-truck area, for example, White bought Euclid, Inc., the hauler division of General Motors, and hoped to increase its market share from 35 to 50% before 1972, when GM could get back into the business after a Justice Dept. ban expired. Realizing that the competition had the advantage since they made their own engines, White tried unsuccessfully to merge with its major diesel supplier, the Cummins Engine Co., and later tried to produce its own engines in an ill-conceived venture that left the corporation with a useless plant in Canton and its prior level of dependence on Cummins. In 1970, White negotiated a merger with White Consolidated Industries, which had a reputation for revitalizing insolvent companies through efficient management. At the time of the proposed merger, White Consolidated was embroiled in a merger fight with Allis-Chalmers, a farm-machinery maker; as a result, the Justice Dept. prohibited the merger, as White Motors had heavy farm-equipment holdings. White Motors then sought a new chief executive who could stop the company's weekly loss of $.5 million, and its falling position in a truck market slowed by recession and a farm market that was dying. The new executive, Semon "Bunkie" Knudsen, a former GM executive at Pontiac and a short-term president of Ford, was skilled in management and engineering. He tightened management, made internal reorganizations, and arranged a $290 million line of credit. Aware that White production differed from Detroit's standardized product, he capitalized on the custom nature of big trucks by offering well-engineered, high-style cabs. Though the company showed a $20 million profit in 1973, his leadership still could not counteract years of mismanagement coupled with changes in the industry, inflation, and recession.

To prevent an inevitable bankruptcy, Knudsen tried to salvage the company by selling off ⅓ of its assets, including the profitable Euclid, Inc., hauler operation. He moved headquarters from Erieview Plaza in downtown Cleveland to Eastlake, and then to Farmington Hills, Mich., and cut employment. By 1978, White announced that it was moving its truck production from its 65-year-old E. 79th St. plant to Virginia, and converting the local plant to parts fabrication. Meanwhile, it sought buyers for its truck operation. It entered into negotiations with Volvo, which resulted in an agreement that Volvo would buy all of White's truck-producing plants except the Cleveland plant (because of its age and its large pension fund liability). In Sept. 1980, the company filed for bankruptcy. Between then and Dec. 1981, it lost $311 million. Despite efforts by the GREATER CLEVELAND GROWTH ASSOC. to keep the Cleveland plant open by negotiating with Volvo, the new company was not interested, and White had to make a pension and benefit settlement with the workers. There was much bitterness among the local long-term employees directed toward White, Volvo, and the UAW over both the plant closing and the retirement arrangements. After a prolonged bankruptcy proceeding, the White Motor Corp. ceased to exist in 1985.

**WHITTLESEY, CHARLES W.** (4 Oct. 1808–17 Oct. 1886), was a noted economic geologist, archeologist, soldier, author, and historian. Whittlesey was born in Southington, Conn., the son of Asaph and Vesta Hart Whittlesey. His family moved to Tallmadge, Ohio, in 1813, where he attended school and worked on his father's farm. He entered West Point in 1827, graduating in 1831. Following graduation, he was stationed at Mackinaw, Ft. Gratiot, and Green Bay, Wis., as a 2d lieutenant in the 5th U.S. Infantry. He later served in the Black Hawk War (1833). Whittlesey resigned his commission and came to Cleveland, where he practiced law until 1837 and served as owner and editor of the *CLEVELAND DAILY GAZETTE* and the *CLEVELAND HERALD & GAZETTE*. Following that, he began working extensively as a geologist. He was appointed assistant geologist of Ohio and in that capacity helped conduct the first geological survey (known as the Mather Survey) in the state. During the next 20 years, Whittlesey participated in or led a number of important surveys, including those of iron and copper ranges in Michigan (1845), the Whitney Survey of Lake Superior and the Upper Mississippi (1847–51), and the "Hall" Survey of Wisconsin (1858–61). He also pursued various archeological explorations at this time, becoming one of the principal investigators of ancient Indian earthworks throughout the state of Ohio.

Following the outbreak of the CIVIL WAR, Whittlesey was appointed assistant quartermaster general by Gov. Dennison. Later, as colonel in the 20th Ohio Volunteer Infantry, he planned and constructed fortifications at Covington, Ky., for the defense of Cincinnati, Ohio. He later commanded a brigade at Ft. Donelson and participated in the Battle of Shiloh in 1862. Whittlesey resigned his commission in Apr. 1862 because of ill health and returned to his geological work. During the postwar years, he became very active as a historian. In 1867 he published *Early History of Cleveland*. In that year, he also helped found the WESTERN RESERVE HISTORICAL SOCIETY, serving as its first president until 1885. In 1869 he published *Contributions to the Geology of Ohio*, one of more than 200 articles, tracts, essays, and reports that he produced during his lifetime, many of which are still invaluable for understanding the prehistory of the Western Reserve. Whittlesey died at his home on Euclid Ave. in 1886. He had married Mary E. Morgan of Oswego, N.Y., in 1858.

Charles Whittlesey Papers, WRHS.

**WHITTLESEY, ELISHA** (19 Oct. 1783–7 Jan. 1863), was a lawyer and politician who served in Congress and as comptroller of the U.S. Treasury. He was a typical conservative state leader of the 19th century. Whittlesey was born in Litchfield County, Conn. Spending his boyhood on his father's farm, he attended rural schools in Salisbury and completed his education in Danbury, where his older brother, Matthew, practiced law. There he met and married Polly Mygatt. Deciding upon a legal career, Whittlesey moved to the village of Canfield in the southeast corner of the WESTERN RESERVE. Soon after reaching Canfield, he was appointed prosecuting attorney for the entire Western Reserve. He served from 1807–23, except during the WAR OF 1812, when he served as an officer and private secretary to Gen. Wm. Henry Harrison. As a lawyer, Whittlesey was the senior partner with Eben Newton in the area's best-known partnership, the proprietor of a 1-room law school, and an early leader of the Ohio bar. As a circuit lawyer specializing in land cases, he earned a reputation for honesty and integrity that brought him considerable business. As a businessman, Whittlesey was only moderately successful, earning a small fortune by slow, steady work. His major interests were handling eastern capital invested in Ohio lands and holding stock in a number of Ohio banks. While speculating in a Maumee Valley land project, he lost a considerable sum in the Panic of 1837. Whittlesey's career in elective office began in 1820 with 2 terms in the Ohio general assembly. Elected to Congress for 8 terms, first as

a Natl. Republican, then later as a Whig, he served from 1 Dec. 1823 until 9 July 1838, when he resigned in favor of Joshua Giddings. Primarily concerned with economic matters affecting the growth of Ohio, Congressman Whittlesey proved a good logician, efficiently performing the unnoticed tasks of committee work and behind-the-scenes politicking. Nicknamed "watchdog of the Treasury," he was recognized as an example of official integrity in government. As a party leader, Whittlesey acted as a conciliator in party rivalries. Active in the American Colonization Society, he believed in expatriation as the answer to the slavery problem. After 1848, Whittlesey served the Taylor, Fillmore, Pierce, and Lincoln administrations as comptroller of the Treasury.

Elisha Whittlesey Papers, WRHS.

*WIADOMOSCI CODZIENNE* (Polish Daily News) was founded in 1914 by S. A. Dangel and Paul Kurdziel. Cleveland's first Polish daily, it was an outgrowth of the weekly *Narodowiec* (Nationalist), 1909–14. Coming under the sole control of Kurdziel by 1921, it was edited by Thos. Siemradski from 1918–37. Under the intellectual Siemradski, the *Wiadomosci* advanced a moderately freethinking viewpoint against the pro-Catholic stance of a rival daily, *MONITOR CLEVELANDSKI*, which it finally absorbed in 1938. It also supported the socialist program of Poland's Joseph Pilsudski and early denounced Germany's Hitler as a "madman and gangster." After the death of Kurdziel in 1940, the *Wiadomosci* passed into the hands of his children. It was published by August J. Kurdziel and edited by Zygmunt Dybowski. In its pages could be found a Polish-speaking "Tarzan" comic strip, as well as a column written by staff members under the pseudonymous byline of "Gwizdafski." Produced in its own plant at 1017 Fairfield Ave., the paper was sold primarily over the counters of stores in Polish neighborhoods. Despite a circulation of 23,183, the *Wiadomosci Codzienne* suspended publication on 15 Oct. 1966, leaving Ohio's Poles without a daily for the first time in over 50 years. Its demise was attributed to the difficulty of recruiting bilingual personnel, as well as to high costs.

**WICKHAM, GERTRUDE VAN RENSSELAER** (20 May 1844–18 Mar. 1930), was a journalist, author, and local historian. She was the first woman to hold an editorial position on a Cleveland newspaper. Wickham was born in Huron and attended Cleveland and Buffalo public schools. She married Capt. Samuel Wickham, of Huron, in 1864. After his death in 1869, Wickham became a principal (of the lower grades) at Huron High School; some accounts claim that she was the first woman to hold such a position in an Ohio public school. She quit after a few years. For the next 3 years, Wickham and her daughter lived on income from her husband's estate. Her entry into journalism resulted from a letter she wrote to the *SUNDAY POST*. The letter was published, drawing a positive public response, and Wickham was asked to contribute on a weekly basis. When the paper folded in 1878, she was picked up by the *CLEVELAND HERALD*. Despite the reluctance of the editors to hire a woman, Wickham was able to persuade them by suggesting that she write a fashion column; such a column, she pointed out, would bring more women into Cleveland (from the nearby rural areas) to shop, and subsequently attract more advertisers to the *Herald*.

The success of Wickham's column led to the creation of a women's department. Her column gradually became more family-oriented. She was also sent to other cities to cover national events. Among these, she was sent to Chicago to cover that city's reception of former president

Grant's return from his world tour. In 1881, Wickham joined the editorial staff of the *CLEVELAND LEADER* when the *Herald* was merged into that paper. Her columns grew increasingly more oriented toward women and children, especially those with needy backgrounds. As a regular feature, she used letters in her column from indigent women and underprivileged children. Concern for the former eventually led her to establish the Woman's Repository (later known as the Woman's Exchange), a place where destitute women could sell their handicrafts. Wickham left the *Leader* in 1884 because of poor health. She continued, however, to provide the Cleveland newspapers with occasional articles and short stories. In 1886 she was one of the charter members of the Women's Press Club (later the CLEVELAND WRITERS' CLUB). In the 1890s, her interests turned to the history of the WESTERN RESERVE. In 1896 she was chosen by the Cleveland Centennial Commission to be historian of the women's department. Her research eventually led to the publication of a book, *Pioneer Women of the Western Reserve*, followed by another book, *Pioneer Families of the Western Reserve*. Wickham's later years, plagued by poor health, were spent collecting important genealogical information on women of the Western Reserve. She was also a prominent member of the Cleveland chapter of the Daughters of the American Revolution.

**WIDDER, MILTON "MILT"** (20 Nov. 1907–15 Dec. 1985), the paragon of Cleveland's gossip columnists, was born in Berlin, Germany, and raised in Hungary. He came to the U.S. with his parents in 1920, graduating from Cleveland Hts. High School and Adelbert College. Although he briefly studied law, he began work as a copy boy for the *CLEVELAND PRESS* in 1926. For 20 years, Widder worked various beats for the *Press*, ranging from police reporting to real-estate news. For 4 years he filled in for the absent ARTHUR LOESSER as the paper's music critic. At the instigation of associate editor Norman Shaw in 1946, Widder was then assigned to do the *Press*'s gossip column. During the next quarter-century, he made his "Sights and Sounds" column into a local institution. Competition among press agents for a "mention" became so intense that Widder needed 2 telephones on his desk to handle the traffic. A "Halo of the Week" award from Widder was one of the community's highest accolades for meritorious public service. Widder's chiding of the Cleveland Trust Co. about the grimy appearance of its headquarters building at Euclid and E. 9th St. became so familiar that the sandblasting, when it came, qualified as a media event. His diet tips were so in demand that the *Press* reprinted them as the "Milt Widder Diet" and distributed more than a million copies. Widder could find news as well as make it. He was the first in the nation to report on the marriage breakup of Howard Hughes and actress Jean Peters. *Press* editors often killed items from his column because they "scooped" stories planned for the front page. A member of the CITY CLUB for over 40 years, Widder was its president in 1969 and a veteran performer in its ANVIL REVUE. In 1932 he married Dorothy Louise Stone, who died in 1980. They had 3 sons—James, John, and Robt. Andrew—and a daughter, Mrs. Barbara Beazle. Failing vision and other health problems forced his retirement from the *Press* in 1972. He died in Cleveland at age 78.

**WIGGERS, CARL JOHN** (28 May 1883–28 Apr. 1963), taught physiology at the Western Reserve University Medical School. Famous for his work in heart and blood-pressure research, he helped to make Cleveland a cardiovascular research center. Wiggers was born in Davenport, Iowa, to George and Margret Kuendal Wiggers. He was educated in the Davenport public schools. He graduated from the University of Michigan with the M.D. degree in 1906 and attended the Institute of Physiology at the University of Munich. He served as an instructor of physiology at the University of Michigan, 1906–11, and as an assistant professor at the Cornell University Medical School, 1911–18. From 1918–53, he was professor and chairman of the Dept. of Physiology at the WRU Medical School. Inspired by the work of Otto Frank at the Institute of Physiology in Munich, Wiggers achieved world recognition for his development of a new method of registering heart and blood pressure; finding the effects of low oxygen pressure on circulation; discovering the effects of valve defects on the functioning of the heart; his studies of the effects of shock; and his pioneering efforts along with Dr. CLAUDE BECK and other associates in the techniques of resuscitation from death in the operating room. He inspired over 100 of his students to forsake private practice to enter medical research. After retiring as professor emeritus in 1953, Wiggers joined the Frank Bunts Institute of the CLEVELAND CLINIC FOUNDATION. Working in medical education, he took part in postgraduate training for student doctors by the institute and in medical and scientific seminars. Wiggers was the first editor of the medical journal *Circulation Research* and authored 7 books and over 300 articles in medical and scientific journals. In 1952, he was presented the Gold Heart Award from the American Heart Assoc. In 1954 he received the Modern Medicine Award, and in 1955 he was given the Albert Lasker Award for distinguished research in cardiovascular research. Wiggers married Minnie E. Berry on 17 Aug. 1907. The Wiggerses had 2 sons, Harold and Raymond.

**WILCOX, FRANK NELSON** (3 Oct. 1887–17 Apr. 1964), was a noted painter, printmaker, and teacher. He was most famous for his watercolors. Wilcox was a native Clevelander. He studied at the Cleveland School of Art with HENRY G. KELLER and FREDERICK C. GOTTWALD, graduating in 1910, then went on to Paris and Europe for more training. In 1913 he began a 40-year teaching career at the CLEVELAND INSTITUTE OF ART. He also taught briefly at the JOHN HUNTINGTON POLYTECHNIC INSTITUTE and BALDWIN-WALLACE COLLEGE. He was founder and past president of the CLEVELAND SOCIETY OF ARTISTS, a member of the American Watercolor Society and the Philadelphia Watercolor Club, and an honorary member of the Artists & Craftsmen Assoc. of Cleveland. Besides garnering 35 awards from the May Show, Wilcox was given the 1920 Penton Medal for sustained excellence. His many other medals were awarded for work in etching, industrial paintings, and oil landscapes. His work can be found in the CLEVELAND MUSEUM OF ART and in museums in Toledo and San Diego. Wilcox was a traditional watercolor painter; his works were a wet blending of restful, romantic moods. He enjoyed working with rural Ohio scenery, the Rocky Mts., and Indian subjects. Wilcox was also a student of Ohio history. He wrote and illustrated *Ohio Indian Trails* in 1933. *Weather Wisdom*, a 1949 limited edition of 24 prints executed by the silkscreen process, was a portfolio illustrating the seasonal moods of nature. He next contributed technical notes to *Seascapes and Landscapes in Watercolor* by Watson Guptill. Wilcox married artist Florence Bard.

**WILEY, AQUILA** (20 Feb. 1835–5 June 1913), was a federal volunteer Army officer who played a central role in Cleveland's military history during the CIVIL WAR. Wiley was born in Mechanicsburg, Pa. He settled in Wooster, Ohio, in 1852. When the Civil War broke out, he was commissioned a 1st lieutenant in the 16th Ohio Volunteer Infantry on 20 Apr. 1861 for 3 months' service. He was promoted to captain on 4 May 1861 and mustered out of service on 18 Aug. 1861. Appointed captain of Co. C, 41st OVI, on 19 Sept. 1861, Wiley trained at Camp Wood in Cleveland. At the Battle of Shiloh he was seriously wounded in the left leg on 7 Apr. 1862. He recovered and was promoted to major on 22 June and to lieutenant colonel on 6 Dec. Advanced to colonel of the 41st, he led the regiment at the Battle of Missionary Ridge on 25 Nov. 1863 and was wounded again in the left leg, seriously enough to necessitate amputation above the knee. Although unfit for full field duty, he was appointed commandant of Camp Cleveland and returned to that city to assume his new responsibilities on 20 Apr. 1864. He successfully oversaw the rendezvous and training of several new infantry regiments by 18 May and received the praise of the adjutant general of Ohio for his efforts. He received a medical discharge on 7 June and left Camp Cleveland on 16 June to return to Wooster. Appointed captain in the 8th Regiment, Veteran Reserve Corps, on 25 Mar. 1865, Wiley rose to the rank of major on 27 Apr. 1865; assigned chief mustering officer at Cleveland, he arrived at Camp Cleveland on 22 May. He served in the dual capacity as provost marshal of the 18th Provost Marshal District until 31 July. He administered the discharge of approximately 11,654 Union troops at Camp Cleveland. Between the end of July and 25 Sept., Wiley served as provost marshal until he was ordered back to the 8th Regiment, then at Cairo, Ill., where he arrived on 24 Oct. Discharged after 18 Nov. 1865, he later was awarded a brevet brigadier generalship, U.S. Volunteers, for his service. Returning to Wooster, Wiley practiced law and served 1 term as probate judge in Wayne County. He was nominated for Congress in 1878. His opponent was Wm. McKinley. A Baptist, he married in 1870 and raised a son and a daughter. He was a member of the Ohio commandery of the Military Order of the Loyal Legion of the U.S.

The **WILKINS EXPEDITION,** led by British major John Wilkins in Nov. 1763, has frequently been erroneously identified as having foundered off ROCKY RIVER and Lakewood Park. Actually, this expedition, which was intended to relieve Ft. Detroit under siege by the Indians of Pontiac's Rebellion, followed the north shore and foundered off Pointe-aux-Pins, Canada, with the loss of 70 men, 20 bateaux, and much supplies and ammunition. This Canadian location is confirmed in the journal of Capt. John Montresor and overrides previous conjecture based on circumstantial evidence, mainly the large number of artifacts found near Rocky River from the 1764 Bradstreet Disaster and the concept of Pointe-aux-Pins being a generic description rather than a specific geographic location.

Marsalek, Daniel E., "The Wilkins Expedition Disaster Site Debate" *Inland Seas Magazine* (1983).
Webster, J. C., *Life of John Montresor* (1928).

**WILLARD, ARCHIBALD MACNEAL** (22 Aug. 1836–11 Oct. 1918), was a prominent American artist who is best remembered for his well-known patriotic painting *SPIRIT OF '76*. Willard was born in BEDFORD, Ohio, the 4th of 7 children of Rev. Samuel R. Willard, a fundamentalist preacher, and his wife, Catherine. The family moved frequently during the early years of Willard's childhood but settled permanently in Wellington, Ohio, in 1855. Willard taught himself to draw. In the early 1860s, he apprenticed himself to E. S. Tripp, a local decorative artist, wheelwright, and wagonmaker, where he began painting vignettes on

wagons and carriages. His work became so well known that he was also asked to paint portraits of several Wellington children and assisted furniture makers with painted designs, as well. In 1863, Willard enlisted as a color sergeant in the 86th Ohio Volunteer Infantry; he served with this unit in Kentucky and Tennessee until Feb. 1864. He returned to Wellington, married Nellie S. Challacombe, and in the same year made contact with Cleveland art dealer JAS. F. RYDER, who photographed and printed several of Willard's Civil War sketches. In 1865 Willard reenlisted, this time in the 176th OVI as a private, and served until June 1865.

Willard returned to Wellington and his work at the Tripp wagon factory. A comical painting he did of his 3 children and the family dog, entitled *Pluck*, was the turning point in his artistic career. At the urging of friends, he sent the painting to Ryder in Cleveland, who displayed it and a second, similar work entitled *Pluck II* in his display window. The paintings were so popular that Ryder had 10,000 pairs of chromolithographs made of them, which he sold for $10 a set. In 1873, Willard went with Ryder to New York for a few weeks and there had his only formal training in painting, with J. O. Eaton. In 1875, at Ryder's request, he began painting a comical 4th of July subject to be made into chromolithographs and sold at the centennial celebration the following year. Because of his father's death in early 1876, Ryder changed the subject of his painting to a more serious work and produced the famous *Spirit of '76*. It was during the creation of this work that he and his family moved to Cleveland and he set up his studio. Willard continued to paint through the remainder of his life and was a prominent force in the development of an artists' colony in Cleveland. He was a founding member and principal director of the ART CLUB, which later developed into the Academy of Art. He instructed students in portraiture and landscape, oil painting, and life drawing classes.

Gordon, Willard F., *"The Spirit of '76": An American Portrait* (1976).

The **WILLARD STORAGE BATTERY COMPANY,** an early leader in the development and manufacture of batteries for automobiles, was founded by Theodore A. Willard. A native of Minnesota, Willard came to Cleveland in 1896 from Norwalk, Ohio, where in 1892 he had formed a battery-manufacturing company in partnership with Dr. Edwin N. Hawley. The Willard Electric & Battery Co. operated a shop at 33 Sheriff (E. 4th) St. in Cleveland in 1896, moving to 49 Wood (E. 3rd) St. the following year. Willard took on jewelers John F. Sipe and Carlton C. Sigler as partners from 1898–1901, but he reorganized the company as the Willard Storage Battery Co. in 1902. The company produced batteries for a variety of uses: by dentists and physicians, in Edison phonographs, and in lighting railroad cars. Willard made his first battery for automobile ignition in 1908; in 1910 the company produced automobile batteries and electric lighting accessories, which it sold to individual automobile owners, unable to convince automobile manufacturers of the viability of these products until 1912. Business grew quickly: after several temporary locations, the company built a 15-acre plant at 274 E. 131st St. in 1915, and by 1918 Willard employed 300 people and had contracts to supply batteries to 85% of the automobile factories in the U.S.

The company grew with the automobile industry and soon began to experiment with other endeavors. After several years of experimental broadcasting, Willard bought Goodyear's radio station WEAR and combined it with its own operation to create WTAM, a 1,500-watt clear-channel radio station in Cleveland, in 1923. In Nov. 1930, Willard was described as the "largest automobile storage battery company in the world," with more than 2,500 employees, additional plants in Toronto and Los Angeles, and distributors in 89 countries. Willard produced batteries for submarines during WORLD WAR II and was a pioneer in the development of small, hand-sized batteries. Despite the founder's death in 1943, the company continued to grow, adding plants in Dallas and Memphis by the company's 50th anniversary in 1952. But employment had fallen to 1,500 by 1952, and the company had become a subsidiary of the Electric Storage Battery Co. of Philadelphia; by 1956 it was a division of that company. In Aug. 1959, Electric Storage Battery announced plans to close its Cleveland manufacturing operations because the plant was too large and could not be adapted to new technology. By 1961, the E. 131st St. plant was vacant, and all that remained of the Willard Storage Battery Co. in Cleveland were offices located at 1717 E. 9th St.

**WILLETT STREET CEMETERY,** located on Cleveland's near west side, is the oldest Jewish cemetery in the city. The Israelitic Society of Cleveland, the community's first congregation, purchased the land for the cemetery on 7 July 1840. The burial ground is now jointly administered by ANSHE CHESED CONGREGATION and the TEMPLE. A high mortality rate during the mid-19th century and the desire for proper Jewish burial were concerns in all fledgling American Jewish communities. In many cities and towns, purchase of cemetery sites preceded establishment of a congregation, although in Cleveland the congregation was formed first. In Apr. 1840, the Israelitic Society requested the city council's permission to purchase a portion of the ERIE ST. CEMETERY, but the request was denied. Three months later, an acre of land at the junction of Willett St. (now Fulton Rd.) and Monroe St. in OHIO CITY was purchased for $100 from JOSIAH BARBER. The cemetery was given its name because it fronted on Willett St. The first interment, of a man named Kanweiler, occurred within a month of the purchase. The Israelitic Society and Anshe Chesed merged in 1845, and administration of the cemetery fell to the newly organized congregation. In 1850, the recently established congregation Tifereth Israel requested to share burial privileges in exchange for sharing maintenance costs. However, an agreement was never reached. Tifereth Israel bought approximately half an acre of land adjoining the Willett St. Cemetery in 1853. A picket fence separated the sections owned by the respective congregations. A second attempt at consolidating the cemeteries failed in 1869. In 1887, Tifereth Israel purchased more than 20 acres fronting Mayfield Rd. in CLEVELAND HTS. for a cemetery. It was named the Mayfield Cemetery. In 1890, the two congregations established the United Jewish Cemeteries, providing for joint ownership of Mayfield Cemetery and Willett St. Many of Cleveland's prominent Jewish pioneers are buried in the Willett St. Cemetery. Among them are SIMSON THORMAN, the city's first permanent Jewish resident; Isaac Hoffman, one of the group of immigrants arriving from Unsleban, Bavaria, in 1839; GUSTAVUS M. COHEN, chazan at Anshe Chesed in the 1860s and 1870s; Rabbi Aaron Hahn of Tifereth Israel; and author MARTHA WOLFENSTEIN.

**WILLEY, JOHN WHEELOCK** (1797–9 July 1841), was Cleveland's first mayor, a prominent jurist, and a land developer who played a part in the early battles between Cleveland and its west side rival, OHIO CITY. Born in New Hampshire, Willey was educated at Dartmouth; after studying law in New York, he was admitted to the bar

there. In 1822 he came to Cleveland. Though he was among the first lawyers in town, the competition was already considerable, which necessitated his aggressive striving for clients. He became known as a witty, sharp debater, a prowess that won him 3 years in the state house of representatives (1827–30) and 3 in the state senate (1830–32) as a Jacksonian Democrat. After leaving public office, he set up a private law practice but became involved in village politics. When Cleveland was chartered as a city in 1836, he became its first mayor, serving 2 terms (1836–37, 1837–38). Willey was responsible for writing the municipal charter as well as many of the original laws and ordinances. He also served on the first board of school managers that planned public education in the city.

Willey was intimately tied to the city of Cleveland but also speculated in real estate in Ohio City. With Jas. Clark and others, he bought a section of the FLATS near the river bend on the east side and planned to transform it into Cleveland Centre, a business and residential district. Next they bought land in the southeast section of Ohio City opposite Columbus St. in Cleveland, named it Willeyville, and built a bridge connecting the 2 sections of Columbus St. This thoroughfare diverted Cleveland-bound traffic that previously had traveled through the WEST SIDE MARKET of Ohio City to the Detroit St. Bridge into Cleveland to the new Willeyville area, and then to Cleveland Centre and CENTRAL MARKET. CLEVELAND CITY COUNCIL, allegedly with the support of Mayor Willey, legislated the removal of the Cleveland section of the Detroit St. Bridge. This action aggravated Ohio City residents and led to the "Bridge War." (see COLUMBUS ST. BRIDGE). Willey was also involved in the proposed construction of the Cleveland-Columbus-Cinncinati and Cleveland, Warren & Pittsburgh railroad lines. He was president of the latter and a member of the board of directors of the early ventures. In 1840, Willey was appointed to serve as presiding judge of the 14th Judicial District. In his short term of service before his death, he developed a reputation as a strong jurist, based on his analytical skills and sound, prompt decisions delivered with humor and flair. Willey married Laura Maria Higby in 1829. They had no children.

The **WILLIAM BINGHAM FOUNDATION** was founded in 1955 by Elizabeth Bingham Blossom after the death of her brother, Wm. Bingham II (1879–1955), from the proceeds of his estate. Elizabeth and Wm. Bingham were the children of CHAS. W. BINGHAM, president of the Standard Tool Co. and Perry-Payne Bldg. Co. Chas. W. Bingham was a graduate of Yale, to which the family donated $1 million for a dormitory, Chas. W. Bingham Hall. Under Mrs. Blossom, wife of DUDLEY S. BLOSSOM, the foundation gave grants only to nonprofit organizations (none to individuals) in the general areas of the fine arts, education, and health and welfare. After the death of Mrs. Blossom in 1970, her estate was added to the foundation, bringing its holdings to $17 million. The foundation in 1985 was in the control of Mrs. Blossom's 7 grandchildren, whose interests have been in the direction of education, welfare, and antinuclear support. In 1983 the assets of the foundation were $14 million, with expenditures of $643,000 for 28 grants. Trustees included C. Bingham Blossom, Dudley S. Blossom III, Laurel Blossom, Benjamin Gale, Mary E. Gale, Thos. Gale, and Elizabeth B. Heffernan.

The **WILLIAM FEATHER COMPANY,** a commercial printing house, was opened in 1916 by Wm. Feather. A *CLEVELAND PRESS* reporter and contributor to *American Mercury* magazine, Feather attracted the attention of H. L. Mencken, who encouraged his literary efforts. Feather, however, pooled his savings, loans, and his wife's inheritance to start a printing company that would publish his own work while providing a steady income. Within 3 years, Feather introduced a magazine that would be syndicated as a house organ for many companies throughout the country. At the request of Karl Niebecker of the Imperial Type Metal Co. of Philadelphia, Feather designed a 24-page pocket-sized magazine that contained his own witty reflections on life within a cover especially designed for Imperial. The idea of having an out-of-house magazine with an in-house touch appealed to many other corporations, who contracted with Feather to produce and print a magazine for them. Readership of the Feather magazines soared to 250,000 by 1950. Among the earliest magazines were *Bagology* for the Chase Bag Co., *Tree-to-Trade* for the Racquette River Paper Co., and *Lab-in-the-Country* for Gregory Farm Lab. The business of the Wm. Feather Co. met immediate success, tripling within the first 5 years. On the edge of the Depression, the company had one of the largest payrolls and plants in the area, but it faced a lean dozen years in the Depression and war economy when the demand for advertising and other commercial printing slumped. Feather's syndicated magazines saved the business, and their numbers grew even in the early 1930s. In 1946, Feather turned the management of the printing business over to his son, Wm., Jr., so he could devote fuller attention to his 30 house magazines and the Wm. Feather magazine that advertised the printing business. He continued to dabble with the magazine until his death in 1981 at 91.

In anticipation of a postwar printing boom, the company under Wm. Feather, Jr., modernized its facilities in the mid-1940s to increase its capacity by 50%. By 1951, all its equipment except its relatively new monotype equipment had been replaced. The plant at 812 Huron in the CAXTON BLDG. had complete art, composition, photoengraving, press, and folding departments to produce catalogs, folders, books, broadsides, annual reports, and the house organs. Feather increased its sales 8-fold between 1946-54. To expand the geographic boundaries of Feather sales west to Chicago and New York, Wm. Feather, Jr., bought several companies between 1954-60, including the Corday, Gross Co., a printing company at 1774 E. 24th St. (1954); the Breman Typographic Co. of Pittsburgh (1956); the D. E. Robinson Co., an offset lithography and mechanical direct-mail company at 1125 Rockwell NE (1957); and the Layden-Hammell Co. of Salem, Ohio (1960). Feather also bought the Copyfier Lithograph Co., a book-printing firm at 1771 E. 24th St. (1971). The out-of-town ventures proved unsuccessful and were sold off. In 1963, Feather made Cleveland prestigious among graphic-arts centers by its purchase of a 5-color web offset press that could produce and fold 25,000 5-color sheets in an hour. The machine increased the company's output by 60% and dramatically increased its sales in northeast Ohio and out-of-town markets. The company and its 300 employees moved to a new building at 9900 Clinton in 1969. In an era when new techniques were revolutionizing printing, Feather tried to retrain its employees, but there was nearly 100% turnover in the workforce within a year. Throughout the 1970s, Feather tried to negotiate with the Graphic Arts Internatl. Union about changing work rules to permit the company to assign personnel in the rapidly changing printing industry to jobs based on qualifications, not seniority. When the union refused after 7 years of negotiations, Feather sadly announced a move of its $17 million business to a new, nonunion plant in Oberlin.

The **WILLIAM O. AND GERTRUDE L. FROHRING FOUNDATION, INC.,** was established in 1958 by Wm.

O. (1893-1959) and Gertrude L. Frohring. Wm. Frohring was born in Cleveland and studied bacteriology and dairy technology at Ohio State University. After graduating in 1915 until 1921, he worked as chief chemist for the TELLING BELLE-VERNON CO. From 1920-40 he was chairman of the SMA Corp., a research-and-development firm that produced synthetic milk products for the special problems of premature and allergic infants. He was also a special consultant to the American Home Prods. Corp., manufacturers of food, drugs, and household products. Frohring was married to Gertrude Lewis, with whom he had 4 children. The purpose of the foundation is to give to established charitable institutions concerned with health, education, and the arts in Geauga County and northern Ohio. In 1962, the Frohring Foundation joined the KULAS FOUNDATION with $355,000 to fund the Frohring Music Bldg. at Hiram College, in addition to the Frohring Art Bldg. The foundation also funded lights for the Blossom Music Ctr. parking lot. No grants are given to individuals or for deficit financing, endowment funds, scholarships and fellowships, matching gifts, or loans. In 1984, assets of the foundation were $2,404,612, with expenditures of $194,714 for 35 grants. Officers included Gertrude L., Glenn H., and Lloyd W. Frohring, Wm. W. Falsgraf, and Elaine A. Szilagyi.

**WILLIAM TAYLOR SON AND COMPANY** was one of Cleveland's leading department stores. The company initiated a retailing trend away from Superior Ave. to Euclid Ave. when 2 Scotchmen, Wm. Taylor and Thos. Kilpatrick, opened a 1-room dry-goods store, known as Taylor, Kilpatrick & Co., on the 1st floor of the Cushing Block at Public Square on 21 Apr. 1870. Taylor and Kilpatrick introduced the revolutionary principle of the 1-price system for selling foods. At first, business was totally retail, but in a few years, a wholesale department was added, with 36 salesmen dealing in clothing, furniture, and jewelry. Taylor quickly made the store a success, building a reputation for himself in the Cleveland business field. He was active in charitable affairs and quite religious: he insisted on strict Sabbath observance; curtains on the display windows were closed and advertising in the newspapers was forbidden on Sundays until 1939. In 1885, Taylor's son, John L. Taylor, joined the partnership. The following year Kilpatrick moved away, and the store assumed the name of Wm. Taylor Son & Co. After Taylor and his son died, John's wife, Sophie Strong Taylor, ably directed the store for over 40 years. The firm became a stock company in 1901. The store continued to grow, and by 1890 it occupied the entire Cushing Block. In 1907, the firm erected a new store, a 5-story building at 630 Euclid Ave. Six years later, 4 stories were added, and employment reached 1,500. In the 1930s, it further expanded its operations by acquiring the adjacent Taylor Arcade and the Clarence Bldg. In 1934, in the midst of the Depression, it completed a $500,000 modernization program and changed its name to Taylor's Dept. Store. In 1939 (when Sophie Taylor's estate was liquidated), the MAY CO. acquired a substantial interest in Taylor's. The store continued to operate independently under its own name. This acquisition was not made known until 1945, when a $2 million expansion program was completed in conjunction with Taylor's 75th anniversary. In 1958, Taylor's moved into the suburbs when it opened a branch store at the SOUTHGATE SHOPPING CTR. in MAPLE HTS. In Oct. 1961, the May Co. decided to close Taylor's because it was no longer feasible to operate 2 major competing department stores in downtown Cleveland. Taylor's officially went out of business on 16 Dec. 1961. Its Southgate store was taken over by May, and in 1964, its downtown store was remodeled into an office building.

Wallen, James, *Cleveland's Golden Story* (1920).

**WILLIAMS, EDWARD CHRISTOPHER** (11 Feb. 1871–24 Dec. 1929), was a distinguished black librarian, teacher, and scholar who laid the foundation for library collections at Western Reserve University and Howard University. Of mixed racial parentage, Williams was born in Cleveland, the son of Daniel P. and Mary Kilkary Williams. He was educated in Cleveland schools and graduated with honors from Adelbert College of WRU in 1892. After a brief stint as a stenographer, he was appointed first assistant librarian of Adelbert College, was made head librarian in 1894, and became university librarian in 1898. Williams took a leave of absence in 1899 to study library science at the New York Library School in Albany. After completing the 2-year course in 1 year, he returned to the university. While at WRU, he more than doubled the library collection and increased its quality, as well. He became a recognized expert on library organization and bibliography. Williams served on the committee that recommended the formation of a school of library science at WRU, and when the school opened in 1904, he taught courses in reference work, bibliography, public documents, and criticism and selection of books, in addition to his library duties. He was a charter member of the Ohio Library Assoc. and was chairman of the committee that drafted its constitution. Williams left Cleveland in 1909 to become principal of M St. High School in Washington, D.C. In 1916, he was appointed university librarian at Howard University. He also directed Howard's library training class, was an instructor in German, and later became head of the Dept. of Romance Languages. In 1929, he took a sabbatical leave from Howard to study for his Ph.D. at Columbia University; however, shortly after he began his studies, he died at age 58. Williams married Ethel P. Chesnutt on 26 Nov. 1902. They had a son, Charles.

**WILLIAMS, WHITING** (11 Mar. 1878–14 Apr. 1975), was an author and lecturer on labor and management problems and a corporate consultant on personnel issues and public relations. Born in Shelby, Ohio, the son of B. J. and Ida Whiting Williams, Williams received a bachelor's degree from Oberlin College in 1899 and continued his studies at the University of Berlin in 1899–1900, returning to the U.S. to study theology at the University of Chicago in 1900–01; he later managed the Bureau of University Travel (1901–04). He rejoined his alma mater as assistant to Oberlin's president (1904–12), taking time to earn a master's degree in 1909. In 1912, Williams moved to Cleveland to become the executive secretary of the Fed. for Charity & Philanthropy; as such, he oversaw the city's first unified charitable fund drive in 1913. In 1916, he joined the Equitable Life Assurance Society as a special group agent; he left in 1918 to serve as personnel director and vice-president of the Hydraulic Steel Co., a post he held for 2 years.

About 1919, Williams set out to experience and study firsthand the working conditions in various countries and the attitudes of workers toward their work. Able to speak French, German, Spanish, and Italian, he worked as a laborer in coal mines and steel plants in the U.S., Germany, France, and Great Britain between 1919–23; between 1925–38, he studied working conditions in Italy, Russia (twice), and Central and South America, and examined unemployment and Prohibition in the American Midwest and Canada. His experiences provided material and insights for lectures throughout the U.S. and Canada and for such books as *What's on the Worker's Mind, By One Who Put On*

*Coveralls to Find Out* (1920), *Full Up and Fed Up: The Worker's Mind in Crowded Britain* (1921), *Horny Hands and Hampered Elbows: The Worker's Mind in Western Europe* (1922), and *Mainsprings of Men* (1925). He authored other books and articles, as well. Williams parlayed his experiences and insights into a role as consultant on labor relations, personnel management, and public relations for a number of large businesses, including General Motors, Western Electric, and B. F. Goodrich. In 1940, he became a member of the Natl. Panel of Arbitrators. He was also active in professional organizations (the Society for the Advancement of Management, the American Management Assoc., the American Economics Assoc., and the Personnel Research Fed.) and local organizations and clubs, from the Chamber of Commerce to the UNION and CITY CLUBs. He was a trustee of both HIRAM HOUSE and the School of Art. Williams was married twice. On 5 Sept. 1906 he married Caroline Harter, who died 2 July 1938. On 4 Aug. 1941 he married Dorothy Rogers.

Whiting Williams Papers, WRHS.

**WILLIAMSON, SAMUEL** (1772–8 Sept. 1834), early settler and businessman; Samuel Williamson, Jr. (1808–14 Jan. 1884), lawyer, public official, and railroad director; and Samuel E. Williamson (1844–21 Feb. 1903), lawyer, judge, and railroad counsel, were members of 3 generations of a distinguished Cleveland family. Samuel Williamson arrived in Cleveland from Crawford County, Pa., in 1810. He built a tannery on St. Clair St., and his first home was on Water (W. 9th) St. Williamson was a trustee of the new village of Cleveland upon its formation in 1815, and he also served as associate judge of the court of common pleas. In 1816 he was one of 8 incorporators of the Bank of Lake Erie, and upon its reorganization in 1832 he became a director. Williamson's wife, Isabella, was one of the charter members of the FIRST PRESBYTERIAN CHURCH of Cleveland (Old Stone), and he was also a staunch member. Williamson built a new brick house on Euclid Ave. at Public Square in 1833, just before his death. He was buried in the ERIE ST. CEMETERY.

Samuel Williamson, Jr., was the eldest son of Samuel Williamson. He graduated from Jefferson College, Washington, Pa., in 1829. He read law in the office of SHERLOCK J. ANDREWS and was admitted to the bar in 1832. He practiced law with LEONARD CASE for 2 years and then with ALBERT G. RIDDLE for nearly 30 years. Among the public offices he held were those of county auditor, city councilman, member of the Board of Education and the Ohio legislature, and prosecuting attorney. Williamson retired from the legal profession in 1866 and was president of the Society for Savings until his death. He was a director and attorney for the Cleveland, Columbus, Cincinnati & Indianapolis Railroad, and one of the incorporators of Case School of Applied Science. Like his father, Samuel, Jr., was an active member of Old Stone Church. His wife was a prominent worker in the Cleveland Ladies Temperance Union, a local movement that resulted in the incorporation of the Women's Christian Temperance Union in 1880, which became a worldwide organization. The family moved from the old Williamson homestead on Euclid Ave. in 1872. Samuel, Jr., had 3 sons, Samuel E., Geo. T., and Jas. D.

Samuel E. Williamson was born in the old homestead on Euclid Ave. He graduated from Western Reserve College in Hudson in 1864, studied law with his father, Samuel, Jr., and completed a course at the Harvard Law School. Samuel E. served as judge of the court of common pleas from 1880–82, when he became legal counsel for the Nickel Plate Railroad. Beginning in 1898, he headed the legal department of the New York Central Railroad until his death in 1903. Samuel E. was one of the founders of UNIVERSITY SCHOOL and a trustee of Western Reserve University, the Society for Savings, and the Old Stone Church. The first Williamson Block bearing the family name was built on the property on the corner of Euclid and Public Square in 1889-90. It suffered a serious fire in 1895, and the second Williamson Bldg., a 16-story steel-framed office skyscraper, was erected on the site in 1899-1900. It was demolished in 1982 for the construction of the Sohio Bldg.

The **WILLOW FREEWAY** was first proposed in 1927 as part of a *T* system of freeways for the city. The horizontal beam of the *T* was to be a freeway running east and west along the city's lakefront (the future MEMORIAL SHOREWAY), while the vertical beam, the Willow Freeway, was to run from downtown south to INDEPENDENCE. It was given the name Willow since its southern terminus would be at the old Willow Station of the B&O Railroad near the Ohio Canal and the CUYAHOGA RIVER. Planning began in May 1935, and WPA funds were committed to the project that same year. Construction began in 1938, with the building of the first "cloverleaf" interchange in the state. The cloverleaf was to bring the new highway (all designated U.S. Rt. 21) over Brookpark/Schaaf roads and provide for an all-direction transfer between the two road systems. It cost $1.175 million and was completed 21 Oct. 1940. Voters supported the freeway in a May 1939 election by approving $4.5 million in tax funding. These monies were to provide for land acquisition and construction of the freeway from the cloverleaf north into downtown Cleveland. The original plans called for the freeway to end near the intersection of Ontario St. and Huron Rd. Two factors slowed progress on the highway's construction. There was dispute over its exact route, and the city hesitated to secure the land needed until the route was finalized. WORLD WAR II then intervened and halted work from Dec. 1941-Nov. 1946.

When construction resumed, the freeway was scheduled to end at Dalton Ave., where it would funnel traffic onto E. 49th St. and then on to Broadway Ave. to downtown. In 1948, however, it was decided to continue construction north to Broadway, and work began in Feb. 1950. By this time, planning was underway for the construction of the downtown INNERBELT FREEWAY, and it was decided that the stretch of the Willow north of Broadway would be tied into that project. The section of the Willow from Broadway across KINGSBURY RUN to the Innerbelt was begun in 1962 and opened to traffic on 17 Jan. 1966. As the federal interstate highway system developed, the existing Willow Freeway was incorporated into plans for I-77, which would run from Cleveland south to Charlotte, N.C. This plan required that the original 4 lanes be expanded to 6. A 7-mi. stretch of the highway, from E. 30th St. to Canal Rd., was brought up to interstate standards. It cost $8.2 million and was completed in Nov. 1973. The last stretch of I-77 work in the county was carrying the renovated Willow across the valley by bridge to connect with the completed stretch running from Rockside Rd. This last segment was opened 29 Oct. 1975. The original Willow Freeway, built at a cost of $15 million, then became the northernmost link of a 168-mi. trans-Ohio superhighway built at a cost of $320 million.

**WILLS, J. WALTER, SR.** (3 June 1874-23 Apr. 1971), was founder and director of the state's largest black-owned funeral business. His leadership in civic and social causes in the black community spanned a period of over 60 years. In 1986, his HOUSE OF WILLS continued to be a major business enterprise in the city. Wills was born and educated in Yellow Springs, Ohio. After graduating from Antioch College, he migrated to Cleveland in 1899. During his early years in the city, he worked as a streecar conductor and insurance salesman while attending law school at night. In 1904 he became a partner in the Gee & Wills Funeral Co. When the partnership dissolved in 1907, Wills formed the J. W. Wills & Sons Co. In 1941, the business moved to 2491 E. 55th St., which in 1986 remained its primary location. As an ardent supporter of the theory that economic self-help was the key to black progress, Wills helped organize the city's first black business organization in 1905, the Cleveland Board of Trade. In 1908, an organization that grew out of the board, the CLEVELAND ASSOC. OF COLORED MEN, affiliated with Booker T. Washington's Natl. Business League. Wills was a leader among a new breed of black businessmen in his day who broke with more traditional integrationist idealism to advocate black solidarity. His civic activities attested to his quest to find a way to end racial discrimination and to improve the lives of BLACKS. Among numerous organizational activities, he was a founder of the local branch of the NAACP, the Negro Welfare Assoc. (URBAN LEAGUE OF CLEVELAND affiliate), and the PHILLIS WHEATLEY ASSOC. Wills was generous with his time as well as his money. He was often called upon to aid the needy as the city's black population expanded. He also donated to MT. ZION CONGREGATIONAL CHURCH, of which he was a member. His interest in the arts was most often expressed through music, as he served as conductor and trainer of choral groups. In 1969, the Community Ctr. at the King-Kennedy Apts. in the Central area was named in his honor.

**WILLSON, HIRAM V.** (Apr. 1808-11 Nov. 1866), was a prominent lawyer and the first judge of the Northern District Court of Ohio. Willson Ave. (E. 55th St.) was named after him. Willson was born in Madison County, N.Y., and graduated from Hamilton College in 1832. He studied law with Jared Willson in Canandaigua, N.Y., and Francis Scott Key in Washington, D.C. He initially supported himself as a teacher. He moved to Painesville and then came to Cleveland, where he opened a law practice with HENRY B. PAYNE in 1833. Payne later retired, and the firm of Payne, Willson & Wade became Willson, Wade & Hitchcock, and later Willson, Wade, & Wade. In 1854, Willson and a group of commissioners from Cleveland and OHIO CITY worked out the details concerning annexing Ohio City to Cleveland. Also in 1854, Willson lobbied for a bill that would divide Ohio into 2 federal court districts. He succeeded, and the U.S. Court for the Northern District of Ohio was formed. Pres. Franklin Pierce appointed Willson the first judge of the Northern District court in 1855. During his term of office, he presided over a number of civil and admiralty cases. In 1859, he presided over the trial of 37 leaders in the OBERLIN-WELLINGTON RESCUE incident who had violated the Fugitive Slave Law. Willson was a director of the CLEVELAND FEMALE SEMINARY in 1854; an officer of the University Hts. Congregational Church in 1859; and one of a group of prominent Cleveland lawyers who contributed to the Cleveland Law Library Assoc. He married Martha Ten Eyck of Detroit, Mich., in 1835.

**WILSON, ELLA GRANT** (1 Sept. 1854-16 Dec. 1939), was a florist and an author who wrote about the famed "Millionaires' Row" located on EUCLID AVE. Wilson was born Ella Grant in Jersey City, N.J., and moved to Cleveland when she was 6. She attended public schools. With $10 saved and $100 borrowed, she started a business of floral decorations. She arranged over 300 weddings and some 1,000 funerals, including JAS. A. GARFIELD's funeral in Cleveland. Her position as an in-demand florist gained her entry into the homes of some of Cleveland's wealthiest and most prominent citizens. This experience proved helpful in later years when she began her writing career. Wilson designed floral arrangements for 18 years for the Chamber of Commerce and the HOLLENDEN HOTEL. When a cyclone destroyed her greenhouse on 22 Apr. 1909 and nearly buried her son alive in the debris, she decided to get out of the business. She again went to work in 1918, as garden editor for the *PLAIN DEALER*, remaining in that position for 6 years. In 1929, at age 75, Wilson began a new career. She had collected and maintained a huge series of scrapbooks of the history of Cleveland and with them began a series of articles in the Sunday magazine of the *Plain Dealer* dealing with old-time Cleveland and Euclid Ave. The articles became the basis of the first of 2 volumes on Millionaires' Row entitled *Famous Old Euclid Avenue*. The first volume contained anecdotes, history, biographies, and geography of Euclid Ave., from E. 30th to E. 79th streets. Her second volume, published in 1937, continued the story to E. 105th St. Wilson was married twice, outliving both husbands, Jas. A. Campbell and Chas. H. Wilson. She had 5 children.

Ella Grant Wilson Scrapbooks, WRHS.

The **WILSON TRANSIT COMPANY** was founded as a freight- transportation business by Capt. Thos. Wilson in 1872. Through several decades, the company was a pioneer in Great Lakes shipping in the use of safety equipment. Capt. Wilson, from a seafaring family in Scotland, started his business with a single ship, the 757-ton *D. M. Wilson*, named after his infant son. Wilson built several more steamers as business prospered, including the *Spokane* in 1886, the lakes' first steel steamer. Wilson, the managing owner and president, died in 1900. At this time the company owned about 14 ships, adding 7 new ones by 1910. The company innovated the use of electric lights on a lake ship, on the *Yakima* in 1887; it was the first to install the gyro-compass in its ships in 1924 and added patented hatch covers the following year. The *William C. Atwater* of the Wilson line was the first lake ship, in 1934, to use a radio telephone. Throughout much of the 20th century, the Wilson Transit Co. specialized in bulk cargo shipping on the Great Lakes. Its ships were characterized by black hulls, a white superstructure, and a large *W* on the stacks. Using larger, more modern ships, it had reduced its fleet to 12 by the 1940s. In 1957 the name was changed to the Wilson Marine Transit Co. In 1967 it became a division of Litton Industries, Inc.

**WINDSOR HOSPITAL** in CHAGRIN FALLS is a 71-bed not-for-profit hospital for the treatment of acute neuro-psychiatric disorders and chemical dependency in adolescents and adults. Windsor Hospital was founded in 1898 by Dr. Christian Sihler, a neurologist and the first chief of staff at Lutheran Hospital. The hospital took its name from its original site on Windsor Ave. in Cleveland, one of the streets that were later linked together to form Chester Ave. Its initial purpose was for the treatment of convalescents, mainly those with minor nerve disorders requiring isolation and rest. When Sihler died in 1919, his son, Herbert Sihler, became the hospital's head. A brother, Paul Sihler, succeeded him as president in 1952. Herbert A. Sihler, Jr., became president in 1964. The hospital was incorporated as a nonprofit corporation in 1956 with a board of 3 trustees, which was later increased to 4. In 1938, Windsor Hos-

pital moved from its original location to a fireproof building on Prospect Ave., where it was renamed Prospect Sanitarium. This facility closed in 1942. Earlier, in 1927, a second site had been purchased in Chagrin Falls. Known as Linden Hall, it offered postoperative care, but it closed shortly after the stock market crash in 1929. It was reopened in 1932 as Windsor Hospital 2 under a third brother, Edmund Sihler. The medical staff was organized under Dr. John H. Nichols, medical director until 1971. He was succeeded by Dr. Guy H. Williams, Jr.

In its early years, Windsor used HYDROTHERAPY as a treatment for typhoid fever and nervous disorders. It began to receive psychiatric patients when hydrotherapy was more widely applied to the treatment of separated nerve endings, believed to be a factor in disturbed emotional states. In the 1920s and 1930s, the hospital in Cleveland cared largely for state psychiatric patients as a result of an overflow from state hospitals, while the hospital in Chagrin Falls treated mainly private patients. This emphasis on the treatment of private patients was continued in Chagrin Falls after the closing of the hospital in Cleveland. From the 1950s, Windsor Hospital experienced a steady shift from long-term to short-term care: a result of the improved treatment of mental illness through the use of psychopharmacological agents. Consequently, the hospital in the 1980s implemented new programs that included adolescent and geriatric programs, a developmental school (for adolescents), and an increased emphasis on the treatment of chemical dependency. In the early 1980s, ST. LUKE'S HOSPITAL, in partnership with Windsor, proposed to build a new $20 million 143-bed hospital on the Windsor Hospital site. The plan was dropped in 1984 because of a downturn in the hospital industry in the Cleveland area.

**WING, MARIE REMINGTON** (5 Nov. 1885–27 Dec. 1982), was a prominent lawyer, feminist, and reformer. Born in Cleveland Wing was the daughter of federal judge Francis J. Wing and Mary Brackett Remington. She attended Cleveland schools and prepared for college at the prestigious MISS MITTLEBERGER'S SCHOOL for Young Ladies. She entered Bryn Mawr college but did not finish because of financial reverses suffered by her father. After returning to Cleveland, Wing found employment with the YWCA, as both industrial secretary and financial secretary. She also served as its general secretary in New York and sat on the board of trustees. She was a member of the Women's Industrial Commission sent to Europe in 1919 under the YWCA Natl. War Work Council. In 1922 Wing left the YWCA and enrolled in the Cleveland Law School, which her father had helped to found. She was elected to CLEVELAND CITY COUNCIL for 2 terms in 1923 and 1925, having previously sat on the charter review that instituted the city manager system in Cleveland. As one of the first 2 women on council, Wing worked to establish a women's bureau in the police department. After admission to the Ohio bar in 1926, she lost a reelection bid in 1927. Active in many local reform groups, Wing served on the executive board of the Cleveland Fed. of Women's Clubs. She also served as the executive secretary of the CONSUMERS LEAGUE OF OHIO, where she worked to pass legislation protecting women and children in industry and providing for a minimum wage. She attempted to form a Women's Union League in Cleveland but was unsuccessful. In 1934 Wing was appointed to the Women's Advisory Committee of the Cleveland Regional Labor Board and headed a special works program committee appointed by the Cuyahoga County Relief Commission. She became the first regional attorney for the Cleveland Social Security office in 1937, continuing in this position until 1953, when she opened a private law practice. In 1956, Wing retired at the age of 71 to live in Mentor, Ohio.

The **WINGS OVER JORDAN CHOIR** was one of the more prominent black choirs in the U.S. It originated in the Gethsemane Baptist Church at E. 30th and Scovill Ave. in 1935 and was known for its interpretations of spirituals. The choir was founded by Rev. Glenn T. Settle. It began performing on radio in July 1937 on the "National Negro Hour" on WGAR. Mrs. Williette Thompson was the pianist for the choir, and Wayne Mack was the announcer. The group performed a program of spirituals and religious music every week. In Jan. 1938 it began broadcasting nationally on the Columbia network, continuing to do so until 1944. In 1940, the choir toured various cities throughout the U.S. The original group disbanded in 1942. A new choir was formed, under the leadership of Hattie Easley, and toured Army camps in Europe in 1944 and 1945. It disbanded after the tour. Rev. Settle tried to organize a new choir in the 1950s, but his attempts were unsuccessful. He died an California in 1967.

**WINTER, H. EDWARD** (14 Oct. 1908–22 July 1976) and **THELMA FRAZIER** (17 Dec. 1903–24 June 1977), were both enamelists. Edward Winter was also a writer, and Thelma a sculptor. They were married in 1939. The Winters studied at the CLEVELAND INSTITUTE OF ART. Thelma went on in 1930 to Ohio State University to study ceramics with Arthur C. Baggs, then to the OSU Medical School for anatomy. She received her B.C. in education in 1935 from Western Reserve University. Edward studied in Vienna, Austria, with Josef Hoffman and Michael Powolny. Although both taught, Edward at the Institute of Art (1935–37) and the Old White Art Colony in West Virginia, and Thelma at LAUREL SCHOOL, the Cleveland Institute of Art, and the CLEVELAND MUSEUM OF ART, the Winters were primarily artists. Edward wrote *Enamel Art on Metals*, *Enameling for Beginners*, and *Enamel Painting Techniques*, and published articles, as did Thelma, in *American Artists Magazine*, *London Studio Magazine*, *American Art*, and *Art & Craft of Ceramic Sculpture*. Edward's style and technique were decorative and abstract expressionism in flora and fauna. He used foil inlay or transparent and opaque surface copper, steel, silver, and aluminum in his enameling process. His work is in the Cleveland and Butler museums of art and New York State's Ceramics Gallery. In 1933, he was commisioned by the FERRO CO. to do a series of murals. They consisted of panels 3½' × 5½' that were designs of large blue angelfish in porcelain enamel, fused onto 18-gauge steel at 1,500 degrees. Edward also drew a special commission in 1944 from the U.S. Army to do educational posters for GIs while he was serving as a technical sergeant. Thelma was the descendant of Morovian immigrants from Gnadenhutten, Ohio. Her media were stylized sculpture, decorative enamels, and ceramics that were also semiabstract. Her work is featured in the Cleveland and Butler museums of art, in the Everson Museum, and at the WESTERN RESERVE HISTORICAL SOCIETY. Her commissions include the *Arisen Christ* for ST. MARY'S ROMANIAN CHURCH of Cleveland and the *Annunciation* and *Last Supper* for the Catholic Diocese. Both of the Winters were awarded many prizes for their works and were represented in many exhibitions nationwide.

**WINTON, ALEXANDER** (20 June 1860–21 June 1932), was an important pioneer in the development and popularization of the automobile, establishing a number of firsts

for the infant industry. Winton was born in Grangemouth, Scotland, where he received a common-school education before coming to the U.S. at age 19. He worked in the Delameter Iron Works in New York for 3 years and was an assistant in a marine engine shop before arriving in Cleveland in 1884. During his career, Winton founded 3 prosperous businesses. He organized the first in 1891 to manufacture an improved bicycle he had designed and patented that year. The Winton Bicycle Co., with Frank L. Alcott as president, Geo. H. Brown as secretary, and plant and offices on Perkins Ave. at the Cleveland & Pittsburgh Railroad, was soon flourishing, but within 10 years Winton abandoned the bicycle business to design and manufacture automobiles. In Sept. 1896, Winton completed his first motor car, and in Mar. 1897 he incorporated the WINTON MOTOR CARRIAGE CO. On 28 July 1897, he began the first reliability run in American autmobile history (the "Cleveland-New York Drive"), a 9-day drive to New York that stimulated investment in his company, permitting construction of 4 more automobiles. The sale of one of these on 24 Mar. 1898 was the first sale of an American-made standard-model gasoline automobile. In 1899 Winton made another, better-publicized 5-day drive to New York that helped boost interest in the automobile and expanded its sales market. He attempted to become the first person to drive cross-country in 1901 but abandoned the effort in the sands of the Nevada desert.

Winton continued to develop new automobile models, including racing cars that set several early speed records; he was also the first to use Daytona Beach, in Fla., for automobile racing. A sharp decline in sales in the early 1920s prompted Winton to liquidate the automobile company and concentrate his resources on his third business venture. Interested in the development of marine engines, Winton organized the Winton Gas Engine & Mfg. Co. in 1912 to produce engines of his own design (see CLEVELAND DIESEL ENGINE DIV. OF GENERAL MOTORS CORP.). In 1913 the company produced the first American diesel engine. Winton guided this company as president and later chairman of the board; he retired after selling the firm to GM in 1930. Winton was active as presiding officer in 2 other companies: the Electric Welding Prods. Co. and the LINDSAY WIRE WEAVING CO. He was a member of the Civil Engineers' Club of Cleveland, the Automobile Club of America, and the Cleveland Automobile Club. Winton was married 4 times. In 1883 he married Jeanie Muir McGlashan, who died in 1903; his 1906 marriage to La Belle McGlashan ended with her death in 1924. He married local actress Marion Campbell in 1927, but they were divorced in 1930; that same year he married Mary Ellen Avery.

Wager, Richard, *Golden Wheels* (1975).

The **WINTON MOTOR CARRIAGE COMPANY**, an early pioneer in the American automobile industry, produced vehicles from its founding in 1897 until Feb. 1924, establishing in that time several firsts for the young industry. The company was founded in Mar. 1897 by Cleveland bicycle manufacturer ALEXANDER WINTON, who had exhibited in October his first car, a 1-cyl., 8-hp vehicle steered with a tiller. Along with Thos. W. Henderson and Geo. H. Brown, Winton established a factory in rented quarters at the corner of Belden and Mason streets. He exhibited his early products on long demonstration runs: in May 1897 he drove a new 2-cyl., 10-hp vehicle to Elyria and back, and in July 1897 he drove one of his automobiles to New York City (the "Cleveland-New York Drive"). Although the latter trip did not receive the publicity Winton had hoped, it stimulated investment in the company, allowing it to construct 4 more automobiles. On 24 Mar. 1898, Winton was the first company to sell a standard American-made gasoline-powered automobile; it was purchased by Robt. Allison of Port Carbon, Pa., for $1,000. The company produced 22 vehicles in 1898. A second drive to New York by Winton received greater publicity in 1899, and orders for vehicles surpassed the company's production capabilities. Soon it was producing 25 cars a week, and the price rose to $2,000. By 1900, the company claimed to have the world's largest automobile factory. Winton made extensive changes in its automobiles as it regularly introduced new models and products. In 1900 a "business wagon deparment" was established to manufacture delivery vehicles, and Winton developed a racing car that competed in a race in France in June, the first American vehicle to compete in a European event. In November the company marketed for $1,200 a 9-hp car with 2 headlamps and a steering wheel. By 1910 it had marketed 18 models of automobiles.

The company grew as it cultivated a market for its classically designed products. In 1902, Winton built a new factory complex at 10601 Berea Rd. and a sales office and garage at 1228 Huron Rd.; the firm employed 700 people that year and had a branch office in New York. Employment increased to 1,500 in 1903, and branches were opened in London, England, in 1904 and in Toronto and Honolulu in 1905. Reorganized as the Winton Motor Car Co. in 1915, the firm produced 2,450 vehicles in 1916. The company's sales were sharply reduced by an economic depression late in 1920; production was halted for a few months early in 1921. Winton had always produced expensive automobiles, and in the early 1920s, having saturated that market, it was unable to adjust to the new market conditions brought about by Henry Ford's less expensive, mass-produced vehicles. The Winton Co. produced only 690 cars in 1922, and on 11 Feb. 1924, it ceased automobile production. Alexander Winton closed the company and concentrated his efforts on the production of diesel engines (see CLEVELAND DIESEL ENGINE DIV. OF GENERAL MOTORS CORP.).

Wager, Richard, *Golden Wheels* (1975).

**WISE, SAMUEL D.** (28 Nov. 1875–25 Mar. 1953), was a well-known civic leader, industrialist, and philanthropist. Dubbed the "Samuel Mather" of the Jewish community, Wise supported such interests as the United Jewish Campaign for Foreign Relief, the Jewish Big Brother Assoc., the Council of Jewish Women, and the Jewish Big Sister Assoc. For his many contributions, he was honored as Cleveland's Distinguished Citizen on 27 May 1931. Born at Walnut Ave. and Erie (E. 9th), Wise was educated in the Cleveland school system. He entered work in 1889 as an office boy and bookkeeper for the Atlantic Refining Co., earning $2.50 a week to start. The firm prospered, making its money in roof coating, lubricating oils, axle grease, and later industrial paints. Wise and some associates acquired all of the company's stock when the owner, Geo. C. Haskell, retired in 1901, and in 1914 the name was changed to the Arco Co. The company's rapid growth continued, and with Wise as president, it became the 3d-largest of the companies in its field after GLIDDEN and the SHERWIN-WILLIAMS CO., making Cleveland "the paint capital of the world." After more than 40 years with Arco, Wise retired in 1936. When Wise left Cleveland for Katonah, in 1951, he had lent his name as contributor and benefactor to a multitude of causes and organizations. He is perhaps best remembered for founding Camp Wise and the Camp Wise Assoc. for children. At the former "Stein's on the Lake," a once-fashionable 20-acre resort located in EUCLID, Wise in 1906 supported the idea of Eugene L. Geismer and Mrs. Beatrice Moss Loeser for building a summer camp for indigent children and their mothers. The success of this venture, which was operated by the Council Educational Alliance, led to the selection of another camp site at Painesville-on-the-Lake, occupying 70 acres of lakefront tract east of Painesville. Wise was an original organizer of the MT. SINAI MEDICAL CTR., giving the principal donation to build its nurses' home and training school. He was also one of the founders of the Jewish Welfare Fund in 1931, and he was a trustee and generous supporter of the Jewish Welfare Fed. Wise donated several art treasures to the CLEVELAND MUSEUM OF ART, of which he was named an honorary trustee. Cultural and needy members of the community still benefit from the Samuel D. & May W. Wise Fund.

**WITT, PETER** (24 July 1869–20 Oct. 1948), was a political leader and transit expert who served in the cabinets of Cleveland mayors TOM L. JOHNSON and NEWTON D. BAKER. Witt was born in Cleveland to Christian and Anna Witt. He attended Orchard Elementary School through the 5th grade, at which time he quit in order to obtain work and assist his family. He first worked in a basket factory, but later became an iron molder and foundryman. Rebellious and outspoken, Witt took part in various union activities and was blacklisted for his actions in 1896. His interest in unions persisted throughout his life, and at one time he served as president of the Cleveland Central Labor Union. A follower of the single-tax philosophy of Henry George, Witt wrote and published *Cleveland before St. Peter*, a spirited pamphlet concerning tax dodging by wealthy Clevelanders. Witt's career as a public servant began in 1900, when he was appointed decennial appraiser for Cleveland. In 1903 he was elected city clerk, under which post he loyally served the administration of Tom L. Johnson. After Johnson's defeat in 1909, Witt temporarily retired from politics to take a position with the Forest City Investment Co. From 1911–15 he served as commissioner of street railways in the administration of Newton D. Baker. Witt's tenure as traction commissioner was both innovative and controversial, as he introduced the "pay-leave" system on city streetcars and eliminated many car stops to reduce running time (see URBAN TRANSPORTATION).

In 1915, Witt ran unsuccessfully for mayor, being defeated by Republican HARRY L. DAVIS. From 1916–23, he spent most of his time serving as a consultant on mass transit for various cities outside of Cleveland. He did, however, play an important role in the successful effort in 1921 to establish a city manager form of government for Cleveland (see CITY MANAGER PLAN). Witt returned to politics in 1923, when he was elected to CLEVELAND CITY COUNCIL as an independent. He served on council until 1927. In 1924 he was an ardent supporter of Robert La Follette, the Progressive presidential candidate. Later he supported the presidential campaigns of Al Smith and Franklin D. Roosevelt. In 1928 Witt ran for Ohio governor but lost to Martin L. Davey. Four years later, following the end of the City Manager Plan, he ran for Cleveland mayor but placed third behind DANIEL MORGAN and RAY T. MILLER. From 1932 until his death, Witt lived in semiretirement, spending much time with his family at a cottage on N. Bass Island. He died of complications following a heart attack in 1948. He was survived by his wife of 56 years, the former Sadie James, and 3 daughters.

Peter Witt Papers, WRHS.

**WITT, STILLMAN** (4 Jan. 1808–29 Apr. 1875), was a railroad president and capitalist and a well-known benefactor of Cleveland charities. Witt was born in Worcester, Mass. At the age of 13, he was taken with his family to Troy, N.Y., where he was employed to run a skiff-ferry for $10 a month. He soon attracted the interest of Canvass White of the U.S. Engineer Corps, who took Witt on as a private pupil. After serving an apprenticeship, Witt was sent by White to take charge of the Cohoes Mfg. Co. Through White, he was next employed to build a bridge at Cohoes Falls on the Mohawk River. He engaged in other building projects as a protege of White, including construction of a bridge across the Susquehanna, and then, still connected with White, he became agent of the Hudson River Steamboat Assoc. in Albany. With the rapid emergence of the railroads in the 1840s, Witt became manager of the Albany & Boston Railroad Co. In the late 1840s, Witt moved to Cleveland, where there was a need for experienced railroad builders. The newly formed firm of Harbach, Stone & Witt was hired to build the road for the Cleveland, Columbus & Cincinnati Railroad, completed in 1851. The firm, later without Harbach, then embarked on the construction of the Cleveland, Painesville & Ashtabula Railroad, and the Chicago & Milwaukee Railroad. Witt then turned his attention to the management of the large interests he had acquired in railroads and other properties. He became director of the above railroad companies, and also the Michigan Southern and Bellefontaine & Indiana railroad companies. He took control of the latter when it was on the verge of bankruptcy, and was credited with regenerating buying interest in the company's stock and thus saving the company. In Cleveland, Witt was, in 1863, one of the incorporators of the Cleveland Rolling Mill Co. He also helped build the Cleveland & Newburgh Railroad in 1868.

In 1873, Witt gave a large sum toward the building of a second boarding home for the Women's Christian Assoc. (later YWCA). A few years earlier, in 1869, the boarding home had opened in a building Witt had bought and donated. In later years it became known as the Stillman Witt Boarding House. Witt was active in many other Cleveland charitable and educational organizations, especially those for women. In the 1850s, he had served on the first directorate of the CLEVELAND FEMALE SEMINARY. Witt married Eliza A. Douglass of Albany in 1834. A daughter, Mrs. Daniel P. Eells, was actively involved in the Women's Christian Assoc. The Witt mansion on Euclid Ave. was torn down in 1884 and replaced by "The Stillman," a hotel and apartment combination. Later, the STILLMAN THEATER occupied the site for many years.

**WITTKE, CARL FREDERICK** (13 Nov. 1892–24 May 1971), was a scholar, historian, author, lecturer, college professor, educational administrator, and authority on American and Canadian history. He was born in Columbus, Ohio, the son of Carl William Oswald and Caroline Kropp Wittke. He received his A.B. degree from Ohio State University (1913) and both an M.A. (1914) and a Ph.D. (1921) from Harvard University. He became an instructor in history at OSU (1916–21), then assistant professor (1921–25) and full professor and chairman of the department (1925–37). He then became professor of history and dean of Oberlin College (1937–48). In 1948 he joined the Western Reserve University faculty as professor of history and dean of the Graduate School. In 1952 he became chairman of the department; in 1959 he was named Elbert Jay Benton Distinguished Professor of History, and in 1961 vice-president

of the university. Wittke received an honorary LL.D. from Lawrence College, Appleton, Wis. (1946); a Litt.D. from Marietta College, Marietta, Ohio (1952); an LL.D. from Fenn College, Cleveland (1955); an L.H.D. from Lake Erie College, Painesville, Ohio (1956); an LL.D. from Denison University, Granville, Ohio (1959); and on 7 June 1963, an L.H.D. from OSU. He retired from WRU in 1963 as dean emeritus of the Graduate School and professor and history department chairman emeritus of the university.

Wittke presented many speeches, wrote over 80 articles for professional journals, edited many historical reviews, and authored over 14 books, including *History of Canada* (1928); *We Who Built America: The Saga of the Immigrant* (1939); *Against the Current: The Life of Karl Heinzen* (1945), for which he received the Ohioana Library Award; and *Refugees of Revolution: The German Forty-eighters in America* (1952). He edited the 6-volume *History of the State of Ohio* and served on the Prentice-Hall editorial board for 15 years. In 1966 he wrote *The First Fifty Years: The Cleveland Museum of Art, 1916–1966*. Wittke was a member of the American Historical Assoc., the Mississippi Valley Historical Assoc. (president, 1940–41), the American Assoc. of University Professors, the Canadian Historical Assoc., the Ohio Academy of History, and the Ohio Archeological & Historical Society, an honorary member of the Deutsche Akademie of Munich, and a fellow of the Royal Historical Society. In 1951 he received the Cleveland B'nai B'rith Sol Fetterman Memorial Award for outstanding achievements in promoting brotherhood and mutual understanding in the community; in 1956 the Brotherhood Award of the Natl. Council of Christians & Jews; in 1961 the "Civil Liberties Man of the Year" award at the City Club by the Cleveland Civil Liberties Union; and in 1963 the Commander's Cross of Order of Merit from the Federal Republic of West Germany. In 1916, Dr. Wittke married Lillian Bowshans; they had 1 son, Carl Francis. Mrs. Wittke died in 1918. On 1 June 1921, Wittke married Lillian Nippert, local artist; she died 12 Feb. 1980.

Cramer, Clarence H., *Carl Frederick Wittke* (1971).

**WOLDMAN, ALBERT A.** (1 Jan. 1897–30 Dec. 1971), was a lawyer, author, and teacher, and served in city and state government. He was most noted as a judge on the CUYAHOGA COUNTY JUVENILE COURT. Born in Russia, Woldman came to Cleveland at the age of 18 months. He attended Mayflower School and CENTRAL HIGH SCHOOL. Graduating with the A.B. degree from Adelbert College in 1917, Woldman attended Western Reserve and Ohio Northern law schools, graduating with the LL.B. degree in 1919. In 1914, he became the youngest probation officer in the juvenile court's history. While in college, he worked as a reporter for the CLEVELAND PRESS and as the assistant state editor for the PLAIN DEALER. Between 1919–41, Woldman maintained his private practice and taught at the John Marshall Law School. In 1941, he became Cleveland's assistant law director. In 1945, he was chosen chairman of the Ohio Bureau of Unemployment Compensation's Board of Review. In 1949, he was appointed director of Ohio's Dept. of Industrial Relations. Gov. Frank Lausche appointed him to the Cuyahoga County Juvenile Court in Aug. 1953. Winning a 2-year term in 1954, Woldman was twice reelected to full 6-year terms. Becoming the court's administrative judge, he was also responsible for the operations of the county juvenile detention home. One of juvenile court's most vigorous judges, Woldman gave numerous speeches before civic groups in addition to handling a full docket and the administrative affairs of the court. He viewed juvenile delinquency as the number-one social problem. His later years on the bench were beset by health problems and increased administrative responsibilities. He had to deal with the discontent and poor morale among court employees because of low pay, as well as professional and public discontent because of delays in construction of a detention home annex. Woldman was an avid student of Abraham Lincoln. His book *Lawyer Lincoln* was an acclaimed study of Lincoln's career as a lawyer and the constitutional problems he faced during the CIVIL WAR. Woldman was president of B'NAI B'RITH of Cleveland, vice-president of the Abraham Lincoln Assoc. of Ohio, a trustee of the Cultural Garden Ctr. and the CLEVELAND BAR ASSOC., and a member of the CUYAHOGA COUNTY BAR ASSOC., the Welfare Fed., and the Mayor's Committee on Juvenile Delinquency. He was married to Lydia Levin. They had 3 children, Robert, Phyllis, and Stuart.

Albert A. Wolman Papers, WRHS.

**WOLF, EDITH ANISFIELD** (1889–23 Jan. 1963), was a published poet, businesswoman, and philanthropist who established 2 awards in honor of her father, clothing manufacturer and philanthropist JOHN ANISFIELD (1860–22 Apr. 1929), and her husband, attorney Eugene E. Wolf (1 Jan. 1884–29 Dec. 1944). Anisfield was born in Cleveland, the daughter of John and Doniella Guttenberg Anisfield. She graduated from East High School and from Women's College (later Flora Stone Mather College). On 7 Aug. 1918, she married another native Clevelander, Eugene E. Wolf. Able to read French, German, and Spanish, Wolf was devoted to literature and charitable work. From her office in downtown Cleveland, she managed her family's estate and wrote poetry. She published several books of poetry, including *Snacks* (1938) and *Balance* (1942), as well as magazine articles. In 1934 she established an annual $1,000 prize for the outstanding book in the field of race relations; the award was named in honor of her father. In 1941 she added a second prize of $1,000 for a creative book that performs "an outstanding service in clarifying the problems of racial relations," and the first award was then designated for the best work of a scientific nature on racial relations. Among the winners of the Anisfield-Wolf awards have been Martin Luther King, Jr., for *Stride toward Freedom* and LANGSTON HUGHES for *Simple Takes a Wife*. In 1943, Wolf was elected by the school board to serve on the board of the CLEVELAND PUBLIC LIBRARY. Upon her death in 1963, she left all of her books to the library; she willed her family home at 1451 East Blvd. to the Cleveland Welfare Fed., and she also left funds to the CLEVELAND FOUNDATION, which were used to establish the $5,000 Anisfield-Wolf Award for community service.

**WOLFENSTEIN, MARTHA** (1869–3 Mar. 1906), was perhaps the first Jewish woman author to write Jewish stories for the secular press. One of 6 children, she was born in Insterburg, Prussia, and was brought to the U.S. as an infant when her father, Samuel Wolfenstein, accepted a position as rabbi of Congregation B'nai El in St. Louis. The family moved to Cleveland in 1878 when Samuel Wolfenstein became superintendent of the JEWISH ORPHAN HOME. They lived at the home, and the children attended Cleveland's public schools. Following the death of her mother from tuberculosis in 1885, Martha became the housekeeper and child-rearer for her father. She also served as matron of the orphan home for a short period of time. Martha's earliest literary endeavor was as a translator of German poetry and stories. She soon began writing short fiction based on her father's reminiscences about his childhood in a Central European ghetto. She published widely in the flourishing secular literary press of the late 19th century, also finding an outlet for her stories in the local Anglo-Jewish press and the *Jewish Orphan Asylum Magazine*. In 1901, the Jewish Publication Society of America published a collection of short fiction that had appeared in *Lippincott's* and *Outlook* under the title *Idylls of the Gass*. Four years later, the society published a collection of stories, *The Renegade and Other Stories*, all of which had appeared in the *Jewish Review & Observer*. Martha was working on a play when she died following a lengthy bout with tuberculosis. The play was never published or performed. A year later, the Council of Jewish Women established a residence for homeless girls, naming it Martha House, after Martha Wolfenstein.

The **WOLPERT FOUNDATION** was founded in 1980 by Samuel A. and Roslyn A. Wolpert. It is a supporting organization of the CLEVELAND FOUNDATION. The purposes of the foundation are for the enhancement of racially integrated community life in CLEVELAND HTS., Jewish affairs in Cleveland, culture, and education. In 1981, the foundation sponsored a multicultural celebration throughout the Cleveland Hts.-University Hts. 10 elementary schools and 1 high school. The foundation also provides support for SHAKER SQUARE. In 1984, assets of the foundation were $525,128, with expenditures of $61,200. Trustees included Robt. D. Gries (Cleveland Foundation), Frances M. King, S. Sterling McMillan, Stanley Pace, and M. Brock Weir, along with Roslyn and Samuel Wolpert.

**WOLSEY, LOUIS** (8 Jan. 1877–4 Mar. 1953), was the first American-born and -trained rabbi to serve Cleveland's ANSHE CHESED CONGREGATION. Born in Midland, Mich., Wolsey received a secular education before attending Hebrew Union College in Cincinnati. He graduated and was ordained in 1899. His first pulpit was Congregation B'nai Israel in Little Rock, Ark., a position he held until 1907. Wolsey was hired by Anshe Chesed in 1907 and began an 18-year tenure. When he became rabbi, the membership of Anshe Chesed stood at 150. By 1925, it had increased to 1,300. He oversaw the move of the congregation from the Scovill Ave. Temple in Woodland to the newly constructed Euclid Ave. Temple at E. 84th and Euclid. Early in his career, Wolsey embraced a conservative view of Reform Judaism, countering the Classical Reform in vogue during the first 2 decades of the century. Soon after his arrival in Cleveland, he engaged in a bitter public debate with Rabbi MOSES J. GRIES of the TEMPLE concerning their respective views of Judaism. Following Gries's death in 1918, Wolsey moved into the mainstream of Classical Reform. Jewish education was a particular interest of Wolsey's. He revitalized the Anshe Chesed Sunday school, which had only 135 pupils in 1908, causing its enrollment to increase to 650 in 1916. He also actively supported the CLEVELAND HEBREW SCHOOLS. Although Wolsey showed some affinity for the fledgling Zionist movement early in his career, he was by 1918 an outspoken critic of political Zionism. Later in his life, he became the leading spokesman for the anti-Zionist cause. In 1943, he founded the American Council for Judaism, an organization of Reform rabbis and lay leaders that formed in opposition to a perceived pro-Zionist stance taken by the Central Conference of American Rabbis. Three years later he renounced his membership in the ACJ, and in 1948 he called for all Jews to give their support to the state of Israel. Wolsey held several key positions in major Reform organizations during his tenure at Anshe Chesed. He was president of the Hebrew Union College Alumni Assoc. from

1914–16. From 1916–24, he served as treasurer, corresponding secretary, and vice-president of the Central Conference of American Rabbis. In 1925, the year he left Cleveland, he was elected president of the conference. He was also a member of the executive board of the Union of American Hebrew Congregations from 1925–29. In 1925, Wolsey accepted the position of rabbi at Rodeph Shalom in Philadelphia, where he remained until his retirement in 1947. He married Florence Weiner, the daughter of a wealthy Cleveland commission merchant, in 1908.

The **WOMAN'S CHRISTIAN TEMPERANCE UNION, NONPARTISAN, OF CLEVELAND** was one of the principal TEMPERANCE reform organizations in the city. Formally organized in 1874 as the Women's Christian Temperance League, the body had its antecedents in the active temperance movement of the pre-Civil War period and in the efforts of praying bands of midwestern women in the 1870s to close down local saloons. Among the leaders of the league were Sarah Fitch, MARY INGHAM, and Sarah Duncan. Although affiliated with the national WCTU only from 1880–85, the group's activities resembled those advocated by the national: praying with saloon owners and patrons, establishing drinking fountains to slake the thirst of Clevelanders, opening reading rooms to promulgate temperance doctrines, supporting social purity reform through mothers' meetings, and kitchen gardens, and attempting the moral reformation of women in the county workhouse. In 1874, the group established Central Friendly Inn, originally a gathering and lodging place for young men and boys and later a social settlement (see FRIENDLY INN SOCIAL SETTLEMENT). After the passage of the Prohibition Amendment (1918), the WCTU NonPartisan continued to maintain Friendly Inn, the RAINEY INSTITUTE, and a training home for girls. In 1926 the group became the Women's Philanthropic Union.

Ingham, Mary, *Women of Cleveland* (1893). Women's Christian Temperance Union Records, WRHS.

The **WOMAN'S CHRISTIAN TEMPERANCE UNION CONVENTION** in Cleveland in 1874 resulted from the TEMPERANCE fervor stirred by the 1873–74 Women's Crusade. On 15 Aug. 1874, an assembly at Chautauqua, N.Y., issued a call to "make permanent the temperance work of the last few months." A letter drafted to national temperance leagues ordered the election of 1 woman from each congressional district to serve as a delegate to the national meeting at Cleveland, 18–20 Nov. 1874. When the convention opened Wednesday, 18 Nov., at the Second Presbyterian Church on Superior St., east of PUBLIC SQUARE, over 200 ladies, visitors, and representatives from all over the country were present. Debates over the voting status of nondelegates resulted in the women's designation as honorary delegates, while men were warned not to interfere with the women's authority and were relegated to separate seats in the "Amen corner." A rousing welcome speech delivered by Dr. L. D. McCabe, president of the Ohio WCTU, reexamined the organization's fundamental principles, endorsed the crusade, and called the women to arms.

The opening sessions established the Committee on Credentials, to which Mrs. MARY INGHAM of Cleveland was appointed treasurer, and the committee to draft a constitution for a national temperance league. A committee to study the feasibility of publishing a temperance organ advocating the women's temperance cause eventually provided directives to produce 2 publications: *Union Signal* and *Young Crusader*. Business got underway on Thursday,

19 Nov., when a "plan of work" for all national local temperance societies was adopted. Directed to the individual, society, religion, home, and the workplace, these guidelines urged national formation of temperance societies; circulation of temperance literature; temperance instruction in schools; juvenile temperance societies; a temperance glee club; abstention pledges; establishment of coffee/reading rooms; use of the pulpit as a soapbox; elimination of wine at religious services; gospel temperance meetings; and home missionary work. Other resolutions were developed that disapproved of intemperate politicians; requested the president, congressmen, and their wives to refrain from using alcoholic beverages; and protested against physicians' and druggists' prescribing alcohol. By Friday, 20 Nov., a preamble and constitution providing an organizational structure and affirming the evils of intemperance were adopted. On this concluding day, the proposed plans and resolutions of the WCTU were ambitious but not wholly impossible. Besides the formal resolutions and construction of a hierarchical authority base, the link established between the national and state temperance societies provided psychological strength and security for its adherents. With the support of the press and the religious community, the union wielded enough power to influence American society for the next generation.

Clark, Norman H., *Deliver Us from Evil* (1976).

**WOMAN'S GENERAL HOSPITAL** was the only hospital in Cleveland entirely founded by women. Although initially devoted to care of women and children, over the years it expanded its services to provide in-patient care in medicine, surgery, and pediatrics. In the 1970s it became widely known for its women's alcoholism rehabilitation unit. Woman's General was founded in 1878 as the Women's & Children's Free Medical & Surgical Dispensary by 2 women physicians, Kate Parsons and MYRA K. MERRICK. Merrick was the first woman to practice medicine in Cleveland. The initial purpose was to give women graduating in medicine an opportunity to obtain clinical experience that was denied them in dispensaries and hospitals of the city, and give needy women an opportunity to be treated by members of their own sex. In its first 4 years, the dispensary operated from a corner of the Homeopathic Medical College on Prospect Ave. A 2-story brick building was purchased in 1882. The dispensary's patients consisted of poor women or women who wanted a female physician. A bed in HURON RD. HOSPITAL was used for the seriously ill. The hospital was incorporated in 1894 as the Women's & Children's Medical & Surgical Dispensary. For many years it was jointly run by a board of trustees composed of medical women, and a board of fiscal trustees composed of men. A prominent woman physician, Sarah Marcus, provided notable leadership during the mid-20th century.

In 1912, under the impetus of Martha A. Canfield, a resolution was adopted to turn the dispensary into a hospital for women and children. This decision was largely in response to a new regulation that allowed only hospital-trained physicians to practice medicine. As a result, Women's Hospital was opened on Cedar Ave. in 1913. In 1915 it moved into a rented building on E. 107th and increased its beds from 12 to 19. A new building was erected on E. 101st at what would later be Chester, in 1918. By 1929, Women's Hospital offered the 3d-largest maternity service in Cleveland. That same year, a new board was established that consisted of both men and women, professional and lay. Large-scale expansion did not begin until 1949, when ground was broken for a new 5-floor facility with beds for medical and surgical patients, an obstetrics and gynecology department, a surgical facility, an x-ray department, and a laboratory. Two additional stories were completed in 1959. In 1964 a 20-year expansion program was announced, but it never fully materialized because of changing economic problems. In 1970 the name was changed to Woman's General Hospital. By 1974 the hospital had an active medical staff of 52, and departments of surgery, medicine, gynecology, pediatrics, radiology, anesthesiology, and pathology. A year later a new wing was opened for women alcoholics, thought to be the first of its kind in the U.S. In the early 1980s, with increasing competition from newer facilities nearby, the hospital suffered declining occupancy. In deep financial trouble, it closed in 1984.

**WOMEN.** Tabitha Stiles, who accompanied her husband on MOSES CLEAVELAND's survey expedition, remained on the shores of Lake Erie and was rewarded with a sizable land grant. She was an exception. Women helped tame the wilderness but seldom held title to it. Nor did many women own the homes, stores, and factories that marked the urban landscape in the 175 years that followed. But women nourished and nurtured the farmers, laborers, and property owners within the privacy of their homes, and they created their own organizations and institutions, which enriched their community with social services and cultural activities. For the first 2 decades, Cleveland's development was slow and precarious. Men built primitive cabins and cleared land for planting. Wives, mothers, and daughters turned the food grown into daily meals and preserved supplies for the long winters. They combed, spun, wove, and sewed the flax grown. Sixteen-year-old daughters taught the younger children between the brief periods of residence of schoolmasters. Female family members nursed the sick—often malaria-ridden—settlers when they themselves did not suffer from "fits and agues." By 1830, the mouth of the Cuyahoga was drained, and health improved. Population, transportation, and commerce grew along with social dislocation, and Cleveland was ripe for evangelical religion, reform, and charity. REBECCA ROUSE and her businessman husband, BENJAMIN ROUSE, arrived that year as agents for the American Bible Society. First they established regular religious services, but quickly Rouse and wives and sisters of the town's business leaders founded the MARTHA WASHINGTON & DORCAS SOCIETY to promote TEMPERANCE and provide poor relief. They founded an orphan asylum and established a branch of the Female Moral Reform Society to rehabilitate prostitutes and assist unmarried pregnant women. Rouse and her friends visited the sick and distributed food and charity. By mid-century, 225 women took part in activities on behalf of poor relief; 1,400 belonged to temperance societies. Only when financial needs outstripped the women's resources were they forced to turn over their benevolent social services to their male relatives, a pattern that would persist.

The property rights of married women were beginning to be questioned and changed at mid-century. Under existing common law, all property and earnings of women belonged to their husbands. New York made significant changes in those practices in 1848; Ohio began soon after, amending all property and contract laws by 1887. Under these slowly changing legal circumstances, women were not just sensitive to the needs of their community, they were also ingenious in their ability to raise money through bazaars, collections, and sale of their handmade products. Fundraising activity reached a significant level in 1864, when thousands of Cleveland women who volunteered their services to the Northern Ohio Soldiers' Aid Society (see SOLDIERS' AID SOCIETY OF NORTHERN OHIO) held a great fair on PUBLIC SQUARE in 1864. Volunteers also

established and staffed a soldiers' home in Cleveland for soldiers en route between home and army base. After the war, the women founded a Free Claims Agency and an employment bureau. By transforming their benevolent societies and church groups into Soldiers' Aid branches, women learned organization and leadership skills in the process of contributing to the war effort.

After the conflict, attention turned to matters at home. In Oct. 1868, 600 women from area churches combined to form the Women's Christian Assoc. of Cleveland. Like the voluntary societies of antebellum Cleveland, the initial motivation was benevolent and religious and focused on the increased mobility of female migrants in search of gainful employment. The association clearly stated its desire to promote "the spiritual welfare of women, especially the young." Within a year of its founding, the organization created a boarding home to meet the needs of working women. Another institution, the Retreat, was quickly established to reform "the tempted and fallen who had already compromised their purity." By the turn of the century, the association, then known as the YWCA, founded additional homes for aged women, for chronically ill women, and for female transients. It also began a number of educational and social programs for working women and for mothers, while establishing other projects that eventually developed into independent organizations, such as the WOMAN'S CHRISTIAN TEMPERANCE UNION and the CLEVELAND DAY NURSERY & FREE KINDERGARTEN ASSOC. For decades the activities of the YWCA became the prototype for a number of other women's associations. The homes for needy women of all ages were replicated by the Non-Partisan WCTU of Cleveland and the SALVATION ARMY, and later by black and immigrant women's clubs and associations. Programs that became the centerpieces of social settlement houses—expanded for mothers and children—were modeled on classes and services first offered by the YWCA.

The dependent women who engaged the attention and concern of the Women's Christian Association were rural migrants and European immigrants who helped double Cleveland's population between 1860-70. They came in search of work and were more successful while the men were away at war. When the men returned and the numbers of female wage earners grew, their economic opportunities narrowed. By 1880, 10,000 Cleveland women were employed, but well over 75% were domestic servants, laundresses, dressmakers, and milliners. At the turn of the century, 20% of Cleveland's labor force was female. By that time, light industries increased, and young women workers clustered in paper box factories, bakeries, cigar and tobacco plants, laundries, men's and ladies' garment shops, and woolen mills. Cleveland's working women were predominantly young and single. Americans and immigrants alike sent their daughters to work. Ethnic background helped determine the kind of employment young women sought, but once employed they could depend on long hours and low wages. A 60-hour week was usual early in the century, and $5 per week was typical pay. Light industrial employment usually was seasonal, and workers experienced periods when no jobs were available. The wages of working daughters were crucial to the family economy, no matter how meager and sporadic. Income was invariably handed over to working-class mothers, who managed the family finances. The mothers contributed to the family coffers by performing many of the rudimentary social services that had characterized the pioneer women a century earlier.

The immigrant neighborhoods became the sites of new social-service institutions by the turn of the century. SETTLEMENT HOUSES originated in Chicago in 1889 and spread rapidly to other cities. Usually founded by well-educated, religious, and middle-class men and women, they became most closely identified with women. FLORA STONE MATHER, wealthy philanthropist who supported a number of YWCA programs, founded Cleveland's Goodrich House (see GOODRICH-GANNETT NEIGHBORHOOD CTR.) in 1897. Programs focused on clubs and classes for women and children. But quickly the Goodrich residents initiated reform and social-service programs: a library branch; music education, which became the CLEVELAND MUSIC SCHOOL SETTLEMENT; a school for crippled children, which became the Sunbeam School; the LEGAL AID SOCIETY; and the CONSUMERS LEAGUE OF OHIO to protect working women. Settlement houses proliferated and reflected the changing profile of Cleveland's population. ALTA HOUSE in LITTLE ITALY responded at first to the needs of Italian working women. The Council Educational Alliance, founded by the Council of Jewish Women as a nonresidential settlement, met the needs of growing Jewish immigration to Cleveland. The PHILLIS WHEATLEY ASSOC. was a tribute to the determination of JANE EDNA HUNTER, who responded to housing and recreational needs of black women migrating from the rural South. This flurry of social-welfare action by Cleveland women was part of an incredible burst of female energy and pride. Mrs. MARY INGHAM wrote a tribute to the educational and philanthropic work of Cleveland's women in 1893. An associate enlisted 216 volunteers to write the early histories of female settlers in as many Western Reserve communities. Their collective tribute was ready for Cleveland's 1896 centennial celebration, at which time a special women's department celebrated its own day during the week-long festivities. The flourishing social feminist activity and sense of femaleness that drew women out of their homes to engage in community building also led to increased attention to political rights.

While Cleveland had hosted women's rights and women's suffrage conventions during the 19th century, concerted efforts on behalf of improving women's legal and political status were few. Improvements in property rights, divorce and child-custody procedures, and related issues had occurred during the century, but primarily in response to pressures exerted from other sections of Ohio. By 1887, the last limitations on women's property rights contracts were removed. In 1894, the Ohio legislature granted women suffrage in schoolboard elections. However, organized efforts on behalf of votes for women did not begin in earnest in Cleveland until 1911. Like the movement nationally, which worked for state-by-state enfranchisement, the Cleveland Suffrage League focused on gaining the vote in Ohio. Leaders and a constantly growing membership organized meetings, trained speakers, distributed publicity, presented pageants, and marched in street demonstrations. They attempted to amend the state constitution and failed; they placed the issue on statewide ballots, but it went down to defeat; and a bill granting presidential suffrage was recalled in a legally questionable referendum. In spite of great effort, Cleveland suffragists were not enfranchised until the 19th Amendment was passed and ratified. Like suffrage associations elsewhere, Cleveland's organizations transformed themselves into the LEAGUE OF WOMEN VOTERS to educate women on issues and voting procedures. The Cleveland league gained national attention with its candidate interviews, the "founding" of the widespread women's peace movement of the interwar years, and the elevation of local president and activist BELLE SHERWIN to head the national league. The Consumers League of Ohio, which had shifted tactics from consumer boycotts of local firms to lobbying for wage, hour, and improved

and protective work standards for women through legislation, also gained national recognition. But the 2 leagues, and other women's associations, did not achieve the successes after the mid-1920s that had marked their earlier efforts.

For Cleveland's working women, female experiences after WORLD WAR I were varied. For immigrant women still coping with a new cultural milieu, the 1920s meant the separation of families because of restrictive immigration legislation. However, the reasonably prosperous decade saw some of their daughters join native-born women in the growing areas of white-collar service jobs. By 1930, 40% of the city's working women were engaged in sales, clerical, and communication-related employment. Black women replaced immigrants at the bottom of the ladder. Few groups escaped the hardships of the 1930s. With its reliance on heavy industry, Cleveland felt the impact of the Depression early. Unemployed steel and auto workers meant extra pressure on work-age daughters to seek increasingly limited employment and forced wives and mothers to find innovative, hard-working methods of homebound "making do." The long tradition of female community nurture and building once more centered on hard-pressed homes. Women's public activities did not cease. Rather, women in organizations ranging from foreign-language branches of the COMMUNIST PARTY to the Consumers League protested against government indifference toward the economically deprived and lobbied on behalf of welfare and relief measures. Working-class women took actions independent of social reformers. In the midst of the labor organizing that followed the formation of the Congress of Industrial Organizations (CIO), thousands of women struck employers and won union representation. Other women played leading roles in the organizing campaigns in heavy industry.

The 1940s brought significant changes to those heavy industries. Conversion to war production and the drafting of men meant tanks rolled off Cleveland's assembly lines and women became a new component of the Cleveland labor force. During WORLD WAR II, the Consumers League was hard-pressed to maintain working and safety standards for the women workers in the face of legislation that undermined work standards. Non-wage-earning sisters and mothers swelled the ranks of the Red Cross, rolling bandages and knitting sweaters while juggling their ration coupons and coping with wartime shortages. Still, given the massive efforts of women at home, at work, and in the community generally, it is significant that no outstanding leadership or organizational bases arose comparable to the Soldiers' Aid Society of the Civil War era or even the short-lived Cleveland Women's Committee of the Council of Natl. Defense of 1917 and 1918. Government agencies filled the roles formerly played by women's voluntary associations and expert advisors.

During the postwar period of inward perspectives, women's collective activities reflected their family-oriented concerns. Parent-teacher associations flourished. League of Women Voters chapters were founded in new suburban communities. The child-rearing mothers of Greater Cleveland communities were the best-educated females in history, and in spite of the pervasive ideology celebrating maternity and domesticity, they looked for voluntary associations that offered intellectual challenge and social companionship. The leagues, with their emphasis on research and discussion, filled a vital need for the women. The issues they studied covered the full range of public concerns, from zoning, enforcement of building codes, and countywide government to support for the United Nations and issues of international trade. Domestic workers rode public transportation each day so that their suburban employers had the leisure to drive to new shopping centers and on to PTA functions and voluntary association meetings. The decreasing and aging membership of other organizations also turned to new issues. The Consumers League focused on the plights of migrant workers and on the country's health needs, advocating national health insurance. Other female activists, older veterans of the vibrant women's movement of the earlier decades of the century, turned their attention to reducing cold war tensions and controlling the growing terrors of nuclear warfare. The post-World War II peace movement never approached the size and female involvement of the one that had flourished in the 1920s and 1930s, but it did engage a number of Cleveland women prior to the antiwar protests and the revived women's movement of the 1960s. And FRANCES PAYNE BOLTON maintained a female presence in the U.S. Congress at a time when women's political visibility was low.

The rebirth of feminism in Greater Cleveland, like the movement nationally, had its roots in civil-rights activism. Unlike in the South, issues involved not Jim Crow laws but rather the de facto segregation that was deeply embedded in residential segregation. Construction of new public schools in the late 1950s, which reinforced educational segregation, aroused the black population and white supporters. The cautious black males who spoke on behalf of the city's NAACP chapters were eclipsed by the female head of the more militant Congress for Racial Equality (CORE), who minced no words in opposing racial inequities in Cleveland. Seemingly overnight, female images and voices were prominent in many areas. The working-class women and CLEVELAND PRESS writers were instrumental in organizing the prototype for the Natl. Committee for Labor Union Women. Middle-class women founded chapters of the NATL. ORGANIZATION FOR WOMEN in a number of communities. The local BUSINESS & PROFESSIONAL WOMEN'S CLUB renewed its efforts on behalf of the Equal Rights Amendment, which made its way out of Congress in 1970. It was joined by the League of Women Voters, which had opposed the amendment for close to half a century because of its threat to special legislation for working women. Together, women mounted a successful assault on the Ohio laws that female reformers had long sought as protective but which new feminist values and goals believed restricted women's economic opportunities. Veteran reformers such as ELIZABETH MAGEE of the Consumers League, however, remained committed to the older vision.

By 1975, Cleveland was a pacesetter in the celebration of INTERNATL. WOMEN'S YEAR. For 3 days in November, tens of women's organizations, hundreds of individual women, and numerous national figures mounted displays, workshops, lectures, and performances in an unprecedented celebration of women, their activities, and the problems they confronted. WOMENSPACE was founded to house the associations—some well-established, most new—ranging from rape crisis centers to employment agencies to legal aid organizations. Female migrations expanded—into nontraditional professional schools, into the labor market, out to more distant suburbs, and out of the area altogether, especially to the Sun Belt. The population loss that had marked the last 2 decades meant that women were leaving the Greater Cleveland area in record numbers, leaving the city all the poorer in the diminished community-building resources that have marked its history. But the women who remained tackled the area's problems from more professional and political as well as volunteer positions of action. As state legislators, county commissioners, and suburban mayors, women continued to attempt to ef-

fect positive change from within power structures on behalf of the metropolitan region.

Lois Scharf
Case Western Reserve University

Abbatt, Virginia Clark, *The History of Women Suffrage and the League of Women Voters in Cuyahoga County, 1911–1945* (1949).
Ingham, Mary A., *Women of Cleveland and Their Work* (1893).
Scharf, Lois, "Cleveland's Labor Force: Women's View, 1880–1930." In *Birth of Modern Cleveland* (1987).
Scharf, Lois, "The Women's Movement in Cleveland from 1850." In *Cleveland: A Tradition of Reform*, ed. David D. Van Tassel and John Grabowski (1986).
Wickham, Gertrude Van Rensselaer, ed., *Memorial to the Pioneer Women of the Western Reserve* (1896–1924).
See also LABOR, PHILANTHROPY, and the names of specific women and women's organizations.

**WOMEN TOGETHER** was formed in the mid-1970s to provide emergency shelter and counseling for battered women. Representatives from social agencies that dealt with female victims of violence, such as the FREE MEDICAL CLINIC, the CLEVELAND RAPE CRISIS CTR., and the Victim Assistance Unit of the Cleveland Municipal Court, and women's groups such as WOMENSPACE and Cleveland Women's Counseling joined forces to form the group and to publicize the need for such a shelter. Among the early members of Women Together were Sandy Scully, Grace Kilbane, Lynne Rosewater, Jan Dickey, Daryl Mittler, and Mary Jo Ginty. By mid-Aug. 1976, the women had found a suitable house and opened an emergency shelter with accommodations for 16 people; women who were victims of abusive partners could escape to this secluded shelter with their children and could begin to put their lives in order. At first the shelter was supported by donations, but within months of opening, it received an initial $17,000 grant from the CLEVELAND FOUNDATION; grants from the GEO. GUND FOUNDATION and the Gerson Foundation followed. Women Together also took over the WomenSpace hotline for battered women and later expanded its operations around the clock. By the spring of 1983, the hotline was receiving about 700 calls a month. In May 1985, Women Together began a new program, Second Step, to provide long-term care and support for women after they left the emergency shelter. The Famicos Foundation renovated a 6-suite apartment building to provide low-cost housing for the women and their children, and Women Together continued to offer counseling services as well as assistance in finding job training or additional education. Women Together became the first battered-women's program in Ohio to offer such a program geared toward helping former battered women establish social and financial independence.

The **WOMEN'S ART CLUB OF CLEVELAND** was founded in Sept. 1912. It was the first art organization in Cleveland to be composed entirely of women and was also known as the Women Artists of Cleveland and Cleveland Women Artists Club. The original club had 25 members, whose goal was the mutual improvement of women artists in Cleveland through exhibitions, sketching trips, life classes, and monthly meetings, which provided a forum for new ideas and innovations. The club originally included women artists working in the fields of design, illustration, oil painting, watercolor, ceramics, and commercial art. The first elected officers of the club were president, Anna Pfenniger, the only woman sculptor in Cleveland, who was also the president of the West End School of Art in Cleveland; vice-president, Caroline G. Williams, a local oil painter; secretary, Mrs. Thos. B. Robinson; and treasurer, Belle Hoffman, at whose studio in the GAGE GALLERY (2258 Euclid Ave.) the monthly meetings, as well as the supplementary life classes, were held. The first exhibition of works by club members was held 18-25 Oct. 1913 at the Gage Gallery. In Nov. 1913, the club relocated to the Bonhard Art Furniture Co. (2054 Euclid Ave.), where the members opened an exhibition and showroom. Another move followed in May 1916, to the Euclid Pt. Bldg. (1272 Euclid Ave.). In 1918, the club was incorporated. Also in 1918, Carrie Robinson donated a lot in GATES MILLS, Ohio, for the erection of a permanent clubhouse and studio building; the new home of the club was officially named Robinwood on 15 June 1918. In Sept. 1921, club members voted to join the FED. OF WOMEN'S CLUBS, and in 1926 they officially joined the American Fed. of Arts.

Because the Gates Mills studio was often inaccessible during the winter, monthly meetings were held at the homes of members or at the CLEVELAND PUBLIC LIBRARY. During the early 1920s, the club rented the 3d-floor rooms at the Gage Gallery to serve as the city headquarters for the group; the city headquarters were later transferred to Mildred Watkins's studio at 10646 Euclid Ave. In 1925, an auxiliary, "the City Division of the Women's Art Club of Cleveland," was established for members who either did not want to or could not travel to the Gates Mills studio. This group was abandoned as unnecessary in 1929. In 1929, the club obtained JEPTHA H. WADE's Lodge property at 1964 E. 40th St. rent-free. The Women's Art Club of Cleveland was, though primarily a social group, very active in the art field, presenting annual shows to the public as well as sending exhibitions to other institutions in the state, including an annual representation of works to the Ohio State Fair in Columbus. In addition, the members maintained close contact with other art groups in the city, often hosting events for the CLEVELAND SOCIETY OF ARTISTS or attending events sponsored by that group. The Women's Art Club of Cleveland numbered 150 members at its height in 1930. The club was active with shows, craft markets, parties, and social events up through the early 1950s.

The **WOMEN'S BUREAU OF THE CLEVELAND POLICE DEPT.** was for nearly 50 years the only area of the department open to women. It provided trained women investigators for a wide variety of functions and duties. While the CPD had employed women as jail matrons since 1893, there were by the 1920s no women police officers. At that time the WOMEN'S CITY CLUB undertook a campaign to create a women's police bureau similar to those already established in other large cities. After considerable lobbying and debate, city council authorized the establishment of the Women's Bureau. While the first policewomen were appointed in 1923, the bureau itself was not officially formed until Dec. 1924. Many of the first women hired were former teachers or social workers. They did not wear uniforms or carry firearms. They were investigators who worked on all police cases in which women or children were involved as either victims or offenders. Emphasis was placed on preventive work. In many instances the women performed as social workers, referring needy women or children to appropriate sources of assistance. By 1932, there were 15 members of the bureau: a captain, a sergeant, and 13 officers. They were responsible for staffing an office 24 hours a day, 365 days a year. They were available to assist detectives whenever requested, to perform undercover details, to escort and protect visiting dignitaries and their families, to guard women prisoners and witnesses, to transport prisoners, to assist the welfare department with

home investigations, to inspect dance halls, and to serve juvenile court warrants.

The first chief of the Women's Bureau was Dorothy Doan Henry, a former social worker, who served from 1924-30. She was succeeded by Alpha Larsen, who had joined the bureau in 1924. Hazel Witt was bureau captain from 1934-65. In 1956, under Capt. Witt, women first attended the police academy. Prior to that time women had received special instruction by academy instructors. By this time the Women's Bureau had grown to 30 members. In 1965, Wilma Neubecker became the first woman to rise completely through the ranks and be promoted to captain and placed in command of the bureau. Under Capt. Neubecker, members of the bureau began to carry firearms. In 1971, Erma Molnar succeeded Neubecker, and she was, in turn, succeeded by Violet Novak in 1973. By 1972, women had successfully lobbied for the right to serve in all units of the CPD. In that year for the first time, women police applicants were required to take the same physical tests as male applicants. More significant, also in 1972 women officers were first assigned to the districts as patrol officers. In 1974, in a reorganization necessitated by a serious personnel shortage, the Women's Bureau was disestablished and its members absorbed into other units. Violet Novak, the last chief of the bureau, later became the first female captain to serve on line duty with the CPD.

The **WOMEN'S CITY CLUB** of Cleveland, located in the Citizens Bldg., 850 Euclid Ave., an organization of (and for) business and professional women as well as homemakers, supports and inaugurates many civic, educational, and cultural projects for the benefit of the city of Cleveland. The idea for a club where public-spirited women, including many suffragettes, "could meet downtown and discuss in a friendly spirit community problems" originated with a group of women that included Mrs. Roger Perkins, Mrs. Edward S. Bassett, Mrs. Morris A. Black, MILDRED CHADSEY, and BELLE SHERWIN. These women held their first planning meeting on 18 Jan. 1916 at the Statler Hilton Hotel (now the Cleveland Plaza). In Feb. 1916, the Downtown Club merged with the new Women's City Club, and on 4 Mar. 1916 the new club was incorporated "for the purpose of promoting a vast acquaintance among women, providing a central meeting place, maintaining an open forum for the discussion of topics of civic and public interest and promoting the welfare of the City of Cleveland." Its clubrooms were those of the Downtown Club in the Flatiron Bldg. In Dec. 1916, the club moved its quarters to the Stillman Bldg. In the fall of 1920, the Women's City Club amended its rules, making it possible for it to actively support and endorse such civil issues and state and federal legislation as were approved by the board of directors. This policy has continued throughout its history. In 1922, the club leased and rebuilt for its own use the Dreamland Dance Hall, 1826 E. 13th St. It remained there until 1933, when it moved to the Bulkley Bldg., 1501 Euclid Ave. in PLAYHOUSE SQUARE. The Women's City Club Foundation was established in Apr. 1948 to foster research relating to the problems of women; it has since been used to initiate and support many civic, educational, and cultural projects. In 1961, the club inaugurated the Creative Fine Arts Awards, giving recognition to Cleveland artists. In July 1971 the Women's City Club and the CITY CLUB moved to the Cleveland Civic House, Women's Federal Bldg., where the two groups shared dining and meeting facilities. In Dec. 1982 the Women's City Club moved to the Citizens Bldg., opening its headquarters in the new location in Jan. 1983.

The **WOMEN'S COUNCIL PEACE PARADE FOR THE PREVENTION OF FUTURE WARS** took place on Sunday, 18 May 1924, when 5,000 women marched down Euclid Ave., from E. 24th St. to E. 3rd and Lakeside. The purpose was to encourage a "will to peace in the world, to prevent war, for peace to reign throughout the world." The parade was organized by the Women's Council for the Prevention of Future Wars, chaired by Mrs. Edward S. Basset, with Mrs. Frances F. Bushea as executive secretary. Participants represented more than 40 organizations and institutions. Controversy surrounded the parade's planning. The American Legion and the Chamber of Commerce opposed it, labeling the women as unpatriotic, Soviet-inspired radicals and writing letters of complaint to the secretary of war. Ex-servicemen countered these complaints by circulating petitions in support of the parade. At 3 P.M. on 18 May, marchers gathered at Euclid Ave. and E. 24th. The groups present included the WOMEN'S CITY CLUB, the Judges & Jurors Assoc., the Polish Singing Society, the Daughters of America, the Daughters of the Civil War, the Campfire Guardians, the Businesswomen's Assoc., more than a dozen Parent-Teacher Associations, and a girls' marching band from Glenville High School. More than 500 university students and many mothers' groups also participated.

The march was led by Cleveland police chief JACOB GRAUL and an escort of several mounted policemen. They were followed by state supreme court judge FLORENCE ALLEN. City councilwoman MARIE WING followed her, wearing a white riding habit and riding a black horse. The Gold Star Mothers followed, wearing blue bonnets. A *Plain Dealer* reporter described them as exemplifying the "mother spirit which had unflinchingly given their sons to wars and now marched to proclaim their objective: no more sons for wars." Little children marched, bearing garlands of rosebuds in their hands. The YWCA represented "Women of All Nations," including a Spanish maiden in crimson lace, a Turkish girl in veils, and girls from Japan, Greece, Czechoslovakia, Austria, and others dressed in their national attire. The Businesswomen's Assoc. wore Red Cross nurses' caps and called themselves the Flanders Poppy Div. They carried poppies in memory of soldiers buried overseas. Turning the corner at E. 6th St., they marched to City Hall, past a reviewing stand filled with city officials, clergy, and elderly women too weak to march, including Mrs. Kate Crocker, widow of a Civil War soldier.

The **WOMEN'S FEDERAL SAVINGS BANK** of Cleveland was the first savings-and-loan association in the nation founded and operated by women. Two of its original officers, CLARA E. WESTROPP and LILLIAN M. WESTROPP, provided direction for the association from the receipt of its charter in 1935 until Clara's death in 1965. Women's Federal developed from an earlier financial institution established by the Westropp sisters. The Women's Savings & Loan Co. was organized by a group of business and professional women who met in Lillian Westropp's law office on 6 Jan. 1922. The company began operations in February with $89,000 in capital. Clara Westropp served as secretary, and after a year of operation, Lillian became president. Women's Savings grew steadily in the 1920s, outgrowing its original offices in the Ulmer Bldg. and moving to new quarters in the Women's City Club building. Between 1932–34, however, it reported losses of half its capital. Although state audits showed the company to be financially sound, "false rumors" about its stability persisted. The directors took advantage of the 1933 Federal Home Owners' Loan Act to reorganize the bank as Women's Federal Savings & Loan. The new bank received its federal charter on 29 May 1935 and a certificate of insurance for its deposits in Aug. 1935. Women's Federal began operations in the Colonial Arcade, but growth forced it to move in 1938 to 320 Superior Ave., a building that it purchased in 1944. By 1950 it was the 97th-largest savings and loan in the country and the 2d-largest in Cuyahoga County, with assets of more than $20 million. Clara Westropp replaced her sister as president in 1957 and oversaw construction of a new office building between Superior and Euclid avenues adjacent to the old site. The new building, opened in June 1963, served as Women's Federal's headquarters until July 1982, when it was sold to the STANDARD OIL CO. and razed. Following his aunt's death in 1965, Thos. C. Westropp became president, taking over a company with $142 million in assets. Lawrence F. Guzowski became president in 1981. After losing money in 1981 and 1982, Women's Federal Savings & Loan became an investor-owned savings bank in June 1983. Investors injected $38 million in new capital into the renamed Women's Federal Savings Bank, returning it to profitability. Assets in June 1983 were more than $576 million.

The **WOMEN'S LAW FUND, INC.**, a nonprofit organization, was the first law firm in the country to limit its practice to sex-discrimination cases. Financed through private grants, WLF opened for business in the Keith Bldg. in Oct. 1972. In 1986, its staff of 2 full-time attorneys handled precedent-setting discrimination cases for both women and men, for which the client was not charged a fee. Professors Jane Picker and Lizabeth Moody of CLEVELAND STATE UNIVERSITY's Cleveland-Marshall College of Law established WLF as an agency for women seeking legal redress in cases of sexual discrimination in employment, education, housing, welfare, credit, and government benefits. Funded by a $140,000 Ford Foundation grant and a $25,000 grant from the CLEVELAND FOUNDATION, WLF originally employed 1 full-time and 3 part-time attorneys. Rita Page Ruess, the first woman assistant U.S. attorney in Cleveland, left her post to join WLF in the full-time position. Picker, a founder, trustee, and litigation chairman for WLF, became interested in the field of sex discrimination through her friend and former Yale Law School classmate Moody. After graduation, Picker specialized in international law, becoming a pioneer in the field of outer-space and communications law while working for the Communications Satellite Corp. in Washington, D.C. Moving to Cleveland in 1969, she entered private practice. Like many other women lawyers, she soon found herself deluged with cases of women unable to find lawyers to take their cases. Working with the aid of Moody, the two established WLF. An outgrowth of WLF is the sex-discrimination clinic headed by Picker for CSU's law students interested in studying discrimination legislation. The year-long course provides students with hands-on experience dealing with actual cases. Utilizing aid from Cleveland-Marshall and a contract with the Equal Employment Opportunities Commission, Picker developed teaching and training materials on sexual-discrimination litigation used even by the EEOC. The WLF has pursued its objectives to the U.S. Supreme Court, where Picker successfully argued on behalf of 2 Cleveland teachers forced to quit when 5 months pregnant. The Court struck down the Cleveland School Board's maternity-leave regulations, ruling that pregnancy could not be used as a deterrence to employment. Among its other accomplishments, WLF succeeded in forcing the CLEVELAND POLICE DEPT. to allow women to enroll in police cadet programs and put women in patrol cars, and has fought for the hiring of more women on the force.

The **WOMEN'S MEDICAL SOCIETY OF CLEVELAND** was founded in 1929 to further the advancement of women in medicine in Cleveland. The first meeting was held at the WOMEN'S CITY CLUB and attended by 19 women. Membership was initially limited to women doctors living or practicing in Cleveland, but in 1931 was broadened to include eligible women doctors from northern Ohio. Sarah Marcus, a prominent Cleveland doctor, was a founding member. The Women's Medical Society met monthly, except during the summer. The monthly dinner meetings in members' homes or at the Women's City Club included a talk generally related to medical problems affecting women, or professional issues concerning women doctors. This format changed little over the years. The number of members remained relatively constant, averaging 20–30. In the late 1950s, in order to generate new interest in the society, women interns and medical students were invited to attend meetings. In the 1970s and 1980s, the society increased its sponsorship of special programs and events, including a symposium on women and exercise in 1980. The society has for many years been affiliated with the Cleveland ACADEMY OF MEDICINE.

The **WOMEN'S PROTECTIVE ASSOCIATION** was established in response to conditions believed responsible for the corruption and exploitation of young women. Formally organized on 9 Mar. 1916, the agency defined its purpose as follows: "to protect and safeguard girls and women against social and moral dangers, to provide them with legal defense when necessary and to render other possible assistance. . . ." Late in 1915, BELLE SHERWIN suggested that Mayor NEWTON D. BAKER appoint a woman as a special investigator to work with women who had been arrested and were scheduled for trial. Sherwin suggested Sabina Marshall, a trained social worker who had graduated from Smith College. Baker and police chief FRED KOHLER approved the idea. Marshall and Sherwin proceeded to organize a board of prominent women to oversee the work. During its first years of operation, the WPA investigated carnivals, patrolled dance halls, and started a movement for women probation officers at police court. During WORLD WAR I, the federal government made the association its agent for the protection of women near army cantonments. An important issue for the WPA was the need to improve women's jail conditions. Marshall felt that women who were being held for investigation, waiting for trial, or waiting for sentence after trial should be kept in a detention home, and not in jail with hardened criminals. In July 1917, CLEVELAND CITY COUNCIL passed an ordinance that permitted the WPA to operate a detention home. The Sterling House, opened in Dec. 1917, was so successful that the association purchased another building for an enlarged home. The old house, renamed the Prospect Club, became a boarding home for girls who needed supervision until permanent residence plans could be made. In 1922 the Big Sister Council, through which volunteer Big Sisters helped promote proper character development in girls, became a part of the WPA. In 1930 the association became the Girls' Bureau. This change reflected the shift of court-oriented work to other agencies, including women's probation services within the juvenile and municipal courts and the creation of the special WOMEN'S BUREAU OF THE CLEVELAND POLICE DEPT. The Girls' Bureau now focused largely on casework. In 1943 the Girls' Bureau expanded its services to include boys and again changed its name, to the Youth Bureau. This agency then became part of what is now known as the CTR. FOR HUMAN SERVICES.

**WOMENSPACE** is a coalition of organizations in Cleveland dedicated to supporting changes for the betterment of women. It is a nonprofit organization run by a board of directors. WomenSpace was founded in 1975 by Jane Campbell. Its purpose was to organize the various women's groups in the area and prevent duplication of effort. By coordinating and uniting the efforts of these groups, WomenSpace sought to attain more influence than each group had by itself. WomenSpace has attempted to accomplish its goals through various programs. Some have been carried out solely by WomenSpace, while others have been coordinated with groups such as UNITED WAY, the Cleveland YWCA, CLEVELAND WOMEN WORKING, and Cuyahoga County. One program, Helpline, is a telephone information service offered to women and their families. Trained staff members offer information and referrals to callers. Another program, Women & Alcohol, is a joint project of WomenSpace and the Cuyahoga County Board of Commissioners. This project not only tries to educate women about alcoholism but also works to ensure that quality services are available to help women in Cuyahoga County. Other projects include Domestic Violence Outreach, Women in Skilled Employment, and Women in Appointed Office. All the projects are oriented toward enabling women to help themselves and to help other women gain control of their lives. In 1986, WomenSpace had its headquarters at 1021 Euclid Ave.

**WOOD, REUBEN** (1792–1 Oct. 1864), was the 16th governor of Ohio (1850–53) and an early Cleveland pioneer, attorney, state senator, judge, and farmer. Wood was born in Middletown, Vt. He moved to Canada at the age of 15, where his studies included law. During the WAR OF 1812, he was conscripted into the Royalist Militia under Gen. Brock. He fled to the U.S. and served briefly in the U.S. Army. He arrived in Cleveland in 1818 and went to Buffalo in the spring of 1819 to accompany his wife and first daughter to Cleveland. After a perilous voyage, the Wood family arrived in Cleveland aboard the first steamship to visit the city, the *WALK-IN-THE-WATER*. He was the city's third attorney; the other two were ALFRED KELLEY and LEONARD CASE. Wood was elected president of the village of Cleveland in 1821. In 1825, he was elected to his first of 3 terms in the Ohio senate. he delivered the address at the opening of the Ohio Canal in 1827. in 1830, he was elected by the general assembly as a judge of the common pleas court for the 3d Circuit; in 1832, he was elected to his first of 2 terms as judge of the Ohio Supreme Court (1833–47); and for the last 3 years of his second term, he served as chief justice. He was defeated for reelection in 1847. Wood was elected governor in 1850. However, in June 1851, the voters approved the new Ohio constitution, which required the election of officials in odd-numbered years, and Wood was again elected governor in 1851. In his 1851 inaugural address, he expressed his abhorrence of the Fugitive Slave Law and urged its repeal. The adoption of the new 1851 Ohio constitution and many related laws was the major accomplishment of his term as governor. Wood narrowly missed being nominated for president at the 1852 Democratic Natl. Convention, losing to Franklin Pierce from New Hampshire. He resigned the governorship in 1853 to accept appointment by Pres. Pierce as consul in Valparaiso, Chile. A year later he returned to Cleveland and resumed his law practice. He spent his later years developing his lakefront farm, known as Evergreen Place, in ROCKPORT, now ROCKY RIVER. Wood married Mary Rice in 1816. They had 2 daughters, Loretta and Mary. Wood and his wife are buried in WOODLAND CEMETERY.

The **WOODLAND AVENUE AND WEST SIDE RAILWAY COMPANY** was the first streetcar line to allow passengers to travel between the east and west sides without requiring a transfer, which would have meant paying a second fare. The line was formed in Feb. 1885 with the merger of the Woodland Ave. and West Side street railway companies. The new line was controlled by Cleveland industrialist MARCUS A. HANNA and his sons. The two lines involved in the merger had been founded by Cleveland omnibus entrepreneur Henry S. Stephens but had changed ownership by the time of the merger. The Woodland Ave. Street Railway was formed in 1859. It carried passengers via horsecars from W. 9th and Superior, around the south side of PUBLIC SQUARE to Ontario, south on Ontario to Woodland, and east on Woodland to E. 55th. It was extended to WOODLAND CEMETERY (E. 65th) in 1862, and later to the Cleveland & Pittsburgh Railroad crossing at E. 79th. A line also operated on Kinsman, to the Cleveland & Pittsburgh tracks at E. 55th. The West Side Railroad Co. was established in Feb. 1863. It was the first streetcar line to run west of the CUYAHOGA RIVER in Cleveland. It carried passengers from Superior and Vineyard St. (which later disappeared when the Terminal Tower complex was built) to the FLATS. The line crossed the river on the Center St. Bridge, climbed the Detroit St. hill, then looped the near west side. Its route went down Detroit to W. 38th, south to Lorain, east on Lorain to W. 25th, then north to Detroit, routing back into the valley. The line acquired the right to use the new SUPERIOR VIADUCT in 1880, eliminating the route through the Flats.

The merged lines entered the era of electrification in the early 1890s, constructing the Viaduct Power House in 1892. Located just north of the Superior Viaduct in the Flats, the structure still stood in 1985, empty and abandoned. Plans to turn it into a shopping boutique in the 1970s were never carried out. The line merged with the Cleveland City Cable Co. in May 1893 and took the name Cleveland City Railway. It was known as the "Little Consolidated" and remained under the Hanna family's control. Its only rival was the CLEVELAND ELECTRIC RAILWAY, or "Big Consolidated," another line formed by mergers of smaller lines. In July 1903, the Big and Little Consolidated merged, as Hanna sold the Cleveland City Railway to the owners of the Cleveland Electric Railway. That effectively left only 1 company that held the Cleveland streetcar monopoly. This company did battle with Cleveland mayor TOM L. JOHNSON over streetcar fares.

Christiansen, Harry, *Trolley Trails through Greater Cleveland and Northern Ohio* (1975).

**WOODLAND CEMETERY** was once the pride of Cleveland's public CEMETERIES. From its start, Woodland differed from other cemeteries that, sensibly named, were functionally laid out. In 1853, Woodland was fashioned in rural cemetery style by New York landscape gardener Howard Daniels. A fancifully poetic description of an unseen Cleveland by Scottish poet Thos. Campbell inspired the name. Woodland's creation derived from a failed real-estate speculation. In 1832, Col. Geo. Bomford, chief of U.S. Army ordnance and master of the Washington, D.C., estate Kalorama, acquired 200 acres in Newburgh Twp. He sold 100 acres to John Whipple, Providence, R.I., and 60 acres to Benjamin F. Butler, Pres. Andrew Jackson's attorney general. The trio divided the land into 40 5-acre lots just before the Panic of 1837. By 1851, the land remained unsold. SAMUEL STARKWEATHER, the local agent, proposed selling Butler's share for the long-sought second city cemetery, an offer accepted by council. Former Ohioan Daniels, who had designed rural cemeteries in Cincinnati (Spring Grove, 1845), Xenia (Woodland, 1847), and

Columbus (Greenlawn, 1849), as well as Dayton's Montgomery County Courthouse (1844), provided a 20-acre plan, "as beautifully prepared for a burial place as fancy and taste could desire." On 14 June 1853, Clevelanders flocked to the dedication complete with sermons, speeches, poetry, and music. Woodland became a popular place for legal and illicit activities. In 1859 the Kinsman Street Railroad went by its gates. During and after the CIVIL WAR, streetcars ran regularly, with extras on Decoration Day. Ohio's last Civil War governor, John Brough, whose grave the city donated, joined other fallen warriors, including the only known Confederate soldier buried in Cleveland, in 1865. Woodland was known to prostitutes, whose presence disconcerted virtuous ladies, and to medical students seeking cadavers. The cemetery for prominent Clevelanders, Woodland was often improved with seasonal plantings, as well as a fountain, a gateway, and a chapel. In the early 20th century, its choice lots sold and Highland Park cemetery being promoted, Woodland declined. The chapel collapsed, and the neighborhood seemed unsafe; in 1953 council debated, then rejected, converting the site to public housing.

**WOODLAND HILLS COMMUNITY (UNION) CHURCH,** located at E. 94th and Ramona Blvd., was the result of a 1925 merger of the Woodland Ave. Presbyterian Church (1872–1925) and the Kinsman-Union Congregational Church (1884–1925), one of the first mergers of these two denominations in the city of Cleveland. Woodland Ave. Presbyterian had its beginnings in the Mayflower Sunday School, which had been organized in 1853 at the corner of Orange and Mayflower streets. In 1855, it became a mission of the Second Presbyterian Church. A building was erected on property given by JOSEPH PERKINS of Euclid Ave. Presbyterian Church. Under the superintendencies of TRUMAN P. HANDY, DANIEL P. EELLS, and Chas. J. Dockstader, the school flourished, and for many years it remained a mission school, becoming one of the largest Sunday schools in the city. Ultimately it resulted in the formation of the Woodland Ave. Presbyterian Church. An organizational meeting was held in the autumn of 1870 at Willson School House. On 18 Jan. 1872, the society was organized at the Cleveland Protestant Orphan Asylum at the corner of Woodland and Willson avenues. A lot was purchased and a chapel erected at E. 46th and Woodland Ave. A Sabbath school was formed, and the Mayflower Mission School was turned over to its care. The church was officially organized on 18 Apr. 1872 with 54 members, some coming from Second Presbyterian and some from Plymouth Congregational Church. When the church was established, the neighborhood was characterized by wide thoroughfares, wide lawns, and homes belonging to many of Cleveland's most affluent citizens. The first elders included Henry N. James, SOLON L. SEVERANCE, John Buchan, John A. Seaton, John Davis, and John Sencabaugh. The first pastor, Rev. E. P. Gardner, was installed on 30 June 1872; he served until 1876.

On 17 Nov. 1878, a new church building was dedicated, and the chapel became the adjoining Sunday school. It became one of the most frequently used meeting places in the city. Prof. ALFRED ARTHUR organized his celebrated Bach Singing Society there. During Dr. Paul Sutphen's pastorate (1886–93), the church grew to be 4th in size among more than 600 Presbyterian churches in Ohio. The period of rapid expansion passed as the neighborhood changed when the congregation moved eastward. In the midst of rapidly changing conditions, the church began a practical ministry to Cleveland's growing immigrant population. Rev. Joel B. Hayden came from Baltimore to assume the pastorate in June 1917, and in Oct. 1918, Rev. FRANK T. BARRY came from Chicago to be assistant pastor. A community ministry among a variety of national and racial groups began in earnest with the formation of the Woodland Ctr. Neighborhood House as an adjunct to the church. Following WORLD WAR I, BLACKS began to move into the area. Rev. Hayden resigned in 1923 to become pastor of FAIRMOUNT PRESBYTERIAN in CLEVELAND HTS. Rev. Barry continued to serve the church until 1925, when the congregation voted to merge with Kinsman Union Congregational Church at 94th and Ramona. Rev. Barry became pastor of the merged church. Woodland Ctr. closed during 1925–27, and Rev. Barry served as its director when it reopened. Woodland Ave. Presbyterian was razed in 1938, but Woodland Ctr. continued to serve the neighborhood until 1941, when it moved to 7100 Kinsman Ave., where it continued a full schedule of social and recreational activities. In 1958, the name of Woodland Ctr. was changed by the Cleveland Presbytery to Garden Valley Neighborhood House. Rev. Barry served Woodland Hills Union Church until 1944, when he retired, but he continued to serve Garden Valley until 1948, when he and his family moved to Florida.

Kinsman-Union Congregational Church had its beginning as the Orange St. Society, organized in 1852. It later became a Congregational church, under the direction of Rev. Frank M. Whitlock (1884–87). Several mergers followed, and in 1895, it became the Kinsman Rd. Congregational Church; in 1914, it merged with the Union Ave. Congregational Church to form Kinsman-Union Church, and a new building was erected on Kinsman Rd. near E. 93rd St. Following the merger with the Woodland Ave. Presbyterian Church, Dr. Frank Barry served as pastor of the merged church from 1925–44. Dr. Guy H. Volpitto served from 1944–51. After a series of pastorates, the congregation voted to close the church 31 Dec. 1976.

**WOODMERE** is a small village in eastern Cuyahoga County just east of the intersection of Chagrin Blvd. and I–271. Occupying less than 1 sq. mi., it is bounded by PEPPER PIKE on the north, BEACHWOOD on the west, and the village of ORANGE on the south. Woodmere was originally part of Orange Twp. Until the 1940s, it was little more than an expanse of farmland. In 1944, voters elected to incorporate the area as the village of Woodmere. The decision was part of a postwar planning project to develop areas of potential growth. Between 1960–66, the population increased from 584 to 1,261, but by 1970 it had decreased to 1,041, and by 1980 to 877. The population is a mixture of nationalities and backgrounds. Woodmere is an integrated community whose residents include older citizens, newer homeowners, and apartment dwellers, the latter constituting the majority of the population. The village was originally zoned for single-family residential dwellings. In order to construct Eaton Square, a shopping center housing 35 shops, a restaurant, and a bank building, Woodmere was rezoned in the 1970s to accommodate general business. The village's primary and secondary schools are part of the Orange School District, which also includes Pepper Pike, MORELAND HILLS, and HUNTING VALLEY. Fire and police protection included 1 full-time and 20 volunteer firemen, and 6 full-time and 4 part-time patrolmen in 1980.

**WOODRUFF MEMORIAL INSTITUTE** (also known as Woodruff Hospital and formerly as Ingleside Hospital), located at 1950 E. 89th St., is a voluntary short-term psychiatric hospital. Ingleside Hospital was established in 1935 in a 15-room mansion at 1906 E. 75th St. (formerly Ingleside Ave.) by Mabel A. Woodruff, a psychiatric social worker. Woodruff served as director of the hospital and was assisted by Geo. H. Holmes. Ingleside was incorporated in 1937 as a nonprofit institution dedicated to the mental health of the people of Cleveland. In 1959 it was listed as one of the nation's top dozen psychiatric hospitals. The hospital moved to the former site of HURON RD. HOSPITAL at 8811 Euclid Ave., which had previously been the residence of Julia Severance Millikin. In 1968, Ingleside experienced severe financial problems brought on by new construction programs. They were exacerbated by a strike of nonprofessional employees of Local 47 of the Building & Service Employees Union seeking union representation, and a dispute between the hospital trustees and the medical staff. The hospital declared bankruptcy and was closed for over a year. It reopened in 1969 and was renamed Woodruff Memorial Institute in honor of its founder. It specialized in alcoholism, drug dependency, and adolescent programs. Ruth Edwards of the CLEVELAND INSTITUTE OF MUSIC pioneered programs in musical therapy for patients. Woodruff also maintained an Eldercare Ctr. in Chardon, Ohio, at 11635 Sherman Rd. In 1986, Woodruff Hospital closed, and its programs were transferred to ST. VINCENT CHARITY HOSPITAL & HEALTH CTR. The building and land were sold to the CLEVELAND CLINIC FOUNDATION.

**WOOLSON, CONSTANCE FENIMORE** (Mar. 1840–24 Jan. 1894), was an author of international repute and a contemporary and friend of Henry James. She was the 6th child of Chas. Jarvis and Hannah Pomeroy Woolson of Claremont, N.H. In 3 short weeks, scarlet fever took the lives of 3 of her siblings. Her father, a partner on a Boston newspaper, moved the family to Cleveland in late 1840 to escape the tragedy and to try his hand at sales. While living in Cleveland, Constance came to know the Lake County region and the Tuscarawas Valley, which would later appear in her books. She graduated from Mme Chegary's School in New York City in 1858. "Two Women," Woolson's first published poem (1862), was a brief start into the literary world. However, it was the death of her father in 1869 that prompted her to discover her roots. Her father was interested in literature, and her great-uncle was Jas. Fenimore Cooper, who, Woolson reported in a letter to her nephew SAMUEL MATHER, was one of the few widely read American authors. In 1871, the remaining family members moved to the South, staying in the Carolinas and Florida. Eight years later, after the death of their mother, Woolson and her sister went to England. Woolson decided to stay in Europe and eventually settled in Venice. There she met Henry James and Wm. Dean Howells. James was the key influence upon her work. Woolson began publishing descriptive articles in magazines (*Harpers, Atlantic Monthly, Galaxy*) a year after her father's death. She wrote a children's book, *The Old Stone House*, under the name Anne March in 1873, but her first book of short stories, *Castle Nowhere: Lake County Sketches*, was not published until 1875. The book consisted of regional stories of the Great Lakes, drawing on the people she had met on family vacations. Her second book of short stories, *Rodman the Keeper: Southern Sketches* (1880), encompassed both southerners and northerners. Woolson's first novel was a great success. It was written in Europe, as were the rest of her books. Published in 1883, *Anne* might well be considered a feminist statement. Woolson wrote 4 more novels, the best being *Horace Chase*, her last, published in 1894; the others were *For the Major, East Angel*, and *Jupiter Lights*. Woolson never married.

The **WORK PROJECTS ADMINISTRATION** in Cleveland was successful in providing needed income for a substantial portion of the city's population, as well as improving and developing the area's transportation network, parks, and recreational facilities. However, it was unable to give jobs to all the able-bodied on the relief rolls, thus putting a burden on the local direct relief programs and heightening the conflicts between city and state officials. The primary purpose of the WPA, passed in Apr. 1935, was to give employment to those on relief, the bulk of whom were unskilled. Upon creation of the federal program, the Cuyahoga County Relief Admin., the Metropolitan Park Board, and officials from the city, county, and suburbs began to design projects, some of which required large capital outlays for land and equipment. The federal government finally decided that its approval would be given to lighter, labor-intensive work-relief projects where the bulk of the money would be used for wages rather than materials or equipment. Local plans had to be revised, and financial resources for the sponsor's share of the projects had to be found. The federal government projected that some 40,000–50,000 people would be employed in Cuyahoga County by Nov. 1935, and about $50 million would be spent in the county. During the first half of 1935, Cleveland's unemployment averaged over 23% of the estimated labor force of 508,870, and that increased when the Federal Emergency Relief Admin. closed down almost 100 projects in July, putting an additional 7,000 workers on the direct relief rolls. The WPA was not fully operational in Cuyahoga County until mid-December, when about 47,000 people were working on projects throughout the county. In order to qualify for WPA jobs, workers on relief rolls had to be certified by the WPA as employable. These lists were used to assign workers to jobs on the projects that had been planned locally and approved by Washington. The local sponsor was expected to provide 10% of the project's cost, and frequently this requirement was met by providing materials or equipment. In Dec. 1936, the sponsor's share was raised to 20%. In the 6 years the program operated, WPA projects included airport and street improvements, the development of the Cleveland Zoo, parks, and city recreation facilities, including the cultural gardens, and the construction of the Nottingham waterworks, the first segment of the shoreway, and public-housing units for the Cleveland Metropolitan Housing Authority. The number of WPA jobs fluctuated during the period according to the size of the relief rolls and the amount of employment available in private industry. Given the changing rates, it was difficult to assure that all able-bodied relief clients would have work. During 1936, local business improved, and unemployment slowly decreased. However, the direct relief rolls did not shrink proportionately, and state figures showed that relief operations for the year in Cuyahoga County were running a deficit as high as $1.5 million. As local business again slowed in 1937, unemployment gradually rose during most of the year and then sharply increased at the beginning of 1938. WPA employment did not reflect this change until later in the year, reaching an all-time high of about 79,000 workers in October. At that time, local plants such as FISHER BODY and Thompson Prods. (see TRW INC.) began calling back their workers, and by Nov. 1939 the WPA employment had been cut back to a little over 30,000. A 1938–39 survey of the WPA in Cleveland showed that approximately 27% of Cleveland's population (comprising workers and their families) benefited from the WPA programs.

Cleveland, which had about 90% of the countywide unemployment, frequently did not have sufficient funds to meet its direct relief obligations, and the state, with its rural-dominated legislature, was reluctant to vote more money for the urban poor. In Nov. 1939, Cleveland mayor

HAROLD BURTON and Ohio Gov. John Bricker engaged in a well-publicized dispute over who was going to pay the city's relief costs. Burton cut 12,000–16,000 from the relief rolls and limited food orders for another 24,000, citing the city's inability to pay more, and insisted that it was the state's responsibility to provide adequate relief. Bricker in turn refused to call a special session of the legislature to vote additional monies for Cleveland, accusing local officials of assigning too many WPA jobs to nonrelief clients instead of using those on the rolls. To help relieve the crisis, the Federal Surplus Commodities Corp. shipped food to Cleveland, and 6,000 additional WPA jobs were promised. Eventually the state government released some funds; the city was able to raise money by selling bonds, and the crisis passed. The business climate continued to improve during 1940, and by 1941 the WPA portion of project costs had been reduced to about 37%. By Mar. 1942, all public works construction was sharply cut back, and WPA jobs were phased out as the defense effort and the war drastically reduced the work-relief rolls and shortages of critical materials developed.

Dunfee, C. Dennis, "Harold H. Burton, Mayor of Cleveland" (Ph.D. diss., Dept. of History, CWRU, 1975).
Green, Howard Whipple, *Unemployment and Relief in Cleveland* (1938).

The **WORK WEAR CORPORATION** was founded in 1915 as the Cleveland Overall Co. by Samuel Rosenthal at 1768 E. 25th St. to manufacture industrial work clothes. In 1919, he bought the Natl. Railway Overall Co., which made bib overalls and other work garments. The company, which changed its name to Work Wear, Inc., in 1961 (and Work Wear Corp., Inc., in 1976), transformed the uniform industry by making stylish, functional work garments available to companies on a rental basis. Before Rosenthal's innovative marketing approach, work clothes were a low-profit item for the manufacturer and for the retailer, whose customer was the tradesman and factory worker. To increase profits and expand the customer base, Rosenthal sold local companies on the concept of providing a new benefit to their employees—rental uniforms that would always be clean, in good repair, and an identifiable company sign. The idea took hold, and to provide the cleaning services, Cleveland Overall capitalized and provided technical assistance to industrial laundries in Cleveland, Akron, Youngstown, and Buffalo, and then throughout the nation, which cleaned the uniforms rented by its customers. As a result of the company's investment in these laundries (which it did not own), its own growth was slow but steady.

The company revolutionized work fashion by designing a durable, comfortable overall that fit better than other off-the-rack work clothes and was available in a variety of colors and styles. In 1941, the company established Buckeye Garment Rental in Cleveland as a research center for further developments in uniform design and manufacture, as well as its first company-owned industrial laundry. During WORLD WAR II, the company produced garments for the military and for wartime production workers at the expense of civilian orders. Many competitors entered the uniform-manufacturing and -service field to cash in on the pent-up demand. Cleveland Overall, to retain its leadership position in the industry, expanded its line to include coveralls, pants, shirts, shop coats, jackets, women's work clothes, and protective clothing. The company also bought a chain of industrial laundries, a venture that required a large supply of capital. Under Leighton Rosenthal, the son of the founder, Cleveland Overall became the publicly held Work Wear, Inc., and stock sales permitted the company to acquire more laundries throughout the 1960s. In 1968, Work Wear came under investigation for its control of the industrial garment manufacture, rental, and clothing industry. Charged with violating the Clayton Anti-Trust Act, the company was ordered to divest itself of either its manufacturing operation or some of its laundries. Work Wear decided to put its domestic laundries under the control of a spin-off corporation, ARA Services, Inc., while keeping direct ownership of its Canadian and other foreign facilities. To continue its role as a preeminent manufacturer of career apparel, Work Wear acquired other manufacturers of work and leisure clothing, as well as companies that make disposable hospital supplies. In 1985, Work Wear employed 6,400 people worldwide and had sales of $165 million; 58% of its sales revenues come from work clothes, 26% from disposable health-care products, and 16% from rental services. Paine Webber Capital, a subsidiary of the Paine Webber Group, Inc., of New York City, acquired Work Wear in Mar. 1986.

The **WORKERS GYMNASTIC UNION,** known by the initials of its name in Czech, Delnicke Telecvicne Jednoty (DTJ), is a Czech gymnastic association that began in Cleveland in 1909. Formed to promote socialism, the DTJ was similar to the Czech Sokol movement in its goal of promoting Czech nationalism, but its socialist outlook led it to oppose the "individualistic" approach of the Sokols and other organizations promoting physical culture; instead, its purpose was "to make it possible for the mass as a whole to rise together to a higher level." The DTJ was first organized in Prague on 22 Aug. 1897. Members of a socialist dramatic and educational club, the Ferdinand Lassalle Society, organized the first American DTJ unit in Cleveland on 16 Jan. 1909, in a meeting at Vahalec's Tavern at Central and E. 77th St. Among its 15 charter members were Frank Vsetecka, Bedrich Plesmit, Frank Cerny, and Vaclav Klier. Units were organized in Chicago and other cities; in 1911, the 6 units across the country formed the Natl. DTJ Council. New units were formed in Cleveland and elsewhere. The Mt. Pleasant unit began in 1911 as an educational club; its 28 charter members included Jaro Sourek, Jan Smetana, Karl Vajgl, and Fred Jenscek, its first president. It began gym classes for boys and girls in a building at Holban Ave. and E. 131st St.; by 1925, its gym classes were being held at Komensky Hall, 3613 E. 131st St., and were attracting more than 200 participants. The unit also offered dramatics and educational activities. The Bedrich Engel Club, organized in 1912 at Ceska Sin Sokol, put on Czech plays and appears to have focused its activities on drama.

The Cleveland DTJs survived attempts at Communist infiltration and expanded their activities in the 1920s to attract 2d-generation Czechs by forming English-Speaking Clubs, such as the Mt. Pleasant DTJ Pleasure Club (1924), the West Side DTJ Club (1926), the Lassalle Jr. Club (1926), and the Maple Hts. DTJ English Speaking Club (1930). The latter was a branch of the Maple Hts. DTJ, which existed from 1929–37. Other DTJ units formed and disappeared more quickly. In 1925, the DTJ District Council began work on Taborville, a 110-acre summer camp and cooperative village near CHAGRIN FALLS. The idea of Czech editor and DTJ gym instructor JOSEPH MARTINEK, Taborville began as a small camp, the construction of which was financed by the sale of surrounding land to DTJ members for cottages. Annual events included July 4th gymnastic exhibitions and harvest festivals in August; the latter, begun in 1934 to raise funds for the *American Labor News*, continued into the 1970s. Taborville also hosted the first American Labor Olympiad in 1936, attracting gymnasts from various countries and about 10,000 spectators. The socialist nature of the DTJ moderated after WORLD WAR II and during the McCarthy era. The Communist takeover of Czechoslovakia split the organization; the moderate Socialists in control expelled those members who supported Communist rule. A new Cleveland unit, the Masaryk Club, was formed in 1958, with many recent immigrants among its charter members. Membership remained constant between 1959–73, with 4 Cleveland-area units and 600 local members.

Frank Bardoun Papers, WRHS.

The **WORKMEN'S CIRCLE,** or Arbeiter Ring, is a secular Jewish fraternal organization founded to build a better world, foster cultural Jewishness, and offer friendships. Part of the national Workmen's Circle, which began in 1900, the first Cleveland branch (#79) was chartered 24 Aug. 1904 to work for social legislation. One of the founders, Morris Gordon, was associated with the Bakers' Union. Almost all the early members were affiliated with unions, for the Workmen's Circle was viewed as an organization of labor unionists, including early Jewish Socialists, although there was no official connection. Early activities included support for labor disputes. Women made dinners and raised funds for strikers. The members demonstrated for social security, unemployment compensation, child labor laws, workmen's compensation, and health security, and supported candidates who supported these issues. In addition, their own candidates ran under the Socialist ticket. From its beginning, the group also provided lectures, poetry readings, and concerts in Yiddish, as well as Yiddish plays and shows. At its height in the 1930s, Cleveland had 4 Yiddish-speaking branches affiliated with the national offices in New York. The region included Akron Branch #587, founded in 1916, and branches in Lorain, Youngstown, Cincinnati, and Columbus. The first English-speaking branch, #1030, was founded in 1939. The group bought its own cemetery in 1920, located at W. 54th St. and Theota in PARMA. Camp Vladek (called the Workmen's Circle Camp) in Rock Creek served as a summer resort for adults and a children's camp from 1950–63, when it was sold. The proceeds were used to build a Workmen's Circle Educational Ctr. on Green Rd. in 1964.

The I. L. Peretz Workmen's Circle School first opened its doors in 1918 on Scovill Ave.; and with the exception of 1 semester in 1952, it has been in continuous operation, moving its location several times before taking up residence at 1980 S. Green Rd. at the Workmen's Circle Educational Ctr. Sender Wajsman served as the school's director from 1953–79. Originally established to provide an education for members' children, the school became a center for reaching the broader community with adult Yiddish classes and Yiddish cultural programming. Since the Holocaust, emphasis has shifted to the preservation, promotion, and perpetuation of Yiddish language and culture. From 1940–60, the organization declined. As a result, a professional director for the Great Lakes Region of the Workmen's Circle, Marilyn Baruch Cagin, was hired by the New York national office in 1973 to expand the organization by membership recruitment, the establishment of benefits, and community service. A Russian-speaking branch for Russian immigrants was established in Sept. 1975. In 1985, there were 5 branches in Cleveland, as well as 1 in Akron.

The **WORLD PUBLISHING COMPANY** was begun in 1902 by Alfred H. Cahen, a Polish immigrant who came to Cleveland via England at the age of 17 and became a major publisher of Bibles, dictionaries, and children's and trade books. Trained as a bookbinder, Cahen was quickly employed by a local bookbinding and printing firm. He also began to gild books from his home and made twice his wages the first week. By 1905, he opened the Commercial Bookbinding Co. in the CAXTON BLDG., and by 1912, he added a printing plant. The facilities were destroyed in a fire in 1920, but his creditors declared a moratorium on his debts while he rebuilt and expanded the plant at W. 110th St. and Western Ave. Gilding continued to be an important service offered by the company, but the printing of Bibles became its major activity. In 1928, Commercial bought out its largest competitor, the World Syndicate Publishing Co. of New York, and assumed the name World Publishing Co. in 1935. When Cahen's son-in-law, Ben Zevin, joined the firm in 1934, he came with a dream of expanding the scope of World's activities to make good literature available to all. At a time when there were only 700 bookstores in the U.S., Zevin sought to sell his books in drugstores and dime stores. In 1940, he introduced Tower Books, a series of 49-cent fiction and nonfiction hardcover titles that sold a million copies the first year. He followed that by introducing moderately priced reprints of classics and children's books that predated the paperback revolution and the firm's entry into that market. At a time when Bibles were selling for $15, he sold them for $1. Unknown to stockholders and directors, Zevin underwrote a staff of researchers to develop the *Webster's New World Dictionary*. After 15 years of research in a warehouse and an expenditure of $1 million, World introduced the volume in 1953. *Webster's New World Dictionary* went through 58 printings and 12 revisions and made the company the 2d-largest publisher of desk dictionaries in the world. Meanwhile, World reigned as the largest printer of Bibles in the country and was an up-and-coming publisher of textbooks. With its purchase of Meridian Books in 1960, World entered the softcover market.

In addition to its success in publishing and printing, World was well known for its enlightened employee relations, its innovations, and the beauty of its books. Especially under the leadership of Zevin, the company promoted equal opportunity for all races and had an integrated workforce, with blacks working all steps of the book-production process even in the 1940s. The company also was a leader in hiring the handicapped. World consistently devoted resources to research and development. Its investments included a rounding and backing machine that increased hourly output from 400 to 2,500 books, and a synthetic glue that was more effective than animal glue. The company could produce 25,000 books every 8 hours. Even the less expensive lines were known for their attractiveness, while its Bibles were proclaimed the most beautiful in the world. In 1963, World was one of 3 American publishers to do their own printing, and annually produced 12 million books from its newly constructed plant in BEDFORD. It was then acquired by Times-Mirror Inc., a newspaper, communications, and graphic-arts firm. The new owner moved the editorial offices from Cleveland to New York twice by 1967, and was unable to operate the company profitably. By 1970, Times-Mirror sought to contract its book-manufacturing business, so in 1971 the local plant was sold to the Bookwalter Co., an affiliate of the Printing Corp. of America, a division of American Can. In 1974, Times-Mirror sold World to Collins Publishing of London and Glasgow. In 1980, the company, known as Collins-World Publishing, announced that it had agreed to the sale of its dictionary line to Simon & Schuster; its children's titles to the Putnam Publishing Group; and its Bible Div. to Riverside Book & Bible House of Iowa Falls, Iowa.

**WORLD WAR I.** With a population of 560,665 on the eve of World War 1, Cleveland stood as the 6th-largest city in the U.S. It thrived economically on the manufacture of iron and steel, paints and varnishes, foundry and machine-shop products, and electrical machinery and supplies. Although recently surpassed by Detroit in automobile production, it still excelled in the making of auto accessories. Proof of the city's financial importance was offered late in 1914, when Cleveland was selected as headquarters for the 4th Federal Reserve District (see FEDERAL RESERVE BANK). The years of U.S. neutrality were bonanza ones for Cleveland's industries, as its workers satisfied contracts for war munitions, automobiles and trucks, uniforms, weapons, and chemicals for explosives. By the fall of 1918, it was estimated that the city had produced $750 million worth of munitions in the 4 years since the war had begun. The issues of the war itself were primarily of interest to the 35% of the city's population (1910 census) that was of foreign birth. War touched the city more directly with the sinking of the *Lusitania* on 8 May 1915, as 7 Clevelanders were listed among the 114 Americans killed on the torpedoed British liner. That fall, Cleveland initiated steps to achieve military preparedness by organizing the Ohio Natl. Guard Military Training School, the first institution of its kind in the nation. By the time Germany resumed unrestricted submarine warfare in Mar. 1917, Clevelanders were packing war meetings in GRAYS ARMORY and aiding the U.S. Naval Reserve in the formation of Lake Erie's "mosquito fleet" of 500 ships.

Upon America's entry into the war on 6 Apr. 1917, a county draft board consisting of DANIEL E. MORGAN, STARR CADWALLADER, and Dr. Walter B. Laffer was named to supervise the local application of the new Selective Service System. By the year's end, 25,000 draftees had joined 8,000 volunteers to raise the area's total of men under arms to 33,000. By war's end, almost 41,000 Clevelanders had joined the services; 1,023 of them were killed in the conflict. Led by Maj. GEO. W. CRILE, Base Hospital Unit No. 4 from Lakeside Hospital had been among the first Americans to reach France as early as May 1917 (see LAKESIDE UNIT). On the home front, Cleveland factories continued to supply the war effort with arms and equipment. The WHITE MOTOR CO. alone produced a total of 18,000 trucks for the use of the U.S. and its allies. As men stepped into the trenches and assembly lines, women were called upon to fill the breach. The Cleveland school system dropped an old ruling that forced female teachers to resign upon marriage. Gertrude Nader greeted Cedar-Fairmount line commuters in 1918 as Cleveland's first streetcar "conductorette," although the female conductors would later lose their jobs as the result of a postwar strike.

To coordinate the city's war activities, Mayor HARRY L. DAVIS appointed a MAYOR'S ADVISORY WAR COMMITTEE to be financed from money from the Red Cross drive. Supervised under the umbrella of the Mayor's Committee were such activities as the war gardens campaign, the "Four Minute Men" speakers' bureau, and local efforts in the Treasury Dept.'s Liberty Loan drives. Clevelanders oversubscribed the first 2 Liberty Loan campaigns by $70 million while also contributing to the support of such local efforts. Nothing was deemed too excessive in the city's desire to flaunt its patriotism. The Board of Education honored one of America's allies by naming a new elementary school after Lafayette. A 1918 Flag Day Pageant in WADE PARK, witnessed by 150,000 Clevelanders, featured a *SPIRIT OF '76* tableau personally directed by ARCHIBALD M. WILLARD. On the negative side, a local branch of the American Protective League was organized to aid the Dept. of Justice in locating draft "slackers," investigating food hoarding, and suppressing alien disturbances. Some violators of the city's first "gasless Sunday" in Sept. 1918 returned to their cars to find the tires slashed.

Despite the outward appearance of 100% Americanism, there were those who objected to the U.S. entry into the war. Members of the city's German and Hungarian communities had hoped for continued neutrality, as did many IRISH, who saw any assistance to the Allies as being assistance to their traditional enemy, the English. Radical political groups, including some Socialists, also advocated neutrality. Socialist Eugene Debs's criticism of the war resulted in his arrest in Cleveland and subsequent imprisonment in 1918 (see DEBS FEDERAL COURT TRIAL). Cleveland's ethnic communities—"hyphenated Americans" in the parlance of the day—came in for their share of patriotic pressure. An Americanization Board was established by the Mayor's Advisory Committee, and naturalization classes were inaugurated under the direction of Dr. RAYMOND MOLEY (see AMERICANIZATION). With the cooperation of the Cleveland Board of Education, free language classes were advertised in 24 different locations. Presumably they might have prevented near-tragedies such as the mobbing of a non-English-speaking man for ripping a Liberty Bond poster from a streetcar, which was cut short only by the discovery that he was reacting to the poster's picturization of the Kaiser rather than its patriotic message. Some ethnic newspapers began printing editorials in English to circumvent a law requiring the filing of translations of war-related copy with the local postmaster.

A particularly intense trial, of course, was reserved for the city's 132,000 residents of German extraction. The German language was dropped from the curriculum of the public elementary schools, although its study was retained on grounds of "military necessity" in the high schools. Local members of the American Protective League, in fact, campaigned to outlaw even the public use of the "enemy" language. A German play production was canceled for lack of an available auditorium, while directors of the German American Savings Bank wisely voted to conduct future business under the less provocative nomenclature of the AMERICAN SAVINGS BANK. So many obstacles were raised for Cleveland's German newspaper *WAECHTER UND ANZEIGER* that one scholar found it surprising that the paper survived the war at all. While the war could not end too soon for the city's German-Americans, its hysteria lingered months beyond Armistice Day for most Clevelanders. Thanks to a premature story appearing in the *CLEVELAND PRESS*, Cleveland celebrated the famous "false armistice" on 7 Nov., as well as the real one 4 days later. More than half a million people still flocked to the Allied War Exposition on the lakefront the following week, where they witnessed a simulated battle and toured 3 mi. of trenches. When the CLEVELAND ORCHESTRA made its debut at Grays Armory on 11 Dec. 1918, there was not yet a single piece by a German composer on the program. Even Cleveland's MAY DAY RIOTS of 1919 can be attributed at least partly to the smoldering embers of World War I patriotism.

Although Cleveland joined in the nation's desire to return to "normalcy," the war had left it changed in at least one major respect. It effectively blocked the flow of immigration from Europe to the nation's urban centers, a change that would be institutionalized in the restrictive immigration legislation of the 1920s. To fill the resultant labor shortages in the country's war industries, employers turned to the disaffected Negro population of the South. Partly as a result of active recruitment and partly from word-of-mouth advertisement, Cleveland's black population grew by 308%, from 8,448 to 34,451, in the decade ending in 1920. One of the local black newspapers, the

*CLEVELAND ADVOCATE*, began a special "Industrial Page" to assist in their adjustment. Unlike their predecessors, who had tended to come from the border states and live in close proximity with other groups, the new arrivals were more likely to come from the Deep South and settle in areas of dense black concentration. "In the midst of a city that had once been proud of its integrationist tradition," observed historian Kenneth L. Kusmer, "a black ghetto was taking shape." (See BLACKS.) World War I thus marked the end of Cleveland's second demographic era, which saw the original New England stock leavened by the influx of the New Immigration. It ushered in a period of transition in which the European immigrants were to be assimilated and succeeded by a third wave of newcomers from the American South.

Judith G. Cetina
Cuyahoga County Archives

J. E. Vacha
Cleveland Public Schools

**WORLD WAR II.** When Japan attacked the U.S. at Pearl Harbor on the morning of 7 Dec. 1941, the ranking American victim was a native Clevelander, Rear Adm. ISSAC C. KIDD, aboard the *Arizona*. Before V-J Day, his death would be followed by those of nearly 4,000 more Clevelanders out of a total of 160,000 called to service. At home, the face of Cleveland would be greatly transformed by the demands of the war effort, while more fundamental changes set in motion by the war would contribute to the city's postwar decline. It did not take Clevelanders long to discover there was a war on. The city's annual Community Fund drive was rechristened the War Chest campaign for the duration. Under Civilian Defense Director WM. A. STINCHCOMB, lighting "blackouts" were being rehearsed by the summer of 1942. A special emphasis on Victory Gardens was incorporated into that year's Home & Flower Show. Rationing was implemented on the local level by 29 War Price & Rationing Boards, which were empowered to issue permits to civilians for such potentially scarce commodities as sugar, meat, and gasoline. Charged with administering the Selective Service Act in Cuyahoga County were 51 local draft boards composed of over 400 volunteers. Meeting several nights a week, board members considered classification appeals and supervised the machinery that called 3,000–4,000 Greater Clevelanders monthly to the armed services.

As young men began departing for military training centers from Union Terminal, an influx of wartime government agencies helped fill the vacuum created by their absence. Contracts with 800 northern Ohio defense plants were placed by the Cleveland Ordnance district office in the Terminal Tower. Operating from the Union Commerce Bldg., the regional office of the War Labor Board became the 3d-busiest in the country, handling 400 cases a week from a 4-state area. In an outdoor exhibit at Euclid and E. 9th St., the War Production Board kept Clevelanders informed of the goals and quotas of the war effort. A focus for the area's wartime activities was provided with the dedication of the War Service Ctr. on PUBLIC SQUARE. Constructed with donated materials and labor, the temporary structure on the northwest quadrant of the Square sheltered recruiting offices, war bond and stamp sellers, and such agencies as the USO, Red Cross, and War Housing Service. Names of Clevelanders who lost their lives in wartime service were painted on the center's walls, which were finally dismantled a year after the war's end. PLAYHOUSE SQUARE was the address of the local branch of the Stage Door Canteen, where servicemen might find hospitality and entertainment. Clevelanders could keep abreast of the war's progress by dropping in at the Telenews Theater, which specialized in continuous showings of newsreels on its Lower Euclid screen.

Cleveland was credited with originating the Block Plan to promote and organize various bond, blood, and scrap drives on the neighborhood level. By the 8th and final war loan drive, county residents had accounted for a total of $2.5 billion worth of bonds. Special goals were set to spur sales, such as the *CLEVELAND NEWS* campaign that raised $320,000 for the purchase of a B–17 Flying Fortress. There were also innumerable rallies, exemplified by the one sponsored in PUBLIC AUDITORIUM on 3 June 1942 to collect money for medical aid to Russia. Even more than bond drives and relief rallies, what Uncle Sam wanted from Cleveland was output of its industrial establishment, ranked 5th in the nation. Steps were taken to expand that industrial base by the construction of such facilities as the Thompson Aircraft (Tapco) plant in EUCLID, which had been started even before the war in 1941. By the war's end, Thompson was Cleveland's largest employer, with a workforce of 21,000. Two large facilities arose in 1942 on the perimeters of Cleveland Municipal Airport. Originally planned for the production of B–29 ("Superfortress") parts, the Fisher Cleveland Aircraft plant underwent successive postwar metamorphoses as the CLEVELAND TANK PLANT and finally the Internatl. Exposition & Trade Ctr. On the other side of the airport, the Natl. Advisory Committee for Aeronautics constructed the world's largest wind tunnel as part of its Aircraft Engine Research Laboratory, which survives as the Natl. Aeronautics & Space Admin. Lewis Research Ctr. (see NASA LEWIS RESEARCH CTR.).

Many local plants recorded distinguished achievements in the war effort. Natl. Acme and Cleveland Twist Drill, later combined as the ACME-CLEVELAND Corp., won 2 of the war's first Army-Navy "Star" awards for production excellence. A double Army-Navy "E" Award went to Cleveland's H. K. Ferguson Co. for erecting Tennessee's Oak Ridge thermal diffusion plant in just 66 days. Perhaps Cleveland's greatest wartime success story was written by Jack & Heinz, an aircraft-parts manufacturer in MAPLE HTS. (see LEAR SIEGLER, INC.) that was singled out after the war by Donald M. Nelson, chairman of the War Production Board, for the following accolade: "By paying exceptionally attractive wages, making sure that working conditions were congenial, developing a strong sense of team play, giving workers full credit for individual and group achievements, stressing the importance of the workers' jobs to the war effort, and appealing to patriotism by explaining the needs of the armed services, this company drove production and earnings to new heights."

Thanks to the impetus of war production, employment in Cleveland by Sept. 1944 had climbed to 34% above its 1940 level. Practically the entire increase had taken place in the manufacturing sector, where employment had risen from 191,000 to 340,000 during the period cited. "Cleveland is one of the Nation's industrial centers which has expanded most since the beginning of the war," concluded the U.S. Bureau of Labor Statistics. While the national index of factory employment in 1944 as compared with 1939 was 156.3, Cleveland's index had leaped to an even more imposing 179.7 (1939=100). Such single-minded application to production was bound to produce strains in other sectors of the community's social fabric. Mayor Frank J. Lausche's War Production Committee was credited with the relative absence of strikes and other labor problems in the city. Cleveland also escaped any major wartime racial outbreaks, though labor demands would contribute to a

75% increase in its black population during the decade (see BLACKS). Careful monitoring of interracial relations was one of the weightiest recommendations of the Post-War Planning Council of Greater Cleveland, an idea that came to fruition in the creation of the CLEVELAND COMMUNITY RELATIONS BOARD.

Commuting and gas rationing combined to tax the city's public transportation facilities. From a Depression low of under 200 million, revenue rides on the newly municipalized Cleveland Transit System peaked at nearly 450 million in 1946, followed by a precipitous postwar decline. Near the end of the war, area engineers revealed a 50-year express highway plan, which envisioned a Cleveland serviced by innerbelt, outerbelt, and crosstown freeways connected by 7 radials converging on downtown. Other experts turned their attention to the demands that increased postwar air travel would make on Cleveland's airport. Without doubt, Cleveland's most vexing homefront problem was housing. Even in 1940, failure to replace aged housing stock during the Depression had resulted in a vacancy rate of only 3%. Wartime building restrictions and in-migrating defense workers drove that down to an infinitesimal 0.5% by Mar. 1943. "Temporary" war housing projects put up in critical areas such as BEREA and Seville could not meet the demand, as the War Housing Service satisfied fewer than half of its 35,000 applicants during its first 2 years. It did not take much studying for the Post-War Planning Council to predict "a splurge of house-building in the suburbs, following the relaxation of artificial war-time restraints upon residential construction." Unless immediate measures were begun to rehabilitate the central city's deteriorating areas and prevent further blight, the council foresaw "wholesale abandonment of older areas and catastrophic losses in investments and tax values." With admirable accuracy, the council concluded that "this boom will set the pattern of Greater Cleveland for the next generation."

As promised and prayed for, victory came on 15 Aug. 1945. Within a month, a victory parade lasting more than 3 hours marched down Superior Ave., where it was viewed by 300,000 Greater Clevelanders and reviewed by Adm. Ernest J. King of Lorain, the area's ranking military officer. For those incapable of marching, a 1,750-bed veterans' hospital in PARMA had been dedicated as Crile General Hospital in 1944. A WAR MEMORIAL FOUNTAIN was promoted by the *CLEVELAND PRESS* and dedicated on the Mall in 1964. Perhaps an even more evocative monument was later provided by the lakefront relocation of the U.S.S. *COD*, a vintage World War II submarine, with its claustrophobic crew quarters and locally built diesel engines. Postwar Cleveland followed the pattern predicted by the Post-War Planning Council, as the exodus began. Space requirements had already dictated suburban locales for the larger plants constructed during the war. Spearheaded by returning veterans taking advantage of government-guaranteed mortgages provided by the GI Bill, the labor force joined the suburban migration. Cleveland's neighborhoods, deserted by a generation that might have rebuilt them, and decimated by implementation of the long-awaited freeway system, were inherited by the elderly and the newer minorities that had arrived to fill wartime labor needs. Largely developed to its capacity before the war, the central city and its remaining denizens were relegated to the backwash of the postwar rush to the suburban frontier.

J. E. Vacha
Cleveland Public Schools

**WORTHINGTON, GEORGE** (21 Sept. 1813–9 Nov. 1871), was a Cleveland businessman and industrialist. He was the founder of the Cleveland Iron & Nail Works, the

Cleveland Iron Mining Co., and the GEO. WORTHING-TON CO., at the time of his death the largest hardware store west of New York City. Worthington was born in Cooperstown, N.Y., to Ralph and Clarissa Clarke Worthington. After completing a common-school education, he started his career in business in 1830 as a hardware store clerk in Utica. After 4 years he moved to the village of Cleveland, where with $500 borrowed from his brother, he started his own hardware business in a 2-story building on Superior at Union Ln. Almost all of Worthington's early business was conducted by barter. At first his goods were carted to him in oxen-drawn wagons. Later they were shipped in by lake schooner from Buffalo. He associated himself with WM. BINGHAM in 1835, and they bought out the stock of Cleveland Sterling & Co. and moved their operations to Superior and Water (W. 9th) St. In 1841, Bingham sold his interests in the company to Worthington. A few years later, Worthington associated with Jas. Barnett and Edward Bingham. By establishing new markets in neighboring towns, the company soon became the largest hardware business in the region, with annual sales of over $1 million. Worthington started plans for the Cleveland Iron & Nail Works ca. 1862. In association with Wm. Bingham, he got company operations underway in 1863. Actively involved in Cleveland's financial life, Worthington helped organize and served as president of the First Natl. Bank of Cleveland, as director of the Ohio Savings & Loan Bank and Hahneman Life, and as vice-president of the Sun Insurance Co. A pioneer in iron manufacturing, he served as president of the Cleveland Iron Mining Co. and as a director of the Cleveland, Columbus & Cincinnati Railroad. Worthington married Maria Blackmar in 1840. The Worthingtons had 8 children, 6 of whom survived to adulthood: Abigail, May, Clarissa, Alice, Ralph, and George. Worthington is buried in LAKE VIEW CEMETERY.

**WRESTLING.** *See* **BOXING AND WRESTLING**

**WRIGHT, ALONZO G.** (30 Apr. 1898–17 Aug. 1976), was a black southern migrant who came to Cleveland as a teenager and eventually became a millionaire as an innovative service-station operator and real-estate financier. Wright was born in a 1-room house in Fayetteville, Tenn., the son of a telephone linesman who was killed on the job when Alonzo was 6. Wright worked as a shoeshine boy and a messenger to help his mother support the family. In the early 1910s, his mother moved to Cleveland and found work in the Eagle Laundry, then sent for her sons. Alonzo attended night school to earn his high school diploma while working as a teamster, a foundry hand, a mail-truck driver, and a garage attendant at the Auditorium Hotel. Wright worked at the hotel garage for 8 years, until his acquaintance with Sohio executive Wallace T. Holliday afforded him opportunity for advancement. Impressed by Wright's work, Sohio's new president learned that Wright aspired to a career in business and arranged for him to become the first black to lease a Sohio station, located at E. 93rd and Cedar. Wright's station was the first Standard Oil station located in a predominantly black neighborhood, and under his leadership it prospered. Customers were attracted by the new services he offered: Wright was credited with being the first station operator to clean windshields regularly and was among the first to offer free tire and radiator checks; his motto was "A Business Built with a Rag." By 1937,

Wright operated 6 stations; his empire grew to 11 stations before he left the business in the mid-1940s.

One of Wright's goals was to create job opportunities for young blacks. By 1940, he was credited with having hired more black youths than any other businessman in the U.S.; he was rewarded with the C. C. Spaulding Business Achievement Award at the annual meeting of the Natl. Negro Business League. As gas rationing slowed sales in the mid-1940s, Wright left the service-station business and in 1943 established Wright's Enterprises, a real-estate investment firm. In 1947 he bought the Carnegie Hotel at 6803 Carnegie Ave., which he planned to make "one of the nicest Negro hotels in the country"; he sold it in 1961. He also bought the Ritzwood Hotel at Woodland and E. 51st, which was destroyed by fire in 1960. In 1960 he transformed an apartment house at 2415 E. 55th St. into the Dunbar Nursing Home. In the 1960s, Wright concentrated his efforts on industrial and residential construction. In its Aug. 1961 issue, *Ebony* touted the millionaire Wright as Cleveland's "richest, most socially prominent Negro." Wright was a member of the GREATER CLEVELAND GROWTH ASSOC. and the CITY CLUB and a trustee of FOREST CITY HOSPITAL. But even as a successful businessman, he felt the stings of racial prejudice. When he moved into an all-white section of CLEVELAND HTS. in the 1930s, his home at 2985 Hampshire Rd. was bombed; in 1947 he moved to a 200-acre estate in Chesterland. In 1961, Wright charged the Lakeside Yacht Club with discrimination after it denied him space at its dock. Wright was married twice—first in 1929, to Henrietta Cheeks, who died in Feb. 1963, and then on 20 Aug. 1964, to Helen Keith.

**WRIGHT AIRLINES, INC.,** was established in 1966 by Jerry Weller and Ernie Rolls to provide service between downtown Cleveland and downtown Detroit. Based at BURKE LAKEFRONT AIRPORT, it served the businessmen of both cities and helped to alleviate congestion at the two major airports. In 1978, Gilbert Singerman became president of Wright. During his tenure, he expanded the company into a leading regional carrier of both freight and passengers. In 1982 he expanded airline service into numerous other cities, and on 1 Oct. 1983, he merged Wright with Aeromech Airlines of Clarksburg, W.Va., to create the 9th-largest regional airline in the U.S. Wright first expanded its services beyond Cleveland and Detroit in 1970. In 1972, it became a certified, scheduled interstate air carrier. It constantly expanded its aircraft fleet; by mid-summer 1984, it had 10 aircraft. In June 1980 it moved part of its operation to CLEVELAND HOPKINS INTERNATL. AIRPORT. Expansion of both service and aircraft, however, was too rapid, and late in 1984, Wright filed for protection under Chap. 11 of the Bankruptcy Law. Two months later, in Nov. 1984, it laid off 240 employees and reduced its schedule to 11 flights between Cleveland and Detroit each day. Nonetheless, Wright Airlines reported in Dec. 1984 that it had lost $170,000. In July 1985, Singerman put up $150,000, causing Bankruptcy Court Judge John Ray to hold off liquidating the company. Wright continued operating by offering 3 round trips to Detroit each day. Bids by Burke Aviation, Inc., and Transystems Services, Inc., to buy the airline were made in Aug. 1985. In Dec. 1985, Wright Airlines was reported to be in Chap. 7 liquidation.

# Y

The **YELLOW CAB COMPANY** became Cleveland's major taxicab service after receiving a monopoly within the city from city council in 1934. It operated profitably until the 1970s, when increases in both competition and costs made the service less in demand and less profitable. A Yellow Cab Co. was organized in Cleveland as early as 1923, operating from E. 49th St. and Superior. It had apparently merged with the Red Top Cab Co. by 1926, altered its name to the Cleveland Yellow Cab Co., and moved into Red Top's former location at 1500–1538 Lakeside Ave. Its officers that year were Wm. G. Beard, president, and Robt. F. Gray (formerly treasurer of Red Top), secretary-treasurer. The company had been reorganized as the Cuyahoga Yellow Cab Co. in 1928 but went out of business that year. By June 1929, Yellow Cab had been taken over by the DeLuxe Cab Co., which had been incorporated in 1927 by Max Ginsburg (formerly president of Red Top), president; Stannard B. Pfahl, vice-president; and Jas. L. Lind, secretary-treasurer. In 1929 Jesse T. Smith became president, and DeLuxe began replacing its fleet with yellow cabs; in 1930 it became the Yellow Cab Co. and moved into a new 400-car garage at 2020 W. 3rd St. Yellow expanded its operations steadily until 3 May 1934, when Taxi Drivers Union Local No. 555 went on strike. The Zone Cab Co., Yellow's major competitor, quickly recognized the striking union and kept its drivers on the street; Yellow Cab charged that the union was controlled by Zone and refused to recognize it. The 11-week strike was marred by vandalism and fighting among drivers; an agreement was finally reached on 19 July. Less than 6 months after the strike, Yellow and Zone announced that they were consolidating their operations in 1 garage. Zone had been organized in 1930 by Daniel Sherby; in 1931, ARTHUR B. "MICKEY" MCBRIDE bought a controlling share of the business and became its president. By Nov. 1934, McBride and Sherby had bought a controlling share of Yellow Cab. Smith remained president of Yellow, and it became the main operating company in the merger, with its garage serving as headquarters. The United Garage Service Corp. was later established as a holding company for the two companies.

Yellow Cab enjoyed a relatively stable and profitable business for the next 3½ decades. In May 1939 it began limousine service between CLEVELAND HOPKINS INTERNATL. AIRPORT and downtown hotels. During WORLD WAR II it employed women drivers as replacements for men, and in Oct. 1944 it became the first cab company to use 2-way radios for dispatch. Between 1946–49, it considered expanding its operations to include a helicopter taxi service between the airports and locations at the downtown lakefront, SHAKER SQUARE, and EUCLID; the plan was dropped because it had become too expensive. In 1947, city council preserved the firm's monopoly on service within the city when it refused to grant taxi permits to a group of veterans who planned to form the G.I. Cab Co. By 1967, there were 481 Yellow and 105 Zone cabs on Cleveland streets. Problems then began to mount. After 27 years, the annual banquet to honor safe drivers was canceled because of complaints about poor service and because of the shortage of available cabs such a celebration created. The extension of the GREATER CLEVELAND REGIONAL TRANSIT AUTHORITY's rapid service to the airport in 1968 contributed to a reduction in Yellow's business; between 1971–74, taxi ridership dropped by 34%, and Yellow and Zone lost $965,413, despite a driver-approved paycut in 1971. A 73% leap in gas costs contributed to these losses; in 1977, the U.S. Environmental Protection Agency formally charged the company with violating clean-air laws by attempts to reduce gas costs by disconnecting air pollution control devices and illegally using leaded gas. Between 1970–76, Yellow and Zone reduced their number of cab drivers from 1,500 to 761, with a fleet of 458 cabs. In 1977, city council granted a rate increase only after Yellow agreed to relax its monopoly and grant unused permits to independent drivers. Yellow then announced that it would not operate any cabs with company-employed drivers but would instead lease its cars to drivers on a daily basis; the announcement prompted a wildcat strike by dissatisfied drivers. By 1979, only 240 cabs worked the city's streets.

**YESHIVATH ADATH B·NAI ISRAEL** (YABI) is an Orthodox Jewish afternoon high school. It was established in 1915 as an afternoon school for all grades, because its founders charged that the existing Talmud Torah was not providing a Jewish education to its pupils. Founders Yehuda Lefkowitz, Joseph Friedman, Shmuel Spero, and Lipa Spero convinced visiting rabbi Pinchus Bleich of New York City to remain in Cleveland and become the education director of a new school. Congregation Shomre Shabbos agreed to let the school use its synagogue at E. 37th St. and Woodland as the first school site. YABI incorporated in 1917 and clearly indicated that its mission was to provide a religious education "according to the rules, regulations, and customs of the Jewish faith." Students learned the Hebrew alphabet while studying Gemorah (commentaries that form part of the Talmud), and the general curriculum included Torah, Talmud, and Jewish ethics. The language of instruction was Yiddish, unlike that of the Talmud Torah, which was Hebrew. YABI changed to Hebrew in the 1940s.

In 1919, YABI's first graduating class included 6 students who went on to attend the Rabbi Yitzhak Elchanan Yeshiva (Yeshiva University) in New York, the most important Orthodox rabbinical seminary in the country. By the mid-1920s, YABI boasted over 600 students at 3 branches in Woodland, Kinsman, and GLENVILLE. In general, school appealed more to the poor East European immigrants, and over 40% of the students attended tuition-free. Funds for the school were raised in the traditional immigrant fashion of door-to-door solicitation, a practice that continued until ca. 1950. In addition, some money was donated by the Orthodox congregations that did not support the Talmud Torah. In 1936, YABI received its first Jewish Welfare Fund subsidy, in large measure through the efforts of Reform rabbi ABBA HILLEL SILVER and wealthy drugstore owner Adolph Weinberger. Ten years later YABI became affiliated with the BUREAU OF JEWISH EDUCATION. During the 1940s, YABI's fortunes began to decline as a result of demographic changes in the community, but also because Congregation Neveh Zedek and the TELSHE YESHIVA established high schools. However, during the late 1940s and 1950s, a period of consolidation of institutions in the community, YABI merged with the high schools of OHEB ZEDEK CONGREGATION, the KINSMAN JEWISH CTR., the Marmarosher Jewish Ctr., and the HEIGHTS JEWISH CTR., and the Telshe Yeshiva school. A merger with the CLEVELAND HEBREW SCHOOLS proposed and actively pushed by the bureau in 1947 led to a long and bitter struggle that eventually was resolved by withdrawal of the proposal. In 1985, YABI was located at 2308 Warrensville Ctr. Rd. and includes an Orthodox congregation.

Yeshivath Adath B'nai Israel Records, WRHS.

Die **YIDDISHE VELT** (Jewish World) was Cleveland's principal Yiddish-language newspaper for over 40 years. It had been preceded by the *Yiddishe Tegliche Presse* (Jewish Daily Press), founded on 1 May 1908 by Samuel Rocker, Adolph Haas, and Jonas Gross. Rocker sold out 2 years later and then brought out the *Jewish World* in 1911. Published as a weekly for the first few months, the *Jewish World* thereafter came out daily except Saturdays. Before the establishment of the Jewish Telegraphic Agency, much of its international news was translated by the editors from the English-language press. Rocker was assisted by his son, Henry, and by Leon Wiesenfeld, a professional journalist who succeeded him as editor of the *World* in 1934. By the time of its silver anniversary in 1936, the *World* had a circulation of 16,000. Copies of its anniversary edition were sent to every Jewish family in Cleveland. A Yiddish rival, *Die Yiddishe Waechter* (Jewish Guardian), had appeared briefly in 1922. Wiesenfeld left the *World* in 1938 to establish a national Yiddish-English weekly here, *Die Yiddishe Stimme* (Jewish Voice). Within 2 years it had evolved into an all-English monthly, then an annual, which finally expired in the 1950s. Acquired from Henry Rocker by Robt. Herwald, the *Jewish World* survived WORLD WAR II but reverted to a weekly schedule in 1945. When it finally halted publication on 22 Feb. 1952, it was said to have been the last of its kind outside of New York City.

The **YODER COMPANY** was the largest manufacturer of electric welded tube and pipe mills and roll-forming mills for the agricultural, automotive, petroleum, appliance, electrical, and aerospace industries. The founders, Carl M. and Henry Yoder, were draftsmen for the Swartwout Mfg. Co., producers of sheet-metal products, in the early 1900s when Carl devised a way to mold scrap sheet steel. The Yoders then started their own business to produce these metalworking machines in the basement of Carl's west side home in 1908. Two years later, it was incorporated as the Yoder Co. In 1913, Yoder went into full production near E. 55th St. and Euclid Ave. During WORLD WAR I, it manufactured all types of special machine tools and contracted a considerable amount of government work for tractors and various machines. At this time, it moved to a plant on Walworth Ave., which burned down in 1922 and was quickly rebuilt. The firm became widely known for its tube and pipe mills, and a growing export business commenced. By WORLD WAR II, 35% of Yoder's output went abroad, mainly to Europe.

After the war, the exports decreased, but the company started to regain its foreign business by granting licenses to foreign manufacturers to produce Yoder's machines and by establishing a French subsidiary in 1950. During World War II and the KOREAN WAR, Yoder produced artillery shells for the U.S. government. In the 1950s, the firm intensified its research program to learn more about the capabilities of its existing products and to develop new equipment. Under Douglas Yoder, the business prospered in the 1950s, employing over 1,000 and reaching $13 million in sales by 1957. With its expanding sales, Yoder constructed a new plant in WESTLAKE in 1958. In the 1960s, it acquired several welding and roll-forming companies, extended it foreign business, and improved its facilities and product line. In 1980, Yoder decided to discard its Westlake plant and consolidate and expand its operations at the Walworth Ave. plant. By this time, though, the company was experiencing financial difficulties, and in 1981 it filed for bankruptcy. Intercole, Inc., of California acquired Yoder and then merged its Cleveland-based Stewart Bolling & Co., Inc. (founded 1929), one of the nation's largest manufacturers of rubber and plastic machines, with Yoder to form the Intercole Bolling Corp., with its operations at Yoder's Walworth Ave. plant. Under Intercole Bolling, Yoder's products continued to maintain their reputation for quality, with $6 million in sales in 1982. In 1985, Intercole Bolling was sold to the Northern Group Investment Co. The Yoder Div. was sold in May 1986 to the Krasny/Kaplan Corp., and the Bolling Div. was also placed on the market.

**YOUNG, DENTON TRUE "CY"** (29 Mar. 1867–4 Nov. 1955), was a major-league BASEBALL pitcher from 1890–11, playing for the CLEVELAND SPIDERS in the Natl. League from 1890–98 and for the Cleveland team in the American League from 1909–11. He won 511 games in his career, a major-league record, and his name personifies good pitching. Young was born at Gilmore, Ohio, and raised on a farm. Until he was 23, he farmed full-time and played baseball locally. After pitching 31 games for Canton in the Tri-State League, his playing contract was sold to the Cleveland Spiders of the NL. For 16 seasons he won 20 or more games, and he averaged 8 innings a game for 22 years. In 1899, Young was switched from Cleveland to St. Louis by Frank DeHaas Robison, who owned both franchises. After 2 years, he signed with the Boston Red Sox in the new AL and received a $600 raise over his $2,400 NL salary. Young pitched in the first World Series and won 2 games as Boston defeated Pittsburgh in 1903. After the 1908 season, his playing contract was sold to Cleveland. Released by the Naps in Aug. 1911, he ended his career that year with Boston of the NL. Young pitched 3 no-hit, no-run games during his career, including a perfect game on 5 May 1904 against Philadelphia. He won 289 games in the NL and 222 in the AL. He appeared in 906 games, a major-league record until Hoyt Wilhelm, a relief pitcher, passed it in 1968. Young was an active farmer in Tuscarawas County until well past the age of 80. He was inducted into the Baseball Hall of Fame in Cooperstown in 1939. He was further recognized when baseball commissioner Ford Frick established the Cy Young Award in 1956 to honor the outstanding pitcher in both leagues. Young married Robba Miller on 8 Nov. 1892. They had no children.

The **YOUNG MEN'S CHRISTIAN ASSOCIATION** was founded in 1854. It operated out of rooms at Superior and W. 3rd streets, offering prayer meetings, a mission Sunday school, a lending library, and lectures. Some of the lectures were delivered by men such as Henry Ward Beecher and Cassius M. Clay. In 1863, the Cleveland YMCA temporarily disbanded because the CIVIL WAR had taken many of the active members. It was reestablished in 1867. Chas. E. Bolton led the movement for reestablishment and was aided in his efforts by SERENO P. FENN, Henry A. Sherwin, and Chas. J. Dockstader. Over the next 20 years, the association grew rapidly. By 1872, it had opened the first railroad YMCA in the country. Directed toward transient railroad workers, it eventually became the Collinwood Branch. During the 1870s, religious and missionary work was intensified, and interest was broadened to include the younger members of the community. In 1875, the YMCA opened a home for "newsboys and bootblacks." In 1879, Joseph B. Merian assumed the presidency of the YMCA. He shifted its emphasis away from reformation and toward development of character. That resulted in the establishment of educational and physical-culture programs in 1881. A Juniors Dept. was added in 1887 as young boys became a part of the association's concerns. In addition to implementing and expanding Merian's new programs, the YMCA's physical plant was greatly enlarged. During the late 19th and early 20th centuries, it built several new main buildings and branches, aided by grants from such men as JOHN D. ROCKEFELLER. The Broadway Branch was established in 1883, the West Side Branch in 1901, and the East End (UNIVERSITY CIRCLE) Branch in 1911. The YMCA built and equipped new central buildings in 1891 and 1912. The latter, located at Prospect Ave. and E. 22nd St., remained the organization's headquarters into the 1980s.

During the first decades of the 20th century, the Cleveland YMCA increased its activities. It worked with the city's social settlements and welfare agencies and actively promoted the Allied cause during WORLD WAR I and a "War Work" fundraising campaign during that conflict. After the war, it continued to add new branches, and increased attention to physical training and work with young boys. In 1921, the educational work of the association was formally organized into the Cleveland School of Technology of the Young Men's Christian Assoc. In 1930, this school was renamed Fenn College, which the association assisted in direction until 1951. In 1967, Fenn College officially became a part of CLEVELAND STATE UNIVERSITY. Despite major financial problems during the Depression, the YMCA continued to offer its standard services as well as employment counseling. Recovery was rapid for the association after WORLD WAR II, when it began its most ambitious expansion programs. By the 1980s, the Cleveland YMCA had over 20 branches and provided residential facilities for men. It also maintained one of the most widely recognized and admired physical-training programs in the U.S.

YMCA of Cleveland Records, WRHS.

The **YOUNG MEN'S SOCIETY**, or the Colored Young Men's Lyceum, was an organization of black men in Cleveland founded in 1839 to advance information on a variety of subjects and to provide for public debate. The society was patterned after the currently popular men's lyceum and literary organizations, with weekly meetings open to the general public. Within a few months of organization, the members established a library and a reading room of about 100 books in the Mechanics Block downtown. The group also supported the small Free School for Blacks during its 3-month terms. Public debates were reported to be stimulating and intelligent, covering such topics as "Would it be sound policy for the U.S. to declare war against Great Britain?" and "Would the principles of the American Anti-Slavery Society benefit colored people more than those of the Colonization Society?" The society exemplified efforts of BLACKS in Cleveland to be accepted on the basis of their merit as good citizens, stating in public resolution that "those who try to help themselves will find friends to help them."

The **YOUNG WOMEN'S CHRISTIAN ASSOCIATION** in Cleveland was founded originally as the Women's Christian Assoc. of Cleveland in Nov. 1868. Its purpose was the promotion of the temporal and spiritual welfare of the growing numbers of self-supporting urban women. Initially located at Superior and W. 3rd streets, the WCA, under the presidency of Sarah Fitch, offered a retreat program directed toward the city's poorer homes, which was coordinated with local Evangelical churches. Any female member of these churches could join the WCA for a fee of $1. The organization also received money from the city council, donations, and interest on its endowment. Over the next 2 decades, the WCA expanded its programs to include industrial training for women and recreational facilities. In 1893, the organization changed its name to the Young Women's Christian Assoc. of Cleveland, Ohio. It was administered by a president, 6 vice-presidents, a secretary, a treasurer, and 18 directors. Each of its activities was governed by a committee. A separate division, the Educational & Industrial Union, concerned itself with the education and recreation of women and girls. The expanded activities were supported by gifts from individuals such as LEONARD CASE, JR., AMASA STONE, JOSEPH PERKINS, and ELIZA JENNINGS. By the end of the 19th century, the YWCA provided boarding houses and employment services for transient women, retreats for "erring" girls, rest homes for the aged, and educational facilities for working women. There was a west side branch, a library, and an educational department staffed by 9 full-time instructors.

During the early 1900s, the association expanded its educational and social services. In 1903 a Committee on Factory Work was established, and an increasing number of women attended the day and evening classes. In 1906, the YWCA built a new building at 1245 Euclid Ave., and the central offices were relocated to Prospect Ave. and E. 18th St. In 1912, the Mary Eells Vacation Farm was opened as a memorial to Mary Eells, past president of the association. Racial and religious restrictions on membership were also dropped during this period. To devote additional resources to education, the Old Age Home and the ELIZA JENNINGS HOME were formally separated from the YWCA in 1922. During the Depression, the association

1077

offered employment services to women by seeking out job opportunities among local businessmen. Since WORLD WAR II, the YWCA has been involved in improving race relations, working for peace through international understanding, and promoting women's activities and rights. By the 1980s it operated 11 branches, 4 of which had been opened since 1938; a central branch at 3201 Euclid Ave.; and a community work project office, and continued to offer educational, recreational, and welfare services to the women of Cleveland.

YWCA Records, WRHS.

**YOUNGLOVE, MOSES C.** (13 Dec. 1811–13 Apr. 1892), was a prominent Cleveland businessman influential in organizing several business enterprises. He was one of the first businessmen west of the Allegheny Mts. to utilize steam-powered machinery. Younglove was born in Cambridge, N.Y., and educated in Greenwich, N.Y. He entered college to study law but abandoned his studies for a career in business, taking a position in his uncle's store in Greenwich. Younglove arrived in Cleveland in Aug. 1836. He worked as a clerk in a dry-goods store for 8 months, then joined with Edward P. Wetmore in 1837 to establish a book and stationery store at 40 Superior St. In 1838, Younglove bought his partner's share of the business and began a job-printing and publishing business in addition to selling books and paper. He sold his book business to 3 of his half-brothers—Caius Cassius, Brutus Junius, and Junius Brutus Cobb—in 1852. Younglove brought several steam-powered machines to Cleveland in the 1840s. In Aug. 1845, he set up a steam-powered printing press in the offices of the *Cleveland Herald*; it was the first such press in Cleveland, and perhaps only the second steam-powered press west of the Allegh-

enies. Younglove used it to print the city's daily papers and to continue his publishing. In 1848, Younglove and John Hoyt established the Cleveland Paper Mill, the first paper mill west of the Alleghenies powered by steam and one of the earliest in the country. They later merged their company with the Lake Erie Paper Co. to form the Cleveland Paper Co. Younglove served as president of the new company until he sold his interest in the firm in 1867.

Younglove was also instrumental in the success of the Cleveland Gas Light & Coke Co. (see EAST OHIO GAS CO). He gained control of the company in 1848 and, unable to obtain sufficient financial support from other Clevelanders, mortgaged everything he owned in order to finance construction of the gas works. He was a director of the company for many years and served as its president in the 1860s. Younglove was involved in other business ventures, as well. He was a founder of the Younglove & Massie Agricultural Works, helped organize the Society for Savings, and served as president of both the Kelley Island Lime & Transport Co. and the Lakeside & Marblehead Railroad Co. He retired from daily business affairs in 1865 but remained a director of the various companies in which he had invested. He was a member of the CLEVELAND ANTI-SLAVERY SOCIETY and of the Cleveland delegation that invited Hungarian revolutionary Louis Kossuth to visit the city in 1852. Younglove was married to Maria Day of Catskill, N.Y. She died in 1886.

**YOUTH DEVELOPMENT CENTER.** *See* **CLEVELAND BOYS' SCHOOL**

**YUGOSLAVS.** *See* **CROATIANS; SLOVENES;** and **SERBIANS**

# Z

**ZANGERLE, JOHN A.** (12 Apr. 1866–1 Oct. 1956), served as Cuyahoga County auditor from 1913–51. The last surviving public official of the TOM L. JOHNSON era, Zangerle, at his retirement, had held a single elective political post longer than anyone else in Cleveland. Zangerle was born in Cleveland to Adam and Maria Reisterer Zangerle. Educated in the Cleveland public schools, he graduated from West High School in 1884. He read law with the firm of Burke & Ingersoll and was admitted to the Ohio bar in 1890. Interested in the sources of wealth, he studied economics at the Univerity of Berlin. Zangerle practiced law with the firm of Zangerle, Higley & Maurer, during which time he helped consolidate a number of breweries into the Cleveland & Sandusky Brewing Co. He was elected to the Cleveland School Board in 1890 and to the Quadrennial Board of Assessors in 1910. Plans for a career in real estate were set aside in 1912 when he won his first election as county auditor. Never aspiring to a higher office, Zangerle became so strong politically that the Republican party often made only token efforts to defeat him. The county auditor's office became responsible for property assessments for taxation purposes in 1917. As auditor, Zangerle established a system of uniform tax appraisals that came to be copied by more than 100 cities nationwide. In the 1930s, he replaced the antiquated equipment in the tax division with efficient mechanical equipment and a new accounting and records system. Zangerle was not afraid to confront prominent individuals or large corporations on the matter of assessments. He secured additional revenues from the STANDARD OIL CO., REPUBLIC STEEL, the Society for Savings, and Sears. He frequently appeared before the Ohio legislature as an advisor concerning taxation matters. He championed a more equitable method of taxation based solely on land values and executed by the state rather than the 88 individual county auditors. From 1951 until his death, Zangerle returned to the practice of law; he was the oldest practicing lawyer in Ohio. He was the author of 3 books on appraising and taxation. Zangerle married Blanche Norton on 10 Nov. 1912. The Zangerles had 3 children, Willis, Hildegard, and Jane Elisabeth.

**ZAPF, NORMAN F.** (14 July 1911–23 June 1974), was a mechanical engineer whose undergraduate research in streamlining led to the design and construction of streamlined steam locomotives. Zapf was born in Cleveland. His family later moved to the western suburbs, where he attended Rocky River High School. He then entered Case School of Applied Science, studying aerodynamics under Dr. Paul Hemke. As an undergraduate, Zapf used the recirculating-type wind tunnel at Case and scale models of steam locomotives to achieve a practical streamlined design that reduced drag 90–100%. At 75 mph, his version required 350 hp less than the unstreamlined form. The findings were part of his senior thesis, entitled "The Streamlining of a Steam Locomotive." He graduated in 1934 with a B.S. degree in mechanical engineering. He married Mildred Anderson in 1935. Zapf took a job with the New York Central Lines but eventually resigned when he failed to procure an engineering position. He returned to Case as a graduate student but soon left to work for a Boston firm that produced hardware for locomotives. In the 1930s, the railroads were searching for ways to improve their image while reducing costs in view of competition from airplanes and automobiles. New streamlined diesel-electric locomotives were introduced, but most railroads already had enormous investments in their steam locomotives. Conclusions from Zapf's thesis were used by the New York Central Lines in the design for their *Commodore Vanderbilt*, the company's first streamlined steam locomotive. Zapf served in the Coast Guard during WORLD WAR II and afterward moved to Florida, where he and his family developed Zapf Groves, Inc.

The **ZARJA SINGING SOCIETY** is the oldest Slovenian chorus outside of Europe. Choral groups were leading forces in the perpetuation of the language and cultural heritage of Cleveland's Slovenian community. By WORLD WAR I, a dozen Slovenian choruses had been active, with varying degrees of success. Zarja (The Dawn) was established in 1916 by 18 members of Lodge 27 of the Jugoslav Socialist Fed., based in Chicago. The men first performed at a 4th of July picnic with folk songs and a Slovenian version of the *Marseillaise*, reflecting their prolabor ideals. Leo Poljsak served as the first president, and John Gombach as director. JOHN IVANUSCH, a student of Franz Lehar, became musical director in 1920 and encouraged the addition of women and expansion into more ambitious musical works. Zarja's unique spring concert at Birk's Hall on St. Clair Ave. was met with popular approval. Other appearances followed, including one at the opening of the SLOVENIAN NATL. HOME, the group's new meeting place.

Early performances were a capella or with piano accompaniment, but by 1926, Zarja was proficient enough to attempt a Slovenian operetta with orchestral accompaniment. Success spurred Ivanusch to find another musical play suitable for talented amateurs; finding none, he wrote a full-length opera based on a work by classical poet France Preseren. *Turjaska Rozamunda* (Rosamund of Turjak) premiered Thanksgiving Day 1928 with a cast of 60 and Ivanusch's wife, Mary Grill, as director, librettist, and female lead. It was the first Slovenian opera presented and the only one composed outside of Europe. An opera from Slovenia, *Urh, Grof Celjski* (Ulrich, Count of Celje), was staged in 1929, with an encore performance at the Theater of Nations festival in PUBLIC AUDITORIUM that received good reviews from the *PLAIN DEALER*. Featured singers included Antoinette Simcic, Frank Plut, and Louis Belle. Many members questioned the need for affiliation with and financial control by the out-of-state parent organization, and a group split from the chorus to form Samostojna (Independent) Zarja, later to be known as GLASBENA MATICA. Ivanusch continued to direct both. The original chorus, renamed the Socialisticna Zarja, lost several capable singers but began to attract young, dedicated members that became the core of the organization into the 1980s. Under Czech director Joseph Krabec from 1933, the group presented concerts, tableaux, and musical plays in Slovenian and English, including Gilbert and Sullivan's *Trial by Jury* and Smetana's *Bartered Bride* in 2 coproductions with the Czech VOJAN SINGING SOCIETY.

Zarja toured, and joint concerts were held with other local choral societies such as Jadran, Slovan, and Sloga. Original dramas by immigrant writers such as Etbin Kristan and Ivan Molek were also staged. Zarja introduced popular songs from Slovenia, as well as partisan songs in the postwar years. Concert proceeds benefited the SLOVENE HOME FOR THE AGED, *CANKARJEV GLASNIK*, and relief efforts in the homeland. The chorus first recorded and appeared on television in 1949. Frequent specialty singers included Victoria Poljsak, Sophie Elersich, Walter Lazar, Frank Kokal, and Frank Elersich. Zarja moved to the Slovenian Society Home in EUCLID in 1961 and enjoyed a revival under the direction of Josephine Turkman. A lighter musical fare and cabaret-style entertainment attracted large audiences and new members. Zarja was invited to perform in Slovenia in 1966, 1972, and 1976 and was given official recognition for upholding musical traditions. It also sponsored 2 choral groups from Slovenia. Zarja's recordings include a collection of wedding and wine songs produced with a grant from the Ohio Arts Council. In the 1980s, the chorus performed semiannually with about 40 members.

**ZION EVANGELICAL LUTHERAN CHURCH,** located at 2062 E. 30th St. and Prospect Ave., often referred to as the "Mother of Churches," has been instrumental in establishing 5 other Lutheran churches of the Missouri Synod in Cleveland. It began on 14 Apr. 1843 when 45 communicants from another congregation organized their own church—Evangelical Lutheran. For 5 years, the congregation worshipped in Concert Hall, located on the 3d floor of a business building on the north side of Superior Ave., between Seneca (W. 3rd) and Bank (W. 6th) streets. Rev. David Schuh, the first pastor, who resigned in Oct. 1844, was succeeded by Rev. August Schmidt on 8 Jan. 1845. In Sept. 1845 the Concert Hall was the site of the first of a series of meetings that subsequently led to the organization (in Chicago) of the Evangelical Lutheran Synod of Missouri, Ohio, and other states; the congregation joined the Missouri Synod in 1852. During Rev. Schmidt's pastorate, the church was incorporated on 17 Mar. 1847 as Zion Evan-

gelical Lutheran Church. That same year, the congregation built a frame church on York St. (Hamilton Ave.) west of E. 9th St.; it was dedicated on 20 Jan. 1848. Rev. Schmidt, who resigned in Apr. 1851, was succeeded by Rev. Henry C. Schwan from Missouri, who was installed in Aug. 1851. On 24 Dec. 1851, Rev. Schwan brought a candle-lit Christmas tree into the sanctuary for the Christmas Eve service. It was one of the first used in a church service in this country. In spite of criticism from Cleveland newspapers and from some parishioners, the tradition continued, and Rev. Schwan served Zion Lutheran for over 30 years.

As German immigration increased in Cleveland, the congregation grew in membership, and in 1853 the church established a mission school in OHIO CITY. (In 1858, this group became an independent congregation, Trinity Evangelical Lutheran Church.) Members of Zion who lived in the NEWBURGH area were released in 1854 in order to organize St. John's Lutheran Church, later located in GARFIELD HTS. The congregation purchased property in 1856 on the south side of Bolivar Ave. east of Erie St. (E. 9th), constructed a school, and in 1865 moved the frame church to the property. Subsequently, a new church was constructed on the northeast corner of Bolivar and Erie streets; it was dedicated in Jan. 1867. In 1870 the congregation formed a school district on Cleveland's east side. A building was constructed on Superior Ave. near Wilson Ave. (E. 55th), and on 1 Sept. 1870 this district of Zion became an independent congregation, St. Paul's Evangelical Lutheran Church. Members of Zion who lived south of the Kingsbury Run area were released in 1878 in order to establish an independent congregation; it later became St. John's Lutheran Church on Cable Ave. In 1883, St. Peter's Evangelical Lutheran Church was organized by members of Zion Church who lived near WOODLAND CEMETERY. Zion sold the property on Bolivar Ave., purchased a lot on Prospect Ave. and Sterling Ave. (E. 30th St.), and in 1901 constructed a school, which remained active until 1974. Subsequently, a sanctuary was built and was dedicated 3 May 1903. Originally services were held only in German, with English being spoken occasionally; English services were introduced by Rev. Carl M. Zorn in 1881, and for many years 2 services were held each Sunday. Services in 1986 were in English, with German services being held only twice a month. In 1974, Zion Evangelical Lutheran Church was designated a Cleveland landmark.

---

*Fiftieth Anniversary of the Dedication of Zion Lutheran Church, 1903–1953 (1953).*

The **ZION MUSICAL SOCIETY** may have been the first public Jewish singing organization during the 19th century in America. The society was formed in 1861 by Rabbi/Cantor GUSTAVE M. COHEN. It not only performed congregational work but also sang outside of the synagogue. Rabbi Cohen was European-born and -educated and, significantly, was the first trained cantor in America. He was the author and composer of the *Sacred Harp of Judah*, published in 3 volumes by Brainard's. His other works of hymns and services include *Family Circle of Worship* and *The Orpheus*, also published in Cleveland. The Melodeon Hall was the site of the first public performance of the Zion Musical Society, on 5 Mar. 1862. The concert consisted of vocal and instrumental sacred music. The society associated with ANSHE CHESED until 1866, when Rabbi Cohen joined Tifereth Israel as Cantor. Sometime between then and 1873, the society dissolved.

The **ZIONIST ORGANIZATION OF AMERICA CONVENTION** (June 1921) was held in Cleveland and represented a turning point in American Zionist history. The leadership of the ZOA changed hands from the pragmatic Brandeisian wing led by Supreme Court Justice Louis Brandeis to a group led by Louis Lipsky and Emanuel Neuman that supported the European ideological Zionism of Chaim Weizman. Brandeis, leader of the ZOA since 1914, believed that political Zionism became obsolete following the issuance of the Balfour Declaration in 1917. He supported practical upbuilding work in Palestine and efficiency in the accounting and management of Zionist funds. Weizman contended that Zionism demanded the primacy of ideology over pragmatism and that Jews in the diaspora had to become nationalists both culturally and politically. The issue that spawned the bitter fight at the 1921 convention was the creation of the Keren Hayesod, established in 1920 as the general fund supporting Zionist work in Palestine. As formed in Europe, the Keren Hayesod managed both the Zionists' general donation fund and the investment of funds. The Brandeis wing demanded the separation of the two functions, thus opposing the proposed creation of an American Keren Hayesod. In 1921, Weizman journeyed to the U.S. for the first time to campaign for the Keren Hayesod and to attend the ZOA convention. Although he had no standing at the convention, his presence was a moral boost to his supporters.

Julian Mack, a Brandeis spokesman and president of the ZOA, opened the convention on 5 June with an explanation of the differences between the two groups. Rabbi Stephen Wise of New York nominated Mack to chair the convention. However, the Lipsky-Neuman forces, which nominated Harry Dannenbaum of Texas, easily carried the election, 139–75. Neuman then presented a resolution to establish the Keren Hayesod in America under the administration of the World Zionist Organization. A full day's debate ensued, with a vote finally taken at 1:30 the next morning. The Weizman faction was victorious by a vote of 153–71. Following the vote on the Keren Hayesod, Mack resigned as president of the ZOA; the national executive committee also resigned. Among those were Felix Frankfurter, Horace Kallen, Rabbis Stephen Wise and Max Heller, and Cleveland's Rabbi ABBA HILLEL SILVER. Lipsky was elected president of the ZOA and led the organization for the next decade. Under his leadership, it suffered serious administrative and financial problems and a drastic drop in membership. At the 1930 ZOA convention, also held in Cleveland, a compromise was reached with the Brandeis forces that vindicated, in part, the latter's views. However, the disunity and loss of strength in the American Zionist movement that began following WORLD WAR I and were hastened by the schism at the 1921 convention were not reversed until the late 1930s, when Arab riots in Palestine, issuance of the British White Paper of 1939, and the persecution of Jews in Europe served to unite the movement.

Urofsky, Melvin I., *American Zionism from Herzl to the Holocaust* (1975).

*Report of the Proceedings of the 24th Annual Convention of the Zionist Organization of America* (1921).

**ZLAMAL, OLDRICH** (4 Apr. 1879–24 Mar. 1955), a longtime pastor of Our Lady of Lourdes Parish in Cleveland, was a leader in Bohemian affairs in both Cleveland and Czechoslovakia. Zlamal was born in Kokory, Moravia, Czechoslovakia. His parents were Anthony and Antoinette Roussila Zlamal. He was educated at Olmutz and Prerov. He came to America as a seminarian and completed his studies at St. Mary Seminary in Cleveland. Bp. IGNATIUS HORSTMANN ordained him on 3 Nov. 1904. Zlamal's first assignment was as pastor of St. Wendelin Church in Cleveland (see ST. WENDELIN PARISH). During his pastorate, he built a school and purchased property for expansion. In 1905 he organized the LAKEWOOD parish of SS. CYRIL & METHODIUS for those SLOVAKS living in eastern Lakewood. In 1908 he was transferred to Youngstown, where he served as pastor of SS. Cyril & Methodius Church. In 1915 he was named pastor of Our Lady of Lourdes Church, succeeding the late Fr. STEPHAN FURDEK. Besides his duties at Our Lady of Lourdes, which had one of the largest Bohemian congregations in the city, Fr. Zlamal was very active in Czech affairs. In 1919 he went to Czechoslovakia at the request of the Natl. Catholic Ward Council. For 6 months he traveled the country, lecturing on democracy and religious topics. In 1938, he organized a war relief committee for the CZECHS. In recognition of his accomplishments, Fr. Zlamal was named a domestic prelate by the Vatican on 1 Dec. 1934 and was given the title of monsignor. He was buried in Calvary Cemetery in Cleveland.

Archives, Diocese of Cleveland.

**ZONING.** Zoning in Greater Cleveland developed quickly between 1920 and the present, paralleling a similar pattern in other parts of the U.S. Several significant zoning cases have emerged from the Cleveland area, including the landmark case that established its constitutionality. Early land planning and development in Greater Cleveland were unconstrained by zoning or other restrictions. The earliest plan for Cleveland was a simple grid design around a town square on the New England model. The 10-acre public square was bisected by 2 wide, straight streets, one running north and south and one running east and west. Using these as axes, a large tract was described by 4 additional streets, which bounded 4 large oblongs along which regular building lots were laid out. These arrangements, surveyed in 1796 by Augustus Porter, became the framework around which the future city was to grow and, to a large extent, still lives. The early design neglected the magnificent lakeside location, but it was neat and orderly, and it facilitated speculative land sales, a compelling motive of land planning and development then as now. The use of land and buildings was controlled only by the doctrine of common-law nuisance: "using your property so as not to injure another's." This approach seemed appropriate to a land-rich country committed to laissez faire economic and social policies, but, in fact, it proved inadequate to the task of maintaining a decent living environment in the explosion of development that characterized the 19th-century industrial city.

American cities reacted to the crowding and disagreeable conditions of industrialization by limiting the areas where the most noxious industries could operate and by legally prohibiting the worst overcrowding through regulations governing the height of buildings. Boston adopted the first height restrictions in the U.S. in 1892, and in 1920 the U.S. Congress adopted similar regulations for Washington, D.C. In Ohio, the enabling legislation (Ohio General Code: Par. 4366-7 to 4366-11) was passed by the general assembly in 1920. Administratively, the city planning commission prepares the comprehensive plans and the zoning plan, which is adopted by city council. The first comprehensive zoning ordinance was adopted by New York City in 1916 after hearings that blended real estate and reform. The need to protect real-estate investments took equal precedence with the need to provide the public with more air and light and to lessen unhealthy congestion in housing. The growth of zoning was phenomenal following passage of the New York City ordinance. In 1924, only 8 years

1081

| Municipality | Charter | Date of Inc. | Plan. Comm. | BOZA | Zoning Ordinance | Gen'l Plan |
|---|---|---|---|---|---|---|
| Bay Village | 1949 | 1903 | 7 | 5 | 1920 | 1969 |
| Beachwood | 1959 | 1915 | 7 | 6 | 1925 | 1958 |
| Bedford | 1932 | 1837 | 5 | 5 | 1935 | 1967 |
| Bedford Hts. | 1951 | 1951 | 5 | 3 | 1951 | 1972 |
| Berea | 1960 | 1850 | 7 | 5 | 1973 | 1975 |
| Bentleyville | Non-Charter | 1929 | 5 | | 1940 | No |
| Bratenahl | Non-Charter | 1904 | 5 | 3 | 1923 | 1983 |
| Brecksville | 1956 | 1921 | 5 | 7 | 1957 | — |
| Broadview Hts. | 1961 | 1926 | 5 | 5 | 1968 | No |
| Brooklyn | 1951 | 1927 | 7 | 5 | 1940 | — |
| Brooklyn Hts. | Non-Charter | 1903 | 5 | | 1949 | — |
| Brookpark | 1966 | 1914 | 7 | 7 | 1957 | No |
| Chagrin Falls | 1962 | 1844 | 5 | 5 | 1932 | 1969 |
| Cleveland | 1915 | 1814 | 7 | 7 | 1929 | 1949 |
| Cleveland Hts. | 1955 | 1900 | 7 | 5 | 1921 | — |
| Cuyahoga Hts. | 1920 | 1918 | 5 | 5 | 1953 | No |
| East Cleveland | 1918 | 1895 | 5 | 5 | 1953 | 1969 |
| Euclid | 1951 | 1903 | 5 | 5 | 1922 | No |
| Fairview Park | 1958 | 1910 | 5 | 5 | 1940 | 1971 |
| Garfield Hts. | 1956 | 1919 | 5 | 5 | 1962 | No |
| Gates Mills | 1972 | 1921 | 9 | | 1926 | — |
| Glenwillow | 1958 | 1914 | 5 | — | 1953 | 1982 |
| Highland Hts. | 1966 | 1920 | 5 | | 1938 | — |
| Hunting Valley | 1968 | 1924 | 3 | 7 | 1938 | 1938 |
| Independence | 1958 | 1914 | 3 | 5 | 1925 | 1980 |
| Lakewood | 1910 | 1903 | 7 | 5 | 1922 | No |
| Linndale | Non-Charter | 1902 | — | — | None | No |
| Lyndhurst | 1951 | 1917 | 5 | 5 | 1926 | No |
| Maple Hts. | 1932 | 1915 | 5 | 3 | 1958 | 1978 |
| Mayfield | 1974 | 1922 | 5 | 5 | 1953 | — |
| Mayfield Hts. | 1951 | 1920 | 5 | 5 | 1929 | 1973 |
| Middleburg Hts. | 1961 | 1927 | 7 | 5 | 1955 | No |
| Moreland Hills | 1929 | 1929 | 5 | 5 | 1973 | 1973 |
| Newburgh Hts. | Non-Charter | 1904 | — | | 1953 | — |
| North Olmsted | 1959 | 1908 | 7 | 5 | 1950 | 1973 |
| North Randall | Non-Charter | 1908 | 3 | | 1956 | No |
| North Royalton | 1952 | 1927 | 5 | 5 | 1930 | 1970 |
| Oakwood | 1968 | 1951 | 5 | 5 | 1971 | 1973 |
| Olmsted Falls | 1972 | 1851 | 5 | 5 | 1975 | 1973 |
| Orange Village | 1977 | 1927 | 5 | | 1942 | 1980 |
| Parma | Non-Charter | 1925 | 5 | 5 | 1940 | No |
| Parma Hts. | 1954 | 1911 | 5 | 3 | 1953 | No |
| Pepper Pike | 1966 | 1924 | 5 | | 1924 | — |
| Richmond Hts. | 1959 | 1917 | 5 | 5 | 1929 | 1972 |
| Rocky River | 1960 | 1904 | 5 | 5 | 1947 | 1968 |
| Seven Hills | 1967 | 1926 | 5 | 5 | 1961 | No |
| Shaker Hts. | 1932 | 1911 | 5 | 5 | 1927 | 1927 |
| Solon | 1954 | 1927 | 3 | | 1950 | 1973 |
| South Euclid | 1953 | 1917 | 5 | 5 | 1923 | No |
| Strongsville | 1960 | 1927 | 7 | 5 | 1927 | 1968 |
| University Hts. | 1941 | 1907 | 3 | 4 | 1956 | 1970 |
| Valley View | Non-Charter | 1919 | 5 | | 1932 | No |
| Walton Hills | Non-Charter | 1951 | 5 | 5 | 1951 | 1951 |
| Warrensvle Hts. | 1958 | 1927 | 5 | 5 | 1931 | — |
| Westlake | 1956 | 1909 | 5 | 5 | 1954 | 1963 |
| Woodmere | 1983 | 1944 | 5 | 7 | 1947 | 1970 |

Data are from a special 1985 survey by Cleveland State University, College of Urban Affairs.

later, the U.S. Dept. of Commerce, under Herbert Hoover, with the assistance of the U.S. Chamber of Commerce, published the *Standard State Zoning Enabling Act*. It sold more than 55,000 copies and was adopted almost verbatim in Ohio and almost half the states. By 1930, 768 municipalities, with 60% of the nation's urban population, had adopted zoning controls, including many in Greater Cleveland, where BAY VILLAGE adopted the area's first zoning ordinance in 1920. Other Cleveland communities soon followed: CLEVELAND HTS. in 1921, LAKEWOOD and EUCLID in 1922, BRATENAHL in 1923, and PEPPER PIKE in 1924. The city of Cleveland, whose city planning commission was created in 1913, adopted its zoning ordinance in 1929. By 1958, almost every municipality in Cuyahoga County had a zoning ordinance. While zoning attained immediate acceptance, city planning and zoning administration lagged. In 1942, 26 Greater Cleveland communities had adopted zoning ordinances; only 1, the city of Cleveland, had any paid administrators. Zoning has received widespread public support. No aspect of local government, with the exception of taxation, has generated as much intense public interest in the post-World War II era. Its administration is carried out by thousands of unpaid citizens who serve on planning commissions, zoning boards, and boards of zoning appeals. In 1970, 25,000 people served in this capacity in the metropolitan areas of the U.S. In 1985, Cuyahoga County had 54 communities with planning commissions, 34 with boards of zoning appeals, and 463 citizens, mostly unpaid, serving on them. The constitutionality of zoning was not tested until 1926, when the celebrated case *VILLAGE OF EUCLID V. AMBLER REALTY CO.* was brought before the U.S. Supreme Court. In deciding *Euclid*, a small village of 10,000 persons immediately east of Cleveland, the Supreme Court held that comprehensive zoning was a constitutional exercise of the police power. The Court's opinion contained 3 principles that have shaped all subsequent zoning litigation. First, the Court emphasized that the scope of the police power is elastic and capable of expansion to meet the complex needs of an urbanizing society. Second, taking challenges based upon dollar loss in property values would not be sustained on that ground alone. Diminution in value henceforth be considered as only one factor in a calculus that weighed the community's interest in orderly development against the land owner's claim to unrestricted property use. Third, the Court extended to zoning enactments a presumption of validity that it had not formerly received. The *Euclid* decision was of such importance that from 1926 when it was decided until late 1973, the Supreme Court accepted only one other zoning case.

As zoning matured from a novelty to an accepted institution, and as the pace of suburban development accelerated after WORLD WAR II, critics began to raise questions about the possible use of zoning to classify and segregate the general population according to income, race, or station in life. These critics pointed to the conflict between the legitimate desire of a community for orderly growth and "preservation of community values" as opposed to the need to provide reasonably priced housing for the region. Noting the extreme racial and economic segregation of Greater Cleveland (2d in the U.S. behind Chicago in 1980), these critics suggested that large-lot or "snob" zoning that protects existing interests in property by making new development more expensive plays a significant role in economic and racial exclusion. Studies lent support to this view: of the 82,500 acres of land in Cuyahoga County zoned for single-family use in 1971, 67% was zoned for 1/2-acre sites or more; 85% of all residentially zoned land in nearby Geauga County required lots of 1 acre or more. Many suburbs either did not permit multifamily housing at all or discouraged apartments by mandating low height and density requirements. Critics feared that such zoning could only raise the price of housing and deepen economic and racial segregation throughout Greater Cleveland. These issues were raised in 2 important Greater Cleveland cases: *United States* v. *City of Parma* and *City of Eastlake* v. *Forest City Enterprises, Inc.*

In June 1980, more than 7 years after the U.S. Justice Dept. brought suit, Judge Frank J. Battisti of the U.S. District Court of Northern Ohio found the city of PARMA liable for violating sections of the Federal Fair Housing Act. The court found that Parma, through a systematic pattern of actions and inaction, had followed a long-standing practice of excluding BLACKS from residing in the city. Included among these actions was the charge that Parma's city council had denied a building permit to a subsidized apartment development, mandated excessive parking requirements in order to raise housing costs, and passed a zoning ordinance sharply restricting height in order to block any subsidized apartments. In the view of the court, land-use regulations were being used for exclusionary and discriminatory purposes. The court-ordered remedy required Parma to promote the development of racially integrated subsidized housing. An unreasonably complex zoning procedure with a possibly exclusionary impact was the issue in the 1976 case of *City of Eastlake* v. *Forest City Enterprises, Inc.* Forest City proposed to rezone 8 acres of its

land from industrial use to high-rise residential. Eastlake's planning commission and city council agreed to the proposal, but opponents demanded a referendum and defeated the rezoning. Subsequently, the city charter was amended to provide that any rezoning application would have to be voted on by the city planning commission, approved by city council, and approved by 55% of the voters at a mandatory referendum. The developer would have to pay the costs of the referendum. The developer brought suit alleging that it was denied due process and that the referendum violated the Ohio constitution. From the perspective of the land owner, the need for a referendum and its cost would obstruct any change in land use by rendering such change so burdensome as to be prohibitive. The majority of the Supreme Court, however, in upholding the amended city charter saw the mandatory referendum procedure as an appropriate extension of town hall democracy.

The concept of direct voter control of zoning has proved to be very popular in Greater Cleveland. Between 1971–77, 21 communities in Cuyahoga County adopted some form of zoning referendum ordinance. That gave the people the direct ability to control growth, protect the "character" of the community, and exclude unpopular land uses. As such, it was a powerful weapon to strengthen the status quo. For example, in STRONGSVILLE, from 1971–77 voters defeated 10 out of 11 proposals for rezoning from single-family to multifamily residential uses. Over the same period in Greater Cleveland, only 1 out of 15 multifamily proposals to go on the ballot passed, and only 2 out of 28 proposals relating to any rezoning change at all were approved by mandatory referendum communities. The possible conflict between home rule and regional responsibility seems likely to underscore future zoning issues. Zoning is a relatively new but very popular modern function in local governmemt. It has been the target of numerous changes and challenges since it appeared in the U.S. and in Greater Cleveland in the early part of this century. Challenges have been mounted by 3 groups: land owners or developers, who typically resist a limitation of their options imposed by the regulations; present residents of communities, who usually seek to impose their vision of desirable community standards through land-use regulations; and surrounding communities and residents of surrounding communities, who are concerned with the adverse regional effects of some restrictive local land-use regulations. Potential residents would like to trade their older environments and public facilities for newer ones; their hopes are not aided by regulations that artificially raise prices or limit racial and economic diversity. The interests of the third group, perhaps best exemplified by the Parma and the Eastlake cases in Greater Cleveland, seem likely to present the region with more frequent challenges in the future. Zoning, which represents a compromise between private rights and the public interest, must be continually modified and broadened to meet these challenges.

Norman Krumholz
Cleveland State University

Cuyahoga Regional Planning Commission, *Land Development Regulations* (Oct. 1974).
Cuyahoga Regional Planning Commission, *Staff Report on Status of Mandatory Referendum Procedures for Land Use Decisions* (11 Apr. 1977).
*Overzoning for Business*, Regional Assoc. of Cleveland, Report No. 5 (Feb. 1939).
*Village of Euclid v. Ambler Realty Co.*, 272 US 365 (1926).

**ZORMAN, IVAN** (1885–7 Aug. 1957), was a prominent local poet and composer of Slovenian descent. Zorman was born in Yugoslavia and moved to the U.S. at the age of 4. He returned to his homeland only once, at the age of 10, and stayed for a year. When he came back to the U.S., he began to study the Slovene language. He attended Central Institute and St. John's College in Minnesota. He later graduated from Western Reserve University with degrees in language, literature, and music. Zorman's major occupation was organist and teacher. He was, for some 40 years, organist at St. Lawrence's Catholic Church. He taught organ, piano, and voice. He directed and composed for many Slovene singing societies. Zorman composed and wrote in the Slovene language. His first 2 books of poetry went largely unnoticed in his homeland. It was not until 1933 that Zorman became acknowledged as a legitimate writer. That same year, "Zorman Night" was declared in the capital city of Ljubljana. His poems were declaimed, his songs were sung, and his life and writing were discussed in lectures. His poems became Slovene schoolroom classics. In 1938, his 5th book of poetry received honorable mention in the Jugoslav University Club at the HOLLENDEN HOTEL. It was appropriately entitled *From the New World*. Zorman eventually wrote 6 volumes of poetry and translated many others. Zorman was again honored in May 1941 at a banquet in the Slovene Society Home in EUCLID as an outstanding poet and composer in America. He became embarrassed, however, at the distribution of Ivan Zorman buttons. Zorman was married to Josephine Maznarsic, who died in 1936. They had 1 child. Two years after Zorman's death, his daughter, Carmen, dedicated a memorial plaque to him in the Yugoslav Cultural Garden.

Ivan Zorman Papers, WRHS.

# Subject Guide to Entries

Cleveland Clearinghouse Assoc., The
Cleveland Cliffs Iron Company
Cleveland Diesel Engine Div. of GM
Cleveland Electric Illuminating Co.
Cleveland Engineering Society, The
Cleveland Greenhouse Veg. Growers' . . .
Cleveland Home Brewing Company, The
Cleveland Insurance Company, The
Cleveland Pneumatic Tool Co, The
Cleveland Provision Company
Cleveland Quarries Company, The
Cleveland Rocket Society, The
Cleveland-Sandusky Brewing Corp, The
Cleveland Tank Plant
Cleveland Union Stockyards Co., The
Cleveland World Trade Assoc., The
Cleveland Worsted Mill Company, The
Clevite Corporation, The
Cole National Corporation, The
Commercial Bank of Lake Erie, The
Connecticut Land Company, The
Continental, a Div. of Dollar Savings Bk.
Convention & Visitors Bureau of Gtr. Cleve.
Cook United Inc.
Cox, Jacob D., Jr.
Crile, George Washington Sr.
Cuyahoga Steam Furnace Company, The
Dauby, Nathan L.
Davy McKee Corporation, The
Delamater, John
Devereux, Henry Kelsey "Harry K."
Devereux, John H.
Diamond Shamrock Corporation, The
Diebolt Brewing Company, The
Dover Vineyards Inc.
Dow, Herbert H.
Dravo Wellman Company, The
Dreher Piano Company, The
East Ohio Gas Company, The
Eaton, Cyrus S.
Eaton Corporation, The
Economy
Eells, Daniel Parmelee
Eisenmann, John
Electrical & Electronics Industries
Elwell Parker Electric Company, The
Empire Savings & Loan, The
Ernst & Whinney
Euclid Inc.
Everett, Sylvester T.
F. B. Stearns Co.
Fawick, Thomas L.
Federal Reserve Bank of Cleveland
Ferro Corporation, The
Figgie International Inc.
First Bank National Association, The
First National Supermarkets, Inc.
Fisher Body Div. GeneralMotors Corp., The
Fisher Foods, Inc.
Fishing Industry
Flagler, Henry M.
Ford, Horatio
Ford Motor Company, The
Forest City Enterprises Inc.
Forest City Publishing Co.
Frasch, Herman
Freiberger, Isadore Fred
Fries & Schuele Company, The
Gabriel Company, The
Garment Industry
General Electric Company, The
George R. Klein News Company, The
George Worthington Company, The
Girdler, Tom Mercer
Glidden Coatings & Resins
Goff, Frederick H.
Gould, Inc.
Grasselli, Caesar Augustin
Grasselli Chemical Company, The
Gray Drugstores, Inc.
Grdina, Anton
Greater Cleveland Growth Assoc., The
Griswold Inc.

Guardian Savings & Trust Co., The
Gund, George
Gund Brewing Company, The
H. W. Beattie & Sons, Inc.
Halle Bros. Company, The
Hamann, Carl August
Handy, Truman P.
Harcourt Brace Jovanovich
Harkness, Stephen V.
Hanna, Marcus Alonzo
Harris Calorific Company, The
Harris Corporation, The
Harshaw Chemical Company, The
Haskell, Coburn
Hauserman Inc.
Hays, Kaufman
Heinen's Inc.
Heise, George W.
Hessenmueller, Edward
Higbee Company, The
Hildebrandt Provision Company, The
Hill Acme Company, The
Holland, Justin Miner
Hollenden Hotel, The
Hopkins, William Rowland
Horsburgh and Scott Company, The
Hotels
Hough Bakeries Inc.
House of Wills, The
Hovorka, Frank
Howe, Charles Sumner
Hoyt, James Madison
Hulett, George H.
Humphrey, George Magoffin
Hunkin-Conkey Construction Co., The
Huntington National Bank of Northeast Ohio
Hupp Corporation, The
Industrial Exposition of 1909, The
Industry
Insurance Board of Cleveland, The
International Management Group, The
International Salt Co., The
J. B. Robinson Co., Inc., The
J. Spang Baking Co., The
Jaycees, The
Jones, David I. and John
Jones & Laughlin Steel Corporation . . .
Jordan, Edward Stanlaw "Ned"
Jordan Motor Car Company, The
Joseph & Feiss Company, The
King Iron Bridge & Mfg. Co.
King Musical Instruments
Kinney and Levan Company, The
Kirby, Josiah
Kirtland, Jared Potter
Klonowski, Stanley J.
Knoble Florists
Korner and Wood
Kronheim Furniture Company, The
Kundtz, Theodor
Kurtz Furniture Company, The
LTV Steel
Lake Carriers Association, The
Lamson and Sessions Company, The
Langley, John W.
Laub Baking Company, The
Laukuff's Bookstore
Lear Siegler Inc. Power Equip. Div.
Leaseway Transportation Corp., The
Leece-Neville Company, The
Leisy Brewing Company, The
Lempco Industries Inc.
Leonard Schlather Brewing Co., The
Leopold Bros. Furniture
Levy and Stearn
Lezius Hiles Company, The
Life Savers
Lincoln, James F.
Lincoln Electric Company, The
Lindsay Wire Weaving Company, The
Lion Knitting Mills, The
Long, William Frew
Lubrizol Corporation, The
MTD Products, Inc.
M. A. Hanna Company
Mabery, Charles F.
McBride, Arthur B. "Mickey"
McDonald & Co. Securities
McGean-Rohco Inc.
McGhee, Norman
Mandelbaum, Maurice (Moses) J.
Markets & Market Houses
Marks, Martin A.

Master Builders
Mather, Samuel
May Company of Cleveland, The
Medusa Corporation, The
Meldrum & Fewsmith
Mercantile National Bank, The
Michelson, Albert Abraham
Midland-Ross Company, The
Miller, Dayton Clarence
Mr. Gasket
Morgan, Garrett A.
Morley, Edward Williams
Murphy-Phoenix Company, The
Musterole Company, The
NASA Lewis Research Center, The
Nassau, Jason J.
National Carbon Company, The
National City Corporation
Nela Park
Newman-Stern Company, The
Norfolk Southern Corporation
Norris Brothers
North American Bank, The
North American Coal Corporation, The
North American Systems Inc.
Northern OH Food Terminal, The
Norton, David Z.
Odenbach, Frederick L. S.J.
Oerlikon Motch Corporation, The
Oglebay Norton Company
Ohio Savings Association, The
O'Neill, Francis Joseph "Steve"
Osborn Engineering Company, The
Osborn Manufacturing Corp., The
Otis, Charles A. Sr.
Otis, William A.
Palmer, William Pendleton
Paramount Distillers Inc.
Park-Ohio Industries, Inc.
Parker Hannifin Corporation, The
Peck, Elihu M.
Peerless Motor Car Company
Penton/IPC
Perkins, Joseph
Pettibone Cleveland
Pickands, James S.
Pickands Mather & Co.
Picker International Inc.
Pilsener Brewing Company, The
Potter and Mellen, Inc.
Preformed Line Products Company, The
Premier Industrial Corporation, The
Prentiss, Francis F.
Prescott Ball & Turben, Inc.
Price Waterhouse
Printing & Publishing in Cleveland
Printz-Biederman Company, The
Progressive Corporation, The
Prutton, Carl F.
Quayle, Thomas
Quincy Savings and Loan, The
Randall Park Mall, The
Ratner, Leonard
Real Property Inventory of Met. Cleve.
Reliance Electric Company, The
Republic Steel Corporation, The
Retail Merchants Board Inc., The
Revco D.S., Inc.
Richman Brothers Company, The
Rockefeller, John D.
Root and McBride Company
Rose, Benjamin
Rosenblum, Max
Ruetenik Gardens
S. Brainard's Sons
St. John, Samuel
Schaefer Body Inc.
Schoenfeld, Frank
Science
Scott, Frank A.
Scott & Fetzer Company, The
Scovill, Philo
Scranton, Joel
Seaway Foods, Inc.
Severance Center
Sheriff Street Market, The
Sherwin-Williams Company, The
Sifco Industries Inc.
Smith, Albert Kelvin
Smith, Albert W.
Smith, Kent H.
Society Corporation, The
Sollmann, Torald Herman
Southgate Shopping Center, The
Spira, Henry
Stager, Anson
Standard Brewing Company, The
Standard Oil Company (Ohio)
Standard Products Company
Standard Trust

State Savings & Loan Company, The
Statler Office Tower, The
Sterling-Lindner Company, The
Stock Exchange
Stone, Amasa
Stouffer, Vernon Bigelow
Stouffer Foods
Stouffer's Inn on the Square
Stout Air Services Inc.
Supreme Life Insurance Company of Amer.
Swasey, Ambrose
TRW Inc.
Taylor Chair Company, The
Technicare Corporation, The
Technology & Industrial Research
Telling-Belle Vernon Company, The
Third Federal Savings & Loan Assoc.
Thomas W. Easton's Sons, Inc.
Thompson, Charles Edwin
Tilley, Madison
Todd, Thomas Wingate
Towmotor Corporation, The
Transohio Savings Bank, The
Tremco Inc.
Treuhaft, William C.
True Temper Corporation, The
URS Dalton
United States Customs Service
United States Dept. of Commerce
United States Steel Corp., The
University Circle, Inc.
Van Dorn Company, The
Van Horn, Frank R.
Van Sweringen, Oris P. & Mantis J.
Vixseboxse Gallery, The
Vlchek Tool Company, The
W. Bingham Company, The
Wade, Jeptha Homer I
Wade, Jeptha Homer II
Warner, Worcester Reed
Warner and Swasey Company, The
Watson, Wilbur J.
Wearn, Joseph T.
Weatherhead Div. of the Dana Corp.
Webb C. Ball Company, The
Weddell, Peter M.
Weddell House, The
West Side Federal Savings & Loan Assoc.
West Side Market, The
Western Electric Company, The
Westinghouse Corporation, The
Westropp, Clara E.
White, Rollin Henry
White, Thomas H.
White, William J.
White Consolidated Industries
White Motor Corporation, The
Willard Storage Battery Company, The
William Feather Company, The
William Taylor Son & Company
Williams, Whiting
Wills, J. Walter, Sr.
Wilson Transit Co., The
Winton, Alexander
Winton Motor Carriage Co., The
Wise, Samuel D.
Witt, Stillman
Women's Federal Savings Bank, The
Work Wear Corporation, The
World Publishing Company, The
Worthington, George
Wright, Alonzo G.
Wright Airlines Inc.
Yellow Cab Company
Yoder Company, The
Younglove, Moses C.
Zapf, Norman F.

# COMMUNICATIONS

*Aliened American,* The
*Americke Delnicke Listy*
*Ameriska Domovina*
Ameritech
Andorn, Sidney Ignatius
Bang, Edward F. "Ed"
Bell, Archie
Bellamy, Paul
Benedict, George A.
Briggs, Joseph W.
Browne, Charles Farrar [Artemus Ward]
*Bystander,* The
*Catholic Universe Bulletin,* The

1087

# IMMIGRATION AND ETHNICITY

Schifflein Christi
Schuplattler & Trachten ...
  Bavaria
Scranton Road Baptist Church, The
Serbs
Shapiro, Ezra Z.
Sherith Jacob Congregation
Sho-Jo-Ji Dancers
Silbert, Samuel
Silver, Abba Hillel
Slavic Village
Slovaks
Slovene Home for the Aged
Slovenes
Slovenian American National
  Council
Slovenian National Home, The
Smetona, Antanas
Spira, Henry
Sokol Cleveland
Sokol Gtr. Cleve. Gymnastic &
  Educ. Org.
Sokol Polski
Statue of Tadeusz ... Kosiuszko
*Svet-American*
Svoboda, Frank J.
*Szabadsag*
Telshe Yeshiva
Temple, Emanu El
Temple, The
Tetiever Ahavath Achim Anshe
  Sfard
Third Federal Savings & Loan
Thorman, Simson
Tong Wars, The
Trentina Club
Ukrainians
Union of Jewish Organizations, The
Union of Poles in America, The
United German Singers
United Hungarian Societies
United Ukrainian Organizations
Villa Sancta Anna Home for the
  Aged
Vlchek Tool Company, The
Vojan Singing Society, The
Vorwaerts Turner Hall, The
*Waechter und Anzeiger*
Walsh (Walaszewicz), Stella
Warrensville Center Synagogue
Weinberg, Joseph Lewis
Welsh Home, The
Western Fraternal Life Assoc., The
*Wiadomosci Codzienne*
Willett Street Cemetery
Wise, Samuel D.
Wolsey, Louis
Workers Gymnastic Union, The
Workmens Circle, The
Yeshivath Adath B'nai Israel (YABI)
*Yiddishe Velt, Die*
Zarja Singing Society
Zion Musical Society
Zionist Org. of America ...
  Convention
Zlamal, Oldrich
Zorman, Ivan

## LABOR

Amalgamated Cloth & Textile
  Workers Union
American Postal Workers Union
  ...
American Socialist Conference, The
Associated Industries of Cleveland
Bandlow, Robert
Brotherhood of Locomotive
  Engineers
CIO "Purge" Convention, The
*Cleveland Citizen, The*
Cleveland Coalition of Labor
  Union Women
Cleveland Federation of Labor,
  The
Cleveland Federation of Musicians
Cleveland Graphite Bronze Seizure
Cleveland Industrial Union Council
Cleveland Newspaper Guild, Local
  1
Cleveland Newspaper Strike of
  1962
Cleveland Rolling Mill Strikes, The
Cleveland Teachers' Union, The
*Cleveland Union Leader*
Cleveland Women Working
Coalition of Black Trade Unionists
Conductors' Strike 1918-19, The
Conference for Progressive Political
  Action
Debs Federal Court Trial, The
Demore, Matthew

Domestic Workers of America, The
Fawick-Airflex Strike, The
Federation of Organized Trades ...
  Convention
Female Protective Union
Fenster, Leo
Foran, Martin A.
Garment Workers' Strike, The
Harrison, Marvin Clinton
Hayes, Max S. (Maximilian
  Sebastian)
Industrial Workers of the World
International Assoc. of Mach. &
  Aerospace ...
International Ladies Garment
  Workers Union
Knights of Labor Dist. Assembly
  No. 47
Labor
Little Steel Strike, The
Long, William Frew
Magee, Elizabeth Stewart
May Day Riots, The
Mechanics Educational Society of
  America
Murphy, Edward F.
O'Malley, Patrick
Peppercorn, Beryl
Presser, William
Ruthenberg, Charles
Socialist Convention, The
Streetcar Strike of 1899, The
Teamsters Union, The
Typographical Workers Union No.
  53
United Auto Workers, The
United Food & Commercial
  Workers
United Labor Agency, The
United Steel Workers
United Transportation Union, The
Wing, Marie Remington
Witt, Peter

## LAW

Andrews, Sherlock James
Arter & Hadden
Backus, Franklin Thomas
Bagby Fugitive Slave Case, The
Baker & Hostetler
Baldwin, Samuel S.
Banks-Baldwin Law Publishing
Black Laws, The
Bolton, Thomas
Brickner-Darrow Debate
Burton, Harold Hitz
Calfee, Halter and Griswold
*City of East Cleveland, Ohio* v.
  *Moore*
Clark, Harold Terry
Clarke, John Hessin
Cleveland Bar Association, The
Cleveland Chapter of the Natl.
  Lawyers Guild
Cleveland Law College, The
Cleveland Survey of Criminal
  Justice
Court of Nisi Prius, The
Cuyahoga County Bar Association,
  The
Cuyahoga County Domestic
  Relations Court
Cuyahoga County Juvenile Court
Day, William L.
Debs Federal Court Trial, The
Dempsey, James Howard
Dunmore, Walter T.
Eastman, Harry Lloyd
Fitch, Zalmon
Garfield, James Rudolph
Gillespie, Chester K.
Ginn, Frank Hadley
Green, John Patterson
Grossman, Mary B.
Hadden, Alexander
Hadden, John A.
Hahn, Edgar A.
Harrison, Marvin Clinton
Herrick, Myron Timothy
Hostetler, Joseph C.
Hoyt, Dustin, & Kelley
*Jacobellis* v. *Ohio*
Jones, Day, Reavis and Pogue
Joseph, Emil
Joseph, Moritz
Lake Erie School of Law, The
Law
Legal Aid Society, The
Levine, Manuel
*Mapp* v. *Ohio*
Meyer, Edward S.

Oberlin-Wellington Rescue
Ohio State & Union Law College,
  The
Payer, Harry Franklin
Ranney, Rufus P.
Sanders, William Brownell
Sawicki, Joseph F.
Sheppard Murder Case, The
Sidlo, Thomas L.
Silbert, Samuel
Spieth, Bell, McCurdy & Newell
  Co.
Squire, Andrew
Squire, Sanders & Dempsey
Sullivan, Jeremiah J.
Tayler, Robert Walker
Thompson, Hine and Flory
Throckmorton, Archibald Hall
Tolles, Hogsett, Ginn, & Morley
*Village of Euclid* v. *Ambler Realty*
War Veterans Bar Association
Westropp, Lillian Mary
Weygandt, Carl V.
White, John Griswold
Whittlesey, Elisha
Willson, Hiram V.
Woldman, Albert A.
Women's Law Fund Inc.

## LIBRARIES AND MUSEUMS

Afro-Amer. Cultural & Hist. Soc.
  Museum
Bay Village Historical Society, The
Bedford Historical Society, The
Benton, Elbert Jay
Brett, William Howard
CAMLS
Cathcart, Wallace Hugh
Chagrin Falls Historical Society,
  The
Cleveland Hall of Fame, The
Cleveland Health Education
  Museum
Cleveland Health Sciences Library,
  The
Cleveland Library Assoc., The
Cleveland Lyceum, The
Cleveland Medical Library Assoc.,
  The
Cleveland Museum of Art, The
Cleveland Museum of Natural
  History
Cleveland Public Library, The
Colket, Meredith Bright Jr.
Cuyahoga County Archives, The
Cuyahoga County Public Library
  System
Eastman, Linda Anne
Gaines, Ervin J.
Great Lakes Historical Society, The
Howard Dittrick Museum of Hist.
  Medicine
Lakewood Historical Society, The
Ledbetter, Eleanor Edwards
Libraries, Archives & Historical
  Societies
Norton, Laurence Harper
Shaker Historical Society, The
Shera, Jesse Hauk
Smythe, Anson
Solon Historical Society, The
South Euclid Historical Society,
  The
Western Reserve Historical Society
White, John Griswold
Whittlesey, Charles W.
Williams, Edward Christopher

## MEDICINE

Academy of Medicine of
  Cleveland, The
Ackley, Horace A.
Allen, Dudley Peter
Allen, Peter
Ambulance Services
American Heart Assoc., Northeast
  Ohio ...
American Red Cross, Cleve
  Chapter, The
Barricelli, Giovanni Alfonso
Beck, Claude Schaeffer
Bill, Arthur Holbrook
Bishop, Robert H. Jr.
Blue Cross & Blue Shield Mutual
  ...
Blue Cross of Northeast Ohio
Blue Rock Spring House

Bolt, Richard Arthur
Booth Memorial Hospital
Brentwood Hospital
Brush Foundation, The
Bundy, Leroy N.
Bunts, Frank E.
Bureau of Child Hygiene, The
Cancer Center Inc. of Northeast
  Ohio
Cassels, John Lang
Casto, Frank M.
Center for Health Affairs-Geater
  Cleve ...
Child Guidance Ctr. of Greater
  Cleve.
Cholera Epidemic of 1832, The
Clement, Kenneth
Cleveland Academy of Natural
  Sciences
Cleveland Academy of Osteopathic
  Medicine
Cleveland Board of Health, The
Cleveland Clinic Disaster, The
Cleveland Clinic Foundation, The
Cleveland Dental Society, The
Cleveland Health Education
  Museum
Cleveland Homeopathic Hospital,
  The
Cleveland Hospital Association,
  The
Cleveland Hospital Service
  Assocation
Cleveland Medical Library
  Assocation
Cleveland Medical Reading Club
Cleveland Medical Society, The
Cleveland Psychiatric Institute, The
Cleveland Society for the Blind,
  The
Cleveland State Hospital, The
Cleveland Water Cure
  Establishment
Community Hospital of Bedford
Corlett, William Thomas
Council for High Blood Pressure,
  The
Crile, George Washington Sr.
Crile Hospital
Cunningham Sanitarium, The
Cushing, Erastus
Cushing, Harvey W.
Cushing, Henry K.
Cutler, Elliot Carr
Cuyahoga County Hospital System,
  The
Cuyahoga County Medical Society,
  The
Cuyahoga County Unit ...
  American Cancer Soc.
Deaconess Hospital of Cleve
Delamater, John
Dentistry
Diabetes Assoc. of Greater
  Cleveland
Doctors Hospital
"Epizootic" or "Canadian Horse
  Epidemic"
Euclid General Hospital
Factory Hospitals
Fairhill Mental Health Center, The
Fairview General Hospital
Forest City Hospital
Fourth General Hospital
Free Medical Clinic of Greater
  Cleveland
Garlick, Theodatus A.
Garvin, Charles H.
Gerstenberger, Henry John
Glaser, Otto
Glenville Health Association, The
Goldblatt, Harry
Grace Hospital Association, The
Greater Cleveland Nurses
  Assocation
Greater Cleveland Poison Control
  Center
Greater Cleveland Volunteer
  Health Plan
Health Hill Hospital for Children
Hillcrest Hospital
Holy Family Cancer Home, The
Homeopathy
Hospice Council of Northern
  Ohio, The
Hospitals & Health Planning
Hough-Norwood Family Health
  Care Center
Howard Dittrick Museum of Hist.
  Medicine
Huron Road Hospital
Hydrotherapy
John, Henry J.

Kaiser Permanente Medical Care
  Program
Kidney Foundation of Ohio Inc.,
  The
Kirtland, Jared Potter
Ladies Hosp. Aid Soc. of East
  Cleveland
Lakeside Unit, The
Lakewood Hospital
Leach, Robert Boyd
Lenhart, Carl H.
Leonards, Jack R.
Long, David
Lower, William Edgar
Lutheran Medical Center
MacLeod, John James
Marine, David
Marymount Hospital
Medical Mutual of Cleveland, Inc.
Medicine
Merrick, Myra King
Metropolitan Health Planning
  Corporation
Moritz, Alan Richards
Mt. Sinai Medical Center, The
Nineteenth Medical District of
  Ohio
Northern Ohio Lung Association,
  The
Nursing
Ohio College of Podiatric Medicine
Parma Community General
  Hospital
Peixotto, Daniel Levi
Perkins, Roger Griswold
Phillips, John
Polyclinic Hospital
Public Health
Railway Hospital
Rammelkamp, Charles Henry Jr.
Richmond Heights General
  Hospital
Robb, Hunter
Rosa, Storm
Rosenwasser, Marcus
St. Alexis Hospital Medical Center
St. John and West Shore Hospital
St. John Hospital
St. Joseph Hospital
Saint Luke's Hospital
Saint Luke's Hospital Assoc., The
Saint Vincent Charity Hosp. &
  Health Ctr.
Salisbury, James Henry
Sanitation
Shaker Medical Center Hospital,
  The
Skeel, Arthur J.
Society of Medical Sciences, The
Sollmann, Torald Herman
Southwest General Hospital
Spenzer, John George
Sports Medicine
Strategic Health Systems
Strickland, Benjamin
Suburban Community Hospital
Todd, Thomas Wingate
Toomey, John A.
Tuckerman, Louis B.
Turnbull, Rupert B. Jr.
United States Marine Hospital, The
University Hospitals of Cleveland
Veteran's Admin. Medical Center
Visiting Nurses Association
Waite, Frederick Clayton
Wearn, Joseph T.
Weber, Gustav C. E.
Wiggers, Carl John
Windsor Hospital
Woman's General Hospital
Women's Medical Society of
  Cleveland
Woodruff Memorial Institute

## MILITARY

Abraham Lincoln's Funeral
Abraham Lincoln's Visit to
  Cleveland
Armstrong, William W.
Barber, Gershom M.
Bauder, Levi F.
Black Military Units
Bliss, Stoughton
Bohm, Edward H.
Brooklyn Artillery, The
Brooks Military School, The
Cadwell, Darius
Central Armory
Civil Defense
Civil War
Civil War Camps in Cleveland

Civil War Regiments
Civil War Roundtables
Clark, Merwin
Cleveland Gatling Gun Battery, The
Cleveland Grays, The
Cleveland Light Artillery, The
Cleveland Medal of Honor
  Winners
Cleveland Tank Plant
Clingman, Andrew R.
Crane, Orrin J.
Creighton, William R.
Crowell, Benedict
Cuyahoga County Military
  Committee
Devereux, John H.
Eighteenth Provost Marshal Dist.
  of Ohio
Eighth Ohio Volunteer Infantry
  Regt.
Eighty-Fourth Ohio Volunteer Inf.
  Regt.
Eleventh Military District of Ohio
Elwell, John Johnson
Fifteenth Ohio National Guard
  Regt.
First Ohio Volunteer Light Artillery
Fitch, Jabez W.
Fort Huntington
Forty-First Ohio Volunteer Inf.
  Regt.
Fourth General Hospital
Frazee, John N.
Garfield, James Abram
Gleason, William J.
Grand Army of the Republic, The
Grays Armory
Greater Cleveland Veterans Council
Halloran, William L.
Hampson, James B.
Hard, Dudley Jackson
Hart, Albert Gailord
Hartman, Charles A.
Hayr, James
Hayward, William Henry
Herrick, John French
Hibernian Guards, The
Hinman, Wilbur F.
Humiston Institute, The
Johnson, Earle L.
Joint Veterans Commission, The
Kidd, Isaac Campbell
King, Woods
Korean War
Kossuth Monument, The
Leland, Jackson Miller
Liberty Row
Lynch, Frank
McQuigg, John Rea
Mayor's Advisory War Committee,
  The
Mexican-American War
Meyer, Edward S.
Molyneaux, Joseph B.
Moses Cleaveland Statue, The
Navy Park
Nike Missile Bases
Nineteenth Ohio Independent
  Battery
Northern Ohio Sanitary Fair, The
Northern Ohio Vietnam Veterans
  of America
150th Ohio Volunteer Infantry
  Regiment
107th Ohio Volunteer Infantry
  Regiment
177th Volunteer Infantry Regiment
103d Ohio Volunteer Infantry
  Regiment
128th Ohio Volunteer Regiment
124th Ohio Volunteer Infantry
  Regiment
Payne, Oliver Hazard
Perry Monument, The
Pickands, James S.
Prentice, Walter M.
Sanford, Alfred S.
Sanford, Junius R.
Scofield, Levi T.
Second Ohio Volunteer Cavalry
Senter, George B.
Seventh Ohio Volunteer Infantry
  Regt.
Shields, Joseph C.
Sixth Ohio Volunteer Cavalry
Sixtieth Ohio Volunteer Infantry
  Regt.
Smith, Charles H.
Smithknight, Louis
Soldiers' Aid Society of Northern
  Ohio
Soldiers & Sailors Monument, The
Soldiers' Home, The

Spangler, Basil L.
Spanish-American War, The
Stager, Anson
Statue of Tadeusz ... Kosciuszko
Streibler, Martin
Tenth Ohio Volunteer Cavalry
Thayer, Lyman C.
Thirty-Seventh Ohio Volunteer Inf.
  Regt.
331st Infantry Regiment
332d Infantry Regiment
Troop A
Twelfth Ohio Volunteer Cavalry
Twentieth Ohio Independent
  Battery
Twenty-Ninth Ohio Volunteer
  Militia
Twenty-Third Ohio Volunteer Inf.
  Regt.
United States Coast Guard
United States General Hospital at
  Cleve.
United States Submarine Veterans
  of WW II
Veterans of Foreign Wars (VFW)
Vietnam War
Walters, Reuben W.
War Memorial Fountain
War of 1812
Whittlesey, Charles W.
Wiley, Aquila
World War I
World War II

## NEIGHBORHOODS AND LANDMARKS

Ambler Heights
Angle, The
Big Italy
Bird's Nest
Blue Rock Spring House
Bluestone Quarries, The
Brooklyn
Buckeye-Woodland
Chagrin River
Clifton Park
Collamer
Collinwood
Coventry Village Business District
Cudell
Cuyahoga River, The
Detroit-Shoreway
Doan Brook
Doan's Corners
Erie Street Cemetery
Euclid Avenue
Fence War of Public Square, The
Five Points
Flats, The
Forest City
Forest Hill
Franklin Circle
Glenville
Green, Howard Whipple
Haymarket, The
Hough
Irishtown Bend
Kamm's Corners
Karlin
Kingsbury Run
Lake View Cemetery
Lincoln Park
Little Italy
Mall, The
Miles Park
Mill Creek
Monroe Street Cemete:y, The
Mount Pleasant
Newburgh
Nine Mile Creek
Nottingham
Ohio City (City of Ohio)
Parkview Village
Public Square
Real Property Inventory of Met.
  Cleve.
Riverside Cemetery
Rockport
Roman Catholic Cemeteries
Shaker Lakes
Shaker Square
Short Vincent
Slavic Village
Social Planning Areas
South Brooklyn
Tinker's Creek
Tremont
University Circle
Wade Park

Warehouse District, The
West Park
Western Reserve
Whiskey Island
Willett Street Cemetery
Woodland Cemetery

## POLITICS AND GOVERNMENT

Abraham Lincoln's Visit to
  Cleveland
Allen, Florence Ellinwood
Allen, John W.
American Socialist Conference, The
Andrews, Sherlock James
Anvil Review, The
Babcock, Brenton D.
Baehr, Herman C.
Baker, Elbert H.
Baker, Newton Diehl
Baldwin, Norman C.
Barber, Josiah
Beidler, Jacob A.
Bemis, Edward W.
Bender, George Harrison
Bernstein, Harry
Bingham, Flavel W.
Blee, Robert E.
Blossom, Dudley S.
Blythin, Edward
Bolton, Chester Castle
Bolton, Frances Payne
Boyd, Albert Duncan "Starlight"
Brownell, Abner
Buhrer, Stephen
Bulkley, Robert Johns
Burke, Thomas A. (Aloysius)
Burnham, Thomas
Burton, Harold Hitz
Burton, Theodore Elijah
Byers, Edgar S.
Castle, William Bainbridge
Cemeteries
Cermak, Albina
Chamber of Commerce-City Plan
  Committee
Chapin, Herman M.
Citizens League, The
City Club of Cleveland, The
City Manager Plan, The
City Planning
Clapp, Nettie MacKenzie
Cleveland City Council, The
Cleveland City Government
Cleveland Community Relations
  Board
Cleveland Convention, The
Cleveland Council on World Affairs
Cleveland-Cuyahoga County Port
  Authority
Cleveland Development
  Foundation, The
Cleveland Little Hoover Comm.,
  The
Cleveland: NOW!
Communist Party, The
Cooley, Harris Reid
Conference for Progressive Political
  Action
Cosmopolitan Democratic League
  of Cuyahoga Ct.
Crosser, Robert
Cuyahoga County Democratic
  Party, The
Cuyahoga County Dept. of Human
  Services
Cuyahoga County Government
Cuyahoga County Juvenile Court,
  The
Cuyahoga County Regional
  Planning Comm.
Cuyahoga County Republican
  Party, The
Cuyahoga Metropolitan Housing
  Authority
Davis, Harry E.
Davis, Harry Lyman
Default
DeMaioribus, Alessandro Louis
  "Sonny"
Dewald, Louise
Dockstader, Nicholas
Dykstra, Clarence Addison

Farley, John Harrington
Fesler, Mayo
Finkle, Herman
Fitzgerald, William Sinton
Fleming, Thomas W. & Lethia
  Cousins
Flint, Edward Sherill
Foran, Martin A.
Franklin Club, The
Free Soil Party, The
Friebolin, Carl David
Gahn, Harry C.
Gardner, George W.
Garfield, James Abram
Gassaway, Harold T.
Glenville Shoot-out
Gongwer, W. Burr
Government
Greater Cleve Regional Transit
  Authority
Greater Cleveland Roundtable, The
Hanna, Marcus Alonzo
Hay, John Milton
Hayward, Nelson
Herbert, Thomas John
Herrick, Myron Timothy
Herrick, Rensselaer Russell
Hilliard, Richard
Hoadley, George
Hodge, Orlando John
Home Rule
Hopkins, William Rowland
Hough Riots
Humphrey, George Magoffin
Huntington, Samuel Jr.
Ingalls, David S.
Ireland, Thomas Sexton Jr.
Irwin, Josephine Saxer
Jackson, Perry B.
Johnson, Tom L.
Kelley, Alfred
Kelley, Daniel
Kelsey, Lorenzo A.
Kentucky Street Reservoir, The
Kohler, Frederick
Local Cleveland
Lord, Richard
McGinty, James J.
McKisson, Robert Erastus
Marshall, John D.
Marshall, Lycurgus Luther
Maschke, Maurice
Masters, Irvine U.
May Day Riots, The
Mayoral Admin. of Anthony J.
  Celebrezze
Mayoral Admin. of Dennis
  Kucinich
Mayoral Admin. of Frank J.
  Lausche
Mayoral Admin. of Ralph Locher
Mayoral Admin. of Ralph J. Perk
Mayoral Admin. of Carl B. Stokes
Mayoral Admin. of George V.
  Voinovich
Miller, Raymond Thomas
Mills, Joshua
Moley, Raymond
Morgan, Daniel Edgar
Mosier, Harold Gerard
Mueller, Jacob
Municipal Ownership
Myers, George
Night in Budapest
Northeast Ohio Areawide
  Coordinating Agency
Norweb, R. Henry
Otis, Charles A. Sr.
Parsons, Richard C.
Payne, Henry B.
Payne, Lawrence O.
Payne, Nathan P.
Pelton, Frederick W.
Politics
Populist Political Parties, The
Porter, Albert S.
Presidential Debate of 1980, The
  Second
Progressive Government Committee
Progressive (Political) Parties
Prohibition Amendment
Prohibition Party, The
Public Housing
Pyke, Bernice Secrest
Raper, John W. "Jack"
Recall Election, The
Regional Government
Republican National Convention of
  1924
Republican National Convention of
  1936
Riddle, Albert G.
Rose, William Grey

Rumbold, Charlotte Margaret
Russell, Jack P.
Salen, Charles P.
Sanitation
Senter, George B.
Socialist Labor Party, The
Spalding (Spaulding), Rufus
Starkweather, Samuel
Stinchcomb, William Albert
Streets
Svoboda, Frank J.
Sweeney, Martin L.
Townes, Clayton C.
Townsend, Amos
United States Customs Service
United States Dept. of Commerce
Vail, Harry L.
Vail, Herman Lansing
Van Aken, William J.
Wade, Edward
Waitt, Maude Comstock
Walworth, Ashbel W.
Walworth, John W.
Water System
Welfare/Relief
Whig Party, The
Willey, John Wheelock
Williamson, Samuel
Witt, Peter
Wood, Reuben
Work Projects Administration, The
Zangerle, John A.
Zoning

## PUBLIC SAFETY

Birns, Alex "Shondor"
Blizzards
Celebrezze, Frank D.
Chadwick, Cassie L.
Cleveland Boys' School in Hudson
Cleveland Clinic Disaster, The
Cleveland Fire Department, The
Cleveland Police Dept., The
Cleveland Workhouse, The
Collinwood School Fire, The
Crime
Cuyahoga River Fire, The
Czolgosz, Leon F.
East Ohio Gas Co. Explosion &
  Fire
Executions
Glenville Shoot-out
Graul, Jacob
Greater Cleveland Safety Council
Greene, Daniel J. "Danny"
Guardian Angels, The
Harvard Club, The
Hough Riots
Kefauver Crime Commission, The
McGannon, William Henry
Maritime Disasters
Mayfield Road Mob, The
Ness, Eliot
Police Athletic League, The
Prohibition Amendment
Prostitution
Public Safety
Safe & Sane Fourth of July
St. Clair Savings & Loan Holdup,
  The
Sheppard Murder Case, The
Torso Murders, The
Wallace, George Alexander Leroy
Waterworks Tunnel Disasters
Women's Bureau . . . Cleve. Police
  Dept.

## RECREATION
## AND POPULAR
## CULTURE

Acacia Country Club, The
Academy of Music, The
Agora, The
Amusement Parks
Anvil Revue, The
Bell, Archie
Bell, Nolan D.
Boating (Recreational)
Brookside Park
Cain Park Theater
Canterbury Golf Club, The
Carroll, Gene
Case Hall
Chagrin Valley Country Club, The
Chagrin Valley Hunt Club, The
Cheshire Cheese Club of Cleveland
Cleveland Air Show

Cleveland Anniversary Celebrations
Cleveland Aquarium, The
Cleveland Arena
Cleveland Athletic Club, The
Cleveland Bicycle Club, The
Cleveland Cinema Club, The
Cleveland Lakefront State Park,
  The
Cleveland Metroparks System, The
Cleveland Metroparks Zoo, The
Cleveland Play House
Cleveland Skating Club, The
Cleveland Theater, The
Cleveland Woman's Club, The
Cleveland Yacht Club, The
Clifton Club, The
College Club of Cleve, The
Colonial Theater, The
Colony Theater, The
Columbia Theater, The
Corrigan, Laura Mae
Cotillion Society of Cleveland, The
Country Club, The
Court of Nisi Prius
Cuyahoga County Centennial, The
Cuyahoga County Fair, The
Cuyahoga Valley Natl. Recreation
  Area
Dance Halls
Dandridge, Dorothy
Dobama Theater, The
Dunham Tavern
Early Settlers Assoc. of the Western
  Reserve
Edgewater Park
Ellsler, Effie
Ellsler, John Adam
Elysium
Embassy Theater, The
English Speaking Union, The
Euclid Avenue Opera House, The
Euclid Beach Park
Euclid Beach Park Riot, The
Excelsior
Fairs & Expositions
Federation of Women's Clubs of
  Gtr. Cleve.
Festival of Freedom, The
Forest Hill Park
Front Row Theater, The
Garden Center of Greater
  Cleveland
Garfield Park
Garfield-Perry Stamp Club, The
German Central Farm, The
Globe Theater, The
Gordon Park
Greater Cleveland Home & Flower
  Show
Great Lakes Exposition
Haltnorth's Gardens
Hanna, Daniel Rhodes, Jr.
Hanna Theater, The
Hartz, Augustus "Gus" Frederic
Harvard Club
Hermit Club, The
Hippodrome Theater, The
Intown Club, The
Italian Hall
Ivan Cankar Dramatic Society, The
Jazz
Junior League of Cleveland, The
Karamu House
Keith's E. 105th St. Theater
Kiwanis Club, The
Lakewood Little Theatre/Beck Ctr.
Leland, Jackson Miller
Luna Park
Lyceum Theater, The
Maison Francaise de Cleveland,
  The
Masons, The
Mayfield Country Club, The
Metropolitan Theater, The
Mid-Day Club, The
Movies filmed in Cleveland
Musicarnival
Novel Club, The
Oakwood Club
Ohio Theater, The
Palace Theater, The
Parks
Patriotic Societies
Philosophical Club of Cleveland,
  The
Playhouse Square
Polkas
Prescott Hunter/Jumper Classic,
  The
Print Club of Cleveland, The
Professional Mens Club of
  Cleveland
Puritas Springs Park

Recreation League of Cleveland,
  The
Rock 'n' Roll
Rockefeller Park
Rotary Club of Cleveland, The
Rowfant Club, The
Roxy Theater, The
Rubinstein Club, The
Shaker Heights Country Club, The
Singing Angels, The
Sissle, Noble
Spitalny, Phil
State Theater, The
Stillman Theater, The
Tavern Club, The
Theater
Town Hall of Cleveland
Union Club of Cleveland, The
University Club, The
Washington Park
Water Street Theater, The
Weidenthal, Leo
White City
Women's City Club, The

## REFORM AND
## PHILANTHROPY

AHS Foundation, The
A. M. McGregor Home, The
Abolitionism
Addison, Hiram M.
Air Foundation, The
Allen, Florence Ellinwood
Alta House
Altenheim, The
Amasa Stone House, The
American Heart Assoc. Northeast
  Ohio
American Women's Suffrage Assoc.,
  The
Animal Protective League, The
Anti-Slavery Societies, Black
Barnett, James
Barry, Frank T.
Bath Houses
Beech Brook, Inc.
Bell Neighborhood Center, The
Bellamy, George Albert
Bellefaire
Benjamin Rose Institute, The
Bethel Union
Bicknell Fund, The
Big Brother/Big Sister Movement,
  The
Bird, Dr. Philip Smead
Birthright Inc.
Blossom, Dudley S.
Blossom Hill School for Girls, The
Bohn, Ernest J.
Bolton Foundation, The
Booth Memorial Hospital
Boy Scouts of America, The
Boystowns
Britton Fund, The
Brown, Anna V.
Cadwallader, Starr
Catherine Horstmann Home, The
Catholic Charities Corporation, The
Center for Human Services, The
Chadsey, Mildred
Charity Organization Society, The
Child Care
Child Guidance Ctr. of Greater
  Cleve.
Children's Aid Society, The
Christchild Society, The
Citizens League of Cleve.
City Mission, The
Clark, Harold Terry
Cleanland, Ohio (Rapid Recovery)
Cleveland Anti-Slavery Society, The
Cleveland Boys' School in Hudson
Cleveland Child Health Assoc., The
Cleveland Comm. on Higher
  Education
Cleveland Council of PTAs, The
Cleveland Council on Soviet Anti-
  Semitism
Cleveland Day Nursery & Free
  Kindergarten . . .
Cleveland Female Orphan Asylum,
  The
Cleveland Foundation, The
Cleveland International Program,
  The
Cleveland Job Corps, The
*Cleveland Liberalist, The*
Cleveland Music School Settlement,
  The
Cleveland: NOW!
Cleveland Rape Crisis Center, The
Cleveland Society for the Blind,
  The
Cleveland Sorosis Society, The
Cleveland Survey of Criminal
  Justice

# RELIGION

Eastman, Linda
Einstein, Ruth
Ellsler, Effie
Fairfax, Florence Bundy
Family Planning
Federation of Women's Clubs of Gtr. Cleve.
Female Protective Union
Florence Crittenton Home, The
Fortnightly Musical Club
Gannett, Alice
Goulder, Grace (Izant)
Greater Cleve. Nurses Association, The
Greve, Bell
Grossman, Mary B.
Guilford, Linda (Lucinda) Thayer
Hamilton, Margaret
Hauser, Elizabeth
Herrick, Maria M.
Horvath, Helen
Hughes, Adella Prentiss
Hunter, Jane Edna Harris
Ingham, Mary Bigelow
Internatl. Women's Yr., Gtr. Cleve. Cong.
Intown Club, The
Irwin, Josephine Saxer
Jennings, Elizabeth (Eliza) Wallace
Jones, Myrta L.

Junior League of Cleveland, The
Ladies Hosp. Aid Soc. of E. Cleveland, The
Ladies Tract Society
League of Women Voters of Cleve., The
Lebanese-Syrian Jr. Women's League
Ledbetter, Eleanor
Magee, Elizabeth Stewart
Martha Washington & Dorcas Society
Martin, Mary Brown
Mather, Flora Stone
Merrick, Myra King
Meyette, Grace E.
Miss Mittleberger's School
Mitchell, L. Pearl
*Mothers and Young Ladies' Guide*
Natl. Council of Jewish Women, Cleve.
Natl. Organization for Women (NOW)
Northern Ohio Sanitary Fair
Norweb, Emery May Holden
Notre Dame College
Novel Club
Nursing
Perkins, Anna ("Newspaper Annie")
Phillis Wheatley Assoc., The

Preterm, Inc.
Progressive Slovene Women of America
Project Eve
Pyke, Bernice S.
Ransom, Caroline L. Ormes
Rouse, Rebecca Cromwell
Rumbold, Charlotte M.
St. Joseph's Orphanage for Girls
St. Mary's Orphan Asylum for Females
Scranton, Irene Hickox (Mrs. Joel)
Severance, Caroline M.
Sherwin, Belle
Sisters of Charity of St. Augustine
Sisters of Notre Dame, The
Sisters of the Good Shepherd, The
Smith, Dorothy
Soldiers' Aid Society of Northern Ohio
Soldiers' Home
Turner, Rachel Walker
Ursuline College
Ursuline Sisters of Cleveland, The
Visiting Nurses Association
Votipka, Thelma
Wagner, Margaret W.
Waitt, Maude Comstock
Walker, Hazel Mountain
Westropp, Clara E.

Westropp, Lillian Mary
Wickham, Gertrude Van Rensselaer
Wilson, Ella Grant
Wing, Marie Remington
Wolf, Edith Anisfield
Wolfenstein, Martha
Woman's Christian Temp. Union Non-Partisan
Woman's Christian Temp. Union Conv.
Woman's General Hospital
Women
Women Together
Women's Art Club
Women's Bureau . . . Cleve. Police Dept.
Women's City Club, The
Women's Council Peace Parade . . . Prevention . . .
Women's Federal Savings Bank, The
Women's Law Fund Inc.
Women's Protective Assoc., The
WomenSpace
Woolson, Constance Fenimore
Young Womens Christian Assoc., The

# Index

Entries in this index are largely limited to names of individuals, places, corporate entities, and events within Cuyahoga County. Corporations and governmental agencies (boards, committees, etc.) are indexed under their variant name forms as used in the text; as these are not consolidated, researchers should check all name forms for an agency when using this index. Entries are keyed to the page number of any article in which they appear or the page number span if the main body of the article is on two or more pages. Boldfacing of page numbers indicates a complete article on the indexed term.

1097

1098

1099

1101

1110

1115